W9-CHG-615

# The World Book Dictionary

## Volume two L-Z

Edited by:
**Clarence L. Barnhart**
**Robert K. Barnhart**

Prepared in Cooperation with
**World Book–Childcraft International, Inc.**
Publishers of
**The World Book Encyclopedia**

**William H. Nault,** Editorial Director
**Robert O. Zeleny,** Executive Editor

A Thorndike-Barnhart Dictionary
Published exclusively for

**World Book–Childcraft International, Inc.**
A subsidiary of The Scott & Fetzer Company
Chicago London Paris Sydney Tokyo Toronto

**1980 Edition**
**The World Book Dictionary**



The World Book Dictionary (previously The World Book Encyclopedia Dictionary) is an integral unit of the Thorndike-Barnhart Dictionary Series, and contains some material in common with other dictionaries in the series:


Printed in the United States of America
ISBN 0-7166-0280-6
Library of Congress Catalog Card Number 79-53618

Trademarks or other proprietary names are entered in this dictionary and so marked; if the proper designation is missing, no legal status should be assumed.

# Contents

# Pronunciation

Say aloud the words *far, fat,* and *face,* and you can hear immediately that there are more sounds in English than letters in the alphabet. To make up the difference, this dictionary uses a special set of symbols that tell you how to pronounce the words you look up. The pronunciation follows the word in this way: **dic|tion|ar|y** (dik′shə ner′ē). Each symbol represents a specific sound, as indicated in the short pronunciation key on almost every right-hand page in this dictionary.

Diacritical marks appear above some symbols. These marks indicate specific sounds for the symbols with which they appear. The diacritical marks are:

*circumflex* (sėr′kəm fleks)—the mark over the ô, as in *order.*

*dieresis* (dī er′ə sis)—two dots over the ä, as in *father,* or the ü, as in *rule.*

*macron* (mā′kron)—the long mark over the ā, as in *age;* the ē, as in *equal;* the ī, as in *ice;* and the ō, as in *open.*

*single dot*—over the ė in the ėr, as in *term,* and over the u̇, as in *full.*

*tilde* (til′də)—the curved mark over the ã, as in *care.*

Stress marks show which syllables to emphasize. A heavy stress mark [′] follows the syllable with primary or strong accent. A light stress mark [′] follows the syllable with secondary or lighter accent.

Some words taken from foreign languages are spoken with sounds that otherwise do not occur in English. Symbols for these sounds are given in the complete pronunciation key on this page.

## Complete pronunciation key

| | | | |
|---|---|---|---|
| a | hat, cap | oi | oil, voice |
| ā | age, face | ou | house, out |
| ã | care, air | p | paper, cup |
| ä | father, far | r | run, try |
| b | bad, rob | s | say, yes |
| ch | child, much | sh | she, rush |
| d | did, red | t | tell, it |
| e | let, best | th | thin, both |
| ē | equal, see | ᴛʜ | then, smooth |
| ėr | term, learn | u | cup, butter |
| f | fat, if | u̇ | full, put |
| g | go, bag | ü | rule, move |
| h | he, how | v | very, save |
| i | it, pin | w | will, woman |
| ī | ice, five | y | young, yet |
| j | jam, enjoy | z | zero, breeze |
| k | kind, seek | zh | measure, seizure |
| l | land, coal | | |
| m | me, am | ə | represents: |
| n | no, in | a | in about |
| ng | long, bring | e | in taken |
| o | hot, rock | i | in pencil |
| ō | open, go | o | in lemon |
| ô | order, all | u | in circus |

**Non-English sounds**

| | |
|---|---|
| ʏ | as in French *du.* Pronounce ē with the lips rounded as for English ü in *rule.* |
| œ | as in French *peu.* Pronounce ā with the lips rounded as for ō. |
| ɴ | as in French *bon.* The ɴ is not pronounced, but shows that the vowel before it is nasal. |
| ʜ | as in German *ach.* Pronounce k without closing the breath passage. |
| à | as in French *ami.* The quality of this vowel is midway between the a of *hat* and the ä of *far,* but closer to the former. |

# Ll

***L¹** or **l** (el), *n.; pl.* **L's** or **Ls**, **l's** or **ls**. **1** the 12th letter of the English alphabet. There are two *l*'s in *ball.* **2** any sound represented by this letter. **3** (used as a symbol for) the 12th, or more usually 11th (of an actual or possible series, either I or J being omitted): *row L in a theater.* **4** the Roman numeral for 50.

**L²** (el), *n., pl.* **L's**. anything shaped like the letter L. An extension to a building at right angles with the main part or a joint connecting two pipes at right angles are L's.

**L³** (el), *n.* an elevated railroad: *The Third Avenue "L" gave up the ghost ... in its seventy-seventh year, leaving no descendants* (New Yorker). Also, **el.** [for *el,* short for *elevated*]

**L-** or **l-**, *combining form.* levo- (left-handed) in configuration: *l-glucose = levoglucose. Most amino acids, including glutamic acid ..., can exist in two forms called D- and L-, distinguished by their effect on polarised light* (New Scientist). [< *l*(evo-)]

**l.** or **l** (no period), an abbreviation for the following:
1 book (Latin, *liber*).
2 latitude.
3 leaf.
4 league.
5 left.
6 length.
7 *pl.* **ll.** line.
8 link.
9 lira or liras; lire (Italian money).
10 liter or liters.
11 locus.
12 low.

**L** (no period), an abbreviation or symbol for the following:
1 *Electricity.* coefficient of self-inductance.
2 Large (especially of garment sizes).
3 Latin.
4 Lebanese (as in *£L,* the Lebanese pound).
5 Libra (constellation).
6 longitude.
7 luminosity (of stellar bodies).

**L.**, an abbreviation for the following:
1 book (Latin, *liber*).
2 Lady.
3 Lake.
4 Latin.
5 left (in stage directions).
6 length.
7 Liberal (Party).
8 line.
9 *Botany.* Linnaeus.
10 lira or liras; lire (Italian money).
11 longitude.

**£**, pound or pounds sterling. [for Latin *libra*]

**la¹** (lä), *n.* the sixth tone of the diatonic scale. [< Latin *labiī.* See etym. under **gamut.**]

**la²** (lä, lô), *interj. Archaic.* an exclamation of surprise. [variant of *lo*]

**la³** (là), *French.* the (feminine singular definite article).

**La** (no period), lanthanum (chemical element).

**La.**, Louisiana.

**LA** (no periods), Louisiana (with postal Zip Code).

**L.A.**, **1** Library Association. **2** Los Angeles.

**laa|ger** (lä′gər), *n., v.* —*n.* a camp or encampment, especially a camp in the open country protected by a circle of wagons: *To South Africa's 17th century settlers, "going into 'laager'" meant forming a circle with their covered wagons to defend themselves against attacks by native tribes. To their present-day descendants, it means turning increasingly to the repressive strictures of 'apartheid' to protect themselves against the nonwhite majority* (Time).
—*v.t., v.i.* to arrange or encamp in a laager. Also, **lager.**
[< Afrikaans *laager,* probably < German *Lager*]

**lab** (lab), *n. Informal.* laboratory: *Rubber research is carried out by a host of firms, and in labs dotted from New England to Southern California* (Wall Street Journal).

**lab.**, **1a** labor. **b** laborer. **2** laboratory.

**Lab.**, **1** Labrador. **2** *British.* **a** Labour (Party). **b** Labourite.

**lab|an** (lab′ən, lä′bən), *n.* a thick, semi-solid or liquid food similar to yogurt, made from curdled milk in parts of North Africa and the Middle East. [< Arabic *laban*]

**La|ban** (lā′bən), *n.* the father of Leah and Rachel, the wives of Jacob (in the Bible, Genesis 29:13-29).

**La|ban|o|ta|tion** (lä′bə nō tā′shən, lā′-), *n.* a method of noting and recording dance movements and arrangements. [< Rudolf von *Laban,* a Hungarian-German dance teacher, who devised and wrote about the method in 1928]

**La|ban system** (lä′bən, lā′bən), = Labanotation.

**lab|a|rum** (lab′ər əm), *n., pl.* **-a|rums, -a|ra** (-ər ə). **1** a banner of purple silk having the monogram of Christ on it, borne at the head of the Roman armies after the conversion of Constantine the Great. **2** a banner or standard borne in ecclesiastical processions of the Roman Catholic Church. **3** any symbolic banner or standard. [< Late Latin *labarum* imperial banner < Latin, a military banner < Greek *lábaron*]

**lab|ba** (lab′ə), *n.* = paca. [< a native name]

**lab|da|num** (lab′də nəm), *n.* a soft, dark-colored gum resin that exudes from various rockroses, much used in perfumery, cosmetics, and formerly in medicines. Also, **ladanum.** [alteration of Latin *lādanum* (influenced by Greek *lábda,* variant of *lámbda* L) < Greek *lādanon* gum from the *lêdon* mastic]

**lab|e|fac|tion** (lab′ə fak′shən), *n.* a shaking or weakening; overthrow; downfall: *labefaction of the government.* [< Late Latin *labefactiō, -ōnis* < Latin *labefacere* shake, loosen < *labāre* to totter + *facere* make]

**la|bel** (lā′bəl), *n., v.,* **-beled, -bel|ing** or (*especially British*) **-belled, -bel|ling.** —*n.* **1** a slip of paper, cardboard, metal, or other material attached to anything and marked to show what or whose it is, or where it is to go: *Can you read the label on the bottle?* **2** a word or short phrase used to describe some person, thing, or idea; epithet: *In winter, Chicago deserves its label of "the Windy City."* **3** a narrow strip of material attached to a document to carry the seal. **4** *U.S.* an identifying mark or brand: *The workers were urged by the delegates not to spread rumors that the brewery and its label were to be sold* (New York Times). **5** a company producing phonograph records: *A new label, Washington Records, has made a noteworthy initial release* (Better Listening). **6** *Architecture.* a dripstone or other molding across the top of a door or window, especially one that also extends downward at the sides. **7** *Archaic.* a narrow band or strip of linen or other cloth, such as a fillet, ribbon, or tassel: *a knit night-cap ... With two long labels button'd to his chin* (Bishop Joseph Hall). **8** *Heraldry.* a narrow band with pendants, used especially to distinguish the oldest son during his father's life.
—*v.t.* **1** to put or write a label on: *The bottle is labeled "Poison."* **SYN:** tag. **2** to describe as; call; name: *He labeled the boastful boy a liar.* **SYN:** designate. **3** to infuse or treat (a substance) with a radioactive chemical or isotope so that its course or activity can be noted: *The movement of sugar in plants was studied in Canada by using sugars "labelled" with radioactive carbon* (*C14*) (Harold William Rickelt).
[< Old French *label;* origin uncertain] —**la′bel|er,** *especially British,* **la′bel|ler,** *n.*

**la|bel|late** (lə bel′āt), *adj.* lipped; labiate. [< Latin *labellum* + English *-ate*¹]

**la belle é|poque** (là bel′ ā pôk′), *French.* **1** the period at the turn of the century: *Was the age of Kipling and the Kaiser, McKinley and Dreyfus, really 'la belle époque,' the sunny Edwardian afternoon it is often nostalgically painted?* (Listener). **2** (literally) the beautiful epoch.

**la belle pro|vince** (là bel′ prô vaɴs′), *French.* **1** (in Canada) a nickname for Quebec. **2** (literally) the beautiful province.

**la|bel|loid** (lə bel′oid), *adj.* shaped like a labellum.

**la|bel|lum** (lə bel′əm), *n., pl.* **-bel|la** (-bel′ə). **1** the large, liplike, middle petal of an orchid, usually different in shape and color from the other two. **2** a liplike part at the tip of the proboscis of various insects, used for lapping up liquids. [< Latin *labellum* (diminutive) < *labium* lip]

**la|bi|a** (lā′bē ə), *n.* plural of **labium.**

**la|bi|al** (lā′bē əl), *adj., n.* —*adj.* **1** of the lips: *vibrations of the labial palps of hawk moths.* **2** having to do with or like a labium. **3** *Phonetics. pronounced with the lips closed, nearly closed, or rounded.* **4** *Music.* having tones produced by the impact of an air current on the edge of a lip, such as that of a flute or an organ flue pipe.
—*n.* **1** *Phonetics.* a sound pronounced with the lips closed, nearly closed, or rounded. *B, p,* and *m* are labials. **2** *Music.* a flue pipe, as distinguished from a reed pipe.
[< Medieval Latin *labialis* < Latin *labium* lip]
—**la′bi|al|ly,** *adv.*

**la|bi|al|ism** (lā′bē ə liz′əm), *n. Phonetics.* a tendency to labialize sounds; labial pronunciation.

**la|bi|al|i|za|tion** (lā′bē ə lə zā′shən), *n. Phonetics.* **1** the action of labializing. **2** the condition of being labialized.

**la|bi|al|ize** (lā′bē ə līz), *v.t.,* **-ized, -iz|ing.** *Phonetics.* **1** to give a labial character to (a sound). **2** to round (a vowel).

**labia ma|jo|ra** (mə jôr′ə, -jōr′-), *Anatomy.* the outer folds at the opening of the vulva. [< New Latin *labia majora* greater lips]

**labia mi|no|ra** (mi nôr′ə, -nōr′-), *Anatomy.* the inner folds at the opening of the vulva. [< New Latin *labia minora* lesser lips]

**la|bi|ate** (lā′bē āt, -it), *adj., n.* —*adj.* **1** having one or more liplike parts. **2** *Botany.* **a** having the corolla or calix divided into two parts suggesting lips. **b** belonging to or having to do with the mint family.
—*n.* a labiate plant.
[< New Latin *labiatus* < Latin *labium* lip]

**la|bi|at|ed** (lā′bē ā′tid), *adj.* = labiate.

**la|bile** (lā′bəl), *adj.* **1** having the tendency to undergo displacement in position or change in nature, form, or composition; unstable: *a labile chemical solution.* **2** likely to lapse: *a labile trust fund.* **3** moving over the part treated. Labile electrodes are used in medical diagnosis. [< Latin *lābilis* < *lābī* to slip, lapse]

**la|bil|i|ty** (lə bil′ə tē), *n., pl.* **-ties.** instability of form or character.

**la|bi|li|za|tion** (lā′bə lə zā′shən), *n.* the process of making or condition of being unstable.

**la|bi|lize** (lā′bə līz), *v.t.,* **-lized, -liz|ing.** to make unstable: *to labilize a chemical compound.*

**labio-**, *combining form.* made with the lips and ___: *Labiodental = made with the lips and teeth.* [< Latin *labium* lip]

**la|bi|o|den|tal** (lā′bē ō den′təl), *adj., n. Phonetics.* —*adj.* made with the lower lip and the upper teeth; made with the lips and teeth.
—*n.* a labiodental sound. *F* and *v* are labiodentals.

**la|bi|o|na|sal** (lā′bē ō nā′zəl), *adj., n. Phonetics.* —*adj.* made with the lips, but with the breath stream passing out through the nose.
—*n.* a labionasal sound. *M* is a labionasal.

**la|bi|o|ve|lar** (lā′bē ō vē′lər), *adj., n. Phonetics.* —*adj.* made with rounded lips and with the back of the tongue toward or against the soft palate.
—*n.* a labiovelar sound. *W* is a labiovelar.

**la|bi|um** (lā′bē əm), *n., pl.* **-bi|a.** **1** a lip or liplike part, such as a portion of the corolla of certain flowers or the organ that constitutes the lower lip of an insect. **2** the inner margin of the opening of a gastropod's shell. [< Latin *labium* lip]

**lab|lab** (lab′lab), *n.* **1** a vine of the pea family, with edible seeds, native to India but widely cultivated in other warm countries; hyacinth bean. **2** any one of various related species. [< Arabic *lablāb*]

**la|bor** (lā′bər), *n., v., adj.* —*n.* **1** effort in doing or making something; work; toil: *The carpenter was well paid for his labor. Labor disgraces no man* (Ulysses S. Grant). **SYN:** exertion, effort. See syn. under **work.** **2** a piece of work to be done; task: *The king gave Hercules twelve labors to perform. Our life is but a little holding, lent to do a mighty labour* (George Meredith). **3a** work, especially manual work, done by skilled and unskilled workers for wages: *Digging ditches is labor.* **b** the work of human beings that produces goods or services. *Land, labor,* and *capital* are the three principal factors of production. *Labor is prior to, and independent of, capital* (Abraham Lincoln).

***L¹**
definition 1

Script letters look like examples of fine penmanship. They appear in many formal uses, such as invitations to social functions.

Ll *Ll*

Handwritten letters, both manuscript or printed (left) and cursive (right), are easy for children to read and to write.

Ll *Ll*

Roman letters have *serifs* (finishing strokes) adapted from the way Roman stonecutters carved their letters. This is *Times Roman* type.

Ll *Ll*

Sans-serif letters are often called *gothic.* They have lines of even width and no serifs. This type face is called *Helvetica.*

Ll *Ll*

Between roman and gothic, some letters have thick and thin lines with slight flares that suggest serifs. This type face is *Optima.*

L

Computer letters can be sensed by machines either from their shapes or from the magnetic ink with which they are printed.

4a skilled and unskilled workers as a group: *Labor favors safe working conditions. Labor's function is to join with ... management in the common enterprise of meeting the needs of the universal consumer* (Emory S. Bogardus). **b** labor unions as a group: *The traditional allies of labor, those who struggle for civil rights, social welfare, the needs of the poor, ... should think of organized labor again as their first call for friends and for continuing significant support* (Victor Gotbaum). **5** the physical exertions of childbirth before delivery: *She was in labor for two hours.* **SYN**: parturition, travail.
—*v.i.* **1** to do work, especially hard work; toil: *He labored all day at the mill.* **2** to move slowly and heavily: *The old car labored as it climbed the steep hill.* **3** to be burdened, troubled, or distressed: *to labor under a mistake or a handicap.* **4** to be long and drawn out; be elaborate. **5** to be in labor during childbirth.
—*v.t.* **1** to elaborate with effort or in detail: *The speaker labored the point so long that we lost interest.* **2** *Archaic.* to till; cultivate. **3** *Archaic.* to work or strive to bring about or achieve.
—*adj.* of or having to do with labor: *a labor shortage, labor leaders.* Also, *Especially British* **labour**.
[< Old French *labour,* learned borrowing from Latin *labor, -ōris* toil, pain]

**la|bo|ra|re est o|ra|re** (lab′ə rãr′ē est ō rãr′ē), *Latin.* **1** work is prayer. **2** (literally) to work is to pray.

**lab|o|ra|to|ri|al** (lab′ər ə tôr′ē əl, -tōr′-; lab′rə-), *adj.* having to do with the laboratory. —**lab′o|ra|to′ri|al|ly**, *adv.*

**lab|o|ra|to|ri|an** (lab′ər ə tôr′ē ən, -tōr′-; lab′rə-), *n., adj.* —*n.* a person who works in a laboratory. —*adj.* = laboratorial.

**lab|o|ra|to|ry** (lab′ər ə tôr′ē, -tōr′-; lab′rə-), *n., pl.* **-ries**, *adj.* —*n.* **1** a place where scientific work is done; a room or building fitted with apparatus for conducting scientific investigations, experiments, or tests: *a chemical laboratory.* **2** a place equipped for manufacturing such products as chemicals, medicines, or explosives. **3** any place, not a classroom or library, equipped for systematic study: *a reading laboratory.*
—*adj.* used or performed in, or having to do with a laboratory: *a laboratory animal, a laboratory experiment. Automation is overtaking even the highly trained medical laboratory technician* (Science News Letter).
[< Medieval Latin *laboratorium* < Latin *labōrāre* to work < *labor, -ōris* work, toil]

**laboratory animal**, any animal commonly used for experiments in a laboratory, such as guinea pigs and mice: *A laboratory animal, such as a rabbit ..., reacts to any protein from a source outside its body in the same way it does to invading disease germs* (Fred W. Emerson).

**laboratory school**, a school for the observation and study of children and evaluation of teaching methods; campus school. It is usually part of the department of education of a university or college.

**labor camp**, **1** a concentration camp for political prisoners in totalitarian countries and for common criminals sentenced to hard labor. **2** a place providing facilities for migratory workers.

**Labor Day**, the first Monday in September, a legal holiday in the United States, Puerto Rico, and Canada in honor of labor and laborers.

**la|bored** (lā′bərd), *adj.* done with much effort; not easy or natural; forced: *labored breathing. ... the trouble is [his] labored writing, which for the most part is as frothy as yesterday's spaghetti* (Clive Barnes). **SYN**: laborious, studied, constrained. See syn. under **elaborate**. —**la′bored|ly**, *adv.* —**la′bored|ness**, *n.*

**la|bor|er** (lā′bər ər), *n.* **1** a person who does work requiring much physical labor: *A field hand on a farm is a laborer.* **2** a worker.

**labor exchange**, an employment office, especially in Great Britain, that helps to find jobs and makes job-payment benefits.

**labor force**, **1** the work force of a country. The labor force of the United States comprises all the employable people 16 years old or over. **2** any work force.

**la|bor|ing** (lā′bər ing), *adj.* **1** that labors, especially that is engaged in manual or mechanical labor: *the laboring man.* **2** struggling, as under difficulty, emotion, stress, or other burden: *an occasional sigh from the laboring heart of the Captain* (Longfellow). **3** rolling or pitching, as a ship. —**la′bor|ing|ly**, *adv.*

**la|bor-in|ten|si|ty** (lā′bər in ten′sə tē), *n.* the condition of being labor-intensive.

**la|bor-in|ten|sive** (lā′bər in ten′siv), *adj.* requiring more money for labor than for machines or materials: *Publishing is a labor-intensive industry. The service sectors have in common the fact that they are disproportionately labor-intensive rather than capital-intensive, even though some sectors (particularly transportation and communication) have extremely high ratios of capital to output* (W. Halder Fisher).

**la|bo|ri|ous** (lə bôr′ē əs, -bōr′-), *adj.* **1** needing or taking much effort; requiring hard work: *Hoeing a garden is laborious.* **SYN**: toilsome, arduous, onerous, wearisome. **2** showing signs of effort; not easy; labored: *The girl who was always late made up laborious excuses.* **3** willing to work hard; industrious: *Bees and ants are laborious workers.* **SYN**: diligent. [< Latin *labōriōsus* < *labor, -ōris* labor] —**la|bo′ri|ous|ly**, *adv.* —**la|bo′ri|ous|ness**, *n.*

**La|bor|ism** (lā′bə riz əm), *n.* **1** the principles or tenets of a Labor Party, especially the British Labour Party. **2** adherence to these principles.

**La|bor|ist** (lā′bər ist), *n.* **1** a supporter of Laborism, especially British Laborism. **2** = Laborite.

**la|bor|is|tic** (lā′bə ris′tik), *adj.* of labor; tending to favor labor: *The production of wealth is almost wholly capitalistic; the distribution of wealth is largely laboristic* (Wall Street Journal).

**la|bor|ite** (lā′bə rīt), *n.* a person who supports the interests of workers.

**La|bor|ite** (lā′bə rīt), *n.* a member of a Labor Party.

**la|bor|less** (lā′bər lis), *adj.* free from labor; doing or requiring no labor.

**labor market**, the supply of labor in relation to the demand for it.

**labor of love**, any work done with eager willingness, either from fondness for the work itself or from affection for the person for whom the work is done.

**la|bor om|ni|a vin|cit** (lā′bôr om′nē ə vin′sit), *Latin.* labor conquers all things (the motto of the state of Oklahoma).

**labor organization**, any group of workers legally empowered to deal with employers on labor disputes, grievances, or conditions of employment, especially as a labor union.

**labor pains**, **1** the muscular contractions and pains of childbirth. **2** the difficulties encountered at the beginning of an endeavor or enterprise: *the labor pains of starting a new book.*

**Labor Party**, any political party organized to protect and promote the interests of workers.

**labor relations**, the study or practice of improving relations between labor and management.

**la|bor-sav|ing** or **la|bor|sav|ing** (lā′bər sā′ving), *adj.* that takes the place of or lessens labor: *A washing machine is a labor-saving device. The neat labor-saving cook-stove had as yet no being* (Harriet Beecher Stowe).

**labor skate**, *U.S. Slang.* a labor unionist: *These were no local cops picking up a labor skate for disturbing the peace* (Newsweek).

**la|bor|some** (lā′bər səm), *adj.* laborious or toilsome. —**la′bor|some|ly**, *adv.*

**labor turnover**, **1** the number of new workers hired in place of workers who have left their jobs. **2** the proportion of new workers hired to the average number of workers an employer has working for him: *In many industries men are "hired and fired" freely, and a labor turnover of 100 per cent in a year has been known to occur* (Emory S. Bogardus).

**labor union**, a group of workers joined to protect and promote their interests, especially by dealing as a group with their employers; union.

**labor unionist**, a member of a labor union: *Labor unionists believe in collective bargaining* (Emory S. Bogardus).

**la|bour** (lā′bər), *n., v.i., v.t., adj. Especially British.* labor. —**la′boured**, *adj.* —**la′bour|er**, *n.* —**la′bour|ing**, *adj.*

**La|bour** (lā′bər), *adj.* of or having to do with the Labour Party: *a Labour politician.*

**La|bour|ite** (lā′bə rīt), *n.* a member of the British Labour Party: *A large majority of the Labourites in Parliament disapproved. Abbr:* Lab.

**Labour Party**, a political party in Great Britain that claims especially to protect the rights and advance the interests of working people. It is one of the two major British political parties and was founded by the trade unions late in the 1800's but has attracted much middle-class and intellectual support.

**La|bour|wal|lah** (lā′bər wol′ə), *n.* (in Kenya and some other parts of eastern Africa) a prominent member of the Labour movement.

**la|bra** (lā′brə, lab′rə), *n.* plural of **labrum**.

**Lab|ra|dor** (lab′rə dôr), *n.* = Labrador retriever.

**Labrador blue**, a very dark blue color.

**Labrador Current**, a current of cold water that rises in the Arctic Ocean and flows along the coast of Labrador to a point near Newfoundland, where it meets the Gulf Stream.

**Labrador duck**, a sea duck of the northern Atlantic coast of North America, extinct since the 1870's, the male of which was black with white head and markings.

**lab|ra|dor|es|cence** (lab′rə dô res′əns), *n.* the brilliant play of colors exhibited by labradorite.

**Lab|ra|dor|i|an** (lab′rə dôr′ē ən), *adj., n.* —*adj.* of or having to do with the peninsula of Labrador, in northeastern North America.
—*n.* a native or inhabitant of Labrador.

**lab|ra|dor|ite** (lab′rə dôr īt, lab′rə dôr′-), *n.* a mineral, a kind of feldspar, that shows a brilliant display of colors when light strikes it. Architects use plates of rock containing labradorite to ornament buildings. [< *Labrador,* where it is found + *-ite*[1]]

**lab|ra|dor|it|ic** (lab′rə dô rit′ik), *adj.* of or like labradorite.

**Labrador retriever**, a medium-sized hunting dog used on land or water to retrieve game. It has a thick, water-resistant coat and is black, chocolate, or yellow in color. The breed originated in Newfoundland.

**Labrador tea**, **1** any of a group of low, evergreen shrubs of the heath family, growing in bogs and swamps of arctic and subarctic regions. **2** tea made with the leaves of a plant of this group.

**la|bral** (lā′brəl, lab′rəl), *adj.* of a labrum or liplike part.

**la|bret** (lā′bret), *n.* an ornament stuck into or through the lip. Labrets are often a piece of wood, stone, bone, or shell worn by certain primitive peoples. [< *labr*(um) + *-et*]

**lab|roid** (lab′roid), *adj., n.* —*adj.* of or having the spiny fins and thick lips characteristic of the family of fishes including the wrasses.
—*n.* any fish belonging to this family.
[< New Latin *Labroidea* the family name < *Labrus* the typical genus < Latin *labrum* lip; see etym. under **labrum**]

**la|brum** (lā′brəm, lab′rəm), *n., pl.* **la|bra** (lā′brə, lab′rə), **1** a lip or liplike part. **2** *Zoology.* **a** the upper lip of insects and certain other arthropods. **b** the outer margin of the opening of a gastropod shell. [< Latin *labrum* lip, related to *labium* labium]

**la|bur|num** (lə bėr′nəm), *n.* a small, poisonous tree or shrub with hanging clusters of bright-yellow flowers. There are several kinds of laburnum, including the golden chain, all belonging to the pea faimily; all are native to Asia or Europe. [< Latin *laburnum*]

**lab|ware** (lab′wãr′), *n.* utensils, as of glass, porcelain, or metal, that are used in a laboratory: *Like all Pyrex labware, these coils are corrosion resistant* (Scientific American). [< *lab* + *ware*]

**Lab|y|rinth** (lab′ə rinth), *n. Greek Mythology.* the maze built by Daedalus for King Minos of Crete to imprison the Minotaur. [< Latin *labyrinthus* < Greek *labýrinthos*]

***lab|y|rinth** (lab′ə rinth), *n.* **1** a number of connecting passages so arranged that it is hard to find one's way from point to point; maze. **2a** any confusing, complicated arrangement, such as of streets or buildings: *We could not find our way out of the labyrinth of dark and narrow streets.* **b** *Figurative.* a confusing, complicated state of affairs: *Undeniably he [Charles de Gaulle] had resurrected French strength by leading the nation out of the colonial labyrinth* (John C. Cairns). **SYN**: intricacy, complexity. **3** *Anatomy.* the inner ear, consisting of a bony and a membranous part. The labyrinth holds the end fibers of the auditory nerves. [< *Labyrinth*] —**lab′y|rinth|like′**, *adj.*

***labyrinth**
definition 1

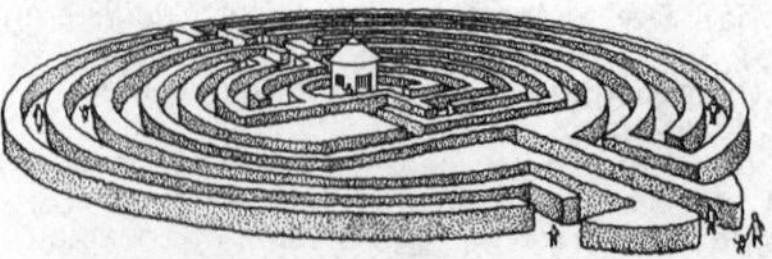

hedge labyrinth

**lay|y|rin|thal** (lab′ə rin′thəl), *adj.* = labyrinthine.

**labyrinth fish**, any tropical fish of a group that is brightly colored and has a cavity above the gills for storing air.

**lab|y|rin|thi|an** (lab′ə rin′thē ən), *adj.* = labyrinthine.

**lab|y|rin|thic** (lab′ə rin′thik), *adj.* = labyrinthine. —**lab′y|rin′thi|cal|ly**, *adv.*

**lab|y|rin|thi|cal** (lab′ə rin′thə kəl), *adj.* = labyrinthine.

**lab|y|rin|thine** (lab′ə rin′thin, -thēn), *adj.* **1** of or forming a labyrinth: *labyrinthine passages.* **2** *Figurative.* confusing and complicated; intricate: *... down the labyrinthine ways Of my own mind* (Francis Thompson). **SYN**: involved, inextricable.

**lab|y|rin|thi|tis** (lab′ə rin thī′tis), *n.* inflammation of the inner ear.

**lab|y|rin|tho|don** (lab′ə rin′thə don), *n.* = labyrinthodont.

**lab|y|rin|tho|dont** (lab′ə rin′thə dont), *adj., n.* —*adj.* **1** having teeth with a labyrinthlike internal

structure. **2** of or having to do with a family of large, sometimes huge, extinct amphibians, with a labyrinthlike tooth structure.
*—n.* a labyrinthodont amphibian: *Some primitive fossil labyrinthodonts probably were ancestral to the oldest reptiles and so to all higher land vertebrates* (Tracy I. Storer).
[< Greek *labýrinthos* + *odoús, odóntos* tooth]

**labyrinth spider**, a spider that spins a tangled web to hide from its prey and a nearly circular web anchored at various points around the circumference in which to catch insects.

**lac**[1] (lak), *n.* a sticky substance deposited on various trees in southern Asia by scale insects. Lac is used especially in making sealing wax, varnish, red dye, and shellac. [< Hindustani *lākh* < Sanskrit *lākṣā*. See related etym. at **lacquer**.]

**lac**[2] (lak), *n., adj.* = lakh.

**lac**[3] (lak), *adj.* of or having to do with the lac operon: *The lac repressor binds to DNA that contains the lac genes but not to DNA without lac genes* (Scientific American). [< *lac*(tose)]

**La|can|don** (lä kän dôn′), *n., pl.* **-don, -do|nes** (-dô′nās). a member of a small primitive tribe of Indians, believed to be descendants of the Mayas, living in southern Mexico near Guatemala.

**lac|cate** (lak′āt), *adj.* having the appearance of being lacquered: *laccate leaves.*

**lac|co|lite** (lak′ə līt), *n.* = laccolith.

**lac|co|lith** (lak′ə lith), *n.* a large mass of igneous rock that has spread on rising from below, causing the overlying strata to bulge upward in a domelike formation. [< Greek *lákkos* storage pit, reservoir, pond + *líthos* stone]

***lace**
definition 1

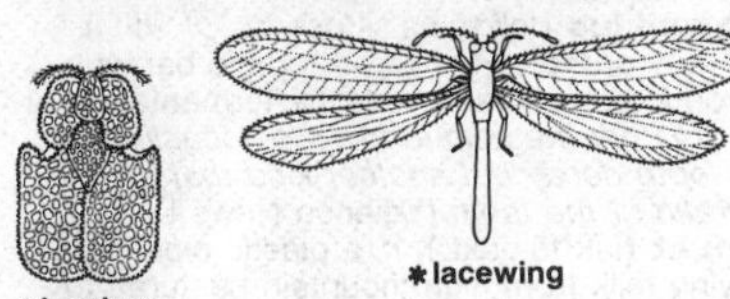

***lacebug** ***lacewing**

***lace** (lās), *n., v.,* **laced, lac|ing.** *—n.* **1** an open weaving or net of fine thread in an ornamental pattern. **2** a cord, string, or leather strip passed through holes to pull or hold together the opposite edges of a shoe, garment, or the like: *These shoes need new laces.* **3** gold or silver braid used for trimming: *Some uniforms have lace on them.* **4** a dash of brandy, whiskey, or other liquor added to such beverages as coffee or tea.
*—v.t.* **1** to trim with lace: *the white-laced collar of a velvet dress.* **2** to put laces through; pull or hold together with a lace or laces: *Lace your shoes.* **3** to adorn or trim with narrow braid: *His uniform was laced with gold.* **4a** to interlace; intertwine: *... a black cotton laced with just enough orlon to keep it from wilting* (New Yorker). *... his oral reports to the F.B.I. were laced with falsehoods* (New York Times). *Though only a story it is laced with many exciting facts about the Revolutionary War.* **b** to mix; blend (with): *... found that sawdust laced with oatmeal makes a much better soil for mushroom farming* (Scientific American). **5** to mark with streaks; streak: *a white petunia laced with purple. A waterfall of foam, lacing the black rocks with a thousand snowy streams* (Charles Kingsley). *Four-lane highways lace the island.* **6** *Informal.* to lash; beat; thrash. **7** to add a dash of brandy, whiskey, or other alcoholic liquor, to (a beverage, especially coffee): *Let's go drink a dish of laced coffee, and talk of the times* (William Wycherley). **SYN**: flavor. **8** to squeeze in the waist of (a person) by drawing the laces of a corset tight. **SYN**: compress. **9** to spread a network over or through: *If any nation were to begin lacing the earth's waters with ... bombs ...* (New Yorker).
*—v.i.* to be laced: *These shoes lace easily.*
**lace into,** *Informal.* **a** to attack by striking again and again; lash: *One of the two quarreling boys suddenly laced into the other, knocking him down.* **b** to criticize severely: *The coach laced into the team for not trying harder to win.*
[< Old French *laz* < Latin *laqueus* noose. See etym. of doublet **lasso.**] **—lace′like′,** *adj.* **—lac′er,** *n.*

**lace|bark** (lās′bärk′), *n.* = lacewood.

***lace|bug** (lās′bug′), *n.* a sucking insect with lacelike markings on the body and wings. It sucks the juices of broadleaf evergreens.

**lace-cur|tain** (lās′kėr′tən), *adj.* **1** fancy; pretentious: *Maybe if I describe the game in another, less lace-curtain, way it will be easier to see* (Scientific American). **2** characteristic of the middle class, sometimes emphazing a pretentious but proper or genteel manner: *He is a man with a strong middle-class provincial, even, lace-curtain ... background* (Harper's).

**Lac|e|dae|mo|ni|an** (las′ə di mō′nē ən), *adj., n.* = Spartan.

**lace fern**, a small fern having the underside of the frond covered with matted wool.

**lace|flow|er** (lās′flou′ər), *n.* **1** a small, delicate blue flower of an Australian plant of the parsley family. **2** the plant.

**lace glass**, a Venetian glass with white lacelike designs contained in the body of clear glass; latticinio.

**lace|leaf** (lās′lēf′), *n., pl.* **-leaves.** = latticeleaf.

**lace|less** (lās′lis), *adj.* without laces: *Loafers and most slippers are laceless shoes.*

**lace|mak|ing** (lās′mā′king), *n.* the art or process of making lace.

**lace paper**, paper cut or stamped in imitation of lace.

**lace pillow**, a round or oval board with a stuffed covering, held on the knees to support the fabric when making pillow lace.

**lac|er|a|bil|i|ty** (las′ər ə bil′ə tē), *n.* the condition of being lacerable.

**lac|er|a|ble** (las′ər ə bəl), *adj.* that can be lacerated.

**lac|er|ate** (*v.* las′ə rāt; *adj.* las′ə rāt, -ər it), *v.,* **-at|ed, -at|ing,** *adj.* *—v.t.* **1** to tear roughly; mangle: *The bear's claws lacerated the hunter's arm.* **SYN**: rend, wound. **2** *Figurative.* to cause pain or suffering to (the feelings, etc.); distress; hurt: *The coach's sharp words lacerated my feelings. The inscription on his tomb in Dublin's St. Patrick's says that "the body of Jonathan Swift is buried here, where fierce indignation ... can lacerate his heart no more"* (Time). **SYN**: harrow, afflict.
*—adj.* **1** deeply or irregularly indented as if torn: *lacerate leaves.* **2** torn; mangled.
[< Latin *lacerāre* (with English *-ate*[1]) < *lacer* mangled]

**lac|er|at|ed** (las′ə rā′tid), *adj.* **1** mangled; torn; hurt: *a lacerated arm.* **2** *Figurative: lacerated pride.*

**lac|er|a|tion** (las′ə rā′shən), *n.* **1** a rough tearing or mangling; process of lacerating. **2** a rough tear; mangled place: *A torn, jagged wound is a laceration.* **SYN**: mutilation.

**lac|er|a|tive** (las′ə rā′tiv), *adj.* having the power to lacerate or tear; tearing.

**lac|er|a|tor** (las′ə rā tər), *n.* a person or thing that lacerates.

**La|cer|ta** (lə sėr′tə), *n., genitive* **La|cer|tae.** a northern constellation near Pegasus. [< Latin *lacerta* lizard]

**La|cer|tae** (lə sėr′tē), *n.* genitive of **Lacerta.**

**la|cer|tian** (lə sėr′shən), *adj., n.* = lacertilian.

**la|cer|tid** (lə sėr′tid), *n.* = lizard.

**lac|er|til|i|an** (las′ər til′ē ən), *adj., n.* *—adj.* **1** of or belonging to the lizards. Lacertilians are a suborder of reptiles that include the geckos, chameleons, and skinks. **2** lizardlike.
*—n.* a lizard or lizardlike reptile.
[< New Latin *Lacertilia* the suborder name (< Latin *lacerta* lizard) + English *-an*]

**la|cer|tine** (lə sėr′tin), *adj.* **1** = lacertilian. **2** consisting of intertwined or curving lizardlike forms in decorative work. [< Latin *lacerta* lizard + English *-ine*[1]]

**lac|er|y** (lā′sər ē), *n., pl.* **-er|ies.** lacelike work.

***lace|wing** (lās′wing′), *n.* an insect with four delicate, lacelike wings and prominent, golden-bronze eyes. Lacewings belong to the same order as the ant lions.

**lace|wood** (lās′wůd′), *n.* the fibrous bark of the currajong tree of Australia.

**lace|work** (lās′wėrk′), *n.* **1** = lace. **2** openwork like lace. **3** *Figurative.* a network: *Saigon ... rests on a lacework of rivers and canals* (Frances Fitzgerald).

**lac|ey** (lā′sē), *adj.,* **lac|i|er, lac|i|est.** = lacy.

**lach|e|na|li|a** (lash′ə nā′lē ə), *n.* any South African plant of a genus of the lily family, bearing yellow, bell-shaped flowers. [< New Latin *Lachenalia* the genus name < *Lachenal,* a Swiss botanist of the 1800's]

**lach|es** (lach′iz), *n., pl.* **lach|es. 1** *Law.* failure to do a thing at the right time; delay in asserting a right, claiming a privilege, or applying for redress: *To decide whether the party applying has not, by laches or misconduct, lost his right to the writ* (London Times). **2** inexcusable negligence: *We may visit on the laches of this ministry the introduction of that new principle and power ... Agitation* (Benjamin Disraeli). [< Anglo-French *lachesse,* Old French *laschesse* < *lasche* negligent < Latin *laxus,* loose, lax]

**Lach|e|sis** (lak′ə sis), *n. Greek and Roman Mythology.* one of the three Fates. Lachesis measures off the thread of human life. [< Latin *Lachesis* < Greek *Láchesis*]

**lach|ry|mal** (lak′rə məl), *adj., n.* *—adj.* **1** of tears; producing tears: *Mostly a salt solution, lachrymal fluid also contains substances that fight bacteria, and proteins that help make the eye immune to infection* (G. W. Beadle). **2** for tears: *Collecting the drops of public sorrow into his volume, as into a lachrymal vase* (Washington Irving). **3** *Anatomy.* lacrimal.
*—n.* = lachrymatory. Also, **lacrimal, lacrymal.**
**lachrymals, a** lacrimal glands. **b** tears: *Something else I said ... made her laugh in the midst of her lachrymals* (Samuel Richardson).
[< Medieval Latin *lachrymalis* < Latin *lacrima* tear[1]]

**lachrymal gland**, = lacrimal gland.

**lach|ry|ma|tion** (lak′rə mā′shən), *n.* the shedding of tears. Also, **lacrimation.**

**lach|ry|ma|tor** (lak′rə mā′tər), *n.* a substance that makes the eyes water, such as tear gas. Also, **lacrimator.**

**lach|ry|ma|to|ry** (lak′rə mə tôr′ē, -tōr′-), *adj., n., pl.* **-ries.** *—adj.* **1** of tears; producing tears. **2** for tears.
*—n.* a small vase with a narrow neck found in ancient Roman tombs and once believed to hold the tears of mourners. Also, **lacrimatory, lacrymatory.**

**lach|ry|mist** (lak′rə mist), *n.* one who is addicted to tears; weeper.

**lach|ry|mose** (lak′rə mōs), *adj.* **1** given to shedding tears; tearful: *lachrymose depressions of spirit.* **SYN**: weeping. **2** suggestive of or tending to cause tears; mournful: *lachrymose poetry.* **SYN**: maudlin, melancholy. [< Latin *lacrimōsus* < *lacrima* tear[1]] **—lach′ry|mose|ly,** *adv.*

**lach|ry|mos|i|ty** (lak′rə mos′ə tē), *n.* = tearfulness.

**lac|i|ly** (lā′sə lē), *adv.* in a lacy way or manner.

**lac|i|ness** (lā′sē nis), *n.* lacy condition or quality.

**lac|ing** (lā′sing), *n.* **1** a cord, string, or the like, for pulling or holding something together: *My boot became loose when its lacing broke.* **2** gold or silver braid used for trimming. **3** streaked coloration, as of flowers or plumage or fur: *pale-rose petals with red-rose lacings.* **4** *Informal.* a lashing; beating; thrashing: *The sound lacing which the young rascal should inevitably receive* (Henry Vizetelly). **5a** a dash of brandy, whiskey, or other alcoholic beverage: *Irish coffee ... has its heart in a goodly lacing of Irish whisky* (Nan Ickeringill). **b** *Figurative: Liberal lacings of sex fail to bring these cardboard characters alive* (Oscar Handlin).

**la|cin|i|a** (lə sin′ē ə), *n.* **1** a slash, as in a leaf or petal. **2** the apex of an insect's maxilla. [< New Latin *lacinia;* see etym. under **laciniate**]

**la|cin|i|ate** (lə sin′ē āt, -it), *adj.* **1** *Botany.* cut into deep and narrow irregular lobes; slashed; jagged. **2** *Anatomy.* shaped or formed like a fringe, as a ligament. [< New Latin *lacinia* a slashed lobe of a petal (< Latin, small piece < *lacer* mangled) + English *-ate*[1]]

**la|cin|i|at|ed** (lə sin′ē ā′tid), *adj.* jagged or fringed; laciniate.

**la|cin|i|a|tion** (lə sin′ē ā′shən), *n.* a lobe or projecting segment; laciniate formation.

**la|cin|i|ose** (lə sin′ē ōs), *adj.* = laciniate.

**lac insect**, a scale insect that attaches itself to the twigs of various trees, inserts its proboscis through the bark, sucks up the sap, and subsequently exudes it to form an amberlike incrustation called lac.

**la|cis** (lā′səs), *n.* = lacework. [< French *lacis*]

**lack** (lak), *v., n.* *—v.t.* **1** to be without; have no: *A homeless person lacks a home. Some guinea pigs lack tails.* **2** to have not enough; need: *A coward lacks courage.*
*—v.i.* **1** to be absent or missing, as something requisite or desirable: *Here lacks but your mother for to say amen* (Shakespeare). **2a** to be short (of). **b** *Obsolete.* to be in want or need: *He that giveth unto the poor shall not lack* (Proverbs 28:27). [< noun]
*—n.* **1** the condition of being without: *Lack of a*

**Pronunciation Key:** hat, āge, cãre, fär; let, ēqual, tėrm; it, īce; hot, ōpen, ôrder; oil, out; cup, pu̇t, rüle; child; long; thin; ᴛʜen; zh, measure;
ə represents **a** in about, **e** in taken, **i** in pencil, **o** in lemon, **u** in circus.

*fire made him cold.* **2** not having enough; shortage: *Lack of rest made her tired. Let his lack of years be no impediment* (Shakespeare). **SYN**: deficiency, deficit, dearth, paucity, scarcity. **3** thing needed: *The campers' main lack was dry wood for a fire.*

**for lack of, a** because of too little: *I sold the business for lack of capital.* **b** for want of; being without: *More than 100 inadequately staffed interagency committees which for lack of authority have ended up doing virtually nothing* (Edmund S. Muskie).

[origin uncertain. Compare Middle Dutch *lac,* Middle Low German *lak.*]

—***Syn.*** *v.t.* **1, 2 Lack, want, need** mean to be without something. **Lack** means to be completely without or without enough of something, good or bad: *A coward lacks courage.* **Want** means to lack something worth having, desired, or, especially, necessary for completeness: *That dress wants a belt.* **Need** means to lack something required for a purpose or that cannot be done without: *He does not have the tools he needs. She needs more sleep.*

**lack|a|dai|si|cal** (lak′ə dā′zə kəl), *adj.* lacking interest or enthusiasm; languid; listless: *A lackadaisical sales staff. The new mayor has worked long and hard and is far from lackadaisical.* **SYN**: spiritless, lethargic, dreamy. [< *lackadaisy,* variant of *lackaday* + *-ic* + *-al*[1]] —**lack′a|dai′si|cal|ly,** *adv.* —**lack′a|dai′si|cal|ness,** *n.*

**lack|a|day** (lak′ə dā′), *interj.* an exclamation of sorrow or regret; alas. [variant of *alackaday!*]

**lack|er** (lak′ər), *n., v.t.* = lacquer. —**lack′er|er,** *n.*

**lack|ey** (lak′ē), *n., pl.* **-eys,** *adj., v.,* **-eyed, -ey|ing.** —***n.*** **1** a male servant; footman: *The nobleman sent one of his lackeys ahead with a message. I saw a gay gilt chariot ... the coachman with a new cockade, and the lackeys with insolence and [illegible] in their countenances* (Sir Richard Steele). **SYN**: flunky. **2** a follower who obeys orders as if he were a servant; toady. **SYN**: sycophant.

—***adj.*** servile; slavish: *a lackey informer.*

—***v.t.*** **1** to wait on: *A thousand liveried angels lacky her* (Milton). **2** to be slavish to.

—***v.i.*** to act or serve as a lackey: *The Navy still lackeys around the clock for the Royal Yacht Squadron and its guests* (Manchester Guardian Weekly).

[< Middle French *laquais* < Spanish *lacayo* foot soldier, perhaps < Arabic *al-qā'id* chief, captain (usually a Moor who occupies a lesser post because he was captured by Christians). Compare etym. under **alcaide.**]

**lack|ing** (lak′ing), *adj., prep.* —***adj.*** **1** not having enough; deficient: *A weak person is lacking in strength.* **2** absent; not here: *Water is lacking because the pipe is broken.*

—***prep.*** without; not having: *Lacking butter, we ate jam on our bread.*

**lack-in-of|fice** (lak′ən ôf′is, -of′-), *n., pl.* **lacks-in-of|fice.** a person who seeks to gain public office; an office seeker.

**lack|land** (lak′land′), *adj., n.* —***adj.*** without land; landless.

—***n.*** a person who has no land.

**lack|lus|ter** (lak′lus′tər), *adj., n.* —***adj.*** lacking brightness; dull and drab: *a lackluster performance of a play. From a gaudy blue to a faint lackluster shade of grey* (Dickens).

—***n.*** *Rare.* the absence of luster or brightness.

**lack|lus|tre** (lak′lus′tər), *adj., n. Especially British.* lackluster.

**lack|wit** (lak′wit′), *n. Informal.* a stupid person.

**La|co|ni|an** (lə kō′nē ən), *adj., n.* —***adj.*** having to do with Laconia, an ancient country in southern Greece whose capital was Sparta, or its inhabitants; Spartan or Lacedaemonian.

—***n.*** an inhabitant of Laconia.

**la|con|ic** (lə kon′ik), *adj.* using few words; brief in speech or expression; concise: *Boccalini ... indicts a laconic writer for speaking that in three words which he might have said in two* (Sir Richard Steele). **SYN**: short, condensed, terse, succinct, pithy, sententious. [< Latin *Lacōnicus* < Greek *Lakōnikós* Spartan < *Lákōn* a Spartan (because Spartans were noted for brevity in speech)] —**la|con′i|cal|ly,** *adv.*

**la|con|i|cism** (lə kon′ə siz əm), *n.* = laconism.

**la|con|i|cum** (lə kon′ə kəm), *n.* the sweating room of an ancient Roman bath. [< Latin *Laconicum,* neuter of *Lacōnicus* (because it was first used by the Spartans); see etym. under **laconic**]

**lac|o|nism** (lak′ə niz əm), *n.* **1** laconic brevity. **2** a loconic speech or expression. [< Greek *lakōnismós* < *lakōnízein* to imitate Lacedaemonians, especially in speech < *Lákōn;* see etym. under **laconic**]

**lac operon,** the operon involved in the metabolism of lactose. It was the first operon isolated in pure form. *The isolation in pure form of a set of six bacterial genes known as the lac operon has been accomplished by a group led by Dr. Jon Beckwith of the Harvard Medical School ...* (Science Journal). [< *lac*(tose)]

**lac|quer** (lak′ər), *n., v.* —***n.*** **1** a varnish used to give a coating or shiny appearance to metals, wood, or paper. Lacquers are made in all colors that are commonly found in paints. Lacquer consists of a solution of pale shellac dissolved in alcohol or some other solvent. Other lacquers are made from the resin of a sumac tree of southeast Asia. **2** articles coated with lacquer; lacquerware. **3** *Obsolete.* lac[1].

—***v.t.*** **1** to coat with or as if with lacquer. **2** *Slang.* to polish; make more presentable: *the Actors Studio, an organization dedicated to lacquering up-and-coming performers* (New York Times).

[< Middle French *lacre* < Portuguese, sealing wax < *lacca* lac < Arabic *lakk* < Persian *lak* lac gum. See related etym. at **lake**[2], **shellac.**] —**lac′quer|er,** *n.*

**lacquer tree,** = varnish tree.

**lac|quer|ware** (lak′ər wãr′), *n.* wooden articles coated with lacquer.

**lac|quer|work** (lak′ər wėrk′), *n.* **1** = lacquerware. **2** the making of lacquerware.

**lac|quey** (lak′ē), *n., pl.* **-queys,** *v.,* **-queyed, -quey|ing.** = lackey.

**lac|ri|mal** or **lac|ry|mal** (lak′rə məl), *adj., n.* —***adj.*** **1** = lachrymal. **2** *Anatomy.* of, having to do with, or near the glands (lacrimal glands) that secrete tears, or the ducts leading from them.

—***n.*** a vessel for tears; lachrymatory.

**lacrimal gland,** either of the two glands one above each eye, that produces tears.

**lac|ri|ma|tion** (lak′rə mā′shən), *n.* = lachrymation.

**lac|ri|ma|tor** (lak′rə mā′tər), *n.* lachrymal substance; lachrymator.

**lac|ri|ma|to|ry** or **lac|ry|ma|to|ry** (lak′rə mə tôr′ē, -tōr′-), *adj., n., pl.* **-ries.** = lachrymatory.

***la|crosse** (lə krôs′, -kros′), *n.* a game played on a field by two teams, usually of 10 players each, with a ball and long-handled rackets with a loose net at one end. The players on one team carry and pass the ball to each other trying to send the ball into the other team's goal. [American English < Canadian French *la crosse* (originally) the racket used in the game; (literally) hooked stick, cross]

***lacrosse**

**lac|ry|ma Chris|ti** (lak′rə mə kris′tē), *pl.* **lac|ry|mae Chris|ti** (lak′rə mē kris′tē). **1** a sweet or dry, white or red wine of southern Italy. **2** a dry, sparkling white wine of northern Italy.

[< New Latin *lacryma Christi* (literally) tears of Christ]

**lact-,** *combining form.* the form of **lacto-** before vowels, as in *lactase.*

**lac|ta|gogue** (lak′tə gôg, -gog), *adj., n.* = galactagogue. [< *lact-* + Greek *-agōgos* a leading]

**lact|al|bu|min** (lak′tal byü′min), *n.* the albumin found in milk. [< *lact-* + *albumin*]

**lac|tam** (lak′tam), *n. Chemistry.* any of a group of compounds containing the NH•CO group. It is a cyclic anhydride of an amino acid, produced by the elimination of water from the amino (-$NH_2$) and carboxyl (-COOH) radicals. [< *lact*(one) + *am*(ino acid)]

**lac|ta|rene** (lak′tə rēn), *n.* a preparation of the casein of milk, used as a color fixative in printing calico. [< Latin *lactārius* having to do with milk (< *lac, lactis* milk) + English *-ene*]

**lac|ta|rine** (lak′tə rin, -rēn), *n.* = lactarene.

**lac|ta|ry** (lak′tər ē), *adj.* of or having to do with milk. [< Latin *lactārius* < *lac, lactis* milk]

**lac|tase** (lak′tās), *n. Biochemistry.* an enzyme in certain yeasts and in the intestines, capable of decomposing lactose into glucose and galactose. [< *lact*(ose) + *-ase*]

**lac|tate**[1] (lak′tāt), *n. Chemistry.* a salt or ester of lactic acid. [< *lact*(ic acid) + *-ate*[2]]

**lac|tate**[2] (lak′tāt), *v.i.,* **-tat|ed, -tat|ing. 1** to secrete milk. **2** to give suck. [< Latin *lactāre* (with English *-ate*[1]) to suckle]

**lactate dehydrogenase,** an enzyme produced in animal tissue that oxidizes lactic acid and is released in increased amounts by cancerous cells. *Abbr:* LDH (no periods).

**lac|ta|tion** (lak tā′shən), *n.* **1** the secretion or formation of milk: *lactation records of cows.* **2** the time during which a mother gives milk. **3** the act of suckling a baby. [< Latin *lactāre* to suckle + English *-ation*]

**lac|ta|tion|al** (lak tā′shə nəl), *adj.* of or having to do with lactation: *a lactational physiologist.* —**lac|ta′tion|al|ly,** *adv.*

**lac|te|al** (lak′tē əl), *adj., n.* —***adj.*** **1** of milk; like milk; milky: *a lacteal secretion.* **2** carrying chyle, a milky liquid formed from digested food: *lacteal vessels.*

—***n.*** any one of the tiny lymphatic vessels that carry chyle from the small intestine to be absorbed by the blood.

[< Latin *lacteus* (< *lac, lactis* milk) + English *-al*[1]] —**lac′te|al|ly,** *adv.*

**lac|te|ous** (lak′tē əs), *adj.* = milky.

**lac|tes|cence** (lak tes′əns), *n.* **1** a milky appearance; milkiness. **2** an abundant flow of sap from a plant when wounded. The sap is commonly white, but sometimes red or yellow.

**lac|tes|cent** (lak tes′ənt), *adj.* **1** becoming milky; having a milky appearance. **2** producing or secreting milk. **3** (of plants and insects) producing a milky fluid. [< Latin *lactēscēns, -entis,* present participle of *lactēscere* become milky, be able to give milk < *lactēre* have milk or juice; suckle < *lac, lactis* milk]

**lac|tic** (lak′tik), *adj.* of milk; from milk, especially sour milk. [< Latin *lac, lactis* milk + English *-ic*]

**lactic acid,** a colorless, odorless, syrupy acid, formed by the action of lactobacilli in sour milk, the fermentation of vegetable juices, etc., and produced by muscle tissue during exercise: *Lactic acid* [*is*] *used normally in the manufacture of such essentials as leather, textiles, foods, and liquors* (Science News Letter). *Formula:* $C_3H_6O_3$

**lactic dehydrogenase,** = lactate dehydrogenase.

**lac|tide** (lak′tīd), *n. Chemistry.* **1** a compound formed by heating lactic acid, and regarded as an anhydride of that acid. **2** any of a class of similar compounds. [< *lact*(ic acid) + *-ide*]

**lac|tif|er|ous** (lak tif′ər əs), *adj.* **1** (of animals or their organs) secreting or conveying milk or a milky fluid. **2** (of plants) yielding a milky juice. [< Latin *lactifer* producing milk or juice (< *lac, lactis* milk + *ferre* to bear) + English *-ous*] —**lac|tif′er|ous|ness,** *n.*

**lac|tif|ic** (lak tif′ik), *adj.* producing milk.

**lac|tiv|o|rous** (lak tiv′ər əs), *adj.* devouring milk.

**lacto-,** *combining form.* **1** milk, as in *lactometer.* **2** lactic acid, as in *lactobacillus.* Also, **lact-** before vowels.

[< Latin *lac, lactis*]

**lac|to|ba|cil|lus** (lak′tō bə sil′əs), *n., pl.* **-cil|li** (-sil′ī). any one of a genus of aerobic bacteria that produces lactic acid with the fermentation of sugar: *It is not the acid-forming lactobacilli that cause tooth decay but another kind that attack the keratin of the teeth* (Science News Letter).

**lac|to|duct** (lak′tō dukt′), *n.* a plastic pipeline conveying milk from high mountain pastures to villages, especially in Switzerland.

**lac|to|fla|vin** (lak′tō flā′vin), *n. Biochemistry.* riboflavin.

**lac|to|gen** (lak′tə jen), *n.* a hormone that stimulates the secretion of milk.

**lac|to|gen|e|sis** (lak′tə jen′ə sis), *n.* the power of initiating milk secretion.

**lac|to|gen|ic** (lak′tə jen′ik), *adj.* stimulating the secretion and flow of milk: *lactogenic hormones.*

**lac|to|glo|bu|lin** (lak′tō glob′yə lin), *n.* the globulin found in milk.

**lac|tom|e|ter** (lak tom′ə tər), *n.* an instrument for testing the purity or richness of milk.

**lac|tone** (lak′tōn), *n. Chemistry.* any of a group of cyclic anhydrides produced by the loss of a molecule of water from the hydroxyl (-OH) and carboxyl (-COOH) radicals of hydroxy acids.

**lac|ton|ic** (lak ton′ik), *adj.* of or having to do with lactone.

**lac|to|phos|phate** (lak′tə fos′fāt), *n.* a lactate and a phosphate in combination.

**lac|to|prene** (lak′tə prēn), *n.* a synthetic rubber with high resistance to oils and heat, made from acrylate and acrylonitrile. [< *lacto-* + (iso)*prene*]

**lac|to|pro|tein** (lak′tə prō′tēn, -tē in), *n.* any protein found in milk.

**lac|to|scope** (lak′tə skōp), *n.* an instrument for testing the purity or richness of milk by its resistance to the passage of light.

**lac|tose** (lak′tōs), *n.* a crystalline sugar, present in milk; milk sugar. It is usually obtained by evaporating whey and converting it into hard, white crystals. Lactose is an isomer of common table sugar. *Formula:* $C_{12}H_{22}O_{11}$ [< French *lactose* < Latin *lac, lactis* milk + French *-ose* -ose]

**lac|to|veg|e|tar|i|an** (lak′tō vej′ə tãr′ē ən), *adj.* consisting of a diet of milk and vegetables.

**la|cu|na** (lə kyü′nə), *n., pl.* **-nae** (-nē), **-nas. 1a** an empty space; gap: *There was a lacuna in the old letter where the ink had faded.* **b** *Figurative:* [*He*] *has sought to fill, with this elegant collection of essays, a serious and regrettable lacuna in Italian* *studies* (Saturday Review). *Every teacher knows that the week before and after vacation is largely lost to study ... This means almost a month's lacuna* (New York Times). **SYN**: hiatus. **2** a tiny cavity or depression in bones or tissues. **3** space in or among the cells of an animal or plant. [< Latin *lacūna* hole, pit < *lacus, -ūs* cistern, lake. See etym. of doublet **lagoon**.]

**la|cu|nal** (lə kyü′nəl), *adj.* **1** of or having to do with a lacuna. **2** having lacunas.

*__la|cu|nar__ (lə kyü′nər), *n., pl.* **la|cu|nars, lac|u|nar-i|a** (lak′yu̇ nãr′ē ə), *adj.* **—*n.*** **1** *Architecture.* a ceiling formed of sunken compartments. **2** one of the compartments; a sunken panel.
**—*adj.*** of a lacuna or consisting of lacunae; lacunal.

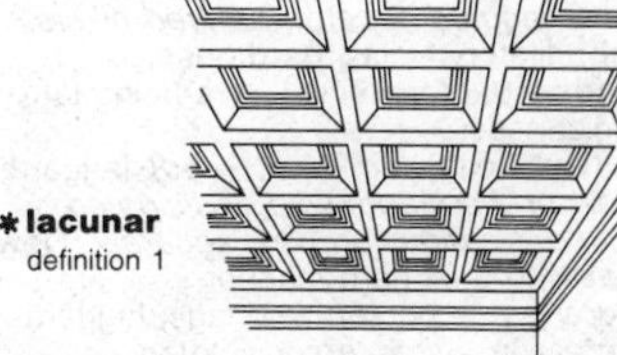
***lacunar**
definition 1

**lac|u|nar|y** (lak′yu̇ ner′ē, lə kyü′nər-), *adj.* = lacunal.

**la|cu|nate** (lə kyü′nit, lak′yu̇ nit; -nāt), *adj.* = lacunal.

**la|cune** (lə kyün′), *n.* = lacuna.

**la|cu|nose** (lə kyü′nōs), *adj.* having lacunas; pitted; furrowed.

**lac|u|nos|i|ty** (lak′yü nos′ə tē), *n.* lacunose quality.

**la|cu|nu|lose** (lə kyü′nyə lōs), *adj.* minutely pitted or furrowed.

**la|cus|tri|an** (lə kus′trē ən), *adj., n.* **—*adj.*** = lacustrine.
**—*n.*** a lake dweller.

**la|cus|trine** (lə kus′trin), *adj.* **1** of lakes: *lacustrine mire.* **2** living or growing in lakes: *lacustrine water fleas.* **3** *Geology.* of or having to do with strata that originated by deposition at the bottom of a lake: *Lacustrine plains are one of the flattest landforms extant.* [ultimately < Latin *lacus, -ūs* lake; receptacle (on analogy of *paluster, -tris* marshy; palustrine) + English *-ine*[1]]

**lac|y** (lā′sē), *adj.,* **lac|i|er, lac|i|est.** **1** of lace: *The little girl wore a lacy frock.* **2** like lace; having an open delicate pattern: *the lacy leaves of a fern.* Also, **lacey.**

**lacy glass,** glass pressed with designs of a lacy appearance, made especially in the United States in the early 1800's.

**lad** (lad), *n.* **1** a boy; youth: *The little lad was playing on the swing. ... he was then a gallant lad on the ready for new ideas* (Lillian Smith). **SYN**: stripling, youngster. **2** *Informal.* a man: *How now, old lad?* (Shakespeare). **SYN**: fellow, chap. [Middle English *ladde* boy, youth; earlier, serving man; origin uncertain]

**La|dak** (lə däk′), *n.* a variety of winter-hardy alfalfa that resists drought, but not wilt. [< *Ladakh,* a region of eastern Kashmir]

**la|dang** (lä′däng), *n.* a system of cultivation practiced by farmers in Indonesia and Malaysia, in which they clear a part of the jungle and farm it until the soil is exhausted, after which they move on to another part and repeat the process. [< Malay *ladang* dry clearing]

**lad|a|num** (lad′ə nəm), *n.* = labdanum.

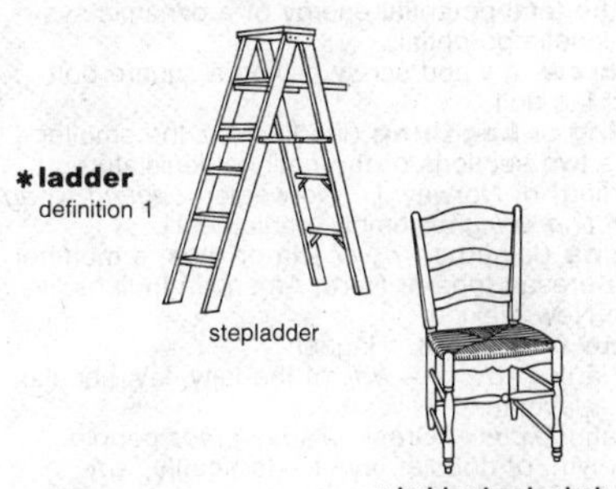
***ladder**
definition 1

stepladder

***ladder-back chair**

*__lad|der__ (lad′ər), *n., v.* **—*n.*** **1** a set of rungs or steps fastened into two long sidepieces of wood, metal, or rope, for use in climbing: *The boys climbed the rope ladder to get into their tree house.* **2** *Figurative.* a means of climbing higher: *Hard work is often a ladder to success.* **3** *Figurative: This company has an elaborate promotion ladder. The mathematician has reached the highest rung on the ladder of human thought* (Havelock Ellis). **4** a series of steps to enable fish to ascend a fall or dam by a succession of leaps; fish ladder. **5** *British.* a run in a stocking or other knitted garment, especially a silk or nylon stocking.
**—*v.i., v.t.*** *British.* to develop runs in (a knitted garment, such as a stocking) as the result of the breaking of a thread.
[Old English *hlǣder*] **—lad′der|less,** *adj.* **—lad′der|like′,** *adj.*

*__lad|der-back chair__ (lad′ər bak′), a chair having a back formed of horizontal pieces of wood between two upright pieces, such as a ladder has.

**lad|der-backed** (lad′ər bakt′), *adj.* having a back formed like the rungs of a ladder: *a ladder-backed armchair.*

**ladder-backed woodpecker,** *U.S.* a North American woodpecker having black-and-white bars on its upper parts.

**lad|dered** (lad′ərd), *adj.* **1** in regular, even sequence, resembling the steps or rungs of a ladder: *See, from the laddered shelves Shakespeare and Swift themselves speak straightly down* (Atlantic). **2** provided with a ladder or ladders.

**ladder polymer,** a polymer made up of double-stranded chains of molecules connected by hydrogen or chemical bonds at regular intervals like the rungs connecting the two sides of a ladder.

**lad|der|proof** (lad′ər prüf′), *adj. British.* resistant to runs: *ladderproof nylon stockings.*

**ladder stitch,** an embroidery stitch made with crossbars between ridges of raised work.

**ladder truck,** a fire engine equipped with extension ladders, fire hooks, and other fire-fighting apparatus.

**lad|der|y** (lad′ə rē), *adj.* resembling a ladder.

**lad|die** (lad′ē), *n. Scottish.* a lad.

**lad|dish** (lad′ish), *adj.* like a lad; boyish; juvenile. **—lad′dish|ness,** *n.*

**lade** (lād), *v.,* **lad|ed, lad|en** or **lad|ed, lad|ing.**
**—*v.t.*** **1** to put a burden on; load, especially a cargo on board (a ship): *Our ships are laden with the harvest of every climate* (Joseph Addison). **SYN**: burden, oppress. **2** to take up (liquid) with a ladle, scoop, or the like; dip: *Like one that ... chides the sea ... saying he'll lade it dry* (Shakespeare). **SYN**: scoop.
**—*v.i.*** **1** to take on a load or cargo. **2** to take up with a ladle, scoop, or the like; bail.
[Old English *hladan.* See related etym. at **last**[4].]

**lad|en**[1] (lā′dən), *adj., v.* **—*adj.*** loaded, burdened, or weighed down: *The laden ship lay low in the water. The laden boughs for you alone shall bear* (John Dryden).
**—*v.*** a past participle of **lade:** *The camels were laden with bundles of silk and rice.*

**lad|en**[2] (lā′dən), *v.t.* to lade; load.

**la-di-da** (lä′dē dä′), *adj., n., v.* **-daed, -da|ing,** *interj. Slang.* **—*adj.*** languidly genteel in speech or manner; affected; pretentious: *What can old Pratt be thinking of, publishing a la-di-da book about men's clothes?* (New Yorker).
**—*n.*** an affected person; fop.
**—*v.i.*** to be snobbish or pretentious.
**—*interj.*** an exclamation ridiculing snobbish or pretentious speech or manners.

**la-di-dah** (lä′dē dä′), *adj., n., v.i.,* **-dahed, -dah-ing,** *interj.* = la-di-da.

**la|dies auxiliary** (lā′dēz), *U.S.* a women's organization associated with a men's club, a fire department, or similar group.

**ladies chain,** a square-dancing figure or call in which the women join hands as they cross over to the men.

**ladies' day,** *U.S.* a day on which a special privilege, such as reduced theater prices or free admission to a sporting event, is given to women.

**ladies' man,** = lady's man.

**ladies' room,** *U.S.* a public lavatory for women.

**ladies' tresses,** = lady's-tresses.

**la|di|fy** (lā′dē fī), *v.t.,* **-fied, -fy|ing.** = ladyfy.

**La|dik** (lä dēk′), *n.* a finely textured Turkish rug woven in or near the town of Ladik, Turkey.

**La|din** (lə dēn′), *n.* **1** a Rhaeto-Romanic dialect spoken in parts of Switzerland and Tyrol, closely related to Romansh. **2** any Rhaeto-Romanic dialect, such as Romansh. **3** one of the people of Switzerland and the Tyrol who speak Ladin. [< Rhaeto-Romanic *Ladin* < Latin *Latīnus* Latin]

**lad|ing** (lā′ding), *n.* **1** the act of loading. **2** load; freight; cargo: *bill of lading.*

**La|di|no** (lə dē′nō), *n., pl.* **-nos.** **1** Also, **ladino.** In Spanish America: **a** a mestizo. **b** a mestizo or other native who adopts Western ways of living. **2** Also, **ladino.** = Ladino clover. **3** the ancient Spanish or Castilian language. **4** a Spanish dialect with Hebrew elements, spoken in Turkey and elsewhere by descendants of Spanish and Portuguese Jews; Judeo-Spanish. [< Spanish *Ladino* (literally) Latin < Latin *Latīnus* Latin]

**Ladino** or **ladino clover,** a variety of giant white clover valuable as a forage crop.

**la|dle** (lā′dəl), *n., v.,* **-dled, -dling.** **—*n.*** a large cup-shaped spoon with a long handle, for dipping out liquids: *We filled our cups with punch from a ladle in the bowl.*
**—*v.t.*** **1** to dip: *Mother ladled out the soup.* **2** to carry in a ladle.
[Old English *hlædel* < *hladan* lade] **—la′dler,** *n.*

**ladle car,** a car into which molten iron is poured from a furnace.

**la|dle|ful** (lā′dəl fu̇l), *n., pl.* **-fuls.** the amount that a ladle holds.

**la dol|ce vi|ta** (lä dōl′chā vē′tä), *Italian.* the sweet life; dolce vita: *Existentialism ... presents an escape from the morass of conformity, la dolce vita, boredom* (Harper's).

**la|drone** (lə drōn′), *n.* (in Spain or Spanish America) a robber; highwayman. [< Spanish *ladrón* < Latin *latrō, -ōnis* bandit; (originally) hired servant]

**la|dy** (lā′dē), *n., pl.* **-dies,** *adj.* **—*n.*** **1a** a woman of good family and high social position: *Here lies a lady of beauty and high degree* (John Crowe Ransom). **SYN**: gentlewoman. See syn. under **woman.** **b** a woman who is looked up to because she has good taste and pleasant manners; well-bred woman: *A lady is polite and courteous to everyone.* **2** a polite term for any woman: *"Ladies" is often used in speaking or writing to a group of women. I stood in front of ... my hostess a married lady* (Holiday). **3** a noblewoman; woman who has the title of Lady: *She is the daughter of an earl, a lady by birth.* **4** a woman who has the rights or authority of a lord; mistress of a household. **5** a woman whom a man loves or is devoted to: *My lady sweet, arise!* (Shakespeare). **SYN**: sweetheart. **6** a wife: *By a former marriage, Mr. Henry Dashwood had one son; by his present lady, three daughters* (Jane Austen). **SYN**: spouse. **7** the bony structure in a lobster's stomach that grinds its food.
**—*adj.*** **1** woman; female: *a lady reporter.* **2** of or having to do with a lady; ladylike.
[Old English *hlǣfdīge* (literally) one who kneads a loaf of bread. See related etym. at **lord.**]
▶ **Lady** is often used in everyday speech to refer to any woman, no matter what her social position or background: *lady cabdriver, lady clerk. "I'm your dustman, lady, come to wish you a Happy New Year"* (Sunday Times). In many cases *woman,* as in *cleaning woman,* might be more appropriate, though *saleslady* and *landlady* are well established. And generally among many women *lady* as a term differentiating job, duty, or office by sex is a complete anathema.

**La|dy** (lā′dē), *n., pl.* **-dies.** a title in speaking to or of women of certain ranks in Great Britain, as: **a** a marchioness, countess, viscountess, or baroness. **b** the daughter of a duke, marquis, or earl. **c** the wife of a man with a courtesy title of Lord. **d** the wife of a baronet or knight.
**Our Lady,** a title of the Virgin Mary: *Low on her knees herself she cast, Before Our Lady murmur'd she* (Tennyson).

**Lady Am|herst's pheasant** (am′ərss), a brightly colored pheasant, native to parts of China and Tibet. [< *Lady Amherst,* a British noblewoman of the 1800's]

**lady apple,** a small, delicate, red, or red and yellow, variety of apple, valued chiefly for its waxy-looking ornamental appearance.

**Lady Baltimore cake,** a white cake of three layers, having a flavored icing which contains chopped figs, nuts, and raisins.

**lady beetle,** = ladybug.

**la|dy|bird** (lā′dē bėrd′), *n.* = ladybug. [< earlier genitive case of (Our) *Lady* + *bird*]

**ladybird beetle,** = ladybug.

**Lady Bountiful,** a kind and gracious, usually well-to-do, woman. [< *Lady Bountiful,* a character in George Farquhar's play *The Beaux' Stratagem*]

**la|dy|bug** (lā′dē bug′), *n.* a small, reddish or yellow beetle that has a rounded back with black or colored spots. Many ladybugs eat certain insects, such as aphids and scale insects, that are harmful to fruit and other crops. See picture under **beetle**[1].

**lady chair,** a kind of seat for a third person, formed by two persons holding each other's hands crossed.

**Lady Chapel** or **chapel,** a chapel dedicated to the Virgin Mary, generally placed behind the high altar in a cathedral or large church.

**lady crab,** any of various crabs, especially a species common on the Atlantic coast of the United States; calico crab.

**lady cracker,** a small firecracker.

**Lady Day,** **1** = Annunciation Day. **2** (formerly)

**Pronunciation Key:** hat, āge, cãre, fär; let, ēqual, tėrm; it, īce; hot, ōpen, ôrder; oil, out; cup, pu̇t, rüle; child; long; thin; ᴛʜen; zh, measure;
ə represents **a** in about, **e** in taken, **i** in pencil, **o** in lemon, **u** in circus.

any festival day honoring the Virgin Mary.
**lady fern**, a fern similar to the spleenwort but having curved spore cases.
**la|dy|fin|ger** (lā′dē fing′gər), *n.* a small sponge cake shaped somewhat like a finger. Also, **lady's-finger**.
**la|dy|fish** (lā′dē fish′), *n., pl.* **-fish|es** or (*collectively*) **-fish**. any one of various small marine game fishes found in the tropical regions of the Atlantic and Pacific Oceans.
**lady friend**, **1** a woman friend or companion. **2** a man's sweetheart; girl friend.
**la|dy|fy** (lā′dē fī), *v.t.,* **-fied, -fy|ing.** to make a lady of; give the title "Lady" to. Also, **ladify**.
**la|dy|hood** (lā′dē hůd), *n.* **1** the condition or character of a lady. **2** ladies as a group.
**lady in waiting**, or **la|dy-in-wait|ing** (lā′dē in-wā′ting), *pl.* **ladies in waiting, la|dies-in-wait|ing.** a lady of the royal household who accompanies or serves a queen or princess.
**la|dy|ish** (lā′dē ish), *adj.* like a lady; having a ladylike quality or character. —**la′dy|ish|ly**, *adv.* —**la′dy|ish|ness**, *n.*
**la|dy-kill|er** (lā′dē kil′ər), *n. Slang.* a man whom women are supposed to find captivating or irresistible.
**la|dy-kill|ing** (lā′dē kil′ing), *n., adj. Slang.* —***n.*** the acts or arts of a lady-killer.
—***adj.*** of or having to do with a lady-killer.
**la|dy|kin** (lā′dē kin), *n.* a little lady.
**la|dy|less** (lā′dē lis), *adj.* without a lady or ladies; unaccompanied by a lady.
**la|dy|like** (lā′dē līk′), *adj.* **1** like a lady; polite and courteous: *a refined, ladylike young woman.* **SYN**: well-bred. **2a** suitable for a lady: *ladylike manners.* **b** effeminate: *fops at all corners, ladylike in mien* (William Cowper). —**la′dy|like′ness**, *n.*
**la|dy|love** (lā′dē luv′), *n.* a woman who is loved by a man; sweetheart.
**lady luck**, chance; good fortune: ... *the large gambling casinos where adventurers have wooed lady luck for generations* (New York Times).
**lady mayoress**, *British.* the wife of a lord mayor.
**lady of the bedchamber**, *British.* a companion or personal attendant upon the queen, not a servant.
**lady of the evening**, = prostitute.
**lady of the house**, the woman who is head of the household: *The salesman asked to speak to the lady of the house.*
**Lady of the Lake**, = Vivian.
**Lady of the Snows, Our**, Canada: *'For we be also a people,' Said our Lady of the Snows* (Rudyard Kipling).
**lady's bedstraw**, a small plant with clusters of white flowers, and fragrant stems and leaves; bedstraw.
**lady's delight**, the common pansy; wild pansy.
**la|dy's-ear|drop** (lā′dēz ir′drop′), *n.* any of various plants with drooping racemes or flowers that suggest eardrops, such as the fuchsia.
**la|dy's-fin|ger** (lā′dēz fing′gər), *n.* = ladyfinger.
**lady's glove**, = foxglove.
**la|dy|ship** (lā′dē ship), *n.* the rank or position of a lady.
**La|dy|ship** (lā′dē ship), *n. British.* a title used in speaking to or of a woman having the rank of Lady: *"Your Ladyship."*
**la|dy-slip|per** (lā′dē slip′ər), *n.* = lady's-slipper.
**lady's maid**, a woman servant who attends a lady in dressing.
**lady's man**, a man who is devoted to the society of women and diligent in his attention to them. Also, **ladies' man**.
**la|dy's-man|tle** (lā′dēz man′təl), *n.* a perennial herb of the rose family. It is an Old-World plant formerly used in medicine as an astringent.
**la|dy-smock** (lā′dē smok′), *n.* = lady's-smock.
**la|dy's-slip|per** (lā′dēz slip′ər), *n.* **1** a wild orchid whose flower looks somewhat like a slipper; moccasin flower. It has a pouch-shaped lip and is terrestrial, growing in temperate regions. **2** any one of various related plants bearing similar flowers, especially a tropical species cultivated in greenhouses.
**la|dy's-smock** (lā′dēz smok′), *n.* = cuckooflower.
**la|dy's-thumb** (lā′dēz thum′), *n.* a common smartweed whose oblong spike suggests a thumb.
**la|dy's-tress|es** (lā′dēz tres′iz), *n.* any one of various low terrestrial orchids, bearing spikes of small, spirally arranged flowers. Also, **ladies' tresses**.
**Laën|nec's cirrhosis** (lā neks′), cirrhosis of the liver. [< René T. H. *Laënnec,* 1781-1826, a French physician]
**La|er|tes** (lā ėr′tēz), *n.* **1** *Greek Legend.* the father of Odysseus. **2** the son of Polonius and brother of Ophelia in Shakespeare's play *Hamlet.*
**Laes|try|go|ni|an** (les′trə gō′nē ən), *n.* a cannibal giant who was one of a mythical race that slew many of Odysseus's companions in Homer's *Odyssey.* Also, **Lestrigonian**.
**Lae|ta|re Sunday** (lē tãr′ē), the fourth and middle Sunday in Lent celebrated in the Roman Catholic Church and named after the beginning of the introit for the day, "Laetare Jerusalem," from Isaiah 66:10. [< Latin *laetāre* be joyful!]
**La|e|trile** (lā′ə tril), *n. Trademark.* a drug extracted from apricot pits and related to amygdalin, widely administered to treat cancer and believed by many to help prevent cancer: *Laetrile ... is not only banned in Canada and the United States but denounced by the Canadian Medical Association as "a cruel fraud"* (Maclean's). *Formula:* $C_{14}H_{15}NO_7$
**laevo-**, *combining form.* a variant of **levo-**, as in *laevorotatory.*
**lae|vo|ro|ta|to|ry** (lē′vō rō′tə tôr′ē, -tōr′-), *adj.* = levorotatory.
**la|fa|yette** (laf′ē et′, lä′fē-), *n.* **1** a small edible fish with spiny fins, living in the waters of the eastern coast of the United States. **2** an oval-shaped fish with a deeply split tail and unelevated fins, abundant along the eastern coast of America. [American English < Marquis de *Lafayette,* 1757-1834, a French general who aided the American Revolution]
**l'af|faire** (là fer′), *n. French.* the affair, especially a political scandal or intrigue: *Since the days of the Dreyfus case, one of the perennial features of French government has been 'l'affaire'—that unique combination of intrigue, scandal and politics that seems to come along at times of great political unrest* (Time).
**La Fleche** (là flesh′), any one of a French breed of chicken with a long body, solid black plumage, and white ear lobes. [< *La Flèche,* a commune in northwestern France]
**LAFTA** (no periods), Latin American Free Trade Association.
**lag**[1] (lag), *v.,* **lagged, lag|ging,** *n., adj.* —***v.i.*** **1** to move too slowly; fall behind: *The child lagged because he was tired.* **SYN**: dawdle, delay, tarry. See syn. under **linger**. **2** to become weaker; flag: *Interest lagged as the speaker droned on.* **3** to toss a marble at a line on the ground to fix the order of shooting in the game of marbles. **4** *Billiards.* to string. —***v.t.*** **1** to cause to lag. **2** *Physics.* (of an electric current) to fall behind (the voltage) in speed of response to alternations. **3** *Economic Statistics.* to follow changes in another variable by a regular interval: *Changes in employment tend to lag changes in wholesale prices.*
—***n.*** **1** the act or fact of lagging; falling behind: *There was a long lag in forwarding mail to us while we were on vacation.* **2a** the amount by which a person or thing falls behind: *There was a month's lag between the order for our car and its delivery.* **b** *Physics.* the retardation, or amount of retardation, in any current or movement. **3** the last or hindmost one (in a race, game, sequence of any kind): *What makes my ram the lag of all the flock?* (Alexander Pope).
—***adj.*** **1** last; hindmost: *The lag end of my life* (Shakespeare). **2** tardy; slow: *An' faith! thou's neither lag nor lame* (Robert Burns).
[origin unknown]
**lag**[2] (lag), *n., v.,* **lagged, lag|ging.** —***n.*** **1** one of the staves or strips that support the cylindrical surfaces of a wooden drum, the casing of a boiler, or the cylinder of a carding machine. **2** a barrel stave.
—***v.t.*** to cover (a boiler or steam pipe) with staves or insulating material. [apparently < Scandinavian (compare Old Icelandic *lögg* barrel rim, Swedish *lagg* stave)]
**lag**[3] (lag), *v.,* **lagged, lag|ging,** *n. Slang.* —***v.t.*** **1** to transport (a convict); send to penal servitude. **2** to arrest.
—***n.*** **1** a convict. **2** a term of transportation or penal servitude.
[origin unknown]
**lag|an** (lag′ən), *n.* goods or wreckage sunk in the sea, but attached to a buoy in order that they may be recovered: *Sir Robert can pick up whenever he likes all the jetsam, flotsam, and lagan that may be washed ashore along this coast* (Manchester Guardian Weekly). Also, **ligan**. [< Old French *lagan,* perhaps < Scandinavian (compare Old Icelandic *lagnir,* plural of *lögn* net laid in the sea)]
**Lag Ba'O|mer** (läg bō′mər), a Jewish holiday, the 18th of Iyar, when the restrictions on weddings and other celebrations in force between Passover and Shabuoth are lifted. Lag Ba'Omer commemorates the end of a plague among students of Rabbi Akiba in Palestine during the 100's C.E. [< Hebrew *lag* 33 (< the numerical value of *l* 30 and *g* 3) + *bə* in + *'Omer* the 49 days from Passover to Shabuoth]
**lag bolt**, = lag screw.
**lag|end** (lag′ənd), *n.* = lagan.
**la|ger**[1] (lä′gər), *n., v.,* —***n.*** = lager beer.
—***v.t.*** to ferment and store (beer) to make it a lager. [American English, short for *lager beer,* half-translation of German *Lagerbier* < *Lager* storehouse + *Bier* beer]
**la|ger**[2] (lä′gər), *n., v.* = laager.
**lager beer**, a beer with a light body that is slowly fermented at a low temperature and stored from six weeks to six months before being used; lager.
**lag fault**, *Geology.* a fault caused by one layer of rock being moved more slowly than another layer of rock.
**lag|gard** (lag′ərd), *n., adj.* —***n.*** a person or thing that moves too slowly or falls behind; loiterer: *Here comes a laggard hanging down his head, Who seems no bolder than a beaten hound* (Tennyson). *Housing is a laggard in the current business recovery* (Wall Street Journal). **SYN**: lingerer, dawdler, lagger. —***adj.*** falling behind; slow; backward: *the laggard pace of the tired hikers.* **SYN**: sluggish, dilatory. —**lag′gard|ness**, *n.*
**lag|gard|li|ness** (lag′ərd lē nis), *n.* a being laggardly; sluggishness.
**lag|gard|ly** (lag′ərd lē), *adj., adv.* —***adj.*** laggard; sluggish: *Few of the actors who participated could sing, and the direction was laggardly* (New Yorker). —***adv.*** in a laggard manner.
**lag|ger**[1] (lag′ər), *n.* a person who lags; laggard.
**lag|ger**[2] (lag′ər), *n. Slang.* a convict; lag.
**lag|ging** (lag′ing), *n.* **1** a lag for a boiler or steam pipe. **2** the act of lagging a boiler or steam pipe. **3** *Architecture.* the narrow cross strips in the centering of an arch.
**lag line**, the line in marble games drawn on the ground toward which the players toss marbles to fix the order of shooting.
**la|gniappe** or **la|gnappe** (lan yap′, lan′yap), *n. U.S.* **1** something given to a customer with a purchase; an extra attraction; prize; bonus: *Dealers have competed fiercely for customers. Some, for example, proposed vacation trips as lagniappe for coy buyers* (Atlantic). **2** a gratuity; tip. [American English < Haitian Creole *lagniappe* < American Spanish *la ñapa,* or *la yapa* the gift < Quechua *yapa* something given into the bargain, an extra]
**lag|o|morph** (lag′ə môrf), *n.* any one of an order of mammals consisting of the rabbits and hares and the pikas. They are similar to rodents, but have two pairs of upper incisor teeth, the second pair, just behind the first, being smaller, and short tails. [< New Latin *Lagomorpha* < Greek *lagôs* hare < *morphē* form, shape]
**lag|o|mor|phic** (lag′ə môr′fik), *adj.* having the form or structure of a lagomorph.
**la|goon** (lə gün′), *n.* **1** a pond or small lake connected with a larger body of water. **2** shallow water separated from the sea by low ridges of sand. A lagoon has salt or brackish water. **3** the water within a ring-shaped coral island. See picture under **bay**[1]. **4** a natural or artificial pond for sewage disposal: *First, the effluent will go into aeration lagoons for biological treatment by bacteria. Then it will go into storage lagoons capable of holding the effluent during the non-irrigation season* (Science News). Also, **lagune**. [< French *lagune* (< Italian) or < Italian *laguna* < Latin *lacūna* pond, hole. See etym. of doublet **lacuna**.]
**la|goon|al** (la gü′nəl), *adj.* of or having to do with a lagoon: *lagoonal areas, lagoonal deposits.*
**La|grang|i|an** (lə gran′jē ən, -grän′-), *adj., n.* —***adj.*** of or having to do with Joseph Louis Lagrange (1736-1813), a French mathematician and astronomer. —***n.*** = Lagrangian function.
**Lagrangian function**, *Physics.* a function equal to the difference between the total kinetic energy and the total potential energy of a dynamic system; kinetic potential.
**lag screw**, a wood screw having a square bolthead; lag bolt.
**Lag|ting** or **Lag|thing** (läg′ting), *n.* the smaller of the two sections of the national legislature (Storting) of Norway. [< Norwegian *Lagting* < *lag* law + *ting, thing* assembly, parliament]
**La|gu|na** (lə gü′nə), *n., pl.* **-na** or **-nas**. a member of a Keresan tribe of North American Indians living in New Mexico.
**la|gune** (lə gün′), *n.* = lagoon.
**la|ic** (lā′ik), *adj., n.* —***adj.*** of the laity; lay; secular. —***n.*** = layman.
[< Latin *lāicus* < Greek *lāïkós* < *lāós* people. See etym. of doublet **lay**[3].] —**la′i|cal|ly**, *adv.*
**la|i|cal** (lā′ə kəl), *adj.* = laic.
**la|i|cism** (lā′ə siz əm), *n.* **1** the power or influence of the laity, especially in politics. **2** the removal of religious influence, especially from political affairs; secularization.
**la|ic|i|ty** (lā is′ə tē), *n., pl.* **-ties**. the rule or influence of the laity.
**la|i|ci|za|tion** (lā′ə sə zā′shən), *n.* a removal from clerical influence or control.
**la|i|cize** (lā′ə sīz), *v.t.,* **-cized, -ciz|ing.** to secularize.
**laid** (lād), *v.* the past tense and past participle of

lay[1]: *He laid down the heavy bundle. Those eggs were laid this morning.*

**laid-back** or **laid|back** (lād′bak′), *adj. Slang.* relaxed; listless; sluggish: *Yates' tenacity in a fight might come as a surprise to those whose judgment is based on his apparent laid-back manner* (Chicago Sun Times). *What's Muscle Shoals like? It's in the country; it's very laid-back* (Rolling Stone).

**laid paper**, paper with a ribbed or lined appearance, from the watermark made by raised parallel wires in the mold.

**laigh** (lāʜ), *adj., adv., n. Scottish.* low[1].

**lain** (lān), *v.* the past participle of **lie**[2]: *The snow has lain on the ground for a week.*

**lair**[1] (lãr), *n., v.* —*n.* **1** the den or resting place of a wild animal: *to rouse the lion from his lair.* **SYN**: shelter, retreat. **2** *Figurative.* a secret or secluded retreat; hideaway: *a pirate's lair.* **3** a place to lie in; bed; couch: *Rising ... he summoned his companions from their warm lairs* (James Fenimore Cooper). **4** *British.* a pen or shelter for cattle.
—*v.i.* to go to or rest in a lair.
[Old English *leger* act or place of lying down, related to *licgan* to lie[2]]

**lair**[2] (lãr), *v.i.* to stick or sink in a mire or bog. [< Scandinavian (compare Old Icelandic *leir* clay, mud)]

**lair|age** (lãr′ij), *n. British.* **1** the placing of cattle in lairs. **2** the space or a place for lairing cattle.

**laird** (lãrd), *n. Scottish.* the owner of land, in ancient times limited to those who held grants immediately from the king. [variant of *lord*]

**laird|ly** (lãrd′lē), *adj.* having the rank or quality of lairds.

**lais|ser-al|ler** (le sā′á lā′), *n. French.* lack of restraint; ease.

**lais|sez faire** or **lais|ser faire** (les′ā fãr′), **1** the principle that trade, business, industry, etc., should operate with a minimum of regulation and interference by government: *After 1945, Belgium stood for laissez faire and orthodox economics, while Holland seemed a model Keynesian economy* (Economist). **2** the principle of letting people do as they please: *Not everyone is sufficiently inner-directed to enjoy laissez faire.* [< French *laissez faire* allow to do (as one pleases)]

**lais|sez-faire** or **lais|ser-faire** (les′ā fãr′), *adj.* of or based on laissez faire; not interfering: *Currency reform and the laissez-faire economic policy adopted by Konrad Adenauer's businessman Government gave Germans a driving incentive to rebuild their factories, buy new machinery on credit, and go without to make the monthly interest payments* (Time).

**lais|sez pas|ser** or **lais|ser pas|ser** (le sā′ pä-sā′), a permit; pass. [< French *laissez passer* allow to pass]

**lai|tance** (lā′təns), *n.* a layer of milky water droplets formed on the upper surface of freshly laid concrete, usually as a result of using too much water in the mixture. [< French *laitance* < *lait* milk (< Latin *lac, lactis*) + *-ance* -ance]

**la|i|ty** (lā′ə tē), *n., pl.* **-ties.** people who are not members of the clergy or of a professional class; laymen collectively: *Doctors use many words that the laity do not understand.*

**La|ius** (lā′əs), *n. Greek Legend.* the king of Thebes and father of Oedipus.

**lak|a|toi** (lak′ə toi), *n.* a sailing boat of New Guinea, made of several dugout canoes with sails shaped like crab claws. [< Papuan *lakatoi*]

**lake**[1] (lāk), *n.* **1a** a body of water entirely or nearly surrounded by land. A lake usually consists of fresh water and is larger than a pond. *Lakes differ from ponds chiefly in size, but this carries with it profound changes in all the principal factors of environment—light, temperature, and dissolved gases, with their effect upon nutrition* (A. Franklin Shull). **b** a wide place in a river. **2** *Figurative.* a pool of liquid: *a lake of oil.* [partly Old English *lacu* < Latin *lacus, -ūs* pond, tank, lake; partly < Old French *lac*, learned borrowing < Latin *lacus, -ūs*]

**lake**[2] (lāk), *n., v.,* **laked, lak|ing.** —*n.* **1** a deep-red or purplish-red coloring matter, obtained from lac or cochineal. **2** an insoluble colored compound formed by combining animal, vegetable, or coal tar coloring matter and metallic salts: *madder lake.*
—*v.t.* to make (blood) lake-colored by diffusion of the hemoglobin in the plasma. —*v.i.* to cause blood to become lake-colored by this means.
[variant of *lac*[1]. See related etym. at **lacquer, shellac.**]

**lake basin**, **1** a depression for a lake. **2** the area drained by the streams that empty into a lake.

**Lake District** or **Country**, a region of beautiful mountains and lakes in northwestern England, associated with William Wordsworth, Samuel Taylor Coleridge, Robert Southey, and other English poets.

**lake dweller**, a person living in a lake dwelling, especially in prehistoric times.

**lake dwelling**, a house built, especially in prehistoric times, on piles driven into a lake or along the shore of a lake: *Remains from the Swiss lake dwellings afford positive evidence that flax was domesticated and its fibers used in weaving* (Beals and Hoijer).

**lake|front** (lāk′frunt′), *n.* the area bordering on a lake: *... a great exposition and convention hall on the Chicago lakefront* (Wall Street Journal).

**lake|head** (lāk′hed′), *n.* the area of a lake nearest its source.

**lake herring**, = cisco.

**lake|land terrier** (lāk′lənd), a terrier with a narrow body, long head, and beard, weighing 15 to 17 pounds. The breed was developed in England for hunting the fox and otter. [< *Lakeland* the Lake District]

**lake|like** (lāk′līk′), *adj.* resembling a lake: *the lakelike glisten of desert sands.*

**La|ken|vel|der** (lä′kən vel′dər), *n.* any of a breed of chicken with black-and-white plumage and white-shelled eggs. It was developed in Germany.

**Lake poets**, William Wordsworth, Samuel Taylor Coleridge, Robert Southey, and other English poets who lived in the Lake District; Laker.

**lak|er** (lā′kər), *n.* **1** a fish living in or taken from a lake, especially a lake trout. **2** a ship or freighter on a lake, especially the Great Lakes: *Giant lakers, previously land-locked on the Great Lakes, can now navigate right down to the Gulf of St. Lawrence* (Maclean's). **3** a person accustomed to living, working, or sailing on a lake.

**Lak|er** (lā′kər), *n.* one of the Lake poets: *The Lakers all ... first despised, and then patronised Walter Scott* (Edward FitzGerald).

**lake salmon**, **1** = lake trout. **2** a landlocked salmon.

**Lake School**, the Lake poets of England and their followers.

**lake|shore** (lāk′shôr′), *n.* = lakeside.

**lake|side** (lāk′sīd′), *n.* the margin or shore of a lake: *the willows and alders by the lakeside.*

**lake sturgeon**, a sturgeon of the Great Lakes and Mississippi Valley waters that reaches a weight of 300 pounds and a length of eight feet; rock sturgeon.

**lake trout**, a large, dark trout with gray or yellowish spots, of the lakes of North America; namaycush.

**lake|ward** (lāk′wərd), *adv., adj.* toward the lake: *Most of the cottages faced lakeward.*

**lakh** (lak), *n., adj.* —*n.* in India: **1** a unit of 100,000, especially a unit of money equivalent to 100,000 rupees. **2** any large number; great amount. —*adj.* 100,000. Also, **lac.** [< Hindustani *lākh* < Sanskrit *lakṣha* 100,000]

**la|kin** (lā′kin), *n. Obsolete.* ladykin (only in *by our lakin,* a form of *by Our Lady*). [< *la*(dy)*kin*]

**La|ko|da** (lə kō′də), *n.* a glossy, amber-colored seal fur obtained from an Alaskan fur seal. [< the name of an area on the Pribilof Islands in the Bering Sea]

**La|ko|ta** (lə kō′tə), *n., pl.* **-ta** or **-tas.** = Dakota.

**Lak|shmi** (luk′shmē), *n.* the Hindu goddess of prosperity and light, wife of Vishnu.

**lak|y** (lā′kē), *adj.* of or like the color of lake; purplish-red. [< *lak*(e)[2] + *-y*[1]]

**la|lang** (lä′läng), *n.* a long, coarse East Indian grass of the jungle. [< Malay *lalang*]

**La|lique glass** (lə lēk′), an ornamental glass decorated in relief with figures or flowers. [< René *Lalique*, 1860-1945, a French designer of glassware and jewelry]

**Lal|lan** (lal′ən), *n., adj. Scottish.* Lowland.

**Lal|lans** (lal′ənz), *n.* the Lowland Scottish dialect; Lowlands: [*He*] *is a solid intelligent Scottish poet who writes partly in English, partly in Lallans* (Observer).

**lal|la|tion** (la lā′shən), *n.* the pronunciation of *r* like *l*, as in *velly* for *very.* [< Latin *lallāre* sing a lullaby + English *-ation*]

**Lal|ly column** (lal′ē), *Trademark.* a steel column filled with concrete: *The adjustment of the houses—a simple shift of stresses on existing uprights and the installation of a Lally column in the center of the dining room—can be accomplished in less than a week* (New Yorker).

**lal|ly|gag** (lal′ē gag), *v.i.,* **-gagged, -gag|ging.** *U.S. Slang.* lollygag: *He was in high spirits after weeks of fishing and lallygagging in Florida ...* (Sports Illustrated).

**lam**[1] (lam), *n., v.,* **lammed, lam|ming.** *Slang.* —*n.* a hurried escape, as from the scene of a crime.
—*v.i.* to escape, especially from an officer of the law; run away; flee.
**on the lam,** in flight; escaping: *When he* [*a bear*] *is on the lam, he can make good time through thickets almost impenetrable to dogs* (Newsweek).
**take it on the lam,** to flee hurriedly; escape: *The heat was on and Antony took it on the lam* (Punch).
[origin uncertain, perhaps < *lam*[2]]

**lam**[2] (lam), *v.t., v.i.,* **lammed, lam|ming.** *Informal.* to beat soundly; thrash; whack: *I bet you I'll lam Sid for that. I'll learn him!* (Mark Twain). [probably < Scandinavian (compare Old Icelandic *lemja* thrash)]

**Lam.,** **1** Lamentations (book of the Old Testament). **2** *Botany.* Lamarck.

**la|ma** (lä′mə), *n.* a Buddhist priest or monk in Tibet and Mongolia. [< Tibetan *blama*]

**La|ma|ism** (lä′mə iz əm), *n.* the religious system of the lamas in Mongolia and in Tibet. It is a form of Mahayana Buddhism and possesses a widespread monastic system and a hierarchical organization headed by the Dalai Lama.

**La|ma|ist** (lä′mə ist), *n., adj.* —*n.* a believer in Lamaism. —*adj.* = Lamaistic.

**La|ma|is|tic** (lä′mə is′tik), *adj.* **1** characteristic of a Lamaist. **2** of or having to do with Lamaism: *the Lamaistic form of Buddhism.*

**La|man|ite** (lā′mə nīt), *n.* one of the ancient Hebrew ancestors of the American Indians according to the Book of Mormon. [< *Laman*, son of Lehi, a Hebrew prophet who supposedly led a group of people to America in the 600's B.C.]

**La|marck|i|an** (lə mär′kē ən), *adj., n.* —*adj.* of the French biologist Jean de Lamarck or Lamarckism. —*n.* person who supports Lamarckism.

**La|marck|i|an|ism** (lə mär′kē ə niz əm), *n.* = Lamarckism.

**La|marck|ism** (lə mär′kiz əm), *n.* the theory of organic evolution proposed by Jean de Lamarck (1744-1829). Lamarckism states that characteristics acquired from the environment by parents tend to be inherited by their descendants.

**la|ma|ser|y** (lä′mə ser′ē), *n., pl.* **-ser|ies.** a monastery of lamas in Mongolia and Tibet. [< French *lamaserie*, apparently < *lama* lama + Persian *serāi*, or *sarāi* inn. Compare etym. under **caravansary.**]

**La|maze** (lə māz′), *adj.* of or having to do with a widely used form of natural childbirth developed in the 1950's by Fernand Lamaze, a French obstetrician: *The method is known as "psychoprophylaxis," or more commonly the Lamaze Method of "natural" childbirth ...* (Sally Olds and Linda Witt).

***lamb** (lam), *n., v.* —*n.* **1** a young sheep: *Mary had a little lamb.* **2** meat from a lamb: *roast lamb.* **3** = lambskin. **4** *Figurative.* a young, innocent, or dear person: *The widow she cried over me and called me a poor lost lamb* (Mark Twain). **5** *Slang, Figurative.* **a** a person who is easily cheated. **b** an inexperienced speculator. **6** *Informal.* = Persian lamb.
—*v.i.* to give birth to a lamb or lambs: *Lambing is always hazardous and is made more difficult by the uncertainty of the weather* (Manchester Guardian Weekly).
—*v.t.* to attend (ewes) which are lambing.
**like a lamb, a** meekly; timidly: *He accepted his defeat like a lamb.* **b** easily fooled: *He was like a lamb in the hands of the swindlers, and they fleeced him of all his savings.*
**the Lamb,** Jesus Christ (in the Bible, John 1:29, 36). *So shows my soul before the Lamb, My spirit before Thee* (Tennyson).
[Old English *lamb*]

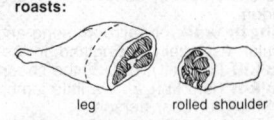

roasts:

leg rolled shoulder

chops:

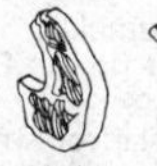
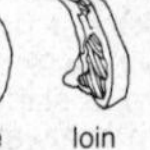
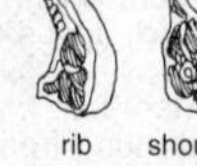

***lamb**
definition 2

blade loin rib shoulder

**lam|bast** (lam bast′), *v.t. Informal.* lambaste.

**lam|baste** (lam bāst′), *v.t.,* **-bast|ed, -bast|ing.** *Informal.* **1** to strike again and again; beat severely; thrash: *The Queen and husband Philip spent the night at Government House, watched the traditional ... drummers lambasting their three-foot drums with ferocious, stout-filled glee* (Time). **2** to scold roughly; denounce violently; condemn: *Apparently the American people expect that in a campaign the two contending parties will lambaste each other unmercifully* (Wall Street Journal). **SYN**: excoriate, revile, score. **3** *Nautical.* to beat with the end of a rope. [perhaps < *lam*[2] + *baste*[3]]

**Pronunciation Key:** hat, āge, cãre, fär; let, ēqual, tėrm; it, īce; hot, ōpen, ôrder; **oi**l, **ou**t; cup, pu̇t, rüle; **ch**ild; lo**ng**; **th**in; ᴛʜen; **zh**, measure; **ə** represents **a** in about, **e** in taken, **i** in pencil, **o** in lemon, **u** in circus.

**✱lamb|da** (lam′də), *n.* the 11th letter of the Greek alphabet. [< Greek *lámbda*]

**✱lambda** Λ capital letter; λ lower-case letter

**lambda particle**, a heavy elementary particle, a form of hyperon, having a neutral charge and decaying very rapidly: *a lambda particle, first discovered in cosmic radiation in 1947* (London Times).

**lambda point**, the temperature, about 2.2 degrees on the Kelvin scale, below which liquid helium becomes a superfluid.

**lamb|doid** (lam′doid), *adj.* **1** shaped like the Greek capital lambda. **2** *Anatomy.* of or noting the suture between the occipital bone and the parietal bones of the skull. [< Middle French *lambdoïde* < Medieval Latin *lambdoides* < Greek *lambdoeidḗs* (medical sense) < *lámbda* lambda + *eîdos* shape]

**lamb|doi|dal** (lam doi′dəl), *adj.* = lambdoid.

**lam|ben|cy** (lam′bən sē), *n., pl.* **-cies.** **1** lambent quality or condition. **2** a flickering light; shimmer: *In the picture, these colors were all different, all smudgy and gray, and the point of this, said Mr. Fowler, was to accent the lambencies of the hair* (New Yorker).

**lam|bent** (lam′bənt), *adj.* **1** moving lightly over a surface: *a lambent flame.* **SYN:** flickering. **2** *Figurative.* playing lightly and brilliantly over a subject: *lambent wit.* **SYN:** playful, lively. **3** *Figurative.* shining with a soft, clear light: *lambent eyes. Moonlight is lambent.* **SYN:** shimmery. [< Latin *lambēns, -entis,* present participle of *lambere* to lick] —**lam′bent|ly,** *adv.*

**lam|bert** (lam′bərt), *n.* the unit of brightness, equivalent to the brightness of a perfectly diffusing surface that emits or reflects one lumen per square centimeter. [< Johann H. *Lambert,* 1728-1777, a German physicist]

**✱Lambert conformal projection** or **Lambert projection**, a map projection in which the meridians are drawn on the surface of a cone and the parallels are spaced mathematically to conform to the actual shape of the features represented. [< Johann H. *Lambert*]

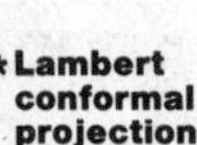

**Lam|beth Conference** (lam′bəth), a meeting of bishops of the Anglican Communion held to discuss church policy about once every ten years in London.

**Lambeth walk**, a ballroom song and dance popular, especially in England, in the late 1930's.

**lamb|kill** (lam′kil′), *n. U.S.* the sheep laurel.

**lamb|kin** (lam′kin), *n.* **1** a little lamb; young lamb. **2** a young or dear person.

**lamb|like** (lam′līk′), *adj.* like a lamb; gentle; meek.

**lamb|ling** (lam′ling), *n.* = lambkin.

**Lamb of God**, Jesus Christ (in the Bible, John 1:29 and 36).

**lam|boys** (lam′boiz), *n.* a skirt of armor, usually steel, which hung from the waist to the knees. It was used chiefly in the 1400's and 1500's. [origin uncertain]

**lam|bre|quin** (lam′brə kin, -bər-), *n.* **1** *U.S.* a drapery covering the top of a window or door, or hanging from a shelf. **2** a scarf worn in medieval times as a covering over a helmet to protect it from heat or dampness. [< Middle French *lambrequin* < Dutch *lamperkÿn* < *lamper* veil + *-kin*]

**lamb|skin** (lam′skin′), *n.* **1** the skin of a lamb, especially with the wool on it: *a heavy coat lined with lambskin.* **2** leather made from the skin of a lamb. **3** parchment made from this skin.

**lamb's-let|tuce** (lamz′let′is), *n.* = corn salad.

**lamb's-quar|ters** or **lambs-quar|ters** (lamz′kwôr′tərz), *n., pl.* **-ters.** a weed of the goosefoot family, a species of pigweed, which is sometimes cultivated and used as a potherb and in salad.

**lambs|wool** or **lamb's wool** (lamz′wu̇l′), *n., adj.* —*n.* **1** a light, soft wool yarn spun from the first shearing of a lamb less than a year old. **2** hot ale mixed with the pulp of roasted apples and sweetened and spiced: *Lay a crab in the fire to roast for lambswool* (George Peele).
—*adj.* made from lambswool: *lambswool blankets, a lambswool shawl.*

**lame¹** (lām), *adj.,* **lam|er, lam|est,** *v.,* **lamed, lam|ing.** —*adj.* **1** not able to walk properly; having an injured leg or foot; crippled: *The soldier limps because he is lame from an old wound.* **SYN:** disabled, halt, game. **2** stiff and sore: *His arm is lame from playing ball.* **3** *Figurative.* poor or weak; not very good: *Sleeping too long is a lame excuse for being late. Santa Croce and the dome of St. Peter's are lame copies after a divine model* (Emerson). **SYN:** imperfect, unconvincing, feeble, unsatisfactory. **4** *U.S. Slang.* not up to date; naive: *Anyone who does not know that he is the positively super-fab lead singer of Paul Revere and the Raiders is obviously lame ... or perhaps just over 25 and into the twilight of life* (Time). **5** *Archaic.* crippled or impaired in any way; unable to move; infirm.
—*v.t.* to make lame; cripple: *The accident lamed him for life.* **SYN:** disable.
—*v.i.* to become lame; go lame.
[Old English *lama*] —**lame′ly,** *adv.* —**lame′ness,** *n.*

**lame²** (lām), *n.* **1** one of numerous thin, small, steel plates laid in an overlapping pattern in making pieces of flexible armor. **2** *Obsolete.* a thin piece of any substance; lamina. [< Old French *lame* < Latin *lāmina,* and *lāmna.* See doublet etym. at **lamina.**]

**la|mé** (la mā′, lä-), *n.* a rich fabric made wholly or partly of metal threads: *Young men in heavy boots stroll the sidewalks with maybe silver lamé inserts in their black shirts* (Patrick O'Donovan). [< French *lamé* a fabric, type of thread; (literally) laminated < Old French *lame* metal leaf]

**lame-brain** (lām′brān′), *n. Informal.* a stupid person: *Only lame-brains and weak sisters resort to handouts* (Wall Street Journal).

**lame-brained** (lām′brānd′), *adj. Informal.* not bright; foolish; stupid.

**la|med** (lä′med), *n.* the twelfth letter of the Hebrew alphabet. [< Hebrew *lamedh* goad]

**lame duck**, **1** *U.S.* a public official, especially a Congressman, who has been defeated for reelection and is serving the last part of his term: *Like a lame-duck President, a Prime Minister who is known to be on the way out cannot command authority* (Manchester Guardian Weekly). **2** a disabled or helpless person or thing: *They started out in convoy, but they had some engine trouble—and you know the rule of the road nowadays: no waiting for lame ducks* (Graham Greene). **3** *Slang.* a person who cannot meet his financial commitments on the stock market.
—**lame′-duck′,** *adj.*

**Lame Duck Amendment**, the 20th Amendment to the United States Constitution, which moved forward the opening of a new Congress to January 3 and the inauguration of a new President to January 20, thus providing the earlier assumption of office by newly elected persons.

**la|mel|la** (lə mel′ə), *n., pl.* **-mel|lae** (-mel′ē), **-mel|las.** **1** a thin plate, scale, or layer, especially of flesh or bone. **2** one of the thin scales or plates composing some shells, as in bivalve mollusks. **3** *Botany.* **a** one of the thin radiating plates or gills forming the spore-bearing layer of a mushroom. **b** one of the erect scales appended to the corolla of some flowers. **c** an erect sheet of cells on the midrib of a leaf in mosses. [< Latin *lāmella* (diminutive) < *lāmina* thin plate, lamina]

**la|mel|lar** (lə mel′ər, lam′ə lər), *adj.* consisting of or arranged in lamellae. —**la|mel′lar|ly,** *adv.*

**lam|el|late** (lam′ə lāt, -lit; lə mel′āt, -it), *adj.* **1** = lamellar. **2** consisting of a flat plate or leaf. **3** platelike or leaflike; flat. **4** = lamellicorn. —**lam′el|late|ly,** *adv.*

**lam|el|lat|ed** (lam′ə lā′tid), *adj.* = lamellate.

**lam|el|la|tion** (lam′ə lā′shən), *n.* lamellate arrangement or structure.

**la|mel|li|branch** (lə mel′ə brangk), *n., adj.* —*n.* a mollusk having thin, platelike gills and a headless body enclosed in a shell whose two parts are connected by a hinge; pelecypod. Lamellibranchs are a class of mollusks that include oysters, clams, and scallops, have a wedge-shaped foot, and are bilaterally symmetrical within a mantle secreted by the shell.
—*adj.* of or belonging to this class of mollusks; lamellibranchiate.
[< New Latin *Lamellibranchia* the class name < Latin *lāmella* lamella + Greek *bránchia* gills, branchia]

**la|mel|li|bran|chi|ate** (lə mel′ə brang′kē āt, -it), *adj., n.* —*adj.* belonging to the lamellibranchs.
—*n.* = lamellibranch.

**la|mel|li|corn** (lə mel′ə kôrn), *adj., n.* —*adj.* **1** of a group of beetles having antennae ending in flattened segments. **2** ending in flattened segments: *lamellicorn antennae.*
—*n.* a cockchafer, dung beetle, scarab, Japanese beetle, or other beetle whose antennae end in flat plates. [< New Latin *Lamellicornes* the group name < Latin *lāmella* lamella + *cornū, -ūs* horn]

**la|mel|li|form** (lə mel′ə fôrm), *adj.* having the shape or structure of a lamella or thin plate.

**la|mel|lose** (lə mel′ōs, lam′ə lōs), *adj.* = lamellar.

**la|ment** (lə ment′), *v., n.* —*v.t.* **1** to sorrow for; mourn aloud for: *We lament the dead.* **SYN:** bewail, deplore. **2** to feel sorrow about; regret: *We lamented his absence. I lamented my own folly ... in attempting a second voyage* (Daniel Defoe).
—*v.i.* to feel or show grief; mourn aloud; weep: *Why does she lament so? The ghost of Freud laments wanly of yet another disservice perpetrated in his name* (Mary O'Reilly). **SYN:** grieve, wail.
—*n.* **1** an expression of grief or sorrow; wail: *The Russian scholars raised a lament against, of all things, the slighting of Latin and Greek in Soviet curriculums* (Newsweek). *Good grandsire, leave these bitter deep laments* (Shakespeare). **2** a poem, song, or tune that expresses grief: *Soon as the dire lament was play'd, It waked the lurking ambuscade* (Scott). **SYN:** elegy, dirge. **3** *Poetic.* the act of lamenting; lamentation.
[< Latin *lāmentārī* < *lāmentum* a wailing, related to *lātrāre* to bark, cry] —**la|ment′er,** *n.* —**la|ment′ing|ly,** *adv.*

**lam|en|ta|ble** (lam′ən tə bəl, lə men′-), *adj.* **1** giving cause for sorrow; to be regretted or pitied: *a lamentable accident. It was a lamentable day when our dog was run over.* **SYN:** pitiable, deplorable. **2** not so good; inferior; pitiful: *a lamentable fake. The singer gave a lamentable performance.* **3** *Archaic.* sorrowful; mournful: *a lamentable voice.*

**lam|en|ta|bly** (lam′ən tə blē, lə men′-), *adv.* to a lamentable degree; regrettably; pitifully: *He was lamentably ignorant about everything except sports.*

**lam|en|ta|tion** (lam′ən tā′shən), *n.* loud grief; cries of sorrow; mourning; wailing: *She tried to forget, but she could not. Her lamentations continued with a strange abundance, a strange persistency* (Lytton Strachey).

**Lam|en|ta|tions** (lam′ən tā′shənz), *n.pl.* a book of the Old Testament, according to tradition, written by Jeremiah. By Christians it is customarily placed among the prophetic books, following Jeremiah, but in the Hebrew Bible it is classed among the sacred writings (Hagiographa) rather than among the Prophets (Nebiim). *Abbr:* Lam.

**la|ment|ed** (lə men′tid), *adj.* **1** mourned for, as one who is dead: *his excellent, learned, and ever lamented friend the late Mr. Yorke* (Edmund Burke). **2** regretted; deplored.

**la|me|ter** (lā′mə tər), *n. Scottish and Northern English.* a lame person; cripple: *You have now, no doubt, friends who will ... not suffer you to devote yourself to a blind lameter like me* (Charlotte Brontë). Also, **lamiter.** [ultimately < *lame¹*]

**la|mi|a** (lā′mē ə), *n., pl.* **-mi|as, -mi|ae** (-mē ē). **1** *Greek and Roman Mythology.* a fabulous monster having the head and breasts of a woman and the body of a serpent, said to lure away children, especially the newborn, to suck their blood. **2** a witch; female demon. [< Latin *lamia* sorceress, a blood-sucking witch < Greek *lámia* flesh-eating monster]

**la|mi|a|ceous** (lā′mē ā′shəs), *adj.* belonging to the mint family. [< New Latin *Lamium* the typical genus (< Latin *lāmium* a barren nettle) + English *-aceous*]

**lam|i|na** (lam′ə nə), *n., pl.* **-nae** (-nē), **-nas.** **1** a thin plate, scale, or layer: *A type of record which occurs widely throughout the world is that of varves, the laminae in certain clays and sands* (G. H. Dury). **2** the flat, wide part of a leaf; blade. **3** *Anatomy.* a thin layer of bone, membrane, or the like. [< Latin *lāmina* thin piece of metal or wood; plate, leaf, layer. See etym. of doublet **lame².**]

**lam|i|na|ble** (lam′ə nə bəl), *adj.* that can be formed into thin plates or layers.

**lam|i|nal** (lam′ə nəl), *adj.* = laminar.

**lam|i|na pro|pri|a** (lam′ə nə prō′prē ə), *pl.* **lam|i|nae pro|pri|ae** (lam′ə nē prō prē ē). *Anatomy.* the thin layer beneath the epithelium of an organ; basement membrane. [< New Latin *lamina propria* (literally) lamina proper]

**lam|i|nar** (lam′ə nər), *adj.* **1** consisting of or arranged in laminae. **2** smooth; streamlined; not turbulent: *The flow of oil for lubrication in bearings is laminar.*

**laminar flow**, a steady flow of a fluid, as opposed to turbulent flow: *When you open the faucet a little bit, the water streams out smoothly in what is known as laminar* (*or streamlined*) *flow* (George Gamow). *Air can flow in the boundary layer in ... orderly paths parallel to the surface of the airplane ... The parallel flow is called laminar flow* (A. Wiley Sherwood). See diagram under **fluid flow.**

**lam|i|nar|i|a|ceous** (lam′ə nãr′ē ā′shəs), *adj.* belonging to a group of brown algae that includes the large kelps. [< New Latin *Laminaria* the genus name (< Latin *lāmina* thin plate) + English *-aceous*]

**lam|i|nar|in** (lam′ə nãr′in), *n.* a sulfated form of starch derived from seaweed, which serves as an anticoagulant. [< New Latin *Laminaria* the genus name + English *-in*]

**lam|i|nate** (*v.* lam′ə nāt; *adj., n.* lam′ə nāt, -nit), *v.,* **-nat|ed, -nat|ing,** *adj., n.* **—** ***v.t.*** **1** to make (plywood, plastics, or glass) by fastening together layer on layer of one or more materials. **2** to beat or roll (metal) into a thin plate. **3** to split into thin layers. **4** to cover with thin plates. **—** ***v.i.*** to separate into thin layers.
**—** ***adj.*** laminated; laminar. **—** ***n.*** laminated plastic. [< Latin *lāmina* lamina + English *-ate*[1]]

**lam|i|nat|ed** (lam′ə nā′tid), *adj.* **1** formed or manufactured in a succession of layers of material: *The magnet must be of laminated construction and is built up from a large number of ½-inch sheets* (L. L. Green). **2** consisting of or arranged in laminae.

**lam|i|na|tion** (lam′ə nā′shən), *n.* **1** the process of laminating or the condition of being laminated: *Lamination consists of gluing thin planks of wood together to make a thick one.* **2** a laminated structure; arrangement in thin layers. **3** a thin layer.

**lam|i|na|tive** (lam′ə nā′tiv), *adj.* of a laminated texture.

**lam|i|na|tor** (lam′ə nā′tər), *n.* a device which protects documents by laminating them between sheets of transparent plastic.

**lam|i|nec|to|my** (lam′ə nek′tə mē), *n., pl.* **-mies.** surgical removal of the posterior arch of a vertebra.

**lam|ing|ton** (lam′ing tən), *n.* (in Australia and New Zealand) a square of sponge cake with a coating of chocolate and coconut. [< Baron *Lamington* (C.W. Baillie), governor of Queensland from 1895 to 1901]

**lam|i|ni|tis** (lam′ə nī′tis), *n.* inflammation of the sensitive laminar structures of a horse's foot; founder. [< New Latin *laminitis* < *lamina* lamina + *-itis* -itis]

**lam|i|nose** (lam′ə nōs), *adj.* consisting of or having the form of laminae.

**lam|i|nous** (lam′ə nəs), *adj.* = laminose.

**lam|is|ter** (lam′ə stər), *n. Slang.* a person who is escaping or hiding from the law; escaped convict; fugitive: *The Irish law was already so well publicized ... that every major British lamister had long since flown the coop* (Time). Also, **lamster.** [< *lam*[1] + *-ster*]

**la|mi|ter** (lā′mə tər), *n.* = lameter.

**Lam|mas** (lam′əs), *n.,* or **Lammas Day, 1** August 1, the day of a harvest festival formerly held in England. **2** August 1, a religious feast in the Roman Catholic Church commemorating the imprisonment and miraculous escape of Saint Peter (in the Bible, Acts 12:4-10). [Old English *hlāfmæsse* < *hlāf* bread + *mæsse* mass (the consecration of loaves of the year's first grain)]

**Lam|mas|tide** (lam′əs tīd′), *n.* the season around August 1 (Lammas).

**lam|mer|gei|er** or **lam|mer|gey|er** (lam′ər gī′ər), *n.* the largest European bird of prey, with a wingspread of nine to ten feet, inhabiting lofty mountains in southern Europe, Asia, and northern Africa; ossifrage; bearded vulture. [< German *Lämmergeier* < *Lämmer,* plural of *Lamm* lamb + *Geier* vulture]

**lam|mer|geir** (lam′ər gīr), *n.* = lammergeier.

**La|mo|na** (lə mō′nə), *n.* any of an American breed of chicken with white plumage and white-shelled eggs.

**lamp** (lamp), *n., v.* **—** ***n.*** **1** a device that gives artificial light. Oil lamps hold oil and a wick by which the oil is burned. A gas or electric light, especially when covered with a glass globe or other shade, is called a lamp. Sometimes anything that gives light, such as a torch or flashlight, is called a lamp. **2** a similar device that gives heat: *a spirit lamp.* **3** *Figurative.* something that suggests the light of a lamp: *the lamp of learning. ... reason, that heav'n-lighted lamp in man* (Edward Young). **4** *Slang.* an eye. **5** one of the heavenly bodies, such as the sun, the moon, a star, or a meteor: *that glorious lamp of heaven, the sun* (Robert Herrick).
**—** ***v.t.*** *Slang.* to eye; look at: *From the corner of his eye, he lamped the woman* (James T. Farrell).
**smell of the lamp,** to suggest long hours of hard work late at night; be stuffy or pedantic: *Hardly any poet smells of the lamp less disagreeably than Spenser* (George E. B. Saintsbury).
[< Old French *lampe* < Latin *lampas, -adis* < Greek *lampás, -ados* < *lámpein* to shine]

**lam|pads** (lam′padz), *n.pl. Poetic.* the seven "lamps of fire" burning before the throne of God (in the Bible, Revelation 4:5). [< Greek *lampás, -ados* lamp]

**lam|pas**[1] (lam′pəs), *n.* an inflammation of the mucous membrane covering the hard palate of the mouth in the horse. [< Old French *lampas*]

**lam|pas**[2] (lam′pəs), *n.* a kind of flowered silk fabric, originally imported from China and usually made into shawls or kerchiefs. [< French *lampas*]

**lamp|black** (lamp′blak′), *n., v.* **—** ***n.*** a fine black soot consisting of almost pure carbon that is deposited when oil, gas, etc., burns incompletely. Lampblack is used as a coloring matter in paint, ink, cement, and in making tires.
**—** ***v.t.*** to paint, smear, or coat with lampblack: *A ... scoundrel who knows no pleasure beyond ... lampblacking signs* (Thomas Brown).

**lamp|brush chromosome** (lamp′brush′), a type of large chromosome found especially in the immature eggs of amphibians, consisting of two long strands that form many brushlike loops along the main axis of the chromosome.

**lam|per eel** (lam′pər), **1** = lamprey. **2** = eelpout (def. 1).

**lam|pers** (lam′pərz), *n.* = lampas[1].

**lamp holder,** *Especially British.* a socket for an electric-light bulb.

**lamp|house** (lamp′hous′), *n.* an enclosure for a source of light, as in a lantern: *This new carbon in its proper lamphouse gives twice as much light as any ... unit previously available* (William F. Kelley).

**lam|pi|on** (lam′pē ən), *n.* a simple small lamp, often of colored glass, used for illumination. [< French *lampion* < Italian *lampione* street or carriage light (augmentative) < *lampa,* probably < Old French *lampe* lamp]

**lamp|light** (lamp′līt′), *n.* the light from a lamp.

**lamp|light|er** (lamp′lī′tər), *n.* **1** a person who lights lamps, especially a person formerly employed to light gas-burning street lamps. **2** *U.S.* (formerly) a torch, twisted paper, or the like, used to light lamps.

**lamp oil, 1** oil used for burning in a lamp. **2** *U.S.* kerosene.

**lam|poon** (lam pün′), *n., v.* **—** ***n.*** a piece of writing, a speech, or a remark that attacks and makes fun of a person in a spiteful or insulting way: *Many popular nursery rhymes probably originated as lampoons on famous people.* **SYN:** satire, pasquinade.
**—** ***v.t.*** to attack and make fun of in a lampoon; ridicule: *It does not pull any punches in lampooning our most august political figures in a program of skits, songs, dialogues, and impersonations of a very high artistic level* (Friedrich Luft).
[< earlier French *lampon* drinking song < *lampons* let us drink (a refrain of a drinking song) < slang *lamper* to drink] **—lam|poon′er,** *n.*

**lam|poon|er|y** (lam pü′nər ē), *n.* **1** the practice of writing lampoons: *The portentous triviality of the questions offered an irresistible cue for lampoonery* (Time). **2** lampooning quality or spirit.

**lam|poon|ist** (lam pü′nist), *n.* a person who writes or makes lampoons.

**lamp|post** (lamp′pōst′), *n.* a post used to support a street lamp.

**lam|prey** (lam′prē), *n., pl.* **-preys.** a marine and freshwater animal having a body like an eel with gill slits like a fish and no jaws but a large, round mouth. Lampreys are vertebrates found throughout the world and are parasitic, some attaching themselves to fishes with their mouths to suck the body fluids. See picture under **eel.** [< Old French *lampreie* < Medieval Latin *lampreda,* uncertain relationship to Late Latin *lampetra* < Latin *lambere* to lick + *petra* rock. See etym. of doublet **limpet.**]

**lamp|shade** (lamp′shād′), *n.* a shade over a lamp to soften or direct the light.

**lamp shell,** = brachiopod.

**lamp|work|ing** (lamp′wėr′king), *n.* the reshaping of glass rods or tubing softened by reheating to make incandescent bulbs, radio tubes, scientific equipment, and decorative objects.

**lam|siek|te** (läm′sēk′tə), *n.* = lamziekte.

**lam|ster** (lam′stər), *n.* = lamister.

**La|mut** (lə müt′), *n., pl.* **-mut** or **-muts. 1** a member of a people of Kamchatka, a peninsula in Siberia, who herd reindeer. **2** their Tungusic language.

**lam|ziek|te** (läm′zēk′tə), *n.* a paralytic disease of cattle in South Africa. It is a form of botulism. [< Afrikaans *lamziekte* < Dutch *lam* lame + *ziekte* disease]

**la|nai** (lä nī′), *n., pl.* **-nais.** a porch or veranda. [< Hawaiian]

**la|nate** (lā′nāt), *adj. Botany, Entomology.* having a woolly covering or surface; lanose. [< Latin *lānātus* < *lāna* wool]

**Lan|cas|ter** (lang′kə stər), *n.* the royal house of England from 1399 to 1461. Its emblem was a red rose. The House of Lancaster was descended from John of Gaunt, Duke of Lancaster. The three kings of this house were Henry IV, Henry V, and Henry VI.

**Lan|cas|te|ri|an** (lang′kə stir′ē ən), *adj.* of or having to do with the English educator Joseph Lancaster (1778-1838) or the system of instruction used by him, in which the younger pupils were taught by the more advanced pupils, who were called monitors.

**Lan|cas|tri|an** (lang kas′trē ən), *n., adj.* **—** ***n.*** **1** (in English history) a supporter or member of the royal house of Lancaster, especially in the Wars of the Roses. **2** a native of Lancashire, county in England.
**—** ***adj.*** of or having to do with the royal house of Lancaster.

**lance**[1] (lans, läns), *n., v.,* **lanced, lanc|ing. —** ***n.*** **1** a long wooden spear with a sharp iron or steel head: *The knights and some cavalry troops carried lances as they rode into battle.* **2** = lancer. **3a** any instrument like a soldier's lance. A spear for harpooning a whale is called a lance. **b** a surgeon's knife; lancet. **4** a metal pipe for supplying oxygen under pressure, used to cut or pierce metal or to oxidize molten iron. **5** a thin paper tube filled with color-producing fireworks. [< Old French *lance* < Latin *lancea* light Spanish spear]
**—** ***v.t.*** **1** to pierce with or as if with a lance: *to lance a fish. They lanced his flesh with knives* (John Bunyan). **SYN:** cut, gash, slit. **2** to cut open with a surgeon's knife: *The dentist lanced the gum where a new tooth had difficulty coming through.* **3** to supply (oxygen) through a lance under pressure in smelting: *Oxygen is lanced into the furnace as it is being tapped. This causes the slag and lead to run* (London Times).
**—** ***v.i.*** to dart, rush, or bound away.
**carry the** (or **a**) **lance for,** defend or argue in favor of: *Miss Butler, carrying a lance for Sarah and the Churchills, charges magnificently up and down the field goring the opposition and reducing Abigail Hill to mincemeat* (London Times).
[< Old French *lancier* < Late Latin *lanceāre* < Latin *lancea.* See etym. of doublet **launch**[1].]

**lance**[2] (lans, läns), *n.* = launce.

**lance corporal, 1** an enlisted man in the United States Marine Corps ranking next below a corporal and next above a private first class. **2** a private in the British Army acting temporarily as a corporal without increase of pay.

**lance knight,** = lansquenet. [< German *Lanzknecht* (< *Lanze* lance), alteration of *Landsknecht*<*Land(e)s*theland's + *Knecht*servant]

**lance|leaf** (lans′lēf′, läns′-), *n., pl.* **-leaves.** a lungwort of western North America, having smooth stems, large leaves, and bell-shaped pink or blue flowers.

**lance|let** (lans′lit, läns′-), *n.* a small, limbless, often translucent, fishlike marine animal, regarded as a link between the vertebrates and the invertebrates, found in the sand under shallow waters; amphioxus; cephalochordate. Lancelets have a thin body, pointed at both ends and no skull. [earlier, a lancet < *lance* + *-let*]

**lance|like** (lans′līk′), *adj.* shaped like a lance; lanceolate: *Strange that so gigantic a tree* [*the sequoia*] *should put out such paltry lancelike leaves* (New Yorker).

**Lan|ce|lot** (lan′sə lət, -lot; län′-), *n.* the bravest of King Arthur's knights of the Round Table. Lancelot was the lover of Queen Guinevere and the father of Sir Galahad.

**lan|ce|o|late** (lan′sē ə lāt, -lit), *adj.* shaped like the head of a lance; tapering from a rounded base toward the apex; lanceolated; lancelike: *a lanceolate leaf.* [< Latin *lanceolātus* < *lanceola* (diminutive) < *lancea* lance] **—lan′ce|o|late|ly,** *adv.*

**lan|ce|o|lat|ed** (lan′sē ə lā′tid), *adj.* = lanceolate.

**lanc|er** (lan′sər, län′-), *n.* a mounted soldier armed with a lance; lance. The **Lancers** are members of a light cavalry unit of the British Army.

**lanc|ers** or **lan|ciers** (lan′sərz, län′-), *n. pl.* **1** a form of square dance or quadrille having figures imitating military drill. **2** the music for it.

**lance sergeant,** a corporal in the British Army, appointed to act temporarily as a sergeant without increase of pay.

**lan|cet** (lan′sit, län′-), *n.* **1** a small pointed knife, usually having two sharp edges, used by doctors and surgeons in opening boils and abscesses and making other small incisions; lance. **2** a lancet arch or lancet window: *Two smaller lancets show red-and-blue designs* (New Yorker). [< Old French *lancette* (diminutive) < *lance* lance < Latin *lancea*]

---

**Pronunciation Key:** hat, āge, cãre, fär; let, ēqual, tėrm; it, īce; hot, ōpen, ôrder; oil, out; cup, pu̇t, rüle; child; long; thin; ᴛʜen; zh, measure; ə represents a in about, e in taken, i in pencil, o in lemon, u in circus.

**lancet arch**, a narrow, sharply pointed arch; lancet.
**lan|cet|ed** (lan′sə tid, län′-), *adj.* having a lancet arch or lancet window.
**lancet fish**, a large, fierce marine fish with a long body, long sharp teeth, and a very long, high dorsal fin.
✱**lancet window**, a high, narrow window with a lancet arch at the top but not divided by tracery; lancet.

✱**lancet window**

**lance|wood** (lans′wu̇d′, läns′-), *n.* **1** a tough, straight-grained, springy wood used especially for fishing rods, carriage shafts, and cabinetwork. **2** any one of various American trees that yield this wood.
**lan|ci|nate** (lan′sə nāt), *v.t.,* **-nat|ed, -nat|ing.** to pierce; tear. [< Latin *lancināre* (with English *-ate*¹) destroy, tear to pieces, related to *lacerāre* lacerate]
**lan|ci|nat|ing** (lan′sə nā′ting), *adj.* piercing; darting: *lancinating pain, lancinating criticism.*
**lan|ci|na|tion** (lan′sə nā′shən), *n.* a sharp, shooting pain.
**land** (land), *n., v.* **—*n.*** **1** the solid part of the earth's surface: *After many weeks at sea, the sailors sighted land.* **2** ground or soil: *This is good land for a garden.* **SYN**: earth. **3a** ground or soil used as property; real estate, such as a piece of ground and everything permanently attached to it: *The farmer invested in land and machinery.* **b** any property interest a person has in land. **4** anything furnished by nature without the help of man, such as soil, mineral deposits, water, or wildlife. *Land, labor,* and *capital* are the three principal factors of production. **5** a country or region: *the explorers traveled north until they reached the Land of the Midnight Sun. Switzerland is a mountainous land.* **6** the people of a country; nation: *He collected folk songs from all the land.* **7** realm; domain: *the land of the living. Soldiers are citizens of death's grey land* (Siegfried Sassoon). **8** one of the strips into which a field is divided by plowing: *I was ploughing in lands, strips across the paddock which widen and eventually join up* (London Times). **9** one of the smooth, raised surfaces between the grooves in the bore of a rifle or other gun with rifling.
**—*v.i.*** **1** to come to land or something solid: *The ship landed at the pier. The crippled airplane landed at an emergency field. The fly landed on the bread.* **2** to go on shore from a ship, boat, or airplane: *The passengers landed.* **3** to come to a stop; arrive: *The thief landed in jail. The car landed in the ditch.*
**—*v.t.*** **1a** to bring to land; set ashore; set on something solid: *The ship landed its passengers. The pilot landed the airplane in Seattle.* **b** to set down from a vehicle: *The bus landed him in front of his house.* **2** to cause to arrive: *This train will land you in London. A combination of circumstances landed the company in bankruptcy.* **3** *Informal.* to get; catch: *to land a job, to land a fish.* **4** *Slang.* to strike with (a blow): *I landed a blow on his chin.*
**how the land lies**, what the state of affairs is: *Uncle Charles's eyes had discovered how the land lay as regarded Rose and himself* (Mary Bridgman).
**lands, a** territorial possessions: *Their lands had been divided by Cromwell among his followers* (Macaulay). **b** those parts of a farm in South Africa on which crops are cultivated: *There are, too, the 'lands' where the mealies and the corn are planted* (Beatrice M. Hicks).
**make land**, to discover or see land as the ship approaches a shore: *We were at sea a full week before we finally made land.*
[Old English *land*]
**Land** (länt), *n., pl.* **Län|der** or **Laen|der** (len′dər). *German.* a state; province: *The Federal Republic of Germany is a federal state composed of ten Länder.*
**land agent**, **1** a manager of a property and its land. **2** real-estate agent.
✱**lan|dau** (lan′dô, -dou), *n.* **1** a four-wheeled carriage with two inside seats facing each other and a top made in two parts that can be folded back. **2** an automobile with a similar top or one that imitates such a top. [< *Landau,* a town in Germany, where it was first made]

✱**landau**
definition 1

**lan|dau|let** or **lan|dau|lette** (lan′dô let′), *n.* **1** a landau with only one seat: *The mistress of a very pretty landaulette* (Jane Austen). **2** an automobile with a single seat and a folding top.
**land bank**, **1** a bank that grants long-term loans on real property in return for mortgages: *As the land bank system developed, it has been able to keep pace with modern farming* (Joseph G. Knapp). **2** *British.* (formerly) a banking institution that issued notes on the security of real property.
**land|bound** (land′bound′), *adj.* **1** bound or limited to the land: *In total nuclear warfare, what can a landbound army do?* (Newsweek). **2** bounded by land: *There are four provinces in Galicia, and we were in Orense—the southernmost and the only one of the four that is landbound* (New Yorker).
**land breeze**, a breeze blowing from the land toward the sea: *The land breeze is usually less developed than the sea breeze; it is shallower, has less speed, and extends only 5 or 6 miles over the sea* (Thomas A. Blair).
**land bridge**, a neck of land connecting two land masses: *Australia may have been settled earlier, when a land bridge still joined that continent to South-East Asia* (Punch).
**land crab**, any one of various large crabs that inhabit the coasts of many tropical countries.
**Land Dyak**, a member of a tribe of Dyaks living inland in Sarawak, in northeastern Borneo. Land Dyaks are distinguished from the Ibans or Sea Dyaks.
**lande** (land; *French* länd), *n.* an uncultivated or unfertile plain covered with heath, broom, ferns, or other undergrowth, as in southwestern France. [< French *lande*]
**land|ed** (lan′did), *adj.* **1** owning land: *the landed aristocracy.* **2** consisting of land: *Landed property is real estate.*
**land|er** (lan′dər), *n.* **1** a person who makes a landing. **2** a person who settles on land. **3** a spacecraft designed for landing instead of orbiting; landing vehicle: *The 30 kg. lander was released from a hovering helicopter and allowed to free fall to the lake bed. In the thin atmosphere of Mars, the lander would be slowed to the same velocity by a six metre parachute; no parachute was used in this test* (Science Journal).
**land|fall** (land′fôl′), *n.* **1** a sighting of land. **2** the land sighted or reached: *When you arrive at Darwin, your landfall in Australia, you are given a form to complete ...* (James Morris). **3** an approach to land; landing: *our landfall on the moon.*
**land|fast** (land′fast′), *adj.* attached to land: *A million years ago the island was either landfast or near the shore.*
**land|fill** (land′fil), *n. U.S.* **1** a place where rubbish or other debris is deposited and covered with earth: *Refuse from Brooklyn and Manhattan ... is dumped in a landfill* (New York Times). **2** this system of rubbish disposal. **3** the material used to fill in low or wet land. **4** a part of a body of water that is drained and filled with earth for use as land: *Building a commercial expressway on landfill along the river's east bank would seriously impair the scenic and historic values of the Hudson highlands* (New York Times).
**land|fill|ing** (land′fil′ing), *n.* the using of landfill.
**land|form** (land′fôrm′), *n.* the physical characteristics of land; irregularities of land: *The principal groups of landforms to be considered, as distinguished by their several characteristic features and degrees of relative relief, are* (*a*) *plains,* (*b*) *plateaus,* (*c*) *hill lands, and* (*d*) *mountains* (Finch and Trewartha).
**land freeze**, a government restriction on the sale and transfer of land.
**land grabber**, a person who acquires land from another by treachery, force, or other means contrary to the spirit of the law.
**land grant**, a grant of land; gift of land by the government for colleges, railroads, roads, or other public projects. Land grant colleges or universities are institutions that receive federal aid in land or money under the Morrill Acts of 1862 and 1890, which permitted each state to use public lands to support at least one agricultural or industrial college.
**land|grave** (land′grāv′), *n.* **1** a German count in the Middle Ages having authority over a considerable territory or over other counts. **2** the title of certain German princes. [ultimately < Middle High German *lantgrāve* < *lant* land + *grāve* count]
**land|hold|er** (land′hōl′dər), *n.* a person who owns or occupies land.
**land|hold|ing** (land′hōl′ding), *adj., n.* **—*adj.*** that owns or occupies land: *a landholding corporation.*
**—*n.*** an owning or occupying of land.
**land|ing** (lan′ding), *n.* **1** a coming to land: *There are many millions of take-offs and landings at the nation's airports each year.* **SYN**: debarkation, disembarkation. **2** a place where persons or goods are landed from a ship, helicopter, or the like; landing place. A wharf, dock, or pier is a landing for boats. **SYN**: port, wharf. **3a** a platform between flights of stairs. **b** the floor at the top or bottom of a staircase. **4** the catching of fish, especially in large amounts by commercial methods: *Halibut landings of 37 million pounds were down six million from the ... catch* (Wall Street Journal). **5** a place where logs are gathered before being transported to a sawmill.
**landing craft**, a boat or ship used for landing troops or equipment on a shore, especially during an assault. Landing craft often have a front that opens or drops to form a ramp and are usually flat-bottomed boats with a very shallow draft.
**landing field**, a field large enough and smooth enough for airplanes to land on and take off from safely.
**landing gear**, wheels, pontoons, or skids which support an aircraft in landing; undercarriage. When on land or water an aircraft rests on its landing gear. See picture under **airplane**.
**landing light**, **1** any of the lights on an aircraft used to see when landing at night. **2** any of the lights of a landing system.
**landing mat**, a mat of meshed steel that can be joined to others to form a smooth landing surface for aircraft on rough ground.
**landing net**, a small net to take fish from the water after they are caught.
**landing party**, **1** any group of people who make a landing. **2** a group of soldiers who make a landing, especially in advance of a main invasion force.
**landing stage**, a floating platform used for loading and unloading people and goods.
**landing strip**, = airstrip.
**landing system**, controls which regulate or assist in the landing of an aircraft: *A jet bomber was safely landed by a ground-based, automatic landing system using radar to track the plane and radio to transmit flight path correction signals to the airplane's auto-pilot* (Science News Letter).
**landing vehicle**, = lander (def. 3).
**land|la|dy** (land′lā′dē), *n., pl.* **-dies. 1** a woman who owns a building or land that she rents to others. **2** a woman who runs an inn or rooming house.
**land|less** (land′lis), *adj.* without land; owning no land: *the landless serfs of the Middle Ages.*
**—land′less|ness,** *n.*
**land|like** (land′līk′), *adj.* like or characteristic of land: *The sea-bottom has landlike hills and valleys.*
**land|line** (land′līn′), *n.* a communication cable that runs on or under the land: *The program, which lasted one hour, was transmitted by a combination of landline and microwave* (New Scientist).
**land|locked** (land′lokt′), *adj.* **1** shut in, or nearly shut in, by land: *the landlocked Great Lakes. The landlocked harbor was protected from the full force of the wind and waves.* **2** living in waters shut off from the sea: *Landlocked salmon must spend their lives in freshwater instead of making the migration to salt water.*
**land|lord** (land′lôrd′), *n.* **1** a person who owns a building or land that he rents to others: *absentee landlords.* **2** a person who runs an inn or rooming house. **SYN**: host, innkeeper.
**land|lord|ism** (land′lôr′diz əm), *n.* **1** the methods or practices of landlords; system of renting from landlords: *... agriculture with low productivity hampered still by the relics of landlordism* (Wall Street Journal). **2** the principle of the supremacy of the landlord class.
**land|lub|ber** (land′lub′ər), *n.* a person not used to being on ships; person who is awkward on board ship because of lack of experience: *The sailors called the landsmen landlubbers in scorn. Their dream, like the dream of so many landlubbers was ... to sail to the South Seas, to leave the world behind* (New York Times).
**land|lub|ber|ly** (land′lub′ər lē), *adj.* confined to or used on land rather than the sea: *landlubberly phrases, landlubberly sports such as cricket and polo.*
**land|lub|bing** (land′lub′ing), *adj., n.* **—*adj.*** living or staying on the land; not seafaring.
**—*n.*** life or activity on land.
**land|mark** (land′märk′), *n., adj., v.* **—*n.*** **1** some-

thing familiar or easily seen, used as a guide: *The hiker did not lose his way in the forest because the rangers' high tower served as a landmark.* **2** *Figurative.* an important fact or event; a happening that stands out above others: *The inventions of the printing press, the telephone, the radio, and television are landmarks in the history of communications.* **3** a historic building, monument, or site: *Under the Landmarks Law, the exterior of a landmark building must be preserved, but there are no restrictions on interior remodeling* (Ada Louise Huxtable). **4** a stone or other object that marks the boundary of a piece of land: *Thou shalt not remove thy neighbour's landmark* (Deuteronomy 19:14).
*—adj.* *U.S.* serving as a guide in future judicial ruling; setting a legal precedent: *a landmark Supreme Court decision.*
*—v.t.* to mark by a landmark; indicate as if by a landmark: *Wakeful and missing little, and landmarking the flylike dance of the planets ...* (Ted Hughes).

**land mass**, or **land|mass** (land′mas′), *n.* a large, unbroken area of land, especially a continent: *Antarctica is the earth's coldest land mass. The Soviet Union and its satellites form a land mass extending from eastern Europe through most of Asia.*

**land measure**, a system of square measure for the area of land.

**land mine**, a container filled with explosives, placed on the ground or lightly covered. It is usually set off by the weight of vehicles or troops passing over it or by magnetic contact.

**Land of Beulah**, the land of rest and happiness just this side of the river of death in John Bunyan's *Pilgrim's Progress.*

**Land of Enchantment**, a nickname for New Mexico.

**land office**, a government office dealing with records of sale and transfer of public lands.

**land-of|fice business** (land′ôf′is, -of′-), *U.S. Informal.* exceedingly active or rapid business: *By day the tomb is thronged with parents and children, and wagons selling ... soft drinks were doing a land-office business* (Saturday Review).

**Land of Lincoln**, a nickname for Illinois.

**land of nod**, sleep. [pun on the *Land of Nod* (in the Bible) the country to which Cain traveled. Genesis 4:16]

**Land of Opportunity**, a nickname for Arkansas.

**Land of Promise**, = Promised Land.

**Land of Shining Mountains**, a nickname for Montana.

**land of the leal**, the dwelling place of the blessed after death; heaven.

**Land of the Midnight Sun**, a nickname for arctic regions, especially the northernmost part of Norway.

**Land of the Rising Sun**, a nickname for Japan.

**land otter**, = river otter.

**land|own|er** (land′ō′nər), *n.* a person who owns land.

**land|own|er|ship** (land′ō′nər ship), *n.* the condition of being a landowner.

**land|own|ing** (land′ō′ning), *adj.* holding or possessing landed estates: *the landowning class.*

**land patent**, *Law.* a deed that gives a private citizen possession of public land.

**land|plane** (land′plān′), *n.* an airplane equipped to land on and take off from land.

**land plaster**, gypsum ground to a powder for use as a fertilizer.

**land-poor** (land′pu̇r′), *adj.* **1** owning much land but needing ready money. **2** poor because of taxes or liens on one's land.

**land power**, **1** military strength in land forces. **2** a nation that maintains large and effective land forces.

**Land|race** (land′rās′), *n.* any one of a breed of large, white hogs introduced from Scandinavia into Great Britain.

**land rail**, = corn crake.

**land reform**, **1** a program of breaking up and redistributing large land holdings, often among the laborers that worked them: *Now all but complete, the land-reform program has freed 98% of Iran's 50,000 villages from landlord control* (Time). **2** any social or economic measure that will benefit farmers.

**land|rise** (land′rīz′), *n.* an uplifting of part of the earth's surface.

**Land Rover**, *Trademark.* an English motor vehicle resembling a jeep but of heavier construction.

**lands** (landz), *n.pl.* See under **land**.

**Land|sat** (land′sat′), *n.* a United States artificial satellite using remote-sensing apparatus to gather data about the earth's natural resources. [< *Land sat*(ellite)]

**land|scape** (land′skāp), *n., v.,* **-scaped, -scap|ing.** *—n.* **1** a view of scenery on land that can be taken in at a glance from one point of view: *From the church tower the two hills with the valley formed a beautiful landscape.* SYN: prospect. **2a** a picture showing a land scene: *an exhibit of landscapes.* **b** the art of painting such scenes: *to study landscape.* **3** *Figurative.* panorama; scene; view: *The landscape of international politics is now very different from what it was* (Listener). SYN: vista.
*—v.t.* to make (land) more pleasant to look at by arranging trees, shrubs, or flowers: *The park is landscaped. ... the beautifully landscaped motels with swimming pools* (Wall Street Journal).
*—v.i.* to be a landscape gardener.
[< Dutch *landschap* < *land* land + *-schap* -ship]
**—land′scap′er**, *n.*

**landscape architect**, a person whose business is designing landscape.

**landscape architecture**, the designing of landscape, as in a city park or along a highway.

**landscape gardener**, a person whose business is landscape gardening.

**landscape gardening**, the arrangement of trees, shrubs, or flowers, to give a pleasing appearance to grounds, parks, or other areas.

**land|scap|ist** (land′skā pist), *n.* **1** a painter of landscapes: *Though Europe has produced a host of great landscapists, from Claude Lorrain to Paul Cézanne, the West's best could have learned much from the Chinese* (Time). **2** a landscape architect or gardener: *In the skillful hands of the Belgian landscapists, the grounds were transformed into a wonderland of light and verdure* (Atlantic).

**land shark**, **1** a dishonest person who cheats or robs seamen on shore: *Flophouse keepers, saloon owners, and other land sharks ... shanghaied [sailors] aboard ship* (Atlantic). **2** *U.S.* a land grabber.

**land|ship** (land′ship), *n.* **1** a ship erected and kept on land for training purposes. **2** a wagon or other vehicle used for transportation on land.

**land|side** (land′sīd′), *n.* the flat side of a plow, which is turned toward the unplowed land.

**land|slide** (land′slīd′), *n., v.,* **-slid** or **-slid|ed, -slid|ing.** *—n.* **1** a sliding down of a mass of soil or rock on a steep slope: *The term landslide usually refers to a rapid movement of earth from side embankments of roadside cuts but can also refer to slow motion movements in which earth gradually slips from roadsides onto the paving* (Science News Letter). **2** the mass that slides down. **3** *Figurative.* an overwhelming number of votes for one political party or candidate in an election: *The enormous vote cast for the President made his election a landslide.* **4** *Figurative.* an event of rapidly developing proportions, especially a disaster: *Along with all their other problems, the two leaders now had to face landslide inflation* (Atlantic).
*—v.i.* to win an election by a landslide.
*—v.t.* to elect by a landslide: *The English electorate ... has landslided the Tomboy Tories in for yet another fun-filled term* (Punch).
[American English]

**land|slip** (land′slip′), *n. British.* landslide (defs. 1 and 2).

**Lands|mål** (läns′môl′), *n.* the more recent of the two varieties of standard, literary Norwegian (contrasted with *Riksmål*); Nynorsk. It incorporates various native dialects. [< Norwegian *Landsmål* < *lands,* genitive of *land* land + *mål* language, speech]

**lands|man** (landz′mən), *n., pl.* **-men. 1** a person who lives or works on land or who has had no experience at sea: *There is nothing so helpless and pitiable an object in the world as a landsman beginning a sailor's life* (Richard Henry Dana). **2** *Nautical.* an inexperienced seaman, below an ordinary seaman in rating.

**land speed**, speed of a vehicle on land or the speed comparable to that of a vehicle on land: *Then the land speed record merely becomes an air speed record at zero altitude* (New Scientist).

**land|spout** (land′spout′), *n.* a funnel-shaped cloud resembling a waterspout but occurring on land. A landspout may be produced by certain severe whirling storms of small extent.

**Lands|raad** (läns′rôd′), *n.* the legislative council of Greenland. [< Danish *Landsraad* < *lands,* genitive of *land* land + *raad* council]

**land's sakes**, an exclamation or expression of surprise, wonder, or mild disgust. [euphemism for *Lord's sakes*]

**Lands|ting** or **Lands|thing** (läns′ting′), *n.* (formerly) the upper house of the Rigsdag or former bicameral parliament of Denmark. [< Danish *Landsting* < *lands,* genitive of *land* land + *ting, thing* assembly, parliament]

**Land|sturm** (länt′shtu̇rm′), *n.* in Germany, Switzerland, and Austria: **1** a general levy in time of war. **2** the force that consists of all men liable to call for military service and not already in the army, navy, or Landwehr. [< German *Landsturm* < *Land* land + *Sturm* storm, military assault]

**lands|wom|an** (landz′wu̇m′ən), *n., pl.* **-wom|en.** a woman who lives or works on land.

**Land|tag** (länt′täk′), *n., pl.* **-ta|ge** (-tä′gə). a diet, or lawmaking body, of a German state or of Liechtenstein. [< German *Landtag* (literally) landday < *Land* land + *Tag* day, assembly]

**land|tied** (land′tīd′), *adj.* joined to the mainland or to other land by the growth of reefs or sand-spits, as islands.

**land-to-land** (land′tə land′), *adj.* launched from land at a target on land: *land-to-land missiles.*

**land|ward** (land′wərd), *adv., adj.* toward the land or shore.

**land|wards** (land′wərdz), *adv.* = landward.

**Land|wehr** (länt′vār′), *n.* (in Germany, Switzerland, and Austria) that part of the organized military forces of the nation that have been trained in regular units for a given period of time and who are required to serve only in time of war. [< German *Landwehr* < *Land* land + *Wehr* defense]

**land wind**, a wind blowing from the land toward the sea.

**land|work|er** (land′wėr′kər), *n.* = farm hand.

**land yacht**, = sand yacht.

**lane**[1] (lān), *n.* **1** a narrow way between hedges, walls, or fences, especially a narrow country road or path or city street: *A carriage drove down the muddy lane. A parish all of fields, high hedges, and deep-rutted lanes* (George Eliot). SYN: passage. **2** a lengthwise division of a highway marked for a single line of traffic: *Center lane for left turn only* (highway sign). *Many four-lane highways cross the country.* **3** a course or route used by ships or aircraft going in the same direction. **4** an alley between buildings. **5** any narrow way or other thing resembling a lane: *The President walked down a lane formed by two lines of soldiers and sailors. The FCC patrols the radio lanes for illegal operations and technical violators* (George O. Gillingham). **6** a bowling alley: *Reflecting the new tone, alleys have become "lanes," and even the gutters that line the alleys are now channels* (Time). **7** one of the narrow alleys on a track, marked by chalked lines, especially one in which a runner must stay during sprint or hurdle races. [Old English *lane*]

**lane**[2] (lān), *adj. Scottish.* lone.

**lane|way** (lān′wā′), *n.* **1** the path or pavement of a lane. **2** = lane.

**lang** (lang, läng), *adj., adv., n. Scottish.* long[1].

**lang.**, language.

**lan|ga|ha** (läng gä′hä), *n.* a snake of Madagascar, having the snout prolonged into a sharply flexible tip. [< the Malagasy name]

**lang|bein|ite** (lang′bī nīt), *n.* a mineral, a sulfate of potassium and magnesium, that occurs in potassium salt deposits and is mined as a source of potassium sulfate. *Formula:* $K_2Mg_2(SO_4)_3$ [< A. *Langbein,* a German chemist of the 1800's + *-ite*[1]]

**Lang|er|hans islands** (läng′ər häns), = islets of Langerhans.

**lang|lauf** (läng′louf′), *n.* the act or sport of cross-country skiing. [< German *Langlauf* (literally) long run]

**lang|läu|fer** (läng′loi′fər), *n., pl.* **-läu|fer** or **-läu|fers.** a cross-country skier; geländeläufer. [< German *Langläufer* (literally) long runner]

**lang|ley** (lang′lē), *n.* a unit of solar radiation equal to 1 small calorie per square centimeter. [< Samuel P. *Langley,* 1834-1906, an American astronomer and physicist]

**Lang|muir probe** (lang′myu̇r), a device to measure plasma density by calculating the potential electric discharge along a probe in a plasma-filled tube. [< Irving *Langmuir,* 1881-1957, an American chemist]

**Lan|go|bard** (lang′gə bärd), *n.* = Lombard.

**Lan|go|bar|di|an** (lang′gō bär′dē ən), *n.* the Germanic language of the Lombards.

**Lan|go|bar|dic** (lang′gə bär′dik), *adj., n.* *—adj.* = Lombardic.
*—n.* = Langobardian.

**lan|gouste** (läɴ güst′), *n. French.* spiny lobster.

**lan|gous|tine** (läɴ güs tēn′), *n. French.* a small lobster.

**lan|grage** or **lan|gridge** (lang′grij), *n.* a kind of scattering shot of nails, bolts, and the like, fastened together or enclosed in a case, formerly used in naval warfare for damaging sails and rigging. [origin unknown]

**lan|grel** (lang′grəl), *n. Obsolete.* langrage.

**Lang|shan** (lang′shan), *n.* any of an Asian breed of large, white-skinned chicken that produces very dark-brown eggs. [< *Langshan,* a locality near Shanghai, China]

**lang syne**, or **lang|syne** (lang′sīn′, -zīn′), *adv.,*

**Pronunciation Key:** hat, āge, cãre, fär; let, ēqual, tėrm; it, īce; hot, ōpen, ôrder; oil, out; cup, pu̇t, rüle; child; long; thin; ᴛʜen; zh, measure; ə represents **a** in about, **e** in taken, **i** in pencil, **o** in lemon, **u** in circus.

*n. Scottish.* —**adv.** long since; long ago: ... *this south-east corner of Scotland, full of memories of men on the march and battles fought lang syne* (London Times).
—**n.** a time long ago, especially in the phrase *auld lang syne.*
[< Scottish *lang* long + *syne* since]

**lan|guage** (lang′gwij), *n.* **1** human speech, spoken or written: *Without language men would be like animals. Language is the basis of man's uniqueness, and the essence of his culture* (Scientific American). *Language is a set of habits. Like other habits, they are easily formed in early life and difficult to change later* (Yuen Ren Chao). **2** the speech used by one nation, tribe, or other similar large group of people; tongue: *the French language, the Navaho language.* **3** a form, style, or kind of language; manner of expression: *bad or strong language, Shakespeare's language. The best language must inevitably be conservative, but it needs no less to be continuously refreshed from the springing well of everyday utterance ...* (Simeon Potter). **SYN**: diction, parlance. **4** wording or words: *in the language of the Lord's Prayer. The lawyer explained to us very carefully the language of the contract.* **5** the special terms used by a science, art, profession, or class of persons: *the language of chemistry. There is one language for the pulpit and another for on board ship* (Frederick Marryat). **SYN**: phraseology, vocabulary, jargon, cant. **6** the expression of thoughts and feelings otherwise than by words: *sign language, the language of reason. A dog's language is made up of barks, whines, growls, and tail-waggings.* **7** = computer language. **8** the study of language or languages; linguistics. **9** a set of assumptions or attitudes, often held by a group: *He just doesn't speak my language. Abbr:* lang. [< Old French *langage* < *langue* tongue, language < Latin *lingua*]
—*Syn.* **2 Language, dialect, idiom** mean the form and pattern of speech of a particular group of people. **Language** applies to the body of words, forms, and patterns of sounds and structure making up the speech of a people, nation, or group of peoples. **Dialect** applies to a form of speech peculiar to one locality or district of the geographical territory of a language: *The dialect of the English language spoken in Boston sounds strange to a Westerner.* **Idiom** applies to a particular language's characteristic manner of using words in phrases and sentences: *The use of prepositions is a striking feature of English idiom.*

**language arts,** *U.S.* training in reading, writing, and speaking, as distinguished from training in literary appreciation and scholarship.

**lan|guaged** (lan′gwijd), *adj.* having or versed in a language or languages: *many-languaged nations.*

**language laboratory,** a schoolroom equipped with tape recorders and similar apparatus to enable students to practice hearing and speaking a foreign language they are studying.

**lan|guage|less** (lang′gwij lis), *adj.* without language or speech.

**language of flowers,** a method of expressing sentiments by means of flowers.

**langue** (läng), *n. Linguistics.* language as a system or code, as distinguished from individual speech; the grammar, vocabulary, and syntax of a language (contrasted with *parole*). [< French *langue* language]

**langue d'oc** (läng′ dôk′), *French.* the Romance dialect spoken in southern France (Provence) in the Middle Ages. It became modern Provençal.

**langue d'o|ïl** (läng′ dô ēl′), *French.* the Romance dialect spoken in northern France in the Middle Ages. It became modern French.

**lan|guet** or **lan|guette** (lang′gwet), *n.* **1** anything shaped like a little tongue. **2** *Music.* a flat plate or tongue fastened opposite the mouth of an organ flue pipe. **3** a tongue-shaped part of any of various implements, as a narrow blade projecting at the edge of a type of spade. [< Middle French *languette* (diminutive) < Old French *langue* tongue < Latin *lingua*]

**lan|guid** (lang′gwid), *adj.* **1** feeling weak; without energy; drooping: *A hot, sticky day makes a person feel languid.* **SYN**: weary, fatigued, exhausted. **2** without interest or enthusiasm; indifferent: *The lazy boy felt too languid to do anything.* **SYN**: listless, spiritless, apathetic. **3** not brisk or lively; sluggish; dull: *languid competition.* **4** without force or effectiveness: *a languid narrative, a languid style.* [< Latin *languidus* < *languēre* be faint, related to *laxus* lax] —**lan′guid|ly,** *adv.* —**lan′guid|ness,** *n.*

**lan|guid|i|ty** (lang gwid′ə tē), *n.* the state of being languid; languor: ... *languidity induced by oppressive heat* (Time).

**lan|guish** (lang′gwish), *v., n.* —**v.i. 1** to grow weak; become weary; droop: *The flowers languished from lack of water.* **SYN**: wither, fade. **2** to become weak or wasted through pain, hunger, or other suffering; suffer under any unfavorable conditions: *The innocent man languished in prison for twenty years. The New York Shakespeare Festival ... is a most important cultural endeavor in the city and should not be allowed to languish and disappear* (New York Times). **3** to grow dull, slack, or less intense: *The sentry's vigilance never languished.* **SYN**: dwindle. **4** to droop with longing; pine with love or grief (for): *She languished for the home she had been forced to leave.* **5** to assume a soft, tender look for effect: *When a visitor comes in, she smiles and languishes, you'd think that butter wouldn't melt in her mouth* (Thackeray).
—**n. 1** the act or state of languishing: *One desperate grief cures with another's languish* (Shakespeare). **2** a tender look or glance: *the warm, dark languish of her eyes* (John Greenleaf Whittier).
[< Old French *languiss-*, stem of *languir* < Vulgar Latin *languīre,* for Latin *languēre* be weary]
—**lan′guish|er,** *n.*

**lan|guish|ing** (lang′gwi shing), *adj.* **1** drooping as with longing. **SYN**: languid, faint, languorous. **2** tender; sentimental; loving: *languishing glances.* **3** lasting; lingering. **4** failing to excite interest. **SYN**: lethargic, spiritless. —**lan′guish|ing|ly,** *adv.*

**lan|guish|ment** (lang′gwish mənt), *n.* **1** a languishing: *Yet do I sometimes feel a languishment For skies Italian* (Keats). **2** a drooping, pining condition. **3** a languishing look or manner.

**lan|guor** (lang′gər), *n., v.* —**n. 1** lack of energy; weakness; weariness: *A long illness caused his languor.* **SYN**: feebleness, fatigue. **2** lack of interest or enthusiasm; indifference: *Languor is not in your heart* (Matthew Arnold). **SYN**: apathy. **3** softness or tenderness of mood. **4** quietness; stillness: *the languor of a summer afternoon.* **5** lack of activity; sluggishness: *The languor of Rome—its weary pavements, its little life* (Hawthorne).
—**v.i.** to grow weak; languish: *to languor with an illness.*
[< Old French *languor,* or *langour* < Latin *languor* < *languēre* be weary]

**lan|guor|ous** (lang′gər əs), *adj.* **1** languid; listless. **2** causing languor: *languorous fragrance.* —**lan′guor|ous|ly,** *adv.* —**lan′guor|ous|ness,** *n.*

**lan|gur** (lung gůr′), *n.* any one of several genera of large, long-tailed, slender monkeys that live in trees in southern Asia, such as the entellus. [< Hindustani *langūr* < Sanskrit *lāṅgūlin* having a long tail < *lāṅgūla* tail]

**lan|iard** (lan′yərd), *n.* = lanyard.

**la|ni|ar|y** (lā′nē er′ē, lan′ē-), *adj.* (of teeth) fitted for tearing, as the canine teeth. [< Latin *laniārius* having to do with a butcher < *lanius* a butcher < *laniāre* to tear]

**la|ni|ate** (lā′nē āt, lan′ē-), *v.t.,* **-at|ed, -at|ing.** to tear apart; rend. [< Latin *laniāre* (with English *-ate*[1]) to tear]

**la|nif|er|ous** (lə nif′ər əs), *adj.* wool-bearing; woolly. [< Latin *lānifer* (< *lāna* wool + *ferre* to bear) + English *-ous*]

**la|nig|er|ous** (lə nij′ər əs), *adj.* = laniferous.

**lank** (langk), *adj.* **1** long and thin; slender: *a lank boy, lank grasses.* **SYN**: skinny, lanky, gaunt. **2** straight and flat; not curly or wavy: *lank locks of hair.* [Old English *hlanc*] —**lank′ly,** *adv.* —**lank′ness,** *n.*

**lank|i|ly** (lang′kə lē), *adv.* in a lanky condition or form.

**lank|i|ness** (lang′kē nis), *n.* the condition of being lanky.

**lank|y** (lang′kē), *adj.,* **lank|i|er, lank|i|est.** awkwardly long and thin; tall and ungraceful: *a lanky boy.*

**lan|ner** (lan′ər), *n.* **1** a falcon found in southern Europe, North Africa, and southern Asia. **2** *Falconry.* a female lanner. [< Old French *lanier,* probably < Vulgar Latin *lanarius,* variant of Latin *laniārius* a type of falcon < *laniāre* tear flesh]

**lan|ner|et** (lan′ə ret), *n. Falconry.* a male lanner, smaller than the female.

**lan|o|lin** (lan′ə lin), *n.* a yellowish, fatty substance obtained from the natural coating on wool fibers; wool fat. Lanolin is purified and mixed with water (hydrous lanolin) and used in cosmetics, ointments, shoe polish, leather dressing, and as a protective coating for metals. [< Latin *lāna* wool + English *-ol*[2] + *-in*]

**lan|o|line** (lan′ə lin, -lēn), *n.* = lanolin.

**la|nose** (lā′nōs), *adj.* woolly; lanate.

**Lans|downe** (lanz′doun), *n. Trademark.* a fine, soft fabric of silk and wool, used for dresses.

**lan|sign** (lan′sīn′), *n.* (in semantics) a word, character, sound, or other language symbol for a thing or idea: *In the 1930s C. K. Ogden, I. A. Richards and A. Korzybski, and more recently C. E. Osgood, D. H. Mowrer and others, tried to show how language symbols and signs* (*lansigns, as they are sometimes called*) *are associated with their referents in much the same way as conditioned stimulus becomes associated with an unconditioned stimulus, as in the classical conditioning theory of Pavlov* (Science Journal). [< *lan*(*guage*) *sign*]

**Lan|sing strain** (lan′sing), one of three known types of virus causing polio. The other two are the Brunhilde and Leon strains. [< *Lansing,* a city in Michigan, home of a victim of the disease]

**lans|que|net** (lans′kə net), *n.* **1** a mercenary foot soldier, commonly armed with a pike or lance. Lansquenets were formerly employed in the German and other Continental armies in the 1600's and 1700's. **2** a card game in which the players bet against the banker. [< Middle French *lansquenet* < German *Landsknecht;* see etym. under **lance knight**]

**lan|ta|na** (lan tā′nə, -tä′-), *n.* any of a group of tropical or subtropical, chiefly American plants of the verbena family, noted for their bright flowers: *Lantana in glowing shades of orange, yellow or rose ...* (New York Times). [< New Latin *Lantana* the genus name]

***lan|tern** (lan′tərn), *n.* **1** a case to protect a light from wind or rain. A lantern has sides of glass, paper, or some other material through which the light can shine and can be carried from place to place. **2a** the room at the top of a lighthouse where the light is. **b** *Obsolete.* a lighthouse. **3a** an upright structure on a roof or dome for letting in light and air or for decoration. **b** a louver on a roof. **4** = magic lantern. **5** = lantern pinion. [< Old French *lanterne* < Latin *lanterna* (with ending patterned on *lūcerna* lamp) < Greek *lamptḗr* torch < *lámpein* to shine]

***lantern**
definitions 1, 3a

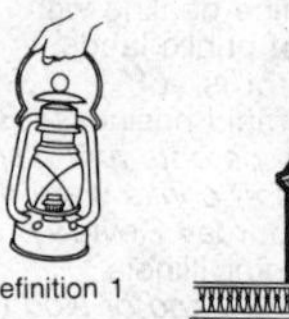

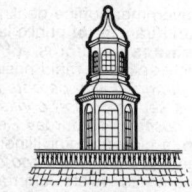

definition 1

definition 3a

**lantern fish,** any of various fishes, chiefly deep-sea, having organs or glands that give off light.

**lantern fly,** any of certain homopterous insects of the tropics; plant hopper. The lantern fly has a long head and was formerly thought to produce light in the dark.

**lantern jaw, 1** a protruding lower jaw: *He has the long, slow step of a countryman, the lantern jaw of a Scotsman ...* (Observer). **2 lantern jaws,** long, thin jaws, giving a hollow appearance to the cheeks.

**lan|tern-jawed** (lan′tərn jôd′), *adj.* having a lantern jaw or lantern jaws.

**lantern pinion** or **wheel,** a kind of gear, used especially in clocks. Lantern pinions have a circular top and bottom connected along the circumferences by staves inserted at equal distances, that serve as teeth; trundle; lantern.

**lantern slide, 1** a small thin sheet of glass with a picture on it that is shown on a screen by a slide projector or a magic lantern.

**lan|tha|nide** (lan′thə nīd, -nid), *n.* any of the rare-earth elements. [< *lanthanum* (first of the rare-earth elements) + *-ide*]

**lanthanide series,** the rare-earth elements: *Cerium is the first of the lanthanide series of the periodic table, so-called because they follow lanthanum in the table* (Science News Letter).

**lan|tha|non** (lan′thə non), *n.* = lanthanide.

***lan|tha|num** (lan′thə nəm), *n.* a soft, malleable, metallic chemical element which occurs in certain rare minerals such as monazite, cerite, and samarskite. Lanthanum is one of the most common of the rare-earth elements, belonging to the cerium metals, and is used in making alloys. Some series do not include lanthanum. [< New Latin *lanthanum* < Greek *lanthánein* lie hidden]

***lanthanum**

| symbol | atomic number | atomic weight | oxidation state |
|---|---|---|---|
| La | 57 | 138.91 | 3 |

**lant|horn** (lant′hôrn, lan′tərn), *n. Archaic.* lantern.

**Lan|tian man** (lan′tyan′), an extinct species of man, thought to be older than Peking man, identified from bones discovered in central China in 1964. [< *Lantien* (county in Shensi province, China, where it was found) + *-ian*]

**la|nu|gi|nose** (lə nü′jə nōs, -nyü′-), *adj.* = lanuginous.

**la|nu|gi|nous** (lə nü′jə nəs, -nyü′-), *adj.* **1** covered with lanugo or soft, downy hairs. **2** like down; downy. [< Latin *lānūginōsus* < *lānūgo, -inis* down, lanugo]

**la|nu|go** (lə nü′gō, -nyü′-), *n. Biology.* a growth of fine soft hair, as on the surface of a leaf or fruit, on the body of an insect, or on the skin of a newborn child.

**lan|yard** (lan′yərd), *n.* **1a** a short rope or cord used on ships to fasten rigging, especially upper rigging, by a tarred rope passed through deadeyes. **b** Also, **knife lanyard.** a loose cord around the neck on which to hang a knife, whistle, or other small tool: *Aboard ship he carried his crutch by a lanyard round his neck* (Robert Louis Stevenson). **c** an ornamented or braided cord worn as a symbol of a military decoration or as part of a uniform. **2** a short cord with a small hook, used in firing certain kinds of cannon. Also, **laniard.** [< French *lanière* thong < Old French *lasniere* < *lasne;* spelling perhaps influenced by English *halyard*]

**La|o** (lä′ō), *n., pl.* **La|o** or **La|os,** *adj.* —*n.* **1** = Laotian. **2** a member of a Sino-Tibetan people of Laos whose Buddhist religion, language, and culture are dominant.
—*adj.* = Laotian.

**La|oc|o|ön** (lā ok′ō on), *n. Greek Legend.* a priest of Apollo at Troy who warned the Trojans against the wooden horse. He and his two sons were killed by two sea serpents sent by Athena.

**La|o|da|mi|a** (lā′ə də mī′ə), *n. Greek Legend.* **1** the wife of Protesilaus, with whom she voluntarily died. **2** the mother of Sarpedon.

**La|od|i|ce|an** (lā od′ə sē′ən), *n., adj.* —*n.* **1** a lukewarm or indifferent Christian. Revelation 3:15-16. **2** a lukewarm or indifferent person.
—*adj.* **1** of or having to do with Laodicea, an ancient city of Phrygia in Asia Minor, or its inhabitants. **2** lukewarm in religion: *Again the humor seems to me painfully grim, and ... in my view Miss O'Connor rewards Laodicean Mrs. Turpin with a vision of herself in hell* (Saturday Review). **3** indifferent.

**La|om|e|don** (lā om′ə don), *n. Greek Legend.* a king of Troy, and father of Priam.

**La|o|size** (lā′ō sīz, lä′-), *v.t.,* **-sized, -siz|ing.** to make Laotian.

**La|o|tian** (lā ō′shən, lä-), *adj., n.* —*adj.* of or having to do with Laos, a country in southeastern Asia, in Indochina, its people, or their language: *Laotian troops.*
—*n.* **1** a person born or living in Laos: *The big problem is how to give Laos back to the Laotians* (Saturday Review). **2** the Thai language spoken by Laotians.

**La|o|tian|ize** (lā ō′shə nīz, lä-), *v.t.,* **-ized, -iz|ing.** = Laosize.

**lap**[1] (lap), *n.* **1** the front part from the waist to the knees of a person sitting down, and the clothing that covers it: *Mother holds the baby on her lap. These advantages would not drop into anyone's lap, and they should not look for easy money* (London Times). **2** the place where anything rests or is cared for: *the lap of the gods. Here rests his head upon the lap of earth* (Thomas Gray). **3** a hollow place thought of as resembling a lap: *The city of Malaga lies in the lap of a fertile valley, surrounded by mountains* (Washington Irving). **4a** a loosely hanging edge of clothing; flap. **b** the front part of a skirt held up to catch or hold something. **5** a long rolled sheet of raw cotton cleaned and ready for carding.
**in the lap of fortune,** fortunate: *She was born in the lap of fortune.*
**in the lap of luxury,** in luxurious circumstances: *He was brought up in the lap of luxury.*
**in the lap of the gods,** out of one's control; beyond anyone's power: *Lord Melchett ... admits that within the present domestic and foreign economic context the new venture is "very much in the lap of the gods"* (Time).
[Old English *læppa*]

**lap**[2] (lap), *v.,* **lapped, lap|ping,** *n.* —*v.i.* **1** to lie together, so as to cover partly; overlap: *The shingles lapped over each other.* **2** to extend out beyond a limit: *The reign of Queen Elizabeth (from 1558 to 1603) lapped over into the 1600's.* **3** to project into or beyond something. **4** to be wound or wrapped around something; be folded. **5a** to get a lap or move ahead in a race. **b** to run or drive a lap at a certain speed or time: *These cars will need to lap at Indianapolis at around 170 m.p.h.* (Manchester Guardian Weekly).
—*v.t.* **1a** to lay together, one thing partly over or beside another: *to lap shingles on a roof.* **b** to put together by overlapping, as a lap joint: *Lap this edge over that.* **2a** to wind or wrap (around); fold (over or about): *He lapped the blanket around him.* **b** to wrap up (in); enwrap: *He lapped himself in a warm blanket.* **3** to envelop or surround: *She was content to be lapped unthinking in this existence* (New Yorker). *For peace her soul was yearning, And now peace laps her round* (Matthew Arnold). **4** to get a lap or more ahead of (other racers) in a race. **5** to cut or polish (gems or metal) with a lap. **6** to enfold as in one's lap; nurse; fondle.
—*n.* **1** the part that laps over. **2** the amount that a part laps over. **3a** one time around a race track: *Who won the first lap of the race? Sunday night at 10:00 o'clock, when the checkered flag drops, the car that has covered the most laps will take the grand prize* (Time). **b** a part of any course traveled: *The last lap of our all-day hike was the toughest. The world would hardly be a safer place if the US pressed forward toward a new and intensified lap in the arms race* (Manchester Guardian Weekly). **4** the act or fact of lapping over. **5** a rotating disk of soft metal or wood to hold polishing powder for cutting and polishing gems or metal.
[< *lap*[1]]

**lap**[3] (lap), *v.,* **lapped, lap|ping,** *n.* —*v.t.* **1** to drink by lifting up with the tongue: *Cats and dogs lap up water.* **2** to move or strike gently against with a lapping sound: *I ... hear the water ... Lapping the steps beneath my feet* (Longfellow).
—*v.i.* **1** to move or beat gently with a lapping; splash gently: *Little waves lapped against the boat.* **2** *Obsolete.* to take up liquid with the tongue.
—*n.* **1** the act of lapping: *With one lap of his tongue the bear finished the honey.* **2** a sound of lapping: *The lap of waves against the boat put me to sleep.* **3** the amount lapped; lick; taste. **4** something that is lapped.
**lap up,** *Informal.* **a** to believe eagerly, especially something untrue: *The boys lapped up the tales about Daniel Boone and the Indians.* **b** to drink or eat greedily or with great pleasure: *The hikers were so hungry after the long hike that they lapped up their dinner.*
[Old English *lapian*]

**lap**[4] (lap), *v. Scottish.* a past tense of **leap.**

**Lap.,** Lapland.

**lap|a|rec|to|my** (lap′ə rek′tə mē), *n., pl.* **-mies.** the surgical removal of a portion of the intestine at the side. [< Greek *lapárā* flank + *ektomē* a cutting out]

**lap|a|ro|cele** (lap′ər ə sēl), *n. Medicine.* hernia in the lumbar regions. [< Greek *lapárā* flank + *kēlē* tumor]

**lap|a|ro|scope** (lap′ə rə skōp), *n.* a tubelike optical instrument for illuminating and examining internal organs from the outside. [< Greek *lapárā* flank + English *-scope*]

**lap|a|ros|co|py** (lap′ə ros′kə pē), *n.* the use of a laparoscope.

**lap|a|rot|o|my** (lap′ə rot′ə mē), *n., pl.* **-mies.** the operation of making an incision into the abdominal wall, especially through the flank. [< Greek *lapárā* flank + *-tomíā* a cutting]

**lap belt,** a safety belt buckled across the lap; seat belt: *The shoulder harnesses, like the lap belts, which are also on all new cars now, are aimed at preventing riders from pitching about in accidents and colliding with the car inside* (New York Times).

**lap|board** (lap′bôrd′, -bōrd′), *n.* a thin flat board held on the lap and used as a table.

**lap dissolve,** the simultaneous fading out of one scene in a motion picture or television show and fading in of another scene.

**lap dog,** **1** a small pet dog. **2** a fawning flatterer; toady.

**lap-dog** (lap′dôg′), *adj.* flattering in a fawning manner: *lap-dog acceptance of his employer's attitudes.*

**la|pel** (lə pel′), *n.* either of the two front parts of a coat folded back just below the collar. [diminutive form of *lap*[1]]

**lap|ful** (lap′fu̇l), *n., pl.* **-fuls.** as much as a lap can hold.

**lap|i|dar|i|an** (lap′ə dãr′ē ən), *n., adj.* = lapidary.

**lap|i|dar|y** (lap′ə der′ē), *n., pl.* **-dar|ies,** *adj.* —*n.* **1a** a person who cuts, polishes, or engraves precious stones. **b** an engraver of stone monuments. **2** the art of cutting precious stones. **3** an expert in precious stones or in the art of cutting them. **4** a piece of jewelry, especially one that shows great workmanship: *The crown ... is revealed as a gorgeous jewel-encrusted, gold piece of lapidary* (New York Times).
—*adj.* **1** having to do with cutting or engraving precious stones. **2** engraved on stone: *In lapidary inscriptions a man is not upon oath* (Samuel Johnson). **3** characteristic of stone inscriptions; brief, precise, and pointed: *... when Samuel Butler attacked Darwin in a series of pamphlets and periodicals, Huxley quoted Goethe's lapidary phrase, "Every whale has its louse"* (New Yorker).
[< Late Latin *lapidārius* working with stone < *lapis, -idis* stone]

**lap|i|date** (lap′ə dāt), *v.t.,* **-dat|ed, -dat|ing.** **1** to throw stones at; pelt with stones. **2** to stone to death. [< Latin *lapidāre* (with English *-ate*[1]) < *lapis, -idis* a stone]

**lap|i|da|tion** (lap′ə dā′shən), *n.* **1** the act of throwing stones at a person. **2** punishment or execution by stoning.

**lap|i|des|cent** (lap′ə des′ənt), *adj.* resembling a stone, especially a stone monument; stonelike: *He is curiously apart, a lapidescent presence, half man, half monument, adored but unapproachable* (Tony Tanner). [< Latin *lapidēscens, -entis,* present participle of *lapidēscere* to become stony < *lapis, -idis* a stone]

**lap|i|dic|o|lous** (lap′ə dik′ə ləs), *adj.* living under or among stones, as beetles or other insects do.

**la|pid|i|fi|ca|tion** (lə pid′ə fə kā′shən), *n.* a turning into stone; petrification.

**la|pid|i|fy** (lə pid′ə fī), *v.,* **-fied, -fy|ing.** —*v.t.* to make or turn into stone.
—*v.i.* to become stone.
[< French *lapidifier* < Latin *lapis, -idis* stone + French *-fier* -fy]

**la|pil|li** (lə pil′ī), *n. pl., sing.* **-pil|lus** (-pil′əs). small stones or pebbles, now especially the fragments of stone ejected from volcanoes. [< Italian *lapilli,* plural < Latin *lapillus* (diminutive) < *lapis, -idis* stone]

**lap|in** (lap′in; *French* lȧ paN′), *n.* **1** a rabbit. **2** rabbit fur. [< French *lapin*]

**la|pis** (lā′pis, lap′is), *n., pl.* **lap|i|des** (lap′ə dēz). *Latin.* a stone (used in phrases, especially in the names of minerals and gems).

**lap|is laz|u|li** (lap′is laz′yə lī, -lē), **1** a deep-blue, opaque, semiprecious stone used chiefly for an ornament and sometimes for preparing the pigment ultramarine. Lapis lazuli contains sodium, aluminum, sulfur, and silicon in a mixture of minerals. *Formula:* $Na_5Al_3Si_3O_{12}S$ **2** deep or azure blue, the color of this stone: *The sun was gold in a sky of lapis lazuli.* [< Medieval Latin *lapis lazuli* < Latin *lapis* stone + Medieval Latin *lazuli,* genitive of *lazulum* lapis lazuli < Arabic *lāzuward* < Persian *lājward.* Compare etym. under **azure.**]

**Lap|ith** (lap′ith), *n., pl.* **Lap|i|thae** (lap′ə thē), **Lapiths.** *Greek Mythology.* one of a people of Thessaly who defeated the centaurs when they tried to carry off the women of the Lapithae at a bridal feast.

**lap joint,** a joint connecting parts of a heavy beam, formed by overlapping the ends of two timbers and bolting, riveting, or strapping them together.

**lap-joint** (lap′joint′), *v.t.* to make a lap joint on; overlap.

**Lap|land|er** (lap′lan dər), *n.* a native or inhabitant of Lapland; Lapp.

**Lap|land longspur** (lap′land), any bird of a variety of longspur with a black throat in the spring plumage, that nests in the Arctic and winters in the United States.

**lap money,** money given to the racer who leads the field at the end of a lap or laps in auto racing.

**Lapp** (lap), *n.* **1** one of a group of people that live in Lapland, a region in northern Norway, Sweden, Finland, and northwestern Soviet Union, who are small, have short, broad heads, and engage in herding reindeer, fishing, and hunting; Laplander: *The Lapps of northerly Scandinavia were formerly classed outright as Mongoloids, but they show perhaps as many Alpine as East Asiatic traits* (Alfred L. Kroeber). **2** the language of the Lapps, a Finno-Ugric language; Lappish. [probably < Swedish *Lapp*]

**lap|pa** (lap′ə), *n., pl.* **-pas.** a long piece of cloth wrapped around the waist, worn as a skirt in Liberia and Sierra Leone. [< a native name in western Africa]

**lap|per**[1] (lap′ər), *n.* one who laps, or takes up (liquid) with the tongue. [< *lap*[3] + *-er*[1]]

**lap|per**[2] (lap′ər), *n.* a person who laps or folds (linen or other cloth). [< *lap*[2] + *-er*[1]]

**lap|pet** (lap′it), *n.* **1** a small flap or fold: *a lappet on a dress.* **2** a loose fold of flesh or membrane. **3** the lobe of the ear. **4** a bird's wattle. [< *lap*[1] + *-et*]

**lappet moth,** a bombycid moth of the eastern United States whose larva has small lobes along its body and feeds on the leaves of many trees, as the apple, oak, and maple.

**Lapp|ish** (lap′ish), *adj., n.* —*adj.* of or having to do with the Lapps or their language.
—*n.* = Lapp (def. 2).

**lap robe,** a blanket, fur robe, or similar covering used to keep the lap and legs warm when riding in an automobile, carriage, or other vehicle.

**laps|a|ble** (lap′sə bəl), *adj.* that can lapse.

**lap|sang souchong** (lap′sang), a fine, smoky

**Pronunciation Key:** hat, āge, cãre, fär; let, ēqual, tėrm; it, īce; hot, ōpen, ôrder; oil, out; cup, pu̇t, rüle; child; long; thin; ᴛʜen; zh, measure; ə represents **a** in about, **e** in taken, **i** in pencil, **o** in lemon, **u** in circus.

variety of souchong (black tea): *He picked up some lapsang souchong, a very smoky tea that he likes to mix with Darjeeling* (New York Times). [< Cantonese *lapsang siu chung*]

**lapse** (laps), *n., v.,* **lapsed, laps|ing.** —*n.* **1** a slight mistake or error: *a lapse of the tongue because of carelessness, a lapse of memory.* **SYN**: slip, fault, indiscretion, misstep. **2** a slipping by; passing away: *A minute is a short lapse of time. Sunny Plaines, And liquid Lapse of murmuring Streams* (Milton). **3a** the act of slipping back; sinking down; slipping into a lower condition: *War is a lapse into savage ways.* **b** the act of falling or passing into any state: *a lapse into silence.* **4** a slipping or falling away from what is right: *a moral lapse. The long strife with evil which began With the first lapse of new-created man* (John Greenleaf Whittier). **5** the ending of a right or privilege because it was not renewed, not used, or otherwise neglected: *the lapse of a lease.* **6** a falling into disuse or ruin: *the lapse of a custom.* **7** an apostatizing from the faith; a falling into heresy. **8** *Meteorology.* a decrease of temperature of the atmosphere with increase of altitude.
—*v.i.* **1** to make a slight mistake or error. **2** to slip by; pass away: *The boy's interest soon lapsed. I saw the river lapsing slowly onward* (Hawthorne). **3a** to slip back; sink down: *The abandoned house lapsed into ruin.* **b** to fall or pass into any specified state: *to lapse into silence. It is difficult to talk to youth today without lapsing into jargon and clichés* (New York Times). **4** to slip or fall away from what is right: *Little boys sometimes lapse from good behavior.* **5** (of a right or privilege) to end because it was not renewed, not used, or otherwise neglected: *His driver's license lapsed when he failed to renew it. If a legal claim is not enforced, it lapses after a certain number of years.* **6** to fall into disuse. **7** to apostatize; forsake one's faith: *He is a lapsed Presbyterian, while Dolores takes her Catholicism very seriously* (Time).
—*v.t.* to allow to lapse; forfeit; lose: *to lapse a right or privilege.*
[< Latin *lāpsus, -ūs* a fall < *lābī* to slip, fall]
—**laps′er**, *n.*

**lapse rate**, the rate of decrease of atmospheric temperature with increase in altitude.

**laps|i|ble** (lap′sə bəl), *adj.* = lapsable.

**lap|strake** (lap′strāk), *adj., n.* —*adj.* constructed with each successive board or plate of a boat overlapping the one below it; clinker-built.
—*n.* a boat that is clinker-built.

**lap|streak** (lap′strēk), *adj., n.* = lapstrake.

**La|pu|ta** (lə pyü′tə), *n.* the flying island in Jonathan Swift's *Gulliver's Travels,* inhabited by philosophers addicted to visionary and absurd projects.

**La|pu|tan** (lə pyü′tən), *adj., n.* —*adj.* **1** of or having to do with Laputa. **2** unpractical; visionary: *Laputan philosophers.*
—*n.* **1** an inhabitant of Laputa. **2** a visionary.

**lap-weld** (lap′weld′), *v.t.* to weld with overlapping edges.

**lap|wing** (lap′wing′), *n.* a plover of Europe, Asia, and northern Africa. the lapwing has a crested head, a slow, irregular flight, and a peculiar wailing cry; pewit; weep. [alteration of Old English *hlēapewince* < *hlēapan* to leap + *-wince* tottering (see related etym. at **wink**); spelling influenced by English *lap*² and *wing*]

**lar** (lär), *n., pl.* **lar|es.** *Latin.* a household god.

**lar|board** (lär′bərd, -bôrd, -bōrd), *n., adj.* —*n.* the side of a ship to the left of a person looking from the stern toward the bow; port.
—*adj.* on the left side of a ship.
[Middle English *ladeborde* (originally) the loading side; influenced by English *starboard*]
▶ In modern nautical use, **larboard** has been replaced by *port.*

**lar|ce|ner** (lär′sə nər), *n.* = larcenist.

**lar|ce|nist** (lär′sə nist), *n.* a person who commits larceny.

**lar|ce|nous** (lär′sə nəs), *adj.* **1** characterized by larceny; guilty of larceny: *Burglary is a larcenous offense.* **2** thievish: *Blue jays are known for their larcenous habits.* —**lar′ce|nous|ly**, *adv.*

**lar|ce|ny** (lär′sə nē), *n., pl.* **-nies.** the unlawful taking, carrying away, and using of the personal property of another person without his consent; theft. **SYN**: robbery, thievery. The distinction between grand larceny and petit larceny, based on the value of the property stolen, still exists in some states of the United States but was abolished in England in 1827.
[< Anglo-French *larcin,* Old French *larrecin* (< Latin *latrōcinium* robbery < *latrō, -ōnis* bandit) + English *-y*³]

**larch** (lärch), *n.* **1** a tree with small, woody cones, and needles that fall off in the autumn. The larches belong to the pine family. See picture under **deciduous. 2** the strong, tough wood of this tree. [< German *Lärche,* ultimately < Latin *larix, -icis*]

**lard** (lärd), *n., v.* —*n.* the fat of pigs or hogs, melted down and made clear. Lard is made especially of the internal fat of the abdomen and is used in cooking. *Mother uses lard in making pies.* (*Figurative.*) *Less taut novels have similar faults concealed beneath the lard* (New York Times).
—*v.t.* **1** to put strips of bacon or salt pork in or on (meat) before cooking. **2** to give variety to; enrich; embellish: *The speaker larded his speech with jokes and stories. The facts ... are still generally unknown, and they have become larded with myths and barroom fantasy* (Newsweek). **SYN**: garnish, interlard. **3** to put lard on or in; grease: *Lard the pan well. Falstaff sweats to death, and Lards the lean earth as he walks along* (Shakespeare). **4** *Obsolete.* to fatten.
**lard in,** to insert or introduce: *Stations try to lard in commercials so they don't interrupt programs* (Maclean's).
[< Old French *lard* bacon fat < Latin *lārdum*]
—**lard′like′**, *adj.*

**lar|da|ceous** (lär dā′shəs), *adj.* **1** of or like lard. **2** *Pathology.* of or having to do with a form of degeneration in which a protein substance (amyloid) is deposited in the tissues, especially those of the abdominal organs.

**lar|der** (lär′dər), *n.* **1** a place where food is kept; pantry. **2** a supply of food: *The hunter's larder included flour, bacon, and what he had shot.* (*Figurative.*) *The most gratifying factor about Canada's restocking of her foreign exchange larder is that January and February are traditionally months that show a drain in reserves* (New York Times). [< Old French *lardier* < Medieval Latin *lardarium* < Latin *lārdum* lard]

**larder beetle**, a kind of small beetle whose larvae are very destructive to stored meat, cheese, and stuffed animals in museums. The larvae are covered with whitish-brown hairs.

**lar|don** (lär′dən), *n.* a narrow strip of bacon fat or salt pork fat inserted in meat in larding. [< Middle French *lardon* < Old French *lard* lard]

**lar|doon** (lär dün′), *n.* = lardon.

**lard-type** (lärd′tīp′), *adj.* raised or bred to turn eaten feed into fat: *a lard-type hog.*

**lard|y** (lär′dē), *adj.,* **lard|i|er, lard|i|est. 1** full of or like lard: *Her face was wide and flat and lardy white* (New Yorker). (*Figurative.*) *The President has sent to Congress a lardy budget* (Time). **2** plump; fat: *a lardy face.*

**lard|y-dard|y** (lär′dē där′dē), *adj. Especially British Slang.* languidly genteel or foppish; affected: *the lardy-dardy school of acting.*

**lar|es** (lâr′ēz), *n., pl. of* **lar.** *Latin.* the household gods of the ancient Romans; the guardian spirits of the house.

**lares and penates**, **1** the household gods of the ancient Romans. The lares were believed to protect the home from outside damage, the penates protecting the interior. **2** the cherished possessions of a family or household. [< Latin *larēs,* plural of *lār,* household god; *penātes,* plural, related to *penus* sanctuary]

**lar|ga|men|te** (lär′gä men′tā), *adv. Music.* in a broad manner. [< Italian *largamente* < *largo* largo]

**lar|gan|do** (lär gän′dō), *adv., adj. Italian.* allargando.

**large** (lärj), *adj.,* **larg|er, larg|est,** *adv., n.* —*adj.* **1** of more than the usual size, amount, or number; big: *America is a large country. A hundred thousand dollars is a large sum of money. Large crowds come to see our team play.* **SYN**: huge, great, vast, enormous, immense, gigantic. See syn. under **great. 2** having much scope or range; broad: *large sympathies. The President should be a man of large experience.* **SYN**: extensive. **3a** on a great scale: *a large employer of labor.* **b** grand or pompous: *to talk in a large way.* **4** *Nautical.* (of the wind) blowing in a favorable direction; fair. **5** *Rare.* extended or lengthy, as speech or writing. **6** *Archaic.* abundant, copious, or ample: *We have yet large day; for scarce the sun Hath finish'd half his journey* (Milton). **7** *Obsolete.* liberal; generous; lavish: *The poor King Reignier whose large style Agrees not with the leanness of his purse* (Shakespeare). **8** *Obsolete.* of speech, actions, or thoughts: **a** lax; free; unrestrained. **b** licentious; improper; gross.
—*adv.* **1** in a large manner: *Do not draw the picture so large.* **2** *Nautical.* with the wind blowing from a favorable direction: *to sail large, to go large.*
—*n.* **at large, a** at liberty; free: *Is the escaped prisoner still at large?* **b** for the most part; altogether: *The people at large want peace.* **c** representing the whole of a state or district, not merely one division of it: *a congressman at large.* **d** in detail; fully: *I ... told him the story at large* (Daniel Defoe).
**in large** or **in the large**, on a big scale: *I have made trial of this method, both in small and in large* (John Smeaton).
**writ large.** See under **writ**².
[< Old French *large* < Latin *lārgus* copious]
—**large′ness**, *n.*

**Large Black**, a large, black hog of a breed with drooping ears, developed in Great Britain.

**large calorie**, the quantity of heat necessary to raise the temperature of a kilogram of water one degree centigrade (Celsius); kilocalorie.

**Large Cloud**, the larger of two Magellanic Clouds, located in the constellation Dorado.

**large cranberry**, a variety of cranberry growing in eastern North America that has berries up to ¾ inch in diameter.

**large-hand|ed** (lärj′han′did), *adj.* **1** having large hands. **2** *Figurative.* bountiful; generous.

**large-heart|ed** (lärj′här′tid), *adj.* generous; liberal. —**large′-heart′ed|ness**, *n.*

**large intestine**, the wide, lower part of the intestines into which the small intestine discharges food that has been digested. It is about five feet long and lies between the small intestine and the anus, consisting of the cecum, colon, and rectum. Water is absorbed and wastes are eliminated in the large intestine. See picture under **intestine.**

**large|ish** (lär′jish), *adj.* rather large; largish: *It is a decorative Tudor house ... and now has a largeish lounge* (Times Educational Supplement).

**large|ly** (lärj′lē), *adv.* **1** to a great extent; mainly: *Success depends largely on working hard. A desert consists largely of sand.* **2** much; in great quantity: *When Simon and his sons had drunk largely* (I Maccabees 16:16).

**large-mind|ed** (lärj′mīn′did), *adj.* having or showing liberal views; tolerant. —**large′-mind′ed|ly**, *adv.* —**large′-mind′ed|ness**, *n.*

**large|mouth** (lärj′mouth′), *n.* = largemouth bass.

**largemouth bass**, a North American fresh water game fish that has a dark-green or almost black color and reaches a weight of over 20 pounds; black bass: *Contrary to popular belief, the largemouth and smallmouth bass are not true bass at all but belong to the sunfish* (Science News Letter).

**large-mouthed black bass** (lärj′mouᴛʜd′, -moutht′), = largemouth bass.

**larg|en** (lär′jən), *v.i.* to become larger: *lateral spread of pattern set up gradually largening movements across the surface like ripples on a still pool* (London Times). —*v.t.* to make larger; enlarge.

**larg|er-than-life** (lär′jər ᴛʜən līf′), *adj.* of heroic or epic dimensions: *larger-than-life adventures. In U.S. folklore, nothing has been more romanticized than guns and the larger-than-life men who wielded them* (Time).

**large-scale** (lärj′skāl′), *adj.* **1** involving many persons or things; great; extensive: *The great Chicago fire of 1871 was a large-scale disaster.* **2** made or drawn to a large scale: *This large-scale map shows many details.*

**large-scale integration**, the use of many integrated circuits in an electronic device, such as a computer.

**lar|gess** or **lar|gesse** (lär′jis), *n.* **1** a generous giving: *Christmas is a day of largess.* **2** a generous gift or gifts: *Largess in the form of research reactors is only one aspect of the use of nuclear science as an instrument of foreign policy* (Bulletin of Atomic Scientists). **3** a generous quality or spirit: *... if he did not exactly sympathize with her temperament and point of view, at least he included her with the largess of his affection* (Theodore Dreiser). [< Old French *largesse* < *large* large]

**large-stat|ured** (lärj′stach′ərd), *adj.* consisting of tall trees and shrubs: *Large-statured forests* (*moist forest of the Temperate Zone, where nutrients are abundant, and certain tropical rain forests*) ... (George W. Woodwell).

**Large White**, a large, white hog of a breed developed in Great Britain.

**lar|ghet|to** (lär get′ō), *adj., adv., n., pl.* **-tos.** *Music.* —*adj.* rather slow; not so slow as largo, but usually slower than andante.
—*adv.* in larghetto tempo; rather slowly.
—*n.* a passage or piece of music in rather slow time.
[< Italian *larghetto* (diminutive) < *largo* largo]

**larg|ish** (lär′jish), *adj.* rather large.

**lar|go** (lär′gō), *adj., adv., n., pl.* **-gos.** *Music.*
—*adj.* slow and dignified; solemn; stately.
—*adv.* in slow and dignified tempo.
—*n.* a slow, stately passage or piece of music.
[< Italian *largo* < Latin *lārgus* large]

**lar|i|at** (lar′ē ət), *n. U.S.* **1** a rope for fastening horses, mules, or other livestock, to a stake while they are grazing. **2** = lasso. [American English < Spanish *la reata* the rope; *reata* < Spanish *re-* again (< Latin *re-*) + *atar* to tie < Latin *aptāre* adjust, adapt. Compare etym. under **riata.**]

**lar|ine** (lar′in, lâr′īn), *adj.* **1** of the family of birds that comprises the gulls. **2** of or like a gull. [< New Latin *Larinae* the subfamily name < *Lari* the former order name < Latin *larus* sea mew < Greek *láros* sea mew, gull]

**la|rith|mic** (lə riᴛʜ′mik), *adj.* of or having to do with larithmics.

**la|rith|mics** (lə riᴛʜ′miks), *n.* the science dealing with population in its quantitative aspects. [< Greek *lāós* people + *arithmós* number + English *-ics*]

**lark**[1] (lärk), *n.* **1** a small songbird of Europe, Asia, America, and northern Africa, with brown feathers and long hind claws. One kind, the skylark, sings while soaring in the air. **2** any one of various similar birds, such as the meadow lark, horned lark, and titlark. [Old English *lāwerce*]

**lark**[2] (lärk), *n., v. Informal.* **—*n.*** something that is good fun; merry or gay time; joke: *The boys went wading just for a lark.* **SYN**: frolic, prank.
**—*v.i.*** **1** to have fun; play pranks; frolic. **2** to ride across country.
**—*v.t.*** to make fun of; tease.
[origin uncertain] **—lark′er,** *n.*

**lark bunting**, a finch of the plains and prairies of western North America. The male is black with a white patch on the wing in its summer plumage.

**lark|ish** (lär′kish), *adj.* = larky. **—lark′ish|ness,** *n.*

**lark's-head** (lärks′hed′), *n.* a knot formed by passing a loop of a rope around an object, and then passing the ends of the rope through the loop; cow hitch. See picture under **hitch**.

**lark|some** (lärk′səm), *adj.* = larky.

**lark sparrow**, a sparrow of central North America with a fan-shaped tail, chestnut markings on the head, and a white breast with a single spot in the center.

**lark|spur** (lärk′spėr), *n.* **1** a plant with clusters of blue, pink, or white flowers on tall stalks. Larkspurs are of the crowfoot family and have a curved, petallike upper sepal shaped like a spur; delphinium. **2** the blue color characteristic of the larkspur: *larkspur, a pastel blue slightly inclining to the mauve* (London Daily Express). [earlier *larkes spur* < genitive of *lark*[1] + *spur*]

**lark|y** (lär′kē), *adj.,* **lark|i|er, lark|i|est.** *Informal.* carefree; frolicsome; gay: *... those oppressed with the weight of wealth as well as those larky with the lack of it* (New York Times).

**lar|moy|ant** (lär moi′ənt), *adj.* tearful; lachrymose: *larmoyant comedy.* [< French *larmoyant,* present participle of *larmoyer* be tearful < *larme* tear[1]]

**lar|nax** (lär′naks), *n., pl.* **-na|kes** (-nə kēz). a box or coffer, especially a boxlike receptacle of clay or terra cotta, often painted, found in early Greek or Mycenaean tombs. [< Greek *lárnax, -akos*]

**lar|oid** (lar′oid), *adj.* **1** belonging to the family of birds that includes the gulls. **2** gull-like. [< New Latin *Lari* (see etym. under **larine**) + English *-oid*]

**lar|ri|gan** (lar′ə gən), *n.* a kind of moccasin shoe or boot of highly oiled leather formerly worn by lumbermen. [American English; origin unknown]

**lar|ri|kin** (lar′ə kin), *n., adj. Especially Australian.* **—*n.*** a rowdy; hoodlum; hooligan: *Given the tempting venue of lonely distances ... it was only natural that the most worthless of the bush larrikins should pass from horse stealing to high robbery and murder* (Kylie Tennant).
**—*adj.*** rough; rowdy; disorderly.
[origin uncertain]

**lar|ri|kin|ism** (lar′ə kə niz′əm), *n. Especially Australian.* rowdy behavior; hooliganism.

**lar|rup** (lar′əp), *v.,* **-ruped, -rup|ing,** *n. Informal.* **—*v.t.*** to beat; thrash: *I ... was larruped with the rope* (Dickens).
**—*n.*** a blow.
[origin uncertain. Compare Dutch *larpen* thrash, box the ears.] **—lar′rup|er,** *n.*

**lar|rup|ing** (lar′əp ing), *adj.* rousing; vigorous: *If possible I want larruping, blunt-nosed accounts of human beings* (Punch).

**lar|um** (lar′əm, lär′-), *n. Archaic.* an alarm; alarum. [short for *alarum*]

**lar|va** (lär′və), *n., pl.* **-vae.** **1** the early form of an insect from the time it leaves the egg until it becomes a pupa. A caterpillar is the larva of a butterfly or moth. A grub is the larva of a beetle. Maggots are the larvae of flies. Larvae look somewhat like worms. They sometimes have short legs but lack compound eyes. Wings, when present in the adult, develop internally during the larval stage. (*Figurative.*) *Every year sees the appearance of fictional contrivances that pause briefly as larvae in book form before butterflying their way onto the screen* (Time). **2** an immature form of certain animals that is different in structure from the adult form and must undergo a change or metamorphosis to become like the parent. A tadpole is the larva of a frog or toad. See picture under **amphibian**. [earlier, a ghost, specter < Latin *lārva* ghost, mask]

**lar|vae** (lär′vē), *n.* plural of **larva**.

**lar|val** (lär′vəl), *adj.* **1** of or having to do with larvae: *larval food.* **2** in the form of a larva: *a larval eel, larval flukes.* **3** characteristic of larvae: *the larval stage of an insect.*

**lar|vi|cid|al** (lär′və sī′dəl), *adj.* of or having to do with killing larvae.

**lar|vi|cide** (lär′və sīd), *n., v.,* **-cid|ed, -cid|ing.** **—*n.*** a substance which kills larvae.
**—*v.t.*** to apply a larvicide to: *... the larviciding of breeding places with DDT* (Scientific American).

**lar|vip|a|rous** (lär vip′ər əs), *adj.* giving birth to young insects that have already passed from the egg to the larval stage. [< *larva* + Latin *parere* to give birth + English *-ous*]

**laryng-**, *combining form.* the form of **laryngo-** before vowels, as in *laryngitis.*

**la|ryn|gal** (lə ring′gəl), *adj., n. Phonetics.* **—*adj.*** produced in the larynx. The Scottish pronunciation of *t* in *bottle* is laryngal. (The same sound occurs in certain pronunciations of American English).
**—*n.*** a laryngal sound.
[< New Latin *larynx, laryngis* larynx + English *-al*[2]]

**la|ryn|ge|al** (lə rin′jē əl), *adj., n.* **—*adj.*** **1** of or having to do with the larynx. **2** produced in the larynx: *a laryngeal sound.* **3** used on the larynx.
**—*n.*** **1** a laryngeal nerve or artery. **2** a laryngeal sound.
[< New Latin *laryngeus* (< *larynx* larynx) + English *-al*[1]]

**lar|yn|gec|to|mee** (lar′ən jek′tə mē′), *n.* a person whose larynx has been removed.

**lar|yn|gec|to|my** (lar′ən jek′tə mē), *n., pl.* **-mies.** the surgical removal of the larynx.

**la|ryn|ges** (lə rin′jēz), *n.* a plural of **larynx**.

**lar|yn|git|ic** (lar′ən jit′ik), *adj., n.* **—*adj.*** of or like laryngitis.
**—*n.*** a person who has laryngitis.

**lar|yn|gi|tis** (lar′ən jī′tis), *n.* inflammation of the larynx, usually accompanied by hoarseness. [< New Latin *laryngitis* < *larynx* larynx + *-itis* inflammation]

**laryngo-**, *combining form.* **1** larynx: *Laryngoscopy = examination of the larynx.*
**2** larynx and ___: *Laryngopharyngeal = having to do with the larynx and the pharynx.* Also, **laryng-** before vowels.
[< Greek *lárynx, láryngos* upper windpipe]

**lar|yn|gol|o|gist** (lar′ing gol′ə jist), *n.* a specialist in laryngology.

**lar|yn|gol|o|gy** (lar′ing gol′ə jē), *n.* the branch of medicine dealing with the larynx and the treatment of its diseases.

**la|ryn|go|pha|ryn|ge|al** (lə ring′gō fə rin′jē əl), *adj.* of or having to do with both the larynx and the pharynx.

**la|ryn|go|phone** (lə ring′gə fōn), *n.* a sound-transmitting apparatus which is applied to the throat to receive the speech sounds directly from the vibration of the larynx.

**la|ryn|go|scope** (lə ring′gə skōp), *n.* an instrument with mirrors for examining the interior of the larynx.

**la|ryn|go|scop|ic** (lə ring′gə skop′ik), *adj.* having to do with a laryngoscope or laryngoscopy.

**la|ryn|go|scop|i|cal** (lə ring′gə skop′ə kəl), *adj.* = laryngoscopic.

**lar|yn|gos|co|py** (lar′ing gos′kə pē), *n., pl.* **-pies.** examination of the larynx, especially with the use of a laryngoscope.

**lar|yn|got|o|my** (lar′ing got′ə mē), *n., pl.* **-mies.** surgical incision into the larynx.

**la|ryn|go|tra|che|i|tis** (lə ring′gō trā′kē ī′tis), *n.* **1** inflammation of the larynx and trachea. **2** a viral, infectious respiratory disease of domestic fowl.

**lar|ynx** (lar′ingks), *n., pl.* **la|ryn|ges** (lə rin′jēz) or **lar|ynx|es.** **1** the upper end of the windpipe in man, where the vocal cords are; voice box. It acts as an organ of speech. See picture under **epiglottis**. **2** a similar organ in other mammals, or the corresponding structure in other animals. **3** (in birds) either of two modifications of the trachea, one at the top and one at the bottom of the windpipe. The syrinx or bottom cavity is the true organ of sound. [< New Latin *larynx* < Greek *lárynx, láryngos* the upper windpipe]

**las|a|ble** (lā′zə bəl), *adj.* capable of being lased: *His scheme is to introduce into the room traces of a "lasable" gas chosen so that its excitation-frequency lies in the invisible ultraviolet, and its emission frequency in the visible* (New Scientist).

**la|sa|gna** (lə zän′yə), *n., pl.* **la|sa|gne** (lə zän′yə). **1** a dish consisting of chopped meat, cheese, and tomato sauce, cooked with layers of wide, flat noodles. **2** a wide, flat noodle. See picture under **pasta**. [< Italian *lasagna* (singular of *lasagne*) < Latin *lasanum* cooking pot < Greek *lásanon* utensil]

**las|car** (las′kər), *n.* a native sailor, army servant, or soldier of the East Indies. [< Portuguese *laschar,* probably < Hindustani *lashkarī* soldier < *lashkar* army, camp < Persian *laskar*]

**las|civ|i|ous** (lə siv′ē əs), *adj.* **1** inclined to or feeling lust: *a lascivious person.* **2** showing lust; lewd; wanton: *He on Eve began to cast lascivious eyes* (Milton). **3** causing lust or wantonness: *He capers nimbly in a lady's chamber To the lascivious pleasing of a lute* (Shakespeare). [< Late Latin *lascīviōsus* < Latin *lascīvia* playfulness < *lascīvus* playful] **—las|civ′i|ous|ly,** *adv.* **—las|civ′i|ous|ness,** *n.*

**lase** (lāz), *v.,* **lased, las|ing.** **—*v.i.*** to emit the intense light beam of a laser: *Many lasers, as I have described, are excited (or "pumped," as we say in the laboratory) by light. Others may be made to lase by radio waves, or by an electric current, or by chemical reactions* (Thomas Meloy).
**—*v.t.*** to subject to the light beams of a laser: *Bean sprouts appeared at the soil surface seven days after planting in the lased samples and nine days in the control sample* (New Scientist).
[back formation < *laser*]

***la|ser** (lā′zər), *n., v.* **—*n.*** a device that produces a very narrow and intense beam of light of only one wavelength going in only one direction; optical maser. Laser beams are used to cut or melt hard materials, remove diseased body tissues, and transmit television signals, among other functions. *A pulsed ruby laser piercing a sapphire crystal is shown on this week's front cover. The laser ... generates energy so intense that it can bore a sixteenth of an inch hole in the sapphire in a thousandth of a second* (Science News Letter). (*Figurative.*) *He brought down the house with the laser wit that has constantly amused his large crowds* (Time).
**—*v.i.*** to act as a laser; lase.
[< *l*(ight) *a*(mplification by) *s*(timulated) *e*(mission of) *r*(adiation)]

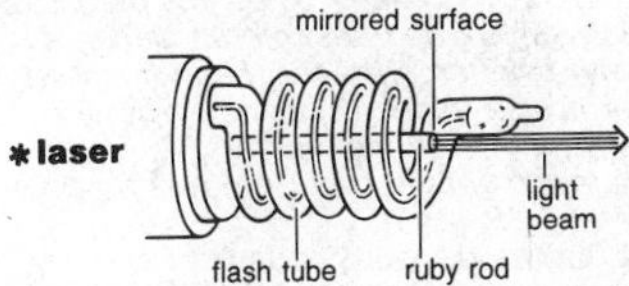


***laser**

**laser surgery**, the destruction of diseased tissue by means of laser beams: *A multi-disciplined team of surgeons, physicists, engineers and technicians is required if laser surgery is to be conducted effectively and safely* (Ronald Brown).

**lash**[1] (lash), *n., v.* **—*n.*** **1** the part of a whip that is not the handle and is usually flexible: *The leather lash cut the side of the horse.* **2** a stroke or blow with a whip, thong, or the like: *I gave my horse a lash that sounded through the forest* (Ann Radcliffe). **3** a sudden, swift movement: *the lash of an animal's tail.* **4** *Figurative.* anything that hurts as a blow from a whip does: *Lest they should fall under the lash of the penal laws* (Jonathan Swift). *How smart a lash that speech doth give my conscience* (Shakespeare). **5** = eyelash.
**—*v.t.*** **1** to beat or drive with a whip: *Yuba Bill ... madly lashed his horses forward* (Bret Harte). **SYN**: flog, scourge. **2** to wave or beat back and forth: *The lion lashed his tail. The wind lashes the sails.* **3** to strike violently; hit: *The rain lashed the windows.* **4** *Figurative.* to attack severely in words; hurt severely: *The captain lashed the lazy crew with a long, angry speech.* **SYN**: castigate, rebuke, berate, scold.
**—*v.i.*** **1** to make strokes with a lash or whip: *The youthful charioteers ... Stoop to the reins, and lash with all their force* (John Dryden). **2** to rush violently; pour: *The rain was still lashing down furiously* (Annie Thomas).
**lash out, a** to strike violently; hit; attack: *The cat lashed out at the dog with its claws.* **b** *Figurative.* to attack severely in words; scold vigorously: *Blunt and outspoken, he* [*Harry S Truman*] *often lashed out with strong language at those who opposed him* (Allan Nevins). *In his latest article he lashes out at modern historians.* **c** *Figurative.* to break forth into violent action, excess, or extravagance: *Yet could not the Duke ... sometimes forbear lashing out into very free expressions* (Charles Cotton).
**under the** (or **one's**) **lash**, under supervision; under the control of someone: *His staff ... behaves itself well enough under Twining's gentle lash* (New York Times).

**Pronunciation Key:** hat, āge, cãre, fär; let, ēqual, tėrm; it, īce; hot, ōpen, ôrder; oil, out; cup, pu̇t, rüle; child; long; thin; ᴛʜen; zh, measure; ə represents **a** in about, **e** in taken, **i** in pencil, **o** in lemon, **u** in circus.

[Middle English *lasshe;* origin uncertain] —**lash′er**, *n.*

**lash**[2] (lash), *v.t.* to tie or fasten with a rope, cord, or the like; secure: *The boy lashed logs together to make a raft.* SYN: bind. [< Old French *lachier,* variant of *lacier* < *laz, lache* a lace]

**LASH or lash**[3] (lash), *n.* a method of transatlantic shipping by means of large vessels carrying lighters (flat-bottomed barges) loaded with cargo. [< *L*(ighter) *A*(board) *SH*(ip)]

**lash|ing**[1] (lash′ing), *n.* **1** the act of a person or thing that lashes. **2** a beating or flogging. **3** *Figurative.* a severe attack in words; sharp scolding.
**lashings,** abundance; great plenty: *Cigars in loads, whiskey in lashings* (Scott).

**lash|ing**[2] (lash′ing), *n.* a rope, cord, or thong used to tie or fasten.

**lash rope,** *Western U.S.* a rope used for lashing a pack on a horse or vehicle.

**lash-up** (lash′up′), *n.* anything put together hastily or offhand; an improvisation; makeshift: *This machine was somewhat of a lash-up of available equipment built on the chassis of a trailer fire-pump* (New Scientist).

**L-as|pa|rag|i|nase** (el′as pə raj′ə nās), *n.* an enzyme effective against leukemia cells by causing the breakdown of L-asparagine, which these cells need for their growth. [< *L-asparagine*]

**L-as|par|a|gine** (el′ə spar′ə jēn, -jin), *n.* the levorotatory form of asparagine.

**lass** (las), *n.* **1** a girl or young woman: *A bonnie lass, I will confess, Is pleasant to the ee* (Robert Burns). **2** a sweetheart: *It was a lover and his lass* (Shakespeare). **3** *Scottish.* a maidservant. [origin uncertain]

**Las|sa fever** (las′ə, lä′sə), a very contagious, usually fatal virus disease characterized by high fever, cardiac infection, and a rash with subcutaneous hemorrhage. It was discovered in Lassa, Nigeria. *The infection, ... Lassa fever, involved almost all the body's organs. The virus produced fever as high as 107 degrees, mouth ulcers, a skin rash with tiny hemorrhages, heart infection and severe muscle aches* (Science News).

**las|sie** (las′ē), *n.* **1** a young lass or girl: *My love she's but a lassie yet* (Robert Burns). **2** a sweetheart.

**las|si|tude** (las′ə tüd, -tyüd), *n.* lack of energy; feeling of weakness; weariness: *Sometimes we feel lassitude on a hot summer day. His anger had evaporated; he felt nothing but utter lassitude* (John Galsworthy). SYN: languor, fatigue. [< Latin *lassitūdō* < *lassus* tired]

***las|so** (las′ō, -ü; la sü′), *n., pl.* **-sos** or **-soes,** *v.,* **-soed, -so|ing.** —*n.* a long rope with a running noose at one end; lariat. A cowboy's lasso, used especially for catching steers and horses, is made of nylon, or formerly of untanned hide, and is from 10 to 30 yards in length.
—*v.t.* to catch with a lasso.
[American English < Spanish *lazo* < Latin *laqueus* noose. See etym. of doublet **lace.**] —**las′so|er,** *n.*

***lasso**

**lasso cell,** *Zoology.* a colloblast.

**las|sock** (las′ək), *n. Scottish.* a little lass. [< *lass* + *-ock,* a diminutive suffix]

**last**[1] (last, läst), *adj., adv., n.* —*adj.* **1a** coming after all others; being at the end; final: *the last page of a book. Z is the last letter of the alphabet.* **b** belonging to the end or final stage. **c** coming after all others in importance or estimation; lowest: *The last of all nations now, though once the first* (William Cowper). **2** latest; most recent: *last Wednesday, last Christmas. I saw him last week.* **3** that remains; being the only remaining: *I was broke after I spent my last dollar. In a desperate last stand against eviction from a doomed apartment house, a building superintendent ... barricaded himself in his basement apartment* (Time). **4** most unlikely; least suitable: *Fighting is the last thing she would expect.* **5** very great; utmost; extreme: *a paper of the last importance, to the last degree.* **6** final and conclusive: *to have the last say on a matter.* SYN: definite. See also **last word.**
—*adv.* **1** after all the others; at the end; finally: *He came last in line. Love thyself last* (Shakespeare). **2** on the latest or most recent occasion: *When did you last see him?* **3** in conclusion; finally.
—*n.* **1** the person or thing that comes after all others: *He was the last in the line. I speak of this last with some hesitation.* **2a** the last part; end: *You have not heard the last of this.* **b** the end of life; death: *Be faithful to the last.*
**at last** or **at long last,** at the end; after a long time; finally: *At last the baby fell asleep. At long last, sometime this month the Los Angeles Public Library is expected to start circulation of discs* (Saturday Review).
**breathe** (or **gasp**) **one's last,** to die: *On his Cross breathing his painful last* (Thomas Ken).
**see the last of,** not to see again: *I'm glad to see the last of this unfriendly place.*
[Old English *latost,* or *lætest,* superlative of *læt* late]
—*Syn. adj.* **1 Last, final, ultimate** mean coming after all others. **Last** applies to that which comes after all others in a series but that is not necessarily the end of the series: *The last person to leave should turn off the light.* **Final** emphasizes the definite end of the series: *The last day of school each year is the final one for graduating seniors.* **Ultimate** emphasizes the last that can ever be reached or found: *The ultimate cause of some diseases is unknown.*
► **Last, latest.** *Last* refers to the final item of a series; *latest,* to the most recent in time of a series that may or may not be continued: *the scholar's latest* (*we hope it won't be his last*) *biography.*
► See **first** for another usage note.

**last**[2] (last, läst), *v., n.* —*v.i.* **1** to go on; hold out; continue to be; endure: *The storm lasted three days. Can you last through the race?* **2** to continue in good condition, force, or the like: *I hope these shoes last a year.* **3** to be enough: *How long will our money last?*
—*v.t.* to be enough for (a person): *This money won't last me a whole week.*
—*n.* power of holding on or out; staying power: *Few have the last to continue long against adversity.*
**last out,** to go or come through safely; survive: *The Puritans lasted out their first winter in New England and began to plant in the spring.*
[Old English *lǣstan* accomplish, carry out, related to *lāst track, last*[3]]
—*Syn. v.i.* **1 Last, continue, endure** mean to go on for a long time. **Last** suggests holding out in good condition or full strength and for an unusually long time: *Those flowers lasted for two weeks.* **Continue** suggests going on and on without an end, usually without a break: *The heavy snow continued all week.* **Endure** implies holding out in spite of adversity or severe trials: *They shall perish, but thou shalt endure* (Psalms 102:26).

***last**[3] (last, läst), *n., v.* —*n.* a block of wood or metal shaped like a person's foot on which shoes are formed or repaired.
—*v.t.* to form (shoes and boots) on a last.
**stick to one's last,** to pay attention to one's own work; mind one's own business: *The cab-driver told the passenger to stick to her last and stop the back-seat driving.*
[Old English *lǣste* < *lāst* track]

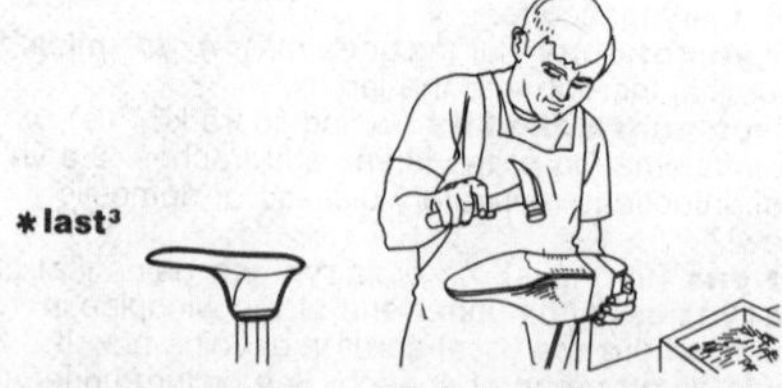
***last**[3]

**last**[4] (last, läst), *n.* a unit of weight or cubic measure, often equal to 4,000 pounds but varying in different localities and for different produce. [Old English *hlæst* a load]

**last-ditch** (last′dich′, läst′-), *adj.* **1** of or serving as a last line of defense; used as a last resort: *a last-ditch effort, a last-ditch stand.* **2** refusing to give in: *the barricades remain in place, with a few new ones which were erected yesterday by last-ditch supporters* (Manchester Guardian).

**last|er**[1] (las′tər, läs′-), *n.* **1** a person who fits the parts of boots or shoes to lasts. **2** a tool used in stretching leather on a last. [< *last*[3] + *-er*[1]]

**last|er**[2] (las′tər, läs′-), *n.* one that lasts (a specified period of time), especially a plant that continues fresh and sound: *Go for the long lasters. The oriental poppies are almost impossible to kill* (London Times). [< *last*[2] + *-er*[1]]

**Las|tex** (las′teks), *n. Trademark.* an elastic yarn made from cotton, rayon, silk, or other fibers, wrapped around a thread of fine rubber. It is woven or knitted into undergarments, bathing suits, or other tight-fitting garments.

**Last Frontier,** a nickname for Alaska.

**last-gasp** (last′gasp′, läst′gäsp′), *adj.* coming as the last effort: *two last-gasp touchdown passes that beat Pittsburgh* (New York Times). *... to carry out missions even at the minimum or last-gasp level* (New Scientist).

**last hurrah,** *U.S.* the final or farewell campaign of a politician: *For Humphrey, it is do or die, a last hurrah at 60 or a gratifying comeback* (Time). [< *The Last Hurrah,* a novel (1956) about an Irish-American politician, by Edwin O'Connor, 1918-1968, an American novelist]

**last in, first out,** = LIFO.

**last|ing** (las′ting, läs′-), *adj., n.* —*adj.* that lasts a long time; that lasts or will last; permanent; durable: *His experience in the war had a lasting effect on him. A just and lasting peace* (Abraham Lincoln). —*n.* **1** staying power. **2** = everlasting (def. 3). —**last′ing|ly,** *adv.* —**last′ing|ness,** *n.*
—*Syn. adj.* **Lasting, enduring, permanent** mean existing or continuing for a long time or forever. **Lasting** emphasizes going on and on indefinitely, long past what would be normal or expected: *The experience had a lasting effect on him.* **Enduring** emphasizes the idea of being able to withstand the attacks of time and circumstance: *All the world hoped for enduring peace.* **Permanent** emphasizes continuing in the same state or position, without changing or being likely to change: *What is your permanent address?*

**Last Judgment, 1** God's final judgment of all mankind at the end of the world. **2** the day of this judging; the Day of Judgment; judgment day.

**last|ly** (last′lē, läst′-), *adv.* in the last place; in conclusion; finally: *Lastly, I want to thank all of you for your help. Sixth and lastly, they have belied a lady* (Shakespeare).

**last-min|ute** (last′min′it), *adj.* at the latest possible time; just before it is too late: *last-minute instructions. The Department stores were crowded with last-minute shoppers at Christmastime.*

**last name,** a person's family name; surname: *Mary Anne's last name is Stone.*

**last offices,** prayers for a dead person.

**last quarter, 1** the period of time between the second half moon and the new moon. **2** the phase of the moon represented by the half moon after full moon.

**last resort,** an attempt to solve a problem beyond which no further attempts are possible: *Force, according to the doctrine of the just war, is to be used only as a last resort* (Listener). *One concept would make the federal government the "employer of last resort"* (A. H. Raskin).

**last rites,** religious rites performed by a priest for a dying or dead person; extreme unction. They include the saying of prayers and the administration of Holy Communion.

**last sleep,** = death.

**last straw,** the last of a series of troublesome things that causes a collapse, outburst, or other final action: *He had been calm through all the day's troubles, but missing the bus was the last straw, and he grew hot with anger.* [from the story in which the last straw broke the laden camel's back]

**Last Supper,** the supper of Jesus and His disciples on the evening before He was betrayed and crucified; Lord's Supper (in the Bible, Matthew 26:20-29). According to the Bible the sacrament of the Eucharist was instituted at the Last Supper (I Corinthians 11:24-25).

**last word, 1** the last thing said: *Why must he always have the last word in an argument?* **2** authority to make the final decision: *... the feeling was that the winner was always able to have the last word* (London Times). **3** *Informal.* the latest thing; most up-to-date style: *Every one thought that ... you were as safe on the last word in liners as in your own bedroom* (A. S. M. Hutchinson). **4** *Informal.* a thing that cannot be improved.

**Las Ve|gas night** (läs vā′gəs), *U.S.* a gambling event based on games of chance, run by a church or other nonprofit organization to raise funds: *Some said their churches would be hesitant about running Las Vegas nights because of the danger that players could lose large sums* (New York Times). [< *Las Vegas,* Nevada, famous for its gambling casinos]

**lat** (lät), *n., pl.* **lats** or **la|tu. 1** a former unit of money in Latvia. **2** a coin representing this unit. [< Latvian *lats* < *Latvija* Latvia]

**lat.,** latitude.

**Lat.,** Latin.

**lat|a|ki|a** or **Lat|a|ki|a** (lat′ə kē′ə), *n.* a fine, highly aromatic variety of Turkish tobacco: *Enveloped in fragrant clouds of Latakia* (Thackeray). [< *Latakia,* a seaport in Syria, near which the tobacco is grown]

**la|ta|ni|a** (lə tā′nē ə), *n.* any one of a group of fan palms native to the Mascarene Islands and much cultivated in greenhouses. [< New Latin *Latania* the genus name < *latanier* the native name]

**latch** (lach), *n., v.* —*n.* a catch for fastening a door, gate, or window, often one not needing a key. It consists of a movable piece of metal or wood that fits into a notch or opening of the adjoining wall. [< verb]
—*v.t., v.i.* to fasten or secure with a latch: *Latch and bar the door.*
**latch on to,** *Informal.* to get as one's own; catch and hold: *She has, in fact, a habit of latching on to men, and she can be extremely tough about relinquishing them* (Wolcott Gibbs).
**on the latch,** not locked, but fastened only by a latch: *The visitors found the door on the latch.*
[Old English *læccan* to grasp]

**latch|er-on** (lach′ər on′), *n. Informal.* a person who attaches himself to others, especially in a habitual or persistent manner.

**latch|et** (lach′it), *n. Archaic.* a strap or lace for fastening a shoe or sandal: *There cometh one ... the latchet of whose shoes I am not worthy to stoop down and unloose* (Mark 1:7). [< Old French *lachet,* dialectal variant of *lacet* (diminutive) < *laz,* or *las* lace]

**latch|key** (lach′kē′), *n.* a key used to draw back or unfasten the latch or other lock on a door.

**latchkey child,** a child left on his own while both parents are working: *Millions of "latchkey" children, for instance, find nobody at home when they get home from school in the afternoon* (New York Times Magazine). *Congress has opened the way for a Federally aided program of day care for the latchkey children of the nation* (New York Times).

**latch|string** (lach′string′), *n.* a string passed through a hole in a door, for raising and unfastening a latch from the outside.
**the latchstring is** (or **hangs**) **out,** visitors are welcome: *The latchstring of English society hangs outside the door for an American* (London Daily News). *Moderate Republicans might therefore serve their cause well by letting Mr. Nixon know their latchstring is out if he wants to come calling* (New York Times).

**late** (lāt), *adj.,* **lat|er** or **lat|ter, lat|est** or **last,** *adv.,* **lat|er, lat|est** or **last.** —*adj.* **1** happening, coming, or developing after the usual or proper time: *We had a late dinner last night.* **2a** happening, coming, or developing near the end: *It was late in the evening.* **b** at an advanced period or stage of development: *the late Cenozoic era.* **3** not long past; recent: *The late storm did much damage. He has been abroad a great deal of late years.* **4** recently dead: *The late Mr. Lee was a good neighbor.* **5** gone out of or retired from office: *Mr. Johnson, the late Mayor, is still working actively in politics.*
—*adv.* **1** after the usual or proper time: *He worked late last night. Better three hours too soon than a minute too late* (Shakespeare). **2** near the end: *It rained late in the afternoon. I was up very late last night. He reached success late in life.* **3** *Poetic.* in recent times; recently: *Those climes where I have late been staying* (Byron). **4** recently but no longer: *John Smith, late of Boston.*
**of late,** a short time ago; recently; lately: *I haven't seen him of late.*
[Old English *læt*] —**late′ness,** *n.*
—*Syn. adj.* **1 Late, tardy** mean happening, coming, or developing after the usual or proper time. **Late** applies whether the delay is avoidable or not: *Because my car broke down, I was late for school.* **Tardy** applies particularly when the delay is due to mere carelessness: *He was tardy again this morning.*
▶ See **first** and **last**[1] for usage notes.

**late blight,** a very widespread, destructive fungous disease of potatoes, tomatoes, and celery, characterized by brown discoloration of the plant.

**late bloomer,** a person whose capacities develop later than normally expected: *But I am still disconcerted when the students I counted on fail me and the least promising prove to be late bloomers* (Harper's). *He hasn't distinguished himself so far this season but he's always a late bloomer* (New York Times).

**late-bloom|ing** (lāt′blü′ming), *adj.* late in developing or reaching full potential.

**late|com|er** (lāt′kum′ər), *n.* a person or group that has arrived late or recently: *The latecomers to the play missed part of the first act.*

**lat|ed** (lā′tid), *adj. Poetic.* belated: *Now spurs the lated traveller apace To gain the timely inn* (Shakespeare).

**la|teen** (la tēn′), *n., adj.* —*n.* lateen sail: *The Romans, like the Greeks, used triangular sails called lateens on their smaller craft* (Lionel Casson).
—*adj.* having a lateen sail. Also, **latteen.**
[< French *latine* < (*voile*) *latine* Latin (sail); because of its use in the Mediterranean]

**la|teen-rigged** (la tēn′rigd′), *adj.* having a lateen sail.

***lateen sail,** a triangular sail held up by a long yard on a short mast. It was introduced into the Mediterranean by the Arabs.

***lateen sail**

**Late Greek,** the Greek language from about 300 to 700 A.D.

**Late Latin,** the Latin language from about 300 to 700 A.D.

**late|ly** (lāt′lē), *adv.* a little while ago; not long ago; recently: *They visited Boston lately. He has not been looking well lately.*

**lat|en** (lā′tən), *v.i., v.t.* to become or make late: *the latening summer season.* [< *lat*(e) + *-en*[1]]

**la|ten|cy** (lā′tən sē), *n.* latent condition or quality: *the latency of disease-producing germs.*

**latency period,** *Psychoanalysis.* a period between early childhood and puberty when heterosexual drives are apparently inactive or sublimated.

**La Tène** (lä ten′), of or having to do with the culture of the late Iron Age in Europe: *His felling ax was ... the first major modification in form of this ancient tool since its prototypes were made in the Basque iron lands during La Tène time, nearly 3,000 years ago* (Scientific American). [< *La Tène,* site on Lake Neuchâtel, Switzerland, where remains of the culture were found]

**la|ten|si|fi|ca|tion** (lā′tən sə fə kā′shən), *n. Photography.* the act or process of latensifying.

**la|ten|si|fy** (lā ten′sə fī), *v.t.,* **-fied, -fy|ing.** *Photography.* to intensify (a latent image) by means of a chemical solution or vapor or with actinic light. [blend of *latent* and *intensify*]

**la|tent** (lā′tənt), *adj., n.* —*adj.* **1** present but not active; hidden; concealed: *latent hostility, latent ability. The power of a grain of wheat to grow into a plant remains latent if it is not planted.* **2** present only in the undeveloped stage of an infection; not yet manifest: *a test to reveal latent tuberculosis.* **3** *Botany.* dormant or undeveloped: *Buds are latent when they are not externally visible until stimulated to grow.* **4** *Psychology.* forming part of the mental content or personality but not apparent in overt acts.
—*n.* a fingerprint not readily visible to the eye: *The police had to take many ... latents which were found at the scene of the crime* (Erle Stanley Gardner).
[< Latin *latēns, -entis,* present participle of *latēre* lie hidden] —**la′tent|ly,** *adv.*
—*Syn. adj.* **1 Latent, potential** mean existing as a possibility or fact, but not showing itself plainly. **Latent** means actually existing as a fact, but lying hidden, not active or plainly to be seen at the present time: *An exertion of a latent genius* (Edmund Burke). **Potential** means existing as a possibility and capable of coming into actual existence or activity if nothing happens to stop development: *That boy has great potential ability in science.*

**latent heat,** *Physics.* the heat required to change a solid to a liquid or a vapor, or to change a liquid to a vapor, without a change of temperature. It is also the heat released in the reverse processes.

**latent image,** an image produced on the chemical emulsion of photographic film by the effect of light, visible only when the film has been developed.

**latent period, 1** *Medicine.* incubation period; the period that elapses between the original infection and the time when a disease can be diagnosed. **2** *Physiology.* the time elapsing between a stimulus and the response to it.

**lat|er** (lā′tər), *adj., adv.* —*adj.* **1** a comparative of **late. 2** more late; more recent: *the later border songs of his own country* (R. H. Hutton).
—*adv.* **1** late in a greater degree: *to stay later than usual.* **2** at a later time or period; subsequently; afterward: *It can be done later.*
**later on,** afterward: *He's busy now, but he'll be free later on.*

**-later,** *combining form.* one who worships ____; one who is devoted to ____: *Idolater = one who worships idols.* [< Greek *-latrēs.* Related to Greek *latreiā;* see etym. under **latria**]

**lat|er|ad** (lat′ər ad), *adv. Anatomy.* toward the side. [< Latin *latus, -eris* side + *ad* to]

**lat|er|al** (lat′ər əl), *adj., n., v.* —*adj.* **1** of the side; at the side; from the side; toward the side: *lateral roots. A lateral fin of a fish grows from its side. A lateral branch of a family is a branch not in the direct line of descent. A river is fed by lateral streams.* **2** *Phonetics.* articulated so that the breath passes out on one or both sides of the tongue, as in pronouncing the English *l.*
—*n.* **1** a lateral part or outgrowth. **2** *Phonetics.* a lateral sound, such as *l.* **3** *Mining.* **a** a drift other than the main drift. **b** a connecting tunnel between main haulage ways. **4** = lateral pass.
—*v.i.* (in football) to throw a lateral pass: *So Gifford lateraled to Center Greg Larson, who looked at the ball and lateraled to Y. A. Tittle* (Time).
[< Latin *laterālis* < *latus, -eris* side]

**lateral chain,** *Chemistry.* side chain (def. 1).

**lateral fissure,** = fissure of Sylvius.

**lat|er|al|i|ty** (lat′ə ral′ə tē), *n., pl.* **-ties. 1** the quality of having distinct sides. **2** the preference of one side to the other: *Crossed laterality* [*is*] *a condition in which the dominant hand and eye are on opposite sides* (London Times).

**lateral line,** the row of connected sensory pores on the heads and sides of fishes, cyclostomes, and certain amphibians by which they detect change in water pressure or current.

**lat|er|al|ly** (lat′ər ə lē), *adv.* **1** in a lateral direction; at the side; sideways. **2** from a lateral branch.

**lateral moraine,** stripes of dirty ice and loose rock along the edge of a glacier. See picture under **glacier.**

**lateral pass,** a pass thrown in football from one player to another in a direction either parallel to or backward toward one's goal line.

**lateral thinking,** a method of solving problems by approaching them indirectly from various angles instead of dwelling on any one aspect at length: *As the name implies, lateral thinking is thinking sideways: not developing a pattern but restructuring a pattern* (Edward de Bono).

**Lat|er|an** (lat′ər ən), *n., adj.* —*n.* **1** the church of Saint John Lateran, the cathedral church in Rome. The Lateran is the official church of the pope. **2** the palace next to it, once the residence of the popes and now a museum..
—*adj.* of or having to do with one of the five general church councils held in the official church of the pope, Church of Saint John Lateran, in Rome.
[< Latin *Laterānus* < (*Plautii*) *Laterānī,* a Roman family, who owned a palace on the site]

**la|ter|a rec|ta** (lā′tər ə rek′tə), plural of **latus rectum.**

**lat|er-born** (lā′tər bôrn′), *adj., n.* —*adj.* born after the first offspring; younger.
—*n.* any child born after the first-born child: *The performance of later-borns was significantly better than that of first-borns or only-borns* (New York Times).

**lat|er|ite** (lat′ə rīt), *n.* a reddish soil rich in iron or aluminum and formed under tropical conditions by the decomposition of rock, common in parts of India, southwestern Asia, Africa, and elsewhere. [< Latin *later, -eris* brick, tile + English *-ite*[1]]

**lat|er|it|ic** (lat′ə rit′ik), *adj.* of or containing laterite: *lateritic ore.*

**lat|er|i|tious** (lat′ə rish′əs), *adj.* **1** having to do with or resembling bricks. **2** of the red color characteristic of bricks. [< Latin *laterītius* < *later, -eris* brick]

**lat|er|iz|a|ble** (lat′ə rī′zə bəl), *adj.* capable of being laterized: *Certain tropical soils ... are laterizable; that is, they may be irreversibly converted to rock as a result of the deprivation of organic matter* (New Yorker).

**lat|er|i|za|tion** (lat′ər ə zā′shən), *n.* the process by which laterite is formed.

**lat|er|ize** (lat′ə rīz), *v.t.,* **-ized, -iz|ing.** to change into laterite; make lateritic or rocklike. [back formation < *laterization*]

**la|tes|cence** (lā tes′əns), *n.* latescent condition or quality.

**la|tes|cent** (lā tes′ənt), *adj.* becoming latent, hidden, or obscure. [< Latin *latēscēns, -entis,* present participle of *latēscere* hide oneself < *latēre* conceal]

**lat|est** (lā′tist), *adj.* **1** the superlative of **late. 2** most late; most recent. **3** *Archaic* or *Poetic.* last; final.
**at the latest,** no later than (the time specified): *I'll see you next week at the latest.*
**the latest,** *Informal.* the most up-to-date thing; the newest style, design, or other popular interest: *The latest the dear girls hereabouts are*

*singing, ... is, "Will he love you as today?"* (Kansas Times and Star).
► See **last**[1] for a usage note.

**late tea,** *British.* supper.

**late|wood** (lāt′wu̇d′), *n.* = summerwood.

**la|tex** (lā′teks), *n., pl.* **lat|i|ces** or **la|tex|es,** *v.* — *n.* **1** a milky fluid found in milkweeds, poppies, and plants yielding rubber. Some kinds of latex harden on exposure to the air and are the source of rubber, chicle, and other products. **2** an emulsion of synthetic rubber or plastic suspended in water, used mainly in paints.
— *v.t.* to add latex to: ... *latexed sisal pads* (Wall Street Journal).
[< Latin *latex, -icis* a liquid]

**lath** (lath, läth), *n., pl.* **laths** (laᴛʜz, laths, läᴛʜz, läths), *v.* — *n.* **1** one of the thin, narrow strips of wood placed over the framework of a wall, ceiling, or roof, formerly used to support plaster or to make a lattice. **2** a wire cloth or sheet metal with holes in it, used in place of laths. **3** a lining or support made of laths. The walls of older frame houses were built with lath and plaster. **4** any thin, narrow, flat piece of wood.
— *v.t.* to cover or line (a wall, ceiling, or roof) with laths.
[Middle English *lathe,* apparently < a variant of Old English *lætt*]

***lathe** (lāᴛʜ), *n., v.* **lathed, lath|ing.** — *n.* **1** a machine for holding pieces of wood, metal, or plastic, and turning them rapidly against a cutting tool used to shape them. **2** the movable swing frame in a loom, consisting of the shuttles, reed, picking apparatus, etc.
— *v.t.* to shape or cut (wood, metal, or plastic) on a lathe. [earlier, scaffolding; origin uncertain; perhaps < Scandinavian (compare Old Icelandic *hlathi* pile, stack)]

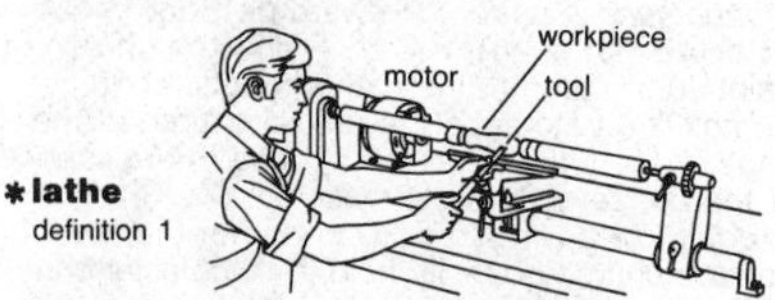

***lathe**
definition 1

**la|thee** (lä′tē), *n.* = lathi.

**lath|er**[1] (laᴛʜ′ər), *n., v.* — *n.* **1** foam made from soap and water. SYN: suds. **2** foam formed in sweating: *the lather of a horse after a race.* SYN: froth. **3** *Slang, Figurative.* a state of great agitation or excitement: *He worked himself into a lather over the final exam. I had been waiting in my room in a lather of anticipation when the telephone rang* (New York Times). [< Old English *lēathor*]
— *v.t.* **1** to put lather on: *He lathers his face before shaving.* **2** *Informal.* to beat; thrash. SYN: flog.
— *v.i.* **1** to form a lather: *This soap lathers well.* **2** to become covered with foam formed in sweating: *The horse lathered from his hard gallop.*
[Middle English *latheren,* alteration of Old English *lēthran* cover with lather] — **lath′er|er,** *n.*

**lath|er**[2] (lath′ər, läth′-), *n.* a workman who puts laths on walls, ceilings, or roofs.

**lath|er|y** (laᴛʜ′ər ē), *adj.* consisting of or covered with lather.

**lath house,** a building for growing plants, made of a frame covered with lath on the top and often the sides, to protect plants from too much sunlight and wind or rain.

**la|thi** (lä′tē), *n.* an iron bar inside a bamboo stick, now used by police and soldiers in India. Also, **lathee.** [< Hindi *lāṭhī*]

**lath|ing** (lath′ing, läth′-), *n.* **1** work consisting of laths; laths collectively. **2** the work of putting laths on walls, ceilings, or roofs.

**lath|work** (lath′wėrk′, läth′-), *n.* = lathing.

**lath|y** (lath′ē, läth′-), *adj.,* **lath|i|er, lath|i|est.** long and slender, like a lath: *a lathy young man.*

**lath|y|rism** (lath′ə riz əm), *n.* a condition in animals and man caused by eating certain plants of the pea family, such as the lupine or vetch. It is characterized by convulsive movements, and sometimes paraplegia, especially in the legs. [< New Latin *Lathyrus* the typical genus, that causes it + English *-ism*]

**lat|i|ces** (lat′ə sēz), *n.* a plural of **latex.**

**la|tic|i|fer** (lā tis′ə fər), *n.* a plant cell which produces latex. [< Latin *latex, -icis* a liquid + *-fer* (< *ferre* to bear)]

**lat|i|cif|er|ous** (lat′ə sif′ər əs), *adj. Botany.* producing latex.

**lat|i|fo|li|ate** (lat′ə fō′lē āt, -it), *adj. Botany.* having broad leaves. [< New Latin *latifoliatus* < Latin *lātus* broad + *folium* leaf]

**lat|i|fo|li|ous** (lat′ə fō′lē əs), *adj.* = latifoliate.

**lat|i|fun|di|o** (lat′ə fun′dē ō; *Spanish* lä′tē fün′dē ō), *n., pl.* **-os.** a large landed estate in any Spanish-speaking country. [< Spanish *latifundio* < Latin *lātifundium*]

**lat|i|fun|dism** (lat′ə fun′diz əm), *n.* the holding of large landed estates.

**lat|i|fun|dist** (lat′ə fun′dist), *n.* the owner of a latifundium: *nine million acres lay idle in the grip of latifundists and private corporations* (New Scientist).

**lat|i|fun|di|um** (lat′ə fun′dē əm), *n., pl.* **-di|a** (-dē ə). a large landed estate: *The low productivity and backwardness of the latifundia of Latin America and the feudal domains of the Middle East* (John Kenneth Galbraith). [< Latin *lātifundium*]

**lat|i|go** (lat′ə gō), *n., pl.* **-gos** or **-goes.** a strong leather strap attached to a saddle, for tightening and fastening the cinch, used in the western United States and Latin America. [American English < Spanish *látigo*]

**lat|i|me|ri|a** (lat′ə mir′ē ə), *n.* any of a group of large coelacanthine fishes of the coast of southeastern Africa. [< New Latin *Latimeria* the genus name < M. *Latimer,* a South African museum curator of the 1900's]

**Lat|in** (lat′ən), *n., adj.* — *n.* **1** the language of the ancient Romans or any one of the later varieties, such as that written by scholars through the Middle Ages. Medieval Latin and New Latin are still used in official documents of the Roman Catholic Church. **2** a member of the peoples whose languages came from Latin: *The Italians, French, Spanish, Portuguese, and Romanians are Latins.* **3** a native or inhabitant of Latium or of ancient Rome. **4** = Roman Catholic. **5** = Latin American: *How does the generality of Latins regard the political status of Puerto Rico?* (Saturday Review).
— *adj.* **1** of Latin; in Latin: *Latin poetry, Latin grammar, a Latin scholar.* **2** of the Latin peoples or their languages. **3** of Latium or its people; ancient Roman. **4** = Roman Catholic. **5** = Latin-American: *Brazil is not just the most important Latin country for us—it's vital to our whole Western Hemisphere ...* (Wall Street Journal). *Abbr:* Lat.
[< Latin *Latīnus* of Latium, an ancient country in Italy that included Rome]

**Lat|in-A|mer|i|can** (lat′ən ə mer′ə kən), *adj.* of or having to do with South America, Central America, Mexico, and most of the West Indies.

**Latin American,** a person born or living in Latin America.

**Lat|in|ate** (lat′ə nāt), *adj.* derived from or having to do with Latin.

**Latin Church,** that part of the Catholic Church that follows the Latin Rite.

**Latin cross,** a cross whose upright is crossed above its center by a shorter, horizontal bar. See the diagram under **cross.**

**La|tin|ic** (la tin′ik), *adj.* **1** of or having to do with the Latin nations, ancient or modern. **2** resembling or coming from Latin: *the prevalent Latinic character of the vocabulary* (J. A. H. Murray).

**Lat|in|ism** (lat′ə niz əm), *n.* **1** a Latin word, idiom, or expression. **2** conformity to Latin models, especially in literary style.

**Lat|in|ist** (lat′ə nist), *n.* a person with much knowledge of the Latin language; Latin scholar.

**La|tin|i|ty** (lə tin′ə tē), *n., pl.* **-ties. 1** the use of Latin idioms or expressions. **2** Latin character or quality: *The broad spectrum of cultural experiences ... constitutes the Latinity—if it may be so called—of Latin America* (New Yorker). **3** a Latin word, idiom, or expression: *The Latinities from which chemical symbols derive were proposed as the bases for the new baptisms, after which, for example, gold would change to aurium, silver to argentium, iron to ferrium ...* (New Scientist).

**Lat|in|i|za|tion** or **lat|in|i|za|tion** (lat′ə nə zā′shən), *n.* **1** a translating into Latin. **2** a making Latin or like Latin. **3** the adapting to or conforming to Latin language or customs: *the Latinization of speech of ancient populations. The Filipinos have had a double dose of colonialism: "Latinization" before "Americanization"* (Saturday Review).

**Lat|in|ize** or **lat|in|ize** (lat′ə nīz), *v.,* **-ized, -iz|ing.** — *v.t.* **1** to translate into Latin. **2** to make like Latin. **3** to make conform to the ideas, customs, or other practices of the Latins or the Latin Church. — *v.i.* to use Latin forms or customs.

**La|ti|no** (lä tē′nō), *adj., n., pl.* **-nos.** — *adj.* = Latin-American: *Latino dancers.*
— *n.* = Latin American. [< Spanish *Latino*]

**Latin Quarter,** a district in Paris, south of the Seine River; Left Bank. Many students and artists live there.

**Latin Rite,** church ceremonies as used in the diocese of Rome; Roman rite.

**Latin school,** *U.S.* a school, especially a private school, in which Latin is emphasized.

**Latin square,** a square divided into a number of cells containing Latin letters so arranged that a letter appears only once in each row and column. It is used especially in statistics to order various elements so as to control variability.

**lat|ish** (lā′tish), *adj., adv.* rather late: *He is in his latish seventies now ... though no one would guess it to look at him* (H. F. Ellis).

***lat|i|tude** (lat′ə tüd, -tyüd), *n.* **1** distance north or south of the equator, measured in degrees. A degree of latitude is about 69 miles. **2** room to act or think; freedom from narrow rules; scope: *You are allowed much latitude in choosing games to play after school. The President had given* [*the Secretary of State*] *wide latitude to decide whether the foreign ministers should meet first or meet concurrently* (New York Times). SYN: range, play, expanse, amplitude. **3** *Astronomy.* **a** = celestial latitude. **b** = galactic latitude. **4** *Photography.* the range between the shortest and the longest exposures that produce good negatives on a given film. **5** transverse dimension; extent as measured from side to side; width of a surface, as opposed to length. *Abbr:* lat.
**latitudes,** a place or region having latitude: *Polar bears live in the cold latitudes.*
[< Latin *lātitūdō, -inis* < *lātus* wide]

***latitude**
definition 1

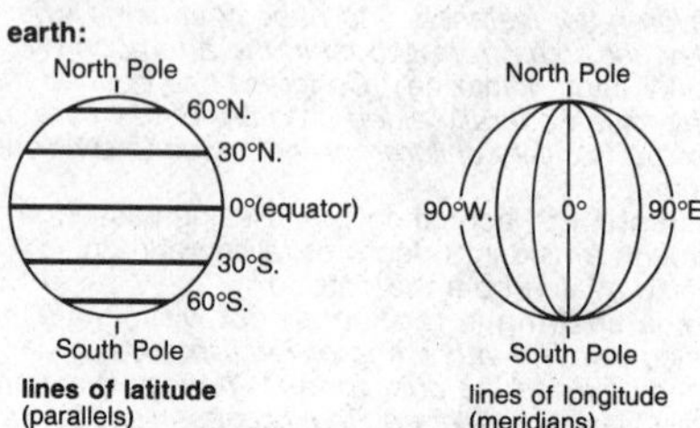


**lat|i|tu|di|nal** (lat′ə tü′də nəl, -tyü′-), *adj.* of or relating to latitude. — **lat′i|tu′di|nal|ly,** *adv.*

**lat|i|tu|di|nar|i|an** (lat′ə tü′də nãr′ē ən, -tyü′-), *adj., n.* — *adj.* allowing others their own beliefs; not insisting on strict adherence to established principles, especially in religious views: *His opinions respecting ecclesiastical polity and modes of worship were latitudinarian* (Macaulay). SYN: broad, liberal, tolerant.
— *n.* a person who holds liberal views and cares little about creeds, doctrines, and forms, especially in religion: *At the other end are what Yale Historian John Morton Blum calls the "latitudinarians": those who, like Lincoln and Wilson, gave wide scope to the Constitution's vague charter* (Time).

**Lat|i|tu|di|nar|i|an** (lat′ə tü′də nãr′ē ən, -tyü′-), *n.* (in the Church of England) one of a school of Episcopal divines who, in the 1600's, strove to unite the dissenters with the Episcopal church by insisting on those doctrines which were held in common by both. They maintained the wisdom of the episcopal form of government and ritual, but denied their divine origin and authority. *Dr. Wilkins, my friend, the Bishop of Chester, is a mighty rising man, as being a Latitudinarian* (Samuel Pepys).

**lat|i|tu|di|nar|i|an|ism** (lat′ə tü′də nãr′ē ə niz′əm, -tyü′-), *n.* the opinions, principles, or practices of latitudinarians or the Latitudinarians.

**La|to|na** (lə tō′nə), *n. Roman Mythology.* the mother of Apollo and Diana, identified with the Greek Leto.

**la|tri|a** (lə trī′ə), *n.* (in the Roman Catholic Church) the supreme worship that can be paid to God alone. [< Late Latin *latrīa* < Greek *latreiā* service (to God) < *latreúein* serve (with prayer)]

**la|trine** (lə trēn′), *n.* a toilet or privy, especially in a camp, factory, or barracks. [< Middle French *latrines,* plural, learned borrowing from Latin *lātrīna,* earlier *lavātrīna* (originally) washbasin, washroom < *lavāre* to wash]

**-latry,** *combining form.* worship of ___; devotion to ___: *Mariolatry = devotion to the Virgin Mary.* [< Greek *-latreia* < *latreiā;* see etym. under **latria**]

**lat|teen** (la tēn′), *adj.* = lateen.

**lat|ten** (lat′ən), *n.* **1** an alloy identical with or closely resembling brass, often hammered into thin sheets, formerly much used for church utensils. **2a** = tin plate. **b** any metal made in thin sheets. [< Middle French *laton, laiton,* Old French *leiton* < Arabic *lāṭūn* copper < dialectal Turkish *altan* gold]

**lat|ter** (lat′ər), *adj.* **1** *a comparative of* **late. 2** the second of two: *Canada and the United States are in North America; the former lies north of the latter.* **3** more recent; toward the end; later: *Friday comes in the latter part of the week.* **4** *Obsolete.* last: *and in his bosom spend my latter gasp* (Shakespeare). [Old English *lætra* later; (originally) slower, comparative of *læt* late]

**lat|ter-day** (lat′ər dā′), *adj.* belonging to recent

times; modern: *latter-day problems, latter-day poets.*

**latter days**, *Archaic.* last days: *In the latter days we shall be tricked by Satan's legates* (R. W. Dixon).

**Latter-day Saint**, = Mormon.

**latter end**, **1** the concluding part: *the latter end of May.* **2** the end of life; death.

**Latter Lammas**, a day that will never arrive because there is no second Lammas in the year.

**lat|ter|ly** (lat′ər lē), *adv.* at a recent time; lately; recently: *He was latterly head of his department until his retirement.*

**lat|ter|most** (lat′ər mōst, -məst), *adj.* last; latest.

**Latter Prophets**, **1** the prophetic books of the Old Testament; the Major and Minor Prophets. **2** the prophets who are believed to have written these books.

**lat|tice** (lat′is), *n., v.,* **-ticed, -tic|ing.** *—n.* **1** wooden or metal strips crossed with open spaces between them: *a cool porch with a vine-covered lattice.* **2** a window, gate, or other opening, having a lattice. **3a** the geometrical pattern of molecules, atoms, or ions in a crystal: *In a crystal all the atoms are distributed in an orderly arrangement throughout the space occupied by the crystal. This is called a lattice* (Science News). **b** = space lattice. **4** a structure in a nuclear reactor, containing fissionable and nonfissionable materials in a regular geometrical pattern: *By suitable choice of the lattice the production of plutonium can be given an optimum value* (M. L. Oliphant). **5** *Mathematics.* a partially ordered set in which any two elements have a least upper bound and a greatest lower bound.
*—v.t.* **1** to furnish with a lattice: *Each window was latticed with iron wire on the outside* (Jonathan Swift). **2** to form into a lattice; make like a lattice: *The cook latticed strips of dough across the pie.*
[< Old French *lattis* < *latte* lath < Germanic (compare Old High German *latta*)] **—lat′tice-like′**, *adj.*

**lattice beam** or **frame**, = lattice girder.

**lattice bridge**, an obsolete type of wooden truss bridge in which top and bottom chord members are connected by closely spaced members fastened across each other at an angle.

**lattice girder**, a girder, especially of a bridge, consisting of top and bottom chord members connected and strengthened by other vertical and diagonal members.

**lat|tice|leaf** (lat′is lēf′), *n., pl.* **-leaves.** any of certain Old-World monocotyledonous water plants remarkable for their skeleton leaves, which lack cellular tissue between the veins; laceleaf.

**lat|tice|work** (lat′is wėrk′), *n.* **1** = lattice. **2** lattices: *Many old New Orleans houses are decorated with wrought-iron latticework.*

**lat|ti|ci|nio** (lat ə chē′nyō), *n., pl.* **-ci|ni** (-chē′nē). = lace glass. [< Italian *latticinio*]

**lat|ti|ci|no** (lat ə chē′nō), *n.* = latticinio.

**la|tu** (lä′tü), *n.* lats; a plural of **lat.**

**la|tus rec|tum** (lā′təs rek′təm), *pl.* **la|ter|a rec|ta.** *Geometry.* a chord of a conic section passing through a focus and perpendicular to the axis of the conic section. [< New Latin *latus rectum* (literally) straight side]

**Latv.**, Latvia.

**Lat|vi|an** (lat′vē ən), *adj., n.* *—adj.* of or having to do with Latvia (Soviet republic in northern Europe, on the Baltic Sea), its people, or their language.
*—n.* **1** a native or inhabitant of Latvia. **2** the Baltic language of Latvia; Lettish: *Lithuanian and Latvian are the only two languages of any social importance in the Baltic branch* (H. A. Gleason, Jr.).

**lau|an** (lou än′), *n.* = Philippine mahogany. [< Tagalog *lauaan*]

**laud** (lôd), *v., n.* *—v.t.* to praise highly; extol: *Our teacher lauded our efforts to read the difficult story.* **SYN**: commend, exalt, eulogize. [< Latin *laudāre* < *laus, laudis* praise]
*—n.* **1** a song or hymn of praise. **2** praise; high commendation: *All glory, laud, and honor to Thee, Redeemer King* (John Mason Neale).
**lauds** or **Lauds**, **a** a morning church service with psalms of praise to God: *To make this the matter of my daily lauds* (Henry Hammond). **b** a prescribed devotional service in the Roman Catholic Church for priests and religious, forming, with matins, the first of the seven canonical hours: *The bell of lauds began to ring, And friars in the chancel 'gan to sing* (Chaucer).
[< Old French *laude,* learned borrowing from Latin *laus, laudis* praise] **—laud′er**, *n.*

**laud|a|bil|i|ty** (lô′də bil′ə tē), *n.* = praiseworthiness.

**laud|a|ble** (lô′də bəl), *adj.* **1** deserving praise; commendable: *Unselfishness is laudable. His desire to help his father in the store is laudable.* **SYN**: praiseworthy, meritorious, creditable. **2** *Medicine, Archaic.* (of secretions, especially pus) healthy; sound. **—laud′a|ble|ness**, *n.*

**laud|a|bly** (lô′də blē), *adv.* in a laudable manner.

**lau|dan|o|sine** (lô dan′ō sēn, -sin), *n.* a toxic, crystalline alkaloid occurring in opium. *Formula:* $C_{21}H_{27}NO_4$

**lau|da|num** (lô′də nəm), *n.* **1** a solution of 10 per cent opium in alcohol and water, used to lessen pain; opium tincture. **2** (formerly) any of various preparations in which opium was the main ingredient. [< New Latin *laudanum,* alteration (perhaps by Paracelsus) of Latin *lādanum;* see etym. under **labdanum**]

**lau|da|tion** (lô dā′shən), *n.* **1** the act of praising: *his very liberal laudation of himself* (Dickens). **2** = praise. **3** the condition of being praised.

**laud|a|tive** (lô′də tiv), *adj.* = laudatory.

**laud|a|to|ry** (lô′də tôr′ē, -tōr′-), *adj.* expressing praise; extolling.

**Laud|i|an** (lô′dē ən), *adj., n.* *—adj.* of or supporting the tenets and practices of Archbishop William Laud (1573-1645) of Canterbury, noted for his persecution of dissenters and nonconformists.
*—n.* a follower of Laud.

**lauds** or **Lauds** (lôdz), *n.pl.* See under **laud.**

**laugh** (laf, läf), *v., n.* *—v.i.* **1** to make the sounds and movements that show one is happy, amused, or feels scorn: *We all laughed at the clown's funny tricks.* **SYN**: chuckle, chortle, giggle. **2** to be gay or lively; seem to laugh: *The wood fire ... laughs broadly through the room* (Hawthorne). **3** to utter a cry or sound like the laughing of a human being, as some birds do.
*—v.t.* **1** to drive, put, or bring about by or with laughing: *The little girl laughed her tears away. His real name which he had never even told ... for fear they would ... have him laughed out of the mob, was Katzenjammer* (Russell Baker). **2** to express with laughter: *to laugh a reply.*
*—n.* **1** the act or sound of laughing: *My father gave a hearty laugh when he saw the clown's tricks. ... gladden this vale of sorrows with a wholesome laugh* (Oliver Wendell Holmes). **2** a cause for laughter: *The funny book had a laugh on every page.* **3** an expression of mirth, derision, or some other feeling, by laughing.
**have the last laugh**, to get the better of (someone) after appearing to lose: *In the race between the hare and the tortoise, the tortoise had the last laugh.*
**laugh at**, to make fun of; ridicule: *The boys laughed at her for believing there were ghosts.*
**laugh off** (or **away**), to pass off or dismiss with a laugh; get out of by laughing: *He laughed off the warning that the ice was not safe and fell through in the middle of the pond.*
**laughs**, *Informal.* fun; diversion; entertainment: *What do you do for laughs here?*
**no laughing matter**, a matter that is serious: *Walking in the woods became no laughing matter when he got lost after dark.*
[Old English *hliehhan*]

**laugh|a|ble** (laf′ə bəl, läf′-), *adj.* causing laughter; amusing; funny: *a laughable mistake.* **SYN**: comical, humorous. See syn. under **funny.** **—laugh′a|ble|ness**, *n.*

**laugh|a|bly** (laf′ə blē, läf′-), *adv.* in a laughable manner; so as to excite laughter: *The clowns were laughably engaged in a pie-throwing scene.*

**laugh|er** (laf′ər, läf′-), *n.* **1** a person who laughs, especially in a hearty manner. **2** a game so overwhelmingly one-sided as to be amusing: *Then, in the fifth, the Orioles sent eleven batters to the plate, scoring six runs, and the game had become a laugher* (New Yorker).

**laugh-in** (laf′in′, läf′-), *n. Informal.* a funny or merry act, entertainment, or the like: *Player conducted a laugh-in on the practice ground, subduing inner feelings about the fate of his father* (London Times).

**laugh|ing** (laf′ing, läf′-), *adj., n.* *—adj.* **1** that laughs or seems to laugh: *a laughing child, the laughing brook.* **2** accompanied by laughter: *a laughing reply.* *—n.* the act of one who laughs; laughter: *The clown's laughing brought smiles to children's faces.*

**laughing death**, = kuru.

**laughing gas**, a colorless, sweet-smelling gas that, when inhaled, usually produces exhilaration, followed by insensibility to pain; nitrous oxide. It is sometimes used as an anesthetic, especially in dentistry. *Formula:* $N_2O$

**laughing gull**, a small gull of temperate and tropical America that has a cry like laughing: *Identify the laughing gull by his coal-black head that looks as if he had dunked it in a big inkwell, his gray back, dark wingtips and squared white tail feathers* (New York Times).

**laughing jackass**, = kookaburra.

**laugh|ing|ly** (laf′ing lē, läf′-), *adv.* in a laughing or merry way; with laughter.

**laugh|ing|stock** (laf′ing stok′, läf′-), *n.* a person or thing that is made fun of: *When he talked, he talked nonsense, and made himself the laughingstock of his hearers* (Macaulay).

**laughing thrush**, any one of a group of large, colorful birds of Asia that resemble thrushes and have a cry that sounds like bursts of laughter.

**laugh line**, **1** a wrinkle at the outer corner of the eye supposedly formed from habitual smiling or laughing: *We sat next to Ralph Brasco, a rangy man with plenty of laugh lines around his eyes* (New Yorker). **2** a brief quip or joke; one-liner: *One of the laugh lines floating around the London headquarters of Amoco (one of the toughest bargainers) is: "Now we know where the Middle East guys learned their trading techniques—from the British* (New Scientist).

**laugh|mak|er** (laf′mā′kər, läf′-), *n. Informal.* a professional humorist or comedian.

**laughs** (lafs, läfs), *n.pl.* See under **laugh.**

**laugh|ter** (laf′tər, läf′-), *n.* **1** the sound of laughing: *Laughter filled the room.* **2** the action of laughing: *The audience rocked with laughter at the clown's foolish antics. Of all the countless folk who have lived ... not one is known ... as having died of laughter* (Max Beerbohm). **3** *Especially Poetic.* a subject or matter for laughter: *Hath Cassius lived To be but mirth and laughter to his Brutus?* (Shakespeare). [Old English *hleahtor*]

**laugh track**, prerecorded laughter dubbed in on the sound track of a filmed television show to enliven the comedy.

**laugh|y** (laf′ē, läf′-), *adj.* inclined to laugh.

**lau ha|la** (lou hä′lə), *n. Hawaiian.* the leaf of the pandanus tree, used in weaving.

**lau|lau** (lou′lou), *n. Hawaiian.* a dish of chopped taro leaves, meat, and fish wrapped in ti palm leaves and steamed.

**launce** (lans, läns), *n.* = sand launce. Also, **lance.**

**launch**[1] (lônch, länch), *v., n.* *—v.t.* **1** to cause to slide into the water; set afloat: *A new ship is launched from the supports on which it was built.* **2** to push out or put forth on the water or into the air: *The satellite was launched in a rocket.* **3** *Figurative.* to start; set going; set out: *His friends launched him in business by lending him money. He had formed his new government in an atmosphere full of the promise of change, of new enterprises launched, of fresh young blood reaching power* (Time). **SYN**: begin, initiate. **4** *Figurative.* to throw; hurl; send out: *A bow launches arrows into the air. The angry man launched wild threats against his enemies.*
*—v.i.* **1** to start; set out: (*Figurative.*) *He used the money to launch into a new business.* (*Figurative.*) *The traveler launched into a long description of his voyage.* **2** to burst; plunge: *The rebels launched into a violent attack on their government.* **3** to push forth or out from land; put to sea: *We launched for the main coast of Africa* (Daniel Defoe).
*—n.* **1** the act of setting an aircraft, rocket, or missile into motion: *The launch of the first space vehicle was a historic event.* **2** the movement of a boat or ship from the land into the water, especially the sliding of a new ship from its platform.
**launch out**, to begin; start: *The small man ... is ... slow to launch out into expense, when things are going well* (Augustus Jessopp).
[< Old North French *lanchier,* Old French *lancier.* See etym. of doublet **lance**[1], verb.]

**launch**[2] (lônch, länch), *n.* **1** a small, more or less open motorboat, used for pleasure trips or carrying passengers to and from larger boats off shore. **2** the largest boat carried by a warship. [< Spanish and Portuguese *lancha,* apparently < Malay *lanchār-an* < *lanchār* quick, agile; spelling influenced by *launch*[1]]

**launch|a|ble** (lôn′chə bəl, län′-), *adj.* that can be launched: *a launchable project; a launchable nuclear stage for a rocket* (Ralph E. Lapp).

**launch complex**, the entire physical arrangement at a rocket or missile launching site, including the launching pad, gantry, fueling devices, communications equipment, and blockhouse.

**launch|er** (lôn′chər, län′-), *n.* **1** a person who launches something. **2** *Military.* **a** a device attached to a rifle that launches a special grenade; grenade launcher. **b** = rocket launcher. **3** = catapult.

***launch|ing pad** (lôn′ching, län′-), **1** surface or platform on which a rocket or missile is prepared for launching and from which it is shot into the air: *Launching pads must withstand high temperatures and high-velocity exhaust blasts. The nuclear-powered missile-carrying submarine ... may well be the most nearly invulnerable launching*

**Pronunciation Key:** h**a**t, **ā**ge, c**ã**re, f**ä**r; l**e**t, **ē**qual, t**ė**rm; **i**t, **ī**ce; h**o**t, **ō**pen, **ô**rder; **oi**l, **ou**t; c**u**p, p**u̇**t, r**ü**le; **ch**ild; lo**ng**; **th**in; **ᴛʜ**en; **zh**, measure; **ə** represents **a** in about, **e** in taken, **i** in pencil, **o** in lemon, **u** in circus.

*pad* (Harper's). **2** *Figurative: ... the conference would be the launching pad for a propaganda drive* (London Times). *Despite the high feelings, the project is not off the launching pad* (Science News).

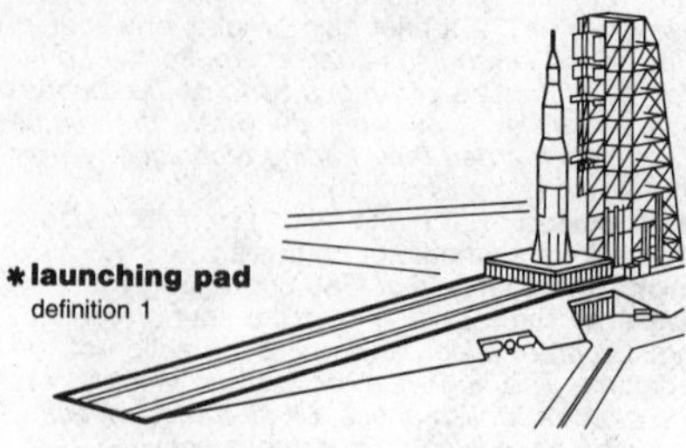

***launching pad** definition 1

**launching platform**, **1** = launching pad. **2** = launching site.
**launching site**, the place at which a rocket or missile is launched.
**launch pad**, = launching pad.
**launch vehicle**, a rocket used to launch a spacecraft or satellite into space.
**launch window**, the conjunction of time and planetary position in a condition that permits successful launching of a spacecraft; window: *The 20-day period centered around the launch date allowing travel between planets on an orbit requiring the least amount of energy. This is the so-called "launch window" used to hurl space vehicles from earth to the moon, or to Venus or Mars* (Science News).
**laun|der** (lôn′dər, län′-) *v., n.* —*v.t.* **1** to wash, or wash and iron, (linens and clothes): *Many homes have machines to launder clothes. These tablecloths and napkins have to be laundered.*
**2** *Figurative.* to rid of any taint; make seem innocent, legitimate, or acceptable: [*He*] *developed the world network of couriers ... that allows the underworld to take profits from illegal enterprises, to send them halfway around the world and then have the money come back laundered clean to be invested in legitimate businesses* (Atlantic). *The newspaper said that the Senator's fund raisers "laundered" large donations from labor unions and other special-interest groups by funneling them through phony re-election committees set up in Washington* (New York Times).
—*v.i.* **1** to be able to be washed; stand washing: *Cotton materials usually launder very well and do not tend to shrink.* **2** to wash, or wash and iron, clothes or linens: *Many housewives launder on Monday.*
—*n.* **1** a trough for water, either cut in the earth or formed of wood or other material. **2** a passage for conveying intermediate products or residues of ore dressing that are suspended in water.
[Middle English *lander* one who washes, earlier *lavender* < Old French *lavandier* < Vulgar Latin *lavandārius* < Latin *lavanda* (things) to be washed < *lavāre* to wash] —**laun′der|er**, *n.*
**laun|der|ette** (lôn′də ret′, län′-), *n.* = laundromat. [< *Launderette,* a trademark for a self-service laundry]
**laun|dress** (lôn′dris, län′-), *n.* a woman whose work is washing and ironing linens or clothes.
**laun|dro|mat** (lôn′drə mat, län′-), *n.* **1 Laundromat,** *Trademark.* a self-service laundry consisting of coin-operated washing machines and dryers. **2** a laundry in which washing and drying machines are operated by workers who charge for the laundry by the pound.
**laun|dry** (lôn′drē, län′-), *n., pl.* **-dries. 1** a room or building where linens, clothes, or other articles, are washed and ironed. **2** linens, clothes, or other articles washed or to be washed. **3** the washing and ironing of linens or clothes.
**laundry list**, *Especially U.S.* a long, itemized list: *The at-large ballot is a bewildering laundry list of 75 names* (Time).
**laun|dry|man** (lôn′drē mən, län′-), *n., pl.* **-men. 1** a man who works in a laundry. **2** a man who collects and delivers laundry.
**laun|dry|wom|an** (lôn′drē wu̇m′ən, län′-), *n., pl.* **-wom|en.** = laundress.
**Laun|fal** (lôn′fəl, län′-), *n.* **Sir**, a knight of the Round Table.
**lau|ra** (lôr′ə), *n., pl.* **lau|ras, lau|rae** (lôr′ē). a form of monastic community among certain early Christians occupying a row or group of detached cells under the authority of a superior. [< Greek *laúrā* lane, passage, alley]
**lau|ra|ceous** (lô rā′shəs), *adj.* of the laurel family of plants. [< New Latin *Lauraceae* the family name < Latin *laurus* laurel tree]
**Lau|ra|sia** (lô rā′zhə, -shə), *n.* a supercontinent comprising North America, Europe, and Asia which is believed to have existed for millions of years before splitting up during the Cenozoic era. [< *Lau*(rentian Mountains of North America) + (Eu)*rasia*]
**Lau|ra|sian** (lô rā′zhən, -shən), *adj.* of or having to do with Laurasia: *Turtles are found in Triassic formation in Laurasia. None are found in Gondwanaland before Cretaceous times. This suggests a Laurasian origin* (Scientific American).
**lau|re|ate** (*adj., n.* lôr′ē it; *v.* lôr′ē āt), *adj., n., v.,* **-at|ed, -at|ing.** —*adj.* **1** crowned with a laurel wreath as a mark of honor: *a laureate head.* **2** honored or distinguished: *a laureate poet.* **3** of laurel: *a laureate crown or wreath.*
—*n.* **1** = poet laureate. **2** a person who is honored or receives a prize for outstanding achievement in a particular field: *a Nobel prize laureate.* **3** a person who praises enthusiastically; panegyrist: *a laureate of Victorian England.*
—*v.t.* **1** to appoint as poet laureate. **2** to crown with laurel in token of honor.
[< Latin *laureātus* < *laurea* laurel tree < *laurus* laurel tree]
**lau|re|ate|ship** (lôr′ē it ship), *n.* **1** the position of poet laureate. **2** the time during which a poet is poet laureate.
**lau|re|a|tion** (lôr′ē ā′shən), *n.* **1** the act of crowning with laurel. **2** the conferring of a university degree; graduation.
**lau|rel** (lôr′əl, lor′-), *n., v.,* **-reled, -rel|ing** or (*especially British*) **-relled, -rel|ling.** —*n.* **1** a shrub or tree of the laurel family, such as a small evergreen tree of the Mediterranean region, with smooth, shiny leaves and many dark-purple berries; bay tree; sweet bay. **2** the leaves of this small evergreen tree. The ancient Greeks and Romans crowned victors with wreaths of laurel. **3** a tree or shrub having evergreen leaves like those of the laurel tree, such as the mountain laurel, sheep laurel, and the great rhododendron. The mountain laurel has pale-pink clusters of blossoms and is the state flower of Connecticut and Pennsylvania.
—*v.t.* to wreathe with laurel; adorn with or as if with laurel.
**laurels, a** high honor; fame: *No other fame can be compared with that of Jesus ... All other laurels wither before his* (William E. Channing). **b** victory: *They neither pant for laurels, nor delight in blood* (Samuel Johnson).
**look to one's laurels,** to guard one's reputation or record, especially from rivals: *The fair widow would be wise to look to her laurels* (J. H. Riddell).
**rest** (or **sit back**) **on one's laurels,** to be satisfied with the honors or achievements one has already won: *One sees no sign that the city has been resting on its laurels ... several activities have been added: notably a nylon factory and plants for making buses* (London Times).
[< Old French *lorier* and *laurier* laurel tree < *lor* laurel < Latin *laurus* laurel tree]
**lau|reled** or **lau|relled** (lôr′əld, lor′-), *adj.* **1** crowned with a laurel wreath. **2** honored: *a great editorial improvement in the paper, deservedly laurelled by the newspaper prize givers as the most improved of the year* (Punch).
**laurel family**, a group of dicotyledonous trees or shrubs, found chiefly in warm regions, where they are evergreen. Many of the plants of this family are aromatic and are used for seasoning. The family includes the laurel, cinnamon, sassafras, avocado, camphor tree, and greenheart.
**Lau|ren|tian** (lô ren′shən), *adj.* **1** of or having to do with the Canadian upland region extending from Labrador past Hudson Bay and north to the Arctic: *The Laurentian area, sometimes called the "Canadian Shield," is the most important mineral-producing section of Canada* (Colby and Foster). **2** of or having to do with the Laurentian Mountains in eastern Canada, between Hudson Bay and the St. Lawrence River: *a Laurentian resort.* **3** of or having to do with the St. Lawrence River and the regions through which it flows: *the Laurentian watershed.* **4** *Geology.* of or having to do with certain granites intrusive in the oldest Pre-Cambrian rocks of southern Canada. [< *Laurentius,* Latin form of Lawrence + *-ian*]
**Laurentian Plateau** or **Shield**, = Canadian Shield.
**lau|res|ti|nus** (lôr′ə stī′nəs), *n.* = laurustinus.
**lau|ric acid** (lôr′ik, lor′-), a fatty acid found in coconut oil and palm oil, used in the manufacture of soap. *Formula:* $C_{12}H_{24}O_2$ [< Latin *laurus* laurel tree + English *-ic*]
**lau|rus|ti|nus** (lôr′ə stī′nəs), *n.* an evergreen shrub of the honeysuckle family, of the Mediterranean region, having clusters of white or pink flowers that bloom in winter in mild regions. Also, **laurestinus.** [< New Latin *laurus tinus* < Latin *laurus* laurel tree, and *tīnus* a kind of plant]
**lau|ryl alcohol** (lôr′əl, lor′-), a crystalline compound used in the manufacture of detergents. *Formula:* $C_{12}H_{24}O$ [< *laur*(ic acid) + *-yl*]
**lav.**, lavatory.
**la|va** (lä′və, lav′ə), *n.* **1** the hot, melted, or molten rock flowing from a volcano or fissure in the earth: *Magma is called lava when it reaches the earth's surface* (Science News Letter). See picture under **volcano. 2** the rock formed by the cooling of this molten rock. Some lavas are hard and glassy; others are light and porous. [< Italian *lava* lava flow < *lavare* to wash < Latin *lavāre*]
**la|va|bo** (lə vā′bō), *n., pl.* **-boes. 1** Also, **Lavabo.** in the Roman Catholic Church: **a** the ritual washing of the celebrant's hands during the Mass, before beginning the Consecration. **b** the passage recited during this ceremony (Psalm 25:6-12 in the Douay Version). **c** the basin used for the washing. **2a** (in many monasteries of the Middle Ages) a trough, or the room in which the trough stood, for washing before religious exercises or meals. **b** = washstand. **3** a small ornamental basin hung on the wall of a hall or living room and sometimes used for holding plants. [< Latin *lavābo* I shall wash (from the first word of the verses said with the ritual)]
**lava cave**, a cave formed when lava hardens at the surface while beneath it flows out from under the hardening crust.
**lava cone**, a volcanic cone built entirely or mainly of lava flows.
**lava dome**, a dome-shaped volcano built up of many lava flows issued from the central vent of a volcano.
**lava field**, a large area of cooled lava: *The excavations at Pompeii and the reclamation of the surrounding marshlands and lava fields were already accomplished facts* (Atlantic).
**lava flow**, **1** the flow of lava from a volcano or fissure: *In 1960, nonexplosive lava flows from Kilauea covered the entire town of Kapoho, and more than 1000 acres were added to the coastline where lava poured into the ocean* (Robert W. Decker). **2** the site of a former lava flow.
**lav|age** (lav′ij; *French.* lȧ vȧzh′), *n., v.,* **-aged, -aging.** —*n.* **1** a laving or washing. **2** *Medicine.* **a** a washing out of the stomach, intestines, or other organs: *gastric lavage.* **b** a cleansing by means of injection, as of a saline solution.
—*v.t. Medicine.* to wash out or cleanse (a wound or organ).
[< Middle French *lavage* < *laver* to wash < Latin *lavāre*]
**la|va-la|va** (lä′vä lä′vä), *n.* a rectangular piece of printed cotton cloth, worn as a skirt or loincloth by the Polynesians: *wrapped in lava-lava skirts.* [< a Samoan word]
**lav|a|liere, lav|a|lier,** or **lav|al|lière** (lav′ə lir′), *n.* **1** an ornament hanging from a small chain, worn around the neck by women. **2** Also, **lavalier microphone.** a small broadcasting microphone worn on a cord about the neck and resting on the chest. [< French *lavallière* < (the *Duchesse de*) *La Vallière,* 1644-1710, a mistress of Louis XIV of France]
**lav|a|ret** (lav′ə ret), *n.* a whitefish that lives in the sea and swims up various European and Asiatic rivers each year. Forms that are landlocked in various European lakes show widely differing characteristics, often being classified in different species. [< French *lavaret*]
**la|vash** (lä′väsh), *n.* a thin, flat bread eaten by Armenians. [< Armenian]
**la|va|tion** (la vā′shən), *n.* **1** the process of washing. **2** water for washing. [< Latin *lavātiō, -ōnis* < *lavāre* to wash]
**la|va|tion|al** (la vā′shə nəl), *adj.* having to do with lavation.
**lav|a|to|ri|al** (lav′ə tôr′ē əl, -tōr′-), *adj.* **1** of or having to do with a bathroom: *the ancient, salty, faintly lavatorial stink of the ocean* (Sunday Times). **2** of or having to do with washing; lavational.
**lav|a|to|ry** (lav′ə tôr′ē, -tōr′-), *n., pl.* **-ries. 1** a bathroom; toilet. **2** a room where a person can wash his hands and face. **3** a bowl or basin to wash in. **4** *Ecclesiastical.* the ritual washing of the celebrant's hands during Communion service just before the consecration of the elements (the lavabo) and (formerly) after the cleansing of the vessels following the communion. **5** *Rare.* a laundry. [< Latin *lavātōrium* < *lavāre* to wash. See etym. of doublet **laver**[1].]
**lave**[1] (lāv), *v.,* **laved, lav|ing.** *Archaic.* —*v.t.* **1** to wash; bathe: *basins and ewers to lave her dainty hands* (Shakespeare). **2** to wash or flow against: *The stream laves its banks.* **3** to pour or throw out, as water; ladle out.
—*v.i.* to bathe.
[Old English *lafian,* ultimately < Latin *lavāre*]
**lave**[2] (lāv), *n. Scottish.* what is left; the remainder; the rest. [Old English *lāf*]
**la|veer** (lə vir′), *v.i. Archaic.* to sail into the wind; tack. [< Dutch *laveeren* < Middle French *loveer* < *lof* windward, probably < Dutch *loef.* Compare etym. under **luff.**]
**lav|en|der** (lav′ən dər), *adj., n., v.* —*adj.* pale-pur-

ple. —*n.* **1** a pale purple. **2a** a plant of the mint family, especially a small shrub native to the Mediterranean region, having spikes of small, fragrant, pale-purple flowers, yielding an oil (lavender oil or oil of lavender) much used in perfumes and in medicine. **b** its dried flowers, leaves, and stalks used to perfume or preserve linens or clothes: *a chest full of lavender and old lace.*
—*v.t.* to perfume with lavender; put lavender among (linen).
[< Anglo-French *lavendre* < Medieval Latin *lavendula,* also *livendula;* origin uncertain]

**lavender cotton**, a small, evergreen, strongly aromatic shrub of the Mediterranean region, with yellow, tubular florets.

**lavender water**, a toilet water or perfume made with oil of lavender.

**la|ver**[1] (lā′vər), *n.* **1** *Archaic.* a bowl or basin to wash in. **2** the large brazen vessel, standing on a pedestal, for the ablutions of the Hebrew priests and the washing of the sacrifices, mentioned in the Bible in the descriptions of the Tabernacle and Solomon's Temple. **3a** *Ecclesiastical.* the water used in baptizing or the font containing it. **b** any spiritually cleansing agency. [< Old French *laveoir,* Old North French *lavur* < Latin *lavātōrium.* See etym. of doublet **lavatory**.]

**la|ver**[2] (lā′vər), *n.* **1** any one of various large, edible, red seaweeds that are widely distributed in the world. **2** such seaweed prepared as food. [< Latin *laver*]

**la|ver|bread** (lā′vər bred′), *n.* a food made from dried seaweed and prepared like bread, eaten in parts of England and Wales.

**lav|er|ock** (lav′ər ək, lāv′rək), *n. Scottish.* a lark: *Now laverocks wake the merry morn* (Robert Burns). Also, **lavrock**. [Middle English *laverokke,* Old English *lāwerce*]

**La|vin|i|a** (lə vin′ē ə), *n. Roman Legend.* the wife of Aeneas.

**lav|ish** (lav′ish), *adj., v.* —*adj.* **1** very free or too free in giving or spending; prodigal: *A very rich person can be lavish with his money. Thank the lavish hand that gives world beauty to our eyes* (Julia Ward Howe). SYN: extravagant. **2** very abundant or too abundant; more than is needed; given or spent freely or too freely: *Mother gave me a lavish helping of ice cream. The lavish, full-skirted velvet gown of the Renaissance period was rich and made with a fabric such as silk or fine cotton* (Bernice G. Chambers). *The lavish gold of her loose hair* (James Russell Lowell). SYN: See syn. under **profuse**.
—*v.t.* to give or spend very freely or too freely; pour out wastefully: *It is a mistake to lavish kindness on ungrateful people. Upon the interior decorations* [*of the castle*] *Albert and Victoria lavished all their care* (Lytton Strachey).
[< Middle French *lavasse* < Old Provençal *lavaci* < Latin *lavātiō;* see etym. under **lavation**] —**lav′ish|er**, *n.* —**lav′ish|ly**, *adv.* —**lav′ish|ness**, *n.*

**lav|rock** (lav′rək), *n.* = laverock.

**law**[1] (lô), *n., v.* —*n.* **1** a rule or regulation made by a country or state for all the people who live there: *Good citizens obey the laws. Organized group control ... is composed of the laws on the statute book and of the attitudes of the people toward these laws. It is the attitudes that count more* (Emory S. Bogardus). **2** the system of rules formed to protect society or some other group: *English law is different from French law. "The rule of law is a lesson learned from centuries of human experience, from many mistakes and much suffering. ... Without it we destroy one another"* (Lord Home). *The Venetian Law cannot impugn you as you do proceed* (Shakespeare). **3** the controlling influence of these rules, or the condition of society brought about by their observance: *The police maintain law and order.* **4** law as a system: *a court of law.* **5** the study concerned with these rules; jurisprudence: *He was design'd to the study of the law* (John Dryden). **6** the body of such rules concerned with a particular subject or derived from a particular source: *commercial law, criminal law, civil law.* **7** the profession of a lawyer: *to enter the law.* **8** *Informal.* a person hired to enforce the law; policeman or detective: *The law came just in time to catch the armed robber.* **9** legal action: *to have recourse to the law.* **10** any act passed upon by the highest legislative body of a State or nation: *a congressional law.* **11** any rule or principle that must be obeyed: *the laws of hospitality, a law of grammar. The laws of the game must be obeyed.* **12** a statement of what always occurs under certain conditions; description of a relation or sequence of phenomena invariable under the same conditions: *the laws of motion, Mendel's law. Physicists* (*and other scientists*) *have a shorthand way of describing natural phenomena. Such shorthand descriptions are termed laws. For instance, there is a law, called the law or principle of Archimedes, describing how far into water a floating body will sink. In physics laws are usually put into mathematical form* (Harper's). **13** a mathematical rule or relationship on which the construction of a curve, a series, etc., depends. **14** *Theology.* **a** a divine rule or commandment. **b** the collective body of precepts held to be received from God; the first five books of the Old Testament: *the Mosaic law.* **c** Often, **Law**. a system or order based on divine dispensation.
—*v.i. Informal.* to go to law; bring a lawsuit: *Your husband's ... given to lawing, they say* (George Eliot).
—*v.t. Dialect or Informal.* to bring a lawsuit against; sue: *One sends me a challenge; another laws me; but I shall keep them all off* (Horatio Nelson).
**go to law**, to appeal to law courts; contest in a lawsuit: *The partners could not agree on splitting their profits and had to go to law to settle the matter.*
**lay down the law**, **a** to give orders that must be obeyed: *There is no official to lay down the law on this question. There is no official ministry view on chastity ... to lay down the law on this subject* (New York Times). **b** to give a scolding: *The teacher laid down the law to the two boys fighting on the playground.*
**read law**, to study to be a lawyer: *He's reading law at Harvard.*
**take the law into one's own hands**, to protect one's rights or punish a crime without appealing to law courts: *The new marshal arrested the vigilantes who had taken the law into their own hands.*
[Old English *lagu* < Scandinavian (compare Old Icelandic *lög* laws)]
—*Syn. n.* **1**, **10 Law, statute** mean a rule or regulation recognized by a state or community as governing the action or procedure of its members. **Law** is the general word applying to any such rule or regulation, written or unwritten, laid down by the highest authority, passed by action of a lawmaking body such as Congress, a state legislature, or a city council, or recognized as custom and enforced by the courts. **Statute** applies to a formally written law passed by a legislative body.

**law**[2] (lô), *adj., adv., n. Obsolete.* low[1].

**Law** (lô), *n.* **the**, **1** the first five books of the Old Testament that contain the Mosaic law. **2a** the Old Testament, as containing the Mosaic law. **b** the part of the Bible setting this forth. **c** the Pentateuch, especially as one of the three recognized divisions of the Hebrew Scripture; Torah.

**law-a|bid|ing** (lô′ə bī′ding), *adj.* obeying the law; peaceful and orderly: *Law-abiding citizens observe the traffic regulations.* —**law′-a|bid′ing|ness**, *n.*

**law and order**, the support or use of stringent measures to suppress crime and violence: *The current emphasis on law and order distresses me because the phrase appears to mean only the stringent regulation of the disadvantaged and rebellious* (R. Hobart Ellis, Jr.).

**law-and-or|der** (lô′ənd ôr′dər), *adj.* supporting or advocating stringent measures to suppress crime and violence, including rioting and other forms of violent demonstrations: [*He*] *was best known for his views on the handling of criminal prosecutions, which had often caused him to be classified as a "law-and-order" judge* (C. Herman Pritchett).

**law|book** (lô′bu̇k′), *n.* a book relating to law, or containing laws or reports of cases.

**law|break|er** (lô′brā′kər), *n.* a person who breaks the law: *All too many lawbreakers and potential lawbreakers are persuaded that they can steal a car ... and get away with it, or with worse crimes* (New York Times).

**law|break|ing** (lô′brā′king), *n., adj.* —*n.* a breaking of the law.
—*adj.* breaking the law: *a lawbreaking offense.*

**law clerk**, an assistant to a judge or lawyer: *Taking a job as a law clerk in Chicago ... he saved enough money to start his own law office* (Wall Street Journal).

**law court**, a place where justice is administered; court of law.

**law day**, a day appointed for the discharge of a bond: *A person who borrows money with a mortgage promises to repay it by law day.*

**Law Day**, *U.S.* May 1, celebrated to emphasize the importance of law in American life.

**law French**, a form of Anglo-French in legal use in England from the time of William the Conqueror to that of Edward III or later, and still surviving in some phrases and expressions.

**law|ful** (lô′fəl), *adj.* **1** according to law; done as the law directs: *a lawful trial, a lawful arrest.* **2** allowed by law; rightful: *lawful demands.* **3** law-abiding: *a lawful man.* —**law′ful|ly**, *adv.* —**law′ful|ness**, *n.*
—*Syn.* **1**, **2 Lawful, legal, legitimate** mean according to law. **Lawful** means in agreement with or not against the laws of the state or community, the laws of a church, or moral law: *To some people gambling is never lawful although it may be legal in some places.* **Legal** means authorized by or according to the actual terms of the legislative acts and other laws of a state or community enforced by the courts: *Divorce is legal in the United States.* **Legitimate** means rightful according to law, recognized authority, or established standards: *Sickness is a legitimate reason for a child's absence from school.*

**law|giv|er** (lô′giv′ər), *n.* a person who prepares and puts into effect a system of laws for a people; legislator; lawmaker.

**law-hand** (lô′hand′), *n.* the style of handwriting in former times customarily used in legal documents: *an immense desert of law-hand and parchments* (Dickens).

**La|wi|ne** (lä vē′nə; *Anglicized* lô′win), *n., pl.* **-nen** (-nən), *German.* an avalanche.

**law|less** (lô′lis), *adj.* **1** paying no attention to the law; breaking the law: *A thief leads a lawless life.* **2** having no laws: *In pioneer days much of the West was a lawless wilderness.* **3** hard to control; disorderly; unruly: *Her lawless hair was caught in a net* (Bret Harte). SYN: uncontrolled, ungovernable. —**law′less|ly**, *adv.* —**law′less|ness**, *n.*

**law lord**, one of the members of the House of Lords qualified to take part in its judicial proceedings: *He's a law lord—a member of our highest appeals court, and thus automatically a life peer* (Norman Kotker).

**law|mak|er** (lô′mā′kər), *n.* a person who helps to make laws of a country; member of a legislature or parliament; legislator; lawgiver: *Congressmen are lawmakers.*

**law|mak|ing** (lô′mā′king), *adj., n.* —*adj.* having the duty and power of making laws; legislative: *Congress is a lawmaking body.*
—*n.* the act or process of making laws; legislation.

**law|man** (lô′mən), *n., pl.* **-men**. a law enforcement officer.

**law merchant**, *pl.* **laws merchant**. **1** the body of principles and rules for the regulation of commerce, drawn chiefly from the customs of merchants; mercantile law. **2** (formerly) the customs that governed legal cases originating in trade or commerce.

**lawn**[1] (lôn), *n., v.* —*n.* **1** land covered with grass kept closely cut, especially near or around a house. **2** *Archaic.* an open space between woods; glade.
—*v.t.* to turn (land) into lawn: *The grounds of the estate are beautifully lawned.*
[< Old French *launde,* also *lande* wooded ground, heath, moor < Celtic (compare Breton *lann,* Irish *laun*)]

**lawn**[2] (lôn), *n.* **1** a thin, sheer linen or cotton cloth, resembling cambric: *A saint in crape is twice a saint in lawn* (Alexander Pope). **2** = lawn sleeves. [apparently < *Laon,* a city in France, long a center of linen manufacture]

**lawn bowling**, the game of bowls.

**lawn chair**, a chair for use outdoors.

**lawn mower**, a machine with revolving blades for cutting the grass on a lawn.

**lawn party**, *U.S.* an informal gathering held on the lawn or in the garden of a house; garden party.

**lawn sleeves**, **1** the sleeves of lawn characterizing the dress of an Anglican bishop. **2a** the position of a bishop. **b** a bishop or bishops.

**lawn tennis**, a game in which a ball is hit back and forth with a racket over a low net. It is played on an open court, sometimes of grass. The game of tennis, as commonly played today, is lawn tennis.

**lawn|y**[1] (lô′nē), *adj.* like a lawn; level and covered with smooth turf: *lawny slopes.* [< *lawn*[1] + *-y*[1]]

**lawn|y**[2] (lô′nē), *adj.* made of or like the cloth lawn. [< *lawn*[2] + *-y*[1]]

**law of averages**, **1** *Statistics.* = law of large numbers. **2** the usual way events turn out or are determined or the customary way people act: *The law of averages can generally be counted upon to catch up with the cheat eventually.*

**law of contradiction**, *Logic.* the law that states that a thing cannot be and not be at the same time or that no statement can be both true and false.

**law of diminishing returns**, = diminishing returns.

**law of gravitation**, *Physics.* statement of the

principle that two bodies attract each other with a force directly proportional to the product of their masses and inversely proportional to the square of the distance between them.

**law of large numbers**, *Statistics.* the rule or theorem that a large number of items chosen at random from a population are bound, on the average, to have the characteristics of the population.

**law of Moses**, = Pentateuch.

**law of nations**, **1** = international law. **2** (in ancient Roman use) the rules common to the law of all nations.

**law of parsimony**, = Occam's Razor.

**law of the jungle**, circumstance that prescribes certain primitive, harsh, or otherwise distasteful conduct to survive: *righteously condemned it as "the law of the jungle" under which "the strong swallow the weak"* (Wall Street Journal).

**law of the land**, law, especially law or accepted rules prevailing in a certain country, profession, or business: *projections of a moral principle to which the Supreme Court has given increasing weight as the law of the land* (New York Times).

**law of the Medes and Persians**, a law that cannot be changed; something unalterable (with allusion to Daniel 6:12).

**law of the sea**, **1** accepted customs of conduct for behavior of seamen or actions of ships' masters and owners. **2** maritime law, especially international maritime law: *The International Convention on the Law of the Sea* (New York Times). **3** what is dictated as necessary to survive at sea.

**Law|ren|cian** (lô ren′shən), *adj.* = Lawrentian.

***law|ren|ci|um** (lô ren′sē əm), *n.* a radioactive, metallic chemical element of the actinide series. Lawrencium is short-lived and artificially produced by bombarding californium with boron ions. [< New Latin *Lawrencium* < Ernest Orlando *Lawrence,* 1901-1958, an American physicist]

| | symbol | atomic number | mass number |
|---|---|---|---|
| ***lawrencium** | Lw | 103 | 256 |

**Law|ren|tian** (lô ren′shən), *adj.* of or characteristic of either the English novelist and poet D. H. Lawrence (1885-1930) or his writings, or the English adventurer T. E. Lawrence (1888-1935) or his writings or adventures.

**Laws of Manu**, = Code of Manu.

**Law|son criterion** (lô′sən), *Nuclear Physics.* a criterion that establishes the point at which a fusion reaction becomes self-sustaining, formulated by the British physicist J. D. Lawson in the 1960's.

**Lawson cypress**, = Port Orford cedar. [< P. *Lawson,* a Scottish horticulturist of the 1800's]

**law|suit** (lô′süt′), *n.* a case in a law court started by one person to claim something from another; application to a court by one person to compel another to do him justice.

**law|yer** (lô′yər), *n.* **1** a person who knows the laws and gives advice about matters of the law or acts for another person in a law court. **2** a scribe; expounder of the Mosaic Law (in the New Testament, Luke 10:25). **3** = burbot. **4** *Australian Dialect.* a long bramble. [< *law*[1] + *-yer,* variant of *-ier*]

► **Lawyer** is a general term for members of the legal profession, such as attorneys, barristers, counselors, solicitors, or advocates.

**law|yer|ing** (lô′yər ing), *n.* the state or condition of being a lawyer: *John W. Davis ... left Wall Street in 1924 to become the Democratic candidate for President; he lost and went back to lawyering* (Time).

**law|yer|ish** (lô′yə rish), *adj.* like that of a lawyer: *lawyerish mannerisms.*

**law|yer|ism** (lô′yə riz əm), *n.* the influence, or principles of lawyers.

**law|yer|like** (lô′yər līk′), *adj.* of or characteristic of a lawyer or lawyers: *Writing slows us down and makes us more grammatical, more lawyerlike* (Saturday Review).

**law|yer|ly** (lô′yər lē), *adj.* of lawyers; lawyerlike.

**lax** (laks), *adj.* **1** not firm or tight; slack: *The package was tied so loosely that the cord was lax.* **SYN**: relaxed, flabby, loose. **2** not strict; careless: *Don't become lax about the schedule you have set for studying. The states have been lax in passing safety regulations requiring seat belts in school buses* (New York Times). **SYN**: negligent, remiss. **3** not exact or precise; vague: *in a lax way of speaking* (Joseph Butler). **4** loose in morals: *Richard [Cromwell] was known to be lax and godless in his conduct* (John Richard Green). **5** loose in texture; loosely cohering or compacted, as of tissue, stone, or soil. **6** *Botany.* loose or open; not compact, as some panicles are. **7** *Phonetics.* pronounced with the muscles of the articulating organs relatively relaxed; wide: *lax vowels.* **8** acting easily; loose, especially of the bowels. [< Latin *laxus* loose] —**lax′ly**, *adv.* —**lax′ness**, *n.*

**lax|a|tion** (lak sā′shən), *n.* **1** a loosening or relaxing. **2** a being loosened or relaxed. **3** a mild purgative; laxative. [< Latin *laxātiō, -ōnis* < *laxāre* loosen < *laxus* loose, lax]

**lax|a|tive** (lak′sə tiv), *n., adj.* —*n.* a medicine that speeds the emptying of the bowels.
—*adj.* **1** helping to empty the bowels; mildly purgative. **2** having the property of relaxing. **3** *Obsolete.* unable to contain one's speech or emotions: *Fellowes of practis'd and most laxative tongues* (Ben Jonson).
[< Latin *laxātīvus* loosening < *laxāre* loosen; see etym. under **laxation**] —**lax′a|tive|ly**, *adv.* —**lax′a|tive|ness**, *n.*

**lax|i|ty** (lak′sə tē), *n.* **1** lax condition or quality; lax conduct: *moral laxity. The newspapers accused local police of laxity in dealing with gamblers.* **2** slackness or want of tension, especially in the muscular or nervous fibers. **3** looseness, especially of the bowels. [< Middle French *laxité,* learned borrowing from Latin *laxitās* < *laxus* loose]

**lay**[1] (lā), *v.,* **laid, lay|ing,** *n.* —*v.t.* **1** to put down; keep down; place in a certain position: *Lay your hat on the table. A shower has laid the dust.* **SYN**: suppress, quash, quell. **2** to bring down; beat down: *A storm laid the crops low.* **SYN**: level. **3a** to place in a lying-down position or a position of rest: *Lay the baby down gently. When, in the evening of her life, the doctors told her that she must return to Europe, she just laid herself down and died* (Observer). **SYN**: deposit. **b** to bury: *He was laid in a quiet churchyard.* **4** to place or set: *Lay your hand on your heart. She lays great emphasis on good manners. That author lays the scenes for most of his stories in faraway places.* **5** to put: *The horse laid his ears back.* **6** to cause to be in a certain situation or condition: *to lay a trap, to lay a table for dinner, to lay a wound open.* **7** to put in place, especially in proper position or in orderly fashion: *to lay bricks, to lay the keel of a new liner. They laid the carpet on the floor.* **8** to smooth down; press: *to lay the nap on cloth.* **9** to devise; arrange: *We have laid our plans for dealing with that situation.* **SYN**: design. **10** to put down as a bet; wager: *I lay five dollars that he will not come.* **11** to impose (something), such as a burden or penalty: *to lay a tax on tea. They laid an embargo on arms shipments.* **12** to bring forward; place before; present: *to lay claim to an estate. I hope you have no objection to laying your case before the uncle* (Oliver Goldsmith). **13** to blame; bring forward as an accusation or charge; impute; attribute: *She laid her failure to her lack of effort. The theft was laid to him.* **SYN**: ascribe. **14** to produce (an egg or eggs): *Birds, fish, and reptiles lay eggs.* **15** to twist yarn or strands together to form (a strand or rope). **16** to make quiet; make disappear: *to lay a ghost. These fears ought now to be laid.* **SYN**: allay.
—*v.i.* **1** to produce eggs: *Hens begin laying about December.* **2** to offer a bet; wager: *I lay I'll keep drier on my own shanks* (M. E. Carter). **3** to apply oneself vigorously: *The men laid to their oars.* **4** to lie: *They found him laying on his back.* **5** *Dialect.* to plan; intend: *... he has laid to arrest me I hear* (Ben Jonson).
—*n.* **1** the way or position in which anything is laid or lies: *The lay of the ground hindered my view of the sea* (Alexander Kinglake). **SYN**: arrangement. **2** the amount and direction of the twist given to the strands or other components of a rope. **3** a share of the profits or of the catch of a whaling or fishing vessel: *All hands, including the captain, received certain shares of the profits called lays* (Herman Melville). **4** *U.S. Dialect.* terms of purchase. **5** *Slang.* a line of business; field of operations; occupation; job: *He's not to be found on his old lay* (Dickens).

**lay about**, to hit out on all sides: *The hunter trapped by a pack of wolves laid about with a heavy stick.*

**lay aside** (or **away**, or **by**), to put away for future use; save: *I laid away a dollar a week toward purchasing a new bicycle. Lay aside that book for me.*

**lay down**, **a** to declare; state: *The umpire laid down the conditions for settling the dispute. It is impossible to lay down what man's needs will be* (Manchester Guardian Weekly). **b** to give; sacrifice: *Many soldiers lay down their lives in battle.* **c** *Slang.* to quit; resign: *Leahy accused the Irish gridders of laying down and, in effect, dubbed them the "Unfighting Irish"* (Tuscaloosa News). **d** to store away for future use: *"His first duty is to his family" and is fulfilled ... by laying down vintages* (Robert Louis Stevenson).

**lay for**, *Informal.* to stay hidden ready to attack: *The bully laid for me on my way home.*

**lay hold of** (or **on**), to seize; grasp: *For Herod has laid hold on John, and bound him, and put him in prison ...* (Matthew 14:3).

**lay in**, to put aside for the future; provide; save: *The trappers laid in a good supply of food for the winter.*

**lay into**, **a** to beat; thrash: *She would lay into Master John with her stick* (George R. Sims). **b** *Informal.* to scold: *Mother laid into me for not doing my homework. ... laying into a politician who was preparing to do something popular which he knew in his heart was wrong* (Economist).

**lay low**. See under **low**[1].

**lay off**, **a** to put aside: *He laid off his coat as he approached the fire.* **b** to put out of work for a time: *Japanese firms try to avoid laying off workers in time of slack business demand* (New York Times). **c** *Informal.* to stop teasing, interfering with, or taking part in, for a time; stop; desist: *The thought of the afternoon's work made Studs gloomy. He thought that he might lay off and go home* (James T. Farrell). *"This song is us, and what we wanna say is: lay off our blue suede shoes, daddy-o"* (Atlantic). **d** to mark off: *The surveyor laid off the boundaries of the lot.*

**lay on**, **a** to apply: *Gold leaf is laid on with white of egg.* **b** to supply; give: *A monumental feast had been laid on for the benefit of myself and of another Scottish friend* (Listener). **c** to strike; beat; inflict: *Lay on, Macduff, And damn'd be him that first cries "Hold, enough!"* (Shakespeare). **d** to utter (flattery), especially in a fulsome manner: *Well said, that was laid on with a trowel* (Shakespeare).

**lay oneself** (or **one**) **open**, to expose oneself or another (to): *He lays himself open to ridicule by his many boasts.*

**lay oneself out**, *Informal.* to make a big effort; take great pains: *He laid himself out to be agreeable.*

**lay open**, **a** to make bare; expose: *The captured spy laid open the whole scheme of the enemy attack.* **b** to make an opening in; wound: *With a swift stroke of his sword, he laid open his attacker.*

**lay out**, **a** to spread out: *Refreshments were laid out in an adjoining room* (H. T. Ellis). **b** to arrange; plan: *The roads had been laid out but were not completed* (J. Bacon). *They lay out experimental pages, ... prepare picture pages, and eventually produce a newspaper* (Saturday Review). **c** *Informal.* to pay out; spend: *I laid out some of my money for purchasing land.* **d** to prepare (a dead body) for burial: *They reverently laid out the corpse* (Elizabeth Gaskell). **e** *Slang.* to scold or punish: *If I didn't bring in my assignment, the teacher would lay me out* (New Yorker). **f** *Slang.* to knock unconscious; put out of the fight: *Never were so many demagogues laid out in one day* (Nation).

**lay over**, **a** to stop for a time in a place: *The stagecoach lay over at the inn until the horses were rested.* **b** to postpone: *At the same time the board laid over indefinitely a proposed allocation of $3,065,000* (New York Times). **c** *Slang.* to be better than; surpass; excel: *They've a street up there in "Roaring," that would lay over any street in Red Dog* (Bret Harte).

**lay to**, **a** to put blame on; ascribe to; impute to: *She laid her failure to her lack of effort.* **b** to head into the wind and stand still: *Because of the heavy fog, the ship laid to until the fog lifted.*

**lay up**, **a** to put away for future use; save: *The prospectors laid up supplies for the long winter ahead.* **b** to cause to stay in bed or indoors because of illness or injury: *The skier is laid up with a broken leg.* **c** to put (a ship) out of service for repairs, cleaning, or by decommissioning: *The Peloponnesians ... laid up their fleet for the rest of the winter* (Connop Thirlwall). *The Navy laid up its old battleships.* **d** to land a golf ball close to but without risking a hazard: *Only five men in a field of eighty-three attempted to carry the pond before the green. With everyone else meekly laying up short of the hazard, the hole completely lacked its old glamour* (New Yorker).
[Middle English *leyen,* Old English *lecgan,* related to *licgan* lie]

► **lay, lie.** In the English of the uneducated and sometimes in the spoken or written English of the educated the work of these two verbs is generally done by one (*lay, lay* or *laid, laid*): *There let him lay. As he came in, he lay his hat on a chair.* In modern standard writing and most educated speech, they have been kept distinct: *lie* (to recline, intransitive), *lay, lain; lay* (to place, transitive), *laid, laid.* You *lie* down for a rest or *lie* down on the job. A farm *lies* in a valley. You *lay* a floor, *lay* a book on the table, *lay* a bet, *lay* out clothes. Now there is some breakdown evidenced. *Her brother lay on the ground near the broken branch.*

**lay²** (lā), *v.* the past tense of **lie²**: *After a long walk I lay down for a rest.*

**lay³** (lā), *adj.* **1** of the people of a church not belonging to the clergy: *The lay preacher this Sunday is a businessman during the week.* SYN: laic, secular. **2** of the people who do not belong to a particular profession: *Doctors feel the lay mind understands little of the causes of diseases.* [< Old French *lai* < Latin *lāicus.* See etym. of doublet **laic.**]

**lay⁴** (lā), *n.* **1** a short lyric or narrative poem, especially one intended to be sung; poem: *The only way to please a minstrel was to listen ... to the lays which he liked best to sing* (Scott). **2** a song or tune. **3** the song of a bird: *The blackbird whistles his lay.* [< Old French *lai,* perhaps < Celtic (compare Irish *laid* poem, chant)]

**lay|a|bout** (lā′ə bout′), *n. British.* a habitually idle person; loafer: *A character the English call a layabout, and we would call a bum, springs forward* (Joel Sayre).

**lay analyst**, a psychoanalyst who is not a doctor of medicine.

**lay|a|way** (lā′ə wā′), *adj., n.* —*adj.* of or having to do with a layaway plan: *layaway buying.*
—*n.* **1** a vat for tanning hides. **2** the liquid in such vats.

**layaway plan**, a method of purchase in which the consumer makes a number of part payments in advance of delivery, and the seller lays away or stores the article until full payment is made.

**lay|back** (lā′bak′), *n.* **1** the backward slant of the body in rowing. **2** the characteristic backward slant of a bulldog's nose.

**lay brother**, a man who has taken the vows and habit of a religious order, but is employed chiefly in manual labor and is exempt from the studies and special religious services of the other members.

**lay-by** (lā′bī′), *n.* **1** *British.* an area off the main highway, where vehicles may stop for repairs without interfering with traffic: *"Lay-by 100 yards ahead," says a sign; this means you will find a safety island into which you can turn for emergency repairs* (Holiday). **2** a similar stopping place for barges on a river or canal. **3** a siding for cars on a railroad, at a mine, etc. **4** *British.* a deposit on goods bought on the layaway plan.

**lay day**, *Commerce.* **1** any one of the total of days specified by a charter party or contract as allowed for loading or unloading a vessel without extra charge. **2** each day allowed a ship to stay in port. **3** a day when competition is suspended during a sailing race.

**lay|er** (lā′ər), *n., v.* —*n.* **1** one thickness or fold: *the layer of clothing next to the skin, a layer of clay between two layers of sand. A cake is often made of two or more layers put together.* **2** a person or thing that lays: *That hen is a champion layer.* **3** *Horticulture.* **a** a branch of a plant bent down and covered with earth so that it will take root and form a new plant while still attached to the parent stock. **b** a plant propagated by layering. **4** = minelayer: *The mines in the Elbe represented the ultimate triumph of layers over sweepers* (Manchester Guardian Weekly). **5** *British Informal.* a layabout.
—*v.i.* to spread by layers. —*v.t.* **1** to form (new plants) by layers: *to layer strawberry runners, to layer carnations.* **2** to form in layers: *Anxiety was layered on anxiety, a child's tower of blocks mounting shakily* (New Yorker).

**lay|er|age** (lā′ər ij), *n.* = layering.

**layer cake**, a cake made in layers put together with filling and often covered with frosting.

**lay|ered** (lā′ərd), *adj.* arranged in or having layers: *In general, the layered rocks are much more open-textured than the crystallines* (Robert M. Garrels).

**layered look**, a fashion in women's clothes in which a variety of garments are worn one over the other: *It was my first overexposure to the so-called "layered look" from Paris—a turtleneck with a blouse, with a sweater, with a vest, with a raincoat, with a cape* (Eli N. Evans).

***layering**

***lay|er|ing** (lā′ər ing), *n. Horticulture.* a method of forming new plants by placing a shoot or twig of a plant in the ground so that it will take root while still attached to the parent stock: *Here I learned about "layering," whereby one grows new roots on a branch while it is still attached to the mother tree or vine* (Katherine Ganes Jackson).

**lay|ette** (lā et′), *n.* a set of clothes and bedding for a newborn baby. [< French *layette* < Middle French, a chest of drawers < *laie* chest]

**lay figure**, **1** a jointed model of the human body. Lay figures are used by artists and in shop windows. **2** *Figurative.* an unimportant, weak, or stupid person; puppet. **3** *Figurative.* a character in fiction destitute of the attributes of reality. [for earlier *layman* < Dutch *leeman* < *lede* limb + *man* man]

**lay|ing on of hands** (lā′ing), the act of placing a hand on a person's head or shoulder in order to bless or transmit grace to him, as practiced by the clergy of some Christian churches. It is traditionally performed in administering baptism, confirmation, ordination, or extreme unction.

**lay|man** (lā′mən), *n., pl.* **-men.** **1** a member of a church who is not a clergyman: *His father is a pastor but he and his brother are laymen.* **2** a person outside any particular profession: *Whether or not scientists wish it, laymen are likely to push the scientists into the position of prophets* (Saturday Review).

**lay|off** (lā′ôf′, -of′), *n.* **1** a dismissing of workmen temporarily: *The majority of those affected will be seasoned employes whose layoff dates will be advanced from one to two months as compared with last year* (Wall Street Journal). **2** a time during which workmen are out of work. **3** a period of little or no activity in business; off-season for professional athletes.

**lay of the land**, **1** the nature of the place; the position of hills, water, woods, or the like: *Scouts were sent out to learn the lay of the land.* **2** the condition of things; state of affairs: *Spies were sent to find out the lay of the land.*

**lay|out** (lā′out′), *n.* **1** an arrangement; plan: *He studied the layout of the city and saw its commercial center surrounded by a girdle of working-class sections* (Edmund Wilson). **2** a plan or design for an advertisement, book, or other printed matter: *Typography and layout are beautiful* (Harper's). **3** something laid or spread out; display. **4** the act of laying out. **5** an outfit; supply; set.

**lay|o|ver** (lā′ō′vər), *n. U.S.* a stopping for a time in a place, especially as an interruption of a trip: *After a twenty-minute layover in Chicago we flew on to Los Angeles.*

**lay reader**, **1** a layman in the Church of England appointed by the bishop to read from the Book of Common Prayer and otherwise assist at services. **2** a layman in the Roman Catholic Church, usually a volunteer, who reads from the Scripture during church services; lector.

**Lay|san** (lī′sän), *adj.* of or inhabiting Laysan, a small island in the central Pacific belonging to Hawaii and noted for its bird life: *Laysan teal, Laysan finches.*

**lay sister**, a woman who occupies a position in a female religious order corresponding to that of a lay brother.

**lay-up** (lā′up′), *n.* **1** *Basketball.* a shot from close under the basket. **2** *Nautical.* the laying up of a ship for repair, cleaning, or storage, especially of small boats: *Some newly-built vessels have gone into immediate lay-up as a result of the depressed shipping market* (Wall Street Journal).

**lay|wom|an** (lā′wu̇m′ən), *n., pl.* **-wom|en.** a woman outside religious orders, the clergy, or a particular profession, especially the law or medicine.

**laz|ar** (laz′ər, lā′zər), *n. Archaic.* a poor or diseased person, especially a leper. [< Medieval Latin *lazarus* a leper < Late Latin *Lazarus,* the beggar in Luke 16:20]

**laz|a|ret** or **laz|a|rette** (laz′ə ret′), *n.* = lazaretto.

**laz|a|ret|to** (laz′ə ret′ō), *n., pl.* **-tos.** **1** a hospital for people having contagious or loathsome diseases; pesthouse. **2** a building or ship used for quarantine purposes. **3** a place in some merchant ships, near the stern, in which supplies are kept. [< Italian *lazzaretto,* blend of *lazzaro* lazar, and the name of a hospital (*Santa Maria di*) *Nazaret* (St. Mary of) Nazareth]

**Laz|a|rist** (laz′ər ist), *n.* a member of the Vincentian order of missionary priests. [< College of St. *Lazare,* Paris (a former center of the order) + *-ist*]

**Laz|a|rus** (laz′ər əs), *n.* **1a** the brother of Mary and Martha, whom Jesus raised from the dead (in the Bible, John 11:1-44). **b** a beggar in one of the parables who suffered on earth but went to heaven (in the Bible, Luke 16:19-25). **2** any diseased beggar, especially a leper.

**laze** (lāz), *v.,* **lazed, laz|ing.** —*v.i.* to be lazy or idle: *As long as there is enough food the lion is quite content to laze all day in the shade of a rock* (Punch).
—*v.t.* to pass (time) lazily (away): *to laze away the summer.*
[back formation < *lazy*]

**la|zi|ly** (lā′zə lē), *adv.* in a lazy manner.

**la|zi|ness** (lā′zē nis), *n.* a dislike of work; unwillingness to work or be active; being lazy. SYN: indolence, sloth, sluggishness.

**laz|u|li** (laz′yə lī, -lē), *n.* = lapis lazuli.

**lazuli bunting**, a finch of western North America, the male of which has a greenish-blue head and back, white and tawny chest, and blackish wings.

**laz|u|lite** (laz′yə līt), *n.* a mineral, hydrous phosphate of aluminum, magnesium, and iron, often found in blue crystals. *Formula:* $(FeMg)Al_2P_2O_8(OH)_2$ [< Medieval Latin *lazulum* lapis lazuli + English *-ite*[1]]

**laz|u|rite** (laz′yə rīt), *n.* a mineral that is the chief component of lapis lazuli. [< Medieval Latin *lazur* azure + English *-ite*[1]]

**la|zy** (lā′zē), *adj.,* **-zi|er, -zi|est,** *v.,* **-zied, -zy|ing.** —*adj.* **1a** not willing to work or be active: *Most bees are workers but the drones are lazy.* SYN: indolent, slothful. **b** characterized by, suggestive of, or conducive to idleness: *a lazy mood, a lazy yawn, a lazy summer day.* **2** moving slowly; not very active: *A lazy stream winds through the meadow.* SYN: sluggish. **3** not functioning up to normal capacity: *lazy eye, lazy heart.* **4** of or having to do with a brand used on livestock that lies on its side instead of upright: *the lazy J brand* (⌣).
—*v.t., v.i.* = laze.
[origin uncertain. Compare Middle Low German *lasich* weak, feeble, tired.]

**la|zy|bones** (lā′zē bōnz′), *n. Informal.* a very lazy person.

**lazy dog**, *Slang.* a fragmentation bomb: *U.S. planes are dropping lazy dogs, which explode in the air and spray the ground with small, razor-sharp projectiles* (Time).

**lazy eye** or **eyes**, = amblyopia.

**la|zy-eye blindness** (lā′zē ī′), = amblyopia.

**la|zy|ish** (lā′zē ish), *adj.* somewhat lazy.

**lazy Susan**, a large revolving tray containing different foods arranged in individual compartments to make them easily accessible for serving.

***lazy tongs**, **1** a device for picking things up, consisting of a series of pairs of crossing pieces, each pair pivoted like scissors and connected with the next pair at the ends. **2** a similar arrangement of crossing pieces used for other purposes.

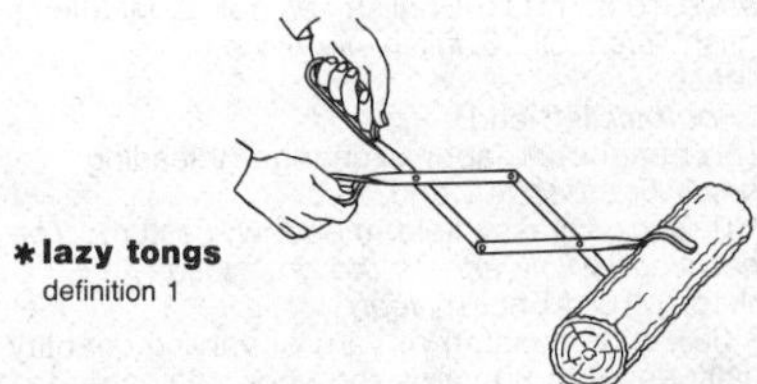
***lazy tongs**
definition 1

**laz|za|ro|ne** (laz′ə rō′nā; *Italian* läd′dzä rō′nā), *n., pl.* **-ni** (-nē; *Italian* -nē). one of a class of very poor persons in Naples, who frequent the streets and live by doing odd jobs or by begging. [< Italian *lazzarone* (augmentative) < *lazzaro* lazar]

**laz|zo** (läd′dzō), *n., pl.* **-zi** (-dzē). *Italian.* a piece of burlesque or comic business in the commedia dell' arte: *These mime plays, or lazzi, as they are properly called, date back to the Italian comedy of the 16th century* (Clive Barnes).

**lb.**, *pl.* **lb.** or **lbs.** pound or pounds: *The same company has developed a miniature direction-finder which weighs only 5 lb.* (New Scientist).

**L.B.**, *U.S.* Bachelor of Letters (Latin, *Litterarum Baccalaureus*).

**L-band** (el′band′), *n.* a UHF band between 390 and 1550 megahertz, used in satellite communications.

**L-bar** (el′bär′), *n.* a metal bar or beam shaped like an L.

**lb. av.**, pound (avoirdupois).

**L-beam** (el′bēm′), *n.* = L-bar.

**lbf** (no periods), pound force: *The hip joint can support steady loads of 300 to 400 lbf* (New Scientist).

**LBJ** (no periods), Lyndon Baines Johnson.

**lbr.**, labor.

**lbs.**, pounds.

**l.c., lc.**, or **lc** (no periods), lower case; in small letters, not capital letters.

**l.c.**, **1** in the place cited (Latin, *loco citato*). **2** left center.

**Pronunciation Key:** hat, āge, cãre, fär; let, ēqual, tėrm; it, īce; hot, ōpen, ôrder; oil, out; cup, pu̇t, rüle; child; long; thin; ᴛʜen; zh, measure; ə represents **a** in about, **e** in taken, **i** in pencil, **o** in lemon, **u** in circus.

**LC** (no periods), landing craft.
**L.C.**, 1 *U.S.* Library of Congress. 2 Lower Canada.
**L.C.C.** or **LCC** (no periods), London County Council: *The LCC is belatedly discouraging any more office development* (Manchester Guardian Weekly).
**l.c.d.** or **L.C.D.**, least common denominator; lowest common denominator.
**LCI** (no periods), landing craft, infantry.
**lcl.**, local.
**L.C.L.** or **l.c.l.**, less than carload lot.
**L clearance**, *U.S.* clearance of atomic information classified as confidential.
**l.c.m.** or **L.C.M.**, least common multiple; lowest common multiple.
**LCPR** (no periods), a small, fast boat used by an underwater demolition team to approach a beach and locate obstacles to an assault. [*l*anding *c*raft *p*ersonnel *r*ubber (boat)]
**l.c.t.**, local civil time.
**L.C.T.**, local civil time.
**ld.**, 1 land. 2 limited.
**Ld.**, 1 limited. 2 lord.
**LD** (no periods), 1 lethal dose. 2 Low Dutch. 3 learning disability.
**L.D.** or **LD.**, Low Dutch.
**L.D.C.** or **LDC** (no periods), less developed country: *The IMF represents virtually all the countries of the free world including the supposedly "financially immature" LDCs* (London Times).
**L. Div.**, Licentiate in Divinity.
**LDL** (no periods), low density lipoprotein: *LDLs carry cholesterol in their core and in man represent the major mode of transporting cholesterol from the liver to cells of various tissues* (New York Times).
**L-do|pa** (el'dō'pə), *n.* a form of the amino acid dopa, used as a drug to relieve the symptoms of Parkinson's disease; levodopa.
**Ldp.**, 1 Ladyship. 2 Lordship.
**ldr.**, leader.
**L-driv|er** (el'drī'vər), *n. British.* a person learning to drive an automobile: *The motorways ... were built specially to carry fast traffic, and from which pedestrians, cyclists, moped riders, and L-drivers are specifically excluded* (Punch). [< *l*(earner)-*driver*]
**L.D.S.**, Latter-day Saints.
**-le**, *suffix.* 1 small (diminutive), as in *icicle, kettle.* 2 again and again (frequentative), as in *crackle, sparkle.* [def. 1, Old English *-el;* def. 2, Middle English *-elen,* Old English *-lian*]
**le.**, lease.
**l.e.**, *Football.* left end.
**LE** (no periods), 1 labor exchange. 2 leading edge. 3 *Football.* left end.
**lea¹** (lē), *n.* a grassy field; meadow; pasture: *The linnet sings wildly across the green lea* (K. T. Hinkson). [Old English *lēah*]
**lea²** (lē), *n.* a measure of yarn of varying quantity, usually equal to 80 yards for wool, 120 yards for cotton and silk, and 300 yards for linen. [perhaps back formation < *leas,* variant of *leash* in sense of "certain quantity of thread"]
**lea³** (lē), *adj., n. Dialect.* —*adj.* (of land) fallow or untilled.
—*n.* fallow or untilled land, usually under grass. [apparently Old English *lǣge-,* as in *lǣghrycg* lea rig]
**LEA** (no periods), Local Education Authority.
**lea.**, 1 league. 2 leather.
**leach¹** (lēch), *v., n.* —*v.t.* 1 to run (water or some other liquid) through slowly; filter: *to leach water through wood ashes.* 2 to dissolve out soluble parts from (ashes, ores, or other matter) by running water or other liquid through slowly: *Wood ashes are leached for potash.* 3 to dissolve out by running water or other liquid through slowly: *to leach sugar from beets. Potash is leached from wood ashes to make soap.* —*v.i.* 1 to lose soluble parts as water or other liquid passes through. 2 (of soil, ashes, or other matter) to be subjected to the action of percolating water.
—*n.* 1 a perforated container for use in leaching. 2 the act, process, or result of leaching.
[apparently Old English *leccan* to wet] —**leach'er**, *n.*
**leach²** (lēch), *n.* = leech².
**leach|a|ble** (lē'chə bəl), *adj.* that can be leached.
**leach|ate** (lē'chāt), *n.* any substance that has undergone leaching: *Leachate from open refuse dumps and poorly engineered landfills has contaminated surface and ground waters* (Richard D. Vaughan).
**Leach's petrel** (lēch'əz), a stormy petrel of the northern Atlantic with a forked tail. [< William *Leach,* a British naturalist of the 1800's]
**leach|y** (lē'chē), *adj.*, **leach|i|er**, **leach|i|est.** that allows water to percolate through.
**lead¹** (lēd), *v.*, **led, lead|ing,** *n., adj.* —*v.t.* 1a to show the way by going along with or in front of; guide: *The usher will lead you to your seats. The Star led the Three Wise Men to Bethlehem.* SYN: conduct. See syn. under **guide. b** to serve to guide: *His cries for help led us to him.* SYN: conduct. See syn. under **guide. 2a** to conduct, as by hand or rope: *He leads the horses to water.* **b** to conduct or bring in a particular channel or course; convey: *to lead water into a basin, lead a wire through an opening. This highway leads most of the traffic into the city.* **c** to bring something to a particular condition or result: *Lack of a willingness to compromise led the country to the point of civil war.* 3 to guide or direct, as in action, policy, or opinion; influence; persuade: *Such actions lead us to distrust him.* SYN: induce, entice. 4 *Figurative.* to go or be first among; have first place; be at the top or head of: *She leads the class in spelling. The elephants led the parade.* 5 to pass or spend (time, life) in some special way: *He leads a quiet life in the country.* 6 to be chief of; command; direct: *A general leads an army. The Archbishop is leading the movement. He leads the community orchestra. A woman led the singing.* SYN: head, manage, control. 7 to begin or open: *She led the dance. He will lead the program.* 8 (in card playing) to begin a trick or round by playing (a card or suit named): *to lead trumps.* 9 *Boxing.* to direct (a blow) at an opponent. 10 to discharge a firearm, arrow, spear, rocket, or other missile at (a moving target), making allowance for the distance it will advance before the shot reaches it; aim in front of: *A flying bird may require to be led several feet.* 11 *Archaic.* to take or bring: *We led them away prisoners.*
—*v.i.* 1 to act as guide; show the way: *Lead, I will follow.* 2 to be a way to a certain condition; be a means of proceeding to or effecting a certain result: *Hard work leads to success. The frequent outbreaks led to civil war.* 3 to form a channel or route: *The drain led into a common sewer. All roads lead to Rome.* 4 to afford passage or way: *Broad steps lead down into the garden.* 5 to be led; submit to being led: *This horse leads easily.* 6 to be chief; direct; act as leader: *And when we think we lead, we are most led* (Byron). 7 *Figurative.* to go first; have the first place: *to lead in a race. In arithmetic he is way down in the class, but in spelling he leads.* 8 to take the leading part; start a dance, begin or open a discussion, etc. 9 to make the first play at cards: *You may lead this time.* 10 *Boxing.* to deal one's opponent the first blow; take the offensive.
—*n.* 1 guidance or direction; leadership; example; precedence: *Many countries in the western world followed the lead of the United States after World War II. Recent work ... using radioisotope techniques ... is giving a new lead on the selective action of weedkillers* (New Scientist). 2 the place of a leader; place in front; position in advance: *He always takes the lead when we plan to do anything.* 3 in card playing: **a** the right to go or begin first: *It is your lead this time.* **b** the card or suit so played: *You should usually return your partner's lead.* **4a** the principal part in a play. **b** the person who plays it. 5 the amount that one is ahead; extent of advance: *He had a lead of 3 yards in the race.* 6 something that leads, as a path, channel, or watercourse. 7 a string, strap, light chain, or rope for leading a dog or other animal; leash: *He had his dog on a lead.* 8 a guiding indication: *He was not sure where to look for the information, but the librarian gave him several good leads.* **9a** the opening paragraph in a newspaper or magazine article. A lead usually summarizes the information in the body of the article. *Once the lead is outlined, the rest of a news story can be quickly written.* **b** the main front-page story in a newspaper. **10a** an insulated conductor conveying electricity. **b** = lead-in. 11 *Boxing.* a taking of the offensive; a first blow directed at an opponent. 12 *Baseball.* a position assumed by a base runner, a short distance off base in the direction of the next base. 13 *Mining.* **a** = lode: *the silver leads of the large mines.* **b** a deposit of gold-bearing gravel along the course of an old river. 14 an open channel through an ice field: *The explorers found a lead which would get them to open water.* 15 *Nautical.* the proper course for a rope, especially in a ship's running rigging: *The lead of each rope was fixed in Harvey's mind* (Rudyard Kipling). **16a** the aiming of a firearm, arrow, spear, rocket, or other missile, in advance of a moving target. **b** the distance allowed in so aiming.
—*adj.* 1 that leads or is used for leading; leading: *the lead violin, a horse on a lead rein.* 2 guided by a lead: *a lead horse.*
**lead off, a** to begin; start: *He led off with his companion in a sort of quickstep* (Harper's). **b** *Baseball.* to be the first player in the batting order or the first to bat in an inning: *He led off with a triple to left field.*
**lead on,** to persuade or entice to follow an unwise course of action; mislead: *I have suspected she is leading him on for his money* (John Ciardi).
**lead up to, a** to prepare the way for: *The harlequinade ... is led up to by a tasteful transformation scene* (Saturday Review). **b** to approach (a subject) in an evasive or gradual manner: *He had guessed what she had to say from the way she'd led up to it* (James T. Farrell).
[Old English *lǣdan*] —**lead'a|ble,** *adj.*
► **lead, led.** *Lead* and *led* show the confusion that English suffers because of representing one sound by different symbols. *Lead* (lēd), the present tense of the verb, gives no trouble; but *led,* the past tense, is often incorrectly spelled with *ea* by analogy with *read* (rēd), *read* (red), or by confusion with the noun *lead* (led): *Please lead the horse away. The culprit was led into the office.*
***lead²** (led), *n., adj., v.* —*n.* 1 a heavy, easily melted, bluish-gray metallic chemical element. It is used to make pipes, machinery, and radiation shields, as a solder, and in alloys. It occurs naturally in galena. 2 something made of lead or one of its alloys. 3 bullets; shot: *a hail of lead.* 4 a long, thin piece of graphite used in pencils. 5 a weight, usually 7 to 14 pounds, on a marked line used to find out the depth of water; plumb; plummet. **6a** a thin metal strip, less than type-high, for widening the space between lines in printing. **b** these strips collectively. **7a** = graphite. **b** = white lead.
—*adj.* made of lead; consisting of lead: *a lead pipe.*
—*v.t.* 1 to cover, frame, or weight with lead. 2 to insert leads between the lines of (print). 3 to mix or impregnate with lead or a compound containing lead: *to lead gasoline.* 4 to set (window glass) within leads. 5 to line or glaze (pottery) with glaze containing lead.
**leads, a** frames of lead in which panes of glass are set, as in stained-glass windows; leading: *It gives the effect of weakness to see large pieces of glass leaded with narrow leads* (F. Miller). **b** strips of lead used to cover roofs; leading: *The tempest crackles on the leads* (Tennyson). **c** a lead roof: *A cat ... whom she used to meet in the evenings, upon the leads of the house* (C. Johnston).
**like a lead balloon.** See under **balloon.**
**swing the lead,** *British Slang.* to shirk work; malinger: *A 30-year-old man might appear to be "swinging the lead" when investigation would show that he had, for example, just come out of a mental hospital* (London Times).
[Old English *lēad*]

***lead²**
definition 1

| symbol | atomic number | atomic weight | oxidation state |
|---|---|---|---|
| Pb | 82 | 207.19 | 2, 4 |

**lead acetate** (led), a colorless or white, poisonous, crystalline compound used as a reagent, in dyeing; sugar of lead. *Formula:* $C_4H_{12}O_7Pb$
**lead-ac|id battery** (led'as'id), a storage battery that produces electricity by chemical reaction between lead electrodes and an electrolyte of dilute sulfuric acid. Most automobiles use a lead-acid battery.
**lead arsenate** (led), a poisonous white, crystalline compound used as an insecticide; arsenate of lead. *Formula:* $Pb_3(AsO_4)_2$
**lead azide** (led), a colorless, crystalline, highly explosive compound handled safely only when immersed in water, and used as a primary detonating agent for high explosives. *Formula:* $Pb(N_3)_2$
**Lead|beat|er's cockatoo** (led'bē'tərz), a white Australian cockatoo with a salmon-pink inner wing; pink cockatoo. [< J. *Leadbeater,* an Australian naturalist of the 1800's]
**Leadbeater's possum,** a small, nearly extinct mammal of Australia, a phalanger, that lives in the hollows of trees and feeds on insects and nectar. [< J. *Leadbeater*]
**lead carbonate** (led), = white lead.
**lead chromate** (led), a yellow, crystalline solid formed by the addition of a chromate to a lead salt, used as chrome yellow. *Formula:* $PbCrO_4$
**lead colic** (led), = painter's colic.
**lead dioxide** (led), a highly toxic crystalline compound, used as an oxidizing agent, as an electrode in storage batteries, as a mordant in textiles, and in the manufacture of explosives; lead peroxide. *Formula:* $PbO_2$
**lead|en** (led'ən), *adj., v.* —*adj.* 1 made of lead: *a leaden coffin.* 2 *Figurative.* heavy; hard to lift or move: *leaden arms tired from working.* SYN: inert. 3 *Figurative.* oppressive; burdensome: *leaden air.* 4 *Figurative.* dull; gloomy: *leaden thoughts.* SYN:

spiritless. **5** bluish-gray; of a dull, cold, pale color: *Do you suppose those leaden clouds may mean snow?* **6** of little value.
— ***v.t.*** to make leaden: (*Figurative.*) *The death of President John Fitzgerald Kennedy leadens the heart with sadness* (Atlanta Constitution). —**lead′en|ly**, *adv.* —**lead′en|ness**, *n.*

**lead|er** (lē′dər), *n.* **1** a person, animal, or thing that leads: *the leader of a band, the leader of a discussion. Brigham Young was the leader of the Mormons. Albert Einstein was a leader in the field of mathematics. Lewis and Clark were leaders of an expedition across America to the Pacific Coast.* **2** a person who is well fitted to lead: *That boy is a born leader.* **3** a horse harnessed at the front of a team: *The whips cracked, the leaders capered, and ... away we rattled* (Charles J. Lever). **4** an important or leading article or editorial in a newspaper: *In 1944, he wrote a blistering leader demanding that the British Government cease toadying to Washington* (Newsweek). **5a** a length of nylon or plastic cord or wire attaching the lure to a fish line. **b** a net placed so as to cause fish to swim into a weir, pound, or trap. **6** a pipe carrying water, oil, or other liquid, especially water from a roof gutter to the ground. **7** an article offered at a low price to attract customers. **8** the concertmaster of an orchestra or vocal group. **9** *Nautical.* a fair-lead.
**leaders**, a row of dots or dashes to guide the eye across a printed page: *There are also two or three em leaders, the number of dots being multiplied according to their length* (American Encyclopedia of Printing).
—**lead′er|less**, *adj.* —**lead′er|less|ness**, *n.*

**lead|ers** (lē′dərz), *n.pl.* See under **leader**.

**lead|er|ship** (lē′dər ship), *n.* **1** the condition of being a leader. **2** the ability to lead: *Leadership is a great asset to an officer.* **3** guidance or direction: *Our group needs some leadership.*

**lead-free** (led′frē′), *adj.* containing no tetraethyl lead; nonleaded: *lead-free gasoline.*

**lead glass** (led), a type of glass, especially crystal, made with lead oxide.

**lead-in** (lēd′in′), *n., adj.* —***n.*** **1** a wire leading from one apparatus or conductor to another, such as the wire connecting the street power lines with a house. **2** the part of a radio or television antenna that connects with the transmitter or receiver. **3** a leading into; introduction: *a lead-in to a television commercial.*
—***adj.*** leading in: *a lead-in wire.*

**lead|ing**[1] (lē′ding), *adj., n.* —***adj.*** **1** showing the way; guiding; directing: *to take the leading hand in a project.* **2** most important; chief; principal: *the leading lady in a play, the town's leading citizen.* **SYN:** main, foremost. **3** that has the front place: **a** that goes first: *the leading end of a pipe.* **b** featured prominently: *a leading article.* [< *lead*[1] + *-ing*[2]]
—***n.*** **1** the act of a person or thing that leads; guidance; direction. **2** (in Quaker use) a spiritual indication of the proper course of action: *a leading from above, a something given* (Wordsworth). [< *lead*[1] + *-ing*[1]]

**lead|ing**[2] (led′ing), *n.* **1** a covering or frame of lead strips, especially for window glass or roofing. **2** *Printing.* **a** the metal strips for widening the space between lines of type. **b** the space provided by these strips.

**lead|ing article** (lē′ding), an important editorial or article in a newspaper; leader.

**lead|ing edge** (lē′ding), *Aeronautics.* the forward edge of an airfoil or propeller blade.

**lead|ing mark** (lē′ding), any object used as a guide in bringing a ship in or out of port.

**lead|ing motive** (lē′ding), = leitmotif.

**lead|ing question** (lē′ding), a question so worded that it suggests the answer desired.

**lead|ing strings** (lē′ding), **1** strings for supporting a child when learning to walk. **2** *Figurative.* close guidance; too close guidance: *A boy of eighteen should not be kept in leading strings by his mother.*

**lead|ing tone** (lē′ding), *Music.* the seventh tone of the diatonic scale, one half step below the tonic, having a melodic tendency up toward the tonic or keynote; subtonic. See picture under **dominant**.

**lead-in wire** (lēd′in′), = lead-in (def. 2).

**lead|less** (led′lis), *adj.* without lead; lead-free.

**lead line** (led), *Nautical.* a sounding line.

**lead monoxide** (led), = litharge.

**lead nitrate** (led), a poisonous metal salt used in medicine, as a fixative in dyeing textiles, and in the manufacture of lead salts and matches. *Formula:* $Pb(NO_3)_2$

**lead|off** (lēd′ôf′, -of′), *n., adj.* —***n.*** **1** an act of beginning or starting something: *The chairman was responsible for the leadoff of the campaign.* **2** *Baseball.* the first player of the batting order or the first to come to bat in an inning.
—***adj.*** that begins or leads off: *a leadoff witness, a leadoff batter.*

**lead oxide** (led), any compound of lead and oxygen, such as litharge.

**lead pencil** (led), a pencil having graphite mixed with fine clay, usually enclosed in wood; an ordinary pencil.

**lead peroxide** (led), = lead dioxide.

**lead-pipe cinch** (led′pīp′), *U.S. Informal.* **1** an absolutely certain thing: *"It's still not a lead-pipe cinch that he'll run," confesses one G.O.P. leader* (Wall Street Journal). **2** an easy thing to do: *Sounds like a headache, but—thanks to xerography—it's turned into a lead-pipe cinch* (Wall Street Journal).

**lead|plant** (led′plant′, -plänt′), *n.* a shrubby North American plant of the pea family with spikes of blue flowers, supposed to indicate the presence of deposits of lead beneath it.

**lead poisoning** (led), **1** a diseased condition caused by ingesting or inhaling lead, or lead compounds in paints or other substances, characterized by abdominal pain, paralysis, and convulsions; plumbism. **2** *U.S. Slang.* death or injury from a gunshot or bullets.

**leads** (ledz), *n.pl.* See under **lead**[2].

**leads|man** (ledz′mən), *n., pl.* **-men.** the man who heaves the lead in taking soundings and calls the depths.

**lead sulfate** (led), a white, crystalline or granular solid formed by adding sulfuric acid to a lead salt, found in nature as anglesite. Lead sulfate is used as an electrode in storage batteries. *Formula:* $PbSO_4$

**lead sulfide** (led), a compound of sulfur and lead in the form of silvery crystals or black powder, found in nature as galena. *Formula:* PbS

**lead|swing|er** (led′swing′ər), *n. British Slang.* a person who shirks work; malingerer.

**lead|swing|ing** (led′swing′ing), *n. British Slang.* the practice of shirking work; malingering.

**lead time** (lēd), the time that elapses, such as the time between the start of or request for a thing and its completion or delivery: *The Russians have cut the lead time that it takes a new plane to progress from the blueprint stage to production* (Drew Pearson).

**lead-up** (lēd′up′), *n.* a leading up to something; preparation or approach: *the lead-up to a story's climax.*

**lead|wort** (led′wėrt′), *n.* any one of a group of herbs of warm regions, usually with blue, white, or reddish-purple flowers; plumbago.

**lead|y** (led′ē), *adj.,* **lead|i|er, lead|i|est.** like lead; leaden.

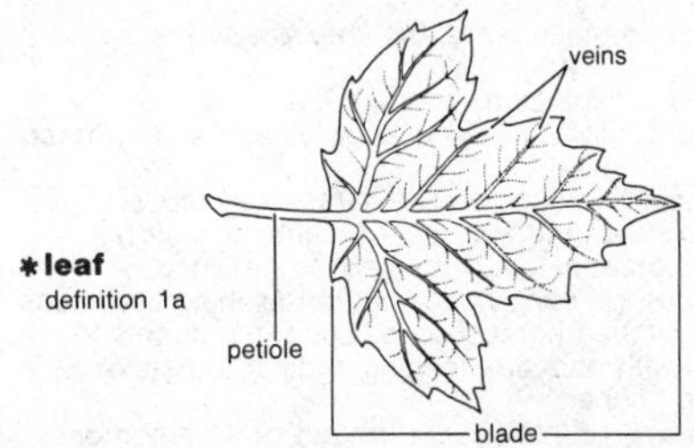

***leaf**
definition 1a

***leaf** (lēf), *n., pl.* **leaves**, *v.* —***n.*** **1a** one of the thin, usually flat, green parts of a tree or other plant, that grows on the stem or grows up from the roots. Leaves are essential organs of most plants and combine carbon dioxide, water, and light to carry on photosynthesis. Some plants are grown primarily for their leaves, such as ornamental trees and shrubs, tobacco and tea plants, or forage grasses. **b** all the leaves of a plant or tree; leafage; leaves: *the fall of the leaf.* **2** a petal of a flower: *a rose leaf.* **3** a sheet of paper. Each side of a leaf is called a page. **4** a very thin sheet of metal, especially gold or silver. **5** a flat movable piece in the top of a table: *We put two extra leaves in the table for the party.* **6** the sliding, hinged, or movable part of a door, shutter, gate, or certain windows. **7** one of the strips of a leaf spring. **8** a layer of leaf fat.
—***v.i.*** **1** to put forth leaves: *The trees along the river leaf earlier than those on the hill.* **2** to turn pages: *to leaf through a book or magazine.*
—***v.t.*** to turn the pages of (a book, magazine, notebook, or other, usually written or printed, matter).
**in leaf**, covered with leaves or foliage: *a sycamore tree in leaf.*
**take a leaf from (one's book)**, to follow one's example; copy one's conduct: *The Third Estate, taking a leaf from the book of the English House of Commons, then declared that it alone represented the nation* (H. G. Wells).
**turn over a new leaf**, to start all over again; try to do or be better in the future: *He promised to turn over a new leaf and study harder.*
[Old English *lēaf*] —**leaf′like′**, *adj.*

**leaf|age** (lē′fij), *n.* leaves; foliage.

**leaf beetle**, any one of a large group of small, round, brilliantly colored beetles that feed on the leaves of potatoes and other plants. See picture under **beetle**[1].

**leaf blight**, a disease caused by various parasitic fungi which attack the leaves of plants and cause them to turn brown and die.

**leaf blister**, a disease of the oak caused by a fungus and marked by the blistering and curling of its leaves.

**leaf bud**, a bud producing a stem with leaves only.

**leaf butterfly**, = Kallima.

**leaf curl**, **1** a disease of fruit trees in which the leaves become curled: *Peach leaf curl must be throttled before buds swell* (New York Times). **2** early blight. **3** leaf roll of potatoes.

**leaf|cut|ter** (lēf′kut′ər), *n.* **1** = leaf-cutter ant. **2** = leaf-cutter bee.

**leaf-cutter ant**, any one of various, largely tropical, American ants that subsist entirely on small mushrooms which they raise underground on a mulch of cut leaves; umbrella ant; parasol ant.

**leaf-cutter bee**, any one of a group of bees that cut oval or round disks from leaves, usually of the rose, to use in preparing their nests.

**leaf-cut|ting ant** (lēf′kut′ing), = leaf-cutter ant.

**leaf-cutting bee**, = leaf-cutter bee.

**leafed** (lēft), *adj.* having a leaf or leaves; leaved.

**leaf|er|y** (lē′fər ē, lēf′rē), *n., pl.* **-er|ies.** = leafage.

**leaf fat**, fat in an animal, especially fat surrounding the kidneys of a hog.

**leaf hopper**, or **leaf|hop|per** (lēf′hop′ər), *n.* any one of various small, leaping homopterous insects that feed on plant juices.

**leaf|i|ness** (lē′fē nis), *n.* leafy condition.

**leaf insect**, any one of various insects found in Africa, southeastern Asia, northern Australia, and in many islands of the South Pacific, remarkable for their resemblance in color and form to the green leaves on which they feed.

**leaf lard**, lard of the best quality, made from the fat around the kidneys of a hog.

**leaf|less** (lēf′lis), *adj.* having no leaves: *the leafless trees of winter.* —**leaf′less|ness**, *n.*

**leaf|let** (lēf′lit), *n., v.,* **-let|ted, -let|ting.** —***n.*** **1** a small, flat or folded sheet of printed matter, or several sheets folded together; circular: *advertising leaflets, leaflets containing Sunday-school lessons.* **SYN:** flier, handbill. **2** a small or young leaf: *the leaflets of early spring.* **3** one of the separate blades or divisions of a compound leaf.
—***v.i.*** to distribute leaflets: *They moved out on to the streets leafletting and selling lapel buttons and bumper stickers* (Sunday Times).

**leaflet bomb**, a bomb which upon explosion scatters leaflets intended to influence the enemy in some way.

**leaf miner**, any one of various insects which, in the larval stage, live and feed between the top and bottom surfaces of a leaf.

**leaf mold**, **1** the partially decomposed leaves which form a surface layer in wooded areas. **2** a mold which attacks foliage.

**leaf mosaic**, an arrangement of the leaves on a tree, bush, or vine in which petiole length and position enable each leaf to receive the maximum amount of sunlight.

**leaf-nosed bat** (lēf′nōzd′), any one of a group of tropical bats with a leaflike projection of skin extending upward from the nose.

**leaf roll**, a stunting disease of potatoes in which the margins of the leaves roll upwards, caused by a virus.

**leaf roller**, any one of various small moths whose larvae roll up leaves to make nests, as a brown and gold moth that is a common apple pest in the northern United States.

**leaf rust**, **1** a rust fungus that attacks the leaves of various cereal grasses, especially wheat. **2** the plant disease caused by this fungus.

**leaf scar**, a mark left on a twig where the stem of a fallen leaf was attached.

**leaf spot**, **1** any one of various plant diseases caused by fungi or bacteria which create discolorations on leaves. **2** the blemish on leaf surfaces caused by leaf spot.

**leaf spring**, a spring, such as one for an automobile, made of layers of curved metal strips.

**leaf|stalk** (lēf′stôk′), *n.* a stalk by which a leaf is attached to a stem; petiole.

**leaf|worm** (lēf′wėrm′), *n.* a moth caterpillar that feeds on the leaves of plants, especially cotton.

**leaf|y** (lē′fē), *adj.,* **leaf|i|er, leaf|i|est.** **1** having

**Pronunciation Key:** hat, āge, cãre, fär; let, ēqual, tėrm; it, īce; hot, ōpen, ôrder; oil, out; cup, pu̇t, rüle; child; long; thin; ᴛʜen; zh, measure; ə represents **a** in about, **e** in taken, **i** in pencil, **o** in lemon, **u** in circus.

many leaves; covered with leaves, especially broad leaves: *the leafy woods.* **2** resembling a leaf; laminate. **3** made or consisting of leaves.

**league**[1] (lēg), *n., v.,* **leagued, lea|guing.** —*n.* **1** a union of persons, parties, or nations formed to help one another. SYN: federation, society. **2** the persons, parties, or countries associated in a league; confederacy. **3** an association of sports clubs or teams: *a baseball league.* **4** any covenant or compact; alliance: *link'd in happy nuptial league* (Milton).
—*v.i., v.t.* to unite in a league; form a union or join, especially without losing separate identity: *The two societies of doctors leagued to force improvements in the local hospital.* SYN: confederate.
**in league with,** associated by agreement with; having a compact with; allied with: *Look you, villains, this fellow is in league with you* (Charles Kingsley).
**in one's league,** *Informal.* in the same category or class with one: [*The*] *quartet is competent, but hardly in his league* (Time).
**out of one's league,** *Informal.* not in one's own class or category: *The amateur musician was out of his league in the professional orchestra. Moon shots and ICBMs are ... clearly out of Canada's scientific and industrial league* (Maclean's).
[< Old French *ligue* < Italian *liga,* variant of *lega* < *legare* to bind < Latin *ligāre*]

**league**[2] (lēg), *n.* **1** a measure of distance, usually about 3 geographical miles, 3.452 statute miles, or 4.8280 kilometers. **2** a unit of measure for land, equal to a square league. [< Late Latin *leuga,* later *leuca* < a Celtic word]

**League of Nations,** an organization intended to promote cooperation among nations and to maintain peace. It was formed in 1920, under the terms of the Treaty of Versailles at the end of World War I. It was dissolved on April 18, 1946, and the United Nations assumed some of its functions.

**League of Women Voters,** a nonpartisan women's political organization founded in 1920. *Abbr:* LWV (no periods).

**lea|guer**[1] (lē′gər), *n.* a member of a league.

**lea|guer**[2] (lē′gər), *v., n. Archaic.* —*v.t.* to besiege; beleaguer: *Two mighty hosts a leaguer'd town embrace* (Alexander Pope). [< noun]
—*n.* **1** a military siege. **2** the camp of a besieging army.
[< Dutch *leger* camp; spelling perhaps influenced by *league*[1]]

**league table,** *British.* **1** a table showing the performance records of two or more athletic leagues. **2** a tabulated comparison of performance in any field.

**Le|ah** (lē′ə), *n.* the older sister of Rachel, and the first wife of Jacob. She was a daughter of Laban. Leah was the mother of Reuben, Simeon, Levi, Judah, Issachar, and Zebulun (in the Bible, Genesis 29:16).

**leak** (lēk), *n., v.* —*n.* **1** a hole or crack not meant to be there that lets something in or out: *a leak in the roof, a leak in a paper bag that lets the sugar run out.* SYN: fissure, breach. **2** the act of leaking; leakage: *a leak of water,* (*Figurative.*) *a leak of information.* **3** a means of escape or loss: *a leak in the treasury.* **4** the escape itself. **5** *Electricity.* **a** an escape of current from a conductor, especially as a result of poor insulation. **b** the point where such escape occurs.
—*v.i.* **1a** to go in or out through a hole or crack not meant to be there: *The gas leaked out of the pipe.* **b** to go in or out through ways suggesting a hole or crack: *Spies leaked into the city.* **2** to let something in which is meant to stay where it is: *My boat leaks and lets water in.* **3** *Figurative.* to become known gradually or indirectly: *The secret leaked out.* **4** *Figurative.* to pass (away) by gradual waste: *The natural resources of our country are leaking away through misuse.*
—*v.t.* **1** to let (something) pass in or out that is meant to stay where it is: *That pipe leaks gas.* **2** *Informal, Figurative.* to make known stealthily or indirectly: *Someone had leaked the company's secret plans to its competitors.*
**spring a leak,** to crack or separate and begin to let water through or in; develop a leak: *One of our pipes sprung a leak and flooded the cellar.*
[probably < Middle Dutch *leken*] —**leak′er,** *n.*

**leak|age** (lē′kij), *n.* **1** the act of leaking; entrance or escape by a leak: *The continuing leakage was the result of a long crack in the pipe.* **2** that which leaks in or out: *the privilege of battening on ... the leakage of the tap-room* (Washington Irving). **3** the amount of leaking: *a leakage of a pailful of water an hour.* **4** *Commerce.* an allowance for waste of fluid by leakage. **5** *Electricity.* = leak. **6** *Informal, Figurative.* a disclosure: *Sometimes leakages of secret information come out in newspaper stories accidentally.*

**leak|proof** (lēk′prüf′), *adj.* that will not leak; free of leaks: *a leakproof flashlight battery, a leakproof hull.*

**leak|y** (lē′kē), *adj.,* **leak|i|er, leak|i|est.** having a leak or leaks; full of leaks; leaking: *The ship was leaky and very much disabled* (Daniel Defoe).
—**leak′i|ness,** *n.*

**leal** (lēl), *adj. Archaic or Scottish.* loyal; faithful; honest; true. [< Old French *leial* < Latin *lēgālis* legal < *lēx, lēgis* law. See etym. of doublets **legal, loyal.**] —**leal′ly,** *adv.*

**le|al|ty** (lē′əl tē), *n., pl.* **-ties.** *Archaic.* loyalty.

**lean**[1] (lēn), *v.,* **leaned** or (*especially British*) **leant** (lent), **lean|ing,** *n.* —*v.i.* **1** to stand slanting, not upright; bend or incline in a particular direction: *The small tree leaned over in the wind.* SYN: slant, slope. **2** to rest sloping or slanting: *Lean against me.* **3** *Figurative.* to depend; rely: *to lean on a friend's advice.* **4** *Figurative.* to bend or turn a little (toward); incline or tend in thought, affection, or conduct: *to lean toward mercy. E'en his failings lean'd to virtue's side* (Oliver Goldsmith). **5** *Obsolete.* to incline (to) for support.
—*v.t.* **1** to set or put in a leaning position; prop: *Lean the ladder against the wall until I am ready for it.* **2** to cause to bend or incline.
—*n.* the act or state of leaning; inclination: *the cracked veranda with a tipsy lean* (John Greenleaf Whittier).
**lean on,** *Slang.* **a** to put pressure or coercion on: *How hard does the Government lean on companies ... to influence their choice of computers?* (London Times). **b** *U.S.* to beat up: *If anybody ever leaned on Kenny the whole gang would pile on him and send him to the hospital* (James T. Farrell).
**lean over backward.** See under **backward.**
**on the lean,** inclining; sloping: *Leaden coffins piled thirty feet high, and all on the lean from their own immense weight* (Peter Cunningham).
[Old English *hleonian*]

**lean**[2] (lēn), *adj., n., v.* —*adj.* **1a** with little or no fat; not fat; thin: *a lean face, lean cattle, a lean and hungry stray dog.* SYN: spare, skinny, gaunt. See syn. under **thin. b** containing little or no fat: *lean meat.* **2** *Figurative.* producing little; poor or meager in quantity or quality; scant; mean: *a lean harvest, a lean diet, a lean year for business.* SYN: meager, barren. **3** (of fuels) low in concentration or ability to produce energy: *Rich gas is cheaper to produce than lean gas—gas of low calorific value* (New Scientist).
—*n.* meat having little fat: *Jack Sprat could eat no fat; his wife could eat no lean* (nursery rhyme).
—*v.t.* to make lean: *His long illness leaned his body.*
—*v.i. Obsolete.* to become lean.
[Old English *hlǣne*] —**lean′ly,** *adv.* —**lean′ness,** *n.*

**Le|an|der** (lē an′dər), *n. Greek Legend.* a lover who swam the Hellespont nightly to visit his sweetheart, Hero, until he was drowned.

**lean|er** (lē′nər), *n.* **1** a person or thing that leans. **2** a pitched horseshoe or quoit that comes to rest with one side leaning against the stake or peg; hobber.

**lean|ing** (lē′ning), *n.* **1** the act of a person or thing that leans; reclining; bending. **2** *Figurative.* tendency; inclination: *political leanings. His leaning was more toward books than baseball.* SYN: proneness, bias, bent, penchant.

**leant** (lent), *v.* leaned; a past tense and a past participle of **lean**[1].

**lean-to** (lēn′tü′), *n., pl.* **-tos,** *adj.* —*n.* **1** a small building attached to another, with a roof sloping downward from the side of the larger building. **2** a crude shelter sometimes built against a tree or post. It is usually open on one of its long sides. *When the rain started, the boy scouts hastily put up a lean-to with ponchos.*
—*adj.* having supports or a roof pitched against or leaning on an adjoining wall or building: *a lean-to shed, a lean-to roof.*

**leap** (lēp), *n., v.,* **leaped** or **leapt** (lept, lēpt), **leaping.** —*n.* **1** a jump or spring; bound: *He went over the fence with a single leap.* **2** something to be jumped over or from: *Lover's Leap.* **3** the distance covered by a jump. [Old English *hlȳp*]
—*v.i.* **1** to jump; spring: *That frog leaps very high. He leaped up the stone steps by two at a time* (George Eliot). SYN: bound. See syn. under **jump. 2** *Figurative.* to pass, come, rise, or take place, as if with a leap or bound: *An idea leaped to his mind.* **3** to fly, shoot, or flash quickly: *The sword leaps from the scabbard. Water, flame, or light leaps up.* **4** to beat vigorously, as the heart: *My heart leaps up when I behold A rainbow in the sky* (Wordsworth).
—*v.t.* **1** to jump over: *He leaped the wall.* (*Figurative.*) *The mind leaps an interval of time.* SYN: vault. **2** to cause to leap: *She leapt her horse over many hurdles as she raced through the forest.*
**a leap in the dark,** a thing done without knowing what its results will be; hazardous undertaking; blind venture: *No doubt ... a great experiment, and "taking a leap in the dark"* (Earl Derby).
**by leaps and bounds,** very fast and very much; swiftly: *The insurrection spread by leaps and bounds.*
[Old English *hlēapan* jump]

**leap|er** (lē′pər), *n.* **1** a person or thing that leaps. **2** = jumping bean.

**leap|frog** (lēp′frog′, -frôg′), *n., v.,* **-frogged, -frogging.** —*n.* **1** a game in which players take turns jumping over the others who are bending over. **2** *Military.* a method of advancing against an enemy in which the most forward unit provides protective fire while the rear unit moves past it.
—*v.i., v.t.* **1** to leap or jump (over) as in the game of leapfrog. **2** (of military units in an attack) to go in advance of each other by turns as boys do when playing leapfrog. **3** to skip over; sidestep; avoid: *The kind of New England summer we elders are accustomed to will leapfrog northern Vermont and New Hampshire* (Harper's).

**leap second,** one or more extra seconds added to clock time each year by international agreement in order to keep the time signals used by navigators synchronized with the actual motion of the earth: *The latest leap second was celebrated New Year's Eve at the stroke of midnight Greenwich Mean Time, when around the world ... radio stations added an extra "beep" to their hourly time signals* (Science News). [patterned on *leap year*]

**leapt** (lept, lēpt), *v.* leaped; a past tense and a past participle of **leap.**

**leap year,** **1** a year having 366 days. The extra day is February 29. A year is a leap year if its number can be divided exactly by four, except years at the end of a century, which must be exactly divisible by 400. *The years 1968 and 2000 are leap years; 1900 and 1969 are not.* **2** a year in any calendar in which there are added days or months.

**Lear** (lir), *n.* the aged king of Britain in Shakespeare's tragedy *King Lear.*

**learn** (lėrn), *v.,* **learned** or **learnt** (lėrnt), **learning.** —*v.i.* **1** to gain knowledge or skill; receive instruction: *Some children learn slowly.* **2** to become informed; hear: *to learn of an occurrence.* —*v.t.* **1** to find out about; gain knowledge of (a subject) or skill in (an art, trade, or other specialty): *to learn French, to learn a new game. She is learning history and geography.* **2** to become able by study or practice: *to learn to fly an airplane. In school we learn to read.* **3** to memorize: *to learn a poem by heart, to learn a song.* **4** to find out; come to know: *He learned the details of the train wreck. He learned that ¼ + ¼ = ½.* **5** *Substandard.* to teach: *After supper she got out her book and learned me about Moses and the Bulrushers* (Mark Twain).
[Old English *leornian*] —**learn′a|ble,** *adj.*
► **learn, teach.** Substandard English often uses *learn* in the sense of *teach: He learned me to play baseball.* Educated usage keeps the distinction: *I learned to play baseball from him. He taught me to play baseball.*

**learn|ed** (lėr′nid), *adj.* showing or requiring knowledge; scholarly; erudite: *a learned professor, learned pursuits.* SYN: educated. —**learn′ed|ly,** *adv.* —**learn′ed|ness,** *n.*

**learned borrowing,** **1** the process of borrowing a classical word into a modern Romance language directly, with slight phonetic alteration. **2** a word borrowed in this way.

**learn|er** (lėr′nər), *n.* **1** a person who is learning: *a slow learner.* SYN: pupil. **2** a beginner: *A learner must get a permit before he can begin to drive.* SYN: novice, neophyte, tyro.

**learn|ing** (lėr′ning), *n.* **1** the gaining of knowledge or skill: *Learning is a more difficult task for some than for others.* **2** the possession of knowledge gained by study; scholarship: *men of learning. A pride there is of rank ... A pride of learning* (Thomas Hood). SYN: education, erudition. **3** knowledge: *A little learning is a dangerous thing* (Alexander Pope). **4** *Psychology.* the relatively permanent modification of responses as a result of experience.

**learning curve,** a graphic representation showing the progress made in learning during successive periods of practice, used in education and in research; growth curve.

**learnt** (lėrnt), *v.* learned; a past tense and a past participle of **learn.**

**lear|y** (lir′ē), *adj.,* **lear|i|er, lear|i|est.** = leery[1].

**leas|a|ble** (lē′sə bəl), *adj.* that can be leased.

**lease** (lēs), *n., v.,* **leased, leas|ing.** —*n.* **1** the right to use property for a certain length of time, usually by paying rent: *The farmer gave a lease on his woodland to a lumber company.* **2** a written statement saying for how long a certain property is rented and how much money shall be paid for it: *We are to meet the landlord on Monday to sign the lease for our new apartment.* **3** the prop-

erty held by a lease. **4** the length of time for which a lease is made. SYN: tenure. **5** the act of giving the right to use property. **6** an allotted period or term, especially of life: *a short lease on life.* [< Anglo-French *les* < *lesser*; see the verb]
**–v.t. 1** to give a lease on; rent: *The Clarks live on the second floor of their house and lease the first floor.* **2** to take a lease on; rent: *We have leased an apartment for one year.*
**–v.i.** to be leased.
**a new lease on** (or **of**) **life**, a chance to live longer, better, or happier: *She was going to have a new lease of life with better health* (Jane Carlyle).
[< Anglo-French *lesser* let, let go < Latin *laxāre* loosen < *laxus* loose] **–leas'er**, *n.*

**lease|back** (lēs'bak'), *n.* = sale and leaseback.

**lease|hold** (lēs'hōld'), *n., adj.* **–n. 1** a holding by a lease. **2** real estate held by a lease.
**–adj.** held by lease.

**lease|hold|er** (lēs'hōl'dər), *n.* a person holding property by a lease.

**lease-lend** (lēs'lend'), *n., v.t.*, **-lent, -lend|ing,** *adj. Especially British.* lend-lease.

**lease-pur|chase** (lēs'pėr'chis), *adj. U.S.* of or having to do with a government program under which money is borrowed from private lenders to finance construction of Federal buildings. The Government takes title to the buildings when the debt is eliminated.

**leash** (lēsh), *n., v.* **–n. 1** a strap or chain for holding a dog or other animal in check: *The boy leads the dog on a leash.* **2** a group of three animals in hunting or judging; a brace and a half, such as three hounds, foxes, or hares. **3** (in hawking) the thong or string which is attached to the jesses to secure the hawk.
**–v.t.** to hold in with a leash; control: *A French poodle leashed to a French-looking woman* (New Yorker). (*Figurative.*) *He leashed his anger and did not say a harsh word.*
**hold** (or **have**) **in leash**, to control; keep in bondage: *Thy low voice ... would ... hold passion in ... leash* (Tennyson).
**on a long** (or **tight**, or **short**) **leash**, with extensive (or restricted) latitude or leeway: *The editor and his editorial writers should be left on a long leash* (Saturday Review). *Its Secretary-General ... had in fact been kept since 1950 on a tight leash by the Security Council and the General Assembly* (Listener).
**strain at the leash**, to be very restless or impatient: *With mankind straining at the leash to reach the moon ...* (Manchester Guardian Weekly).
[Middle English *leese* < Old French *laisse,* and *lesse* < Latin *laxa,* feminine of *laxus* loose]

**leas|ing** (lē'zing), *n. Scottish.* **1** lying; falsehood. **2** a lie; a falsehood: *Thou shalt destroy them that speak leasing* (Psalms 5:6). [Old English *lēasung* < *lēasian* to lie < *lēas* false]

**least** (lēst), *adj., n., adv.* **–adj. 1** less than any other; smallest; slightest: *The least bit of dirt in a watch may make it stop. Ten cents is a little money; five cents is less; one cent is least.* SYN: minimal. **2** *Archaic.* lowest in power or position; meanest: *He that is least among you all, the same shall be great* (Luke 9:48).
**–n.** the smallest amount; smallest thing: *The least you can do is to thank her.* SYN: minimum.
**–adv.** to the smallest extent or degree: *I liked that book least of all.*
**at** (or **at the**) **least, a** at the lowest estimate: *Yesterday was very hot; the temperature must have been 95 degrees at least.* **b** at any rate; in any case: *He may have been late, but at least he came. At least we'll die with harness on our back* (Shakespeare).
**not in the least**, not at all: *a thing not in the least likely.*
**to say the least**, at the lowest estimate; at least: *I find many of the standards the referees use, to say the least, curious* (Maclean's).
[Old English *lǣst* and *lǣsest,* superlative of *lȳtel* small, little]

**least bittern**, a small wading bird of temperate America with brownish-yellow body and black back and crown. It is the smallest of the herons.

**least common denominator**, the least common multiple of the denominators of a group of fractions: *30 is the least common denominator of 2/3, 4/5, and 1/6.* Also, **lowest common denominator**. *Abbr:* l.c.d. or L.C.D.

**least common multiple**, the smallest quantity that contains two or more given quantities without a remainder: *12 is the least common multiple of 3 and 4 and 6. Abbr:* l.c.m. Also, **lowest common multiple**.

**least darter**, the smallest of the darters, about one inch in length.

**least|est** (lēs'təst), *n. Slang.* **the leastest**. the least amount or number of something; the least: *I suppose the better mousetrap has some advantages ... if "advantage" may be said of the ability to kill the mostest for the leastest* (Milton Mayer).

**least flycatcher**, a small flycatcher of Canada and the northern United States, often seen about farms and open woods; chebec.

**least grebe**, a small, gray grebe, found from southern Texas to South America.

**least sandpiper**, a small brownish sandpiper of eastern North America.

**least squares**, *Statistics.* a method of determining the trend of a group of data when that trend can be represented on a graph by a straight line.

**least tern**, a small, gray and white American tern, about nine inches long, that has yellow legs and bill in the summer; fairy bird.

**least|ways** (lēst'wāz'), *adv. Informal.* leastwise.

**least weasel**, a small, brown and white weasel of northern regions of the world that turns all white in the winter. It is the smallest living carnivorous animal, weighing from 1 to 2½ ounces.

**least|wise** (lēst'wīz'), *adv. Informal.* at least; at any rate: *It was a sign that his money would come to light again, or leastwise that the robber would be made to answer for it* (George Eliot).

**leath|er** (leᴛʜ'ər), *n., adj., v.* **–n. 1** a material made from the skins of animals by removing the hair and flesh, and then tanning them: *Shoes are made of leather.* **2** an article made of leather. **3** the loose hanging part of a dog's ear.
**–adj. 1** made of leather: *leather gloves.* **2** like leather; leathery.
**–v.t. 1** to furnish or cover with leather; use leather on. **2** *Informal.* to beat with a strap; thrash: *I'd like to leather 'im black and blue* (Tennyson).
**hellbent** (or **hell-bent**) **for leather**, *Slang.* as fast as possible; very fast: *General Tolson said that he had told his commanders to advance cautiously. "The worst trap we could get into here would be to go hell-bent for leather, thinking we've got it easy," he said* (New York Times).
[Old English *lether*]

**leath|er|back** (leᴛʜ'ər bak'), *n.* a large sea turtle of tropical waters, having a flexible, leathery shell studded with small bony plates. It is the largest living turtle, often weighing over 1,000 pounds.

**leath|er|board** (leᴛʜ'ər bōrd', -bōrd'), *n.* an imitation leather made of leather scraps, paper, wood chips, or sawdust, pressed together, used especially in shoemaking.

**leather carp**, any one of a scaleless or nearly scaleless variety of carp which was developed through special breeding.

**leath|er|cloth** (leᴛʜ'ər klôth', -kloth'), *n.* cloth coated on one side with a waterproof varnish.

**leath|er|coat** (leᴛʜ'ər kōt'), *n.* a russet apple.

**leath|er|craft** (leᴛʜ'ər kraft', -kräft'), *n.* **1** things made out of leather. **2** the art of making things out of leather.

**leath|er|ette** (leᴛʜ'ə ret'), *n.* **1** imitation leather, made of paper and cloth. **2 Leatherette**. a trademark for this.

**leath|er|jack|et** (leᴛʜ'ər jak'it), *n. British.* the larva of a crane fly.

**leath|er|leaf** (leᴛʜ'ər lēf'), *n., pl.* **-leaves**. an evergreen shrub of the heath family that has leathery leaves and is found in boggy areas of the northern Temperate Zone.

**leath|er-lunged** (leᴛʜ'ər lungd'), *adj. Informal.* having powerful lungs; speaking or able to speak very loudly or at great length.

**leath|ern** (leᴛʜ'ərn), *adj.* **1** made of leather: *a leathern belt* (Hawthorne). **2** like leather; leathery: *the weak-eyed bat ... flits by on leathern wing* (William Collins). [Old English *letheren* < *lether* leather]

**leath|er|neck** (leᴛʜ'ər nek'), *n. Slang.* a United States marine.

**Leath|er|oid** (leᴛʜ'ə roid), *n. Trademark.* imitation leather made of paper treated with chemicals.

**leath|er|wood** (leᴛʜ'ər wu̇d'), *n.* **1** any shrub of a group with strong, flexible branches, especially a species grown in eastern North America for ornament, having yellow flowers and a very tough bark; wicopy. **2** a shrub of the southeastern United States cultivated for its fragrant white flowers and the autumn colors of its foliage.

**leath|er|work** (leᴛʜ'ər wėrk'), *n.* **1** things made out of leather. **2** a making things out of leather.

**leath|er|work|er** (leᴛʜ'ər wer'kər), *n.* a person who makes things out of leather.

**leath|er|y** (leᴛʜ'ər ē), *adj.* like leather; tough: *A huge grin spread across the old man's leathery face* (Time). **–leath'er|i|ness**, *n.*

**leathery turtle**, = leatherback.

**leave¹** (lēv), *v.*, **left, leav|ing**. **–v.i. 1** to go away; depart: *We leave on our trip tonight.* SYN: See syn. under **go**. **2** *Obsolete.* to cease; desist; stop: *... and began at the eldest, and left at the youngest* (Genesis 44:12).
**–v.t. 1** to go away from; depart from: *They left the room.* SYN: depart, relinquish. See syn. under **go**. **2a** to stop living in, belonging to, or working at or for; go away from permanently: *to leave the country, to leave the Boy Scouts, to leave a job.* SYN: depart, relinquish. **b** to abandon; forsake: *He has left his home and friends and gone to sea.* SYN: depart, relinquish. **3** to go without taking; let stay behind: *I left a book on the table. Business and ambition take up men's thoughts too much to leave room for philosophy* (Sir Richard Steele). **4** to let stay (in a certain condition): *to leave a thing unsaid, to leave a window open. The story left him unmoved. Being now on that part of his life which I am obliged to leave almost a blank* (Samuel Taylor Coleridge). **5** to let (a person or thing) alone; let be: *The potatoes must be left to boil for half an hour. Leave me to settle the matter.* **6** to give (to family, friends, some establishment, or charity) when one dies; let remain; bequeath: *He left a large fortune to his children.* **7** to give or hand over (to someone else) to do: *Leave the matter to me. I left the cooking to my sister.* **8** not to attend to: *I left my homework until tomorrow. Nothing in the Revolution ... was left to accident* (Edmund Burke). **9** to let remain, as uneaten, unused, or unremoved: *There is some cake left.* **10** to yield as a remainder after subtraction: *4 from 10 leaves 6. And take from seventy springs a score, It only leaves me fifty more* (A. E. Housman). **11** to give to be kept; deposit; give: *I left my suitcase in the station while I walked around the town. He left word that he would soon be home* (Dickens). **12** *Archaic.* to stop; leave off.
**leave alone**. See under **alone**.
**leave in**, (in bridge) to permit the bid of (one's partner) to stand: *Having poor support for my partner's trumps, I left in his bid of three diamonds.*
**leave off, a** to stop; interrupt, or discontinue: *Continue the story from where you left off. He left off smoking.* **b** *Archaic.* to give up; forsake: *He would send her sufficient to enable her to leave off her shop* (Daniel Defoe).
**leave out**, to not say, do, or put in; omit: *She left out two words when she read the sentence.*
[Old English *lǣfan*]
▶ See **let¹** for usage note.

**leave²** (lēv), *n.* **1** consent; permission: *Have I your leave to go? I desired leave of this prince to see the curiosities of the island* (Jonathan Swift). **2a** permission to be absent from duty: *The judge gave the doctor leave from jury duty.* **b** the length of time one has such leave: *Our annual leave is thirty days.* **3** an act of parting; farewell.
**on leave**, absent from or off duty with permission: *He was going on leave, after some years of service, to see his kindred at Remiremont* (Charles Reade).
**take leave of**, to say good-by to: *The soldier took leave of his family before he returned to the front.*
[Old English *lēaf*]

**leave³** (lēv), *v.i.*, **leaved, leav|ing**. to put forth leaves; leaf: *Trees leave in the spring.*
**be leaved out**, *U.S.* to be filled with leaves: *The poplars were leaved out* (Popular Science Monthly).
[Middle English *levien,* variant of *leaf,* verb]

**leaved** (lēvd), *adj.* **1** having leaves or foliage; in leaf. **2** having leaves or foliage (of a specified number or kind).

**leav|en** (lev'ən), *n., v.* **–n. 1** any substance, such as yeast, that will cause fermentation and raise dough. **2** a small amount of fermenting dough kept for this purpose. **3** *Figurative.* an influence that, spreading silently and strongly, changes conditions or opinions: *The leaven of reform was working.* **4** *Figurative.* a tempering or modifying element; a tinge or admixture: *to mix a leaven of charity in one's judgments. He had a leaven of the old man in him which showed that he was his true-born son* (Washington Irving). **5** *Figurative.* character; sort: *two men of the same leaven.*
**–v.t. 1** to raise with or as with a leaven; make (dough) light or lighter: *Know ye not that a little leaven leaveneth the whole lump?* (I Corinthians 5:6). **2** *Figurative.* to spread through and transform. SYN: permeate, pervade. **3** *Figurative.* to blend or temper with some modifying element.
**–v.i.** *Figurative.* to become transformed or modified under some strong influence: *The play ultimately leavens according to the power and magic of the actress playing Joan* (Saturday Review).
[< Old French *levain* < Latin *levāmen* a lifting < *levāre* to raise < *levis* light²]

**Pronunciation Key:** hat, āge, cãre, fär; let, ēqual, tėrm; it, īce; hot, ōpen, ôrder; oil, out; cup, pu̇t, rüle; child; long; thin; ᴛʜen; zh, measure; ə represents **a** in about, **e** in taken, **i** in pencil, **o** in lemon, **u** in circus.

**leav|en|ing** (lev′ə ning), *n.* **1** something that leavens; leaven. **2** the act of causing to ferment by leaven.

**leave of absence**, **1** official permission to stay away from one's work, school, or military duty. **2** the length of time that this lasts.

**leav|er** (lē′vər), *n.* **1** a person or thing that leaves. **2** *British.* a student who leaves school, usually to seek employment.

**leaves**[1] (lēvz), *n.* plural of **leaf**.

**leaves**[2] (lēvz), *v.* third person singular present tense of **leave**[1]: *He leaves for work at 8:00* A.M.

**leaves**[3] (lēvz), *n.* plural of **leave**[2].

**leaves**[4] (lēvz), *v.* third person singular present tense of **leave**[3]: *Which tree leaves first?*

**leave-tak|ing** (lēv′tā′king), *n.* the act of taking leave; saying good-by.

**leav|ings** (lē′vingz), *n.pl.* things left; leftovers; remnants; residue: *The leavings of the meal were given to the dog.* SYN: remains, residuum.

**leav|y** (lē′vē), *adj.*, **leav|i|er**, **leav|i|est**. leafy: *the leavy beech* (Tennyson).

**Leb|a|nese** (leb′ə nēz′, -nēs′), *adj., n., pl.* **-nese**. —*adj.* of or having to do with Lebanon or its people.
—*n.* a person born or living in Lebanon.

**Le|bens|raum** or **le|bens|raum** (lā′bəns roum′), *n.* **1** (in Nazi theory) the additional territory that a nation must control in order to expand economically. **2** additional room that is needed, as to function or be less densely populated. **3** freedom of action. [< German *Lebensraum* (literally) living space]

**le|bes** (lē′bēz), *n.* a basinlike or bowllike vessel of ancient Greece, commonly of metal, with a rounded base. [< Greek *lébēs* kettle, cauldron]

**Leb|ku|chen** (lāp′kü′кнən), *n., pl.* **-chen**. *German.* a kind of spice cake often made with honey and bits of fruit, traditionally prepared around Christmastide.

**lech** (lech), *v., n., adj. Informal.* —*v.i.* to be a lecher; to lust.
—*n.* **1** a lecherous desire; lust. **2** lecher.
—*adj.* lecherous.
[back formation < *lecher* and *lechery*]

**le|cha|te|lier|ite** (lə shä′tə lir′īt), *n.* the amorphous form of silica produced by the heat of lightning or meteoric impact. [< Henry Louis *Le Chatelier,* 1850-1936, a French chemist + *-ite*[1]]

**le|che cas|pi** (lā′chā käs′pē), **1** the latex from a Peruvian tree which when coagulated and purified is used as a gum base in making chewing gum. **2** the tree itself. [< American Spanish *leche caspi* (literally) milk core]

**lech|er** (lech′ər), *n.* a man who indulges in lechery. [< Old French *lecheor* licker < *lechier* to lick, ultimately < Germanic (compare Old High German *lëchōn*)]

**lech|er|ous** (lech′ər əs, lech′rəs), *adj.* lewd; lustful. SYN: lascivious, libidinous. —**lech′er|ous|ly**, *adv.* —**lech′er|ous|ness**, *n.*

**Lech|er wires** (leн′ər), *Electronics.* parallel wires used to measure the wave length of currents having high frequencies, as those produced by radio waves. [< Ernst *Lecher,* 1856-1926, a German physicist]

**lech|er|y** (lech′ər ē, lech′rē), *n.* gross indulgence of lust; lewdness.

**lech|we** (lēch′wē), *n.,* or **lechwe antelope**, an African antelope related to the waterbuck that frequents swamps or other wet places. [probably < Sesuto *letsa* antelope]

**lec|i|thin** (les′ə thin), *n.* any one of a group of fatty substances found in plant or animal tissues. Lecithins are obtained especially from egg yolk, soybeans, and corn. They are used in candy, drugs, cosmetics, and paints. Lecithin is composed of nitrogen and phosphorus and is found especially in nerve cells and brain tissue. [< Greek *lékithos* egg yolk + English *-in*]

**lec|i|thin|ase** (les′ə thə nās, lə sith′ə nās), *n.* an enzyme capable of hydrolyzing lecithin or its components.

**Le|Conte** (lə kont′), *n.* a large, yellow pear that is a cross between the common pear and the sand pear, grown in the central and southern United States. [< the proper name *LeConte*]

**Le|conte's sparrow** (lə konts′), a striped, yellowish-brown sparrow of the prairie marshes of central North America. [< John *LeConte,* 1818-1891, an American physician and educator]

**lect.**, lecture.

***lec|tern** (lek′tərn), *n.* **1** a reading desk in a church, especially the desk from which the lessons are read at daily prayer. **2** a reading desk or stand. [Middle English *lectryne,* alteration of earlier *lettorne* < Old French *lettrun,* learned borrowing from Medieval Latin *lectrum* < Latin *legere* read]

**lec|tin** (lek′tin), *n.* a substance that causes agglutination of cells, especially red blood cells, obtained from the seeds and other parts of certain plants. [< Latin *lectus* (past participle of *legere* to select, read) + English *-in*]

**lec|tion** (lek′shən), *n.* **1** a reading of a text found in a particular copy or edition. **2** a portion of a sacred writing appointed to be read in church, usually at a given time of year; lesson. [< Latin *lēctiō, -ōnis* < *legere* read. See etym. of doublet **lesson**.]

**lec|tion|ar|y** (lek′shə ner′ē), *n., pl.* **-ar|ies**. **1** a book containing lessons or portions of Scripture appointed to be read at divine service. **2** a list of passages appointed to be read at divine service.

**lec|tor** (lek′tər, -tôr), *n.* **1** a person in minor orders who reads passages in a church service. **2** a university reader or lecturer (chiefly in Scandinavia and Germany). **3** = lay reader. [< Latin *lēctor* < *legere* read]

**lec|tor|ate** (lek′tər it), *n.* = lectorship.

**lec|tor|ship** (lek′tər ship), *n.* the office of lector.

**lec|ture** (lek′chər), *n., v.,* **-tured**, **-tur|ing**. —*n.* **1a** a speech; planned talk on a chosen subject: *I can spare the college bell, And the learned lecture well* (Emerson). **b** such a speech or talk written down or printed: *Two lectures ... appear in appendixes* (New Yorker). **2** a scolding: *My mother gives me a lecture when I come home late for supper.*
—*v.i.* to give a lecture or lectures: *The explorer lectured on life in the Arctic.*
—*v.t.* **1** to instruct or entertain by a lecture. **2** to scold; reprove: *Those whom he had lectured withdrew full of resentment* (Macaulay). SYN: admonish, rebuke, reprimand.
[< Late Latin *lēctūra* < *legere* read]

**lec|tur|er** (lek′chər ər), *n.* **1** a person who gives a lecture or lectures. **2** a person in a college or university who gives lectures or performs other academic duties but does not have the rank or title of professor. **3** *British.* a teaching position in a university, ranking below professor and reader.

**lec|ture|ship** (lek′chər ship), *n.* the office of lecturer.

**lec|tur|ette** (lek′chə ret′), *n.* a short lecture.

**lec|y|thus** (les′ə thəs), *n., pl.* **-thi** (-thī). a tall, slender, narrow-necked vase with a handle, for holding oil, unguents, and other liquids, used in ancient Greece. Also, **lekythos**. [< Greek *lḗkythos*]

**led** (led), *v.* past tense and past participle of **lead**[1]: *The policeman led the child across the street. That blind man is led by his dog.*
▶ See **lead**[1] for usage note.

**LED** (no periods), light-emitting diode (a tiny crystalline semiconducting device that glows with a bright red light when current flows through it, used especially in electronic displays).

**Le|da** (lē′də), *n. Greek and Roman Mythology.* the wife of Tyndareus of Sparta, the mother by him of Clytemnestra. Zeus visited Leda in the form of a swan, and she was the mother by him of Castor and Pollux and Helen of Troy.

**led captain** (led), a hanger-on; henchman.

**le|der|ho|sen** (lā′dər hō′zən), *n.pl.* leather breeches usually with suspenders and colorfully embroidered, worn especially in Bavaria and the Tirol. [< German *Lederhosen* leather trousers]

**ledge** (lej), *n.* **1** a narrow shelf: *a window ledge.* **2a** a shelf or ridge of rock: *He climbed up the side of the chasm to gain the ledge above* (Frederick Marryat). **b** such a ridge of rocks near the shore beneath the surface of the sea: *the Maldives, a famous ledge of islands* (Daniel Defoe). **3** a layer or mass of metal-bearing rock; lode or vein. [Middle English *legge* crossbar on a door, perhaps < *leggen* lay[1], or perhaps Old English *lecg* some part of a short sword] —**ledge′less**, *adj.*

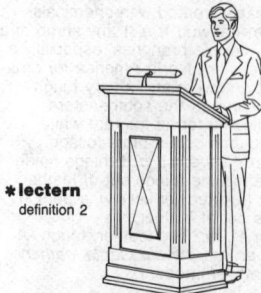

***lectern**
definition 2

**ledg|er** (lej′ər), *n., v.* —*n.* **1a** a book of accounts in which a business keeps a record of all money transactions. **b** the book of final entry in bookkeeping and accounting, where a complete record of all assets, liabilities, and proprietorship items are kept. It shows the changes that occur in these items during the month as a result of business operations carried on, by means of debits and credits. **2** a flat stone slab covering a grave. **3** a horizontal member of a scaffold, attached to the uprights and supporting the putlogs. **4a** Also, **leger**. = ledger bait. **b** = ledger tackle.
—*v.i.* to fish with a ledger.
[probably Middle English *leggen* lay[1]. Compare Dutch *ligger, legger* ledger.]

**ledger bait**, bait for fishing fixed so that it stays in one place, usually on the bottom.

**ledger board**, the horizontal board which forms the top of a fence or balustrade, often serving as a handrail or guard.

***ledger line**, **1** *Music.* a short line added above or below the staff for notes that are too high or too low to be put on the staff. **2** = ledger tackle. Also, **leger line**.

***ledger line**
definition 1

**ledger paper**, writing paper of the kind used in ledgers, having a hard, easily erasable finish.

**ledger tackle**, fishing tackle arranged to keep bait in one place.

**ledg|y** (lej′ē), *adj.*, **ledg|i|er**, **ledg|i|est**. having ledges.

**lee**[1] (lē), *n., adj.* —*n.* **1** shelter; protection: *The bear's cave was under the lee of a fallen pine.* **2** the side or part sheltered or away from the wind: *The wind was so fierce that we ran to the lee of the house.* **3** *Nautical.* the direction toward which the wind is blowing.
—*adj.* **1** sheltered or away from the wind: *the lee side of a ship.* **2** *Nautical.* in the direction toward which the wind is blowing.
[Old English *hlēo* shelter]

**lee**[2] (lē), *n. Obsolete.* sediment; dregs. See **lees**. [< Old French *lie;* see etym. under **lees**]

**lee|an|gle** (lē′ang′gəl), *n.* a heavy club with a bent and pointed end, used by Australian aborigines. [< an Australian native word]

***lee|board** (lē′bôrd′, -bōrd′), *n.* a large, flat board lowered vertically into the water on the lee side of a sailboat to keep the boat from drifting sideways.

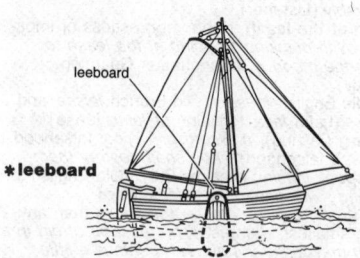

leeboard

***leeboard**

**leech**[1] (lēch), *n., v.* —*n.* **1** a worm, living especially in ponds and streams, that sucks the blood of animals. There is usually a sucker at each end of the body. Doctors formerly used leeches to suck blood from sick people. Leeches are annelids. **2** *Figurative.* a person who tries persistently to get what he can from others without doing anything to earn it; parasite: *The spendthrift, and the leech that sucks him* (William Cowper). **3** *Archaic.* a doctor: *Thither came The King's own leech to look into his hurt* (Tennyson). **4** an instrument to draw blood for medical purposes.
—*v.t.* **1** *Archaic.* to bleed with leeches for medical purposes; doctor. **2** *Figurative.* to hang on to and drain (a person or his resources) like a leech: *to leech someone's strength. Her relatives leeched her for her money like parasites.*
—*v.i. Figurative.* to hang on to a person or thing like a leech: *to leech on to another's fortune.*
[Old English *lǣce* physician; Old English *lǣce* leech, may be the same word] —**leech′like′**, *adj.*

**leech**[2] (lēch), *n.* **1** either of the vertical edges of a square sail. **2** the after edge of a fore-and-aft sail. Also, **leach**. [Middle English *lyche.* Compare Swedish *lik* bolt rope.]

**lee|chee** (lē′chē), *n.* = litchi.

**leek** (lēk), *n.* **1** a vegetable somewhat like a long, thick, green onion. A leek has larger leaves, a smaller bulb shaped like a cylinder, and a milder flavor than an onion. It is the national emblem of Wales. See picture under **amaryllis family**. **2** any one of several related vegetables. [Old English *lēac.* Compare etym. under **garlic**.]

**leek-green** (lēk′grēn′), *adj.* of the dull, bluish-green color of the leek.

**leer**[1] (lir), *n., v.* —*n.* a sly, nasty look to the side; evil glance: *She gives the leer of invitation* (Shakespeare). *Damn with faint praise, assent with civil leer* (Alexander Pope). [< verb]

—*v.i.* to give a sly, evil glance.
[perhaps < *leer*³] —**leer′ing|ly,** *adv.*

**leer²** (lir), *adj. Dialect.* **1** empty; unburdened. **2** hungry. Also, **leery.** [compare Old English *lǣrnes* emptiness]

**leer|y¹** (lir′ē), *adj.,* **leer|i|er, leer|i|est.** *Informal.* **1** suspicious; wary; doubtful: *We are leery of his advice.* **2** sly; wide-awake; knowing: *You're a very leery cove, by the look of you* (Arthur Conan Doyle). Also, **leary.** —**leer′i|ly,** *adv.* —**leer′i·ness,** *n.*

**leer|y²** (lir′ē), *adj. Dialect.* leer; empty.

**lees** (lēz), *n.pl.* **1** the most worthless part of anything; dregs: *I will drink Life to the lees* (Tennyson). **2** the sediment deposited in the container by wine and some other liquids. [< Old French *lias,* plural of *lie,* probably < Late Latin (Gaul) *lia,* perhaps < a Celtic word]

**Lee's Birthday** (lēz), *U.S.* January 19, the anniversary of Robert E. Lee's birthday, a legal holiday in most Southern states.

**lee shore,** the shore toward which the wind is blowing, especially in relation to a ship.

**leet** (lēt), *n. English History.* **1** a court held annually or semiannually in certain manors; court-leet. **2** its jurisdiction. **3** the day on which it met. [< Anglo-French *lete;* origin uncertain]

**lee tide,** a tide running in the direction toward which the wind blows.

**lee|ward** (lē′wərd; *Nautical* lü′ərd), *adj., adv., n.* —*adj., adv.* **1** on the side away from the wind; lee: *We stood leeward of the wind on the sheltered side of the house* (adv.). **2** in the direction toward which the wind is blowing: *leeward shore* (adj.).
—*n.* the side away from the wind; lee.

**lee wave,** *Meteorology.* a stationary atmospheric wave, formed on the lee or downwind sides of mountains and often marked by the presence of an apparently motionless cloud.

**lee|way** (lē′wā′), *n.* **1** the sideways movement or drift of a ship or aircraft to leeward, out of its course. **2** *Figurative.* extra space at the side; time, money, or other commodity, more than is needed; margin of safety: *If you take $10 more than you think you will need on a trip, you are allowing yourself a leeway of $10.* **3** *Figurative.* convenient room or scope for action: *leeway in planning.*

**left¹** (left), *adj., adv., n.* —*adj.* **1a** belonging to the side of the less used hand (in most people); of the side of anything that is turned west when the main side is turned north; opposite of right: *A person who usually uses his right hand has a slightly larger right hand than left hand. John lost his left shoe while wading through the brook.* **b** on this side when viewed from in front; having this relation to the front of any object: *the left wing of an army.* **2** situated nearer the observer's or speaker's left hand than his right: *Take a left turn at the next light.* **3** Often, **Left.** having liberal or radical views.
—*adv.* on, to, or toward the left side: *to turn left.*
—*n.* **1** the left side or hand: *He sat at my left.* **2** what is on the left side. **3** Often, **Left. a** the part of a lawmaking body consisting of the more liberal or radical groups. In some European legislative assemblies this group sits on the left side of the chamber as seen by the presiding officer. **b** *Figurative.* the persons or parties holding liberal or radical views. **4** *Sports.* a blow struck with the left hand.
[Middle English *left,* variant of *lift, luft,* Old English *lyft* weak]

**left²** (left), *v.* past tense and past participle of **leave**¹: *He left his hat in the hall. Milk is left at our door. She left at four o'clock.*
**be left,** to remain: *If you do not make haste to return, there will be little left to greet you, of me, or mine* (Charles Lamb).
**get left,** *Slang, Figurative.* **a** to be left behind or outdone, as in a contest or rivalry: *The horse got left at the post.* **b** to be disappointed in one's attempts or expectations: *He got left twice, but made the team on his third try.*

**left-arm|er** (left′är′mər), *n. British.* a left-handed bowler in cricket; left-hander.

**Left Bank,** the Bohemian section of Paris, on the left bank of the Seine river.

**left bower,** the jack that has the same color as the jack of trumps in certain card games.

**left-cen|ter** (left′sen′tər), *adj., n.* —*adj.* of or belonging to the liberal or radical segment of a political party or group of the center.
—*n.* a left-center party, group, or position.

**left face,** a 90-degree turn to the left, made by pivoting on the left heel in military drill.

**left field,** *Baseball.* **1** the section of the outfield behind third base. **2** the position of the player in this area. *Abbr:* lf. or l.f.
**out in left field,** *U.S. Slang.* wrong; mistaken; out of order: *His argument is way out in left field.*

**left fielder,** the baseball player whose position is in left field.

**left-foot|ed** (left′fu̇t′id), *adj.* **1** using the left foot more easily and readily than the right. **2** *Figurative.* awkward; clumsy: *a left-footed recruit.*
—**left′-foot′ed|ness,** *n.*

**left-hand** (left′hand′), *adj.* **1** on or to the left: *a left-hand turn.* **2** of or for the left hand; with the left hand; left-handed: *a left-hand glove.*

**left-hand|ed** (left′han′did), *adj., adv.* —*adj.* **1** using the left hand more easily and readily than the right: *A left-handed person who sews, often has trouble with regular scissors.* **2** done with the left hand: *a left-handed catch.* **3** made to be used with the left hand or placed on the left hand. **4** turning from right to left: *a left-handed screw.* **5** *Figurative.* awkward; clumsy: *It seems to me as if murder and massacre were but a very left-handed way of producing civilization and love* (William Godwin). **6** doubtful or insincere; ambiguous: *a left-handed compliment.* **7** (in scientific and technical use) characterized by a direction or rotation to the left; producing such a rotation in the plane of a polarized ray. **8** morganatic (from the custom at German morganatic weddings of the bridegroom's giving the bride his left hand rather than his right).
—*adv.* toward the left; with the left hand.
—**left′-hand′ed|ly,** *adv.* —**left′-hand′ed|ness,** *n.*

**left-hand|er** (left′han′dər), *n.* **1** a left-handed person: *The left-hander has a long way to travel before he catches up with the right-handed majority* (New York Times). **2** *Baseball.* a left-handed pitcher; southpaw. **3** *Cricket.* a left-handed bowler. **4** a blow with the left hand.

**left|ism** or **Left|ism** (lef′tiz əm), *n.* adherence or tendency to adhere to liberal or radical views in politics: *Leftism seems everywhere in a majority ... but nowhere is it in effective control* (H. G. Wells).

**left|ist** or **Left|ist** (lef′tist), *n., adj.* —*n.* **1** a person who has liberal or radical ideas in politics. **2** a member of a liberal or radical political organization. **3** *U.S. Informal.* a left-handed person.
—*adj.* having liberal or radical ideas.

**left-lug|gage office** (left′lug′ij), *British.* a checkroom.

**left-of-cen|ter** (left′əv sen′tər), *adj.* occupying a position on the left side of those in the center; holding a leftist view in politics; left-wing: *a left-of-center candidate.*

**left|o|ver** (left′ō′vər), *n., adj.* —*n.* a thing that is left. Scraps of food from a meal are leftovers.
—*adj.* that is left; remaining: *leftover parts, to make sandwiches from leftover roast beef. I did carry a handful of leftover flowers around* (R. M. Stuart).

**left|ward** (left′wərd), *adj., adv.* on or toward the left.

**left|wards** (left′wərdz), *adv.* = leftward.

**left wing, 1** Often, **Left Wing.** the liberal or radical members, especially of a political party. **2** persons or parties holding liberal or radical views.

**left-wing** (left′wing′), *adj.* belonging to or like the left wing.

**left-wing|er** (left′wing′ər), *n.* a left-wing member of a political party or a supporter of left-wing political views.

**left-wing|ism** (left′wing′iz əm), *n.* the doctrines or practices of left-wingers: *The Bill of Rights ... smacked of the most extreme left-wingism at the time* (Atlanta Constitution).

**left|y** (lef′tē), *n., pl.* **left|ies. 1** *U.S. Informal.* a left-handed person: *Of the six hurlers, Burnside, a tall lefty, turned in the best stint, allowing only one strike* (New York Times). **2** *British Informal.* a liberal or radical; leftist: *No one likes economic cuts, but ... even Labour's lefties had to admit that cutting back was necessary* (Punch).

***leg** (leg), *n., v.,* **legged, leg|ging.** —*n.* **1** one of the limbs on which people and animals stand and walk: *Dogs stand on their four legs. A person uses his two legs in walking and running.* **2** the part of a garment that covers a leg: *He fell and tore his pants' leg.* **3** anything shaped or used like a leg; any support that is much longer than it is wide: *a table leg. One leg of a compass holds the pencil. A rainbow, therefore ... plunges one of its legs down to the river* (Thomas Jefferson). **4** one of the parts or stages of any course: *the last leg of a trip. A runner fell in the first leg of the relay and his team lost the race.* **5** a side of a triangle that is not the base or hypotenuse. **6** *Nautical.* **a** the course or run made on one tack by a sailing vessel. **b** each of the straight courses or parts of a sailing race from point to point. **7** *Cricket.* **a** that part of the field to the left of and behind a right-handed batsman as he faces the bowler. **b** the fielder placed there. **8** *Archaic.* an obeisance made by drawing back one leg and bending the other; scrape: *He is one that cannot make a good leg* (Longfellow).
—*v.i. Informal.* Usually, **leg it. 1** to walk or run: *We could not get a ride, so we had to leg it.* **2** to do the work of a legman: *[The] syndicated celebrity columnist ... has been legging it for 35 years* (Time).
**a leg up, a** assistance in climbing or getting over an obstacle, as in mounting a horse: *The wall is very low, Sir, and your servant will give you a leg up* (Dickens). **b** *Figurative.* encouragement; support: *He might see fit to change his mind ... if the Government would at last give a leg up to the languishing ... bill, for which he has long and devotedly battled* (New Yorker). **c** *Figurative.* an advantage: *The consensus in the labor field is that [he] has a "leg up" on his rival* (New York Times).
**get on one's hind legs,** to go into a rage: *"Don't get on your hind legs," returned Betty composedly* (London Daily News).
**have not a leg to stand on,** *Informal.* to have no defense or reason: *When he is through adding up his last column of figures, the ... notion of a coup d'état pulled off by big city bondholders hasn't a leg to stand on* (Wall Street Journal).
**legs,** timbers used to support a ship upright when dried out.
**on one's last legs,** about to fail, collapse, or die; at the end of one's resources: *After the suppression of the revolutionary movement the Second Republic was on its last legs* (Manchester Guardian Weekly).
**pull one's leg,** *Informal.* to fool, trick, or make fun of one: *"When you write your piece," she giggled, "I won't mind if you pull my leg—just a little"* (Maclean's).
**shake a leg,** *Slang.* **a** hurry up!: *You'd better shake a leg or we'll miss our bus.* **b** to dance: *The bandleader urged the couples to get up and shake a leg.*
**stretch one's legs,** to take a walk; get exercise by walking: *The passengers got off the bus to stretch their legs after the long ride.*
[< Scandinavian (compare Old Icelandic *leggr*)]

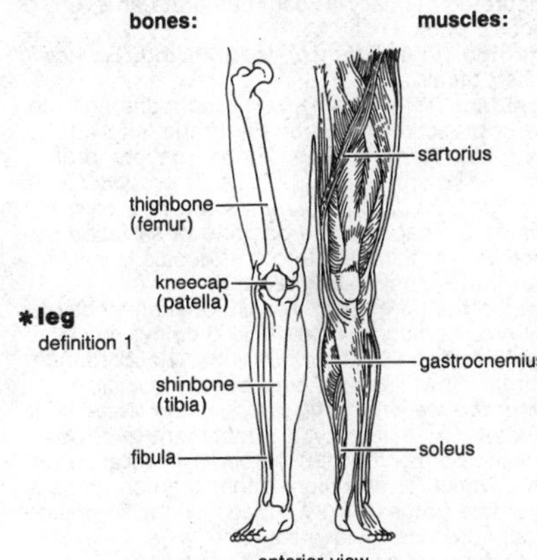


***leg**
definition 1

anterior view

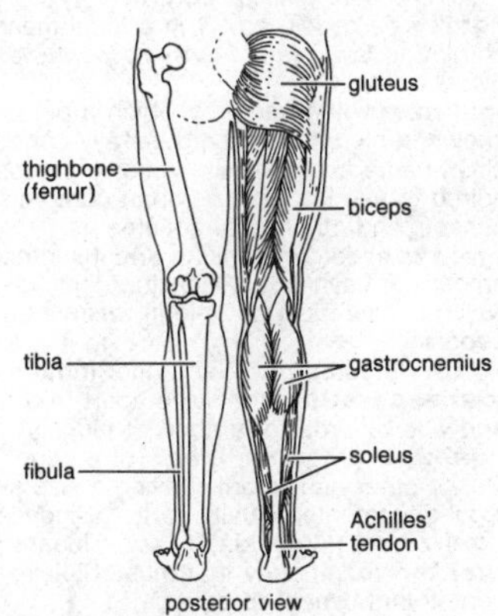


posterior view

**leg.,** an abbreviation for the following:
**1** legal.
**2** legate.
**3** *Music.* legato.
**4** legislative.
**5** legislature.

**Pronunciation Key:** hat, āge, cãre, fär; let, ēqual, tėrm; it, īce; hot, ōpen, ôrder; oil, out; cup, pu̇t, rüle; child; long; thin; ᴛʜen; zh, measure; ə represents **a** in about, **e** in taken, **i** in pencil, **o** in lemon, **u** in circus.

**leg|a|cy** (leg′ə sē), *n., pl.* **-cies. 1** money or other property left to a person by the will of someone who has died; bequest: *The two sisters got all their brother had which amounted to a legacy of several thousand dollars.* **SYN**: inheritance. **2** *Figurative.* something that has been handed down from an ancestor or predecessor: *the legacy of freedom. Books are the legacies that a great genius leaves to mankind* (Joseph Addison). **SYN**: heritage. [< Anglo-French *legacie* bequest, Old French, legateship, legate's office < Medieval Latin *legatia* < Latin *lēgātum* bequest < *lēgāre* bequeath]

**le|gal** (lē′gəl), *adj., n.* **—adj. 1** of law: *legal knowledge.* **2** of a lawyer or lawyers: *legal advice.* **3** according to law; lawful: *a legal guardian, legal incapacity. Hunting is legal only during certain seasons.* **SYN**: See syn. under **lawful. 4** valid in or recognized by law rather than equity. **5a** of Mosaic law. **b** based on Mosaic law. **c** having to do with salvation by good works rather than free grace.
**—n.** a legal notice.
**legals**, securities in which savings banks, trustees, and other investors under legal regulation may invest as authorized by law: *the purchase of legals by investors.*
[< Middle French *légal*, learned borrowing from Latin *lēgal, lēgālis* < *lēx, lēgis* law. See etym. of doublets **leal, loyal.**]

**legal age**, the age at which a person attains full legal rights and responsibilities; majority.

**legal aid society**, an organization of citizens offering legal services at no cost for those who cannot afford to hire a lawyer.

**legal cap**, *U.S.* writing paper in double sheets of 14 X 8½ inches, used by lawyers.

**le|gal|ese** (lē′gə lēz′, -lēs′), *n. Informal.* legal jargon.

**legal fiction**, = fiction (def. 5).

**legal holiday**, a day set by law or statute as exempt from normal labor or business activities and celebrated annually to commemorate an event or honor a person.

**le|gal|ise** (lē′gə līz), *v.t.,* **-ised, -is|ing.** *Especially British.* legalize.

**le|gal|ism** (lē′gə liz əm), *n.* **1** strict adherence to law or prescription, especially to the letter of the law rather than the spirit. **2** legal matters, problems, or complications: *... heavily occupied with civil rights legalisms during his two-year tenure* (Time). **3** *Theology.* the doctrine of salvation by good works; adherence to the Mosaic law rather than the Gospel. **—le′gal|ist,** *n.*

**le|gal|is|tic** (lē′gə lis′tik), *adj.* adhering strictly to law or prescription. **—le′gal|is′ti|cal|ly,** *adv.*

**le|gal|i|ty** (li gal′ə tē), *n., pl.* **-ties. 1** accordance with law; lawfulness: *They raised a question about the legality of the appointment* (New York Times). **SYN**: legitimacy. **2** attachment to or observance of law or rule. **3** *Theology.* reliance on good works for salvation, rather than on grace.

**le|gal|ize** (lē′gə līz), *v.t.,* **-ized, -iz|ing.** to make legal; authorize by law; sanction: *The American people have been unwilling to legalize ... extensive gambling* (Edward C. Devereux, Jr.). **SYN**: legitimize. **—le′gal|i|za′tion,** *n.*

**le|gal|ly** (lē′gə lē), *adv.* **1** in a legal manner. **2** according to law: *He is legally responsible for his wife's debts.*

**legal name**, the name by which a person is known in his community, generally consisting of a given name and a family name. A person is required to use his legal name in contracts, licenses, and other legal documents.

**legal reserve**, (in banking and insurance) the amount of cash or certain other liquid assets which by law must be held in reserve against deposits.

**le|gals** (lē′gəlz), *n.pl.* See under **legal.**

**legal separation**, the living apart of a husband and wife by order of a court or judge.

**le|gal-size** (lē′gəl sīz′), *adj.* (of a page, folder, file, or other equipment) having a size suitable for legal documents, usually up to 14 inches long.

**le|gal-sized** (lē′gəl sīzd′), *adj.* = legal-size.

**legal tender**, money that must, by law, be accepted in payment of debts.

**leg|ate** (leg′it), *n.* **1** a representative of the Pope: *The Lord Cardinal Pole, sent here as legate From our most Holy Father Julius, Pope* (Tennyson). **2** an ambassador or representative; messenger: *the legates from Utrecht* (John L. Motley). **3** in ancient Rome: **a** an assistant or deputy to a general or to the governor of a province. **b** (under the empire) the governor of a province. [< Old French *legat*, learned borrowing from Latin *lēgātus* (originally) provided with a contract < *lēgāre* bequeath < *lēx, lēgis* contract]

**leg|a|tee** (leg′ə tē′), *n.* a person to whom a legacy is left.
▶ See **heir** for usage note.

**leg|ate|ship** (leg′it ship), *n.* the dignity and office of a legate.

**leg|a|tine** (leg′ə tin, -tīn), *adj.* **1** of or having to do with a legate. **2** having the authority of a legate.

**le|ga|tion** (li gā′shən), *n.* **1** a diplomatic representative of a country and his staff of assistants. A legation ranks next below an embassy and is now usually headed by a minister. **2** the official residence or offices of such a representative in a foreign country. **3** the office, position, or dignity of a legate. **4** the act of sending a deputy or representative, especially a papal legate. **5** the fact of his being sent. **6** the object for which an ambassador or legate is sent; his mission or commission. [< Old French *legation*, learned borrowing from Latin *lēgātiō, -ōnis* < *lēgāre* to dispatch (with a commission) < *lēx, lēgis* law]

**le|ga|tion|ar|y** (li gā′shə ner′ē), *adj.* **1** of or having to do with a legation. **2** qualified or ready to go on a legation.

**le|ga|to** (li gä′tō), *adj., adv., n., pl.* **-tos.** *Music.* **—adj., adv.** smooth and connected; without breaks between successive tones.
**—n.** a legato performance or style.
[< Italian *legato* bound < Latin *ligātus*, past participle of *ligāre* to bind]

**le|ga|tor** (li gā′tər, leg′ə tôr′), *n.* a person who leaves something by will; testator.

**leg|a|to|ri|al** (leg′ə tôr′ē əl, -tōr′-), *adj.* of or having to do with a legator or testator.

**leg before wicket**, *Cricket.* the action of stopping a ball that would have hit the wicket with the leg or other part of the batsman's body, except the hand. It usually results in an out.

**leg break**, *Cricket.* a ball pitched on or breaking from the side of the field that lies in a line with the batsman.

**leg bye**, *Cricket.* a run made on a ball touching any part of the batsman's body except his hand.

**leg|end** (lej′ənd), *n.* **1** a story coming down from the past, which many people have believed: *The stories about King Arthur and his knights of the Round Table are legends, not history. Listen to this Indian Legend, To this Song of Hiawatha* (Longfellow). **SYN**: saga. **2** such stories as a group; the legends of certain peoples: *a hero of Irish legend, a spot rich in legend.* **SYN**: folklore. **3** what is written on a coin or medal: *Read the legend on a five-cent piece.* **SYN**: motto. **4** words accompanying a picture or diagram, usually explaining something about it; caption: *The legend underneath the picture identified the man as General Custer.* **5** in the Middle Ages: **a** a story of the life of a saint. **b** a collection of saints' lives or inspirational stories. [< Old French *legende*, learned borrowing from Medieval Latin *legenda* (things) to be read < Latin, neuter plural gerundive of *legere* read]
▶ **legend, myth.** *Legend* applies particularly to a story associated with some period in the history of a people or nation, often containing an element of fact but sometimes wholly untrue. Legends are intended to glorify, especially a hero, saint, object, or belief, and tell marvelous deeds he or it supposedly performed or caused to happen. *Myth* applies particularly to a story connected with the religion of a primitive or early civilization. Myths are told about gods or superhuman beings and are invented to explain beliefs or rituals or something in nature.

**leg|end|ar|y** (lej′ən der′ē), *adj., n., pl.* **-ar|ies.** **—adj. 1** of a legend or legends; like a legend; not historical: *Robin Hood is a legendary person. His legendary song ... Of ancient deeds so long forgot* (Scott). **2** celebrated or described in legend: *a legendary hero or event.* **3** relating legends: *a legendary writer.*
**—n.** a collection of legends, especially of lives of saints. **—leg′end|ar′i|ly,** *adv.*

**leg|end|ry** (lej′ən drē), *n., pl.* **-ries.** legends collectively.

**leg|er** (lej′ər), *n.* = ledger (def. 4).

**leg|er|de|main** (lej′ər də mān′), *n.* **1** sleight of hand; conjuring tricks; jugglery: *A common trick of legerdemain is to take rabbits from an apparently empty hat.* **SYN**: prestidigitation. **2** *Figurative.* trickery; deception; hocus-pocus: *In a remarkable bit of legerdemain, he transferred his popular film personality to his singing style* (Time). **3** *Obsolete.* artful trick; juggle. [< Middle French *léger de main* quick of hand < Vulgar Latin *leviārius* (< Latin *levis* light), Latin *dē* of, and *mānus* hand]

**leg|er|de|main|ist** (lej′ər də mā′nist), *n.* a person who practices legerdemain.

**le|ger|i|ty** (lə jer′ə tē), *n.* lightness; nimbleness: *Alighting with the legerity of a cat, he ... was off, like a streak of lightning* (New Yorker). [< Middle French *légèreté* < *léger* quick (see etym. under **legerdemain**) + *-eté* -ity]

**leger line**, = ledger line.

**le|ges** (lē′jēz), *n. Latin.* plural of **lex.**

**-legged**, *combining form.* having ____ legs: *Long-legged = having long legs.*

**leg|ging** (leg′ing), *n.* one of a pair of leggings.

**leg|gings** (leg′ingz), *n.pl.* extra outer coverings of cloth or leather for the legs, for use out of doors. **SYN**: puttees.

**leg|gy** (leg′ē), *adj.,* **-gi|er, -gi|est. 1** having long legs: *a leggy, gun-totin' singer at the Dirty Shame saloon* (Time). **2** having awkwardly long legs: *Slapper's long-tailed leggy mare* (Thackeray). **3** long-stemmed (often said of plants that have grown too tall and thin from being crowded): *The white meeting-house, and the row of youthful and leggy trees before it* (Oliver Wendell Holmes). **4** *Informal.* having shapely legs.

**leg hit**, *Cricket.* a hit that sends the ball to leg.

**leg|horn** (leg′hôrn, -ərn), *n.* **1** a hat made of fine, smooth, yellow braided straw or an imitation of it. **2** this straw, made from cut and bleached green wheat. [< *Leghorn*, a seaport in Italy]

**Leg|horn** (leg′hôrn, -ərn), *n.* a rather small chicken which produces large numbers of eggs. Leghorns are white, brown, buff, black, or silver with a yellow skin. This breed of domestic fowl originated in Italy. [see *leghorn*]

**leg|i|bil|i|ty** (lej′ə bil′ə tē), *n.* legible condition or quality; clearness of print or writing: *words emblazoned in all the legibility of gilt letters* (Dickens).

**leg|i|ble** (lej′ə bəl), *adj.* **1** that can be read: (*Figurative.*) *the trouble legible in my countenance* (Charles Lamb). **SYN**: readable. **2** easy to read; plain and clear: *Her handwriting is both beautiful and legible.* **SYN**: distinct. [< Late Latin *legibilis* < Latin *legere* read] **—leg′i|ble|ness,** *n.*

**leg|i|bly** (lej′ə blē), *adv.* clearly; readably: *The next time you make a list, write more legibly.*

**le|gion** (lē′jən), *n.* **1** a division of the ancient Roman army containing several thousand foot soldiers and several hundred horsemen. **2** a large body of soldiers; army: *Nor knew great Hector how his legions yield* (Alexander Pope). **3** a great many; very large number: *a legion of difficulties, a legion of supporters. Legions of grasshoppers destroyed the crops. The number of his supporters is legion.* **SYN**: multitude. **4** Often, **Legion,** any one of various military or honorary groups or societies, especially a national organization of former servicemen: *the Royal Canadian Legion.*
**one's name is legion,** there are a great many others of the same kind: *My name is Legion: for we are many* (Mark 5:9). *She could be reached, be helped, at least in theory. Her name is indeed legion* (Robert Coles).
[< Old French *legion*, learned borrowing from Latin *legiō, -ōnis* < *legere* choose]

**Le|gion** (lē′jən), *n.* **1** the American Legion. **2** the French Foreign Legion.

**le|gion|ar|y** (lē′jə ner′ē), *adj., n., pl.* **-ar|ies.**
**—adj. 1** of or belonging to a legion. **2** organized as or formed of a legion or legions.
**—n. 1** a soldier of a legion; legionnaire. **2** *British.* a member of the British Legion (a veterans' organization).

**legionary ant**, an army ant of North and South America.

**le|gioned** (lē′jənd), *adj.* arrayed in legions.

**le|gion|naire** (lē′jə nãr′), *n.* **1** a member of the American Legion or any other group using the title of Legion. **2** a soldier of a legion. [< French *légionnaire* < Old French *legion* legion]

**legionnaires'** or **legionnaire's disease**, a serious and sometimes fatal form of pneumonia caused by bacterial infection, characterized by high fever, abdominal pain, and lung congestion. [from the outbreak at an American Legion convention in 1976 in Philadelphia]

**Legion of Honor**, an honorary society founded by Napoleon in 1802. Membership is given as a reward for great services to France.

**Legion of Merit**, *U.S.* a military award conferred by the President on Americans and people of friendly foreign nations, for exceptional services.

**Legis.**, Legislature.

**leg|is|late** (lej′is lāt), *v.,* **-lat|ed, -lat|ing. —v.i.** to make laws: *Congress legislates for the United States.*
**—v.t.** to force by legislation; bring about by legislation: *The council legislated him out of office.*
[apparently back formation < *legislator*]

**leg|is|la|tion** (lej′is lā′shən), *n.* **1** the act or process of making laws: *Congress has the power of legislation.* **SYN**: lawmaking. **2** the laws made: *Important legislation is reported in the newspaper.*

**leg|is|la|tive** (lej′is lā′tiv), *adj., n.* **—adj. 1** having to do with making laws: *legislative reforms.* **2** having the duty and power of making laws: *Congress is a legislative body.* **3** ordered by law; made to be as it is by legislation: *a legislative decree. Legislative approval is necessary before a corporation can come into existence in New York State* (New York Times). **4** suitable to a legislature: *a legislative hall.*
**—n.** the branch of government which makes laws. **—leg′is|la′tive|ly,** *adv.*

**legislative assembly** or **Legislative Assembly**, **1** the lower branch of the legislature in some states of the United States. **2** the bicameral legislature of certain states of the United States.

**Legislative Assembly**, **1** the popularly elected legislature of a Canadian province. **2** the legislature of France from 1791 to 1792, during the French Revolution.

**legislative council**, a committee of members from both houses that advises some State legislatures of the United States on all matters of law.

**Legislative Council**, (in Canada) the former upper house of the legislature of Quebec. It was abolished in 1968.

**leg|is|la|tor** (lej′is lā′tər), *n.* a person who makes laws; member of a group that makes laws; lawmaker. Senators and representatives are legislators. [< Latin (originally) *lēgislātor* proposer of a law < *lēx, lēgis* law + *lātus,* past participle of *ferre* bring, bear]

**leg|is|la|to|ri|al** (lej′is lə tôr′ē əl, -tōr′-), *adj.* **1** of or having to do with a legislator or legislature. **2** functioning as a legislator or legislature. —**leg′is|la|to′ri|al|ly,** *adv.*

**leg|is|la|tor|ship** (lej′is lā′tər ship), *n.* the office or function of a legislator.

**leg|is|la|tress** (lej′is lā′tris), *n.* a woman legislator.

**leg|is|la|trix** (lej′is lā′triks), *n.* = legislatress.

**leg|is|la|ture** (lej′is lā′chər), *n.* a group of persons that has the duty and power of making laws for a state or country. Each state of the United States has a legislature.

**le|gist** (lē′jist), *n.* an expert in law. [< Old French *legiste,* learned borrowing from Medieval Latin *legista* < Latin *lēx, lēgis* law]

**le|git** (lə jit′), *adj., n. Slang.* —***adj.*** legitimate: *Is it legit to draw two cards at once? I'm a legit playwright* (Saturday Review).
—*n.* legitimate drama; the legitimate theater.

**leg|i|tim** (lej′ə tim), *n. Civil and Scots Law.* the portion of the estate of a deceased person to which his children are legally entitled. [< Old French *legitime,* learned borrowing from Latin *lēgitimus* lawful < *lēx, lēgis* law]

**le|git|i|ma|cy** (lə jit′ə mə sē), *n.* the fact or condition of being legitimate or lawful.

**le|git|i|mate** (*adj.* lə jit′ə mit; *v.* lə jit′ə māt), *adj., v.,* **-mat|ed, -mat|ing.** —***adj.*** **1** allowed or admitted by law; rightful; lawful: *a legitimate claim.* **SYN:** See syn. under **lawful. 2** allowed; valid, logical, or acceptable: *a legitimate conclusion. Sickness is a legitimate reason for a child's being absent from school.* **3** born of parents who are married: *a legitimate child.* **4** conforming to accepted standards; normal; regular: *legitimate business practices.* **5** resting on, or ruling by, the principle of hereditary right: *the legitimate title to a throne, a legitimate ruler.* **6** of the legitimate theater: *a legitimate playwright.* **7** *Obsolete.* genuine; real.
—***v.t.*** **1** to make or declare lawful. **2** to affirm or show to be legitimate; authorize or justify by word or example: *Necessity legitimates my advice; for it is the only way to save our lives* (Daniel Defoe).
[< Medieval Latin *legitimatus,* past participle of *legitimare* < Latin *lēgitimus* lawful < *lēx, lēgis* law] —**le|git′i|mate|ly,** *adv.* —**le|git′i|mate|ness,** *n.* —**le|git′i|ma′tion,** *n.*

**legitimate drama, 1** the body of plays of recognized merit. **2** = legitimate theater.

**legitimate stage,** = legitimate theater.

**legitimate theater,** drama acted on the stage as opposed to motion pictures, vaudeville, musical comedy, and the like.

**le|git|i|ma|tize** (lə jit′ə mə tīz), *v.t.,* **-tized, -tiz|ing.** = legitimize.

**le|git|i|mism** (lə jit′ə miz əm), *n.* the principles or views of legitimists; support of legitimate authority, especially of a claim to a throne based on direct descent.

**le|git|i|mist** (lə jit′ə mist), *n., adj.* —*n.* **1** a supporter of legitimate authority, especially of claims to rule based on direct descent. **2** Also, **Legitimist.** (In Europe in the 1800's), a member of any one of various monarchist or reactionary groups, such as the supporters of Metternich in Austria or of the Bourbons, or Hapsburgs.
—***adj.*** of or having to do with legitimists; expressing the views of legitimists.

**le|git|i|mize** (lə jit′ə mīz), *v.t.,* **-mized, -miz|ing.** to make or declare to be legitimate: *The notary's stamp legitimized the deed.* —**le|git′i|mi|za′tion,** *n.*

**leg|less** (leg′lis), *adj.* having no legs; without legs. —**leg′less|ness,** *n.*

**leg|man** (leg′man′), *n., pl.* **-men. 1** a newspaper reporter who gathers information by going to the scene of the news: *Where editors once sent legmen out chasing ambulances ... some of them are sending their best men out to dig up the background to the news* (Maclean's). **2** a person who delivers messages, gathers information, or does other legwork: *He was an older attorney's legman* (Time).

∗**leg-of-mut|ton** (leg′əv mut′ən), *adj.* having the shape of a leg of mutton; wide at one end and narrow at the other: *a leg-of-mutton sleeve.*

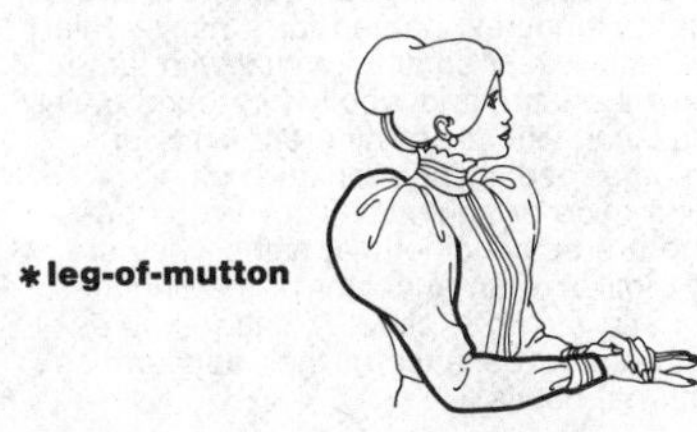
∗**leg-of-mutton**

**leg-of-mutton sail,** a triangular sail having its head at the masthead, and not set on a gaff or yard.

**leg-o'-mut|ton** (leg′ə mut′ən), *adj.* = leg-of-mutton.

**le|gong** or **Le|gong** (le′gông), *n.* a classical Balinese dance which tells a story. The dance is performed by two small girls. [< Balinese *légong*]

**leg-pull** (leg′pu̇l′), *n. Informal.* an act of fooling, tricking, or ridiculing; hoax; practical joke: *He found it hard to persuade them that his call for help was not another leg-pull* (New Scientist).

**leg-pull|er** (leg′pu̇l′ər), *n. Informal.* a person who engages in leg-pulling.

**leg-pull|ing** (leg′pu̇l′ing), *n. Informal.* the act or practice of fooling, tricking, or ridiculing.

**leg|room** (leg′rüm′, -ru̇m′), *n.* enough space to extend one's legs when seated, especially in an automobile, airplane, or the like: *The middle person in the front or back seat will have full legroom* (Time).

**legs** (legz), *n.pl.* See under **leg.**

**leg stump,** *Cricket.* the stump nearest the batsman.

**leg|ume** (leg′yüm, li gyüm′), *n.* **1** a plant which bears pods containing a number of seeds. Beans and peas are legumes; they belong to the pea family. Many legumes can absorb nitrogen from the air and convert it into nitrates by means of bacteria present in nodules on the roots of the plants. **2a** the pod of such a plant. **b** the fruit or edible portion of such a pod. A peanut is really a legume, not a nut. **3** *Botany.* a dry, several-seeded fruit, characteristic of plants of the pea family. It is formed of a single carpel, which is dehiscent by both sutures and so divides into two valves, the seeds being borne at the inner or ventral suture only.
**legumes,** vegetables, especially those of the pea family, used for food: *The dry edible fruit and other species of food, which we call by the general name of legumes* (Benjamin Jowett).
[< Middle French *légume,* learned borrowing from Latin *legūmen*]

**le|gu|min** (li gyü′min), *n. Biochemistry.* a globulin found in leguminous seeds.

**le|gu|mi|nous** (li gyü′mə nəs), *adj.* **1** of or bearing legumes. **2** of or belonging to the same group of plants as beans and peas; of the pea family.

**leg-up** (leg′up′), *n. Informal.* help; assistance: *Other sections of the shipping industry ... are not scheduled to receive any ... financial leg-up from the government* (New Yorker).

**leg|work** (leg′wėrk′), *n.,* or **leg work,** work which involves much moving about or traveling, usually in pursuit of information; the work of a legman: *Government agencies revealed they were spending around $10 million annually to assist the Washington press corps with its legwork* (Newsweek).

**Le|hi** (lē′hī), *n.* (in the Book of Mormon) a Hebrew prophet who led a group of people to the west coast of America about 600 B.C. by divine command to found a colony. After his death, the colony grew into two nations, the Nephites and the Lamanites.

**lehr** (lir), *n.* an oven used for annealing glass. [origin uncertain]

**le|hu|a** (lā hü′ä), *n.* **1** a hardwood tree of the myrtle family, found in Hawaii, Samoa, and other Pacific islands, having clusters of bright-red flowers. **2** its flower. [< Hawaiian *lehua*]

**lei¹** (lā), *n., pl.* **leis.** a wreath of flowers or leaves, or an imitation of them, worn as an ornament around the neck or on the head: *He came ashore to a rousing welcome, complete with ... hula dancers, a lei of red carnations ...* (Time). [< Hawaiian *lei*]

**lei²** (lā), *n.* plural of **leu.**

**Leib|niz|i|an** or **Leib|nitz|i|an** (līp nit′sē ən), *adj.* of or having to do with the philosophy and works of Gottfried Wilhelm von Leibniz (or Leibnitz) (1646-1716).

**Leib|niz|i|an|ism** or **Leib|nitz|i|an|ism** (līp nit′sē ə niz′əm), *n.* the philosophy of Gottfried Wilhelm von Leibniz (or Leibnitz), including the theory of monadism and the doctrine of optimism, as based on his idea that the structure of the human mind determines man's view of reality.

**Leices|ter** (les′tər), *n.* any long-wooled sheep of a breed originally of Leicestershire, England.

**Lei Day,** May 1, a holiday in Hawaii in which leis are worn and competitions for the most attractive leis are held.

**lei|o|my|o|ma** (lī′ō mī ō′mə), *n., pl.* **-mas, -ma|ta** (-mə tə). a benign tumor composed of smooth muscle fiber. [< Greek *leîos* smooth + English *myoma*]

**Leish|man-Don|o|van body** (lēsh′mən don′ə vən), a small, oval protozoan which is transmitted by insects to the human bloodstream in various forms of leishmaniasis. [< William B. *Leishman* and Charles *Donovan*]

**leish|man|i|a** (lēsh man′ē ə, -mā′nē-), *n.* any one of a genus of protozoan flagellates that are parasitic in vertebrate tissues and cause leishmaniasis: *Leishmanias ... are responsible for oriental sore and potentially fatal kala-azar* (New Scientist).

**leish|man|i|a|sis** (lēsh′mə nī′ə sis), *n., pl.* **-ses** (-sēz). a disease most common in tropical areas, causing lesions and sores of the skin and mucous membranes. It is caused by a protozoan in the bloodstream, and a more serious form, kala-azar, attacks internal organs. [< William B. *Leishman,* 1865-1926, a British army surgeon, who described it + *-iasis*]

**leis|ter** (lēs′tər), *n., v.* —***n.*** a rod with three or more prongs on the end, used for spearing fish.
—***v.t.*** to spear (fish) with such a rod.
[< Scandinavian (compare Danish *lyster,* Old Icelandic *ljōstr* < *ljōsta* strike)] —**leis′ter|er,** *n.*

**lei|sur|a|ble** (lē′zhər ə bəl, lezh′ər-), *adj.* leisurely; deliberate. —**lei′sur|a|bly,** *adv.*

**lei|sure** (lē′zhər, lezh′ər), *n., adj.* —***n.*** **1** time free from required work, in which a person may rest, amuse himself, and do the things he likes to do: *A busy man hasn't much leisure. She spends at least a part of her leisure in reading. 'Zounds! how has he the leisure to be sick In such a justling time?* (Shakespeare). **2** the condition of having time free from required work: *a gentleman of leisure.*
—***adj.*** **1** free; not busy: *leisure hours. A whole leisure Saturday afternoon was before him* (Longfellow). **2** = leisured.
**at leisure, a** free; not busy: *to be at leisure to see a caller.* **b** without hurry; taking plenty of time: *to proceed at leisure.*
**at one's leisure,** when one has leisure; at one's convenience: *Write me at your leisure.*
[< Old French *leisir,* noun use of infinitive < Latin *licēre* be allowed; influenced by English *measure*]

**lei|sured** (lē′zhərd, lezh′ərd), *adj.* **1** having ample leisure: *the leisured class of society.* **2** leisurely: *He walked at a leisured pace.*

**lei|sure|ly** (lē′zhər lē, lezh′ər-), *adj., adv.* without hurry; taking plenty of time; deliberate: *a leisurely person* (adj.), *to stroll leisurely through the park* (adv.). **SYN:** See syn. under **slow.** —**lei′sure|li|ness,** *n.*

**leisure suit,** a man's suit consisting of a light, shirt-styled jacket and matching trousers, designed especially for leisure-time wear.

**lei|sure|wear** (lē′zhər wãr′, lezh′ər-), *n.* casual clothes for leisure-time wear.

**leit|mo|tif** or **leit|mo|tiv** (līt′mō tēf′), *n.* **1** a short passage in a musical composition, associated throughout the work with a certain person, situation, or idea. Franz Liszt developed the leitmotif used later by Richard Wagner in his operas. **2** *Figurative.* any recurrent theme or motif: *This is the leitmotif of the three novels, the stories of three tormented men* (Scientific American). [< German *Leitmotiv* (literally) leading motive]

**lek¹** (lek), *n.* the unit of money of Albania, equal to 100 qintar. [< Albanian *lek*]

**lek²** (lek), *n., v.,* **lekked, lek|king.** —***n.*** a meeting ground of male birds for display and courtship: *The prairie chicken has ... a kind of ruff, displayed while courting, and its courtship is invariably conducted on a lek* (Peter Matthiessen).
—***v.i.*** to gather at a lek: *the curious lekking habit of blackcock—when the birds foregather for what seems to be half a tournament, quarter a display dance, and quarter a social meeting for boastful crowing* (J. D. U. Ward).
[< Swedish *lek* mating, pairing; game, sport]

**lek|y|thos** (lek′ə thos), *n., pl.* **-thoi** (-thoi). = lecythus.

**Pronunciation Key:** hat, āge, cãre, fär; let, ēqual, tėrm; it, īce; hot, ōpen, ôrder; oil, out; cup, pu̇t, rüle; child; long; thin; ᴛʜen; zh, measure; ə represents **a** in about, **e** in taken, **i** in pencil, **o** in lemon, **u** in circus.

**LEM** (lem), *n.* = lunar excursion module.

**lem|an** (lem′ən, lē′mən), *n. Archaic.* **1** a lover; sweetheart: *He ... offered kingdoms unto her in view, To be his Leman and his Lady true* (Edmund Spenser). **2** an unlawful lover or mistress. [Middle English *leofman* < Old English *lēof* dear + *man* person]

**lem|el|o** (lem′ə lō), *n., pl.* **-los.** a hybrid fruit produced by crossing the grapefruit and the lemon. [< *lem*(on) + (pom)*elo*]

**lem|ma**[1] (lem′ə), *n., pl.* **lem|mas, lem|ma|ta** (lem′ə tə). **1** *Mathematics.* a subsidiary or auxiliary proposition to be used in the proof of a main proposition. **2** an argument, theme, subject, or gloss. [< Greek *lêmma, -atos* < *lēm-,* perfect stem of *lambánein* to take]

**lem|ma**[2] (lem′ə), *n. Botany.* the lower bract of the pair enclosing the flower in a spikelet of grass. [< Greek *lémma* < *lépein* to peel]

**lem|mer** (lem′ər), *n.* a person who cuts the meat and bones from the bodies of whales. [origin unknown]

**lem|ming** (lem′ing), *n.* a small, mouselike arctic rodent, having a short tail and furry feet. At certain times, when food is scarce, lemmings migrate in great masses. Some reach the sea where they swim a short distance, and usually drown. [< Norwegian *lemming*]

**Lem|ni|an earth** or **bole** (lem′nē ən), a soft, astringent, clayey substance found on the island of Lemnos, in the northern Aegean Sea, and formerly much used for medicinal purposes; terra sigillata; sphragide.

**lem|nis|cate** (lem nis′kit), *n. Geometry.* a closed curve consisting of two symmetrical loops meeting at a node and generally resembling a horizontal figure 8. [< New Latin *lemniscata* < Latin *lēmniscāta,* feminine of *lēmniscātus* adorned with ribbons < *lēmniscus* a hanging ribbon < Greek *lēmnískos*]

**lem|nis|cus** (lem nis′kəs), *n., pl.* **-nis|ci** (-nis′ī). *Anatomy.* a band of nerve fibers in the mesencephalon. [< New Latin *lemniscus* < Latin *lēmniscus* a hanging ribbon < Greek *lēmnískos*]

**lem|on** (lem′ən), *n., adj.* **—*n.*** **1** a sour, light-yellow citrus fruit that grows in warm climates. The juice is much used for flavoring and for making lemonade, and yields citric acid; the rind yields oil or essence of lemons, which is used in cookery and perfumery. **2** the thorny tree that bears this fruit. It belongs to the rue family. **3** a pale yellow. **4** *Slang, Figurative.* something or someone that is worthless or unpleasant: *A car, fan, refrigerator, or other manufactured product that does not work very well most of the time is sometimes referred to as a lemon.*
**—*adj.*** **1** pale-yellow; lemon-colored: *a creamy lemon complexion.* **2** flavored with lemon: *lemon ice.*
[< Old French *limon* < Arabic *līmūn* < Persian] **—lem′on|like′,** *adj.*

**lem|on|ade** (lem′ə nād′), *n.* a drink made of lemon juice, sugar, and water. It is usually served cold. [< French *limonade* < Old French *limon;* see etym. under **lemon**]

**lemon balm, 1** an herb of the mint family whose leaves have a flavor like that of lemon. **2** the leaves of this herb, used for seasoning.

**lem|on-col|ored** (lem′ən kul′ərd), *adj.* having a pale-yellow color.

**lemon drop,** a small, hard candy made of sugar and flavored with lemon.

**lemon geranium,** a common garden geranium, whose leaves have a lemonlike odor.

**lemon grass,** or **lem|on|grass** (lem′ən gras′, -gräs′), *n.* a cultivated perennial grass, the source of an essential oil, lemon grass oil, used especially in perfumes and flavorings for its strong scent of fresh lemon.

**lem|on|ish** (lem′ə nish), *adj.* = lemony.

**lemon oil,** an essential oil obtained from the rind of lemons.

**lemon shark,** a common, yellowish shark of warm, shallow waters on the Atlantic coasts of North and South America.

**lemon sole,** any one of various soles or flatfishes used for food, especially a small variety of European sole.

**lemon squash,** *British.* lemonade made with carbonated water.

**lemon verbena,** a small South American garden shrub of the verbena family, whose long, slender leaves have a lemonlike odor.

**lem|on|wood** (lem′ən wu̇d′), *n.* **1a** a tropical American tree of the madder family with hard, strong wood. **b** its wood, used especially for making bows. **2** an evergreen shrub or tree of South Africa, belonging to the madder family, sometimes growing to a height of 20 to 30 feet and having a hard, tough wood. **3** = tarata.

**lem|on|y** (lem′ə nē), *adj.* lemonlike, as in taste or smell: *lemony iced tea* (New Yorker).

**lemon yellow,** a pale-yellow color; lemon.

**lem|on-yel|low** (lem′ən yel′ō), *adj.* pale-yellow; lemon-colored.

**lem|pi|ra** (lem pē′rä), *n.* the unit of money of Honduras, a note or coin equal to 100 centavos. [< American Spanish *lempira* < *Lempira,* a department in Honduras, named for a native chief]

***le|mur** (lē′mər), *n.* a small mammal with large eyes, a foxlike face, and woolly fur, found mainly in Madagascar. There are different kinds of lemurs, some resembling monkeys, others resembling mice or squirrels. They live in trees and some are active chiefly at night. They are probably similar to an ancestor of the primates. [< New Latin *lemures,* plural < Latin *lemurēs* specters, ghosts (because of their appearance and nocturnal habits)]

***lemur**

**lem|u|res** (lem′yə rēz), *n.pl. Roman Mythology.* the spirits of the departed; nocturnal spirits. [< Latin *lemurēs;* see etym. under **lemur**]

**lem|u|roid** (lem′yə roid), *adj., n.* **—*adj.*** of or like the lemurs.
**—*n.*** = lemur.

**Len|a|pe** (len′ə pē; lə nä′pē), *n., pl.* **-pe** or **-pes.** = Delaware (defs. 1a, b).

**Le|nard rays** (lā′närt), cathode rays which have passed through the window of a Lenard tube. [< Philipp von *Lenard,* 1862-1947, a German physicist]

**Lenard tube,** a special form of vacuum tube containing a diaphragm or window of aluminum through which cathode rays pass to the outside.

**lend** (lend), *v.,* **lent, lend|ing,** *n.* **—*v.t.*** **1** to let another have or use for a time: *Will you lend me your bicycle for an hour?* **2** to give the use of (money) for a fixed or specified amount of payment: *Banks lend money and charge interest.* **3** to give for a time; give; add: *A becoming dress lends charm to a girl. The Salvation Army is quick to lend aid in time of disaster.* **SYN:** bestow, impart, afford, grant.
**—*v.i.*** to make a loan or loans: *A person who borrows should be willing to lend.*
**—*n.*** *Informal.* a loan: *He got the lend of my best suit of clothes* (John Galt).
**lend itself** (or **oneself**) **to,** to help or be suitable for: *to lend oneself to the schemes of others. This subject lends itself admirably to dramatic treatment.*
[Middle English *lenen,* Old English *lǣnan* < *lǣn* loan; the *-d* is < *lende,* the Middle English past tense, influenced by *rend, send*] **—lend′a|ble,** *adj.* **—lend′er,** *n.*
► See **loan** for usage note.

**lend|ing library** (len′ding), a public library that permits books to be borrowed.

**lend-lease** (lend′lēs′), *n., v.,* **-leased, -leas|ing,** *adj.* **—*n.*** a policy of making a loan to an allied country of certain equipment in which the lender is superior, and of receiving some service or material in return. The United States used this policy in World War II to bolster the strength of its allies.
**—*v.t.*** to send as a loan under such a policy.
**—*adj.*** of or having to do with such a policy: *lend-lease supplies.*

**le|nes** (lē′nēz), *n.* plural of **lenis.**

**length** (lengkth, length), *n.* **1** how long a thing is; what a thing measures from end to end; the longest way a thing can be measured: *the length of your arm, the length of a room, eight inches in length. The carp ... will grow to a very great bigness and length* (Izaak Walton). **2** how long something lasts or goes on; extent in time; duration: *the length of an hour, the length of a visit, the length of a performance.* **3** the distance a thing extends: *The length of the race is one mile. I might ... have gone the length of a ... street* (Daniel Defoe). **4** a long stretch or extent: *Quite a length of hair hung down in a braid. Large lengths of seas and shores Between my father and my mother lay* (Shakespeare). **5** a piece or portion of given length: *a length of rope, a dress length of silk.* **6** the distance from end to end, as of a boat or horse, as a unit of measurement in racing: *The gray horse finished the race two lengths ahead of the brown one.* **7** the quality or fact of being long: *a book noted for its length. Such customs have their force, only from length of time* (Thomas Hobbes). **8** *Prosody.* the force with which a syllable or vowel is spoken, or the way it is pronounced. **9** *Phonetics.* **a** duration of sounds; quantity. **b** vowel distinction, as between the *a* represented in *ate* and that represented in *at.*
**at full length,** with the body fully stretched out flat: *The snake lay at full length on the rock, sunning itself.*
**at length, a** at last; finally: *At length, after many delays, the meeting started. They ... pressed for admittance ... which at length was granted them* (George Washington). **b** with all the details; in full: *He told of his adventures at length.*
**go (to) any length** or **lengths,** to do everything possible: *I will go to any length to help you. He would go ... any lengths for his party* (Benjamin Disraeli).
**keep at arm's length.** See under **arm**[1].
**measure one's length,** to fall, be thrown, or lie flat on the ground: *He lost his balance and measured his length upon the ground* (Dickens).
[Old English *length* < *lang* long[1]]
► The pronunciations (lenth) and (strenth) for **length** and **strength** occur both in America and in Great Britain, but are rare in educated use. Spellings reflecting this type of pronunciation are found as early as the 1300's; in the 1800's it was sometimes described as largely peculiar to Irish and Scottish speech.

**length|en** (lengk′thən, leng′-), *v.t.* to make longer: *A tailor can lengthen your trousers.* **—*v.i.*** to become or grow longer: *the shadows lengthening as the vapours rise* (John Dryden). *Your legs have lengthened a great deal since you were five years old.* **—length′en|er,** *n.*
**—*Syn.* *v.t., v.i.*** **Lengthen, extend, prolong** mean to make or become longer. **Lengthen** means to make or become longer in space or time: *There is no way to lengthen a day.* **Extend** means to stretch out beyond the present point or limits: *We had to extend the table for Thanksgiving.* It often applies to measurements in addition to length (*The ranch extends beyond the horizon*) and is frequently used metaphorically (*Reading can extend one's knowledge*). **Prolong** means to lengthen in time beyond the usual or expected limit: *She prolonged her visit.*

**length|ways** (lengkth′wāz′, length′-), *adv., adj.* = lengthwise.

**length|wise** (lengkth′wīz′, length′-), *adv., adj.* **—*adv.*** in the direction of the length: *She cut the cloth lengthwise.*
**—*adj.*** following the direction of the length; longitudinal: *The tailor made a lengthwise cut in the cloth.*

**length|y** (lengk′thē, leng′-), *adj.,* **length|i|er, length|i|est. 1a** having unusually great length; long. **b** (of speeches, a speaker, a writer, or the like) too long; long-winded; tedious: *His directions were so lengthy that everybody lost interest.* **SYN:** prolix. **2** very tall (a humorous use). **3** (in technical use, of some animals) long in the body. [American English < *length* + *-y*[1]] **—length′i|ly,** *adv.* **—length′i|ness,** *n.*

**len|ience** (lēn′yəns, lē′nē əns), *n.* = leniency.

**len|ien|cy** (lēn′yən sē, lē′nē ən-), *n.* lenient quality; mildness; gentleness; mercy: *When you have gone too far to recede, do not sue to me for leniency* (Dickens). **SYN:** indulgence, tolerance.

**len|ient** (lēn′yənt, lē′nē ənt), *adj.* **1** mild or gentle; not harsh or stern; merciful; tolerant: *a lenient judge, lenient punishment. My father was always very strict about how I talked to Mother, but he was more lenient if I yelled at my brother.* **SYN:** compassionate, forbearing, indulgent. **2** *Archaic.* softening, soothing, or relaxing: *Old Time ... upon these wounds hath laid His lenient touches* (Wordsworth). **SYN:** emollient. [< Latin *lēniēns, -entis,* present participle of *lēnīre* soften < *lēnis* mild] **—len′ient|ly,** *adv.*

**Len|i-Len|a|pe** (len′ē len′ə pē, -lə nä′pē), *n., pl.* **-pe** or **-pes.** = Lenape.

**Len|in|ism** (len′i niz əm), *n.* the political and economic principles of Lenin, developed from Marxism and forming the basis of the communist policies and practices of the Soviet Union. Leninism stresses the belief that, although communism is historically inevitable as Marx thought, it must be guided by a well-disciplined core of "professional revolutionaries." [< Vladimir I. *Lenin* (born Ulyanov), also called Nikolai *Lenin,* 1870-1924, a Russian revolutionary leader, and chief founder of the Soviet Union + *-ism*]

**Len|in|ist** (len′i nist), *n., adj.* **—*n.*** a believer in or supporter of Leninism.
**—*adj.*** believing in or supporting Leninism: *Tossed into discard was the Leninist tenet that while capitalism exists, wars are an inevitability* (Newsweek).

**Len|in|ite** (len′i nīt), *n., adj.* = Leninist.

**Len|in|ol|a|try** (len′in ol′ə trē), *n.* idolization of Lenin. [< *Lenin* + (id)*olatry*]

**le|nis** (lē′nis), *adj., n., pl.* **le|nes** (lē′nēz). *Phonetics.* **—*adj.*** articulated with relatively little muscular tension and force. In English, *b, d, v, z* are

generally lenis in comparison with *p, t, f,* and *s,* which are fortis.
—*n.* a lenis consonant.
[earlier *lene* < Latin *lēnis* smooth, soft]

**le|ni|tion** (li nish′ən), *n. Phonetics.* the gradual lessening of the force with which a consonant is articulated, sometimes leading to change or loss. [< German *Lenition* < Latin *lēnīre* soften]

**len|i|tive** (len′ə tiv), *adj., n.* —*adj.* **1** softening; mitigating. **2** tending to relieve; soothing: *Aspirin is a lenitive medicine.* **3** mildly laxative.
—*n.* **1** anything that soothes or softens; palliative. **2** a soothing medicine or application: *Tranquilizers are lenitives.* **3** a mild laxative.
[< Medieval Latin *lenitivus* < Latin *lēnīre* soften]

**len|i|ty** (len′ə tē), *n., pl.* **-ties. 1** mildness; gentleness; mercifulness; leniency: *His Majesty gave many marks of his great lenity, often ... endeavouring to extenuate your crimes* (Jonathan Swift). **2** an instance of this. [< Middle French *lénité,* learned borrowing from Latin *lēnitās* < *lēnis* mild]

**Len|ni-Len|a|pe** (len′ē len′ə pē, -lə nä′pē), *n., pl.* **-pe** or **-pes.** = Lenape.

**le|no** (lē′nō), *n.* **1** a textile weave in which the warp threads alone intersect and are bound in position by the weft threads; gauze weave. **2** an open-weave cotton gauze used for such items as caps, veils, and curtains. [perhaps alteration of French *linon*]

*__lens__ (lenz), *n., pl.* **lens|es. 1** a curved piece of glass, or something like glass, that will bring closer together or send wider apart the rays of light passing through it. The lens of a camera forms images. The lenses of a telescope make things look larger and nearer. Lenses have two opposite surfaces, either both plane or one plane and one curved, and are used alone or in combination in optical instruments. **2** a combination of two or more of these pieces, especially as used in a camera, microscope, or telescope. **3** the part of the eye that directs light rays upon the retina. The lens is a clear, oval structure behind the iris. **4** a device to focus radiations other than those of light. **5** *Geology.* a layer of uniform sedimentary material that becomes progessively thinner along its edges. [< Latin *lēns, lentis* lentil (which has a biconvex shape)] —**lens′less,** *adj.*

*__lens__
definition 1

**converging lenses:**

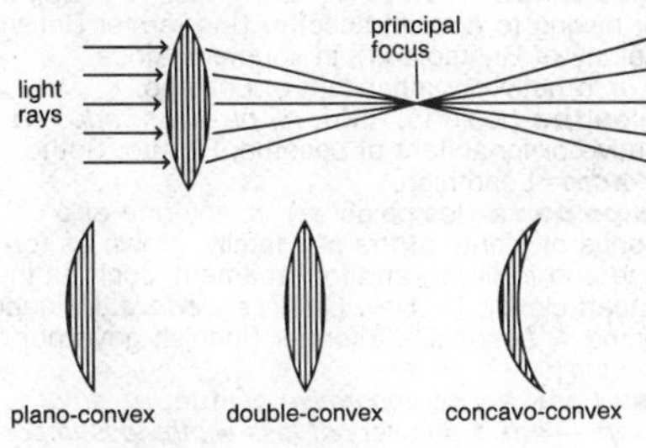


**diverging lenses:**

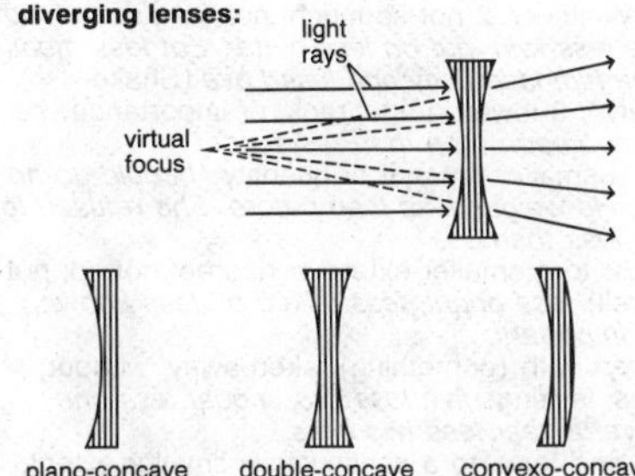


**lensed** (lenzd), *adj.* having a lens or lenses.

**lens hood,** *Photography.* a tube-shaped device with a blackened inside surface, attached to a lens to keep stray light from striking it.

**lens|let** (lenz′lit), *n.* a small lens.

**lens|man** (lenz′mən), *n., pl.* **-men.** *Informal.* a photographer: *amateur lensmen.*

**lens shade,** = lens hood.

**lent** (lent), *v.* the past tense and past participle of **lend**: *I lent you my pencil. He had lent me his knife.*

**Lent** (lent), *n.* **1** the forty weekdays between Ash Wednesday and Easter, observed in many Christian churches as a time for fasting and repenting of sins; Quadragesima. **2** *Obsolete.* (in the Middle Ages) any season of religious fasting. [Old English *lencten* spring < *lang* long[1] (probably because of its lengthening days)]

**len|ta|men|te** (len′tə men′tā), *adv. Music.* slowly (used as a direction). [< Italian *lentamente* < *lento* lento]

**len|tan|do** (len tän′dō), *adj. Music.* becoming slower (used as a direction). Also, **slentando.** [< Italian *lentando* (literally) present participle of *lentare* slow down, ultimately < Latin *lentus* slow]

**Lent|en** or **lent|en** (len′tən), *adj.* **1** of Lent; during Lent; suitable for Lent. **2** such as may be used in Lent; meager; plain; dismal or somber. [Old English *lencten;* see etym. under **Lent**]

**Lenten rose,** a perennial herb of the crowfoot family, native to Asia Minor, with showy green to purple flowers that bloom before spring.

**len|tic** (len′tik), *adj. Ecology.* of or living in standing or stagnant water, such as ponds and swamps (contrasted with *lotic*). [< Latin *lentus* slow + English *-ic*]

**len|ti|cel** (len′tə sel′), *n. Botany.* a usually lens-shaped body of cells formed in the corky layer of bark, which serves as a pore for the exchange of gases between the plant and the atmosphere. [< French *lenticelle,* or New Latin *lenticella* (diminutive) < Latin *lēns, lentis* lentil (because of its shape)]

**len|ti|cel|late** (len′tə sel′āt), *adj.* producing lenticels.

**len|tic|u|lar** (len tik′yə lər), *adj.* **1** having the form of a lens, especially a double-convex lens, as some seeds do; convexo-convex; biconvex. **2** resembling a lentil or double-convex lens in size or form. **3** of or having to do with a lens, especially that of the eye. [< Latin *lenticulāris* < Latin *lenticula* (diminutive) < *lēns, lentis* lentil] —**len|tic′u|lar|ly,** *adv.*

**lenticular cloud,** a stationary cloud shaped like a lens, formed especially above hills and mountains.

**lenticular nucleus,** *Anatomy.* the lower gray nucleus in the corpus striatum at the base of the brain.

**len|tic|u|late** (len tik′yə lāt), *v.t.,* **-lat|ed, -lat|ing.** to furnish (film) with lenticules.

**len|ti|cule** (len′tə kyül), *n.* one of a large number of cylindrical embossings on black-and-white film that act as lenses to reproduce color images under certain kinds of projection, especially for television. [< Latin *lenticula;* see etym. under **lenticular**]

**len|tig|i|nous** (len tij′ə nəs), *adj. Medicine.* freckled.

**len|ti|go** (len tī′gō), *n., pl.* **-tig|i|nes** (-tij′ə nēz). *Medicine.* **1** a freckle. **2** a freckly condition. [< Latin *lentīgo, -inis* freckle, round red spot < *lēns, lentis* lentil]

*__len|til__ (len′təl), *n.* **1** an annual plant having pods that contain small, flat seeds. It belongs to the pea family and grows mostly in southern Europe, Egypt, Asia, and the United States. **2** a vegetable much like a bean; the seed of the lentil. Lentils are cooked like peas and are often eaten in soup. [< Old French *lentille* < Vulgar Latin *lentīcula* < Latin *lenticula* (diminutive) < *lēns, lentis* lentil]

*__lentil__
definition 1

lentil pods

**len|tis|cus** (len tis′kəs), *n., pl.* **-tis|cus|es, -tis|ci** (-tis′ī). the mastic tree. [< Latin *lentiscus*]

**len|tis|si|mo** (len tis′ə mō), *adj., adv. Music.*
—*adj.* very slow (used as a direction).
—*adv.* very slowly.
[< Italian *lentissimo,* superlative of *lento* lento]

**len|to** (len′tō), *adj., adv. Music.* —*adj.* slow (used as a direction).
—*adv.* slowly.
[< Italian *lento* slow < Latin *lentus* slow, lasting, flexible]

**len|toid** (len′toid), *adj.* lens-shaped. [< Latin *lēns, lentis* (see etym. under **lens**) + English *-oid*]

**l'en|voi** or **l'en|voy** (len′voi, len voi′), *n.* = envoy[2]. [< Middle French *l'envoi* < *le* the + *envoi* a sending]

**Lenz's law** (len′zəz, lent′səz), *Physics.* the law that an induced electric current creates a magnetic field that opposes the action of the force that produces the current. [< Heinrich F. E. *Lenz,* a German physicist of the 1800's, who formulated the law]

**Le|o** (lē′ō), *n. genitive* (def. 1) **Le|o|nis. 1** a northern constellation between Cancer and Virgo, seen by ancient astronomers as having the rough outline of a lion. **2** the fifth sign of the zodiac; Lion. The sun enters Leo about July 22. **3** a person born under the sign of Leo. [< Latin *Leō, -ōnis* (literally) the lion < Greek *léōn, léontos*]

**Leo Minor,** *genitive* **Le|o|nis Mi|no|ris.** a northern constellation south of Ursa Major.

**Le|o|nar|desque** (lē′ə när desk′), *adj.* in or resembling the style of Leonardo da Vinci (1452-1519).

**le|o|ne** (lē ō′nē), *n.* the unit of money of Sierra Leone, a note equal to 100 Sierra Leone cents.

**Le|o|nid** (lē′ə nid), *n., pl.* **Le|o|nids, Le|on|i|des** (li on′ə dēz). one of a shower of meteors occurring about November 14. The Leonids seem to radiate from the constellation Leo.

**le|o|nine** (lē′ə nīn), *adj.* of a lion; like a lion: *The dog's tawny color and heavy coat gave him an almost leonine appearance.* [< Latin *leōnīnus* < *leō, -ōnis* lion; see etym. under **Leo**]

**Le|o|nine** (lē′ə nīn), *adj.* of or having to do with some person named Leo, Leonius, or Leoninus.

**leonine partnership,** a partnership in which one partner has all the profits and none of the losses.

**Le|o|nines** (lē′ə nīnz), *n.pl.* = Leonine verse.

**Leonine verse,** a kind of Latin verse consisting of hexameters or alternate hexameters and pentameters, in which the last word of the line rhymes with the word immediately preceding the middle caesura.

**Le|o|nis** (lē ō′nis), *n.* genitive of **Leo** (the constellation).

**Leonis Mi|no|ris** (mi nôr′is, -nōr′-), genitive of **Leo Minor.**

**Le|on strain** (lē′on), one of the three known types of virus causing polio. The other two are the Brunhilde and Lansing strains. [< *Leon,* the name of a young victim of the disease]

**le|on|ti|a|sis** (lē′on tī′ə sis), *n., pl.* **-ses** (-sēz). *Medicine.* a form of leprosy in which the face becomes bloated and wrinkled, thus appearing more or less leonine. [< Greek *léōn, léontos* lion + English *-iasis*]

*__leop|ard__ (lep′ərd), *n.* **1** a large, fierce animal of Africa and Asia, usually having a dull-yellowish fur spotted with black. It is a mammal of the cat family. Some leopards are black and may be called panthers. See the picture below on the following page. **2** any one of various animals related to the leopard, such as the jaguar or American leopard, the cheetah or hunting leopard, and the ounce or snow leopard. **3** the fur of any of these leopards. **4** *Heraldry.* a lion shown walking with the dexter front paw raised and looking directly at the spectator, as in the royal arms of England.
**the leopard cannot change its spots,** it is impossible to change inborn traits or inveterate habits (in allusion to Jeremiah 13:23): *[They] have maintained in effect that the leopard cannot change its spots and that the new Germany was really no different from the old* (New York Times).
[< Old French *leupart, lebard,* learned borrowing from Late Latin *leopardus* < Greek *leópardos* < *léōn* lion + *párdos* leopard, pard[1]]

**leopard cat, 1** a wild, spotted cat of India and the Malay Archipelago. **2** = ocelot.

**leop|ard|ess** (lep′ər dis), *n.* a female leopard.

**leopard frog,** a spotted frog common in North America and found as far south as Panama; grass frog. See picture under **frog**[1].

**leopard lily, 1** a very tall lily with reddish-orange flowers spotted with purple, found along the west coast of the United States. **2** a spotted yellow and red lily of South Africa.

**leopard man,** any one of a group of fanatic or ritual murderers of western Africa who mutilate their victims as if by a leopard's claws.

**leop|ard's-bane** (lep′ərdz bān′), *n.* a composite herb with yellow flowers; doronicum.

**leopard seal,** = sea leopard.

**leopard shark, 1** a small, light-colored shark with dark spots, common along the coast of California. **2** = tiger shark.

**le|o|tard** (lē′ə tärd), *n.* **1** a tight-fitting, one-piece garment, with or without sleeves, worn by dancers and acrobats. **2** Also, **leotards.** = tights. [< French *léotard* < Jules *Léotard,* a French aerialist of the 1800's]

**Lep|cha** (lep′chə), *n., pl.* **-cha** or **-chas.** a member of an aboriginal people of Mongoloid extraction living in Sikkim, a small state in the Himalayas.

**lep|er** (lep′ər), *n.* a person who has leprosy. [Middle English *lepre* leprosy < Old French, learned borrowing from Late Latin *leprae,* plural < Latin *lepra* < Greek *lépra* < *lépein* to peel, scale off]

**leper house,** a hospital or asylum for lepers.

**le|pid|o|lite** (lə pid′ə līt, lep′ə də-), *n.* a mineral, a variety of mica containing lithium, commonly occurring in lilac, rose-colored, or grayish-white scaly masses. [< Greek *lepis, -idos* scale[1] + English *-lite*]

**Pronunciation Key:** hat, āge, cãre, fär; let, ēqual, tėrm; it, īce; hot, ōpen, ôrder; **oi**l, **ou**t; cup, půt, rüle; **ch**ild; lo**ng**; **th**in; **ŦH**en; **zh**, measure; **ə** represents **a** in about, **e** in taken, **i** in pencil, **o** in lemon, **u** in circus.

**lep|i|dop|ter** (lep′ə dop′tər), *n.* a lepidopterous insect.

**lep|i|dop|ter|al** (lep′ə dop′tər əl), *adj.* = lepidopterous.

**lep|i|dop|ter|an** (lep′ə dop′tər ən), *adj., n.* —*adj.* = lepidopterous. —*n.* a lepidopterous insect.

**lep|i|dop|ter|ist** (lep′ə dop′tər ist), *n.* an expert on, or collector of, moths and butterflies.

**lep|i|dop|ter|o|log|i|cal** (lep′ə dop′tər ə loj′ə kəl), *adj.* of or having to do with the scientific study or collection of moths and butterflies. —**lep′i|dop′ter|o|log′i|cal|ly,** *adv.*

**lep|i|dop|ter|ol|o|gy** (lep′ə dop′tə rol′ə jē), *n.* the scientific study of moths and butterflies.

**lep|i|dop|ter|on** (lep′ə dop′tər on), *n., pl.* **-ter|a** (-tər ə). = lepidopter.

**lep|i|dop|ter|ous** (lep′ə dop′tər əs), *adj.* belonging to the large order of insects including butterflies and moths. The larvae are wormlike and are called caterpillars. The adults have four broad, membranous wings more or less covered with small, sometimes colorful, overlapping scales, and a coiled proboscis for sucking. [< New Latin *Lepidoptera* the order name (< Greek *lepís, -idos* a scale[1] + *pterón* wing, feather) + English *-ous*]

**lep|i|dop|ter|y** (lep′ə dop′tər ē), *n.* the collection of moths and butterflies; the art or practice of a lepidopterist.

**lep|i|do|si|ren** (lep′ə dō sī′rən), *n.* any one of various eellike lungfishes of South American swamps. [< Greek *lepís, -ídos* a scale[1] + English *siren*]

**lep|i|dote** (lep′ə dōt), *adj. Botany.* covered with scurfy scales; leprose. [< New Latin *lepidotus* < Greek *lepidōtós* < *lepís, -ídos* a scale[1] < *lépein* to peel]

**lep|o|rid** (lep′ər id), *n.* any one of the group of mammals which consists of the rabbits and hares. [< New Latin *Leporidae* the family name < Latin *lepus, -oris* hare]

**lep|o|rine** (lep′ə rīn, -ər in), *adj.* of or like a hare. [< Latin *leporīnus* < *lepus, -oris* hare]

**Lep|o|ris** (lep′ər is), *n.* genitive of **Lepus.**

**lep|o|spon|dyl** (lep′ə spon′dəl), *n.* any one of an order of extinct amphibians of the Paleozoic, whose backbone consisted of a thin shell of bone surrounding a rodlike band of cells. [< New Latin *Lepospondyli* the name of the order < Greek *lepís, -idos* a scale[1] + *spóndylos* vertebra]

**lep|re|chaun** (lep′rə kôn), *n. Irish Legend.* an elf resembling a little old man, believed to possess hidden gold and who can be made to reveal it if he is caught: *But now all the leprechauns and all the four-leafed clover could not stop the destruction wrought by the English* (London Times). [< Irish *lupracan*]

**lep|rol|o|gist** (lep rol′ə jist), *n.* an expert in leprous diseases.

**lep|rol|o|gy** (lep rol′ə jē), *n.* the scientific study of leprosy.

**lep|ro|sar|i|um** (lep′rə sãr′ē əm), *n., pl.* **-sar|i|ums, -sar|i|a** (-sãr′ē ə). **1** a hospital or institution for the care and treatment of lepers: *The Salvation Army maintains shelters for men, women, and children, hospitals, military canteens, leprosaria, and schools* (New York Times). **2** a leper colony. [< Medieval Latin *leprosarium* < Late Latin *leprōsus;* see etym. under **leprous**]

**lep|rose** (lep′rōs), *adj. Botany.* having a scaly or scurfy appearance, as certain lichens in which the thallus adheres to trees or stones like a scurf; lepidote. [< Late Latin *leprōsus* < Latin *lepra;* see etym. under **leper**]

**lep|ro|sy** (lep′rə sē), *n., pl.* **-sies. 1** a mildly infectious disease caused by certain rod-shaped bacteria that develop open sores and white, scaly scabs; Hansen's disease. Leprosy attacks the skin and nerves, causing weakening and wasting of muscles, and may lead to tuberculosis or other diseases. If not treated, the injury to the nerves results in loss of feeling, paralysis, and deformity. **2** *Figurative.* a wasting or decadent condition, as of the mind or spirit: ... *the moral leprosy of the world we live in* (Emanuel Litvinoff). [perhaps < *leprous,* or noun use of Medieval Latin *leprosius,* Late Latin *leprōsus* leprous]

**lep|rot|ic** (le prot′ik), *adj.* = leprous.

**lep|rous** (lep′rəs), *adj.* **1** having leprosy: *a leprous person.* **2** of or like leprosy: *white, leprous scales.* **3** scaly or scurfy: *One old leprous screen of faded Indian leather* (Dickens). **4** causing leprosy. **5** *Botany.* leprose. [< Old French *leprous,* learned borrowing from Late Latin *leprōsus* < Latin *lepra* leprosy; see etym. under **leper**] —**lep′rous|ly,** *adv.* —**lep′rous|ness,** *n.*

**lep|to|ceph|a|lus** (lep′tə sef′ə ləs), *n., pl.* **-li** (-lī). the narrow-headed, transparent larva of various freshwater eels. [< New Latin *leptocephalus* < Greek *leptós* thin + *kephalḗ* head]

**lep|to|dac|tyl** (lep′tə dak′təl), *adj.* (of a bird) having slender toes. [< Greek *leptós* thin + *dáktylos* toe]

**lep|to|dac|ty|lous** (lep′tə dak′tə ləs), *adj.* = leptodactyl.

**lep|ton** (lep′ton), *n., pl.* **-tons** *for 1;* **-ta** (-tə) *for 2.* **1a** any one of a class of light elementary particles that includes the neutrino, electron, and mumesons. Leptons interact weakly with other particles. **b** any weakly interacting particle, regardless of mass: *a hypothetical group of heavy leptons.* **2** a unit of money in modern Greece, a coin worth 1/100 of a drachma. [< Greek *leptón* (*nómisma*) small (coin), neuter of *leptós* thin]

**lep|ton|ic** (lep ton′ik), *adj.* of or having to do with leptons.

**lep|tor|rhine** (lep′tər in), *adj. Anthropology.* having a long, narrow nose. [< Greek *leptós* thin + *rhīs, rhīnós* nose]

**lep|to|some** (lep′tə sōm), *n., adj.* —*n.* a person having a tall and spare build; an ectomorph.
—*adj.* tall and spare; asthenic; ectomorphic: *A strain in the living population of East Africa ... is most characterized by great attenuation: enormous stature, spindly legs, leptosome proportions, and delicate lines throughout* (Alfred L. Kroeber). [< Greek *leptós* thin + *sôma* body]

**lep|to|spi|ral** (lep′tə spī′rəl), *adj.* of or like leptospires: *a leptospiral organism.*

**lep|to|spire** (lep′tə spīr), *n.* the spirochete that causes leptospirosis. [< New Latin *Leptospira;* see etym. under **leptospirosis**]

**lep|to|spi|ro|sis** (lep′tō spī rō′sis), *n.* an often fatal disease of livestock, dogs, rats, and other animals, that can be transmitted to man. It is caused by a spirochete and takes the form of a fever and, usually, infectious jaundice. [< New Latin *Leptospira* the genus of spirochetes that cause the disease (< Greek *leptós* thin + *speîra* coil) + English *-osis*]

**lep|to|tene** (lep′tə tēn), *n. Biology.* the stage of the prophase of meiosis just before the paired chromosomes unite. The chromosomes have the form of separate thin threads. [< Greek *leptós* thin + *tainiā́* band]

**lep|tus** (lep′təs), *n., pl.* **-tus|es, -ti** (-tī). any one of certain mites during the first larval stage when they have six legs. [< New Latin *Leptus* the genus name < Greek *leptós* thin, small]

**Le|pus** (lē′pəs), *n., genitive* **Lep|o|ris.** a southern constellation south of Orion. [< Latin *Lepus, -oris* (originally) hare]

**Ler|nae|an** (lėr nē′ən), *adj. Greek Mythology.* of Lake Lerna and the marshy district near Argos, Greece, the abode of the Hydra.

**le roi est mort, vive le roi!** (lə rwȧ′ e môr′ vēv′ lə rwȧ′), *French.* the king is dead, long live the king!

**le roi le veut** (lə rwȧ′ lə vœ′), *French.* the king wills it.

**LES** (no periods), *Aeronautics.* launch escape system.

**Les|bi|an** (lez′bē ən), *n., adj.* —*n.* **1** Also, **lesbian. 1** a homosexual woman. **2** a native or inhabitant of the Greek island of Lesbos.
—*adj.* **1** Also, **lesbian.** having to do with homosexuality in women. **2** of or having to do with the island of Lesbos. **3** = erotic.
[< *Lesbos* + *-ian* (because of the reputed homosexuality of the inhabitants there)]

**Les|bi|an|ism** or **les|bi|an|ism** (lez′bē ə niz′əm), *n.* homosexual relations between women.

**Lesch-Ny|han syndrome** (lesh′nī′hən), a genetic disorder of male children characterized by mental retardation and involuntary writhing motions. [< M. *Lesch,* born 1939, and W. L. *Nyhan,* born 1926, American pediatricians, who first described it in 1964]

**lèse-ma|jes|té** (lez′mȧ zhes tā′), *n. French.* lese-majesty.

**lese-maj|es|ty** (lēz′maj′ə stē), *n.,* or **lese majesty,** any crime or offense against the sovereign power in a state; high treason. [< Middle French *lèse-majesté,* learned borrowing from Latin (*crīmen*) *laesae majestātis* (crime) of insulted sovereignty; *laesa,* feminine past participle of *laedere* to damage; *majestās* majesty]

**le|sion** (lē′zhən), *n.* **1** an injury; hurt. **2** an abnormal change in the structure of an organ or body tissue, caused by disease or injury. [< Latin *laesiō, -ōnis* injury < *laedere* to strike, damage]

**le|sioned** (lē′zhənd), *adj.* having a lesion; injured: *lesioned tissue, a lesioned area.*

**Le|so|than** (lə sō′tən, -thən), *adj., n.* = Lesothian.

**Le|so|thi|an** (lə sō′tē ən, -thē-), *adj., n.* —*adj.* of or having to do with Lesotho (the former British colony of Basutoland), in southern Africa.
—*n.* a native or inhabitant of Lesotho.

**Le|so|tho** (lə sō′tō, -thō), *n., pl.* **-thos,** *adj.* —*n.* a native or inhabitant of Lesotho; Basuto; Sotho.
—*adj.* = Lesothian.

**les|pe|de|za** (les′pə dē′zə), *n.* any one of a genus of plants of the pea family, grown as forage and fertilizer, and for ornament, such as the Japan clover. [< New Latin *Lespedeza* the genus name < *Lespedez,* a former Spanish governor of Florida]

**less** (les), *adj., comparative of* **little,** *n., adv., prep.* —*adj.* **1** smaller: *of less width, less importance. Never be thy shadow less* (John Greenleaf Whittier). **2** not so much; not so much of: *to have less rain, put on less butter. Eat less meat. I owe him little Duty and less Love* (Shakespeare). **3** lower in age, rank, or importance: *no less a person than the President.*
—*n.* a smaller amount or quantity: *I could do no less. He weighs less than before. She refused to take less than $5.*
—*adv.* to a smaller extent or degree; not so; not so well: *less bright, less talked of, less known, less important.*
—*prep.* with (something) taken away; without; minus; lacking: *five less two, a coat less one sleeve, a year less two days.*
**less and less,** to a continuously smaller extent; progressively less: *Our colleagues are less and less convinced, though, that any such factors ... really do exist* (Claude Lévi-Strauss).
**none the less,** nevertheless: *Though Michelet's way was as alien as possible from their ways, his work remained valid none the less* (Edmund Wilson).
**the less, a** something smaller (of two things compared): *Thou ... wouldst ... teach me how To name the bigger light, and how the less, That burn by day and night* (Shakespeare). **b** he who is or they who are less, especially less important: *The less is blessed of the better* (Hebrews 7:7).
[Old English *lǣssa,* adjective; *lǣs,* adverb]
—**less′ness,** *n.*

► **less, lesser.** Both are used as comparatives (of *little*), *less* more usually referring to size or quantity: *less time, less food; lesser,* a formal word, referring to value or importance: *a lesser writer.*

***leopard**
definitions 1, 2

▶ See **fewer** for another usage note.
**-less**, *suffix forming adjectives.* **1** (*added to nouns*) without a ___; that has no ___: *Homeless = without a home.*
**2** (*added to verbs*) that does not ___: *Tireless = that does not tire. Ceaseless = that does not cease.*
**3** (*added to verbs*) that cannot be ___ed: *Countless = that cannot be counted.*
[Old English *-lēas* < *lēas* free from, without]
**les|see** (le sē′), *n.* a person to whom a lease is granted; a tenant under a lease.
**les|see|ship** (le sē′ship), *n.* the condition or position of a lessee.
**less|en** (les′ən), *v.i.* to grow less or apparently less; diminish: *The fever lessened during the night.* — ***v.t.*** **1** to make less, especially in size; decrease; shrink. **2** to represent as less; minimize; belittle: *to lessen the achievements of a rival.*
**less|er** (les′ər), *adj.* **1** smaller; less: *I have seen the cuckoo chased by lesser fowl* (Tennyson). **2** less important: *Both laziness and lying are wrong, but the first is clearly the lesser of the two evils.*
▶ See **less** for usage note.
**lesser Bairam**, a Moslem festival lasting three days that celebrates the breaking of the fast of Ramadan; Lesser Festival; Little Bairam.
**Lesser Bear**, = Ursa Minor.
**lesser Canada goose**, a goose weighing about five pounds, which nests from Alaska to Hudson Bay and winters in Washington, California, and northern Mexico.
**lesser celandine**, = celandine (def. 2).
**Lesser Dog**, = Canis Minor.
**Lesser Festival**, = lesser Bairam.
**less|er-known** (les′ər nōn′), *adj.* very little known; quite unfamiliar: *His book ... brings alive lesser-known atomic scientists and places them in perspective* (Time).
**Lesser Lion**, = Leo Minor.
**lesser omentum**, a fold of the peritoneum between the stomach and the liver.
**lesser panda**, a slender, reddish-brown mammal of the Himalayas, related to and resembling the raccoon; Himalayan raccoon; panda.
**lesser prairie chicken**, a variety of prairie chicken having pale plumage, found from Kansas south to western central Texas.
**lesser scaup duck**, a freshwater diving duck found especially along the lakes and coasts of North America. The males have heads that give off a purplish luster.
**lesser yellowlegs**, a shore bird related to the sandpiper, which breeds in Canada and Alaska, having a length of about 11 inches and similar in appearance to the greater yellowlegs.
**les|son** (les′ən), *n., v.* — ***n.*** **1** something to be learned, taught, or studied: *Children study many different lessons in school.* **2** a unit of teaching or learning; what is to be studied or taught at one time: *to give a music lesson, to prepare a French lesson. Tomorrow we take the tenth lesson.* **3** an instructive experience serving to encourage or warn: *The accident taught me a lesson: always look before you leap. On my heart Deeply hath sunk the lesson thou has given* (William Cullen Bryant). **4** a selection from the Bible or other sacred writing, read as part of a church service. **5** *Figurative.* a rebuke or punishment intended to prevent repetition of an offense; lecture: *The judge read the speeding driver a stiff lesson.* **SYN**: reprimand, admonition.
— ***v.t.*** **1** to give a lesson or lessons to; instruct; teach: *Well hast thou lesson'd us; this shall we do* (Shakespeare). **2** *Figurative.* to rebuke; admonish. **SYN**: discipline.
[< Old French *leçon* < Latin *lēctiō, -ōnis* a reading < *legere* read. See etym. of doublet **lection**.]
**les|sor** (les′ôr, le sôr′), *n.* a person who grants a lease; a person who leases property to another.
**lest** (lest), *conj.* **1** for fear that: *Be careful lest you fall from that tree.* **2** that (after words meaning fear or danger): *I was afraid lest he should come too late to save us.* [Old English (*thȳ*) *lǣs the* (literally) whereby less that]
**Les|tri|go|ni|an** (les′trə gō′nē ən), *n.* = Laestrygonian.
**le style, c'est l'homme** (lə stēl′, se lôm′), *French.* the style is the man (shows what he really is).
**let**[1] (let), *v.,* **let, let|ting,** *n.* — ***v.t.*** **1** to not stop from doing or having something; allow; permit: *Let the dog have a bone. She plumes her feathers, and lets grow her wings* (Milton). **2** to allow to pass, go, or come: *They let the visitor on board the ship.* **3** to allow to run out; allow (something) to escape: *Doctors used to let blood from people to lessen a fever.* **4a** to rent; hire out: *to let a boat by the hour. The woman lets rooms to college students.* **b** to give out (a job) by contract: *to let work to a builder. In connection with the letting of private contracts for demolition of the Third Avenue Elevated Line ...* (New York Times). **5** *Let* is used in giving suggestions or giving commands, as an auxiliary verb: *"Let's go home" means "I suggest that we go home." Let every man do his duty.* **6** to suppose; assume: *Let the two lines be parallel.* **7** *Obsolete.* to quit; abandon; forsake.
— ***v.i.*** to be rented; be hired out: *This room lets for $80 a month.*
— ***n.*** *British.* a letting for hire or rent: *The sign said "House For Let."*
**let alone.** See under **alone**.
**let be.** See under **be**.
**let down, a** to lower: *He let the box down from the roof.* **b** to slow up: *As her interest wore off, she began to let down.* **c** to disappoint: *Don't let us down today; we're counting on you to win. Losing the job was bad enough, but even worse was the feeling that I had let my family down.* **d** to humiliate: *Nothing in the world lets down a character more than that wrong turn* (Lord Chesterfield).
**let go.** See under **go**[1].
**let in,** to permit to enter; admit: *Let in some fresh air. I was let in at the back gate of a lovely house* (Sir Richard Steele).
**let in for,** to open the way to; cause (trouble, unpleasantness, or the like): *He let his friends in for a lot of questioning when he left town so suddenly.*
**let in on,** to share a confidence or secret with: *Once a strong voice in favor of tightly guarding U.S. scientific secrets, physicist Edward Teller ... now thinks everyone should be let in on most classified information* (Time).
**let know.** See under **know**.
**let loose,** to set free; release; let go: *... like so many bedlamites and demoniacs let loose* (Washington Irving). *He was let loose among the woods as soon as he was able to ride on horseback* (Joseph Addison).
**let off, a** to permit to go free; excuse from punishment, service, or other obligation: *He was let off with a warning to do better in the future. I will let Clavering off from that bargain* (Thackeray). **b** to discharge; allow to get off: *This train stops to let off passengers on signal.* **c** to fire; explode: *On 1 August the Americans let off a hydrogen bomb* (New Scientist).
**let on,** *Informal.* **a** to allow to be known; reveal one's knowledge of: *He didn't let on his surprise at the news. The kids know too, but they never let on* (Time). **b** to make believe; pretend: *He let on that he did not see me.*
**let out, a** to permit to go out or escape; set free; release: *They let me out of the hospital too soon.* **b** to make larger or longer: *Let out the hem on this skirt.* **c** to rent: *Has the room been let out yet?* **d** *Informal.* to dismiss or be dismissed: *When does your class let out?* **e** to make known; disclose; divulge: *to let out a secret.*
**let up,** *Informal.* to stop or pause: *They refused to let up in the fight. We can go out when the storm lets up.*
**let well enough alone,** to be satisfied with existing conditions and not try to make them better or different: *He is the kind of worker who cannot leave well enough alone but must do each job perfectly.*
[Old English *lǣtan*]
▶ **let, leave.** A common substandard idiom is the use of *leave* in the sense of "allow," where formal and informal English use *let. Examples: Leave us go. Leave him be. Leave us not fight. Let* should be used in each of these sentences.
**let**[2] (let), *n., v.,* **let|ted** or **let, let|ting.** — ***n.*** **1** an interference with the ball in tennis and similar games, especially a serve that hits the net. The ball or point must be played over again. **2a** *Archaic.* prevention; hindrance; stoppage; obstruction. **b** something that hinders; an impediment: *That I may know the let, why gentle Peace Should not expel these inconveniences* (Shakespeare).
— ***v.t.*** *Archaic.* to stand in the way of; prevent; hinder; obstruct: *Mine ancient wound is hardly whole, And lets me from the saddle* (Tennyson).
**without let or hindrance,** with nothing to prevent, hinder, or obstruct: *He may hunt for his own amusement, without let or hindrance, throughout the year until September* (Atlantic).
[Old English *lettan* hinder < *lǣt* late]
**-let,** *suffix added to nouns to form other nouns.*
**1** little ___: *Booklet = a little book.*
**2** thing worn as a band on ___: *Anklet = a band worn around the ankle.*
**3** other meanings, as in *couplet, gauntlet, ringlet.*
[< Old French *-elet* < *-el* (< Latin *-ellus,* diminutive suffix, or < Latin *-ale* -al[1]) + *-et* -et]
**l'é|tat, c'est moi** (lā tȧ′ se mwȧ′), *French.* the state, it is I; I am the state (attributed to Louis XIV of France).
**letch** (lech), *n.* a yen; yearning; desire: *He develops a letch for an attractive Circassian lady* (New Yorker). [origin uncertain, perhaps a back formation from *lecher*]
**let|down** (let′doun′), *n., adj.* — ***n.*** **1** a slowing up: *Middle age often brings a letdown in vitality. The talked about letdown in copper buying has not yet appeared* (Wall Street Journal). **2** a disappointment: *Losing the contest was a big letdown for him.* **3** humiliation. **4** the approach of an aircraft toward a landing.
— ***adj.*** characterized by depression or dejection: *a letdown sensation.*
**Let|ga|li** (let gä′lē), *n.pl.* a people who occupied the eastern half of present-day Latvia before A.D. 1200, and of whom the Letts are descendants.
**le|thal** (lē′thəl), *adj., n.* — ***adj.*** causing death; deadly; mortal: *lethal weapons, a lethal dose of a drug.* **SYN**: fatal.
— ***n.*** a lethal thing, especially a lethal factor or gene.
[< Latin *lēthālis* < *lētum* death] — **le′thal|ly,** *adv.*
**lethal chamber, 1** a chamber in which animals are put painlessly to death, as with deadly gases. **2** the death chamber, as used in legal executions of criminals by means of gas.
**lethal factor** or **gene,** *Biology.* any gene, either dominant or recessive, which results in the premature death of the organism bearing it.
**le|thal|i|ty** (li thal′ə tē), *n.* the quality of being lethal; ability to cause death; deadliness: *Means may be found to increase or decrease the lethality of the rays* (Science News Letter).
**le|thar|gic** (lə thär′jik), *adj.* **1** unnaturally drowsy; sluggish; dull: *A hot, humid day makes most people feel lethargic.* **SYN**: apathetic. **2** producing lethargy. — **le|thar′gi|cal|ly,** *adv.*
**lethargic encephalitis,** a form of inflammation of the brain believed to be caused by a virus, characterized by extreme drowsiness or lethargy, sometimes followed by stupor or paralysis; sleeping sickness; encephalitis lethargica.
**leth|ar|gy** (leth′ər jē), *n., pl.* **-gies. 1** drowsy dullness; lack of energy; sluggish inactivity: *to rouse the nation from its lethargy, to sink into the lethargy of indifference.* **SYN**: torpor, apathy, stupor. **2** *Medicine.* a state of prolonged unconsciousness resembling deep sleep, from which the person can be roused but immediately loses consciousness again. [< Late Latin *lēthargia* < Greek *lēthargiā* < *lēthargos* forgetful < *lēthē* forgetfulness (see etym. under **Lethe**) + *argós* undone, unmade < *an* not + *érgon* work]
**Le|the** (lē′thē), *n.* **1** *Greek Mythology.* a river in Hades. Drinking its water caused forgetfulness of the past. **2** *Figurative.* forgetfulness; oblivion: *Till that the conquering wine hath steeped our sense In soft and delicate Lethe* (Shakespeare). [< Latin *Lēthē* < Greek *lēthē* oblivion < *lanthanésthai* escape notice, forget]
**Le|the|an** (li thē′ən), *adj.* **1** having to do with Lethe or its water. **2** causing forgetfulness: *daily labour's dull, Lethaean spring* (Matthew Arnold).
**le|thif|er|ous** (li thif′ər əs), *adj.* that causes or results in death; deadly: *lethiferous diseases.* [< Latin *lethifer* (< *lētum* death + *ferre* to carry, bring) + English *-ous*]
**Le|to** (lē′tō), *n. Greek Mythology.* the mother of Apollo and Artemis by Zeus. The Romans called her Latona.
**let-off** (let′ôf′, -of′), *n.* a letting off; release; exemption: *A light let-off that will be for the murderer* (Punch).
**l'é|toile du nord** (lā twäl′ dʏ nôr′), *French.* the star of the north (Minnesota state motto).
**let-out** (let′out′), *n. British.* a means of escape or release; loophole: *This terminology gives a useful let-out in the event of a conflict* (Manchester Guardian Weekly).
**le tout en|sem|ble** (lə tü tän sän′blə), *French.* everything considered together.
**let's** (lets), let us.
**Lett** (let), *n.* **1** a member of a group of people living in Latvia, Lithuania, Estonia, and Germany, related to the Lithuanians. **2** their language; Lettish.
**let|ta|ble** (let′ə bəl), *adj.* that can be let or leased: *lettable floor space* (London Times).
**let|ter**[1] (let′ər), *n., v.* — ***n.*** **1** a mark or sign that stands for any one of the sounds that make up words. There are 26 letters in our alphabet. **2** a written or printed message: *He told me about his vacation in a letter. Put a stamp on that letter. I'd teach them to ... write their own letters, and read letters that are written to them* (Harriet Beecher Stowe). **3** the exact wording; actual terms; literal

---

**Pronunciation Key:** hat, āge, cãre, fär; let, ēqual, tėrm; it, īce; hot, ōpen, ôrder; **oi**l, **ou**t; cup, pu̇t, rüle; **ch**ild; lo**ng**; **th**in; **ᴛʜ**en; **zh**, measure; **ə** represents **a** in about, **e** in taken, **i** in pencil, **o** in lemon, **u** in circus.

meaning, as of a statement: *He kept the letter of the law but not the spirit.* **4** *Printing.* **a** a block of type bearing a letter; a type. **b** types; type. **c** a particular style of type. **5** the initial of a school, college, or other institution given as an award or trophy to members of a sports team. It is usually made of cloth and sewn to a garment. *He is a 3-letter man; he has letters in football, basketball, and track.* **6** a size of paper. **7** an official document granting some right or privilege: *a letter of attorney.*
–***v.t.*** **1** to mark with letters: *Letter your answers from A through H.* **2** to inscribe (something) in letters: *Please letter a new sign.*
–***v.i.*** to make letters (on).
**letters, a** literature; belles-lettres: *men of letters. He has devoted his life to philosophy and letters. "The Revival of Letters" was the old term for the Renaissance.* **b** knowledge of literature; literary culture; learning: *Deign on the passing world to turn thine eyes, And pause awhile from letters to be wise* (Samuel Johnson). **c** the profession of an author: *Letters kept pace with art* (William H. Prescott).
**to the letter,** just as one has been told; very exactly: *I carried out your orders to the letter.*
[< Old French *lettre* < Latin *littera*] –**let′ter|er,** *n.* –**let′ter|less,** *adj.*
–***Syn.*** *n.* **2 Letter, epistle** mean a written message. **Letter,** the general word, applies to any written, typed, or printed message, either personal, business, or official: *Please mail this letter for me.* **Epistle,** chiefly literary, applies to a long letter written in formal or elegant language, intended to teach or advise: *This year we are studying the epistles of some famous poets. Such Epistles of the New Testament as Corinthians and Colossians are Saint Paul's letters of advice to newly founded Christian churches.*

**let|ter**[2] (let′ər), *n.* a person who lets, especially a person who rents something. [< *let*[1] + *-er*[1]]

**letter board,** *Printing.* a board to arrange type on.

**letter bomb,** an envelope containing an explosive set to detonate on opening, used especially by terrorists: *All the letter bombs received in the London and Paris embassies had been posted in Amsterdam* (London Times).

**letter book,** a book in which letters are filed, or in which copies of letters are kept for reference.

**letter box, 1** a box in which letters are mailed or delivered; mailbox. **2** a box in which letters are kept.

**letter carrier,** a person who collects or delivers mail; mailman; postman.

**letter contract,** = letter of intent.

**let|tered** (let′ərd), *adj.* **1** marked with letters. **2** able to read and write; educated; literate: *lettered coxcombs without good breeding* (Sir Richard Steele). **3** having or characterized by learning or literary culture; learned.

**let|ter|form** (let′ər fôrm′), *n.* **1** the shape, design, or type face of a letter of the alphabet: *a sans-serif letterform.* **2** a sheet of stationery for writing letters.

**let|ter|gram** (let′ər gram), *n.* a long telegram sent at a low rate because it is subject to the priority of regular telegrams; day letter or night letter. [< *letter* + (tele)*gram*]

**let|ter|head** (let′ər hed′), *n.* **1** words printed at the top of a sheet of paper, usually a name and address. **2** a sheet or sheets of paper printed with such a heading.

**let|ter|head|ing** (let′ər hed′ing), *n.* = letterhead.

**let|ter|ing** (let′ər ing), *n.* **1** letters drawn, painted, or stamped. **2** the act of lettering; marking with letters; making letters.

**let|ter|man** (let′ər man′), *n., pl.* **-men.** an athlete who has won his letter in a sport.

**letter of advice,** a letter notifying the person addressed that: **a** a consignment of goods has been made to him, or giving other specific information concerning a commercial shipment. **b** a bill (of exchange) has been issued against him.

**letter of credence,** = letters of credence.

**letter of credit, 1** a document issued by a bank, allowing the person named in it to draw money up to a certain amount from other specified banks. **2** a document issued, as by a banker, at one place, authorizing the person to whom it is addressed to draw money up to a certain amount upon the issuer at another place, and promising to be responsible for the credit so extended.

**letter of intent,** a letter in which the signer declares his intention to buy, produce, or deliver, issued in advance of a formal contract: *Boeing has sold 134 [jet planes] to 11 airlines, either on firm contract or letter of intent* (Time).

**letter of marque,** = letters of marque.

**let|ter-per|fect** (let′ər pėr′fikt), *adj.* **1** knowing one's part or lesson perfectly: *He practiced his part in the play until he was letter-perfect.* **2** correct in every detail: *letter-perfect copies.*

**letter post,** *British.* first-class matter.

**let|ter|press** (let′ər pres′), *n.* **1** printed words, as distinguished from illustrations, and other matter; print. **2** printing from type, or from relief plates, as distinguished from offset, lithography, or photogravure, and the like; relief printing.

**letter press,** a machine for making copies of letters.

**let|ters** (let′ərz), *n.pl.* See under **letter**[1].

**letters credential,** = letters of credence.

**letters of administration,** *Law.* an instrument issued by a court or government official, giving an administrator of a dead person's estate authority to act.

**letters of credence,** a document accrediting a diplomatic agent to the government to which he is assigned.

**letters of marque** or **letters of marque and reprisal,** an official document giving a person permission from a government to capture the merchant ships of an enemy; marque.

**letters patent,** an official document giving a person authority from a government to do some act or to have some right, such as the exclusive rights to an invention.

**letters testamentary,** *Law.* an instrument issued by a court or government official giving an executor of a will authority to act.

**letter stock,** an unregistered stock which a company does not offer on the open market for fear of driving down the price of the company's publicly-traded stock.

**letter telegram,** = lettergram.

**let|ter|wood** (let′ər wu̇d′), *n.* **1** a South American tree with a beautifully mottled hard wood. **2** the wood itself.

**let|ter-writ|er** (let′ər rī′tər), *n.* a person who writes letters as a profession or avocation: ... *that inveterate letter-writer Saint Paul* (Manchester Guardian Weekly).

**Let|tic** (let′ik), *adj., n.* –***adj.*** **1** of or having to do with the Letts; Lettish. **2** of or denoting the group of Indo-European languages that includes Lettish, Lithuanian, and Old Prussian; Baltic.
–***n.*** **1** the Lettish language. **2** the Baltic division of Indo-European languages.

**Let|tish** (let′ish), *adj., n.* –***adj.*** of or having to do with the Letts or their language.
–***n.*** the Baltic language of the Letts.

**let|tre de ca|chet** (let′rə də kȧ shā′), *French.* **1** a letter under the seal of the king of France, especially one ordering someone to be sent to prison or exile without a trial or hearing. **2** an informer's letter.

**let|tre de change** (let′rə də shäNzh′), *French.* a bill of exchange.

**let|tre de cré|ance** (let′rə də krā äNs′), *French.* a letter of credit.

**✱let|tuce** (let′is), *n.* **1** the large, crisp, green leaves of a garden plant that are used in salad. **2** the plant itself. It belongs to the composite family. There are many types of lettuce, including loose-leaved and head varieties. **3** any one of various plants resembling lettuce. **4** *Slang.* paper money: *It takes a lot of lettuce these days just to bring home the bacon* (Maclean's). [< Old French *laituës,* plural of *laituë* < Latin *lactūca* lettuce < *lac, lactis* milk (because of the milky juice of the plant)]

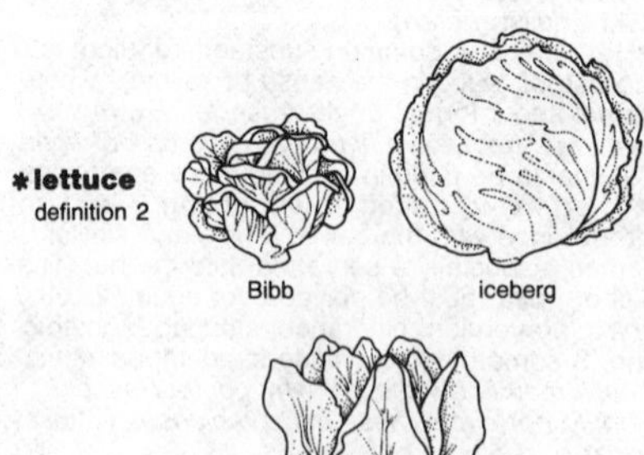

**✱lettuce** definition 2

**let|up** (let′up′), *n. Informal.* a stop or pause: *There is going to be no letup in the kinds of pressure now going on until something is done* (New York Times). [American English < *let up,* verb phrase]

**le|u** (le′ü), *n., pl.* **lei** (lā). the unit of money of Romania, a coin or note equal to 100 bani. Also, **ley.** [< Romanian *leu* (literally) lion < Latin *leō, -ōnis*]

**leuc-,** *combining form.* the form of **leuco-** before vowels, as in *leucine.* Also, **leuk-.**

**leu|ce|mi|a** (lü sē′mē ə, -sēm′yə), *n.* = leukemia.

**leu|cine** (lü′sēn, -sin), *n. Biochemistry.* a white, crystalline amino acid produced in several ways, especially by the digestion of proteins by the pancreatic enzymes. Leucine is essential in nutrition. *Formula:* $C_6H_{13}NO_2$ [< *leuc-* + *-ine*[2]]

**leu|cite** (lü′sīt), *n.* a white or grayish mineral, a silicate of potassium and aluminum, found in certain volcanic rocks. *Formula:* $KAlSi_2O_6$ [< obsolete German *Leucit* < Greek *leukós* white + German *-it* -ite[1]]

**leu|cit|ic** (lü sit′ik), *adj.* of or like leucite.

**leu|co** (lü′kō), *adj. Chemistry.* of or designating a colorless or slightly colored substance formed by the reduction of a dye. It can be reconverted into the dye by the action of oxidizing agents: *a leuco base.* [< *leuco-*]

**leuco-,** *combining form.* white; without color: *Leucocyte = a white corpuscle or blood cell.* Also, **leuko-.** [< Greek *leukós*]

**leu|co|ci|din** (lü kō′sə din, lü′kə sī′-), *n.* a substance produced by staphylococci and certain other bacteria, that destroys white blood cells. [< *leuco-* + *-cide*[1] + *-in*]

**leu|co|cyte** (lü′kə sīt), *n.* one of the tiny, colorless cells in the blood that has a nucleus and destroys disease germs; white blood cell; white corpuscle. Normal blood contains five recognized types, the neutrophil, eosinophil, basophil, lymphocyte, and monocyte. Also, **leukocyte.**

**leu|co|cy|thae|mi|a** or **leu|co|cy|the|mi|a** (lü′kō sī thē′mē ə), *n.* = leukemia. [< *leuco-* + Greek *kýtos* -cyte + *haîma* blood]

**leu|co|cyt|ic** (lü′kə sit′ik), *adj.* **1** of or having to do with leucocytes. **2** characterized by an excess of leucocytes. Also, **leukocytic.**

**leu|co|cy|to|sis** (lü′kō sī tō′sis), *n.* an increase in the number of leucocytes or white blood cells. [< New Latin *leucocytosis* < English *leucocyte* + *-osis*]

**leu|co|cy|tot|ic** (lü′kō sī tot′ik), *adj.* of or having to do with leucocytosis.

**leu|co|cy|to|zo|on infection** (lü′kə sī′tə zō′on), a blood disease of domestic and wild birds, caused by an infection with a parasitic protozoan. [< *leucocyte* + Greek *zôion* small animal]

**leu|co|der|ma** (lü′kə dėr′mə), *n.* unnatural whiteness or white patches in the skin due to a deficiency of pigment. [< *leuco-* + Greek *dérma* skin]

**leu|co|der|mic** (lü′kə dėr′mik), *adj.* of or like leucoderma.

**leu|co|dys|tro|phy** (lü′kō dis′trə fē), *n.* = leukodystrophy.

**leu|co|ma** (lü kō′mə), *n.* a white opacity in the cornea of the eye, caused by inflammation, a wound, etc. [< Greek *leúkōma* < *leukós* white]

**leu|co|ma|ine** (lü kō′mə ēn, -in), *n. Biochemistry.* any one of a group of poisonous basic substances normally formed in living animal tissue as metabolic products.

**leu|co|pe|ni|a** (lü′kə pē′nē ə), *n.* an abnormal decrease in the number of leucocytes or white blood corpuscles. [< *leuco-* + Greek *peniā* poverty]

**leu|co|plast** (lü′kə plast), *n. Botany.* one of the colorless plastids in the cytoplasm of plant cells that functions in the formation and storage of starch. [< *leuco-* + Greek *plastós* something molded]

**leu|co|plas|tid** (lü′kə plas′tid), *n.* = leucoplast.

**leu|co|poi|e|sis** (lü′kə poi ē′sis), *n.* the production of leucocytes or white blood corpuscles. [< *leuco-* + Greek *poiēsis* production]

**leu|cor|rhe|a** or **leu|cor|rhoe|a** (lü′kə rē′ə), *n.* a whitish discharge of mucus or pus from the female genital organs. [< New Latin *leucorrhea* < Greek *leukós* white + *rhoiā* flux < *rheîn* to flow]

**leu|co|sis** (lü kō′sis), *n., pl.* **-ses** (-sēz). **1** a virus disease of poultry, often characterized by paralysis, swelling of the liver and spleen, poor bone formation, blindness, or leukemia. **2** = leukemia. Also, **leukosis.** [< New Latin *leucosis* < Greek *leúkōsis* < *leukós* white]

**leu|co|stic|te** (lü′kə stik′tē), *n.* = rosy finch. [< New Latin *Leucosticte* the genus name < Greek *leukós* white + *stiktós* pricked]

**leu|cot|o|mize** (lü kot′ə mīz), *v.t., v.i.,* **-mized, -miz|ing.** = lobotomize.

**leu|cot|o|my** (lü kot′ə mē), *n., pl.* **-mies.** = lobotomy. [< New Latin *leucotomia* < *leuco-* lobe of the brain (< Greek *leukós* white) + *-tomia* a cutting < Greek *-tomiā*]

**leud** (lüd), *n., pl.* **leuds, leu|des** (lü′dēz). a vassal in the Frankish kingdoms during the Middle Ages. [< Medieval Latin *leudes* < Old High German *liudi*]

**leuk-,** *combining form.* the form of **leuko-** before vowels.

**leu|ke|mi|a** or **leu|kae|mi|a** (lü kē′mē ə, -kēm′yə), *n.* a rare, usually fatal, disease characterized by a large excess of white blood cells. It is a kind of cancer. In some types there is an enlargement of the spleen, the lymph nodes, and other organs. Also, **leucemia.** [< New Latin *leukemia* < Greek *leukós* white + *haîma* blood]

**leu|ke|mic** or **leu|kae|mic** (lü kē′mik), *adj., n.* —***adj.*** of or having to do with leukemia: *In leukemia small doses of radiation administered to the whole body can kill many of the leukemic cells and relieve the distress of the disease* (Scientific American).
—***n.*** a person having leukemia: *Nineteen of the 24 leukaemics were positive, one was doubtful, and four were negative* (New Scientist).

**leu|ke|mo|gen|ic** (lü kē′mə jen′ik), *adj.* causing leukemia.

**leu|ke|moid** (lü kē′moid), *adj.* like leukemia; having symptoms resembling leukemia: *a leukemoid disease.* [< *leukem*(ia) + *-oid*]

**leuko-**, *combining form.* = leuco-.

**leu|ko|cyte** (lü′kə sīt), *n.* = leucocyte.

**leu|ko|cyt|ic** (lü′kə sit′ik), *adj.* = leucocytic.

**leu|ko|dys|tro|phy** (lü′kō dis′trə fē), *n.* a genetic disorder, often fatal, characterized by the progressive degeneration of the white matter of the brain. Also, **leucodystrophy**. [< *leuko-* + *dystrophy*]

**leu|ko|pla|ki|a** (lü′kə plā′kē ə), *n.* a condition of the mouth and throat marked by the presence of small white nodules or patches, that may become malignant. [< New Latin *leukoplakia* < Greek *leukós* white + *pláx, plakós* something flat]

**leu|ko|sis** (lü kō′sis), *n., pl.* **-ses** (-sēz). = leucosis.

**lev** (lef), *n., pl.* **le|va** (le′və). the unit of money of Bulgaria, a coin equal to 100 stotinki. [< Bulgarian *lev,* variant of *lŭv* lion < Old Slavic *lĭvŭ,* ultimately < Greek *léōn* lion]

**lev-**, *combining form.* the form of **levo-** before vowels, as in *levarterenol.*

**Lev.**, Leviticus (book of the Old Testament).

**Le|val|loi|si|an** (lə val wä′zē ən), *adj. Anthropology.* of, having to do with, or characteristic of an early period in man's culture characterized by a new method of making stone tools and weapons by flaking. [< *Levallois*-Perret, a town in France, where these relics were found + *-ian*]

**lev|al|lor|phan** (lev′ə lôr′fən), *n.* a white, odorless, crystalline powder, used as an antidote to morphine poisoning. *Formula:* $C_{23}H_{31}NO_6$ [< *lev-* + *all*(yl) + (m)*orph*(ine) + *-an,* variant of *-ane*]

**lev|an** (lev′ən), *n.* a naturally occurring polysaccharide of fructose, found in the leaves of various grasses. *Formula:* $(C_6H_{10}O_5)_n$ [< Latin *laevus* left[1] (because of its levorotatory properties)]

**Le|vant** (lə vant′), *n.* **1** the countries about the eastern Mediterranean Sea from Greece to Egypt, especially Syria, Lebanon, and Israel. **2** *Obsolete.* the East; Orient. [< Middle French *levant,* present participle of (*se*) *lever* rise < Latin *levāre* < *levis* light[2] (from its position relative to the rising sun)]

**le|vant**[1] (lə vant′), *n.* **1** = Levant morocco. **2** = Levanter. [< *Levant*]

**le|vant**[2] (lə vant′), *v.i.* to run away or abscond, especially to avoid paying debts. [perhaps < Spanish *levantar* get up, raise < *levar* to lift < Latin *levāre*]

**Levant dollar**, an Austrian silver dollar used in trade, bearing the image of Maria Theresa, first issued in Austria and still made for circulation in the Near East.

**Le|vant|er** or **le|vant|er**[1] (lə van′tər), *n.* a strong and raw easterly wind on the Mediterranean, associated especially with the Strait of Gibraltar and with the channel between Spain and Morocco.

**le|van|ter**[2] (lə van′tər), *n.* a person who levants.

**le|van|tine** (lə van′tən; lev′ən tīn, -tēn), *n.* a sturdy, twilled silk cloth. [< French *levantine*]

**Le|van|tine** (lə van′tən; lev′ən tīn, -tēn), *adj., n.* —***adj.*** of the Levant.
—***n.*** **1** a person born or living in the Levant. **2** a ship of the Levant.

**Levant morocco**, a large-grained morocco of finest quality, used in bookbinding.

**Levant wormseed**, an Asiatic shrub of the composite family cultivated in the western United States and in Russia. Its dried flower heads are a source of santonin and limonene.

**lev|a|pad** (lev′ə pad′), *n.* a device for supporting an air cushion vehicle, consisting of a perforated flat plate through which air up to 100 pounds per square inch is forced under pressure. [< Latin *levāre* to lift, raise + English *pad*[1]]

**lev|ar|ter|en|ol** (lev′är tir′ə nol), *n.* levorotatory norepinephrine, a crystalline compound found in the adrenal glands and synthesized for use in medicine as a vasoconstrictor. [< *lev-* + *arterenol*]

**le|va|tor** (lə vā′tər, -tôr), *n., pl.* **le|va|to|res** (lev′ə tôr′ēz, -tōr′-). **1** a muscle that raises some part of the body, such as the one that opens the eye. **2** a surgical instrument used to raise a depressed part of the skull. [< Late Latin *levātor* a "lifter," thief < Latin *levāre* to raise < *levis* light[2]]

**lev|ee**[1] (lev′ē), *n., v.,* **lev|eed, lev|ee|ing.** —***n.*** **1** a bank built to keep a river from overflowing: *There are levees in many places along the lower Mississippi River.* SYN: embankment. **2** a landing place for boats, such as a quay or pier. **3** a raised bank along a river, occurring naturally as the result of deposits left during successive floods: *The Yellow River in China has high levees.* See picture under **valley**. **4** a ridge around a piece of irrigated land.
—***v.t.*** *U.S.* to provide with a levee or levees: *An act to authorize the leveeing of Blue River, in Shelby County* (Indiana Senate Journal).
[American English < French *levée* < *lever* to raise < Latin *levāre* < *levis* light[2]]

**lev|ee**[2] or **lev|ée** (lev′ē, le vē′), *n.* **1** a reception. French kings used to hold levees in the morning while they were getting up and dressing. **2** *U.S.* one of the President's receptions. **3** (in Great Britian and Ireland) an assembly held in the early afternoon by the sovereign or his representative, for men only: *I think an English gentleman never appears to such disadvantage as at the levee of a minister* (Tobias Smollett). [< French *levé* (or *lever,* noun use of infinitive) < *lever* to raise; see etym. under **levee**[1]]

***lev|el** (lev′əl), *adj., n., v.,* **-eled, -el|ing** or (*especially British*) **-elled, -el|ling,** *adv.* —***adj.*** **1** having the same height everywhere; flat; even: *a level floor, a level field.* **2** lying in a plane parallel to the plane of the horizon; horizontal: *a level stretch of railroad.* **3** of equal height; lying in or reaching the same horizontal plane: *The table is level with the sill of the window.* **4** *Figurative.* of equal importance, rank, or ability: *Those five students are about level in ability. Young boys and girls are level now with men* (Shakespeare). **5** *Figurative.* even; uniform; steady: *a calm and level tone, level colors.* **6** *Figurative.* well-balanced; sensible: *a level head.* **7** *Physics.* lying in such a surface that no work is gained or lost in the transportation of a particle from one point of it to any other; equipotential. [< noun]
—***n.*** **1a** something that is level; even or flat surface, such as a tract of land: *The lake overflowed its banks, and all the level of the valley was covered with the inundation* (Samuel Johnson). *In the far distance, across the vast level, something ... is moving this way* (George W. Cable). **b** one of the floors within a building: *Local trains leave on the lower level of this station. The modern house on that hillside has three levels.* **2** an instrument for showing whether a surface is level, such as a spirit level. **3** the measuring of differences in height with such an instrument. **4** level position or condition: *a river whose course is more upon a level* (Jonathan Swift). **5** height: *The flood rose to a level of 60 feet. To the level of his ear Leaning with parted lips, some words she spake* (Keats). **6** *Figurative.* **a** position or standard from a social, moral, or intellectual point of view: *His work is not up to a professional level. To degrade human kind to a level with brute beasts* (George Berkeley). **b** the standard amount of something; normal quantity or quality: *... getting blood samples from people with advanced malnutrition, to determine serum-protein and cholesterol levels at three stages* (New Yorker). **7** a horizontal passage in a mine: *Water trapped the men working the face on the 1200-foot level. The explosion occurred on the third level near the working face.*
—***v.t.*** **1** to make level; put on the same level: *to level freshly poured concrete. The contractor leveled the ground with a bulldozer.* **2** to bring to a level: *They leveled the tennis court by rolling it.* **3** to lay low; bring (something) to the level of the ground: *The tornado leveled every house in the valley.* **4** to raise and hold level for shooting; aim: *The soldier leveled his rifle at the target. ... to guard all the passes to his valley with the point of his levelled spear* (Herman Melville). **5** *Figurative.* to aim or direct (words, intentions, or glances): *This fellow's writings ... are levelled at the clergy* (Henry Fielding). *Others were levelling their looks at her* (Byron). **6** *Figurative.* to remove or reduce (as differences); make uniform: *The mercantile spirit levels all distinctions* (Charles Lamb). *The colors must be leveled before they can be used.* **7** *Surveying.* to find the relative heights of different points in (land).
—***v.i.*** **1** to aim with a weapon: *They level: a volley, a smoke and the clearing of smoke* (Robert Browning). **2** to bring things or persons to a common level: (*Figurative.*) *Your levellers wish to level down as far as themselves; but they cannot bear levelling up to themselves* (Samuel Johnson). **3** *Figurative.* to direct one's words or attention: *The author ... levels at Nero* (Richard Brinsley Sheridan). **4** *Surveying.* to make measurements of levels.
—***adv.*** *Archaic.* in a level manner; directly: *It shall as level to your judgement pierce as day does to your eye* (Shakespeare).
**find** (or **seek**) **one's level**, to arrive at the natural or proper level: *Water seeks its own level.*
**level off, a** to come to an equilibrium; even off; steady; come to the end of a rise or decline in something: *The money-supply situation hasn't eased up any recently, so that's just one more force working toward a leveling off in capital spending* (Newsweek). **b** to return (an airplane) to a horizontal position in landing or after a climb or dive: *The plane leveled off.*
**level out**, to level off: *The effects of the "credit squeeze" would now appear to be levelling out, but it is impossible to forecast the future* (London Times).
**level with**, *Slang.* to be honest with; tell the truth: *She was tempted to squirm out of it, but instead she leveled with him and felt better for it.*
**one's level best**. See under **best**.
**on the level**, *Informal.* fair and straightforward; honest; legitimate: *In 1957 members became worried about the scheme, but she thought it was on the level and told them so* (Cape Times).
[< Old French *livel* < Vulgar Latin *lībellum* < Latin *lībella* (diminutive) < *lībra* a balance, scale]
—**lev′el|ness**, *n.*
—***Syn.*** *adj.* **1 Level, even, smooth** mean flat or having a flat surface. **Level** means not sloping and having no noticeably high or low places on the surface: *We built our house on level ground.* **Even** means having a uniformly flat, but not necessarily level, surface with no irregular places: *The top of that card table is not even.* **Smooth** means perfectly even, without a trace of roughness to be seen or felt: *We sandpapered the shelves until they were smooth.*

***level**
*n.,* definition 2

spirit level

**level crossing**. *British.* a grade crossing.

**lev|el|er** (lev′ə lər), *n.* **1** a person or thing that levels: *It has been said that Death is the great leveler.* **2** *Figurative.* a person who would abolish all social and other distinctions and bring all people to a common level. **3** a surveyor who uses a surveyor's level.

**lev|el-head|ed** (lev′əl hed′id), *adj.* having good common sense or good judgment; sensible: *This is a level-headed and practical book* (Scientific American). SYN: judicious. [American English < earlier *level head* + *-ed*[2]] —**lev′el-head′ed|ly**, *adv.* —**lev′el-head′ed|ness**, *n.*

**lev|el|ing** (lev′ə ling), *n.* **1** the act of one who or that which levels. **2** *Surveying.* the process or art of finding the relative elevation of points on the earth's surface, as with a surveyor's level and leveling rod, or of determining horizontal lines, grades, or the like, by such a method.

**leveling rod** or **staff**, a graduated rod or staff used with a level to determine heights in surveying.

**leveling screw**, a screw at the base of a surveyor's transit that can be turned to make the instrument level.

**lev|el|ler** (lev′ə lər), *n. Especially British.* leveler.

**Lev|el|ler** (lev′ə lər), *n. Historical.* a member of a political party which arose in the army of the Long Parliament about 1647 with the aim of leveling all ranks and establishing equality in titles and estates.

**lev|el|ly** (lev′əl lē, -ə lē), *adv.* **1** in a level manner or position; on a level. **2** *Figurative.* in an unemotional manner: *He eyed his accuser levelly for a moment before replying.*

**lev|el-peg** (lev′əl peg′), *v.i.,* **-pegged, -peg|ging.** *British.* to maintain a balanced condition or position, as between rivals: *England and Wales have met 74 times, and it is as nearly level-pegging between them as makes no odds, with 32 victories to England, 31 to Wales, and 11 drawn* (U. A. Titley).

**level stress**, the indication of two primary accents in the pronunciation of a word, usually a compound, as in *well-to-do* (wel′tə dü′) and *home-grown* (hōm′grōn′). Level stress is usually used to represent stress variation, or a combination of primary and secondary stresses, in a compound.

**level wind** (wīnd), a device on a bait-casting reel that prevents backlash and winds the fish line on the spool evenly.

***lev|er** (lev′ər, lē′vər), *n., v.* —***n.*** **1a** a bar which

---

**Pronunciation Key:** hat, āge, cãre, fär; let, ēqual, tėrm; it, īce; hot, ōpen, ôrder; **oi**l, **ou**t; cup, pu̇t, rüle; **ch**ild; lo**ng**; **th**in; **ᴛʜ**en; **zh**, measure; **ə** represents **a** in about, **e** in taken, **i** in pencil, **o** in lemon, **u** in circus.

rests on a fixed support called a fulcrum and is used to transmit force and motion especially by moving a weight at one end in response to the force of pushing down at the other end, much like the action of a seesaw. The lever is a simple machine. **b** a bar working on the same principle as the lever, used to control machinery, such as the throttle of a locomotive or the gearshift lever in an automobile. **2** any bar working on an axis for support, such as a crowbar or handspike, used to pry: *the brake lever of an automobile.* **3** *Figurative.* a means of exerting control or achieving a purpose: *to use the threat of a strike as a lever to obtain better wages from a company. They believed that they had discovered the levers by which to regulate the processes of human society* (Edmund Wilson).
— ***v.t.*** to move, lift, or push, with a lever: *It was partly buried in the sand and they were trying to lever it up with rusty iron bars, found on the beach* (London Times). — ***v.i.*** to use a lever.
[< Old French *leveor* < *lever* to raise < Latin *levāre* < *levis* light[2]]

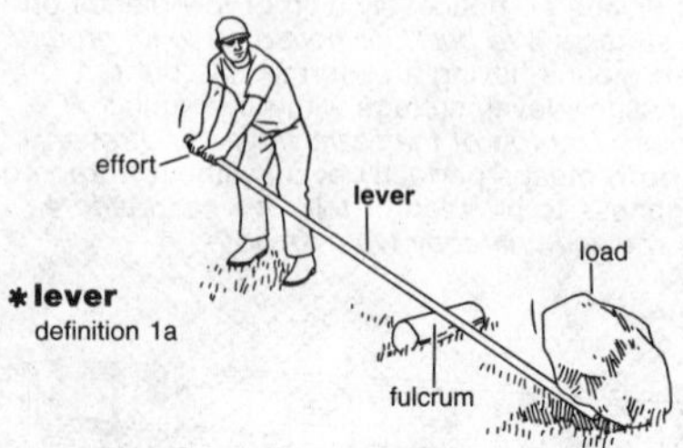


***lever**
definition 1a

**lev|er|age** (lev′ər ij, lē′vər-; lev′rij), *n., v.,* **-aged, -ag|ing.** —*n.* **1** the action of a lever. **2** the advantage or power gained by using a lever. **3** *Figurative.* increased power of action; advantage for accomplishing a purpose. **4** *U.S. Finance.* the use of borrowed money in the expectation that the profits made on the money will exceed the interest rate.
— ***v.i., v.t.*** *U.S. Finance.* to speculate or cause to speculate on borrowed money in the expectation that the profits will exceed the interest rate.

**lev|er|et** (lev′ər it), *n.* a young hare, especially one in its first year. [< Old French *levrete* (diminutive) < *levre* < Latin *lepus, -oris* hare]

**Le|vi** (lē′vī), *n.* **1** a son of Jacob and ancestor of the Levites (in the Bible, Genesis 29:34). **2** the tribe that claimed to be descended from him, from which the priests and the Levites were drawn.

**lev|i|a|ble** (lev′ē ə bəl), *adj.* **1** that can be levied. **2** liable or subject to a levy.

**le|vi|a|than** (lə vī′ə thən), *n., adj.* —*n.* **1** a huge sea monster in Canaanite myths. It was originally defeated in combat with God but will break forth again at doomsday when He will finally defeat it (in the Bible, Isaiah 27:1). **2** a whale or other large marine animal. **3** a huge ship: *the oak leviathans* (Byron). **4** *Figurative.* any great and powerful person or thing: *The indispensable state remains always a leviathan to be watched with suspicion* (Canada Month).
— ***adj.*** huge; monstrous: *a leviathan hall, a leviathan industry.*
[< Late Latin *leviathan* < Hebrew *liwyåthån* dragon, crocodile]

**lev|i|er** (lev′ē ər), *n.* a person who levies.

**lev|i|gate** (lev′ə gāt), *v.,* **-gat|ed, -gat|ing,** *adj.*
— ***v.t.*** **1** to make into a fine powder by rubbing or grinding: *to levigate mortar.* **2** to mix into a smooth paste. **3** *Chemistry.* to mix so as to make homogeneous. **4** *Obsolete.* to make smooth; polish.
— ***adj.*** smooth, as if polished.
[< Latin *lēvigāre* (with English *-ate*[1]) < *lēvis* smooth + *agere* do, make] — **lev′i|ga|ble,** *adj.*
— **lev′i|ga′tion,** *n.*

**lev|in** (lev′in), *n. Archaic.* lightning: *the flashing Levin* (Edmund Spenser). [Middle English *levene;* origin unknown]

**lev|i|rate** (lev′ər it, -ə rāt; lē′vər it, -ə rāt), *n.* a custom among many patrilineal societies, including the ancient Jews and other Semitic peoples, of binding the brother or nearest patrilineal kinsman of a dead man under certain circumstances to cohabit with his widow, in order to beget children who will be designated legally begotten offspring of the deceased (in the Bible, Deuteronomy 25:5-10). [< Latin *lēvir* brother-in-law + English *-ate*[3]]

**lev|i|rat|ic** (lev′ə rat′ik, lē′və-), *adj.* having to do with or according to the levirate.

**Le|vi's** (lē′vīz), *n.pl.* **1** *Trademark.* tight-fitting, heavy blue denim trousers reinforced at strain points with copper rivets or extra stitching. **2 levis,** = blue jeans. [American English < *Levi* Strauss and Company, an American manufacturer]

**Levit.,** Leviticus (book of the Old Testament).

**lev|i|tate** (lev′ə tāt), *v.,* **-tat|ed, -tat|ing.** — ***v.i.*** to rise or float in the air. — ***v.t.*** to cause to rise or float in the air: *The magician appeared to levitate a large chair without touching it.*
[< Latin *levitās, -ātis* lightness, levity + English *-ate*[1]; after English *gravitate*] — **lev′i|ta′tor,** *n.*

**lev|i|ta|tion** (lev′ə tā′shən), *n.* **1** the act or process of levitating. **2** the act or process of rising, or raising (a body), from the ground by spiritualistic means: *He claimed to have seen Hindu fakirs perform unbelievable feats of levitation.*

**lev|i|ta|tion|al** (lev′ə tā′shə nəl), *adj.* of or having to do with levitation.

**lev|i|ta|tive** (lev′ə tā′tiv), *adj.* that can levitate.

**Le|vite** (lē′vīt), *n.* a member of the tribe of Levi, from which assistants to the Jewish priests were chosen (in the Bible, Numbers 18:2, 6). [< Latin *levīta,* or *levītēs* < Greek *Leuītēs* < Hebrew *Lewi* Levi]

**Le|vit|ic** (lə vit′ik), *adj.* = Levitical.

**Le|vit|i|cal** (lə vit′ə kəl), *adj.* **1** of or having to do with the Levites. **2** of or having to do with Leviticus or the law contained in it. — **Le|vit′i|cal|ly,** *adv.*

**Levitical degrees,** degrees of kindred within which persons were forbidden to marry (in the Bible, Leviticus 18:6-18).

**Le|vit|i|cus** (lə vit′ə kəs), *n.* the third book of the Old Testament, containing the laws for the priests and Levites and the ritual for Jewish rites and ceremonies. *Abbr:* Lev. [< Late Latin *Leviticus* (*liber*) (The Book) of the Levites < Greek *Leuītikós* < *Leuītēs* Levite]

**lev|i|ty** (lev′ə tē), *n., pl.* **-ties. 1** lightness of mind, character, or behavior; lack of proper seriousness or earnestness: *Giggling in church shows levity. Our graver business Frowns at this levity* (Shakespeare). *Nothing like a little judicious levity* (Robert Louis Stevenson). **SYN:** flippancy, frivolity. **2** instability; fickleness; inconstancy. **3** lightness in weight: ... *ingenious contrivances to facilitate motion, and unite levity with strength* (Samuel Johnson). [< Latin *levitās* < *levis* light[2]]

**lev|o** (lev′ō), *adj. Chemistry.* turning or turned to the left; levorotatory: *Dextro and levo ... testosterone molecules are ... each a mirror image of the other* (Science News Letter). [< Latin *laevus* left]

**levo-,** *combining form.* **1** toward the left: *Levorotatory = rotatory toward the left.*
**2** levorotatory: *Levoglucose = levorotatory glucose.* Also, **lev-** before vowels. Also, **laevo-.** [< Latin *laevus* left]

**le|vo|do|pa** (lē′vō dō′pə), *n.* = L-dopa.

**le|vo|glu|cose** (lē′vō glü′kōs), *n.* a form of glucose, levorotatory to polarized light.

**le|vo|gy|rate** (lē′vō jī′rāt), *adj.* = levorotatory.

**le|vo|ro|ta|tion** (lē′vō rō tā′shən), *n.* **1** rotation toward the left. **2** *Chemistry, Physics.* rotation of the plane of polarization of light to the left when the observer is looking toward the source of light.

**le|vo|ro|ta|to|ry** (lē′vō rō′tə tôr′ē, -tōr′-), *adj.* **1** turning or causing to turn toward the left or in a counterclockwise direction. **2** *Chemistry, Physics.* characterized by turning the plane of polarization of light to the left, as a crystal, lens, or compound in solution (contrasted with *dextrorotatory*). Also, **laevorotatory.**

**lev|u|lin** (lev′yə lin), *n.* a substance resembling dextrin, obtained from the roots of certain composite plants. It forms levulose on hydrolysis. *Formula:* $(C_6H_{10}O_5)_n$ [< *levul*(ose) + *-in*]

**lev|u|lin|ic acid** (lev′yə lin′ik), an acid obtained chiefly by treating sugar with hydrochloric acid, used in the manufacture of plastics, nylon, etc. *Formula:* $C_5H_8O_3$

**lev|u|lose** (lev′yə lōs), *n.* a form of sugar in honey, many fruits, and drugs; fruit sugar; fructose. Levulose is levorotatory to polarized light. It is sweeter than glucose or sucrose. *Formula:* $C_6H_{12}O_6$ [< *lev-* *-ul*(e) + *-ose*]

**lev|y** (lev′ē), *v.,* **lev|ied, lev|y|ing,** *n., pl.* **lev|ies.**
— ***v.t.*** **1** to order to be paid: *The government levies taxes to pay its expenses.* **SYN:** assess. **2** to collect (men) for an army: *Troops are levied in time of war.* **SYN:** conscript. **3** to seize by law for unpaid debts.
— ***v.i.*** **1** to make a levy. **2** to seize property by law for unpaid debts: *They levied on his property for unpaid rent.* [< noun]
— ***n.*** **1** money collected by authority or force: *The tax levy paid for local school improvements.* **SYN:** tax. **2** men collected for an army: *a levy produced by a national draft.* **3** the act of levying.

**levy war on** (or **against**), to make war on; start a war against: *Treason against the United States shall consist only in levying war against them* (Constitution of the United States).
[< Middle French *levée* < *lever* to raise; see etym. under **levee**[1]]

**levy en masse,** a collecting of civilian men of a country to bear arms and resist invasion. [partial translation of French *levée en masse;* see etym. under **levy.** Compare etym. under **en masse.**]

**lewd** (lüd), *adj.* **1** not decent; obscene; lustful: *lewd stories, a lewd song.* **SYN:** lascivious, lecherous. **2** *Obsolete.* **a** unlearned; ignorant. **b** base; vile; wicked. **c** worthless; unprincipled. [Old English *lǣwede* unlearned; (originally) laic] — **lewd′ly,** *adv.* — **lewd′ness,** *n.*

**lew|is** (lü′is), *n.* a wedge or tenon fitted into a dovetail recess or mortise in a block of stone, and having a hoisting ring for lifting the stone. [perhaps < the name *Lewis*]

**lew|is|i|a** (lü is′ē ə), *n.* any perennial evergreen herb of a group of the purslane family, native to western North America. It is widely planted in rock gardens for its narrow, woolly leaves and handsome rose-colored flowers that open only in sunshine. One kind is called *bitterroot.* [< New Latin *Lewisia* the genus name < Meriwether *Lewis,* 1774-1809, an American explorer]

**Lew|is|i|an** (lü is′ē ən), *adj.* of or having to do with the oldest rocks in Scotland, consisting chiefly of gneisses similar to the Laurentian types of North America, or the geologic period when they were formed, occurring at the beginning of the Archeozoic era. [< the island of *Lewis,* in the Hebrides]

**lew|is|ite** (lü′ə sīt), *n.* a colorless liquid with an odor like geraniums, that causes extreme injury to the skin and lungs, used in warfare as a poison gas. *Formula:* $C_2H_2AsCl_3$ [< W. Lee *Lewis,* 1878-1943, an American chemist + *-ite*[1]]

**Lew|is machine gun** (lü′is), a light machine gun with a circular magazine, in which the bolt is worked by compressed gas. [< Colonel Isaac N. *Lewis,* 1858-1931, United States Army, who invented it]

**lew|is|son** (lü′ə sən), *n.* = lewis.

**Lew|is's woodpecker** (lü′is əz), a woodpecker of western North America with greenish-black back and tail, crimson forehead, face, and throat, and light-red chest. [< Meriwether *Lewis,* 1774-1809, an American explorer]

**lex** (leks), *n., pl.* **le|ges.** *Latin.* law, especially in reference to a legislative measure enacted by the assembly of the whole Roman people.

**lex.,** lexicon.

**lex|eme** (lek′sēm), *n. Linguistics.* a minimum meaningful element in the vocabulary of a language. *Example: Lifesaver* is a lexeme consisting of the morphemes *life, save,* and *-er.* [< Greek *léxis* word + *-eme,* as in *morpheme*]

**lex fo|ri** (leks′ fôr′ī, fōr′-), *Latin.* law of the court; the law of the jurisdiction where an action is pending.

**lex|i|cal** (lek′sə kəl), *adj.* **1** of or having to do with words or vocabulary especially of a language, dialect, group, or author: *"Lifesaver" is a lexical form composed of the words "life" and "saver."* **2** having to do with or like a lexicon or dictionary. [< Greek *lexikós* of words + English *-al*[1]] — **lex′i|cal|ly,** *adv.*

**lex|i|cal|i|ty** (lek′sə kal′ə tē), *n.* the quality or condition of being lexical.

**lexical meaning,** *Linguistics.* the meaning common to the linguistic forms belonging to a paradigm, as distinguished from grammatical meaning. The words *am, are,* and *is* all have the lexical meaning of "be," although the grammatical meanings are different (person, tense, mood).

**lexicog.,** **1** lexicographer. **2** lexicographical. **3** lexicography.

**lex|i|cog|ra|pher** (lek′sə kog′rə fər), *n.* a writer or maker of a dictionary: *His new dictionary is the result of thirty years of that faithful drudgery which is the lot of every true lexicographer* (New Scientist). [< Greek *lexikográphos* < *lexikón* wordbook, lexicon + *gráphein* to write]

**lex|i|co|graph|ic** (lek′sə kə graf′ik), *adj.* = lexicographical.

**lex|i|co|graph|i|cal** (leks′sə kə graf′ə kəl), *adj.* of or having to do with lexicography: *lengthy lexicographical research.* — **lex′i|co|graph′i|cal|ly,** *adv.*

**lex|i|cog|ra|phy** (lek′sə kog′rə fē), *n.* the writing or making of dictionaries.

**lex|i|col|o|gist** (lek′sə kol′ə jist), *n.* a person who is skilled in lexicology.

**lex|i|col|o|gy** (lek′sə kol′ə jē), *n.* the study of the form, history, and meaning of words.

**lex|i|con** (lek′sə kən, -kon), *n.* **1** a dictionary, especially of Greek, Latin, or Hebrew. **SYN:** wordbook. **2** the vocabulary of a language or of a certain subject, group, or activity: *In the lexicon of youth ... there is no such word As —fail!* (Edward Bulwer-Lytton). **3** *Linguistics.* the total stock of morphemes in a given language. [< Greek *lexikón* (*biblíon*) wordbook, neuter of *lexikós* of words < *léxis* word < *leg-,* stem of *légein* say]

**lex|i|co|stat|is|tic** (lek′sə kō stə tis′tik), *adj.* of or having to do with lexicostatistics: *studies in lexicostatistic theory.*

**lex|i|co|sta|tis|tics** (lek′sə kō stə tis′tiks), *n. Linguistics.* a method of dating languages, or the separation of related languages, by making statistical comparisons of their basic vocabularies; glottochronology.

**lex|i|gram** (lek′sə gram), *n.* a geometric form or other symbol that stands for a word. Lexigrams are used to teach animals, such as chimpanzees, to communicate with humans.

**lex|i|graph|ic** (lek′sə graf′ik), *adj.* having to do with or characterized by lexigraphy. —**lex′i-graph′i|cal|ly,** *adv.*

**lex|i|graph|i|cal** (lek′sə graf′ə kəl), *adj.* = lexigraphic.

**lex|ig|ra|phy** (lek sig′rə fē), *n.* a system of writing, such as the Chinese, in which each character represents a word.

**lex|is** (lek′səs), *n.* vocabulary; lexicon. [< Greek *léxis* word, speech]

**lex la|ta** (leks′ lā′tə), *Latin.* existing law.

**lex lo|ci** (leks lō′sī), *Latin.* the law of the place where an event occurred.

**lex non scrip|ta** (leks non skrip′tə), *Latin.* unwritten law.

**Lex Sa|li|ca** (leks sal′ə kə), *Latin.* the Salic law.

**lex scrip|ta** (leks skrip′tə), *Latin.* written law; statutory law.

**lex ta|li|o|nis** (leks tal′ē ō′nis), *Latin.* the law of retaliation ("an eye for an eye, a tooth for a tooth"). See also **talion.**

**ley**[1] (lē, lā), *n.* a meadow; pasture; lea. [variant of *lea*[1]]

**ley**[2] (lā), *n.* = leu.

**Ley|den jar** (lī′dən), a device for storing an electric charge, consisting essentially of a glass jar lined inside and outside, for most of its height, with tin or aluminum foil and sealed with a stopper containing a metal rod. The rod is connected to the internal coating. [earlier *Leyden phial,* translation of Dutch *Leidsche flesch* < *Leiden,* Netherlands, where it was invented]

**Ley|dig cell** (lī′dig), any one of the interstitial cells of the testicle, thought to be the producers of male sex hormones. [< F. von *Leydig,* 1821-1908, a German biologist]

**leze-maj|es|ty** (lēz′maj′ə stē), *n.,* or **leze majesty,** = lese-majesty.

**lf.,** 1 *Baseball.* **a** left field. **b** left fielder. **2** lightface (type).

**l.f.,** 1 left field. **2** left fielder.

**LF** (no periods), **L.F.,** or **l.f.,** low frequency.

**l.f.b.,** *Soccer and Field Hockey.* left fullback.

**L-form** (el′fôrm′), *n.* **1** a variant form of bacteria developed by subjecting bacterial cultures to various treatments, especially with antibiotics: *The L-forms are completely insensitive to penicillin and are, in fact, often produced under the influence of the antibiotic* (New Scientist). **2** a naturally occurring variant bacterial form similar to the cultivated form, found in certain infections. [< *L*(ister Institute of Preventive Medicine), in London, where these forms were first observed in 1934 + *form*]

**lg.,** long.

**l.g.,** 1 *Football.* left guard. **2** lifeguard.

**LG** (no periods), **L.G.,** or **LG.,** Low German.

**lge.,** large.

**LGk.** or **L.GK.,** Late Greek.

**LGP** (no periods), *British.* liquefied petroleum gas. The abbreviation in the United States is *LPG.*

**lgr.,** larger.

**lgth.,** length.

**l.h.,** *Music.* left hand.

**LH** (no periods), luteinizing hormone.

**L.H.A.,** Lord High Admiral.

**Lha|sa ap|so** (lä′sə ap′sō), a small dog with a heavy, usually light-brown, coat and much hair over the eyes. It is native to Tibet, where for 800 years it was trained as a watchdog. [< *Lhasa,* the capital of Tibet + Tibetan *apso* (*seng kye*) sentinel (lion dog)]

**l.h.b.,** *Football.* left halfback.

**L.H.C.,** Lord High Chancellor.

**L.H.D.,** Doctor of the Humanities; Doctor of Humane Letters (Latin, *Litterarum Humaniorum Doctor*).

**L-head engine** (el′hed′), a type of internal-combustion engine having cylinders with both intake and exhaust valves on one side in the cylinder block.

**L.H.T.,** Lord High Treasurer.

**li** (lē), *n., pl.* **li.** Chinese unit of linear measure, equal to about one third of a mile. [< Chinese *li*]

**Li** (no period), lithium (chemical element).

**L.I.,** Long Island.

**li|a|bil|i|ty** (lī′ə bil′ə tē), *n., pl.* **-ties. 1** the state of being susceptible: *liability to disease.* **SYN:** susceptibility. **2** the state of being under obligation: *liability for a debt.* **3** something that is to one's disadvantage: *His poor handwriting is a liability in getting a job as a clerk.* **SYN:** handicap, impediment.

**liabilities,** the debts or other financial obligations of a business, for money, goods, or services received: *A business with more liabilities than assets is bound to fail.*

**liability insurance,** insurance taken out against injury, damage, or loss to others: *Liability insurance will pay the bill if your car pushes over a pedestrian. It won't pay for damage to your own car* (Wall Street Journal).

**li|a|ble** (lī′ə bəl, lī′bəl), *adj.* **1** likely; unpleasantly likely: *That glass is liable to break. You are liable to slip on ice.* **SYN:** apt. **2** in danger of having or doing: *We are all liable to diseases.* **3** bound by law to pay; responsible: *The Postal Service is not liable for damage to a parcel unless it is insured.* **SYN:** accountable, answerable. **4** under obligation; subject: *Citizens are liable to jury duty.* [< Old French *lier* bind (< Latin *ligāre*) + English *-able*] —**li′a|ble|ness,** *n.*

▶ See **likely** for usage note.

**li|aise** (lē āz′), *v.i.,* **-aised, -ais|ing.** to form a liaison; make a connection: *Throughout this period I liaised with, and fought alongside, no fewer than three companies of the Kenya regiment* (Manchester Guardian). [back formation < *liaison*]

**li|ai|son** (lē′ā zon′; lē ā′zon, lē′ə-), *n., v.* —*n.* **1a** the connection between parts of an army, branches of a service, or the like, to secure proper cooperation: *His job was to maintain liaison between the regular army and the company building the tanks.* **b** a similar connection between persons or groups to secure cooperation, such as that between a customer and a manufacturer, a sales force and an engineering department, schools within a district, or departments of a government: *A need for some closer liaison between business and government was expressed* (Raymond Daniell). **c** a person who establishes or maintains such a connection: *In recent years he served as the … company's liaison with European scientific centers* (New York Times). **2** an illicit intimacy between a man and a woman. **3** (in speaking French and other languages) joining a usually silent final consonant to a following word that begins with a vowel or mute *h.* **4** the act or fact of thickening sauces, soups, or other liquid food by the addition of eggs, flour, or other thickeners.

—*v.i.* to form a liaison; liaise: *a half-day of conventional sightseeing or shopping, then half-the-night* (*depending on one's constitution*) *liaisoning with the natives at nightclubs* (Jon Ruddy). [< Old French *liaison* < Latin *ligātiō, -ōnis* < *ligāre* to bind]

**li|a|na** (lē ä′nə, -an′ə), *n.* a general name for a climbing plant or vine, especially one of those having woody stems that twine around the trunk of trees of tropical forests. [alteration of French *liane,* earlier *liorne,* alteration of *viorne* < Latin *vīburnum* the wayfaring-tree]

**li|ane** (lē än′), *n.* = liana.

**liang** (lyäng), *n., pl.* **liang.** a Chinese unit of weight, equal to a hectogram. 16 liang equal 1 catty. [< Mandarin *liang*]

**Liao** (lyou), *n.* the dynasty of Khitans which ruled northern China from A.D. 905 to 1122.

**li|ar** (lī′ər), *n.* a person who tells lies; person who says what is not true: *He's … an infinite and endless liar, an hourly promise-breaker* (Shakespeare). **SYN:** prevaricator.

**liard** (lyär), *n.* a small copper coin formerly used in France, worth one fourth of a sou. [< French *liard,* apparently < a proper name]

**li|as** (lī′əs), *n.* a compact blue limestone rock. [< Old French *liois,* or *liais,* probably < *lias,* plural of *lie* lee[2] (because of its darkish color)]

**Li|as** (lī′əs), *n. Geology.* **1** the earliest epoch of the European Jurassic system, characterized by clayey rocks with fossils. **2** the rocks of this epoch. [< *lias*]

**Li|as|sic** (lī as′ik), *adj. Geology.* of or having to do with the Lias.

**lib** or **Lib** (lib), *adj., n. Informal.* —*adj.* of or having to do with liberationists: *the students' lib movement.*

—*n.* a liberationist group or organization: *men's lib.*

**lib.,** 1 book (Latin, *liber*). **2** librarian. **3** library.

**Lib.,** 1 Liberal. **2** Liberia.

**li|ba|tion** (lī bā′shən), *n.* **1** the action of pouring out wine, water, or other liquid to drink, as an offering to a god. **2** the wine, water, or other liquid, offered in this way: *The goblet then she took … Sprinkling the first libations on the ground* (John Dryden). **3** *Informal.* any liquid poured out to be drunk; drink; potation. [< Latin *lībātiō, -ōnis* < *lībāre* pour out]

**li|ba|tion|ar|y** (lī bā′shə ner′ē), *adj.* = libatory.

**li|ba|to|ry** (lī′bə tôr′ē, -tōr′-), *adj.* having to do with libation.

**lib|ber** (lib′ər), *n. Informal.* a liberationist: *For some men's libbers, a limited solution to their anxiety seems to lie in a partial retreat from women* (Time). [< *lib* + *-er*[1]]

**li|bec|cio** (lē bet′chō), *n. Italian.* the southwest wind.

**li|bel** (lī′bəl), *n., v.,* **-beled, -bel|ing** or (*especially British*) **-belled, -bel|ling.** —*n.* **1** a written or published statement, picture, etc., that is likely to harm the reputation of the person about whom it is made; false or damaging statement. **SYN:** calumny. **2** the act or crime of writing or publishing such a statement, picture, etc. **3** any false or damaging statement or implication about a person: *His conversation is a perpetual libel on all his acquaintance* (Richard Brinsley Sheridan). **SYN:** slander, vilification. **4** (in admiralty, ecclesiastical, and Scottish law) a formal written declaration of the allegations of a plaintiff and the grounds for his suit.

—*v.t.* **1** to write or publish a libel about, such as a statement or picture. **2** to make false or damaging statements about. **SYN:** malign. **3** to institute suit against by means of a libel, as in an admiralty court.

[Middle English *libel* a formal written statement, little book < Old French *libel,* or *libelle,* learned borrowing from Latin *libellus* (diminutive) < *liber* book]

▶ See **slander** for usage note.

**li|bel|ant** (lī′bə lənt), *n. Law.* a person who institutes a suit by means of a libel.

**li|bel|ee** (lī′bə lē′), *n.* a person against whom a libel instituting a suit has been filed.

**li|bel|er** or **li|bel|ler** (lī′bə lər), *n.* a person who libels another.

**li|bel|ist** (lī′bə list), *n.* = libeler.

**li|bel|lous** (lī′bə ləs), *adj. Especially British.* libelous.

**li|bel|ous** (lī′bə ləs), *adj.* **1** containing injurious statements or other libel about a person; like a libel. **2** spreading libels: *a libelous tongue.* —**li′bel-ous|ly,** *adv.*

**li|ber** (lī′bər), *n. Botany.* the inner bark of exogens; phloem. [< Latin *liber* book; bark[1]]

**lib|er|al** (lib′ər əl, lib′rəl), *adj., n.* —*adj.* **1a** generous; having or giving freely: *a liberal donation. A liberal giver gives much. The bearers … are persons to whom you cannot be too liberal* (Dickens). *Wisely liberal of his money for comfort and pleasure* (John Ruskin). **SYN:** bountiful. **b** plentiful; abundant: *We put in a liberal supply of fuel for the winter.* **SYN:** ample, large. **2a** tolerant; not narrow in one's ideas and views; broad-minded: *a liberal thinker, liberal theology.* **b** not strict; not rigorous: *a liberal interpretation of a rule.* **3** favoring progress and reforms: *a liberal political program.* **4** giving the general thought; not a word-for-word rendering; broad and sympathetic as opposed to literal and pedantic: *a liberal translation.* **5** of or having to do with the liberal arts or a liberal education. **6** *Obsolete.* **a** free from restraint; free in speech or action. **b** licentious.

—*n.* a person favorable to progress and reforms. [< Old French *liberal,* learned borrowing from Latin *līberālis* befitting free men < *līber* free] —**lib′er|al|ly,** *adv.* —**lib′er|al|ness,** *n.*

**Lib|er|al** (lib′ər əl, lib′rəl), *adj., n.* —*adj.* of or belonging to a political party, especially the Liberal Party of Great Britain, that favors progress and reforms.

—*n.* a member of a Liberal Party.

**liberal arts,** 1 subjects studied for their cultural and intellectual value rather than for immediate practical use. Literature, languages, history, and philosophy are some of the liberal arts. **2** (in ancient Rome and in the Middle Ages) grammar, rhetoric, and logic (the trivium) and arithmetic, geometry, astronomy, and music (the quadrivium). [translation of Latin *artēs līberālēs* the arts befitting *līberī* free men]

**liberal education,** 1 education for cultural and intellectual development rather than as a preparation for a business or profession; education in the liberal arts: *A liberal education develops the mind broadly.* **2** wide education or experience: *The son of a banker, he had received a liberal education in finance.*

**lib|er|al|ise** (lib′ər ə līz, lib′rə-), *v.t., v.i.,* **-ised, -is-ing.** *Especially British.* liberalize.

**lib|er|al|ism** (lib′ər ə liz′əm, lib′rə liz-), *n.* **1** liberal views or opinions; belief in progress and reforms. **2** Also, **Liberalism.** the principles and practices of liberal political parties, especially of the Liberal Party in Great Britain. **3** *Theology.* a recent movement in Protestantism stressing the ethical nature of religion rather than its authoritarian and formal aspects. It emphasizes the freedom of the mind to satisfy its own spiritual needs. —**lib′er|al-ist,** *n.*

---

**Pronunciation Key:** hat, āge, cãre, fär; let, ēqual, tėrm; it, īce; hot, ōpen, ôrder; oil, out; cup, pu̇t, rüle; child; long; thin; ᴛʜen; zh, measure; ə represents **a** in about, **e** in taken, **i** in pencil, **o** in lemon, **u** in circus.

**lib|er|al|is|tic** (lib′ər ə lis′tik, lib′rə-), *adj.* of or characterized by liberalism.

**lib|er|al|i|ty** (lib′ə ral′ə tē), *n., pl.* **-ties.** 1 generosity; generous act or behavior: *His liberality knew no bottom but an empty purse* (Thomas Fuller). **SYN**: munificence, bounty. 2 a liberal gift. 3 a tolerant and progressive nature; being broad-minded: *Where look for liberality, if men of science are illiberal to their brethren?* (Edward Bulwer-Lytton). **SYN**: largess.

**lib|er|al|ize** (lib′ər ə līz, lib′rə-), *v.t., v.i.,* **-ized, -iz|ing.** to make or become liberal; remove restrictions from: *French and Italian economic and political representatives reached tentative agreement to liberalize trade* (Wall Street Journal). **—lib′er|al|i|za′tion,** *n.* **—lib′er|al|iz′er,** *n.*

**Liberal Party,** 1 a political party that favors progress and reforms. 2 a political party in Great Britain formed about 1830. 3 one of the principal political parties of Canada.

**lib|er|ate** (lib′ə rāt), *v.t.,* **-at|ed, -at|ing.** 1 to set free; free: *Lincoln liberated the slaves. Allied troops moved in swiftly to liberate the occupied towns.* **SYN**: release, emancipate. 2 to free from social biases or restrictions, especially those based on sexual differences: *In nearly half a dozen cities, women swept past headwaiters to "liberate" all-male bars and restaurants* (Time). 3 *Chemistry.* to set free from combination: *to liberate a gas.* 4 *Slang.* to rob or plunder, especially in wartime: *A handful of Mukti Bahini carrying World War I rifles made a nighttime foray into a roadside village, firing a few stray bullets, ... and liberating the [railroad] station safe of 23 rupees, 80 paisa (about three dollars)* (Atlantic). [< Latin *līberāre* (with English *-ate*[1]) < *līber* free]

**lib|er|a|tion** (lib′ə rā′shən), *n.* 1 the action of setting free: *As the troops withdrew, the entire city celebrated the liberation.* 2 the condition of being set free.

**lib|er|a|tion|ist** (lib′ə rā′shə nist), *n., adj.* **—*n.*** a person, especially a woman, advocating freedom from social biases or restrictions: *The demand on the part of the liberationists for equal pay for equal work is a sound one yet to be realized in many professional areas* (Jacqueline Wexler).
**—*adj.*** advocating freedom from social biases and restrictions: *a liberationist group, a liberationist magazine.*

**lib|er|a|tive** (lib′ə rā′tiv), *adj.* that liberates or favors liberation.

**lib|er|a|tor** (lib′ə rā′tər), *n.* a person or thing that liberates; deliverer.

**lib|er|a|to|ry** (lib′ə rə tôr′ē, -tōr′-), *adj.* = liberative.

**Li|be|ri|an** (lī bir′ē ən), *adj., n.* **—*adj.*** of or having to do with Liberia or its people.
**—*n.*** a native or inhabitant of Liberia.

**Li|ber|man|ism** (lē′bər mə niz′əm), *n.* the economic theories and ideas of the Soviet economist, Yevsei Grigorievich Liberman (born 1897), stressing the role of profit motive and individual incentive in increasing production.

**lib|er|tar|i|an** (lib′ər tãr′ē ən), *n., adj.* **—*n.*** 1 a person who advocates liberty, especially in thought or conduct: *Mencken was first and foremost a libertarian. That explains his unceasing warfare against censorship and prohibition* (Newsweek). 2 a person who maintains the doctrine of the freedom of the will.
**—*adj.*** 1 of or having to do with liberty or libertarians: *It is the modern libertarian idea that a man is accountable only to himself for what he thinks and what he says* (New Yorker). 2 advocating the doctrine of free will.

**lib|er|tar|i|an|ism** (lib′ər tãr′ē ə niz′əm), *n.* the principles or doctrines of libertarians.

**li|ber|té, é|ga|li|té, fra|ter|ni|té** (lē ber tā′ ā gȧ lē tā′ frȧ ter nē tā′), *French.* liberty, equality, fraternity.

**li|ber|ti|cid|al** (li bėr′tə sī′dəl), *adj.* = liberticide[1].

**li|ber|ti|cide**[1] (li bėr′tə sīd), *n., adj.* **—*n.*** a destroyer of liberty. **—*adj.*** destructive of liberty.

**li|ber|ti|cide**[2] (li bėr′tə sīd), *n.* the destruction of liberty.

**lib|er|tin|age** (lib′ər tə nij), *n.* = libertinism.

**lib|er|tine** (lib′ər tēn), *n., adj.* **—*n.*** 1 a person without moral restraints; immoral or licentious person; man who does not respect women. **SYN**: rake, debauchee. 2 a person or thing that goes its own way; one not restricted or confined: *When he speaks, The air, a charter'd libertine, is still* (Shakespeare). 3 a person who holds free or loose opinions about religion; freethinker. 4 a freedman in ancient Rome.
**—*adj.*** 1 without moral restraints; dissolute; licentious. 2 free or unrestrained: *He is free and libertine, Pouring of his power the wine To every age, to every race* (Emerson). 3 freethinking opinions about religion.
[< Latin *lībertīnus* freedman < *lībertus* made free < *līber* free]

**lib|er|tin|ism** (lib′ər tē niz′əm, -tə-), *n.* 1 libertine practices or habits of life. 2 libertine views in religious matters.

**lib|er|ty** (lib′ər tē), *n., pl.* **-ties.** 1 freedom; the condition of being free from captivity, imprisonment, or slavery; independence: *Lincoln granted liberty to slaves. The American colonies won their liberty. A university should be a place of light, of liberty, and of learning* (Benjamin Disraeli). **SYN**: emancipation. See syn. under **freedom.** 2 the right or power to do as one pleases; power or opportunity to do something: *liberty of speech, liberty of action.* 3a permission granted to a sailor to go ashore, usually for not more than 48 hours: *His liberty's stopped for getting drunk* (Frederick Marryat). **b** permission; consent; leave: *You have my full liberty to publish them* (Henry Fielding). 4 the right of being in, using, or otherwise having freedom (of): *We give our dog the liberty of the yard. They allowed him the liberty of the town* (Daniel Defoe). 5 a privilege or right granted by a government. 6 too great freedom; setting aside rules and manners: *The novelist allowed himself liberties of fact that no historian could assume.* 7 *Philosophy.* (of the will) the condition of being free from the control of fate or necessity.
**at liberty, a** free: *You are at liberty to go whenever you wish.* **b** allowed; permitted: *You are at liberty to make any choice you please. She is at liberty to be married to whom she will* (I Corinthians 7:39). **c** not busy: *The principal will see us as soon as she is at liberty after her next appointment.*
**take liberty** (or **liberties**), **a** to act or speak freely, especially beyond the bounds of decorum: *He was repeatedly provoked into striking those who had taken liberties with him* (Macaulay). **b** to be unduly or improperly familiar: *The poor man had taken liberty with a wench* (Daniel Defoe).
[< Old French *liberte,* learned borrowing from Latin *lībertās* < *līber* free]

**Liberty bond,** *U.S.* a government bond issued during World War I to help finance the cost of the war.

**liberty cap,** a soft, cone-shaped cap worn as a symbol of liberty. In Roman times emancipated slaves were given such a cap, and it was adopted as a symbol by the opponents of the monarchy at the start of the French Revolution.

**liberty horse,** a horse trained to perform in a circus without a rider.

**Liberty Party,** the first American political party to oppose the extension of slavery into the territories. It existed from 1840 to 1848.

**liberty pole,** a tall pole with the liberty cap or other symbol of liberty on it, used as a flagstaff.

**Liberty ship,** a cargo ship of about 10,000 gross tons, built in large numbers, mostly in prefabricated sections, by the United States during World War II.

**li|be|rum ve|to** (lib′ə rəm vē′tō), the power of a single member of a legislature to veto a proposed law: *... it could lead to legislative paralysis, like the notorious "liberum veto" by means of which a single deputy could stop the proceedings in the old Polish parliament* (Wall Street Journal). [< Latin *līberum,* accusative of *līber* free, unrestricted + English *veto*]

**li|bid|i|nal** (lə bid′ə nəl), *adj.* of or having to do with the libido: *libidinal energy* (Time). **—li|bid′i|nal|ly,** *adv.*

**li|bid|i|nous** (lə bid′ə nəs), *adj.* lustful; lecherous; lewd: *Bare arms were long considered indecent and even in the libidinous court of Charles II, the upper arm was prudently covered* (Newsweek). **SYN**: lascivious. [< Latin *libīdinōsus* < *libīdō, -inis;* see etym. under **libido**] **—li|bid′i|nous|ly,** *adv.* **—li|bid′i|nous|ness,** *n.*

**li|bi|do** (lə bē′dō, -bī′-), *n.* 1 sexual energy or desire. 2 the energy associated with instincts generally; vital impulse; force motivating mental life: *Libido ... is now very commonly, though not invariably, used to mean the ... vital impetus of the individual* (F. G. H. Coster). [< Latin *libīdō, -inis* desire < *libēre* be pleasing]

**Lib-Lab** (lib′lab′), *adj. British.* of, having to do with, or involving both the Liberal Party and the Labour Party: *We have rejected timorous and defeatist proposals for a Lib-Lab alliance* (Manchester Guardian Weekly).

**Lib.-Lab.,** Liberal-Labour (British politics of the early 1900's).

**Lib-Lab|ber|y** (lib′lab′ər ē, -lab′rē), *n. British.* alliance between the Liberal Party and the Labour Party. [< *Lib-Lab* + *-ery*]

**li|bra**[1] (lī′brə), *n., pl.* **-brae** (-brē). the ancient Roman pound, equal to about 7/10 of a pound avoirdupois. [< Latin *lībra* balance; a weight]

**li|bra**[2] (lē′brä), *n., pl.* **-bras** (-bräs). a former Peruvian monetary unit or gold coin replaced by the sol. [< American Spanish *libra* pound < Latin *lībra* balance; a weight]

**Li|bra** (lē′brə, lī′-), *n., genitive* (def. 1) **Li|brae.** 1 a southern constellation between Virgo and Scorpio, seen by ancient astronomers as having the rough outline of a pair of scales. 2 the seventh sign of the zodiac; Scales. The sun enters Libra about September 23. 3 a person born under the sign of Libra. [< Latin *Lībra* (originally) balance]

**Li|brae** (lē′brē, lī′-), *n.* genitive of **Libra** (the constellation).

**li|brar|i|an** (lī brãr′ē ən), *n.* 1 a person in charge of a library or part of a library: *The librarian had several helpers to work at the desk checking books in and out.* 2 a person trained for work in a library: *Several librarians were needed to check in books, and decide where they should be placed in the library.*

**li|brar|i|an|ship** (lī brãr′ē ən ship), *n.* 1 the profession, authority, and duties of a librarian. 2 the management of a library.

**li|brar|y** (lī′brer ē, -brər-), *n., pl.* **-brar|ies.** 1a a collection of books: *Those two girls have libraries all their own. Good as it is to inherit a library, it is better to collect one* (Augustine Birrell). **b** a room or building where a collection of books, periodicals, manuscripts, and other materials, is kept. A public library that lends books to members for a certain time is called a lending, circulating, or free library. *He goes to the public library to borrow and return books every Saturday. Reference books may be read only in the reference library.* 2 = rental library. 3a any classified group of objects, collected and arranged for use or study: *a library of classical records, a film library, a stamp library.* **b** any room or building where such a collection is kept: *There are a hundred and fifty species of barnacle on file in the library* (New Yorker). 4 a series of books similar in some respect and issued by the same publisher: *The Complete Home Library of Classics.* [< Latin *librārium* a chest for books < *liber* book; (originally) bark[1]]

**library card,** a card entitling the holder to borrow books from a circulating library.

**library paste,** a white, thick paste for paper and cardboard, used in libraries, offices, and schools.

**library science,** the science of organizing, administering, and maintaining libraries, including the techniques of collecting, cataloging, and circulating books and other materials for reading or reference.

**li|brate** (lī′brāt), *v.i.,* **-brat|ed, -brat|ing.** 1 to move from side to side or up and down; sway; oscillate. 2 to be balanced or poised, as a bird. [< Latin *lībrāre* (with English *-ate*[1]) to weigh, balance < *lībra* a balance]

**li|bra|tion** (lī brā′shən), *n.* 1 *Astronomy.* a real or apparent oscillatory motion of a planet or satellite in its orbit. 2 the act of librating; swaying to and fro. 3 a being balanced; equipoise; balance.

**li|bra|to|ry** (lī′brə tôr′ē, -tōr′-), *adj.* librating; oscillatory.

**li|bret|tist** (lə bret′ist), *n.* the writer of a libretto.

**li|bret|to** (lə bret′ō), *n., pl.* **-tos, -ti** (-tē). 1 the words of an opera or other long musical composition: *a clever and yet beautiful libretto.* 2 a book containing the words: *a beautifully bound libretto.* [< Italian *libretto* (diminutive) < *libro* book < Latin *liber, librī*]

**li|bri|form** (lī′brə fôrm), *adj. Botany.* having the form of or resembling liber or bast; elongated, thick-walled, and woody, as certain cells. [< Latin *liber, librī* book; bark[1] + English *-form*]

**Lib|ri|um** (lib′rē əm), *n. Trademark.* chlordiazepoxide.

**Lib|y|an** (lib′ē ən), *adj., n.* **—*adj.*** of or having to do with Libya or its people.
**—*n.*** 1 a native or inhabitant of Libya. 2 ancient or modern Berber, or the group of Hamitic languages to which Berber belongs.

**lice** (līs), *n.* plural of **louse.**

**li|cence** (lī′səns), *n., v.t.,* **-cenced, -cenc|ing.** = license.

**li|cen|cee** (lī′sən sē′), *n.* = licensee.

**li|cense** (lī′səns), *n., v.,* **-censed, -cens|ing.** **—*n.*** 1 permission given by law to do something: *A license to drive an automobile is issued by the state. The man passed the tests and has a license to be a plumber.* 2 a paper, card, or plate, showing such permission: *The policeman asked the reckless driver for his license.* 3 the fact or condition of being allowed to do something: *The farmer gave us license to use his road and to fish in his brook.* 4 freedom of action, speech, thought, or other expression or activity, that is permitted or conceded. Poetic license is the freedom from rules that is permitted in poetry and other arts. *He ... had obtained for himself a sort of license for the tongue* (James F. Cooper). 5 too much liberty; lack of proper control; abuse of liberty: *License they mean when they cry liberty* (Milton). 6 formal permission; authorization: *His majesty ... was pleased to give me his license to depart* (Jonathan Swift).
**—*v.t.*** 1 to give a license to; permit by law: *A*

*doctor is licensed to practice medicine.* **2** to give permission to do something; allow freedom of action to: *They were licensed to make bold with any of his things* (John Bunyan).
[< Old French *licence,* learned borrowing from Latin *licentia* < *licēre* be allowed] —**li′cens|a|ble,** *adj.* —**li′cense|less,** *adj.*

**li|cen|see** (lī′sən sē′), *n.* **1** a person to whom a license is given. **2** *Law.* a person having the right to enter or be on property belonging to someone else.

**license plate,** a metal plate on an automobile, truck, or other vehicle, bearing numbers and letters that identify the vehicle.

**li|cens|er** or **li|cen|sor** (lī′sən sər), *n. Law.* a person who is authorized to grant licenses.

**li|cen|sure** (lī′sən shůr), *n.* a licensing, especially to practice a profession.

**li|cen|ti|ate** (lī sen′shē it, -āt), *n.* **1** a person who has a license or permit to practice an art or profession: *An attorney is a licentiate in law.* **2** a person who holds a certain degree between that of bachelor and that of doctor in certain European universities. [< Medieval Latin *licentiatus,* ultimately < Latin *licentia* license < *licēre* be allowed]

**li|cen|ti|ate|ship** (lī sen′shē it ship, -āt-), *n.* the rank or status of a licentiate.

**li|cen|tious** (lī sen′shəs), *adj.* **1** loose in sexual activities; immoral. **SYN**: lewd, lustful, lascivious, sensual, wanton. **2** disregarding commonly accepted rules or principles; lawless. [< Latin *licentiōsus* < *licentia;* see etym. under **license**] —**li|cen′tious|ly,** *adv.* —**li|cen′tious|ness,** *n.*

**lich** (lich), *n. Archaic.* a dead body; corpse. Also, **lych.** [Old English *līc*]

**li|chee** (lē′chē), *n.* = litchi.

**li|chen** (lī′kən), *n., v.* —*n.* **1** a plant without roots, stems, leaves, or flowers that grows on rocks, trees, and other surfaces. Lichens are gray, yellow, brown, black, or green. A lichen consists of a fungus and an alga growing together so that they look like one plant. The alga provides the food, and the fungus provides the water and protection. **2** a skin disease characterized by itching and reddish pimples in a small area.
—*v.t.* to cover with lichens: *weathered, lichened grave-stones* (New Yorker).
[< Latin *līchēn* < Greek *leichên, -ênos* (originally) what eats around itself < *leíchein* lick]

**li|chen|in** (lī′kə nin), *n.* a white gelatinous carbohydrate, a polysaccharide, obtained from Iceland moss and other lichens. *Formula:* $C_6H_{10}O_5$ [< *lichen* + *-in*]

**li|chen|ize** (lī′kə nīz), *v.t.,* **-ized, -iz|ing. 1** to unite (a fungus) with an alga so as to form a lichen. **2** to cover with lichens.

**li|chen|oid** (lī′kə noid), *adj.* like a lichen: *lichenoid eczema.*

**li|chen|ol|o|gist** (lī′kə nol′ə jist), *n.* a person who studies lichenology.

**li|chen|ol|o|gy** (lī′kə nol′ə jē), *n.* the branch of botany dealing with lichens.

**li|chen|o|met|ric** (lī′kə nə met′rik), *adj.* of, having to do with, or based on lichenometry: *lichenometric dating.*

**li|chen|om|e|try** (lī′kə nom′ə trē), *n.* the measurement of the diameter of lichens to establish their age or the age of the area in which they grow: *Although not as precise or reliable as other methods of dating neoglacial moraines, lichenometry has proved to be particularly useful in certain non-forested arctic and alpine regions and, under ideal circumstances, is applicable over intervals as great as 4,000 years* (Scientific American).

**li|chen|ose** (lī′kə nōs), *adj.* = lichenous.

**li|chen|ous** (lī′kə nəs), *adj.* of, like, or covered with lichens.

**lich gate** (lich), a roofed gate to a churchyard, under which a bier was set down to await the coming of the clergyman. Also, **lych gate.** [< *lich* corpse + *gate*]

**li|chi** (lē′chē), *n., pl.* **-chis.** = litchi.

**licht** (liHt), *n., adj., v.t., v.i.* Scottish. light.

**lic|it** (lis′it), *adj.* lawful; permitted. **SYN**: legitimate, legal. [< Latin *licitus* < *licēre* be allowed] —**lic′it|ly,** *adv.* —**lic′it|ness,** *n.*

**lick** (lik), *v., n.* —*v.t.* **1** to pass the tongue over: *to lick a stamp. He licked the ice-cream cone.* **2** to lap up with the tongue: *Cats and dogs lick water to drink it.* **3** to make or bring by using the tongue: *The cat licked the plate clean.* **4** to pass about or play over like a tongue: *The flames were licking the roof of the burning building.* **5** *Informal.* to beat or thrash: *to lick the dickens out of a boy.* **6** *Informal.* to defeat in a fight; conquer; overcome: *I could lick you with one hand tied behind me, if I wanted to* (Mark Twain). *The washing machine filter ... licked a rust problem* (Scientific American).
—*n.* **1** a stroke of the tongue over something: *He gave the ice-cream cone a big lick.* **2** a place where natural salt is found and where animals go to lick it up: *shot down like deer standing at a lick* (James F. Cooper). **3** *Informal.* a blow: *He gave his horse a few gentle licks with his hand. That rascal of a boy gave me a devil of a lick on the shoulder* (Frederick Marryat). **4** a small quantity; as much as may be had by licking: *She didn't do a lick of work. Flamingo ... was so badly upset ... that he couldn't run a lick* (New Yorker). **5** *Informal.* a brief stroke of activity or effort: *to take a lick at a piece of work. Mr. Saxon is expected to get in his licks before the Committee today* (Wall Street Journal). **6** *Informal.* speed: *to go at full lick.* **7** *Slang.* an improvised part, derived from the main melody, played at the beginning of a jazz composition.
**lick and a promise,** *Informal.* slight or hasty work as if with a promise of doing better later: *I wash the dishes, give the house a "lick and promise," except on Friday morning, when I clean into every nook and cranny* (Christian Science Monitor).
**lick into shape.** See under **shape.**
**lick one's chops.** See under **chop**[2].
**lick the boots of.** See under **boot**[1].
**lick the dust.** See under **dust.**
[Old English *liccian*] —**lick′er,** *n.*

**lick|er|ish** (lik′ər ish), *adj.* **1** fond of choice food. **2** greedy. **3** lecherous; lustful. **4** *Obsolete.* tempting; choice; dainty. Also, **liquorish.** [alteration of Middle English *lickerous* < an Anglo-French equivalent of Old French *lecheros* lecherous, greedy < *lecheor;* see etym. under **lecher**] —**lick′er|ish|ly,** *adv.* —**lick′er|ish|ness,** *n.*

**lick|e|ty-split** (lik′ə tē split′), *adv., adj. Informal.* at full speed; headlong; rapid; rapidly: *... the lickety-split growth of trailer parks across the land* (Wall Street Journal).

**lick|ing** (lik′ing), *n. Informal.* **1** a beating; thrashing: *The bigger boy gave Billy quite a licking.* **2** a setback; reverse: *Business took a bad licking during the recession.*

**lick|spit** (lik′spit′), *n.* = lickspittle.

**lick|spit|tle** (lik′spit′əl), *n.* a contemptible flatterer; parasite; toady: *... a parcel of sneaks, a set of lickspittles* (Thackeray).

**lic|o|rice** (lik′ər is, lik′ris; -ər ish, -rish), *n.* **1** a sweet-tasting substance obtained from the roots of a European and Asiatic plant, used as a flavoring in medicine, tobacco, soft drinks, and candy. **2** candy flavored with this substance. **3** the plant that yields this substance. It is a perennial plant that belongs to the pea family. Licorice has pinnate leaves and bluish pealike flowers in spikes. **4** its root. **5** any one of various plants whose roots resemble or are used as substitutes for licorice. Also, **liquorice, liquorish.** [< Anglo-French *lycorys* < Late Latin *liquirītia* < Latin *glycyrrhīza* < Greek *glykyrrhîzā* < *glykýs* sweet + *rhîzā* root]

**licorice fern,** any one of several polypodies with a sweet rootstock.

**lic|tor** (lik′tər), *n.* one of the group of attendants on a public official in ancient Rome who punished offenders at the official's orders. The lictors carried the fasces. [< Latin *līctor,* related to *ligāre* to bind (from the fasces he carried)]

**lic|u|a|la palm** (lik′yə wä′lə), a dwarf fan palm with large flowers and leaves arranged in a circle. [*licuala* < a native name in Celebes, Indonesia]

**lid** (lid), *n.* **1** a movable cover; top: *the lid of a box, the lid of a pot, a stove lid on a wood-burning stove.* **2** a cover of skin that is moved in opening and shutting the eye; eyelid: *She was alone again in the darkness behind her lids* (Graham Greene). **3** *Slang.* a hat or cap. **4** *Informal, Figurative.* a restraint; check; curb: *to put the lid on gambling. A protest against the secrecy lid was made by Governor Harriman* (New York Times). **5** *Botany.* **a** the upper section of a pyxidium which separates transversely. **b** (in mosses) the coverlike part on the theca. **6** *U.S. Slang.* a small package containing from 22 grams to one ounce of marijuana.
**blow (or flip) one's lid,** *U.S. Slang.* to get very angry or excited: *I showed up with my hair all straggly and no makeup on and Hillyer took a look at me and blew his lid* (New Yorker).
**blow (lift or take) the lid off,** *U.S. Slang.* to expose (illegal or secret activities or those engaging in such activities): *The ensuing investigation achieved nationwide notoriety as the "Summerdale Police Scandal" and blew the lid off the Chicago Police Department* (O. W. Wilson).
[Old English *hlid*]

**li|dar** (lī′där), *n.* a radar that uses laser light beams instead of radio waves: *Meteorological lidar [is] a laser "radar" system using high-power pulses of coherent light to portray cloud patterns and atmospheric aberrations* (New Scientist). [< *li*(ght) (ra)*dar*]

**lid|ded** (lid′id), *adj.* having a lid; covered with or as if with a lid.

**-lidded,** *combining form.* having _____(eye)lids: *Heavy-lidded = having heavy (eye)lids.*

**lid|less** (lid′lis), *adj.* **1** having no lid or lids. **2** having no eyelids. **3** *Poetic.* watchful.

**li|do** (lē′dō), *n., pl.* **-dos.** a fashionable resort: *On beaches, mountains, roads, cruising liners and lidos you will find cricket-lovers* (Punch). [< the *Lido,* a fashionable resort at Venice < Italian *lido* shore < Latin *lītus, -oris*]

**lid|o|caine** (lid′ə kān, lī′də-), *n.* a yellowish-white, crystalline compound used in the form of its hydrochloride salt as a local anesthetic. *Formula:* $C_{14}H_{22}N_2O$ [< (ani)*lid*(e) + (c)*ocaine*]

**lie**[1] (lī), *n., v.,* **lied, ly|ing.** —*n.* **1** something that is not true, said to deceive; false statement known to be false by the person who makes it: *A lie which is half a truth is ever the blackest of lies* (Tennyson). **2** something that gives or is intended to give a false impression: *My life was all a lie* (William Godwin). **3** a false statement: *Women love the lie that saves their pride, but never an unflattering truth* (Gertrude Atherton). [Old English *lyge*]
—*v.i.* **1** to tell a lie or lies: *A faithful witness will not lie* (Proverbs 14:5). **2** to make a false statement. **3** to give a false impression; mislead: (*Figurative*) *That clock must be lying; it isn't noon yet.* (*Figurative.*) *The sun, who never lies, Foretells the change of weather in the skies* (John Dryden).
—*v.t.* to get, bring, put, or otherwise maneuver, by lying: *to lie oneself out of a difficulty.*
**give the lie to, a** to call a liar; accuse of lying: *to give each other the lie in a tavern brawl* (Robert Louis Stevenson). **b** to show to be false; belie: *His actions gave the lie to his statement.*
[Old English *lēogan*]
—*Syn. n.* **1 Lie, falsehood, fib** mean an untruthful statement. **Lie** applies to an untruthful statement deliberately made with the knowledge that it is untruthful and with the purpose of deceiving, sometimes of hurting, others: *Saying his friend stole the money was a lie.* **Falsehood** means an untruthful statement made for a purpose, but can apply to one made when the truth would be undesirable or impossible: *Since he did not want to hurt his sister's feelings, he told a falsehood and said he didn't know.* **Fib** means a lie or excusable falsehood about something unimportant: *Many people tell fibs to get out of embarrassing situations.*

**lie**[2] (lī), *v.,* **lay, lain, ly|ing,** *n.* —*v.i.* **1** to have one's body in a flat position along the ground or other surface: *to lie on the grass, to lie in bed.* **SYN**: recline, repose. **2** to assume such a position: *to lie down on the couch. From off the wold I came, and lay Upon the freshly-flower'd slope* (Tennyson). **3** to be in a horizontal or flat position; rest (on a surface): *The book was lying on the table.* **4** to be kept or stay in a given state: *to lie idle, to lie hidden, to lie unused, to lie asleep.* **5a** to be; be placed: *a lake that lies to the south of us, a road that lies among the trees. The ship is lying at anchor. At Wakefield, six miles off, lay three thousand of the enemy* (Lord Fairfax). *Our course lay along the valley of the Rhone* (Thomas Carlyle). **b** *Figurative.* to exist; be found to be; have its place; belong: *The cure for ignorance lies in education. What a future lies before him!* **6** to be in the grave; be buried: *His body lies in Plymouth.* **7** (of the wind) to remain in a specified quarter. **8** *Archaic.* to spend the night; lodge: *He lay that night at the deanery* (Macaulay). **9** *Law.* to be sustainable or admissible.
—*n.* **1a** the manner, position, or direction in which something lies: *I was able from this position to get a very good idea of the general lie of the Italian eastern front* (H. G. Wells). **b** the state, position, or aspect (as of affairs). See also **lie of the land. 2** the place where an animal is accustomed to lie or lurk. **3** *Golf.* the position of the ball after a drive, in regard to obstacles on the ground or accessibility to the green: *His ball landed in an unplayable lie. His second drive landed in the same woods* (New York Times).
**lie back, a** to lean backwards against some support: *I shipped the oars and lay back thinking* (Samuel R. Crockett). **b** to hold back; keep from exerting oneself: *Landy ran through his carefully planned routine. He lay back, just off the pace* (Time).
**lie by, a** to keep quiet; remain inactive: rest: *I must go below, and lie by for a day or two* (Richard Henry Dana). **b** to remain unused; be laid up

**Pronunciation Key:** hat, āge, cãre, fär; let, ēqual, tėrm; it, īce; hot, ōpen, ôrder; **oi**l, **ou**t; cup, pu̇t, rüle; **ch**ild; lo**ng**; **th**in; **ᴛʜ**en; **zh**, measure; **ə** represents **a** in about, **e** in taken, **i** in pencil, **o** in lemon, **u** in circus.

in store: *I had ... pillows lying by of no use* (Jane Carlyle).
**lie down, a** to give up; succumb: *You could say a man like me ought to be expected to lie down and quit the picture* (Saul Bellow). **b** to neglect; shirk: *to lie down on the job.* **c** to die: ... *"the opium of the people." Some of the dear dead phrases won't lie down* (Norman Shrapnel).
**d** See **take lying down** below.
**lie in**, to be confined in childbirth: *Five hungry children, and a wife lying in of a sixth* (Henry Fielding).
**lie low**. See under **low**[1].
**lie off**, to stay not far from the shore or some other craft: *Intending to lie off at Ramsey for contraband rum* (Hall Caine).
**lie over, a** to be left waiting until a later time: *That matter can just as well lie over until fall.*
**b** to suspend traveling; stop: *We arrived there too late for the morning cars. We had, therefore, to lie over a day* (John R. Bartlett).
**lie to**, to come almost to a stop, facing the wind: *During the storm, the sailing ship lay to.*
**lie up, a** to go into or remain in retreat; remain inactive: *A small herd are shown leaving one of the pools of mud in which they lie up during the day* (New Scientist). **b** to go into dock: *There they [ships] must lie up, or be three or four years in their return from a place which may be sailed in six weeks* (William Dampier).
**lie with**, to be up to; be the province of: *It lies now with Turkey to take the initiative* (Manchester Examiner).
**take (something) lying down**, to yield to (something); not stand up to (something): *That was an insult he just couldn't take lying down, and he demanded an apology.*
[Middle English *lien,* Old English *licgan*]
▶ See **lay** for usage note.

**lie-a|bed** (lī′ə bed′), *n.* a person who lies late in bed; late riser; sluggard.

**Lie algebra** (lē), an algebraic system that reduces independent quantities to groupings whose relationships are then subject to algebraic operation, used especially in studying the behavior of fundamental atomic structures. [< Marius Sophus *Lie,* 1842-1899, a Norwegian mathematician, who developed the system]

**Lieb|frau|milch** (lēp′frou milн′), *n. German.* a light-colored Rhine wine.

**Lie|big condenser** (lē′big), a condenser used in distilling liquids. [< Baron Justus Von *Liebig,* 1803-1873, a German chemist]

**lied**[1] (līd), *v.* the past tense and past participle of **lie**[1]: *That boy lied about his work. He has lied before.*

**lied**[2] (lēd; *German* lēt), *n., pl.* **lie|der** (lē′dər). a German song or ballad, especially one of the songs of Franz Schubert or Robert Schumann or one of similar character. [< German *Lied*]

**lie|der|kranz** (lē′dər kränts′), *n.* **1** a smooth cheese resembling Camembert in texture but with a stronger flavor and odor. **2 Liederkranz.** *Trademark.* a name for this cheese. **3** Also, **Liederkranz. a** a German male singing society. **b** a collection of songs. [American English < German *Liederkranz* garland of songs]

**lie detector**, a device that records the physical reactions of an emotion felt by a person when asked questions; polygraph. It is used especially in crime detection to determine whether a person is lying or telling the truth.

**lie-down** (lī′doun′), *n.* = lie-in.

**lief** (lēf), *adv., adj.* **—adv.** willingly: *I would as lief go hungry as eat that nasty mess.*
**—*adj.*** *Archaic.* **1** beloved; dear; precious: *I charge thee, quickly go again, as thou are lief and dear* (Tennyson). **2** willing; glad: *He up arose, however lief or loth, And swore to him true fealtie for aye* (Edmund Spenser). Also, **lieve**.
[Old English *lēof* dear]

**lief|ly** (lēf′lē), *adv.* gladly; willingly.

**liege** (lēj), *n., adj.* **—*n.*** the relation between a lord and his vassals in the Middle Ages: **a** a lord having a right to the homage and loyal service of his vassals; liege lord: *The young knight knelt and swore loyalty to his liege.* **b** a vassal obliged to give homage and loyal service to his lord; liegeman.
**—*adj.*** **1** having a right to the homage and loyal service of vassals. **2** obliged to give homage and loyal service to a lord: *every liege subject* (Scott). **3** of or having to do with the relationship between vassal and lord. **4a** *Rare.* loyal; faithful.
**b** *Obsolete.* entitled and bound to mutual fidelity.
[< Old French *liege,* or *lige* < Frankish (compare Old High German *ledig*)]

**liege|man** (lēj′mən), *n., pl.* **-men. 1** = vassal.
**2** *Figurative.* a faithful follower: *sworn liegemen of the Cross* (John Keble).

**Lie group** (lē), a mathematical group with a continuous operation in which it is possible to label the group elements by a finite number of coordinates. [< Marius Sophus *Lie;* see etym. under **Lie algebra**]

**lie-in** (lī′in′), *n.* a lying down of a group of people in a public place to disrupt traffic, business, or other affairs, as a form of protest or demonstration; lie-down: *Pollution protesters staged a lie-in at government offices in Tokyo* (Time).

**lien** (lēn), *n.* a claim on the property of another for payment of a debt: *The garage owner has a lien upon my automobile until I pay his bill.* [< Old French *lien* < Latin *ligāmen* bond < *ligāre* bind]

**li|e|nal** (lī ē′nəl), *adj.* of or having to do with the spleen; splenic. [< Latin *liēn* the spleen + English *-al*[1]]

**li|e|ni|tis** (lī′ə nī′tis), *n. Medicine.* inflammation of the spleen; splenitis. [< Latin *liēn* the spleen + English *-itis*]

**lien|or** (lē′nər, -nôr), *n. Law.* a person who holds a lien.

**li|en|ter|ic** (lī′ən ter′ik), *adj.* relating, having to do with, or affected with lientery.

**li|en|ter|y** (lī′ən ter′ē), *n. Medicine.* a form of diarrhea in which the food is discharged partially or wholly undigested. [< Middle French *lienterie* < Medieval Latin *lienteria* < Greek *leienteriā* < *leîos* slippery, smooth + *éntera* the bowels]

**lie of the land, 1** the way in which the land is laid out. **2** *Figurative.* the condition in which things are. See also **lay of the land**.

**li|er** (lī′ər), *n.* a person who lies (down, in wait, or the like).

**li|erne** (lē ėrn′), *n. Architecture.* a minor rib used as a tie between main vaulting ribs and not springing from the impost of the vault. [< French *lierne*]

**Lie theory**, = Lie algebra.

**lieu** (lü), *n.* place; stead.
**in lieu of**, in place of; instead of: *He was jailed ... and is being held in lieu of $30,000 in property bonds* (New York Times).
[< Old French *lieu* < Latin *locus*]

**Lieut.**, Lieutenant.

**lieu|ten|an|cy** (lü ten′ən sē; *British usage,* lef-ten′ən sē, *except for the navy* lə ten′ən sē), *n., pl.* **-cies.** the rank, commission, or authority of a lieutenant.

**lieu|ten|ant** (lü ten′ənt; *British usage,* lef ten′ənt, *except for the navy* lə ten′ənt), *n.* **1** a person who acts in the place of someone above him in authority: *The scoutmaster used the two older boys as his lieutenants.* **2** a commissioned officer in the army, air force, or Marine Corps ranking next below a captain; a first lieutenant or a second lieutenant. **3** a commissioned officer in the navy ranking next below a lieutenant commander and next above a lieutenant junior grade. **4** an officer in a police or fire department, usually ranking next below a captain and next above a sergeant. *Abbr:* Lt. [< Middle French *lieutenant* substitute, (literally) place-holder < *lieu,* or *luef* a place (< Latin *locus*) + *tenant,* present participle of *tenir* to hold < Latin *tenēre*]

**lieutenant colonel**, a commissioned officer in the army, air force, or Marine Corps ranking next below a colonel and next above a major. *Abbr:* Lt. Col.

**lieutenant commander**, a commissioned officer in the navy ranking next below a commander and next above a lieutenant. *Abbr:* Lt. Comdr.

**lieutenant general**, a commissioned officer in the army, air force, or Marine Corps ranking next below a general and next above a major general. *Abbr:* Lt. Gen.

**lieutenant governor, 1** *U.S.* a public official next in rank to the governor of a state. In case of the governor's absence, resignation, or death, the lieutenant governor takes his place. **2** the official head of a provincial government in Canada, appointed by the governor general as the representative of the Crown in a province. *Abbr:* Lt. Gov.

**lieutenant junior grade**, a commissioned officer in the navy ranking next below a lieutenant and next above an ensign. *Abbr:* Lt. jg.

**lieve** (lēv), *adv., adj.,* **liev|er, liev|est.** = lief.

**life** (līf), *n., pl.* **lives** (līvz), *adj.* **—*n.*** **1a** living; being alive. People, animals, and plants have life; rocks, dirt, and metals do not. Life is shown by growing and reproducing. *Life is seen in organized bodies only, and it is in living bodies only that organization is seen* (Ronald Knox). SYN: being, existence. **b** a state, existence, or principle of existence conceived as belonging to the soul, especially in Biblical and religious use: *the spiritual life, eternal life.* **2** the time of being alive; existence of an individual: *a day of one's life, a short life, food enough to sustain life. During his life he was an outstanding doctor.* **3** how long something lasts; time of existence or action of inanimate things; period of being in power or able to operate: *a machine's life, the life of a lease. The life of the Roman Empire was long.* **4** a living being; person: *Five lives were lost.* **5** living beings considered together: *The desert island had almost no animal or vegetable life.* **6** a way of living: *a country life, a dull life, a blameless life.* **7** an account of a person's life; biography: *Several lives of Lincoln have been written.*
**8** spirit; vigor: *Put more life into your work.* SYN: animation, liveliness, vivacity. **9** a source of activity or liveliness: *the life of the party. Definiteness is the life of preaching* (Cardinal Newman).
**10** existence in the world of affairs or society: *young people on the threshold of life.* **11** the living form or model, especially as represented in art. **12 Life,** (in the belief of Christian Scientists) God.
**—*adj.*** for a lifetime: *a life member, a life sentence.* **2** having to do with life or one's life: *a life span. Botany is a life science.* **3** affecting the life of an individual: *a life decision.* **4** painted, drawn, or sculptured, from life: *A life portrait is a painting for which the subject has actually sat.*
**(as) big** (or **large**) **as life, a** just as in life and so not lacking in detail; in reality: *There half-way down was my own name, in print, large as life* (Graham Greene). **b** in person: *There he stood, as large as life.*
**bring to life, a** to revive; restore to consciousness: *The prompt use of artificial respiration can often bring to life a victim of drowning.* **b** cause to live; give life to: *His novels bring to life the Victorian age.*
**come to life, a** to be revived; be restored to consciousness: *A drooping plant comes to life in water.* **b** to be or become vivid: *There are moments when this lethargic and mannered story threatens to come to life* (Orville Prescott).
**for dear life**, to save one's life: *to run for dear life. The gripping spectacle unfolded of Swallow driving the master to the limit of his powers and making him hang on for dear life at the end of the third game* (London Times).
**for life**, during the rest of one's life: *sentenced to hard labor for life.*
**for the life of me**, *Informal.* if my life depended on it: *I can't for the life of me see why you do it.*
**from life**, using a living model: *This was painted from life, not from a photograph.*
**not on your life**, *Informal.* not at all; on no account: *The congressman was asked if there had been any gambling during the trip. "Not on your life," he said* (New York Evening Post).
**see life**, to get experience, especially of the exciting features of human activities: *Does a man want ... to see life in metropolitan boulevards and continental spas?* (Edward Garrett).
**take (a) life**, to kill (someone): *He was sentenced to death for taking a life.*
**take one's life in one's hands, a** to take the risk of causing one's own death: *The man who sails far from land during the hurricane season is taking his life in his hands.* **b** to take any serious risk: *A Republican is taking his life in his hands if he enters the primary in Wisconsin* (Barry Goldwater).
**take one's (own) life**, to kill oneself: *In a moment of deep dejection she thought of taking her own life.*
**to the life**, like the model; exactly; perfectly: *The portrait is my uncle to the life.*
**true to life**, true to reality; as in real life: *Though many of Shakespeare's plays are not historically accurate, most of his characters are true to life.*
[Old English *līf*]

**life adjustment**, *U.S.* an educational theory and program stressing adjustment to society through a system of progressive education.

**life-and-death** (līf′ən deth′), *adj.* involving life and death; crucial; decisive; critical: *the life-and-death power of dispensation of water rights* (William O. Douglas). Also, **life-or-death**.

**life assurance**, *British.* life insurance.

**life belt**, a life preserver made like a belt.

**life|blood** (līf′blud′), *n.* **1** the blood necessary to life: *Fear at my heart, as at a cup, My lifeblood seem'd to sip* (Samuel Taylor Coleridge).
**2** *Figurative.* a source of strength and energy; the vital part or vitalizing influence: *Field work is the lifeblood of anthropology. Opportunities for investment ... are economic lifeblood* (Harper's).

***lifeboat**
definition 2

***life|boat** (līf′bōt′), *n.* **1** a strong boat specially built for saving lives at sea or along a coast. **2** a boat carried on davits on a ship for use by the

passengers in an emergency.
**lifeboat ethic**, a principle of conduct which asserts that in a situation of peril priorities should be assigned according to urgency or expediency: *The Age of Scarcity and accompanying new 'lifeboat ethic' threatens some basic American beliefs . . . and heightens the conflict between rich and poor* (Richard J. Barnet).
**life|boat|man** (līf′bōt′mən), *n., pl.* **-men.** a member of a lifeboat's crew.
**life buoy**, a cork or plastic ring, belt, or jacket used as a life preserver; buoy to keep a person afloat until rescued.
**life cycle**, *Biology.* the successive stages of development that a living thing passes through from a particular stage in one generation to the same stage in the next. See picture under **amphibian.**
**life-ev|er|last|ing** (līf′ev′ər las′ting, -läs′-), *n.* any one of certain species of everlasting and cudweed, especially a fragrant herb common in the eastern United States.
**life expectancy**, the average number of remaining years that a person at a given age can expect to live.
**life force**, the vital or creative force in life; vital force: *Jung . . . holds that primal libido, or life force, is composed of both sexual and nonsexual energy* (Time).
**life|ful** (līf′fəl), *adj. Rare.* **1** full of life; animated. **2** = life-giving.
**life|giv|er** (līf′giv′ər), *n.* a person or thing that gives life.
**life-giv|ing** (līf′giv′ing), *adj.* giving life; vivifying.
**life|guard** (līf′gärd′), *n.* a person employed on a bathing beach or at a swimming pool to help in case of accident or danger to bathers. Lifeguards are trained in lifesaving. [American English < *life* + *guard*]
**Life Guards**, two British cavalry regiments whose duty is to guard the king and queen of England.
**life history**, **1** *Biology.* **a** the successive stages of development of an organism from its inception to death. **b** one series of such stages, often equivalent to a life cycle. **2** *Sociology.* a record, based on personal documents or interviews, of an individual's most important experiences in life. **3** = biography.
**life insurance**, **1** a system by which a person pays a small sum regularly to have a large sum paid to his family or heirs at his death. **2** the sum paid by the insurance company at death. **3** the payments made to the insurance company. **4** a combination of life insurance and endowment insurance.
**life jacket**, a sleeveless jacket which is filled with a light material such as cork or kapok, or inflated with air, and worn as a life preserver.
**life|less** (līf′lis), *adj.* **1** not living; without life: *a lifeless planet, a lifeless stone. My doll, poor lifeless thing, was no comfort.* **SYN:** inanimate. **2** dead: *The lifeless body of the drowned sailor floated ashore.* **SYN:** See syn. under **dead. 3** dull: *a lifeless performance. It was a lifeless party until she came.* **SYN:** sluggish, torpid. **4** (of food) containing no nourishment. **—life′less|ly,** *adv.* **—life′less|ness,** *n.*
**life|like** (līf′līk′), *adj.* like life; looking as if alive; like the real thing: *a lifelike portrait, a lifelike description.* **—life′like′ness,** *n.*
**life|line** (līf′līn′), *n.,* or **life line**, **1** a rope for saving life, such as one thrown to a person in the water or a line fired across a ship to haul aboard a breeches buoy. **2** a line across a deck or passageway of a ship to grab to prevent falling or being washed overboard. **3** a diver's signaling line. **4** *Figurative.* anything that maintains or helps to maintain something, such as a remote military position, that cannot exist by itself.
**life|long** (līf′lông′, -long′), *adj.* lasting all one's life: *a lifelong commitment. The two old men have been lifelong friends.*
**life|man** (līf′mən), *n., pl.* **-men.** *Informal.* a personwho practices lifemanship.
**life|man|ship** (līf′mən ship), *n. Informal.* the skill or act of making others feel inferior so as to gain an advantage. [(coined by Stephen Potter, born 1900, an English author) < *life* + *-manship*]
**life mask**, a likeness made from a cast taken from the face of a living person.
**Life Master**, *U.S.* a player of contract bridge who earns 300 points or more in the national tournaments.
**life net**, a strong net or sheet of canvas, used to catch people jumping from burning buildings. [American English < *life* + *net*]
**life of Ri|ley** (rī′lē), *U.S. Slang.* a carefree, easy life, often with a degree of luxury.
**life-or-death** (līf′ər deth′), *adj.* involving life and death; crucial; decisive; critical: *Water was another life-or-death commodity* (Time).
**life peer**, a British peer whose title is only for his lifetime and is not hereditary.
**life peerage**, the rank of a life peer.
**life peeress**, a woman who is a life peer.
***life preserver**, **1** a wide belt, jacket, or circular tube, usually made of cloth filled with cork, kapok, or air, to keep a person afloat in the water; something to keep a person afloat until rescued. **2** *British.* a short stick with a heavy head or a blackjack used for self-defense.

***life preserver**
definition 1

**life president** or **Life President**, a president, especially the president of any of various African republics, elected to his office for life.
**lif|er** (lī′fər), *n. Slang.* **1** a convict in prison for life. **2** a career officer or soldier: *The old ones, the lifers, know everyone in the Army, from four-star generals on down* (Ward Just).
**life raft**, a raft for saving lives in a shipwreck or the wreck of an aircraft at sea.
**life|sav|er** (līf′sā′vər), *n.* **1a** a person who saves people from drowning. **b** a circular tube, usually made of cork or kapok, used as a life preserver. **2** = lifeguard. **3** *Informal.* a person or thing that saves someone from trouble, discomfort, embarrassment, or the like.
**life|sav|ing** (līf′sā′ving), *n., adj.* **—*n.*** the act of saving people's lives; keeping people from drowning. **—*adj.*** **1** saving people's lives; keeping people from drowning: *a lifesaving service.* **2** designed or used to save people's lives.
**life science**, any one of the sciences dealing with living matter, including biology, biochemistry, medicine, psychology, and the like.
**life scientist**, a scientist who specializes in one or more of the life sciences.
**life sentence**, a decree by a judge or court condemning a person to be imprisoned for the rest of his life.
**life-size** (līf′sīz′), *adj.* of the same size as the living thing: *a life-size statue.*
**life-sized** (līf′sīzd′), *adj.* = life-size.
**life span**, **1a** the length of time that it is possible for a member of a given animal or plant species to live: *Modern medicine has increased man's life span.* **b** the length of time that such a member lives. **2** the actual or potential duration of existence of anything: *The average life span of Governments in the Fourth Republic . . .* (New York Times).
**life style**, a person's or group's characteristic manner of living; one's style of life: *The tastes, ideas, cultural preferences and life styles preferred by many Jews are coming to be shared by non-Jews* (Time).
**life-sup|port system** (līf′sə pôrt′, -pōrt′), the equipment necessary to maintain human life where a normal environment is lacking. A spacecraft's life-support system enables the crew to live outside the earth's atmosphere. *Each astronaut has a life-support system to supply him with breathing and suit-pressurizing oxygen and water for the liquid-cooled garment* (Science News). *All submersibles require life-support systems* (E. S. Arentzen). *. . . the energy that runs the life-support systems of the biosphere* (Scientific American).
**life table**, a table showing the number of individuals that may be expected to live up to certain ages, used in insurance, medical research, and other statistical surveys; mortality table.
**life|time** (līf′tīm′), *n., adj.* **—*n.*** **1** the time of being alive; period during which a life lasts: *My grandfather has seen many changes during his lifetime.* **2** the length of the time anything lasts, is enforced, or is useful: *the lifetime of an electronic system. It is permitted for the lifetime of the contract to import free of duty* (New York Times). **—*adj.*** for life; during one's life: *a lifetime friend, a lifetime investment.*
**life vest**, = life jacket.
**life|way** (līf′wā′), *n.* = way of life.
**life|work** (līf′wėrk′), *n.* work that takes or lasts a whole lifetime; main work in life. **SYN:** career.
**life zone**, a region that generally has a uniform type of plant or animal life, and a single type of climate. Because of environment, the plants in one life zone usually differ from the plants in another zone. *During the growth of the last continental ice sheet . . . the climatic belts and the life zones were gradually pressed southward in front of the ice* (New Yorker).
**LIFO** (lī′fō), *n.* last in, first out (a method of valuing inventory which assumes items in stock are those purchased earliest and values them at prices charged in earliest orders).
**lift**[1] (lift), *v., n.* **—*v.t.*** **1** to raise up higher; raise into the air; take up; pick up; raise: *to lift a chair. Mother lifts the baby from the bed. He lifted his eyes from his work.* **SYN:** See syn. under **raise. 2** to hold up; display on high: *The mountain lifts its head above the clouds. As through a night of storm some tall Strong lighthouse lifts its steady flame* (John Greenleaf Whittier). **3** *Figurative.* to raise, as in rank, condition, estimation, or spirits: elevate; exalt: *to lift a person out of squalor. Battle-fields where thousands bleed To lift one hero into fame* (Longfellow). **4** to send up loudly: *to lift a cry, lift one's voice.* **5** to bring above the horizon by approaching, as at sea. **6** *Informal.* **a** to pick or take up; steal: *to lift things from a store.* **b** = plagiarize. **7** to tighten the skin and erase the wrinkles of (a person's face) through surgery: *She decided to have her face lifted, hoping that it would make her look younger.* **8** *U.S.* to pay off: *to lift a mortgage.* **9** to take up out of the ground, as crops or treasure. **10** *Dialect.* to take up or collect (rents or moneys due). **11** to pick up or loft (a ball) with a golf club.
**—*v.i.*** **1** to rise and go; go away: *the darkness lifts. The fog lifted at dawn.* **2** to yield to an effort to raise something; go up; be raised: *This window will not lift.* **3** to rise: *The island peaks lifted above the horizon. The big liner rolled and lifted* (Rudyard Kipling). **4** to pull or tug upward: *to lift at a heavy box.*
**—*n.*** **1** an elevating influence or effect: *The promotion gave him a lift. . . . without one thrill of inspiration, or one lift above the dust of earth* (Harriet Beecher Stowe). **2** the act of lifting, raising, or rising: *the lift of a helping hand, a lift of the fog.* **3** the distance through which a thing is lifted or moved: *It required a lift of three feet to get the piano in.* **4** *Figurative.* an act of helping; helping hand; assistance: *Give me a lift with this job.* **5** a ride in a vehicle given to a traveler on foot; free ride: *He often gave the neighbor's boy a lift to school.* **6** *British.* an elevator. **7** one of the layers of leather in the heel of a shoe or boot. **8** *Figurative.* a rise, such as in position or condition; promotion; advancement: *a lift of one's fortunes.* **9** elevated carriage (as of the head, neck, or eyes): *a haughty lift of the chin.* **10** a rise of ground. **11** the quantity or weight that can be lifted at one time: *A lift of fifty pounds was all the boy could manage.* **12** a cable or rope with seats or attachments for holding on, to raise a skier to the top of a slope: *Ski slopes for all, lifts, well-marked trails* (Atlantic). **13** *Aeronautics.* **a** the upward reaction of an aircraft into an area of less dense air flowing over its airfoil, such as a wing or rotor blade. See the diagram under **airfoil. b** the upward tendency of an airship or balloon caused by the gas it contains. **14** the ore mined in one operation. **15** *Nautical.* a rope connecting an end of a yard with a masthead and serving to raise, support, square, or trim the yard. **16** the catch of fish brought up in the raising of a net.
[< Scandinavian (compare Old Icelandic *lypta* raise < *lopt* air, sky, loft)]
**lift**[2] (lift), *n. Especially Scottish or Poetic.* the sky; upper regions. [Old English *lyft*]
**lift|a|ble** (lif′tə bəl), *adj.* that can be lifted.
**lift bridge**, a kind of drawbridge of which part may be lifted to permit the passage of boats.
**lift|er** (lif′tər), *n.* **1** a person or thing that lifts. **2** a weight lifter. **3** a thing used for lifting.
**lift|ing body** (lif′ting), = aerospace plane.
**lift|man** (lift′mən), *n., pl.* **-men.** *British.* an elevator operator.
**lift|off** (lift′ôf′, -of′), *n.* the firing or launching of a rocket.
**lift pump**, any pump that lifts a liquid without forcing it out under pressure.
**lift-slab** (lift′slab′), *adj.* of or having to do with preformed concrete slabs, as of flooring, lifted into place by hydraulic jacks, especially in the construction of tall buildings.
**lift truck**, = fork-lift truck.
***lig|a|ment** (lig′ə mənt), *n.* **1** a band of strong, flexible, white tissue that connects bones or holds parts of the body in place: *to strain a ligament.* **2** *Figurative.* a connecting tie; bond of union or attachment: *By such slight ligaments are we bound to prosperity or ruin* (Mary W. Shelley).

**Pronunciation Key:** hat, āge, cãre, fär; let, ēqual, tėrm; it, īce; hot, ōpen, ôrder; **oi**l, **ou**t; cup, pu̇t, rüle; **ch**ild; lo**ng**; **th**in; ᴛʜen; **zh**, measure; ə represents **a** in about, **e** in taken, **i** in pencil, **o** in lemon, **u** in circus.

3 *Obsolete.* a band; bandage; ligature. [< Latin *ligāmentum* < *ligāre* bind]

***ligament**
definition 1

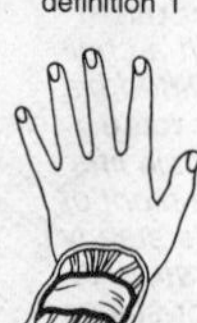
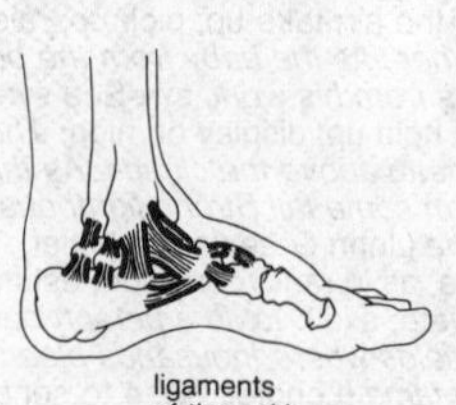
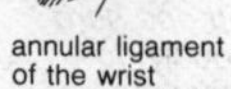
annular ligament of the wrist
ligaments of the ankle

**lig|a|men|tal** (lig′ə men′təl), *adj.* = ligamentous.
**lig|a|men|ta|ry** (lig′ə men′tər ē), *adj.* = ligamentous.
**lig|a|men|tous** (lig′ə men′təs), *adj.* having to do with, of the nature of, or forming a ligament.
**lig|a|men|tum** (lig′ə men′təm), *n., pl.* **-ta** (-tə). *Anatomy.* ligament. [< Latin *ligāmentum*]
**li|gan** (lī′gən), *n.* = lagan.
**lig|and** (lig′ənd), *n. Chemistry.* an ion, molecule, or the like, that forms complex compounds (chelates) by establishing a coordinate bond with the ion of a metal. [< Latin *ligāndum,* neuter gerundive of *ligāre* bind]
**lig|ase** (lig′ās, lī′gās), *n.* an enzyme that joins nucleic acid molecules, used in the synthesis of DNA; synthetase: *All newly made DNA is synthesized in a discontinuous manner. These discontinuous segments are then joined by an enzyme, ligase, to produce a continuous strand* (James C. Copeland).
[< Latin *ligāre* bind + English *-ase*]
**li|gate** (lī′gāt), *v.t.,* **-gat|ed, -gat|ing.** to tie up or bind with a ligature: *to ligate a bleeding artery.* [< Latin *ligāre* (with English *-ate*[1]) bind]
**li|ga|tion** (lī gā′shən), *n.* **1** the act of ligating, especially in surgery. **2** the condition of being bound. **3** something used in binding, as a ligature. **4** place of tying.
***lig|a|ture** (lig′ə chůr, -chər), *n., v.,* **-tured, -tur|ing.** **—*n.*** **1** anything used to bind or tie up, such as a band, bandage, or cord; tie. **2** a thread, wire, or string, used by surgeons to tie up a bleeding artery or vein or to remove a tumor by strangulation, etc. **3** the act of binding or tying up.
**4** *Music.* **a** a slur or a group of notes connected by a slur, showing a succession of notes sung to one syllable or in one breath, or played with one stroke of the bow. **b** = tie. **c** (in some medieval music) one of various compound note forms designed to indicate groups of two or more tones which were to be sung to a single syllable.
**5a** two or three letters joined in printing to form one character. **b** a mark connecting two letters. **—*v.t.*** to bind, tie up, or connect with a ligature. [< Late Latin *ligātūra* < Latin *ligāre* bind]

***ligature**
definitions 4a, 5a

music

ff ffi ffl fi fl
printing

**li|geance** (lī′jəns, lē′-), *n. Law.* **1** obedience of a subject to his sovereign, a citizen to his government, etc. **2** the territories subject to a sovereign. [< Old French *ligeance* < *lige;* see etym. under **liege**]
**li|ger** (lī′gər), *n.* a hybrid animal, the offspring of a lion and a tigress. See **tiglon.** [< *li*(on) + (ti)*ger*]
**light**[1] (līt), *n., adj., v.,* **light|ed** or **lit, light|ing.** **—*n.*** **1a** that by which we see; form of radiant energy that acts on the retina of the eye. Light consists of electromagnetic waves that travel at about 186,282 miles per second. *The sun gives light to the earth.* **b** a similar form of radiant energy which does not affect the retina, such as ultraviolet rays or infrared rays. **2** anything that gives light, such as the sun, a lamp, a lighthouse, or a burning candle: *the Sandy Hook light. We saw the lights of the city. In the house light after light went out* (Tennyson). **3** supply of light: *A tall building cuts off our light.* **4** brightness; clearness; illumination; particular case of this: *a strong or dim light. The light of a standard candle at the distance of one foot is used as a unit of illumination. A good light is needed for reading if eyestrain is to be avoided.* **SYN:** radiance, luminosity. **5** a bright part: *light and shade in a painting. The Italian masters universally make the horizon the chief light of their picture* (John Ruskin). *When the ripe colours soften and unite, And sweetly melt into just shade and light* (Alexander Pope). **6** daytime; time of daylight: *the light of day.* **7** dawn; daybreak: *The workman gets up before light.* **8** a means of letting in light; window or part of a window: *a mullioned window of three lights.* **9** a thing with which to start something burning, such as a match: *He wanted a light for his cigar.* **10** *Figurative.* knowledge; information; mental or spiritual illumination: *We need more light on this subject. ... the men ... of light and leading in England* (Edmund Burke). *God is light* (I John 1:5). **SYN:** understanding, enlightenment.
**11** *Figurative.* public knowledge; open view.
**12** *Figurative.* the aspect in which a thing is viewed: *The principal put the matter in the right light for the students. We have to interpret his words in a modern light* (Graham Greene). **13** *Figurative.* a gleam or sparkle in the eye, expressing lively feeling: *He has the light of battle in his eyes.* **14** *Figurative.* a shining model or example: *George Washington is one of the lights of history.* **15** = traffic light. **16** favor; approval: *the light of his countenance.* **17** *Archaic.* the power of sight; vision: *His ministers with point of piercing sword put out my light for ever* (R. W. Dixon). **—*adj.*** **1** having light: *the lightest room in the house.* **2** bright; clear: *This moonlight night is as light as day.* **3** pale in color; approaching white: *light hair, light blue, the light green of larch trees in the spring.*
**—*v.t.*** **1** to cause to give light: *She lighted the lamp.* **2** to give light to; fill with light: *The room is lighted by six windows.* **3** *Figurative.* to make lively; make bright or clear; brighten: *Her face was lighted by a smile. His style is lighted up with flashes of wit.* **4** to show (a person) the way by means of a light: *Here is a candle to light you to bed.* **5** to set fire to; kindle; ignite: *She lighted the candles.*
**—*v.i.*** **1** to become light; be lighted up: *The sky lights up at dawn.* **2** to take fire; become ignited: *Matches light when you scratch them.* **3** *Figurative.* to become bright with animation, eagerness, or happiness: *Her face lit up with satisfaction.*
**bring to light,** to reveal; expose: *The reporter brought to light bribery in the city government.*
**by** (or **according to**) **one's** (**own**) **lights,** following one's own ideas, intelligence, and conscience in the best way that one knows: *In communities like Hull, Mass., the citizens do what they can by their own lights* (Newsweek).
**come to light,** to be revealed or exposed: *When his prison record came to light, he lost his job.*
**hide one's light under a bushel,** to shy from the display of one's own talent; hide one's skills; be too modest: *With typical modesty they have hidden their light under a bushel, refusing to brag even to their own people* (New York Times).
**in** (**the**) **light of, a** because of; considering: *In the light of all these facts, what he did was completely right. We would judge in the light of all the circumstances as to whether or not the situation was out of hand* (Wall Street Journal).
**b** from the standpoint of: *He views progress in the light of scientific achievement.*
**see the light** (**of day**), **a** to be born: *The helpless infant sees the light* (David Hume). **b** *Figurative.* to be made public: *Had not the doctrines offended France, they had long since seen the light* (William Petty). **c** *Figurative.* to get the right idea: *He had the gardener tell Alexandra ... that he had finally seen the light and invited her to a New Year's Party* (Edmund Wilson).
**shed** (or **throw, cast**) **light on,** to make clear; explain: *The space age has cast new light on natural radiation initially in the discovery of the Van Allen belts* (Harper's).
**stand in one's own light,** to oppose one's own interest; frustrate one's purpose: *Even from the first You stood in your own light and darken'd mine* (Tennyson).
**strike a light,** to make a light: *We had implements to strike a light* (Washington Irving).
[Old English *lēoht,* noun, and adjective]
▶ **lighted, lit.** Both forms are in good use as the past tense and past participle of *light. Lighted* is the more common form of the attributive adjective: *She carried a lighted lamp.* The predicate adjective is either *lighted* or *lit: The room was well lighted* (or *lit*).
**light**[2] (līt), *adj., adv.* **—*adj.*** **1** easy to carry; not heavy: *a light load.* **2** having little weight for its size; of low specific gravity: *a light metal. Feathers are light.* **3a** having less than usual or normal weight: *Many men wear light suits in summer.* **b** below the standard or legal weight: *light coin.* **4** less than usual in amount or force: *a light sleep, a light rain, a light meal.* **5** easy to bear or do; not hard or severe: *light housekeeping, light punishment, a light task, light taxes. The service will be light and easy* (Benjamin Franklin). **6** not looking heavy; graceful; delicate: *a light bridge, light carving.* **7** moving easily; nimble: *a light step, light on one's feet.* **SYN:** agile, active. **8** *Figurative.* cheerfully careless; happy; gay: *a light laugh, light spirits.* **SYN:** buoyant. **9** *Figurative.* not serious enough; fickle: *a light mind, light of purpose.* **10** *Figurative.* aiming to entertain; not serious: *light reading, light music.* **11** *Figurative.* not important: *light losses.* **SYN:** slight, trivial, unimportant. **12** *Figurative.* careless in morals; wanton; unchaste: *a light woman.* **13** not dense: *a light fog, a light snow.* **14** sandy; porous: *a light soil.* **15a** containing little alcohol: *a light wine.* **b** that has risen properly; not soggy: *light dough.* **16a** lightly armed or equipped: *light infantry, in light marching order.* **b** of small size, caliber, or capacity: *light weapons.* **17** built small and without much weight; adapted for light loads and for swift movement: *a light truck.* **18a** carrying a small or comparatively small load. **b** (of a vessel) with little or no cargo. **19** having a velocity of 7 miles per hour or less (on the Beaufort scale, force 1 and 2): *a light wind.* **20** (of a vowel or syllable) not stressed or accented.
**—*adv.*** in a light manner; lightly: *to travel light.*
**light in the head.** See under **head.**
**make light of,** to treat as of little importance: *Making light of what ought to be serious ...* (Jane Austen).
[Old English *lēoht, līht*]
**light**[3] (līt), *v.i.,* **light|ed** or **lit, light|ing. 1** to come down to the ground; alight: *He lighted from his horse.* **2** to come down from flight: *A bird lighted on the branch.* **3** to come by chance: *My eye lighted upon a coin in the road.* **4** to fall suddenly: *The blow lit on his head.*
**light into,** *Slang.* **a** to attack: *Then he lit into Congress for its "passion for economy regardless of the consequences"* (Newsweek). **b** to scold: *The librarian lit into the boys who were making all the noise.* **c** *Obsolete.* to come by chance; be brought or drawn: *When the Hierarchy of England shall light into the hands of busy and audacious men ... much mischief is like to ensue* (Milton).
**light out,** *Slang.* to leave suddenly; go away quickly: *And so when I couldn't stand it no longer, I lit out* (Mark Twain).
[Old English *līhtan* < *līht* light[2]]
**light-a|dapt** (līt′ə dapt′), *v.t.* to adjust to increasing light or brightness: *As the human becomes light-adapted, ... colour discrimination becomes possible* (New Scientist).
**light adaptation,** the adjustment of the pupils of the eyes to increasing light or brightness. Light adaptation occurs when a person steps out of a dark theater into a sunny street.
**light air,** *Meteorology.* a condition in which the wind has a velocity of 1-3 miles per hour (on the Beaufort scale, force 1).
**light-armed** (līt′ärmd′), *adj.* equipped with light weapons.
**light|boat** (līt′bōt′), *n.* = lightship.
**light breeze,** *Meteorology.* a condition in which the wind has a velocity of 4-7 miles per hour (on the Beaufort scale, force 2).
**light bulb,** = incandescent lamp.
**light chain,** any one of the pair of short polypeptide chains in an antibody molecule. Each such molecule contains two light chains (each about 200 amino acids long) and two heavy chains.
**light|clav|i|er** (līt′klə vir′), *n.* an instrument similar to the clavilux, used especially in the 1800's.
**light colonel,** *U.S. Slang.* a lieutenant colonel.
**light curve,** the plotted curve which shows the variations in magnitude of a star's light at different times.
**light-day** (līt′dā′), *n.* the distance that light travels in one day; about 16 billion (16,000,000,000) miles.
**light due** or **duty,** a toll on ships to maintain lighthouses and lightships.
**light|en**[1] (lī′tən), *v.i.* **1** to grow light; become brighter: *The sky lightens before the dawn.* **2** *Figurative.* to brighten: *Her face lightened.* **3** to become lighter in color. **4** to flash with lightning: *It thundered and lightened outside.* **—*v.t.*** **1** to make light; give light to: *Dawn lightens the sky. The city had no need of the sun ... for the glory of God did lighten it* (Revelation 21:23). **2** *Figurative.* to brighten (as the face or eyes). **3** to make lighter in color. **4** to flash like lightning: *Now she lightens scorn At him that mars her plan* (Tennyson). **5** *Archaic.* to enlighten or illuminate spiritually: *Now the Lord lighten thee! Thou art a great fool* (Shakespeare). [Middle English *lighten* < *light*[1]] **—light′en|er,** *n.*
**light|en**[2] (lī′tən), *v.t.* **1** to reduce the load of (a ship or other carrier or a container) or lessen the weight of (a load or quantity); make lighter: *The airplane was lightened when we removed some of the cargo. We lightened the load of the airplane.* (*Figurative.*) *I was lightened of my purse, in which was almost every farthing I had* (Washington Irving). **2** to make less of a burden: *to lighten the burden of his work, lighten taxes.* **SYN:** alleviate, mitigate. **3** *Figurative.* to make more

cheerful: *The good news lightened our hearts.*
— ***v.i.*** **1** to have the load reduced; become lighter. **2** to become less of a burden: *Their luggage … lightened every day* (Daniel Defoe). **3** *Figurative.* to become more cheerful: *Their spirits lightened as summer vacation drew near.* [Middle English *lighten* < *light*²] —**light′en|er**, *n.*

**light|en|ing hole** (lī′tə ning), a hole cut in a beam or structure to lighten it.

**light|er**¹ (lī′tər), *n.* **1** a thing used to set something else on fire, such as the various devices for lighting cigarettes. **2** a person who lights or kindles. [< *light*¹, verb + *-er*¹]

**light|er**² (lī′tər), *n., v.* —***n.*** a flat-bottomed barge used for loading and unloading ships, usually offshore, or for carrying cargo over a short route.
— ***v.t.*** to carry (goods) in a flat-bottomed barge: *All day long the surfboats move back and forth between the shore and the freighters at anchor, lightering cargo* (New Yorker).
[< *light*³ (in earlier sense of "unload"), or perhaps < Dutch *lichter*]

**light|er|age** (lī′tər ij), *n.* **1** the loading, unloading, or carrying of goods in a lighter. **2** the charge for this.

**light|er|man** (lī′tər man′, -mən), *n., pl.* **-men.** **1** a person who works on or manages a flat-bottomed barge. **2** a flat-bottomed barge; lighter.

**light|er-than-air** (lī′tər ᴛʜən ãr′), *adj.* **1** having less weight than the air and depending for support on the buoyancy of the air around it, as gas-filled balloons or airships do. **2** of or having to do with balloons or airships.

***light|face** (līt′fās′), *n., adj.* —***n.*** printing type that has thin, light lines. *Abbr:* lf. —***adj.*** = lightfaced.

***lightface**

The World Book Dictionary

**light|faced** (līt′fāst′), *adj.* (of type) having thin, light lines.

**light-fast** (līt′fast′, -fäst′), *adj.* dyed or treated to resist fading when exposed to light, especially sunlight: *light-fast textiles.* —**light′-fast′ness**, *n.*

**light-fin|gered** (līt′fing′gərd), *adj.* **1** skillful at picking pockets; thievish. **2** having light and nimble fingers. —**light′-fin′gered|ness**, *n.*

**light-foot** (līt′fu̇t′), *adj. Poetic.* light-footed: *light-foot Iris* (Tennyson).

**light-foot|ed** (līt′fu̇t′id), *adj.* stepping lightly; active; nimble. —**light′-foot′ed|ly**, *adv.* —**light′-foot′ed|ness**, *n.*

**light gun**, = biscuit gun.

**light-hand|ed** (līt′hand′id), *adj.* **1** having a light hand or touch; dexterous. **2** having little in the hand. **3** short-handed, as a factory. —**light′-hand′ed|ness**, *n.*

**light harness horse**, any horse bred as a trotter or pacer, especially for use in harness racing. Standardbreds and Morgans are light harness horses.

**light-head|ed** (līt′hed′id), *adj.* **1** dizzy: *A second glass of wine made him light-headed.* **2** out of one's head; delirious: *The sick man was light-headed from fever.* **3** silly; thoughtless; frivolous; empty-headed; flighty: *That frivolous, light-headed girl thinks of nothing but parties and clothes.* ꜱʏɴ: changeable, fickle. —**light′-head′ed|ly**, *adv.* —**light′-head′ed|ness**, *n.*

**light-heart|ed** (līt′här′tid), *adj.* without worry; carefree; cheerful; gay: *light-hearted lads, a light-hearted laugh.* —**light′-heart′ed|ly**, *adv.* —**light′-heart′ed|ness**, *n.*

**light heavyweight**, a boxer or wrestler who weighs 161 to 175 pounds.

**light-heeled** (līt′hēld′), *adj.* light-footed; nimble: *The villain is much lighter-heel'd than I: I follow'd fast but faster he did fly* (Shakespeare).

**light horse**, cavalry that carries light weapons and equipment.

**light-horse|man** (līt′hôrs′mən), *n., pl.* **-men.** a cavalryman who carries light weapons and equipment.

**light|house** (līt′hous′), *n.* a tower or framework with a bright light that usually revolves or flashes and shines far over the water. It is often located at a dangerous place to warn and guide ships. See picture under **beacon**.

**light industry**, industry that manufactures products, such as shoes or food, for use by consumers.

**light infantry**, infantry that carries light arms and equipment.

**light|ing** (lī′ting), *n.* **1** the act or fact of giving light; providing with light; illumination: *The lighting in the library is inadequate.* **2** the way in which lights are arranged: *Indirect lighting is used in many modern homes.* **3** a starting to burn; kindling; ignition. **4** the way the light falls in a picture: *The photographer was careless in the lighting and the picture had many shadows.*

**light|ish** (lī′tish), *adj.* rather light, as in color, weight, or substance.

**light|less** (līt′lis), *adj.* without light: *His undetected offence of riding a lightless bicycle after dark* (London Daily Chronicle). —**light′less|ness**, *n.*

**light|ly** (līt′lē), *adv., v.,* **-lied, -ly|ing.** —***adv.*** **1** with little weight or force; gently; superficially: *Cares rested lightly on the little girl. The sea gull rested lightly on the waves.* **2** to a small degree or extent; not much; to no great amount: *lightly clad.* **3** in an airy way: *flags floating lightly.* **4** quickly; easily; nimbly: *She jumped lightly aside.* **5** cheerfully or with cheerful unconcern; gaily: *to take bad news lightly.* **6** in a slighting way; indifferently: *Don't speak lightly of her because she is poor.* **7** thoughtlessly; carelessly; frivolously: *to behave lightly, an offer not lightly to be refused. These are opinions that I have not lightly formed, or that I can lightly quit* (Edmund Burke). **8a** *Archaic.* readily: *Credulous people believe lightly whatever they hear* (Lord Chesterfield). **b** *Obsolete.* immediately; at once. **9** *Obsolete.* not chastely.
— ***v.t.*** *Especially Scottish.* to make light of; despise; disparage.

**light machine gun**, a machine gun of .30 caliber or smaller, especially a lightweight, air-cooled, .30-caliber machine gun.

**light meson**, a meson resulting from the decay of heavy mesons, having a rest mass or weight about 273 times that of an electron; L-meson.

**light meter**, **1** an instrument for measuring the intensity of light, such as the photoelectric exposure meter. **2** a device to measure and record the amount of electricity used.

**light-mind|ed** (līt′mīn′did), *adj.* empty-headed; thoughtless; frivolous. —**light′-mind′ed|ly**, *adv.* —**light′-mind′ed|ness**, *n.*

**light-month** (līt′munth′), *n.* the distance that light travels in one month; about 500 billion (500,000,000,000) miles.

**light|ness**¹ (līt′nis), *n.* **1** the condition of being lighted; brightness; clearness; illumination. **2** paleness; light color; whitishness. **3** amount of light: *The lightness of the sky showed that the rain was really over.* [Old English *līhtnes* < *lēoht* light¹]

**light|ness**² (līt′nis), *n.* **1** the condition of being light; not being heavy: *The lightness of this load is a relief after the heavy one I was carrying.* **2** the condition of not being hard or severe. **3** gracefulness; delicacy. **4** agility; nimbleness; swiftness: *lightness of step.* **5** *Figurative.* the condition of being gay or cheerful: *lightness of spirits.* **6** *Figurative.* lack of proper seriousness; fickleness; frivolity: *Such lightness of conduct is not to be permitted in church.* **7** *Obsolete.* wantonness; lewdness; incontinence. [< *light*² + *-ness*]

**light|ning** (līt′ning), *n., adj., v.* —***n.*** **1** a flash of light in the sky caused by a discharge of electricity between clouds, between parts of a cloud, or between a cloud and the earth's surface. The sound that it makes is thunder. **2** the discharge of electricity causing this. **3** a flash of light: *The great brand Made lightnings in the splendour of the moon* (Tennyson). **4** any one of a class of racing sloops that are 19 feet long and have movable keels.
— ***adj.*** quick as lightning; very rapid: *Scores often came in lightning succession* (Wall Street Journal).
— ***v.i.*** to emit flashes of lightning: *The overcast sky suddenly lightninged.*
[Middle English *lightening* < *lighten*¹ + *-ing*¹]

**lightning arrester**, a device to protect electrical apparatus from damage by lightning by carrying to the ground the excess voltage produced by lightning discharges.

**lightning ball**, = St. Elmo's fire.

**lightning beetle**, = firefly.

**lightning bug**, = firefly.

**lightning chess**, a game of chess in which the players receive only about ten seconds for each move.

**lightning rod**, a metal rod fixed on a building or ship to conduct lightning into the earth or water.

**light-o'-love** (līt′ə luv′), *n.* **1** a woman capricious or inconstant in love; coquette. **2** a wanton; harlot.

**light opera**, = operetta.

**light pen**, a photosensitive device shaped like a large fountain pen, used to send messages to a computer in response to light impulses displayed by the computer on a cathode-ray tube: *The engineer in charge can … correct the diagram with a single light-pen, and the machine will retranslate the diagram into numbers* (Jean-Jacques Servan-Schreiber).

**light|proof** (līt′prüf′), *adj.* that will not let light through: *a lightproof changing bag.*

**light quantum**, *Physics.* a photon.

**light railway**, **1** a railroad with light equipment. **2** a narrow-gauge railway.

**light ruby silver**, = proustite.

**lights** (līts), *n.pl.* the lungs, as of sheep or pigs, used as food. [< *light*² (from their lack of weight). Compare etym. under **lung**.]

***light|ship** (līt′ship′), *n.* a ship with a bright light that shines far over the water, anchored at a dangerous place to warn and guide ships where it is impractical to build a lighthouse or beacon.

***lightship**

**light show**, a display of colored lights and films in kaleidoscopic patterns usually accompanied by music: *psychedelic light shows.*

**light soil**, a loose, easily workable soil containing more sand than clay.

**light|some**¹ (līt′səm), *adj.* **1** nimble; lively; quick: *lightsome feet.* **2** *Figurative.* happy; gay; cheerful: *a lightsome heart.* **3** *Figurative.* frivolous; flighty. [< *light*² + *-some*¹] —**light′some|ly**, *adv.* —**light′some|ness**, *n.*

**light|some**² (līt′səm), *adj.* **1** radiant with light; light-giving; luminous. **2** well-lighted; bright; illuminated. [< *light*¹ + *-some*¹] —**light′some|ness**, *n.*

**lights-out** (līts′out′), *n.* a signal at which lights must be put out.

**light-struck** (līt′struk′), *adj.* (of photographic film, plates, prints, or X-ray pictures) injured or fogged by unintentional exposure to light or radiation.

**light tank**, any military tank weighing less than 25 tons.

**light-tight** (līt′tīt′), *adj.* that will not let light in: *a light-tight film package.*

**light trap**, a device for trapping insects by means of a mercury vapor lamp or other light source that attracts insects.

**light water**, ordinary water, $H_2O$, as distinguished from heavy water (deuterium oxide, $D_2O$).

**light-wa|ter** (līt′wôt′er, -wot′-), *adj.* of, having to do with, or using light water: *light-water reactors.*

**light-week** (līt′wēk′), *n.* the distance that light travels in one week; 115 billion (115,000,000,000) miles.

**light|weight** (līt′wāt′), *n., adj.* —***n.*** **1** a person, animal, or thing of less than average weight. **2** a boxer or wrestler who weighs 126 to 135 pounds. **3** *Informal, Figurative.* a person who has little intelligence, importance, or influence.
— ***adj.*** **1** light in weight: *The hat … is made of lightweight leather* (London Daily Chronicle). **2** *Figurative.* unimportant; insignificant: *They were written [as] lightweight affairs with humorous entertainment as their object* (New Yorker).

**light|well** (līt′wel′), *n.* a narrow space or shaft admitting light within or between buildings.

**light whiskey**, an American whiskey of a lighter body and fewer natural flavor components than traditional whiskeys.

**light|wood** (līt′wu̇d′), *n.* a dry wood, especially very resinous pine wood, used in the southern United States in lighting a fire.

**light-year** (līt′yir′), *n.* **1** the distance that light travels in one year at a speed of 186,282 miles per second; about six trillion (6,000,000,000,000) miles. It is used to measure astronomical distances. **2** *Figurative.* **a** a very great distance; immeasurably far: *Orthodoxy is still light-years away from any union with Rome* (Time). **b** a very long time; aeon: *That was 1962—light-years ago in political time* (New Yorker).

**lign|al|oes** (līn′al′ōz, lig nal′-), *n.pl.* **1** aloes wood. **2** the bitter drug aloes. [< Late Latin *lignum aloēs* wood of the aloe]

**lig|ne|ous** (lig′nē əs), *adj.* of or like wood; woody. [< Latin *ligneus* (with English *-ous*) < *lignum* wood]

**lig|nic|o|lous** (lig nik′ə ləs), *adj.* **1** living or growing on wood, as fungi. **2** living in wood, as shipworms. [< Latin *lignum* wood + *colere* to inhabit + English *-ous*]

**lig|ni|fi|ca|tion** (lig′nə fə kā′shən), *n.* **1** the act of lignifying. **2** the state of being lignified.

**lig|ni|form** (lig′nə fôrm), *adj.* having the form of wood; resembling wood, as a variety of asbestos. [< Latin *lignum* wood + English *-form*]

**lig|ni|fy** (lig′nə fī), *v.,* **-fied, -fy|ing.** —***v.t.*** to change into wood.
— ***v.i.*** to become wood, as cells whose walls

**Pronunciation Key:** hat, āge, cãre, fär; let, ēqual, tėrm; it, īce; hot, ōpen, ôrder; oil, out; cup, pu̇t, rüle; child; long; thin; ᴛʜen; zh, measure; ə represents **a** in about, **e** in taken, **i** in pencil, **o** in lemon, **u** in circus.

have been thickened and indurated by the deposit of lignin.
[< Latin *lignum* wood + English *-fy*]

**lig|nin** (lig′nin), *n. Botany.* an organic substance which, together with cellulose, forms the essential part of woody tissue, making the greater part of the weight of dry wood. [< Latin *lignum* wood + English *-in*]

**lig|nite** (lig′nīt), *n.* a dark-brown coal in which the texture of the wood can be seen; brown coal; wood coal. In lignite, decomposition of vegetable matter has proceeded farther than in peat but not so far as in bituminous coal. [< French *lignite* < Latin *lignum* wood + French *-ite* -ite[1]]

**lig|nit|ic** (lig nit′ik), *adj.* **1** of or having to do with lignite. **2** containing lignite.

**lig|niv|o|rous** (lig niv′ər əs), *adj.* eating wood, as the larvae of many insects. [< Latin *lignum* wood + *vorāre* devour + English *-ous*]

**lig|no|cel|lu|lose** (lig′nə sel′yə lōs), *n. Botany.* lignin combined with cellulose, forming an essential constituent of woody tissue, as in jute fiber.

**lig|no|sul|fo|nate** (lig′nə sul′fə nāt), *n.* a brown or tan powder obtained from lignin in the process of converting wood into pulp.

**lig|num vi|tae** (lig′nəm vī′tē), **1** an extremely heavy and hard wood used especially for making pulleys, rulers, and other things that get much use and hard wear. **2** the guaiacum tree of tropical America from which it comes. **3** any one of several other trees having similar wood. [< New Latin *lignum vitae* (literally) wood of life]

**lig|ro|in** or **lig|ro|ine** (lig′rō in), *n. Chemistry.* a volatile, inflammable liquid mixture of hydrocarbons obtained by the fractional distillation of petroleum, used as a solvent; petroleum ether. [origin unknown]

**lig|u|la** (lig′yə lə), *n., pl.* **-lae** (-lē), **-las.** **1** *Zoology.* the terminal or dorsal part of the labium of an insect. **2** = ligule. [< Latin *ligula* strap, tonguelike part, variant of *lingula* (diminutive) < *lingua* tongue]

**lig|u|lar** (lig′yə lər), *adj.* of or like a ligula.

**lig|u|late** (lig′yə lit, -lāt), *adj.* **1** having a ligule or ligules. **2** *Botany.* strap-shaped.

**lig|u|lat|ed** (lig′yə lā′tid), *adj.* = ligulate.

**lig|ule** (lig′yül), *n. Botany.* any one of several strap-shaped organs or parts, such as the flattened corolla in the ray florets of composites or the projection from the top of the leaf sheath in many grasses. [< Latin *ligula;* see etym. under **ligula**]

**lig|ure** (lig′yu̇r), *n.* an unidentified precious stone in the breastplate of the high priest, thought to be the jacinth (in the Bible, Exodus 28:19). [< Late Latin *ligurius* < Greek *ligýrion* (diminutive) < *ligyros* a kind of precious stone]

**Li|gu|ri|an** (li gyu̇r′ē ən), *adj., n.* —***adj.*** of Liguria, a district in northwest Italy, or its people.
—*n.* a native or inhabitant of Liguria.

**lik|a|bil|i|ty** (lī′kə bil′ə tē), *n.* the quality or condition of being likable.

**lik|a|ble** (lī′kə bəl), *adj.* having qualities that win good will or friendship; pleasing; popular: *the most likable boy in school.* **SYN:** agreeable. —**lik′a|ble|ness,** *n.*

**like[1]** (līk), *prep., adj.,* **lik|er, lik|est,** *adv., n., conj., v.,* **liked, lik|ing.** —***prep.*** **1** similar; similar to; resembling something or each other: *Mary is like her sister. Our house is like theirs. A critic like you is one who fights the good fight, contending with stupidity* (Robert Louis Stevenson). **2** in like manner with; similarly to; in the same way as; as well as: *She can sing like a bird. She works like a beaver.* **3** such as one would expect of; characteristic of: *His jaw closed like a steel trap. Isn't that just like a boy? It would be like his impudence ... to dare to think of such a thing* (Dickens). **4** in the right condition or frame of mind for: *On Mondays I always feel like going fishing.* **5** giving promise or indication of: *It looks like rain.* **6** *Informal.* such as: *On our trip we will visit cities like Paris, London, and Rome.*
—***adj.*** **1** similar; resembling something or each other: *His uncle promised him $10 if he could earn a like sum. She enjoys drawing, painting, and like arts. Like events will follow like actions* (Thomas Hobbes). *It was very like and very laughable, but hardly caricatured* (Hawthorne). **2** *Archaic.* likely; probable: *The king is sick and like to die. 'Tis like that they will know us* (Shakespeare). **3** *Dialect.* about: *He seemed like to choke.*
—***adv.*** **1** *Informal.* probably: *Like enough it will rain.* **2** in like manner: *Like as a father pitieth his children, so the Lord pitieth them that fear him* (Psalms 103:13). **3** *Archaic.* to a like extent or degree: *The enterprise ... Shall be to you, as us, like glorious* (Shakespeare). **4** *Dialect.* as it were; so to speak; somewhat: *They say she was out of her mind like for six weeks or more* (Thackeray).
—***n.*** **1** a person or thing like another; match; counterpart or equal: *We shall not see his like again.* **2** something of similar nature.
—***conj.*** *Informal.* **1** as if: *He acted like he was afraid. Drive it like you hate it, it's cheaper than psychiatry* (New York Times). **2** in the same way as; as: *It was just like he said it was. Unfortunately few have observed like you have done* (Charles Darwin). **3** as if to say; so to speak: *Afterward, a girl came up to me and said, "You look kinda interested in this; did you know there are civil rights for women?" And I thought like wow, this is for me* (Kate Millett).
—***v.t.*** *Obsolete.* to compare. —***v.i.*** *Dialect.* to come near: *He liked to have choked.*
**and the like, a** and so forth: *He studied music, painting, and the like.* **b** and other like things: *We went to the zoo and saw tigers, lions, bears, and the like.*
**had like,** *Dialect.* came near; was about: *He had like to have been killed.*
**like crazy.** See under **crazy.**
**like to,** *U.S. Dialect.* sort of; in a way: *Valda, she dropped the baby, and I like to fainted* (Michael Lydon).
**nothing like,** not nearly: *I have had nothing like a bad fall lately* (G. Gambado).
**or the like,** or other like things: *Legends glorify heroes, saints, animals, or the like.*
**something like,** about; almost: *The soldiers of the Guard ... killed something like a thousand people* (Edmund Wilson).
**tell it** (or **say it**) **like it is,** *U.S. Slang.* to speak out frankly or candidly; tell the facts without evasion or deception: *The [TV] series' intention, says Griffith, is "to tell it like it is for the young people while remaining palatable to older audiences"* (Time).
**the like(s) of,** such a person or thing as: *Are there no harems still left in Stamboul for the likes of thee to sweep and clean?* (George du Maurier).
[Middle English *liche,* Old English *gelīc*]
▶ **like, as.** In written or formal English *as* and *as if* (not *like*) are preferred to introduce clauses of comparison: *He writes as* (not *like*) *he used to when he was a child. Act as if* (not *like*) *you were accustomed to being here.* In spoken or informal English *like* is often used instead of *as* and *as if: He writes like he used to. Act like you know what you are doing.* Although historically both *like* and *as* are justified, custom in certain circles has made *as* the preferred form in introducing clauses in written and formal English.

**like[2]** (līk), *v.,* **liked, lik|ing,** *n.* —***v.t.*** **1** to be pleased with; be satisfied with; find agreeable or congenial: *to like a place, to like a person. Baby likes milk. He shall dwell ... where it liketh him best* (Deuteronomy 23:16). **2** to wish for; wish to have: *I should like more time to finish my work.*
—***v.i.*** **1** to feel inclined; wish: *Boys like to play. Come whenever you like.* **2** *Archaic.* to please; be pleasing; suit a person: *They ... looking liked, and liking loved* (Scott).
—***n.*** **likes,** likings; preferences: *Mother knows all of my likes and dislikes.*
[Old English *līcian* to please. See related etym. at **like[1]**.] —**lik′er,** *n.*
▶ **Like, love** are generally not considered interchangeable. *Like* means to find pleasure or satisfaction in something or someone, or to have friendly feelings for a person, but does not suggest strong feelings or emotion: *I like books. Boys like to play. Love* emphasizes strong feelings and deep attachment, and is used to express the emotion of love: *She loves her mother. He loves music* (suggests deep attachment).

**-like,** *suffix added to nouns to form adjectives.*
**1** like; similar to: *Daisylike* = *like a daisy. Doglike* = *similar to a dog. Wolflike* = *like a wolf.*
**2** like that of; characteristic of: *Childlike* = *like that of a child.*
**3** suited to; fit or proper for: *Businesslike* = *suited to business.*
[< *like[1]*, adjective]
▶ **-like** is a living suffix, freely used to form adjectives of nouns and sometimes to form adverbs of adjectives. Words ending in *-like* are usually not hyphenated unless three *l's* come together: *springlike, fall-like.*

**like|a|bil|i|ty** (lī′kə bil′ə tē), *n.* = likability.

**like|a|ble** (lī′kə bəl), *adj.* = likable. —**like′a|ble|ness,** *n.*

**like|li|hood** (līk′lē hu̇d), *n.* **1** the quality or fact of being likely or probable; probability. **2** a probability or chance of something: *Is there any great likelihood of rain this afternoon?* **3** *Obsolete.* an indication; sign: *Many likelihoods informed me of this before* (Shakespeare).

**like|li|ness** (līk′lē nis), *n.* the condition or quality of being likely.

**like|ly** (līk′lē), *adj.,* **-li|er, -li|est,** *adv.* —***adj.*** **1** probable: *One likely result of this heavy rain is the rising of the river.* **2** to be expected: *It is likely to be hot in August.* **3** appearing to be true; believable: *a likely story.* **4** suitable: *Is this a likely place to fish?* **5** giving promise of success or excellence; promising: *a likely boy.*
—***adv.*** probably; in all probability: *I shall very likely be at home all day.*
[< Scandinavian (compare Old Icelandic *līkligr*)]
▶ **Likely, apt, liable** indicate possibility but not in the same way. *Likely* implies probability: *It is likely to rain tonight. Apt* implies natural or habitual tendency: *Children are apt to be noisy at play. Liable* implies risk or danger: *Because he doesn't study, he is liable to fail.*

**like-mind|ed** (līk′mīn′did), *adj.* **1** in agreement or accord. **2** that thinks along the same lines: *And the Presidential nominee ... should resign his nomination ... if he does not get the like-minded Vice Presidential running-mate he wants* (New York Times). —**like′-mind′ed|ly,** *adv.* —**like′-mind′ed|ness,** *n.*

**lik|en** (lī′kən), *v.t.* to represent as like; compare: *The kingdom of heaven is likened unto a man which sowed good seed in his field* (Matthew 13:24).

**like|ness** (līk′nis), *n.* **1** a resembling; a being alike: *The boy's likeness to his father was striking.* **2** something that is like; copy; picture: *to have one's likeness painted. The stamp has a good likeness of Lincoln on it.* **SYN:** counterpart, image, portrait. **3** appearance; shape: *His fairy godmother came to him in the likeness of a bird.*

**likes** (līks), *n.pl.* See under **like[2]**.

**like|wise** (līk′wīz′), *adv.* **1** the same; similarly: *See what I do. Now you do likewise.* **2** also; moreover; too; as well: *I must go home now, and she likewise.*

**li|kin** (lē′kēn′), *n.* a Chinese provincial duty on goods in transit. [< Mandarin *li-chin* < *li* a small coin + *chin* money]

**lik|ing** (lī′king), *n.* **1** preference; fondness; kindly feeling: *a liking for apples, a liking for children. Friendships begin with liking* (George Eliot). **2** taste; pleasure: *food to your liking. James Binnie had found the Continental life pretty much to his liking* (Thackeray). [Old English *līcung* < *līcian* to please, like[2]]

**lik|ker** (lik′ər), *n. U.S. Dialect.* liquor: *corn likker.*

**li|ku|ta** (li kü′tə), *n., pl.* **ma|ku|ta.** a unit of money of Zaire, equal to 1/100 of a zaire.

**li|lac** (lī′lək, -lak, -läk), *n., adj.* —***n.*** **1** a shrub with clusters of tiny, fragrant, usually pale pinkish-purple or white flowers that belongs to the olive family. Its blossom is the floral emblem of New Hampshire. See picture under **olive family. 2** a cluster of these flowers. **3** a pale pinkish purple.
—***adj.*** pale pinkish-purple: *a lilac dress.*
[< obsolete French *lilac* < Spanish < Arabic *līlak* < Persian, variant of *nīlak* bluish < *nīl* indigo. Compare etym. under **anil.**]

**li|la|ceous** (lī lā′shəs), *adj.* of or resembling the pinkish-purple of most lilacs.

**li|lan|ge|ni** (li läng′gə nē), *n., pl.* **emalangeni.** the unit of money of Swaziland, equal in value with the South African rand. [< siSwati *lilangeni*]

**lil|i|a|ceous** (lil′ē ā′shəs), *adj.* **1** of or characteristic of lilies. **2** belonging to the lily family. [< Late Latin *līliāceus* (with English *-ous*) lilylike < Latin *līlium* lily]

**lil|ied** (lil′ēd), *adj.* **1** resembling a lily in fairness of complexion; white. **2** covered with or full of lilies.

**Lil|ith** (lil′ith, lī′lith), *n.* **1** *Semitic Mythology.* a female demon who consorts with men in their dreams. In later legend she was a vampire who dwelt in deserted places and preyed on children. **2** (in Jewish folklore) Adam's first wife, before Eve was created.

**Lil|li|put** (lil′ə put, -pət), *n.* an imaginary island described in Jonathan Swift's *Gulliver's Travels* (1726). Its tiny people are represented as being about six inches tall.

**Lil|li|pu|tian** (lil′ə pyü′shən), *adj., n.* —***adj.*** **1** of or suitable for Lilliput or its inhabitants. **2** very small; tiny; petty: *A four-inch fort, with crenellated walls and a ramp, concealing ten Lilliputian soldiers in its base* (New Yorker).
—*n.* **1** an inhabitant of Lilliput. **2** a person of little size, character, or mind; a very small person.

**li|lo** (lī′lō), *n., pl.* **-los.** *British.* an air mattress. [alteration of *lie low*]

**lilt** (lilt), *v., n.* —***v.t.*** to sing or play (a tune) in a light, tripping manner: *She tripped merrily on, lilting a tune to supply the lack of conversation* (Emily Brontë).
—***v.i.*** **1** to sing or play in a light, tripping manner. **2** to move in a light, springing manner.
—***n.*** **1** a lively song or tune with a swing. **2** rhythmical cadence or swing: *The lines go with a lilt* (Robert Louis Stevenson). **3** a springing action; a lively, springing movement: *She walks with a lilt.*
[Middle English *lulten, lylten;* origin uncertain]
—**lilt′ing|ly,** *adv.*

**lil|y** (lil′ē), *n., pl.* **lil|ies,** *adj.* —***n.*** **1** a plant with flowers that are usually large, bell-shaped, and beautiful, and are often divided into six parts. It grows from a bulb and belongs to the lily family.

**2** the flower. The white lily is a symbol of purity. **3** the bulb. **4** any one of various related or similar plants, such as the calla lily, day lily, or water lily. **5** *Heraldry.* the fleur-de-lis.
— ***adj.*** **1** like a white lily; pure and lovely; delicate: *Elaine, the lily maid of Astolat* (Tennyson). **2** pallid; colorless; bloodless.
**gild the lily,** to ornament or overstate something that is already good or pleasing: *Apparently acknowledging that Mr. Ford had made his point, Commissioner Ploscowe soon cut off the questioning, saying "I don't know why you're gilding the lily"* (New York Times).
[Old English *lilie* < Latin *līlium*] — **lil′y|like′,** *adj.*

**∗lily family,** a group of monocotyledonous herbs, shrubs, and trees, that usually have flowers with six parts, grow from fleshy rootstocks or bulbs, and have stemless leaves. Lilies, tulips, hyacinths, trilliums, asparagus, smilax, and aloes belong to the lily family.

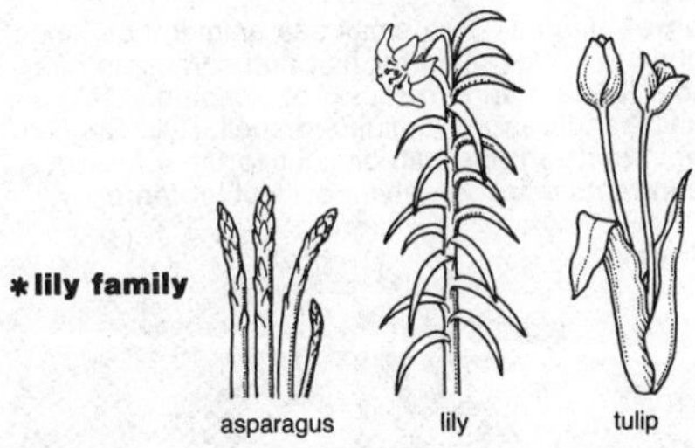

**∗lily family**

**lily iron,** a harpoon with a detachable head used in killing swordfish.

**lil|y-liv|ered** (lil′ē liv′ərd), *adj.* cowardly: *thou lily-livered boy* (Shakespeare).

**lily of the valley,** *pl.* **lilies of the valley.** **1** a plant having tiny, sweet-smelling, bell-shaped, white flowers arranged up and down a single stem. It belongs to the lily family. **2** its flowers.

**lily pad,** *U.S.* the broad, flat floating leaf of a water lily: *Huge moccasin darting away beneath the dense reeds and lily pads of the swamp* (Knickerbocker Magazine).

**lil|y-white** (lil′ē hwīt′), *adj.* **1** clean; free of stigma: *There was no justification for the "war" that was going on ... "It should end," he declared, "Neither one is lily-white"* (New York Times). **2** pure white; white as a lily: *And, as with my lily-white hands I knock up an extra wing in which to house them* (Punch). **3** *U.S.* excluding or seeking to exclude Negroes: *a lily-white country club.* — **lil′y-white′ness,** *n.*

**Lil|y-white** (lil′ē hwīt′), *n., adj.* — ***n.*** a member of a faction of Republicans in the southern United States seeking to exclude Negroes from political affairs.
— ***adj.*** of or having to do with the Lily-whites.

**lim.,** limit.

**L.I.M.** or **LIM** (no periods), linear induction motor.

**Li|ma** (lē′mə), *n.* **1** *U.S.* a code name for the letter *l,* used in transmitting radio messages. **2** = Lima bean.

**Lima bean,** **1** a broad, flat, pale-green or white bean used as a vegetable: *[The] Lima bean is the most nutritious member of the pea family. It is high in protein value, and rich in vitamin B* (Arthur J. Pratt). **2** the plant that it grows on. [< *Lima,* the capital of Peru]

**li|mac|i|form** (lī mas′ə fôrm), *adj.* having the form of a slug; snaillike: *limaciform larvae.* [< Latin *līmāx, -ācis* snail, slug + English *-form*]

**lim|a|cine** (lim′ə sīn, -sin; lī′mə-), *adj.* **1** of or having to do with the family of mollusks comprising the slugs. **2** resembling the slugs. [< New Latin *Limacinae* a subfamily of snails < Latin *līmāx, -ācis* snail, slug < Greek *leímāx, -akos*]

**lim|a|con** or **lim|a|çon** (lim′ə son, lē mə sôɴ′), *n.* **1** *Geometry.* a curve, invented and named by Pascal, generated from a circle by adding a constant length to all the radii vectores drawn from a point of its circumference as an origin. The limacon has three varieties, one of which is the cardioid. **2** a snail or its shell; univalve. [< French *limaçon* snail < Latin *līmāx, -ācis* snail, slug]

**limb**[1] (lim), *n., v.* — ***n.*** **1** a leg, arm, or wing: *That man with one arm lost his other limb in an airplane crash.* **2** a large branch: *They sawed the dead limb off the tree.* **SYN:** See syn. under **branch.** **3** a part that projects, such as a section of a building: *the four limbs of a cross.* **SYN:** arm, shoot. **4** a person or thing thought of as a branch or offshoot: *The housing committee is a limb of the city council. Television is a limb of the electronics industry* (Punch). **5** a mischievous child; scamp: *I always hated young uns, and this ere's a perfect little limb* (Harriet Beecher Stowe). **6** a member or clause of a sentence. **7** a spur of a mountain range. **8** one of the pieces of a gunlock.
— ***v.t.*** to pull limb from limb; dismember.
**go out on a limb,** *Informal.* to put oneself in a dangerous or vulnerable position: *He went out on a limb for his wayward brother by recommending him to a friend for a job. The candidate went out on a limb on the budget issue.*
**limb from limb,** completely apart; entirely to pieces: *They pulled down ... their houses, and pulled them ... limb from limb* (Daniel Defoe).
[Old English *lim*] — **limb′less,** *adj.*

**limb**[2] (lim), *n.* **1** the edge or boundary of a surface, especially: **a** the graduated edge of a quadrant or similar instrument. **b** the edge of the disk of a heavenly body: *the sun's lower limb was just free of the hill* (Thomas Hardy). **2** *Botany.* the expanded flat part of a structure, such as the upper part of a gamopetalous corolla or the blade of a leaf. **3** *Archery.* either part of a bow above or below the grip or handle. [< Latin *limbus* border, edge. See etym. of doublets **limbo, limbus.**]

**lim|ba** (lim′bə), *n.* **1** = afara. **2** the wood of the afara. [< a native word]

**lim|bate** (lim′bāt), *adj. Biology.* having a border; bordered, as a flower having an edging of a different color from the rest. [< Late Latin *limbātus* bordered, edged < Latin *limbus* edge, limbus]

**-limbed,** *combining form.* having ____limbs: *Straight-limbed = having straight limbs.*

**lim|ber**[1] (lim′bər), *adj., v.* — ***adj.*** **1** bending or moving easily; flexible: *Willow is a limber wood. A piano player should have limber fingers.* **SYN:** supple, nimble, pliant, lithe. See syn. under **flexible.** **2** *Figurative.* yielding readily to strain or influence: *You put me off with limber vows* (Shakespeare).
— ***v.t.*** to make limber.
— ***v.i.*** to become limber: *He is stiff when he begins to skate, but limbers up easily.*
[perhaps < *limb*[1]] — **lim′ber|ly,** *adv.* — **lim′berness,** *n.*

**lim|ber**[2] (lim′bər), *n., v.* — ***n.*** the detachable front part of the carriage of a horse-drawn field gun.
— ***v.t., v.i.*** to attach the limber (to) in preparing to move.
[alteration of Middle English *lymour,* or *limmer,* perhaps < Middle French *limonière* wagon with shafts < Old French *limon* shaft]

**lim|ber|neck** (lim′bər nek′), *n.* botulism of domestic poultry.

**limber pine,** a white pine with a short trunk, a wide, round-topped head, and pliable wood, found on the northwestern coast of North America.

**lim|bers** (lim′bərz), *n.pl.* holes or channels through which water may pass to the pump well of a ship. [perhaps < French *lumière* hole; (literally) light]

**lim|bic** (lim′bik), *adj.* **1** of or having the character of a limbus or border; bordering; marginal. **2** of or having to do with the limbic lobes or the limbic system: *the limbic cortex.*

**limbic lobe,** *Anatomy.* either of two lobes of the brain, one in each hemisphere.

**limbic system,** *Anatomy.* a group of interconnected neural structures in the rudimentary cortex of the brain, which surround the midline surfaces of the cerebral hemispheres and pass into the brain stem. The limbic system is believed to control various emotional patterns of behavior.

**lim|bo** (lim′bō), *n.* **1** Often, **Limbo.** (in Roman Catholic theology) a region for souls of people who die unbaptized but do not deserve the punishment of sinners. The souls of righteous people who died before the coming of Christ were kept in limbo until after the Resurrection. **2** *Figurative.* a place for people and things forgotten, cast aside, or out of date: *The belief that the earth is flat belongs to the limbo of outworn ideas. Vast tracts of land will go into a kind of limbo which may or may not mean permanent socialization* (Wall Street Journal). **3** *Figurative.* prison; jail; confinement: *I should be better satisfied if you were in limbo, with a rope about your neck, and a comfortable bird's-eye prospect to the gallows* (William Godwin). **4** a West Indian calypso dance in which each participant dances his way under a rod held up horizontally, bending backward to avoid touching the rod as it is progressively lowered: *And when the limbo dancers perform their dazzling gyrations and move their incredibly supple bodies under the low, flaming pole, you will gasp with admiration and excitement* (New Yorker). [< Latin *(in) limbō* (on) the edge, ablative of *limbus.* See etym. of doublets **limb**[2], **limbus.**]

**Lim|burg|er** (lim′bėr gər), *n.* a soft white cheese with a strong smell. [< German *Limburger* < *Limbourg,* a province in Belgium]

**lim|bus** (lim′bəs), *n., pl.* **-bi** (-bī). **1** a border or edge differentiated by color or formation, as in some flowers and shells. **2** a place on the border of hell; limbo. [< Latin *limbus* border, edge (in Medieval Latin, limbo). See etym. of doublets **limb**[2], **limbo.**]

**lime**[1] (līm), *n., adj., v.,* **limed, lim|ing.** — ***n.*** **1a** a white substance obtained by burning limestone, shells, or bones; calcium oxide; quicklime. Lime is strongly alkaline and is used in making mortar, cement, and glass, in tanning, and on fields to improve the soil. *Formula:* CaO **b** any one of various other compounds containing calcium that are used for soil improvement. **2** = birdlime.
— ***adj.*** having to do with or containing lime: *lime pits, a lime ointment.*
— ***v.t.*** **1** to put lime on; treat with lime: *He drained the land and limed it.* **2** to smear (branches or twigs) with birdlime. **3** to catch (birds) with or as if with birdlime. **4** *Figurative.* to entangle; ensnare: *O limed soul, that struggling to be free, Art more engaged!* (Shakespeare). **5** to cement: *I will not ruinate my father's house, Who gave his blood to lime the stones together* (Shakespeare).
[Old English *līm*]

**lime**[2] (līm), *n., adj.* — ***n.*** **1** a juicy citrus fruit much like a lemon. A lime is green, and smaller and sourer than a lemon. Its juice is used as a flavoring and as a source of vitamin C. **2** the tree it grows on, native to Asia. It is a small tropical tree that belongs to the rue family.
— ***adj.*** **1** of the color of lime: *lime green.* **2** of lime; containing lime: *a lime flavor, a lime drink.*
[< French *lime* < Spanish *lima* < Arabic *līma,* back formation of *līmūn* (< Persian), with *-ūn* taken as an ending. Compare etym. under **lemon.**]

**lime**[3] (līm), *n.* the linden tree of Europe, often used for shade. [variant of earlier *line,* Old English *lind* linden]

**lime|ade** (līm′ād′), *n.* a drink made of lime juice, sugar, and water.

**lime|burn|er** (līm′bėr′nər), *n.* **1** a person who makes lime by burning or calcining limestone. **2** a container for burning or calcining limestone.

**lime glass,** a type of inexpensive glass containing a large amount of calcium oxide, introduced in the 1860's.

**lime juice,** the juice of limes, used in flavoring beverages or food and once used especially by seamen and arctic explorers to prevent scurvy.

**lime|juic|er** (līm′jü′sər), *n. Slang.* a British sailor or ship.

**lime|kiln** (līm′kil′, -kiln′), *n.* a furnace for making lime, as by burning limestone, shells, and bones.

**lime|light** (līm′līt′), *n., v.,* **-light|ed** or **-lit, -lighting.** — ***n.*** **1** the center of public interest or glare of public attention: *Some people are never happy unless they are in the limelight showing off. German bonds took the limelight in the foreign land market* (London Times). **2a** a strong light thrown upon the stage of a theater to light up certain persons or objects and draw attention to them; oxycalcium light; calcium light. **b** the fixture used to produce such a stage light by directing an oxyhydrogen flame against a block of lime. **c** the part of the stage thus lighted, usually the center.
— ***v.t.*** to illuminate by or as if by limelight; make the center of attention: *Louis MacNiece was a poet's poet. He never sought the easy limelit road to a mass audience* (London Times).

**li|men** (lī′men), *n. Psychology, Physiology.* a threshold, especially of perception. [< Latin *līmen, -inis* threshold]

**lim|er|ick** (lim′ər ik, lim′rik), *n.* a kind of humorous verse of five lines. *Example:*
"There was a young lady from Lynn
Who was so exceedingly thin
That when she essayed
To drink lemonade
She slid down the straw and fell in."
A limerick has a rhyme scheme with lines 1, 2, and 5 having three feet, and 3 and 4 having two feet. [apparently from a song that mentioned *Limerick,* a county and city in Ireland]

**li|mes** (lī′mēz), *n., pl.* **lim|i|tes.** a boundary or line of fortifications, especially in ancient Rome. [< Latin *līmes, -itis* boundary]

**lime saltpeter,** = calcium nitrate.

**lime|stone** (līm′stōn′), *n.* a rock consisting mostly of calcium carbonate, used for building and for making lime. Marble is a kind of limestone.

**lime sulfur,** a solution of lime, sulfur, and water boiled together, used as a fungicide and insecticide.

**lime tree,** **1** any linden tree (used more commonly in Europe than America). **2** a tupelo or sour gum, found in the southern United States.

---

**Pronunciation Key:** hat, āge, cãre, fär; let, ēqual, tėrm; it, īce; hot, ōpen, ôrder; oil, out; cup, pu̇t, rüle; child; long; thin; ᴛʜen; zh, measure; ə represents **a** in about, **e** in taken, **i** in pencil, **o** in lemon, **u** in circus.

3 a tree that bears limes.

**lime twig**, 1 a twig smeared with birdlime for catching birds. 2 *Figurative.* anything used to ensnare: *Catch fools with lime twigs dipt with pardons* (Thomas Dekker).

**lime|wash** (līm′wosh′, -wôsh′), *n., v.* —*n.* a mixture of lime and water, used for coating walls, woodwork, or other surfaces.
—*v.t.* to whitewash with such a mixture.

**lime|wa|ter** (līm′wô′tər, -wot′ər), *n.* 1 a solution of slaked lime in water. It is used to counteract an acid condition in the digestive tract. 2 water that contains naturally a large amount of either calcium carbonate or calcium sulfate.

**lim|ey**[1] (lī′mē), *n., pl.* **-eys**, *adj. Slang.* —*n.* 1 any Englishman, especially a sailor or soldier. 2 an English ship.
—*adj.* English: *Naples was the first port this limey ship made* (New Yorker). Also, **limy**.
[American English < *limejuicer* < the use of *lime juice* on British vessels to control scurvy]

**lim|ey**[2] (lī′mē), *adj.* = limy[1].

**li|mic|o|line** (lī mik′ə līn, -lin), *adj.* of or having to do with certain shore birds or wading birds, such as the plovers, snipes, and sandpipers. [< Late Latin *līmicola* a dweller in mud (< *līmus* mud + *colere* inhabit) + English *-ine*[1]]

**li|mic|o|lous** (lī mik′ə ləs), *adj.* living in mud. [< Late Latin *līmicola* (see etym. under **limicoline**) + English *-ous*]

**lim|i|nal** (lim′ə nəl, lī′mə-), *adj.* 1 *Psychology, Physiology.* of or having to do with a limen or threshold, especially of perception. 2 *Rare.* of or having to do with the threshold or initial stage of a process. [< Latin *līmen, -inis* threshold; limen + English *-al*[1]]

**lim|it** (lim′it), *n., v.* —*n.* 1 the farthest edge or boundary; where something ends or must end; final point, such as to extent, amount, or procedure: *the limit of vision. I have reached the limit of my patience. Laws put a limit on the authority of policemen, judges, and other officials.* SYN: border, bound. 2 *Mathematics.* a value toward which terms of a sequence or values of a function approach indefinitely near. 3 an established maximum amount: *to catch the legal limit of five fish per day.* 4 the agreed maximum amount of any bet or raise in betting games. 5 *Obsolete.* the tract or region defined by a boundary.
—*v.t.* 1 to set a limit to; restrict: *We must limit the expense to $10. Her food was limited to bread and water.* SYN: restrain, check. 2 *Law.* to assign definitely: *to limit an estate over to someone.*
**limits, a** bounds: *Keep within the limits of the school grounds. As things stand now, Michaels is a healthy man, within limits* (Newsweek). **b** territories or regions: *At length into the limits of the north They came* (Milton).
**the limit**, *Slang.* as much as, or more than, one can stand: *You naughty little boy, you are really the limit!*
[< Middle French *limite,* learned borrowing from Latin *līmes, -itis* boundary] —**lim′it|a|ble**, *adj.* —**lim′it|a|ble|ness**, *n.*

**lim|i|tar|y** (lim′ə ter′ē), *adj.* 1 subject to limits; limited. 2 of or having to do with a limit; serving as a limit. 3 of or situated on a boundary.

**lim|i|ta|tion** (lim′ə tā′shən), *n.* 1 the action of limiting: *the limitation of armaments.* 2 limited condition: *The import limitation has been reduced to $100 per person.* 3a that which limits; limiting rule or circumstance; restriction: *His hunting suffered from two limitations, a cheap gun and poor eyesight. This was a severe limitation upon some of the historians* (London Times). SYN: hindrance, handicap. **b** *Figurative.* lack of understanding or imagination: *The work of that dull fellow suffers from his severe limitations.* 4 a period of time set by law, after which a claim cannot be enforced.

**lim|i|ta|tive** (lim′ə tā′tiv), *adj.* tending to limit; limiting; restrictive.

**lim|it|ed** (lim′ə tid), *adj., n.* —*adj.* 1a kept within limits; restricted: *a limited space, a limited number of seats, limited resources.* SYN: circumscribed, confined. **b** *Figurative.* lacking understanding or imagination: *He is quite limited and able to do only the most routine jobs.* 2 traveling fast and making only a few stops: *This limited train has only sleeping cars, and makes very few stops.* 3 with legal responsibility only to a limited or restricted extent, usually the nominal stock or shares insofar as it is not yet paid up: *a limited liability. Abbr:* Ltd. 4 *English Law.* assigned by a conveyance or settlement: *property limited to a person for life.*
—*n.* a train or bus that travels fast and makes only a few stops: *The Twentieth Century Limited.* —**lim′it|ed|ly**, *adv.* —**lim′it|ed|ness**, *n.*

**lim|it|ed-ac|cess** (lim′ə tid ak′ses), *adj.* (of highways) having access roads at relatively few points.

**limited company**, a company in which the liability of stockholders is limited to the amount of money they invested in the company.

**limited edition**, a special edition of a book printed in a limited number of copies. A limited edition is often printed and bound differently, if there is a popular edition.

**limited monarchy**, = constitutional monarchy.

**limited payment insurance**, life insurance for which the insured pays a higher premium for a fixed number of years, after which the policy is fully paid.

**limited policy**, an insurance policy that covers only a limited number of risks or contingencies.

**limited war**, a war confined to a limited area, usually of strategic importance: *... the ability to fight either an all-out or a limited war* (Vernon D. Tate).

**lim|it|er** (lim′ə tər), *n.* 1 a person or thing that limits. 2 *Physics.* a transducer.

**lim|i|tes** (lim′ə tēz), *n.* plural of **limes**.

**lim|it|ing** (lim′ə ting), *adj.* 1 that limits. 2 serving to restrict the meaning of the word modified: *a limiting adjective.*

**lim|it|less** (lim′it lis), *adj.* without limits; boundless; infinite: *the limitless expanse of space, limitless ambition.* SYN: illimitable, unlimited. —**lim′it|less|ly**, *adv.* —**lim′it|less|ness**, *n.*

**limit point**, *Mathematics.* the limit of any sequence of points in a set. The limit point of the sequence 5, 4, 3, 2, 1, ½, ... is zero.

**lim|i|trophe** (lim′ə trōf), *adj.* situated on the frontier; bordering on or adjacent to (another country): *the countries limitrophe to India.* [< French *limitrophe* < Latin *līmes, -itis* boundary + Greek *-tróphos* supporting, feeding]

**lim|its** (lim′its), *n.pl.* See under **limit**.

**lim|mer** (lim′ər), *n. Scottish.* 1a a worthless woman; strumpet. **b** a minx. 2 *Obsolete.* a rogue; scoundrel. [origin uncertain]

**limn** (lim), *v.t.,* **limned, limn|ing.** 1 to paint (a picture). 2 to portray or depict (a subject) in a painting, drawing, or description. 3 *Figurative.* to portray in words; describe: *Beatrice was a reticent woman and had too much taste to bare all these grubby secret details, but she limned a general picture for him* (New Yorker). 4 to illuminate (a manuscript). [Middle English *lymnen,* variant of *luminen* < Old French *luminer;* see etym. under **lumine**]

**lim|ner** (lim′nər, lim′ər), *n.* a person who limns.

**lim|net|ic** (lim net′ik), *adj.* 1 inhabiting the open water of lakes, as various animals and plants. 2 having to do with life or organisms in the open water of lakes.

**lim|no|log|i|cal** (lim′nə loj′ə kəl), *adj.* of or having to do with limnology: *the limnological study of the Danube* (New Scientist). —**lim′no|log′i|cal|ly**, *adv.*

**lim|nol|o|gist** (lim nol′ə jist), *n.* an expert in limnology.

**lim|nol|o|gy** (lim nol′ə jē), *n.* the scientific study of inland bodies of fresh water, such as lakes and ponds, especially with reference to their physical and biological features. [< Greek *límnē* lake, marsh + English *-logy*]

**lim|o** (lim′ō), *n., pl.* **lim|os.** *Informal.* a limousine: *Start packing—there'll be a limo there in an hour to put you on the noon flight to L.A.* (New Yorker).

**Li|moges** (li mōzh′), *n.* porcelain made at Limoges, a city in central France.

**lim|o|nene** (lim′ə nēn), *n.* a terpene having an odor like that of lemons. Limonene is found in three optically different forms, the dextrorotatory one occurring in the essential oils of lemon, orange, and other citrus fruit. *Formula:* $C_{10}H_{16}$ [< New Latin *limonum* lemon + English *-ene*]

**li|mo|nite** (lī′mə nīt), *n.* a mineral, varying in color from dark brown to yellow, used as an iron ore and yellow pigment; hydrous ferric oxide. It is found in lakes and marshes. *Formula:* $2Fe_2{\cdot}O_3{\cdot}3H_2O$ [< German *Limonit* < Greek *leimṓn* meadow]

**li|mo|nit|ic** (lī′mə nit′ik), *adj.* consisting of or resembling limonite.

**Li|mou|sin** (lim′ə zēn′; *French* lē mü zaN′), *n.* a hardy, fawn-colored breed of beef cattle. [< *Limousin,* a region in central France]

**lim|ou|sine** (lim′ə zēn′, lim′ə zēn), *n.* 1 a usually closed automobile, seating from three to five passengers, with a driver's seat separated from the passengers by a partition. 2 a large closed automobile, often luxuriously appointed and driven by a chauffeur. 3 a large closed automobile used to transport passengers to or from an airport, railroad station, or bus terminal. [< French *limousine* < *Limousin,* a region in central France]

**limousine liberal**, *Informal.* a wealthy liberal.

**limp**[1] (limp), *n., v.* —*n.* a lame step or walk. [< verb]
—*v.i.* 1 to walk with a limp: *After falling down the stairs, he limped for several days.* SYN: hobble. 2 *Figurative.* to proceed slowly and with difficulty: *The plane limped toward the airfield.*
[origin uncertain. Compare Old English *lemphealt* lame] —**limp′er**, *n.* —**limp′ing|ly**, *adv.*

**limp**[2] (limp), *adj.* 1 not at all stiff; ready to bend or droop; lacking stiffness: *limp flowers, a limp body. This starched collar soon gets limp in hot weather.* 2 *Figurative.* lacking firmness, force, energy, or the like: *I am so tired I feel as limp as a rag.* [origin uncertain. Compare Icelandic *lempinn* pliable, gentle] —**limp′ly**, *adv.* —**limp′ness**, *n.*
—*Syn.* 1, 2 **Limp, flabby** mean lacking firmness, both literally and figuratively. **Limp** suggests drooping or hanging loosely or, figuratively, lacking firmness and strength: *My clothes hung limp in the humid weather. Hot weather always makes me feel limp.* **Flabby** suggests being soft and weak, flapping or shaking easily or, figuratively, lacking forcefulness and vigor: *She is so fat her flesh is flabby. He showed a flabby weakness of purpose.*

***lim|pet** (lim′pit), *n.* a small sea animal that clings tightly to rocks, used for bait and sometimes for food. It is a marine mollusk, of the same class as snails, and has a tent-shaped shell. [Old English *lempedu* (perhaps with diminutive *-t*) < Medieval Latin *lampreda.* See etym. of doublet **lamprey**.]

***limpet**

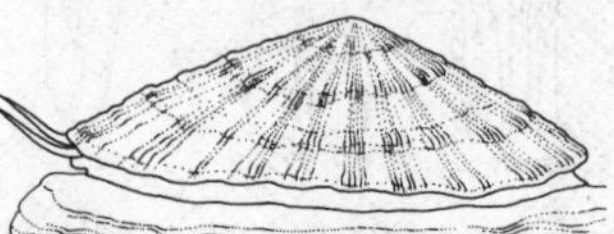

**lim|pid** (lim′pid), *adj.* clear or transparent: *a spring of limpid water, limpid eyes.* SYN: pellucid. [< Latin *limpidus*] —**lim′pid|ly**, *adv.* —**lim′pid|ness**, *n.*

**lim|pid|i|ty** (lim pid′ə tē), *n.* limpid quality or condition. SYN: clearness, transparence.

**limp|kin** (limp′kin), *n.* a brown wading bird of tropical America, related to the cranes and rails, but being the only living member of its family; courlan. [American English < *limp*[1], verb + *-kin* (because of its halting gait)]

**limp|sy** (limp′sē), *adj. Dialect.* limp.

**lim|u|loid** (lim′yə loid), *adj., n.* —*adj.* of or having to do with the king crabs.
—*n.* a king crab.
[< *limul*(us) + *-oid*]

**lim|u|lus** (lim′yə ləs), *n., pl.* **-li** (-lī). a king crab or horseshoe crab. [< New Latin *Limulus* the genus name < Latin *līmulus* a bit askance (diminutive) < *līmus* askew]

**lim|y**[1] (lī′mē), *adj.,* **lim|i|er, lim|i|est.** 1 of or containing lime; resembling lime. 2 smeared with birdlime. Also, **limey**.

**lim|y**[2] (lī′mē), *n., pl.* **lim|ies**, *adj.* = limey[1].

**lin.**, 1 lineal. 2 linear.

**lin|a|ble** (lī′nə bəl), *adj.* ranged in a straight line. Also, **lineable**.

**lin|ac** (lin′ak), *n.* = linear accelerator. [< *lin*(ear) *ac*(celerator)]

**lin|age** (lī′nij), *n.* 1 = alignment. 2a a quantity of printed or written matter estimated in number of lines: *Advertising space is usually figured in linage.* **b** the charge or rate of charge for a line. Also, **lineage**.

**lin|al|o|ol** (li nal′ō ōl, -ol; lin′ə lül′), *n. Chemistry.* an unsaturated, open-chain, liquid alcohol, related to the terpenes, occurring in various essential oils and used in perfumes. *Formula:* $C_{10}H_{18}O$ [< Spanish *lináloe* (< *lignáloe* < Late Latin *lignum aloēs* wood of aloe) + English *-ol*[1]]

**lin|a|ma|rin** (lin′ə mãr′in), *n.* a glucoside present in flax that helps to protect it against wilt. *Formula:* $C_{10}H_{17}NO_6$ [< Latin *līnum* flax + *amārus* bitter + English *-in*]

**lin|ar** (lī′när), *n.* a radio star that emits waves at wavelengths characteristic of the spectral line of certain chemical compounds. [< *lin*(e) + *-ar,* as in *quasar, pulsar*]

**li|na|ri|a** (lī nãr′ē ə), *n.* = toadflax. [< New Latin *Linaria* < Latin *līnum* flax]

**linch|pin** (linch′pin′), *n.* 1 a pin inserted through a hole in the end of an axle to keep the wheel on. 2 *Figurative.* that which keeps something from falling; a critical point: *The small station of Kohima in the Burma Campaign suddenly became the linchpin in the defense of India* (Listener). Also, **lynchpin**. [alteration of Middle English *linspin* < Old English *lynis* linchpin + Middle English *pin* pin]

**Lin|coln** (ling′kən), *n.* any long-wooled sheep of a breed originating in Lincolnshire, England.

**Lin|coln|esque** (ling′kə nesk′), *adj.* like or characteristic of Abraham Lincoln.

**Lin|coln|i|an** (ling kō′nē ən), *adj.* of, having to do with, or characteristic of Abraham Lincoln (1809-1865): *The Republicans might be tempted to* *abandon the last vestiges of their Lincolnian heritage and to fight the election on a frankly reactionary ticket* (Manchester Guardian Weekly).

**Lin|coln|i|a|na** (ling kō′nē ä′nə, -an′ə, -ā′nə), *n.pl.* a collection of objects, documents, books, facts, and other material about or belonging to Abraham Lincoln.

**Lincoln Red**, any reddish cow of a British breed related to the shorthorn.

**Lincoln's Birthday**, February 12, the anniversary of Abraham Lincoln's birthday, a legal holiday in some states of the United States.

**Lincoln's sparrow**, a striped sparrow of Canada and the northern United States, similar to the song sparrow, living in boggy, brushy areas. [< Thomas *Lincoln*, 1812-1883, an American farmer and friend of Audubon]

**lin|co|my|cin** (ling′kə mī′sən), *n.* an antibiotic derived from a kind of streptomyces, found effective against certain bacteria that are resistant to penicillin. [< *linco*(lnensis), name of the variety of streptomyces from which the drug is derived + (strepto)*mycin*]

**lin|crus|ta** (lin krus′tə), *n.* a wall or ceiling covering made like linoleum. [< *Lincrusta* Walton, a trademark for this covering < *lin*(oleum) + Latin *crusta* crust]

**linc|tus** (lingk′təs), *n.* a cough syrup or similar liquid to soothe the throat. [< Latin *linctus* a licking < *lingere* to lick]

**lin|dane** (lin′dān), *n.* a benzene compound used as an insecticide in place of DDT. *Formula:* $C_6H_6Cl_6$ [< T. van der *Linden*, a Dutch chemist of the 1900's + *-ane*]

**lin|den** (lin′dən), *n.* **1** a shade tree with heart-shaped leaves and clusters of small, sweet-smelling, yellowish flowers; lime tree; linn. The lindens include the basswood of eastern North America and a common European species. **2** the soft, white wood of any of these trees. [Old English *linden*, adjective < *lind* linden, lime[3]]

**linden looper**, a measuring worm that eats the leaves of trees, especially the linden.

**Linde process** (lind), a method of liquefying gases in which the gas is first cooled by contact with another liquefied gas and then freely expanded. [< Carl von *Linde*, 1842-1934, a German engineer, who developed it]

**Lin|dy** (lin′dē), *n., pl.* **-dies**, *v.,* **-died**, **-dy|ing**.
—*n.* a kind of jitterbug, especially popular in the 1930's and 1940's.
—*v.i.* to dance the Lindy.
[< Charles A. *Lindbergh*, 1902-1974, an American aviator (because of the fame attached to his flying exploits)]

**Lin|dy-hop** (lin′dē hop′), *v.i.,* **-hopped**, **-hop|ping**. = Lindy.

**Lindy Hop** or **hop**, = Lindy.

**line**[1] (līn), *n., v.,* **lined**, **lin|ing**. —*n.* **1** a piece of rope, cord, string, thread, or wire: *a telegraph line, to hang wash on a line. Reins are sometimes called lines.* **2** a cord for measuring or making level. A plumb line has a plumb at the end of a line and is used to find the depth of water or to see if a wall is vertical. **3** a cord with a hook for catching fish. **4** a long narrow mark: *Draw two lines along the margin.* **SYN**: stroke, scratch, streak, dash. **5** anything that is like a long narrow mark: *the lines in a rock, the lines in your face.* **6** a straight line: *to draw a line with a ruler.* **7** a circle of the terrestrial or celestial sphere: *the equinoctial line.* **8** *Mathematics.* the path traced by a moving point. It has length but no breadth or thickness. **9** the use of lines in drawing: *a picture in line, clearness of line in an artist's work.* **10** an edge or boundary: *the line between Texas and Mexico.* **SYN**: limit. **11** a row of persons or things: *a line of chairs, a line of trees.* **SYN**: rank. **12** a row of words on a page or in a column: *a column of 40 lines.* **13** a short letter; note: *Drop me a line.* **14** a connected series of persons or things following one another in time: *to trace back one's family line. The Stuarts were a line of English kings.* **15** family or lineage: *of noble line.* **16** course, track, or direction; route: *the line of march of an army.* **SYN**: way. **17** *Figurative.* a certain way of doing; course of action, conduct, or thought: *a line of policy, the Communist party line. Please proceed on these lines till further notice. The State Department denied today any aggressive intent ... saying that was an old propaganda line* (New York Times). **18** a front row of trenches or other defenses: *a line extending along a five-mile front, the Siegfried Line.* **19a** a formation of soldiers or ships placed side by side. **b** the arrangement of an army or fleet for battle. **20a** a wire or network of wires connecting points or stations in a telegraph or telephone system, radar warning operation, or the like. **b** the system itself. **21** any rope, wire, pipe, hose, or tube running from one point to another: *a steam line, to tie up a boat with the forward line.* **22** a long fiber of flax, hemp, or the like, prepared for spinning by hackling. **23** a single track of railroad. **24a** one branch of a system of transportation: *the main line of a railroad.* **b** a whole system of transportation or conveyance: *the Grand Trunk Line, the municipal bus line.* **25** a branch of business; kind of activity: *the dry-goods line. This kind of work is not my line.* **26** a kind or branch of goods: *a good line of hardware. He carries the best line of shoes in town.* **27** the part of a poem or lyric that is usually written on one line; verse of poetry. **28a** talk, usually intended to deceive or confuse: *She fell for the playboy's line and eloped with him. The burglar tried to hand the police a line, but two witnesses saw him break into the house.* **b** a joke, remark, or story, used frequently by a person, often by an entertainer, for identification. **29** one of the horizontal lines that make a staff in music. **30** *Sports.* any boundary that limits or divides a court, field, rink, track, lane, or other playing area: *a finish line, a foul line, a scrimmage line.* **31** *Football.* **a** = scrimmage line. **b** the players along the scrimmage line at the start of a play. Usually the offensive team has seven men in the line, and the defensive team has four to seven. **32** *Bowling.* a complete game of ten frames. **33** *Television.* a single scanning line. **34** a measure of buttons equal to 1/40 inch. *Abbr:* l.
—*v.t.* **1** to mark with lines: *to line a column in red and one in green. Please line your paper with a pencil and ruler.* **2** to cover with lines: *a face lined with age.* **3** to arrange in a line; bring into a line or row; align: *Line your shoes along the edge of the shelf.* **4** to form a line along; arrange a line along: *to line a frontier with soldiers. Cars lined the road for a mile. The rebels ... lined the hedges leading to the town* (Macaulay). **5** to measure or test with a line. **6** *Baseball.* to hit (a line drive): *Wilson ... capped a four-run outburst in the sixth ... by lining the ball over the 365-foot marker* (New York Times).
—*v.i.* **1** to form a line; take a position in a line; range. **2** *Baseball.* to line out: *The batter lined to the first baseman.*

**all along the line**, at every point; everywhere: *This car has given us trouble all along the line. ... has therefore been compelled to lower its sights all along the line* (New Yorker).

**bring into line**, to cause to agree or conform: *to bring a theory into line with the facts.*

**come into line**, to agree; conform: *The radical wing of the party came into line as soon as financial support of their candidate was threatened.*

**down the line**, the whole way; as far as possible; to the end: *Many Democrats ... have promised to fight him down the line on these [proposals]* (New York Times).

**draw a** (or **the**) **line**, to set a limit: *They know how to draw the line between private and public feeling* (London Examiner).

**get** (or **have**) **a line on**, *Informal.* to get or have information about: *The "economic diagnosticians" have been busy ... studying the consumer ... to get a line both on what is happening and what may happen* (Petroleum and Chemical Transporter).

**hold the line**, to prevent or resist successfully a threatened change, such as an increase in prices: *Space officials, for the first time in six years, plan to hold the line or even trim budget requests for new funds* (Wall Street Journal).

**in line**, **a** in alignment; in a row: *The children are all in line.* **b** *Figurative.* in agreement: *Our thoughts on this subject are pretty much in line.* **c** *Figurative.* ready: *in line for action.* **d** in order; in succession: *next in line.*

**in line with**, in agreement with: *This plan is in line with their thinking.*

**lay** (or **put**) **on the line**, *U.S. Slang.* **a** to produce or present fully, without suppressing anything: *Next time a full-scale hearing will be laid on the line* (New York Times). **b** to speak frankly; say openly: *An art instructor laid it on the line: "Children don't have prejudices"* (Time).

**line one's pocket**. See under **pocket**.

**line out**, **a** (1) *Baseball.* to hit a line drive which is caught: *Mantle lined out to the shortstop.* (2) *Rugby.* to put the ball in play by a lineout: *The forward must always be ready to line out and face his man.* **b** to draw a line or lines to indicate an outline: *to line out a picture. It ... must be lined out into oblong squares* (Patrick Browne). **c** to transplant (seedlings) from the seedbed to rows in the forest or nursery: *The tomato plants were lined out neatly.* **d** to read or sing out (a hymn or folk song) a line or two at a time for repetition in singing: *The preacher was lining out a hymn. He lined out two lines, everybody sung it ... and so on* (Mark Twain).

**lines**, **a** outline; contour: *a car of fine lines.* **b** a plan of construction: *two books written along the same lines.* **c** a double row (front and rear rank) of soldiers: *The lines of infantry are being disbanded.* **d** poetry; verses: *Lines forty thousand, cantos twenty-five* (Byron). **e** words that an actor speaks in a play: *to forget one's lines.* **f** one's lot in life: *The lines are fallen unto me in pleasant places* (Psalms 16:6). **g** *Informal.* a marriage certificate: *"How should a child like you know that the marriage was irregular?" "Because I had no lines!" cries Caroline* (Thackeray). **h** a system of curves and straight lines used by naval architects to trace the outline of the shape of a ship: *Her extravagant poop ..., and her lines like a cocked hat reversed* (Charles Reade).

**line up**, **a** to form a line; form into a line: *Cars are lined up along the road for a mile. The horses lined up for the start of the race.* **b** to make available or accessible: *The theater agent lined up backers for the new show.*

**on a line**, even; level: *The walk is on a line with the road.*

**on the line**, **a** in between; neither one thing nor the other: *Politically, he is on the line, choosing to avoid both the right and the left.* **b** approximately on a level with the eye: *a painting hung on the line.* **c** *Slang, Figurative.* at once; readily: *Paying on the line is cheaper than on credit.*

**out of line**, **a** in disagreement; not in harmony: *For some time it has been felt that the share capital of the Company was out of line with the capital employed in the business* (London Times). **b** behaving improperly: *The new boy was impertinent and almost always out of line.*

**read between the lines**, to get more from the words than they say; find a hidden meaning: *They do not say as much to their secret selves; but you can read between the lines these words—"What a weariness it is!"* (Charles H. Spurgeon).

**the line**, **a** the equator: *The sun crosses the line at the equinoxes. We were in the latitude of 12 degrees 35 minutes south of the line* (Daniel Defoe). **b** the regular army or navy; the soldiers or ships that do all the fighting: *to serve in the line, go into the line.* **c** the group of officers in charge of such forces: *The combatant officers in the navy are called officers of the line* (Thomas A. Wilhelm).

**toe the line** (or **mark**), **a** to conform to a certain standard of duty, conduct, or performance: *The other satellite Communist leaders ... are all toeing the line and employing terror to extinguish opposition* (Newsweek). **b** to stand with the tips of the toes touching a certain line or mark, as before a race or contest: *The child toed the line, ready to jump.*
[fusion of Old English *līne* line, rope, and Middle English *ligne* line < Old French; both ultimately < Latin *līnea* line; linen thread < *līnum* flax] —**line′less**, *adj.*

**line**[2] (līn), *v.,* **lined**, **lin|ing**, *n.* —*v.t.* **1** to put a layer of material, such as paper, cloth, or felt, inside of (a dress, hat, box, bag, or other article); cover the inner side of with something: *to line a coat with sheepskin, to line a fireplace with brick. ... a great library all lined with books* (Robert Louis Stevenson). **2** to fill: *to line one's pockets with money.* **3** to serve as a lining for: *This piece of silk would line your coat very nicely.*
—*n.* the long parallel fibers of flax, used in making fine linen.
[Old English *līn* flax, linen thread or cloth]

**line|a|ble** (lī′nə bəl), *adj.* = linable.

**lin|e|age**[1] (lin′ē ij), *n.* **1** descent in a direct line from an ancestor: *... he was of the house and lineage of David* (Luke 2:4). **SYN**: ancestry. **2** a family or race: *The Lords of Douglas ... are second to no lineage in Scotland in the antiquity of their descent* (Scott). **SYN**: stock, extraction. **3** the descendants through exclusively male or exclusively female links of a specified ancestor. [alteration (influenced by *line*[1]) of Middle English *lynage* < Old French *lignage* < *ligne* line[1] < Latin *līnea*]

**line|age**[2] (lī′nij), *n.* = linage.

**lin|e|al** (lin′ē əl), *adj.* **1** in the direct line of descent: *A grandson is a lineal descendant of his grandfather.* **2** having to do with such descent; hereditary: *a lineal right.* **SYN**: ancestral. **3** of or like a line; linear. [< Late Latin *līneālis* < Latin *līnea* line[1]] —**lin′e|al|ly**, *adv.*

**lin|e|al|i|ty** (lin′ē al′ə tē), *n.* = linearity.

**lin|e|a|ment** (lin′ē ə mənt), *n.* **1** a part or feature, especially a part or feature of a face, with attention to its outline: *He was pensively tracing in my countenance the early lineaments of my mother* (Washington Irving). **2** a part or feature; distinctive characteristic: *The style of Denman is more*

**Pronunciation Key:** hat, āge, cãre, fär; let, ēqual, tėrm; it, īce; hot, ōpen, ôrder; **oil**, **out**; cup, pu̇t, rüle; **ch**ild; lo**ng**; **th**in; **ᴛʜ**en; **zh**, measure; **ə** represents **a** in about, **e** in taken, **i** in pencil, **o** in lemon, **u** in circus.

*lofty, and impressed with stronger lineaments of sincerity* (John Galt). **3** an outline: *lineaments of its subject* (Scientific American). [< Latin *līneamentum* < *lineāre* reduce to a line < *līnea* line¹]

**lin|e|ar** (lin′ē ər), *adj.* **1** of a line or lines: *The royal crown is passed from father to son in a linear succession.* **2** made of lines; making use of lines: *a linear design.* **3** in a line or lines: *a linear series.* **4** of length: *An inch is a linear measure.* **5** like a line; long and narrow: *A pine tree has linear leaves.* **6** proportional: *There is a linear relationship between the size of a star and its luminosity.* [< Latin *līneāris* < *līnea* line¹] —**lin′e-ar|ly,** *adv.*

**Linear A,** an ancient language used on Crete from about 1800-1500 B.C., found on clay tablets. The writing is derived from a cuneiform Arcadian script written in a syllabary form.

**linear accelerator,** *Electronics.* a device for accelerating charged particles in a straight line through a vacuum tube or series of tubes by means of alternating negative and positive impulses from electric fields.

**linear algebra,** *Mathematics.* the study of the algebraic properties of vectors, especially of a set of vectors over a field of scalars or real numbers.

**Linear B,** an ancient language used on Crete and found on clay tablets especially at Knossos and Mycenae. It is an archaic Greek written in a syllabary form.

**linear equation,** *Mathematics.* an equation whose terms involving variables are of the first degree. *Example:* $y = 4x + 20$

**linear function,** *Mathematics.* a function in which the variables are of the first degree.

***linear induction motor,** an electric motor that produces thrust directly by means of the linear impelling force of the magnetic field rather than by the rotating force or torque: *A linear induction motor is like a regular rotary motor that has been sliced open and laid out flat* (Lowell K. Bridwell).

***linear induction motor**

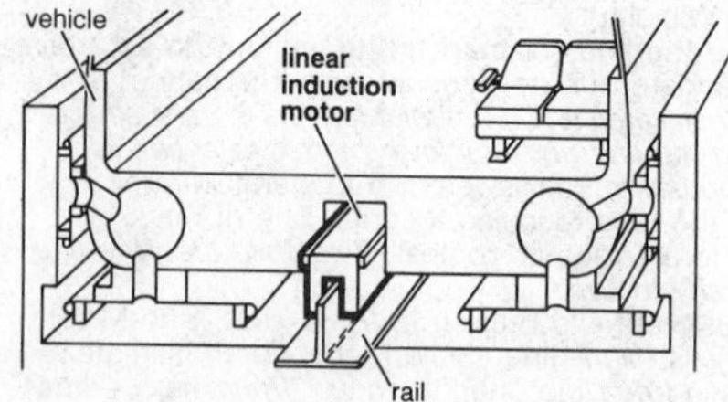


**lin|e|ar|i|ty** (lin′ē ar′ə tē), *n.* the quality or state of being linear; a linear arrangement or form.

**lin|e|ar|ize** (lin′ē ə rīz), *v.t.,* **-ized, -iz|ing.** to represent in linear form, or by means of lines. —**lin′e|ar|i|za′tion,** *n.*

**linear measure, 1** measure of length. **2** a system for measuring length.

English system

| | |
|---|---|
| 12 inches = 1 foot | 8 furlongs = 1 mile |
| 3 feet = 1 yard | 1,760 yards = 1 mile |
| 5½ yards = 1 rod | 5,280 feet = 1 mile |
| 40 rods = 1 furlong | 3 miles = 1 league |

Metric system

10 millimeters = 1 centimeter
100 centimeters = 1 meter
1000 meters = 1 kilometer
1 kilometer = 3,280.8 feet (or about 0.6 mile)

**linear motor,** = linear induction motor.

**linear perspective,** the branch of perspective that is concerned with the apparent form, magnitude, and position of visual objects.

**linear program,** a program used in a teaching machine in which every student answers the same questions, instead of the questions being determined by the individual's answers. In a linear program the questions are worded to help the student make a correct response.

**linear programming,** a method of solving operational problems by stating a number of variables simultaneously in the form of linear equations and calculating the optimal solution within the given limitations.

**lin|e|ate** (lin′ē it, -āt), *adj.* marked with lines, especially longitudinal and parallel lines. [< Latin *līneātus,* past participle of *līneāre* to reduce to a line < *līnea* line¹]

**lin|e|a|tion** (lin′ē ā′shən), *n.* **1** the act or process of drawing lines or marking with lines. **2** a division into lines. **3** a line; outline. **4** a marking or line on a surface, as of the skin. **5** an arrangement or group of lines.

**line|back|er** (līn′bak′ər), *n.* a defensive football player whose position is directly behind the line.

**line|back|ing** (līn′bak′ing), *n.* the act or fact of serving as a linebacker.

**line-breed** (līn′brēd′), *v.t.,* **-bred, -breed|ing.** to breed within one line or strain of stock in order to develop certain favorable characteristics.

**line breeding,** breeding within one line or strain of stock in order to develop certain favorable characteristics.

**line|cast|er** (līn′kas′tər, -käs′-), *n.* a linecasting machine.

**line|cast|ing** (līn′kas′ting, -käs′-), *n., adj.* —*n.* the act or process of casting lines of printing type in one piece, as with a Linotype.
—***adj.*** designed for casting lines of type in one piece: *a linecasting machine.*

**line drawing,** a drawing done with a pen, pencil, or charcoal, completely in lines, including the shading, if any, and often made especially to be engraved for an illustration.

**line drive,** a baseball hit so that it travels in almost a straight line, usually close to the ground; liner.

**line engraver,** a person who makes line engravings.

**line engraving, 1** *Fine Arts.* lines cut in a plate or block with a tool, as distinguished from etching or mezzotint. **2** *Printing.* photoengraved work in line or flat areas, as distinguished from halftone. **3** a plate so engraved. **4** the impression or print made from it.

**line gauge,** a printer's ruler, usually divided into picas and nonpareils on one edge and inches on the other.

**line graph,** a graph in which points representing quantities are plotted and then connected by a series of short straight lines, usually forming a jagged or smooth curve. See picture under **graph**¹.

**line judge,** a person who watches for fouls in various sports, especially football.

**line|man** (līn′mən), *n., pl.* **-men. 1** a man who sets up or repairs telegraph, telephone, or electric wires; linesman. **2** *Football.* a player in the line; center, guard, tackle, or end: *The entire cadet backfield and three linemen played sixty minutes* (New York Times). **3** a man who inspects railroad tracks. **4** a man who carries the line in surveying.

**lin|en** (lin′ən), *n., adj.* —*n.* **1** cloth, thread, or yarn made from flax fiber. **2** articles made of linen or some substitute. Tablecloths, napkins, sheets, towels, shirts, and collars are all called linen even when they are made of some substitute. **3** Also, **linen paper.** writing paper of very fine quality. It was formerly paper made from linen rags.
—***adj.*** **1** made of linen: *a linen dress.* **2** made of flax: *linen thread, linen fabric.*
**wash one's dirty linen in public,** to mention publicly one's quarrels or difficulties: *I never saw a company wash its dirty linen in public this way* (Wall Street Journal).
[Old English *linnen, līnen,* adjective < *līn* flax, linen thread or cloth]

**lin|en|fold** (lin′ən fōld′), *adj., n.* —***adj.*** of or forming a linen scroll: *a linenfold carving. The walls are lined with linenfold panelling* (Manchester Guardian Weekly).
—*n.* a linen scroll.

**linen scroll** or **pattern,** *Architecture.* a form of decorative ornament suggesting the convolutions of rolled or folded linen, used to fill panels, especially during the Tudor period in England.

**lin|en|y** (lin′ə nē), *adj.* similar to linen.

**line of ap|si|des** (ap′sə dēz), the straight line that joins the two points in the elliptical orbit of a planetary body.

**line of battle,** soldiers or ships in battle formation; battle line: *Cochrane sighted three merchantmen who turned out to be French line-of-battle ships* (Wall Street Journal).

**line of credit,** the quantity of credit granted by a store or bank to one of its customers.

**line of duty,** performance of duty or service, especially military duty.
**in the line of duty,** while performing one's duty, especially in military service: *The guard was injured in the line of duty while serving at headquarters.*

**line officer,** a commissioned officer in the army or navy commanding a combat unit or force.

**line of fire,** the path of a bullet, shell, rocket, or other missile.

***line of force,** *Physics.* a line in a field of electric or magnetic force that indicates the direction in which the force is acting.

**line of position,** the charted course on which an aircraft or ship is traveling, as determined by visual sightings, as of a railroad, or by radio or celestial means. When an intersecting line is obtained, the exact position of the craft can be determined.

**line of scrimmage,** = scrimmage line.

**line of sight, 1** the straight line from the eye to the object it is looking at, such as a target in shooting or bombing. **2** the straight line of the beam from a radar antenna. —**line′-of-sight′,** *adj.*

**line of vision,** a straight line from the fovea of the retina to the point on which vision is fixed.

**lin|e|o|late** (lin′ē ə lāt), *adj. Biology.* marked with minute lines; finely lineate. [< Latin *līneola* (diminutive) < *līnea* line¹; + English *-ate*¹]

**lin|e|o|lat|ed** (lin′ē ə lā′tid), *adj.* = lineolate.

**line|out** (līn′out′), *n. Rugby.* the putting of the ball in play from the sideline.

**line printer,** a computer output device that prints out a complete line of type in one printing cycle.

**lin|er**¹ (lī′nər), *n.* **1** a ship or airplane belonging to a transportation system: *During the First World War Kendall commanded HMS Calgarian, a luxury liner serving as a cruiser* (Maclean's). **2a** a person who makes lines, such as a person who keeps the lines in football. **b** an instrument, tool, or device for marking lines or stripes. **3** a baseball hit so that it travels nearly parallel to the ground; line drive: *Reese followed with a liner high off the left field wall for a double* (New York Times).

**lin|er**² (lī′nər), *n.* **1** a person who lines or fits a lining to anything. **2** something that serves as a lining, such as: **a** an inside cylinder, or a vessel placed inside another. **b** a thin slip of metal or other material placed between two parts to adjust them; shim. **3** a short passage usually on the cover of a phonograph record giving information about the record.

**lin|er|board** (lī′nər bôrd, -bōrd), *n.* a paper product, the principal material used in making corrugated boxes.

**liner notes,** the text on a phonograph record cover.

**lines** (līnz), *n.pl.* See under **line**¹.

**line segment,** any finite section between two points on a line; segment.

**lines|man** (līnz′mən), *n., pl.* **-men. 1** a telephone, telegraph, or electric company lineman. **2** (in lawn tennis, football, and certain other games) an official who watches the lines that mark out the field, court, rink, track, lane, or other playing area, and assists the umpire or referee. **3** the official in football who watches the scrimmage for violation of the rules. **4** one of the forwards, center, guard, tackle, or end, in football.

**line spectrum,** a spectrum produced by a luminous gas or vapor in which distinct lines characteristic of an element are emitted by its atoms.

**line squall,** *Meteorology.* a thunderstorm or other severe local storm appearing along a cold front.

**line storm,** a storm or gale occurring at or near an equinox; equinoctial.

**line-up** or **line|up** (līn′up′), *n.* **1** a formation of persons or things into a line or file. A police lineup is the arrangement of a group of individuals for identification. **2a** a list of players who will take part or are taking part in a game of football, baseball, or certain other games. **b** the players themselves. **3** any alignment of persons or groups for a common purpose: *With the present lineup, the balance of power in the commission has shifted from conservative to progressive* (New York Times).

**ling**¹ (ling), *n., pl.* **lings** or (*collectively*) **ling. 1** any one of a number of marine fishes of the North Atlantic, related to the cod, and having an elongated body, largely used for food, either salted or split and dried. **2** the freshwater burbot of Europe and North America. **3** any one of several other fishes. [Middle English *lenge,* perhaps < earlier Dutch *lenghe,* or *linghe*]

**ling**² (ling), *n.* any one of various heaths, especially the common heather. [< Scandinavian (compare Old Icelandic *lyng*)]

***line of force**

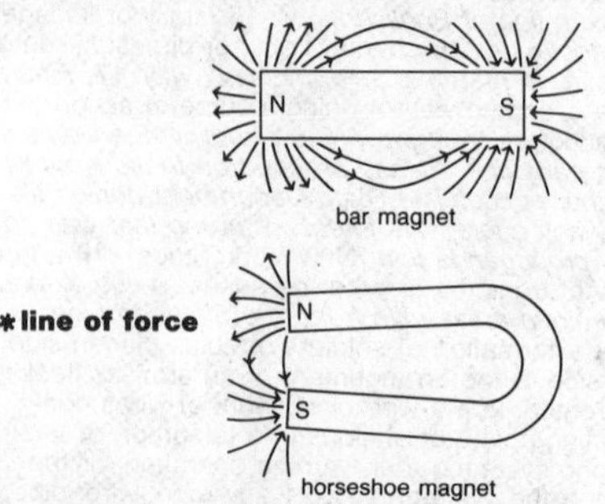

bar magnet
horseshoe magnet

**-ling,** *suffix forming nouns.* **1** little; unimportant: *Duckling* = *a little duck.* **2** one that is ___: *Underling* = *one that is under.*

3 one belonging to or concerned with: *Earthling = one belonging to the earth.*
[Old English *-ling*]
**ling.**, linguistics.
**lin|ga** (ling′gə), *n.* = lingam.
**Lin|ga|la** (ling gäl′ə), *n.* a lingua franca much used in the Congo (Zaire), consisting of Swahili and several Bantu dialects.
**lin|gam** (ling′gəm), *n.* a Hindu phallic symbol representing the male generative principle and used in the worship of Siva. [< Sanskrit *linga* (nominative *lingam*)]
**Lin|ga|yat** (ling gä′yət), *n.* a member of a Hindu sect of southern India devoted to the worship of Siva.
**ling cod**, a food fish of the North American Pacific coast; cultus.
**lin|ger** (ling′gər), *v.i.* **1** to stay on or go slowly, as if unwilling to leave: *She lingered after the others had left.* **2** to be slow to pass away or disappear: *Daylight lingers long in the summertime.* **3** to be slow or late in doing or beginning anything; hesitate; delay; dawdle: *By no remonstrance . . . could he prevail upon his allies to be early in the field . . . Everyone of them lingered, and wondered why the rest were lingering* (Macaulay). **4** to continue alive, in spite of weakness, sickness, or other adverse conditions: *I would not have thee linger in thy pain* (Shakespeare). *—v.t.* to draw out, prolong, or protract by lingering: (*Figurative.*) *How slow This old moon wanes! She lingers my desires* (Shakespeare).
**linger away**, to waste by lingering: *Better to rush at once to shades below Than linger life away* (Alexander Pope).
**linger on**, to continue to linger; live although near death: *He lingered on in a comatose state.*
[Middle English *lengeren* (frequentative) < *lengen* delay, Old English *lengan* < *lang* long[1]] —**lin′ger|er**, *n.* —**lin′ger|ing|ly**, *adv.*
*—Syn. v.i.* **1, 3 Linger, loiter, lag** mean to delay in starting or along the way. **Linger** emphasizes delay in starting, and suggests reluctance to leave: *The children lingered at the zoo until closing time, then hurried home for supper.* **Loiter** emphasizes delaying along the way, and suggests moving slowly and aimlessly: *She loitered downtown, looking into all the shopwindows.* **Lag** emphasizes falling behind others or in one's work, and suggests failing to keep up the necessary speed or pace: *The child lagged because he was tired.*
**lin|ge|rie** (lan′zhə rē′, län′jə rā′), *n.* **1** women's underwear, nightgowns, and the like. **2** linen articles. [< Middle French *lingerie* linen articles < Old French *linge* linen < Latin *līneus,* adjective < *līnum* flax]
**lin|go** (ling′gō), *n., pl.* **-goes**. *Used humorously or in contempt.* **1** language, especially foreign speech or language. **2** any speech that sounds strange or is not understood, such as the jargon of some special group: *Writers about baseball use a strange lingo.* [< Provençal *lengo* < Latin *lingua* language, tongue; influenced by *lingua franca*]
**lin|goe** (ling′gō), *n., pl.* **-goes**. a metal weight hanging from the bottom of each cord of a Jacquard loom. [apparently < French *lingot* ingot]
**lin|gon|ber|ry** (ling′gən ber′ē), *n., pl.* **-ries**. **1** a low shrub of the heath family growing in the northern parts of North America, Asia, and Europe; cowberry. **2** its berry, similar to, and used in place of, the common cranberry. [< Swedish *lingon* lingonberry + English *berry*]
**lin|gua** (ling′gwə), *n., pl.* **-guae** (-gwē). a tongue or tonguelike organ, such as the ligula of some insects and the proboscis of butterflies and moths. [< Latin *lingua* tongue]
**lin|gua fran|ca** (ling′gwə frang′kə), *pl.* **lin|gua fran|cas**. **1** a hybrid language, consisting of Italian mixed with French, Spanish, Greek, Arabic, and Turkish, used especially by traders in the eastern Mediterranean region: *A . . . voice . . . pronounced these words . . . in the lingua franca, mutually understood by Christians and Saracens* (Scott). **2** any language, especially a hybrid language, used as a trade or communication medium by people speaking different languages: *During the whole 500 years . . . of the Abbasid Caliphate's existence, Arabic was the lingua franca of the whole area extending from Soviet Central Asia to Spain and Portugal inclusive* (Arnold Toynbee). [< Italian *lingua franca* (literally) Frankish language]
**Lin|gua Ge|ral** (ling′gwə zhə räl′), a language based on Tupi-Guarani and widely spoken in the Amazon region of Brazil. [< Portuguese *lingua* language, *geral* general]
**lin|gual** (ling′gwəl), *adj., n.* *—adj.* **1** of the tongue: *a lingual nerve, a lingual defect.* **2** *Phonetics.* formed with the aid of the tongue, particularly the tip, as *t* and *d.* **3** having to do with language or languages.
*—n. Phonetics.* a lingual sound.
[< Medieval Latin *lingualis* < Latin *lingua* tongue] —**lin′gual|ly**, *adv.*
**lingual tonsil**, a mass of lymphoid tissue located at the back of the tongue.
**lin|gua Ro|ma|na** (ling′gwərō mä′nə), the vernacular language of the Romans; Vulgar Latin.
**lin|gui|fo rm** (ling′gwə fôrm), *adj.* tongue-shaped; lingulate; ligulate.
**lin|gui|ne** (ling gwē′nē), *n.* a kind of pasta, long and thin like spaghetti, but flat: *The kitchen produces first-rate linguine with clam sauce* (Craig Claiborne). [< Italian *linguine,* plural of *linguina* (diminutive) < *lingua* tongue]
**lin|guist** (ling′gwist), *n.* **1** a person who studies the history and structure of language; expert in languages or linguistics: *The linguist collects and records utterances, and by comparing these one with another abstracts the way or modes of speaking which, as we have said, constitute the language of the speech community* (Beals and Hoijer). **2** a person skilled in a number of languages besides his own; polyglot; multilingual person. [< Latin *lingua* tongue, language]
**lin|guis|tic** (ling gwis′tik), *adj.* having to do with language or the study of languages. —**lin|guis′ti|cal|ly**, *adv.*
**lin|guis|ti|cal** (ling gwis′tə kəl), *adj.* = linguistic.
**linguistic analysis**, **1** *Linguistics.* the breaking down of the elements of a language into basic units, such as phonemes, morphemes, immediate constituents, and the like, to find out the structure of the language. **2** *Philosophy.* the analysis of the ways language is used by examining and classifying different statements; philosophical analysis.
**linguistic analyst**, a person who engages in linguistic analysis.
**linguistic atlas**, a book, usually of maps, describing dialect features and their boundaries; dialect atlas.
**linguistic form**, any meaningful unit of speech, such as a sentence, phrase, word, or morpheme; speech form.
**linguistic geographer**, a person who studies linguistic geography.
**linguistic geography**, the study of the geographical distribution of dialect features and of local variations in dialect; dialect geography.
**lin|guis|ti|cian** (ling′gwə stish′ən), *n.* = linguist (def. 1).
**lin|guis|tics** (ling gwis′tiks), *n.* the science of language; comparative study of languages, including the study of speech sounds, language structures, and the history and historical relationship of languages and linguistic forms.
**linguistic stock**, **1** a group of related languages together with the parent language from which they are derived. **2** all the people that speak languages of such a related group.
**lin|gu|late** (ling′gyə lāt), *adj.* tongue-shaped; ligulate; linguiform. [< Latin *lingulātus* < *lingula* (diminutive) < *lingua* tongue]
**lin|i|ment** (lin′ə mənt), *n.* a soothing liquid which is rubbed on the skin to relieve the pain of sore muscles, sprains, and bruises, or one that acts as a counterirritant. SYN: embrocation. [< Late Latin *linīmentum* < Latin *linere* anoint, smear]
**li|nin** (lī′nin), *n.* **1** *Chemistry.* a crystallizable bitter principle obtained from a European species of flax, used as a purgative. *Formula:* $C_{23}H_{23}O_9$
**2** *Biology.* a substance now considered to be an artificial product of fixation, but formerly thought to be the achromatic substance composing the network that encloses the granules of chromatin in the nucleus of a cell. [< Latin *līnum* flax + English *-in*]
**lin|ing** (lī′ning), *n., v.* *—n.* **1** a layer of material covering the inner surface of something: *the lining of a coat, the lining of a stove.* **2** the material reinforcing the back of a book. **3** *Figurative.* contents, as of the pocket or purse: *the lining of his coffers shall make coats To deck our soldiers* (Shakespeare). **4** the act of providing with a lining: *In making a coat, lining is the process that is most difficult for an inexperienced seamstress.* **5** concrete or steel applied to the interior of shafts and tunnels for smoothness and strength.
*—v.* present participle of **line**[2].
**link**[1] (lingk), *n., v., adj.* *—n.* **1** one ring or loop of a chain: *The tractor pulled the log with a chain that had very heavy links.* **2a** anything that joins as a link joins: *a cuff link. I had severed the link between myself and my former condition* (Frederick Marryat). *Labour thus helped to create a link of friendship between the rising peoples* (London Times). **b** a part or parts so joined: *links of sausage.* **3** *Figurative.* a fact or thought that connects others: *a link in a chain of evidence.* **4** the hundredth part of a surveyor's chain, used as a measure of length, equal to 7.92 inches. **5** a rod, bar, or similar piece connected at its ends to two parts of a machine and transmitting motion from one to the other. **6** *Electricity.* the part of a fuse that melts when too strong a current goes through it. **7** *Chemistry.* = bond.
*—v.t.* to join as a link does; unite or connect: *to link arms. Your fortunes and his are linked together* (Charles Kingsley). *—v.i.* to be coupled, joined , or connected: *Your story links up with his.*
*—adj.* arranged in or connected by links: *link sausages.*
[apparently < Scandinavian (compare Swedish *länk* )] —**link′er**, *n.*
**link**[2] (lingk), *n.* a torch, especially one made of tow and pitch, formerly used to light people's way along the streets. [origin uncertain]
**link**[3] (lingk), *v.i. Scottish.* to move nimbly; pass quickly along; trip. [compare Norwegian *linka* to give a toss, bend]
**link|age** (ling′kij), *n.* **1** the act or process of linking. **2** the state of being linked. **3** an arrangement or system of links. **4** the policy or practice of having some aspect of the relations between two countries dependent upon the success or failure of another aspect of their relations: **5** *Biology.* the association of two or more genes or their characteristics on the same chromosome so that they are transmitted together. **6** any one of various devices consisting of a number of bars linked or pivoted together, used to produce a desired motion in a machine part, or for tracing lines. **7** *Electricity.* the product of the magnetic flux going through a coil and the number of turns in the coil. It serves as a measure of the voltage that can be induced in the coil.
**linkage group**, *Biology.* a group of genes or hereditary characteristics that are transmitted together.
**link|boy** (lingk′boi′), *n.* a boy who used to be employed to carry a link or torch to light the way for a person along the streets.
**linked** (lingkt), *adj.* **1** connected by or like links. **2** *Biology.* exhibiting linkage.
**link|ing r** (ling′king), *Phonetics.* (in dialects in which *r* is not pronounced in final and preconsonantal position) the final *r-* sound preserved before a word with an initial vowel, as in *far off* with a linking *r* (contrasted with *far* with no *r-* sound).
**linking verb**, a verb, with little or no meaning of its own, used to connect a subject with a predicate noun or predicate adjective; copula. *Be* and *seem* are the most common linking verbs. In "The men are soldiers," *are* is a linking verb.
▶See **copula** for usage note.
**link|man** (lingk′mən), *n., pl.* **-men**. **1** a man formerly employed to carry a link or torch to light the way for a person along the street. **2** a player who acts as a link between the center forwards and backs in soccer, Rugby, and field hockey. **3** *British.* **a** a moderator or coordinator, especially of a radio or television discussion program. **b** an intermediary; a go-between.
**link motion**, **1** a valve gear in a steam engine for controlling (including reversing) the valve motion, consisting of a series of links connecting the eccentrics to the block that operates the valve. **2** any system of links that connects, and regulates the motion of, two parts, one of which drives the other.
**links** (lingks), *n.pl.* **1** = golf course. **2** *Scottish.* **a** a comparatively level or gently rolling sandy ground near the seashore, covered with turf or coarse grass. **b** the windings of a stream. **c** the ground lying along such windings. [Old English *hlinc* rising ground]
▶**Links** is used as either singular or plural: *Do you know of a links where we can play tomorrow? The Sunnyview Links are always crowded.*
**links|land** (lingks′land′, -lənd), *n.* a stretch of sandy soil deposited by the ocean and formed into dunes and sand hills by the winds.
**links|man** (lingks′mən), *n., pl.* **-men**. a golfer.
**Link trainer**, *Trademark.* **1** *Aeronautics.* a ground training device in which flight conditions are simulated. **2** a training device for drivers in which road conditions are simulated.
**link-up** (lingk′up′), *n.* **1** connection; affiliation; tie. **2** a rendezvous of space vehicles with physical connections, as by tethers, but not docking.
**link|work** (lingk′wėrk′), *n.* **1** work composed of or arranged in links. **2** a mechanism using links to transmit motion.
**linn**[1] (lin), *n. Especially Scottish.* **1** a waterfall. **2** a pool, especially one beneath a waterfall. **3a** a precipice. **b** a steep ravine. [perhaps fusion of Old English *hlynn* torrent, and Gaelic *linne* pool]
**linn**[2] (lin), *n.* = linden. [altered form of Old English *lind* linden]

**Pronunciation Key:** hat, āge, cãre, fär; let, ēqual, tėrm; it, īce; hot, ōpen, ôrder; **oi**l, **ou**t; cup, pu̇t, rüle; **ch**ild; lo**ng**; **th**in; ᴛʜen; **zh**, measure; ə represents **a** in about, **e** in taken, **i** in pencil, **o** in lemon, **u** in circus.

**Lin|ne|an** or **Lin|nae|an** (li nē′ən), *adj.* **1** of Carolus Linnaeus (1707-1778). The Linnean system of naming animals uses two words, the first for the genus and the second for the species. **2** of the earlier system of plant classification introduced by Linnaeus, dividing plants into 24 classes.

**lin|net** (lin′it), *n.* **1** a small songbird of Europe, Asia, and Africa. It has brown or gray plumage, the color changing at different ages and seasons. The linnet is a kind of finch. **2** any one of certain allied birds, such as the pine siskin or pine linnet, of North America. **3** = redpoll (def. 1). [perhaps Old English *līnetwigle,* or *līnete* < *līn* flax, ultimately < Latin *līnum* (flaxseed forms much of the bird's diet)]

**li|no** (lī′nō), *n., pl.* **-nos.** *Informal.* **1** linoleum. **2a** a linotype. **b** a linotypist.

**li|no|cut** (lī′nə kut′), *n.* **1** a design cut in relief on a block of linoleum. **2** a print obtained from this.

**Li|no|film** (lī′nə film), *n. Trademark.* a machine which sets type photographically, consisting chiefly of a keyboard unit which produces a copy on perforated tape and a photographic unit into which the tape is automatically fed to be put on film.

**lin|o|le|ic acid** (lin′ə lē′ik, lə nō′lē-), an unsaturated acid essential to the human diet, found as a glyceride in linseed and other oils, and used as a drying agent in paint and varnish. *Formula:* $C_{18}H_{32}O_2$

**lin|o|le|nic acid** (lin′ə lē′nik, -len′ik), an unsaturated fatty acid essential to the human diet, found as a glyceride in linseed and other oils. It is also used as a drying agent in paint and varnish. *Linolenic acid inhibits thrombosis* (Observer). *Formula:* $C_{18}H_{30}O_2$

**li|no|le|um** (lə nō′lē əm), *n.* **1** a floor covering made by putting a hard surface of ground cork mixed with linseed oil on a canvas or burlap back. **2** any similar floor covering. **3** linseed oil oxidized until hard. [< Latin *līnum* flax + *oleum* oil]

**lin|on** (lin′on; *French* lē nôɴ′), *n.* lawn, a linen or cotton fabric. [< French *linon*]

**li|no|type** (lī′nə tīp), *n., v.,* **-typed, -typ|ing.** *—n.* **1** a typesetting machine that is operated like a typewriter and that casts each line of type in one piece. **2 Linotype.** *Trademark.* a name for a machine of this kind.
*—v.t.* to set with a linotype.
[American English (originally) *line o'type* line of type] **—li′no|typ′er,** *n.* **—li′no|typ′ist,** *n.*

**lin|sang** (lin′sang), *n.* any one of various catlike, carnivorous mammals of the East Indies and Africa, having a very long tail and retractile claws. [< Javanese *linsang*]

**lin|seed** (lin′sēd′), *n.* the seed of flax; flaxseed. [Old English *līnsǣd* flaxseed]

**linseed oil,** a yellowish oil obtained by pressing the seed of flax. It is used in making paints, printing inks, and linoleum.

**lin|sey** (lin′zē), *n., pl.* **-seys.** = linsey-woolsey.

**lin|sey-wool|sey** (lin′zē wůl′zē), *n., pl.* **-wool-seys. 1** a strong, coarse fabric made of linen and wool or of cotton and wool. **2** *Figurative.* any poor or incongruous mixture. [Middle English *linsey* a linen fabric (< *lin-,* Old English *līn* linen) + English *wool;* with a rhyming ending]

**lin|stock** (lin′stok), *n.* a stick with a forked end, formerly used to hold a fuze or match in firing a cannon. [alteration of Dutch *lontstok* < *lont* match (originally made of tow) + *stock* stock, stick]

**lint** (lint), *n.* **1** a soft down or fleecy material obtained by scraping linen. Formerly lint was put on wounds to keep out air and dirt. **2** tiny bits of thread or fluff of any material: *Lint collects on the carpet.* **3** raw cotton that has been ginned and is ready for baling. **4** *Scottish.* the flax plant. [Middle English *linnet,* probably ultimately Old English *līn* flax, or < Latin *līnum*] **—lint′less,** *adj.*

**lin|tel** (lin′təl), *n.* a horizontal beam or stone above a door or window to support the structure above it. [< Old French *lintel* threshold, ultimately < Latin *līmes, -itis* limit]

**lint|er** (lin′tər), *n. U.S.* a machine for stripping off the short cotton fibers remaining on the cotton-seed after ginning.
**linters,** the cotton fibers so removed: *Linters may be used for cotton batting, the manufacture of rayon, and the making of paper and guncotton.*

**lint|white** (lint′hwīt′), *n. Especially Scottish.* the linnet.

**lint|y** (lin′tē), *adj.,* **lint|i|er, lint|i|est. 1** full of or marked with lint. **2** like lint: *the linty seeds of dandelion.*

**li|num** (lī′nəm), *n.* any dicotyledonous herb of the genus that includes flax, especially the ornamental species. [< Latin *līnum* flax]

**Li|nus** (lī′nəs), *n.* **1** *Greek Mythology.* a son of Apollo who became a skillful musician and taught Orpheus. **2** Also, **Linus song.** a lamentation sung in ancient Greece.

**lin|y** (lī′nē), *adj.,* **lin|i|er, lin|i|est. 1** full of or marked with lines. **2** linelike.

**li|on** (lī′ən), *n.* **1** a large, strong animal of Africa and southern Asia that has a dull-yellowish coat. Lions are carnivorous mammals and members of the cat family. The male has a full, flowing mane of coarse hair. **2** any one of various related animals, especially the puma. **3** *Figurative.* **a** a very brave or strong person. **b** a famous man; celebrity. **4a** the lion as the national emblem of Great Britain. **b** the British nation itself.
**beard the lion in his den,** to defy a person in his home, office, or other usual place of work or living: *And dar'st thou then to beard the lion in his den, the Douglas in his hall?* (Scott).
**put one's head in the lion's mouth.** See under **head.**
**throw** (or **feed**) **to the lions,** to cast into ruin or destruction, usually by withdrawing support from or otherwise abandoning: *On the other side there is also the shadow of ... old-established enterprises disappearing and of their older employees being thrown to the lions* (London Times).
**twist the lion's tail,** to say or do something intended to excite the resentment of some government or other authority, especially the government or people of Great Britain: *Encroachment on that land would twist the lion's tail.*
[< Old French *lion* < Latin *leō, -ōnis* < Greek *léōn, léontos*] **—li′on|like′,** *adj.*

**Li|on** (lī′ən), *n.* **1** a constellation and the fifth sign of the zodiac; Leo. **2** a member of a local organization of the International Association of Lions Clubs, founded in 1917 for community service. [< *lion*]

**li|on|ess** (lī′ə nis), *n.* a female lion.

**li|on|et** (lī′ə net), *n.* a little or young lion.

**li|on|fish** (lī′ən fish′), *n., pl.* **-fish|es** or (*collectively*) **-fish.** a tropical marine fish with patterned light and dark fins, found in the Indian Ocean and in the Pacific around the East Indies; turkey fish. The lionfish has very poisonous dorsal spines.

**li|on|heart** (lī′ən härt′), *n.* a person of great courage.

**li|on-heart|ed** (lī′ən här′tid), *adj.* brave; courageous. **SYN:** dauntless, valiant. **—li′on-heart′ed-ness,** *n.*

**li|on|ize** (lī′ə nīz), *v.t.,* **-ized, -iz|ing. 1** to treat (a person) as very important: *Never, never have I been so lionized! I assure you, I was cock of the walk* (Henry James). **SYN:** adulate, glorify. **2** to visit the sights of (a place); visit or go over (a place of interest). **—li′on|i|za′tion,** *n.* **—li′on|iz′-er,** *n.*

**li|on|ly** (lī′ən lē), *adj.* resembling a lion.

**lion's share,** the biggest or best part: *The liberal publications have the major influence* [*and*] *get the lion's share of attention* (New York Times).

**lion's tooth,** = dandelion.

**lip** (lip), *n., adj., v.,* **lipped, lip|ping.** *—n.* **1** either one of the two fleshy movable edges of the mouth, especially in man and some other animals: *When the baby fell she bit her lip.* **2** the folding or bent-out edge of any opening: *the lip of a pitcher, the lip of a crater, one of the lips of a wound.* **3** *Music.* **a** the mouthpiece of a musical instrument. **b** the manner of shaping the mouth to play a wind instrument. **c** the edges above and below the mouth of a flue pipe of an organ. **4** *Slang.* impudent talk: *"Don't you give me none o' your lip," says he* (Mark Twain). **5** *Botany.* **a** either one of the two parts of a labiate corolla or calyx, the upper lip being closest to the axis of the inflorescence and the lower lip farthest away from the axis. **b** = labellum (in an orchid). **6** *Zoology.* = labium. **7** an edge of the opening of a gastropod shell. **8** the spiral blade on the end of an auger.
*—adj.* **1** not heartfelt or deep, but just on the surface: *lip worship.* See also **lip service. SYN:** superficial, insincere. **2** of a lip or lips. **3** *Phonetics.* formed or produced by the lips; labial.
*—v.t.* **1** to touch with the lips: *after the final adjustment of the mouthpiece, lipping the instrument* (Samuel Lover). **2** to pronounce with the lips only; murmur softly: *I heard my name Most fondly lipp'd* (Keats). **3** to kiss: *A hand that kings Have lipp'd, and trembled kissing* (Shakespeare). **4** to hit a golf ball so that it touches but does not drop in (the hole).
*—v.i.* to use the lips in playing a wind instrument.
**curl one's lip,** to raise the upper lip as an expression of contempt or scorn: *He always curled his lip in pronouncing the name of an enemy.*
**hang on the lips of,** to listen to with great attentiveness and admiration: *The audience hung on the lips of the orator.*
**keep a stiff upper lip, a** to be brave or firm; show no fear or discouragement: *What's the use o' boohooin'? ... Keep a stiff upper lip; no bones broke* (John Neal). **b** to be very reserved; show no feeling: *The British male is popularly supposed to keep a stiff upper lip and shun all displays of emotion whatever the cause* (Punch).
**lips, a** the mouth: *Her lips formed a perfect bow.* **b** the lips as organs of speech: *His lips are very mild and meek* (Tennyson).
**smack one's lips, a** to open the lips with a sharp sound, especially as a sign of pleasure: *He smacked his lips over the wine.* **b** *Figurative.* to express enjoyment or pleasurable anticipation over something: [*The airline*] *has been smacking its lips over the prospect of a $145 million windfall* (Time).
[Old English *lippa*] **—lip′like′,** *adj.*

**lip|a|roid** (lip′ə roid), *adj. Rare.* lipoid; fatty. [< Greek *liparós* shiny, greasy]

**li|pase** (lī′pās, lip′ās), *n.* any one of a class of enzymes occurring especially in the pancreatic and gastric juices and certain seeds, that can change fats into fatty acids, glycerin, and sugar. [< Greek *lípos* fat, noun + English *-ase*]

**li|pec|to|my** (li pek′tə mē), *n., pl.* **-mies.** surgical removal of fat, as in cases of obesity. [< Greek *lípos* fat + *ektomē* a cutting out]

**li|pe|mi|a** (li pē′mē ə), *n.* the presence of an excessive quantity of fat in the blood; hyperlipemia. [< New Latin *lipemia* < Greek *lípos* fat + *haîma* blood]

**lip|id** (lip′id, lī′pid), *n.* any one of a group of organic compounds including the fats, oils, waxes, and sterols. They are characterized by an oily feeling, solubility in fat solvents such as chloroform, benzene, or ether, and insolubility in water. [< Greek *lípos* fat, noun + English *-id*(e)]

**lip|ide** (lip′īd, -id; lī′pīd, -pid), *n.* = lipid.

**li|pin** (lī′pin, lip′in), *n.* = lipid.

**Lip|iz|zan** (lip′ə zän), *n.* = Lipizzaner.

**Lip|iz|za|ner** (lip′ə zä′nər), *n.* a horse bred in Europe since the 1500's for use in the Spanish Riding School, in Austria. Lipizzaners are born with dark coats that turn white after three to seven years.

**lip|less** (lip′lis), *adj.* having no lips.

**lip|o|ca|ic** (lip′ə kā′ik), *n.* a lipotropic substance found in the pancreas. [< Greek *lípos* fat, noun + *kaíein* to burn + English *-ic*]

**lip|o|chrome** (lip′ə krōm), *n.* any of a group of fat-soluble pigments, such as the carotenoids, occurring in animals and plants. They produce the bright red or yellow plumage of birds. [< Greek *lípos* fat, noun + *chrôma* color]

**lip|o|gen|e|sis** (lip′ə jen′ə sis), *n.* the formation of fat in the body. [< Greek *lípos* fat + English *genesis*]

**lip|o|gen|ic** (lip′ə jen′ik), *adj.* tending to produce fat.

**lip|o|gram** (lip′ə gram, lī′pə-), *n.* a writing from which all words containing a particular letter or letters are omitted: *an ancient Greek lipogram.* [< Greek *lip-,* stem of *leípein* to be wanting + English *-gram*]

**li|po|ic acid** (li pō′ik), = thioctic acid.

**lip|oid** (lip′oid, lī′poid), *adj., n. Biochemistry.*
*—adj.* like fat or oil.
*—n.* any one of a group of nitrogenous fatlike substances, such as the lecithins.
[< Greek *lípos* fat, noun + English *-oid*]

**lip|oi|dal** (lip oi′dəl, lī′poi dəl), *adj.* = lipoid.

**lip|oid|o|sis** (lip′oi dō′sis, lī′poi-), *n.* the abnormal deposition of fat in some part of the body.

**li|pol|y|sis** (li pol′ə sis), *n. Chemistry.* the breakdown or dissolution of a fat, as by the action of lipase.

**lip|o|lyt|ic** (lip′ə lit′ik), *adj.* of, having to do with, or of the nature of lipolysis.

**li|po|ma** (li pō′mə), *n., pl.* **-mas, -ma|ta** (-mə tə). a tumor, usually benign and painless, composed of fat cells. [< New Latin *lipoma* < Greek *lípos* fat, noun]

**li|pom|a|tous** (li pom′ə təs), *adj.* having to do with or of the nature of a lipoma.

**lip|o|phil|ic** (lip′ə fil′ik), *adj.* having an affinity for lipids.

**lip|o|pol|y|sac|cha|ride** (lip′ə pol′ē sak′ə rīd, -ər-id), *n.* a compound formed by a lipid and a polysaccharide: *bacterial lipopolysaccharides.*

**lip|o|pro|tein** (lip′ə prō′tēn, -tē in), *n. Biochemistry.* any one of a class of proteins, one of the components of which is a lipid.

**lip|o|trop|ic** (lip′ə trop′ik), *adj. Biochemistry.* **1** having an affinity for lipids. **2** reducing the accumulation of fat.

**lip|o|trop|ism** (lip′ə trop′iz əm), *n.* lipotropic tendency or property.

**lipped** (lipt), *adj.* **1** having a lip or lips. **2** *Botany.* labiate.

**-lipped,** *combining form.* having ___ lips: *Thin-lipped = having thin lips.*

**lip|pen** (lip′ən), *Scottish and British Dialect.* *—v.i.* to confide; rely; trust.
*—v.t.* to expect with confidence. [origin uncertain]

**lip|per** (lip′ər), *n. Nautical.* a slightly rough or rippling sea. [probably imitative]

**Lip|pes loop**, (lip′əs), a loop-shaped plastic intrauterine device. [< Jack *Lippes,* an American physician of the 1900's, who invented it]

**Lip|pi|zan** (lip′ə zän), *n.* = Lipizzaner.

**Lip|pi|za|ner** (lip′ə zä′nər), *n.* = Lipizzaner.

**lip print**, the impression made by the lines of the lips on a surface.

**lip|py** (lip′ē), *adj.* **1** *Informal.* having a large or protruding lip or lips. **2** *Slang.* impertinent: *Out with all the officials who are lippy* (Maclean's).

**lip-read** (lip′rēd′), *v.i. v.t.,* **-read, -read|ing.** to understand speech by watching the movements of the speaker's lips.

**lip reader**, a person who lip-reads.

**lip reading**, the understanding of speech by watching the movements of the speaker's lips; speech reading.

**lips** (lips), *n.pl.* See under **lip**.

**lip service**, service with the lips or words only; insincere profession of devotion or good will: *The Conservatives have realized that they must pay at least lip service to Labour's policy* (London Times).

**lip|stick** (lip′stik′), *n.* a small stick of a waxlike cosmetic, used for coloring the lips.

**lip sync**, **1** synchronization of lip movements with sound previously recorded: *Pantomiming to a record... is a convenient ruse known as "lip sync"* (Time). **2** synchronization of a voice with lip movements filmed previously, as in the preparation of a dubbed, native-language version of a foreign film.

**liq.**, **1** liquid. **2** liquor.

**li|quate** (lī′kwāt), *v.t.,* **-quat|ed, -quat|ing.** **1** liquefy. **2** to separate (a metal) in a liquid state from impurities or from other less fusible metals in a solid form by heating. **3** to heat (a metal) to produce such separation. [< Latin *liquāre* (with English *-ate*[1]) melt, related to *liquor* liquor]

**li|qua|tion** (lī kwā′shən), *n.* **1** the process of liquating. **2** the separation of metals by fusion.

**liq|ue|fa|cient** (lik′wə fā′shənt), *n.* something that serves to liquefy.

**liq|ue|fac|tion** (lik′wə fak′shən), *n.* **1** the process of changing into a liquid, especially of changing a gas by the application of pressure and cooling. **2** liquefied condition.

**liq|ue|fac|tive** (lik′wə fak′tiv), *adj.* causing liquefaction.

**liq|ue|fied petroleum gas** (lik′wə fīd), bottled gas; LP gas: *The gas companies may also remove lighter hydrocarbons, such as propane and butane, from natural gas. These gas fuels are sometimes called liquefied petroleum gases* (Harlan W. Nelson). *Abbr:* LPG (no periods).

**liq|ue|fy** (lik′wə fī), *v.t., v.i.,* **-fied, -fy|ing.** to change into a liquid; make or become liquid: *Liquefied air is extremely cold.* [< Middle French *liquéfier,* learned borrowing from Latin *liquefacere* < *liquēre* be fluid + *facere* make] **—liq′ue|fi′a|ble,** *adj.* **—liq′ue|fi′er,** *n.*

**li|ques|cence** (li kwes′əns), *n.* liquescent condition.

**li|ques|cent** (li kwes′ənt), *adj.* **1** becoming liquid. **2** apt to become liquid. [< Latin *liquēscēns, -entis,* present participle of *liquēscere* begin to be(come) liquid < *liquēre* be(come) liquid]

**li|queur** (li kėr′, -kyůr′), *n., v.* **—*n.*** a strong, sweet, highly flavored alcoholic liquor, often served after dinner.

**—*v.t.*** to treat or flavor with liqueur.

[< French *liqueur* < Old French *licour* liquid. See etym. of doublet **liquor**.]

**liq|uid** (lik′wid), *n., adj.* **—*n.*** **1** any substance that is not a solid or a gas; substance that flows freely like water. Liquids and gases are classed together as fluids. Mercury is a liquid at room temperature. A liquid is composed of molecules that move freely over each other so that a mass has the shape of its container, like a gas, but, unlike a gas, it has a definite volume. **2** *Phonetics.* the sound of *l* or *r;* liquid consonant.

**—*adj.*** **1** in the form of a liquid; melted: *butter heated until it is liquid. Many shampoos are made of liquid soap.* **2** flowing or capable of flowing like water. **3** *Figurative.* clear and bright like water: *a beautiful young girl with liquid eyes.* **4** *Figurative.* clear and smooth-flowing in sound: *the liquid notes of a bird. Italian is the most liquid ... language that can possibly be imagined* (David Hume). **5** *Phonetics.* **a** having the nature of a liquid. **b** (of consonants, especially *l* or *n,* as in Spanish) palatalized. **6** *Figurative.* smooth and easy in movement; graceful. **7** *Figurative.* easily turned into cash: *liquid assets.*

[< Latin *liquidus* < *liquēre* to be(come) fluid] **—liq′uid|ly,** *adv.* **—liq′uid|ness,** *n.*

**—*Syn:*** *n.* **1 Liquid, fluid** mean a substance that flows. **Liquid** applies only to a substance that is neither a solid nor a gas: *Milk and oil are liquids; oxygen is not a liquid.* **Fluid** applies to anything that flows in any way, either a liquid or a gas: *Milk, water, and oxygen are fluids.*

**liquid air**, an intensely cold, transparent liquid formed by putting air under very great pressure and then cooling it. It is used mainly as a refrigerant and as a source of nitrogen and oxygen.

**liq|uid|am|bar** (lik′wid am′bər, -bär), *n.* **1** any one of a small group of trees related to the witch hazel, especially the sweet gum tree of North America, that in warm regions exudes a gum used in the preparation of chewing gum and in medicine, and a species of Asia Minor that yields the balsam known as liquid storax. **2** Also, **liquid amber.** the resinous gum that exudes from the bark of the sweet gum. [< New Latin *Liquidambar* the genus name < Latin *liquidus* liquid + Medieval Latin *ambar* amber]

**liq|ui|date** (lik′wə dāt), *v.,* **-dat|ed, -dat|ing.** **—*v.t.*** **1** to pay (a debt): *to liquidate a mortgage.* **2** to settle the accounts of (a business, foundation, or estate) by distributing the assets; clear up the affairs of (a bankrupt). **3** to get rid of (an undesirable person or thing): *The French Revolution liquidated the nobility.* **4** to kill ruthlessly; exterminate. **5** to convert into cash. **6** *Law.* to determine and apportion by agreement or litigation the amount of (indebtedness or damages).

**—*v.i.*** to liquidate debts, assets, or accounts.

[< Late Latin *liquidāre* (with English *-ate*[1]) < Latin *liquidus* liquid]

**liq|ui|da|tion** (lik′wə dā′shən), *n.* **1** the act of liquidating a company's assets or the like. **2** the state or condition of being liquidated: *to go into liquidation.* **3** the elimination of an undesirable person, idea, or institution: *He advocated the gradual liquidation of the German standing army* (Edmund Wilson).

**liq|ui|da|tor** (lik′wə dā′tər), *n.* a person who liquidates, especially one appointed, as by a court, to conduct the liquidation of a company.

**liquid crystal**, a substance that flows like a liquid but has some of the properties of a crystal within a certain temperature range. Many types of brightly colored liquid crystals have the property of changing colors because of small changes in temperature.

**liquid fire**, a flaming oil or chemical usually hurled from flame throwers.

**li|quid|i|ty** (li kwid′ə tē), *n.* liquid condition or quality.

**liq|uid|ize** (lik′wə dīz), *v.t.,* **-ized, -iz|ing.** to make liquid. **—liq′uid|iz′er,** *n.*

**liquid measure**, **1** the measurement of liquids. **2** a system for measuring liquids.

English system
4 ounces = 1 gill
4 gills = 1 pint = 28.875 cubic inches
2 pints = 1 quart = 57.75 cubic inches
4 quarts = 1 gallon = 231 cubic inches
31½ gallons = 1 barrel = 7276.5 cubic inches
2 barrels (63 gallons) = 1 hogshead = 14,553 cubic inches

Metric system
10 milliliters = 1 centiliter
100 centiliters = 1 liter
100 liters = 1 hectoliter

**liquid membrane**, a thin film either of oil forming a surface around a globule of water, or of water around a globule of oil, the film being stabilized by the surrounding molecules of an agent that reduces surface tension. A liquid membrane is either a barrier or a permeable film depending on its chemical composition or surface structure. *The team tested both aspirin and phenobarbital and found that liquid membrane ... will remove 95 percent of each drug within five minutes from acidic solutions* (Science News).

**liquid oxygen**, an intensely cold, transparent liquid formed by putting oxygen under very great pressure and then cooling it; lox. It is used as a rocket fuel.

**liquid paraffin**, = mineral oil.

**liquid petrolatum**, = mineral oil.

**liquid propellant**, a liquid fuel used in a rocket engine. It contains its own oxygen or combines with oxygen usually released from a separate tank.

**liquid protein**, a preparation of concentrated protein processed mainly from gelatin, as in cowhide, and once recommended as a food substitute to reduce weight: *Analyses of liquid protein products ... suggest a deficiency of essential minerals and nutrients would occur if the products were consumed in place of natural foods* (Julie Ann Miller).

**liquid storax**, = storax (def. 4).

**liq|uor** (lik′ər), *n., v.* **—*n.*** **1** an alcoholic drink, especially brandy, whiskey, gin, or rum: *The old trapper always carried a bottle of liquor in his pack to pour down his throat to help fight the cold or to pour over a cut to help fight infection.* **SYN:** spirits. **2** any liquid, especially: **a** the liquid in which food is packaged, canned, or cooked: *Pickles are put up in a salty liquor.* **b** *Pharmaceutics.* a solution of medicinal substances in water: *liquor ammoniae.* **c** a liquid or a prepared solution used in many industrial processes.

**—*v.t.*** **1** (in various industrial arts) to steep in or soak with a liquor. **2** to dress (leather, boots, or shoes) with oil or grease. **3** *Slang.* to supply with liquor to drink; ply with liquor: *Many of the men came back liquored up, and started scrapping on the way* (New Yorker). **4** *Rare.* to cover or smear with a liquor, especially to lubricate.

**—*v.i.*** *Slang.* to drink alcoholic liquor.

**in liquor**, in a state of intoxication; drunk: *I smoke like a furnace— I'm always in liquor, A ruffian— a bully— a sot* (W. S. Gilbert).

[< Old French *licour* liquid, learned borrowing from Latin *liquor* liquid, liquidity < *liquēre* to be(come) fluid. See etym. of doublet **liqueur**.]

**liq|uo|rice** (lik′ər is, lik′ris; -ər ish, -rish), *n.* = licorice.

**liq|uor|ish**[1] (lik′ər ish), *n. Dialect.* licorice.

**liq|uor|ish**[2] (lik′ər ish), *adj.* = lickerish.

**li|ra** (lir′ə), *n., pl.* **li|re** (lir′ā), **li|ras,** or *for 3* **li|rot** (lē′rōt). **1a** the unit of money of Italy, equal to 100 centesimi. **b** a coin or note worth a lira. **2** a unit of money or gold coin of Turkey, equal to 100 kurus; Turkish pound. **3** a unit of money of Israel, worth 100 agorot; the Israeli pound. [< Italian *lira* < Latin *lībra* pound (the weight); balance, scales]

**lir|i|o|den|dron** (lir′ē ə den′drən), *n., pl.* **-dra** (-drə). any tree of a small group of the magnolia family, especially the tulip tree of North America. [< New Latin *Liriodendron* the typical genus < Greek *leírion* lily + *déndron* tree]

**lir|i|pipe** (lir′ə pīp), *n.* the long tail of a graduate's hood in early academic costume. [< Medieval Latin *liripipium,* or *leropipium* tippet, shoelace]

**lis** (lis), *n., pl.* **li|tes.** *Law.* litigation; lawsuit. [< Latin *līs;* see etym. under **litigate**]

**lisle** (līl), *n., adj.* **—*n.*** **1** a fine, hard-twisted, strong, linen or cotton thread, used for making stockings, gloves, shirts, etc. **2** a fabric or garment knit or woven of this thread.

**—*adj.*** made of lisle: *lisle stockings.*

[< French *Lisle,* earlier spelling of *Lille,* a town in France, where this cloth was originally made]

**lisp** (lisp), *v., n.* **—*v.i.*** **1** to use the sound of *th* in *thin* and *then* instead of the sound of *s* in *bus* and *is* when speaking: *A person who lisps might say, "Thing a thong of thixpenth" for "Sing a song of sixpence."* **2** to speak imperfectly: *Children usually lisp until they are three or four.*

**—*v.t.*** **1** to pronounce with a lisp. **2** to pronounce imperfectly, as in a simple, childlike way.

**—*n.*** the act, habit, or sound of saying a sound represented by *th* for a sound represented by *s* and *z: He spoke with a lisp.*

[Old English *-wlispian*] **—lisp′er,** *n.*

**lis pen|dens** (lis pen′denz), *Latin, Law.* **1** a lawsuit that is pending. **2** the jurisdiction or control of a court over property involved in litigation.

**lis|som** (lis′əm), *adj.* = lissome. **—lis′som|ness,** *n.*

**lis|some** (lis′əm), *adj.* **1** bending easily; lithe; limber; supple: *a daughter of our meadows ... straight, but as lissome as a hazel wand* (Tennyson). **2** nimble; active. [variant of *lithesome*] **—lis′some|ly,** *adv.* **—lis′some|ness,** *n.*

**lis|sot|ri|chous** (li sot′rə kəs), *adj. Anthropology.* having smooth hair. [< Greek *lissós* smooth + *thrix, trichós* hair + English *-ous*]

**list**[1] (list), *n., v.* **—*n.*** **1** a series of names, numbers, words, or phrases; catalog or roll usually consisting of a column or series of names, figures, words, or the like: *a shopping list.* **2** all the stocks or other securities officially entered and traded on a stock exchange.

**—*v.t.*** **1** to make a list of; enter in a list: *A dictionary lists words in alphabetical order. I shall list my errands on a card.* **2** to enter (a stock or other securities) on the list of those traded on an exchange. **3** to enroll (soldiers); enlist.

**—*v.i.*** **1** to be listed. **2** to have one's name entered upon the list of a military body; enlist.

[< French *liste,* ultimately < Germanic (compare Old High German *līsta* strip border, English *list*[2])] **—list′a|ble,** *adj.*

**—*Syn:*** *n.* **1 List, catalog, roll** mean a series of names of items. **List** is the general word applying to a series of names, figures, or words: *This is the list of the people who are going to the picnic.* **Catalog** applies to a complete list arranged alphabetically or according to some other system, often with short descriptions of the items: *Has the new mail-order catalog come?* **Roll** applies to a list of the names of all members of a group: *His name is on the honor roll.*

**list**[2] (list), *n., adj., v.* —***n.*** **1** the edge of cloth where the material is a little different; selvage. **2** a cheap fabric made out of such edges. **3** any strip of fabric. **4** a narrow strip of wood cut from the edge of a plank, especially sapwood. **5** *Architecture.* a square molding; fillet. **6** a stripe of color: *Gartered with a red and blue list* (Shakespeare). **7** *U.S.* a strip of ground, especially one of the ridges or furrows made by a lister. **8** one of the divisions of a head of hair or of a beard. **9** *Obsolete.* **a** a border, hem, or bordering strip (of anything). **b** a limit; bound; boundary. **c** an encircling palisade; railed or staked enclosure.
—***adj.*** made of list: *a list carpet. ... her quiet tread muffled in a list slipper* (Charlotte Brontë).
—***v.t.*** **1** to put list around the edges of; border or edge. **2** to cover an object with list. **3** to cut a narrow strip from the edge of (a plank); shape (a block) by chopping. **4** *U.S. Dialect.* to prepare (land), especially for a crop of corn or cotton, with a lister or by making alternate strips and beds.
[Old English *līste*]

**list**[3] (list), *n., v.* —***n.*** the act or condition of tipping to one side, as caused by unequal distribution of weight in a ship; tilt: *The sinking ship had a list that was so far over water lapped its decks.*
—***v.i.*** to tip to one side, as a ship; careen; heel; tilt: *The sinking ship had listed so far that water lapped its decks.*
—***v.t.*** to cause a tipping or list in (a ship): *The shifting cargo had listed the storm-tossed freighter.*
[perhaps extended use of *list*[4], noun]

**list**[4] (list), *v., n. Archaic.* —***v.t.*** to be pleasing to; please: *Me lists not to speak. When it listeth him to call them to an account* (Sir Walter Raleigh).
—***v.i.*** to like; wish: *The enemy plundered where they listed.*
—***n.*** appetite; desire; longing; inclination: *I had little list or leisure to write* (Thomas Fuller).
[Old English *lystan* < *lust* pleasure]

**list**[5] (list), *Archaic.* —***v.i.*** to listen: *Go forth, under the open sky, and list to Nature's teachings* (William Cullen Bryant). *List, list; I hear Some far off hallo break the silent air* (Milton).
—***v.t.*** to listen to; hear: *Elves, list your names* (Shakespeare).
[Old English *hlystan,* related to *hlyst* hearing. Compare etym. under **listen.**]

**list|ed** (lis′tid), *adj.* **1** set down or entered in a list. **2** (of securities) entered in or admitted to the regular list of securities which may be traded on a stock exchange.

**list|ee** (lis tē′), *n.* a person who is listed in a directory, registry, or other list of names.

**lis|tel** (lis′təl), *n. Architecture.* a narrow list or fillet. [< French *listel* < Italian *listello* (diminutive) < *lista* border < a Germanic word. Compare etym. under **list**[1].]

**lis|ten** (lis′ən), *v., n.* —***v.i.*** **1** to try to hear; attend with the ears so as to hear: *The mother listens for her baby's cry. I like to listen to music.* **SYN:** See syn. under **hear. 2** to give heed (to advice, temptation, etc.); pay attention: *Ye who listen with credulity to the whispers of fancy ...* (Samuel Johnson).
—***v.t.*** *Archaic.* to hear attentively; pay attention to (a person speaking or what is said).
—***n.*** the act of listening.
**listen in, a** to listen to others talking, especially on a telephone; eavesdrop: *If you want to hear what he says, listen in on the extension.* **b** to listen to the radio: *Listen in next week for the exciting conclusion of our story.*
[Old English *hlysnan.* Compare etym. under **list**[5].]
—**lis′ten|er,** *n.*

**lis|ten|a|bil|i|ty** (lis′ə nə bil′ə tē, lis′nə-), *n.* listenable quality or condition.

**lis|ten|a|ble** (lis′ə nə bəl, lis′nə-), *adj.* pleasant to listen to; worth listening to: *... the more listenable current melodies* (Harper's).

**lis|ten|er-in** (lis′ə nər in′, lis′nər-), *n., pl.* **lis|ten-ers-in. 1** a person who listens in; eavesdropper. **2** a device for listening in: *I heard this as Ernest handed me the listener-in on the phone* (A. J. Heal).

**lis|ten|er|ship** (lis′ə nər ship, lis′nər-), *n.* the number of people who listen (to a radio or television program, record, or other sound transmission): *From bitter experience, all broadcasters know that a routine political speech by a routine politician has a low-low rating in listenership* (Time).

**lis|ten|ing post** (lis′ə ning, lis′ning), **1** any position that serves as a center of information or communication, especially on foreign political and economic trends: *Germany is one of the best listening posts for what goes on in Russia* (New York Times). **2** *Military.* an outpost in front of a postion, for detecting and warning of enemy movement.

**list|er**[1] (lis′tər), *n.* a plow with a double moldboard, used especially in corn and beet culture, that throws the dirt to both sides of the furrow. Some kinds plant and cover seeds at the same time. [American English < *list*[2], verb + *-er*[1]]

**list|er**[2] (lis′tər), *n.* one who makes out a list.

**lis|te|ri|o|sis** (lis tir′ē ō′sis), *n.* = circling disease. [< New Latin *Listeria* genus name of the organism that causes the disease (< Joseph *Lister,* 1827-1912, an English physician) + English *-osis*]

**Lis|ter|ism** (lis′tə riz əm), *n.* the system of antiseptic surgery originated by Joseph Lister.

**list|ing** (lis′ting), *n.* **1** the fact or condition of being on a list, especially one that represents exclusive membership in some group, association, or club: *to apply for a listing on the stock exchange.* **2** an item on a list: *There is no listing under his name in the telephone directory.* **3** a list: *New listings of prices have been drawn up.*

**list|less** (list′lis), *adj.* seeming too tired to care about anything; not interested in things; not caring to be active: *a dull and listless mood, listless movements.* **SYN:** indifferent, languid. [< *list*[4], noun + *-less*] —**list′less|ly,** *adv.* —**list′less|ness,** *n.*

**list price,** a price of an article published in a catalog, advertisement, or list. Discounts are figured from it.

**lists** (lists), *n.pl.* **1a** a place where knights fought in tournaments or tilts. **b** the barriers enclosing such a place. **2** *Figurative.* any place or scene of combat or contest.
**enter the lists,** to join in a contest; take part in a fight or argument: *The Royal Society ... contained few individuals capable of ... entering the lists against his ... assailants* (David Brewster).
[blend of *list*[2], and Old French *lice,* or *lisse* place of combat < a Germanic word]

**list system,** a system of proportional representation in which each political party offers a list of candidates, and the voter marks his ballot for the party he chooses, not the individual candidates. Thus if a party receives 40 per cent of the total vote, it receives 40 per cent of the available seats in the legislature.

**Liszt|i|an** (lis′tē ən), *adj.* of or characteristic of the Hungarian composer and pianist Franz Liszt (1811-1886): *a Lisztian exercise in orchestral mastery* (Atlantic).

**lit**[1] (lit), *v., adj.* —***v.*** lighted; a past tense and a past participle of **light**[1] and **light**[3]: *Have you lit the candles? She lit the lamp. Two birds lit on my window sill. His eye lit upon a sentence.*
—***adj.*** *Slang.* Often, **lit up.** intoxicated; drunk.
▶ Both **lighted** and **lit** are in good use as the past tense and past participle. *Lit,* however, is rarely employed as a participial adjective before a substantive: *a lighted candle* rather than *a lit candle.*

**lit**[2] (lit), *n.* = litas.

**lit.,** an abbreviation for the following:
**1** liter or liters.
**2a** literal. **b** literally.
**3** literary.
**4** literature.

**lit|a|ny** (lit′ə nē), *n., pl.* **-nies. 1a** a prayer consisting of a series of supplications said by the minister or priest, and responses said by the people. **b** Often, **Litany.** a prayer in similar form, the "general supplication" appointed for use in the Book of Common Prayer. **2** a repeated series: *a litany of curses.* [< Old French *letanie,* and *litanie,* learned borrowings from Late Latin *litanīa* < Greek *litaneiā* litany; an entreating < *litê* prayer, entreaty < *litesthai* entreat, pray, beg]

**li|tas** (lē′täs), *n., pl.* **-tai** (-tī), **-tu.** the former unit of money or gold coin of Lithuania. Also, **lit.** [< Lithuanian *litas*]

**Lit. B.,** Bachelor of Letters (Latin, *Litterarum Baccalaureus*).

**li|tchi** (lē′chē), *n., pl.* **-tchis. 1** a small, nut-shaped fruit with a thin, brittle, rough, red shell. Inside the shell is a sweet, white, edible, jellylike pulp with a single brown seed. **2** the Chinese tree of the soapberry family that it grows on, now cultivated in warm regions throughout the world. Aso, **leechee, lichi.** [< Cantonese *laichi*]

**litchi nut,** the litchi fruit when dried. It is of a brownish or black color and is edible.

**Lit. D.,** Doctor of Letters (Latin, *Litterarum Doctor*).

**-lite,** *combining form.* stone; rock; mineral, as in *chrysolite. Aerolite = a meteorite made of stone.* [< French *-lite,* earlier *-lithe* < Greek *lithos* a stone]

✱**li|ter** (lē′tər), *n.* the basic measure of capacity in France, Germany, and other countries that use the metric system. A liter equals 1 cubic decimeter or 1,000 cubic centimeters, and is usually defined as the volume of a kilogram of water at its maximum density. One liter equals 1.0567 quarts U.S. liquid measure, or .908 quart U.S. dry measure. *Abbr:* l. Also, *especially British,* **litre.** [< French *litre* < *litron,* an obsolete measure of capacity < Medieval Latin *litra* < Greek *lītrā* pound (of 12 ounces)]

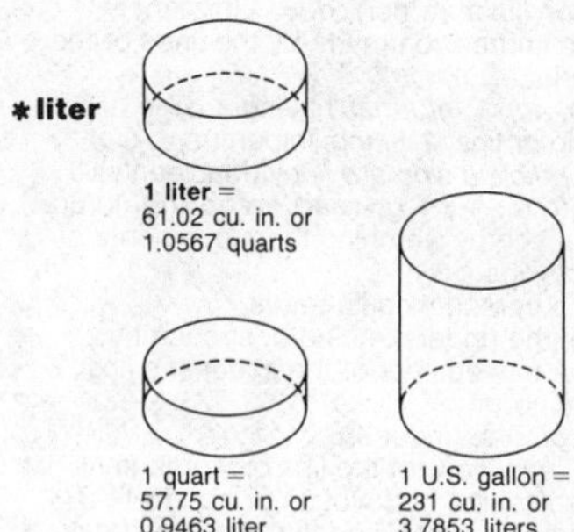


**lit|er|a|cy** (lit′ər ə sē), *n.* the ability to read and write; quality or state of being literate.

**literacy test,** a test to determine whether a person's ability to read and write meets voting or other requirements: *By 1917, a literacy test had been required for adult immigrants and virtually all Asians were excluded* (New York Times).

**lit|er|al** (lit′ər əl), *adj., n.* —***adj.*** **1** following the exact words of the original: *a literal translation.* **SYN:** verbatim. **2** taking words in their usual meaning, without exaggeration or imagination; matter-of-fact: *the literal meaning of a phrase, a literal type of mind, a literal interpretation of the Bible stories.* **SYN:** prosaic. **3** true to fact; not exaggerated: *a literal account.* **4** of letters of the alphabet; expressed by letters.
—***n.*** *Printing.* a typographical error or misprint in a letter or letters of the alphabet.
[< Late Latin *litterālis* of the characters (of the alphabet) < Latin *littera* letter] —**lit′er|al|ness,** *n.*

**lit|er|al|ism** (lit′ər ə liz′əm), *n.* **1** a keeping to the literal meaning in translation or interpretation. **2** *Fine Arts.* the faithfully unaltered representation or interpretation of objects without any idealization. —**lit′er|al|ist,** *n.*

**lit|er|al|is|tic** (lit′ər ə lis′tik), *adj.* **1** having to do with or characteristic of literalism.

**lit|er|al|i|ty** (lit′ə ral′ə tē), *n., pl.* **-ties. 1** the quality or fact of being literal. **2** an instance of this.

**lit|er|al|ize** (lit′ər ə līz), *v.t.,* **-ized, -iz|ing.** to make literal; represent or accept as literal. —**lit′er|al|i|za′tion,** *n.* —**lit′er|al|iz′er,** *n.*

**lit|er|al|ly** (lit′ər ə lē), *adv.* **1** word for word: *to translate literally. Abbr:* lit. **2a** in a literal sense; without exaggeration; without imagination: *Is this literally true? Write the story literally as it happened. I am literally penniless.* **b** actually: *He is literally without fear.* **3** *Informal.* in effect, though not actually; virtually: *The champion runner literally flew around the track. He is literally coining money with his new business.*

**lit|er|ar|ism** (lit′ər ə riz′əm), *n.* emphasis on literary or humanistic values.

**lit|er|ar|y** (lit′ə rer′ē), *adj.* **1** having to do with literature: *literary annals.* **2** knowing much about literature: *a literary authority.* **3** engaged in literature as a profession: *some gentlemen of the literary fraternity* (Thackeray). —**lit′er|ar′i|ly,** *adv.* —**lit′er|ar′i|ness,** *n.*

**lit|er|ate** (lit′ər it), *adj., n.* —***adj.*** **1** able to read and write: *The literate person can find out from books what the person who cannot read must find out for himself or be told.* **2** acquainted with literature; educated; literary. **SYN:** lettered.
—***n.*** **1** a person who can read and write: *The number of literates in the United States has been increasing until most can now read and write.* **2** an educated person.
[< Latin *litterātus* < *littera* letter (in the plural, literature, learning)] —**lit′er|ate|ly,** *adv.* —**lit′er|ate-ness,** *n.*

**lit|e|ra|ti** (lit′ə rä′tē, -rā′tī), *n., pl. of* **literatus.** men and women of letters; scholarly or literary people: *the enlightened literati, who turn over the pages of history* (Washington Irving). [< Latin *litterātī,* plural of *litterātus,* (literally) lettered; see etym. under **literate**]

**lit|e|ra|tim** (lit′ə rā′tim), *adv.* letter for letter; exactly as written: *to reproduce a text literatim.* Also, **litteratim.** [< Medieval Latin *litteratim* < Latin *littera* letter]

**lit|er|a|tor** (lit′ə rā′tər), *n.* a literary man; littérateur.

**lit|er|a|ture** (lit′ər ə chůr, -chər; lit′rə-), *n.* **1** the writings of a period, language, or country, especially those kept alive by their beauty of style or thought: *the literature of Greece. Shakespeare is a great name in English literature. The particular concern of the literature of the last two centuries has been with the self in its standing quarrel with culture* (Newsweek). **SYN:** belles-lettres. **2** all the books and articles on a subject: *the literature of stamp collecting.* **3** writing books as a profession; literary production: *Never pursue literature as a trade* (Samuel Taylor Coleridge). **4** the study of literature: *I shall take literature and mathematics this spring. Hoagland spent some time as a cagehand with the circus, when he was not studying literature at Harvard* (Newsweek). **5** *Informal.* printed matter of any kind: *election campaign literature.* **6** *Rare.* acquaintance with the world of letters or books; literary culture: *another person of infinite literature* (John Selden). [< Middle French *literature* teaching of letters; writing < Latin *litterātūra* writing < *littera* letter (in the plural, literature, learning)]

**lit|e|ra|tus** (lit′ə rā′təs, -rä′-), *n., pl.* **-ti.** a man of learning or scholarship.

**li|tes** (lī′tēz), *n.* plural of **lis.**

**lith** (lith), *n. Archaic.* **1** a limb. **2** a joint. [Old English *lith*]

**lith-**, *combining form.* the form of **litho-** before vowels, as in *lithiasis.*

**-lith**, *combining form.* stone; rock, as in *megalith, laccolith.* [< Greek *líthos* stone]

**lith.**, **1** lithograph. **2** lithography.

**Lith.**, **1** Lithuania. **2** Lithuanian.

**li|thae|mi|a** (li thē′mē ə), *n.* = lithemia.

**li|thae|mic** (li thē′mik), *adj.* = lithemic.

**lith|arge** (lith′ärj, li thärj′), *n.* **1** a yellow or reddish oxide of lead, used in making glass, glazes for pottery, and driers for paints and varnishes; lead monoxide. *Formula:* PbO **2** (sometimes) any form of lead monoxide, such as massicot, which is produced with less heat than litharge. [< Old French *litarge,* also *litargire* < Latin *lithargyrus* < Greek *lithárgyros* < *líthos* stone + *árgyros* silver]

**lithe** (līᴛʜ), *adj.* bending easily; supple: *lithe limbs, a lithe willow. An athlete should be lithe of body.* **SYN:** flexible, limber, pliant, lithesome, lissome, willowy. [Old English *līthe* soft, mild] — **lithe′ly,** *adv.* — **lithe′ness,** *n.*

**li|the|mi|a** (li thē′mē ə), *n. Medicine.* an excessive amount of uric acid in the blood. [< New Latin *lithaemia* < Greek *líthos* stone + *haîma* blood]

**li|the|mic** (li thē′mik), *adj.* of or affected with lithemia.

**lith|er** (liᴛʜ′ər), *adj.* **1** *British Dialect and Scottish.* lazy; sluggish; spiritless. **2** *British Dialect.* active or nimble. **3** *Archaic.* pliant; supple: *the lither sky* (Shakespeare). **4** *Obsolete.* **a** bad or wicked. **b** poor, sorry, or worthless. **c** withered. [Old English *lȳthre* bad]

**lithe|some** (līᴛʜ′səm), *adj.* = lithe.

**lith|i|a** (lith′ē ə), *n.* a white oxide of lithium, soluble in water, and forming an acrid and caustic solution. *Formula:* $Li_2O$
[< New Latin *lithia,* alteration (after *soda,* etc.) of earlier *lithion* < Greek *líthos* stone (because of its mineral origin)]

**li|thi|a|sis** (li thī′ə sis), *n. Medicine.* the formation of calculi or stony concretions in the body, especially in the gall bladder and urinary tract.

**lithia water**, a mineral water, natural or artificial, containing lithium salts.

**lith|ic¹** (lith′ik), *adj.* **1** consisting of stone or rock. **2** *Medicine.* of or having to do with stone or stony concretions formed within the body, especially in the bladder. [< Greek *lithikós* < *líthos* stone]

**lith|ic²** (lith′ik), *adj. Chemistry.* of, having to do with, or consisting of lithium. [< *lith*(ium) + *-ic*]

**lithic acid**, = uric acid.

**lith|i|fi|ca|tion** (lith′ə fə kā′shən), *n.* the process by which rocks are formed from sediment.

**lith|i|fy** (lith′ə fī), *v.t.,* **-fied, -fy|ing.** to change into rock.

***lith|i|um** (lith′ē əm), *n.* **1** a soft, silver-white chemical element which occurs in small quantities in various minerals. Lithium is the lightest known metal and is similar to sodium. *Lithium's use in lubricants, ceramics, and chemical processes is growing* (Wall Street Journal). **2** = lithium carbonate. [< New Latin *lithium* < *lithia* lithia < Greek *líthos* stone]

***lithium**

| symbol | atomic number | atomic weight | oxidation state |
|---|---|---|---|
| Li | 3 | 6.939 | 1 |

**lithium carbonate**, a white, crystalline powder used in the manufacture of ceramics, glass, and luminescent paints, and in medicine as a psychotherapeutic drug. *Formula:* $Li_2CO_3$

**lithium chloride**, a crystalline salt soluble in water or alcohol, used especially as a dehumidifier in air conditioning and as a flux in soldering and welding. *Formula:* LiCl

**lithium fluoride**, a white powder used in ceramics, as a flux in soldering and welding, and, in the form of synthetic crystals, in the construction of devices for detecting and measuring radiation. *Formula:* LiF

**lith|o** (lith′ō), *adj., n., pl.* **lith|os.** — *adj.* = lithographic: *litho printing.* — *n.* = lithograph.

**litho-**, *combining form.* stone or stones, as in *lithography, lithology.* Also, **lith-** before vowels. [< Greek *litho-* < *líthos* stone]

**litho.** or **lithog.**, **1** lithograph. **2** lithography.

**li|tho|did** (li thō′did), *n.* any one of various crabs with a triangular carapace and the fifth pair of legs much reduced. [< New Latin *Lithodidae* the family name < Greek *lithṓdēs* stonelike < *líthos* stone + *eîdos* form]

**lith|o|fa|cies** (lith′ə fā′shiz), *n.* a record of the rock strata and deposition of a given area.

**li|thog|e|nous** (li thoj′ə nəs), *adj.* produced by or originating from stone or rock.

**lith|o|graph** (lith′ə graf, -gräf), *n., v.* — *n.* a print made from a flat, specially prepared stone or metal plate.
— *v.t.* to print from such a stone or plate.

**li|thog|ra|pher** (li thog′rə fər), *n.* a person who makes lithographs.

**lith|o|graph|ic** (lith′ə graf′ik), *adj.* **1** of a lithograph. **2** made by lithography. — **lith′o|graph′i|cal|ly,** *adv.*

**lith|o|graph|i|cal** (lith′ə graf′ə kəl), *adj.* = lithographic.

**li|thog|ra|phy** (li thog′rə fē), *n.* the art or process of printing from a smooth, flat stone or metal plate on which the picture or design is made with a greasy material that will hold printing ink, the rest of the surface being made ink-repellent with water.

**lith|oid** (lith′oid), *adj.* of the nature or structure of stone.

**li|thoi|dal** (li thoi′dəl), *adj.* = lithoid.

**lith|o|log|ic** (lith′ə loj′ik), *adj.* **1** of or having to do with lithology. **2** concerning the nature or composition of stone; petrographic. — **lith′o|log′i|cal|ly,** *adv.*

**lith|o|log|i|cal** (lith′ə loj′ə kəl), *adj.* = lithologic.

**li|thol|o|gy** (li thol′ə jē), *n.* **1** the science of rocks and their composition. **2** the branch of medicine dealing with calculi in the human body.

**lith|o|marge** (lith′ə märj), *n.* any one of several kinds of soft, claylike minerals, including kaolin. [< New Latin *lithomarga* < Greek *líthos* stone + Latin *marga* marl]

**lith|o|phile** (lith′ə fīl), *adj. Geology.* having an affinity for the stony material of the earth's crust: *Lithophile ... elements ... tend to associate with silicate and oxide material* (Scientific American).

**li|thoph|i|lous** (li thof′ə ləs), *adj.* **1** *Botany.* growing on rocks. **2** *Entomology.* living in stony places.

**lith|o|phyte** (lith′ə fīt), *n. Botany.* a plant that grows among stone or rock. [< *litho-* + Greek *phytón* plant]

**lith|o|phyt|ic** (lith′ə fit′ik), *adj. Botany.* growing among stone or rock.

**lith|o|pone** (lith′ə pōn), *n.* a dry, white pigment used in paints, made from a mixture of zinc sulfide, barium sulfate, and zinc oxide. [< *litho-,* perhaps + Latin *ponere* to put, place]

**lith|o|print** (lith′ə print′), *n., v.* — *n.* a print reproduced by lithography: *His enchanting drawings (transformed into big, clear-coloured lithoprints in limited editions of 100 each) are in a gallery run by his mother* (Sunday Times).
— *v.t.* to print by lithography: *The several hundred local natural history publications, often duplicated or lithoprinted, offer an easy outlet for young artists* (Jon Tinker).

**lith|o|sphere** (lith′ə sfir), *n.* the solid portion of the earth as opposed to the atmosphere and the hydrosphere; geosphere.

**lith|o|spher|ic** (lith′ə sfir′ik), *adj.* of or having to do with the lithosphere.

**li|thot|o|my** (li thot′ə mē), *n., pl.* **-mies.** the surgical removal of stones from the bladder. [< Late Latin *lithotomia* < Greek *lithotomiā* < *líthos* stone + *témnein* to cut]

**lith|o|trite** (lith′ə trīt), *n.* a surgical instrument used to perform lithotrity.

**li|thot|ri|tist** (li thot′rə tist), *n.* a person who practices lithotrity.

**li|thot|ri|ty** (li thot′rə tē), *n., pl.* **-ties.** the surgical operation of crushing stones in the bladder into pieces small enough to pass out. [< French *lithotriteur* lithotrite (ultimately < Greek *líthos* stone + *thrýptein* crush small) + English *-y*³]

**Lith|u|a|ni|an** (lith′ů ā′nē ən), *adj., n.* — *adj.* belonging or relating to Lithuania, its people, or their language.
— *n.* **1** a native or inhabitant of Lithuania. **2** the Baltic language of Lithuania.

**lith|y** (lī′ᴛʜē, liᴛʜ′ē), *adj. Archaic.* flexible; supple; lithe. [Old English *lithig*]

**lit|i|ga|ble** (lit′ə gə bəl), *adj.* that can be made the subject of a suit in a law court.

**lit|i|gant** (lit′ə gənt), *n., adj.* — *n.* a person engaged in a lawsuit.
— *adj.* **1** engaging in a lawsuit. **2** inclined to go to law. [< Latin *lītigāns, -antis,* present participle of *lītigāre* litigate]

**lit|i|gate** (lit′ə gāt), *v.,* **-gat|ed, -gat|ing.** — *v.i.* to engage in a lawsuit. — *v.t.* to contest in a lawsuit; make the subject of a lawsuit.
[< Latin *lītigāre* (with English *-ate*¹) < *līs, lītis* lawsuit + *agere* drive, conduct]

**lit|i|ga|tion** (lit′ə gā′shən), *n.* **1** the action of carrying on a lawsuit. **2** the action of going to law. **3** a lawsuit or legal proceeding: *Title litigation scared off the drillers until a recent court decision awarded the mineral rights to the government* (Time). **4** *Rare.* disputation.

**lit|i|ga|tor** (lit′ə gā′tər), *n.* a person who litigates.

**li|ti|gious** (lə tij′əs), *adj.* **1** having the habit of going to law: *They are very litigious ... They will persevere in a lawsuit until they are ruined* (Mountstuart Elphinstone). **2** offering material for a lawsuit; that can be disputed in a court of law. **SYN:** litigable. **3** of or having to do with litigation. [< Latin *lītigiōsus* < *lītigium* dispute < *lītigāre;* see etym. under **litigate**] — **li|ti′gious|ly,** *adv.* — **li|ti′gious|ness,** *n.*

**lit|mus** (lit′məs), *n.* a blue coloring matter obtained from various lichens. Litmus is used in litmus paper as a chemical indicator. [< Scandinavian (compare Old Icelandic *litmosi* < *litr* color, dye + *mosi* moss)] — **lit′mus|less,** *adj.*

**litmus paper**, unsized paper treated with litmus. Blue litmus paper will turn red if put into an acid; red litmus paper will turn blue when put into an alkali. Litmus paper is used as an indicator of the ion concentration in solutions.

**litmus test**, a decisive test; acid test: *The litmus test of a liberal regime must surely be the freedom of the individual from arbitrary arrest and punishment* (Edward Mortimer).

**lit|o|ral** (lit′ər əl), *adj., n.* = littoral.

**li|to|tes** (lī′tə tēz, lit′ə-), *n.* a figure of speech that makes an assertion by denying its opposite. *Example:* "This was no small storm" means that the storm was quite violent. [< Greek *lītótēs* < *lītós* small, plain, simple]

**li|tre** (lē′tər), *n. Especially British.* liter.

**Litt.B.**, Bachelor of Letters (Latin, *Litterarum Baccalaureus*).

**Litt.D.**, Doctor of Literature; Doctor of Letters (Latin, *Litterarum Doctor*).

**lit|ten** (lit′ən), *adj. Poetic.* lighted: *And travellers now within that valley, Through red-litten windows, see vast forms* (Edgar Allan Poe).

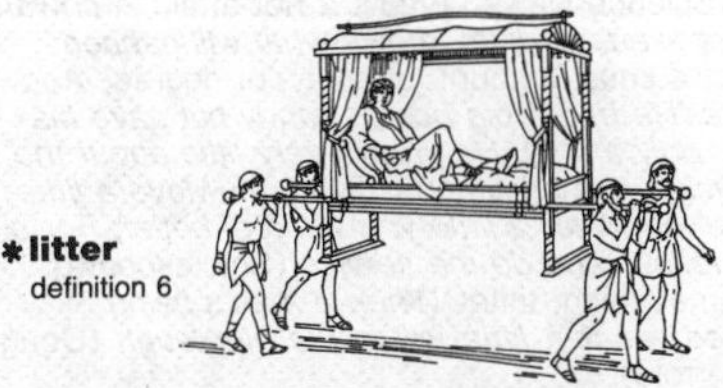

***litter**
definition 6

***lit|ter** (lit′ər), *n., v.* — *n.* **1** little bits left about in disorder; things scattered about: *Children should pick up their own litter. The kitchen was covered with the litter of dressmakers preparing for the wedding* (Hall Caine). **SYN:** trash, debris. **2** a state of disorder or untidiness: *She was ashamed to be seen in such a pickle ... her house was in such a litter* (Henry Fielding). **3** the young animals produced by an animal at one time: *a litter of puppies.* **4a** straw or hay used as bedding for animals, or for other purposes, such as the protection of plants. **b** the surface layer of decaying leaves and other organic matter on the floor of a forest: *This is the ladderlike arrangement of litter, understory, and overstory that naturally builds up, with time, in the forest* (New Yorker). **5** a stretcher for carrying a sick or wounded person. **6** a framework to be carried on men's shoulders or by beasts of burden, with a couch usually enclosed by curtains: *I have sent a message ... saying that thou wast a little feeble and would need a litter* (Rudyard Kipling). **SYN:** palanquin.
— *v.t.* **1** to scatter (things) about; leave (odds and ends) lying around: *He littered the Sunday paper all over the floor.* **SYN:** strew. **2** to make untidy or disordered: *She littered her room with books and papers.* **SYN:** disarrange. **3** to give birth to (young animals). **4a** to make a bed for (an animal) with straw or hay. **b** to cover with litter: *The floor of the stable had just been littered with fresh straw.*
— *v.i.* (of an animal) to bring forth a litter of young.
[< Anglo-French *litere,* Old French *litiere,* learned

**Pronunciation Key:** hat, āge, cãre, fär; let, ēqual, tėrm; it, īce; hot, ōpen, ôrder; oil, out; cup, půt, rüle; child; long; thin; ᴛʜen; zh, measure; ə represents **a** in about, **e** in taken, **i** in pencil, **o** in lemon, **u** in circus.

borrowing from Medieval Latin *lectaria, literia,* for Latin *lectīca* litter; sedan < *lectus* bed, couch] —**lit′ter|er**, *n.*

**lit|te|rae hu|ma|ni|o|res** (lit′ə rē hyü man′ē ō′-rēz), *Latin.* the field of humanities.

**lit|té|ra|teur** or **lit|te|ra|teur** (lit′ər ə tėr′), *n.* a literary person; writer or critic of literature. [< French *littérateur,* learned borrowing from Latin *lītterator* < *littera* letter]

**lit|te|ra|tim** (lit′ə rā′tim), *adv.* = literatim.

**litter bag**, *U.S.* a usually small plastic or paper bag for litter.

**lit|ter|bin** (lit′ər bin′), *n. British.* a public trash basket, as on a street; litter basket.

**lit|ter|bug** (lit′ər bug′), *n., v.,* **-bugged, -bug|ging.** *U.S.* —***n.*** a person who throws down trash along a highway, sidewalk, in a park, or other public place: *At Yellowstone, the cost of cleaning up after the litterbugs runs to $400 a day* (Newsweek).
—***v.i.*** to be a litterbug: *He ... was arrested for litterbugging and fined $50* (Time).

**litter mate**, an animal born and raised in the same litter as another or others.

**lit|ter|y** (lit′ər ē), *adj.* consisting of litter; covered with litter; untidy.

**lit|tle** (lit′əl), *adj.,* **less** or **less|er, least;** or **lit|tler, lit|tlest;** *adv.,* **less, least;** *n.* —***adj.*** **1** not great or big; small. A grain of sand is little. *She was called tall and gawky by some ... of her own sex, who prefer littler women* (Thackeray). **2** short; not long in time or distance; brief: *Wait a little while and I'll go a little way with you.* **3** not much: **a** small in number: *a little army. In the realm of mere letters, Voltaire is one of the little band of great monarchs* (Christopher Morley). **b** small in amount: *a little money. A very sick child has little strength and can eat only a little food.* **c** small in degree: *little hope. He has but little ability.* **d** small in importance or interest; trifling; trivial: *Every little discontent appears to him to portend a revolution* (Macaulay). **4** small in mind, feeling, nature, or power; mean; narrow-minded: *He was so little he would not take time to help a blind man across the street.*
—***adv.*** **1** in a small amount or degree; slightly: *The teacher read from an interesting book that was little known to us. A zeal little tempered by humanity* (Macaulay). *They live in a little-known town. Little-known metals are now coming into use* (Science News Letter). **2** not at all: *A coward is little liked. He little knows what will happen.*
—***n.*** **1** a small amount, quantity, or degree: *Add a little. He had a big box of candy but gave his sister only a little. He knows very little about the subject.* **2** a short time or distance: *Move a little to the left. After a little you will feel better. For a little follow, and do me service* (Shakespeare). **3** a small thing; trifle: *When a man's being shaved, what a little will make him laugh* (Douglas Jerrold).
**in little**, on a small scale; in miniature: *to paint in little. A miniature of loveliness, all grace summ'd up ... in little* (Tennyson).
**little by little**, by a small amount at a time; slowly; gradually: *Weak and dead for hunger, I went little by little up the street* (David Rowland).
**make little of**, to treat as of little importance: *She made little of her troubles.*
**not a little**, a great deal; much; extremely; very: *We are not a little upset by the incident.*
**think little of**, **a** to not value much; consider as unimportant or worthless: *the critic thought little of the painting.* **b** to not hesitate about: *He thought little of commuting to Washington.*
[Old English *lȳtel*] —**lit′tle|ness**, *n.*
—***Syn.*** *adj.* **1 Little, small, diminutive** mean not big or large. **Little** sometimes suggests affection or sympathy for what it describes: *a cozy little cottage. He is a funny little boy.* **Small**, often used interchangeably with *little,* means relatively not large or great, and often suggests being below average: *He is small for his age.* **Diminutive** means very small in size: *Cinderella's feet were diminutive.*
▶ **Littler** and **littlest** are usually restricted to familiar or affectionate use: *the sweetest, littlest baby in the world.*
▶ See **less** for another usage note.

**little auk**, = dovekie (def. 1).

**Little Bairam**, = lesser Bairam.

**Little Bear**, = Ursa Minor.

**lit|tle|-bit|ty** (lit′əl bit′ē), *adj. Informal.* very small; itsy-bitsy: [*They*] *scored twin touchdowns on little-bitty three-yard runs* (Time).

**little blue heron**, a dark blue, medium-sized heron of the southeastern United States that is snowy white in its immature stage.

**little bluestem**, a bluestem grass from two to four feet high that grows abundantly throughout the United States, especially in Kansas and Oklahoma.

**little brown crane**, a crane of North America with brown plumage and a small patch of red skin on its forehead. It breeds in the icy region of the Arctic Circle and spends the winter in the southwestern United States and Mexico.

**little chief hare**, the pika of North America.

**Little Christmas**, = Epiphany.

**Little Dipper**, the group of seven bright stars in the constellation Ursa Minor (the Little Bear) shaped like a dipper with the North Star at the end of the dipper's handle. See picture under **constellation**.

**Little Dog**, = Canis Minor.

**lit|tle-ease** (lit′əl ēz′), *n.* a narrow place of confinement, such as the stocks or pillory or a very small dungeon. [< *Little Ease,* a dungeon in the Tower of London]

**Lit|tle-end|i|an** or **lit|tle-end|i|an** (lit′əl en′dē-ən), *n.* **1** a member of the orthodox religious party in Lilliput (in Jonathan Swift's *Gulliver's Travels*) who maintained, in opposition to the Big-endians, that eggs should be broken at the little end. **2** *Figurative.* a disputer about trifles.

**Little Englander**, an opponent of the territorial enlargement of the British Empire, especially in the 1800's.

**Little Eng|land|ism** (ing′glən diz əm), the policies or views of Little Englanders: *To me it is ... a curiously heartless piece of Little Englandism to refuse help to a recently independent Commonwealth partner for whom we were so long responsible* (Manchester Guardian Weekly).

**little finger**, the finger farthest from the thumb; smallest finger.

**Little Fox**, = Vulpecula.

**little go**, *British Informal.* the first examination for the degree of B.A. at Cambridge University; Previous Examination.

**little goblet**, = chanterelle[1].

**little grebe**, = dabchick.

**little green heron**, a small heron that ranges from tropical America to Canada.

**little gull**, a very small, white and grayish European gull living along the New England coast and around the Great Lakes.

**Little Horse**, = Equuleus.

**little hours**, the canonical hours of prime, tierce, sext, and nones, and sometimes vespers and complin in the Roman Catholic Church.

**Little It|a|ly** (it′ə lē), *pl.* **-lys** or **-lies.** *U.S.* the section of a city where Italians live.

**lit|tle|leaf disease** (lit′əl lēf′), any one of various diseases of plants in which the leaves become small and yellow, especially a disease of pines caused by a parasitic fungus related to the one that causes late blight.

**Little League**, **1** a group of baseball clubs for children twelve years old and under. Before 1974, the Little League included only boys. **2** one of these clubs.

**Little Leaguer**, a member of a Little League club.

**little magazine** or **review**, a small magazine devoted to printing experimental or occasional writing.

**little music**, that part of Scottish music that includes marches and music for dancing.

**lit|tle|neck** (lit′əl nek′), *n.,* or **littleneck clam**, **1** a young quahog, larger than a cherry stone, usually eaten raw. **2** any one of certain similar clams. [< *Little Neck,* Long Island, New York]

**little Neddy**, *British Slang.* a committee affiliated with Neddy (NEDC) that deals with the development of a particular sector of the national economy.

**little office**, a Roman Catholic service honoring the Virgin Mary, similar to the daily prescribed office, but shorter.

**little people**, fairies.

**Little Rho|dy** (rō′dē), a nickname for Rhode Island.

**Little Russian**, **1** a Ukrainian or Ruthenian. **2** the Ukrainian or Ruthenian language.

**little slam**, *Bridge.* a hand in which one side takes all the tricks but one; small slam.

**little theater**, **1** a small theater, especially one that produces experimental or amateur plays. **2** the plays produced in such a theater.

**lit|to|ral** (lit′ər əl), *adj., n.* —***adj.*** **1** of a shore. **2** on or near the shore, especially living near the shore.
—***n.*** a region along the shore: *the Mediterranean littoral of France.* Also, **litoral**.
[< Latin *lītorālis* < *lītus* shore]

**li|tu** (lē′tü), *n.* a plural of **litas**.

**li|tur|gic** (lə tėr′jik), *adj.* = liturgical.

**li|tur|gi|cal** (lə tėr′jə kəl), *adj.* **1** of liturgies. **2** used in liturgics. **3** of or having to do with the Communion or Eucharistic service. [< Late Latin *lītūrgicus* (< Greek *leitourgikós* < *leitourgiā* liturgy) + English *-al*[1]] —**li|tur′gi|cal|ly**, *adv.*

**li|tur|gics** (lə tėr′jiks), *n.* **1** the branch of theology dealing with the conduct of public worship. **2** the study of liturgies.

**li|tur|gi|ol|o|gist** (lə tėr′jē ol′ə jist), *n.* a specialist in the study of liturgies.

**li|tur|gi|ol|o|gy** (lə tėr′jē ol′ə jē), *n.* the science or study of liturgies.

**lit|ur|gist** (lit′ər jist), *n.* **1a** an expert on liturgies. **b** a compiler of a liturgy or liturgies. **2** a person who uses, or favors the use of, a liturgy.

**lit|ur|gy** (lit′ər jē), *n., pl.* **-gies.** **1a** a form of public worship. Different churches use different liturgies. **SYN**: ritual. **b** a collection of such forms. **2** a Communion service, especially in the Eastern Church.
**the liturgy** (or **Liturgy**), **a** (in the Episcopal Church) the Book of Common Prayer: *It was Sunday ... and I happened to be reading the Liturgy* (George Borrow). **b** (in the Eastern Church) Communion service: *They use the Liturgy of Saint Chrysostome* (Ephraim Pagitt).
[< Late Latin *lītūrgia* < Greek *leitourgiā,* ultimately < *lāós* people + *érgon* work]

**liv|a|bil|i|ty** (liv′ə bil′ə tē), *n.* **1** Also, **liveability**. the condition of being fit to live in; livable state. **2** the ability of poultry to survive various conditions and diseases.

**liv|a|ble** (liv′ə bəl), *adj.* **1** fit to live in: *a livable house.* **SYN**: habitable. **2** easy to live with: *a livable person.* **SYN**: companionable, sociable. **3** worth living; endurable. Also, **liveable**. —**liv′a-ble|ness**, *n.*

**live**[1] (liv), *v.,* **lived** (livd), **liv|ing.** —***v.i.*** **1** to have life; be alive; exist: *All creatures have an equal right to live.* **2** to remain alive: *to live long, if I live till May.* **3** *Figurative.* to last; endure: *His good name will live forever.* **4** to keep up life: *to live by one's wits. Most men live by working. She and her mother now had nothing to live on but a small government pension* (Edmund Wilson). **5** to feed or subsist: *Lions live upon other animals. The Chinese live largely on rice.* **6** to pass life in a particular manner: *to live well, live in peace, live extravagantly.* **7** to dwell; reside: *to live in the country. Who lives in this house? Here lived I, but now live here no more* (Shakespeare). **SYN**: sojourn, lodge, abide. **8** to have a rich and full life: *To-morrow do thy worst, for I have liv'd today* (John Dryden). **9** *Figurative.* to remain afloat or exist through danger, as a ship: *It blew so hard ... that I could not suppose their boat could live, or that they ever reached to their own coast* (Daniel Defoe).
—***v.t.*** **1** to pass (life): *to live a life of ease. And each half lives a hundred different lives* (Matthew Arnold). **2** to carry out or show in life: *to live one's ideals, to live one's religion. He ... lived himself the truth he taught* (Whittier).
**live down**, **a** to live so worthily that (some fault or sin of the past) is overlooked or forgotten: *How long do you think it will take in New York society for a girl with sixty thousand dollars a year to live anything down?* (Archibald C. Gunter). **b** to outlive (a fashion, custom, or the like): *It is very probable that your cousin will live down his fancy* (H. Rider Haggard).
**live in**, to dwell in the house where one works as a servant: *The domestics in that house live in.*
**live it up**, *U.S. Slang.* to enjoy life to the full: *Life is short. Live it up. See all you can. Hear all you can and go all you can* (New York Times).
**live out**, **a** to stay alive or hold out through; last through: *He was not expected to live out the night.* **b** to dwell away from the house where one works as a servant: *Their maid lives out.* **c** to live through; experience: *American national life is being ever more fully reflected—or perhaps lived out—in the university* (London Times).
**live up to**, to act according to; do (what is expected or promised): *It can be so much easier to make a reputation than live up to one* (London Times).
**live with**, *Informal.* to accept without protest; resign to; put up with: *The employers will have "to live with the new pacts"* (Wall Street Journal).
[Old English *lifian,* or *libban*]

**live**[2] (līv), *adj., adv.* —***adj.*** **1** having life; alive: *a live dog. I brought two live plants in flower pots* (Jane Carlyle). **2a** burning or glowing: *live coals, a live cigar.* **b** *Figurative.* heated; angry: *a live quarrel.* **3** *Figurative.* full of energy or activity: *a live person.* **4** *Figurative.* **a** up-to-date: *live ideas.* **b** cheerful; gay: *a live party.* **5** *U.S., Figurative.* of present interest or importance: *a live question.* **6** still in use or to be used; still having power: *live steam, live printing type.* **7** being in play: *a live football.* **8** carrying an electric current: *The electrician checked to see whether the wire was live.* **9a** loaded; not fired or exploded: *a live cartridge.* **b** not yet lit: *a live match.* **10a** broadcast or presented at the actual time of performance, not as recorded on tape or film: *a live television show. Lacking live opera, try a good phonograph record* (Newsweek). **b** being present at a performance: *a live audience.* **c** performed by living persons or animals; taken from nature; not animated: *a live film about safety.* **11** moving or imparting motion: *live wheels, a live axle.* **12** in the native state; not mined or quarried: *live metal, live rocks.* **13** *Figurative.* bright; vivid: *a live color.* **14** *Figurative.* of or belonging to a living being: *All the live murmur of a summer's day* (Matthew Arnold). **15** living, or containing a living organism, but not able to cause infection: *The live virus polio vaccine may soon make its debut* (Science News Letter).

—***adv.*** with the actual performance or event shown; as it takes place: *The game will be telecast live.*

[variant of *alive*] —**live′ness,** *n.*

**live|a|bil|i|ty** (liv′ə bil′ə tē), *n.* = livability.

**live|a|ble** (liv′ə bəl), *adj.* = livable. —**live′a|ble-ness,** *n.*

**live-bear|er** (līv′bãr′ər), *n.* a fish that brings forth live young; a viviparous fish.

**live|born** (līv′bôrn′), *adj.* born alive; not stillborn: *a liveborn baby.*

**live-box** (līv′boks′), *n.* a box immersed in water, as on a fishing boat, used for keeping fish alive.

**live center** (līv), a revolving center or point that holds the work on the spindle of a lathe or on some other machine tool.

**-lived** (līvd), *combining form.* having a ____ life: *Long-lived = having a long life.*

**live-for|ev|er** (liv′fər ev′ər), *n.* either of two garden plants of the orpine family with thick, juicy stems, widespread in Europe and Asia and naturalized in North America.

**live-in** (liv′in′), *adj., n.* —***adj.*** **1a** living in the place where one works: *The Hetheringtons have no live-in maid. A woman comes three days a week to clean* (Anthony Bailey). **b** that requires one to live at the place where one works: *She said she had an off-campus live-in job* (New York Times). **2** of or having to do with living in a particular place as an inhabitant or resident: *Dr. Jastrow went on from a discussion of the moon to a discussion of the live-in prospects on Mars* (New Yorker).

—***n.*** the act or fact of inhabiting one's place of work as a form of protest: *Twenty-two social workers ... have been staging a protest live-in at the office of the City Department of Labor* (New York Times).

**live|li|hood** (līv′lē hu̇d), *n.* a means of living; what is needed to support life; a living: *to write for a livelihood. He earned his livelihood by working for a farmer.* **SYN**: See syn. under **living.** [Old English *līflād* < *līf* life + *lād* (see etym. under **load**); influenced by obsolete *livelihood* liveliness]

**live|li|ly** (līv′lə lē), *adv.* in a lively manner; briskly; vigorously.

**live|li|ness** (līv′lē nis), *n.* lively quality or condition; vigor; activity; gaiety; vividness.

**live load** (līv), **1** the load that a bridge, floor, or other structure must support in addition to its own weight, such as the load of vehicles, people, or furniture. **2** a temporary moving load on a structure.

**live|long** (liv′lông′, -long′), *adj.* **1** whole length of; whole; entire: *She is busy the livelong day.* **2** *Obsolete.* lasting: *Thou ... Hast built thyself a livelong monument* (Milton). [alteration (taken as < *live,* verb) of Middle English *lefe longe* lief long[1]]

**live|ly** (līv′lē), *adj.,* **-li|er, -li|est,** *adv., n., pl.* **-lies.** —***adj.*** **1** full of life and spirit; active; vigorous: *A good night's sleep made us all lively again.* **SYN**: brisk, energetic, animated, spirited, vivacious. **2** exciting: *We had a lively time during the hurricane.* **3** *Figurative.* bright; vivid: *lively colors.* **4** *Figurative.* cheerful; gay: *a lively conversation.* **SYN**: blithe, buoyant. **5** bouncing well and quickly: *a lively baseball.* **6** (of air) fresh; invigorating. **7** lifelike, as an image or picture. **8** (of a ship) riding the waves buoyantly but with plenty of motion. **9** brisk or sparkling, as liquors.

—***adv.*** in a lively manner; briskly; nimbly; vigorously.

—***n.*** a lively fellow (used of sailors).

[Old English *līflīc* living]

**liv|en** (lī′vən), *v.t.* to make more lively; put life into; cheer up: *A brisk discussion livened the dull conversation.* —***v.i.*** to become more lively; brighten: *As he grew well, his spirits began to liven again.* —**liv′en|er,** *n.*

**live oak** (līv), **1** an evergreen oak of the United States; encina. It has heavy, hard, strong, durable wood and is valued as a shade tree. **2** its wood, formerly used especially in shipbuilding. **3** any one of various other evergreen oaks.

**live-out** (liv′out′), *adj.* not living in the place where one works: *a live-out cook.*

**live parking** (līv), *U.S.* parking in which the parked vehicle's operator remains in attendance.

***liv|er[1]** (liv′ər), *n.* **1a** a large reddish-brown organ in animals with backbones that makes bile, converts sugars into glycogen that it stores, and aids in the absorption of food. The liver breaks down waste matter in the blood and manufactures blood proteins. A person's liver was once thought to be the source of his emotions. **b** a large gland in some animals without backbones that secretes into the digestive tract. **2** the liver of an animal used as food: *Calves' liver and chicken livers are considered delicacies by many.* [Old English *lifer*]

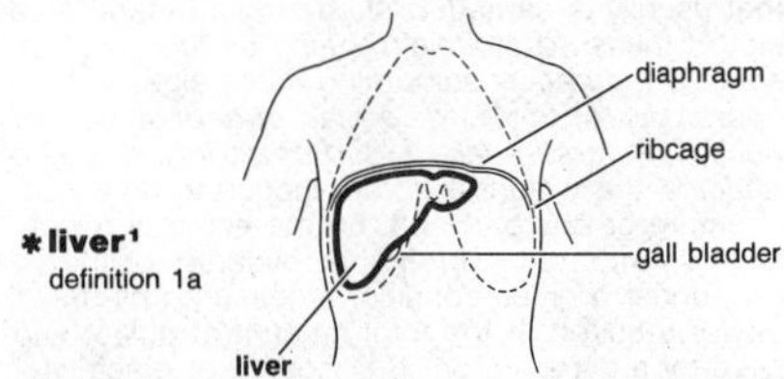


***liver[1]**
definition 1a

**liv|er[2]** (liv′ər), *n.* **1** a person who lives: *a long liver, evil livers.* **2** *Especially U.S.* an inhabitant; dweller: *a liver in the country.* [< *liv*(e)[1] + *-er*[1]]

**liver color,** a dark, reddish-brown color.

**-livered,** *combining form.* **1** having a ____ liver or livers: *Fat-livered codfish = codfish that have fat livers.*

**2** having the characteristics (formerly attributed to a state of the liver) of: *Lily-livered = having the characteristics of a lily* (*cowardly*).

**liver extract,** an extract made from the liver of mammals, used to increase the red corpuscles or blood cells in treating anemia.

**liver fluke,** any one of certain leaf-shaped flukes infesting the liver of various mammals.

**liver fungus,** a bright-red fungus that lives on the stumps of dead trees, much valued as food; vegetable beefsteak.

**liv|er|ied** (liv′ər id, liv′rid), *adj.* clothed in a livery, as servants.

**liv|er|ish** (liv′ər ish), *adj. Informal.* having the symptoms attributed to a disordered liver, especially a disagreeable disposition; testy; cross. —**liv′er|ish|ness,** *n.*

**liv|er|leaf** (liv′ər lēf′), *n.* any one of a group of herbs of the crowfoot family, with delicate white to purple flowers; hepatica.

**liv|er|pool** (liv′ər pül′), *n.* a jumping hurdle in steeplechasing, usually consisting of a bar, a ditch, and a hedge. [probably < *Liverpool,* England]

**Liv|er|pud|li|an** (liv′ər pud′lē ən), *adj., n.* —***adj.*** of or belonging to Liverpool, a seaport in western England. —***n.*** a native or inhabitant of Liverpool. [< *Liver*(pool) + *puddle* (humorous substitute for *pool*) + *-ian*]

**liv|er|wort** (liv′ər wėrt′), *n.* **1** any one of various small, green plants closely related to the mosses, that grow mostly on damp ground, the trunks of trees, on rocks and bark, and sometimes in water. Liverworts comprise a class of bryophytes. **2** = hepatica. [< *liver*[1] + *wort,* translation of Medieval Latin *hepatica* hepatica (because of the shape of some of its parts)]

**liv|er|wurst** (liv′ər wėrst′, -wu̇rst′), *n.* a sausage consisting largely of liver. [American English, half-translation of German *Leberwurst* liver sausage]

**liv|er|y** (liv′ər ē, liv′rē), *n., pl.* **-er|ies. 1** any uniform provided for servants, or adopted by a group or profession: *A nurse's livery is often white.* **2** *Figurative.* any characteristic dress, garb, or outward appearance: *trees in summer livery.* **3** the feeding and care of horses for pay. **4** the hiring out of horses and carriages. **5** the keeping of cars, boats, bicycles, or other vehicles, for hire. **6** = livery stable. **7** *Law.* the delivery of legal possession of property. **8** *Obsolete.* liveried retainers or servants as a group. **9** *Obsolete.* **a** the dispensing of food, provisions, or clothing to retainers or servants. **b** the food or provisions so dispensed. **c** an allowance of provender for horses. [Middle English *livere* servants' rations < Old French *livree,* past participle of *livrer* dispense < Latin *līberāre* liberate < *līber* free]

**livery company,** one of the London City companies or guilds which had formerly a distinctive costume for special occasions.

**liv|er|y|man** (liv′ər ē mən, liv′rē-), *n., pl.* **-men. 1** a person who works in or keeps a livery stable. **2** a person wearing livery. **3** *British.* a freeman who was a member of a guild or livery company of London and entitled to wear its livery.

**livery stable,** a stable where horses are cared for for pay or hired out.

**lives** (līvz), *n.* plural of **life.**

**live steam,** **1** steam coming from a boiler at full pressure. **2** steam under pressure: *Researchers said that five full minutes ... in live steam was needed to kill the hepatitis virus* (New York Times).

**live|stock** (līv′stok′), *n.* farm animals; domestic animals raised for their working ability or for their value as a source of food and other products. Cows, horses, sheep, poultry, and pigs are livestock.

**live weight** (līv), the weight of an animal while living.

**live wire** (līv), **1** a wire having a connection to a source of electricity, especially such a wire in which an electric current is flowing. **2** *Informal, Figurative.* an energetic, wide-awake person: *Weaver had earned something of a reputation for himself as a live wire* (New Yorker).

**liv|id** (liv′id), *adj.* **1a** having a dull-bluish or grayish color: *a livid sea, the livid face of a dead man.* **b** very pale; grayish-white: *livid with rage.* **SYN**: ashen, ashy. **2** discolored by a bruise; black-and-blue: *the livid marks of blows on his arm.* [< Latin *līvidus* < *līvēre* be bluish] —**liv′id|ly,** *adv.* —**liv′id|ness,** *n.*

**li|vid|i|ty** (li vid′ə tē), *n.* the condition of being livid; discoloration.

**liv|ing** (liv′ing), *adj., n., v.* —***adj.*** **1** having life; being alive: *a living plant.* **2** full of life; vigorous; strong; active: *a living faith; the living question of the hour* (Oliver Wendell Holmes). **SYN**: lively. **3** in actual existence; still in use; alive: *a living language.* **4** true to life; vivid; lifelike: *a living portrait, a picture which is the living image of a person.* **5** of life; to sustain life: *The tramp's life is one of poor living conditions. My living expenses had been considerably larger than my total receipts* (Atlantic). **6** sufficient to live on: *a living pension.* **7** for living in; for use by a family: *a living area, a living unit.* **8** of or having to do with human beings: *within living memory.* **9** burning; flaming; live: *living coals.* **10** refreshing, as water: *... they have forsaken me the fountain of living waters* (Jeremiah 2:13).

—***n.*** **1** the condition of being alive: *the pleasures of living in the country. The old man is tired of living.* **2** the means of keeping alive; livelihood: *What does he do for a living? He earns his living as a grocer.* **3** manner of life: *The preacher urged the importance of right living. Plain living and high thinking are no more* (Wordsworth). **4** (in Great Britain) a position in the church with the income attached; benefice. **5** *Obsolete.* property in general, especially a landed estate.

—***v.*** the present participle of **live**[1]. —**liv′ing|ly,** *adv.* —**liv′ing|ness,** *n.*

—***Syn.*** *n.* **2 Living, livelihood, support** mean a person's means of providing shelter, food, and other necessities for himself. **Living,** the general word, applies to what he earns and how he does so: *to earn a bare living, to work hard for one's living.* **Livelihood** applies particularly to the kind of work he does: *Painting, once merely a hobby, became her livelihood.* **Support** applies particularly to what is provided for another's living: *to depend on one's parents for support.*

**living death,** a state of misery not deserving the name of life: *Hopelessness makes the future a living death.*

**living fossil,** a plant or animal that is one of the last living species of a group or family which was once very common.

**living picture,** = tableau vivant.

**living quarters,** a place to live.

**living room,** a room for general family use, usually during leisure hours and for entertaining; sitting room.

**liv|ing|ry** (liv′ing rē), *n.* the development of better living conditions through technology: *He prefers livingry to weaponry* (Manchester Guardian Weekly).

**living standard,** = standard of living.

**living wage,** a wage sufficient to provide a worker and his or her dependents with the necessities and comforts required for their well-being.

**living will,** a formal document expressing a person's wishes as to how he should be treated medically if he were to become permanently brain-damaged, comatose, or the like: *"Living wills" prepared in advance of illness ... typically state the conditions under which the future patient would like life-prolonging treatment to be omitted and death-hastening treatments* (*narcotics*) *to be used* (Diana Crane).

**li|vre** (lē′vər), *n.* an old French silver coin or money of account that differed in value according to the place of issue. [< Old French *livre* < Latin *lībra* pound (weight), scale, balance]

**li|wa** (lē′wə), *n.* one of the administrative districts or provinces into which Iraq is divided. [< Arabic *liwā*]

**lix|iv|i|ate** (lik siv′ē āt), *v.t.,* **-at|ed, -at|ing. 1** to impregnate with lixivium or lye. **2** to subject to lixiviation. [< *lixivi*(um) + *-ate*[1]]

**lix|iv|i|a|tion** (lik siv′ē ā′shən), *n.* the separating of a soluble substance from one that is insoluble by the percolation of water, as alkaline salts from

**Pronunciation Key:** hat, āge, cãre, fär; let, ēqual, tėrm; it, īce; hot, ōpen, ôrder; oil, out; cup, pu̇t, rüle; child; long; thin; ᴛʜen; zh, measure; ə represents **a** in about, **e** in taken, **i** in pencil, **o** in lemon, **u** in circus.

wood ashes.

**lix|iv|i|um** (lik siv′ē əm), *n., pl.* **-i|ums, -i|a** (-ē ə). water impregnated with salts extracted by lixiviation, as lye from wood ashes. [< Late Latin *lixīvium,* variant of Latin *lixīvia* < *lixīvius* or *lixīvus* made into lye < *lixa* lye-ashes]

***liz|ard** (liz′ərd), *n.* **1** a reptile with dry, scaly skin. Lizards have long bodies, a long tail, and movable eyelids. They usually have four legs. Some lizards have no legs and look much like snakes. The iguana, chameleon, horned toad, and glass snake are lizards. **2** any of certain similar reptiles, especially of large size, such as the crocodiles and dinosaurs. **3** *Slang, Figurative.* an idler or lounger in places of social enjoyment: *a parlor lizard.* [< Old French *lesard,* or *laisarde,* feminine < Latin *lacertus,* or *lacerta*] **—liz′ard|like′,** *adj.*

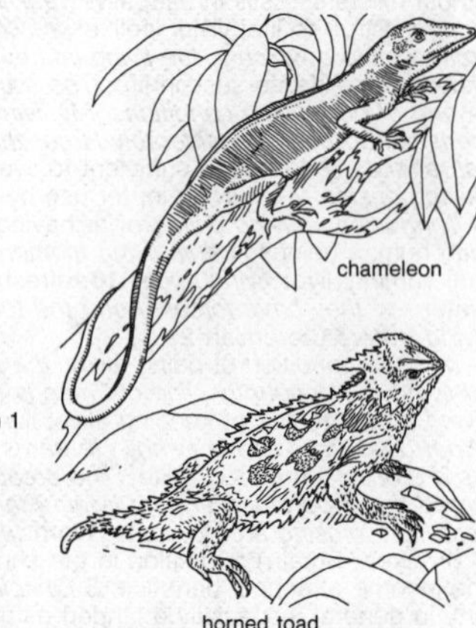


***lizard**
definition 1

**lizard fish**, any one of various large-mouthed fishes with lizardlike heads, especially a species of the Atlantic Ocean.

**liz|ard's-tail** (liz′ərdz tāl′), *n.* a perennial herb having taillike spikes of small white flowers, growing in wet areas of the eastern and southern United States.

**LL** (no periods), **L.L.**, or **LL.**, **1** Late Latin. **2** Low Latin.

**ll.**, lines.

***lla|ma** (lä′mə), *n., pl.* **-mas** or (*especially collectively*) **-ma. 1** a South American mammal somewhat like a camel, but smaller and without a hump. Llamas chew the cud and have woolly hair. They are used as beasts of burden in Peru and other countries of the Andes. **2** the wool of the llama or a fabric made from this: *Her* [*the Lady Mayoress's*] *petticoat was of llama and gold* (Tuer and Fagan). [< Spanish *llama* < Quechua (Peru)]

**lla|ne|ro** (lyä nā′rō, yä-), *n. Spanish.* a plainsman.

**lla|no** (lä′nō), *n., pl.* **-nos.** *Spanish America and Southwestern U.S.* a broad, almost treeless, grassy plain. [American English < Spanish *llano* < Latin *plānus* level]

**LL.B.**, Bachelor of Laws (Latin, *Legum Baccalaureus*).

**LL.D.**, Doctor of Laws (Latin, *Legum Doctor*).

**LL.M.**, Master of Laws (Latin, *Legum Magister*).

**Lloyd's** (loidz), *n.* an association of businessmen in London dealing in many kinds of insurance, especially marine insurance. Lloyd's is unique in that the risks are borne by the individual underwriters rather than by the corporation.

**Lloyd's Register**, a publication containing the age, tonnage, classification, and other data, of merchant ships and yachts, and other shipping information, published by a nonprofit society allied to Lloyd's, that establishes standards of shipping construction.

**Llyr** (lir), *n. Celtic Mythology.* the personification of the sea and father of Bran.

**lm.**, lumen.

**LM** (no periods), lunar module.

**L.M.**, **1** Licentiate in Medicine. **2** Licentiate in Midwifery.

**L-mes|on** (el′mes′on, -mez′-; -mē′son, -zon), *n.* = light meson.

**lmn.**, lineman.

**l.m.t.**, local mean time.

**ln.**, **1** liaison. **2** loan.

**Ln** (no period), lanthanide.

**LNG** (no periods), liquefied natural gas.

**lo** (lō), *interj.* look! see! behold!

**lo and behold**, look and see (used as an expression of great surprise): *And then—lo and behold—it was there all the time* (J. B. Priestley). [Old English *lā*]

**loach** (lōch), *n., pl.* **loach|es** or (*collectively*) **loach.** any one of a family of small European and Asian freshwater fishes related to the minnows. [< Old French *loche*]

**load** (lōd), *n., v.* **—*n.* 1** what one is carrying; burden: *The cart has a load of hay.* **2a** the amount that usually is carried. **b** such amount taken as a unit of measure or weight: *Send us four loads of sand.* **3** *Figurative.* something that weighs down, oppresses, or impedes: *a load of debt, a load of guilt. The nurse bears a load of anxiety.* **4** *Mechanics.* the weight or force supported by a structure or any part of it. **5a** the external resistance overcome by an engine, dynamo, or the like, under a given condition, measured by the power required. **b** the total amount of power supplied by a dynamo, or other source of electricity in a given time. **6** the amount of work that a person, business, or machine is expected to perform: *A medical student carries a very heavy load of work through school.* **7** one charge of powder and shot for a gun. **8** one cubic yard of earth or gravel. **9** the sales charge levied on a purchaser of mutual fund shares. **10** = genetic load. **11** *Slang.* enough liquor to make one drunk. **—*v.t.* 1** to place on or in something for conveyance; heap or pile on: *to load grain.* **2** to put

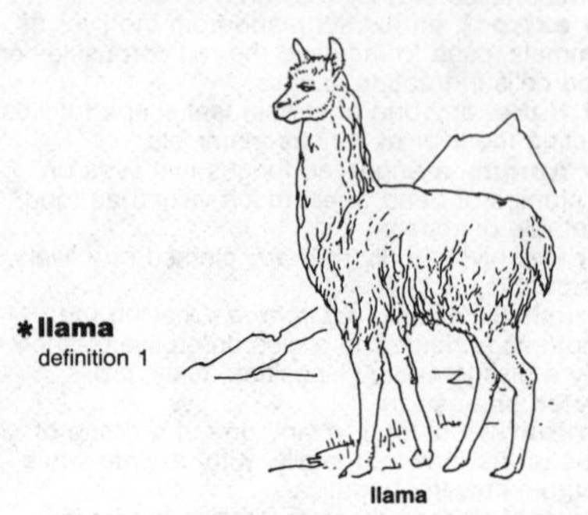


***llama**
definition 1

**resembles a llama:**

whatever is to be carried in or on: *to load a ship. He loaded the camera with film.* **3** *Figurative.* to burden; oppress: *to load the mind with worries, load the stomach with sweets.* **4** to alter or add to, making inferior or impure: *Silk was formerly loaded with chemicals which made it appear heavier and of better quality than it really was.* **5** to add to the weight of: *to load dice fraudulently so as to regulate the fall after a roll, to load a thin wine to give it greater body.* **6** *Figurative.* to influence unfairly; slant: *Sir Joseph complained that the theme of the programme was "loaded to give viewers the impression that the police are ... 'bent'"* (London Times). **7** to supply amply or in excess: *to load a person with gifts. They loaded her with compliments on her singing.* **8** to put a charge in (a gun): *The pioneer loaded his musket with powder and shot.* **9** to increase (an insurance premium) by adding an extra charge as a provision against contingencies. **10** *Baseball.* to cause runners to occupy (first, second, and third bases): *He ... retired three Orioles in a row after loading the bases* (New York Times).
**—*v.i.* 1** to take on a load or cargo: *The ship loaded in five days.* **2** to provide a gun with a charge, bullet, or shell.

**get a load of**, *U.S. Slang.* take note of; notice; observe: *When the boss gets a load of that* [*fancy car*] *parked next to his own heap, he fires the hero on the spot* (Time).

**loads**, *Informal.* **a** a great quantity or number: *loads of money, loads of people.* **b** very much: *I like you loads.*
[Old English *lād* way, course, carrying, related to *lǣdan* lead[1]; influenced in meaning by *lade.* See doublet etym. at **lode.**]
**—*Syn.* *n.* 1, 3 Load, burden** mean what one is carrying. **Load**, the general word, applies literally to whatever is carried by a person or animal or in a vehicle, boat, or plane, and figuratively to something that weighs heavily on the mind or spirit: *That is a heavy load of groceries. That's a load off my mind.* **Burden** means something borne, and now, except in a few phrases, is used only figuratively, applying to sorrow, care, duty, or work: *She had too heavy a burden and became sick.*

**load arm**, the distance from the load to the fulcrum of a lever.

**load displacement**, the displacement of a ship carrying a full load.

**load|ed** (lō′did), *adj.* **1** carrying a load: *a loaded barge. The loaded apple trees in the orchard* (John Ruskin). **2** with a charge in it. **3** weighted, especially with lead or the like: *a loaded stick or whip.* **4** *Informal, Figurative.* full of meaning and implications: *a loaded question.* **5** *U.S. Slang.* having plenty of money; rich: *This money will make me a millionaire. I'll be loaded* (New Yorker). **6** *U.S. Slang.* drunk.

**load|er** (lō′dər), *n.* **1** a person who loads. **2** a loading machine.

**load factor**, **1** *Electricity.* the ratio of the average to the maximum load of production or consumption. **2** *Aviation.* the ratio of the average number of seats occupied to the maximum seating capacity.

**load|ing** (lō′ding), *n.* **1** the act of a person or thing that loads: *Freight-car loadings continue to slack off* (Newsweek). **2** *Electricity.* the introduction of additional inductances, as to a telephone circuit or an antenna. **3** an addition to the net insurance premium, derived from statistics, to provide for expenses, fluctuations in the death rate, and other contingencies. **4** the weight imposed on a given supporting component, expressed by dividing the gross weight of an airplane by factors of flight, as engine power (power loading), wing span (span loading), or wing area (wing loading).

**loading coil**, a coil introduced into an electric circuit to increase its inductance.

**load line**, a line painted amidships on the side of a ship that marks the water line under a full load.

**load|mas|ter** (lōd′mas′tər, -mäs′-), *n.* a person in charge of an aircrew loading and unloading an aircraft.

**loads** (lōdz), *n.pl.* See under **load.**

**load-shed|ding** (lōd′shed′ing), *n.* the cutting off of electric power in a particular area especially as a means of preventing a widespread blackout.

**load|star** (lōd′stär′), *n.* = lodestar.

**load|stone** (lōd′stōn′), *n.* **1** a hard, black stone that attracts iron and steel as a magnet does. It is a kind of magnetite. **2** *Figurative.* something that attracts: *Gold was the loadstone that drew men to Alaska.* Also, **lodestone.** [< earlier *load* or *lode* way, course + *stone*]

**loaf[1]** (lōf), *n., pl.* **loaves. 1** bread baked as one piece: *The loaf came apart easily from the loaves it was baked with.* **2** a rather large cake, often baked in the shape of a loaf of bread. **3** anything like a loaf in shape, especially food shaped like a loaf of bread. Meat loaf is meat chopped and mixed with other things and then baked. **4** a cone-shaped mass of sugar. **5** *Dialect.* bread. **6** *Slang.* head; brains.

**half a loaf**, *Informal.* half of something desired or deserved: *Urban Negroes ... tend to regard the housing provisions in the rights bill as less than half a loaf* (New York Times).
[Old English *hlāf* loaf, bread]

**loaf[2]** (lōf), *v.i.* to spend time idly; do nothing: *I can loaf all day Saturday.* **—*v.t.*** to idle (away): *to loaf one's life away.* [American English; origin uncertain]

**loaf|er** (lō′fər), *n.* **1** a person who loafs; idler. **2a** a shoe resembling a moccasin, but with sole and heel stitched to the upper. **b Loafer**, a trademark for such a shoe.

**loaf sugar**, **1** a cone-shaped mass of sugar. **2** sugar in lumps.

**loam** (lōm), *n., v.* —*n.* **1a** soil that is between sandy soil and clay soil in texture; rich, fertile earth in which decaying leaves and other organic matter are mixed with clay and sand and is therefore easy to work. **b** *Figurative: College novels ... were once filled with japes, walks, clubs, sports, and cliques—rich loam for the industrious novelist* (New Yorker). **2** a mixture of clay, sand, and straw used to make molds for large metal castings, and also to plaster walls, stop up holes, and the like. **3** *Archaic.* earth; ground; soil.
—*v.t.* to cover or fill with loam.
[Old English *lām* clayey earth. See related etym. at **lime**[1].] —**loam′less**, *adj.*

**loam|y** (lō′mē), *adj.,* **loam|i|er, loam|i|est.** of or like loam. —**loam′i|ness**, *n.*

**loan**[1] (lōn), *n., v.* —*n.* **1** the act of lending: *She asked for the loan of his pen.* **2** money lent: *He asked his brother for a small loan.* **3** anything that is lent: *The bicycle was only a loan from a friend and had to be returned that afternoon.* **4** = loan word.
—*v.t.* to make a loan of; lend: *His brother loaned him the money.* —*v.i.* to make a loan.
[< Scandinavian (compare Old Icelandic *lān*)] —**loan′a|ble**, *adj.* —**loan′er**, *n.*
▶ **loan, lend.** In standard British English *loan* is a noun and *lend* a verb. But in American English *loan* and *lend* are verbs, and *loan* is both a verb and a noun: *I loaned* (*or lent*) *him my tuxedo. He asked me for a loan of five dollars.*

**loan**[2] (lōn), *n. Scottish.* **1** a lane; by-road. **2** an open, uncultivated piece of ground near a farmhouse or village, on which cows are milked. [Middle English *lone,* variant of *lane* lane]

**loan company**, an organization that lends money to individuals, especially a finance company that makes small loans.

**loan office**, **1** *U.S. Historical.* an office for receiving subscriptions to a government loan, such as those established during the American Revolutionary War. **2** = pawnshop.

**loan shark**, *U.S. Informal.* a person who lends money at an extremely high or unlawful rate of interest.

**loan-shark|ing** (lōn′shär′king), *n. U.S. Informal.* moneylending at extremely high or unlawful interest rates: *The bill would make "extortionate extensions of credit," or loan-sharking, subject to a maximum penalty of $10,000 and 20 years' imprisonment* (New York Times).

**loan translation**, an expression that is a literal translation of a foreign expression, such as *marriage of convenience* from French *mariage de convenance.*

**loan word**, a word borrowed from another language, especially a foreign word that has become naturalized. *Examples:* khaki, intelligentsia. [translation of German *Lehnwort*]

**loath** (lōth), *adj., n.* —*adj.* **1** unwilling or reluctant; averse: *The little girl was loath to leave her mother. They are loath to admit that their son had run away.* **SYN**: See syn. under **reluctant**. **2** *Obsolete.* repulsive; hateful; loathsome.
—*n. Obsolete.* loathing. Also, **loth**.
**nothing loath**, willing; willingly: *He pulled out a chair beside his desk and Greta sat down in it, nothing loath* (Michael Strange).
[Old English *lāth* hostile] —**loath′ness**, *n.*

**loathe** (lōᴛʜ), *v.t.,* **loathed, loath|ing.** to hate very much; feel strong dislike and disgust for; abhor: *We loathe rotten food or a nasty smell. I loathe cockroaches. He knew the model boy very well though—and loathed him* (Mark Twain). **SYN**: abominate, detest. [Old English *lāthian* to hate < *lāth* hostile, loath] —**loath′er**, *n.*

**loath|ful** (lōᴛʜ′fəl), *adj.* that is an object of loathing or disgust; hateful; loathsome: *the loathful behavior of a cheat.*

**loath|ing** (lō′ᴛʜing), *n., adj.* —*n.* a very great hatred; strong dislike and disgust; intense aversion: *They looked upon the Creature with a loathing undisguised;—It wasn't Disinfected and it wasn't Sterilized* (Arthur Guiterman). **SYN**: antipathy, repugnance.
—*adj.* that feels an intense aversion. —**loath′ing|ly**, *adv.*

**loath|ly**[1] (lōᴛʜ′lē), *adj.* = loathsome. [Old English *lāthlīc* < *lāth* hostile]

**loath|ly**[2] (lōth′lē, lōᴛʜ′-), *adv.* unwillingly; reluctantly. Also, **lothly**. [Old English *lāthlīce* < *lāth* hostile]

**loath|some** (lōᴛʜ′səm), *adj.* very hateful; disgusting; making one feel sick: *a loathsome smell. Some of the details are loathsome.* **SYN**: abominable, detestable, repulsive, nauseating, odious. Also, **lothsome**. —**loath′some|ly**, *adv.* —**loath′some|ness**, *n.*

**loaves** (lōvz), *n.* plural of **loaf**[1].

**lob**[1] (lob), *n., v.,* **lobbed, lob|bing.** —*n.* **1** a ball, especially a tennis ball, hit in a high arc, usually to the back of the opponent's court. **2** an artillery shell, rock, or other object shot or thrown in a high arc. **3** a slow underhand throw in cricket. [< verb]
—*v.t.* **1** to hit (a ball, especially a tennis ball) in a high arc, usually to the back of an opponent's court. **2** to throw (an artillery shell, a rock, or other object) in a high arc: *mainland shore batteries occasionally lob shells at Quemoy* (New York Times). **3** to throw (a cricket ball) with a slow underhand movement. **4** to throw heavily or clumsily. —*v.i.* **1** to hit a lob, as in tennis. **2** to throw a lob, as of an artillery shell or a rock. **3** to move heavily or clumsily.
[Middle English *lobben.* Probably related to **lubber**.] —**lob′ber**, *n.*

**lob**[2] (lob), *n.* **1** = lugworm. **2** *Dialect.* a country bumpkin; lout. [compare Danish *lobbes* clown, bumpkin]

**lo|bar** (lō′bər), *adj.* of or affecting a lobe or lobes: *lobar pneumonia.*

**lo|bate** (lō′bāt), *adj.* **1** having a lobe or lobes. **2** having the form of a lobe: *The liver is lobate.* **3** of or having to do with a bird's foot that is adapted for paddling by having lobes or flaps along the sides of the toes, as in the coot. [< New Latin *lobatus* < Late Latin *lobus* < Greek *lobós*] —**lo′bate|ly**, *adv.*

**lo|bat|ed** (lō′bā tid), *adj.* = lobate.

**lo|ba|tion** (lō bā′shən), *n.* **1** lobate formation or state. **2** = lobe.

**lob|by** (lob′ē), *n., pl.* **-bies**, *v.,* **-bied, -by|ing.** —*n.* **1** an entrance hall connected with one or more rooms in a building and used as a passageway or anteroom: *the lobby of a theater. A hotel lobby usually has chairs and couches to sit on.* **SYN**: foyer. **2** a room or hall outside a legislative chamber, open to the public. The lobby of the British House of Commons serves chiefly for interviews between members and persons not belonging to the House. **3** a person or persons that try to influence members of a lawmaking body; body of lobbyists: *The governor conceded the legislative proposals probably will be strongly opposed by business interests. An aide said business lobbies had indicated almost "uniform resistance"* (Wall Street Journal).
—*v.i.* to try to influence members of a lawmaking body in their votes: *The cotton farmers from the South lobbied against a law to allow importing cotton from Egypt. The jewelry industry has been lobbying against a low tariff on watches.*
—*v.t.* **1** to get or try to get (a bill) passed by lobbying: *The group tried to lobby the bill through.* **2** to influence (legislators) in their votes: *Aircraft workers might decide to lobby their M.P.s within the next two or three weeks* (London Times).
[< Medieval Latin *lobium, lobia* covered walk < Germanic (compare Old High German *louba* hall, roof). See etym. of doublets **lodge, loge, loggia**.] —**lob′by|er**, *n.*

**lob|by-fod|der** (lob′ē fod′ər), *n. Especially British.* a politician or politicians regarded as primarily serving the needs of lobbyists.

**lob|by|ism** (lob′ē iz əm), *n.* the system or practice of lobbying.

**lob|by|ist** (lob′ē ist), *n.* a person who tries to influence members of a lawmaking body in their votes, or executives in their administration of laws, especially a member of a group (lobby) having special interests or favoring particular legislation: *Among the principal lobbyists for this clause at the time were the oil, textile, and coal industries* (London Times).

**lobe** (lōb), *n.* a rounded projecting part, as of a leaf, the lungs, the brain, or a gland. The lobe of the ear is the lower rounded end. [< Middle French *lobe,* learned borrowing from Late Latin *lobus* < Greek *lobós*]

**lo|bec|to|my** (lō bek′tə mē), *n., pl.* **-mies**. the removal of a lobe of the lung.

**lobed** (lōbd), *adj.* having a lobe or lobes.

**lobe|fin** (lōb′fin′), *n.,* or **lobefin fish**, = lobe-finned fish.

**lobe-finned fish** (lōb′find′), any one of a group of fishes having rounded scales and lobed fins. The coelacanth is a lobe-finned fish.

**lobe|less** (lōb′lis), *adj.* having no lobes.

**lo|bel|ia** (lō bēl′yə), *n.* a plant with small blue, red, yellow, purple, or white flowers. It belongs to the lobelia family and may be wild or cultivated. [< New Latin *Lobelia* < Matthias de *Lobel,* 1538-1616, a Flemish botanist]

**lo|be|li|a|ceous** (lō bē′lē ā′shəs), *adj.* belonging to the lobelia family of plants.

**lobelia family**, a group of widely distributed, mainly herbaceous, dicotyledonous plants often grown for their showy flowers. The family includes the cardinal flower and Indian tobacco.

**lo|be|line** (lō′bə lēn), *n.* a poisonous alkaloid obtained from a variety of lobelia, used as a respiratory stimulant and smoking deterrent. *Formula:* $C_{22}H_{27}NO_2$

**Lo|bi** (lō′bē), *n.pl.* a Moslem people of Upper Volta.

**lob|lol|ly** (lob′lol′ē), *n., pl.* **-lies**. **1a** a pine tree of the southern United States that has a thick bark, long needles, and cones with spiny tips. It grows in swampy soils. *Skinny pines, including a kind rather pleasantly known as the loblolly, grew thick as weeds over some 35 million acres* (Time). **b** its coarse wood. **2** *U.S.* thick mud; swamp. **3** *Dialect.* thick gruel or other liquid food. [American English; apparently special use as "mud, bog" of British English, thick gruel or stew, perhaps < dialectal *lob* bubble up + *lolly* broth, stew]

**loblolly bay**, an ornamental, white-flowered shrub or small tree of the southern United States. The loblolly bay belongs to the tea family.

**loblolly boy**, *Obsolete.* the assistant of a ship's surgeon. [probably < *loblolly* thick gruel or stew]

**loblolly pine**, = loblolly (def. 1).

**lo|bo** (lō′bō), *n., pl.* **-bos**. the timber wolf; gray wolf. [American English < Spanish *lobo* < Latin *lupus*]

**lo|bo|la** (lō′bə lə), *n.* a dowry paid by a native South African for his bride. [< Zulu *lobola*]

**lo|bot|o|mize** (lō bot′ə mīz), *v.t., v.i.,* **-mized, -miz|ing.** to perform a lobotomy (on).

**lo|bot|o|my** (lō bot′ə mē), *n., pl.* **-mies**. surgical incision into a lobe of the brain, especially to cut nerve fibers in the treatment of certain mental disorders. [< *lobe* + Greek *-tomiā* a cutting]

**lob|scouse** (lob′skous′), *n.* a stew chiefly of meat, vegetables, and hardtack, formerly eaten by sailors. [variant of *lob's couse;* origin uncertain. Compare *loblolly* gruel, *lob* boil with lumps (like porridge).]

**Lob's pound** (lobz), **1** *British Dialect.* jail or prison. **2** any situation of embarrassment or difficulty. [perhaps < *lob*[2] clown, bumpkin]

∗**lob|ster** (lob′stər), *n.* **1a** a sea animal about a foot long with two big claws and eight legs. Its shell turns a bright red when a lobster is boiled for food. Lobsters are crustaceans with compound eyes that grow on thick stalks. **b** the flesh of a lobster, used as food. **2** any one of various related crustaceans that lack an enlarged pair of claws, such as the spiny lobsters. **3** *Historical.* a British soldier; redcoat. **4a** *Slang.* a gullible, foolish, or stupid person. **b** a red-faced person. [Old English *loppestre,* probably alteration of Latin *lōcusta* locust, lobster]

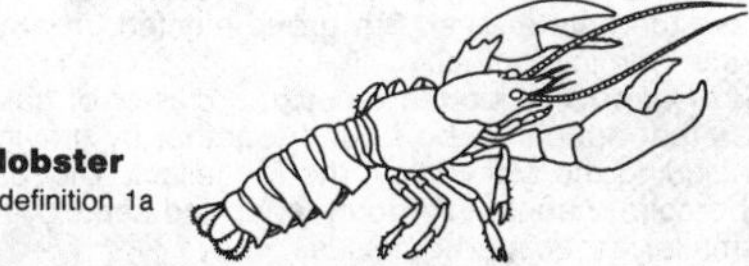

∗**lobster**
definition 1a

**lob|ster|back** (lob′stər bak′), *n. Historical.* a redcoat; lobster: *British lobsterbacks burned the original Capitol in 1814* (Time).

**lob|ster|ing** (lob′stər ing), *n.* the process or business of catching lobsters.

**lob|ster|man** (lob′stər mən), *n., pl.* **-men**. a man who catches lobsters for a living or for sport.

**lobster Newburg**, a hot dish of lobster meat cut in chunks, prepared with cheese sauce and sherry.

**lobster pot**, = lobster trap.

**lobster shift**, *U.S. Informal.* graveyard shift: *I was assigned the lobster shift, from midnight until eight in the morning* (New Yorker).

**lobster thermidor**, a dish of boiled lobster cut up in cream sauce, often with mushrooms and sherry, baked with a covering of grated cheese in a lobster shell.

**lobster trap**, a trap for catching lobsters, consisting of a box made of slats and a hole of funnel-shaped net through which the lobster crawls to get into the baited box.

**lob|u|lar** (lob′yə lər), *adj.* **1** having the form of a lobule or small lobe. **2** of or having to do with lobules: *a lobular vein.*

**lob|u|late** (lob′yə lit), *adj.* = lobulated.

**lob|u|lat|ed** (lob′yə lā′tid), *adj.* consisting of or separated into lobules: *lobulated kidneys.*

**lob|u|la|tion** (lob′yə lā′shən), *n.* separation into lobules.

**lob|ule** (lob′yül), *n.* **1** a small lobe. **2** a part of a lobe. [< New Latin *lobulus* < Late Latin *lobus;* see etym. under **lobe**]

**lob|worm** (lob′wėrm′), *n.* = lugworm.

**loc.**, local.

**lo|cal**[1] (lō′kəl), *adj., n.* —*adj.* **1** of a place: *New*

**Pronunciation Key:** hat, āge, cãre, fär; let, ēqual, tėrm; it, īce; hot, ōpen, ôrder; oil, out; cup, pu̇t, rüle; child; long; thin; ᴛʜen; zh, measure; ə represents **a** in about, **e** in taken, **i** in pencil, **o** in lemon, **u** in circus.

*Jersey is a local name.* **2** having to do with a certain place or places: *the local doctor, local news, local self-government. A local thing called Christianity* (Thomas Hardy). **3** of just one part of the body; affecting a particular organ of the body: *a local pain, local disease, local application of a remedy.* **4** making all or almost all stops: *a local train.* **5** of or concerned with position in space: *The poet's pen ... gives to airy nothing A local habitation and a name* (Shakespeare).
— *n.* **1** a train, bus, or airplane that stops at all, or almost all, of the stations on its route. **2** a local inhabitant. **3** a branch or chapter of a labor union, fraternity, or other group: *The local would not agree with the national decision to strike.* **4** a newspaper item of interest to a particular area: *As a young reporter, he covered the locals.* **5** *British.* a local tavern; pub.
[< Latin *locālis* < *locus* place]

**lo|cal**[2] (lō kal′), *n.* = locale.

**local action**, **1** the electrical action set up between different parts of a plate of conducting material when it is immersed in an electrolyte. **2** a legal action which must be brought in the particular locality where the cause of action arose, such as an action to recover lands.

**local anesthesia**, anesthesia that causes a loss of feeling in a given area of the body but does not cause unconsciousness. It is used especially during minor operations and dental work.

**local authority**, *British.* an elected body for the administration of local affairs in a town, county, or other district.

**local color**, **1** the distinctive customs, peculiarities, or other characteristics of a certain place or period, used in stories and plays to add realism: *He ... found plenty of local color in the little Puritan metropolis* (Henry James). **2** the color that is natural to each object or part of a picture independently of the general color scheme or the distribution of light and shade.

**lo|cale** (lō kal′), *n.* a place, especially with reference to events or circumstances connected with it: *The locale of "Don Quixote" is Spain in the 1600's. Author Bowles brings the Moroccan locale to life with meticulous realism* (Time). [< French *local,* noun use of adjective, local, learned borrowing from Latin *locālis*]

**local government**, **1a** the administration of local affairs in a town, city, or other place, by its own people. **b** *U.S.* any type of government at less than state level. **2** a group elected for any such administration.

**local group** or **Local Group**, a cluster of galaxies that appear to be bound together by gravity, including the Milky Way, the Magellanic Clouds, the spiral nebula in Andromeda, and some smaller associated galaxies.

**lo|cal|ise** (lō′kə līz), *v.t., v.i.,* **-ised, -is|ing.** *Especially British.* localize.

**lo|cal|ism** (lō′kə liz əm), *n.* **1** a local expression, custom, or other characteristic: *To be sure, some of the varieties of speech are mere localisms* (Scientific American). **2** = sectionalism. **3** attachment to a certain place.

**lo|cal|ist** (lō′kə list), *n.* a person who is greatly or unduly concerned with local conditions or affairs; sectionalist.

**lo|cal|ite** (lō′kə līt), *n.* a local inhabitant; local.

**lo|cal|i|ty** (lō kal′ə tē), *n., pl.* **-ties. 1** place; one place and the places near it; region, district, or neighborhood: *the locality of a mineral, the locality of a crime. He knows many people in the locality of Boston. A sense of locality enables a person to find his way.* **SYN**: section, vicinity. **2** *Phrenology.* the faculty of recognizing and remembering places and locations.

**lo|cal|ize** (lō′kə līz), *v.,* **-ized, -iz|ing.** — *v.t.* to make local; fix in, assign, or limit to a particular place or locality: *The infection seemed to be localized in the foot.* **SYN**: place.
— *v.i.* to become localized. — **lo′cal|iz′a|ble,** *adj.* — **lo′cal|i|za′tion,** *n.* — **lo′cal|iz′er,** *n.*

**lo|cal|ly** (lō′kə lē), *adv.* **1** in a local manner or respect; with regard to place: *to be far separated locally.* **2** in one place or in a number of places; not everywhere; not widely: *Outbreaks of the disease occurred locally.* **3** in respect to position in space.

**local mean time**, = local time.

**local metamorphism**, = contact metamorphism.

**local option**, the right granted by the legislature of a country or state to the inhabitants of a political district to decide by vote certain matters, especially whether the sale of liquor shall be permitted within the district.

**local time**, time measured from the instant of passing of the mean sun over the particular meridian of a place. *Abbr:* l.t.

**lo|cat|a|ble** (lō kā′tə bəl), *adj.* that can be located.

**lo|cate** (lō′kāt, lō kāt′), *v.,* **-cat|ed, -cat|ing.** — *v.t.* **1** to establish in a place; settle: *He located his new store on Main Street.* **2** to find out the exact position of: *The general tried to locate the enemy's camp. We followed the stream until we located its source.* **3** to state or show the position of: *Can you locate Africa on the globe?* **4a** to establish the boundaries or rights of: *to locate a claim.* **b** to fix the site, path, or alignment of: *to locate a building, to locate a highway or railroad.*
— *v.i.* to establish oneself in a place: *Early settlers located where there was water.*
**be located,** to be situated; lie: *The capital is located on a river.*
[< Latin *locāre* (with English *-ate*[1]) < *locus* place] — **lo′cat|er,** *n.*

**lo|ca|tion** (lō kā′shən), *n.* **1** the act of locating or condition of being located: *The scouts disputed about the location of the camp.* **2** position or place: *a house in a fine location, a location for a mill. The camp was in a bad location as there was no water near it.* **SYN**: locality. See syn. under **place. 3** a plot of ground marked out by boundaries; lot: *a mining location.* **4** a place outside a studio, used in making all or part of a motion picture: *to shoot a film on location.* **5** (in South Africa) the quarters set apart for natives. **6** (in Australia) a farm or station. **7** *Civil and Scots Law.* the act of letting or leasing for hire, or a contract by which a thing or person is hired. **8** a minor civil division in New Hampshire. **9** a position in the memory of a digital computer storing one word or unit of meaning.

**lo|ca|tion|al** (lō kā′shə nəl), *adj.* of or having to do with location: *New England is at a locational disadvantage in reaching the rapidly expanding markets of the southeast and the southwest* (Atlantic). — **lo|ca′tion|al|ly,** *adv.*

**loc|a|tive** (lok′ə tiv), *adj., n. Grammar.* — *adj.* indicating place.
— *n.* **1** a case used to indicate place in which. **2** a word in this case, such as Latin *domi,* "at home."
[< New Latin *locativus* < Latin *locāre;* see etym. under **locate**]

**lo|ca|tor** (lō′kā tər, lō kā′-), *n.* **1** *U.S.* a person who marks the boundaries of or takes possession of land or a mining claim. **2** a person who locates alignment especially of roads and railroads. **3** = radiolocator. [American English < *locate* + *-er*[1]]

**loc. cit.**, in the place cited (Latin, *loco citato*).

**loch** (lok, loн), *n. Scottish.* **1** a lake: *Loch Lomond.* **2** an arm of the sea, especially when narrow or partly landlocked. [< Scottish Gaelic *loch*]

**lo|chi|a** (lō′kē ə, lok′ē-), *n.pl.* the discharge of fluid from the vagina after childbirth. [< New Latin *lochia* < Greek *lóchia,* neuter plural of *lóchios* < *lóchos* childbirth]

**lo|ci** (lō′sī), *n.* plural of **locus.**

***lock**[1] (lok), *n., v.* — *n.* **1** a means of fastening (doors, boxes, windows, and similar things), consisting of a bolt and usually needing a key of special shape to open it: *Our front door has a lock. But what can Miss Emily want with a box ... without any locks?* (Walter de la Mare). **2** a part of a canal or dock in which the level of the water can be changed by letting water in or out, to raise or lower ships. **3a** the part of a gun by means of which it if fired; gunlock: *When the lock jammed the rifle failed to go off.* **b** a safety on a gun. **4** a device to keep a wheel from turning. A lock is used when a vehicle is parked facing downhill. *For a car of this size the lock is excellent* (London Times). **5** an airtight chamber admitting to a compartment in which there is compressed air; air lock. **6** a kind of hold in wrestling: *a hammer lock.* **7** the action of locking together; interlocking.
— *v.t.* **1** to fasten with a lock: *Lock and bar the door.* **2** to shut (something in or out or up): *to lock something in a closet, to lock a building up for the night. We lock up jewels in a safe. Where'er she lie, Locked up from mortal eye* (Richard Crashaw). **3** to hold fast: *The ship was locked in ice.* (*Figurative.*) *The secret was locked in her heart.* **4** to join, fit, jam, or link together: *The girls locked arms and walked down the street together. When the brakes locked the wheels the car skidded to a stop.* **5** to make or set fast; fasten. **6** to fasten (a wheel) to keep from turning. **7** *Printing.* to fasten (type or blocks in a chase) for printing or plating. **8a** to embrace closely: *Lock'd in each other's arms we stood* (Matthew Arnold). **b** to grapple in combat: *one glance ... showed me Hands and his companion locked together in deadly wrestle* (Robert Louis Stevenson). **9** to move (a ship) by means of a lock. **10** to furnish (a river, canal, or dam) with locks. **11** to shut off (a portion of a river or canal) by means of a lock. **12** to invest (capital) in something that is not easily convertible into money.
— *v.i.* **1** to be locked; be capable of being locked: *The door will not lock with his key.* **2** to become fixed or set fast; become locked: *This gear has locked. Two cars locked together in passing.* **3** to go or pass by means of a lock. **4** to provide locks for the passage of vessels.
**lock on, a** (of a radar) to fix upon and automatically follow a moving object: *The radar locked on the missile and tracked it until it landed in the desert.* **b** to aim missiles, shells, or bombs at (a target), as by radar: *The 1,500-mph Nike, a target-seeking missile that "locks on" the radar image of a plane ...* (John Hall Thompson).
**lock out,** to refuse to give work to (workers) until they accept the employer's terms: *Large funds are subscribed, out of which labourers on strike or locked out are supported* (James E. Rogers).
**lock, stock, and barrel,** *Informal.* completely; entirely: *It is thus the only foreign city in the world run lock, stock, and barrel by the U.S. Navy* (Time).
**lock the wheels** (or **brakes**). See under **wheel.**
**under lock and key,** locked up; in a place that is locked: *Under lock and key, in the ... store room* (H. Stuart).
[Old English *loc*] — **lock′a|ble,** *adj.* — **lock′less,** *adj.*

***lock**[1]
definition 2

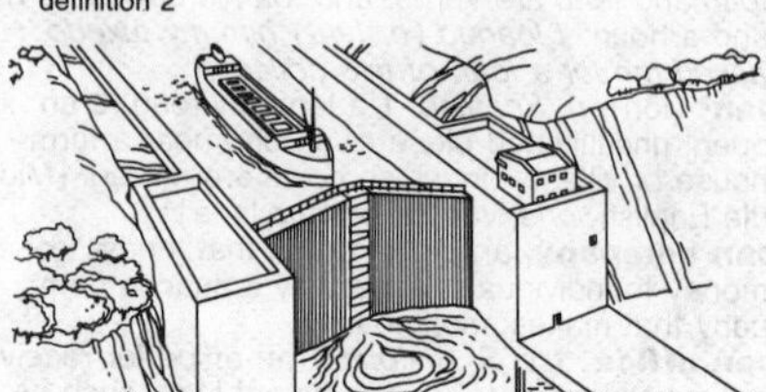

**lock**[2] (lok), *n.* **1** a curl of hair of the head: *Like the white lock of Whistler* (G. K. Chesterton). **SYN**: ringlet. **2** a small portion of hair, wool, flax, or cotton.
**locks,** the hair of the head: *The child has curly locks.*
[Old English *locc*]

**lock|age** (lok′ij), *n.* **1** the construction, use, or operation of locks in canals or streams. **2** the passing of ships through a lock or series of locks. **3a** the walls, gates, or other parts, forming a lock or locks. **b** a system of locks or the locks in such a system. **4** the amount of elevation and descent effected by a lock or locks. **5** a toll paid for passage through a lock or locks.

**lock-a|way** (lok′ə wā′), *n. British.* a long-term security: *At this level and in view of the prospects the shares should be regarded as a widows' and orphans' lock-away rather than a performance stock* (London Times).

**lock-box** (lok′boks′), *n.* **1** a box with a lock. **2** a coin-operated public locker.

**Lock|e|an** (lok′ē ən), *adj.* of, having to do with, or characteristic of the English philosopher John Locke (1632-1704): *He dismisses ... Lockean representative government as irrelevant to the problems of large-scale industrial societies* (New Yorker).

**Lock|e|an|ism** (lok′ē ə niz′əm), *n.* the philosophical doctrines of John Locke (1632-1704) or his followers.

**locked-in** (lokt′in′), *adj.* **1** closed to outside influence or control; exclusive: *a locked-in commercial enterprise.* **2a** (of an investor) holding on to securities, especially to avoid payment of high capital gains taxes. **b** (of securities) not sold or traded on the market; static.

**lock|er** (lok′ər), *n.* **1** a chest, drawer, small closet, cupboard, or other compartment that can be locked. Ships have lockers for storing equipment and supplies. **2** a refrigerated compartment for storing frozen foods. **3** a person or thing that locks.

**locker room**, **1** a room with lockers near a gymnasium or athletic field, or in a clubhouse, bowling alley or skating rink, for dressing and for storing sports equipment: *After football practice he was always down in the locker room* (New Yorker). **2** a room with lockers for storage: *the locker room of a frozen-food plant.*

**lock|et** (lok′it), *n.* a small, ornamental case of gold or silver, for holding a picture of someone or a lock of hair. It is usually worn around the neck on a chain. A locket often has a hinged cover. [< Old French *locquet* latch (diminutive) < Old French *loc* < Germanic (compare Old Low German *lok* lock)]

**lock|gate** (lok′gāt′), *n.* one of the gates of a canal lock.

**lock-in** (lok′in′), *n.* a protest demonstration in which a group locks itself within a building, office, or other enclosed area: *They decided last week* *to stage a lock-in to draw attention to their case* (Sunday Times).

**lock|jaw** (lok′jô′), *n.* **1** a form of tetanus in which the jaws become firmly closed. **2** = tetanus.

**lock|keep|er** (lok′kē′pər), *n.* the supervisor of a lock.

**lock|mas|ter** (lok′mas′tər), *n.* a person who operates a lock: *The lockmaster in his control station closes the lower gates by pressing a button* (Alexander Laing).

**lock|nut** (lok′nut′), *n.* **1** a nut that can be screwed down on another to keep it securely in place. **2** a nut that locks in place when tightly screwed.

**lock-on** (lok′on′), *n.* the action of locking on to an object by radar.

**lock|out** (lok′out′), *n.* **1** a refusal of an employer to give work to employees until they accept his terms; shut-out: *The lockout was ordered yesterday evening, following a clash between a section of workers and some representatives of the management* (Times of India). **2** an underwater compartment in which the air pressure is sufficient to prevent water from entering through the compartment's open port: *Some of the modifications which are being considered are as follows: a lockout which will allow entry and exit of divers at work sites down to 1000 feet* (New Scientist).

**lock|ram** (lok′rəm), *n.* a linen fabric or cloth formerly made in England for garments and household use. [< French *locrenan* < *Locronan,* a village in Brittany, where it was made]

**locks** (loks), *n.pl.* See under **lock**[2].

**lock|smith** (lok′smith′), *n.* a person who makes or repairs locks and keys.

**lock|smith|er|y** (lok′smith′ər ē), *n., pl.* **-er|ies.** the work or craft of a locksmith.

**lock|smith|ing** (lok′smith′ing), *n.* = locksmithery.

**lock|step** (lok′step′), *n., adj.* **—*n.*** **1** a way of marching in step very close together, with the legs of each person nearly touching those of the person in front and back. **2** *Figurative.* a rigid pattern or arrangement: *When Manning came to Stanford in 1964, he was determined to break the traditional lockstep of three-year law school curriculums* (Time).

**—*adj.*** rigid; unbending: *Mrs. Handy's lockstep methods (copy the great novelists, read the "Masters of the Far East," stay away from girls) produced a handful of published novels* (New Yorker).

**lock stitch,** a sewing-machine stitch in which two threads are fastened together at short intervals.

**lock|up** (lok′up′), *n.* **1a** a house or room for the temporary detention of persons under arrest. **b** = jail. **2** the act of locking up. **3** the state of being locked up.

**lock washer,** any one of various types of steel washers placed under a nut to keep it from working loose.

**lo|co**[1] (lō′kō), *adj., n., pl.* **-cos,** *v.,* **-coed, -co|ing.** *U.S.* **—*adj.*** *Slang.* crazy.

**—*n.*** **1** locoweed. **2** a disease caused by eating this weed; loco disease.

**—*v.t.*** **1** to poison with locoweed. **2** *Slang.* to make insane.

[American English < Spanish *loco* insane; locoweed, perhaps < Italian *locco* fool < *alocco* owl < Latin *ulucus* < *ululāre* howl]

**lo|co**[2] (lō′kō), *n., adj. British Informal.* **—*n.*** a locomotive.

**—*adj.*** of or having to do with locomotives: *loco engineering.*

**lo|co ci|ta|to** (lō′kō sī tā′tō), *Latin.* in the place cited or passage quoted previously. *Abbr:* loc. cit.

**loco disease,** a disease in horses, cattle, and sheep, affecting the brain, caused by eating locoweed; loco.

**lo|co|fo|co** (lō′kō fō′kō), *n. Obsolete.* a type of friction match. [perhaps < *loco-* (misunderstood as meaning "self-"), as in *locomotive* + *foco,* rhyming alteration < Italian *fuoco* fire]

**Lo|co|fo|co** (lō′kō fō′kō), *n. U.S.* a member of the independent or radical section of the Democratic Party (about 1835) which opposed monopolies and advocated hard money, election by direct popular vote, direct taxes, and free trade. [< the use of *locofoco* matches as emergency lighting at one of their meetings]

**lo|co|ism** (lō′kō iz əm), *n.* = loco disease.

**lo|co|mo|bile** (lō′kə mə bēl′; -mō′bəl, -bēl), *adj.* able to move from place to place under its own power; self-propelled. [< Latin *locō* (see etym. under **locomotion**) + *mobilis* mobile]

**lo|co|mote** (lō′kə mōt′), *v.i.,* **-mot|ed, -mot|ing.** to move from place to place: *She was a driven traveller, locomoting restlessly on her indomitable energy* (New Yorker). [back formation < *locomotion*]

**lo|co|mo|tion** (lō′kə mō′shən), *n.* the act or power of moving from place to place. Walking, swimming, and flying are common forms of locomotion. *I have no taste whatever for locomotion, by earth, air, or sea* (Jane W. Carlyle). [< Latin *locō* from a place, ablative of *locus* + English *motion*]

**lo|co|mo|tive** (lō′kə mō′tiv), *n., adj.* **—*n.*** **1** an engine that goes from place to place on its own power, especially used to pull railroad trains. **2** *U.S. Slang.* a group cheer that imitates a railroad engine by starting up slowly and gradually gathering speed.

**—*adj.*** **1** moving from place to place; having the power of locomotion: *locomotive bacteria.* **2** of or designating locomotion by means of a vehicle, engine, or other mechanical device. **3** having to do with the power to move from place to place: *In these locomotive days one is too apt to forget one's neighbours* (Sir Arthur Helps). **—lo′co|mo′tive|ly,** *adv.* **—lo′co|mo′tive|ness,** *n.*

**lo|co|mo|tor** (lō′kə mō′tər), *n., adj.* **—*n.*** a person, animal, or thing that is capable of locomotion.

**—*adj.*** of or having to do with locomotion.

**locomotor ataxia,** a degenerative disease of the spinal cord marked by loss of control over walking and certain other voluntary movements, and severe pains in the internal organs; tabes dorsalis. It is often associated with syphilis.

**lo|co|mo|to|ry** (lō′kə mō′tər ē), *adj.* having to do with or having locomotive power.

**lo|co|weed** (lō′kō wēd′), *n., pl.* **-weeds** or (collectively) **-weed.** a plant of the western United States that affects the brain of horses, sheep, and other grazing animals that eat it. Locoweed comprises various herbs of the pea family.

**Lo|cri|an** (lō′krē ən), *adj., n.* **—*adj.*** of or having to do with Locris, a city in Greece.

**—*n.*** an inhabitant of Locris.

**Lo|crine** (lō′krīn), *n.* a mythical king of England, father of Sabrina.

**loc|u|lar** (lok′yə lər), *adj.* having one or more locules (used chiefly in compounds, such as *bilocular, trilocular*).

**loc|u|late** (lok′yə lāt, -lit), *adj.* having locules.

**loc|u|lat|ed** (lok′yə lā′tid), *adj.* = loculate.

**loc|u|la|tion** (lok′yə lā′shən), *n.* separation into locules.

**loc|ule** (lok′yül), *n.* a small cavity or cell in animal or plant tissue, separated from another locule by a septum, such as a compartment in an ovary, fruit, or anther. [< Latin *loculus* chest, compartment; (literally) small place (diminutive) < *locus* place, locus]

**loc|u|li|cid|al** (lok′yə lə sī′dəl), *adj. Botany.* splitting lengthwise through the back or dorsal suture of each loculus or carpel of a capsule, as in the seed pod of the iris. [< Latin *loculus* loculus + *caedere* to cut + English *-al*[1]] **—loc′u|li|cid′al|ly,** *adv.*

**loc|u|lose** (lok′yə lōs), *adj.* divided into locules or cells.

**loc|u|lous** (lok′yə ləs), *adj.* = loculose.

**loc|u|lus** (lok′yə ləs), *n., pl.* **-li** (-lī). = locule.

**lo|cum** (lō′kəm), *n. Informal.* locum tenens.

**locum te|nen|cy** (tē′nən sē), *pl.* **locum te|nen|cies. 1** the office of employment of a locum tenens. **2** the holding of a place by temporary substitution.

**locum te|nens** (tē′nenz), *pl.* **locum te|nen|tes** (tə nen′tēz), a person temporarily holding the place or office of another; deputy; substitute: *There's this locum tenens I was going to take up in the North* (A. S. M. Hutchinson). [< Medieval Latin *locum tenens* < Latin *locum,* accusative of *locus* place, and *tenēns,* present participle of *tenēre* to hold. Compare etym. under **lieutenant.**]

**lo|cus** (lō′kəs), *n., pl.* **-ci. 1** place or locality. **2** *Mathematics.* a curve, surface, or other figure that contains all the points, and only those points, that satisfy a given condition. The locus of all the points 1 ft. distant from a given point is the surface of a sphere having a radius of 1 ft. **3** *Genetics.* the position of a gene on a chromosome. **4** a shortened form for various Latin phrases, especially *locus classicus.* [< Latin *locus* place]

**lo|cus clas|si|cus** (lō′kəs klas′ə kəs), *pl.* **lo|ci clas|si|ci** (lō′sī klas′ə sī). *Latin.* a classical passage, usually cited for illustration or explanation of a particular word or subject.

**lo|cus si|gil|li** (lō′kəs si jil′ī), *pl.* **lo|ci si|gil|li** (lō′sī si jil′ī). *Latin.* the place of the seal (on official papers or documents). *Abbr:* L.S.

**lo|cus stan|di** (lō′kəs stan′dī), *pl.* **lo|ci stan|di** (lō′sī stan′dī). *Latin.* place of standing; a right of place in court; the right to appear and be heard before a tribunal.

**lo|cust** (lō′kəst), *n.* **1** a kind of grasshopper with short antennae. Sometimes locusts come in great swarms destroying crops. *The white ant can destroy fleets and cities, and the locusts can erase a province* (Benjamin Disraeli). (*Figurative.*) *Those locusts called middle-men ... who live ... out of the labour of the producer and the consumer* (William Cobbett). See picture under **grasshopper. 2** = cicada. **3a** an American tree with small, rounded leaflets and clusters of sweet-smelling white or rose-colored flowers. It belongs to the pea family. **b** its hard wood that resists decay. **4** any one of several other leguminous trees, such as the carob and the honey locust. [< Latin *lōcusta* locust, crab, lobster]

**lo|cus|ta** (lō kus′tə), *n., pl.* **-tae** (-tē). *Botany.* the inflorescence or spikelet of grasses. [< New Latin *locusta* < Latin *lōcusta* locust (supposedly from the shape)]

**locust bean,** the fruit of the carob.

**locust bread,** a bread made from the meal of the locust bean.

**locust years,** years of deprivation and hardship: *Those were terrible years—'the locust years,' Churchill has called them* (Hans Koningsberger). [in reference to Joel 2:25 in the Bible]

**lo|cu|tion** (lō kyü′shən), *n.* **1** style of speech; manner of expression: *to be accustomed to the rustic locution.* **2** a form of expression or phraseology: *unfamiliar locutions, foreign locutions.* **SYN:** idiom. **3** *Obsolete.* speech as the expression of thought; discourse. [< Latin *locūtiō, -ōnis* < *loquī* speak]

**loc|u|to|ry** (lok′yə tôr′ē, -tōr′-), *n., pl.* **-ries.** a room or place in a monastery set apart for conversation. [< Medieval Latin *locutorium* < Latin *locūtor* one who speaks < *loquī* speak]

**lode** (lōd), *n.* **1a** a vein of metal ore: *The miners struck a rich lode of copper.* **b** any mineral deposit filling a fissure in the rock. **2** *British.* a watercourse; aqueduct, channel, or open drain. [Old English *lād* course, way, carrying. See etym. of doublet **load.**]

**lo|den** (lō′dən), *n.* **1** a waterproof woolen cloth with a thick pile. **2** a garment, especially an overcoat, made of loden. [< German *Loden* < Old High German *lodo*]

**lode|star** (lōd′stär′), *n.* **1** a star that shows the way. **2** the North Star; polestar. **3** *Figurative.* a guiding principle or center of attraction. Also, **loadstar.** [< *lode,* and *load* + *star*]

**lode|stone** (lōd′stōn′), *n.* = loadstone.

**lodge** (loj), *v.,* **lodged, lodg|ing,** *n.* **—*v.i.*** **1** to live in a place for a time: *We lodged in motels on our trip.* **SYN:** dwell, reside. **2** to live in a rented room in another's house: *We are merely lodging at present.* **3** to get caught or stay in a place without falling or going farther: *The boy's kite lodged in the branches of a big tree.*

**—*v.t.*** **1** to supply with a place to sleep or live in for a time: *Can you lodge us for the weekend?* **2** to rent a room or rooms to. **3** to put or send into a particular place: *The marksman lodged a bullet in the center of the target.* **4** to put for safekeeping: *to lodge money in a bank. I lay all night in the cave where I had lodged my provisions* (Jonathan Swift). **5** to put before some authority: *We lodged a complaint with the police.* **6** to put (power, authority, or privilege) in a person or thing: *The authority to arrest criminals is lodged with the police.* **SYN:** vest. **7** to beat down or lay flat, as crops by rain or wind. **8** to search out the lair of (a deer).

**—*n.*** **1a** a place to live in: *There is a lodge down the road that rents rooms to travelers.* **b** a small or temporary house, such as one used during the hunting season or in summer: *My uncle rents a lodge in the mountains for the summer.* **c** a cottage on an estate or the like, such as one for a caretaker or gardener: *The porter of my father's lodge* (Emily Dickinson). **2a** a branch of a secret society: *The lodge holds its meetings on Tuesday nights.* **b** the place where it meets: *No one but a member is allowed in the lodge.* **3** the den of an animal, especially the large structure built near or in the water by a beaver or an otter. **4** *U.S.* **a** a wigwam, tepee, or other dwelling of a North American Indian. **b** the number of Indians living in one dwelling. **5** the residence of the head of a college at Cambridge University, England, or the vice-chancellor's residence at certain other schools.

[< Old French *loge* arbor, covered walk < Germanic (compare Old High German *louba* hall, roof). See etym. of doublets **lobby, loge, loggia.**] **—lodge′a|ble,** *adj.*

**lodge|ment** (loj′mənt), *n. Especially British.* lodgment.

**lodge|pole pine** (loj′pōl′), **1** a tall pine tree of western North America with yellow-green needles in clusters of two, used once especially for poles, railroad ties, and in insulation board. **2** its wood.

**lodg|er** (loj′ər), *n.* **1** a person who lives in a rented room or rooms in another's house; roomer: *I'm now no more than a mere lodger in*

**Pronunciation Key:** hat, āge, cãre, fär; let, ēqual, tėrm; it, īce; hot, ōpen, ôrder; oil, out; cup, pu̇t, rüle; child; long; thin; ᴛʜen; zh, measure; ə represents **a** in about, **e** in taken, **i** in pencil, **o** in lemon, **u** in circus.

*my own house* (Oliver Goldsmith). **2** *Archaic.* **a** a person who stays in a place; occupant; inhabitant: *Queer Street's full of lodgers just now* (Dickens). **b** a person who sleeps or passes the night in a place.

**lodg|ing** (loj′ing), *n.* **1** a place where one is living only for a time: *a lodging for the night.* **SYN**: accommodation. **2** *Obsolete.* a dwelling; abode.
**lodgings,** a rented room or rooms in a house, not in a hotel: *Life in lodgings, at the best of times, is not a peculiarly exhilarating state of existence* (J. H. Riddell).

**lodging house,** a house in which rooms are rented, not a hotel.

**lodg|ment** (loj′mənt), *n.* **1** the act of lodging. **2** the condition of being lodged: *the lodgment of a claim against a company.* **3** something lodged or deposited: *a lodgment of earth on a ledge of rock.* **4** *Military.* **a** a position gained; foothold. **b** an entrenchment built temporarily on a position gained from the enemy. **5** *Law.* the action of depositing (a sum of money, securities, or other assets). **6** a lodging place; lodging house; lodgings. Also, **lodgement**.

**lod|i|cule** (lod′ə kyül), *n. Botany.* one of the small scales in the flowers of most grasses, close to the base of the ovary. [< Latin *lōdīcula* (diminutive) < *lōdix, -īcis* coverlet, blanket]

**lo|ess** (lō′is, lœs), *n.* a fine, yellowish-brown loam usually deposited by the wind. It consists of tiny mineral particles, picked up by the wind from deserts and former glaciated areas, and brought to the places where they are now found, such as the central United States. [< German *Löss*, apparently < Swiss German *lösen* pour out of a vessel]

**lo|ess|i|al** (lō es′ē əl), *adj.* of or having to do with loess: *loessial soil, loessial plains.*

**lo-fi** (lō′fī′), *adj., n. Informal.* —*adj.* of a standard or inferior quality of sound reproduction; not hi-fi: *the nation's strictly lo-fi TV sets* (Time).
—*n.* lo-fi sound, reproduction, or equipment.
[< *lo*(w)-*fi*(delity), patterned after *hi-fi*]

**loft** (lôft, loft), *n., v.* —*n.* **1** the space just below the roof in a cabin; attic: *Abe Lincoln slept in a loft as a boy.* **SYN**: garret. **2** the room under the roof of a barn: *This loft is full of hay.* **3** a gallery in a church or hall: *a choir loft.* **4** an upper floor of a business building or warehouse: *Many small businesses are located in the lofts of our large business buildings.* **5a** the backward slope of the face of a golf club. **b** a stroke that drives a golf ball upward. **c** the act of driving a golf ball upward. **6** *Bowling.* the throwing of the ball into the air so that it drops on the alley beyond the foul line. **7a** a pigeon house. **b** a flock of pigeons.
—*v.t.* **1** to throw or hit (a ball, stone, or other object) high in the air. **2a** to hit (a golf ball) high up, especially to clear an obstacle. **b** to slant back the face of (a golf club). **3** to throw (a bowling ball) into the air so that it drops on the alley beyond the foul line. **4** to launch into space: *The more I hear about the ... plan for lofting communications satellites into space in order to extend the scope of Educational TV broadcasting, the more I wish it ... well* (Michael Arlen). **5** to keep (pigeons) in a loft or flock. **6** *Obsolete.* **a** to build (a building) with a loft or upper story. **b** to store (goods) in a loft.
—*v.i.* **1** to throw or hit a ball, stone, or other object, high in the air. **2** to hit a golf ball high up. **3** to throw a bowling ball into the air so that it drops on the alley beyond the foul line.
[Old English *loft* sky, upper region < Scandinavian (compare Old Icelandic *lopt* air, sky; loft, upper room)]

**LOFT** (lôft, loft), *n.* low frequency radio telescope: *LOFT would be designed for observation at frequencies between 0.5 and 10 megahertz, a range that is reflected by the ionosphere and cannot be observed from the ground* (Science News).

**loft-bomb|ing** (lôft′bom′ing, loft′-), *n.* a method of releasing bombs while the bomber is rising almost vertically, causing the bomb to travel through a long arc and explode after the plane is safely out of range; over-the-shoulder bombing.

**loft|er** (lôf′tər, lof′-), *n.* = lofting iron.

**loft|i|ly** (lôf′tə lē, lof′-), *adv.* in a lofty manner.

**loft|i|ness** (lôf′tē nis, lof′-), *n.* lofty quality or condition.

**loft|ing** (lôf′ting, lof′-), *n.* **1** the action of throwing or hitting a ball, stone, or other object, high in the air. **2** a difficult shot in the game of marbles in which a player shoots in an arc through the air to hit a marble.

**lofting iron,** an iron golf club used to make the ball rise over an obstacle.

**loft|y** (lôf′tē, lof′-), *adj.,* **loft|i|er, loft|i|est.** **1** very high; towering: *lofty mountains.* **SYN**: tall. See syn. under **high**. **2** *Figurative.* exalted or dignified; grand: *lofty aims.* **SYN**: sublime, stately. **3** *Figurative.* proud; haughty; overweening: *a lofty sneer. He had a lofty contempt for others.* **SYN**: arrogant.

**log** (lôg, log), *n., adj., v.,* **logged, log|ging.** —*n.* **1** a length of wood just as it comes from the tree: *We burn logs in our fireplace.* **2a** the daily record of a ship's voyage, kept in a logbook: *The captain wrote the log each evening.* **b** a similar record of an airplane trip: *The log was never completed because the airplane crashed.* **c** a record of the operation or performance of an engine or other device. **d** any daily record of activity: *a log of meetings, a log of telephone calls. The Presidential log of this ... day started at two o'clock this morning* (Manchester Guardian Weekly). **3** a float for measuring the speed of a ship, such as a chip log or patent log: *A sailor threw the log overboard each day and the mate took the reading.*
—*adj.* made of logs: *a log house.*
—*v.i.* to cut down trees, cut them into logs, and move them out of the forest.
—*v.t.* **1** to cut (trees) into logs; cut down and trim (trees). **2** to cut down trees on (land). **3a** to enter in the log of a ship or airplane. **b** to enter name and offense of (a sailor) in a ship's log. **c** to keep in a daily record of activity. **4** to travel (a distance or length of time), especially as indicated by the rate of speed registered by a log: *One plane logged 150 hours in the sky between July 31 and August 15* (Wall Street Journal).
**log in,** to register, especially with a computer as an authorized operator: *The user gives his password ... and the machine logs him in and reports the number of seconds used by the central processor in the exchange* (Scientific American).
**sleep like a log,** to sleep soundly and heavily: *Exhausted by the day's activities, he slept like a log.*
[Middle English *logge;* origin uncertain] —**log′like′**, *adj.*

**log** (no period) or **log.,** logarithm.

**lo|gan|ber|ry** (lō′gən ber′ē), *n., pl.* **-ries.** **1** a large, purplish-red fruit of a bramble developed in California, from a cross between a blackberry and a red raspberry. **2** the plant it grows on. [American English < J. H. *Logan,* 1841-1928, an American jurist and horticulturist, who developed it + *berry*]

**lo|ga|ni|a|ceous** (lō gā′nē ā′shəs), *adj.* belonging to a family of tropical and subtropical dicotyledonous plants that includes the nux vomica, buddleia, and gelsemium. [< New Latin *Loganiaceae* the family name (< James *Logan,* an Irish botanist of the 1700's) + English *-ous*]

**log|an stone** (lôg′ən, log′-), a rock so balanced on its base that it rocks to and fro readily, as under pressure of the hand or of the wind; rocking stone. [perhaps imitative. Compare earlier *log* to rock to and fro.]

**log|a|oe|dic** (log′ə ē′dik), *adj., n.* —*adj.* of poetry: **1** composed of meter combining dactyls and trochees, or anapests and iambs, producing a movement somewhat suggestive of prose. **2** composed of any mixture of meters.
—*n.* a logaoedic verse.
[< Late Latin *logaoedicus* < Greek *logaoidikós* between prose and poetry < *lógos* speech (< *légein* speak) + *aoidē* song < *aeidein* sing]

***log|a|rithm** (lôg′ə riᴛʜ əm, log′-), *n. Mathematics.* **1** the power to which a fixed number or base (usually 10) must be raised in order to produce a given number. If the fixed number or base is 10, the logarithm of 1,000 is 3; the logarithm of 10,000 is 4; the logarithm of 100,000 is 5. *Abbr:* log (no period). **2** one of a system of such numbers used to shorten calculations in mathematics. [< New Latin *logarithmus* < Greek *lógos* proportion, calculation; word (< *légein* speak, select words) + *arithmós* a number]


***logarithm** definition 1

**log|a|rith|mic** (lôg′ə riᴛʜ′mik, log′-), *adj.* **1** of or having to do with a logarithm or logarithms. **2** that can be expressed in terms of a logarithm: *the logarithmic function y = log x.* —**log′a|rith′mi|cal|ly**, *adv.*

**log|a|rith|mi|cal** (lôg′ə riᴛʜ′mə kəl, log′-), *adj.* = logarithmic.

**log|book** (lôg′bu̇k′, log′-), *n.* **1** a book in which a daily record of a ship's voyage is kept. **2** a book for records of an airplane's trip. **3** a journal of travel or of any other activity.

**log chip,** thin piece of wood of a chip log. Also, **log ship.**

**loge** (lōzh), *n.* **1** a box in a theater or opera house. **2** a booth or stall, such as one at a fair. [< French *loge* < Old French. See etym. of doublets **lodge, lobby, loggia.**]

**log|gan stone** (lôg′ən, log′-), = logan stone.

**log|gats** or **log|gets** (log′əts), *n.* an old English game in which pieces of wood were thrown at a stake fixed into the ground, and the person throwing nearest to the stake won. [apparently a derivative of *log*]

**logged** (lôgd, logd), *adj.* **1** cut into logs, as trees. **2** cleared, as land by the cutting of timber. **3** inert or unwieldly, like a log. **4** = water-logged: *a logged vessel.* **5** = stagnant: *logged water.*

**log|ger¹** (lôg′ər, log′-), *n.* **1** a person whose work is logging; lumberjack: *Rains and late snows have kept loggers out of the woods* (Wall Street Journal). **2** a machine for loading or hauling logs, such as a donkey engine attached to a boom or a tractor to drag logs from the forest. **3** an electronic device that automatically records or logs physical processes and events. [< *log* + *-er¹*]

**log|ger²** (lôg′ər, log′-), *adj. Dialect.* thick, heavy, or stupid. [perhaps back formation < *loggerhead*]

**log|ger|head** (lôg′ər hed′, log′-), *n.* **1** a stupid person; blockhead. **2** Also, **loggerhead turtle.** a large-headed sea turtle of the tropical Atlantic and Pacific oceans. It is meat-eating. **3** an iron instrument with a long handle and a ball or bulb at the end, used, when heated in the fire, for melting pitch and for heating liquids. **4** an upright piece near the stern of a whaleboat, around which the harpoon line is passed. **5** Also, **loggerhead shrike.** a bluish-gray shrike of eastern North America, with a white breast, black-and-white wings and tail, and two black bars on the side of the head meeting at the forehead.
**at loggerheads,** at enmity; disputing: *The politicians and the generals were at loggerheads over the advisability of ever starting the business* (London Times).
[< *logger,* variant of *log* + *head*]

***log|gia** (loj′ə, loj′ē ə; lô′-; *Italian* lôd′jä), *n., pl.* **log|gias,** *Italian,* **log|gie** (lôd′jā). a gallery or arcade open to the air on at least one side. **SYN**: piazza. [< Italian *loggia* < Old French *loge.* See etym. of doublets **lodge, loge, lobby.**]

***loggia**

**log|ging** (lôg′ing, log′-), *n.* the work of cutting down trees, sawing them into logs, and moving the logs out of the forest: *Paul Bunyan is a legend of American logging.* [American English]

**log|i|a** (log′ē ə), *n.pl., sing.* **-i|on.** **1** the sayings or maxims attributed to a religious teacher or sage. **2** Often, **Logia.** the sayings of Jesus, especially those contained in collections supposed to have been among the sources of the present Gospels or those in the Agrapha, attributed to Jesus but not in the Bible. [< Greek *lógia,* plural of *lógion* oracle < *lógos* word]

**log|ic** (loj′ik), *n., adj.* —*n.* **1** the branch of philosophy dealing with the principles of reasoning and inference: **a** the science of proof: *Logic is not the science of Belief, but the science of Proof, or Evidence* (John Stuart Mill). **b** the science of reasoning: *The Grape that can with Logic absolute The Two-and-Seventy jarring Sects confute* (Edward FitzGerald). *Logic, or the science of the general principles of good and bad reasoning* (Adam Smith). **2a** a particular system or theory of logic: *The metaphysical logic of Hegel, the empirical logic of Mill, the formal logic of Kant* (Robert Adamson). **b** the science of reasoning as applied to some particular branch of knowledge or study: *The logic of taste, if I may be allowed the expression* (Edmund Burke). **3** a book on logic. **4a** the use of argument; reasoning: *Vociferated logic kills me quite* (William Cowper). *She could not cope with Lancelot's quaint logic* (Charles Kingsley). **b** a means of convincing or proving: *The logic of his argument persuaded us that he was right.* **5** reason; sound sense: *There is much logic in what he says.* **6** the logical outcome or effect; inevitable result: *The logic of events proved them wrong.* **7a** the nonarithmetical operations in a computer; logical operations. **b** the electronic circuitry performing such operations: *The computer logic is so fast that it has to loaf at several intervals while the input and output devices—the peripherals—are printing information* (New Yorker).
—*adj.* of or having to do with logical operations in a computer: *logic circuits, a logic element.*
**chop logic,** to exchange logical arguments and terms; bandy logic; argue: *A man must not presume to use his reason, unless he has studied the categories, and can chop logic* (Tobias Smollett).
[< Late Latin *logicē* < Greek *logikḗ* (*téchnē*) rea-

soning (art) < *lógos* word, idea < *légein* speak, select words]

**log|i|cal** (loj′ə kəl), *adj.* **1** having to do with logic; according to the principles of logic: *logical reasoning. The scientific quest is grounded in reason and logical inference from known facts* (John E. Owen). **2** reasonably expected; reasonable: *A failing grade was the logical result of his frequent absences from school. War was the logical consequence of these conditions.* SYN: consistent. **3** reasoning correctly or capable of reasoning correctly: *a logical man, a clear and logical mind.* SYN: rational, sound. —**log′i|cal|ly**, *adv.* —**log′i-cal|ness**, *n.*

**log|i|cal|i|ty** (loj′ə kal′ə tē), *n.* the quality of being logical; logicalness.

**logical operations**, the nonarithmetical operations in a computer, such as comparing, selecting, making references, matching, and sorting.

**logical positivism**, a philosophical school influenced by positivism and symbolic logic, that accepts as meaningful only the analytic propositions of logic and mathematics and propositions that can be verified by empirical procedures. —**logical positivist**

**lo|gi|cian** (lō jish′ən), *n.* an expert in logic.

**log|i|on** (log′ē on), *n.* singular of **logia**.

**lo|gis|tic** (lō jis′tik), *adj.* **1** of or having to do with logistics. **2** = logarithmic. **3** = sexagesimal. [< Medieval Latin *logisticus* < Greek *logistikós,* ultimately < *lógos* reckoning, reason] —**lo|gis′ti|cal-ly**, *adv.*

**lo|gis|ti|cal** (lō jis′tə kəl), *adj.* = logistic.

**lo|gis|ti|cian** (lō′jə stish′ən), *n.* an expert in logistics.

**lo|gis|tics** (lō jis′tiks), *n.* **1a** the art of planning and carrying out military movement, evacuation, and supply. **b** the planning and carrying out of any complex or large-scale operation or activity: *The logistics were staggering, and in fact, the trip was postponed several times before we finally got all the artists organized and together* (New Yorker). **2** the art of arithmetical calculation. [< French *logistique* (with English *-ics*) < Old French *logis* lodgement or *loger* to lodge; probably influenced by Old French *logistique* < Medieval Latin *logisticus;* see etym. under **logistic**]

**log|jam** (lôg′jam′, log′-), *n., v.,* **-jammed, -jam-ming.** —*n.* **1** the act or fact of blocking the downstream movement of logs, causing a jumbled overcrowding of the timber in the river. **2** a deadlock; delay; standstill: *The Yugoslavs might break the logjam that has stalled formal talks* (Wall Street Journal). **3** the act or fact of jamming; mass; congestion: *Yesterday's appointments and prospective appointments represented in part a break in a logjam of unfilled positions* (New York Times).
—*v.t., v.i.* **1** to crowd or block by crowding: *On the day of the sale customers logjammed the aisles of the store.* **2** to delay, obstruct, or block by confusion or overloading.

**log line**, the line attached to the float for measuring the speed of a ship.

**log|nor|mal** (lôg′nôr′məl, log′-), *adj.* having a normal or symmetrical logarithmic distribution: *Distributions that are not normal come in for genuine attention* (*although not enough time is spent on the lognormal case*) (Scientific American). [< *log* (arithm) + *normal*]

**log|o** (lôg′ō, log′ō), *n., pl.* **log|os.** = logotype.

**log|o|dae|da|ly** (lôg′ə dē′də lē, -ded′ə-; log′-), *n.* verbal legerdemain; a playing with words, as by passing from one meaning of them to another. [ultimately < Greek *lógos* word + *daídalos* skillfully wrought]

**log|o|gram** (lôg′ə gram, log′-), *n.* a single character or a combination of characters regarded as a unit, representing a whole word, as in shorthand. [< Greek *lógos* word + English *-gram*]

**log|o|gram|mat|ic** (lôg′ə grə mat′ik, log′-), *adj.* having to do with logograms.

**log|o|graph** (lôg′ə graf, -gräf; log′-), *n.* = logogram.

**log|o|graph|ic** (lôg′ə graf′ik, log′-), *adj.* **1** of or having to do with logography. **2** consisting of characters or signs each representing a single word. —**log′o|graph′i|cal|ly**, *adv.*

**log|o|graph|i|cal** (lôg′ə graf′ə kəl, log′-), *adj.* = logographic.

**lo|gog|ra|phy** (lō gog′rə fē), *n.* **1** *Printing.* the use of logotypes. **2** a former method of longhand reporting, in which several reporters each took down a few words in succession. **3** a system of writing that uses logographs (logograms). [< Greek *logographía* < *logográphos* speech-writer < *lógos* word, speech + *gráphein* write]

**log|o|griph** (lôg′ə grif, log′-), *n.* **1** an anagram, or a puzzle involving anagrams. **2** a puzzle in which a hidden word must be guessed from other words formed from its letters, these words often being themselves discovered by indirect clues, verse, or the like, as in a charade. [< Greek *lógos* word + *grîphos* riddle]

**log|o|mach|ic** (lôg′ə mak′ik, log′-), *adj.* of or given to logomachy.

**lo|gom|a|chist** (lō gom′ə kist), *n.* a person who contends about words; person who disputes about verbal subtleties.

**lo|gom|a|chy** (lō gom′ə kē), *n., pl.* **-chies.** contention about words or in words only. **2** a game, similar to anagrams, in which words are formed from single letters. [< Greek *logomachíā* < *lógos* word + *máchēa* fight, contest < *máchesthai* to fight]

**log|o|pe|dics** (lôg′ə pē′diks, log′-), *n.* the study, analysis, and treatment of defective speech. [< Greek *lógos* word + (ortho)*pedics* ]

**log|or|rhe|a** (lôg′ə rē′ə, log′-), *n.* **1** the habit of talking too much. **2** a great flow of words. **3** excessive volubility accompanying some forms of insanity. [< Greek *lógos* word + *rheîn* to flow]

**log|or|rhe|ic** (lôg′ə rē′ik, log′-), *adj.* characterized by logorrhea; excessively talkative.

**Log|os** (log′os), *n.* **1** *Theology.* Jesus, the Word of God; the second person of the Trinity; the revelation of God to men (in the Bible, John 1:1-18). **2** Also, **logos**. *Philosophy.* mind or reason as a universal principle. [< Greek *lógos* word, discourse; (active principles of) reason < *légein* say, select words]

**log|o|thete** (lôg′ə thēt, log′-), *n.* one of the administrative officials of the Byzantine Empire. [< Greek *logothétēs* one who audits accounts < *lógos* word; account + *the-*, stem of *tithénai* to set (down)]

**log|o|type** (lôg′ə tīp, log′-), *n.* **1** *Printing.* a single type on which two or more letters are cast (but not connected), to facilitate the printing of combinations frequently used, as *Co.* **2** a trademark or other figure frequently associated with an enterprise: *KLM changed the sloping diagonal lines of its trademark, or logotype, to horizontal ones because they gave a greater feeling of security* (Listener). [< Greek *lógos* word + English *type*]

**log|o|typ|y** (lôg′ə tī′pē, log′-), *n.* = logography.

**log perch**, the largest of the darters, about six to eight inches long, found in the streams and lakes to the south and east of Lake Superior.

**log pond**, a pond of water next to a sawmill, in which logs are stored before entering the mill.

**log reel**, the reel by which a float for measuring the speed of a ship is unwound.

**log|roll** (lôg′rōl′, log′-), *Informal.* —*v.t.* to get (a bill) passed by logrolling.
—*v.i.* to take part in logrolling.
[American English; back formation < *logrolling*] —**log′roll′er**, *n.*

**log|roll|ing** (lôg′rō′ling, log′-), *n.* **1** the act of giving political aid in return for a like favor, especially in order to pass legislation: *Our logrolling, our stumps and their politics . . . are yet unsung* (Emerson). **2a** the act of rolling floating logs, especially by treading on them. It is a sport often engaged in by lumberjacks, in which two men standing on a floating log try to upset each other by spinning the log with their feet. **b** a gathering at which lumberjacks roll logs, either to move them to a required place or for sport. [American English; earlier, a gathering of neighbors to help someone clear land < *log* + *rolling*]

**log rule**, **1** a table showing the amount of lumber that can be cut from logs of various sizes. **2** a graduated stick for measuring the diameters of logs.

**log ship**, = log chip.

**log|way** (lôg′wā′, log′-), *n.* a gangway for logs.

**log|wood** (lôg′wůd′, log′-), *n.* **1** the heavy, hard, brownish-red wood of a tropical American tree, used in dyeing. **2** the tree itself. It belongs to the pea family.

**lo|gy** (lō′gē), *adj.,* **-gi|er, -gi|est.** heavy, sluggish, or dull. SYN: lethargic. Also, **loggy.** [Compare Dutch *log* heavy, dull]

**-logy**, *combining form.* **1** doctrine, study, or science of: *Biology = the science of life.*
**2** speech or discussion, as in *tautology, eulogy.*
**3** special meanings, as in *analogy, tetralogy, anthology.*
[< Greek *-logíā,* sometimes < *lógos* a discourse, but mainly < *lógos* one treating of < *légein* speak (of), recount]

**Lo|hen|grin** (lō′ən grin), *n. German Legend.* a knight of the Holy Grail and son of Parsifal.

**loi** (no periods), lunar orbit insertion.

**loi-ca|dre** (lwä′kä′drə), *n.* a law providing a framework for the gradual establishment of home rule in a territory, protectorate, or other district that is striving for self-government, especially in the French Community. [< French *loi-cadre* (literally) law framework]

**loid** (loid), *n., v. Slang.* —*n.* a strip of celluloid used by a burglar to push back the bolt of a spring lock. —*v.t.* to unlock (a door) with a loid. [< (cellu)*loid*]

**loin** (loin), *n.* a piece of meat from the front and upper part of a hindquarter, without the flank: *a loin of pork.*

**gird (up) one's loins**, to get ready for action: *With the electricity dispute* (*more or less*) *out of the way the Government is girding its loins as other public sector workers come knocking loudly on the door* (Manchester Guardian Weekly).

**loins, a** the part of the body between the ribs and the hipbones. The loins are on both sides of the backbone and nearer to it than the flanks. **b** this part of the body, especially the pelvic or pubic area, regarded as the seat of physical strength and generative power: *Kings shall come out of thy loins* (Genesis 35:11).
[< Old French *loigne* < Vulgar Latin *lumbea* < Latin *lumbus*]

**loin|cloth** (loin′klôth′, -kloth′), *n.* a piece of cloth worn around the hips and between the thighs by natives, especially men, of warm countries, often as the only garment.

**loin guard**, the part of a suit of armor which protects the loins.

**loi|ter** (loi′tər), *v.i.* **1** to linger idly; stop along the way: *She loitered along the street, looking into all the shop windows.* SYN: delay, tarry, lag, dawdle. See syn. under **linger.** **2** to waste time in idleness; idle; loaf. —*v.t.* to spend (time) idly: *to loiter the hours away.* [< Dutch *leuteren* be loose, erratic; shake, totter] —**loi′ter|er**, *n.* —**loi′-ter|ing|ly**, *adv.*

**Lo|ki** (lō′kē), *n.* the Norse god of destruction and mischief, the brother of Odin. Because he caused the death of Balder he was chained to a rock where he must remain to the end of the world, when he will break loose and fight with the giants against the gods.

**Lok Sab|ha** (lôk sub′hä), the lower house of the parliament of India: *The parliament consists of the Lok Sabha* (*House of the People*) *and the Rajya Sabha* (*Council of States*) (R. I. Crane).

**lol|i|gin|id** (lol′ə jin′id) *adj.* of or belonging to a family of long-bodied cylindrical squids. [< New Latin *Loliginidae* the family name < Latin *lōlīgo, -inis* cuttlefish]

**loll** (lol), *v., n.* —*v.i.* **1** to recline or lean in a lazy manner; *to loll on a sofa.* **2** to hang loosely or droop; dangle: *A dog's tongue lolls out in hot weather. . . . babies with their little round heads lolling forward* (George Eliot). —*v.t.* to allow to hang or droop: *A dog lolls out his tongue.*
—*n.* **1** the act of lolling. **2** a person or thing that lolls.
[Middle English *lollen.* Compare Dutch *lollen* loll.] —**loll′er**, *n.*

**lol|la|pa|loo|sa** (lol′ə pə lü′zə), *n. U.S. Slang.* a very striking person or remarkable thing; corker. [origin uncertain]

**Lol|lard** (lol′ərd), *n.* one of the followers of John Wycliffe's religious teachings from the late 1300's to the early 1400's; Wycliffite. The Lollards advocated certain religious, political, and economic reforms, and were persecuted as heretics. [< Middle Dutch *lollaerd* mumbler < *lollen* mumble]

**Lol|lard|ism** (lol′ərd iz əm), *n.* the beliefs and practices of the Lollards.

**Lol|lard|ry** (lol′ərd rē), *n.* = Lollardism.

**lol|li|pop** or **lol|ly|pop** (lol′ē pop), *n.* **1** a piece of hard candy, usually on the end of a small stick. **2** *British.* a pole with a stop sign, used by a crossing guard to stop traffic. [origin uncertain]

**lol|lop** (lol′əp), *v.i.,* **-loped, -lop|ing.** *Informal.* **1** to lounge or sprawl; lounge indolently. **2** to bob up and down; go with clumsy movements. [< *loll* + *-op,* as in *wallop*]

**lol|ly** (lol′ē), *n., pl.* **-lies.** *British.* **1** a lollipop. **2** *Slang.* money.

**lol|ly|gag** (lol′ē gag), *v.i.,* **-gagged, -gag|ging.** *U.S. Slang.* to while away time idly.

**Lom|bard** (lom′bärd, -bərd; lum′-), *n., adj.* —*n.* **1** a member of a Germanic tribe which in A.D. 568 invaded Italy. The Lombards settled in the part of northern Italy since known as Lombardy. **2** a native or inhabitant of Lombardy. **3** *Obsolete.* **a** a native of Lombardy engaged as a banker, moneychanger, or pawnbroker. **b** any person carrying on any of these businesses.
—*adj.* of or having to do with the Lombards or Lombardy; Lombardic. Also, **Longobard.**
[< Old French *lombard* < Italian *lombardo* < Late Latin *Langobardus* < Germanic elements meaning "long beard"]

**Lom|bar|dic** (lom bär′dik), *adj.* = Lombard.

**Lombard Street**, the London money market or financiers. [< *Lombard* Street, London, famous as a financial center]

**Lom|bard|y poplar** (lom′bər dē, lum′-), a tall, slender poplar with branches that curve upward.

**Pronunciation Key:** hat, āge, cãre, fär; let, ēqual, tėrm; it, īce; hot, ōpen, ôrder; oil, out; cup, pu̇t, rüle; child; long; thin; ᴛʜen; zh, measure; ə represents **a** in about, **e** in taken, **i** in pencil, **o** in lemon, **u** in circus.

It is often planted along roads and drives.
**Lom|bro|sian** (lom brō′zhən), *adj.* of or having to do with the theories and methods of Cesare Lombroso (1836-1909), who believed in the existence of a criminal type.
**lo|ment** (lō′ment), *n. Botany.* a leguminous fruit which is contracted in the spaces between the seeds, breaking up when mature into one-seeded segments, as in the tick trefoil. [Middle English *lomente* bean meal < Latin *lōmentum;* see etym. under **lomentum**]
**lo|men|ta|ceous** (lō′mən tā′shəs), *adj. Botany.* **1** of or like a loment. **2** bearing loments.
**lo|men|tum** (lō men′təm), *n., pl.* **-ta** (-tə). *Botany.* a loment. [< Latin *lōmentum* bean meal; a cleansing mixture made of it < a stem related to *-luere,* and *lavāre* to wash]
**lo|mi salmon** (lō′mē), a Hawaiian dish of salmon kneaded with the fingers, mixed with onions, and seasoned. [< Hawaiian *lomi* knead, mash]
**lon.**, longitude.
**Lon|don broil** (lun′dən), broiled flank steak cut into thin diagonal slices.
**Lon|don|er** (lun′də nər), *n.* a native or inhabitant of London, England.
**London plane tree**, a large shade tree that is a cross between a buttonwood and another species of plane tree. It is commonly grown along city streets because of its resistance to air pollution and drought.
**London smoke**, a dark, dull gray color.
**lone** (lōn), *adj., n.* —*adj.* **1** without others; alone; solitary: *The lone traveler was glad to reach home. The explorer was the lone survivor of his expedition to the North Pole.* **SYN:** single. **2** lonesome; lonely: *They lived a lone life after their children grew up and moved away. The lone nights are the worst.* **3** single or widowed: *a poor lone woman* (Shakespeare). **4a** standing apart; isolated: *a lone house.* **b** lonely; unfrequented: *Bokhara and lone Khiva in the waste* (Matthew Arnold).
—*n.* **Lone**, **1** a member of the Girl Guides of Canada who is physically disabled or lives in a remote area and cannot attend troop meetings. **2** a member of the Boy Scouts of America who has no group near him.
[variant of *alone*]
**lone|li|ly** (lōn′lə lē), *adv.* in a lonely manner.
**lone|li|ness** (lōn′lē nis), *n.* the condition or the feeling of being lonely; solitude.
**lone|ly** (lōn′lē), *adj.,* **-li|er, -li|est,** *n.* —*adj.* **1** feeling oneself alone and longing for company or friends; lonesome: *He was lonely while his brother was away. Now a lonely man Wifeless and heirless* (Tennyson). **2** without many people; desolate: *a lonely road, a lonely spot, lonely seas.* **SYN:** secluded. **3a** alone; isolated: *a lonely tree.* **b** unaccompanied; solitary: *I go alone, Like to a lonely dragon, that his fen Makes fear'd and talk'd of more than seen* (Shakespeare).
—*n.* **1** a lonely person. **2** = loner.
**lonely hearts**, unmarried persons who seek to meet eligible members of the opposite sex by consulting matchmakers, joining special clubs, or advertising in newspaper personal columns: *In a bouncy, daffy romantic ... musical, matchmaker Carol Channing juggles lonely hearts and sassily wangles one for herself* (Time).
**lone|ness** (lōn′nis), *n.* = loneliness.
**lon|er** (lō′nər), *n. Informal.* **1** a person who is or prefers to be alone; one who lives or works alone: *the loners who like to listen to music in solitude, the professional loner.* **2** an independent person: *a political loner.*
**lone|some** (lōn′səm), *adj.,* **-som|er, -som|est,** *n.* —*adj.* **1** feeling lonely or forlorn: *The lonesome sailor was all alone in a strange town far across the sea from his home.* **2** making one feel lonely: *a lonesome journey.* **3** unfrequented; desolate: *a lonesome road.* **4** solitary: *One lonesome pine stood in the yard.*
—*n. Informal.* **one's lonesome**, oneself: *He is sitting home all by his lonesome.*
—**lone′some|ly,** *adv.* —**lone′some|ness,** *n.*
**Lone Star State**, a nickname for Texas (from the single star on its flag and seal).
**lone wolf**, **1** *Informal.* **a** a person who works or prefers to work alone: *More than most of today's scientists, she is a lone wolf investigator, living for the excitement of finding things out* (Atlantic). **b** a person who remains to himself, especially in opinions: *He is obviously not an individualist or a lone wolf* (New Scientist). **2** a wolf that lives and hunts alone.
**long¹** (lông, long), *adj.,* **long|er, long|est,** *adv., n.* —*adj.* **1a** that measures much, or more than usual, from end to end in space or time: *a long distance, a long speech, a long list. An inch is short; a mile is long. A year is a long time. He told a long story.* **SYN:** extended, prolonged. **b** having a long, narrow, or thin shape: *a long board. Like all lank men, my long friend had an appetite of his own* (Herman Melville). **c** continuing too long; lengthy; tedious: *long hours of waiting.* **SYN:** extended, prolonged. **d** beyond the normal quantity: *a long dozen.* **2** in length; having a specified length in space or time or in a series: *two hours long, a speech five pages long. My table is three feet long.* **3** *Figurative.* extending to a great distance in space or time; far-reaching: *a long memory, a long look ahead.* **4** involving considerable risk, liability to error, or possibility of failure: *a long chance.* **5** (of vowels or syllables) taking a comparatively long time to speak; like *a* in *late, e* in *be,* or *o* in *note: In American English "e" is usually longer in "pen" than in "pet".* **6a** well supplied (with some commodity): *long in salt.* **b** depending on a rise in prices for profit. **7** *Especially Law.* (of a date) distant; remote.
—*adv.* **1** for its whole length: *all night long.* **2** for a long time: *a reform long advocated. I can't stay long.* **3** at a point of time far distant from the time indicated: *long since. It happened long before you were born.*
—*n.* **1** a long time: *I am going away but not for long.* **2** a long sound or syllable. **3** a size of garment for people who are taller than average. **4** a person who buys or holds more goods or stock than he needs, generally depending on a rise in prices for profit.
**as** (or **so**) **long as**, provided that: *As long as that's the case, we'll go.*
**before long**, soon; in a short time: *Summer will come before long.*
**long on**, well furnished or highly endowed with: *... prancing about in an English comedy that is long on eccentricity and short on wit* (New Yorker). *Most advertising today is long on the big promise* (Harper's).
**the long and the short of it**, the sum total (of something); substance; upshot: *The long and the short of it ... is that you must pay me this money* (Walter Besant).
[Old English *lang*]
**long²** (lông, long), *v.i.* to wish very much; desire greatly: *He longed for his mother. She longed to see him. I long'd so heartily then and there, To give him the grasp of fellowship* (Tennyson). **SYN:** yearn, crave. [Old English *langian* < *lang* long¹]
**long³** (lông, long), *adj. Dialect.* along.
**long⁴** (lông, long), *v.i.* **1** *Archaic.* to be fitting; be appropriate to: *... such feast as 'longed unto a mighty king* (William Morris). **2** *Obsolete.* to be the property or rightful possession; belong. [short for Old English *gelang* at hand, dependent on]
**long.**, longitude.
**long-a|go** (lông′ə gō′, long′-), *adj., n.* —*adj.* that has long gone by; that belongs to the distant past: *Hiroshima today is obsessed by that long-ago mushroom cloud* (Time).
—*n.* the distant past or its events: *Time is always apt to paint the long-ago in fresh colours* (Augustus Hare).
**lon|gan** (long′gən), *n.* **1** a Chinese evergreen tree of the soapberry family, related to the litchi and bearing a similar but smaller and less palatable fruit. **2** its fruit. Also, **lungan.** [< Cantonese *lung-ngan* (literally) dragon's eye]
**lon|ga|nim|i|ty** (long′gə nim′ə tē), *n.* long-suffering; forbearance or patience, as under provocation. [< Latin *longanimitās* < *longanimus* patient < *longus* long + *animus* mind]
**lon|gan|i|mous** (long gan′ə məs), *adj.* long-suffering; patient.
**long|beard** (lông′bird′, long′-), *n.* **1** a man with a long beard. **2** = bellarmine. **3** = Spanish moss.
**long-billed curlew** (lông′bild′, long′-), a curlew of western North America, about two feet long, with a short, rounded tail, and very long, decurved bill.
**long-billed marsh wren**, a wren of eastern and central North America with a long, slightly curved bill, that nests among reeds and cattails in marshes.
**long|boat** (lông′bōt′, long′-), *n.* the largest and strongest boat carried by a sailing ship.
**long|bow** (lông′bō′, long′-), *n.* a large bow drawn by hand, for shooting a long, feathered arrow.
**draw** (or **pull**) **the longbow**, *Informal.* to tell exaggerated stories: *At speaking truth perhaps they are less clever, But draw the longbow better now than ever* (Byron).
**long|bow|man** (lông′bō′mən, long′-), *n., pl.* **-men.** an archer who uses a longbow.
**long|case clock** (lông′kās′, long′-), *British.* a grandfather clock.
**long-chain** (lông′chān′, long′-), *adj.* consisting of or denoting molecules containing a long chain of atoms: *The nucleic acids* (*known as DNA and RNA*) [*are*] *long-chain molecules* (Scientific American).
**long clam** = soft clam.
**long|cloth** (lông′klôth′, long′kloth′), *n.* a kind of fine, soft, cotton cloth, often used for underwear.
**long-day plant** (lông′dā′, long′-), a plant that flowers only when exposed to light for a relatively long period of time each day.
**long distance**, an operator or exchange that takes care of long-distance calls.
**long-dis|tance** (lông′dis′təns, long′-), *adj., adv., v.,* **-tanced, -tanc|ing.** —*adj.* **1** of or having to do with telephone service to another town, city, or other place out of one's area: *a long-distance call from Chicago to Los Angeles.* **2** for or over great distances: *a long-distance moving van.*
—*adv.* **1** by long-distance telephone: *She called us long-distance from Hawaii to tell us she was coming to New York to visit us.* **2** over a great distance: *They ship the cars long-distance by freight.*
—*v.t.* to call by long distance: *As soon as he reached the hotel, he long-distanced his wife.*
[American English < phrase *long distance telephone*]
**long division**, a method of dividing numbers in which each step of the division is written out. It is used to divide large numbers. See picture under **division**.
**long dog**, = lurcher (def. 1).
**long dozen**, = thirteen.
**long-drawn** (lông′drôn′, long′-), *adj.* lasting a long time; prolonged to great length: *a long-drawn tale, a long-drawn scream.*
**long-drawn-out** (lông′drôn′out′, long′-), *adj.* = long-drawn.
**longe** (lunj), *n., v.,* **longed, longe|ing.** = lunge².
**long-eared** (lông′ird′, long′-), *adj.* **1** having long ears or earlike parts. **2** *Figurative.* asinine.
**long-eared owl**, a crow-sized owl with long ear tufts, found in woodlands of temperate North America.
**lon|ge|ron** (lon′jər ən; *French* lônzh rôn′), *n.* one of the main longitudinal stays or metal girders of an airplane, found especially in the fuselage and nacelle. It is heavier than a stringer. [< French *longéron*]
**lon|geur** (lông gėr′), *n.* = longueur.
**lon|ge|val** (lon jē′vəl), *adj.* living to a great age; long-lived. [< Latin *longaevus* long-lived + English *-al*¹]
**lon|gev|i|ty** (lon jev′ə tē), *n.* **1** long life: *Good eating habits promote longevity. ... a medicine that shall preserve him ... until the utmost term of patriarchal longevity* (Hawthorne). **2** length or duration of life: *the average longevity of human beings.* **3** length or duration of service. [< Latin *longaevitās* < *longaevus* long-lived < *longus* long + *aevum* age]
**lon|ge|vous** (lon jē′vəs), *adj.* = longeval. [< Latin *longaevus* (with English *-ous*)]
**long face**, a sad or unhappy expression: *"You people always skate out on ice with long faces, ready to lose"* (New Yorker).
**long green**, *U.S. Slang.* paper money.
**long gun**, *U.S.* a rifle or shotgun: *The bill would require all persons owning or buying long guns to obtain a license from a new Firearms Control Board and to register them* (New York Times).
**long|hair** (lông′hãr′, long′-), *n., adj. Slang.* —*n.* **1** a person who enjoys, performs, or composes classical music: *The ... radio network has a scheme for attracting longhairs: a chain of classical-music stations to extend from Virginia to Maine* (Time). **2** an intellectual: *Such current terms as "longhair" and "egghead," he felt, were contributing factors to the U.S.'s inability to obtain good teachers and scientists* (Newsweek). **3** a person wearing long hair, especially a male hippie: *Rampaging hardhats ... have been hunting down longhairs in the canyons of downtown Manhattan* (New York Times).
—*adj.* classical or intellectual; long-haired: *longhair music, longhair literature.*
**longhair cat**, a breed of domestic cat that is a crossbreed of a Persian cat and an Angora cat.
**long-haired** (lông′hãrd′, long′-), *adj.* **1** having long hair: *The long-haired animals come from tropical Africa* (Science News Letter). **2** *Slang.* **a** intellectual: *... long-haired idealists* (New Yorker). *Industry and business were not concerned with these preoccupations of the long-haired scientist* (Science News Letter). **b** enjoying, performing, or composing classical music.
**long|hand** (lông′hand′, long′-), *n.* ordinary handwriting, not shorthand or typewriting: *We were always a week or two behind when we worked by longhand* (Wall Street Journal).
**long haul**, **1** the transportation of goods over relatively great distances. **2** *Figurative.* any difficult activity extending over a long period of time: *We have a long haul in front of us, and not just a short spurt* (London Times).
**for** (or **over**) **the long haul**, *Informal.* in the long run: *But executives are almost unanimous in contending that over the long haul it's better business ...* (Wall Street Journal).
**long-haul** (lông′hôl′, long′-), *adj.* **1** of or having to do with long hauls: *long-haul truckers, long-*

*haul air routes.* **2** *Figurative.* extending over a long period of time; long-run: *long-haul opportunities, long-haul strategy.*

**long|head** (lôngʹhed′, longʹ-), *n.* **1** a person having a long head; dolichocephalic person. **2** a head whose breadth is less than four-fifths of its length.

**long-head|ed** (lôngʹhedʹid, longʹ-), *adj.* **1** having a long head; dolichocephalic. **2** *Figurative.* shrewd; far-sighted: *a long-headed deal; long-headed customers* (Dickens). *That's a short-handed way of expressing a long-headed idea* (Newsweek). — **longʹ-headʹed|ness,** *n.*

**long-hop** (lôngʹhop′, longʹ-), *n. Cricket.* a ball that hits the ground, bounces, and then travels some distance before reaching the batsman or wicketkeeper.

**long|horn** (lôngʹhôrn′, longʹ-), *n.* any cow of a breed that has very long horns and was raised for beef; Texas longhorn. They were formerly common in the southwestern United States and Mexico and descended from Spanish stock.

**long-horned beetle** (lôngʹhôrnd′, longʹ-), any wood-boring beetle of a group with extremely long, heavy antennae, injurious to trees, shrubs, and wooden lawn furniture.

**long-horned grasshopper**, any grasshopper of a group with antennae as long as the body, including the katydid and others that cause heavy damage to crops.

**long horse**, a side horse having one end curved upwards for vaulting.

**long house**, a large communal dwelling of certain North American Indians, especially the Iroquois, and various tribal societies in southeastern Asia, Borneo, New Guinea, and elsewhere. Many families live together in one long, usually rectangular, house.

**long hundredweight**, the British hundredweight, equal to 112 pounds.

**lon|gi|corn** (lonʹjə kôrn), *adj., n.* —*adj.* **1** having long antennae. **2** of or belonging to a family of beetles that often have very long antennae.
—*n.* = long-horned beetle.
[< Latin *longus* long + *cornū* horn]

**long|ies** (lôngʹēz, longʹ-), *n.pl.* **1** long underwear. **2** long winter pants for boys.

**long|ing** (lôngʹing, longʹ-), *n., adj.* —*n.* earnest desire: *a longing for home; the restless, unsatisfied longing* (Longfellow). **SYN:** craving, yearning, pining. See syn. under **desire.**
—*adj.* having or showing earnest desire: *a child's longing look at a window full of toys.* — **longʹing|ly,** *adv.*

**lon|gi|pen|nate** (lonʹjə penʹāt), *adj.* having long wings. [< Latin *longus* long + English *pennate*]

**long iron**, a golf club with a steel head inclined at a relatively small angle to its long shaft, suitable for low, long-distance shots.

**long|ish** (lôngʹish, longʹ-), *adj.* somewhat long.

***lon|gi|tude** (lonʹjə tüd, -tyüd), *n.* **1a** distance east or west on the earth's surface, measured in degrees from a certain meridian (line from the North to the South Pole). Usually the meridian through Greenwich, England, is used. **b** *Astronomy.* celestial longitude. **c** = galactic longitude. *Abbr:* long., lon. **2** *Humorous, Figurative.* length: *a rusty sword of immense longitude* (Hawthorne).
[< Latin *longitūdō, -inis* length < *longus* long]

***longitude**
definition 1a

**earth:**

North Pole
90°W. 0° 90°E.
South Pole

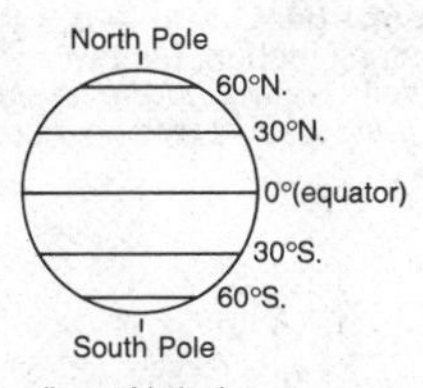


**lines of longitude** (meridians)

lines of latitude (parallels)

**lon|gi|tu|di|nal** (lonʹjə tüʹdə nəl, -tyüʹ-), *adj.* **1** of length; in length: *longitudinal measurements.* **2** running lengthwise: *The flag of the United States has longitudinal stripes.* **3** of longitude: *The longitudinal difference between New York and San Francisco is about 50 degrees.* — **lon′gi-tuʹdi|nal|ly,** *adv.*

**longitudinal wave**, *Physics.* a wave in which individual particles of a medium move back and forth in the same direction the wave moves (distinguished from a *transverse wave* in which they move across the direction of wave motion); compression wave.

**long johns** (jonz), *U.S. Slang.* long, warm underwear: *Everyone wore long johns, ate porridge and preserves, and kids were so lovingly bundled up they couldn't move* (Maclean's).

**long jump**, = broad jump.

**long|leaf pine**, or **long|leaf** (lôngʹlēf′, longʹ-), *n.* **1** a pine tree of the southeastern United States, with very long needles; Georgia pine. It is an important source of tar, pitch, turpentine, and resin, and its hard, durable, reddish wood is much used in shipbuilding and construction. **2** its wood.

**long-leg|ged** (lôngʹlegʹid, longʹ-), *adj.* having long legs.

**long|legs** (lôngʹlegz′, longʹ-), *n.* **1** a long-legged person or animal. **2** a daddy longlegs.

**long-line fishing** (lôngʹlīn′, longʹ-), = long-lining.

**long-lin|er** (lôngʹlīʹnər, longʹ-), *n.* **1** a person who engages in long-lining: *Some fishermen fear that long-liners are depleting the stock of swordfish* (New York Times). **2** a fishing boat used in long-lining.

**long-lin|ing** (lôngʹlīʹning, longʹ-), *n.* a form of fishing using a very long fish line with many baited hooks; long-line fishing.

**long-lived** (lôngʹlīvdʹ, -livdʹ; longʹ-), *adj.* living or lasting a long time: *long-lived legends. Strontium-90 is a long-lived element* (Science News Letter). — **longʹ-livedʹness,** *n.*

**long|ly** (lôngʹlē, longʹ-), *adv.* at or to a great or considerable length.

**long measure**, = linear measure.

**long moss**, = Spanish moss.

**long|ness** (lôngʹnis, longʹ-), *n.* = length.

**long|nose gar** (lôngʹnōz′, longʹ-), a North American gar with extremely long jaws, used in preying upon other fish.

**Lon|go|bard** (longʹgə bärd), *n., adj.* = Lombard.

**Lon|go|bar|di** (longʹgə bärʹdī), *n.pl.* Lombards.

**Lon|go|bar|dic** (longʹgə bärʹdik), *adj.* = Lombard.

**long-pe|ri|od variable** (lôngʹpirʹē əd, longʹ-), a variable star whose period from one peak of brightness to the next is over 100 days.

**long pig**, a human body (from the words used by cannibals of the South Seas).

**long|play** (lôngʹplā′, longʹ-), *n.* = long-playing record.

**long-play|er** (lôngʹplāʹər, longʹ-), *n.* **1** = long-playing record. **2** a phonograph that plays long-playing records.

**long-play|ing record** (lôngʹplāʹing, longʹ-), **1** a phonograph record playing at 33⅓ revolutions per minute. A long-playing record 12 inches in diameter provides about 25 minutes of sound on each side. **2** any phonograph record that plays at less than 33⅓ revolutions per minute, but especially at 16 or 8 revolutions.

**long primer**, a size of printing type (10 point).

**long-pull** (lôngʹpu̇lʹ, longʹ-), *adj. Informal.* long-term; long-range: *long-pull prospects.*

**long-range** (lôngʹrānjʹ, longʹ-), *adj.* **1a** looking ahead; prospective; future: *long-range plans. In the decade since World War II the U.S. has found itself assuming, ... partly as a matter of long-range policy, responsibility for aid to peoples all around the globe* (Scientific American). **b** of or for a long period; long-term: *long-range effects, long-range returns, a long-range trend toward inflation.* **2** having a long range; covering a great distance: *long-range airliners, a long-range ballistic missile.*

**long-run** (lôngʹrunʹ, longʹ-), *adj.* **1** happening or continuing over a long period of time; occurring after a long period of time: *long-run developments, a long-run play, a long-run objective.* **2** maturing over a long period of time: *long-run securities.*

**long|shanks** (lôngʹshangks′, longʹ-), *n.* **1** a long-legged person. **2** = stilt (def. 3).

**long ship**, a swift, narrow vessel up to 80 feet long, used by the Vikings between the 700's and the late 1000's.

**long|shore** (lôngʹshôr′, longʹ-; -shōr′), *adj.* **1** existing, found, or employed along the shore: *longshore fisheries, longshore laborers.* **2** of or having to do with the waterfront or with longshoremen: *a longshore union. The recent longshore dispute ... resulted in what was regarded by unionists as a favorable contract* (Wall Street Journal). [< *alongshore*]

**long|shore|man** (lôngʹshôrʹmən, longʹ-; -shōrʹ-), *n., pl.* **-men.** a man whose work is loading and unloading ships; stevedore.

**long|shor|ing** (lôngʹshôrʹing, longʹ-; -shōrʹ-), *n.* the work of loading and unloading ships: *Longshoring ... remains a high hazard industry* (New York Times).

**long shot**, *Informal.* **1** an attempt at something difficult. **2** anything, such as a venture, experiment, racehorse or other contestant or candidate, unlikely to succeed but rewarding if it should: *to bet on a long shot. I made the first test very simple, because the whole idea seemed a long shot* (Scientific American).
**not by a long shot**, not at all: *This one is not as good as the other by a long shot. He couldn't count on making it—not by a long shot* (New Yorker).

**long-sight|ed** (lôngʹsīʹtid, longʹ-), *adj.* **1** seeing distant things more clearly than near ones; far-sighted. **2** *Figurative.* having foresight; wise: *Her long-sighted notion of a society not solely based on war and agriculture ...* (Manchester Guardian). — **longʹ-sightʹed|ness,** *n.*

**long|some** (lôngʹsəm, longʹ-), *adj. Archaic.* long; lengthy; tedious: *the way there was a little longsome* (Robert Louis Stevenson).

**long|spur** (lôngʹspėr′, longʹ-), *n.* any of certain finches having long hind claws, found in northern climates, as the Lapland longspur.

**long-stand|ing** (lôngʹstanʹding, longʹ-), *adj.* having lasted for a long time: *a long-standing feud, a long-standing friendship.*

**long-sta|ple** (lôngʹstāʹpəl, longʹ-), *n.* = long-staple cotton.

**long-staple cotton**, cotton with fibers averaging more than 1⅛ inches in length.

**long-stop** (lôngʹstop′, longʹ-), *n.* **1** *Cricket.* a fielder who stands behind the wicketkeeper to stop balls that pass him. **2** *British, Figurative.* a person or thing that serves to hold back or prevent something undesirable: *Session after session major Bills are sent to the Lords so late that the peers cannot be expected to act as efficient long-stops* (London Times).

**long-suf|fer|ance** (lôngʹsufʹər əns, longʹ-), *n. Archaic.* long-suffering.

**long-suf|fer|ing** or **long|suf|fer|ing** (lôngʹsufʹər ing, -sufʹring; longʹ-), *adj., n.* —*adj.* enduring trouble, pain, or injury long and patiently: *Various were the excesses committed by the insubordinate troops ... upon the long-suffering inhabitants* (John L. Motley).
—*n.* long and patient endurance of trouble, pain, or injury: *Put on therefore, as the elect of God ... humbleness of mind, meekness, longsuffering* (Colossians 3:12).

**long suit**, **1** the suit in card games in which one has most cards. **2** *Figurative.* a strong point: *Patience is his long suit. Frankly, I discount the wisdom of the elder generation unless it comes from their long suit—experience* (Harper's).

**long sweetening**, *U.S. Dialect.* molasses.

**long-tailed jaeger** (lôngʹtāldʹ), a jaeger of arctic regions with a long forked tail.

**long-tailed tit**, a common titmouse with plumage of black, white, and pink, found in parts of Europe, Africa, and Asia.

**long-tailed weasel**, a large brown weasel with a white body and long black-tipped tail, common from Central America to the Arctic.

**long-term** (lôngʹtėrm′, longʹ-), *adj.* **1** of or for a long period of time: *long-term goals.* **2** falling due after a long time: *a long-term loan.*

**long-term bond** or **note**, a bond or note that will not be redeemed for two years or more.

**long-term|er** (lôngʹtėrʹmər, longʹ-), *n.* a person who is serving a long prison term.

**long-time** (lôngʹtīm′, longʹ-), *adj.* **1** for a long time: *a long-time companion, a long-time Democrat.* **2** lasting a long time: *a long-time feud.*

**long-tom** (lôngʹtomʹ, longʹ-), *n. Australian.* a needlefish (def. 1).

**long tom**, a cradle for washing gold.

**Long Tom**, **1** any large cannon having a long range. **2** a large, long-range gun carried on the deck of small warships.

**long ton**, the British ton, 2,240 pounds or 1,016.05 kilograms.

**long-tongued** (lôngʹtungdʹ, longʹ-), *adj.* **1** having a long tongue. **2** *Figurative.* talking much or too much: *a long-tongued babbling gossip* (Shakespeare).

**long-tongued bat**, a leaf-nosed bat with a long pointed snout and a long tongue, that feeds on pollen and nectar and is found in southeastern Asia and the Pacific islands.

**lon|guette** (lông getʹ), *n.* a dress, skirt, or other garment for women that reaches to the calf; midi. [< French *longuette,* adjective, somewhat long, longish]

**lon|gueur** (lông gėrʹ), *n.* a long or tedious passage in a book, play, piece of music, or film. Also, **longeur.** [< French *longueur* length]

**long vacation**, *British.* the long summer vacation observed in law courts and universities.

**long view**, a point of view or perspective that covers a long period of time; long-term view: *He takes the long view. And, according to that view, eventually governments in many parts of the world may grow tired of American guidance* (Wall Street Journal).

**long-waist|ed** (lôngʹwāsʹtid, longʹ-), *adj.* comparatively long from neck to waistline: *a long-waisted dress, a long-waisted girl.*

**Pronunciation Key:** hat, āge, cãre, fär; let, ēqual, tėrm; it, īce; hot, ōpen, ôrder; oil, out; cup, pu̇t, rüle; child; long; thin; ᴛʜen; zh, measure; ə represents a in about, e in taken, i in pencil, o in lemon, u in circus.

**long|wall** (lông′wôl′, long′-), *adj.* of or designating a system of mining in which the whole seam of coal or ore is removed and nothing is left to support the roof except the shaft pillars.

**long wave**, a radio wave having a wave length above 545 or 600 meters.

**long-wave** (lông′wāv′, long′-), *adj.* of, for, or by means of long waves.

**long|ways** (lông′wāz′, long′-), *adv.* in the direction of the length; lengthwise.

**long-wind|ed** (lông′win′did, long′-), *adj.* **1** talking or writing at great lengths; tiresome: *a long-winded speaker, a long-winded sermon.* **2** capable of long effort without getting out of breath: *A long-distance runner must be long-winded. These horses are ... remarkably stout and long-winded* (Washington Irving). **—long′-wind′ed|ly**, *adv.* **—long′-wind′ed|ness**, *n.*

**long|wise** (lông′wīz′, long′-), *adv.* in the direction of the length; lengthwise; longways.

**long wool**, wool from four to eight inches long, produced by Lincoln, Leicester, Cotswold, and some other sheep.

**long|yi** (long′gē), *n.* = lungi.

**loo**[1] (lü), *n., pl.* **loos**, *v.,* **looed** (lüd), **loo|ing.** **—*n.*** **1** a card game in which players who fail to take a trick pay forfeits into a pool. **2** the forfeit paid. **3** an instance of being looed.
**—*v.t.*** to cause to pay into a pool after failing to take a trick at loo.
[short for *lanterloo* < French *lanturelu,* a word in an old refrain]

**loo**[2] (lü), *n. Scottish.* love.

**loo**[3] (lü), *n., pl.* **loos.** *British Informal.* toilet; bathroom. [origin uncertain]

**loo|by** (lü′bē), *n., pl.* **-bies.** *British.* a lazy, hulking fellow; lout. [compare etym. under **lob**[2]]

**loof**[1] (lüf), *n. Scottish.* the palm of the hand. [< Scandinavian (compare Old Icelandic *lōfe*)]

**loof**[2] (lüf), *v.i., n.* = luff.

**loo|fah** (lü′fə), *n.* **1** any one of a group of tropical plants of the gourd family. **2** the fruit of such a plant, containing a mass of coarse, strong fibers. **3** these dried fibers, used as a sponge. Also, **luffa.** [< Arabic *lūfah*]

**look** (lu̇k), *v., n.* **—*v.i.*** **1a** to turn the eyes; try to see; see: *Look at the pictures. He looked this way. I looked, and, lo, a Lamb stood on the mount Sion* (Revelation 14:1). *It's all his imagining. I've never looked at another man* (John Strange). **SYN:** gaze, stare, observe, glance. **b** to look hard; stare; glance or gaze in a certain way: *to look questioningly or kindly at a person. Looking at one another like cat and dog* (Henry Kingsley). **2** to search: *I looked through the drawer to see if I could find my keys.* **3** *Figurative.* to pay attention; examine: *You must look at all the facts.* **4** to have a view; face: *The house looks to the south upon a garden. These windows look to the north.* **5** to show how one feels by one's appearance; seem; appear: *She looks pale. Flowers look pretty. It looks as if it might rain.* **6** to expect; anticipate. **7** *Figurative.* to tend; point; indicate: *The facts look to this decision.*
**—*v.t.*** **1** to direct a look at: *to look one in the eyes.* **2** to express or suggest by looks: *He said nothing but looked his disappointment. The old lady ... looked carving-knives at the ... delinquent* (Dickens). **3** to appear as befits or accords with (one's character, condition, age, or other station); appear equal to: *He doesn't look his age.* **4** *Figurative.* to affect by looking in a certain way: *to look down insubordination.* **5** *British and Scottish.* to view; inspect; examine.
**—*n.*** **1** the act of looking; glance or gaze of the eyes; seeing: *a mother's loving look at her baby.* **2** a search; examination: *Take a quick look around the house before you leave.* **3** appearance; aspect: *a kind look. A deserted house has a desolate look.*

**look after, a** to attend to; take care of: *She looked after her little brother. Of course they looked after her on the boat* (Graham Greene). *The investor should look after his own interests* (Law Times). **b** to follow (a departing person or thing) with the eye: *Every man at his tent door ... looked after Moses, until he was gone into the tabernacle* (Exodus 33:8).

**look alive**, hurry up! be quick!: *Look alive! Keep moving!*

**look back**, to think about the past; recollect: *An era in its history has ended. It may be worthwhile at this moment to look back and try to see what has happened* (Edmund Wilson).

**look down on**, to despise; scorn: *The miser looked down on all beggars.*

**look down one's nose at.** See under **nose.**

**look for**, to expect; anticipate: *to look for a coming Messiah. We'll look for you tonight.*

**look forward to**, to expect with pleasure; be eager for: *The children are looking forward to the picnic.*

**look in**, to make a short visit: *Look in this afternoon. I just wanted to tell him he'd be welcome to look in* (Graham Greene).

**look into**, to examine; inspect; investigate: *The president of our club is looking into the problem.*

**look on, a** to watch without taking part: *The teacher conducted the experiment while we looked on. He himself was largely forced to look on* (Edmund Wilson). **b** to regard; consider: *I look on him as a very able man. Although the experiments ... have been looked on with interest ...* (Observer).

**look oneself**, to seem like oneself; seem well: *But what's the matter, George? ... you don't look yourself* (Dickens).

**look out**, to be careful; watch out: *Look out for cars as you cross the street.*

**look over**, to examine; inspect: *The policeman looked over my license.*

**looks, a** personal appearance: *Good looks means a good appearance. His looks are against him.* **b** *Informal.* attractive personal appearance: *He has looks as well as money.* **c** *Informal.* appearance; aspect: *I don't like the looks of this place.*

**look to, a** to attend to; take care of: *The treasurer has to look to paying the bills of our club. A man who has the affairs of such a great bank as ours to look to, must be up with the lark* (Thackeray). **b** *Figurative.* to turn to for help: *The defeated army looked to its exiled leaders for help.* **c** *Figurative.* to look forward to; expect: *I look to hear from you soon.*

**look up, a** to search for; refer to; find: *He looked up the unfamiliar word in a dictionary.* **b** *Informal.* to call on; visit: *Look me up when you come to town. You'd better look him up at his hotel* (Harper's). **c** *Informal.* to get better; improve: *Things are looking up for me since I got the new job. [He] also reported that Pennsy's earnings were looking up* (Time).

**look upon**, to regard; consider: *Many parents look upon fireworks as a nuisance if not dangerous.*

**look up to**, to respect; admire: *We look up to Washington as a founder of our country. Sweden looks up to British agriculture as the model for imitation* (Journal of the Royal Agricultural Society).

[Old English *lōcian*]

► **look.** When used as verb of complete meaning (use the eyes, gaze), *look* is modified by an adverb: *look searchingly, look sharp.* As a linking verb, equivalent to *appear, look* is followed by an adjective which modifies the subject: *He looks well, or healthy, or tired.*

**look-a|like** (lu̇k′ə līk′), *n., adj. U.S. Informal.* **—*n.*** one of a pair or a set that look just alike: *Pre-engineered metal buildings were rather plain look-alikes* (Wall Street Journal).
**—*adj.*** looking just alike; very similar: *They wore look-alike silks* (Time).

**look|er** (lu̇k′ər), *n.* **1** a person who looks. **2** *U.S. Slang.* a person who is good-looking.

**look|er-on** (lu̇k′ər on′, -ôn′), *n., pl.* **look|ers-on.** a person who watches without taking part; spectator; onlooker.

**look-in** (lu̇k′in′), *n.* **1** a glance in; hasty look. **2** a brief visit. **3** *Slang.* a chance of success, as in a horse race. **4** *Slang.* a chance to participate, as in some venture.

**look|ing glass** (lu̇k′ing), **1** = mirror. **2** the glass used in mirrors.

**look|ing-glass** (lu̇k′ing glas′, -gläs′), *adj. Informal.* completely inverted or reversed; topsy-turvy: *the looking-glass world of white supremacy south of the Zambesi* (Manchester Guardian Weekly). [< *Through the Looking-Glass,* a fantasy (1871), by Lewis Carroll, 1832-98, an English writer]

**look|out** (lu̇k′out′), *n.* **1** a careful watch for someone to come or for something to happen: *Keep a sharp lookout for mother. Be on the lookout for a signal.* **2** a place from which to watch. A tower or a crow's-nest is a lookout. **3** a person or group that has the duty of watching: *The lookout cried, "Land Ho!" There was nothing to do but steer the ship, and relieve the lookouts at the mast-heads* (Herman Melville). **4** *Figurative.* what one sees ahead; outlook; prospect: *See those clouds! A poor lookout for our picnic.* **5** *Informal.* a thing to be cared for or worried about: *Never you mind what I took her for, that's my lookout* (Dickens).

**look-o|ver** (lu̇k′ō′vər), *n. Informal.* an inspection or evaluation.

**looks** (lu̇ks), *n. pl.* See under **look.**

**look-say method** (lu̇k′sā′), = word method.

**look-see** (lu̇k′sē′), *n. Slang.* a look, survey, inspection, or search: *a quick look-see. The aim is to take a broad look-see and prepare a "white paper" on the findings* (New Scientist).

***loom**[1] (lüm), *n., v.* **—*n.*** **1** a frame or machine for weaving yarn or thread into cloth by interlacing the warp and the woof threads: *Weave no more silks, ye Lyons looms* (Julia Ward Howe). See picture below. **2** the art, process, or business of weaving: *a splendid silk of foreign loom* (Tennyson). **3** the part of an oar between the blade and the handle or the part between the oarlock and the hand.
**—*v.t.*** to weave on a loom.
[Middle English *lome,* Old English *gelōma* implement]

**loom**[2] (lüm), *v., n.* **—*v.i.*** to appear dimly or vaguely; appear as large and dangerous: *A large iceberg loomed through the thick, gray fog.* (*Figurative.*) *War loomed ahead.* (*Figurative.*) *Little things loom large to an anxious mind.*
**—*n.*** **1** an indistinct appearance or outline of a thing seen vaguely at a distance or through a fog. **2** the reflection on the clouds when the light from a lighthouse is below the horizon.
[origin uncertain. Compare dialectal Swedish *loma* to move slowly.]

**loom**[3] (lüm), *n.* **1** = loon[1]. **2** = guillemot. [< Scandinavian (compare Old Icelandic *lōmr*)]

**L.O.O.M.**, Loyal Order of Moose.

**loom|er|y** (lü′mər ē), *n., pl.* **-er|ies.** a breeding place of loons or guillemots. [< *loom*[3]]

**loon**[1] (lün), *n,* a large, web-footed diving bird. Loons have a loud, wild cry and live in northern regions. They comprise the only living group of their order. *Visitors to ... the United States will probably never forget the cry of the loon sounding ... like the hysterical laughter of a lunatic* (A. M. Winchester). [alteration of *loom*[3]]

**loon**[2] (lün), *n.* **1** a worthless or stupid person: *thou cream-faced loon* (Shakespeare). **2** *Scottish.* a boor; lout: *The lairds are as bad as the loons* (Scott). **3** *Scottish.* a boy; lad. **4** *Scottish.* a worthless or loose woman. **5** *Archaic.* a man of low birth or condition. Also, **loun, lown.** [origin uncertain]

**loon|ey** (lü′nē), *adj.,* **loon|i|er, loon|i|est,** *n., pl.* **loon|ies.** = loony.

**loon|y** (lü′nē), *adj.,* **loon|i|er, loon|i|est,** *n., pl.* **loon|ies.** *Slang.* **—*adj.*** crazy, foolish, or silly.
**—*n.*** a crazy person; lunatic. Also, **luny.**
[variant of earlier *luny* < *lunatic;* probably influenced by *loon*[2]] **—loon′i|ness,** *n.*

**loony bin**, *Slang.* an insane asylum.

***loop**[1] (lüp), *n., v.* **—*n.*** **1** the shape of a curved string, ribbon, bent wire, or cord that crosses itself: *He wound the garden hose in loops and hung it up.* **2** a thing, bend, course, or motion

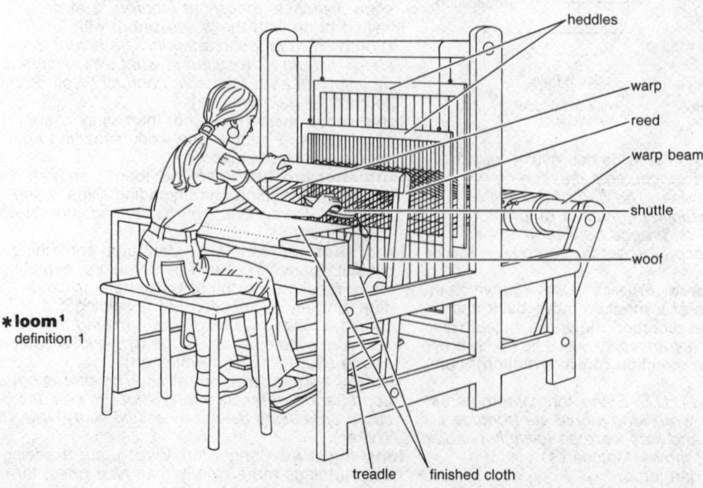


***loom**[1]
definition 1

shaped like a loop. In writing, *b* and *g* and *h* and *l* have loops. *The road makes a wide loop around the lake. Write a more distinct current hand ... open the loops of your l's* (Scott). **3** a fastening or ornament formed of cord bent and crossed: *The heavy velvet curtains were held back by satin loops.* **4** a turn like the letter *l*, especially one made by an airplane. **5** a ring or curved piece of metal or plastic, used for the insertion of something or as a handle. **6** *Physics.* **a** the portion of a vibrating string, column of air in an organ pipe, etc., between two nodes; antinode. **b** the middle point of such a part. **7** *Electricity.* **a** a complete or closed electric circuit. **b** = hysteresis loop. **8** in electronic computers or computing systems: **a** the repetition of instructions in a program. **b** the carrying out of instructions for a fixed number of times. **9** *U.S. Slang. Sports.* a league: *The teams involved are engaged in a tussle for fourth place in the loop* (New York Times). **10** an intrauterine contraceptive device; Lippes loop.

*—v.t.* **1** to make a loop of: *to loop the rope and tie the ends.* **2** to make loops in: *to loop the rope and fasten it over the pole.* **3** to fasten with a loop: *to loop the rope around the pole.* **4** to encircle with a loop. **5** to cause (an airplane) to fly in a loop or loops. **6** *Electricity.* to join (conductors) so as to form a loop.

*—v.t.* **1** to form a loop or loops: *This yarn loops easily for knitting.* **2** to move by forming loops in crawling: *The currant worms went looping and devouring from twig to twig* (Atlantic Monthly). **3** to perform a loop, as an airplane.

**knock for a loop**, *U.S. Slang.* **a** to knock out: *The contender knocked him for a loop in their championship bout.* **b** *Figurative.* to put something out of operation; diminish; make ineffectual: *His testimony confirmed the Chambers story in an essential matter and knocked the Hiss claims for a loop* (Saturday Review). **c** *Figurative.* to impress strongly; overwhelm: *He would have knocked the girls at Bradley for a loop* (Harper's).

**loop the loop**, to turn over and over; make a loop in the air: *The kite looped the loop in a sudden gust of wind.*

[Middle English *loupe,* perhaps < Celtic (compare Gaelic *lùb* bend)]

***loop[1]** definitions 2, 4

definition 2 definition 4

**loop[2]** (lüp), *n. Archaic.* an opening in a wall; loophole: *Stop all sight-holes, every loop* (Shakespeare). [Middle English *loupe,* perhaps < Middle Dutch *lūpen* to peer, watch]

**loop[3]** (lüp), *n., v. —n.* a ball-shaped, pasty mass of iron before it is made into a bloom; ball.

*—v.i.* to form such a mass.

[< French *loupe*]

**loop aerial** or **antenna**, an aerial or antenna made of several turns of wire looped around a frame, used instead of an outdoor aerial or antenna.

**looped** (lüpt), *adj. Slang.* drunk.

**loop|er** (lü'pər), *n.* **1** a person or thing that loops or forms loops. **2** = measuring worm. **3** the part that carries the thread in a sewing machine.

**loop|hole** (lüp'hōl'), *n., v.,* **-holed, -hol|ing.** *—n.* **1** a small opening in a wall for looking through, or letting in air and light, or for firing through at an enemy outside: *... barred with care All the windows, and doors, and loopholes there* (Robert Southey). **2** *Figurative.* a means of escape: *The clever lawyer found a loophole in the law to save his client. The bill has been watered down somewhat by amendments providing loopholes and escape clauses in favor of special interests* (New York Times).

*—v.t.* to provide with loopholes: *a stout loghouse ... loopholed for musketry on every side* (Robert Louis Stevenson).

**loop knot**, **1** a single knot tied in a doubled cord, so as to leave a loop beyond the knot; overhand loop. **2** *Obsolete.* a square knot.

**loop of Hen|le** (hen'lē), = Henle's loop.

**loop stitch**, **1** = blanket stitch. **2** a fancy stitch consisting of loops.

**loop|worm** (lüp'wėrm'), *n.* = measuring worm.

**loop|y** (lü'pē), *adj.,* **loop|i|er, loop|i|est.** **1** full of loops. **2** *Scottish.* crafty; deceitful. **3** *Slang.* crazy; intoxicated.

**loose** (lüs), *adj.,* **loos|er, loos|est,** *v.,* **loosed, loos|ing,** *adv., n.* *—adj.* **1** not fastened: *a loose thread.* **SYN:** unbound, unfastened, untied. **2** not tight: *loose clothing, loose reins.* **SYN:** slack. **3** not firmly set or fastened in: *a loose tooth, loose planks on a bridge.* **4** not bound together: *loose papers.* **5** not put up in a box, can, or other container: *loose coffee.* **6** not shut in or up; free: *The dog has been loose all night.* **7** not pressed close together; having spaces between the parts; open: *loose earth, cloth with a loose weave.* **8** *Figurative.* not strict, close, or exact: *a loose account of the accident, a loose translation from another language, loose thinking. His loose grammar was the fruit of careless habit, not ignorance* (Mark Twain). **SYN:** vague, indefinite, careless. **9** *Figurative.* moving too freely; not retentive: *a loose tongue; a good deal of loose information* (Thomas Carlyle). *A kind of men so loose of soul, That in their sleeps will mutter their affairs* (Shakespeare). **10** *Figurative.* careless about morals or conduct: *a loose character. The loose political morality of Fox presented a remarkable contrast to the ostentatious purity of Pitt* (Macaulay). **SYN:** wanton, immoral. **11** *Informal.* not tense; relaxed. **12** *Informal.* not employed; not appropriated: *loose hours, loose funds.* **13** (of a chemical element) free; uncombined.

*—v.t.* **1** to set free; let go: *He loosed my arm from his grip. Ye shall find a colt tied ...; loose him, and bring him* (Mark 11:2). **2** to shoot (an arrow, shot from a gun, or other missile): *The attacking Indians loosed a volley of arrows against the fort.* (*Figurative.*) [*The*] *Agriculture Secretary loosed a blast at Congressional critics of his farm program* (Wall Street Journal). **3** to make loose; untie; unfasten: *to loose a knot.* **4** to make less tight; relax; slacken: *The coxswain loosed his grip upon the shrouds* (Robert Louis Stevenson).

*—v.i.* **1** to become loose. **2** to shoot an arrow, shot from a gun, or other missile.

*—adv.* in a loose manner; loosely: *Our manners set more loose upon us* (Joseph Addison).

*—n.* **give a loose** (or **loose**) **to,** to give freedom or full vent to: *Give a loose to your fancy, indulge your imagination* (Jane Austen). *He would not give loose to passion* (George Eliot).

**in the loose**, *British.* in open formation or play, as in Rugby: *In the loose, however, the Scottish forwards were yards quicker about the field* (Sunday Times).

**let** (or **set, turn**) **loose**. See under **let[1]**, **set**, and **turn**.

**on the loose**, *Informal.* **a** without restraint; free: *The puppy is out on the loose.* **b** on a spree: *The visitors are on the loose in the town.*

[Middle English *los* < Scandinavian (compare Old Icelandic *lauss*)] **—loose'ly,** *adv.* **—loose'ness,** *n.* **—loos'er,** *n.*

**loose-box** (lüs'boks'), *n. British.* box stall.

**loose-cou|pler** (lüs'kup'lər), *n.* a coupler or transformer in which the primary coil and the secondary coil are associated without close inductive relation, as by being well separated from each other.

**loose ends**, bits of unfinished business: *She added that the loose ends left were disturbing and she thought the whole inquiry procedure unsatisfactory* (London Times).

**at loose ends**, See under **end[1]**.

**loose-joint|ed** (lüs'join'tid), *adj.* **1** able to move very freely: *a tall, shambling, loose-jointed man* (Harriet Beecher Stowe). **2** having loose joints; loosely built. **—loose'-joint'ed|ness,** *n.*

**loose-leaf** (lüs'lēf'), *adj.* having pages or sheets that can be taken out and replaced: *a loose-leaf notebook.*

**loos|en** (lü'sən), *v.t.* to make loose or looser; untie; unfasten: *The doctor loosened the stricken man's collar.* (*Figurative.*) *What liberty A loosened spirit brings* (Emily Dickinson). *—v.i.* to become loose or looser: *The collar loosened around his neck.* [< *loose,* adjective + *-en[1]*] **—loos'en|er,** *n.*

**loose sentence**, a sentence which is grammatically complete and makes sense before its end.

**loose smut**, a disease of cereals, caused by a smut fungus, in which the heads change into loose masses of spores.

**loose|strife** (lüs'strīf'), *n.* **1** any plant of a group of herbs of the loosestrife family characterized by a cylindrical calyx tube and a capsule included within the calyx, such as the purple loosestrife. **2** any one of various erect or creeping herbs of the primrose family, such as a common species bearing clusters of yellow flowers, the moneywort. [< *loose,* verb + *strife,* translation of Latin *lysimachia* < Greek *lysimácheios* < *Lysímachos,* the supposed discoverer]

**loosestrife family**, a group of dicotyledonous herbs, shrubs, and trees most common in tropical America, and including some species often grown as ornamentals, such as the crape myrtle, henna, and purple loosestrife.

**loose-tongued** (lüs'tungd'), *adj.* talking too freely; blabbing: *He knew how loose-tongued is calumny* (Charles Reade).

**loot[1]** (lüt), *n., v. —n.* **1** things taken in plundering; spoils; booty: *loot taken by soldiers from a captured town.* **SYN:** See syn. under **plunder**. **2** anything taken illegally, especially by force or with violence: *burglar's loot.* **3** *Slang.* money or other capital: *That's a lot of loot to spend for a record player!*

*—v.t.* **1** to plunder; rob: *The burglar looted the jewelry store.* **SYN:** sack, rifle. **2** to carry off as loot.

*—v.i.* to take booty; pillage; plunder; rob. **SYN:** sack, rifle.

[Anglo-Indian < Hindustani *lūṭ* < Sanskrit *loptram* < *lupati* breaks, plunders] **—loot'er,** *n.*

**loot[2]** (lüt), *v. Scottish.* past tense of **let[1]**.

**lop[1]** (lop), *v.,* **lopped, lop|ping,** *n. —v.t.* **1** to cut off; cut: *to lop the dead branches from a tree, to lop off the legs of a table.* **2** to cut branches, twigs, or stems from; trim. **3** to remove parts as if by cutting: *Expunge the whole or lop the excrescent parts* (Alexander Pope). *...they had lopped off the sentimentality and fantasy which had surrounded the practical perceptions of the utopians* (Edmund Wilson).

*—n.* **1** the smaller branches and twigs of trees. **2** a part or parts lopped off.

[Middle English *loppen;* origin uncertain]

**lop[2]** (lop), *v.,* **lopped, lop|ping,** *adj. —v.i.* **1** to hang loosely or limply; droop: *The sleeping man's hand lopped over the arm of the chair.* **2** to flop: *She ... cried about it, she did, and lopped round, as if she'd lost every friend she had* (Harriet Beecher Stowe).

*—v.t.* to let hang or droop.

*—adj.* hanging loosely; drooping.

[compare etym. under **lob[1]**]

**lope** (lōp), *v.,* **loped, lop|ing,** *n. —v.i., v.t.* to run with a long, easy stride: *The horse loped along the trail in an easy gallop. I loped my cayuse full tilt by Mr. Snake* (Owen Wister).

*—n.* a long, easy stride: *Now and then a Shawanee passed us, riding his little shaggy pony at a "lope"* (Francis Parkman).

[Middle English *lopen* < Scandinavian (compare Old Icelandic *hlaupa* to leap, run)] **—lop'er,** *n.*

**lop-eared** (lop'ird'), *adj.* having ears that hang loosely or droop: *a lop-eared rabbit.*

**lop-eared cat**, = pendulous-eared cat.

**lo|pho|branch** (lō'fə brangk, lof'ə-), *adj., n.* *—adj.* of or belonging to an order of teleost marine fishes having tuftlike gills, including the sea horses and pipefishes.

*—n.* a lophobranch fish.

[< New Latin *Lophobranchii* the former order name < Greek *lóphos* crest, tuft + *bránchia* gills]

**lo|pho|bran|chi|ate** (lō'fə brang'kē āt, -it; lof'ə-), *adj., n.* = lophobranch.

**lo|pho|phore** (lō'fə fôr, -fōr; lof'ə-), *n.* a structure having rows of ciliated tentacles, used to set up currents which carry tiny particles of food into the mouth, as in brachiopods, bryozoans, and certain other animals. [< Greek *lóphos* crest + English *-phore*]

**lop|o|lith** (lop'ə lith), *n.* a large intrusive mass of molten rock that has cooled and hardened, characterized by a basin-shaped upper and lower surface (contrasted with *batholith*). [< Greek *lopós* bent backward, convex + *líthos* stone]

**lop|per[1]** (lop'ər), *n.* a person who lops (trees or plants). [< *lop[1]* + *-er[1]*]

**lop|per[2]** (lop'ər), *v., n. Scottish. —v.i., v.t.* to curdle, as milk.

*—n.* **1** something curdled, such as milk or blood. **2** partly melted snow; slush. Also, **lapper.**

[perhaps < Scandinavian (compare Old Icelandic *hloup* coagulation)]

**lop|py** (lop'ē), *adj.,* **-pi|er, -pi|est.** hanging loosely; drooping; limp.

**lop|sid|ed** (lop'sī'did), *adj.* larger or heavier on one side than the other; unevenly balanced; leaning to one side: *a lopsided load, a lopsided score.* (*Figurative.*) *... the lopsided economy of Malta, so largely dependent on the dockyard* (London Times). **—lop'sid'ed|ly,** *adv.* **—lop'sid'ed|ness,** *n.*

**loq.**, he, she, or it speaks (Latin, *loquitur*).

**lo|qua|cious** (lō kwā'shəs), *adj.* **1** talking much; fond of talking: *Jack became loquacious on his favourite topic* (Frederick Marryat). **SYN:** See syn. under **talkative**. **2** making sounds as of much talking: *loquacious birds or frogs, loquacious water.* [< Latin *loquāx, -ācis* (with English *-ous*) talkative < *loquī* speak, talk] **—lo|qua'cious|ly,** *adv.* **—lo|qua'cious|ness,** *n.*

**lo|quac|i|ty** (lō kwas'ə tē), *n.* an inclination to talk a great deal; talkativeness: *The only limit to his loquacity was his strength* (Henry T. Buckle). *The*

**Pronunciation Key:** hat, āge, cãre, fär; let, ēqual, tėrm; it, īce; hot, ōpen, ôrder; oil, out; cup, pu̇t, rüle; child; long; thin; ᴛʜen; zh, measure; ə represents **a** in about, **e** in taken, **i** in pencil, **o** in lemon, **u** in circus.

*songs ... help to compensate for the loquacity* (New Yorker). **SYN**: garrulity, volubility. [< Latin *loquācitās* < *loquāx, -ācis* talkative < *loquī* to talk]

**lo|quat** (lō′kwot, -kwat), *n.* **1** a small evergreen tree with small, yellow, plumlike fruit, native to China and Japan but grown in North America since the late 1700's. It belongs to the rose family. **2** its rather tart fruit, which is good to eat. [< Cantonese *lo-kwat* (literally) rush orange]

**lo|qui|tur** (lok′wə tər), *Latin.* he, she, or it speaks (often used as a stage direction).

**lor|al** (lôr′əl, lōr′-), *adj.* = loreal.

**lo|ran** (lôr′an, lōr′-), *n.* a system that helps the navigator of an aircraft or ship find his geographical position quickly in any kind of weather by means of signals sent out from two or more fixed radio stations. It is effective up to about 800 miles during the day and 1,600 miles at night. *The new knowledge of the Gulf Stream was due in great part to the use of loran* (Science News Letter). [< *lo*(ng) *ra*(nge) *n*(avigation)]

**lo|ran|tha|ceous** (lôr′an thā′shəs, lōr′-), *adj.* belonging to a family of largely tropical, parasitic plants typified by the mistletoe. [< New Latin *Loranthaceae* the mistletoe family (< *Loranthus* the typical genus < Latin *lōrum* strap + Greek *ánthos* flower) + English *-ous*]

**lor|cha** (lôr′chə), *n.* a light Chinese sailing ship built somewhat like a European model, but rigged like a junk. [< Portuguese *lorcha*]

**lord** (lôrd), *n., v.* —*n.* **1** an owner, ruler, or master; person or animal that has the power: *Lions and elephants are lords of the jungle.* **2** a feudal superior; owner of a manor. **3** (in Great Britian) a man of any one of certain high ranks; peer of the realm; person entitled by courtesy to the title of Lord. **4** *Archaic.* a husband: *Ye lords of ladies intellectual ... have they not henpeck'd you all?* (Byron). **5** *Astrology.* the planet that has a dominant influence over an event, period, or region.

—*v.i.* to behave like a lord; rule proudly or absolutely; domineer: *I am not one to be lorded over by a man no better than myself* (Richard Blackmore).

—*v.t.* to raise to the rank of lord; ennoble.

**lord it over**, to domineer over; boss: *He was the oldest and lorded it over the rest of us.*

[Old English *hlāford* < *hlāf* loaf + *weard* keeper, ward. Compare etym. under **lady**.] —**lord′less**, *adj.*

**Lord** (lôrd), *n.* **1** God: *Know ye that the Lord he is God: it is he that hath made us, and not we ourselves* (Psalms 100:3). **2** Jesus Christ: *the year of our Lord. Unto you is born this day ... a Saviour which is Christ the Lord* (Luke 2:11). **3** in Great Britian: **a** a titled nobleman or peer of the realm belonging to the House of Lords, the upper of the two branches of the British Parliament. **b** a title used in speaking or writing about men of certain high ranks: *Lord Tennyson. The son of a duke or marquis is called a Lord.* **c** a title given by courtesy to men holding certain positions: *A bishop is called a Lord. Although clothed in impressive robes and addressed as "My Lord," the judge is still a human being* (Maclean's).

**the Lords**, **a** the House of Lords; the upper house of the British Parliament: *In the Lords, there were but 12 to 106* (Horace Walpole). **b** members of the House of Lords.

**Lord Chamberlain**, the official in charge of the royal household of Great Britain.

**Lord Chancellor** or **Lord High Chancellor**, the highest judicial official of the United Kingdom, who ranks above all peers except royal princes and the Archbishop of Canterbury. He is Keeper of the Great Seal and chairman of the House of Lords. In theory he presides over the chancery division of the High Court of Justice, though in practice he rarely sits there. He recommends or advises on the appointment of most judges. His office, unlike that of other judges, is political and changes with the government.

**Lord Chief Justice**, (in Great Britain) the officer who presides over the King's Bench division of the High Court of Justice and, usually, over the Court of Criminal Appeal. Formerly, the Courts of King's Bench and Common Pleas each had its own Chief Justice, the Chief Justice of the King's Bench sometimes being referred to as the Lord Chief Justice.

**Lord High Admiral**, (formerly) a high officer at the head of Great Britain's naval administration.

**Lord High Treasurer**, (formerly) a high officer of the British Crown who was in charge of the government's revenue.

**lord|ing** (lôr′ding), *n.* **1** = lordling. **2** *Archaic.* a lord or master (used as a form of address).

**Lord in Waiting**, a nobleman holding an office in attendance on a British sovereign.

**Lord Lieutenancy**, the position or office of a Lord Lieutenant.

**Lord Lieutenant**, *pl.* **Lords Lieutenant**. *British.* **1** a county official who controls the appointment of justices of the peace. **2** the former English viceroy of Ireland.

**lord|li|ness** (lôrd′lē nis), *n.* **1** the state of being lordly; high station. **2** lordly pride; haughtiness.

**lord|ling** (lôrd′ling), *n.* a little or unimportant lord.

**lord|ly** (lôrd′lē), *adj.*, **-li|er**, **-li|est**, *adv.* —*adj.* **1** like a lord; suitable for a lord; grand; magnificent: *He saw at a distance the lordly Hudson, far, far below him* (Washington Irving). **SYN**: noble, aristocratic. **2** haughty; insolent; scornful: *His lordly airs annoyed his country cousins.* **SYN**: arrogant, proud, overbearing. **3** of or having to do with a lord or lords; consisting of lords: *a lordly gathering.*

—*adv.* in a lordly manner.

**Lord Mayor**, the title of the mayors of London and some other large English cities.

**Lord of Hosts**, God; Jehovah as Lord of the heavenly hosts and as director of the armies of Israel or as God over all mankind.

**Lord of Misrule**, = Abbot of Misrule.

**lor|do|sis** (lôr dō′sis), *n., pl.* **-ses** (-sēz). **1** a forward curvature of the spine that appears to bend the upper body slightly backward. **2** any abnormal curvature of the bones, especially one associated with tetanus or rabies. [< Greek *lórdōsis* < *lordós* bent backward]

**lor|dot|ic** (lôr dot′ik), *adj.* having to do with or affected with lordosis.

**Lord Privy Seal**, the official, usually a member of the British cabinet, who is Keeper of the Privy Seal.

**lord proprietor**, *pl.* **lords proprietors**, an English nobleman granted a charter by the king to settle and govern a colony in North America.

**Lord Protector**, the title used by Oliver Cromwell as head of the English government, 1653-1658, and his son Richard, 1658-1659.

**Lord Provost**, the chief magistrate of a Scottish burgh, equal to a mayor.

**Lords** (lôrdz), *n.pl.* **the**. See under **Lord**.

**lords-and-la|dies** (lôrdz′ən lā′dēz), *n.* a common European arum; wake-robin.

**Lord's Anointed**, the Messiah or Christ.

**Lord's Day**, = Sunday (in Christian nations).

**lord|ship** (lôrd′ship), *n.* **1** the rank or position of a lord. **2** Often, **Lordship**. *British.* the title used in speaking to or of a man having the rank of Lord: *Your Lordship, his Lordship.* **3** rule; authority; ownership: *His lordship over these lands is not questioned. They which are accounted to rule over the Gentiles exercise lordship over them* (Mark 10:42). **4** the land or domain of a lord: *From many a lordship forth they rode* (William Morris).

**Lord's Prayer**, a prayer given by Jesus to His disciples. It begins with the words "Our Father Who art in Heaven" (in the Bible, Matthew 6:9-13; Luke 11:2-4).

**Lords Spiritual** or **lords spiritual**, *British.* the bishops and archbishops in the House of Lords.

**Lord's Supper**, **1** Jesus' last supper with His disciples before His crucifixion; Last Supper. **2** the church service in memory of this; Holy Communion.

**Lord's Table**, the altar on which the elements of the Eucharist are placed; Communion table.

**Lords Temporal** or **lords temporal**, *British.* the members of the House of Lords other than bishops and archbishops; lay peers.

**Lord Steward**, the official in charge of the finances of the royal household of Great Britain.

**Lord|y** (lôr′dē), *interj.* an exclamation of surprise or wonder: *Lordy, but it was hot!* (E. S. Field).

**lore**[1] (lôr, lōr), *n.* **1** the facts and stories about a certain subject: *fairy lore, bird lore, Greek lore.* **2** learning; knowledge: *cobwebs of scholastic lore* (John Greenleaf Whittier); *... many a quaint and curious volume of forgotten lore* (Edgar Allan Poe). **3** *Archaic.* teaching or something taught: *The subtle fiend his lore Soon learn'd* (Milton). **4** *Archaic.* advice; counsel. [Old English *lār*. See related etym. at **learn**.]

**lore**[2] (lôr, lōr), *n. Zoology.* **1** a space between the eye and the side of the superior mandible of a bird. **2** an area between the eye and the nostril of a snake or other reptile. **3** a corresponding space or area in fishes. Also, **lorum**. [< New Latin *lorum* < Latin *lōrum* strap, thong]

**lor|e|al** (lôr′ē əl, lōr′-), *adj. Zoology.* of or having to do with a lore. Also, **loral**.

**Lor|e|lei** (lôr′ə lī, lor′-), *n. German Legend.* a siren of the Rhine whose beauty and singing distracted sailors and caused them to wreck their ships: *The voices from the East echoed hauntingly, like the lure of the legendary Lorelei* (Newsweek). Also, **Lurlei**.

**Lo|rentz force** (lôr′ents, lōr′-), *Physics.* a force acting on an electrically charged particle moving through a magnetic field: *Lorentz force ... tends to make a charged particle entering a magnetic field travel at right angles to both the direction of its original motion and the lines of force* (Scientific American). [< Hendrik Antoon *Lorentz*, 1853-1928, a Dutch physicist]

**Lorentz transformation**, *Physics.* any one of a series of equations that show the relationship between uniformly moving bodies and how such bodies are deformed by motion.

**lo|rette** (lô ret′), *n.* (in France) a courtesan of the more elegant or pretentious kind. [< French *lorette*]

***lor|gnette** (lôr nyet′), *n.* eyeglasses or opera glasses mounted on a handle to hold in the hand. [< French *lorgnette* < *lorgner* look sidelong at, to eye < Old French *lorgne* squinting]

***lorgnette**

**lor|gnon** (lôr nyôN′), *n.* **1** an eyeglass or a pair of eyeglasses, especially a pince-nez. **2** = opera glass. [< French *lorgnon* earlier, eyeglass, opera glasses < *lorgner;* see etym. under **lorgnette**]

**lo|ri|ca** (lô rī′kə, lō-), *n., pl.* **-cae** (-sē). **1** *Zoology.* **a** a hard, thickened body wall, as of a rotifer. **b** a protective case or sheath, as of a protozoan. **2** a leather cuirass or corselet worn by the ancient Romans. [< Latin *lōrīca* leather cuirass < *lōrum* strap, thong]

**lor|i|cate** (lôr′ə kāt, lor′-), *adj., n. Zoology.* —*adj.* having a lorica.

—*n.* a loricate animal.

**lor|i|cat|ed** (lôr′ə kā′tid, lor′-), *adj.* = loricate.

**lor|i|keet** (lôr′ə kēt, lor′-; lôr′ə kēt′, lor′-), *n.* any one of various small parrots, a kind of lory having a brushlike tongue: *Lories, which include the lorikeets, are among the most beautiful parrots* (R. Meyer de Schauensee). [< *lory* + (para)*keet*]

**lo|ris** (lôr′is, lōr′-), *n., pl.* **-ris|es** or (*collectively*) **-ris**. **1** either of two small, slow-moving nocturnal lemurs of southern Asia, the slender loris and slow loris. They have very large eyes and no tail, and live mostly in trees. **2** a larger lemur of India and Malaya. [< French *loris,* perhaps < Dutch *loeris* booby]

**lorn** (lôrn), *adj. Archaic.* **1** forsaken; forlorn: *Lorn stream, whose sullen tide no sedge-crown'd sisters now attend* (William Collins). *I am a lone lorn creetur'* (Dickens). **2** lost; ruined: *If thou readest, thou art lorn! Better hadst thou ne'er been born* (Scott). [Middle English *lorn*, Old English *-loren*, past participle of *-lēosan* lose. See related etym. at **forlorn**.]

**Lor|raine cross** (lə rān′; *French* lô ren′), a cross having two horizontal arms, the upper shorter than the lower. See diagram under **cross**. [< *Lorraine*, a region in France]

**lor|ry** (lôr′ē, lor′-), *n., pl.* **-ries**, *v.*, **-ried**, **-ry|ing**. —*n.* **1** *British.* a motor truck: *At least once ... a week they must take down their large machines, pack them on lorries, drive to the next fairground and put them up again* (Economist). **2** a long, flat, horse-drawn wagon with or without sides, set on four low wheels. **3** a car or other vehicle running on rails, as in a mine.

—*v.t.* to transport in a lorry: *In Northern Rhodesia there is no such protection and the smaller game is being lorried out to safety* (Sunday Times).

[compare dialectal *lurry* to pull, lug]

**lor|ry|load** (lôr′ē lōd, lor′-), *n. British.* as much or as many as a lorry can hold.

**lo|rum** (lô′rəm, lō′-), *n., pl.* **-ra** (-rə). **1** a long, narrow scarf worn by the emperor or empress in Byzantine times instead of a paludament. **2** *Zoology.* = lore[2]. [< Latin *lōrum* strap, thong]

**lo|ry** (lôr′ē, lōr′-), *n., pl.* **-ries**. any one of various small, bright-colored parrots with a bristled tongue adapted to their diet of nectar, found in Australia and nearby islands. [earlier, *lourey* < Malay *luri*]

**LOS** (no periods), **1** line of scrimmage. **2** loss of signal.

**los|a|ble** (lü′zə bəl), *adj.* that can be lost.

**Los An|ge|le|no** (lôs an′jə lē′nō, los), a native or inhabitant of Los Angeles; Angeleno.

**lose** (lüz), *v.*, **lost**, **los|ing**. —*v.t.* **1** to not have any longer; have taken away from one by accident, carelessness, parting, or death: *to lose a finger, to lose a dollar, to lose a friend, to lose one's life.* **2** to be unable to find: *to lose a book, to lose an address.* **3** to fail to keep, preserve, or maintain; cease to have: *to lose patience, to lose your temper, to lose one's mind.* **4** *Figurative.* to fail to follow with eye, hearing, or mind: *to lose words here and there in a speech, to lose a face in a crowd.* **5** to miss; fail to have, get, or catch: *to lose a sale, to lose a train.* **6** to fail to win: *to lose the prize, to lose a bet or game.* **7** to bring

to destruction or ruin: *The ship and its crew were lost.* **8** to spend or let go by without any result; waste: *to lose a chance, to lose time waiting. The hint was not lost on me.* **9** to cause the loss of: *Delay lost the battle.* **10** to cause to lose: *That one act of misconduct lost him his job.* **11** to leave far behind in a race, pursuit, or other contest: *The sly fox lost the dogs.*
*—v.i.* **1** to be defeated: *Our team lost. The battle's loss may profit those who lose* (Shelley). **2a** to suffer loss: *to lose on a contract. Thus, by gaining abroad, he lost at home* (John Dryden). **b** to be or become worse off in money, numbers, property, or possessions: *The army lost heavily in yesterday's battle. The gambler lost heavily at poker.*
**lose ground.** See under **ground**[1].
**lose oneself, a** to let oneself go astray; become bewildered: *He finally lost himself in the maze of income tax figures.* **b** to become absorbed or engrossed: *He seemed to lose himself in thought* (Joseph Conrad). *As I pace the darkened chamber and lose myself in melancholy musings* (Washington Irving).
**lose one's heart (to).** See under **heart.**
**lose out,** *U.S.* to be unsuccessful; fail: *He lost out in the election.*
[Old English *losian* be lost < *los* destruction, loss]

**lo|sel** (lō′zəl, lü′-; loz′əl), *n., adj. Archaic.* —*n.* a worthless person; profligate; scoundrel. **SYN:** rake, ragamuffin.
*—adj.* good-for-nothing; worthless: *those losel scouts* (Washington Irving).
[Middle English *losel,* apparently alteration of Old English *-losen,* alternate past participle of *-lēosan* lose. Compare etym. under **lorn.**]

**los|er** (lü′zər), *n.* **1** a person who loses something: *The loser of the purse was told to come to the office and claim her property.* **2** a person or animal that is beaten in a race, game, or battle: *The losers had to pick up the game and put it away.* **3** *U.S. Informal.* a person who habitually loses or fails.

**los|ing** (lü′zing), *adj., n.* —*adj.* that cannot win or be won: *You are playing a losing game if you are not careful crossing streets.*
*—n.* **losings,** losses, especially in gambling.
*—***los′ing|ly,** *adv.*

**loss** (lôs, los), *n.* **1a** the action of losing or having lost something: *The loss of health is serious, but the loss of a pencil is not.* **b** the fact or condition of being lost: *Thou hast ... quitted all to save A world from utter loss* (Milton). **2** a person or thing lost: *His house was a complete loss to the fire. The death of the statesman was a great loss to his country.* **3** the amount lost. **4** the value of the thing lost; harm or disadvantage caused by losing something: *Our losses by the fire amounted to $10,000.* **5** a defeat: *Our team had two losses and one tie out of ten games played.* **6** *Military.* the losing of soldiers by death, capture, or wounding. **7** *Insurance.* the occurrence of death, property damage, or other contingency against which a person is insured, under circumstances that make the insurer liable under the contract. **8** *Electricity.* the reduction in power, measured by the difference between the power input and power output, in an electric circuit, device, or system, corresponding to the transformation of electric energy into heat.
**at a loss, a** not sure; puzzled; in difficulty: *He was embarrassed and at a loss as to how to act.* **b** embarrassed for want of something: *at a loss for words or for information.*
**at a loss to,** unable to: *at a loss to understand, imagine, or explain.*
**losses, a** the number of soldiers dead, wounded, or captured: *The losses in that war were great.* **b** *Accounting.* the excess of money spent or invested over money gained in any business transaction, manufacturing operation, or other venture: *The losses put them in the red.* **c** *Accounting.* the ratio of monetary loss to the amount of capital invested, especially for a fiscal year or other stated period of time: *The firm reported losses in excess of a million.*
[Old English *los*]

**loss leader,** *Commerce.* an article of trade sold below cost to attract customers: *Retailers are meeting the new competition with such old weapons as special loss leaders, or with price reductions* (Time).

**loss|mak|er** (lôs′mā′kər, los′-), *n. British.* a business or industry that shows consistent losses or deficits: *What happens, when two companies, both lossmakers, merge into one? The answer, as often as not, is one big lossmaker* (Manchester Guardian Weekly).

**loss|mak|ing** (lôs′mā′king, los′-), *adj. British.* showing consistent losses or deficits.

**loss ratio,** *Insurance.* the ratio of the amounts paid out to insured parties to the value of the premiums received during a given period.

**loss|y** (lôs′ē, los′-), *adj. Electronics.* tending to lose or dissipate energy: *At optical frequencies a metal transmission line structure would be very lossy and only transparent dielectric materials such as glass can be considered* (Science Journal).

**lost** (lôst, lost), *v., adj.* —*v.* a past tense and past participle of **lose:** *I lost my new pencil. I had already lost my ruler.*
*—adj.* **1** no longer possessed or retained: *lost friends.* **2** no longer to be found; missing: *lost books.* **SYN:** astray. **3** met with defeat; not won: *a lost battle, a lost prize.* **4** not used to good purpose; wasted: *lost time.* **5** *Figurative.* having gone astray: *a lost child.* **6** destroyed or ruined: *a lost soul, a lost cause.* **7** *Figurative.* bewildered: *a lost expression.*
**be lost on** (or **upon**), to have no effect on; fail to influence: *Your kindness is not lost upon me* (Harriet Martineau).
**lost in, a** so taken up with (something) that one fails to notice anything else; completely absorbed or interested in: *lost in contemplation. He was lost in a book and failed to hear us come in.* **b** hidden or obscured in: *outlines lost in the fog.* **c** merged in or obscured by (something else): *a ball lost in the sun. Her small contribution was lost in the grand total.*
**lost to, a** no longer possible or open to: *The opportunity was lost to him.* **b** no longer belonging to: *He realized that she was lost to him.* **c** insensible to: *The deserting soldier was lost to all sense of duty to his country.*
*—***lost′ness,** *n.*

**lost cause,** a cause that is defeated already or sure to be defeated: *... the idealized heroic Lost Cause of the Confederacy* (New York Times).

**Lost Generation,** the young people, especially writers and artists, who emerged from World War I (1914-1918) disillusioned and without roots.

**lost tribes,** the ten Hebrew tribes inhabiting the northern kingdom of Israel, who were taken into captivity by Sargon of Assyria in 721 B.C. and are believed never to have returned to their tribal lands.

**lost-wax** (lôst′waks′, lost′-), *adj.* = cire-perdue.

**lot** (lot), *n., v.,* **lot|ted, lot|ting,** *adv.* —*n.* **1** one of a set of objects, such as bits of paper or wood, used to decide something by chance. The winner or loser is decided by the size of the lot chosen by him from a set held so that they appear to be equal. **2** such a method of deciding: *to divide property by lot. It was settled by lot.* **3** the choice made in this way: *The lot fell to me.* **4** what a person gets by lot; one's share or portion: *This then was the lot of the tribe ... of Judah ... even to the border of Edom* (Joshua 15:1). **SYN:** allotment, part, parcel. **5** *Figurative.* a person's destiny; fate; fortune: *a happy lot. A policeman's lot is not a happy one!* (W. S. Gilbert). *We will submit to whatever lot a wise Providence may send us* (Hawthorne). **SYN:** doom. **6** a plot or portion of ground: *His house is between two empty lots.* **7** a motion-picture studio and its grounds. **8** a portion or part: *Some of the bread in that last lot was moldy. He divided the fruit into ten lots.* **9** a number of persons or things considered as a group; collection; set: *a fine lot of boys. This lot of oranges is better than the last.* **10** *Informal.* a great many; a good deal: *a lot of books. I have a lot of marbles.* **11** *Informal.* a person of a certain kind: *He is a bad lot.*
*—v.t.* **1** to divide into lots, as land. **2** to assign to someone as his share or portion, or as his lot or destiny: *Who ... were lotted their shares in a quarrel not theirs* (Thomas Hardy). **3** to cast lots for; divide, apportion, or distribute by lot.
*—v.i.* to cast lots.
*—adv.* **a lot,** *Informal.* a great deal; much: *I feel a lot better.*
**cast** (or **throw**) **in one's lot with,** to share the fate of; become a partner with: *I intended to go along with this good man, and to cast in my lot with him* (John Bunyan).
**draw** (or **cast**) **lots,** to use lots to decide something: *We drew lots to decide who should be captain.*
**lots,** *Informal.* **a** a great many; a good deal: *lots of time, lots of money.* **b** very much: *I like you lots. I feel lots better.*
**the lot,** *Especially British.* everyone or everything; all: *Painting, wallpapering, carpeting, roof-tiling—the lot* (Punch).
[Old English *hlot*]
► **a lot, a lot of, lots, lots of.** Formal English avoids using *lots* and *lots of* in the sense of a considerable quantity or number. Informal: *He tried lots of* (or *a lot of*) *different shots, but lost.* Formal: *He tried a variety of* (or *a great many different*) *shots, but lost.*

**Lot** (lot), *n.* a righteous man, the nephew of Abraham, who was allowed to escape from Sodom with his wife before God destroyed it. His wife looked back, and was changed into a pillar of salt (in the Bible, Genesis 19:1-26).

**lo|ta** or **lo|tah** (lō′tə), *n.* a round water pot, usually of polished brass, used especially in India and the East Indies. [< Hindi *loṭa*]

**lote** (lōt), *n. Archaic.* lotus.

**loth** (lōth), *adj., n.* = loath.

**Lo|thar|i|o** (lō thãr′ē ō), *n., pl.* **-i|os.** a man who makes love to many women; libertine. **SYN:** rake. [< *Lothario,* a character in *The Fair Penitent* by Nicholas Rowe, 1674-1718, an English dramatist]

**loth|ly** (lōth′lē, lōŦH′-), *adv.* = loathly[2].

**loth|some** (lōŦH′səm), *adj.* = loathsome.

**lo|tic** (lō′tik), *adj. Ecology.* of, living in, or designating rapidly flowing water, such as a stream (contrasted with *lentic*). [< Latin *lōtus* (a past participle of *lavāre* to wash) + English *-ic*]

**lo|ti|form** (lō′tə fôrm), *adj.* shaped like or resembling a lotus, especially in form. [< *lotus* + *-form*]

**lo|tion** (lō′shən), *n., v.* —*n.* **1** a liquid containing medicine or a cosmetic. Lotions are applied to the skin to relieve pain or to heal, cleanse, perfume, or beautify the skin. *Among products that can now be packaged in ... squeeze bottles are ... complexion lotions* (Newsweek). **2** *Obsolete.* the act of washing (the body); ablution.
*—v.t.* to put lotion on: *Lotion your hands anytime* (New Yorker).
[< Latin *lōtiō, -ōnis* a washing, ultimately < *lavāre* to wash]

**lo|to** (lō′tō), *n.* = lotto.

**Lo|toph|a|gi** (lō tof′ə jī), *n.pl. Greek Legend.* lotus-eaters. [< Latin *Lōtophagi* < Greek *Lōtophágoi* < *lōtós* lotus + *phageîn* eat]

**lo|tos** (lō′təs), *n.* = lotus.

**lo|tos-eat|er** (lō′təs ē′tər), *n.* = lotus-eater.

**lots** (lots), *n.pl.* See under **lot.**

**lot|ter|y** (lot′ər ē), *n., pl.* **-ter|ies. 1** a scheme for distributing prizes by lot or chance. In a lottery a large number of tickets are sold, some of which draw prizes. **2** a similar scheme used to determine the order in which men are drafted into a country's armed forces; draft lottery. **3** *Figurative. They thought themselves unfortunate in the lottery of life* (Tobias Smollett). **4** *Obsolete.* **a** chance. **b** the issue of events as determined by chance. [< Italian *lotteria* < *lotto;* see etym. under **lotto**]

**lottery wheel,** the wheel used for shuffling the numbers on lottery tickets.

**lot|to** (lot′ō), *n.* a game played by drawing numbered disks from a bag or box and covering the corresponding numbers on cards. The first player to complete a blank row is the winner. Also, **loto.** [< Italian *lotto* lot, ultimately < Germanic. Compare *lot.*]

***lo|tus** (lō′təs), *n.* **1** a water plant having large, often floating leaves, and showy flowers. It belongs to the water-lily family. The lotus was commonly represented in the decorative art of the Hindus and the Egyptians: **a** one of two African water lilies, a white-flowered species and a blue-flowered species. **b** a perennial plant with large, fragrant rose or pink flowers; sacred lotus of India. **2** a shrubby plant bearing red, pink, or white flowers, such as the bird's-foot trefoil. It belongs to the pea family. **3a** a plant whose fruit was supposed by the ancient Greeks to cause a dreamy mental state in which one forgets real life and loses all desire to return home. **b** the fruit itself. **4** *Architecture.* an ornament representing the Egyptian water lily. Also, **lotos.** [< Latin *lōtus* < Greek *lōtós*]

***lotus**
definitions 1, 4

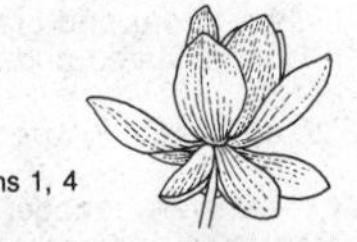
flower

ornament

**lo|tus-eat|er** (lō′təs ē′tər), *n.* **1** a person who leads a life of dreamy, indolent ease. **2** *Greek Legend.* a person who lived on the fruit of the lotus, and became content and indolent, having no desire to return home. Also, **lotos-eater.**

**lo|tus|land** (lō′təs land′), *n.* **1** a land of idleness and delight: *Oxford, that lotusland, saps the willpower, the power of action* (New Yorker). **2** the land of the lotus-eaters.

**lotus position,** a sitting position with the legs folded and the arms resting on the knees, used in yoga. [in allusion to the lotus leaf which, though it rests on water, does not become wet,

---

**Pronunciation Key:** hat, āge, cãre, fär; let, ēqual, tėrm; it, īce; hot, ōpen, ôrder; **oi**l, **ou**t; cup, pu̇t, rüle; **ch**ild; lo**ng**; **th**in; ŦHen; **zh**, measure; **ə** represents **a** in about, **e** in taken, **i** in pencil, **o** in lemon, **u** in circus.

and thus symbolizes detachment]

**lotus tree**, **1** a kind of jujube of northern Africa and southern Europe, supposed by many to have produced the lotus fruit in Greek myth. **2** a nettle tree of Europe, also associated with this myth.

**louche** (lüsh), *adj.* oblique; not straightforward; sinister; shady: ... *a bank hold-up by three louche gentlemen who arrive by train on this most fatal Saturday* (London Times). [< French *louche,* ultimately < Latin *luscus* having one eye]

**loud** (loud), *adj., adv.* —*adj.* **1** making a great sound; not quiet or soft: *a loud bang, a loud voice. The door slammed with a loud noise.* **2** noisy; resounding: *loud music, a loud place to study. When all is gay With lamps, and loud With sport and song* (Tennyson). **SYN:** deafening. **3** *Figurative.* clamorous; insistent: *to be loud in demands.* **4** *Informal.* showy in dress or manner: *loud clothes.* **5** *Informal.* obtrusive; somewhat vulgar: *a loud person.*
—*adv.* in a loud manner; with a loud noise or voice; aloud; loudly: *The hunter called loud and long.*
[Old English *hlūd*] —**loud′ness**, *n.*
—*Syn. adj.* **1, 2 Loud, noisy** mean making much or intense sound. **Loud** suggests strength or intensity of sound, but not necessarily disagreeableness: *The speaker's voice was loud, clear, and pleasing.* **Noisy** always suggests disagreeable loudness and sometimes implies that it is constant or habitual: *The people next door are noisy.*

**loud|en** (lou′dən), *v.i.* to become loud or louder: *As the radio loudened tenants began slamming down windows.* —*v.t.* to make loud or louder.

**loud|hail|er** (loud′hā′lər), *n. Especially British.* a loudspeaker: *The Rev. James Bevels ... used a police loudhailer to address the crowds* (London Times).

**loud|ish** (lou′dish), *adj.* somewhat loud: *A superplump guest in a loudish cape and an oversize Homburg hat stands at the desk* (Alexander Woollcott).

**loud|ly** (loud′lē), *adv.* **1** with much noise. **2** in a loud voice: *He spoke so loudly it startled everyone.*

**loud|mouth** (loud′mouth′), *n. Slang.* a loudmouthed person, especially one who is boastful or disparaging.

**loud|mouthed** (loud′mouᴛʜd′, -moutht′), *adj.* **1** talking loudly; irritatingly or offensively noisy: *Yet, though his loudmouthed tabloids spiel sex, crime, and the workingman's cause ...* (Time). **SYN:** vociferous, blatant, clamorous. **2** talking too much; not discreet.

**loud|speak|er** (loud′spē′kər), *n.* a device for making sounds louder, especially in a radio or phonograph or a public-address system: *Horn type loudspeakers ... for all parts of the audio range ...* (Roy J. Hoopes).

**lough** (loʜ), *n. Anglo-Irish.* **1** a lake. **2** an arm of the sea. **3** *Obsolete.* any body of water. [Middle English *lough.* Compare etym. under **loch.**]

**lou|is** (lü′ē), *n., pl.* **lou|is** (lü′ēz). = louis d'or.

**lou|is d'or** (lü′ē dôr′), **1** a French gold coin issued 1640-1795, worth from about $4 to about $4.60 at various times. **2** a later French gold coin, worth 20 francs. [< French *louis d'or* (literally) gold louis; *louis* < proper name of several French kings]

**Lou|is heel** (lü′ē), a curved heel on a woman's shoe about 1½ inches high and flared at the base. [< King *Louis* XV of France]

**Lou|i|si|an|a heron** (lů ē′zē an′ə, lü′i-), a grayish-purple heron with a white throat and breast, common in the southern United States and south to Brazil.

**Lou|i|si|an|an** (lů ē′zē an′ən, lü′i-), *adj., n.* = Louisianian.

**Louisiana tanager,** = western tanager.

**Louisiana water thrush,** a brownish warbler with a striped breast, found in wooded areas of North America, especially along small streams.

**Lou|i|si|an|i|an** (lů ē′zē an′ē ən, lü′i-), *adj., n.* —*adj.* of or having to do with Louisiana, a Southern state of the United States.
—*n.* a native or inhabitant of Louisiana.

***Louis Qua|torze** (kȧ tôrz′), the French title of Louis XIV of France, used to designate the styles in architecture, furniture, decorative art, and the like, characteristic of his reign (1643-1715) or of approximately that period.

***Louis Quinze** (kaɴz), the French title of Louis XV of France, used to designate the styles in architecture, furniture, decorative art, and the like, characteristic of his reign (1715-1774) or of approximately that period: *a Louis Quinze chair.*

***Louis Seize** (sez), the French title of Louis XVI of France, used to designate the styles in architecture, furniture, decorative art, and the like, characteristic of his reign (1774-1792) or of approximately that period.

***Louis Treize** (trez), the French title of Louis XIII of France, used to designate the styles in architecture, furniture, decorative art, and the like, characteristic of his reign (1610-1643) or of approximately that period. See picture below.

**lou|koum** (lü küm′), *n., pl.* **-kou|mi** (-kü′mē). = fig paste. [< Turkish *lokum*]

**loun** (lün), *n.* = loon[2].

**lounge** (lounj), *v.,* **lounged, loung|ing,** *n.* —*v.i.* **1** to stand, stroll, sit, or lie at ease in a lazy way; loll: *He lounged in an old chair. I lounged on the beach.* **2** to pass time lazily; idle at one's ease.
—*v.t.* to pass (time) away with lounging: *She lounged away the weekend.*
—*n.* **1** a comfortable and informal room in which one can lounge and be at ease: *a theater lounge.* **2** a sofa, couch, or other article of furniture, used for reclining. **3** an act or state of lounging: *We went for a lounge in the park after dinner.* **4** a lounging gait or manner of reclining: *tall, raw-boned Kentuckians ... with the easy lounge peculiar to the race* (Harriet Beecher Stowe).
[origin uncertain; perhaps < Old French *longis* drowsy laggard] —**loung′er**, *n.*

**lounge car,** a special railroad passenger car equipped with lounge seats, sofas, and bar.

**lounge lizard,** *U.S. Slang.* a lady's man.

**lounge suit,** *British.* a business suit.

**lounge|wear** (lounj′wãr′), *n.* leisurewear for lounging indoors.

**loup**[1] (loup, lōp, lüp), *n., v.i., v.t. Scottish.* leap: *The horses gave a sudden loup* (John Galt). [variant of *leap*]

**loup**[2] (lü), *n.* a light mask or half mask of silk or velvet, worn by women. [< French *loup* (literally) wolf < Latin *lupus*]

**loup-cer|vier** (lü′ser vyā′), *n., pl.* **loup-cer|viers** (lü′ser vyā′). = Canada lynx. [< French *loup-cervier* < Latin *lupus cervārius* lynx that hunts stags < *lupus* wolf, *cervus* stag]

**loup de mer** (lü′ də mer′), a food fish of European waters similar to the sea bass, valued as a delicacy. [< French *loup de mer* (literally) sea wolf]

***loupe** (lüp), *n.* a small eyepiece fitted with a powerful magnifying lens, used especially by jewelers and watchmakers: *Finally, Mr. Cohen took out a loupe, a diamond man's magnifying glass, and studied the stone* (New Yorker). [< French *loupe*]

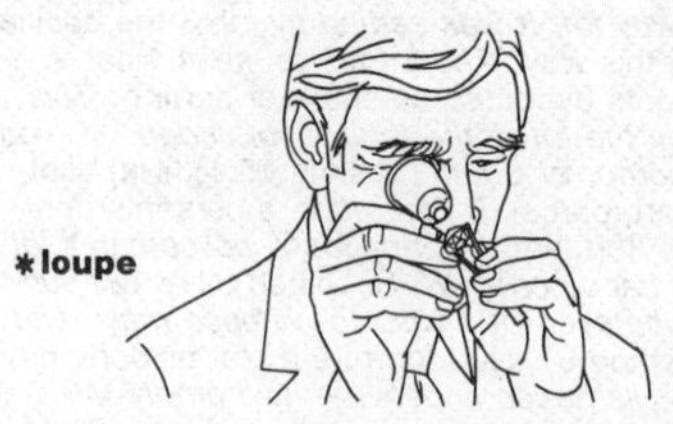
***loupe**

**loup-ga|rou** (lü′gə rü′), *n., pl.* **loups-ga|rous** (lü′gə rü′). a werewolf; lycanthrope. [< Old French *loup-garou* < *loup* wolf (see etym. under **loup**[2]) + *garou,* earlier *garoul* werewolf < Germanic (compare Middle High German *wërwolf*)]

**loup|ing ill** (lou′ping), an acute, infectious nervous and paralytic disease of sheep, caused by a tick-borne virus and characterized by involuntary leaping; trembles.

**lour** (lour), *v.i., n.* = lower[2].

**lour|ing** (lour′ing), *adj.* = lowering. —**lour′ing|ly**, *adv.*

**lour|y** (lour′ē), *adj.* = lowery.

**louse** (lous), *n., pl.* **lice** *for 1, 2, 3,* **lous|es** *for 4, v.,* **loused, lous|ing.** —*n.* **1** a small, wingless insect that infests the hair or skin of people and animals, causing great irritation. It has a flat body and sucks blood. *a body louse, a crab louse.* (*Figurative*) ... *a louse in the locks of literature* (Tennyson). **2** any one of various other insects that infest animals or plants, such as the bee louse and the plant louse or aphid: *We spray plants to kill the lice.* **3** any one of certain other superficially similar arthropods, such as the book louse or the wood louse. **4** *Slang, Figurative.* a mean, contemptible person.
—*v.t.* to remove lice from; delouse.
**louse up.** *Slang.* to spoil; get (something) all confused or in a mess: *to louse up a song, joke, or deal.*
[Old English *lūs*]

**louse|ber|ry** (lous′ber′ē, -bər-), *n., pl.* **-ries.** a spindle tree common in Europe, whose powdered berries were reputed to destroy lice.

**louse|wort** (lous′wėrt′), *n.* any herbaceous plant of a large group of the figwort family, formerly believed to breed lice in sheep and other livestock that feed on them; wood betony.

**lous|y** (lou′zē), *adj.,* **lous|i|er, lous|i|est.** **1** infested with lice. **2** *Slang, Figurative.* **a** bad; poor; of low quality: *The thing about bridge is that nobody can play it well. It's so hard that everybody's lousy at it* (New Yorker). **b** dirty; disgusting; mean. **3** *Slang, Figurative.* well supplied: *lousy with money. MacEachern looked up to discover the area was, as he puts it, "lousy with lobsters"* (Maclean's). —**lous′i|ly**, *adv.* —**lous′i|ness**, *n.*

**lout**[1] (lout), *n., v.* —*n.* an awkward, stupid fellow; boor; bumpkin: *Grimes is a rough rustic lout* (William Godwin).
—*v.t. Obsolete.* to treat with contempt; mock.
[probably < *lout*[2]. Compare Old Icelandic *lūtr* bent down, stooping, *lūta* to stoop.]

**lout**[2] (lout), *Archaic.* —*v.i.* **1** to bend; bow; make obeisance: *He fair the knight saluted, louting low* (Edmund Spenser). **2** to stoop.
—*v.t.* to bow (the head).
[Old English *lūtan*]

**lout|ish** (lou′tish), *adj.* awkward and stupid; boorish. —**lout′ish|ly**, *adv.* —**lout′ish|ness**, *n.*

**lou|troph|o|ros** (lü trof′ər əs), *n., pl.* **-o|roi** (-ər oi). a tall, long-necked vase for carrying water for a bath, especially for a ceremonial nuptial bath in ancient Greece. It was often placed upon the tomb of a young person who died unmarried. [< Greek *loutrophóros*]

***lou|ver** (lü′vər), *n.* **1** = louver board. **2** a window or other opening covered with louver boards. **3** a ventilating slit, especially for the escape of heat, as one in the hood of an automobile or the bulkhead of a ship. **4** a turret or lantern constructed on a roof, as in medieval architecture, to supply ventilation or light or allow smoke to escape. Also, **louvre.** [< Old French *lover* < Germanic (compare Old High German *louba* upper roof)]

***louver**
definition 2

**louver board,** any one of several overlapping strips of wood or other material set slanting in a window or other opening, so as to keep out rain but provide ventilation and light.

**lou|vered** (lü′vərd), *adj.* **1** provided with a louver or louvers. **2** arranged like louvers.

**louver fence,** a fence made of louver boards, providing privacy and ventilation.

**lou|vre** (lü′vər), *n. British.* louver.

**lov|a|bil|i|ty** (luv′ə bil′ə tē), *n.* the quality of being lovable. Also, **loveability.**

**lov|a|ble** (luv′ə bəl), *adj.* worthy of being loved; endearing: *She was a most lovable person, al-*

***Louis Treize**

***Louis Quatorze**

***Louis Quinze**

***Louis Seize**

*ways kind and thoughtful.* SYN: likeable, winning, pleasing, amiable. Also, **loveable.** —**lov′a|ble-ness**, *n.* —**lov′a|bly**, *adv.*

**lov|age** (luv′ij), *n.* a perennial herb of the parsley family, native to southern Europe, grown in herb gardens for its aromatic seeds and leaves. [Middle English *loveache*, alteration of Old French *luvesche*, or *levesche* < Late Latin *levisticum*, apparently alteration of Latin *ligusticum* of Liguria]

**lov|at** (luv′ət), *n.* a brownish-green color mixture often blended with other colors in fabrics. [< *Lovat*, a Scottish proper name]

**love** (luv), *n., v.,* **loved, lov|ing.** —*n.* **1** fond or tender feeling; warm liking; affection; attachment: *He had a deep love for his parents.* **2** strong or passionate affection for a person of the opposite sex: *But we loved with a love that was more than love* (Edgar Allan Poe). **3** an instance of such feeling; being in love: *I suppose, the Colonel was crossed in his first love* (Jonathan Swift). **4** this feeling as a subject for books or as a personified influence: *There is no love. The whole plot is political* (Macaulay). *I bow before thine altar, Love* (Tobias Smollett). **5** strong liking: *a love of books, a love of freedom.* **6** a person who is loved, especially a sweetheart: *Live with me and be my love* (Christopher Marlowe). *The young May moon is beaming, love* (Thomas Moore). **7** *Informal.* something charming or delightful: *What a love of a bracelet! The garden is quite a love* (Jane Austen). **8** the kindly feeling or benevolence of God for His creatures, or the reverent devotion due from them to God, or the kindly affection they should have for each other: *Ye have not the love of God in you* (John 5:42). **9** no score for a player or side in tennis and certain other games, such as bridge: *West was the dealer at love all* (Manchester Guardian Weekly). [Old English *lufu*]

—*v.t.* **1** to be very fond of; hold dear: *I love my country. She loves her mother.* **2** to have a lover's strong or passionate affection for; be in love with; feel love for: *And I will love thee still, my dear, Till a' the seas gang dry* (Robert Burns). **3** to like very much; take great pleasure in: *He loves music. Most children love ice cream. All that hate contentions, and love quietness, and virtue, and angling* (Izaak Walton). **4** to embrace affectionately.

—*v.i.* **1** to have affection: *He can hate but cannot love.* **2** to be in love; fall in love: *One that loved not wisely, but too well* (Shakespeare).

**fall in love,** to begin to love; come to feel love: *The young couple fell in love at first sight.*

**for love, a** for nothing; without pay: *He did the work for love.* **b** for pleasure; not for money: *They played the game for love.* **c** by reason of love; out of affection: *It is commonly a weak man who marries for love* (Samuel Johnson).

**for love or money, a** on any terms: *He would not do the work for love or money.* **b** at any price; by any means: *... Anglo-Saxon texts not elsewhere to be had for love or money* (Francis A. March).

**for the love of,** for the sake of; because of: *He did it for the love of his country. For the love of God, peace* (Shakespeare).

**in love,** feeling love: *My sister is in love and wants to get married.*

**in love with, a** feeling love for: *Romeo was in love with Juliet.* **b** very fond of; enamored of: *He is in love with his profession.*

**make love, a** to caress or kiss, and do as lovers do; pay loving attention (to); woo: *Demetrius ... made love to Nedar's daughter* (Shakespeare). **b** to have sexual intercourse (with).

**no love lost between, a** dislike between persons: *There was no love lost between the two ladies* (Thackeray). **b** no love lacking, as between persons who love each other: *We grumble a little now and then ... But there's no love lost between us* (Oliver Goldsmith). [Old English *lufian*]

—SYN: *n.* **1 Love, affection** mean a feeling of warm liking and tender attachment. **Love** applies to a strong attachment that suggests tenderness, as for a child or parent, and devotion and loyalty, as to friends or family: *Every person needs to give and receive love.* **Affection** applies to a less strong feeling, suggesting warm fondness: *I like my teacher, but feel no affection for her.*

▶See **like** for usage note.

**Love** (luv), *n.* **1** the god or goddess of love: **a** Venus. **b** Cupid or Eros. **2** (in the belief of Christian Scientists) God.

**love|a|bil|i|ty** (luv′ə bil′ə tē), *n.* = lovability.

**love|a|ble** (luv′ə bəl), *adj.* = lovable. —**love′a|ble-ness**, *n.* —**love′a|bly**, *adv.*

**love affair, 1** a particular experience of being in love; amour. **2** an affinity, as between two persons or groups: *The love affair between the Administration and Pakistan worries many people in Britain* (Harper's).

**love apple,** an old name for the tomato.

**love beads,** a long string or chain of beads worn around the neck as a love symbol or for ornament.

**love|bird** (luv′bėrd′), *n.* **1** a small tropical parrot that shows great affection for its mate. Lovebirds are often kept in cages as pets. **2** *Informal.* a person in love.

**love-bomb|ing** (luv′bom′ing), *n.* the practice of overwhelming potential recruits into a cult with a show of warm fellowship, concern, and affection: *The attractant consists of deception in the form of love-bombing and a contrived appeal to the subject's idealistic and altruistic impulses* (Melvin S. Finstein).

**love child,** an illegitimate child.

**love feast, 1** a meal eaten together by the early Christians as a symbol of brotherly love, apparently originally in connection with the Eucharistic celebration. **2** a religious ceremony imitating this. **3** any banquet or other gathering to promote good feeling: *There will be a great Democratic love feast in which a thousand Democratic editors will take part* (Charleston News and Courier).

**love game,** a game won in tennis or certain other sports without any score having been made by the opponent.

**love grass,** any one of a group of grasses with delicate flower spikes, often grown for pasturage and hay.

**love-in** (luv′in′), *n.* a gathering of hippies, flower children, or the like, for the purpose of celebrating or expressing love.

**love-in-a-mist** (luv′in ə mist′), *n.* a garden plant of the crowfoot family, native to southern Europe, having feathery leaves and pale-blue flowers; fennelflower; devil-in-the-bush.

**love-in-i|dle|ness** (luv′in ī′dəl nis), *n.* = wild pansy.

**love knot,** an ornamental knot or bow of ribbons as a symbol or token of love.

**love|less** (luv′lis), *adj.* **1** without love; feeling no love; not loving: *a loveless heart.* SYN: unloving. **2** receiving no love; not loved: *a loveless child.* SYN: unloved. —**love′less|ly**, *adv.* —**love′less-ness**, *n.*

**love letter,** a letter expressing love for another.

**love-lies-bleed|ing** (luv′līz blē′ding), *n.* an amaranth with long spikes of crimson flowers that often droop.

**love|light** (luv′līt′), *n.* a gleam or sparkle in the eye, expressing love.

**love|li|ly** (luv′lə lē), *adv.* in a lovely manner.

**love|li|ness** (luv′lē nis), *n.* = beauty.

**love|lock** (luv′lok′), *n.* **1** any conspicuous lock of hair, especially a curl worn on the forehead. **2** a long, flowing lock dressed separately from the rest of the hair, worn by courtiers in the time of Elizabeth I and James I.

**love|lorn** (luv′lôrn′), *adj.* suffering because of love; forsaken by the person whom one loves. —**love′lorn′ness**, *n.*

**love|ly** (luv′lē), *adj.,* **-li|er, -li|est,** *n., pl.* **-lies.** —*adj.* **1** beautiful in mind, appearance, or character; beautiful; lovable: *She is one of the loveliest girls we know.* SYN: See syn. under **beautiful**. **2** *Informal.* very pleasing; delightful: *We had a lovely holiday.* **3** *Obsolete.* loving; affectionate. —*n. Informal.* a pretty girl: *Two local lovelies whom he and his friend had met in the afternoon, arrived at the pier* (Harper's).

**love-mak|ing** (luv′mā′king), *n.* **1** attentions or caresses between lovers; wooing; courtship. **2** sexual intercourse.

**love match,** a marriage for love, not for money or social position.

**love-nest** (luv′nest′), *n.* a place where lovers dwell or keep a tryst.

**love potion,** a potion intended to induce love; philter.

**lov|er** (luv′ər), *n.* **1** a person who loves. **2** a person who is in love with another, especially a man who is in love with a woman: *The young princess chose her husband from among many lovers.* SYN: suitor, admirer, beau. **3** a person who loves illicitly; paramour. **4** a person having a strong liking: *a lover of music, a lover of books.*

**lovers,** a man and a woman who are in love with each other: *Hero and Leander were lovers.* —**lov′er|like′**, *adj.*

**lov|er|ly** (luv′ər lē), *adj., adv.* —*adj.* like a lover: *loverly attentions.* —*adv.* in the manner of a lover.

**love seat,** a seat or small sofa for two persons.

**love set,** a set won in tennis and certain other games without the opponent's winning a game.

**love|sick** (luv′sik′), *adj.* **1** languishing because of love. **2** expressing a languishing caused by love: *a lovesick song.* —**love′sick′ness**, *n.*

**love|some** (luv′səm), *adj. Archaic.* **1** lovable. **2** lovely; beautiful: *One praised her ankles ... One her dark hair and lovesome mien* (Tennyson). **3** loving; friendly. **4** amorous. —**love′some-ness**, *n.*

**love spoon,** a wooden spoon with twin bowls at the end of a handle, formerly part of Welsh courtship custom, given by a man to his sweetheart.

**love story,** a story whose main theme is the affection existing between lovers.

**love|struck** (luv′struk′), *adj.* affected strongly with love: *a lovestruck couple.*

**love tern** = fairy tern.

**love vine,** = dodder.

**Love wave,** a seismic wave that travels across the earth's surface in a horizontal motion. [< A. E. H. *Love*, 1863-1940, an English mathematician, who discovered it]

**love|y-dove|y** (luv′ē duv′ē), *n., adj. Informal.* —*n.* darling. —*adj.* weakly sentimental.

**lov|ing** (luv′ing), *adj.* feeling or showing love; affectionate; fond: *loving hearts, loving glances.* —**lov′ing|ly**, *adv.* —**lov′ing|ness**, *n.*

**loving cup, 1** a large cup with two or more handles, passed around for all to drink from, as at the close of a banquet: *Tonight the loving cup we'll drain* (Henry Newbolt). **2** such a cup awarded as a trophy.

**lov|ing-kind|ness** (luv′ing kīnd′nis), *n.* kindness coming from love; affectionate tenderness and consideration: *the loving-kindness of God's mercies.* SYN: kindliness, benevolence.

**low¹** (lō), *adj., adv., n.* —*adj.* **1** not high or tall; short: *low walls, a low hedge. This footstool is very low.* **2a** near the ground, the floor, or a base; close to the earth: *a low shelf, a low jump, a low bow.* **b** near the horizon: *the low evening sun.* **c** prostrate or dead: *And wilt thou weep when I am low?* (Byron). **3** rising only slightly from the general or usual level or lying below it: *low hills, low carving, low ground near the sea.* **4** *Figurative.* **a** below others; inferior; lowly: *of a low grade. She had a rather low position as a kitchen maid. One law for gentlemen, another for low people* (Jeremy Bentham). SYN: obscure. **b** not advanced in organization: *Bacteria are low organisms.* **5** *Figurative.* less than usual; small; moderate: *a low price, low temperature, low speed, a low diet of few calories.* **6** of less than ordinary height, depth, or quantity, or nearly used up: *The well is getting low. The dry summer made all the streams too low for fishing. Our supplies were low.* **7** *Figurative.* unfavorable; poor: *The boys had a low opinion of cowards. I have a low regard for his judgment.* SYN: disapproving, disparaging. **8** *Figurative.* mean or base; coarse; vulgar; degraded: *low company, low thoughts. A person hears some low talk in saloons.* SYN: See syn. under **base²**. **9** *Figurative.* **a** feeble; weak: *a low state of health. The sick man's resistance is very low. The lights were low.* **b** depressed or dejected: *low spirits. I am low and dejected at times* (Edmund Burke). **10** far down in a scale or series: **a** deep in pitch; not high in the musical scale: *a low note.* **b** near the equator: *low latitudes.* **c** designating an arrangement of gears that gives the lowest speed and the greatest power. In low gear the ratio of the drive shaft to that of the crankshaft is smallest. **11** not loud; soft: *a low whisper.* **12** cut low; low-necked: *I'm sorry you've come in such low dresses* (Anthony Trollope). **13** *Phonetics.* pronounced with the tongue far from the palate. The *a* in *fat* and the *o* in *got* are low vowels. **14** relatively recent: *His dating of the burial seems too low considering the primitive character of the pottery.* **15** maintaining Low-Church practices.

—*adv.* **1a** at or to a low point, place, rank, amount, degree, price, or other condition: *Supplies are running low.* **b** near the horizon: *The sun sank low.* **2** near the ground, floor, or base: *to fly low. Party fights are won by aiming low* (Oliver W. Holmes). *The spotted pack, with tails high mounted, ears hung low* (William Cowper). **3** *Figurative.* meanly; humbly: *You value yourself too low.* **4a** softly; quietly; not loudly: *Lucia, speak low, he is retired to rest* (Joseph Addison). **b** at a low pitch on the musical scale. **5** near the equator. **6** lately; at a comparatively recent date.

—*n.* **1** that which is low, or something or someone in a low position: *We take the rough with the smooth, the low with the high. The poor and the low have their way of expressing the last facts of philosophy as well as you* (Emerson). *From the light, flutey high notes, where sopranos often lose character, to rich, viola-like lows* (Time). **2** an arrangement of the gears to give the lowest speed and greatest power in an automobile and similar machines. **3** *Meteorology.* an area of com-

**Pronunciation Key:** hat, āge, cãre, fär; let, ēqual, tėrm; it, īce; hot, ōpen, ôrder; oil, out; cup, pu̇t, rüle; child; long; thin; ᴛʜen; zh, measure; ə represents **a** in about, **e** in taken, **i** in pencil, **o** in lemon, **u** in circus.

paratively low barometric pressure; cyclone: *Winds in a low rotate counterclockwise in the Northern Hemisphere* [*and*] *clockwise in the Southern Hemisphere* (James E. Miller). **4a** the lowest trump card in certain games. **b** the lowest score, number, or rank, or the player who makes it in a sport or game. **5** the lowest point reached in output, prices, business transactions, or the like; a minimum: *Many stocks fell to new lows after the news was received.*
**lay low, a** to knock down: *The boxer laid low his opponent.* (*Figurative.*) [*The senator*] *was laid low by a serious attack of shingles, and had to withdraw from the race* (Time). **b** to kill: *The enemy was laid low.*
**lie low,** to stay hidden; keep still: *After the third robbery, the thieves decided to lie low for a time. I shall lie low and pretend to know nothing about it. Brer Fox, he lay low* (Joel Chandler Harris).
[< Scandinavian (compare Old Icelandic *lāgr*)]
—**low′ness,** *n.*

**low²** (lō), *v., n.* —*v.i., v.t.* to make the sound of a cow; moo: *The lowing herd winds slowly o'er the lea* (Thomas Gray).
—*n.* the sound a cow makes; mooing.
[Old English *hlōwan*]

**low³** (lō), *n., v. Especially Scottish.* —*n.* **1** a flame; blaze. **2** a lantern, torch, or candle.
—*v.i.* to flame, blaze, or glow. Also, **lowe.**
[< Scandinavian (compare Old Icelandic *loge*)]

**low beam,** the less intense of the two beams in an automobile headlight.

**low blood pressure,** = hypotension.

**low blow,** a foul blow; unfair treatment.

**low blueberry,** = lowbush blueberry.

**low|born** (lō′bôrn′), *adj.* of humble birth. **SYN:** plebeian.

**low|boy** (lō′boi′), *n. U.S.* a low chest of drawers, usually having legs.

**low brass,** = red brass.

**low|bred** (lō′bred′), *adj.* coarse; vulgar: *a lowbred fellow, lowbred manners.*

**low|brow** (lō′brou′), *n., adj. Informal.* —*n.* a person who is not cultured or intellectual: *Ben ... said this powerful play was too powerful for a bunch of lowbrows like us* (H. L. Wilson).
—*adj.* **1** of or suitable for a lowbrow: *Generalizations about the proportion of support for highbrow and lowbrow activity in any community must of course be carefully checked* (Harper's). **2** being a lowbrow; incapable of culture.

**low-browed** (lō′broud′), *adj.* **1** having a low forehead. **2** *Informal, Figurative.* lowbrow.

**low|bush blueberry** (lō′bůsh′), **1** any one of several eastern North American bushes growing to a height of one or two feet, with small clusters of greenish-white flowers and a sweet, dark-blue berry; low blueberry. **2** its berry.

**Low-Church** (lō′chėrch′), *adj.* of or having to do with a party in the Anglican Communion that lays little stress on church authority and ceremonies, emphasizing the evangelical rather than the priestly or Catholic character of the Church; more like other Protestant denominations and less like the Roman Catholic Church.

**Low Church,** a party maintaining Low-Church practices.

**Low Churchman,** a person who favors Low-Church practices.

**low comedy,** comedy of a broad rather than a subtle nature, relying more on boisterous physical action and ludicrous situations than on witty dialogue.

**low-cost** (lō′kôst′, -kost′), *adj.* = inexpensive.

**low-coun|try** (lō′kun′trē), *adj.* of the Low Countries; having to do with the Netherlands, Belgium, and Luxembourg.

**low-cut** (lō′kut′), *adj.* **1** cut low: *a low-cut neckline.* **2** low-necked: *low-cut dresses.*

**low-down¹** (lō′doun′), *adj. Informal.* **1** low; mean; contemptible: *a low-down neighborhood. Giving me a broken pen in the trade was a low-down trick.* **2** earthy: *Delightful low-down musical about Broadway's floating crap games* (Time). [American English; in earlier British English, previous, low in space]

**low-down²** or **low|down** (lō′doun′), *n. Slang.* the actual facts or truth: *In an undertone he gave me the lowdown on them, contemptuously* (Saul Bellow). [American English; origin uncertain]

**lowe** (lō), *n., v.i.,* **lowed, low|ing.** = low³.

**low-en|er|gy** (lō′en′ər jē), *adj.* of or having to do with the energy of elementary particles that have not been accelerated in particle accelerators; not high-energy: *low-energy electrons or neutrons, low-energy physics.*

**low|er¹** (lō′ər), *v., adj., adv.* —*v.t.* **1** to let down or haul down: *We lower the flag at night.* **2** to make lower: *to lower the water in a canal, to lower the volume of the radio,* (*Figurative.*) *to lower the price of a car, to lower the steam pressure in a boiler.* (*Figurative.*) *The fan soon lowered the temperature of the room.* **SYN:** decrease, diminish. **3** *Figurative.* to bring down in rank, station, or estimation; degrade; dishonor. **4** *Music.* to depress in pitch.
—*v.i.* to sink or become lower: *The sun lowered slowly.* **SYN:** descend, fall.
[< adjective]
—*adj., comparative of* **low¹**. **1** more low; below others on a comparative scale: (*Figurative.*) *lower organisms,* (*Figurative.*) *lower prices.* **2** consisting of representatives usually elected by popular vote: *the lower branch of a legislature.* **3** Usually, **Lower.** *Geology.* being or relating to an earlier division of a period, system, or the like: *Lower Cretaceous.*
—*adv.* comparative of **low¹**.
[< *low¹* + *-er³*]

**low|er²** (lou′ər), *v., n.* —*v.i.* **1** to look dark and threatening: *Dark lowers the tempest overhead* (Longfellow). **SYN:** menace. **2** to look angry or sullen; frown; scowl. **SYN:** glower.
—*n.* **1** a dark and threatening look; gloominess. **2** an angry or sullen look; frown; scowl. Also, **lour.**
[Middle English *louren*]

**lower bound,** *Mathematics.* a number less than or equal to a given function.

**Lower Carboniferous,** *Geology.* the name outside of North America for the Mississippian period of Carboniferous time.

***lower case,** *Printing.* **1** small letters, not capitals. *Abbr:* l.c. **2** the frame or frames in which small letters are kept for hand setting.

***lower case** definition 1 — abc (lower-case letters) — ABC (capital letters)

**low|er-case** (lō′ər kās′), *adj., v.,* **-cased, -cas|ing.** *Printing.* —*adj.* **1** in small letters, not capitals. **2** kept in or having to do with the lower case.
—*v.t.* to print in small letters.

**lower class,** a class of society below the middle class, comprising unskilled and some semiskilled laborers, people who are chronically unemployed, and (sometimes) the working class in general: *Until a few decades ago the urban lower class was almost entirely white; every ethnic group, including the Anglo-Saxon Protestant one, contributed to it, and its outlook and style of life were strikingly similar to those of the present Negro lower class* (Edward C. Banfield).

**low|er-class** (lō′ər klas′, -kläs′), *adj.* **1** of, having to do with, or included in the lower class: *lower-class neighborhoods.* **2** of or having to do with the freshman and sophomore classes in a college, university, or high school.

**low|er|class|man** (lō′ər klas′mən, -kläs′-), *n., pl.* **-men.** a freshman or sophomore in a college, university, or high school; underclassman.

**lower criticism,** the critical physical study of a text, especially of the Bible, having in view the correction of copyists' errors, omissions, and additions, and other corruptions which have crept into the text since it was first written; textual criticism.

**Lower House** or **lower house,** the more representative branch of a lawmaking body that has two branches, made up of members usually elected by popular vote. The House of Representatives is the Lower House in the United States Congress.

**low|er|ing** (lou′ər ing), *adj.* **1** dark and threatening; gloomy: *a gloomy and lowering day* (Francis Parkman). **2** frowning; scowling; angry-looking. Also, **louring.** —**low′er|ing|ly,** *adv.*

**lower mast,** the lowest section of a mainmast, on which the mainsail is carried.

**low|er|most** (lō′ər mōst), *adj.* = lowest.

**lower regions,** hell; Hades.

**low|er-sense arts** (lō′ər sens′), arts, such as the making of perfume and cooking, that are not usually considered fine arts.

**lower transit,** *Astronomy.* the passage of a heavenly body across the part of the meridian that lies below the pole.

**lower world, 1** the abode of the dead; hell; Hades. **2** the earth.

**low|er|y** (lou′ər ē), *adj.* dull; gloomy; threatening. Also, **loury.**

**low|est common denominator** (lō′ist), **1** *Mathematics.* = least common denominator. **2** that which most fully expresses the feelings or opinions of a large number of persons or a group in general.

**lowest common multiple,** = least common multiple.

**Lowes|toft** (lōs′toft, -təft), *n.* **1** a softly colored blue-and-white china produced in England in the second half of the 1700's. **2** porcelain made in China for foreign export, especially to England and America, mistakenly thought to have been made at Lowestoft in England. [< *Lowestoft,* a seaport in Suffolk, England]

**low explosive,** an explosive used as a propellant, as for the shell in a gun, rather than to destroy by its own force.

**low-fre|quen|cy** (lō′frē′kwən sē), *adj.* of or having to do with a frequency ranging from 30 to 300 kilohertz: *low-frequency radio receivers, low-frequency sound waves. Abbr:* LF (no periods).

**low gear,** the gear that gives the greatest force and the least speed, especially in an automobile; low.

**Low German, 1** the Germanic speech of the Low Countries (Dutch, Flemish, etc.). **2** the German dialect of northern Germany; Plattdeutsch.

**low-grade** (lō′grād′), *adj.* of poor quality; inferior: *low-grade ores.*

**low hurdles,** a race in which the runners jump over hurdles 2½ feet high.

**low-key** (lō′kē′), *adj.* understated; played down: *To take account of French feelings, the British are reported to be willing to settle for a very low-key communiqué that would not present the nuclear force as a great new development of NATO* (New York Times).

**low-keyed** (lō′kēd′), *adj.* = low-key.

**low|land** (lō′lənd), *n., adj.* —*n.* land that is lower and flatter than the neighboring country.
—*adj.* of or in the lowlands: *a lowland farm.*

**Low|land** (lō′lənd), *n., adj.* —*n.* Also, **Lowlands.** a low, flat region in southern and eastern Scotland.
—*adj.* of, belonging to, or characteristic of the Lowlands of Scotland.
**Lowlands,** the Lowland (Scottish) dialect: *The Scottish word for Lowlands is Lallans.*

**low|land|er** (lō′lən dər), *n.* a person born or living in a lowland.

**Low|land|er** (lō′lən dər), *n.* a person born or living in the Lowlands of Scotland.

**lowland fir** or **lowland white fir,** a large fir of the western coast of the United States and Canada, having long, curved branches, dark foliage, and soft wood suitable for lumber, boxes, and pulp; grand fir; white fir.

**lowland rice,** rice that grows on flooded or irrigated land.

**Low Latin,** Latin as spoken in the post-Classical period.

**low-lev|el** (lō′lev′əl), *adj.* **1** having or occurring at a low level of altitude: *low-level explosions, low-level flights, a low-level bridge.* **2** low in content; containing a relatively small amount of something: *Much of this refuse from fission is low-level and short-lived* (Newsweek). *Mice were given low-level doses of streptomycin* (Science News Letter). **3** at the lowest level of authority, rank, quality, or condition: *a low-level official.* **4** soft; hard to hear: *The recording is low-level, faint, and poor in definition* (New York Times).

**low|life** (lō′līf′), *n., pl.* **-lifes,** *adj.* —*n. Slang.* **1** a vicious, degenerate, or vile person; a criminal: *... a scattering of lowlifes whose crimes include an attempted kidnaping* (New Yorker). **2** immoral people or environment: *The salacious, raucously funny bestiary of Roman lowlife* (Time).
—*adj.* **1** characteristic of a lowlife; immoral; degenerate: *The guys are a lowlife lot who peddle dope, steal, and double-cross each other* (New Yorker). **2** unrefined; cheap; crude; mean: *The bands that played jazz were considered lowlife and vulgar* (Saturday Review).

**low|li|head** (lō′lē hed), *n. Archaic.* humility; lowliness.

**low|li|ly** (lō′lə lē), *adv.* in a lowly manner; humbly.

**low|li|ness** (lō′lē nis), *n.* humbleness of feeling or behavior; humble station in life.

**low-lived** (lō′līvd′), *adj. Informal.* belonging in or characteristic of a low order of life or society; vulgar; mean: *low-lived manners.*

**low|ly** (lō′lē), *adj.,* **-li|er, -li|est,** *adv.* —*adj.* **1** low in rank, station, position, or development: *a lowly corporal, a lowly occupation, the lowly protozoan.* **SYN:** inferior. **2** modest in feeling, behavior, or condition; humble; meek: *He held a lowly opinion of himself. I am meek and lowly in heart* (Matthew 11:29). **SYN:** unassuming. See syn. under **humble.**
—*adv.* **1** humbly; meekly. **2** in a low manner, degree, or position. **3** in a low voice.

**low-ly|ing** (lō′lī′ing), *adj.* **1** lying below the normal level or elevation: *Within a few hours the low-lying island city was overrun by the raging waters of the Gulf of Mexico* (New Yorker). **2** lying close to the ground: *low-lying foothills.*

**Low Mass,** a simplified form of High Mass in the Roman Catholic Church, conducted by one priest assisted by altar boys. There is no chanting in Low Mass.

**low-mind|ed** (lō′mīn′did), *adj.* having or showing a coarse or low mind; mean; vulgar. —**low′-mind′ed|ly,** *adv.* —**low′-mind′ed|ness,** *n.*

**lown**[1] (loun), *adj., n., v. Scottish.* **—*adj., n.*** calm; quiet. **—*v.i., v.t.*** to calm; lull. [< Scandinavian (compare Icelandic *lygn*, Swedish *lugn*)]

**lown**[2] (lün), *n.* = loon[2].

**low-necked** (lō′nekt′), *adj.* (of a dress, blouse, or sweater) cut low so as to show the neck, part of the bosom, and shoulders or back; décolleté.

**low-oc|tane** (lō′ok′tān), *adj.* **1** (of gasoline) having a low octane number, or percentage of octane. **2** *Figurative.* dull; weak; uninspiring: . . . *an hour and a half of low-octane merriment, brightened by an occasional lively vignette* (Maclean's).

**low-pitched** (lō′picht′), *adj.* **1a** of low tone or sound; deep. **b** little elevated: (*Figurative.*) *poor and low-pitched desires* (Milton). **2** having little slope: *a low-pitched roof.* **3** having little height between floor and ceiling.

**low-pres|sure** (lō′presh′ər), *adj.* **1** having or using less than the usual pressure. **2** having a low barometric pressure: *During the seasons in question the coastal low-pressure troughs were farther west than usual* (Scientific American). **3** *Figurative.* easygoing; that does not arouse or annoy: *a low-pressure salesman. His books are quiet, low-pressure, and frequently on the edge of becoming pedestrian* (New Yorker).

**low profile, 1** manner, behavior, style, performance, or the like, that is inconspicuous, moderate, or unexceptional: *Japan today simply stands too tall and too rich to maintain a low profile* (Time). **2** a person who shows or cultivates a low profile: *We now have a government of "low profiles," gray men who represent no identifiable place, no region, no program* (Harper's).

**low-pro|file** (lō′prō′fīl), *adj.* played down; low-key: *Dim lights, small tables, and low-profile recorded music* (New Yorker).

**low profile tire,** a tire wider (from side wall to side wall) than it is high (from tread to wheel rim), designed to put more tread into contact with the road than do regular tires.

**low relief,** sculpture in which the figures stand out only slightly from the background; bas-relief.

**low|rid|er** (lō′rī′dər), *n.* a person who takes part in lowriding.

**low|rid|ing** (lō′rī′ding), *n.* a practice of lowering the clearance of a car to within a few inches of the ground. The style is to cruise slowly and exhibit a lavishly decorated automobile.

**low-rise** (lō′rīz′), *adj.* having few stories; not high-rise: *low-rise housing developments, a low-rise building without elevators.*

**lows** (lōz), *adj., v.t., v.i., adv. Obsolete.* loose.

**low silhouette,** = low profile.

**low-slung** (lō′slung′), *adj.* built low; standing close to the ground: *It was a low-slung contraption which looked as if it had been built of bed slats* (Atlantic).

**low-spir|it|ed** (lō′spir′ə tid), *adj.* sad; depressed; dejected. **SYN:** dispirited, morose. **—low′-spir′it|ed|ly,** *adv.* **—low′-spir′it|ed|ness,** *n.*

**low spirits,** a condition of little energy or joy; sadness; depression; dejection.

**Low Sunday,** the Sunday after Easter.

**low-ten|sion** (lō′ten′shən), *adj.* **1** (of an electrical device or circuit) having, using, or for use at a low voltage, usually of fewer than 750 volts. **2** (of a winding of a transformer) to be used at a low voltage.

**low-test** (lō′test′), *adj.* having a relatively high boiling point: *low-test gasoline.*

**low tide, 1** the lowest level of the ocean on the shore. See picture under **tide**[1]. **2** the time when the ocean is lowest on the shore. **3** *Figurative.* the lowest point of anything.

**low-volt|age** (lō′vōl′tij), *adj.* designed to operate at a voltage of fewer than 750 volts.

**low water, 1** the lowest level of water, as in a channel. **2** low tide.

**low-wa|ter mark** (lō′wôt′ər, -wot′ər), **1a** the lowest level reached by a body of water. **b** the mark showing low water. **2** *Figurative.* any lowest point: *The low-water mark in the Tories' fortunes was reached at the county council elections* (Economist).

**low wine,** wine of low percentage of alcohol.

**low-yield** (lō′yēld′), *adj.* yielding little, as of ore.

**lox**[1] (loks), *n.* a kind of smoked salmon. [< Yiddish *laks* < Middle High German *lacs* salmon]

**lox**[2] or **LOX** (loks), *n.* = liquid oxygen.

**lox|o|drome** (lok′sə drōm), *n.* a loxodromic curve; rhumb line. [back formation < *loxodromic*]

**lox|o|drom|ic** (lok′sə drom′ik), *adj.* having to do with sailing obliquely across meridians on a rhumb line. [< Greek *loxós* oblique + *drómos* a course + English *-ic*] **—lox′o|drom′i|cal|ly,** *adv.*

**lox|o|drom|i|cal** (lok′sə drom′ə kəl), *adj.* = loxodromic.

**loxodromic curve** or **line,** a line on the surface of a sphere cutting all meridians at the same angle, such as that formed by the path of a ship whose course is constantly directed to the same point of the compass in a direction oblique to the equator; rhumb line.

**lox|o|drom|ics** (lok′sə drom′iks), *n.* the art of sailing obliquely across meridians on a rhumb line.

**lox|od|ro|my** (lok sod′rə mē), *n.* = loxodromics.

**loy|al** (loi′əl), *adj.* **1** true and faithful to love, promise, duty, or other obligations: *a loyal worker, loyal conductor sentiments, loyal devotion. I will remain The loyal'st husband that did e'er plight troth* (Shakespeare). **SYN:** constant. See syn. under **faithful. 2** faithful to one's king, government, or country: *a loyal citizen.* **3** *Obsolete.* legal; legitimate. [< Middle French *loyal*, Old French *loial*, and *leial* < Latin *lēgālis* legal < *lēx, lēgis* law. See etym. of doublets **leal, legal.**] **—loy′al|ly,** *adv.*

**loy|al|ist** (loi′ə list), *n.* a person who supports his king or the existing government, especially in time of revolt. **—loy′al|ism,** *n.*

**Loy|al|ist** (loi′ə list), *n.* **1** an American colonist who opposed independence for the American colonies at the time of the American Revolutionary War; Tory. **2** a person loyal to the Republic and opposed to Franco and the Falangists during the civil war in Spain from 1936 to 1939. **3** = United Empire Loyalist (in Canada). **4** a person opposing political separation of Northern Ireland from Great Britain: *The Loyalist coalition . . . want majority rule in Ulster, and to remain part of the United Kingdom* (Listener).

**loy|al|ty** (loi′əl tē), *n., pl.* **-ties.** loyal feeling or behavior; faithfulness: *Loyalty, like love, cannot be forced. In its essence loyalty is love for a person, a group, a cause. . . . group loyalty cannot be obtained by force, but group disloyalty can be restrained by force* (Emory S. Bogardus). **SYN:** fidelity, constancy.

**loyalty oath,** an oath pledging loyalty to a government or constitution: *Each has been required to swear a loyalty oath with this ominous clause: "If I betray this oath, I agree to suffer the punishment of a traitor"* (Newsweek).

***loz|enge** (loz′inj), *n.* **1** a design or figure shaped like a diamond; rhombus. It has four equal sides, two acute angles, and two obtuse angles. **2** a small tablet of any shape used as medicine or candy. Cough drops are sometimes called lozenges. [< Old French *losenge*, ultimately < Late Latin *lausa* slab]

***lozenge**
definition 1

**loz|enged** (loz′injd), *adj.* **1** having the shape of a lozenge: *the lozenged panes of a very small latticed window* (Charlotte Brontë). **2** divided into or ornamented with figures in the shape of lozenges, especially of alternate colors.

**LP** (no periods), **1** a long-playing phonograph record: *All five LP versions of the Concerto for Orchestra are excellent* (Atlantic). **2** *Trademark.* a name for a phonograph record of this type. **3** low pressure.

**L.P.,** low pressure.

**LPG** (no periods), liquefied petroleum gas.

**LP gas,** or **LP-gas** (el′pē′gas′), *n.* liquefied petroleum gas.

**L plate,** *British.* a plate affixed to the vehicle of a person learning to drive. [< *L*(earner) *plate*]

**L.P.O.** or **LPO** (no periods), **1** London Philharmonic Orchestra. **2** lunar parking orbit.

**L.P.S.,** Lord Privy Seal.

**lr.,** lira.

**Lr** (no period), lawrencium (chemical element).

**LR** (no periods), long range.

**L.R.,** Lloyd's Register.

**LRL** (no periods), Lunar Receiving Laboratory (a sealed, germ-free building where astronauts and lunar samples are quarantined for a given period after returning from the moon).

**LRV** (no periods), lunar roving vehicle.

**L.S., 1** *British.* Leading Seaman. **2** Licentiate in Surgery. **3** the place of the seal (Latin, *locus sigilli*).

**LSA** (no periods), Linguistic Society of America.

**L.S.D.** or **l.s.d.,** pounds, shillings, and pence (Latin, *librae, solidi, denarii*).

**LSD** (no periods), **1** landing ship, dock. **2** lysergic acid diethylamide: *LSD . . . is a chemical that produces hallucinations and delusions in healthy persons like those in mental sickness* (Science News Letter).

**L.S.E.** or **LSE** (no periods), London School of Economics.

**LSI** (no periods), large-scale integration: *LSI . . . involves building up very complex electronic networks on tiny chips* (Irwin Stambler).

**LSM** (no periods), landing ship, medium.

**L.S.O.** or **LSO** (no periods), London Symphony Orchestra.

**L.S.S.,** Lifesaving Service.

**l.s.t.,** local standard time.

**LST** (no periods), landing ship, tank.

**L.S.T.,** local standard time.

**l.t,** an abbreviation for the following:
1 lawn tennis.
2 left tackle (in football).
3 local time.
4 long ton.
5 low tension.

**Lt.,** lieutenant.

**L.T.A.,** Lawn Tennis Association.

**Lt. Col.,** lieutenant colonel.

**Lt. Comdr.,** lieutenant commander.

**Ltd.** or **ltd.,** limited.

**Lt. Gen.,** lieutenant general.

**Lt. Gov.,** lieutenant governor.

**LtH** (no periods), luteotrophic hormone.

**L. Th.,** Licentiate in Theology.

**lthr.,** leather.

**ltr.,** letter.

**Lu** (no period), lutetium (chemical element).

**lu|au** (lü′ou), *n.* a feast, especially in Hawaii, generally held outdoors, with roast pig as the main dish. [< Hawaiian *lū'au*]

**lub.,** lubricate.

**lub|ber** (lub′ər), *n., adj.* **—*n.* 1** a big, clumsy, stupid fellow; lout: *the rude tricks of an overgrown lubber* (William Godwin). **SYN:** dolt, bumpkin. **2** an inexperienced or clumsy sailor: *He swore woundily at the lieutenant, and called him . . . swab and lubber* (Tobias Smollett). **—*adj.*** loutish; clumsy; stupid; coarse. [Middle English *lober*. Compare dialectal Swedish *lubber* fat, lazy fellow.]

**lubber grasshopper,** a large, short-horned, short-winged grasshopper that cannot fly.

**lub|ber|ly** (lub′ər lē), *adj., adv.* **—*adj.* 1** loutish; clumsy; stupid. **SYN:** bungling, gawky. **2** awkward in the work of a sailor: *Such was Rope Yarn; of all land-lubbers the most lubberly and most miserable* (Herman Melville). **—*adv.*** in a lubberly manner; clumsily. **—lub′ber|li|ness,** *n.*

**lubber's hole,** an opening in the platform or top at the head of a lower mast, through which an inexperienced sailor may pass, while an expert seaman goes around the outside.

**lubber's knot,** = granny knot.

**lubber's line, mark,** or **point,** *Nautical.* a vertical line on the forward inner surface of a compass bowl in line with the bow, which indicates the direction in which the ship's head is swinging, to assist the helmsman in keeping course at sea.

**lube** (lüb), *n.,* or **lube oil,** *Informal.* lubricant; heavy petroleum oil used to lubricate machinery: *Cleaning and relubricating with a thinner lube is called for* (Roy Hoopes). [short for *lubricating oil*]

**lu|bra** (lü′brə), *n. Australian.* female aborigine; gin.

**lu|bric** (lü′brik), *adj. Archaic.* smooth and slippery: *This lubric and adult'rate age* (John Dryden). [< Latin *lūbricus* slippery]

**lu|bri|cal** (lü′brə kəl), *adj. Archaic.* lubric.

**lu|bri|cant** (lü′brə kənt), *n., adj.* **—*n.*** oil, grease, graphite, or detergents for putting on parts of machines that move against one another, to make them smooth and slippery so that they will work easily. **—*adj.*** lubricating.

**lu|bri|cate** (lü′brə kāt), *v.,* **-cat|ed, -cat|ing.** **—*v.t.* 1** to make (machinery) smooth and easy to work by putting on oil or grease. **2** *Figurative.* to make slippery or smooth; expedite: *Dinner lubricates business* (Lord Stowell). **—*v.i.*** to act as a lubricant. [< Latin *lūbricāre* (with English *-ate*[1]) < *lūbricus* slippery]

**lu|bri|ca|tion** (lü′brə kā′shən), *n.* **1** the act or process of lubricating or oiling. **2** the state of being lubricated or oiled.

**lu|bri|ca|tion|al** (lü′brə kā′shə nəl), *adj.* of or having to do with lubrication.

**lu|bri|ca|tive** (lü′brə kā′tiv), *adj.* having the property of lubricating.

**lu|bri|ca|tor** (lü′brə kā′tər), *n.* **1** a person or thing that lubricates. **2** a device for lubricating machinery. **3** a lubricating substance; lubricant.

**lu|bri|ca|to|ri|um** (lü′brə kə tôr′ē əm, -tōr′-), *n.* a place or establishment where motor vehicles are lubricated. [< *lubricat*(e) + (emp)*orium*]

**lu|bri|cious** (lü brish′əs), *adj.* = lubricous. **—lu|bri′cious|ly,** *adv.*

**lu|bric|i|ty** (lü bris′ə tē), *n., pl.* **-ties. 1** oily smoothness; slipperiness: *this . . . lubricity of all objects, which lets them slip through our fingers then when we clutch hardest* (Emerson). **2** shiftiness; unsteadiness. **SYN:** instability, elusiveness. **3** lasciviousness; lewdness; wantonness. [< Late Latin *lūbricitās* < Latin *lūbricus* slippery]

**lu|bri|cous** (lü′brə kəs), *adj.* **1** slippery; smooth;

---

**Pronunciation Key:** hat, āge, cãre, fär; let, ēqual, tėrm; it, īce; hot, ōpen, ôrder; **oi**l, **ou**t; cup, pu̇t, rüle; **ch**ild; lo**ng**; **th**in; ᴛʜen; **zh**, measure; ə represents **a** in about, **e** in taken, **i** in pencil, **o** in lemon, **u** in circus.

slimy; oily. **2** shifty; unstable; elusive. **3** wanton; lewd. [< Latin *lūbricus* (with English *-ous*)]

**lu|bri|to|ri|um** (lü′brə tôr′ē əm, -tōr′-), *n.* = lubricatorium.

**lu|carne** (lü kärn′), *n.* an opening in a roof, such as a skylight or dormer window. [< Old French *lucane,* perhaps < a Germanic word]

**Lu|ca|yan** (lü kä′yən), *adj.* of or having to do with the Lucayo, or their language.

**Lu|ca|yo** (lü kä′yō), *n., pl.* **-yo** or **-yos.** **1** a member of an extinct Arawakan tribe of American Indians that inhabited the Bahamas at the time of Columbus. The Lucayo had the bow and arrow but used it for fishing. **2** the language of this tribe.

**luce** (lüs), *n.* a pike (fish), especially when fully grown. [< Old French *lus, luis* < Late Latin *lūcius*]

**lu|cen|cy** (lü′sən sē), *n.* brilliance; luminosity.

**lu|cent** (lü′sənt), *adj.* **1** bright or shining; luminous: *the sun's lucent orb* (Milton). **2** letting the light through; clear; translucent; lucid. [< Latin *lūcēns, -entis,* present participle of *lūcēre* to shine] **—lu′cent|ly,** *adv.*

**lu|cern** (lü sėrn′), *n.* = lucerne.

**lu|cerne** (lü sėrn′), *n. Especially British.* alfalfa. [< French *luzerne,* or *lucerne* < Provençal *luzerno,* ultimately < Latin *lūx, lūcis* light[1], related to *lūcēre* to shine (because of the shiny appearance of the grains)]

**lu|ces** (lü′sēz), *n.* luxes; a plural of **lux.**

**lu|cid** (lü′sid), *adj.* **1** easy to follow or understand: *A good explanation is lucid. The tangled weights and measures of old France gave place to the simple and lucid decimal system* (H. G. Wells). **SYN:** plain. **2** clear in intellect; sane; rational: *An insane person sometimes has lucid intervals.* **3** clear; translucent or transparent: *a lucid stream.* **SYN:** pellucid, limpid. **4** shining; bright. **SYN:** luminous. [< Latin *lūcidus* < *lūx, lūcis* light[1], related to *lūcēre* to shine] **—lu′cid|ly,** *adv.* **—lu′cid|ness,** *n.*

**lu|cid|i|ty** (lü sid′ə tē), *n.* lucid quality or condition; clearness, especially of thought, expression, perception, or the like: *The lucidity and accuracy of French had, both in style and in thought, served him well* (New Yorker).

**Lu|ci|fer** (lü′sə fər), *n.* **1** the chief rebel angel who was cast out of heaven; Satan; the Devil. **2** *Poetic.* the planet Venus when it is the morning star. [< Latin *lūcifer* the morning star, (literally) light-bringing < *lūx, lūcis* light[1] + *ferre* bring]

**lu|ci|fer** (lü′sə fər), *n.,* or **lucifer match,** a match that lights by friction. [< *Lucifer*]

**lu|cif|er|ase** (lü sif′ə rās), *n. Biochemistry.* an enzyme found in the cells of luminescent organisms, which acts on luciferin to produce luminosity.

**Lu|ci|fer|i|an** (lü′sə fir′ē ən), *adj.* like Lucifer; evil; diabolic.

**lu|cif|er|in** (lü sif′ər in), *n. Biochemistry.* a chemical substance found in the cells of luminescent organisms, such as fireflies, which, when acted on by luciferase, undergoes oxidation producing heatless light.

**lu|cif|er|ous** (lü sif′ər əs), *adj.* **1** bringing illumination or insight; illuminating. **2** that brings, conveys, or emits light.

**lu|cif|u|gous** (lü sif′yə gəs), *adj.* shunning the light, as bats and cockroaches do. [< Latin *lūcifugus* (with English *-ous*) < *lūx, lūcis* light[1] + *fugere* to flee]

**Lu|ci|na** (lü sī′nə), *n. Roman Mythology.* the goddess of childbirth, identified with Juno or sometimes Diana.

**Lu|cite** (lü′sīt), *n. Trademark.* a plastic, an acrylic resin, used instead of glass for airplane windows, lighting fixtures, camera lenses, automobile tail lights, and surgical and scientific instruments; methyl methacrylate.

**lu|ci|vee** (lü′sə vē), *n. U.S. Dialect and Canada.* the Canada lynx. [apparently < French *loup cervier* < Latin *lupus cervārius;* see etym. under **loup-cervier**]

**luck** (luk), *n., v.* **—*n.*** **1** that which seems to happen or come to one by chance; fortune; chance: *Luck favored me, and I won. There is no luck in literary reputation* (Emerson). **2** good luck; success, prosperity, or advantage coming by chance: *to wish one luck, to have luck in fishing. She gave me a penny for luck. She had the luck to win first prize.* **SYN:** success. **3** some object on which good fortune is supposed to depend.
**—*v.i., v.t.*** *Informal.* to come by sheerest chance or luck: *I will admit that a number of them have lucked in on me while I was backing good, sensible 30-1 shots, but I have never let that affect my basic thinking about horse racing* (New Yorker).
**as luck would have it,** as it happened; just by chance: *[She] fell in love with Mexico and, as luck would have it, an elegant band of Mexicans reciprocated* (New York Times).
**down on one's luck,** *Informal.* having bad luck; unlucky: *He would not hesitate to give money to anyone down on his luck* (London Times).
**in luck,** having good luck; fortunate; lucky: *I am in luck today; I found a quarter.*
**out of luck,** having bad luck; unlucky: *In the big storm, the fishermen were out of luck.*
**push one's luck,** *Informal.* to carry one's advantage too far: *Would you, I asked, pushing my luck, admit His Imperial Majesty Haile Selassie, Emperor of Ethiopia?* (Punch).
**try one's luck,** to see what one can do: *He tried his luck at various jobs until he found one that suited him.*
**worse luck,** unfortunately: *Worse luck, it rained.*
[< Middle Dutch *gheluc,* earlier *luk* or Middle Low German *gelucke*]

**luck|i|ly** (luk′ə lē), *adv.* by good luck; fortunately.

**luck|i|ness** (luk′ē nis), *n.* the quality or condition of being lucky; fortunateness.

**luck|less** (luk′lis), *adj.* having bad luck; bringing bad luck; unlucky; unfortunate. **—luck′less|ly,** *adv.* **—luck′less|ness,** *n.*

**luck penny,** *British.* **1** a penny or other coin kept or given to bring good luck. **2** a small sum given back for luck by the seller to the purchaser in a business transaction.

**luck|y** (luk′ē), *adj.,* **luck|i|er, luck|i|est.** **1** having good luck: *a lucky person.* **SYN:** happy. See syn. under **fortunate.** **2** bringing good luck: *a person's lucky star, a lucky charm, a lucky meeting. This is a lucky day.* **SYN:** happy. See syn. under **fortunate.**

**lu|cra|tive** (lü′krə tiv), *adj.* bringing in money; yielding gain or profit; profitable: *a lucrative profession, a lucrative investment.* **SYN:** gainful, remunerative. [< Latin *lucrātīvus* < *lūcrārī* to gain < *lucrum* gain] **—lu′cra|tive|ly,** *adv.* **—lu′cra|tive|ness,** *n.*

**lu|cre** (lü′kər), *n.* money considered as a bad or degrading influence; gain viewed as a low motive for action: *not greedy of filthy lucre* (I Timothy 3:3). **SYN:** pelf, mammon. [< Latin *lucrum* gain]

**Lu|cre|tian** (lü krē′shən), *adj.* having to do with Lucretius (about 94-about 55 B.C.), the Roman poet and Epicurean philosopher, or with his philosophical doctrines.

**lu|cu|brate** (lü′kyə brāt), *v.i.,* **-brat|ed, -brat|ing.** **1** to work by artificial light. **2** to produce lucubrations; discourse learnedly in writing. [< Latin *lūcubrāre* (with English *-ate*[1]) work at night, related to *lūcēre* to shine] **—lu′cu|bra′tor,** *n.*

**lu|cu|bra|tion** (lü′kyə brā′shən), *n.* **1** laborious study: *Absolute measure, which always inspired the lucubrations of the Greeks, was never popular in Greek trade* (Atlantic). **2** a learned or carefully written production, especially one that is labored and dull. **3** study carried on late at night: *the well-earned harvest of ... many a midnight lucubration* (Edward Gibbon).

**lu|cu|lent** (lü′kyə lənt), *adj.* **1** clear, convincing, or lucid, as of evidence, arguments, or explanations. **2** full of light; bright; luminous. [< Latin *lūculentus* < *lūx, lūcis* light[1]] **—lu′cu|lent|ly,** *adv.*

**Lu|cul|lan** (lü kul′ən), *adj.* = Lucullian.

**Lu|cul|li|an** (lü kul′ē ən), *adj.* rich; magnificent; luxurious: *a Lucullian feast.* [< *Lucullus,* about 110-57 B.C., a Roman general famous for wealth and luxury + English *-ian*]

**lu|cus a non lu|cen|do** (lü′kəs ā non lü sen′dō), *Latin.* **1** a grove, so called from not being light. **2** an absurd derivation; illogical reasoning.

**Lu|cy Ston|er** (lü′sē stō′nər), a woman who believes in keeping and using her maiden name after marriage: *Whoever thought a Lucy Stoner would be so girlishly sensitive as Jane Grant about being called a "newshen"?* (Time). [< *Lucy Stone,* 1818-1893, an American woman suffragist]

**Lud|dism** (lud′iz əm), *n.* **1** the principles and practices of the Luddites. **2** strong opposition to increased mechanization or automation in any field: *There is the Dataf low project, aimed at increasing their productivity: "Though systems men are just as susceptible to Luddism as anyone else," McQuaker comments* (Sunday Times).

**Lud|dite** (lud′īt), *n., adj.* **—*n.*** **1** a member of any one of the organized bands of workmen in England (1811-16) who set about destroying manufacturing equipment because they believed that it lessened employment. **2** a person who is strongly opposed to increased mechanization or automation in any field.
**—*adj.*** of or having to do with the Luddites or with Luddism: *Luddite riots. In American estimates, however, port capacity can be greatly increased by quick installation of modern equipment—if the Indian Government is really determined to override the Luddite resistance of the wharf labour* (London Times).
[perhaps < Ned *Lud,* a weak-minded person, who destroyed equipment in a Leicestershire village about 1779 + *-ite*[1]]

**Lud|dit|ish** (lud′īt′ish), *adj.* characteristic of a Luddite; showing Ludditism: *Not many years ago it was considered regressive and Ludditish even to suggest the need for control of technology* (Wilbur H. Ferry).

**Lud|dit|ism** (lud′ə tiz′əm), *n.* = Luddism.

**lu|dic** (lü′dik), *adj.* of or having to do with play; playful: *Despite the time-worn example of kittens chasing blown leaves as if they were mice, it remains to be proved that "ludic behaviour" (play) is directly related to superiority in the adult animal* (New Scientist). [< Latin *lūdus* game, play + English *-ic*]

**lu|di|crous** (lü′də krəs), *adj.* absurd but amusing; causing derisive laughter; ridiculous: *the ludicrous acts of a clown.* **SYN:** laughable, droll, comical. [< Latin *lūdicrus* (with English *-ous*) < *lūdus* sport] **—lu′di|crous|ly,** *adv.* **—lu′di|crous|ness,** *n.*

**Lud|low** (lud′lō), *n.* a style of sans-serif printing type. [< *Ludlow,* trademark for a linecasting machine]

**lu|do** (lü′dō), n. *Especially British.* a game resembling pachisi, played with dice and counters on a special board. [< Latin *lūdo* I play]

**lu|es** (lü′ēz), *n.* = syphilis. [< Latin *luēs, luis* plague < *luere* loosen, decompose]

**lu|et|ic** (lü et′ik), *adj.* having to do with lues; affected with lues; syphilitic. [< Latin *luēs* plague; patterned on *herpetic*] **—lu|et′i|cal|ly,** *adv.*

**luff** (luf), *v., n.* **—*v.i.*** to turn the bow of a ship toward the wind; sail into the wind: *Now, my hearty, luff* (Robert Louis Stevenson). [< noun]
**—*n.*** **1** the act of turning the bow of a ship toward the wind. **2** the forward edge of a fore-and-aft sail. **3** the fullest and broadest part of a ship's bow. Also, **loof.**
[Middle English *lof,* perhaps < Dutch *loef*]

**luf|fa** (luf′ə), *n.* = loofah.

**Luft|waf|fe** (lụft′väf′ə), *n. German.* **1** the German air force, especially under the Nazis in World War II. **2** (literally) air weapon.

**lug**[1] (lug), *v.,* **lugged, lug|ging,** *n.* **—*v.t.*** **1** to pull along or carry with effort; drag: *We lugged the rug to the yard to clean it. The children lugged home a big Christmas tree.* **2** *Figurative.* to introduce irrelevantly or without appropriateness: *He always had to lug in some reference to his ancestors.* **3** (of a ship) to carry (sail) beyond the limit of safety in a strong wind.
**—*v.i.*** **1** to pull or tug. **2** to veer or bear toward the rail in a horse race: *Mark-Ye-Well, who was ridden by Arcaro, lugged toward the rails and got himself boxed in* (New Yorker).
**—*n.*** **1** the act of pulling or carrying something heavy; a rough pull. **2** *U.S. Informal.* something heavy to be carried, dragged, or tugged.
[perhaps < Scandinavian (compare Swedish *lugga* pull by the hair)] **—lug′ger,** *n.*

**lug**[2] (lug), *n.* **1** a projecting part used to hold or grip something, such as a handle on a pitcher or bowl, or a leather loop on the side of the harness saddle in which the shaft rests. **2** *Scottish.* the ear. **3** *Slang.* a clumsy or stupid person. [origin uncertain. Compare Swedish *lugg* forelock.]

**lug**[3] (lug), *n.* = lugsail.

**lug**[4] (lug), *n.* = lugworm.

**Lu|gan|da** (lü gan′də), *n.* the language of the Baganda.

**lug|bait** (lug′bāt′), *n.* = lugworm.

***luge** (lüzh), *n., v.,* **luged, luge|ing.** **—*n.*** a small coasting sled steered by short iron-pointed sticks, used especially in Switzerland.
**—*v.i.*** to coast or race in a luge: *Lugeing isn't merely a competitive sport. In Europe there are 30,000 registered lugers, backed by a vanguard of thousands who luge for the fun of it* (New York Times).
[< French *luge* < Swiss dialect (Grisons)] **—lug′er,** *n.*

***luge**

**lu|ger** or **Lu|ger** (lü′gər), *n.* an automatic pistol made in Germany: *We both carried Lugers, which were more fashionable with American troops than American weapons* (New Yorker). [< George *Luger,* a German engineer of the late 1800's]

**lug|gage** (lug′ij), *n.* **1** baggage, especially of a traveler or passenger; suitcases and the like: *I left my servant at the railway looking after the luggage* (Dickens). **2** *British.* the baggage of an army. [< *lug*[1] + *-age*] **—lug′gage|less,** *adj.*

**luggage van,** *British.* a baggage car.

**lug|ger** (lug′ər), *n.* a boat rigged with lugsails: *In 1952 there were 130 luggers working out of Australian ports* (New York Times). [perhaps < *lug*$^{3}$ + *-er*$^{1}$. Compare Dutch *logger.*]

**lug|gie** (lug′ē, lu̇g′-; lü′gē), *n. Scottish.* a small wooden vessel with a lug (handle).

**lug|sail** (lug′sāl′; *Nautical* lug′səl), *n.* a four-cornered sail held by a hoisting yard that slants across the mast at one third of its length. [perhaps < *lug*$^{1}$ or *lug*$^{2}$ + *sail*]

**lu|gu|bri|ous** (lü gü′brē əs, -gyü′-), *adj.* too sad; overly mournful; sorrowful: *A dog set up a long, lugubrious howl* (Mark Twain). **SYN**: dismal, doleful, melancholy. [< Latin *lūgubris* (with English *-ous*) < *lūgēre* mourn] — **lu|gu′bri|ous|ly**, *adv.* — **lu|gu′bri|ous|ness**, *n.*

**lug|worm** (lug′wėrm′), *n.* a kind of worm that burrows in sand along the seashore; lobworm; lugbait. Lugworms are large marine polychaete worms having a reduced head and a row of gills in pairs along the back. They are largely used for bait. [< *lug*$^{4}$ lugworm (compare Dutch *log* slow, heavy) + *worm*]

**Luing** (ling), *n.* a breed of beef cattle produced on the island of Luing off the west coast of Scotland by interbreeding Shorthorn bulls and purebred Highland cows.

**Luke** (lük), *n.* **1** a physician in the Bible who was the companion of the Apostle Paul and is traditionally believed to have written the third Gospel and the Acts of the Apostles. **2** the third book of the New Testament, telling the story of the life of Christ. It is one of the Synoptic Gospels.

**luke|warm** (lük′wôrm′), *adj.* **1** neither hot nor cold; moderately warm: *a lukewarm bath.* **SYN**: tepid. **2** *Figurative.* showing little enthusiasm; half-hearted: *a lukewarm greeting, a lukewarm supporter, lukewarm obedience.* **SYN**: indifferent, unconcerned. [perhaps < Middle Dutch *leuk* tepid + English *warm*] — **luke′warm′ly**, *adv.* — **luke′warm′ness**, *n.*

**luke|warmth** (lük′wôrmth′), *n.* = lukewarmness.

**Lu|ki|ko** (lü kē′kō), *n.* the native council or parliament of Buganda, a former kingdom and province of Uganda. [< a Luganda word]

**lu|lab** (lü′läb), *n., pl.* **lu|labs, lu|la|bim** (lü lä bēm′). *Judaism.* a green palm branch, with attached boughs of myrtle and willow, used together with the ethrog during the Sukkoth morning services. [< Hebrew *lūlābh*]

**lu|lav** (lü′lôv, -ləv), *n., pl.* **lu|lavs, lu|la|vim** (lü lô′vim, -lô vēm′). = lulab.

**lull** (lul), *v., n.* — *v.t.* **1** to soothe with sounds or caresses; hush to sleep: *The mother lulled the crying baby.* **2** *Figurative.* to quiet; make calm or more nearly calm; make peaceful or tranquil: *to lull one's suspicions. The captain lulled our fears.*
— *v.i.* to become calm or more nearly calm: *The wind lulled.*
— *n.* **1** a period of less noise or violence; brief calm: *We ran home during a lull in the storm.* **SYN**: respite. **2** *Figurative.* a period of reduced activity: *a lull in trade.* **3** something which lulls; a lulling sound or motion: *the lull of falling waters.*
[Middle English *lullen,* probably imitative. Compare Swedish *lulla* lull to sleep, Dutch *lullen.*] — **lull′er**, *n.*

**lul|la|by** (lul′ə bī), *n., pl.* **-bies**, *v.,* **-bied, -by|ing.** — *n.* **1** a soft song to lull a baby to sleep; song for singing to a child in a cradle; cradlesong. **2** any song which soothes to rest: *The bees have hummed their noontide lullaby* (Samuel Rogers). **3** *Obsolete.* farewell; good night.
— *v.t.* to soothe with a lullaby; sing to sleep.
— *v.i.* to sing a lullaby or lullabies: *Platformed six feet above the orchestra, the Mothers were lullabying away* (Time).
[< earlier *lulla* < *lull*]

**lu|lu**$^{1}$ (lü′lü), *n. U.S. Slang.* an unusual thing or striking person: *The thunderstorm was a lulu. They've just one gap left to fill from last February's floods, but it's a lulu—more than 30 feet deep and over 400 feet long* (Wall Street Journal).

**lu|lu**$^{2}$ (lü′lü), *n. U.S. Slang.* an allowance paid to a legislator in lieu of expenses, which he does not have to itemize: ... *the redistribution of three committee "plums" in the Senate that carry "lulus"* (New York Times). [reduplication of *lieu*]

**lum** (lum, lu̇m), *n. Scottish.* a chimney. [origin uncertain]

**lum|ba|go** (lum bā′gō), *n., pl.* **-gos.** a pain in the muscles of the small of the back and in the loins. It is a form of rheumatism. [< Late Latin *lumbāgō* < Latin *lumbus* loin]

**lum|bar** (lum′bər), *adj., n.* — *adj.* of the loin or loins: *the lumbar region.*
— *n.* a lumbar vertebra, artery, nerve, or the like. [< New Latin *lumbaris* < Latin *lumbus* loin]

**lum|ber**$^{1}$ (lum′bər), *n., v.* — *n.* **1** timber that has been roughly cut into boards, planks, or beams and prepared for use: *Since 1920, the center of the lumber industry has been in the Pacific Northwest, with the South running a close second* (Stanley M. Jepsen). **2** household articles no longer in use; old furniture and other useless things that take up room. **3** *Figurative.* useless material: *The bookful blockhead, ignorantly read, With loads of learned lumber in his head* (Alexander Pope).
— *v.i.* to cut and prepare lumber.
— *v.t.* **1** to obtain lumber from (land). **2** to fill up or obstruct by taking space that is wanted for something else; encumber: *Do not lumber up my shelf with your collection of stones and insects. Empty bottles lumbered the bottom of every closet* (Washington Irving). **3** to heap together in disorder.
[originally, useless goods, perhaps early variant of *lombard* pawnshop]

**lum|ber**$^{2}$ (lum′bər), *v., n.* — *v.i.* **1** to move along heavily and noisily; roll along with difficulty: *to lumber along like an elephant. The old stagecoach lumbered down the road.* **2** to rumble; make a rumbling noise.
— *n.* a rumbling noise.
[Middle English *lomeren;* origin uncertain. Compare dialectal Swedish *loma* walk heavily.]

**lum|ber|er** (lum′bər ər), *n.* = lumberjack.

**lum|ber|ing**$^{1}$ (lum′bər ing, -bring), *n.* the act or business of cutting and preparing timber for use. [< *lumber*$^{1}$ + *-ing*$^{1}$]

**lum|ber|ing**$^{2}$ (lum′bər ing, -bring), *adj.* **1** ponderous in movement; inconveniently bulky: *Air coach passengers on various lines now ride a variety of planes, ranging from lumbering 220-mile-an-hour DC-4's to a sprinkling of Super Constellations* (Wall Street Journal). **2** *Obsolete.* rumbling. [< *lumber*$^{2}$ + *-ing*$^{2}$] — **lum′ber|ing|ly**, *adv.*

**lum|ber|jack** (lum′bər jak′), *n., v.* — *n.* a man whose work is cutting down trees and getting out the logs; woodsman; logger: *Among the hopeful immigrants are four lumberjacks, their wallets bulging after seven hard years in Alaska* (Punch).
— *v.i.* to do the work of a lumberjack.

**lumber jacket**, a short, straight jacket usually of heavy wool or leather, worn especially by men and boys outdoors.

**lum|ber|ly** (lum′bər lē), *adj.* clumsy; lumbering.

**lum|ber|man** (lum′bər mən), *n., pl.* **-men. 1** = lumberjack. **2** a man whose work is cutting and preparing timber for use. **3** a man whose work is buying and selling timber or lumber.

**lumber mill**, = sawmill.

**lumber port**, a porthole or opening in the bow or stern of a vessel, for use in loading and unloading lumber.

**lumber room**, a room for lumber, or articles not in use.

**lum|ber|yard** (lum′bər yärd′), *n.* a place where lumber and building supplies are stored and sold.

**lum|bo|sa|cral** (lum′bō sā′krəl), *adj.* or or having to do with both the lumbar and sacral regions or parts of the body: *Lumbosacral subluxation [is] a condition in which there is forward slipping of the fifth lumbar vertebra on the sacrum* (John S. Batchelor).

**lum|bri|cal** (lum′brə kəl), *n., adj.* — *n.* any one of four small muscles in either the hand or the foot that help move the fingers or toes.
— *adj.* of or having to do with these muscles.
[< New Latin *lumbricalis* < Latin *lumbrīcus* (parasitic) worm, earthworm]

**lum|bri|ca|lis** (lum′brə kā′lis), *n., pl.* **-les** (-lēz). = lumbrical.

**lum|bri|coid** (lum′brə koid), *adj.* **1** like an earthworm. **2** of a kind of roundworm common as an intestinal parasite in man. [< New Latin *lumbricoides* the roundworm species < Latin *lumbrīcus;* see etym. under **lumbrical**]

*__lu|men__ (lü′mən), *n., pl.* **-mi|na** (-mə nə), **-mens.** **1** *Physics.* a unit of light, equivalent to the amount of light given out per second, through an angle by a point source of one candela radiating equally in all directions. It is the unit of luminous flux. *Electric lights today are usually compared by lumens instead of by candle power* (Karl Lark-Horovitz). **2** *Anatomy.* the space within a tubular organ, such as a blood vessel: *These were then diluted with physiological saline and were injected directly into the lumen of the gizzard of groups of 3-day old white Leghorn chicks* (Science). **3** *Botany.* the central cavity or space within the wall of a cell. [< Latin *lūmen, -inis* light$^{1}$; opening in a tube]

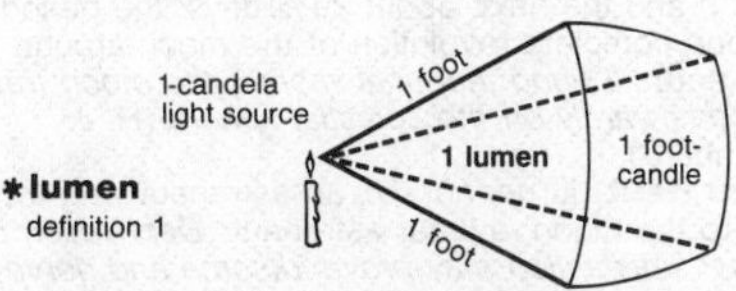


*__lumen__
definition 1

**lu|men na|tu|ra|le** (lü′men nä′tü rä′lā), *Latin.* **1** natural intelligence. **2** (literally) natural light.

**lu|mi|naire** (lü′mə när′), *n.* a lighting unit complete with all the necessary parts and accessories such as reflector and socket. [< French *luminaire* < Late Latin *lūminarium;* see etym. under **luminary**]

**lu|mi|nal** (lü′mə nəl), *adj.* of or belonging to a lumen (defs. 2,3). [< Latin *lūmen, -inis* light$^{1}$ + English *-al*$^{1}$]

**Lu|mi|nal** (lü′mə nəl, -nal), *n. Trademark.* phenobarbital.

**luminal art**, a form of art that uses the arrangement or projection of colored electric lights to create images, moving patterns, and flashing designs; luminist art: *Kinetic art deals with movement, with which a great deal of contemporary work—including most luminal art—is concerned, directly or indirectly* (Benjamin de Brie Taylor).

**luminal artist**, a person who produces luminal art; luminist.

**lu|mi|nance** (lü′mə nəns), *n.* the intensity of light in relation to the area of its source; luminosity: *The sensitivity of the eye to differences in luminance decreases as the luminance increases* (New Scientist).

**lu|mi|nant** (lü′mə nənt), *adj., n.* — *adj.* illuminating; luminous.
— *n.* an illuminating agent; illuminant.

**lu|mi|nar|ist** (lü′mə nər ist), *n.* a painter who treats light effectively, or whose color is luminous; luminist.

**lu|mi|nar|y** (lü′mə ner′ē), *n., pl.* **-nar|ies**, *adj.* — *n.* **1** a heavenly body that gives or reflects light; the sun, moon, or other light-giving body: *If the earth's orbit were perfectly circular, the earth's movement around the great central luminary would be uniform* (H. J. Bernhard). **2** *Figurative.* a famous person. **SYN**: celebrity, notable. **3** anything that gives light.
— *adj.* having to do with light.
[< Late Latin *lūminarium* light, lamp < Latin *lūmen, -inis* light$^{1}$]

**lu|mine** (lü′mən), *v.t.,* **-mined, -min|ing.** *Obsolete.* to light up; illumine. [< Old French *luminer,* learned borrowing from Latin *lūmināre* < *lūmen, -inis* light$^{1}$]

**lu|mi|nesce** (lü′mə nes′), *v.i.,* **-nesced, -nesc|ing.** to exhibit luminescence: *Green plants were found to luminesce like fireflies, although on a small scale* (Science News Letter).

**lu|mi|nes|cence** (lü′mə nes′əns), *n.* an emission of light occurring at a temperature below that of incandescent bodies. Luminescence includes phosphorescence and fluorescence, and may result from biological or chemical processes. *The intensity of the luminescence that some rocks give off when heated is an indication of their geologic age* (Science News Letter).

**lu|mi|nes|cent** (lü′mə nes′ənt), *adj.* **1** giving out light without being much heated. **2** having to do with luminescence. [< Latin *lūmen, -inis* light$^{1}$ + *-escent*]

**lu|mi|nif|er|ous** (lü′mə nif′ər əs), *adj.* producing or transmitting light: *The firefly is a luminiferous insect.* [< Latin *lūmen, -inis* light$^{1}$ + English *-ferous*]

**lu|mi|nism** (lü′mə niz əm), *n.* the art or style of a group of impressionist painters of the late 1800's who made a scientific study of light and color and employed new methods to depict light, chiefly in landscapes.

**lu|mi|nist** (lü′mə nist), *n., adj.* — *n.* **1** = luminarist. **2** a painter using the style of luminism. **3** = luminal artist.
— *adj.* of luminists or luminism: *luminist art, luminist landscapes.*

**lu|mi|nom|e|ter** (lü′mə nom′ə tər), *n.* an instrument for measuring the intensity of illumination.

**lu|mi|nos|i|ty** (lü′mə nos′ə tē), *n., pl.* **-ties.** **1** luminous quality or condition. **2** something luminous; a luminous point or area. **3** the amount of energy in the form of light emitted by the sun or a star.

**lu|mi|nous** (lü′mə nəs), *adj.* **1a** shining by its own light: *The sun and stars are luminous bodies. Certain animals and plants are luminous.* **b** emitting a certain amount of light, regardless of its distance: *Many stars are more luminous than the sun.* **2** full of light; shining; bright: *a luminous sunset.* **SYN**: glowing, effulgent, refulgent. **3** *Figurative.* easily understood; clear; enlightening: *Goethe's wide and luminous view* (Matthew Arnold); *luminous eloquence* (Macaulay). *The whole performance was luminous and moving* (New York Times). **SYN**: perspicuous, lucid. **4** well lighted: *The church of Ashbourne ... is one of the ... most luminous that I have seen* (James

**Pronunciation Key:** hat, āge, cãre, fär; let, ēqual, tėrm; it, īce; hot, ōpen, ôrder; oil, out; cup, pu̇t, rüle; child; long; thin; ᴛʜen; zh, measure; ə represents a in about, e in taken, i in pencil, o in lemon, u in circus.

Boswell). [< Latin *lūminōsus* < *lūmen, -inis* light¹] —**lu′mi|nous|ly**, *adv.* —**lu′mi|nous|ness**, *n.*

**luminous energy**, = light¹ (def. 1).

**luminous flux**, the rate at which light (luminous energy) is transmitted. Its unit is the lumen. *Radiant flux, evaluated with respect to its capacity to evoke the sensation of brightness, is called luminous flux* (Sears and Zemansky).

**luminous intensity**, a measure of the strength of a source of light, equivalent to the luminous flux given out per unit solid angle in a given direction.

**lum|me** (lum′ē), *interj. British Slang.* an exclamation of surprise: *Lumme, they're going to charge for going over the bridge* (London Times). [altered pronunciation of (God) *love me*]

**lum|mox** (lum′əks), *n. Informal.* an awkward, stupid person: *A thoughtful weighing of all aspects would surely convince them that the big lummoxes get their money's worth out of the silliest purchase* (Saturday Evening Post). [origin uncertain, apparently related to dialectal *lummock* move heavily]

**lump¹** (lump), *n., v., adj.* —*n.* **1** a solid mass of no particular shape, often small: *a lump of coal; a great lump of beeswax ... which weighed above half a hundred weight* (Daniel Defoe). **2** a swelling; bump: *There is a lump on my head where I bumped it.* **3** a lot; mass; heap: *a lump of money.* **4** *Informal.* a stupid person. **5** *Informal.* a big, sturdy person: *a brave lump of a boy* (Samuel Lover). *When we were lumps of lads* (Hall Caine). **6** *Obsolete.* a collection; clump; cluster.
—*v.i.* **1** to form into a lump or lumps: *The cornstarch lumped because we cooked it too fast. The low-humidity atmosphere keeps the sugar from lumping* (Wall Street Journal). **2** to move heavily. **3** to rise in a lump or lumps. **4** to act as a lumper or longshoreman.
—*v.t.* **1** to make lumps of, on, or in: *He lumped the salt by carelessly getting water into it.* **2** to put together; deal with in a mass or as a whole: *to lump all of one's effort in a single project. We will lump all our expenses.*
—*adj.* **1** in lumps; in a lump: *lump sugar, lump coal.* **2** including a number of items: *The girls will be given a lump sum of $10 to pay all their expenses.*
**a lump in one's throat**, a feeling of inability to swallow, caused by pity, sorrow, or other strong emotion: *The sad story gave her a lump in her throat.*
**in the lump**, in the mass; as a whole: *He praises or dispraises in the lump* (Joseph Addison).
**lumps**, *Informal.* a beating; punishment: *The Sooners had ... regularly taken their lumps from the likes of Texas (7-40)* (Time).
[Middle English *lumpe.* Compare earlier Dutch *lompe* mass, chunk, piece.]

**lump²** (lump), *v.t. Informal.* to put up with; endure: *If you don't like what I am doing, you can lump it.* [American English; origin uncertain]

**Lum|pa** (lu̇m′pä, lum′pə), *n., pl.* **-pas.** a member of a militant religious sect of Zambia (the former Northern Rhodesia), opposed to the government both before and after independence from the British.

**lump|ec|to|my** (lum pek′tə mē), *n., pl.* **-mies.** the surgical removal of a cancerous lump in the breast: *For certain of her patients in cases in which early diagnosis has been made, she favors "lumpectomy," the removal of the cancer alone rather than the entire breast* (Time). [< *lump*¹ + (mast)*ectomy*]

**lum|pen** (lu̇m′pən), *adj.* lacking class-consciousness: *a lumpen intellectual. When it comes to voting time ... the lumpen aristocracy, too, just shuffle mindlessly past the ballot box* (Punch). [back formation < *lumpenproletariat*]

**lum|pen|pro|le|tar|i|at** (lu̇m′pən prō′lə tãr′ē ət), *n.* the section of the proletariat that lacks class-consciousness: *These are not the real working class. These are the lumpenproletariat, tainted by petty-bourgeois ideology* (New Yorker). [< German *Lumpenproletariat* < *Lumpen*(volk) rabble (< *Lump* ragamuffin < *Lumpen* rag) + *Proletariat* proletariat]

**lump|er** (lum′pər), *n.* **1** a laborer employed to load and unload ships; longshoreman. **2** a person who lumps things together or deals with things in the lump or mass.

**lump|fish** (lump′fish′), *n., pl.* **-fish|es** or (*collectively*) **-fish.** a clumsy, spiny-finned fish of the northern Atlantic, with a high, ridged back and a sucker on the belly formed by the ventral fins; lumpsucker.

**lump|i|ly** (lum′pə lē), *adv.* in a lumpy manner; in lumps.

**lump|i|ness** (lum′pē nis), *n.* the condition of being lumpy or full of lumps.

**lump|ish** (lum′pish), *adj.* **1** like a lump; heavy and clumsy: *The six-story blocks of flats are lumpish, with ponderously silly little balconies* (Wall Street Journal). **SYN**: unwieldy. **2** heavy and dull; stupid; stolid: *She expects to be paid off ... for her lumpish efforts in behalf of the party* (Harper's). **SYN**: lumbering. **3** *Obsolete.* low-spirited. —**lump′ish|ly**, *adv.* —**lump′ish|ness**, *n.*

**lumps** (lumps), *n.pl.* See under **lump**¹.

**lump|suck|er** (lump′suk′ər), *n.* = lumpfish.

**lump|y** (lum′pē), *adj.,* **lump|i|er, lump|i|est.** **1** full of lumps: *lumpy gravy, lumpy sugar.* **2** covered with lumps: *lumpy ground.* **3** heavy and clumsy: *a lumpy animal.* **SYN**: lumpish. **4** rough, with the surface cut up by the wind into small waves; choppy: *lumpy water.*

**lumpy jaw** = actinomycosis.

**Lu|mumb|ist** (lə mum′bist), *n., adj.* —*n.* a follower of Patrice Lumumba (1925-1961), first prime minister of the Congo (the former Belgian Congo), or of his policies.
—*adj.* of or having to do with Lumumbists.

**lu|na** (lü′nə), *n.* **1** *Heraldry.* argent, in the blazonry of sovereign princes. **2** *Obsolete.* silver. [< Latin *lūna* moon (because of the silvery light)]

**Lu|na** (lü′nə), *n.* **1** the Roman goddess of the moon. The Greeks called her Selene. **2** the moon.

**lu|na|base** (lü′nə bās′), *adj.* having to do with or designating the low, flat surfaces of the moon: *The lunabase valleys have parted the mountains, and the overlay of ash, clearly visible on the foothills, is absent from them* (V. Axel Firsoff).

**lu|na|cy** (lü′nə sē), *n., pl.* **-cies.** **1** insanity, especially intermittent insanity, formerly supposed to be brought about by the changes of the moon: *In one of these fits of lunacy or distraction ... I fell down, and struck my face* (Daniel Defoe). **2** *Figurative.* extreme folly: *It is lunacy to cross the Atlantic in a rowboat.*

**luna moth** or **Luna moth**, a large North American moth having light-green wings with a crescent-shaped spot on each wing and a long tail on each hind wing.

**lu|na|naut** (lü′nə nôt), *n.* = lunarnaut. [< Latin *lūna* moon + English (astro)*naut*]

**lu|nar** (lü′nər), *adj.* **1a** of the moon: *a lunar eclipse, lunar rock samples.* **b** on the moon: *lunar soil, lunar mountains.* **2** like the moon: *the lunar glow of faraway street lights.* **3** of or containing silver. **4** *Figurative.* pale or pallid: *Even the lustre of Partridge [in "Tom Jones"] is pallid and lunar beside the noontide glory of Micawber* (Algernon Charles Swinburne). [< Latin *lūnāris* < *lūna* moon]

**lunar caustic**, fused silver nitrate, prepared in sticks for use in cauterizing. *Formula:* $AgNO_3$

**lunar cycle**, = Metonic cycle.

**lunar day**, **1** the interval between two successive crossings of the same meridian by the moon: *Tidal rhythms are related to the lunar day of 24 hours, 50 minutes* (Science News Letter). **2** the time it takes the moon to make one rotation on its axis; about 27 days, 7 hours, and 43 minutes.

**lunar eclipse**, the total or partial cutting off of the light of the full moon by the earth's shadow. It occurs when the sun, earth, and moon are in, or almost in, a straight line. See diagram under **eclipse**.

**lunar excursion module**, = lunar module.

**lu|nar|i|an** (lü nãr′ē ən), *n.* **1** a student of lunar phenomena. **2** a supposed inhabitant of the moon.

**lu|na|rite** (lü′nə rīt), *adj.* having to do with or designating the upland surfaces of the moon: *The least four of the largest craters in the ... lunarite mountain flows are conical or "dimple" craters, which suggests collapse following withdrawal of lava* (Ian Ridpath).

**lu|nar|i|um** (lü nãr′ē əm), *n.* an instrument representing the phases and motions of the moon. [< New Latin *lunarium* < Latin *lūnāris* lunar]

**lunar module**, a module used to land on the moon after separating from an orbiting spacecraft near the lunar surface: *The lunar module is the first of its kind, a new generation of spacecraft too weak to lift itself from the earth, too vulnerable to fly through the atmosphere without burning up. So specialized is the strange vehicle that it even is designed in two sections—one to land on the moon and the other to take off again* (Science News). *Abbr:* LM (no periods).

**lunar month**, the interval between one new moon and the next, about 29½ days; the period of one complete revolution of the moon around the earth: *During the lunar month, the moon travels eastwardly on the celestial sphere* (H. J. Bernhard).

**lu|nar|naut** (lü′nər nôt), *n.* an astronaut who travels to the moon; a lunar astronaut: *Deprivation of nasal satisfaction may prove irksome and nerve-ragging to future long-stay lunarnauts and the provision of an interesting aromatic background may be as necessary to their well-being as the maintenance of an artificial atmosphere* (New Scientist). [< *lunar* + (astro)*naut*] Also, **lunanaut.**

**lunar probe**, **1** the launching of a space vehicle which passes near the moon and records information about it. **2** space vehicle thus launched.

**lunar rainbow**, = moonbow.

**lunar rover** or **lunar roving vehicle**, a vehicle for exploratory travel on the moon's surface; moon rover: *Apollo 15 was first of three missions to transport heavier payloads than the earlier flights and to carry an electric-powered vehicle resembling a golf cart, called Lunar Rover* (William Hines). *Abbr:* LRV (no periods).

**lu|nar|scape** (lü′nər skāp), *n.* a view of the lunar surface; moonscape.

**lu|na|ry¹** (lü′nər ē), *adj.* = lunar.

**lu|na|ry²** (lü′nər ē), *n., pl.* **-ries.** **1** = honesty (def. 3). **2** = moonwort (def. 1). [< Medieval Latin *lunaria* < Latin *lūna* moon]

**lunar year**, a period of 12 lunar months, about 354⅓ days.

**lu|nate** (lü′nāt), *adj., n.* —*adj.* **1** crescent-shaped; luniform. **2** *Anatomy.* of a crescent-shaped bone of the human wrist, in the proximal row of carpal bones.
—*n.* the lunate bone.
[< Latin *lūnātus,* past participle of *lūnāre* to bend into a crescent < *lūna* moon] —**lu′nate|ly**, *adv.*

**lu|nat|ed** (lü′nā tid), *adj.* = lunate.

**lu|na|tic** (lü′nə tik), *n., adj.* —*n.* **1** an insane person: *Lunatics are often put in insane asylums.* **2** *Figurative.* an extremely foolish person.
—*adj.* **1** insane: *a lunatic man.* **2** for insane people: *a lunatic asylum.* **3** *Figurative.* extremely foolish; mad; idiotic: *a lunatic search for buried treasure, a lunatic policy.*
[< Late Latin *lūnāticus* < Latin *lūna* moon, because it was once thought that insanity was brought about by the changes of the moon] —**lu-nat′i|cal|ly**, *adv.*

**lunatic fringe**, *Informal.* those whose zeal in some cause, movement, or ism goes beyond reasonable limits: *the lunatic fringe in all reform movements* (Theodore Roosevelt).

**lu|na|tion** (lü nā′shən), *n.* the time from one new moon to the next, about 29½ days; lunar month.

**lunch** (lunch), *n., v.* —*n.* **1** a light meal between breakfast and dinner, or breakfast and supper: *We usually have lunch at noon.* **2** a light meal: *The scientist survived only on lunches as long as he was working on his experiment.* **3** food for a lunch. **4** *Scottish.* a thick piece; lump: *An' cheese an' bread ... Was dealt about in lunches* (Robert Burns).
—*v.i.* to eat lunch: *She ... made excursions to New York with them, and lunched in fashionable restaurants* (Winston Churchill).
—*v.t. Informal.* to provide lunch for.
**out to lunch**, *U.S. Slang.* out of date; behind the times or the latest trend; not with-it: *"He's smart enough to know that if he gets involved with ... that crowd, he's out to lunch"* (Harper's).
[short for *luncheon*] —**lunch′er**, *n.* —**lunch′less**, *adj.*

**lunch counter**, a long table or counter, as in a restaurant, at which persons sit on stools or stand while eating.

**lunch|eon** (lun′chən), *n., v.* —*n.* **1** = lunch. **2** a formal lunch: *a luncheon of the ladies' auxiliary at the church.* **3** *Scottish.* a thick piece or lump of food: *Little Benjie ... was cramming a huge luncheon of pie crust into his mouth* (Scott).
—*v.i.* to eat lunch.
[earlier, a lump; origin uncertain, probably influenced by dialectal *nuncheon* lunch]

**lunch|eon|ette** (lun′chə net′), *n.* **1** a restaurant in which light meals are served. **2** a light lunch.

**lunch|room** (lunch′rüm′, -ru̇m′), *n.* **1** a restaurant in which light meals are served. **2** a room, as in a school, factory, or office building, in which to eat lunch.

**lunch|time** (lunch′tīm′), *n.* the time at which lunch is eaten or served.

**Lun|da** (lün′də, lu̇n-), *n., pl.* **-da** or **-das.** **1** a member of a Negroid people living in the northeastern district of Angola. **2** the Bantu language of this people.

***lune¹** (lün), *n.* **1** a crescent-shaped figure on a plane or sphere bounded by two arcs of circles. **2** anything shaped like a crescent or a half moon. [< French *lune* < Latin *lūna* moon]

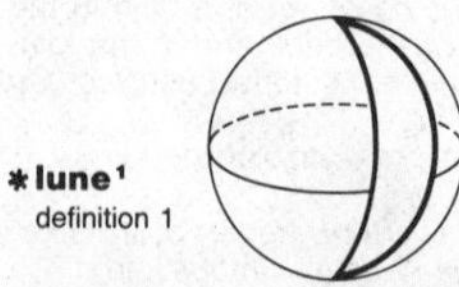

***lune¹** definition 1

**lune²** (lün), *n.* a leash for a hawk. [variant of Middle English *loigne* < Old French < Medieval Latin *longia* halter for a horse < Latin *longus* long]

**lunes** (lünz), *n.pl. Archaic.* fits of lunacy; tantrums: *Why, woman, your husband is in his old lunes again* (Shakespeare). [< Medieval Latin *luna* (literally) moon; fit of lunacy < Latin *lūna* moon]
**lu|net** (lü′nit), *n. Obsolete.* lunette.
✱**lu|nette** (lü net′), *n.* **1a** a crescent-shaped opening or space in a vaulted ceiling, dome, wall, or the like. **b** a painting or other decoration filling this space. **2** an arched or rounded opening, window, or the like, as in a vault: *The top story has no regular windows but, instead, circular lunettes* (New Yorker). **3** a projecting part of a rampart, shaped somewhat like a pointed arch. **4** a ring in the back of a towed vehicle, especially the trail of a field gun, to which the towing apparatus is attached. [< Old French *lunette* (diminutive) < *lune* moon, crescent < Latin *lūna*]

✱**lunette**
definitions 1a, 3

in a wall    on a rampart

✱**lung** (lung), *n.* **1** one of the pair of organs for breathing, found in the chest of most animals that breathe air and have backbones. The lungs absorb oxygen from the air and give the blood the oxygen it needs, and relieve it of carbon dioxide. A lung is composed of masses of spongy tissue containing many millions of tiny air sacs or alveoli, each with its own network of capillaries. *The two lungs fill almost the whole chest cavity except the part filled by the heart and windpipe* (Beauchamp, Mayfield, and West). **2** a similar organ in certain invertebrates, such as snails and spiders. **3** any device aiding respiration, such as a respirator or an iron lung. **4** *Especially British, Figurative.* an open space in a town or city, where housing and traffic are not permitted: *Nowadays, with ... planners opening up new urban "lungs," the old town parks have a faintly period look* (Manchester Guardian Weekly).
**at the top of one's lungs**, in the loudest voice possible: *I doggedly plowed through pronoun declensions and conjugated verbs at the top of my lungs* (New Yorker).
[Old English *lungen*] —**lung′like′**, *adj.*

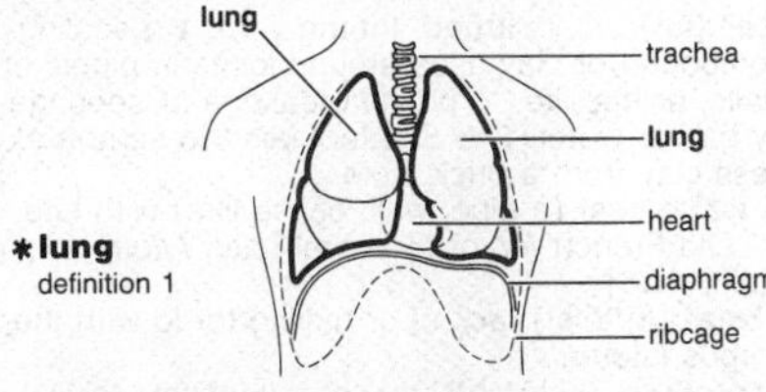


✱**lung**
definition 1

**lun|gan** (lung′gən), *n.* = longan.
**lunge**[1] (lunj), *n., v.,* **lunged, lung|ing.** —*n.* **1** any sudden forward movement; plunge; lurch: *At no time shall I be surprised to see a sudden lunge forward on that front* (H. G. Wells). **2** a thrust, such as with a sword or other weapon.
—*v.i., v.t.* **1** to move suddenly forward: *the dog lunged at the stranger.* **2** to thrust: *to lunge a poker into the fire.*
[short for earlier *allonge* < Old French *allonger* to lunge; (originally) to lengthen < *a-* a-[3] + *long* long < Latin *longus*]
**lunge**[2] (lunj), *n., v.,* **lunged, lung|ing.** —*n.* **1** a long rope used in training or exercising a horse. **2** the use of this rope in training a horse. **3** a ring or circular track for training a horse.
—*v.t.* to train or exercise (a horse) by the use of a rope or in a ring.
—*v.i.* (of a horse) to move in a circle within a ring or at the end of a rope. Also, **longe**.
[< French *longe* a cord, halter < Old French *loigne;* see etym. under **lune**[2]]
**lunge**[3] or **'lunge** (lunj), *n. Informal.* muskellunge.
**-lunged**, *combining form.* having ____ lungs: *Weak-lunged = having weak lungs.*
**lun|gee** (lůng′gē), *n.* = lungi.
**lun|geous** (lun′jəs), *adj. Dialect.* **1** rough or violent (in play). **2** tending to do harm; spiteful; mischievous. [< *lunge*[1] + *-ous*]
**lung|er**[1] (lung′ər), *n. Slang.* a person who has tuberculosis of the lungs. [< *lung* + *-er*[1]]
**lung|er**[2] (lun′jər), *n.* a person who lunges.
**lung|fish** (lung′fish′), *n., pl.* **-fish|es** or (*collectively*) **-fish**. a freshwater fish having a lunglike sac in addition to gills, enabling it to obtain oxygen both in and out of water, by gulping air through the mouth as well as by passing water through its gills; dipnoan. Lungfishes are found in Australia, Africa, and South America. *The lungfishes were formerly abundant, and there are many fossil forms dating as far back as the Devonian* (John D. Black).
**lung fluke**, a parasitic flatworm that lives in the lungs of human beings and animals. Lung flukes often enter the body when improperly cooked fish or crab meat is eaten.
**lung|ful** (lung′fůl), *n., pl.* **-fuls**. as much as the lungs will hold: *to breathe in a lungful of air.*
**lun|gi** (lůng′gē), *n.* **1** a long strip of cloth worn as a loincloth in India. **2** a long strip of cloth worn as a skirt, scarf, or other garment in Burma, India, and Pakistan. **3** a headdress worn in many styles in the northwest districts of India. Also, **longyi, lungee, lungyi**. [< Hindi *lungī*]
**lung|worm** (lung′wėrm′), *n.* any one of several nematode worms parasitic in the lungs of various vertebrates. One kind infests the lungs of sheep.
**lung|wort** (lung′wėrt′), *n.* **1** a European plant of the borage family, with small purple flowers and leaves spotted with white. It was once a popular remedy for lung disease. **2** an American plant of the same family, having blue flowers; Virginia cowslip. **3** a lichen.
**lun|gyi** (lůng′gē), *n.* = lungi.
**lu|ni|form** (lü′nə fôrm), *adj.* lunate; crescent-shaped.
**lu|nik** (lü′nik), *n.* a lunar probe of the Soviet Union: *... Soviet sputniks and luniks flashing through space* (New York Times Magazine). [< Russian *lunnik* < *luna* moon + *-nik* a suffix meaning one that does or is connected with]
**lu|ni|log|i|cal** (lü′nə loj′ə kəl), *adj.* of or having to do with study of the moon, especially its geology.
**l'u|nion fait la force** (ly nyôN′ fe lȧ fôrs′), *French.* union makes strength (the motto of Belgium).
**lu|ni|so|lar** (lü′nə sō′lər), *adj. Astronomy.* having to do with the mutual relations or joint action of the moon and sun: *lunisolar attraction.* [< Latin *lūna* moon + English *solar*]
**lu|ni|tid|al** (lü′nə tī′dəl), *adj.* having to do with the movements of the tide dependent on the moon. [< Latin *lūna* moon + English *tidal*]
**lunitidal interval**, the time between the transit of the moon and the next lunar high tide.
**lunk** (lungk), *n. U.S. Informal.* a lunkhead.
**lun|ker** (lung′kər), *n. Informal.* something uncommonly large of its kind, especially a game fish: *The lunkers* [*are*] *... much too sophisticated to be caught by the first stray dude from Peoria or Westmount* (Maclean's). [origin uncertain]
**lunk|head** (lungk′hed′), *n. U.S. Informal.* a blockhead. [American English; origin uncertain]
**Lu|no|khod** (lü′nə hōt′), *n.* a vehicle powered by solar cells and directed by radio signals from earth, designed by Soviet scientists for exploration on the lunar surface. [< Russian *Lunokkhod* (literally) moonwalker]
**lunt** (lunt, lůnt), *n., v. Scottish.* —*n.* **1** a slow match. **2** a torch. **3** smoke; smoke with flame. **4** pipe smoke.
—*v.i.* **1** to flame. **2** to emit smoke. **3** to smoke a pipe.
—*v.t.* **1** to kindle; light. **2** to smoke (a pipe).
**set lunt to**, to set fire to: *The gardener set lunt to the dead leaves.*
[< Dutch *lont* a match[1]]
**lu|nu|la** (lü′nyə lə), *n., pl.* **-lae** (-lē). **1** a crescent-shaped mark or spot, especially such a white mark at the base of the human fingernail. **2** = lune. [< Latin *lūnula* (diminutive) < *lūna* moon]
**lu|nu|lar** (lü′nyə lər), *adj.* having to do with a lune or lunula; crescent-shaped.
**lu|nu|late** (lü′nyə lāt, -lit), *adj.* **1** marked with crescent-shaped spots. **2** crescent-shaped.
**lu|nule** (lü′nyül), *n.* = lunula.
**lu|nu|let** (lü′nyə lit), *n. Zoology.* a small crescent-shaped mark; lunula.
**lun|y** (lü′nē), *adj.,* **lun|i|er, lun|i|est,** *n., pl.* **lun|ies**. = loony.
**Lu|o** (lü ō′), *n., pl.* **Lu|o**. **1** a member of one of the principal Negro tribes in Kenya. **2** the Nilotic language of this tribe.
**lu|pa|nar** (lü pā′nər), *n.* a brothel: *... a gamin from the streets of Ménilmontant, educated in barracks and lupanars* (Saturday Review). [< Latin *lupānar* < *lupa* prostitute, she-wolf, feminine of *lupus* wolf]
**Lu|per|cal** (lü′pər kal), *n.* **1** singular of **Lupercalia**. **2** a cave in the Palatine Hill, sacred to Lupercus.
**Lu|per|ca|li|a** (lü′pər kā′lē ə), *n.pl.* an ancient Roman fertility festival celebrated on February 15 in honor of Lupercus. Women were struck with thongs to insure easy childbirth.
**Lu|per|ca|li|an** (lü′pər kā′lē ən), *adj.* of or having to do with the Lupercalia.
**Lu|per|ci** (lü pėr′sī), *n.pl.* the priests of Lupercus or Faunus.
**Lu|per|cus** (lü pėr′kəs), *n.* a Roman rural god, the protector of the flocks, identified with Faunus and Pan.
**Lu|pi** (lü′pī), *n.* genitive of **Lupus**.
**lu|pine**[1] or **lu|pin** (lü′pən), *n.* **1** a plant that has long spikes of flowers, clusters of hairy leaflets, and flat pods with bean-shaped seeds. It belongs to the pea family and is grown for its showy flowers and as a food and cover crop. **2** the seeds, often used for food. [< Latin *lupīnus,* or *lupīnum* lupine[2]]
**lu|pine**[2] (lü′pīn), *adj.* **1** of or like a wolf; ravenous; fierce. **SYN**: wolflike, wolfish, savage. **2** related to the wolf. [< Latin *lupīnus* < *lupus* wolf]
**lu|pu|lin** (lü′pyə lin), *n.* **1** a fine, yellow powder consisting of the small, round glands found on the stipules and fruit of hops, formerly used as an aromatic bitter and a sedative. **2** a crystalline substance regarded as the bitter principle of the hop. [American English < Medieval Latin *lupulus* the hop (diminutive) < Latin *lupus* + English *-in*]
**lu|pus** (lü′pəs), *n.* **1** a skin disease caused by the tubercle bacillus, that often scars the face. **2** any one of several other skin diseases. [< Medieval Latin *lupus* < Latin, wolf (apparently from its rapid eating away of the affected part)]
**Lu|pus** (lü′pəs), *n., genitive* **Lu|pi**. a southern constellation near Centaurus. [< Latin *Lupus* (originally) wolf]
**lupus er|y|them|a|to|sus** (er′ə them′ə tō′sis), a disease that attacks the skin and connective tissues, resulting in a condition similar to rheumatoid arthritis and often in its acute form leading to disability and death.
**lupus vul|ga|ris** (vul gãr′is), = lupus (def. 1).
**lur** (lůr), *n.* a large, curved, bronze trumpet of Scandinavia, used in prehistoric times: *From the Bronze Age are a pair of spiraling, S-shaped lurs that represent two of the world's earliest wind instruments* (Science News Letter). [< Scandinavian (compare Old Icelandic *lūthr* trumpet)]
**Lur** (lůr), *n., pl.* **Lur** or **Lurs**. a member of a nomadic tribe speaking a Persian dialect and living in the mountainous regions of western Iran.
**lurch**[1] (lėrch), *n., v.* —*n.* **1** a sudden leaning or roll to one side, like that of a ship, a car, or a staggering person: *The car gave a lurch and upset.* **2** a swaying motion or gait; stagger.
—*v.i.* to lean or roll suddenly to one side; make a lurch; stagger: *The wounded man lurched forward.* **SYN**: pitch, sway, lunge. —**lurch′ing|ly**, *adv.*
**lurch**[2] (lėrch), *n., v.* —*n.* **1** a condition in which one player in certain games, such as cribbage, scores nothing or is badly beaten. **2** a game ending in this way.
—*v.t.* to beat badly in a game: *Lurched ... before you have gained six points* (R. Hardie).
**leave in the lurch**, to leave in a helpless condition or difficult situation: *Dutton ... a debauched fellow ... leaving Win in the lurch, ran away with another man's bride* (Tobias Smollett).
[< French *lourche,* name of a game]
**lurch**[3] (lėrch), *v.t.* **1** to catch (game) using a lurcher. **2** *Archaic.* **a** to prevent (a person) from obtaining a fair share of food, profit, or other advantage, by getting a start before him. **b** to cheat; rob. **3** *Obsolete.* to pilfer; steal. —*v.i. British Dialect.* to lurk; prowl; sneak. [variant of *lurk*]
**lurch|er** (lėr′chər), *n.* **1** a kind of crossbred hunting dog much used by poachers. **2** a prowler; petty thief; poacher.
**lur|dan** or **lur|dane** (lėr′dən), *n., adj. Archaic.*
—*n.* a lazy, stupid person; worthless loafer: *A fine thing it would be for me ... to be afraid of a fat lurdane* (Scott).
—*adj.* lazy; worthless: *lurdane knights* (Tennyson).
[< Old French *lourdin* < *lourd* heavy]
**lure** (lůr), *n., v.,* **lured, lur|ing.** —*n.* **1** the power of attracting or fascinating; charm; allure; attraction: *Many people feel the lure of the sea. Monarchs, whom the lure of honour draws* (William Cowper). **2** something that allures, entices, or tempts: *that grand lure in the eyes of the savage, a pocket mirror* (Washington Irving). **3** a decoy or bait, especially an artificial bait used in fishing: [*He*] *asked the sailor if he had ever tried deep-sea fishing with an artificial lure instead of bait* (Newsweek). **4** a bunch of feathers, often with meat attached, tossed or swung at the end of a long cord or thong, used as a decoy in falconry to recall a hawk to its perch. **5** a bulb or tassellike process dangling over the head from the first dorsal ray of an angler or related fish.
—*v.t.* **1** to lead away or into something by arous-

**Pronunciation Key:** hat, āge, cãre, fär; let, ēqual, tėrm; it, īce; hot, ōpen, ôrder; oil, out; cup, půt, rüle; child; long; thin; ᴛʜen; zh, measure; ə represents **a** in about, **e** in taken, **i** in pencil, **o** in lemon, **u** in circus.

ing desire; allure; entice; tempt: *Bees are lured by the scent of flowers. Pixies; don't go near 'em, child; they'll lure you on, Lord knows where* (Henry Kingsley). SYN: attract. **2** to attract with a bait: *We lured the fox into a trap.* **3** to recall (a hawk) with a lure.
[< Old French *leurre* < Germanic (compare Middle High German *luoder* bait)] —**lur'er**, *n.* —**lur'ing|ly**, *adv.*
—*Syn. v.t.* **1 Lure, allure, entice** mean to attract or tempt. **Lure**, commonly in a bad sense, means to tempt by rousing desire and usually to lead into something bad or not to one's advantage: *The hope of high profits lured him into questionable dealings.* **Allure**, seldom in a bad sense, means to tempt by appealing to the senses and feelings and by offering pleasure or advantage: *Hawaii allures many tourists.* **Entice**, in a good or bad sense, means to tempt by appealing to hopes and desires and by using persuasion: *We enticed the kitten from the tree.*

**lure|ment** (lůr'mənt), *n.* = allurement.

**lu|rid** (lůr'id), *adj.* **1a** lighted up with a red or fiery glare: *lurid flashes of lightning. The sky was lurid with the flames of the burning city.* **b** glaring in brightness or color: *a lurid red; a cheap lurid print* (Thomas B. Aldrich). **2** *Figurative.* terrible; sensational; startling; ghastly: *lurid crimes. The detective told some lurid stories.* **3** pale and dismal in color; wan and sallow. **4** *Biology.* dirty brown. [< Latin *lūridus* pale yellow, ghastly] —**lu'rid|ly**, *adv.* —**lu'rid|ness**, *n.*

**lurk** (lėrk), *v.i.* **1** to stay about without arousing attention; wait out of sight: *A tiger was lurking in the jungle outside the village. The spy lurked in the shadows.* **2** *Figurative.* to be hidden; be unsuspected or latent: *A cunning politician often lurks under the clerical robe* (Washington Irving). *A fever lurked in my veins* (Charles Brockden Brown). **3** to move about in a secret and sly manner: *The thief was caught lurking near the house. ... the main thoroughfare ... by which cook lurks down before daylight to scour her pots and pans* (Thackeray). [Middle English *lurken,* apparently < *louren* lower[2]] —**lurk'er**, *n.* —**lurk'ing|ly**, *adv.*
—*Syn.* **1, 3 Lurk, skulk** mean to keep out of sight or move in a secret or furtive way. **Lurk** often but not always suggests an evil purpose: *A stray dog was seen lurking about the house.* **Skulk**, implying sneakiness, cowardice, or shame, always suggests an evil purpose: *The cattle thieves skulked in the woods until the posse had passed.*

**Lur|lei** (lůr'lī), *n.* = Lorelei.

**Lu|sa|ti|an** (lü sā'shē ən, -shən), *adj., n.* —*adj.* of or having to do with Lusatia, a region in northern Europe, or its people.
—*n.* **1** a native or inhabitant of Lusatia. **2** = Wendish.

**lus|cious** (lush'əs), *adj.* **1** very pleasing to taste; richly sweet; delicious: *a luscious peach.* SYN: See syn. under **delicious**. **2** *Figurative.* very pleasing to smell, hear, see, or feel: *the luscious tones of a cello, a luscious view of a garden, a luscious description.* **3** too sweet; cloying; sickly. [perhaps variant of *licious,* a back formation < *delicious*] —**lus'cious|ly**, *adv.* —**lus'cious|ness**, *n.*

**lush[1]** (lush), *adj.* **1** tender and juicy; growing thick and green: *Lush grass grows along the riverbank.* SYN: succulent. **2** characterized by abundant growth; producing abundantly: *As the year Grows lush in juicy stalks* (Keats). **3** *Figurative.* luxurious; abundant: *the lush life of a millionaire.* **4** very rich; too ornamented; flowery; extravagant: *lush description.* [Middle English *lache,* perhaps imitative variant of Old French *lasche* lax, soft, succulent (as young shoots) < *lascher* be careless < Vulgar Latin *lascāre* weaken < Latin *laxāre* < *laxus* lax] —**lush'ly**, *adv.* —**lush'ness**, *n.*

**lush[2]** (lush), *n., v. Slang.* —*n.* **1** liquor; drink. **2** a person who drinks too much: *Daddy figured him for forty-forty-five and something of a lush maybe* (Maclean's).
—*v.t.* **1** to supply with drink. **2** to drink: *some of the richest sort you ever lushed* (Dickens).
—*v.i.* to drink liquor; drink.
[perhaps humorous use of *lush*[1] in sense of "watery"]

**lush|y** (lush'ē), *adj.,* **lush|i|er, lush|i|est.** tender; soft; lush.

**Lu|si|ta|ni|an** (lü'sə tā'nē ən), *adj., n.* —*adj.* **1** of or having to do with Lusitania, an ancient country comprising parts of Portugal and western Spain. **2** Portuguese.
—*n.* **1** a native of Lusitania. **2** a Portuguese.

**Lu|si|ta|no-A|mer|i|can** (lü'sə tā'nō ə mer'ə kən), *n., adj.* —*n.* a Brazilian of Portuguese descent.
—*adj.* of or having to do with Brazilians of Portuguese descent: *Lusitano-American society.* [< Portuguese *Lusitano* Lusitanian + English *American*]

**Lu|so-Bra|zil|ian** (lü'sō brə zil'yən), *n., adj.* = Lusitano-American. [< Portuguese *Luso* (short for *Lusitano* Lusitanian) + English *Brazilian*]

**lust** (lust), *n., v.* —*n.* **1** strong desire: *lust for power, lust for gold. That mere lust of fighting, common to man and animals* (Charles Kingsley). **2** desire for indulgence of sex, especially excessive sexual desire. **3** bad desire or appetite. **4** *Obsolete.* desire; inclination: *gazing upon the Greeks with little lust* (Shakespeare). **5** *Obsolete.* pleasure; delight: *If you would consider your estate, you would have little lust to sing* (Beaumont and Fletcher). **6** *Obsolete.* vigor; fertility: *a plant that cometh of the lust of the earth* (Francis Bacon).
—*v.i.* **1** to have a strong desire: *A miser lusts after gold. The fruits that thy soul lusted after are departed from thee* (Revelation 18:14). **2** to have excessive sexual desire.
[Old English *lust* desire, pleasure]

**lus|ter[1]** (lus'tər), *n., v.* —*n.* **1** a bright shine on the surface: *the luster of pearls. Beetles, glittering with metallic luster* (Francis Parkman). SYN: sheen, gloss. See syn. under **polish**. **2** brightness; radiance: *Her eyes lost their luster. The sun's mild luster warms the vital air* (Alexander Pope). *His countenance, radiant with health and the luster of innocence* (Benjamin Disraeli). **3** *Figurative.* fame; glory; brilliance: *The deeds of heroes add luster to a nation's history. The virtues of Claudius ... place him in that short list of emperors who added luster to the Roman purple* (Edward Gibbon). **4a** a shiny, metallic, often iridescent surface on pottery or china. **b** = luster ware: *pink luster teacups.* **5** *Mineralogy.* the appearance of the surface of a mineral due to the reflection of light: *Cut a piece of lead or zinc, and observe the luster of its fresh surface* (Thomas Huxley). **6** a thin, light fabric of cotton and wool that has a lustrous surface, used for dresses and lining. **7a** a chandelier with glass pendants: *The luster, which had been lighted for dinner, filled the room with a festal breadth of light* (Charlotte Brontë). **b** one of the glass pendants of such a chandelier. **8** something used to give a shine or gloss, such as to manufactured articles or furs. **9** a bright light; shining body or form.
—*v.t.* to finish with a luster or gloss.
—*v.i.* to shine with luster. Also, **lustre**.
[< Middle French *lustre* < Italian *lustro* < *lustrare* < Latin *lūstrāre* illuminate; (originally) purify by sacrifice < *lūstrum* a sacrifice]

**lus|ter[2]** (lus'tər), *n.* a period of five years; lustrum: *So it will be the turn of you young folks, come eight more lusters, and your heads will be bald like mine* (Thackeray). [< Latin *lūstrum* lustrum]

**lus|ter|less** (lus'tər lis), *adj.* without luster; dull; colorless: *What Dr. Ostwald calls a "flat" voice is a smudged, lusterless, hesitant way of speaking* (Science News Letter).

**luster painting**, a form of decoration on pottery or glass consisting of painting with a metallic pigment on a white glaze, practiced in the Middle East and Spain from the 800's to the 1600's.

**luster ware**, or **lus|ter|ware** (lus'tər wãr'), *n.* a kind of china or pottery that has a lustrous, metallic, often iridescent surface.

**lust|ful** (lust'fəl), *adj.* **1** full of lust or desire; desiring indulgence of sex; sensual; lewd. SYN: lecherous, lascivious. **2** *Archaic.* vigorous; lusty. —**lust'ful|ly**, *adv.* —**lust'ful|ness**, *n.*

**lust|i|head** (lus'tē hed), *n. Archaic.* lustiness.

**lust|i|hood** (lus'tē hůd), *n. Archaic.* lustiness.

**lust|i|ly** (lus'tə lē), *adv.* in a lusty manner; vigorously; heartily.

**lust|i|ness** (lus'tē nis), *n.* the fact or condition of being lusty; vigor; robustness.

**lus|tra** (lus'trə), *n.* lustrums; a plural of **lustrum**.

**lus|tral** (lus'trəl), *adj.* **1** of or used in ceremonial purification: *The assistants were sprinkled with lustral water* (Edward Gibbon). *At one entrance to this building was a sunken "lustral area," where visitors made formal ablutions* (Scientific American). **2** occurring every five years. [< Latin *lūstrālis* < *lūstrum* lustrum]

**lus|trate** (lus'trāt), *v.t.,* **-trat|ed, -trat|ing.** to purify by offering a sacrifice or by any ceremonial method. [< Latin *lūstrāre* (with English *-ate*[1]) brighten; purify by sacrifice < *lūstrum* lustrum]

**lus|tra|tion** (lus trā'shən), *n.* **1** a ceremonial washing or purification: *The offender having ceased to exist, the lustration which the laws of knight-errantry prescribe was rendered impossible* (William Godwin). **2** *Humorous.* a washing.

**lus|tre[1]** (lus'tər), *n.* = luster.

**lus|tre[2]** (lus'tər), *n. Especially British.* lustrum.

**lus|tring** (lus'tring), *n.* a glossy silk fabric; lutestring. [alteration of French *lustrine* < Middle French *lustre* luster[1]]

**lus|trous** (lus'trəs), *adj.* **1** having luster; shining; glossy: *lustrous satin.* **2** bright; brilliant; splendid: (*Figurative.*) *The great scientist has a lustrous record of achievement.* —**lus'trous|ly**, *adv.* —**lus'trous|ness**, *n.*

**lus|trum** (lus'trəm), *n., pl.* **-trums** or **-tra**. **1** a ceremonial purification of the ancient Romans, performed every five years, after the taking of the census. **2** the ancient Roman census. **3** a period of five years. [< Latin *lūstrum*]

**lust|y** (lus'tē), *adj.,* **lust|i|er, lust|i|est.** **1** strong and healthy; full of vigor: *a lusty boy. The churches ringing out the lustiest peals he had ever heard* (Dickens). *The savage ... a stout, lusty fellow ... had thrown him down* (Daniel Defoe). SYN: robust, sturdy, vigorous, hearty. **2** *Archaic.* merry; cheerful: *a lusty heart* (Chaucer); *lusty banqueting* (Scott). **3** *Obsolete.* pleasing; agreeable: *some lusty grove* (Christopher Marlowe). **4** *Obsolete.* beautiful; handsome.

**lu|sus** (lü'səs), *n.* = lusus naturae.

**lusus na|tu|rae** (nə tůr'ē, -tyůr'-), something, such as a plant or animal, that deviates greatly from the normal; freak of nature. [< Latin *lūsus nātūrae* a jest of nature; *lūsus, -ūs* a playing < *lūdere* to play]

**lu|ta|nist** (lü'tə nist), *n.* a player on the lute: *I have heard Gog-Owza, the lutanist, playing his lute* (Lord Dunsany). Also, **lutenist**. [< Medieval Latin *lutanista* < *lutana* lute]

***lute[1]** (lüt), *n., v.,* **lut|ed, lut|ing.** —*n.* a stringed musical instrument, much used in former times, having a long neck and a hollow, resonant body. It is like a large mandolin and is played by plucking the strings with the fingers of one hand or with a plectrum.
—*v.i.* **1** to play on a lute. **2** *Poetic.* to sound like a lute: *Her new voice luting soft, Cried, "Lycius!"* (Keats).
—*v.t. Poetic.* to express with or as if with the music of a lute: *Knaves are men, that lute and flute fantastic tenderness* (Tennyson).
[< Old French *lut,* or *leüt* < Old Provençal *laüt* < Arabic *al-'ūd* the lute]

***lute[1]**

**lute[2]** (lüt), *n., v.,* **lut|ed, lut|ing.** —*n.* **1** a sealing compound of clay used around joints in pipes, on walls, or the like, to prevent leakage or seepage by gas or water. **2** *U.S.* a tool used to scrape excess clay from a brick mold.
—*v.t.* to seal (a pipe, wall, or the like) with lute.
[< Old French *lut,* or Medieval Latin *lutum* < Latin, mud]

**lu|te|al** (lü'tē əl), *adj.* of or having to do with the corpus luteum.

**lu|te|ci|um** (lü tē'shē əm), *n.* = lutetium.

**lu|te|in** (lü'tē in), *n.* **1** a yellow pigment obtained from the corpus luteum. **2** = xanthophyll.

**lu|te|in|ize** (lü'tē ə nīz), *v.i., v.t.,* **-ized, -iz|ing.** to stimulate the production of a corpus luteum (in the ovary).

**lu|te|in|iz|ing hormone** (lü'tē ə nī zing), a hormone produced by the anterior lobe of the pituitary gland, which in the female stimulates the development of the corpus luteum and in the male stimulates the interstitial cells of the testicles to produce testosterone. *Abbr:* LH (no periods).

**lu|te|nist** (lü'tə nist), *n.* = lutanist.

**lu|te|o|lin** (lü'tē ə lin), *n.* a yellow, crystalline coloring matter present in a great many plants and used in dyeing. *Formula:* $C_{15}H_{10}O_6$ [< French *lutéoline* < New Latin *luteola* weld[2] < Latin *lūteolus* (diminutive) < *lūteus;* see etym. under **luteous**]

**lu|te|o|ly|sin** (lü'tē ō lī'sən), *n.* a chemical substance which destroys the corpus luteum even if an egg has been fertilized, studied to develop an effective contraceptive pill. [< (corpus) *luteum* + *lysin*[1]]

**lu|te|o|troph|ic** (lü'tē ə trof'ik), *adj.* that stimulates the corpus luteum. [< (corpus) *luteum* + *trophic*]

**luteotrophic hormone**, = prolactin.

**lu|te|o|troph|in** (lü'tē ə trof'in), *n.* = prolactin.

**lu|te|ous** (lü'tē əs), *adj.* golden-yellow; orange-yellow. [< Latin *lūteus* (with English *-ous*) deep yellow < *lūtum* weld[2], a plant from which the yellow used by dyers was obtained]

**lu|tes|cent** (lü tes'ənt), *adj.* tending to yellow; yellowish. [< Latin *lūteus* yellow + English *-escent*]

**lute|string** (lüt′string′), *n.* **1** = lustring. **2** a ribbon, especially for attaching eyeglasses.

**Lu|te|tian** (lü tē′shən), *adj.* of or having to do with ancient Lutetia or Paris; Parisian.

***lu|te|ti|um** (lü tē′shē əm), *n.* a metallic chemical element which usually occurs in nature with ytterbium. It is one of the rare-earth metals. Also, **lutecium**. [< New Latin *lutecium* < Latin *Lutetia,* or *-cia* Paris]

***lutetium**

| symbol | atomic number | atomic weight | oxidation state |
|---|---|---|---|
| Lu | 71 | 174.97 | 3 |

**lut|fisk** (lüt′fisk′), *n.* fish soaked in a lye solution and boiled, forming one of the main dishes at a Swedish Christmas dinner. [< Swedish *lutfisk* < *luta* to wash in lye + *fisk* fish]

**Luth.**, Lutheran.

**Lu|ther|an** (lü′thər ən, lüth′rən), *adj., n.* —*adj.* having to do with Martin Luther (1483-1546), or the church and doctrines that were named for him. —*n.* a member of the Lutheran Church.

**Lu|ther|an|ism** (lü′thər ə niz′əm, lüth′rə niz-), *n.* the doctrine, organization, and manner of worship of the Lutheran Church, characterized by a belief in justification by faith alone, denial of the material presence of Christ in the Eucharist, and lack of an organized hierarchy.

**lu|thern** (lü′thərn), *n.* = dormer window. [perhaps alteration of *lucarne*]

**lut|ing** (lü′ting), *n.* **1** a seal of lute. **2** the material used; lute. **3** the act or process of sealing with lute.

**lut|ist** (lü′tist), *n.* **1** a lute player. **2** a maker of lutes.

**lu|trine** (lü′trin), *adj.* of or like the otter; otterlike. [< New Latin *lutrinus* < Latin *lutra* otter]

**lutz** (lu̇tz), *n.* a jump in figure skating in which the skater leaps from the outside back edge of one skate, rotates in the air, and lands on the outside back edge of the other skate: *[She] presented a dramatic programme of great athletic merit in which the only mistake was a faulty double lutz* (London Times). [origin uncertain]

**luv** (luv), *n. Especially British Slang.* darling; dear; loved one. [alteration of *love*]

**Lu|wi|an** (lü′ē ən), *n., adj.* —*n.* **1** a member of an ancient people who lived in the southern part of Asia Minor during the 2000's B.C. **2** the Anatolian language of this people, known only through cuneiform writings and related to Hittite. —*adj.* of or having to do with the Luwians or their language. [< *Luwi,* the name of the Luwian people + *-an*]

**lux** (luks), *n., pl.* **lux|es** or **lu|ces**. the international unit of illumination, equivalent to the amount of light falling on a surface which is situated, at all points, one meter from a point source of one candela. A lux equals one lumen per square meter. [< Latin *lūx, lūcis* light[1]]

**Lux.**, Luxembourg.

**lux|ate** (luk′sāt), *v.t.,* **-at|ed, -at|ing.** to put out of joint; dislocate. [< Latin *luxāre* (with English *-ate*[1]) dislocate < *luxus* out of place]

**lux|a|tion** (luk sā′shən), *n.* dislocation, as of bones at a joint.

**luxe** (lu̇ks, luks; *French* lyks), *n., adj.* —*n.* very fine quality; luxury; elegance. —*adj.* luxurious; elegant; deluxe: *I found myself staying at a luxe hotel* (Blair Fraser). *The trip promised to be gorgeously luxe* (Harper's). [< French *luxe* < Latin *luxus, -ūs* abundance, excess]

**Lux|em|bourg|er** or **Lux|em|burg|er** (luk′səm bėr′gər), *n.* a person born or living in the grand duchy or city of Luxembourg.

**Lux|em|bourg|i|an** or **Lux|em|burg|i|an** (luk′-səm bėr′gē ən), *adj., n.* —*adj.* of or having to do with Luxembourg, its people, or their language. —*n.* the Germanic language of Luxembourg.

**lux|u|ri|ance** (lug zhu̇r′ē əns, luk shu̇r′-), *n.* luxuriant growth or productiveness; rich abundance: *the faults which grow out of the luxuriance of freedom* (Edmund Burke). **SYN**: richness. profusion.

**lux|u|ri|an|cy** (lug zhu̇r′ē ən sē, luk shu̇r′-), *n.* = luxuriance.

**lux|u|ri|ant** (lug zhu̇r′ē ənt, luk shu̇r′-), *adj.* **1** growing thick and green: *luxuriant jungle growth.* **SYN**: lush. **2** producing abundantly: *rich, luxuriant soil.* **SYN**: fertile. **3** richly abundant; profuse. **4** rich in ornament: *a luxuriant tapestry.* **SYN**: florid. [< Latin *luxuriāns, -antis,* present participle of *luxuriāre* luxuriate] —**lux|u′ri|ant|ly**, *adv.*

**lux|u|ri|ate** (lug zhu̇r′ē āt, luk shu̇r′-), *v.i.,* **-at|ed, -at|ing.** **1** to indulge in luxury. **2** to take great delight; enjoy oneself; revel: *The explorer planned to luxuriate in hot baths and clean clothes when he came home. You luxuriate in the contemplation of nature ... I in my snuff-box* (Frederick Marryat). **SYN**: bask. **3** to grow very abundantly. [< Latin *luxuriāre* (with English *-ate*[1]) < *luxuria* luxury]

**lux|u|ri|a|tion** (lug zhu̇r′ē ā′shən, luk shu̇r′-), *n.* the act or process of luxuriating.

**lux|u|ri|ous** (lug zhu̇r′ē əs, luk shu̇r′-), *adj.* **1** fond of luxury; tending toward luxury; self-indulgent: *a luxurious taste for food, a luxurious city. She is too proud, too luxurious, to marry a beggar* (Charles Kingsley). **2** giving luxury; very comfortable and beautiful: *a deep, luxurious arm-chair* (Hawthorne). *Luxurious cruise ships sail to the Caribbean and Mediterranean seas and other warm areas* (Lionel Casson). —**lux|u′ri|ous|ly**, *adv.* —**lux|u′ri|ous|ness**, *n.*

**lux|u|ry** (luk′shər ē, lug′zhər-), *n., pl.* **-ries**, *adj.* —*n.* **1** the comforts and beauties of life beyond what is really necessary: *Even very poor people today live in what would have been considered luxury 1,000 years ago. The world declined to support the lady in luxury for nothing* (George Meredith). **SYN**: luxuriousness. **2** the use of the best and most costly food, clothes, houses, furniture, and amusements: *The movie star was accustomed to luxury.* **SYN**: extravagance. **3** a thing that one enjoys, usually something choice and costly: *He saves some money for luxuries such as fine paintings.* **4** a thing that is pleasant but not necessary: *Candy is a luxury. Nancy had treated herself to an expensive luxury in the shape of a husband* (Harriet Beecher Stowe). **5** any form or means of enjoyment or self-gratification: *Learn the luxury of doing good* (Oliver Goldsmith). *I had learned ... not to indulge in the luxury of discontent* (William Godwin). —*adj.* providing lavish comfort and enjoyment; luxurious: *a luxury hotel. The luxury liners Constitution and Independence are your floating hotels, replete with shops, pools, theaters, restaurants* (Harper's). [< Latin *luxuria* < *luxus, -ūs* excess, abundance]

**luxury tax**, a tax put on the sale, manufacture, purchase, or use of luxury goods and services.

**lv.**, **1** leave or leaves. **2** livre or livres.

**lve.**, leave or leaves.

**lvs.**, *Botany.* leaves.

**Lw** (no period), lawrencium (chemical element).

**L wave**, *Physics.* a long wave.

**L.W.F.** or **LWF** (no periods), Lutheran World Federation.

**l.w.l.**, load waterline.

**l.w.m.**, low-water mark.

**LWR** (no periods), light-water reactor.

**LWV** (no periods), League of Women Voters.

**LXX** (no periods), Septuagint (Greek translation of the Old Testament).

**-ly**[1], *suffix added to adjectives to form adverbs.*
**1** in a ___ manner: *Cheerfully = in a cheerful manner. Slightly = in a slight manner.*
**2** in ___ ways or respects: *Financially = in financial respects.*
**3** to a ___ degree or extent: *Greatly = to a great degree.*
**4** in, to, or from a ___ direction: *Northwardly = to or from the north.*
**5** in the ___ place: *Thirdly = in the third place.*
**6** at a ___ time: *Recently = at a recent time.*
[Middle English *-ly,* and *-li,* short for *-liche,* and *-like,* Old English *-licē* < *līc* -ly[2] + *-e,* adverb suffix]

▶ **-ly.** A few adjectives end in **-ly** (*comely, kindly, lovely*), but *-ly* is more distinctly an ending for adverbs. The suffix *-ly* is a living suffix and is freely added to adjectives to form adverbs.

**-ly**[2], *suffix added to nouns to form adjectives.*
**1** like a ___: *Ghostly = like a ghost.*
**2** like that of a ___; characteristic of a ___: *Brotherly = like that of a brother.*
**3** suited to a ___; fit or proper for a ___: *Womanly = suited to a woman.*
**4** of each or every ___; occurring once per ___: *Daily = of every day.*
**5** being a ___; that is a ___: *Heavenly = that is a heaven.*
[Middle English *-ly,* and *-li,* reduction of *-lich,* and *-lik,* Old English *-līc* < *līc* body]

**ly|am-hound** (lī′əm hound′), *n.* = bloodhound. Also, **lyme-hound**. [< Old French *liem* a leash, (ultimately < Latin *līgare* to bind) + English *hound*]

**ly|ard** (lī′ərd), *adj. Scottish.* **1** having white or silver-gray spots: *a lyard horse.* **2** gray; silvery gray: *lyard hair.* [< Old French *liart,* perhaps < *lie* lee[2]]

**ly|art** (lī′ərt), *adj.* = lyard.

**ly|can|thrope** (lī′kən thrōp, lī kan′-), *n.* **1** a person affected with lycanthropy. **2** = werewolf.

**ly|can|throp|ic** (lī′kən throp′ik), *adj.* of, having to do with, or characteristic of lycanthropy.

**ly|can|thro|py** (lī kan′thrə pē), *n.* **1** a mental disturbance, associated with schizophrenia, in which a person thinks he is a wolf. **2** the supposed ability of a human being to turn into a wolf by witchcraft. [< Late Latin *lycanthrōpia* < Greek *lykanthrōpiā* < *lykánthrōpos* one who imagines himself a wolf < *lýkos* wolf + *ánthrōpos* man]

**Ly|ca|on** (lī kā′on), *n. Greek Legend.* a king of Arcadia who tested the divinity of Zeus by offering him human flesh to eat, and was changed into a wolf as punishment.

**ly|cée** (lē sā′), *n.* a French secondary school maintained by the government: *... far more eligible candidates than the nation's lycées could possibly handle* (Time). [< French *lycée,* learned borrowing from Latin *Lycēum.* See etym. of doublet **Lyceum.**]

**ly|cé|en** (lē sā′ən), *n.* a student of a lycée: *We shall expect him to appreciate the French masters as sensitively as any Parisian lycéen* (London Times). [< French *lycéen*]

**Ly|ce|um** (lī sē′əm, lī′sē-), *n.* **1** an ancient outdoor grove and gymnasium near Athens, where Aristotle taught. **2** the Aristotelian school of philosophy. [< Latin *Lycēum* < Greek *Lýkeion* (from the nearby temple of *Apollo lýkeios*). See etym. of doublet **lycée.**]

**ly|ce|um** (lī sē′əm, lī′sē-), *n.* **1** a place where popular lectures are given; lecture hall. **2** an association for instruction and entertainment through lectures, debates, and concerts, popular during the middle part of the 1800's: *Their appearances were scheduled by one or another of several lyceum bureaus* (Emory S. Bogardus). **3** = lycée. [< *Lyceum*]

**lych** (lich), *n.* = lich.

**ly|chee** (lē′chē), *n.* = litchi.

**lych gate**, = lich gate.

**lych|nis** (lik′nis), *n.* any one of a group of plants of the pink family having showy red or white flowers, such as the rose campion and the ragged robin. [< Latin *lychnis* < Greek *lychnís* some kind of brilliant red flower < *lýchnos* lamp]

**Ly|ci|an** (lish′ē ən), *adj., n.* —*adj.* of or having to do with Lycia, an ancient district in Asia Minor. —*n.* **1** a native or inhabitant of Lycia. **2** the Anatolian language of ancient Lycia.

**ly|co|pene** (lī′kə pēn), *n.* a red pigment, a carotenoid, occurring in ripe fruit, especially tomatoes. [< New Latin *Lycop(ersicon)* genus name of the tomato plant + English *-ene*]

**ly|co|pod** (lī′kə pod), *n.* = club moss.

**ly|co|po|di|a|ceous** (lī′kə pō′dē ā′shəs), *adj.* of or belonging to the family of plants typified by the lycopodium or club moss.

**ly|co|po|di|um** (lī′kə pō′dē əm), *n.* **1** = club moss. **2** a fine, yellow, inflammable powder made from the spores of certain club mosses, used especially in fireworks and in surgery. [< New Latin *Lycopodium* the genus name of the club moss < Greek *lýkos* wolf + *poús, podós* foot]

**Ly|cra** (lī′krə), *n. Trademark.* a spandex fiber having the elastic characteristics of rubber, used especially in swimming suits and foundation garments.

**lydd|ite** (lid′īt), *n.* a high explosive, consisting chiefly of picric acid. [< *Lydd,* a town in Kent, England, where it was first manufactured and tested + *-ite*[1]]

**Lyd|i|an** (lid′ē ən), *adj., n.* —*adj.* **1** of Lydia (an ancient country in western Asia Minor famous for its wealth and luxury), its people, or their language: *American scientists found an inscription in the little known Lydian tongue* (Science News Letter). **2** of the Lydian mode; soft; gentle; effeminate: *Soft Lydian airs, Married to immortal verse* (Milton). *Softly sweet, in Lydian measures, Soon he sooth'd his soul to pleasures* (John Dryden). —*n.* **1** a native or inhabitant of Lydia. **2** the language of Lydia. **3** a style of sans-serif printing type with distinctive hairlines.

**Lydian mode**, **1** one of the modes in ancient Greek music, characterized as soft and effeminate. **2** a mode of medieval church music, beginning and ending on the note F.

**lye** (lī), *n., v.,* **lyed, ly|ing.** —*n.* **1** any strong alkaline solution used in making soap and in cleaning. Sodium hydroxide and potassium hydroxide are kinds of lye. **2** an alkaline solution made by leaching wood or other vegetable ashes: *soap lye, soda lye.* **3** a crude or impure caustic soda, used especially for scouring. —*v.t.* to treat with lye. [Old English *lēag.* See related etym. at **lave, lather.**]

**ly|go|di|um** (lī gō′dē əm), *n.* a delicate climbing fern with palmately lobed fronds, native to the eastern United States. [< New Latin *Lygodium* the genus name < Greek *lygṓdēs* like a willow < *lýgos* withy + *eîdos* form]

**ly|gus bug** (lī′gəs), a common hemipterous insect that feeds on the flowers, buds, and seeds of various plants, and is especially destructive of

**Pronunciation Key:** hat, āge, cãre, fär; let, ēqual, tėrm; it, īce; hot, ōpen, ôrder; oil, out; cup, pu̇t, rüle; child; long; thin; ᴛʜen; zh, measure; ə represents **a** in about, **e** in taken, **i** in pencil, **o** in lemon, **u** in circus.

alfalfa. [< New Latin *Lygus* the genus name]

**ly|ing¹** (lī′ing), *n., adj., v.* —*n.* the act of telling a lie; the habit of telling lies. SYN: mendacity, prevarication.
—***adj.*** false; not truthful.
—***v.*** present participle of **lie¹**: *I was not lying; I told the truth.* —**ly′ing|ly,** *adv.*

**ly|ing²** (lī′ing), *v.* present participle of **lie²**: *He was lying on the ground.*

**ly|ing-in** (lī′ing in′), *n., adj.* —*n.* confinement in childbirth; giving birth to a child. —***adj.*** of or having to do with childbirth: *a lying-in hospital.*

**Lyman alpha,** or **Ly|man-al|pha** (lī′mən al′fə), *adj.* of or having to do with the Lyman-alpha line. [< E. M. *Lyman,* born 1910, American physicist]

**Lyman-alpha line** or **Lyman alpha line,** a line of hydrogen in the extreme ultraviolet range of the emission spectrum of the sun, representing a large part of the sun's ultraviolet radiation.

**Lyme arthritis** (līm), a form of arthritis accompanied by large reddened areas of the skin, believed to be caused by a virus carried by ticks: *Alerted by the Connecticut data, doctors in Massachusetts, Rhode Island and New York have since discovered instances of Lyme arthritis in their own areas* (Time). [< *Lyme,* Connecticut, where the illness was widespread]

**lyme-hound** (līm′hound′), *n.* = lyam-hound.

**lymph** (limf), *n.* **1** a nearly colorless liquid in the tissues of the body, somewhat like blood without the red corpuscles. Lymph is derived from parts of the blood which have filtered through blood capillary walls and is conveyed back to the bloodstream by the lymphatic vessels. It has a slightly alkaline quality. *The lymph carries with it most of the blood substances which can be dissolved in water* (A. F. Shull). **2** *Medicine.* any diseased matter taken from a person or animal for use in inoculation, especially against smallpox. **3** *Archaic.* pure, clean water or a stream of it: *I drink the virgin lymph, pure and crystalline as it gushes from the rock* (Tobias Smollett). [< New Latin *lympha* < Latin, clear water; water nymph < Greek *nýmphē* nymph]

**lym|phad** (lim′fad), *n.* a former type of galley with a single mast. [alteration of Gaelic *longfhada*]

**lym|phad|e|nec|to|my** (lim fad′ə nek′tə mē), *n., pl.* **-mies.** the surgical removal of a lymph node.
[< New Latin *lympha* lymph + Greek *adēn* gland, kernel + English *-ectomy*]

**lym|phad|e|ni|tis** (lim fad′ə nī′tis, lim′ fə də-), *n.* inflammation of a lymph node or gland. [< New Latin *lympha* lymph + Greek *adēn* gland, kernel + English *-itis*]

**lym|phan|gi|al** (lim fan′jē əl), *adj.* of or having to do with the lymphatic vessels. [< New Latin *lympha* lymph + Greek *angeîon* vessel + English *-al¹*]

**lym|phan|gi|i|tis** (lim fan′jē ī′tis), *n.* inflammation of the lymphatic vessels. [< New Latin *lympha* lymph + Greek *angeîon* vessel + English *-itis*]

**lym|phan|gi|og|ra|phy** (lim fan′jē og′rə fē), *n.* the X-raying of the lymphatic vessels: *In another procedure, called lymphangiography, a radiopaque dye is injected into a lymph vessel* (Irwin H. Krakoff). Also, **lymphography.** [< *lymphangial* + *-graphy*]

**lym|phan|gi|tis** (lim′fan jī′tis), *n.* = lymphangiitis.

**lym|phat|ic** (lim fat′ik), *adj., n.* —***adj.*** **1** of, carrying, or secreting lymph: *the lymphatic system, a lymphatic disease.* **2** sluggish; lacking energy; pale. A lymphatic appearance or temperament was formerly thought to be due to having too much lymph in the body.
—***n.*** = lymphatic vessel.
[< Latin *lymphāticus* frenzied; the meaning is < New Latin *lympha* lymph] —**lym|phat′i|cal|ly,** *adv.*

**lymphatic gland,** = lymph gland.

***lymphatic system,** the network of small vessels, resembling blood vessels, by which lymph circulates throughout the body carrying food from the blood to the cells, picking up fats from the small intestines, and carrying body wastes to the blood; lymph system.

**lymphatic vessel,** a tube or canal through which lymph circulates to different parts of the body.

**lymph cell,** = lymphocyte.

**lymph corpuscle,** = lymphocyte.

**lymph|e|de|ma** (lim′fi dē′mə), *n.* edema caused by the abnormal accumulation of lymph fluid: *In lymphedema there is insufficient drainage of fluid, and proteins* (Scientific American). [< New Latin *lympha* lymph + *edema*]

**lymph gland,** any one of the bean-shaped, glandlike bodies occurring along the paths of the lymphatic vessel. A lymph gland is composed of a network of connective tissue and is active as a source of lymphocytes. Lymph glands filter out bacteria and other harmful microorganisms from lymph. *Tonsils ... have at last been pin-pointed as the primary site of polio infection, along with similar lymph glands in the small intestine* (Science News Letter).

**lymph node,** = lymph gland.

**lympho-,** *combining form.* lymph: *Lymphocyte* = *a lymph cell.* [< New Latin *lympha;* see etym. under **lymph**]

**lym|pho|blast** (lim′fə blast), *n.* a lymphocyte in an early stage of development. [< *lympho-* + Greek *blastós* germ sprout]

**lym|pho|blas|tic** (lim′fə blas′tik), *adj.* of a lymphoblast.

**lym|pho|cyte** (lim′fə sīt), *n.* one of the nearly colorless cells of the blood and lymphatic system, produced by lymph glands; lymph cell. Lymphocytes have a nucleus and are believed to serve a regenerative function, forming new leucocytes and red blood cells. *The lymphocytes in leukemia, unlike normal lymphocytes, can break down the adrenal hormone, cortisone, into five compounds* (Science News Letter). [< *lympho-* + *-cyte*]

**lym|pho|cyt|ic** (lim′fə sit′ik), *adj.* of or having to do with a lymphocyte or lymphocytes.

**lym|pho|cy|to|sis** (lim′fō sī tō′sis), *n.* an excessive number of lymphocytes in the blood.

**lym|pho|cy|tot|ic** (lim′fō sī tot′ik), *adj.* of a lymphocyte.

**lym|pho|gran|u|lo|ma** (lim′fō gran′yə lō′mə), *n.* **1** a venereal disease caused by a filterable virus, characterized by swelling in the groin, usually followed by ulceration leading to disturbance of the lymph nodes. **2** = Hodgkin's disease. [< *lympho-* + *granuloma*]

**lym|pho|gran|u|lo|ma|to|sis** (lim′fō gran′yə lō′mə tō′sis), *n.* = Hodgkin's disease.

**lymphogranuloma ve|ne|re|um** (və nir′ē əm), = lymphogranuloma (def. 1). [< New Latin *lymphogranuloma venereum* venereal lymphogranuloma]

**lym|phog|ra|phy** (lim fog′rə fē), *n.* = lymphangiography.

**lymph|oid** (lim′foid), *adj.* **1** of or having to do with lymph or lymphocytes; like lymph or lymphocytes. **2** of or having to do with the tissue of the lymph glands; like the tissue of the lymph glands. [< *lymph*(o)- + *-oid*]

**lymphoid tissue,** the tissue that forms most of the lymph glands and thymus gland, consisting of connective tissue containing lymphocytes.

**lym|pho|ma** (lim fō′mə), *n., pl.* **-mas, -ma|ta** (-mə tə). any one of various malignant tumors of the lymphatic tissue, such as Hodgkin's disease and lymphosarcoma: *The spread of the lesions and the size of the lymphomas were much larger at sea level than at high altitude* (Science News Letter).

**lym|pho|ma|to|sis** (lim′fō mə tō′sis), *n., pl.* **-ses** (-sēz). any one of several forms of the avian leucosis complex, characterized by enlargement of the liver, paralysis, blindness, or enlargement of the bones.

**lym|pho|poi|e|sis** (lim′fō poi ē′sis), *n.* **1** the formation of lymphocytes. **2** the production of lymph. [< *lympho-* + Greek *poíēsis* formation, composition]

**lym|pho|sar|co|ma** (lim′fō sär kō′mə), *n.* a sarcoma of the lymphatic tissue, characterized by enlargement of the lymph nodes: *Two of the four had lymphosarcoma, which attacks the blood-forming organs* (New York Times). [< *lympho-* + *sarcoma*]

**lymph system,** = lymphatic system.

**lyn|ce|an** (lin sē′ən), *adj.* like a lynx; keen or sharp-sighted. [< Latin *lyncēus* (< Greek *lýnkeios* < *lýnx* lynx) + English *-an*]

**lynch** (linch), *v.t.* to put (an accused person) to death, usually by hanging, without a lawful trial: *The angry mob lynched an innocent man.* [American English < *lynch* (law)] —**lynch′er,** *n.*

**lyn|chet** (lin′chet), *n. British.* **1** a strip of green land between two pieces of plowed land: *The small rectangular fields are divided from one another by lynchets* (London Times). **2** a slope or terrace along the face of a chalk down: *There was a series of clearly defined lynchets, suggesting that intensive cultivation was practised on these downs* (Manchester Guardian Weekly). [<

***lymphatic system**

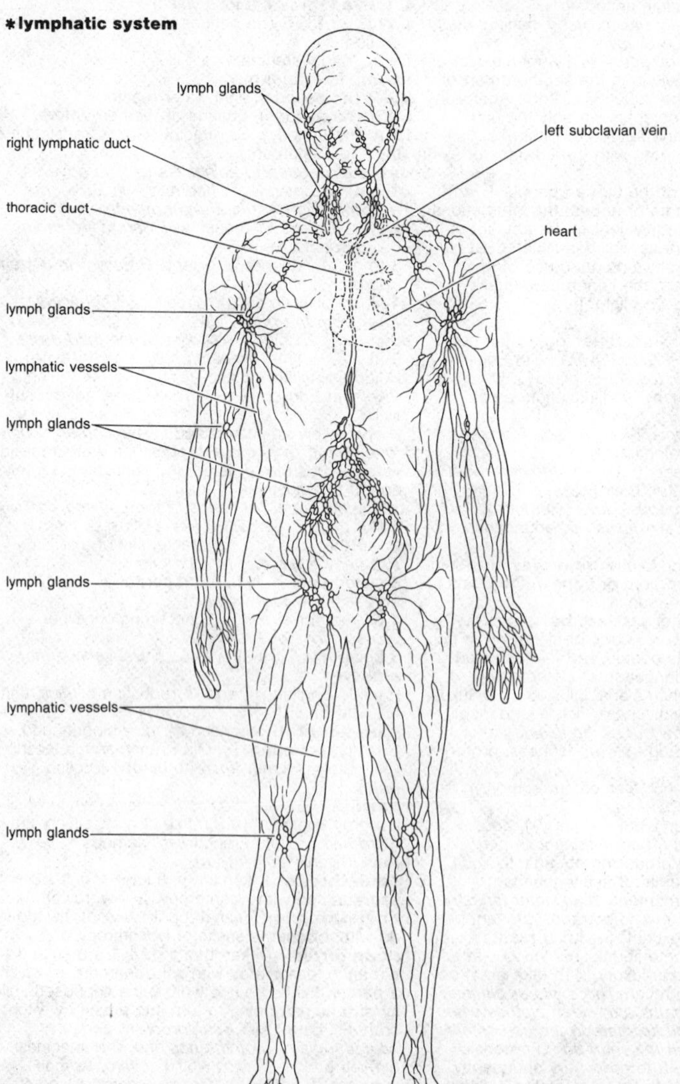

earlier *linch* ridge, ledge (variant of *link*[1]) + *-et*]

**lynch law**, a putting an accused person to death without a lawful trial. [American English; (originally) *Lynch's law,* apparently from Charles *Lynch,* 1736-1796, a planter of Virginia, who drew up a vigilante compact with his neighbors]

**lynch|pin** (linch′pin′), *n.* = linchpin.

**Lyn|cis** (lin′sis), *n.* genitive of **Lynx**.

***lynx** (lingks), *n., pl.* **lynx|es** or (*collectively*) **lynx**. any one of certain wildcats of the Northern Hemisphere having a short tail, rather long legs, and tufts of hair at the ends of their ears. Lynxes include the Canada lynx and bobcat of North America, and several Old World varieties. [< Latin *lynx* < Greek *lýnx*] —**lynx′like′**, *adj.*

***lynx**

Canada lynx — bobcat

**Lynx** (lingks), *n., genitive* **Lyn|cis**. a northern constellation near Ursa Major.

**lynx eye**, a sharp eye, such as the lynx is supposed to have: *His lynx eye immediately perceives the paper* (Edgar Allan Poe).

**lynx-eyed** (lingks′īd′), *adj.* having sharp eyes or keen sight; sharp-sighted.

**ly|on|naise** (lī′ə nāz′), *adj.* fried with pieces of onion: *lyonnaise potatoes.* [< French *lyonnaise,* feminine of *lyonnais* of *Lyon,* a city in France]

**Ly|on|nesse** (lī′ə nes′), *n.* a legendary region off southwestern England, near Cornwall, associated with Arthurian legend and supposed to have sunk beneath the sea.

**ly|o|phile** (lī′ə fīl), *adj.* = lyophilic.

**ly|o|phil|ic** (lī′ə fil′ik), *adj. Chemistry.* characterized by strong attraction between the colloid and the dispersion medium of a colloidal system: *Lyophilic colloidal systems are affected very little by electrolytes* (W. N. Jones). [< Greek *lyyén* to loosen + English *-phil* + *-ic*]

**ly|oph|i|li|za|tion** (lī of′ə lə zā′shən), *n.* the process of lyophilizing substances for preservation: *Refrigeration, freezing and lyophilization, the methods used almost exclusively for preserving plasma, are also the best methods for preserving viruses* (Science News Letter).

**ly|oph|i|lize** (lī of′ə līz), *v.t.,* **-lized, -liz|ing**. to dehydrate (a frozen material) for storage by converting its water content to a gaseous state in a vacuum, leaving it as a porous solid.

**ly|o|pho|bic** (lī′ə fō′bik, -fob′ik), *adj. Chemistry.* characterized by a lack of attraction between the colloid and the dispersion medium of a colloidal system. [< Greek *lyyén* to loosen + English *-phobe* + *-ic*]

**Ly|ra** (lī′rə), *n., genitive* **Ly|rae**. a small northern constellation that was seen by ancient astronomers as having the rough outline of the lyre of Mercury or Orpheus. It contains Vega, the fifth brightest star, excluding the sun. *The brightest star of the early summer evenings, however, is Vega, which is high in the east, part of Lyra, the lyre* (Science News Letter). Also, **Lyre**. [< Latin *Lyra* < Greek *Lýrā* (literally) the lyre]

**Ly|rae** (lī′rē), *n.* genitive of **Lyra**.

**ly|rate** (lī′rāt), *adj.* shaped like a lyre, as the tail of certain birds or a leaf. [< New Latin *lyratus* < Latin *lyra* lyre]

**ly|rat|ed** (lī′rā tid), *adj.* = lyrate.

***lyre** definition 1

***lyrebird**

***lyre** (līr), *n.* **1** an ancient stringed musical instrument somewhat like a small harp. It was used by the ancient Greeks as accompaniment for singing and reciting. **2** *Figurative.* the medium of a poet's expression: *Milton's golden lyre* (Mark Akenside). *Here Poesy might wake her heav'n-taught lyre* (Robert Burns). [< Old French *lire,* and *lyre,* learned borrowing from Latin *lyra* < Greek *lýrā*]

**Lyre** (līr), *n.* = Lyra.

***lyre|bird** (līr′bėrd′), *n.* either of two Australian birds about the size of a rooster. The male has a long tail that resembles the shape of a lyre when spread. The lyrebird is a perching bird and exhibits elaborate courtship behavior.

**lyre crab**, a variety of crab with a thick, round body and a shell shaped somewhat like a lyre.

**lyr|ic** (lir′ik), *n., adj.* —*n.* **1** a short poem expressing personal emotion. A love poem, a patriotic song, a lament, and a hymn might all be lyrics. **2** a lyric poet.

—*adj.* **1** having to do with such poems: *a lyric poet.* **2** characterized by a spontaneous expression of feeling: *Elegies, sonnets, and odes are kinds of lyric poetry.* **3** of, expressed in, or suitable for song. SYN: melodious. **4a** tender, light in volume, and often used in the higher register: *Sopranos and tenors have lyric singing voices.* **b** (of a singer) having such a voice. **5** of or for the lyre.

**lyrics**, the words for a song, especially a popular song: *He wanted to use some Italian lyrics written for a Johann Strauss melody* (New Yorker). [< Latin *lyricus* < Greek *lyrikós* of a lyre < *lýrā* lyre]

**lyr|i|cal** (lir′ə kəl), *adj.* **1** emotional; poetic; having the qualities or characteristics of lyric poetry: *a lyrical landscape and still-life painter. She became almost lyrical when she described the scenery.* **2** = lyric. —**lyr′i|cal|ly**, *adv.* —**lyr′i|cal|ness**, *n.*

**lyr|i|cism** (lir′ə siz əm), *n.* **1** lyric character or style: *the lyricism of Donne's songs and sonnets.* **2** a lyric form or expression. **3** lyric outpouring of feeling; emotionally expressed enthusiasm.

**lyr|i|cist** (lir′ə sist), *n.* **1** a person who writes the words for a song, especially in a musical comedy; writer of lyrics: *The cards also list the song titles, the composer and lyricist* (New Yorker). **2** a lyric poet.

**lyr|i|cize** (lir′ə sīz), *v.,* **-cized, -ciz|ing**. —*v.i.* **1** to sing lyrics. **2** to compose lyrics.

—*v.t.* **1** to treat in a lyric style. **2** to express in an emotional way.

**lyr|i|co-dra|mat|ic** (lir′ə kō drə mat′ik), *adj.* combining the characteristics of lyric and dramatic poetry.

**lyr|i|co-ep|ic** (lir′ə kō ep′ik), *adj.* having the characteristics of lyric and epic poetry.

**lyr|ics** (lir′iks), *n.pl.* See under **lyric**.

**lyric tenor**, **1** a light, high tenor voice. **2** a man with such a voice.

**lyric theater**, any form of theatrical production in which dance, music, and spoken words are combined.

**lyr|i|form** (līr′ə fôrm), *adj.* shaped like a lyre.

**lyr|ism** (lir′iz əm *for 1;* līr′iz əm, lir′- *for 2*), *n.* **1** lyricism; lyrical enthusiasm. **2** performance on a lyre; musical performance; singing: *The lyrism ... had gradually assumed a rather deafening and complex character* (George Eliot).

**lyr|ist** (lir′ist *for 1;* līr′ist, lir′- *for 2*), *n.* **1** a lyric poet: *They ... are both tolerably well acquainted with the minor Elizabethan lyrists* (Listener). **2** a person who plays on the lyre; person who plays and sings to an accompaniment on the lyre.

**ly|sate** (lī′sāt), *n.* the product resulting from the destruction of a cell by a lysin or lysins: *A lysate ... may contain over a hundred thousand million bacteriophage particles* (Science News Letter).

**lyse** (līs), *v.,* **lysed, lys|ing**. —*v.t.* to bring about the dissolution of red blood cells by lysins; subject to lysis: *These viruses prevent bacterial growth and division, eventually lysing the cells* (Science).

—*v.i.* to undergo lysis.

[< *lysis*]

**Ly|sen|ko|ism** (lə seng′kō iz əm), *n.* the theory of heredity maintained by Trofim D. Lysenko (born 1898), a Russian geneticist, that acquired characteristics are inheritable, not accepted by most geneticists: *Biology has of course been made —and is still being made—nonsensical by Lysenkoism* (Alastair Mackenzie).

**Ly|sen|ko|ist** (lə seng′kō ist), *n., adj.* —*n.* a follower of Lysenko or Lysenkoism: *He was arraigned by the Lysenkoists because he had refused to compromise with their phoney science* (New Scientist).

—*adj.* of, having to do with, or characteristic of Lysenkoism.

**ly|ser|gic acid** (lī sėr′jik), a chemical produced synthetically or extracted from ergot, with properties similar to lysergic acid diethylamide. *Formula:* $C_{16}H_{16}N_2O_2$ [*lysergic* < *lys*(is) + *erg*(ot) + *-ic*]

**lysergic acid di|eth|yl|am|ide** (dī eth′ə lam′-īd), a hallucinogenic compound of lysergic acid that produces temporary symptoms of schizophrenia. It is a derivative of an acid obtained from ergot. *Formula:* $C_{20}H_{25}N_3O$ *Abbr.:* LSD (no periods).

**ly|sim|e|ter** (lī sim′ə tər), *n.* an instrument for measuring the quantity of matter dissolved in a liquid. [< Greek *lýsis* a loosening]

**ly|sin**[1] (lī′sin), *n.* an antibody that can dissolve bacteria, red blood cells, and other cellular elements. Lysins are developed in blood serum. [special use of *lysin*[2]]

**ly|sin**[2] (lī′sin), *n.* = lysine.

**ly|sine** (lī′sēn, -sin), *n.* a basic amino acid essential for growth, formed by the hydrolysis of various proteins. *Formula:* $C_6H_{14}N_2O_2$ [< Greek *lýsis* a loosening + English *-ine*[2]]

**ly|sis** (lī′sis), *n., pl.* **-ses** (-sēz). **1** the destruction of a cell by dissolution of the cell membrane, as by a lysin or a virus: *For some considerable distance around the mold growth, the staphylococcal colonies were undergoing lysis* (*being dissolved*) (Marguerite Clark). **2** the gradual ending of an acute disease (contrasted with *crisis*). [< Latin *lysis* < Greek *lýsis* a loosening < *lyyén* to loosen]

**ly|so|cline** (lī′sə klīn), *n.* a layer of water in the sea where certain chemical substances undergo dissolution: *When marine organisms die and sink to about 4,000 meters, they cross the "lysocline," below which calcium carbonate redissolves because of the high pressure* (Scientific American). [< Greek *lýsis* a loosening + *klīnein* to slope]

**ly|so|ge|na|tion** (lī′sə jə nā′shən), *n.* = lysogenization.

**ly|so|gen|ic** (lī′sə jen′ik), *adj.* **1** causing the destruction of cells by dissolution of the cell membrane. **2** carrying a prophage within the cell: *a lysogenic bacterium.*

**ly|sog|e|ni|za|tion** (lī soj′ə nə zā′shən), *n.* the process of lysogenizing; fusion of the genetic material of a virus with that of a host bacterium.

**ly|sog|e|nize** (lī soj′ə nīz), *v.t.,* **-nized, -niz|ing**. to make lysogenic; cause (bacteria) to carry a prophage within the cell.

**ly|sog|e|ny** (lī soj′ə nē), *n.* **1** the production of a lysin or lysins. **2** the initiation of the process of lysis. **3** = lysogenization.

**Ly|sol** (lī′sōl, -sol), *n. Trademark.* a brown, oily liquid containing cresols and soap, used as a disinfectant and antiseptic.

**ly|so|lec|i|thin** (lī′sə les′ə thin), *n.* a substance that is highly destructive of red blood cells, obtained by the action of snake venom on lecithin.

**ly|so|som|al** (lī′sə sō′məl), *adj.* of or having to do with lysosomes: *The membrane serves to protect the rest of the cell from the contents of lysosomes, because uninhibited action of lysosomal enzymes causes cell death* (London Times).

**ly|so|some** (lī′sə sōm), *n.* a particle in the cytoplasm of most cells that contains destructive, hydrolytic enzymes: *The lysosomes function in many ways as the digestive system of the cell* (Scientific American). See picture under **cell**. [< Greek *lýsis* a loosening + *sôma* body]

**ly|so|staph|in** (lī′sə staf′ən), *n.* an enzyme that destroys staphylococcal bacteria by disintegrating the bacterial cell wall. [< Greek *lýsis* a loosening + English *staph*(ylococci) + *-in*]

**ly|so|zyme** (lī′sə zīm, -zim), *n.* an enzymelike substance that is capable of destroying many kinds of bacteria. It is found in egg white, human tears, and most body fluids. *As early as 1922, researchers have known that the enzyme lysozyme, found in nasal secretions, has important bacteria-destroying powers* (Science News Letter). [< Greek *lýsis* a loosening + English (en)*zyme*]

**lys|sa** (lis′ə), *n.* = rabies. [< Greek *lýssa*]

**lys|sic** (lis′ik), *adj.* having to do with lyssa or rabies.

**lys|so|pho|bi|a** (lis′ə fō′bē ə), *n.* an abnormal fear of rabies, which sometimes simulates its symptoms; pseudorabies. [< Greek *lýssa* rage, rabies + English *-phobia*]

**Lys|tro|sau|rus** (lis′trə sôr′əs), *n., pl.* **-sau|ri** (-sôr′ī). a small herbivorous reptile of the Triassic period whose remains were discovered in South Africa and Asia, and, recently, in Antarctica. [< New Latin *Lystro* + Greek *saûros* lizard]

**lyth|ra|ceous** (lith rā′shəs, lī thrā′-), *adj.* of or belonging to the loosestrife family of plants. [< New Latin *Lythraceae* the family name (< *Lythrum* the typical genus < Greek *lýthron* gore) + English *-ous*]

**lyt|ic** (lit′ik), *adj.* **1** having to do with or producing lysis. **2** of or having to do with a lysin.

**lyt|ta** (lit′ə), *n., pl.* **lyt|tae** (lit′ē). a long, worm-shaped cartilage in the tongue of dogs and other carnivorous animals. [< New Latin *lytta* < Greek *lýtta,* variant of *lýssa* rabies, rage]

**LZ** (no periods) or **L.Z.**, landing zone.

---

**Pronunciation Key:** hat, āge, cãre, fär; let, ēqual, tėrm; it, īce; hot, ōpen, ôrder; oil, out; cup, pu̇t, rüle; child; long; thin; ᴛʜen; zh, measure; ə represents a in about, e in taken, i in pencil, o in lemon, u in circus.

# Mm

***M**[1] or **m** (em), *n., pl.* **M's** or **Ms, m's** or **ms**. **1** the 13th letter of the English alphabet. There are three *m*'s in *mammoth.* **2** any sound represented by this letter. **3** (used as a symbol for) the 13th, or more usually the 12th (of an actual or possible series, either I or J being omitted): *row M in a theater.* **4** the Roman numeral for 1,000. **5** *Printing.* an em, the square of any size of type.

**M**[2] (em), *n., pl.* **M's**. anything shaped like an M.

**m-**, *prefix.* variant of **meta-** in chemical terms.

**m.** or **m** (no period), an abbreviation for the following:
**1** male.
**2** manual.
**3** mark (in German money).
**4** married.
**5** masculine.
**6** *Physics.* mass.
**7** medicine.
**8** medium.
**9** meridian.
**10** meridional.
**11** metal.
**12** meter or meters.
**13** midnight.
**14** mile or miles.
**15** mill or mills.
**16** milli- (one thousandth).
**17** million.
**18** minim.
**19** minute or minutes.
**20** mist.
**21** *Mathematics.* modulus.
**22** month.
**23** moon.
**24** morning.
**25** mountain.
**26** muscle.
**27** noon (Latin *meridies*).

**M** (no period), an abbreviation for the following:
**1** Mach.
**2** *Physics.* magnetization.
**3** *Physics.* mass.
**4** Mature (for adult audiences).
**5** medium.
**6** mega- (one million).
**7** *Linguistics.* Middle; Medieval.
**8** missile.
**9** *Economics.* money.
**10** morphine.
**11** *British.* motorway: *M1.*

**M.**, an abbreviation for the following:
**1** majesty.
**2** Manitoba.
**3** *Music.* manual.
**4** mark (unit of German money).
**5** marquis.
**6** mass.
**7** medical.
**8** medicine.
**9** member.
**10** midnight.
**11** militia.
**12** Monday.
**13** Monsieur.
**14** mountain.
**15** noon (Latin, *meridies*).

**M-1** or **$M_1$** (emʹwunʹ), *n. Economics.* currency and demand deposits.

**M-2** or **$M_2$** (emʹtüʹ), *n. Economics.* M-1 plus time deposits and certificates of deposit.

**ma** (mä, mô), *n. Informal.* mamma; mother.

**ma.**, milliampere.

**mA.**, milliangstrom.

**Ma** (no period), masurium (chemical element).

**MA** (no periods), **1** machine accountant. **2** Maritime Administration. **3** Massachusetts (with postal Zip Code). **4** mental age.

**M.A.**, **1** Master of Arts (Latin, *Magister Artium*). Also, **A.M. 2** Military Academy.

**MAA** (no periods), Medical Assistance for the Aged.

**MAAG** (no periods), Military Assistance Advisory Group.

**maʹal|lem** (mə alʹim), *n.* an Arab teacher or scholar. [< Arabic *mu'allim*]

**maʹam** (mam, mäm), *n. Informal.* madam.

**maar** (mär), *n. Geology.* the crater of a volcano formed by an explosion but with no flow of lava. [< German *maar*]

**Mab** (mab), *n.* See **Queen Mab**.

**Ma|ba|an** (mä bä änʹ), *n.* a member of an African tribe in southeastern Sudan who live in virtual silence and are mainly vegetarians: *Coronary heart disease and hypertension are unknown among the Mabaans, and at age 75 their hearing is still acute* (Samuel Rosen).

**Ma Bell**, *U.S.* a nickname for the telephone company. [< the *Bell* System (of telephone companies) < Alexander Graham *Bell,* inventor of the telephone]

**mac** (mak), *n. British Informal.* a mackintosh: *The raincoat, or mac, is as essential to an Englishman as his teeth* (H. Allen Smith).

**Mac** (mak), *n.* **1** son of (used in Scottish and Irish family names): *Her Macs let Scotland boast* (Henry Fielding). **2** *U.S. Slang.* fellow (used as a form of direct address): *"If you don't like the way the subway's being run, Mac, why don't you buy it?"* (New Yorker). [< *Mac-*]

**MAC** (mak), *n.,* or **M.A.C.**, **1** Military Airlift Command (a unit of the U.S. Air Force). **2** multiple-access computer (a computer system which allows simultaneous use from several inputs). **3** = Big Mac.

**Mac-**, *prefix.* son of (used in Scottish and Irish family names). Also, **Mc-**. [< Scottish Gaelic, and Irish *mac* son]

**Mac.**, Maccabees (books of the Apocrypha).

**ma|ca|ber** (mə käʹbər), *adj.* = macabre.

**ma|ca|bre** (mə käʹbrə, -bər), *adj.* **1** causing horror; gruesome; horrible; ghastly. **SYN**: grim. **2** having to do with or suggestive of the danse macabre (dance of death): *Jörgenson ... without being exactly macabre, behaved more like an indifferent but restless corpse* (Joseph Conrad). [< French *macabre* < Middle French (*danse*) *macabré* (dance of) death; origin uncertain] —**ma|caʹbre|ly**, *adv.*

**ma|ca|co**[1] (mə kāʹkō), *n., pl.* **-cos**. = macaque. [< Portuguese *macaco* < an African (Congo) word; see etym. under **macaque**]

**ma|ca|co**[2] (mə kāʹkō), *n., pl.* **-cos**. a black, short-tailed lemur of Madagascar. [< French *mococo;* origin uncertain]

**mac|ad|am** (mə kadʹəm), *n.* **1** small, broken stones. Layers of macadam are rolled until solid and smooth to make roads. **2** a road or pavement made of this. [< John L. *McAdam,* 1756-1836, a Scottish engineer, who invented this kind of road]

**mac|a|da|mi|a** (makʹə dāʹmē ə), *n.* **1** any one of a genus of trees or tall shrubs native to eastern Australia and cultivated in Hawaii. **2** the nut of this tree; macadamia nut. [< New Latin *Macadamia* the genus name < John *Macadam,* 1827-1865, an Australian scientist]

**macadamia nut**, the large, smooth nut of the macadamia; Queensland nut. It is rich in oil and has a sweet flavor.

**mac|ad|am|ise** (mə kadʹə mīz), *v.t.,* **-ised**, **-is|ing**. *Especially British.* macadamize.

**mac|ad|am|ize** (mə kadʹə mīz), *v.t.,* **-ized**, **-iz|ing**. to make or cover (a road) with macadam. **SYN**: pave. —**mac|adʹam|i|zaʹtion**, *n.*

**ma|caque** (mə käkʹ), *n.* any one of a group of hardy monkeys of Asia, the East Indies, and northern Africa, that includes the Barbary ape and the rhesus. [< French *macaque* < Portuguese *macaco;* see etym. under **macaco**[1]]

**mac|a|rize** (makʹə rīz), *v.t.,* **-rized**, **-riz|ing**. to call happy; consider blessed. [< Greek *makarízein* < *mákar* happy]

**mac|a|ro|ni** (makʹə rōʹnē), *n., pl.* **-nis** or **-nies**. **1** wheat flour paste that has been dried, usually in the form of hollow tubes, to be cooked for food. See picture under **pasta**. **2** a fashionable English dandy of the 1700's who affectedly followed French or Italian fashions in dress, food, and manners. **3** a fop; dandy: *the pigmy macaronies of these degenerate days* (Washington Irving). Also, **maccaroni**. [< earlier Italian *maccaroni,* plural of *maccarone,* perhaps ultimately < Late Greek *makariā* barley broth]

**mac|a|ron|ic** (makʹə ronʹik), *adj., n.* —*adj.* **1** characterized by a mixture of Latin words with words from another language, or with non-Latin words that are given Latin endings: *macaronic verse.* **2** involving a mixture of languages. **3** mixed; jumbled.
—*n.* a macaronic composition; a confused heap or mixture of several things.
**macaronics**, macaronic verses.
[< New Latin *macaronicus* mixed (verse) < Italian *maccheronico,* < *maccarone;* see etym. under **macaroni**] —**macʹa|ronʹi|cal|ly**, *adv.*

**macaroni wheat**, a variety of wheat, such as durum, used to make macaroni, spaghetti, and the like.

**mac|a|roon** (makʹə rünʹ), *n.* **1** a small, very sweet cookie made of whites of eggs, sugar, and ground almonds, or coconut. **2** a mixture of eggs, sugar, and lemon juice, used as a topping for cakes. [< French *macaron* < Italian *maccarone;* see etym. under **macaroni**]

**Ma|cas|sar oil** (mə kasʹər), an oily substance much used during the 1800's to dress the hair. [< *Macassar,* a seaport in Celebes, Indonesia, the alleged place of origin]

**ma|caw** (mə kôʹ), *n.* a large parrot of South and Central America with a long tail, brilliant feathers, and a harsh voice. There are several kinds. [< Portuguese *macao,* perhaps < a Brazilian name (compare Tupi *macavuana*)]

**Mac|beth** (mək bethʹ, mak-), *n.* **1** a tragedy by Shakespeare, first printed in 1623. **2** the principal character in this play, who murders his king and becomes king himself. His wife, Lady Macbeth, helps him to do this.

**Macc.**, Maccabees (books of the Apocrypha).

**Mac|ca|be|an** (makʹə bēʹən), *adj.* of or having to do with Judas Maccabeus or the Maccabees.

**Mac|ca|bees** (makʹə bēz), *n.pl.* **1** the supporters or successors of Judas Maccabeus, the leader of a successful revolt of Jewish patriots against Syria in 166 B.C. The members of his family ruled Palestine as a dynasty from about 141 B.C. to 37 B.C. **2** two historical books of the Old Testament Apocrypha that tell about the revolt. *Abbr:* Macc. **3** a fraternal and benevolent organization founded in London, Ontario, in 1878, until 1914, called the Knights of the Maccabees.

**mac|ca|boy** (makʹə boi), *n.* a semiwet, highly flavored type of snuff. [< *Macouba,* a district in Martinique]

**mac|ca|ro|ni** (makʹə rōʹnē), *n., pl.* **-nis** or **-nies**. = macaroni.

**mace**[1] (mās), *n.* **1** a club with a heavy metal head, often spiked, used as a weapon in the Middle Ages to smash armor. **2** a staff carried by or before certain officials as a symbol of their authority. **SYN**: truncheon. **3** = mace-bearer. **4** a light stick with a flat head, formerly used in billiards instead of a cue. [< Old French *mace,* also *masse* < Vulgar Latin *mattea* < Latin *matteola,* variant of *mateola* a digging tool]

**mace**[2] (mās), *n.* a spice made from the dried outer covering of nutmegs. [Middle English *mace,* taken as singular of *macis* < Old French *macis* < Latin *macir* a fragrant resin < Greek *mákir*]

**mace**[3] (mās), *n., v.* **maced**, **mac|ing**. *Slang.* —*n.* **1** swindling. **2** a swindler.
—*v.t.* **1** to swindle. **2** to dun; make demands upon; extort from: ... *indicted on graft and corruption charges for passing out illegal contracts and macing state employees for political contributions* (Time).
[origin unknown]

**mace**[4] (mās), *n., v.,* **maced**, **mac|ing**. —*n.* **1** any liquid chemical irritant, especially liquid tear gas: *a cartridge of mace.* **2** a device for firing or releasing mace: *The new arsenal includes maces that fire up to 50 rounds of tear gas in 50 seconds, each harmlessly incapacitating* (Donald Janson).
—*v.t.* to attack or disable with mace.
[< *Mace*]

**Mace** (mās), *n. Trademark.* a liquid tear gas usually sprayed from a pressurized container, such as an aerosol bomb, used especially in riot control; Chemical Mace: *Mace temporarily incapacitates, but it contains no toxic ingredients other than tear gas and the risk with Mace is negligible when compared with conventional weapons, the team reported* (New York Times).

**mace-bear|er** (māsʹbārʹər), *n.* a person who car-

***M**[1]
definition 1

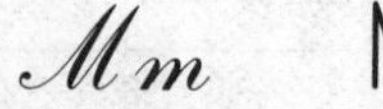

Script letters look like examples of fine penmanship. They appear in many formal uses, such as invitations to social functions.

Mm *Mm*

Handwritten letters, both manuscript or printed (left) and cursive (right), are easy for children to read and to write.

Mm *Mm*

Roman letters have *serifs* (finishing strokes) adapted from the way Roman stonecutters carved their letters. This is *Times Roman* type.

Mm *Mm*

Sans-serif letters are often called *gothic.* They have lines of even width and no serifs. This type face is called *Helvetica.*

Mm *Mm*

Between roman and gothic, some letters have thick and thin lines with slight flares that suggest serifs. This type face is *Optima.*

M

Computer letters can be sensed by machines either from their shapes or from the magnetic ink with which they are printed.

ries a mace as a symbol of authority before some high official.

**Maced.**, Macedonia.

**mac|é|doine** (mas'ā dwän'), *n.* a mixture of vegetables or fruits, sometimes in jelly, served as a salad, garnish, dessert, or appetizer. [< French *macédoine* (literally) Macedonian, apparently a reference to Macedonia as a land of many peoples, therefore a mixture]

**Mac|e|do|ni|an** (mas'ə dō'nē ən), *adj., n.* —*adj.* of or having to do with Macedonia, its people, or their language.
—*n.* **1** a native or inhabitant of Macedonia. **2** the Slavic language of modern Macedonia. **3** the Indo-European language of ancient Macedonia.

**mac|er** (mā'sər), *n.* **1** = mace-bearer. **2** (in Scotland) an officer who keeps order, calls the rolls, and performs other such duties, in a law court. [< Old French *maissier* < *masse* mace[1]]

**mac|er|ate** (mas'ə rāt), *v.,* **-at|ed, -at|ing.** —*v.t.* **1** to soften or separate the parts of (a substance) by soaking for some time. Flowers are macerated to extract their perfume. SYN: ret. **2** to break up or soften (food) by the digestive process. **3** to cause to grow thin. SYN: emaciate. **4** *Archaic.* to oppress; vex; worry.
—*v.i.* **1** to be softened, as by soaking. **2** to become thin; waste away. [< Latin *mācerāre* (with English *-ate*[1]) soften] —**mac'er|at'er, mac'er|a'tor,** *n.* —**mac'er|a'tion,** *n.*

**Mach** (mäk, mak), *n. Aeronautics.* Mach number.

**mach.**, **1** machine. **2** machinery. **3** machinist.

**Mach|a|bees** (mak'ə bēz), *n.pl.* (in the Douay Bible) Maccabees.

**ma|chan** (mə chän'), *n. Anglo-Indian.* a platform built into a tree, used by hunters to await a tiger driven toward them by beaters. [< Hindustani *machān*]

**ma chère** (mȧ sher'), *French.* my dear (used in addressing a woman or girl).

***ma|chet|e** (mə shet'ē, -shet'; *Spanish* mä chā'tā), *n.* a large, heavy knife, used as a tool for cutting brush or sugar cane and as a weapon in South America, Central America, and the West Indies. [American English < Spanish *machete* (diminutive) < *macho* sledge hammer, mallet, ax, probably dialectal variant of *maza* < Vulgar Latin *mattea;* see etym. under **mace**[1]]

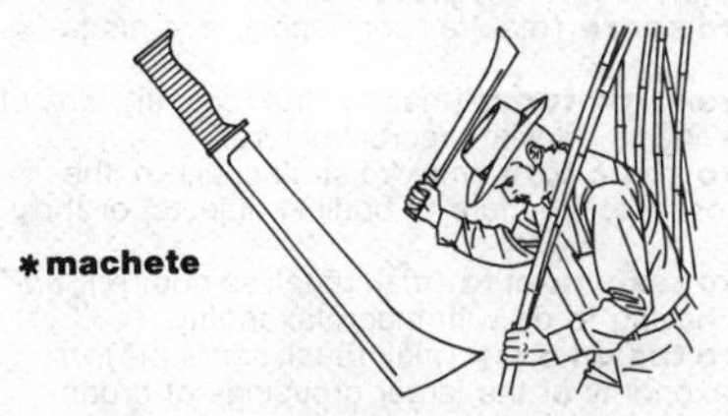

***machete**

**Mach|i|an** (mä'kē ən, mak'ē ən), *adj., n.* —*adj.* of or having to do with the theories of the Austrian physicist and philosopher Ernst Mach (1838-1916): *The Machian criticism of the relations between matter and motion had been held to reduce the reality of matter* (New Scientist).
—*n.* a student or follower of Ernst Mach.

**Mach|i|a|vel** (mak'ē ə vel), *n.* a Machiavellian person.

**Mach|i|a|vel|li|an** or **Mach|i|a|vel|i|an** (mak'ē-ə vel'ē ən), *adj., n.* —*adj.* **1** of or having to do with the Italian statesman and student of politics Niccolò Machiavelli (1469-1527) or his political theories and principles, especially the idea that a ruler must use any means, no matter how unscrupulous, to keep in power: *Educated in the Machiavellian ... school of politics, she was versed in that "dissimulation" to which liberal Anglo-Saxons give a shorter name* (John L. Motley). **2** characterized by subtle or unscrupulous cunning; crafty. SYN: wily, astute.
—*n.* a follower of the crafty political methods of Machiavelli.

**Mach|i|a|vel|li|an|ism** (mak'ē ə vel'ē ə niz'əm), *n.* the principles and practices of Machiavelli or his followers; unscrupulous political cunning.

**Mach|i|a|vel|lism** (mak'ē ə vel'iz əm), *n.* = Machiavellianism.

**ma|chic|o|late** (mə chik'ə lāt), *v.t.,* **-lat|ed, -lat|ing.** to build or decorate with machicolations. [< Medieval Latin *machicolare* (with English *-ate*[1]), Latinization of Old French *machicoler* < Old Provençal *machacol* projection, balcony < *macar* to crush (< a Germanic word) + *col* neck < Latin *collum*]

**ma|chic|o|lat|ed** (mə chik'ə lā'tid), *adj.* having machicolations.

**ma|chic|o|la|tion** (mə chik'ə lā'shən), *n. Architecture.* **1** an opening in the floor of a projecting gallery or parapet, or in the roof of an entrance, through which missiles, hot liquids, or stones might be cast upon attackers. Machicolations were much used in medieval fortified structures. **2** a projecting gallery or parapet with such openings.

**ma|chin|a|bil|i|ty** (mə shē'nə bil'ə tē), *n.* the ability to be worked by a machine; ease of operation by machine.

**ma|chin|a|ble** (mə shē'nə bəl), —*adj.* that can be worked or tooled by machine.

**mach|i|nate** (mak'ə nāt), *v.i., v.t.,* **-nat|ed, -nat|ing.** to contrive or devise artfully or with evil purpose; plot; intrigue. [< Latin *māchinārī* (with English *-ate*[1]) < *māchina;* see etym. under **machine**]

**mach|i|na|tion** (mak'ə nā'shən), *n.* **1** evil or artful plotting; scheming against authority; intrigue. SYN: conspiracy, cabal. **2** Usually, **machinations.** an evil plot; secret or cunning scheme: *The election of our candidate was almost prevented by the machinations of his opponent.*

**mach|i|na|tor** (mak'ə nā'tər), *n.* a person who machinates; schemer; plotter.

**ma|chine** (mə shēn'), *n., adj., v.,* **-chined, -chin|ing.** —*n.* **1** an arrangement of fixed and moving parts for doing work, each part having some special thing to do; mechanical apparatus or device: *Sewing machines and washing machines make housework easier.* **2** any device for applying or changing the direction of power, force, or motion. Levers and pulleys are simple machines. SYN: mechanism. **3** = automobile. SYN: motorcar. **4** = airplane. SYN: aircraft. **5** *Figurative.* a person or group that acts without thinking: *Public hacknies in the schooling trade ... Machines themselves, and governed by a clock* (William Cowper). SYN: automaton. **6** *Figurative.* a group of people controlling a political party or other organization: *the Democratic machine, the boss of a state machine.* **7a** a contrivance in the ancient theater for producing stage effects. **b** a contrivance, such as a supernatural power or person, introduced into a literary work for effect. **8** *Archaic.* the human or animal body. **9** any structure or contrivance: *There was not a bed ... except one oldfashioned machine, with a high-gilt tester* (Tobias Smollett). **10** *Obsolete.* any vehicle, such as a stagecoach.
—*adj.* **1** of or having to do with a machine or machines: *machine action, a machine politician, the machine age.* **2** by or with a machine, not by hand: *machine printing.* **3** *Figurative.* like that of a machine; mechanical or stereotyped.
—*v.t.* to make, prepare, or finish with a machine: *Bessemer steel normally contains more sulfur and phosphorus, and therefore is easier to machine, or cut* (Max D. Howell).
[< Middle French *machine,* learned borrowing from Latin *māchina* < Greek *mēchanē* a device < *mêchos* means, expedient]

**ma|chine|a|ble** (mə shē'nə bəl), *adj.* = machinable.

**machine art**, a form of art that uses mechanical, electronic, magnetic, or similar objects or devices as works of art.

**machine bolt**, a bolt with a thread and a square or hexagonal head. See picture under **bolt**[1].

**machine gun**, a gun that can keep up a rapid fire of bullets. A machine gun fires small-arms ammunition automatically.

**ma|chine-gun** (mə shēn'gun'), *v.,* **-gunned, -gun|ning,** *adj.* —*v.t.* to fire at with a machine gun; kill or wound with a machine gun: *The undefended Basque city of Guernica was systematically bombed and machine-gunned by German planes* (Time).
—*adj.* **1** of or having to do with a machine gun: *machine-gun fire.* **2** *Figurative.* rapid and staccato, like the action of a machine gun: *Speaking in either language at a machine-gun pace ...* (New York Times). —**machine gunner.**

**machine language**, **1** the coding system that a computer uses to process information: *Machine languages are typically specific to a particular class or type of computer and frequently are entirely numeric, thus difficult for a human to understand* (Van Court Hare, Jr.). **2** information or instructions in the physical form which a computer can handle without conversion or translation.

**ma|chine|like** (mə shēn'līk'), *adj.* resembling a machine in structure or operation; steady, automatic, and unvarying: (*Figurative.*) *machinelike repetition.*

**ma|chine-made** (mə shēn'mād'), *adj.* made by machinery, not by hand.

**ma|chine-read|a|ble** (mə shēn'rē'də bəl), *adj.* able to be processed directly by a computer: *With current bibliographic information available in machine-readable form ..., library users will eventually be able to disregard the traditional card catalog* (Harold Borko).

**ma|chin|er|y** (mə shē'nər ē, -shēn'rē), *n., pl.* **-er|ies. 1** machines: *construction machinery. A factory contains much machinery.* **2** the parts or works of a machine; mechanism: *Machinery is oiled to keep it running smoothly.* **3** *Figurative.* any combination of persons or things by which something is kept going or something is done; system: *Judges and courts are part of the machinery of the law.* **4** persons, incidents, and background, used in the plot of a literary work.

**machine screw**, a threaded metal rod (¼ inch or less in diameter), usually with a slotted head, used in holes tapped in metal parts.

**machine sculpture**, a three-dimensional figure in the form of a machine or machinelike object or device.

**machine shop**, a workshop where people make or repair machines or parts of machines.

**machine time**, the amount of time a computer or other machine is in operation on a specific assignment.

**machine tool**, an automatic, power-driven tool or machine used to form metal, wood, or other material into desired shapes by cutting, hammering, or squeezing: *Machine tools perform the heavy grinding and milling chores in metal working shops* (Wall Street Journal).

**ma|chine-tool** (mə shēn'tül'), *v.t.* to produce, especially to mass-produce, by or as if by a machine tool; produce automatically or with regular precision.

**machine translation**, **1** translation from one language into another by a computer. **2** the result of this process.

**ma|chin|ist** (mə shē'nist), *n.* **1** a worker skilled with machine tools. **2** a person who runs a machine. **3** a person who makes or repairs machinery. **4** a warrant officer who acts as assistant to an engineer officer in the United States Navy.

**machinist's hammer**, a hammer having a straight or rounded peen.

**ma|chis|mo** (mä chēs'mō, -chēz'-), *n.* (in Spanish America) manly self-assurance; masculine drive; virility: *Having many sons is proof of virility, of machismo ..., that quality prized above all others in Latin America* (Gladys Delmas). [< American Spanish *machismo* < *macho;* see etym. under **macho**]

**Mach|me|ter** or **mach|me|ter** (mäk'mē'tər, mak'-), *n.* a device that indicates the speed of an aircraft relative to the speed of sound. [< *Mach* (*number*) + *-meter*]

**Mach number** (mäk, mak), a number expressing in decimals the ratio of the speed of an object to the speed of sound in the same medium. An aircraft traveling at the speed of sound has a Mach number of 1; at half the speed of sound its Mach number is 0.5, or subsonic; at twice the speed of sound its Mach number is 2, or supersonic. *The use of swept-back wings raises the critical Mach number for the aircraft* (Science News). Also, **Mach.** [< Ernst *Mach,* 1838-1916, an Austrian physicist]

**ma|cho** (mä'chō), *n., pl.* **-chos,** *adj.* in Spanish America: —*n.* a virile, manly male: *the one who knows how to fight and win is a real "macho"* (Sergio Gutierrez-Olivos).
—*adj.* virile; manly: *Tequila, the macho drink of Mexico* (London Times).
[< Spanish *macho* (literally) male (noun and adjective)]

**Mach One**, *Aeronautics.* the speed of sound.

**ma|chree** (mə krē'), *n. Irish.* dear; darling. [< Irish Gaelic *mo croidhe* (literally) my heart]

**Macht|po|li|tik** (mäHt'pō'lē tēk'), *n. German.* power politics.

**mac|in|tosh** (mak'ən tosh), *n.* = mackintosh.

**mack** (mak) *n. British Informal.* a mackintosh (raincoat).

**mack|er|el** (mak'ər əl, mak'rəl), *n., pl.* **-el** or (*occasionally, especially with reference to different species*) **-els. 1** a saltwater fish of the North Atlantic, much used for food. It is blue-green with dark bands on the back and silver below, and grows to about 18 inches long. **2** any one of various related fishes, such as the Spanish mackerel of the Atlantic coasts of North and South America. [< Old French *maquerel*]

**mackerel clouds**, small, fleecy, white clouds that resemble the wavy markings on the back of a mackerel.

**mackerel gull**, = common tern.

**mackerel shark**, any one of a group of large, voracious sharks of northern waters, such as the porbeagle.

**mackerel sky**, a sky spotted with mackerel clouds.

**mack|i|naw** (mak'ə nô), *n.* **1** Also, **Mackinaw coat.** a kind of short coat made of heavy woolen cloth, often in a plaid pattern. **2** Also, **Mackinaw blanket.** a kind of thick woolen blanket, often with bars of color, used in the northern and west-

---

**Pronunciation Key:** hat, āge, cãre, fär; let, ēqual, tėrm; it, īce; hot, ōpen, ôrder; oil, out; cup, pu̇t, rüle; child; long; thin; ᴛʜen; zh, measure; ə represents **a** in about, **e** in taken, **i** in pencil, **o** in lemon, **u** in circus.

ern United States and in Canada by Indians, lumbermen, and others. **3** = Mackinaw boat. [American English < earlier *Mackinac,* a place name, now Mackinaw City, Michigan < Canadian French *michili-mackinac* < Algonkian (Ojibwa) *mitchi makinâk* large turtle]

**Mackinaw boat**, a large, heavy, flat-bottomed boat with a sharp prow and square stern, formerly used on the Great Lakes.

**Mackinaw trout**, = namaycush.

**mack|in|tosh** (mak′ən tosh), *n.* **1** a waterproof raincoat: *He put on his mackintosh and went out again in the rain* (Graham Greene). **2** the waterproof cloth it is made of. Also, **macintosh**. [< Charles *Macintosh,* 1766-1843, the inventor of the waterproofing process]

**mack|in|toshed** (mak′ən toshd), *adj.* wearing a mackintosh.

**mack|le** (mak′əl), *n., v.* **-led, -ling.** *Printing.* **—*n.*** a blur, such as from a double impression.
**—*v.t., v.i.*** to blur or become blurred, as from a double impression. Also, **macule**. [< Middle French *macule;* see etym. under **macule**]

**Mac|lau|rin's series** (mə klôr′inz), *Mathematics.* a Taylor's series in which the reference point (*a*) is replaced by zero. [< Colin *Maclaurin,* 1698-1746, a Scottish mathematician]

**ma|cle** (mak′əl), *n.* **1** a twinned crystal: *Crystals of ice, like macles of snow, were observed to form near the bottom* (Matthew F. Maury). **2** a dark spot in a mineral. **3** = chiastolite. [< French *macle,* Old French *mascle,* perhaps < Medieval Latin *mascula* mesh of a net < Latin *macula* a spot, stain]

**mac|ra|mé** (mak′rə mā), *n.,* or **macramé lace**, a coarse lace or fringe, made by knotting thread or cord in patterns. [apparently < Turkish *makrama* napkin < Arabic *maḥrama* handkerchief]

**mac|ro** (mak′rō), *adj., n., pl.* **-ros.** **—*adj.*** of great or comprehensive scope; large-scale: *The macro approach to human problems tends to the notion of the individual not as a unit, but as a fraction, a percentage of some whole* (Sunday Times).
**—*n.*** **1** anything very large among its kind, such as a large molecule or one of the larger butterflies. **2** = macroinstruction.
[< *macro-*]

**macro-**, *combining form.* **1** large or long: *Macromolecule = large molecule.*
**2** abnormally large: *Macrocephalic = having an abnormally large head.*
[< Greek *makro-* < *makrós* long, large]

**mac|ro|bi|ot|ic** (mak′rō bī ot′ik), *adj., n.* **—*adj.*** **1** = long-lived. **2** tending to prolong life. **3** of or having to do with macrobiotics: *macrobiotic diet.*
**—*n.*** a follower or adherent of macrobiotics: *Most macrobiotics, as Ohsawa's devotees call themselves, try to follow his other nine diets, which are graduated from six to minus three to include increasing amounts of fish and vegetables—organically grown—along with brown rice* (Time).
[< Greek *makrobíotos* long-lived, prolonging life (< *makrós* long + *bíotos* life) + English *-ic*]

**mac|ro|bi|ot|ics** (mak′rō bī ot′iks), *n.* a dietary system derived from Zen Buddhism, based on the opposite qualities of yin and yang in various foods, and consisting chiefly of organically grown fruits, vegetables, and fish, usually accompanied by brown rice.

**mac|ro|ce|phal|ic** (mak′rō sə fal′ik), *adj.* having an abnormally large head or skull. [< Greek *makroképhalos* (< *makrós* long + *kephalē̂* head) + English *-ic*]

**mac|ro|ceph|a|lous** (mak′rə sef′ə ləs), *adj.* = macrocephalic.

**mac|ro|ceph|a|ly** (mak′rə sef′ə lē), *n.* a condition in which the head or skull is abnormally large.

**mac|ro|chem|i|cal** (mak′rō kem′ə kəl), *adj.* of or having to do with macrochemistry.

**mac|ro|chem|is|try** (mak′rō kem′ə strē), *n.* the branch of chemistry that deals with substances or reactions observed by the unassisted eye or without a microscope.

**mac|ro|cli|mate** (mak′rō klī′mit), *n.* the climate of a large region.

**mac|ro|cosm** (mak′rə koz əm), *n.* the whole universe; cosmos: *The microcosm repeats the macrocosm* (Thomas Huxley). [< Old French *macrocosme,* learned borrowing from Medieval Latin *macrocosmus* < Greek *makrós* great + *kósmos* world order, universe; (originally) order; ornament]

**mac|ro|cos|mic** (mak′rə koz′mik), *adj.* of or having to do with the macrocosm; immense; comprehensive. **—mac′ro|cos′mi|cal|ly**, *adv.*

**mac|ro|cy|clic** (mak′rə sī′klik, -sik′lik), *adj. Chemistry.* containing an atomic ring structure of large size: *a macrocyclic antibiotic.*

**mac|ro|cyst** (mak′rə sist), *n.* a large cyst or spore, such as certain resting forms of slime molds.

**mac|ro|cys|tis** (mak′rə sis′tis), *n.* a brown seaweed of the southern seas and the northern Pacific coasts. It has the longest stems known in the vegetable kingdom, sometimes reaching a length of 700 feet. [< New Latin *Macrocystis* the genus name < Greek *makrós* long + *kýstis* bladder]

**mac|ro|cyte** (mak′rə sīt), *n.* an abnormally large red corpuscle found in the blood, especially in pernicious anemia.

**mac|ro|cyt|ic** (mak′rə sit′ik), *adj.* marked by the presence of macrocytes: *Macrocytic anemia occurs not only as pernicious anemia but also with liver disease, pregnancy, sprue, and pellagra* (Science News Letter).

**mac|ro|dome** (mak′rə dōm), *n. Crystallography.* a dome whose planes are parallel to the longer lateral axis.

**mac|ro|e|co|nom|ic** (mak′rō ē′kə nom′ik, -ek′ə-), *adj.* of or having to do with macroeconomics: *macroeconomic planning.*

**mac|ro|e|co|nom|ics** (mak′rō ē′kə nom′iks, -ek′ə-), *n.* economics dealing with those statistics that can be taken as controlling factors in the economy as a whole.

**mac|ro|e|con|o|mist** (mak′rō i kon′ə mist), *n.* a person who studies macroeconomics.

**mac|ro|ev|o|lu|tion** (mak′rō ev′ə lü′shən), *n.* the evolution of animals and plants on a large scale, resulting in new classifications at the species level or in large groupings.

**mac|ro|ev|o|lu|tion|ar|y** (mak′rō ev′ə lü′shə ner′ē), *adj.* of or having to do with macroevolution.

**mac|ro|fau|na** (mak′rō fô′nə), *n., pl.* **-na, -nae** (-nē). the macroscopic animals of a given habitat.

**mac|ro|flo|ra** (mak′rō flôr′ə, -flōr′-), *n., pl.* **-flo|ras, -flo|rae** (-flôr′ē, -flōr′-). the macroscopic plants of a given habitat.

**mac|ro|fos|sil** (mak′rō fos′əl), *n.* a macroscopic fossil; a plant or animal fossil that is large enough to be seen and examined without a microscope.

**mac|ro|ga|mete** (mak′rō gə mēt′, -gam′ēt), *n.* the larger, usually the female, of two gametes of an organism which reproduces by the union of unlike gametes; megagamete.

**mac|ro|glob|u|lin** (mak′rō glob′yə lin), *n.* a globulin with an abnormally high molecular weight, found in the blood plasma of persons suffering from rheumatoid arthritis.

**mac|ro|glob|u|lin|e|mi|a** (mak′rō glob′yə lə nē′mē ə), *n.* a disorder, such as rheumatoid arthritis, characterized by the presence of macroglobulins in the blood plasma. [< *macroglobulin* + *-emia*]

**mac|ro|graph** (mak′rə graf, -gräf), *n.* a photograph, drawing, or other reproduction of an object that is magnified very little or not at all.

**ma|crog|ra|phy** (mə krog′rə fē), *n.* **1** abnormally large writing, especially as a symptom of nervous disorder. **2** examination and preparation of work, particularly in engineering and metallurgy, at low magnification or without use of a microscope.

**mac|ro|in|struc|tion** (mak′rō in struk′shən), *n.* a series of computer operations contained in a single instruction.

**mac|ro|lep|i|dop|ter|on** (mak′rō lep′ə dop′tər on), *n., pl.* **-ter|a** (-tər ə). a large lepidopterous insect, such as the monarch butterfly and the swallowtail.

**mac|ro|lide** (mak′rə līd), *n.* any one of a class of antibiotics made by certain species of streptomyces, characterized by a ring structure of large size. [probably < *macro-* + *-ol*[2] + *-ide*]

**mac|ro|mere** (mak′rə mir), *n. Embryology.* a blastomere of large size.

**mac|ro|mod|el** (mak′rō mod′əl), *n.* a large-scale model: *We do not shy away from constructing macromodels, applicable to whole countries or to the entire world* (Gunnar Myrdal).

**mac|ro|mo|lec|u|lar** (mak′rō mə lek′yə lər), *adj.* of or characteristic of macromolecules: *macromolecular chemistry.*

**mac|ro|mol|e|cule** (mak′rō mol′ə kyül), *n.* a large and complex molecule made up of many smaller molecules linked together, as in a resin or polymer.

***ma|cron** (mā′kron, mak′ron; mā′krən, mak′rən), *n.* a straight, horizontal line placed over a vowel to show that it is long or is pronounced in a certain way. Examples: *āge, ēqual, īce, ōpen, ūse.* [< Greek *makrón,* neuter, long]

***macron** | — | is kōld āl

**mac|ro|nu|cle|us** (mak′rō nü′klē əs, -nyü′-), *n., pl.* **-cle|i** (-klē ī), **-cle|us|es.** the larger of two types of nuclei present in various ciliate protozoans, which controls metabolic functions inside the cell.

**mac|ro|nu|tri|ent** (mak′rō nü′trē ənt, -nyü′-), *n.* a nutrient element of which large amounts are necessary for plant growth: *In contrast to the macronutrients, such as calcium, phosphorus, sulfur, sodium and potassium that are needed in relatively large amounts, the trace elements are required only in very small amounts* (Science News Letter).

**mac|ro|phage** (mak′rə fāj), *n.* any one of several types of large phagocytes, especially in connective tissue.

**mac|ro|phag|ic** (mak′rə faj′ik), *adj.* of or having to do with macrophages.

**mac|ro|pho|to|graph** (mak′rō fō′tə graf, -gräf), *n.* a photograph of an object that is magnified very little or not at all; a macrograph made by photography.

**mac|ro|pho|tog|ra|phy** (mak′rō fə tog′rə fē), *n.* the photographing of objects upon an actual or slightly magnified scale.

**mac|ro|phys|ics** (mak′rō fiz′iks), *n.* the branch of physics that deals with bodies that are large enough to be observed and measured.

**mac|ro|phyte** (mak′rə fīt), *n.* a macroscopic plant.

**mac|ro|phyt|ic** (mak′rə fit′ik), *adj.* of or having to do with macrophytes.

**mac|rop|ter|ous** (ma krop′tər əs), *adj.* having very large wings or fins. [< Greek *makrópteros* (with English *-ous*) < *makrós* long + *pterón* wing]

**mac|ro|scale** (mak′rə skāl′), *n., adj.* **—*n.*** a scale or standard involving very large amounts or measurements.
**—*adj.*** of or designating large-scale atmospheric phenomena, such as hurricanes.

**mac|ro|scop|ic** (mak′rə skop′ik), *adj.* visible to the naked eye. **—ma′cro|scop′i|cal|ly**, *adv.*

**mac|ro|scop|i|cal** (mak′rə skop′ə kəl), *adj.* = macroscopic.

**mac|ros|mat|ic** (mak′roz mat′ik), *adj.* having the organs of smell well developed.

**mac|ro|so|ci|o|log|i|cal** (mak′rō sō′sē ə loj′ə kəl, -shē-), *adj.* of or having to do with macrosociology: *macrosociological studies.*

**mac|ro|so|ci|ol|o|gy** (mak′rō sō′sē ol′ə jē, -shē-), *n.* sociology dealing with whole human societies, such as agrarian, maritime, and industrial societies.

**mac|ro|spo|ran|gi|um** (mak′rə spə ran′jē əm), *n., pl.* **-gi|a** (-jē ə). = megasporangium.

**mac|ro|spore** (mak′rə spôr, -spōr), *n.* = megaspore.

**mac|ro|struc|tur|al** (mak′rō struk′chər əl), *adj.* of or having to do with macrostructure.

**mac|ro|struc|ture** (mak′rō struk′chər), *n.* the macroscopic structure of bodies, objects, or the like.

**mac|ro|tax|o|nom|ic** (mak′rō tak sə nom′ik), *adj.* of or having to do with macrotaxonomy.

**mac|ro|tax|on|o|my** (mak′rō tak son′ə mē), *n.* the taxonomy of the larger groupings of organisms, such as family or order.

**ma|cru|ran** (mə krür′ən), *n., adj.* **—*n.*** a macrurous crustacean.
**—*adj.*** = macrurous.

**ma|cru|rous** (mə krür′əs), *adj.* of or belonging to a group of crustaceans that have ten legs and well-developed abdomens, including the lobsters, prawns, and shrimps. [< New Latin *Macrura* the suborder name (< Greek *makrós* long + *ourā́* tail) + *-ous*]

**mac|u|la** (mak′yə lə), *n., pl.* **-lae** (-lē). **1** a spot on the skin which is unlike the surrounding tissues. **2** = macule (def. 1). **3** = sunspot. **4** = macula lutea. [< Latin *macula* spot, stain]

**macula lu|te|a** (lü′tē ə), *pl.* **maculae lu|te|ae** (lü′tē ē). a yellowish spot surrounding the fovea centralis in the retina of certain vertebrates. [< New Latin *macula lutea*]

**mac|u|lar** (mak′yə lər), *adj.* **1** of or having to do with the macula lutea. **2** or or characteristic of a macula or maculae. **3** having maculae; spotted.

**mac|u|late** (*v.* mak′yə lāt; *adj.* mak′yə lit), *v.,* **-lat|ed, -lat|ing,** *adj.* **—*v.t.*** to spot; stain; soil; defile.
**—*adj.*** spotted; stained; soiled.
[< Latin *maculāre* (with English *-ate*[1]) < *macula* a spot]

**mac|u|la|tion** (mak′yə lā′shən), *n.* **1** the act or process of spotting or soiling. **2** the state of being spotted or defiled. **3** the pattern of spots on an animal or plant.

**mac|ule** (mak′yül), *n., v.,* **-uled, -ul|ing.** **—*n.*** **1** a spot, stain, or blotch on the skin which is not raised above the surface. **2** = macula (def. 1). **3** *Printing.* mackle.
**—*v.t., v.i. Printing.*** to mackle; make or become blurred.
[< Middle French *macule,* learned borrowing from Latin *macula* spot, stain]

**ma|cush|la** (mə küsh′lə), *n. Irish.* dear; darling. [< Irish Gaelic *mo cuishle* (literally) my blood]

**MACV** (mak vē′), *n.* **1** Military Assistance Command, Vietnam. **2** multi-purpose airmobile combat-support vehicle.

**mad** (mad), *adj.*, **mad|der, mad|dest,** *v.*, **mad-ded, mad|ding,** *n.* **—*adj.*** **1** out of one's mind; crazy; insane: *A man must be mad to cut himself on purpose.* **SYN:** See syn. under **crazy**. **2** *Informal.* very angry; furious: *Mother was mad at me for coming home late for dinner. The insult made him mad.* **3** much excited; wild: *The dog made mad efforts to catch up with the automobile.* **SYN:** frenzied, frantic. **4** foolish; unwise: *a mad undertaking. . . . the same trash mad mortals wish for here* (Alexander Pope). *The maddest voyage, and the most unlikely to be performed, that ever was undertaken* (Daniel Defoe). **SYN:** rash. **5a** blindly and unreasonably fond: *mad about skiing. Some girls are mad about going to dances.* **SYN:** infatuated. **b** wildly gay or merry: *Tomorrow will be the maddest, merriest day of the year.* **6** having rabies. A mad dog often foams at the mouth and may bite people.
**—*v.t.*** , ***v.i.*** *Archaic.* to be or become mad; madden: *At the same time it madded some of the Republicans* (Marietta Holley).
**—*n.*** **1** anger; rage. **2** *Slang.* a fit of bad temper; sullen mood: *to have a mad on.*
**like mad,** *Informal.* furiously; very hard or fast: *I ran like mad to catch the train.*
**mad as a hatter.** See under **hatter**.
**mad as a March hare.** See under **hare**.
[Old English *gemǣded* rendered insane]
▶**mad, angry.** Although *mad* is often substituted for *angry* in informal English, this usage is not regarded as standard in all quarters.

**Mad.,** madam.

**MAD** (mad), *n.* mutual assured destruction: *Called MAD. . . the doctrine holds that peace is best maintained by threatening to obliterate an entire enemy society in retaliation for a nuclear attack* (Time).

**Mad|a|gas|can** (mad′ə gas′kən), *n., adj.* = Malagasy.

**Mad|a|gas|car jasmine** (mad′ə gas′kər), a tropical twining shrub of Madagascar and neighboring areas, with thick, dark-green leaves and fragrant, waxy flowers, often cultivated in hothouses; stephanotis [< *Madagascar,* a large island in the Indian Ocean opposite southeastern Africa]

**ma|da|ke** (mä dä′kä), *n.* a long-jointed bamboo of Japan. [< Japanese *madake*]

**mad|am** (mad′əm), *n., pl.* **mad|ams** or **mesdames,** *v.* **—*n.*** **1** a polite title used in speaking to a woman or of a woman: *Madam, will you take my seat?* **2** a woman who runs a brothel.
**—*v.t.*** to address as "madam": *. . . the sparring scene between her and Mrs. Chatterley, wherein they "Madam" each other with genteel petulance* (Examiner).
[< Old French *ma dame* my lady < Latin *mea* my, and *domina* mistress, lady]
▶As a form of address, Madam or Dear Madam is appropriate for either a married or an unmarried woman.

**mad|ame** (mad′əm; *French* mȧ dȧm′), *n., pl.* **mesdames. 1** a French title for a married woman; Mrs. **2** a title often used by women singers, artists, or performers. *Abbr:* Mme. **3** = madam (def. 2). [< Old French *ma dame;* see etym. under **madam**]

**mad|a|pol|lam** (mad′ə pol′əm), *n.* a soft cotton cloth intermediate in quality between calico and muslin. [< *Madapollam,* a town in India where it was first manufactured]

**ma|dar** (mə där′), *n.* **1** either of two tropical Asian or African shrubs of the milkweed family whose juice and root bark yield a drug. **2** a latex obtained from this shrub, used as a substitute for gutta-percha. **3** a fine silky fiber obtained from the madar. Also, **mudar**. [< Hindi *madār*]

**mad-brained** (mad′brānd′), *adj.* hot-headed; uncontrolled; rash.

**mad|cap** (mad′kap′), *n., adj.* **—*n.*** a person who goes ahead and carries out wild ideas without stopping to think first; very impulsive person. **SYN:** rattlebrain.
**—*adj.*** wild; hasty; impulsive: *Their going along was nothing more than a madcap frolic* (Herman Melville). **SYN:** reckless, precipitate.

**mad|den** (mad′ən), *v.t.* **1** to make very angry or excited; irritate greatly: *The crowd was maddened by the umpire's decision.* **SYN:** enrage, infuriate. **2** to make crazy: *The shipwrecked sailors were nearly maddened by cold and hunger when the rescuers found them.* **SYN:** derange. **—*v.i.*** to become crazy; act crazy: *All Bedlam, or Parnassus, is let out . . . They rave, recite, and madden round the land* (Alexander Pope).

**mad|den|ing** (mad′ə ning), *adj.* **1** very annoying; irritating: *maddening delays.* **2** raging; furious: *All the people rushed along with maddening eagerness to the anticipated solace* (Thomas De Quincey). **—mad′den|ing|ly,** *adv.*

**mad|der** (mad′ər), *n., v.* **—*n.*** **1** a European and Asian vine with prickly leaves and small greenish-yellow flowers. **2** its red root, used for making dyes. **3** a red dye made from these roots. **4** red; crimson. **—*v.t.*** to treat or dye with madder. [Old English *mædere* some plant used in dyeing]

**∗madder family,** a group of dicotyledonous, chiefly tropical trees, shrubs, or herbs closely related to the honeysuckle family. The family includes the madder, cinchona, coffee, gardenia, bedstraw, and partridgeberry.

**∗madder family**

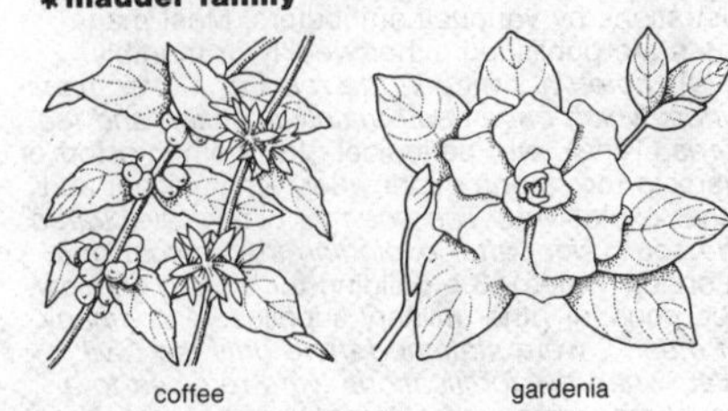


**mad|ding** (mad′ing), *adj.* **1** mad; acting as if mad: *Far from the madding crowd's ignoble strife* (Thomas Gray). **2** making mad; maddening: *the distraction of this madding fever* (Shakespeare).

**mad|dish** (mad′ish), *adj.* somewhat mad.

**made** (mād), *v., adj.* **—*v.*** past tense and past participle of **make:** *The cook made the cake. It was made of flour, milk, butter, eggs, and sugar.*
**—*adj.*** **1** built; constructed; formed: *a strongly made swing.* **2** specially prepared: *made gravy, a made dish.* **3** artificially produced: *made land.* **4** invented; made-up: *a made word.* **5** certain of success; successful: *a made man.*
**have (got) it made,** *U.S. Informal.* to be assured of success: *"The Odd Couple" [a play] has it made* (New York Times). *Most Western Republicans think that . . . their boy Barry's got it made* (Wall Street Journal).

**Ma|dei|ra** or **ma|dei|ra** (mə dir′ə), *n.* a kind of fortified wine made on the island of Madeira, ranging from quite pale and dry to brownish and sweet.

**Madeira vine,** a basellaceous climbing plant of tropical America, with bright-green leaves and long clusters of small, fragrant, white flowers.

**made|leine** (mȧd len′), *n.* a small, sweet cake resembling a pound cake and usually spread with jam, icing, nuts, or fruits. [< French *madeleine*]

**mad|e|moi|selle** (mad′ə mə zel′; *French* mȧd-mwȧ zel′), *n., pl.* **mes|de|moi|selles. 1** the French title for an unmarried woman; Miss. **2** a French governess. *Abbr:* Mlle. [< French *mademoiselle* < Old French *ma demoiselle* my demoiselle, young lady]

**made-to-meas|ure** (mād′tů mezh′ər), *adj.* made according to the buyer's measurements: *a made-to-measure suit.*

**made-to-or|der** (mād′tů ôr′dər), *adj.* made according to the buyer's wishes: *made-to-order clothing.*

**made-up** (mād′up′), *adj.* **1** not real; imaginary; invented: *a made-up story.* **SYN:** fabricated, untrue. **2** having on rouge, powder, or other cosmetics: *made-up lips.* **3** put together: *The made-up sandwiches were stacked to be ready for lunch customers.* **SYN:** constructed. **4** resolved; decided: *a made-up mind.*

**made-work** (mād′wėrk′), *adj.* devised to make jobs, sometimes unimportant or unnecessary, especially in public works originated during periods of economic distress: *a made-work project.*

**Mad Hatter's disease,** = hatter's shakes.

**mad|house** (mad′hous′), *n.* **1** an asylum for insane people. **2** a place of uproar and confusion: *The arena was a madhouse after the home team won the championship game.*

**Mad|i|son Avenue** (mad′ə sən), **1** a street in New York City, the chief advertising center of the United States. **2** the advertising industry of the United States.

**Mad|i|so|ni|an** (mad′ə sō′nē ən), *adj.* of or having to do with James Madison (1751-1836), fourth president of the United States: *. . . our attempt to combine the Madisonian system of checks and balances with the Jeffersonian concept of majority rule under parties* (Harper's).

**mad itch,** = pseudorabies.

**mad|ly** (mad′lē), *adv.* **1** = insanely. **2** = furiously. **3** = foolishly.

**mad|man** (mad′man′, -mən), *n., pl.* **-men. 1** an insane man; person who is crazy: *The explosion was probably the act of a madman.* **2** a person who behaves madly; wildly foolish person: *I have been a madman and a fool* (David Bethune).

**mad money,** *U.S. Slang.* **1** money carried by a girl or woman to use for small expenses. **2** money carried by a girl or woman so that she is not dependent on an escort for transportation home, in the event of a quarrel or other cause for leaving him.

**mad|ness** (mad′nis), *n.* **1** the fact or condition of being crazy; insane condition; loss of one's mind: *Great wits are sure to madness near allied* (John Dryden). **SYN:** insanity. **2** great anger; rage; fury: *In his madness he kicked the fence post. The madness of the people soon subsided* (Edward Gibbon). **SYN:** wrath. **3** folly: *It would be madness to try to sail a boat in this storm.* **SYN:** idiocy. **4** extravagant enthusiasm. **5** = rabies.

**ma|don|na** (mə don′ə), *n.* a former Italian title for a married woman equivalent to *madame* (*signora* is now used). [< Italian *madonna* < *ma,* short for *mia* my (< Latin *mea*) + *donna* lady < Latin *domina*]

**Ma|don|na** (mə don′ə), *n.* **1** Mary, the mother of Jesus. **2** a picture or statue of her.

**Madonna lily,** a common, early-blooming lily whose white blossom is a symbol of purity.

**mad|ras** (mad′rəs; mə dras′, -dräs′), *n.* **1** a closely woven cotton cloth with a design on plain background, used for shirts, dresses, and similar clothing. **2** a thin cloth, often with a design or pattern, used for such items as curtains and draperies. **3** a brightly colored kerchief of silk and cotton. [< *Madras,* a city in India]

**ma|dras|ah** (mə dras′ə), *n.* a Moslem school or college. Also, **medresseh**. [< Arabic *madrasa*]

**MADRE** (mad′rə), *n.* magnetic drum receiving equipment.

**mad|re|po|rar|i|an** (mad′rə pô rãr′ē ən, -pō-), *adj., n.* **—*adj.*** of or belonging to a group of anthozoans with a continuous calcareous skeleton, including most of the stony corals.
**—*n.*** a madreporarian anthozoan.

**mad|re|pore** (mad′rə pôr, -pōr), *n.* any one of an order of stony corals that often form reefs in tropical seas. [< French *madrépore* < Italian *madrepora* < *madre* mother (< Latin *māter*) + *poro,* ultimately < Greek *pôros* kind of stone]

**mad|re|por|i|an** (mad′rə pôr′ē ən, -pōr′-), *adj.* = madreporic.

**mad|re|por|ic** (mad′rə pôr′ik, -pōr′-), *adj.* **1** of or having to do with madrepores. **2** of or having to do with a madreporite.

**mad|re|por|ite** (mad′rə pə rīt; mad′rə pôr′īt, -pōr′-), *n.* the external opening of the stone canal in an echinoderm. [< *madrepor*(e) + *-ite*[1]]

**mad|ri|gal** (mad′rə gəl), *n.* **1** a short poem, often about love, that can be set to music. **2** a song with parts for several voices, usually sung without instrumental accompaniment. **3** *Figurative.* any song. [< Italian *madrigale,* ultimately < Latin *mātrīcālis* original, invented < *mātrīx* womb; see etym. under **matrix**]

**mad|ri|gal|i|an** (mad′rə gal′ē ən), *adj.* of or having to do with madrigals: *madrigalian counterpoint.*

**mad|ri|gal|ist** (mad′rə gə list), *n.* a composer or singer of madrigals.

**mad|ri|lene** or **mad|ri|lène** (mad′rə len, mad′rə-len′), *n.* a consommé flavored with tomato, usually served chilled or jellied. [< French *madrilène* of Madrid, Spain < Spanish *madrileño*]

**Ma|dri|le|ño** (mä′drə lān′yō), *n., pl.* **-ños.** a native or inhabitant of Madrid, Spain. [< Spanish *madrileño*]

**ma|dro|ña** (mə drōn′yə), *n.* an evergreen tree or shrub of the heath family, growing especially in western North America and in other parts of the world. It has a very hard wood and a smooth, reddish bark, and bears a rough, berrylike fruit that has mealy flesh and hard seeds. [< American English < Spanish *madroño* arbutus]

**madroña apple,** the berry of the madroña.

**ma|dro|ne** (mə drō′nə), *n.* = madroña.

**ma|dro|ño** (mə drōn′yō), *n., pl.* **-ños.** = madroña.

**mad|stone** (mad′stōn′), *n. U.S.* a concretion of mineral salts found in the stomach and intestines of deer, formerly thought to relieve or cure the effects of a poisonous bite when placed on the wound. [< *mad* (because it was supposed to cure the madness caused by the bite of a rabid animal) + *stone*]

**mad|tom** (mad′tom′), *n.* any one of a large group of small catfish with a poison gland at the base of the pectoral spine, found in lakes and streams.

**Ma|du|ra foot** (mə důr′ə), mycetoma of the foot, a fungous disease. [< *Madura,* a city in southern India]

**ma|du|ro** (mə důr′ō), *adj., n., pl.* **-ros. —*adj.*** made with dark and strong tobacco.
**—*n.*** a maduro cigar. [< Spanish *maduro* mature < Latin *mātūrus*]

**mad|wom|an** (mad′wům′ən), *n., pl.* **-wom|en. 1** a woman who is insane. **2** a wildly foolish woman.

---

**Pronunciation Key:** hat, āge, cãre, fär; let, ēqual, tėrm; it, īce; hot, ōpen, ôrder; oil, out; cup, pův, rüle; child; long; thin; ŦHen; zh, measure; ə represents **a** in about, **e** in taken, **i** in pencil, **o** in lemon, **u** in circus.

**mad|wort** (mad′wėrt′), *n.* **1** any one of a group of low, branching herbs of the mustard family, such as the gold-of-pleasure; alyssum. **2** a low, weedy herb of the borage family native to Europe.

**M.A.E.** or **MAE** (no periods), **1** Master of Aeronautical Engineering. Also, **M.Aero.E. 2** Master of Art Education. **3** Master of Arts in Education. Also, **M.A.Ed.**

**Mae|ce|nas** (mi sē′nəs), *n.* a generous patron of literature or art: *Are you not called ... a mock Maecenas to second-hand authors?* (Richard Brinsley Sheridan). [< *Maecenas,* a Roman statesman, about 74-8 B.C., patron of literature and friend of Horace and Virgil]

**M.A.Ed.**, Master of Arts in Education.

**mael|strom** (māl′strəm), *n.* **1** a great or turbulent whirlpool. **2** *Figurative.* a violent confusion of feelings, ideas, or conditions: *The poor man lived always in the whirl of a perfect Maelstrom of promises and engagements* (Harriet Beecher Stowe).
[< earlier Dutch *maelstrom* < *malen* to grind + *stroom* stream]

**mae|nad** (mē′nad), *n.* **1** *Greek and Roman Mythology.* a woman attendant or worshiper of Bacchus; bacchante. **2** *Figurative.* a woman who is extremely excited or in a frenzy. Also, **menad.** [< Latin *Maenas, -adis* < Greek *mainás, -ádos* a mad woman, especially a bacchante < *mainesthai* to rage, be mad]

**mae|nad|ic** (mi nad′ik), *adj.* of or like the maenads; frenzied. **SYN:** raving, frantic. Also, **menadic.**

**M.Aero.E.**, Master of Aeronautical Engineering.

**ma|es|to|so** (mä′es tō′sō), *adj., adv. Music.* with majesty or dignity; stately. [< Italian *maestoso* majestic < *maesta,* or *maestate* majesty, learned borrowing from Latin *mājestās*]

**maes|tro** (mīs′trō; *Italian* mä es′trō), *n., pl.* **maes|tros,** *Italian* **ma|es|tri** (mä es′trē). **1** a great composer, teacher, or conductor of music: *His appearance in the dual role of pianist and maestro, was nevertheless an impressive demonstration of a remarkable musical talent* (New Yorker). **2** a master of any art: ... *a maestro in the field of travel and gastronomy* (Atlantic). [< Italian *maestro* < Latin *magister* a master]

**Mae West** (mā′ west′), an inflatable vest worn as a life preserver by an aviator in flying over water. [< *Mae West,* born 1892, an American actress (from a whimsical comparison of inflated vest to her celebrated bust size)]

**Maf|fe|i galaxy** (mä fā′ē), either of two large galaxies which are part of the Local Group, discovered in 1971. One is an elliptical and the other a spiral galaxy; they are about 3 million light-years away from earth. *The Maffei galaxies, obscured by the Milky Way dust, appear as small, diffuse patches* (Hyron Spinrad). [< Paolo *Maffei,* an Italian astrophysicist, who first called attention to them in 1968]

**maf|fick** (maf′ik), *v., n. British.* —*v.i.* to celebrate a national victory with great demonstrations of joy.
—*n.* an act of mafficking.
[back formation < earlier *mafficking,* used as if a present participle, alteration of *Mafeking,* South Africa (from the kind of celebrations following the end of the siege there, on May 17, 1900)]
—**maf′fick|er,** *n.*

**ma|fi|a** or **maf|fi|a** (mä′fē ä), *n.* the spirit of popular hostility to the law, manifesting itself frequently in criminal acts. [< Italian *mafia*]

**Ma|fi|a** or **Maf|fi|a** (mä′fē ä), *n.* **1** a secret organization of criminals supposed to control underworld activities in various parts of the world. **2** a secret Sicilian society hostile to the law and practicing terrorism. **3** Also, **mafia.** any secret society or exclusive set, circle or clique: *the Diplomatic Mafia. The composers' Mafia, with its dedication to atonality* ... (New Yorker). [see *mafia*]

**maf|ic** (maf′ik), *adj. Geology.* of or having to do with magnesium and iron: *mafic rocks.* [< *ma*(gnesium) + Latin *f*(errum) iron + English *-ic*]

**Ma|fi|o|so** or **ma|fi|o|so** (ma′fē ō′sō), *n., pl.* **-si** (-sē). a member of the Mafia: *A jailed mafioso traded his influence over the waterfront gangs for a remission of sentence* (Manchester Guardian Weekly). [< Italian *mafioso* < *mafia* mafia]

**ma foi** (mȧ fwȧ′), *French.* **1** upon my word! indeed! **2** (literally) my faith.

**mag**[1] (mag), *n. British Slang.* a halfpenny. [origin uncertain]

**mag**[2] (mag), *n., v.,* **magged, mag|ging.** *British Dialect.* —*n.* chatter; talk.
—*v.i.* to chatter: *I'll snap your backbone across my knee if you mag half a second more* (James Runciman). [shortened form of *magpie*]

**mag.**, an abbreviation for the following:
**1** magazine.
**2** *British.* magister (Latin, used as a title for a university master).
**3** magnetism.
**4** magnitude.

**Mag|a|rac** (mag′ə rak), *n.* **Joe,** a legendary hero of the steel mills in American folklore.

**mag|a|zine** (mag′ə zēn′, mag′ə zēn), *n., v.,* **-zined, -zin|ing.** —*n.* **1** a publication appearing regularly and containing stories, articles, and illustrations by various contributors. Most magazines are published either weekly or monthly. [*He*] *noted a switch in the roles of ... the magazines, which once dealt mainly in fiction and features* (Time). **SYN:** periodical. **2** a room in a fort or warship for storing gunpowder, ammunition, and other explosives: *The enemy ... have evacuated the south side, after exploding their magazines* (London Times). **3** a building for storing gunpowder, guns, or other military supplies: *A company of men ... were stationed there until the Civil War, when the fortifications were reduced to a naval magazine with a complement of five* (New Yorker). **4** a place in a repeating rifle, a revolver, or an automatic gun from which cartridges are fed into the firing chamber: *Carruthers ... took a box of cartridges from a niche in the wall, and proceeded to recharge his magazine* (Boyd Cable). **5** a place for holding a roll or reel of film in a camera or projector: *A new 35-mm camera ... featured interchangeable film magazines* (F. E. Fenner). **6** a place or region rich in natural or commercial products: *This district is a magazine of mineral wealth.* **7** a storehouse; warehouse: *a magazine of flesh, milk, butter and cheese* (Daniel Defoe). (*Figurative.*) *The mind of man in a long life will become a magazine of wisdom or folly* (Sir Richard Steele).
—*v.t.* to store in or as if in a magazine.
[< Old French *magazin* < Italian *magazzino,* ultimately < Arabic *makhāzin,* plural of *makhzan* storehouse]

**mag|a|zin|ist** (mag′ə zē′nist), *n.* a person who writes for, edits, or produces a magazine or magazines.

**Mag|da|len** (mag′də lən), *n.* = Magdalene.

**Mag|da|lene** (mag′də lēn), *n.* See **Mary Magdalene.**

**mag|da|lene** (mag′də lēn), *n.* **1** a woman who has reformed from a sinful life; repentant prostitute. **2** a home or reformatory for prostitutes. [< *Magdalene*]

**Mag|da|le|ni|an** (mag′də lē′nē ən), *adj.* belonging to or denoting a late paleolithic period represented by remains found at La Madeleine, Dordogne, France: *Magdalenian art involves portable objects and mural decorations on the walls of caves* (Beals and Hoijer). [< French *magdalénian,* Latinization of French *La Madeleine,* in Dordogne, France, a site containing remains of the period]

**Mag|de|burg hemispheres** (mag′də bėrg′), an early experimental apparatus for illustrating air pressure, consisting of two closely fitting hemispherical cups from which the air could be evacuated. [< *Magdeburg,* Germany, where its inventor (Otto von Guericke) was born]

**mage** (māj), *n. Archaic.* **1** a magician: *And there I saw mage Merlin* (Tennyson). **2** a wise person. [< Latin *magus;* see etym. under **Magi**]

**Mag|el|lan|ic** (maj′ə lan′ik), *adj.* having to do with or named after Ferdinand Magellan (1480?-1521).

**Magellanic Cloud**, either of two faintly luminous patches in the heavens south of the equator. They are the two galaxies nearest to our own and consist of multitudes of stars.

**ma|gen Da|vid** (mô′gən dô′vid, mä gän′ dä-vēd′), a Jewish emblem, consisting of a six-pointed star formed of two interlaced triangles; Star of David. [< Hebrew *māgēn dāvīd* shield of David]

**ma|gen|ta** (mə jen′tə), *n., adj.* —*n.* **1** a purplish-red aniline dye; fuchsin. **2** a purplish red.
—*adj.* purplish-red.
[< the Battle of *Magenta,* Italy, 1859 (because it was discovered in that year)]

**mag|got** (mag′ət), *n.* **1** the legless larva of any one of various kinds of flies. Maggots usually live in decaying matter. **2** *Figurative.* a queer notion; whim: *I thought she'd got some maggot in her head* (George Eliot). **SYN:** fancy. [Middle English *magot;* origin uncertain, perhaps related to Middle English *maddock,* ultimately < Old Icelandic]

**mag|got|y** (mag′ə tē), *adj.* **1** full of maggots: *maggoty biscuits* (Maclean's). **2** *Figurative.* full of queer notions; whimsical.

**ma|gi** (mā′jī, maj′ī), *n.* plural of **magus.**

**Ma|gi** (mā′jī, maj′ī), *n., pl. of* **Magus. 1** the Three Wise Men who followed the star to Bethlehem and brought gifts to the infant Jesus (in the Bible, Matthew 2:1 and 2:7-13). **2** the priests of an ancient Persian religion, famous as astrologers, and supposed to have supernatural powers. [< Latin *magī,* plural of *magus* < Greek *mágos* Persian priest or astrologer < Old Persian *magu* member of a priestly clan of Media]

**ma|gi|an** (mā′jē ən), *adj. Poetic.* magic.

**Ma|gi|an** (mā′jē ən), *adj., n.* —*adj.* of or having to do with the Magi or priests of ancient Persia.
—*n.* one of the Magi.

**mag|ic** (maj′ik), *n., adj., v.,* **-icked, -ick|ing.** —*n.* **1** the pretended or supposed art of using secret charms and spirits to make unnatural things happen: *The fairy's magic changed the brothers into swans. In simple cultures, magic is often closely related to religion* (John Mulholland). **SYN:** sorcery, necromancy, witchcraft. **2** *Figurative.* something that produces results as if by magic; mysterious influence; unexplained power: *the magic of music. The magic of her voice charmed the audience.* **3** the art or skill of creating illusions, especially by sleight of hand: *An entertainer performed magic at the children's birthday party. All these appearances could be nothing else but necromancy and magic* (Jonathan Swift). *Science is not a form of black magic* (Polykarp Kusch).
—*adj.* **1** done by magic or as if by magic: *A magic palace stood in place of their hut.* **2** of magic; used in magic: ... *the spell of certain magic words or phrases* (James B. Conant). **3** *Figurative.* magical; mysterious.
—*v.t.* to obtain, get rid of, or otherwise do, by or as if by magic: ... *the voluptuous wealth that could be magicked out of water colours* (Manchester Guardian Weekly).
**like magic,** at once; with incredible swiftness: *The waiter appeared like magic from the kitchen with a steaming hot lunch.*
[< Latin *magicē* < Greek *magikḗ,* feminine of *magikós* < *mágos;* see etym. under **Magi**]

**mag|i|cal** (maj′ə kəl), *adj.* **1** done by magic or as if by magic: *The waving of the fairy's wand produced a magical effect.* **SYN:** occult. **2** *Figurative.* like magic; mysterious; unexplained: *a magical feeling.* **SYN:** enchanting. —**mag′i|cal|ly,** *adv.*

**magic carpet**, **1** a magically propelled carpet used for riding through the air by characters in *The Arabian Nights.* **2** any means of transporting a person to strange and exotic places through the imagination.

**ma|gi|cian** (mə jish′ən), *n.* **1** a person who can use magic: *The wicked magician cast a spell over the princess.* **SYN:** sorcerer, necromancer. **2** a person who entertains by magic tricks; person skilled in sleight of hand: *The magician pulled—not one, but three rabbits out of his top hat!* **SYN:** conjuror. [< Old French *magicien* < *magique* magic]

**magic lantern**, an early type of projector for showing slides on a screen.

**Magic Marker**, *Trademark.* an instrument for marking and drawing, consisting of a metal tube which holds quick-drying, waterproof ink and a thick felt tip which transmits the ink onto a surface.

**magic number**, the number of neutrons or protons in a nucleus which has a closed or completed shell. Magic numbers, 2, 8, 20, 50, 82, and 126, indicate that the nucleus containing them is highly stable.

**mag|i|co-re|li|gious** (maj′ə kō ri lij′əs), *adj.* of or having to do with magic and religion, especially in the use of magic to seek the intervention of a deity or deities in the events of the natural world.

**magic realism**, a form of painting in which symbolic or mythical subjects are painted in a highly realistic manner.

**magic realist**, a painter in the style of magic realism.

***magic square**, a square figure formed by a series of numbers so arranged in parallel and equal ranks that the sum of each row or line taken perpendicularly, horizontally, or diagonally, is constant.

| 2 | 7 | 6 |
|---|---|---|
| 9 | 5 | 1 |
| 4 | 3 | 8 |

***magic square**

**ma|gilp** (mə gilp′), *n.* = megilp.

**Ma|gi|not Line** (mazh′ə nō), an elaborate system of defense built by France against Germany after the First World War. The German Army swept around through Belgium in 1940 and completely outflanked it. The line was overhauled in the 1950's for possible use in case of atomic war. [< French *la ligne Maginot* < André *Maginot,* 1877-1932, a former French minister of war]

**mag|is|te|ri|al** (maj′ə stir′ē əl), *adj.* **1a** of a magistrate; suited to a magistrate: *A judge has magisterial rank.* **b** (of persons) holding the office of a magistrate. **2** showing authority: *The captain spoke with a magisterial voice.* **SYN**: authoritative. **3** imperious; domineering; overbearing: *He paced up and down the room with a magisterial stride.* **SYN**: dictatorial, haughty, arrogant. [< Medieval Latin *magisterialis* < Late Latin *magisterius* < Latin *magister* a master] — **mag′is\|te′ri\|al\|ly**, *adv.* — **mag′is\|te′ri\|al\|ness**, *n.*

**mag\|is\|te\|ri\|ous\|ly** (maj′ə stir′ē əs lē), *adv.* in a magisterial or imperious manner; with an assumption of authority.

**mag\|is\|te\|ri\|um** (maj′ə stir′ē əm), *n.* the teaching function or authority of the Roman Catholic Church. [< Middle Latin *magisterium;* see etym. under **magistery**]

**mag\|is\|ter\|y** (maj′ə ster′ē), *n., pl.* **-ter\|ies.** (in alchemy and medieval medicine) a substance, remedy, or other concoction, believed to be effective in curing or transmuting. [< Medieval Latin *magisterium* < Latin, office of a *magister* master]

**mag\|is\|tra\|cy** (maj′ə strə sē), *n., pl.* **-cies. 1** the position, rank, or duties of a magistrate: *A political executive magistracy ... is a great trust* (Edmund Burke). **2** magistrates as a group: *He went from city to city, advising with the magistracies* (John L. Motley). **3** the district under a magistrate.

**mag\|is\|tral** (maj′ə strəl, mə jis′trəl), *adj., n.* — *adj.* **1** *Pharmacy.* prescribed or prepared for a particular occasion: *a magistral prescription.* **2** of or like a magistral line; principal: *The principal or magistral gallery runs all round the work* (J. M. Spearman). **3** magisterial; authoritative; dogmatic: *Magistral powers ... of the forceful and free over the weak and servile elements of life* (John Ruskin).
— *n.* = magistral line.
[< Latin *magistrālis* < *magister* a master. See etym. of doublet **mistral.**] — **mag′is\|tral\|ly**, *adv.*

**magistral line**, the principal line of a military defense, from which the position of all other lines is determined.

**mag\|is\|trate** (maj′ə strāt, -strit), *n.* **1** an officer of a government who has power to apply the law and put it into force. The President is the chief magistrate of the United States. **2** a judge in a minor court. A justice of the peace is a magistrate. [< Latin *magistrātus, -ūs* < *magistrāre* serve as a magistrate < *magister* a master]

**mag\|is\|trate\|ship** (maj′ə strāt ship, -strit-), *n.* the position, duties, or term of office of a magistrate.

**mag\|is\|tra\|ture** (maj′ə strā′chər), *n.* = magistrateship.

**Mag\|le\|mo\|sian** or **Mag\|le\|mo\|sean** (mag′lə-mō′zhən), *adj.* belonging to or denoting a Mesolithic period represented by artifacts found in Denmark: *The best known culture of Boreal times in northern Europe is the Maglemosian, which extended from Denmark across the North Sea to Britain* (New Scientist). [< *Maglemose,* the name of the typical site on the island of Zeeland, Denmark + English *-ian*]

**mag\|lev** or **mag-lev** (mag′lev), *n.* a high-speed train supported above the ground and guided by a system of superconducting electromagnets. [< *mag*(netic) *lev*(itation)]

**mag\|ma** (mag′mə), *n., pl.* **-ma\|ta** (-mə tə), **-mas. 1** the molten material beneath the earth's crust from which igneous rock is formed: *The liquefied material forms a fluid mass, called magma, that is lighter than the overlying rocks and tends to rise at an opening* (Science News Letter). **2** any crude mixture of mineral or organic substances in the form of a thin paste. **3** *Pharmacy.* a suspension of insoluble or nearly insoluble material in water: *Magnesia magma is the technical term for milk of magnesia.* [< Latin *magma* dregs of an unguent < Greek *mágma* an unguent, ultimately < *mássein* to knead, mold]

**mag\|mat\|ic** (mag mat′ik), *adj.* of or having to do with a magma.

**Mag\|na Char\|ta** or **Mag\|na Car\|ta** (mag′nə kär′-tə), **1** the great charter which the English barons forcibly secured from King John at Runnymede on June 15, 1215. The Magna Charta provided a basis for guaranteeing the personal and political liberties of the people of England, and placed the king under the rule of the law and decisively checked his power. *For many years, the document was commonly known as Magna Charta, but in 1946 the British government officially adopted the Latin spelling, Magna Carta* (Bryce Lyon). **2** any fundamental constitution guaranteeing civil and political rights. [< Medieval Latin *magna carta* (literally) great charter < feminine singular of Latin *magnus* great, and *charta* chart]

**mag\|na cum lau\|de** (mag′nə kům lou′də, kum lô′dē), with high honors (the second highest degree of merit on the diplomas of superior students): *to graduate magna cum laude.* [< Latin *magnā cum laude* with great praise]

**mag\|nal\|i\|um** (mag nā′lē əm), *n.* a strong alloy of aluminum and magnesium having increased hardness and good machinability, used for airplane parts and scientific instruments.

**Mag\|na\|my\|cin** (mag′nə mī′sin), *n. Trademark.* = carbomycin.

**mag\|na\|nim\|i\|ty** (mag′nə nim′ə tē), *n., pl.* **-ties. 1** magnanimous nature or quality; nobility of soul or mind: *The soldiers showed magnanimity by treating their prisoners well. Magnanimity in politics is not seldom the truest wisdom* (Edmund Burke). **SYN**: generosity. **2** a magnanimous act.

**mag\|nan\|i\|mous** (mag nan′ə məs), *adj.* **1** noble in soul or mind; generous in forgiving; free from mean or petty feelings or acts: *a magnanimous adversary.* **SYN**: high-minded, unselfish. **2** showing or arising from a generous spirit: *a magnanimous attitude toward a conquered enemy. He spoke ... with the magnanimous frankness of a man who had done great things, and could well afford to acknowledge some deficiencies* (Macaulay). [< Latin *magnanimus* (with English *-ous*) < *magnus* great + *animus* spirit, soul] — **mag\|nan′i\|mous\|ly**, *adv.* — **mag\|nan′i\|mous\|ness**, *n.*

**mag\|nate** (mag′nāt), *n.* **1** an important, powerful, or prominent person: *a railroad magnate. My grandfather, a well-to-do farmer, was one of the chief magnates of the village* (Harriet Beecher Stowe). **2** a member of the upper house of the former Hungarian or Polish parliaments. [< Late Latin *magnās, -ātis* < Latin *magnus* great]

**mag\|ne\|sia** (mag nē′shə, -zhə), *n.* **1** a white, tasteless powder; magnesium oxide. Magnesia is slightly alkaline and is used in medicine as an antacid and a laxative, and in industry in making fertilizers and heat-resistant building materials. *Formula:* MgO **2** = magnesium. [< Medieval Latin *magnesia* < Greek *hē Magnēsiā líthos* loadstone; also, probably talc; (literally) the Magnesian stone (from *Magnesia,* a region in Thessaly)]

**mag\|ne\|sian** (mag nē′shən, -zhən), *adj.* of or like magnesia.

**magnesian limestone**, = dolomite.

**mag\|ne\|sic** (mag nē′sik), *adj.* of or containing magnesium.

**mag\|ne\|site** (mag′nə sīt), *n.* a mineral, carbonate of magnesium, occurring either in compact, white masses or crystalline, used for lining furnaces and in making steel. *Formula:* $MgCO_3$ [< *magnes*(ium) + *-ite*[1]]

* **mag\|ne\|si\|um** (mag nē′shē əm, -zhē-), *n.* a very light, silver-white metal that burns with a dazzling white light. Magnesium is a chemical element. It is noted for its ductility and malleability. It is stable in dry air but tarnishes when exposed to moisture. It is used in photography, fireworks, and metal alloys. [< New Latin *magnesium* < Medieval Latin *magnesia;* see etym. under **magnesia**]

***magnesium**

| symbol | atomic number | atomic weight | oxidation state |
|---|---|---|---|
| Mg | 12 | 24.312 | 2 |

**magnesium carbonate**, carbonate of magnesium, occurring in dolomite or naturally as magnesite. *Formula:* $MgCO_3$

**magnesium chloride**, a colorless, crystalline, deliquescent salt found in salt water, used as a source of magnesium. *Formula:* $MgCl_2$

**magnesium hydroxide**, a white, odorless powder which, when suspended in water, is milk of magnesia. *Formula:* $Mg(OH)_2$

**magnesium light**, the brilliant white light produced by the burning of magnesium, used in flares, photography, and fireworks.

**magnesium oxide**, = magnesia.

**magnesium pemoline**, a combination of the stimulant pemoline and magnesium hydroxide, used as a drug to stimulate the nervous system.

**magnesium sulfate**, **1** a white salt used in medicine and in making textiles, leather, and other goods. *Formula:* $MgSO_4$ **2** hydrated magnesium sulfate; Epsom salt.

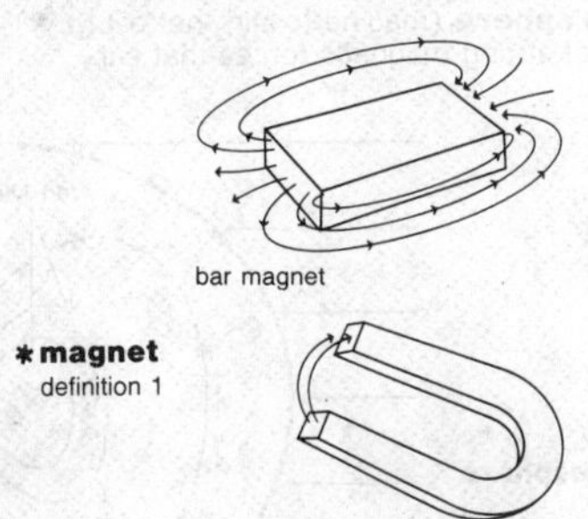

bar magnet

***magnet**
definition 1

horseshoe magnet

* **mag\|net** (mag′nit), *n.* **1** a piece of iron, steel, or stone that attracts or draws to it bits of iron or steel. A loadstone is a natural magnet. Bar magnets and horseshoe magnets are steel magnets which retain their magnetism for a long time. **2** *Figurative.* anything that attracts: *The rabbits in our back yard were a magnet that attracted all the children in the neighborhood. The actor was the magnet that drew great audiences.* [< Old French *magnete* < Latin *magnēs, -ētis* < Greek *Mágnēs* (*líthos*) Magnesian (stone). Compare etym. under **magnesia.**]

**mag\|net\|ic** (mag net′ik), *adj.* **1** having the properties of a magnet: *the magnetic needle of a compass.* **2a** of or having something to do with a magnet or magnetism: *a magnetic axis.* **b** producing, caused by, or operating by means of magnetism: *a magnetic circuit.* **3** of or having to do with the earth's magnetism: *the magnetic meridian.* **4** capable of being magnetized or of being attracted by a magnet: *magnetic nickel.* **5** *Figurative.* very attractive: *Many stars of stage and screen are liked because they have magnetic personalities. Sympathy, the magnetic virtue ... was extinct* (William Godwin). **SYN**: winning, charming. **6** of or caused by hypnotism; mesmeric. — **mag\|net′i\|cal\|ly**, *adv.*

**mag\|net\|i\|cal** (mag net′ə kəl), *adj.* = magnetic.

**magnetic amplifier**, a device consisting of two wires wound around an iron core, used to control large amounts of electric power, such as the speed of large motors or the brightness of airport runway lights; saturable reactor.

**magnetic anomaly**, *Geology.* a pattern of alternating bands of rock having normal and reversed magnetization.

**magnetic axis**, *Physics.* the straight line joining the poles of a magnet.

**magnetic bottle**, *Nuclear Physics.* any arrangement of magnetic fields for confining or constricting charged particles in a controlled thermonuclear reaction. Magnetic bottles are formed in the pinch effect, in mirror machines, and in stellarators.

**magnetic bubble**, a magnetic domain formed in an orthoferrite, used chiefly as a miniature computer processing unit and as a telephone switching unit.

**magnetic circuit**, the closed path taken by the magnetic flux.

**magnetic compass**, a device for indicating directions along the lines of the earth's magnetic field, consisting of a freely suspended magnetized pointer on a pivot.

**magnetic core**, a tiny metal ring which can be magnetized in either of two directions to represent symbols used by a computer; memory core.

**mag\|net\|ic-core memory** (mag net′ik kôr′, -kōr′), an array of magnetic cores used for storing information for a computer; core memory.

**magnetic course**, the course (especially of a ship or airplane) with reference to the north magnetic pole instead of the north geographic pole.

**magnetic domain**, an area or portion of a ferromagnetic substance in which all the electrons spin in the same direction, forming a miniature magnet.

**magnetic drum**, a rapidly rotating cylinder coated with a magnetic material on which information may be stored in a computer as small polarized spots; memory drum.

**magnetic equator**, the line around the earth at which a magnetic needle balances horizontally without dipping. See diagram under **aclinic line.**

**magnetic field**, **1** the space around a magnet in which its power of attraction is effective; space around an electric current in which the magnetic force of the current is felt. **2** the magnetic forces present in such a space.

**magnetic flux**, **1** the total number of magnetic lines of force passing through a specified area, generally expressed in maxwells or webers. **2** the result of dividing the magnetomotive force by the reluctance.

**magnetic head**, a device in a recording apparatus for converting electrical impulses into magnetic impulses, for changing stored magnetic impulses back to electrical impulses, or for erasing such impulses already converted or stored, as in a tape or wire recorder; recording head.

**magnetic induction**, **1** the amount of magnetic flux in a unit area taken perpendicular to the direction of the magnetic flux. **2** the process by which a substance (such as iron or steel) becomes magnetized by a magnetic field.

**magnetic ink**, a specially prepared ink whose metallic properties activate electronic machines.

**Pronunciation Key:** hat, āge, cãre, fär; let, ēqual, tėrm; it, īce; hot, ōpen, ôrder; oil, out; cup, pu̇t, rüle; child; long; thin; ᴛʜen; zh, measure; ə represents **a** in about, **e** in taken, **i** in pencil, **o** in lemon, **u** in circus.

It is useful in check processing, account coding, and other banking procedures.

**magnetic meridian**, a line passing through both magnetic poles that represents the force exerted by the earth's magnetic field.

**magnetic mine**, an underwater mine which is exploded by the action of the metal parts of an approaching ship upon a magnetic needle; influence mine.

**magnetic moment**, **1** the product of the pole strength of a magnet and the distance between the poles. **2** a magnetic force between two opposite charges in an electron or other elementary particle, associated with the spin and orbital motion of the particle.

**magnetic monopole**, *Physics.* a hypothetical particle having only one pole of magnetic charge instead of the two possessed by ordinary magnetic bodies: *Long particle track is claimed to be possible evidence of a magnetic monopole* (Science News).

**magnetic needle**, a slender bar of magnetized metal used as a compass. When mounted so that it turns easily, it points approximately north and south toward the earth's magnetic poles.

**magnetic north**, the direction shown by the magnetic needle of a compass, differing in most places from the true north.

**magnetic pole**, **1** one of the two poles of a magnet. **2** one of the two poles of the earth toward which a compass needle points. The north magnetic pole is in the Arctic, and the south magnetic pole is in Antarctica: *The north magnetic pole is south of the geographic North Pole.*

**magnetic pyrites**, = pyrrhotite.

**magnetic recorder**, **1** = tape recorder. **2** = wire recorder.

**magnetic recording**, **1** = tape recording. **2** = wire recording.

**mag|net|ics** (mag net′iks), *n.* the science of magnetism.

**magnetic storm**, a marked disturbance or variation of the earth's magnetic field, associated with solar flares.

**magnetic tape**, **1** a thin metal, plastic, or paper strip, usually coated or impregnated with iron oxide, on which (in a tape recorder or electronic computer) a magnetic effect is produced so that sounds or other electrical signals can be recorded on it in the form of fluctuations in the magnetism of the tape. **2** a tape used in television to record both sound and image.

**magnetic variation**, the deviation of the needle of a compass, declination.

**magnetic wire**, the fine steel wire used in a wire recorder.

**mag|net|ise** (mag′nə tīz), *v.t., v.i.,* **-ised, -is|ing.** *Especially British.* magnetize. — **mag′net|is′er**, *n.*

**mag|net|ism** (mag′nə tiz əm), *n.* **1** the properties or qualities of a magnet; the showing of magnetic properties: *the magnetism of iron and steel.* **2** the branch of physics dealing with magnets and magnetic properties. **3** *Figurative.* the power to attract or charm: *A person with magnetism has many friends and admirers. Suddenly the face softened and shone with all its old magnetism* (Mrs. Humphry Ward). **4** hypnotic power; mesmerism.

**mag|net|ite** (mag′nə tīt), *n.* an important iron ore that is strongly attracted by a magnet; black iron oxide. Magnetite that possesses polarity is called loadstone. *Formula:* $Fe_3O_4$ [< German *Magnetit*]

**mag|net|iz|a|bil|i|ty** (mag′nə tī′zə bil′ə tē), *n.* the power or capacity of being magnetized.

**mag|net|iz|a|ble** (mag′nə tī′zə bəl), *adj.* that can be magnetized.

**mag|net|i|za|tion** (mag′nə tə zā′shən), *n.* **1** the act of magnetizing. **2** the state of being magnetized.

**mag|net|ize** (mag′nə tīz), *v.,* **-ized, -iz|ing.** — *v.t.* **1** to give the properties or qualities of a magnet to: *You can magnetize a needle by rubbing it with a magnet. An electric current in a coil around a bar of iron will magnetize the bar.* **2** *Figurative.* to attract or influence (a person); win by personal charm: *The singer's beautiful voice magnetized the audience. His wife was a woman ... who, coming under the dominion of a stronger nature, was perfectly magnetized by it* (Harriet Beecher Stowe). **3** to mesmerize; hypnotize: *The little white building magnetized him, as though concealed there was his only companionship* (Graham Greene).
— *v.i.* to become magnetic. — **mag′net|iz′er**, *n.*

**mag|ne|to** (mag nē′tō), *n., pl.* **-tos.** a small generator with permanent magnets which uses a magnetic field to produce an electric current. In some gasoline engines, a magneto supplies an electric spark to explode the gasoline vapor. [short for *magnetoelectric* (machine)]

**magneto-**, *combining form.* magnetism; magnetic forces; magnets: *Magnetometer = an instrument for measuring magnetic forces.* [< Greek *mágnēs, -ētis* magnet]

**mag|ne|to|car|di|o|gram** (mag nē′tō kär′dē ə gram), *n.* the record or tracing made by a magnetocardiograph.

**mag|ne|to|car|di|o|graph** (mag nē′tō kär′dē ə graf, -gräf), *n.* a cardiograph that records heart action in the magnetic field around the heart.

**mag|ne|to|chem|i|cal** (mag nē′tō kem′ə kəl), *adj.* of or having to do with magnetochemistry.

**mag|ne|to|chem|is|try** (mag nē′tō kem′ə strē), *n.* the science dealing with the relations between magnetism and chemistry.

**mag|ne|to|e|lec|tric** (mag nē′tō i lek′trik), *adj.* of or characterized by electricity produced by magnets: *A magneto is a magnetoelectric generator.*

**mag|ne|to|e|lec|tric|i|ty** (mag nē′tō i lek′tris′ə tē), *n.* **1** electricity produced by the action of magnets. **2** the science dealing with electricity and magnetism.

**mag|ne|to|gas|dy|nam|ics** (mag nē′tō gas′dī nam′iks), *n.* = magnetohydrodynamics.

**mag|ne|to|gen|er|a|tor** (mag nē′tō jen′ə rā′tər), *n.* = magneto.

**mag|ne|to|gram** (mag nē′tə gram), *n.* the record made by a magnetograph.

**mag|ne|to|graph** (mag nē′tə graf, -gräf), *n.* a device consisting of three variometers and a recording mechanism, used for detecting variations in the direction and intensity of magnetic fields.

**mag|ne|to|hy|dro|dy|nam|ic** (mag nē′tō hī′drō dī nam′ik), *adj.* of or having to do with magnetohydrodynamics: *magnetohydrodynamic insulation.*

**mag|ne|to|hy|dro|dy|nam|i|cal** (mag′nē tō hī′drō dī nam′ə kəl), *adj.* = magnetohydrodynamic.

**mag|ne|to|hy|dro|dy|nam|ics** (mag nē′tō hī′drō dī nam′iks), *n.* the study of the interaction of magnetic fields and electrically conducting liquids and gases, such as the highly ionized airflow about a spacecraft on reentry into the atmosphere. *Abbr:* MHD (no periods).

**mag|ne|tom|e|ter** (mag′nə tom′ə tər), *n.* an instrument for measuring the intensity and direction of magnetic forces.

**mag|ne|tom|e|try** (mag′nə tom′ə trē), *n.* the measurement of magnetic forces with a magnetometer.

**mag|ne|to|mo|tive** (mag nē′tə mō′tiv), *adj.* producing magnetic effects; having to do with the production of such effects.

**magnetomotive force**, **1** magnetizing force or influence which produces a magnetic flux through a magnetic circuit, analogous to the electromotive force which produces an electric current or flux in an electric circuit; the quantity which, divided by the magnetic reluctance, or resistance, gives the intensity of magnetization. It is equal to the work necessary to move a magnetic pole of unit strength around a closed path of magnetic flux. **2** the force required to produce magnetic flux in a magnetic circuit, measured in gilberts.

**mag|ne|ton** (mag′nə ton), *n. Physics.* **1** the unit of magnetic moment. **2** a theoretical ultimate magnetic particle. **3** *Obsolete.* an electron moving in a circle with the velocity of light. [< French *magnéton* < *magnétique* magnetic; influenced by English *electron*]

**mag|ne|to|op|tic** (mag nē′tō op′tik), *adj.* of or having to do with magnetooptics.

**mag|ne|to|op|ti|cal** (mag nē′tō op′tə kəl), *adj.* = magnetooptic.

**mag|ne|to|op|tics** (mag nē′tō op′tiks), *n.* that branch of physics which deals with the influence of a magnet upon light.

**mag|net|o|pause** (mag nē′tə pôz, -net′ə-), *n.* the upper limits of the magnetosphere.

**mag|ne|to|plas|ma|dy|nam|ic** (mag nē′tō plaz′mə dī nam′ik), *adj.* using highly ionized gas in magnetic fields to generate power: *a magnetoplasmadynamic spacecraft engine.*

**mag|ne|to|re|sis|tance** (mag nē′tō ri zis′təns), *n.* a change in the electrical resistance of a metal with the increase or decrease of the strength of a magnetic field applied to it.

*** mag|ne|to|sphere** (mag nē′tə sfir, -net′ə-), *n.* **1** a zone of strong magnetic forces that surrounds the earth and extends outward about 40,000 miles, trapping within the earth's magnetic field electrons, protons, and other particles radiating from outer space. The Van Allen radiation belts are part of the magnetosphere. *The moon, unlike the earth, is not protected from the solar wind—it has no magnetic field and, therefore, no shielding magnetosphere* (Science News). **2** any similar zone around a heavenly body: *If the pulsars are magnetic neutron stars spinning in a vacuum ... such a star must have a magnetosphere, a plasma-filled region surrounding the star* (Jeremiah P. Ostriker).

**mag|ne|to|spher|ic** (mag nē′tə sfer′ik, -net′ə-), *adj.* of, having to do with, or characteristic of the magnetosphere.

**mag|ne|to|stric|tion** (mag nē′tə strik′shən), *n.* **1** a change in the dimensions of a ferromagnetic substance when subjected to an intense magnetic field (especially characteristic of nickel). **2** a change in the magnetic properties of a body subjected to mechanical stress.

**mag|ne|to|stric|tive** (mag nē′tə strik′tiv), *adj.* of, having to do with, or utilizing magnetostriction.

**mag|ne|to|tel|lur|ic** (mag nē′tə te lùr′ik), *adj.* of or having to do with the magnetic areas of the earth. [< *magneto-* + *telluric*[1]]

**mag|ne|tron** (mag′nə tron), *n.* a vacuum tube in which the flow of electrons from the heated cathode to the anode is regulated by an external magnetic field. It is used to produce microwaves.

**magnet school**, *U.S.* a large, central school with a broad curriculum, designed to attract students from small neighborhood or district schools: *Each magnet school, in addition to offering regular courses, specialized in an area of learning, such as vocational training or performing arts* (Charles W. Theisen).

**mag|ni|cide** (mag′nə sīd), *n.* the killing of an important person, especially a ruler or leader. [< Latin *magnus* great + English *-cide*[2]]

**mag|nif|ic** (mag nif′ik), *adj. Archaic.* **1** magnificent; splendid; imposing: *Power ... God's gift magnific* (Robert Browning). **2** pompous; grandiloquent. **3** = eulogistic. [< Old French *magnifique,* learned borrowing from Latin *magnificus* < *magnus* great + *facere* to make] — **mag|nif′i|cal|ly,** *adv.*

**mag|nif|i|cal** (mag nif′ə kəl), *adj. Archaic.* magnific.

**Mag|nif|i|cat** (mag nif′ə kat), *n.* **1** the hymn of the Virgin Mary, beginning *Magnificat anima mea Dominum* ("My soul doth magnify the Lord"), used as a canticle at evensong or vespers (in the Bible, Luke 1:46-55). **2** music for this hymn. [< Latin *magnificat* it magnifies, 3rd singular present indicative of *magnificāre* glorify, extol, magnify]

**mag|ni|fi|ca|tion** (mag′nə fə kā′shən), *n.* **1** the act of magnifying. **2** magnified condition. **3** the power to magnify. **4** a magnified copy, model, or picture.

**mag|nif|i|cence** (mag nif′ə səns), *n.* richness of material, color, and ornament; grand beauty; splendor: *We were dazzled by the magnificence of the mountain scenery.* **SYN:** majesty. [< Old French *magnificence,* learned borrowing from Latin *magnificentia* < *magnificus* noble; see etym. under **magnific**]

**mag|nif|i|cent** (mag nif′ə sənt), *adj.* **1** richly colored or decorated; making a splendid appearance; grand; stately: *the magnificent palace of a king, the magnificent jewels of a queen, a magnificent spectacle.* **2** impressive; noble; exalted: *magnificent words, magnificent ideas.* **3** extraordinarily fine; superb: *a magnificent view of the mountains.*
**the Magnificent**, a title of certain historic persons: *Lorenzo the Magnificent was the greatest of the Medicis.*
[< Old French *magnificent* < *magnificence;* see etym. under **magnificence**] — **mag|nif′i|cent|ly,** *adv.*
— *Syn.* **1, 2, 3. Magnificent, splendid, superb** mean impressive in dignity and beauty, brilliance, or excellence. **Magnificent** emphasizes impres-

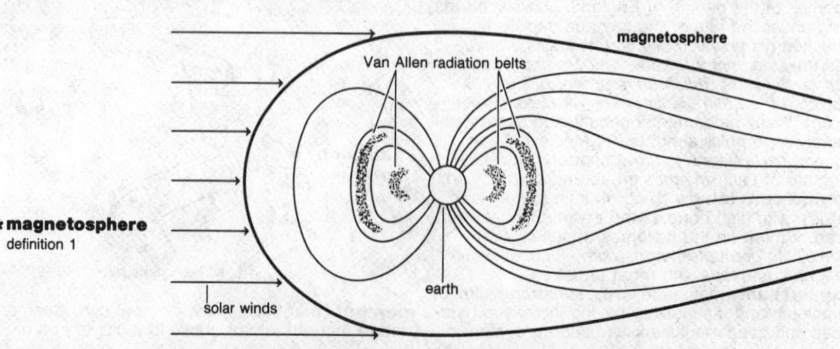


*** magnetosphere**
definition 1

sive beauty and costly richness or stateliness of things like surroundings, jewels, or buildings, and noble greatness of ideas: *The palace at Versailles is magnificent.* **Splendid** emphasizes impressive brilliance or shining brightness in appearance or character of things, people, or deeds: *The queen wore a splendid gown glittering with jewels. He made a splendid record in the army.* **Superb** means of the highest possible excellence, magnificence, splendor, richness, etc.: *We had a superb view of the ocean.*

**mag|nif|i|co** (mag nif′ə kō), *n., pl.* **-coes. 1** a Venetian nobleman: *The duke himself, and the magnificoes of greatest port* (Shakespeare). **2** a person in an exalted position or one of great importance: *Rockingham, a virtuous magnifico, ... resolved to revive something of the pristine purity ... of the old Whig connection* (Benjamin Disraeli). [< Italian *magnifico* < Latin *magnificus* magnific]

**mag|ni|fi|er** (mag′nə fī′ər), *n.* **1** one that magnifies. **2** a lens that magnifies things; magnifying glass. **3** a small eyepiece attached to a camera to permit examination of the sharpness of focus of the image seen in the viewfinder.

**mag|ni|fy** (mag′nə fī), *v.,* **-fied, -fy|ing.** — *v.t.* **1a** to cause to look larger than the real size: *A microscope magnifies bacteria so that they can be seen and studied.* **SYN**: enlarge, amplify.
**b** *Figurative.* to make too much of; go beyond the truth in telling: *She not only tells tales on her brother, but she magnifies them. My wife ... used every art to magnify the merit of her daughter* (Oliver Goldsmith). **SYN**: exaggerate, overstate.
**2** *Archaic.* to praise highly; glorify; extol: *My soul doth magnify the Lord* (Luke 1:46). *When the high heart we magnify ... Ourselves are great* (John Drinkwater).
— *v.i.* to increase the apparent size of an object.
[< Latin *magnificāre* esteem greatly < *magnificus* magnific]

**mag|ni|fy|ing glass** (mag′nə fī′ing), a lens or combination of lenses that causes things to look larger than they really are.

**magnifying power, 1** the ratio of the size of an image when viewed through an optical instrument to the size of the object when seen with the unaided eye. **2** the ratio of the focal length of the objective to that of the eyepiece in a telescope.

**mag|nil|o|quence** (mag nil′ə kwəns), *n.* **1** the use of big and unusual words and elaborate phrases; high-flown, lofty style of speaking or writing: *Cibber ... foisted his own bombast into the company of Shakespeare's magniloquence* (Cowden Clarke). **SYN**: bombast. **2** boastfulness. [< Latin *magniloquentia* < *magnus* great + *loquēns, -entis,* present participle of *loquī* speak]

**mag|nil|o|quent** (mag nil′ə kwənt), *adj.* **1** using big and unusual words; expressed in high-flown language. **SYN**: grandiloquent. **2** boastful: *She was a trifle more magniloquent than usual, and entertained us with stories of colonial governors and their ladies* (Thackeray). — **mag|nil′o|quent|ly,** *adv.*

**mag|ni|tude** (mag′nə tüd, -tyüd), *n.* **1** greatness of size: *the height, strength, and magnitude of a building.* **SYN**: amplitude. **2** great importance, effect, or consequence: *The war brought problems of very great magnitude to many nations.* **SYN**: moment. **3** size, whether great or small. **4** the measure of the brightness of a star. The brightest stars are of the first magnitude. Each degree is 2.512 times brighter than the next degree. *The scale of apparent magnitude ... goes on up to the sixth magnitude which is the faintest that the eye alone can see* (George W. Gray). **5** the number expressing this. **6** *Geometry.* the measure or extent of a particular line, area, volume, or angle. **7** *Mathematics.* a number given to a quantity so that it may be compared with similar quantities. **8** the measurement of the force of an earthquake, expressed on a scale of 0 to 10. *Abbr:* mag. **9** *Obsolete.* greatness of character, rank, or position.
**of the first magnitude,** very great in some respect; excellent; overwhelming; very serious: *Thou liar of the first magnitude* (William Congreve).
[< Latin *magnitūdō* < *magnus* large]

**mag|no|lia** (mag nōl′yə), *n.* **1** a North American or Asian tree or shrub with large, generally fragrant, white, pink, or purplish flowers. There are several kinds. They belong to the magnolia family. The blossom of one variety is the state flower of Louisiana and Mississippi. **2** its flower. [< New Latin *Magnolia* the genus name < Pierre *Magnol,* 1638-1715, a French botanist]

**mag|no|li|a|ceous** (mag nō′lē ā′shəs), *adj.* belonging to the magnolia family.

**magnolia family,** a group of dicotyledonous trees and shrubs, found in tropical and temperate regions of North America and Asia, and including the magnolia, tulip tree, and umbrella tree.

**Magnolia State,** a nickname for Mississippi.

**magnolia warbler,** an American warbler having black back, wings, and tail banded with white, and yellow breast striped with black.

**mag|non** (mag′non), *n. Nuclear Physics.* a wave propagated by the deviation of a nuclear spin in a magnetic field. [< *magn*(etic) + *-on*]

**mag|nox** (mag′noks), *n.* a British type of nuclear reactor fueled by rods of natural uranium encased in magnesium alloy cans. [< *Magnox,* trade name of the magnesium alloy]

**mag|num** (mag′nəm), *n., pl.* **-nums** *for 1, 2;* **-na** (-nə) *for 3.* **1** a bottle that holds about two quarts of wine or alcoholic liquor. **2** the amount that it holds: *He ... declared that we must have wine, and sent for a magnum of the best* (Robert Louis Stevenson). **3** a heavy load used in certain firearms: *.357 magnum, magnum loads for shotguns.* **4** *Anatomy.* the capitate bone. [< Latin *magnum,* neuter, great]

**magnum o|pus** (ō′pəs), **1** a large or important work of literature or art: *He himself said that what he had in him was short essays rather than a magnum opus* (London Times). **2** a person's greatest work: *Darwin turned to his friends Lyell and Hooker, who knew the many years he had been laboring upon his magnum opus* (Scientific American). **SYN**: masterpiece. [< Latin *magnum* great, and *opus* work]

**mag|nus hitch** (mag′nəs), a hitch or knot with one more turn than a clove hitch. [probably < the name *Magnus*]

**Ma|gog** (mā′gog), *n.* **1** a son of Japheth (in the Bible, Genesis 10:2). **2** a people descended from him (in the Bible, Ezekiel 38-39). **3** one of the two nations (**Gog and Magog**) that make war against the kingdom of God at Armageddon (in the Bible, Revelation 20:8).

**mag|ot** (mag′ət, mä gō′), *n.* **1** the Barbary ape. **2** a small, grotesque figure of porcelain or ivory, common in Chinese and Japanese art: *Her rooms were crowded with hideous China magots* (Thackeray). [< French *magot*]

**mag|pie** (mag′pī), *n., adj.* — *n.* **1** a noisy black-and-white bird with a long tail and short wings. Magpies are related to the crows and jays. **2** a person who chatters. **SYN**: chatterbox, chatterer, babbler.
— *adj.* of or like a magpie; characterized by the habit of hoarding ascribed to magpies: *magpie gleanings; ... Yeats's magpie fascination with collecting ... all sorts of symbols and myths* (Canadian Forum).
[< *Mag,* nickname for *Margaret* + *pie*[2]]

**magpie lark,** a black-and-white bird of Australia, similar to but smaller than a magpie; peewee.

**M.Agr.,** *U.S.* Master of Agriculture.

**mags|man** (magz′mən), *n., pl.* **-men.** *British Slang.* a swindler. [< *mag*[2] + *man*]

**ma|gua|ri** (mə gwä′rē), *n.* a large white stork with black on its wings and tail, red feet, and a forked tail, found in South America. [< Portuguese *maguari* < Tupi]

**mag|uey** (mag′wā; *Spanish* mä gā′), *n.* **1** any one of various agaves with pointed, fleshy leaves, found especially in Mexico, and used in making a fiber and the intoxicating drinks mescal, tequila, and pulque. The century plant is a maguey. **2** the fiber. [< Spanish *maguey* < Arawak (West Indies)]

**ma|gus** (mā′gəs), *n., pl.* **ma|gi.** an astrologer or magician: *Simon Magus* (Acts 8:9-24).

**Ma|gus** (mā′gəs), *n., pl.* **Ma|gi. 1** one of the Magi or Three Wise Men. **2** an ancient Persian priest. [< Latin *magus;* see *Magi*]

**Mag|yar** (mag′yär; *Hungarian* mu′dyur), *n., adj.* — *n.* **1** a member of the chief group of people living in Hungary. **2** their Finno-Ugric language; Hungarian.
— *adj.* of the Magyars or their language; Hungarian.
[< Hungarian *Magyar*]

**Mag|yar|ize** (mag′yä rīz) *v.t.,* **-ized, -iz|ing.** to make Hungarian in habits, language, customs, or character. — **Mag′yar|i|za′tion,** *n.*

**Ma|ha|bha|ra|ta** (mə hä′bä′rə tə), *n.* the earlier of the two great ancient epics of Hinduism (the *Ramayana* is the other), written in Sanskrit between about 200 B.C. and 200 A.D. and combining a fabulous account of a dynastic struggle of 1200 B.C. with moral lessons in politics, law and religion, and other topics.
[< Sanskrit *Mahābhārata* < *mahā* great + *Bharata,* a tribal designation]

**ma|ha|lo** (mä hä′lō), *n. Hawaiian.* thanks.

**ma|hant** (mə hunt′), *n.* a religious superior in India. [< Hindi *mahant*]

**ma|ha|ra|ja** or **ma|ha|ra|jah** (mä′hə rä′jə), *n.* **1** a former ruling prince in India, especially one who ruled a state. **2** a person holding this title. [< Sanskrit *mahārāja* < *mahā* great + *rājan* rajah]

**ma|ha|ra|nee** or **ma|ha|ra|ni** (mä′hə rä′nē), *n.* **1** the wife of a maharaja. **2** a former ruling princess in India, especially one who ruled a state. [< Hindustani *mahārānī* < *mahā* great (< Sanskrit) + *rānī* queen < Sanskrit *rājñī*]

**Ma|ha|rash|tra** (mə hä′räsh′trə), *n.* a people of India, related to the Mahratta. [< Sanskrit *Mahārāṣtra;* see etym. under **Mahratta**]

**Ma|ha|ri|shi** (mä′hə rē′shē), *n.* **1** the title of a Hindu guru or spiritual guide. **2** Also, **maharishi.** any guru. [< Sanskrit *mahā* great + *rishi* sage, seer]

**ma|hat|ma** (mə hät′mə, -hat′-), *n.* **1** (in India) a wise and holy person who has extraordinary powers. **2** any person thought of as resembling a mahatma in wisdom, manner, or practice.
**the Mahatma,** Mohandas K. Gandhi (1869-1948), Hindu political, social, and religious leader: *followers of the Mahatma.*
[< Sanskrit *mahātman* < *mahā* great + *ātman* soul]

**ma|hat|ma|ism** (mə hät′mə iz əm, -hat′-), *n.* the principles and practice of mahatmas.

**Ma|ha|ya|na** (mä′hə yä′nə, mə hä′yä′nə), *n.* a form of Buddhism, now predominant in Japan, China, Korea, Tibet, and Mongolia, which worships Buddha as a divine being. [< Sanskrit *mahāyāna* < *mahā* great + *yāna* vehicle, way]

**Ma|ha|ya|nist** (mä′hə yä′nist), *adj., n.* — *adj.* of or having to do with Mahayana.
— *n.* a believer in Mahayana.

**Mah|di** (mä′dē), *n., pl.* **-dis. 1** the leader expected by Moslems to come and establish a reign of righteousness. **2** a person claiming to be this leader. [< Arabic *mahdīy* one who is guided aright < *hadā* he led aright]

**Mah|dism** (mä′diz əm), *n.* **1** the doctrine of the coming of the Mahdi. **2** adherence to or support of a person who claims this title.

**Mah|dist** (mä′dist), *n.* an adherent of a person claiming to be the Mahdi.

**Ma|hi|can** (mə hē′kən), *n.* **1** a confederacy or tribe of Algonkian Indians who once lived in or near the upper valley of the Hudson. **2** a member of this confederacy. See also **Mohegan, Mohican.** [American English < Algonkian *maingan* wolf]

**ma|hi|ma|hi** (mä′hē mä′hē), *n. Hawaiian.* a dolphin, a saltwater fish popular as food.

**mah-jongg** or **mah-jong** (mä′jông′, -jong′), *n.* a game of Chinese origin played by four people with small tiles resembling dominoes. Each player tries to form winning combinations by drawing or discarding from many pieces, usually 144 in the Orient and a varying number elsewhere. [< Shanghai dialectal Chinese *ma chiang* (literally) hemp birds, sparrows (from a design on the pieces)]

**Mah|ler|i|an** (mä lir′ē ən), *adj., n.* — *adj.* of or having to do with the Bohemian composer Gustav Mahler (1860-1911) or his music.
— *n.* a follower, interpreter, or admirer of Mahler's music.

**mahl|stick** (mäl′stik′, môl′-), *n.* a light stick used by painters as a support for the painting hand and held in the other. Also, **maulstick.** [< Dutch *maalstok* < *malen* to paint + *stok* stick]

**ma|hoe** (mə hō′), *n.* a tropical shrub or tree of the mallow family, important as a source of fiber especially for cord and sails. [apparently < Carib *mahou*]

**ma|hog|a|nize** (mə hog′ə nīz, -hôg′-), *v.t.,* **-nized, -niz|ing.** to stain or finish (wood) to resemble mahogany.

**ma|hog|a|ny** (mə hog′ə nē, -hôg′-), *n., pl.* **-nies,** *adj.* — *n.* **1** a hard, fine-grained, reddish-brown wood of a tree growing in tropical America and in Africa. Because mahogany takes a very high polish, it is much used in making fine furniture. **2** the tree itself. It is a large evergreen which belongs to the mahogany family. **3** any one of various related or similar trees or woods. **4** a dark reddish brown. **5** *Figurative.* a table, especially a dinner table: *I had hoped ... to have seen you three gentlemen ... with your legs under the mahogany in my humble parlour* (Dickens).
— *adj.* **1** made of mahogany: *a mahogany chest of drawers.* **2** dark reddish-brown.
[< obsolete Spanish *mahogani,* perhaps < the Maya (Honduras) name]

**mahogany family,** a group of dicotyledonous tropical trees and shrubs with hard wood, frequently scented, including the mahogany and chinaberry.

**Ma|hom|et|an** (mə hom′ə tən), *adj., n.* = Mohammedan.

**Ma|hom|et|an|ism** (mə hom′ə tə niz′əm), *n.* = Mohammedanism.

**ma|ho|nia** (mə hōn′yə), *n.* any one of a group of

shrubs of the barberry family, having evergreen, pinnate leaves and dense racemes of yellow flowers, such as the Oregon grape. [< New Latin *Mahonia* the typical genus < Bernard Mc*Mahon,* 1775-1816, an American horticulturist]

**Ma|hound** (mə hound′), *n.* **1** *Archaic.* Mohammed, especially when thought of as a false prophet. **2** *Scottish.* the Devil; Satan. [Middle English *Mahun* < Old French < *Mahomet* Mahomet]

**ma|hout** (mə hout′), *n.* the keeper and driver of an elephant in India and the East Indies. [< Hindustani *mahāut*]

**Mah|rat|ta** (mə rat′ə), *n.* a member of a Hindu people who live in the central and southwestern parts of India. Also, **Maratha.** [< Hindi *Marhaṭṭa* < Sanskrit *Mahārāṣṭra* < *mahā* great + *rāṣṭra* kingdom]

**Mah|rat|ti** (mə rat′ē), *n.* the Indic language of the Mahrattas. Also, **Marathi.**

**mah|seer** or **mah|sir** (mä′sər), *n.* a large freshwater cyprinoid fish of India, resembling the barbel. [< Hindi *mahāsīr*]

**ma|hua** (mä′wä), *n.* a south Asian tree of the sapodilla family. Its seeds yield an oil used especially in cooking and in making soap, and its flowers are used for food and in making an intoxicating drink. [< Hindi *mahwa* < Sanskrit *madhūka* < *madhu* sweet]

**mah|zor** (mäн zōr′, mäн′zər), *n., pl.* **mah|zo|rim** (mäн′zō rēm′), **mah|zors.** a Jewish prayer book with the prayers and devotional poetry used on festivals and holidays. [< Hebrew *mahazōr* cycle]

**Ma|ia** (mā′ə, mī′-), *n. Greek Mythology.* the eldest of the Pleiades, who was loved by Zeus and became the mother of Hermes by him.

**maid** (mād), *n.* **1** a young unmarried woman; girl: *Many a youth, and many a maid, Dancing in the chequer'd shade* (Milton). **2** an unmarried woman: *Good old English reading ... makes* (*if the worst come to the worst*) *most incomparable old maids* (Charles Lamb). SYN: spinster. **3** a woman servant. **4** *Archaic.* a virgin.

**the Maid,** Joan of Arc (1412-1431), French heroine who led armies against invading England: *Rumours of the ... miracles of the Maid were repeated even in the English camp* (J. Gairdner).

[Middle English *meide,* short for *meiden,* Old English *mægden* maiden]

**mai|dan** (mī dän′), *n.* a level, open space in or near a town in India and countries of southeast Asia; esplanade. [< Persian *maidān*]

**maid|en** (mā′dən), *n., adj.* —*n.* **1** a young unmarried woman; maid; girl: *Here's to the maiden of bashful fifteen* (Richard B. Sheridan). **2a** a horse that has never won a race. **b** a race or prize for such horses. **3** *Cricket.* a maiden over. **4** *Archaic.* **a** a virgin. **b** a spinster.

—*adj.* **1** of or befitting a maiden: *maiden grace.* **2** unmarried; virgin: *a maiden aunt.* SYN: single. **3** *Figurative.* **a** new; fresh; untried; unused: *maiden ground. Full bravely hast thou fleshed Thy maiden sword* (Shakespeare). SYN: virgin. **b** made or used for the first time; first: *a ship's maiden voyage.* SYN: initial. **4a** (of a horse or apprentice jockey) being a maiden. **b** (of a race or prize) for maiden horses: *... the winner of a mile maiden race at Epsom* (London Times).

[Old English *mægden*]

**Maid|en** (mā′dən), *n.* an instrument similar to a guillotine, formerly used in Scotland for beheading criminals.

**maid|en|hair** (mā′dən hãr′), *n.,* or **maidenhair fern,** a fern with very slender, dark, shining stems and delicate, finely divided fronds.

**maidenhair tree,** = ginkgo.

**maid|en|head** (mā′dən hed), *n.* **1** = hymen. **2** *Archaic.* virginity; maidenhood.

**maid|en|hood** (mā′dən hůd), *n.* **1** the condition of being a maiden or time when one is a maiden: *There is ... a very pleasant atmosphere of maidenhood about her* (Hawthorne). SYN: virginity. **2** *Figurative.* freshness.

**maid|en|li|ness** (mā′dən lē nis), *n.* maidenly quality or behavior.

**maid|en|ly** (mā′dən lē), *adj., adv.* —*adj.* **1** of a maiden. **2** like a maiden; gentle; modest. **3** suited to a maiden: *maidenly reserve.*

—*adv.* after the fashion of a maiden; modestly: *Her looks turned maidenly to ground* (Elizabeth Barrett Browning).

**maiden name,** a woman's surname before her marriage.

**maiden over,** *Cricket.* an over in which no runs are scored.

**maiden speech,** the first speech delivered by a member of a legislative assembly, especially one delivered in the House of Commons by a member of Parliament.

**maid|hood** (mād′hůd), *n.* = maidenhood.

**maid in waiting,** or **maid-in|wait|ing** (mād′in-wā′ting), *n., pl.* **maids in waiting, maids-in-waiting.** an unmarried noble lady who attends a queen or princess.

**Maid Marian, 1** a character in old English May Day games and morris dances. **2** Robin Hood's companion and sweetheart.

**maid of honor, 1** an unmarried woman who is the chief attendant of the bride at a wedding: *The maid of honor adjusted the bride's veil.* **2** an unmarried noble lady who attends a queen or princess: *The daughters of several noblemen served as the Queen's maids of honor.*

**maid|serv|ant** (mād′sėr′vənt), *n.* a woman servant: *The maidservant met me at the front door* (Jane Carlyle). SYN: maid, bonne.

**Mai|du** (mī′dü), *n., pl.* **-du** or **-dus. 1** a member of a tribe of American Indians that once lived in the Feather and American river valleys of north-central California. **2** the Penutian language of this tribe.

**ma|ieu|tic** (mā yü′tik), *adj.* **1** of or having to do with the Socratic method of helping a person to bring out ideas latent in the mind. **2** having to do with midwifery. [< Greek *maieutikós* (literally) obstetric < *maîa* midwife]

**ma|ieu|tics** (mā yü′tiks), *n.* the maieutic art, especially as practiced by Socrates.

**mai|gre** (mā′gər), *adj., n., adv.* —*adj.* **1** having neither flesh nor its juices and therefore permissible on days of religious abstinence: *a maigre soup.* **2** characterized by such abstinence in diet.

—*n.* a large food fish, common in the Mediterranean.

—*adv.* using no meat in preparation of a food: *At last he* [*the doctor*] *consented on condition that I should ... live maigre and drink no wine* (Hannah More).

[< French *maigre* lean. See etym. of doublet **meager.**]

**mai|hem** (mā′hem), *n.* = mayhem.

**mail$^1$** (māl), *n., v., adj.* —*n.* **1** letters, postcards, papers, and parcels to be sent by post: *The postman rested his sack of mail on the ledge under the mailbox.* **2** the system by which such mail is sent; post. It is managed in the United States by the U.S. Postal Service, formerly the Post Office Department. *You can pay most bills by mail.* **3** all that comes by one post or delivery: *The morning mail is full of advertisements.* **4** a train, boat, airplane, or person that carries mail: *Most of us disdained all coaches except his majesty's mail* (Thomas De Quincey). **5** *U.S.* the collection, dispatch, or delivery of postal matter at a particular time: *the 10 o'clock mail.* **6** *Scottish.* a bag; traveling bag.

—*v.t.* to send by mail; put in a mailbox; post: *He mailed the letter for his mother.*

—*adj.* **1** of or for mail. **2** employed to carry the mail.

[< Old French *male* wallet, bag < Germanic (compare Old High German *malha*)]

► In American use, **mail** is more common than **post.** In British use, **post** is the ordinary term, except for def. 4 of the noun and some uses of def. 1 of the adjective, such as *mail train.*

***mail$^2$** (māl), *n., v.* —*n.* **1** a flexible armor made of metal rings or small loops of chain linked together, or of overlapping plates, for protecting the body against the enemy's arrows or spears. **2** any armor. **3** the protective shell or scales of certain animals, such as the tortoise or the lobster.

—*v.t.* to cover or protect with or as if with mail.

[< Old French *maille* < Latin *macula* a mesh in a net; (originally) spot, mark] —**mail′less,** *adj.*

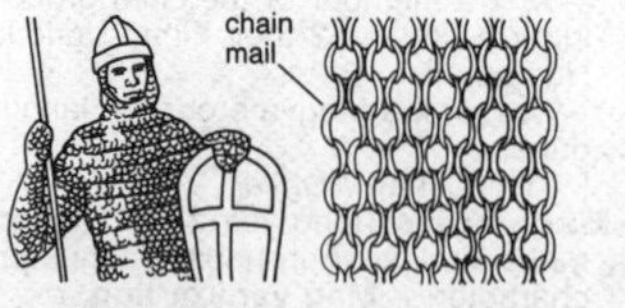

chain mail

***mail$^2$** definition 1

**mail$^3$** (māl), *n. Obsolete or Scottish.* payment; tax; rent. [Old English *māl*]

**mail|a|bil|i|ty** (mā′lə bil′ə tē), *n.* the condition of being legally acceptable for mailing.

**mail|a|ble** (mā′lə bəl), *adj.* that can be mailed.

**mail|bag** (māl′bag′), *n.* a large bag for carrying mail.

**mail|boat** (māl′bōt′), *n.* a boat or ship that carries mail.

**mail|box** (māl′boks′), *n.* **1** a public box from which mail is collected: *We walked down to the corner mailbox to post the letters.* **2** a private box to which mail is delivered: *Everybody in the apartment building went to their mailbox each morning.* [American English < *mail$^1$* + *box$^1$*]

**mail call,** the distribution of mail, especially in the armed forces.

**mail car,** a railroad car in which mail is sorted and transported.

**mail carrier,** = mailman.

**mail|chute** (māl′shüt′), *n.* a chute for depositing mail, situated in a corridor on each floor in office buildings.

**mail clerk,** an office worker who takes care of the receiving, sorting, and distributing, and frequently the sending, of mail.

**mail cover,** *U.S.* the screening and holding of certain types of mail by postal officials: *When a person is subjected to a mail cover, the Post Office records the name and address of anyone sending mail to him, as well as the postmarking and the class of mail* (New York Times).

**mail drop,** an address used only for purposes of receiving mail: *... Shakespeare and Company served as their club, mail drop, meeting-house, and forum* (New Yorker).

**mailed** (māld), *adj.* **1** covered, armed, or protected with mail. **2** (of animals) having a protective covering resembling armor or mail.

**mailed fist,** force of arms; military power: *The massive helms are symbolic of the knight's dauntless courage, as the mailed fist is of his might* (Time). —**mailed′-fist′,** *adj.*

**mail|er** (mā′lər), *n.* **1** a person who mails. **2** = mailing machine. **3** a reinforced container in which to mail photographs, maps, or other material, especially to keep it from being bent or damaged. **4** a vessel that carries mail.

**mail|gram** (māl′gram), *n. U.S.* a letter transmitted electronically from a telegraph office to a local post office for delivery to the addressee.

**mail|ing$^1$** (mā′ling), *n.* **1** the sending of mail. **2** something sent by mail. **3** a batch of mail sent at one time. [< *mail$^1$* + *-ing$^1$*]

**mail|ing$^2$** (mā′ling), *n. Scottish.* **1** a rented farm. **2** the rent paid for a farm: *Let the creatures stay at a moderate mailing* (Scott). [< *mail$^3$* + *-ing$^1$*]

**mailing list,** a list of names, such as those of people or businesses, to whom circulars, advertisements, or other matter are distributed by mail.

**mailing machine,** a machine for addressing and stamping mail.

**mailing piece,** a catalog, circular, or other advertising matter to be distributed by mail.

**mailing tube,** a cardboard tube into which papers, maps, or photographs are rolled for mailing, to prevent creasing or other damage.

**maill** or **maille** (māl), *n. Obsolete.* mail (tax).

**mail|lot** (mȧ yō′), *n. French.* **1** a one-piece, close-fitting garment resembling a bathing suit, worn especially by dancers and acrobats. **2** a one-piece bathing suit.

**mail|man** (māl′man′), *n., pl.* **-men.** a man who carries or delivers mail; postman.

**mail order,** an order sent by mail for goods that are to be shipped by mail or other means.

**mail-or|der** (māl′ôr′dər), *adj., v.* —*adj.* of or having to do with mail orders or a mail-order house.

—*v.t., v.i.* to send (merchandise) upon receiving orders by mail: *More than $40,000 worth of tickets were mail-ordered before the box office opened* (Time).

**mail-order catalog,** a catalog for the advertisement of goods sold by mail order.

**mail-order house,** a business firm that receives orders and sends goods by mail.

**mail|room** (māl′rüm′, -rům′), *n.* a room used for receiving and distributing mail, as in an office.

**maim** (mām), *v., n., adj.* —*v.t.* **1** to cut off or make useless an arm, leg, ear, or the like, of; cripple; disable: *He lost two toes in the accident, but we were glad that he was not more seriously maimed.* SYN: mutilate, mangle. **2** *Figurative.* to make defective or powerless: *You maim'd the jurisdiction of all bishops* (Shakespeare).

—*n.* **1** a crippling or wounding of the body; injury. **2** *Figurative.* a serious defect, blemish, or hurt.

—*adj.* maimed.

[Middle English *maimen,* or *maheimen* < Old French *mahaignier,* perhaps < a Frankish word] —**maim′er,** *n.*

**maim|ed|ness** (mā′mid nis, māmd′-), *n.* maimed condition.

**main$^1$** (mān), *adj., n., adv., v.* —*adj.* **1** most important; largest: *the main dish at dinner, the main street of a town, the main line of a railway, the main branches of a river. No more than an interlude in the main business of his life* (Hawthorne). SYN: principal, leading, chief. **2** exerted to the utmost; full; sheer: *by main strength.* **3** designating a considerable stretch of water, land, or, sometimes, sky: *Over all the face of earth main ocean flowed* (Milton). **4** *Nautical.* of or having to do with the mainmast or mainsail. **5** *British and Scottish Dialect.* remarkable: *a main crop of apples. It were a main place for pirates once* (Robert Louis Stevenson). **6** *Archaic.* mighty: *Soaring on main wing* (Milton).

—*n.* **1a** a large pipe or conductor which carries water, gas, sewage, or electricity to or from smaller branches: *When the water main broke, the houses on our block had no water.* **b** *British.* an electrical outlet. **2** the open sea; ocean: *Forced from their homes ... To traverse climes* *beyond the western main* (Oliver Goldsmith). **3** *Nautical.* a mainmast or mainsail. **4** a main line of a railroad. **5** *Archaic.* mainland: ... *the land they saw from our island was not the main, but an island* (Robert Louis Stevenson). **6** *Archaic.* physical strength, force, or power. **7** *Obsolete.* a broad expanse.

—*adv.* *British and Scottish Dialect.* exceedingly; very: *I am main sorry to displease your worship* (William Godwin).

—*v.t.* *Slang.* to inject (heroin or a similar drug) into a vein; mainline.

**in the main**, for the most part; chiefly; mostly: *Her grades are excellent in the main. Milly ... is an excellent girl in the main* (James Fenimore Cooper).

**with might and main.** See under **might**[2].

[Old English *mægen-* < *mægen* power]

**main**[2] (mān), *n.* **1** a match between gamecocks. **2** a number called by the caster before throwing the dice in the game of hazard: *He likes to throw a main of an evening* (Thackeray). **3** a throw, match, or stake at dice. [origin uncertain]

**main|brace** (mān′brās′), *n.* *Nautical.* the brace attached to the lower yard of the mainmast.

**splice the mainbrace**, *British Informal.* to serve alcoholic beverages; drink freely: *Mr. Falcon, splice the mainbrace, and call the watch* (Frederick Marryat).

**main chance**, the chance or probability of greatest importance or advantage to oneself: *He knew that the ladies of the stage have an ear for flattery, and an eye to the main chance* (Reade).

**main clause**, *Grammar.* a clause in a complex sentence that can act by itself as a sentence; independent clause: [Main clause] *There are differences of opinion on the matter* [subordinate clause] *which cause a great deal of disharmony.*

**main course**, *Nautical.* the square sail attached to the lowest yard of the mainmast of a square-rigged vessel.

**main-de-fer** (maɴ′də fer′), *n.* a defensive covering of iron for the hand, used in medieval tournaments. [< Old French *main de fer* hand of iron]

**main drag**, *Slang.* = main stem.

**Main|er** (mā′nər), *n.* a native or inhabitant of the state of Maine.

**main-force** (mān′fôrs′, -fōrs′), *adj.* *U.S. Military.* belonging to the regular army; not guerrilla or paramilitary: *a main-force battalion.*

**main|frame** (mān′frām′), *n.,* or **main frame**, the central processor and immediate access store of a computer.

**main|land** (mān′land′, -lənd), *n., adj.* —*n.* the main part of a continent or land mass, apart from outlying islands or peninsulas.

—*adj.* of or belonging to the mainland: *the mainland states of the United States. The Chinese who really count ... are the seven hundred million mainland Chinese* (Maclean's).

**main|land|er** (mān′lən dər, -lan′-), *n.* a person who lives on the mainland.

**main|line** (mān′līn′), *adj., v.,* **-lined, -lin|ing.** —*adj.* traveling on or situated along a main line: *mainline towns.*

—*v.i., v.t.* *U.S. Slang.* to inject a narcotic, especially heroin, directly into a vein.

**main line**, **1** a principal route of a railroad, airline, bus or trucking firm, as distinguished from a branch line. **2** (of railroads) a through track, as distinguished from local or yard tracks.

**main|lin|er** (mān′lī′nər), *n.* **1** a railroad, train, airplane, boat, bus, or truck that travels the mainline route. **2** *U.S. Slang.* a drug addict who mainlines.

**main|ly** (mān′lē), *adv.* **1** for the most part; chiefly; mostly: *He is interested mainly in sports and neglects his schoolwork.* SYN: principally. **2** *Obsolete.* mightily; greatly: *I think we should suit one another mainly* (Charles Lamb).

**main|mast** (mān′mast′, -mäst′; *Nautical* mān′-məst), *n.* **1** the principal mast of a ship. **2** the second mast from the bow on a brig, schooner, or other large sailing vessel. See picture under **mast**[1]. **3** the mast nearer the bow in a yawl or ketch.

**mains** (mānz), *n.pl.* *Scottish.* the farm attached to the main house of an estate; a home farm. [short for *domains*]

**main|sail** (mān′sāl′; *Nautical* mān′səl), *n.* the largest sail of a ship on the mainmast. See picture under **sail**.

**main sequence**, the group of stars which, when plotted according to luminosity and spectral class on the Russell diagram, fall in a narrow diagonal band from the upper left to the lower right. Most stars fall in this sequence, showing that there is a correlation between luminosity and spectral type, and, by extension, luminosity and size.

**main-se|quence star** (mān′sē′kwens), any star in the main sequence, such as the sun.

**main|sheet** (mān′shēt′), *n.* the rope or tackle that controls the angle at which the mainsail is set.

**main|spring** (mān′spring′), *n.* **1** the principal spring of a clock or watch: *The broken mainspring prevents the watch from working at all.* **2** *Figurative.* the main cause, motive, or influence: *The Opposition is still searching for a mainspring* (New York Times).

**main|stay** (mān′stā′), *n.* **1** a rope or wire supporting the mainmast. The mainstay extends forward and down to the bow. **2** *Figurative.* a main support: *Loyal friends are a person's mainstay in time of trouble.* SYN: prop, backbone.

**main stem**, *U.S. Slang.* the busiest or chief street of a city or town; a main artery.

**main|stream** (mān′strēm′), *n., adj., v.* —*n.* a main course or direction in the historical development of an organization, branch of government, legal system, art form, idea, country, or any other institution or thing: *Kabuki continues to form the mainstream of the Japanese theater* (Atlantic).

—*adj.* belonging in the main direction or course of development; not tributary or marginal: *mainstream jazz, mainstream literature.*

—*v.t., v.i.* *U.S.* to integrate (handicapped children) with other schoolchildren by transferring them from special classes to regular classrooms, usually on a gradual or part-time basis: *That children will be mainstreamed without backup services is always a danger in times of financial stress* (Myron Brenton).

**main|street** (mān′strēt′), *v.i.* *U.S. and Canada.* to campaign for election along the main streets of towns and districts: *Boston has witnessed a merry binge of mainstreeting, leafletting, and parties with some of the excitement of a mayoral election* (Time). —**main′street′er**, *n.*

**Main Street**, **1** the chief street, usually the business section, in a small town. **2** *Figurative.* the typical behavior, point of view, and opinions found in a small town; limited experience and outlook; provincial attitude: *Arriving in Paris, he felt that he had finally parted with Main Street.*

**main|tain** (mān tān′), *v.t.* **1** to keep; keep up; carry on: *to maintain a business, to maintain one's health. One must maintain a footing in a tug of war. Policemen assist in maintaining order. Maintain your hold.* SYN: continue, preserve. **2** to support; uphold: *to maintain an opinion. He had a reputation to maintain.* SYN: defend. See syn. under **support**. **3** to bear the expenses of; provide for: *He maintains his family.* **4** to keep in repair or supplied or equipped: *This apartment house is maintained very well. He employs a mechanic to maintain his fleet of trucks.* **5** to declare to be true: *He maintains that he is innocent. She maintained that war did not pay.* **6** to assert against opposition; affirm: *He maintains his innocence.* SYN: contend. **7** to keep or hold against attack: *to maintain one's ground.* [< Old French *maintenir* < Latin *manū tenēre* hold by the hand; *manū,* ablative of *manus, -ūs* hand] —**main|tain′a|ble**, *adj.* —**main-tain′er**, *n.*

**main|tain|a|bil|i|ty** (mān tā′nə bil′ə tē), *n.* the fact or condition of being maintainable.

**main|tained school** (mān tānd′), *British.* a school maintained by public funds, such as a council school.

**main|te|nance** (mān′tə nəns), *n.* **1** the act or process of maintaining: *Maintenance of quiet is necessary in a hospital.* **2** the condition of being maintained; support: *A government collects taxes to pay for its maintenance.* **3** the act or fact of keeping up or in repair; upkeep: *the maintenance of an automobile. A state devotes much time to the maintenance of roads.* **4** enough to support life; means of living: *His small farm provides a maintenance, but not much more.* SYN: subsistence, livelihood. **5** *Law.* meddling in a lawsuit by helping either party with money or other means to prosecute or defend it: *Champerty is but a particular modification of this sin of maintenance* (Jeremy Bentham).

**maintenance man**, **1** a man hired to clean a store, offices, or other building; janitor. **2** a man whose work is repairing, cleaning, or renovating machines; repairman.

**maintenance of membership**, a clause in a union contract requiring all employees to remain paid-up members for the life of the contract or be dismissed by the employer: *The union's 650,000 basic steel workers are demanding ... a union shop to replace an existing maintenance of membership clause* (Tuscaloosa News).

**main|top** (mān′top′), *n.* a platform at the head of the lower mainmast.

**main|top|gal|lant** (mān′top gal′ənt; *Nautical* mān′tə gal′ənt), *n.* the mast, sail, or yard above the maintopmast.

**main|top|gal|lant|mast** (mān′top gal′ənt mast′, -mäst′; *Nautical* mān′tə gal′ənt məst), *n.* the mast next above the maintopmast.

**main|top|gal|lant|sail** (mān′top gal′ənt sāl′; *Nautical* mān′tə gal′ənt səl), *n.* the sail belonging to the maintopgallantmast.

**main|top|gal|lant|yard** (mān′top gal′ənt yärd′; *Nautical* mān′tə gal′ənt yärd′), *n.* a beam or pole that supports the maintopgallantsail. See picture under **mast**[1].

**main|top|mast** (mān′top′mast′, -mäst′; *Nautical* mān′top′məst), *n.* the second section of the mainmast above the deck.

**main|top|sail** (mān′top′sāl′; *Nautical* mān′top′-səl), *n.* the sail above the mainsail.

**main yard**, the beam or pole fastened across the mainmast to support the mainsail. See picture under **mast**[1].

**mai|oid** (mā′oid), *adj., n.* —*adj.* of, belonging to, or like a large group of ten-footed crustaceans, typified by the spider crab.

—*n.* any crab of this group, especially a spider crab.

[< New Latin *Maia* the genus name (< Latin *maia* a kind of crab < Greek *maîa*) + English *-oid*]

**ma|iol|i|ca** (mə yol′ə kə), *n.* = majolica.

**mair** or **maire** (mār), *adj., n., adv.* *Scottish.* more.

**mai|son de cou|ture** (me zôɴ′ də kü tyr′), *pl.* **mai|sons de cou|ture** (me zôɴ′ də kü tyr′). *French.* house of fashion; fashion salon.

**mai|son de san|té** (me zôɴ′ də säɴ tā′), *pl.* **mai-sons de san|té** (me zôɴ′ də säɴ tā′). *French.* a private hospital or sanitarium.

**mai|son|ette** or **mai|son|nette** (mā′zə net′), *n.* *British.* **1** a house divided into apartments: *An historic house modernised and divided into flat and maisonette ...* (Observer). **2** an apartment, especially a duplex: *New modern Maisonettes for sale* (New York Times). [< French *maisonnette* (diminutive) < Old French *maison* house; see etym. under **mansion**]

**maist** (māst), *adj., n., adv.* *Scottish.* most.

**mai tai** (mī′ tī′), a drink made from assorted rums, lime, sugar, and pineapple. [< Hawaiian *mai tai*]

**maî|tre** (me′trə), *n.* *French.* the master or leader of something; a teacher; mentor.

**maî|tre d′** (mā′trə dē′, mā′tər dē′), *Informal.* a maître d'hôtel (def. 1 and 3).

**maî|tre de bal|let** (me′trə də ba lā′), *French.* a ballet teacher.

**maî|tre d'hô|tel** (me′trə dō tel′), *pl.* **maî|tres d'hô|tel** (me′trəz dō tel′). **1** a headwaiter. **2** a butler or steward; major-domo. **3** a hotel manager: *The attentive maître d'hôtel flew past us and threw open the door of a splendid apartment* (R. H. Savage). **4** with a sauce of creamed butter, chopped parsley, and lemon juice or vinegar. [< Middle French *maître d'hôtel* (literally) master of the house; *maître* < Old French *maistre* master]

**maize** (māz), *n.* **1** corn; Indian corn. **2** the color of ripe corn; yellow. [< Spanish *maíz,* earlier *mahiz, mahis,* or *mayz* < Arawak (Haiti) *mahiz*]

**Maj.**, major.

**ma|ja** (mä′hä), *n.* a Spanish woman of the lower classes who dresses gaily and is a belle in her circle. [< Spanish *maja,* feminine of *majo*]

**ma|jes|tic** (mə jes′tik), *adj.* of or having majesty; grand; noble; dignified: *His face ... Majestic though in ruin* (Milton). *In more lengthen'd notes and slow, The deep, majestic, solemn organs blow* (Alexander Pope). SYN: kingly, stately, regal, august, imposing. —**ma|jes′ti|cal|ly**, *adv.*

**ma|jes|ti|cal** (mə jes′tə kəl), *adj.* = majestic.

**maj|es|ty** (maj′ə stē), *n., pl.* **-ties.** **1** stately appearance; royal dignity; nobility; grandeur: *the majesty of the starry heavens.* SYN: sublimity. **2** supreme power or authority: *Policemen and judges uphold the majesty of the law.* SYN: sovereignty. [< Old French *majeste* < Latin *mājestās* < *mājor,* earlier *mājus,* comparative of *magnus* great]

**Maj|es|ty** (maj′ə stē), *n., pl.* **-ties.** a title used in speaking to or of a king, queen, emperor, empress, or the like: *Your Majesty, His Majesty, Her Majesty, Their Royal Majesties.*

**Maj. Gen.**, major general.

**Maj|lis** or **maj|lis** (maj lēs′), *n.* **1** the National Assembly of Iran, one of two houses of the legislative branch of the government: *The draft agreement ... has been submitted to the Persian Majlis for its approval* (Economist). **2** the legislature of the Maldives. Also, **Mejlis.** [< Persian *majlis*]

**ma|jo** (mä′hō), *n., pl.* **-jos.** a gaily dressed Spanish dandy of the lower classes: *The Majo glitters in velvets and filigree buttons, tags, and tassels* (Richard Ford). [< Spanish *majo* (literally) gay, fine]

**Pronunciation Key:** hat, āge, cãre, fär; let, ēqual, tėrm; it, īce; hot, ōpen, ôrder; oil, out; cup, pu̇t, rüle; child; long; thin; ᴛʜen; zh, measure; ə represents **a** in about, **e** in taken, **i** in pencil, **o** in lemon, **u** in circus.

**ma|jol|i|ca** (mə jol′ə kə, -yol′-), *n.* **1** a kind of enameled Italian pottery richly decorated in colors: *The finest majolica was painted during the greatest days of European painting* (George Savage). **2** any similar pottery made elsewhere: *Majolica was made in [the] U.S. in Pennsylvania and Maryland* (Carl W. Drepperd). Also, **maiolica**. [< Italian *maiolica* < Majorca, where the earliest specimens reputedly came from]

**ma|jor** (mā′jər), *adj., n., v.* —***adj.*** **1** more important; larger; greater: *A major part of a baby's life is spent in sleeping. Take the major share of the profits.* **2** of the first rank or order: *Robert Frost and T. S. Eliot are major poets. New York is a major American port.* **3** of the legal age of responsibility (18 or 21 years). **4** *Music.* **a** greater by a half step than the corresponding minor interval: *A major chord.* **b** noting a scale or key having half steps after the third and seventh tones: *the C major scale or key.* **c** (of a chord, especially a triad) containing a major third (two whole steps) between the root and the second tone or note. **5** *U.S.* of, having to do with, or designating a student's principal subject or course of study. **6** *Logic.* broader or more extensive. **7** elder or senior: *Cato Major.*
—***n.*** **1** an officer of the army, air force, or marines, ranking next above a captain and next below a lieutenant colonel. *Abbr:* Maj. **2** a person of the legal age of responsibility. **3** *Music.* a major interval, chord, scale, or key: *The scale of C major has neither sharps nor flats.* **4** *U.S.* **a** a subject or course of study to which a student gives most of his time and attention: *His major is mathematics.* **b** a student engaged in such a course of study: *She is a mathematics major.* **5** *Logic.* a major premise or term. **6** a person of superior rank in a certain class: *Babe Ruth was a major among baseball players.*
—***v.i.*** *U.S. and Canada.* **major in,** to have or take as a major subject of study: *He will major in mathematics. Bulbous-headed adolescents who have majored in English descend in shoals* (Publishers' Weekly).
**the majors, 1** *U.S. Sports.* the major leagues, especially as a representation of professional baseball in the United States. **2** the large international oil-producing companies: *For years independents have been silently resentful of the majors' overseas investments—aiding the Arabs and themselves at the expense of production at home* (Atlantic).
[< Latin *mājor,* comparative of *magnus* great. See etym. of doublet **mayor**.]

**major arc,** *Mathematics.* an arc that is greater than half a circle.

**major axis,** *Mathematics.* the diameter of an ellipse which passes through its foci.

**Ma|jor|can** (mə jôr′kən), *adj., n.* —***adj.*** of or having to do with Majorca (the largest of the Balearic Islands).
—***n.*** **1** a native or inhabitant of Majorca. **2** the language of the Majorcans, related to Provençal.

**ma|jor-do|mo** (mā′jər dō′mō), *n., pl.* **-mos. 1** a man in charge of a royal or noble household: *Sir John ... seemed to be mingling the roles of major-domo and Prime Minister* (Lytton Strachey). **2** a butler or steward: *Whose designs are so humble, as not to aspire above a major-domo, or some such domestic preferment* (Government Tongue). [< Spanish *mayordomo,* or Italian *maggiordomo* < Medieval Latin *major domus* chief of the household < Latin *mājor* (see etym. under **major**), *domūs,* genitive of *domus* house(hold)]

**ma|jor|ette** (mā′jə ret′), *n. U.S.* drum majorette.

**major general,** an officer of the army, air forces, or marines ranking next above a brigadier general and next below a lieutenant general.

**ma|jor-gen|er|al|cy** (mā′jər jen′ər əl sē), *n., pl.* **-cies.** the rank or position of a major general.

**ma|jor-gen|er|al|ship** (mā′jər jen′ər əl ship), *n.* = major-generalcy.

**ma|jor|i|tar|i|an** (mə jôr′ə tãr′ē ən, -jōr′-), *n., adj.* —***n.*** a person who favors majority rule.
—***adj.*** having to do with or characteristic of majoritarians or majority rule: *majoritarian excesses.*

**Ma|jor|i|tar|i|an** (mə jôr′ə tãr′ē ən, -jōr′-), *n. U.S.* a person belonging to the Silent Majority.

**ma|jor|i|tar|i|an|ism** (mə jôr′ə tãr′ē ə niz′əm, -jōr′-), *n.* belief in or advocacy of majority rule.

**ma|jor|i|ty** (mə jôr′ə tē, -jor′-), *n., pl.* **-ties,** *adj.* —***n.*** **1** the larger number; greater part; more than half: *A majority of the children chose red covers for the books that they had made. The will of the majority should prevail* (Thomas Jefferson). **2** the number by which the votes on one side are more than those on the other; larger number of votes than all the rest: *If Smith received 12,000 votes, Adams 7,000, and White 3,000, Smith had a majority of 2,000 and a plurality of 5,000.* **3** the legal age of responsibility. Under the varying laws of the states of the United States, a person may reach his majority at the age of 18 or 21. *A person who is 21 years old or over has reached his majority and may manage his own affairs.* **4** the rank or position of an army major. **5** a party or group having the larger number of votes in an assembly, electoral body, or the like. **6** *Obsolete.* superiority; preponderance.
—***adj.*** **1** of or constituting a majority: *a majority vote.* **2** representing or belonging to a majority: *the majority leader of the Senate. The court's majority opinion was delivered by Chief Justice Taft* (Manchester Guardian).
**go** (or **pass**) **over to** (or **join**) **the majority,** to die: *Mirabeau's work then is done ... He has gone over to the majority* (Thomas Carlyle).

**majority rule,** a principle of democratic government or organization whereby laws, rules, or decisions are made according to the will of the greatest number of people, and that they will be binding on all the people.

**major key,** a musical key or mode based on the major scale.

**major league,** either of the two chief leagues in American professional baseball, the National League or the American League.

**ma|jor-league** (mā′jər lēg′), *adj.* **1** of, having to do with, or in the major leagues: *a major-league ballplayer.* **2** top-ranking; first-class: *Handy Associates is strictly major-league* (New Yorker).

**ma|jor-lea|guer** (mā′jər lē′gər), *n.* a major-league ballplayer.

**ma|jor-med|i|cal** (mā′jər med′ə kəl), *n. U.S.* a broad form of health insurance, providing coverage for large surgical, hospital, and other medical expenses.

**major mode,** = major key.

**major orders,** = holy orders.

**major penalty,** a five-minute penalty put on a player in ice hockey for a serious breaking of the rules, such as striking another player with the stick held high or for starting a fight.

**major piece,** *Chess.* a queen or a rook.

**major premise,** *Logic.* the more inclusive or general premise of a syllogism.

**Major Prophets, 1** the more important of the prophetic books of the Old Testament, including Isaiah, Jeremiah, and Ezekiel. **2** the prophets who are believed to have written these books.

**major scale,** a musical scale having eight notes, with half steps instead of whole steps after the third and seventh notes.

**major suit,** spades or hearts, the suits having greater scoring value in auction and contract bridge.

**major term,** *Logic.* the term that is the predicate at the conclusion of a syllogism.

**ma|jus|cu|lar** (mə jus′kyə lər), *adj.* of or like a majuscule; large: *In the beverage bold Let's renew us and grow muscular; And for those who're getting old, Glasses get of size majuscular* (Leigh Hunt).

**ma|jus|cule** (mə jus′kyül), *n., adj.* —***n.*** a large letter in medieval writing, capital or uncial.
—***adj.*** **1** (of a letter) large. **2** written in majuscules.
[< French *majuscule,* learned borrowing from Latin *mājusculus* somewhat larger (diminutive) < *mājor;* see etym. under **major**]

**mak|a|ble** (mā′kə bəl), *adj.* that can be made. Also, **makeable**.

**ma|kai** (mä kī′), *adv., adj. Hawaiian.* toward the ocean; seaward.

**mak|ar** (mak′ər), *n. Scottish.* a poet. [Middle English *makar* maker, poet]

**make[1]** (māk), *v.,* **made, mak|ing,** *n.* —***v.t.*** **1** to bring into being; put together; build; form; shape: *to make a new dress, to make a boat, to make jelly, to make a fire, to make a will. God made the country, and man made the town* (William Cowper). **SYN:** create. **2** to have the qualities needed for: *Wood makes a good fire.* **3** to cause; bring about: *to make trouble, to make peace, to make a noise, to make a bargain. Haste makes waste.* **4** to force to; cause to: *Make him stop hitting me. He made me go. You can lead a horse to water but you cannot make him drink.* **5a** to cause to be or become; cause oneself to be: *to make a room warm, to make a fool of oneself. A sight to make an old man young* (Tennyson). **b** to appoint; constitute; render: *Who made thee a ruler and a judge over us?* (Acts 7:27). **6** to turn out to be; become: *She will make a good teacher.* **7** to put into condition for use; arrange: *I make my own bed.* **8** to get; obtain; earn: *to make a fortune, to make one's living, to make good grades at school, to make friends.* **SYN:** acquire. **9** to do; perform: *to make an attempt, to make a mistake, to make a speech. Don't make a move.* **10** to amount to; add up to; count as: *Two and two make four. That makes 40 cents you owe me. One good verse doesn't make a poet.* **11** to think of as; figure to be: *I make the distance across the room 15 feet. What do you make of him?* **12** to reach; arrive at: *Will the ship make harbor? The opposing parties made a settlement.* **13** to reach or keep up a speed of: *Some airplanes can make more than 1,500 miles an hour.* **SYN:** go, travel. **14** to cause the success of: *One big business deal made the young man.* **15** *Informal.* to get on; get a place on: *He made the football team.* **16** in card games: **a** to win (a trick). **b** to state (the trump or bid). **c** to win a trick with (a card). **d** to shuffle (the cards). **17** *Electricity.* **a** to complete (a circuit) and so allow the current to flow. **b** to cause (a current) to flow by doing this. **18** to score in a sport or game; have a score of. **19** *Slang.* to win the favor of (a person of the opposite sex); seduce.
—***v.i.*** **1** to cause something to be in a certain condition: *to make sure, to make ready.* **2** to behave or act in a certain way: *to make merry, to make bold. He beckons, and makes as he would speak* (Longfellow). **3** to attempt; start: *He made to stop me.* **4** to move in a certain direction; proceed: *to make straight toward the barn, a boat making upstream.* **5** to be effective: *All these facts make in his favor.* **6** to flow toward the land; rise: *About nine o'clock at night, the tide making, we weighed anchor* (Charles Carrol). **7** to construct or form something: *He can neither make nor mar. God makes; man mars.*
—***n.*** **1** the way in which a thing is made; build or style; fashion: *Do you like the make of that coat?* **2** kind; brand: *What make of car is this?* **3** nature; character: *To my natural make and my temper Painful the task is I do* (Longfellow). **4** the act or process of making. **5** the amount made; yield; output. **6** the closing of an electric circuit; completion of a circuit: *Since this rate is larger on the "break" of the circuit than on the "make," the secondary voltage is much larger in one direction* (Sears and Zemansky). **7** in card games: **a** the naming of the trump suit. **b** the trump suit named.
**make after,** to follow; chase; pursue: *At the signal, the hounds made after the fox.*
**make as if** or **as though,** to pretend that; act as if: *to make as if one is afraid.*
**make away with, a** to kill: *The trap made away with the rat.* **b** to steal: *The treasurer made away with the club's funds.* **c** to get rid of: *I will make away with my castle and dowry to support the cause* (David Williams).
**make believe.** See under **believe**.
**make bold.** See under **bold**.
**make book.** See under **book**.
**make (both) ends meet.** See under **end[1]**.
**make do,** to get along; manage; be contented (with): *I shall make do quite happily on biscuits and cheese* (Punch).
**make eyes at.** See under **eye**.
**make fast,** to attach firmly: *Make the boat fast to the dock.*
**make for, a** to go toward: *Make for the hills!* **b** to rush at; attack: *The watchdog made for the robber.* **c** to help bring about; favor: *The new facts made for the prisoner's acquittal.*
**make fun of.** See under **fun**.
**make good.** See under **good**.
**make hay.** See under **hay[1]**.
**make head.** See under **head**.
**make it,** *U.S. Slang.* **a** to attain success: *I was thirty-seven and I wanted to make it as a writer* (Alex Haley). **b** to make love: *She was the sniffling ... girl who wanted to make it with Arlo* (New Yorker).
**make light of.** See under **light[2]**.
**make like,** *U.S. Informal.* **a** to imitate; act the part of: *The clown made like a monkey to amuse the children.* **b** to perform the services of: *to make like a cook.*
**make love.** See under **love**.
**make much of.** See under **much**.
**make no bones.** See under **bone[1]**.
**make off,** to run away; leave suddenly: *Just before the storm everybody made off for home.*
**make off with,** to steal; take without permission: *He made off with some apples.*
**make one's own,** to consider (something or someone) as one's own: *He never succeeded in his own life but he made his son's success his own.*
**make or break,** to cause to succeed or fail: *... a critique written by one of the men in New York who make or break plays* (George E. Sokolsky).
**make out, a** to write out: *She made out a marketing list.* **b** to show to be; prove: *to make out a strong case.* **c** to try to prove; declare to be: *Your accusation that I never share my candy makes me out most selfish. They aren't as rich as they make out.* **d** to understand: *to make out what someone says. The boy had a hard time making out the problem.* **e** to see with difficulty: *I can barely make out three ships near the horizon.* **f** to complete; fill out: *We need two more eggs to make out a dozen.* **g** *Informal.* to get

along; manage or succeed: *We must try to make out with what we have. How did you make out with your interview? You made out well with that dinner* (Harriet Beecher Stowe).
**make over, a** to alter; make different: *She had to make over her dress because it was too big.* **b** to hand over; transfer ownership of: *He made over his business to his son.*
**make sail**. See under **sail**.
**make time**. See under **time**.
**make tracks**. See under **track**.
**make up, a** to put together: *to make up cloth into a dress, to make up a prescription.* **b** to invent: *to make up a story.* **c** to settle (a dispute, etc.); reconcile: *to make up one's differences. The two gentlemen should ... try to make matters up* (Macaulay). **d** to pay for; compensate: *to make up a loss. The school said it would make up all expenses the team had going to the county track meet.* **e** to become friends again after a quarrel: *There we were quarreling and making up by turns.* **f** to put rouge, lipstick, powder, or other cosmetics on the face: *They have skins that would make a lemon look white; ... but the maid makes them up; and people say how handsome they are* (New Review). **g** to prepare for a part on the stage by putting on suitable clothing, cosmetics, etc.: *to make up as a beggar.* **h** *Printing.* to arrange; set up: *to make up a page of type.* **i** to decide: *Make up your mind.* **j** to go to form or produce; constitute: *Girls make up most of that class.* **k** to take (a test or course failed) for the second time; take (an examination missed) at a later time: *He dropped out of school for a term, which he will have to make up if he wants to graduate.* **l** to add up and balance; adjust: *to make up a statement of accounts.*
**make up for**, to give or do in place of: *to make up for lost time.*
**make up to**, to try to get the friendship of; flatter: *We all made up to the new boy the first day. If Lady Elinor was a widow, I should certainly make up to her* (Edward G. Bulwer-Lytton).
**make water**. See under **water**.
**make way**. See under **way**.
**make with (the)**, *U.S. Slang.* **a** to use in the usual way: *Make with the piano!* **b** to produce; offer: *Finally, he made with the coffee.*
**on the make**, *Slang.* trying for success, profit, status, or the like: *... "What Makes Sammy Run?", Budd Schulberg's vitriolic story of a young heel on the make* (Time).
[Old English *macian*]
—*Syn. v.t.* **1 Make, construct, fashion** mean to put together or give form to something. **Make** is the general word meaning to bring something into existence by forming or shaping it or putting it together: *She made a cake.* **Construct** means to put parts together in proper order, and suggests a plan or design: *They constructed a bridge.* **Fashion** means to give a definite form, shape, or figure to something and usually suggests that the maker is inventive or resourceful: *He fashions beautiful bowls out of myrtle wood.*

**make²** (māk), *n. British Dialect.* **1** a mate; companion; friend: *like a widow having lost her make* (Sir Philip Sidney). **2** a match; equal. [Old English *gemaca*]

**make|a|ble** (mā′kə bəl), *adj.* = makable.

**make|bate** or **make|bait** (māk′bāt′), *n. Archaic.* a person or thing that causes great trouble, leads to fighting, or the like. [< *make¹* + (de)*bate*, confused with *bait*, verb]

**make-be|lieve** (māk′bi lēv′), *n., adj.* —*n.* **1** pretense: *Fairies live in the land of make-believe. His friendships with important people are all make-believe.* **2** a person who pretends; pretender.
—*adj.* pretended; imaginary: *Children often have make-believe playmates.*

**make-do** (māk′dü′), *n., adj.* —*n.* a temporary substitute, usually of an inferior kind.
—*adj.* used as a make-do; characterized by makeshift methods: *When ... prices steadily mounted to their peak, thousands of careful housewives adopted ... a make-do policy* (London Daily Mail).

**make|fast** (māk′fast′, -fäst′), *n.* a buoy, piling, or other mooring, to which a ship can be tied.

**make-or-break** (māk′ər brāk′), *adj.* that can be either a complete success or a complete failure: *a make-or-break year for the British economy* (Manchester Guardian Weekly).

**make-peace** (māk′pēs′), *n.* = peacemaker.

**mak|er** (mā′kər), *n.* **1** a person or thing that makes; manufacturer: *Who was the maker of this stove?* **2** *Law.* a person who signs a promissory note or other document: *The maker should have a lawyer examine any document that he does not completely understand* (Robert W. Merry). **3** the player who first names the trump in card games; declarer. **4** *Archaic.* a poet.

**Mak|er** (mā′kər), *n.* God: *And three firm friends, more sure than day and night,—Himself, his Maker, and the angel Death* (Samuel Taylor Coleridge).
**gone to (meet** or **join) one's Maker**, dead: *The old man has gone to his Maker.*

**make|read|y** or **make-read|y** (māk′red′ē), *n.* **1** the preparation of a form for printing by leveling the type or plates with underlays or overlays to insure an even impression or arranging negatives of film for making plates. **2** the underlays or overlays used.

**mak|er-up** (mā kər up′), *n., pl.* **mak|ers-up**. **1** *British.* a maker or manufacturer of garments. **2** a person who makes up type, pictures, or film for printing.

**make|shift** (māk′shift′), *n., adj.* —*n.* something made to use for a time instead of the right thing; temporary substitute: *When the electric lights went out, we used candles as a makeshift. Spools and buttons were the child's makeshifts for toys.* —*adj.* **1** used for a time instead of the right thing: *drowsing in the scant shade of makeshift awnings* (Mark Twain). **2** characterized by makeshifts: *makeshift endeavors.*

**make|shift|y** (māk′shif′tē), *adj.* = makeshift.

**mak|est** (mā′kist), *v.* archaic form of the second person singular of **make**.

**mak|eth** (mā′kith), *v. Archaic.* makes.

**make|up** or **make-up** (māk′up′), *n.* **1** the way in which a thing is made up or put together: *The novelty of the orchestra's size and makeup ...* (Maclean's). **SYN**: composition, constitution. **2** nature; disposition: *People of a nervous makeup are excitable.* **3a** the way in which an actor is dressed and painted in order to look his part. **b** the clothes, cosmetics, wigs, or other costume used by an actor to look his part. **4** rouge, lipstick, powder, cream, or other preparation to adorn the face; cosmetics: *When you have plenty of makeup on, you always get served faster* (New Yorker). **5a** the arrangement of type, pictures, and illustrations in a book, paper, or magazine. **b** the result of this: *That book has good makeup.* **6** an examination, course, or procedure, taken to make up for having missed or failed a previous one: *Make-up injections will be given to another 300 children at the health center* (New York Times). **7** a person who makes up pages of type; compositor.

**makeup** or **make-up man**, **1** a man whose business is making up actors and actresses or other people appearing before an audience. **2** a man who arranges type, pictures, and illustrations in a book, paper, or magazine.

**make|weight** (māk′wāt′), *n.* **1** anything added to make up for some lack: *Even a "good" Budget next month may prove no more than a temporary makeweight* (Sunday Times). **SYN**: offset. **2** something put on a scale to complete a required weight; counterpoise.

**make-work** (māk′wėrk′), *n., adj.* —*n. U.S.* **1** the contriving of unnecessary activity; featherbedding. **2** the providing of work for unemployed people.
—*adj.* **1** of or used for unnecessary work. **2** devised to make jobs: *Top Administration planners view a huge make-work program as the last ditch move to perk up the economy* (Wall Street Journal).

**ma|ki|mo|no** (mä′kə mō′nō), *n., pl.* **-nos**. a Japanese picture or writing on silk, paper, or other material that is kept rolled up, and not suspended as a kakemono. [< Japanese *makimono* < *maki* scroll + *mono* thing]

**mak|ing** (mā′king), *n.* **1** the cause of a person's success; means of advancement: *Early hardships were the making of him.* **2** Often, **makings**. the material needed. **3** the qualities needed: *I see in him the making of a hero.* **4** something made. **5** the amount made at one time.
**in the making**, in the process of being made; not fully developed: *Our plans are still in the making.*
**makings**, *U.S. Slang.* paper and tobacco for rolling cigarettes: *He had the makings for a whole pack.*

**ma|ko** (mä′kō), *n., pl.* **-kos**. = mako shark. [< Maori *mako*]

**mako shark**, a shark of warm waters that reaches a length of 12 feet and is highly regarded as a game fish.

**ma|ku|ta** (mə kü′tə), *n.* plural of **likuta**.

**mal-**, *combining form.* bad or badly; poor or poorly; unlawful; not ____: *Malodorous = smelling bad. Maladjusted = badly adjusted. Malnutrition = poor nutrition. Malcontent = not content.* Also, **male-**. [< French *mal-* < *mal*, adverb (< Latin *male* badly), or adjective < Latin *malus* bad]

**Mal.**, **1** Malachi (book of the Old Testament). **2** Malayan.

**mal|ab|sorp|tion** (mal′ab sôrp′shən, -zôrp′-), *n. Medicine.* poor or abnormal absorption of food by the body: *malabsorption of carbohydrates.*

**Ma|lac|ca cane** (mə lak′ə), a light walking stick made of the stem of an East Indian rattan palm. [< *Malacca*, a state in the Malay Peninsula]

**Malacca pern**, a pern of the East Indies that hunts at dusk and can catch a bat on the wing.

**ma|la|ceous** (mə lā′shəs), *adj.* of or belonging to a group of plants now generally classified with the rose family, as the apple and pear. [< New Latin *Malaceae* the family name (< Latin *mālum* apple) + English *-ous*]

**Mal|a|chi** (mal′ə kī), *n.* **1** a Hebrew prophet who lived about 450 B.C. He was the last of the Minor Prophets. **2** the last book of the Old Testament, attributed to him. *Abbr:* Mal.

**Mal|a|chi|as** (mal′ə kī′əs), *n.* Malachi in the Douay Bible.

**mal|a|chite** (mal′ə kīt), *n.* a green mineral that is an ore of copper and is used for ornamental articles. It is a basic carbonate of copper. *Formula:* $CuCO_3 \cdot Cu(OH)_2$ [< French *malachite* < Greek *maláchē* mallow (because of the similar color)]

**mal|a|co|log|i|cal** (mal′ə kə loj′ə kəl), *adj.* of or having to do with malacology.

**mal|a|col|o|gist** (mal′ə kol′ə jist), *n.* an expert in malacology.

**mal|a|col|o|gy** (mal′ə kol′ə jē), *n.* the branch of zoology that deals with mollusks. [< French *malacologie*, short for *malacozoologie* < *malaco-* (< Greek *malakós* soft) + *zoologie* zoology]

**mal|a|cop|ter|yg|i|an** (mal′ə kop′tə rij′ē ən), *adj.* of or having to do with a group of soft-finned, teleost fishes, in older classifications. [< New Latin *Malacopterygii* the division name (< Greek *malakós* soft + *ptéryx, -ygos* wing, fin < *pterón* wing) + English *-an*]

**mal|a|cos|tra|can** (mal′ə kos′trə kən), *adj., n.* —*adj.* of or having to do with a subclass of crustaceans usually having many appendages on the thorax and abdomen. Lobsters, crabs, and shrimps belong to this subclass.
—*n.* a malacostracan crustacean.
[< New Latin *Malacostraca* the order name, ultimately < Greek *malakós* soft + *óstrakon* shell + English *-an*]

**mal|a|cos|tra|cous** (mal′ə kos′trə kəs), *adj.* = malacostracan.

**mal|a|dap|ta|tion** (mal′ə dap tā′shən), *n.* poor adaptation; lack of adaptation: *But there is a direct maladaptation between our inherited nature and culture that brings social disorganization* (Ogburn and Nimkoff).

**mal|a|dapt|ed** (mal′ə dap′tid), *adj.* **1** = maladjusted: *... the "maladapted" delinquent* (Listener). **2** poorly adapted; ill-suited: *work maladapted to the assembly line.*

**mal|a|dap|tive** (mal′ə dap′tiv), *adj.* poorly adapting; exhibiting maladaptation: *a maladaptive response to stress.*

**mal|a|dive** (mal′ə div), *adj.* of or affected with sickness; sickly: *The magnificent Prescott* [*a singer*] *is nearly overgrown by a chorus of maladive voices, like a tree engulfed by poison ivy* (New Yorker). [< Old French *maladif* < *malade* ill; see etym. under **malady**]

**mal|ad|just|ed** (mal′ə jus′tid), *adj.* badly adjusted; not in a healthy or harmonious relation with one's environment.

**mal|ad|just|ment** (mal′ə just′mənt), *n.* poor or unsatisfactory adjustment; lack of adaptation: *... a first line of defense against delinquency, as well as against personal maladjustment and unhappiness* (New York Times).

**mal|ad|min|is|ter** (mal′əd min′ə stər), *v.t.* to administer badly; manage inefficiently or dishonestly: *We will never allow the cry of party to be used ... in the defense of a man who maladministers the law* (Atlantic).

**mal|ad|min|is|tra|tion** (mal′əd min′ə strā′shən), *n.* bad administration; inefficient or dishonest management: *The Whigs had repeatedly assailed the maladministration of the Prince* (William E. H. Lecky). **SYN**: misrule, misgovernment.

**mal|ad|min|is|tra|tor** (mal′əd min′ə strā′tər), *n.* a person guilty of maladministration.

**mal|a|droit** (mal′ə droit′), *adj.* unskillful; awkward; clumsy. **SYN**: blundering, bungling. [< French *maladroit* < *mal-* mal- + *adroit* adroit] —**mal′a|droit′ly**, *adv.* —**mal′a|droit′ness**, *n.*

**mal|a|dy** (mal′ə dē), *n., pl.* **-dies**. **1** any bodily disorder or disease, especially one that is chronic or deep-seated: *Cancer and malaria are serious maladies.* **SYN**: sickness, illness. **2** *Figurative.* any unwholesome or disordered condition: *Poverty and slums are social maladies.* [< Old French *maladie* < *malade* ill < Latin *male habitus* feeling unwell < *male* bad, and *habitus*, past participle of *habēre* have]

**Pronunciation Key:** hat, āge, cãre, fär; let, ēqual, tėrm; it, īce; hot, ōpen, ôrder; oil, out; cup, pu̇t, rüle; child; long; thin; ᴛʜen; zh, measure; ə represents **a** in about, **e** in taken, **i** in pencil, **o** in lemon, **u** in circus.

**ma|la fi|de** (mā′lə fī′dē), *Latin.* in bad faith; with or by fraud.
**ma|la fi|des** (mā′lə fī′dēz), *Latin.* bad faith.
**Mal|a|ga** (mal′ə gə), *n.* **1** a large, oval, firm, sweet, white grape, grown in Spain and in California. **2** a white dessert wine originally made in Málaga, Spain. [< *Málaga,* a province in Spain]
**Mal|a|gas|y** (mal′ə gas′ē), *n., pl.* **-gas|y** or **-gas-ies,** *adj.* **—*n.*** **1** a native of the Malagasy Republic (former name, 1958–75, of Madagascar); Madagascan. **2** the language of Madagascar.
**—*adj.*** of or having to do with Madagascar, its people, or their language; Madagascan.
**ma|la|gue|ña** (mä′lä gā′nyä), *n. Spanish.* a kind of fandango originating from Málaga, Spain.
**mal|aise** (ma lāz′), *n.* **1** an uneasy, disturbed, or disordered condition: *The loss of highly trained scientists is more a symptom of an underlying malaise than the cause* (Manchester Guardian Weekly). **2** vague bodily discomfort; uneasiness, often before sickness: *It was afflicting him with a general malaise, it was affecting his energy, his temper* (H. G. Wells). [< French *malaise* < *mal-* imperfect (see etym. under **mal-**) + *aise* ease]
**ma|la|mute** (mä′lə myüt), *n.* = Alaskan malamute. Also, **malemute.**
**mal|an|ders** (mal′ən dərz), *n.* a dry, scabby rash behind the knee in horses. [< Old French *malandre* a sore on a horse's knee, learned borrowing from Latin *malandria* sores on a horse's neck]
**ma|lang|a** (mə läng′gə), *n.* = taro. [< American Spanish *malanga*]
**mal|a|pert** (mal′ə pėrt), *adj., n. Archaic.* **—*adj.*** too bold; pert; saucy: *His malapert boldness might peradventure be punished* (Sir Thomas More).
**—*n.*** a person who is too bold, pert, or saucy. [< Middle French *malapert* < *mal-* badly, mal- + *apert* adroit, expert < Latin *apertus* open] **—mal′-a|pert′ly,** *adv.* **—mal′a|pert′ness,** *n.*
**mal|ap|por|tioned** (mal′ə pôr′shənd, -pōr′-), *adj. U.S.* wrongly or unfairly apportioned: *At stake was the necessity of readjusting Georgia's outrageously malapportioned U.S. congressional districts* (Time).
**mal|ap|por|tion|ment** (mal′ə pôr′shən mənt, -pōr′-), *n. U.S.* wrong or unfair assignment of representation in a legislature: *In a landmark case, Baker vs. Carr, the Court held, 7-2, that federal courts may hear claims that malapportionment of state legislatures violates the equal-protection clause of the Fourteenth Amendment* (Milton Greenberg).
**Mal|a|prop** (mal′ə prop), *n.* **Mrs.,** a character in Richard Brinsley Sheridan's play *The Rivals,* noted for her ridiculous misuse of words. [< *malapropos*]
**mal|a|prop|ism** (mal′ə prop iz′əm), *n.* **1** a ridiculous misuse of words, especially a confusion of two words somewhat similar in sound but different in meaning, such as a musical *progeny* for a musical *prodigy.* Malapropisms are often used for humorous effect. **2** an instance of this; misused word: *Lemaitre has reproached Shakespeare for his love of malapropisms* (Harper's). [earlier *malaprop* < Mrs. *Malaprop*]
**mal|ap|ro|pos** (mal′ap rə pō′), *adv., adj.* at the wrong time or place: *a joke told malapropos* (adv.); *a malapropos comment* (adj.). [< French *mal à propos* badly for the purpose < *mal* (see etym. under **mal-**) + *à propos* apropos]
**ma|lar** (mā′lər), *adj., n.* **—*adj.*** of or having to do with the cheekbone or cheek.
**—*n.*** = cheekbone.
[< New Latin *malaris* < Latin *māla* jaw, cheek, cheekbone]
**ma|lar|i|a** (mə lãr′ē ə), *n.* **1** a disease that causes chills, fever, and sweating. Malaria is transmitted by the bite of anopheles mosquitoes which have previously bitten infected persons. It is caused by minute parasitic animals in the red blood corpuscles. **2** unwholesome or poisonous air, especially from marshes; miasma. [< Italian *malaria,* for *mala aria* (literally) bad air; *aria* < Latin *āēr, āēris* < Greek *āēr, āēros*]
**ma|lar|i|al** (mə lãr′ē əl), *adj.* **1** having malaria: *In this circulation of the contagion the presence of malarial man is indispensable* (British Medical Journal). **2** of or like malaria. **3** likely to cause, or associated with, malaria: *malarial swamps, malarial parasites.*
**ma|lar|i|an** (mə lãr′ē ən), *adj.* = malarial.
**ma|lar|i|ol|o|gist** (mə lãr′ē ol′ə jist), *n.* a person skilled in malariology.
**ma|lar|i|ol|o|gy** (mə lãr′ē ol′ə jē), *n.* the study of malaria, especially the relationship between malarial parasites and their hosts.
**ma|lar|i|ous** (mə lãr′ē əs), *adj.* = malarial.
**ma|lar|key** or **ma|lar|ky** (mə lär′kē), *n. U.S. Slang.* nonsense; baloney: *But this yogi business— ... sheer nonsense. Pure malarkey* (New Yorker).
**mal|ate** (mal′āt, mā′lāt), *n.* a salt or ester of malic acid. [< *mal*(ic acid) + *-ate*[2]]
**mal|a|thi|on** (mal′ə thī′on), *n.* a residual organic phosphate widely used against many types of insect pests. *Formula:* $C_{10}H_{19}O_6PS_2$ [< *mal*(ic) *a*(cid) + *thion*(ic)]
**Ma|la|wi|an** (mä lä′wē ən), *adj., n.* **—*adj.*** of or having to do with the republic of Malawi (the former Nyasaland) or its people.
**—*n.*** a native or inhabitant of Malawi.
**mal|ax|ate** (mal′ək sāt), *v.t.,* **-at|ed, -at|ing.** to soften by kneading, rubbing, mixing, making into a paste, or the like. [< Latin *malaxāre* (with English *-ate*[1]) < Greek *malássein*] **—mal′ax|a′tion,** *n.* **—mal′ax|a′tor,** *n.*
**Ma|lay** (mā′lā, mə lā′), *n., adj.* **—*n.*** **1** a member of a brown-skinned people living in the Malay Peninsula and nearby islands. **2** their Indonesian language. **3** any one of a breed of chicken originating in India, having a long, muscular body and red and black plumage.
**—*adj.*** of the Malays, their country, or their language.
**Mal|a|ya|lam** (mal′ə yä′ləm), *n.* the Dravidian language spoken on the southwestern coast of India.
**Ma|lay|an** (mə lā′ən), *n., adj.* = Malay.
**Malayan bear,** = sun bear.
**Malay cat,** any one of a rare breed of cats having white fur and a curled tail.
**Ma|lay|o-Pol|y|ne|sian** (mə lā′ō pol′ə nē′zhən, -shən), *adj.* of or having to do with the Malays and Polynesians and the languages they speak; Austronesian.
**Ma|lay|sian** (mə lā′zhən, -shən), *adj., n.* **—*adj.*** of or having to do with Malaysia, its people, or their languages.
**—*n.*** a person born or living in Malaysia.
**mal|con|duct** (mal kon′dukt), *n.* bad or improper conduct, especially in office.
**mal|con|for|ma|tion** (mal′kon fôr mā′shən, -fər-), *n.* imperfect or faulty conformation, as of parts.
**mal|con|tent** (mal′kən tent′), *adj., n.* **—*adj.*** discontented; dissatisfied; rebellious: *A project was even formed by the malcontent troops to deliver Harlem into the hands of Orange* (John Lothrop Motley).
**—*n.*** a discontented or rebellious person: *It was pointed out that the Exhibition would serve as a rallying point ... for all the malcontents in Europe* (Lytton Strachey).
[< Old French *malcontent* < *mal-* mal- + *content* content[2]]
**mal|con|ten|ted** (mal′kən ten′tid), *adj.* discontented; malcontent: *"We are anxious to give the best possible service, and malcontented guests will be welcome to call at the office"* (Sunday Times). **—mal′con|tent′ed|ly,** *adv.* **—mal′con-tent′ed|ness,** *n.*
**mal de mer** (mȧl′ də mer′), *French.* seasickness.
**mal de ra|quette** (mȧl′ də rȧ ket′), *Canadian French.* snowshoe sickness.
**mal de siè|cle** (mȧl′ də sye′klə), sickness of the age: *All the belief systems that have served society for hundreds of years have gone, resulting in the modern mal de siècle* (New Scientist). [alteration of French *mal du siècle*]
**mal|de|vel|op|ment** (mal′di vel′əp mənt), *n.* the improper growth or maturity of an organ, nerve, or other part of an organism: *Babies are occasionally exposed to critical stresses which initiate many of the maldevelopments not seen until birth* (Scientific American).
**mal|dis|tri|bu|tion** (mal′dis trə byü′shən), *n.* improper or ineffective arrangement or apportionment: *Overproduction plus maldistribution equals bootlegging* (Wall Street Journal).
**Mal|div|i|an** (mal div′ē ən), *adj., n.* **—*adj.*** of or having to do with the Maldives, an island country in the Indian Ocean.
**—*n.*** a native or inhabitant of the Maldives.
**mal du pays** (mȧl′ dʏ pā ē′), *French.* homesickness.
**mal du siè|cle** (mȧl′ dʏ sye′klə), *French.* sickness of the age.
**male** (māl), *n., adj.* **—*n.*** **1** a man or boy; male human being. Males belong to the sex that, when mature, produce sperm. **2** any animal of the same sex as a man or boy. A rooster is a male. **3a** a flower having a stamen or stamens but no pistils. **b** a plant bearing only flowers with stamens.
**—*adj.*** **1a** of or having to do with men or boys: *the male love of fighting.* **b** composed or consisting of men or boys: *a male chorus.* **2** of or belonging to the sex that can father young: *a male dog. Bucks, bulls, and roosters are all male animals.* **3** *Botany.* **a** (of seed plants) having flowers which contain stamens but not pistils; staminate. **b** able to fertilize the female. The same plant may have both male and female flowers. **4** designating the projecting part of a connection, machine, or the like, which fits inside a corresponding part: *a male plug.* **5** of superior strength or vigor: *He is the most male of all these performers because he never weeps* (Edmund Wilson). [< Old French *male, masle,* and *mascle* < Latin *masculus* masculine (diminutive) < *mās, maris* male] **—male′ness,** *n.*
**—*Syn.*** *adj.* **1, 2, 3 Male, masculine, manly** mean having to do with men or the sex to which they belong. **Male** applies to plants, animals, or persons, and suggests only sex: *We have a male kitten.* **Masculine** applies to persons, things, or qualities, and suggests the characteristics (especially strength or vigor) more commonly associated with men and boys than women or girls: *She had a brisk, masculine stride.* **Manly** suggests admirable characteristics such as courage and honor more likely to be found in a mature man than in a boy: *The boy fought back with manly courage.*
**male-,** *combining form.* a variant of **mal-,** especially in borrowings from Latin, as in *maledict.*
**ma|le|ate** (mə lē′ət), *n.* a salt or ester of maleic acid.
**male chauvinism,** excessive male pride or exaggerated loyalty to members of the male sex: *Historically hampered by archaic laws and antique moral codes, European women ... taking a cue from their more combative sisters across the Atlantic, have launched their attack on male chauvinism* (Time).
**male chauvinist,** a person who exhibits male chauvinism; a man who regards himself as superior to women.
**Mal|e|cite** (mal′ə sīt), *n., pl.* **-cite** or **-cites.** an Indian of the Abnaki group of the Algonkian linguistic stock, living in New Brunswick, Canada.
**mal|e|dict** (mal′ə dikt), *adj., v. Archaic.* **—*adj.*** accursed: *As the wings of starlings bear them on In the cold season in large band and full, So doth that blast the spirits maledict* (Longfellow).
**—*v.t.*** to curse.
[< Latin *maledictus,* past participle of *maledīcere* < *male* ill, wrongly + *dīcere* speak]
**mal|e|dic|tion** (mal′ə dik′shən), *n.* a speaking evil of or to a person; curse: *menaces and maledictions against king and nobles* (Shakespeare). SYN: slander, execration, imprecation. [< Latin *maledictiō, -ōnis* < *maledīcere;* see etym. under **maledict.** See etym. of doublet **malison.**]
**mal|e|dic|to|ry** (mal′ə dik′tər ē), *adj.* characterized by or like malediction.
**mal|e|fac|tion** (mal′ə fak′shən), *n.* a crime; evil deed: *Guilty creatures ... have proclaimed their malefactions* (Shakespeare). [< Latin *malefactiō, -ōnis* < *malefacere* to do wrong < *male* wrongly + *facere* do]
**mal|e|fac|tor** (mal′ə fak′tər), *n.* a criminal; evildoer: *Rank and fortune were offered to any malefactor who would compass the murder* (John L. Motley). [< Latin *malefactor* < *malefacere* < *male* badly + *facere* do]
**mal|e|fac|tress** (mal′ə fak′tris), *n.* a woman malefactor.
**male fern,** a fern whose rhizomes and stipes yield an oleoresin used medically to eradicate the tapeworm.
**ma|lef|ic** (mə lef′ik), *adj.* producing evil or harm; baleful. [< Latin *maleficus,* related to *malefacere;* see etym. under **malefactor**]
**ma|lef|i|cence** (mə lef′ə səns), *n.* **1** the act or fact of doing evil or harm; harm; evil: *Who the perpetrator of this Parisian maleficence was, remained dark* (Thomas Carlyle). **2** evil character; harmfulness. [< Latin *maleficentia* < *maleficus* wicked < *male* badly + *facere* do]
**ma|lef|i|cent** (mə lef′ə sənt), *adj.* doing evil or harm; harmful; evil. [< *maleficence,* perhaps based on *beneficent*]
**male fig,** = caprifig.
**ma|le|ic acid** (mə lē′ik), a colorless, crystalline acid, isomeric with fumaric acid, produced by the distillation of malic acid. It is used in dyeing and in organic synthesis. *Formula:* $C_4H_4O_4$ [ultimately < *malic acid*]
**maleic anhydride,** a chemical used in making paints, synthetic resins, and dyes. *Formula:* $C_4H_2O_3$
**maleic hydrazide,** a hydrazine compound that affects the growth of plants. It is used to prevent the sprouting of stored potatoes and onions, retard leaf or flower development, and kill weeds. *Formula:* $C_4H_4N_2O_2$
**mal|e|kized rice** (mal′ə kīzd), a process of parboiling rice to retain its minerals and vitamins and preserve it for a longer time. [< *Malekized,* a trademark]
**ma|le|mute** or **ma|le|miut** (mä′lə myüt), *n.* = Alaskan malamute.
**mal|en|ten|du** (mȧl än tän dʏ′), *n., adj. French.*
**—*n.*** a misunderstanding; misinterpretation.
**—*adj.*** mistaken; misapprehended.
**male screw,** = external screw.
**male-ster|ile** (māl′ster′əl), *adj.* not having or producing male reproductive cells: *An advanced technique of breeding, using male-sterile parents*

*on one side has been employed to produce the desired hybrids* (London Times).

**ma|lev|o|lence** (mə lev′ə ləns), *n.* the wish that evil may happen to others; ill will; spite.

**ma|lev|o|lent** (mə lev′ə lənt), *adj.* wishing evil to happen to others; showing ill will; spiteful: *at the mercy of one whose purposes could not be other than malevolent* (Hawthorne). [< Old French *malivolent,* learned borrowing from Latin *malevolēns, -entis* < *male* ill + *volēns, -entis,* present participle of *velle* to wish] —**ma|lev′o|lent|ly,** *adv.*

**mal|fea|sance** (mal fē′zəns), *n.* official misconduct; violation of a public trust or duty: *A judge is guilty of malfeasance if he accepts a bribe.* [< French *malfaisance* < *mal-* badly, mal- + *faisant,* present participle of *faire* to do < Latin *facere*]
► See **feasance** for usage note.

**mal|fea|sant** (mal fē′zənt), *adj., n.* —*adj.* doing evil.
—*n.* an evildoer; malefactor.

**mal|for|ma|tion** (mal′fôr mā′shən), *n.* distorted or abnormal shape; faulty structure: *A hunchback has a malformation of the spine.*

**mal|formed** (mal fôrmd′), *adj.* badly shaped; having a faulty structure.

**mal|func|tion** (mal′fungk′shən), *n., v.* —*n.* **1** an improper functioning; failure to work or perform: *a malfunction of the body or in a machine. "Malfunction" is the most feared word a rocket scientist can hear* (Scientific American). **2** a disorder (of the body); sickness: *a gastrointestinal malfunction.*
—*v.i.* to function badly; work or perform improperly: *They are full of delicate pumps and valves that often malfunction* (Time).

**mal|gré** (mȧl grā′), *prep. French.* in spite of.

**mal|gré lui** (mȧl grā lwē′), *French.* in spite of himself: *He sat the war out, a "slacker malgré lui"* (Time).

**Ma|li|an** (mä′lē ən), *adj., n.* —*adj.* of or having to do with the republic of Mali (the former French Sudan) or its people.
—*n.* a native or inhabitant of Mali.

**mal|i|bu board** (mal′ə bü), a streamlined plastic surfboard, usually about 9 feet long. [< *Malibu* Beach, on the Pacific, in southern California]

**mal|ic** (mal′ik, mā′lik), *adj.* **1** of, having to do with, or obtained from apples. **2** of or having to do with malic acid. [< French *malique* < Latin *mālum* apple (< Doric Greek *mâlon*) + French *-ique* -ic]

**malic acid,** a colorless, crystalline acid found in apples and numerous other fruits, used in making certain salts and for aging wine. *Formula:* $C_4H_6O_5$

**mal|ice** (mal′is), *n.* **1** a wish to hurt or make suffer; active ill will; spite: *Lincoln asked the people of the North to act "with malice toward none, with charity for all." I never bore malice to a brave enemy for having done me an injury* (Scott). SYN: spitefulness, grudge, rancor. See syn. under **spite. 2** *Law.* intent to commit an act which will result in harm to another person without justification. [< Old French *malice,* learned borrowing from Latin *malitia* < *malus* evil]

**malice aforethought,** *Law.* malice (def. 2).

**ma|li|cious** (mə lish′əs), *adj.* **1** showing ill will; wishing to hurt or make suffer; spiteful: *I think that story is nothing more than malicious gossip. He cursed that blind and malicious power which delighted to cross his most deep-laid schemes* (William Godwin). **2** proceeding from malice: *malicious mischief.* [< Old French *malicius* (with English *-ous*) < Latin *malitiōsus* < *malitia;* see etym. under **malice**] —**ma|li′cious|ly,** *adv.* —**ma|li′cious|ness,** *n.*

**malicious mischief,** *Law.* damage to property without cause: *Vandals usually are guilty of malicious mischief.*

**ma|lif|er|ous** (mə lif′ər əs), *adj.* bringing evil; producing bad effects; unwholesome; unhealthful. [< Latin *malus* bad + English *-ferous*]

**ma|lign** (mə līn′), *v., adj.* —*v.t.* to speak evil of; slander: *You malign a generous person when you call him stingy. Have I not taken your part when you were maligned?* (Thackeray). [< Old French *malignier* < Late Latin *malignāre* < Latin *malignus;* see the adjective]
—*adj.* **1** evil; injurious: *Gambling often has a malign influence.* **2** hateful; malicious: *The devil ... with jealous leer malign Eyed them askance* (Milton). **3** very harmful; threatening to be fatal; cancerous: *a malign tumor.* [< Old French *maligne,* learned borrowing from Latin *malignus,* for *male genus* < *malus* evil, and *genus* < root of *gignere* beget] —**ma|lign′er,** *n.* —**ma|lign′ly,** *adv.*

**ma|lig|nance** (mə lig′nəns), *n.* = malignancy.

**ma|lig|nan|cy** (mə lig′nən sē), *n., pl.* **-cies. 1** malignant quality or tendency: *The malignancy of my fate might perhaps distemper yours* (Shakespeare). **2** *Medicine.* something malignant or diseased, such as a tumor.

**ma|lig|nant** (mə lig′nənt), *adj., n.* —*adj.* **1** very evil; very hateful; very malicious: *Events were fatally to prove ... that there are natures too malignant to be trusted or to be tamed* (John L. Motley). **2** very harmful; having an evil influence: *Unless the next word ... Have some malignant power upon my life* (Shakespeare). **3** very dangerous; causing or threatening to cause death: *A cancer is a malignant growth.* **4** *Archaic.* disaffected; malcontent.
—*n.* a malcontent: *The supporters of the Stuarts during the English Civil War were called malignants by their opponents.*
[< Late Latin *malignāns, -antis* acting from malice, present participle of *malignāre* to injure < Latin *malignus;* see etym. under **malign,** adjective] —**ma|lig′nant|ly,** *adv.*

**malignant hypertension,** essential hypertension characterized by a sudden and severe onset, which progresses rapidly.

**ma|lig|ni|ty** (mə lig′nə tē), *n., pl.* **-ties. 1** great malice; extreme hate or ill will: *Iago's soliloquy, the motive-hunting of a motiveless malignity—how awful it is!* (Samuel Taylor Coleridge). SYN: enmity. **2** great harmfulness; dangerous quality; deadliness: *the malignity of cancer.* **3** a malignant feeling or act. [< Old French *malignite,* learned borrowing from Latin *malignitās* < *malignus;* see etym. under **malign,** adjective]

**ma|li|hi|ni** (mä′li hē′nē), *n. Hawaiian.* a newcomer or visitor: *Soon after he arrives in Hawaii, a sweet lassitude creeps over the malihini* (Time).

**ma|lik** (mä′lik), *n.* a tribal chief in Pakistan. [ultimately < Arabic *mālik*]

**ma|lines** or **ma|line** (mə lēn′; *French* mȧ lēn′), *n.* **1** = Mechlin lace. **2** a thin, stiff, silk net used especially in dressmaking and in making women's hats. [< French *malines* < *Malines,* or *Mechlin,* a town in Belgium]

**ma|lin|ger** (mə ling′gər), *v.i.* to pretend to be sick or injured in order to escape work or duty; shirk: *Hastie examined him; and ... knew not ... whether the man was sick or malingering* (Robert Louis Stevenson). [< French *malingre* sickly < Old French, a proper name, perhaps < *mal-* mal- + *heingre* or *haingre* sick, haggard] —**ma|lin′ger|er,** *n.*

**Ma|lin|ke** or **Ma|lin|ké** (mə ling′kē, -kā), *n., pl.* **-ke** or **-ké, -kes** or **-kés. 1** a member of a Negro people of western Africa. **2** their Mandingo language. Also, **Mandinka.**

**mal|i|son** (mal′ə zən, -sən), *n. Archaic.* a malediction; curse: *Farewell, and my malison abide with thee!* (Charles Kingsley). [< Old French *maleïson,* or *maleïçon* < Latin *maledictiō, -ōnis.* See etym. of doublet **malediction.**]

**mal|kin** (mô′kin), *n. British Dialect.* **1** an untidy woman; a slut; slattern. **2** a scarecrow. **3** a cat. **4** a mop. **5** *Scottish.* a hare. Also, **maukin, mawkin.** [diminutive form of *Maud,* a proper name]

**mall**[1] (môl, mal), *n.* **1** a shaded walk; public walk or promenade. **2** a central walk in a shopping center. **3a** the mallet used to strike the ball in the game of pall-mall. **b** the game pall-mall. **c** the alley on which the game is played. [< Old French *mail, and maul* mallet < Latin *malleus* hammer. Compare etym. under **maul.**]

**mall**[2] (môl), *n., v.t.* = maul.

**mal|lard** (mal′ərd), *n., pl.* **-lards** or (*collectively*) **-lard.** a wild duck found in Europe, northern Asia, and North America. The male has a greenish-black head and a white band around its neck. Many domestic ducks are descended from mallards. [< Old French *mallart,* apparently < *male;* see etym. under **male**]

**mal|le|a|bil|i|ty** (mal′ē ə bil′ə tē), *n.* malleable quality or condition: *Manganese increases the malleability of steel.* (*Figurative.*) *The Japanese, individually and socially, has a malleability which makes it possible for him to incorporate ... varied elements* (Atlantic).

**mal|le|a|ble** (mal′ē ə bəl), *adj.* **1** that can be hammered or pressed in various shapes without being broken. Gold, silver, copper, and tin are malleable; they can be beaten into thin sheets. **2** *Figurative.* adaptable; yielding: *A malleable person can adjust to changed plans. Human nature is often malleable ... where religious interests are concerned* (John Lothrop Motley). [< Old French *malleable* < Latin *malleus* hammer + Old French *-able* -able] —**mal′le|a|ble|ness,** *n.*

**malleable cast iron,** white cast iron made tough and malleable by long heating at a high temperature followed by slow cooling.

**malleable iron, 1** = malleable cast iron. **2** = wrought iron.

**mal|lee** (mal′ē), *n.* **1** any eucalyptus of several dwarf Australian kinds that sometimes form large areas of brushwood. **2** such brushwood. [< the Australian name]

**mal|le|in** (mal′ē ən), *n.* a product of the glanders bacillus, used in the mallein test. [< New Latin *malleus* glanders (< Latin *malleus* hammer) + English *-in*]

**mallein test,** a test for glanders in which mallein is injected into the animal's eye. If the animal is diseased, inflammation of the eye covering occurs with a pussy discharge.

**mal|le|muck** (mal′ə muk), *n.* any one of various large sea birds, such as the fulmar or the albatross. [< Dutch *mallemok,* perhaps < *mal* foolish < *mok* gull; or perhaps alteration of a Greenland Eskimo word]

**mal|le|o|lar** (mə lē′ə lər), *adj.* of or having to do with the malleolus.

**mal|le|o|lus** (mə lē′ə ləs), *n., pl.* **-li** (-lī). the bony part that sticks out on either side of the ankle. [< Latin *malleolus* (diminutive) < *malleus* hammer]

**mal|let** (mal′it), *n.* a kind of hammer with a head of wood or hard rubber, used to drive a chisel or other tool. Specially shaped mallets are used to play croquet and polo. Light mallets are used to play some musical instruments. [< Old French *maillet* (diminutive) < *mail* < Latin *malleus* hammer. Compare etym. under **mall**[1], **maul.**]

**mal|le|us** (mal′ē əs), *n., pl.* **mal|le|i** (mal′ē ī). the outermost of the three small bones in the middle ear of mammals, shaped like a hammer; hammer. See picture under **ear**[1]. [< Latin *malleus* hammer]

**mal|low** (mal′ō), *n.* **1** an ornamental plant with purple, pink, or white, five-petaled flowers, and hairy leaves and stems. **2** any one of various other plants of the mallow family, such as the marsh mallow. [Old English *mealwe* < Latin *malva.* See etym. of doublet **mauve.**]

***mallow family,** a group of dicotyledonous herbs, shrubs, and trees, most of which have sticky, gummy juice, and flowers shaped like those of the hollyhock. The family includes the mallow, hollyhock, cotton, okra, hibiscus, and althea.

***mallow family**

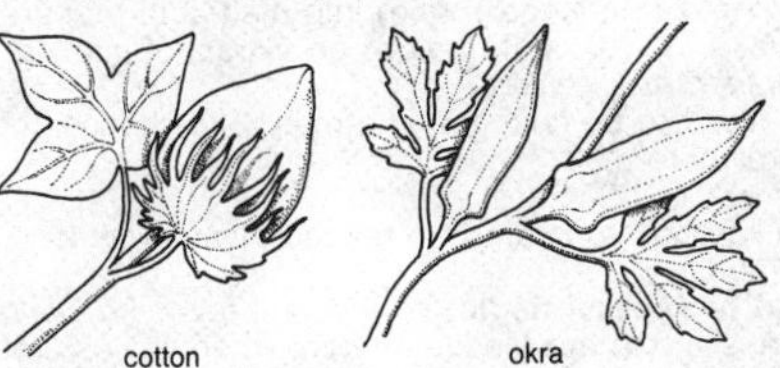


**mallow rose,** any one of certain plants of the mallow family having rose-colored flowers; rose mallow.

**malm** (mäm), *n. British.* **1** a soft, friable, grayish limestone. **2** *Dialect.* a light, loamy soil containing chalk. [Old English *mealm-,* in *mealmstān* malm stone. See related etym. at **meal**[2].]

**malm|sey** (mäm′zē), *n.* a strong, sweet wine, originally made in Greece. [< Medieval Latin *malmasia,* alteration of Greek *Monembasia,* a Greek seaport. See etym. of doublets **malvasia, malvoisie.**]

**mal|nour|ished** (mal nėr′isht), *adj.* improperly nourished: *The malnourished American eats virtually no breakfast, has a light lunch and gorges on his evening meal* (Science News Letter).

**mal|nu|tri|tion** (mal′nü trish′ən, -nyü-), *n.* a poorly nourished condition. People suffer from malnutrition because of eating the wrong kinds of food as well as from lack of food.

**mal|nu|tri|tioned** (mal′nü trish′ənd, -nyü-), *adj.* suffering from malnutrition; malnourished.

**mal|oc|clu|sion** (mal′ə klü′zhən), *n.* failure of teeth opposite each other in the upper and lower jaws to close or meet properly against each other. [< *mal-* + *occlusion*]

**mal|o|dor** (mal ō′dər), *n.* a bad smell; stench. [< *mal-* + *odor*]

**mal|o|dor|ous** (mal ō′dər əs), *adj.* smelling bad: *A pestilent, malodorous home of dirt and disease* (The Century). SYN: unsavory, fetid. —**mal|o′dor|ous|ly,** *adv.* —**mal|o′dor|ous|ness,** *n.*

**ma|lo|nic acid** (mə lō′nik, -lon′ik), a white, crystalline dicarboxylic acid readily decomposed by heat, derived from malic acid by oxidation. *Formula:* $C_3H_4O_4$ [< French *malonique,* alteration of *malique* (*acide*) malic (acid)]

**malonic ester,** a colorless liquid used as a chemical intermediate. *Formula:* $C_7H_{12}O_4$

**mal|pais** (mal′pīs), *n.* a volcanic rock formation characterized by a rough and jagged surface. [American English < Spanish *mal país* bad country, ultimately < Latin *malus* bad, and *pāgus* district]

**mal|pigh|i|a|ceous** (mal pig′ē ā′shəs), *adj.* belonging to a family of dicotyledonous tropical

---

**Pronunciation Key:** hat, āge, cãre, fär; let, ēqual, tėrm; it, īce; hot, ōpen, ôrder; oil, out; cup, pu̇t, rüle; child; long; thin; ᴛʜen; zh, measure; ə represents **a** in about, **e** in taken, **i** in pencil, **o** in lemon, **u** in circus.

trees and shrubs with yellow or red flowers, some of which are grown for ornament. [< New Latin *Malpighiaceae* the order name (< *Malpighia* the typical genus < Marcello *Malpighi,* 1628-1694, an Italian anatomist) + English *-ous*]

**Mal|pigh|i|an** (mal pig′ē ən), *adj.* of, having to do with, or discovered by Marcello Malpighi (1628-1694), an Italian anatomist.

**Malpighian body** or **corpuscle,** = renal corpuscle.

**Malpighian layer,** the deeper part of the epidermis, consisting of living cells which have not become hardened.

**Malpighian tube, tubule,** or **vessel,** a tube-shaped gland in insects and arachnids that is connected to the alimentary canal and serves as an excretory organ.

**Malpighian tuft,** a tuft of capillaries in the kidney.

**mal|posed** (mal pōzd′), *adj.* badly placed: *teeth malposed in the jaw* (Lancet).

**mal|po|si|tion** (mal′pə zish′ən), *n.* a faulty or wrong position, especially of a part or organ of the body or of a fetus in the uterus.

**mal|prac|tice** (mal prak′tis), *n.* **1** criminal neglect or wrong treatment of a patient by a doctor or dentist: *A professional brother, prosecuted for malpractice, is always sure you will do what you can to clear him* (Josiah G. Holland). **2** wrong practice or conduct in any official or professional position; misconduct: *We took pains ... to correct the malpractice of the men* (John Colborne).

**mal|prac|ti|tion|er** (mal′prak tish′ə nər), *n.* a person guilty of malpractice.

**malt** (môlt), *n., v., adj.* —*n.* **1** barley or other grain soaked in water until it sprouts, and then dried and aged. Malt has a sweet taste and is used in making beer and ale. **2** *Informal.* beer or ale.
—*v.t.* **1** to change (grain) into malt. **2** to prepare, make, or treat with malt or an extract of malt: *a malted milk shake.*
—*v.i.* **1** to be changed into malt. **2** to change grain into malt.
—*adj.* of or containing malt.
[Old English *mealt.* See related etym. at **melt, smelt.**]

**Mal|ta fever** (môl′tə), = undulant fever. [< *Malta,* an island in the Mediterranean, where it was first studied in goats]

**malt|ase** (môl′tās), *n.* an enzyme, present in saliva and other body juices and in yeast, that changes maltose to dextrose.

**malt|ed milk** (môl′tid), **1** a soluble powder made of dried milk, malted barley, and wheat flour. **2** a drink prepared by mixing this powder with milk and flavoring, and often ice cream.

**Mal|tese** (mol tēz′, -tēs′), *n., pl.* **-tese,** *adj.* —*n.* **1** a person born or living in Malta, an island in the Mediterranean, south of Sicily. **2** the native language of Malta. It is a form of Arabic with many Italian words. **3** any one of a breed of small dogs with long, silky, white hair and usually weighing between 2 and 7 pounds. It was popular as a lap dog among well-to-do Greeks and Romans.
—*adj.* **1** of Malta, its people, or their language. **2** of or having to do with the religious and military order of the Knights of Malta.

**Maltese cat,** a kind of short-haired, bluish-gray domestic cat.

**Maltese cross, 1** a type of cross with four equal arms resembling arrowheads pointed toward the center. See diagram under **cross. 2** = scarlet lychnis.

**Maltese fever,** = Malta fever.

**Maltese goat,** any one of a breed of goats native to Malta, raised for their milk.

**Maltese lace, 1** a pillow lace of silk or linen of the guipure kind. **2** a machine-made lace of coarse cotton thread.

**malt extract,** a sugary substance obtained by soaking malt in water.

**mal|tha** (mal′thə), *n.* **1** any one of various cements or mortars, especially one containing bitumen. **2** any one of various natural mixtures of hydrocarbons, such as ozocerite. **3** a black, tar-like substance formed from the drying of petroleum. [< Latin *maltha* < Greek *máltha,* or *málthē*]

**Mal|thu|sian** (mal thü′zhən, -zē ən), *adj., n.*
—*adj.* of or having to do with Malthus or his theory that the world's population tends to increase faster than the food supply, and that poverty and misery are inevitable unless this trend is checked by war, famine, birth control, or other means.
—*n.* a believer in this theory.
[< Thomas R. *Malthus,* 1766-1834, an English social economist + *-ian*]

**Mal|thu|sian|ism** (mal thü′zhə niz əm, -zē ə-), *n.* the theories of Malthus and his followers.

**malt liquor,** beer, ale, or other alcoholic liquor made with malt.

**malt|ose** (môl′tōs), *n.* a white, crystalline sugar made by the action of various enzymes on starch; malt sugar. It is formed in the body during digestion. Maltose is used commercially in brewing and distilling alcoholic liquors. *Formula:* $C_{12}H_{22}O_{11}\cdot H_2O$ [< French *maltose* < *malt* (< English *malt*) + *-ose* -ose[2]]

**mal|treat** (mal trēt′), *v.t.* to treat roughly or cruelly; abuse: *Only very mean persons maltreat animals. Many monasteries were robbed, many clerical persons maimed and maltreated* (John L. Motley). [< French *maltraiter* < *mal-* mal- + Old French *traiter* to treat]

**mal|treat|ment** (mal trēt′mənt), *n.* rough or cruel treatment; abuse.

**malt|ster** (môlt′stər), *n.* a person who makes or sells malt.

**malt sugar,** = maltose.

**malt|y** (môl′tē), *adj.,* **malt|i|er, malt|i|est. 1** of or like malt: *The bread would be soft, clammy, greyish and malty* (Michael Donovan). **2** addicted to the use of malt liquor. **3** *Slang.* drunk.

**mal|va|ceous** (mal vā′shəs), *adj.* of or belonging to the mallow family. [< Latin *malvāceus* < *malva* a mallow]

**mal|va|si|a** (mal′və sē′ə), *n.* **1** a variety of sweet grape used to make malmsey. **2** = malmsey. [< Italian < *malvasia,* alteration of Greek *Monembasia* a Greek seaport. See etym. of doublets **malmsey, malvoisie.**]

**mal|va|si|an** (mal′və sē′ən), *adj.* of, made from, or containing malvasia or malmsey: *malvasian liquor.*

**mal|ver|sa|tion** (mal′vər sā′shən), *n.* corrupt conduct in a position of trust, as extortion or fraud: *Cardonnel was turned out of the House of Commons for malversation of public money* (Thackeray). [< Middle French *malversation* < *malverser* behave wrongly (in office) < *mal-* mal- + *verser* < Latin *versārī* conduct oneself, be active in]

**mal|voi|sie** (mal′voi zē, -və-), *n.* **1** = malmsey. **2** = malvasia (def. 1). [alteration of Middle English *malevesie* < Old French < alteration of Greek *Monembasia.* See etym. of doublets **malvasia, malmsey.**]

**ma|ma** (mä′mə; *especially British* mə mä′), *n.* mother: *Mama, it was all your own fault* (Oliver Goldsmith). [compare etym. under **mamma[1]**]

**ma|man** (má mäɴ′), *n. French.* mother; mama.

**ma|ma-san** (mä′mə sän′), *n., pl.* **-san** or **-sans.** a matronly native woman in Japan, Korea, Vietnam, or certain other countries of Asia, often the head of a family or other group. [< Japanese *mama* mama, mother + *-san,* an honorific title]

**mama's boy,** *U.S. Informal.* a boy or man lacking normal masculine interests or unwilling to accept the responsibilities of manhood; sissy. Also, **mamma's boy.**

**mam|ba** (mam′bə), *n.* any one of a genus of long, slender snakes of Central and South Africa, whose bite is poisonous. Mambas belong to the same family as the cobras but are hoodless. [< Kaffir *imamba*]

**mam|bo** (mäm′bō), *n., pl.* **-bos,** *v.,* **-boed, -bo|ing.** —*n.* **1** a kind of rumba of Caribbean origin with a syncopated four-beat rhythm, the accent on the third beat. **2** the music for this dance, with a heavy beat.
—*v.i.* to dance the mambo: *I mamboed into the kitchen* (Atlantic).
[< Cuban Spanish *mambo*]

**mam|e|luke** (mam′ə lük), *n.* a slave in Moslem countries.

**Mam|e|luke** (mam′ə lük), *n.* a member of a military group that ruled Egypt from about 1250 to 1517 and had great power until 1811. The Mamelukes were originally slaves. [< Arabic *mamlūk* slave]

**ma|mey** (ma mā′, -mē′), *n.* = mammee.

**Mam|luk** (mam′lük), *n.* = Mameluke.

**mam|ma[1]** (mä′mə; *especially British* mə mä′), *n.* = mother. [reduplication of infantile sound. Compare Latin *mamma,* Greek *mámmē.*]

**mam|ma[2]** (mam′ə), *n., pl.* **mam|mae** (mam′ē). = mammary gland. [< Latin *mamma* breast]

**mam|mal** (mam′əl), *n.* any one of a class of animals that are warm-blooded, that have a backbone, that usually have hair, and that feed their young with milk from the mothers' breasts. Human beings, horses, cattle, dogs, lions, bats, rats, cats, and whales are mammals. [(originally) mammals, Anglicization of *Mammalia,* plural, ultimately < Latin *mamma* breast]

**Mam|ma|li|a** (ma mā′lē ə, -māl′yə), *n. pl.* the class of vertebrates comprising the mammals.

**mam|ma|li|an** (ma mā′lē ən, -māl′yən), *adj., n.*
—*adj.* of or belonging to the mammals.
—*n.* one of the mammals.

**mam|mal|o|gist** (ma mal′ə jist), *n.* an expert in mammalogy.

**mam|mal|o|gy** (ma mal′ə jē), *n.* the branch of zoology that deals with mammals.

**mam|ma mi|a** (mäm′mä mē′ä), *Italian.* **1** an exclamation, as of surprise, alarm, or frustration: *There are tax forms, statements of account, car registration papers, insurance policies, mamma mia, everything to be filled in and checked* (Manchester Guardian Weekly). **2** (literally) mother of mine.

**mam|ma|ry** (mam′ər ē), *adj.* of or having to do with the mammae or breasts.

**mammary gland,** the milk-producing gland of female mammals; mamma.

**mamma's boy,** = mama's boy.

**mam|ma|to-cu|mu|lus** or **mam|ma|to|cu|mu|lus** (ma mā′tō kyü′myə ləs), *n., pl.* **-li** (-lī). a cumulus cloud with rounded protuberances or festoons on the lower surface. It is usually a sign of rain. [< Latin *mammātus* (literally) having mammae + English *cumulus*]

**mam|mee** (ma mē′, -mā′), *n.* **1** a tall, tropical American tree with fragrant white flowers and a large, edible fruit. **2** the large, edible fruit of this tree. **3** the sapodilla. **4** the marmalade tree or its fruit. Also, **mamey.** [< Spanish *mamey* < Arawak (Haiti)]

**mammee apple,** the fruit of the mammee.

**mam|mer** (mam′ər), *British Dialect.* —*v.i.* to mutter; stammer; hesitate in speech or in thought: *I wonder ... What you would ask me, that I should deny, Or stand so mammering on* (Shakespeare).
—*v.t.* to confuse; perplex.
[imitative]

**mam|met** (mam′it), *n.* = maumet.

**mam|mif|er|ous** (ma mif′ər əs), *adj.* having mammae or breasts; mammalian. [< Latin *mamma* breast + English *-ferous*]

**mam|mil|la** (ma mil′ə), *n., pl.* **-mil|lae** (-mil′ē). **1** the nipple of the female breast; teat. **2** any nipple-shaped organ or protuberance. [< Latin *mamilla* (diminutive) < *mamma* mamma[2]]

**mam|mil|lar|y** (mam′ə ler′ē), *adj.* **1** of, having to do with, or like a mammilla. **2** having rounded protuberances, as a mineral.

**mam|mil|late** (mam′ə lāt), *adj.* having mammillae or nipples, or nipple-shaped protuberances.

**mam|mil|lat|ed** (mam′ə lā′tid), *adj.* = mammillate.

**mam|mock** (mam′ək), *n., v.* —*n. Archaic or British Dialect.* a scrap; fragment; shred.
—*v.t.* to break, cut, or tear into mammocks.
[origin uncertain]

**mam|mo|gram** (mam′ə gram), *n.* an X-ray picture of the breast. [< Latin *mamma* breast + English *-gram[1]*]

**mam|mo|graph** (mam′ə graf, -gräf), *n.* = mammogram.

**mam|mog|ra|phy** (ma mog′rə fē), *n.* X-ray examination of the breast.

**mam|mon** (mam′ən), *n.* riches thought of as an evil; material wealth: *the worship of mammon.* [< Latin *mammōna* < Greek *mamōnâs* < Aramaic *māmōnā* riches]

**Mam|mon** (mam′ən), *n.* a personification of riches as an evil spirit or god, or a soulless wordly force: *Mammon wins his way where Seraphs might despair* (Byron).

**mam|mon|ism** (mam′ə niz əm), *n.* devotion to the pursuit of riches; greed for wealth.

**Mam|mon|ism** (mam′ə niz əm), *n.* the worship of Mammon: *It was necessary to protect the Lord's Day against Mammonism* (London Daily News).

**mam|mon|ist** (mam′ə nist), *n.* a person devoted to the pursuit of riches.

**mam|mon|ite** (mam′ə nīt), *n.* = mammonist.

**mam|mo|plas|ty** (mam′ə plas′tē), *n.* plastic surgery of the breast. [< Latin *mamma* breast + English *-plasty*]

**mam|moth** (mam′əth), *n., adj.* —*n.* **1** a very large kind of elephant with a hairy skin and long curved tusks. The last mammoth died about 10,000 years ago. Mammoths lived during the Pleistocene. **2** *Figurative.* anything huge or gigantic: *Year by year such mammoths as Boulder Dam pile up the sediment that makes their reservoirs shallower* (Harper's).
—*adj.* huge; gigantic: *Digging the Panama Canal was a mammoth undertaking.* **SYN:** colossal, immense.
[< earlier Russian *mamot*]

**mam|mo|troph|ic** (mam′ə trôf′ik), *adj.* stimulating the mammary glands to give milk. [< Latin *mamma* breast + English *trophic*]

**mammotrophic hormone,** = prolactin.

**mam|my** (mam′ē), *n., pl.* **-mies. 1** mamma; mother (used especially in the Appalachians): *These too were greeted ... "daddy and mammy"* (Southern Literary Messenger). **2** a Negro woman who takes care of white children, or is a servant in a white household: *Like most Southern children, I was brought up and cared for by a "black mammy"* (R. D. Evans).

**mammy wagon,** a light truck used as a bus in the rural areas of western Africa.

**mam|pa|lon** (mam′pə lon), *n.* a small, otterlike, viverrine animal of Borneo, having webbed feet and living in and out of water. [probably < a native name]

**man** (man), *n., pl.* **men,** *v.,* **manned, man|ning,** *adj., interj.* —*n.* **1** an adult male person. When a boy grows up, he becomes a man. *When I became a man, I put away childish things* (I Corinthians 13:11). **2** a human being; person: *All men are created equal* (Declaration of Independence). *No man can be sure of the future.* SYN: individual, being, mortal. **3** the human race; all human beings: *Man likes company. Man has existed for thousands of years. Man shall not live by bread alone* (Matthew 4:4). SYN: humanity, mankind. **4** *Zoology.* a human being classified as belonging to the genus *Homo,* of which there is now only one species, *Homo sapiens,* characterized by high mental development. **5** a male follower, servant, or employee: *Robin Hood and his merry men; the men at the factory.* SYN: valet, attendant. **6a** a husband: *man and wife.* **b** a male lover; suitor. **7** one of the pieces that is moved about on the board in such games as chess, checkers, or backgammon. **8** a person characterized by manly qualities: *He was every inch a man. His life was gentle, and the elements So mix'd in him that Nature might stand up and say to all the world, "This was a man!"* (Shakespeare). **9** manly character or courage. **10** a form of address formerly implying contempt, impatience, or the like, but now largely of no emotional coloration: *Here, read it, read it, man* (Benjamin Disraeli). **11** *Archaic.* a vassal; liegeman.
—*v.t.* **1** to supply with men: *Sailors man a ship.* **2** to serve or operate; get ready to operate: *Man the guns.* **3** *Figurative.* to make courageous or strong; brace: *The captive manned himself to endure torture.* **4** (in falconry) to accustom (a hawk) to the presence of men; tame.
—*adj.* male: *a man dancer.*
—*interj. Informal.* an exclamation of surprise, joy, excitement, or other emotion, or for effect: *Man, what a player! Man, that's some car!*
**act the man,** to be courageous: *The young sailor acted the man in every way.*
**as a man,** from a human point of view: *He spoke as a man, not merely as a soldier.*
**as one man,** with complete agreement; unanimously: *The crowd voted as one man.*
**be one's own man, a** to be free to do as one pleases: *So Constance Nevill may marry whom she pleases, and Tony Lumpkin is his own man again* (Oliver Goldsmith). **b** to have complete control of oneself: *The Royal progress on Saturday will be as a sign ... that the King is indeed his own man again* (London Daily Graphic).
**man alive!** *U.S. Informal.* an exclamation or mild oath: *Man alive! What an exciting ball game!*
**man and boy,** from boyhood on; as a youth and as an adult: *... had been a peace officer, man and boy, for half a century* (Dickens).
**man for man,** without exception; to a man: *The top Indian civil servants impressed me as man for man the ablest people in any civil service with which I have had experience* (Milton Friedman).
**men,** the common soldiers or sailors, as distinguished from the officers: *The English had lost more than 2,400 officers and men* (James T. Wheeler).
**my good man,** a condescending form of address, as to an inferior: *Come here, my good man.*
**the man** or **the Man, a** the essential human being: *Style is less important than the man.* **b** *U.S. Slang.* the police: *Look out, here comes the man!* **c** *U.S. Slang.* the white man; white society: *The demonstrations, I think, suggested to "the man" that tokenism won't make it and that he has to come to grips with the problem right now* (New York Times).
**to a man,** without exception; all: *They obeyed him, to a man.*
**wise man of Gotham.** See under **Gotham.**
[Old English *mann* human being]
▶ **man, gentleman.** *Man* is now generally preferred to the more pretentious *gentleman,* unless a note of special courtesy or respect is desired.

**man.,** manual.

**Man.,** 1 Manila (paper). 2 Manitoba.

**ma|na** (mä′nä), *n.* (in the mythology of the Pacific Islands) an impersonal supernatural power or influence that flowed through objects, persons, or places. A man who succeeded at a difficult task had a large amount of mana. [< Maori *mana*]

**man-a|bout-town** (man′ə bout toun′), *n., pl.* **men-a|bout-town.** a man who spends much of his time in clubs, theaters, fashionable restaurants, and other places high society frequents.

**man|a|cle** (man′ə kəl), *n., v.,* **-cled, -cling.** —*n.* **1** Often, **manacles.** a handcuff; fetter for the hands: *We'll put you ... in manacles, Then reason safely with you* (Shakespeare). **2** *Figurative.* anything that fetters; restraint: *The manacles of the all-building law* (Shakespeare).
—*v.t.* **1** to put manacles on; handcuff: *The pirates manacled their prisoners.* **2** *Figurative.* to restrain; hamper; fetter.
[< Old French *manicle* < Latin *manicula* (diminutive) < *manicae* sleeves, manacles < *manus, -ūs* hand]

**ma|na|da** (mə nä′də), *n. Southwestern U.S.* **1** a drove of horses, especially breeding mares. **2** a herd of cattle. [< Spanish *manada*]

**man|age** (man′ij), *v.,* **-aged, -ag|ing,** *n.*
—*v.t.* **1** to guide or handle with skill or authority; control; direct: *They hired a man to manage the business. A good rider manages his horse well. Only his mother could manage him.* **2** to succeed in doing something; contrive; arrange: *I shall manage to keep warm with this blanket. How did you manage to paint the whole house in a week? The clumsy waiter managed to spill the soup. He had managed to remain poor all of his life* (Edmund Wilson). **3** to make use of: *He manages tools well.* **4** to get one's way with (a person) by craft or by flattering: *He thoroughly understood the art of managing men, particularly his superiors* (John L. Motley). **5** to use or change for one's own purpose; manipulate: *There has never been an administration ... so studiously engaged in trying to manage news* (Columbia University Forum). **6** to train or handle (a horse) in the manège. **7** *Archaic.* to treat carefully; use sparingly; husband: *to manage one's health, to manage resources.*
—*v.i.* **1** to conduct affairs. **2** to get along: *We managed on very little money. He managed a whole year upon the proceeds* (William Dean Howells).
—*n.* **1** = manège. **2** *Archaic.* management.
[earlier *manege* < Italian *maneggiare* handle or train (horses) < *mano* hand < Latin *manus*]
—*Syn. v.t.* **1 Manage, conduct, direct** mean to guide or handle with authority. **Manage** emphasizes the idea of skillful handling of people and details so as to get results: *He manages a large department store.* **Conduct** emphasizes the idea of supervising the action of a group working together for something: *The teacher conducted the class on a tour of the museum.* **Direct** emphasizes the idea of guiding the affairs or actions of a group by giving advice and instructions to be followed: *An ornithologist directed our bird conservation program.*

**man|age|a|bil|i|ty** (man′i jə bil′ə tē), *n.* the condition or quality of being manageable.

**man|age|a|ble** (man′i jə bəl), *adj.* that can be managed; controllable: *a package of manageable size. A meek and manageable child* (Elizabeth Barrett Browning). SYN: tractable, wieldy. —**man′age|a|ble|ness,** *n.* —**man′age|a|bly,** *adv.*

**man|aged currency** (man′ijd), currency whose purchasing power is regulated by government.

**man|age|ment** (man′ij mənt), *n.* **1** a managing or handling; control; direction: *Bad management caused the bank's failure.* SYN: guidance, regulation. **2** the persons who manage a business or an institution: *a dispute between labor and management. The management of the store decided to increase the size of the parking lot.* SYN: administration. **3** administrative skill; skillful dealing or use: *Mark with what management their tribes divide* (John Dryden). *In the management of the heroic couplet Dryden has never been equalled* (Macaulay).

**man|age|men|tal** (man′ij men′təl), *adj.* of or having to do with management; managerial.

**management consultant,** a person hired by a business firm to study its system of management and recommend necessary changes in it.

**management engineer,** = industrial engineer. —**management engineering.**

**man|ag|er** (man′i jər), *n.* **1** a person who manages: *the manager of a baseball team.* **2** a person in charge of the management of a business or an institution: *a bank manager.* SYN: director, executive, administrator. *Abbr:* Mgr. **3** a person skilled in managing such things as affairs, time, or money: *She was neat, honest, and a good manager.* **4** *British.* a theatrical producer.

**man|ag|er|ess** (man′i jər is), *n.* a woman manager.

**man|a|ge|ri|al** (man′ə jir′ē əl), *adj.* of a manager; having to do with management: *Executives are given training in managerial methods.* —**man′a|ge′ri|al|ly,** *adv.*

**man|a|ge|ri|al|ist** (man′ə jir′ē ə list), *n.* a person who believes in managerial planning or control in business, government, or other organizations.

**man|ag|er|ship** (man′i jər ship), *n.* the position or control of a manager.

**man|ag|ing editor** (man′i jing), the executive in charge of the practical management of a publishing company or publication, such as of a newspaper, magazine, or encyclopedia. The editors of the different production departments are usually responsible to the managing editor.

**man|a|kin** (man′ə kin), *n.* **1** any one of various small, bright-colored, songless birds of tropical America. **2** = manikin. [variant of *manikin*]

**man amplifier,** a mechanical device attached to a person's body enabling him to exert much greater strength or force than usual.

**ma|ña|na** (mä nyä′nä), *n., adv. Southwestern U.S.* tomorrow; some time: *Business will await, meetings, friends, jobs will be for mañana* (New Yorker). [American English < Spanish *mañana* < Latin *māne* morning]

**man-ape** (man′āp′), *n.* a primitive fossil man of the early Pleistocene, having both human and subhuman characteristics.

**Ma|nas|seh** (mə nas′ə), *n.* **1** Joseph's elder son (in the Bible, Genesis 41:50-51). **2** an Israelite tribe that descended from him (in the Bible, Joshua 17:1-6). **3** a king of ancient Judah who ruled from about 692 to 638 B.C. (in the Bible, II Kings 21:1-18).

**man-at-arms** (man′ət ärmz′), *n., pl.* **men-at-arms.** **1** = soldier. **2** a heavily armed soldier on horseback.

**man|a|tee** (man′ə tē′), *n.* a large water mammal with two flippers and a flat, oval tail; sea cow. Manatees live in the warm, shallow waters of the Atlantic near the coasts of tropical America and Africa and feed on water plants. They belong to the same order as the dugong. *The manatee ... by its quiet breathing and gentle breasts probably originated the haunting mermaid legends* (Punch). [< Spanish *manati* < Carib (perhaps West Indies) *manati* (female) breast]

**ma|nav|el|ins** or **ma|nav|il|ins** (mə nav′ə linz), *n.pl. Nautical Slang.* miscellaneous gear or equipment. [origin uncertain]

**Man|ches|ter terrier** (man′ches′tər, -chə stər), any one of a breed of slender, lively dogs, originally developed in England to catch rats, having a short, shiny-black coat marked with tan. There is a toy variety, weighing under 12 pounds, and a standard variety, from 12 to 22 pounds. [< *Manchester,* a city in England]

**man|chet** (man′chit), *n. Archaic.* **1** bread made of the finest white flour. **2** a small loaf or roll of such bread. [origin uncertain]

**man-child** (man′chīld′), *n., pl.* **men-chil|dren.** a male child: *Bring forth men-children only* (Shakespeare).

**man|chi|neel** (man′chə nēl′), *n.* a tropical American tree of the spurge family, having a milky, poisonous sap, and a bitter, poisonous fruit somewhat like an apple. [< French *mancenille* < Spanish *manzanilla* (diminutive) < *manzana* apple, alteration of Old Spanish *mazana* < Latin *matiāna* (*māla*), plural, Matian fruit, probably < C. *Matius* Calvena, author of a work on cookery]

**Man|chu** (man′chü), *n., adj.* —*n.* **1** a member of a Mongoloid people living in Manchuria, who conquered China in 1644 and ruled it until 1912. **2** their Ural-Altaic language.
—*adj.* of the Manchus, their country, or their language.

**Man|chu|ri|an** (man chür′ē ən), *adj., n.* —*adj.* of or having to do with Manchuria, a region in northeastern China, or its people.
—*n.* a person born or living in Manchuria, a region in northeastern China.

**man|ci|ple** (man′sə pəl), *n.* a person who buys provisions for a college or other institution; steward. [< Old French *manciple, mancipe,* learned borrowing from Latin *mancipium* acquisition; a purchase, slave < *manceps, -cipis* purchaser < *manū capere* to take in hand]

**Man|cu|ni|an** (mang kyü′nē ən), *adj., n.* —*adj.* of or belonging to Manchester, a city in western England.
—*n.* a native or inhabitant of Manchester, England.
[< Latin *Mancunium* Manchester + English *-an*]

**Man|dae|an** (man dē′ən), *n., adj.* —*n.* **1** a follower of an ancient religious sect, holding Gnostic beliefs with many Jewish and Zoroastrian elements, still surviving in Iraq. **2** an Aramaic dialect used in the writings of this sect.
—*adj.* of the Mandaeans or Mandaean. Also, **Mandean.**
[< Aramaic *mandayyā* (translation of Greek *Gnōstikoi* the knowing ones, Gnostics) < *mandā* knowledge]

**man|da|la** (man′də lə), *n.* the symbol of contemplation or meditation in Buddhism and Hinduism. It is represented by a square within a circle. [< Sanskrit *maṇḍala* circle]

**man|da|mus** (man dā′məs), *n., v.,* **-mused, -mus|ing.** —*n. Law.* **1** a written order from a higher court to a lower court, an official, a city, a corporation, or other body or group, directing that a certain act be done: *He sought ... an order of*

**Pronunciation Key:** hat, āge, cãre, fär; let, ēqual, tėrm; it, īce; hot, ōpen, ôrder; oil, out; cup, pu̇t, rüle; child; long; thin; ᴛʜen; zh, measure; ə represents a in about, e in taken, i in pencil, o in lemon, u in circus.

*mandamus to restore his name to the register* (London Times). **2** any one of various writs or mandates formerly issued by an English sovereign, directing that certain acts be performed.
—***v.t.*** *Informal.* to serve or threaten with a mandamus.
[< Latin *mandāmus* we order, 1st plural present indicative active of *mandāre*]

**Man|dan** (man′dan), *n., pl.* **-dan** or **dans. 1** a member of a western plains tribe of North American Indians, famous as traders. **2** the Siouan language of this tribe.

**man|da|rin** (man′dər in), *n., adj.* —***n.*** **1** an official of high rank under the Chinese Empire. There were nine ranks, distinguished by the color of a certain button worn on the cap. **2** a person important in political or intellectual circles, who is usually elderly or conservative: *In their first week in office they have had some cool advice from the mandarins of British administration, the top civil servants* (Anthony Lewis). **3** a small, sweet, spicy citrus fruit with a thin, orange-colored, very loose peel and segments that separate easily. **4** the small tree or shrub it grows on. **5** a bright, reddish-orange dye.
—***adj.*** of, or characteristic of, mandarins; especially intellectual and conservative: *a mandarin style, mandarin coteries. The future of Vietnam does not belong to a mandarin type of leadership* (London Times).
[< Portuguese *mandarim* < Malay *mantri* < Hindustani < Sanskrit *mantrin* advisor < a root *man-* to think]

**Man|da|rin** (man′dər in), *n.* **1** the main dialect of the Chinese language under the Manchu dynasty, spoken by officials and educated people. **2** the chief Chinese dialect, spoken in northern China, especially the dialect of Peking.

**man|da|rin|ate** (man′dər ə nāt), *n.* **1** the office or authority of a mandarin. **2** mandarins as a group. **3** government by mandarins.

***mandarin coat**, a woman's long, brocaded coat for evening wear, usually of silk, having slits on the sides, elbow-length sleeves, a mandarin collar, and fastened with frogs or buttons. It is patterned after the coats worn formerly by mandarins.

***mandarin coat**

**mandarin collar**, a narrow, turned-up collar of uniform width, with a slightly tapered split at the front.

**mandarin duck**, a crested duck with variegated plumage of purple, green, chestnut, and white, native to China, where it is a symbol of conjugal affection.

**man|da|rin|ic** (man′də rin′ik), *adj.* having to do with or characteristic of a mandarin: *The first business of any writer, especially of any critical writer, is not to be mandarinic and tedious* (London Times).

**man|da|rin|ism** (man′də rə niz′əm), *n.* **1** the qualities or characteristics of mandarins, especially intellectualism or conservatism: *French literature as a whole has not fallen into mandarinism [but] has remained in close touch with life and society* (Francis Steegmuller). **2** a mandarin style or form of expression: ... *the exquisite mandarinisms of the centuries-old Peking opera* (Time).

**mandarin orange**, = mandarin (def. 3).

**man|da|tar|y** (man′də ter′ē), *n., pl.* **-tar|ies. 1** a nation to which a mandate over another country has been given. **2** *Law.* a person to whom a mandate is given. [< Late Latin *mandātārius* < Latin *mandātum* a mandate]

**man|date** (*n.* man′dāt, -dit; *v.* man′dāt), *n., v.,* **-dat|ed, -dat|ing.** —***n.*** **1** a command or order: *a royal mandate. The mandate of God to His creature man is: Work!* (Thomas Carlyle). **SYN:** edict, behest, injunction. **2** an order from a higher court or official to a lower one: *Towards the close of Adams's term, Georgia had bid defiance to the mandates of the Supreme Court* (Theodore Roosevelt). **3** a direction or authority given to a government by the votes of the people in an election: *After his election the governor said he had a mandate to increase taxes.* **4** a commission given to one nation by a group of nations to administer the government and affairs of a territory or colony. The system of mandates established after World War I was administered by the League of Nations. *The character of the Mandate must differ according to the stage of the development of the people* (League of Nations Covenant). **5** a mandated territory or colony. **6** an order issued by the Pope stating that a certain person should be given a benefice. **7** a contract in Roman and civil law, by which one person requests another to act for him gratuitously, agreeing to indemnify him against losses. **8** any contract of agency. **9** a command in ancient Rome from the emperor, especially to the governor of a province.
—***v.t.*** to put (a territory or colony) under the administration of another nation: *The result of the late war has been to eliminate Germany from the map, her territories being mandated to the British and other nations* (Times Literary Supplement).
[< Latin *mandātum,* noun use of neuter past participle of *mandāre* to order]

**man|da|tor** (man dā′tər), *n.* the giver of a mandate.

**man|da|to|ry** (man′də tôr′ē, -tōr′-), *adj., n., pl.* **-ries.** —***adj.*** **1** of or containing a mandate; giving a command or order: *a mandatory statement.* **2** required by a command or order: *a mandatory sentence for manslaughter.* **3** of, having to do with, or having received a mandate, as a nation commissioned to take care of a dependent territory.
—***n.*** = mandatary. —**man′da|to′ri|ly,** *adv.*

**man-day** (man′dā′), *n.* one day of one man's work, used as a unit in figuring cost, time, or other constituent, of production.

**Man|de** (män′dā), *n., pl.* **-de** or **-des,** *adj.* = Mandingo.

**Man|de|an** (man dē′ən), *n., adj.* = Mandaean.

**man|di|ble** (man′də bəl), *n.* **1** an organ in insects for seizing and biting: *The ant seized the dead fly with its mandibles.* **2** either part of a bird's beak. **3** a jaw, especially the lower jaw. See picture under **face.** [< Late Latin *mandibula* < Latin *mandere* to chew]

**man|dib|u|lar** (man dib′yə lər), *adj., n.* —***adj.*** of, having to do with, or like a mandible.
—***n.*** = mandible (def. 3).

**man|dib|u|late** (man dib′yə lit, -lāt), *adj., n.* —***adj.*** **1** having a mandible or mandibles; having jaws, as most animals. **2** adapted for chewing.
—***n.*** a mandibulate insect.

**Man|din|gan** (man ding′gən), *adj., n.* —***adj.*** of or having to do with the Mandingo or their language.
—***n.*** **1** = Mandingo. **2** the language of the Mandingo.

**Man|din|go** (man ding′gō), *n., pl.* **-go, -gos,** or **-goes,** *adj.* —***n.*** **1** a member of a group of Negro peoples forming a linguistic group in western Africa. **2** any one of the languages spoken by these peoples, forming a branch of the Niger-Congo language group.
—***adj.*** of or having to do with the Mandingo or their languages.

**Man|din|ka** (man ding′kā, -kə), *n., pl.* **-ka** or **-kas.** = Malinke.

**man|di|o|ca** (man′dē ō′kə), *n.* **1** the edible root of the manioc, a staple starch foodstuff of tropical South America. **2** the manioc or cassava plant. [< Portuguese *mandioca* < Tupi (Brazil) *manioca.* Compare etym. under **manioc.**]

**man|do|la** (man dō′lə), *n.* a small lute of the 1600's and 1700's with a slightly curved handle where the tuning pegs were placed. [< Italian *mandola;* see etym. under **mandolin**]

***man|do|lin** (man′də lin, man′də lin′), *n.* a musical instrument with a pear-shaped body. It has four to six pairs of metal strings played with a pick, and a fretted neck. [< French *mandoline* < Italian *mandolino* (diminutive) < *mandola,* variant of *mandora* < Latin *pandūra* < Greek *pandoûrā* three-stringed instrument]

***mandolin**

**man|do|lin|ist** (man′də lə nist, man′də lin′ist), *n.* a player on the mandolin.

**man|dor|la** (man dôr′lə; *Italian* män′dôr lä), *n., pl.* **-las,** *Italian* **-le** (-lā). **1** an almond-shaped or pointed oval panel, space, or piece, used as decoration. **2** = vesica piscis. [< Italian *mandorla* (literally) almond]

**man|drag|o|ra** (man drag′ər ə), *n.* = mandrake. [< Latin *mandragoras* < Greek *mandragóras*]

**man|drake** (man′drāk), *n.* **1** a poisonous herb having a very short stem and a thick, often forked root thought to resemble the human form. There are several kinds all belonging to the nightshade family and native to southern Europe and Asia. The mandrake was formerly used in medicine because of its emetic and narcotic properties. **2** the root, supposed in legend to cry out when pulled up from the ground. Eating the root was believed to aid in conceiving a child. *And shrieks like mandrakes torn out of the earth* (Shakespeare). **3** *U.S.* the May apple. [alteration (perhaps by folk etymology, with *man* and *drake*[2]) of Middle English *mandragge,* short for *mandragora* < Latin *mandragoras* < Greek *mandragóras*]

**man|drel** or **man|dril** (man′drəl), *n.* **1** a spindle or bar of a lathe that supports the material being turned. **2** a rod or core around which metal or other material is shaped. [< alteration of French *mandrin*]

**man|drill** (man′drəl), *n.* a large, fierce baboon of western Africa. The face of the male mandrill is marked with blue and scarlet. See picture under **monkey.** [perhaps < *man* + *drill*[4] baboon]

**Mandt's guillemot** (mänts), a variety of guillemot that lives in the arctic regions of America. [< Martin W. von *Mandt,* a German naturalist of the 1800's]

**mane** (mān), *n.* **1** the long, heavy hair on the back of or around the neck of a horse, lion, and certain other animals. **2** a person's hair when long and thick. [Old English *manu*]

**man-eat|er** (man′ē′tər), *n.* **1** = cannibal. **2** a lion, tiger, shark, or other animal that attacks or is supposed to attack human beings for food. **3** *Figurative.* **a** a woman who is very aggressive toward men: *He is half-heartedly fighting off the advances of a man-eater named Margaret* (Time). **b** any very aggressive person: *a corporate man-eater.*

**man-eat|ing** (man′ē′ting), *adj.* **1** eating or devouring human beings: *a man-eating shark.* **2** *Figurative.* that is a man-eater; very aggressive: *a man-eating woman, a man-eating politician.*

**ma|neb** (man′eb), *n.* an organic brown powder used as a fungicide on the leaves of fruit trees, vegetables, and cereal grasses. [< *man*(ganese) *e*(thylene)*b*(isdithiocarbamate), its chemical composition]

**maned** (mānd), *adj.* having a mane: *a maned animal.*

**maned wolf**, a long-legged animal resembling a red fox, found in the plains of Argentina, Paraguay, and Brazil.

**ma|nège** or **ma|nege** (mə nezh′, -nāzh′), *n.* **1** the art of training and riding horses; horsemanship. **2** the movements of a trained horse. **3** a school for training horses and teaching horsemanship; riding school. [< French *manège* < Italian *maneggio* < *maneggiare* to manage, handle]

**ma|nes** or **Ma|nes** (mā′nēz), *n.pl.* **1** (in ancient Roman belief) the deified souls of dead ancestors, together with the gods of the lower world. **2** the spirit or shade of a particular dead person. [< Latin *mānēs,* plural, related to *mānus* good]

**ma|neu|ver** (mə nü′vər), *n., v.,* **-vered, -ver|ing.**
—***n.*** **1** a planned movement of troops, warships, or tanks: *Every year the army and navy hold maneuvers for practice.* **2** *Figurative.* a skillful plan or movement; clever trick: *When we refused to use his idea, he tried to force it on us by a series of maneuvers.* **3** *Figurative.* the management of affairs by scheming: *when corruption shall be added to intrigue and maneuver in elections* (John Adams).
—***v.i.*** **1** to perform maneuvers: *The tanks maneuvered toward the front lines.* **2** *Figurative.* to plan skillfully; use clever tricks; scheme: *A scheming person is always maneuvering for some advantage.*
—***v.t.*** **1** to cause (troops, warships, or tanks) to perform maneuvers: *The admiral maneuvered his ships in the battle plan.* **2** *Figurative.* to force by skillful plans; get by clever tricks: *She maneuvered her lazy brother out of bed.* **3** *Figurative.* to move or manipulate skillfully: *He maneuvered his car through the heavy traffic with ease.* Also, *especially British,* **manoeuvre.**
**maneuvers**, a training exercise between two or more military or naval units, simulating combat situations: *The new soldiers were divided into opposing teams and went out on maneuvers in the field.*
[< French *manœuvre* manipulation, Old French *maneuvre* < Vulgar Latin *manuopera* < *manuoperāre* < Latin *manūoperārī* to work by hand. See etym. of doublet **manure.**] —**ma|neu′ver|er,** *n.*

**ma|neu|ver|a|bil|i|ty** (mə nü′vər ə bil′ə tē), *n.* the quality or power of being maneuverable: *The paraboloid type of antenna has many advantages, especially maneuverability in scanning the sky* (Scientific American).

**ma|neu|ver|a|ble** (mə nü′vər ə bəl), *adj.* that can

be maneuvered: *maneuverable scenery, a maneuverable gearshift.*

**ma|neu|vra|bil|i|ty** (mə nü′vrə bil′ə tē), *n.* = maneuverability.

**ma|neu|vra|ble** (mə nü′vrə bəl), *adj.* = maneuverable.

**man-for-man** (man′fər man′), *adj.* = man-to-man (def. 2).

**man Friday**, **1** a faithful servant or indispensable assistant. **2** Robinson Crusoe's servant, whom he called *"my man Friday."*

**man|ful** (man′fəl), *adj.* manly; brave; resolute: *explorers' manful attempts to reach the summit.* —**man′ful|ly**, *adv.* —**man′ful|ness**, *n.*

**mang|a|bey** (mang′gə bā), *n.* a tropical African monkey having a very long tail, noted for the ease with which it is domesticated. [< *Mangabey*, Madagascar]

**man|ga|nate** (mang′gə nāt), *n.* a salt of manganic acid. [< *mangan*(ic acid) + *-ate*[2]]

***man|ga|nese** (mang′gə nēs, -nēz), *n.* a hard, brittle, grayish-white, metallic chemical element. It resembles iron but is not magnetic and is softer. Manganese is used chiefly in making alloys of steel, fertilizers, paints, insecticides, and industrial chemicals. [< French *manganèse* < Italian *manganese*, alteration of Medieval Latin *magnesia;* see etym. under **magnesia**]

***manganese**

| symbol | atomic number | atomic weight | oxidation state |
|---|---|---|---|
| Mn | 25 | 54.9380 | 2, 3, 4, 7 |

**manganese dioxide**, a black crystal, or brownish-black powder, used especially in making dyes, paints, and dry-cell batteries, as an oxidizing agent. *Formula:* $MnO_2$

**manganese spar**, = rhodonite.

**manganese steel**, a tough, durable cast steel containing up to 14 per cent of manganese.

**manganese sulfate**, a white salt or rose-colored crystals derived by the action of sulfuric acid on manganese dioxide, used in fungicides, paints, dyes, and especially as an ingredient in fertilizers. *Formula:* $MnSO_4$

**man|gan|ic** (man gan′ik, mang gan′-), *adj.* **1** of or like manganese. **2** containing manganese, especially with a valence of six.

**manganic acid**, an acid known only in the form of its salts. *Formula:* $H_2MnO_4$

**man|ga|nif|er|ous** (mang′gə nif′ər əs), *adj.* containing manganese.

**Man|ga|nin** (mang′gə nin), *n. Trademark.* an alloy of copper, manganese, and nickel, widely used in making various types of resistors.

**man|ga|nite** (mang′gə nīt), *n.* **1** a mineral, a hydrated oxide of manganese, occurring in steel-gray or iron-black masses or crystals. *Formula:* $Mn_2O_3{\cdot}H_2O$ **2** any salt of a group containing manganese with a valence of four, formed from several manganese hydroxides, and considered to be an acid.

**man|ga|nous** (mang′gə nəs, man gan′əs), *adj.* containing manganese, especially with a valence of two.

**mange** (mānj), *n.* a skin disease of dogs, horses, sheep and cattle, caused by parasitic mites. It is much like the itch in man. Tiny skin sores form, and the hair or wool falls out in patches. [< Old French *manjüe*, or *mangeue* the itch < *mangier* to eat < Latin *mandūcāre* to chew < *mandere*]

**man|gel** (mang′gəl), *n.* = mangel-wurzel.

**man|gel-wur|zel** (mang′gəl wėr′zəl), *n.* a large, coarse variety of beet, used as food for cattle. [< German *Mangelwurzel*, variant of *Mangoldwurzel* beet root]

**man|ger** (mān′jər), *n.* **1** a box or trough in a barn or stable, built against the wall at the right height for horses or cattle to eat from: *And she ... wrapped him in swaddling clothes, and laid him in a manger; because there was no room for them in the inn* (Luke 2:7). *His hay storage ... equipped with a movable manger, reduces labor* (Newsweek). **2** *Nautical.* a small space at the forward end of a deck, divided off by a bulkhead or board to shut off any water entering by the hawseholes.
[< Old French *mangeoire*, or *maingeure* < Vulgar Latin *mandūcātoria* feeding trough < Latin *mandūcāre* to chew < *mandere*]

**man|gle**[1] (mang′gəl), *v.t.*, **-gled, -gling. 1** to cut or tear (the flesh) roughly: *The two cats bit and clawed until both were much mangled.* **SYN**: lacerate, mutilate. **2** *Figurative.* to spoil; ruin: *The child mangled the music because it was too difficult for her to play. My mangled youth lies dead beneath the heap* (Francis Thompson). [< Anglo-French *mangler*, perhaps < *mahangler* (frequentative) < Old French *mahaigner* to maim < *mahaigne* injury] —**man′gler**, *n.*

**man|gle**[2] (mang′gəl), *n., v.*, **-gled, -gling.** —*n.* a machine with rollers for pressing and smoothing sheets, towels, and other flat things after washing.
—*v.t.* to press or make smooth in a mangle.
[< Dutch *mangel* < Middle Dutch *mange* < Late Latin *manganum* < Greek *mánganon* contrivance] —**man′gler**, *n.*

**man|go** (mang′gō), *n., pl.* **-goes** or **-gos. 1** a slightly sour, juicy, oval fruit with a thick, yellowish-red rind. Mangoes are eaten ripe or pickled when green. **2** the tropical evergreen tree that it grows on. The mango belongs to the cashew family. See picture under **cashew family**. [< Portuguese *manga* < Malay *mangga* < Tamil *mānkāy*]

**man-god** (man′god′), *n., pl.* **men-gods. 1** one who is both a man and a god: *Prometheus, in the eyes of the Greek, was a man-god* (North American Review). **2** a deified man: *The Christian world was sunk in the worship ... of men-gods* (Thomas P. Thompson). **3** a god having the form of a man: *The old idolaters cut down a tree and made a man-god ... out of it* (North American Review).

**man|gold** (mang′gəld), *n.* = mangel-wurzel.

**man|go|nel** (mang′gə nel), *n.* a machine formerly used in war for throwing large stones or other objects. [< Old French *mangonel* < Vulgar Latin *manganellum* (diminutive) < Late Latin *manganum;* see etym. under **mangle**[2]]

**man|go|steen** (mang′gə stēn), *n.* **1** a juicy, edible fruit with a thick, reddish-purple rind. **2** the tree of southeast Asia that it grows on. [< Malay *mangqustan*]

***man|grove** (mang′grōv), *n.* **1** any one of a genus of tropical trees and shrubs having branches that send down many roots that look like additional trunks. Mangroves grow in coastal swamps and along the banks of brackish rivers. **2** any one of several similar plants or trees of tropical America and the southern coast of the United States, whose flowers are rich in nectar. [< Spanish *mangle*, earlier *mangue;* origin uncertain; spelling influenced by English *grove*]

***mangrove**
definition 1

**man|gy** (mān′jē), *adj.*, **-gi|er, -gi|est. 1** having or caused by the mange; like the mange; with the hair falling out. **2** shabby and dirty: *a mangy dog.* **3** *Informal, Figurative.* mean; contemptible. —**man′gi|ly**, *adv.* —**man′gi|ness**, *n.*

**man|han|dle** (man′han′dəl), *v.t.*, **-dled, -dling. 1** to treat roughly; pull or push about: *If you worry me ... I'll catch you and manhandle you, and you'll die* (Rudyard Kipling). **2** to move by human strength, without mechanical appliances: *The larger weapons will be marked by electricity, but are also capable of being manhandled* (London Times).

**Man|hat|tan** (man hat′ən), *n.* a cocktail consisting of rye whiskey, sweet vermouth, and usually bitters. [< *Manhattan*, a borough of New York]

**Man|hat|tan|ese** (man hat′ə nēz′, -nēs′), *adj., n., pl.* **-ese.** —*adj.* of the borough of Manhattan; having to do with Manhattan, New York, or its inhabitants: *I was Manhattanese, friendly, and proud* (Walt Whitman). —*n.* = Manhattanite.

**Man|hat|tan|ite** (man hat′ə nīt), *n.* a native or inhabitant of the borough of Manhattan: *Even a Manhattanite can find his subway way to the Coney Island Aquarium* (New York Times).

**Manhattan Project**, the code name for the secret project of the Manhattan District, an organization originally responsible for atomic research on the atomic bomb: *The Manhattan Project was initiated because the physicists had come up with a revolutionary new concept (namely the nuclear chain reaction)* (Wall Street Journal).

**man|hole** (man′hōl′), *n.* a hole through which a workman can enter a sewer, steam boiler, or underground chamber containing street wiring, gas or water mains, or telephone lines, to inspect or repair them.

**man|hood** (man′hu̇d), *n.* **1** the condition or time of being a man: *The boy was about to enter manhood. The disappointment of manhood succeeds to the delusion of youth* (Benjamin Disraeli). **2** courage; manliness; character or qualities of a man: *Some civic manhood firm against the crowd* (Tennyson). *Peace hath higher tests of manhood than battle ever knew* (John Greenleaf Whittier). **SYN**: virility, bravery. **3** men as a group: *the manhood of the United States.* **4** the state or condition of being human; human nature: *Yea, Manhood hath a wider span And larger privilege of life than man* (James Russell Lowell).

**man-hour** (man′our′), *n.* one hour of work done by one man, used as a time unit in industry: *If progress continues, the materials used in clothing will not involve the man-hours of labor traditional in the industry* (Atlantic).

**man|hunt** (man′hunt′), *n.* **1** a widespread search for a criminal, escaped prisoner, or hostage: *It ended a manhunt conducted by hundreds of persons, including about 175 state patrolmen, FBI agents, sheriffs' deputies ...* (Chicago Tribune). **2** a dramatic entertainment based upon such a search.

**ma|ni|a** (mā′nē ə), *n.* **1** a kind of insanity characterized by great excitement; form or phase of mental disorder, characterized by extremes of joy or rage, uncontrolled and often violent activity, extravagant and irregular speech, and the like, often followed by depression. It is a recurring state in manic-depressive psychosis. **2** an unusual or unreasonable fondness; craze: *a mania for gardening, a mania for dancing. He has a mania for collecting old bottles.* [< Latin *mania* < Greek *maniā* madness < *mainesthai* rage, be mad]

**ma|ni|ac** (mā′nē ak), *n., adj.* —*n.* an insane person; raving lunatic; madman: *His eyes rolled like that of a maniac in his fever fit* (Scott).
—*adj.* insane; raving: *a maniac world.*
[< Late Latin *maniacus* < Latin *mania;* see etym. under **mania**]

**MANIAC** (mā′nē ak), *n.* a complex electronic computer used in the development of the hydrogen bomb and in other projects. [< *M*(athematical) *A*(nalyzer) *N*(umerical) *I*(ntegrator) *A*(nd) *C*(omputer)]

**ma|ni|a|cal** (mə nī′ə kəl), *adj.* **1** insane; raving. **2** of or characteristic of mania or a maniac: *His industry grew almost maniacal* (Lytton Strachey). —**ma|ni′a|cal|ly**, *adv.*

**ma|ni|a|kis** (mə nī′ə kis), *n.* a wide jeweled collar worn by the empress of the Byzantine empire in the Middle Ages. [< Greek *maniákēs* necklace]

**ma|nic** (mā′nik, man′ik), *adj.* **1** of or like mania: *to be in a manic phase.* **2** suffering from mania. [< Greek *manikos* mad < *maniā* madness, mania]

**man|ic-de|pres|sive** (man′ik di pres′iv), *adj., n.* —*adj.* having or characterized by alternating attacks of mania and depression: *manic-depressive psychosis.*
—*n.* a person who has this condition: *The man is a manic-depressive who brawls in his manic phases* (New Yorker).

**Man|i|che|an** or **Man|i|chae|an** (man′ə kē′ən), *n., adj.* —*n.* a member of a Gnostic sect, arising in Persia in the 200's A.D., compounded of Christian, Buddhistic, Zoroastrian, and other beliefs, and maintaining a theological dualism in which the body and matter were identified with darkness and evil, and the soul, striving to liberate itself, was identified with light and goodness.
—*adj.* of or having to do with the Manicheans or their doctrines.
[< Late Latin *Manichaeus* (< Late Greek *Manichaîos* < *Manichaîos* of Mani, founder of the sect) + English *-an*]

**Man|i|che|an|ism** or **Man|i|chae|an|ism** (man′ə kē′ə niz əm), *n.* = Manicheism.

**Man|i|chee** (man′ə kē), *n.* = Manichean.

**Man|i|che|ism** or **Man|i|chae|ism** (man′ə kē′iz əm), *n.* the doctrines of the Manicheans.

**man|i|cot|ti** (man′ə kot′ē), *n.* macaroni stuffed with cheese and baked in tomato sauce. [< Italian *manicotti*]

**man|i|cure** (man′ə kyu̇r), *v.*, **-cured, -cur|ing**, *n.* —*v.t., v.i.* **1** to care for (the hands and fingernails); trim, clean, and polish (the fingernails): *The lady manicured her hands after working in the garden.* **2** *Figurative.* to trim (a hedge, grounds, or other landscaping) carefully: *... showed him lounging in his weeds and his neighbors slavishly manicuring their lawns* (Maclean's).
—*n.* **1** the care of the hands and fingernails, especially trimming, cleaning, and polishing the fingernails: *The lady gave her hands a manicure after working in the garden.* **2** a single such treatment: *She went to the beauty parlor for a manicure.* **3** = manicurist.
[< French *manicure* < Latin *manus*, *-ūs* hand + *cūra* care]

**man|i|cur|ist** (man′ə kyu̇r′ist), *n.* a person whose work is caring for the hands and the fingernails.

**man|i|fest** (man′ə fest), *adj., v., n.* —*adj.* apparent to the eye or to the mind; plain; clear: *His*

**Pronunciation Key:** hat, āge, cãre, fär; let, ēqual, tėrm; it, īce; hot, ōpen, ôrder; oil, out; cup, pu̇t, rüle; child; long; thin; ᴛʜen; zh, measure; ə represents **a** in about, **e** in taken, **i** in pencil, **o** in lemon, **u** in circus.

*guilt was manifest. For nothing is secret, that shall not be made manifest* (Luke 8:17). SYN: obvious, evident, unmistakable.

—*v.t.* **1** to show plainly; display: *to manifest interest. There is nothing hid, which shall not be manifested* (Mark 4:22). SYN: exhibit, disclose, evidence, reveal. **2** to put beyond doubt; prove: *His dress ... manifested the economy of its owner by the number and nature of its repairs* (James Fenimore Cooper). **3a** to record (an item) in a ship's manifest. **b** to present the manifest of (a ship's cargo).

—*n.* **1** a list of the cargo of a ship or aircraft: *The line's manifests made interesting reading* (New York Times). **2** = bill of lading. **3a** manifestation; expression: *Jan Kadar and Elmar Klos ... have constructed a human drama that is a moving manifest of the dark dilemma that confronted all people who were caught as witnesses to Hitler's terrible crime* (Bosley Crowther). **b** = manifesto. **4** *Railroading.* a fast freight train; hot-shot. [< Latin *manifestus* palpable < *manus, ūs* hand + *-festus* (able to be) seized] —**man′i|fest′ly**, *adv.* —**man′i|fest′ness**, *n.*

**man|i|fes|tant** (man′ə fes′tənt), *n.* a person who takes part in a public demonstration.

**man|i|fes|ta|tion** (man′ə fes tā′shən), *n.* **1** the act or process of showing; making manifest. **2** the fact or condition of being manifested. **3** a thing or act that shows or proves: *Entering the burning building was a manifestation of his courage.* **4** a public demonstration by a government, political party, or other group, intended as a display of its power and determination to enforce some demand: *The manifestation planned by the party in power got off to a bad start. The principal manifestation of the British power was directed against Rangoon* (H. H. Wilson). **5** an occurrence or occasion in spiritualism in which a spiritual materialization is supposed to be demonstrated: *No manifestation occurred at the first séance.*

**manifest destiny**, *U.S. Historical.* the belief in the 1840's in the inevitable territorial expansion of the United States, especially as advocated by southern slaveholders who wished to extend slavery into new territories.

**man|i|fes|to** (man′ə fes′tō), *n., pl.* **-toes** or **-tos**, *v.,* **-toed, to|ing.** —*n.* a public declaration of intentions, purposes, or motives by an important person or group; proclamation: *The emperor issued a manifesto. A Labour Government ... would (as stated in the party's election manifesto) set up a new Ministry of Social Welfare* (London Times).

—*v.i.* to put forth a manifesto.

[< Italian *manifesto* < Latin *manifestus* manifest]

**man|i|fold** (man′ə fōld), *adj., n., v.* —*adj.* **1** of many kinds; many and various: *manifold duties. Attractions manifold* (Wordsworth). SYN: varied. **2** having many parts, features, or forms: *the manifold wisdom of God* (Ephesians 3:10); *a music strange and manifold* (Tennyson). *This changeful life, So manifold in cares* (William Cowper). **3** doing many things at the same time. **4** *Archaic.* being such in many ways: *a manifold fool.*

—*n.* **1** a pipe with several openings for connection with other pipes. **2** a pipe in an internal-combustion engine, connecting the cylinders in the engine with a main inlet or outlet. **3** one of many copies; copy made by a manifolder. **4** *Mathematics.* a topological space or surface: *Manifolds are objects of primary interest in present-day topology. They are spaces built by pasting together pieces that look like ordinary Euclidean space. If the dimension of the Euclidean space is n, the manifold is called n-dimensional. One way to study a manifold is to try to break it into simple pieces resembling triangles; if the procedure is successful, it is said that the manifold has been triangulated* (Irving Kaplansky).

—*v.t.* **1** to make many copies of. **2** to make manifold; multiply.

[Old English *manigfeald* < *manig* many + *feald* -fold] —**man′i|fold′ly**, *adv.* —**man′i|fold′ness**, *n.*

► See **manyfold** for usage note.

**man|i|fold|er** (man′ə fōl′dər), *n.* **1** a device for making copies of a letter, document, or the like, as with carbon paper. **2** a person who makes such copies.

**man|i|hot** (man′ə hot), *n.* any tropical American plant of a group of the spurge family, including the cassava and several varieties which yield a rubber. [< New Latin *Manihot* the genus name < French *manihot;* see etym. under **manioc**]

**man|i|kin** (man′ə kin), *n.* **1** a little man; dwarf. **2** = mannequin. **3** a model of the human body, used for teaching anatomy, surgery, or other physiological studies. Also, **manakin, mannikin.** [< Dutch *manneken* (diminutive) < *man* man]

**ma|nil|a** (mə nil′ə), *n.* **1** = Manila hemp. **2** = Manila paper. [< *Manila,* a city in the Philippines]

**Manila hemp**, a strong fiber made from the leaves of a Philippine plant, used especially for making ropes and fabrics; abaca.

**Manila paper**, a strong, brown or brownish-yellow paper, originally made from Manila hemp, used especially for wrapping and sketching.

**Manila rope**, a strong rope made from Manila hemp.

**ma|nil|la[1]** (mə nil′ə), *n.* = manila.

**ma|nil|la[2]** (mə nil′ə), *n.* the next to highest trump in some card games. [alteration of Spanish *malilla* (diminutive) < *mala,* feminine, (originally) bad]

**ma|nille** (mə nil′), *n.* = manilla[2].

**man in blue**, a policeman: *The middle classes especially ... used to regard the man in blue as the trusty guardian of their property* (Sunday Times).

**man in the middle**, the arbiter in a dispute.

**man in the moon**, a figure in the disk of the full moon popularly believed to resemble a man's face: *I was the Man in th' Moon, when time was* (Shakespeare).

**not know one from the man in the moon**, not to know one at all: *I don't know him from the man in the moon.*

**man in the street**, *U.S.* the average person, especially as typifying public opinion: *It was not read solely by naturalists and other scientists. The man in the street read it* (Science News Letter).

**man|i|oc** (man′ē ok, mā′nē-), *n.* = cassava. [< French *manioc,* and *manihot* < Tupi (Brazil) *manioca*]

**man|i|ple** (man′ə pəl), *n.* **1** a subdivision of the ancient Roman legion, containing 120 or 60 men. **2** a Eucharistic vestment, consisting of an ornamental band or strip of cloth worn on the left arm near the wrist. [< Latin *manipulus* (literally) a handful < *manus, -ūs* hand + root of *plēre* to fill]

**ma|nip|u|la|bil|i|ty** (mə nip′yə lə bil′ə tē), *n.* the quality or power of being manipulable.

**ma|nip|u|la|ble** (mə nip′yə lə bəl), *adj.* that can be manipulated: *Film is manipulable* (Walter Kerr). *Their tendency [is] to see society in terms of large manipulable masses of people* (John W. Aldridge).

**ma|nip|u|lar** (mə nip′yə lər), *adj., n.* —*adj.* **1** of or having to do with an ancient Roman maniple. **2** of or having to do with manipulation.

—*n.* a Roman soldier belonging to a maniple.

**ma|nip|u|lat|a|ble** (mə nip′yə lā′tə bəl), *adj.* = manipulable.

**ma|nip|u|late** (mə nip′yə lāt), *v.t.,* **-lat|ed, -lat|ing.** **1** to handle or treat, especially with skill: *The driver of an automobile manipulates the steering wheel and pedals. A sailboat is steered by manipulating the sails. A clever writer manipulates his characters and plot to create interest.* **2** *Figurative.* to manage by clever use of influence, especially unfair influence: *He so manipulated the ball team that he was elected captain although they really thought his brother would be a better leader. At 70, he was fighting price wars and manipulating stocks to form railroad combinations* (W. H. Baughn). **3** *Figurative.* to treat unfairly or dishonestly; change for one's own purpose or advantage: *That clerk stole money from the firm and manipulated the accounts to conceal his theft.* [< French *manipuler* (with English *-ate*[1]) < *maniple,* learned borrowing from Latin *manipulus* handful; see etym. under **maniple**]

**ma|nip|u|la|tion** (mə nip′yə lā′shən), *n.* **1** skillful handling or treatment: *Sometimes the individual must be anesthetized to straighten a fixed joint thru manipulation* (Chicago Tribune). **2** *Figurative.* clever use of influence, especially unfair influence. **3** a change made for one's own purpose or advantage.

**ma|nip|u|la|tive** (mə nip′yə lā′tiv), *adj.* **1** of or having to do with manipulation. **2** done by manipulation. —**ma|nip′u|la′tive|ly**, *adv.*

**ma|nip|u|la|tor** (mə nip′yə lā′tər), *n.* a person or thing that manipulates: (*Figurative.*) *I don't think they are reliable people. ... They are sophisticated, clever manipulators* (Wall Street Journal).

**ma|nip|u|la|to|ry** (mə nip′yə lə tôr′ē, -tōr′-), *adj.* = manipulative.

**man|i|to** (man′ə tō), *n., pl.* **-tos.** **1** a spirit worshiped by Algonkian Indians as a force of nature with supernatural powers; Great Spirit. **2** a supernatural or magic power believed by the Algonkians to be contained in every object and being. [< Algonkian (probably Narragansett) *manito* supernatural power]

**Man|i|to|ban** (man′ə tō′bən), *adj., n.* —*adj.* of or having to do with Manitoba, a province in Canada.

—*n.* a native or inhabitant of Manitoba.

**man|i|tou** or **man|i|tu** (man′ə tü), *n.* = manito.

**man jack**, *Slang.* a man: *While I realize there isn't a man jack alive who doesn't know the plot ...* (New Yorker).

**every man jack**, every one; every single one (referring to a man): *Send them all to bed—every man jack of them* (Charles Lamb).

**man|jak** or **man|jack** (man′jak), *n.* a form of bitumen found in Barbados and elsewhere, used especially in making varnish and for insulating electric cables. [< a native word]

**man-kill|er** (man′kil′ər), *n.* **1** something that kills people: *What is striking about lung cancer as a man-killer is its sudden rise* (Canada Month). **2** *Slang.* a femme fatale.

**man|kind** (man′kīnd′ *for 1;* man′kīnd′ *for 2*), *n.* **1** the human race; all human beings: *Let observation with extensive view Survey mankind from China to Peru* (Samuel Johnson). *To live in mankind is far more than to live in a name* (Vachel Lindsay). *The history of language is the history of mankind* (Greenough and Kittredge). **2** men; the male sex: *Mankind and womankind both like praise.*

**man|less** (man′lis), *adj.* **1** having no man. **2** without men.

**man|like** (man′līk′), *adj.* **1** like a man: *Under his forming hands a creature grew, Manlike, but different sex* (Milton). **2** suitable for a man: *From long association with men she had learnt a manlike reticence* (H. S. Merriman).

**man|li|ly** (man′lə lē), *adv.* in a manly manner.

**man|li|ness** (man′lē nis), *n.* manly quality; manly behavior.

**man lock**, an air lock or decompression chamber.

**man|ly** (man′lē), *adj.,* **-li|er, -li|est,** *adv.* —*adj.* **1** like a man; as a man should be; strong, frank, brave, noble, independent, and honorable: *On his father's death, the boy set to work in a manly way. Now clear the ring, for, hand to hand, The manly wrestlers take their stand* (Scott). *My aunt was a lady of large frame, strong mind, and great resolution ... a very manly woman* (Washington Irving). SYN: See syn. under **male**. **2** suitable for a man; masculine: *Boxing is a manly sport.*

—*adv. Archaic.* in a manly manner.

**man-made** (man′mād′), *adj.* made by man; not natural; artificial: *man-made laws, man-made radioactivity, a man-made satellite, man-made fibers and diamonds.*

**man|na** (man′ə), *n.* **1** the food miraculously supplied to the Israelites in the wilderness (in the Bible, Exodus 16:14-36). **2** *Figurative.* food for the soul or mind: *To some coffee-house I stray For news, the manna of a day* (Matthew Green). **3** *Figurative.* a much needed thing that is unexpectedly supplied: *Her inheritance came as manna from heaven.* **4** a sweet, pale-yellow, or whitish substance obtained from the bark of certain European ash trees, formerly used as a laxative. [Old English *manna* < Late Latin < Greek *mánna* < Hebrew *mān*]

**manna grass**, any one of a group of mostly aquatic grasses, grown as forage for cattle; meadow grass.

**manna gum**, an Australian eucalyptus tree that yields a crumblike, sugary substance.

**man|nan** (man′an, -ən), *n.* a polysaccharide found in plants which yields mannose upon hydrolysis. [< *mann*(ose) + *-an*]

**manned** (mand), *adj. Aeronautics.* **1** occupied by one or more persons assigned to control flight: *a manned aircraft, a manned bomber.* **2** occupied by one or more persons, but not under their control or guidance: *a manned satellite, a manned space vehicle.*

**man|ne|quin** (man′ə kin), *n.* **1** a figure of a person used by tailors, artists, and stores. **2** a woman whose work is wearing new clothes to show them to customers. Also, **manikin, mannikin.** [< French *mannequin* < Dutch *manneken;* see etym. under **manikin**]

**man|ner** (man′ər), *n.* **1** a way of doing, being done, or happening: *The trouble arose in this manner.* SYN: fashion. See syn. under **way**. **2** a way of acting or behaving: *an arrogant manner. She has a kind manner. Urbanity of manner* (G. K. Chesterton). *Her manner made me sensible that we stood upon no real terms of confidence* (Hawthorne). SYN: bearing, demeanor, deportment. **3** kind or kinds: *We saw all manner of birds in the forest. What manner of man art thou?* (Samuel Taylor Coleridge). **4** a characteristic or customary way; mode; fashion: *a house decorated in the Italian manner.* **5** a distinguished or fashionable air: *We country persons can have no manner at all* (Oliver Goldsmith). **6a** personal style, as in art, music, or writing: *an operatic manner of singing.* **b** a style characteristic of a particular artist, school, or period: *a painting in the manner of Picasso.* **c** affectation in style; mannerism.

**by all manner of means**, most certainly: *Yes, in God's name, and by all manner of means* (John Ruskin).

**by no manner of means**, not at all; under no circumstances: *"Basil" is by no manner of* *means an impeccable work of imperishable art* (Algernon Charles Swinburne).

**in a manner,** after a fashion; in one way; in one sense: *The bread is in a manner common* (I Samuel 21:5).

**in a manner of speaking,** as one might say; so to speak: *The cattle ... has been, in a manner of speaking, neglected* (Rolfe Boldrewood).

**make one's manners,** *U.S. Dialect.* to show one's good manners by a bow, curtsy, or handshake: *good children ... who made their manners when they came into her house* (Harriet Beecher Stowe).

**manners, a** polite ways of behaving: *He has no manners at the table. Oh! ... return to us again; And give us manners, virtue, freedom, power* (Wordsworth). **b** ways of behaving: *good manners, bad manners.* **c** customs; ways of living: *a comedy of manners.*

**to the manner born, a** accustomed since birth to some way or condition: *Though I am native here And to the manner born* (Shakespeare). **b** seeming to be naturally fitted for something: *a chef to the manner born.*

[< Anglo-French *manere,* Old French *maniere* way or mode of handling, ultimately < Latin *manuārius* belonging to the hand < *manus, -ūs* hand]

**man|nered** (man′ərd), *adj.* having many mannerisms; affected; artificial: *a mannered style of writing.*

**-mannered,** *combining form.* having ___ manners: *Well-mannered = having good manners. Mild-mannered = having mild manners.*

**man|ner|ism** (man′ə riz əm), *n.* **1** too much use of some manner in speaking, writing, or behaving: *In his official contacts [he] has been handicapped by the mannerism of the lecture hall* (New York Times). SYN: affectation. **2** an odd little trick; queer habit; peculiar way of acting: *the same little dainty mannerisms, the same quick turns and movements* (Charlotte Brontë). SYN: peculiarity.

**Man|ner|ism** (man′ə riz əm), *n.* a style of painting and architecture of the 1500's, chiefly Italian, which attempted to break away from the classical forms of the Renaissance by distorting scale, perspective, lighting effect, and the like, within a formal framework. Mannerism is characterized by graceful lines, elongated and abstract forms, and metallic colors with white highlights. Its rediscovery in the early part of the 1900's was due to its affinity with some movements in modern art.

**man|ner|ist** (man′ər ist), *n.* a person given to mannerism, especially an artist, musician, or writer.

**Man|ner|ist** (man′ər ist), *n., adj.* —*n.* a painter or architect whose work is characterized by Mannerism: *Tintoretto and El Greco are sometimes referred to as essentially Mannerists.*
—*adj.* of or representing Mannerism: *a Mannerist painting, a Mannerist architect.*

**man|ner|is|tic** (man′ər is′tik), *adj.* characterized by mannerisms. —**man′ner|is′ti|cal|ly,** *adv.*

**man|ner|less** (man′ər lis), *adj.* without good manners.

**man|ner|ly** (man′ər lē), *adj., adv.* —*adj.* having or showing good manners; polite: *It is not mannerly to contradict one's parents. Here is mannerly forbearance* (Shakespeare). SYN: courteous, civil, well-behaved.
—*adv.* politely; courteously: *When we have supp'd, We'll mannerly demand thee of thy story* (Shakespeare). —**man′ner|li|ness,** *n.*

**man|ners** (man′ərz), *n.pl.* See under **manner.**

**man|ni|kin** (man′ə kin), *n.* **1** = manikin. **2** = mannequin.

**man|nish** (man′ish), *adj.* **1** characteristic of a man: *a mannish way of holding a baby, a mannish argument.* **2** like a man, not a woman; imitating a man; masculine: *a mannish style of dress, a woman with a mannish walk.* —**man′nish|ly,** *adv.* —**man′nish|ness,** *n.*

**man|nite** (man′īt), *n.* = mannitol. [< *manna* + *-ite*[2]]

**man|nit|ic** (mə nit′ik), *adj.* of, containing, or derived from mannite, or mannitol.

**man|ni|tol** (man′ə tōl, -tol), *n.* a white, odorless, crystalline alcohol obtained from glucose, seaweed, or a variety of ash tree, occurring in three optically different forms. *Formula:* $C_6H_{14}O_6$ [< *mannit*(e) + *-ol*[1]]

**man|no|ga|lac|tan** (man′ō′gə lak′tən), *n.* the gum obtained from the seeds of the guar; guar gum. [< *manno*(se) + *galact*(ose) + (guar)*an* another name of the gum (because it contains large percentages of mannose and galactose)]

**man|nose** (man′ōs), *n.* a simple sugar, a hexose, obtained from the plant substance manna or by oxidation of mannitol. *Formula:* $C_6H_{12}O_6$ [< *manna* + *ose*[2]]

**ma|no** (mä′nō), *n. Southwestern U.S.* a hand grinding stone used by Mexicans and Indians. [American English < Spanish *mano* < Latin *manus* hand]

**ma|noeu|vre** (mə nü′vər), *n., v.i., v.t.,* **-vred, -vring.** *Especially British.* maneuver.

**Man of Galilee,** Jesus Christ.

**man of God, 1** a holy man; saint; prophet. **2** = clergyman.

**man of letters, 1** = writer. **2** a person who has a wide knowledge of literature.

**Man of Sorrows,** Jesus Christ (by traditional inference) (in the Bible, Isaiah 53:3).

**man of straw,** an imaginary person whose arguments can easily be proved wrong.

**man of the cloth,** = clergyman.

**man-of-the-earth** (man′əv ᴛʜē ėrth′), *n., pl.* **men-of-the-earth.** a trailing plant of the morning-glory family of the eastern United States having a very large root. [< the shape of the root]

**man of the house,** the man who is head of the household.

**man of the world,** a man who knows people and customs, and is tolerant of both: *Temple was a man of the world among men of letters* (Macaulay).

**man-of-war** (man′əv wôr′), *n., pl.* **men-of-war. 1** a warship of a type used in former times: *All the men-of-war were burnt during the night* (London Times). **2** = Portuguese man-of-war. Also, **man-o'-war.**

**man-of-war bird** or **hawk,** = frigate bird. Also, **man-o'-war bird** or **hawk.**

**ma|nom|e|ter** (mə nom′ə tər), *n.* **1** an instrument for measuring the pressure of gases or vapors. **2** an instrument for determining blood pressure; sphygmomanometer. [< French *manomètre* < Greek *mānós* thin + French *-mètre* -meter]

**man|o|met|ric** (man′ə met′rik), *adj.* **1** having to do with or obtained with a manometer. **2** having to do with the measurement of gaseous pressure. —**man′o|met′ri|cal|ly,** *adv.*

**man|o|met|ri|cal** (man′ə met′rə kəl), *adj.* = manometric.

**manometric flame,** a gas flame which fluctuates in response to the movements of a diaphragm placed in an opening in the wall of an organ pipe or other resonator. The varying amounts of fluctuation are used to measure the sound vibrations in the pipe.

**ma|nom|e|try** (mə nom′ə trē), *n.* the measurement of the pressure of gases or vapors by means of a manometer.

**man on horseback,** a military leader whose influence over the people threatens the government.

**man-on-man** (man′on man′, -ôn-), *adv., adj. U.S. and Canada.* (in team sports) of or in a defensive position in which one defensive player is assigned to one offensive player: *They were forced into single man-on-man coverage by the blitzing tactics of the Kansas City linebackers* (Time).

**man|or** (man′ər), *n.* **1** (in the Middle Ages) a large estate, part of which was set aside for the lord and the rest divided among his peasants, who paid the owner rent in goods, services, or money. If the lord sold his manor, the peasants or serfs were sold with it. **2** a large estate. **3** a tract of land in colonial America within which the owner had a similar arrangement. **4** the main house or mansion of an estate. [< Old French *manoir,* earlier *maneir,* noun use of infinitive < Latin *manēre* to stay, abide]

**manor house,** the house of the owner of a manor.

**ma|no|ri|al** (mə nôr′ē əl, -nōr′-), *adj.* **1** of or having to do with a manor: *manorial rights.* **2** forming a manor: *a manorial estate.*

**ma|no|ri|al|ism** (mə nôr′ē əl iz′əm, -nōr′-), *n.* the economic relationship of a feudal lord and his peasants by which they made a living from land.

**man-o'-war** (man′ə wôr′), *n., pl.* **men-o'-war.** = man-of-war.

**man-o'-war bird** or **hawk,** = frigate bird.

**man|pack** (man′pak′), *adj.* that may be carried by one person: *a manpack radio set.*

**man|pow|er** (man′pou′ər), *n., adj.* —*n.* **1** power supplied by the physical work of people. **2** strength thought of in terms of the number of persons needed or available: *China has great potential military manpower.* **3a** a unit equivalent to the rate at which a man can do work, equal to 1/10 horsepower. **b** work done, expressed in terms of this unit.
—*adj.* of or having to do with manpower: *the manpower problem, a manpower shortage.*

**man|qué** (män kā′), *adj. French.* defective or abortive; unfulfilled, unrealized, or frustrated: *a poet manqué, an adventure manqué. At heart every masseur is a doctor manqué* (New Yorker).

**man|quée** (män kā′), *adj. French.* the feminine form of **manqué.**

**man-rate** (man′rāt′), *v.t.,* **-rat|ed, -rat|ing.** to certify (a rocket or spacecraft) as safe for manned flight: *The lunar module ... was man-rated after one flight* (Birmingham, Alabama, News).

**man|rope** (man′rōp′), *n.* a rope used as a handrail at the side of a ladder, gangway, or platform.

***man|sard** (man′särd), *n.* **1** Also, **mansard roof.** a four-sided roof with two slopes on each side. The lower slopes are nearly vertical and the upper slopes nearly flat, allowing greater headway throughout the top story. *The splendid mansard roof, with its double tier of dormers and fancy iron crestings* (New Yorker). **2** the story under such a roof. [< French *mansarde,* adjective < François *Mansard,* 1598-1666, a French architect]

***mansard** definition 1

**manse** (mans), *n.* **1** a minister's house; parsonage, especially of a Presbyterian minister in Scotland: *The pastor may remain on salary and continue to reside in the manse* (Chicago Tribune). **2** *Obsolete.* land sufficient to support a family. **3** *Obsolete.* a mansion. [< Medieval Latin *mansa* a dwelling < Latin *manēre* to stay, abide]

**man|serv|ant** (man′sėr′vənt), *n., pl.* **men|servants.** a male servant.

**man-shift** (man′shift′), *n.* the shift a man works each day, used as a unit in figuring cost, output, or other constituent of production: *The increase in productivity, as measured by output per man-shift ... has averaged two per cent per annum cumulatively* (London Times).

**-manship,** *combining form.* the art or skill of being, doing, or using (something) to one's own advantage: *Companies find that premium-manship is more convincing than quality control* (Saturday Review). [abstracted from *gamesmanship, lifemanship,* and *one-upmanship,* terms coined by the English author Stephen Potter, born 1900]

**man|sion** (man′shən), *n.* **1** a large house; stately residence: *the governor's mansion.* **2** = manor house. **3** *Archaic.* a place to live in; abiding place: *the village preacher's modest mansion* (Oliver Goldsmith). **4a** the sign of the zodiac in which the sun or a planet has its special residence: *Phebus the sun ... was ... in his mansion In Aries* (Chaucer). **b** one of the twenty-eight divisions of the moon's monthly path, according to Oriental and medieval astronomy. **5** *Obsolete.* a staying in a place; sojourn.

**mansions,** *British.* an apartment house or apartment: *The inhabitants of Cornwall Mansions ... have petitioned the Kensington Council to change the name to Cornwall-place* (London Daily Chronicle).

[< Old French *mansion,* learned borrowing from Latin *mānsiō, -ōnis* < *manēre* to stay, abide. Compare etym. under **manse, manor.**]

**man-size** (man′sīz′), *adj.* = man-sized.

**man-sized** (man′sīzd′), *adj.* **1** suitable for a full-grown man; large: *man-sized tools, man-sized portions.* **2** *Informal.* requiring a grown man's strength or maturity of judgment: *man-sized responsibilities.*

**man|slaugh|ter** (man′slô′tər), *n.* **1** the killing of a human being or beings: *The Indian massacre at Deerfield was nothing more nor less than manslaughter.* **2** *Law.* the killing of a human being unlawfully but without deliberate intent or under strong provocation: *The charge against the prisoner was changed from murder to manslaughter. He was indicted for involuntary manslaughter and reckless driving* (Time).

**man|slay|er** (man′slā′ər), *n.* **1** a person who kills a human being. **2** a person who commits manslaughter.

**man|slay|ing** (man′slā′ing), *n., adj.* —*n.* the act of killing a human being; homicide.
—*adj.* that kills a human being; homicidal.

**man|stop|per** (man′stop′ər), *n.* a manstopping bullet.

**man|stop|ping** (man′stop′ing), *adj.* having great force; designed to inflict a wound that will stop an advancing soldier: *a manstopping bullet.*

**man|suete** (man swēt′), *adj. Archaic.* gentle; meek; mild. [< Latin *mansuētus,* past participle of *mansuēscere* become tame < *manus* hand + *suēscere* to accustom]

**Pronunciation Key:** hat, āge, cãre, fär; let, ēqual, tėrm; it, īce; hot, ōpen, ôrder; oil, out; cup, pu̇t, rüle; child; long; thin; ᴛʜen; zh, measure; ə represents **a** in about, **e** in taken, **i** in pencil, **o** in lemon, **u** in circus.

**man|sue|tude** (man′swə tüd, -tyüd), *n. Archaic.* gentleness; meekness; mildness: *our Lord Himself, made all of mansuetude* (Robert Browning). [< Latin *mansuētūdo* < *mansuēscere;* see etym. under **mansuete**]

***man|ta** (man′tə), *n.* **1** a piece of cloth used as a cloak or wrap by women in Spain and Latin America. **2** a kind of horse blanket. **3** *Military.* a movable shelter formerly used by attacking soldiers for protection; mantelet: *Seizing their mantas ... they made a gallant assault* (Washington Irving). **4** = devilfish. [< Spanish *manta* < Vulgar Latin < Late Latin *mantum,* back formation < Latin *mantellum* cloak, mantle]

***manta**
definition 1

***manteau**
definition 1

***mantilla**
definition 1

**man-tai|lored** (man′tā′lərd), *adj.* (of women's coats, suits, or other garments) tailored in the manner or style of men's clothing.

**manta ray,** = devilfish.

***man|teau** (man′tō; *French* mäɴ tō′), *n., pl.* **-teaus, -teaux** (-tōz; *French* -tō′). **1** a mantle or cloak. **2a** a gown open in front to show the petticoat, formerly worn by women. **b** a loose upper garment: *Tell my gentlewoman to bring my black scarf and manteau* (Scott). **c** = mantua. [< French *manteau* < Old French *mantel* mantle]

**man|tel** (man′təl), *n.* **1** a shelf above a fireplace with its supports. *The fireplace looked very plain after we removed the mantel.* **2** the shelf itself; mantelpiece: *The picture above the fireplace fell to the mantel.* **3** the decorative framework around a fireplace: *a mantel of tile.* [spelling variant of *mantle*[2]]

**man|tel|et** (man′tə let, mant′lit), *n.* **1** a short mantle or cape: *a lady in a little lace mantelet* (Thackeray). **2** = manta (def. 3). **3** = devilfish. [< Old French *mantelet* (diminutive) < *mantel* mantle]

**man|tel|let|ta** (man′tə let′ə), *n.* a sleeveless, knee-length vestment of silk or wool, worn by cardinals, bishops, abbots, and other dignitaries of the Roman Catholic Church. [< Italian *mantelletta* (diminutive) < *mantello* < Latin *mantellum* mantle]

**man|tel|piece** (man′təl pēs′), *n.* = mantel (def. 2); chimney piece.

**man|tel|shelf** (man′təl shelf′), *n.* = mantel (def. 2).

**man|tel|tree** (man′təl trē′), *n.* **1** = mantel (def. 1). **2** = mantelpiece.

**man|tic** (man′tik), *adj.* **1** of or having to do with divination. **2** having the power of divination; prophetic. [< Greek *mantikós* < *mántis* prophet; see etym. under **mantis**]

**man|ti|core** (man′ti kôr, -kōr), *n.* a fabulous monster having the body of a lion, the head of a man, and the tail or sting of a scorpion. [< Latin *manticora* < Greek *mantichōras,* apparently < an old Persian word for "man-eater"]

**man|tid** (man′tid), *n.* = mantis.

***man|til|la** (man til′ə), *n.* **1** a veil or scarf, often of lace, covering the hair and falling down over the shoulders. Spanish and Latin-American women often wear mantillas. *Her rosepoint lace veil was arranged mantilla fashion* (New York Times). **2** a short mantle or cape. [< Spanish *mantilla* (diminutive) < *manta* woolen blanket < *manto* cloak, mantle < Late Latin *mantus, -ūs*]

**man|tis** (man′tis), *n., pl.* **-tis|es, -tes** (-tēz). a large insect that holds its forelegs doubled up as if praying; praying mantis. It eats other insects. [< New Latin *Mantis* the genus name < Greek *mántis* prophet < *maínesthai* be inspired]

**mantis crab** or **shrimp,** = squilla.

**man|tis|sa** (man tis′ə), *n.* the decimal part of a logarithm. In the logarithm 2.95424, the characteristic is 2 and the mantissa is .95424. [< Latin *mantissa,* variant of *mantīsa* addition < Etruscan, apparently < Celtic]

**man|tle¹** (man′təl), *n., v.,* **-tled, -tling.** —*n.* **1** a loose cloak without sleeves: *a mantle thrown over his shoulders.* **2** *Figurative.* anything that covers like a mantle: *The ground had a mantle of snow.* **3** a lacelike tube around a gas flame that gets so hot it glows and gives light. **4** *Zoology.* **a** the fold of the body wall of a mollusk that lines the shell and secretes the material which forms the shell; pallium. It often serves largely for respiration. **b** a pair of similar folds that secrete the shell of a brachiopod. **c** the soft tissue that lines the shell of a tunicate or barnacle. **5** the folded wings and back feathers of a bird that enclose the body like a cloak. **6** *Geology.* the part of the earth beneath the crust and above the outer core: *Conditions within the earth's thin crust are controlled from the mantle* (New York Times). See picture under **core¹**. **7** a steel structure which supports the stack of a blast furnace.
—*v.t.* **1** to cover with or as if with a mantle: *a small stagnant stream, mantled over with bright green mosses* (Scott). **2** *Figurative.* to cover or conceal; obscure; cloak: *Clouds mantled the moon.*
—*v.i.* **1** to blush; flush; redden: *Her face mantled with shame.* **2** *Figurative.* to spread out like a mantle: *The rosy blush of dawn began to mantle in the east* (Washington Irving). **3** to be or become covered with a coating or scum: *The pond has mantled.* **4** to spread first one wing and then the other over the corresponding outstretched leg for exercise, as a perched hawk does in falconry.
[fusion of Old English *maentel* < Latin *mantellum,* and of Middle English *mantel* < Old French < Latin *mantellum*]

**man|tle²** (man′təl), *n.* = mantel.

**mantle rock,** the layer of soil and loose rock fragments overlying solid rock; regolith.

**mant|let** (mant′lit), *n.* = mantelet.

**man|tling** (mant′ling), *n. Heraldry.* the ornamental accessory of drapery or scrollwork frequently depicted behind and around an escutcheon.

**man-to-man** (man′tə man′), *adj., adv.* —*adj.* **1** frank; straightforward; direct. **2** (in team sports) having to do with or denoting a pattern of defense in which one player guards only his opponent, and not a certain zone; man-for-man; man-on-man: *man-to-man defensive tactics.*
—*adv.* frankly; in a straightforward manner.

**Man|toux test** (man′tü), a test for tuberculosis in which old tuberculin in a diluted mixture is injected between the layers of the skin. [< Charles *Mantoux,* 1877-1947, a French physician, who developed it]

**man|tra** (man′trə), *n.* (in Hinduism and Mahayana Buddhism) a prayer or invocation, sometimes held to have magical power. [< Sanskrit *mantra* (literally) instrument of thought < a root *man-* think]

**man-trap** (man′trap′), *n.* **1** a trap for catching trespassers in private grounds. **2** *Figurative.* anything that is likely to cause injury or trouble to the unwary; trap.

**man|tu|a** (man′chủ ə), *n.* **1** a loose gown or cloak, worn by women in the 1600's and 1700's. **2** = mantle. [altered < French *manteau,* by confusion with *Mantua,* a city in Italy]

**Man|tu|an** (man′chủ ən), *adj., n.* —*adj.* of or having to do with Mantua, a city in northern Italy.
—*n.* a native or inhabitant of Mantua: *Virgil was known as "the Mantuan."*

**Man|u** (man′ü), *n. Hindu Mythology.* **1** a legendary being, a son of the sun god, and father of the human race. He is ascribed to be the author of the system of laws known as the Code of Manu. **2** one of a group of supernatural beings, each of whom presides over a cycle of time.

**man|u|al** (man′yủ əl), *adj., n.* —*adj.* **1a** of the hands; done with the hands: *manual labor.* **b** powered by hand and not by electricity: *a manual typewriter.* **2** like a manual or handbook: *to follow the manual procedure.*
—*n.* **1** a book that helps its readers to understand or use something; handbook. A cookbook is a manual. *The workbook has a teachers' manual.* **2** a drill in handling a rifle or other weapons, especially at formal military ceremonies. **3** an organ keyboard played with the hands: *Most church organs have two to four manuals* (Wall Street Journal). See picture at **organ.**
[< Old French *manuel,* learned borrowing from Latin *manuālis* < *manus, -ūs* hand] —**man′u|al|ly,** *adv.*

**manual alphabet,** = finger alphabet.

**manual training,** training in work done with the hands; practice in various arts and crafts, especially in making things out of wood, metal, or plastic.

**ma|nu|bri|um** (mə nü′brē əm, -nyü′-), *n., pl.* **-bri|a** (-brē ə). **1** a process or part of a bone or other bodily structure, that is shaped like a handle. **2a** the broad upper division of the sternum of mammals, with which the two first ribs articulate; episternum. See diagram under **skeleton. b** a small, tapering, curved or twisted process of the malleus of the ear. [< Latin *manūbrium* a handle, haft < *manus, -ūs* hand]

**man|u|duc|tion** (man′yə duk′shən), *n.* a leading by or as if by the hand; guidance. [< Medieval Latin *manuductio, -onis* < Latin *manū dūcere* to lead by hand]

**man|u|duc|to|ry** (man′yə duk′tər ē), *adj.* leading by or as if by the hand; guiding.

**manuf.,** **1** manufacture. **2** manufacturer. **3** manufacturing.

**man|u|fac|to|ry** (man′yə fak′tər ē), *n., pl.* **-ries.** = factory.

**man|u|fac|tur|a|ble** (man′yə fak′chə rə bəl), *adj.* that can be manufactured.

**man|u|fac|ture** (man′yə fak′chər), *v.,* **-tured, -turing,** *n.* —*v.t.* **1** to make by hand or by machine. A big factory manufactures goods in large quantities by using machines and dividing the work up among many people. **2** to make into something useful: *to manufacture aluminum into kitchenware, manufacture steel into rails.* **3** *Figurative.* to make up; invent: *The lazy boy manufactured excuses. The dishonest lawyer manufactured evidence.* **4** *Figurative.* to produce (literary work, a film, or the like) mechanically: *If the music is useful and effective, it also sounds manufactured* (Manchester Guardian Weekly). [< noun]
—*n.* **1** the act or process of making articles by hand or by machine, especially in large quantities. *Abbr:* mfr. **2** a thing manufactured. **3** *Figurative.* something produced mechanically, such as a story.
[< Middle French *manufacture,* learned borrowing from Medieval Latin *manufactura* < Latin *manū facere* make by hand]

**man|u|fac|tur|er** (man′yə fak′chər ər), *n.* a person or company whose business is manufacturing; an owner of a factory: *The manufacturer guaranteed to replace any defective product.*

**ma|nu|ka** (mə nü′kə; *Maori* mä′nủ kä), *n.* any one of several Australasian trees and shrubs of the myrtle family, yielding a very hard, dark, close-grained wood, and an aromatic leaf sometimes used as a substitute for tea. [< Maori *mánuka*]

**man|u|mis|sion** (man′yə mish′ən), *n.* **1** the act of freeing from slavery. **2** the condition of being freed from slavery: *Perhaps he remembers his ancestor from the Congo, who would not leave the state even for his manumission* (Time). [< Latin *manūmissiō, -ōnis* < *manūmittere;* see etym. under **manumit**]

**man|u|mit** (man′yə mit′), *v.t.,* **-mit|ted, -mit|ting.** to set free from slavery or bondage: *The Christian masters were not bound to manumit their slaves, and yet were commended if they did so* (Jeremy Taylor). [< Latin *manūmittere* < *manū* *mittere* release from control < *manū,* ablative of *manus* hand + *ēmittere* send out, release < *ex-* from + *mittere* to send]

**ma|nure** (mə nủr′, -nyủr′), *n., v.,* **-nured, -nur|ing.** —*n.* a substance put in or on the soil as fertilizer. Dung or refuse from stables is a kind of manure. *The histories of the most primitive agricultural peoples show that they knew the value of various kinds of manures* (Fred W. Emerson). [< verb]
—*v.t.* to put manure in or on.
[< Anglo-French *maynoverer,* Old French *manouvrer* work with the hands < *maneuvre* hand work. See etym. of doublet **maneuver.**] —**ma|nur′er,** *n.*

**manure worm,** = brandling (def. 1).

**ma|nu|ri|al** (mə nủr′ē əl, -nyủr′-), *adj.* having to do with or of the nature of manure.

**ma|nus** (mā′nəs), *n., pl.* **-nus.** **1** the distal part of the forelimb of a vertebrate, including the carpus or wrist, and the forefoot or hand. **2** power or authority of a husband over his wife in Roman law. [< Latin *manus, -ūs* hand]

**man|u|script** (man′yə skript), *n., adj.* —*n.* **1** a book, article, or paper written by hand or with a typewriter. Before printing was invented, all books and papers were handwritten manuscripts. *Abbr:* MS. **2** handwritten or typewritten condition: *His last book was three years in manuscript.*
—*adj.* written by hand or with a typewriter.
[< Latin *manū scriptus* written by hand < *manū,* ablative of *manus* hand + *scriptus,* past participle of *scrībere* to write]

**man|u|script|al** (man′yə skrip′təl), *adj.* **1** of or like a manuscript or manuscripts. **2** found in a manuscript or manuscripts.

**man|ward** (man′wərd), *adv., adj.* —*adv.* toward man; in relation to man.
—*adj.* directed toward man.

**man|wards** (man′wərdz), *adv.* = manward.

**man|wise** (man′wīz′), *adv.* in the manner of a man.

**Manx** (mangks), *adj., n.* —*adj.* of the Isle of Man, its people, or their language. The Isle of Man is a small island west of northern England in the Irish Sea. —*n.* **1** the people of the Isle of Man. **2** the Celtic language spoken on the Isle of Man. [earlier, *maniske,* perhaps < a Scandinavian word < the Celtic name of the island (compare Old Irish *Manu*)]
▶ **Manx**, meaning the people of the Isle of Man, is plural in use: *The Manx are hardworking people. Manx,* meaning the language of these people, is singular in use: *Manx is nearly extinct.*

**Manx** or **manx cat**, a breed of domestic cat that has no tail or only the stump of a tail.

**Manx|man** (mangks′mən), *n., pl.* **-men.** a native or inhabitant of the Isle of Man.

**Manx shearwater**, a small shearwater which nests on islands of the North Atlantic and Mediterranean.

**man|y** (men′ē), *adj.,* **more, most,** *n.* —*adj.* consisting of a great number; numerous: *many years ago. There are many children in the city.*
—*n.* **1** a great number: *many of us. Do you know many of them?* **2** a large number of people or things: *There were many at the dance. Many be called, but few chosen* (Matthew 20:16). *Never ... was so much owed by so many to so few* (Sir Winston Churchill).
**a good many**, a fairly large number: *A few failed the test but a good many got perfect scores.*
**a great many**, a very large number: *A great many gathered at the scene.*
**how many**, what number of: *How many days until school is out?*
**one too many (for)**, **a** more than a match for: *We were one too many for the enemy.* **b** too much for one's own good, especially of alcoholic beverage: *Our friend has had one too many at the party.*
**the many**, **a** most people: *The many fail* (Tennyson). **b** the common people: *The folly and foolish self-opinion of the half-instructed many* (Samuel Taylor Coleridge).
[Middle English *moni,* or *mani,* Old English *manig*]
—*Syn. adj.* **Many**, **innumerable** mean consisting of a large number. **Many** is the general word: *Were many people there?* **Innumerable** means more than can be counted, or so many that counting would be very hard: *He has given innumerable excuses for being late.*

**man-year** (man′yir′), *n.* one year of work by one man, used as a unit in figuring cost, time, output, or other constituent of production: *Deaths in World War II produced a loss of 3 million man-years.*

**man|y-fac|et|ed** (men′ē fas′ə tid), *adj.* having many facets; many-sided.

**man|y|fold** (men′ē fōld′), *adv.* many times; to a great extent: *During the past five years the number of weapons has increased manyfold* (Lewis L. Strauss).
▶ **Manyfold** is a compound recently formed on the analogy of such compounds as *twofold* and *threefold,* which denote the number of times an action recurs: *The population of our city has increased manyfold.* **Manifold** appeared in Old English about the same time as *twofold* and *threefold* but, unlike them, it does not function as an adverb and is limited to expressing kind and variety, never time and duration: *His responsibilities are manifold.*

**man|y|plies** (men′ē plīz′), *n.* the third stomach of a cow or other ruminant animal; omasum; psalterium. [< *many* + *plies,* plural of *ply,* noun]

**man|y-sid|ed** (men′ē sī′did), *adj.* **1** having many sides. **2** *Figurative.* having many interests or abilities; versatile: *Benjamin Franklin was a many-sided person.* **3** *Figurative.* having many aspects, possibilities, or capacities: *Flying to the moon is a many-sided problem.* —**man′y-sid′ed|ness**, *n.*

**man|y-val|ued** (men′ē val′yüd), *adj. Mathematics.* having many values; multivalued.

**man|za|nil|la** (man′zə nil′ə), *n.* a dry, light Spanish sherry with a somewhat bitter flavor. [< Spanish *manzanilla* (originally) camomile (diminutive) < *manzana* apple; see etym. under **manchineel**]

**man|za|ni|ta** (man′zə nē′tə), *n.* **1** any one of various evergreen shrubs or trees of the heath family that grow in western North America, such as the bearberry. **2** the fruit of any one of these plants. [American English < American Spanish *manzanita* (diminutive) < *manzana* apple; see etym. under **manchineel**]

**Mao** (mou), *n., pl.* **Maos.** = Mao jacket.

**MAO** (no periods), monoamine oxidase.

**Mao|cra|cy** (mou′krə sē), *n.* a ruling body or class made up of Maoists. [< *Mao* Tse-tung + *-cracy,* as in *aristocracy*]

**Mao flu**, = Hong Kong flu. [< *Mao* Tse-tung]

**Mao|ism** (mou′iz əm), *n.* the principles and practices of Mao Tse-tung, Chinese Communist leader, characterized by rigid adherence to Marxian doctrine: *They seek to make of Maoism a powerful faith that would unite, guide, and inspire future generations* (London Times).

**Mao|ist** (mou′ist), *adj., n.* —*adj.* of or having to do with Mao Tse-tung or Maoism: *According to Maoist precepts, people thinking and acting together can achieve any goal, no matter how primitive their tools* (Seymour Topping).
—*n.* a follower or supporter of Mao Tse-tung or of Maoism: *The young Maoists, more influenced by the idea of Götterdämmerung than perhaps they know, are for burning down and starting over* (New York Times).

**Mao|ize** (mou′īz), *v.t.,* **-ized, -iz|ing.** to bring under the influence of Mao Tse-tung; convert to Maoism. —**Mao′i|za′tion**, *n.*

**Mao jacket** or **coat**, a narrow jacket or coat with a mandarin collar. [< *Mao* Tse-tung]

**Ma|o|ri** (mä′ō rē, mou′rē), *n., pl.* **-ris,** *adj.* —*n.* **1** a member of the native Polynesian people of New Zealand. **2** their Polynesian language.
—*adj.* of the Maoris or their language.

**Ma|o|ri|land|er** (mä′ō rē lan′dər, mou′rē-), *n.* = New Zealander. [< *Maoriland* a name for New Zealand + *-er*[1]]

**Ma|o|ri|tan|ga** (mä′ō rē tang′gə, mou′rē-), *n.* the art, customs, traditions, or other cultural aspects of the Maoris. [< Maori]

**mao tai** (mou′ tī′), a Chinese liquor, like vodka, distilled from millet. [< Chinese *mao t'ai*]

**map** (map), *n., v.,* **mapped, map|ping.** —*n.* **1** a drawing of the earth's surface or of part of it, usually showing countries, cities, rivers, seas, lakes, and mountains: *We looked over several maps to find the best route to drive to Canada.* **2** a drawing of the sky or of part of it, showing the position of the stars and the planets: *The map of the heavens showed all the northern constellations.* **3** a maplike drawing of anything: *a highway map, a weather map.* **4** = genetic map.
—*v.t.* **1** to make a map of; show on a map: *Surveyors gradually mapped the United States as the frontier moved west.* **2** to collect information for a map by exploring or surveying (a region or other geographical area or feature). **3** *Figurative.* to arrange in detail; plan: *Each Monday we map out the week's work. I set to work to map out a new career* (Mark Twain). **4** *Mathematics.* to cause an element in (one set) to correspond to an element in the same or another set. **5** *Genetics.* to place (a gene or genes) in a particular arrangement on a chromosome.
**put on the map**, to give importance or prominence to; make well-known: *He [Gene Krupa] is credited with putting jazz drumming on the map* (New Yorker).
[< Medieval Latin *mappa* map (for earlier *mappa mundi* map of the world) < Latin *mappa* napkin, cloth (on which maps were once drawn)] —**map′like′**, *adj.* —**map′per**, *n.*
—*Syn. n.* **1 Map, chart** mean a drawing representing a surface or area. **Map** applies particularly to a representation of some part of the earth's surface or an area of land, showing relative geographical positions, shape, size, or other physical characteristics of certain places or features: *A map of a city shows streets and parks.* **Chart** applies particularly to a map used especially in sea or air navigation, showing deep and shallow places, islands, channels, or obstacles in a body of water, or air currents, airlanes, or the like, for flying: *The reef that the ship struck is on the chart.*

**ma|ple** (mā′pəl), *n.* **1** a tree grown for shade, ornament, its wood, or its sap. There are many kinds of maples, but all have dry fruits with two wings, and opposite leaves without stipules. **2** its hard, fine-grained, light-colored wood, used especially for furniture and flooring. **3** the flavor of maple sugar or maple syrup. [Old English *mapeltrēow* maple tree] —**ma′ple|like′**, *adj.*

**maple family**, a group of dicotyledonous trees and shrubs with dry, two-winged fruit, found in mountainous, northern countries, and cultivated widely for shade and ornament.

**maple leaf**, **1** a leaf of the maple tree. **2** this leaf as the official Canadian emblem.

**maple sugar**, a pale-brown sugar made by boiling the sap of the maple, usually the sugar maple, until much of the water has evaporated.

**maple syrup**, syrup made by boiling the sap of the maple, usually the sugar maple.

**map|mak|er** (map′mā′kər), *n.* = cartographer.

**map|mak|ing** (map′mā′king), *n.* = cartography.

**map|pa|ble** (map′ə bəl), *adj.* that can be mapped: *a genetically mappable gene.*

**map|per|y** (map′ər ē), *n.* the process of making maps; cartography.

**map|pist** (map′ist), *n.* = mapmaker.

**ma|qua|hui|tl** (mä′kwə wē′təl), *n.* an Aztec sword made of hard wood, usually inlaid with carvings or mosaic work, and having both edges set with sharp, rectangular pieces of obsidian. [< Nahuatl *maquahuitl*]

**ma|quette** (ma ket′), *n.* a preliminary sketch or model in clay or wax of a painting, monument, building, or sculpture: *The eleven maquettes on display were selected from 199 entries by a jury* (New York Times). [< French *maquette* < Italian *macchietta* (diminutive) < *macchia* sketch, spot]

**ma|quil|lage** (mȧ kē yȧzh′), *n. French.* cosmetics applied to the face; makeup.

**ma|quil|leur** (mȧ kē yœr′), *n. French.* a makeup man.

**Ma|quis** (mȧ kē′), *n., pl.* **-quis,** *adj.* —*n.* **1** the French underground resistance movement against the Germans in World War II. **2** a member of this: *At a tank stop the train was boarded by a gang of armed Maquis* (Time). **3** an underground resistance movement in Algeria during French occupation.
—*adj.* of, resembling in tactics, or having to do with the Maquis.
[< French *maquis* (originally) scrub forest, thicket < Italian *macchia* thicket, as cover for bandits < Latin *macula* spot, cluster. Compare etym. under **macula, macule, mail**[2].]

**Ma|qui|sard** (mȧ kē zärd′), *n. French.* a member of the Maquis.

**mar** (mär), *v.,* **marred, mar|ring,** *n.* —*v.t.* **1** to spoil the beauty of; damage; injure: *The nails in the workmen's shoes have marred our newly finished floors. Weeds mar a garden. ... hideously marred about the face* (Herman Melville). SYN: disfigure. **2** to spoil or ruin: *Grant us felicity ... nor let our sweet delight be marred by aught* (William Morris). SYN: impair.
—*n.* something that mars; blemish; drawback.
[Old English *merran* to waste, spoil]

**MAR** (mär), *n.* multifunction array radar (a radar system using electronic switching instead of mechanical rotation to scan the horizon, designed especially for operation at antiballistic missile sites).

**mar.**, **1** marine. **2** maritime. **3** married.

**Mar.**, March.

**ma|ra** (mə rä′), *n.* a large South American rodent having long ears and long, thin legs; Patagonian cavy or hare. [< American Spanish *mará*]

**Ma|ra** (mä′rə), *n.* the devil who tempted Gautama Buddha, according to the early Buddhists.

**mar|a|bou** or **mar|a|bout**[1] (mar′ə bü), *n.* **1** any one of several varieties of large, white-bodied storks of Africa and Asia; adjutant. **2** a furlike trimming made from its soft, white, downy feathers, used especially on women's hats, dresses, and boas. **3a** a silk that is nearly pure-white in the raw state. **b** a delicate cloth made from it. [< *marabout*[2] (because the bird appears reflective)]

**mar|a|bout**[2] (mar′ə büt), *n.* **1** a Moslem holy man or ascetic of northern Africa. **2** the tomb of such a holy man, serving as a shrine. [< French *marabout* < Arabic *murābiṭ* hermit]

**ma|ra|ca** (mə rä′kə, -rak′ə), *n.* a percussion instrument, consisting of seeds, pebbles, or lead shot enclosed in a dry gourd or gourd-shaped body and shaken like a rattle. Maracas are usually played in pairs. [American English < Portuguese *maracá* < the Brazilian name for a gourd]

**ma|rae** (mə rī′), *n., pl.* **-rae** or **-raes. 1** a temple, altar, or sacred enclosure at which Polynesians worship. **2** an enclosed space or yard in front of a Maori house. [< Polynesian]

**mar|ag|ing steel** (mär′ā′jing), a very strong, corrosion-resistant, low-carbon alloy of iron, chromium, nickel, titanium, silicon, and manganese, often used in spacecraft parts. [< *mar*(tensite) *aging*]

**Ma|rah** (mā′rə, mär′ə), *n.* **1** the place where the Israelites in their wanderings found only bitter water (in the Bible, Exodus 15:23). **2** (in the Bible) a well or stream of bitter water. [< Hebrew *mārā* bitter]

**ma|rah** (mā′rə, mär′ə), *n.* bitter water; bitterness: *The wasting famine of the heart they fed, And slaked its thirst with marah of their tears* (Longfellow). [< *Marah*]

**Mar|a|nao** (mar′ə nou′), *n., pl.* **-nao** or **-naos. 1** a member of a Malay people of Mindanao, in the Philippines, and of northern Borneo (Sabah). **2** the Austronesian language of this people.

**mar|a|nath|a** (mar′ə nath′ə), *n.* = anathema. [<

**Pronunciation Key:** hat, āge, cãre, fär; let, ēqual, tėrm; it, īce; hot, ōpen, ôrder; oil, out; cup, pu̇t, rüle; child; long; thin; ᴛʜen; zh, measure; ə represents **a** in about, **e** in taken, **i** in pencil, **o** in lemon, **u** in circus.

Greek *maranathá*. Compare etym. under **anathema**.]

**ma|ran|ta** (mə ran′tə), *n.* any one of various tropical herbs commonly grown under glass for their showy foliage; arrowroot. [< New Latin *Maranta* the genus name < Bartolomeo *Maranta*, an Italian physician and botanist of the 1500's]

**mar|an|ta|ceous** (mar′an tā′shəs), *adj.* belonging to the family of plants typified by the arrowroot.

**ma|ran|tic** (mə ran′tik), *adj.* = marasmic.

**ma|ras|ca** (mə ras′kə), *n.* a small black cherry whose sour fruit is the source of maraschino. [< Italian *marasca*, short for *amarasca* < *amaro* bitter, sour < Latin *amārus*]

**mar|a|schi|no** (mar′ə skē′nō, -shē′-), *n.* a strong liqueur made from the fermented juice of a small, bitter black cherry. [< Italian *maraschino* < *marasca*; see etym. under **marasca**]

**maraschino cherry**, a cherry preserved in a sweet syrup. It is used to decorate and to add flavor to drinks and desserts.

**ma|ras|mic** (mə raz′mik), *adj.* of or having to do with marasmus.

**ma|ras|mus** (mə raz′məs), *n.* a wasting away of the body, especially due to malnutrition or old age, rather than disease. [< New Latin *marasmus* < Greek *marasmós*, alteration of *máransis* < *maraínein* put out (a fire), die away slowly]

**Ma|ra|tha** (mə rä′tə), *n.* = Mahratta.

**Ma|ra|thi** (mə rä′tē, -rat′ē), *n.* = Mahratti.

**Mar|a|thon** (mar′ə thon), *n.* a plain in Greece about 25 miles northeast of Athens. After the Athenians defeated the Persians there in 490 B.C., a runner ran all the way to Athens with the news of the victory.

**mar|a|thon** (mar′ə thon), *n.* **1** a foot race of 26 miles, 385 yards. It was introduced in 1896 with the revival of the Olympic Games, in memory of the runner who carried the news to Athens that the Athenians had defeated the Persians in the battle of Marathon (490 B.C.). **2** any race over a long distance. **3** *Figurative.* any activity that calls for endurance: *The litigation ... turned out to be a marathon affair* (New Yorker).

**Mar|a|tho|ni|an** (mar′ə thō′nē ən), *adj., n.* —*adj.* of or having to do with Marathon or the battle of Marathon. —*n.* a native of Marathon.

**ma|raud** (mə rôd′), *v., n.* —*v.i.* to go about in search of plunder: *The Saxon stern, the pagan Dane, Maraud on Britain's shores again* (Scott).
—*v.t.* to make raids on for booty; plunder.
—*n.* a marauding expedition; raid.
[< French *marauder* < Middle French *maraud* rascal (perhaps as a prowler); (originally) tomcat; apparently imitative < *marau* meow]

**ma|raud|er** (mə rô′dər), *n.* a person or animal that goes about in search of plunder: *Tigers and leopards are night marauders of the jungle.*

**ma|raud|ing** (mə rô′ding), *adj.* going about in search of plunder; making raids for booty: *The marauding pirates blocked the harbor and attacked the city.*

**mar|a|ve|di** (mar′ə vā′dē), *n., pl.* **-dis. 1** a gold coin used by the Moors in Spain during the 1000's and 1100's. **2** a former Spanish copper coin. [< Spanish *maravedí* < Arabic *Murābiṭīn*, plural, a Moorish dynasty at Cordoba, 1087-1147. Compare etym. under **marabout**[2].]

**mar|ble** (mär′bəl), *n., adj., v.,* **-bled, -bling.** —*n.* **1** a hard limestone, white or colored, that can take a beautiful polish. Marble lasts as long as granite and is much softer to work. Marble is much used for statues and in buildings. **2** a piece, block, or slab of marble, especially one that has been cut or shaped by man. **3** a small ball of clay, glass, or stone, used in games. **4** a pattern or color that looks like marble. **5** *Figurative.* something as cold and hard as marble: *a heart of marble.*
—*adj.* **1** made of marble: *a marble vase.* **2** *Figurative.* like marble; white, hard, cold, or unfeeling: *a marble heart.* **3** having a pattern like marble; mottled.
—*v.t.* to color in imitation of the patterns in marble: *Binders marble the edges of some books. The horizon bounded by a propitious sky, azure, marbled with pearly white* (Charlotte Brontë).
**marbles, a** a game played with small, usually colored balls. Each player uses a larger marble to knock the smaller marbles out of a ring. *There was the floor on which ... I had played at marbles* (R. Chambers). **b** a collection of sculptures: *the Elgin Marbles.* **c** *Slang.* common sense; reason: *I think he's lost his marbles.*
**pick up one's marbles,** *Informal.* to give up; quit: *He hoped the committee [Citizens Committee for Children] would not "just pick up its marbles and thus penalize the children of New York"* (New York Times).
[< Old French *marble*, and *marbre* < Latin *marmor, -oris* < Greek *mármoros* marble, gleaming stone] —**mar′ble|like′**, *adj.*
► **Marbles**, the game, is plural in form and singular in use: *Marbles is played by many boys.*

**marble bones**, = osteopetrosis.

**marble cake**, a cake with streaks of dark and light, made by filling the pan with alternate spoonfuls of dark and light batter.

**mar|bled** (mär′bəld), *adj.* **1** decorated or covered with marble: *a marbled column.* **2** having a pattern like marble; mottled; dappled: *a marbled duck, a marbled cat.* **3** having the lean streaked with thin layers of fat: *finely marbled meat, a well-marbled roast of beef.*

**marbled godwit**, a large brownish shore bird with an upturned bill that nests in central North America.

**mar|ble|ize** (mar′bə līz), *v.t.,* **-ized, -iz|ing.** to make like marble in pattern, grain, or color.

**mar|bling** (mär′bling), *n.* **1** a coloring, graining, or marking that suggests marble: *beefsteak with a marbling of fat.* **2** a pattern of coloring, graining, or marking on book edges or bindings in imitation of the patterns of marble. **3** the staining of paper with colors in imitation of marble.

**mar|bly** (mär′blē), *adj.,* **-bli|er, -bli|est.** like marble.

**Mar|burg disease** (mär′bėrg), a contagious, often fatal, virus disease characterized by high fever and hemorrhaging. It was discovered in Marburg, Germany among technicians handling green monkeys: *A new virus related to the so-called Marburg, or green monkey, disease spread in Sudan and Zaire* (Richard H. Pfaff).

**marc** (märk; *French* mȧr), *n.* **1** the refuse that remains after pressing grapes or other fruits: *Wine made by pressing the marc or refuse that remains after all the sound grape juice has been squeezed from the grapes* (London Times). **2** brandy derived from this: *France's alcoholism consists mostly of excess wine drinking ... with some help from spirits like marc, Calvados, cognac* (New Yorker). **3** the residue that remains, as after extracting oil or the like, from plants, seeds, or nuts by means of a solvent. [< Middle French *marc*, verbal noun of *marcher* trample under foot; see etym. under **march**[1]]

**MARC** (märk), *n.* a computerized system for cataloging bibliographical data on magnetic tapes for use by libraries. [< *ma*(chine)-*r*(eadable) *c*(atalog)]

**mar|ca|site** (mär′kə sīt), *n.* **1** a whitish-yellow mineral with a metallic luster, a native iron disulfide, similar to and of the same composition as ordinary pyrite; white iron pyrites. *Formula:* $FeS_2$ **2** any crystallized iron pyrites used in the 1700's for ornaments. **3** a crystallized piece cut and polished as an ornament: *Marcasites are among the staple stones of costume jewelry* (London Times). [< Medieval Latin *marcasita* < Arabic *marqashītā* < Aramaic]

**mar|ca|sit|i|cal** (mär′kə sit′ə kəl), *adj.* having to do with or containing marcasite.

**mar|ca|to** (mär kä′tō), *adj., adv. Music.* —*adj.* with strong emphasis; accentuated; marked: *The beautiful, languid tune ... was played in quite strict time and in almost marcato rhythm* (London Times). —*adv.* in a marcato manner.
[< Italian *marcato* (literally) marked, past participle of *marcare* to mark]

**mar|cel** (mär sel′), *n., v.,* **-celled, -cel|ling.** —*n.* Also, **marcel wave.** a series of regular waves put in the hair.
—*v.t.* to set (the hair) with such waves.
[< *Marcel* Grateau, 1852-1936, a French hairdresser, who originated the style] —**mar|cel′ler**, *n.*

**mar|ces|cence** (mär ses′əns), *n.* marcescent condition.

**mar|ces|cent** (mär ses′ənt), *adj.* withering but not falling off, as a part of a plant. [< Latin *marcēscēns, -entis*, present participle of *marcēscere* to wither away < *marcēre* be faint, languid]

**march**[1] (märch), *v., n.* —*v.i.* **1** to walk as soldiers do, in time and with steps of the same length: *The members of the band marched in the parade to the beat of the drums.* **2** to walk or go on steadily; advance: *The boy marched to the front of the room and began his speech. The minister marched to the altar. Miss Ophelia marched straight to her own chamber* (Harriet Beecher Stowe). **3** *Figurative.* to proceed steadily; advance: *History marches on.* **4** to demonstrate or protest by marching: *Their first realization that the school was being marched on came when the demonstrating students ... formed ranks around the building and [began] chants of "Strike! Strike! Strike!"* (New Yorker).
—*v.t.* **1** to cause to march or go: *The teacher marched the children out to the playground. The policeman marched the thief off to jail. March the regiment to the barracks.* **2** to pass over, across, or through in marching.
—*n.* **1** the act or fact of marching: *The news of the enemy's march made whole villages flee.* **2** a manner of marching: *a slow march.* **3** music meant for marching; piece of music with a rhythm suited to accompany marching: *We enjoyed listening to marches.* **4** the distance marched; distance covered in a single course of marching: *The camp is a day's march away.* **5** a long, hard walk. **6** a forward movement; advance; progress: *History records the march of events. We may resume the march of our existence* (Byron). **7** a demonstration or protest by marching: *The leaders of the march on Washington would meet in the next days to assess the results of the demonstration* (New York Times).
**on the march,** making progress; going ahead; advancing: *The National Farmers Organization, many of its members freed by winter from their daily chores, is on the march again* (New York Times). *The Tories are at least on the march* (Manchester Guardian Weekly).
**steal a march,** to gain an advantage without being noticed: *to steal a march on one's competitors. We must be off early ... and steal a long march upon them* (Frederick Marryat).
[< Middle French *marcher*, earlier, to trample, ultimately < Late Latin *marcus* hammer < Latin *marculus* small hammer]

**march**[2] (märch), *n., v.* —*n.* the land along the border of a country; frontier: *Those low and barren tracts were the outlying marches of the empire* (John L. Motley). SYN: boundary.
—*v.i.* to border (on).
**the Marches,** the districts along the border between England and Scotland, or between England and Wales: *... then occupying those parts which we now call the middle Marches, between the English and Scots* (William Warner).
[< Old French *marche* < Germanic (compare Old High German *marcha*, English *mark*[1]). Compare etym. under **marquis**.]

**March** (märch), *n.* the third month of the year. It has 31 days. *Abbr:* Mar. [< Old French *marche* < Latin *Martius* (*mēnsis*) (month) of Mars]

**March.,** marchioness.

**M. Arch.,** Master of Architecture.

**Mär|chen** (mer′ʜən), *n., pl.* **Mär|chen.** *German.* **1** a fairy tale or folk tale. **2** any story or tale.

**march|er**[1] (mär′chər), *n.* a person who marches or walks.

**march|er**[2] (mär′chər), *n.* **1** an inhabitant of a march. **2** an officer or lord having jurisdiction over border territory.

**marcher lord,** any one of the barons granted control of the Marches under William the Conqueror.

**March|es** (mär′chiz), **the.** See under **march**[2].

**mar|che|sa** (mär kā′zä), *n., pl.* **-che|se** (-kā′zā). *Italian.* the wife or widow of a marchese; marchioness.

**mar|che|se** (mär kā′zā), *n., pl.* **-che|si** (-kā′zē). *Italian.* a nobleman ranking next above a count and next below a prince.

**March fly,** any one of a group of dark-colored flies, sometimes marked with red or yellow, which appear in the spring and feed on the roots of plants and decaying vegetable matter.

**march|ing orders** (mär′ching), **1** *Military.* orders to proceed or to begin a march. **2** *Informal, Figurative.* notice to an employee that he has been discharged: *He referred to a recent case where the directors of a company gave the guilty executives their "marching orders"* (London Times).

**mar|chion|ess** (mär′shə nis), *n.* **1** the wife or widow of a marquis. **2** a lady equal in rank to a marquis. [< Medieval Latin *marchionissa* < *marchio, -onis* marquis < *marche* march[2]. Compare etym. under **march**[2].]

**march|land** (märch′land′, -lənd), *n.* a border territory; frontier district.

**March of Dimes,** *U.S.* an annual appeal for and collection of money, originally for research on poliomyelitis and rehabilitation of victims of it, and now for combating other diseases as well.

**march|pane** (märch′pān′), *n.* = marzipan. [< Italian *marzapane*; see etym. under **marzipan**]

**march-past** (märch′past′, -päst′), *n.* a parade or march, especially by troops, past a reviewing stand.

**Mar|cion|ism** (mär′shə niz əm), *n.* the beliefs and doctrines of the Marcionites.

**Mar|cion|ist** (mär′shə nist), *n., adj.* = Marcionite.

**Mar|cion|ite** (mär′shə nīt), *n., adj.* —*n.* a member or adherent of a Gnostic sect founded in Rome in the 100's A.D., which rejected most of the Bible and regarded the Biblical God as an imperfect divinity, the supreme God being manifested in Jesus Christ.
—*adj.* of or having to do with the Marcionites or Marcionism: *Marcionite heresies.*
[< *Marcion*, a Christian Gnostic of the 100's A.D., who founded the sect + *-ite*[1]]

**Mar|co|ni** (mär kō′nē), *adj.* of or designating the system of wireless telegraphy devised by Guglielmo Marconi (1874-1937), an Italian engineer who helped to perfect wireless telegraphy.

**mar·co·ni·gram** (mär kō′nē gram), *n.* a wireless telegram; radiogram.

***Marconi rig**, a rig for a sailboat having one or more jibs and a large fore-and-aft sail hoisted on a tall mast with the foot set on a boom; Bermuda rig.

***Marconi rig**

**Marco Polo sheep**, a large wild sheep, a variety of argali, native to the plateaus of central Asia; Pamir sheep; Tian-shan sheep.

**Mar·cu·si·an** or **Mar·cu·se·an** (mär kü′zē ən), *adj., n.* —*adj.* of or having to do with the ideas and theories of Herbert Marcuse (born 1898), a German-born American philosopher.
—*n.* a follower or supporter of Marcuse or of his ideas: *But there too were the extreme Marcusians, ... students who demanded democratic participation in the running of research laboratories and scientific foundations* (Punch).

**Mar·di gras** (mär′dē grä′), or **Mardi Gras**, the last day before Lent; Shrove Tuesday. It is celebrated in New Orleans and other cities with parades and festivities. [< French *mardi gras* fat (that is, meat-eating) Tuesday; *mardis* < Latin *Martis* (*dies*) (day) of Mars, Tuesday; *gras* < Latin *crassus*]

**Mar·duk** (mär′dük), *n.* the chief god of the Babylonians, originally a god of the city of Babylon only.

**mare**[1] (mãr), *n.* a female horse or donkey, especially when mature: *In two and a half hours, sixteen yearlings and 23 brood mares were auctioned off* (Newsweek). [Middle English *mare,* Old English *mearh* horse]

**mare**[2] (mãr), *n. Obsolete.* **1** a goblin once believed to cause nightmares by sitting on the chest of the sleeper. **2** the nightmare itself. [Old English *mare*]

**ma·re**[3] (mär′ē, mãr′ē), *n., pl.* **ma·ri·a.** **1** *Astronomy.* **a** a broad, flat, dark area on the moon: ... *these dark areas appear as smooth gray plains, so uniform that Galileo and his contemporaries thought they might be seas and accordingly called them maria* (John Charles Duncan). **b** a similar dark region on any planet. **2** *Latin.* a sea.

**ma·re clau·sum** (mär′ē klô′səm; mãr′ē), *Latin.* a closed sea; waters within the sphere of control of one nation.

**Mar·ek's disease** (mãr′iks), a contagious disease of the lymph system of chickens, caused by a herpesvirus and resulting in paralysis, blindness, and tumors; fowl paralysis. It is the most common form of the avian leucosis complex. [< Jacob *Marek,* a German veterinarian of the 1900's]

**ma·re li·be·rum** (mär′ē lib′ər əm; mãr′ē), *Latin.* open sea; the high seas.

**ma·rem·ma** (mə rem′ə), *n., pl.* **-rem·me** (-rem′ē). **1** a low, marshy, unhealthful region by the seashore. **2** the miasma of such a region. [< Italian *maremma* < Latin *maritima,* feminine of *maritimus* maritime]

**ma·re nos·trum** (mär′ē nos′trəm; mãr′ē), *Latin.* our sea: *The Mediterranean ... Rome's mare nostrum* (Time).

**mar·e·schal** (mar′ə shəl), *n. Obsolete or Archaic.* marshal.

**mare's-nest** (mãrz′nest′), *n.* **1** a supposedly great discovery that turns out to be a mistake or hoax: *In Mr. Sutliff's opinion, Mr. Kraushauer had run off after a mare's-nest* (John Stephen Strange). **2** a condition of great disorder or confusion.

**mare's-tail** (mãrz′tāl′), *n.* **1** a long, feathery cirrus cloud shaped somewhat like a horse's tail. **2** a water plant, with many circles of narrow, hairlike leaves around the stems. **3** = horsetail (def. 2).

**Ma·re·zine** (mãr′ə zēn, -zin), *n. Trademark.* = cyclizine.

**Mar·fan's syndrome** (mär′fänz), a congenital and hereditary condition characterized by abnormal length and slenderness of the arms, legs, fingers, and toes. [< Bernard-Jean *Marfan,* 1858-1942, a French pediatrician, who first recognized the syndrome]

**marg** (märj), *n. Informal.* margarine.

**marg.**, **1** margin. **2** marginal.

**mar·gar·ic acid** (mär gar′ik, -gär′-; mär′gər-), a white, crystalline, fatty acid found in lichens and produced artificially, resembling palmitic and stearic acids. *Formula:* $C_{17}H_{34}O_2$ [< French *acide margarique* < Greek *márgaron* pearl (from the appearance of its crystals)]

**mar·ga·rin** (mär′jər in), *n.* = margarine.

**mar·ga·rine** (mär′jə rin, -jə rēn; -gər in, -gə rēn), *n.* a substitute for butter made from cottonseed oil, soybean oil, and other vegetable oils; oleomargarine: *We like margarine on bread. Modern margarine is made from refined vegetable oils ... grown on American farms, plus cultured skim milk* (Time). [< French *margarine* < *margarique;* see etym. under **margaric acid**]

**mar·ga·ri·ta** (mär′gə rē′tə), *n.* a cocktail made of tequila, orange-flavored liqueur, and lime (or lemon) juice, usually served in a glass whose rim is treated with salt. [< Mexican Spanish *margarita* < Spanish *Margarita* Margaret, or < *margarita* a daisy]

**mar·ga·rite** (mär′gə rīt), *n.* **1** a hydrated calcium aluminum silicate, occurring as scales with a pearly luster. *Formula:* $H_2CaAl_4Si_2O_{12}$ **2** *Archaic.* a pearl. [< Latin *margarīta* < Greek *margarī́tēs* (pearl) stone < *márgaron* pearl]

**Mar·gaux** (mär gō′), *n.* a claret produced in the commune of Margaux, in the region near Bordeaux.

**mar·gay** (mär′gā), *n.* a small, long-tailed, spotted wildcat of the same genus as and similar to the ocelot, found from Texas south to Brazil: *The elusive Texas margay ... has only been taken one time, back in the last century* (Science News Letter). [< French *margay,* alteration of *margaia* < Tupi (Brazil) *mbaracaïa*]

**marge**[1] (märj), *n. Archaic.* a margin; edge; border: *the illuminated marge of some old book* (James Russell Lowell). *The plashy brink Of weedy lake, or marge of river wide* (William Cullen Bryant). [< Middle French *marge,* learned borrowing from Latin *margō, -inis* margin]

**marge**[2] (märj), *n. Informal.* margarine.

**mar·gent** (mär′jənt), *n. Archaic.* margin: *Across the margent of the world I fled* (Francis Thompson). [alteration of *margin*]

**mar·gin** (mär′jən), *n., v.* —*n.* **1** an edge or border: *the margin of a lake. A step or two farther brought him to one margin of a little clearing* (Robert Louis Stevenson). *Over the margin, After it, follow it, Follow the Gleam* (Tennyson). **SYN:** brim, brink, rim, verge. **2** the space around a page that has no writing or printing on it: *Do not write in the margin.* (*Figurative.*) *I love a broad margin to my life* (Thoreau). **3** *Figurative.* an extra amount; amount beyond what is necessary; difference: *a margin for error. We allow a margin of 15 minutes in catching a train.* **4** the difference between the cost and selling price, as of stocks. **5** *Finance.* **a** the money or securities deposited with a broker to protect him from loss on transactions undertaken for the real buyer or seller. **b** the amount of such a deposit: *The reserve board raised margins from 50 to 60 per cent* (New York Times). **c** the transaction itself, financed by both the broker and his customer: *When you buy on margin you put up only part of the total cost and the broker lends you the remainder.* **d** the customer's profit or loss in such a transaction. **6** the point at which an economic activity yields just enough return to cover its costs and below which the activity will result in a loss. **7** a condition beyond which something ceases to exist or be possible; limit: *the margin of subsistence, the margin of consciousness. Abbr:* marg.
—*v.t.* **1** to provide with a margin; border: *The shore ... was margined with foam* (Herman Melville). **2** to enter (notes, comments, figures, or sketches) in the margin. **3** to provide (a book or article) with marginal notes. **4** *Finance.* **a** to deposit a margin upon (stock or other securities). **b** to secure by a margin: *Probably 45 per cent of all purchases on the Stock Exchange are margined* (New York Times).
[< Latin *margō, marginis* edge]

**mar·gin·al** (mär′jə nəl), *adj., n.* —*adj.* **1** written or printed in a margin: *a marginal comment.* **2** of or in a margin: *marginal space.* **3** on or near the margin: *Marginal land is barely fit for farming.* **4** *Figurative.* existing or occurring on the fringes of anything established; only partly taken in: *a marginal culture.* **5a** barely producing or capable of producing, as goods or crops, at a profitable rate: *The small, inefficient or marginal farmer* (New Yorker). **b** of, having to do with, or obtained from goods or crops that are so produced and marketed: *marginal income. Britain's current economic problem is marginal* (Newsweek). **6** *Sociology.* only partially assimilated in a social group: *The marginal man is the person who belongs to two or more cultures but is not fully accepted in any* (Emory S. Bogardus).
—*n. Especially British.* a constituency where the results of an election might favor either party: *Of five by-elections pending, two are in marginals* (Sunday Times).
[< New Latin *marginalis* < Latin *margō;* see etym. under **margin**] —**mar′gin·al·ly,** *adv.*

**mar·gi·na·li·a** (mär′jə nā′lē ə), *n.pl.* marginal notes. [< New Latin *marginalia,* neuter plural of *marginalis* marginal]

**mar·gin·al·i·ty** (mär′jə nal′ə tē), *n.* the quality or condition of being marginal.

**mar·gin·al·ize** (mär′jə nə līz), *v.t.,* **-ized, -iz·ing.** to make marginal; leave on the fringes of society: ... *towering economic and social problems which effectively leave half the populations marginalized* (Richard Wigg). —**mar′gin·al·i·za′tion,** *n.*

**marginal utility**, the utility derived, or expected, from a unit of a commodity which a buyer is just barely willing to purchase at the prevailing price.

**mar·gin·ate** (mär′jə nāt), *v.,* **-at·ed, -at·ing,** *adj.* —*v.t.* to provide with a margin; border.
—*adj.* having a margin.
[< Latin *margināre* (with English *-ate*[1]) furnish with a margin < *margō, marginis* margin] —**mar′gin·a′tion,** *n.*

**mar·gin·at·ed** (mär′jə nā′tid), *adj.* = marginate.

**mar·go·sa** (mär gō′sə), *n.* an East Indian tree of the mahogany family whose oil and bitter bark are used in medicine. [< Portuguese *amargosa,* feminine of *amargoso* bitter]

**mar·gra·vate** (mär′grə vāt), *n.* = margraviate.

**mar·grave** (mär′grāv), *n.* **1** a title of certain princes of Germany or the Holy Roman Empire. **2** the military governor of a German border province in former times. [earlier *marcgrave* < Middle Dutch *markgrave* count of the marches]

**mar·gra·vi·al** (mär grā′vē əl), *adj.* of or having to do with a margrave or a margraviate.

**mar·gra·vi·ate** (mär grā′vē āt, -it), *n.* the territory ruled by a margrave.

**mar·gra·vine** (mär′grə vēn), *n.* the wife or widow of a margrave.

**mar·gue·rite** (mär′gə rēt′), *n.* **1** a kind of daisy with white petals and a yellow center, such as the oxeye daisy. **2** any one of several kinds of chrysanthemums with daisylike flowers. [< French *marguerite* pearl < Old French *margarite;* see etym. under **margarite**]

**Ma·ri** (mä′rē), *n., pl.* **-ri** or **-ris.** a member of a Finno-Ugric people of the Volga Valley of the Soviet Union.

**ma·ri·a** (mär′ē ə, mãr′ē ə), *n.* plural of **mare**[3].

**ma·ri·a·chi** (mär′ē äch′ē), *n., pl.* **-chis.** **1** a member of a Mexican band of strolling singers and musicians: *Professional mariarchis in old times were wandering minstrels* (Saturday Review). **2** a band of mariachis. **3** music played by such a band: *Several informal groups of musicians were playing mariachi* (Harper's). [< Mexican Spanish *mariachi,* probably < French *mariage* marriage (because they originally played at weddings)]

**ma·ri·age de con·ve·nance** (mȧ ryȧzh′ də kôɴvnäɴs′), *French.* a marriage of convenience or expediency, especially to gain prestige, wealth, or other advantage.

**Mar·i·an** (mãr′ē ən), *adj., n.* —*adj.* **1** of or having to do with the Virgin Mary. **2** of or having to do with some other Mary, such as Mary, Queen of Scots.
—*n.* **1** a worshiper of the Virgin Mary. **2** a supporter of Mary, Queen of Scots.

**Mar·i·an·ism** (mãr′ē ə niz′əm), *n.* **1** the worship of the Virgin Mary. **2** the theory or belief concerning this worship: *The differences between Protestants and Roman Catholics are normally defined in terms of doctrine—papal infallibility, Marianism, the nature of the church* (Time).

**Mar·i·anne** (mãr′ē an′), *n.* the republic of France personified as a woman in flowing robes and wearing a liberty cap.

**Mar·i·a·nol·o·gy** (mãr′ē ən ol′ə jē), *n.* the body of knowledge and opinion relating to the Virgin Mary; Mariology.

**Ma·ri·a The·re·sa dollar** or **thaler** (mə rē′ə tə-rā′sə), = Levant dollar. [< *Maria Theresa,* 1717-1780, queen of Bohemia and Hungary from 1740 to 1780]

**ma·ri com·plai·sant** (mȧ rē′ kôɴ ple zäɴ′), *French.* **1** a husband who puts up with an unfaithful wife; cuckold. **2** (literally) complaisant husband.

**Mar·i·co·pa** (mar′ə kō′pə), *n., pl.* **-pa** or **-pas.** **1** a member of a North American Indian tribe inhabiting the Gila River valley in Arizona. **2** the Hokan language of this tribe.

**mar·i·cul·ture** (mar′ə kul′chər), *n.* the cultivation of marine plants and animals for food and raw materials; sea farming; marine farming: *If we are very optimistic and assume for a moment that the yield of the traditional fishery will not change,*

**Pronunciation Key:** hat, āge, cãre, fär; let, ēqual, tėrm; it, īce; hot, ōpen, ôrder; **oi**l, **ou**t; cup, pu̇t, rüle; **ch**ild; lo**ng**; **th**in; ᴛʜen; **zh**, measure; **ə** represents **a** in about, **e** in taken, **i** in pencil, **o** in lemon, **u** in circus.

*mariculture could perhaps lead to an increment in the crop produced from the sea from the present 1% to 1.1%* (Pieter Korringa). [< Latin *maris* sea + *cultūra* culture]

▶ The related term *aquaculture* encompasses all bodies of water, including the sea.

**mar|i|cul|tur|ist** (mar′ə kul′chər ist), *n.* a person who engages in mariculture.

**mar|i|gold** (mar′ə gōld), *n.* **1** a plant with yellow, orange, brownish, or red flowers. It belongs to the composite family. See picture under **composite family**. **2** any calendula, especially the pot marigold. **3** the flower of any of these plants. [Middle English *mary-goulden* < (the Virgin) *Mary* + *gold*]

***mar|i|jua|na** or **mar|i|hua|na** (mar′ə wä′nə), *n.* **1** the hemp plant; Indian hemp; cannabis. **2** a drug made from its dried leaves and flowers, smoked in cigarettes to produce a narcotic-like effect; hashish. [American English < Mexican Spanish *mariguana, marihuana*]

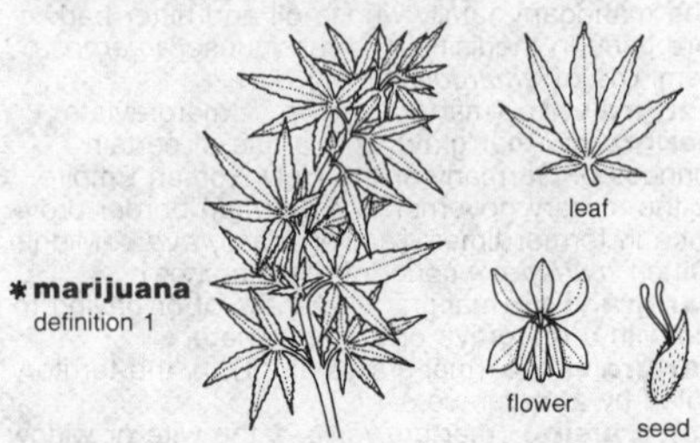

***marijuana** definition 1

**ma|rim|ba** (mə rim′bə), *n.* a musical instrument somewhat like a xylophone. It consists of small bars of hard wood that produce different sounds when they are struck with mallets. [ultimately < a Bantu word]

**ma|ri|na** (mə rē′nə), *n.* a dock where moorings and supplies are available, having a service station for small boats. It frequently has other facilities such as sleeping accommodations, restaurant, stores, and amusements. [< Spanish, or Italian *marina* shore, coast < Latin *marīna;* see etym. under **marine**]

**mar|i|nade** (*n.* mar′ə nād′; *v.* mar′ə nād), *n., v.,* **-nad|ed, -nad|ing.** —*n.* **1** a spiced vinegar, wine, or oil used to pickle meat or fish. **2** meat or fish pickled in this.
—*v.t.* = marinate. [< French *marinade* < *mariner* to marinate]

**ma|ri|na|ra** (mar′ə nar′ə), *n.* a sauce flavored with tomatoes and garlic, used in Italian cuisine: *The spaghetti, a great specialty, is presented with the usual sauces—mushroom, meat, marinara, tomato* (New York Times). [< Italian *marinare* to marinate < French *mariner;* see etym. under **marinate**]

**mar|i|nate** (mar′ə nāt), *v.,* **-nat|ed, -nat|ing.**
—*v.t.* **1** to soak (food) in brine or marinade. **2** to soak in oil and vinegar. **3** *Figurative: Our faculty have to learn to write English, a rare skill among people who have been marinated in academic jargon* (John Fischer).
—*v.i.* to be or become marinated: *The meat marinated in the brine for two days.* (*Figurative.*) *During the 1968 campaign it was said by Republicans that R.M.N. had somehow, during his eight long years in political exile, marinated from an "old" Nixon into a "new" Nixon* (Time). [< French *mariner* (with English *-ate*[1]) to pickle in (sea) brine < Old French *marin,* adjective, marine] —**mar′i|na′tion,** *n.*

**ma|rine** (mə rēn′), *adj., n.* —*adj.* **1** of the sea; found in the sea; produced by the sea: *Seals and whales are marine animals.* **SYN:** pelagic, oceanic. **2** of shipping; maritime: *marine law.* **3** of the navy; naval: *marine power.* **4** for use at sea or on a ship: *marine supplies, a marine engine.* **5a** of or having to do with ships, sailors, or other aspects of the sea: *marine lore.* **b** of or having to do with navigation at sea: *a marine compass.* **6a** of or having to do with a marine or marines. **b** serving or trained to serve as a marine. **7** = underwater: *marine salvage.*
—*n.* **1** shipping; fleet: *our merchant marine.* **2a** a soldier formerly serving only at sea, now also serving on land and in the air. **b** Also, **Marine.** a person serving in the Marine Corps. **3** a picture of the sea, seashore, or ships at sea; seascape: *His first solo show in five years comprises portraits, landscapes, and marines* (New Yorker). **4** the government department of naval affairs in France and some other European countries.
**marines,** the Marine Corps.
**tell that to the marines,** *Informal.* an expression of contemptuous disbelief, originally implying an amount of credulity on the part of marines that would not be found in sailors: *Tell that to the marines—the sailors won't believe it* (Scott).
[< Old French *marin* < Latin *marīnus* of the sea < *mare, maris* sea]

**marine biologist,** a person who studies marine biology.

**marine biology,** a branch of biology dealing with the living organisms of the sea.

**marine blue,** a navy blue that is somewhat purple or green in hue.

**Marine Corps,** a separate branch of the Armed Forces of the United States. Its members are trained especially for landing operations. The Marine Corps has its own air, sea, and land units and is independently responsible to the Secretary of the Navy.

**marine engineering,** a branch of engineering that deals with the design of ships and submarines and their propulsion system.

**marine farming,** = mariculture.

**marine glue,** a glue used in ship carpentry, consisting of rubber, shellac, and pitch.

**marine iguana,** an iguana of the Galapagos Islands that feeds on seaweed in the surf.

**marine insurance,** insurance against damage to goods in transit and their means of transportation, especially in regard to shipwrecks or disasters at sea.

**marine league,** a measure of nautical distance equal to three nautical miles.

**marine leg,** a device consisting of a chute containing electrically operated buckets that convey grain between the hold of a ship and the cupola of a grain elevator.

**mar|i|ner** (mar′ə nər), *n.* **1** a person who navigates or assists in navigating a ship; sailor; seaman: *... as reassuring a beacon as a lighthouse to a lost mariner* (New Yorker). **2** *Law.* any person employed on a ship. [< Anglo-French *mariner,* Old French *marinier* < *marin* marine]

**mariner's compass,** a sensitive, accurate compass on a ship or boat, supported in a box or bowl on gimbals, placed for the helmsman to steer by.

**marine science,** the sciences dealing with the sea and its environment, including marine biology, oceanography, and similar specializations.

**marine son|o|probe** (son′ə prōb′), an instrument used in the exploration for oil to analyze offshore subsurface formations by means of reflected sound waves.

**Mar|i|ol|a|ter** (mãr′ē ol′ə tər), *n.* a worshiper of the Virgin Mary.

**Ma|ri|ol|a|trous** (mãr′ē ol′ə trəs), *adj.* characterized by Mariolatry.

**Mar|i|ol|a|try** (mãr′ē ol′ə trē), *n.* worship of the Virgin Mary. [< Greek *Maríā* + *latreíā* worship]

**Mar|i|o|log|i|cal** (mãr′ē ə loj′ə kəl), *adj.* of or having to do with Mariology.

**Mar|i|ol|o|gy** (mãr′ē ol′ə jē), *n.* = Marianology.

**Mar|i|on beauty ivy** (mar′ē ən), a variety of ivy with trailing stems and lush green leaves, often kept as a house plant.

***mar|i|o|nette** (mar′ē ə net′), *n.* a doll or puppet moved by strings or by the hands, often on a little stage: *At the end of the living room, a couple who worked a marionette show were dismantling their stage* (New Yorker). [< French *marionnette* < *Marion* (diminutive) < *Marie* Mary]

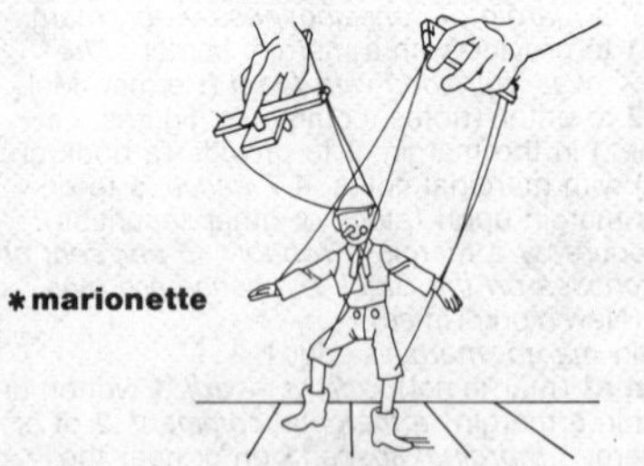
***marionette**

**Mar|i|otte's law** (mar′ē ots′), = Boyle's law (in continental Europe). [< Edme *Mariotte,* 1620-1684, a French physicist]

**mar|i|po|sa** or **Mar|i|po|sa lily** or **tulip** (mar′ə-pō′sə, -zə), **1** any one of a genus of plants of the lily family with tuliplike yellow, white, blue, or lilac flowers, growing in the western United States and in Mexico. **2** the flower. [American English < Spanish *mariposa* butterfly]

**Mar|i|sat** (mar′ə sat′), *n.* any one of a group of United States communications satellites positioned over the Atlantic, Pacific, and Indian oceans to transmit maritime weather conditions. [< *Mari*(time) + *sat*(ellite)]

**mar|ish** (mar′ish), *n., adj. Archaic.* —*n.* a marsh. —*adj.* **1** marshy. **2** such as is found in marshes: *a matted, marish vegetation* (Robert Louis Stevenson). [Middle English *mareis* < Old French *marais;* origin uncertain]

**Mar|ist** (mãr′ist), *n., adj.* —*n.* a member of a Roman Catholic missionary and teaching order, founded in 1816, devoted to the Virgin Mary.
—*adj.* of or belonging to the Marists. [< French *Mariste* < *Marie* the Virgin Mary]

**mar|i|tal** (mar′ə təl), *adj.* **1** of or having to do with marriage: *A man and woman take marital vows when they marry.* **SYN:** matrimonial, connubial. **2** *Archaic.* of a husband. [< Latin *marītālis* < *marītus* married man] —**mar′i|tal|ly,** *adv.*

**marital deduction,** a tax deduction in the United States of up to one-half the net value of an estate which a deceased leaves entirely to his spouse.

**mar|i|time** (mar′ə tīm), *adj.* **1** of the sea; having something to do with shipping and sailing; nautical: *Ships and sailors are governed by maritime laws.* **2** on the sea; near the sea: *Boston is a maritime city.* **3** living near the sea: *Many maritime peoples are fishermen.* **4** characteristic of a seaman; nautical: *Solomon Gills ... was far from having a maritime appearance* (Dickens). [< Latin *maritimus* < *mare, maris* sea]

**Mar|i|time** (mar′ə tīm), *adj., n.* —*adj.* of, having to do with, or characteristic of the Maritime Provinces along the Atlantic coast of Canada.
—*n.* a Maritime Province.

**maritime law,** the branch of law dealing with affairs of the sea or other navigable waters, of boats and ships, and of cargo; admiralty law.

**maritime pine,** = pinaster.

**Mar|i|tim|er** (mar′ə tī′mər), *n.* a native or inhabitant of the Maritime Provinces.

**mar|jo|ram** (mär′jə rəm), *n.* **1** any one of a genus of fragrant herbs of the mint family related to the oregano. Sweet marjoram is used as flavoring in cooking. **2** = oregano. [< unrecorded Old French *marjorane,* alteration of *maiorane,* learned borrowing from Medieval Latin *majorana,* also *majoraca,* perhaps < Latin *amāracus* bitter < Greek *amárakos*]

**mark**[1] (märk), *n., v.* —*n.* **1** a trace or impression made by some object on the surface of another. A line, dot, spot, stain, dent, or scar is a mark. *The old soldier showed me the mark of an old wound.* **2a** a line or dot to show position: *the high-water mark. This mark shows how far you jumped.* **b** the line where a race starts: *On the mark; get set; go! The race will start from the mark.* **3** something that shows what or whose a thing is; sign; indication: *a laundry mark. Courtesy is a mark of good breeding.* **4** a tag with a mark on it: *Remove the price mark from your new suit.* **5** a written or printed stroke or sign: *punctuation marks. She took up her pen and made a few marks on the paper.* **6** a letter or number to show how well one has done; grade or rating: *My mark in arithmetic was B.* **7** a cross or other sign made by a person who cannot write, instead of signing his name: *Make your mark here. Dost thou sign thy name or make thy mark?* (Herman Melville). **8** something to be aimed at; target: *Standing there, the lion was an easy mark. Both balls had passed through the lungs—the true mark in shooting buffalo* (Francis Parkman). (*Figurative.*) *So I was a mark for plunder at once, And lost my cash* (Rudyard Kipling). **SYN:** goal. **9** *Figurative.* what is usual, proper, or expected; standard: *A tired person does not feel up to the mark.* **10** *Figurative.* influence; impression: *A great man leaves his mark on whatever he does.* **11** *Figurative.* eminence; importance; distinction: *That doctor is a man of mark. And left me in reputeless banishment, A fellow of no mark nor likelihood* (Shakespeare). *There was nothing of high mark in this* (Dickens). **12** *Nautical.* **a** a piece of bunting, bit of leather, knot, or other material or device, used to mark depths on a lead line. **b** = Plimsoll mark. **13** the jack or its position in the game of bowls. **14** *British.* a model or class: *a heavy machine gun* (*Mark IV*). **15** *Boxing.* the solar plexus. **16** *British.* a registration of the sale of stocks. **17** *Slang.* a person marked as good pickings; sucker: *I teased my way into the pockets of a thousand marks or two* (Newsweek). **18** *Archaic.* a border or frontier. **19** *Obsolete.* a landmark. **20** *Obsolete.* a memorial stone.
—*v.t.* **1** to give grades to; rate: *The teacher marked our examination papers.* **2** to make a mark on or put one's name on to show whose a thing is. **3** to make a mark on by stamping, cutting, or writing: *Be careful not to mark the table.* **4** to trace or form by marks or as if by marks. **5** to show by a mark: (*Figurative.*) *They never marked a man for death* (Rudyard Kipling). (*Figurative.*) *Melancholy mark'd him for her own* (Thomas Gray). **6** to show clearly; indicate; manifest: *A tall pine marks the beginning of the trail. A frown marked her disapproval.* **7** *Figurative.* to distinguish; set off; characterize: *Many important discoveries mark the last 150 years. His character was marked by profligacy, insolence, and ingratitude* (James Boswell). **8** *Figurative.* to give

attention to; notice; observe; see: *Mark how carefully he moves. Mark my words; his plan will fail. Full well I mark'd the features of his face* (Alexander Pope). *Mark my bidding, and be safe* (Charles Brockden Brown). SYN: note, heed, regard, consider. **9** to put in a pin or make a line to show where a place is: *Mark all of the large cities on this map.* **10** to keep (the score); record. **11** to put a price mark on; tag: *All goods are plainly marked for sale.* **12** to register: *The thermometer marked 90° F.* **13** *British.* to register (a sale of stocks) so as to put it on the official price list: *On Tuesday 823 bargains were marked* (Economist).
—*v.i.* **1** to make a mark or marks. **2** *Figurative.* to pay attention; take notice; consider: *Mark, I pray you, and see how this man seeketh mischief* (I Kings 20:7). **3** to keep score in a game.
**beside the mark, a** not hitting the thing aimed at: *The bullet went beside the mark.* **b** *Figurative.* not to the point; off the subject; not relevant: *To reason with such a writer is like talking to a deaf man, who catches at a stray word, makes answer beside the mark* (Macaulay).
**hit the mark, a** to succeed in doing what one tried to do: *He hit the mark when he became president of the class.* **b** to be exactly right: *Venerable name was found ... luckily hitting the mark, as a title neither too high nor too low* (Thomas Fuller).
**make one's mark,** to succeed; become well known: *That boy is a hard worker, he'll make his mark. That fellow's a gentleman's son ... and he'll make his mark* (Ella L. Dorsey).
**mark down, a** to write down; note down: *to mark down an appointment in a datebook.* **b** to mark for sale at a lower price: *We have selected over $30,000 of our elegant stock and marked them down 50 per cent* (Chicago Tribune). **c** to note where (game) has gone to cover: *It is no good to talk of having marked birds down, unless you have distinctly seen a certain toss up of the wings as they pitch* (Cornhill Magazine).
**mark off** or **out, a** to make lines to show the position of or to separate: *We marked out the tennis court. The hedge marks off one yard from another.* **b** *Figurative.* to differentiate; distinguish: *Thus, in the last resort, what marks human history off from natural history is the fact that it is—quite deliberately—man-centered* (New Yorker).
**mark out for,** to set aside for; select for: *He seemed marked out for trouble.*
**mark up, a** to deface or disfigure: *Don't mark up the desks.* **b** to add; put: *to mark up the score.* **c** to mark for sale at a higher price: *The prices of venison and other game was so far "marked up" that gold ... was charged for salmon* (American Naturalist). **d** to revise a legislative bill to put it in final form: *The budget committee is marking up the new bill before presenting it to Congress.*
**miss the mark, a** to fail to do what one tried to do: *Many a preacher misses the mark because, though he knows books, he does not know men* (John Stalker). **b** to be not exactly right: *His answer to the arithmetic problem missed the mark.*
**off the mark, a** missing the desired object or end: *The projections of the Government on these outlays, ... turned out to be pretty far off the mark* (Wall Street Journal). **b** off the subject; inaccurate: *I leave it to them equally to decide whether my very brief and necessarily incomplete summary of Bruner's ideas is as far off the mark as he claims* (New Yorker).
**save** (or **bless**) **the mark,** an exclamation of deprecation, apology, impatience, or contempt: *The best of my talents* (*bless the mark*) *shut up even from my own poor view* (Thomas Carlyle).
**toe the mark, a** to stand with the tips of the toes touching a certain line or mark, as before a race or contest: *The chief mate ... marked a line on the deck, brought the two boys up to it, making them toe the mark* (Richard H. Dana, Jr.). **b** *Figurative.* to conform to a certain standard, as of duty or conduct: *He began to think it was high time to toe the mark* (James K. Paulding).
**wide of the mark, a** missing the thing aimed at by a considerable margin: *The shot fell wide of the mark.* **b** *Figurative.* irrelevant: *It may, however, be ... very wide of the mark when applied to the case* (John R. McCulloch).
[Old English *mearc* boundary, mark, limit of space or time. Compare etym. under **march**².]
—***Syn.*** *n.* **3 Mark, sign, token,** mean an indication of something not visible or readily apparent. **Mark** particularly suggests an indication of the character of something: *Generosity is a mark of greatness.* **Sign** is the general word, applying to any indication, mark, or token, such as of quality, idea, or mental or physical state: *We could see no signs of life.* **Token** applies especially to something that stands as a reminder or promise of something else, as of a feeling or an event: *This gift is a token of my love.*

**mark²** (märk), *n.* **1** a German unit of money. The mark is now called the Deutsche mark, and is equal to 100 pfennigs. **2** a coin or paper note equal to the mark. *Abbr:* M. **3** an old weight for gold and silver, equal to 8 ounces. **4** = markka. **5** a former Scottish silver coin, worth slightly more than 13 shillings. [Old English *mearc,* perhaps < Germanic (compare Middle High German *marke*)]

**Mark** (märk), *n.* **1** one of the four Evangelists, a fellow worker with the Apostle Paul and the Apostle Peter; Saint Mark. **2** the second book of the New Testament, attributed to the Apostle Mark. It tells the story of the life of Christ. **3 King,** *Arthurian Legend.* a king of Cornwall, the uncle of Tristan and husband of Iseult. [< Latin *Mārcus,* a Roman praenomen]

**mark|down** (märk′doun′), *n., adj.* —*n.* **1** a decrease in the price of an article: *Spurts of selling—mostly in small blocks—touched off almost hourly markdowns* (Wall Street Journal). **2** the amount of this decrease.
—*adj.* of, having to do with, or characteristic of a markdown: *markdown prices.*

**marked** (märkt), *adj.* **1** having a mark or marks: *a marked table, marked money.* **2** *Figurative.* very noticeable; very plain; easily recognized: *There are marked differences between apples and oranges.* SYN: prominent, conspicuous, outstanding. **3** *Figurative.* distinguished or singled out as if by a mark: *Even as a youth he was marked for success.* **4** made note of as an object of suspicion, hatred, or vengeance: *When the gang discovered his hiding place, he knew he was a marked man.* **5** *Linguistics.* that indicates a distinctive class, function, or other feature. *Examples:* In the pair of phonemes *d* and *t, d* is marked for voicing. The suffix *-s* in boys is marked for plurality.

**mark|ed|ly** (mär′kid lē), *adv.* in a marked manner or degree; conspicuously; noticeably; plainly: *After this, the air temperature is known to rise markedly* (New Scientist).

**mark|ed|ness** (mär′kid nis), *n.* marked quality or condition.

**mark|er** (mär′kər), *n.* **1** a person or thing that marks: *Holding a black marker in his hand, the clerk numbered each carton as he counted them.* **2** a person or device that keeps the score in a game. **3** *Sports.* **a** a line or mark indicating position on a playing field: ... *went over standing up from the 7-yard marker* (New York Times). **b** score: ... *accounted for the first West Point marker on a 2-yard plunge* (New York Times). **4** a counter used in card games. **5** = bookmark: *Put a marker in that book ... page seventy-four* (Samuel Lover). **6** *U.S. Slang.* a pledge of payment, especially of a gambling debt; an I.O.U. **7** *Linguistics.* any unit that indicates a distinctive class, function, or other feature: *a number marker, a person marker, the plural marker -s.* **8** = genetic marker. **9** a machine formerly used to cut grooves in square patterns in ice covering a stream, pond, or lake, so that blocks could be cut for commercial use.

**mar|ket** (mär′kit), *n., v., adj.* —*n.* **1** a meeting of people for buying and selling: *To market, to market, To buy a fat pig* (Nursery Rhyme). **2** the people at such a meeting: *Excitement stirred the market.* **3** an open space or covered building in which food, cattle, and other things are shown for sale: ... *the busy market square, where piles of vari-colored fruits and vegetables gleam* (Atlantic). **4** a store for the sale of food: *a meat market.* **5** trade or traders, especially as regards a particular article: *the cotton market, the grain market, the best shoes in the market.* **6** the demand (for something); price offered: *a rising market for automobiles. The drought created a high market for corn.* **7** a region where goods may be sold; center of trade: *South America is a market for American automobiles.* **8** a chance to sell or buy: *to lose one's market. There is always a market for wheat. Do you know, Considering the market, there are more Poems produced than any other thing?* (Robert Frost).
—*v.t.* to sell: *The farmer cannot market all of his wheat.* **2** to carry or send to market: *The peasants marketed all their surplus produce.*
—*v.i.* to buy or sell in a market.
—*adj.* of, having to do with, or characteristic of a market: *Canned food bargains, dumped into the housewife's market basket ...* (Wall Street Journal).
**at the market,** at the price current when a broker sells or buys for a customer: *Jackson found that brokers had put in orders to buy 77,000 shares at the market* (New Yorker).
**be in the market for,** to be a possible buyer of: *If you are in the market for a used car, that dealer has some fine bargains.*
**glut the market,** to offer on a market a quantity, as of a commodity or stock, so greatly in excess of demand as to make the item unsalable except at a very low price: *The price for wheat dropped when the market was glutted with it.*
**play the market,** to speculate on the stock exchange: *He has been playing the market on tips.*
**price out of the market,** to lose business by setting a price above that of competitors or above what buyers will pay: *Many U.S. firms are pricing themselves out of the Far Eastern Market because of high prices and their reluctance to accept deferred payments.* (Wall Street Journal).
[< Old North French *market,* Old French *marchiet* < Latin *mercātus, -ūs* trade, market < *mercārī* to trade, deal in < *merx, mercis* merchandise]

**mar|ket|a|bil|i|ty** (mär′kə tə bil′ə tē), *n.* the quality of being marketable: *Voting rights would substantially increase the marketability of the shares* (Wall Street Journal).

**mar|ket|a|ble** (mär′kə tə bəl), *adj.* **1** that can be sold; salable: *Farmers therefore use less time and less food to bring stock to marketable weight* (Science News). **2** of or having to do with buying or selling. —**mar′ket|a|bly,** *adv.*

**market analysis,** the study of the extent, characteristics, and potential of a given market.
—**market analyst.**

**market economy,** an economic system based on free enterprise; capitalism: *This switch to a kind of market economy apparently has made East German industry much more efficient* (New York Times).

**mar|ke|teer** (mär′kə tir′), *n.* a person who sells in a market.

**mar|ket|er** (mär′kə tər), *n.* **1** a person who goes to market: *They could not walk side by side in that throng of marketers—women with shopping baskets, women pushing ...* (New Yorker). **2** a person who buys or sells in a market: *Happily for the marketers, Americans by nature seem to relish learning to want new things* (Atlantic).

**market garden,** a farm or garden where vegetables are grown for market; truck farm: *The market gardens of the kolkhoz, which provide all Ashkhabad with vegetables, are right outside the city* (Atlantic).

**market gardener,** a person who operates a market garden; truck farmer.

**market gardening,** the business of operating a market garden; truck farming.

**mar|ket|ing** (mär′kə ting), *n., adj.* —*n.* **1** the act or fact of trading in a market; buying or selling: *Marketings for the first two days of the week dwindled to the lowest point for a like period in more than three years* (Wall Street Journal). **2** something bought or sold in a market. **3** the bringing of merchandise, livestock, or other commodity to market. **4** the action of shopping for groceries, small items, and the like: *Sometimes we took her cakes for tea, or a pot of soup, or did her marketing* (New Yorker).
—*adj.* of, having to do with, or characteristic of marketing: *marketing research, marketing men.*

**market letter,** *U.S.* a newsletter containing information and advice on the stock market, issued by a stockbroker or investment advisory firm to its customers.

**mar|ket|man** (mär′kit man′), *n., pl.* **-men. 1** a man who sells in a market. **2** a person who buys in a market.

**market order,** an order to buy or sell a commodity, stock, or other security at whatever price may be current when the transaction is completed.

**market place,** or **mar|ket|place** (mär′kit plās′), *n.* **1** the place where a market is held, usually an open space or a square in a town: *In open market place produced they me, To be a public spectacle to all* (Shakespeare). **2** the world of commerce: *"The inexorable law of the market place," he argued, "is that a business which cannot compete, cannot survive"* (Wall Street Journal).

**market price,** the price that an article brings when sold; current price.

**market research,** the study of what makes people buy or not buy a product, when they do it, how long they may continue, and other similar buying habits.

**market town,** a town in which markets are held at stated times, by privilege, as in England.

**market value,** the probable price at which an article would be bought or sold at a given time on the open market: *The discovery that the painting of St. Jerome is the work of the Flemish master has "vastly increased the market value" of the work, according to Edgar P. Richardson,*

**Pronunciation Key:** hat, āge, cãre, fär; let, ēqual, tėrm; it, īce; hot, ōpen, ôrder; oil, out; cup, pu̇t, rüle; child; long; thin; ᴛʜen; zh, measure; ə represents a in about, e in taken, i in pencil, o in lemon, u in circus.

*director of the institute* (New York Times).

**mar|ket|wise** (mär′kit wīz′), *adv.* **1** with regard to the stock market: *The steel news yesterday had virtually no effect marketwise* (Baltimore Sun). **2** in the market; commercially: *Mr. Morgan ... hopes that chemical products* (*other than cellulose*) *derived from wood may become valuable marketwise* (Wall Street Journal).

**mar|khor** (mär′kôr), *n.* a large, wild goat of the Himalayas, with long, spirally twisted horns. [< Persian *mārkhōr*]

**mark|ing** (mär′king), *n.* **1** a mark or marks: *The marking on the wall was childish and unsightly.* **2** an arrangement of marks: *the traditional marking of a tiger.* **3** the act of a person or thing that marks.

**mark|ka** (märk′kä), *n., pl.* **-kaa** (-kä). the unit of money of Finland, equal to 100 pennia; mark. [< Finnish *markka* < Swedish *mark,* probably < Old Icelandic *mork*]

**Mark Master**, a Mason of the first degree of the York Rite.

**mark of cadency**, *Heraldry.* an additional device used on a shield when more than one individual claims the same coat of arms. The file or label is the mark of cadency of the eldest son.

**Mar|kov chain** (mär′kôf), *Statistics.* a succession of random events each of which is determined by the event immediately preceding it: *In its simplest form, a Markov chain states that the probability of a succeeding event occurring is dependent upon the fact that a preceding event occurred. For example, if the letter Q is known to exist, what is the probability of it being followed by the letter U?* (John P. Dowds). [< Andrei *Markov,* 1856-1922, a Russian mathematician]

**Mar|kov|i|an** (mär kō′vē ən, -kô′-), *adj.* of, having to do with, or based on a Markov chain or Markov process: *On the average, only about one-sixth of a stock's price change is due to a common market factor. This type of process is said to be "Markovian" because it has no memory* (New Scientist).

**Markov process**, any process based on a Markov chain: *The interconnection between classical potential theory and Brownian motion depends heavily on the fact that Brownian motion is a Markov process, that is, its present behavior is not influenced by its past behavior* (Scientific American).

**marks|man** (märks′mən), *n., pl.* **-men.** **1a** a person who shoots well at a target: *He is noted as a marksman.* **b** a person who shoots at a target: *Some marksmen shoot badly.* **2** a soldier in the United States Army having the lowest range of qualifying scores in firing a weapon.

**marks|man|ship** (märks′mən ship), *n.* the art or skill of a marksman; skill in shooting at targets.

**marks|wom|an** (märks′wům′ən), *n., pl.* **-women.** a woman who shoots or is skilled in shooting at a target.

**mark|up** (märk′up′), *n.* **1** an increase in the price of an article: *The concern is getting a slightly higher gross markup on shoes this year* (Wall Street Journal). **2** the amount of this increase. **3** the percentage or amount added to the cost of an article to determine the selling price. The markup takes care of profit and overhead. *Many large firms are able to work on narrow markups because of enormous turnover.* **4** *U.S.* the act or process of putting a legislative bill in final form.

**mark|wor|thy** (märk′wėr′ᴛʜē), *adj.* worthy to be marked or noticed; noteworthy.

**marl¹** (märl), *n., v.* —*n.* **1** a loose, crumbly soil consisting usually of clay, sand, and calcium carbonate, used in making cement and as a fertilizer. **2** *Archaic.* earth: *to seize upon his foe flat lying on the marl* (Edmund Spenser).
—*v.t.* to fertilize with marl.
[< Old French *marle* < Medieval Latin *margila* < Latin *marga,* probably < a Celtic word]

**marl²** (märl), *v.t.* to wind, cover, or fasten with marline. [< Dutch *marlen* (apparently frequentative) < Middle Dutch *merren* to tie]

**mar|la|ceous** (mär lā′shəs), *adj.* of or resembling marl.

**mar|lin¹** (mär′lən), *n., pl.* **-lins** or (*collectively*) **-lin.** **1** a large sea fish related to the swordfish and the sailfish: *The Wanderer ... was damaged by the sword of a blue marlin as they lay becalmed off the Azores* (London Times). **2** = spearfish. [short for *marlinespike* (because of its long snout)]

**mar|line** or **mar|lin²** (mär′lən), *n.* a small cord wound around the ends of a rope to keep it from fraying. It has two loosely twisted strands. [< Dutch *marlijin* < *marren* to tie + *lijn* line]

**mar|line|spike** or **mar|lin|spike** (mär′lən spīk′), *n.* a pointed iron tool used by sailors to separate the strands of a rope in splicing.

**mar|ling¹** (mär′ling), *n.* = marline.

**marl|ing²** (mär′ling), *n.* fertilization with marl.

**mar|ling|spike** (mär′ling spīk′), *n.* = marlinespike.

**marl|ite** (mär′līt), *n.* a variety of marl that resists the action of the air.

**marl|it|ic** (mär lit′ik), *adj.* of or like marlite.

**Mar|lo|vi|an** (mär lō′vē ən), *adj.* of or characteristic of the English dramatist and poet Christopher Marlowe (1564-1593) or his work: *He is too eager in straining for Marlovian echoes in Shakespeare* (Manchester Guardian Weekly).

**marl|stone** (märl′stōn′), *n.* a rock consisting of a hardened mixture of clay, calcium carbonate, and other minerals: ... *the marlstone formations of the Colorado region* (Gerald L. Farrar).

**marl|y** (mär′lē), *adj.,* **marl|i|er, marl|i|est.** of, like, or full of marl.

**mar|ma|lade** (mär′mə lād), *n.* a preserve similar to jam, made of oranges or of other fruit. The peel is usually sliced up and boiled with the fruit. [< Middle French *marmelade* < Portuguese *marmelada* < *marmelo* quince < Latin *melimēlum* < Greek *melimēlon* < *méli* honey + *mêlon* apple]

**marmalade cat**, a tabby cat with stripes of an orange color like that of marmalade.

**marmalade tree**, an evergreen Central American tree of the sapodilla family that yields a fruit whose pulp resembles marmalade. The fruit is used in preserves.

**Mar|mes man** (mär′mis), a prehistoric man whose fossil bone fragments were discovered in 1965 in the state of Washington and dated as being over 11,000 years old: *Marmes man was a Mongoloid, having a broad-cheeked, flat face* (Bert Salween). [< R. J. *Marmes,* a rancher on whose property the bones were discovered]

**mar|mite** (mär′mīt, mär mēt′), *n.* **1** an earthenware pot in which soups are made and served. **2** a yeast extract that has a rich vitamin content and acts as an antineuritic agent. [< French *marmite*]

**mar|mo|re|al** (mär môr′ē əl, -mōr′-), *adj.* **1** of marble. **2** like marble; cold, smooth, or white: *The thronging constellations rush in crowds, Paving with fire the sky and the marmoreal floods* (Shelley). [< Latin *marmoreus* (< *marmor, -oris* marble) + English *-al¹*] —**mar|mo′re|al|ly,** *adv.*

**mar|mo|re|an** (mär môr′ē ən, -mōr′-), *adj.* = marmoreal.

**mar|mo|set** (mär′mə zet), *n.* a very small monkey of Central or South America having soft, thick fur and a long, bushy tail. See picture under **monkey.** [< Old French *marmouset* grotesque figurine < *merme* under age < Latin *minimus* very small; influenced by Greek *mormōtós* fearful]

**mar|mot** (mär′mət), *n.* a rodent related to the squirrels, having a thick body and a bushy tail. Woodchucks are marmots. [< French *marmotte* < unrecorded Old French *murmont* < Vulgar Latin *mūrem montis* mouse of the mountain < Latin *mūs, mūris* mouse, and *mōns, montis* mountain]

**mar|o|cain** (mar′ə kān), *n.* a dress fabric of silk and wool or cotton, having a texture like crepe. [< French *maroquin* (originally) having to do with Morocco < *Maroc* Morocco]

**Mar|o|nite** (mar′ə nīt), *n.* one of a group of Syrian Christians in communion with the Roman Catholic Church: *The Maronite congregation conducts its services in Syriac* (London Times). [< Late Latin *Marōnīta* < *Marōn,* who founded the sect during the 300's]

**ma|roon¹** (mə rün′), *adj., n.* —*adj.* very dark brownish-red.
—*n.* a very dark brownish red.
[< Middle French *marron* < Italian *marrone* chestnut]

**ma|roon²** (mə rün′), *v., n.* —*v.t.* **1** to put (a person) ashore in a desolate place and leave him: *Pirates used to maroon people on desert islands.* **2** *Figurative.* to leave in a lonely, helpless position: *During the storm we were marooned in a cabin miles from town.*
—*v.i. Southern U.S.* to camp out for several days. [American English, (originally) to camp out < noun]
—*n.* **1** a descendant of escaped Negro slaves living in the West Indies and Surinam. **2** an escaped Negro slave, an ancestor of these people. **3** a person who is marooned.
[< French *marron,* perhaps < American Spanish *cimarrón* wild; seeking refuge in the bushes on the mountains < Old Spanish *cimarra* bushes < *cima* summit < Latin *cȳma* swelling, cyma]

**mar|plot** (mär′plot′), *n.* a person who spoils some plan by meddling or blundering. [< *mar* + *plot*]

**Marq.**, **1** marquess. **2** marquis.

**marque¹** (märk), *n.* **1** official permission from a government to capture enemy merchant ships. Governments used to issue letters of marque to individuals authorizing them to plunder an enemy's shipping. **2** *Obsolete.* reprisal. [< dialectal Middle French *marque* < Old Provençal *marca* reprisal < *marcar* seize as a pledge, ultimately < a Germanic word]

**marque²** (märk), *n. British.* a mark; make; brand: *Pride of ownership has for decades made this dignified marque the choice of the discriminating motorist ...* (Sunday Times). [< French *marque*]

∗**mar|quee** (mär kē′), *n.* **1** a rooflike shelter over an entrance, especially of a theater or hotel. Theater marquees usually display the names of shows being featured. *At eight o'clock I'd been waiting fifteen minutes under the marquee of the Bellevue theatre* (Maclean's). **2** *Especially British.* a large tent with sides that can be rolled up, often put up for some outdoor entertainment or exhibition. [new singular < French *marquise* < Old French (*tente*) *marquise* large tent for officers, (literally) for a marquis]

∗**marquee** definition 1

**Mar|que|san** (mär kā′zən, -sən), *adj., n.* —*adj.* of or having to do with the Marquesas Islands, in the South Pacific.
—*n.* a native or inhabitant of the Marquesas Islands.

**mar|quess** (mär′kwis), *n. Especially British.* marquis.

**mar|quess|ate** (mär′kwə sāt), *n. Especially British.* marquisate.

**mar|que|te|rie** (mär′kə trē), *n.* = marquetry.

**mar|que|try** (mär′kə trē), *n., pl.* **-tries.** decoration made with thin pieces of wood, ivory, metal, tortoise shell, or the like, fitted together to form a design on furniture: *a marquetry writing desk* (New Yorker). [< Middle French *marqueterie* < *marqueter* to inlay < *marque* mark¹]

**mar|quis** (mär′kwis, mär kē′), *n., pl.* **mar|quis|es, mar|quis** (mär kē′). a nobleman ranking below a duke and above an earl or count. [< Old French *marquis,* alteration of earlier *marchis* < Medieval Latin *marchensis* (count) of the marches < *marcha* march²]

**mar|quis|ate** (mär′kwə zit), *n.* **1** the position or rank of marquis. **2** the territory governed by a marquis.

**mar|quise** (mär kēz′), *n.* **1** the wife or widow of a marquis. **2** a woman equal in rank to a marquis. **3a** a pointed oval shape into which diamonds or other gems are frequently cut. See picture under **gem.** **b** a ring setting of this shape. **4** = marquee. **5** an upholstered love seat. [< French *marquise,* Old French *marchise,* feminine of *marquis* marquis]

**mar|qui|sette** (mär′kə zet′, -kwə-), *n.* a very thin fabric with square meshes, made of cotton, silk, or synthetic fabric. It is often used for window draperies. [< French *marquisette* (diminutive) < *marquise* marquise]

**Marquis of Queens|ber|ry rules** (kwēnz′ber′ē, -bər-), **1** the standard rules and provisions of modern boxing, sponsored by the Marquis of Queensberry in 1867. **2** any similar set of rules governing a game, contest, or other competition: *We are forced to fight by Marquis of Queensberry rules while the criminals are permitted to gouge and bite* (Time).

**mar|ram grass** (mar′əm), a tall, coarse, perennial beach grass native to Europe, sometimes sown to prevent the drifting of sand masses. [< Scandinavian (compare Old Icelandic *maralmr* < *marr* sea + *halmr* haulm)]

**mar|ra|no** (mə rä′nō), *n., pl.* **-nos.** a Christianized Jew or Moor of medieval Spain, especially one who only professed conversion to escape persecution by the Inquisition. [< Spanish *marrano* pig < Arabic *maḥrām* forbidden thing (because Jewish and Moslem law forbid the eating of pork)]

**mar|riage** (mar′ij), *n.* **1** the act or fact of living together as husband and wife; relation between husband and wife; married life; wedlock: *We wished the bride and groom a happy marriage.* [*Their*] *marriage certainly did not seem made in heaven* (Time). **2** the condition of being a husband or wife. **3** the ceremony of being married; a marrying; a wedding. **4** *Figurative.* a close union: *the marriage of music and drama in opera. The marriage of words and melody in that song was unusually effective.* **5** the king and queen of the same suit in pinochle, bezique, and some other card games. **6** the merger of two business firms, or the acquisition of one by the other: *This major bank marriage is the fourth in less than six months* (Wall Street Journal). [< Old French *mariage* < *marier;* see etym. under **marry¹**]

—*Syn.* 1, 2, 3 **Marriage, matrimony, wedding** mean the state of being married or the act of marrying. **Marriage** emphasizes the legal union of a man and woman: *The marriage took place on June 26, 1975.* **Matrimony** is the formal and religious word, and applies especially to the spiritual or religious bond established by the union: *They were wedded in holy matrimony.* **Wedding** is the common word for the ceremony or celebration: *It was a beautiful wedding.*

**mar|riage|a|bil|i|ty** (mar′i jə bil′ə tē), *n.* the condition of being marriageable.

**mar|riage|a|ble** (mar′i jə bəl), *adj.* fit for marriage; old enough to marry: *a girl of marriageable age.* SYN: nubile. —**mar′riage|a|ble|ness**, *n.*

**marriage broker**, a person whose business is to arrange marriages.

**marriage brokerage** or **brokage**, the business of a marriage broker.

**marriage bureau**, the office or agency of a marriage broker: *Many marriage bureaus were in essence offering clients, in consideration of a fee, introductions to prospective partners* (London Times).

**marriage of convenience**, = mariage de convenance.

**marriage portion**, = dowry.

**mar|ried** (mar′ēd), *adj., n.* —*adj.* **1** living together as husband and wife: *a married couple.* **2** having a husband or wife: *a married man. Abbr:* m. **3** of marriage; of husbands and wives: *Married life has many rewards.* SYN: connubial, matrimonial. **4** *Figurative.* closely united.
—*n.* **marrieds**, a married couple: *newly marrieds.*

**mar|ri|er** (mar′ē ər), *n.* a person who marries.

**mar|ron** (mar′ən; *French* mȧ rôɴ′), *n.* a large sweet European chestnut, often used in cooking, or candied or preserved in syrup. [< French *marron* < Italian *marrone.* Compare etym. under **maroon**[1].]

**mar|rons gla|cés** (mȧ rôɴ′ glȧ sā′), *French.* marrons glazed with sugar or preserved in a sugar syrup: *Her admirers sent her boxes of marrons glacés* (Punch).

**mar|row**[1] (mar′ō), *n.* **1** the soft substance that fills the hollow central part of most bones; medulla. Marrow is the source of red blood cells and many white blood cells. **2** this substance obtained from animal bones and used as food. **3** *Figurative.* the inmost or important part: *The icy wind chilled me to the marrow.* **4** *Figurative.* vitality; strength: *It takes the marrow out of a man* (Benjamin Disraeli). **5** = vegetable marrow. [Old English *mearg*]

**mar|row**[2] (mar′ō), *n. Scottish and British Dialect.* **1** a mate; companion; associate. **2** an equal; match. [origin uncertain]

**mar|row|bone** (mar′ō bōn′), *n.* a bone containing marrow which can be eaten.
**marrowbones, a** the knees: *I jest flopped down on my marrowbones* (John Hay). **b** = crossbones: *I ... sailed under the black flag and marrowbones* (Scott).

**mar|row|fat** (mar′ō fat′), *n.*, or **marrowfat pea**, **1** a tall, late variety of pea having a large, rich seed. **2** its seed, used for food.

**mar|row|less** (mar′ō lis), *adj.* having no marrow: *Thy bones are marrowless, thy blood is cold* (Shakespeare).

**marrow pea**, = marrowfat.

**marrow squash**, = vegetable marrow.

**mar|row|y** (mar′ō ē), *adj.* of, like, or full of marrow.

**mar|ry**[1] (mar′ē), *v.*, **-ried, -ry|ing.** —*v.t.* **1** to join as husband and wife: *The minister married them.* **2** to take as husband or wife: *He plans to marry her soon.* **3** to give in marriage: *He married his daughter to a young lawyer.* **4** *Figurative.* to bring together in any close union; unite closely; blend: *Great cognacs are achieved by marrying fine old brandies* (London Times). **5** *Nautical.* to sew together or join (two ropes) without increasing the diameter.
—*v.i.* **1** to take a husband or wife; become married: *She married late in life.* **2** *Figurative.* to become closely united: *By that old bridge where the waters marry* (Tennyson).
**marry into**, to become part of (a family) through marriage: *"Curly, ... I'd almost give you the truck, like it stands, not to marry into us"* (Eudora Welty).
**marry off**, to give away in marriage: *... the casket-maker Ioannidis with the six ugly sisters he can never hope to marry off* (Harry M. Petrakis).
**marry up**, *Figurative.* to join up; combine or unite: *The Fast Deployment Logistics Ships* [*are*] *needed to haul the Army's tanks and trucks, artillery and ammunition, and "marry up" with the airborne troops* (Time).
[< Old French *marier* < Latin *marītāre* < *marītus* husband]

**mar|ry**[2] (mar′ē), *interj. Archaic.* an exclamation showing surprise, indignation, or other emotion: *Marry, hang the idiot ... to bring me such stuff* (Oliver Goldsmith). [< (the Virgin) *Mary*]

***Mars** (märz), *n.* **1** *Roman Mythology.* the god of war, son of Jupiter and Juno and husband or lover of Venus. The Greeks called him Ares. **2** = war. **3** the planet next in order beyond the earth and the fourth in distance from the sun. Its orbit about the sun lies between those of the earth and Jupiter and takes 687 days to complete, at an average distance from the sun of about 141,500,000 miles. It is the seventh largest planet in the solar system, with a mean diameter of 4,220 miles. *Mars is notable among the planets and stars for its red color* (John C. Duncan). See diagram under **solar system**.

***Mars** definition 3 ♂ symbol

**Mar|sa|la** (mär sä′lä), *n.* a light wine resembling sherry, originating in Marsala, Sicily.

**Mar|seil|laise** (mär′sə lāz′; *French* mȧr se yez′), *n.* the French national anthem, written in 1792 during the French Revolution by Claude Joseph Rouget de Lisle. [< French (*chanson*) *marseillaise* < the city of *Marseilles* (because first sung by a group from there)]

**mar|seilles** (mär sālz′), *n.* a thick, stiff cotton cloth woven in figures or stripes, used for bedspreads, curtains, and upholstery. [< *Marseilles,* a city in France]

**marsh** (märsh), *n., adj.* —*n.* low land covered at times by water; soft, wet land; swamp. Such plants as reeds, rushes, and sedges grow in marshes. SYN: bog, fen.
—*adj.* **1** marshy. **2** living in marshes: *a marsh plant.*
[Old English *mersc,* related to *mere* lake, mere[2]]

**mar|shal** (mär′shəl), *n., v.*, **-shaled, -shal|ing** or (*especially British*) **-shalled, -shal|ling.** —*n.* **1a** an officer of various kinds, especially a police officer. A United States marshal is an officer of a Federal court whose duties are like those of a sheriff. **b** a police officer in a city or town in some states with duties similar to those of a sheriff or constable, including serving processes. **c** the chief of police or head of the fire department in some cities. **2** a high officer in an army. A Marshal of France is a general of the highest rank in the French Army. **3** a person who arranges the order of march in a parade: *The marshal rode at the head of the parade.* **4** a person in charge of events or ceremonies: *The dean of the school acts as marshal of graduation exercises.* **5** one of the highest officials of a royal household or court, responsible in the Middle Ages for military affairs.
—*v.t.* **1** to arrange in proper order: *He took great care in marshaling his facts for the debate. So to the office in the evening to marshal my papers* (Samuel Pepys). **2** to conduct with ceremony; lead formally; usher: *The foreign visitor was marshaled into the presence of the king. The abbot marshalled him to the door of Augustine's chamber* (Scott). **3** to arrange in military order; prepare for war. **4** *Heraldry.* **a** to combine (two or more coats of arms) upon one shield so as to form a single composition. **b** to associate (accessories) with a shield of arms so as to form a complete composition. —*v.i.* to take up positions in proper order: *no marshaling troop, no bivouac song* (Joaquin Miller).
[< Old French *mareschal* < Late Latin *mariscalcus* groom < Germanic (compare Old High German *marahscalc* < *marah* horse + *scalc* servant)] —**mar′shal|er**, *especially British,* **mar′shal|ler**, *n.*

**mar|shal|cy** (mär′shəl sē), *n., pl.* **-cies.** the office, rank, or position of a marshal.

**marshaling yard** = classification yard.

**Mar|shal|lese** (mär′shə lēz′, -lēs′), *adj., n., pl.* **-ese.** —*adj.* of or having to do with the Marshall Islands, a group of islands in the north Pacific, under U.S. trusteeship: *the Marshallese people.* —*n.* **1** a native or inhabitant of the Marshall Islands. **2** the Austronesian language of the Marshallese people.

**Mar|shall Plan** (mär′shəl), a program for economic recovery of Europe after World War II. It ended in 1951. [< George C. *Marshall,* 1880-1959, Secretary of State 1947-1949, who advanced the plan]

**Marshal of the Royal Air Force**, the officer of highest rank in the Royal Air Force, equivalent to a United States General of the Air Force.

**Mar|shal|sea** (mär′shəl sē), *n.* a court held by the steward and marshal of the British royal household, originally for the king's servants, abolished in 1849. [alteration of Middle English *mareschalcie* < Anglo-French, Old French *mareschaucie* < Late Latin *mariscalcus;* see etym. under **marshal**]

**mar|shal|ship** (mär′shəl ship), *n.* = marshalcy.

**Marsh Arab**, an Arab living in the marshes of southern Iraq.

**marsh bird's-foot**, any plant of a species of trefoil common in damp meadowland.

**marsh|buck** (märsh′buk′), *n., pl.* **-bucks** or (*collectively*) **-buck.** = sitatunga.

***marsh buggy**, an amphibious vehicle somewhat like a tractor, which can travel on land or through low water, mud, and swamp.

***marsh buggy**

**marsh calla**, = water arum.

**marsh cress**, a North American plant of the mustard family that grows in moist places.

**marsh deer**, any one of a kind of deer of South America, growing about four feet high and living in the swampy plains and forests of Brazil, Paraguay, and Uruguay; swamp deer.

**marsh elder**, **1** any one of a group of herbs or shrubs of the composite family with heads of greenish-white flowers, growing in coastal marshes and sands. **2** = cranberry tree (def. 2).

**marsh|fire** (märsh′fīr′), *n.* = ignis fatuus.

**marsh gas**, a gas formed by the decomposition of organic substances in marshes; methane.

**Marsh grapefruit**, a commercial variety of seedless grapefruit.

**marsh hare**, *U.S.* a muskrat.

**marsh harrier**, **1** a large reddish-brown harrier of the Old World that lives in marshes and feeds on small animals. **2** = marsh hawk.

**marsh hawk**, the only harrier in North America, gray or brownish with a white patch on the rump. It lives in open and marshy regions and feeds mainly on mice, frogs, and snakes.

**marsh hen**, any one of certain birds that live in marshes, such as the coot and bittern.

**marsh|i|ness** (mär′shē nis), *n.* marshy state.

**marsh|land** (märsh′land′, -lənd), *n.* marshy land.

**marsh mallow**, a shrublike plant that grows in marshy places. It has pink flowers and a root that is used in medicine to soothe or protect irritated mucous tissues. It belongs to the mallow family.

**marsh|mal|low** (märsh′mal′ō, -mel′-), *n.* **1** a soft, white, spongy candy, covered with powdered sugar. It is made from corn syrup, sugar, starch, and gelatin. Originally it was made from the root of the marsh mallow. **2** = marsh mallow. [Old English *merscmealwe* the marsh mallow plant]

**marsh|mal|low|y** (märsh′mal′ō ē, -mel′-), *adj.* resembling or suggesting marshmallow, as in appearance or sweetness: *wave to them cheerily from the marshmallowy cliffs* (Mary McCarthy).

**marsh marigold**, a plant with bright yellow flowers that grows in moist meadows and swamps; cowslip. It belongs to the crowfoot family.

**marsh rabbit**, **1** *U.S.* a muskrat. **2** a coarse-furred rabbit, a species of cottontail, that lives in wet areas of the southeastern United States.

**marsh wren**, any one of certain American wrens that breed in marshes, such as the long-billed marsh wren.

**marsh|y** (mär′shē), *adj.*, **marsh|i|er, marsh|i|est.** **1** soft and wet like a marsh: *a marshy field.* **2** having many marshes; swampy: *a marshy region.* **3** of marshes: *a marshy odor.*

**Mar|sil|id** (mär sil′id), *n. Trademark.* iproniazid.

**mar|si|po|branch** (mär′si pə brangk), *adj., n.* = cyclostome. [< New Latin *Marsipobranchii* the class name < Greek *mársipos* pouch + *bránchia* gills]

**Mar|so|khod** (mär′sə ʜôt′), *n.* a vehicle like the Lunokhod designed by Soviet scientists for exploration of the surface of Mars. [< Russian *Marsokhod* (literally) Mars walker]

**Mars|quake** (märz′kwāk′), *n.* a shaking or sliding on or beneath the surface of the planet Mars, similar to an earthquake: *The instrument can give information on the location of Marsquakes by comparing the data from both landers' seismometers* (J. Kelly Beatty).

**mar|su|pi|al** (mär sü′pē əl), *n., adj.* —*n.* a mammal that carries its young in a pouch. Kangaroos,

opossums, and wombats are marsupials. The pouch covers the mammary glands on the abdomen, and the incompletely developed young are nursed as well as carried in it. *Today, pouched animals, or marsupials, are found only in North and South America, Australia and Tasmania* (Science News Letter).
—*adj.* **1** of the marsupials. **2** having a pouch for carrying the young. **3** having to do with or like a pouch.
[< New Latin *marsupialis* < Latin *marsūpium;* see etym. under **marsupium**]

**marsupial mouse**, any one of several Australian desert animals, related to the dasyure, that somewhat resemble a mouse or rat. Marsupial mice live mainly on insects.

**mar|su|pi|um** (mär sü′pē əm), *n., pl.* **-pi|a** (-pē ə). **1** a pouch or fold of skin on the abdomen of a female marsupial for carrying its young. **2** a similar pouch in certain fishes and crustaceans. [< Latin *marsūpium* < variant of Greek *marsípion* (diminutive) < *mársipos* pouch]

**mart**[1] (märt), *n.* **1** a center of trade; market: *New York and London are two great marts of the world. Lisbon outshone Venice as a mart for oriental spices* (H. G. Wells). **SYN**: emporium. **2** *Archaic.* a fair. [< *mart,* dialectal form of Dutch *markt* market]

**mart**[2] (märt), *n. Scottish.* an ox or cow fattened for slaughter, especially at Martinmas. [< Gaelic *mart*]

**mar|ta|gon** (mär′tə gən), *n.* = Turk's-cap lily. [< Middle French *martagon* < Turkish *martagan* a kind of turban]

**mar|tel** (mär′tel), *n. Archaic.* a hammer, especially one used as a weapon in war. [< Old French *martel*]

**mar|tel|la|to** (mär′tə lä′tō), *adj., adv. Music.* —*adj.* strongly accented (used as a direction for bowed stringed instruments and piano music).
—*adv.* in a martellato manner.
[< Italian *martellato* (literally) hammered, past participle of *martellare* to hammer]

**Mar|tel|lo tower**, or **mar|tel|lo** (mär tel′ō), *n.* a circular tower, formerly used mostly for coastal defense. [alteration (influenced by Italian *martello* hammer) of Cape *Mortella,* where one of these towers was located]

**mar|ten** (mär′tən), *n., pl.* **-tens** or (*collectively*) **-ten**. **1** a slender carnivorous mammal like a weasel and of the same family, but larger, found in forest areas of Asia, Europe, and northern and western North America. There are various kinds. Several species are valued for their brown fur. **2** the fur. [< Old French *martrine,* feminine of *martrin* of marten < *martre* a marten < Germanic (compare Old High German *mardar*)]

**mar|tens|ite** (mär′tən zīt), *n.* a hard, brittle, solid solution of up to 2 per cent of carbon in alpha iron, a constituent of steel which is quenched rapidly. [< Adolf *Martens,* 1850-1914, a German metallurgist + *-ite*[1]]

**mar|tens|it|ic** (mär′tən zit′ik), *adj.* having to do with or consisting of martensite: *martensitic steel.*

**Mar|tha** (mär′thə), *n.* the sister of Lazarus and Mary; Jesus was her guest. She is often taken to represent the vigorous housekeeper (in the Bible, Luke 10:38-42).

**mar|tial** (mär′shəl), *adj.* **1** of war; suitable for war: *martial music.* **SYN**: See syn. under **military**. **2** such as war requires; brave; valiant: *a martial spirit.* **SYN**: See syn. under **military**. **3** given to fighting; warlike: *a martial nation.* **4** of or having to do with the army and navy. **5** *Obsolete.* of or containing iron. [< Latin *Mārtiālis* of Mars < *Mārs, Mārtis* Mars, Roman god of battle] —**mar′tial|ly**, *adv.* —**mar′tial|ness**, *n.*

**Mar|tial** (mär′shəl), *n.* **1** *Astronomy.* Martian. **2** *Astrology.* subject to the influence of Mars, as a poisonous plant or animal.

**martial art**, any one of the Oriental arts of fighting or self-defense, such as karate and aikido.

**martial artist**, a practitioner of one or more of the martial arts.

**martial eagle**, a large eagle of the African plains that feeds especially on hyraxes.

**mar|tial|ism** (mär′shə liz əm), *n.* martial or warlike character or spirit.

**mar|tial|ist** (mär′shə list), *n.* a warrior.

**martial law**, rule by the army in a time of trouble or of war instead of by the ordinary civil authorities.

**Mar|tian** (mär′shən), *adj., n.* —*adj.* **1** of the planet Mars: *the Martian year lasts six hundred and eighty-seven days* (New Yorker). **2** of Mars, the god of war.
—*n.* a supposed inhabitant of the planet Mars.
[< Latin *Mārtius* of Mars + English *-an*]

**Mar|tian|ol|o|gist** (mär′shə nol′ə jist), *n.* a person who engages in scientific study of the planet Mars.

**mar|tin** (mär′tən), *n.* any one of several swallows with a short beak, long, pointed wings, and a forked tail. The purple martin is a large, blue and black martin of North America. [apparently < French *martin* < *Martin,* a proper name]

**mar|ti|net** (mär′tə net′, mär′tə net), *n.* **1** a person who enforces very strict discipline on those under him: *They soon discovered that the new teacher was a martinet.* **SYN**: disciplinarian. **2** a military or naval officer who imposes very strict discipline: *The commander-in-chief was a little of a martinet* (James Fenimore Cooper). [< Colonel *Martinet,* a French general and drillmaster of the 1600's]

**mar|ti|net|ish** (mär′tə net′ish), *adj.* of, belonging to, or characteristic of a martinet.

**mar|ti|net|ism** (mär′tə net′iz əm), *n.* the spirit or methods of a martinet.

**mar|tin|gal** (mär′tən gal), *n.* = martingale.

**mar|tin|gale** (mär′tən gāl), *n.* **1** a strap of a horse's harness that prevents the horse from rising on its hind legs or throwing back its head; pole strap. **2a** a rope or stay that holds down the jib boom on a ship. **b** a short spar to which the stay or rope is attached; dolphin striker. **3** a system of betting in which the wager is doubled after each loss. [< Middle French *martingale* < Provençal *martengalo,* feminine of *martengo* inhabitant of *Martigues,* a small town near Marseilles, France]

**mar|ti|ni** (mär tē′nē), *n., pl.* **-nis**. a cocktail consisting of gin or vodka and dry vermouth, usually served with a green olive or a twisted strip of lemon peel. [< *Martini* and Rossi, an Italian company that manufactures vermouth]

**Mar|ti|ni|can** (mär′tə nē′kən), *n., adj.* —*n.* a native or inhabitant of Martinique.
—*adj.* of or having to do with Martinique or Martinicans.

**Mar|ti|nique** (mär′tə nēk′), *n.* = Gros Michel. [< *Martinique,* an island in the West Indies]

**Mar|tin|mas** (mär′tən məs), *n.* November 11, a Roman Catholic church festival in honor of Saint Martin; St. Martin's Day.

**mart|let** (märt′lit), *n.* **1** the European house martin. **2** *Heraldry.* a bearing depicting a bird without visible feet. [< Middle French *martelet,* probably alteration of *martinet* (diminutive) < *martin;* see etym. under **martin**]

**mar|tyr** (mär′tər), *n., v.* —*n.* **1** a person who is put to death or made to suffer greatly because of his religion or other beliefs; person who chooses to die or suffer rather than renounce his faith or principles. Many of the early Christians were martyrs. **2** *Figurative.* a person who suffers greatly: *She is a martyr to dyspepsia and bad cooking* (Francis A. Kemble).
—*v.t.* **1** to put (a person) to death or torture because of his religion or other beliefs. **2** *Figurative.* to cause to suffer greatly; torture: *She was ever at my side ... martyring me by the insufferable annoyance of her vulgar loquacity* (Charles Lever). **SYN**: torment, persecute.
[Old English *martyr* < Latin < Greek *mártyr* witness] —**mar′tyr|like′**, *adj.*

**mar|tyr|dom** (mär′tər dəm), *n.* **1** the death or suffering of a martyr: *Like all rebellions, this one had its ... moments of bravery, martyrdom, and sacrifice* (Newsweek). **2** the state of being a martyr. **3** *Figurative.* great suffering; torment.

**mar|tyr|i|za|tion** (mär′tər ə zā′shən), *n.* **1** the action of martyrizing. **2** the state of being martyrized.

**mar|tyr|ize** (mär′tə rīz), *v.,* **-ized, -iz|ing**. —*v.t.* **1** to make a martyr of. **2** *Figurative.* to torment.
—*v.i.* to be or become a martyr.

**mar|tyr|ol|a|try** (mär′tə rol′ə trē), *n.* worship of martyrs.

**mar|tyr|o|log|i|cal** (mär′tər ə loj′ə kəl), *adj.* of or having to do with martyrology.

**mar|tyr|ol|o|gist** (mär′tə rol′ə jist), *n.* a writer of martyrology.

**mar|tyr|ol|o|gy** (mär′tə rol′ə jē), *n., pl.* **-gies**. **1** a list or register of martyrs, usually with an account of their lives. **2** such accounts as a group. **3** the part of church history or literature dealing with martyrs.

**mar|tyr|y** (mär′tər ē), *n., pl.* **-tyr|ies**. a shrine, chapel, or other monument erected in honor of a martyr. [< Late Latin *martyrium* suffering, < Greek *martýrion* < *mártyr* witness]

**MARV** (märv), *n., v.* —*n.* **1** a long-range missile with nuclear warheads that can be maneuvered after reentry into the earth's atmosphere to evade interception by defensive missiles. **2** any one of the warheads on this missile. —*v.t.* to equip with a MARV: *The U.S. has already MIRVed a good number of its missiles and hopes eventually to MARV others* (Time).
[< *MA*(neuverable) *R*(eentry) *V*(ehicle)]

**mar|vel** (mär′vəl), *n., v.,* **-veled, -vel|ing** or (*especially British*) **-velled, -vel|ling**. —*n.* **1** something wonderful; astonishing thing; a wonder: *The airplane and television are among the marvels of science. The book is a marvel of accuracy.* **2** *Archaic.* astonishment; wonder: *The vast acquirements of the new governor were the theme of marvel among the simple burghers* (Washington Irving).
—*v.i.* **1** to be filled with wonder; be astonished: *I marvel at your boldness. She marveled at the beautiful sunset. Lancelot marvell'd at the wordless man* (Tennyson). **2** to feel astonished curiousity: *I marvel how men toil and fare* (Andrew Lang). —*v.t.* **1** to wonder at: *We marveled that no one had been injured in the accident. And the people ... marvelled that he tarried so long in the temple* (Luke 1:21). **2** to wonder or be curious about: *I marvel what kin thou and thy daughters are* (Shakespeare).
[< Old French *merveille* < Vulgar Latin *miribilia,* for Latin *mīrābilia* wonders, neuter plural of *mīrābilis* strange, wonderful < *mīrārī* to wonder at < *mīrus* wonderful]

**mar|vel|lous** (mär′və ləs), *adj. Especially British.* marvelous. —**mar′vel|lous|ly**, *adv.* —**mar′vel-lous|ness**, *n.*

**mar|vel-of-Pe|ru** (mär′vəl əv pə rü′), *n.* = four-o'clock (def. 1).

**mar|vel|ous** (mär′və ləs), *adj.* **1** causing wonder; extraordinary: *I thought of Chatterton, the marvelous boy* (Wordsworth). **SYN**: astonishing, surprising. See syn. under **wonderful**. **2** improbable; incredible: *Children like tales of marvelous things, like that of Aladdin and his lamp.* **3** *Informal.* excellent; splendid; fine: *a marvelous time.* —**mar′vel|ous|ly**, *adv.* —**mar′vel|ous|ness**, *n.*

**mar|ver** (mär′vər), *n., v.* —*n.* a slab or tablet, originally of marble, but now generally of metal, on which a gather of glass is rolled, shaped, and cooled in glassmaking.
—*v.t.* to shape on a marver.
[< French *marbre* marble; see etym. under **marble**]

**mar|vie** or **mar|vy** (mär′vē), *interj. U.S. Slang.* marvelous: *"O Sad Arthur, how marvie!" cried the entranced Lambie* (Roger Angell).

**Marx|i|an** (märk′sē ən), *adj., n.* —*adj.* of or having to do with Karl Marx (1818-1883) or his theories: *They have dug up a classic Marxian dogma for the occasion* (New York Times).
—*n.* a follower of Marx; believer in the theories of Marx.

**Marx|i|an|ism** (märk′sē ə niz′əm), *n.* = Marxism.

**Marx|ism** (märk′siz əm), *n.* the political and economic theories of Karl Marx and Friedrich Engels. They interpreted history as a continuing economic class struggle and believed that the eventual result would be the establishment of a classless society and communal ownership of all natural and industrial resources. *Mounting unemployment with attendant sliding toward Marxism is another result of too many people in too circumscribed areas* (Bulletin of Atomic Scientists).

**Marx|ism-Len|in|ism** (märk′siz əm len′i niz əm), *n.* the political and economic theories of Marxism as expanded and augmented by those of Nikolai Lenin: *This fatuous optimism overlooks the peculiar character of Marxism-Leninism as a secular religion* (New York Times).

**Marx|ist** (märk′sist), *n., adj.* —*n.* a follower of Karl Marx; believer in his theories: *China's leaders are devoted Marxists* (Atlantic).
—*adj.* of Marx or his theories; Marxian.

**Marx|ist-Len|in|ist** (märk′sist len′i nist), *adj.* of, having to do with, or characteristic of the theories of Marxism-Leninism.

**Mar|y** (mãr′ē), *n.* **1** the mother of Jesus (in the Bible, Matthew 1:18-25). **2** the sister of Lazarus and Martha (in the Bible, Luke 10:38-42). **3** = Mary Magdalene. [Old English *Maria* < Late Latin < Greek *Mariā,* variant of *Mariám* < Hebrew *Miryām*]

**mar|y|jane** (mãr′ē jān′), *n. Slang.* marijuana.

***Mary Jane**, **1** *Trademark.* a patent leather shoe for young girls with a low heel and a strap across the instep. **2** *Slang.* marijuana.

***Mary Jane**
definition 1

**Mar|y|knoll|er** (mãr′ē nōl′ər), *n.* a member of the Maryknoll Fathers, a society of Roman Catholic priests.

**Mar|y|land** (mer′ə lənd), *n.* **1** a breed of hogs developed in the United States by cross-breeding two or more breeds in order to obtain improved meat qualities. **2** an air-cured tobacco known for

its burning qualities, used primarily in the manufacture of cigarettes.
**Mar|y|land|er** (mer′ə lən dər), *n.* a native or inhabitant of the state of Maryland.
**Maryland yellowthroat**, a North American warbler with olive-brown upper parts, yellow throat, and, in the male, a black mask across the face.
**Mary Magdalene**, a woman from whom Jesus cast out seven devils (in the Bible, Luke 8:2). She is commonly supposed to be the repentant sinner forgiven by Jesus (Luke 7:37-50).
**mar|zi|pan** (mär′zə pan), *n.* a confection made of ground almonds and sugar, molded into various forms: *marzipan shaped and colored to look like strawberries, apples, and pears.* Also, **marchpane.** [< German *Marzipan* < Italian *marzapane,* perhaps < Medieval Latin *matapanus* Venetian coin bearing image of a seated Christ < Arabic *mauṭabān* a seated king; porcelain container]
**ma|sa** (mä′sä), *n. Spanish.* the corn flour or dough with which tortillas and tamales are made: *Most of the supermarkets here carry a broad array of the basics of Spanish-American cooking including . . . masa for tamales* (New York Times).
**Ma|sai** (mä sī′), *n., pl.* **-sai** or **-sais. 1** a member of a tribe of tall cattle-raising and hunting natives of East Africa. **2** their Nilo-Hamitic language.
**masc.**, masculine.
**mas|car|a** (mas kar′ə), *n.* a preparation used for coloring the eyelashes and eyebrows, made in various dark colors. [< Spanish *máscara* disguise, mask < Arabic *maskharah* buffoon]
**mas|car|aed** (mas kar′id), *adj.* colored with mascara: *mascaraed lashes.*
**mas|ca|ron** (mas′kər ən), *n.* a decorative ornament in the form of a grotesque face or head. [< French *mascaron* < Italian *mascherone* < *maschera;* see etym. under **mask**]
**mas|cle** (mas′kəl), *n.* **1** *Heraldry.* a bearing shaped like a voided lozenge. **2** a small, perforated, lozenge-shaped metal plate used in making medieval armor. [< Anglo-French *mascle* (in French, *macle* mackle), probably < Germanic (compare Middle Dutch *masche*)]
**mas|con** (mas′kon), *n.* **1** a massive concentration of dense material lying below the lunar surface and characterized by a higher-than-average gravity: *Most scientists believe that the moon has mascons . . . which alter the orbital paths of spacecraft* (Science News). **2** a similar feature on the planets or their moons: *We have already noted the detection on the Martian surface of mascons, analogous to the lunar areas of especially high gravity* (New Scientist and Science Journal). [< *mas*(s) *con*(centration)]
**mas|cot** (mas′kot), *n.* an animal, person, or thing supposed to bring good luck: *The boys kept the stray dog as a mascot.* [< French *mascotte* < Provençal *mascoto* sorcery, a fetish < *masco* witch < Old Provençal *masca*]
**mas|cotte** (mas′kot), *n.* = mascot.
**mas|cu|line** (mas′kyə lin), *adj., n.* **—*adj.* 1** of men or boys; male: *masculine traits.* **SYN:** See syn. under **male. 2** like that of a man: *masculine courage, masculine strength.* **SYN:** manly, strong, vigorous, virile. See syn. under **male. 3** having qualities, tastes, or the like, suited to a man; mannish: *a masculine woman.* **4** of or belonging to the male sex. **5** *Grammar.* of the gender to which nouns and adjectives referring to males belong. "Boy," "nephew," "king," and "bull" are masculine nouns.
**—*n.* 1** *Grammar.* **a** the masculine gender. **b** a word or form in the masculine gender. *Abbr:* masc. **2** something that is male; male: *She flounced out of the room and left the masculines to themselves* (F. W. Robinson).
[< Latin *masculīnus* < *masculus* < *mās, maris* male. See etym. of doublet **male.**] **—mas′cu|line|ly,** *adv.* **—mas′cu|line|ness,** *n.*
**masculine cadence**, *Music.* a cadence in which the final chord falls on the strong beat.
**masculine rhyme**, a rhyme in which the final syllables are stressed, as in *disdain* and *complain, recline* and *divine.*
**mas|cu|lin|ist** (mas′kyə lə nist), *n.* a person who favors or demands male rights or privileges. [patterned on *feminist*]
**mas|cu|lin|i|ty** (mas′kyə lin′ə tē), *n.* masculine quality or condition.
**mas|cu|lin|ize** (mas′kyə lə nīz), *v.t.,* **-ized, -iz|ing.** to produce masculine characteristics in (a female). **—mas′cu|lin|i|za′tion,** *n.*
**mase** (māz), *v.i.,* **mased, mas|ing.** to behave like a maser; generate and amplify microwaves. [back formation < *maser*]
**ma|ser** (mā′zər), *n.* a device which amplifies or generates electromagnetic waves, especially microwaves, with great stability and accuracy. Masers operate at temperatures near absolute zero. Their primary uses are in long-distance radar and radio astronomy. *Low-noise amplifiers using solid-state masers may well become important in space research* (New Science). [< *m*(icrowave) *a*(mplification by) *s*(timulated) *e*(mission of) *r*(adiation)]
**mash¹** (mash), *n., v.* **—*n.* 1** a soft mixture; soft mass: *He beat the potato into a mash before eating it. A mash of snow covered the walk.* **2a** a warm mixture of bran or meal and water for horses and other animals. **b** any one of various mixtures of ground grain, often supplemented with proteins, antibiotics, or other additives, used as feed for poultry, livestock, and pets.
**3a** crushed malt or meal soaked in hot water for making beer or ale. **b** a similar preparation of rye, corn, barley, or other grain, used to make whiskey. **4** *Figurative.* a confused mixture; muddle.
**—*v.t.* 1** to beat into a soft mass; crush to a uniform mass: *I'll mash the potatoes.* **2** to mix (crushed malt or meal) with hot water in brewing.
[Old English *māsc-, māx-,* in *māx-wyrt* mash-wort]
**mash²** (mash), *v., n. Slang.* **—*v.t.*, *v.i.*** to look (at) with amorous desire; flirt (with); ogle: *Shan't I just mash the men!* (Arnold Bennett).
**—*n.*** a person, especially a woman, who is looked at in this way.
[origin uncertain]
**MASH** (no periods) or **M.A.S.H.**, mobile army surgical hospital.
**mash|er¹** (mash′ər), *n.* a person or thing that mashes: *a potato masher.*
**mash|er²** (mash′ər), *n. Slang.* a man who tries to make advances to women: *. . . police-women assigned to ride the subways and arrest such shady characters as mashers* (New Yorker). [< *mash*² + *-er*¹]
**mash|gi|ach** (mäsh gē′äн), *n., pl.* **-gi|chim** (-gē-нēm′). an inspector appointed to supervise the observance of Jewish law in the preparation of kosher food. [< Hebrew *mashgiāh* (literally) overseer]
**mash|ie** or **mash|y** (mash′ē), *n., pl.* **mash|ies.** a golf club with a short, sloping, steel face, used especially for long approach shots. It is usually called a "number 5 iron." [perhaps < alteration of Old French *massue* club < Vulgar Latin *matteuca* < *mattea;* see etym. under **mace**¹]
**mashie niblick**, a golf club with a steel face that slopes more than that of a mashie, but less than that of a niblick, used especially for short approach shots. It is usually called a "number 6 iron."
**Ma|sho|na** (mə shō′nə), *n., pl.* **-na** or **-nas. 1** a member of a Bantu tribe now inhabiting the northeastern part of Rhodesia. **2** the language of the tribe. Also, **Shona.**
**mas|jid** (mus′jid), *n.* = mosque. [< Arabic *masjid;* see etym. under **mosque**]

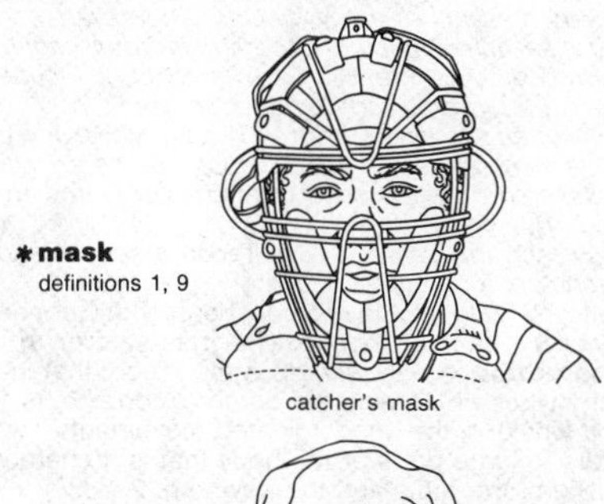

***mask**
definitions 1, 9

catcher's mask

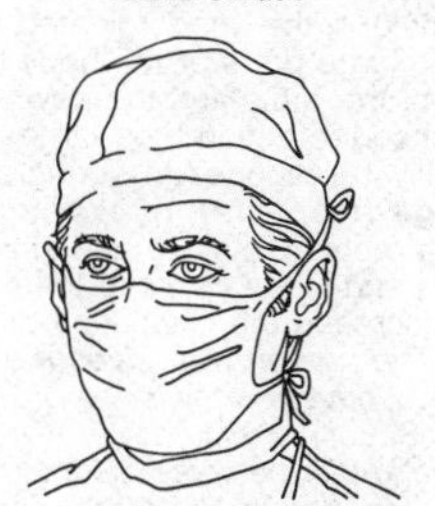

surgeon's mask

***mask** (mask, mäsk), *n., v.* **—*n.* 1** a covering to hide or protect the face: *The burglar wore a mask. Fencers and baseball catchers wear masks.* **2** a false face worn for amusement, as at Halloween, a masquerade, or carnival. **3** *Figurative.* something that hides or disguises; disguise: *The fox hid his plans under a mask of friendship.* **SYN:** pretense, cloak. **4** a person wearing a mask: *A mask, in the character of an old woman, joined them* (Henry Fielding). **5** a clay, wax, or plaster likeness of a person's face. **6** the hollow figure of a human head worn by Greek and Roman actors to identify the character represented and increase the volume of the voice. **7** = masque. **8** a carved or molded face or head, usually grotesque, used as an architectural ornament. **9** a piece of fine gauze worn over the mouth and nose of surgeons, nurses, and the like, during operations. **10** any similar covering, such as one used to aid in breathing. **11** *Military.* a screen of earth, brush, or camouflage, used to hide or protect a battery or any military operation. **12** the pattern for the components of an integrated circuit: *If one is designing the mask for an integrated electronic circuit, the objects to be represented are the transistors, resistors, gates, wiring and other elementary components from which the circuit is to be built* (Scientific American).
**—*v.t.* 1** to cover (the face) with a mask.
**2** *Figurative.* to hide or disguise: *A smile masked his disappointment.* **3** *Military.* to hide (a battery or military operation) from the sight of the enemy.
**—*v.i.*** to cover or conceal anything with a mask; put on or wear a mask.
[< Middle French *masque* < Italian *maschera* < Arabic *maskhara* laughingstock < *sakhira* to ridicule]
**mas|ka|longe** (mas′kə lonj), *n.* = muskellunge.
**mas|ka|nonge** (mas′kə nonj), *n.* = muskellunge.
**mask crab**, a crab that has markings on its carapace suggestive of a mask.
**mask diver**, a person who engages in mask diving.
**mask diving**, skin diving in which the diver uses a face mask and, usually, a snorkel.
**masked** (maskt, mäskt), *adj.* **1** wearing or provided with a mask or masks. **2** *Figurative.* disguised; concealed. **3** *Zoology.* **a** marked on the face or head as if wearing a mask. **b** having the wings, legs, etc., of the future image indicated in outline beneath the integument, as certain insect pupae. **4** *Botany.* personate.
**masked ball**, a dance at which masks are worn.
**masked shrew**, a shrew usually found near marshes and streams in the northern United States and in Canada.
**mask|er** (mas′kər, mäs′-), *n.* a person who wears a mask, especially at a masked ball, masquerade, or masque. Also, **masquer.**
**mas|kil** (mäs′kēl), *n., pl.* **mas|ki|lim** (mäs kē-lēm′). a modern Jewish intellectual, especially one devoted to the Hebrew language, literature, and culture. [< Hebrew *maskīl* (literally) enlightened]
**mask|ing** (mas′king, mäs′-), *n.* a thing that masks or conceals something from view: *[He] contended he had tripped on a piece of masking covering a worn rug* (New York Times).
**masking tape**, a gummed tape used to mask or protect surfaces not to be treated, painted, or sprayed while work is being done on adjacent areas.
**mas|lin** (maz′lən), *n. Dialect.* **1** a mixture of grains, especially rye and wheat. **2** bread made of it. **3** a mixture or medley. [< Old French *mesteillon,* ultimately < Latin *miscēre* mix]
**mas|och|ism** (mas′ə kiz əm, maz′-), *n.* **1** abnormal sexual pleasure derived from being dominated or physically abused. **2** any enjoyment derived from being dominated or made to suffer. [< Leopold von Sacher-*Masoch,* 1836-1895, an Austrian novelist, who described it in his stories + *-ism*]
**mas|och|ist** (mas′ə kist, maz′-), *n.* a person who derives pleasure from being dominated or physically abused; person who enjoys suffering: *Then . . . come the masochists whose only longing is to suffer, in real or in symbolic form, humiliations and tortures at the hands of the loved object* (Sigmund Freud).
**mas|och|is|tic** (mas′ə kis′tik, maz′-), *adj.* of or having to do with masochists or masochism: *as masochistic as the wintertime spectacle of Polar Club dunkers* (Newsweek). **—mas′och|is′ti|cal|ly,** *adv.*
**ma|son** (mā′sən), *n., v.* **—*n.*** a man whose work is building with stone, brick, or similar materials; stonemason or bricklayer.
**—*v.t.*** to build of brick, stone, or similar materials; strengthen with masonry: *the masoned house* (Robert Louis Stevenson).
[< Old French *masson,* earlier *maçon* < Late Latin *machiō, machiōnis,* also *maciō* < Germanic (compare Old High German *steinmezzo* stonemason)]
**Ma|son** (mā′sən), *n.* a member of the worldwide secret society of Freemasons; Freemason.
**Mason and Dix|on's Line** (dik′sənz), = Mason-Dixon line.
**mason bee**, a solitary bee that builds its nest of mud.

**Pronunciation Key:** hat, āge, cãre, fär; let, ēqual, tėrm; it, īce; hot, ōpen, ôrder; **oil, out;** cup, pu̇t, rüle; **ch**ild; lo**ng**; **th**in; **ᴛʜ**en; **zh**, measure; **ə** represents **a** in about, **e** in taken, **i** in pencil, **o** in lemon, **u** in circus.

**Ma|son-Dix|on line** (mā′sən dik′sən), the boundary between Pennsylvania and Maryland, formerly thought of as separating the free states of the North from the slave states of the South. It was surveyed between 1763 and 1767 by Charles Mason and Jeremiah Dixon.

**ma|son|ic** or **Ma|son|ic** (mə son′ik), *adj.* **1** of Masons or Masonry; having to do with the society of Freemasons or Freemasonry: *In those expert hands the trowel seemed to assume the qualities of some lofty masonic symbol* (Lytton Strachey). **2** in the spirit of Freemasonry; giving sympathetic understanding: *In some voiceless, masonic way, most people in that saloon had become aware that something was in process of happening* (Owen Wister).

**Ma|son|ite** (mā′sə nīt), *n. Trademark.* a type of hard fiberboard given a smooth finish on one side, used for partitions, panels, and the like.

**Mason jar**, a glass jar with a metal cover that can be screwed on tightly, used in home canning: *The Mason jar is the most commonly used canning jar today* (Helen Marley). [< John *Mason,* an American inventor, who patented it in 1858]

**ma|son|ry** (mā′sən rē), *n., pl.* **-ries. 1** a wall, foundation, or part of a building built by a mason; stonework or brickwork: *Stone fell from the walls as the masonry of the old castle began to crumble over the years.* **2** the trade or skill of a mason: *Masonry is a lost skill among farmers today.* **3** Often, **Masonry. a** the principles or doctrines of Freemasons; Freemasonry. **b** the members of this society.

**mason wasp**, a solitary wasp that builds its nest of mud.

**Ma|so|ra** or **Ma|so|rah** (mə sôr′ə, -sōr′-), *n.* **1** the tradition, compiled by Jewish critics and scholars in the 900's and earlier, regarding the correct text of the Hebrew Bible. **2a** the marginal notes to the Biblical text preserving this information. **b** a book containing these. Also, **Massora, Massorah.** [earlier *Masoreth* < Hebrew *māsōrāh,* alteration of earlier *massôreth* tradition]

**Mas|o|rete** (mas′ə rēt), *n.* **1** a Hebrew scholar who is skilled in the study of the Masora. **2** one of the Jewish scholars who wrote the Masora. Also, **Massorete, Massorite.**

**Mas|o|ret|ic** (mas′ə ret′ik), *adj.* of or having to do with the Masora or the Masoretes.

**masque** (mask, mäsk), *n.* **1** an amateur dramatic entertainment in which fine costumes, scenery, music, and dancing are more important than the story. Masques were so named because the performers wore masks. They were much given in England in the 1500's and 1600's, at court and at the homes of nobles, often outdoors. *Masque is not opera: nor for that matter is it drama or ballet. It is something of them all* (London Times). **2** a play written for such an entertainment: *Milton's "Comus" is a masque.* **3** a masked ball; masquerade. Also, **mask.** [< Middle French *masque;* see etym. under **mask**]

**mas|quer** (mas′kər, mäs′-), *n.* = masker.

**mas|quer|ade** (mas′kə rād′), *v.,* **-ad|ed, -ad|ing,** *n.* —*v.i.* **1** to disguise oneself; go about under false pretenses: *The king masqueraded as a beggar to find out if his people really liked him.* **2** to take part in a masquerade.
—*n.* **1** a party or dance at which masks and fancy costumes are worn: *Gaily dressed revelers ... drumming carnival bands ... magnificent masquerade parties* (Time). **2** the costume and mask worn at such a party or dance. **3** *Figurative.* false pretense; disguise: *And, after all, what is a lie? It is but the truth in masquerade* (Bryon). **4** *Figurative.* the act or fact of going about or acting under false pretenses.
[< French *mascarade* < Italian *mascarata,* variant of *mascherata* < *maschera;* see etym. under **mask**] —**mas′quer|ad′er,** *n.*

**mass**[1] (mas), *n., v., adj.* —*n.* **1** a lump; piece or amount of anything without any clear shape or size: *a mass of dough.* **2** a large quantity together; great amount or number: *a mass of flowers, a mass of treasure, a mass of books.* **SYN:** aggregate, accumulation. **3** the greater part; main body; majority: *The great mass of men consider themselves healthy.* **4** bulk or size: *the sheer mass of an iceberg.* **5** the quantity of matter anything contains; the property of a physical body which gives it inertia. Mass is a constant not dependent on gravity and is obtained either by dividing the weight of the body by the acceleration of gravity or by comparing an unknown mass with a known mass, as on a balance. *The mass of a piece of lead is not changed by melting it. Isotopes are atoms of the same element that differ in atomic weight, or mass* (R. L. Thornton). **6** = mass number. **7** an expanse, as of color or shade, in a painting. **8** *Pharmacy.* thick, pasty preparation from which pills are made.
—*v.t., v.i.* to form or collect into a mass; assemble: *It would look better to mass the peonies behind the roses than to mix them. The great bands of caribou ... mass up on the edge of the woods* (W. Pike). **SYN:** gather.
—*adj.* **1** of or by many people: *a mass protest.* **2** on a large scale: *mass buying.* **3** of or having to do with the masses: *mass culture.*
**in the mass**, as a whole; without distinguishing parts or individuals: *It is difficult to speak accurately of mankind in the mass.*
**the masses**, the common people; the working classes; the lower classes of society: *The masses rebelled against the monarchy during the French Revolution.*
[< Middle French *masse,* learned borrowing from Latin *massa* kneaded dough, lump < Greek *mâza* barley bread, related to *mássein* to knead]

**Mass** or **mass**[2] (mas), *n.* **1** the main religious service of worship in the Roman Catholic Church and in some other churches; Holy Eucharist as a sacrifice. The Mass consists of many prayers and ceremonies. *The principal parts of the Mass are the Offertory, the Consecration, and the Communion* (Fulton J. Sheen). **2** a particular celebration of the Eucharist. **3** music written for certain parts of it: *Bach's Mass in B Minor.* [Old English *mæsse* < Late Latin *missa* < Latin *mittere* to send away]

**Mass.**, Massachusetts.

**mas|sa** (mas′ə), *n.* an old southern Negro form of **master**.

**Mas|sa|chu|set** (mas′ə chü′sit, -zit), *n., pl.* **-set** or **-sets. 1** a member of a tribe of Algonkian Indians who formerly lived near Massachusetts Bay. **2** their Algonkian language.

**Mas|sa|chu|setts** (mas′ə chü′sits, -zits), *n., pl.* **-setts.** = Massachuset.

**mas|sa|cre** (mas′ə kər), *n., v.,* **-cred, -cring.** —*n.* **1** wholesale, pitiless slaughter of people or animals: *The hunters came from the East to massacre the buffalo of the plains, killing several million in a short time.* **SYN:** butchery, carnage. **2** *Figurative: ... the specter of automation causing a wholesale massacre of jobs* (Wall Street Journal). *Highways ... are responsible for the massacre of the countryside* (Ada Louise Huxtable).
—*v.t.* **1** to kill (many people or animals) needlessly or cruelly; slaughter in large numbers: *The cavalry massacred many Indians. The savages had massacred many of the garrison after capitulation* (Benjamin Franklin). **SYN:** butcher. **2** *Figurative: ... a big brawling demagogue, who massacred the king's English* (Saturday Review). *Once more a really funny ... book has been massacred on the screen* (Manchester Guardian Weekly).
[< French *massacre* < Old French *macecle,* and *mache-col* a shambles, butchery, perhaps ultimately < Vulgar Latin *maccāre* beat (< a Germanic word) + Latin *collum* neck] —**mas′sa|crer,** *n.*

**mass action**, **1** *Psychology.* **a** the theory that in many types of learning the cerebral cortex acts as a whole. **b** the uncoordinated movements involving large parts of the body that is a characteristic of the fetus and the newborn. **2** *Sociology.* concerted action by a large group of people, especially in response to strong opposition.

**mas|sage** (mə säzh′), *n., v.,* **-saged, -sag|ing.**
—*n.* **1** a rubbing, striking and kneading of the muscles and joints to make them work better and to increase the circulation of blood; rubdown: *The person who gives the massage should ... have a knowledge of human anatomy* (W. W. Bauer). **2** *Figurative: A weak one will accept the kudos because his indifferent performance ... creates in him a real need for ego massage* (New Yorker).
—*v.t.* **1** to give a massage to: *Let me massage your back for you.* **2** *Figurative: "Sometimes in the past," he said, "this convention has seemed to me just to massage the prejudices of the delegates"* (New York Times).
[< French *massage* friction, kneading < Middle French *masse* dough, mass[1]] —**mas|sag′er,** *n.*

**massage parlor**, **1** a place where massages are given. **2** a house of prostitution: *Organized crime, says a Washington official, dominates the traditional porn industry, as well as massage parlors* (Time).

**mas|sa|sau|ga** (mas′ə sô′gə), *n.* a very small rattlesnake of the southern United States. [American English < the *Missisauga* river < Algonkian (Ojibwa) (literally) < *misi* great + *sâg,* or *sauk* river mouth]

**Mass card**, a card informing the family of a deceased person that the sender has arranged for a Mass or Masses to be offered in his memory.

**mass communication**, communication through the mass media.

**mass|cult** (mas′kult′), *n.* the culture created by the influence of radio, television, and other mass media.

**mass defect**, the difference between the atomic weight of an atom when determined by totaling the atomic weights of the neutrons and protons comprising the atom, and the atomic weight of the atom as a whole; packing effect. The mass defect is considered as a measure of the binding energy of the atom. *The "mass defect" ... refers to the fact that the mass of the nucleus is slightly smaller than the sum of the masses of the particles combined in it* (Scientific American).

**mas|sé** (ma sā′), *n.,* or **massé shot**, a stroke in billiards in which the cue ball is hit with the cue held almost vertically and with a sharp downward motion. [< French *massé,* past participle of *masser* to make such a stroke < *masse* a cue, club < Old French *mace* mace]

**masse|cuite** (màs kwēt′), *n.* (in sugar making) the juice of the sugar cane, a mixture of molasses and sugar crystals, after concentration by boiling. [< French *masse cuite* mass cooked]

**mass-en|er|gy equation** (mas′en′ər jē), an equation expressing the relation of mass and energy, formulated by Albert Einstein in 1905: $E = mc^2$; Einstein equation. $E$ = the energy in ergs; $m$ = the mass in grams; $c$ = the velocity of light in centimeters per second. *What happens in the Bevatron confirms Einstein's famous mass-energy equation which says that energy can be converted into mass and mass into energy* (New York Times).

**mas|se|ter** (ma sē′tər), *n.* a muscle that raises the lower jaw in chewing. See diagram under **face.** [< New Latin *masseter* < Greek *masētḗr* (*mŷs*) chewer (muscle) < *masâsthai* to chew]

**mas|se|ter|ic** (mas′ə ter′ik), *adj.* of or having to do with the masseter.

**mas|seur** (ma sœr′), *n.* a man whose work is massaging people. [< French *masseur* < *masser* to massage]

**mas|seuse** (ma sœz′), *n.* a woman whose work is massaging people. [< French *masseuse,* feminine of *masseur* masseur]

**mas|si|cot** (mas′ə kot), *n.* a yellow powder, an unfused monoxide of lead, used as a pigment and drier. *Formula:* PbO [< Old French *massicot* < Italian *marzacotta* a potter's glaze < Spanish *mazacote* mortar; earlier, soda < Arabic *mashaqunyā*]

**mas|sif** (mas′if; *French* mà sēf′), *n.* **1** the main part of a mountain range, surrounded by valleys: *The Rocky massif was already splotched with golden aspens* (Time). **2** a large block of the earth's crust shifted upward or downward as a unit and bounded by faults. [< Middle French *massif* massive]

**mas|sive** (mas′iv), *adj.* **1** big and heavy; large and solid; huge: *a massive rock, a massive building, a massive wrestler.* **SYN:** weighty, ponderous, bulky. **2** giving the impression of being large and broad: *a massive forehead.* **3** *Figurative.* imposing; impressive: *Beethoven's Ninth Symphony is a massive work.* **4** in or by great numbers; broad in scope; extensive: *a massive assault, massive retaliation.* **5** (of gold, silver, or plate) solid rather than hollow: *a chain of massive gold* (Scott). **6a** affecting a large area of bodily tissue: *a massive hemorrhage.* **b** much larger or more than usual: *a massive dose.* **7** *Mineralogy.* not definitely crystalline. **8** *Geology.* without definite structural divisions. [< Middle French *massive,* feminine of *massif* < *masse* mass[1]] —**mas′sive|ly,** *adv.* —**mas′sive|ness,** *n.*

**mas|siv|i|ty** (ma siv′ə tē), *n.* the fact or condition of being massive.

**mass|less** (mas′lis), *adj.* lacking mass; having a mass of zero: *The neutrino is a massless particle.*

**mass man**, man conceived not as an individual but as representing the anonymous multitudes of people in a mass society: *The mass man loses his independence, and more importantly, he loses the desire to be independent* (Bulletin of Atomic Scientists).

**mass medium**, *pl.* **mass media**, any form of communication, such as the press, television, radio, and motion pictures, which reaches large numbers of people: *A good deal of adult education has been accomplished by the mass media* (Bulletin of Atomic Scientists).

**mass meeting**, a large public gathering of people to hear or discuss some matter of common interest.

**mass noun**, a noun which does not form a plural. Mass nouns usually refer to something uncountable and cannot be preceded by the articles *a* or *an.* Abstract nouns are usually mass nouns. *Examples:* physics, riches.

**Pronunciation Key:** hat, āge, cãre, fär; let, ēqual, tėrm; it, īce; hot, ōpen, ôrder; oil, out; cup, pu̇t, rüle; child; long; thin; ᴛʜen; zh, measure; ə represents **a** in about, **e** in taken, **i** in pencil, **o** in lemon, **u** in circus.

**mass number**, the whole number that most closely indicates the atomic weight of an isotope. It is equal to the sum of the protons and neutrons in the nucleus. *For some elements that do not occur in nature, especially the radioactive elements, the term mass number is used instead of atomic weight* (George Bush and Ralph Lapp). *Symbol:* A (no period).

**mass observation**, *British.* a method of studying and recording the attitudes, opinions, and habits of a large segment of the population by means of a system of surveys, interviews, and documentary analyses.

**Mas|so|ra** or **Mas|so|rah** (mə sôr′ə, -sōr′-), *n.* = Masora.

**Mas|so|rete** (mas′ə rēt), *n.* = Masorete.

**mas|so|ther|a|py** (mas′ō ther′ə pē), *n.* the treatment of a disease by massage. [< French *masser* massage + English *therapy*]

**mass-pro|duce** (mas′prə düs′, -dyüs′), *v.t.*, **-duced, -duc|ing.** to make (any product) in large quantities, especially by machinery: *the lathe factory in Moscow which already mass-produces the cheapest lathes in the world* (New Scientist).
— **mass′-pro|duc′er**, *n.*

**mass production**, **1** the making of goods in large quantities, especially by machinery and with division of labor: *the mass production of automobiles.* **2** *Figurative: the mass production of entertainment.*

**mass ratio**, the ratio of the weight of a fully loaded space vehicle to its weight after its fuel is consumed and after sections no longer required have been separated.

**mass society**, a large, highly organized, and impersonal society consisting of masses of anonymous individuals; the society of the mass man.

**mass spectrograph**, an apparatus for determining the mass numbers of isotopes by passing streams of ions through electric and magnetic fields which separate ions of different masses. The results are recorded on a photographic plate. *The mass spectrograph has been used to compare the ratios of mass to charge in the electron and positron* (Science News).

**mass spectrometer**, an apparatus similar to the mass spectrograph except that its results are recorded electrically.

**mass-spec|tro|met|ric** (mas′spek′trə met′rik), *adj.* of or having to do with a mass spectrometer.

**mass spectrometry**, study with or use of the mass spectrometer.

**mass spectroscope**, any one of various devices utilizing magnetic fields, electric fields, or both, and used especially for separating, weighing indirectly, and studying isotopes, and atomic particles. The mass spectrograph and the mass spectrometer are two types of mass spectroscopes. *In the simplest mass spectroscope, electrons bombard a gas at low pressure* (Alfred O. Nier).

**mass spectroscopy**, study with or use of a mass spectroscope.

**mass spectrum**, the band of charged particles of different masses formed when a beam of ions is passed through the deflecting fields of a mass spectrograph or a mass spectrometer.

**mass|y** (mas′ē), *adj.*, **mass|i|er, mass|i|est.** **1** bulky and heavy; massive: *We closed all the massy shutters of our old building* (Edgar Allan Poe). **2** *Figurative.* great; impressive. **3** solid, rather than hollow or plated, as metal.

✱**mast**[1] (mast, mäst), *n., v.* — *n.* **1** a long pole of wood or metal set upright on a ship or boat to support the sails and rigging. SYN: spar. See picture below. **2** any tall, upright pole: *the mast of a derrick.*
— *v.t.* to equip or rig with a mast or masts.
**abaft the mast**, *British.* in a position of authority: *He was not satisfied unless he was abaft the mast.*
**before the mast**, **a** serving as a common sailor, because such sailors used to sleep in the forward part of a ship: *He sailed for two years before the mast.* **b** in front of the foremast; in the forecastle: *Common sailors used to be berthed before the mast.*
[Old English *mæst*] — **mast′less**, *adj.* — **mast′-like′**, *adj.*

**mast**[2] (mast, mäst), *n.* acorns, chestnuts, beechnuts, and other tree fruits on the ground; the fruit of certain forest trees, especially as food for swine: *Pigs eat mast.* [Old English *mæst*]

**mas|ta|ba** or **mas|ta|bah** (mas′tə bə), *n.* an ancient Egyptian tomb set over a mummy chamber burrowed in rock. It was rectangular with a flat top and sides sloping outward to the base. [< Arabic *maṣṭaba* (literally) bench]

**mast cell**, a large cell in connective tissue that has a very granular cytoplasm. Under certain conditions it releases histamine and an anticoagulant, heparin. [*mast* < German *masten* fatten]

**mas|tec|to|my** (mas tek′tə mē), *n., pl.* **-mies.** the surgical removal of a woman's breast, as when cancerous. [< Greek *mastós* breast + *ektomḗ* a cutting out]

**-masted**, *combining form.* having a ___ mast or masts: *A three-masted ship = a ship having three masts.*

**mas|ter** (mas′tər, mäs′-), *n., adj., v.* — *n.* **1** a person who has power or authority over others, such as the head of a household, a school, or a ship; one in control; owner, employer, or director. SYN: chief, ruler, commander. **2** a person who has the power to control, use, or dispose of something at will: *to be master of a situation. He ... was a perfect master of both languages* (Jonathan Swift). **3** a male teacher, especially in private schools: *The village master taught his little school* (Oliver Goldsmith). **4** an artist, musician, or author of the highest rank. **5** a picture, painting, or sculpture by a great artist: *an old master.* **6** a person who knows all there is to know about his work; expert, such as a great artist or skilled workman: *a master of the violin.* **7** a skilled worker, qualified to teach apprentices; craftsman in business for himself. **8a** a title of respect for a boy: *First prize goes to Master Henry Adams.* **b** a young gentleman; boy. **9** Also, **Master. a** a person who has taken a degree above bachelor and below doctor at a college or university. **b** = Master of Arts. **c** = Master of Science. **10** a person who overcomes another; victor: *They have marched from far away ... And the morning saw them masters of Cremona* (Sir Arthur Conan Doyle). **11** an owner of a slave or a horse or dog. **12** (in general) an owner; possessor: ... *those qualities of the mind he was master of* (Jonathan Swift). **13** a court officer appointed to assist the judge. **14** (in Scotland) the title of the heir apparent to a rank of the peerage lower than earl. **15** a rank of excellence in contract bridge tournament play: ... *contests for individuals, pairs and teams, in both masters' and non-masters' classifications* (New York Times). **16** a high-quality initial copy or original, as of a recording or tape, used as a source for duplications: *to make thousands of long-playing records from a master, to prepare masters of the semester exams.*
— *adj.* **1** being master of; of a master; by a master: *O let me be the tune-swept fiddlestring That feels the Master Melody* (John G. Neihardt). **2** main: *the master bedroom of a house.* **3** qualified to teach apprentices and carry on his trade independently; highly skilled: *a master printer.* **4** controlling or standardizing the operation of other mechanisms or parts: *a master plan, a master switch.* **5** serving as the source for duplication: *a master tape, a master test.*
— *v.t.* **1** to become the master of; conquer; control: *She learned to master her anger.* SYN: overcome, subjugate, subdue. **2** to become expert in; become skillful at; learn: *He has mastered riding his bicycle. He mastered whatever was not worth the knowing* (James Russell Lowell). **3** to rule or direct as a master.
**(the) Master**, Jesus Christ: *Closer drew the twelve disciples to their Master's side* (Nathaniel P. Willis).
**the Masters**, a golf tournament held annually at Augusta, Georgia, for the top professional and amateur players: *Between 1963 and 1973 Jack Nicklaus won the Masters four times.*
[fusion of Old English *mægester* (< Latin *magister*), and Middle English *meistre* < Old French *maistre* < Latin *magister*]

**mas|ter-at-arms** (mas′tər ət ärmz′, mäs′-), *n., pl.* **mas|ters-at-arms.** a petty officer on a ship who keeps order and takes charge of prisoners. The rating survives in the Royal Navy, and has recently been reactivated in the United States Navy.

**master builder**, **1** = architect. **2** a building contractor.

**mas|ter|ful** (mas′tər fəl, mäs′-), *adj.* **1** fond of power or authority; domineering: *She was attracted by his masterful ways.* SYN: imperious, lordly, overbearing. **2** expert or very skillful; masterly: *a masterful performance.* — **mas′ter|ful|ly**, *adv.* — **mas′ter|ful|ness**, *n.*

**master gland**, = pituitary gland.

**master gunnery sergeant**, a noncommissioned officer in the Marine Corps, ranking above a sergeant major.

**mas|ter-hand** (mas′tər hand′, mäs′-), *n.* **1** a highly skilled craftsman; expert: *Chaucer was a master-hand at getting comic or satiric or emotional effects* (Atlantic). **2** a high degree of skill or excellence; expertise.

**mas|ter|hood** (mas′tər hu̇d, mäs′-), *n.* the condition or character of being a master.

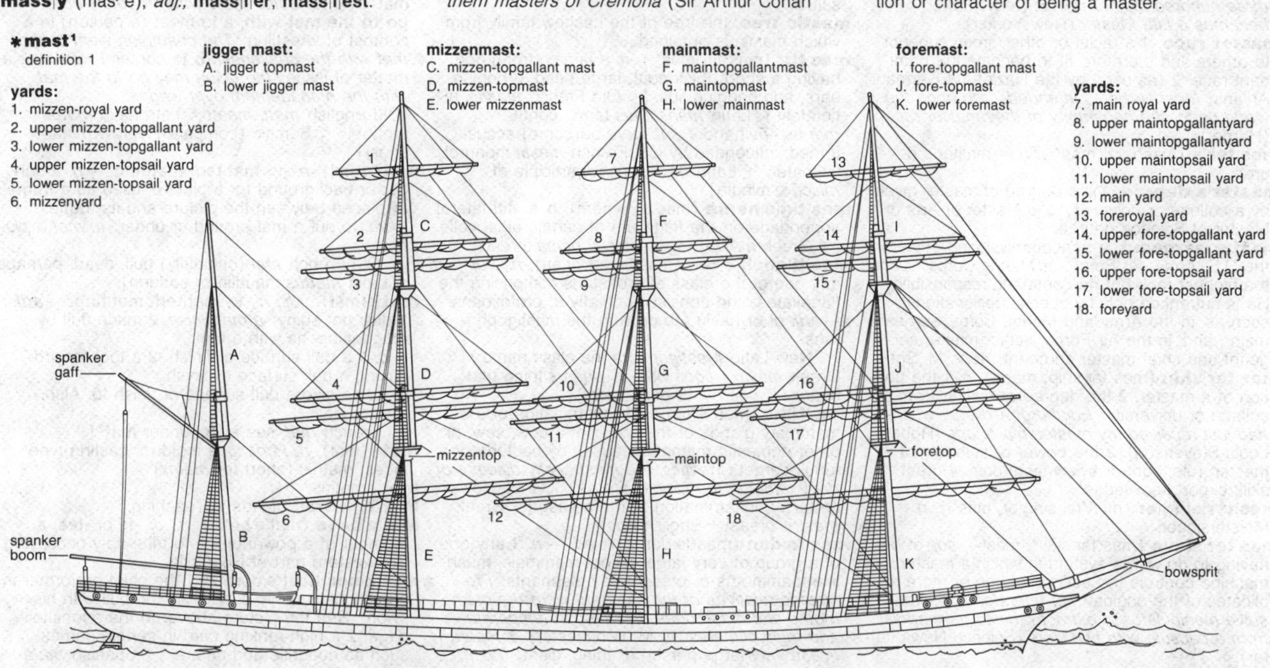

**master key**, 1 a key that opens all the different locks of a set. 2 a key that will open many different locks of a similar type.

**mas|ter|less** (mas′tər lis, mäs′-), *adj.* having no master; uncontrolled or unprotected by a master: *Many a town must now be masterless, And women's voices rule* (William Morris).

**mas|ter|li|ness** (mas′tər lē nis, mäs′-), *n.* the quality or condition of being masterly.

**mas|ter|ly** (mas′tər lē, mäs′-), *adj., adv.* —*adj.* expert; very skillful: *a masterly piece of work. Rembrandt was a masterly painter.* **SYN**: proficient, finished, excellent.
—*adv.* in an expert or very skillful way.

**master mason**, 1 a skilled mason who can direct the work of others. 2 Often, **Master Mason**. a fully qualified Freemason, who has passed the 3rd degree.

**master mechanic**, a skilled mechanic who can direct the work of others.

**mas|ter|mind** (mas′tər mīnd′, mäs′-), *n., v.* —*n.* a person who plans and supervises a scheme or operation, usually from behind the scenes or in the background: *Soustelle, the political mastermind of the Algiers uprising that swept DeGaulle back to power ...* (Wall Street Journal). —*v.t.* to devise and conduct (a plan of action), usually from behind the scenes or in the background: *The statement gave Burgess the credit for masterminding their escape to Russia* (Time).

**Master of Arts**, 1 a degree given by a college or university to a person who has completed a graduate course of study in the liberal arts or humanities, or as an honor. *Abbr:* M.A. or A.M. 2 a person who has had the degree of Master of Arts conferred upon him.

**master of ceremonies**, a person in charge of a ceremony or entertainment, who makes sure that all parts of it take place in the proper order. He usually welcomes guests and introduces speakers or performers.

**Master of Science**, 1 a degree given by a college or university to a person who has completed a graduate course of study in science, or as an honor. *Abbr:* M.S. or M.Sc. 2 a person who has had the degree of Master of Science conferred upon him.

**mas|ter|piece** (mas′tər pēs′, mäs′-), *n.* 1 anything done or made with wonderful skill; perfect piece of art or workmanship: *This plan of setting our enemies to destroy one another seemed to us a masterpiece of policy* (Francis Parkman). 2 a person's greatest piece of work: *The Ninth Symphony was Beethoven's masterpiece.*

**mas|ter-plan** (mas′tər plan′, mäs′-), *v.t., v.i.,* **-planned, -plan|ning.** to devise or design according to a master plan.

**master plan**, any general plan or design, especially one used as a blueprint for a large building project: *He helped to develop the council's master plan for hospitals in the city* (New York Times).

**master point**, *U.S.* a point awarded to a player of contract bridge who wins or ranks high in a national tournament: *A player with a total of three hundred master points, he went on, becomes a Life Master* (New Yorker).

**master race**, 1 a racial or other group superior to others and therefore fit to become the dominant race. 2 (as used by the Nazis) the German Aryans: *Most Nazis ... intended ... to bring the world under the hegemony of their master race* (Harper's).

**mas|ter's** (mas′tərz, mäs′-), *n.* = master's degree.

**master's degree**, 1 the degree of master given by a college or university. 2 a Master of Arts or Master of Science degree.

**master sergeant**, a noncommissioned officer in the U.S. Army, Air Force, or Marine Corps having the highest rank but no command responsibility. He is outranked only by special designations, such as, in the Army and Marine Corps, sergeant major, and, in the Air Force, senior master sergeant and chief master sergeant. *Abbr:* M. Sgt.

**mas|ter|ship** (mas′tər ship, mäs′-), *n.* 1 the position of a master. 2 the degree of master from a college or university: *Edinburgh College, where I had just received my mastership of arts* (Robert Louis Stevenson). 3 the power or authority of a master; rule; control. **SYN**: masterdom. 4 great skill; expert knowledge.

**mas|ter|sing|er** (mas′tər sing′ər, mäs′-), *n.* = Meistersinger.

**mas|ter|slave** (mas′tər slāv′, mäs′-), *adj.* of or having to do with a system in which a master machine controls the actions of one or more duplicates of the original: *He operates a master-slave manipulator to extract radioactive material from a capsule with tweezers* (Science News Letter).

**mas|ter-stream nozzle** (mas′tər strēm′, mäs′-), a large nozzle used in fire fighting that is usually mounted on a truck and attached to a large hose line.

**master stroke**, or **mas|ter|stroke** (mas′tər-strōk′, mäs′-), *n.* a very skillful act or achievement.

**mas|ter|work** (mas′tər wėrk′, mäs′-), *n.* = masterpiece.

**master workman**, 1 a person very skilled in a trade or craft. 2 = foreman.

**mas|ter|y** (mas′tər ē, -trē; mäs′-), *n., pl.* **-ter|ies.** 1 power such as a master has; rule; control: *So far humanity has shown itself most unfit for a rational mastery of its own future* (Science News). **SYN**: command, sway. 2 the upper hand; victory: *The two teams vied for mastery. Four champions fierce, Strive here for mastery* (Milton). **SYN**: triumph. 3 very great skill or knowledge: *a mastery over musical instruments. The teacher had a mastery of his subject. This consummate military leader ... was distinguished by ... a mastery of method rarely surpassed* (Benjamin Disraeli). **SYN**: command, grasp.

**mast|head** (mast′hed′, mäst′-), *n., v.* —*n.* 1 the top of a ship's mast. A crow's-nest near the masthead of the lower mast is used as a lookout. 2 the part of a newspaper or magazine that gives the title, owner, address, staff members, rates, and other information: *The biggest category on Time's masthead ... is that of its sixty-two girl editorial researchers* (New Yorker).
—*v.t.* 1 to raise (as a flag or yard) to the masthead. 2 to send to the masthead as a punishment: *One of the midshipmen was mastheaded ... for not waiting on deck until he was relieved* (Frederick Marryat).

**mas|tic** (mas′tik), *n.* 1 a yellowish resin obtained from the bark of a small Mediterranean evergreen tree. It is used in making varnish, chewing gum, and incense, and as an astringent. 2 the tree it comes from. It belongs to the cashew family. 3 a distilled liquor flavored with this resin. 4 any one of various cements or mortars having a pasty texture. [< Old French *mastic* < Late Latin *mastichum* < *masticha* < Greek *mastíchē* < *masâsthai* chew]

**mas|ti|ca|ble** (mas′tə kə bəl), *adj.* that can be masticated.

**mas|ti|cate** (mas′tə kāt), *v.t., v.i.,* **-cat|ed, -cat|ing.** 1 to grind (food) to a pulp with the teeth; chew: *Americans now masticate 86 million pounds of meat every day* (Wall Street Journal). 2 to crush or knead (rubber or other unrefined substance) to a pulp. [< Late Latin *masticāre* (with English *-ate*) < Greek *mastichân* gnash the teeth < *mástax, -akos* mouth, jaws < *masâsthai* chew]

**mas|ti|ca|tion** (mas′tə kā′shən), *n.* the act or process of masticating.

**mas|ti|ca|tor** (mas′tə kā′tər), *n.* 1 a person, animal, or organ that chews. 2 a machine for cutting or grinding things into small pieces.

**mas|ti|ca|to|ry** (mas′tə kə tôr′ē, -tōr′-), *adj., n., pl.* **-ries.** —*adj.* of, having to do with, or used in chewing: *the masticatory muscles.*
—*n.* a substance chewed to increase the flow of saliva.

**mastic tree**, the tree of the cashew family from which mastic is obtained.

**mas|tiff** (mas′tif, mäs′-), *n.* a large, strong dog having a short, thick coat, large head, drooping ears, and hanging lips. [< Old French *mastin,* ultimately < Latin *mānsuētus* tame, gentle < *manus, -ūs* hand + *suēscere* be(come) accustomed; influenced by Old French *mestif* mongrel, ultimately < Latin *mixtus,* past participle of *miscēre* mingle]

**mas|tig|o|neme** (mas tig′ə nēm), *n.* a stiff lateral appendage on the flagellum of certain algal cells. [< Greek *mástix, -tigos* whip + *nêma* thread]

**mas|ti|goph|o|ran** (mas′tə gof′ər ən), *n., adj.* —*n.* any one of the class of protistans comprising the flagellates, and consisting chiefly of protozoans.
—*adj.* of or having to do with the mastigophorans.
[< New Latin *Mastigophora* the class name < Greek *mástix, -tigos* whip + *-phóros* thing that bears (< *phérein* to bear, carry)]

**mas|ti|tis** (mas tī′tis), *n.* 1 inflammation of the mammary glands or the udder of a cow, sow, or other domestic mammal, caused by bacteria or fungi; garget: *Mastitis, the most costly disease of dairy cattle in the United States* (Science News Letter). 2 inflammation of the breast. [< Greek *mastós* breast + English *-itis*]

**mas|to|don** (mas′tə don), *n., adj.* —*n.* 1 any one of a group of very large extinct mammals, much like mammoths or present-day elephants: *Prehistoric relatives of the elephant were the mammoths and mastodons that lived in temperate and frigid climates* (A. M. Winchester). 2 *Figurative.* a very large person or thing; giant: *It is romantic nonsense to think in terms of world-wide strikes to bring the mastodons of industry to their knees* (A. H. Raskin).
—*adj.* very large; gigantic: *Stone has brought forth a mastodon volume, "The Passions of the Mind"* (Atlantic). **SYN**: mammoth.
[< French *mastodonte* < New Latin *Mastodon* the genus name < Greek *mastós* breast + *odoús, odóntos* tooth (from the nipplelike projections on its teeth)]

**mas|to|don|ic** (mas′tə don′ik), *adj.* gigantic; immense.

**mas|to|dont** (mas′tə dont), *n., adj.* = mastodon.

**mas|toid** (mas′toid), *n., adj.* —*n.* 1 a projection of bone behind the ear of many mammals. 2 *Informal.* mastoiditis.
—*adj.* 1 of or near the mastoid: *the mastoid bone. The mastoid process may be felt as the hard area just behind and below the ear* (William V. Mayer). 2 of or designating certain air cells near the mastoid. 3 shaped like a breast or nipple.
[< Greek *mastoeidês* < *mastós* breast + *eîdos* form]

**mas|toid|ec|to|my** (mas′toi dek′tə mē), *n., pl.* **-mies.** removal of the mastoid.

**mas|toid|i|tis** (mas′toi dī′tis), *n.* inflammation of the mastoid.

**mas|tur|bate** (mas′tər bāt), *v.,* **-bat|ed, -bat|ing.**
—*v.i.* to engage in masturbation.
—*v.t.* to subject to masturbation.
[< Latin *māsturbārī* (with English *-ate*[1]), perhaps < *manus, -ūs* hand + *stuprāre* defile < *stuprum* defilement] —**mas′tur|ba′tor,** *n.*

**mas|tur|ba|tion** (mas′tər bā′shən), *n.* the stimulation of sexual organs by practices other than sexual intercourse, especially manual self-stimulation; self-abuse; onanism; autoeroticism.

**mas|tur|ba|tion|al** (mas′tər bā′shə nəl), *adj.* = masturbatory.

**mas|tur|ba|to|ry** (mas′tər bə tôr′ē, -tōr′-), *adj.* of or having to do with masturbation.

**ma|su|ri|um** (mə zůr′ē əm), *n.* the former name of the chemical element technetium. [< New Latin *masurium* < *Masuria,* former district in East Prussia]

**mat**[1] (mat), *n., v.,* **mat|ted, mat|ting.** —*n.* 1 a piece of coarse fabric made of woven grass, straw, rope, or fiber, used for floor covering or for wiping mud from shoes. A mat is like a small rug. *I didn't fancy that the red carpet would be out; some form of mat, perhaps* (Sunday Times). 2 a smaller piece of material, often ornamental, to put under a dish, vase, lamp, or the like. A mat is put under a hot dish when it is brought to the table. 3 a large, thick pad covering part of a floor, used to protect wrestlers or gymnasts. 4 anything growing thickly packed or tangled together: *a mat of weeds.* 5 a bag made of matting, used to hold coffee, sugar, spices, or other produce.
—*v.t.* 1 to cover with mats or matting: *This vine ... has clothed and matted with its many branches the four walls* (Cardinal Newman). 2 to pack or tangle thickly (together): *The swimmer's wet hair was matted together. Willow and cottonwood trees, so closely interlocked and matted together, as to be nearly impassable* (Washington Irving). —*v.i.* to pack or tangle together like a mat: *The fur collar mats when it gets wet.*
**go to the mat with, a** to meet (a person) in a contest of wrestling: *The champion went to the mat with the challenger.* **b** to contend with over a matter of issue: *the union may go to the mat with the management over wages.*
[Old English *matt, meatt* < Late Latin *matta,* probably < Semitic (compare Hebrew *miṭṭāh* floor)]

**mat**[2] (mat), *n., v.,* **mat|ted, mat|ting.** —*n.* a border or background for a picture, used as a frame or placed between the picture and its frame.
—*v.t.* to put a mat around or under: *to mat a picture.*
[< Old French *mat* (originally) dull, dead, perhaps < Latin *mattus* maudlin or sodden]

**mat**[3] (mat), *adj., n., v.,* **mat|ted, mat|ting.** —*adj.* 1 dull; not shiny: *a mat finish.* 2 made dull by roughening, as with a tool.
—*n.* 1 a dull surface or finish. 2 a tool for producing a dull surface or finish.
—*v.t.* to give a dull surface or finish to. Also, **matte.**
[< French *mat;* see etym. under **mat**[2]]

**mat**[4] (mat), *n. Printing.* a mold for casting type faces; matrix. [short for *matrix*]

**mat.,** matins.

**M.A.T.,** Master of Arts in Teaching.

**Mat|a|be|le** (mat′ə bē′lē), *n., pl.* **-le** or **-les.** a member of a powerful Bantu tribe now occupying the western part of Rhodesia.

* **mat|a|dor** (mat′ə dôr), *n.* 1 the chief performer in a bullfight. It is his duty to kill the bull with his sword. See the picture above on the opposite page. 2 a high-ranking card in certain games such as quadrille and ombre. [< Spanish *mata-*

*dor* killer < Latin *mactātor* one who sacrifices < *mactāre* sacrifice (originally) honor (a god) by offerings]

**✱matador** definition 1

**Ma|ta Ha|ri** (mä′tə hä′rē, mat′ə har′ē), a woman spy, especially one who seduces men to obtain military secrets: ... *a Mata Hari from Minnesota who worked for British Intelligence* (Time). [< *Mata Hari* (Gertrud Margarete Zelle), 1876-1917, a Dutch dancer who lived in France and spied for the Germans during World War I]

**ma|tai** (mä′tī), *n., pl.* **-tai** or **-tais.** the hereditary chief or head of a Samoan tribe or family group. [< Samoan *matai*]

**match[1]** (mach), *n.* **1** a short, slender piece of wood or pasteboard tipped with a mixture that takes fire when rubbed on a rough or specially prepared surface: *The heads of matches have, at the very tip, a chemical called phosphorus sulfide.* **2** a cord or wick prepared to burn at a uniform rate, formerly used for firing guns and cannon. **3** *Obsolete.* a piece of cord, cloth, paper or wood, dipped in melted sulfur, ignited by the use of a tinderbox. [< Old French *meiche,* probably < Latin *myxa* < Greek *mýxa* lamp wick; (originally) mucus, slime; influenced by Vulgar Latin *muccāre* to snuff (a candle) < Latin *muccus* mucus]

**match[2]** (mach), *n., v.* — *n.* **1** a person able to contend or compete with another as an equal; an equal: *to meet one's match. A boy is not a match for a man.* **2** a person or thing equal to another or much like another in some respect: *a period without its match in history.* **3** a person or thing that is like or forms an exact pair with another; a mate: *The all-seeing sun Ne'er saw her match* (Shakespeare). **4** two persons or things that are alike or go well together: *Those two horses make a good match.* **5a** a game; contest: *a tennis match, a boxing match.* **SYN**: competition, tournament, tourney. **b** an engagement for a game or contest. **6** a marriage: *The match between the duke's daughter and the prince was arranged by the duke and the king.* **7** a person considered as a possible husband or wife: *That young man is a good match.* **8** *Obsolete.* an agreement; compact; bargain: *A match! 'tis done* (Shakespeare).
— *v.t.* **1** to be equal to in a contest; be a match for: *No one could match the skill of the unknown archer. The event cannot ... match the expectation* (Charlotte Brontë). **2** to be the same as: *The color of the skirt does not match that of the coat.* **3** to make like; fit together: *To match our spirits to our day And make a joy of duty* (John Greenleaf Whittier). **4** to find the equal of or one exactly like: *to match a vase so as to have a pair. To match this scenery you must go a long distance. Modern craftsmen have been unable so far to match objects produced by some of the ancient lost arts.* **5** to arrange a match for; marry: *the duke matched his daughter with the king's son.* **6** to try (one's skill or strength against); oppose: *He matched his strength against his brother's.* **7** to pair as opponents or competitors; provide with an opponent or competitor of equal power: *The champions of each league were matched for a game. A heavyweight and a lightweight cannot be matched.*
— *v.i.* **1** to be alike; go well together: *The rugs and the wallpaper match.* **2** = marry.
[Old English *mæcca* < *gemæcca* companion. See related etym. at **make[2]**.] — **match′er,** *n.*

**match|a|ble** (mach′ə bəl), *adj.* that can be matched.

**match|board** (mach′bôrd′, -bōrd′), *n.* a board with a tongue cut along one edge and a groove along the opposite edge, so as to fit together with similar boards, used in floors and siding.

**match|book** (mach′bůk′), *n.* a folder of safety matches, especially a folder of two rows of safety matches, with a surface for striking at the bottom.

**match|box** (mach′boks′), *n.* a cardboard box for holding or carrying matches, usually with a striking surface on one side.

**matched order** (macht), an instruction to a broker to buy and sell an equal amount of a certain commodity, stock, or other security, at the same price.

**match|ing fund** (mach′ing), a sum of money given by some individual, institution, or government, usually in proportion to that raised by contribution. The matching fund is an inducement to obtain enough money in total to pay for some project.

**match|less** (mach′lis), *adj.* so great or wonderful that it cannot be equaled: *Daniel Boone had matchless courage.* **SYN**: unequaled, peerless, unparalleled, unrivaled. — **match′less|ly,** *adv.* — **match′less|ness,** *n.*

**match|lock** (mach′lok′), *n.* **1** an old form of gun fired by lighting the charge of powder with a wick or cord. **2** a gunlock on such gun.

**match|make** (mach′māk′), *v.,* **-made, -mak|ing.** — *v.i.* to arrange or try to arrange a marriage: *Nor did I matchmake for Rose, who was quite able to find her own young men* (Harper's).
— *v.t.* to arrange a marriage for: *Capitol busybodies have tried to matchmake widow Smith with Georgia's Senator Richard B. Russell* (Time).

**match|mak|er[1]** (mach′mā′kər), *n.* **1** a person who arranges, or tries to arrange, marriages for others. **2** a person who arranges contests, prize fights, races, or the like: *Sam Silverman, matchmaker for the independent Andy Callahan ... booked the fifteen-round match for Boston Garden* (New York Times).

**match|mak|er[2]** (mach′mā′kər), *n.* a person who makes matches for burning.

**match|mak|ing[1]** (mach′mā′king), *n., adj.* — *n.* **1** the practice of trying to arrange marriages. **2** the business of arranging or making matches for prize fighters, or of arranging other contests.
— *adj.* having to do with matchmakers or matchmaking.

**match|mak|ing[2]** (mach′mā′king), *n., adj.* — *n.* the business of making matches for burning.
— *adj.* having to do with matchmakers or matchmaking.

**match-plate pattern** (mach′plāt′), a pattern in casting split in two halves, used to make molds consisting of several matching parts.

**match play,** **1** a way of playing golf in which the player or side that wins the greatest number of holes is the winner, regardless of total strokes. **2** a play in any match, as in handball or tennis.

**match point,** **1** the concluding point that is needed to win a match, as in tennis. **2** *Especially British.* a point scored in a sports match.

**match|safe** (mach′sāf′), *n.* a box for holding matches; matchbox.

**match|stick** (mach′stik′), *n.* a stick or slender piece of wood, of which a match is made.

**match-up** (mach′up′), *n.* the fact or process of matching two persons or things; pairing.

**match|wood** (mach′wůd′), *n.* **1** wood for making matches. **2** splinters; tiny pieces.

**mate[1]** (māt), *n., v.,* **mat|ed, mat|ing.** — *n.* **1** one of a pair: *Where is the mate to this glove?* **2** a husband or wife; spouse: *The widow mourned for her dead mate.* **3** one of a pair of animals that is mated: *The pigeon and its mate spent much time billing and cooing.* **4a** a deck officer of a merchant ship, next below the captain; first mate: *The mate took command when the captain fell sick.* **b** any one of various other deck officers in the line of command: *a second mate.* **5** an assistant to a specialist on a ship: *a carpenter's mate, a cook's mate.* **6** a companion; fellow worker: *Hand me a hammer, mate.* **SYN**: comrade, crony. **7** a petty officer who assists a warrant officer in the United States Navy: *a gunner's mate.* **8** *Archaic.* an equal; match: *I know you proud to bear your name, Your pride is yet no mate for mine* (Tennyson).
— *v.t., v.i.* **1** to join in a pair; couple; pair. **2** (of animals) to pair; breed: *Birds mate in the spring.* **3** to join as husband and wife; marry: *She's above mating with such as I* (Thomas Hardy). **4** *Obsolete.* to match.
[apparently < Middle Low German *mate* messmate. Compare etym. under **meat.**]

**mate[2]** (māt), *n., v.t.,* **mat|ed, mat|ing,** *interj.* = checkmate. [< Old French *mater* to checkmate < *mat* checkmated, defeated < Arabic *māta* he died]

**ma|té** or **ma|te[3]** (mä′tā, mat′ā), *n.* **1** a kind of tea made from the dried leaves and twigs of a South American holly. Maté is a popular drink in Argentina and Uruguay. **2** the plant itself. **3** its leaves. Also, **Paraguay tea.** [< Spanish *mate* (originally) the cup holding the drink < Quechua (Peru) *mati* calabash dish; *maté,* probably < French *maté* < Spanish *mate*]

**mat|e|lasse** (mat′ə las), *n.* = matelassé.

**mate|las|sé** (mát lá sā′), *adj., n.* — *adj.* (of fabrics) woven with a raised pattern, as if quilted.
— *n.* a matelassé fabric, as of silk, or of silk and wool: *Brocades and matelassés are at their best for these loose and voluminous evening wraps* (London Times). [< French *matelassé*]

**mate|less** (māt′lis), *adj.* without a mate or companion.

**mate|lot** (mát lō′), *n.* **1** *French.* a sailor. **2** a sailor-type blouse [< French *matelot*]

**mat|e|lote** (mat′ə lōt), *n.* a fish stew cooked in red or white wine instead of water, with onions and herbs as flavoring. [< French *matelote* < *matelot* sailor]

**ma|ter** (mā′tər), *n. Especially British Informal.* mother: *You're the kid whose mater kissed him goodbye, aren't you?* (New Yorker). [< Latin *māter, mātris*]

**Ma|ter Do|lo|ro|sa** (mā′tər dō′lə rō′sə), *Latin.* **1** the Virgin Mary. **2** a picture or statue of Mary grieving over the crucified Christ. **3** (literally) sorrowful mother.

**ma|ter|fa|mil|i|as** (mā′tər fə mil′ē əs), *n. Latin.* the mother of a household; woman head of a house.

**ma|te|ri|al** (mə tir′ē əl), *n., adj.* — *n.* **1** what a thing is made from; substance of anything manufactured or built: *building materials.* **SYN**: See syn. under **substance.** **2** cloth: *dress material.* **3** *Figurative:* *the materials of which history is made. His files contain enough notes, facts, ideas, and other material for a score of books.*
— *adj.* **1** of matter or things; physical: *the material world.* **2** of the body: *Food and shelter are material comforts.* **SYN**: bodily. **3** leaving out or forgetting the spiritual side of things; worldly: *a material point of view.* **4** that matters greatly; important: *The baking is a material factor in making cake. Hard work was a material factor in his success.* **SYN**: essential, pertinent. **5** *Law.* providing or likely to provide information that might determine the decision of a case: *material evidence, a material witness.* **6** *Philosophy.* of or having to do with matter as distinguished from form.
**materials,** articles necessary for making or doing something: *writing materials, teaching materials.*
[< Latin *māteriālis* < *māteria* substance, matter <*māter* source, origin; mother. Compare etym. under **matter.** See etym. of doublet **materiel.**]
— **ma|te′ri|al|ness,** *n.*

**ma|te|ri|al|ise** (mə tir′ē ə līz), *v.i., v.t.,* **-ised, -is|ing.** *Especially British.* materialize.

**ma|te|ri|al|ism** (mə tir′ē ə liz′əm), *n.* **1** the belief that all action, thought, and feeling is made up of material things and not of ideas: *In the latter half of the 1800's, materialism severely challenged the traditional spiritual view of man* (Science). **2** the tendency to leave out or forget the spiritual side of things; worldliness: *Our materialism has produced too much dependence upon industry* (Atlantic). **3** the ethical doctrine that material self-interest should and does determine conduct.

**ma|te|ri|al|ist** (mə tir′ē ə list), *n., adj.* — *n.* **1** a believer in materialism: ... *the current split between the materialists and the idealists* (London Times). **2** a person who leaves out or forgets the spiritual side of things.
— *adj.* of or having to do with materialism; materialistic.

**ma|te|ri|al|is|tic** (mə tir′ē ə lis′tik), *adj.* of materialism or materialists; characterized by materialism. — **ma|te′ri|al|is′ti|cal|ly,** *adv.*

**ma|te|ri|al|i|ty** (mə tir′ē al′ə tē), *n., pl.* **-ties. 1** the quality of being material. **2** material nature of character. **3** something that is material.

**ma|te|ri|al|ize** (mə tir′ē ə līz), *v.,* **-ized, -iz|ing.** — *v.i.* **1** to become an actual fact; be realized: *Our plans for the party did not materialize.* **2** to appear in material or bodily form: *A spirit materialized from the smoke of the magician's fire. Wang vanished from the scene, to materialize presently in front of the house* (Joseph Conrad).
— *v.t.* **1** to give material form to: *The inventor materialized his ideas by building a model.* **2** to cause to appear in material or bodily form: *If you materialize angels in that way, where are you going to stop?* (James M. Barrie). **3** to make materialistic: *The system ... tends to materialize our upper class, vulgarize our middle class, brutalize our lower class* (Matthew Arnold). — **ma|te′ri|al|i|za′tion,** *n.* — **ma|te′ri|al|iz′er,** *n.*

**ma|te|ri|al|ly** (mə tir′ē ə lē), *adv.* **1** with regard to material things; physically: *He improved materially and morally.* **2** considerably; greatly: *The tide helped the progress of the boat materially.* **SYN**: substantially. **3** in matter or substance; not in form: *What is formally correct may be materially false* (Charles S. C. Bowen).

---

**Pronunciation Key:** hat, āge, cãre, fär; let, ēqual, tėrm; it, īce; hot, ōpen, ôrder; oil, out; cup, půt, rüle; child; long; thin; ᴛʜen; zh, measure; ə represents a in about, e in taken, i in pencil, o in lemon, u in circus.

**ma|te|ri|als** (mə tir′ē əlz), *n.pl.* See under **material**

**materials science**, a branch of metallurgy dealing with semiconductors, plastics, organic solids, and glass. —**materials scientist**.

**ma|te|ri|a med|i|ca** (mə tir′ē ə med′ə kə), **1** the drugs or other substances used in medicine. **2** the branch of medical science dealing with these drugs and substances. [< New Latin *materia medica* healing matter]

**ma|te|ri|el** or **ma|té|ri|el** (mə tir′ē el′), *n.* everything used by an army, organization, or undertaking; equipment: *The general said the Iron Curtain countries had vast resources in manpower and matériel* (New York Times). [< French *matériel* material, learned borrowing of Latin *māteriālis*. See etym. of doublet **material**.]

**ma|ter|nal** (mə tėr′nəl), *adj.* **1** of or like a mother; motherly: *maternal kindness.* **2** related on the mother's side of the family: *Everyone has two maternal grandparents and two paternal grandparents.* **3** received or inherited from one's mother: *His blue eyes were a maternal inheritance.* [< Middle French *maternel*, learned borrowing from Vulgar Latin *māternālis* < Latin *māternus* maternal < *māter, mātris* mother]
—**ma|ter′nal|ly**, *adv.*

**ma|ter|nal|ism** (mə tėr′nə liz əm), *n.* maternal quality or condition; motherliness.

**ma|ter|ni|ty** (mə tėr′nə tē), *n., adj.* —*n.* **1** the condition of being a mother; motherhood. **2** the qualities of a mother; motherliness.
—***adj.*** **1** for a woman soon to have a baby: *maternity clothes.* **2** for women in or after childbirth: *maternity care, a maternity ward.*

**mate|ship** (māt′ship), *n.* **1** comradeship; fellowship. **2** (in Australia) fellowship based on equal opportunity for all.

**mat|ey** (mā′tē), *adj., n., pl.* **-eys**. *British Informal.*
—***adj.*** friendly; sociable; companionable.
—***n.*** mate; fellow worker. —**mat′ey|ness**, *n.*

**math**[1] (math), *n. Informal.* mathematics.

**math**[2] (math), *n. Obsolete.* the amount of a crop mowed; a mowing. [Old English *mǣth*]

**math.**, **1** mathematical. **2** mathematician. **3** mathematics.

**math|e|mat|ic** (math′ə mat′ik, math mat′-), *adj., n.* —***adj.*** = mathematical.
—***n.*** = mathematics.
[Middle English *mathematique* < Old French < Latin *mathēmatica* (*ars*) mathematical science < Greek *mathēmatikḗ* (*téchnē*), feminine singular of *mathēmatikós* relating to knowledge < *máthēma, -atos* science < *math-*, stem of *manthánein* to learn]

**math|e|mat|i|cal** (math′ə mat′ə kəl, math mat′-), *adj.* **1** of mathematics; having something to do with mathematics: *Mathematical problems are not always easy.* **2** exact; accurate: *mathematical measurements.* SYN: precise.

**mathematical logic**, = symbolic logic.

**math|e|mat|i|cal|ly**(math′ə mat′ə klē,math mat′-), *adv.* **1** according to mathematics. **2** in a mathematical manner; exactly; precisely; accurately.

**math|e|ma|ti|cian** (math′ə mə tish′ən, math′mə-), *n.* a person skilled in mathematics.

**math|e|mat|ics** (math′ə mat′iks, math mat′-), *n.* the study of numbers, measurements, and space; science dealing with the measurement, properties, and relationships of quantities, as expressed in numbers or symbols. Mathematics includes arithmetic, algebra, geometry, and calculus. *Abbr:* math. [see etym. under **mathematic**]

**math|e|mat|ize** (math′ə mə tīz, math′mə-), *v.t., v.i.,* **-ized**, **-iz|ing**. to formulate something into mathematical terms. —**math′e|ma|ti|za′tion**, *n.* —**math′e|mat|iz′er**, *n.*

**ma|thet|ic** (mə thet′ik), *adj.* of or having to do with learning: ... *mathetic programming* (Harper's). [< Greek *mathētikós* < *manthánein* to learn]

**maths** (maths), *n. British Informal.* mathematics.

**mat|ie** (mā′tē), *n.* a herring having the roe or milt perfectly but not largely developed. [< Dutch *maatjes* (*haring*), literally, maiden (herring)]

**ma|tière** (mà tyer′), *n.* artistic material. [< French *matière*]

**mat|i|ly** (mā′tə lē), *adv. British Informal.* in a matey manner; sociably.

**mat|in** (mat′ən), *n., adj.* —***n.*** **1** *Poetic.* a morning call or song, as of birds: *The sprightly lark's shrill matin wakes the morn* (Edward Young). **2** = matins. **3** *Obsolete.* the morning: *The glow-worm shows the matin to be near, And 'gins to pale his uneffectual fire* (Shakespeare).
—***adj.*** having to do with or occurring in the early morning.
[< Old French *matin;* see etym. under **matins**]

**mat|in|al** (mat′ə nəl), *adj.* **1** early; morning. **2** early-rising.

**mat|i|nee** or **mat|i|née** (mat′ə nā′; *especially British* mat′ə nā), *n., pl.* **-nees** or **-nées**, *adj.* —***n.*** a dramatic or musical performance held in the afternoon.
—***adj.*** of a matinee: *a matinee audience.*
[< French *matinée* < Old French *matin* morning (that is, daytime); see etym. under **matins**]

**matinee** or **matinée idol**, a handsome actor attractive especially to women who attend matinees: *"The Four Horsemen of the Apocalypse" brought fame to Rudolph Valentino, the matinee idol of the day* (Eric Johnston).

**mat|i|ness** (mā′tē nis), *n. British Informal.* the quality or condition of being matey.

**mat|ing** (mā′ting), *n.* **1** the act or fact of matching. **2** the act or fact of marrying. **3** the act or fact of pairing, as of birds.

**mating call**, the special call or noise made, as by an animal or insect in trying to attract a mate.

**mat|ins** or **Mat|ins** (mat′ənz), *n. pl.* **1** a church service held at dawn or in the morning. Matins properly starts at midnight but is often said as a dawn service and joined to lauds. **2** the first of the seven canonical hours in the breviary of the Roman Catholic Church. **3** the order for public morning prayer in the Anglican Church; mattins. **4** a morning song; matin. [< Old French *matines* < *matin* < Latin *mātūtīnus* of, or in, the morning < *Mātūta* a dawn goddess]

**mat|rass** (mat′rəs), *n.* **1** a small glass tube with one end closed, used by chemists in blowpipe analysis. **2** a round or oval glass vessel with a long neck, formerly used especially for distilling or evaporating; bolthead. Also, **mattrass**. [< Middle French *matheras*, perhaps < Arabic *maṭara* vase, bottle]

**ma|tri|arch** (mā′trē ärk), *n.* **1** a mother who is the ruler of a family or tribe: *a crowded company of more than fifty persons, with the imperial matriarch in their midst* (Lytton Strachey). **2** a venerable woman, especially one who dominates the group of which she is a member: *Mrs. Astor was the matriarch of New York society for many years.* [< Latin *māter, mātris* mother + English (patri)*arch*]

**ma|tri|ar|chal** (mā′trē är′kəl), *adj.* **1** of a matriarch or matriarchy. **2** suitable for a matriarch.

**ma|tri|ar|chal|ism** (mā′trē är′kə liz əm), *n.* **1** the fact or condition of being matriarchal. **2** matriarchal customs or practices.

**ma|tri|ar|chate** (mā′trē är′kit, -kāt), *n.* **1** a family or community governed by a matriarch. **2** a matriarchal system.

**ma|tri|ar|chic** (mā′trē är′kik), *adj.* = matriarchal.

**ma|tri|ar|chy** (mā′trē är′kē), *n., pl.* **-chies**. **1** a form of social organization in which the mother is the ruler of a family or tribe, descent being traced through the mother: *Matriarchy* (*absolute rule by women*) *and patriarchy* (*absolute rule by men*) *are exceedingly rare extremes* (Beals and Hoijer). **2** government by women; matriarchate.

**ma|tric** (mə trik′), *n. British Informal.* matriculation; a matriculation examination.

**ma|tri|cal** (mat′rə kəl), *adj.* having to do with a matrix.

**mat|ri|car|i|a** (mat′rə kãr′ē ə), *n.* **1** the feverfew plant. **2a** any one of a group of daisylike plants of the composite family found chiefly in the Old World, such as the camomile. **b** the dried flower heads of the camomile used in medicine. [< Medieval Latin *matricaria* < Latin *mātrīx, -īcis* womb (for its supposed medicinal qualities)]

**mat|ri|cen|tric** (mat′rə sen′trik), *adj.* having or recognizing the mother as the center of the family: *Many lower-class ... families are matricentric families: a woman and her children, with only vague or temporary associations with adult males* (Scientific American).

**ma|tri|ces** (mā′trə sēz, mat′rə-), *n.* a plural of **matrix**.

**ma|tri|cid|al** (mā′trə sī′dəl, mat′rə-), *adj.* of or having to do with a matricide.

**ma|tri|cide**[1] (mā′trə sīd, mat′rə-), *n.* the act of killing one's mother. [< Latin *mātricīdium* < *māter* mother + *-cīdium* act of killing, -cide[2]]

**ma|tri|cide**[2] (mā′trə sīd, mat′rə-), *n.* a person who kills his mother. [< Latin *mātricīda* < *māter* mother + *-cīda* killer, -cide[1]]

**ma|tric|u|lant** (mə trik′yə lənt), *n.* a person who matriculates; candidate for matriculation.

**ma|tric|u|late** (*v.* mə trik′yə lāt; *n.* mə trik′yə lit), *v.,* **-lat|ed**, **-lat|ing**, *n.* —***v.t.***, ***v.i.*** to enroll as a student; admit or be admitted to membership and privileges in a college or university by enrolling: *Three years later he matriculated for advance study* (Harper's).
—***n.*** a person who has been matriculated.
[< Latin *mātrīcula* a public register (diminutive) < *mātrīx, -īcis* register, loan-translation of Greek *mētrā* register of property + English *-ate*[1]]

**ma|tric|u|la|tion** (mə trik′yə lā′shən), *n.* the action of matriculating; enrollment as a student or candidate for a degree.

**ma|tric|u|la|tor** (mə trik′yə lā′tər), *n.* a person who matriculates.

**mat|ri|lat|er|al** (mat′rə lat′ər əl), *adj.* = maternal.

**mat|ri|lin|e|age** (mat′rə lin′ē ij), *n.* the line of descent from a female ancestor or the maternal side of a family, clan, tribe, or other group.

**mat|ri|lin|e|al** (mat′rə lin′ē əl), *adj.* having or maintaining relationship through the female line of a family, clan, tribe, or other group: *In most of Nyasaland the tribes are ... matrilineal and uxorilocal; rights in land descend in the female line, and when a man marries he goes to live in his wife's village* (Manchester Guardian). [< Latin *māter, mātris* mother + English *lineal*] —**mat′ri|lin′e|al|ly**, *adv.*

**mat|ri|lin|e|ar** (mat′rə lin′ē ər), *adj.* = matrilineal.

**mat|ri|li|ny** (mat′rə lī′nē), *n.* the taking of relationship and descent through the female line.

**mat|ri|lo|cal** (mat′rə lō′kəl), *adj.* having its focus in the home of the wife's family; uxorilocal: *The Zuni have matrilocal residence which means that newlyweds make their home with the parents of the bride* (Ogburn and Nimkoff). [< Latin *māter, mātris* mother + *locus* place + English *-al*[1]]

**mat|ri|lo|cal|i|ty** (mat′rə lō kal′ə tē), *n.* residence in or near the home of the wife's family.

**mat|ri|mo|ni|al** (mat′rə mō′nē əl), *adj.* of or having to do with marriage: *matrimonial vows, matrimonial agencies.* SYN: nuptial, connubial. —**mat′ri|mo′ni|al|ly**, *adv.*

**mat|ri|mo|ny** (mat′rə mō′nē), *n., pl.* **-nies**. **1** married life; marriage: *The young man proposed matrimony and she accepted.* **2** the rite or ceremony of marriage; act of marrying. SYN: See syn. under **marriage**. **3** the relation between married persons; wedlock: *to unite in holy matrimony.* SYN: See syn. under **marriage**. **4a** a card game in which players score for holding certain combinations of cards. **b** a king or queen of the same suit; marriage. [< Old French *matrimoine*, learned borrowing from Latin *mātrimōnium* < *māter, mātris* mother]

**matrimony vine**, = boxthorn.

**ma|trix** (mā′triks, mat′riks), *n., pl.* **-tri|ces** or **-trix|es**, *v.,* **-trixed** or **trixt**, **-trix|ing**. —***n.*** **1** something that gives origin or form to something enclosed within it: **a** a mold for a casting. **b** the rock in which crystallized minerals, gems, or fossils are embedded: *By etching away the limestone matrix in dilute acid, the silicified fossils, which are not affected by the acid, are freed from the rock* (Raymond Cecil Moore). **c** *Figurative: The tradition of the Renaissance still hung about Marx and Engels: they had only partly emerged from its matrix* (Edmund Wilson). **2** *Printing.* a mold for casting type faces. **3** = womb. **4a** *Anatomy.* the formative part of an organ, such as the skin beneath a fingernail or toenail. **b** *Biology.* the intercellular substance of a tissue. **5** *Mathematics.* a set of quantities in a rectangular array, subject to operations such as multiplication or inversion according to specified rules. **6** *Statistics.* an ordered table or two-dimensional array of variables: *Dr. Warner's group has ... set up "matrix"—a device for statistical analysis—that comprises some thirty-five different disease entities and fifty-seven symptoms known to be associated with congenital defects* (New York Times). **7** an array of circuit elements designed to perform a particular function in a computer: *The diodes on each character unit are connected to a matrix of seven horizontal wires ... In this way, any one diode can be switched on individually by applying a voltage across selected horizontal wires and vertical wires in the matrix* (Science Journal).
—***v.i.***, ***v.t.*** to arrange or organize in a matrix: *The four channels can be recorded separately as four tracks on a disc, or any one of a number of matrixing techniques can be used to combine two or more channels on a single track* (New Scientist and Science Journal).
[< Latin *mātrīx, -īcis* womb, breeding animal < *māter, mātris* mother]

**matrix algebra**, algebra in which the symbols are placed in a rectangular set of compartments in which an unoccupied space represents a zero.

**matrix isolation**, *Chemistry.* the trapping of molecules in an inert solid material to observe them in isolation.

**matrix mechanics**, *Physics.* a formulation of quantum mechanics using spectroscopic data and matrix algebra, developed by Werner Heisenberg. It is mathematically equivalent to the theory of wave mechanics.

**matrix sentence**, *Linguistics.* a sentence within which another sentence is embedded. In the sentence "That boy who hit the ball is my brother," the matrix sentence is "That boy is my brother." A matrix sentence is usually equivalent to a main clause in traditional grammar.

**ma|tron** (mā′trən), *n.* **1** wife or widow, especially a mother or married woman: *a department store that caters to young matrons.* **2** a woman who manages the household matters or supervises the inmates of a school, hospital, dormitory, or other institution. A police matron has charge of the women in a jail. [< Old French *matrone,* learned borrowing from Latin *mātrōna* < *māter, mātris* mother] — **ma′tron|like′**, *adj.*

**ma|tron|age** (mā′trə nij, mat′rə-), *n.* **1** matrons as a group. **2** guardianship by a matron. **3** the state of being a matron.

**ma|tron|al** (mā′trə nəl), *adj.* **1** of or having to do with a matron. **2** suitable to a matron. **3** = matronly.

**ma|tron|hood** (mā′trən hu̇d), *n.* the condition of being a matron.

**ma|tron|ize** (mā′trə nīz, mat′rə-), *v.t.*, **-ized, -iz|ing.** **1** to make matronly. **2** = chaperon.

**ma|tron|ly** (mā′trən lē), *adj., adv.* — *adj.* like a matron; suitable for a matron; dignified: *a plain, matronly woman, neat matronly attire.*
— *adv.* in the manner of a matron. — **ma′tron|li|ness**, *n.*

**matron of honor**, a married woman who is the chief attendant of the bride at a wedding.

**ma|tron|ship** (mā′trən ship), *n.* the condition or position of a matron.

**mat|ro|nym|ic** (mat′rə nim′ik), *adj., n.* = metronymic.

**Mats.**, matinees.

**MATS** (no periods) or **M.A.T.S.**, *U.S.* Military Air Transport Service.

**mat|su** (mat′sü), *n.* the most common tree of Japan, a pine that grows for a very long time and becomes very large. Its wood is valuable for household carpentry and furniture. [< Japanese *matsu*]

**matt** (mat), *adj., n., v.t.* = mat³.

**Matt.**, Matthew (book of the New Testament).

**matte** (mat), *adj., n., v.*, **mat|ted, mat|ting.** — *adj.* not shiny; dull; mat.
— *n.* **1** an impure and unfinished product, a mixture of sulfides, of the smelting of various sulfide ores, especially those of copper. **2** a dull surface or finish; mat.
— *v.t.* to give a dull surface or finish to; mat.
[< French *matte;* see etym. under **mat²**]

**mat|ted¹** (mat′id), *adj.* **1** formed into a mat; entangled in a thick mass: *a matted growth of shrubs.* **2** covered with mats or matting.

**mat|ted²** (mat′id), *adj.* having a dull finish.

**mat|ter** (mat′ər), *n., v.* — *n.* **1** what things are made of; material; substance. Matter occupies space, has weight, and can exist as a solid, liquid, or gas. Animals and plants are organic matter; minerals and water are inorganic matter. *All matter is mostly vacuum, thinly populated with minute particles such as electrons and protons* (John R. Pierce). **SYN**: stuff. See syn. under **substance**. **2a** the substance of the material world; the opposite of mind or spirit. **b** a specific substance or body: *foreign matter, coloring matter, printed matter.* **3** an affair; thing to do; concern: *business matters, a matter of life and death. They order, said I, this matter better in France* (Laurence Sterne). **SYN**: activity. **4** what is said or written, thought of apart from the way in which it is said or written: *There was very little matter of interest in his speech.* **SYN**: topic, subject. **5** reason or grounds; occasion; cause; basis: *If a man is robbed, he has matter for complaint to the police. Neither can he that mindeth but his own business find much matter for envy* (Francis Bacon). **6** an instance or case; thing or things: *a matter of record, a matter of accident.* **7** an amount; quantity: *a matter of two days, a matter of 20 miles. The matter of a fortnight* (Thomas Carlyle). **8** importance; significance: *Let it go since it is of no matter.* **SYN**: moment, concern. **9** things written or printed: *reading matter.* **10** mail: *Second-class matter requires less postage than first-class matter.* **11** *Printing.* **a** something to be printed; copy. **b** type that has been composed. **12** *Law.* something to be tried or proved; statements or allegations coming before the court; something in a document. **13** a substance secreted by a living body, especially pus.
— *v.i.* **1** to be important: *Nothing seems to matter when you are sick. What they said matters little* (Bret Harte). **2** to form or discharge pus; suppurate.

**for that matter**, so far as that is concerned: *For that matter, we did not know what we were doing.*

**no laughing matter**. See under **laughing**.

**no matter, a** regardless of: *No matter what excuse he gives, I will not forgive him for standing me up.* **b** never mind; it is not important: *"He has lost his key to the trunk...." "No matter; we can break it open"* (Maria Edgeworth).

**not mince matters**, to speak plainly and frankly: *A candid ferocity, if the case calls for it, is in him; he does not mince matters!* (Thomas Carlyle).

**what is the matter?** what is wrong?: *What is the matter with the child?*

[< Old French *matiere* < Latin *māteria* substance, matter, growing layer in trees < *māter, mātris* mother. Compare etym. under **material**.]
— **mat′ter|less**, *adj.*

**matter of course**, something to be expected: *to accept daily chores as a matter of course.*

**mat|ter-of-course** (mat′ər əv kôrs′, -kōrs′), *adj.* **1** to be expected; normal. **2** accepting things as a matter of course: *the cool matter-of-course manner of this reply.*

**matter of fact**, something that is so; fact as contrasted with opinion, probability, or inference: *I was going to say when Truth broke in With all her matter of fact ...* (Robert Frost).

**as a matter of fact**, in truth; in reality: actually: *As a matter of fact, you are quite right* (J. K. Jerome).

**mat|ter-of-fact** (mat′ər əv fakt′), *adj.* dealing with facts; not fanciful; unimaginative; prosaic: *Iranian acceptance of these long-overdue exchanges has been calm and matter-of-fact* (Atlantic). — **mat′ter-of-fact′ly**, *adv.* — **mat′ter-of-fact′ness**, *n.*

**mat|ter|y** (mat′ər ē), *adj.* full of pus; purulent.

**Mat|the|an** (mə thē′ən), *adj.* of or characteristic of the Evangelist Matthew or his gospel.

**Mat|thew** (math′yü), *n.* **1** (in the Bible) one of Christ's twelve Apostles. He was a tax collector who became one of the four Evangelists. **2** the first book of the New Testament, attributed to him. It tells the story of the life of Christ. *Abbr:* Matt. [< French *Mathieu* < Late Latin *Matthaeus* < Greek *Matthaîos* < Hebrew *Mattīthyāh*]

**Mat|thi|as** (mə thī′əs), *n.* a disciple chosen by lot to replace Judas Iscariot as one of the twelve Apostles (in the Bible, Acts 1:26).

**mat|ting¹** (mat′ing), *n.* **1** a fabric of grass, straw, hemp, or other fiber, for covering floors, for mats, or for wrapping material. **2** mats. **3** the making of mats.

**mat|ting²** (mat′ing), *n.* the process of producing a mat surface, or such a surface itself, especially on metal articles.

**mat|tins** (mat′ənz), *n.pl.* = matins (the form preferred in the Anglican Church).

*** mat|tock** (mat′ək), *n.* a large tool with a steel head like a pickax, but having a flat blade on one side or flat blades on both sides, used for loosening soil and cutting roots. [Old English *mattuc*]

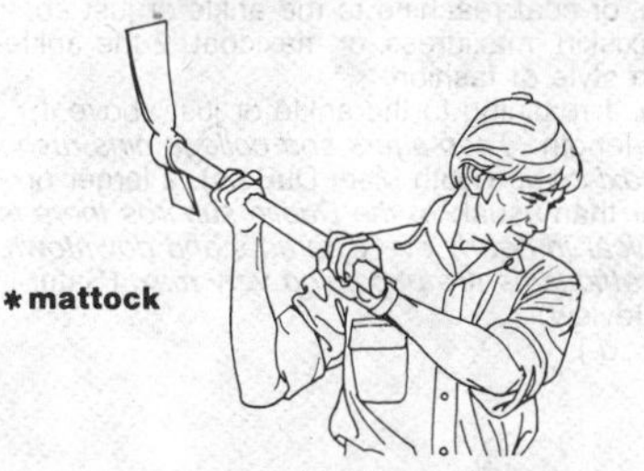

*** mattock**

**mat|trass** (mat′rəs), *n.* = matrass.

**mat|tress** (mat′ris), *n.* **1** a casing of strong cloth stuffed with hair, cotton, straw, foam rubber, or some other material. It is used on a bed or as a bed. *Many mattresses have springs inside.* **2** a strong mat consisting especially of brush and rods or poles, bound or twisted together, used to protect dikes, embankments, and dams from erosion. **3** = air mattress. [< Old French *materas* < Italian *materasso* < Arabic *al-maṭraḥ* the cushion]

**Ma|tu|ra diamond** (mä′tə rə, mat′-), = jargon². [< *Matura,* a town in Sri Lanka]

**mat|u|rate** (mach′u̇ rāt), *v.i.*, **-rat|ed, -rat|ing.** **1** to ripen; mature. **2** to discharge pus; suppurate. [< Latin *mātūrāre* (with English *-ate¹*) < *mātūrus* ripe]

**mat|u|ra|tion** (mach′u̇ rā′shən), *n.* **1** the process of growing and developing; ripening or maturing: (*Figurative.*) *the germination and maturation of some truth* (Cardinal Newman). **2** Biology. **a** the final stages in the preparation of germ cells for fertilization, including meiosis and various changes in the cytoplasm: *At the close of the growth period, the reproductive cells undergo two special maturation divisions* (Beals and Hoijer). **b** the development of a germ cell prior to meiosis. **c** the last stage of differentiation in cellular growth. **3** a formation of pus; suppuration.

**mat|u|ra|tion|al** (mach′u̇ rā′shə nəl), *adj.* of or having to do with maturation.

**ma|tur|a|tive** (mə chu̇r′ə tiv, mach′ə rā′-), *adj.* **1** producing maturity; conducive to ripening. **2** causing suppuration.

**ma|ture** (mə tu̇r′, -tyu̇r′, -chu̇r′), *adj., v.*, **-tured, -tur|ing.** — *adj.* **1a** ripe or full-grown: *a mature plant, a mature fruit. Grain is harvested when it is mature. Fifty is a mature age.* **b** fully developed in body and mind: *a mature person.* **c** brought by time or treatment to the condition of full excellence: *mature wine, mature cheese.* **d** characteristic of full development: *a mature appearance, mature wisdom.* **e** *Figurative.* fully worked out; carefully thought out; fully developed: *mature plans.* **2** due; payable: *a mature note, a mature savings bond.* **3** *Geology.* **a** so long subjected to erosion as to show mainly smooth slopes: *mature land.* **b** fully adjusted to rock formations: *a mature stream.* **4** in a state of suppuration.
— *v.i.* **1** to come to full growth; ripen: *These apples are maturing fast.* **2** to fall due: *This note to the bank matured yesterday.*
— *v.t.* **1** to bring to full growth or development: *His prudence was matured by experience* (Edward Gibbon). **2** *Figurative.* to work out carefully: *He matured his plans for the long trip.*
[< Latin *mātūrus* ripe] — **ma|ture′ly**, *adv.* — **ma|ture′ness**, *n.* — **ma|tur′er**, *n.*

**ma|tu|ri|ty** (mə tu̇r′ə tē, -tyu̇r′-, -chu̇r′-), *n., pl.* **-ties.** **1** full development; ripeness: *She had reached maturity by the time she was twenty.* **SYN**: adultness. **2** the condition of being completed or ready: (*Figurative.*) *When their plans reached maturity, they were able to begin.* **SYN**: readiness. **3** Also, **maturities**. **a** the act or fact of falling due: *U.S. Government obligations lost ground, particularly in the longer maturities, though trading volume continued quiet* (Wall Street Journal). **b** the time a debt or note is payable. **4** *Geology.* a stage in the evolutionary erosion of land areas where the flat uplands have been widely dissected by deep river valleys.

**ma|tur|i|ty-on|set diabetes** (mə tu̇r′ə tē on′set′; -tyu̇r′-, -chu̇r′-; ôn′-), the widespread form of diabetes, occurring in adults usually after the age of 40. It is believed to be hereditary. *When one member of identical twins has documented maturity-onset diabetes, the other member is also found almost always to have diabetes* (George F. Cahill, Jr.).

**ma|tu|ti|nal** (mə tü′tə nəl, -tyü′-), *adj.* **1** occurring in the morning; early in the day; having to do with the morning: *A thundering sound of cowhide boots on the stairs announced that Sol's matutinal toilet was complete* (Harriet Beecher Stowe). **2** early-rising. [< Late Latin *mātūtīnālis* < Latin *mātūtīnus* of, or in, the morning; see etym. under **matins**] — **ma|tu′ti|nal|ly**, *adv.*

**mat|zah** (mät′sə), *n., pl.* **-zahs** or (*collectively*) **-zah.** = matzo.

**mat|zo** (mät′sō), *n., pl.* **mat|zoth** (mät′sōth), **mat|zos** (mät′sōs, -səz), or (*collectively*) **mat|zo.** a thin piece of unleavened bread, eaten especially during the Jewish holiday of Passover. [< Yiddish *matse* < Hebrew *maṣṣāh* cake of unleavened bread]

**matzo ball**, a ball-shaped dumpling made from ground matzo, usually served in chicken soup.

**mat|zoh** (mät′sō), *n., pl.* **mat|zoth** (mät′sōth), **mat|zohs** (mät′sōs, -səz), or (*collectively*) **mat|zoh.** = matzo.

**maud** (môd), *n.* **1** a gray woolen plaid worn in southern Scotland. **2** a small blanket or shawl of similar material. [origin uncertain]

**maud|lin** (môd′lən), *adj.* **1** sentimental in a weak, silly way: *We saw a maudlin movie about a boy who lost his dog. Sympathy for criminals if often maudlin.* **SYN**: mawkish. **2** tearfully silly because of drunkenness or excitement: *It is but yonder empty glass That makes me maudlin-moral* (Tennyson). [Middle English *Maudlin, Maudelen* < pronunciation of (Mary) *Magdalene,* often painted as weeping] — **maud′lin|ly**, *adv.* — **maud′lin|ness**, *n.*

**mau|gre** or **mau|ger** (mô′gər), *prep. Archaic.* in spite of. [< Old French *maugre,* earlier *malgré* (originally) ill will, spite < Latin *malō grātō* in spite of displeasure; (literally) with no thanks]

**Mau|i** (mou′ē), *n.* a Polynesian demigod, the creator of the Hawaiian Islands.

**mau|ka** (mou′kə), *adv., adj. Hawaiian.* toward the mountains.

**mau|kin** (mô′kin), *n. Dialect.* malkin.

**maul** (môl), *n., v.* — *n.* **1** a very heavy hammer or mallet. It is used for driving stakes, piles, or wedges. **2** *Archaic.* a heavy club or mace. **3** *Rugby.* a struggle for the ball when it is carried across the goal line.
— *v.t.* **1** to beat and pull about; handle roughly or carelessly; bruise: *The lion mauled its keeper badly. He seized the gunwale, but the knives of our rowers so mauled his wrists that he was forced to quit his hold* (Herman Melville). **2** *Figurative: The ... novel was mauled by the New York critics* (Manchester Guardian Weekly). **3** *U.S.* to split (rails) with a maul and wedge. [variant of Middle English *malle;* see etym. under **mall¹**] — **maul′er**, *n.*

**maul|stick** (môl′stik′), *n.* = mahlstick.

**Mau Mau** (mou′ mou′), a secret society of Afri-

**Pronunciation Key:** hat, āge, cãre, fär; let, ēqual, tėrm; it, īce; hot, ōpen, ôrder; oil, out; cup, pu̇t, rüle; child; long; thin; ᴛʜen; zh, measure; ə represents **a** in about, **e** in taken, **i** in pencil, **o** in lemon, **u** in circus.

can, chiefly Kikuyu, tribesmen sworn to expel Europeans from Kenya by violent means. It was active during the 1950's.

**mau-mau** (mou'mou'), *v.t.*, **-maued, -mau|ing.** *U.S. Slang.* to terrorize: *Going downtown to mau-mau the bureaucrats got to be the routine practice in San Francisco* (Tom Wolfe). [< *Mau Mau*]

**mau|met** (mô'mit), *n.* **1** *British Dialect.* a dressed-up figure such as a doll or puppet. **2** *Obsolete.* a false god; idol. Also, **mammet.** [< Old French *mahumet* idol < *Mahumet* Mahomet (from the old belief that he was considered divine)]

**maun** (mon, môn), *v.i. Scottish.* must: *Folk maun do something for their bread* (Robert Burns). [Middle English *man* < Scandinavian (compare Old Icelandic *man,* present tense of *munu* shall, will)]

**maund** (mônd), *n.* a unit of weight used in India and parts of the Middle East, usually equal to 82.28 pounds, but in some localities varying from 23 to 28 pounds: *The duty on raw jute is increased by one rupee a maund* (London Times). [earlier, *mana* < Hindi *mān* < Sanskrit *mā* measure]

**maun|der** (môn'dər), *v.i.* **1** to talk in a rambling, foolish way: *People who maunder talk much but say little.* SYN: drivel. **2** to move or act in an aimless or confused manner: *The injured man maundered about in a daze. The drunken man maundered along the street.* **3** *Obsolete.* to grumble; mutter. [origin uncertain. Compare etym. under **meander.**] —**maun'der|er,** *n.* —**maun'der|ing|ly,** *adv.*

**maun|dy** (môn'dē), *n., pl.* **-dies. 1** an old ceremony of washing the feet of a number of poor people to commemorate the Last Supper and Christ's washing the feet of His disciples, performed as a religious rite, as by a sovereign or an ecclesiastic, on the Thursday before Good Friday (in the Bible, John 13:5, 14, 34). **2** alms distributed at the ceremony or on this day: *In addition to the specially minted maundy coins there was a surprise for each recipient* (London Times). [< Old French *mande* < Latin *mandātum* a command, < *mandāre;* (*mandātum* is the first word of the service for that day)]

**Maun|dy** (môn'dē), *n., pl.* **-dies.** the celebration of Maundy Thursday, in which the feet of the poor are washed and Maundy money given out.

**Maundy Thursday,** the Thursday before Easter.

**Mau|resque** (mə resk'), *adj., n.* = Moresque.

**Mau|ri|ta|ni|an** (môr'ə tā'nē ən, -tān'yən), *adj., n.* —*adj.* of or having to do with Mauritania, a republic in West Africa.
—*n.* a native or inhabitant of Mauritania.

**Mau|ri|tian** (mô rish'ən), *adj., n.* —*adj.* of or having to do with Mauritius, an island country in the Indian Ocean.
—*n.* a native or inhabitant of Mauritius.

**Mauritian hemp, 1** a plant of the amaryllis family grown in Mauritius, that yields a tough fiber used to make heavy cord and coarse cloth. **2** the fibers of this plant.

**Mau|ry|a** (mou'rē ə), *n.* a member of the ancient Indian people who established an empire in northern India from about 321 B.C. to 184 B.C.

**Mau|ry|an** (mou'rē ən), *adj.* of or having to do with the Mauryas or their civilization: *a Mauryan dynasty, the Mauryan empire.*

**Mau|ser** (mou'zər), *n. Trademark.* a powerful repeating rifle or pistol. [< Paul *Mauser,* 1838-1914, a German inventor]

**mau|so|le|an** (mô'sə lē'ən), *adj.* of or having to do with a mausoleum; monumental.

**Mau|so|le|um** (mô'sə lē'əm), *n.* a magnificent tomb in southwest Asia Minor, at Halicarnassus, built in the 300's B.C. It was one of the seven wonders of the ancient world. [< Latin *Mausōlēum* < Greek *Mausōleîon* (tomb) of *Maúsōlos,* a king of Caria]

**mau|so|le|um** (mô'sə lē'əm), *n., pl.* **-le|ums, -le|a** (-lē'ə). **1** a large, magnificent tomb, especially one above ground: *a ponderous mausoleum with a front wall of reinforced concrete* (Newsweek). **2** *Informal, Figurative.* any large structure, building, or room similar to the Mausoleum. [< *Mausoleum*]

**mau|vaise honte** (mō vez' ôɴt'), *French.* excessive modesty or shame; bashfulness.

**mauve** (mōv), *adj., n.* —*adj.* delicate pale-purple. SYN: violet, lilac, lavender.
—*n.* **1** a delicate, pale purple. **2** a purple dye obtained from coal tar chemicals or aniline: *The beautiful purple dye mauve, synthesized by Perkin in 1856, was not found in animal and plant material* (Atlantic).
[< French *mauve* < Old French, *mallow* < Latin *malva.* See etym. of doublet **mallow.**]

**mauve|ine** (mō'vin, -vēn), *n.* the dye mauve or its color: *mauveine, the first synthetic organic dye* (Scientific American). [< *mauve* + *-ine*[2]]

**mav|er|ick** (mav'ər ik), *n., adj.* —*n. U.S.* **1** a calf or other animal not marked with an owner's brand. A maverick on the open range formerly became the property of anyone who branded him. **2** *Informal, Figurative.* **a** a person who refuses to affiliate or who breaks with a regular political party: *A maverick tried unsuccessfully to unseat Mayor Edward Kelly* (Wall Street Journal). **b** any person or organization which is unconventional in its actions or behavior: *All around town, there are entrancing mavericks that may have no great significance and follow no trend* (New Yorker).
—*adj.* unconventional; refusing to be bound by normal procedures: *For years these maverick merchants have flourished by following a simple formula* (Wall Street Journal).
[American English < Samuel *Maverick,* 1803-1870, a Texas cattle owner who did not brand the calves of one of his herds]

**ma|vin** or **ma|ven** (mā'vən), *n. U.S. Slang.* an expert or connoisseur. [< Yiddish *meyvn* < Hebrew *mēbhīn*]

**ma|vis** (mā'vis), *n.* = song thrush (def. 2). [< Old French *mauvis,* perhaps < a Celtic word]

**ma|vour|neen** or **ma|vour|nin** (mə vůr'nēn, -vôr'-, -vōr'-), *n. Irish.* my darling. [< Irish *mo mhuirnīn* my treasure]

**maw** (mô), *n.* **1** the mouth, throat, or gullet, especially of a meat-eating animal, as concerned in devouring: *a lion's maw.* **2** *Figurative: Nations continue to pour wealth into the maw of war.* **3** = stomach. SYN: craw. **4** the crop of a bird. [Old English *maga*]

**maw|kin** (mô'kin), *n.* = malkin.

**mawk|ish** (mô'kish), *adj.* **1** sickly sentimental; weakly emotional: *The portrait of Lady Mendl is sharp without being unkind and sentimental without being mawkish* (Harper's). **2** sickening; nauseating: *If I would drink water, I must quaff the mawkish contents of an open aqueduct* (Tobias Smollett). [< Middle English *mawke* maggot < Scandinavian (compare Old Icelandic *mathkr*) + *-ish*] —**mawk'ish|ly,** *adv.* —**mawk'ish|ness,** *n.*

**max.,** 1 maxim. 2 maximum.

***max|i** (mak'sē), *n., pl.* **max|is,** *adj.* —*n.* **1** a skirt, dress, or coat reaching to the ankle or just above it; maxiskirt, maxidress, or maxicoat. **2** the ankle-length style of fashion.
—*adj.* **1** reaching to the ankle or just above it; ankle-length: *Teen-agers and college girls rushed for maxi coats* (Ruth Mary DuBois). **2** larger or longer than usual: *In the Dublin suburbs there is a minicar in nearly every garage, and downtown the traffic jams are becoming very maxi* (Saturday Review).
[< *maxi-*]

***maxi**
definition 1

**maxi-,** *prefix.* **1** reaching down to the ankle; long, as in *maxicoat, maxidress, maxilength, maxiskirt.* **2** very large, as in *maxi-order, maxi-taxi.* [< *maxi*(mum)]

**max|il|la** (mak sil'ə), *n., pl.* **max|il|lae** (mak sil'ē), **max|il|las. 1** the jaw or jawbone, especially the upper jawbone. See diagram under **face. 2** either of the pair of appendages just behind the mandibles of insects or crabs and other crustaceans. [< Latin *maxilla* (upper) jaw < *māla* cheekbone, jaw]

**max|il|lar|y** (mak'sə ler'ē), *adj., n., pl.* **-lar|ies.** —*adj.* of or having to do with the jaw or jawbone, especially the upper jawbone.
—*n.* = maxilla.

**max|il|li|ped** (mak sil'ə ped), *n.* = foot jaw. [< *maxilla* + Latin *pēs, pedis foot*]

**max|il|lo|fa|cial** (mak sil'ə fā'shel), *adj.* of or having to do with the lower half of the face: *maxillofacial prosthetics.* [< *maxilla* + *facial*]

**max|im** (mak'səm), *n.* **1** a short rule of conduct; proverb: *"A stitch in time saves nine" and "Look before you leap" are maxims. That maxim of the heathen, "Enjoy the present, trust nothing to the future"* (Cardinal Newman). *My maxim is to obey orders* (James Fenimore Cooper). SYN: adage. **2** a statement expressing some general truth: *The trite maxim that every Englishman's house is his castle* (William E. H. Lecky). SYN: aphorism, apothegm. [< Middle French *maxime,* learned borrowing from Late Latin *maxima* (*prōpositiō*) axiom; (literally) greatest premise; see etym. under **maximum**]

**max|i|ma** (mak'sə mə), *n.* maximums; a plural of **maximum.**

**max|i|mal** (mak'sə məl), *adj.* of or being a maximum; greatest possible; highest: *an insistence on maximal loyalty.* —**max'i|mal|ly,** *adv.*

**Max|i|mal|ism** or **max|i|mal|ism** (mak'sə mə liz'-əm), *n.* the doctrines, methods, or procedure of Maximalists.

**Max|i|mal|ist** (mak'sə mə list), *n.* **1** a member of the radical section of the Social Revolutionary Party in Russia about 1903. **2** a radical section or a radical in any party.

**max|i|mate** (mak'sə māt), *v.t.,* **-mat|ed, -mat|ing.** = maximize.

**Max|im gun** (mak'səm), a type of water-cooled machine gun, in which the bolt is operated by the recoil. [< Sir Hiram S. *Maxim,* 1840-1916, a British inventor, born in the United States]

**max|i|min** (mak'sə min), *n.* that strategy in the theory of games which provides the maximum of a player's minimum possible gains (contrasted with *minimax*): *Maximin is like a philosophy of complete pessimism except that the decision is based on the decision-maker's possible payoffs rather than losses* (New Scientist). [< *maxi-*(mum) + *min*(imum)]

**max|i|mise** (mak'sə mīz), *v.t., v.i.,* **-mised, -mis|ing.** *Especially British.* maximize.

**max|im|ite** (mak'sə mīt), *n.* a powerful explosive consisting chiefly of picric acid, formerly used in shells for piercing armor. [< Hudson *Maxim,* 1853-1927, an American engineer and inventor + *-ite*[1]]

**max|i|mize** (mak'sə mīz), *v.,* **-mized, -miz|ing.** —*v.t.* to increase or magnify to the highest possible amount or degree: *to maximize sales or profits. Instead of maximizing facilities for motorcars, we should maximize the advantages of urban life* (New Yorker).
—*v.i.* to maintain the most rigorous or comprehensive interpretation possible of a theological doctrine or an obligation. [< *maxim*(um) + *-ize*] —**max'i|mi|za'tion,** *n.* —**max'i|miz'er,** *n.*

**max|i|mum** (mak'sə məm), *n., pl.* **-mums, -ma** (-mə), *adj.* —*n.* **1** the largest or highest amount; greatest possible amount; highest point or degree: *Sixteen miles in a day was the maximum that any of our club walked last summer. Drivers must not exceed a maximum of 55 miles an hour.* SYN: limit. **2** = relative maximum.
—*adj.* **1** greatest possible; largest or highest: *The maximum score on the test is 100.* **2** having to do with a maximum or maximums: *a maximum period.*
[< Latin *maximum,* neuter of *maximus* greatest, superlative of *magnus* great]

**ma|xi|xe** (mə shē'shə, mak sēks'), *n.* a lively dance, originally Brazilian, formerly popular in Europe and the United States. [< Portuguese *maxixe*]

**max|well** (maks'wel, -wəl), *n.* the unit of magnetic flux in the centimeter-gram-second system; the flux through one square centimeter normal to a magnetic field, the intensity of which is one gauss. [< James Clerk *Maxwell,* 1831-1879, a Scottish physicist]

**Max|well-Boltz|mann distribution** (maks'wəl-bôlts'män, -wel-; -mən), *Physics.* a theory dealing with the distribution of velocities among gas particles in equilibrium and the statistical probabilities associated with these. [< James Clerk *Maxwell,* 1831-1879, and Ludwig *Boltzmann,* 1844-1906, the two physicists who formulated the theory]

**may**[1] (mā), *v., pres. indic. sing.* **may,** (*Archaic*) **may|est** or **mayst, may,** *pl.* **may;** *past tense* **might. —auxiliary. v. 1** to be permitted or allowed to: *May I have an apple? You may go now.* **2** to be possible that it will: *It may rain tomorrow.* **3** it is hoped that: *May you have a pleasant trip.*
**4** *May* is used to express contingency, condition, concession, purpose, result, and the like: *I write that you may know my plans.* **5** ability or power (more commonly *can*). **6** *Law.* must; shall (as interpreted by courts in documents, laws, and the like). —*v.i. Obsolete.* to be able; have power. [Old English *mæg*]
▶ See **can** for usage note.

**may**[2] (mā), *n.* **1** the hawthorn. It blooms in May. **2** any spiraea that blooms in May. [< *May*]

**may**[3] (mā), *n. Archaic.* a maiden; virgin: *For ill beseems in a reverend friar, The love of a mortal may* (Thomas L. Peacock). [perhaps Old English *mæg* kinswoman]

**May** (mā), *n.* **1** the fifth month of the year. It has 31 days. **2** *Figurative.* the springtime; prime of life; prime: *the May of my years* (Philip Sidney). **3** the festivities of May Day: *I'm to be Queen o' the May, mother* (Tennyson). [Old English *maius* (< Latin), and Middle English *mai* < Old French < Latin *Māius* (*mēnsis*) (month) of May, probably related to *Māia,* an earth goddess]

**ma|ya** (mä'yä), *n. Hinduism.* illusion or deceptive appearance: *Reality, says the classic Vedanta doctrine is one—hence all plurality is illusion* (*maya*) (Time). [< Sanskrit *māyā*]

**Ma|ya** (mä'yə), *n.* **1** one of an ancient Indian people who lived in Central America and Mexico. The Mayas had a high degree of civilization from the 200's A.D. to the 800's, but declined long before they were discovered by the Spaniards. **2** their language; Mayan.

**Ma|yan** (mä′yən), *adj., n.* —***adj.*** of or having to do with the Mayas, their language, or the language family to which it belongs. —***n.*** **1** one of the Mayas. **2** the language of the Mayas or the language family to which it belongs.

**May apple**, **1** a North American perennial plant of the barberry family with a large, white flower, and poisonous leaves and roots; mandrake. It blooms in May. **2** its yellowish, slightly acid, egg-shaped fruit, which is sometimes eaten.

**may|be** (mā′bē), *adv., n.* —***adv.*** it may be; possibly; perhaps: *Maybe you'll have better luck later.* —***n.*** a possibility or probability; uncertainty: *There are lots of maybes in this glittering promise* (New York Times).

► **maybe, may be.** *Maybe* is an adverb or noun; *may be* is a verb form: *Maybe I'll get a new bike for my birthday. He may be the next mayor.*

**May beetle**, **1** = cockchafer. **2** = June bug.

**May blob**, = marsh marigold.

**May bug**, = May beetle.

**May bush**, = hawthorn.

**May Day**, the first day of May, often celebrated by crowning a girl honored as the queen of May, dancing around the Maypole, and other festivities. In some parts of the world, labor parades and meetings are held on May Day.

**May|day** (mā′dā′), *n.*, or **May Day**, the international radiotelephone call for help, used by a ship or aircraft when in distress. [< French *m'aidez* help me!]

**may|est** (mā′əst), *v. Archaic.* may. "Thou mayest" means "you may." Also, **mayst**.

**May|fair** (mā′fãr′), *n.* **1** a fashionable section of London. **2** fashionable London society.

**may|flow|er** (mā′flou′ər), *n.* any one of several plants whose flowers blossom in May; the trailing arbutus, spring beauty, and certain hepaticas and anemones (in the United States); the hawthorn, cowslip, and marsh marigold (in England).

**May fly**, or **may|fly** (mā′flī′), *n.* **1** a slender insect with lacy front wings, which are much larger than the hind wings; ephemerid; drake; dun; shadfly. It dies soon after reaching the adult stage. May flies comprise an order of insects. **2** an artificial fishing fly tied to resemble this insect.

**may|hap** (mā′hap′, mā′hap), *adv. Archaic.* perhaps; perchance. [< earlier *it may hap*]

**may|hap|pen** (mā′hap′ən), *adv.* = mayhap.

**May|haw** (mā′hô′), *n.* a small hawthorn common in the southern United States. [because the fruit ripens in May]

**may|hem** (mā′hem, -əm), *n.* **1** the crime of intentionally maiming a person or injuring him so that he is less able to defend himself. **2** any violence inflicted upon another person, especially that which causes permanent physical injury: *Professional wrestling ... has become so popular in Japan that scores of youngsters who have attempted to imitate their favorites' make-believe mayhem have wound up in hospitals* (Newsweek). **3** a state of general confusion and, often violent, disorder. Also, **maihem**. [< Anglo-French *mahem, mahaigne,* or *meshaigne,* related to *mahaignier* to maim]

**May|ing** (mā′ing), *n.* the celebration of May Day; taking part in May festivities.

**may|n't** (mā′ənt, mānt), may not.

► See **can't** for usage note.

**may|o** (mā′ō), *n. Informal.* mayonnaise.

**may|on|naise** (mā′ə nāz′, mā′ə nāz), *n.* a dressing made of egg yolks, oil, vinegar or lemon juice, and seasoning, beaten together until thick. It is used on salads, fish, vegetables, and other foods. [< French *mayonnaise,* ultimately < *Mahon,* a seaport in Minorca, captured by the Duc de Richelieu, whose chef introduced the *Mahonnaise* after his master's victory]

**may|or** (mā′ər, mãr), *n.* the person at the head of a city or town government; chief official, usually elected, of a city or town: *The mayor led the town meeting about taxes.* [< Old French *maire,* and *maor* < Latin *mājor.* See etym. of doublet **major**.]

**may|or|al** (mā′ər əl, mãr′-), *adj.* of, having to do with, or characteristic of a mayor: *mayoral robes, mayoral duties.*

**may|or|al|ty** (mā′ər əl tē, mãr′-), *n., pl.* **-ties.** **1** the position of mayor. **2** the term of office of a mayor.

**may|or-coun|cil** (mā′ər koun′səl, mãr′-), *adj.* of or having to do with a system of municipal government in which a popularly elected mayor and council are in charge of the city administration.

**may|or|ess** (mā′ər is, mãr′-), *n.* **1** a woman mayor. **2** *British.* the wife of a mayor.

**may|or|ship** (mā′ər ship, mãr′-), *n.* the office or dignity of mayor.

**May|pole** or **may|pole** (mā′pōl′), *n.* **1** a high pole, usually decorated with flowers or ribbons, around which merrymakers dance on May Day. **2** *Figurative.* a tall, slender person: *the daughter, ... a trapesing, trolloping, talkative maypole* (Oliver Goldsmith).

**may|pop** (mā′pop′), *n.* **1** the small, edible, yellow fruit of a passionflower growing in the southern United States. **2** the plant itself. [American English, earlier *maycock,* alteration of *maracock* < Algonkian (perhaps Powhatan) *mäkäk, mäkaku* a hollow receptacle; a variety of cucurbita]

**May queen**, a girl crowned with flowers and honored as queen on May Day.

**mayst** (māst), *v. Archaic.* may. "Thou mayst" means "you may."

**may|thorn** (mā′thôrn′), *n.* = hawthorn.

**May|tide** (mā′tīd′), *n.* = Maytime.

**May|time** (mā′tīm′), *n.* the month of May.

**may tree**, *British.* the hawthorn.

**may|weed** (mā′wēd′), *n.* a weed of the composite family found in Europe, Asia, and America, having flower heads with a yellow disk and white rays and ill-smelling foliage; dog fennel. [< unrecorded *maythe-weed* < obsolete *maythe,* the same plant, Old English *mægtha, magethe*]

**May wine**, a punch made from a mixture of white wine, sugar, and woodruff herbs.

**maz|ard** (maz′ərd), *n.* **1** *Archaic.* the head or face: *knocked about the mazard with a sexton's spade* (Shakespeare). **2** *Obsolete.* mazer. Also, **mazzard**. [alteration of *mazer*]

**maz|a|rine** (maz′ə rēn′), *n., adj.*, or **mazarine blue**. —***n.*** a deep, rich blue.
—***adj.*** of this color; deep-blue: *There are stars in the mazarine sky* (New Yorker).
[perhaps < French *Mazarin,* a proper name]

**Maz|da|ism** or **Maz|de|ism** (maz′də iz əm), *n.* the religion of ancient Persia; Zoroastrianism. [< Avestan *mazda* the principle of good. Compare etym. under **Ormazd**.]

**Maz|da|ist** or **Maz|de|ist** (maz′də ist), *n.* a believer in Mazdaism.

**maze** (māz), *n., v.,* **mazed, maz|ing.** —***n.*** **1a** a network of paths through which it is hard to find one's way: *A guide led us through the maze of tunnels in the cave. He turned short into one of the mazes of the wood* (Scott). SYN: labyrinth. **b** *Figurative.* any complicated arrangement, such as of streets or buildings: *Bath was then a maze of only four or five hundred houses* (Macaulay). **c** *Figurative.* intricate windings; intricacy: *a maze of errors. Here would the good Peter ... watch the mazes of the dance* (Washington Irving). **2** *Figurative.* a state of confusion; muddled condition: *He was in such a maze that he couldn't speak.* SYN: perplexity, bewilderment.
—***v.t.*** *Archaic.* **1** to stupefy; daze: *Finding This tumult 'bout my door ... It somewhat maz'd me* (Ben Jonson). **2** to bewilder; perplex.
[variant of *amaze*] —**maze′like′**, *adj.*

**ma|zel tov** (mä′zəl tōv′), *interj. Hebrew.* congratulations; good luck.

**ma|zer** (mā′zər), *n. Obsolete.* a large goblet without a foot, originally made of a hard wood, often richly carved or ornamented. Also, **mazard**. [< Old French *masere* < Germanic (compare Old High German *maser* gall on a tree; drinking cup)]

**ma|zu|ma** (mə zü′mə), *n. Slang.* money. [< Yiddish *mazuma* < Hebrew *məzumon*]

**ma|zur|ka** or **ma|zour|ka** (mə zėr′kə, -zůr′-), *n.* **1** a lively Polish folk dance. **2** music for it, usually in 3/4 or 6/8 time. [< alteration of Polish *mazurek* (literally) dance of *Mazovia,* a region in Poland]

**maz|y** (mā′zē), *adj.,* **maz|i|er, maz|i|est.** **1** like a maze; full of intricate windings; intricate: *Five miles meandering with a mazy motion Through wood and dale the sacred river ran* (Samuel Taylor Coleridge). SYN: devious. **2** *Dialect.* dizzy; confused. —**maz′i|ly**, *adv.* —**maz′i|ness**, *n.*

**maz|zard** (maz′ərd), *n.* **1** a sweet cherry, especially a wild sweet cherry used as a stock for breeding varieties of sweet and of sour cherries. **2** = mazard. [origin uncertain; perhaps Middle English *mazer,* later *mazard* a wood used for cups; a cup < Old French *masere;* see etym. under **mazer**]

**mb.**, *Meteorology.* millibar or millibars.

**M.B.**, **1** *British.* Bachelor of Medicine (Latin, *Medicinae Baccalaureus*). **2** Bachelor of Music (Latin, *Musicae Baccalaureus*).

**M.B.A.** or **MBA** (no periods), *U.S.* Master of Business Administration.

**M.B.E.**, Member of the Order of the British Empire.

**m|bi|ra** (em bir′ə), *n.* an African musical instrument consisting of a hollow piece of wood, usually about eight inches long, with metal strips, inserted lengthwise, that vibrate when played with the thumb. The instrument is tuned to play tribal music while held in both hands with the palms upward. [< a Bantu word]

**M. b. m.**, thousand feet board measure.

**MBS** (no periods), Mutual Broadcasting System.

**M|bu|ti** (em bü′tē), *n., pl.* **-ti** or **-tis.** a member of certain Negroid pygmy people native to equatorial Africa and the Congo forests.

**m.c.** (em′sē′), *v.t., v.i.,* **m.c.'d, m.c.'ing.** *Informal.* to act as master of ceremonies (for): *[He] wrote it, produced it, m.c.'d it, and, he now says, loved every minute of it* (New Yorker).

**Mc-** *prefix.* a variant of **Mac** ("son of"), as in *McDonald.*

**mc** (no period), **1** megacycle or megacycles. **2** millicurie or millicuries.

**mc.**, megacycle or megacycles.

**m.c.** or **MC** (no periods), master of ceremonies.

**M.C.**, an abbreviation for the following:
**1** Master Commandant.
**2** master of ceremonies.
**3** Medical Corps.
**4** Member of Congress.
**5** *British.* Military Cross.

**Mc|Car|thy|ism** (mə kär′thē iz əm), *n.* **1** the policy or practice of publicly accusing individuals or groups of political disloyalty and subversion, usually without sufficient evidence: *McCarthyism breeds fear, suspicion and unrest. It turns neighbor against neighbor* (New York Times). *So McCarthyism—a synonym for reckless accusation—was born* (Life). **2** the public investigation of Communist activities in the United States in the early 1950's, conducted in sensational public hearings: *While this was going on, McCarthyism and attendant mental ills were preventing researchers here from even acknowledging that Russia possessed competent scientists* (New Scientist). [< Senator Joseph R. *McCarthy,* 1908-1957, chairman of the U.S. Senate Permanent Investigations Committee + *-ism*]

**Mc|Car|thy|ite** (mə kär′thē īt), *n., adj.* —***n.*** a follower of Senator Joseph McCarthy or a believer in McCarthyism: *The Administration will not allow itself to be hamstrung by the McCarthyites and isolationists* (Newsweek).
—***adj.*** characteristic of McCarthyism.

**Mc|Coy** (mə koi′), *n. U.S. Informal.* Usually, **the real McCoy.** the genuine article; the real thing: *You can't fake this cigar; it's the real McCoy.* [American English < the Scottish phrase *the real Mackay,* probably < *Mackay,* a Scotch whisky exported to the U.S. and Canada by A. and M. Mackay of Glasgow; influenced by Kid *McCoy,* a celebrated boxer of the late 1800's, who was sometimes confused with another, less popular boxer called McCoy]

**M.C.E.**, Master of Civil Engineering.

**Mcfd** (no periods) or **M.C.F.D.**, thousands of cubic feet per day.

**M.Ch.**, Master of Surgery (Latin, *Magister Chirurgiae*).

**mcht.**, merchant.

**Mc|In|tosh** (mak′ən tosh), *n.*, or **McIntosh Red**, a bright-red, early fall variety of eating apple. [< John *McIntosh,* of Ontario, Canada, who cultivated it in the 1700's]

**M.C.L.**, **1** Master of Civil Law. **2** Master of Comparative Law.

**Mc|Lu|han|ism** (mə klü′ə niz əm), *n.* **1** the ideas and theories of the Canadian writer and communications specialist Marshall McLuhan, born 1911, especially his emphasis on the influence of electronic communications and the mass communications media in radically reshaping society. **2** a word or expression peculiar to Marshall McLuhan: *These movies are all "non-linear," to use a favorite McLuhanism; they refuse to follow A-to-Z patterns* (Marshall Delaney).

**Mc|Lu|han|ist** (mə klü′ə nist), *n.* = McLuhanite.

**Mc|Lu|han|ite** (mə klü′ə nīt), *n.* a follower or supporter of Marshall McLuhan and his ideas.

**MCM** (no periods), 1,000 circular mils. 1MCM = 0.000785 sq. in.

**Mc|Naugh|ten Rule** (mək nô′tən), = M'Naghten Rule.

**MCP** (no periods), *Informal.* male chauvinist pig: *A Doll's House, one of the genuine Ibsen masterpieces, was ... rescued by Claire Bloom and Anthony Hopkins as Nora and her MCP husband Torvald* (National Review).

**MCPA** (no periods), a widely used herbicide for controlling broad-leaved weeds, especially in cereal crops. *Formula:* $C_9H_9ClO_3$ [< *m*(ethyl)-*c*(hloro)-*p*(henoxyacetic) *a*(cid)]

**mc/s** or **Mc/s** (no periods), megacycles per second.

**M.C.S.**, Master of Commercial Science.

**mcy sec** (no periods), megacycles per second.

**m/d** (no periods) or **m.d.**, *Commerce.* month's

---

**Pronunciation Key:** hat, āge, cãre, fär; let, ēqual, tėrm; it, īce; hot, ōpen, ôrder; oil, out; cup, pu̇t, rüle; child; long; thin; ᴛʜen; zh, measure; ə represents **a** in about, **e** in taken, **i** in pencil, **o** in lemon, **u** in circus.

date; months after date.
**Md** (no period), mendelevium (chemical element).
**Md.**, Maryland.
**MD** (no periods), **1** Doctor of Medicine (Latin, *Medicinae Doctor*). **2** Maryland (with postal Zip Code). **3** muscular dystrophy.
**M/D** (no periods), *Banking.* memorandum of deposit.
**M.D.**, **1** Doctor of Medicine (Latin, *Medicinae Doctor*). **2** Medical Department. **3** *Banking.* memorandum of deposit.
**MDAP** (no periods), Mutual Defense Assistance Program.
**M-day** (em′dā′), *n.* mobilization day; the day on which the armed forces are officially mobilized.
**MDC** (no periods), more developed country: *The MDCs should make research facilities and technical and industrial institutions available to the LDCs* (Annual Register).
**Mdlle.**, Mademoiselle.
**mdm.**, madam.
**Mdme.**, Madame.
**M.D.S.**, Master of Dental Surgery.
**mdse.**, *U.S.* merchandise.
**me** (mē; *unstressed* mi), *pron. I* and *me* mean the person speaking. *Me* is the objective case of *I. She said "Give the dog to me. I like it and it likes me."* [Old English *mē*]
**take it from me**. See under **take**.
▶ **it's I, it's me**. The first of these is formal English, the second now established in good use on the informal conversational level. The objective case of the other personal pronouns after the forms of *to be* has less status, though many speakers do not avoid locutions like *it's her, it was us,* since the nominative sounds somewhat stilted.
**m.e.**, marbled edges (in book manufacturing).
**Me** (no period), *Chemistry.* methyl.
**Me.**, Maine.
**ME** (no periods), **1** Maine (with postal Zip Code). **2** Also, **ME.** Middle English.
**M.E.**, an abbreviation for the following:
**1** marine engineer.
**2** Master of Engineering.
**3** mechanical engineer.
**4** Methodist Episcopal.
**5** Middle English.
**6** mining engineer.
**me|a cul|pa** (mē′ə kul′pə), **1** (by) my fault: ... *I plead guilty. Mea culpa* (New Yorker). **2** a plea or confession of guilt: ... *polemics, Party speeches and resolutions, mea culpas of penitents confessing to scientific error* (Bulletin of the Atomic Scientists). **3** an apology: *a cringing mea culpa.* **4** a recantation, especially of a political ideology: *Since his mea culpa, [he] has been outspoken against Communism* (New Yorker). [< Latin *mea culpa* (it is) my fault]
**mead**[1] (mēd), *n. Archaic.* a meadow: *Downward sloped The path through yellow meads* (James Russell Lowell). [Old English *mǣd*]
**mead**[2] (mēd), *n.* **1** an alcoholic drink made from fermented honey and water, especially in Anglo-Saxon days. **2** *U.S. Obsolete.* a soft drink of carbonated water and flavoring. [Old English *medu*]
**mead|ow** (med′ō), *n.* **1** a piece of grassy land, especially one used for growing hay or as a pasture for grazing animals. **2** low, grassy land near a stream or river. [Old English *mǣdwe,* oblique case of *mǣd* mead[1]]
**meadow beauty**, any North American herb of a group of low perennials with showy, crimson or rose flowers.
**meadow brown**, any brown or grayish butterfly of a family that has eyespots on the wings; satyr.
**meadow fescue**, a tall grass grown in Europe and America for pasture and for hay.
**meadow grass**, **1** any one of a group of grasses, such as the Kentucky bluegrass of the United States. **2** *U.S.* manna grass.
**mead|ow|land** (med′ō land′, -lənd), *n.* land used as a meadow.
**meadow lark**, or **mead|ow|lark** (med′ō lärk′), *n.* a songbird of North America about as big as a robin, having a thick body, short tail, and a yellow breast marked with black; field lark. Meadow larks are related to the orioles.
**meadow lily**, = Canada lily.
**meadow mouse**, any one of various short-tailed voles living in fields and meadows; field mouse.
**meadow mushroom**, the common edible mushroom.
**meadow rue**, any plant of a group of the crowfoot family with leaves like those of the rue.
**meadow saffron**, = colchicum.
**meadow snipe**, **1** = American snipe. **2** = pectoral sandpiper.
**mead|ow|sweet** (med′ō swēt′), *n.* **1** a shrub, a species of spiraea, with dense clusters of small, fragrant, pink or white flowers. **2** any one of a genus of tall herbs of the rose family, having many small white, pink, or purple flowers.
**meadow violet**, a long-stemmed violet with heart-shaped leaves, commonly with a purple flower, found in wet lands in eastern North America; hooded violet.
**meadow vole**, = meadow mouse.
**mead|ow|y** (med′ō ē), *adj.* **1** like a meadow. **2** of meadows: *meadowy land.*
**mea|ger** or **mea|gre** (mē′gər), *adj.* **1** poor or scanty: *a meager meal.* **SYN**: sparse. See syn. under **scanty**. **2** thin; lean: *a meager face. A small, meagre man* (John L. Motley). *Shaggy, meager little ponies* (Francis Parkman). **3** without fullness or richness; deficient in quality or quantity: *The report that first reached us through the newspapers was meagre and contradictory* (Thomas B. Aldrich). [< French, Old French *maigre* < Latin *macer* thin. See etym. of doublet **maigre**.]
—**mea′ger|ly, mea′gre|ly**, *adv.* —**mea′ger|ness, mea′gre|ness**, *n.*
**meal**[1] (mēl), *n.* **1** one of the regular, daily occasions of eating, such as a breakfast, lunch, dinner, supper, or tea: *Come to the meal and join the family.* **SYN**: repast. **2** the food served or eaten at any one time: *We enjoyed the hot meal after being out in the rain.* **SYN**: repast.
**make a meal of**, *British Informal.* to get full satisfaction or advantage from: *Shaletta appeared on their wide outside, making a meal of the conditions* (London Times).
[Old English *mǣl* appointed time; meal]
**meal**[2] (mēl), *n.* **1** grain ground up; grain that is coarsely ground and not sifted, especially corn meal: *enough meal to make muffins.* **2** anything ground to a powder: *linseed meal.* [Old English *melu.* See related etym. at **mill**.]
**meal|ie** (mē′lē), *n.* in South Africa: **a** an ear of corn. **b** corn: *In her hand she held the paper carrier containing the bag of mealie and the sugar and coffee that the Welfare people doled out* (New Yorker).
**mealies**, corn: *a sack of mealies.*
[< Afrikaans *milje* < Portuguese *milho* (*da India*) (Indian) corn < Latin *milium;* origin uncertain]
**meal moth**, a small, grayish-brown moth whose larvae feed on Indian meal.
**meals on wheels**, a service that brings a hot meal daily to an elderly or disabled person in his home. It is usually a private service subsidized by the government.
**meal ticket**, **1** a ticket authorizing a person to obtain a meal: *We ... were permitted to buy our meal tickets for seven shillings and sixpence* (Harper's). **2** *Informal.* a person or thing that is a source of money: *Thomas Harrow is loved more as a meal ticket than as the man and creative genius he is* (Wall Street Journal).
**meal|time** (mēl′tīm′), *n.* time for eating a meal.
**meal worm**, or **meal|worm** (mēl′wėrm′), *n.* a beetle larva that feeds on flour and meal. Meal worms are raised as food for cage birds.
**meal|y**[1] (mē′lē), *adj.*, **meal|i|er, meal|i|est**. **1** like meal; dry and powdery: *mealy potatoes.* **2** of or containing meal: *the mealy treasures of the harvest bin* (James W. Riley). **SYN**: farinaceous. **3** covered with meal: *the miller's mealy hands.* **4** as if dusted with flour; pale: *a mealy complexion. I only know two sorts of boys. Mealy boys, and beef-faced boys* (Dickens). **5** = mealy-mouthed. **6** flecked as if with meal; spotty. [< *meal*[2] + *-y*[1]] —**meal′i|ness**, *n.*
**meal|y**[2] (mē′lē), *n., pl.* **meal|ies**. = mealie. [< *meal*[2] + *-y*[2]]
**mealy bug**, or **meal|y|bug** (mē′lē bug′), *n.* a small, soft-bodied scale insect which covers itself with a whitish secretion. It causes considerable damage by sucking the juices of citrus trees and other plants. They comprise a family of insects.
**meal|y-mouthed** (mē′lē mouᴛʜd′, -moutht′), *adj.* unwilling to tell the straight truth in plain words; using soft words insincerely: *a mealy-mouthed politician.* **SYN**: hollow, insincere, equivocating.
**mean**[1] (mēn), *v.*, **meant, mean|ing**. —*v.t.* **1** to have as its thought; signify: *Can you make out what this sentence means? What does this word mean? A poem should not mean but be* (Archibald MacLeish). **SYN**: import, denote. **2** to intend to say or indicate: *Keep out; that means you. Say what you mean.* **3** to have as a purpose; have in mind; intend: *Do you think they mean to fight us? Do you mean to use the chops for dinner? It's no use waiting any longer, if you mean to go at all, today* (William D. Howells). **SYN**: design, purpose. See syn. under **intend**. **4** to set aside for a definite purpose; destine: *Fate meant us for each other. He was meant for a soldier.*
—*v.i.* to have intentions of some kind; be minded or disposed: *She means well.*
**mean well by**, to have kindly feelings toward: *The manager means well by his workers.*
[Old English *mǣnan* mean, tell, say]
**mean**[2] (mēn), *adj.* **1** not noble; petty; unkind; small-minded: *It is mean to spread gossip about others.* **SYN**: base, contemptible, despicable, ignoble. **2** low in quality or grade; poor: *the meanest of gifts.* **3** low in social position or rank; humble: *A peasant is of mean birth; a king is of noble birth.* **SYN**: common, plebeian. **4** of little importance or value: *the meanest flower. Rightly viewed no meanest object is insignificant* (Thomas Carlyle). **SYN**: insignificant, paltry, petty. **5** of poor appearance; shabby: *The poor widow lived in a mean hut.* **6** stingy or selfish; close-fisted: *A miser is mean about money.* **SYN**: miserly. **7** *U.S. Informal.* humiliated; ashamed: *to feel mean.* **8** *U.S. Informal.* **a** hard to manage; troublesome; bad-tempered: *a mean horse.* **b** selfish and ill-tempered; vicious; cruel: *Tell me where you hid my hat; don't be so mean!* **9a** *Informal.* in poor physical condition; unwell: *I feel mean today.* **b** stubborn and annoying: *a mean cold.* **10** *Informal.* that attracts notice, especially because it is done well or one is very good or clever: *"I bet you play a mean ukulele," she said* (Punch). *Daddy was a real mean cook when he had something to work with* (Louise Meriwether). **SYN**: excellent.
**no mean**, very good: *That scholar is no mean worker, writing several articles a year.*
[Middle English *mene,* Old English *gemǣne* common]
✱**mean**[3] (mēn), *adj., n.* —*adj.* **1** halfway between two extremes: *the mean annual air temperature. 6 is the mean number between 3 and 9.* **2** intermediate in kind, quality, or degree. **SYN**: medium, average. **3** *Mathematics.* having a value intermediate between the values of other quantities: *a mean diameter.*
—*n.* **1** a condition, quality, or course of action halfway between two extremes: *Eight hours is a happy mean between too much sleep and too little.* **2** *Mathematics.* **a** a quantity having a value intermediate between the values of other quantities, especially the average obtained by dividing the sum of all the quantities by the total number of quantities: *6 is the mean of 3, 7, and 8.* **b** either the second or third term of a proportion of four terms. See picture below. **3** *Logic.* the middle term of a syllogism. **4** See also **means**.
[< Old French *meien* < Latin *mediānus* (of the) middle < *medius* middle (of). See etym. of doublet **median**.]
**me|an|der** (mē an′dər), *v, n.* —*v.i.* **1** to follow a winding course: *A brook meanders through the meadow.* **2** *Figurative.* to wander aimlessly: *We meandered through the park. Paris is built for meandering, and for getting lost* (John O'Hara). **SYN**: ramble, saunter.
—*v.t.* to make (one's way) or follow (a course) by meandering. [< noun]
—*n.* **1** an aimless wandering: *After the sun got so hot, the hike turned into a meander along the edge of a stream.* **2** a winding course or path: *the meanders of the law* (John Arbuthnot). **3** an intricate variety of fret or fretwork. **4** a looplike, winding turn in a river or stream.
[< Latin *Maeander* < Greek *Maiandros,* a winding river in Asia Minor (now the *Menderes* River in western Turkey)] —**me|an′der|ing|ly**, *adv.*
**mean deviation**, *Statistics.* a measure of dispersion obtained by taking the average of the absolute values of the differences between individual

✱**mean**[3]
*n.*, definition 2a

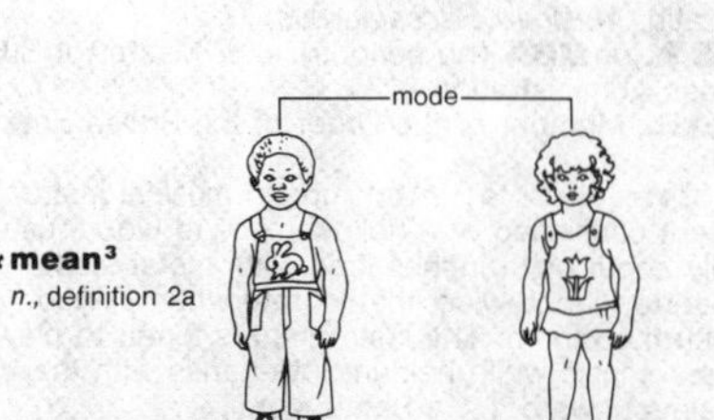

2 years old 2 years old

4 years old

5 years old

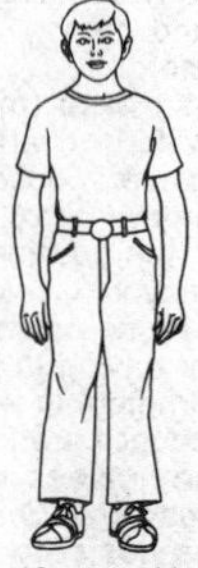
12 years old

numbers or scores and their mean.

**mean distance**, **1** the average of the distances of the aphelion and perihelion of a planet from the sun, one of the data necessary to determine the orbit of a planet: *The earth's mean distance from the sun is about 92,900,000 miles* (Robert H. Baker). **2** the average of the greatest and least distances of any heavenly body, such as a star or a satellite, from the focus of its orbit.

**me|an|drous** (mē an′drəs), *adj.* meandering; winding: (*Figurative.*) *an introspective, meandrous excursion through his own mind* (New Yorker).

**mean free path**, the average distance a molecule of a gas or other substance can travel before it collides with another molecule. The distance will vary according to altitude in the case of a gas. *In a gas the mean free path may be as large as a few hundred angstroms, or much larger than the size of the atom itself* (Scientific American).

**mean|ing** (mē′ning), *n., adj.* —*n.* **1** that which is meant or intended; significance: *the meaning of a story, the meaning of a sermon. The meaning of that sentence is clear.* **2** *Archaic.* intention or purpose: *I am no honest man if there by any good meaning towards you* (Shakespeare).
—*adj.* **1** that means something; expressive; significant: *a meaning look.* **2** having purpose; intending: *well meaning.* —**mean′ing|ly**, *adv.* —**mean′ing|ness**, *n.*
—*Syn. n.* **1 Meaning, sense, purport** mean what is expressed or meant to be. **Meaning** is the general word, applying to anything that is subject to explanation or interpretation, such as a word, statement, gesture, action, or painting: *What is the meaning of such behavior?* **Sense** applies especially to a particular meaning of a word: *He used the word "lady" in the special sense of "a British noblewoman." In other senses this word is not a synonym of "meaning."* **Purport**, formal, applies to the main idea or general drift of a longer statement: *That was the purport of the president's address.*

**mean|ing|ful** (mē′ning fəl), *adj.* full of meaning; having much meaning; significant: *History must be made more meaningful to the individual* (New York Times). —**mean′ing|ful|ly**, *adv.* —**mean′ing|ful|ness**, *n.*

**mean|ing|less** (mē′ning lis), *adj.* without meaning; not making sense; not significant: *Words such as "purpose" are ... scientifically meaningless* (Science News). **SYN**: senseless, insignificant. —**mean′ing|less|ly**, *adv.* —**mean′ing|less|ness**, *n.*

**mean|ly** (mēn′lē), *adv.* in a mean manner; poorly, basely, or stingily.

**mean|ness** (mēn′nis), *n.* **1** the fact or state of being mean in grade or quality; poorness. **2** the fact or state of being selfish in small things; stinginess. **3** a mean act.

**mean noon**, the time when the mean sun is on the meridian of the observer.

**mean proportional**, *Mathematics.* the means in a proportion when they are equal. *Example:* In a:b = b:c, b is the mean proportional.

**means** (mēnz), *n.pl.* **1** what something is done by or the way something is brought about; agency; method: *We won the game by fair means. His quick thinking was the means of saving her life. There are no means that I will not resort to, to discover this infamous plot* (Frederick Marryat). **SYN**: device, instrumentality, expedient, shift, way. **2** wealth; resources: *a man of means, to live beyond one's means.* **SYN**: funds, income, property.
**by all means**, certainly; in any possible way; without fail: *By all means I must visit my sick friend. I must by all means keep this feast* (Acts 18:21).
**by any means**, at all; in any possible way; at any cost: *None of them can by any means redeem his brother* (Psalms 49:7).
**by means of**, by the use of; through; with: *I found my lost dog by means of a notice in the paper.*
**by no means**, certainly not; not at all; in no way: *Mother by no means shared our idea of spending all afternoon looking at television. But her other uncle by no means shared her sentiments* (Lytton Strachey).
**means to an end**, a way of getting or doing something: *This job is only a means to an end for him; he needs the experience to start his own business.*
▶ **Means**, meaning what a thing is done by, is plural in form and singular or plural in use: *A means of communication is lacking. The means of helping others are never lacking. Means,* meaning wealth, is plural in form and in use: *His means permit him to live comfortably.*

**mean solar day**, a day of twenty-four hours, measured from midnight to midnight; civil day.

**mean solar time**, = mean time.

**mean-spir|it|ed** (mēn′spir′ə tid), *adj.* having a mean spirit; small-minded: *Only a very mean-spirited reader would grudge the price of these victories* (Listener).

**means test**, *British.* an examination of a person's financial resources to determine whether he is eligible for financial assistance, such as a scholarship, welfare support, or the like.

**means-test** (mēnz′test′), *v.t. British.* to subject to a means test: *Anyone who qualifies for free welfare milk will not have to be separately means-tested for ophthalmic or dental treatment or for free prescription charges* (Manchester Guardian Weekly).

**mean sun**, a hypothetical sun in various astronomical calculations that moves uniformly along the celestial equator at the mean speed with which the real sun apparently moves along the ecliptic.

**meant** (ment), *v.* past tense and past participle of **mean**[1]: *He explained what he meant. That sign was meant as a warning.*

**mean|time** (mēn′tīm′), *n., adv.* —*n.* the time between. **SYN**: interim, interval.
—*adv.* **1** in the time between. **2** at the same time.

**mean time**, time according to the hour angle of the mean sun, constituting the "ordinary time" or "clock time" of daily life.

**mean|while** (mēn′hwīl′), *n., adv.* = meantime.

**Mearns'** or **Mearns's quail** (mérnz), a small quail of the southwestern United States and Mexico having a multicolored face and no crest. [< Edgar *Mearns,* an American naturalist of the 1900's]

**meas.**, **1** measurable. **2** measure.

**mea|sle** (mē′zəl), *n.* one of the tapeworm larvae that produce measles in pigs and other animals. [singular of *measles*]

**mea|sled** (mē′zeld), *adj.* infected with measles; measly.

**mea|sles** (mē′zelz), *n.* **1** a contagious disease caused by a virus, characterized by the symptoms of a bad cold, fever, and a breaking out of small, red spots on the skin; rubeola. Measles is a disease that is much more common in children than in grown-ups. *What seems to be a cold ... often turns out to be the beginning of measles* (Newsweek). **2** a less severe disease with a similar breaking out; German measles. **3a** a disease of hogs and cattle caused by the larvae of tapeworms. **b** the larvae that cause this disease. [Middle English *maseles* blood blisters; probably influenced by *mezel* leprous < Old French < Latin *misellus* wretch < *miser* wretched]
▶ **Measles** is plural in form but usually singular in use: *Measles is a children's disease.*

**mea|sly** (mē′zlē), *adj.*, **-sli|er**, **-sli|est**. **1** of or like measles. **2** having measles: *measly pork.* **3** *Informal.* scanty; meager: *a measly portion, a measly bit of work.*

**meas|ur|a|bil|i|ty** (mezh′ər ə bil′ə tē, mā′zhər-), *n.* the quality or condition of being measurable.

**meas|ur|a|ble** (mezh′ər ə bəl, mā′zhər-), *adj.* that can be measured. —**meas′ur|a|ble|ness**, *n.*

**meas|ur|a|bly** (mezh′ər ə blē, mā′zhər-), *adv.* to an amount or degree that can be measured; perceptibly: *The sick man has improved measurably since yesterday.* **SYN**: appreciably, discernibly.

**meas|ure** (mezh′ər, mā′zhər), *v.*, **-ured**, **-ur|ing**, *n.* —*v.t.* **1a** to find the size or amount of (anything); find how long, wide, deep, large, or much (a thing) is: *We measured the room and found it was 20 feet long and 15 feet wide. We measured the pail by finding out how many quarts of water it would hold.* **b** to estimate by some standard: *I would measure this room at about 12 by 16 feet.* **2** to mark off or out (in inches, feet, quarts, or some other unit); get, take, or set apart by measuring: *Measure out a bushel of potatoes. Measure off 2 yards of this cloth.* **3** to compare with a standard or with some other person or thing by estimating, judging, or acting: *I measured my swimming ability with his by racing him across the pool. The soldier measured his strength with that of his enemy in a hand-to-hand fight.* **4** to have a measurement of: *The tree measures 40 feet in height.* **5** to serve as a measure of: *A clock measures time.* **6** to adjust; suit: *to measure one's behavior by the company one is in. Measure your needs to your income.* **7** *Archaic.* to travel over; traverse: *She turned back into the room and measured its length with a restless step* (Henry James). **8** *Poetic.* to delimit: *A cloud to measure out their march by day* (William Cowper).
—*v.i.* **1** to be of a certain size or amount: *Buy some paper that measures 8 by 10 inches.* **2** to take measurements; find out size or amount: *Can he measure accurately?* **3** to admit of measurement.
[< Old French *mesurer* < Late Latin *mēnsūrāre* < Latin *mēnsūra:* see the noun]
—*n.* **1** the size, dimensions, quantity, or amount obtained by measuring: *His waist measure is 32 inches.* **2** the act or process of finding the extent, size, quantity, capacity, or other amount, of something, especially by comparison with a standard. **3** something with which to measure. A foot rule, a yardstick, a pint measure, a quart dipper, and a bushel basket are common measures. **4** a unit or standard of measure, such as an inch, a foot, or a meter, a mile or a kilometer, a quart or a liter. Some other common measures are a pound, a gallon, an acre, a peck, and an hour. **5** a system of measurement: *liquid measure, dry measure, square measure.* **6** any standard of comparison, estimation, or judgment; criterion: *Man is the measure of all things. Some ... make themselves the measure of mankind* (Alexander Pope). **7** a quantity or degree that should not be exceeded; limit; bound: *Her joy knew no measure. The bad news distressed him beyond measure.* **8** quantity, degree, or proportion: *a measure of relief. Sickness is in great measure preventable. Carelessness is in large measure responsible for many accidents.* **9** a particular movement or arrangement in poetry or music; time: *the measure in which a poem or song is written.* **10** a metrical unit; foot of verse: *the stately measures of blank verse.* **11** a bar of music. **12** a dance or dance movement, especially when slow and stately: *the measures of a minuet.* **13** an action meant as a means to an end; procedure: *To adopt measures to relieve suffering. What measures shall we take to solve this very puzzling mystery?* **14** a law or proposed law: *This measure has passed the Senate.* **15** *Mathematics.* a number or quantity contained in another some number of times without remainder; factor. **16** a definite quantity measured out: *to drink a measure.* **17** *Poetic.* an air; tune; melody.
**for good measure**, as something extra; as something not necessarily expected: *... while for good measure there are five plays instead of the usual three* (London Times).
**in a measure**, to some degree; partly: *The story was funny in a measure, but it had its serious side, too.*
**measure out, a** to divide; apportion; distribute: *I ... Have known the evenings, mornings, afternoons, I have measured out my life with coffee spoons* (T. S. Eliot). **b** to mete or deal out: *Sermons were measured out with no grudging hand* (Leslie Stephen).
**measures**, strata or beds of a mineral: *The coal measures were found deep in the mine.*
**measure up**, to have the necessary qualifications: *He did not get the job because he just did not measure up.*
**measure up to**, to match: *The party did not measure up to her expectations.*
**take measures**, to do something; act: *The Security Council has taken measures to avert a major crisis.*
**take one's measure**, to judge one's character: *I have encountered a good many of these gentlemen in actual service, and have taken their measure* (Benjamin Jowett).
**tread a measure**, to dance: *Let us gaily tread a measure* (Sir William S. Gilbert).
[< Old French *mesure* < Latin *mēnsūra,* noun < *mēnsus,* past participle of *mētīrī* to measure]
—**meas′ur|er**, *n.*

**meas|ured** (mezh′ərd, mā′zhərd), *adj.* **1** regular; uniform: *the measured march of soldiers, measured portions of food. She hears the measured beating of our horses' hoofs* (Thomas De Quincey). **SYN**: regulated. **2** rhythmical: *measured beats.* **3** written in poetry, not in prose; metrical: *measured lines of poetry. For the unquiet heart and brain, A use in measured language lies* (Tennyson). **4** deliberate and restrained; not hasty or careless: *The angry old man spoke to the boys with measured speech.* **SYN**: moderate, temperate. —**meas′ured|ly**, *adv.*

**measured mile**, a course exactly a mile long, either on land or water, used to check the calibration of an automobile speedometer and mileage indicator, a ship's log, or other device.

**meas|ure|less** (mezh′ər lis, mā′zhər-), *adj.* too great to be measured; unlimited; vast: *the measureless ocean, the measureless prairie.* **SYN**: infinite, immeasurable. —**meas′ure|less|ly**, *adv.* —**meas′ure|less|ness**, *n.*

**meas|ure|ment** (mezh′ər mənt, mā′zhər-), *n.* **1** a way of measuring; way of finding the size, quantity, or amount: *Clocks give us a measurement of time.* **SYN**: gauge. **2** the act or fact of measuring; finding the size, quantity, or amount:

---

**Pronunciation Key:** hat, āge, cãre, fär; let, ēqual, tėrm; it, īce; hot, ōpen, ôrder; oil, out; cup, pu̇t, rüle; child; long; thin; ᴛʜen; zh, measure; ə represents a in about, e in taken, i in pencil, o in lemon, u in circus.

*The measurement of length by a yardstick is easy.* **SYN**: computation, reckoning. **3** size, quantity, or amount found by measuring; dimension: *The measurements of this room are 10 by 15 feet.* **SYN**: extent, capacity. **4** a system of measuring or of measures: *Metric measurement is used in most countries of the world.*

**measurement ton** = freight ton.

**meas|ur|ing rod** (mezh′ər ing, mā′zhər-), yardstick: (*Figurative.*) *By this measuring rod the United States has been moving steadily backward* (Harper's).

**measuring worm**, the larva of certain moths; inchworm. It moves by bringing the rear end of its body forward, forming a loop, and then advancing the front end.

**meat** (mēt), *n.* **1** animal flesh used for food. Fish and poultry are not usually called meat. **2** food of any kind, especially solid food: *meat and drink.* **3** the part of anything that can be eaten: *The meat of the walnut is tasty. Thy head is as full of quarrels as an egg is full of meat* (Shakespeare). **4** *Figurative.* the essential part or parts; food for thought; substance: *the meat of an argument. But the real meat of the book is in the depiction of the moral conflicts keenly felt by these men* (Bulletin of Atomic Scientists). **SYN**: gist. **5** *Slang, Figurative.* something a person finds easy and pleasant to do: *... peninsular warfare is traditionally the Navy's meat* (Time). **6** *Archaic.* a meal, especially the principal meal: *Say grace before meat.* [Old English *mete* food; any item of food; a meal]

**meat and potatoes**, *Informal.* the principal part; foundation; basis: *Textbooks remain the meat and potatoes of publishing in Canada* (Maclean's).

**meat-and-po|ta|toes** (mēt′ən pə tā′tōz), *adj. Informal.* basic; fundamental: *One would like to urge [him] to leave the meat-and-potatoes repertory for which his style of playing is not best suited for more contemporary cuisine* (New York Times).

**meat ax** or **axe**, **1** a butcher's cleaver used to chop roughly through meat and bone. **2** *Figurative.* a ruthless and sometimes indiscriminate hacking away: *The House assaulted the Administration's defense request with meat axes, lopped off some $2.5 billion* (Time).

**meat ball**, or **meat|ball** (mēt′bôl′), *n.* **1** a ball of chopped or ground meat, cooked and usually served in gravy or sauce, especially with spaghetti: *a spicy Italian meat ball.* **2** *Slang.* an uninteresting and uninspired person: *"What have these meat balls been handing you?" he inquired* (New Yorker). **3** *Naval.* **a** the target aimed at by an airplane landing on an aircraft carrier in a mirror landing system. It is a ball of light focused upon a mirror from four different sources. **b** *Slang.* a battle efficiency pennant.

**meat bird**, or **meat|bird** (mēt′bėrd′), *n.* = Canada jay.

**meat-eat|er** (mēt′ē′tər), *n.* **1** a carnivore. **2** a person who includes meat in his diet.

**meat|head** (mēt′hed′), *n. Slang.* a stupid person.

**meat|less** (mēt′lis), *adj.* **1** without meat. **2** on which no meat is sold or eaten: *meatless Tuesday.*

**meat|man** (mēt′man′), *n., pl.* **-men.** a man who sells meat; butcher.

**meat packing**, the business of slaughtering animals and preparing their meat for transportation and sale: *Poor returns on pork have cut earnings of the meat packing industry* (Wall Street Journal).

**meat-safe** (mēt′sāf′), *n.* a cupboard with walls of wire gauze, perforated zinc, or the like, for storing food.

**meat tea**, *British.* a tea at which meat is served; high tea.

**meat-type** (mēt′tīp′), *adj.* raised or bred to turn feed into meat instead of extra fat: *a meat-type hog.*

**me|a|tus** (mē ā′təs), *n., pl.* **-tus|es** or **-tus.** a passage, duct, or opening in the body, as in the ear. [< Latin *meātus* path < *meāre* to pass]

**meat wagon**, *Slang.* an ambulance.

**meat|work|er** (mēt′wėr′kər), *n.* a slaughterhouse or packing-house worker in Australia.

**meat|works** (mēt′wėrks′), *n.* a slaughterhouse or packing house in Australia.

**meat|y** (mē′tē), *adj.,* **meat|i|er, meat|i|est.** **1** of meat; having the flavor of meat: *some choice meaty bits.* **2** like meat: *a meaty texture.* **3** full of meat; fleshy: *a meaty roast with little bone.* **4** *Figurative.* full of substance; giving food for thought; pithy: *The speech was very meaty; it contained many valuable ideas.* — **meat′i|ly,** *adv.* — **meat′i|ness,** *n.*

**me|ca|myl|a|mine** (mek′ə mil′ə mēn), *n.* **1** a nerve-blocking drug used in controlling high blood pressure. *Formula:* $C_{11}H_{21}N$ **2** *Mecamylamine.* a trademark for this drug.

**Mec|ca** or **mec|ca** (mek′ə), *n.* **1** a place that many people visit: *[The] Duquesne Club, lunchtime Mecca for some of the nation's top businessmen ...* (Wall Street Journal). **2** *Figurative.* a place that a person longs to visit. **3** *Figurative.* the goal of one's desires or ambitions. Also, **Mekka.** [< *Mecca,* the sacred city of Islam, in Saudi Arabia, where Moslems go on pilgrimages]

**Mec|can** (mek′ən), *adj., n.* — *adj.* of or having to do with Mecca.
— *n.* a native or inhabitant of Mecca.

**mech.,** **1** mechanical. **2** mechanics. **3** mechanism.

**me|chan|ic** (mə kan′ik), *n., adj.* — *n.* **1** a workman skilled with tools, especially one who makes, repairs, and uses machines: *a typewriter mechanic, an automobile mechanic.* **2** *Archaic.* a person who works with his hands; artisan.
— *adj.* = mechanical. [< Latin *mēchanicus* < Greek *mēchanikós* < *mēchanē* machine < *mêchos* a means, expedient]

**me|chan|i|cal** (mə kan′ə kəl), *adj., n.* — *adj.* **1** of or having something to do with machinery: *Mechanical problems are usually more interesting to boys than to girls.* **2** made or worked by machinery. **3** *Figurative.* like a machine; automatic; without expression or feeling: *Her reading is very mechanical.* **SYN**: stereotyped. **4** having to do with or in accordance with the science of mechanics: *a mechanical law.* **5** *Archaic.* of or having to do with artisans.
— *n.* **1** a mechanical part or object: *The basic mechanicals—artwork, films, and so on—were ... produced in Italy* (Murry Leask). **2** *Printing.* a finished piece of copy ready for photomechanical reproduction. — **me|chan′i|cal|ness,** *n.*

**mechanical advantage**, the ratio of resistance or load to the force or effort that is applied in a machine. Mechanical advantage is shown by the number of times a machine increases the force exerted on it. *We call the amount of help we get from a machine its mechanical advantage.*

**mechanical drawing**, drawing of machines, tools, other devices, and buildings, done to exact scale with instruments such as rulers, squares, compasses, triangles, templates, and curves.

**mechanical efficiency**, the ratio of the horsepower of an engine actually produced to the horsepower it could theoretically produce.

**mechanical energy**, **1** the energy transmitted by a machine or machinery; energy in the form of mechanical power: *The largest single loss ... occurs when heat energy is converted into mechanical energy* (New Scientist). **2** *Physics.* the kinetic plus the potential energy of a body: *Provided there are no frictional or other dissipative effects, the total mechanical energy of a system of bodies remains constant* (Shortley and Williams).

**mechanical engineer**, a person skilled in mechanical engineering.

**mechanical engineering**, the branch of engineering that deals with the production and use of mechanical power and machinery.

**me|chan|i|cal|ize** (mə kan′ə kə līz), *v.t.,* **-ized, -iz|ing.** to make mechanical.

**mechanical laughter**, laughter recorded to accompany the sound track of a television or radio program: *Producers believe "mechanical laughter" creates a responsive mood in the living room for watching a comedy or variety show* (Jack Gould).

**me|chan|i|cal|ly** (mə kan′ə klē), *adv.* **1** in a mechanical manner: (*Figurative.*) *He greeted us mechanically.* **2** in mechanical respects: *That new engine is mechanically perfect.* **3** toward mechanics: *Boys are usually more mechanically inclined than girls.*

**mechanical mixture**, a mixture in which the several ingredients have not entered into chemical combination, but still retain their identity and can be separated by mechanical means.

**mechanical mule**, a low-built vehicle used by the United States Army for transporting men and supplies.

**mech|a|ni|cian** (mek′ə nish′ən), *n.* = mechanic.

**me|chan|ics** (mə kan′iks), *n.* **1** the branch of physics dealing with the action of forces on solids, liquids, and gases at rest or in motion. Mechanics includes kinetics, statics, and kinematics. **2** knowledge dealing with machinery: *Any auto mechanic must be familiar with mechanics.* **3** the mechanical part; technique: *The mechanics of playing the piano are easy for some people to acquire.*

**mechanic's lien**, **1** a claim for materials or labor furnished by a contractor in the construction of a building. **2** any claim against property for work or services provided on the property.

**mech|a|nise** (mek′ə nīz), *v.t.,* **-nised, -nis|ing.** *Especially British.* mechanize.

**mech|a|nism** (mek′ə niz əm), *n.* **1** a machine or its working parts: *the mechanism of a watch. Something is wrong with the mechanism of our refrigerator. An automobile engine is a complex mechanism.* **2** a system of parts working together as the parts of a machine do: *The bones and muscles are parts of the mechanism of the body.* **3** the means or way by which something is done; machinery: *The mechanism of human speech,* (*Figurative.*) *the ancient mechanisms of the law grinding toward justice.* **4** the mechanical part; technique, as in painting or music. **5** *Psychology.* **a** the arrangements in the mind or brain that determine thought, feeling, or action in regular and predictable ways. **b** a response unconsciously selected to protect oneself or find satisfaction for an unfulfilled desire: *a defense mechanism.* **6** *Philosophy.* the theory that everything in the universe is produced and can be explained by mechanical or material forces: *the influence of mechanism and materialism in science* (Science News).

**mech|a|nist** (mek′ə nist), *n., adj.* — *n.* **1** a person who believes in the philosophical theory of mechanism. **2** *Archaic.* a mechanic.
— *adj.* mechanistic: *mechanist philosophy, a mechanist approach to language.*

**mech|a|nis|tic** (mek′ə nis′tik), *adj.* **1** of or having to do with mechanics or mechanical theories: *We may regard Newton's laws of motion as the supreme model of mechanistic determinism* (Scientific American). **2** of or having to do with the belief that everything in the universe is produced by and can be explained by mechanical or material forces. — **mech′a|nis′ti|cal|ly,** *adv.*

**mech|a|nize** (mek′ə nīz), *v.t.,* **-nized, -niz|ing.** **1** to do by machinery, rather than by hand: *Much housework can be mechanized.* **2** to replace men or animals by machinery in (a business or other enterprise): *to mechanize a factory.* **3** to make mechanical: *Raphael paints wisdom; Handel sings it, ... Shakespeare writes it, ... Watt mechanizes it* (Emerson). **4** to equip (a military unit) with armored vehicles, tanks, and other machines. — **mech′a|niz′a|ble,** *adj.* — **mech′a|ni|za′tion,** *n.* — **mech′a|niz′er,** *n.*

**mech|a|no|car|di|og|ra|phy** (mek′ə nō kär′dē og′rə fē), *n.* a method of measuring the rate at which blood is pumped from the heart by the combined use of an electrocardiograph and X ray.

**mech|a|no|chem|i|cal** (mek′ə nō kem′ə kəl), *adj.* of or having to do with mechanochemistry.

**mech|a|no|chem|is|try** (mek′ə nō kem′ə strē), *n.* the study of the means by which chemical substances can be used to produce mechanical energy.

**mech|a|no|mor|phic** (mek′ə nō môr′fik), *adj.* of or having to do with mechanomorphism: *mechanomorphic psychology.*

**mech|a|no|mor|phism** (mek′ə nō môr′fiz əm), *n.* any doctrine or theory that conceives of or explains something only in mechanistic terms.

**mech|a|no|re|cep|tion** (mek′ə nō ri sep′shən), *n.* response to mechanical stimuli by a sense organ: *the mechanoreception of chordotonal organs.*

**mech|a|no|re|cep|tor** (mek′ə nō ri sep′tər), *n.* a sense organ that responds to mechanical stimuli: *The mechanoreceptors in muscle respond to ... stimuli such as stretching and pressure* (Scientific American).

**mech|a|no|ther|a|pist** (mek′ə nō ther′ə pist), *n.* a person who is skilled in or performs mechanotherapy: *The mechanotherapist aids nature with mechanical methods such as movement or exercise* (W. W. Bauer).

**mech|a|no|ther|a|py** (mek′ə nō ther′ə pē), *n.* therapy by mechanical means, as for relieving muscle stiffness: *Mechanotherapy includes gymnastics and massage* (W. W. Bauer). [< Greek *mēchanē* machine + English *therapy*]

**mé|chant** (mā shän′), *adj. French.* malicious; mischievous; naughty; bad: *Mr. Pendennis was wicked, méchant, perfectly abominable* (Thackeray).

**mé|chante** (mā shänt′), *adj. French.* the feminine form of **méchant.**

***Mech|lin** (mek′lən), *n.,* or **Mechlin lace,** a fine lace with the pattern clearly outlined by a distinct thread; malines. [< *Mechlin,* a city in Belgium, where it is made]

***Mechlin**

**mec|li|zine** (mek′lə zēn), *n.* = Bonine.

**me|con|ic** (mi kon′ik), *adj.* of or derived from

the poppy. [< Greek *mēkōn* poppy]

**meconic acid**, a white crystalline acid derived from opium. It is used in medicine. *Formula:* $C_7H_4O_7$

**me|co|ni|um** (mə kō′nē əm), *n.* a green material discharged from the fetal intestine after birth. [< Latin *meconium* < Greek *mēkōnion* (diminutive) < *mēkōn* poppy]

**mec|o|nop|sis** (mek′ə nop′sis), *n., pl.* **-ses** (-sēz). any one of a group of plants of the poppy family with a style bearing from four to six radiating stigmas. [< Greek *mēkōn* poppy + *ópsis* appearance]

**med.**, an abbreviation for the following:
**1** median.
**2a** medical. **b** medicine.
**3** medieval.
**4** medium.

**Med.**, **1** medieval. **2** Mediterranean.

**M.Ed.**, Master of Education.

**med|al** (med′əl), *n., v.,* **-aled, -al|ing** or (*especially British*) **-alled, -al|ling.** — ***n.*** a piece of metal like a coin, with a figure or inscription stamped on it, given as an award for achievement or to celebrate an important event. Other medals are sometimes worn to invoke the favor of a saint. *The captain won a medal for bravery. She won the gold medal for having the highest marks in the school. The medal is in silver and bears on the obverse an effigy of the Queen* (London Times).
— ***v.t.*** to decorate or honor with a medal: *Irving went home, medalled by the king* (Thackeray).
[< Middle French *médaille* < Italian *medaglia* < Vulgar Latin *metallea* < Latin *metallum* metal, medal < Greek *métallon* mine, quarry, metal]

**Medal for Merit**, a decoration given by the United States to a civilian for exceptional or outstanding service to the country.

**med|al|ist** (med′ə list), *n.* **1** a person who designs or makes medals. **2** a person who has won a medal.

**me|dal|lic** (mə dal′ik), *adj.* having to do with or like a medal.

**me|dal|lion** (mə dal′yən), *n.* **1** a large medal. **2** a design or ornament shaped like a medal. A design on a book or a pattern in lace may be called a medallion. **3** *U.S.* **a** a license or permit to operate a taxicab, issued in the form of a medallion which is purchased by the licensee: *A government contract is awarded to the bidder who will best serve the government's interest or to the one who submits the lowest bid. The theory is extended to taxicab medallions and turnpike concessions* (Charles A. Reich). **b** a taxicab operated with such a license. [< French *médaillon* < Italian *medaglione* large medal < *medaglia* medal]

**me|dal|lioned** (mə dal′yənd), *adj.* ornamented with a medallion or medallions; formed into a medallion.

**me|dal|lion|ist** (mə dal′yə nist), *n.* a maker of medallions.

**med|al|list** (med′ə list), *n. Especially British.* medalist.

**Medal of Freedom**, = Presidential Medal of Freedom.

**Medal of Honor**, the highest military decoration of the United States, given by Congress to members of the armed forces for bravery in combat at the risk of their lives and beyond the call of duty.

**medal play**, a form of golf in which the player or side that scores the lowest number of strokes is the winner; stroke play.

**med|dle** (med′əl), *v.i.,* **-dled, -dling. 1** to busy oneself with other people's things or affairs without being asked or needed: *Don't meddle with my books or my toys. That busybody has been meddling in my business.* **2** *Obsolete.* to fight; contend. **3** *Obsolete.* to associate; mingle. [< Old French *medler,* ultimately < Latin *miscēre* to mix]
— ***Syn.* 1 Meddle, tamper, interfere** mean to concern oneself unnecessarily or unduly with someone or something. **Meddle** implies busying oneself, without right or permission, with something not one's own affair: *One country should not meddle in the internal affairs of another.* **Tamper** suggests meddling in order to experiment with a thing or improperly influence a person: *Don't tamper with electrical appliances.* **Interfere** suggests meddling in a way that disturbs or hinders: *She interferes when we scold the children.*

**med|dler** (med′lər), *n.* a person who interferes or meddles.

**med|dle|some** (med′əl səm), *adj.* likely to meddle in other people's affairs; meddling; interfering: *He was curious, meddlesome, gossipy* (Atlantic). **SYN:** officious. — **med′dle|some|ly,** *adv.* — **med′dle|some|ness,** *n.*

**Mede** (mēd), *n.* a person who was born or lived in Media, an ancient country in southwestern Asia.

**Me|de|a** (mi dē′ə), *n.* **1** *Greek Legend.* an enchantress who helped Jason win the Golden Fleece. She eloped with Jason and was later deserted by him. **2a** a play by Euripides. **b** the heroine of this play.

**med|e|vac** or **Med|e|vac** (med′i vak′), *n., v.,* **-vacked, -vack|ing.** *U.S.* — ***n.*** a helicopter for evacuating the wounded from a combat zone.
— ***v.t.*** to transport by a medevac.
[< *med*(ical) *evac*(uation)]

**Med|fly** (med′flī′), *n., pl.* **-flies.** = Mediterranean fruit fly.

**me|di|a**[1] (mē′dē ə), *n.* **1** a plural of **medium**: *Newspapers, magazines, and billboards are important media for advertising.* **2** = medium (def. 2). **3** = mass media.
► See **medium** for usage note.

**me|di|a**[2] (mē′dē ə), *n., pl.* **-di|ae** (-dē ē). **1** the middle layer of the wall of a blood or lymphatic vessel. **2** *Phonetics.* a voiced stop, such as *b, d,* or *g.* [< Latin *media,* feminine of *medius* middle]

**me|di|a|cy** (mē′dē ə sē), *n.* **1** a being mediate. **2** *Obsolete.* mediation.

**me|di|ad** (mē′dē ad), *adv.* toward the middle line or plane (of a body).

**me|di|ae|val** (mē′dē ē′vəl, med′ē-), *adj.* = medieval. — **me′di|ae′val|ly,** *adv.*

**me|di|ae|val|ism** (mē′dē ē′və liz əm, med′ē-), *n.* = medievalism. — **me′di|ae′val|ist,** *n.*

**media event**, an event especially arranged to be publicized through the news media; pseudo-event: *His travels today ... were only the first leg of an elaborately extensive, two-day, 950-mile media event* (New York Times).

**me|di|a|gen|ic** (mē′dē ə jen′ik), *adj.* suitable for the communications media; having an attractive or appealing public image: [*He*] *hopes to find someone young and mediagenic, politically moderate to balance his own brand of midwest conservatism* (Newsweek). [patterned on *photogenic*]

**me|di|al** (mē′dē əl), *adj., n.* — ***adj.*** **1** in the middle; middle. **SYN:** intermediate, median. **2** having to do with a mathematical mean or average. **3** average; ordinary. **4** *Phonetics.* occurring in the middle of or within a word: *In "dairy" the "i" is in medial position.*
— ***n.*** **1** a medial letter. **2** a form of a letter used in the middle of a word.
[< Late Latin *mediālis* (of the) middle < Latin *medius* middle]

**me|di|al|ly** (mē′dē ə lē), *adv.* in the middle; in a medial position.

**medial moraine**, the moraine that occurs when the lateral moraines of two glaciers meet and merge.

**me|di|a|man** (mē′dē ə mən), *n., pl.* **-men.** an employee of an advertising agency who evaluates and selects media for carrying the advertisements of clients.

**me|di|an** (mē′dē ən), *adj., n.* — ***adj.*** **1** of or in the middle; middle: *the median vein of a leaf.* **2** having to do with or designating the plane that divides something into two equal parts, especially one dividing a symmetrical animal into right and left halves. **3** of a median; having as many above as below a certain number: *The median age of the population was found to be 21* (*that is, there were as many persons above 21 as below it*), *while the average age was found to be 25.*
— ***n.*** **1** the middle number of a series. If the sequence has an even number of values, the median is the average of the two middle values. *Examples:* the median of 1, 3, 4, 8, 9 is 4. The median of 1, 3, 4, 8, 9, 10 is 6. **2a** a line from a vertex of a triangle to the midpoint of the opposite side. **b** the line joining the midpoints of the nonparallel sides of a trapezoid. *Abbr:* med. **3** = median strip. *Abbr:* med.
[< Latin *mediānus* of the middle < *medius* middle. See etym. of doublet **mean**[3].] — **me′di|an|ly,** *adv.*

**Me|di|an** (mē′dē ən), *adj., n.* — ***adj.*** of Media or the Medes. — ***n.*** = Mede.

**median strip**, the strip of land, usually grass-covered or landscaped, between the lanes for traffic going in opposite directions on some modern highways and expressways.

**me|di|ant** (mē′dē ənt), *n.* the third note or tone of a diatonic musical scale, halfway from the tonic or keynote to the dominant. See picture under **dominant.** [< Italian *mediante* < Late Latin *mediāns, -antis,* present participle of *mediārī;* see etym. under **mediate**]

**me|di|as|ti|nal** (mē′dē as tī′nəl), *adj.* or or having to do with the mediastinum.

**me|di|as|ti|num** (mē′dē as tī′nəm), *n., pl.* **-na** (-nə). **1** a middle partition between two body cavities or parts. **2** a partition formed by the two pleurae between the lungs, including the enclosed space in which are all the viscera of the thorax except the lungs. [< New Latin *mediastinum* < Medieval Latin *mediastinus* intermediate; the meaning is < Latin *medius* middle; the form is < Latin *mediastīnus* inferior servant < *mediānus;* see etym. under **median**]

**me|di|ate** (*v.* mē′dē āt; *adj.* mē′dē it), *v.,* **-at|ed, -at|ing,** *adj.* — ***v.i.*** **1** to come in to help settle a dispute; be a go-between; act in order to bring about an agreement between persons or sides: *Mother mediated in the quarrel between the two boys. The mayor tried to mediate between the bus company and its employees.* **2** to occupy an intermediate place or position.
— ***v.t.*** **1** to effect by intervening; settle by intervening: *to mediate an agreement, to mediate a strike.* **2** to be a connecting link between. **3** to be the medium for effecting (a result), for conveying (a gift), or for communicating (knowledge).
— ***adj.*** **1** connected, but not directly; connected through some other person or thing: *A vassal's relation with his king was mediate through the lord on whose estate he lived.* **2** intermediate: *After many mediate preferments ... at last he became Archbishop of Canterbury* (Thomas Fuller).
[< Late Latin *mediārī* (with English *-ate*[1]) to be in the middle, intervene < Latin *medius* middle]
— **me′di|ate|ly,** *adv.* — **me′di|ate|ness,** *n.*

**me|di|a|tion** (mē′dē ā′shən), *n.* the action of mediating; effecting an agreement; friendly intervention, especially to effect an agreement or reconciliation: *the mediation of friendly nations.*

**me|di|a|tive** (mē′dē ā′tiv), *adj.* = mediatory.

**me|di|a|tize** (mē′dē ə tīz), *v.t.,* **-tized, -tiz|ing. 1** (in the Holy Roman Empire) to reduce (a prince, principality, or other entity) from a position of direct or immediate vassalage to the empire to one of indirect or mediate vassalage. **2** to annex (a principality) to another state while leaving some rights of government to its former sovereign. **3** to make mediate in position. — **me′di|a|ti|za′tion,** *n.*

**me|di|a|tor** (mē′dē ā′tər), *n.* a person or group that mediates: *Mother acts as a mediator when the children quarrel. The unions ... had refused to accept the intervention of an official mediator* (London Times).

**me|di|a|to|ri|al** (mē′dē ə tôr′ē əl, -tōr′-), *adj.* = mediatory.

**me|di|a|tor|ship** (mē′dē ā′tər ship), *n.* the office or function of a mediator.

**me|di|a|to|ry** (mē′dē ə tôr′ē, -tōr′-), *adj.* of or having to do with mediation; mediating.

**me|di|a|tress** (mē′dē ā′tris), *n.* = mediatrix.

**me|di|a|trice** (mē′dē ā′tris), *n.* = mediatrix.

**me|di|a|trix** (mē′dē ā′triks), *n., pl.* **-tri|ces** or **-trix|es.** a woman mediator. [< Latin *mediātrix,* feminine of *mediātor* mediator]

**med|ic**[1] (med′ik), *n. Informal.* **1** a soldier or sailor in the medical corps who is trained to perform medical services, especially giving first aid in combat: *Army medics knocked out their* [*Korean POWs'*] *malaria* (Newsweek). **2** a medical student. **3** a physician. [< Latin *medicus* physician; adjective, healing < *medērī* to heal]

**med|ic**[2] (med′ik), *n.* any one of a genus of herbs of the pea family, with purple or yellow flowers. Alfalfa is a kind of medic. [< Latin *Medica* < Greek (*póa*) *Medikē* Median (herb), lucerne]

**med|i|ca|ble** (med′ə kə bəl), *adj.* that can be cured or relieved by medical treatment; curable. [< Latin *medicābilis* < *medicārī* to heal < *medicus;* see etym. under **medic**[1]]

**Med|i|caid** or **med|i|caid** (med′ə kād), *n. U.S.* a program sponsored by the federal, state, and local governments, providing medical benefits for needy or disabled persons not covered by social security: *While Medicare covers persons over 65 ... Medicaid is a federal-state-local venture to help the "medically indigent" regardless of age* (Time). [< *medic*(al) *aid*]

**med|i|cal** (med′ə kəl), *adj., n.* — ***adj.*** **1** of or having to do with healing or with the science and practice of medicine: *medical advice, a medical school, medical treatment. Abbr:* med. **2** curative; medicinal.
— ***n.*** **1** a medical examination: *... the door was flung open and a warden shouted "Get ready for your medicals"* (Punch). **2** *Informal.* a medical student or a doctor: *I remain as skeptical as most medicals about male pattern baldness* (Maclean's).
[< French *médical,* learned borrowing from Late Latin *medicālis* < Latin *medicus* doctor; see etym. under **medic**[1]] — **med′i|cal|ly,** *adv.*

**medical examiner**, **1** an official, especially a doctor or coroner, appointed by a local government to examine the bodies of persons who died by suicide, murder, or otherwise violently, perform autopsies, and attempt to determine the circumstances of death. **2** a doctor who is in charge of

---

**Pronunciation Key:** hat, āge, cãre, fär; let, ēqual, tėrm; it, īce; hot, ōpen, ôrder; oil, out; cup, pu̇t, rüle; child; long; thin; ᴛʜen; zh, measure; ə represents **a** in about, **e** in taken, **i** in pencil, **o** in lemon, **u** in circus.

examining persons applying for accident insurance, workmen's compensation, and the like: *Medical examiners can and should ... consider the kind and location of the applicant's cancer* (Science News Letter).

**medical geography**, the study of the influence of geography and natural environment on health, vital functions, and diseases.

**medical jurisprudence**, = forensic medicine.

**me|dic|a|ment** (mə dik′ə mənt, med′ə kə-), *n., v.* —*n.* a substance used to cure or heal; medicine. —*v.t.* to treat with medicine; medicate: *He ... had been treated and medicamented as the doctor ordained* (Thackeray).
[< Latin *medicāmentum* < *medicārī* to heal < *medicus* healing; a doctor; see etym. under **medic**[1]]

**med|i|ca|men|tal** (med′ə kə men′təl), *adj.* of or like a medicament; medicinal.

**med|i|ca|men|ta|ry** (med′ə kə men′tər ē), *adj.* = medicamental.

**med|i|ca|men|tous** (med′ə kə men′təs), *adj.* = medicamental.

**Med|i|care** or **med|i|care** (med′ə kãr′), *n.* **1** *U.S.* a program of medical care and hospital services sponsored by the federal government for persons sixty-five years old or older. **2** *Canada.* a government-sponsored program of health insurance. [< *medi*(cal) *care*]

**med|i|cas|ter** (med′ə kas′tər), *n.* a pretender to medical skill; quack: *Impostors and visionaries and swindlers and medicasters ... hastened to Rome* (Hendrik Van Loon). [< Latin *medicus* physician + *-aster,* a diminutive suffix]

**med|i|cate** (med′ə kāt), *v.t.,* **-cat|ed, -cat|ing.** **1** to treat with medicine: *to medicate a cold.* **2** to put medicine on or in: *The doctor medicated the gauze before applying the bandage.* [< Latin *medicārī* (with English *-ate*[1]) < *medicus* healing; a doctor; see etym. under **medic**[1]]

**med|i|cat|ed** (med′ə kā′tid), *adj.* containing medicine: *medicated gauze. Cough drops are medicated.*

**med|i|ca|tion** (med′ə kā′shən), *n.* **1** treatment with medicine. **2** the act of putting medicine on or in. **3** = medicament.

**med|i|ca|tive** (med′ə kā′tiv), *adj.* curative or healing; medicinal.

**Med|i|ce|an** (med′ə sē′ən, -chē′-), *adj.* of, having to do with, or like the Medici, a wealthy and powerful Florentine family from the 1400's to the 1600's, famous as rulers of Tuscany and as patrons of many artists, sculptors, and writers: *He lived a life of ... Medicean splendor* (Harper's).

**med|i|chair** (med′ə chãr′), *n.* a chair with electronic sensors to monitor the physiological activity of a person: *Scientists have developed an instrumented chair that gives a person a quick basic medical check-up in one sitting ... This medichair was demonstrated for the first time ... at the opening session of the annual meeting of the Aero-space Medical Association* (New York Times). [< *medi*(cal) *chair*]

**me|dic|i|na|ble** (mə dis′ə nə bəl), *adj. Archaic.* curative; medicinal: (*Figurative.*) *Some griefs are med'cinable; that is one of them, For it doth physic love* (Shakespeare).

**me|dic|i|nal** (mə dis′ə nəl), *adj.; n.* —*adj.* having value as medicine; healing; helping; relieving: *the medicinal effect of soaking a strained muscle.* (*Figurative.*) *Clearing one's conscience is medicinal for the soul.*
—*n.* something which is or can be used as a medicine.

**medicinal leech**, a European leech, about four inches long, formerly used for taking blood from sick people.

**me|dic|i|nal|ly** (mə dis′ə nə lē), *adv.* as medicine.

**med|i|cine** (med′ə sən), *n., v.,* **-cined, -cin|ing.** —*n.* **1** any substance, such as a drug, used to treat, prevent, or cure disease or improve health: *The sick boy has to take his medicine three times a day.* (*Figurative.*) *The miserable have no other medicine but only hope* (Shakespeare). **2** the science of treating, preventing, or curing disease; study or practice of maintaining and improving health: *The young doctor had studied medicine for a number of years.* **3** the field of medicine, especially internal medicine, as distinguished from surgery or obstetrics. **4a** any object or ceremony, such as a spell, charm, or fetish, that certain primitive peoples believe has magic power over disease, evil spirits, or unfavorable circumstances. **b** the magic power that primitive peoples believe certain men have over disease, evil spirits, and other things. **5** *Figurative.* any influence that effects an improvement: *Another tax cut could well be regarded as just the right medicine* (New York Times). **6** = medicine man. **7** *Obsolete.* a drug, love potion, or poison: *If the rascal have not given me medicines to make me love him, I'll be hanged* (Shakespeare).
—*v.t.* to give medicine to; affect by or as if by medicine.
**take one's medicine**, to do what one must; do something one dislikes to do: *Canada can do nothing—she must take her medicine and make the best of it* (New York Times).
[< Old French *medicine, medecine,* learned borrowings from Latin *medicīna* (originally) of a doctor < *medicus* physician; see etym. under **medic**[1]]

**medicine ball**, a large, heavy, stuffed leather ball tossed from one person to another for exercise.

**medicine dance**, a ceremonial dance of primitive peoples to cure disease or produce magic.

**medicine lodge**, a lodge used by North American Indians for medicine dances and other rites.

**medicine man**, a man supposed by the early North American Indians and certain primitive peoples to have magic power over diseases, evil spirits, and other things; shaman.

**med|i|cin|er** (med′ə sə nər), *n. Archaic.* a physician: *It is unbecoming a mediciner of thine eminence to interfere with the practice of another* (Scott).

**medicine show**, *U.S.* a traveling show at which patent medicines, remedies, and cure-alls were formerly advertised and sold: *The days of the medicine show are over* (Maclean's).

**med|i|co** (med′ə kō), *n., pl.* **-cos.** *Informal.* **1** a doctor; physician: *The medico held my chin in the usual way, and examined my throat* (Alexander W. Kinglake). **2** a medical student. [< Italian *medico,* or Spanish *médico* physician, learned borrowings from Latin *medicus;* see etym. under **medic**[1]]

**medico-**, *combining form.* medical and ____, as in *medicolegal.* [< New Latin *medico-* < Latin *medicus* physician]

**med|i|co|chi|rur|gi|cal** (med′ə kō kī rėr′jə kəl), *adj.* having to do with both medicine and surgery.

**med|i|co|le|gal** (med′ə kō lē′gəl), *adj.* of or having to do with forensic medicine; medical and legal: *... medicolegal problems such as the determination of disputed paternity, based on the inheritance of the various blood groups and types* (Lawrence H. Snyder).

**me|di|e|val** (mē′dē ē′vəl, med′ē-), *adj.* **1** belonging to or having to do with the Middle Ages (the years from about 500 to about 1450 A.D.): *The Cathedral Church of Saint Peter ... is the largest medieval cathedral in England* (Newsweek). *Abbr:* med. **2** like that of the Middle Ages. Also, **mediaeval.** [< Latin *medium,* neuter, middle + *aevum* age + English *-al*[1]] —**me′di|e′val|ly,** *adv.*

**Medieval Greek**, the Greek language during the Middle Ages, from about 700 A.D. to about 1500 A.D.; Middle Greek.

**me|di|e|val|ism** (mē′dē ē′və liz əm, med′ē-), *n.* **1** the spirit, ideals, and customs of the Middle Ages; medieval thought, religion, and art. **2** devotion to medieval ideals; adoption of medieval customs. **3** a medieval belief, custom, or idea. Also, **mediaevalism.**

**me|di|e|val|ist** (mē′dē ē′və list, med′ē-), *n.* **1** an expert on the Middle Ages: *a Cambridge University medievalist* (New Yorker). **2** a person who is in sympathy with medieval ideals or customs. Also, **mediaevalist.**

**Medieval Latin**, the Latin language during the Middle Ages, from about 700 A.D. to about 1500 A.D.; Middle Latin.

**me|di|na** (mə dē′nə), *n.* the native Arab quarter of a city in North Africa: *the medina of Marrakech, the Casablanca medina.* [< Arabic *madīna* town]

**me|di|o|cre** (mē′dē ō′kər, mē′dē ō′-), *adj.* of average quality: neither bad nor good; ordinary: *a mediocre book, a mediocre student, a mediocre performance, a person of mediocre abilities.* SYN: medium, commonplace, indifferent. [< Old French *mediocre,* learned borrowing from Latin *mediocris* (originally) halfway up < *medius* middle (of) + *ocris* jagged mountain]

**me|di|oc|ri|ty** (mē′dē ok′rə tē), *n., pl.* **-ties.** **1** quality that is neither good nor bad; mediocre quality: *Mediocrity knows nothing higher than itself, but talent instantly recognizes genius* (Sir Arthur Conan Doyle). **2** a mediocre ability or accomplishment. **3** a mediocre person.

**Medit.**, Mediterranean.

**med|i|tate** (med′ə tāt), *v.,* **-tat|ed, -tat|ing.** —*v.i.* to think quietly; engage in deep and serious thought; reflect: *In some orders monks and nuns meditate on holy things for hours at a time. He quitted her presence to meditate upon revenge* (Frederick Marryat). SYN: ponder, muse, cogitate. See syn. under **think.**
—*v.t.* **1** to think about; consider; plan; intend: *They are meditating a reimposition of the tax on corn* (Manchester Examiner). *All men that meditate peace, be allowed safe conduct* (Thomas Hobbes). **2** to observe intently: *The ready spaniel ... meditates the prey* (Alexander Pope).
[< Latin *meditārī* (with English *-ate*[1])]

**med|i|ta|tion** (med′ə tā′shən), *n.* **1** quiet thought; reflection. **2** contemplation on sacred or solemn subjects, especially as a devotional exercise. **3** a contemplative or devotional writing or talk.

**med|i|ta|tive** (med′ə tā′tiv), *adj.* **1** fond of meditating; inclined to meditate; thoughtful: *I'm just not the meditative type* (New Yorker). **2** expressing meditation: *a meditative manner, a meditative essay.* **3** engaged or lost in meditation: *He was gazing, rapt and meditative, at the hallway to the kitchen* (Elizabeth Cullinan). —**med′i|ta′tive|ly,** *adv.* —**med′i|ta′tive|ness,** *n.*

**med|i|ta|tor** (med′ə tā′tər), *n.* a person who meditates.

**med|i|ter|ra|ne|an** (med′ə tə rā′nē ən, -rān′yən), *adj.* nearly or entirely enclosed by land; landlocked. [< Latin *mediterrāneus* (< *medius* middle (of) + *terra* land, earth) + English *-an*]

**Med|i|ter|ra|ne|an** (med′ə tə rā′nē ən, -rān′yən), *adj., n.* —*adj.* of or having to do with the Mediterranean Sea or the lands around it. **2** of or having to do with a class of chicken that includes Leghorns, Blue Andalusians, and Minorcas.
—*n.* **1** one of the generally recognized principal subgroups of the Caucasoid or Caucasian racial group, chiefly found on the shores of the Mediterranean Sea, and characterized by dark eyes, hair, and skin, narrow nose and head, and relatively short stature. **2** a member of this group.
[< Late Latin (*mare*) *Mediterrāneum* Mediterranean (Sea)]

**Mediterranean anemia**, = thalassemia.

**Mediterranean fever**, = undulant fever.

**Mediterranean flour moth**, = flour moth.

**Mediterranean fruit fly**, a very destructive fly, about the size of the common housefly, whose larvae attack fruits and vegetables. It is found in warm regions of the world. Also, **Medfly.**

**me|di|um** (mē′dē əm), *adj., n., pl.* **-di|ums** or (*also for 2, 3, and 4*) **-di|a.** —*adj.* having a middle position, quality, or condition; moderate: *Eggs can be cooked hard, soft, or medium. Five feet eight inches is a medium height for a man. A medium frequency is intermediate between the high and low frequencies.*
—*n.* **1** something that is in the middle; neither one extreme nor the other; middle condition: *a happy medium between city and country life.* **2** a substance or agent through which anything acts or an effect is produced; a means: *Copper wire is a medium of electric transmission. Television and radio are media of communication. A newspaper is a medium of communication and also an advertising medium. Waves behave differently when they move from one medium to another ... or when other waves are also present in the medium* (L. Wallace Dean). *A negotiation was opened through the medium of the ambassador, Sam* (Charlotte Brontë). **3** a substance in which something can live; environment: *Water is the natural medium in which most fish live.* **4a** a nutritive substance, either liquid or solid, such as agar-agar or gelatin, in or upon which bacteria, fungi, and other microorganisms are grown for study; culture medium. **b** a substance used for displaying, or preserving organic specimens. **5a** a liquid with which pigments are mixed for painting. **b** a type of painting: *His best medium is oil painting.* **6** a person through whom messages from the spirits of the dead are supposedly sent to the living.
[< Latin *medium,* neuter, middle]
► The plural is always **mediums** in the sense of def. 6, and also in that of def. 1, although in this sense the plural rarely occurs. In other senses both *mediums* and **media** are used, but *media* is more common in technical and scientific work.

**medium frequency**, *Electronics.* a frequency ranging from 300 to 3000 kilohertz.

**me|di|um|is|tic** (mē′dē ə mis′tik), *adj.* of or having to do with a spiritualistic medium.

**medium of exchange**, money or anything used as money.

**me|di|um-priced** (mē′dē əm prīst′), *adj.* (of a line of products) having a price ranging approximately between the cheapest and the most expensive of its kind.

**me|di|um-range** (mē′dē əm rānj′), *adj.* effective or operable over a moderate range.

**me|di|um-sized** (mē′dē əm sīzd′), *adj.* neither large nor small of its kind.

**me|di|um-term** (mē′dē əm tėrm′), *adj.* of or for a period of time intermediate between long-term and short-term: *This medium-term coverage expands the short-term export insurance offered since February* (Wall Street Journal).

**med|lar** (med′lər), *n.* **1** a fruit that looks like a small brown apple; mespil. It is picked after frost and ripened, and usually preserved. *You'll be rotten before you are half ripe, and that's the right virtue of a medlar* (Shakespeare). **2** the small, bushy tree of the rose family that it grows on. **3** any one of various related trees or their fruit.

[< Old French *medler,* earlier *meslier* the medlar (tree) < *mesle* medlar (fruit), also *mesple* < Latin *mespila* < Greek *méspīlon*]

**Med|lars** or **MEDLARS** (med′lərz), *n.* a computerized system for processing and retrieving bibliographical data compiled from articles published in medical journals. [< *Med*(ical) *L*(iterature) *A*(nalysis) and *R*(etrieval) *S*(ystem)]

**med|ley** (med′lē), *n., pl.* **-leys,** *adj., v.,* **-leyed** or **-lied, -ley|ing.** *—n.* **1** a mixture of things, often ones that ordinarily do not belong together: *The United States grew and thrived on its medley of peoples from Europe, Asia, and Africa.* **SYN**: hodgepodge, jumble. **2** a piece of music made up of parts from other pieces: *a medley of songs from several shows on Broadway.* **3** *Archaic.* hand-to-hand fighting; melee.
*—adj.* made up of parts that are not alike; mixed: *a medley air of cunning and of impudence* (Wordsworth). **SYN**: mingled, motley.
*—v.t.* to mix as in a medley.
[< Old French *medlee,* earlier *meslee,* feminine past participle of *medler,* or *mesler* to mix, ultimately < Latin *miscēre* to mix. See etym. of doublet **melee.**]

**medley relay,** **1** a relay race in swimming between several teams, each of which consists of three or four swimmers who take turns swimming a different stroke for each third or fourth of the course. **2** a relay race between several teams of runners, each of whom runs a certain distance out of the total required.

**Mé|doc** or **Me|doc** (mā dôk′), *n.* a red wine, a kind of Bordeaux or claret. [< *Médoc,* a district in France, where it is made]

**me|dres|seh** (mə dras′e), *n.* = madrasah.

**me|dul|la** (mi dul′ə), *n., pl.* **-dul|las** or (*especially for 1, 2*) **-dul|lae** (-dul′ē). **1** = medulla oblongata. **2** the marrow of bones. **3** the inner substance of an organ or structure, as of the kidney. **4** the pith of plants. **5** the central core of the shaft of hair in most mammals. [< Latin *medulla* marrow; origin uncertain]

**medulla ob|lon|ga|ta** (ob′long gā′tə, -gä′-), the lowest part of the brain, at the top end of the spinal cord, containing nerve centers which control breathing and other involuntary functions. See picture under **brain.**

**med|ul|lar|y** (med′ə ler′ē, mi dul′ər-), *adj.* of, having to do with, or like medulla or the medulla oblongata.

**medullary ray,** one of the radiating vertical bands of woody tissue which divide the vascular bundles and connect the pith with the bark in the stems of exogenous plants; wood ray.

**medullary sheath,** **1** a narrow ring comprising the innermost layer of woody tissue that surrounds the pith in certain plants. **2** = myelin.

**med|ul|lat|ed** (med′ə lā′tid, mi dul′ā-), *adj.* having a medullary sheath: *a medullated nerve fiber.*

**me|dul|lin** (mə dul′ən), *n.* a prostaglandin isolated from the medulla of the kidney, used in the treatment of high blood pressure.

**Me|du|sa** (mə dü′sə, -dyü′; -zə), *n., pl.* **-sas.** *Greek Legend.* one of the three Gorgons or horrible monsters with snakes for hair. Anyone who looked upon her was turned to stone. She was slain by Perseus, and her head fixed on the shield of Athena. *Cast not thine eye upon Medusa* (John Gower). **— Me|du′sa|like′,** *adj.*

***me|du|sa** (mə dü′sə, -dyü′-; -zə), *n., pl.* **-sas, -sae** (-sē, -zē). a jellyfish, especially a free-swimming type. [< New Latin *Medusa* the genus name < Latin *Medūsa* Medusa (because one species has feelers that look like the snake hair of Medusa)]

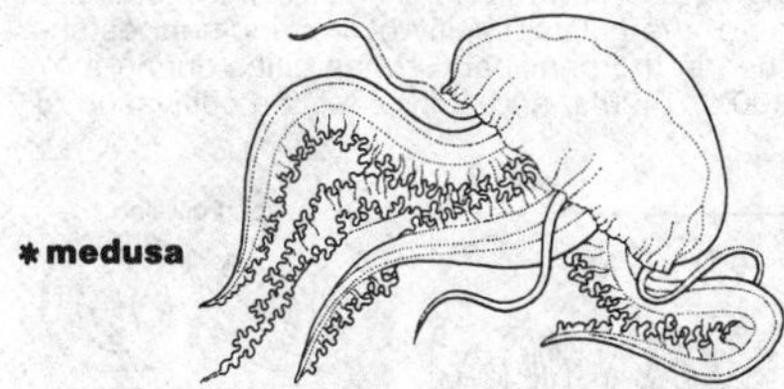
***medusa**

**me|du|san** (mə dü′sən, -dyü′-; -zən), *adj., n.*
*—adj.* of or having to do with a medusa or jellyfish.
*—n.* a medusa or jellyfish.

**me|du|soid** (mə dü′soid, -dyü′-), *adj., n.* *—adj.* of or like a medusa or jellyfish: *The bracts, swimming bells, and gonophores are constructed on a medusoid plan* (A. Franklin Shull).
*—n.* = jellyfish.

**meed** (mēd), *n.* **1** *Archaic.* what one deserves or has earned; reward: *a meed of praise, the meed of victory.* **2** *Obsolete.* a gift. **3** *Obsolete.* corrupt gain; bribery. **4** *Obsolete.* merit; worth: *My meed hath got me fame* (Shakespeare). [Old English *mēd*]

**meek** (mēk), *adj., adv.* *—adj.* **1** not easily angered; mild; patient: *Even the man Moses, the meekest of men, was wrathful sometimes* (George Eliot). **SYN**: mild, forbearing. See syn. under **gentle.** **2** submitting tamely when ordered about or injured by others: *The little boy was meek as a lamb after he was punished.* **SYN**: yielding, docile, submissive. See syn. under **humble.** **3** *Obsolete.* **a** gentle; courteous; kind. **b** (of a superior) merciful; compassionate.
*—adv. Obsolete.* in a meek manner; meekly.
[< Scandinavian (compare Old Icelandic *mjūkr* (originally) soft)] **— meek′ly,** *adv.* **— meek′ness,** *n.*

**meek|en** (mē′kən), *v.t., v.i.* to make or become meek. [< *meek* + *-en*[1]]

**meer|kat** (mir′kat), *n.* a small South African carnivorous animal allied to the mongoose; suricate: *Tortoise eggs are much sought after by jackals, meerkats and muishonds* (Cape Times). [< Afrikaans *meerkat* < Dutch *meer* sea + *kat* cat]

**meer|schaum** (mir′shəm, -shôm), *n.* **1** a very soft, white, clayey mineral, used especially to make tobacco pipes; sepiolite. It is a hydrous silicate of magnesium. *He dried the meerschaum mug and put it back in the cabinet* (New Yorker). *Formula:* $H_4Mg_2Si_3O_{10}$ **2** a tobacco pipe with a bowl made of this material. Meerschaums are valued for the rich brown color they gain after continued use. [< German *Meerschaum* (literally) sea foam (compare etym. under **mere**[2]), translation of Persian *kef-i-daryā* foam of (the) sea]

**meet**[1] (mēt), *v.,* **met, meet|ing,** *n.* *—v.t.* **1a** to come face to face with (something or someone coming from the other direction): *Our car met another car on a narrow road.* **SYN**: confront, encounter. **b** to receive and welcome on arrival; be present at the arrival of: *to meet a plane. I must go to the station to meet my mother.* **2a** to come together with; come into contact or connection with: *Sword met sword in battle.* **b** to join; intersect: *The accident occurred where Oak Street meets Main Street.* **3** to come into company with; be together with: *The hosts met their guests at the restaurant.* **4** to keep an appointment with: *Meet me at one o'clock.* **5** to be introduced to; become acquainted with: *Have you met my sister?* **6** to be perceived by; be seen or heard by: *There is more to this matter than meets the eye. Of Forests, and enchantments drear, Where more is meant than meets the ear* (Milton). **7** to fulfill; put an end to; satisfy: *to meet obligations. The explorers starved because they did not take enough food to meet their needs for the long journey over ice and snow.* **SYN**: settle. **8** to pay (one's debts) when due: *He did not have enough money to meet his bills.* **SYN**: settle. **9** to fight with; deal with; oppose: *to meet an enemy in battle, to meet threats with defiance.* **10** to face directly: *He met her glance with a smile.* **11** to experience: *He met open scorn before he won fame.* **12** to conform to (a person's wishes or opinions).
*—v.i.* **1** to come face to face: *Their cars met on the narrow road.* **2** to assemble: *Congress will meet next month. When shall we three meet again?* (Shakespeare). **3** to come together; come into contact or connection; join: *The two roads met near the church.* **4** to be united; join in harmony: *His is a nature in which courage and caution meet.*
*—n.* **1** a meeting; gathering: *an athletic meet.* **2** the people at a meeting. **3** the place of meeting.
**meet up with,** to meet with: *He meets up with a Bohemian sort of girl* (Atlantic).
**meet with, a** to come across; light upon: *We met with bad weather.* **b** to have; get: *The plan met with approval and was quickly put into practice.*
[Old English *mētan* < *mōt* meeting, moot]
**— meet′er,** *n.*

**meet**[2] (mēt), *adj., adv.* *—adj. Archaic.* **1** fitting; becoming: *It is meet and right so to do* (Book of Common Prayer). **2** suitable; proper: *It is meet that you should help your friends.*
*—adv. Obsolete.* in a meet or proper manner; fitly.
[Old English *gemǣte*] **— meet′ness,** *n.*

**meet|ing** (mē′ting), *n.* **1** the act or fact of coming together: *a meeting of minds, a chance meeting with an old friend.* **2** the act or fact of coming together or assembling for worship: *a Quaker meeting, a prayer meeting.* **3** any act of coming together or assembly of people: *an open meeting of a Congressional committee. Our club held a meeting. He* [*Mr. Gladstone*] *speaks to me as if I was a public meeting* (Queen Victoria). **4** a place where things meet; junction: *a meeting of roads, the meeting of the Ohio and the Mississippi.* **5** a hostile encounter; duel: *The meeting, was set for the next morning; the weapons: pistols at thirty paces.* **6** a schedule of or gathering for horse races lasting several days or weeks.
*— Syn.* **3 Meeting, assembly, gathering** mean a coming together of a group of people. **Meeting** applies especially when the purpose is to discuss or arrange business or action: *The directors of the bank held a meeting.* **Assembly** often applies when the purpose is less explicit but suggests that the occasion is rather formal: *The principal called an assembly.* **Gathering** suggests that the occasion is less formal or organized and that it may be for social pleasure: *There was a large gathering at her house.*

**meeting ground,** a place where different elements meet or come together: *New York City is a meeting ground of people from almost every part of the world.*

**meeting house,** or **meet|ing|house** (mē′ting-hous′), *n.* **1** any place of worship; church. **2a** a building used for worship in the Quaker fashion. **b** *British.* any nonconformist house of worship; conventicle.

**meet|ly** (mēt′lē), *adv.* in a meet manner; suitably; properly: *... where change should meetly fall* (Robert Browning).

**meg-,** *combining form.* the form of **mega-** before vowels, as in *megohm.*

**mega-,** *combining form.* **1** large: *Megaspore = large spore.*
**2** one million: *Megacycle = one million cycles. Megaton = one million tons.* Also, **meg-** before vowels.
[< Greek *mégas, megálou* great]

**meg|a|bar** (meg′ə bär), *n.* a unit of pressure equal to one million bars. [< *mega-* + *bar*[3]]

**meg|a|bit** (meg′ə bit), *n.* a unit of information equivalent to one million bits or binary digits. [< *mega-* + *bit*[4]]

**meg|a|buck** (meg′ə buk′), *n. U.S. Slang.* a million dollars: *A fifty megabuck ($50,000,000) laboratory is today a commonplace* (New York Times Magazine). [< *mega-* + *buck*[5]]

**meg|a|ce|phal|ic** (meg′ə sə fal′ik), *adj.* **1** large-headed. **2** *Anthropology.* having a skull with a cranial capacity exceeding the average for modern man (about 1,600 cubic centimeters). [< *mega-* + *cephalic*]

**meg|a|ceph|a|lous** (meg′ə sef′ə ləs), *adj.* = megacephalic.

**meg|a|ceph|a|ly** (meg′ə sef′ə lē), *n.* the condition of being megacephalic.

**meg|a|cit|y** (meg′ə sit′ē), *n., pl.* **-cit|ies.** a city with a population of more than a million: *The United States has evolved a way to concentrate in its "megacities" vast numbers of people to optimize economic proficiency* (New Scientist).

**meg|a|cu|rie** (meg′ə kyůr′ē), *n.* a million curies: *Since each megacurie is roughly as potent as 2,200 lbs. of pure radium, this is a large amount of radioactivity* (Time).

**meg|a|cy|cle** (meg′ə sī′kəl), *n.* **1** one million cycles: *The oscillation frequency used is 200 megacycles per second* (Science News). **2** one million cycles per second, used formerly to express the frequency of radio waves, now expressed in megahertz. *Abbr:* mc.

**meg|a|death** (meg′ə deth′), *n.* the death of one million persons, such as could result from nuclear warfare: *The Kremlin can now destroy nearly 40 per cent of our industry and take a toll of 13 megadeaths* (Birmingham News).

**meg|a|dyne** (meg′ə dīn′), *n.* a million dynes.

**Me|gae|ra** (mə jē′rə), *n. Greek and Roman Mythology.* one of the three Furies (Erinyes), Alecto and Tisiphone being the other two.

**meg|a|gam|ete** (meg′ə gam′ēt, -gə mēt′), *n. Biology.* = macrogamete.

**meg|a|hertz** (meg′ə hėrts′), *n.* a unit of frequency equal to one million hertz, used to express the frequency of radio waves. *Abbr:* MHz (no periods). [< *mega-* + *hertz* one cycle per second]

**meg|a|jet** (meg′ə jet′), *n.* a jet aircraft larger and faster than a jumbo jet.

**meg|a|joule** (meg′ə joul′, -jül′), *n.* a unit of work or energy, equivalent to a million joules.

**meg|a|kar|y|o|cyte** (meg′ə kar′ē ə sīt), *n. Biology.* a large cell of bone marrow with a lobulated nucleus that gives rise to blood platelets. [< *mega-* + *karyo-* + *-cyte*]

**Meg|a|le|sian Games** (meg′ə lē′zhən), a festival in ancient Rome with a stately procession, feasting, and performances in the theater, held in April in honor of the goddess Rhea. [< Latin *Megalēsia(lūdī)* Megalesian games < Greek *mégas, megálou* great]

**meg|a|lith** (meg′ə lith), *n.* a stone of great size,

---

**Pronunciation Key:** hat, āge, cãre, fär; let, ēqual, tėrm; it, īce; hot, ōpen, ôrder; oil, out; cup, půt, rüle; child; long; thin; ᴛʜen; zh, measure; ə represents a in about, e in taken, i in pencil, o in lemon, u in circus.

especially in ancient construction or in monuments left by people of prehistoric times. [< *mega-* + Greek *líthos* stone]

**meg|a|lith|ic** (meg′ə lith′ik), *adj.* **1** having to do with megaliths. **2** of or having to do with a culture in western Europe in the late neolithic period, characterized by rough stone monuments and tombs of large stones.

**meg|a|lo|blast** (meg′ə lō blast′, -bläst′), *n.* a nucleated red blood cell, of abnormally large size, found in the blood of anemic persons. [< Greek *mégas, megálou* great + *blastós* sprout, germ]

**meg|a|lo|blas|tic** (meg′ə lō blas′tik, -bläs′-), *adj.* of or having megaloblasts; characterized by the presence of megaloblasts in the blood: *megaloblastic anemia.*

**meg|a|lo|ce|phal|ic** (meg′ə lō sə fal′ik), *adj.* = megacephalic.

**meg|a|lo|ceph|a|lous** (meg′ə lō sef′ə ləs), *adj.* = megacephalic.

**meg|a|lo|ceph|a|ly** (meg′ə lō sef′ə lē), *n.* = megacephaly.

**meg|a|lo|ma|ni|a** (meg′ə lō mā′nē ə), *n.* a mental disorder marked by delusions of great personal power, importance, or wealth. It is associated with schizophrenia and other disorders. [< Greek *mégas, megálou* great + English *mania*]

**meg|a|lo|ma|ni|ac** (meg′ə lō mā′nē ak), *n., adj.* — ***n.*** a person who has megalomania.
— ***adj.*** = megalomaniacal.

**meg|a|lo|ma|ni|a|cal** (meg′ə lō mə nī′ə kəl), *adj.* of or having to do with megalomania or with a person afflicted with megalomania.

**meg|a|lop|o|lis** (meg′ə lop′ə lis), *n.* **1** a city of enormous size, especially when thought of as the center of power, wealth, or culture in a country or the world: *This grim vignette symbolizes the crushing weight of the modern industrial megalopolis* (Atlantic). **2** a large metropolitan area, often including several cities with little or no intervening countryside. [< Greek *mégas, megálou* great + *pólis* city]

**meg|a|lo|pol|i|tan** (meg′ə lə pol′ə tən), *adj., n.* — ***adj.*** of or having to do with a megalopolis: *megalopolitan jungles such as New York and Chicago* (Harper's).
— ***n.*** a person living in a megalopolis.

**meg|a|lops** (meg′ə lops), *n.* the final larval stage of a crab, a small organism with large, stalked eyes that swims to the shore and digs a hole in the sand where it molts into a tiny crab. [< New Latin *megalops* < Greek *megalṓpōs* large-eyed < *mégas, megálou* great + *ṓps, ōpós* eye]

**meg|a|lo|saur** (meg′ə lə sôr), *n.* any one of an extinct group of gigantic terrestrial, carnivorous reptiles. [< New Latin *Megalosaurus* the genus name < Greek *mégas, megálou* great + *saûros* lizard]

**meg|a|lo|sau|ri|an** (meg′ə lə sôr′ē ən), *adj., n.* — ***adj.*** having the characteristics of a megalosaur.
— ***n.*** = megalosaur.

**meg|a|lo|sau|rus** (meg′ə lō sôr′əs), *n.* = megalosaur.

**meg|a|ma|chine** (meg′ə mə shēn′), *n.* a social system so dominated by technology that it resembles a gigantic machine which functions without any regard for human needs and objectives: *What is needed to save mankind from the megamachine—or whatever controls the megamachine—is to displace the mechanical world picture with an organic world picture, in the center of which stands man himself* (Lewis Mumford).

**meg|a|par|sec** (meg′ə pär′sek), *n.* a unit of distance, equivalent to one million parsecs.

**meg|a|phone** (meg′ə fōn), *n., v.,* **-phoned, -phoning.** — ***n.*** a large, funnel-shaped horn used to increase the loudness of the voice or the distance at which it can be heard: *The cheerleader at the football game yelled through a megaphone. The megaphone has gone electronic* (Science News Letter).
— ***v.t., v.i.*** **1** to magnify or direct (sound) by means of a megaphone: *In desperation, Kendall megaphoned to the Storstad, "Go full speed astern!"* (Maclean's). **2** to speak very loudly. [American English < *mega-* + *phone*]

**meg|a|phon|ic** (meg′ə fon′ik), *adj.* increasing the loudness of sound or the distance at which it can be heard: *She had escaped even the microscopic research and the megaphonic talk of a small country place like Highwood* (Mrs. Lynn Linton).

**meg|a|pod** (meg′ə pod), *adj., n.* — ***adj.*** having a large foot or feet.
— ***n.*** = megapode.

**meg|a|pode** (meg′ə pōd), *n.* any one of a family of large-footed, fowllike birds of Australia and Indonesia, that scratch up mounds, usually of decaying vegetation, in which they bury their eggs and leave them to hatch; moundbird; mound builder. [< New Latin *Megapodius* < Greek *mégas* great + *poús, podós* foot]

**meg|a|rad** (meg′ə rad′), *n.* a unit for measuring absorbed doses of radiation, equivalent to one million rads.

**meg|a|ron** (meg′ə ron), *n.* the central room of an ancient Greek house, having a hearth and used as a kitchen and living room. [< Greek *mégaron*]

**meg|a|scop|ic** (meg′ə skop′ik), *adj.* **1** enlarged or magnified. **2** = macroscopic. — **meg′a|scop′i|cal|ly,** *adv.*

**meg|a|seism** (meg′ə sī zəm, -səm), *n.* a great or severe earthquake. [< *mega-* + Greek *seismós* earthquake]

**meg|a|seis|mic** (meg′ə sīz′mik, -sīs′-), *adj.* **1** of or having to do with a severe earthquake. **2** caused by a severe earthquake.

**meg|a|spo|ran|gi|um** (meg′ə spə ran′jē əm), *n., pl.* **-gi|a** (-jē ə). a sporangium containing megaspores: *The megasporangium usually produces only four megaspores* (Fred W. Emerson). Also, **macrosporangium.** [< *mega*(spore) + *sporangium*]

**meg|a|spore** (meg′ə spôr, -spōr), *n.* **1** an asexually produced spore of comparatively large size that gives rise to the female gametophyte in certain ferns. **2** the embryo sac in seed plants: *Within the nucleus is found the embryo sac or megaspore* (Heber W. Youngken). Also, **macrospore.**

**meg|a|spo|ro|phyll** (meg′ə spôr′ə fil, -spōr′-), *n. Botany.* **1** a sporophyll bearing only megasporangia. **2** = carpel.

**me|gass** or **me|gasse** (mə gas′), *n.* = bagasse.

**meg|a|struc|ture** (meg′ə struk′chər), *n.* a very large building: *Arcology ... is a total planned environment—dwellings, factories, utilities, cultural centers—within a single megastructure 1-2 miles wide and up to 300 stories high* (Estie Stoll).

**meg|a|tech|nics** (meg′ə tek′niks), *n.* large-scale technology: *Under the impulsion of unprecedented "megatechnics"—"nuclear energy, supersonic transportation, cybernetic intelligence, and instantaneous distant communication"—the far-flung settlement patterns of Megalopolis are resistlessly expanding in many parts of the world, transforming man and the earth* (Allan Temko).

**meg|a|there** (meg′ə thir), *n.* any one of an extinct group of huge, plant-eating mammals of the Pleistocene, resembling the sloths, the fossil remains of which have been found in South America. [< New Latin (Cuvier) *Megatherium* < Greek *mégas* large + *thēríon* wild animal]

**meg|a|the|ri|um** (meg′ə thir′ē əm), *n.* = megathere.

**meg|a|ton** (meg′ə tun′), *n.* **1** a measure of atomic power equivalent to the energy released by one million tons of high explosive, specifically TNT: *Most estimates suggest that each megaton of dirty bomb would cause a few thousand deaths from leukaemia* (Manchester Guardian). **2** a measure of weight equal to one million tons. *Abbr:* mt.

**meg|a|ton|nage** (meg′ə tun′ij), *n.* the total amount of atomic power in megatons.

**meg|a|ver|si|ty** (meg′ə vėr sə tē), *n., pl.* **-ties.** a very large university, with an enrollment of many thousands of students. [< *mega-* + (uni)*versity*]

**meg|a|vi|ta|min** (meg′ə vī′tə min), *adj.* of or based on the use of very large doses of vitamins to control disease: *Megavitamin treatment for schizophrenia* (Science News). *It is my opinion that in the course of time it will be found possible to control hundreds of diseases by megavitamin therapy* (Linus Pauling).

**meg|a|volt** (meg′ə vōlt′), *n.* a unit of electromotive force equivalent to one million volts.

**meg|a|watt** (meg′ə wot′), *n.* a million watts; thousand kilowatts.

**me|gil|lah** (mə gil′ə), *n. Slang.* a long story or account: *I talked the whole megillah over with Cassius and he reckons you'd be a better draw* (Punch). [< Hebrew *megīllah* scroll (especially the scroll of the Book of Esther, which is unrolled and read in the synagogue during the festival of Purim)]

**Me|gil|lot** (mə gi lot′), *n. Judaism.* the five books of the Hagiographa consisting of the Song of Solomon, Ruth, Lamentations, Ecclesiastes, and Esther, read in the synagogue on certain festivals. [< Hebrew *megīlloth* scrolls, plural of *megīllah*]

**me|gilp** (mə gilp′), *n.* a jellylike preparation (consisting usually of a mixture of linseed oil with turpentine or mastic varnish) used by artists as a vehicle for oil colors. Also, **magilp.** [origin unknown]

**Meg|i|mide** (meg′ə mīd), *n. Trademark.* a drug that counteracts the influence of barbiturates, used in treating persons who have taken an overdose of sleeping pills: *Megimide ... brings sleeping-pill victims out of dangerous comas in a few minutes* (Newsweek). *Formula:* $C_8H_{13}NO_2$

**meg|ohm** (meg′ōm′), *n.* a unit of electrical resistance, equivalent to one million ohms. [< *meg-* one million + *ohm*]

**meg|ohm|me|ter** (meg′ōm mē′tər), *n.* an instrument for measuring the electrical resistance of a conductor in megohms. [< *megohm* + *-meter*]

**me|grim** (mē′grim), *n.* **1** = migraine. **2** *Figurative.* a passing fancy; whim; caprice: *It was a pity she should take such megrims into her head* (George Eliot). *The hamlet ... has no patience with urban megrims* (J. W. R. Scott).

**megrims, a** morbid low spirits; attack of the blues: *suffering from a mountainous attack of the mental megrims* (John Moyes). *She was neurotic and addicted to the megrims.* **b** the staggers in animals: *The poor mare was suddenly seized with megrims* (Peter Hawker).
[earlier variant of *mygreyn* migraine. Compare etym. under **hemicrania.**]

**Mei|ji** (mā′jē), *n.* the reign (1868-1912) of Emperor Mutsuhito of Japan: *There was some attempt at systematic development in the Meiji era* (London Times). [< Japanese *Meiji* (literally) enlightened rule]

**mein|ie** or **mein|y** (mā′nē), *n., pl.* **mein|ies.** **1** *Scottish.* a great number; multitude. **2** *Obsolete.* a body of feudal dependents or retainers; retinue; train: *They summon'd up their meiny, straight took horse* (Shakespeare). [< Old French *meyne,* earlier *mesnede* < Vulgar Latin *mansiōnāta* < Latin *mansiō, -ōnis* mansion]

***mei|o|sis¹** (mī ō′sis), *n., pl.* **-ses** (-sēz). **1** *Biology.* the process by which the number of chromosomes in reproductive cells of sexually reproducing organisms is reduced to half the original number, resulting in the production of gametes or spores; reduction division. Meiosis consists essentially of two cell divisions. In the first, the homologous chromosomes separate equally into the two new cells so that each contains the haploid number, or half the diploid number. In the second cell division, the pairs of chromosomes split, one of each kind of chromosome going to the four new cells. Thus each new cell again contains the haploid number of chromosomes. See picture below. **2** = litotes. Also, **miosis.** [< New Latin *meiosis* < Greek *meíōsis* a lessening < *meioûn* lessen < *meíōn* less]

**mei|o|sis²** (mī ō′sis), *n., pl.* **-ses** (-sēz). = miosis¹.

**mei|ot|ic** (mī ot′ik), *adj.* of or having to do with meiosis. — **mei|ot′i|cal|ly,** *adv.*

**Meis|sen ware** or **china** (mī′sən), = Dresden china. [< *Meissen,* Saxony, where it was first made]

**Meis|ter|sing|er** or **meis|ter|sing|er** (mīs′tər-sing′ər; *German* mīs′tər zing′ər), *n.* a member of one of the guilds, chiefly of workingmen, established in the principal German cities during the 1300's, 1400's, and 1500's for the cultivation of

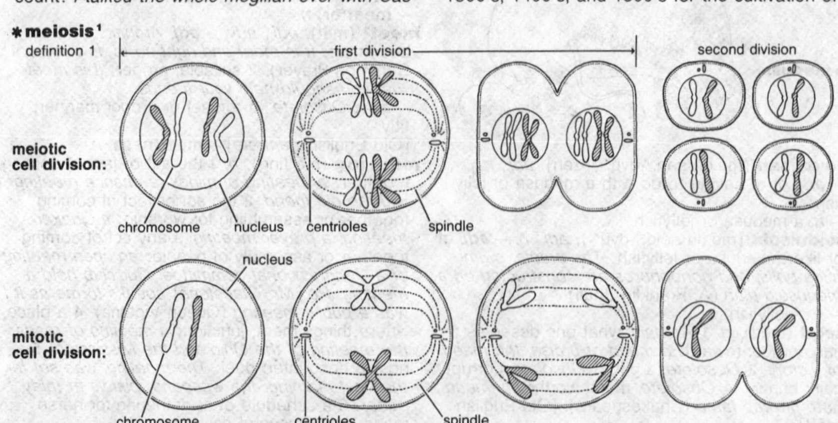

poetry and music. Also, **mastersinger**. [< German *Meistersinger* < *Meister* master (of a guild) + *Singer* singer]

**Mej|lis** (mej lēs′), *n.* = Majlis.

**me|ke** (mā′kē), *n.* a Fijian war dance: *They stripped down to palm skirts and battle paint to demonstrate ... mekes* (Time). [< Fijian]

**Mek|ka** (mek′ə), *n.* = Mecca.

**mel** (mel), *n. Pharmacology.* honey. [< Latin *mel*]

**mel|a|mine** (mel′ə mēn, -min; mel′ə mēn′), *n., adj.* —*n.* **1** a colorless, crystalline substance derived from dicyandiamide. Melamine reacts with formaldehyde to form a group of resins which are used for coatings, insulators, and plastics. *Formula:* $C_3H_6N_6$ **2** the resin formed with this substance and formaldehyde.
—*adj.* of or having to do with melamine: *melamine dinnerware, melamine resin, a melamine finish.*
[< *mel*(am), a chemical compound + *amine*]

**mel|an|cho|li|a** (mel′ən kō′lē ə), *n.* a functional mental disorder characterized by great depression of spirits and activity, and gloomy thoughts and fears often accompanied by vivid delusions. [< Late Latin *melancholia* < Greek *melancholía* < *mélās, -anos* black + *cholḗ* bile]

**mel|an|cho|li|ac** (mel′ən kō′lē ak), *adj., n.* —*adj.* affected with melancholia.
—*n.* a person affected with melancholia.

**mel|an|chol|ic** (mel′ən kol′ik), *adj., n.* —*adj.* **1** melancholy; gloomy; emotionally depressed. **2** having to do with, like, or suffering from melancholia.
—*n.* a person who is melancholic; gloomy person. —**mel′an|chol′i|cal|ly**, *adv.*

**mel|an|chol|i|ly** (mel′ən kol′ə lē), *adv.* in a melancholy manner.

**mel|an|chol|i|ness** (mel′ən kol′ē nis), *n.* the condition of being melancholy.

**mel|an|chol|y** (mel′ən kol′ē), *n., pl.* **-chol|ies**, *adj.* —*n.* **1** low spirits; sadness; tendency to be sad: *The chronic melancholy which is taking hold of the civilized races ...* (Thomas Hardy). SYN: depression, dejection, gloominess. **2** sober thoughtfulness; pensiveness: *I ... began, Wrapp'd in a pleasing fit of melancholy, To meditate my rural minstrelsy* (Milton). **3** one of the four humors, thought in ancient and medieval physiology to be secreted by the kidney or spleen and to be the cause of such conditions as depression and gloominess; black bile: *to purge melancholy* (Shakespeare).
—*adj.* **1** sad; gloomy; depressed in spirits: *A melancholy person is not very good company.* SYN: depressed, despondent, downcast. **2** causing sadness; depressing; dismal: *a melancholy scene.* **3** expressive of sadness: *a melancholy smile.* **4** lamentable; deplorable: *a melancholy fact.* **5** soberly thoughtful or pensive: *to refresh his mind with a melancholy walk* (Anthony Wood). **6** *Obsolete.* having to do with or affected with melancholia.
[< Old French *melancolie*, and *malencollie*, learned borrowings from Late Latin *melancholia*; see etym. under **melancholia**]

**Mel|a|ne|sian** (mel′ə nē′zhən, -shən), *adj., n.* —*adj.* of Melanesia, its people, or their languages.
—*n.* **1** a member of any one of the dark-skinned peoples living in Melanesia, one of the three main groups of islands in the Pacific, northeast of Australia, including New Caledonia and Fiji: *Authorities include the Melanesians ... with the Negro group* (Ogburn and Nimkoff). **2** any of the related languages of Melanesia, or the group that they constitute.

**mé|lange** (mā länzh′), *n.* a mixture; medley: *Every nationality of the Soviet Union seemed to be represented in the mélange of peoples that paraded today before the leaders of the local Communist party and government* (New York Times). SYN: jumble, hodgepodge, miscellany. [< Middle French *mélange* < *mêler* to mix < Old French *mesler* < Late Latin *misculāre* < Latin *miscēre*]

**me|lan|ic** (mə lan′ik), *adj.* **1** having to do with or showing melanism. **2** affected by melanosis; melanotic.

**mel|a|nin** (mel′ə nin), *n.* any one of a class of dark pigments, especially the black pigment in the skin, hair, and eyes of human beings and many animals, or one developed in certain diseases. Large amounts of melanin help protect the skin from sunburn and improve vision in bright sunlight. See diagram under **skin**. [< Greek *mélās, -anos* black + English *-in*]

**mel|a|nism** (mel′ə niz əm), *n.* **1** darkness of color resulting from an abnormal development of melanin in the skin, hair, and eyes of a human being, or in the skin, coat, or plumage of an animal. **2** darkness, especially near blackness, of skin, hair, and eyes, as a characteristic of certain peoples. [< Greek *mélās, -anos* black + English *-ism*]

**mel|a|nis|tic** (mel′ə nis′tik), *adj.* characterized by melanism.

**mel|a|nite** (mel′ə nīt), *n.* a velvet-black variety of garnet. [< Greek *mélās, -anos* black + English *-ite*[1]]

**mel|a|ni|za|tion** (mel′ə nə zā′shən), *n.* **1** the act or process of melanizing. **2** the condition of being melanized.

**mel|a|nize** (mel′ə nīz), *v.t.*, **-nized, -niz|ing.** to produce melanism in.

**mel|a|no** (mel′ə nō), *n.* a person or animal characterized by melanism. [< Greek *mélās, -anos* black]

**mel|a|no|blast** (mel′ə nə blast), *n.* a cell which is capable of developing into a melanophore: *The melanomas so produced contain almost a pure culture of melanoblasts, the cells characteristic of both mouse and human black cancers* (Science News Letter). [< Greek *mélās, -anos* black + *blastós* germ, sprout]

**mel|a|no|blas|to|ma** (mel′ə nō blas tō′mə), *n., pl.* **-mas, -ma|ta** (-mə tə). a malignant tumor formed from melanophores, characterized by dark coloring and rapid growth; black cancer.

**mel|a|no|car|ci|no|ma** (mel′ə nō kär′sə nō′mə), *n.* = melanoblastoma.

**Mel|a|noch|ro|i** (mel′ə nok′rō ī), *n.pl.* a subdivision of the Caucasian peoples having dark hair and pale complexions. [< New Latin *Melanochroi* (coined by Thomas H. Huxley) < Greek *mélās, -anos* black + *ōchrós* pale (yellow)]

**Mel|a|no|chro|ic** (mel′ə nō krō′ik), *adj.* = Melanochroid.

**Mel|a|noch|roid** (mel′ə nok′roid), *adj.* having to do with or like the Melanochroi.

**mel|a|no|cyte** (mel′ə nə sīt), *n.* **1** a lymphocyte which contains black pigment. **2** a cell which synthesizes melanin, found in the skin, the choroid of the eye, and the hair. [< Greek *mélās, -anos* black + English *-cyte*]

**mel|a|no|cyte-stim|u|lat|ing hormone** (mel′ə nə sīt stim′yə lā′ting), a pituitary hormone that controls pigmentation; intermedin. *Abbr:* MSH (no periods).

**mel|a|no|gen|e|sis** (mel′ə nō jen′ə sis), *n.* the formation and development of melanin. [< Greek *mélās, -anos* black + Latin *genesis*]

**mel|a|noid** (mel′ə noid), *adj.* **1** of, affected by, or like melanosis. **2** like the color of melanin; darkly pigmented; blackish.

**mel|a|no|ma** (mel′ə nō′mə), *n., pl.* **-mas, -ma|ta** (-mə tə). **1** a dark-colored or blackish tumor arising in the skin or in the pigmented layers of the eye; melanoblastoma. **2** a benign tumor developed from a birthmark. [< New Latin *melanoma* < Greek *mélās, -anos* black + *-oma* -oma]

**mel|a|no|phore** (mel′ə nə fôr, -fōr), *n.* a chromatophore which contains a black or brown pigment, melanin.

**mel|a|nose** (mel′ə nōs), *n.* a common fungal disease of grapefruit that destroys the leaves and spoils the appearance of the fruit. [perhaps back formation < *melanosis*]

**mel|a|no|sis** (mel′ə nō′sis), *n., pl.* **-ses** (-sēz). **1** an abnormal deposit or development of melanin in various parts of the body, sometimes leading to the production of malignant pigmented tumors. **2** a discoloration caused by this. [< New Latin *melanosis* < Late Greek *melánōsis* blackening < *melanoûsthai* become black < *mélās, -anos* black]

**mel|a|not|ic** (mel′ə not′ik), *adj.* **1** characterized by or having to do with melanosis. **2** = melanistic.

**mel|a|nous** (mel′ə nəs), *adj.* **1** = melanic. **2** = melanoid.

**mel|an|tha|ceous** (mel′ən thā′shəs), *adj.* belonging to a group of bulbless plants now generally classified in the lily family, including the bellwort and white hellebore. [< New Latin *Melanthaceae* the family name (< Greek *mélās, -anos* black + *ánthos* flower) + English *-ous*]

**mel|a|phyre** (mel′ə fīr), *n.* any one of various dark-colored igneous rocks of porphyritic texture. [< French *mélaphyre* < Greek *mélas* black + French *porphyre* porphyry]

**mel|a|to|nin** (mel′ə tō′nin), *n.* a hormone, the first to be isolated from the pineal gland: *Melatonin ... appeared to lighten the amphibian skin by causing the aggregation of melanin granules within the cells* (Scientific American). *Melatonin ... affects the maturing of the sex glands in certain species of young animals* (Will G. Ryan). [< Greek *mélas* black + English *tone*, verb + *-in* (from its effect on melanocytes)]

**Mel|ba toast** (mel′bə), a kind of very crisp, evenly browned toast made from extremely thin slices of slightly stale white bread. [perhaps < Dame Nellie *Melba*, 1861-1931, an Australian soprano]

**Mel|bur|ni|an** or **Mel|bour|ni|an** (mel bėr′nē ən), *n., adj.* —*n.* a native or inhabitant of Melbourne, Australia.
—*adj.* of or having to do with Melbourne or its people.

**Mel|chi|or** (mel′kē ôr), *n.* one of the Three Wise Men, according to medieval legend.

**Mel|chite** (mel′kīt), *n., adj.* —*n.* **1** (formerly, in Syria, Palestine, and Egypt) an orthodox Eastern Christian, originally as distinguished from a Monophysite or a Nestorian. **2** one of the Uniat Christians of these countries.
—*adj.* of or having to do with the Melchites. Also, **Melkite**.
[< New Greek *Melchîtai* (literally) royalists < a Syriac word]

**Mel|chiz|e|dek** (mel kiz′ə dek), *n.* **1** a priest and king of ancient Salem, who blessed Abraham (in the Bible, Genesis 14:18). **2** the higher order of priests in the Mormon Church that has the primary responsibility of carrying out the church ordinances.

**meld**[1] (meld), *v., n.* —*v.t., v.i.* to announce and show (cards for a score) in rummy, canasta, pinochle, or certain other card games: *The veteran newspaperman melded the eight kings for a score of 800* (Charlottesville Daily Progress).
—*n.* **1** the act of melding. **2** any grouping of cards that can be melded.
[American English < German *melden* announce]

**meld**[2] (meld), *v.t., v.i.* to unite; merge: *Then comes a melding of fur and flower* (New Yorker). [perhaps a blend of *melt* and *weld*]

**mel|e** (mel′e), *n.* a native Hawaiian song or melody. [< Hawaiian *mele*]

**Mel|e|a|ger** (mel′ē ā′jər), *n. Greek Legend.* the hero who killed the Calydonian boar. He was one of the Argonauts.

**me|lee** or **mê|lée** (mā′lā, mā lā′, mel′ā), *n.* **1** a confused fight; hand-to-hand fight among a number of fighters: *Placing himself at the head of his handful of cavalry, he dashed into the mêlée* (John L. Motley). **2** any fracas: *... the unions felt they must join in the general mêlée* (London Times). [< French *mêlée* < Old French *meslee*. See etym. of doublet **medley**.]

**me|li|a|ceous** (mē′lē ā′shəs), *adj.* belonging to the mahogany family of trees and shrubs. [< New Latin *Meliaceae* the family name < *Melia* the typical genus < Greek *meliā* ash tree + English *-ous*]

**Me|li|an** (mē′lē ən, mēl′yən), *adj., n.* —*adj.* of or having to do with the Greek island of Melos, in the southern Aegean.
—*n.* a native or inhabitant of Melos.

**mel|ic** (mel′ik), *adj.* **1** intended to be sung. **2** of or having to do with an elaborate type of Greek lyric poetry, composed in strophes, as distinguished from iambic and elegiac poetry (originally by Terpander in the 600's B.C.). [< Greek *melikós* < *mélos* song]

**melic grass**, any grass of a group widely distributed in temperate regions but of no great agricultural value. [< New Latin *Melica* the genus name < Italian *melica* sorghum < Latin *mel* honey]

**mel|i|lot** (mel′ə lot), *n.* any cloverlike herb of a group of the pea family, with racemes of small, white or yellow flowers, such as the sweet clover. [< Middle French *melilot* < Latin *melilōtos* < Greek *melílōtos* a sweet clover < *méli* honey + *lōtós* clover, lotus]

**me|line** (mē′lin, -līn), *adj.* having to do with the badger; badgerlike. [< Latin *mēlīnus* < *mēlēs* badger, marten]

**mel|i|nite** (mel′ə nīt), *n.* a powerful explosive very similar to lyddite, consisting essentially of picric acid and guncotton. [< French *mélinite* < Greek *mḗlinos* quince-yellow (< *mêlon* quince; any kind of tree fruit) + French *-ite* ite[1]]

**Mel|ior** (mēl′yər), *n.* a style of modern printing type.

**mel|io|ra|ble** (mēl′yər ə bəl, mē′lē ər-), *adj.* that can be improved.

**mel|io|rate** (mēl′yə rāt, mē′lē ə-), *v.t., v.i.*, **-rat|ed, -rat|ing.** to make or become better or more bearable; improve; ameliorate. [< Late Latin *meliōrāre* (with English *-ate*[1]) < Latin *melior* better, comparative of *bonus* good] —**mel′io|ra′tion**, *n.* —**mel′io|ra′tor**, *n.*

**mel|io|ra|tive** (mēl′yə rā′tiv, mē′lē ə-), *adj.* tending to improve; improving.

**mel|io|rism** (mēl′yə riz əm, mē′lē ə-), *n.* the doctrine or belief, fundamental to some systems of ethics, that the world tends naturally to become better or is capable of being made better by human effort, a mean between pessimism and optimism: *Meliorism is ... to proceed according to sociological principles and to educate the young* *to a higher level of intelligence and morality* (Hinkle and Hinkle). [< Latin *melior* better + English *-ism*]

**mel|io|rist** (mēl′yər ist, mē′lē ər-), *n., adj.* **—*n.*** a person who holds the doctrine of meliorism **—*adj.*** = melioristic.

**mel|io|ris|tic** (mēl′yə ris′tik, mē′lē ə-), *adj.* of or having to do with meliorism.

**mel|ior|i|ty** (mēl yôr′ə tē, -yor′-; mē′lē ôr′-, -or′-), *n.* the quality or condition of being better; superiority.

**me|lis|ma** (mə liz′mə), *n., pl.* **-mas, -ma|ta** (-mə tə). *Music.* **1** a song, melody, or air, as contrasted with a recitative or declamatory passage. **2a** a long, florid melodic passage sung on one syllable, especially in Gregorian chant. **b** any melodic decoration, grace, fioritura, or roulade. **3** = cadenza. [< Greek *mélisma*]

**mel|is|mat|ic** (mel′iz mat′ik), *adj.* ornate or florid in melody: *Davy's "In honore summae matris" was extremely melismatic, so that it was easy to realize the force of clerical objection to such ways of setting sacred texts* (London Times). **—mel′is|mat′i|cal|ly,** *adv.*

**mel|is|mat|ics** (mel′iz mat′iks), *n.* the art of florid or ornate vocalization.

**me|lit|tin** (mə lit′ən), *n.* an antibiotic substance extracted from the poison of honeybees: *They found the antibacterial effect of one milligram of the bee substance, called "melittin," was the equivalent of as much as 93 units of penicillin* (New York Times). [< Greek *mélitta* honeybee + English *-in*]

**Mel|kite** (mel′kīt), *n., adj.* = Melchite.

**mell** (mel), *Archaic.* **—*v.t.*** to mix; mingle; combine; blend.
**—*v.i.*** **1** to interfere; meddle. **2** to join or engage in combat: *They are too many to mell with in the open field* (Scott). [< Old French *meller,* variant of *mesler;* see etym. under **meddle**]

**mel|lah** (mel′ə), *n.* (in Morocco) the Jewish quarter of a city. [origin uncertain]

**mel|ler** (mel′ər), *n. Slang.* melodrama (def. 1): *The better prose doesn't conceal the fact that the story is a lurid meller* (New York Times). [shortening and alteration of *melodrama*]

**mel|lif|er|ous** (mə lif′ər əs), *adj.* yielding or producing honey. [< Latin *mellifer* (< *mel, mellis* honey + *ferre* to bear, produce) + English *-ous*]

**mel|lif|lu|ence** (mə lif′lu̇ əns), *n.* sweet sound; smooth flow, as of words, poetry, or a voice.

**mel|lif|lu|ent** (mə lif′lu̇ ənt), *adj.* = mellifluous: *He is a mellifluent preacher* (Newsweek). [< Late Latin *mellifluēns, -entis* < *mel, mellis* honey + *fluēns, -entis,* present participle of *fluere* flow] **—mel|lif′lu|ent|ly,** *adv.*

**mel|lif|lu|ous** (mə lif′lu̇ əs), *adj.* **1** sweetly or smoothly flowing: *mellifluous tones. We enjoyed the mellifluous speech of the orator.* **2** flowing with honey; made sweet with or as if with honey: *mellifluous flowers.* [< Late Latin *mellifluus* (with English *-ous*) < Latin *mel, mellis* honey + *fluere* to flow] **—mel|lif′lu|ous|ly,** *adv.* **—mel|lif′lu|ous|ness,** *n.*

**mel|lo|phone** (mel′ə fōn), *n.* a type of althorn similar to a French horn; cor. See picture under **French horn.** [< *mello*(w) + *-phone*]

**mel|lo|rine** (mel′ə rēn), *n.* an imitation ice cream in which vegetable fats replace butterfat. [probably < *mello*(w) + (marga)*rine*]

**mel|lo|tron** (mel′ə tron), *n.* an electronic musical instrument programed by computer: *... the cold, windswept string tone of the mellotron, a keyboard instrument which simulates—but not quite—the sound of an orchestra* (Richard Williams). [apparently < *mello*(w) + (elec)*tron*(ic)]

**mel|low** (mel′ō), *adj., v.* **—*adj.*** **1** ripe, soft, and with good flavor; sweet and juicy: *a mellow apple.* **2** fully matured: *a mellow wine.* **3** soft and rich; full and pure without harshness: *a violin with a mellow tone, a mellow light in a picture, velvet with a mellow color.* **4** soft, rich, and loamy: *mellow soil.* **5** *Figurative.* softened and made wise by age or experience: *The baronet was ... as merry and mellow an old bachelor as ever followed a hound* (Washington Irving). **6** affected by liquor or drinking; slightly tipsy: *The party got gloriously mellow* (Herman Melville).
**—*v.t., v.i.*** to make or become mellow: *The apples mellowed after we picked them.* (*Figurative.*) *Time had mellowed his youthful temper.*
[Middle English *melwe.* See related etym. at **mild, malt.**] **—mel′low|ly,** *adv.* **—mel′low|ness,** *n.*

**me|lo|de|on** (mə lō′dē ən), *n.* **1** a small reed organ in which air is sucked inward by a bellows, an American predecessor of the harmonium. **2** a kind of accordion. [American English, variant of earlier *melodium* < *melody*]

**me|lo|di|a** (mə lō′dē ə), *n.* an 8-foot organ stop with wooden flue pipes, having a flutelike tone. [< Late Latin *melōdia* melody]

**me|lod|ic** (mə lod′ik), *adj.* **1** having to do with melody, especially as distinguished from harmony and rhythm. **2** = melodious. [< Late Latin *melōdicus* < Greek *melōidikós* < *melōidíā* melody] **—me|lod′i|cal|ly,** *adv.*

**me|lod|i|ca** (mə lod′ə kə), *n., pl.* **-cas.** a small wind instrument resembling a harmonica but having a pianolike keyboard. [< Late Latin *melōdica,* feminine of *melōdicus* melodic]

**melodic minor,** a version of the minor scale having the sixth and seventh steps raised in its ascending form. See picture under **minor scale.**

**me|lod|ics** (mə lod′iks), *n.* the branch of musical science concerned with melody; melodic theory.

**me|lo|di|ous** (mə lō′dē əs), *adj.* **1** sweet-sounding; pleasing to the ear; musical: *a melodious voice. Man ... forges the subtile ... air into wise and melodious words* (Emerson). **SYN:** melodic, tuneful, harmonious. **2** producing melody; singing sweetly: *melodious birds.* **3** having a melody; having to do with or of the nature of melody. **—me|lo′di|ous|ly,** *adv.* **—me|lo′di|ous|ness,** *n.*

**mel|o|dist** (mel′ə dist), *n.* a composer or singer of melodies: *Bellini was certainly one of the greatest melodists who have ever lived* (New Yorker).

**mel|o|dize** (mel′ə dīz), *v.,* **-dized, -diz|ing.** **—*v.t.*** **1** to make melodious. **2** to compose a melody for (a song). **—*v.i.*** **1** to blend melodiously: *Such a strain ... Might melodize with each tumultuous sound* (Scott). **2** to make melody or compose melodies. **—mel′o|diz′er,** *n.*

**mel|o|dra|ma** (mel′ə drä′mə, -dram′ə), *n.* **1** a sensational drama with exaggerated appeal to the emotions and, usually, a happy ending: *Most mystery shows are melodramas. It is the custom on the stage, in all good murderous melodramas to present the tragic and the comic scenes, in ... regular alternation* (Dickens). **2** any sensational writing, speech, or action with exaggerated appeal to the emotions: *If you can identify the murderer in Agatha Christie's melodrama, you probably belong on the police force yourself* (New Yorker). **3** (in the late 1700's and early 1800's) a romantic stage play with music interspersed. [< French *mélodrame* < Greek *mélos* music + *drâma* drama]

**mel|o|dra|mat|ic** (mel′ə drə mat′ik), *adj., n.* **—*adj.*** of, like, or suitable for melodrama; sensational and exaggerated: *His soldiers, who, save for a few rare melodramatic encounters, saw nothing of him, idolized their "Little Corporal"* (H. G. Wells). **SYN:** See syn. under **dramatic.**
**—*n.*** **melodramatics,** melodramatic actions: *Her tears and other melodramatics did not keep her father from saying "no."*
**—mel′o|dra|mat′i|cal|ly,** *adv.*

**mel|o|dram|a|tist** (mel′ə dram′ə tist, -drä′mə-), *n.* a writer of melodrama.

**mel|o|dram|a|tize** (mel′ə dram′ə tīz, -drä′mə-), *v.t.,* **-tized, -tiz|ing.** **1** to make into a melodrama. **2** to make melodramatic.

**mel|o|dy** (mel′ə dē), *n., pl.* **-dies.** **1** sweet music; any sweet sound: *The birds chant melody on every bush* (Shakespeare). **2** musical quality: *the melody of a voice, the melody of verse.* **3** a succession of single tones in music; tune. Most music has melody, harmony, and rhythm. *She sang some sweet old melodies.* **4** the main tune in music with harmony; air. **SYN:** theme. **5** a poem suitable for singing: *Thomas Moore's "Irish Melodies."* [< Old French *melodie,* learned borrowing from Late Latin *melōdia* < Greek *melōidíā* < *mélos* song + *ōidḗ* song < *aeídein* sing]

**mel|oid** (mel′oid), *n., adj.* **—*n.*** any beetle of a family that includes the blister beetles.
**—*adj.*** of or like these beetles.
[< New Latin *Meloïdae* the family name < *Meloē* the typical genus; origin uncertain]

**mel|o|lon|thine** (mel′ə lon′thīn, -thin), *adj., n.* **—*adj.*** of or having to do with a subfamily of beetles, including the June bugs and chafers.
**—*n.*** a melolonthine beetle.
[< New Latin *Melolontha* the typical genus (< Greek *mēlolónthē* cockchafer) + English *-ine*[1]]

**mel|o|mane** (mel′ə mān), *n.* = melomaniac. [< French *mélomane*]

**mel|o|ma|ni|a** (mel′ə mā′nē ə), *n.* a mania for music. [< French *mélomanie* < Greek *mélos* song + *maniā* madness]

**mel|o|ma|ni|ac** (mel′ə mā′nē ak), *n.* a person who has a mania for music.

**mel|on** (mel′ən), *n.* **1** the large, juicy fruit of a vine much like the pumpkin, squash, and cucumber. It belongs to the gourd family. Watermelons and muskmelons are different kinds. **2** a deep-pink color. **3** a round mass of blubber at the top of the head of certain cetaceans, such as the dolphin. **4** *U.S. Slang.* a sum of money representing an excess of profits, political or criminal loot, or other monetary gain, for sharing by the owners of or the participants in an enterprise.
**cut** (or **split**) **a melon,** *U.S. Slang.* to divide extra profits among those considered to have a claim on them: *The corporation cut a melon for its stockholders at the end of the year.*
[< Old French *melon* < Late Latin *mēlō, -ōnis,* short for Latin *mēlopepō* < Greek *mēlopépōn* < *mêlon* apple + *pépōn* gourd] **—mel′on|like′,** *adj.*

**melon aphid,** an aphid that attacks cucumber and cotton plants and spreads mosaic disease.

**melon fly,** a fly whose larvae bore into melons, cucumbers, and tomatoes, related to the fruit fly.

**melon shell,** the shell of a marine gastropod, such as the bailer, so called from the shape.

**mel|o|plas|ty** (mel′ə plas′tē), *n., pl.* **-ties.** plastic surgery of the cheek. [< Greek *mêlon* apple; later, cheek + English *-plasty*]

**mel|os** (mel′os, mē′los), *n. Music.* melody: *The singer repeated endlessly a short phrase of melos* (London Times). [< Greek *mélos* song]

**Me|lox|ine** (me lok′sin), *n. Trademark.* a drug which increases the resistance of the skin to sunburn, taken orally in pill form; methoxsalen. *Formula:* $C_{12}H_8O_4$

**Mel|pom|e|ne** (mel pom′ə nē), *n. Greek Mythology.* the Muse of tragedy.

**melt** (melt), *v.,* **melt|ed, melt|ed** or **mol|ten, melt|ing,** *n.* **—*v.t.*** **1** to change from a solid to a liquid by applying heat: *to melt ice or butter. Great heat melts iron.* **2** to dissolve: *to melt sugar in water.* **3** *Figurative.* to cause to disappear gradually; disperse: *The noon sun will melt away the fog. These our actors ... were all spirits, and Are melted into air* (Shakespeare). **4** *Figurative.* to change very gradually; blend; merge: *Dusk melted the colors of the hill into a soft gray.* **5** *Figurative.* to make tender or gentle; soften: *Pity melted her heart.* **SYN:** mollify.
**—*v.i.*** **1** to be changed from a solid to a liquid by applying heat: *The ice on the sidewalks had melted in the sunshine.* **2** to dissolve; appear to disintegrate: *Sugar melts in water.* **3** *Figurative.* to disappear gradually; vanish; disappear: *The clouds melted away, and the sun came out. The crowd melted away.* **4** *Figurative.* to waste away; dwindle: *His wealth melted away.* **5** *Figurative.* to change very gradually; blend; merge: *In the rainbow, the green melts into blue, the blue into violet.* **6** *Figurative.* to become softened; be made gentle; soften: *I had a good deal melted towards our enemy* (Robert Louis Stevenson). **7** to suffer from the heat: *You will melt if you sit so close to the fire.* **8** *Obsolete.* to be overwhelmed by grief.
**—*n.*** **1** the act or process of melting. **2** the state of being melted. **3** a melted metal. **4** a quantity of metal melted at one operation or over a specified period, especially a single charge in smelting: *A number of melters using both pig iron and scrap have begun to use more pig iron in their melt* (Baltimore Sun). **5** the spleen; milt.
[fusion of Old English *meltan* to melt, and *mieltan* make liquid] **—melt′er,** *n.* **—melt′ing|ly,** *adv.*
**—*Syn. v.t.* 1, 2. Melt, dissolve, thaw, fuse** mean to change from a solid state. **Melt** suggests either a gradual change caused by heat, by which a solid softens, loses shape, and finally becomes liquid (*The warm air melted the butter*) or the change of a solid going into solution in a liquid composed of another substance and becoming a part of it (*The lump of sugar melted in the cup of coffee*). **Dissolve** also has both these meanings, although the second is far more frequent: *The candle dissolved into a pool of wax as it burned. Dissolve some salt in a glass of water.* **Thaw,** used only of frozen things, means to change to the unfrozen state, either liquid or less hard and stiff: *She thawed the frozen fruit.* **Fuse** means to reduce a solid substance to a fluid state by subjecting it to a high temperature and is used especially of the blending together of metals into a combination which persists when they again solidify: *to fuse copper and tin.*

**melt|a|bil|i|ty** (mel′tə bil′ə tē), *n.* the capacity of being melted.

**melt|a|ble** (mel′tə bəl), *adj.* that can be melted.

**melt|down** (melt′doun′), *n.* a condition in which the radioactive fuel of a nuclear reactor melts through its insulation and is released because of a breakdown of its cooling system: *If there were to be a meltdown, the release of radioactivity would be retarded by the very strong reactor vessel* (Scientific American).

**mel|te|mi** (mel tā′mē), *n.* the northerly summer wind in the eastern Mediterranean and the Aegean Sea. [< New Greek *meltémi* < Turkish *meltem*]

**melt|ing point** (mel′ting), the temperature at which a solid substance melts, especially under a pressure of one atmosphere; fusing point. Different substances have different melting points. Tungsten has the highest melting point of all metallic elements. *Abbr:* m.p.

**melting pot,** **1** a country or city thought of as a place in which various races or sorts of people are assimilated: *America is the New World, where there are no races and nations any more; She is the melting pot, from which we will cast* *the better state* (H. G. Wells). **2** a pot in which metals or other substances are melted; crucible.

**mel|ton** (mel′tən), *n.* a smooth, heavy woolen cloth, used especially for overcoats: *Melton is generally made dark and plain in color* (Bernice G. Chambers). [< *Melton* Mowbray, in Leicestershire, England, a hunting center]

**melt|wa|ter** (melt′wôt′ər, -wot′-), *n.* water formed from melting ice or snow, especially from a glacier: *A valley glacier ... is far wider and thicker than the corresponding stream of meltwater* (Science News).

**mem**[1] (mem), *n.* the thirteenth letter of the Hebrew alphabet. [< Hebrew *mem*]

**mem**[2] (mem), *n. British Informal.* madam. [alteration of *ma'am*]

**mem.**, an abbreviation for the following:
**1** member.
**2** memoir.
**3** memorandum.
**4** memorial.

**mem|ber** (mem′bər), *n.* **1** a person, animal, or thing belonging to a group: *Every member of the family came home for Mother's Day. Our church has over five hundred members. The lion is a member of the cat family.* **2** a part or organ of a plant, animal, or human body, especially a leg, arm, wing, or branch. **3** a constituent part of a whole: *a member of a logical proposition.* **SYN**: component. **4** *Mathematics.* **a** a quantity that belongs to a set; element of a set. **b** the expression on either side of an equation. **5** a rafter, column, or other structural unit of a building. **6** a person elected to participate in the proceedings of a legislative body (used especially as a form of direct address by a colleague): **a** *U.S.* a member of the Congress of the United States, especially of the House of Representatives. **b** *British.* a member of the House of Commons. [< Old French *membre* < Latin *membrum* limb, part] —**mem′ber|less**, *adj.*

**-membered**, *combining form.* having ___ members: *Many-membered = having many members.*

**mem|ber|ship** (mem′bər ship), *n.* **1** the fact or state of being a member: *Do you enjoy your membership in the Boy Scouts?* **2** members as a group: *All of the club's membership was present.* **3** the number of members: *We have a large membership in our club this year.*

**mem|bral** (mem′brəl), *adj.* of or having to do with a member, especially a member of the body.

**mem|brane** (mem′brān), *n.* **1** a thin, soft skin, sheet, or layer of animal tissue, lining, covering, separating, or connecting some part of the body: *Living cells are enclosed in membranes through which they obtain their food* (K. S. Spiegler). **2** a similar layer of vegetable tissue. **3** a similar layer of some synthetic substance. The semipermeable plastic sheets used in electrodialysis are called membranes. **4** a skin of parchment forming part of a roll. [< Latin *membrāna* a (covering) membrane of skin < *membrum* member]

**membrane bone**, a bone that originates in membranous connective tissue, instead of being developed or preformed in cartilage.

**mem|bra|no|phone** (mem brā′nə fōn′), *n.* any musical instrument that produces its sound when a membrane stretched tightly over its frame is struck or rubbed. A drum is a kind of membranophone. [< Latin *membrāna* membrane + English *-phone*]

**mem|bra|nous** (mem′brə nəs, mem brā′-), *adj.* **1** of or like membrane: *The hind pair* [*of wings*] *are membranous and are used in flying* (A. M. Winchester). **2** characterized by the formation of a membrane or a lining like a membrane: *Diphtheria is a membranous disease.* —**mem′bra|nous|ly**, *adv.*

**membranous croup**, a form of croup in which a deposit similar to a membrane forms in the throat and hinders breathing.

**membranous labyrinth**, the membranous part of the inner ear.

**Me|men|to** (mə men′tō), *n.* (in the Roman Catholic Church) either of two prayers beginning "Memento" ("Remember") in the canon of the Mass, in which the living and the dead respectively are commemorated. [< Latin *mementō* remember, imperative of *meminisse* to remember]

**me|men|to** (mə men′tō), *n., pl.* **-tos** or **-toes**. **1** something serving as a reminder, warning, or remembrance: *These post cards are mementos of our trip abroad. This ring is a memento of an old friend.* **2** *Archaic.* a reminder, warning, or hint as to conduct or with regard to future events. [< *Memento*]

**me|men|to mo|ri** (mə men′tō môr′ī, mōr′ī), **1** *Latin.* remember that you must die. **2** an object or emblem used as a reminder that all men are mortal.

**Mem|non** (mem′non), *n.* **1** *Greek Legend.* an Ethiopian king killed during the Trojan War by Achilles and made immortal by Zeus. **2** a huge statue of an Egyptian king at Thebes, Egypt.

**Mem|no|ni|an** (mem nō′nē ən), *adj.* of, having to do with, or resembling Memnon.

**mem|o** (mem′ō), *n., pl.* **mem|os**. *Informal.* a memorandum: *The memo contains all the ideas being discussed at that time* (Bulletin of Atomic Scientists).

**mem|oir** (mem′wär, -wôr), *n.* **1** a biography, now especially a relatively short or limited one; biographical note. **2** a report of a scientific or scholarly study made to a learned society.
**memoirs, a** a record of facts and events written from personal knowledge or special information: *memoirs of the Scottish clans.* **b** a record of a person's own life and experiences; autobiography: *General Marshall rejected offers up to $1 million for his memoirs* (Newsweek).
[< Middle French *mémoire,* masculine < Old French *memoire,* feminine, memory. See etym. of doublet **memory**.]

**mem|oir|ist** (mem′wär ist, -wôr-), *n.* a person who writes or has written a memoir or memoirs: *Sargent has been characterized by some memoirists as a dull man* (New Yorker).

**mem|o|ra|bil|i|a** (mem′ər ə bil′ē ə), *n.pl.* **1** things or events worth remembering; noteworthy things: *a full disclosure of the memorabilia of my life* (Charles J. Lever). **2** an account of such things: *A man of gelid reserve who ... left no paper trail of written memorabilia* (New Yorker). [< Latin *memorābilia,* neuter plural of *memorābilis;* see etym. under **memorable**]

**mem|o|ra|bil|i|ty** (mem′ər ə bil′ə tē), *n., pl.* **-ties**. **1** the quality of being memorable; memorableness. **2** a person or thing worth remembering.

**mem|o|ra|ble** (mem′ər ə bəl), *adj., n.* —*adj.* worth remembering; not to be forgotten; notable: *The play "Peter Pan" has many memorable scenes. He nothing common did or mean Upon that memorable scene* (Andrew Marvell). **SYN**: remarkable, extraordinary.
—*n.* Often, **memorables**. a memorable or notable thing: *When I take up my pen to record the memorables of this Ann. Dom.* (John Galt).
[< Latin *memorābilis* < *memorāre* to remind < *memor, -oris* mindful] —**mem′o|ra|ble|ness**, *n.*

**mem|o|ra|bly** (mem′ər ə blē), *adv.* in a memorable manner; so as to be remembered.

**mem|o|ran|da** (mem′ə ran′də), *n.* memorandums; a plural of **memorandum**.

**mem|o|ran|dum** (mem′ə ran′dəm), *n., pl.* **-dums** or **-da**. **1** a short written statement for future use; note to aid one's memory: *Mother made a memorandum of the groceries needed. A memorandum on his desk reminded him that it was his wife's birthday. "The horror of that moment," the Kind went on, "I shall never, never forget!" "You will, though," the Queen said, "if you don't make a memorandum of it"* (Lewis Carroll). **2** an informal letter, note, or report: *I contented myself ... to write down only the most remarkable events of my life, without continuing a memorandum of other things* (Daniel Defoe). **3** *Law.* a writing containing the terms of a transaction. **4** (in diplomacy) a summary of facts and arguments on some issue or arrangement that concerns two or more governments. **5** *Commerce.* a written statement of the terms under which a shipment of goods is made, authorizing their return if they are not sold within a specified time: *Sollazzo then took to peddling jewelry ... obtaining his wares on memorandum* (New Yorker). [< Latin *memorandum* (thing) to be remembered, neuter singular of *memorandus,* gerundive of *memorāre;* see etym. under **memorable**]

**me|mo|ri|al** (mə môr′ē əl, -mōr′-), *n., adj.* —*n.* **1** something that is a reminder of some event or person, such as a statue, an arch or column, a book, a holiday, or a park: *These stones shall be for a memorial unto the children of Israel forever* (Joshua 4:7). **2** a statement sent to a government or person in authority, usually giving facts and asking that some wrong be corrected. **3** (in diplomacy) any one of various informal state papers.
—*adj.* **1** helping people to remember some person, thing, or event; commemorative: *a memorial window in a church, memorial services.* **2** of or having to do with memory.
[< Latin *memoriālis* < *memoria;* see etym. under **memory**] —**me|mo′ri|al|ly**, *adv.*

**Memorial Day**, a day for honoring American servicemen who died for their country, observed by decorating graves and memorials; Decoration Day. In most states it is a legal holiday that falls on the last Monday in May. See also **Confederate Memorial Day**.

**me|mo|ri|al|ist** (mə môr′ē ə list, -mōr′-), *n.* **1** a writer of biographical or historical memorials: *the Duc de Saint-Simon, France's amplest secret memorialist and most illuminating historical gossip* (New Yorker). **2** a person who presents a memorial.

**me|mo|ri|al|ize** (mə môr′ē ə līz, -mōr′-), *v.t.,* **-ized, -iz|ing**. **1** to preserve the memory of; be a memorial of; commemorate. **2** to submit a memorial to; petition. —**me|mo′ri|al|i|za′tion**, *n.* —**me|mo′ri|al|iz′er**, *n.*

**memorial park**, *U.S.* a cemetery.

**me|mo|ri|a tech|ni|ca** (mə môr′ē ə tek′nə kə, -mōr′-), a method of aiding the memory by a form of words or other device; system of mnemonics. [< New Latin *memoria technica* technical (artificial) memory]

**mem|o|ried** (mem′ər ēd), *adj.* filled or associated with memories: *a memoried castle.*

**-memoried**, *combining form.* having a ___ memory: *Long-memoried = having a long memory.*

**mem|o|rise** (mem′ə rīz), *v.t.,* **-rised, -ris|ing**. *Especially British.* memorize.

**me|mo|ri|ter** (mə mor′ə tər), *adv. Latin.* from memory; by heart.

**mem|o|riz|a|ble** (mem′ə rī′zə bəl), *adj.* that can be memorized.

**mem|o|ri|za|tion** (mem′ər ə zā′shən), *n.* the act of memorizing: *... mere memorization of fact or a formula* (Science News).

**mem|o|rize** (mem′ə rīz), *v.t.,* **-rized, -riz|ing**. to commit to memory; learn by heart: *We have all memorized the alphabet. He memorized his lines for the play.* —**mem′o|riz′er**, *n.*

**mem|o|ry** (mem′ər ē, mem′rē), *n., pl.* **-ries**. **1** the ability to remember or keep in the mind; capacity to retain or recall that which is learned or experienced: *She has a better memory than her sister has.* **2** the act or fact of remembering; remembrance; recollection: *the memory of things past. That vacation lives in her memory.* **3** a person, thing, or event that is remembered: *His mother died when he was small; she is only a memory to him now.* **4** all that a person remembers; what can be recalled to mind: *to examine one's memory carefully.* **5** the length of past time that is remembered: *This has been the hottest summer within my memory.* **6** reputation after death; *ancient heroes of noble memory.* **7a** any device or equipment in a computer, such as a magnetic core or magnetic drum, in which information can be stored and extracted at a later time: *A thin-film superconducting memory that can store 16,384 "bits" of computer information in an area ... only 120 millionth of an inch thick has been developed* (New Scientist). **b** the amount of information that a memory or a computer can store: *a 500,000-bit memory. Another important feature ... is the machine's ability to take its instructions immediately from its 1,024 "word" electronic memory* (Wall Street Journal).
**commit to memory**, to learn by heart; memorize: *... no longer compelled to commit to memory many thousand verses* (Benjamin Jowett).
**in memory of**, to help in remembering; as a reminder of: *I sent this card in memory of our happy summer together.*
[< Old French *memorie,* learned borrowing from Latin *memoria* < *memor, -oris* mindful. See etym. of doublet **memoir**.]
—*Syn.* **2. Memory, recollection** mean the act or fact of remembering. **Memory** emphasizes keeping in mind something once learned or experienced: *Her memory of the incident is still fresh.* **Recollection** emphasizes calling back to mind, often with effort, something not thought of for a long time: *I have little recollection of my childhood.*

**memory bank**, the data stored in a computer memory; databank: *By pushing buttons on a console, the clerk queries a regional computer's "memory bank" and gets an instant reading on what seats are available. Customers then can have their tickets printed electronically on the spot* (Time).

**memory core**, = magnetic core: *One possibility from work with superconductors is smaller and faster memory cores for computers* (Wall Street Journal).

**memory drum**, = magnetic drum: *The memory drum of a computer at a medical college holds millions of pieces of evidence regarding the results of certain types of treatment based on particular symptoms* (Walter Buckingham).

**memory switch**, an Ovonic device which remains in a semiconducting state until a pulse of electricity is applied to close it.

**memory television**, a device that can record and play back televised pictures, either attached to or incorporated in a standard television set: *Memory television ... has a refreshable memory capable of storing one or more frames of a*

---

**Pronunciation Key:** hat, āge, cãre, fär; let, ēqual, tėrm; it, īce; hot, ōpen, ôrder; oil, out; cup, pu̇t, rüle; child; long; thin; ᴛʜen; zh, measure; ə represents a in about, e in taken, i in pencil, o in lemon, u in circus.

*television signal* (Kimio Ito).

**memory trace**, a chemical change occurring in the brain when new information is absorbed and remembered: *The two most popular chemical contenders for this elusive "memory trace" ... have been ribonucleic acid (RNA) and protein. The learning process is assumed to produce changes in these molecules which then, on recall, alter in some way the properties of the neural synapses and allow the memory to be expressed* (New Scientist).

**Mem|phi|an** (mem′fē ən), *adj.* **1** having to do with Memphis in ancient Egypt. **2** of Egypt; Egyptian.

**Mem|phite** (mem′fīt), *n.* **1** a native or inhabitant of Memphis in ancient Egypt. **2** the Coptic dialect spoken in the neighborhood of ancient Memphis, or, formerly, the dialect spoken in the neighborhood of Alexandria.

**Mem|phit|ic** (mem fit′ik), *adj.* = Memphian.

**mem|sa|hib** (mem′sä′ib), *n.* a term of respect for a European woman in colonial India, used by native servants: *Throughout most of the tropics it was below the dignity of the sahib, and especially the memsahib, to do physical labor* (Harper's). [Anglo-Indian *mem-sāhib* < *mem* (< English *ma'am*) + *sāhib* master < Arabic *ṣaḥib*]

**men** (men), *n.* **1** plural of **man**. Boys grow up to be men. **2** human beings; persons in general: *"All men are created equal." Men and animals have some things in common. The best laid schemes o' mice and men Gang aft a-gley* (Robert Burns). *It is impossible to find any exact physical basis for the division of apes from men* (Observer).

**men|ace** (men′is), *n., v.,* **-aced, -ac|ing.** —*n.* something that threatens; threat: *In dry weather, forest fires are a great menace. A whispering menace that chilled brain and blood* (Walter de la Mare).
—*v.t.* to threaten: *Floods menaced the valley towns with destruction.* SYN: See syn. under **threaten**.
—*v.i.* to be threatening: *Earth below shook; heaven above menaced* (Edmund Burke).
[< Old French *menace* < Vulgar Latin *mināciа*, singular of Latin *mināciae*, ultimately < *minae* threats, projecting points] —**men′ac|er**, *n.* —**men′ac|ing|ly**, *adv.*

**me|nad** (mē′nad), *n.* = maenad.

**me|nad|ic** (mi nad′ik), *adj.* = maenadic.

**mé|nage** or **me|nage** (mā näzh′), *n.* **1** a domestic establishment; household. **2** the management of a household: *Nothing tended to make ladies so ... inefficient in the menage as the study of dead languages* (Hannah More). [< Old French *menage* < Vulgar Latin *mansiōnāticus* household < Latin *mānsiō, -ōnis;* see etym. under **mansion**]

**mé|nage à trois** (mā näzh′ à trwä′), *French.* **1** a household comprising a married couple and the lover of one of them. **2** (literally) household of three.

**me|nag|er|ie** (mə naj′ər ē, -nazh′-), *n.* **1** a collection of wild animals kept in cages, especially for exhibition, as in a zoo or a circus: *The menagerie becomes ruthless at mealtime.* **2** the place where such animals are kept: *The menagerie was cleaned out once a day.* **3** a curious assortment or collection of people: *An old quack doctor ... completed this strange menagerie* (Macaulay). [< French *ménagerie* (literally) management of a household < *ménage;* see etym. under **ménage**]

**me|nar|che** (mə när′kē, me-), *n.* the beginning of menstruation; first menstrual period. [< Greek *mên* month + *archê* a beginning]

**men|a|zon** (men′ə zon), *n.* a systemic insecticide used widely because of its low toxicity to mammals. *Formula:* $C_6H_{12}N_5O_2PS_2$ [apparently irregular formation < (di)*me*(thyl) + (tri)*az*(in) + (thi)*on*(ate)]

**men-chil|dren** (men′chil′drən), *n.* plural of **man-child**.

**Menck|e|ni|an** (meng kē′nē ən), *adj., n.* —*adj.* of, having to do with, or characteristic of the American author, journalist, and critic H. L. Mencken (1880-1956) or his writings; sharply critical of existing institutions; iconoclastic: *Menckenian satire.*
—*n.* an admirer or follower of H. L. Mencken or his works.

**mend** (mend), *v., n.* —*v.t.* **1** to put in good condition again; make whole; repair: *to mend a road, to mend a broken doll, to mend stockings.* **2** to remove or correct faults in: *He should mend his manners.* SYN: better. **3** to remove (a fault); correct (a defect): *to mend an error.* SYN: rectify. **4** to restore to proper condition by any action: *to mend a fire by adding fuel.* **5** to set right; improve: *Try to mend matters with her.* **6** to make better; improve; advance: *He ... mended his worldly prospects by a matrimonial union with a widow lady of large property* (Harriet Beecher Stowe). **7** *Informal.* to improve on; surpass.
—*v.i.* **1** to get back one's health: *The child will soon mend if she has enough to eat.* **2** to become better; improve: *There is no prospect of matters mending.* **3** to make amends: *Least said, soonest mended.*
—*n.* **1** a place that has been mended: *The mend in your dress scarcely shows.* **2** a mending; improvement.
**on the mend, a** improving: *Home trade in finished linens is perhaps on the mend* (London Daily News). **b** getting well: *My health is on the mend.*
[Middle English *menden,* probably variant of *amenden* amend] —**mend′er**, *n.*
—*Syn. v.t.* **1 Mend, repair, patch** mean to put in good or usable condition again. **Mend** means to restore something that has been broken, torn, or worn, but is now seldom used of large things: *She mended the broken cup with cement.* **Repair** means to make right again something damaged, run down, decayed, or weakened: *He repaired the old barn.* **Patch** means to mend by putting a piece (or amount) of material on or in a hole, tear, or worn place: *His mother patched his torn trousers.*

**mend|a|ble** (men′də bəl), *adj.* that can be mended.

**men|da|cious** (men dā′shəs), *adj.* **1** lying; untruthful; given to telling lies. *The mendacious beggar told a different tale of woe at every house.* SYN: dishonest. **2** false; untrue: *a mendacious report, mendacious rumors.* SYN: spurious. [< Latin *mendāx, -ācis* lying + English *-ous*] —**men|da′cious|ly**, *adv.* —**men|da′cious|ness**, *n.*

**men|dac|i|ty** (men das′ə tē), *n., pl.* **-ties. 1** the habit of telling lies; untruthfulness: *The natural mendacity of fishermen is epitomized in "the bigger one that got away."* **2** = lie. SYN: falsehood.

**Men|de** (men′dē), *n., pl.* **-de** or **-des. 1** a member of a tribe of west African people living in the central and southeastern part of Sierra Leone. **2** the Mandingo language of this people.

**Men|de|le|ev's** or **Men|de|ley|ev's law** (men′də lā′əfs), *Chemistry.* the periodic law. [< Dmitri *Mendeleev,* 1834-1907, a Russian chemist, who formulated it]

***men|de|le|vi|um** (men′də lē′vē əm, -lā′-), *n.* a rare, highly radioactive, metallic chemical element, produced artificially from einsteinium: *Element 101, mendelevium, was first made in 1955, by Dr. Glenn Seaborg* (Science News Letter). [< New Latin *mendelivium* < Dmitri *Mendeleev;* see etym. under **Mendeleev's law**]

***mendelevium**

| symbol | atomic number | mass number |
|---|---|---|
| Md | 101 | 256 |

**Men|de|li|an** (men dē′lē ən), *adj., n.* —*adj.* **1** of or having to do with Gregor Johann Mendel or Mendel's laws: *Any heredity is now considered Mendelian if it is dependent on chromosomes* (A. Franklin Shull). **2** inherited in accordance with Mendel's laws: *Phenylketonuria is a metabolic defect transmitted genetically as a Mendelian recessive factor* (Saturday Review).
—*n.* a follower of Mendel or supporter of his theories.

**Men|de|li|an|ism** (men dē′lē ə niz′əm), *n.* = Mendelism.

**Men|del|ism** (men′də liz əm), *n.* the doctrines of Gregor Johann Mendel.

**Men|del's laws** (men′dəlz), the laws or principles governing the inheritance of certain characteristics by plants and animals, formulated by Gregor Johann Mendel (1822-1884), an Austrian monk and botanist, in experiments with peas. They state that each characteristic is inherited independently, that characteristics show dominant and recessive forms, and that successive generations of crossbred offspring exhibit inherited characteristics in different combinations, each combination in a specific proportion of individuals. *Ideas of dominance, and of independent units, together with a third, usually referred to as segregation, have come to be called Mendel's Laws* (Fred W. Emerson).

**men|di|can|cy** (men′də kən sē), *n.* **1** the act of begging: *Mendicancy in the East is regarded as no disgrace.* **2** the state of being a beggar: *After a riotous youth, ill health and bad habits reduced him to mendicancy.*

**men|di|cant** (men′də kənt), *adj., n.* —*adj.* begging: *Mendicant friars ask alms for charity. And with that dejected air and mendicant voice* (Samuel Richardson).
—*n.* **1** a beggar: *We were surrounded by mendicants asking for money.* **2** a member of a mendicant religious order.
[< Latin *mendīcāns, -antis,* present participle of *mendīcāre* beg < *mendīcus* beggar]

**men|dic|i|ty** (men dis′ə tē), *n.* beggary; mendicancy: *Among the poor, and in times of great strife among all that are displaced, mendicity becomes a way of life.* [< Middle French *mendicité,* learned borrowing from Latin *mendīcitās, -ātis* < *mendicus* beggar]

**men|e|hu|ne** (men′ə hü′nə), *n., pl.* **-ne** or **-nes.** a legendary Polynesian dwarf or elf who worked only at night, building ponds, roads, and similar projects. [< Hawaiian *menehune*]

**Men|e|la|us** (men′ə lā′əs), *n. Greek Legend.* a king of Sparta, husband of Helen of Troy, and brother of Agamemnon. He was the son of Atreus.

**men|folk** (men′fōk′), *n.pl.* **1** men. **2** the male members of a family or other group: ... *a nation of 2.5 million whose menfolk often work abroad* (Economist).

**men|folks** (men′fōks′), *n.pl.* = menfolk.

**men-gods** (men′godz′), *n.* plural of **man-god**.

**men|ha|den** (men hā′dən), *n., pl.* **-den.** a sea fish common along the eastern coast of the United States, used for making oil, meal, and fertilizer; pogy; mossbunker. The menhaden belongs to the same family as the herring and has the appearance of a shad but with a more compressed body. [American English < Algonkian (probably Narragansett) *munnawhateaûg* a fish like a herring; (literally) they fertilize]

**men|hir** (men′hir), *n. Archaeology.* an upright monumental stone (megalith) standing either alone or with others, typical of the monuments of the megalithic culture of western Europe. [< French *menhir* < Breton *men hir* < *men* stone + *hir* long]

**me|ni|al** (mē′nē əl, mēn′yəl), *adj., n.* —*adj.* belonging to or suited to a servant; low; mean: *Cinderella had to do menial tasks. Her ladyship was of humble, I have even heard menial, station originally* (Thackeray). SYN: servile, slavish.
—*n.* **1** a servant who does the humblest and most unpleasant tasks: *I worked for a menial's hire, Only to learn, dismayed, That any wage I had asked for Life, Life would have paid* (Jessie B. Rittenhouse). **2** a low, mean, or servile person; flunky.
[< Anglo-French *menial* < *meiniée,* variant of Old French *meisniee* household < Vulgar Latin *mansiōnāta* < Latin *mānsiō, -ōnis* habitation; see etym. under **mansion**] —**me′ni|al|ly**, *adv.*

**Mé|nière's** or **Me|nier's disease** or **syndrome** (mā nyārz′), a disease of the inner ear which causes dizziness and may lead to deafness. [< Prosper *Ménière,* 1799-1862, a French physician who first described it]

**me|nin|ge|al** (mə nin′jē əl), *adj.* of or having to do with the meninges.

**me|nin|ges** (mə nin′jēz), *n., pl. of* **me|ninx.** the three protective membranes that surround the brain and spinal cord. They are the pia mater, arachnoid membrane, and dura mater. [< New Latin *meninges* < Greek *mêninx, -ingos* (body) membrane]

**me|nin|gi|o|ma** (mə nin′jē ō′mə), *n., pl.* **-mas, -ma|ta** (-mə tə). a tumor situated in the meninges that grows by expansion, causing damage to the brain: *Meningioma ... can often be cured by surgery* (Sunday Times). [< *mening*(es) + *-oma*]

**men|in|git|ic** (men′in jit′ik), *adj.* relating to, having to do with, or affected by meningitis.

**men|in|gi|tis** (men′in jī′tis), *n.* a very serious infectious disease in which the membranes surrounding the brain or spinal cord are inflamed. Meningitis is usually caused by a bacterium or virus and results in acute, sometimes fatal, illness. *In meningitis, several or all of the following symptoms may appear: headache, vomiting, dizziness, stiff neck, sore throat* (Sidonie M. Gruenberg). [< *mening*(es) + *-itis*]

**me|nin|go|coc|cal** (mə ning′gə kok′əl), *adj.* having to do with or caused by meningococci.

**me|nin|go|coc|cic** (mə ning′gə kok′sik), *adj.* = meningococcal.

**me|nin|go|coc|cus** (mə ning′gə kok′əs), *n., pl.* **-ci** (-sī). a bacterium or coccus that causes cerebrospinal meningitis. [< *mening*(es) + *coccus*]

**me|ninx** (mē′ningks), *n.* singular of **meninges**.

**me|nis|coid** (mə nis′koid), *adj.* like a meniscus; cresent-shaped: concavo-convex.

***me|nis|cus** (mə nis′kəs), *n., pl.* **-nis|cus|es, -nis|ci** (-nis′ī). **1** *Physics.* the curved upper surface of a column of liquid, caused by capillarity. It is concave when the walls of the container are moistened, convex when they are dry. *Most liquids wet glass, and therefore have a concave meniscus* (W. N. Jones). **2** a lens, convex on one side and concave on the other. A meniscus is thicker in the center so that it has a crescent-shaped section. **3** a crescent or crescent-shaped body.

[< New Latin *meniscus* < Greek *mēnískos* (diminutive) of *mēnē* moon]

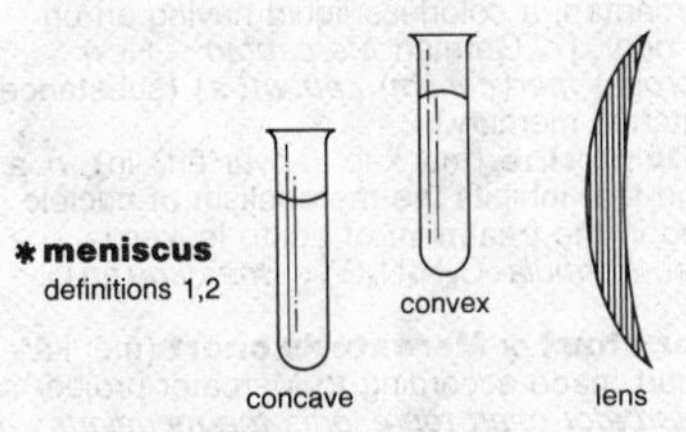

***meniscus**
definitions 1,2

**men|i|sper|ma|ceous** (men′ə spėr mā′shəs), *adj.* belonging to a family of dicotyledonous, chiefly tropical, woody, climbing plants, having small, usually three-parted flowers, and possessing narcotic properties, typified by the moonseed. [< New Latin *Menispermaceae* the family name (< *Menispermum* the typical genus < Greek *mēnē* moon + *spérma* seed) + English *-ous* (because of their crescent-shaped seeds)]

**Men|non|ist** (men′ə nist), *n.* = Mennonite.

**Men|non|ite** (men′ə nīt), *n.* a member of a Christian church opposed to infant baptism, taking oaths, holding public office that requires use of force, and military service. The Mennonites often wear very plain clothes and live simply. They are descended from an Anabaptist church that originated in the 1530's in Friesland and Holland. [< *Menno* Simons, of Friesland, 1492-1559, a leader of the original church + *-ite*[1]]

**me|no** (mā′nō), *adv. Music.* less (used as a direction, always with another word). [< Italian *meno* (literally) less < Latin *minus* less]

**men|o|branch** (men′ə brangk), *n.* any salamander of a group characterized by persistent gills forming external tufts, and by four limbs, each having four well-developed digits. [< New Latin *Menobranchus* the typical genus < Greek *ménein* remain + *bránchia* gills]

**men-of-war** (men′əv wôr′), *n.* plural of **man-of-war.**

**me|nol|o|gy** (mi nol′ə jē), *n., pl.* **-gies. 1** an annotated calendar of the months. **2** the calendar of the Greek Church with lives of the saints in the order of their festivals. **3** a series of saints' biographies arranged according to the calendar. [< New Latin *menologium* < Late Greek *mēnológion* < *mên* month + *lógos* an account, treatment < *légein* to tell]

**Me|nom|i|nee** (mə nom′ə nē), *n., pl.* **-nees** or **-nee. 1** a member of a tribe of Indians living in Wisconsin, northern Michigan, and northern Illinois, of Algonkian stock. **2** the Algonkian language of this tribe.

**Menominee whitefish**, a commercially valuable whitefish found in the lakes of New England and the Adirondacks, in the Great Lakes, and in Alaskan waters.

**me|no mos|so** (mā′nō môs′sō), *Music.* not so fast; slower (used as a direction). [< Italian *meno mosso*]

**men|o|paus|al** (men′ə pô′zəl), *adj.* = menopausic.

**men|o|pause** (men′ə pôz), *n.* the final cessation of the menses, occurring normally between the ages of 45 and 50; change of life; climacteric: *Menstrual periods ... continue from the onset of puberty until the menopause* (Harbaugh and Goodrich). [< Greek *mēn* month + *paûsis* cessation]

**men|o|paus|ic** (men′ə pô′zik), *adj.* having symptoms of the menopause.

**men|o|pome** (men′ə pōm), *n.* any one of the amphibians, such as the hellbender, with persistent branchial apertures. [< New Latin *Menopoma* the typical genus < Greek *ménein* remain + *pôma* lid]

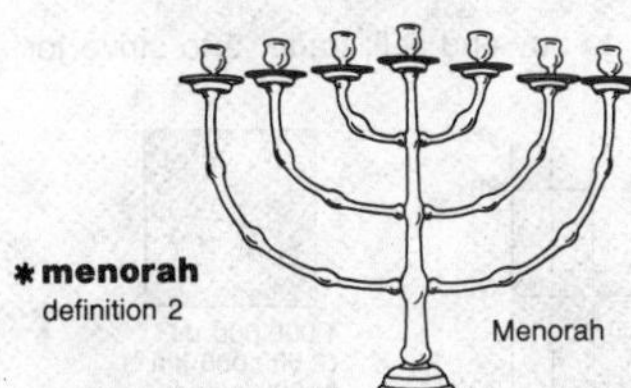

***menorah**
definition 2

***me|nor|ah** (mə nôr′ə, -nōr′-), *n.* **1** Also, **Menorah.** a candlestick with eight branches, used during the Jewish festival of Hanukkah. Many menorahs have a ninth branch for the shames, or extra candle, used to light the others. Each night an additional candle is lit until finally all are lit on the last night. **2 Menorah**, a candlestick having seven branches, in the ancient Temple at Jerusalem, whose flame was fed by consecrated oil. According to the Apocrypha, when the Temple was rededicated after Judas Maccabaeus and his brothers overthrew the Syrians (about 165 B.C.) the Menorah burned for eight days with only a single day's supply of oil. [< Hebrew *manorah*]

**men|or|rha|gi|a** (men′ə rā′jē ə), *n.* excessive menstrual discharge. [< New Latin *menorrhagia* < Greek *mênes* the menses + *rhēgnýnai* burst forth, flood]

**Men|sa**[1] (men′sə), *n., genitive* **Men|sae.** a southern constellation.

**Men|sa**[2] (men′sə), *n.* an international club for people of superior intelligence who must take a series of intelligence tests before being accepted as members. [< Latin *mēnsa* table]

**Men|sae** (men′sē), *n.* genitive of **Mensa**[1].

**men|sal**[1] (men′səl), *adj.* = monthly. [< Latin *mēnsis* month + English *-al*[1]]

**men|sal**[2] (men′səl), *adj.* of, having to do with, or used at the table. [< Latin *mēnsālis* < *mēnsa* table]

**mensch** (mench), *n., pl.* **men|schen** (men′chən). *U.S. Slang.* a respected person; decent human being: *The seedy Dallas strip-joint owner ... yearned to be a mensch, a pillar of the community* (Time). [< Yiddish *mentsh* (literally) a person, human being < German *Mensch*]

**mense** (mens), *n. Scottish.* **1** propriety; decorum. **2** neatness; tidiness. [< Scandinavian (compare Old Icelandic *mennska* humanity; kindness)]

**mense|ful** (mens′fəl), *adj. Scottish.* **1** proper; decorous. **2** neat; tidy.

**mense|less** (mens′lis), *adj. Scottish.* lacking propriety or decorum.

**men|serv|ants** (men′sėr′vənts), *n.* plural of **manservant.**

**men|ses** (men′sēz), *n.pl.* the discharge of bloody fluid from the uterus that normally occurs approximately every four weeks between puberty and the menopause. [< Latin *mēnses*, plural of *mēnsis* month]

**Men|she|vik** (men′shə vik), *n., pl.* **Men|she|viks, Men|she|vi|ki** (men′shə vē′kē). a member of the less radical wing of the Russian Social Democratic Party, opposed to the Bolsheviks from 1903 to 1917. [< Russian *men'shevik* < *men'shij* lesser (because of their temporary minority within the party; so named by V. I. Lenin at a party congress in 1903)]

**Men|she|vism** or **men|she|vism** (men′shə vizəm), *n.* the doctrines or principles of the Mensheviks.

**Men|she|vist** or **men|she|vist** (men′shə vist), *n., adj.* **—*n.*** = Menshevik.
**—*adj.*** of the Mensheviks or Menshevism.

**Men's Lib** or **Men's Liberation**, *U.S.* a group or movement of males whose aim is to free men from their traditional image and role in society: *The member of Men's Lib say they are tired of "having to prove our masculinity twenty-four hours a day"* (New Yorker). [patterned on *Women's Lib, Women's Liberation*]

**mens re|a** (menz rē′ə), *Law.* criminal intent: *One is not anxious to multiply criminal offences in which there is no mens rea* (London Times). [< Latin *mēns rea* a guilty mind]

**men's room**, *U.S.* a public lavatory for men.

**mens sa|na in cor|po|re sa|no** (menz sā′nə in kôr′pə rē sā′nō), *Latin.* a sound mind in a sound body.

**men|stru|al** (men′strü əl), *adj.* **1** of or having to do with the menses: *the menstrual discharge.* **2** = monthly.

**men|stru|ate** (men′strü āt), *v.i.,* **-at|ed, -at|ing.** to have a discharge of bloody fluid from the uterus, normally at intervals of approximately four weeks. [< Late Latin *mēnstruāre* (with English *-ate*[1]) < Latin *mēnstrua* the menses < *mēnsis* month; see etym. under **menses**]

**men|stru|a|tion** (men′strü ā′shən), *n.* the act or period of menstruating: *The interval from ovulation to menstruation is about two weeks* (Sidonie Gruenberg).

**men|stru|ous** (men′strü əs), *adj.* **1** menstruating. **2** = menstrual. [< Late Latin *mēnstruōsus,* or < Latin *mēnstruus* (with English *-ous*) < *mēnsis* month]

**men|stru|um** (men′strü əm), *n., pl.* **-stru|ums, -stru|a** (-strü ə). *Archaic.* any liquid substance that dissolves a solid; solvent. [< Medieval Latin *menstruum,* neuter of Latin *mēnstruus* menstrual, monthly; see etym. under **menstruous** (from the medieval alchemists' reputed belief in the dissolving capacity of the menses)]

**men|su|ra|bil|i|ty** (men′shər ə bil′ə tē), *n.* the property of being mensurable.

**men|su|ra|ble** (men′shər ə bəl), *adj.* **1** = measurable. **2** having assigned limits. [< Late Latin *mēnsūrābilis* < Latin *mēnsūrāre* to measure]

**men|su|ral** (men′shər əl), *adj.* having to do with measure.

**men|su|rate** (men′shə rāt), *v.t.,* **-rat|ed, -rat|ing.** = measure.

**men|su|ra|tion** (men′shə rā′shən), *n.* **1** the act, art, or process of measuring. **2** the branch of mathematics that deals with finding lengths, areas, and volumes. [< Late Latin *mensūrātiō, -ōnis* < *mēnsūrāre* to measure < Latin *mēnsūra* a measure]

**men|su|ra|tive** (men′shə rā′tiv), *adj.* adapted for or concerned with measuring.

**mens|wear** (menz′wãr′), *n., adj.* **—*n.* 1** clothing for men. **2** cloth characteristically used in making suits for men.
**—*adj.*** of or made from this cloth: *menswear flannel.*

**-ment**, *suffix added to verbs to form nouns.* **1** the act or state or fact of ___ing: *Enjoyment = the act of enjoying.*
**2** the condition of being ___ed: *Amazement = the condition of being amazed.*
**3** the product or result of ___ing: *Pavement = the product of paving. Measurement = the result of measuring.*
**4** thing that ___s: *Inducement = a thing that induces.*
**5** two or more of these meanings, as in *improvement, measurement, settlement.*
**6** other meanings, as in *ailment, basement.*
[< Old French *-ment* < Latin *-mentum* result of]

**men|tal**[1] (men′təl), *adj.* **1** of the mind: *a mental test, mental illness.* **2** for the mind: *a mental reminder.* **3** done by or existing in the mind; without the use of written figures: *mental arithmetic.*
**4a** having a mental disease or weakness: *a mental patient.* **b** for people having a disease of the mind or a mental deficiency: *a mental hospital.*
**5** concerned with the mind and its phenomena: *a mental specialist.* [< Middle French *mental,* learned borrowing from Late Latin *mentālis* < Latin *mēns, mentis* mind]

**men|tal**[2] (men′təl), *adj.* of, having to do with, or in the region of the chin. [< Latin *mentum* chin + English *-al*[1]]

**mental age**, *Psychology.* a measure of the mental development or general intelligence of an individual in terms of the average performance of normal individuals of various ages. It is determined by a series of tests that are prepared to show natural intelligence rather than the result of education.

**mental deficiency**, a lack of ordinary intelligence such as to place the individual at a disadvantage in school and adult life, ranging from mild (with an intelligence quotient between 70 and 85) to severe or profound (with an intelligence quotient below 50); feeble-mindedness: *Mental deficiency, or feeble-mindedness, is an arrested development of the brain* (Marguerite Clark).

**mental health**, the state of being well mentally, characterized by soundness of thought and outlook, adaptability to one's environment, and balanced behavior: *On all sides we see the signs of an anxious, awakened interest in this grave problem of mental health* (New York Times).

**mental hygiene**, the science that deals with the preservation of mental health.

**mental illness**, any sickness or disorder of the mind, ranging from mild emotional disturbances, such as a neurosis, to severe personality disorders such as psychosis and schizophrenia: *There are probably as many different kinds of mental illnesses as there are kinds of physical illnesses* (Sidonie M. Gruenberg).

**men|tal|ism** (men′tə liz əm), *n.* the doctrine that mental processes are valid subjects of scientific study and experimentation: *When the behaviorists threw out mentalism, they made stimuli and responses the critical elements* (New Scientist).

**men|tal|ist** (men′tə list), *n.* **1** a person who believes in mentalism. **2** a mind reader or telepathist: *Dunninger, who says he is a mentalist, put his eyes up against the camera and, he said, transmitted a thought to those tuned in* (New York Times).

**men|tal|is|tic** (men′tə lis′tik), *adj.* arising from or having to do with the mind or its processes as opposed to purely physical reality or biological processes: *Bloomfield strove vigorously to avoid mentalistic terms ... in the statement of his linguistic materials and believed that every truly "scientific statement is made in physical terms"* (Charles C. Fries).

**men|tal|i|ty** (men tal′ə tē), *n., pl.* **-ties. 1** mental capacity; mind: *An idiot has a very low mentality.* **2** an attitude or outlook: *a childish mentality.*

**men|tal|ly** (men′tə lē), *adv.* **1** in the mind; with the mind; by a mental operation: *He is strong physically, but weak mentally.* **2** with regard to

**Pronunciation Key:** hat, āge, cãre, fär; let, ēqual, tėrm; it, īce; hot, ōpen, ôrder; oil, out; cup, pu̇t, rüle; child; long; thin; ᴛʜen; zh, measure; ə represents a in about, e in taken, i in pencil, o in lemon, u in circus.

the mind: *Police said the bomb thrower was mentally unbalanced.*

**mental reservation**, an unexpressed qualification of a statement.

**mental retardation**, a condition in which intelligence does not develop normally because of some anomaly during pregnancy, genetic defect, disease, or physical injury: *Research in mental retardation involves many fields of study, including medicine, genetics, neurology, physiology, education, psychology, and social work* (Harriet E. Blodgett).

**mental telepathy**, = extrasensory perception.

**men|ta|tion** (men tā′shən), *n.* mental action.

**men|tha|ceous** (men thā′shəs), *adj.* belonging to the mint family of plants. [< New Latin *Menthaceae* the family name (< *Mentha* the typical genus < Latin *mentha,* variant of *menta* mint[1]) + English *-ous*]

**men|thene** (men′thēn), *n.* a colorless, liquid hydrocarbon, produced by the dehydration of menthol. *Formula:* $C_{10}H_{18}$ [< German *Menthen* < Latin *menta* mint[1]]

**men|thol** (men′thol, -thôl), *n.* a white, crystalline substance obtained from oil of peppermint, used in making medicine, in making perfumes, and in confectionery. *Formula:* $C_{10}H_{19}OH$ [< German *Menthol* < Latin *menta* mint[1] + *oleum* oil]

**men|tho|lat|ed** (men′thə lā′tid), *adj.* **1** containing menthol. **2** treated with menthol.

**men|ti|cide** (men′tə sīd), *n.* = brainwashing: *It was proposed that menticide, or political intervention in the individual human mind to force confessions or impose an ideology, should be declared an international crime* (Science News Letter). [< Latin *mēns, mentis* mind + English *-cide*[2]]

**men|tion** (men′shən), *v., n.* **—*v.t.*** to speak about; refer to: *Do not mention the accident before the children.* [< noun]

**—*n.*** a short statement; a mentioning; reference: *There was mention of our school party in the newspaper. He grows peevish at any mention of business* (Samuel Johnson).

**make mention of,** to speak of; refer to: *He made mention of a book he had read recently.*

**not to mention,** not even considering; besides: *The hotel's sports activities included boating and fishing, not to mention swimming, tennis, and golf.*

[< Old French *mention,* learned borrowing from Latin *mentiō, -ōnis* < *mēns, mentis* mind] **—men′tion|er,** *n.*

**men|tion|a|ble** (men′shə nə bəl), *adj.* that can be mentioned; worthy of mention.

***men|ton|nière** (men′tə nyãr′; *French* mäN tô-nyer′), *n.* a piece of armor for protecting the chin or lower part of the face and neck, used only on occasions of special danger. [< French *mentonnière* < *menton* chin < Latin *mentum*]

***mentonnière**

**Men|tor** (men′tər), *n. Greek Legend.* a faithful friend of Odysseus. When Odysseus went to fight the Trojans, he left his son with Mentor to be taught and advised.

**men|tor** (men′tər), *n.* a wise and trusted adviser. [< *Mentor*]

**men|tor|ship** (men′tər ship), *n.* the office of mentor.

**men|u** (men′yü, mā′nyü), *n.* **1** a list of the food served at a meal; bill of fare: *The waiter handed each guest a menu.* **2** the food served: *Everyone enjoyed the fine menu.* [< French *menu* < Middle French, small, detailed < Latin *minūtus* made small. See etym. of doublet **minute**[2].]

**me|nu|et** (mə ny e′), *n. French.* minuet (used in musical scores).

**Me|o** (mē′ō), *n., pl.* **Me|o** or **Me|os. 1** a member of a Sino-Tibetan people of the mountain slopes of Laos, Thailand, and Vietnam. **2** the language of this people.

**me|ow** (mē ou′), *n., interj., v.* **—*n., interj.*** a sound made by a cat or kitten: *The meow told me our hungry cat was outside the door.*

**—*v.i.*** to make this sound: *The hungry cat meowed and we let it in.*

**—*v.t.*** to sing or utter with a voice like that of a cat. Also, **mew, miaow, miaou, miaul.** [imitative]

**m.e.p.,** mean effective pressure.

**mep|a|crine** (mep′ə krin, -krēn), *n. British.* Atabrine.

**me|per|i|dine hydrochloride** (mə per′ə dēn), a synthetic drug used as a sedative and pain reliever; pethidine. It is not as powerful as morphine but can also cause addiction. *Formula:* $C_{15}H_{21}NO_2{\cdot}HCl$ [< *me*(thyl) (carbethoxypi)*peridine*]

**me|phen|e|sin** (mə fen′ə sin), *n.* a drug that relaxes the muscles and helps to relieve nervous tension. *Formula:* $C_{10}H_{14}O_3$ [< *me*(thyl), *phen*(oxy), (cr)*es*(yl), parts of its chemical name]

**Me|phis|to** (mi fis′tō), *n.* = Mephistopheles.

**Meph|i|stoph|e|les** (mef′ə stof′ə lēz), *n.* **1** the devil of the Faust legend. Mephistopheles was one of the chief evil spirits of medieval European demonology. **2** a powerful evil spirit; crafty devil. [< German *Mephistopheles;* origin uncertain]

**Meph|is|to|phe|li|an** or **Meph|is|to|phe|le|an** (mef′ə stə fē′lē ən), *adj.* **1** like Mephistopheles; wicked and crafty; sardonic; scoffing. **2** of or having to do with Mephistopheles.

**me|phit|ic** (mi fit′ik), *adj.* **1** having a nasty smell. **SYN:** fetid. **2** noxious; poisonous; pestilential. **SYN:** pestiferous. [< Late Latin *mephīticus* < Latin *mephītis* stench] **—me|phit′i|cal|ly,** *adv.*

**me|phi|tis** (mi fī′tis), *n.* **1** a foul or nasty smell. **SYN:** stench. **2** a noxious or pestilential vapor, especially from the earth. **SYN:** miasma. [< Latin *mephītis*]

**me|pro|ba|mate** (mə prō′bə māt), *n.* a synthetic drug widely used as a tranquilizer; Miltown; Equanil: *The ... associate professor refers to seven reports of overdoses of meprobamate and their poisoning effects* (Science News Letter). *Formula:* $C_9H_{18}N_2O_4$ [< *me*(thyl), *pro*(pyl), (dicar)*bamate,* parts of its chemical name]

**meq.,** milliequivalent.

**mer., 1** mercury. **2a** meridian. **b** meridional.

**Me|rak** (mē′rak), *n.* one of two stars (the other being Dubhe) in the Big Dipper pointing toward the North Star. Merak is the farther of the two from the North Star.

**Mer|a|tran** (mer′ə tran), *n. Trademark.* pipradol.

**mer|bro|min** (mər brō′min), *n.* = Mercurochrome.

**Mer|cal|li scale** (mer kä′lē), a scale for measuring the intensity of an earthquake, ranging from 1 to 12. [< Giuseppe *Mercalli,* an Italian scientist of the 1800's, who devised it]

**mer|can|tile** (mėr′kən til, -tīl), *adj.* **1** of merchants or trade; commercial: *a successful mercantile venture, mercantile law.* **2** engaged in trade or commerce: *a mercantile firm.* **3** of or having to do with mercantilism (def. 1). [< French *mercantile* < Italian, < *mercante* merchant < Latin *mercāns, -antis* (literally) trading < *mercārī* to trade < *merx, mercis* wares]

**mercantile agency,** = commercial agency.

**mercantile law,** = law merchant (def. 1).

**mercantile marine,** = merchant marine.

**mercantile paper,** transferable paper, such as promissory notes given by merchants for merchandise purchased or drafts drawn against purchasers of merchandise.

**mercantile system,** = mercantilism (def. 1).

**mer|can|til|ism** (mėr′kən ti liz′əm, -tī-), *n.* **1** the economic system prevailing in Europe in the 1500's and 1600's, which favored a balance of exports over imports, national wealth being measured by the amount of gold and silver possessed. A nation's agriculture, industry, and trade were regulated with that end in view. **2** the principles or practice characteristic of trade or commerce; commercialism.

**mer|can|til|ist** (mėr′kən ti list, -tī-), *n., adj.* **—*n.*** **1** an advocate of mercantilism (def. 1) or of some similar theory. **2** a believer in the supreme importance of trade and commerce.

**—*adj.*** = mercantilistic.

**mer|can|ti|lis|tic** (mėr′kən ti lis′tik, -tī-), *adj.* of or having to do with mercantilism or mercantilists: *the mercantilistic policies of Louis XIV.*

**mer|cap|tan** (mər kap′tan), *n.* any organic compound of a series having the general formula RSH, resembling the alcohols and phenols, but containing sulfur in place of oxygen, especially ethyl mercaptan, a colorless liquid having an unpleasant odor. [< German *Mercaptan* < New Latin (*corpus*) *mer*(*curium*) *captan*(*s*) (substance) which catches mercury]

**mer|cap|to|pu|rine** (mər kap′tō pyůr′ēn, -in), *n.* a compound that inhibits the metabolism of nucleic acid, used in the treatment of acute leukemia; Purinethol. *Formula:* $C_5H_4N_4S$ [< *mercapt*(an) + *purine*]

**Mer|ca|tor chart** or **Mercator's chart** (mėr kā′tər), a chart made according to Mercator projection. *A Mercator chart represents the meridians and parallels of latitude as straight lines.*

***Mercator projection** or **Mercator's projection,** a method of drawing maps with parallel straight lines instead of curved lines for latitude and longitude. Mercator projection is useful in navigation, but the areas near the poles appear disproportionately large, because the latitudes increase in distance from each other as they approach the poles. *The Mercator projection ... is conformal, i.e., taking any small area, the shape of the regions is the same as on the globe* (Erwin Raisz). See diagram below. [< Gerhardus *Mercator,* 1512-1594, a Flemish cartographer]

**mer|ce|nar|i|ly** (mėr′sə ner′ə lē), *adv.* in a mercenary manner.

**mer|ce|nar|i|ness** (mėr′sə ner′ē nis), *n.* the character of being mercenary.

**mer|ce|nar|y** (mėr′sə ner′ē), *adj., n., pl.* **-nar|ies. —*adj.*** **1** working for money only; acting with money as the motive: *Such wretches are kept in pay by some mercenary bookseller* (Oliver Goldsmith). **SYN:** hireling, grasping. **2** done for money or gain: *a mercenary marriage.* **SYN:** venal. **3** hired to fight for a foreign ruler, army, or cause: *These ... Followed their mercenary calling And took their wages and are dead* (A. E. Housman).

**—*n.*** **1** a soldier serving for pay in a foreign army: *Persia, Greece, and Rome all employed mercenaries, but mercenaries became most prominent from the 1200's to the 1500's, when Swiss and German soldiers were in great demand* (Theodore Ropp). **2** a person who works merely for pay.

[< Latin *mercēnārius* < *mercēs, -edis* wages < *merx, mercis* wares, merchandise]

**mer|cer** (mėr′sər), *n.* a dealer in cloth, originally in silks, velvets, and other costly fabrics, but now commonly in cloth of any kind. **SYN:** draper. [< Old French *mercier* < *merz* wares < Latin *merx, mercis*]

**mer|cer|ise** (mėr′sə rīz), *v.t.,* **-ised, -is|ing.** *Especially British.* = mercerize.

**mer|cer|i|za|tion** (mėr′sər ə zā′shən), *n.* the process of mercerizing: *Mercerization increases luster and strength, and enables dye to penetrate the cloth more easily* (H. B. Strahan).

**mer|cer|ize** (mėr′sə rīz), *v.t.,* **-ized, -iz|ing.** to treat (cotton thread or cloth) with a solution of sodium hydroxide that strengthens the cotton, makes it hold dyes better, and gives it a silky luster. [< John *Mercer,* 1791-1866, an English calico printer, who patented the process + *-ize*]

**mer|cer|y** (mėr′sər ē), *n., pl.* **-cer|ies.** *British.* **1** the place of business of a mercer. **2** the ware sold by a mercer: *He left outlandish merceries stored up With many a brazen bowl and silver cup* (William Morris). [< Old French *mercerie* merchandise in general < *mercier* mercer]

**mer|chan|dis|a|bil|i|ty** (mėr′chən dī′zə bil′ə tē), *n.* = merchantability.

**mer|chan|dis|a|ble** (mėr′chən dī′zə bəl), *adj.* = merchantable.

**mer|chan|dise** (*n.* mėr′chən dīz, -dīs; *v.* mėr′chən dīz), *n., v.,* **-dised, -dis|ing. —*n.*** **1** goods for sale; articles bought and sold; wares. *Abbr:* mdse. **SYN:** stock. **2** *Archaic.* commercial business; trade.

**—*v.t., v.i.*** **1** to buy and sell; trade. **2** to strive for

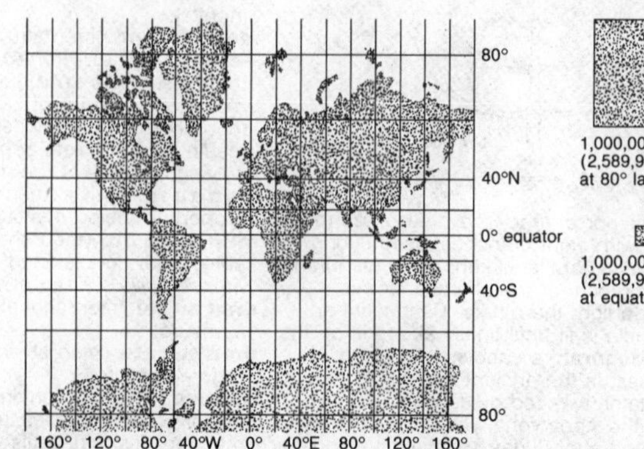


***Mercator projection**

increased sales (of goods and services) by attractive display, advertising, and other methods. [< Old French *marchandise* < *marchand,* earlier *marchëant* merchant] —**mer′chan|dis′er,** *n.*

**mer|chan|dis|ing** (mėr′chən dī′zing), *n.* the planning of sales programs, including research, packaging, advertising, and other forms of promotion directed toward creating a market demand for a product.

**mer|chan|dize** (mėr′chən dīz), *n., v.t., v.i.,* **-dized, -diz|ing.** = merchandise.

**mer|chant** (mėr′chənt), *n., adj., v.* —*n.* **1** a person who buys and sells for profit; trader. Many merchants now deal on a relatively large scale. *The business of some merchants is mostly with foreign countries.* **SYN:** dealer. **2** a storekeeper; retail shopkeeper: *The local merchants try to encourage business in town among the shops.*
—*adj.* **1** having to do with trade; trading; commercial; mercantile: *merchant ships, a merchant town.* **2** of or having to do with the merchant marine: *a merchant seaman.*
—*v.i.* to buy and sell commodities for profit.
—*v.t.* to trade or sell as a commodity: *They never quite believe in the great causes that they merchant to the plain people* (Time).
[< Old French *marchëant,* later *marchand* < Vulgar Latin *mercātans, -antis,* present participle of *mercātāre* (frequentative) < Latin *mercārī* to trade < *merx, mercis* wares]

**mer|chant|a|bil|i|ty** (mėr′chən tə bil′ə tē), *n.* merchantable quality or condition; marketability.

**mer|chant|a|ble** (mėr′chən tə bəl), *adj.* marketable; salable. **SYN:** vendible.

**merchant adventurer,** a person, especially a member of a commercial company, engaged in the sending out of trading expeditions to foreign parts and the establishment there of factories and trading stations.

**merchant bank,** (in Great Britain) a banking firm that engages in accepting bills of exchange and issuing stocks and shares for British industry; acceptance house.

**merchant banker,** a person who manages or represents a merchant bank.

**merchant flag,** a flag flown by a merchant ship.

**mer|chant|man** (mėr′chənt mən), *n., pl.* **-men.** **1** a ship used in commerce; trading vessel: *a stout merchantman of 350 tons. He dresses up as an ordinary seaman and sails on a merchantman* (Graham Greene). **2** *Archaic.* a merchant (def. 1).

**merchant marine, 1** ships used in commerce; trading ships of a nation: *Japan is building up a large merchant marine.* **2** the body of officers and sailors who serve on such ships: *His brother is in the merchant marine.*

**merchant navy,** *British.* merchant marine.

**merchant of death,** a manufacturer or seller of military weapons: *Quarrels between poor countries serve no other interests than those of the big powers and the merchants of death that, to mankind's shame, they have become* (Manchester Guardian Weekly).

**mer|chant|ry** (mėr′chən trē), *n.* **1** the business of a merchant; trade. **2** merchants as a group.

**merchant seaman,** a seaman who works on a ship used in commerce or trade.

**merchant ship** or **vessel,** a trading vessel; merchantman.

**merchant tailor,** a tailor who furnishes the cloth for the garments that he fits and makes to order.

**mer|ci** (mer sē′), *interj. French.* thank you; thanks.

**Mer|cian** (mėr′shən, -shē ən), *adj., n.* —*adj.* of Mercia, an ancient Anglo-Saxon kingdom in central England, its people, or their dialect: *a Mercian king, a Mercian legend.*
—*n.* **1** a native or inhabitant of Mercia: *The warlike Mercians ...* (Spenser). **2** the Old English dialect spoken in Mercia.

**mer|ci beau|coup** (mer sē′ bō kü′), *French.* thank you very much; many thanks.

**mer|ci|ful** (mėr′si fəl), *adj.* having mercy; showing or feeling mercy; full of mercy: *God be merciful to me a sinner* (Luke 18:13). **SYN:** compassionate, clement, kind, lenient. —**mer′ci|ful|ly,** *adv.* —**mer′ci|ful|ness,** *n.*

**mer|ci|less** (mėr′si lis), *adj.* without pity; having no mercy; showing no mercy: *The soldiers' cruelty was merciless. ... a stern prince, merciless in his exactions* (William H. Prescott). **SYN:** relentless, implacable, pitiless, ruthless. —**mer′ci|less|ly,** *adv.* —**mer′ci|less|ness,** *n.*

**mer|cu|rate** (mėr′kyə rāt), *v.t.,* **-rat|ed, -rat|ing.** **1** to combine or treat with mercury or a salt of mercury. **2** to subject to the action of mercury. [< *mercur(y)* + *-ate*[1]]

**mer|cu|ri|al** (mər kyůr′ē əl), *adj., n.* —*adj.* **1a** sprightly and animated; quick: *I was ardent in my temperament; quick, mercurial, impetuous* (Washington Irving). **SYN:** agile. **b** changeable; fickle: *mercurial breezes. Mercurial currency exchange rates are proving to be of dollars-and-cents significance* (Wall Street Journal). **SYN:** variable, volatile. **2** caused by the use of mercury: *mercurial poisoning.* **3** containing mercury: *a mercurial ointment.*
—*n.* a drug containing mercury.
[< Latin *mercuriālis* < *Mercurius* Mercury (originally) the god; the planet] —**mer|cu′ri|al|ly,** *adv.* —**mer|cu′ri|al|ness,** *n.*

**mer|cu|ri|al|ism** (mər kyůr′ē ə liz′əm), *n.* poisoning caused by the absorption of mercury: *Chronic mercury poisoning, or mercurialism, was well known ... since the first Christian century* (New Yorker).

**mer|cu|ri|al|ize** (mər kyůr′ē ə līz), *v.t.,* **-ized, -iz|ing.** **1** to make mercurial in quality. **2** to treat or impregnate with mercury or one of its compounds. **3** *Medicine.* to affect with or subject to the action of mercury. —**mer|cu′ri|al|i|za′tion,** *n.*

**Mer|cu|ri|an** (mėr kyůr′ē ən), *adj., n.* —*adj.* of or having to do with the planet Mercury: *Mercurian climate.*
—*n.* a hypothetical native or inhabitant of Mercury.

**mer|cu|ric** (mər kyůr′ik), *adj.* **1** of mercury. **2** containing mercury, especially with a valence of two: *a mercuric compound.*

**mercuric chloride,** = corrosive sublimate.

**mercuric oxide,** a yellow or orange-red powder which dissolves in acids, but not in water, used in the manufacture of mercury salts, pigments, paints, and pottery, and also in ointments for the treatment of parasitic skin diseases and eye diseases. *Formula:* $HgO$

**mercuric sulfide,** = cinnabar.

**Mer|cu|ro|chrome** (mər kyůr′ə krōm), *n. Trademark.* a red compound containing mercury, formed by the solution of a greenish mercury derivative in water, used externally as an antiseptic; merbromin. *Formula:* $C_{20}H_8Br_2HgNa_2O_6$

**mer|cu|rous** (mər kyůr′əs, mėr′kyər-), *adj.* **1** of mercury. **2** containing mercury, especially with a valence of one: *a mercurous compound.*

**mercurous chloride,** = calomel.

***Mer|cu|ry** (mėr′kyər ē), *n.* **1** *Roman Mythology.* the god who served as the messenger for the other gods. He was the god of commerce, of skill of hands, quickness of wit, eloquence, and thievery. The Greeks called him Hermes. **2** the smallest planet in the solar system, and the one nearest to the sun. Its orbit about the sun takes 88 days to complete, at a mean distance of almost 36,000,000 miles. Mercury goes around the sun about four times while the earth is going around once. See diagram under **solar system.** **3** a messenger or bearer of news: *But what says she to me? Be brief, my good She-Mercury* (Shakespeare). [< Latin *Mercurius*]

***Mercury** definition 2
☿
symbol

***mer|cu|ry** (mėr′kyər ē), *n., pl.* **-ries.** **1** a heavy, silver-white, metallic chemical element that is liquid at ordinary temperatures; quicksilver. It occurs naturally in the mineral cinnabar and combines with most other metals to form amalgams. **2** the column of mercury in a thermometer or barometer, especially with reference to the temperature or the state of the atmosphere shown by it: *The mercury dropped below freezing last night.* **3** a go-between, especially in amorous affairs. **4** a guide. **5** any one of a group of herbs of the spurge family, especially dog's mercury, a poisonous European weed. [< Medieval Latin *mercurius* the metal < Latin *Mercurius* Mercury]

***mercury**
definition 1

| symbol | atomic number | atomic weight | oxidation state |
|---|---|---|---|
| Hg | 80 | 200.59 | 1,2 |

**mercury chloride,** = corrosive sublimate.

**mercury fulminate,** a grayish powder, the mercury salt of fulminic acid, exploding readily when dry, used in making detonators. *Formula:* $Hg(CNO)_2$

**mercury glass,** a kind of glass with a silvery appearance obtained by pouring a mercury alloy between the thin walls of a piece of glassware and then sealing the opening to make the piece airtight; silvered glass.

**mercury lamp,** = mercury-vapor lamp.

**mer|cu|ry-pool rectifier** (mėr′kyə rē pül′), a rectifier in which the cathode consists of a pool of mercury in a metal container whose top holds an insulated anode. The current ionizes the mercury vapor and electrons flow to the anode. Mercury-pool rectifiers, such as the ignitron, are used especially when currents as large as 1,000 amperes must be rectified.

**mercury switch,** a silent electrical switch, especially a wall switch, in which mercury is used to open and close the circuit.

**mercury vacuum pump,** a pump which produces a vacuum by using mercury as a piston.

**mer|cu|ry-va|por lamp** (mėr′kyə rē vā′pər), an apparatus consisting essentially of a glass or quartz discharge tube containing mercury vapor, that produces a bright greenish-yellow illumination when an electric current is passed through it, used for street lighting and in sunlamps, and to treat physical ailments, and kill bacteria.

**Mer|cu|ti|o** (mėr kyü′shē ō), *n.* the dashing friend of Romeo in Shakespeare's play *Romeo and Juliet.*

**mer|cy** mėr′sē), *n., pl.* **-cies.** **1** more kindness than justice requires; kindness beyond what can be claimed or expected: *The judge showed mercy to the young offender.* **2** kindly treatment; pity: *deeds of mercy.* **3** something to be thankful for; blessing: *We thank the Lord for all His mercies. It's a mercy that you weren't injured in the accident. I say that we are wound with mercy round and round As if with air* (Gerard Manley Hopkins).
**at the mercy of,** in the power of: *at the mercy of the elements. The poor lunatic ... was at the mercy of his servants, who robbed, laughed at, and neglected him* (Frederick Marryat).
[< Old French *merci* < *mercit* < Latin *mercēs, -ēdis* reward, wages < *merx, mercis* wares, merchandise]
—*Syn.* **1 Mercy, clemency** mean kindness or mildness shown to an enemy or offender. **Mercy** suggests kind feeling, sympathy, or compassion for those in trouble: *The women showed mercy to the hungry beggar and gave him some food.* **Clemency** suggests a mild nature or disposition, rather than sympathy, in someone with the right or duty to be severe: *That judge's clemency is well known.*

**mercy killing,** = euthanasia: *A doctor has no right to speed a patient's end by euthanasia, or "mercy killing," no matter how hopeless his condition* (Time).

**mercy seat, 1** a cover of gold above the Ark of the Covenant in the ancient Hebrew temple, with cherubim at either end, regarded as the place of God's presence and on which the high priest sprinkled the blood of the sin offering (in the Bible, Exodus 25; Leviticus 16). **2** the throne of God in heaven.

**merde** (merd), *n. French.* excrement; filth.

**mere**[1] (mir), *adj., superl.* **mer|est.** **1** nothing else than; simple; only: *The cut was the merest scratch. The mere sight of a dog makes him afraid. Even when a mere child I began my travels* (Washington Irving). **SYN:** bare, sheer. **2** *Law.* done, performed, or exercised by a person or the persons specified, without any influence or help. **3** *Obsolete.* pure; unmixed: *mere wine.* [< Anglo-French *meer* unaided (in law) < Latin *merus* pure, unmixed]

**mere**[2] (mir), *n. Archaic.* a lake or pond: *lonely mountain-meres* (Tennyson). [Old English *mere* a body of water]

**mere**[3] (mir), *n. Archaic.* a boundary. [Old English *gemǣre*]

**mère** (mer), *n. French.* mother.

**-mere,** *combining form.* part; division; segment, as in *metamere.* [< Greek *méros* portion, share]

**mere|ly** (mir′lē), *adv.* **1** and nothing more; and that is all; simply; only: *merely as a matter of form. The multitudes Who read merely for the sake of talking* (Joseph Butler). **SYN:** solely. **2** *Obsolete.* without admixture; purely. **3** *Obsolete.* absolutely.

**me|ren|gue** (me reng′gā), *n., v.,* **-gued, -gu|ing.** —*n.* **1** a fast, gay dance of the West Indies, especially the Dominican Republic and Haiti, where it originated. Its main characteristic is a limping side step. *The merengue corresponds to the rumba of Cuba or samba of Brazil* (Newsweek). **2** music for such a dance: *The band played a merengue.*
—*v.i.* to dance the merengue.
[< Spanish (West Indies) *merengue*]

**mer|e|tri|cious** (mer′ə trish′əs), *adj.* **1** attractive in a showy way; alluring by false charms: *A wooden building painted to look like marble is meretricious. There is nothing showy or meretricious about the man* (William Dean Howells). *The actual broadcasts have also combined the sublime and the ridiculous, the serious and the meretricious, in the kind of melange ... found to*

**Pronunciation Key:** hat, āge, cãre, fär; let, ēqual, tėrm; it, īce; hot, ōpen, ôrder; oil, out; cup, půt, rüle; child; long; thin; ᴛʜen; zh, measure; ə represents **a** in about, **e** in taken, **i** in pencil, **o** in lemon, **u** in circus.

*be commercially profitable* (New Yorker). **2** having to do with or characteristic of a prostitute. [< Latin *meretrīcius* (with English *-ous*) < *meretrīx, -īcis* prostitute < *merērī* to earn (money)] —**mer'e|tri'cious|ly**, *adv.* —**mer'e|tri'cious|ness**, *n.*

**mer|gan|ser** (mər gan'sər), *n., pl.* **-sers** or (*collectively*) **-ser.** any one of several kinds of large, fish-eating ducks having long, slender, serrated bills hooked at the tip, and great diving powers; sheldrake. They are found in many parts of the world. Mergansers often have crested heads. [< New Latin *merganser* < Latin *mergus* waterfowl, diver (< *mergere* to dip, immerse) + *ānser* goose]

**merge** (mėrj), *v.,* **merged, merg|ing.** —*v.t.* **1** to cause to be swallowed up or absorbed so as to lose its own character or identity; combine or consolidate: *The big company merged various small businesses.* SYN: fuse. **2** *Obsolete.* to immerse; sink (in): *the same forces which merged the Dane in the Englishman* (John R. Green).
—*v.i.* to become swallowed up or absorbed in something else: *The two railroads merged into one. The twilight merged into darkness.*
[< Latin *mergere* dip]

**merg|ee** (mėr'jē'), *n.* one party to a merger.

**mer|gence** (mėr'jəns), *n.* a merging or being merged.

**merg|er** (mėr'jər), *n.* **1** the act of merging or the condition of being merged; consolidation; combination: *One big company was formed by the merger of four small ones.* SYN: coalition, amalgamation, absorption. **2** a person or thing that merges.

**mer|i|carp** (mer'ə kärp), *n.* one of the two single-seeded halves of the schizocarp, the fruit of most plants of the parsley family or of the maple. [< French *méricarpe* < Greek *méros* part + *karpós* fruit]

***me|rid|i|an** (mə rid'ē ən), *n., adj.* —*n.* **1** an imaginary circle passing through any place on the earth's surface and through the North and South Poles. **2** the half of such a circle from pole to pole. All the places on the same meridian have the same longitude. *All places within one half-hour's time east and west of the 75th longitude line, or meridian, have Eastern Standard Time.* **3** the highest point that the sun or any star reaches in the sky. **4** *Figurative.* the highest point; period of highest development or perfection; culmination: *The meridian of life is the prime of life. I imagined my fortune had passed its meridian, and must now decline* (Charlotte Brontë).
—*adj.* **1** highest; greatest: *Athens reached its meridian glory in the age of Pericles.* **2** of or having to do with a meridian. **3** at or from the zenith: *the sun's meridian beams. The meridian moon shone full into the hovel* (Jane Porter). **4** of or having to do with noon: *the meridian hour.*
[Middle English *meridien* midday < Latin *merīdiānus* of noon, ultimately < *medius* middle + *diēs* day]

***meridian**
definition 2

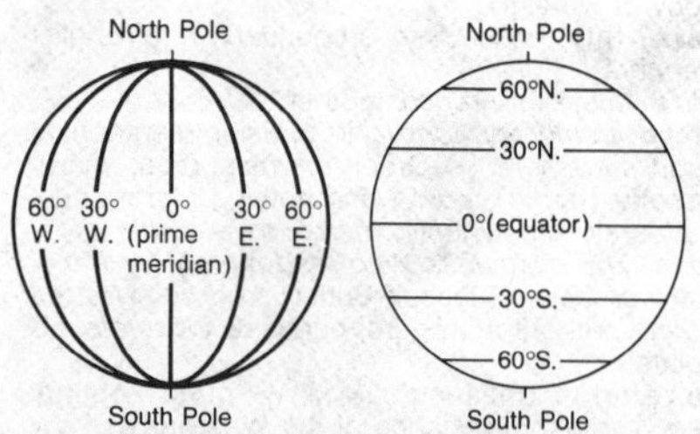


**meridians (lines of longitude)** parallels (lines of latitude)

**meridian of Greenwich,** = prime meridian.

**me|rid|i|o|nal** (mə rid'ē ə nəl), *adj., n.* —*adj.* **1** having to do with or characteristic of the south or people living there, especially of southern France: *foremost among the Spanish grandees ... stood ... a man of meridional aspect with coal-black hair and beard* (John L. Motley). **2** situated in the south; southern. **3** of or having to do with a meridian. **4** along a meridian; in a north-south direction: *a meridional flow of air, a meridional chain of weather stations.*
—*n.* an inhabitant of the south, especially the south of France.
[< Late Latin *merīdiōnālis* < Latin *merīdiēs* noon, south (< *medius* middle + *diēs* day), on the pattern of *septentriōnālis* northern] —**me|rid'i|o|nal|ly**, *adv.*

**me|ringue**[1] (mə rang'), *n.* **1** a mixture made of egg whites beaten stiff and sweetened with sugar, often flavored. Meringue is often made into shells for ice cream or other filling, or spread on pies or puddings, and lightly browned in the oven. **2** a small shell made of this mixture and filled with fruit, whipped cream, ice cream, or other filling. [< French *meringue*]

**mé|ringue** or **me|ringue**[2] (mā rang'), *n.* a variant of the merengue, danced in Haiti. [< Creole *méringue* < Spanish (West Indies) *merengue*]

**me|ri|no** (mə rē'nō), *n., pl.* **-nos,** *adj.* —*n.* **1** Often, **Merino.** any one of a breed of sheep with long, fine wool and (on the full-grown male) large, spiral horns. It is of Spanish origin. **2** the wool of this sheep. **3** a soft woolen yarn made from it. **4** a thin, soft, woolen fabric made from this yarn or some substitute.
—*adj.* made of this wool, yarn, or fabric.
[< Spanish *merino,* apparently < the name of a Moorish tribe, whose sheep were imported in order to improve the local breed]

**mer|i|stem** (mer'ə stem), *n. Botany.* the undifferentiated, growing cellular tissue of the younger parts of plants; actively dividing cell tissue. [< Greek *meristós* divisible, divided (< *merízein* divide < *méros* part) + *-ēma,* a noun suffix]

**mer|i|ste|mat|ic** (mer'ə stə mat'ik), *adj.* of or having to do with the meristem.

**me|ris|tic** (mə ris'tik), *adj. Biology.* of or having to do with the number or arrangement of body parts or segments: *meristic variation.* [< Greek *meristós* divisible + English *-ic*] —**me|ris'ti|cal|ly**, *adv.*

**mer|it** (mer'it), *n., v.* —*n.* **1** goodness; worth; value: *Each child will get a mark according to the merit of his work. Reputation is ... oft got without merit, and Lost without deserving* (Shakespeare). **2** something that deserves praise or reward; commendable quality.
—*v.t.* **1** to be worthy of; deserve: *a hard-working boy merits praise.* **2** to earn by commendable action.
—*v.i.* to deserve: *a simple, religious fanatic, who felt sure that ... he was meriting well of God and his king* (John L. Motley).
**make a merit of,** to represent (some action, circumstance, or quality) as deserving of reward or praise: *the party felon whose unblushing face ... coolly makes a merit of disgrace* (John Greenleaf Whittier).
**merits,** real facts or qualities, whether good or bad: *The judge will consider the case on its merits.*
[< Old French *merite,* learned borrowing from Latin *meritum* earned < *merēre* to earn, deserve] —**mer'it|a|ble**, *adj.*
—*Syn. n.* **1 Merit, worth** mean the goodness or value of someone or something. **Merit** implies achieved rather than inherent excellence, and often suggests practical value: *The merits of your plan outweigh the defects.* **Worth** implies excellence or value belonging to the person or thing by its very nature, apart from any connections or conditions affecting its usefulness, value, or importance: *The worth of the new drugs is certain, although all their uses are not yet known.*

**mer|it|ed** (mer'ə tid), *adj.* deserved; well-earned. —**mer'it|ed|ly**, *adv.*

**mer|it|less** (mer'it lis), *adj.* without merit; without excellence or commendable qualities; undeserving.

**mer|i|toc|ra|cy** (mer'ə tok'rə sē), *n.* **1** a class of people distinguished for their high intellect or talent. **2** a system of education which stresses advancement of those who are most talented or have the highest intellect: *Selection of pupils by ability is not so much a device of meritocracy as an accepted method of increasing teaching productivity* (London Times). [< *merit* + *-ocracy,* as in *aristocracy*]

**mer|i|to|crat** (mer'ə tə krat), *n.* a person who belongs to a meritocracy: *It urges a programme of action for ... the potential drop-outs who are too often ignored in an education system which often seems devoted only to the able and the clever—the meritocrats* (Brian MacArthur).

**mer|i|to|crat|ic** (mer'ə tə krat'ik), *adj.* **1** having to do with a meritocracy: *a meritocratic society.* **2** based solely upon intellectual achievement: *Higher education in Britain is in danger of becoming a "meritocratic treadmill"* (London Times). —**mer'i|to|crat'i|cal|ly**, *adv.*

**mer|i|to|ri|ous** (mer'ə tôr'ē əs, -tōr'-), *adj.* deserving reward or praise; having merit; worthy: *His work at school was meritorious but not brilliant.* SYN: commendable, praiseworthy. [< Latin *meritōrius* (with English *-ous*) of use in, or connected with, the earning of money < *merēre* to earn, deserve] —**mer'i|to'ri|ous|ly**, *adv.* —**mer'i|to'ri|ous|ness**, *n.*

**merit system,** the system in which appointments and promotions in the civil service are made on the basis of the merit or good performance of the employees rather than on allegiance to a political party.

**merle** or **merl** (mėrl), *n. Archaic.* the common European blackbird. [< Old French *merle* < Latin *merula*]

**mer|lin** (mėr'lən), *n.* **1** a kind of small falcon, one of the smallest European birds of prey, and one of the boldest, that does not hesitate to attack birds of twice its own size. **2** any one of certain closely allied birds, such as the North American pigeon hawk. [Middle English *merlyon* < Anglo-French *merilun,* Old French *esmerillon* (diminutive) < *esmeril,* probably < Germanic (compare Old High German *smirl*)]

**Mer|lin** (mėr'lən), *n.* (in medieval legends and romances), a powerful magician who helped King Arthur.

**mer|lon** (mėr'lən), *n.* the solid part between two openings in a battlement. [< French *merlon* < Italian *merlone* < *merlo* battlement, perhaps < Latin *mergae,* plural, (two-pronged) pitchfork]

**mer|maid** (mėr'mād'), *n.* **1** an imaginary sea maiden having the head and upper body of a woman, and the form of a fish from the waist down: *a mermaid fair, Singing alone, Combing her hair Under the sea* (Tennyson). **2** an expert woman swimmer. [< *mere*[2] in the sense of "sea" + *maid*]

**mer|maid|en** (mėr'mā'dən), *n.* = mermaid.

**mermaid's purse,** = skatebarrow.

**mer|man** (mėr'man'), *n., pl.* **-men. 1** an imaginary man of the sea having the head and upper body of a man, and the form of a fish from the waist down. **2** an expert male swimmer. [< *mere*[2] (see etym. under **mermaid**) + *man*]

**mer|o|blast** (mer'ə blast), *n. Embryology.* an ovum whose contents consist of considerable nutritive as well as formative or germinal matter. [< Greek *méros* part + *blastós* germ, sprout]

**mer|o|blas|tic** (mer'ə blas'tik), *adj. Embryology.* (of an ovum) containing nutritive as well as germinal matter and therefore undergoing only partial segmentation, as in birds, reptiles, and most fishes: *meroblastic cleavage.*

**me|rog|o|ny** (mə rog'ə nē), *n.* the development of an embryo from a portion of an egg. [< Greek *méros* part + *-goniā* a begetting]

**Mer|o|ite** (mer'ə īt), *n.* an inhabitant of Meroë, the capital city of the ancient African state of Kush, which flourished as a center of art and trade from about 300 B.C. to about 200 A.D.

**Mer|o|pe** (mer'ō pē), *n. Greek Mythology.* one of the Pleiades. In some accounts of the story, Merope became the seventh or faint star because she married a mortal.

**mer|o|sym|met|ri|cal** (mer'ə si met'rə kəl), *adj.* being partially symmetrical.

**mer|o|sym|me|try** (mer'ə sim'ə trē), *n.* (in crystallography) partial symmetry. [< Greek *méros* part + English *symmetry*]

**Mer|o|vin|gi|an** (mer'ə vin'jē ən), *adj., n.* —*adj.* of or having to do with the first Frankish line of kings, which reigned in Gaul or France from about A.D. 486 to 751.
—*n.* one of these kings.

**mer|ri|ly** (mer'ə lē), *adv.* in merry manner; laughing and gay.

**mer|ri|ment** (mer'ē mənt), *n.* laughter and gaiety; merry enjoyment; fun; mirth: *Albert was of course delighted, and his merriment at the family gathering was more pronounced than ever* (Lytton Strachey). SYN: jollity, hilarity.

**mer|ri|ness** (mer'ē nis), *n.* the quality or condition of being merry.

**mer|ry** (mer'ē), *adj.,* **-ri|er, -ri|est. 1** laughing and gay; full of fun: *merry talk, merry laughter.* SYN: jolly, jovial. See syn. under **gay. 2** gay; joyful; characterized by festivity and rejoicing: *a merry Christmas. I am never merry when I hear sweet music* (Shakespeare). **3** *Archaic.* **a** (of things) pleasant; agreeable: *the merry month of May.* **b** (of music) delightful; sweet. **c** (of a wind) favorable. **4** *Archaic.* **a** amusing: *a merry jest.* **b** facetious: *His lordship is but merry with me* (Shakespeare).
**make merry,** to laugh and be gay; have fun.
[Middle English *meri,* Old English *merge, myrge* pleasing, agreeable]

**mer|ry-an|drew** or **Mer|ry-An|drew** (mer'ē an'drü), *n.* a clown or buffoon. SYN: harlequin, punchinello.

***merry-go-round**
definition 1

***mer|ry-go-round** (mer'ē gō round'), *n.* **1** a set of animal figures and seats on a platform that goes round and round by machinery to lively music; carousel. Children ride on them for fun. *The opera itself was tuneful as a merry-go-round* (Time). **2** a round platform that is made to revolve by pushing with the feet. It is used by children in a playground. **3** *Figurative.* any whirl or rapid round: *The holidays were a merry-go-round of parties.*

**mer|ry-make** (mer′ē māk′), *v.i.,* **-made, -making.** to make merry; hold festivities.

**mer|ry|mak|er** (mer′ē mā′kər), *n.* a person who is being merry; person engaged in merrymaking.

**mer|ry|mak|ing** (mer′ē mā′king), *n., adj.* —*n.* **1** laughter and gaiety; fun. **SYN:** conviviality. **2** a gay festival; merry entertainment.
—*adj.* gay and full of fun; having a merry time.

**mer|ry|thought** (mer′ē thôt′), *n.* = wishbone.

**Mer|thi|o|late** (mər thī′ə lāt), *n. Trademark.* thimerosal.

**mer|y|chip|pus** (mer′i kip′əs), *n.* any one of an extinct group of horses believed to be an ancestor of the modern horse. Merychippus lived about 26 million years ago, had three toes on each foot, and grew about 40 inches high. [< New Latin *Merychippus* the genus name < Greek *mērykázein* to chew the cud + *hippos* horse]

**mes-,** *combining form.* the form of **meso-** before vowels, as in *mesencephalon.*

**me|sa** (mā′sə), *n.* a small, isolated, high plateau with a flat top and steep, rocky sides, common in dry regions of the western and southwestern United States: *Some of the most prominent cliffs and mesas of the Colorado Plateau country are made by these Jurassic sandstones* (Raymond C. Moore). [American English < Spanish *mesa* < Latin *mēnsa* table < *metīrī* to measure]

**mé|sal|li|ance** (mā zal′ē əns; *French* mā zȧ-lyäɴs′), *n.* marriage with a person of lower social position; misalliance. [< French *mésalliance* < *mes-* mis- + Old French *alliance* alliance]

**Me|san|to|in** (mə san′tō in), *n. Trademark.* a drug which depresses the nervous system, used especially to decrease the number and intensity of epileptic fits. *Formula:* $C_{12}H_{14}N_2O_2$

**mes|cal** (mes kal′), *n.* **1** an alcoholic drink of Mexico made from the fermented juice of certain agaves, especially the maguey. **2** any one of the plants yielding this. **3** a small cactus of northern Mexico and the southwestern United States, whose buttonlike tops are dried and chewed as a stimulant and hallucinogen by some tribes of Indians during religious ceremonies; peyote. [American English < Mexican Spanish *mescal* < Nahuatl *mexcalli* a fermented drink of maguey]

**mescal button,** any one of the small, buttonlike tops of the mescal plant.

**Mes|ca|le|ro** (mes′kə lãr′ō), *n., pl.* **-ros** or **-ro.** a member of a tribe of Apaches living chiefly in New Mexico, formerly noted for their use of mescal: *The Mescaleros ... have had their reservation here [in New Mexico] since it was established by President Grant on May 27, 1873* (New York Times).

**mes|cal|in** (mes′kə lin), *n.* = mescaline.

**mes|cal|ine** (mes′kə lēn, -lin), *n.* a stimulating drug contained in the small buttonlike tops of the mescal; peyote. It induces hallucinations and reactions associated with psychosis. *Formula:* $C_{11}H_{17}NO_3$ [< *mescal* + *-ine*[2]]

**mes|dames** (mā däm′; *French* mā dȧm′), *n.* **1** a plural of **madam. 2** *French.* plural of **madame.** *Abbr:* Mmes.

► **Mesdames** is used to supply a plural for *Mrs.,* particularly in reports of social affairs: *The bazaar is being organized by Mesdames Howard, Clarkson, and Reed.* In most kinds of writing, however, *Mesdames* is avoided by the repetition of *Mrs.* before each name.

**mes|de|moi|selles** (mād mwȧ zel′), *n. French.* plural of **mademoiselle.**

**me|seems** (mi sēmz′), *v., past tense* **meseemed.** *Archaic.* it seems to me.

**mes|en|ce|phal|ic** (mes′en sə fal′ik), *adj.* **1** of or having to do with the mesencephalon: *the mesencephalic segment of the brain.* **2** situated in the midst of the encephalon, as the midbrain.

**mes|en|ceph|a|lon** (mes′en sef′ə lon), *n.* the middle section of the brain, lying between the cerebellum and pons, and the forebrain; midbrain. [< Greek *mésos* middle + *enképhalon* encephalon]

**mes|en|chy|ma** (mes eng′kə mə), *n.* = mesenchyme.

**mes|en|chy|mal** (mes eng′kə məl), *adj.* having to do with, consisting of, or derived from mesenchyme: *mesenchymal cells.*

**mes|en|chym|a|tous** (mes′eng kim′ə təs), *adj.* = mesenchymal.

**mes|en|chyme** (mes′eng kim), *n.* that portion of the mesoderm, consisting of cells set in a gelatinous matrix, from which the connective tissues, bone, cartilage, vascular system, and lymphatic vessels develop. [< New Latin *mesenchyma* < Greek *mésos* middle + *enchýma* infusion < *en* in + *cheîn* pour. Compare etym. under **chyme.**]

**mes|en|ter|ic** (mes′ən ter′ik), *adj.* of or having to do with a mesentery.

**mes|en|ter|i|tis** (mes en′tə rī′tis), *n.* inflammation of the mesentery.

**mes|en|ter|on** (mes en′tə ron), *n., pl.* **-ter|a** (-tər ə). *Embryology.* the interior of the primitive intestine (archenteron), bounded by endoderm. [< New Latin *mesenteron* < Greek *mésos* middle + *énteron* enteron]

**mes|en|ter|on|ic** (mes en′tə ron′ik), *adj.* of or having to do with the mesenteron.

**mes|en|ter|y** (mes′ən ter′ē), *n., pl.* **-ter|ies.** a membrane that enfolds and supports an internal organ, attaching it to the body wall or to another organ. [< Medieval Latin *mesenterium* < Greek *mesentérion* < *mésos* middle + *énteron* intestine, enteron]

**mesh** (mesh), *n., v.* —*n.* **1** one of the open spaces of a net, sieve, or screen: *This net has half-inch meshes. An 80-mesh screen has 80 meshes to the inch.* **2** the cord or wire used in a net or screen: *We found an old fly swatter made of wire mesh.* **3** a means of catching or holding fast; network; net: *Here in her hairs the painter plays the spider and hath woven a golden mesh to entrap the hearts of men* (Shakespeare). **4** the engagement or fitting together of gear teeth.
—*v.t., v.i.* **1** to catch or be caught in a net: *The fish was so deeply meshed in the net it could not wriggle free.* **2** to engage or become engaged. The teeth of the small gear mesh with the teeth of the larger one. **3** *Figurative.* to bring closely together; fit together; blend; integrate: *The [organization] never had a chance to ... mesh all its supporters into a strong party* (Canada Month). *Both ... plans need study to find how they might best be meshed* (Wall Street Journal).
**in mesh,** in gear; fitted together: *The machinery is in mesh.*
**meshes, a** a network; net: *A fish was entangled in the meshes.* **b** *Figurative.* snares: *The spy was entangled in the meshes of his own plot to steal defense secrets. Greece has extricated it from the meshes of diplomacy* (William E. Gladstone).
[compare Old English *mǣscre* net]

**Me|shach** (mē′shak), *n.* one of the three Hebrews cast into the fiery furnace by Nebuchadnezzar (in the Bible, Daniel 3:12-30).

**meshed** (mesht), *adj.* having meshes; reticulated: *meshed carpet.*

**me|shug|ga** or **me|shug|ga** (mə shu̇g′ə), *adj. Slang.* crazy: *This man is meshugga ... [he] read science-fiction while awaiting trial* (Time). [< Yiddish *meshuge* < Hebrew *mĕshuggā′*]

**mesh|work** (mesh′wėrk′), *n.* a structure consisting of meshes; network.

**mesh|y** (mesh′ē), *adj.,* **mesh|i|er, mesh|i|est.** formed with meshes; meshed; reticulated.

**me|si|al** (mē′zē əl, mes′ē-), *adj.* having to do with, situated in, or directed toward the middle line of a body; median. [< Greek *mésos* middle + English *-ial*] —**me′si|al|ly,** *adv.*

**mes|ic atom** (mez′ik, mes′-; mē′zik, -sik), an atom in which an electron has been replaced by a negatively charged meson.

**me|sit|y|lene** (mə sit′ə lēn, mes′ə tə-), *n.* an oily, colorless, aromatic, liquid hydrocarbon obtained by the action of sulfuric acid on acetone. *Formula:* $C_9H_{12}$ [< obsolete *mesite* acetic ether (< Greek *mesítēs* go-between < *mésos* middle) + *-yl* + *-ene*]

**mes|mer|ic** (mes mer′ik, mez-), *adj.* = hypnotic. —**mes|mer′i|cal|ly,** *adv.*

**mes|mer|ism** (mes′mə riz əm, mez′-), *n.* = hypnotism. [< Franz *Mesmer,* 1734-1815, an Austrian physician who popularized the doctrine of animal magnetism + *-ism*]

**mes|mer|ist** (mes′mər ist, mez′-), *n.* = hypnotist.

**mes|mer|ize** (mes′mə rīz, mez′-), *v.t., v.i.,* **-ized, -iz|ing.** = hypnotize. —**mes′mer|i|za′tion,** *n.* —**mes′mer|iz′er,** *n.*

**mesn|al|ty** (mē′nəl tē), *n., pl.* **-ties. 1** the estate of a mesne lord. **2** the condition of being a mesne lord. [< law French *mesnalte* < Old French *mene, meien;* see etym. under **mesne**]

**mesne** (mēn), *adj. Law.* middle; intermediate; intervening: *A feudal lord with vassals, but himself a vassal of a superior, was a mesne lord.* [< law French *mesne,* alteration of Anglo-French *meen,* Old French *mein, meien* mean[3]]

**meso-,** *combining form.* middle; halfway; midway; intermediate: *Mesoderm = middle layer of cells.* Also, **mes-** before vowels. [< Greek *mésos*]

**Mes|o|a|mer|i|can** (mes′ō ə mer′ə kən, mē′sō-), *adj., n.* —**adj.** of or having to do with Mesoamerica, the central part of the American continent extending from northern Mexico through Central America to the Isthmus of Panama.
—*n.* a native or inhabitant of Mesoamerica, especially in prehistoric times: *... the complex histories of Mesoamericans, especially the Aztec and Maya* (New Scientist).

**mes|o|blast** (mes′ə blast, mē′sə-), *n.* mesoderm in an embryo. [< *meso-* + Greek *blastós* germ, sprout]

**mes|o|blas|tic** (mes′ə blas′tik, mē′sə-), *adj.* of or having to do with the mesoblast: *a mesoblastic cell, the mesoblastic layer.*

**mes|o|carp** (mes′ə kärp, mē′sə-), *n.* the middle layer of the pericarp of a fruit or ripened ovary, such as the fleshy part of a peach or plum. See diagram under **fruit.** [< *meso-* + Greek *karpós* fruit]

**mes|o|ce|phal|ic** (mes′ō sə fal′ik, mē′sō-), *adj.* **1** *Anthropology.* **a** having a skull with a cranial capacity of from 1,350 to 1,450 cubic centimeters, intermediate between dolichocephalic and brachycephalic. **b** having a skull of medium proportion. **2** *Anatomy.* of or having to do with the mesencephalon. [< *meso-* + *cephalic*]

**mes|o|crat|ic** (mes′ə krat′ik, mē′sə-), *adj.* (of rock) composed of light and dark minerals in about equal proportions. [< *meso-* + Greek *krateîn* to rule, prevail + English *-ic*]

**mes|o|derm** (mes′ə dėrm, mē′sə-), *n.* **1** the middle layer of cells formed during the development of the embryo of an animal: *There is a third body layer, the mesoderm, that must be produced in order to lay the foundation for the body parts that are to develop later* (A. M. Winchester). **2** the tissues derived from this layer of cells, such as the muscles, bones, circulatory system, and connective tissue. [< *meso-* + Greek *dérma* skin]

**mes|o|der|mal** (mes′ə dėr′məl, mē′sə-), *adj.* of or having to do with the mesoderm in plants or animals.

**mes|o|der|mic** (mes′ə dėr′mik, mē′sə-), *adj.* = mesodermal.

**mes|o|fau|na** (mes′ə fô′nə, mē′sə-), *n., pl.* **-nas, -nae** (-nē). the animals of a given habitat that are of intermediate size. [< *meso-* + *fauna*]

**mes|o|gas|tric** (mes′ə gas′trik, mē′sə-), *adj.* of or having to do with the mesogastrium; umbilical.

**mes|o|gas|tri|um** (mes′ə gas′trē əm, mē′sə-), *n.* **1** the umbilical region of the abdomen. **2** (in an embryo) one of the two mesenteries of the stomach. [< New Latin *mesogastrium* < Greek *mésos* middle + *gastḗr, gastrós* stomach]

**mes|o|gloe|a** or **mes|o|gle|a** (mes′ə glē′ə, mē′sə-), *n.* a gelatinous or fibrous layer that connects the outer and inner cell layers of a coelenterate. [< *meso-* + Greek *gloiā́* glue]

**mes|o|gloe|al** or **mes|o|gle|al** (mes′ə glē′əl, mē′sə-), *adj.* consisting of, having to do with, or resembling mesogloea.

**me|sog|na|thism** (mi sog′nə thiz əm), *n.* = mesognathy.

**me|sog|na|thous** (mi sog′nə thəs), *adj.* **1** having jaws that are of moderate size and project only slightly. **2** having a moderate facial angle (80 to 85 degrees); having a gnathic index that ranges between 98 and 103. [< *meso-* + Greek *gnáthos* jaw + English *-ous*]

**me|sog|na|thy** (mi sog′nə thē), *n.* the character or state of being mesognathous.

**mes|o|hip|pus** (mes′ō hip′əs), *n.* any one of an extinct group of horses believed to be an ancestor of the modern horse. It lived in North America about 30 million years ago. About 24 inches in height, it had long slender legs and three toes on each foot. [< New Latin *Mesohippus* the genus name < Greek *mésos* middle + *hippos* horse]

**mes|o|lith|ic** or **Mes|o|lith|ic** (mes′ə lith′ik, mē′sə-), *adj., n.* —**adj.** of or having to do with the middle part of the Stone Age, transitional between the neolithic and paleolithic periods: *We know from the middens of mesolithic Man that shellfish for long remained a favourite food* (New Scientist).
—*n.* this period.
[< *meso-* + Greek *líthos* stone + English *-ic*]

**mes|o|me|te|or|o|log|i|cal** (mes′ə mē′tē ər ə loj′ə kəl, mē′sə-), *adj.* of or having to do with mesometeorology.

**mes|o|me|te|or|ol|o|gy** (mes′ə mē′tē ə rol′ə jē, mē′sə-), *n.* the branch of meteorology that deals with atmospheric phenomena of an intermediate range, such as storms affecting an area of several tens of miles.

***mes|o|morph** (mes′ə môrf, mē′sə-), *n.* **1** a meso-

**Pronunciation Key:** hat, āge, cãre, fär; let, ēqual, tėrm; it, īce; hot, ōpen, ôrder; oil, out; cup, pu̇t, rüle; child; long; thin; ᴛʜen; zh, measure; ə represents **a** in about, **e** in taken, **i** in pencil, **o** in lemon, **u** in circus.

morphic person. **2** a mesomorphic body structure.

***mesomorph**
definition 2

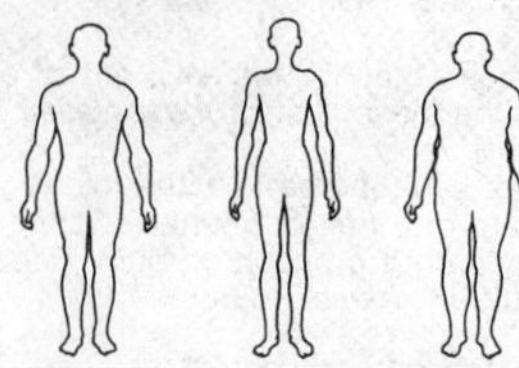


**mes|o|mor|phic** (mes′ə môr′fik, mē′sə-), *adj.* of or designating the muscular physical type, characterized by predominance of bone, muscle, and other structures developed from the mesodermal layer of the embryo. [< *meso-* + Greek *morphḗ* form + English *-ic*] —**mes′o|mor′phi|cal|ly,** *adv.*

**mes|o|mor|phy** (mes′ə môr′fē, mē′sə-), *n.* the character or state of being mesomorphic.

**mes|on** (mes′on, mez′-; mē′son, -zon), *n.* a highly unstable particle found in the nucleus of an atom, having a mass greater than that of an electron and less than that of a proton and a very short lifetime (about a millionth of a second or less). A meson may have a positive, negative, or neutral charge. *Mesons are particles believed to act as the glue that binds atomic nuclei* (Science News Letter). [< Greek *mésos* middle + English *-on,* as in *electron*] —**mes′on|like′,** *adj.*

**mes|o|neph|ric** (mes′ə nef′rik, mē′sə-), *adj.* of or having to do with the mesonephros.

**mesonephric duct,** the embryonic genital or reproductive tract of male animals in vertebrate animals; Wolffian duct.

**mes|o|neph|ros** (mes′ə nef′ros, mē′sə-), *n., pl.* **-roi** (-roi). the middle division of the primitive kidney of vertebrate embryos, the pronephros and the metanephros being the anterior and posterior divisions, respectively; Wolffian body. The mesonephros becomes part of the permanent kidney in fishes and amphibians. [< *meso-* + Greek *nephrós* kidney (because it develops between the pronephros and metanephros)]

**meson factory,** a particle accelerator designed to produce intense beams of mesons with which to probe atomic nuclei.

**mes|o|pause** (mes′ə pôz′, mē′sə-), *n.* the area of atmospheric demarcation between the mesosphere and the exosphere: *Near the mesopause there is a change in the nature of the air motion and tidal effects begin to dominate* (New Scientist).

**mes|o|phase** (mes′ə fāz′, mē′sə-), *n.* a semicrystalline phase of some substances, such as liquid crystals.

**mes|o|phile** (mes′ə fīl′, -fil′; mē′sə-), *adj.* = mesophilic.

**mes|o|phil|ic** (mes′ə fil′ik, mē′sə-), *adj.* requiring moderate temperatures for development: *They studied ... flagella from mesophilic bacteria that live under more temperate conditions* (Science News Letter). [< *meso-* + *-phil* + *-ic*]

**mes|o|phyll** or **mes|o|phyl** (mes′ə fil, mē′sə-), *n.* the inner green tissue of a leaf, lying between the upper and lower layers of epidermis; parenchyma of a leaf. [< *meso-* + Greek *phýllon* leaf]

**mes|o|phyte** (mes′ə fīt, mē′sə-), *n.* a plant that grows under conditions of average moisture and dryness. Mesophytes are intermediate between hydrophytes and xerophytes. [< *meso-* + Greek *phytón* plant]

**mes|o|phyt|ic** (mes′ə fit′ik, mē′sə-), *adj.* of or having to do with a mesophyte.

**Mes|o|po|ta|mi|an** (mes′ə pə tā′mē ən, -tām′yən), *adj., n.* —***adj.*** of or having to do with Mesopotamia (an ancient country in southwestern Asia between the Tigris and Euphrates rivers).
—***n.*** a native or inhabitant of Mesopotamia.

**mes|o|scale** (mes′ə skāl′, mē′sə-), *adj.* of or having to do with atmospheric phenomena intermediate between microscale and macroscale: *Mesoscale meteorology* [*is*] *the meteorology of areas 10 to 20 miles in diameter, or about the size of many urban areas* (Science News).

**mes|o|scaph** or **mes|o|scaphe** (mes′ə skaf, -skāf; mē′sə-), *n.* an apparatus similar to the bathyscaph, used to explore the middle depths of the ocean: *The existence of these many portholes, with the possibility of looking in virtually every direction, is a principal characteristic of the mesoscaph and distinguishes her from naval or combatant submarines* (Jacques Piccard). [< French *mésoscaphe,* coined by its inventor, the French deep-sea explorer Jacques Piccard, born 1922, < Greek *mésos* middle + *skáphē* vessel]

**mes|o|seis|mal** (mes′ō sīz′məl, -sīs′-; mē′sō-), *adj.* having to do with the center of intensity of an earthquake.

**mes|o|some** (mes′ə sōm, mē′sə-), *n.* a structure on cell membranes which has to do with the formation of the cross wall when a cell divides: *The mesosome* [*is*] *a structure which can be observed in electron micrographs of bacteria ... It is the point at which DNA is attached to the cell membrane* (New Scientist). [< *meso-* + *-some*[3]]

**mes|o|sphere** (mes′ə sfir, mē′sə-), *n.* **1** the region of the earth's atmosphere between the stratosphere and the ionosphere, which extends from about 20 to 50 miles above the earth's surface. Most of the ozone in the atmosphere is created in the mesosphere, and there is almost no variation in the temperature. See diagram under **atmosphere. 2** the region of the earth's atmosphere between the ionosphere and the exosphere.

**mes|o|spher|ic** (mes′ə sfer′ik, mē′sə-), *adj.* of or having to do with the mesosphere.

**mes|o|the|li|al** (mes′ə thē′lē əl, mē′sə-), *adj.* of or having to do with mesothelium.

**mes|o|the|li|o|ma** (mes′ə thē′lē ō′mə, mē′sə-), *n., pl.* **-mas, -ma|ta** (-mə tə). a malignant tumor of the mesothelial tissue of the pleura or peritoneum, usually associated with excessive exposure to asbestos.

**mes|o|the|li|um** (mes′ə thē′lē əm, mē′sə-), *n., pl.* **-li|ums, -li|a** (-lē ə). that part of the mesoderm that lines the primitive body cavity of a vertebrate embryo. [< New Latin *mesothelium* < *meso-(derma)* mesoderm + (*epi*)*thelium* epithelium]

**mes|o|ther|mal** (mes′ə thėr′məl, mē′sə-), *adj.* of or having to do with a moderate or intermediate temperature range. [< Greek *mésos* middle + English *thermal*]

**mes|o|tho|rac|ic** (mes′ə thô ras′ik, -thō-; mē′sə-), *adj.* of or having to do with the mesothorax of an insect.

**mes|o|tho|rax** (mes′ə thôr′aks, -thōr′-; mē′sə-), *n., pl.* **-rax|es, -ra|ces** (-rə sēz). the middle of the three divisions of the thorax of an insect, typically bearing the first pair of wings and the middle pair of legs. [< *meso-* + *thorax*]

**mes|o|tho|ri|um** (mes′ə thôr′ē əm, -thōr′-; mez′-), *n.* either of two radioactive isotopes, mesothorium I (*at.no.:* 88; *half-life:* 6.7 years), an isotope of radium, formed from thorium and yielding mesothorium II (*at.no.:* 89; *half-life:* 6.13 hours), an isotope of actinium. Both isotopes have an atomic weight of 228, and are intermediate between thorium and radiothorium. [< *meso-* + *thorium*]

**mes|o|tron** (mes′ə tron, mē′sə-), *n.* = meson.

**mes|o|var|i|um** (mes′ō vãr′ē əm, mē′sō-), *n.* the fold of peritoneum that suspends the ovary. [< *meso-* + Latin *ōvārium* ovary]

**Me|so|zo|ic** (mes′ə zō′ik, mē′sə-), *n., adj.* —***n.*** **1** the geological era before the present era; Age of Reptiles. It was characterized by the development of mammals, flying reptiles, birds, and flowering plants, and the appearance and death of dinosaurs. It comprises the Triassic, Jurassic, and Cretaceous periods. The Mesozoic began about 225 million years ago. **2** the rocks formed in this era.
—***adj.*** of this era or these rocks.
[< *meso-* + Greek *zōē* life + English *-ic*]

**mes|pil** (mes′pəl), *n.* = medlar. [< Latin *mespilus*]

***mes|quite** or **mes|quit** (mes kēt′, mes′kēt), *n.* **1** a deep-rooted tree or shrub, common in the southwestern United States and Mexico, that often grows in dense clumps or thickets; algaroba. It belongs to the pea family. Its beanlike pods contain much sugar, and furnish a valuable food for cattle. Its wood is used as fuel and lumber. *Here and there are patches of a lush green shrub—the mesquite* (Scientific American). **2** any closely related plant, especially the screw bean. [American English < Mexican Spanish *mezquite* < Nahuatl *mizquitl*]

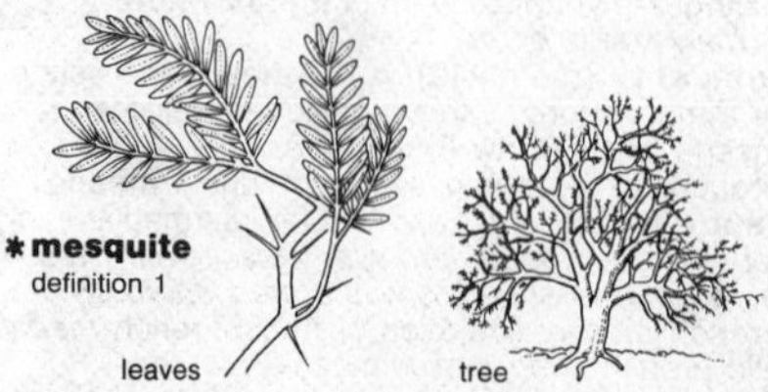


***mesquite**
definition 1

**mess** (mes), *n., v.* —***n.*** **1a** a dirty or untidy mass or group of things; dirty or untidy condition: *Look what a mess you have made of your dress, playing in that dirt. The children kept the house in a mess.* **b** *Informal.* a person or thing in a poor or untidy condition: *"Isn't he a mess," said Melanie. The wall had scraped raw patches on Edward's forehead and palms and shins* (Joanna Ostrow). *In 1914 Russia was, politically and economically, a mess* (Colin Simpson). **2** confusion or difficulty: *His business affairs are in a mess.* **3** *Figurative.* an unpleasant or unsuccessful affair or state of affairs: *He made a mess of his final examinations. Then maybe he would a locked her up, and this awful mess wouldn't ever happened* (Mark Twain). **4a** a group of people who take meals together regularly, especially such a group in the armed forces: *The sailor found the mess a congenial lot.* **b** a meal for such a group: *The officers are at mess now.* **c** a place where such a group eats; mess hall: *When he is not dining out, he eats in the White House mess* (Time). **5a** a portion of food, especially a portion of soft food: *a mess of oatmeal.* **b** a quantity of some edible item sufficient for a meal or meals: *He caught a large mess of fish.* **6** food that does not look or taste good: *The first edge of hunger blunted, I perceived I had got in hand a nauseous mess* (Charlotte Brontë). **7** *Informal.* a lot, especially a disagreeable or bothersome lot: *How about cleanin' up de whole mess of 'em and sta'tin' all over ag'in wid some new kind of animal?* (Marc Connelly).
—***v.t.*** **1** to make dirty or untidy: *He messed up his book by scribbling on the pages.* **2** to make a failure of; spoil: *He messed up his chances of winning the race.* **3** to supply with meals, as soldiers or sailors.
—***v.i.*** to take one's meals (with): *We turned in to bunk and mess with the crew forward* (Richard H. Dana).
**mess about** or **around,** to busy oneself without seeming to accomplish anything: *On my vacation I read and messed about with my stamp collection. I mess about my flowers and read snatches of French* (Lynn Linton).
**mess around** (or **about**) **with,** *Informal.* to tamper with: *I don't want the school messing around in something I have been doing* (Sheila H. Kieran). [*She*] *is determined that one piece of tradition shall not be messed about with* (Manchester Guardian).
[< Old French *mes* < Late Latin *missus, -ūs* a course at dinner, (literally) thing put (that is, on the table) < Latin *mittere* send]

**mes|sage** (mes′ij), *n., v.,* **-saged, -sag|ing.** —***n.*** **1** words sent from one person or group to another: *a radio message, a message of welcome.* SYN: communication, letter, note. **2** an official speech or writing: *the President's message to Congress.* **3** a lesson or moral contained in a story, a motion picture, a play, or a speech: *Films with a message sometimes run the risk of spoiling good plots.* **4** inspired words: *the message of a prophet.* **5** the business entrusted to a messenger; mission; errand: *His message completed, he went on his way.* **6** a unit of the genetic code which specifies the order or sequence in which amino acids synthesize a particular protein: *The genetic message is carried from the nucleus to the cytoplasm in the form of messenger ribonucleic acid* (*messenger RNA*) (Science Journal).
—***v.t.*** to inform or communicate through a message: *We messaged him that everything was going well.*
—***v.i.*** to send a message: *The Philippine Coast Guard cutter Anemone messaged briefly that all towns on the tiny southern island were deserted* (Charlottesville Daily Progress).
**get the message,** *Informal.* to grasp the significance, implication, etc., of something: *Disgusted Detroit fans littered the ice with rubber balls and garbage, and the Red Wings got the message* (Time).
[< Old French *message* < Medieval Latin *missaticum* < Latin *missus,* past participle of *mittere* to send]

**message service,** a large public service by a spiritualist church or group at which a séance or séances are held.

**message unit,** *U.S.* a unit used by a telephone company to charge for its service, based on the number of calls made in a given period. Regular telephone service allows for the equivalent of about 50 message units.

**mes|sa|line** (mes′ə lēn′, mes′ə lēn), *n.* a thin, soft silk cloth with a surface like satin. [< French *messaline*]

**mes|san** or **mes|sin** (mes′ən), *n. Scottish.* **1** a lap dog. **2** a miserable cur (applied to a person as a term of abuse). [perhaps < Gaelic *measan*]

**mess boy,** = messman.

**mes|sei|gneurs** (mes′ā nyėrz′; *French* mā senyœr′), *n.* plural of **monseigneur.**

**mes|sen|ger** (mes′ən jər), *n.* **1a** a person who carries a message or goes on an errand: *The dying man asked his nurse to be the messenger to his family.* **b** a person whose job it is to carry messages, run errands, and the like: *a telegraph messenger.* **2** *Figurative.* anything thought of as sent on an errand: *Each bullet was a messenger of death.* **3** *Figurative.* a sign that something is coming; forerunner; herald: *Dawn is the messenger of day. ... yon gray lines That fret the clouds are messengers of day* (Shakespeare). **4** a government official employed to carry dispatches; courier: *... messenger at the British embassy in Washington* (Time). **5** a chemical substance which carries or transmits genetic information. **6** *Obsolete.* a servant sent forward to prepare the way. [Middle English *messanger,* earlier *messager* < Old French *messagier* < *message* message]

**messenger RNA**, a ribonucleic acid which carries genetic messages from the DNA (deoxyribonucleic acid) in the nucleus of a cell to the ribosomes in the cytoplasm, specifying the particular protein or enzyme to be synthesized.

**Mes|se|ni|an** (mə sē′nē ən), *n.* an inhabitant of Messenia, an area in ancient southwestern Greece.

**Mes|ser|schmitt** (mes′ər shmit′), *n.* a German fighter plane. [< Willy *Messerschmitt,* born 1898, a German industrialist, who built it]

**mess hall**, a place where a group of people eat together regularly, especially such a place on a military post.

**Mes|si|ah** (mə sī′ə), *n.* **1** the leader and liberator of the Jews, promised by the prophets and looked for as the restorer of the theocracy. **2** Often, **messiah.** any person hailed as or thought of as a savior, liberator, or deliverer.
**the Messiah,** (in Christian use) Jesus, as fulfilling the prophecy of the Lord's Anointed: *At thy nativity, a glorious quire Of angels, in the fields of Bethlehem, sung To shepherds, ... And told them the Messiah now was born* (Milton).
[variant of Middle English *messias* < Greek *Messîās* < Hebrew *māshiaḥ*]

**Mes|si|ah|ship** or **mes|si|ah|ship** (mə sī′ə-ship), *n.* the character or office of a Messiah.

**Mes|si|an|ic** (mes′ē an′ik), *adj.* **1** of or having to do with a Messiah or the Messiah: *the Messianic kingdom, a Messianic prophecy.* **2** Often, **messianic.** of or characteristic of a Messiah or savior: *He is possessed by a Messianic zeal to reform mankind.*

**Messianic Age**, the time when peace and freedom will reign on earth, especially in the belief of Conservative and Reform Jews.

**Mes|si|an|ism** (mə sī′ə niz əm), *n.* **1** the belief in a Messiah and his coming. **2** the belief in the betterment of mankind in preparation for or anticipation of the Messianic Age. **3** Often, **messianism.** a visionary outlook; utopianism: *In 1925 ... the Bolshevik Revolution turned its face away from the West, abandoned Marxist messianism, and became Russianised* (Manchester Guardian).

**Mes|si|an|ist** (mə sī′ə nist), *n.* **1** a person who advocates or supports Messianism. **2** Often, **messianist.** a person who advocates a utopian or visionary outlook.

**Mes|si|as** (mə sī′əs), *n.* = Messiah.

**Mes|si|dor** (me sē dôr′), *n.* the tenth month of the French Revolutionary calendar, extending from June 19 to July 18. [< French *Messidor* < Latin *messis* harvest (< *metere* to reap) + Greek *dôron* gift]

**mes|sieurs** (mes′ərz; *French* mā syœ′), *n.* plural of **monsieur.** *Abbr.:* MM.
► See **Messrs.** for usage note.

**mess|i|ly** (mes′ə lē), *adv.* in a messy manner.

**mess|i|ness** (mes′ē nis), *n.* messy condition.

**mess jacket**, a man's short, usually white jacket, open in front and reaching to the waist, worn especially by military and naval officers as part of a semiformal dress uniform.

*** mess kit**, **1** a shallow metal container like a skillet that folds in on itself, containing a fork, spoon, and (usually) a knife, and also a large metal cup, used especially by a soldier in the field or a camper. **2** the stove, pots and pans, and serving equipment of a field kitchen, military mess, or the like.

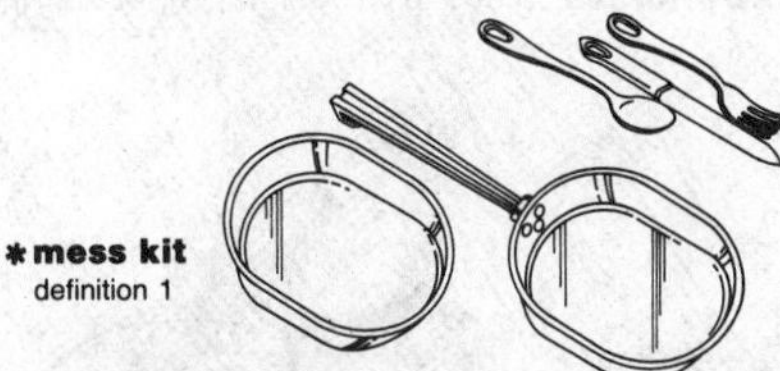

***mess kit**
definition 1

**mess|man** (mes′mən), *n., pl.* **-men.** a person who serves food on a ship.

**mess|mate** (mes′māt′), *n.* **1** one of a group of people who eat together regularly: *He would be more comfortable aboard a ship in which he had many old messmates and friends* (Frederick Marryat). **2** (in Australia) any one of several species of eucalyptus trees.

**mess|room** (mes′rüm′, -rům′), *n.* the mess hall of a ship or naval base.

**Messrs.**, Messieurs.
► **Messrs.** is used as the plural of *Mr.* (*Messrs. Kennedy and Nixon*) and sometimes, though rarely now in American usage, in addressing firms (*Messrs. Brown, Hubbell, and Company*).

**mes|suage** (mes′wij), *n. Law.* a dwelling house with its adjacent buildings and the land assigned to the use of those who live in it: *They wedded her to sixty thousand pounds, To lands in Kent and messuages in York* (Tennyson). [< Anglo-French *messuage,* ultimately < Latin *manēre* remain, dwell]

**mess|y** (mes′ē), *adj.,* **mess|i|er, mess|i|est. 1** in a mess; like a mess; in disorder; untidy: *a messy desk.* **2** covered with dirt; dirty: *messy hands.*

**mes|tee** (mes tē′), *n.* = mustee. [< variant pronunciation of Spanish *mestizo* mestizo]

**mes|ti|za** (mes tē′zə), *n.* a female mestizo. [< Spanish *mestiza*]

**mes|ti|zo** (mes tē′zō), *n., pl.* **-zos** or **-zoes.** a person of mixed blood: **a** (in Spanish America) a person of Spanish and American Indian descent: *He was a big, simple mestizo, and his Spanish and Indian blood was evident in his dark-skinned face* (New Yorker). **b** (in the Philippines) a person of Chinese and native descent. **c** (in Asia and Africa) a person of European and East Indian, Negro, or Malay descent. [< Spanish *mestizo* < Late Latin *mixtīcius* < Latin *mixtus* mixed, past participle of *miscēre* mix]

**met** (met), *v.* the past tense and past participle of **meet**[1]: *My father met us this morning at ten. We were met at the gate by our three dogs.*

**met-**, *combining form.* the form of **meta-** before vowels, as in *metempirics, metempsychosis, metestrum.*

**met.**, an abbreviation for the following:
**1** metaphor.
**2** metaphysics.
**3** metronome.
**4** metropolitan.

**meta-**, *prefix.* **1** between; among, as in *metacarpus.*
**2** change of place or state, as in *metathesis, metabolism.*
**3** behind; after, as in *metathorax.*
**4** reciprocal, as in *metacenter.*
**5** beyond, as in *metagalaxy, metalinguistics.*
**6** similar in chemical composition to, as in *metaphosphate.* Also, **met-** before vowels.
[< Greek *metá* with, after]

**me|tab|a|sis** (mə tab′ə sis), *n., pl.* **-ses** (-sēz). transition, as from one subject to another. [< Greek *metábasis,* related to *metabaínein* change one's place < *meta-* meta- + *baínein* go]

**met|a|bi|o|log|i|cal** (met′ə bī ə loj′ə kəl), *adj.* of or having to do with metabiology.

**met|a|bi|ol|o|gy** (met′ə bī ol′ə jē), *n.* a theory or philosophy of knowledge based on established biological principles.

**met|a|bol|ic** (met′ə bol′ik), *adj.* having to do with or produced by metabolism: *The hormone was used to treat both hypothyroidism and metabolic insufficiency* (Science News Letter). **— met′a|bol′i|cal|ly,** *adv.*

**me|tab|o|lism** (mə tab′ə liz əm), *n.* **1** the process by which all living things turn food into energy and living tissue. In metabolism food is broken down to produce energy, which is then used by the body to build up new cells and tissues, provide heat, and engage in physical activity. Growth and action depend on metabolism. *Only living matter is able to carry on metabolism* (A. M. Winchester). **2** the metamorphosis of an insect. [< Greek *metabolḗ* change + English *-ism*]

**me|tab|o|lite** (mə tab′ə līt), *n.* a substance produced by metabolism.

**me|tab|o|lize** (mə tab′ə līz), *v.,* **-lized, -liz|ing.**
**— *v.t.*** to alter by or subject to metabolism.
**— *v.i.*** to function in or undergo metabolism: *Before the seed can metabolize, all the enzymes ... must become active* (Science News). **— me-tab′o|liz′a|ble,** *adj.*

**met|a|car|pal** (met′ə kär′pəl), *adj., n.* **— *adj.*** of or having to do with the metacarpus.
**— *n.*** a bone of the metacarpus: *Five metacarpals support the palm of the hand* (Harbough and Goodrich). See picture under **hand.**

**met|a|car|pus** (met′ə kär′pəs), *n., pl.* **-pi** (-pī). **1** the part of the hand, especially the bones, between the wrist and the fingers, comprising five bones in man. **2** the corresponding part of the forefoot of a quadruped, between the carpus and the phalanges. [< New Latin *metacarpus* < Greek *metakárpion* < *metá* after + *karpós* wrist]

**met|a|cen|ter** (met′ə sen′tər), *n.* the intersecting point of the vertical line passing through the center of buoyancy of a floating body, such as a ship, when in perfect equilibrium, and the vertical line passing through the center of buoyancy when the floating body is out of equilibrium. The floating body is stable if this point is above the center of gravity, and lacks stability if it is below. [< French *métacentre* < *méta-* meta- + *centre*]

**met|a|cen|tre** (met′ə sen′tər), *n. Especially British.* metacenter.

**met|a|cen|tric** (met′ə sen′trik), *adj.* of or having to do with the metacenter.

**met|a|chro|mat|ic** (met′ə krō mat′ik), *adj.* **1** of or having to do with metachromatism. **2** *Anatomy.* assuming a different color from that of other tissues, when stained with a dye.

**met|a|chro|ma|tism** (met′ə krō′mə tiz əm), *n.* change or variation of color, especially as a result of change of temperature or other physical condition.

**met|a|chrome** (met′ə krōm), *n.* a body or substance that changes color. [< *meta-* + Greek *chrôma* color]

**met|a|cor|tan|dra|cin** (met′ə kôr tan′drə sin), *n.* = prednisone.

**met|a|cor|tan|dra|lone** (met′ə kôr tan′drə lōn), *n.* = prednisolone.

**met|a|di|hy|drox|y|ben|zene** (met′ə dī′hī drok′-sē ben′zēn), *n.* = resorcinol.

**met|a|ga|lac|tic** (met′ə gə lak′tik), *adj.* of or having to do with the metagalaxy.

**met|a|gal|ax|y** (met′ə gal′ək sē), *n., pl.* **-ax|ies.** the whole system of known galaxies, especially those outside the Milky Way: *The metagalaxy ... is essentially the measurable material universe* (New Scientist).

**met|age** (mē′tij), *n.* **1** the official measurement of contents or weight. **2** the charge for it. [< *met*(e)[1] + *-age*]

**met|a|gen|e|sis** (met′ə jen′ə sis), *n. Biology.* alternation of sexual and asexual generations, such as occurs in some coelenterates.

**met|a|ge|net|ic** (met′ə jə net′ik), *adj.* having to do with, characterized by, or resulting from metagenesis.

**me|tag|na|thous** (mə tag′nə thəs), *adj.* (of a bird) having the upper and lower tips of the mandibles crossed, as the crossbills. [< *meta-* + Greek *gnáthos* jaw + English *-ous*]

**met|al** (met′əl), *n., adj., v.,* **-aled, -al|ing** or (*especially British*) **-alled, -al|ling. — *n.* 1a** any one of a group of chemical elements, such as iron, gold, silver, copper, lead, and tin. Metals usually have a shiny surface, are good conductors of heat and electricity, and can be melted or fused, hammered into thin sheets, or drawn out into wires. They also form alloys with each other. *Very few metals ... exist in the earth's crust in metallic form* (Science News). **b** any alloy or fused mixture of these, such as steel, bronze, brass, or pewter. **c** the constituent matter of a metal or of metals collectively; metallic substance: *a mirror of polished metal.* **2** *Chemistry.* any chemical element or mixture of chemical elements which lose electrons from their atoms in most chemical reactions and react with certain acids to form salts. In the salt the metal takes on a positive charge. *The positive valency of metals, and the fact that they form positive ions in solution, indicate that the atoms of a metal will part readily with one or more of their outer electrons* (Sears and Zemansky). **3** an object made of metal, such as one of the rails of a railroad: *He had fallen from an engine, And been dragged along the metals* (William E. Henley). **4** broken stone, cinders, or rubble used for roads or as ballast for roadbeds or railroad tracks; road metal. **5** the melted material that becomes glass or pottery, or the glaze on pottery. **6** *Figurative.* **a** basic stuff; material; substance: *Cowards are not made of the same metal as heroes. ... the native metal of a man* (James Russell Lowell). **b** = mettle. **7** *Printing.* **a** = type metal. **b** the state of being set or composed in type. **8** the aggregate number, mass, or power of the guns of a warship. **9** *Heraldry.* one of the three kinds of tincture (the other two being color and fur). The two heraldic metals are or (gold) and argent (silver).
**— *adj.*** made of metal: *a metal container, a metal coin. Quonset huts are usually covered with metal sheeting.*
**— *v.t.*** to furnish, cover, or fit with metal.
[< Old French *metal,* learned borrowing from Latin *metallum* metal, mine < Greek *métallon* (originally) mine] **— met′al|like′,** *adj.*

**metal.**, metallurgy.

**Metal Age**, the period including the Copper Age, Bronze Age, and Iron Age; period when copper, bronze, and iron were used for making weapons and tools.

**Pronunciation Key:** hat, āge, cãre, fär; let, ēqual, tėrm; it, īce; hot, ōpen, ôrder; oil, out; cup, pu̇t, rüle; child; long; thin; ᴛʜen; zh, measure; ə represents a in about, e in taken, i in pencil, o in lemon, u in circus.

**met|a|lan|guage** (met′ə lang′gwij), *n.* any language used to analyze or make assertions about another language: *The language of metaphysics is the metalanguage of science* (New Scientist).

**met|a|law** (met′ə lô′), *n.* any system of law beyond the present human frame of reference: *Metalaw is the system for dealing with the beings we will encounter in our exploration of the vast beyond* (Science News Letter).

**met|al|clad** (met′əl klad′), *adj.* coated or plated with metal: *metalclad switchgear.*

**metal fatigue**, the cracking, disintegration, or other failure of a metal caused by small but repeated stress, such as continuous vibration or tapping.

**met|a|lin|guis|tic** (met′ə ling gwis′tik), *adj.* of or having to do with metalinguistics; exolinguistic.

**met|a|lin|guis|tics** (met′ə ling gwis′tiks), *n.* a branch of linguistics that studies social, educational, and other cultural factors related to or involving language; exolinguistics.

**met|al|ist** (met′ə list), *n.* **1** a worker in metals. **2** a person skilled in the knowledge of metals.

**met|al|ize** (met′ə līz), *v.t.,* **-ized, -iz|ing.** **1** to make metallic; give the appearance or other characteristics of metal to. **2** to cover or treat with a metal or a compound containing a metal. —**met′al|i|za′tion**, *n.*

**metall.**, metallurgy.

**me|tal|lic** (mə tal′ik), *adj.* **1** of metal; containing metal; consisting of a metal or metals: *a metallic substance, metallic reactions, metallic vaults.* **2** like metal; characteristic of metal; that suggests metal: *the metallic luster of a Japanese beetle.* **3** resembling the sound produced when metal is struck: *a metallic voice. The bird ... broke into a gush of melody ... rich, full, and metallic* (Henry Kingsley). **4** *Chemistry.* having the form or outward characteristics of a metal (usually said of a metal when occurring uncombined with other substances): *metallic iron.* —**me|tal′li|cal|ly**, *adv.*

**met|al|lide** (met′ə līd), *v.t.,* **-lid|ed, -lid|ing.** to subject (a metal) to metalliding: *Molybdenum, for example, is a relatively soft metal; when boron is metallided into it, the resulting surface alloy is apparently second in hardness only to diamond* (Science News).

**met|al|lid|ing** (met′ə lī ding), *n.* a process of strengthening the surface of metals by diffusing the atoms of one metal through high-temperature electrolysis into the surface of another. The resulting surface alloy is harder than any mechanically applied coating or plating. [< *Metalliding,* a trademark]

**met|al|lif|er|ous** (met′ə lif′ər əs), *adj.* containing or yielding metal: *metalliferous rocks, metalliferous mines.* [< Latin *metallifer* (< *metallum* metal + *ferre* to bear) + English *-ous*]

**met|al|line** (met′ə lin, -līn), *adj.* **1** = metallic. **2** containing one or more metals or metallic salts.

**met|al|lise** (met′ə līz), *v.t.,* **-lised, -lis|ing.** *Especially British.* metalize.

**met|al|list** (met′ə list), *n.* = metalist.

**met|al|lize** (met′ə līz), *v.t.,* **-lized, -liz|ing.** = metalize. —**met′al|li|za′tion**, *n.*

**me|tal|lo|ge|net|ic** (mə tal′ə jə net′ik), *adj.* producing metals: *The world's chief tin fields can be resolved into a few groups, which can be conveniently termed "metallogenetic tin provinces"* (W. R. Jones).

**me|tal|lo|graph** (mə tal′ə graf′, -gräf′), *n.* a microscope for investigating the structure of metals and alloys.

**met|al|log|ra|pher** (met′ə log′rə fər), *n.* an expert in metallography: *Metallographers use microscopes and X rays to explore the effects of heat on metal.*

**me|tal|lo|graph|ic** (mə tal′ə graf′ik), *adj.* of or having to do with metallography. —**me|tal′lo|graph′i|cal|ly**, *adv.*

**me|tal|lo|graph|i|cal** (mə tal′ə graf′ə kəl), *adj.* = metallographic.

**met|al|log|ra|phy** (met′ə log′rə fē), *n.* **1** the study of metals and alloys, chiefly with the aid of a microscope. **2** an art or process allied to lithography, in which metal plates are used instead of stones. [< Greek *métallon* metal + *gráphein* draw, write]

**met|al|loid** (met′ə loid), *n., adj.* —*n.* Chemistry. **1** an element having properties of both a metal and a nonmetal, such as arsenic, antimony, or silicon. **2** = nonmetal.
—*adj.* **1** of or having to do with metalloids. **2** of the nature of or like a metalloid. **3** having the form or appearance of a metal.

**me|tal|lo|phone** (mə tal′ə fōn), *n.* **1** a musical instrument similar to the xylophone but having metal bars in place of wooden ones: *a troupe of Balinese dancers, accompanied by their orchestra of gongs, gong-chimes, metallophones and drums* (New York Times). **2** a musical instrument similar to the piano but having metal bars rather than strings. [< Greek *métallon* metal + English *-phone*]

**me|tal|lo|ther|a|py** (mə tal′ō ther′ə pē), *n.* the use of metals, especially certain metallic salts, in the treatment of disease. [< Greek *métallon* metal + English *therapy*]

**met|al|lur|gic** (met′ə lėr′jik), *adj.* = metallurgical.

**met|al|lur|gi|cal** (met′ə lėr′jə kəl), *adj.* of or having to do with metallurgy: *metallurgical coal, a metallurgical engineer.* —**met′al|lur′gi|cal|ly**, *adv.*

**met|al|lur|gist** (met′ə lėr′jist), *n.* an expert in metallurgy.

**met|al|lur|gy** (met′ə lėr′jē), *n.* the science or art of metals. It includes the study of their properties and structure, the separation and refining of metals from their ores, the production of alloys, and the shaping and treatment of metals by heat and rolling. *Metallurgy is very important in rocket building* (Science News). [< New Latin *metallurgia,* ultimately < Greek *métallon* metal + *érgon* work]

**met|al|mark** (met′əl märk′), *n.* any one of a family of colorful butterflies having metallike dots on their wings.

**met|al|smith** (met′əl smith′), *n.* a person skilled in metalworking.

**met|al|ware** (met′əl wãr′), *n.* articles or utensils made of metal.

**met|al|work** (met′əl wėrk′), *n.* **1** things, especially artistic things, made out of metal. **2** a making things out of metal.

**met|al|work|er** (met′əl wėr′kər), *n.* a person who makes things out of metal.

**met|al|work|ing** (met′əl wėr′king), *n.* the act or process of making things out of metal: *Unitron also has companion instruments for the metalworking industries* (Science).

**met|a|math|e|mat|i|cal** (met′ə math′ə mat′ə kəl), *adj.* of or having to do with metamathematics.

**met|a|math|e|mat|ics** (met′ə math′ə mat′iks), *n.* the branch of mathematics that deals with the logic and consistency of mathematical proof, formulas, and equations. [< German *Metamathematik*]

**met|a|mer** (met′ə mər), *n. Chemistry.* a compound that is metameric with another.

**met|a|mere** (met′ə mir), *n.* any of a longitudinal series of more or less similar parts or segments composing the body of various animals, such as the earthworm; somite. [< *meta-* + *-mere*]

**met|a|mer|ic** (met′ə mer′ik), *adj.* **1** *Chemistry.* (of compounds) having the same molecular weight and the same elements combined in the same proportion but with their radicals in different positions, and hence differing in structure and chemical properties. *Example:* $CH_3{\cdot}CH_2{\cdot}CH_2{\cdot}CHO$, an aldehyde, and $CH_3{\cdot}CH_2{\cdot}CO{\cdot}CH_3$, a ketone. **2** *Zoology.* of or having to do with a metamere or metameres; segmental: *metameric segmentation.* —**met′a|mer′i|cal|ly**, adv.

**me|tam|er|ism** (mə tam′ə riz əm), *n.* **1** *Zoology.* the condition of consisting of metameres: *Animals exhibiting metamerism are composed of a linear series of body segments* (A. Franklin Shull). **2** segmentation into metameres, typically with some repetition of organs. **3** *Chemistry.* the state of being metameric; isomerism.

**met|a|mor|phic** (met′ə môr′fik), *adj.* **1** characterized by change of form; having to do with change of form; exhibiting metamorphosis. **2** *Geology.* changed in structure by heat, moisture, and pressure; formed by metamorphism. Slate is metamorphic rock that is formed from shale, a sedimentary rock. *Metamorphic rocks are classified by their texture and composition. Most metamorphic rocks are very old* (Ernest E. Wahlstrom).

**met|a|mor|phism** (met′ə môr′fiz əm), *n.* **1** change of form; metamorphosis. SYN: transmutation. **2** change in the structure of a rock caused by pressure, heat, and moisture, especially when the rock becomes harder and more crystalline.

**met|a|mor|phose** (met′ə môr′fōz, -fōs), *v.,* **-phosed, -phos|ing.** —*v.t.* **1** to change in form, structure, or substance by or as if by witchcraft; transform: *The witch metamorphosed people into animals.* SYN: transmute. **2** to change the form or structure of by metamorphosis or metamorphism: *Metamorphosed sandstone is called quartzite* (Ernest E. Wahlstrom).
—*v.i.* to undergo metamorphosis or metamorphism.

***met|a|mor|pho|sis** (met′ə môr′fə sis), *n., pl.* **-ses** (-sēz). **1** a change of form, structure, or substance. **2** *Figurative.* a noticeable or complete change in appearance, character, circumstances, or condition: *His visage ... changed as from a mask to a face. ... I know not that I have ever seen in any other human face an equal metamorphosis* (Charlotte Brontë). **3** a change in form, shape, or substance by or as if by witchcraft; transformation: *Metamorphosis is a favorite game in fairy tales: princes into swans, ogres into dragons, mice into horses, and a pumpkin into a coach.* **4** the changed form resulting from any such change. **5** a marked change in the form, and usually the habits, of an animal in its development after the embryonic stage. Tadpoles become frogs by metamorphosis; they lose their tails and grow legs. *It is the process of losing the larval organs and gaining the missing adult organs which is called metamorphosis* (A. Franklin Shull). See picture below. **6** the structural or functional modification of a plant organ or structure during the course of its development. **7** *Physiology.* metabolism. [< Latin *metamorphōsis* < Greek *metamórphōsis,* ultimately < *metá* (change) over + *morphḗ* form]

**met|a|neph|ric** (met′ə nef′rik), *adj.* of or having to do with the metanephros.

**met|a|neph|ros** (met′ə nef′ros), *n.* the posterior division of the primitive renal organ or kidney of vertebrate embryos, the mesonephros and pronephros being the middle and anterior divisions, respectively. The adult kidney develops from the metanephros. [< *meta-* + Greek *nephrós* kidney (because it develops after the pronephros and mesonephros)]

**metaph.**, **1** metaphor. **2** metaphysics.

**met|a|phase** (met′ə fāz), *n.* the second stage in mitosis, characterized by the arrangement of the chromosomes along the middle of the spindle: *In the metaphase ... double chromosomes group together near the equator of the cell* (Fred W. Emerson). See diagram at **mitosis**.

**Met|a|phen** (met′ə fen), *n. Trademark.* a preparation containing mercury and used in ointment form as an antiseptic for the eyes, skin, or mucous membranes and in solution or tincture as a disinfectant. *Formula:* $C_7H_5HgNO_3$

**met|a|phlo|em** (met′ə flō′em), *n. Botany.* the primary phloem which is formed from the procambium after the protophloem; the last primary phloem to be developed. [< *meta-* + *phloem*]

**met|a|phor** (met′ə fər, -fôr), *n.* an implied comparison between two different things; figure of speech in which a word or phrase that ordinarily means one thing is applied to another thing in order to suggest a likeness between the two. *Examples:* "a copper sky," "a heart of stone."
**mix metaphors**, to confuse two or more metaphors in the same expression. *Example:* "He embarked early on the sea of public life, where he climbed at last to the very summit of success."
[< Old French *metaphore,* learned borrowing from Latin *metaphora* < Greek *metaphorā́* a transfer, ultimately < *meta-* over, across + *phérein* to carry]
► **Metaphors** and **similes** both make comparisons, but in a *metaphor* the comparison is implied and in a *simile* it is indicated by *like* or *as.* "The sea of life" is a metaphor. "Life is like a sea" is a simile.

**met|a|phor|ic** (met′ə fôr′ik, -for′-), *adj.* = metaphorical.

**met|a|phor|i|cal** (met′ə fôr′ə kəl, -for′-), *adj.* using metaphors; figurative. —**met′a|phor′i|cal|ly**, *adv.*

**met|a|phor|ist** (met′ə fər ist, -fôr′-), *n.* a person who coins or uses metaphors.

**met|a|phor|ize** (met′ə fə rīz, -fôr′īz), *v.,* **-ized, -iz-**

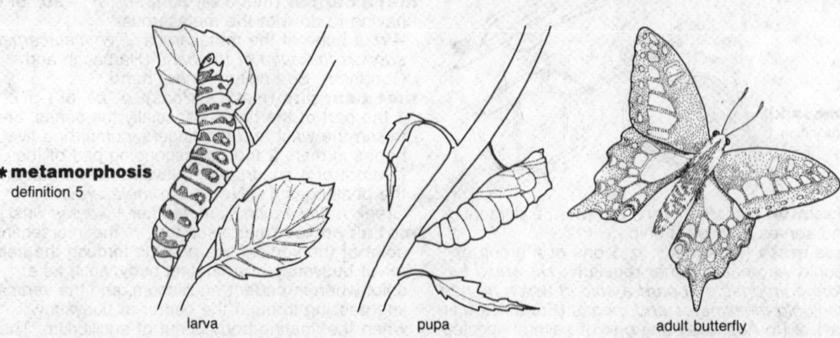


***metamorphosis**
definition 5

ing. —*v.i.* to use metaphor or metaphors; speak in or reason from metaphor.

—*v.t.* **1** to change metaphorically (into): ... *dewdrops, metaphorized into pearls* (T. Twining). **2** to ply with metaphors.

**met|a|phos|phate** (met′ə fos′fāt), *n.* a salt of metaphosphoric acid.

**met|a|phos|phor|ic acid** (met′ə fos fôr′ik, -for′-), an acid obtained by treating a phosphorous oxide with water and by other methods. It contains one molecule of water less than phosphoric acid. *Formula:* $HPO_3$

**met|a|phrase** (met′ə frāz), *n., v.,* **-phrased, -phras|ing.** —*n.* a translation, especially a word-for-word translation as distinguished from a paraphrase.

—*v.t.* **1** to translate, especially word for word. **2** to change the phrasing or literary form of. [< Greek *metáphrasis* < *meta-* + *phrázein* translate, explain; declare]

**met|a|phrast** (met′ə frast), *n.* a person who changes a composition into a different literary form, as prose into verse. [< Greek *metaphrástēs* < *metaphrázein* translate]

**met|a|phras|tic** (met′ə fras′tik), *adj.* close or literal in translation.

**met|a|phys|ic** (met′ə fiz′ik), *n., adj.* —*n.* metaphysics. —*adj.* = metaphysical: *He knew what's what, and that's as high As metaphysic wit can fly* (Samuel Butler).

**met|a|phys|i|cal** (met′ə fiz′ə kəl), *adj.* **1** of metaphysics; about the real nature of things. **2** highly abstract; hard to understand: *When the engineer struggles with Einstein's idea of time and space, technology becomes almost metaphysical* (Edward Weeks). **SYN:** abstruse. **3** of or having to do with a group of English poets of the 1600's whose verse is characterized by hard-to-understand metaphors and fanciful, elaborate imagery. The metaphysical poets included John Donne, Abraham Cowley, George Herbert, and Richard Crashaw. **4** philosophical; theoretical: *wars ... waged for points of metaphysical right* (Scott). **5** concerned with abstract thought or subjects: *a metaphysical mind.* **6** *Archaic.* supernatural: *metaphysical aid* (Shakespeare). **7** *Archaic.* fanciful; imaginary. —**met′a|phys′i|cal|ly,** *adv.*

**met|a|phy|si|cian** (met′ə fə zish′ən), *n.* a person skilled in or familiar with metaphysics: *It is a type of argument that was beloved by metaphysicians of an older generation* (Science News).

**met|a|phys|ics** (met′ə fiz′iks), *n.* **1** the branch of philosophy that tries to explain reality and knowledge; study of the real nature of things. Metaphysics includes epistemology (the theory of knowledge), ontology (the study of the nature of reality), and cosmology (the theory of the origin of the universe and its laws). *Youth is the time ... to circumnavigate the metaphysics* (Robert Louis Stevenson). **2** the more abstruse or speculative divisions of philosophy, thought of as a unit. **3** any process of reasoning thought of as abstruse or extremely subtle. [plural of earlier *metaphysic,* translation of Medieval Latin *metaphysica* < Medieval Greek (*tà*) *metaphysiká* for Greek *tà metà tà physiká* the (works) after the Physics (referring to the order of the works of Aristotle)]

**met|a|pla|sia** (met′ə plā′zhə), *n.* the direct formation of one type of adult tissue from another, as of bone from cartilage. [< New Latin *metaplasia* < Greek *metaplássein* transform; see etym. under **metaplasm**]

**met|a|plasm** (met′ə plaz əm), *n.* **1** carbohydrates, pigment, or other lifeless matter in the protoplasm of a cell. **2** *Grammar.* the alteration of a word by addition, removal, or transposition of sounds or letters. [< Latin *metaplasmus* (rhetorical) transposition < Greek *metaplasmós* (grammatical) formation from a different stem < *metaplássein* transform < *meta-* over, changed + *plássein* mold]

**met|a|plas|mic** (met′ə plaz′mik), *adj.* **1** of or having to do with the metaplasm of a cell. **2** of or having to do with metaplasm of words.

**met|a|po|di|us** (met′ə pō′dē əs), *n., pl.* **-di|i** (-dē ī). a large carnivorous bug abundant in the southern United States and an important enemy of the cotton worm and the army worm. [< New Latin *Metapodius* the genus name < Greek *metá* after + *poús, podós* foot]

**met|a|po|lit|i|cal** (met′ə pə lit′ə kəl), *adj.* of or having to do with metapolitics.

**met|a|pol|i|tics** (met′ə pol′ə tiks), *n.* the study of political science on a philosophical level.

**met|a|pro|tein** (met′ə prō′tēn, -tē in), *n.* any one of a group of products of the hydrolytic decomposition (resulting from the action of acids or alkalis) of proteins. Metaproteins are insoluble in water but soluble in acids or alkalis. [< *meta-* + *protein*]

**met|a|psy|chics** (met′ə sī′kiks), *n.* = parapsychology.

**met|a|psy|cho|log|i|cal** (met′ə sī′kə loj′ə kəl), *adj.* of or having to do with metapsychology.

**met|a|psy|chol|o|gy** (met′ə sī kol′ə jē), *n.* a systematic or philosophic speculation on the origin, structure, or function of the mind, and on the connection between mental and physical responses or actions.

**met|a|schiz|o|the|ri|um** (met′ə skiz′ō thir′ē əm), *n.* a large extinct mammal related to the rhinoceros, having five toes on each foot and teeth like those of hooved mammals. [< New Latin *Metaschizotherium* the genus name < Greek *meta-* + *schízein* to split + *thēríōn* wild animal (because of the form of the feet)]

**met|a|so|mat|ic** (met′ə sō mat′ik), *adj.* having to do with or resulting from metasomatism. —**met′a|so|mat′i|cal|ly,** *adv.*

**met|a|so|ma|tism** (met′ə sō′mə tiz əm), *n.* the process by which the chemical constitution of a rock is changed, as of limestone into granite. [< *meta-* + Greek *sôma, sómatos* body + English *-ism*]

**met|a|so|ma|to|sis** (met′ə sō′mə tō′sis), *n.* = metasomatism.

**met|a|sta|bil|i|ty** (met′ə stə bil′ə tē), *n.* the quality or condition of being metastable: *The scientists sought stability then, not mere metastability, not the top-heavy balancing rock on which we all breathlessly sit* (Scientific American).

**met|a|sta|ble** (met′ə stā′bəl), *adj.* relatively stable; intermediate between stable and unstable, as when an excited atom requires further stimulation or an interval of time before emitting its radiation and returning to its normal state: *a metastable compound.* (*Figurative.*) *a world-wide metastable equilibrium of uncertain permanency* (Bulletin of Atomic Scientists).

**me|tas|ta|sis** (mə tas′tə sis), *n., pl.* **-ses** (-sēz). **1** the transfer, as through the blood vessels or the lymphatics, or by contact, of a function, pain, or disease from one organ or part to another, especially such a transfer of cancerous cells. **2** a cancerous growth or tumor that has been so transferred. **3** transformation, as in radioactive disintegration when an alpha particle is emitted. **4** = metabolism. **5** *Rhetoric.* a rapid transition, as from one subject to another. [< Late Latin *metastasis* < Greek *metástasis* removal < *methistánai* to remove, change < *meta-* changed, over + *histánai* place]

**me|tas|ta|sise** (mə tas′tə sīz), *v.i.,* **-sised, -sis|ing.** *Especially British.* metastasize.

**me|tas|ta|size** (mə tas′tə sīz), *v.i.,* **-sized, -siz|ing.** (of a function, pain, or disease) to spread by or undergo metastasis. Cancer cells sometimes metastasize.

**met|a|stat|ic** (met′ə stat′ik), *adj.* of, having to do with, or characterized by metastasis. —**met′a|stat′i|cal|ly,** *adv.*

**met|a|tar|sal** (met′ə tär′səl), *adj., n.* —*adj.* of or having to do with the metatarsus: *metatarsal bones.*

—*n.* a bone of the metatarsus. See picture under **foot.** —**met′a|tar′sal|ly,** *adv.*

**metatarsal arch,** the arch formed by bones across the ball of the foot.

**met|a|tar|sus** (met′ə tär′səs), *n., pl.* **-si** (-sī). **1** the part of the foot, especially the bones, between the ankle and the toes, comprising five bones in man. **2** the corresponding part of the hind foot of a quadruped, between the tarsus and the phalanges. **3** a leg bone of a bird, consisting of both tarsal and metatarsal elements, extending from the tibia to the phalanges; tarsometatarsus. **4** the most basal segment of an insect's tarsus when strongly differentiated from the following segments. [< New Latin *metatarsus* < Greek *meta-* after + *tarsós* tarsal (bones), flat (of the foot)]

**me|ta|te** (mā tä′tā), *n.* a stone with a flat or concave upper surface, and sometimes with legs beneath, on which corn or the like is ground by hand by means of a smaller stone, used in Mexico and the southwestern United States: *A basalt metate was found in the hearth* (Science). [< Mexican Spanish *metate* < Nahuatl *metatl*]

**me|tath|e|sis** (mə tath′ə sis), *n., pl.* **-ses** (-sēz). **1** the transposition of sounds, syllables, or letters in a word, as in English *bird,* Old English *bridd: By inversion of sounds, called "metathesis", many speakers change apron to apern* (Scientific American). **2** the interchange of radicals between two compounds in a chemical reaction. **3** a change or reversal of condition. **SYN:** transposition. [earlier, (grammatical) interchange < Late Latin *metathesis* < Greek *metáthesis* transposition < *metatithénai* to transpose < *meta-* changed, over + *tithénai* to set]

**met|a|thet|ic** (met′ə thet′ik), *adj.* of the nature of or containing metathesis.

**met|a|thet|i|cal** (met′ə thet′ə kəl), *adj.* = metathetic.

**met|a|tho|rac|ic** (met′ə thô ras′ik, -thō-), *adj.* of or having to do with the metathorax of an insect: *The flies ... each have a pair of clubbed threads ... in place of the metathoracic wings* (Hegner and Stiles).

**met|a|tho|rax** (met′ə thôr′aks, -thōr′-), *n., pl.* **-rax|es, -ra|ces** (-rə sēz). the posterior of the three segments of the thorax of an insect, bearing the third pair of legs and the second pair of wings.

**met|a-tor|ber|nite** (met′ə tôr′bər nīt), *n.* an altered form of torbernite that serves as an uranium ore.

**met|a|xy|lem** (met′ə zī′ləm), *n. Botany.* the primary xylem that is formed from the procambium after the protoxylem; last primary xylem to be developed: *When elongation has ceased, metaxylem ... is formed* (Fred W. Emerson).

**mé|tay|age** (me tā′yäzh, *French* mā te yȧzh′), *n.* the métayer system of agriculture. [< French *métayage*]

**mé|tay|er** (me tā′ər; *French* mā te yā′), *n.* a farmer who cultivates land for a share of the produce, usually a half, the owner usually furnishing the stock, seed, and tools. [< French *métayer* < Medieval Latin *medietasius* < Latin *medietās* half]

**met|a|zo|a** (met′ə zō′ə), *n.* plural of **metazoon.**

**Met|a|zo|a** (met′ə zō′ə), *n.pl.* the subkingdom of animals that comprises the metazoans.

**met|a|zo|al** (met′ə zō′əl), *adj.* = metazoan.

**met|a|zo|an** (met′ə zō′ən), *n., adj.* —*n.* any one of a large subkingdom of animals, comprising all animals except the protozoans (or animallike protistans), having the body made up of many cells arranged in tissues, developing from a single cell. Many scientists do not include the sponges in this subkingdom.

—*adj.* of or belonging to the metazoans. [< New Latin *Metazoa* (ultimately < Greek *meta-* after + *zôia,* neuter plural of *zôion* animal) + English *-an*]

**met|a|zo|ic** (met′ə zō′ik), *adj.* = metazoan.

**met|a|zo|on** (met′ə zō′on, -ən), *n., pl.* **-zo|a.** = metazoan.

**mete**[1] (mēt), *v.t.,* **met|ed, met|ing. 1** to give to each a share of; give to each what is due him; distribute; allot: *The judges will mete out praise and blame. Chance has meted you a measure of happiness* (Charlotte Brontë). **SYN:** apportion. **2** *Archaic.* to measure. [Old English *metan*]

**mete**[2] (mēt), *n.* **1** = boundary. **SYN:** limit. **2** a boundary stone. [< Old French *mete* < Latin *meta* boundary (mark) or limit]

**met|em|pir|ic** (met′em pir′ik), *n., adj.* —*n.* **1** = metempirics. **2** a supporter of the metempirical philosophy.

—*adj.* = metempirical.

**met|em|pir|i|cal** (met′əm pir′ə kəl), *adj.* **1** beyond, or outside of, the field of experience: *If then the Empirical designates the province we include within the range of Science, the province we exclude may fitly be styled the metempirical* (George H. Lewes). **2** of or having to do with metempirics.

**met|em|pir|i|cism** (met′em pir′ə siz əm), *n.* metempirical philosophy.

**met|em|pir|ics** (met′em pir′iks), *n.* a branch of philosophy closely related to the transcendentalism of Immanuel Kant, Johann Fichte, and Georg Hegel, concerned with things outside the field of experience, but not beyond human knowledge. [< *met-* + *empir*(ic) + *-ics*]

**met|em|psy|chic** (met′əm sī′kik), *adj.* of or having to do with metempsychosis.

**met|em|psy|cho|sis** (met′əm sī kō′sis, mə temp′sə-), *n., pl.* **-ses** (-sēz). the passing of the soul at death from one body into another body; transmigration of the soul. Some Oriental philosophies teach that by metempsychosis a person's soul lives again in an animal's body. The belief in metempsychosis is a characterizing feature of most animistic religions, and has reached a high degree of sophistication in Buddhism and Hinduism. [< Latin *metempsȳchōsis* < Greek *metempsȳchōsis* < *meta-* over, changed + *en-* in + *psȳchōsis* a livening < *psȳchē* soul]

**met|en|ce|phal|ic** (met′en sə fal′ik), *adj.* of or having to do with the metencephalon.

**met|en|ceph|a|lon** (met′en sef′ə lon), *n., pl.* **-la** (-lə). a section of the brain of the vertebrate embryo, the anterior part of the rhombencephalon or hindbrain, which comprises the cerebellum and pons. [< *met-* + *encephalon*]

**me|te|or** (mē′tē ər), *n.* **1** a mass of stone or metal that enters the earth's atmosphere from outer space with enormous speed; falling star;

shooting star. Meteors become so hot from rushing through the air that they glow and often burn up. A trail of hot gas forms in the meteor's wake. **2** *Obsolete.* any atmospheric phenomenon, such as winds, rain, a rainbow, or lightning: *In starry flake, and pellicle, All day the hoary meteor* [*snow*] *fell* (John Greenleaf Whittier). [< Late Latin *meteōrum* < Greek *metéōron* (thing) in the air < *meta-* up + *aeírein* lift]

**meteor.**, meteorology.

**me|te|or|ic** (mē′tē ôr′ik, -or′-), *adj.* **1** of meteors: *meteoric dust, meteoric gases.* **2** *Figurative.* flashing like a meteor; brilliant and soon ended; swift: *a man's meteoric rise to fame.* **SYN**: dazzling. **3** of the atmosphere; meteorological: *Wind and rain are meteoric phenomena.* —**me′te|or′i|cal|ly**, *adv.*

**meteoric shower**, = meteor shower.

**meteoric water**, ground water that filters through the soil after a rain or seeps into the ground from rivers and lakes: *Meteoric water makes up most of the 2 million cubic miles of ground water in the earth* (Ray K. Linsley).

**me|te|or|ite** (mē′tē ə rīt), *n.* **1** a mass of stone or metal that has reached the earth from outer space without burning up; fallen meteor: *Meteorites are deceptive because some are predominantly iron while others are largely stone* (Hubert J. Bernhard). **2** a meteor or meteoroid.

**me|te|or|it|ic** (mē′tē ə rit′ik), *adj.* of or having to do with a meteorite or meteorites.

**me|te|or|it|i|cist** (mē′tē ə rit′ə sist), *n.* a person who studies meteorites, especially their structure and frequency.

**me|te|or|o|graph** (mē′tē ər ə graf, -gräf; mē′tē-ôr′-, -or′-), *n.* an instrument for automatically recording various meteorological conditions, as barometric pressure, temperature, and humidity, at the same time, especially one carried aloft by a balloon or airplane; aerograph.

**me|te|or|o|graph|ic** (mē′tē ər ə graf′ik, -ôr′-; -or′-), *adj.* of or having to do with the meteorograph.

**me|te|or|oid** (mē′tē ə roid), *n.* any one of the many small bodies, believed often to be the remains of disintegrated comets, that travel through space and become meteors or shooting stars when they enter the earth's atmosphere.

**meteorol.**, meteorology.

**me|te|or|o|lite** (mē′tē ər ə līt), *n.* = meteorite.

**me|te|or|o|log|ic** (mē′tē ər ə loj′ik), *adj.* = meteorological.

**me|te|or|o|log|i|cal** (mē′tē ər ə loj′ə kəl), *adj.* **1** of or having to do with the atmosphere, atmospheric phenomena, or weather. **2** having to do with meteorology.

**me|te|or|o|log|i|cal|ly** (mē′tē ər ə loj′ə klē), *adv.* in meteorological respects; by meteorology; according to meteorology.

**me|te|or|ol|o|gist** (mē′tē ə rol′ə jist), *n.* a person who studies meteorology.

**me|te|or|ol|o|gy** (mē′tē ə rol′ə jē), *n.* **1** the science dealing with the atmosphere and weather. The study of atmospheric conditions, such as winds, moisture, and temperature, and forecasts of the weather are part of meteorology. **2** meteorological condition; atmosphere, atmospheric phenomena, or weather: *Little can be said about the meteorology of deserts* (Science News). [< Greek *meteōrologíā* < *meteōron* (thing) in the air + *-logos* treating of]

**me|te|or|ous** (mē′tē ər əs), *adj.* = meteoric.

**meteor shower**, a large number of meteors entering and burning up in the earth's atmosphere, occurring when the earth encounters a meteor swarm or a comet: *Meteor showers begin in earnest in mid-July* (New York Times).

**meteor swarm**, a large group of meteors that orbit together about the sun, considered to be the remains of a disintegrated comet.

***me|ter¹** (mē′tər), *n.* **1** the basic measure of length in the metric system, approximately equal to 39.37 inches. It was intended to be, and very nearly is, equal to one ten-millionth of the distance from the equator to either pole measured on a meridian, but actually is equal to 1,650,-763.73 wave lengths of the orange-red light from the isotope krypton 86. This standard was adopted in 1960. *Abbr:* m. **2a** any kind of poetic rhythm; the arrangement of beats or accents in a line of poetry: *The meter of "Jack and Jill went up the hill" is not the meter of "One, two, buckle my shoe."* **b** a specific kind of rhythm in verse, depending on the kind and number of feet of which the verse consists: *iambic meter, dactylic meter.* **c** (in English hymns) the rhythmical pattern of a stanza or strophe, determined by the kind and number of lines: *short meter, long meter, common meter.* **3** the arrangement of beats in music as divided into parts or measures of a uniform length of time; musical rhythm: *Three-fourths meter is waltz time.* Also, *especially British and Canadian,* **metre**. [(definition 1) < French *mètre,* learned borrowing from Latin *metrum* measure < Greek *métron* measure; (definitions 2,3) < Old French *metre,* learned borrowing from Latin *metrum* measure]

***meter¹**
definition 1

1 meter = 3.28 feet or 39.37 inches

1 yard = 3 feet or 36 inches

1 foot = 12 inches

**me|ter²** (mē′tər), *n., v.* —*n.* **1** a device for measuring. **2** a device for measuring and recording the amount of something used, such as gas, water, or electricity. **3** a person who measures, especially one whose duty or office is to see that commodities are of the proper measure.
—*v.t., v.i.* to measure or record with a meter.
[< *met(e)*¹ + *-er*¹; probably influenced by *-meter*]
▶ **meter, metre.** *Meter* is the preferred spelling of this word in both U.S. and British use.

**-meter**, *combining form.* **1** a device for measuring ____: *Speedometer = a device for measuring speed.*
**2** meter (39.37 inches): *Kilometer = one thousand meters. Millimeter = one thousandth of a meter.*
**3** having ____ metrical feet: *Tetrameter = having four metrical feet.*
[< New Latin *-metrum* < Greek *métron* a measure]

**me|ter|age** (mē′tər ij), *n.* **1** the act of measuring. **2** the measurement itself. **3** the price paid for measurement.

**meter candle**, a unit of illumination equal to one lux; candle meter.

**me|tered mail** (mē′tərd), mail that has the amount to be paid for postage stamped on it by a machine. The post office controls the machines and collects the amounts from the senders.

**me|ter-kil|o|gram-sec|ond** (mē′tər kil′ə gram-sek′ənd), *adj.* having to do with a system of measurement in which the meter is the unit of length, the kilogram is the unit of mass, and the second is the unit of time. *Abbr:* M.K.S.

**meter maid**, *U.S.* a woman assigned to issue tickets for violations of parking regulations.

**met|es|trum** (met es′trəm, -ēs′-), *n.* Zoology. the period of regressive changes following the estrous cycle. [< *met-* + *estrum*]

**mete|wand** (mēt′wänd′), *n. Archaic.* a measuring stick or yardstick.

**meth** (meth), *n. U.S. Slang.* methamphetamine.

**Meth.**, Methodist.

**meth|ac|ry|late** (me thak′rə lāt), *n.* a salt or ester of methacrylic acid.

**meth|a|cryl|ic acid** (meth′ə kril′ik), a colorless liquid obtained artificially. Its esters are used in the manufacture of plastics. *Formula:* $C_4H_6O_2$ [< *meth*(yl) + *acrylic*]

**meth|a|don** (meth′ə don), *n.* = methadone.

**meth|a|done** (meth′ə dōn), *n.* a synthetic narcotic used to relieve pain and to aid in curing heroin addiction: *The Army is finding methadone a satisfactory substitute for morphine* (Newsweek). *Formula:* $C_{21}H_{27}NO \cdot HCl$ [< (di)*meth*(yl)-*a*(mino) + *d*(iphenyl) + (heptan)*one*]

**met|hae|mo|glo|bin** (met hē′mə glō′bin, -hem′ə-; me thē′-), *n.* = methemoglobin.

**meth|am|phet|a|mine** (meth′am fet′ə mēn, -min), *n.* a drug that is a powerful stimulant of the central nervous system, used to combat fatigue and mental depression and often prescribed in the treatment of obesity to reduce the appetite; Methedrine. It is not physically addictive but its misuse by drug users is dangerous. *Formula:* $C_{10}H_{15}N \cdot HCl$ [< *meth*(yl) + *amphetamine*]

***methane**

H
|
H — C — H
|
H

formula

***meth|ane** (meth′ān), *n.* a colorless, odorless, flammable gas, the simplest of the hydrocarbons, and commercially important as a fuel; marsh gas. Methane is formed naturally by the decomposition of plant or other organic matter in marshes, petroleum wells, volcanoes, and coal mines. It is the principal constituent of natural gas and of firedamp in coal mines. *Formula:* $CH_4$

**methane series**, a homologous series of saturated, open-chain (aliphatic) hydrocarbons, with the group formula $C_nH_{2n+2}$ (*n* standing for the number of carbon atoms in the molecule); alkanes. The methane series includes a larger number of known compounds than any other chain series, many of which, as methane, ethane, butane, and propane, are commercially important.

**meth|an|o|gen** (mə than′ə jən, -thā′nə-), *n.* one of the archaebacteria, microorganisms that are genetically distinct: *In this study the surprised scientists found that the methanogens' RNA sequences were unlike any others they had ever seen ... Microbiologist Wolfe detected chemicals inside the methanogens that are different from any in common bacteria* (Newsweek). [< *methane* + *-gen*]

**meth|a|nol** (meth′ə nōl, -nol), *n.* = methyl alcohol. *Formula:* $CH_3OH$

**meth|an|the|line** (mə than′thə lēn), *n.* a white, nearly odorless powder with a very bitter taste, used to inhibit cholinergic and secretory action in the treatment of various conditions; Banthine. *Formula:* $C_{21}H_{26}BrNO_3$

**Meth|e|drine** (meth′ə drin, -drēn), *n. Trademark.* methamphetamine.

**me|theg|lin** (mə theg′lin), *n.* an alcoholic drink made from fermented honey and water; a kind of mead, originally a spiced kind made in Wales. [< Welsh *meddyglyn* < *meddyg-* healing (< Latin *medicus;* see etym. under **medic**) + *llyn* liquor]

**met|he|mo|glo|bin** (met hē′mə glō′bin, -hem′ə-; me thē′-), *n.* a brownish substance formed in the blood when the hematin of oxyhemoglobin is oxidized, either by spontaneous decomposition of the blood or by the action of an oxidizing agent, as potassium chlorate. [< German *Methemoglobin* < Greek *meth-*, variant of *meta-* meta- + New Latin *haemoglobin* hemoglobin]

**met|he|mo|glo|bi|ne|mi|a** (met hē′mə glō′bə nē′-mē ə), *n.* the presence of methemoglobin in the blood: *Dr. Singley knew that he was dealing with methemoglobinemia, in which poisoned red cells carry no oxygen, and other cells cannot deliver enough, to the tissues* (Time).

**me|the|na|mine** (me thē′nə mēn, -min), *n.* a colorless or white, crystalline substance produced from ammonia and formaldehyde, used especially as a urinary antiseptic, chemical agent, and in making plastics and explosives. *Formula:* $C_6H_{12}N_4$ [< *methen*(e) + *amine*]

**meth|ene** (meth′ēn), *n.* = methylene.

**meth|er** (meᴛʜ′ər), *n.* a square wooden drinking vessel, formerly in common use in Ireland. [< Irish *meadar*]

**meth|i|cil|lin** (meth′ə sil′ən), *n.* a synthetic penicillin used against staphylococci that have developed resistance to natural penicillin.

**me|thinks** (mi thingks′), *v., past tense* **methought**. *Archaic.* it seems to me: *The lady doth protest too much, methinks* (Shakespeare). [Old English *mē thyncth* it seems to me]

**me|thi|o|nine** (me thī′ə nēn, -nin), *n.* an amino acid containing sulfur, indispensable to human life, occurring in various proteins, such as in casein, yeast, and egg whites: *Methionine is one of the eight essential amino acids* (Science News Letter). *Formula:* $C_5H_{11}NO_2S$ [< *met-* + Greek *theîon* sulfur + *-ine*²]

**meth|od** (meth′əd), *n.* **1** way of doing something, especially according to a defined plan: *a method of teaching music. Roasting is one method of cooking meat.* **SYN**: mode, manner. See syn. under **way**. **2** the habit of acting according to plan; order or system in getting things done or in thinking: *If you used more method, you wouldn't waste so much time.* **3** orderly arrangement of ideas and topics in writing.

**method in one's madness**, system and sense in apparent folly: *There was method in Portia's madness when she disguised herself as a doctor of law in "The Merchant of Venice."*
[< Latin *methodus* < Greek *méthodos* (originally) pursuit, following after < *meta-* after + *hodós* a traveling, road, way]

**Meth|od** (meth′əd), *n.* **the**, = Stanislavsky method.

**me|thod|ic** (mə thod′ik), *adj.* = methodical.

**me|thod|i|cal** (mə thod′ə kəl), *adj.* **1** done according to a method; orderly; systematic: *a methodical check of one's work.* **SYN**: See syn. under **orderly**. **2** acting with method or order: *A scientist is usually a methodical person.* —**me-thod′i|cal|ly**, *adv.* —**me|thod′i|cal|ness**, *n.*

**meth|od|ism** (meth′ə diz əm), *n.* adherence to a fixed method or methods.

**Meth|od|ism** (meth′ə diz əm), *n.* the doctrine, organization, and manner of worship of the Methodist Church.

**meth|od|ist** (meth′ə dist), *n.* a person who attaches great importance to method.

**Meth|od|ist** (meth′ə dist), *n., adj.* —*n.* a member of a church that had its origin in the teachings and work of John Wesley; adherent of Methodism; Wesleyan.
—*adj.* of the Methodists or Methodism.

**Meth|od|is|tic** (meth′ə dis′tik), *adj.* of or like the Methodists.

**Meth|od|is|ti|cal** (meth′ə dis′tə kəl), *adj.* = Methodistic.

**meth|od|ize** (meth′ə dīz), *v.t.*, **-ized, -iz|ing.** to reduce to a method; arrange with method: *I endeavored to arrange and methodize my ideas on the subject.* **SYN:** organize. —**meth′od|iz′er,** *n.*

**meth|od|less** (meth′əd lis), *adj.* lacking method, order, or regularity.

**meth|od|o|log|i|cal** (meth′ə də loj′ə kəl), *adj.* of or having to do with methodology: *methodological tools, methodological questions.* —**meth′od|o|log′i|cal|ly,** *adv.*

**meth|od|ol|o|gist** (meth′ə dol′ə jist), *n.* a person who deals with or is trained in methodology.

**meth|od|ol|o|gy** (meth′ə dol′ə jē), *n., pl.* **-gies.** **1** the system of methods or procedures used in any field: *the methodology of the modern historian.* **2** a branch of logic dealing with the application of its principles in any field of knowledge. **3** the methods of teaching; the branch of education dealing with the means and ways of instruction. [< New Latin *methodologia* < Greek *méthodos* method + *-logiā* science, system, treatment < *légein* speak]

**meth|o|trex|ate** (meth′ə trek′sāt), *n.* = amethopterin.

**me|thought** (mi thôt′), *v. Archaic.* the past tense of **methinks.**

**meth|ox|sal|en** (me thok′sə lən), *n.* = Meloxine.

**meth|ox|y|chlor** (me thok′sə klôr, -klōr), *n.* a chlorinated hydrocarbon insecticide less toxic than DDT. *Formula:* $C_{16}H_{15}Cl_3O_2$

**meths** (meths), *n.pl. British Informal.* methylated spirits.

**Me|thu|se|lah** (mə thü′zə lə), *n.* **1** a son of Enoch, said to have lived 969 years, the longest life span attributed to anyone in the Bible (Genesis 5:27). **2** a very old man. **3** Also, **methuselah.** a champagne bottle holding 208 ounces, equivalent to eight standard bottles.

**meth|yl** (meth′əl), *n.* a univalent hydrocarbon radical, occurring in methane, members of the methane series, and many other organic compounds. *Formula:* $-CH_3$ [< French *méthyle,* back formation < *méthylène* methylene]

**methyl acetate,** a fragrant, colorless, inflammable, volatile liquid obtained by the action of sulfuric acid on methyl alcohol and acetic acid in the presence of heat, used as a solvent, in making perfumes, and as a flavoring agent. *Formula:* $C_3H_6O_2$

**meth|yl|al** (meth′ə lal′, meth′ə lal), *n.* a volatile, inflammable liquid having a pleasant, ethereal odor. It is used in artificial resins, for extracting odors in making perfume, and in certain chemical tests. *Formula:* $C_3H_8O_2$ [< *methyl* + *al*(cohol)]

**methyl alcohol,** a colorless, volatile, flammable, poisonous liquid made by the destructive distillation of wood or by the combination of carbon monoxide and hydrogen in the presence of a catalyst, used especially in making formaldehyde, in organic synthesis, as a solvent, and as a fuel; methanol; wood alcohol: *Methyl alcohol is sometimes used as a rubbing compound* (Science News Letter). *Formula:* $CH_3OH$

**meth|yl|a|mine** (meth′ə lə mēn′, -lam′in), *n.* a colorless, inflammable, gaseous compound with an odor like that of ammonia. It is formed by the combination of methanol and ammonia in the presence of a catalyst, and is used in organic synthesis, tanning, and dyeing. *Formula:* $CH_3NH_2$ [< *methyl* + *amine*]

**meth|yl|ate** (meth′ə lāt), *n., v.,* **-at|ed, -at|ing.** —*n.* a compound derived from methyl alcohol by substituting a metal for the hydrogen of the hydroxyl group.
—*v.t.* **1** to add the radical methyl ($-CH_3$) to. **2** to mix or saturate with methyl alcohol.

**meth|yl|at|ed spirit** (meth′ə lā′tid), ordinary alcohol mixed with methyl alcohol so as to render it unfit for drinking.

**meth|yl|a|tion** (meth′ə lā′shən), *n.* the substitution of the radical methyl ($-CH_3$) for an atom of hydrogen.

**methyl atropine,** a chemical compound that inhibits the transmission of nerve impulses: *Smith and his colleagues applied methyl atropine to the lateral hypothalami of killer rats. This chemical, which blocks the action of acetylcholine, turned the formerly deadly rats into harmless pacifists* (New Scientist). *Formula:* $C_{18}H_{26}N_{20}O_6$

**meth|yl|ben|zene** (meth′əl ben′zēn, -ben zēn′), *n.* = toluene.

**methyl bromide,** a colorless liquid produced from methyl alcohol and bromine, used to extinguish fires and to fumigate grain, fruit, and other produce. *Formula:* $CH_3Br$

**methyl cellulose,** a white substance prepared from wood pulp or cotton, used especially as a thickening agent, laxative, and adhesive.

**methyl chloride,** a colorless liquefiable gas produced from hydrochloric acid and methyl alcohol, used especially as a refrigerant, anesthetic, and solvent: *Methyl chloride is used to produce butyl rubber* (Wall Street Journal). *Formula:* $CH_3Cl$

**meth|yl|chol|an|threne** (meth′əl kə lan′thrēn), *n.* a chemical used experimentally to produce cancer in animals. *Formula:* $C_{21}H_{16}$

**meth|yl|ene** (meth′ə lēn), *n.* **1** *Chemistry.* a bivalent hydrocarbon radical occurring only in combination, and regarded as derived from methane. *Formula:* $-CH_2-$ **2** (in commercial use) = methyl alcohol. [< French *méthylène* < Greek *méthy* wine + *hȳlē* wood, substance + French *-ène* -ene]

**methylene blue,** a dark-green, crystalline compound used as a dye, as a stain in bacteriology, in medicine as an antidote for cyanide poisoning, and in the treatment of various diseases: *The methylene blue test on a milk sample measures one type of bacterial activity* (Science News). *Formula:* $C_{16}H_{18}ClN_3S{\cdot}3H_2O$

**methylene chloride,** a colorless nonflammable liquid used as a solvent, refrigerant, and local anesthetic. *Formula:* $CH_2Cl_2$

**me|thyl|ic** (mə thil′ik), *adj. Chemistry.* containing, relating to, or derived from the radical methyl ($-CH_3$).

**meth|yl|mer|cu|ry** (meth′əl mėr′kyər ē), *n.,* or **methyl mercury,** a highly toxic compound used as a seed disinfectant, fungicide, and pesticide.

**methyl methacrylate,** a tough, transparent plastic obtained by the polymerization of the methyl ester of methacrylic acid. It is sold under various trade names, such as Plexiglas and Lucite.

**meth|yl|naph|tha|lene** (meth′əl naf′thə lēn, -nap′-), *n.* a compound obtained from coal tar, used (in the liquid alpha form) in ascertaining the cetane number of a fuel. *Formula:* $C_{11}H_{10}$

**meth|y|lo|sis** (meth′ə lō′sis), *n. Geology.* that variety of metamorphism which involves change of chemical substance. [< New Latin *methylosis* < Greek *meta-* change + *hȳlē* wood, substance + *-osis* condition]

**meth|yl|pen|ty|nol** (meth′əl pen′tə nol), *n.* a drug used as a sedative and hypnotic, as during childbirth and dental operations. *Formula:* $C_6H_{10}O$

**meth|yl|phen|i|date** (meth′əl fen′ə dāt), *n.* a drug used as a stimulant in the treatment of various mental disorders and depressive states; Ritalin: *The idea that hyperactivity has a biological basis is further strengthened by the dramatic change in behavior produced in many of these children by a stimulating drug (such as amphetamine or methylphenidate)* (Scientific American). *Formula:* $C_{14}H_{19}NO_2$

**meth|yl|pred|nis|o|lone** (meth′əl pred nis′ə lōn), *n.* a drug having uses similar to those of cortisone, such as the treatment of inflammations, asthma, and allergies. *Formula:* $C_{22}H_{30}O_5$

**methyl salicylate,** a heavy, volatile liquid either obtained from the leaves and bark of certain plants or prepared synthetically; oil of wintergreen. It is used in perfumes, as a food flavoring, and medicinally in liniments. *Formula:* $C_8H_8O_3$

**methyl styrene,** or **meth|yl|sty|rene** (meth′əl stī′rēn, -stir′ēn), *n.* a monomer used in the production of various polymers, such as heat-resistant plastics. *Formula:* $C_9H_{10}$

**meth|yl|tes|tos|ter|one** (meth′əl tes tos′tə rōn), *n.* a synthetic male sex hormone used especially in the treatment of glandular deficiency, breast cancer, and disorders of the uterus. *Formula:* $C_{20}H_{30}O_2$

**meth|y|ser|gide** (meth′ə sėr′jīd), *n.* a drug derived from the fungal nerve poison ergot: *Methysergide ... is effective in reducing the number and severity of migraine headaches in about 70 per cent of patients* (Jane E. Brody). *Formula:* $C_{21}H_{27}N_3O_2$ [< *methy*(l) + (ly)*serg*(ic acid) + *-ide*]

**met|ic** (met′ik), *n.* a resident alien in an ancient Greek city, having some of the privileges of citizenship: *A metic, or foreigner, could not be naturalized as an Athenian citizen, nor could his children become citizens* (William F. McDonald). [< Late Latin *metycus* < Greek *metoikos* < *metá* meta- + *oîkos* dwelling]

**Met|i|cor|te|lone** (met′ə kôr′tə lōn), *n. Trademark.* prednisolone.

**Met|i|cor|ten** (met′ə kôr′tən), *n. Trademark.* prednisone.

**me|tic|u|los|i|ty** (mə tik′yə los′ə tē), *n.* the quality of being meticulous.

**me|tic|u|lous** (mə tik′yə ləs), *adj.* extremely or excessively careful about small details: *He had throughout been almost worryingly meticulous in his business formalities* (Arnold Bennett). **SYN:** scrupulous. [earlier, fearful < Latin *meticulōsus* < *metus, -ūs* fear] —**me|tic′u|lous|ly,** *adv.*

**me|tic|u|lous|ness** (mə tik′yə ləs nis), *n.* extreme care about minute details; scrupulousness: *Only the auditor's meticulousness uncovered the embezzling teller.*

**mé|tier** (mā tyā′), *n.* **1** a trade; profession. **2** a kind of work for which a person has special ability: *a Yale boy who's finally found his métier* (New Yorker). **SYN:** specialty. [< French *métier* < Old French *mestier* < earlier *menestier* < Latin *ministerium.* See etym. of doublet **ministry.**]

**mé|tis** (mā tēs′), *n., pl.* **-tis.** **1** a person of mixed descent: *There was distinct advantage in being a métis—the offspring of a foreigner and a Vietnamese* (Time). **2** *U.S.* an octoroon. **3** (in Canada) a person of white (especially French) and American Indian descent. [< French *métis* < Old French *mestiz* < Late Latin *mixtīcius;* see etym. under **mestizo**]

**Me|tis** (mē′tis), *n. Greek Mythology.* a goddess personifying wisdom whom Zeus swallowed after hearing a prophecy that said she would bear him a child wiser than he. The child, Athena, was born through Zeus's forehead.

**mé|tisse** (mā tēs′), *n.* a female métis. [< French *métisse*]

**METO** (no periods), Middle East Treaty Organization.

**Me|tol** (mē′tōl, -tol), *n. Trademark.* a soluble, whitish powder, much used as the base for photographic developers. *Formula:* $C_{14}H_{20}N_2O_6S$

**meton.,** metonymy.

**Me|ton|ic** (mi ton′ik), *adj.* of or having to do with Meton, an Athenian astronomer of the 400's B.C.

**Metonic cycle,** a cycle of 19 years or 235 lunar months, after which the phases of the moon recur on the same days of the calendar as in the previous cycle.

**met|o|nym** (met′ə nim), *n.* a word used in a transferred sense. [see etym. under **metonymy**]

**met|o|nym|ic** (met′ə nim′ik), *adj.* = metonymical.

**met|o|nym|i|cal** (met′ə nim′ə kəl), *adj.* having to do with or involving metonymy. —**met′o|nym′i|cal|ly,** *adv.*

**me|ton|y|my** (mə ton′ə mē), *n.* a figure of speech that consists in substituting for the name of a thing an attribute of it or something which it naturally suggests. *Example:* The *pen* (power of literature) is mightier than the *sword* (force). [< Late Latin *metōnymia* < Greek *metōnymiā* (literally) change of name < *meta-* change, over + *ónyma* name]

**me-too** (mē′tü′), *adj., v.,* **-tooed, -too|ing.** *Informal.* —*adj.* (in politics) characterized by metooism; adopting the successful ideas of an opponent expediently: *a me-too platform, candidate, or policy.*
—*v.t., v.i.* to say "me-too" about, in favor of, or against a political proposal, doctrine, or the like; imitate or adopt (an opponent's political platform): *A senator has little to gain politically merely by me-tooing the liberality of the House* (Newsweek). —**me′-too′er,** *n.*

**me-too|ism** (mē′tü′iz əm), *n. Informal.* the adoption of the political line of the opposition.

**met|o|pe** (met′ə pē, -ōp), *n.* one of the square spaces, decorated or plain, between the triglyphs in a Doric frieze. [< Latin *metopa* < Greek *metópē* < *meta-* between + *ópai,* plural of *ópē* holes for beams in a frieze]

**me|top|ic** (mi top′ik), *adj.* of or having to do with the forehead; frontal. [< Greek *métōpon* forehead]

**met|o|pon** (met′ə pon), *n.* a narcotic derived from morphine. *Formula:* $C_{18}H_{21}NO_3{\cdot}HCl$ [< *met*(hyl) + (dihydr)*o* + (mor)*p*(hine) + *-on*(e)]

**me|tral|gi|a** (mi tral′jē ə), *n.* pain in the uterus. [< New Latin *metralgia* < Greek *mētrā* the cervix; (originally) uterus, related to *mḗtēr* mother + *-algiā* < *álgos* pain]

**Met|ra|zol** (met′rə zōl, -zol), *n. Trademark.* pentylenetetrazol.

**me|tre** (mē′tər), *n. Especially British and Canadian.* meter[1].

**Met|re|cal** (met′rə kal), *n. Trademark.* a low-calorie food substitute.

**met|ric** (met′rik), *adj., n.* —*adj.* **1** of the meter or the metric system: *metric measurements. The gram is a metric unit.* **2** using or used to a metric system of measurement: *In a metric Britain, Manchester will be 296 km from London, not 184 miles* (New Scientist). **3** = metrical.
—*n.* metrical style, composition, or arrangement: *A new metric, a new emphasis on narrative, ... distinguish Dickey's maturity from his early work* (Peter Davison).
**go metric,** to adopt the metric system of measurement: *Going metric will not deprive us of the use of fractions where they are convenient: we can continue to count in halves and quarters as well as in twos, tens, and dozens* (Manchester

**Pronunciation Key:** hat, āge, cãre, fär; let, ēqual, tėrm; it, īce; hot, ōpen, ôrder; oil, out; cup, pu̇t, rüle; child; long; thin; ᴛʜen; zh, measure; ə represents **a** in about, **e** in taken, **i** in pencil, **o** in lemon, **u** in circus.

Guardian Weekly).
[(adj. defs. 1 and 2) < French *métrique* < *mètre* meter[1]; (adj. def. 3 and n.) < Latin *metricus* metrical < Greek *metrikós* < *métron* measure, poetic meter]

**met|ri|cal** (met′rə kəl), *adj.* **1** of meter; having a regular arrangement of accents; written in verse, not in prose: *a metrical translation of Homer.* **2** of, having to do with, or used in measurement; metric.

**met|ri|cal|ly** (met′rə klē), *adv.* in meter; according to meter.

**met|ri|cate** (met′rə kāt), *v.t., v.i.,* **-cat|ed, -cat|ing.** to change to the metric system: *Nine-tenths of the world is already metricated, or going metric* (New Scientist).

**met|ri|ca|tion** (met′rə kā′shən), *n.* the act or process of changing to the metric system.

**met|ri|ca|tor** or **met|ri|ca|ter** (met′rə kā′tər), *n. British.* a supporter of metrication.

**metric hundredweight,** 50 kilograms.

**me|tri|cian** (me trish′ən), *n.* a person who studies the subject of poetic meters; metrist.

**met|ri|cism** (met′rə siz əm), *n.* the quality or condition of being metric.

**met|ri|cize** (met′rə sīz), *v.t.,* **-cized, -ciz|ing.** to put into metrical form; make or compose in meter.

**metric mile,** (in swimming and track competition) 1,500 meters, or 120 yards short of a statute mile.

**met|rics** (met′riks), *n.* the science or art of meter; art of metrical composition.

*** metric system,** a decimal system of weights and measures, or one which counts by tens. It is based on the meter as its unit of length, the gram as its unit of mass or weight, and the liter as its unit of volume. A cubic centimeter of water weighs approximately one gram.

***metric system**

**length:**

1 kilometer = 1,000 meters
1 meter
1 centimeter = 0.01 meter
1 millimeter = 0.001 meter

**area:**

1 square kilometer = 1,000,000 square meters
1 square centimeter = 0.0001 square meter
1 square millimeter = 0.000,001 square meter

**volume:**

1 cubic centimeter = 0.000,001 cubic meter
1 cubic millimeter = 0.000,000,001 cubic meter

**capacity:**

1 hectoliter = 100 liters
1 decaliter = 10 liters
1 liter
1 deciliter = 0.1 liter
1 centiliter = 0.01 liter
1 milliliter = 0.001 liter

**weight:**

1 metric ton = 1,000 kilograms
1 kilogram = 1,000 grams
1 gram
1 centigram = 0.01 gram
1 milligram = 0.001 gram

**metric ton,** a measure of weight equal to 1,000 kilograms or about 2,204.62 pounds. *Abbr:* M.T.

**met|ri|fi|ca|tion** (met′rə fə kā′shən), *n.* **1** the making of verses. **2** *British.* metrication: *the metrification of weights and measures.*

**met|ri|fi|er** (met′rə fī′ər), *n.* a person skilled in poetic meter, especially one who writes verse.

**met|ri|fy**[1] (met′rə fī), *v.t., v.i.,* **-fied, -fy|ing.** to put into meter; make verse. [< Middle French *métrifier* < Medieval Latin *metrificare* < Latin *metrum* meter[1] + *facere* make]

**met|ri|fy**[2] (met′rə fī), *v.t., v.i.,* **-fied, -fy|ing.** *British.* metricate. [< *metri(c)* + *-fy*]

**met|rist** (met′rist, mē′trist), *n.* a person skilled in the use of poetic meters.

**me|tri|tis** (mi trī′tis), *n.* inflammation of the uterus. [< New Latin *metritis* < Greek *mētrā* uterus, cervix + New Latin *-itis* inflammation]

**Met|ro** or **met|ro** (met′rō), *n., adj. U.S. and Canada.* — *n.* a form of municipal government whose powers extend over a metropolitan area and usually encompass a group of smaller municipalities: *Metro has amalgamated some of the services shared by all, such as police, water, conservation ... and town planning* (Canada Month).
— *adj.* **1** of such a form of government. **2** extending over a metropolitan area: *Metro Toronto.*
[< *metro*(politan) area]

**Mét|ro** or **mét|ro** (met′rō), *n., pl.* **-ros.** (in Paris and certain other French-speaking cities) the subway system; subway: *Even the buses and Métro trains are flying the tricolor* (New Yorker). [< French *métro,* short for (*chemin de fer*) *métropolitain* metropolitan (railroad)]

**Met|ro|li|ner** (met′rō lī′nər), *n. U.S.* a high-speed train of the Amtrak railroad network: *Metroliners are capable of speeds up to 160 mph but cruise at 120 mph* (Walter E. Jessup).

**met|ro|log|i|cal** (met′rə loj′ə kəl), *adj.* of or having to do with metrology. — **met′ro|log′i|cal|ly,** *adv.*

**me|trol|o|gist** (mi trol′ə jist), *n.* a person who studies metrology.

**me|trol|o|gy** (mi trol′ə jē), *n., pl.* **-gies. 1** a system of measures and weights. [< Greek *métron* measure + English *-logy*]

**met|ro|ma|ni|a** (met′rə mā′nē ə), *n.* a mania for writing verse. [< Greek *métron* measure + English *mania*]

**met|ro|ma|ni|ac** (met′rə mā′nē ak), *n.* a person excessively fond of writing verse.

**met|ro|nome** (met′rə nōm), *n.* a clocklike device with a pendulum that can be adjusted to make loud ticking sounds at different speeds. Metronomes are used especially to mark time for persons practicing on musical instruments. [< Greek *métron* measure + *nómos* regulation, law, rule]

**met|ro|nom|ic** (met′rə nom′ik), *adj.* **1** of or like a metronome. **2** having to do with tempo as indicated by a metronome: (*Figurative.*) *a short, discreet, honest, and rather metronomic autobiography* (New Yorker). — **met′ro|nom′i|cal|ly,** *adv.*

**me|tro|nym** (mē′trə nim, met′rə-), *n.* a metronymic name.

**me|tro|nym|ic** (mē′trə nim′ik, met′rə-), *adj., n.* — *adj.* derived from the name of a mother or other female ancestor.
— *n.* a metronymic name. Also, **matronymic.**
[< Greek *mētrōnymikós* < *mḗtēr, mētros* mother + dialectal *ónyma* name]

**met|ro|pole** (met′rə pōl), *n.* a metropolis, now especially an ecclesiastical metropolis.

**me|trop|o|lis** (mə trop′ə lis), *n.* **1** the most important city of a country or region. It is usually (but not always) the one in which the government is carried on. *New York is the metropolis of the United States.* **2** a large city; important center, especially the center of some activity: *a financial metropolis. Chicago is a busy metropolis.* **3** the chief diocese of a church province; the see of a metropolitan bishop. **4** the mother city or parent state of a colony, especially of an ancient Greek colony. [< Latin *Metropolis,* a place name < Greek *mētrópolis* < *mḗtēr* mother + *pólis* city]

**met|ro|pol|i|tan** (met′rə pol′ə tən), *adj., n.* — *adj.* **1** of a large city; belonging to large cities: *metropolitan newspapers.* **2** constituting a metropolis: *a metropolitan center.* **3** of or having to do with a metropolitan of the church, or his see or province. **4** constituting the mother city or the mainland territory of the parent state: *metropolitan France. The political connection between the people of the metropolitan country and their colonies* (James Fenimore Cooper).
— *n.* **1** a person who lives in a large city and knows its ways. **2** the chief bishop of an ecclesiastical province, having authority over the bishops (suffragans) within the territory: **a** (in the Roman Catholic Church) an archbishop presiding over a church province. **b** (in the Eastern Orthodox Church) a prelate ranking above an archbishop and below a patriarch. **3** a citizen of the mother city or parent state of a colony.

**metropolitan area,** the area or region including a large city and its suburbs: *The metropolitan area of New York goes over into New Jersey, up the Hudson River, and into Long Island* (Baltimore Sun).

**met|ro|pol|i|tan|ate** (met′rə pol′ə tə nāt), *n.* the office or see of a metropolitan bishop.

**met|ro|pol|i|tan|ism** (met′rə pol′ə tə niz′əm), *n.* **1** the characteristics and manners of metropolitan living, especially as distinguished from provincialism; sophistication; urbanity: *The new metropolitanism is affecting most of our social institutions* (Science News Letter). **2** *Sociology.* the social influence or control exerted by a central city over those who live in or on the fringes of a metropolitan area.

**met|ro|pol|i|tan|ize** (met′rə pol′ə tə nīz), *v.t., v.i.,* **-ized, -iz|ing. 1** to make or become metropolitan. **2** to incorporate into a metropolitan area. — **met′ro|pol′i|tan|i|za′tion,** *n.*

**met|ro|po|lit|i|cal** (met′rə pə lit′ə kəl), *adj.* of or having to do with a metropolitan of the church, or his see or province: *Metropolitical responsibility for the diocese of Hongkong and Macao, which the then Archbishop of Canterbury accepted in 1952, has been transferred ...* (London Times).

**me|tror|rha|gi|a** (mē′trə rā′jē ə, met′rə-), *n.* a hemorrhage from the uterus not associated with menstruation. [< New Latin *metrorrhagia* < Greek *mētrā* uterus, cervix + *rhēgnýnai* to flow]

**-metry,** *combining form.* the process or art of measuring ___: *Biometry = the process or art of measuring life.* [< Greek *-metriā* a measuring < *métron* a measure]

**met|sat** (met′sat′), *n.* = met-satellite.

**met-sat|el|lite** (met′sat′ə līt), *n.* = weather satellite. [< *met*(eorological) *satellite*]

**met|teur en scène** (me tœr′ äɴ sen′), *pl.* **metteurs en scène** (me tœr′ äɴ sen′). *French.* a stage director.

**met|tle** (met′əl), *n.* **1** quality of disposition or temperament: *to try a man's mettle.* **2** spirit; courage: *They ... tell me flatly I am ... a lad of mettle* (Shakespeare). **SYN:** pluck, fortitude.
**be on** (or **upon**) **one's mettle,** to be ready or anxious to do one's best: *They would have to contend against cavalry, who would be upon their mettle to show their superiority over the cyclists* (London Times).
**put on one's mettle,** to challenge; inspire: *Her children's faith put her on her mettle to do her best by them. A whiff of ... hostility in the atmosphere put him on his mettle* (George Meredith).
[variant of *metal*]

**met|tled** (met′əld), *adj.* having mettle; spirited; mettlesome.

**met|tle|some** (met′əl səm), *adj.* full of mettle; spirited; courageous: *a mettlesome horse.* **SYN:** ardent, fiery.

**Mett|wurst** (met′vůrst′), *n. German.* a pork sausage with high fat content.

**me|um et tu|um** (mē′əm et tü′əm, tyü′-), *Latin.* mine and thine; what is my property and what is yours, thought of as expressing the universal and fundamental division of all property: *He seems to confuse meum et tuum in making out his accounts.*

**Mev** or **mev** (mev), *n.* a million electron volts, used as a measure of energy in nuclear physics. [< *m*(illion) *e*(lectron) *v*(olts)]

**Mev.,** million electron volts.

**MeV.,** *British.* million electron volts.

**mev|a|lon|ic acid** (mev′ə lon′ik), a chemical compound important in the biosynthesis of steroids, carotenoids, and terpenes. *Formula:* $C_6H_{12}O_4$ [< *me*(thyl) + *val*(eric acid) + (lact)*on*(e) + *-ic*]

**mew**[1] (myü), *n., v.t., v.i.* = meow. [probably imitative]

**mew**[2] (myü), *n.* a gull, especially the common European gull; sea mew. [Old English *mǣw*]

**mew**[3] (myü), *n., v.* — *n.* **1** a cage or building in which hawks are kept, especially while molting. **2** *Dialect.* a breeding cage for any of various small, tame birds. **3** a place of retirement or concealment; secret place; den. **4** See **mews.**
— *v.t.* **1** to shut up in a cage; confine; conceal: (*Figurative.*) *to mew us up here until our lives' end* (Scott). **2** to cage (a hawk), especially at molting time. **3** *Archaic.* to change (feathers); molt. — *v.i. Archaic.* to molt.
[< Old French *müe* < *muer* to molt < Latin *mutāre* to change]

**mewl** (myül), *v., n.* — *v.i., v.t.* to cry like a baby; make a feeble, whining noise; whimper: *The infant, Mewling and puking in the nurse's arms* (Shakespeare).
— *n.* the cry of a baby. [imitative]

**mews** (myüz), *n.pl.* (*often sing. in use*). **1a** a group of stables or garages built around a court or alley. **b** a street or alley that was formerly part of a mews: *a mews house in Mayfair—one of those London surprises where a plain front conceals an almost Mediterranean courtyard* (Manchester Guardian). **2** (in English history) the royal stables at London (so called because they were built on the site of the royal mews for hawks). [(originally) plural of *mew*[3]]

**Mex.,** **1** Mexican. **2** Mexico.

**Mex|i|can** (mek′sə kən), *adj., n.* — *adj.* of Mexico or its people.
— *n.* a person born or living in Mexico.

**Mexican bean beetle,** a large, brownish-yellow ladybug of North America with eight black dots on each wing cover, that is very destructive to bean plants.

**Mexican earflower,** = sacred earflower.

**Mexican fruit fly,** a fly native to Mexico and found as far south as Panama and north to southern Texas, which infests the crops of citrus and other fruits.

**Mexican hairless**, any dog of a very old Mexican breed, approximately as large as a small fox terrier, having no hair except for a tuft on the head and sometimes a little fuzz on the lower part of the tail.

**Mex|i|can|ize** (mek′sə kə nīz), *v.t., v.i.,* **-ized, -iz|ing.** to make or become Mexican in habits, customs, character, or ownership. —**Mex′i|can|i|za′tion,** *n.*

**Mexican jumping bean,** = jumping bean.

**Mexican onyx,** = onyx marble.

**Mexican poppy,** a prickly poppy bearing orange, yellow, or white flowers.

**Mexican Spanish,** the dialect of Spanish spoken in Mexico.

**mez|cal** (mes kal′), *n.* = mescal (def. 1).

**Me|zen|tian** (mə zen′shən), *adj.* having to do with or suggestive of Mezentius, a legendary Etruscan king who is said to have had living men bound face to face with corpses and then left to die: *That fatal and Mezentian oath which binds the Irish to the English Church* (Sydney Smith).

**me|ze|re|on** (mi zir′ē on), *n. Especially British.* mezereum.

**me|ze|re|um** (mi zir′ē əm), *n.* **1** a European and Asiatic shrub, having fragrant, purplish or white flowers which appear in early spring before the leaves. **2** the dried bark of this plant and related species, formerly used in pharmacy. [< New Latin *mezereum,* alteration of Medieval Latin *mezereon* < Arabic *māzaryūn*]

**mezereum family,** a family of dicotyledonous plants, mostly trees and shrubs, including the leatherwood and daphne.

**me|zu|zah** or **me|zu|za** (me zü′zä), *n., pl.* **-zoth** (-zōth), **-zahs, -za.** *Judaism.* a parchment scroll inserted in a small tube or box, usually of wood or metal, and attached by Orthodox Jews to the right-hand doorposts of their homes, in obedience to the Biblical injunction in Deuteronomy 6:4-9 and 11:13-21, both passages being inscribed on one side of the parchment. On the other side is written "Shaddai," an ancient name of God, that is visible through a small window cut in the container.
[< Hebrew *məzuzå* doorpost]

**Mezz.,** mezzanine (of a theater).

**mez|za** (met′sä, mez′ə), *adj.* the feminine form of **mezzo.**

**mez|za|nine** (mez′ə nēn), *n.* a low story, usually extending above a part of the main floor to form a balcony; entresol. In a theater the lowest balcony is often called a mezzanine. In a hotel the upper part of the lobby is often surrounded by a mezzanine. [< French *mezzanine* < Italian *mezzanino* < *mezzano* middle < Latin *mediānus;* see etym. under **median**]

**mez|za-vo|ce** (med′zä vō′chā), *n. Italian.* a medium voice; voice with a medium fullness of sound: *Her voice was nevertheless sufficiently ample to fill Town Hall, even when she sang—as she often did—in a safe mezza-voce* (New Yorker).

**mez|zo** (met′sō, mez′ō), *adj., n., pl.* **-zos.** *Music.*
—***adj.*** middle; medium; half, as to the dynamics or range.
—***n.*** = mezzo-soprano: *Mezzo or not, her voice ascends to a good, strong high B* (Harper's).
[< Italian *mezzo* < Latin *medius* middle]

**mez|zo-for|te** (met′sō fôr′tā, mez′ō-), *adj., adv.,* or **mezzo forte,** *Music.* half as loud as forte; moderately loud (used as a direction). *Abbr:* mf.
[< Italian *mezzo forte*]

**mezzo pi|a|no** (pē ä′nō), *Music.* moderately soft or low (used as a direction).

**mez|zo-re|lie|vo** (met′sō ri lē′vō), *n., pl.* **-vos.** relief in which the figures project half their true proportions from the surface on which they are carved; half relief; demirelief. [< Italian *mezzo-rilievo* < *mezzo* middle + *rilievo* relievo]

**mez|zo-ri|lie|vo** (med′zō rē lye′vō), *n., pl.* **mez|zi-ri|lie|vi** (med′zē rē lye′vē), *Italian.* mezzo-relievo.

**mez|zo-so|pran|o** (met′sō sə pran′ō, -prä′nō), *n., pl.* **-pran|os,** *adj.* —***n.*** **1** a voice or part between soprano and contralto. **2** a singer having such a voice.
—***adj.*** of, for, or having to do with a mezzo-soprano.
[< Italian *mezzo-soprano* < *mezzo* middle + *soprano* soprano]

**mez|zo|tint** (met′sō tint′, mez′ō-), *n., v., adj.* —***n.*** **1** an engraving on copper or steel made by polishing and scraping away parts of a roughened surface, so as to produce the effect of light and shade. **2** a print made from such an engraving: *All that I own is a print, An etching, a mezzotint* (Robert Browning). **3** this method of etching or engraving pictures.
—***v.t.*** to engrave in mezzotint.
—***adj.*** of, having to do with, or produced by mezzotint: *mezzotint engravings.*
[< Italian *mezzotinto* (literally) half-tint < *mezzo* mezzo + *tinto* < Latin *tinctus*] —**mez′zo|tint′er,** *n.*

**mez|zo|tin|to** (met′sō tin′tō, mez′ō-), *n., pl.* **-tos,** *v.t.,* **-toed, -to|ing.** = mezzotint.

**mf.** or **mf** (no period), **1** *Music.* mezzoforte. **2** microfarad. **3** millifarad.

**MF** (no periods), **1** medium frequency. **2** Middle French.

**M.F.** or **MF.,** Middle French.

**M.F.A.,** Master of Fine Arts.

**mfd.,** **1** manufactured. **2** microfarad.

**mfg.,** manufacturing.

**MFH** (no periods) or **M.F.H.,** master of foxhounds.

**MFN** (no periods), most favored nation.

**mfr.,** **1** manufacture. **2** manufacturer.

**mfrs.,** manufacturers.

**M.F.S.,** **1** Master of Food Science. **2** Master of Foreign Study.

**mg.** or **mg** (no period), milligram or milligrams.

**Mg** (no period), magnesium (chemical element).

**MG** (no periods), **1** machine gun. **2** Military Government.

**MGB** (no periods), the Ministry of State Security of the Soviet Union. The MGB now reportedly conducts espionage and counterespionage.

**m.g.d.** or **mgd** (no periods), million gallons per day.

**Mgr.,** **1** Manager. **2** Monseigneur. **3** Monsignor.

**mh.** or **mh** (no period), millihenry.

**MH** (no periods), Medal of Honor.

**M.H.,** **1** Master of Humanities. **2** Master of Hygiene. **3** Medal of Honor.

**MHD** (no periods), **1** magnetohydrodynamic. **2** magnetohydrodynamics.

**MHG** (no periods), **MHG.,** or **M.H.G.,** Middle High German.

**M.H.L.,** Master of Hebrew Literature.

**mho** (mō), *n., pl.* **mhos.** a unit of electrical conductance, equivalent to the conductance of a body through which one ampere of current flows when the difference of potential is one volt. It is the reciprocal of the ohm. [reversed spelling of *ohm*]

**M.Hort.,** Master of Horticulture.

**M.H.R.,** Member of the House of Representatives.

**m.h.w.,** mean high water.

**MHz** (no periods), megahertz.

**mi** (mē), *n. Music.* the third tone of the diatonic scale. [< Medieval Latin *mi;* see etym. under **gamut**]

**mi.,** **1** mile or miles. **2** mill or mills.

**MI** (no periods), **1** Michigan (with postal Zip Code). **2** Military Intelligence.

**M.I.,** Military Intelligence.

**M.I.5,** the division of British Military Intelligence concerned with counterespionage and security in Great Britain.

**M.I.A.,** missing in action.

**mi|a|cis** (mī′ə sis), *n.* a prehistoric carnivorous ancestor of the dog and cat, about the size of a weasel, having a long body, short legs, and a long tail. [< New Latin *Miacis* the genus name]

**Mi|am|i** (mī am′ē, -ə), *n., pl.* **-am|i** or **-am|is.** **1** a member of a tribe of Algonkian Indians, formerly in the Green Bay region of Wisconsin. **2** their language, a dialect of Illinois.

**Mi|am|i|an** (mī am′ē ən), *n.* a native or inhabitant of Miami, Florida.

**mi|aow** or **mi|aou** (mē ou′), *n., interj., v.i., v.t.* = meow.

**mi|asm** (mī′az əm), *n.* = miasma.

**mi|as|ma** (mī az′mə, mē-), *n., pl.* **-mas, -ma|ta** (-mə tə). **1** a bad-smelling vapor rising from decaying matter on the earth. The miasma of swamps was formerly supposed to cause disease. ... *far enough from the Dead Sea to escape its miasma* (London Times). **2** *Figurative.* anything considered to resemble this in its ability to spread and poison: *a miasma of fear.* [< New Latin *miasma* < Greek *míasma* pollution < *miaínein* to pollute]

**mi|as|mal** (mī az′məl, mē-), *adj.* containing miasma; noxious: *miasmal swamps.*

**mi|as|mat|ic** (mī′az mat′ik), *adj.* = miasmal.

**mi|as|mat|i|cal** (mī′az mat′ə kəl), *adj.* = miasmal.

**mi|as|mic** (mī az′mik, mē-), *adj.* = miasmal.

**mi|aul** (mē oul′, -ôl′), *n., interj., v.i., v.t.* = meow: *a miauling kitten* (Scott).

**mib** (mib), *n.* a marble, especially one used as the object of a shot.
**mibs,** the game of marbles.
[perhaps alteration of *marbles*]

**Mic.,** Micah (book of the Old Testament).

**MIC** (no periods), military-industrial complex: *Representatives of the big firms, sometimes called MICs* (*for military-industrial complex*), *are often corporate vice presidents* (Time).

**mi|ca** (mī′kə), *n.* a mineral that divides into thin, partly transparent layers; isinglass. Mica is highly resistant to heat and is used in electric fuses and formerly in stove doors and lanterns, where the heat might break glass. Mica is composed essentially of silicate of aluminum, of potassium, or of other metals, occurring in minute, glittering plates or scales in granite and other rocks, or in crystals that separate. *An outcrop of sandstone and schist with secondary white mica* (Science News). [< Latin *mīca* grain, crumb; perhaps influenced by *micāre* to shine]

**mi|ca|ceous** (mī kā′shəs), *adj.* **1** consisting of, containing, or like mica: *micaceous minerals.* **2** of or having to do with mica.

**Mi|cah** (mī′kə), *n.* **1** a Hebrew prophet of the 700's B.C. **2** a book of the Old Testament attributed to him, placed among the Minor Prophets. *Abbr:* Mic.

**Mi-Ca|rême** (mē kȧ rem′), *n. French.* Mid-Lent.

**Mi|caw|ber** (mə kô′bər), *n.* **1 Wilkins,** an optimistic character in Charles Dickens' novel *David Copperfield,* who is seldom able to pay his bills and is always expecting "that something will turn up." **2** any person resembling Micawber in character or habits.

**Mi|caw|ber|ish** (mə kô′bər ish), *adj.* characteristic of a Micawber; improvident but habitually optimistic: *For years, the nation's biggest city has followed a Micawberish routine of using reserves and loans to meet ever-rising operating costs* (Time). —**Mi|caw′ber|ish|ly,** *adv.*

**Mi|caw|ber|ism** (mə kô′bər iz əm), *n.* the quality or condition of being Micawberish: *My own fear is that the present Micawberism will leave us wide open ... to a humiliating series of defeats* (London Times).

**mice** (mīs), *n.* plural of **mouse.**

**mi|cel|la** (mi sel′ə, mī-), *n., pl.* **-cel|lae** (-sel′ē). = micelle.

**mi|celle** or **mi|cell** (mi sel′), *n.* a colloidal particle, especially one in a soap solution. [< New Latin *micella* (diminutive) < Latin *mīca;* see etym. under **mica**]

**Mich.,** **1** Michaelmas. **2** Michigan.

**Mi|chael** (mī′kəl), *n.* **Saint,** the archangel who led the loyal angels in defeating the revolt of Satan (in the Bible, Revelation 12:7-9).

**Mi|chae|lis constant** (mī kā′lis, mī′kə lis), *Biochemistry.* a measure of the affinity of an enzyme for its substrate, equal to the substrate concentration at which the enzyme-catalyzed reaction proceeds at half of its maximal rate. [< Leonor *Michaelis,* 1875-1949, an American chemist]

**Mich|ael|mas** (mik′əl məs), *n.* **1** an annual church festival honoring the archangel Michael and all the angels. Michaelmas is held on September 29 in the Roman Catholic and Anglican churches and on November 8 in the Greek, Armenian, and Coptic churches. **2** Also, **Michaelmas Day.** September 29, the date of this festival and one of the quarter days in England.

**Michaelmas daisy,** **1** a common wild aster often grown in gardens, that blooms near Michaelmas. **2** any one of several garden asters of a shrubby habit and bearing masses of small, purplish flowers.

**miche** (mich), *v.,* **miched, mich|ing.** *Dialect.*
—***v.i.*** **1** to lurk out of sight; skulk. **2** to play truant. **3** to grumble; whine.
—***v.t.*** to pilfer. [< Old French *muchier, mucier* skulk, hide, perhaps < Celtic (compare Old Irish *mūchaim* stifle)] —**mich′er,** *n.*

**Mi|che|as** (mī kē′əs), *n.* Micah in the Douay Bible.

**Mich|e|ga|me|a** (mish′ə gə mē′ə), *n., pl.* **-me|a** or **-me|as.** **1** a member of a woodland tribe of North American Indians, once constituting a part of the Illinois confederacy, who lived in eastern Arkansas. **2** the language of this tribe, a dialect of Illinois.

**Mi|chel|an|gel|esque** (mī′kəl an′jə lesk′, mik′əl-), *adj.* of or characteristic of Michelangelo or his work: *There is, in fact, something genuinely Michelangelesque about many of his paintings and drawings* (London Times). [< *Michelangelo* Buonarroti, 1475-1564, the Italian painter, sculptor, architect, and poet + *-esque*]

**Mich|i|gan** (mich′ə gən), *n.* = newmarket (def. 2). [< *Michigan,* the state]

**Mich|i|gan|der** (mish′ə gan′dər), *n.* a native or inhabitant of the state of Michigan. [American English; blend of *Michigan* and *gander,* originally the nickname of Lewis Cass, 1782-1866, an American soldier and politician who was the governor of Michigan Territory]

**Mich|i|gan|ite** (mish′ə gə nīt), *n.* = Michigander.

**mi|chron** (mī′kron), *n.* the time of vibration of a wave of one micron. [< Greek *mī*(*krós*) small + *chrón*(*os*) time]

**mick** (mik), *n. U.S. Slang.* an easy or simple college course: *Despite the best efforts of administrators to stamp them out, U.S. universities still*

**Pronunciation Key:** hat, āge, cãre, fär; let, ēqual, tėrm; it, īce; hot, ōpen, ôrder; oil, out; cup, pu̇t, rüle; child; long; thin; ᴛʜen; zh, measure; ə represents **a** in about, **e** in taken, **i** in pencil, **o** in lemon, **u** in circus.

*have their share of "micks" (Mickey Mouse courses)* (Time). [< *Mick*(ey Mouse)]

**Mick|ey** or **mick|ey** (mik′ē), *n., pl.* **-eys.** = Mickey Finn.

**take the mickey out of,** *British Slang.* to make fun of; ridicule: *Miss Grenfell ... helped to give us a happy satire on broadcasting itself and took the mickey out of certain familiar programmes* (London Times).

**Mickey Finn** or **mickey finn** (fin′), *U.S. Slang.* a drugged alcoholic drink intended to make the person who unsuspectingly drinks it incapable of defending himself or of continuing whatever he may be doing.

**Mickey Mouse,** *U.S. Slang.* **1** anything unnecessary or unimportant: *A central concern now is ... the antimilitary atmosphere in the country, the low pay, and (for the younger men) the anachronistic spit-and-polish, the Mickey Mouse* (Atlantic). **2** a muddled situation; foul-up: *Logistically so far, the only big Mickey Mouse, in G.I. parlance, was a brief shortage of canvas-and-rubber jungle boots* (Time). **3a** an easy or simple college course: *Some popular opinion persists, of course, that college courses in "the movies" are a kind of trade-school apprenticeship or something easy to relax with ("Mickey Mouse" in today's campus parlance)* (Harper's). **b** simple; easy; unimportant: *"This is no Mickey Mouse business," [he] said ... "In the old days you put together a funhouse for $3,000, now it can cost $40,000"* (New York Times).
[< *Mickey Mouse,* an animated cartoon character, in allusion to its childish appeal, its simplicity and triviality]

**mick|ey-mouse** (mik′ē mous′), *v.i.,* **-moused, -mous|ing.** *Informal.* to synchronize the background music with the action, as in an animated cartoon: *The choreography ... is the feeblest element in the film, with too much unimaginative "Mickey-mousing", matching each note in the score with some movement rather than creating an overall style of dance* (London Times).

**mick|le** (mik′əl), *adj., adv., n. Dialect.* much. [Old English *micel,* also *mycel*]

**Mic|mac** (mik′mak), *n., pl.* **-mac** or **-macs.** an Indian of an Algonkian tribe living in the Maritime Provinces of Canada.

**micr-,** *combining form.* the form of **micro-** before vowels, as in *microhm.*

**MICR** (no periods), magnetic ink character recognition (a technique for sensing type faces by computer, used especially in processing bank checks and in printing).

**mi|cra** (mī′krə), *n.* microns; a plural of **micron.**

**mi|cri|fy** (mī′krə fī), *v.t.,* **-fied, -fy|ing.** to make small or insignificant. [< *micr-* + *-fy,* perhaps patterned on *magnify*]

**mi|cro** (mī′krō), *adj., n.* —*adj.* shorter than mini; mid-thigh or higher: *The hem was the same place it was last year—everywhere. Couturiers pegged it all the way from micro to floor level* (Edith R. Locke). —*n.* a skirt, dress, or other garment that is shorter than mini: *Hemlines go to all lengths. In extremes, there are micros* (Gloria Emerson). [< *micro-*]

**micro-,** *combining form.* **1** small; very small; microscopic: *Microorganism = a microscopic organism. Microphotograph = a very small photograph.*
**2** abnormally small: *Microcephalic = having an abnormally small head.*
**3** done with, or involving the use of, a microscope: *Microscopy = investigation done under a microscope.*
**4** one millionth of a ____: *Microfarad = one millionth of a farad.*
**5** that magnifies small ____: *Microphone = an instrument that magnifies small sounds.* Also, **micr-** before vowels.
[< Greek *mīkrós* small]

**mi|cro|am|me|ter** (mī′krō am′ē′tər), *n.* an instrument which measures an electric current in microamperes.

**mi|cro|am|pere** (mī′krō am′pir), *n.* a unit of electrical current, equivalent to one millionth of an ampere.

**mi|cro|a|nal|y|sis** (mī′krō ə nal′ə sis), *n., pl.* **-ses** (-sēz). *Chemistry.* the analysis of very small quantities of matter.

**mi|cro|an|a|lyst** (mī′krō an′ə list), *n.* a person who is skilled in or practices microanalysis.

**mi|cro|an|a|lyt|ic** (mī′krō an′ə lit′ik), *adj.* = microanalytical.

**mi|cro|an|a|lyt|i|cal** (mī′krō an′ə lit′ə kəl), *adj.* of or having to do with microanalysis.

**mi|cro|an|a|lyze** (mī′krō an′ə līz), *v.t.,* **-lyzed, -lyz|ing.** to carry out microanalysis on (a substance).

**mi|cro|an|a|lyz|er** (mī′krō an′ə līz′ər), *n.* an apparatus for microanalysis: *An ion microanalyzer provided instant photomicrographs of a specimen's chemical distribution by combining a mass spectrometer with an ion-emission microscope* (Jacob Kastner).

**mi|cro|a|nat|o|my** (mī′krō ə nat′ə mē), *n.* the anatomy of microscopic structures.

**mi|cro|bal|ance** (mī′krō bal′əns), *n.* a very sensitive scale used to weigh minute quantities (one milligram or less) of chemicals or other substances: *microbalances that weigh lift and drag in terms of millionths of a gram* (Scientific American).

**mi|cro|bar** (mī′krō bär), *n.* a unit of pressure equal to one millionth of a bar. [< *micro-* + *bar*³]

**mi|cro|barn** (mī′krō bärn), *n. Nuclear Physics.* one millionth of a barn: *One microbarn is $10^{-30}$ square centimeters or about a millionth of the cross section of an atomic nucleus* (Science News). [< *micro-* + *barn* (def. 4)]

**mi|cro|bar|o|graph** (mī′krō bar′ə graf, -gräf), *n.* an instrument for recording very small fluctuations of atmospheric pressure.

**mi|crobe** (mī′krōb), *n.* **1** a living organism of very small size; germ; microorganism. **2** a bacterium, especially one causing diseases or fermentation: *Pasteur, Koch, and Lister proved conclusively that germs, or microbes, were the cause of certain diseases.* [< French *microbe* < Greek *mīkrós* small + *bíos* life]

**mi|cro|beam** (mī′krō bēm′), *n.* a finely focused electron beam: *Chromosome mapping and investigations of chromosome structure could be extended by the laser microbeam* (Scientific American).

**mi|cro|bi|al** (mī krō′bē əl), *adj.* of, having to do with, or caused by microbes: *microbial disease, microbial parasites.*

**mi|cro|bic** (mī krō′bik), *adj.* = microbial.

**mi|cro|bi|cid|al** (mī krō′bə sī′dəl), *adj.* having to do with the killing of microbes.

**mi|cro|bi|cide** (mī krō′bə sīd), *n.* something that kills microbes; germicide. [< *microbe* + *-cide*¹]

**mi|cro|bi|o|log|i|cal** (mī′krō bī′ə loj′ə kəl), *adj.* **1** of or having to do with microbiology: *microbiological research.* **2** of, having to do with, or utilizing microorganisms: *microbiological experiments.* —**mi′cro|bi′o|log′i|cal|ly,** *adv.*

**mi|cro|bi|ol|o|gist** (mī′krō bī ol′ə jist), *n.* an expert in microbiology.

**mi|cro|bi|ol|o|gy** (mī′krō bī ol′ə jē), *n.* the science dealing with microorganisms; study of microbes.

**mi|cro|bi|on** (mī krō′bē on), *n., pl.* **-bi|a** (-bē ə). = microbe. [< New Latin *microbion*]

**mi|cro|blade** (mī′krō blād′), *n. Archaeology.* a thin sliver chipped delicately from a prepared flint core, usually with parallel edges, used especially in the paleolithic and mesolithic periods: *Commonly inserted as "side blades" into lateral grooves in antler and bone projectile points, such "microblades" lacerated the flesh of wounded game animals and thus promoted free bleeding and rapid death* (Charles E. Borden).

**mi|cro|bod|y** (mī′krō bod′ē), *n., pl.* **-bod|ies.** *Biology.* a tiny cellular particle containing an enzyme system; microsome.

**micro book,** a very small book which requires the use of a magnifying glass for reading.

**mi|cro|bus** (mī′krə bus′), *n.* a passenger van or truck seating about twelve people.

**mi|cro|cal|o|rie** (mī′krō kal′ər ē), *n.* one millionth of a calorie: *The heat flux of the moon is about two-tenths to three-tenths of a microcalorie per square centimeter per second, or about a sixth to a third that of the earth* (Science News).

**mi|cro|cap|sule** (mī′krō kap′səl, -syül), *n.* a very small or microscopic capsule of a chemical substance or drug: *Chang showed that his microcapsules of asparaginase broke down asparagine when suspended in an asparagine solution* (New Scientist and Science Journal).

**mi|cro|card** (mī′krō kärd′), *n.* a card-sized photographic print containing pages of books, newspapers, records, or other printed matter, greatly reduced in size. It is used to facilitate storage and transportation of such materials. *Sets of microcards containing weather information* (Science News Letter).

**mi|cro|ce|phal|ic** (mī′krō sə fal′ik), *adj.* **1** having a cranial capacity of less than 1,350 cubic centimeters. **2** having an abnormally small head, especially as a result of a congenital defect, as certain idiots.

**mi|cro|ceph|a|lous** (mī′krō sef′ə ləs), *adj.* = microcephalic.

**mi|cro|ceph|a|ly** (mī′krō sef′ə lē), *n.* the condition of having a small or imperfectly developed head.

**mi|cro|chem|i|cal** (mī′krō kem′ə kəl), *adj.* of or having to do with microchemistry: *microchemical reactions.*

**mi|cro|chem|is|try** (mī′krō kem′ə strē), *n.* chemical analysis or investigation carried on by working with exceptionally small samples, often weighing only about one milligram.

**mi|cro|cin|e|ma|tog|ra|phy** (mī′krō sin′ə mə tog′rə fē), *n.* the art of obtaining motion pictures of microscopic objects on a magnified scale.

**mi|cro|cir|cuit** (mī′krō sėr′kit), *n.* a highly miniaturized electronic circuit, usually formed of microcromodules; integrated circuit: *Microcircuits ... are replacing miniaturized circuits just as transistors replaced vacuum tubes* (Scientific American).

**mi|cro|cir|cuit|ry** (mī′krō sėr′kə trē), *n.* **1** the study of microcircuits. **2** the components of a microcircuit; integrated circuitry. **3** microscopic circuits: *Ganglion cells, however, fall into certain classes, indicating considerable order in the microcircuitry between them and the receptor cells* (Peter Gouras).

**mi|cro|cir|cu|la|tion** (mī′krō sėr′kyə lā′shən), *n.* circulation of the blood through the capillary vessels.

**mi|cro|cli|mate** (mī′krō klī′mit), *n.* the climate of a very small, specific area such as a glacier, valley bottom, cornfield, or animal burrow.

**mi|cro|cli|mat|ic** (mī′krō klī mat′ik), *adj.* of or having to do with a microclimate or microclimatology: *Where ample water is available, redistribution ... can cause beneficial microclimatic changes* (Bulletin of Atomic Scientists).

**mi|cro|cli|ma|tol|o|gy** (mī′krō klī′mə tol′ə jē), *n.* the branch of climatology dealing with the climatic conditions of small areas.

**mi|cro|cline** (mī′krə klīn), *n.* a potash feldspar similar to orthoclase, white, yellow, red, or green in color. [< German *Mikroklin* < Greek *mīkrós* small + *klīnein* to incline]

**mi|cro|coc|cal** (mī′krə kok′əl), *adj.* relating to or caused by micrococci.

**mi|cro|coc|cic** (mī′krə kok′sik), *adj.* = micrococcal.

**mi|cro|coc|cus** (mī′krə kok′əs), *n., pl.* **-coc|ci** (-kok′sī). any one of a genus of spherical or egg-shaped, parasitic or saprophytic bacteria, aggregating in various ways. Certain micrococci cause disease; others produce fermentation. [< New Latin *Micrococcus* the genus name < Greek *mīkrós* small + *kókkos* berry, seed, grain]

**mi|cro|com|put|er** (mī′krō kəm pyü′tər), *n.* a tiny electronic computer; microprocessor: *Because its single chips were complete systems or major portions of systems that could now be changed at will, the microcomputer offered a previously unknown flexibility for thousands of machines, instruments, and other devices* (Gene Bylinsky).

**mi|cro|cop|y** (mī′krə kop′ē), *n., pl.* **-cop|ies,** *v.,* **-cop|ied, -cop|y|ing.** —*n.* a copy of a book or other printed work made on microfilm.
—*v.t.* to make a copy of on microfilm.

**mi|cro-cor|ne|al lens** (mī′krō kôr′nē əl), a contact lens covering part of the cornea of the eye.

**mi|cro|cosm** (mī′krə koz əm), *n.* **1** a little world; universe in miniature; community or the like regarded as an epitome of the world: *The circus comes as close to being the world in microcosm as anything I know* (New Yorker). **2** man thought of as a miniature representation of the universe.
[< Old French *microcosme* < Late Latin *microcosmus* < Late Greek *mīkròs kósmos* little world]

**mi|cro|cos|mic** (mī′krə koz′mik), *adj.* of, having to do with, or of the nature of a microcosm.

**mi|cro|cos|mi|cal** (mī′krə koz′mə kəl), *adj.* = microcosmic.

**microcosmic salt,** a colorless, crystalline compound, a phosphate of sodium and ammonium, originally derived from human urine. It is used as a reagent in chemical analyses, especially of metallic oxides. *Formula:* $NaNH_4HPO_4 \cdot 4H_2O$

**mi|cro|cos|mos** (mī′krə koz′məs, -mos), *n.* = microcosm.

**mi|cro|cou|lomb** (mī′krō kü′lom), *n.* one millionth of a coulomb.

**mi|cro|crack** (mī′krō krak′), *n., v.* —*n.* a microscopic crack in a material such as glass or chrome: *The low strength of glass is attributed to the presence of microcracks in the glass surface which drastically reduce the overall stress needed to cause fracture* (New Scientist).
—*v.i., v.t.* to produce microcracks (in a material).

**mi|cro|crys|tal** (mī′krō kris′təl), *n.* a minute or microscopic crystal.

**mi|cro|crys|tal|line** (mī′krō kris′tə lin, -līn), *adj.* formed of microscopic crystals: *microcrystalline wax.*

**mi|cro|cul|ture** (mī′krō kul′chər), *n.* **1** a small, narrowly confined geographical area, whose inhabitants are considered to have their own ways and fashions that form a cultural unit within a nation or other larger area. **2** a culture of microscopic organisms, tissue, or other living matter.

**mi|cro|cu|rie** (mī′krō kyůr′ē), *n.* a unit of radioactivity, equivalent to one millionth of a curie.

**mi|cro|cyte** (mī′krə sīt), *n.* an abnormally small red blood cell. [< *micro-* + *-cyte*]

**mi|cro|de|gree** (mī′krə di grē′), *n.* one millionth of a degree.

**mi|cro|den|si|tom|e|ter** (mī′krō den′sə tom′ə tər), *n.* an instrument for measuring the density of very small areas of a photographic negative: *Mapping was accomplished by ... analysis of brightness changes measured with a microdensitometer* (Donald F. Eschman). [< *micro-* + *densitometer*]

**mi|cro|de|tec|tor** (mī′krō di tek′tər), *n.* an instrument used to detect small quantities or changes, especially a sensitive galvanometer used to detect slight changes in electric current.

**mi|cro|dis|sec|tion** (mī′krō di sek′shən), *n.* dissection done under a microscope.

**mi|cro|dont** (mī′krə dont), *adj., n.* —*adj.* having very small teeth.
—*n.* a very small tooth. [< *micr-* + Greek *odoús, odóntos* tooth]

**mi|cro|don|tous** (mī′krə don′təs), *adj.* = microdont.

**mi|cro|dot** (mī′krō dot′), *n.* **1** a photograph of a letter, page, or other document, reduced in size to a dot for purposes of secrecy or economy in processing or storage: *A male Russian agent ... gave Mintkenbaugh a 35-mm. camera, along with a quick course in developing microdots and hiding microfilm* (Time). **2** *Slang.* a small pill containing the hallucinogenic drug LSD in highly concentrated form.

**mi|cro|dyne** (mī′krə dīn), *n.* one millionth of a dyne.

**mi|cro|earth|quake** (mī′krō ėrth′kwāk), *n.* a small earthquake, of magnitude of less than 2.5 on the Richter scale: *Before a volcano erupts it generates microearthquakes, which we are able to detect on our seismographs* (New York Times).

**mi|cro|e|col|o|gy** (mī′krō i kol′ə jē), *n.* a branch of ecology dealing with environmental conditions in very small areas.

**mi|cro|e|co|nom|ic** (mī′krō ē′kə nom′ik, -ek′ə-), *adj.* of or having to do with microeconomics: *microeconomic planning, microeconomic analysis.*

**mi|cro|e|co|nom|ics** (mī′krō ē′kə nom′iks, -ek′ə-), *n.* economics that deals with individual units in the economy, such as a family or a corporation.

**mi|cro|e|lec|tric** (mī′krō i lek′trik), *adj.* of or having to do with very small electric quantities.

**mi|cro|e|lec|trode** (mī′krō i lek′trōd), *n.* a very fine electrode, especially one used to detect electrical impulses of nerve cells and muscle fibers.

**mi|cro|e|lec|tron|ic** (mī′krō i lek′tron′ik, -ē lek′-), *adj.* of or having to do with microelectronics: *Without the voracious demand of the computer industry we would not have seen such a rapid advance in electronic, and especially microelectronic, technology* (Science Journal). —**mi′cro|e|lec′tron′i|cal|ly,** *adv.*

**mi|cro|e|lec|tron|ics** (mī′krō i lek′tron′iks, -ē′lek-), *n.* the branch of electronics dealing with microminiaturization: *Microelectronics, the use of extremely small circuits to replace larger and more costly tubes and transistors, will make ... throw-away devices "economically useful"* (Science News Letter).

**mi|cro|e|lec|tro|pho|re|sis** (mī′krō i lek′trō fə rē′sis), *n.* a technique for observing the electrophoresis of very small individual particles through a microscope or ultramicroscope.

**mi|cro|e|lec|tro|pho|ret|ic** (mī′krō i lek′trō fə ret′ik), *adj.* having to do with or produced by microelectrophoresis: *He has developed an elegant microelectrophoretic technique that makes it possible to determine the base composition of very small amounts of RNA* (Scientific American).

**mi|cro|el|e|ment** (mī′krō el′ə mənt), *n.* a chemical element found only in very small amounts.

**mi|cro|en|cap|su|late** (mī′krō en kap′sə lāt), *v.t.,* **-lat|ed, -lat|ing.** to enclose (something small) in a microcapsule: *Attempts ... are being made to microencapsulate enzymes for therapy* (New Scientist and Science Journal).

**mi|cro|en|cap|su|la|tion** (mī′krō en kap′sə lā′shən), *n.* encapsulation in microcapsules: *Copying paper that needs no carbon, or drugs that taste pleasant yet later (according to a precisely designed time schedule) release unpalatable medicants into the body, or packaged perfume painted invisibly on to paper for release months or years later ... all owe their existence to microencapsulation* (Science Journal).

**mi|cro|en|vi|ron|ment** (mī′krō en vī′rən mənt), *n.* the environment of a very small area, especially the isolated habitat of a particular species of plant or animal: *The Himalayan microenvironment shows great temperature contrasts between localities only a few inches apart* (Lawrence W. Swan).

**mi|cro|en|vi|ron|ment|al** (mī′krō en vī′rən men′təl), *adj.* of or having to do with a microenvironment.

**mi|cro|ev|o|lu|tion** (mī′krō ev′ə lü′shən), *n.* the evolution of animals and plants on the level of species or subspecies due to a succession of small genetic variations.

**mi|cro|ev|o|lu|tion|ar|y** (mī′krō ev′ə lü′shə ner′ē), *adj.* of or having to do with microevolution.

**mi|cro|far|ad** (mī′krō far′əd, -ad), *n.* a unit of electrical capacity, equal to one millionth of a farad.

**mi|cro|fau|na** (mī′krō fô′nə), *n., pl.* **-na, -nae** (-nē). the microscopic animals of a given habitat, as in a stream. [< *micro-* + *fauna*]

**mi|cro|fau|nal** (mī′krō fô′nəl), *adj.* of or having to do with a microfauna.

**mi|cro|fi|bril** (mī′krō fī′brəl), *n.* a microscopic fibril.

***mi|cro|fiche** (mī′krə fēsh′), *n., pl.* **-fich|es, -fiche** (-fēsh′). a plastic card or sheet, usually about 4 by 6 inches, containing a strip of microfilm which has been cut into short pieces. A single microfiche may contain microimages of over 100 pages of a standard-size book. [< *micro-* + French *fiche* card]

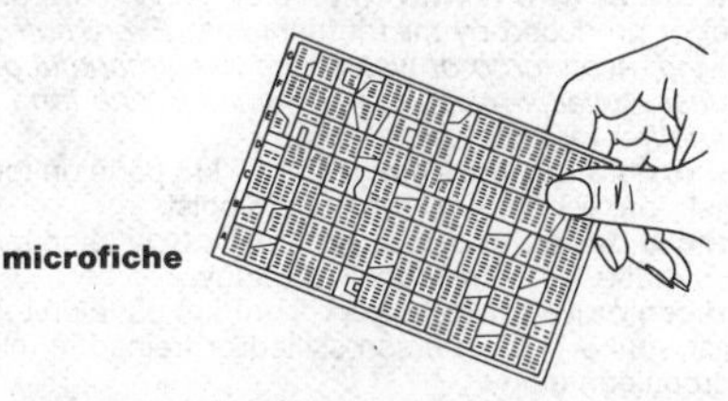

***microfiche**

**mi|cro|fi|lar|i|a** (mī′krō fi lãr′ē ə), *n., pl.* **-lar|i|ae** (-lãr′ē ē). the larva of a filaria: *The tiny young larvae, called microfilariae, pour out of the mother and are transported via the lymphatic vessels to the bloodstream* (Scientific American).

**mi|cro|film** (mī′krə film′), *n., v.* —*n.* **1** a fine-grained film for making very small photographs of pages of a book, newspapers, records, and other printed matter, to preserve them in a very small space. **2** a photograph made on such film.
—*v.t., v.i.* to photograph on microfilm: *allow ... the Treasury to microfilm tax returns* (Wall Street Journal).

**mi|cro|flo|ra** (mī′krō flôr′ə, -flōr′-), *n., pl.* **-flo|ras, -flo|rae** (-flôr′ē, -flōr′-). the microscopic plants of a given habitat, as in a cow's stomach: *the wild yeast microflora.* [< *micro-* + *flora*]

**mi|cro|flo|ral** (mī′krō flôr′əl, -flōr′-), *adj.* of or having to do with a microflora.

**mi|cro|form** (mī′krə fôrm′), *n., v.* —*n.* any material on which something can be reproduced in greatly reduced form: *The master files of the more than 3.2 million patents issued since 1790 will be put on microfilm, videotape, or another microform for quick retrieval and public sale* (Stacy V. Jones).
—*v.t.* to reproduce on microfilm or other material; make copies of on microfilm: *The Massachusetts Institute of Technology ... is planning to "microform" its entire engineering library* (New York Times).

**mi|cro|fos|sil** (mī′krō fos′əl), *n.* a microscopic plant or animal fossil, such as of foraminifera or a pollen grain, used in oil exploration and in determining early conditions on the earth.

**mi|cro|fun|gus** (mī′krō fung′gəs), *n., pl.* **-gi** (-jī), **-gus|es.** a microscopic fungus: *... a filamentous microfungus is grown on a carbohydrate substrate* (New Scientist).

**mi|cro|ga|mete** (mī′krō gə mēt′, -gam′ēt), *n.* the smaller, typically the male, of two gametes of an organism that reproduces by the union of unlike gametes.

**mi|cro|gauss** (mī′krə gous), *n.* one millionth of a gauss: *The earth's magnetic field is about one microgauss near the magnetic poles* (Scientific American).

**mi|cro|gram** (mī′krō gram), *n.* a unit of mass equal to one millionth of a gram.

**mi|cro|gramme** (mī′krō gram), *n. British.* microgram.

**mi|cro|graph** (mī′krə graf, -gräf), *n.* **1** a photograph, drawing, or other representation of an object as seen through a microscope: *Other micrographs are described as showing the effects of multiple dislocations on the growth of the crystals* (Science News). **2** an instrument that produces very small writing or engraving. **3** a device that measures and records extremely small movements by means of the corresponding movements of a diaphragm. [< *micro-* + *-graph*]

**mi|cro|graph|ic** (mī′krə graf′ik), *adj.* **1** having to do with the description of microscopic objects. **2** of or having to do with the writing of very small characters; minutely written.

**mi|crog|ra|phy** (mī krog′rə fē), *n.* **1** the description of microscopic objects. **2** examination or study with the microscope. **3** the art of writing in very small letters.

**mi|cro|groove** (mī′krə grüv′), *n.* **1** a very narrow groove used on phonograph records, especially records designed for playing speeds of 45, 33⅓, or 16 revolutions per minute, typically requiring the use of a needle measuring 1/1000 of an inch in width at the tip: *The long-playing microgroove record ... [is] now known familiarly to phonograph fans as "LP"* (Newsweek). **2 Microgroove,** *Trademark.* a record having such grooves: *These two symphonies have been committed to Microgroove at least twenty-two times apiece* (Atlantic).

**mi|cro|hab|i|tat** (mī′krō hab′ə tat), *n.* = microenvironment.

**mi|cro|hard|ness** (mī′krō härd′nis), *n.* the degree of hardness of a metal, determined by measuring a very small indenture made on its surface.

**mi|crohm** (mī′krōm), *n.* one millionth of an ohm.

**mi|cro|im|age** (mī′krō im′ij), *n.* an image or reproduction made by microphotography: *The Bible was reproduced by what ... the company's head of research calls photochromic microimages* (Time).

**mi|cro|inch** (mī′krō inch′), *n.* a unit of linear measure equal to one millionth of an inch.

**mi|cro|in|jec|tion** (mī′krō in jek′shən), *n.* injection of substances into microscopic bodies by using a micropipette: *Biologists can manipulate cells, introduce chemicals by microinjection* (Scientific American).

**mi|cro|in|struc|tion** (mī′krō in struk′shən), *n.* a single brief instruction to a computer, such as "add" or "delete."

**mi|cro|lens** (mī′krə lenz′), *n.* a lens for photography on a microscopic scale: *[He] used microlenses and extreme slow motion to get awesome footage of mayflies living out their brief lives* (Time).

**mi|cro|lep|i|dop|ter|on** (mī′krō lep′ə dop′tər on), *n., pl.* **-ter|a** (-tər ə). a small lepidopterous insect, such as the clothes moth.

**mi|cro|li|ter** (mī′krō lē′tər), *n.* one millionth of a liter.

**mi|cro|lith** (mī′krə lith), *n.* a tiny, pointed blade or chip of stone, usually flint, such as those used on arrows and tools during periods of the Stone Age. [< *micro-* + Greek *lithos* stone]

**mi|cro|lith|ic** (mī′krə lith′ik), *adj.* of, having to do with, or characterized by the use of microliths.

**mi|cro|li|tre** (mī′krō lē′tər), *n. British.* microliter.

**mi|cro|log|ic** (mī′krə loj′ik), *adj.* = micrological.

**mi|cro|log|i|cal** (mī′krə loj′ə kəl), *adj.* characterized by minuteness of investigation or discussion.

**mi|crol|o|gy** (mī krol′ə jē), *n.* the discussion or investigation of trivial things or petty affairs; hairsplitting. [< Greek *mīkrologiā* hairsplitting < *mīkrós* small + *-logiā* system, treatment < *légein* speak]

**mi|cro|ma|chin|ing** (mī′krō mə shē′ning), *n.* the machining of very small parts, such as the components of microcircuits: *Micromachining has received much publicity in the past ... An example of this would be the drilling of a very fine hole in a hard material to a depth many times the diameter* (New Scientist).

**mi|cro|ma|nip|u|la|tion** (mī′krō mə nip′yə lā′shən), *n.* the technique of performing delicate operations on microscopic bodies and structures such as cells, subcellular structures, crystals, and fibers.

**mi|cro|ma|nip|u|la|tor** (mī′krō mə nip′yə lā′tər), *n.* a device or instrument used in micromanipulation to move tiny needles, scalpels, and other tools. The operations are performed under a microscope. *With a pair of micromanipulators we were able to tease off the outer layers* (Scientific American).

**mi|cro|map** (mī′krə map′), *v.t.,* **-mapped, -mapping.** to map microscopic parts or details of: *This effect makes it possible to locate—or micromap—the distribution of uranium and thorium in different samples* (Robert M. Walker).

**mi|cro|me|te|or** (mī′krō mē′tē ər), *n.* = micrometeorite.

**mi|cro|me|te|or|ic** (mī′krō mē′tē ôr′ik, -or′-), *adj.* of or having to do with micrometeorites: *micrometeoric dust.*

**mi|cro|me|te|or|ite** (mī′krō mē′tē ə rīt), *n.* a tiny particle of meteoritic dust, so small that it does not burn as it falls to earth from outer space. Micrometeorites range from a few microns to about 100 microns in diameter. The impact of micrometeorites on the surface of space vehicles is the subject of much research by space scientists. *The metallized fabric balloons are susceptible to puncturing by micrometeorites* (New Scientist).

---

**Pronunciation Key:** hat, āge, cãre, fär; let, ēqual, tėrm; it, īce; hot, ōpen, ôrder; oil, out; cup, pu̇t, rüle; child; long; thin; ᴛʜen; zh, measure;
ə represents **a** in about, **e** in taken, **i** in pencil, **o** in lemon, **u** in circus.

**mi|cro|me|te|or|oid** (mī′krō mē′tē ə roid), *n.* = micrometeorite.

**mi|cro|me|te|or|ol|o|gy** (mī′krō mē′tē ə rol′ə jē), *n.* the branch of meteorology that deals with the atmospheric phenomena of very small areas.

**mi|crom|e|ter¹** (mī krom′ə tər), *n.* **1** an instrument for measuring very small distances, angles, and objects. Certain kinds are used with a microscope or telescope. **2** = micrometer caliper. **3** = micrometer screw. [< French *micromètre* < *micro-* micro- + *-mètre* -meter]

**mi|cro|me|ter²** (mī′krō mē′tər), *n.* one millionth of a meter; micron. [< *micro-* + *-meter*]

**micrometer caliper**, a caliper having a screw with a very fine thread, used for very accurate measurement, such as in working on or with machine tools or in watchmaking.

**micrometer screw**, a screw with very fine, precisely cut threads and a head graduated so that the distance traveled by the screw from its base setting may be exactly ascertained. Measurements in units as small as 1/10,000 of an inch can be made with a micrometer screw.

**mi|cro|met|ric** (mī′krə met′rik), *adj.* of, having to do with, or made with the micrometer: (*Figurative.*) *a micrometric crispness of control.* —**mi′cro-met′ri|cal|ly**, *adv.*

**mi|cro|met|ri|cal** (mī′krə met′rə kəl), *adj.* = micrometric.

**mi|crom|e|try** (mī krom′ə trē), *n.* the measurement of minute objects with a micrometer.

**mi|cro|mi|cro|cu|rie** (mī′krō mī′krō kyůr′ē), *n.* one millionth of one millionth of a curie.

**mi|cro|mi|cro|far|ad** (mī′krō mī′krō far′əd, -ad), *n.* one millionth of one millionth of a farad.

***mi|cro|mi|cron** (mī′krō mī′kron), *n.* one millionth of a micron.

***micromicron** μμ symbol

***micron** definition 1 μ symbol

**mi|cro|mil|li|me|ter** (mī′krō mil′ə mē′tər), *n.* **1** one millionth of a millimeter; millicron. **2** = micron.

**mi|cro|mil|li|me|tre** (mī′krō mil′ə mē′tər), *n. British.* micromillimeter.

**mi|cro|min|i|a|ture** (mī′krō min′ē ə chər), *adj.* smaller than miniature; extremely small.

**mi|cro|min|i|a|tur|i|za|tion** (mī′krō min′ē ə chər-ə zā′shən), *n.* the process of developing and producing microminiature electronic circuits or similar devices.

**mi|cro|min|i|a|tur|ize** (mī′krō min′ē ə chə rīz, -min′ə chə-), *v.t.*, **-ized, -iz|ing.** to reduce (electronic circuits or similar devices) to a size smaller than miniature: *The transistorized lock ... could be microminiaturized and adapted to any number of combinations* (New York Times).

**mi|cro|mod|ule** (mī′krō moj′ül), *n.* a small chip or wafer of insulation material, usually ceramic, in which an element of a microminiature electronic circuit has been deposited.

**mi|cro|mole** (mī′krə mōl), *n. Chemistry.* one millionth of a gram molecule: *Enzyme activity is expressed in micromoles of substrate metabolized per hour per gram* (Science). [< *micro-* + *mole⁵*]

**mi|cro|mor|pho|log|i|cal** (mī′krō môr′fə loj′ə-kəl), *adj.* of or having to do with micromorphology.

**mi|cro|mor|phol|o|gy** (mī′krō môr fol′ə jē), *n.* the morphology of microscopic structures or bodies: *studies in the micromorphology of soil.*

**mi|cro|mo|tion** (mī′krō mō′shən), *n.* an exceedingly short (in duration or length) motion or series of motions.

**mi|cro|mount** (mī′krə mount′), *n.* a small specimen, such as of a mineral or similar object, mounted for display in a small box or kept for viewing under a low-power microscope.

***mi|cron** (mī′kron), *n., pl.* **-crons** or **-cra.** **1** a unit of length equal to one millionth of a meter. **2** a colloidal particle with a diameter ranging from 1/100 to 1/5000 of a millimeter. Also, **mikron.** [< Greek *mīkrón*, neuter of *mīkrós* small]

**mi|cro|nee|dle** (mī′krō nē′dəl), *n.* a fine glass needle used in micromanipulation.

**Mi|cro|ne|sian** (mī′krə nē′zhən, -shən), *adj., n.* —*adj.* of or having to do with Micronesia (a group of small islands in the Pacific, east of the Philippines), its people, or their languages.
—*n.* **1** one of the natives of Micronesia, of mixed Melanesian, Polynesian, and Malay stock. **2** any one of the Austronesian languages spoken by these people.
[< Greek *mīkrós* small + *nêsos* island + English *-ian;* probably patterned on *Polynesian*]

**mi|cro|nu|cle|us** (mī′krō nü′klē əs, -nyü′-), *n., pl.* **-cle|i** (-klē ī), **-cle|us|es.** the smaller of two kinds of nuclei of ciliate protozoans, containing chromatin materials necessary for reproduction. There can be one or more micronuclei in a cell. *The nuclei are 2 in number, a large macronucleus concerned with vegetative functions, and a smaller micronucleus that is important in reproduction* (Hegner and Stiles).

**mi|cro|nu|tri|ent** (mī′krō nü′trē ənt, -nyü′-), *n.* = trace element.

**mi|cro|or|gan|ism** (mī′krō ôr′gə niz əm), *n.* an animal or vegetable organism too small to be seen except with a microscope. Bacteria are microorganisms. SYN: microbe.

**mi|cro|or|gan|is|mal** (mī′krō ôr′gə niz′məl), *adj.* of or produced by microorganisms: *Every puff of wind, every drop of water, and every handful of dust contains microorganismal life in one form or another* (Joshua Lederberg).

**mi|cro|pa|lae|on|tol|o|gist** (mī′krō pā′lē on tol′ə-jist, -pal′ē-), *n.* = micropaleontologist.

**mi|cro|pa|lae|on|tol|o|gy** (mī′kro pā′lē on tol′ə-jē, -pal′ē-), *n.* = micropaleontology.

**mi|cro|pa|le|on|tol|o|gist** (mī′krō pā′lē on tol′ə-jist, -pal′ē-), *n.* a person skilled or trained in micropaleontology.

**mi|cro|pa|le|on|tol|o|gy** (mī′krō pā′lē on tol′ə jē, -pal′ē-), *n.* the branch of paleontology which studies fossils of microscopic size. It is of great importance in oil exploration.

**mi|cro|par|a|site** (mī′krō par′ə sīt), *n.* a parasitic microorganism.

**mi|cro|par|a|sit|ic** (mī′krō par′ə sit′ik), *adj.* having the character of, having to do with, or caused by microparasites: *microparasitic diseases.*

**mi|cro|pho|bi|a** (mī′krə fō′bē ə), *n.* an abnormal fear of bacteria, parasites, or small objects.

***mi|cro|phone** (mī′krə fōn), *n.* an instrument for magnifying small sounds or for transmitting sounds. Microphones change sound waves into variations of an electric current. Radio and television stations use microphones for broadcasting. The mouthpiece of a telephone contains a microphone. [< *micro-* + *phone*]

***microphone**

floor microphone

hand-held microphone

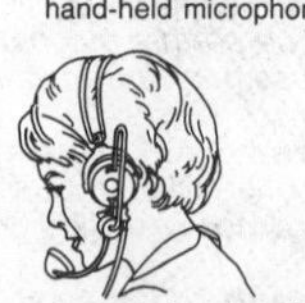

telephone operator's microphone

**mi|cro|phon|ic** (mī′krə fon′ik), *adj.* having to do with a microphone; serving to magnify small sounds.

**mi|cro|phon|ics** (mī′krə fon′iks), *n.* **1** the science of magnifying small sounds. **2** noise caused by mechanical shocks or vibrations.

**mi|cro|pho|to|graph** (mī′krō fō′tə graf, -gräf), *n., v.* —*n.* **1** a photograph too small to be deciphered by the naked eye. It has to be enlarged for viewing. **2** a photograph made on, or printed from, microfilm. **3** = photomicrograph.
—*v.t.* to make a microphotograph of: *Although the capsule is relatively large, its restricted space will require all printed information to be microphotographed* (Science News).

**mi|cro|pho|to|graph|ic** (mī′krō fō′tə graf′ik), *adj.* having to do with or connected with microphotography. —**mi′cro|pho′to|graph′i|cal|ly**, *adv.*

**mi|cro|pho|tog|ra|phy** (mī′krō fə tog′rə fē), *n.* the photographing of objects of any size upon a microscopic or very small scale.

**mi|cro|pho|tom|e|ter** (mī′krō fō tom′ə tər), *n.* a type of densitometer that measures and analyzes light passed through a photographic negative. It is particularly useful in detecting cancerous tissue and in determining the magnitude of stars: *The light the cells give off can be measured with a microphotometer* (Science News Letter).

**mi|cro|pho|to|met|ric** (mī′krō fō′tə met′rik), *adj.* of or having to do with a microphotometer. —**mi′-cro|pho′to|met′ri|cal|ly**, *adv.*

**mi|cro|phys|i|cal** (mī′krō fiz′ə kəl), *adj.* of or having to do with microphysics.

**mi|cro|phys|ics** (mī′krō fiz′iks), *n.* the branch of physics concerned with minute masses or the ultimate particles and structure of matter.

**mi|cro|phyte** (mī′krə fīt), *n.* a microscopic plant, especially a bacterium. [< *micro-* + Greek *phytón* plant]

**mi|cro|phyt|ic** (mī′krə fit′ik), *adj.* having to do with or caused by microphytes: *microphytic diseases.*

**mi|cro|pi|pette** (mī′krō pī pet′, -pi-), *n.* a very fine pipette used in micromanipulation.

**mi|cro|pop|u|la|tion** (mī′krō pop′yə lā′shən), *n.* the population of microorganisms living in a particular habitat: *the micropopulation of soil and water.*

**mi|cro|po|rous** (mī′krə pôr′əs, -pōr′-), *adj.* having very small pores: *These have high absorbency and a microporous structure that makes them extremely suitable for use as molecular sieves* (New Scientist).

**mi|cro|print** (mī′krə print′), *n.* a microphotograph of newspapers, records, or other printed matter, having such small dimensions that it must be read with a magnifying device.

**mi|cro|probe** (mī′krə prōb′), *n.* an instrument using a very fine-focused electron beam, usually in combination with optical apparatus, to microanalyze the chemical composition of rocks, minerals, glasses, and alloys.

**mi|cro|proc|es|sor** (mī′krō pros′əs ər; *especially British* -prō′səs-), *n.* an electronic computer or processor contained in a chip as small as a quarter of an inch square and able to perform the sensing, communication, and control functions of a standard-sized computer or processor: *The microprocessor is basically a grouping of thousands of tiny transistors and other electronic components ... Together, they form a miniature computer that can govern the use of fuels to their maximum efficiency* (New York Times).

**mi|cro|pro|gram** (mī′krə prō′gram, -grəm), *n., v.,* **-grammed, -gram|ming** or **-gramed, -gram|ing.**
—*n.* a routine stored in the memory of a computer, used as part of a more complex program or to control the operations of a subordinate computer: *In the 1970s, Babcock believes, writable control stores and loadable microprograms will become common* (New Scientist and Science Journal).
—*v.t.* to provide (a computer) with a microprogram.

**mi|cro|pro|gram|ma|ble** (mī′krə prō′grə mə bəl), *adj.* capable of being microprogrammed.

**mi|cro|pro|jec|tion** (mī′krō prə jek′shən), *n.* the projecting of a greatly enlarged image of a minute object on a screen by means of a microprojector: *"Discovery '63" covers ... microprojection of tiny objects and organisms* (Time).

**mi|cro|pro|jec|tor** (mī′krō prə jek′tər), *n.* an apparatus, consisting of a microscope lens system and an illuminator, that projects enlarged images of minute objects on a screen.

**mi|crop|ter|ism** (mī krop′tə riz əm), *n. Zoology.* abnormally small wing or fin development.

**mi|crop|ter|ous** (mī krop′tər əs), *adj. Zoology.* having small wings or fins. [< Greek *mīkrópteros* (with English *-ous*) < *mīkrós* small + *pterón* wing]

**mi|cro|pul|sa|tion** (mī′krō pul sā′shən), *n.* an extremely small fluctuation in the earth's magnetic field.

**mi|cro|py|lar** (mī′krə pī′lər), *adj.* having to do with or characteristic of a micropyle: *the micropylar end of the embryo sac.*

**mi|cro|pyle** (mī′krə pīl), *n.* **1** any one of the minute holes in the membrane covering the ovum of certain animals, through which spermatozoa enter. **2** the minute opening in the outer layer or layers of an ovule, through which pollen enters. [< French *micropyle* < Greek *mīkrós* small + *pýlē* gate]

**mi|cro|py|rom|e|ter** (mī′krō pī rom′ə tər), *n.* an optical instrument used in determining the temperature of very small glowing bodies. [< *micro-* + *pyrometer*]

**mi|cro|ra|di|o|graph** (mī′krō rā′dē ə graf, -gräf), *n.* an enlarged radiographic image of a small specimen.

**mi|cro|ra|di|o|graph|ic** (mī′krō rā′dē ə graf′ik), *adj.* of or having to do with a microradiograph or microradiography: *a microradiographic image, a microradiographic laboratory.*

**mi|cro|ra|di|og|ra|phy** (mī′krō rā′dē og′rə fē), *n.* the technique of producing microradiographs, used in examinations, such as of metal structure, body tissue, and paint density.

**mi|cro|read|er** (mī′krō rē′dər), *n.* a device that projects an enlarged image of a microphotograph on a screen to make its content readable or recognizable with the naked eye.

**mi|cro|roent|gen** (mī′krō rent′gən), *n.* one millionth of a roentgen.

**micros.**, microscopy.

**mi|cro|scale** (mī′krə skāl′), *n., adj.* **—*n.*** a scale or standard involving very small amounts or measurements: *These materials are ... crude on a microscale* (New Scientist).
**—*adj.*** of or designating small-scale atmospheric phenomena, such as water-vapor condensation and accretion of raindrops or snowflakes: *the microscale processes involved in clear-air turbulence.*

***mi|cro|scope** (mī′krə skōp), *n.* an instrument with a lens or a combination of lenses for making small things look larger. Bacteria, blood cells, and other objects not visible to the naked eye are clearly visible through a microscope. The simple microscope is merely a convex lens placed in a frame; the compound microscope consists essentially of two lenses, or systems of lenses, one of which, the objective or object glass, forms an enlarged inverted image of the object, and the other, the eyepiece or ocular, magnifies this image. *The microscope showed us the existence of small living organisms whose existence had not been suspected* (Atlantic). [< New Latin *microscopium* < Greek *mīkrós* small + *skopeîn* look at]

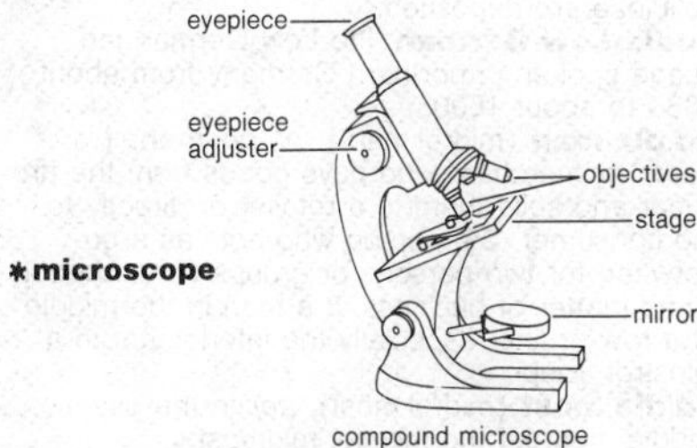

***microscope**
compound microscope

**mi|cro|scop|ic** (mī′krə skop′ik), *adj.* **1** that cannot be seen without using a microscope; extremely small; tiny; minute: *microscopic germs.* **2** like a microscope; suggesting a microscope: *a microscopic eye for mistakes, microscopic inquiry.* **3a** of a microscope: *a microscopic lens.* **b** with a microscope: *She made a microscopic examination of a fly's wing.* **4** having to do with microscopy.

**mi|cro|scop|i|cal** (mī′krə skop′ə kəl), *adj.* = microscopic.

**mi|cro|scop|i|cal|ly** (mī′krə skop′ə klē), *adv.* **1** by the use of the microscope. **2** as if with a microscope; in great detail.

**Mi|cro|sco|pi|i** (mī′krō skō′pē ī), *n.* genitive of **Microscopium.**

**mi|cros|co|pist** (mī kros′kə pist, mī′krə skō′-), *n.* an expert in microscopy; person trained in the use of the microscope.

**Mi|cro|sco|pi|um** (mī′krō skō′pē əm), *n., genitive* **Mi|cro|sco|pi|i.** a southern constellation.

**mi|cros|co|py** (mī kros′kə pē, mī′krə skō′-), *n.* the use of a microscope; microscopic investigation.

**mi|cro|sec|ond** (mī′krō sek′ənd), *n.* a unit of time equal to one millionth of a second.

**mi|cro|sec|tion** (mī′krō sek′shən), *n.* a very small section of animal tissue, mineral, or the like, prepared for microscopic examination.

**mi|cro|seism** (mī′krə sī zəm, -səm), *n.* a faint earthquake tremor, detectable only with seismographs: *Microseisms that travel about half a mile a second are the clue to changes in Great Lakes' weather detected in New York* (Science News Letter). [< *micro-* + Greek *seismós* a shaking, an earthquake < *seíein* to shake]

**mi|cro|seis|mic** (mī′krə sīz′mik, -sīs′-), *adj.* having to do with or of the nature of a faint earth tremor.

**mi|cro|seis|mi|cal** (mī′krə sīz′mə kəl, -sīs′-), *adj.* = microseismic.

**mi|cro|seis|mom|e|ter** (mī′krə sīz mom′ə tər, -sīs-), *n.* a seismograph for detecting microseisms.

**mi|cro|skirt** (mī′krə skėrt′), *n.* a skirt that is shorter than a miniskirt.

**mi|cro|sleep** (mī′krə slēp′), *n.* a momentary blackout beset by a sense of disorientation occurring to people deprived of sleep for a few days: *The subjects developed serious anomalies in brain wave pattern accompanied by 'microsleep'—a compulsive tendency to drop off unless kept constantly active* (Science Journal).

**mi|cro|slide** (mī′krə slīd′), *n.* a microscopic slide used in ultramicroscopic study.

**mi|cros|mat|ic** (mī′krəs mat′ik), *adj.* having small or feebly developed organs of smell. [< *micro-* + *osmatic*]

**mi|cro|so|ci|ol|o|gy** (mī′krō sō′sē ol′ə jē, -shē-), *n.* sociology concerned with the smallest social units.

**mi|cro|so|mal** (mī′krə sō′məl), *adj.* of or having to do with a microsome or microsomes: *a microsomal enzyme, microsomal protein synthesis.*

**mi|cro|some** (mī′krə sōm), *n.* one of the submicroscopic bodies found in the cytoplasm of cells, composed of lipid and nucleoprotein, and found to be the site of enzyme activity: *Microsomes are the tiny "protein factories" within all living cells* (Science News Letter). [< New Latin *microsoma* < Greek *mīkrós* small + *sôma* body]

**mi|cro|spec|tro|pho|tom|e|ter** (mī′krō spek′trō fō tom′ə tər), *n.* a spectrophotometer used for the examination of light reflected by very small specimens: *All three made direct measurements of the light reflected by individual cone cells in the retina, using a special microspectrophotometer* (Lorus J. Milne).

**mi|cro|spec|tro|pho|tom|e|try** (mī′krō spek′trō fō tom′ə trē), *n.* **1** the science that deals with the use of the microspectrophotometer. **2** the use of the microspectrophotometer.

**mi|cro|spec|tro|scope** (mī′krō spek′trə skōp), *n.* a combination of the microscope and the spectroscope, for the examination of minute traces of substances.

**mi|cro|spec|tro|scop|ic** (mī′krō spek′trə skop′ik), *adj.* of or having to do with the microspectroscope.

**mi|cro|sphere** (mī′krə sfir′), *n.* a very small sphere; tiny drop; globule: *The microspheres are about four times the size of human red blood cells and are labeled just prior to injection* (Science News).

**mi|cro|spo|ran|gi|um** (mī′krō spə ran′jē əm), *n., pl.* **-gi|a** (-jē ə). *Botany.* a sporangium containing microspores, homologous with the sac containing the pollen in flowering plants: *A microsporangium contains several hundred microspores* (Fred W. Emerson). [< New Latin *microsporangium* < *micro-* micro- + *sporangium* sporangium]

**mi|cro|spore** (mī′krə spôr′, -spōr′), *n.* **1** an asexually produced spore of comparatively small size from which a male gametophyte develops in certain ferns. **2** a pollen grain in seed plants.

**mi|cro|spo|ro|phyll** or **mi|cro|spo|ro|phyl** (mī′krə spôr′ə fil, -spōr′-), *n. Botany.* a leaf or other structure bearing microsporangia.

**mi|cro|state** (mī′krə stāt′), *n.* a very small country; ministate: *Other events included ... proposals that a special UN membership category be created for "microstates"* (Neville M. Hunnings).

**mi|cro|stom|a|tous** (mī′krə stom′ə təs, -stō′mə-), *adj.* having an extremely small mouth. [< *micro-* + Greek *stóma, stómatos* mouth + English *-ous*]

**mi|cros|to|mous** (mī kros′tə məs), *adj.* = microstomatous.

**mi|cro|struc|tur|al** (mī′krə struk′chər əl), *adj.* of or having to do with microstructure.

**mi|cro|struc|ture** (mī′krə struk′chər), *n.* the microscopic structure of bodies or objects, such as cells or minerals: *Scientists ... have been studying the microstructure of the insect eye* (Scientific American).

**mi|cro|sur|geon** (mī′krō sėr′jən), *n.* a person skilled in microsurgery.

**mi|cro|sur|ger|y** (mī′krō sėr′jər ē), *n.* surgery performed on very small or minute structures of the body: *The microsurgery of classical embryology is now extended by the powerful techniques of biochemistry* (Scientific American).

**mi|cro|sur|gi|cal** (mī′krō sėr′jə kəl), *adj.* having to do with microsurgery.

**mi|cro|switch** (mī′krō swich′), *n.* an electric switch used in circuits of low voltage and current: *The sleeper can turn the sound off by activating a microswitch that has been taped to his hand* (Science News Letter).

**mi|cro|tek|tite** (mī′krō tek′tīt), *n.* a microscopic variety of tektite found deep in ocean sediments: *Microtektites ... are reckoned to be the fine-grained components of the so-called "strewn fields" of larger tektites* (New Scientist and Science Journal).

**mi|cro|ther|mom|e|ter** (mī′krō thər mom′ə tər), *n.* a thermometer for measuring minute variations of temperature.

**mi|cro|tome** (mī′krə tōm), *n.* an instrument for cutting extremely thin sections of tissues for microscopic examinations. [< *micro-* + Greek *-tomos* that cuts]

**mi|cro|tom|ic** (mī′krə tom′ik), *adj.* of or having to do with the microtome or microtomy.

**mi|cro|tom|i|cal** (mī′krə tom′ə kəl), *adj.* = microtomic.

**mi|crot|o|mist** (mī krot′ə mist), *n.* a person expert in the use of the microtome.

**mi|crot|o|my** (mī krot′ə mē), *n.* the preparation of objects for microscopic examination, especially tissue examination with sectioning done with a microtome.

**mi|cro|ton|al** (mī′krə tō′nəl), *adj.* having to do with or consisting of a microtone or microtones. **—mi′cro|ton′al|ly,** *adv.*

**mi|cro|tone** (mī′krə tōn′), *n. Music.* an interval smaller than a semitone: *The composer's restless quest for new forms of expression led him to forecast microtones and electronic music and much else long before these things descended on us* (Sunday Times).

**mi|cro|tu|bule** (mī′krō tü′byül), *n.* a long, straight tubular structure, of uncertain function, in many cells of the body: *The microtubules are very fine tubes averaging 250 angstroms in diameter. They are found in cilia, in the tail of sperm cells, in the mitotic spindle of a dividing cell and in the cytoplasm of many types of cell* (Scientific American).

**mi|cro|vas|cu|lar** (mī′krō vas′kyə lər), *adj.* of or having to do with the very small vessels of the circulatory system, such as the capillaries: *Precise formations of the microvascular system and other spaces in organs of dead animals are revealed in detail when this liquid silicone compound is injected* (Science News).

**mi|cro|vil|lus** (mī′krō vil′əs), *n., pl.* **-vil|li** (-vil′ī). a microscopic hairlike part growing on the surface of a cell or cell particle: *Partly digested food is finally broken down on the surface of the small intestine which ... forms a "living porous reactor", the pores being formed by microvilli, where adsorbed enzymes complete the process of hydrolysis* (Science Journal).

**mi|cro|volt** (mī′krō vōlt′), *n.* a unit of electrical voltage, equivalent to one millionth of a volt: *The short term drift is less than 10 microvolts* (New Scientist).

**mi|cro|watt** (mī′krō wot′), *n.* a unit of electrical power, equivalent to one millionth of a watt.

**mi|cro|wave** (mī′krō wāv′), *n.* a high-frequency electromagnetic wave, usually having a wave length from one millimeter to thirty centimeters: *The biological effects of microwaves include structural or functional changes to the ... central nervous system, all due to the heating caused by microwave absorption* (New Scientist).

**microwave oven,** an oven for baking food with heat produced by microwaves: *Although microwave ovens take 50 per cent more power than conventional ovens, the microwaves are nevertheless the cheaper servants. A five-pound roast can be cooked in a microwave oven in one-fifth the time required by a conventional oven and with one-half the energy* (Saturday Review).

**mi|cro|zo|on** (mī′krə zō′on), *n., pl.* **-zo|a** (-zō′ə). a microscopic animal, especially a protozoan. [< *micro-* + Greek *zôion* animal]

**mi|cro|zyme** (mī′krə zīm), *n.* any microorganism supposed to act like a ferment in producing disease. [< *micro-* + Greek *zýmē* leaven]

**mi|crur|gi|cal** (mī krėr′jə kəl), *adj.* having to do with micrurgy.

**mi|crur|gy** (mī′krėr jē), *n.* = micromanipulation.

**Mic|tlan** (mik tlän′), *n. Aztec Mythology.* the underworld; abode of the dead.

**Mic|tlan|chi|hua|tl** (mik tlan′chē wä′təl), *n.* the Aztec goddess of the underworld.

**Mic|tlan|te|cuh|tli** (mik tlan′tə kü′tlē), *n.* the Aztec god of the underworld.

**mic|tu|rate** (mik′chə rāt), *v.i.,* **-rat|ed, -rat|ing.** = urinate. [< *mictur*(ition) + *-ate*[1]]

**mic|tu|ri|tion** (mik′chə rish′ən), *n.* **1** the act of urinating; urination. **2** (formerly) abnormally frequent passage of urine, caused by disease. **3** *Obsolete.* the wish to urinate. [< Latin *micturīre* desire to make water (< *mingere* to urinate) + English *-tion*]

**mid**[1] (mid), *adj., n.* **—*adj.*** **1** in the middle of; middle: *the mid days of autumn* (Keats). **2** designating the middle or a middle: *the mid sea* (Milton). **3** *Phonetics.* articulated with the tongue midway between high and low position, as English *e* in *bet, u* in *but.*
**—*n.*** *Obsolete.* middle: *the mid of night* (Shakespeare).
[Old English *midd,* adjective (found only in inflected forms)]

**mid**[2] or **'mid** (mid), *prep. Archaic.* amid: *'Mid pleasures and palaces though we may roam*

**Pronunciation Key:** hat, āge, cãre, fär; let, ēqual, tėrm; it, īce; hot, ōpen, ôrder; oil, out; cup, pu̇t, rüle; child; long; thin; ᴛʜen; zh, measure; ə represents a in about, e in taken, i in pencil, o in lemon, u in circus.

(John H. Payne). [variant of *amid;* influenced by *mid*¹]

**mid-**, *prefix.* **1** the middle point or part of ______: *Midcontinent = the middle part of a continent.* **2** of, in, or near the middle of ______: *Midsummer = in the middle of summer.*
[< *mid*¹]

**mid.**, **1** middle. **2** midshipman.

**mid|af|ter|noon** (mid′af′tər nün′, -äf′-), *n., adj.* —***n.*** the middle of the afternoon: *The judges, gourmets all, couldn't tear themselves away from a magnificent lunch until midafternoon* (Maclean's).
—***adj.*** occurring at, or having to do with, the middle of the afternoon: *a midafternoon snack.*

**mid|air** (mid′ãr′), *n., adj.* —***n.*** **1** the middle of the air; air above the ground: *The acrobat made a somersault in midair. ... each of these rockets either failed to leave the pad or was destroyed in midair* (New Yorker). *This small sample is melted by electromagnetic induction while held suspended in midair by a magnetic field* (Science News Letter). **2** doubt; uncertainty: *... the idea of changing the traditional Block Island race rules and the argument was left hanging in midair* (New York Times).
—***adj.*** Also, **mid-air**, in midair.

**Mi|das** (mī′dəs), *n.* **1** *Greek Legend.* a king of Phrygia who had the power to turn everything he touched into gold. Having transformed even his food and his daughter, he was permitted to wash away his detested magic touch. **2** *Figurative.* a man of great wealth or of great moneymaking ability.
**the Midas touch**, the ability to profit or make money from every enterprise: *The same people who hopefully predicted that my father would lose his shirt now say that he had the Midas touch* (New Yorker).
—**Mi′das|like′**, *adj.*

**mid|brain** (mid′brān′), *n.* the middle part of the brain; mesencephalon. See picture under **brain**.

**mid|chan|nel** (mid′chan′əl), *n.* the middle part of a channel.

**mid|con|ti|nent** (mid′kon′tə nənt), *n.* the middle part of a continent.

**mid|course** (mid′kôrs′, -kōrs′), *adj., n.* —***adj.*** for or during the middle part of the course of a spacecraft, aircraft, or ship: *During the uneventful, 73-hour coast* [*of Apollo 11 toward the moon*], *only one of the four planned midcourse corrections was necessary* (William J. Cromie).
—***n.*** the middle part of the trip of a spacecraft, aircraft, or ship: *The small rocket engine which can manoeuvre the spacecraft slightly in midcourse was needed only to direct Ranger to the sunny rather than the dark side of the moon* (London Times).

**mid|court** (mid′kôrt′, -kōrt′), *n., adj.* —***n.*** the middle of a tennis court, basketball court, or other playing area in court games: *His volleying from midcourt was confident* (London Times).
—***adj.*** in or from midcourt: *a midcourt pass, a midcourt shot.*

**mid|cult** (mid′kult′), *n.* cultural characteristics associated with the middle class, typified by conventional and moderately intellectual values and ideas. [< *mid*(dle-class) *cult*(ure)]

**mid|day** (mid′dā′), *n., adj.* —***n.*** the middle of the day; noon.
—***adj.*** of midday: *a midday meal.*
[Old English *middæg*]

**mid|den** (mid′ən), *n.* **1** = kitchen midden. **2** *Dialect.* a dunghill; refuse heap. [Middle English *myddyng,* apparently < Scandinavian (compare Danish *møding,* alteration of *møgdynge* muck heap)]

**mid|dle** (mid′əl), *n., adj., v.,* **-dled, -dling.** —***n.*** **1** the point or part that is the same distance from each end or side; center: *the middle of the road.* **2** the middle part of a person's body; waist.
—***adj.*** **1** halfway between; in the center; at the same distance from either end or side: *the middle house in the row, the middle point of a line.* **2** in between; medium: *a man of middle size. O, beware the middle mind That purrs and never shows a tooth* (Elinor H. Wylie). SYN: intermediate. **3** *Grammar.* intermediate between active and passive, as a voice of Greek verbs which represents the subject as acting on or for itself. **4** *Phonetics.* medial.
—***v.t.*** **1** to set or place in the middle. **2** to fold in the middle; double, as a rope.
[Old English *middel*]
—***Syn.*** ***n.*** **1 Middle, center** mean a point or part halfway between certain limits. **Middle** most commonly means the part more or less the same distance from each end, side, or other limit of a thing or between the beginning and end of a period or action: *the middle of the room. He came in the middle of the day.* **Center** applies to the point in the exact middle of something having a definite outline or shape, such as a circle, sphere, or square, or to something thought of as the point from, to, or around which everything moves: *the center of a circle. Washington is the center of our government.*

**Mid|dle** (mid′əl), *adj.* **1** between ancient and modern, or old or new: *the Middle Ages, the Middle Kingdom.* **2** of or having to do with a period in the history of a language intermediate between the periods called "Old" and "Modern" (or "New"): *Middle English.* **3** *Geology.* of or having to do with an intermediate principal division of a period, system, or the like, between the upper and lower divisions: *Middle Cambrian.*

**middle age**, the time of life between youth and old age, between about 40 and 65: *He was past youth, but had not reached middle age; perhaps he might be thirty-five* (Charlotte Brontë). *Middle age has always seemed to us one of the hardest spans of life to pin down statistically* (New Yorker).

**mid|dle-aged** (mid′əl ājd′), *adj.* **1** neither young nor old; between youth and old age; being of middle age: *a middle-aged parent.* **2** characteristic of people in middle age.

**mid|dle-ag|er** (mid′əl ā′jər), *n.* a person in his or her middle age: *In "The Odd Couple," a pair of poker-playing middle-agers fled their wives to room together in bachelor bliss* (Time).

**Middle Ages**, the period in European history between ancient and modern times, from about 500 A.D. to about 1450.

**mid|dle-ag|ing** (mid′əl ā′jing), *adj.* inclined to middle age; becoming middle-aged.

**mid|dle-aisle** (mid′əl īl′), *v.t.,* **-aisled, -aisl|ing.** *U.S. Slang.* to marry.

**Middle America**, **1** the middle class of America: *The decline in stock prices is cutting painfully into the hopes and fortunes of Middle America* (Time). **2** the Middle Western section of the United States: *A major industrial center plopped down on the placid, undulating farmland of southwestern Ohio, Dayton is about as Middle America as you can get* (Paul Hemphill). **3** the region between the United States and South America which includes Mexico, Central America, and the West Indies.

**Middle American**, **1** a middle-class American. **2** of or having to do with Middle Americans. **3** of or having to do with Middle America.

**mid|dle-break|er** (mid′əl brā′kər), *n.* = lister¹.

**mid|dle|brow** (mid′əl brou′), *n., adj. Informal.* —***n.*** a person who is somewhat interested in education and culture, and is therefore about midway between a highbrow and a lowbrow: *Griffith is a discontented middlebrow* (Harper's).
—***adj.*** of or suitable for a middlebrow; characteristic of a middlebrow: *A professional mixture ... it is skilfully angled at the middlebrow audience* (Punch).

**mid|dle|bust|er** (mid′əl bus′tər), *n.* a lister, especially such a plow used for planting cotton seeds.

✱**middle C**, the musical note on the first added line below the treble staff and the first above the bass staff.

✱**middle C**

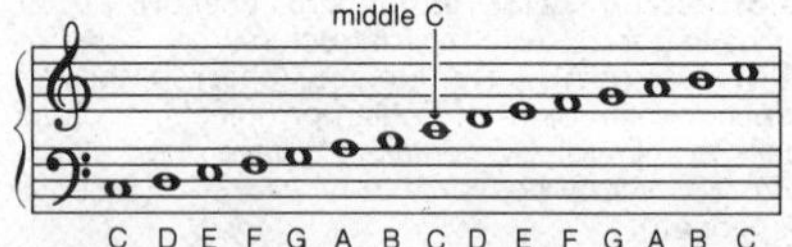


**middle class**, the class of people between the very wealthy class and the class of unskilled laborers and unemployed people. The middle class includes businessmen, professional people, office workers, and many skilled workers. In Great Britain, it includes the class socially and conventionally between the aristocratic class and the laboring class, such as professional men, bankers, owners of businesses, and small gentry.

**mid|dle-class** (mid′əl klas′, -kläs′), *adj.* of, or characteristic of, the middle class; bourgeois: *She was the most obnoxious variety of snob: the middle-class woman who has married into the fringe of society* (Leonard Merrick).

**middle distance**, **1** the part midway between the foreground and the remote region, as in a painting or the like. **2** any race from 440 yards up to and sometimes including the mile.

**Middle Dutch**, the Dutch language from about 1100 to about 1500.

**middle ear**, the hollow space between the eardrum and the inner ear; tympanum. In human beings it contains three small bones which pass on sound waves from the eardrum to the inner ear. See diagram under **ear**¹.

**Middle Eastern**, of or having to do with the Middle East, the region where Asia, Africa, and Europe meet.

**Middle English**, **1** the period in the development of the English language between Old English and Modern English, lasting from about 1100 to about 1500. **2** the English language of this period. Chaucer wrote in Middle English. *Abbr:* ME (no periods).

**middle finger**, the third finger of the hand, between the forefinger and the ring finger.

**Middle French**, the French language from about 1400 to about 1600. *Abbr:* MF (no periods).

**middle game**, the middle of a game of chess, during which the most intricate moves are made: *As the middle game looms, Black, content to hold his own, leaves White with the choice of standing pat or overreaching himself* (New York Times).

**Middle Greek**, = Medieval Greek.

**middle ground**, **1** a course between two extremes: *Between these two concepts there is no middle ground, no halfway house* (Wall Street Journal). **2** a shallow place, such as a bank or bar: *Where a middle ground exists in a channel, each end of it will be marked by a buoy* (Sailor's Pocket Book). **3** = middle distance (def. 1).

**Middle High German**, the High German language spoken in central and southern Germany from about 1050 to about 1500. *Abbr:* MHG (no periods).

**mid|dle-in|come** (mid′əl in′kum), *adj.* **1** being between the wealthy and the poor; belonging to the middle class: *The surprise was the mayor's strength in the populous outer boroughs, with their heavy concentrations of middle-income whites* (Time). **2** of or for middle-income people: *middle-income housing.*

**Middle Irish**, the Irish language from about 900 to about 1400.

**middle lamella**, *Botany.* the primary layer of a plant cell wall, composed chiefly of calcium pectate, on which, in older cells, secondary layers of cellulose are deposited.

**Middle Low German**, the Low German language spoken in northern Germany from about 1050 to about 1500.

**mid|dle|man** (mid′əl man′), *n., pl.* **-men.** **1** a trader or merchant who buys goods from the producer and sells them to a retailer or directly to the consumer. **2** a person who acts as a go-between for two persons or groups concerned in some matter of business. **3** a man in the middle of a row or line, especially the interlocutor in a minstrel troupe.

**mid|dle|most** (mid′əl mōst), *adj.* in the exact middle; nearest the middle; midmost.

**middle name**, **1** a name often following a first name and preceding a family or last name. **2** *Figurative.* a well-known characteristic: *Service is that company's middle name.*

**mid|dle-of-the-road** (mid′əl əv ᴛʜə rōd′), *adj.* **1** moderate, especially in politics; shunning extremes: *... the drift of the South away from its ancient conservatism toward a more middle-of-the-road variety of politics* (Harper's). **2** *U.S.* of or having to do with a style of performing popular music that appeals to a broad audience: *preferring the greater craft and professionalism of such middle-of-the-road singers as the Carpenters* (William Livingstone).

**mid|dle-of-the-road|er** (mid′əl əv ᴛʜə rō′dər), *n.* a moderate, especially in politics: *Middle-of-the-roaders try to strike a balance between pleasing Washington and following their own line of thought and research* (New Yorker).

**middle passage**, the passage across the Atlantic Ocean formerly made by ships carrying slaves from West Africa to the West Indies or America.

**middle register**, the range of a voice midway between the head and chest registers, especially in singing.

**mid|dle-road** (mid′əl rōd′), *adj.* = middle-of-the-road.

**mid|dle-road|er** (mid′əl rō′dər), *n.* = middle-of-the-roader.

**middle school**, any school intermediate between elementary school and senior high school.

**Middle Temple**, one of the Inns of Court in London.

**middle term**, *Logic.* the term in the major and minor premises of a syllogism but not in the conclusion.

**middle voice**, *Grammar.* the form of the verb, in Greek and some other languages, which is regularly passive in form but active in meaning, and that normally expresses reflexive or reciprocal action that affects the subject or intransitive conditions.

**mid|dle|ware** (mid′əl wãr′), *n.* computer software designed for the particular needs of a system: *The available computer has only one large file store. By appropriate middleware, which extends the file handling facilities in the control programs, a situation can be created in which the application programs are able to behave as if they each had their own separate file* (Science Journal).

**middle way**, a course between extremes.

**mid|dle|weight** (mid′əl wāt′), *n.* **1** a person, especially a man, of average weight. **2** a boxer or wrestler who weighs more than 147 pounds and less than 160.

**Middle Western**, of or having to do with the Middle West, a part of the United States west of the Appalachian Mountains, east of the Rocky Mountains, north of the Ohio River and the southern boundaries of Missouri and Kansas.

**Middle Westerner**, a native or inhabitant of the Middle West, a part of the United States, west of the Appalachian Mountains, east of the Rocky Mountains, north of the Ohio river and the southern boundaries of Missouri and Kansas.

**mid|dling** (mid′ling), *adj., adv., n.* —***adj.*** **1** medium in size, quality, grade, or other characteristic; ordinary; average: *the abundant consumption of middling literature* (Matthew Arnold). **2** mediocre; second-rate.
—***adv.*** *Informal or Dialect.* moderately; fairly: *I've got a middlin' tight grip, sir, On the handful o' things I know* (John Hay).
—***n.*** **middlings, a** products of medium size, quality, grade, or price: *There are often middlings in a coal-washing process* (Science News). **b** coarse particles of ground wheat mixed with bran, used in making a very nutritious flour: *The smaller chunks go to purifiers that remove the bran by means of air currents. The purified endosperm, called middlings at this stage, is ground and sifted to produce white flour* (W. B. Dohoney). **c** *Dialect.* pork or bacon from between the ham and shoulder: *The price of middlings has gone up this week.*
[< Scottish *middling,* probably < *mid* [1], adjective + *-ling*] —**mid′dling|ly**, *adv.*

**mid|dy** (mid′ē), *n., pl.* **-dies. 1** *Informal.* a midshipman. **2** = middy blouse.

*** middy blouse**, a loose blouse like a sailor's, having a collar with a broad flap at the back, worn by children and young girls.

*** middy blouse**

**Mid|east** (mid′ēst′), *adj.* = Middle Eastern.

**Mid|east|ern** (mid′ē′stərn), *adj.* = Middle Eastern.

**mid|field** (mid′fēld′), *n.* the middle of a sports field.

**mid|field|er** (mid′fēl′dər), *n.* a lacrosse player stationed in midfield.

**mid-flight** (mid′flīt′), *n.* **1** the middle of flight: *When bats are caught in mid-flight, their wings are often broken* (Science News Letter). **2** the middle of any action or procedure: *a career in mid-flight, music in mid-flight.*

**Mid|gard** (mid′gärd), *n. Norse Mythology.* the earth, placed between heaven and hell, and connected with heaven by a rainbow. Also, **Midgarth, Mithgarthr.**

**Mid|garth** (mid′gärᴛʜ), *n.* = Midgard.

**midge** (mij), *n.* **1** any one of various very small insects; gnat: *Of course, I just call them black flies, but the guides call them midges* (New York Times). **2** a very small person, such as a child. [Old English *mycg*]

**midg|et** (mij′it), *n., adj.* —***n.*** **1** a person very much smaller than normal; tiny person: *We saw midgets in the circus. Parson Kendall's a little midget of a man* (Harriet Beecher Stowe). **SYN:** See syn. under **dwarf. 2** anything much smaller than the usual size for its type or kind.
—***adj.*** very small; miniature; diminutive: *a midget car.*

**midget moth**, any one of a family of tiny moths with wing spans of less than one-eighth inch.

**mid|gut** (mid′gut′), *n.* the middle section of the embryonic alimentary canal.

**mid|heav|en** (mid′hev′ən), *n.* **1** the middle of the sky. **2** *Astronomy.* the meridian of a place.

*** midi**
definition 1

*** mid|i** (mid′ē), *n., pl.* **mid|is,** *adj.* —***n.*** **1** a skirt, dress, or other garment reaching to the calf, usually the mid-calf; longuette. **2** the style or length characterized by hemlines at the calf.
—***adj.*** reaching to the calf, usually the mid-calf: *a midi coat.*
[< *mid* [1] + *-i,* as in *mini* and *maxi*]

**Mi|di** (mē dē′), *n.* the south, especially the south of France. [< French *midi* (originally) the south, midday < Old French; *mi* < Latin *medius* middle; *-di* < Latin *diēs* day. Compare etym. under **meridian.**]

**Mid|i|an** (mid′ē ən), *n.* one of Abraham's sons (in the Bible, Genesis 25:2).

**Mid|i|an|ite** (mid′ē ə nīt), *n.* a member of a wandering tribe of northwestern Arabia, said to be descended from Midian. They fought against the Israelites (in the Bible, Numbers 31:1-9).

**mid|i|nette** (mid′ə net′; *French* mē dē net′), *n.* a girl who works in a Paris store, dressmaking establishment, or the like: *It is the season to look at the little shopgirls and midinettes* (New Yorker). [< French *midinette,* perhaps < (*qui fait la*) *dînette* (*à*) *midi* one who takes a little dinner at midday]

**mid|i|ron** (mid′ī′ərn), *n.* a golf club with a steel or iron head having a face of small slope, used for long approach shots. It is usually called a "number 2 iron."

**mid|land** (mid′lənd), *n. adj.* —***n.*** **1** the middle part of a country; the interior: *The stranger had come from the midland and never seen the sea.* **2 Midlands,** the central part of England.
—***adj.*** **1** in or of the midland; inland: *midland plains.* **2** surrounded by land; mediterranean.

**Mid|land** (mid′lənd), *adj.* **1** belonging to the Midlands. **2** General American, the variety of English spoken in most of the United States. **3** the dialect of English spoken in the midland of England especially in the Middle English period.

**Mid|land|er** (mid′lən dər), *n.* an inhabitant of the Midland counties of England.

**Midland man**, an early North American human, probably predating the Folsom man.

**mid|leg** (mid′leg′), *n.* **1** the middle of the leg. **2** one of the middle or second pair of legs of an insect.

**Mid-Lent** (mid′lent′), *n.* the middle of Lent.

**mid|line** (mid′līn′), *n.* a line marking the middle of a body or object: *the midline of an organ, embryo, or hoof.*

**mid mashie**, a golf club with a steel head having a hitting surface sloped more than that of a midiron, but less than that of a mashie. It is usually called a "number 3 iron."

**mid|morn|ing** (mid′môr′ning), *n., adj.* —***n.*** the middle of the morning: *He reached Chicago in midmorning after two nights on the train* (New Yorker).
—***adj.*** occurring at, or having to do with, the middle of the morning: *midmorning coffee break.*

**mid|most** (mid′mōst), *adj., adv., prep.* —***adj.*** **1** in the exact middle; nearest the middle; middle. **SYN:** middlemost. **2** most intimate.
—***adv.*** in the midmost part; in the midst.
—***prep.*** in the midst of.

**mid|night** (mid′nīt′), *n., adj.* —***n.*** twelve o'clock at night, when the old day ends and the new one begins; the middle of the night: *We have heard the chimes at midnight* (Shakespeare).
—***adj.*** **1** of or at midnight. **2** dark as midnight.
**burn the midnight oil.** See under **oil.**

**mid|night|ly** (mid′nīt′lē), *adj., adv.* —***adj.*** occurring at midnight or every midnight.
—***adv.*** at midnight; every midnight.

**midnight sun**, the sun seen throughout the day and night in the arctic and antarctic regions during their summers: *The midnight sun is an example of a circumpolar star* (Robert H. Baker).

**mid|noon** (mid′nün′), *n.* the middle of the day; noon: *Gentlewomen ... who begin their morning at midnoon* (John Lyly).

**mid-o|cean** (mid′ō′shən), *n.* the middle of the ocean: *stable mid-ocean research platforms* (Scientific American).

**mid-ocean ridge**, any one of the large ridges running through the middle of the Atlantic Ocean and across the Pacific Ocean. Their existence is thought to support the theory of continental drift.

**mid-off** (mid′ôf′, -of′), *n. Cricket.* the fieldsman or the area to the left of the wicket.

**mid-on** (mid′on′, -ôn′), *n. Cricket.* the fieldsman or the area to the right of the wicket.

**mid|phrase** (mid′frāz′), *n.* the midpoint of a phrase of music or speech: *In the awesomely beautiful open-air arena at Persepolis he* [*Artur Rubinstein*] *rehearses the sublime opening of the last movement of the Appassionata Sonata, and in midphrase looks up and laughs* (Manchester Guardian Weekly).

**mid|point** (mid′point′), *n.* the middle part of anything; midway point: *the midpoint of a journey.*

**Mid|rash** (mid′rash), *n.* the whole body of Jewish traditional Scriptural exegesis, partly of a legal nature, but mostly of a homiletic character. [< Hebrew *midrash* commentary]

**mid|rash** (mid′rash), *n., pl.* **mid|ra|shim** (mid rä′shēm) or **-shoth** (-shōth). *Judaism.* an exposition of the Scriptures or a part of them. [< *Midrash*]

**mid|rash|ic** (mid rash′ik), *adj.* of or having to do with a midrash or the Midrash: *His latest venture is into the vast and cloudy hinterland of Jewish midrashic lore* (Sunday Times).

**mid|rib** (mid′rib′), *n.* the main vein of a leaf, continuous with the petiole, extending through the central part of the blade of the leaf.

**mid|riff** (mid′rif), *n., adj.* —***n.*** **1a** the diaphragm separating the chest cavity from the abdomen. **b** the middle portion of the human body: *a bare midriff, a punch in the midriff.* **2** a woman's or girl's garment, often made in two pieces, that leaves the middle portion of the body bare.
—***adj.*** made so as to expose the middle part of the body: *a midriff bathing suit.*
[Old English *midhrif* < *midd* mid + *hrif* belly]

**mid|sea|son** (mid′sē′zən), *n., adj.* —***n.*** the middle of a season; the busy or active part of the season in a particular business, sport, or field of entertainment: *The hotel rates were high during midseason.*
—***adj.*** in or for the midseason: *Counted out of the league after a disastrous midseason slump* ... (Time).

**mid|sec|tion** (mid′sek′shən), *n.* **1** the middle part of something: *The cold air pouring down into the country's midsection and Southeast is sure to shift in March* (Science News Letter). **2** the middle part of the body; midriff: *The midsection is a bit on the heavy side and the hair is gray and thinned* (New York Times).

**mid|ship** (mid′ship′), *adj.* in, of, or belonging to the middle part of a ship.

**mid|ship|man** (mid′ship′mən), *n., pl.* **-men. 1a** a student at the United States Naval Academy at Annapolis or any other school for training officers for the U.S. Navy or Marine Corps. **b** the rank held by such a student, immediately below that of a commissioned officer. **2a** a graduate of British naval schools until he is made sublieutenant. **b** an officer of the same rank in training on a ship. **3** a boy or young man who assisted the officers of a ship in former times.

**mid|ship|mite** (mid′ship′mīt), *n. Slang.* midshipman: *This linen also serves for one-piece hostess pajamas with brass ball buttons, bell-bottom trousers, and the look of a midshipmite* (New Yorker).

**mid|ships** (mid′ships′), *adv.* = amidships.

**midst**[1] (midst), *n., adv.* —***n.*** the middle point or part; center; middle.
—***adv.*** in the middle place: *To extol him first, him last, him midst, and without end* (Milton).
**in our midst,** among us: *a traitor in our midst.*
**in the midst of, a** in the middle of; surrounded by; among: *in the midst of a forest. And Jesus called a little child unto him, and set him in the midst of them* [*His disciples*] (Matthew 18:2). **b** in the thick of; during: *in the midst of a day's work.*
[perhaps < phrase *amidst of* (with *a-* taken as preposition)]

**midst**[2] or **'midst** (midst), *prep.* in the midst of; amidst; amid: *They left me 'midst my enemies* (Shakespeare). [short for *amidst*]

**mid|stream** (mid′strēm′), *n., adj., adv.* —***n.*** the middle of a stream: *The boat was kept in midstream.* (*Figurative.*) *the midstream of history.*
—***adj., adv.*** in midstream: *The two boats collided midstream* (adv.). *The two boats were in a midstream collision* (adj.).

**mid|sum|mer** (mid′sum′ər), *n., adj.* —***n.*** **1** the middle of summer: *the intense heat of midsummer.* **2** the time of the summer solstice, about June 21: *the sun at midsummer.*
—***adj.*** in the middle of the summer: *a midsummer festival.*

**Midsummer Day**, (in England) June 24, one of the quarter days.

**midsummer madness**, the height of madness: *Why, this is very midsummer madness* (Shakespeare).

**mid|term** (mid′tėrm′), *n., adj.* —***n.*** **1** the middle of a term of office, school, or appointment: *Kennedy at midterm had changed. No longer did one think of him first as the youngest President elected by his countrymen* (John L. Steele). **2** *U.S. Informal.* an examination held during the middle of a school term.
—***adj.*** occurring at, or having to do with, midterm: *The university was in midterm recess* (Time).

**mid|town** (mid′toun′), *n., adj.* —***n.*** the middle

**Pronunciation Key:** hat, āge, cãre, fär; let, ēqual, tėrm; it, īce; hot, ōpen, ôrder; oil, out; cup, pu̇t, rüle; child; long; thin; ᴛʜen; zh, measure; ə represents a in about, e in taken, i in pencil, o in lemon, u in circus.

section of a city or town, between downtown and uptown: *He had reached midtown before he remembered the package.*
—**adj.** of or located in midtown.

**mid-Vic|to|ri|an** (mid′vik tôr′ē ən, -tōr′-), *adj., n.* —**adj.** 1 of the middle period of Queen Victoria's reign in Great Britain, or from about 1850 to 1890: *mid-Victorian architecture, a mid-Victorian novel.* 2 like this period; strict in morals; old-fashioned. SYN: prudish.
—**n.** 1 a person who lived during the middle period of Queen Victoria's reign. 2 a person with old-fashioned ideas and tastes, and strict in morals.

**mid|wa|ter trawl** (mid′wôt′ər, -wot′-), a trawl dragged by two boats for snaring such fish as herring and cod.

**mid|way** (mid′wā′), *adj., adv., n.* —**adj.** in the middle; halfway: *a midway position.*
—**adv.** halfway: *midway between the hill and the city.*
—**n.** 1 a middle way or course: *no midway 'Twixt these extremes at all* (Shakespeare). 2 a place for games, rides, and other amusements at a fair or exposition: *the clamor and excitement of the midway.*
[Old English *midweg;* (noun, def. 2) < the *Midway Plaisance,* a boulevard area, site of the amusements at the Columbian Exposition in 1893 at Chicago, Illinois]

**mid|week** (mid′wēk′), *n., adj.* —**n.** the middle of the week: *By midweek the newspapers found it necessary to give short "missiles for the layman" courses* (New York Times).
—**adj.** in the middle of the week.

**Mid|week** (mid′wēk′), *n.* Wednesday. It is so called by the Quakers.

**mid|week|ly** (mid′wēk′lē), *adv., adj.* in the middle of the week.

**Mid|west** (mid′west′), *adj.* = Middle Western.

**Mid|west|ern** (mid′wes′tərn), *adj.* = Middle Western.

**Mid|west|ern|er** (mid′wes′tər nər), *n.* a person who lives in the Middle West; Middle Westerner.

**mid|wife** (mid′wīf′), *n., pl.* **-wives,** *v.,* **-wifed, -wif|ing** or **-wived** (-wivd), **-wiv|ing.** —**n.** 1 a woman who helps women in childbirth, especially a woman trained by schooling or experience.
2 *Figurative.* a person who helps to bring forth something new: *This remarkable machine has been giving its midwives—among others—some headaches ... since it came into operation* (New Scientist).
—**v.t.** to help bring forth (something new): *Down the years since W. C. Handy midwifed the blues* ... (Time). *Central banks might take a hand ... in midwiving such an operation* (London Times).
[Middle English *midwyf* < Old English *mid* with + *wīf* woman]

**mid|wife|ry** (mid′wī′fər ē, -wīf′rē), *n.* the art or practice of helping women in childbirth; obstetrics.

**midwife toad,** either of two small toads about two inches long of central and southwestern Europe; obstetrical toad.

**mid-wing** (mid′wing′), *adj.* of or having to do with an airplane having the wings attached halfway up the side of the fuselage: *a mid-wing design.*

**mid|win|ter** (mid′win′tər), *n., adj.* —**n.** 1 the middle of winter: *the chill of midwinter.* 2 the time of the winter solstice, about December 21: *the low sun at midwinter.* 3 (formerly) Christmas.
—**adj.** in the middle of the winter: *midwinter chill.*

**mid world,** = Midgard.

**mid|year** (mid′yir′), *adj., n.* —**adj.** happening in the middle of a year: *a midyear dividend, a midyear examination.*
—**n.** **midyears,** *Informal.* **a** midyear examinations: *The student passed all his midyears.* **b** the period during which these examinations are held: *I'd breezed through the fall semester, been on Dean's List at midyears, ... and now was failing* (New Yorker).

**M.I.E.E.,** *British.* Member of the Institute of Electrical Engineers.

**mien** (mēn), *n.* the manner of holding the head and body; way of acting and looking: *George Washington had the mien of a soldier.* SYN: bearing, demeanor, appearance. [probably short for obsolete *demean,* noun; influenced by Middle French *mine* appearance, expression of the face, perhaps < Breton *min* muzzle, beak]

**miff** (mif), *n., v. Informal.* —**n.** a peevish fit; petty quarrel: ... *a little quarrel, or miff, as it is vulgarly called, rose between them* (Henry Fielding). SYN: huff, tiff.
—**v.i.** to be offended; have a petty quarrel.
—**v.t.** to offend: *She was miffed at the idea that she could be mistaken.*
[origin uncertain; perhaps imitative]

**miff|y** (mif′ē), *adj.,* **miff|i|er, miff|i|est.** *Informal.* easily offended; touchy.

**mig** or **migg** (mig), *n. Dialect.* a marble, especially one used as the object in the game of marbles. [origin unknown]

**MIG** or **Mig** (mig), *n.* any one of various Russian-designed jet fighter planes (the type and model being indicated by a number): *The MIG-21J is ... the most advanced aircraft in the MIG series and is able to fly at supersonic speeds at sea level* (New Scientist). [< Artem *Mi*(koyan) and Mikhail *G*(urevich) Russian airplane designers of the 1900's]

**might**[1] (mīt), *v.* the past tense of **may**[1]: *Mother said that we might play in the barn. He might have done it when you were not looking.* [Old English *mihte, meahte*]
▶ See **could** for usage note.

**might**[2] (mīt), *n.* 1 great power; strength: *Work with all your might.* 2 operative power (whether great or small): *To the measure of his might each fashions his desires* (Wordsworth).
**with might and main,** with all one's strength: *They fell to work and belabored each other with might and main* (Washington Irving).
[Old English *miht*]

**might-have-been** (mīt′həv bin′, -əv-), *n.* 1 something that might have happened: ... *a junk heap of might-have-beens, the unfulfilled promises of worlds that never were* (New Yorker). 2 a person or thing that might have been greater or more eminent: *Gustav Mahler, when he died in 1911, left behind one of the most tantalising might-have-beens in musical history: his unfinished Tenth Symphony* (Sunday Times).

**might|i|ly** (mī′tə lē), *adv.* 1 in a mighty manner; powerfully; vigorously: *Samson strove mightily and pulled the pillars down.* 2 very much; greatly: *We were mightily pleased at winning.*

**might|i|ness** (mī′tē nis), *n.* 1 power; strength. 2 Often, **Mightiness.** as with *your, his,* or *her,* and often preceded by *high,* a title of dignity (now used ironically).

**might|less** (mīt′lis), *adj.* without might; powerless; impotent.

**might|y** (mī′tē), *adj.,* **might|i|er, might|i|est,** *adv., n., pl.* **might|ies.** —**adj.** 1 showing strength or power; powerful; strong: *a mighty ruler, mighty force.* 2 very great: *a mighty famine, a mighty dinner.* SYN: extraordinary.
—**adv.** *Informal.* very: *a mighty long time.*
—**n.** a mighty or powerful person: *Eleazar ... who was one of the three mighties* (I Chronicles 11:12).
—**Syn.** *adj.* 1 **Mighty, powerful** mean strong. **Mighty** suggests great strength and size but not necessarily effective force: *The mighty battleship was so badly damaged that it had to be scuttled.* **Powerful** suggests the strength, energy, or authority to exert great force: *The battleship was a powerful weapon.*

**mig|ma|tite** (mig′mə tīt), *n. Geology.* a common type of rock formed of a complex mixture of igneous and metamorphic rocks, characterized chiefly by gneissic bands and crosscutting veins. [< Greek *mígma, -atos* compound + English *-ite*[1]]

**mi|gnon** (min′yon; *French* mē nyôN′), *adj.* delicately formed; small and pretty; dainty. [< French *mignon*]

**mi|gnon|ette** (min′yə net′), *n.* 1 a common garden plant having long, pointed clusters of small, fragrant, greenish-white flowers with prominent, golden-brown anthers. 2 a yellowish-green or grayish-green color; reseda. [< Middle French *mignonnette* < *mignon* mignon]

**mi|graine** (mī′grān; *especially British* mē′grān), *n.* a severe headache, usually recurrent, on one side of the head only, and accompanied by nausea; sick headache; megrim. [< Old French *migraigne* < Late Latin (*hē*)*micrānia* < Greek *hēmikrāniā* < *hēmi-* half + *krānion* headache; (originally) skull. See etym. of doublet **hemicrania.**]

**mi|grain|ous** (mī grā′nəs), *adj.* having to do with or suffering from migraines: *Migrainous subjects have been found to have a disordered function in the arteries that supply the head and brain* (New Scientist).

**mi|gran|cy** (mī′grən sē), *n.* the state or condition of being migrant: *Until we see the connection between migrancy ... the despairing, destitute families groping for a way to live, and the bountiful supply of fruits and vegetables on every corner fruit stand or in every supermarket, no change will come* (Atlantic).

**mi|grant** (mī′grənt), *adj., n.* —**adj.** migrating; roving; migratory: *a migrant worker.*
—**n.** a person, animal, bird, or plant that migrates: *The western United States was settled by migrants from all over the world.*

**mi|grate** (mī′grāt), *v.i.,* **-grat|ed, -grat|ing.** 1 to move from one place to settle in another: *Pioneers from New England migrated to all parts of the United States.* 2 to go from one region to another with the change in the seasons. Most birds migrate to warmer climates to spend the winter. 3 to spread from one localized area to another or larger area: *The wind helps trees migrate by carrying their seeds beyond the forest ... Forests can migrate over fairly level land but not across oceans or mountain ranges* (Martin H. Zimmermann). [< Latin *migrāre* (with English *-ate*[1])]

**mi|gra|tion** (mī grā′shən), *n.* 1 the action of moving from one place or region to another; migrating: *Those almighty instincts that propel the migrations of the swallow and the lemming* (Thomas De Quincey). *If migration offers little by way of a solution of the world's demographic problems, why is it so often mentioned?* (Wall Street Journal). 2 a number of people or animals migrating together. 3a a movement of one or more atoms from one place to another within the molecule. **b** the movement of ions between the two electrodes during electrolysis.
▶ **Migration** of people includes both *emigration* (the movement out of an area) and *immigration* (the movement into an area).

**mi|gra|tion|al** (mī grā′shə nəl), *adj.* of or having to do with migration or movement to another place: *migrational ability of birds.*

**mi|gra|tor** (mī′grā tər), *n.* 1 a person or thing that migrates. 2 a migratory bird.

**mi|gra|to|ry** (mī′grə tôr′ē, -tōr′-), *adj.* 1 moving from one place to another; that migrates; migrating: *migratory laborers, migratory birds.* 2 of or having to do with migration: *the migratory pattern of elephants.* 3 wandering: *a migratory pain.*

**migratory locust,** any one of the grasshoppers which have short antennae and migrate in great swarms, destroying crops and other vegetation in their path.

**mih|rab** (mē′rəb), *n.* a niche in a Moslem mosque, which points to Mecca. [< Arabic *miḥrāb*]

**mi|ka|do** or **Mi|ka|do** (mə kä′dō), *n., pl.* **-dos.** a former title of the emperor of Japan. The Japanese seldom use this title except in poetry, and it is now decreasingly used by foreigners. [< Japanese *mikado* < *mi* honorable + *kado* gate]

**mike** (mīk), *n., v.,* **miked, mik|ing.** *Informal.* —**n.** a microphone.
—**v.t.** to transmit on a microphone: *The most important things at the convention ... happen on the podium and in the miked statements from the delegations* (Harper's).
—**v.i.** to use a microphone: *Jolas specifically asks the viola to stand up in concertante passages, ... though miking may well have justified it to radio listeners* (London Times).

**Mike** (mīk), *n. U.S.* a code name for the letter *m,* used in transmitting radio messages.

**mi|kron** (mī′kron), *n., pl.* **-krons, -kra** (-krə). = micron.

**mik|vah** (mik′və), *n.* a Jewish ritual bath used in ceremonies of purification, such as the bathing of women following menstruation, and the dipping of new dishes before use: *Rabbis want to know why the mikvah attendance has fallen off* (Maclean's). [< Hebrew *mikvah*]

**mil** (mil), *n.* 1 a measure of length equal to 0.001 of an inch. It is used in measuring the diameter of wires. 2 a unit of angular measure used in adjusting the aim of a piece of artillery, equal to 1/6400 of a complete circle or about 1/18 of a degree. 3 *Pharmacy.* a milliliter. 4 an Israeli bronze coin, worth 1/1000 of a pound. [< Latin *mīlle* thousand; the modern senses are short for *mīllēsimum* thousandth]

**mil.,** 1 military. 2 militia.

**mi|la|dy** or **mi|la|di** (mi lā′dē), *n., pl.* **-dies.** 1 my lady: *The spittoon, once a fixture even in banks, ought to be replaced by a wall mirror so milady can look her best* (Wall Street Journal). 2 an English lady or noblewoman.
▶ **Milady** originated as an appellation used by continental Europeans in speaking to or of an English noblewoman or great lady. In fashionable European hotels, shops, and the like, it is often applied to any English-speaking woman whose manner, dress, or purchases are deemed to justify it: *Would milady care to pay now, or later?*

**mil|age** (mī′lij), *n. U.S.* mileage.

**Mi|lan** or **mi|lan** (mi lan′, mil′ən), *n.* a fine, closely woven straw used in the manufacture of women's hats: *a hat of red Milan* (New Yorker). [< *Milan,* a city in Italy, where it is made]

**Mil|a|nese** (mil′ə nēz′, -nēs′), *adj., n., pl.* **-nese.** —**adj.** of or having to do with Milan, a city in northern Italy, or its people: *a Milanese painter.*
—**n.** a native or inhabitant of Milan.

**milch** (milch), *adj.* giving milk; kept for the milk it gives: *a milch cow.* [Old English *-milce* a milking < *mioluc* milk]

**milch|er** (mil′chər), *n.* a milch animal, such as a cow.

**mil|chig** (mil′ʜik), *adj.* (in Jewish dietary law) restricted to dairy foods or products: *a milchig meal, milchig dishes.* [< Yiddish *milkhig* (literally) milky]

**mild** (mīld), *adj., n.* —**adj.** 1 gentle or kind: *a mild*

*old gentleman, a mild tone of voice.* **SYN**: tender, lenient, merciful. See syn. under **gentle**. **2** calm; warm; temperate; moderate; not harsh or severe: *a mild climate, a mild winter.* **SYN**: clement, pleasant, bland. **3** soft or sweet to the senses; not sharp, sour, bitter, or strong in taste: *a mild cheese, a mild cigar.*
*—n. British Informal.* mild ale or beer: *Bill Flanagan, with whom I took a glass of mild at the Canonbury Working Men's Institute yesterday ...* (Punch).
[Old English *milde* mild, generous] — **mild′ly**, *adv.* — **mild′ness**, *n.*

**Mild** (mīld), *n.* coffee grown outside of Brazil.

**mild|en** (mīl′dən), *v.t., v.i.* to make or become mild or milder.

**mil|dew** (mil′dü, -dyü), *n., v. —n.* **1** a kind of fungus that appears on plants or on paper, clothes, or leather during damp weather. Mildew is a minute, parasitic fungus that produces a whitish coating or a discoloration. *Mildew killed the rosebuds in our garden.* **2** the coating or discoloration, or the diseased condition, produced by such a fungus: *Damp clothes left in a pile will show mildew in a few days.* **3** any similar discoloration caused by a fungus, such as on cotton and linen fabrics, paper, or leather.
*—v.t., v.i.* to cover or become covered with mildew: *A pile of damp clothes in his closet mildewed.*
[Old English *mildēaw, meledēaw* honeydew]

**mil|dew|cide** (mil′dü sīd, -dyü-), *n.* a substance for preventing or destroying mildew: *The improved "mildewcides," products which contain mercury derivatives, are now on the market* (New York Times). [< *mildew* + *-cide*[1]]

**mil|dewed** (mil′düd, -dyüd), *adj.* **1** tainted with mildew: *mildewed books.* **2** *Figurative.* affected from lack of use; outmoded: *"Too True To Be Good," by George Bernard Shaw, is substandard ... full of mildewed seventyish garrulities on religion, militarism, and the idle rich* (Time).

**mil|dew|y** (mil′dü ē, -dyü-), *adj.* of, like, or affected with mildew: *There is a mildewy odor from that old trunk.*

**mild steel**, = soft steel.

***mile** (mīl), *n.* **1** a measure of distance equal to 5,280 feet; statute mile: *After running out of gas we walked two miles to the filling station.* **2** a measure of length equal to about 6,080 feet, used especially at sea. It is theoretically equal to the distance traversed along one minute of a degree of a great circle of the earth: *The fishing boats were several miles out at sea.* **3** an international unit of linear measure for sea and air navigation, equal to 1.852 kilometers or 6,076.1154 feet (international nautical mile). **4** the ancient Roman mile, equal to 4,860 feet. **5** the modern Swedish mile, equal to 10 kilometers. *Abbr:* mi. [Old English *mīl* < Latin *mīlia* (*passuum*) a thousand (Roman paces), plural of *mīlle; passuum,* genitive plural of *passus, -ūs* the legionary's double pace]

***mile**
definitions 1, 3

1 statute mile = 5,280 feet or 1.6093 kilometers

1 nautical mile = 6,076.11549 feet or 1.852 kilometers

1 kilometer = 3,280.8 feet

**mile|age** (mī′lij), *n.* **1** miles covered or traveled: *Our mileage was 350 yesterday. The mileage of this car is 50,000.* **2** miles traveled per gallon of gasoline: *Do you get good mileage with your car?* **3** length, extent, or distance in miles. The mileage of a railroad is its total number of miles of roadbed. **4** an allowance for traveling expenses at so much a mile: *Congressmen are given mileage between their homes and Washington, D.C.* **5** a rate charged per mile, as on a toll highway or for a rented car. **6** a mileage ticket or mileage book. **7** *Informal, Figurative.* benefit; use; gain: *The situation is not without humor but the politicians say there is no mileage in it either way* (Birmingham News). Also, **milage**.

**mileage book**, a book of mileage tickets or coupons.

**mileage ticket**, a ticket or coupon that entitles the bearer to a certain number of miles of railroad travel.

**mile|post** (mīl′pōst′), *n.* a post set up on a road or railroad to show the distance in miles to a certain place or the distance covered: *A milepost showed that we were 38 miles from Chicago.*

**mil|er** (mī′lər), *n.* a person or animal, such as a horse, competing in or trained for a mile race: *The number of sprinters and milers has increased* (Observer).

**mi|les glo|ri|o|sus** (mī′lēz glôr′ē ō′səs, glōr′-), *pl.* **mi|li|tes glo|ri|o|si** (mil′ə tēz glôr′ē ō′sī, glōr′-). *Latin.* a vain and boastful soldier (from the title and hero of a comedy by Plautus).

**Mi|le|sian**[1] (mī lē′zhən, -shən; mə-), *adj., n. —adj.* Irish: *a racy Milesian brogue* (Herman Melville).
*—n.* a native of Ireland.
[< *Milesius,* a fabled Spanish king whose sons supposedly conquered ancient Ireland + *-ian*]

**Mi|le|sian**[2] (mī lē′zhən, -shən; mə-), *adj., n. —adj.* of or having to do with Miletus, an ancient Greek city of Ionia on the western coast of Asia Minor: *In 499 B.C., the Milesian ruler Aristagoras led the Ionian Greeks in an unsuccessful revolt* [*against the Persians*] (Donald W. Bradeen).
*—n.* a native or inhabitant of Miletus.

**mile|stone** (mīl′stōn′), *n., v.,* **-stoned, -ston|ing.**
*—n.* **1** a stone set up on a road to show the distance in miles to a certain place: *The old milestones along the railroad had fallen over.*
**2** *Figurative.* an important event: *The invention of printing was a milestone in human progress.*
*—v.t.* to mark with milestones: (*Figurative.*) *The road was milestoned by the parched hides ... of horses, mules, and oxen* (J. H. M. Abbott).

**mil|foil** (mil′foil), *n.* = yarrow. [< Old French *milfoil,* learned borrowing from Latin *mīllefolium* < *mīlle* thousand + *folium* leaf]

**mil|i|ar|i|a** (mil′ē ãr′ē ə), *n.* an acute, inflammatory skin disease, located about the sweat glands, characterized by an eruption of spots or blisters resembling millet seeds, accompanied by itching and considerable perspiration, and occurring especially in tropical climates; prickly heat; miliary fever. [< New Latin *miliaria,* feminine of Latin *miliārius* miliary]

**mil|i|ar|y** (mil′ē er′ē, mil′yər ē), *adj.* **1** like a millet seed in size or form. **2** (of a disease) characterized as by eruptions and lesions resembling millet seeds. [< Latin *miliārius* < *milium* millet]

**miliary fever**, **1** = miliaria. **2** = sweating sickness.

**miliary tuberculosis**, tuberculosis characterized by the appearance in various parts of the body of spherical lesions about the size of a millet seed (miliary tubercles), that are caused by tubercle bacilli carried by the bloodstream.

**Mi|li|bis** (mī′lə bis), *n. Trademark.* an arsenical powder administered orally in the treatment of intestinal amebiasis. *Formula:* $C_6H_9AsBiNO_6$

**mi|lieu** (mē lyœ′), *n., pl.* **mi|lieus** (mē lyœz′), **milieux** (mē lyœ′). surroundings; environment: *He* [*man*] *takes the milieu in which he finds himself for granted* (H. G. Wells). [< French *milieu* < *mi* (< Latin *medius* middle) + *lieu* (< Latin *locus* place)]

**mil|i|o|lite** (mil′ē ə līt), *n.* a fossil foraminifer, the minute shells of which, occurring in immense numbers in some strata, are the chief constituent of certain limestones. [< New Latin *Miliola* the genus name (diminutive) < Latin *milium* millet + English *-ite*[1]]

**milit.**, military.

**mil|i|tan|cy** (mil′ə tən sē), *n.* warlike behavior or tendency; militant spirit or policy: *The union is having trouble holding the rising militancy within bounds* (Wall Street Journal).

**mil|i|tant** (mil′ə tənt), *adj., n. —adj.* **1** aggressive; fighting; warlike: *a militant nature. The American Indians became very militant as settlers began to move west.* **SYN**: combative. **2** engaged in warfare; warring. **3** active in serving a cause or in spreading a belief: *a militant churchman, a militant pacifist.* *—n.* a militant person.
[< Latin *mīlitāns, -antis* serving as a soldier, present participle of *mīlitāre* serve as a soldier < *mīles, mīlitis* soldier] — **mil′i|tant|ly**, *adv.* — **mil′i|tant|ness**, *n.*

**mil|i|tar|i|a** (mil′ə ter′ē ə), *n.pl.* a collection of objects having to do with the military, such as firearms, decorations, and uniforms: *During his last years he spent much of his time in trying to gather together writings, militaria, and other possessions left by the Field-Marshal* (London Times). [< Latin *mīlitāria,* neuter plural of *mīlitāris* military]

**mil|i|tar|i|ly** (mil′ə ter′ə lē), *adv.* in a military manner: *This nation will aid these islands militarily if they are threatened* (Wall Street Journal).

**mil|i|tar|i|ness** (mil′ə ter′ē nis), *n.* the state or condition of being military.

**mil|i|ta|rism** (mil′ə tə riz′əm), *n.* **1a** the policy of making military organization and power very strong. **b** the political condition in which the military interest is predominant in government or administration. **2** military spirit and ideals.

**mil|i|ta|rist** (mil′ə tər ist), *n., adj. —n.* **1** a person who believes in a very powerful military organization or the predominance of military interests.
**2** an expert in warfare and military matters.
*—adj.* = militaristic.

**mil|i|ta|ris|tic** (mil′ə tə ris′tik), *adj.* of or having to do with militarists or militarism; characterized by militarism: *militaristic empires.* — **mil′i|ta|ris′ti|cal|ly**, *adv.*

**mil|i|ta|ri|za|tion** (mil′ə tər ə zā′shən), *n.* **1** the act of militarizing: *Superior air power is ... a bulwark against the militarization of society* (Bulletin of Atomic Scientists). **2** the state of being militarized.

**mil|i|ta|rize** (mil′ə tə rīz), *v.t.,* **-rized, -riz|ing.** **1** to make the military organization of (a country) very powerful. **2** to fill with military spirit and ideals.

**mil|i|tar|y** (mil′ə ter′ē), *adj., n. —adj.* **1** of soldiers or war: *military training, military history.* **2** done by soldiers: *military maneuvers.* **3** fit for soldiers: *military discipline.* **4** suitable for war; warlike: *military valor.* **5** supported by armed force: *a military government.*
*—n.* **the military, a** the army; soldiers: *an officer of the military. Haven't you any aquaintances among the military to whom you could show your model* [*of a cannon*]*?* (William D. Howells). **b** the armed forces; military establishment of a country or countries: *Their government is now being run by the military.*
[< Latin *mīlitāris* < *mīles, mīlitis* soldier]
*—Syn. adj.* **1, 4 Military, martial, warlike** mean having to do with war. **Military** emphasizes the idea of war as a serious business, and describes anything having to do with affairs of war or the armed forces (especially the army): *military strength, a military bearing.* **Martial** emphasizes the glory and pomp or the gallantry of fighting men: *martial music.* **Warlike** is applied particularly to aggressive acts or to sentiments that lead to war: *a warlike demonstration. The Iroquois were a warlike people.*

**military attaché**, an officer in one of the armed services serving on the staff of an ambassador, minister, or other diplomat, in a foreign country.

**military fold**, the formal method of folding the United States flag twice lengthwise and then a series of triangular folds.

**mil|i|tar|y-in|dus|tri|al complex** (mil′ə ter′ē in-dus′trē əl), the military branch of a government and all of the businesses supplying its needs: *We hear many dark mutterings about the vested interest of the military-industrial complex in war ...* (Harper's).

**military law**, a system of rules regulating the government of armed forces and the discipline and control of persons employed in military service.
► **military law, martial law.** *Military law* is limited only to military personnel. *Martial law* applies to both citizens and soldiers, and operates in place of civil law when civil courts are prevented from functioning.

**military police**, soldiers or marines who act as police for the Army or Marine Corps. *Abbr:* M.P., MP (no periods).

**military press**, a weight-lifting exercise in which the bar is lifted from the floor, brought to rest against the chest, and raised above the head at the signal from the referee.

**military school**, a private school run like a military post.

**military science**, the study of tactics, strategy, logistics, engineering, and communications, and other aspects of conducting war.

**mil|i|tate** (mil′ə tāt), *v.i.,* **-tat|ed, -tat|ing.** **1** to have or exert force; act; work; operate (against or in favor of): *Bad weather militated against the success of the picnic. Passion, in him, comprehended many of the worst emotions which militate against human happiness* (Edward G. Bulwer-Lytton). **SYN**: contend. **2** *Obsolete.* to serve in an army; be a soldier. [< Latin *mīlitāre* (with English *-ate*[1]) serve as a soldier < *mīles, mīlitis* soldier]

**mil|i|ta|tion** (mil′ə tā′shən), *n.* = conflict.

**mi|li|tia** (mə lish′ə), *n.* **1** a military force; army of citizens who are not regular soldiers but who undergo training for emergency duty or national defense. Every state of the United States has a militia called the National Guard. **2** an authorized but unorganized military force consisting of the entire body of able-bodied men in the United States or its territories who have reached the age of 18 and are not more than 45, who are or propose to become citizens, and who are not members of a National Guard or any of the regular armed services. **3** any citizens' army; any nonprofessional armed force organized or summoned to duty in an emergency. [earlier the military art; later, administration < Latin *mīlitia* < *mīles, mīlitis* soldier]

**mi|li|tia|man** (mə lish′ə mən), *n., pl.* **-men.** a soldier in the militia.

**Pronunciation Key:** hat, āge, cãre, fär; let, ēqual, tėrm; it, īce; hot, ōpen, ôrder; oil, out; cup, pu̇t, rüle; child; long; thin; ᴛʜen; zh, measure; ə represents **a** in about, **e** in taken, **i** in pencil, **o** in lemon, **u** in circus.

**mil|i|um** (mil′ē əm), *n.* a hard, white or yellow tubercle in the skin resembling a millet seed, produced by the retention of a sebaceous secretion. [< New Latin *milium* < Latin, millet]

**Mil|i|um** (mil′ē əm), *n. Trademark.* a fabric sprayed with a metal solution, especially of aluminum, used as a lining to insulate against cold.

**milk** (milk), *n., v.* **—*n.*** **1** the white liquid secreted by female mammals for the nourishment of their young, especially cow's milk, which we drink and use in cooking. Milk is the source of butter, cheese, and cream. **2** any kind of liquid resembling this, such as the white juice of a plant, tree, or nut: *the milk of the coconut.*
**—*v.t.*** **1a** to draw milk from (a cow, goat, ewe, or other mammal); secure the milk available in the udder of (a cow, goat, ewe, or other mammal). **b** to extract or draw (milk): *12 quarts were milked from that cow.* **2** *Figurative.* to drain contents, strength, information, wealth, or other resource from; exploit: *to milk a company of its resources. The dishonest treasurer milked the club treasury.* **3** to draw juice, poison, or other liquid, from: *to milk a snake.*
**—*v.i.*** to yield or produce milk.
**cry over spilt milk,** to waste sorrow or regret on what has happened and cannot be remedied: *The money is lost, so there's no use in crying over spilt milk.*
[Old English *mioluc, milc*]

**milk adder,** = milk snake.

**milk-and-wa|ter** (milk′ən wô′tər, -wot′ər), *adj.* weak or insipid, like milk diluted with water; wishy-washy.

**milk bar,** a food counter specializing in dairy drinks and dairy products, such as ice cream or yogurt; soda fountain: *Even alcoholic Paris, thank Heaven, is being infiltrated with milk bars* (Harper's).

**milk car,** a railroad tank car used to transport milk.

**milk chocolate,** a chocolate candy whose basic ingredients are chocolate liquor, whole milk solids, and granulated sugar.

**milk|er** (mil′kər), *n.* **1** a person who milks. **2** a machine that milks. **3** any animal that gives milk, especially a cow.

**milk fat,** fat in milk containing vitamins A, D, E, and K, traces of lecithin and cholesterol, and carotene; butterfat: *Milk fat ... provides energy and essential fatty acids that our bodies cannot make* (Glenn H. Beck).

**milk fever,** **1** a slight fever sometimes occurring in women about the beginning of lactation, originally believed to be caused by a great accumulation of milk in the breasts, now thought to be caused by an infection. **2** a disease occurring in milch cows, especially before or after calving, characterized by low sugar and calcium content of the blood and paralysis (actually not a fever).

**milk|fish** (milk′fish′), *n., pl.* **-fish|es** or (*collectively*) **-fish.** an edible fish of the South Pacific, related to the herrings and having a small, toothless mouth and a length of up to 4 feet.

**milk float,** *British.* a light wagon or cart, usually pulled by a horse or run by an electric motor, used to carry and deliver milk.

**milk glass,** = opal glass.

**milk|house** (milk′hous′), *n.* a room or building in a dairy where fresh milk is stored.

**milk|i|ly** (mil′kə lē), *adv.* in a milky manner; with a milky appearance.

**milk|i|ness** (mil′kē nis), *n.* the condition of being milky or of resembling milk in appearance or quality.

**milk|ing** (mil′king), *n.* the amount of milk obtained at one time.

**milking machine,** an apparatus for milking cows mechanically.

**Milking Shorthorn,** any one of a breed of dairy cattle developed from the shorthorn cattle.

**milking stool,** a stool for sitting on while milking a cow or other animal.

**milk leg,** or **milk-leg** (milk′leg′), *n.* a painful swelling of the leg caused by clots in the veins, usually due to an inflammation after childbirth.

**milk|less** (milk′lis), *adj.* without milk; not secreting milk.

**milk-liv|ered** (milk′liv′ərd), *adj.* cowardly; white-livered: *Milk-liver'd man! That bear'st a cheek for blows* (Shakespeare).

**milk|maid** (milk′mād′), *n.* **1** a woman who milks cows: *The cow kicked the milkmaid.* **2** a woman who works in a dairy: *The milkmaids made the cheese.* **SYN:** dairymaid.

**milk name,** the third name customarily given in a Chinese family, corresponding to a given name.

**milk|man** (milk′man′), *n., pl.* **-men.** a man who sells milk or delivers it to customers.

**milk|o** (mil′kō), *n. Australian Slang.* a milkman.

**milk of human kindness,** natural sympathy and affection.

**milk of magnesia,** a milk-white medicine used as a mild laxative and antacid. It consists of magnesium hydroxide suspended in water.

**milk punch,** alcoholic liquor such as whiskey or brandy, mixed with milk, sugar, and other flavorings.

**milk room,** a cool room in which milk and other food or stores of a household are kept.

**milk run,** *Slang.* a routine flight, especially a short reconnaissance or supply mission.

**milk shake,** a beverage consisting of milk, flavoring, and often ice cream, shaken or beaten until frothy.

**milk|shed** (milk′shed′), *n.* **1** the region from which a city or an area receives its milk supply: *the New York City milkshed.* **2** a shed where cows are milked. [< *milk* + *shed,* as in *watershed*]

**milk sickness,** a disease, formerly common in the western United States, characterized by weakness, trembling, and vomiting, and caused by the consumption of dairy products or meat from cattle that have eaten any one of various poisonous plants, especially the white snakeroot; trembles.

**milk snake,** any one of several harmless, tricolored, blotched or ringed snakes of North America, which are constrictors of the same genus as the king snakes. One kind is sometimes confused with the copperhead. Milk snakes are traditionally, but wrongly, supposed to milk cows; house snake.

**milk|sop** (milk′sop′), *n.* an unmanly fellow; coward: *He was no milksop; he rode, and shot, and fenced* (Lytton Strachey). **SYN:** mollycoddle. [< *milk* + *sop*]

**milk|sop|ism** (milk′sop′iz əm), *n.* the character of a milksop; effeminacy.

**milk sugar,** = lactose.

**milk|toast** (milk′tōst′), *n.* = milquetoast.

**milk toast,** toast served with or in (usually hot) milk.

**milk tooth,** *pl.* **milk teeth.** one of the first set of teeth, of which man has twenty; temporary tooth of a young child or animal.

**milk train,** *U.S.* a train that carries milk to the market, usually very early in the morning.

**milk tusk,** either one of a young elephant's tusks which never grow more than two inches long and are shed before it is two years old.

**milk vetch,** **1** a European herb of the pea family, thought to increase the amount of milk secreted by goats feeding upon it. **2** any of several allied herbs.

**milk|weed** (milk′wēd′), *n.* **1** a weed with white juice that looks like milk and seeds tufted with long, silky hairs; silkweed. Milkweed is an herb of North America and Africa. *One of the most attractive milkweeds is the brilliant butterfly weed* (Earl L. Core). **2** any one of various other plants having a milky juice, such as the butterfly weed.

**milkweed butterfly,** **1** = monarch butterfly. **2** any one of the related butterflies whose larvae feed on milkweed.

**milkweed family,** a large group of dicotyledonous herbs and shrubs, typically having a milky juice and bearing flowers in clusters. The family includes the milkweed, anglepod, and waxplant.

**milk-white** (milk′hwīt′), *adj.* white as milk.

**milk|wort** (milk′wėrt′), *n.* **1** any one of a group of showy-flowered plants, formerly thought to increase the secretion of milk in women; polygala: *I was equally glad to see and photograph the orange milkwort* (New York Times). **2** a plant of the primrose family, common on the seacoast and in salt marshes, having small, purplish-white flowers; sea milkwort.

**milk|y** (mil′kē), *adj.,* **milk|i|er, milk|i|est.** **1** like milk; white as milk; whitish: *Milky dribbles of melting vanilla ice cream ran down his cone.* **2** of milk; containing milk: *the milkweed with its milky autumn pods.* **3** *Figurative.* mild; weak; timid: *They made ... me* (*the milkiest of men*) *a satirist* (Byron).

**milky disease,** a disease that kills the larvae of Japanese beetles and other scarabaeids, caused by a type of bacteria that sporulates in the soil.

**Milky Way,** **1** a broad band of faint light that stretches across the sky at night. It is made up of countless stars and luminous clouds of gas, too far away to be seen separately without a telescope. *The Milky Way is an island universe composed of millions of stars grouped in the shape of a flat disc that turns like a great wheel in space* (Scientific American). **2** the galaxy in which these countless stars are found; Galaxy. The earth, sun, and all the planets around the sun are part of the Milky Way. [translation of Latin *Via Lactea; Via* way; *lactea,* feminine of *lacteus* < *lac, lactis* milk]

**mill[1]** (mil), *n., v.* **—*n.*** **1** a machine for grinding grain into flour or meal: *the crush of grain between the heavy stones of the mill.* **2** a building specially designed and fitted with machinery for the grinding of grain into flour: *A dusty miller appeared at a window of the mill.* **3a** any machine for crushing or grinding: *a coffee mill, a pepper mill.* **b** a machine designed to extract juices by grinding or crushing: *a cider mill.* **4** a building where manufacturing is done: *Cotton cloth is made in a cotton mill.* **5** a roller of hardened steel having impressed upon it a pattern that is transferred by pressure to a cylinder (for printing cloth) or plate (for printing currency, bonds, and the like). **6** a machine that performs its work by rotary motion, especially one used by lapidaries in polishing precious stones. **7** a machine with rotary cutters or rollers for working metal. **8** any one of various other machines for performing certain operations upon material in the process of manufacture. **9** *Slang.* a fight with the fists.
**—*v.t.*** **1** to grind (grain) into flour or meal: *The Indians pounded grain to mill it into flour.* **2** to grind into powder or pulp; grind very fine: *The passing cars milled the leaves that fell on the road.* **3** to manufacture. **4** to cut a series of fine notches or ridges on the edge of (a coin): *A dime is milled; a nickel is not.*
**—*v.i.*** **1** to move about in a circle in a confused way: *Cattle sometimes mill around when they are frightened.* **2** *Slang.* to fight with the fists; box.
**go through the mill,** *Informal.* **a** to get a thorough training or experience: *He is an excellent soldier, having gone through the mill at military school.* **b** to learn by hard or painful experience: *He went through the mill in that business undertaking.*
**put through the mill,** *Informal.* **a** to test; examine; try out: *The new car was put through the mill.* **b** to teach by hard or painful experience: *He was put through the military mill during basic training.*
[Old English *mylen* < Late Latin *molīna, molīnum,* (originally) adjectives, Latin *molīnus* having to do with a mill < *mola* millstone, mill]

**mill[2]** (mil), *n.* $.001, or 1/10 of a cent, used especially in expressing tax rates. Mills are used in figuring but not as coins. [American English, short for Latin *millēsimus* one thousandth < *mīlle* thousand]

**mill|a|ble** (mil′ə bəl), *adj.* that can be milled; suitable for milling: *It also put out last week its first guide prices for ... millable wheat* (London Times).

**mill|age** (mil′ij), *n.* a rate of taxation expressed in mills per dollar.

**mill|board** (mil′bôrd′, -bōrd′), *n.* a stout board made of wastepaper or pulp, used for the covers of books.

**mill cake,** the cake or mass resulting from the incorporation of the ingredients of gunpowder, preliminary to granulation.

**mill|course** (mil′kôrs′, -kōrs′), *n.* = millrace.

**mill|dam** (mil′dam′), *n.* **1** a dam built across a stream to supply water power for a mill. **2** a pond made by such a dam; millpond.

**mille** (mēl), *n.* an Arabic unit of linear measure, equal to 119 miles. [< Arabic *mīl*]

**milled** (mild), *adj.* made or formed by milling.

**mille|feuille** (mēl′fœy′), *n.* a thin, crusty, sweet French pastry made in several layers with flour, butter, and eggs and with a cream filling between each layer; napoleon. [< French *mille-feuille*]

**mil|le|fi|o|ri glass** (mil′ə fē ôr′ē, -ōr′-), ornamental glassware made by fusing small glass tubes or rods of various colors together lengthwise and cutting the fused mass into cross sections that are then embedded in clear glass or treated in some other way. [< Italian *mille-fiori* (literally) thousand flowers]

**mille|fleurs[1]** (mēl′flœr′), *adj.* showing a design or pattern of many flowers, as of cloth, paintings, or tapestries: *A rare Gothic Flemish tapestry of the "millefleurs" type, a weaving closely studded with bluebells, columbines, and other flowers ...* (New Yorker). [< French *mille-fleurs* (literally) a thousand flowers]

**mille|fleurs[2]** (mēl′flœr′), *n.* a perfume containing extracts from a variety of flowers. [< French (*eau de*) *mille-fleurs* (water of) a thousand flowers]

**mil|le|nar|i|an** (mil′ə nãr′ē ən), *adj., n.* **—*adj.*** **1** of or relating to a thousand. **2** *Theology.* of or having to do with the prophesied millennium.
**—*n.*** *Theology.* a believer in the millennium, especially one who believes it will come soon; chiliast.

**mil|le|nar|i|an|ism** (mil′ə nãr′ē ə niz′əm), *n.* the doctrine of or belief in the millennium.

**mil|le|nar|y** (mil′ə ner′ē), *adj., n., pl.* **-nar|ies.**
**—*adj.*** **1** consisting of or having to do with a thousand, especially a period of a thousand years. **2** *Theology.* of or having to do with the millennium or millenarians.
**—*n.*** **1a** an aggregate of one thousand, especially a continuous period of one thousand years: *We danced through three nights, dancing the old millenary out, dancing the new millenary in* (Cardinal Newman). **b** a thousandth anniversary or the celebration of such an anniversary. **2** *Theol-*

*ogy.* **a** a millennium; the millennium. **b** = millenarian.
[< Late Latin *mīllēnārius* < *mīllēnī* a thousand each < *mīlle* a thousand]

**mil|len|ni|al** (mə len′ē əl), *adj., n.* —*adj.* **1** of a thousand years. **2** *Theology.* having to do with a millennium, especially the prophesied millennium. **3** *Figurative.* like that of the millennium; fit for the millennium: *There was to be a millennial abundance of new gates ... and returns of ten per cent* (George Eliot).
—*n.* a thousandth anniversary or its celebration; millenary. —**mil|len′ni|al|ly,** *adv.*

**Millennial Church,** the Shakers.

**mil|len|ni|al|ist** (mə len′ē ə list), *n.* = millenarian.

**mil|len|ni|an|ism** (mə len′ē ə niz′əm), *n.* = millenarianism: *Always, each outburst of millennianism has its prophetic leader* (London Times).

**mil|len|ni|a|ry** (mə len′ē ə rē), *adj.* = millennial.

**mil|len|ni|um** (mə len′ē əm), *n., pl.* **-len|ni|ums, -len|ni|a** (-len′ē ə). **1a** a period of one thousand years: *The Christian Era is less than two millenniums old; the world is many millenniums old.* **b** a thousandth anniversary. **2** the period of a thousand years during which, according to the Bible, Christ is expected to reign on earth. **3** *Figurative.* a period of righteousness and happiness, of just government, or of peace and prosperity: *a catastrophic climax which would be followed by something in the nature of a millennium* (Edmund Wilson). [< New Latin *millennium* < Latin *mīlle* thousand + *annus* year, patterned on English *biennium*]

**mil|le|ped** (mil′ə ped), *n.* = millipede.

**mil|le|pede** (mil′ə pēd), *n.* = millipede.

**mil|le|pore** (mil′ə pôr, -pōr), *n.* any one of various corallike hydrozoans covered with very small openings and bearing tentacles with powerful stings. [< New Latin *millepora* < Latin *mīlle* thousand + *porus* pore]

**mil|le|po|rine** (mil′ə pôr′in, -pōr′-), *adj.* having to do with the millepores or having their characteristics.

**mill|er** (mil′ər), *n.* **1a** a person who owns or runs a mill, especially a flour mill. **b** a person who operates any machine called a mill. **2** a moth whose wings look as if they were powdered with flour. **3a** = milling machine. **b** a tool used in a milling machine.

**mill|er|ite** (mil′ə rīt), *n.* a mineral, nickel sulfide, usually occurring in brassy or bronze crystals or in incrustations. *Formula:* NiS [< German *Millerit* < W. H. *Miller,* 1801-1880, a British mineralogist + *-it* -ite[1]]

**Mill|er|ite** (mil′ə rīt), *n.* an Adventist following the doctrine of William Miller, an American preacher, who foretold the second coming of Christ and the beginning of the millennium which would occur in the immediate future: *The Millerites ... believed that the world would be destroyed by fire in 1843* (New Yorker).

**mill|er's-thumb** (mil′ərz thum′), *n.* any one of various small, spiny-finned, freshwater fishes; sculpin.

**mil|les|i|mal** (mə les′ə məl), *adj., n.* —*adj.* **1** = thousandth. **2** consisting of thousandth parts. **3** dealing with thousandths.
—*n.* a thousandth part.
[< Latin *mīllēsimus* a thousandth (< *mīlle* thousand) + English *-al*[1]] —**mil|les′i|mal|ly,** *adv.*

**mil|let** (mil′it), *n.* **1** a very small grain used for food in Europe, Asia, and Africa. **2** the plant that it grows on. In the United States and Europe, millet is used for hay. Millet is an annual cereal grass bearing a large crop of nutritious seeds on a drooping terminal panicle. It is probably native to India, but has been extensively cultivated throughout history as a food grain. **2** any one of various other grasses grown for their seeds or for forage, such as durra or Indian millet, pearl millet, or Italian millet. **3** the grain or seed of any of these plants. [< Middle French *millet* (diminutive) < *mil* millet < Latin *milium*]

**mill hand,** a worker in any type of mill; millman: *The Pacific Northwest's great experiment in turning plywood mill hands into capitalists* (Wall Street Journal).

**mill|house** (mil′hous′), *n.* a building in which milling is done.

**milli-,** *combining form.* one thousandth of a ______: *Millimeter = one thousandth of a meter.* [< Latin *mīlli-* < *mīlle*]

**mil|li|am|me|ter** (mil′ē am′mē′tər), *n.* an ammeter which measures thousandths of amperes: *A milliammeter, used to measure small electric currents, is constructed so that blind persons can feel its raised dial markings* (Science News Letter).

**mil|li|amp** (mil′ē amp′), *n.* = milliampere.

**mil|li|am|pere** (mil′ē am′pir), *n.* a unit for measuring electric current equal to one thousandth of an ampere. *Abbr:* ma.

**mil|li|ang|strom** (mil′ə ang′strəm), *n.* one thousandth of an angstrom. *Abbr:* mA.

**mil|liard** (mil′yərd, -yärd), *n. British.* a thousand millions; billion; 1,000,000,000. [< Middle French *milliard,* alteration of *million,* influenced by Latin *mīlliārius* containing a thousand < *mīlle* thousand]
▶ **Milliard** is the usual term for this number in Great Britain and most of Europe. The term *billion* is synonymous with *milliard* in the French system, and is applied by the British, Germans, and others, to the number 1,000,000,000,000, known as a *trillion* in the United States and France.

**mil|li|ar|y** (mil′ē er′ē), *adj., n., pl.* **-ar|ies.** —*adj.* of, having to do with, or using the ancient Roman mile of a thousand paces.
—*n.* = milestone.
[< Latin *mīlliārium* a mile (stone), neuter adjective < *mīlle* (*passuum*); see etym. under **mile**]

**mil|li|bar** (mil′ə bär), *n.* a measure of atmospheric pressure equal to 1,000 dynes per square centimeter. Standard atmospheric pressure at sea level is about 1,013 millibars or 14.69 pounds per square inch. Thirty-four millibars are about equal to one inch of mercury. *Abbr:* mb. [< *milli-* + *bar*[3]]

**mil|li|barn** (mil′ə bärn′), *n. Nuclear Physics.* one thousandth of a barn. [< *milli-* + *barn* (def. 4)]

**mil|li|cron** (mil′ə kron), *n.* = micromillimeter.

**mil|li|cu|rie** (mil′ə kyůr′ē), *n.* one thousandth of a curie: *One millicurie of radium expels thirty million alpha particles per second* (Science News). *Abbr:* mc (no period).

**mil|li|de|gree** (mil′ə di′grē), *n.* one thousandth of a degree: *... procedures capable of lowering the temperature range accessible for research to within millidegrees of absolute zero* (Scientific American).

**mil|lieme** (mēl yem′), *n.* a unit of money in Egypt, Libya, and the Sudan, worth one thousandth of the country's basic monetary unit. [< French *millième* < Latin *millesimus* thousandth]

**mil|li|e|quiv|a|lent** (mil′ē i kwiv′ə lənt), *n.* one thousandth of the value of an equivalent weight. *Abbr:* meq.

**mil|lier** (mēl yā′), *n.* = metric ton. [< French *millier* < Old French, having 1,000 < *mille* a thousand < Latin *mīlia,* plural of *mīlle*]

**mil|li|far|ad** (mil′ə far′əd, -ad), *n.* one thousandth of a farad. *Abbr:* mf.

**mil|li|gal** (mil′ə gal), *n.* a measure of gravity, one thousandth of a gal, equal to an acceleration of one thousandth of a centimeter per second.

**mil|li|gram** (mil′ə gram), *n.* one thousandth of a gram, equal to 0.0154 of a grain, or about two millionths of a pound. *Abbr:* mg.

**mil|li|gramme** (mil′ə gram), *n. British.* milligram.

**mil|li|hen|ry** (mil′ə hen′rē), *n., pl.* **-ries** or **-rys.** one thousandth of a henry. *Abbr:* mh.

**mil|li|li|ter** (mil′ə lē′tər), *n.* one thousandth of a liter, equal to 1.000027 cubic centimeters, 0.061 cubic inch, or 0.0338 fluid ounce. *Abbr:* ml.

**mil|li|li|tre** (mil′ə lē′tər), *n. British.* milliliter.

**mil|lime** (mil′im, -ēm), *n.* a unit of money in Tunisia, equal to 1/1000 dinar. [alteration of French *millième* thousandth, millieme]

**mil|li|me|ter** (mil′ə mē′tər), *n.* one thousandth of a meter, equal to 0.03937 inch. *Abbr:* mm (no period). See picture under **inch**[1].

**mil|li|me|tre** (mil′ə mē′tər), *n. British.* millimeter.

**mil|li|met|ric** (mil′ə met′rik), *adj.* of or having to do with the millimeter or any system of measurement based on it.

**mil|li|mi|cron** (mil′ə mī′kron), *n., pl.* **-crons, -cra** (-krə). a unit of length equal to one thousandth of a micron.

**mil|li|mi|cro|sec|ond** (mil′ə mī′krō sek′ənd), *n.* one thousandth of a microsecond: *Accuracy is said to be within a fraction of a millimicrosecond* (Science News Letter).

**mil|li|mole** (mil′ə mōl′), *n. Chemistry.* one thousandth of a gram molecule. [< *milli-* + *mole*[5]]

**mil|line** (mil′līn′), *n. U.S.* a unit used in buying and selling advertising space, representing one 5½-point (agate) line, one column wide, in one million copies of a newspaper, magazine, or similar publication. [< *mil*(lion) + *line*]

**mil|li|ner** (mil′ə nər), *n.* **1** a person who makes, trims, or sells women's hats. **2** *Obsolete.* a dealer in fancy wares and articles of apparel, especially those originally of Milan manufacture. [earlier *myllener,* variant of *Milaner,* a dealer in goods from *Milan,* Italy, famous for its straw work]

**mil|li|ner|y** (mil′ə ner′ē, -nər-), *n., pl.* **-ner|ies.** **1** women's hats: *Some women use elaborate millinery to attract attention.* **2** the business of making, trimming, or selling women's hats: *The capital of millinery is still Paris.* **3** articles made or sold by milliners.

**mill|ing** (mil′ing), *n.* **1** the business of grinding grain in a mill. **2** manufacturing. **3** the act or process of cutting notches or ridges on the edge of a coin. **4** such notches or ridges. **5** *Slang.* a thrashing.

**milling machine,** a machine tool with rotary cutters for working metal.

**mil|li|ohm** (mil′ē ōm′), *n.* one thousandth of an ohm.

**mil|lion** (mil′yən), *n., adj.* —*n.* **1** one thousand thousand; 1,000,000: *1 million days is 2,740 years. Abbr:* m. **2** a very large number; very many: *millions of fish. She can always think of millions of reasons for not helping with the dishes.* **3** a million coins or units of money of account of some understood value, especially a million dollars or British pounds: *He left an estate of over a million.*
—*adj.* **1** one thousand thousand; 1,000,000. **2** very large number of; very many: *a million thanks.*
**the million,** the multitude; the masses: *The play ... pleased not the million* (Shakespeare).
[Old French *million* < Italian *milione* < *mille* thousand < Latin *mīlle*]

**mil|lion|aire** or **mil|lion|naire** (mil′yə nãr′), *n.* **1** a person whose wealth amounts to a million or more dollars, pounds, francs, or the like. **2** a very wealthy person: *Only a millionaire could afford these prices.* SYN: Croesus, Midas.

**mil|lion|aire|dom** or **mil|lion|naire|dom** (mil′yə-nãr′dəm), *n.* **1** the condition of being a millionaire. **2** millionaires considered as a group.

**mil|lion|air|ess** or **mil|lion|nair|ess** (mil′yə nãr′-is), *n.* a woman millionaire.

**mil|lion|ar|y** (mil′yə ner′ē; *especially British* mil′-yə nər ē), *adj., n., pl.* **-aries.** —*adj.* possessing millions, as of money: *these millionary people* (Rudyard Kipling).
—*n.* = millionaire.

**mil|lioned** (mil′yənd), *adj.* **1** numbered by the million. **2** possessed of millions, as of money.

**mil|lion|fold** (mil′yən fōld′), *adv., adj.* a million times as much or as many: *a millionfold increase* (adj.), *to increase a millionfold* (adv.).

**mil|lionth** (mil′yənth), *adj., n.* **1** last in a series of one million. **2** one, or being one, of a million equal parts.

**mil|li|ped** (mil′ə ped), *n.* = millipede.

***mil|li|pede** (mil′ə pēd), *n.* any one of a class of small, wormlike arthropods having a body consisting of many segments, most of which bear two pairs of legs; diplopod: *Millipedes do not rank as a major agricultural pest* (Science News). Also, **milleped, millepede, milliped.** [< Latin *mīllepeda* < *mīlle* thousand + *pēs, pedis* foot]

***millipede**

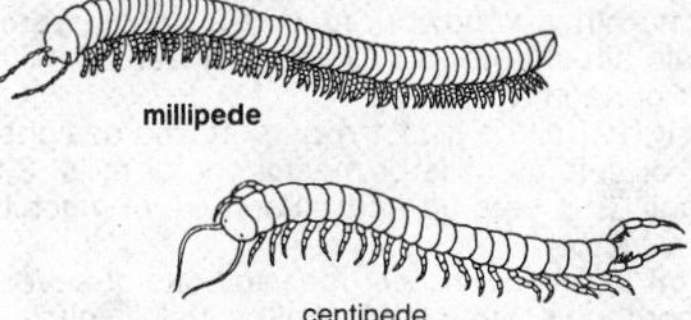


**Mil|li|pore** (mil′ə pôr, -pōr), *n. Trademark.* a plastic, semipermeable membrane of molecular dimension, used to filter bacteria from water, air, or other fluid, and in surgical operations to repair and protect tissues: *The apparatus consisted of a Millipore filter soaked in haemoglobin solution* (New Scientist).

**mil|li|pound** (mil′ə pound′), *n.* one thousandth of a pound: *NASA has ... determined that the 6.3 millipound-thrust ion engine would not interfere with radio transmission* (Science News).

**mil|li|rad** (mil′ə rad), *n.* one thousandth of a rad.

**mil|li|rem** (mil′ə rem), *n.* one thousandth of a rem.

**mil|li|roent|gen** (mil′ə rent′gən), *n.* one thousandth of a roentgen: *The present level of radiostrontium in the bones of young children ... is about two milliroentgens per year* (Science News Letter).

**mil|li|sec** (mil′ə sek), *n.* = millisecond.

**mil|li|sec|ond** (mil′ə sek′ənd), *n.* one thousandth of a second: *delayed in time by several hundred milliseconds* (Science News). *Abbr:* ms (no period).

**mil|li|stere** (mil′ə stir), *n.* a unit of volume in the metric system, equal to one thousandth of a stere, or one cubic decimeter.

**mil|li|volt** (mil′ə vōlt′), *n.* a unit of electrical voltage, equivalent to one thousandth of a volt.

**mil|li|watt** (mil′ə wot′), *n.* one thousandth of a watt.

**mill|man** (mil′man′, -mən), *n., pl.* **-men.** **1** a

**Pronunciation Key:** hat, āge, cãre, fär; let, ēqual, tėrm; it, īce; hot, ōpen, ôrder; oil, out; cup, půt, rüle; child; long; thin; ᴛʜen; zh, measure; ə represents **a** in about, **e** in taken, **i** in pencil, **o** in lemon, **u** in circus.

worker in any type of mill: *Miners and millmen agreed to return to work after negotiation of a new one-year contract* (Wall Street Journal).
**2** Also, **mill man.** *Informal.* a person who owns or operates a mill.

**✱mill|pond** (mil′pond′), *n.* **1** a pond supplying water to drive a mill wheel, especially such a pond formed by a milldam. See picture below. **2** the Atlantic, especially that part of the ocean crossed by ships passing between Great Britain and North America (used in a humorous way).

**✱mill|race** (mil′rās′), *n.* **1** the current of water that drives a mill wheel: *The millrace is fast enough to run a large wheel.* **2** the trough in which the water flows to the mill: *The millrace collapsed under the weight of the ice.* **SYN**: sluice. See picture below.

**Mills bomb** or **grenade** (milz), a type of hand grenade long standard in the British and many other armies, about the size and shape of a goose egg and weighing about 1½ pounds: *Our retaliation was to put twelve Mills bombs into the building* (Lord Louis Mountbatten). [< Sir William *Mills,* 1856-1932, a British inventor]

**✱mill|stone** (mil′stōn′), *n.* **1** either of a pair of round, flat stones used for grinding corn, wheat, or other grain. The upper millstone rotates upon the lower millstone. *An enormous millstone, a relic of the original mill, is imbedded in the terrace* (Wall Street Journal). See picture below. **2** a type of stone, especially a hard sandstone suitable for the making of millstones. **3** *Figurative.* a heavy burden: *The widow worked hard to carry the millstone of a large family.* **4** *Figurative.* anything that grinds or crushes: *the millstone of war.*

**mill|stream** (mil′strēm′), *n.* the stream in a millrace.

**✱mill wheel,** a wheel that is turned by water and supplies power for a mill.

**✱mill wheel**

**mill|work** (mil′wėrk′), *n.* **1** doors, windows, moldings, and other woodwork made separately from the main structure of a building in a planing mill. **2** work done in a mill.

**mill|wright** (mil′rīt′), *n.* **1** a person who designs, builds, or sets up mills or machinery for mills. **2** a mechanic who sets up and takes care of machinery in a factory.

**mi|lo** (mī′lo, mil′ō), *n., pl.* **-los.** any one of several grain sorghums with slender, pithy stalks, introduced into the United States soon after 1880, and cultivated for grain and forage. [< Sesotho *maili*]

**mil|om|e|ter** (mī lom′ə tər), *n. British.* an instrument that registers the number of miles traveled by an automobile or other motor vehicle. [< *mil*(e) + *-ometer,* as in *speedometer*]

**Mi|lon|tin** (mī lon′tin), *n. Trademark.* an anticonvulsant administered orally in the treatment of petit mal. *Formula:* $C_{11}H_{11}NO_2$

**mi|lor** (mi lôr′), *n.* = milord.

**mi|lord** (mi lôrd′, -lôr′), *n.* **1** my lord. **2** an English lord, nobleman, or gentleman. [< French *milord* < English *my lord,* a phrase of address]
► **Milord** originated as an appellation used by continental Europeans in speaking to or of an English lord, and subsequently came to be applied to any wealthy Englishman. A further general extension to any well-to-do, or seemingly well-to-do, English-speaking male, paralleling the development of **milady,** has not taken place.

**mil|pa** (mil′pä), *n.* a field in Central America made by clearing the jungle, farmed for only a few seasons, after which it is abandoned. [< Mexican Spanish *milpa*]

**milque|toast** or **Milque|toast** (milk′tōst′), *n.* an extremely timid person: *Foreign policy planners fear the U.S. gets a Milquetoast reputation abroad* (Wall Street Journal). [< the comic strip character, Caspar *Milquetoast,* probably < *milk toast*]

**mil|reis** (mil′rās′), *n., pl.* **-reis. 1** a former Brazilian silver coin and monetary unit, worth 1,000 reis. **2** an old Portuguese gold coin. [< Portuguese *milreis* (literally) a thousand reis < *mil* (< Latin *mīlle* a thousand) + *reis,* plural of *real* (literally) regal, or royal (coin) < Latin *regālis*]

**milt¹** (milt), *n., v.* — *n.* **1** the sperm cells of male fishes with the milky fluid containing them. **2** the reproductive gland in male fishes when containing this fluid.
— *v.t.* to impregnate (fish eggs) with milt.
[perhaps < Middle Dutch *milte* milt of fish, spleen; influenced by Middle English *milk* milt of fish]

**milt²** (milt), *n.* = spleen. [Old English *milte*]

**milt|er** (mil′tər), *n.* a male fish in breeding season.

**Mil|to|ni|an** (mil tō′nē ən), *adj.* = Miltonic.

**Mil|ton|ic** (mil ton′ik), *adj.* **1** of or having to do with John Milton (1608-1674). **2** resembling Milton's literary style; solemn and majestic.

**Mil|town** (mil′toun), *n. Trademark.* meprobamate.

**mil|vine** (mil′vīn, -vin), *adj.* having to do with or resembling the kites (birds). [< Latin *milvus* kite + English *-ine*¹]

**Mil|wau|kee|an** (mil wô′kē ən), *n.* a native or inhabitant of Milwaukee, Wisconsin.

**mim** (mim), *adj. Dialect.* primly quiet; affectedly modest; prim. [imitative]

**✱mim|bar** (mim′bär), *n.* the pulpit in a mosque. [< Arabic *minbar*]

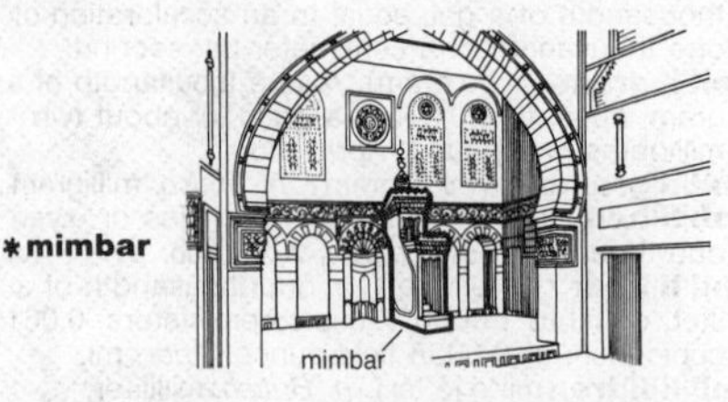

**✱mimbar**

**mime** (mīm), *n., v.,* **mimed, mim|ing.** — *n.* **1** a mimic, jester, clown, or buffoon: *Della Scala stood among his courtiers with mimes and buffoons ... making him heartily merry* (Thomas Carlyle). **2** among the ancient Greeks and Romans: **a** a farce using funny actions and gestures and the ludicrous representation of familiar types and events: *No more shall wayward grief abuse The genial hour with mask and mime* (Tennyson). **b** an actor in such a farce. **c** a dialogue written for it. **3** an actor or dancer. **4a** = pantomimist. **b** = pantomime: *the art of mime.*
— *v.t.* **1** to imitate; mimic: *miming Chinese laundrymen, Swedish servant girls and balloon-pants Dutch comics* (Time). **2** to act or play (a part), usually without words: *A gang of leaping fiends ... introduced a horrid wizard (mimed by Frederick Ashton)* (Time).
— *v.i.* to act without using words; act in a pantomime.
[< Latin *mīmus* < Greek *mîmos*] — **mim′er,** *n.*

**mim|e|o** (mim′ē ō), *n., v.* **mim|e|oed, mim|e|o|ing.** *Informal.* — *n.* a mimeographed bulletin, newsletter, memorandum, or other copy.
— *v.t.* to mimeograph: *We learn later that the statement was mimeoed* (Harper's).
[short for *mimeograph*]

**mim|e|o|graph** (mim′ē ə graf, -gräf), *n., v.* — *n.* a machine for making copies of written or typewritten materials by means of stencils.
— *v.t.* to make (copies) with a mimeograph: *A resolution ... was mimeographed on official conference stationery* (New York Times).
[< American English *Mimeograph* (originally a trademark) < Greek *mīmeîsthai* imitate + English *-graph*]

**mi|me|sis** (mi mē′sis, mī-), *n.* **1** imitation; mimicry. **2** resemblance of one animal to another or to its surroundings, which gives protection; mimicry. **3** Also, **mimosis.** the assuming by one disease of the symptoms of another. **4** imitation or reproduction of the supposed words of another, in order to represent his character. **5** the representation, by means of details from ordinary life, of reality in works of literature or art: *It implies an attempt to deny that art itself is art, a mimesis, a make-believe* (Atlantic). [< Greek *mī́mēsis* < *mīmeîsthai* imitate < *mîmos* mime]

**mi|met|ic** (mi met′ik, mī-), *adj.* **1** imitative: *mimetic gestures.* **2** mimic or make-believe: *mimetic games of children.* **3** having to do with or exhibiting mimicry: *It is difficult for dancing to portray the beauty of physical rapture ... since it must not be mimetic* (London Times). [< Greek *mīmētikós* < *mīmeîsthai* imitate < *mîmos* mime] — **mi|met′i|cal|ly,** *adv.*

**mim|e|tite** (mim′ə tīt, mī′mə-), *n.* a mineral arsenate and chloride of lead, of a yellow to brown color, usually occurring in crystals. *Formula:* $Pb_5As_3O_{12}Cl$ [< Greek *mīmētḗs* imitator (because it resembles pyromorphite)]

**mim|ic** (mim′ik), *v.,* **-icked, -ick|ing,** *n., adj.* — *v.t.* **1** to make fun of by imitating or copying (a person, his speech, or his manner): *We like to get him to mimic our music teacher.* **2** to copy closely; imitate; ape: *A parrot can mimic a person's voice.* **3** to represent imitatively, as by drawing; simulate. **4** to be an imitation of: *Fresh carved cedar, mimicking a glade Of palm and plantain* (Keats). **5** to resemble (something else) closely in form, color, or other aspect: *Some insects mimic leaves.* [< noun]
— *n.* **1** a person skillful in imitating or mimicking: *The audience cheered for more as the mimic imitated first one public figure and then another.* **2** one that imitates another: *Cunning is the only mimic of discretion* (Joseph Addison). **3** *Obsolete.* a mime. [< adjective]
— *adj.* **1** not real, but imitated or pretended for some purpose: *The soldiers staged a mimic battle for the visiting general.* **2** imitative: *mimic gestures or expression.*
[< Latin *mīmicus* < Greek *mīmikós* < *mîmos* a mime]

**mim|i|cal** (mim′ə kəl), *adj.* = mimic.

**mim|ick|er** (mim′ə kər), *n.* a person or thing that mimics.

**mim|ic|ry** (mim′ik rē), *n., pl.* **-ries. 1** the act or practice of mimicking: *By the talent of mimicry ... I could copy their pronunciation of the English language* (William Godwin). **2** an instance, performance, or result of mimicking: *an imitation and mimicry of good nature* (Joseph Addison). **3** the close outward resemblance of an animal to its surroundings or to some different animal, especially for protection or concealment.

**Mi|mir** (mē′mir), *n. Norse Mythology.* the giant who guarded the spring of wisdom beneath the ash tree Yggdrasil and who knew the past and the future. His head was taken by Odin to be used as an oracle.

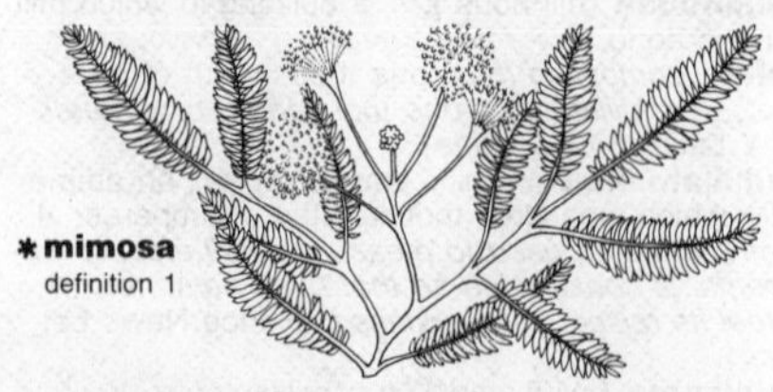
**✱mimosa**
definition 1

**✱mi|mo|sa** (mi mō′sə, -zə), *n.* **1** a tree, shrub, or herb growing in warm regions, and usually having fernlike leaves and heads or spikes of small pink, yellow, or white flowers. The tropical American plant called the sensitive plant is a mimosa.

**✱millpond**
definition 1

**✱millstone**
definition 1

Mimosas belong to the pea family. **2** = acacia. **3** the flower of any of these plants. [< New Latin *Mimosa* the genus name < Latin *mīmus* mime (< Greek *mîmos*) + *-ōsa*, feminine -ose[1] (because it mimics animal reactions)]

**mim|o|sa|ceous** (mim′ə sā′shəs, mī′mə-), *adj.* of or like the mimosa.

**mi|mo|sis** (mi mō′sis, mī-), *n.* = mimesis.

**mim|sy** (mim′zē), *adj.*, **-si|er, -si|est.** *British Informal.* prim; prudish. [< *mim* + *-sy,* as in *clumsy*] —**mim′si|ness,** *n.*

**mim|u|lus** (mim′yə ləs), *n.* a monkey flower. [< New Latin *mimulus* (diminutive) < Latin *mīmus* mime]

**min.**, an abbreviation for the following:
**1a** mineralogical. **b** mineralogy.
**2** minim or minims.
**3** minimum.
**4** mining.
**5** minister.
**6** minor.
**7** minute or minutes.

**mi|na[1]** (mī′nə), *n., pl.* **-nae** (-nē), **-nas.** a unit of weight and value used by the ancient Greeks, Egyptians, and others, equal to 1/60 of a talent or about one pound. [< Latin *mina* < Greek *mnâ, mnâs* < Semitic (compare Babylonian *manū*)]

**mi|na[2]** (mī′nə), *n.* = myna.

**min|a|ble** (mī′nə bəl), *adj.* that can be mined: *minable ores.* Also, **mineable.**

**mi|na|cious** (mi nā′shəs), *adj.* threatening; menacing. **SYN**: minatory. [< Latin *mināx, minācis* (with English *-ous*) < *minārī* to threaten < *minae* projecting points, threats, menaces] —**mi|na′cious|ly,** *adv.* —**mi|na′cious|ness,** *n.*

**mi|nac|i|ty** (mi nas′ə tē), *n.* disposition to threaten.

**Min|a|ma|ta disease** (min′ə mä′tə), poisoning by ingestion of mercury from contaminated fish and shellfish: *Minamata disease, as it came to be called, produced progressive weakening of the muscles, loss of vision, impairment of other cerebral functions, eventual paralysis and in some cases coma and death. The victims had suffered structural injury to the brain* (Scientific American). [< *Minamata* Bay, in western Kyushu, Japan, where it was first identified]

★**min|a|ret** (min′ə ret′, min′ə ret), *n.* a slender, high tower attached to a Moslem mosque, with one or more projecting balconies, from which a crier calls the people to prayer: *The minaret is one of the most typical features of Islamic architecture and one of the most beautiful* (Kenneth J. Conant). [< French *minaret,* or Spanish *minarete,* probably < Turkish *minare* < Arabic *manārah* lighthouse]

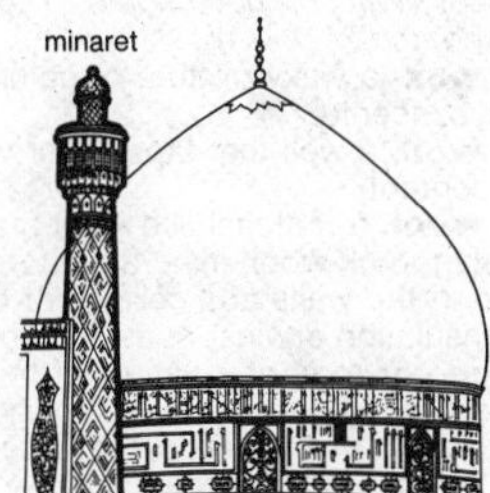

★**minaret**

**min|a|ret|ed** or **min|a|ret|ted** (min′ə ret′id, min′ə ret′-), *adj.* having a minaret or minarets: *a mintareted mosque.*

**min|a|to|ri|al** (min′ə tôr′ē əl, -tōr′-), *adj.* threatening; minatory.

**min|a|to|ry** (min′ə tôr′ē, -tōr′-), *adj.* that threatens; menacing: *a minatory gesture.* **SYN**: threatening. [< Late Latin *minātōrius* < Latin *minārī* threaten] —**min′a|to′ri|ly,** *adv.*

**mi|nau|dière** (mē nō dyer′), *n.* a small metal case, often jeweled, in which a woman carries cosmetics and other small items. [< French *minaudière* (literally) coquettish]

**mince** (mins), *v.,* **minced, minc|ing,** *n.* —*v.t.* **1** to cut or chop up (meat or other food) into very small pieces; shred: *All vegetables used in this recipe are to be minced very fine.* **SYN**: hash. **2** to cut up; subdivide minutely: *The scientists extracted the gene material by mincing the cells* (Science News Letter). **3** to speak or do in an affectedly polite or elegant manner. **4** to make little of; disparage. **5** *Figurative.* to minimize in representation; soften or moderate (words), as in stating unpleasant facts: *The judge, in addressing the jury, spoke bluntly, mincing no words.*
—*v.i.* **1** to put on fine airs in speaking or walking: *Vanity, vanity! ... the same sentiment that sets a lassie mincing to her glass* (Robert Louis Stevenson). **2** to walk with short, dainty steps: *The daughters of Zion are haughty, and walk with stretched forth necks ... mincing as they go* (Isaiah 3:16).
—*n.* **1** meat or other food cut up into very small pieces; a dish of minced meat or the like: *a mince of chicken. They dined on mince and slices of quince* (Edward Lear). **2** = mincemeat. [< Old French *mincier* < Vulgar Latin *minūtiāre* < Latin *minūtus* small; see etym. under **minute[1]**] —**minc′er,** *n.*

**mince|meat** (mins′mēt′), *n.* **1** a cooked mixture of apples, suet, raisins, currants, and spices, usually with chopped meat, used as a filling for pies. **2** *British.* meat cut up into very small pieces.
**make mincemeat of,** to reduce as if into little pieces; cut down; defeat overwhelmingly: *The Yankees were making mincemeat of the rest of the league.*

**mince pie,** a pie filled with mincemeat.

**minc|ing** (min′sing), *adj.* **1** putting on dainty and refined airs; too polite; too nice: *a mincing voice.* **2** affectedly delicate or dainty: *I'll turn two mincing steps into a manly stride* (Shakespeare). —**minc′ing|ly,** *adv.* —**minc′ing|ness,** *n.*

**mind[1]** (mīnd), *n., v.* —*n.* **1** the part of a person that knows and thinks and feels and wishes and chooses: *the powers or processes of the mind, an anxious state of mind, peace of mind.* **2** the intellect or understanding; mental ability; intelligence: *explanations adapted to the popular mind. To learn arithmetic easily, you must have a good mind. An upright heart and cultivated mind* (William Cowper). **3** a person who has intelligence: *the greatest minds of the period. A mind for ever Voyaging through strange seas of Thought, alone* (Wordsworth). **4** reason; sanity: *to lose one's mind.* **5** mental or physical activity in general, as opposed to matter. **6** a conscious or intelligent agency or being: *the doctrine of a mind creating the universe. A pulse in the eternal mind* (Rupert Brooke). **7** a way of thinking and feeling; opinion; view. **8** tendency of thinking or feeling in social or moral respects; spirit; temper: *But the war is not ended; the hostile mind continues in full vigour* (Edmund Burke). **9** desire, purpose, intention, or will. **10** attention; thought; mental effort: *to give one's mind to a new occupation. Keep your mind on your work.* **11** remembrance or recollection; memory: *out of sight, out of mind.* **12** commemoration. **13** *Psychology.* the organized total of all conscious experience of the individual. **14 Mind,** (in the belief of Christian Scientists) God.
—*v.t.* **1** to bear in mind; give heed to: *Mind my words! Mind you, it is clear that, as always, Stratford has not forgotten its summer audience* (Canadian Saturday Night). **2** to be careful concerning: *Mind the step. Mind that you come on time.* **3** to look after; take care of; tend: *Please mind the baby.* **4** to obey: *Mind your father and mother.* **5** to object to; feel bad about: *Do you mind closing the door for me? I mind parting from my friends. Some people don't mind cold weather.* **6** to trouble oneself about; be concerned about: *I am rather faint ... but don't mind me* (Dickens). **7** to turn one's attention to; apply oneself to: *Mind your own business. Bidding him be a good child and mind his book* (Joseph Addison). **8** *Dialect.* to notice; perceive; be aware of: *Will he mind the way we are, and not tidied or washed cleanly at all?* (John M. Synge). **9** *Dialect.* to remember: *I mind being there when I was a lad* (Robert Louis Stevenson). **10** *Dialect.* to remind: *They mind us of the time we made bricks in Egypt* (Tennyson). **11** *Dialect.* to intend; contemplate.
—*v.i.* **1** to take notice; observe: *Now mind, these are not my ideas.* **2** to be obedient: *to train a dog to mind.* **3** to be careful: *If you don't mind, you'll get hurt.* **4** to feel concern; care; object: *Father was furious, but Mother didn't mind.* **5** *Dialect.* to remember.

**bear in mind,** to keep one's attention on; remember: *He promised to bear the subject in mind* (Macaulay).
**be of one** (or **a**) **mind,** to have the same opinion; agree: *Why should we quarrel when we are both of one mind?*
**blow one's mind,** *Slang.* **a** to experience or cause to have drug-induced hallucinations: *He regularly turned on with marijuana or blew his mind with LSD* (New York Times). *In one episode, some hippies offer him coffee and "blow his mind" with the new mind-expanding drug* (Maclean's). **b** to cause to lose control over one's mind; excite, stir, or shock to an extreme degree: *The film was meant to blow the minds of the viewers, but they blew their cool instead. Some raced around trying to pull the plugs of the projectors* (Time).
**bring** (or **call**) **to mind, a** to recall: *This brings to mind a story.* **b** to remember: *I cannot call it to mind.*
**change one's mind, a** to alter one's purpose. *Her first impulse was to change her mind and not go after all* (Francis M. Crawford). **b** to alter one's way of thinking, opinion, or attitude: *I have lived to change my mind, and am almost of the contrary opinion* (John Duncombe).
**cross one's mind,** to occur to one; come into one's thoughts suddenly: *Such an idea never crossed ... our minds* (Thomas Medwin).
**have a mind of one's own,** to have definite or decided opinions, inclinations, or purposes: *He has a mind of his own and will not be persuaded by what others think.*
**have a mind to,** to intend to; think of doing: *He thought that he could do as he had a mind to with his own books.*
**have half a mind to,** to be somewhat inclined to; have some desire to: *I have half a mind to go.*
**have in mind, a** to remember: *Others forgot her, but he still had her in mind.* **b** to take into account; think of; consider: *We should have in mind the benefits of the journey as well as the difficulties we might encounter.* **c** to intend; plan: *She has in mind a trip to Europe next summer.*
**in two (many, etc.) minds,** vacillating between two (many, etc.) intentions: *Last week Moscow sources found the Central Committee in two minds about how to deal with the youth problem* (Time).
**keep in mind,** to remember: *Keep the rules in mind. It was hard to deal realistically with the immediate situation and yet keep in mind the ultimate goal* (Edmund Wilson).
**know one's own mind,** to know what one really thinks, intends, or wishes: *They are both very young and may not know their own minds* (Henry Kingsley).
**make up one's mind,** to decide; resolve: *I made up my mind to study harder and get better grades. We had all quietly made up our minds to treat him like one of ourselves* (Robert Louis Stevenson).
**mind one's p's and q's.** See under **P.**
**never mind, a** don't let it trouble you; it does not matter: *Never mind, Mother, I'll buy the dress myself.* **b** *Informal.* not to speak of; let alone: *New York politics are confusing enough to New Yorkers, never mind outsiders* (Manchester Guardian Weekly).
**of two (many, etc.) minds,** vacillating between two (many, etc.) intentions: *The half-hearted way MacDonald tells the story makes one wonder whether he wasn't of two minds about its chilling outcome* (New Yorker).
**on one's mind,** in one's mind; in one's thoughts; troubling one: *My aunt has something of importance on her mind.*
**out of one's mind,** crazy; insane: *On my first hunt, I thought I'd go out of my mind through fear* (Norman Elder). *A lot of people ... think that anyone who likes to see three or more movies a week has to be clean out of his mind* (Maclean's).
**pass out of mind,** to be forgotten: *When they are out of sight, they soon pass out of mind.*
**pay no mind,** *Dialect.* to pay no attention to; ignore: *Pay his insults no mind!*
**piece of one's mind.** See under **piece.**
**put one in mind of,** to remind one of: *Your joke puts me in mind of a joke my uncle told me. Many of Mr. Rutherford's contributors do somewho put one in mind of a gang of beachcombers making the best of what a storm has washed ashore* (Dan Jacobson).
**put one's mind to,** to want very much; be strongly inclined to: *It is a pity he has not written the book ... he could have written had he put his mind to it* (Hans J. Morgenthau).
**put out of one's mind,** to avoid thinking about: *Resolutely, I put the $500 out of my mind* (Meyer Levin).
**set one's mind on,** to want very much: *He set his mind on becoming a great lawyer.*
**speak one's mind,** to give one's frank opinion; speak plainly or freely: *Speak your mind freely. Give me leave to speak my mind* (Shakespeare).
**take one's mind off,** to distract one's attention from; divert from (something unpleasant): *The music took his mind off his troubles.*
**to one's mind, a** to one's way of thinking; in one's opinion: *To my mind, he is very rude.* **b** according to one's wishes or whims: *It was ... some time before we could get a ship to our minds* (Daniel Defoe).
[Old English *gemynd* memory; thinking]
—***Syn.*** *n.* **1 2 Mind, intellect** mean the part of a human being that enables him to know, think, and act effectively. **Mind** in general usage is the

**Pronunciation Key:** hat, āge, cãre, fär; let, ēqual, tėrm; it, īce; hot, ōpen, ôrder; oil, out; cup, pu̇t, rüle; child; long; thin; ᴛʜen; zh, measure; ə represents **a** in about, **e** in taken, **i** in pencil, **o** in lemon, **u** in circus.

inclusive word, meaning the part that knows, thinks, feels, wills, or remembers, thought of as distinct from the body: *To develop properly, the mind needs training and exercise.* **Intellect** applies to the knowing and thinking powers of the mind, as distinct from the powers of feeling and will: *Many motion pictures appeal to the feelings instead of the intellect.*

**mind²** (mind), *n. Archaeology.* a diadem or crescent-shaped ornament found in Ireland. [< Middle Irish *mind*]

**mind-bend|er** (mīnd′ben′dər), *n. Slang.* **1** a hallucinogenic drug: *The active ingredient is mescaline, the cactus-derived mind-bender* (Science News). **2** a user of drugs, especially hallucinogenic drugs: *In recent years, youthful mind-benders have tripped* (*or thought they did*) *on everything from airplane glue to morning-glory seeds* (Time). **3** something which boggles the mind. **4** a person who uses subtle means to influence or persuade: *What the ... mind-benders are thinking about is individualized communication—computerized mail and telephone on a scale new to politics—and subtle use of television* (Harper's).

**mind-bend|ing** (mīnd′ben′ding), *adj. Slang.* **1** causing hallucinations; hallucinogenic: *a mind-bending admixture of hemp and the inner bark of dogwood* (Time). **2** distorting the perception; causing mental stupor or derangement: *Already "mind-bending" gases for military purposes are said to be at an advanced stage of development* (New Scientist). **3** boggling the mind; overwhelming: *The theoretical mathematics of the situation* [*mining metals*] *are positively mind-bending* (Sunday Times).

**mind-blow** (mīnd′blō′), *v.t.*, **-blew, -blown, -blow|ing.** *Slang.* to blow the mind of; excite, stir, or shock: *It can mind-blow a long-haired GI to know he'll have to live straighter to survive in Sweden than in the Army or in America* (Listener).

**mind blower,** *Slang.* **1** a hallucinogenic drug. **2** a user of drugs, especially hallucinogenic drugs. **3** a mind-blowing experience.

**mind-blow|ing** (mīnd′blō′ing), *adj., n. Slang.* —***adj.*** **1** hallucinogenic. **2** exciting, stirring, or shocking to an extreme degree.
—***n.*** the act of blowing one's mind.

**mind|ed** (mīn′did), *adj.* **1** having a certain kind of mind: *high-minded, strong-minded.* **2** inclined; disposed: *She was minded to argue with the teacher about her mark. Come a little early, if you are so minded.* —**mind′ed|ness,** *n.*

**Min|del** (min′dəl), *n. Geology.* the second glaciation of the Pleistocene in Europe. [< *Mindel* River, Bavaria]

**mind|er** (mīn′dər), *n.* **1** a person whose business is to mind or attend to something. **2** *British.* a child, especially an orphan or one whose parents are unable to support him, who is committed to a special school or home.

**mind-ex|pand|er** (mīnd′ek span′dər), *n.* a mind-expanding or hallucinogenic drug: *The effects of Vietnamese marijuana were sometimes surprisingly similar to those induced by hallucinogenic and psychotogenic agents such as L.S.D., mescaline, and other so-called mind-expanders* (London Times).

**mind-ex|pand|ing** (mīnd′ek span′ding), *adj.* intensifying and distorting perception; psychedelic: *A Buffalo scientist reported ... evidence ... that the "mind-expanding" drug LSD might be damaging the users' chromosomes* (New York Times).

**mind|ful** (mīnd′fəl), *adj.* **1** having in mind; heedful (of); thinking; being aware: *Mindful of your advice, I went slowly. What is man, that thou art mindful of him?* (Psalms 8:4). **SYN:** aware, cognizant. **2** taking thought; careful (of): *We had to be mindful of every step we took on the slippery sidewalk.* **SYN:** attentive. —**mind′ful|ly,** *adv.*
—**mind′ful|ness,** *n.*

**mind|less** (mīnd′lis), *adj.* **1** without mind or intelligence: *the shrieking of the mindless wind* (John Greenleaf Whittier). **2** not taking thought; forgetful; careless: *Cursed Athens, mindless of thy worth, Forgetting thy great deeds* (Shakespeare). —**mind′less|ly,** *adv.* —**mind′less|ness,** *n.*

**mind reader,** a person who can guess the thoughts of others.

**mind reading,** the ability or act of guessing the thoughts of others: *It is quite legitimate for a scientist to investigate whether such phenomena as ... mind reading or divination ... do exist* (Bulletin of Atomic Scientists). —**mind′-read′ing,** *adj.*

**mind-set** (mīnd′set′), *n.* frame of mind; mental or intellectual climate: *Whatever the explanation, the national mind-set in Sweden clearly makes major reform easier than it is in most countries* (Saturday Review).

**mind's eye,** mental view or vision; imagination: *And now crossing my mind's eye were the visions that had gone with the name* (New Yorker).

**mine¹** (mīn), *pron., adj.* —***pron.*** *Possessive form of* **I.** **1** belonging to me: *This book is mine. Such as you were, I took you for mine* (Robert Browning). **2** the one or ones belonging to me: *Your shoes are black, mine are brown. Please lend me your pen; I have lost mine.* **3** those who are mine, especially my family or kindred: *me and mine.*
—***adj.*** *Archaic.* my (used only before a vowel or *h*, or after a noun): *mine own, mine heart, mine eyes, sister mine.*
[Old English *mīn*]

**mine²** (mīn), *n., v.,* **mined, min|ing.** —***n.*** **1** a large hole or space dug in the earth to get out ores, precious stones, coal, salt, or anything valuable: *a gold mine, a coal mine.* **2** a deposit of mineral or ore, either under the ground or at its surface. **3** *Figurative.* a rich or plentiful source: *The book proved to be a mine of information about radio.* **4** an underground passage in which an explosive is placed to blow up the enemy's entrenchment, forts, or the like. **5** an explosive device put under water, laid on the ground, or shallowly buried to blow up enemy troops or equipment. An underwater mine can be exploded by the vibrations of a ship's propeller, by changes in water pressure, or by magnetic attraction. A land mine is exploded by contact with a vehicle or person, by remote control or by a time fuse. **6** a kind of firework, consisting of a series of separate charges that scatter high in the air and explode simultaneously or in sequence.
—***v.i.*** **1** to make a hole or space in the earth in order to get out ores, coal, or anything valuable; dig a mine; get ores, coal, or anything valuable from a mine: *to mine for gold. The government controls mining in that area.* **2** to work in a mine: *He retired after mining for forty years.* **3** to make a passage, hole, or space, below the surface of the earth; dig or lay explosive mines: *The ships mined along the entrance to the harbor.*
—***v.t.*** **1** to get from a mine: *to mine coal, to mine gold.* **2** to dig into for ores, precious stones, coal, salt, or other minerals: *to mine the earth.* **3** to dig in; make (passages) by digging or burrowing. **4** to lay explosive mines in or under: *to mine the mouth of a harbor.* **5** *Figurative.* to destroy secretly; ruin slowly; undermine.
**go down the mine,** *Surfing Slang.* to miss the proper take-off point in a wave and be thrown in front of the wave: *His board hit him when he went down the mine.*
**spring a mine,** to cause the gunpowder or other explosive in a mine to explode: *Be prepared to spring the mines in these bridges if the enemy should advance* (Duke of Wellington).
[< Old French *mine* < unrecorded Gaulish *meina* unrefined metal]

**mine|a|ble** (mī′nə bəl), *adj.* = minable.

**mine detector,** an electromagnetic device used to locate explosive mines, primarily those placed underground in wartime.

**mine|field** (mīn′fēld′), *n. Military.* **1** an area throughout which explosive mines have been laid. **2** the pattern or arrangement of mines in an area.

**mine|hunt|er** (mīn′hun′tər), *n. British.* a ship equipped to locate explosive mines.

**mine|lay|er** (mīn′lā′ər), *n.* a surface vessel or submarine designed or equipped for laying underwater mines.

**min|er** (mī′nər), *n.* **1** one who works in a mine: *a coal miner.* (*Figurative.*) *... the mole, the miner of the soil* (William Cowper). **2** a soldier who digs to lay mines; sapper. **3** a machine used for mining. **4** an insect that, in the larval stage, lives between the surfaces of a leaf; leaf miner.

**min|er|al** (min′ər əl, min′rəl), *n., adj.* —***n.*** **1a** a substance obtained by mining or digging in the earth: *Coal, quartz, feldspar, mica, and asphalt are minerals. It is easier to identify minerals than rocks, because minerals have certain definite properties that we can more or less accurately determine* (Frederick H. Pough). **b** an inorganic substance found in nature, of uniform constituents in regular crystalline form: *Coal is not a true mineral, diamond is.* **2** *Mining.* an ore. **3** any substance neither plant nor animal. Salt and sand are minerals. **4** *British.* mineral water.
—***adj.*** **1** of minerals. **2** like a mineral or minerals. **3** containing minerals: *mineral water.* **4** neither animal nor vegetable; inorganic.
**minerals,** *British.* mineral waters; soft drinks: *There will be ... supper with ale and minerals at Osborne's Hotel* (Glasgow Herald).
[< Medieval Latin *minerale,* neuter adjective < *minera* a mine < Old French *minere* < *mine;* see etym. under **mine²**]

**mineral cotton,** = mineral wool.

**mineral dressing,** an initial process in the refining of an ore, in which the ore is crushed and ground into tiny particles which are, by flotation or some other process, then separated into mineral concentrates and waste materials.

**mineral fuel,** coal, petroleum, or gas.

**mineral hammer,** a hammer that has both square and pointed ends for pounding and loosening mineral specimens embedded in solid rock.

**min|er|al|ize** (min′ər ə līz, min′rə-), *v.,* **-ized, -iz|ing.** —***v.t.*** **1** to convert into mineral substance; transform (metal) into an ore. **2** to impregnate or supply with a mineral substance or substances.
—***v.i.*** to search for minerals. —**min′er|al|i|za′tion,** *n.* —**min′er|al|iz′er,** *n.*

**mineral jelly,** a kind of petrolatum that is mixed with certain explosives to make them less sensitive to shock, heat, or dampness, and thus easier to handle, ship, and store.

**mineral kingdom,** all minerals, as distinguished from plants and animals.

**min|er|al|o|cor|ti|coid** (min′ər ə lō kôr′tə koid), *n.* any steroid hormone of a group produced by the adrenal cortex, which plays an important part in metabolism, especially in controlling the salt and water balance in the body. [< *mineral* + *corticoid*]

**min|er|a|log|i|cal** (min′ər ə loj′ə kəl), *adj.* of or having to do with mineralogy. —**min′er|a|log′i|cal|ly,** *adv.*

**min|er|al|o|gist** (min′ə rol′ə jist, -ral′-), *n.* a person who studies mineralogy.

**min|er|al|o|gy** (min′ə rol′ə jē, -ral′-), *n.* **1** the science of minerals. **2** a book about this science.

**mineral oil,** **1** any oil derived from minerals, such as petroleum. **2** a colorless, odorless, tasteless oil obtained from petroleum, used especially as a laxative; liquid petrolatum.

**mineral pitch,** = asphalt.

**mineral right,** a right to the mineral content of a certain area of land.

**min|er|als** (min′ər əlz, min′rəlz), *n.pl.* See under **mineral.**

**mineral salt,** a salt which occurs as, or is derived from, a mineral: *Over-irrigation led to the depositing of mineral salts on the soil to such an extent that crop yields were reduced sharply* (Science News Letter).

**mineral spirits,** a flammable petroleum fraction used as a thinner in paints and varnishes.

**mineral spring,** a spring that yields mineral water.

**mineral tallow,** a soft, waxy mineral substance found in Wales and Scotland; hatchettin.

**mineral tar,** a semiliquid variety of bitumen; maltha.

**mineral water,** water containing mineral salts or gases. People drink various mineral waters for their health.
**mineral waters,** *British.* soft drinks; effervescent nonalcoholic beverages, such as soda water or ginger beer: *Will you have some mineral waters with your lunch?*

**mineral wax,** a waxy mixture of natural hydrocarbons; ozocerite.

**mineral well,** a well that taps water with a high mineral content.

**mineral wool,** a material like wool made from melted slag; rock wool; mineral cotton; slag wool. It is used in the walls and ceilings of buildings to provide insulation against heat and cold.

**miner bee,** any one of a variety of bees that dig tunnels and make their nests in the ground.

**miner's asthma,** **1** a lung disease caused by inhalation of coal dust; anthracosis. **2** = pneumoconiosis.

**miner's cramp,** = heat cramp.

**Mi|ner|va** (mə nėr′və), *n. Roman Mythology.* the goddess of wisdom, the arts, and defensive war. The Greeks called her Athena.

**min|e|stro|ne** (min′ə strō′nē), *n.* a thick soup containing vegetables, vermicelli, and, sometimes, meat. [< Italian *minestrone* < *minestra* soup < *minestrare* minister to < Latin *ministrāre* minister to < *minister;* see etym. under **minister**]

**mine|sweep|er** (mīn′swē′pər), *n.* a ship used for dragging a harbor, the sea, or other area, to remove, disarm, or harmlessly explode mines laid by an enemy.

**mine|sweep|ing** (mīn′swē′ping), *n.* the process of dragging a harbor, the sea, or other area, to remove underwater mines laid by an enemy.

**mine thrower,** = trench mortar.

**mine|work|er** (mīn′wėr′kər), *n.* = miner.

**Ming** (ming), *n.* **1** the ruling Chinese dynasty from 1368 to 1644, known especially for the exquisitely decorated ceramics and paintings produced under it. **2** a piece of fine porcelain made in China under this dynasty. [< Chinese *Ming* (literally) bright]

**min|gle** (ming′gəl), *v.,* **-gled, -gling.** —***v.t.*** **1** to combine in a mixture; mix; blend: *Two rivers that join mingle their waters.* **SYN:** fuse. **2** to bring together or associate; unite or join in company: *Their families are mingled by marriage.* **3** to form by mixing various ingredients; concoct: *men of strength to mingle strong drink* (Isaiah 5:22).
—***v.i.*** **1** to be or become mingled; mix; blend:

*The blood of all nations is mingling with our own* (Longfellow). SYN: fuse. **2** to associate: *to mingle with important people. He is very shy and does not mingle much with the children at school.* [Middle English *mengelen* (perhaps frequentative) < Old English *mengan* to mix. Compare Middle Dutch *mengelen.*] **—min′gle|ment,** *n.* **—min′gler,** *n.*

**min|go** (ming′gō), *n., pl.* **-gos.** a chief of the Chickasaw. [< Chickasaw *mingo*]

**Ming tree, 1** a dwarfed tree; bonsai. **2** an imitation of a dwarf tree made by gluing several gnarled branches or twigs together into the form of a windswept tree, often decorated with moss or lichens. [probably < *Ming*]

**min|gy** (min′jē), *adj.,* **-gi|er, -gi|est.** *Informal.* niggardly; stingy: *We weren't mingy with our music; everybody . . . got an earful* (Punch). [perhaps < *m*(ean) + (st)*ingy*]

**min|i** (min′ē), *adj.,* **min|i|er, min|i|est,** *n., pl.* **minis.** **—*adj.* 1** reaching well above the knee; very short: *The maxi coat, worn over the mini dress, was symbolic of the times* (Ruth Mary DuBois). **2** small for its kind; miniature: *A waiter serves me with three mini-sandwiches* (Punch).
**—*n.* 1** a short skirt, dress, or coat, especially one ending two to four inches above the knee; miniskirt or minidress: *The passing girls, dressed in . . . conservatively cut suits, look as if they were afraid to wear minis* (Atlantic). **2** anything miniature in size: *The Micro 16 does not pretend to be a pale imitation of a large machine: it is intended to be, and indeed is, a highly effective mini* (New Scientist and Science Journal). **3** the style or length of fashions characteristic of the miniskirt: *"The midi will get time, but not equal time with the mini"* (Time). **4** = minicar: *you see him zipping by in the family mini* (London Times).
[< *mini-*]

**mini-,** *combining form.* **1** small for its kind; miniature, as in *minicar, mini-ski, minisub.*
**2** reaching well above the knee; very short, as in *minicoat, minidress.*
[< *mini*(ature)]

**min|i|ate** (*adj.* min′ē it; *v.* min′ē āt), *adj., v.,* **-at|ed, -at|ing.** **—*adj.*** of the color of minium; orange-red.
**—*v.t.*** to color or paint with minium; rubricate or illuminate (a manuscript or the like).
[< Latin *miniāre* (with English *-ate*[1]) paint red]

**min|i|a|ture** (min′ē ə chər, min′ə chər), *n., adj.* **—*n.* 1** anything represented on a very small scale; a reduced image or likeness: *She is a miniature of her mother. In the museum there is a miniature of the ship "Mayflower." Tragedy is the miniature of human life* (John Dryden). **2** a very small painting, usually a portrait: *His [Holbein's] miniatures have all the strength of oil colors joined to the most finished delicacy* (Horace Walpole). **3** the art of painting these. **4** a picture in an illuminated manuscript.
**—*adj.*** done or made on a very small scale; tiny: *The little girl had miniature furniture for her doll house; her brother had miniature knights for his toy castle.* SYN: diminutive.
**in miniature,** on a very small scale; reduced in size: *I run over the whole history of my life in miniature, or by abridgment* (Daniel Defoe).
[< Italian *miniatura* < Medieval Latin *miniare* to rubricate, illuminate (a manuscript) in red < Latin *miniāre* paint red < *minium* red lead; later taken as related to Latin *minūtus* small]

**miniature camera,** a camera using narrow film (35-millimeter or less), suitable especially for taking action photographs and informal snapshots.

**miniature golf,** a game based on golf, played on a small obstacle course.

**miniature pinscher,** a German toy dog of the terrier family that resembles the Doberman pinscher.

**miniature schnauzer,** the smallest of the three schnauzer dog breeds, about 12 inches high.

**min|i|a|tur|ist** (min′ē ə chər ist, min′ə chər-), *n.* a painter of miniatures.

**min|i|a|tur|ize** (min′ē ə chə rīz, min′ə chə-), *v.t.,* **-ized, -iz|ing.** to reduce to a very small size, especially as an improved replacement for a much larger type: *The technological skills that produced miniature radios and computers . . . should be equally successful in miniaturizing artificial organs* (Atlantic). **—min′i|a|tur|i|za′tion,** *n.* **—min′i|a|tur|iz′er,** *n.*

**min|i|bike** (min′ē bīk′), *n. U.S.* a small motorcycle.

**min|i|bus** (min′ē bus′), *n., pl.* **-bus|es** or **-bus|ses.** *Especially British.* any passenger van or truck seating about twelve people.

**min|i|cab** (min′ē kab′), *n. British.* a minicar used as a taxicab.

**min|i|cal|cu|la|tor** (min′ē kal′kyə lā′tər), *n.* a pocket-size, battery-operated, electronic calculating machine with a numerical keyboard and a register in which the results of calculations are automatically displayed.

**min|i|cam** (min′ē kam), *n.* = miniature camera. [< *mini*(ature) *cam*(era)]

**min|i|car** (min′ē kär′), *n. British.* a compact car seating two persons.

**min|i|cell** (min′ē sel′), *n.* a small bacterial cell produced by an abnormal division process and able to transfer episomes from and into normal cells.

**min|i|com|put|er** (min′ē kəm pyü′tər), *n.* a small, low-cost, general-purpose computer.

**min|i|dress** (min′ē dres′), *n.* a very short dress, above the knee.

**Min|i|é ball** or **bullet** (min′ē ā, min′ē), a conical bullet with a hollow base which expands, when fired, to fit the rifling of the gun. [< Captain Claude E. *Minié,* 1814-1879, a French inventor]

**min|i|fi|ca|tion** (min′ə fə kā′shən), *n.* the act or process of making smaller; lessening.

**min|i|fy** (min′ə fī), *v.t.,* **-fied, -fy|ing.** to make less: *The pliancy of Congress . . . during the past two sessions has greatly minified the importance of that body in the eyes of the public* (Baltimore Sun). [< Latin *minor,* masculine of *minus* less (see etym. under **minus**) + English *-fy*]

**min|i|kin** (min′ə kin), *n., adj.* **—*n.* 1** *Archaic.* a small or insignificant thing; a diminutive creature. **2** *Obsolete.* a pretty girl.
**—*adj.* 1** dainty; elegant. **2** affected; mincing. **3** diminutive; miniature; tiny: *In the distance . . . the farmsteads [have become] minikin as if they were the fairy-finest to be packed in a box* (John Ruskin).
[alteration of earlier Dutch *minneken* small, frail thing (diminutive) < *minne* love + *-ken* - kin]

**min|im** (min′əm), *n., adj.* **—*n.* 1** the smallest unit of liquid measure, equal to of a fluid dram, or about a drop, or 0.0616 milliliter. **2** *British.* a half note in music. **3** a very small amount; the least possible portion; jot. **4** a very small or insignificant person or thing: *Not all minims of nature; some of serpent kind, Wondrous in length and corpulence* (Milton). **5** a single stroke made vertically downward in writing by hand, as either of the two strokes in *n.*
**—*adj.*** extremely small; smallest.
[< Latin *minimus* smallest, superlative of *minus* less; see etym. under **minus**]

**Min|im** (min′əm), *n.* a mendicant friar of the Order of Least Hermits, founded in the 1400's by Saint Francis of Paula (1416-1507). [< *minim*]

**min|i|ma** (min′ə mə), *n.* minimums; a plural of **minimum.**

**min|i|mal** (min′ə məl), *adj., n.* **—*adj.* 1** least possible; very small; having to do with a minimum: *minimal damage, a minimal cost.* **2** of or having to do with minimal art: *Minimal forms still massively demand their unrewarding space* (Time).
**—*n.* 1** = minimal art. **2** a work of minimal art.
[< Latin *minimus* smallest (see etym. under **minim**) + English *-al*[1]] **—min′i|mal|ly,** *adv.*

**minimal art,** a form of painting and sculpture in which the simplest or most basic shapes, colors, or materials are used: *Sculptors have produced forms in aluminum, plastics, and other industrial materials which remain severely geometrical, deliberately anonymous, and almost totally impersonal. Such work has been called minimal art* (Sir Herbert Read).

**minimal artist,** = minimalist.

**mi|ni|mal|ism** (min′ə mə liz′əm), *n.* = minimal art.

**mi|ni|mal|ist** (min′ə mə list), *n., adj.* **—*n.*** a person who produces minimal art: *Minimalists do the minimum. That's it with the minimum waste of words* (Sunday Times).
**—*adj.*** of or having to do with minimalists or minimal art: *Tony Smith, usually taken as the original minimalist sculptor (after the pyramids and Goethe's sphere on a cube) is well represented by large sculptures* (Manchester Guardian Weekly).

**Min|i|mal|ist** (min′ə mə list), *n.* a member of a less radical section of the former Social Revolutionary Party in Russia about 1903. [translation of Russian *men'shevik* Menshevik]

**min|i|max** (min′ē maks), *n., adj., v.* **—*n.* 1** that strategy in the theory of games which provides the minimum of a player's maximum possible losses (contrasted with *maximin*). **2** = minimax theorem.
**—*adj.*** of or having to do with or based on the minimax theorem: *They [moves in mathematical games] will depend not on chance but on decisions by the players, each of whom is trying to minimize his opponent's utility (that is, payoff) and maximize his own . . . This decision rule is known as the minimax rule* (Scientific American).
**—*v.i.*** to apply the minimax theorem: *Each player, then, is minimaxing— minimising maximum loss, or maximising minimum profit* (Listener).
[< *mini*(mum) + *maxi*(mum)]

**minimax theorem,** a principle in the theory of games which states that in an optimal strategy one player plays so as to minimize his maximum losses and the other plays so as to maximize his minimum gains: *It was not until 1926 that John von Neumann gave his proof of the minimax theorem, the fundamental theorem of game theory* (Scientific American).

**min|i|mi** (min′ə mī), *n.* plural of **minimus.**

**min|i|mise** (min′ə mīz), *v.t.,* **-mised, -mis|ing.** *Especially British.* minimize.

**min|i|mize** (min′ə mīz), *v.t.,* **-mized, -miz|ing.** **1** to reduce to the least possible amount or degree: *The polar explorers took every precaution to minimize the dangers of their trip.* **2** to state or represent at the lowest possible estimate; make the least of: *An ungrateful person minimizes the help others have given him.* SYN: belittle. **—min′i|mi|za′tion,** *n.* **—min′i|miz′er,** *n.*

**min|i|mum** (min′ə məm), *n., pl.* **-mums** or **-ma,** *adj.* **—*n.* 1a** the least possible amount; lowest amount: *Each of the children had to drink some milk at breakfast; half a glass was the minimum.* **b** the lowest amount of variation attained or recorded. **2** *Mathematics.* a value of a function less than any values close to it.
**—*adj.* 1** least possible: *Eighteen is the minimum age for voting in most states.* **2** lowest: *the minimum rate.*
[< Latin *minimum* smallest thing, neuter of *minimus;* see etym. under **minim**]
▶**Minimum** has two plurals: *minimums* and *minima.* The first is more common in informal English.

**minimum wage, 1** the wage agreed upon or fixed by law as the lowest payable to certain employees: *The men wanted a minimum wage of two dollars an hour.* **2** = living wage.

**min|i|mus** (min′ə məs), *n., pl.* **-mi.** a very small or insignificant creature: *Get you gone, you dwarf, You minimus* (Shakespeare). [< Latin *minimus;* see etym. under **minim**]

**min|ing** (mī′ning), *n.* **1** the working of mines for ores, coal, or other minerals: *Mining is very dangerous work.* **2** the business of digging coal or ores from mines: *Mining is a very profitable business.* **3** the laying of explosive mines: *The mining of a harbor can be a defense against enemy attack or an attack against the enemy's harbor.*

**mining engineering,** a branch of engineering that deals with the discovery of mineral deposits, their removal from the earth, and the preparation of minerals for commercial use.

**min|ion** (min′yən), *n., adj.* **—*n.* 1** a servant or follower willing to do whatever he is ordered to do by his master; henchman: *It is no wonder if he helps himself from the city treasury and allows his minions to do so* (James Bryce). *Let us be Diana's foresters . . . minions of the moon* (Shakespeare). SYN: lackey. **2** a favorite person or animal; darling; beloved; idol (a contemptuous use): (*Figurative.*) *A son . . . Who is sweet Fortune's minion and her pride* (Shakespeare). **3** a size of printing type; 7 point. **4** *Obsolete.* a lady love, especially a mistress or paramour.
**—*adj.*** dainty; elegant.
[< Middle French *mignon* petite, dainty; favorite. Compare etym. under **mignon.**]

**minion of the law,** a policeman.

**min|i|pill** (min′ē pil′), *n.* a pill containing a very low dose of a drug, especially an oral contraceptive having only one-tenth of the progesterone and none of the estrogen present in larger pills.

**min|is|cule** (min′ə skyül), *adj., n.* **—*adj.*** = minuscule. **—*n.*** = miniature.

**min|i|se|ries** (min′ē sir′ēz), *n., pl.* **-ries.** a short serial, especially on television: *Miniseries— a series of programs that would end after six, eight, 10 or whatever number [of programs] the writers feel necessary. . .to tell one complete story* (TV Guide).

**min|ish** (min′ish), *Archaic.* **—*v.t.*** to make less or fewer; diminish: *Ye shall not minish ought from your bricks of your daily task* (Exodus 5:19).
**—*v.i.*** to become less; diminish. [alteration of Middle English *menusen,* ultimately < Old French *menuis-,* stem of *mincier* make small; see etym. under **mince**]

**min|i-ski** (min′ē skē′), *n., pl.* **-skis** or **-ski.** a short ski worn by beginners or in ski bobbing.

**min|i|skirt** (min′ē skėrt′), *n.* **1** a very short skirt, several inches above the knee. **2** a dress with such a skirt; minidress: *A lady of forty-eight doesn't look as good or as fresh in miniskirts as a girl of eighteen* (Irving Howe).

**min|i|skirt|ed** (min′ē skėr′tid), *adj.* wearing a miniskirt.

**min|i|state** (min′ē stāt′), *n.* a very small country, especially one of the newer independent small states of Africa and Asia; microstate: *South Africa's economic predominance radiates . . . to the three ministates of Botswana, Lesotho, and*

**Pronunciation Key:** hat, āge, cãre, fär; let, ēqual, tėrm; it, īce; hot, ōpen, ôrder; oil, out; cup, pu̇t, rüle; child; long; thin; ᴛʜen; zh, measure; ə represents **a** in about, **e** in taken, **i** in pencil, **o** in lemon, **u** in circus.

*Swaziland* (New York Times).

**min|is|ter** (min′ə stər), *n., v.* —*n.* **1** a clergyman serving a church, especially a Protestant church; spiritual guide; pastor: *The minister always gives a good sermon.* **2** a person who is given charge of a department of the government: *the Minister of Finance.* **3** a person sent to a foreign country to represent his own government, especially a diplomat ranking below an ambassador: *the United States Minister to Switzerland.* **4** a person or thing employed in carrying out a purpose or the will of another; agent: *The storm which killed the murderer seemed the minister of God's vengeance.* **5** *Archaic.* a servant or attendant: *A multitude of cooks, and inferior ministers, employed in the service of the kitchens* (Edward Gibbon).
—*v.i.* **1** to attend (to comfort or wants); act as a servant or nurse; be of service: *She ministers to the sick man's wants. For even the Son of man came not to be ministered unto, but to minister, and to give his life a ransom for many* (Mark 10:45). **SYN**: serve. **2** to be helpful; give aid; contribute: *My lord's clearness of mind ... had not ceased to minister to my amazement* (Robert Louis Stevenson). **SYN**: help, assist.
—*v.t.* **1** *Archaic.* to furnish; supply: *I will endeavour most faithfully not to minister any occasion of strife* (Scott). **2** *Obsolete.* to dispense or administer (a sacrament). **3** *Obsolete.* to apply or administer (something healing).
[< Old French *ministre,* learned borrowing from Latin *minister, -trī* servant < *minus* less; see etym. under **minus**]

**min|is|te|ri|al** (min′ə stir′ē əl), *adj.* **1** of a minister; having to do with a minister. **2** of the ministry. **3** suited to a clergyman: *a ministerial manner.* **4** executive; administrative: *a ministerial act.* **5** acting as an agent; instrumental. **SYN**: ancillary. —**min′is|te′ri|al|ly,** *adv.*

**min|is|te|ri|al|ist** (min′ə stir′ē ə list), *n. British.* a supporter of the ministry in political office.

**minister plenipotentiary,** *pl.* **ministers plenipotentiary.** a diplomatic agent given full powers by his government; plenipotentiary.

**minister president,** *pl.* **ministers president** or **minister presidents.** a head of government of certain countries, especially of East Germany.

**minister resident,** a diplomatic agent to a minor country.

**min|is|ter|ship** (min′ə stər ship), *n.* the office of a minister.

**minister without portfolio,** a minister in a government who does not have the position and duties of a cabinet member or minister of state, but usually acts in some special capacity as the personal agent of the chief executive.

**min|is|trant** (min′ə strənt), *adj., n.* —*adj.* that ministers; ministering: *angels ministrant* (Milton).
—*n.* a person who ministers: *I was chosen to act as ministrant and carry the cross* (New Yorker).
[< Latin *ministrāns, -antis,* present participle of *ministrāre* to minister to < *minister;* see etym. under **minister**]

**min|is|tra|tion** (min′ə strā′shən), *n.* **1** service as a minister of a church. **2** help; aid: *to give ministration to the poor; in sore extremity, when she most needed the ministration of her own sex* (Francis Bret Harte).

**min|is|tra|tive** (min′ə strā′tiv), *adj.* ministering; giving service.

**min|is|try** (min′ə strē), *n., pl.* **-tries. 1** the office, duties, or time of service of a minister: *The clergyman's ministry covered a period of fifty years.* **2** the ministers of a church; clergy: *Many of the ministry of the Roman Catholic Church met in Rome.* **SYN**: ecclesiastics. **3** the ministers of a government, especially of the British or a European government. Ministers of a government are often equivalent to cabinet members in the United States. **4** in Great Britain and in Europe: **a** a government department under a minister. **b** the offices of such a department. **5** the act of ministering or serving: *My idea of heaven is the perpetual ministry of one soul to another* (Tennyson). **SYN**: ministration. **6** agency; instrumentality.
[< Latin *ministerium* office, service < *minister;* see etym. under **minister**. See etym. of doublet **métier**.]

**min|i|sub** (min′ē sub′), *n.* a very small research submarine equipped to explore and monitor the underwater environment.

**min|i|tank|er** (min′ē tang′kər), *n.* a small ship or truck carrying some liquid; small tanker.

**Min|i|ta|ri** (min′ə tä′rē), *n., pl.* **-ri** or **-ris.** = Hidatsa.

**min|i|track** (min′ē trak′), *n.* an electronic system for following the course of satellites and rockets by means of radio signals transmitted from the satellite or rocket to receiving stations on the ground, which pool their plottings of each reading of its position. [< *mini*(mum weight) + *track*(ing)]

**min|i|um** (min′ē əm), *n.* **1** = vermilion (def. 1). **2** = red lead. [< Latin *minium* red lead]

**min|i|van** (min′ē van′), *n. British.* a small van or pickup truck.

**min|i|ver** (min′ə vər), *n.* **1** a fur or combination of furs formerly much used for lining and trimming garments, especially ceremonial costumes. Miniver includes spotted white and gray fur, white fur symmetrically adorned with bits of dark fur, plain white fur, and ermine. **2** *British.* any pure white fur, especially ermine. [< Old French *menu vair* small vair; *menu* < Latin *minūtus* (see etym. under **minute**[2]); *vair* < Latin *varius* variegated]

**mink** (mingk), *n., pl.* **minks** or (*collectively*) **mink. 1** a small animal like a weasel that lives in water part of the time. It is found in North America, and the northern part of Europe and Asia. **2** its valuable fur. It is most commonly a deep, lustrous brown, but occurs in other shades in certain varieties of the animal. **3** a coat or jacket made from this fur. [apparently < Swedish *mänk*] —**mink′like′,** *adj.*

**Minn.,** Minnesota.

**min|ne|lied** or **Min|ne|lied** (min′ə lēd, *German* -lēt), *n., pl.* **-lie|der** (-lē′lər). **1** = minnesong. **2** any song similar to a minnesong. **3** any love song. [< German *Minnelied* < Middle High German *Minneliet* < *minne* love + *liet* song]

**Min|ne|o|la** (min′ē ō′lə), *n., pl.* **-las.** a variety of tangelo grown in the United States.

**min|ne|sang** (min′ə säng, -zäng), *n.* = minnesong. [< German *Minnesang;* see etym. under **minnesinger**]

**min|ne|sing|er** or **Min|ne|sing|er** (min′ə sing′ər), *n.* one of a class of German lyrical poets and singers of the 1100's to the 1300's. The chief theme of their songs was love. [< German *Minnesinger,* variant of *Minnesänger* < *Minnesang* minnesong < Middle High German *minne* love + *sanc* song]

**min|ne|song** or **Min|ne|song** (min′ə sông, -song), *n.* **1** one of the songs of the minnesingers; minnelied: *All the Minnesongs, even the most diversified, seem still to resemble each other* (Longfellow). **2** such songs collectively: *English works on the subject of the German Minnesong are ... scanty in number* (F. C. Nicholson). [< German *Minnesang;* see etym. under **minnesinger**]

**Min|ne|so|ta** (min′ə sō′tə), *n.* a breed of hogs developed in the United States by cross-breeding two or more breeds in order to obtain improved meat qualities.

**Minnesota Multiphasic Personality Inventory.** See **MMPI.**

**Min|ne|so|tan** (min′ə sō′tən), *adj., n.* —*adj.* of or having to do with the state of Minnesota.
—*n.* a native or inhabitant of Minnesota.

**min|now** (min′ō), *n., pl.* **-nows** or (*collectively*) **-now. 1** a very small freshwater fish, especially one belonging to the same family as the carp, and certain of the killifishes. **2** any very tiny fish. [Middle English *minwe.* Compare Old English *myne* (apparently) minnow.]

**Mi|no|an** (mi nō′ən), *adj., n.* —*adj.* of or having to do with the civilization of Crete from about 3500 to 1400 B.C.: *Excavations by the local department of antiquities at the site of Eraclea, a city of the Minoan period, have been completed* (London Times).
—*n.* a native or inhabitant of Minoan Crete: *The origin of the Minoans ... remains in darkness* (New Yorker). [< *Mino*(s) + *-an*]

**mi|nor** (mī′nər), *adj., n., v.* —*adj.* **1** smaller; less important; lesser: *a minor fault, a minor poet, a minor gain, a minor political party. Correct the important errors in your paper before you bother with the minor ones.* **SYN**: subordinate, secondary, lower, inferior. **2** under legal age of responsibility. **3** *Music.* **a** less by a half step than the corresponding major interval: *a minor seventh, a minor chord.* **b** denoting a scale, key, or mode whose third tone is minor in relation to the fundamental tone: *the C minor scale or key.* **4** *U.S.* of, having to do with, or designating a minor in education: *a minor subject.* **5** *Logic.* less broad; less extensive: *a minor premise.* **6** (in English boys' schools) of the younger (in age or standing) of two pupils who have the same surname.
—*n.* **1** a person under the legal age of responsibility. Under the varying laws of the States of the United States, a person may be a minor until he reaches 18 or 21. **2** *Music.* a minor key, scale, chord, or interval. **3** a subject or course of study to which a student gives much time and attention, but less than to his major subject: *His minor is French; his major is English.* **4** *Mathematics.* the determinant of next lower order in a matrix, obtained by crossing out the row and column containing the given element. **5** *U.S. Sports.* a minor league.
—*v.i.* **minor in,** to have or take as a minor subject of study: *He will minor in French.*
[< Latin *minor* lesser, comparative of *parvus* small]

**Mi|nor** (mī′nər), *n.* a member of the Friars Minor; Minorite.

**minor arc,** *Mathematics.* an arc that is less than half a circle.

**minor axis,** the diameter of an ellipse perpendicular to its major axis.

**Mi|nor|ca** (mə nôr′kə), *n., pl.* **-cas.** any one of a breed of chickens of moderate size with black, buff, or white plumage and white earlobes, notable for prolific laying. [< *Minorca,* an island in the Mediterranean < Spanish *Menorca* < Latin *minor* smaller, minor]

**Mi|nor|can** (mə nôr′kən), *adj., n.* —*adj.* of or having to do with the island of Minorca, an island in the Mediterranean.
—*n.* a native or inhabitant of Minorca.

**minor element,** = trace element.

**Mi|nor|ite** (mī′nə rīt), *n.* a member of the Friars Minor; Franciscan friar.

**mi|nor|i|ty** (mə nôr′ə tē, -nor′-; mī-), *n., pl.* **-ties,** *adj.* —*n.* **1a** the smaller number or part; less than half: *The minority must often do what the majority decides to do. A minority of the children wanted a party, but the majority chose a picnic; as a result we had a big picnic.* **b** a group within a country, state, or community that differs in race, religion, or national origin from the larger part of the population; minority group: *They represent a growing nationwide effort to develop ... classroom literature that depicts blacks and other minorities in a different and more equal perspective* (New York Times). **2** the condition or time of being under the legal age of responsibility: *the long minority of Henry the Sixth, who was a boy nine months old at his father's death* (John R. Green). **SYN**: nonage.
—*adj.* **1** of or constituting a minority: *a minority vote, a minority party.* **2** representing or belonging to a minority: *a minority opinion, the minority leader of the senate.*

**minority group,** any group, especially a racial or ethnic group, occupying a subordinate position in a community and often subjected to discriminatory or unequal treatment: *More than 60% of [the company's] new employees in recent years have come from "minority groups"—the euphemism embracing blacks, Spanish-speaking people, American Indians, and Orientals* (Time). *As the term is often used, a minority group ... refers to a category of people who can be identified by a sizable segment of the population as objects for prejudice or discrimination* (George and Achilles Theodorson).

**minor key,** a musical key or mode based on the minor scale.

**minor league,** any professional sports league or association, especially in baseball, other than the major leagues.

**mi|nor-league** (mī′nər lēg′), *adj.* **1** of or having to do with a minor league or the minor leagues: *We went to see two excellent minor-league teams play a double-header* (New Yorker). **2** *Informal, Figurative.* not first-class; inferior, cheap, or undistinguished: *a minor-league writer, a minor-league politician.*

**minor leaguer, 1** a person in a minor league, especially a minor-league ballplayer. **2** *Informal, Figurative.* a person who is undistinguished, especially in a particular field of endeavor.

**minor mode,** = minor key.

**minor orders,** the lesser degrees or grades of clerical office. In the Roman Catholic Church, the minor orders are acolyte, exorcist, reader, and doorkeeper.

**minor penalty,** a two-minute penalty put on a player in ice hockey for a minor breaking of the rules, such as hooking or slashing with the stick.

**minor piece,** *Chess.* a bishop or a knight.

**minor planet,** = asteroid.

**minor premise,** the premise that refers to a particular case in a syllogism.

**Minor Prophets, 1** the less important of the prophetic books of the Old Testament, including Hosea, Joel, Amos, Obadiah, Jonah, Micah, Nahum, Habakkuk, Zephaniah, Haggai, Zechariah, and Malachi. **2** the prophets who are believed to have written these books.

***minor scale**

harmonic minor

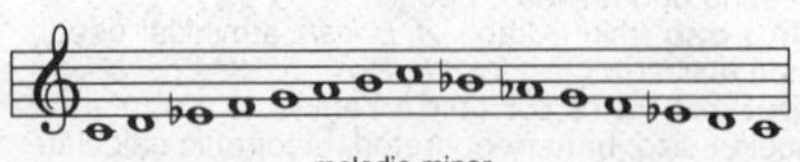

melodic minor

***minor scale,** a musical scale having eight notes, with half steps instead of whole steps after the second and fifth notes. It is a natural scale, but in the harmonic minor the seventh step is raised to a leading tone, and in the melodic minor both the sixth and seventh steps are raised in ascending, but natural in descending.

**minor suit**, diamonds or clubs, the suits of lesser scoring value in auction and contract bridge.

**minor term**, the subject of the conclusion of a syllogism.

**Mi|nos** (mī′nəs, -nos), *n. Greek Legend.* **1** a king and lawgiver of Crete, the son of Zeus and Europa, who became one of the three judges in Hades. **2** his grandson, who built the Labyrinth at Crete and kept the Minotaur in it.

**Min|o|taur** (min′ə tôr), *n. Greek Legend.* a monster with a bull's head and a man's body (or, in some accounts, with a man's head and a bull's body), kept in the Labyrinth at Crete, where every year it devoured seven Athenian youths and seven maidens offered in tribute. Theseus killed the Minotaur. [< Latin *Mīnōtaurus* < Greek *Minōtauros* < *Mínos* Minos + *taûros* bull]

**min|ster** (min′stər), *n.* **1** the church of a monastery. **2** a large or important church; cathedral. [Old English *mynster* < Vulgar Latin *monistērium,* for Late Latin *monastērium.* See etym. of doublet **monastery.**]

**min|strel** (min′strəl), *n.* **1** a singer or musician in the Middle Ages who entertained in the household of a lord: *Here to the harp did minstrels sing* (Scott). **2** a singer or musician in the Middle Ages who went about and sang or recited poems, often of his own making, to the accompaniment of a harp or other instrument: *A wandering minstrel I—a thing of shreds and patches, of ballades, songs, and snatches* (William S. Gilbert). **3** a member of a group or company of actors performing songs, dancing, jokes, and the like, supposed to have come from the Negroes; member of a minstrel show. **4** a musician, singer, or poet. [< Old French *menestrel* < Late Latin *ministeriālis* < Latin *ministerium;* see etym. under **ministry**]

**minstrel show**, a show or entertainment in which the performers blackened their faces and hands with burnt cork and played music, sang songs, and told jokes. Minstrel shows were very popular until the end of the 1800's.

**min|strel|sy** (min′strəl sē), *n., pl.* **-sies. 1** the art or practice of a minstrel: *From minstrelsy to ragtime and jazz was only a short hop, skip and jump for the banjo* (Wall Street Journal). **2** a collection of songs and ballads. **3** a company of minstrels: *Nodding their heads before her goes the merry minstrelsy* (Samuel Taylor Coleridge).

**mint¹** (mint), *n.* **1** a sweet-smelling herb often used for flavoring. Peppermint and spearmint are well-known kinds of mint. The mints comprise a genus of the mint family. **2** any other plant of the mint family. **3** a piece of candy, usually flavored with peppermint, often eaten after dinner: *Pass the chocolate-covered mints, please.* [Old English *minte,* ultimately < Latin *menta*]

**mint²** (mint), *n., v., adj.* **—*n.* 1** a place where money is coined by public authority: *There are several mints in the United States, all part of the Federal government.* **2** a large amount: *A million dollars is a mint of money. He has a mint of reasons* (Tennyson). **3** *Figurative.* a place where anything is made or fabricated. **4** *Obsolete.* a piece of money; coin.
—***v.t.* 1** to coin (money): *The Federal government is the only agency allowed to mint money in the United States.* **2** *Figurative.* to make or fabricate; originate: *to mint words or phrases.* **SYN**: invent.
—***adj.* 1** (of a stamp) in the condition of issue by the Post Office. **2** *Figurative.* without a blemish; as good as new: *an antique car in mint condition.*
[Old English *mynet* a coin, ultimately < Latin *monēta* mint. See etym. of doublet **money.**]
**—mint′er,** *n.*

**mint³** (mint), *Archaic.* **—*v.t.* 1** to intend. **2** to attempt. **3** to aim (a blow): *I will cleave to the brisket the first man that mints another stroke* (Scott). **4** to hint at; insinuate.
—***v.i.* 1** to aim a blow; take aim in shooting. **2** to hint.
[Old English *myntan*]

**mint|age** (min′tij), *n.* **1** the act or process of minting; coinage. **2** the product of minting; output of a mint. **3** a charge for coining; cost of coining. **4** the stamp or character impressed in minting.

***mint family**, a large group of dicotyledonous herbs and shrubs having square stems and opposite or whorled, aromatic leaves which usually contain a volatile, aromatic oil. The family includes many herbs used in preparing food, such as the mints, sage, thyme, and basil.

***mint family**

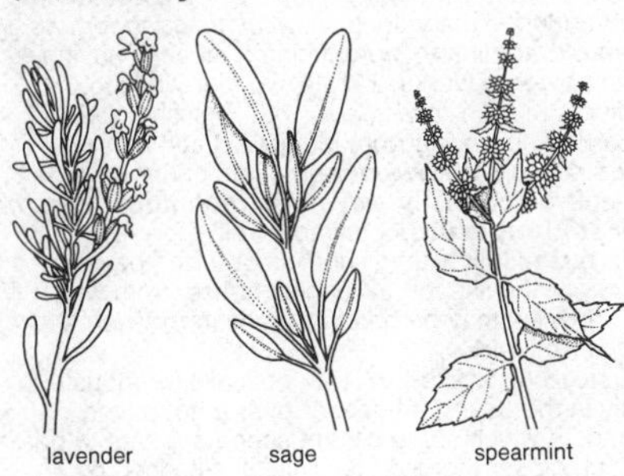


**mint julep**, *U.S.* an alcoholic beverage of bourbon, sugar, crushed ice, and fresh mint, served in a frosted glass.

**mint|y** (min′tē), *adj.,* **mint|i|er, mint|i|est.** of or like that of mint.

**min|u|end** (min′yu̇ end), *n.* a number or quantity from which another is to be subtracted: *In 100 − 23 = 77, the minuend is 100.* [< Latin *minuendus* (*numerus*) (number) to be made smaller, gerundive of *minuere* diminish < *minus;* see etym. under **minus**]

**min|u|et** (min′yu̇ et′), *n., v.* **—*n.* 1** a slow, stately dance in triple time with complex figures. It is of French origin and was fashionable in the 1600's and 1700's. *A French ball in the time of the last French kings usually opened with a minuet.* **2** music for it.
—***v.i.*** to dance a minuet.
[< French *menuet* < Old French (diminutive) < *menu* small < Latin *minūtus;* see etym. under **minute²**]

**mi|nus** (mī′nəs), *prep., adj., n.* **—*prep.* 1** less; decreased by: *gross earnings minus costs. 5 minus 2 leaves 3.* **2** without; lacking: *a book minus its cover.*
—***adj.* 1** less than: *A mark of B minus is not so high as B.* **2** showing subtraction: *a minus sign.* **3a** less than zero: *If you have no money, and owe someone 10¢, you have minus 10¢.* **b** negative in quantity. **4** *Botany.* of or having to do with the strain of heterothallic fungi which acts as the female in reproduction.
—***n.* 1** the sign (−) meaning that the quantity following is to be subtracted: *There is a minus before the number to be subtracted.* **2** a negative quantity. **3** any deficiency or shortcoming; lack.
[< Latin *minus* less, neuter of *minor,* comparative of *parvus* small]

**mi|nus|cu|lar** (mi nus′kyə lər), *adj.* **1** like a minuscule; small. **2** consisting of minuscules.

***mi|nus|cule** (mi nus′kyül), *adj., n.* **—*adj.* 1** extremely small: *a minuscule person.* **2a** (of a letter) small: *Legal-size pages of written material in minuscule letters that can be blown up to reading size* (Wall Street Journal). **b** written in minuscules.
—***n.* 1** a small letter in medieval writing, neither capital nor uncial. **2** a lower-case letter.
[< French *minuscule,* learned borrowing from Latin *minuscula* (*littera*) slightly smaller (letters) < *minus* less; see etym. under **minus**]

***minuscule**
definition 1

a b c d e — A B C D E
minuscules — majuscules

***minus sign**, the sign indicating that the quantity following is to be subtracted, or is a negative quantity.

***minus sign**

— 16 − 3 = 13

***min|ute¹** (min′it), *n., v.,* **-ut|ed, -ut|ing. —*n.* 1** one sixtieth of an hour; sixty seconds: *ten minutes to six. Abbr:* min. **2** a short time; instant: *I'll be there in a minute.* **3** an exact point of time: *Come here this minute. The minute you see him coming, please tell me.* **4** one sixtieth of a degree. 10° 10′ means ten degrees and ten minutes.
—***v.t.* 1** to record in the minutes of a meeting or other proceeding. **2** to draft (a document, report, or the like); summarize in a memorandum: *I ... told them the story ... just as I have since minuted it down* (Daniel Defoe). **3** to time exactly, as movements or speed.

**at the last minute,** at the latest possible time; just before the last opportunity to do something: *Labor Secretary Wirtz stepped in at the last minute to halt a strike ... which threatened opening day at the ball park* (New York Times).

**minutes, a** a written summary of what happened, such as at a meeting of a society, board, or committee, kept by the secretary: *The meeting started with some disagreement as to whether executive-committee minutes should be read* (Newsweek). **b** a rough draft or written summary; note; memorandum: *Glossin had made careful minutes of the information derived from these examinations* (Scott).

**up to the minute,** up to date: *She keeps her clothes up to the minute. We brought him up to the minute on the developments.*

[< Old French *minute* < Late Latin *minūta* minute, small part < Latin *minūta,* feminine of *minūtus;* see etym. under **minute²**]

—*Syn. n.* **2, 3 Minute, moment, instant** mean a point or extremely short period of time. When **minute** is less definite in meaning than "sixty seconds," it is interchangeable with **moment,** both suggesting a brief time of noticeable duration: *May I rest a minute? I'll be with you in a moment.* **Instant** suggests a point of time, a period too brief to be noticed: *I recognized him the instant I saw him.*

***minute¹**
definition 4

′ 54° 40′

**mi|nute²** (mī nüt′, -nyüt′; mə-), *adj.* **1** very small: *a minute speck of dust, minute animals, minute portions, minute variations.* **SYN**: tiny, diminutive, little. **2** going into very small details; very precise or particular: *a minute observer. He gave me minute instructions about how to do my work.* **SYN**: detailed. **3** of very little consequence or importance; trifling; petty: *to involve the minutest details of a case.* [< Latin *minūtus* made small, past participle of *minuere* diminish < *minus* less; see etym. under **minus.** See etym. of doublet **menu.**] **—mi|nute′ness,** *n.*

**min|ute gun** (min′it), **1** the firing of a gun, especially a cannon, once a minute as a signal of distress or formal indication of mourning. **2** a gun used for this.

**minute hand**, the longer hand on a clock or watch, that indicates minutes. It moves around the whole dial once in an hour.

**min|ute|ly¹** (min′it lē), *adj., adv.* **—*adj.*** happening every minute; continually occurring; unceasing.
—***adv.*** every minute; minute by minute.
[< *minute¹* + *-ly*]

**mi|nute|ly²** (mī nüt′lē, -nyüt′-; mə-), *adv.* in minute manner, form, degree, or detail. [< *minute²* + *-ly*]

**min|ute|man** (min′it man′), *n., pl.* **-men.** a member of the American militia just before and during the Revolutionary War. The minutemen kept themselves ready for military service at very short notice. [American English < *minute¹* + *man*]

**Min|ute|man** (min′it man′), *n., pl.* **-men.** *U.S.* **1** a member of a secret reactionary organization formed in 1961 to prepare militarily against a communist uprising or invasion it believes to be imminent: *The prisoners and weapons belonged to bands of Minutemen, a right-wing group* (New York Times). **2** a three-stage, solid-fueled intercontinental ballistic missile, launched from underground silos. [< *minuteman*]

**min|ute of arc** (min′it), 1/60 of a degree.

**min|utes** (min′its), *n.pl.* See under **minute¹.**

**min|ute steak** (min′it), a thin, small piece of steak cut from the top round, often scored or cubed, that can be cooked very quickly.

**mi|nu|ti|a** (mi nü′shē ə, -nyü′-), *n.* singular of **minutiae.**

**mi|nu|ti|ae** (mi nü′shē ē, -nyü′-), *n.pl.* very small matters; trifling details: *scientific minutiae. They waited ... for the exchange of pass-words, the delivery of keys, and all the slow minutiae attendant upon the movements of a garrison in a well-guarded fortress* (Scott). [< Latin *minūtiae* trifles, plural of *minūtia* smallness < *minūtus;* see etym. under **minute²**]

**minx** (mingks), *n.* **1** a pert girl; hussy: *She liked the notion of humbling the haughty minx* (Cardi-

**Pronunciation Key:** hat, āge, cãre, fär; let, ēqual, tėrm; it, īce; hot, ōpen, ôrder; oil, out; cup, pu̇t, rüle; child; long; thin; ᴛʜen; zh, measure; ə represents a in about, e in taken, i in pencil, o in lemon, u in circus.

nal Newman). **2** *Obsolete.* a lewd or wanton woman. [origin uncertain. Compare Low German *minsk* person.]

**min|yan** (min′yən), *n., pl.* **min|ya|nim** (min′yə nēm′), **min|yans.** the minimum of ten male Jews over thirteen years old required by Jewish law in order to hold a religious service or to form a congregation. In Conservative Judaism, women may be included in the minyan. [< Hebrew *minyan*]

**min|yo** (min′yō′), *n. Japanese.* folk song; ballad.

**Mi|o|cene** (mī′ə sēn), *n., adj.* **—*n.*** **1** the fourth epoch of the Tertiary period of the Cenozoic, after the Oligocene and before the Pliocene. During the Miocene, grasses developed and grazing mammals flourished. **2** the rocks formed in this epoch. **—*adj.*** of this epoch or these rocks. [< Greek *meiōn* less + *kainós* new, recent]

**mi|o|hip|pus** (mī′ō hip′əs), *n.* any one of an extinct group of horses of North America, closely related to mesohippus but somewhat larger. See picture under **evolution.** [< New Latin *miohippus* < Greek *meíōn* less + *híppos* horse]

**mi|o|sis**[1] (mī ō′sis), *n., pl.* **-ses** (-sēz). excessive contraction of the pupil of the eye. Also, **meiosis, myosis.** [< Greek *myein* to shut (the eyes)]

**mi|o|sis**[2] (mī ō′sis), *n., pl.* **-ses** (-sēz). = meiosis.

**mi|ot|ic**[1] (mī ot′ik), *adj., n.* **—*adj.*** having to do with, suffering from, or causing miosis. **—*n.*** a drug that causes miosis. Also, **myotic.**

**mi|ot|ic**[2] (mī ot′ik), *adj.* = meiotic.

**MIP** (no periods), Monthly Investment Plan (a plan for purchasing listed securities by investing a fixed amount on a regular or monthly basis).

**miq|ue|let** (mik′ə lit), *n.* **1** a Spanish guerrilla soldier who fought against the French in Spain from 1808 to 1814. **2** a soldier belonging to any one of certain regiments of Spanish militia, used especially for local escort duty. [< French *miquelet* < Spanish *miquelete*]

**mir** (mēr), *n.* a self-governing farming community that existed in Russia in the middle 1800's. [< Russian *mir*]

**Mi|ra** (mī′rə), *n.* the brightest and first variable star discovered, one of the largest of all stars, in the constellation Cetus. [< New Latin *Mira* < Latin *m īra,* feminine of *m īrus* wonderful]

**mir|a|belle** (mir′ə bəl), *n.* **1** a kind of European plum. **2** a colorless plum brandy made from it. [< French *mirabelle*]

**mi|ra|bi|le dic|tu** (mi rab′ə lē dik′tü, -tyü), *Latin.* wonderful to relate; amazing as it may seem: *Mirabile dictu, the price hasn't gone up by so much as a penny* (New Yorker).

**mi|ra|bi|li|a** (mir′ə bil′ē ə), *n.pl. Latin.* miracles; wonderful things; wonders.

**mi|ra|cid|i|um** (mī′rə sid′ē əm), *n., pl.* **-i|a** (-ē ə). the minute, ciliated aquatic larva which hatches from the egg of a fluke and infects the snail, the intermediate host, in the development of the fluke. [< New Latin *miracidium* < Greek *meirakídion* little boy (diminutive) < *meirákion* boy]

**mir|a|cle** (mir′ə kəl), *n.* **1** a wonderful happening that is beyond the known laws of nature: *It would be a miracle if the sun stood still in the heavens for an hour. The greatest miracle in the New Testament is the resurrection of Jesus Christ* (Bernard Ramm). **2** something marvelous; a wonder: *It was a miracle you weren't hurt in that accident.* **3** a remarkable example: *an engineering miracle. Mother is a miracle of patience to answer all the questions that the children ask. What hymns are sung, what praises said For homemade miracles of bread?* (Louis Untermeyer). **4** = miracle play. [<Old French *miracle <Latin mīrāculum <mīrārī* marvel at *<mīrus* wonderful]

**miracle drug,** a drug, especially an antibiotic, considered to be a marvelous relief or cure for a disease; wonder drug.

**miracle fruit,** an African fruit that is tasteless by itself but becomes sweet when mixed with a sour substance: *Miracle fruit comes from a wild shrub, in tropical West Africa* (New Scientist). Also, **miraculous fruit.**

**miracle man, 1** *Informal.* a man who accomplishes something unusually difficult or previously thought impossible. **2** a man who performs miracles; wonder-worker.

**miracle play,** a play based on Bible stories, especially on the life of Christ, or on the legends of the saints, produced during the Middle Ages.

**miracle rice,** a hybrid rice seed whose yield is twice or three times traditional varieties.

**mi|rac|u|lin** (mə rak′yə lin), *n.* the taste-modifying protein of the miracle fruit, isolated for use as a sweetener and for research into the mechanism of taste: *A glycoprotein of comparatively small molecular size, ... miraculin possesses no taste itself. If, however, a person ingests miraculin and then sometime later eats a sour, acid food, that food will taste sweet* (Magnus Pyke). [< *miracul(ous)* + *-in*[2]]

**mi|rac|u|lous** (mə rak′yə ləs), *adj.* **1** going against the known laws of nature: *In the story, the miraculous tree grew up again in an hour after it was cut down. Christ's raising of Lazarus from the dead was miraculous.* SYN: supernatural. **2** wonderful; marvelous: *miraculous good fortune.* SYN: extraordinary. **3** producing a miracle; having the power to work miracles; wonder-working. [< Middle French *miraculeux* (with English *-ous*), learned borrowing from Medieval Latin *miraculosus* < Latin *mīrāculum;* see etym. under **miracle**] **—mi|rac′u|lous|ly,** *adv.* **—mi|rac′u|lous|ness,** *n.*

**miraculous fruit,** = miracle fruit.

**mir|a|dor** (mir′ə dôr′, -dōr′), *n.* a turret, bay window, or the like, on a Spanish house, from which a fine view may be had. [< Spanish *mirador* < *mirar* to look]

**mi|rage** (mə räzh′), *n.* **1** an optical illusion, usually in the desert, at sea, or over a hot paved road, in which some distant scene appears to be much closer than it actually is. It is caused by the refraction of light rays from the distant scene by air layers of different temperatures. Often what is reflected is seen upside down or as something other than it is. Travelers on the desert may see a mirage of palm trees and water. *The sweet mirage that lured me on its track* (William W. Story). **2** *Figurative.* anything that does not exist; illusion. [< French *mirage* < *mirer* look at carefully < Latin *mīrāre,* variant of *mīrārī* wonder at < *mīrus* wonderful]

**Mi|ran|da card** (mi ran′də), *U.S.* a card carried by police on which is printed the constitutional rights read to an accused person, usually upon arrest: *Police used a Miranda card to read a Mexican immigrant his rights before arresting him in connection with the barroom slaying* (New York Post). [< Ernesto *Miranda,* 1942-1976, the defendant in a case (1966) in which the U.S. Supreme Court ruled a defendant must be informed of his rights prior to questioning]

**mire** (mīr), *n., v.,* **mired, mir|ing.** **—*n.*** **1** soft, deep mud; slush: *I sink in deep mire, where there is no standing* (Psalms 69:2). **2** wet, swampy ground; bog; swamp. **—*v.t.*** **1** to get stuck in mire: *He mired his horses and had to go for help.* **2** to soil with mud or mire: (*Figurative.*) *smeared thus and mired with infamy* (Shakespeare). SYN: defile. **3** *Figurative.* to involve in difficulties; entangle. SYN: embroil. **—*v.i.*** to stick in mire; be bogged: *A path ... that is so muddy that one mires afore he sets out* (James Fenimore Cooper). [< Scandinavian (compare Old Icelandic *mýrr* bog, swamp)]

**mire|poix** (mir pwä′), *n., pl.* **-poix.** a mixture of chopped vegetables, herbs, seasonings, and bits of fat meat placed under meat or fish for braising. [< French *mirepoix,* probably < the duke of *Mirepoix,* a French diplomat of the 1700's]

**Mi|ri|am** (mir′ē əm), *n.* a Hebrew prophetess, the sister of Moses and Aaron (in the Bible, Exodus 15:20).

**mir|i|ness** (mīr′ē nis), *n.* miry condition.

**mirk** (mėrk), *n., adj.* = murk.

**mirk|y** (mėr′kē), *adj.,* **mirk|i|er, mirk|i|est.** = murky.

**mir|ror** (mir′ər), *n., v.* **—*n.*** **1** a glass in which you can see yourself; looking glass: *Mirrors showing stained and aging faces* (Ford Madox Ford). *The reflecting microscope ... was made largely for the sheer fun of making a microscope with mirrors instead of lenses* (Science News). **2** any surface that reflects light. **3** *Figurative.* whatever reflects or gives a true description: *This book is a mirror of the life of the pioneers.* **4** *Figurative.* something to be imitated; a model; example; pattern: *That knight was a mirror of chivalry.* **5** *Archaic.* a glass or crystal used in magic art: *With a single drop of ink for a mirror, The Egyptian sorcerer undertakes to reveal ... visions of the past* (George Eliot). **—*v.t.*** **1** to reflect as a mirror does: *The water was so still that it mirrored the trees along the bank.* **2** to convert (glass) into a mirror by plating. **with mirrors, a** by the use of mirrors to create an optical illusion: *The magician pulled off that trick with mirrors.* **b** *Figurative.* by the use of magic or trickery: *It is Wizard of Oz economics — all done with mirrors* (New Scientist). [< Old French *mireor,* or *mirour* < *mirer* wonder at < Latin *mīrāre;* see etym. under **mirage**] **—mir′ror|like′,** *adj.*

**mirror carp,** any one of a variety of carp having shining scales of various sizes, the larger ones being below the dorsal fin and near the tail.

**mir|rored** (mir′ərd), *adj.* having a mirror or mirrors: *a mirrored hall.*

**mirror image,** an image in reverse; reflection: *The two ridges are roughly mirror images of each other, showing that the motion was uniform on each side* (Scientific American).

**mir|ror|phone** (mir′ər fōn′), *n.* a device in which language students watch their mouth movements and compare them with those of a speaker.

**mirror sextant,** the common sextant having a horizon glass and an index glass.

**mirror writing,** writing reversed from the usual order, as if seen reflected in a mirror. Mirror writing is sometimes a symptom of aphasia or nervous disease.

**mirth** (mėrth), *n.* merry fun; being joyous or gay; laughter: *a sudden outburst of mirth. His sides shook with mirth. Then I commended mirth, because a man hath no better thing under the sun, than to eat, and to drink, and to be merry* (Ecclesiastes 8:15). SYN: merriment, merrymaking, jollity, gaiety, glee, hilarity. [Old English *myrgth* joy, pleasure, related to *myrge* merry]

**mirth|ful** (mėrth′fəl), *adj.* merry; jolly; joyous or gay; laughing. SYN: amused. **—mirth′ful|ly,** *adv.* **—mirth′ful|ness,** *n.*

**mirth|less** (mėrth′lis), *adj.* without mirth; joyless; gloomy. SYN: cheerless. **—mirth′less|ly,** *adv.* **—mirth′less|ness,** *n.*

**MIRV** (mėrv), *n., v.* **—*n.*** **1** a long-range missile having multiple warheads that can be guided from beyond the atmosphere to different targets so as to penetrate an enemy's antiballistic missile shield. **2** any one of the warheads on this missile. **—*v.t.*** to equip with a MIRV. [< *M*(ultiple) *I*(ndependently-targeted) *R*(eentry) *V*(ehicle)]

**mir|y** (mīr′ē), *adj.,* **mir|i|er, mir|i|est.** **1** muddy; slushy. **2** swampy; boggy; marshy: *The miry defiles ... of the mountains* (Washington Irving). **3** *Figurative.* dirty; filthy.

**mir|za** (mir′zə, mēr′zä), *n.* in Iran: **1** a royal prince (as a title, placed after the name). **2** a standard title of honor, placed before the surname. [< Persian *mīrzād* < *mīr* prince, chief (< Arabic *amīr* emir) + *zādah* born]

**mis-,** *prefix.* **1** bad: *Misgovernment* = *bad government.* **2** badly: *Misbehave* = *behave badly.* **3** wrong: *Mispronunciation* = *wrong pronunciation.* **4** wrongly: *Misapply* = *apply wrongly.* [Old English *mis-,* or in borrowed words < Old French *mes-* < Old High German *missi-, missa-*]

**mis|ad|dress** (mis′ə dres′), *v.t.* to address improperly or incorrectly.

**mis|ad|ven|ture** (mis′əd ven′chər), *n.* an unfortunate accident; bad luck; mishap. SYN: misfortune. [alteration of Middle English *misaventure* < Old French *mesaventure* < *mesavenir* turn out badly; patterned on *aventure* adventure]

**mis|ad|ven|tur|ous** (mis′əd ven′chər əs), *adj.* unfortunate; unlucky.

**mis|ad|vise** (mis′əd vīz′), *v.t.,* **-vised, -vis|ing.** to advise wrongly or incorrectly.

**mis|a|lign** (mis′ə līn′), *v.t.* **1** to align incorrectly: *Doors will work even if misaligned* (Science News Letter). **2** to put out of alignment: *I ... had broken the glass of my watch and misaligned the hands* (London Times). **—mis′a|lign′ment,** *n.*

**mis|al|li|ance** (mis′ə lī′əns), *n.* an unsuitable alliance or association, especially in marriage. [< *mis-* + *alliance,* patterned on French *mésalliance*]

**mis|al|lo|cate** (mis al′ə kāt), *v.t.,* **-cat|ed, -cat|ing.** to distribute (money, time, or other resources) incorrectly or poorly; misappropriate or misapply: *The tendency ... is to misallocate managerial skills* (Sunday Times). **—mis′al|lo|ca′tion,** *n.*

**mis|al|ly** (mis′ə lī′), *v.t.,* **-lied, -ly|ing.** to ally inappropriately; join unsuitably.

**mis|an|dry** (mi′san drē, mī′-), *n.* hatred of men. [< Greek *mīsandríā* < *mīsandros* man hating < *mîsos* hatred + *anḗr, andrós* man]

**mis|an|thrope** (mis′ən thrōp, miz′-), *n.* a person who dislikes or distrusts people in general; hater of mankind: *He was also a lonely misanthrope who saw the world and himself with intolerable clarity* (Time). [< Greek *mīsánthrōpos* < *miseîn* to hate + *ánthrōpos* man]

**mis|an|throp|ic** (mis′ən throp′ik), *adj.* of or like a misanthrope: *scowling on all the world from his misanthropic seclusion* (Francis Parkman). **—mis′an|throp′i|cal|ly,** *adv.*

**mis|an|throp|i|cal** (mis′ən throp′ə kəl), *adj.* = misanthropic.

**mis|an|thro|pist** (mis an′thrə pist), *n.* = misanthrope.

**mis|an|thro|py** (mis an′thrə pē), *n.* hatred, dislike, or distrust of people in general: *The outcry was so great that it ... may well have been responsible in part for Degas's subsequent misanthropy* (New Yorker).

**mis|ap|pli|ca|tion** (mis′ap lə kā′shən), *n.* a misapplying or being misapplied; wrong application.

**mis|ap|plied** (mis′ə plīd′), *adj.* put to a wrong use; applied wrongly.

**mis|ap|ply** (mis′ə plī′), *v.t.,* **-plied, -ply|ing.** to put to a wrong use; apply wrongly.

**mis|ap|prais|al** (mis′ə prā′zəl), *n.* an incorrect appraisal.

**mis|ap|pre|hend** (mis′ap ri hend′), *v.t.* = misunderstand. SYN: misconstrue.

**mis|ap|pre|hen|sion** (mis′ap ri hen′shən), *n.* a misunderstanding; misconception.

**mis|ap|pre|hen|sive** (mis′ap ri hen′siv), *adj.*

misapprehending; apt to misapprehend. — **mis′ap-pre|hen′sive|ly**, *adv.*

**mis|ap|pro|pri|ate** (*v.* mis′ə prō′prē āt; *adj.* mis′ə-prō′prē it), *v.*, **-at|ed**, **-at|ing**, *adj.* — ***v.t.*** **1** to use dishonestly as one's own: *The treasurer had misappropriated the club funds.* **2** to put to a wrong use. SYN: misapply.
— ***adj.*** = inappropriate. — **mis′ap|pro|pri|a′tion**, *n.*

**mis|as|sign** (mis′ə sīn′), *v.t.* to assign to the wrong person or category.

**mis|at|trib|ute** (mis′ə trib′yüt), *v.t.*, **-ut|ed**, **-ut|ing**. to attribute incorrectly: *Acts of anonymous attack ... may be misattributed as to source and so lead to a world holocaust* (Bulletin of Atomic Scientists). — **mis′at|tri|bu′tion**, *n.*

**mis|be|come** (mis′bi kum′), *v.t.*, **-came**, **-come**, **-com|ing**. to be unbecoming to; be unfit for: *Profanity misbecomes a lady.*

**mis|be|gat** (mis′bi gat′), *v. Archaic.* misbegot; a past tense of **misbeget**.

**mis|be|get** (mis′bi get′), *v.t.*, **-got** or (*Archaic*) **-gat**, **-got|ten** or **-got**, **-get|ting**. to beget unlawfully.

**mis|be|got** (mis′bi got′), *adj.*, *v.* — ***adj.*** = misbegotten.
— ***v.*** a past tense and a past participle of **misbeget**.

**mis|be|got|ten** (mis′bi got′ən), *adj.*, *v.* — ***adj.*** **1** unlawfully or improperly begotten; illegitimate. **2** *Informal.* rascally: *Three misbegotten knaves in Kendal green* (Shakespeare).
— ***v.*** a past participle of **misbeget**.

**mis|be|have** (mis′bi hāv′), *v.i.*, *v.t.*, **-haved**, **-hav-ing**. to behave badly; conduct oneself improperly: *She was not the woman to misbehave towards her betters* (George Eliot).

**mis|be|hav|ior** (mis′bi hāv′yər), *n.* bad behavior. SYN: misconduct.

**mis|be|hav|iour** (mis′bi hāv′yər), *n. Especially British.* misbehavior.

**mis|be|lief** (mis′bi lēf′), *n.* a wrong or erroneous belief, especially an unorthodox or heretical religious belief.

**mis|be|lieve** (mis′bi lēv′), *v.i.*, **-lieved**, **-liev|ing**. to hold an erroneous belief, especially an unorthodox or heretical religious belief. — **mis′be-liev′er**, *n.*

**mis|be|stow** (mis′bi stō′), *v.t.* to bestow improperly.

**mis|brand** (mis brand′), *v.t.* **1** to brand or mark incorrectly. **2** to label improperly or falsely, especially with the brand name or trademark of another: *The Federal Trade Commission still is studying whether his textile companies misbranded their products* (Wall Street Journal).

**misc.**, **1** miscellaneous. **2** miscellany.

**mis|cal|cu|late** (mis kal′kyə lāt), *v.t.*, *v.i.*, **-lat|ed**, **-lat|ing**. to calculate wrongly or incorrectly.

**mis|cal|cu|la|tion** (mis′kal kyə lā′shən), *n.* a wrong or incorrect calculation: [*Hitler's*] *miscalculation was not in respect of Russia; ... his miscalculation was in respect of Britain* (Atlantic).

**mis|call** (mis kôl′), *v.t.* to call by a wrong or incorrect name; misname.

**mis|car|riage** (mis kar′ij), *n.* **1** a failure, especially to achieve the proper result: *Because the judge was unfair, that trial resulted in a miscarriage of justice. With infinite difficulty and repeated miscarriages I at length effected my purpose* (William Godwin). SYN: breakdown. **2** failure to arrive or deliver: *the miscarriage of a letter, a miscarriage of freight.* **3** the birth of a baby before it is able to live; birth of a fetus before it can live, especially before the twentieth week of pregnancy. SYN: abortion.

**mis|car|ry** (mis kar′ē), *v.i.*, **-ried**, **-ry|ing**. **1** to go wrong; be unsuccessful: *My plans miscarried and I could not go on vacation. His letters to his son are a mixture of excited admiration and apprehension lest Karl's genius miscarry* (Edmund Wilson). **2** to fail to arrive: *My letter to mother must have miscarried, for she never received it.* **3** to have a miscarriage; give birth to a baby before it is able to live. **4** to be born before being developed enough to live. **5** *Obsolete.* to go astray.

**mis|cast** (mis kast′, -käst′), *v.t.*, **-cast**, **-cast|ing**. to put in a role for which one is not suited: *The soft-spoken actor was badly miscast as Iago.*

**mis|ce|ge|na|tion** (mi sej′ə nā′shən, mis′ə jə-), *n.* an intermarriage or interbreeding between different races, especially, in the United States, between whites and blacks. [American English < Latin *miscēre* mix + *genus* race + English *-ation*]

**mis|ce|ge|net|ic** (mis′ə jə net′ik), *adj.* of or constituting miscegenation: *The rule voiding miscegenetic marriages creates another disturbing problem* (Atlantic).

**mis|cel|la|ne|a** (mis′ə lā′nē ə), *n.pl.* a miscellaneous collection, especially of literary compositions; miscellany. [< Latin *miscellānea* a meat hash; a (literary) medley, neuter plural of *miscellāneus* miscellaneous]

**mis|cel|la|ne|i|ty** (mis′ə lə nē′ə tē), *n.* the condition of being miscellaneous: *... lost in the general impression of fragmentation and miscellaneity* (Manchester Guardian Weekly).

**mis|cel|la|ne|ous** (mis′ə lā′nē əs), *adj.* **1** not all of one kind or nature; of mixed composition or character: *The boy had a miscellaneous collection of stones, butterflies, marbles, stamps, birds' nests, and many other things. My second boy ... received a sort of miscellaneous education* (Oliver Goldsmith). **2** dealing with various subjects; many-sided: *a miscellaneous writer. Abbr:* misc. [< Latin *miscellāneus* (with English *-ous*) < *miscellus* mixed < *miscēre* to mix] — **mis′cel|la′-ne|ous|ly**, *adv.* — **mis′cel|la′ne|ous|ness**, *n.*
— ***Syn.* 1 Miscellaneous, indiscriminate** mean including various things or kinds, without plan or order in selection. **Miscellaneous** emphasizes the varied or mixed nature of the things gathered together: *A person's miscellaneous expenses include stamps and haircuts.* **Indiscriminate** emphasizes the lack of judgment or taste in selection and always suggests disapproval: *Indiscriminate buying is wasteful.*

**Mis|cel|la|ne|ous** (mis′ə lā′nē əs), *adj.* of or having to do with a class of chickens that are raised especially for show purposes.

**mis|cel|la|nist** (mis′ə lā′nist, -lə-; mi sel′ə-), *n.* a writer of miscellanies.

**mis|cel|la|ny** (mis′ə lā′nē, mi sel′ə-), *n., pl.* **-nies**. a miscellaneous collection; mixture: *A man who takes notes these days soon finds himself drowning in his own miscellany* (New Yorker). SYN: medley, mélange.
**miscellanies**, a collection of miscellaneous articles in one book: *He has published a volume of miscellanies.*
[< Latin *miscellānea*, neuter plural of *miscellāneus;* see etym. under **miscellaneous**]

**misch** (mish), *n.* a mixture of rare-earth metals, primarily cerium and lanthanum, used to make flints for cigarette lighters and as an ingredient in alloys. Also, **misch metal**. [< German *mischen* to mix, ultimately < Latin *miscēre*]

**mis|chance** (mis chans′, -chäns′), *n.* **1** bad luck; misfortune: *By some mischance he didn't receive my telegram.* SYN: misadventure. **2** a piece of bad luck; unlucky accident: *... the vicissitudes and mischances of sublunary affairs* (Hawthorne). [alteration of Middle English *meschaunce* < Old French *mescheance* < *mes-* mis- + *cheance* chance]

**mis|char|ac|ter|ize** (mis kar′ik tə rīz), *v.t.*, **-ized**, **-iz|ing**. to characterize incorrectly.

**mis|chief** (mis′chif), *n.* **1** conduct that causes harm or trouble, often without meaning it: *A child's mischief may cause a serious fire.* **2** injury, usually done by some person; harm: *Why are you angry? He did you no mischief. The devil is seldom out of call when he is wanted for any mischief* (Daniel Defoe). *The mischief of flattery is ... that it suppresses the influence of honest ambition* (Samuel Johnson). SYN: damage, hurt. **3** a person who does harm or causes annoyance, often just in fun: *You little mischief! You have untied my apron.* **4** merry teasing: *Her eyes were full of mischief.*
**raise (the) mischief**, *Informal.* to make a disturbance; create an uproar or confusion: *The head editor has been in here raising the mischief and tearing his hair* (Mark Twain).
[< Old French *meschief* < *meschever* to come (or bring) to grief < *mes-* badly, mis- + *chever* to come to an end < *chief* the head or end < Latin *caput, -itis*]

**mis|chief-mak|er** (mis′chif mā′kər), *n.* a person who makes mischief; person who stirs up trouble, as by gossiping or talebearing.

**mis|chief-mak|ing** (mis′chif mā′king), *adj.*, *n.*
— ***adj.*** causing trouble or quarrels.
— ***n.*** the act or practice of stirring up trouble or quarrels.

**mis|chie|vous** (mis′chə vəs), *adj.* **1** full of mischief; causing annoyance; naughty: *mischievous behavior.* **2** harmful or injurious: *mischievous gossip.* SYN: hurtful. **3** full of pranks and teasing fun: *mischievous children.* SYN: playful, teasing, roguish. — **mis′chie|vous|ly**, *adv.* — **mis′chie|vous-ness**, *n.*
► In nonstandard speech **mischievous** is frequently pronounced (mis chē′vi əs).

**misch metal**, = misch.

**mis|ci|bil|i|ty** (mis′ə bil′ə tē), *n.* the quality or condition of being miscible.

**mis|ci|ble** (mis′ə bəl), *adj.* that can be mixed: *Water is not miscible with oil.* [< Latin *miscēre* mix + English *-ible*]

**mis|cite** (mis sīt′), *v.t.*, **-cit|ed**, **-cit|ing**. to cite erroneously; misquote. — **mis′ci|ta′tion**, *n.*

**mis|clas|si|fi|ca|tion** (mis′klas ə fə kā′shən), *n.* incorrect or false classification.

**mis|clas|si|fy** (mis klas′ə fī), *v.t.*, **-fied**, **-fy|ing**. to classify incorrectly or falsely: *... misclassifying car buyers into higher risk categories and charging them stiffer premiums* (Wall Street Journal).

**mis|code** (mis kōd′), *v.t.*, **-cod|ed**, **-cod|ing**. to provide with a wrong or faulty genetic code.

**mis|col|or** (mis kul′ər), *v.t.* to give an inaccurate color to.

**mis|col|our** (mis kul′ər), *v.t. Especially British.* miscolor.

**mis|com|mu|ni|cate** (mis′kə myü′nə kāt), *v.t.*, *v.i.*, **-cat|ed**, **-cat|ing**. to communicate wrongly or incorrectly: *miscommunicated military orders.*

**mis|com|pre|hend** (mis′kom pri hend′), *v.t.* = misunderstand.

**mis|com|pre|hen|sion** (mis′kom pri hen′shən), *n.* wrong comprehension; mistaken meaning; misunderstanding: *A comedy of miscomprehension that explodes into sudden tragedy* (Time).

**mis|con|ceive** (mis′kən sēv′), *v.t.*, *v.i.*, **-ceived**, **-ceiv|ing**. to have wrong ideas about; misunderstand: *Things which, for want of due consideration ... they misconceived* (Richard Hooker).
— **mis′con|ceiv′er**, *n.*

**mis|con|cep|tion** (mis′kən sep′shən), *n.* a mistaken idea or notion; wrong conception: *The great errors and dangers that may result out of a misconception of the names of things* (William Harvey).

**mis|con|duct** (*n.* mis kon′dukt; *v.* mis′kən dukt′), *n.*, *v.* — ***n.*** **1** bad behavior; improper conduct: *The misconduct of the children resulted in their being punished.* **2** bad management; mismanagement: *The misconduct of that business nearly ruined it.* **3** *Law.* **a** adultery. **b** malfeasance.
— ***v.t.*** **1** to manage badly; mismanage: *The owner misconducted his business, running it quickly into bankruptcy.* **2** to behave badly: *The boys misconducted themselves at the movies with loud talk and laughter.*

**mis|con|struc|tion** (mis′kən struk′shən), *n.* a wrong or mistaken meaning; misunderstanding: *What you said was open to misconstruction.* SYN: misinterpretation.

**mis|con|strue** (mis′kən strü′), *v.t.*, **-strued**, **-stru-ing**. to take in a wrong or mistaken sense; misunderstand: *The little girl's shyness was sometimes misconstrued as rudeness.* SYN: misinterpret.

**mis|cop|y** (mis kop′ē), *v.*, **-cop|ied**, **-cop|y|ing**, *n., pl.* **-cop|ies**. — ***v.t.*** to copy incorrectly.
— ***n.*** **1** an incorrect copy. **2** an error in copying.

**mis|coun|sel** (mis koun′səl), *v.*, **-seled**, **-sel|ing** or (*especially British*) **-selled**, **-sel|ling**, *n.* — ***v.t.*** to counsel wrongly; misadvise.
— ***n.*** wrong counsel.

**mis|count** (*v.* mis kount′; *n.* mis′kount′), *v.*, *n.*
— ***v.t.***, ***v.i.*** to count wrongly or incorrectly; miscalculate; misreckon: *I miscounted the number of guests for lunch which meant several sandwiches were left over.*
— ***n.*** a wrong or incorrect count: *A miscount of the cookies led to a disagreement.*

**mis|cre|ant** (mis′krē ənt), *adj.*, *n.* — ***adj.*** **1** having very bad morals; wicked; base; depraved: *a miscreant gang of criminals.* SYN: vile, detestable. **2** *Archaic.* unbelieving; heretical.
— ***n.*** **1** a base or wicked person; villain: *He belongs to a ... gang of miscreants sworn against all order and peace* (Edward G. E. L. Bulwer-Lytton). **2** *Archaic.* an unbeliever; heretic.
[< Old French *mescreant* < *mes-* wrongly, mis- + *creant,* present participle of *creire* believe < Latin *crēdere*]

**mis|cre|ate** (*v.* mis′krē āt′; *adj.* mis′krē it, -āt′), *v.*, **-at|ed**, **-at|ing**, *adj.* — ***v.t.***, ***v.i.*** to create amiss; misform.
— ***adj.*** created or formed improperly or unnaturally; misshapen. — **mis′cre|a′tion**, *n.*

**mis|cue** (mis kyü′), *n.*, *v.*, **-cued**, **-cu|ing**. — ***n.*** **1** a stroke in billiards or pool in which the cue slips, causing it to miss the ball or not to hit it squarely. **2** *Informal, Figurative.* an error; slip; mistake: *The miscues gave the* [*Cincinnati*] *Redlegs five unearned runs* (New York Times).
— ***v.i.*** **1** to make a miscue in billiards or pool. **2** *Theater.* to miss one's cue; respond to a wrong cue.

**mis|date** (mis dāt′), *v.*, **-dat|ed**, **-dat|ing**, *n.* — ***v.t.*** to date wrongly or incorrectly; assign or affix an incorrect date to: *Friday's newspaper was misdated as Saturday.*
— ***n.*** a wrong or incorrect date.

**mis|deal** (*v.* mis dēl′; *n.* mis′dēl′), *v.*, **-dealt**, **-deal|ing**, *n.* — ***v.t.***, ***v.i.*** to deal wrongly at cards.
— ***n.*** a wrong deal at cards. — **mis|deal′er**, *n.*

**mis|deed** (mis dēd′, mis′dēd′), *n.* a bad act; wicked deed. SYN: misdemeanor, offense. [Old English *misdǣd*]

---

**Pronunciation Key:** hat, āge, cãre, fär; let, ēqual, tėrm; it, īce; hot, ōpen, ôrder; oil, out; cup, pu̇t, rüle; child; long; thin; ᴛʜen; zh, measure; ə represents **a** in about, **e** in taken, **i** in pencil, **o** in lemon, **u** in circus.

**mis|deem** (mis dēm′), *v.i.* to deem or judge wrongly.
— ***v.t.*** to have a wrong opinion of.

**mis|de|mean** (mis′di mēn′), *v.t., v.i.* to behave badly; misbehave.

**mis|de|mean|ant** (mis′di mē′nənt), *n.* **1** *Law.* a person convicted of a misdemeanor. **2** a person guilty of misconduct.

**mis|de|mean|or** (mis′di mē′nər), *n.* **1** *Law.* an act of breaking the criminal law, not so serious as a felony: *The theft of a small amount of money is a misdemeanor.* **2** a wrong deed. **SYN**: misdeed. **3** bad behavior; misconduct. **SYN**: misbehavior.

**mis|de|mean|our** (mis′di mē′nər), *n. Especially British.* misdemeanor.

**mis|de|rive** (mis′di rīv′), *v.t.,* **-rived, -riv|ing.** to derive incorrectly; assign an incorrect derivation to. — **mis′der|i|va′tion,** *n.*

**mis|de|scribe** (mis′di skrīb′), *v.t.,* **-scribed, -scrib|ing.** to describe incorrectly or falsely.

**mis|de|scrip|tion** (mis′di skrip′shən), *n.* an incorrect description.

**mis|des|ig|nate** (mis dez′ig nāt), *v.t.,* **-nat|ed, -nat|ing.** to designate wrongly; miscall; misname.

**mis|di|ag|nose** (mis′dī əg nōs′, -nōz′), *v.t.,* **-nosed, -nos|ing.** to diagnose incorrectly.

**mis|di|ag|no|sis** (mis′dī əg nō′sis), *n., pl.* **-ses** (-sēz). an incorrect diagnosis: *Even in recent years this same misdiagnosis has been made, and patients have been committed to mental institutions as having childhood schizophrenia when in reality they have phenylketonuria* (Atlantic).

**mis|did** (mis did′), *v.* the past tense of **misdo.**

**mis|di|rect** (mis′də rekt′, -dī-), *v.t.* to direct wrongly; give wrong directions to: *Great interests ... which might be affected by a misdirected or careless inheritance of the colossal Walter empire* (Time). *In the hurry of a trial the ablest judge may mistake the law and misdirect the jury* (William Blackstone). **SYN**: mislead.

**mis|di|rec|tion** (mis′də rek′shən, -dī-), *n.* **1** wrong direction; improper guidance. **2** direction to an incorrect address: *misdirection of a letter.* **3** *Law.* an error made by a judge in his charge to a jury.

**mis|di|vide** (mis′də vīd′), *v.t.,* **-vid|ed, -vid|ing.** to divide incorrectly.

**mis|di|vi|sion** (mis′də vizh′ən), *n.* an incorrect division.

**mis|do** (mis dü′), *v.t., v.i.,* **-did, -done, -do|ing.** to do wrongly; perform improperly; do amiss: *I have misdone, and I endure the smart* (John Dryden). [Old English *misdōn*] — **mis|do′er,** *n.*

**mis|do|ing** (mis dü′ing), *n.* **1** = wrongdoing. **2** = misdeed.

**mis|done** (mis dun′), *v.* the past participle of **misdo.**

**mis|doubt** (mis dout′), *v., n.* — ***v.t., v.i.*** **1** to have doubts about; be distrustful of; suspect; distrust: *I do not misdoubt my wife* (Shakespeare). *We do injuriously ... to misdoubt her [truth's] strength* (Milton). **2** to fear.
— ***n.*** **1** suspicion; distrust; doubt. **2** fear of evil: *Change misdoubt to resolution* (Shakespeare).

**mise** (mēz, mīz), *n.* **1** a settlement by agreement. **2** *Law.* the main point or issue in a writ of right. [< Anglo-French, Old French *mise* < *mettre* set, place < Latin *mittere*]

**mis|ease** (mis ēz′), *n. Archaic.* **1** uneasiness; disquiet. **2** distress; affliction. **SYN**: discomfort, suffering. [< Old French *mesaise* < *mes-* ill, mis- + *aise* ease]

**mis|ed|u|cate** (mis ej′u kāt), *v.t.,* **-cat|ed, -cat|ing.** to educate improperly.

**mis|ed|u|ca|tion** (mis′ej u kā′shən), *n.* improper education.

**mise en scène** (mē′ zäN sen′), *French.* **1** the scenery, properties, and the like, for a play: *The tasteful handling of the mise en scène and the subtle use of color ... made the performance a joy to watch* (New Yorker). **2** the placing of scenery and actors in a scene. **3** *Figurative.* setting; surroundings; milieu: *The train whistles in the background add to the mise en scène* (Harper's).

**mis|em|ploy** (mis′em ploi′), *v.t.* to use wrongly or improperly. **SYN**: misuse. — **mis′em|ploy′ment,** *n.*

**mi|ser** (mī′zər), *n.* **1a** a person who loves money for its own sake; one who lives poorly in order to save money and keep it. A miser dislikes to spend money for anything, except to gain more money. *Even to the old The hours are as a miser's coins* (Thomas B. Aldrich). **SYN**: skinflint, niggard. **b** any grasping person. **2** *Obsolete.* a miserable wretch. [< Latin *miser* wretched]

**mis|er|a|ble** (miz′ər ə bəl, miz′rə-), *adj., n.* — ***adj.*** **1** very unhappy; unfortunate or uncomfortable: *A sick child is often miserable.* **SYN**: See syn. under **wretched. 2** causing trouble, unhappiness, or discomfort: *miserable damp weather. I have a miserable cold. O, I have passed a miserable night, so full of ugly sights, of ghastly dreams* (Shakespeare). **3a** poor; mean; wretched: *The ragged child lives in miserable surroundings.* **SYN**: sordid. **b** pitiful; deplorable; sorry: *a miserable failure, miserable sinners.*
— ***n.*** a person who is in misery or great want.
[< Old French *miserable,* learned borrowing from Latin *miserābilis* < *miserārī* to lament < *miser* wretched] — **mis′er|a|ble|ness,** *n.* — **mis′er|a|bly,** *adv.*

**Mis|e|re|re** (miz′ə rãr′ē, -rir′-), *n.* **1** the 51st Psalm in the Revised and Authorized versions of the Bible; the 50th Psalm in the Douay Version of the Bible. **2** a musical setting for this psalm. [< Latin *miserēre* have pity, singular imperative of *miserērī* (the first word of this psalm in the Vulgate)]

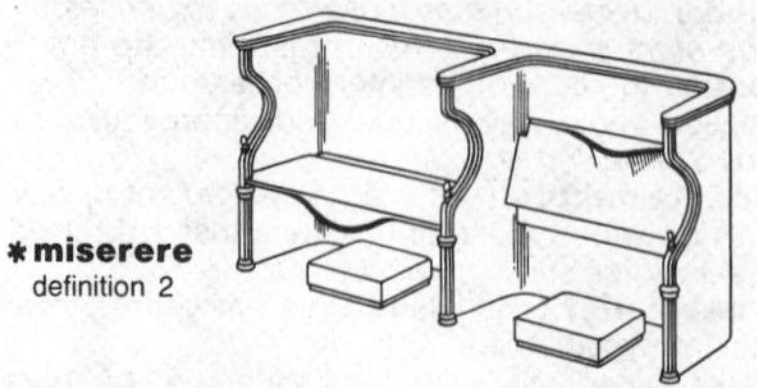

***miserere** definition 2

***mis|e|re|re** (miz′ə rãr′ē, -rir′-), *n.* **1** a prayer asking mercy. **2** a bracket on the under side of a hinged seat in a church stall, so arranged that when the seat is turned up a person standing in the stall could lean against it for support. [< *Miserere*]

**mis|er|i|cord** or **mis|er|i|corde** (miz′ər ə kôrd′, mi zer′ə kôrd), *n.* **1** a specially permitted relaxation of monastic rule, as in dress or food. **2** a room in a monastery in which certain relaxations of the rule are permitted, especially those relating to food. **3** = miserere (def. 2). **4** (in the Middle Ages) a dagger used to give the death blow to a wounded foe. [< Latin *misericordia* < *misericors, -cordis* < *miserērī* to have pity on (< *miser* wretched) + *cor, cordis* heart]

**mi|se|ri|cor|di|a** (miz′ər ə kôr′dē ə), *n. Latin.* compassion; pity.

**mi|ser|li|ness** (mī′zər lē nis), *n.* the condition or quality of being miserly; avariciousness; niggardliness; penuriousness.

**mi|ser|ly** (mī′zər lē), *adj.* of, like, or suited to a miser; stingy: *miserly habits, a miserly wretch.* **SYN**: niggardly, close, penurious.

**mis|er|y** (miz′ər ē, miz′rē), *n., pl.* **-er|ies. 1** a miserable, unhappy state of mind: *Think of the misery of having no home or friends. It is acknowledged that rage, envy, resentment, are in themselves mere misery* (Samuel Butler). **SYN**: wretchedness, woe, distress. **2** poor, mean, miserable circumstances: *the misery of poverty, companions in misery. The very poor live in misery without beauty or comfort around them.* **3** a miserable condition or circumstance; a cause or source of wretchedness: *The explorer was exposed to unthinkable miseries and hardships. That packet of assorted miseries which we call a ship* (Rudyard Kipling). **4** *U.S.* bodily pain: *He had the worst "misery in his back" that he had ever suffered* (George W. Cable). [< Latin *miseria* < *miser* wretched]

**mis|es|teem** (mis′es tēm′), *v., n.* — ***v.t.*** to hold improperly in low esteem.
— ***n.*** want of esteem or respect; disesteem.

**mis|es|ti|mate** (*v.* mis es′tə māt; *n.* mis es′tə-mit), *v.,* **-mat|ed, -mat|ing,** *n.*
— ***v.t.*** to make an incorrect estimate of.
— ***n.*** an incorrect estimate or valuation. — **mis′es-ti|ma′tion,** *n.*

**mis|fea|sance** (mis fē′zəns), *n.* **1** the wrongful performance of a lawful act; wrongful and injurious exercise of lawful authority. **SYN**: malfeasance. **2** any wrong done; trespass: *General denunciation, embellished with assorted charges of misfeasance and high misdemeanors* (New York Times). **SYN**: misdeed. [< Middle French *mesfaisance* < Old French *mesfaire* to misdo < *mes-* wrong, mis- + *faire* do < Latin *facere*]

**mis|fea|sor** (mis fē′zər), *n. Law.* a person guilty of misfeasance.

**mis|file** (mis fīl′), *v.t.,* **-filed, -fil|ing.** to file incorrectly: *a misfiled memorandum.*

**mis|fire** (mis fīr′), *v.,* **-fired, -fir|ing,** *n.* — ***v.i.*** **1** to fail to fire or explode properly: *The pistol misfired. The firings were the first of the Talos since October 15 when the missile's booster misfired shortly after takeoff* (Wall Street Journal). **2** to go wrong; fail: *The robber's scheme misfired and he went to jail. The play as a whole misfires* (New Yorker).
— ***n.*** failure to discharge or start.

**mis|fit** (*n.* mis′fit′; *v.* mis fit′), *n., v.,* **-fit|ted, -fit|ting.** — ***n.*** **1** a person who does not fit in a job or group; maladjusted individual: *The old farmer sure was a misfit among all those fancy businessmen.* **2** a bad fit; a garment or other article which does not fit: *Do not buy shoes which are misfits.*
— ***v.t., v.i.*** to fit badly: *His clothes are completely misfitting.*

**mis|form** (mis fôrm′), *v.t.* to form amiss; misshape.

**mis|for|ma|tion** (mis′fôr mā′shən), *n.* = malformation.

**mis|for|tune** (mis fôr′chən), *n.* **1** bad luck; bad or adverse fortune: *Misfortune has a habit of striking when it's least expected.* **2** a piece of bad luck; unlucky accident: *The misfortunes hardest to bear are those which never come* (James Russell Lowell). *By misfortunes was my life prolong'd, To tell sad stories of my own mishaps* (Shakespeare).
— ***Syn.*** **1, 2 Misfortune, adversity, mishap** mean something unlucky. **Misfortune** applies to an unfortunate condition that is not one's own fault: *She had the misfortune to be born lame.* **Adversity** applies chiefly to misfortune marked by a series of accidents or hardships: *Displaced persons have experienced adversity.* **Mishap** applies to a minor accident or unlucky incident: *Breaking a dish is a mishap. By some mishap the letter went astray.*

**mis|gauge** (mis gāj′), *v.t.,* **-gauged, -gaug|ing.** to gauge incorrectly; misestimate: *No diplomatic response has fueled aggression as has appeasement—the act of misgauging the imperialist's appetite* (Wall Street Journal).

**mis|give** (mis giv′), *v.,* **-gave, -giv|en, -giv|ing.**
— ***v.t.*** to cause to feel doubt, suspicion, or anxiety: *My mind misgives me that we are lost.*
— ***v.i.*** to have misgivings.

**mis|giv|ing** (mis giv′ing), *n.* a feeling of doubt, suspicion, or anxiety: *We started off through the storm with some misgivings.* **SYN**: foreboding, apprehension.

**mis|gov|ern** (mis guv′ərn), *v.t.* to govern or manage badly.

**mis|gov|ern|ment** (mis guv′ərn mənt, -ər-), *n.* bad government or management.

**mis|guid|ance** (mis gī′dəns), *n.* bad or wrong guidance; faulty or improper direction; misdirection.

**mis|guide** (mis gīd′), *v.t.,* **-guid|ed, -guid|ing.** to lead into mistakes or wrongdoing; mislead. **SYN**: misdirect. — **mis|guid′er,** *n.*

**mis|guid|ed** (mis gī′did), *adj.* led into mistakes or wrongdoing; misled: *The misguided boy joined a gang of thieves.* — **mis|guid′ed|ly,** *adv.* — **mis-guid′ed|ness,** *n.*

**mis|han|dle** (mis han′dəl), *v.t.,* **-dled, -dling. 1** to handle badly or roughly; maltreat: *It is a shame to see how they have mishandled the old man among them* (Scott). **2** to manage badly; mismanage: *to mishandle accounts.*

**mi|shan|ter** (mi shan′tər), *n. Scottish.* misadventure; mishap. [variant of earlier *misaunter,* contraction of *misaventure* misadventure]

**mis|hap** (mis′hap, mis hap′), *n.* **1** an unlucky accident; misadventure: *By some mishap the letter went astray. ... secure from worldly chances and mishaps* (Shakespeare). **SYN**: See syn. under **misfortune. 2** bad luck; misfortune. **SYN**: See syn. under **misfortune.**

**mis|hear** (mis hir′), *v.t., v.i.,* **-heard** (-hėrd′), **-hear|ing.** to hear incorrectly or imperfectly.

**mis|hit** (*n.* mis′hit′; *v.* mis hit′), *n., v.,* **-hit, -hit-ting.** — ***n.*** a faulty or bad hit: *A club is thrown wildly away after a mishit* (Punch).
— ***v.t.*** to hit badly: *Father Urban watched Father Feld mishit his second shot, saw it ... roll back down ten yards—into a bad lie* (J. F. Powers).

**mish|mash** (mish′mash′), *n., v.* — ***n.*** a confused mixture; hodgepodge; jumble: *a mishmash of unrelated facts and figures. A gastronomical mishmash of grilled and roasted and fried fishes and meats* (Atlantic).
— ***v.t.*** to make a mishmash of.
[probably imitative reduplication of *mash*[1]. Compare German *Mischmasch* < *mischen* to mix.]

**Mish|nah** or **Mish|na** (mish′nə), *n.* **1** the collection of interpretations and discussions of the law of Moses by the rabbis, codified about 200 A.D.; oral law of the Jews. The Mishnah is written in Hebrew and forms the basic part of the Talmud. **2** a section or paragraph of this collection. [< Hebrew *mishnāh* instruction < *shānāh* he learned; earlier, he repeated]

**Mish|na|ic** (mish nā′ik), *adj.* **1** having to do with or relating to the Mishnah. **2** characteristic of the Mishnah: *Mishnaic Hebrew.*

**mis|i|den|ti|fi|ca|tion** (mis′ī den′tə fə kā′shən), *n.* wrong or mistaken identification.

**mis|i|den|ti|fy** (mis′ī den′tə fī), *v.t.,* **-fied, -fy|ing.** to identify wrongly or mistakenly: *Members of the crowd loudly misidentify the ministers* (London Times).

**mis|im|pres|sion** (mis′im presh′ən), *n.* a mistaken impression or idea.

**mis|in|form** (mis′in fôrm′), *v.t.* to give wrong or misleading information to. — ***v.i.*** to make a false statement about someone or something. — **mis′in|form′er**, *n.*

**mis|in|form|ant** (mis′in fôr′mənt), *n.* a person who gives wrong or misleading information.

**mis|in|for|ma|tion** (mis′in fər mā′shən), *n.* wrong or misleading information.

**mis|in|ter|pret** (mis′in tėr′prit), *v.t., v.i.* to interpret or explain wrongly; misunderstand. **SYN**: misconstrue. — **mis′in|ter′pre|ta′tion**, *n.* — **mis′in|ter′pret|er**, *n.*

**mis|join|der** (mis join′dər), *n. Law.* a joining of parties in an action, or of causes of action in a suit, that ought not to be so joined.

**mis|judge** (mis juj′), *v.*, **-judged, -judg|ing.** — ***v.t.*** **1** to judge wrongly: *The archer misjudged the distance to the target, and his arrow fell short.* **2** to judge unjustly: *The teacher soon discovered that she had misjudged the girl's character.* — ***v.i.*** to form wrong opinions.

**mis|judge|ment** (mis juj′mənt), *n. Especially British.* misjudgment.

**mis|judg|ment** (mis juj′mənt), *n.* wrong or unjust judgment.

**Mis|ki|to** (mis kē′tō), *n., pl.* **-tos** or **-to.** **1** a member of a people of mixed American Indian and Negro descent, living on the eastern coast of Nicaragua and Honduras. **2** the language of this people. Also, **Mosquito.**

**mis|know** (mis nō′), *v.t.*, **-knew** (-nü′ or -nyü′), **-known, -know|ing. 1** to misapprehend; misunderstand. **2** *Scottish.* to not recognize (a person).

**mis|knowl|edge** (mis nol′ij), *n.* faulty knowledge; misapprehension of truth or fact.

**mis|la|bel** (mis lā′bəl), *v.t.*, **-beled, -bel|ing** or (*especially British*) **-belled, -bel|ling.** to label falsely or incorrectly: *horsemeat mislabeled as beef* (New York Times).

**mis|laid** (mis lād′), *v.* the past tense and past participle of **mislay**: *The boy mislaid my books. I have mislaid my pen.*

**mis|lay** (mis lā′), *v.t.*, **-laid, -lay|ing. 1** to put in a place and then forget where it is; lose temporarily: *Mother is always mislaying her glasses. Was ever anything so provoking—to mislay my own jewels, and force me to wear her trumpery* (Oliver Goldsmith). **2** to put in an incorrect place. — **mis|lay′er**, *n.*

**mis|lead** (mis lēd′), *v.t.*, **-led, -lead|ing. 1** to cause to go in the wrong direction; lead astray: *Our guide misled us in the woods, and we got lost.* **SYN**: misguide, misdirect. **2** to cause to do wrong; lead into wrongdoing: *He is a good boy, but bad companions misled him.* **3** to lead to think what is not so; deceive: *His lies misled me. Misled by fancy's meteor ray, By passion driven* (Robert Burns). **SYN**: delude, beguile, dupe. — **mis|lead′er**, *n.*

**mis|lead|ing** (mis lē′ding), *adj.* **1** causing wrong conclusions; deceiving: *The detectives found that the false clue was misleading.* **2** causing mistakes or wrongdoing: *Bad advice can be misleading.* — **mis|lead′ing|ly**, *adv.* — **mis|lead′ing|ness**, *n.*

**mis|leared** (mis lird′), *adj. Scottish.* unmannerly; ill-bred. [< *mis-* + Middle English *leared,* past participle of *leren* teach, Old English *lǣran*]

**mis|led** (mis led′), *v.* the past tense and past participle of **mislead**: *The boy was misled by bad companions. ... by ambition far misled* (Scott).

**mis|like** (mis līk′), *v.*, **-liked, -lik|ing,** *n.* — ***v.t.*** **1** to disapprove of; dislike: *Mislike me not for my complexion* (Shakespeare). **2** to displease; offend.
— ***n.*** aversion; dislike; distaste: *Julian's mislike of the rising faith* (Richard C. Trench). — **mis|lik′er**, *n.*

**mis|man|age** (mis man′ij), *v.t., v.i.*, **aged, -ag|ing.** to manage badly or improperly: *If you mismanage the business, you will lose money.* — **mis|man′age|ment**, *n.* — **mis|man′ag|er**, *n.*

**mis|mar|riage** (mis mar′ij), *n.* an unsuitable marriage; unwise marriage; mismatch.

**mis|match** (mis mach′), *v., n.* — ***v.t.*** to match badly or unsuitably, especially in marriage: (*Figurative.*) *These seemingly mismatched mergers are not as ill-matched as they appear* (Wall Street Journal).
— ***n.*** a bad, unwise, or unsuitable match.

**mis|mate** (mis māt′), *v.t., v.i.*, **-mat|ed, -mat|ing.** to mate unsuitably.

**mis|move** (mis müv′), *n.* **1** *U.S.* a faulty move or step in action; misstep. **2** any wrong move, as in a game.

**mis|name** (mis nām′), *v.t.*, **-named, -nam|ing.** to call by a wrong name; miscall: *That lazy, careless boy is misnamed Ernest.*

**mis|no|mer** (mis nō′mər), *n.* **1** a name that describes wrongly; wrong designation: *"Lightning" is a misnomer for that slow, old horse.* **2** an error in naming; misapplication of a term. **3** *Law.* a mistake in naming a person in a legal instrument. [< Middle French *mesnommer* < *mes-* wrongly, mis- + *nommer* to name < Latin *nomināre* < *nomen, -inis* name]

**mis|no|mered** (mis nō′mərd), *adj.* wrongly named: *the misnomered "low-priced" field* (Wall Street Journal).

**mi|so** (mē′sō), *n.* a Japanese vegetable paste made from fermented soybean curds: *Thick, heavy miso [is] used for anything from a basis for soup to a marinade for beef* (Manchester Guardian Weekly). [< Japanese *miso*]

**mi|sog|a|mist** (mi sog′ə mist, mī-), *n.* a person who hates marriage.

**mi|sog|a|my** (mi sog′ə mē, mī-), *n.* hatred of marriage. [< Greek *mîsos* hatred + *gámos* marriage]

**mis|o|gyn|ic** (mis′ə jin′ik, mī′sə-), *adj.* misogynous.

**mi|sog|y|nism** (mi soj′ə niz əm), *n.* hatred of women; misogyny.

**mi|sog|y|nist** (mi soj′ə nist, mī-), *n.* a hater of women.

**mi|sog|y|nis|tic** (mi soj′ə nis′tik, mī-), *n.* characteristic of misogynism or misogynists: *The misogynistic lament that "Adam ever lost a rib"* (Harper's).

**mi|sog|y|nous** (mi soj′ə nəs, mī-), *adj.* hating women.

**mi|sog|y|ny** (mi soj′ə nē, mī-), *n.* hatred of women. [< Greek *mīsogyniā* < *mīsogýnēs* woman hater < *mîsos* hatred + *gynḗ* woman]

**mi|sol|o|gist** (mi sol′ə jist, mī-), *n.* **1** a hater of reason or discussion. **2** a hater of learning.

**mi|sol|o|gy** (mi sol′ə jē, mī-), *n.* **1** hatred of reason or discussion. **2** hatred of learning. [< Greek *mīsologiā* < *mîsos* hatred + *lógos* reason, discussion]

**mis|o|ne|ism** (mis′ə nē′iz əm, mī′sə-), *n.* hatred or dislike of what is new; strong opposition to change. [< Italian *misoneismo* < Greek *mîsos* hatred + *néos* new + Italian *-ismo* -ism] — **mis′o|ne′ist**, *n.*

**mis|o|ne|is|tic** (mis′ə nē is′tik, mī′sə-), *adj.* hating what is new.

**mis|o|ri|ent** (mis ôr′ē ent, -ōr′-), *v.t.* to place in the wrong direction; arrange or position badly; misdirect: *Adjacent grains are misoriented with respect to one another* (New Scientist).

**mis|o|ri|en|tate** (mis ôr′ē en tāt, -ōr′-), *v.t.*, **-tat|ed, -tat|ing.** = misorient.

**mis|o|ri|en|ta|tion** (mis ôr′ē en tā′shən, -ōr′-), *n.* wrong or improper orientation.

**mis|per|ceive** (mis′pər sēv′), *v.t.*, **-ceived, -ceiv|ing.** to perceive imperfectly or erroneously: *From the very beginning, you have grossly misperceived our situation* (Donald Barthelme).

**mis|per|cep|tion** (mis′pər sep′shən), *n.* imperfect or erroneous perception.

**mis|pick|el** (mis′pik′əl), *n.* = arsenopyrite. [< German *Mispickel*]

**mis|place** (mis plās′), *v.t.*, **-placed, -plac|ing. 1** *Informal.* to put in a place and then forget where it is; mislay: *I have misplaced my pencil.* **2** to put in a wrong place: *misplaced acts of foolery* (Charles Lamb). **3** to give (one's love or trust) to the wrong person, especially to one who is unworthy: *His affections have been misplaced in a fickle admirer.* — **mis|place′ment**, *n.*

**mis|play** (mis plā′), *n., v.* — ***n.*** a wrong play, especially one not permitted by the rules of a game.
— ***v.t., v.i.*** to play wrongly: *She misplayed her hand in cards.*
[American English < *mis-* + *play*]

**mis|plead** (mis plēd′), *v.t., v.i. Law.* to plead wrongly.

**mis|plead|ing** (mis plē′ding), *n. Law.* an error in pleading, as through the omission of something essential to the case.

**mis|praise** (mis prāz′), *v.t.*, **-praised, -prais|ing. 1** to praise mistakenly or imprudently: *They, whom I have so mispraised, are the worse in the sight of God for my overpraising* (John Donne). **2** to dispraise; blame.

**mis|print** (*n.* mis′print′; *v.* mis print′), *n., v.* — ***n.*** a mistake in printing: *Several misprints in the directory led to wrong telephone numbers.* **SYN**: erratum.
— ***v.t.*** to print wrongly: *They misprinted the book's title, upside down.*

**mis|prise** (mis prīz′), *v.t.*, **-prised, -pris|ing.** = misprize.

**mis|pri|sion[1]** (mis prizh′ən), *n.* **1a** a wrongful action or omission, especially by a public official. **b** *Law.* failure to give to the proper authority information which to a person's knowledge may lead to the apprehension of a felon: *misprision of treason.* **2** *Archaic.* the mistaking of a thing, word, or other item or object, for another; misunderstanding. **SYN**: misapprehension, mistake. [< Old French *mesprision* < *mesprendre* to mistake, act wrongly < *mes-* mis- + *prendre* take < Latin *prehendere*]

**mis|pri|sion[2]** (mis prizh′ən), *n. Archaic.* contempt; scorn: *those unhappy persons, who ... have their hearts barred against conviction by prejudice and misprision* (Scott). [< *misprize* + *-ion;* influenced by *misprision*[1]]

**mis|prize** (mis prīz′), *v.t.*, **-prized, -priz|ing. 1** to value too little; undervalue; slight: *Not that I have any call to misprize the event ... since it launched me upon a commercial career* (New Yorker). **2** to despise; scorn: *It sorrows me that you misprize my love* (Thomas Heywood). [< Old French *mesprisier* < *mes-* mis- + *prisier,* variant of *preisier* praise, prize[3]]

**mis|pro|nounce** (mis′prə nouns′), *v.t., v.i.*, **-nounced, -nounc|ing.** to pronounce incorrectly: *Many people mispronounce the word "mischievous."*

**mis|pro|nun|ci|a|tion** (mis′prə nun′sē ā′shən), *n.* an incorrect pronunciation.

**mis|proud** (mis proud′), *adj. Archaic.* wrongly or wickedly proud; arrogant.

**mis|punc|tu|ate** (mis pungk′chů āt), *v.t.*, **-at|ed, -at|ing.** to punctuate incorrectly. — **mis′punc|tu|a′tion**, *n.*

**mis|quo|ta|tion** (mis′kwō tā′shən), *n.* **1** an incorrect quotation. **2** inaccuracy in quoting.

**mis|quote** (mis kwōt′), *v.t., v.i.*, **-quot|ed, -quot|ing.** to quote incorrectly: *With just enough of learning to misquote* (Byron).

**mis|read[1]** (mis rēd′), *v.t.*, **-read, -read|ing. 1** to read incorrectly: *He misread the label and poured sugar instead of salt into the saltshaker.* **2** to interpret wrongly; misunderstand: *She misread the recipe and spoiled the cake.* **SYN**: misconceive. [< *mis-* + *read*[1]]

**mis|read[2]** (mis red′), *v.* the past tense and past participle of **misread[1]**.

**mis|reck|on** (mis rek′ən), *v.t., v.i.* to miscalculate; miscount.

**mis|re|mem|ber** (mis′ri mem′bər), *v.t., v.i.* **1** to remember wrongly, imperfectly, or incorrectly. **2** *Dialect.* to forget.

**mis|re|port** (mis′ri pôrt′, -pōrt′), *v., n.* — ***v.t.*** to report (anything) incorrectly or falsely.
— ***n.*** a false or erroneous report. — **mis′re|port′er**, *n.*

**mis|rep|re|sent** (mis′rep ri zent′), *v.t.* **1** to represent falsely; give a wrong idea of: *He misrepresented the value of the automobile when he said it was in good condition.* **2** to fail to represent correctly or adequately as agent or official representative. — ***v.i.*** to make false or misleading statements. — **mis′rep|re|sent′er**, *n.*

**mis|rep|re|sen|ta|tion** (mis′rep ri zen tā′shən), *n.* **1** a false representation: *He obtained the position by misrepresentation.* **2** an incorrect story or explanation: *The report is a misrepresentation of the facts in the case.*

**mis|rep|re|sent|a|tive** (mis′rep ri zen′tə tiv), *adj.* misrepresenting; conveying a false impression.

**mis|route** (mis rüt′, -rout′), *v.t.*, **-rout|ed, -rout|ing.** to route incorrectly; send by the wrong route: *The parcels ... were misrouted on the railways* (London Times).

**mis|rule** (mis rül′), *n., v.*, **-ruled, -rul|ing.** — ***n.*** **1** bad or unwise rule; misgovernment: *the misrule of a dishonest government official.* **SYN**: maladministration. **2** a condition of disorder, anarchy, or rebellion: *the misrule of mobs* (Lytton Strachey).
— ***v.t.*** to rule or govern badly: *The people elected a mayor who misruled for his entire term of office.* **SYN**: misgovern. — **mis|rul′er**, *n.*

**miss[1]** (mis), *v., n.* — ***v.t.*** **1** to fail to hit or strike: *to miss a target in shooting. He hammers away, but half the time he misses the nail.* **2a** to fail to find, get, or meet: *I set out to meet my father, but in the dark I missed him.* **b** to fail to catch: *to miss a train.* **c** to leave out: *to miss a word in reading.* **d** to fail to hear, understand, or grasp: *to miss the point of a remark. What did you say? I missed a word or two.* **e** to fail to keep, do, or be present at: *I missed my music lesson today.* **3** to let slip by; not seize: *I missed the chance of a ride to town.* **4** to escape or avoid: *to barely miss being hit, to miss death by a hair.* **5** to notice the absence or loss of; feel keenly the absence of: *I did not miss my purse till I got home. He missed his mother when she went away.*
— ***v.i.*** to fail to hit: *He fired twice, but both shots missed.*
— ***n.*** **1** a failure to hit or reach: *to make more misses than hits.* **2** *Obsolete.* loss; lack: *Aged people feel the miss of children* (George Eliot).
**a miss is as good as a mile,** a close miss has the same effect as a wide miss: *He was very near being a poet—but a miss is as good as a mile, and he always fell short of the mark* (Scott).
**miss fire.** See under **fire.**

**Pronunciation Key:** hat, āge, cãre, fär; let, ēqual, tėrm; it, īce; hot, ōpen, ôrder; oil, out; cup, pu̇t, rüle; child; long; thin; ᴛʜen; zh, measure; ə represents a in about, e in taken, i in pencil, o in lemon, u in circus.

**miss of**, *Archaic.* to fail to hit, meet, obtain, or attain; miss: *A project which ... had very narrowly missed of success* (Macaulay).
**miss out on**, to fail to grasp: *He is also repetitive, misses out on detail, ... and is often inaccurate* (Listener).
**miss the boat**. See under **boat**.
[Old English *missan*]
**miss²** (mis), *n., pl.* **miss|es**. a young unmarried woman; girl: *an arch little miss ... to whom we strove to make ourselves particularly agreeable* (Herman Melville).
**misses**, a size of clothing for girls or women with average-developed figures. Misses' sizes usually run from 8 to 16.
[short for *mistress*]
**Miss** (mis), *n., pl.* **Miss|es**. **1** a title given to a girl or to a woman who is not married: *Miss Brown.* **2** a term of address used to a young woman; young lady: *Excuse me, Miss, are you one of the salesladies?* **3** a title given to a girl or unmarried woman representing the thing named: *Miss Florida, Miss Teen-Age America.*
▶ **Miss**. Plural *Misses* is sometimes pronounced mis′ez or mis′ēz to distinguish from mis′iz (Mrs.): *the Misses Angel and Joyce.* Of the two plural forms used in referring to unmarried women of the same family, *the Misses Thorne* is more formal than *the Miss Thornes.*
**Miss.**, Mississippi.
**mis|sa can|ta|ta** (mis′ə kən tä′tə), a Mass intermediate between High Mass and Low Mass, especially a Low Mass accompanied by choral chants; Sung Mass: *The service for the President was a "missa cantata," a black-vestmented Low Mass, sung in Latin* (New York Times). [< Medieval Latin *missa cantata* sung mass]
**mis|said** (mis sed′), *v.* the past tense and past participle of **missay**.
**mis|sal** (mis′əl), *n.* **1** a book containing the prayers and other devotional matter for celebrating Roman Catholic Mass throughout the year: *The religious were intent on their missals, following the recital of Mass* (Time). **2** a devotional book: *Expert bookmen think the Pierpont Morgan Library purchase, a missal, or book of devotions, was an earlier experimental project of Johannes Gutenberg* (Helen T. Geer). [< Medieval Latin *missale* < Late Latin *missa* Mass]
**Mis|sa So|lem|nis** (mis′ə sə lem′nis), = High Mass. [< Medieval Latin *missa solemnis*]
**mis|say** (mis sā′), *v.*, **-said, -say|ing**. — ***v.i.*** to speak wrongly.
— ***v.t.*** **1** to say wrongly. **2** *Archaic.* to speak ill of; slander. — **mis|say′er**, *n.*
**mis|see** (mis sē′), *v.t., v.i.*, **-saw, -seen, -see|ing**. to see wrongly.
**mis|seem** (mis sēm′), *v.t.* to be unseemly for; misbecome.
**mis|sel thrush** (mis′əl), a large European thrush that feeds on the berries of the mistletoe. [< obsolete *missel* mistletoe, Old English *mistel*]
**mis|send** (mis send′), *v.t.*, **-sent, -send|ing**. to send amiss; send to a wrong place or person.
**mis|sense** (mis′sens′), *adj. Genetics.* having to do with or resulting from specifying the wrong amino acid in the genetic code: *Missense mutant is one in which the codon is mutated to one incorporating a different amino acid, making an inactive or perhaps unstable enzyme* (Scientific American). [< *mis-* + *sense*, as in *nonsense*]
**mis|sent** (mis sent′), *v.* the past tense and past participle of **missend**.
**mis|ses** (mis′əs). See under **miss²**.
**mis|set** (mis set′), *v.t.*, **-set, -set|ting**. to set incorrectly; misplace: *One of these misset relays activated a circuit breaker* (New York Times).
**mis|shape** (mis shāp′), *v.t.*, **-shaped, -shaped** or **-shap|en, -shap|ing**. to make in the wrong shape; shape badly; deform. SYN: distort.
**mis|shap|en** (mis shā′pən), *adj., v.* — ***adj.*** badly shaped; deformed: *This fork got bent and is misshapen. ... the misshapen hairy Scandinavian troll* (Emerson). (*Figurative.*) *Crooked and misshapen minds* (John Florio).
— ***v.*** misshaped; a past participle of **misshape**.
— **mis|shap′en|ly**, *adv.* — **mis|shap′en|ness**, *n.*
**mis|sile** (mis′əl), *n., adj.* — ***n.*** **1** any object that is thrown, hurled, or shot, such as a stone, an arrow, a bullet, or a lance: *David hurled a missile at Goliath.* **2** a self-propelled bomb or rocket. There are ballistic missiles and guided missiles. Missiles can be launched from land, ships, or airplanes. *In our diversified family of missiles, we have weapons adapted to every kind of distance, launching, and use* (Wall Street Journal).
— ***adj.*** **1** capable of or adapted to use as a missile: *We ... bend the bow, or wing the missile dart* (Alexander Pope). **2** that discharges missiles: *long-bows, slings, and other missile weapons* (Scott).
[< Latin *missile*, neuter < *mittere* to send]
**mis|sil|eer** (mis′ə lir′), *n.* = missileman.
**mis|sile|man** (mis′əl man′), *n., pl.* **-men**. a person who works with missiles or rockets, either in construction or in use and maintenance.
**missile range**, a particular course or area, marked out beforehand, over which missiles are test-flown under observation.
**mis|sile|ry** (mis′əl rē), *n.* **1** the science or art having to do with the design, manufacture, and operation of missiles and rockets: *In the fast-maturing age of missilery, a world of new wonders was in the making* (Time). **2** missiles collectively: *The advent of intercontinental missilery with its only multi-minute warning time ... poses a severe dilemma for long-range civil defense planning* (Bulletin of Atomic Scientists).
**mis|sil|ry** (mis′əl rē), *n.* = missilery.
**miss|ing** (mis′ing), *adj.* **1** lacking or wanting: *It was a good cake but something was missing.* **2** out of its usual place; lost; gone: *The missing ring was found under the dresser. One of the books was missing.* **3** absent: *Four children were missing from class today.*
**missing link**, **1** a hypothetical creature assumed to have been the connecting link between man and the anthropoid apes. **2** something lacking from a series: *A small bit of evidence—an old shoe—proved to be the missing link in the murder case.*
**mis|si|ol|o|gy** (mis′ē ol′ə jē), *n.* the study of religious missions and missionary work. [< Latin *missiō, -ōnis* mission + *-logia* -logy]
**mis|sion** (mish′ən), *n., adj., v.* — ***n.*** **1** the action of sending or fact of being sent on some special work or service; errand: *He was sent on a mission to a foreign government.* **2** a group of persons sent on some special business, as to conduct negotiations: *He was one of a mission sent by our government to France.* SYN: commission, delegation. **3** a permanent diplomatic establishment, embassy, or legation. **4** a task or function assigned to a military or naval unit, especially a combat operation by one or more aircraft. **5** a group of persons sent by a religious organization into other parts of the world to spread its beliefs: *A mission was sent to Africa by the Baptist Church.* **6** the business on which a mission is sent: *The diplomats successfully carried out the mission on which they were sent by their government. Hast thou perform'd my mission which I gave?* (Tennyson). SYN: message, charge, duty, trust. **7** the station or headquarters of a religious mission, as the center of missionary effort in a particular area: *a mission in the slums.* **8** a special series of religious services to revive, stimulate, or create religious feeling. **9** a congregation or district assigned to a priest or pastor from a neighboring parish. **10** one's business or purpose in life; one's calling: *It seemed to be her mission to care for her brother's children. When one's all right, he's prone to spite The doctor's peaceful mission* (Eugene Field).
— ***adj.*** of or having to do with a mission or missions.
— ***v.t.*** **1** to conduct a religious mission among (a people) or in (a district). **2** to send (a person) on a mission.
**missions**, an organized effort by a religious group to set up churches, schools, hospitals, or other charitable agencies: *foreign missions.*
[< Latin *missiō, -ōnis* < *mittere* to send]
**mis|sion|al** (mish′ə nəl), *adj.* of or having to do with a mission.
**mis|sion|a|rize** (mish′ə nə rīz), *v.i., v.t.*, **-rized, -riz|ing**. = missionize.
**mis|sion|ar|y** (mish′ə ner′ē), *n., pl.* **-ar|ies**, *adj.* — ***n.*** **1** a person sent on the work of a religious mission: *the missionary went to Africa to convert people to Christianity.* **2** a person who works to advance some cause or idea. **3** *Obsolete.* an emissary.
— ***adj.*** **1** of religious missions or missionaries: *missionary enthusiasm.* **2** sent on a mission; engaged in missionary work: *a missionary priest, a missionary society.*
**mission control**, the spacecraft center on the ground that controls a mission or flight into outer space.
**mission furniture**, a kind of heavy, plain, dark furniture, resembling the furniture used in the old Spanish missions in California.
**mis|sion|ize** (mish′ə nīz), *v.*, **-ized, -iz|ing**. — ***v.i.*** to send missionaries or missions; establish a religious mission or missions: *All three religions ... have been actively missionizing* (Alfred L. Kroeber).
— ***v.t.*** to send missionaries or missions to; convert through evangelizing: *to missionize a pagan people.*
**mis|sions** (mish′ənz), *n.pl.* See under **mission**.
**mis|sis** (mis′iz, -is), *n. Dialect.* **1** a wife: *And how is the missis these days?* **2** the mistress of a household: *Missis and the young ladies and Master John are going out to tea this afternoon* (Charlotte Brontë). Also, **missus**. [variant of *mistress*]
**miss|ish** (mis′ish), *adj.* prim; prudish; affected: *You are not going to be missish, I hope, and pretend to be affronted at an idle report* (Jane Austen). [< *miss²* + *-ish*] — **miss′ish|ness**, *n.*
**Mis|sis|sip|pi|an** (mis′ə sip′ē ən), *n., adj.* — ***n.*** **1** a native or inhabitant of Mississippi. **2** the earlier of the two periods into which the Carboniferous is divided, after the Devonian and before the Pennsylvanian, characterized by the appearance of fern and lichen forests; Lower Carboniferous (the name used outside North America). **3** the rocks formed in this period.
— ***adj.*** **1** of or having to do with Mississippi or the Mississippi River. **2** of or having to do with the Mississippian or its rocks.
**Mississippi kite**, a graceful, falconlike hawk with grayish plumage and black tail, found in the southeastern and central United States.
**Mis|si|sau|ga** (mis′ə sô′gə), *n., pl.* **-ga** or **-gas**. a member of a tribe of Algonkian Indians inhabiting central Ontario and Quebec, first encountered by the French in 1634.
**mis|sive** (mis′iv), *n., adj.* — ***n.*** a written message; letter: *You ... with taunts Did gibe my missive out of audience* (Shakespeare). SYN: dispatch.
— ***adj.*** *Obsolete.* **1** that is or is intended to be sent. **2** sent as a message: *a letter missive.*
[< Medieval Latin *missivus* < Latin *mittere* to send]
**Mis|sou|ri** (mə zůr′ē, -ə), *n., pl.* **-ri** or **-ris**. **1** a member of a Siouan tribe of North American Indians, formerly living in central and western Missouri. **2** the language of this tribe.
**from Missouri**, *Informal.* not convinced until shown clear proof; skeptical; doubtful: *The legislators, for the most part, have said that they are from Missouri* (New Yorker).
[American English < French *Missouri* < the Algonkian name of the tribe, which lived near the mouth of the Missouri River; probably meaning people who have dugout or wooden canoes]
**Mis|sou|ri|an** (mə zůr′ē ən), *adj., n.* — ***adj.*** of Missouri or its people.
— ***n.*** a native or inhabitant of Missouri.
**Missouri flowering currant**, = golden currant.
**mis|speak** (mis spēk′), *v.t., v.i.*, **-spoke, -spo|ken, -speak|ing**. to speak, utter, or pronounce wrongly or incorrectly.
**mis|speech** (mis spēch′), *n.* faulty or incorrect speech.
**mis|spell** (mis spel′), *v.t., v.i.*, **-spelled** or **-spelt, -spell|ing**. to spell incorrectly.
**mis|spell|ing** (mis spel′ing), *n.* an incorrect spelling.
**mis|spelt** (mis spelt′), *adj., v.* — ***adj.*** misspelled.
— ***v.*** misspelled; a past tense and a past participle of **misspell**.
**mis|spend** (mis spend′), *v.t.*, **-spent, -spend|ing**. to spend foolishly or wrongly; waste.
**mis|spent** (mis spent′), *adj., v.* — ***adj.*** spent foolishly or wrongly; wasted: *a misspent fortune, a misspent, ruined life.*
— ***v.*** the past tense and past participle of **misspend**.
**mis|spoke** (mis spōk′), *v.* the past tense of **misspeak**.
**mis|spo|ken** (mis spō′kən), *v.* the past participle of **misspeak**.
**mis|state** (mis stāt′), *v.t.*, **-stat|ed, -stat|ing**. to state wrongly or incorrectly. SYN: misrepresent, distort, falsify. — **mis|state′ment**, *n.*
**mis|step** (mis step′, mis′step′), *n.* **1** a wrong step: *A misstep to the right or left was fatal.* **2** an error or slip in conduct; faux pas.
**mis|sus** (mis′iz, -is), *n.* = missis.
**miss|y** (mis′ē), *n., pl.* **miss|ies**. *Informal.* little miss; miss.
**mist** (mist), *n., v.* — ***n.*** **1** a cloud of very fine drops of water in the air; fog; haze: *As the sun rose it burned off the clouds of low mist in the valleys.* **2** *U.S.* a fine drizzle. **3** a cloud of very fine drops of any liquid in the air: *A mist of perfume issued from the atomizer.* **4** *Figurative.* anything that dims, blurs, or obscures: *She did not cry, but a mist came over her eyes. A mist of prejudice spoiled his judgment. Things view'd ... through the mist of fear* (Thomas Carlyle).
— ***v.i.*** **1** to come down in mist; rain in very fine drops; drizzle: *It is misting.* **2** to become covered with mist; become dim: *The windows are misting.*
— ***v.t.*** to cover with a mist; put a mist before; make dim: *Tears misted her eyes. The composer gazed absently out of the misted window* (London Times).
[Old English *mist*] — **mist′less**, *adj.* — **mist′like′**, *adj.*
**mis|tak|a|ble** (mis tā′kə bəl), *adj.* that may be mistaken or misunderstood. SYN: ambiguous.
**mis|take** (mis tāk′), *n., v.*, **-took, -tak|en, -tak|ing**. — ***n.*** **1** an error in action, thought, or judgment; blunder: *It was a mistake to leave before the snow stopped. I used your towel by mistake.* SYN:

fault, oversight, slip. See syn. under **error**. **2** a misunderstanding of a thing's meaning: *a mistake in interpretation.* [< verb]
— ***v.t.*** **1** to misunderstand (what is seen or heard); take in a wrong sense: *You have mistaken the meaning of the letter.* **2** to take wrongly; take (to be some other person or thing): *to mistake a fixed star for a planet. I mistook that stick for a snake. You can't mistake him for his brother. There's no mistaking his real motive.* **3** to estimate wrongly: *to mistake one's own strength.*
— ***v.i.*** Archaic. to make a mistake; be in error.
**and no mistake,** without a doubt; surely: *Mary Ann was mad, and no mistake* (Harper's).
**make no mistake (about it),** you may be sure; have no doubt: *Whitehall, make no mistake, is gravely alarmed and fearful* (Manchester Guardian Weekly). *Make no mistake about it ... we are going to win* (Atlantic).
[< Scandinavian (compare Old Icelandic *mistaka*)]
— **mis|tak′er,** *n.*

**mis|tak|en** (mis tā′kən), *adj., v.* — ***adj.*** **1** wrong in opinion; having made a mistake: *A mistaken person should admit that he was wrong.* **2** wrongly judged; wrong; misplaced: *a mistaken opinion. It was a mistaken kindness to give that boy more candy; it will make him sick.* **SYN:** erroneous.
— ***v.*** the past participle of **mistake**: *She was mistaken for the queen.* — **mis|tak′en|ly,** *adv.* — **mis|tak′en|ness,** *n.*

**mis|taught** (mis tôt′), *v.* the past tense and past participle of **misteach**: *He was mistaught in the lower grades.*

**mis|teach** (mis tēch′), *v.t.,* **-taught, -teach|ing.** to teach badly or wrongly.

**mis|ter** (mis′tər), *n., v.* — ***n.*** *Informal.* sir: *"Good morning, mister," said Dominicus* (Hawthorne).
— ***v.t.*** *Informal.* to address as "mister."
[variant of *master*]
▶ **Mister** (spelled out in writing) is sometimes used alone as a word of address, especially by a superior officer speaking to another officer under his command, as a ship's master. Except for such traditional uses, *mister* without a name or title following is largely confined to informal English: *What's the time, mister?*

**Mis|ter** (mis′tər), *n.* Mr., a title put before a man's name or the name of his office or occupation: *Mr. Smith, Mr. President.*

**Mister Charlie** or **Mister Charley,** *U.S. Slang.* the white man: *He is an "Uncle Tom," the most dread and spirit-shattering of epithets, ... because he laughs at Mister Charlie's jokes* (Atlantic). Also, **Mr. Charlie** or **Mr. Charley.**

**mis|ter|i|o|so** (mis tir′ē ō′sō), *adv., adj. Music.*
— ***adv.*** mysteriously.
— ***adj.*** mysterious: *The composition went into dance rhythms that turned misterioso with a ululating vibraphone* (Time).
[< Italian *misterioso* mysterious]

**mis|term** (mis tėrm′), *v.t.* to term wrongly or incorrectly.

**mist|flow|er** (mist′flou′ər), *n.* a North American composite herb whose blue flower heads resemble those of the ageratum, but are smaller.

**mis|think** (mis thingk′), *v.,* **-thought, -think|ing.**
— ***v.i.*** **1** to think mistakenly. **2** *Obsolete.* to think unfavorably.
— ***v.t.*** *Obsolete.* to have a bad opinion of.

**mis|thought** (mis thôt′), *v.* the past tense and past participle of **misthink.**

**mist|i|ly** (mis′tə lē), *adv.* in a misty manner.

**mis|time** (mis tīm′), *v.t.,* **-timed, -tim|ing. 1** to say or do at the wrong time: *to mistime a move or a remark.* **2** to miscalculate or misstate the time of.

**mist|i|ness** (mis′tē nis), *n.* misty condition.

**mis|tle** (mis′əl), *n.,* or **mistle thrush,** = missel thrush.

***mistletoe**
definition 1

***mis|tle|toe** (mis′əl tō), *n.* **1** a plant with small, waxy, white berries and yellow flowers, that grows mostly as a parasite on trees, but produces some chlorophyll and is capable of photosynthesis. **2** a sprig of mistletoe, often used as a Christmas decoration: *The mistletoe is still hung up in farm-houses and kitchens at Christmas; and the young men have the privilege of kissing the girls under it* (Washington Irving). [Old English *mistiltān* < *mistel* mistletoe + *tān* twig]

**mis|took** (mis tu̇k′), *v.* the past tense of **mistake**: *I mistook you for your sister yesterday.*

**mis|tral** (mis′trəl, mis träl′), *n.* a cold, dry, northerly wind common in the Mediterranean provinces of France and neighboring regions. [< French *mistral* < Provençal, (originally) dominant < Latin *magistrālis* < *magister* master. See etym. of doublet **magistral.**]

**mis|trans|late** (mis′trans lāt′, -tranz-; mis trans′-lāt, -tranz′-), *v.t., v.i.,* **-lat|ed, -lat|ing.** to translate incorrectly.

**mis|trans|la|tion** (mis′trans lā′shən, -tranz-), *n.* an incorrect translation.

**mis|treat** (mis trēt′), *v.t.* to treat badly or wrongly; ill-treat: *The boy was punished for mistreating his dog.* **SYN:** maltreat, abuse.

**mis|treat|ment** (mis trēt′mənt), *n.* bad treatment; ill-treatment. **SYN:** maltreatment.

**mis|tress** (mis′tris), *n.* **1** the woman who is at the head of a household: *Mistress Gilpin (careful soul!)* (William Cowper). **2** *Figurative.* a woman, country, or idea that is in control or can rule: *Great Britain was sometimes called mistress of the seas. There always lurked the hope that around the corner ... he would encounter ... his long-lost mistress, Inspiration* (John Updike). **3** a woman owner or possessor: *The dog's mistress walks him every day. I show more mirth than I am mistress of* (Shakespeare). **4** a woman who has a thorough knowledge or mastery: *She is a complete mistress of the art of cookery.* **5** a woman teaching in a school, or at the head of a school, or giving lessons in a special subject: *the dancing mistress.* **6** *Archaic.* a woman loved and courted by a man: *O! mistress mine, where are you roaming? O! stay and hear; your true love's coming* (Shakespeare). **7** a woman who lives as a wife with a man without being married to him. **8** *Archaic or Dialect.* Mrs., Madam, or Miss. [< Old French *maistresse,* feminine of *maistre;* see etym. under **master**]

**Mis|tress** (mis′tris), *n. Archaic.* a title of courtesy for a woman, now superseded by *Mrs., Madam,* or *Miss.*

**mistress of ceremonies,** a woman in charge of a ceremony or entertainment.

**mistress of the robe,** *British.* the chief attendant to the queen.

**mis|tri|al** (mis trī′əl), *n.* **1** an inconclusive trial, especially a trial in which the jury cannot agree on a verdict. **2** a trial having no effect in law because of some error in the proceedings: *The decrepit barrister ... has defended his simple little murderer so badly that he saves his life by perpetrating a mistrial* (Listener).

**mis|trust** (mis trust′), *v., n.* — ***v.t.*** **1** to feel no confidence in; suspect the intentions or motives of; distrust; doubt: *She mistrusted her ability to learn to swim.* **SYN:** suspect. **2** to have forebodings about: *The old woman gravely mistrusted the future.*
— ***v.i.*** to be distrustful, suspicious, or without confidence.
— ***n.*** lack of trust or confidence; suspicion; distrust: *He looked with mistrust at the stranger. Hate and mistrust are the children of blindness* (Sir William Watson). **SYN:** doubt. — **mis|trust′er,** *n.* — **mis|trust′ing|ly,** *adv.*

**mis|trust|ful** (mis trust′fəl), *adj.* lacking confidence; distrustful; doubting; suspicious. — **mis-trust′ful|ly,** *adv.* — **mis|trust′ful|ness,** *n.*

**mist|y** (mis′tē), *adj.,* **mist|i|er, mist|i|est. 1** of mist. **2** full of or covered with mist: *misty hills, misty air.* **3** not clearly seen or outlined: *The ghost was just a misty outline.* **4** *Figurative.* as if seen through a mist; vague; indistinct: *a misty notion.* [Old English *mistig*]

**mist|y-eyed** (mis′tē īd′), *adj.* **1** close to tears: *... bowed misty-eyed to the packed hall* (Time). **2** *Figurative.* sentimental to the point of tears: *a misty-eyed speech, misty-eyed farewells.* **3** *Figurative.* having dreamy eyes: *a misty-eyed youth.*

**mis|un|der|stand** (mis′un dər stand′), *v.t., v.i.,* **-stood, -stand|ing. 1** to understand wrongly; not comprehend rightly; misconceive: *He misunderstood the question and got the answer wrong.* **SYN:** misapprehend. **2** to take in a wrong sense; give the wrong meaning to: *Don't misunderstand me; I'm only trying to help, not to pry.* **SYN:** misinterpret. — **mis′un|der|stand′er,** *n.*

**mis|un|der|stand|ing** (mis′un dər stan′ding), *n.* **1** wrong understanding; failure to understand; mistake as to meaning: *I shall speak in simple words that there may be no misunderstanding.* **SYN:** misconception, misinterpretation. **2** a disagreement; quarrel: *After their misunderstanding they scarcely spoke to each other. Some little pique or misunderstanding between them* (George Eliot). **SYN:** dissension.

**mis|un|der|stood** (mis′un dər stu̇d′), *v., adj.* — ***v.*** the past tense and past participle of **misunderstand**: *She misunderstood what the teacher said and did the wrong homework.*
— ***adj.*** **1** not properly understood; taken in a wrong sense. **2** not properly appreciated: *There came a time in her life when she felt herself grievously misunderstood.*

**mis|us|age** (mis yü′sij, -zij), *n.* **1** a wrong or improper usage; misuse. **2** bad treatment; maltreatment; ill-usage.

**mis|use** (*v.* mis yüz′; *n.* mis yüs′), *v.,* **-used, -us|ing,** *n.* — ***v.t.*** **1** to use for the wrong purpose; use improperly: *He misuses his knife at the table by lifting food with it.* **SYN:** misapply. **2** to treat badly; abuse; mistreat: *He misuses his horses by giving them loads that are too heavy. Men deal with life as children with their play, Who first misuse, then cast their toys away* (William Cowper). **SYN:** maltreat, ill-treat.
— ***n.*** **1** a wrong or improper use; misapplication: *I notice a misuse of the word "who" in your letter.* **2** *Obsolete.* ill-usage. **3** *Obsolete.* evil conduct.

**mis|us|er** (mis yü′zər), *n.* **1** *Law.* unlawful use of a liberty, benefit, or power. **2** a person who misuses.

**mis|val|ue** (mis val′yü), *v.t.,* **-ued, -u|ing. 1** to value falsely or wrongly. **2** = undervalue. — **mis′-val|u|a′tion,** *n.*

**mis|ven|ture** (mis ven′chər), *n.* an unfortunate adventure; mischance.

**mis|word** (mis wėrd′), *v.t.* to word (a message or other statement) incorrectly.

**mis|write** (mis rīt′), *v.t.,* **-wrote, -writ|ten, -writ-ing.** to write improperly; make a mistake in writing (a word or statement).

**mis|writ|ten** (mis rit′ən), *v.* the past participle of **miswrite.**

**mis|wrote** (mis rōt′), *v.* the past tense of **mis-write.**

**M.I.T.,** Massachusetts Institute of Technology.

**Mi|tan|ni|an** (mi tan′ē ən), *n.* a member of an ancient people who ruled the area north of Syria from about 2000 to about 1300 B.C.

**Mitchell grass,** any one of various perennial grasses of Australia, much used as fodder.

**mite**[1] (mīt), *n.* a very tiny animal, related to the spider, that lives in foods, on plants, or on other animals. Mites are related to the ticks and sometimes are found as free-living scavengers in soil or water. Mites are arachnids. [Old English *mīte*]

**mite**[2] (mīt), *n., adv.* — ***n.*** **1** anything very small; little bit: *I can't eat even a mite of supper. He doesn't care a mite.* **SYN:** particle, iota, jot, whit. **2** a coin of very small value. **3** a very small sum of money: *Though poor, she gave her mite to charity.* **4** a very small child: *What a mite she is!* **SYN:** tot.
— ***adv.*** *Informal.* little; a bit: *It is a mite easier to make reservations for Europe this year* (Saturday Review).
[< Middle Dutch *mite,* ultimately of same origin as *mite*[1]]

**mi|ter**[1] (mī′tər), *n., v.* — ***n.*** **1** a tall, pointed, folded cap worn by bishops during sacred ceremonies. **2** the office or dignity of bishop; episcopal rank. **3** *Judaism.* the official headdress or ceremonial turban of the ancient Jewish high priest. **4** a headband or fillet worn by women in ancient Greece.
— ***v.t.*** to bestow a miter on; make a bishop. Also, *especially British,* **mitre.**
[< Middle French *mitre* < Latin *mitra* < Greek *mitrā* headband]

**mi|ter**[2] (mī′tər), *n., v.* — ***n.*** **1** = miter joint. **2** the bevel on either of the pieces in a miter joint. **3** = miter square.
— ***v.t.*** **1** to join with a miter joint. The corners of a picture frame are mitered. **2** to prepare (ends of wood) for joining in a miter joint. Also, *especially British,* **mitre.**
[perhaps special use of *miter*[1]]

***miter box,** an apparatus used to cut wood for a miter joint, having cuts to guide the saw.

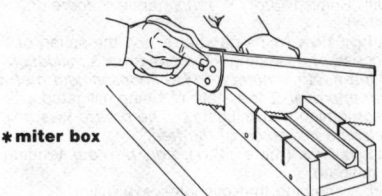

***miter box**

**mi|tered**[1] (mī′tərd), *adj.* having a miter joint.

**mi|tered**[2] (mī′tərd), *adj.* **1** wearing or privileged to wear a bishop's miter: *a mitered abbot.*

**Pronunciation Key:** hat, āge, cãre, fär; let, ēqual, tėrm; it, īce; hot, ōpen, ôrder; oil, out; cup, pu̇t, rüle; child; long; thin; ᴛʜen; zh, measure; ə represents **a** in about, **e** in taken, **i** in pencil, **o** in lemon, **u** in circus.

2 shaped like a bishop's miter.

**miter gear**, a pair of beveled gear wheels of equal diameter whose axles are at right angles, and which have their teeth set at an angle of 45 degrees.

**miter joint**, a kind of joint or corner where two pieces of wood are fitted together at right angles with the ends cut slanting, as at the corners of a picture frame.

**miter shell**, the fusiform shell of any of various gastropods, mostly of warm seas (so called from the shape of the spire).

**miter square**, **1** a carpenter's square having one arm fixed at a right angle to the other. **2** a similar square having an arm adjustable to any angle.

**miter wheels**, the gear wheels of a miter gear.

**mi|ter|wort** (mī′tər wėrt′), *n.* **1** any one of a group of low perennial plants of the saxifrage family, having a capsule that suggests a bishop's miter; bishop's-cap. **2** an annual plant of the southeastern United States, with small white flowers and a capsule shaped like a miter. Also, *especially British,* **mitrewort**.

**Mith|gar|thr** (miᴛʜ′gär′ᴛʜər), *n.* = Midgard.

**Mith|ra** (mith′rə), *n.* = Mithras.

**Mith|rae|um** (mith rē′əm), *n., pl.* **-rae|a** (-rē′ə). a Mithraic temple. [< New Latin *Mithraeum* < Latin *Mithrās* Mithras]

**Mith|ra|ic** (mith rā′ik), *adj.* of, having to do with, or connected with Mithras or his worship.

**Mith|ra|i|cism** (mith rā′ə siz əm), *n.* = Mithraism.

**Mith|ra|ism** (mith′rā iz əm), *n.* the religion of the worshipers of Mithras: *Mithraism took on the form of a mystery religion, with elaborate rites and ceremonies* (C. E. Olmstead).

**Mith|ra|ist** (mith′rā ist), *n.* a worshiper of or believer in Mithras.

**Mith|ra|is|tic** (mith′rā is′tik), *adj.* = Mithraic.

**mith|ra|my|cin** (mith′rə mī′sən), *n.* a highly toxic antibiotic derived from a species of streptomyces, used in the treatment of various cancerous tumors. [< Medieval Latin *mithr*(idatum) an antidote + English (strepto)*mycin*]

**Mith|ras** (mith′ras), *n.* the Persian and Aryan god of light, truth, and justice, who opposed Ahriman, the power of evil and darkness. Mithras became the subject of an extensive cult during the late Roman Empire.

**mith|ri|date** (mith′rə dāt), *n.* an antidote against poison, especially a compound of many ingredients, supposed to be an antidote against all poisons. [< Medieval Latin *mithridatum,* ultimately < *Mithridates* VI, King of Pontus, who supposedly immunized himself against poison]

**mith|ri|dat|ic** (mith′rə dat′ik), *adj.* of or having to do with a mithridate or mithridatism.

**mith|ri|da|tism** (mith′rə dā′tiz əm), *n.* resistance to a poison produced by taking the poison in gradually increased doses.

**mi|ti|cid|al** (mit′ə sī′dəl), *adj.* that destroys mites: *a miticidal agent.*

**mi|ti|cide** (mī′tə sīd), *n.* a substance for killing mites. [< *mite*[1] + *-cide*[1]]

**mit|i|ga|ble** (mit′ə gə bəl), *adj.* that can be mitigated.

**mit|i|gant** (mit′ə gənt), *adj.* mitigating.

**mit|i|gate** (mit′ə gāt), *v.,* **-gat|ed, -gat|ing.** — *v.t.* **1** to make (wrath, harshness, severity, or adversity) less in force or degree: *The American genius for compromise could be invoked ... to mitigate possible dangers* (Bulletin of Atomic Scientists). **2** to make less severe; make more bearable; temper; moderate: *A cool breeze mitigated the scorching heat of the day. Aspirin mitigated the pain of his headache in about half an hour.* **3** to make less harsh: *The principal mitigated the punishment that the teacher had given the boy in anger.* — *v.i.* to become mild; become milder or less harsh; soften. [< Latin *mītigāre* (with English *-ate*[1]) < *mītis* gentle + *agere* do, make]

**mit|i|ga|tion** (mit′ə gā′shən), *n.* **1** the action or process of mitigating: *The Governor's mitigation of the death sentence to life imprisonment met with approval.* **2** the state of being mitigated. **3** something that mitigates: *The breeze was a welcome mitigation of the heat.*

**mit|i|ga|tive** (mit′ə gā′tiv), *adj., n.* — *adj.* tending to mitigate.
— *n.* something that mitigates. SYN: balm.

**mit|i|ga|tor** (mit′ə gā′tər), *n.* a person or thing that mitigates.

**mit|i|ga|to|ry** (mit′ə gə tôr′ē, -tōr′-), *adj., n., pl.* **-ries.** — *adj.* mitigative.
— *n.* something which serves to mitigate.

**mi|tis** (mī′tis, mē′-), *n.* = mitis casting (def. 2). [a coined word < Latin *mītis* mild]

**mitis casting**, **1** a method of producing malleable iron castings by fusing wrought iron with a minute quantity of aluminum. **2** a casting so made.

**mitis metal**, = mitis casting (def. 2).

**Mit|nag|ge|dim** (mit′nä gə dēm′, mis näg′dim), *n., pl. of* **Mit|nag|ged** (mit nä ged′, mis nä′gid). **1** the Orthodox Jews of Russia and Lithuania who opposed the Hasidim during the 1700's and 1800's. **2** all Orthodox Jews who are not Hasidim. [< Hebrew *mithnăggədim* opponents]

**mi|to|chon|dri|a** (mī′tə kon′drē ə), *n., pl. of* **mitochondrion.** minute sausage-shaped structures found in the cytoplasm of cells, containing many enzymes important for cell metabolism. They produce most of the energy required by the cells. Mitochondria often change their shape under certain conditions although their number in each cell remains about the same. See the diagram under **cell.**
[< Greek *mítos* a thread + *chóndros* lump]

**mi|to|chon|dri|al** (mī′tə kon′drē əl), *adj.* of or having to do with the mitochondria.

**mi|to|chon|dri|on** (mit′ə kon′drē ən), *n., pl.* **-dri|a.** singular of **mitochondria**: *The mitochondrion ... is frequently a spherical body about 1-2 microns in diameter* (New Scientist).

**mi|to|ge|net|ic** (mī′tə jə net′ik), *adj.* = mitogenic.

**mi|to|gen|ic** (mī′tə jen′ik), *adj.* that promotes or induces mitosis: *mitogenic agents.*

**mi|to|my|cin** (mī′tə mī′sin), *n.* an antibiotic substance obtained from a species of streptomyces, used to treat malignant tumors. [< Greek *mítos* thread + English (strepto)*mycin*]

***mi|to|sis** (mi tō′sis, mī-), *n. Biology.* the process by which a cell of a plant or animal divides to form two new cells, each containing the same number of chromosomes as the original cell; cell division. Mitosis is typically divided into four stages: *prophase,* in which the chromatin of the nucleus forms into a thread that separates into segments or chromosomes, each of which in turn separates longitudinally into two parts; *metaphase,* in which the nuclear membrane disappears and the chromosomes line up near the middle of the cell; *anaphase,* in which one chromosome of each pair moves toward each end of the cell; and *telophase,* in which the chromosomes lose their threadlike shape and again become chromatin, two new nuclear membranes form around the chromatin, and the cytoplasm draws together in the middle, divides, and two new cells exist. See diagram below. [< New Latin *mitosis* < Greek *mítos* thread + English *-osis*]

**mi|tot|ic** (mi tot′ik, mī-), *adj.* of mitosis. — **mi|tot′i|cal|ly,** *adv.*

**Mit|ra** (mit′rə), *n. Hindu Mythology.* a sun god and ruler of the day who, according to the Rig-Veda, jointly rules the universe with Varuna.

**mi|trail|leur** (mē trä yœr′), *n. French.* **1** a machine gunner. **2** a soldier who operated a mitrailleuse. **3** = mitrailleuse.

**mi|trail|leuse** (mē trä yoez′), *n. French.* **1** an early type of machine gun consisting of a cluster of breechloading barrels around a central axis which could be fired simultaneously or in sequence. **2** any machine gun.

**mi|tral** (mī′trəl), *adj.* **1** of, having to do with, or like a miter. **2** of the mitral valve.

**mitral stenosis**, the hardening or narrowing of the mitral valve, caused by rheumatic fever.

**mitral valve**, the valve of the heart between the left auricle and left ventricle, which prevents the blood from flowing back into the auricle; bicuspid valve. See the diagram under **heart.**

**mi|tre** (mī′tər), *n., v.t.,* **-tred, -tring.** *Especially British.* miter[1] and miter[2].

**mi|tred** (mī′tərd), *adj. Especially British.* mitered[1] and mitered[2].

**mi|tre|wort** (mī′tər wėrt′), *n. Especially British.* miterwort.

**mitt** (mit), *n.* **1** a kind of long glove without fingers or with very short fingers. **2** a baseball glove with a big pad over the palm and fingers: *a catcher's mitt.* **3** = mitten. **4** *U.S. Slang.* a hand. [short for *mitten*]

**Mit|tel|schu|le** (mit′əl shü′lə), *n., pl.* **-len** (-lən). a German or Austrian secondary school that emphasizes science and modern languages in preparation for the university or higher technical school. [< German *Mittelschule* (literally) middle school]

**mit|ten** (mit′ən), *n.* **1** a kind of winter glove covering the four fingers together and the thumb separately: *So long as the thumb is in the right place mittens can fit on either hand.* **2** a long glove; mitt. **3** *Slang.* a boxing glove.
**get the mitten,** *Slang.* **a** to be refused as a lover: *Young gentlemen that have got the mitten ... always sigh* (Joseph C. Neal). **b** to be dismissed from any office or position: *Lifeboat hands who are found shrinking get ... the mitten* (Punch).
**give the mitten to,** *Slang.* **a** to refuse as a lover: *Some said that Susan had given her young man the mitten* (Oliver Wendell Holmes). **b** to dismiss: *Here comes Dana, ... who'll be going to write what'll never be written till the Muse, ere he thinks of it, gives him the mitten* (James Russell Lowell).
[< Old French *mitaine* mitten, half glove < *mite* mitten. Compare Medieval Latin *mitanna.*]

**mit|ti|mus** (mit′ə məs), *n. Law.* **1** a warrant committing someone to prison. **2** (formerly) a writ for transferring a record from one court to another. [< Latin *mittimus* we send]

**Mit|ty** (mit′ē), *n., pl.* **-ties.** a timid person who in his fantasies is a fabulous hero; a daydreaming milquetoast: *The hero of "Stern," a flabby Jewish Mitty, has ... an imagination that flowers with persecution mania* (Manchester Guardian Weekly). [< Walter *Mitty,* the hero of the short story *The Secret Life of Walter Mitty,* by James Thurber]

**Mit|ty|esque** (mit′ē esk′), *adj.* characteristic of a Mitty; like an extravagant daydream: *... a ticket-office attendant given to Mittyesque fantasies* (London Times).

**mitz|vah** (mits′vä, -və), *n., pl.* **-voth** (-vōth), **-vahs.** *Judaism.* **1** a religious obligation or commandment; act enjoined by the Bible or the rabbis. **2** an act fulfilling a religious or ethical duty; good deed; kind act. [< Hebrew *miṣwāh* commandment]

**mix** (miks), *v.,* **mixed** or **mixt, mix|ing,** *n.* — *v.t.* **1** to put together; stir well together: *We mix butter, sugar, milk, and flour for a cake.* **2** to prepare by putting different things together: *to mix a cake.* **3** to carry on at the same time; join: *to mix business and pleasure. You mix your sadness with some fear* (Shakespeare). **4** to cross in breeding.
— *v.i.* **1** to be mixed: *Oil and water will not mix.* **2** to associate together; get along together: *She likes people and mixes well in almost any group.* SYN: fraternize. **3** to be crossed in breeding.
— *n.* **1** a mixture: *Having no experience as a bartender, he was uncertain about the mix.* **2** a preparation that is already mixed, such as the dry ingredients for a cake or pudding, packaged and sold together: *a cake mix.* **3** *Informal.* a mixed or muddled condition; mess.
**mix it (up),** *Slang.* to fight, especially (of boxers) actively and without clinching: *If a hundred children are put to the fiddle and another hundred are made to mix it, ... the second group will turn out some unusual bruisers* (New Yorker).
**mix up, a** to confuse: *She always manages to mix up instructions. I was so mixed up that I used the wrong method in that problem.* **b** to involve; concern: *He was mixed up in a plot to kill the king. Don't mix yourself up in other folks' affairs!*
[back formation < earlier *mixt* mixed < Middle French *mixte,* learned borrowing from Latin *mix-*

***mitosis**

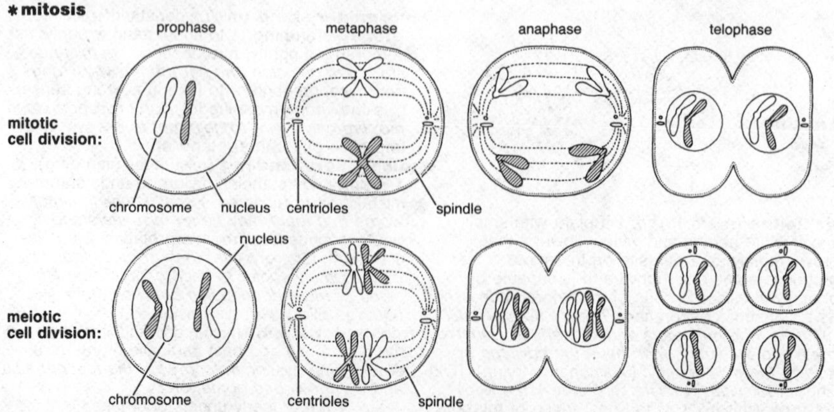

*tus,* past participle of *miscēre* to mix] —**mix'a|ble,** *adj.*

—*Syn. v.t.* **1 Mix, blend** mean to put two or more ingredients together. **Mix** applies particularly when the ingredients retain all or some of their distinct identities: *to mix gravel and cement.* **Blend** implies a thorough mixing so that the ingredients lose their identities and the resulting whole has the qualities of both or all elements: *to blend teas. Blend the flour into the melted butter.*

**mix|age** (mik'sij), *n.* the editing of motion-picture film.

**mixed** (mikst), *adj.* **1** put together or formed of different kinds: *mixed candies, a mixed drink, mixed emotions, a mixed response or blessing.* **2** of different classes, kinds, status, character, etc.; not exclusive: *a mixed society.* **3** of or for both men and women: *a mixed chorus. What Shakespeare judged could safely be absorbed by mixed company in sixteenth-century London can evidently be taken in stride by succeeding generations also* (Saturday Review). **4** of or for different races; racially integrated: *a mixed housing development, to attend mixed classes.* **5** *Informal.* mentally confused, especially muddled with drink. **6** *Botany.* (of an inflorescence) combining both determinate and indeterminate arrangements, as a thyrsus does. **7** *Anatomy.* consisting of both sensory and motor fibers: *a mixed nerve.* **8** *Law.* involving two or more kinds of legal characteristics, issues, rights, etc.: *Mixed property is property that is partly real and partly personal.* **9** *Business, Commerce.* (of stock prices) some rising and some falling from previous levels: *Prices were mixed on the New York Stock Exchange.* **10** *Phonetics.* central; neither front nor back.

**mixed art**, an artistic medium combining several art forms: *The theater is sometimes a mixed art because it combines the script of the playwright, the scenic background of the architect and painter, and the speech and movement of the actors* (Oscar G. and Lenyth Brockett).

**mixed bag**, *Informal.* a mixture; medley; miscellany: *a mixed bag of projects, a mixed bag of ill-assorted characters, a mixed bag of emotions.*

**mixed blood**, *U.S.* **1** descent from two or more races. **2** a person of mixed blood.

**mixed-blood** (mikst'blud'), *adj.* **1** (of a person or persons) descended from two or more races. **2** consisting largely or entirely of such people: *a mixed-blood nation, a mixed-blood population.* **3** = interracial.

**mixed-blood|ed** (mikst'blud'id), *adj. U.S.* descended from two or more races.

**mixed bud**, a bud producing both foliage and flower.

**mixed doubles**, doubles played with a man and a woman on each team.

**mixed economy**, an economy that is partly capitalistic, partly socialistic: [*In*] *a mixed economy ... cooperative private business, commercial private business, and government business compete openly and honestly in meeting the needs of the people* (Emory S. Bogardus).

**mixed farming**, the practice of using a farm for multiple purposes, such as cattle-raising, fruit-growing, and producing grain for sale and for livestock food.

**mixed feed**, a feed designed to provide a balanced diet for livestock, consisting typically of a mixture of grain, meal, and grasses with vitamins and other additives.

**mixed grill**, an assortment of grilled meats and vegetables served together.

**mix|ed|ly** (mik'sid lē, mikst'lē), *adv.* in a mixed manner; like a mixture.

**mixed-manned** (mikst'mand'), *adj.* (of a supranational military force or unit) supplied with men representing member nations; multinational or multilateral.

**mixed marriage**, a marriage in which the husband and wife are of different religions or races.

**mixed media**, the simultaneous use of motion pictures, tapes, phonograph records, and the like, to produce an artistic work or exhibition; multimedia: *Miss Caldwell used a "mixed media" technique, with photographs and movies projected on bits of backdrop while the action was going on* (New Yorker).

**mixed-me|di|a** (mikst'mē'dē ə), *adj.* using mixed media: *More galleries experimented with mixed-media exhibitions making use of the wonders of modern technology* (Sandra Millikin).

**mixed metaphor**, an incongruous combination of metaphors. *Example:* "He set forth early on the stream of public life, where he climbed to the peak of success."

**mixed number**, a number consisting of a whole number and a fraction, such as 16⅔.

**mixed tide**, a tide that does not flow and ebb regularly twice a day: *Some Pacific islands have mixed tides, such as two high tides daily, with only a little ebb between, and then a very low tide* (Robert O. Reid).

**mixed-up** (mikst'up'), *adj. U.S.* confused; unstable; emotionally immature: *Some people think we're a bunch of crazy mixed-up kids because we give our client a hard time* (New York Times).

**mix|er** (mik'sər), *n.* **1** a thing that mixes: *a bread mixer, an electric mixer.* **2** a person who mixes. A person who gets along well with others is called a good mixer. **3** *U.S.* an informal social gathering or dance. **4** soda, juice, syrup, or water, used with alcoholic liquors for mixing drinks. **5** *Electronics.* **a** a device used for sound in television and motion pictures, consisting of two or more signal inputs and a common output. It combines the outputs of individual microphones linearly and in the desired proportions, to produce the final audio output signal. **b** a similar device which combines the outputs of two or more cameras, used in television and motion pictures. **6** a person who blends the individual sound tracks for the dialogue, music, and sound effects of a motion picture or television show.

**mix|ing bowl** (mik'sing), a bowl in which foods or ingredients are mixed before cooking or serving.

**mixing faucet**, a faucet attached to a hot and a cold water pipe each controlled by a mixing valve. See picture under **faucet**.

**mixing valve**, a valve that automatically controls the flow of hot and cold water out of a common spout, usually thermostatically and by pressure.

**mix|ol|o|gist** (mik sol'ə jist), *n. Slang.* a skilled mixer of drinks; bartender.

**mix|ol|o|gy** (mik sol'ə jē), *n. Slang.* the art or skill of mixing alcoholic drinks.

**mix|o|lyd|i|an** (mik'sə lid'ē ən), *adj.* of or having to do with the mixolydian mode: *mixolydian chords. The song is recognizably mixolydian* (London Times).

**mixolydian mode**, **1** the highest in pitch of the modes in ancient Greek music. **2** a mode of medieval church music, beginning and ending on the note G. [< Greek *mixolýdios* half-Lydian + English *-an*]

**mixt** (mikst), *v.* mixed; a past tense and a past participle of **mix**.

**Mix|tec** (mēs'tek), *n., pl.* **-tecs** or **-tec**, *adj.* —*n.* **1** a member of a large, pre-Toltec American Indian people living in southern Mexico since before the Spanish Conquest. **2** the language of this people; Mixtecan.
—*adj.* of or having to do with the ancient culture of the Mixtecs: *the Mixtec Empire, Mixtec mythology.*

**Mix|tec|an** (mēs tek'ən), *n., adj.* —*n.* the language of the Mixtecs.
—*adj.* of the Mixtecs or their civilization: *the Mixtecan civilization.*

**mix|ture** (miks'chər), *n.* **1** the action or fact of mixing: *The mixture of the paints took three hours.* SYN: blending, fusing. **2** a mixed condition: *His mixture of relief and disappointment left him speechless.* **3** something that has been mixed; product of mixing: *Orange is a mixture of yellow and red. Many teas and tobaccos are mixtures. This suit is made of a mixture of Dacron and wool.* SYN: blend. **4** *Chemistry, Physics.* the product of two or more substances mixed together, but not chemically combined. **5** a fabric woven of variegated or mottled yarns: *an oxford mixture.* [< Latin *mixtūra* < *miscēre* to mix]

**mix-up** (miks'up'), *n.* **1** confusion; mess; muddle. **2** *Informal.* a confused fight: *The son took no part in the mix-up.*

**Mi|zar** (mī'zär), *n.* a bright star in the handle of the Big Dipper. With its companion, Alcor, it forms a visual binary.

**miz|zen** or **miz|en** (miz'ən), *n., adj.* —*n.* **1** a fore-and-aft sail on the mizzenmast; spanker. **2** = mizzenmast. —*adj.* of or on the mizzenmast. [< Middle French *misaine* foresail, foremast < Italian *mezzana* mizzen sail < Latin *mediānus* (in the) middle < *medius* middle]

**miz|zen|mast** (miz'ən mast', -mäst'; *Nautical* miz'ən məst), *n.* the mast nearest the stern in a two-masted or three-masted ship, or the third mast from the bow in a ship having four or more masts. See picture under **mast**[1].

**miz|zen-roy|al mast, sail, yard** (miz'ən roi'əl), the mast, sail, yard, etc., near the top of the mizzenmast of a square-rigged vessel next above the mizzen-topgallant mast, sail, yard.

**miz|zen|sheet** (miz'ən shēt'), *n.* a rope used to control a fore-and-aft mizzen or spanker.

**miz|zen|stay** (miz'ən stā'), *n.* the fore-and-aft stay which helps support a mizzen lower mast.

**miz|zen|stay|sail** (miz'ən stā'sāl'; *Nautical* miz'ən stā'səl), *n.* a triangular sail set on the mizzenstay.

**miz|zen|top** (miz'ən top'), *n.* a platform on a mizzenmast, just below the mizzen-topmast.

**miz|zen-top|gal|lant mast, sail, yard** (miz'ən-top gal'ənt; *Nautical* miz'ən tə gal'ənt), the mast, sail, yard, etc., on the mizzen-topmast, mizzen-topsail, topsail yard.

**miz|zen-top|mast** (miz'ən top'mast', -mäst'; *Nautical* miz'ən top'məst), *n.* the mast on the mizzenmast next above the lower mast, especially on a square-rigged vessel.

**miz|zen-top|sail** or **yard** (miz'ən top'sāl'; *Nautical* miz'ən top'səl), the sail or yard, or either of two sails or yards, on the mizzen-top.

**miz|zen|yard** (miz'ən yärd'), *n.* the yard holding the mizzen on the lower section of the mizzenmast of a square rigged vessel; crossjack yard.

**miz|zle**[1] (miz'əl), *n., v.,* **-zled, -zling.** *Dialect.* —*n.* a drizzle: *The rain, a mere mizzle when I left the restaurant ... had got heavier* (New Yorker).
—*v.i.* to drizzle: *It is mizzling.*
—*v.t.* (of a cloud) to send down in a drizzle.
[origin uncertain. Compare Low German *miseln.*]

**miz|zle**[2] (miz'əl), *v.i.,* **-zled, -zling.** *British Slang.* to disappear suddenly; decamp; vanish: *Bealby had not "mizzled" although he was conspicuously not in evidence about the camp* (H. G. Wells). [origin uncertain]

**miz|zly** (miz'lē), *adj.,* **-zli|er, -zli|est.** *Dialect.* drizzly; misty.

**Mjol|nir** (myôl'nir), *n. Norse Mythology.* Thor's hammer, made for him by the dwarfs.

**mk.**, *pl.* **mks. 1** mark[2] (unit of money). **2** markka.

**MKS** (no periods), **mks** (no periods), or **M.K.S.**, meter-kilogram-second.

**MKS system**, a system of units in which the meter, kilogram, and second are considered as the basic units of length, mass, and time.

**mkt.**, market.

**ml.**, milliliter or milliliters.

**Ml.**, *British.* mail.

**ML** (no periods) or **ML.**, **1** Medieval Latin. **2** Mortar Locator (a radar system that tracks enemy mortar shells).

**M.L.** or **ML.**, Medieval Latin.

**MLA** (no periods) or **M.L.A.**, **1** Modern Language Association. **2** (in Canada) Member of the Legislative Assembly.

**MLD** (no periods) or **m.l.d.**, minimum lethal dose.

**MLF** (no periods) or **M.L.F.**, multilateral force (a proposed mixed-manned fleet of surface ships armed with nuclear weapons).

**MLG** (no periods) or **MLG.**, Middle Low German.

**Mlle.**, Mademoiselle.

**Mlles.**, Mesdemoiselles (plural of *Mademoiselle*).

**MLS** (no periods), Macrowave Landing System.

**M.L.S.**, Master of Library Science.

**mm.** or **mm** (no period), **1** millimeter or millimeters. **2** thousands (Latin, *millia*).

**mm.**$^2$ or **mm**$^2$ (no period), square millimeter.

**mm.**$^3$ or **mm**$^3$ (no period), cubic millimeter.

**MM.**, **1** (Their) Majesties. **2** Messieurs.
▶ See **Messrs.** for usage note.

**M.M.**, Master of Music.

**Mme.**, Madame.

**M.M.Ed.**, Master of Music Education.

**Mmes.**, Mesdames (plural of *Madame*).

**mmf** (no periods) or **m.m.f.**, magnetomotive force.

**mmfd** (no period) or **mmfd.**, micromicrofarad.

**MMPI** (no periods), Minnesota Multiphasic Personality Inventory (a personality test originally designed to sort out the mentally ill).

**M.Mus.**, Master of Music.

**M.Mus.Ed.**, Master of Music Education.

**Mn** (no period), manganese (chemical element).

**MN** (no periods), Minnesota (with postal Zip Code).

**M'Nagh|ten Rule** (mə nä'tən, -nô'-, -na'-; mək-), *Law.* the rule that an accused person is not criminally responsible if at the time of committing the crime he was unable to distinguish between right and wrong: *The old M'Naghten Rule* [*is*] *still used in the majority of states* (Science News Letter). Also, **McNaughten Rule.** [< the name of the defendant in a trial held in England in 1843, at which the rule was formulated]

**mne|mon|ic** (ni mon'ik), *adj., n.* —*adj.* **1** aiding the memory. **2** intended to aid the memory: *The strongly mnemonic nature of the catchword system certainly supports the idea that the writing grew out of a memory-aid device* (Scientific American). **3** of or having to do with the memory.
—*n.* **1** a mnemonic device. **2** = mnemonics.
[< Greek *mnēmonikós* < *mnâsthai* remember]
—**mne|mon'i|cal|ly**, *adv.*

**mne|mon|i|cal** (ni mon'ə kəl), *adj.* = mnemonic.

**mne|mon|ics** (ni mon'iks), *n.* **1** (*singular in use*) the art of improving or developing the memory. **2** (*plural in use*) mnemonic aids or devices.

---

**Pronunciation Key:** hat, āge, cãre, fär; let, ēqual, tėrm; it, īce; hot, ōpen, ôrder; oil, out; cup, pu̇t, rüle; child; long; thin; ᴛʜen; zh, measure; ə represents a in about, e in taken, i in pencil, o in lemon, u in circus.

**Mne|mos|y|ne** (ni mos′ə nē), *n. Greek Mythology.* the goddess of memory, daughter of Uranus and Gaea, and mother of the Muses by Zeus.

**Mngr.**, **1** Monseigneur. **2** Monsignor.

**MNS** (no periods), a blood group system in human beings. Blood groups M and N are common among Asians and Europeans.

**mo** (mō), *adj., n., adv. Obsolete.* more¹. [Old English *mā*]

**mo.**, month or months.

**m.o.**, **1** mail order. **2** money order.

**Mo** (no period), molybdenum (chemical element).

**Mo.**, **1** Missouri. **2** Monday.

**MO** (no periods), **1** medical officer. **2** Missouri (with postal Zip Code).

**M.O.**, **1** mail order. **2** modus operandi. **3** money order.

**mo|a** (mō′ə), *n.* any one of various extinct, flightless birds of New Zealand, somewhat like an ostrich, but varying in size from that of a turkey to 12 feet high. [< a Maori word]

**Mo|ab|ite** (mō′ə bīt), *n., adj.* —*n.* a native or inhabitant of Moab, an ancient kingdom in Syria.
—*adj.* of Moab or its people.

**Mo|ab|it|ess** (mō′ə bī′tis), *n.* a female Moabite.

**Moabite stone**, a slab of black basalt bearing an inscription in Hebrew-Phoenician characters, which records the victories of Mesha, king of Moab, over the Israelites. It was discovered in 1868, and for a time was the oldest known monument, 800's B.C., of the Semitic alphabet.

**Mo|ab|it|ic** (mō′ə bit′ik), *adj.* = Moabite.

**Mo|ab|it|ish** (mō′ə bī′tish), *adj.* = Moabite.

**moan** (mōn), *n., v.* —*n.* **1** a long, low sound of suffering: *So is mortal life, A moan, a sigh, a sob, a storm, a strife* (Sir Edwin Arnold). **2** any similar sound: *the moan of the winter wind. The moan of doves in immemorial elms* (Tennyson). **3** complaint; lamentation: *Unheard ... Their English mother made her moan* (James Russell Lowell). **4** an instance of this: *Her moan was only that she had not been invited.*
—*v.i.* **1** to make moans: *The sick man moaned in his sleep.* SYN: wail. See syn. under **groan**. **2** to complain; lament; grieve.
—*v.t.* **1** to utter with a moan: *"I'm so stiff I can't move," she moaned.* **2** to complain about; grieve for: *He is always moaning his luck.* SYN: bemoan, bewail.
[Middle English *mone* a moan. Compare Old English *mǣnan* to complain.] —**moan′ing|ly**, *adv.*

**Mo|ap|a** (mō ap′ə), *n.* a variety of alfalfa grown especially in the extreme southern and southwestern United States.

**moat** (mōt), *n., v.* —*n.* a deep, wide ditch dug around a castle or town as a protection against enemies. Moats were usually kept filled with water. See picture under **castle**.
—*v.t.* to surround with or as if with a moat: *Beyond the crossroads lay a big farm with an immense, moated farmhouse* (New Yorker).
[earlier *mote* mound, embankment < Old French *mote* mound, fortified height; origin uncertain]

**mob** (mob), *n., v.,* **mobbed, mob|bing.** —*n.* **1** a lawless crowd, easily moved to act without thinking: *The mob is man voluntarily descending to the nature of the beast* (Emerson). *The destruction and damage caused by the mobs were more extensive than was originally reported* (London Times). **2** a large number of people; crowd: *Streets were crowded with mobs of workers going home after work.* **3** *Informal.* a group of criminals who work together; gang. **4** (in Australia) a group of animals, such as a flock of sheep or a herd of cattle or horses.
—*v.t.* **1** to crowd around, especially in curiosity or anger: *The eager children mobbed the candy man the moment he appeared.* **2** to attack with violence, as a mob does: *He was mobbed as soon as he left the prison gates.*
**the mob, a** the common mass of people, thought of as lacking taste, culture, and social niceties; the masses: *jokes at which the mob laughs* (G. K. Chesterton); *our supreme governors, the mob* (Horace Walpole). **b** the lawless part of the populace; the rabble. **c** *U.S. Slang.* the dominant group in the underworld of a city, state, or other area: *The metropolis had been ruled by the mob for twenty years.*
[short for earlier *mobile* < Latin *mōbile* (*vulgus*) the fickle (common people) < *mōbilis;* see etym. under **mobile**] —**mob′like′**, *adj.*

**mob|bish** (mob′ish), *adj.* moblike; riotous.

**mob|bist** (mob′ist), *n.* a member of a mob.

**mob|cap** (mob′kap′), *n.* a large, loose cap, fitting down over the ears, originally worn indoors by women in the 1700's and early 1800's. [< obsolete *mob* an indoor cap + *cap*]

**mob|dom** (mob′dəm), *n.* = gangsterdom.

**mo|bile** (*adj.* mō′bəl, mō bēl′; *n.* mō bēl′, mō′bəl), *adj., n.* —*adj.* **1a** that can move; easy to move; movable: *a mobile hospital unit. The arms and legs are mobile.* **b** tending to be naturally fluid: *Mercury is a mobile metal.* **2** moving easily; changing easily: *a face with mobile features. A mobile mind is one that is easily moved by ideas or feeling.* **3** versatile: *mobile talents.* **4** *Sociology.* **a** characterized by mobility: *a mobile class of society.* **b** upward-mobile.
—*n.* a piece of sculpture or a decoration composed of strips or pieces, such as of wire, paper, cloth, and wood, in balance with each other, usually suspended on wires or threads so that the various parts may shift in currents of air to form different patterns: *An American sculptor, Alexander Calder, was the first to create the true mobile, in which movement is the basic aesthetic purpose* (Bernard Frazier).
[< Latin *mōbilis* movable < *movēre* to move]

***mobile home**, a house trailer, especially a large one set on a more or less permanent site.

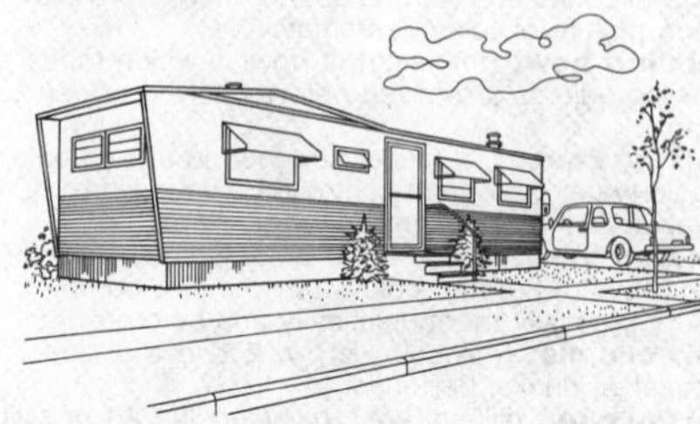
***mobile home**

**mobile library**, a traveling branch of a library; bookmobile.

**mobile unit**, a specially equipped vehicle performing on-the-spot services for a larger enterprise: *Mobile units ... offered food, clothing, and medical aid* (Time).

**mo|bi|lise** (mō′bə līz), *v.t., v.i.,* **-lised, -lis|ing.** *Especially British.* mobilize.

**mo|bi|lis|tic** (mō′bə lis′tik), *adj.* of mobility; having to do with being mobile.

**mo|bil|i|ty** (mō bil′ə tē), *n., pl.* **-ties. 1** the ability or readiness to move or be moved; being mobile: *Reciprocity enables us to find this potential in terms of the mobilities of the ions present* (Science News). **2** *Sociology.* a movement of people from one social group or status to another: *the downward mobility of the unemployed, the upward mobility of second-generation Americans.*

**mo|bi|li|za|tion** (mō′bə lə zā′shən), *n.* **1** the act of mobilizing; calling troops, ships, or other units into active military service. **2** the condition of being mobilized.

**mo|bi|lize** (mō′bə līz), *v.,* **-lized, -liz|ing.** —*v.t.* **1a** to call (troops, ships, or other units) into active military service; organize for war. **b** to organize or call to take part, usually during an emergency: *to mobilize Red Cross or defense units during a violent storm, to mobilize industry in time of national crisis.* **2** to put into motion or active use: *to mobilize the wealth of a country.* **3** to make movable: *The doctor was able to mobilize the patient's stiff elbow joint.*
—*v.i.* **1** to assemble and prepare for war: *The troops mobilized quickly.* **2** to organize or assemble in an emergency.
[< French *mobiliser* (with English *-ize*) < *mobile* mobile, learned borrowing from Latin *mōbilis* mobile] —**mo′bi|liz′a|ble**, *adj.* —**mo′bi|liz′er**, *n.*

***Mö|bi|us strip** or **band** (mœ′bē əs, mō′-), *Geometry.* a strip of paper or other material which is given a half twist and then joined at the ends, thus having only one side. [< August F. *Möbius*, 1790-1868, a German mathematician]

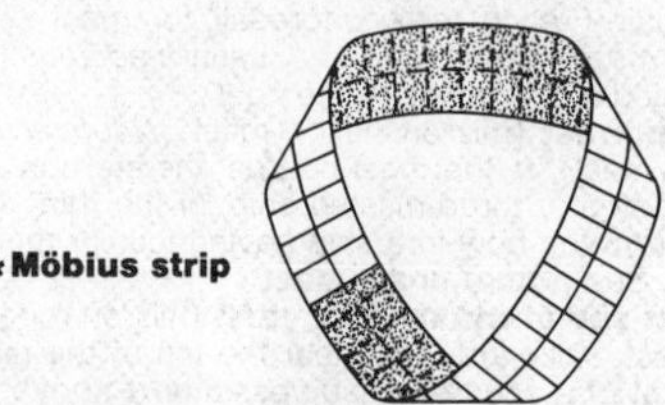
***Möbius strip**

**mob|oc|ra|cy** (mob ok′rə sē), *n., pl.* **-cies. 1** political control by a mob; mob rule: *If Congress ... refuses to appropriate money to maintain the judiciary and executive departments, the result is mobocracy* (Baltimore Sun). **2** the mob as a ruling class.

**mob|o|crat** (mob′ə krat), *n.* **1** a supporter of mobocracy. **2** a leader of the mob; demagogue.

**mob|o|crat|ic** (mob′ə krat′ik), *adj.* **1** having to do with mobocracy. **2** like a mobocracy. **3** that advocates mobocracy.

**mob rule**, rule or political control by a mob: *The President pointed out ...* [*that*] *"mob rule cannot be allowed to override the decisions of the courts"* (Wall Street Journal).

**MOBS** (mobz), *n.* Multiple Orbital Bombardment System (a nuclear-weapon system in which earth satellites carry warheads that may be released from space upon earth targets, thus escaping detection by conventional radar).

**mob|ster** (mob′stər), *n.* a chronic lawbreaker, especially a person who specializes in crimes of violence; criminal; gangster: *I will not allow work on the piers to go to hoodlums and mobsters from New York* (New York Times).

**mo|camp** (mō kamp′), *n.* a tourist camp providing various facilities for campers. [< *mo*(torist) *camp*]

***moc|ca|sin** (mok′ə sən), *n.* **1** a soft shoe, often made from the skin of a deer. Moccasins were originally worn by North American Indians, and are typically without heels, having the sole and the sides stitched to the upper or vamp with rawhide. **2** a poisonous snake of the southeastern United States; the copperhead or especially the water moccasin. [American English < Algonkian (probably a Virginia tribe). Compare Powhatan *mäkäsĭn.*]

***moccasin**
definition 1

**moccasin flower**, a pink or white orchid shaped somewhat like a slipper; pink or white North American lady's-slipper.

**mo|cha** (mō′kə), *n., adj.* —*n.* **1** a choice variety of coffee originally coming from southwestern Arabia, in what is now Yemen. **2** a mixture of coffee and chocolate, used as a flavoring in drinks, cakes, and other foods: *Strong American coffee ... is converted into mocha by adding a tablespoon of chocolate syrup and a dab of unsweetened whipped cream* (New York Times). **3** a kind of soft, thin leather used for gloves, usually made from Arabian goatskin.
—*adj.* flavored with coffee, or with chocolate and coffee: *a mocha frosting, mocha cake.*
[< *Mocha,* a seaport in Yemen]

**Mocha stone**, a kind of agate having dendritic markings due to the presence of metallic oxides; moss agate.

**Mocha ware**, a white pottery formerly produced in England for household use, decorated with dendritic or treelike designs on a tinted ground.

**Mo|chi|ca** (mō chē′kə), *n., pl.* **-ca** or **-cas**, *adj.* —*n.* a member of a civilization that dominated the coast of northern Peru for about a thousand years, until the 1000's A.D. The Mochica were noted for achievements in architecture and ceramics.
—*adj.* of or having to do with this civilization.

**mo|chi|la** (mō chē′lə), *n.* a leather flap that covers a saddletree. [American English < Spanish *mochila* knapsack, caparison < Latin *mutīla* shortened (thing)]

**mock** (mok, môk), *v., adj., adv., n.* —*v.t.* **1** to laugh at; make fun of; ridicule: *Little children ... mocked him, and said ... Go up, thou bald head* (II Kings 2:23). SYN: deride, taunt. See syn. under **ridicule**. **2** to make fun of by copying or imitating: *The thoughtless children mocked the different speech of the new boy.* **3** to imitate; copy: *Prepare To see the life as lively mock'd as ever still sleep mock'd death* (Shakespeare). SYN: mimic, ape. **4** to make light of; pay no attention to; disregard: *health that mocks the doctor's rules* (John Greenleaf Whittier). **5** *Figurative.* to deceive or disappoint: *Mind is a light which the Gods mock us with, to lead those false who trust it* (Matthew Arnold). SYN: delude, fool.
—*v.i.* to scoff; jeer. SYN: gibe.
—*adj.* not real; imitation; copying; sham: *a mock king, a mock battle, mock modesty.* SYN: feigned, pretended, counterfeit, false.
—*adv.* in a feigned or false manner; feignedly; falsely (usually in compounds such as *a mock-modest person, a mock-pompous statement*).
—*n.* **1** an action or speech that mocks: *His bullying made a mock of all the fine things he had said about kindness to others.* **2** a person or thing scorned or deserving scorn. **3** an imitation; counterfeit; copy. **4** derision; mockery.
[< Middle French, Old French *mocquer;* origin uncertain]

**mock|a|ble** (mok′ə bəl, môk′-), *adj.* that can be mocked; subject to mockery.

**mock|er** (mok′ər, môk′-), *n.* **1** a person who mocks. **2** = mockingbird.

**mock|er|nut hickory** (mok′ər nut′, môk′-), any one of a variety of hickories growing in the southern United States.

**mock|er|y** (mok′ər ē, môk′-), *n., pl.* **-er|ies.** **1** a making fun; ridicule; derision: *Their mockery of her hat hurt her feelings.* **2** a person, thing, or action to be made fun of; laughingstock: *Through his foolishness he became a mockery in the village.* **3** a bad copy or imitation: *The little girl's pie was a mockery of her mother's cooking.* **4a** a wasted or useless thing; naught: *The unfair trial was a mockery of justice.* **b** something insultingly or absurdly unfitting: *In her bitterness she felt that all rejoicing was a mockery* (George Eliot).

**mock-he|ro|ic** (mok′hi rō′ik, môk′-), *adj., n.* **—*adj.*** imitating or burlesquing the heroic style or character: *Alexander Pope's "Rape of the Lock" is a mock-heroic poem.*
**—*n.*** an imitation or burlesque of what is heroic.
**—mock′-he|ro′i|cal|ly,** *adv.*

**mock|ing** (mok′ing, môk′-), *adj.* **1** that mocks; deriding; mimicking: *a mocking voice.* **SYN**: imitating. **2** *Figurative.* deluding: *a mocking mirage.*
**—mock′ing|ly,** *adv.*

**mock|ing|bird** (mok′ing bėrd′, môk′-), *n.* **1** a grayish songbird, especially of southern North America, and Central and South America, that imitates the notes of other birds. It belongs to the same family as the catbird. *The mockingbird, whose song once charmed only the Southland, has been gradually spreading out toward the north* (Science News Letter). **2** any one of certain similar or related birds. [American English < *mocking* + *bird*]

**mock moon,** = paraselene.

**mock orange,** = syringa.

**mock sun,** a parhelion; sundog.

**mock turtle soup,** a soup made with calf's head in imitation of green turtle soup.

**mock-up** (mok′up′, môk′-), *n.* a full-sized model of an airplane, machine, or other device, used for teaching purposes, for testing, or for studying details or new features of design. A mock-up is usually built to scale out of some material such as plywood, plaster, or clay. *The investigators sought to recover every possible part of the fallen plane for a mock-up on chickenwire of sections, or even all of the craft* (Wall Street Journal).

**mo|co** (mə kō′), *n., pl.* **-cos.** a large South American rodent belonging to the same family as the cavy. [< Portuguese *mocó* < Tupi]

**mod**[1] (mod), *adj., n. Informal.* **—*adj.*** very up-to-date and fashionable in style, as of clothes, makeup, music, and art; very stylish: *Their eyes are also very much on the present. This gives the show a mod look* (Dan Sullivan). *Both appeared wearing ... white shirts and mod ties* (Don McDonagh). *More often than not, the music that enhances these mod liturgies comes from an electric guitar pulsating to a rock beat* (Time).
**—*n.*** **1** a person who is very stylish or up-to-date: *From mod to teenybopper, all and sundry must see the error of our ways* (Maclean's). **2** extremely modern or fashionable style: *The look of "chic mod" she says she is trying to achieve ...* (New York Times).
[< *Mod*]

**Mod** or **mod**[2] (mod), *n. British.* one of a group of teen-agers of the 1960's affecting extreme neatness of appearance and a foppish liking for very fine or stylish clothes. [< *mod*(ern)]

**mod.,** an abbreviation for the following:
**1** moderate.
**2** *Music.* moderato; in moderate time.
**3** modern.
**4** modulus.

**MOD** (no periods), Ministry of Defence (in Great Britain).

**mod|a|cryl|ic** (mod′ə kril′ik), *adj.* having to do with or designating a type of synthetic fiber formed from long-chain polymers consisting chiefly of acrylonitrile, and used for making carpets, imitation furs, and draperies: *modacrylic fabrics. Dynel is a modacrylic fiber.* [< *mod*(ified) *acrylic*]

**mo|dal** (mō′dəl), *adj.* **1** of or having to do with mode, manner, or form, as contrasted with substance. **2** *Grammar.* **a** of or having to do with the mood of a verb. **b** denoting manner or modality. **3** *Music.* of or having to do with a mode, especially any of the medieval church modes: *One must pause before attempting to define this new music of Claude Debussy in all its tonal attributes, modal developments, and techniques* (Atlantic). **4** *Philosophy.* of, consisting in, or relating to formal manifestation as contrasted with basic substance. **5** *Law.* (of a legacy, contract, or other instrument) containing provisions defining the manner in which it is to take effect. **6** *Logic.* displaying modality. **7** *Physics.* of or having to do with a mode of vibration. [< Medieval Latin *modalis* < Latin *modus* a measure. Compare etym. under **mode**[1].] **—mo′dal|ly,** *adv.*

**modal auxiliary,** one of a set of auxiliary verbs in English, including words like *may, can, must, would,* and *should,* that indicates the mood of the verb with which it is used.

**mo|dal|i|ty** (mō dal′ə tē), *n., pl.* **-ties.** **1** the quality or fact of being modal. **2** a modal attribute or circumstance; mode. **3** *Medicine.* a form, method, or apparatus of therapy, especially physiotherapy or electrotherapy. **4** *Logic.* the character of a proposition as asserting or denying necessarily, possibly, or without such qualification.

**mod. con.,** *pl.* **mod. cons.** *British.* modern convenience: *We live in a small flat with all mod. cons.* (Punch).

**mode**[1] (mōd), *n.* **1** the manner or way in which a thing is done; method: *Riding on a donkey is a slow mode of travel.* **2** the manner or state of existence of a thing: *Heat is a mode of motion. Reflection is a mode of consciousness. The present transition of the Greenlanders' mode of life from seal-hunting to cod-fishing* (Science News). **3** *Grammar.* **a** the property of verbs that indicates whether the act or state is thought of as a fact, command, or wish; mood: *the indicative mode, the imperative mode, the subjunctive mode.* **b** a distinctive verb form (or set of forms) or verb phrases thus used. **4** *Music.* **a** any of various arrangements of the tones of an octave. **b** either of the two classes (major and minor) of keys. **c** any of the various scales used in ancient Greek and medieval music, having the intervals differently arranged. **d** a rhythmical pattern, especially in medieval mensurable music. **5** *Statistics.* the value of the variable with the highest frequency in a set of data. **6** *Logic.* **a** the form of a proposition with reference to the necessity, contingency, possibility, or impossibility of its content. **b** any one of the various forms of valid syllogisms, depending on the quantity and quality of their constituent propositions. **7** the actual mineral composition of a rock, stated quantitatively in percentages by weight. **8** *Physics.* any one of various patterns in which vibration may occur. In a freely vibrating system, oscillation is restricted to certain characteristic patterns of motion at certain characteristic frequencies. **9** *Philosophy.* a formal manifestation or particularized scheme of arrangement necessarily assumed by anything as an essential of its real existence. [< Latin *modus* measure, manner]

**mode**[2] (mōd), *n.* the style, fashion, or custom that is current; the way most people are behaving, talking, or dressing: *Bobbed hair became the mode around 1920.* **SYN**: vogue. [< Middle French *mode,* (originally) feminine, learned borrowing from Latin *modus* mode[1]]

**mod|el** (mod′əl), *n., v.,* **-eled, -el|ing** or (*especially British*) **-elled, -el|ling,** *adj.* **—*n.*** **1** a small copy: *a model of a ship or an engine, a model of an island.* **2a** an object or figure made in clay, wax, or the like, that is to be copied in marble, bronze, or other material: *a model for a statue.* **b** a design or representation of anything made to scale: *a model of the DNA molecule, a model of a stage set.* **3** the way in which a thing is made; design; style: *an airplane of an advanced model. Our car is a late model. I want a dress like yours, for that model is becoming to me.* **4** any formula, diagram, or scheme used to explain or describe relationships: *a mathematical model of communications, the mechanistic model of the universe. A tree is often used as a model showing the relationship between languages.* **5** *Figurative.* a thing or person to be copied or imitated; exemplar: *a model of courage. Make your father your model, and you will become a fine man.* **6** a person who poses for artists and photographers: *Nearly every individual of their number might have been taken for a sculptor's model* (Herman Melville). **7** a person, especially a woman, who wears new clothes in a clothing store, at a fashion show, or the like, in order to show customers how the clothes look; mannequin.
**—*v.t.*** **1** to make, shape, or fashion; design or plan: *Model a horse in clay.* **2** to follow as a model; form (something) after a particular model: (*Figurative.*) *Model yourself on your father.* **3** to wear as a model: *to model a dress.* **4** (in drawing or painting) to give an appearance of natural relief to: *Model the trees by shading.*
**—*v.i.*** **1** to make models; design: *She models in plaster as a hobby.* **2** to be a model; pose: *She models for an illustrator.* **3** (of the portions of a drawing in progress) to assume the appearance of natural relief: *The trees model as you add shading.*
**—*adj.*** **1** just right or perfect, especially in conduct; exemplary: *She is a model child.* **2** serving as a model: *a model house. A model home is being prepared for display by the middle of June* (New York Times).
[< French *modèle* < Italian *modello* (diminutive) < *modo* mode[1] < Latin *modus* measure, manner] **—mod′el|er,** *especially British,* **mod′el|ler,** *n.*
**—*Syn.*** *n.* **5 Model, example, pattern** mean someone or something to be copied or followed. **Model** implies especially a quality of conduct or character worth copying or imitating: *The saint was a model of unselfishness.* **Example** implies especially action or conduct, good or bad, that one is likely to follow or copy: *Children follow the example set by their parents.* **Pattern** applies particularly to any example or model that is followed or copied very closely: *The family's pattern of living has not changed in generations.*

**mod|el|ing** (mod′ə ling), *n.* **1** the act or art of a person who models: *Miss Carter ... said she would like to take up modeling as a profession* (Baltimore Sun). **2** the production of designs in some plastic material, such as clay or wax, especially for reproduction in a more durable material, such as marble or bronze. **3** the representation of solid form, as in sculpture. **4** the bringing of surfaces into proper relief, as in carving. **5** the rendering of the appearance of relief, as in painting.

**mod|el|ling** (mod′ə ling), *n. Especially British.* modeling.

**mo|del|lo** (mō del′ō), *n., pl.* **-los.** a finished sketch or other study for a large picture or decoration: *A series of modellos by the Baroque painters brings down to a scale convenient for appreciation the compositions with which they covered vast spaces of wall and ceiling* (London Times). [< Italian *modello;* see etym. under **model**]

**mode-locked** (mōd′lokt′), *adj.* having the light phases of a laser modulated to produce pulses of extremely short duration.

***Model T,** **1** *Trademark.* an automobile manufactured by the Ford Motor Company from 1908 to 1927. It began the era of mass-produced automobiles in the United States. **2** *Figurative.* any early or outdated type or model: *The present plants being planned will soon be the Model T's of the atomic power field* (New York Times).
**—Mod′el-T′,** *adj.*

***Model T**
definition 1

**mod|em** (mod′əm, mō′dem), *n.* a device used in telecommunications to convert digital signals to analogue form and vice versa: *Modems ... adapt alphanumeric information* (*letters and numerals*) *for transmission over standard voice channels* (Scientific American). [blend of *mod*(*ulator*) and *dem*(*odulator*)]

**mod|er|an|tism** (mod′ə rən tiz′əm), *n.* a moderate political policy, especially during the French Revolution. [< French *modérantisme* < *modérant,* present participle of *modérer* to moderate < Latin *moderāre*]

**mod|er|ate** (*adj., n.* mod′ər it; *v.* mod′ə rāt), *adj., n., v.,* **-at|ed, -at|ing.** **—*adj.*** **1** kept or keeping within proper bounds; not extreme: *moderate expenses, moderate styles.* **2** not violent, severe, or intense; calm: *moderate in speech or opinion.* **3** fair; medium; not very large or good: *to make a moderate profit.* **4** (in the U.S. Weather Service wind scale) denoting a breeze having a velocity of 13-18 miles per hour (on the Beaufort scale, force 4), or a gale of 32-38 miles per hour (Beaufort force 7).
**—*n.*** **1** a person who holds moderate opinions, especially in politics or religion. **2** Usually, **Moderate.** a member of a political party whose aims are considered moderate.
**—*v.t.*** **1** to make less violent, severe, or intense: *He ... did what he could to moderate the grief of his friend* (Anthony Trollope). **SYN**: diminish, lessen. **2** to act in as moderator; preside over: *The commissioner moderated the public meeting.* **3** *Nuclear Physics.* to slow down or lower the energy of (a particle, especially a neutron).
**—*v.i.*** **1** to become less extreme or violent: *The wind is moderating.* **SYN**: diminish, lessen. **2** to act as moderator; preside.
[< Latin *moderātus,* past participle of *moderāre* to regulate < *modus* measure, mode[1]] **—mod′er|ate|ly,** *adv.* **—mod′er|ate|ness,** *n.*

**Pronunciation Key:** hat, āge, cãre, fär; let, ēqual, tėrm; it, īce; hot, ōpen, ôrder; oil, out; cup, pu̇t, rüle; child; long; thin; ᴛʜen; zh, measure; ə represents **a** in about, **e** in taken, **i** in pencil, **o** in lemon, **u** in circus.

*–Syn. adj.* 1, 2 **Moderate, temperate** mean not extreme in any way. **Moderate** emphasizes freedom from excess, not going beyond or above the proper, right, or reasonable limit: *moderate speed. He is a moderate eater.* **Temperate** emphasizes deliberate restraint, holding back within limits, especially with regard to the feelings or appetites: *a temperate reply to an angry attack.*

**mod|er|a|tion** (mod′ə rā′shən), *n.* **1** the action or fact of moderating: *We all welcomed the moderation of the uncomfortably hot weather.* **2** freedom from excess; proper restraint; temperance: *The government adopted a policy of moderation during the crisis.* **3** calmness; lack of violence: *By common understanding, by tolerance and by the virtue of moderation* (New York Times).
**in moderation**, within limits; not going to extremes: *The doctor advised him to eat and drink in moderation.*
**Moderations**, *British.* (at Oxford University) the first public examination for the degree of B.A., informally called Mods: *The Tutor or Lecturer ... will be expected to teach for Honour Moderations* (Economist).

**mod|e|ra|to** (mod′ə rä′tō), *adj., adv. Music.* in moderate time (a direction). [< Italian *moderato* < Latin *moderātus* moderate]

**mod|er|a|tor** (mod′ə rā′tər), *n.* **1** a presiding officer; chairman: *the moderator of a town meeting, the moderator of a church assembly.* **2** an arbitrator; mediator. **SYN**: arbiter, umpire, judge. **3** *Physics.* a material, such as graphite, used in a reactor to reduce the speed of neutrons, making them more efficient in splitting atomic nuclei: *In the Florida reactor, the moderator will be heavy water, which does not absorb the atomic particles* (Wall Street Journal).

**mod|er|a|to|ri|al** (mod′ər ə tôr′ē əl, -tōr′-), *adj.* of or having to do with a moderator.

**mod|er|a|tor|ship** (mod′ə rā′tər ship), *n.* the office of moderator: *His service was fittingly crowned by a Double Moderatorship of the General Assembly* (London Times).

***mod|ern** (mod′ərn), *adj., n.* *–adj.* **1** of the present time; of times not long past: *Color television is a modern invention. All modern American literature comes from one book ... Huckleberry Finn* (Ernest Hemingway). **SYN**: See syn. under **new**. **2** up-to-date; not old-fashioned: *modern views. The Justice ... Full of wise saws and modern instances* (Shakespeare).
*–n.* **1** a person of modern times: *Some in ancient books delight; Others prefer what moderns write* (Matthew Prior). **2** a person who has modern ideas and tastes. **3** *Printing.* any one of various styles of type, such as Bodoni, characterized by thin serifs and hairlines, heavy downstrokes, and greater symmetry and precision of cut.
[earlier, extant < Late Latin *modernus* < Latin *modō* just now; (originally) in a (certain) manner, ablative of *modus* measure, mode[1]] *–***mod′ern|ly**, *adv.* *–***mod′ern|ness**, *n.*

***modern**
definition 3

The World Book Dictionary

**Mod|ern** (mod′ərn), *adj.* designating the form of a language now in use, in contrast to an earlier form; New: *Modern Arabic.*

**modern dance**, dancing as an art form based on the principle of expression through natural bodily movements and rhythms.

**mod|ern-dress** (mod′ərn dres′), *adj.* **1** (of a play) produced or performed with the actors dressed in modern fashion, or with modern scenery in the background to make it up-to-date: *a modern-dress version of Hamlet.* **2** (of a literary work, especially fiction) up-to-date, as in setting or characterization; in or having a modern setting: *Faulkner's "A Fable" is a modern-dress account of the Passion of Jesus.*

**mo|derne** (mō dārn′), *adj.* conspicuously or ostentatiously modern: *Its grandeur ... seems moderne rather than modern* (Harper's). [< French *moderne* modern < Late Latin *modernus;* see etym. under **modern**]

**Modern English**, **1** a period in the development of the English language from about 1500 through the present. It is sometimes subdivided into Early Modern, 1500-1700, and Late Modern, 1700 to the present. **2** the English language of this period.

**Modern French**, the French language from about 1600 to the present.

**Modern Greek**, = New Greek.

**Modern Hebrew**, the language of modern Israel, a revived form of ancient Hebrew; New Hebrew.

**modern history**, **1** history from about 1450 to the present time. **2** history from the end of the Roman Empire to the present time.

**mod|ern|ise** (mod′ər nīz), *v.t., v.i.,* **-ised, -is|ing.** *Especially British.* modernize. *–***mod′ern|is′er**, *n.*

**mod|ern|ism** (mod′ər niz əm), *n.* **1** modern attitudes or methods; sympathy with what is modern: *Modernism entered Japanese poetry with the wave of Western influence which began late in the 19th Century* (Atlantic). **2** a tendency in religion to interpret the teachings of the Bible or the church in accordance with modern scientific theories. **3** a modern word, phrase, or usage.

**Mod|ern|ism** (mod′ər niz əm), *n.* **1** a movement among Roman Catholics to modify the teachings and tenets of the Church in the direction of the scientific, literary, and philosophic opinions of the 1800's and 1900's. It was condemned by Pope Pius X in 1907. **2** = modernism (def. 2).

**mod|ern|ist** (mod′ər nist), *n., adj.* *–n.* **1** a person who holds modern views or uses modern methods: *The contemporary modernists rebel only with the established forms of Expressionism and Abstractionism* (New Yorker). **2** a person who supports the study of modern subjects in preference to the ancient classics. **3** a person who interprets religious teachings in a modern way: *Christianity for the modernist is a life, not a doctrine* (Newsweek).
*–adj.* of or having to do with modernists or modernism.

**mod|ern|is|tic** (mod′ər nis′tik), *adj.* **1a** having or suggesting a modern quality or appearance: *a modernistic building, a modernistic painting.* **b** = modern. **2** having to do with modernism or modernists. *–***mod′ern|is′ti|cal|ly**, *adv.*

**mo|der|ni|ty** (mə dėr′nə tē, mō-), *n., pl.* **-ties.** **1** the quality of being modern: *Modernity, natural disaster, war, and hard times have ... seriously affected many Buddhist sects* (Atlantic). **2** something modern.

**mod|ern|i|za|tion** (mod′ər nə zā′shən), *n.* **1** the act of modernizing; bringing up to the present ways or standards: *The government ... is pouring $1.4 billion worth of British pounds sterling into mechanization and modernization of mining* (Wall Street Journal). **2** the state of being modernized.

**mod|ern|ize** (mod′ər nīz), *v.,* **-ized, -iz|ing.** *–v.t.* to make modern; bring up to present ways or standards: *Much expenditure has been incurred in extending, modernizing and improving the plants* (Manchester Guardian).
*–v.i.* to become modern. *–***mod′ern|iz′er**, *n.*

**modern jazz**, a style of jazz characterized by intricate improvisation, stress on contrapuntal rhythms, and complicated harmonic development. *–***mod′ern-jazz′**, *adj.*

**Modern Latin**, = New Latin.

**modern pentathlon**, a five-event competition in the Olympic Games, consisting of horseback riding, fencing, pistol shooting, swimming, and running.

**mod|est** (mod′ist), *adj.* **1** not thinking too highly of oneself; not vain; humble: *In spite of the honors he received, the scientist remained a modest man.* **SYN**: unpretentious, unassuming. **2** bashful; shy; held back by a sense of what is fit and proper; not bold or forward: *a modest girl, modest pride. The Victorian definition of a modest woman is clearly outmoded.* **SYN**: diffident. **3a** not calling attention to one's body; decent: *a modest bathing suit.* **b** having or showing decency of actions or thoughts: *modest behavior.* **4** not too great; not asking too much: *a modest request.* **5** not conspicuous; not gaudy; humble in appearance; quiet: *a modest little house, modest decorations.* [< Latin *modestus* in due measure, moderate < *modus* measure] *–***mod′est|ly**, *adv.*
*–Syn.* **2 Modest, demure** mean not bold or forward. **Modest** emphasizes a sense of what is fit and proper, a holding back from calling attention to oneself: *I like a modest girl, who is neither shy nor loud.* **Demure** often suggests undue modesty or pretended shyness thought to be attractive and put on for effect: *She sipped her soda and looked demure.*

**mod|es|ty** (mod′ə stē), *n., pl.* **-ties.** **1** freedom from vanity; being modest or humble: *Few "letters home" of successful men or women display the graces of modesty and self-forgetfulness* (H. G. Wells). **SYN**: humility. **2** the quality of being shy or bashful. **SYN**: diffidence, shyness, bashfulness. **3** the quality of being decent or chaste; not calling attention to one's body: *Modesty, then, appears to be a culturally determined function of clothing, and very likely not a fundamental or original purpose* (Beals and Hoijer).

**mod|es|ty-bit** (mod′ə stē bit′), *n.* = modesty-piece.

**mod|es|ty-piece** (mod′ə stē pēs′), *n.* a piece or article of lace, net, embroidered muslin, or the like, worn by women over the bosom with a low-cut or open bodice.

**Mo|di** (mō′dē), *n. Norse Mythology.* the son of Thor.

**mod|i|cum** (mod′ə kəm), *n., pl.* **-cums.** a small quantity; moderate amount: *She is so bright that even with a modicum of effort she does excellent work.* [< Latin *modicum,* neuter of *modicus* moderate < *modus* measure, mode[1]]

**mod|i|fi|a|bil|i|ty** (mod′ə fī′ə bil′ə tē), *n.* the quality of being modifiable.

**mod|i|fi|a|ble** (mod′ə fī′ə bəl), *adj.* that can be modified. *–***mod′i|fi′a|ble|ness**, *n.*

**mod|i|fi|ca|tion** (mod′ə fə kā′shən), *n.* **1** a partial alteration or change: *With some modifications your essay will do for the school paper. Every modification of accepted house plans means additional cost.* **2** the act or process of modifying or condition of being modified; making less severe, strong, or otherwise striking in some characteristic; toning down: *The modification of his anger made him able to think clearly again.* **3a** limitation of meaning; qualification. **b** an instance or result of this. **c** a change in the form of a linguistic element when it is part of a construction. **4** a modified form; variety: *This car is a modification of last year's model.* **5** *Biology.* a change in an organism resulting from external influences, and not inheritable.

**mod|i|fi|ca|tive** (mod′ə fə kā′tiv), *adj.* = modificatory.

**mod|i|fi|ca|to|ry** (mod′ə fə kā′tər ē), *adj.* modifying; tending to modify.

**mod|i|fi|er** (mod′ə fī′ər), *n.* **1** a word or group of words that limits or qualifies the meaning of another word or group of words. In "a very tight coat," the adjective *tight* is a modifier of *coat,* and the adverb *very* is a modifier of *tight.* **2** a person or thing that modifies.

**mod|i|fy** (mod′ə fī), *v.,* **-fied, -fy|ing.** *–v.t.* **1** to make partial changes in; change somewhat: *to modify the design of an automobile, to modify the terms of a lease.* **SYN**: alter. **2** to make less; make less severe or strong; tone down: *He has modified his demands.* **SYN**: temper. **3** to limit the meaning of; qualify. Adverbs modify verbs, adjectives, and other adverbs. **4** to change (a vowel) by umlaut.
*–v.i.* to be subjected to modification; make a modification.
[< Latin *modificāre* to limit, be moderate < *modus* measure, mode[1] + *facere* to make]

**mo|dil|lion** (mō dil′yən, mə-), *n. Architecture.* **1** one of a series of ornamental blocks or brackets placed under the corona of a cornice in the Corinthian and other orders. **2** a block or bracket similarly used in medieval and modern styles. [earlier *modiglion* < Italian *modiglione,* ultimately < Latin *mūtulus*]

**mo|di|o|lar** (mō dī′ə lər, mə-), *adj.* resembling a modiolus.

**mo|di|o|lus** (mō dī′ə ləs, mə-), *n., pl.* **-li** (-lī). *Anatomy.* the central conical axis around which the cochlea of the ear winds. [< New Latin *modiolus* < Latin, nave of a wheel; a vessel or container < *modius* a Roman measure; also, a socket < *modus* mode[1]]

**mod|ish** (mō′dish), *adj.* fashionable; stylish. *–***mod′ish|ly**, *adv.* *–***mod′ish|ness**, *n.*

**mo|diste** (mō dēst′), *n.* a person who makes or sells fashionable women's dresses, hats, and accessories; dressmaker. [< French *modiste* < *mode* mode[2]]

**mo|di|us** (mō′dē əs), *n., pl.* **-di|i** (-dē ī). **1** an ancient Roman dry measure, equal to about a peck. **2** a tall, cylindrical headdress worn by certain divinities as represented in ancient art. [< Latin *modius* < *modus* mode[1]]

**Mo|doc** (mō′dok), *n., pl.* **-doc** or **-docs.** a member of a small tribe of American Indians of southwestern Oregon and northern California, closely related to the Klamath Indians.

**Mo|dred** (mō′dred), *n. Arthurian Legend.* King Arthur's nephew, and one of the knights of the Round Table. He was a traitor and led a rebellion against Arthur. Also, **Mordred**.

**Mods** (modz), *n.pl. British Informal.* Moderations, the first public examination for the B.A. at Oxford: *They have scarcely opened a classical text since they got their first in Mods* (London Times).

**mod|u|lar** (moj′ů lər), *adj.* **1** of or having to do with a module or modules: *Modular construction [is] based on the use of prefabricated and stacked concrete apartment boxes* (Mary E. Jessup). **2** made or built in units or pieces that can be interchanged to meet various needs, as furniture or building materials: *The console has three modular units that can be arranged in the room as one wishes. Basically it is an analogue computer, built up on the modular system and therefore extremely versatile* (New Scientist). **3** of or having to do with furniture, building materials, or any parts that can be interchanged: *a modular plan, a modular pattern.* **4** *Mathematics, Physics.* of or having to do with a modulus or moduli.

**modular arithmetic**, a form of arithmetic dealing with the remainders after a set of numbers are divided by a single number, the modulus.

**mod|u|lar|i|ty** (moj′ů lar′ə tē), *n.* the use of modules in building computers and other machines: *Digital transmitters directly adaptable to digital computers ... will be of more complex construction than existing equipment and impose the need for modularity in design to ease servicing* (London Times).

**mod|u|lar|ize** (moj′ů lə rīz), *v.t.*, **-ized, -iz|ing.** to make modular; build with modules: *to modularize machinery or equipment.*

**mod|u|late** (moj′ů lāt), *v.*, **-lat|ed, -lat|ing.** *—v.t.* **1** to regulate or adjust; tone down; soften. **2** to alter (the voice) in pitch, tone, or volume for expression; inflect: *He had a really noble voice which he could modulate with great skill* (Alexander Kinglake). **3** *Music.* **a** to attune (as sounds) to a certain pitch or key. **b** to cause to change from one key or note to another. **4** to vary the frequency of (electromagnetic waves): *A light-beam modulated at a frequency of 8.2 megacycles per second* (Science News). **5** *Radio.* to cause (a carrier wave) to vary by adding sound waves to it in accordance with the signal being sent, the effect of one sound wave being spread over a considerable number of oscillations of the carrier wave. **6** to intone (as a prayer or response); sing softly.

*—v.i.* **1** to undergo modulation. **2** *Music.* to change from one key to another, according to the laws of harmony. **3** to vary electrical waves by producing oscillations. **4** to produce modulation in a radio carrier wave.

[< Latin *modulārī* (with English *-ate*[1]) < *modulus* small measure (diminutive) < *modus* measure]

**mod|u|la|tion** (moj′ů lā′shən), *n.* **1** the act or process of modulating: *Modulation ... includes the patterns of stress and intonation which frequently accompany utterances or parts of utterances* (Beals and Hoijer). **2** the quality or condition of being modulated. **3** a change from one key to another in the course of a piece of music, especially with a certain succession of chords: *He went to his organ and improvised with learned modulations* (Lytton Strachey). **4** *Electronics.* **a** a varying of high-frequency waves. **b** variation of the amplitude, frequency, or phase of the carrier wave in accordance with the sound wave or other signal being sent.

**mod|u|la|tor** (moj′ů lā′tər), *n.* **1** a person or thing that modulates. **2** a device, such as a vacuum tube, for changing a radio current by adding sound waves to it.

**mod|u|la|to|ry** (moj′ů lə tôr′ē, -tōr′-), *adj.* serving to modulate; that modulates.

**mod|ule** (moj′ül), *n.* **1** a standard or basic unit for measuring: *Many high schools are now programming their students' day in 20 minute modules. Houses of the future may all be built using a four-inch cube called a module as the structural "atom"* (Science News Letter). **2** *Architecture.* **a** the size of some part taken as a unit of measure for other parts, especially a dimension of some part, such as a column, used as a unit of measure throughout a structure, to bring all parts into correct proportion. **b** a prefabricated dwelling unit: *The house is a two-story boxlike structure consisting of four factory-produced modules equipped with plumbing, heating, lighting, kitchen equipment, and wall-to-wall carpeting* (New Yorker). **3** any standardized or interchangeable piece or part; modular unit: **a** a self-contained unit in an aircraft or spacecraft, designed to serve a particular function: *a spacecraft's command and service modules, a lunar module. An operational crew module which could be used in an emergency for escape and survival is to be fitted to the American F-111 fighter-bomber* (London Times). **b** a self-contained, standardized, and interchangeable unit or component in a computer or other machine: *One reason why Sigma 5 gets more efficient as it grows larger is that when memory modules are added interleave and overlap occur* (Scientific American). **4** = micromodule. [earlier, a scale < Latin *modulus* (diminutive) < *modus* a measure, mode[1]]

**mod|u|lo** (moj′ə lō), *adv. Mathematics.* with respect to a (specified) modulus. *Example:* 18 is congruent to 42 modulo 12, because both 18 and 42 leave 6 as a remainder when divided by 12. [< Latin, ablative of *modulus*]

**mod|u|lus** (moj′ů ləs), *n., pl.* **-li** (-lī). **1** *Physics.* a quantity expressing the measure of some function, property, or the like, especially under conditions where the measure is unity. **2** *Mathematics.* **a** a number by which two given numbers can be divided to leave the same remainders. *Example:* the modulus of 7 and 9 is 2, written as 7 = 9 (modulus 2). **b** the factor by which a logarithm in one system is multiplied to change it to a logarithm in another system. **c** = absolute value. [< Latin *modulus;* see etym. under **module**]

► **modulus, coefficient.** *Modulus* is used generally in describing physical relations; *coefficient* is more common for mathematical relations.

**mo|dus** (mō′dəs), *n., pl.* **-di** (-dī). manner or method of procedure; mode. [< Latin *modus*]

**mo|dus o|pe|ran|di** (mō′dəs op′ə ran′dī), *Latin.* method or manner of working; mode of operation: *Her modus operandi in arriving at her conclusions was simplicity itself: she talked to people about politics* (Harper's). *Abbr:* M.O.

**mo|dus vi|ven|di** (mō′dəs vi ven′dī), *Latin.* mode of living; way of getting along; temporary arrangement while waiting for a final settlement: *Détente is a modus vivendi between East and West.*

**Moe|bi|us strip** or **band** (mœ′bē əs, mō′-), = Möbius strip.

**Moe|ra** (mir′ə), *n., pl.* **Moe|rae** (mir′ē). *Greek Mythology.* the goddess of Fate. Also, **Moira. Moerae,** the Fates.

**Moe|so|goth** (mē′sə goth), *n.* of a Gothic tribe which settled in Moesia, an ancient Roman province corresponding nearly to modern Bulgaria and Serbia.

**Moe|so|goth|ic** (mē′sə goth′ik), *adj., n.* *—adj.* of or having to do with the Moesogoths or their language.

*—n.* the language of the Moesogoths.

**moeurs** (mœrs), *n.pl. French.* mores: *She ... transformed a historical subject ... by endowing her characters with the moral conceptions and moeurs of her time* (Listener).

**mo|fette** or **mof|fette** (mō fet′), *n.* **1** an opening or fissure in the earth from which gases, especially carbon dioxide, emanate. **2** an emanation from such an opening. [< French *mofette* < Italian *mofetta.* Compare etym. under **mephitic.**]

**mog** (mog), *v.,* **mogged, mog|ging.** *Dialect.* *—v.i.* **1** to move on; depart; decamp. **2** to move along slowly but steadily; jog.

*—v.t.* to move (something); cause to go. [origin unknown]

**mog|gie** or **mog|gy** (mog′ē), *n., pl.* **-gies. 1** *British Slang.* **a** a cat. **b** an untidy woman or girl. **2** *British Dialect.* a calf or cow. [perhaps alteration of the name *Maggie*]

**Mo|ghul** (mō′gul, mō gul′), *n.* = Mogul.

**Mo|gol|lon** (mō′gə yōn′), *n., pl.* **-lon** or **-lons.** a member of a tribe of North American Indians which once lived in the southwestern United States, thought to be predecessors of the Hopi and Zuñi Indians.

**Mo|gul** (mō′gul, mō gul′), *n.* **1** a Mongol or Mongolian. **2a** one of the Mongol conquerors of India in the 1500's. **b** one of their descendants. [< Persian and Arabic *mughal, mughul,* alteration of *Mongol,* the native name]

**mo|gul**[1] (mō′gul, mō gul′), *n.* **1** an important or powerful person: *The ruthless industrial giants of the 1800's were the moguls of American society.* **2** a steam locomotive used especially in the late 1800's and early 1900's for hauling freight trains. [< *Mogul*]

**mo|gul**[2] (mō′gəl), *n.* a moundlike elevation on a ski slope: *Easily, solid on her skis, she swung down among the moguls and wind-bared ice, and became small, and again waited* (John Updike). [probably < Norwegian *muge, mugje* (feminine *muga*) a heap or mound; form influenced by English *mogul*[1]]

**mo|hair** (mō′hãr), *n.* **1** cloth made from the long, silky hair of the Angora goat; Angora. **2** a similar cloth made of wool and cotton or rayon, used for upholstery and clothing. **3** a garment of mohair. **4** the hair of the Angora goat. [earlier *mocayare,* ultimately < Arabic *mukhayyar;* influenced by English *hair*]

**Moham.,** Mohammedan.

**Mo|ham|med|an** (mō ham′ə dən), *adj., n.* *—adj.* of the Arabian prophet Mohammed (570?-632) or the religion founded by him; Moslem.

*—n.* a follower of Mohammed; believer in the religion founded by him; Moslem. Also, **Mahometan, Muhammadan.**

**Mohammedan calendar,** = Islamic calendar.

**Mo|ham|med|an|ism** (mō ham′ə də niz′əm), *n.* = Islam: *In its essence Mohammedanism ... holds to the doctrine of the unity and omnipotence of Allah, and of the responsibility of every human being to Allah* (Emory S. Bogardus). Also, **Mahometanism, Muhammadanism.**

**Mo|ham|med|an|ize** (mō ham′ə də nīz), *v.t.,* **-ized, -iz|ing.** = Islamize.

**Mo|har|ram** (mō har′əm), *n.* = Muharram.

**Mo|ha|ve** (mō hä′vē), *n., pl.* **-ve** or **-ves. 1** a member of a tribe of North American Indians dwelling chiefly in California, Nevada, and Arizona. **2** the Hokan language of this tribe. Also, **Mojave.** [American English < Yuman (Mohave) *hamakhava* (literally) the three mountains]

**Mo|hawk** (mō′hôk), *n., pl.* **-hawk** or **-hawks. 1** a member of a tribe of North American Indians formerly living in central New York State, the most powerful of the Six Nations or Iroquois. **2** the Iroquoian language of the Mohawks. [American English < the Algonkian (Algonkin) name *mowak* or *mowawak* (literally) they eat living things]

**Mo|he|gan** (mō hē′gən), *n., pl.* **-gan** or **-gans. 1** a member of a tribe of North American Indians related to the Mohicans, formerly living in western Connecticut. **2** = Mahican. [American English, variant of *Mahican*]

**mo|hel** (mō′hel), *n., pl.* **mo|he|lim** (mō′he lēm′). a Jewish ritual circumciser. [< Hebrew *mōhēl*]

**Mo|hi|can** (mō hē′kən), *n., pl.* **-can** or **-cans.** a member of either of two tribes of North American Indians formerly living in the upper Hudson valley and in Connecticut. Also, **Mahican.** [American English, variant of *Mahican*]

**Moh|ism** (mō′iz əm), *n.* the moral teachings of Mo Ti (or Mo-Tzu), a Chinese philosopher of the 400's B.C. Mohism emphasized universal love and opposed the traditional teachings of Confucianism. Also, **Moism.**

**Moh|ist** (mō′ist), *n., adj.* *—n.* an adherent of Mohism.

*—adj.* of, having to do with, or like Mohism. Also, **Moist.**

**Mo|ho** (mō′hō), *n.* = Mohorovicic discontinuity.

**Mo|hock** (mō′hok), *n.* **1** one of a class of ruffians, often aristocrats, who roamed the streets of London at night early in the 1700's. **3** *Obsolete.* Mohawk. [variant of *Mohawk*]

**Mo|hock|ism** (mō′hok iz əm), *n.* the practices of the Mohocks.

**Mo|hole** (mō′hōl), *n.* an experimental drilling project to bore into the earth's mantle to obtain geological specimens and to verify the Mohorovicic discontinuity. The project was financed by the United States government and ended by Congress in 1966. [< *Moho*(rovicic) discontinuity + (ho)*le*]

**Mo|ho|ro|vic|ic discontinuity** (mō′hō rō vē′chēch), the boundary between the earth's crust and mantle, the depth of which varies from approximately 6 to 8 miles under ocean basins, to 20 to 22 miles under the continents. [< A. *Mohorovičić,* a Yugoslav geophysicist, who discovered it in 1909 from studies of earthquake records]

***Mohs** or **Mohs' scale** (mōz), **1** a scale for classifying the relative hardness of minerals, as follows: talc 1; gypsum 2; calcite 3; fluorite 4; apatite 5; feldspar 6; quartz 7; topaz 8; corundum 9; diamond 10. **2** a modified form of this scale, arranged as follows: talc 1; gypsum 2; calcite 3; fluorite 4; apatite 5; orthoclase 6; vitreous silica 7; quartz 8; topaz 9; garnet 10; fused zirconia 11; fused alumina 12; silicon carbide 13; boron carbide 14; diamond 15. [< Friedrich *Mohs,* 1773-1839, a German mineralogist, who invented it]

***Mohs scale**
definition 1

| mineral | hardness | common tests |
|---|---|---|
| talc | 1 | scratched by a fingernail |
| gypsum | 2 | |
| calcite | 3 | scratched by a copper coin |
| fluorite | 4 | scratched by a knife blade or window glass |
| apatite | 5 | |
| feldspar | 6 | scratches a knife blade or window glass |
| quartz | 7 | |
| topaz | 8 | |
| corundum | 9 | |
| diamond | 10 | scratches all common materials |

**mo|hur** (mō′hər, -hůr), *n.* **1** a former gold coin of India. It was equal to 15 rupees. **2** the rupee of Nepal. [< Hindi *muhr* < Persian]

**moh|wa** (mō′wä), *n.* = mahua.

**M.O.I.,** Ministry of Information (an agency of the British government during World War II, since replaced by the Central Office of Information and the British Information Service).

**moi|dore** (moi′dôr, -dōr), *n.* a former gold coin of Portugal and Brazil, worth about $6.50. [< Portuguese *moeda d'ouro* coin of gold < Latin *monēta* coin, money, *de* of, *aurum* gold]

**moi|e|ty** (moi′ə tē), *n., pl.* **-ties. 1** half: *War, pestilence, and famine, had consumed ... the moiety of the human species* (Edward Gibbon). **2** part: *Only a small moiety of college students win scholarships.* **3** a person's share or portion. **4** *Anthropology.* each of the two strictly comparable major sections of a single society. Typically, as common among Australian aborigines, each moiety is exogamous so that all the members of any one moiety must find their spouses in the other. [earlier *moitie* < Old French *meitiet* < Late Latin *medietās* half < Latin, (coined by Cicero for Greek *mesótēs*) the middle < *medius* middle]

**Pronunciation Key:** hat, āge, cãre, fär; let, ēqual, tėrm; it, īce; hot, ōpen, ôrder; **oi**l, **ou**t; cup, půt, rüle; **ch**ild; lo**ng**; **th**in; **ᴛʜ**en; **zh**, measure; **ə** represents **a** in about, **e** in taken, **i** in pencil, **o** in lemon, **u** in circus.

**moil**[1] (moil), *v., n.* — *v.i.* **1** to work hard; drudge. **2** to be in a turmoil; agitate.
— *v.t. Archaic.* **1** to wet; moisten. **2** to soil; bedaub; make dirty.
— *n.* **1** hard work; drudgery. **2** confusion, turmoil, or trouble.
[< Old French *moillier* to moisten (as in soup), ultimately < Latin *mollis* soft] — **moil′er,** *n.*

**moil**[2] (moil), *n.* the glass that adheres to the blowpipe or a piece of glassware after the piece has been blown and cracked off. [origin uncertain]

**Moing|we|na** (moing wē′nə), *n., pl.* **-na** or **-nas.** **1** a member of a woodland tribe of North American Indians, once constituting a part of the Illinois confederacy, who lived in central Iowa. **2** the language of this tribe, a dialect of Illinois.

**Moi|ra** (moi′rə), *n., pl.* **-rai** (-rī), **-rae** (-rē). *Greek Mythology.* **1** any one of the three Fates. **2** Also, **moira.** a person's fate, or the kind of life he has been decreed by the Fates to live: *I am going through my end, moira, my allotted part* (Atlantic).

**moire** (mwär; mwä rā′, mô-, mō-), *n.* **1** any textile fabric, especially silk, rayon, or acetate, to which a watered appearance or wavelike pattern is given by pressing it between engraved rollers; watered fabric: *This ... gown is made of satin finished silk organdy, with a moire sash* (New York Times). **2** (originally) a kind of watered silk. [< French *moire,* earlier *mouaire,* apparently alteration of English *mohair*]

✱**moi|ré** (mwä rā′, mô-, mō-), *n., adj.* — *n.* **1** = moire: *... weaving the stuff into a fine mesh or engine-turning it into something resembling silk moiré* (New Yorker). **2** a variegated or clouded appearance like that of watered silk, especially on metals for ornamentation. **3** Also, **moiré pattern.** a pattern of lines resulting from two other patterns overlapping: *Moirés are what one sees when viewing two overlapping figures that each have a regular pattern, such as picket fences, concentric circles, radial lines and the like* (New York Times). *In the typical moiré pattern the ... effect materializes when two sets of straight lines are superposed so that they intersect at a small angle* (Scientific American).
— *adj.* **1** (of silk, paper, or metal) having a wavelike pattern or clouded appearance; watered: *moiré silk.* **2** (of a stamp) printed on the paper surface with an intricate wavy pattern to prevent forgery.
[< French *moiré* < *moirer* to give a watered look to < *moire* moire]

✱**moiré**
definition 3

**moire antique,** silk watered in a large pattern. [< French *moire antique*]

**Mo|ism** (mō′iz əm), *n.* = Mohism.

**Mo|ist** (mō′ist), *n., adj.* = Mohist.

**moist** (moist), *adj.* **1a** slightly wet; not dry; damp: *a moist cloth, a moist cellar, a moist dressing for an infection.* SYN: humid, dank. See syn. under **damp. b** (of the eyes) wet with tears; tearful. **2** rainy; wet: *The weather is moist and raw* (Dickens). **3** associated or connected with liquid, as a disease marked by a discharge of matter or phlegm. [< Old French *moiste,* perhaps < Late Latin *muscidus* moss (< Latin *muscus* moss), blended with Latin *mūcidus* slimy, musty < *mūcus* slime, mucus] — **moist′ly,** *adv.* — **moist′ness,** *n.*

**moist|en** (moi′sən), *v.t.* to make moist; dampen: *Moisten the flap of the envelope to seal it.* — *v.i.* to become moist: *Her eyes moistened with tears.* — **moist′en|er,** *n.*

**moist gangrene,** gangrene characterized by the presence of blisters, oozing fluid, and a bad odor. Bacteria which cause the flesh to decay are active in moist gangrene.

**mois|ture** (mois′chər), *n.* slight wetness; water or other liquid spread in very small drops in the air or on a surface. Dew is moisture that collects at night on the grass. [< Old French *moistour* < *moiste* moist] — **mois′ture|less,** *adj.*

**mois|tur|ize** (mois′chə rīz), *v.t.,* **-ized, -iz|ing.** to supply with moisture by means of some agent: *An invisible protective film that moisturizes skin, leaving it smoother, younger-looking* (New Yorker). — **mois′tur|iz′er,** *n.*

**moist|y** (mois′tē), *adj.* **moist|i|er, moist|i|est.** moist; damp.

**mo|jar|ra** (mō hä′rə), *n., pl.* **-ras** or (*collectively*) **-ra.** any one of a group of warm-water fishes found in shallow waters on both coasts of the Americas, of small size and silvery coloration. [< American Spanish *mojarra*]

**Mo|ja|ve** (mō hä′vē), *n., pl.* **-ve** or **-ves.** = Mohave.

**moke** (mōk), *n. Slang.* **1** a donkey: *You too could ride around on this patient moke* (Sunday Times). **2** a stupid fellow; dolt. [origin unknown]

**mol** (mōl), *n.* = mole[5].

**MOL** (no periods) or **M.O.L.,** Manned Orbiting Laboratory.

**mo|la** (mō′lə), *n., pl.* **-las** or (*collectively*) **-la.** = ocean sunfish. [< New Latin *Mola* the genus name < Latin *mola* millstone]

**mo|lal** (mō′ləl), *adj.* **1** of or having to do with a mole or gram molecule. **2** (of a solution) having one mole of solute in 1,000 grams of solvent.

**mo|lal|i|ty** (mō lal′ə tē), *n.* the molal concentration of a solution. It is expressed as the number of moles of solute in 1,000 grams of solvent.

**mo|lar**[1] (mō′lər), *n., adj.* — *n.* a tooth with a broad surface for grinding, having somewhat flattened points; grinder. The twelve permanent back teeth in man are molars.
— *adj.* **1** adapted for grinding. **2** of the molar teeth.
[< Latin *molāris* grinding < *mola* millstone]

**mo|lar**[2] (mō′lər), *adj.* **1** *Physics.* of mass or a body as a whole; acting on or by means of large masses of matter. **2** *Chemistry.* having one mole of solute in a liter of solution. [< Latin *mōlēs* mass + English *-ar*]

**mo|lar|i|ty** (mō lar′ə tē), *n.* **1** *Chemistry.* the molar concentration of a solution. It is expressed as the number of moles of solute in a liter of solution. **2** *Physics.* mass.

**mo|las|ses** (mə las′iz), *n.* a sweet, brown syrup obtained in the process of making sugar from sugar cane, or from raw sugar or sorghum; treacle. [< Portuguese *melaço* < Late Latin *mellāceum* must[2] < Latin *mellāceus* honeylike < *mel, mellis* honey]

**mold**[1] (mōld), *n., v.* — *n.* **1** a hollow shape in which anything is formed or cast: *Melted metal is poured into a mold to harden into shape. The gelatin was left in a mold to stiffen.* **2** the shape or form which is given by a mold: *iron of an ancient mold. The molds of ice cream were turkeys and pumpkins.* **3** *Figurative.* the model according to which anything is shaped: *He is cast in his father's mold.* **4** something shaped in a mold: *a mold of pudding.* **5** *Figurative.* nature; character: *a man of base mold.* **6** the shape or frame on or about which something is made: *a basket mold.* **7** an impression or cavity made in earth by the convex side of a fossil shell.
— *v.t.* **1** to form; shape: *Children mold figures out of clay. I would mold a world of fire and dew* (William Butler Yeats). **2** to make or form into shape: *to mold dough into loaves. We mold wax into candles. Her character was molded by the trials she went through.* **3** to produce a mold of or from, so as to obtain a casting. **4** to form into, or decorate with, moldings. **5** to ornament by shaping or carving. Also, *especially British,* **mould.**
[< Old French *modle,* also *molle* < Latin *modulus.* See etym. of doublet **module.**]

**mold**[2] (mōld), *n., v.* — *n.* **1** a woolly or furry growth, often greenish or whitish in color, that appears on food and other animal or vegetable substances when they are left too long in a warm, moist place or when they are decaying. Mold is a fungus. **2** any fungus that forms mycelium covering the surface of its structure; mold fungus.
— *v.i.* to become covered with mold: *The cheese molded in the damp cellar.*
— *v.t.* to cover with mold. Also, *especially British,* **mould.**
[probably < past participle of Middle English *moulen,* or *muwlen* grow moldy]

**mold**[3] (mōld), *n.* **1** loose earth; fine, soft, rich soil. Mold is rich in decayed leaves, manure, or other organic matter and is suitable for the cultivation of plants. *Many wild flowers grow in the forest mold.* SYN: topsoil, humus. **2** *Archaic.* earth as the material of the human body. **3** *Archaic.* **a** ground; earth, especially as used for a grave. **b** a grave. Also, *especially British,* **mould.** [Old English *molde*]

**mold|a|bil|i|ty** (mōl′də bil′ə tē), *n.* the ability to be easily molded.

**mold|a|ble** (mōl′də bəl), *adj.* that can be molded or formed: *The moldable character of a child is usually shaped by the adults he sees.*

**Mol|da|vi|an** (mol dā′vē ən, -dāv′yən), *adj., n.* — *adj.* of or having to do with Moldavia, a Soviet republic in the southwestern Soviet Union, or its inhabitants.
— *n.* a native or inhabitant of Moldavia.

**mol|da|vite** (mol′də vīt), *n.* a dull-green glass similar to obsidian. [< *Moldavia,* a region of Rumania, where it is found + *-ite*[1]]

**mold|board** (mōld′bôrd′, -bōrd′), *n.* **1** a curved metal plate in a plow, that turns over the earth from the furrow. **2** one of the boards forming the sides of a concrete mold.
[alteration of Middle English *moldebred* < *mold*[3] + *bred* board, tablet]

**mold|er**[1] (mōl′dər), *v.i.* to break up gradually into dust by natural decay; crumble; waste away: *John Brown's body lies a-moldering in the grave* (Charles Sprague Hall).
[probably < *mold*[3]. Compare dialectal Norwegian *muldra* crumble.]

**mold|er**[2] (mōl′dər), *n.* **1** a person who shapes something. **2** a maker of molds. **3** *Printing.* an electrotype plate from which duplicate electrotypes are made. [< *mold*[1] + *-er*[1]]

**mold fungus,** any fungus producing a woolly or furry growth that is often greenish in color and appears especially on decaying matter; mold.

**mold|i|ness** (mōl′dē nis), *n.* the condition of being moldy.

**mold|ing** (mōl′ding), *n.* **1** the act of shaping: *the molding of dishes from clay.* **2** something molded. **3a** a strip, usually of wood, around the upper walls of a room, used to support pictures, to cover electric wires, or for decoration. **b** a decorative variety of contour or outline given to cornices, jambs, strips of woodwork, and the like.

**molding board,** a board used for kneading bread pastry dough.

**mold loft,** a large room (usually a loft) in a shipyard, on the floor of which the lines of a ship are drawn in full size, in plan and elevation, from the designer's drawings.

**mold|warp** (mōld′wôrp′), *n. British Dialect.* mouldwarp.

**mold|y** (mōl′dē), *adj.,* **mold|i|er, mold|i|est.** **1** covered with mold: *a moldy crust of bread, moldy cheese.* **2** musty, as from decay or age: a moldy smell. **3** *Figurative.* stale: *a moldy joke.* **4** of or like mold.

**moldy fig,** *U.S. Slang.* an old-fashioned or outmoded person or thing.

**mole**[1] (mōl), *n.* **1** a spot on the skin, usually brown: *Upon one cheek he had a mole not unbecoming* (Robert Louis Stevenson). **2** = nevus. [Old English *māl*]

**mole**[2] (mōl), *n.* **1** a small animal that lives underground most of the time eating the insects, worms, and larvae, that it finds there. Moles have dark, velvety fur, very small eyes that cannot see well, and forelimbs adapted for digging. The moles comprise a family of mammals. **2** *Figurative.* a person who works in obscurity, especially one who works patiently and painstakingly. **3** a machine for boring through the earth, especially to make tunnels: *A giant mole* [*was*] *used to drill a tunnel for a Navajo Indian irrigation project in New Mexico* (New York Times). [Middle English *molle,* or *molde;* origin uncertain; perhaps short for *moldwarp*]

**mole**[3] (mōl), *n.* **1** a barrier built of stone to break the force of the waves and sometimes serving as a pier; breakwater. **2** the harbor formed by it. [< Latin *mōlēs, -is* a mass, dam]

**mole**[4] (mōl), *n.* a fleshy or bloody mass occurring in the uterus. [< French *môle* < Old French *mole,* learned borrowing from Latin *mola* misconception < Greek *mýlē* tumor on the womb]

**mole**[5] (mōl), *n.* the molecular weight of a substance expressed in grams; gram molecule. Also, **mol.** [< German *Mole*(*kül*) molecule < New Latin *molecula*]

**mo|le**[6] (mō′lā), *n.* a Mexican sauce made of chocolate, chili, sesame seed, and spices, often served with meat and fowl. [< Mexican Spanish *mole* < Nahuatl *molli* sauce]

**mole|cast** (mōl′kast, -käst), *n.* = molehill.

**Mo|lech** (mō′lek), *n.* = Moloch.

**mol|e|chism** or **mol|e|cism** (mol′ə kiz′əm), *n.* any virus, viewed as an infective agent possessing the characteristics of both a living microorganism and a nonliving molecule; organule. [*molechism* < *mole*(cule) + *ch*(emical) + (organ)*ism; molecism* < *molec*(ule) + (organ)*ism*]

**mole crab,** a small crustacean which buries itself in the sand under the ocean surf and gathers food with its feathery antennae.

**mole cricket,** a large insect having velvety hair and stout forelegs adapted for burrowing in the ground. It is found throughout the tropical and temperate world, feeding on insect larvae, earthworms, and root and tuber crops, including potatoes and sugar cane.

**mo|lec|u|lar** (mə lek′yə lər), *adj.* **1** having to do with molecules: *Some progress has been made towards interpreting the ... theorem in molecular terms* (Science News). **2** consisting of molecules: *Molecular ions of deuterium are injected from an accelerating machine into a large magnetic bottle* (New Scientist). **3** caused by molecules: *A heavy metal ball in a vessel of water ... will be lifted to* *the surface by a concentration of molecular impulses* (T. Fursdon Crang). —**mo|lec'u|lar|ly**, *adv.*

**molecular astronomy**, the study of the chemical molecules found in interstellar space.

**molecular beam** or **ray**, a stream of molecules moving in about the same direction and at approximately the same speed.

**molecular biologist**, a person who studies molecular biology: *Molecular biologists are mainly interested in the structure and function of genes and enzymes and the interaction between the two* (Max Perutz).

**molecular biology**, the branch of biology dealing with the chemical processes of life at the molecular level, especially the mechanism of the replication of cells, and the transmission of genetic information.

**molecular film**, = monomolecular film.

**molecular formula**, a chemical formula that shows the number and kinds of atoms in a molecule without indicating how the atoms are arranged.

**molecular fossil**, a molecule of organic material extracted from rocks other than the oldest known fossils, used to study the early evolution of life on earth: *The exciting studies of ... "molecular fossils," have not, however, firmly established the biogenic nature of these substances* (Science Journal).

**molecular gas constant**, = Boltzmann constant.

**molecular genetics**, genetics that accounts for heredity in terms of nucleotide base sequences.

**mo|lec|u|lar|i|ty** (mə lek'yə lar'ə tē), *n.* molecular condition or quality.

**molecular sieve**, a zeolite whose crystalline structure is honeycombed with regularly spaced holes of uniform size that can be used to filter out molecules: *New ... air separation methods used molecular sieves to separate nitrogen from the oxygen in the air* (Marshall Sittig).

**molecular weight**, the weight of a molecule, now usually expressed on a scale on which an isotope of carbon weighs exactly 12.0000 units; the sum of the atomic weights of all the atoms in a molecule. *Abbr:* mol. wt.

***mol|e|cule** (mol'ə kyül), *n.* **1** the smallest particle into which a substance can be divided without chemical change. A molecule of an element consists of one or more atoms that are alike; a molecule of a compound consists of two or more different atoms. *The rate of escape from a solid to a surrounding vapor depends on the intensity of the molecules' motion* (Scientific American). **2** that quantity of a substance whose weight is equivalent to the molecular weight; gram molecule. **3** a very small particle. [< New Latin *molecula* (diminutive) < Latin *mōlēs* mass, burden]

***molecule**
definition 1

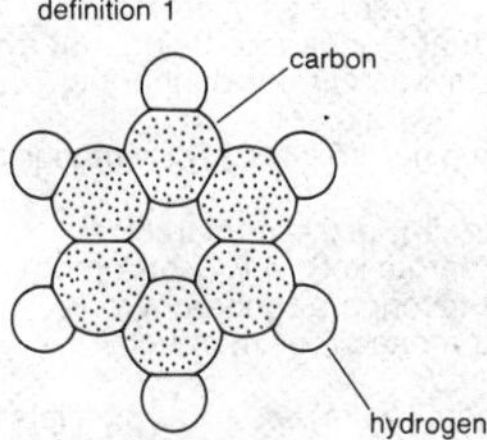

benzene molecule

**mole|hill** (mōl'hil'), *n.* **1** a small mound or ridge of earth raised up by moles burrowing under the ground. **2** something insignificant.
**make a mountain (out) of a molehill.** See under **mountain**.

**mole|like** (mōl'līk'), *adj.* resembling a mole.

**mole rat**, any one of various Old World molelike rodents, which live underground and burrow extensively.

**mole|skin** (mōl'skin'), *n.* **1a** the skin of the mole used as fur. **b** other skins dressed so as to resemble this. **2** a strong, thick cotton fabric used for sportsmen's and laborers' clothing.
**moleskins**, garments, especially trousers, made of a strong, thick cotton fabric: *It is not unlikely that the resumption of football by his famous backfield partner ... will accentuate a desire to don the so-called moleskins and emulate Blanchard's achievements* (Baltimore Sun).

**mo|lest** (mə lest'), *v.t.* **1** to meddle with and injure; interfere with and trouble; disturb: *We did not molest the big dog, because we were afraid of him.* **SYN:** harass, harry, worry, annoy. **2** to interfere with improperly or indecently, especially by making sexual advances. [< Old French *molester*, learned borrowing from Latin *molestāre* < *molestus* troublesome, related to *mōlēs*, *-is* burden, mass] —**mo|lest'er**, *n.*

**mo|les|ta|tion** (mō'les tā'shən, mol'es-), *n.* **1** the act of molesting. **2** the fact or condition of being molested; annoying or hostile interference: *He is not solitary by nature, but his way of life and his desire to continue it without molestation impose this penalty upon him* (Harper's). **3** *Obsolete.* vexation; distress.

**mo|line** (mō'lin, mə līn'), *adj. Heraldry.* having arms which terminate in two branches resembling the rynd of a millstone: *A cross moline is the mark of an eighth son.* See the diagram under **cross**. [probably < unrecorded Anglo-French *moliné* < Old French *molin* mill]

**Mo|li|nism** (mō'lə niz əm, mol'ə-), *n.* the religious doctrine of quietism. [< Miguel de *Molinos*, 1627-1696, a Spanish priest, who propounded it + *-ism*] —**Mo'li|nist**, *n.*

**moll** (mol), *n. Slang.* **1** a female companion of a gangster, gunman, or other criminal or of a vagrant. **2** = prostitute. [short for *Molly*, familiar variant of *Mary*]

**mol|lah** (mol'ə), *n.* = mullah.

**mol|les|cence** (mə les'əns), *n.* a tendency toward softness.

**mol|les|cent** (mə les'ənt), *adj.* tending to become soft. [< Latin *mollēscēns*, *-entis*, present participle of *mollēscere* become soft < *mollīre* soften < *mollis* soft]

**mol|lie** (mol'ē), *n.* a small, brightly colored or black freshwater fish of tropical America, related to the guppy and commonly raised in aquariums. Also, **molly**. [< New Latin *Mollie(nisia)* the genus name < François N. *Mollien*, 1758-1850, a French nobleman]

**mol|li|fi|a|ble** (mol'ə fī'ə bəl), *adj.* that can be mollified, softened, or soothed.

**mol|li|fi|ca|tion** (mol'ə fə kā'shən), *n.* **1** the act of mollifying or softening: *For induration, or mollification, it is to be enquired what will make metals harder and harder, and what will make them softer and softer* (Francis Bacon). **2** pacification; an appeasing: *No mollification of his wife's anger appeared likely.* **3** something that will soothe: *Some mollification for your giant, sweet lady* (Shakespeare).

**mol|li|fy** (mol'ə fī), *v.*, **-fied, -fy|ing.** —*v.t.* **1** to soften, especially in temper; appease; mitigate: *He tried to mollify his father's anger by apologizing.* **SYN:** allay, pacify, calm. **2** to make soft or supple.
—*v.i. Obsolete.* **1** to become less angry; relent. **2** to become soft or tender. [< Late Latin *mollificāre* < *mollis* soft + *facere* make] —**mol'li|fi'er**, *n.* —**mol'li|fy'ing|ly**, *adv.*

**mol|lusc** (mol'əsk), *n.* = mollusk.

**Mol|lus|ca** (mə lus'kə), *n.pl.* the phylum of invertebrates comprising the mollusks.

**mol|lus|can** (mə lus'kən), *adj., n.* —*adj.* of or having to do with mollusks.
—*n.* = mollusk.

**mol|lus|ci|cid|al** (mə lus'kə sī'dəl), *adj.* of or by means of molluscicides.

**mol|lus|ci|cide** (mə lus'kə sīd), *n.* a substance for killing mollusks, especially one used to destroy the snails which are vectors of schistosomiasis. [< *mollusc* + *-cide*[1]]

**mol|lus|coid** (mə lus'koid), *adj., n.* —*adj.* resembling a mollusk.
—*n.* an animal similar to a mollusk.

**mol|lus|cous** (mə lus'kəs), *adj.* **1** belonging to or resembling the mollusks. **2** *Figurative.* spineless; flabby; soft; weak.

**mol|lus|cum con|ta|gi|o|sum** (mə lus'kəm kən tā'jē ō'səm), an infectious skin disease of humans in which tubercles containing cheesy matter appear on the face. It is caused by a virus. [< New Latin *molluscum* a skin disease (< Latin *molluscus* soft-bodied), *contagiosum* contagious]

***mollusk**

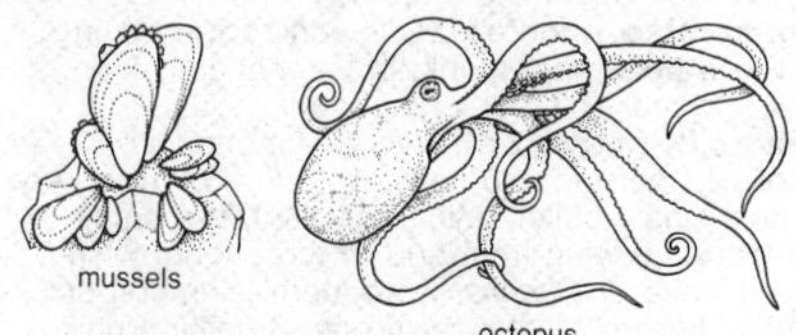


***mol|lusk** (mol'əsk), *n.* any one of a large group of animals having no backbone, soft bodies not composed of segments, and usually covered with a hard shell of one or more parts. The shell of mollusks is secreted by a covering mantle and is formed on snails, clams, oysters, whelks, and mussels. Slugs, octopuses, and squids have no shell. Mollusks make up a phylum in the animal kingdom. Also, **mollusc**. [< French *mollusque*, learned borrowing from New Latin *Mollusca* a Linnean order, (originally) neuter plural of Latin *molluscus* soft-bodied < *mollis* soft]

**mol|lus|kan** (mə lus'kən), *adj., n.* = molluscan.

**Moll|wei|de projection** (môl'vī'də), a type of homolographic map projection in which the surface of the earth is represented as an ellipse, with the equator and parallels of latitude as straight lines. [< Karl *Mollweide*, 1774-1825, a German mathematician and astronomer, who devised it]

**mol|ly**[1] (mol'ē), *n., pl.* **-lies.** *Informal.* an effeminate man or boy; mollycoddle.

**mol|ly**[2] (mol'ē), *n., pl.* **-lies.** = mallemuck. [alteration of *mallemuck*]

**mol|ly**[3] (mol'ē), *n., pl.* **-lies.** = mollie.

**mol|ly|cod|dle** (mol'ē kod'əl), *n., v.*, **-dled, -dling.** —*n.* a person, especially a boy or man, accustomed to being fussed over and pampered; milksop: *You have been bred up as a mollycoddle, Pen, and spoilt by the women* (Thackeray).
—*v.t.* to coddle; pamper.
[perhaps < *Molly* (compare etym. under **moll**) + *coddle*] —**mol'ly|cod'dler**, *n.*

**Mol|ly Ma|guires** (mol'ē mə gwīrz'), **1** a secret society organized in Ireland about 1843 for resisting payment of rent during the famine. Its members diguised themselves as women when attacking rent collectors and other officials. **2** a group in the mining regions of Pennsylvania, formed to press the cause of the miners against the abuses of the owners, suppressed in 1877. [< *Molly Maguire*, a common Irish name]

**mol|ly|mawk** (môl'ē môk), *n.* = mallemuck.

**Mo|loch** (mō'lok), *n.* **1** a fire god of ancient times whose worship was marked by the sacrifice of children as burnt offerings, especially first-born males, by their parents. Moloch was a Semitic deity. He is mentioned in the Bible as a Canaanite god whom the Israelites worshiped secretly. **2** *Figurative.* anything thought of as requiring frightful sacrifice: *War is a Moloch.* Also, **Molech**.

**mo|loch** (mō'lok), *n.* a spiny Australian lizard; horned lizard. [< New Latin *Moloch* the genus name < English *Moloch* (because of its ugly appearance)]

**Mo|lo|tov cocktail** (mô'lə tôf, -tôv; mol'ə-, mō'lə-), a crude type of hand grenade, consisting of a bottle filled with gasoline, and having a rag as a wick. It was used in Spain by the opponents of Franco during the civil war of the late 1930's, and in World War II by various irregular or partisan troops. [< Vyacheslav *Molotov*, born 1890, a Russian diplomat (because it was used during the Spanish Civil War, when Molotov was involved in Russian international affairs)]

**molt** (mōlt), *v., n.* —*v.i.* to shed feathers, skin, hair, shell, antlers, or other growths, before a new growth. Birds, snakes, insects, and crustaceans molt.
—*v.t.* to shed (feathers, skin, or other growths): *We saw the snake molt its skin.*
—*n.* **1** the act or process of molting. **2** skin, hair, antlers, or other growths, shed in molting. Also, **moult**.
[alteration of Middle English *mouten*, Old English *-mūtian* (as in *bemūtian* exchange for), ultimately < Latin *mūtāre* to change] —**molt'er**, *n.*

**mol|ten** (mōl'tən), *adj., v.* —*adj.* **1** made liquid by heat; melted: *molten steel.* **2** made by melting and casting into a mold; cast: *a molten image.*
—*v.* melted; a past participle of **melt**. —**mol'ten|ly**, *adv.*

**molten sea**, = brazen sea.

**mol|to** (mōl'tō), *adv. Music.* much; very (used with other directions): *molto allegro.* [< Italian *molto* much; very < Latin *multum*]

**Mo|luc|can** (mō luk'ən), *adj., n.* —*adj.* of or having to do with the Moluccas or Spice Islands, their people, or their language.
—*n.* native or inhabitant of the Moluccas.

**mol. wt.**, molecular weight.

**mo|ly**[1] (mō'lē), *n., pl.* **-lies. 1** *Greek Legend.* an herb with a milk-white flower and a black root, having magic properties. Hermes gave Odysseus moly to counteract the spells of Circe. **2** a wild garlic of Europe. [< Latin *mōly* < Greek *mōly*]

**mol|y**[2] (mol'ē), *n. Informal.* molybdenum.

**mo|lyb|date** (mə lib'dāt), *n.* a salt of molybdic acid.

**mo|lyb|de|nite** (mə lib'də nīt, mol'ib dē'-), *n.* a soft native sulfide of molybdenum that resembles graphite. It is the chief ore of molybdenum. *Formula:* $MoS_2$

**mo|lyb|de|nous** (mə lib'də nəs, mol'ib dē'-), *adj.* **1** of molybdenum. **2** containing molybdenum, especially with a valence of two; molybdous.

***mo|lyb|de|num** (mə lib'də nəm, mol'ib dē'-), *n.* a heavy, hard, grayish or silver-white metallic

**Pronunciation Key:** hat, āge, cãre, fär; let, ēqual, tėrm; it, īce; hot, ōpen, ôrder; oil, out; cup, pu̇t, rüle; child; long; thin; ᴛʜen; zh, measure; ə represents a in about, e in taken, i in pencil, o in lemon, u in circus.

chemical element. Molybdenum can be hammered or pressed into various shapes without being broken, but fuses with difficulty, and occurs in combination, as in molybdenite or wulfenite. It is much used to strengthen and harden steel alloys. [earlier *molybdena* any of several ores of lead < Latin *molybdaena* < Greek *molýbdaina* < *mólybdos* lead]

***molybdenum**

| symbol | atomic number | atomic weight | oxidation state |
|---|---|---|---|
| Mo | 42 | 95.94 | 6 |

**molybdenum disulfide**, a black powder that is a compound of molybdenum and sulfur, used especially as a lubricant in greases and in dispersion of oils. *Formula:* $MoS_2$

**molybdenum trioxide**, a yellowish white powder that is a compound of molybdenum and oxygen, used as a source material for preparation of molybdenum compounds and for increasing the adhesion of enamels for coating metals. *Formula:* $MoO_3$

**mo|lyb|dic** (mə lib′dik), *adj.* **1** of molybdenum. **2** containing molybdenum, especially with a valence of six.

**molybdic acid**, any of certain acids containing molybdenum.

**mo|lyb|dous** (mə lib′dəs), *adj.* containing molybdenum (in larger proportion than a corresponding molybdic compound).

**mom** (mom), *n. Informal.* mother.

**mom and pop store**, *U.S.* a small retail store owned and operated, often under a franchise, by a husband and wife: *Though this would include even mom and pop grocery stores, Congressional backers of the proposal would like to insert a provision to exempt such tiny businesses* (Wall Street Journal).

**mome** (mōm), *n. Archaic.* a blockhead; dolt.

**mo|ment** (mō′mənt), *n.* **1** a very short space of time; instant: *In a moment the house was in flames. Won't you stay for a moment? Do not delay; the golden moments fly* (Longfellow). **SYN**: second. See syn. under **minute. 2a** a particular point of time: *We both arrived at the same moment. I could not recall his name at the moment.* **b** a definite stage, period, or turning point in a course of events. **3** importance; weight: *The President is busy on a matter of moment.* **SYN**: consequence, significance. **4** a tendency to cause rotation around a point or axis: *Evidence is accumulating to suggest that the biosphere has its own specificity for spin and moment which may well be critical* (Atlantic). **5** the product of a (specified) physical quantity and the length of the perpendicular from a point or axis. The moment of a force about a point is the product of the magnitude of the force and the length of the perpendicular distance from the point to the line of action of the force. **6** *Philosophy.* a cause, motive, or stage of a logically developing process of thought or action; momentum. **7** *Statistics.* any one of several values derived from sums of powers of the variables in a set of data. [< Latin *mōmentum* movement < *movēre* to move. See etym. of doublet **momentum.**]

**mo|men|ta** (mō men′tə), *n.* a plural of **momentum.**

**mo|men|tar|i|ly** (mō′mən ter′ə lē, mō′mən ter′-), *adv.* **1** for a moment: *He hesitated momentarily.* **2** at every moment; from moment to moment: *The danger was increasing momentarily.* **3** at any moment: *We were expecting the postman momentarily.*

**mo|men|tar|i|ness** (mō′mən ter′ē nis), *n.* the state of being momentary.

**mo|men|tar|y** (mō′mən ter′ē), *adj.* **1** lasting only a moment; fleeting: *momentary hesitation.* **SYN**: transitory, temporary. **2** occurring or present every moment: *momentary interruptions.* **3** occurring at any moment: *to live in fear of momentary exposure.* **4** *Archaic.* (of living beings) ephemeral.

**mo|ment|ly** (mō′mənt lē), *adv.* **1** from moment to moment; every moment: *The throng momently increased* (Edgar Allan Poe). **2** at any moment; on the instant. **3** for the moment; for a single moment: *The attack was stopped—but only momently.*

**moment of inertia**, *Physics.* a measure of the resistance of a body to angular acceleration, equal to the sum of the products of each particle of a rotating body multiplied by the squares of the distances of the particles from the axis of rotation: *The moon's ... moment of inertia varies according to the axis of hypothetical rotation one calculates it for* (Science News).

**moment of truth**, **1** the point in time when a harsh truth must be faced; a moment of direct confrontation with some unpleasant fact or circumstance: *It was a shaking moment of truth for the Government and for the British public, who suddenly received a lightning, unflattering intimation of exactly how solid a risk they looked to the neighbors* (New Yorker). *As the excruciatingly painful moment of truth nears on voting a half-billion dollars of new taxes, a rash of substitute proposals can be expected from lawmakers* (New York Times). **2** the moment in a bullfight when the matador faces the bull with the final sword thrust. [translation of Spanish *momento de la verdad*]

**mo|men|tous** (mō men′təs), *adj.* very important; of great consequence; weighty: *Choosing between peace and war is a momentous decision. Momentous To himself, as I to me, Hath each man been* (Sir William Watson). **SYN**: serious, critical. **—mo|men′tous|ly**, *adv.* **—mo|men′tous-ness**, *n.*

**mo|men|tum** (mō men′təm), *n., pl.* **-tums** or **-ta.** **1** the force with which a body moves, equal to its mass multiplied by its velocity: *A falling object gains momentum as it falls.* **2** impetus resulting from movement: *The runner's momentum carried him over the finish line when he stumbled just before the end of the race. The runner stumbled just before the end of the race but his momentum carried him over the finish line.* (*Figurative.*) *Jazz rhythms create what can only be called momentum* (Harper's). **SYN**: impulse, force. **3** *Philosophy.* a moment.
[< Latin *mōmentum* moving power. See etym. of doublet **moment.**]

**mom|ism** (mom′iz əm), *n. Informal.* the emotional domination of a son by his mother. [(coined by Philip Wylie) < *mom* + *-ism*]

**mom|ma** (mom′ə), *n.* mamma; mother.

**mom|me** (mom′ē), *n., pl.* **-me.** a Japanese unit of weight, equal to 3.75 grams: *Everybody else in the world was weighing pearls in momme, the traditional Japanese unit, while Japan was determinedly using the gramme* (New Scientist). [< Japanese]

**mom|my** (mom′ē), *n., pl.* **-mies.** *Informal.* mother.

**Mo|mus** (mō′məs), *n.* **1** *Greek Mythology.* the god of ridicule, who was banished from heaven for his censures upon the gods. **2** a faultfinder; critic. [< Latin *Mōmus* < Greek *Mômos* god of ridicule; later, ridicule, criticism]

**mon¹** (mon), *n. Scottish.* man.

**mon²** (mon), *n.* a Japanese personal or family device or insignia. [< Japanese *mon*]

**Mon** (mōn), *n., pl.* **Mons** or **Mon. 1** a member of a people living in southeastern Burma, culturally not related to the native Burmese. **2** the Mon-Khmer language of this people.

**mon-**, *prefix.* the form of **mono-** before vowels, as in *monatomic, monism.*

**mon.**, **1** monastery. **2** monetary.

**Mon.**, an abbreviation for the following:
**1** Monaco.
**2** Monday.
**3** Monsignor.
**4** Montana.
**5** Monument.

**MON** (no periods), motor octane number.

**mo|na** (mō′nə), *n.* a small, long-tailed African monkey of docile disposition, often kept in captivity. [< Spanish, Portuguese *mona,* feminine of *mono* monkey]

**Mon|a|can** (mon′ə kən, mə nä′kən), *adj., n.* **—adj.** of or having to do with Monaco, a small country on the French Riviera coast of the Mediterranean Sea, or its inhabitants.
**—n.** a native or inhabitant of Monaco. Also, *French,* **Monégasque.**

**mon|a|chal** (mon′ə kəl), *adj.* = monastic. [< Late Latin *monachālis* < *monăchus* monk]

**mon|a|chism** (mon′ə kiz əm), *n.* = monasticism.

**mon|a|chi|za|tion** (mon′ə kə zā′shən), *n.* the act or event of becoming a monk.

**mon|a|chize** (mon′ə kīz), *v.,* **-chized, -chiz|ing.**
**—v.i.** to become a monk; live a monastic life.
**—v.t.** to make (a person) a monk.

**mon|ac|id** (mon as′id), *adj., n.* = monoacid.

**mon|ad** (mon′ad, mō′nad), *n., adj.* **—n. 1a** a very simple single-celled animal or plant. **b** a small protozoan having from one to three long, whiplike flagella. **2** *Chemistry.* an atom, element, or radical having a valence of one. **3** unity; a unit. **4** *Philosophy.* an absolutely simple entity, conceived as the ultimate unit of being.
**—adj.** of or having the nature of a monad.
[< Late Latin *monas, -adis* < Greek *monás, -ádos* unit < *mónos* alone, single]

**mon|a|del|phous** (mon′ə del′fəs), *adj.* having stamens united by their filaments into one group, as in various legumes and mallows. [< Greek *mónos* one, single + *adelphós* brother; (literally) from the womb + English *-ous*]

**mon|a|des** (mon′ə dēz), *n.* plural of **monas.**

**mo|nad|ic** (mə nad′ik), *adj.* **1** having to do with monads. **2** of the nature of a monad. **3** composed of monads. **—mo|nad′i|cal|ly**, *adv.*

**mo|nad|i|cal** (mə nad′ə kəl), *adj.* = monadic.

**mon|ad|ism** (mon′ə diz əm, mō′nə-), *n.* **1** the philosophical theory that the universe is composed of and controlled by minute, simple entities. **2** a system based on this theory.

**mon|ad|is|tic** (mon′ə dis′tik), *adj.* of or having to do with monadism.

**mo|nad|nock** (mə nad′nok), *n.* an isolated hill or mountain of resistant rock standing in an area that is almost level from erosion. [< Mt. *Monadnock,* in New Hampshire]

**mon|ad|o|log|i|cal** (mon′ə də loj′ə kəl, mō′nə-), *adj.* of or having to do with monadology or the doctrine of monads.

**mon|ad|ol|o|gy** (mon′ə dol′ə jē, mō′nə-), *n. Philosophy.* the doctrine of monads.

**mon|a|ker** (mon′ə kər), *n.* = moniker.

**mo|nal** (mə nol′), *n.* = monaul.

**mon|al|pha|bet|ic** (mon′al′fə bet′ik), *adj.* = monoalphabetic.

**mo|nan|drous** (mə nan′drəs), *adj.* **1** having only one husband at a time; characterized by monandry: *a monandrous society.* **2** having only one stamen: *a monandrous flower.* **3** having such flowers: *a monandrous plant.* [< Greek *mónandros* (with English *-ous*) < *mónos* single, one + *anḗr, andrós* husband]

**mo|nan|dry** (mə nan′drē), *n.* **1** the custom or condition of having only one husband at a time. **2** *Botany.* the condition of having but one perfect stamen.

**mo|nan|thous** (mə nan′thəs), *adj.* (of a plant) single-flowered; bearing one flower on each stalk. [< Greek *mónos* single + *ánthos* flower + English *-ous*]

**mon|arch** (mon′ərk), *n.* **1** a king, queen, emperor, empress, or other ruler. A monarch is usually a hereditary sovereign with more or less limited powers, but more often had sole and absolute powers in earlier times. **2** *Figurative.* a person or thing like a monarch: *The tall, solitary pine was monarch of the forest. The lion is the monarch of the jungle. Mont Blanc is the monarch of mountains* (Byron). **3** = monarch butterfly. [< Late Latin *monarcha* < Greek *mónarchos* < *mónos* alone + *árchein* to rule]

**mo|nar|chal** (mə när′kəl), *adj.* **1** of or having to do with a monarch or monarchy: *monarchal power, a monarchal retinue.* **2** favoring a monarchy. **3** characteristic of a monarch: *a monarchal aloofness.* **4** suitable for a monarch: *monarchal ceremony.* **5** having the status of a monarch: *monarchal rank.* **—mo|nar′chal|ly**, *adv.*

**monarch butterfly**, a large, orange-and-black butterfly whose larvae feed on milkweed. The monarch butterfly is widely distributed and migrates south each fall.

**mon|ar|chess** (mon′ər kis), *n.* a woman monarch.

**mo|nar|chi|al** (mə när′kē əl), *adj.* = monarchal.

**mo|nar|chi|an** (mə när′kē ən), *n.* an early Christian believer in monarchianism.

**mo|nar|chi|an|ism** (mə när′kē ə niz′əm), *n.* the theological doctrine that God is one being, not a Trinity. Monarchianism was current during the 100's and 200's A.D.

**mo|nar|chi|an|ist** (mə när′kē ə nist), *n.* = monarchian.

**mo|nar|chic** (mə när′kik), *adj.* = monarchical.

**mo|nar|chi|cal** (mə när′kə kəl), *adj.* **1** of a monarch or monarchy. **2** favoring a monarchy or monarchism. **3** like a monarch or monarchy.
**—mo|nar′chi|cal|ly**, *adv.*

**mon|ar|chism** (mon′ər kiz əm), *n.* **1** the principles of monarchy. **2** the advocacy of monarchical principles.

**mon|ar|chist** (mon′ər kist), *n., adj.* **—n.** a person who supports or favors government by a monarch.
**—adj.** = monarchistic.

**mon|ar|chis|tic** (mon′ər kis′tik), *adj.* of or having to do with monarchism. **—mon′ar|chis′ti|cal|ly**, *adv.*

**mon|ar|chize** (mon′ər kīz), *v.i., v.t.,* **-chized, -chiz|ing.** to rule as or like a monarch.

**mon|ar|chy** (mon′ər kē), *n., pl.* **-chies. 1** government by a monarch. In a monarchy the power to rule is formally vested in a single person. Denmark and Sweden have limited monarchies; Great Britain is a constitutional monarchy. *There were those who accused him of wanting to establish a monarchy with himself as king* (Newsweek). **2** a nation governed by a monarch: *The British monarchy once ruled most of the world's oceans.* **3** *Obsolete.* absolute rule by a single person. [< Middle French *monarchie,* learned borrowing from Late Latin *monarchia* < Greek *monarchíā* < *mónos* alone, single + *árchein* to rule]

**mo|nar|da** (mə när′də), *n.* any one of a group of North American aromatic herbs of the mint family, such as the Oswego tea; horsemint. [American English < New Latin *Monarda* the genus name < N. *Monardes,* 1493-1588, a Spanish botanist]

**mon|as** (mon′as, mō′nas), *n., pl.* **mon|a|des.** = monad. [< Late Latin *monas* monad]

**mon|as|te|ri|al** (mon′ə stir′ē əl), *adj.* of or characteristic of a monastery.

**mon|as|ter|y** (mon′ə ster′ē), *n., pl.* **-ter|ies. 1** a building or buildings where (usually) monks or (sometimes) nuns live by themselves in a contemplative life according to fixed rules and under religious vows. SYN: cloister, convent. **2** the group of persons living in such a place: *a monastery of 85.* [< Late Latin *monastērium* < Greek *monastḗrion* < *monázein* to live alone. See etym. of doublet **minster**.]

**mo|nas|tic** (mə nas′tik), *adj., n.* **—*adj.* 1** of monks or nuns: *monastic vows of poverty, chastity, and obedience.* **2** of monasteries: *monastic architecture. He had visited . . . some monastic ruins in the county of Dumfries* (Scott). **3** like that of monks or nuns; ascetic.
**—*n.*** a member of a monastic order; monk: *monastics . . . who have retired to the sacred sites of Palestine* (Alexander Kinglake).
[< Late Latin *monasticus* < Late Greek *monastikós* solitary, ultimately < *mónos* alone, single]
**—mo|nas′ti|cal|ly,** *adv.*

**mo|nas|ti|cal** (mə nas′tə kəl), *adj.* = monastic.

**mo|nas|ti|cism** (mə nas′tə siz əm), *n.* **1** the system or condition of living a monastic life according to fixed rules, in groups shut off from the world, and devoted to religion: *Here the Virgin sits serenely with hands folded across her breast in a gesture that sums up one of the great credos of monasticism: "Thy will be done"* (Time). **2** the system of monasterial communities.

**mo|nas|ti|cize** (mə nas′tə sīz), *v.t.,* **-cized, -cizing.** to make monastic.

**mon|a|tom|ic** (mon′ə tom′ik), *adj. Chemistry.* **1** having one atom in the molecule. **2** having one replaceable atom or group of atoms. **3** = univalent.

**mo|naul** (mə nôl′), *n.* any one of several East Indian pheasants. Also, **monal.** [< Hindustani *munāl*]

**mon|au|ral** (mon ôr′əl), *adj.* **1** = monophonic: *monaural recordings, monaural record players.* **2** of, with, or for one ear: *a monaural hearing aid.* **—mon|au′ral|ly,** *adv.*

**mon|ax|i|al** (mon ak′sē əl), *adj.* **1** having but one axis; uniaxial. **2** *Botany.* having flowers growing directly from the main axis.

**mon|ax|on** (mon ak′son), *n.* a tiny, rod-shaped spicule found in sponges.

**mon|a|zite** (mon′ə zīt), *n.* a phosphate of cerium and related rare-earth metals, found in small reddish or brownish crystals. [< German *Monazit* < Greek *monázein* be solitary (< *mónos* alone) + German *-it* -ite[1]]

**mon cher** (môɴ sher′), *French.* my dear (masculine).

**mon|dain** (môɴ daɴ′), *adj., n. French.* **—*adj.*** worldly; mundane. **—*n.*** a mundane person.

**mon|daine** (môɴ den′), *n. French.* a woman of the fashionable world or of society.

**Mon|day** (mun′dē, -dā), *n.* the second day of the week; the day after Sunday. *Abbr:* Mon. [Old English *mōnan dæg* the moon's day]

**Mon|day|ish** (mun′dē ish, -dā-), *adj.* affected with the indisposition typical of a Monday; exhausted or depressed. **—Mon′day|ish|ness,** *n.*

**Monday morning quarterback,** *U.S. Slang.* **1** a person who criticizes the errors of a football team after the game is over. **2** *Figurative.* a person who offers advice on how to avoid an error after the error has been committed.

**monde** (môɴd), *n. French.* **1** the world. **2** the world of society; the fashionable world. **3** a particular social group or stratum: *haut monde.*

**mon Dieu** (môɴ dyœ′), *French.* my God (used as a mild interjection).

**mo|ne|cious** (mə nē′shəs), *adj.* = monoecious.

**Mo|né|gasque** (mô nā gàsk′), *adj., n. French.* Monacan.

**mo|nen|sin** (mō nen′sən), *n.* a product of fermentation resulting from the action of a species of streptomyces. Monensin is used as an additive to feed for beef cattle to inhibit the formation of certain gases which promotes the absorption of energy from feed. It is also noted for its ability to carry ions across lipid barriers. *Monensin and DES can reduce total feed requirements by as much as 25 percent* (Science). [< (*Streptomyces cinna*) *monensis,* the species of streptomyces + *-in*[2]]

**mo|ne|ran** (mə nir′ən), *n.* any plant or animal, such as bacteria and blue-green algae, that does not have a nucleus. [< New Latin *Monera,* plural (< Greek *monērēs* individual, solitary < *mónos* alone, single) + English *-an*]

**mon|e|tar|i|ly** (mon′ə ter′ə lē, mun′-), *adv.* as regards monetary affairs; from a monetary point of view; financially.

**mon|e|tar|ism** (mon′ə ter iz′əm, mun′-), *n. Economics.* the theory that the money supply of a country determines the shape of its economy.

**mon|e|tar|ist** (mon′ə ter ist, mun′-), *n., adj.* **—*n.*** a person who favors or advocates monetarism: *[He] there reveals himself as an uncompromising monetarist . . . , insisting that "as John Stuart Mill once said, nothing is more important than money"* (London Times).
**—*adj.*** of monetarists or monetarism: *Broadly, the monetarist school remains confident that a recovery cannot be far off, since the monetary policy of the Federal Reserve Board remains expansionary* (Manchester Guardian Weekly).

**mon|e|tar|y** (mon′ə ter′ē, mun′-), *adj.* **1** of the money of a country; having to do with coinage or currency: *The American monetary system was formerly based on the gold standard.* **2** of money; pecuniary: *a monetary reward.* SYN: See syn. under **financial.** [< Late Latin *mōnetārius* < Latin *monēta;* see etym. under **money**]

**monetary unit,** the unit of a currency taken as the standard of comparative value for that currency, such as the dollar in the United States and Canada, and the pound in Great Britian.

**mon|e|ti|za|tion** (mon′ə tə zā′shən, mun′-), *n.* the act or process of monetizing.

**mon|e|tize** (mon′ə tīz, mun′-), *v.t.,* **-tized, -tiz|ing. 1** to legalize as money; assign a specified value to (silver, gold, or other metal) in the currency of a country. **2** to coin into money: *to monetize gold or silver.*

**mon|ey** (mun′ē), *n., pl.* **mon|eys** or **mon|ies. 1** current coin; gold, silver, or other metal made into coins for use in buying and selling, or paper bills that represent gold, silver, or other assets issued by a government or authorized public authority: *an exhibit of money from different countries.* **2** a particular form or denomination of money. **3** a sum of money used for a particular purpose or belonging to a particular person: *Come back when your money's spent* (Rudyard Kipling). **4** wealth; property of any kind having value that can be expressed in terms of money: *He is a man of money. There is money in this contract. He agreed to pay the bill when certain moneys were realized. Wealth and money . . . are, in common language, considered in every respect synonymous* (Adam Smith). **5** any object or material serving as a medium of exchange and a measure of value, such as checks drawn on a bank, or nuggets or the dust of a precious metal: *Money in the United States consists primarily of checking accounts in the nation's banks* (Warren W. Shearer). **6** = money of account.
**coin money,** *Informal.* to become rich; have a prospering business: *The owners of horses and mules were coining money, transporting people to the fairground* (Charles Dudley Warner).
**for my money,** *Informal.* for my choice; in my opinion; as I see it: *Miss Day is, for our money, the most fetching star in screen musicals today* (Baltimore Sun).
**in the money,** *Slang.* **a** in a winning position in a contest, especially in first, second, or third place in a horse or dog race: *That's too fast a pace for that kind of horse. She'll be lucky to finish in the money* (New York Times). **b** having plenty of money: *Had it never occurred to him, as to most writers and artists who suddenly find themselves "in the money," to keep a reserve for tax purposes?* (Sunday Telegram).
**make money, a** to get money: *He made money in the stock market. The War Office ought not to make money out of, any more than they should subsidize, the rifle clubs* (Spectator). **b** to become rich: *His ambition is to make money and retire young.*
**money for jam,** *British Slang.* something, especially money, that is very easily come by: *The task for the British salesman ought to be money for jam* (Homer Bigart).
**out of the money,** *Slang.* not in a winning position, especially in a horse or dog race: *Determine and Poona II . . . finished out of the money* (New Yorker).
[< Old French *moneie* < Latin *monēta* mint, money < *Jūnō Monēta* Juno the protectress (< *monēre* to warn), in whose temple money was coined. See etym. of doublet **mint**[2].]
▶**money.** Exact sums of money are usually written in figures: *72¢; $4.98; $5; $168.75; $42,810.* Round sums are more likely to be written in words: *two hundred dollars, a million and a half dollars.* In factual writing with frequent references to sums of money, figures are often used throughout.

**mon|ey|bag** (mun′ē bag′), *n.* a bag for money. **moneybags,** *Informal.* **a** a wealthy or avaricious person. **b** wealth; riches.
▶**Moneybags,** meaning wealth, is plural in form and use. When *moneybags* means a wealthy person, it is plural in form and singular in use: *Old moneybags is finally giving a little money to charity.*

**money belt,** a belt with an inner flap or fold in which money can be secretly carried, usually under a person's clothing.

**mon|ey|chang|er** (mun′ē chān′jər), *n.* **1** a person whose business it is to exchange money at a fixed or authorized rate, usually that of one country for that of another: *And Jesus went into the temple of God . . . and overthrew the tables of the money changers* (Matthew 21:12). **2** a banker or financier.

**money cowry,** the shell of a marine gastropod, used as money in parts of Asia and Africa.

**money crop,** *U.S.* a cash crop.

**mon|eyed** (mun′ēd), *adj.* **1** having money; wealthy: *the not too gracious bounty of moneyed relatives* (Thomas Carlyle). SYN: rich. **2** consisting of or representing money; derived from money: *moneyed resources.* Also, **monied.**

**mon|ey|er** (mun′ē ər), *n.* **1** a person authorized to coin money; minter. **2** *Archaic.* a banker or financier: *F. B. moves among moneyers and City nobs* (Thackeray).

**mon|ey|grub|ber** (mun′ē grub′ər), *n.* a person sordidly devoted to making money or gaining wealth: *Emlen is a boor and an unscrupulous moneygrubber* (Atlantic).

**mon|ey|grub|bing** (mun′ē grub′ing), *n., adj.* **—*n.*** the amassing of money: *Schiller's plot shows . . . the bourgeois world of social climbing and moneygrubbing* (London Times).
**—*adj.*** bent on amassing money: *She . . . brought up her child to be "more cultured, less moneygrubbing, more spontaneous and creative" than she herself was brought up to be* (Time).

**mon|ey|lend|er** (mun′ē len′dər), *n.* a person whose business is lending money at interest: *Understandably, the spurned student becomes a rich and ruthless moneylender* (Newsweek).

**mon|ey|lend|ing** (mun′ē len′ding), *n., adj.* **—*n.*** the lending of money at interest.
**—*adj.*** having to do with or engaged in moneylending: *moneylending activities, a moneylending institution.*

**mon|ey|less** (mun′ē lis), *adj.* without money; impecunious: *Her public coffers are moneyless* (R. Aastler).

**mon|ey-mak|er** or **mon|ey|mak|er** (mun′ē mā′kər), *n.* **1** a person who is skilled in earning money or building a fortune; one who is well paid: *the country's No. 2 professional golf money-maker* (New York Times). **2** a thing which yields pecuniary profit.

**mon|ey-mak|ing** or **mon|ey|mak|ing** (mun′ē-mā′king), *n., adj.* **—*n.*** the acquisition of money. **—*adj.* 1** occupied in gaining wealth. **2** yielding money; lucrative: *He sees the task of putting the slim, pale monthly on a money-making basis* (Time).

**mon|ey|man** (mun′ē man′), *n., pl.* **-men.** *Informal.* **1** a person involved in finance; financier or banker: *The moneymen of world finance are meeting in Washington for an accounting of the way their various governments have handled their monetary affairs* (Wall Street Journal). **2** a financial backer; angel: *The rumpled character caught in the crush . . . had one of the most important parts in the show: he was the moneyman* (Time).

**money market, 1** the market or field for the investment of money; the district or sphere within which financial operations are carried on: *Commercial paper is the money-market term for short-term borrowings of companies* (Wall Street Journal). **2** the body of persons carrying on such operations.

**mon|ey|mon|ger** (mun′ē mung′gər, -mong′-), *n.* a dealer in money; moneylender.

**money of account,** a monetary denomination used in reckoning, especially one not issued as a coin. In the United States, the mill is a money of account but not a coin. The nickel is a coin, but not a money of account.

**money order,** an order for the payment of money. You can buy a money order at the post office, a bank, or certain commercial establishments, and send it to a person in another city, who can get the money at the post office, bank, or certain commercial establishments, there.

**money shell,** a large, edible clam of the Pacific coast of the United States; butter clam.

**money spider,** a small spider supposed to bring good luck in money or other matters to the person over whom it crawls.

**money spinner,** *British Informal.* a person, thing, or activity that brings in a lot of money: *The trees have a reputation as money spinners because of quick maturity at high prices* (London Times).

**mon|ey|wise**[1] (mun′ē wīz), *adv.* so far as money is concerned: *It expects the semiconductor market ... to shrink moneywise* (New Scientist and Science Journal). [< *money* + *-wise*]

**mon|ey|wise**[2] (mun′ē wīz′), *adj.* wise about money: *To help lure back some of the country's moneywise mulattoes—as well as other investors and tourists—Papa Doc* [*Duvalier*] *called a rare press conference* (Time). [< *money* + *wise*[1]]

**mon|ey|wort** (mun′ē wėrt′), *n.* a creeping perennial plant of the primrose family, having roundish leaves and solitary, yellow, dark-spotted flowers; creeping Charlie; creeping Jennie. It is native to Europe and naturalized in the eastern United States.

**mong** (mong), *Australian Slang.* a dog of mixed breed; mongrel.

**'mong** (mung), *prep. Poetic.* among.

**mon|ger** (mung′gər, mong′-), *v., n.* —*v.t.* **1** to deal or traffic in. **2** to spread (pernicious gossip, ill will, or other evil).
—*n.* a person who mongers; trafficker.
[back formation < *mongering*]

**-monger**, *combining form.* **1** a dealer in ____; person who sells ____: *Fishmonger = a dealer in fish.*
**2** a person who traffics in ____; person who spreads or busies himself with ____: *Scandalmonger = a person who spreads scandal.*
[Old English *mangere,* ultimately < Latin *mangō, -ōnis* trader]

**mon|ger|ing** (mung′gər ing, mong′-), *n.* trading; trafficking (used especially as a second element in compounds): *All these ... militant mongerings of moral half-truths* (Robert Louis Stevenson).

**mon|ging** (mung′ing), *n.* = mongering.

**mon|go** (mong′gō), *n., pl.* **-gos.** a unit of money of the Mongolian People's Republic, equal to 1/100 of a tugrik. [< Mongolian *mongo*]

**Mon|gol** (mong′gəl, -gol, -gōl), *n., adj.* —*n.* **1** a member of the Asiatic people now inhabiting Mongolia and nearby parts of China and Siberia. Mongols formerly lived also in eastern Europe. **2** = Mongolian. **3** the language of the Mongols; Mongolian. **4** = Mongoloid.
—*adj.* **1** of this people. **2** = Mongolian.

**Mon|go|li|an** (mong gō′lē ən), *adj., n.* —*adj.* **1** of Mongolia, the Mongolians, or their languages. **2** of or belonging to the yellow-skinned, straight-haired race of mankind; Mongoloid. **3** displaying characteristics of Mongolism; Mongoloid.
—*n.* **1** a member of the Mongoloid or yellow race living in Asia. Mongolians are traditionally characterized as having slanting eyes, prominent cheekbones, a short, broad nose, and straight hair that is dark brown to brown-black. The Chinese, Japanese, Tartars, and Eskimos are Mongolians. **2** their language or languages. **3** a person born or living in Mongolia; Mongol. **4** a person who has Mongolism; Mongoloid.

**Mongolian fold**, = epicanthic fold.

**Mongolian gerbil**, a gerbil of Mongolia and nearby parts of China that is often used for laboratory experiments: *It is the Mongolian gerbil, a creature about half the size of a rat, gray-brown in color, with a long, furry tail and large dark eyes* (Science News Letter).

**Mongolian idiocy**, = Mongolism.

**Mon|go|li|an|ism** (mong gō′lē ə niz′əm), *n.* = Mongolism.

**Mongolian race**, the Mongolians.

**Mon|gol|ic** (mong gol′ik), *adj., n.* —*adj.* = Mongolian.
—*n.* the Mongolian language.

**Mon|gol|ism** (mong′gə liz əm), *n.* a form of mental deficiency characterized by certain body abnormalities, including a flattened face with slanting eyes and a short nose, a small, round head, broad hands and feet, and stubby fingers with the little finger often turned inward; Down's syndrome. It is caused by an imbalance or abnormality in the chromosomes.

**Mon|gol|oid** (mong′gə loid), *adj., n.* —*adj.* **1** resembling the Mongols or Mongolians; belonging to the race that is traditionally characterized as having yellowish skin, slanting eyes, prominent cheekbones, a short, broad nose, and straight hair that is dark brown to brown-black. **2** having characteristics of Mongolism: *the inferior mental growth of a Mongoloid child.*
—*n.* **1** a person of Mongoloid race. **2** a person suffering from Mongolism: *Few Mongoloids have a mental age greater than that of a 4-year-old child* (George A. Ulett).

**mon|goose** or **mon|goos** (mong′güs), *n., pl.* **-goos|es.** a slender, flesh-eating mammal of Africa and Asia, like a ferret. There are various kinds, comprising more than one genus. It is often kept as a pet for destroying rats, and is noted for its ability to kill cobras and certain other poisonous snakes without being harmed. *The mongoose ... is not immune to the venom of the cobra it fights* (Scientific American). Also, **mungoos, mungoose.** [< Marathi *mangūs*]

**mon|grel** (mung′grəl, mong′-), *n., adj.* —*n.* **1** an animal or plant of mixed breed, especially a dog: *Our pet dog is a mongrel of no particular breed.* **2** a person of mixed breed (used in an unfriendly way). **3** *Figurative.* anything of a haphazardly mixed nature.
—*adj.* of mixed breed, race, origin, or nature: (*Figurative.*) *a mongrel speech that is half Spanish and half Indian. These mongrel pamphlets, part true, part false* (Thomas Fuller).
[earlier *mengrell;* perhaps influenced by obsolete *mong* mixture, Old English *gemang* mixture (compare etym. under **among**) < *mengan* mix]

**mon|grel|ism** (mung′grə liz əm, mong′-), *n.* a mixture of different breeds; the condition of being of mixed breeds.

**mon|grel|ize** (mung′grə līz, mong′-), *v.t.,* **-ized, -iz|ing.** to mix various elements, especially the characteristics of racial groups, supposedly to the injury of a dominant group of people (used in an unfriendly way). —**mon′grel|i|za′tion,** *n.*

**mon|grel|ly** (mung′grə lē, mong′-), *adj.* of or like a mongrel.

**'mongst** (mungst), *prep. Poetic.* amongst.

**mon|ied** (mun′ēd), *adj.* = moneyed.

**mon|ies** (mun′ēz), *n.pl.* sums of money: *authorized by the charter to pay out monies.*

**mon|i|ker** or **mon|ick|er** (mon′ə kər), *n. Informal.* **1** a person's name or signature. **2** = nickname. **3** any mark or sign used as identification by a tramp. Also, **monaker.** [origin unknown]

**mo|nil|i|al** (mō nil′ē əl), *adj.* caused by one of a genus of pathogenic fungi: *monilial vaginitis.* [< Latin *monīle* necklace + English *-ial*]

**mon|i|li|a|sis** (mon′ə lī′ə sis, mō′nə-), *n.* **1** an infection caused by a type of fungus, affecting different parts of the body, including the skin, mucous membrane, lungs, vagina, and gastrointestinal tract; candidiasis. Thrush is a form of moniliasis. **2** mycosis of the digestive tract of poultry. [< Latin *monīle* necklace + English *-iasis* (because of the beaded appearance of the diseased tissue)]

**mo|nil|i|form** (mō nil′ə fôrm), *adj.* resembling a string of beads, as certain roots or pods, which have a series of swellings alternating regularly with contractions. [< Latin *monīle* necklace + English *-form*] —**mo|nil′i|form|ly,** *adv.*

**mon|ish** (mon′ish), *v.t. Archaic.* to admonish.

**mon|ism** (mon′iz əm, mō′niz-), *n. Philosophy.* **1** the doctrine that the universe can be explained by one substance or principle, such as matter, mind, or some other single thing or force. **2** the doctrine that reality is an indivisible, universal organism. [< New Latin *monismus* < Greek *mónos* single]

**mon|ist** (mon′ist, mō′nist), *n.* a person who believes in monism.

**mo|nis|tic** (mō nis′tik), *adj.* of or having to do with monism. —**mo|nis′ti|cal|ly,** *adv.*

**mo|nis|ti|cal** (mō nis′tə kəl), *adj.* = monistic.

**mo|ni|tion** (mō nish′ən), *n.* **1** admonition; warning: *sage monitions from his friends* (Jonathan Swift); *the monitions of Christianity* (Herman Melville). **2** an official or legal notice: **a** a formal court order or summons to appear and answer, as after a complaint has been filed, or to confirm title and silence adverse claims, or to commence a suit. **b** a formal notice from a bishop to one of his subordinates to require the amendment of some ecclesiastical offense: *The bishop sent a monition to three clergymen.* [< Old French *monition,* learned borrowing from Latin *monitiō, -ōnis* < *monēre* to warn]

**mon|i|tor** (mon′ə tər), *n., v.* —*n.* **1** a pupil in school with special duties, such as helping to keep order and taking attendance: *Several of the older boys in school serve as monitors on the playground.* **2** a person who gives advice or warning: *The Teamsters Union, which has been battling to rid itself of court-appointed monitors* (Wall Street Journal). **3** something that reminds or gives warning: *Conscience ... a most importunate monitor, paying no respect to persons and making cowards of us all* (Frederick Marryat). **4** a low, armored warship having one or more revolving turrets, each with one or two heavy guns. It was used chiefly in the late 1800's. **5** any one of a family of large, carnivorous lizards of Africa, southern Asia, Australia, Indonesia, New Guinea, and the Solomon Islands. Monitors are from 4 to 10 feet long, have a forked tongue and the habit of swallowing their prey without chewing it, and exhibit other snakelike characteristics. They are the only living genus of their family, the dragon lizard or dragon of Komodo being the most familiar, and are known to have lived in America from the fossils found in Wyoming. *All of the zoo's tenants were at their best, but the ... giant lizards or monitors virtually stole the show* (New York Times). **6** a receiver or other device used for checking and listening to radio or television transmissions, telephone messages, or other electronic signals as they are recorded or broadcast: *When a monitor or headphone connection is provided, it will be "live" even during recording* (Roy J. Hoopes).
—*v.t., v.i.* **1a** to check and listen to (radio or television transmissions, telephone messages, or other electronic signals) by using a monitor, especially to check the quality, wave frequency, or the like. **b** to listen to (broadcasts or telephone messages) for censorship, military significance, or other surveillance: *He noted that agency investigators have been monitoring broadcasts and telecasts since last fall* (Wall Street Journal). **2** *Physics.* to test the intensity of radiations, especially of radiations produced by radioactivity. **3** to check in order to control something: *Hearing aids now play a life-saving role in the operating room by monitoring the breathing of unconscious surgical patients* (Science News Letter).
[< Latin *monitor, -ōris* < *monēre* to admonish, warn]

**mon|i|to|ri|al** (mon′ə tôr′ē əl, -tōr′-), *adj.* **1** of or having to do with a monitor: *monitorial duties.* **2** using monitors. **3** serving to admonish or warn. —**mon′i|to′ri|al|ly,** *adv.*

**mon|i|tor|ship** (mon′ə tər ship), *n.* the office, work, or period of service of a monitor: *He was compelled to raise the legal point because ... he could not continue to serve while doubting the legality of the entire monitorship procedure* (Wall Street Journal).

**mon|i|to|ry** (mon′ə tôr′ē, -tōr′-), *adj., n., pl.* **-ries.** —*adj.* admonishing; warning: *the monitory growl of a dog. The mottoes of their families are monitory proverbs* (Emerson). **SYN:** admonitory.
—*n.* a letter containing admonition, as from the Pope or a bishop; monitory letter.
[< Latin *monitōrius* < *monitor, -ōris* monitor]

**monitory letter**, a monitory; letter containing admonition, sent by the Pope or a bishop.

**mon|i|tress** (mon′ə tris), *n.* **1** a girl who is a monitor at school. **2** a girl or woman who gives advice or warning. [< *monitor* + *-ess*]

**monk** (mungk), *n.* a man who gives up everything else for religion and enters a monastery to live a life of prayer and worship. Monks live either in solitude as hermits or as members of a religious order and are bound by the vows of poverty, celibacy, and obedience to a superior. **SYN:** cenobite. [Old English *munuc* < Late Latin *monachus* < Late Greek *monachós* monk < Greek, individual, solitary < *mónos* alone, single]
► Though the terms **monk** and **friar** are often used as synonyms, a *monk* specifically is a member of an order living a cloistered life; a *friar* is properly a member of a mendicant order.

**monk|er|y** (mung′kər ē), *n., pl.* **-er|ies.** **1** = monasticism. **2** = monastery. **3** monks as a group.
**monkeries**, monastic practices or customs.

***mon|key** (mung′kē), *n., pl.* **-keys,** *v.,* **-keyed, -key|ing.** —*n.* **1** an animal of the group most like man. Monkeys are mammals and range from the anthropoid apes to the marmosets, but exclude man and, usually, the lemurs. **2** one of the smaller mammals in this group, usually having a

***monkey**
definition 1

long tail. Monkeys are distinguished from the chimpanzee, gorilla, or other large ape. **3** *Figurative.* a person, especially a child, who is full of mischief: *That little monkey ate a piece of pie while my back was turned.* **4** the fur of various long-haired monkeys, often used as trimming. **5** any one of various machines or implements, especially the heavy hammer or ram of a pile driver. **6** a small passageway in a coal mine.
– ***v.i.*** *Informal.* **1** to play in a mischievous way; fool; trifle: *Don't monkey with the television.* **2** to meddle or tinker: *He didn't think much of the thing, and never monkeyed with it* (Harper's).
– ***v.t.*** to copy, as monkeys do; mimic; ape.
**make a monkey (out) of,** *Informal.* to make (a person) look foolish; make a fool of: *He had mocked the laws and made monkeys out of the lawmen* (Time).
**monkey on one's back,** *U.S. Slang.* **a** the burden of drug addiction: *The patient goes back on drugs again ..., more convinced than ever that the monkey on his back can't be removed by any means* (Wall Street Journal). **b** any strong addiction viewed as a burden: *Smokers may not have a full-sized monkey on their back but what they do have is just as hard to get rid of* (New Yorker). **c** any intolerable burden: *Sometimes the pseudoliberal can become a monkey on your back* (Floyd McKissick).
[probably < Middle Low German *Moneke,* son of Martin the Ape in the *Romance of Reynard*]
– **mon'key\|like',** *adj.*

**monkey bars,** *Informal.* jungle gym.

**monkey board,** a platform high in an oil derrick, on which a worker helps with the drilling operation.

**monkey bread,** **1** the fruit of the baobab, eaten by monkeys. **2** the tree itself.

**monkey business,** *U.S. Slang.* trickery; fraud; deceit.

**monkey cup,** a pitcher plant of the Old World.

**monkey dog,** = affenpinscher.

**mon\|key-eat\|ing eagle** (mung'kē ē'ting), a large eagle of the Philippines, similar to the harpy eagle, that feeds on large birds and monkeys.

**monkey engine,** **1** a form of pile driver having a ram or monkey working in a wooden frame. **2** the engine which lifts such a ram or monkey.

**mon\|key-faced owl** (mung'kē fāst'), = barn owl.

**monkey flower,** any one of a group of plants and small shrubs of the figwort family, often grown for their brilliant flowers, which are spotted so as to suggest a grimace, as a Chilean species with deep-yellow flowers and the musk plant, native to the western United States.

**mon\|key\|ish** (mung'kē ish), *adj.* like a monkey, especially in imitativeness or mischievousness: *He drinks and smokes in a monkeyish way* (Dickens).

**mon\|key\|ism** (mung'kē iz əm), *n.* monkeylike character or behavior.

**monkey jacket,** a short, close-fitting jacket of heavy, coarse material, formerly worn by sailors.

**monkey nut,** *British.* the peanut.

**mon\|key\|pod** (mung'kē pod'), *n.* **1** a tropical shade tree of the pea family that may spread as much as 100 feet across; rain tree. It grows from southern Florida to Brazil and has a stout trunk, pink and white flowers, and leaves that fold up at night and on cloudy days. **2** the wood of this tree.

**mon\|key\|pot** (mung'kē pot'), *n.* **1** the large, woody, urn-shaped fruit, containing several edible seeds, of any one of various large tropical trees. **2** any one of these trees, related to the Brazil-nut tree.

**monkey puzzle,** an evergreen tree, a variety of araucaria native to Chile, having stiff, twisted branches and edible nuts; Chile pine.

**mon\|key\|shine** (mung'kē shīn'), *n. Slang.* a mischievous trick; clownish joke: *Recent weather monkeyshines hereabouts suggest that the polar air blanket may have moved south already* (Baltimore Sun).

**monkey suit,** *U.S. Slang.* **1** a uniform: *... busboys in scarlet monkey suits* (Time). **2** a dress suit: *[He] buys [a] monkey suit to serve as best man* (Saturday Review).

**monkey wrench,** a wrench with a movable jaw that can be adjusted to fit different sizes of nuts.
**throw a monkey wrench into,** *Informal.* to interfere with; subvert; destroy: *The amiable, blubber-eating Eskimos throw a monkey wrench into the dietary fat theory. In Alaska, they live for months at a time on the fat of island seal and whale, but even among their oldsters fatal atherosclerosis is rare* (Time).

**monk fish,** = goosefish.

**Mon-Khmer** (mōn'kmer'), *adj.* of or belonging to a linguistic family of monosyllabic languages of southeastern Asia, including Khmer, spoken in Cambodia. Annamese, spoken in Vietnam, shows strong Mon-Khmer influence.

**monk\|hood** (mungk'hu̇d), *n.* **1** the condition or profession of a monk. **2** monks as a group.

**monk\|ish** (mung'kish), *adj.* **1** of a monk; having to do with monks or monasticism. **2** like a monk; characteristic of a monk. **3** like monks or their way of life (often used in an unfriendly way): *William of Occam was a monkish philosopher* (Sunday Times). – **monk'ish\|ly,** *adv.* – **monk'ish-ness,** *n.*

**monk's cloth,** **1** a heavy worsted fabric in a basket weave, used for monks' garments. **2** a similar fabric of cotton used especially for draperies and the like.

**monks\|hood** (mungks'hu̇d'), *n.* a kind of aconite grown for its purple or white hooded flowers. Its roots are the source of the drug aconite.

**mon\|ny** (mon'ē), *n., pl.* **-nies.** a shooting marble; taw; glassy. [origin unknown]

**mon\|o**[1] (mon'ō), *adj., n., pl.* **mon\|os.** – ***adj.*** = monophonic (def. 4).
– ***n.*** **1** monophonic sound reproduction: *The sound ... remains good despite the fact that it is only in mono* (London Times). **2** a monophonic record.

**mon\|o**[2] (mon'ō), *n. Slang.* mononucleosis.

**mono-,** *prefix.* **1** having one ____: *Monosyllabic = having one syllable.*
**2** a single ____: *Monorail = a single rail.*
**3** containing one atom or other constituent of the substance specified, as in *monosulfide.* Also, sometimes **mon-** before vowels.
[< Greek *mónos* single, one]

**mon\|o\|ac\|id** (mon'ō as'id), *adj., n.* – ***adj.*** **1** (of a base or alcohol) having one hydroxyl (-OH) group that can be replaced by an atom or radical of an acid to form a salt or ester. **2** having one acid atom of hydrogen per molecule.
– ***n.*** an acid containing only one replaceable hydrogen atom. Also, **monacid.**

**mon\|o\|a\|cid\|ic** (mon'ō ə sid'ik), *adj.* = monoacid.

**mon\|o\|al\|pha\|bet\|ic** (mon'ō al'fə bet'ik), *adj. Cryptography.* having to do with or using a single cipher alphabet: *the ancient cryptographic technique of monoalphabetic substitution, in which only one letter is substituted for another to encipher a message* (Scientific American). Also, **monalphabetic.** – **mon'o\|al'pha\|bet'i\|cal\|ly,** *adv.*

**mon\|o\|a\|mine** (mon'ō ə mēn', -am'in), *n.* an amine which contains one amino group: *Monoamines play a considerable part in regulating the central nervous system* (New Scientist).

**monoamine oxidase,** an enzyme present in the cells of most animal and plant tissue which oxidizes and destroys amines such as norepinephrine and serotonin. *Abbr:* MAO (no periods).

**mon\|o\|a\|mine-ox\|i\|dase inhibitor** (mon'ō ə-mēn'ok'sə dās, -am'in-), any one of various drugs that inhibit the action of monoamine oxidase, used to reduce high blood pressure and mental depression.

**mon\|o\|ba\|sic** (mon'ō bā'sik), *adj.* **1a** (of an acid) having but one atom of hydrogen that can be replaced by an atom or radical of a base in forming salts. **b** having one basic hydroxyl (-OH) radical per molecule. **c** (of a salt) having one basic atom or radical which can replace a hydrogen atom of an acid. **2** *Biology.* being the sole type of its group; monotypic.

**mon\|o\|bath** (mon'ə bath', -bäth'), *n. Photography.* a solution in which film can be developed and fixed in one continuous procedure.

**mon\|o-block** (mon'ō blok'), *adj.* made by or having to do with a process of cold-working and strengthening metal cast in one piece, especially gun barrels, by using internal pressure to compress the inner layers of the metal.

**mon\|o\|ca\|ble** (mon'ə kā'bəl), *n.* **1** a single cable serving as a complete track. **2** an aerial railway having such a cable.

**mon\|o\|carp** (mon'ə kärp), *n.* a plant that bears fruit only once during its lifetime. [< *mono-* + Greek *karpós* fruit]

**mon\|o\|car\|pel\|lar\|y** (mon'ə kär'pə ler'ē), *adj. Botany.* having or consisting of a single carpel.

**mon\|o\|car\|pic** (mon'ə kär'pik), *adj.* producing fruit but once, then dying: *All annual and biennial plants are monocarpic.*

**mon\|o\|car\|pous** (mon'ə kär'pəs), *adj.* **1** (of a flower) having a gynoecium that forms only a single ovary. **2** = monocarpic.

**Mo\|noc\|er\|os** (mə nos'ər əs), *n., genitive* **Mo\|no\|cer\|o\|tis.** a constellation near Orion. [< Latin *monoceros* (literally) unicorn]

**Mo\|noc\|er\|o\|tis** (mə nos'ə rō'tis), *n.* genitive of **Monoceros.**

**mon\|o\|cha\|si\|al** (mon'ə kā'zhē əl, -zē-), *adj.* having to do with or like a monochasium.

**mon\|o\|cha\|si\|um** (mon'ə kā'zhē əm, -zē-), *n., pl.* **-si\|a** (-zhē ə, -zē ə). *Botany.* a cyme in which the main axis produces only a single branch. [< New Latin *monochasium* < Greek *mónos* one + *chásis* chasm, separation < *chainein* to yawn]

**mon\|o\|chlo\|ride** (mon'ə klôr'īd, -id; -klōr'-), *n.* a chloride having one chlorine atom per molecule.

**mon\|o\|chord** (mon'ə kôrd), *n.* an instrument composed of a sounding board with a single string stretched over a bridge that can be moved along a graduated scale, used for the mathematical determination of musical intervals by the division of the string into two separately vibrating parts. [< Middle French *monocorde* < Late Latin *monochordos* < Greek *mónos* one + *chordḗ* string, chord[1]]

**mon\|o\|chro\|ic** (mon'ə krō'ik), *adj.* of one color; monochromatic: *Arterial blood is monochroic* (James Cagney). [< Greek *monóchroos* having one color (< *mónos* one + *chróā* color) + English *-ic*]

**mon\|o\|chro\|mat** (mon'ə krō'mat), *n.* a person having monochromatism.

**mon\|o\|chro\|mat\|ic** (mon'ə krō mat'ik), *adj.* **1** having or showing one color only. **2** (of light) consisting of one wave length: *The use of monochromatic light ... does not improve the acuity of the eye to more than a very small extent* (Science News). **3** producing such light. – **mon'-o\|chro\|mat'i\|cal\|ly,** *adv.*

**mon\|o\|chro\|ma\|tic\|i\|ty** (mon'ə krō'mə tis'ə tē), *n.* the state, degree, or quality of being monochromatic.

**mon\|o\|chro\|ma\|tism** (mon'ə krō'mə tiz əm), *n.* color blindness in which none of the primary colors can be seen; total color blindness.

**mon\|o\|chro\|ma\|tor** (mon'ə krō'mə tər), *n.* an instrument which can isolate and transmit a beam of monochromatic, or nearly monochromatic, light, especially useful in analyzing radiation spectra: *The filtering element in my coronagraph is a quartz monochromator* (Scientific American).

**mon\|o\|chrome** (mon'ə krōm), *n., adj.* – ***n.*** **1** a painting, drawing, print, or design in a single color or shades of a single color; monotint: *The Elgin frieze is a monochrome in a state of transition to sculpture* (John Ruskin). **2** a stretch or mass of a single color: *A profile was visible against the dull monochrome of cloud around her* (Thomas Hardy). **3** the art of representation in one color.
– ***adj.*** **1** having or providing one color only: *a monochrome picture.* **2** black and white: *monochrome television.*
[< Medieval Latin *monochroma* < Greek *monochrômos* < *mónos* single + *chrôma* color; complexion; skin]

**mon\|o\|chro\|mic** (mon'ə krō'mik), *adj.* of a single color.

**mon\|o\|chro\|mist** (mon'ə krō'mist), *n.* a person who paints or draws in monochrome.

***mon\|o\|cle** (mon'ə kəl), *n.* an eyeglass for one eye. [< French *monocle,* learned borrowing from Late Latin *monoculus* one-eyed < Greek *mónos* single + Latin *oculus* eye]

***monocle**

**mon\|o\|cled** (mon'ə kəld), *adj.* wearing a monocle.

**mon\|o\|cli\|nal** (mon'ə klī'nəl), *adj., n. Geology.* – ***adj.*** **1** (of strata) dipping or sloping in one direction. **2** of or having to do with strata that dip in the same direction: *monoclinal valleys.*
– ***n.*** = monocline.
[< *mono-* + Greek *klīnein* to slope, bend + English *-al*[1]] – **mon'o\|cli'nal\|ly,** *adv.*

**mon\|o\|cline** (mon'ə klīn), *n.* a monoclinal rock formation or fold, such as the oblique portion of a belt of strata at the place where it changes from one horizontal position to another of different level.

**mon\|o\|clin\|ic** (mon'ə klin'ik), *adj.* (of crystals or crystallization) characterized by three unequal axes with one oblique intersection. See picture under **crystal.**

**mon\|o\|cli\|nous** (mon'ə klī'nəs, mon'ə klī'-), *adj.* **1** (of a plant) having both stamens and pistils in the same flower. **2** (of a flower) having both stamens and pistils. [< French *monocline* (< Greek *mónos* one + *klīnē* bed < *klīnein* to recline, slope) + English *-ous*]

**mo\|no\|coque** (mô nô kôk'), *n.* a type of structure, originally used in aircraft fuselages and now also in truck trailers, which relies on a stiffened, lightweight shell of metal, veneer, or plastic, to bear the principal stresses. [< French *monocoque* < *mono-* + *coque* shell]

**mon|o|cot** (mon′ə kot), *n.* = monocotyledon.

**mon|o|cot|yl** (mon′ə kot′əl), *n.* = monocotyledon.

**mon|o|cot|y|le|don** (mon′ə kot′ə lē′dən), *n.* a plant with only one cotyledon. The monocotyledons, which include grasses, palms, lilies, and irises, are angiosperms, one of the two large subclasses of plants that have the seeds enclosed in an ovary. They have leaves with parallel veins and flower parts in threes. *Botanists are impressed with the fact that the Polynesians divided the plant world into monocotyledons and dicotyledons* (Scientific American). See picture under **cotyledon.** [< *mono-* + *cotyledon*]

**mon|o|cot|y|le|don|ous** (mon′ə kot′ə lē′də nəs, -led′ə-), *adj.* having only one cotyledon: *monocotyledonous plants.*

**mo|noc|ra|cy** (mə nok′rə sē), *n., pl.* **-cies.** government by one person; autocracy.

**mon|o|crat** (mon′ə krat), *n.* **1** an autocrat. **2** a supporter of monocracy or monarchy. [American English (apparently coined by Thomas Jefferson to describe extreme Federalists) < Greek *monokratês* ruling alone < *mónos* alone + *krateîn* rule]

**mon|o|crat|ic** (mon′ə krat′ik), *adj.* having to do with monocracy.

**mon|o|crys|tal** (mon′ə kris′təl), *n.* a very strong filament made of a single piece of synthetic crystal.

**mon|o|crys|tal|line** (mon′ə kris′tə lēn), *adj.* composed of monocrystals.

**mo|noc|u|lar** (mə nok′yə lər), *adj., n.* —*adj.* **1** having to do with or intended for use by one eye only: *The bird's perception of depth and distance was believed to be entirely dependent upon monocular cues* (Scientific American). **2** having only one eye or eyepiece.
—*n.* any monocular instrument.
[< Late Latin *monoculus* one-eyed (< Greek *mónos* single + Latin *oculus* eye) + English *-ar*]
—**mo|noc′u|lar|ly**, *adv.*

**mon|o|cul|tur|al** (mon′ə kul′chər əl), *adj.* having to do with or characteristic of monoculture. —**mon′o|cul′tur|al|ly**, *adv.*

**mon|o|cul|ture** (mon′ə kul′chər), *n.* the growing of only one product: *Concentrate on grain monoculture and you are looking for trouble* (Cape Times).

**mon|o|cy|cle** (mon′ə sī′kəl), *n.* = unicycle.

**mon|o|cy|clic** (mon′ə sī′klik, -sik′lik), *adj.* **1** having a single circle or cycle. **2** *Biology.* having a single whorl or series of parts, as certain crinoids with a single circlet of basal plates. **3** *Chemistry.* having one ring (of atoms).

**mon|o|cyte** (mon′ə sīt), *n.* one of the major types of leucocytes in the blood, being the largest in size and comprising about 3 to 8 per cent of the total white blood cells. It is a phagocyte with a single, well-defined nucleus. [< *mono-* + *-cyte*]

**mon|o|cyt|ic** (mon′ə sit′ik), *adj.* of, having to do with, or characteristic of a monocyte.

**mon|o|cy|to|sis** (mon′ə sī tō′sis), *n.* a fatal disease of domestic fowl, characterized by cyanosis of the comb and wattles; blue comb. [< *monocyt*(e) + *-osis*]

**mon|o|dac|tyl** (mon′ə dak′təl), *adj.* = monodactylous.

**mon|o|dac|ty|lous** (mon′ə dak′tə ləs), *adj.* having only one finger, toe, or claw. [< Greek *monodáktylos* (with English *-ous*) < *mónos* single + *dáktylos* finger]

**mo|nod|ic** (mə nod′ik), *adj.* having to do with or like a monody; homophonic. [< Greek *monōdikós* < *monōidiā* monody] —**mo|nod′i|cal|ly**, *adv.*

**mo|nod|i|cal** (mə nod′ə kəl), *adj.* = monodic.

**mon|o|dra|ma** (mon′ə drä′mə, -dram′ə), *n.* a play or other dramatic piece for a single performer.

**mon|o|dra|mat|ic** (mon′ə drə mat′ik), *adj.* of or characteristic of a monodrama.

**mon|o|dy** (mon′ə dē), *n., pl.* **-dies. 1** a mournful song; lament; dirge. **2** a plaintive poem in which one person laments another's death: *In this Monody the Author bewails a learned Friend, unfortunately drowned* (Milton). **3a** a style of musical composition in which one part or melody predominates; homophony. **b** a composition written in this style. **4** a Greek ode sung by a single voice, as by an actor in a tragedy. [< Late Latin *monōdia* < Greek *monōidiā* < *monodós* singing alone < *mónos* single + *ōidê* ode]

**mo|noe|cious** (mə nē′shəs, mō-), *adj.* **1** *Botany.* having the stamens and pistils in separate flowers on the same plant: *Corn, birches, and walnuts are monoecious plants.* **2** *Zoology.* having both male and female organs in the same individual; hermaphroditic. Also, **monecious.** [< New Latin *Monoecia* the class name (< Greek *mónos* single + *oikiā* dwelling place < *oîkos* property, house) + English *-ous*]

**mo|noe|cism** (mə nē′siz əm), *n.* monoecious condition.

**mon|o|en|er|get|ic** (mon′ō en′ər jet′ik), *adj. Nuclear Physics.* (of radiation particles) having the same or nearly the same energy.

**mon|o|eth|a|nol|a|mine** (mon′ə eth′ə nol′ə mēn, -nə lam′in), *n.* = ethanolamine.

**mon|o|fil|a|ment** (mon′ə fil′ə mənt), *n.* a strand of yarn, plastic, wire, or the like, composed of a single filament only, regardless of its thickness or weight.

**mon|o|gam|ic** (mon′ə gam′ik), *adj.* = monogamous.

**mo|nog|a|mist** (mə nog′ə mist), *n., adj.* —*n.* a person who practices, advocates, or believes in monogamy.
—*adj.* = monogamous.

**mo|nog|a|mis|tic** (mə nog′ə mis′tik), *adj.* = monogamous.

**mo|nog|a|mous** (mə nog′ə məs), *adj.* **1** practicing or advocating monogamy: *We may now return to the criteria to be applied in drawing judgments concerning polygamous as against monogamous families* (Melville J. Herskovits). **2** of or having to do with monogamy. —**mo|nog′a|mous|ly**, *adv.* —**mo|nog′a|mous|ness**, *n.*

**mo|nog|a|my** (mə nog′ə mē), *n.* **1** the practice or condition of being married to only one person at a time: *Monogamy ... has been and is the leading type of marriage* (Emory S. Bogardus). **2** the habit among some animals of having only one mate during a lifetime. **3** *Rare.* the custom or principle of marrying only once. [< Latin *monogamia* < Greek *monogamiā* < *mónos* single + *gámos* marriage]

**mon|o|gen|e|sis** (mon′ə jen′ə sis), *n.* the theory that all living things derive from a single, common origin.

**mon|o|ge|net|ic** (mon′ə jə net′ik), *adj.* **1** of or having to do with monogenesis or monogenism; monogenic. **2** having only a single host during the life cycle, as certain trematode worms. **3** formed by one geological process: *a monogenetic mountain range.*

**mon|o|gen|ic** (mon′ə jen′ik), *adj.* **1** *Biology.* monogenetic. **2** *Zoology.* reproducing by only one method.

**mo|nog|e|nism** (mə noj′ə niz əm), *n.* the theory that all human beings have descended from a single pair.

**mo|nog|e|nist** (mə noj′ə nist), *n.* a believer in monogenism.

**mon|o|germ** (mon′ə jėrm′), *adj.* being or containing a single seed which develops into an isolated plant: *monogerm sugar beet varieties.*

**mon|o|glot** (mon′ə glot), *adj., n.* —*adj.* **1** using or understanding only one language. **2** written in only one language.
—*n.* a person who knows only one language.
[< Greek *monóglōttos* < *mónos* single + *glôtta* tongue]

**mon|o|glyc|er|ide** (mon′ə glis′ə rīd, -ər id), *n.* any one of various glycerides containing a single hydroxyl or acid molecule, used as an emulsifier in bread and other products.

**monogr.**, monograph.

***mon|o|gram** (mon′ə gram), *n., v.,* **-grammed, -gram|ming.** —*n.* a person's initials combined in one design. Monograms are used on note paper, table linen, clothing, and jewelry.
—*v.t.* to print, sew, or engrave a monogram on.
[< Late Latin *monogramma* < Late Greek *monogrammon,* neuter, consisting of a single letter < Greek *mónos* single + *grámma* letter]

***monogram**

**mon|o|gram|mat|ic** (mon′ə grə mat′ik), *adj.* having to do with or in the form of a monogram.

**mon|o|grammed** (mon′ə gramd), *adj.* bearing a monogram.

**mon|o|graph** (mon′ə graf, -gräf), *n., v.* —*n.* a book or article, especially a scholarly one, about a particular subject: *D. O. Hebb's recent monograph on behaviour theory was an attempt to build a bridge between physiology and psychology* (F. H. George). **SYN:** treatise.
—*v.t.* to write a monograph on; treat in a monograph: *This extraordinary object ... has been monographed, mapped, measured, figured, and photographed* (A. M. Clerke).
[< *mono-* + *-graph*]

**mo|nog|ra|pher** (mə nog′rə fər), *n.* a writer of a monograph or monographs.

**mon|o|graph|ic** (mon′ə graf′ik), *adj.* **1** having to do with or like a monograph. **2** = monogrammatic. —**mon′o|graph′i|cal|ly**, *adv.*

**mo|nog|y|nous** (mə noj′ə nəs), *adj.* **1** having but one wife at a time. **2** characterized by monogyny: *a monogynous condition.* **3** *Botany.* **a** (of a flower) having only one pistil or style. **b** (of a plant) having such flowers.

**mo|nog|y|ny** (mə noj′ə nē), *n.* the practice or the condition of having only one wife at a time. [< *mono-* + Greek *gynê* woman, female + *-y*[3]]

**mon|o|hull** (mon′ə hul′), *n.* a sailing vessel with a single hull.

**mon|o|hy|brid** (mon′ə hī′brid), *n., adj.* —*n.* the offspring of parents who differ in a single gene or character.
—*adj.* of or having to do with a monohybrid.

**mon|o|hy|drate** (mon′ə hī′drāt), *n.* a chemical compound in which each molecule unites with one molecule of water.

**mon|o|hy|dric** (mon′ə hī′drik), *adj.* **1** containing a single hydroxyl (-OH) group, as an alcohol. **2** containing one replaceable atom of hydrogen.

**mon|o|hy|drox|y** (mon′ə hī drok′sē), *adj. Chemistry.* having one hydroxyl (-OH) radical.

**mon|o|ki|ni** (mon′ə kē′nē), *n.* a very scant one-piece bathing suit. [< French *monokini* < *mono-* + (bi)*kini*]

**mo|nol|a|ter** (mə nol′ə tər), *n.* a person who practices monolatry; henotheist. [< *monolatry;* patterned on *idolater*]

**mo|nol|a|trist** (mə nol′ə trist), *n.* = monolater.

**mo|nol|a|trous** (mə nol′ə trəs), *adj.* of or having to do with monolatry.

**mo|nol|a|try** (mə nol′ə trē), *n.* the worship of but one god when other gods are nonetheless believed to exist; henotheism. [< *mono-* + Greek *latreiā* worship]

**mon|o|lay|er** (mon′ə lā′ər), *n., adj.* —*n.* a monomolecular layer.
—*adj.* = monomolecular.

**mon|o|lin|gual** (mon′ə ling′gwəl), *adj.* limited to the knowledge or use of only one language: *a monolingual dictionary.* [< *mono-* + Latin *lingua* tongue + English *-al*[1]]

**mon|o|lith** (mon′ə lith), *n.* **1** a single large block of stone, especially one forming a monument or used for building or sculpture: *Beacon Rock, an 850-foot monolith* (New York Times). **2** a monument, column, statue, etc., formed of a single large block of stone. **3** *Figurative.* a nation, political party, culture, or organization that in its rigid and unyielding attitudes and policies suggests a massive block of stone: *Here is a world in which Russia is a constant, a monolith, at best an enigma* (Economist). [< Latin *monolithus,* adjective < Greek *monólithos* < *mónos* single + *líthos* stone]

**mon|o|lith|ic** (mon′ə lith′ik), *adj., n.* —*adj.* **1** of a monolith; being a monolith. **2** consisting of monoliths: *a monolithic circle.* **3** having to do with or using a single piece of material, such as a silicon chip or wafer, in fabricating microcircuits: *a monolithic electronic device, a monolithic computer system.* **4** *Figurative.* massively uniform, as when individuals are absolutely subservient to the state: *a monolithic society, a monolithic state.*
—*n.* a monolithic circuit: *Monolithics are also used as storage devices in the high-speed buffer memories* (London Times). —**mon′o|lith′i|cal|ly**, *adv.*

**monolithic circuit**, = integrated circuit.

**monolithic integrated circuit**, = integrated circuit.

**mon|o|log** (mon′ə lôg, -log), *n.* = monologue.

**mon|o|log|ic** (mon′ə loj′ik), *adj.* of or characterized by a monologue. —**mon′o|log′i|cal|ly**, *adv.*

**mon|o|log|i|cal** (mon′ə loj′ə kəl), *adj.* = monologic.

**mon|o|log|ist** (mon′ə lôg′ist, -log′-), *n.* **1** a person who talks or acts in monologue, or delivers monologues. **2** a person who monopolizes conversation.

**mo|nol|o|gize** (mə nol′ə jīz), *v.i.,* **-gized, -giz|ing.** to talk in monologue; give a monologue.

**mon|o|logue** (mon′ə lôg, -log), *n.* **1** a long speech by one person in a group; speech that monopolizes conversation: *Mrs. Ellison's monologue ran on with scarcely a break from Kitty* (William Dean Howells). **2** an entertainment by a single speaker: *The comedian gives a monologue each night.* **3** a play for a single actor: *The monologue was playing in a small theater.* **4** a scene or part of a play in which a single actor speaks alone: *Shakespeare wrote many monologues into his plays about history.* **5** a poem or other composition in which a single person speaks alone: *Browning was master of the dramatic monologue.* [< French *monologue* < Medieval Greek *monologos* < Greek *mónos* single + *lógos* speech, discourse]

**mon|o|logu|ist** (mon′ə lôg′ist, -log′-), *n.* = monologist.

**mon|o|logu|ize** (mon′ə lôg′īz, -log′-), *v.i.,* **-ized, -iz|ing.** = monologize.

**mo|nol|o|gy** (mə nol′ə jē), *n., pl.* **-gies. 1** the habit of talking to oneself. **2** *Obsolete.* monologue.

**mon|o|ma|ni|a** (mon′ə mā′nē ə), *n.* **1** mental disorder in which a person is obsessed or controlled by a single idea or emotion: *In "Moby Dick," Captain Ahab's pursuit of the white whale is an example of monomania.* **2** an interest or tendency so strong and obsessive as to seem almost insane. **3** a dominant interest: *I call it my monomania, it is such a subject of mine* (Dickens). [< *mono-* + *mania;* patterned on French *monomanie*]

**mon|o|ma|ni|ac** (mon′ə mā′nē ak), *n., adj.* —*n.* a person whose behavior is characterized by monomania.
—*adj.* = monomaniacal.

**mon|o|ma|ni|a|cal** (mon′ə mə nī′ə kəl), *adj.* **1** of or having to do with monomania. **2** characterized by monomania. —**mon′o|ma|ni′a|cal|ly,** *adv.*

**mon|o|mer** (mon′ə mər), *n.* **1** a single molecule that can combine with others to form a polymer. **2** a chemical compound existing in unpolymerized form. [< *mono-* + Greek *méros* part]

**mon|o|mer|ic** (mon′ə mer′ik), *adj.* of or like a monomer.

**mo|nom|er|ous** (mə nom′ər əs), *adj.* (of a flower) having one member in each whorl (sometimes written *1-merous*). [< Greek *monomerḗs* < *mónos* single + *méros* part]

**mon|o|me|tal|lic** (mon′ə mə tal′ik), *adj.* **1** using one metal only. **2** of or having to do with monometallism.

**mon|o|met|al|lism** (mon′ə met′ə liz əm), *n.* **1** the use of one metal only, such as gold or silver, as the standard of money values. **2** beliefs or policies in support of such a use.

**mon|o|met|al|list** (mon′ə met′ə list), *n.* an advocate of monometallism.

**mo|nom|e|ter** (mə nom′ə tər), *n. Prosody.* **1** a line of verse having one foot. **2** (in Greek and Latin poetry) a verse containing one dipody (two feet). [< Late Latin *monometrus* < Greek *monómetros* < *mónos* single + *métron* a measure]

**mon|o|met|ric** (mon′ə met′rik), *adj.* **1** *Prosody.* consisting of one foot or dipody. **2** *Crystallography.* isometric.

**mon|o|met|ri|cal** (mon′ə met′rə kəl), *adj. Prosody.* = monometric.

*** mo|no|mi|al** (mō nō′mē əl), *adj., n.* —*adj.* **1** *Algebra.* consisting of a single term. **2** *Biology.* (of a name) consisting of a single word.
—*n.* **1** *Algebra.* an expression consisting of a single term. **2** *Biology.* a scientific name of a plant or animal consisting of a single word.
[< *mono-* + *-nomial,* as in *binomial*]

***monomial** definition 1 — 3, 3x, $3x^2$, 3ab — monomials

**mon|o|mo|lec|u|lar** (mon′ō mə lek′yə lər), *adj.* of or having to do with one molecule; that is one molecule in thickness: *a monomolecular layer.* —**mon′o|mo|lec′u|lar|ly,** *adv.*

**monomolecular film,** a film one molecule thick; molecular film.

**mon|o|mor|phic** (mon′ə môr′fik), *adj. Biology.* having only one form; having the same form throughout development.

**mon|o|mor|phism** (mon′ə môr′fiz əm), *n.* monomorphic condition or character.

**mon|o|mor|phous** (mon′ə môr′fəs), *adj.* = monomorphic.

**mon|o|nu|cle|ar** (mon′ə nü′klē ər, -nyü′-), *adj.* **1** having only a single nucleus; mononucleate. **2** *Chemistry.* = monocyclic.

**mon|o|nu|cle|ate** (mon′ə nü′klē āt, -nyü′-), *adj.* having only one nucleus: *mononucleate cells.*

**mon|o|nu|cle|o|sis** (mon′ə nü′klē ō′sis, -nyü′-), *n.* **1** a condition characterized by an abnormal increase in the number of mononuclear leucocytes in the blood: *Every couple of years he comes down with mononucleosis, a disease that is generally attributed to fatigue* (New Yorker). **2** = infectious mononucleosis.

**mon|o|nu|cle|o|tide** (mon′ə nü′klē ə tīd, -nyü′-), *n.* a principal constituent of nucleic acid; nucleotide.

**mon|o|pet|al|ous** (mon′ə pet′ə ləs), *adj. Botany.* **1** having the corolla composed of united petals, as in the morning-glory; gamopetalous. **2** (of a corolla) having only a single petal.

**mo|noph|a|gous** (mə nof′ə gəs), *adj. Zoology.* eating only one kind of food.

**mo|noph|a|gy** (mə nof′ə jē), *n. Zoology.* the habit of feeding on only one kind of food.

**mon|o|phase** (mon′ə fāz), *adj. Electricity.* single-phase.

**mon|o|pho|bi|a** (mon′ə fō′bē ə), *n.* an abnormal fear of being alone. [< *mono-* + *-phobia*]

**mon|o|phon|ic** (mon′ə fon′ik), *adj., n.* —*adj.* **1** designating music sung or played in unison without accompaniment. **2** = monodic. **3** = homophonic. **4** having to do with or characterizing the transmission or reproduction of sound by means of a single channel, without auditory perspective; monaural: *Stereo aims at a more full-bodied representation of sound than the older-type monophonic record gives* (Wall Street Journal).
—*n.* **1** monophonic sound reproduction. **2** a monophonic phonograph record.
[< *mono-* + Greek *phōnḗ* voice + English *-ic*]
—**mon′o|phon′i|cal|ly,** *adv.*

**mo|noph|o|ny** (mə nof′ə nē), *n.* **1** a monophonic sound reproduction; monophonic: *Stereo has a compulsive force that monophony has not; you are made to want to turn toward the source of the music* (Atlantic). **2** = homophony.

**mon|oph|thong** (mon′əf thông, -thong), *n.* a single, simple vowel sound showing little or no change in quality throughout its duration. *Example: i* in *pin.* [< Greek *monóphthongos* with one sound < *mónos* single + *phthóngos* sound, voice]

**mon|oph|thon|gal** (mon′əf thông′gəl, -thong′-), *adj.* having to do with or consisting of a monophthong.

**mon|oph|thong|ize** (mon′əf thông īz, -thong-), *v.t.,* **-ized, -iz|ing.** to make into a monophthong.

**mon|o|phy|let|ic** (mon′ə fī let′ik), *adj.* descended from a single, common ancestral species, usually of the same type as the extant group: *monophyletic animals.* [< *mono-* + *phyletic*] —**mon′o|phy|let′i|cal|ly,** *adv.*

**mon|o|phyl|lous** (mon′ə fil′əs), *adj. Botany.* **1** consisting of one leaf: *a monophyllous calyx.* **2** having only one leaf. [< Greek *monóphyllos* < *mónos* single + *phýllon* leaf (with English *-ous*)]

**Mo|noph|y|site** (mə nof′ə sīt), *n.* a person who believes that Christ has but one nature, or a single composite nature that is both divine and human: *The Coptic Church in Egypt ... has been an independent Monophysite Church since the fifth century* (London Times). [< Late Latin *Monophysīta* < Late Greek *Monophysī́tēs* a believer in the "one nature" < Greek *mónos* one + *phýsis* nature]

**Mon|o|phy|sit|ic** (mon′ə fə sit′ik), *adj.* of or having to do with the Monophysites or their doctrines.

**Mo|noph|y|sit|ism** (mə nof′ə sī′tiz əm), *n.* the doctrines of the Monophysites.

**mon|o|pla|coph|o|ran** (mon′ō plə kof′ə rən), *n.* any one of a class of mollusks having a single flat shell, several pairs of gills, six or more pairs of kidneys, and many nerve centers. Monoplacophorans live in the deepest parts of the oceans. [< New Latin *Monoplacophora* (< *mono-* + Greek *pláx, plakós* flat surface + *-phóros* bearer, carrier) + English *-an*]

*** mon|o|plane** (mon′ə plān), *n.* an airplane with only one pair of wings. Most modern airplanes are monoplanes.

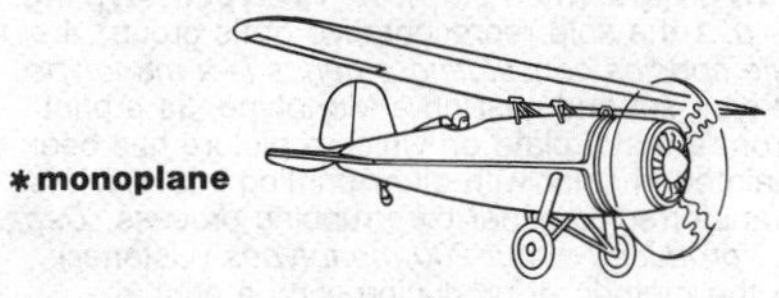

***monoplane**

**mon|o|plan|ist** (mon′ə plā′nist), *n.* the pilot of a monoplane.

**mon|o|ple|gi|a** (mon′ə plē′jē ə), *n.* paralysis of only one limb or a single muscle or muscle group. [< New Latin *monoplegia* < Greek *mónos* one + *-plegiā* < *plēgḗ* stroke]

**mon|o|pleg|ic** (mon′ə plej′ik, -plē′jik), *adj.* of or characterized by monoplegia.

**mon|o|ploid** (mon′ə ploid), *adj., n. Biology.* —*adj.* having one set of unpaired chromosomes; haploid.
—*n.* a monoploid organism or cell.
[< *mono-* + *-ploid,* as in *haploid*]

**mon|o|pode** (mon′ə pōd), *adj., n.* —*adj.* having only one foot.
—*n.* **1** a creature having only one foot or footlike organ. **2** = monopodium.
[< Late Latin *monopodius* with one foot < Greek *monópous* < *mónos* single + *poús, podós* foot]

**mon|o|po|di|al** (mon′ə pō′dē əl), *adj.* of or like a monopodium.

**mon|o|po|di|um** (mon′ə pō′dē əm), *n., pl.* **-di|a** (-dē ə). *Botany.* a single main axis which continues to extend at the apex in the original line of growth, producing lateral branches beneath, such as the trunk of a pine tree. [< New Latin *monopodium,* neuter (diminutive) < Late Latin *monopodius;* see etym. under **monopode**]

**mon|o|pole** (mon′ə pōl′), *n.* = magnetic monopole.

**mo|nop|o|lise** (mə nop′ə līz), *v.t.,* **-lised, -lis|ing.** *Especially British.* monopolize.

**mo|nop|o|lism** (mə nop′ə liz əm), *n.* the existence or prevalence of monopolies.

**mo|nop|o|list** (mə nop′ə list), *n.* **1** a person who has a monopoly: *to raise the value of the possessions in the hands of the great private monopolists* (Edmund Burke). **2** a person who favors monopoly.

**mo|nop|o|lis|tic** (mə nop′ə lis′tik), *adj.* **1** that monopolizes: *The federal government and most of the states have laws that forbid monopolistic combinations of capital* (John A. Appleman). **2** having to do with monopolies or monopolists: *To curb monopolistic abuses, the Interstate Commerce Act was passed in 1887* (Wall Street Journal). —**mo|nop′o|lis′ti|cal|ly,** *adv.*

**mo|nop|o|lize** (mə nop′ə līz), *v.t.,* **-lized, -liz|ing.** **1** to have or get exclusive possession or control of: *This firm monopolizes the production of linen thread.* **2** to occupy wholly; keep entirely to oneself: *to monopolize a person's time. The few tolerable rooms are monopolized by the friends and favourites of the house* (Tobias Smollett). —**mo|nop′o|li|za′tion,** *n.* —**mo|nop′o|liz′er,** *n.*

**mo|nop|o|ly** (mə nop′ə lē), *n., pl.* **-lies.** **1** the exclusive control of a commodity or service: *In most communities, the telephone company has a monopoly. You have, in this Kingdom, an advantage in lead, that amounts to a monopoly* (Edmund Burke). **2** such a control granted by a government: *An inventor has a monopoly on his invention for a certain number of years. Raleigh held a monopoly of cards, Essex a monopoly of sweet wines* (Macaulay). **3** control that is not exclusive but which enables the person or company to fix prices. **4** a commercial product or service that is exclusively controlled or nearly so. **5** a person or company that has a monopoly on some commodity or service: *The pilots' association was now the compactest monopoly in the world* (Mark Twain). **6** the exclusive possession or control of something intangible: *a monopoly of a person's time. No one person has a monopoly of virtue. Neither side has a monopoly of right or wrong* (Edward A. Freeman). [< Latin *monopōlium* < Greek *monopṓlion* < *mónos* single + *pōleîn* to sell]

**Mo|nop|o|ly** (mə nop′ə lē), *n. Trademark.* a game played upon a board, in which the players try to accumulate token real-estate parcels and put each other out of business.

**mon|o|pol|y|logue** (mon′ə pol′ə lôg, -log), *n.* an entertainment in which a single actor plays many parts: *Miss Emma Stanley, the celebrated entertainer ... made her third appearance in her "monopolylogue"* (Times of India). [< *mono-* + *poly-* + Greek *-logos* < *légein* speak]

**mon|o|pro|pel|lant** (mon′ō prə pel′ənt), *n.* a propellant for a rocket, such as hydrogen peroxide, which contains its own oxidizer and requires no additional air or oxygen for ignition.

**mo|nop|so|ny** (mə nop′sə nē), *n.* exclusive control of the demand for a product by a single purchaser of that product. [< *mon-* + Greek *opsōniā* purchase of food]

**mo|nop|ter|al** (mə nop′tər əl), *adj. Architecture.* (of a temple) having a single row of columns arranged in a circle, either about a cella or, often, without a cella. [< Greek *monópteros* (< *mónos* single + *pterón* wing, row of columns) + English *-al*[1]]

**mon|o|rail** (mon′ə rāl′), *n., adj.* —*n.* **1** a single rail serving as a complete track. **2** a railway in which cars run on a single rail, either balanced on it or suspended from it.
—*adj.* of or having to do with a monorail: *a monorail system.*

**mon|o|rhyme** or **mon|o|rime** (mon′ə rīm), *n.* a stanza or poem in which all the lines end in the same rhyme.

**mon|o|sac|cha|ride** (mon′ə sak′ə rīd, -ər id), *n.* any one of a class of simple sugars, such as glucose, fructose, and arabinose, that occur naturally or are formed by hydrolyzing polysaccharides or glycosides: *Monosaccharides ... are made up of a chain of five or six carbon atoms, which cannot be broken down by enzymes or dilute acids* (Dexter French). [< *mono-* + *saccharide*]

**mon|o|sep|al|ous** (mon′ə sep′ə ləs), *adj. Botany.* **1** having the sepals united; gamosepalous. **2** having only one sepal: *a monosepalous calyx.*

**mon|o|sex|u|al** (mon′ə sek′shü əl), *adj.* of or for one sex only: *monosexual dances.* —**mon′o|sex′u|al|ly,** *adv.*

**mon|o|so|di|um glutamate** (mon′ə sō′dē əm), a salt of glutamic acid, derived from any of a number of vegetable proteins, as corn gluten or certain sugar-beet products, and marketed as a white, crystalline powder, which has little taste of its own but is used to enhance and point up the

**Pronunciation Key:** hat, āge, cãre, fär; let, ēqual, tėrm; it, īce; hot, ōpen, ôrder; **oi**l, **ou**t; cup, pu̇t, rüle; **ch**ild; lo**ng**; **th**in; **ŧʜ**en; **zh**, measure; **ə** represents **a** in about, **e** in taken, **i** in pencil, **o** in lemon, **u** in circus.

flavor of foods. *Formula:* $C_5H_8NNaO_4$

**mon|o|some** (mon′ə sōm), *n.* **1** an impaired chromosome. **2** a monosomic individual. **3** a single, isolated ribosome. [< *mono-* + *-some*³]

**mon|o|so|mic** (mon′ə sō′mik), *adj.* having less than the usual number of chromosomes.

**mon|o|sper|mal** (mon′ə spėr′məl), *adj. Botany.* one-seeded; monospermous.

**mon|o|sper|mous** (mon′ə spėr′məs), *adj. Botany.* containing only one seed.

**mon|o|stich** (mon′ə stik), *n.* **1** a poem or epigram consisting of a single metrical line. **2** a single line of poetry. [< Greek *monóstichon,* neuter of *monóstichos;* see etym. under **monostichous**]

**mo|nos|ti|chous** (mə nos′tə kəs), *adj. Botany.* arranged in a single vertical row on one side of an axis, as flowers. [< Greek *monóstichos* (with English *-ous*) made up of one row < *mónos* single + *stíchos* row, line]

**mon|o|stome** (mon′ə stōm), *adj.* = monostomous.

**mo|nos|to|mous** (mə nos′tə məs, mon′ə stō′-), *adj. Zoology.* having a single mouth or mouthlike part: *Many jellyfish are monostomous.* [< Greek *monóstomos* < *mónos* one + *stóma* mouth]

**mo|nos|tro|phe** (mə nos′trə fē, mon′ə strōf), *n.* a poem in which all the stanzas have the same metrical form. [< Greek *monóstrophos,* adjective < *mónos* single + *strophḗ* strophe]

**mon|o|stroph|ic** (mon′ə strof′ik), *adj.* of or like a monostrophe.

**mon|o|sty|lous** (mon′ə stī′ləs), *adj. Botany.* having only one style.

**mon|o|sub|sti|tut|ed** (mon′ə sub′stə tü′tid, -tyü′-), *adj.* having one substituent: *a monosubstituted chemical compound.*

**mon|o|sul|fide** (mon′ə sul′fīd, -fid), *n. Chemistry.* a sulfide in which one atom of sulfur is combined with the other element or radical.

**mon|o|syl|lab|ic** (mon′ə sə lab′ik), *adj.* **1** having only one syllable: *a monosyllabic word.* **2** consisting of a word or words of one syllable: *"No, not now" is a monosyllabic reply.* **3** using or speaking in monosyllables: *Lothair ... was ... somewhat monosyllabic and absent* (Benjamin Disraeli). —**mon′o|syl|lab′i|cal|ly,** *adv.*

**mon|o|syl|la|bism** (mon′ə sil′ə biz əm), *n.* the use of monosyllables; monosyllabic character.

**mon|o|syl|la|ble** (mon′ə sil′ə bəl), *n.* a word of one syllable. *Yes* and *no, man* and *child* are monosyllables.

**mon|o|sym|met|ric** (mon′ə si met′rik), *adj.* **1** = monoclinic. **2** *Botany.* bilaterally symmetrical; zygomorphic. —**mon′o|sym|met′ri|cal|ly,** *adv.*

**mon|o|sym|met|ri|cal** (mon′ə si met′rə kəl), *adj.* = monosymmetric.

**mon|o|sym|me|try** (mon′ə sim′ə trē), *n. Botany.* the condition of being monosymmetric.

**mon|o|syn|ap|tic** (mon′ə si nap′tik), *adj. Biology.* consisting of a single synapse: *The simplest reflex pathway in the spinal cord ... is a monosynaptic, or two-neuron, arc consisting of a fiber from a sensory neuron forming a synapse with a motoneuron* (Scientific American).

**mon|o|tech|nic** (mon′ə tek′nik), *adj., n.* —*adj.* specializing in one discipline or field of endeavor: *a monotechnic school or college.*
—*n.* a monotechnic school.

**mon|o|the|ism** (mon′ə thē iz′əm), *n.* the doctrine or belief that there is only one God; worship of one God: *While monotheism ... was achieved by a few primitive peoples, a number of advanced groups like the Egyptians, Greeks, and Romans had polytheism, a hierarchy of gods* (Ogburn and Nimkoff). [< *mono-* + Greek *theós* god + English *-ism*]

**mon|o|the|ist** (mon′ə thē′ist), *n., adj.* —*n.* a believer in only one God.
—*adj.* = monotheistic.

**mon|o|the|is|tic** (mon′ə thē is′tik), *adj.* **1** believing in only one God. **2** having to do with belief in only one God. —**mon′o|the|is′ti|cal|ly,** *adv.*

**mon|o|the|is|ti|cal** (mon′ə thē is′tə kəl), *adj.* = monotheistic.

**mon|o|the|mat|ic** (mon′ə thē mat′ik), *adj. Music.* having a single theme: *a monothematic symphony.*

**mon|o|thet|ic** (mon′ə thet′ik), *adj.* positing or supposing a single essential element: *"Monothetic" ... means that all the elements allocated to one class must share the character or characters under consideration. Thus the members of the class of "soluble substances" must in fact be soluble* (Scientific American). [< *mono-* + *thetic*]

**mon|o|tint** (mon′ə tint), *n.* **1** a single color. **2** a picture in one color.

**mon|o|tone** (mon′ə tōn), *n., adj., v.,* **-toned, -ton|ing.** —*n.* **1** sameness of tone, of style of writing, or of color: *the annoying blaring monotone of a stuck car horn.* (*Figurative.*) *Its* [*science's*] *history is a monotone of endurance and destruction* (John Ruskin). **2** a manner of speaking or singing without change of pitch; unvaried sound or repetition of sounds: *Don't speak in a monotone; use expression.* **3** *Music.* **a** a single tone without change of pitch. **b** recitative singing, especially of liturgy, in such a tone. **4** a person who sings or speaks in a monotone.
—*adj.* continuing on one tone; of one tone, style, or color; monotonous: *The dark figure of a watchman soldier pacing his weary round through the monotone snow, appeared the only living object* (C. P. Smyth). **SYN:** uniform.
—*v.t., v.i.* to recite in monotone: *He generally seized the opportunity ... to monotone long extracts* (Eclectic Magazine).
[< Greek *monótonos;* see etym. under **monotonous**]

**mon|o|ton|ic** (mon′ə ton′ik), *adj.* **1** of a montone; uttered in a montone. **2** *Mathematics.* either always increasing or always decreasing: *a monotonic quantity.* —**mon′o|ton′i|cal|ly,** *adv.*

**mo|not|o|nous** (mə not′ə nəs), *adj.* **1** continuing in the same tone or pitch: *She spoke in a monotonous voice. ... the monotonous ... chant of a Gaelic song* (Scott). **SYN:** singsong. **2** *Figurative.* not varying; without change: *monotonous food; dull straight streets of monotonous houses* (John R. Green). **SYN:** unvarying, uniform. **3** *Figurative.* wearying because of its sameness: *monotonous work.* **SYN:** tedious, humdrum. [< Greek *monótonos* (with English *-ous*) of one tone < *mónos* single + *tónos* something stretched] —**mo|not′o|nous|ly,** *adv.* —**mo|not′o|nous|ness,** *n.*

**mo|not|o|ny** (mə not′ə nē), *n.* **1** sameness of tone or pitch: *The monotony of the man's voice was irritating.* **2** *Figurative.* lack of variety: *the monotony of the desert.* **3** wearisome sameness: *At sea, everything that breaks the monotony of the surrounding expanse, attracts attention* (Washington Irving). [< Late Greek *monotoniā* < Greek *monótonos* monotonous]

**mon|o|trem|a|tous** (mon′ə trem′ə təs, -trē′mə-), *adj.* of or belonging to the monotremes.

**mon|o|treme** (mon′ə trēm), *n.* any member of the lowest order of mammals, comprising the duckbill and the echidnas, which lay eggs and have a common opening for the genital and urinary organs and the digestive tract. [< *mono-* + Greek *trêma, -atos* hole]

**mo|not|ri|chous** (mə not′rə kəs), *adj.* having a single flagellum at one end: *monotrichous bacteria.* [< Greek *mónos* single + *thrix, trichós* hair]

**mon|o|tri|glyph** (mon′ə trī′glif), *adj. Architecture.* having only one triglyph in the portion of the frieze over the space between two columns, as is usual in the Doric order.

**mon|o|tri|glyph|ic** (mon′ə trī glif′ik), *adj.* = monotriglyph.

**mon|o|type** (mon′ə tīp), *n., v.,* **-typed, -typ|ing.** —*n.* **1** the sole representative of its group: *A single species constituting a genus is a monotype.* **2** type set and cast on a Monotype. **3a** a print from a metal plate on which a picture has been painted in color with oil or printing ink, which is transferred to paper by a rubbing process: *Degas ... produced about 200 monotypes* (Listener). **b** the method of producing such a print.
—*v.t.* to set (type) with a Monotype.

**Mon|o|type** (mon′ə tīp), *n. Trademark.* a set of two machines (a keyboard machine and a casting machine) for setting and casting type in separate letters.

**mon|o|typ|ic** (mon′ə tip′ik), *adj. Biology.* **1** being the sole representative of its group: *a monotypic form.* **2** (of a genus) having only one species; monobasic. **3** having only one type or representative.

**mon|o|un|sat|u|rate** (mon′ō un sach′ər it, -ə rāt), *n.* a monounsaturated oil or fat, such as peanut or olive oil.

**mon|o|un|sat|u|rat|ed** (mon′ō un sach′ə rā′tid), *adj.* (of a fat or oil) free of hydrogen bonds at one point in its carbon chain.

**mon|o|va|lence** (mon′ə vā′ləns, mə nov′ə-), *n.* monovalent character or state.

**mon|o|va|len|cy** (mon′ə vā′lən sē, mə nov′ə-), *n.* = monovalence.

**mon|o|va|lent** (mon′ə vā′lənt, mə nov′ə-), *adj.* **1** *Chemistry.* having a valence of one; univalent: *a monovalent ion.* **2** *Bacteriology.* containing antibodies to only one antigen.

**mon|ox|ide** (mon ok′sīd, -sid; mə nok′-), *n.* an oxide containing one oxygen atom in each molecule.

**mon|o|zy|got|ic** (mon′ə zī got′ik), *adj.* produced by the splitting of a single fertilized ovum; identical: *monozygotic twins.*

**Mon|roe Doctrine** (mən rō′), the doctrine that European nations should not interfere with American nations or try to acquire more territory in the Western Hemisphere. The Monroe Doctrine was derived from President Monroe's message to Congress on Dec. 2, 1823, and became a part of United States foreign policy.

**mons** (monz), *n., pl.* **mon|tes.** a rounded, fatty eminence on the lower abdomen where the pubic bones meet, usually covered with hair after puberty. It is called *mons pubis* in the male and *mons veneris* in the female. [< Latin *mōns, montis* mountain]

**Mons.,** **1** Monsieur. **2** Monsignor.

**Mon|sei|gneur** or **mon|sei|gneur** (mon sēn′yər; *French* môɴ se nyœr′), *n., pl.* **Mes|sei|gneurs** or **mes|sei|gneurs.** **1** a French title of honor meaning "My Lord." It is given to princes, bishops, and other persons of importance. *Abbr:* Mgr. **2** a person having this title. [< Old French *monseigneur* my lord < *mon* my (< Latin *meum*) + *seigneur* lord, learned borrowing from Latin *senior* elder, senior. See etym. of doublet **monsieur.**]

**mon|sieur** (mə syėr′; *French* mə syœ′), *n., pl.* **mes|sieurs.** the French title of courtesy for a man; Mr.; Sir. *Abbr:* M. [< Old French *monsieur,* earlier *mon sieur* my lord; *mon* < Latin *meum; sieur* < Latin *senior* senior. See etym. of doublet **Monseigneur.**]

**Monsig.,** Monsignor.

**Mon|si|gnor** or **mon|si|gnor** (mon sēn′yər; *Italian* mōn′sē nyōr′), *n., pl.* **-gnors,** *Italian* **-gno|ri** (-nyō′rē). **1** a title given to certain dignitaries in the Roman Catholic Church. *Abbr:* Msgr. **2** a person having this title. [< Italian *monsignore,* half-translation of Old French *monseigneur* monseigneur. See related etym. at **Monseigneur.**]

**Mon|si|gno|re** or **mon|si|gno|re** (mōn′sē nyō′rā), *n., pl.* **-ri** (-rē). *Italian.* Monsignor.

**mon|soon** (mon sün′), *n.* **1** a seasonal wind of the Indian Ocean and southern Asia. It blows from the southwest from April to October and from the northeast from October to April. **2** a season during which this wind blows from the southwest, usually accompanied by heavy rains. **3** any wind that has seasonal reversals of direction. [apparently < Portuguese *monção* < Arabic *mausim* appropriate season]

**mon|soon|al** (mon sü′nəl), *adj.* of, having to do with, or characteristic of a monsoon: *monsoonal rains.*

**mons pubis,** the mons in the human male.

**mon|ster** (mon′stər), *n., adj.* —*n.* **1** an imaginary creature having parts of different animals. Centaurs, sphinxes, griffins, and mermaids are monsters. **2** an imaginary animal of strange and horrible appearance: *His imagination transformed shadows into monsters* (Charles Brockden Brown). **3** *Figurative.* a person too wicked to be considered human: *He is a monster of cruelty.* **4** an animal or plant that is very unlike those usually found in nature. A cow with two heads is a monster. **SYN:** monstrosity. **5** *Figurative.* a huge creature or thing: *The moving van is a monster of a truck.* **SYN:** giant. **6** *Medicine.* a congenitally malformed infant with extremely abnormal physical structure; an anomaly.
—*adj.* huge; enormous: *The purpose of the resignation is believed to be to stage a monster demonstration* (London Times). **SYN:** gigantic.
[< Old French *monstre,* learned borrowing from Latin *mōnstrum* portent; (originally) divine warning, related to *monēre* to warn] —**mon′ster|like′,** *adj.*

***mon|strance** (mon′strəns), *n.* a receptacle in which the consecrated Host is shown for adoration or is carried in procession. [< Medieval Latin *monstrantia,* showing, review (of troops) < Latin *mōnstrāre* to show < *mōnstrum* divine warning; see etym. under **monster**]

***monstrance**

**mon|stre sa|cré** (mōɴ′strə sȧ krā′), *pl.* **mon|stres sa|crés** (mōɴ′strə sȧ krā). a celebrity whose eccentric or unconventional behavior is excused or admired by the public: *Picasso* [*was*] *as much of an individualist and a monstre sacré as Cocteau himself* (Saturday Review). [< French *monstre sacré* (literally) sacred monster]

**mon|stros|i|ty** (mon stros′ə tē), *n., pl.* **-ties.** **1** = monster. **2** the state or character of being monstrous: (*Figurative.*) ... *the multitude ... that numerous piece of monstrosity, which, taken asunder, seem men, and the reasonable creatures of God, but, confused together, make but one great beast and monstrosity more prodigious than Hydra* (Sir Thomas Browne). [< Late Latin *mōnstrōsitās* < Latin *mōnstrōsus* monstrous]

**mon|strous** (mon′strəs), *adj., adv.* —*adj.* **1** huge; enormous: *a monstrous wolf, a monstrous sum.*

*Even while I gazed, this current acquired a monstrous velocity* (Edgar Allan Poe). SYN: gigantic, immense, colossal, prodigious, stupendous.
**2** having the nature or appearance of a monster of fable or legend: *With monstrous head and sickening cry And ears like errant wings* (G. K. Chesterton). **3** *Figurative.* so wrong or absurd as to be almost unheard of: *a monstrous lie.*
**4** *Figurative.* shocking; horrible; dreadful: *There was no excess too monstrous for them to commit* (Nicholas P. S. Wiseman). SYN: atrocious.
**5** wrongly or abnormally formed or shaped; like a monster. **6** *Obsolete.* full of monsters: *Where thou, perhaps, under the whelming tide, Visit'st the bottom of the monstrous world* (Milton).
**—*adv.*** *Archaic.* very; extremely.
[< Old French *monstreux* (with English *-ous*), learned borrowing from Latin *mōnstrōsus* < *mōnstrum;* see etym. under **monster**] **—mon′strous|ly,** *adv.* **—mon′strous|ness,** *n.*

**mons ve|ne|ris** (ven′ər is), the mons in the human female.

**Mont.,** Montana.

**mon|tage** (mon täzh′), *n., v.,* **-taged, -tag|ing.** **—*n.*** **1** the combination of several distinct pictures to make a composite picture. Montage is frequently used in photography. **2** a composite picture so made: *These dramatic photographs ... were only montages* (Newsweek). **3** in motion pictures and television: **a** the use of a rapid succession of pictures, especially to suggest a train of thought. **b** the use of a combination of images on the screen at once, often revolving or otherwise moving around or toward a focal point. **c** a part of a motion picture using either of these devices. **4** *Radio.* a rapid sequence of separate or blended voices and sound effects which suggest varying states of mind. **5** any combining or blending of different elements: *His latest novel is a montage of biography, history, and fiction.*
**—*v.t.*** to make (pictures, scenes, voices, or other images, sounds, or elements) into a montage: *to montage a theatrical set.*
[< French *montage* a mounting < Old French *monter* to mount[1]]

**Mon|ta|gnais** (mon′tə nyā′), *n., pl.* **-gnais** (-nyā′, -nyāz′), **-gnaises** (-nyāz′). **1** a member of an Indian tribe of northern Quebec. **2** the Cree dialect spoken by this tribe. **3** = Chipewyan. [< French *Montagnais* < *montagne* mountain]

**Mon|ta|gnard** or **mon|ta|gnard** (mon′tən yärd′), *n., pl.* **-gnards** or **-gnard,** *adj.* **—*n.*** any one of a large group of dark-skinned, aboriginal tribesmen living in the mountainous regions of Vietnam.
**—*adj.*** of or belonging to the Montagnards.
[< French *montagnard* (literally) mountaineer]

**Mon|ta|gue** (mon′tə gyü), *n.* a member of Romeo's family in Shakespeare's play *Romeo and Juliet.*

**mon|ta|ña** (mon ta′nyä), *n.* the forested region of the upper Amazon, on the eastern slopes of the Andes. [< Spanish *montaña* mountain < Latin *montānus;* see etym. under **montane**]

**Mon|tan|an** (mon tan′ən), *adj., n.* **—*adj.*** of or having to do with the state of Montana.
**—*n.*** a person born or living in Montana.

**mon|tane** (mon′tān), *adj., n.* **—*adj.*** of, or having to do with, or inhabiting mountains. **—*n.*** the zone of plant growth on mountains below the subalpine zone. [< Latin *montānus* < *mōns, montis* mountain. See etym. of doublet **mountain.**]

**mon|ta|ni sem|per li|be|ri** (mon tā′nī sem′pər lib′ə rī), *Latin.* mountaineers are always free (the motto of West Virginia).

**Mon|ta|nism** (mon′tə niz əm), *n.* the teachings of a heretical Christian sect of the 100's A.D. whose followers believed in the prophetic inspiration of Montanus and practiced rigorous asceticism. [< *Montanus* of Phrygia, the founder of the sect + *-ism*] **—Mon′ta|nist,** *n., adj.*

**mon|tan wax** (mon′tan), a dark-brown hydrocarbon wax extracted from various lignites and peat, used especially in making polishes, candles, and carbon paper. [apparently < German *Montan* < Latin *montānus* mountain]

**mont-de-pié|té** (môɴ′də pyā tā′), *n., pl.* **monts-de-pié|té** (môɴ′də pyā tā′). **1** a former state-controlled pawnshop in certain European countries that lent money at low interest to the poor. **2** any pawnshop. [< French *mont-de-piété,* translation of Italian *monte di pietà* (literally) hill of pity]

**mon|te** (mon′tē), *n.* a Spanish and Spanish-American gambling game, played with the Spanish deck of 40 cards. [American English < Spanish *monte* (originally) heap (that is, the "bank[2]"), mountain < Latin *mōns, montis*]

**Mon|te Car|lo method** (mon′tē kär′lō), any one of various methods involving statistical techniques, such as the use of random samples, for finding solutions to mathematical and physical problems. [< *Monte Carlo,* Monaco, noted as a gambling resort (so called because of the element of chance in such methods)]

**mon|teith** (mon tēth′), *n.* a large bowl, usually silver, with a scalloped or notched rim from which stemmed glasses can be hung by the foot so as to cool in the water inside the bowl. It is also used as a punch bowl. [supposedly < a proper name]

**Mon|te|ne|grin** (mon′tə nē′grin), *adj., n.* **—*adj.*** of or having to do with Montenegro or its people.
**—*n.*** a native or inhabitant of Montenegro.

**Mon|te|rey cypress** (mon′tə rā′), a cypress tree of the Pacific coast of North America, having long, massive limbs that spread and grow in unusual shapes. [< *Monterey,* a city on the coast of California]

**Monterey pine,** a pine tree of the Pacific coast, growing 40 to 60 feet in height, and widely cultivated for shelter and ornament.

**mon|te|ro** (mon tãr′ō; *Spanish* môn tā′rō), *n., pl.* **-te|ros** (-tãr′ōz; *Spanish* -tā′rōs). a cap with a round crown and a flap to draw over the ears, worn by huntsmen. [< Spanish *montera* < *montero* a hunter; (literally) a mountaineer < *monte* mountain; see etym. under **monte**]

**mon|tes** (mon′tēz), *n.* plural of **mons.**

**Mon|tes|so|ri|an** (mon′tə sôr′ē ən, -sōr′-), *n., adj.* **—*n.*** a follower of the Montessori method.
**—*adj.*** of or having to do with the Montessori method.

**Mon|tes|so|ri method** or **system** (mon′tə sôr′ē, -sōr′-), a system for teaching young children that stresses training of the senses and self-education, developed by Maria Montessori (1870-1952), Italian educator.

**mont|gol|fi|er** (mont gol′fē ər), *n.* a balloon raised by heated air from a fire in the lower part; fire balloon. [< the French brothers *Montgolfier,* who in 1783 sent up the first balloon]

***month** (munth), *n.* **1** one of the 12 periods of time into which the year is divided; calendar month. April, June, September, and November have 30 days; February has 28 days except in leap years, when it has 29; all the other months have 31 days. *Abbr:* mo. **2** the time from any day of one calendar month to the corresponding day of the next month. **3** *Astronomy.* **a** the time it takes the moon to make one complete revolution around the earth; lunar month. **b** the time from one new moon to the next, about 29.53 days; synodical month. **c** one twelfth of a solar year, about 30.41 days; solar month. **d** a sidereal month.
[Old English *mōnath.* See related etym. at **moon.**]
▶ **months.** In technical and informal writing, the names of months with more than four letters are abbreviated in dates: *Jan. 21, 1977; Aug. 16, 1984.* But: *May 1, 1978; July 4, 1976.* When only the month or the month and year are given, abbreviations are rarely used: *January, 1970. He held office from September to February.* In formal writing, the names of the months are not abbreviated at all.

**month|ly** (munth′lē), *adj., adv., n., pl.* **-lies.** **—*adj.*** **1** of a month; for a month: *a monthly report, a monthly salary.* **2** lasting a month: *a monthly supply.* **3** done, happening, or payable once a month or every month: *a monthly meeting, a monthly examination, monthly bills.* **4** = menstrual.
**—*adv.*** once a month; every month; month by month: *Some magazines come monthly.*
**—*n.*** a magazine or other periodical published once a month.
**monthlies,** = menses: *The issue is not at the usual time of the monthlies* (James G. Murphy).

**month's mind, 1** the commemoration of a dead person by a Requiem, a month after death.
**2** *British Dialect.* a mind; inclination; fancy: *Clinker has a month's mind to play the fool ... with Mrs. Winifred Jenkins* (Tobias Smollett).

**mon|ti|cule** (mon′tə kyül), *n.* **1** a small hill; mound. **2** a minor cone of a volcano. [< Middle French *monticule,* learned borrowing from Late Latin *monticulus* (diminutive) < Latin *mōns, montis* mountain]

**mont|mo|ril|lon|ite** (mont′mə ril′ə nīt), *n.* one of a group of mineral clays, a silicate of aluminum and certain other elements, used because of its absorbent structure for various industrial purposes and for safely disposing of radioactive waste materials. [< *Montmorillon,* a town in France, where it is found + *-ite*[1]]

**Mont|re|al|er** (mon′trē ô′lər), *n.* a native or inhabitant of Montreal, Canada.

**mon|tu|no** (mon′tü nō), *n.* a loose, long-sleeved, embroidered shirt made of coarse white cotton worn over short, fringed trousers by men in Panama. [American Spanish *montuno* < Spanish *montuno* (adjective) rustic, peasant]

**mon|u|ment** (mon′yə mənt), *n.* **1** an object or structure set up to keep a person or an event from being forgotten. A monument may be a building, pillar, arch, statue, tomb, or stone.
**2** anything that keeps alive the memory of a person, civilization, period, or event. SYN: memorial.
**3** a permanent or prominent instance or example: *The Hoover Dam is a monument of engineering. The professor's researches were monuments of learning.* **4** *U.S. Law.* any permanent object, natural or artificial, serving to mark a boundary. **5** any area or site officially designated by a government as having special historical or natural significance. **6** something written or done by a person, regarded as his memorial after death: *Except some unpublished despatches ... and a few detached sayings, he has left no monument behind him* (William E. H. Lecky).
**7** *Obsolete.* a sepulcher; tomb: *Her body sleeps in Capel's monument* (Shakespeare). **8** *Obsolete.* an effigy. [< Latin *monumentum* < *monēre* to remind, warn]

**mon|u|men|tal** (mon′yə men′təl), *adj.* **1** of or having to do with a monument or monuments: *monumental decorations.* **2** serving as a monument or memorial: *a monumental chapel. He hath given her his monumental ring* (Shakespeare). **3** like a monument; having great size: *a monumental mountain peak.* **4** weighty and lasting; historically prominent and significant; important: *a monumental decision. The Constitution of the United States is a monumental document. A great encyclopedia is a monumental production.* SYN: impressive, notable. **5** very great; colossal: *monumental ignorance.* **6** (of a statue or portrait) larger than life-size. **—mon′u|men′tal|ly,** *adv.*

**mon|u|men|tal|ism** (mon′yə men′tə liz əm), *n.* monumental style or construction.

**mon|u|men|tal|ist** (mon′yə men′tə list), *n., adj.* **—*n.*** a painter, writer, or other artist who works on a grand or monumental scale.
**—*adj.*** of or having to do with a monumentalist or monumentalism: *monumentalist sculpture.*

**mon|u|men|tal|i|ty** (mon′yə men tal′ə tē), *n.* the state or quality of being monumental.

***month** definition 1

| Roman months: | Julian months: | Gregorian months: |
|---|---|---|
| Jānuārius | Jānuārius | January |
| Februārius | Februārius | February |
| (Intercalaris) | Martius | March |
| Martius | Aprīlis | April |
| Aprīlis | Māius | May |
| Māius | Jūnius | June |
| Jūnius | Jūlius | July |
| Quintīlis | Augustus | August |
| Sextīlis | September | September |
| September | Octōber | October |
| Octōber | November | November |
| November | December | December |
| December | | |
| (plus Intercalaris in a leap year) | | |

| Jewish months: | French Revolutionary months: |
|---|---|
| Tishri | Vendémiaire |
| Heshvan | Brumaire |
| Kislev | Frimaire |
| Tebet | Nivôse |
| Shebat | Pluviôse |
| Adar | Ventôse |
| (Veadar) | Germinal |
| Nisan | Floréal |
| Iyar | Prairial |
| Sivan | Messidor |
| Tammuz | Thermidor |
| Ab | Fructidor |
| Elul | |
| (plus Veadar in a leap year) | |

**Pronunciation Key:** hat, āge, cãre, fär; let, ēqual, tėrm; it, īce; hot, ōpen, ôrder; oil, out; cup, pu̇t, rüle; child; long; thin; ᴛʜen; zh, measure; ə represents **a** in about, **e** in taken, **i** in pencil, **o** in lemon, **u** in circus.

**mon|u|men|tal|ize** (mon′yə men′tə līz), *v.t.*, **-ized, -iz|ing.** to establish a lasting memorial or record of. — **mon′u|men′tal|i|za′tion**, *n.*

**mon|zo|nite** (mon′zə nīt), *n.* an igneous rock composed of nearly equal amounts of plagioclase and orthoclase, plus other minerals, intermediate in composition between syenite and diorite. [< German *Monzonit* < *Monzoni*, a mountain in Tyrol + *-it* -ite[1]]

**mon|zo|nit|ic** (mon′zə nit′ik), *adj.* of or consisting of monzonite.

**moo** (mü), *n., pl.* **moos**, *v.*, **mooed, moo|ing.** — ***n.*** the sound made by a cow; a lowing. — ***v.i.*** to make the sound of a cow; low: *The cow mooed in the barn.* [imitative]

**mooch** (müch), *Slang.* — ***v.t.*** **1** to get from another by begging or sponging; beg: *He mooches a couple of cigarettes off me every day.* **2** to pilfer; steal. — ***v.i.*** **1** to sponge or beg shamelessly. **2** to sneak; skulk; rove about: *They sort of mooched after me, and I tells a policeman* (Lord Dunsany). Also, **mouch.** [earlier *mowche* (originally) to pretend poverty; origin uncertain. Perhaps related to **miche.**] — **mooch′er**, *n.*

**mood**[1] (müd), *n.* **1** state of mind or feelings: *Are you in the mood to listen to music? I am in the mood to play now; I don't want to study.* **2** *Obsolete.* bad temper; anger.
**moods,** fits of depression, irritation, or bad temper: *Then turn'd Sir Torre, and being in his moods left them* (Tennyson).
[Old English *mōd* mind, heart, courage]
— ***Syn.*** **1 Mood, humor** mean a person's state of mind or feeling at a particular time. **Mood** applies to a state of mind determined by some emotion or desire that affects everything a person says and does while in this frame of mind: *I am not in the mood to read just now; I want to watch television.* **Humor** applies to a state of mind and spirits determined by a person's natural disposition or the way he feels physically, and suggests the likelihood of changing suddenly or without apparent reason: *He is in a good humor today.*

**mood**[2] (müd), *n.* **1** the form of a verb or verb phrase which shows whether the act or state it expresses is thought of as a fact, condition, command, or a wish; mode. In "I am hungry," *am* is in the indicative mood. In "I demand that she answer," *answer* is in the subjunctive mood. In "Open the window," *open* is in the imperative mood. *In English, modern grammar experts usually limit the term mood to the indicative, subjunctive, and imperative forms* (Paul Roberts). **2** *Logic.* = mode. [alteration of *mode*[2]; influenced by *mood*[1]]

**mood drug**, a drug, such as a stimulant or tranquilizer, that affects one's state of mind.

**mood|i|ly** (mü′də lē), *adv.* in a moody manner.

**mood|i|ness** (mü′dē nis), *n.* moody condition.

**mood|ing** (mü′ding), *n.* the process of roughly shaping metal with a hammer, as in making a spoon or the blade of a knife. [< *mood*, verb, an English dialectal variant of *mold*[1]]

**mood music**, **1** music used to evoke or sustain a particular mood, as in connection with passages in a play or other dramatic presentation. **2** unobtrusive instrumental music played to provide a pleasant atmosphere for eating, drinking, or talking, as in a restaurant; wallpaper music.

**moods** (müdz), *n.pl.* See under **mood**[1].

**mood stone**, an artificial gem that is supposed to change color to reflect the mood of the wearer, made of quartz incorporating liquid crystals.

**mood|y** (mü′dē), *adj.*, **mood|i|er, mood|i|est.** **1** likely to have changes of mood: *It is difficult to predict his reaction because he is so moody.* **2** often having gloomy moods: *a dour, moody person. She has been moody ever since she lost her job.* **3** sunk in sadness; gloomy; sullen: *The little girl sat in moody silence.* **SYN:** melancholy, sad. **4** expressive of a mood, especially a bad mood: *a moody remark.*

**Moog synthesizer** (mōg, müg), an electronic keyboard instrument for generating a large variety of sounds. [< Robert A. *Moog*, an American engineer, who invented it]

**mool** (mül), *n. Scottish.* **1** mold; earth; soil. **2** the grave. [variant of *mold*[2]]

**moo|la** or **moo|lah** (mü′lə, -lä), *n. U.S. Slang.* money: *She is going back to stuffing our moola in the mattress* (Atlantic). [origin unknown]

∗**moon** (mün), *n., v.* — ***n.*** **1** a heavenly body that revolves around the earth once in about 29½ days at a mean distance of 238,857 miles or 384,403 kilometers. The moon shines in the sky at night and looks bright because it reflects the sun's light. It is a natural satellite of the earth and is held in orbit by the earth's gravity. The moon's diameter is about 2,160 miles, and its volume about 1/50 that of the earth. The force of the moon's gravity on the earth causes tides in the ocean. **2** the moon as it looks at a certain period of time. The half moon appears as a half circle, the full moon as a circle, and the old moon as a waning crescent. In technical usage, what is often called the "new moon" is properly a waxing crescent and the actual new moon is almost invisible. **3** a lunar month; about a month or 29½ days. The Indians counted time by moons. *A young and tender suckling—under a moon old* (Charles Lamb). **4** = moonlight. **5** something shaped like the moon in any of its appearances: *a great moon of a face.* **6** a satellite of any planet: *the moons of Jupiter.* **7** an artificial earth satellite.
— ***v.i.*** **1** to wander about idly; gaze in a dreamy way: *to go mooning about the house and stables* (Thomas Bailey Aldrich). *If you moon at me in that stupid way ... I shall certainly end in an insane asylum* (William Dean Howells). **2** to shine as a moon does.
— ***v.t.*** **1** to spend (time) idly. **2** to expose (something) to the moon's rays.
**bark at the moon,** to clamor or agitate to no effect: *Those who protested against the dictator's ruthless actions were barking at the moon, since they were few and powerless.*
**once in a blue moon.** See under **blue moon.**
[Old English *mōna.* See related etym. at **month.**]
— **moon′er**, *n.* — **moon′like′**, *adj.*

∗**moon**
definitions 1, 2

earth; moon's orbit; 1–8

**phases as seen from the earth:**
1 new moon; 2 waxing crescent; 3 first quarter; 4 waxing gibbous; 5 full moon; 6 waning gibbous; 7 last quarter; 8 waning crescent

**moon|beam** (mün′bēm′), *n.* a ray of moonlight.

**moon bear**, an Asiatic black bear, so called because of the white, crescentlike mark on its chest.

**moon-blind** (mün′blīnd′), *adj.* suffering from moon blindness.

**moon blindness**, **1** an intermittent inflammation of the eyes in horses, usually resulting in blindness; mooneye. **2** = night blindness.

**moon|bow** (mün′bō′), *n.* a rainbow formed by moonlight; lunar rainbow: *Moonbows are due to the same cause as rainbows, but since the reflected light from the moon does not contain all the colors of sunlight the bow appears silver* (London Times).

**moon|calf** (mün′kaf′, -käf′), *n., pl.* **-calves. 1** a congenital idiot. **2** a foolish person; fool; dolt. **3** a person who moons. **4** *Archaic.* a monstrosity.

**moon car**, = lunar rover.

**moon|child** (mün′chīld′), *n., pl.* **-chil|dren.** a person born under the zodiacal sign of Cancer. [so called because the moon is supposed to rule the house or sign of Cancer]

**moon|craft** (mün′kraft′, -kräft′), *n., pl.* **-craft.** a spacecraft for traveling to the moon; moonship.

**moon crawler**, = lunar rover.

**moon|creep|er** (mün′krē′pər), *n.* = moonflower.

**moon daisy**, = oxeye daisy.

**mooned** (münd; *Poetic* mü′nid), *adj.* **1** moon-shaped. **2** ornamented with moons or crescents.

**moon|eye** (mün′ī′), *n.* **1** an eye affected with moon blindness. **2** = moon blindness.

**moon|eyed** (mün′īd′), *adj.* **1** having round, wide-open eyes, as from terror or surprise. **2** = moon-blind.

**moon|face** (mün′fās′), *n.* **1** a round, moonlike face: *As he neared the top, he turned his happy moonface* (Time). **2** an abnormal obesity of the face caused by various diseases.

**moon|faced** (mün′fāst′), *adj.* having a round face like a full moon: *a moonfaced clock, a moonfaced baby.*

**moon|fish** (mün′fish′), *n., pl.* **-fish|es** or (*collectively*) **-fish.** any of a number of fishes that suggest the moon by the silvery or yellowish color of their body, as various carangoids, opahs, and a Mexican top minnow.

**moon|flight** (mün′flīt′), *n.* space flight to the moon.

**moon|flow|er** (mün′flou′ər), *n.* **1** a tropical plant of the morning-glory family, having large, fragrant white flowers that open in the evening. **2** any one of various related plants. **3** *Especially British.* the oxeye daisy.

**moon|gate** (mün′gāt′), *n.* a circular gateway through a wall, as in a Chinese temple.

**moon|glow** (mün′glō′), *n.* = moonlight.

**Moon|ie** (mü′nē), *n.* a follower of Sun Myung Moon, born 1921, a Korean evangelist preaching a blend of fundamentalist Christianity and Eastern mysticism: *Young Moonies, who also are encouraged to donate their personal possessions and bank accounts to the movement, receive no pay* (New York Sunday News).

**moon|i|ly** (mü′nə lē), *adv.* in a moony manner.

**moon|i|ness** (mü′nē nis), *n.* moony quality or condition.

**moon|ish** (mü′nish), *adj.* **1** like the moon; changeable; fickle: *at which time would I, being but a moonish youth, ... be effeminate, changeable* (Shakespeare). **2** caused by the moon. — **moon′ish|ly**, *adv.*

**moon jellyfish**, the most common jellyfish, disk-shaped and white or bluish, found along the Atlantic and Pacific coasts.

**moon|less** (mün′lis), *adj.* **1** having no moon: *It is by no means improbable that Mars was originally moonless* (H. C. Macpherson). **2** not lit up by the moon: *a moonless night.*

**moon|let** (mün′lit), *n.* **1** a little moon: *I pledge thee in the silver horn Of yonder moonlet bright* (William Motherwell). **2** a small artificial earth satellite: *man-made moonlets circle the earth.*

**moon|light** (mün′līt′), *n., adj., v.* — ***n.*** the light of the moon: *Moonlight has a considerable influence on the activity of insects at night* (Science News).
— ***adj.*** **1** having the light of the moon; moonlit: *a moonlight night.* **2** while the moon is shining; at or by night: *a moonlight swim.*
— ***v.i.*** *U.S. Informal.* to work at a second job, often at night, in order to supplement the wages earned at a regular job: *Workers moonlight to live on a higher plane than otherwise is possible* (Chicago Daily News). — **moon′light′er**, *n.*

**moonlight flit**, *British Slang.* the action of absconding at night to escape creditors.

**moon|light|ing** (mün′lī′ting), *n. U.S. Informal.* the practice of holding or working at a second job, usually at night, in addition to a regular daytime job.

**moon|lit** (mün′lit′), *adj.* lighted by the moon: *moonlit woods.*

**moon|man** (mün′man′, -mən), *n., pl.* **-men. 1** a person skilled in or trained for moonflight: *Then, according to the theory, the moonmen take off, orbit, rendezvous and couple with the mother ship* (Harper's). **2** a person engaged in research and other projects concerned with moonflight.

**moon|port** (mün′pôrt′, -pōrt′), *n.* a launch complex for preparing spacecraft to travel to the moon.

**moon probe**, = lunar probe.

**moon|quake** (mün′kwāk′), *n.* a quake or series of vibrations on the moon analogous to an earthquake.

**moon|rak|er** (mün′rā′kər), *n.* **1** a stupid or silly person. **2** = moonsail.

**moon|rise** (mün′rīz′), *n.* **1** the rising of the moon: *watching a chilly autumnal moonrise over the stubbles of the cornfield* (Mrs. Humphry Ward). **2** the time when the moon rises: *The wolves began to howl about an hour after moonrise.*

**moon|rock** (mün′rok′), *n.* a rock sample from the moon, such as ferropseudobrookite.

**moon rover**, = lunar rover.

**moon|sail** (mün′sāl′; *Nautical* mün′səl), *n.* a light sail set above a skysail; moonraker.

**moon|scape** (mün′skāp), *n.* **1** a view of the surface of the moon. **2** the surface viewed. **3** a view or landscape on earth which looks as rugged as a moonscape. [< *moon* + (land)*scape*]

**moon|seed** (mün′sēd′), *n.* any climbing plant of a group having panicles of greenish-white flowers and crescent-shaped seeds, especially a variety of eastern North America grown on walls and arbors.

**moon|set** (mün′set′), *n.* **1** the setting of the moon. **2** the time of setting of the moon.

**moon shell**, **1** = moon snail. **2** the shell of this snail.

**moon|shine** (mün′shīn′), *n.* **1** *Informal.* intoxicating liquor made unlawfully or smuggled: *Moonshine making may be on the rise again, revenue sleuths fear* (Wall Street Journal). **2** *Figurative.* empty talk; foolish talk or ideas; nonsense: *Making every allowance for Communist statistical moonshine ...* (Time). **3** = moonlight.

**moon|shin|er** (mün′shī′nər), *n. Informal.* **1** a person who distills intoxicating liquor, especially of corn whiskey, contrary to law. **2** a person who follows an unlawful trade at night.

**moon|shin|ing** (mün′shī′ning), *n., adj.* — ***n.*** the unlawful distilling of intoxicating liquor.
— ***adj.*** of or having to do with moonshining.

**moon|shin|y** (mün′shī′nē), *adj.* **1** like moonlight. **2** lighted by the moon. **3** unreal.

**moon|ship** (mün′ship′), *n.* = mooncraft.

**moon shoot**, = moon shot.

**moon shot**, the act or process of launching a

rocket or missile toward the moon.
**moon snail**, a predatory, carnivorous marine snail with a rounded shell; natica: *The moon snail is a blind creature ... with an immense foot, which it uses effectively in digging and in grasping its prey, while with its radula it drills a neat round hole in the shell* (New Yorker).
**moon|stone** (mün′stōn′), *n.* a whitish, translucent gem with a pearly luster. Moonstone is a variety of feldspar.
**moon|struck** (mün′struk′), *adj.* affected in mind, supposedly through the influence of the moon; dazed, crazed, or confused: *Deform'd in body, and Of moonstruck mind* (Robert Bridges). **SYN**: lunatic.
**Moon type**, **1** a system of printing for blind people, the letters being represented by nine basic characters placed in different positions, which may be read by touch. **2** the letters themselves. [< William *Moon*, a British inventor of the 1900's]
**moon|walk** (mün′wôk′), *n.* an exploratory walk on the moon's surface: *During their first moonwalk Captain Cernan and Dr. Schmitt gathered 29 lb. of lunar rock and soil* (London Times).
**moon|walk|er** (mün′wô′kər), *n.* a person who takes a moonwalk; moon explorer: *... Earth's first moonwalker, Neil Armstrong* (Science Journal).
**moon|ward** (mün′wərd), *adv., adj.* —*adv.* toward the moon: *The first serious attempts to send rockets moonward were made by the Americans in 1958* (Listener).
—*adj.* directed toward the moon: *... balloon-launched moonward rockets* (Time).
**moon|wort** (mün′wėrt′), *n.* **1** any fern of a group having fronds with crescent-shaped leaflets. **2** = honesty (def. 3).
**moon|y** (mü′nē), *adj.*, **moon|i|er, moon|i|est. 1** of or belonging to the moon. **2** like the moon; crescent-shaped; round: *... nor lift the moony shield* (John Dryden). **3** mooning; dreamy; listless: *moony dreamings over inscrutable beautiful eyes* (George Meredith). **4** illuminated by the moon; moonlit. **5** resembling moonlight.
**moor[1]** (mu̇r), *v.t.* **1** to put or keep (a ship or boat) in place by means of ropes or chains fastened to the shore or to anchors: *The ship was moored in the harbor to unload cargo.* **2** *Figurative.* to fix firmly; secure. —*v.i.* **1** to tie up a ship or boat. **2** *Figurative.* to be made secure. [earlier *moren.* Compare Old English *mǣrels* mooring rope.]
**moor[2]** (mu̇r), *n.* **1** open wasteland, especially if heather or coarse grasses grow on it; heath: *Wind and mist blew across the stark moor.* **2** a game preserve consisting of such land. [Old English *mōr*]
**Moor** (mu̇r), *n.* a member of a Moslem people of mixed Arab and Berber stock living in northwestern Africa. The Moors invaded and conquered Spain in the 700's A.D. They were driven out in 1492. *Under the Moors, Spain became more civilized than most other European countries* (Walter C. Langsam). [< Old French *More,* later *Maure* < Latin *Maurus* < Greek *Maûros*]
**moor|age** (mu̇r′ij), *n.* **1** a mooring or being moored. **2** a place for mooring. **3** the charge for its use.
**moor|ber|ry** (mu̇r′ber′ē, -bər-), *n., pl.* **-ries. 1** = bilberry. **2** a small cranberry.
**moor cock**, the male red grouse.
**moor|fowl** (mu̇r′foul′), *n.* = red grouse.
**moor hen**, **1** the female red grouse; gorhen. **2** any one of various wading birds, such as the gallinule, rail, and coot.
**moor|ing** (mu̇r′ing), *n.* **1** the act of tying up or securing a ship or boat. **2** Also, **moorings.** a place where a ship or boat is or may be tied up. **3** Also, **moorings.** *Figurative.* anything to which a person or thing is attached or fastened.
**moorings**, ropes, cables, or anchors by which a ship or boat is made fast: *The ship snapped its moorings and drifted away.*
**mooring mast** or **tower**, a mast or tower to which an airship can be moored.
**moor|ish** (mu̇r′ish), *adj.* **1** of or like a moor. **2** full of moors; covered with moors: *moorish hills.*

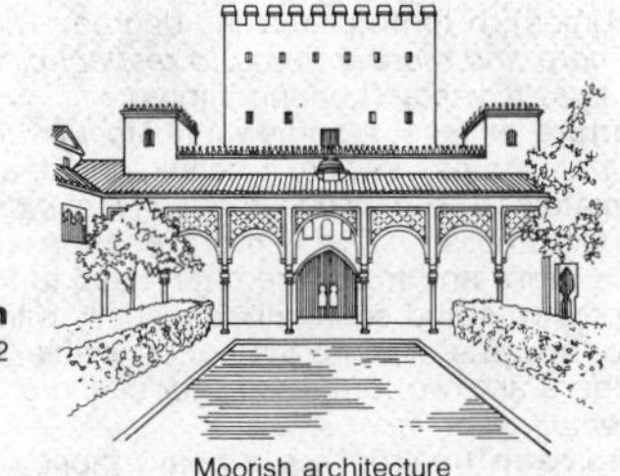
***Moorish** definition 2

Moorish architecture

***Moor|ish** (mu̇r′ish), *adj.* **1** of the Moors. **2** in the style of the Moors.
**moor|land** (mu̇r′land′, -lənd), *n., adj. Especially British.* —*n.* land covered with heather; moor: *... opportunities for studying the ecology of moorlands* (A. W. Haslett).
—*adj.* of moorland.
**moor|wort** (mu̇r′wėrt′), *n.* a low evergreen shrub of the heath family, growing chiefly in bogs in north temperate regions.
**moor|y** (mu̇r′ē), *adj.*, **moor|i|er, moor|i|est.** = moorish.
**moose** (müs), *n., pl.* **moose. 1** a large cud-chewing animal of the same family as the deer, living in wooded areas of Canada and the northern part of the United States. The moose is a mammal, the male of which has a heavy build, large head, and broad antlers. See picture under **deer. 2** the European elk. [American English < Algonkian (compare Narraganset *moos,* apparently < *moosu* he strips bark of young trees as food)]
**moose|wood** (müs′wu̇d′), *n.* a small, slender maple tree having a green bark with white stripes.
**moot** (müt), *adj., v., n.* —*adj.* that is doubtful or debatable; that can be argued: *a moot point.* [< noun]
—*v.t.* **1** to bring forward (a point, subject, question, or case) for discussion: *The project of this conference was first mooted about two years ago* (Bulletin of Atomic Scientists). **2** *Archaic.* to argue, discuss, or debate (a point, subject, question, or case). —*v.i.* **1** to argue; dispute. **2** to debate a hypothetical case of law, as was done by students in the Inns of Court.
[Old English *mōtian* < *gemōt;* see the noun]
—*n.* **1** (in early English history) an assembly of the people of an administrative division for discussing local judicial and political affairs. **2a** a discussion of a hypothetical law case by students for practice. **b** a hypothetical case that may be used for this.
[Old English *gemōt* a meeting. See related etym. at **meet[1]**.] —**moot′er**, *n.*
**moot court**, a mock court held in a law school to give students practice.
**moot hall**, (in early English history) a hall in which a moot was held.
**mop[1]** (mop), *n., v.,* **mopped, mop|ping.** —*n.* **1** a bundle of coarse yarn, rags, cloth, or the like, or a sponge, fastened at the end of a stick, for cleaning floors, dishes, or other things: *The janitor pushed a mop over the dirty floor.* **2** a thick, tangled, or unruly mass: *a mop of hair not a little resembling the shag of a Newfoundland dog* (Washington Irving). **3** any one of various small instruments resembling a mop, especially one used in surgery to apply medicated fluids or to remove infected matter.
—*v.t.* **1** to wash or wipe up; clean with a mop: *to mop the floor.* **2** to wipe sweat or tears from: *He mopped his brow.* —*v.i.* to use a mop.
**mop up, a** to clean up with a mop. **b** *Informal.* to finish: *Tom ... will follow the fireballer, and Johnny Sain will mop up* (New York Times). **c** *Military.* to clear out or rid (an area) of scattered or remaining enemy troops: *The mopping up, after an unexpected quick victory ..., may be long and difficult* (New York Times).
[earlier *mappe,* perhaps < French (Walloon) *mappe* < Latin, or directly < Latin *mappa* napkin]
**mop[2]** (mop), *v.,* **mopped, mop|ping,** *n.* —*v.i.* to make a wry face; grimace.
—*n.* a grimace.
**mop and mow**, to make faces; grimace: *At the circus, the clowns mopped and mowed.*
[perhaps imitative. Compare Dutch *moppen* to pout.]
**mo|pa|ni** (mō pä′nē), *n.* a medium-sized tree of the pea family found in tropical Africa, used for lumber and as a source of copal. [< a native word]
**mop|board** (mop′bôrd′, -bōrd′), *n. U.S.* a baseboard.
**mope** (mōp), *v.,* **moped, mop|ing,** *n.* —*v.i.* to be dull, silent, and sad; be gloomy: *Went moping under the long shadows at sunset* (D. G. Mitchell). **SYN**: sulk.
—*v.t.* to cause to mope.
—*n.* a person who allows himself to be dull, silent, and sad: *She is no mope, only thoughtful and quiet* (M. C. Jackson).
**the mopes**, low spirits; the blues; the dumps: *Master [is] still in the mopes* (Thackeray).
[perhaps related to **mop[2]**. Compare Low German *mopen* to sulk.] —**mop′er**, *n.* —**mop′ing|ly**, *adv.*
**mo|ped** (mō′ped), *n.* a heavily built bicycle with a low-powered auxiliary engine; motorbicycle: *Since it ... can be propelled by the pedals alone, the moped is clearly no motorcycle. It might best be called the effortless bike* (Time). [< *mo*(tor) + *ped*(al)]
**mop|er|y** (mō′pər ē), *n., pl.* **-er|ies.** mopish action or behavior.
**mop|head** (mop′hed′), *n.* **1** *Informal.* a person with a thick or bushy head of hair. **2** the bundle or sponge fastened at the end of a mop.
**mop|ish** (mō′pish), *adj.* inclined to mope; listless and dejected. —**mop′ish|ly**, *adv.* —**mop′ish-ness**, *n.*
**mo|poke** (mō pōk′), *n.* any one of several Australian birds, especially a kind of goatsucker or a small owl. Also, **morepork.** [probably imitative]
**mop|per** (mop′ər), *n.* a person who mops.
**mop|per-up** (mop′ər up′), *n., pl.* **mop|pers-up. 1** *Informal.* a person who cleans up or finishes off something. **2** *Military.* a soldier who takes part in a mop-up action.
**mop|pet** (mop′it), *n.* **1** a little child: *Additional moppets over five travel at $1 a head extra* (Wall Street Journal). **2** *Archaic.* darling, a term of endearment for a baby or little girl, or a rag doll. [< obsolete *mop* doll + *-et*]
**mop|ping-up** (mop′ing up′), *adj.* = mop-up.
**mop|py** (mop′ē), *adj.,* **-pi|er, -pi|est.** like a mop: *moppy hair.*
**mop-up** (mop′up′), *n., adj.* —*n. Informal.* **1** the act or process of cleaning up; a wiping out: *It was the first county in which a mop-up of gambling was ordered* (New York Times). **2** the systematic killing or capture of defeated troops left in an area after a major battle or war: *As the mop-up continued, casualties mounted* (Time).
—*adj.* of or having to do with a mop-up: *Terrorists struck at British mop-up patrols with homemade bombs and rifle fire* (Newsweek).
**mop|y** (mō′pē), *adj.,* **mop|i|er, mop|i|est.** = mopish.
**mo|quette** (mō ket′), *n.* a thick, velvety carpet or upholstery fabric made of wool and hemp or linen. [< French *moquette,* earlier *moucade;* origin uncertain]
**mor** (mōr), *n.* a peaty kind of humus, poor in lime and nitrogen, and unsuitable for plant growth. [< Scandinavian (compare Icelandic *mor* peat soil)]
**mor.**, morocco (leather).
**Mor.**, Morocco.
***mo|ra** (môr′ə, mōr′-), *n., pl.* **mo|rae** (môr′ē, mōr′-), **mo|ras. 1** a unit of meter, equivalent to a short syllable. **2** *Law.* a negligent delay. [< Latin *mora* pause, delay]

***mora** definition 1

I sing of arms and the hero

**mo|ra|ceous** (mô rā′shəs, mō-), *adj.* belonging to the mulberry family: *The fig, hop, hemp, and the Osage orange are moraceous plants.* [< New Latin *Moraceae* the mulberry family (< Latin *mōrum* mulberry, or *mōrus* mulberry tree) + English *-ous*]
**mo|rain|al** (mə rā′nəl), *adj.* of or having to do with a moraine.
**mo|raine** (mə rān′), *n.* **1** a mass or ridge of rocks, dirt, and other natural debris, deposited at the side or end of a glacier, or beneath the ice as the glacier melts. The material is scraped up by the glacier as it moves along. **2** a raised border or ridge formed chiefly of stones on which plants are grown: *The one essential of the moraine is drainage of the most perfect description* (L. B. Meredith). [< French *moraine,* perhaps < Provençal *mourenne;* origin uncertain]
**mo|rain|ic** (mə rā′nik), *adj.* = morainal.
**mor|al** (môr′əl, mor′-), *adj., n., v.,* **-aled, -al|ing** or (*especially British*) **-alled, -al|ling.** —*adj.* **1** good in character or conduct; virtuous according to civilized standards of right and wrong; right; just: *a moral act, a moral man.* **2** capable of understanding right and wrong: *A little baby is not a moral being.* **3** having to do with character or with the difference between right and wrong: *Whether finding should be keeping is a moral question. The Abolitionists felt a moral responsibility to free the slaves.* **4** based on the principles of right conduct rather than on law or custom. **5** teaching a good lesson; having a good influence: *a moral book.* **6** proper in sexual relations; not lewd; virtuous. **7** based upon considerations of what generally occurs; resting upon grounds of probability: *a moral certainty.*
—*n.* **1** the lesson, inner meaning, or teaching of a fable, a story, or an event: *The moral of the story was "Look before you leap."* **2** the type of something; embodiment: *She is the very moral of old-fashioned prejudice* (Hawthorne). **3** the image

**Pronunciation Key:** hat, āge, cãre, fär; let, ēqual, tėrm; it, īce; hot, ōpen, ôrder; oil, out; cup, pu̇t, rüle; child; long; thin; ᴛʜen; zh, measure; ə represents **a** in about, **e** in taken, **i** in pencil, **o** in lemon, **u** in circus.

or counterpart of a person or thing: *They said I was the very moral of Lady Richmanstone, but not so pale* (Tobias Smollett).
—*v.i. Archaic.* to moralize: *When I did hear the motley fool thus moral on the time* (Shakespeare).
**morals, a** principles of conduct; ethics; moral philosophy: *In morals the action is judged by the intention* (Algernon Charles Swinburne). **b** principles, habits, character, or behavior in matters of right and wrong: *George Washington's morals were excellent.*
[< Latin *mōrālis* < *mōs, mōris* custom, *mōrēs* manners]
—***Syn.*** *adj.* **1 Moral, ethical** mean in agreement with a standard of what is right and good in character or conduct. **Moral** implies conformity to the customary rules and accepted standards of society: *He leads a moral life.* **Ethical** implies conformity to the principles of right conduct expressed in a formal system or code, such as that of a profession or business: *It is not considered ethical for doctors to advertise.*
▶ **moral, morale.** A common error is writing *moral* (concerning right conduct) when *morale* (mental condition as regards courage, confidence, or enthusiasm) is the word intended.

**mo|rale** (mə ral′, -räl′), *n.* **1** moral or mental condition in regard to courage, confidence, or enthusiasm: *the morale of troops. The morale of the team was low after its defeat.* **2** morality; morals: *Here the ... traveller may see more of the habits and morale of the Turkish women than he can hope to do elsewhere* (Julia S. H. Pardoe). [< French *morale,* feminine of Old French *moral* moral, learned borrowing from Latin *mōrālis*] ▶ See **moral** for usage note.

**moral hazard,** the risk taken by an insurer that the insured may not be trustworthy.

**mor|al|ise** (môr′ə līz, mor′-), *v.i., v.t.,* **-ised, -is|ing.** *Especially British.* moralize.

**mor|al|ism** (môr′ə liz əm, mor′-), *n.* **1** the action of moralizing; moral counsel or advice. **2** a moral maxim. **3** good morals as distinct from religion.

**mor|al|ist** (môr′ə list, mor′-), *n.* **1** a person who thinks much about moral duties, sees the moral side of things, and leads a moral life. **2** a person who teaches, studies, or writes about morals: *Writers of satires are usually moralists, because they wish to improve human conditions.* **3** a person who believes in regulating the morals of others.

**mor|al|is|tic** (môr′ə lis′tik, mor′-), *adj.* **1** teaching the difference between right and wrong; moralizing. **2** of or having to do with a moralist or moral teaching. **3** narrow-minded or self-righteous in moral judgment or beliefs: *the moralistic bossiness of provincial politicians* (Santha Rama Rau). —**mor′al|is′ti|cal|ly,** *adv.*

**mo|ral|i|ty** (mə ral′ə tē), *n., pl.* **-ties. 1** the right or wrong of an action: *They argued about the morality of dancing on Sunday.* **2** doing right; virtue: *He ranks very high in both intelligence and morality.* **3** a system of morals; set of rules or principles of conduct: *Doctor Johnson's morality was as English an article as beefsteak* (Hawthorne). **4** a moral lesson or precept; moral instruction: *A genial optimist, who daily drew from what he saw his quaint moralities* (William Cullen Bryant). **5** = morality play.

**morality play,** a type of drama popular during the 1400's and 1500's, in which the characters were personifications of abstract qualities, such as vice, virtue, wealth, poverty, knowledge, or ignorance.

**mor|al|ize** (môr′ə līz, mor′-), *v.,* **-ized, -iz|ing.** —*v.i.* to think, talk, or write about questions of right and wrong: *... no one can moralize better after a misfortune has taken place* (Washington Irving).
—*v.t.* **1** to point out the lesson or inner meaning of: *But what said Jaques? Did he not moralize this spectacle?* (Shakespeare). **2** to improve the morals of: *... a social life passed in peaceful occupation is positively moralizing* (Herbert Spencer). —**mor′al|i|za′tion,** *n.* —**mor′al|iz′er,** *n.* —**mor′al|iz′ing|ly,** *adv.*

**mor|al|ly** (môr′ə lē, mor′-), *adv.* **1** in a moral manner; virtuously: *He tried to behave morally.* **2** in morals; as to morals: *The king was a good man morally, but too stupid for a position of importance.* **3** from a moral point of view; ethically: *things morally considered, morally speaking. What he did was morally wrong.* **4** practically; virtually: *I am morally sure that I locked the door.*

**moral philosophy,** = ethics.

**Moral Re-Armament,** a religious movement of the 1900's advocating a personal form of Christianity based on ethical and moral precepts; Buchmanism.

**Moral Re-Armer,** a supporter of Moral Re-Armament; Buchmanite.

**mor|als** (môr′əlz, mor′-), *n.pl.* See under **moral.**

**moral support,** approval but not active help: *We gave moral support to the team by cheering them enthusiastically.*

**moral turpitude,** *Law.* low or depraved conduct; conduct that offends the moral sense of a community or society.

**moral victory,** a defeat that has the effect on the mind that a victory would have: *Labor party increased its share of the vote and therefore claimed a moral victory* (New York Times).

**mo|rass** (mə ras′), *n.* **1** a piece of soft, low, wet ground; swamp; marsh: *The towing path was a morass of sticky brown mud* (Arnold Bennett). **SYN:** bog. **2** *Figurative.* a difficult, confused, or entangled state of affairs; puzzling mess: *The odd programme ... generally floundered in a morass of ineptitude* (Canadian Saturday Night). [< Dutch *moeras* < Old French *marais,* perhaps < Germanic (compare Old High German *marī*)]

**mo|rass|y** (mə ras′ē), *adj.* of or like a morass; marshy; swamp.

**mo|rat** (môr′at, mōr′-), *n.* an old-time drink made of honey flavored with mulberries. [< Medieval Latin *moratum* < Latin *mōrus* mulberry tree]

**mor|a|to|ri|um** (môr′ə tôr′ē əm, -tōr′-; mor′-), *n., pl.* **-to|ri|ums, -to|ri|a** (-tôr′ē ə, -tōr′-). **1** a legal authorization to delay payments of money due, as during an emergency. **2** the period during which such authorization is in effect. **3** a voluntary or negotiated temporary cessation of action on any issue: *... it is suggested that a moratorium on mechanical invention be declared until the lags of society have caught up* (Ogburn and Nimkoff).
[< New Latin *moratorium,* neuter of Latin *morātōrius;* see etym. under **moratory**]

**mor|a|to|ry** (môr′ə tôr′ē, -tōr′-; mor′-), *adj.* authorizing delay in payment: *a moratory bill or law in regard to mortgages.* [< Latin *morātōrius* tending to delay < *morārī* to delay < *mora* a delay, pause]

**Mo|ra|vi|an** (mô rā′vē ən, mō-), *adj., n.* —*adj.* **1** of or having to do with Moravia, its Slavic inhabitants, or their language. **2** of or having to do with the Protestant church organized in Moravia and Bohemia and based on the teachings of John Huss.
—*n.* **1** a native or inhabitant of Moravia. **2** the Slavic language of Moravia, a dialect of Czech. **3** a member of the Moravian Church.

**mo|ray** (môr′ā, mōr′-; mô rā′, mō-), *n.* any one of various fierce, often brilliantly colored eels of the tropical seas; muraena. One kind, found in the Mediterranean, is used as food. See picture under **eel.** [< Portuguese *moreia* < Latin *murēna,* variant of *muraena* < Greek *mýraina,* feminine of *mýros*]

**mor|bid** (môr′bid), *adj.* **1** unhealthy; not wholesome; sickly: *morbid fancies, a morbid look. A liking for horrors is morbid.* **SYN:** unsound, unwholesome. **2** caused by disease; characteristic of disease; diseased: *Cancer is a morbid growth.* **3** having to do with diseased parts: *morbid anatomy.* **4** horrible; gruesome; grisly: *the morbid details of a murder.* [< Latin *morbidus* < *morbus* disease] —**mor′bid|ly,** *adv.* —**mor′bid|ness,** *n.*

**mor|bi|dez|za** (môr′bē dāt′sä), *n. Italian.* the soft delicacy of living flesh as represented in painting or other forms of art.

**mor|bid|i|ty** (môr bid′ə tē), *n.* **1** morbid condition or quality: *He has been criticized for cynicism or coldness, as Zola was for morbidity and clinical detachment* (Observer). **2** the proportion of sickness in a certain group or locality: *Morbidity records show the health of the men in the armed forces at an all-time high* (New York Times).

**mor|bif|ic** (môr bif′ik), *adj.* causing disease: *morbific agents.* [< Late Latin *morbificus* < Latin *morbus* disease + *facere* make, cause] —**mor|bif′i|cal|ly,** *adv.*

**mor|ceau** (môr sō′), *n., pl.* **-ceaux** (-sō′). *French.* **1** a short literary or musical composition: *He sat down and produced the following morceau* (Tobias Smollett). **2** (literally) a small piece; morsel.

**mor|cel|late** (môr′sə lāt), *v.t.,* **-lat|ed, -lat|ing.** to divide into many pieces; break up. [< French *morceler* (with English *-ate*[1]) < *morceau* small piece < Old French *morsel;* see etym. under **morsel**] —**mor′cel|la′tion,** *n.*

**mor|da|cious** (môr dā′shəs), *adj.* **1** given to biting; biting: *They likewise assured us the bats were very mordacious* (George Forster). **2** *Figurative.* caustic; mordant: *A repose freed from ... mordacious malignity* (Isaac D'Israeli). [< Latin *mordāx, -ācis* (with English *-ous*) < *mordēre* to bite] —**mor|da′cious|ly,** *adv.*

**mor|dac|i|ty** (môr das′ə tē), *n.* = mordancy.

**mor|dan|cy** (môr′dən sē), *n.* mordant or biting quality: *Speeches denouncing Mr. Gladstone ... none of them equal in mordancy to the Duke of Somerset's recent jet of vitriol* (The Echo).

**mor|dant** (môr′dənt), *adj., n., v.* —*adj.* **1** biting; cutting; sarcastic: *a mordant sense of humor. The mordant criticism hurt his feelings. Restraining his tongue from mordant allusions to that "prancing, red-haired fellow"* (John Galsworthy). **SYN:** caustic. **2** that fixes colors in dyeing. **3** acute; burning: *mordant pain.* **4** = corrosive.
—*n.* **1** a substance that fixes colors in dyeing, such as tannic acid or a salt of a metal or metallic compound. A mordant acts by combining in a chemical reaction with a dye to form an insoluble compound that will not wash from the fibers, as of cloth or leather. **2** an acid that eats into metal, used in etching.
—*v.t.* to treat with a mordant: *The cloth may be ... mordanted as usual with tin, and then dyed* (Ernest Spon).
[< Old French *mordant,* present participle of *mordre* to bite < Latin *mordēre.* See etym. of doublet **mordent.**] —**mor′dant|ly,** *adv.*

**Mor|de|cai** (môr′də kī), *n.* the cousin of Esther, who helped her save the Jews from being destroyed by Haman (in the Bible, Esther 2-10).

***mor|dent** (môr′dənt), *n. Music.* **1** a grace note or embellishment consisting of the rapid alternation of a tone with another tone usually a half step below it. There are two kinds: the single (short) with one alternation, and the double (long) with two or more. **2** = pralltriller. [< German *Mordent* < Italian *mordente,* present participle of *mordere* to bite < Latin *mordēre.* See etym. of doublet **mordant.**]

***mordent**
definitions 1,2

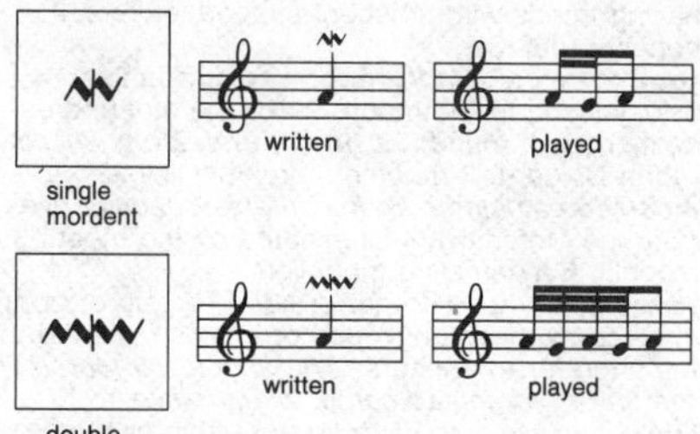


pralltriller:

**Mor|do|vi|an** (môr dō′vē ən), *n.* a member of a Finno-Ugric people of the Volga Valley of the Soviet Union.

**Mor|dred** (môr′dred), *n.* = Modred.

**more** (môr, mōr), *adj.* (*used as comparative of* **much** *and* **many,** *with the superlative* **most**), *n., adv.* —*adj.* **1** greater in quantity, amount, degree, number, or importance: *more cold, more men, more help. A foot is more than an inch.* **2** further; additional: *This plant needs more sun. Take more time if you need it.* **3** greater: *The more fool you, to believe such a tale.*
—*n.* **1** a greater quantity, amount, degree, or number: *The more they have, the more they want. Ten boys will not be enough for the football team; we will need more.* **2** an additional amount: *Tell me more about your camping trip.* **3** something of greater importance: *Kind hearts are more than coronets* (Tennyson).
—*adv.* **1** in a higher degree; to a greater extent: *A burn hurts more than a scratch does.* **2** in addition; farther; longer; again: *Take one step more. Sing once more.* **3** besides: *Drink a glass more.*
**be no more,** to be dead: *Cassius is no more* (Shakespeare).
**more and more, a** increasingly more: *A spokesman said that more and more vehicles were taking to the highways every year* (New York Times). **b** to an increasing degree: *The public is more and more growing to respect cleanliness and efficiency* (London Times).
**more or less, a** somewhat: *Most people are more or less selfish.* **b** nearly; about; approximately: *The distance is fifty miles, more or less.*
[Old English *māra*] —**more′ness,** *n.*
▶ **More** and **most** are often used to form comparatives and superlatives, usually with adjectives or adverbs of more than one syllable. For many there are two forms: *emptier* or *more empty; emptiest* or *most empty.*

**mo|reen** (mə rēn′), *n.* a heavy fabric of wool, or wool and cotton, usually with a watered or embossed finish, used especially for draperies and upholstery. [compare etym. under **moire**]

**mo|rel**[1] (mə rel′), *n.* any one of various small edible mushrooms, eaten as a table delicacy by gourmets. Morels have brown, spongy, pitted caps. [< French *morille* < Germanic (compare German *Morchel* < Old High German *morhila*)]

**mo|rel**[2] or **mo|relle** (mə rel′), *n.* any one of several nightshades, especially the black nightshade. [< Old French *morele,* perhaps ultimately < Latin *mōrum* mulberry]

**mo|rel|lo** (mə rel′ō), *n., pl.* **-los.** a kind of sour cherry having dark-red fruit and juice. [origin uncertain; perhaps < Flemish *amarelle* < Italian *amarella* (diminutive) < *amaro* bitter < Latin *amārus;* probably influenced by Italian *morello* dark-colored]

**mo|ren|do** (mō ren′dō), *adj. Music.* dying away; diminuendo at the end of a cadence. [< Italian *morendo,* present participle of *morire* to die < Latin *morī*]

**more|o|ver** (môr ō′vər, mōr-), *adv.* also; besides; in addition to that: *I don't want to go skating and, moreover, the ice is too thin. His power is absolute and, moreover, hereditary. The proposal was not well thought out; moreover, it would have been very expensive.* **SYN**: furthermore, further.

**more|pork** (môr pôrk′, mōr pōrk′), *n.* = mopoke.

**mo|res** (môr′āz, -ēz; mōr′-), *n.pl.* the traditional rules and customs of a group of people or a society; ways; manners. They are accepted as right and morally binding. *TV ... is having its inevitable effect on local manners and mores around the world* (Newsweek). **SYN**: folkways. [< Latin *mōrēs* manners, plural of *mōs, mōris* custom]

**Mo|resque** or **mo|resque** (mə resk′), *adj., n.* —*adj.* in the Moorish style; Moorish: *Moresque architecture, colorful moresque rugs.*
—*n.* Moorish design or decoration, as in architecture. Also, **Mauresque.**
[< French *moresque* < Italian *moresco* < *Moro* Moor < Latin *Maurus;* see etym. under **Moor**]

**Mor|gain le Fay** (môr′gān lə fā′, môr′gən), or **Morgain,** *n.* = Morgan le Fay.

**Mor|gan** (môr′gən), *n.* any one of an American breed of sturdy, relatively light horses that originated in Vermont, used as trotting horses and for work on farms. [< Justin *Morgan,* 1748-1798, of Vermont, who owned the first of the breed]

**Mor|ga|na** (môr gä′nə), *n.* = Morgan le Fay.

**mor|ga|nat|ic** (môr′gə nat′ik), *adj.* having to do with a form of marriage in which a man of high rank, such as a king or duke, marries a woman of lower rank with an agreement that neither she nor her children shall have any claim to his rank or property. [< New Latin *morganaticus* < Medieval Latin (*matrimonium ad*) *morganaticam* (marriage with) morning gift (instead of a share in the husband's possessions), ultimately an adaptation of Old High German *morgangeba* < *morgan* morning + *geba* gift] —**mor′ga|nat′i|cal|ly,** *adv.*

**mor|gan|ite** (môr′gə nīt), *n.* a rose-colored beryl. [< J. P. *Morgan,* 1837-1913, an American financier + *-ite*[1]]

**Mor|gan le Fay** (môr′gən lə fā′), *Arthurian Legend.* the half sister of King Arthur. She is usually represented as a scheming, evil fairy who seeks King Arthur's death. [< Old French *Morgain la Fee* Morgan the fairy (see etym. under **fay**[1]), probably translation of Italian *Fata Morgana*]

**mor|gen** (môr′gən), *n., pl.* **-gen** or **-gens. 1** a unit of land measure used in South Africa, and formerly used in the Netherlands and the Dutch colonies, hence in early New York, equal to about two acres. **2** a unit of land measure formerly used in Prussia, Norway, and Denmark, equal to about 2/3 of an acre. [American English < Dutch *morgen*]

**morgue** (môrg), *n.* **1** a place in which the bodies of persons unidentified or killed by accident or violence are kept until they can be identified or for investigation: *The* [*police*] *headquarters contains ... a morgue* (New York Times). **2** a reference library, especially of a newspaper or magazine office, in which clippings and other materials are kept. [< French *morgue* (originally) a building in Paris used as a morgue; origin uncertain]

**mor|i|bund** (môr′ə bund, mor′-), *adj., n.* —*adj.* at the point of death or extinction; dying: *a moribund person,* (*Figurative.*) *a moribund political party.*
—*n.* a dying person.
[< Latin *moribundus* < *morī* to die] —**mor′i|bund|ly,** *adv.*

**mor|i|bun|di|ty** (môr′ə bun′də tē, mor′-), *n.* moribund condition.

**mo|rin** (môr′in, mōr′-), *n.* a substance obtained from fustic wood, used as a yellow dye, and in chemistry as a highly reliable test reagent for aluminum. *Formula:* $C_{15}H_{10}O_7$ [< French *morine* < Latin *mōrus* mulberry + French *-ine* -in]

**mo|ri|on**[1] (môr′ē on, mōr′-), *n.* a helmet without a visor, shaped like a hat, with a comb-shaped crest and an upturned rim forming a peak in front, worn especially by Spanish foot soldiers in the 1500's and 1600's. [< French *morion* < Spanish *morrion* < *morra* top of the head; origin uncertain]

**mo|ri|on**[2] (môr′ē on, mōr′-), *n.* a dark-brown or nearly black, smoky quartz. [< a misreading of Latin *mormorion,* in early editions of Pliny's *Natural History*]

**Mo|ri|o|ri** (mō′rē ō′rē), *n., pl.* **-ri** or **-ris.** a member of an extinct aboriginal people of New Zealand related to the Maoris and other Polynesians. The Moriori were conquered by the Maoris between A.D. 950 and 1350.

**Mo|ris|co** (mə ris′kō), *adj., n., pl.* **-cos** or **-coes.** —*adj.* Moorish; Moresque: *It was of a composite architecture, between the Morisco and the Spanish* (Frederick Marryat).
—*n.* a Moor, especially one of the Moors in Spain.
[< Spanish *morisco* < *moro* Moor < Latin *Maurus;* see etym. under **Moor**]

**mo|ri|tu|ri te sa|lu|ta|mus** (môr′ə tyůr′ī tē sal′yə tā′məs, mōr′-), *Latin.* we who are about to die salute thee (the salute of Roman gladiators).

**Mor|mon** (môr′mən), *n., adj.* —*n.* a member of the Church of Jesus Christ of Latter-day Saints, founded by Joseph Smith in 1830. One of the sacred books of this church is called the Book of Mormon.
—*adj.* of or having to do with the Mormons or their religion.
[American English < *Mormon,* the name according to Mormons of the author of "The Book of Mormon"]

**mormon** or **Mormon cricket,** a type of grasshopper (rather than a true cricket), dark-brown to black, two inches long, and highly destructive to all crops. It is native to the western United States. *Hoppers and Mormon crickets chewed up $37 million of ... crops* (Wall Street Journal).

**Mor|mon|ism** (môr′mə niz əm), *n.* the religious system of the Mormons.

**mor|my|rid** (mor mī′rid), *n., adj.* —*n.* any one of a group of African freshwater teleost fishes with a long snout bent downward and electric organs in the tail.
—*adj.* of or having to do with mormyrids.
[< New Latin *Mormyridae* the family name < Latin *mormyrus* a sea fish]

**morn** (môrn), *n.* **1** *Archaic.* morning: *the golden light of morn* (Thomas Hood). **2** *Scottish.* the next day; morrow. [Middle English *morwen,* Old English *morgen*]

**mor|nay sauce,** or **mor|nay** (môr nā′), *n.* a white sauce flavored with sharp cheese. [< Philippe de *Mornay,* 1549-1623, a French Protestant leader]

**morn|ing** (môr′ning), *n., adj.* —*n.* **1** the early part of the day, ending at noon: *We spent the morning studying; then went to lunch and took a walk in the afternoon.* **2** *Figurative.* the first or early part of anything: *the morning of life. A king lived long ago, in the morning of the world* (Robert Browning). **SYN**: dawn. **3** the dawn; daybreak: *Far up the solitary morning smote the streaks of virgin snow* (Tennyson). **4** the first part of the next day or morrow: *Wait until morning. I'll come in the morning.*
—*adj.* **1** of or in the morning: *a morning walk, the morning paper.* **2** of the first or early part of anything: *Young he appear'd, for on his cheek there shone the morning glow of health* (Robert Southey).
[Middle English *morwening* < *morwen* morn + *-ing*[1]; patterned on *evening*]

**morn|ing-af|ter** (môr′ning af′tər, -äf′-), *n., pl.* **morn|ings-af|ter.** *Informal.* the morning following a night of heavy drinking of alcoholic liquor; hangover.

**morning-after pill,** an oral contraceptive that prevents pregnancy after fertilization by stopping the fertilized egg from reaching or becoming attached to the uterus.

**morning coat,** = cutaway.

**morn|ing-glo|ry** (môr′ning glôr′ē, -glōr′-), *n., pl.* **-ries. 1** a climbing vine with heart-shaped leaves and funnel-shaped flowers of blue, purple, red, pink, or white. Morning-glories bloom early in the day. **2** the flower.

* **morning-glory family,** a group of dicotyledonous herbs, shrubs, and small trees, having alternate leaves, bisexual, regular flowers, and often a milky juice. The family includes the morning-glory, sweet potato, dodder, and convolvulus.

**morning gown,** = dressing gown.

**morning gun,** a gun fired, usually at dawn, as a signal for reveille or the raising of the flag.

**morning line,** *Informal.* the probable odds against the horses running at any track, published the morning of the race.

**morning prayer,** a service for morning worship in the Church of England and the Episcopal Church; matins.

**morning room,** a room used as a sitting room during the early part of the day.

**morn|ings** (môr′ningz), *adv. Informal.* during the morning; in the morning: [*He*] *trains the colt and gallops him mornings* (New Yorker).

**morning sickness,** nausea and vomiting in the morning, a common symptom of pregnancy.

**morning star, 1** a bright planet, especially Venus, when seen in the eastern sky before sunrise; daystar: *Venus, the familiar morning and evening star, is the brightest of the planets* (Robert H. Baker). **2** an old form of weapon consisting of a ball of metal, usually set with spikes, either mounted upon a long handle or staff or slung to one by a thong or chain.

**morn|ing|tide** (môr′ning tīd′), *n. Poetic.* morning.

**Mo|ro** (môr′ō, mōr′-), *n., pl.* **-ros,** *adj.* —*n.* **1** a member of any one of the Moslem Malay tribes in Mindanao and other southern Philippine Islands. **2** any one of the Austronesian languages of these tribes.
—*adj.* of or having to do with these people or their languages.
[< Spanish *moro* a Moor < Latin *Maurus;* see etym. under **Moor**]

**Mo|roc|can** (mə rok′ən), *adj., n.* —*adj.* of or having to do with Morocco or its people.
—*n.* a native or inhabitant of Morocco.

**mo|roc|co** (mə rok′ō), *n., pl.* **-cos. 1** a fine leather made from goatskin tanned with vegetable extracts, used in binding books. **2** leather made in imitation of this. [< *Morocco,* a country in Africa, where it was first made]

**morocco leather,** = morocco.

**mo|ron** (môr′on, mōr′-), *n.* **1** a person born with such a weak mind that he can be trained to do only routine tasks, but probably can be trained to read; person who does not develop beyond the mental age of eight to twelve years. A moron is less mentally deficient than an imbecile or idiot. **2** *Informal.* a stupid or annoyingly ignorant person; dullard; dunce. [American English < Greek *mōron,* neuter of *mōrós* foolish, dull]

**mo|ron|ic** (mə ron′ik), *adj.* of or like a moron: *Miss Winters goes about her moronic chores quite convincingly* (New Yorker). —**mo|ron′i|cal|ly,** *adv.*

**mo|ron|ism** (môr′on iz əm, mōr′-), *n.* the condition of being a moron; moronity.

**mo|ron|i|ty** (mə ron′ə tē), *n.* = moronism.

**mo|rose** (mə rōs′), *adj.* **1** gloomy; sullen; ill-humored: *a morose person, a morose scowl.* **SYN**: moody, surly, gruff. **2** harsh: *morose doctrines.* [< Latin *mōrōsus* (originally) set in one's ways < *mōs, mōris* habit, custom] —**mo|rose′ly,** *adv.* —**mo|rose′ness,** *n.*

**mo|ros|i|ty** (mə ros′ə tē), *n.* the state of being morose; moroseness.

**morph**[1] (môrf), *n.* a minimum meaningful unit or group of speech sounds: *Any morph can be recorded as a phoneme or a pattern of phonemes* (George P. Faust). [apparently back formation < *morpheme*]

**morph**[2] (môrf), *n. Biology.* a variant form of an animal or plant species: *There were also differences between the various "morphs", i.e., winged or wingless, viviparous or oviparous* (New Scientist). [< Greek *morphḗ* form]

**morph.,** morphology.

**mor|phac|tin** (môr fak′tin), *n.* any one of a group of chemical compounds derived from fluorene and carboxylic acid that affect the morphogenesis of higher plants, inhibiting plant growth when applied in certain concentrations or promoting the development of ovaries into fruit without pollination. [< *morph*(ogenesis) + *act*(ive) + *-in*]

* **morning-glory family**

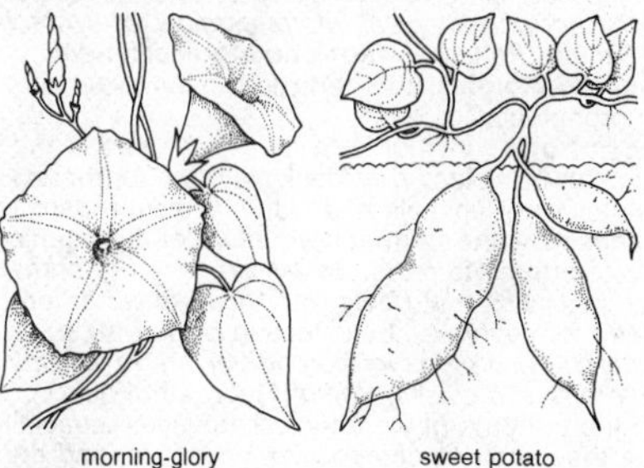

morning-glory    sweet potato

**Mor|phe|an** (môr′fē ən), *adj.* of or belonging to Morpheus.

**mor|pheme** (môr′fēm), *n. Linguistics.* the small-

**Pronunciation Key:** hat, āge, cãre, fär; let, ēqual, tėrm; it, īce; hot, ōpen, ôrder; oil, out; cup, půt, rüle; child; long; thin; ᴛʜen; zh, measure; ə represents **a** in about, **e** in taken, **i** in pencil, **o** in lemon, **u** in circus.

est part of a word that has meaning of its own. Morphemes may be words, prefixes, suffixes, or endings that show inflection. In the word *carelessness,* the morphemes are *care, -less,* and *-ness. A morpheme does not necessarily* CONSIST *of phonemes, but all morphemes are statable in terms of phonemes* (H. A. Gleason, Jr.). [< French *morphème* < Greek *morphḗ* form; patterned on French *phonème* phoneme]

**mor|phe|mic** (môr fē′mik), *adj.* of, having to do with, or characteristic of a morpheme: *These three bound forms /iz, s, z/ may be termed allomorphs or morphemic variants* (Simeon Potter). —**mor|phe′mi|cal|ly,** *adv.*

**mor|phe|mics** (môr fē′miks), *n. Linguistics.* the systematic study of the minimum meaningful elements of language and their characteristics in living speech.

**Mor|phe|us** (môr′fē əs, -fyüs), *n. Greek Mythology.* the god of dreams; popularly, the god of sleep. The name was first used by Ovid and is popular in literary references.
**in the arms of Morpheus,** asleep; sleeping: *He was so tired that within minutes of lying down he was in the arms of Morpheus.*
[< Latin *Morpheus,* proper name meaning "fashioner" or "molder," coined by Ovid from Greek *morphḗ* form, shape (alluding to the forms seen in dreams)]

**mor|phi|a** (môr′fē ə), *n.* = morphine.

**mor|phic** (môr′fik), *adj.* = morphological.

**mor|phine** (môr′fēn, -fin), *n.* a drug made from opium, used in medicine to dull pain and to cause sleep. It is a bitter, colorless or white, crystalline alkaloid. *Morphine and heroin, for example, do not give normal persons the "kick" and pleasant sensations they are supposed to give* (Science News Letter). *Formula:* $C_{17}H_{19}NO_3{\cdot}H_2O$ [< French *morphine,* or German *Morphin* < Latin *Morpheus* Morpheus (because of its sleep-inducing properties)]

**mor|phin|ism** (môr′fə niz əm), *n.* **1** a disordered condition caused by the habitual use of morphine. **2** the morphine habit; addiction to the use of morphine.

**mor|phin|ist** (môr′fə nist), *n.* a habitual user of morphine; morphine addict.

**mor|phi|no|ma|ni|a** (môr′fə nə mā′nē ə), *n.* uncontrollable craving for morphine.

**mor|pho** (môr′fō), *n., pl.* **-phos** or **-phoes.** a large South American butterfly with iridescent colors, especially a brilliant blue, on the wings. [< New Latin *Morpho* the genus name < Greek *Morphṓ,* an epithet of Aphrodite, (literally) shapely < *morphḗ* form, shape]

**mor|pho|gen|e|sis** (môr′fə jen′ə sis), *n. Biology.* the origin and evolution of morphological characters; the growth and differentiation of cells and tissues during development.

**mor|pho|ge|net|ic** (môr′fə jə net′ik), *adj.* of or having to do with morphogenesis. —**mor′pho|ge|net′i|cal|ly,** *adv.*

**mor|pho|ge|net|i|cist** (môr′fə jə net′ə sist), *n.* a person who studies morphogenesis.

**mor|pho|gen|ic** (môr′fə jen′ik), *adj.* = morphogenetic.

**mor|pho|line** (môr′fə lēn, -lin), *n.* a viscous liquid of basic properties, used as a solvent for dyes, waxes, and resins, as a reagent, and as an emulsifying agent. *Formula:* $C_4H_9ON$

**mor|pho|log|ic** (môr′fə loj′ik), *adj.* = morphological.

**mor|pho|log|i|cal** (môr′fə loj′ə kəl), *adj.* of or having to do with morphology; relating to form; structural: *Every segment of every effective utterance has some degree of meaning at all levels, whether phonological, morphological, or syntactic* (Simeon Potter). —**mor′pho|log′i|cal|ly,** *adv.*

**mor|phol|o|gist** (môr fol′ə jist), *n.* an expert in morphology.

**mor|phol|o|gy** (môr fol′ə jē), *n., pl.* **-gies. 1** the branch of biology that deals with the form and structure of animals and plants without regard to function. **2** the form and structure of an organism or of one of its parts. **3a** the branch of grammar or linguistics that deals with forms of words and their formation, as by inflection or derivation: *... the first two steps in morphology are to identify morphs and classify them* (George P. Faust). **b** the patterns of words in a language, especially as they apply to composition, inflection, and derivation: *So likewise, the syntax must be stated in terms of the morpheme sequences described in the morphology* (H. A. Gleason, Jr.). **4** the study of forms in any science, as in physical geography or geology. [< Greek *morphḗ* form + English *-logy*]

**mor|pho|met|ric** (môr′fə met′rik), *adj.* of or having to do with morphometry.

**mor|phom|e|try** (môr fom′ə trē), *n.* the measurement of the external form of any object: *... has worked out in detail the morphometry of the Lake of Geneva* (Nature). [< Greek *morphḗ* form + English *-metry*]

**mor|pho|pho|neme** (môr′fə fō′nēm), *n.* any one of a set of phonemes that is a variant of a morpheme. *Example:* The phonemes *-s, -z,* and *-iz* are morphophonemes of the plural morpheme *-s* in such words as *books, dogs,* and *houses.*

**mor|pho|pho|ne|mic** (môr′fō fə nē′mik), *adj.* **1** of or having to do with morphophonemes or the phonemic variations of morphemes: *The plurals of substantives and the third person present singular forms of verbs show interesting morphophonemic features in English* (Simeon Potter). **2** of or having to do with morphophonemics. —**mor′pho|pho|ne′mi|cal|ly,** *adv.*

**mor|pho|pho|ne|mics** (môr′fō fə nē′miks), *n.* the study of the variations in the phonemic structure of morphemes.

**mor|pho|pho|no|log|i|cal** (môr′fə fō′nə loj′ə kəl), *adj.* of, having to do with or characteristic of morphophonology.

**mor|pho|pho|nol|o|gy** (môr′fə fō nol′ə jē), *n.* the study of the phonological variations occurring in morphemes.

**mor|pho|sis** (môr fō′sis), *n., pl.* **-ses** (-sēz). *Biology.* the manner of formation or development of an organism or part. [< New Latin *morphosis* < Greek *mórphōsis* < *morphoûn* to form (< *morphḗ* form) + *-ōsis* -osis]

**mor|ral** (mə ral′), *n. Southwestern U.S.* a feedbag. [< Spanish *morral*]

**mor|ris** (môr′is, mor′-), *n.* = morris dance.

***morris** or **Morris chair,** an armchair with removable cushions and an adjustable back. [< William *Morris,* 1834-1896, an English artist and poet, who invented it]

***morris chair**

**morris dance,** an old English folk dance performed chiefly on May Day by people in fancy, traditional costume. The dancers frequently represented Friar Tuck, Maid Marian, and other characters of the Robin Hood legend. [earlier *moreys,* variant of *Moorish*]

**mor|ris-pike** (môr′is pīk′, mor′-), *n.* a kind of pike (military weapon), no longer in use. [< obsolete *morys,* a variant of *Moorish*]

**Morris Plan Bank,** *U.S.* a private industrial bank that lends small amounts of money upon a note signed by the borrower and two acceptable endorsers, without other security than prospective wages. Only a few Morris Plan Banks still operate.

**mor|ro** (mor′ō; *Spanish* môr′rō), *n., pl.* **mor|ros** (mor′ōz; *Spanish* môr′rōs). a round hill, hillock, or promontory. [< Spanish *morro* round object]

**mor|row** (môr′ō, mor′-), *n.* **1** the following day: *Whereas ye know not what shall be on the morrow* (James 4:14). **2** *Figurative.* the time immediately following a particular event: *On the morrow of a long and costly war ...* (John Fiske). **3** *Archaic.* morning. [Middle English *morwe,* variant of *morwen* morn]

**Mors** (môrz), *n.* death personified as a god by the ancient Romans, identified with the Greek Thanatos. [< Latin *Mors*]

**morse¹** (môrs), *n.* a clasp or fastening, as of a cope, often made of gold or silver and set with jewels. [< Old French *mors* < Latin *morsus* buckle clasp < *mordēre* bite]

**morse²** (môrs), *n.* = walrus. [< Lapp *morsa,* or Finnish *mursu*]

**Morse** (môrs), *adj., n.* —***adj.* 1** designating or having to do with the Morse code or a telegraph system using it. **2** having to do with a telegraphic code similar to Morse code.
—*n.* **1** = Morse code. **2** any similar code.
[< Samuel F. B. *Morse,* 1791-1872, American inventor of the telegraph]

***Morse** or **morse code,** a system by which letters, numbers, punctuation, and other signs are expressed by dots, dashes, and spaces or by wigwags of a flag, long and short sounds, or flashes of light. Morse code is now used mainly in signaling, and in some telegraphy. See picture below.

**mor|sel** (môr′səl), *n., v.,* **-seled, -sel|ing** or (*especially British*) **-selled, -sel|ling.** —*n.* **1** a small bite; mouthful: *having not eaten a morsel for some hours* (Jonathan Swift). *Take a morsel of our bread and cheese* (Hawthorne). **2** a small piece; fragment; bit; scrap: *a morsel of chalk, a morsel of earth.* SYN: mite, particle. **3** a dish of food; tidbit: *a dainty morsel.* **4** *Figurative.* something to be enjoyed, disposed of, or endured: *to find a person a tough morsel. This decision was a bitter morsel.*
—*v.t.* to divide into small pieces; distribute (property) in small parcels.
[< Old French *morsel* (diminutive) < *mors* a bite, ultimately < Latin *mordēre* to bite]

**Morse lamp,** a blinking lamp for flashing signals that stand for the dots, dashes, and spaces used in the Morse code.

**Morse telegraph,** the electric telegraph in general use.

**mort¹** (môrt), *n.* **1** a note sounded on a hunting horn at the death of a deer. **2** *Obsolete.* death. [< Old French *mort* death (< Latin *mors, mortis*) and *morte* dead < Latin *mortuus*]

**mort²** (môrt), *n., adv. British Dialect.* —*n.* a great quantity or number. [origin uncertain; perhaps < adjective use of *mortal*]

**mort³** (môrt), *n.* a salmon in its third year. [origin unknown]

**mor|ta|del|la** (môr′tə del′ə), *n.* a large cooked and smoked sausage made of chopped beef, pork, and pork fat and seasoned with garlic and pepper. [< Italian *mortadella* (diminutive) < Latin *murtātum* a kind of sausage]

**mor|tal** (môr′təl), *adj., n., adv.* —***adj.* 1** sure to die sometime: *all mortal creatures. Do you think your daughter is not mortal like other people?* (Charles Reade). **2** of man; of mortals: *Mortal flesh has many pains and diseases.* SYN: human. **3** of or characterized by death: *a mortal year.* **4** causing death; deadly; fatal: *a mortal wound, a mortal illness.* SYN: lethal. See syn. under **fatal. 5** to the death; implacable; relentless: *a mortal enemy, a mortal battle, mortal hatred.* **6** *Figurative.* very great; deadly; dire: *The spy lived in mortal fear of being discovered.* **7** causing death of the soul (in Roman Catholic use): *Murdering your brother would be a mortal sin.* **8** *Informal.* **a** long and tedious: *And so on for 940 mortal pages* (Edward G. Bulwer-Lytton). **b** conceivable: *By no mortal means* (Ben Jonson).
—*n.* **1** a being that is sure to die sometime. All living creatures are mortals. **2** a human being; man; person: *No mortal could have survived the fire. No mortal should strive against God. What fools these mortals be* (Shakespeare).
—***adv.*** *Dialect.* extremely; excessively: *Missis was mortal angry* (Thackeray).
[< Latin *mortālis* < *mors, mortis* death]

**mor|tal|i|ty** (môr tal′ə tē), *n., pl.* **-ties. 1** the condition of being sure to die sometime; mortal nature, character, or existence: *Life's gayest scenes speak man's mortality* (Edward Young). **2** loss of life on a large scale; frequency of death: *The mortality from automobile accidents is very serious. Years of dearth ... are generally among the common people, years of sickness and mortality* (Adam Smith). **3** the number of deaths in proportion to the population or to a specified part of a population; death rate: *The mortality from typhoid fever is decreasing.* **4** deadliness; power to kill. **5** the human race; humanity: *Young Sir Harry is about as puny and feeble a little bit of mortality as I ever saw* (Harriet Beecher Stowe). **6** *Obsolete.* death: *Here on my knee I beg mortality* (Shakespeare).

**mortality table,** a table stating the number of people of a given age that may be expected to die during a given period, survive to a certain age, etc.; life table.

**mor|tal|ize** (môr′tə līz), *v.t.,* **-ized, iz|ing.** to make mortal; consider or represent as mortal: *In later times he [Faunus] was mortalized like all the*

**continental code or international Morse code**

·— a  —··· b  —·—· c  —·· d  · e  ··—· f  ——· g
···· h  ·· i  ·——— j  —·— k  ·—·· l  —— m  —· n
——— o  ·——· p  ——·— q  ·—· r  ··· s  — t  ··— u
···— v  ·—— w  —··— x  —·—— y  ——·· z

***Morse code**

*other Italian gods* (Thomas Keightley).

**mor|tal|ly** (môr′tə lē), *adv.* **1** so as to cause death; fatally: *mortally wounded.* **2** bitterly; grievously: *mortally offended. Whoe'er it be That tells my faults, I hate him mortally* (Alexander Pope). **3** *Informal.* very greatly; extremely; exceedingly: *mortally ugly.* **4** as a mortal: *Yet I was mortally brought forth, and am No other than I appear* (Shakespeare).

**mortal mind**, **1** (in Christian Science) the erroneous beliefs of people unguided by Christian Science. **2** human intelligence and feelings.

**mortal sin**, (in Christian theology) a sin so bad that it causes the death of the soul: *Murder and blasphemy are mortal sins.*

**mor|tar[1]** (môr′tər), *n., v.* —*n.* a mixture of sand and water with lime, cement, or often both, for holding bricks or stones together.
—*v.t.* to plaster with mortar; fix or hold together with mortar: (*Figurative*). *There was a real danger that the U.S.-British-French united front that Herter mortared together ... might show cracks* (Time).
[< Old French *mortier* < Latin *mortārium* vessel for mixing or pounding; the material prepared in it]

***mor|tar[2]** (môr′tər), *n., v.* —*n.* **1** a bowl of porcelain, glass, brass, hardwood, or other very hard material in which substances may be pounded to a powder with a pestle. **2** any one of various mechanical devices in which limestone, shale, or other substances may be pounded or ground. **3a** a very short cannon for shooting shells at high angles over a short range, so as to drop on the target from above. Mortars have a wide, unrifled barrel and a low muzzle velocity. The most common type of mortar in use today is the trench mortar. **b** a similar apparatus for shooting fireworks or lifelines.
—*v.t.* to fire mortars at; to hit with mortar fire: *An airborne battalion ... got badly mortared* (New Yorker).
—*v.i.* to fire mortars.
[noun (def. 1) Old English *mortere* < Latin *mortārium;* see etym. under **mortar**[1]; (def. 2) < Middle French, Old French *mortier* < Latin; (def. 3) < Old French *mortier* cannon]

***mortar[2]**
definition 1

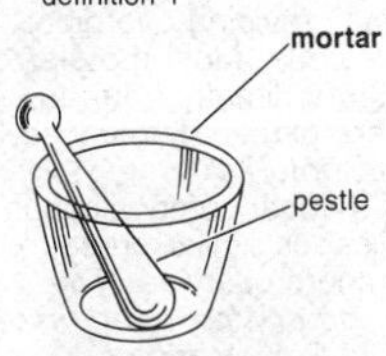


***mor|tar|board** (môr′tər bôrd′, -bōrd′), *n.* **1** a flat, square board used by masons to hold mortar while working with it. **2** an academic cap with a close-fitting crown topped by a stiff, flat, cloth-covered square piece from which a tassel usually hangs, worn at graduation exercises and on other academic occasions.

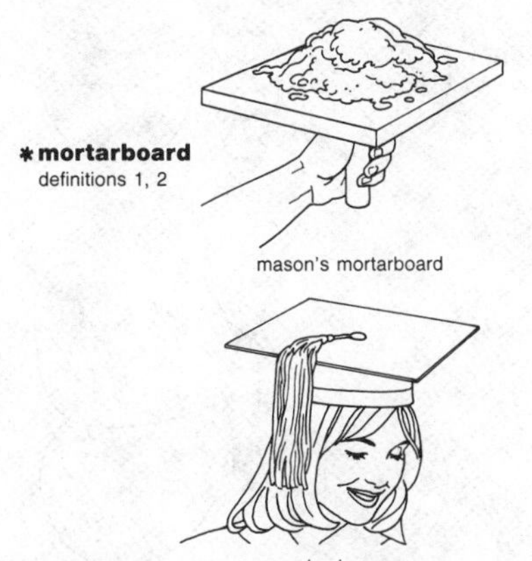


***mortarboard**
definitions 1, 2

**mort|gage** (môr′gij), *n., v.,* **-gaged, -gag|ing.** —*n.* **1** a claim on property, given as security to a person, bank, or firm that has loaned money, in case the money is not repaid when due. **2** the formal document that gives such a claim. **3** the rights conferred by it, or the state of the property conveyed.
—*v.t.* **1** to give a lender a claim to (one's property) in case a debt is not paid when due: *to mortgage a house.* **2** *Figurative.* to put under some obligation; pledge: *Faust mortgaged his soul to the Devil. He would not mortgage an inch of his independence by asking a favour from a minister* (Edward G. Bulwer-Lytton).
[< Old French *mortgage* < *mort* dead (see etym. under **mort**[1]) + *gage* pledge, gage[1]]

**mort|ga|gee** (môr′gi jē′), *n.* a person to whom property is mortgaged; the holder of a mortgage.

**mort|gag|er** or **mort|ga|gor** (môr′gi jər), *n.* a person who mortgages his property.

**mor|tice** (môr′tis), *n., v.t.,* **-ticed, -tic|ing.** = mortise.

**mor|ti|cian** (môr tish′ən), *n.* = undertaker.
[American English < *mort*(uary) + *-ician,* as in *logician*]

**mor|tif|er|ous** (môr tif′ər əs), *adj.* bringing or producing death; deadly. —**mor|tif′er|ous|ly,** *adv.* —**mor|tif′er|ous|ness,** *n.*

**mor|ti|fi|ca|tion** (môr′tə fə kā′shən), *n.* **1** a feeling of shame; humiliation; chagrin: *mortification at having spilled food on the tablecloth.* SYN: embarrassment. **2** a cause or source of shame, humiliation, or chagrin: *It is one of the vexatious mortifications of a studious man to have his thoughts disordered by a tedious wit* (Roger L'Estrange). **3** the action of mortifying or state of being mortified: *the mortification of the body by fasting. I intend to live in continual mortification* (Jonathan Edwards). **4** the death of tissues in one part of the body only; gangrene; necrosis: *His leg had to be amputated because mortification had set in.*

**mor|ti|fy** (môr′tə fī), *v.,* **-fied, -fy|ing.** —*v.t.* **1** to wound (a person's feelings); make (a person) feel humbled and ashamed; humiliate: *He mortified his parents with his bad behavior.* SYN: chagrin, embarrass. See syn. under **ashamed.** **2** to overcome (bodily desires and feelings) by pain and going without things: *The saint mortified his body.* **3** to cause (a part of the body) to become affected with gangrene or necrosis. **4** *Obsolete.* to reduce in strength or force; weaken. —*v.i.* **1** to become gangrenous; die or decay: *The injured foot has mortified and must be amputated. We had ... their fingers and toes to thaw, and take care of, lest they should mortify and fall off* (Daniel Defoe). **2** to overcome bodily desires and feelings by pain and going without things: *Imagine him mortifying with his barrel of oysters in dreary solitude* (Jane Austen). [< Old French *mortifier* < Latin *mortificare* to kill, subdue < *mors, mortis* death + *facere* make] —**mor′ti|fi′er,** *n.* —**mor′ti|fy|ing|ly,** *adv.*

**mor|tise** (môr′tis), *n., v.,* **-tised, -tis|ing.** —*n.* **1** a hole cut in or through one piece of wood to receive the tenon on another piece so as to form a joint. **2** a groove or slot, as for the reception or passage of a rope or an adjustable pin.
—*v.t.* **1** to fasten by a mortise and tenon: *Good furniture is mortised together, not nailed.* **2** to fasten or join securely. **3** to cut a mortise in; provide with a mortise.
[< Old French *mortaise,* perhaps < Arabic *murtazz* be fastened]

**mort|main** (môrt′mān), *n. Law.* **1** the condition of lands or tenements held without the right to sell or give them away; inalienable possession. **2** the possession, usually perpetual, of land by a church, school, or similar corporate body. [< Middle French *morte mayn,* Old French *mortemain,* loan translation of Medieval Latin *mortus manus* dead hand (referring to corporations not being persons)]

**mor|tu|ar|y** (môr′chů er′ē), *n., pl.* **-ar|ies,** *adj.* —*n.* **1** a building or room where dead bodies are kept until burial or cremation. **2** = morgue. **3** a gift to the priest of a parish from the estate of a dead parishioner.
—*adj.* **1** of death, burial, or mourning: *a mortuary service or chapel.* **2** *Figurative.* sad; gloomy; funereal: *The cities are drab, but the countryside is mortuary* (Harper's).
[< Latin *mortuārius* having to do with the dead < *mortuus* dead, past participle of *morī* to die, related to *mors, mortis* death]

**mortuary science**, the methods and techniques used in embalming corpses.

**mor|u|la** (môr′yů lə, -ů-), *n., pl.* **-lae** (-lē). the spherical mass of blastomeres forming the embryo of many animals, just after the segmentation of the ovum and before the formation of a blastula. [< New Latin *morula* (diminutive) < Latin *mōrum* mulberry]

**mor|u|lar** (môr′yů lər, -ů-), *adj.* of or having to do with a morula.

**mor|u|la|tion** (môr′yů lā′shən, -ů-), *n.* the formation of a morula.

**mos.**, months.

**MOS** (no periods), **1** *U.S.* an army military occupational specialty (designated in the service record of a soldier by a serial number or numbers). **2** metal oxide semiconductor (used in integrated circuits, especially of the large-scale integration type).

**mo|sa|ic** (mō zā′ik), *n., adj., v.,* **-icked, -ick|ing.** —*n.* **1** decoration made of small pieces of stone, glass, or wood of different colors, inlaid to form a picture or design: *Most of the mosaic with its dozens of pictures had chipped out of the floor of the ancient temple.* **2** such a picture or design. Mosaics are used in the floors, walls, or ceilings of buildings, for tabletops, etc. **3** the art or process of making such a picture or design: *This reflected the inferior role the Venetians had been forced to accept in all the arts but mosaic* (New Yorker). **4** *Figurative.* anything like a mosaic: *His music is a mosaic of folk melodies.* **5** a group of aerial photographs put together to form a continuous photograph of an area. **6** mosaic disease.
—*adj.* formed by, having to do with, or resembling a mosaic.
—*v.t.* **1** to combine, as in mosaic. **2** to form like mosaic. **3** to decorate with or as if with mosaics: *... brilliantly mosaicked piles of folded Persian rugs* (Atlantic).
[< Medieval Latin *mosaicus,* variant of *musaicus* having to do with music, the Muses; artistic]
—**mo|sa′i|cal|ly,** *adv.*

**Mo|sa|ic** (mō zā′ik), *adj.* of or having to do with Moses or the Mosaic law. [< New Latin *Mosaicus* < Latin *Mōsēs* < Greek *Mōsês* < Hebrew *moshe*]

**Mo|sa|i|cal** (mō zā′ə kəl), *adj.* = Mosaic.

**mosaic disease**, any one of various virus diseases of tobacco and other plants in which the leaves become spotted or mottled.

**mosaic gold**, **1** a yellow compound, stannic sulfide, used in gilding. *Formula:* $SnS_2$ **2** = ormolu.

**mo|sa|i|cism** (mō zā′ə siz əm), *n. Biology.* the presence of different or antagonistic genetic characteristics in adjacent cells of the body, chiefly due to faulty cell division.

**mo|sa|i|cist** (mō zā′ə sist), *n.* a maker or seller of mosaics.

**Mosaic law**, **1** the ancient law of the Israelites, ascribed to Moses and contained chiefly in the Pentateuch or the Torah. **2** the part of the Bible where these laws are stated; Pentateuch.

**mosaic vision**, the manner of vision of compound eyes, as of insects or other arthropods, in which the visual impression is composed of the impressions of a number of the individual facets of the eye.

**mo|sa|saur** (mō′sə sôr, mos′ə-), *n.* a prehistoric marine lizard which reached forty feet in length.
[< New Latin *Mosasaurus* the genus name < Latin *Mosa,* the river *Meuse* (close to Maastricht, site of the fossil remains) + Greek *saûros* lizard]

**mo|sa|sau|rus** (mō′sə sôr′əs), *n., pl.* **-sau|ri** (-sôr′ī). = mosasaur.

**mos|chate** (mos′kāt, -kit), *adj.* smelling like musk; musky. [< New Latin *moschatus,* variant of Late Latin *muscatus* < Latin *muscus* musk]

**mos|cha|tel** (mos′kə tel′, mos′kə tel), *n.* an inconspicuous perennial plant of uncertain classification but related to the honeysuckle, having greenish or yellowish flowers with a musky smell. [< French *moscatelle* < Italian *moscatella* < *moscato* musk < Late Latin *muscus.* See related etym. at **muscatel.**]

**Mos|co|vite** (mos′kə vīt), *n. Especially British.* Muscovite.

**Mo|sel** (mō′zəl), *n. German.* Moselle.

**Mo|selle** or **mo|selle** (mō zel′), *n.* a white wine, usually light and dry, produced along the Moselle river in Germany: *Her preference in wines is a light and sweet one such as moselle or sauterne* (Sunday Times). Also, *German* **Mosel.**

**Mo|ses** (mō′ziz, -zis), *n.***1** the great leader and lawgiver of the Israelites, who led them out of Egypt and through the desert to within sight of the Promised Land, and received the Ten Commandments from God on Mount Sinai. The last four books of the Pentateuch tell the life and achievements of Moses. **2** a person like Moses; great leader or lawgiver. [< Latin *Mōsēs;* see etym. under **Mosaic**]

**Moses basket**, *Especially British.* a bassinet. [so called from the small ark into which Moses was put as a baby by his mother (in the Bible, Exodus 2:3-5)]

**mo|sey** (mō′zē), *v.i.,* **-seyed, -sey|ing.** *U.S. Slang.* to move along or away slowly; saunter; amble: *I'll mosey along now* (Mark Twain). [American English; origin uncertain]

**mo|shav** (mō shäv′), *n., pl.* **-sha|vim** (-shä vēm′). an Israeli cooperative settlement with independent farms of equal size. [< Hebrew *mōshābh* (literally) dwelling place]

**Mos|lem** (moz′ləm, mos′-), *n., pl.* **-lems** or **-lem,** *adj.* —*n.* a follower of Mohammed; believer in Is-

---

**Pronunciation Key:** hat, āge, cãre, fär; let, ēqual, tėrm; it, īce; hot, ōpen, ôrder; oil, out; cup, půt, rüle; child; long; thin; ᴛʜen; zh, measure; ə represents **a** in about, **e** in taken, **i** in pencil, **o** in lemon, **u** in circus.

lam, the religion founded by him.
—*adj.* of Mohammed, his followers, or Islam, the religion founded by him; Mohammedan: *The Moslem world today presents a complex pattern* (Newsweek). SYN: Islamic. Also, **Muslem, Muslim, Mussulman.**
[< Arabic *muslim* one who submits. See related etym. at **Islam, salaam.** See etym. of doublet **Mussulman.**]

**Mos|lem|ic** (moz lem′ik, mos-), *adj.* = Moslem.

**Mos|lem|ism** (moz′lə miz əm, mos′-), *n.* the practice of the religion of Islam, followed by Moslems; Mohammedanism.

**Mos|lem|ize** (moz′lə mīz, mos′-), *v.t.,* **-ized, -iz|ing.** to convert to Islam, the religion of Moslems; Islamize: *The Berbers were Moslemized during the Arab invasions ... in the 700's* (Time).

***mosque** (mosk), *n.* a place of public worship for Moslems: *A Mohammedan mosque is as much a place of rest and refuge as of prayer ... the houseless Arab may take shelter there by night or day* (Amelia B. Edwards). Also, **masjid, musjid.** [< Middle French *mosquée* < Italian *moschea* < Arabic *masjid*]

***mosque**

***mos|qui|to** (mə skē′tō), *n., pl.* **-toes** or **-tos.** a small, slender insect with two wings. There are various kinds, making up a family of insects. The females have mouthparts that can pierce the skin of human beings and animals and draw blood, causing itching. Certain mosquitoes are carriers of malaria, others of yellow fever, and others of encephalitis. *Fish are the chief enemies of mosquitoes* (Carl L. Hubbs). [< Spanish *mosquito* (diminutive) < *mosca* fly < Latin *musca*]

***mosquito**
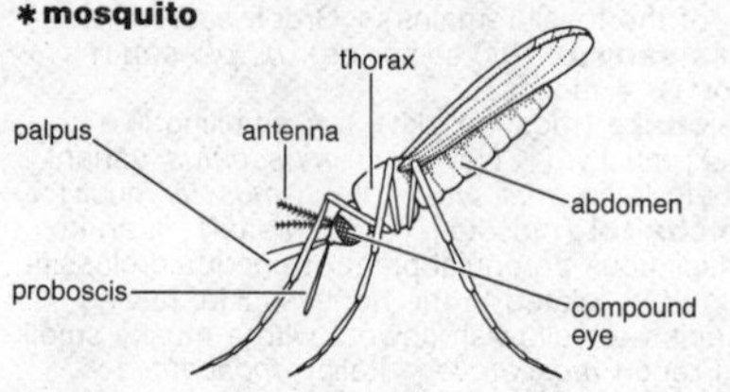


**Mos|qui|to** (mə skē′tō), *n., pl.* **-tos** or **-to.** = Miskito.

**mosquito bar,** = mosquito net.

**mosquito boat,** a fast motorboat carrying a gun and torpedoes, now called a PT boat.

**mos|qui|to|ey** (mə skē′tō ē), *adj.* of or like a mosquito.

**mosquito fish,** a small freshwater fish of the southern United States, that feeds on the larvae of mosquitoes; gambusia.

**mosquito fleet,** a fleet of mosquito boats, used to chase and destroy submarines and do scout and fast patrol duty.

**mosquito hawk,** 1 = dragonfly. 2 = nighthawk (def. 1).

**mosquito net,** a piece of mosquito netting that can be hung on a frame, as over a bed or chair, to keep off mosquitoes.

**mosquito netting,** a coarse cotton fabric with small meshes, used for mosquito nets.

**moss** (môs, mos), *n., v.* —*n.* **1** very small, soft, green or brown plants that grow close together like a carpet on the ground, on rocks, or on trees. There are various kinds, making up a class of plants. Mosses have small stems and numerous, generally narrow leaves. They are bryophytic plants. **2** a matted mass of such plants growing together. **3** any one of several other plants which grow close together like mosses, such as certain lichens, club mosses, and liverworts. **4** *Scottish.* a bog or swamp, especially a peat bog: *With anxious eye he wander'd o'er Mountain and meadow, moss and moor* (Scott).
—*v.t.* to cover with a growth of moss: *an oak whose boughs were moss'd with age* (Shakespeare).
[Old English *mos* bog; later, moss. See related etym. at **mire.**] —**moss′like′,** *adj.*

**moss agate,** a variety of agate with dark green, brownish, or black markings that resemble a moss.

**moss|back** (môs′bak′, mos′-), *n.* **1** *U.S. Slang.* a person whose ideas are out of date; extreme conservative; fogy: *He says Major Garnet means well, only he's a mossback* (George Washington Cable). **2** *U.S.* a large and old fish or turtle with a growth of algae on its back. [American English < *moss* + *back,* noun]

**moss|backed** (môs′bakt′, mos′-), *adj. U.S.* behind the times; conservative; unchanging: *... there were some who tried to dismiss the whole matter as a mossbacked anachronism* (Time).

**Moss|bau|er** or **Möss|bau|er effect** (môs′bou ər, mos′-, mœs′-), *Physics.* a method of producing gamma rays with a precise wave length that makes measurements by gamma radiation possible: *The experimental apparatus that employs the Mössbauer effect consists of an aluminum turntable, on the spindle of which is mounted a photon emitter, a radioactive isotope of iron* (Scientific American). [< Rudolf Ludwig *Mössbauer,* born 1929, a German physicist, who discovered it]

**moss|bunk|er** (môs′bung′kər, mos′-), *n. U.S. Dialect.* the menhaden. [American English, probably < Dutch *marsbanker,* earlier *masbank*]

**moss campion,** any one of several low, mosslike campions, having reddish, purplish, or white flowers and growing in arctic and mountainous regions.

**moss-grown** (môs′grōn′, mos′-), *adj.* **1** overgrown with moss: *moss-grown towers* (Shakespeare). **2** *Figurative.* antiquated.

**moss hag,** *Scottish.* **1** a hollow in a bog. **2** a hole or pit from which peat has been dug.

**Mos|si** (mos′ē), *n., pl.* **-si** or **-sis,** *adj.* —*n.* **1** a member of the largest tribe of Upper Volta, a country in western Africa. **2** the Gur language of this tribe.
—*adj.* of or belonging to the Mossi: *the Mossi kingdom.*

**mos|so** (môs′sō), *adj. Music.* rapid (used as a direction). [< Italian *mosso* movement < *muovere* to move < Latin *movēre*]

**moss pink,** a low-growing phlox of the eastern United States, with pink, white, or lavender flowers; ground pink.

**moss rose,** a cultivated cabbage rose with mosslike growth on the calyx and stem.

**moss-troop|er** (môs′trü′pər, mos′-), *n.* **1** a marauder of the Scottish border during the 1600's. **2** a raider; brigand.

**moss-troop|er|y** (môs′trü′pər ē, mos′-), *n., pl.* **-er|ies. 1** the condition of being moss-troopers. **2** the acts of moss-troopers.

**moss-troop|ing** (môs′trü′ping, mos′-), *adj.* freebooting; marauding.

**moss|y** (môs′ē, mos′-), *adj.,* **moss|i|er, moss|i|est. 1** covered with moss or a mosslike substance: *a mossy bank. A wood of mossy distorted trees* (Francis Parkman). **2** like moss: *mossy green.* **3** covered as if with moss; downy; velvety: *the mossy antlers of a deer.* —**moss′i|ness,** *n.*

**moss|y-cup oak** (môs′ē kup′, mos′-), = bur oak.

**most** (mōst), *adj.* (*used as superlative of* **much** *and* **many,** *with the comparative* **more**), *n., adv.*
—*adj.* **1** greatest in quantity, amount, measure, degree, or number: *The winner gets the most money.* **2** almost all: *Most children like candy.*
—*n.* **1** the greatest quantity, amount, degree, or number: *He did most of the work. Who gave the most? Most of my books are old.* **2** the greatest number of persons; the majority: *He has a better appetite than most.*
—*adv.* **1** in the highest degree; to the greatest extent: *This tooth hurts most.* **2** as a superlative: *most kind, most kindly, most truly, most easily, most rapid, most curious.* **3** Also, **'most.** *Informal.* almost; nearly: *I felt so lonesome I most wished I was dead* (Mark Twain).
**at (the) most,** not more than; at the utmost extent; at furthest; at the outside: *Within an hour at most I will tell you. They [the works of the great poets] have only been read as the multitude read the stars, at most astrologically, not astronomically* (Thoreau).
**for the most part.** See under **part.**
**make the most of,** to make the best use of; use to the best advantage: *making the most of an opportunity. Ah, make the most of what we yet may spend* (Edward FitzGerald).
**the most,** *Slang.* the ultimate; the absolute superlative (used predicatively): *Last week the general and even the Pentagon conceded that the bop campaign was the most, to say the least* (Time).
[Old English *māst,* and *mǣst*]
► **most, almost.** *Most* is the common, informal clip of *almost: A drop in prices will appeal to most everybody.* It would be used in writing conversation and in informal style, but is ordinarily out of place in written English.
► See **more** for another usage note.

**'most** (mōst), *adv.* most (def. 3).

**-most,** *suffix forming superlatives of adjectives and adverbs.* greatest in amount, degree, or number, as in *foremost, inmost, outmost, hithermost, topmost, uttermost.* [alteration (influenced by *most*) of Middle English *-mest* < Old English *-mo,* or *-ma* + *-est,* both superlative suffixes]

**moste** (mōst), *v.* past tense of **mote**[2].

**most|est** (mōs′tist), *n. Slang.* the most: *the hostess with the mostest.*

**Most Excellent Master,** a Mason of the third degree of the York Rite.

**most favored nation,** the nation receiving from another nation the most advantageous terms in respect to duties, tariffs, and quotas of commodities. Terms granted to the most favored nation are frequently taken as the standard fixing the terms to be granted by the other nation to a third, in treaties or trade agreements. —**most′-fa′vored-na′tion,** *adj.*

**most|ly** (mōst′lē), *adv.* almost all; for the most part; mainly; chiefly: *The work is mostly done. All afternoon we sat together, mostly in silence* (Robert Louis Stevenson). SYN: principally.

**mot** (mō *for 1;* mot *for 2*), *n.* **1** a clever or witty remark: *He moved easily and with a certain pleasure in political circles, loving to note down mots of Balfour and others* (London Times). SYN: witticism. **2** *Archaic.* a note sounded on a bugle, huntsman's horn, or the like: *Three mots on this bugle will ... bring round, at our need, a jolly band of yonder honest yeomen* (Scott). [< Old French *mot* < Vulgar Latin *mottum* < Latin *muttum* grunt, word. See etym. of doublet **motto.**]

**MOT** (no periods), Ministry of Transport (of Great Britain).

**mote**[1] (mōt), *n.* **1** a speck of dust: *thick as motes in the sunbeam* (Chaucer). **2** *Figurative.* any very small thing: *And why beholdest thou the mote that is in thy brother's eye* (Matthew 7:3). [Old English *mot*]

**mote**[2] (mōt), *v.i., past tense* **moste. 1** *Archaic.* may or might: *Was never knight on ground mote be with him compared* (James Thomson). **2** *Obsolete.* must: *At last their ways so fell, that they mote part* (Edmund Spenser). [Old English *mōtan*]

**mot|ed** (mō′tid), *adj.* full of motes: *the moted sunlight* (John Greenleaf Whittier).

**mo|tel** (mō tel′), *n.* a roadside hotel or group of furnished cottages or cabins providing overnight lodging for motorists; motor court. Most motels have units that can be entered directly from an outdoor court where cars are parked. [American English; blend of *motor* and *hotel*]

**mo|tet** (mō tet′), *n. Music.* a vocal composition in polyphonic style, on a Biblical or similar prose text, intended for use in a church service: *The boy and I again to the singing of Mr. Porter's motets* (Samuel Pepys). [< Old French *motet* (diminutive) < *mot* word; see etym. under **mot**]

***moth**
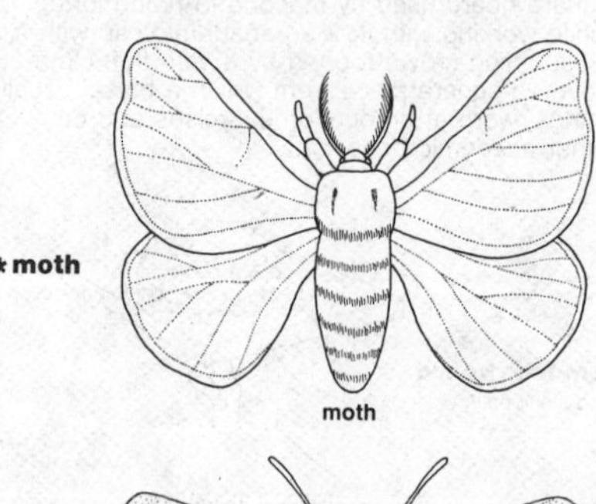
moth

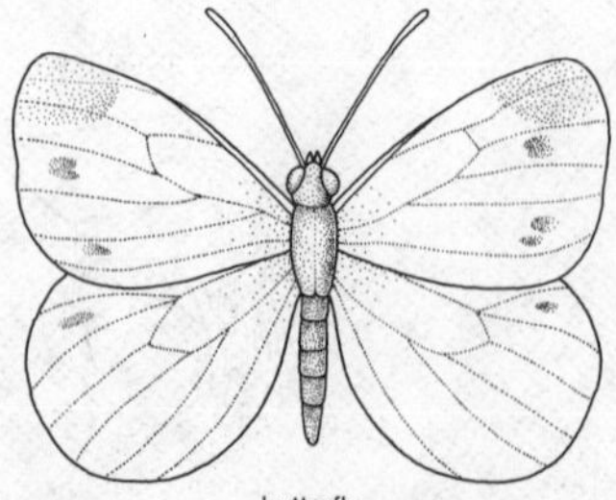
butterfly

***moth** (môth, moth), *n., pl.* **moths** (môᴛʜz, moᴛʜz, môths, moths). a winged insect very much like a butterfly, but lacking knobs at the ends of the antennae, having less brightly colored wings, and flying mostly at night. There are various kinds, of the same order of insects as the butterfly. Moths are destructive only in the larval stage. The clothes moth lays eggs in cloth and fur, and its larvae eat holes in the material. Some larvae, such as the silkworm, are useful to man. [Old English *moththe*]

**moth ball**, or **moth|ball** (môth′bôl′, moth′-), *n.* a small ball of naphthalene or camphor, used to keep moths away from wool, silk, fur, and other types of clothing or blankets.
**in** (or **into**) **moth balls**, in or into storage protected against deterioration or damage: *The Navy has 3 carriers of the Midway class, ... and 24 of the Essex class, of which 9 are in active service and 15 in moth balls* (Newsweek).

**moth-ball** or **moth|ball** (môth′bôl′, moth′-), *v., adj.* — ***v.t.*** *U.S.* to store (as a ship, tank, or machinery) protected against deterioration: *The Navy should moth-ball battleships and similar outdated ships of the line* (Time). — ***adj.*** mothballed; stored in a state protecting against deterioration: *moth-ball vessels, the mothball fleet, moth-ball wheat.*

**moth-eat|en** (môth′ē′tən, moth′-), *adj.* **1** eaten by moths; having holes made by moths. **2** *Figurative.* looking as if eaten into by moths; worn-out; out-of-date: *the moth-eaten battlecries of an old revolutionary.* **SYN**: passé.

**moth|er¹** (muᴛʜ′ər), *n., v., adj.* — ***n.*** **1** a woman who has given birth to a child: *The mother and father were very proud of their new baby.* **2** a female parent: *The puppies have lost their mother.* **3** *Figurative.* the cause or source of anything: *Necessity is the mother of invention. France, the mother of ideas* (Walter Besant). **4** the head of a large community of religious women; mother superior. **5** a woman exercising control and responsibility like that of a mother. **6** a familiar name for an old woman. **7** a female ancestor. **8** the qualities characteristic of a mother; maternal affection: ... *the mother in her soul awakes* (Alexander Pope). **9** *Archaic.* hysteria: *She is ... much subject to fits of the mother* (Tobias Smollett).
— ***v.t.*** **1** to take care of; be mother of; act as mother to: *She mothers her baby sister.* **2** to acknowledge oneself mother of or assume as one's own. **3** to give birth to; produce as a mother: (*Figurative.*) *The floods were mothered by another hurricane* (Time).
— ***adj.*** **1** that is a mother: *a mother bear.* **2** like a mother; that bears or produces others: *a mother vein from which many ores are derived, the mother cathedral of England, a mother nucleus.* **3** of a mother: *mother love, mother pain.* **4** *Figurative.* native: *English is our mother tongue. The poet, Robert Frost, was a product of his New England mother culture.* **5** that carries another or others: *a mother plane, a mother craft.*
[alteration of Old English *mōdor.* Compare etym. under **father**.]

**moth|er²** (muᴛʜ′ər), *n.* a stringy, sticky substance formed in vinegar or on the surface of liquids that are turning to vinegar; mother of vinegar. Mother consists of bacteria. Sometimes mother is added to liquids to cause them to turn to vinegar. [perhaps special use of *mother*¹, or perhaps < Middle Dutch *moeder,* or *moder*]

**Mother Car|ey's chicken** (kãr′iz), **1** = stormy petrel. **2** any one of various other petrels, such as Wilson's petrel. [spelling for altered pronunciation of Latin *Māter cāra* dear Mother, an expression of Levantine sailors (the entire expression meant "snow," perhaps referring to the white of petrel feathers)]

**mother cell**, *Biology.* the cell from which daughter cells are formed by cell division.

**mother church**, a church from which or by which others have been formed.

**mother cloud**, the cloud from which the funnel of a tornado descends.

**mother country**, **1** the country where a person was born. **2** a country in relation to its colonies or its natives.

**moth|er|craft** (muᴛʜ′ər kraft′, -kräft′), *n. British.* a mother's duties in the family; the craft or business of a mother: *Against all the rules of mothercraft, she picked herself a favourite* (London Times).

**mother earth**, the earth personified as the mother of its inhabitants and its products: ... *the unbounded treasures of mother earth* (Rolf Boldrewood).

**mother element**, the radioactive element whose decay gives rise to a daughter element.

**mother figure**, **1** *Psychoanalysis.* a person imaginatively substituted for one's real mother and made the object of responses originally developed toward the mother. **2** a maternal figure; a kindly or warmhearted person.

**Mother Goose**, **1** the pretended author of a book of fairy tales by Charles Perrault, published in 1697. **2** the pretended author of a book of English nursery rhymes published about 1760.

**moth|er|hood** (muᴛʜ′ər hu̇d), *n.* **1** the condition or fact of being a mother: *The young wife was proud of her motherhood and her new baby.* **2** the qualities or spirit of a mother: *Faithful motherhood is an important factor in a child's life.* **3** mothers: *All the motherhood of the town came to the exhibition of prize babies.*

**mother house**, **1** the monastery or convent in which the superior of a religious congregation or order lives. **2** the original monastery or convent of a congregation or order.

**Mother Hub|bard** (hub′ərd), **1** a full, loose garment worn by women, especially for housework. **2** the old woman who is the subject of a well-known Mother Goose nursery rhyme, beginning "Old Mother Hubbard went to the cupboard...."

**mother image**, = mother figure.

**Moth|er|ing Sunday** (muᴛʜ′ər ing), *British.* the Sunday in mid-Lent on which it is customary to visit one's parents and to give or receive presents; Laetare Sunday.

**moth|er-in-law** (muᴛʜ′ər in lô′), *n., pl.* **moth|ers-in-law**. **1** the mother of one's husband or wife: *His wife called the husband's mother and asked her mother-in-law to tea.* **2** *British Informal.* a stepmother.

**moth|er|land** (muᴛʜ′ər land′), *n.* **1** one's native country. **2** the land of one's ancestors. **3** a country as the mother or producer of anything.

**moth|er|less** (muᴛʜ′ər lis), *adj.* having no mother; having no living mother: *a motherless child.* — **moth′er|less|ness**, *n.*

**moth|er|li|ness** (muᴛʜ′ər lē nis), *n.* motherly quality.

**mother liquor**, *Chemistry, Pharmacy.* the liquid that remains after the removal of crystallizing substances from a solution.

**mother lode**, a rich or main vein of ore in an area, or in a mine.

**moth|er|ly** (muᴛʜ′ər lē), *adj.* **1** like a mother; like a mother's; kindly: *motherly person, motherly action.* **2** of a mother: *motherly affection. You from motherly lap the bright girl can sever* (Robert Ellis).

**moth|er-na|ked** (muᴛʜ′ər nā′kid), *adj.* naked as at birth; stark naked.

**Mother Nature**, nature personified as the mother of all things except those made by man; Nature.

**mother of game**, a woman in certain American Indian dances, who was supposed to bring animals to the hunters.

**Mother of God**, the Virgin Mary (a title officially defined by the Council of Ephesus in A.D. 431).

**moth|er-of-pearl** (muᴛʜ′ər əv pėrl′), *n., adj.* — ***n.*** the hard, smooth, glossy lining of the shell of the pearl oyster and certain other shells of mollusks, such as the mussel and abalone; nacre. It changes colors as the light changes and is used to make ornaments and buttons. — ***adj.*** made of or like this substance.

**mother-of-pearl cloud**, = nacreous cloud.

**moth|er-of-thyme** (muᴛʜ′ər əv tīm′), *n.* = wild thyme.

**mother of vinegar**, = mother².

**mother's boy**, = mama's boy.

**Mother's Day**, **1** the second Sunday in May set apart in the United States and Canada in honor of mothers. **2** *British.* = Mothering Sunday.

**mother ship**, **1** an aircraft that carries aloft another aircraft, drone, or rocket, and launches it, and sometimes directs its flight. **2** a ship which guards, escorts, or acts as a base for, one or more torpedo boats, submarines, or the like.

**moth|er-sib** (muᴛʜ′ər sib′), *n. U.S., Anthropology.* a group or clan whose members trace their descent from a common ancestor through the line of the mother.

**mother superior**, a woman who is the head of a convent of nuns; mother.

**moth|er-to-be** (muᴛʜ′ər tu̇ bē′), *n., pl.* **moth|ers-to-be**. an expectant mother.

**mother tongue**, **1** one's native language. **2** an original language to which other languages owe their origin.

**mother wit**, natural intelligence; common sense. **SYN**: sagacity.

**moth|er|wort** (muᴛʜ′ər wėrt′), *n.* a bitter European plant of the mint family, whose notched leaves have whorls of purple flowers in their axils.

**moth|er|y** (muᴛʜ′ər ē), *adj.* containing or resembling mother: *mothery vinegar.* [< *mother*² + *-y*¹]

**moth fly**, a small fly having wings covered with short hairs that make it look like a tiny moth. Moth flies are commonly found around sewage plants, septic tanks, and the like.

**moth mullein**, a biennial mullein native to Europe, with smooth leaves, racemes of solitary yellow or whitish flowers, and purple, hairy filaments.

**moth|proof** (môth′prüf′, moth′-), *adj., v.* — ***adj.*** **1** repellent to moths or resistant to the attack of their larvae: *mothproof wool.* **2** impervious to moths: *a mothproof closet.*
— ***v.t.*** to make resistant to attack by the larvae of moths.

**moth|y** (môth′ē, moth′-), *adj.,* **moth|i|er, moth|i|est.** infested by moths; moth-eaten.

**mo|tif** (mō tēf′), *n.* **1** a subject for development or treatment in art, literature, or music; principal idea or feature; motive; theme: *This opera contains a love motif.* **2** a distinctive figure in a design, painting, or decoration. **3** *Music.* motive. [< French *motif* < Middle French, adjective < Late Latin *mōtīvus* moving. See etym. of doublet **motive**.]

**mo|tile** (mō′təl), *adj., n.* — ***adj.*** *Biology.* moving or able to move by itself: *motile cells, motile spores.*
— ***n.*** *Psychology.* a person whose mental images are chiefly motor.
[< Latin *mōtus* moved, past participle of *movēre* + *-ilis* of, like]

**mo|til|i|ty** (mō til′ə tē), *n.* motile quality: *A very small lesion may produce very decided impairment of motility* (A. M. Hamilton).

**mo|tion** (mō′shən), *n., v.* — ***n.*** **1** change of position or place; movement; moving. Anything is in motion which is not at rest. *a sudden motion. Can you feel the motion of the ship? Avoid unnecessary motion of your hand while you are writing.* **2** a formal suggestion made in a meeting or legislative body, to be voted on: *The motion to adjourn was carried.* **3** *Law.* an application made to a court or judge for an order, ruling, or other action. **4** a mental or emotional impulse; inclination; volition: *He signed the agreement of his own motion.* **5a** a mechanical apparatus that moves, causes motion, or modifies motion. **b** the action of a mechanical apparatus or any of its parts. **6** *Music.* **a** the melodic progression of a single part or voice from one pitch to another. **b** the progression of two or more parts or voices with relation to each other. **7** *Obsolete.* **a** a puppet show. **b** a puppet.
— ***v.i.*** to make a movement, such as one of the hand or head, to show one's meaning: *He motioned to show us the way.* **SYN**: gesticulate.
— ***v.t.*** to show (a person) what to do by such a motion: *He motioned me out.*
**go through the motions**, to do something only from habit or as a ritual or formality: *The Republicans don't really hope or want to take over New York's City Hall, but ... they just go through the motions every four years* (New York Times).
**in motion**, moving; going: *to set the wheels of industry in motion. The price increases ... set in motion demands for further wage increases* (John Kenneth Galbraith).
**motions**, movements; actions; activities: *Mr. Glossin was well aware that such a hint was of power sufficient to decide the motions of his ... colleague* (Scott).
[< Old French *motion,* learned borrowing from Latin *mōtiō, -ōnis* < *movēre* to move]
— ***Syn.*** ***n.*** **1 Motion, movement** mean change of place or position. **Motion** emphasizes the state of not being at rest or the process of moving, especially as thought of apart from any particular thing or definite action: *We study the laws of motion.* **Movement** emphasizes a definite moving in a particular direction and regular way: *the movement of the earth.*

**mo|tion|al** (mō′shə nəl), *adj.* **1** of or having to do with motion. **2** characterized by particular motions, as certain diseases.

**mo|tion|less** (mō′shən lis), *adj.* not moving; incapable of motion: *Some sat on horseback, motionless as equestrian statues* (Francis Parkman). **SYN**: inert, stationary, still, quiet. — **mo′tion|less|ly**, *adv.* — **mo′tion|less|ness**, *n.*

**motion picture**, **1** a series of pictures on a strip of film recording very slight changes in position of persons or things, and projected on a screen at such a speed that the viewer gets the impression that the persons or things pictured are moving: *The motion picture began to attract attention in the United States at the close of the last century* (Emory S. Bogardus). Also called **moving picture**, **cinema**, **film**, or (*in Great Britain*) **pictures**. **2** a story or drama told by means of this; photoplay.

**mo|tion-pic|ture** (mō′shən pik′chər), *adj.* of, having to do with, or characteristic of motion pictures: *One of the most characteristic products of the American motion-picture industry is the Western* (Saturday Review).

**mo|tions** (mō′shənz), *n.pl.* See under **motion**.

**motion sickness**, a condition characterized by nausea, vomiting, and dizziness, caused by motion or visual disorientation, as in traveling by car, plane, or ship or by watching a motion picture.

**mo|ti|vate** (mō′tə vāt), *v.t.,* **-vat|ed, -vat|ing.** to

**Pronunciation Key:** hat, āge, cãre, fär; let, ēqual, tėrm; it, īce; hot, ōpen, ôrder; **oi**l, **ou**t; cup, pu̇t, rüle; **ch**ild; lo**ng**; **th**in; ᴛʜen; **zh**, measure; ə represents **a** in about, **e** in taken, **i** in pencil, **o** in lemon, **u** in circus.

provide with a motive or incentive; induce to act; act upon as a motive. SYN: incite.
**mo|ti|va|tion** (mō′tə vā′shən), *n.* the act or process of furnishing with an incentive or inducement to action: *Man's motivations emerge from his entire experience* (Atlantic).
**mo|ti|va|tion|al** (mō′tə vā′shə nəl), *adj.* **1** of or having to do with motivation: *motivational analysis.* **2** motivating: *those motivational drives that lead us to write to editors, to vote, to ...* (Wall Street Journal). — **mo′ti|va′tion|al|ly**, *adv.*
**motivational** or **motivation research**, the study of what conscious or subconscious influences actually induce people to choose or reject a course of action, especially all the factors that make potential customers buy or refrain from buying a particular commodity or brand: *Motivational research procedures already developed have proved that in many cases they can be used to boost a product's saleability* (Wall Street Journal).
**mo|ti|va|tive** (mō′tə vā′tiv), *adj.* that motivates or tends to motivate.
**mo|ti|va|tor** (mō′tə vā′tər), *n.* a person or thing that motivates.
**mo|tive** (mō′tiv), *n., adj., v.,* **-tived, -tiv|ing.** — *n.* **1** a thought or feeling that makes a person act; moving consideration or reason: *His motive in going away was a wish to travel. The poor savages ... had merely gathered together through motives of curiosity* (Washington Irving). SYN: incentive. See syn. under **reason. 2** a motif in art, literature, or music: *a beautiful motive of festoons.* **3** *Music.* **a** the briefest intelligible melodic or rhythmic fragment of a theme or subject. **b** = subject. **c** = leitmotif.
— *adj.* that makes something move. See also **motive power.**
— *v.t.* to provide with a motive; supply a motive to.
[< Late Latin *mōtīvus* moving, impelling < Latin *movēre* to move. See etym. of doublet **motif.**]
— **mo′tive|less**, *adj.*
**motive power**, **1** power used to impart motion; source of mechanical energy: *For many years the motive power of trains was steam.* (*Figurative.*) *Public reputation is a motive power* (Benjamin Disraeli). **2** all the locomotives and other self-propelled vehicles of a railroad.
**mo|tiv|ic** (mō tiv′ik), *adj. Music.* of or characteristic of a motif: *motivic themes.*
**mo|tiv|i|ty** (mō tiv′ə tē), *n.* **1** the power of initiating or producing motion. **2** = kinetic energy.
**mot juste** (mō zhʏst′), *pl.* **mots justes** (mō zhʏst′). *French.* a word or phrase that exactly fits the case: *Such was the general enthusiasm for her that she was credited with mots justes and insights* (New Yorker).
**mot|ley** (mot′lē), *adj., n., pl.* **-leys.** — *adj.* **1** made up of different things or kinds: *a motley crowd, a motley collection of butterflies, shells, and stamps.* SYN: heterogeneous. **2** of different colors like a clown's suit: *dressed in the motley garb that jesters wear* (Longfellow). SYN: variegated, harlequin. **3** wearing motley: *a motley fool* (Shakespeare).
— *n.* **1** a mixture of things that are different. SYN: medley, mélange. **2** a suit of more than one color worn by clowns: *At the party he wore motley. Old-time fools and jesters wore motley.* **3** a jester; fool: *I have gone here and there and made myself a motley to the view* (Shakespeare). **4** a woolen fabric of mixed colors, used for clothing from the 1300's to 1600's, especially in England.
[Middle English *motteley,* apparently < unrecorded Anglo-French *motelé* < Old English *mot* mote[1]] — **mot′ley|ness**, *n.*
**mot|mot** (mot′mot), *n.* any one of various tropical birds, related to the kingfishers, having a serrate bill, greenish and bluish feathers, and a tail with long feathers spread like a tennis racket, found in wooded areas of Central and South America. [< New Latin *momot;* apparently imitative]
**mo|to|car** (mō′tō kär′), *n.* = motorcar. [American English, variant of *motorcar*]
**mo|to-cross** (mō′tō krôs′), *n.* a cross-country motorcycle race. [< French *moto-cross* < *moto* motorcycle + *cross*(-country) < English]
**mo|to|neu|ron** (mō′tə nůr′on, -nyůr′-), *n.* a motor neuron: *Nerve impulses generated by the motoneuron activate the muscle to which the stretch receptor is attached* (Scientific American).
***mo|tor** (mō′tər), *n., adj., v.* — *n.* **1** an engine that makes a machine go: *an electric motor, a gasoline motor.* **2** an apparatus that converts electrical into mechanical energy by the inducing of an electrodynamic response which causes a part (the armature) of the apparatus to revolve. **3** = internal-combustion engine. **4** an apparatus that adapts the energy of some natural agent, such as water or wind, or force, such as compression, to mechanical use; prime mover, such as a water wheel or steam engine. **5** an automobile; motorcar: *The younger generation ... is habituated to motors and cinemas* (J. W. R. Scott). **6** a person or thing that imparts motion or compels action.
— *adj.* **1** run by a motor: *a motor cart, a motor mechanism.* **2** having to do with or by means of automobiles: *a motor tour.* **3** causing or having to do with motion or action; functioning like a motor. **4a** (of nerves) conveying or imparting an impulse from the central nervous system to a muscle or organ which results in motion or activity. **b** (of muscles, impulses, and centers) concerned with or involving motion or activity. **c** designating the effect of stimuli from the central nervous system causing motion or action. **5** *Psychology.* of, having to do with, or involving muscular or glandular activity: *a motor response.*
— *v.i.* to travel by automobile; ride in an automobile: *The two spent their time ... motoring and walking on the Downs* (John Galsworthy).
— *v.t. Especially British.* to drive by automobile; take in an automobile: *He motored his wife to the station.*
[< Latin *mōtor* mover < *movēre* to move]

***motor**
definition 2

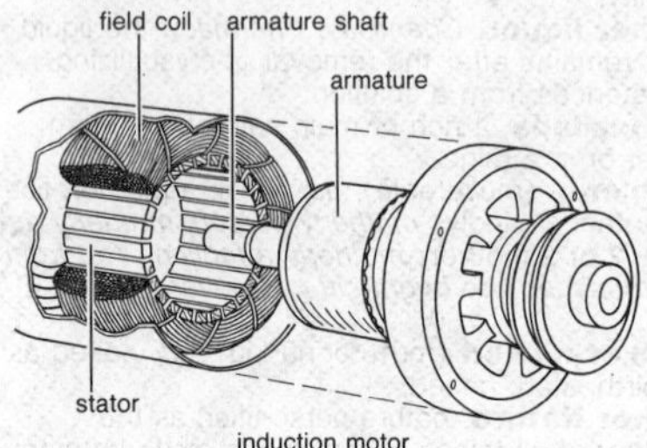


**mo|tor|a|ble** (mō′tər ə bəl), *adj.* that can be traveled over by a motor vehicle: *motorable roads.*
**mo|tor|bi|cy|cle** (mō′tər bī′sə kəl), *n.* **1** a bicycle with an auxiliary motor. **2** a light motorcycle.
**mo|tor|bike** (mō′tər bīk′), *n. Informal.* a motorbicycle: *The motorbike lay on the other side of the road, its wheels in the air, like a dead bug* (Atlantic).
**mo|tor|bik|er** (mō′tər bī′kər), *n. Informal.* **1** a motorcyclist. **2** a rider of a motorbicycle.
***mo|tor|boat** (mō′tər bōt′), *n.* a boat that is run by a motor.

***motorboat**

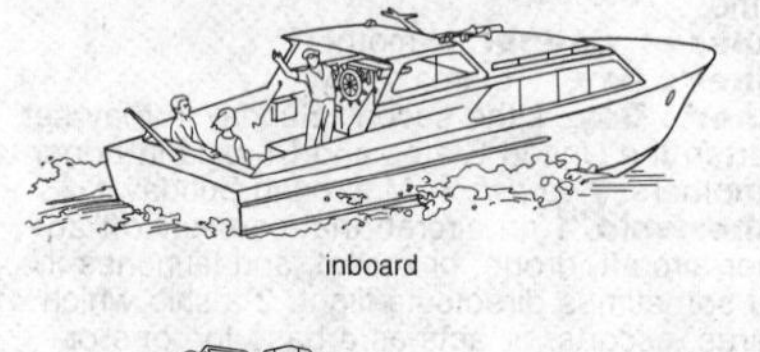


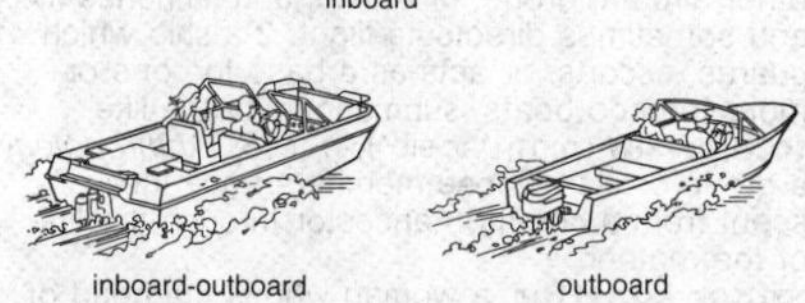


**mo|tor|boat|er** (mō′tər bō′tər), *n.* a person who engages in motorboating.
**mo|tor|boat|ing** (mō′tər bō′ting), *n.* the sport of riding in a motorboat: *Motorboating did not become practical or popular until the gasoline engine was perfected in the early 1900's* (William W. Robinson).
**mo|tor|bus** (mō′tər bus′), *n.* a bus run by a motor.
**mo|tor|cade** (mō′tər kād), *n., v.,* **-cad|ed, -cad|ing.** — *n.* a procession or long line of automobiles: *The crowd ... had gathered to greet Mr. Nehru's motorcade* (Times of India).
— *v.i. Informal.* to travel in or with a large group of automobiles: *But in Flint and Jackson, where he motorcaded through the streets ...* (Nashville Tennessean).
[American English < *motor* + *-cade*]
**mo|tor|car** (mō′tər kär′), *n.* **1** = automobile. **2** Also, **motor car.** a motor-driven railroad car.
**motor carrier**, a truck or bus line that carries passengers or freight.
**mo|tor|coach** (mō′tər kōch′), *n.,* or **motor coach**, = motorbus.
**motor court**, *U.S.* a motel.
**mo|tor|cy|cle** (mō′tər sī′kəl), *n., v.,* **-cled, -cling.** — *n.* a vehicle like a bicycle but larger and heavier, run by a motor. Sometimes a sidecar is attached to it, with a third wheel to support it.
— *v.i.* to travel by motorcycle.
**mo′tor|cy|clist** (mō′tər sī′klist), *n.* a person who rides a motorcycle.
**motor drive**, an electric motor used for operating a machine or machines.
**mo|tor-driv|en** (mō′tər driv′ən), *adj.* driven by a motor or motors.
**mo|tor|drome** (mō′tər drōm′), *n.* a rounded course or track, often rising at an angle or in a curve toward its outer edge, upon which automobile and motorcycle races are run.
**mo|tored** (mō′tərd), *adj.* having a motor or motors.
**motor generator** or **motor generator set**, an apparatus consisting of a combination of one or more motors and one or more generators, used especially to transform electric currents or to lower voltage.
**motor hotel**, a motel that provides full hotel service, especially one with garage space, in the downtown section of a city: *... a new seven-story motor hotel, to serve the tourist and convention trade* (Wall Street Journal). Also, **motor inn, motor lodge.**
**mo|to|ri|al** (mō tôr′ē əl, -tōr′-), *adj.* **1** of or having to do with motion. **2** of or having to do with a motor nerve.
**mo|tor|ic** (mō tôr′ik, -tōr′-), *adj.* having to do with or causing motion or action: *motoric rhythm.*
**mo|tor|ing** (mō′tər ing), *n.* riding in a vehicle operated by a motor.
**motor inn**, = motor hotel.
**mo|tor|ise** (mō′tə rīz), *v.t.,* **-ised, -is|ing.** *Especially British.* motorize.
**mo|tor|ist** (mō′tər ist), *n.* a person who drives or travels in an automobile, especially one who does it a great deal: *Visiting motorists could cross the frontier at Brest-Litovsk and drive to Moscow* (Manchester Guardian).
**mo|to|ri|um** (mō tôr′ē əm, -tōr′-), *n., pl.* **-to|ri|a** (-tôr′ē ə, -tōr′-). the part of an organism which is concerned with motion. [< New Latin *motorium* < Late Latin, power of motion < Latin *mōtor;* see etym. under **motor**]
**mo|tor|i|za|tion** (mō′tər ə zā′shən), *n.* **1** the act or process of motorizing. **2** the state of being motorized.
**mo|tor|ize** (mō′tə rīz), *v.t.,* **-ized, -iz|ing.** **1** to furnish with a motor or motors: *The Danville voyageurs ... rode in a motorized "box car"* (Baltimore Sun). **2** to equip with motor-driven vehicles in place of horses and horse-drawn vehicles. **3** to equip (infantry) with motor-driven transport vehicles, especially trucks, but not to alter the nature of their weapons.
**mo|tor|less** (mō′tər lis), *adj.* having no motor; without a motor: *motorless aircraft.*
**motor lodge**, = motor hotel.
**motor lorry**, *British.* a motor truck.
**mo|tor|man** (mō′tər mən), *n., pl.* **-men.** **1** a man who runs an electric train, streetcar, or monorail. **2** a man who runs a motor.
**motor mower**, a motor-driven lawn mower; power lawn mower: *Now—the light motor mower that has everything!* (Sunday Times).
**motor pool**, a group of automobiles or other motor vehicles held by an organization for temporary use, as needed, by individuals, but not permanently assigned.
**motor sailer**, a sailboat with a motor, usually an inboard motor.
**motor scooter**, a vehicle like a child's scooter, except that the driver is seated. It is run by a motor. *They can out-sell us with cars, motor scooters, typewriters—not because their efficiency is high but their wage-bill is low* (Scottish Sunday Express).
**mo|tor|ship** (mō′tər ship′), *n.* a ship whose engine is driven by a motor, usually a diesel engine. *Abbr:* M.S.
**motor spirit**, *British.* gasoline: *The Government clapped a whacking increase onto the duty on oil and motor spirit* (New Yorker).
**motor torpedo boat**, a small, very fast, and highly maneuverable boat, having little or no armor, equipped with torpedoes, depth charges, anti-aircraft guns, and smoke-screen equipment.
**motor truck**, a truck with an engine, frame, and wheels made for carrying heavy loads.
**motor vehicle**, a motor-driven vehicle for use on roads and highways, such as an automobile, truck, or bus.
**mo|tor|way** (mō′tər wā′), *n. British.* a highway with high speed limits and no cross traffic.
**mo|to|ry** (mō′tər ē), *adj.* = motor.
**mott** or **motte**[1] (mot), *n. Southwestern U.S.* a clump of trees in a prairie. [< Mexican Spanish *mata*]
**motte**[2] (mot), *n.* an earthen mound on which a wooden castle was built in early Norman times. [< Old French *motte* mound. See related etym. at **moat.**]
**mot|tet|to** (mōt tet′tō), *n., pl.* **-ti** (-tē). *Italian.* a motet.

**mot|tle** (mot′əl), *v.*, **-tled, -tling,** *n.* — *v.t.* to mark with spots or streaks of different colors or shades: *the gray stone parapet, mottled with the green and gold of innumerable mosses* (Mrs. Humphry Ward). **SYN**: dapple.
— *n.* **1** a mottled coloring or pattern; mottling. **2** a spot, blotch, or streak on a mottled surface. **SYN**: variegation.
[apparently < unrecorded Anglo-French *moteler* to speckle < Old English *mot* speck, mote[1]. Compare etym. under **motley**.]

**mot|tled** (mot′əld), *adj.* spotted or streaked with different colors or shades; dappled; marbled.

**mottled enamel**, streaked or spotted enamel of the teeth, caused by continued use of water with excessive fluorine during the time the teeth are forming.

**mottle figure**, a pattern in the grain of wood formed by spots and cloudiness and producing a dappled effect.

**mot|tler** (mot′lər), *n.* a person or thing that mottles.

**mot|tling** (mot′ling), *n.* mottled coloring.

**mot|to** (mot′ō), *n., pl.* **-toes** or **-tos. 1** a brief sentence adopted as a rule of conduct: *"Think before you speak" is a good motto.* **SYN**: proverb, adage, saying. **2** a word, sentence, or phrase written or engraved on some object. **3** = motto theme. [< Italian *motto* < Vulgar Latin *mottum* < Latin *muttum* grunt, word. See etym. of doublet **mot**.]

**motto theme**, a recurrent and sometimes transformed symbolic theme in a piece of music; leitmotif.

**mo|tu pro|pri|o** (mō′tü prō′prē ō, mō′tyü), *Latin.* **1** independently; of one's own accord. **2** (literally) by one's own motion.

**mouch** (müch), *v.t., v.i.* = mooch.

**mou|chard** (mü shär′), *n. French.* a police spy; informer: *I think the fellow's a cursed mouchard —some Government spy* (Charles Kingsley).

**mou|choir** (mü shwär′), *n.* a handkerchief: *A mouchoir with musk his spirits to cheer* (London Magazine). [< Middle French *mouchoir* < Old French *moucher* blow, wipe the nose < Vulgar Latin *muccāre* < Latin *muccus,* variant of *mūcus* mucus]

**moue** (mü), *n.* a grimace; pout: *Her pleasantly assembled features ... can be compressed on stage into an alarming and comical moue* (New York Times). [< French *moue*]

**mouf|flon** (müf′lon), *n., pl.* **-flons** or (*collectively*) **-flon.** = mouflon.

**mouf|lon** (müf′lon), *n., pl.* **-lons** or (*collectively*) **-lon. 1** a small wild sheep of the mountainous regions of Sardinia and Corsica, the male of which has large, curving horns: *In the game-rich Gennargentu mountains there are boar, deer, and mouflon* (Atlantic). **2** its wool, used for fur. **3** any one of various similar wild sheep. [< French *mouflon* < Italian *muflone,* alteration of Late Latin *mufrō, -ōnis*]

**mought** (mout), *v. Archaic or Dialect.* might[1].
▶ **Mought** survives in nonstandard, rustic speech, chiefly in the southern United States.

**mouil|lé** (mü yā′), *adj. Phonetics.* **1** palatalized by a following *y*-sound, as *l* in *million.* **2** pronounced as palatal or palatalized, as the sounds represented in Spanish by *ll, ñ,* in Italian by *gl, gn,* and in French by *gn.* **3** pronounced as a *y*- sound but spelled *l* or *ll,* as in certain French words. [< French *mouillé,* past participle of Old French *mouiller* to wet, moisten < Vulgar Latin *molliāre* to soften, for Latin *mollīre* < *mollis* soft]

**mou|jik** (mü zhik′, mü′zhik), *n.* = muzhik.

**mou|lage** (mü läzh′), *n.* **1** the making of molds, in plaster of Paris or the like, of objects involved in a crime, or their outlines, as a footprint or tire track, for use especially in identification and as evidence. **2** such a mold. **3** a plaster, wax, or rubber imitation of an injury of the body, used in medical therapy or training. [< French *moulage* a casting < Middle French *mollage* < Old French *mouler* to mold, cast < *modle* a mold[1]]

**mould** (mōld), *n., v.t., v.i. Especially British.* mold[1], mold[2], and mold[3].

**mould|a|ble** (mōl′də bəl), *adj. Especially British.* moldable.

**mould|board** (mōld′bôrd′, -bōrd′), *n. Especially British.* moldboard.

**mould|er** (mōl′dər), *v.i., n. Especially British.* molder[1] and molder[2].

**mould|ing** (mōl′ding), *n. Especially British.* molding.

**mould|warp** (mōld′wôrp′), *n. British Dialect.* the common mole of the Old World. Also, **moldwarp.** [Middle English *mouldwarp, moldwarp* < Old English *molde* earth, dust, mold[3] + *weorpan* throw]

**mould|y** (mōl′dē), *adj.,* **mould|i|er, mould|i|est.** *Especially British.* moldy.

**mou|lin** (mü laN′), *n.* a nearly vertical shaft or cavity worn in a glacier by surface water falling through a crack in the ice. [< French *moulin* (literally) a mill < Old French *molin;* see etym. under **moline**]

**moult** (mōlt), *v.i., v.t., n. Especially British.* molt.
— **moult′er,** *n.*

**mound**[1] (mound), *n., v.* — *n.* **1** a bank or heap of earth, stones, or other material: *a mound of hay.* **SYN**: pile. **2** a small hill; hillock: *The explorers climbed a mound to survey the land around them.* **SYN**: knoll. **3** the slightly elevated ground from which a baseball pitcher pitches: *Dean, coming to the mound from center field, got the side out with only one of the runners scoring* (Tishomingo Capital-Democrat).
— *v.t.* **1** to heap up: *to mound earth.* **2** to enclose with a mound or embankment: *A sand-built ridge of heaped hills that mound the sea* (Tennyson). **3** *Dialect.* to enclose with a fence.
[origin uncertain]

**mound**[2] (mound), *n.* a globe of gold or other precious material, intended to represent the earth, often surmounted by a cross and forming part of the insignia of royalty. [< Old French *monde,* learned borrowing from Latin *mundus* earth]

**mound|bird** (mound′bėrd′), *n.,* or **mound bird,** = megapode.

**mound builder,** = megapode.

**Mound Builders,** a largely prehistoric group of agricultural Indians who lived in central and eastern North America, especially in the valleys of the Mississippi and Ohio rivers and the Great Lakes region. They built mounds of earth as burial places, to hold temples or chiefs' houses, or for defense.

**mounds|man** (moundz′mən), *n., pl.* **-men.** *Baseball.* a pitcher.

**mount**[1] (mount), *v., n.* — *v.t.* **1** to go up on or climb up; ascend: *to mount a hill, mount a ladder, mount stairs. It was our design to mount the head-waters of the Hudson, to the neighbourhood of Crown Point* (Robert Louis Stevenson). **SYN**: See syn. under **climb. 2a** to get up on: *to mount a platform.* **b** to get on for riding: *to mount a horse, to mount a motorcycle.* **3** to put on a horse; furnish with a horse: *Many policemen in this city are mounted.* **4a** to put in proper position or order for use: *to mount specimens on a slide, to mount a piece of artillery.* **b** to prepare (a slide). **5** to fix in a setting, backing, or support: *to mount gems in gold, to mount a picture on cardboard.* **6** to have or carry (guns), as a fortress or ship does: *The ship mounts eight guns.* **7** to provide (a play) with scenery, costumes, and properties. **8a** to assign (a guard) as a sentry or watch. **b** to go on duty as (a guard or watch). **9** to set or place upon an elevation: *a small house mounted on poles. No wonder we see more than the ancients, because we are mounted upon their shoulders* (Cardinal Newman). **10** to put on; show oneself as wearing: *He found Dick mounting a large top-coat, and muffling up* (Samuel Lover). *It was then that I mounted the turban* (Herman Melville).
— *v.i.* **1** to move or proceed upward: *A flush mounts to the brow. They shall mount up with wings as eagles* (Isaiah 40:31). **2** to rise in amount; increase; rise: *The cost of living mounts steadily. The rage of each had mounted to delirium* (Frederick Marryat). **3** to get on a horse; get up on something: *to mount on the motorbike and ride away. Paul Revere mounted in haste.*
— *n.* **1** a horse or other animal, or a bicycle or motorcycle for riding: *The riding instructor had an excellent mount. There was not another mount in the stable* (George Eliot). **2** something in or on which anything is mounted; setting; backing; support: *the mount for a picture. A mount for microscopic examination is a slide.* **3** an act or occasion of riding a horse, especially in a race. **4** the act or manner of mounting. **5** *Especially British.* a mat: *a picture mount.*
[< Old French *monter,* or *munter* < Vulgar Latin *montāre* < Latin *mōns, montis* mountain]
— **mount′er,** *n.*

**mount**[2] (mount), *n.* **1** a mountain; high hill. *Mount* is often used before the names of mountains: *Mount Rainier, Mount Everest, Mount Olympus. Abbr:* Mt. **2** (in palmistry) a significant prominence in the palm of the hand. **3** *Archaic.* a defensive rampart of earth. **4** *Obsolete.* a mound. [partly Old English *munt* < Latin *mōns, montis,* and partly < Old French *mont* < Latin]

**mount|a|ble** (moun′tə bəl), *adj.* that can be mounted.

***moun|tain** (moun′tən), *n., adj.* — *n.* **1** a very high hill; a natural elevation of the earth's surface rising high above the surrounding level in a massive and conspicuous way: *The distant mountains were covered with snow and the tops hidden in the clouds.* **SYN**: peak. See picture on the following page. **2** a very large heap or pile of anything; something like a mountain or high hill: *a mountain of rubbish.* **3** *Figurative.* a huge amount: *a mountain of money. The crippled man overcame a mountain of difficulties.*
— *adj.* **1** of or having something to do with mountains: *mountain air, mountain scenery.* **2** living, growing, or found on mountains: *mountain plants.* **3** resembling or suggesting a mountain.
**make a mountain (out) of a molehill,** to give great importance to something which is really insignificant: *She was only five minutes late, but he made a mountain out of a molehill about it.*
**mountains,** a series of very high hills: *Mountains interposed make enemies of nations* (William Cowper).
**the Mountain,** an extreme revolutionary party, led by Danton and Robespierre, in the Legislative Assembly and the National Convention of the French Revolution.
[< Old French *montaigne* < Late Latin *montānea,* feminine of Latin *montānus* mountainous < *mōns, montis* mountain. See etym. of doublet **montane**.]
▶ **Mountain** regularly implies a much larger and higher elevation than **hill**; but in a particular region *mountain* may designate an elevation which would be considered a *hill* elsewhere.

**mountain arnica,** the common variety of arnica.

**mountain ash, 1** any one of a genus of trees and shrubs of the rose family, having delicate pinnate leaves, white flowers, and bright-red to orange-brown berries. They grow in Europe and from Newfoundland to northern Georgia. **2** any one of various Australian eucalyptus trees.

**mountain avens,** a low evergreen plant of the rose family with erect yellow or white flowers, growing on mountains and in arctic regions.

**mountain beaver,** an animal with a short, thick body, short legs, and small eyes and ears. The mountain beaver is a rodent, but not a beaver, that lives in colonies and makes its home in tunnels dug in the banks of streams along the Pacific coast and in nearby mountains.

**mountain blacksnake,** = blacksnake (def. 1b).

**mountain bluebird,** an American bluebird of the western United States.

**mountain caribou,** the largest of the woodland caribous.

**mountain cat, 1** = cougar. **2** = bobcat.

**mountain chain, 1** a connected series of mountains or mountain ranges. **2** = mountain system. See picture under **mountain**.

**mountain chickadee,** a variety of chickadee of the western United States: *The mountain chickadee has a black cap, but has a white line over each eye* (Arthur A. Allen).

**mountain climber,** = mountaineer.

**mountain cork,** a variety of asbestos.

**mountain cranberry,** an evergreen shrub of the heath family, growing in North America, with an edible, very tart, red berry; lingonberry.

**mountain damson,** a West Indian tree of the quassia family, the bark of whose root is used in medicine as a tonic and astringent.

**mountain dew,** *Slang.* illegally distilled whiskey.

**mountain eagle,** = golden eagle.

**moun|tained** (moun′tənd), *adj. Poetic.* **1** set on or as if on a mountain: *Like old Deucalion mountain'd o'er the flood* (Keats). **2** covered with mountains; mountainous.

**moun|tain|eer** (moun′tə nir′), *n., v.* — *n.* **1** a person skilled in mountain climbing; alpinist: *Fitzpatrick was a hardy and experienced mountaineer, and knew all the passes and defiles* (Washington Irving). **2** a person who lives in the mountains: *a Kentucky mountaineer.*
— *v.i.* to climb mountains: *Those who mountaineer in regions where the heights are undetermined must not depend on aneroids alone* (C. T. Dent).

**moun|tain|eer|ing** (moun′tə nir′ing), *n.* the art or sport of mountain climbing; alpinism: *Mountaineering is all ... patience, deliberate skill, and exaltation after long endurance* (Scientific American).

**mountain goat,** a white, goat antelope of the Rocky Mountains, with slender, backward-curving black horns; Rocky Mountain goat.

**mountain gorilla,** a gorilla of the mountain forests of the Congo and western Uganda, in central Africa. It is larger and has longer and thicker hair than other gorillas.

**mountain hemlock,** a large hemlock of the western United States that yields a hard lumber.

**mountain laurel,** an evergreen shrub with glossy leaves and pale-pink or white flowers, found in eastern North America. It belongs to the heath family. Mountain laurel is the state flower of Connecticut and Pennsylvania.

---

**Pronunciation Key:** hat, āge, cãre, fär; let, ēqual, tėrm; it, īce; hot, ōpen, ôrder; **oi**l, **ou**t; cup, pu̇t, rüle; **ch**ild; lo**ng**; **th**in; **ᴛʜ**en; **zh**, measure; ə represents **a** in about, **e** in taken, **i** in pencil, **o** in lemon, **u** in circus.

**mountain lion**, a large North American wildcat; cougar; puma: *Largest and probably most widely scattered of the native cats is the mountain lion* (Science News Letter).
**mountain mahogany**, a shrub of the rose family found in the Rocky Mountains.
**mountain man**, a person who lives in the mountains; mountaineer.
**mountain maple**, a shrublike maple of eastern North America, with greenish-yellow flowers growing in erect, downy spikes.
**moun|tain|meal** (moun′tən mēl′), *n.* = bergmehl. [translation of German *Bergmehl*]
**mountain nestor**, = kea. [< New Latin *Nestor* the genus name]
**moun|tain|ous** (moun′tə nəs), *adj.* **1** covered with mountain ranges: *mountainous country.* **2** like a mountain; large and high; huge: *mountainous waves.* SYN: enormous. — **moun′tain|ous|ly**, *adv.* — **moun′tain|ous|ness**, *n.*
**mountain pass**, a natural passageway over or through a mountain barrier.
**mountain peony**, = tree peony.
**mountain plover**, a plover of the plains of the western United States, resembling the killdeer but smaller and without the black rings across the breast.
**mountain quail**, a grayish-brown quail with chestnut markings and a crest formed by two black feathers, found along the Pacific coast of the United States.
**mountain range**, **1** a row of connected mountains: *The Rockies is one of the great mountain ranges of the western United States.* **2** a group of mountains. See picture under **mountain**.
**mountain rose bay**, any shrub of a species of rhododendron found in Virginia and having brilliant lilac-purple flowers.
**moun|tains** (moun′tənz), *n.pl.* See under **mountain.**
**moun|tain|scape** (moun′tən skāp′), *n.* a scene or view of mountains, pictured or in nature: *The most trivial but eye-stopping addition to the mountainscape is the seedy tangle of billboards* (Maclean's).
**mountain sheep**, **1** = bighorn. **2** any one of several other wild sheep inhabiting mountains.
**mountain sickness**, sickness caused by the rarefied air at high altitudes. The common symptoms are difficulty in breathing, headache, and nausea.
**moun|tain|side** (moun′tən sīd′), *n.* the side or slope of a mountain below the summit: *snow-draped mountainsides* (Wall Street Journal).
**Mountain Standard Time**, the standard time in the Rocky Mountain regions of the United States and Canada. It is seven hours behind Greenwich Time. Noon coincides with the apparent passage of the sun over the 105th west meridian. *Abbr:* MST
**Mountain State**, a nickname for West Virginia.
**mountain sumac**, = dwarf sumac.
**mountain system**, a group of geographically related mountain ranges.
**Mountain time**, Mountain Standard Time.
**mountain tobacco**, a perennial herb of the composite family, used as the source of the medicine arnica.
**moun|tain|top** (moun′tən top′), *n.* the top or summit of a mountain.
**mountain trout**, = cutthroat trout.
**moun|tain|ward** (moun′tən wərd), *adv., adj.* toward the mountain or mountains.
**moun|tain|wards** (moun′tən wərdz), *adv.* = mountainward.
**mountain whitefish**, a variety of whitefish found in the western mountain streams of North America.
**moun|te|bank** (moun′tə bangk), *n., v.* — *n.* **1** anybody who tries to deceive people by tricks, stories, and jokes; charlatan: *He has a reputation as one of the most corrupt and unimaginative mountebanks in Brazilian politics* (New Republic). *I am a natural-born mountebank* (George Bernard Shaw). **2** a person who sells quack medicines in public, appealing to his audience by means of tricks, stories, and jokes: *an impudent mountebank who sold pills which ... were very good against an earthquake* (Joseph Addison).
— *v.i.* to play the mountebank.
[< Italian *montambanco* for *monta in banco* (literally) mount on bench (because such quacks usually spoke from an elevated platform)]
**moun|te|bank|er|y** (moun′tə bang′kər ē), *n., pl.* **-er|ies**. the practice of a mountebank; action characteristic of or suited to a mountebank: *It fills the stage with mountebankery that is broad and funny* (New York Times).
**mount|ed** (moun′tid), *adj.* **1** on a horse, mule, bicycle, or other animal or vehicle. **2** serving on

**∗mountain**
definition 1

horseback or motorcycle: *mounted police, mounted infantry.* **3** in a position for use: *a mounted camera, a mounted gun.* **4** on a support; in a setting: *a mounted diamond.*

**Mount|ie** (moun′tē), *n. Informal.* a member of the Royal Canadian Mounted Police, a force maintained by the government of Canada.

**mount|ing** (moun′ting), *n.* **1** a support, setting, or the like. The mounting of a photograph is the paper or cardboard on which it is pasted. **2** the act of a person or thing that mounts.

**mounting block**, a block, usually of stone, from which to mount a horse or step into and out of a carriage.

**mourn** (môrn, mōrn), *v.i.* **1** to feel or express deep sorrow or grief; grieve: *I left them to mourn over my folly, and now I am left to mourn under the consequence of it* (Daniel Defoe). **SYN**: lament, sorrow. **2** to show the conventional signs of grief following the death of a person; go into mourning: *We mourn in black* (Shakespeare). **3** to make a low sound indicative of pain or grief: *The dove mourned in the pine, Sad prophetess of sorrows not her own* (Shelley). —***v.t.*** **1** to feel or show grief over: *to mourn a person's death. She mourned her lost doll. But she must die ... and all the world shall mourn her* (Shakespeare). **SYN**: lament, bewail, bemoan. **2** to utter in a very sorrowful manner: *Where the love-lorn nightingale Nightly to thee her sad song mourneth well* (Milton). [Old English *murnan* to mourn; to be anxious]

**mourn|er** (môr′nər, mōr′-), *n.* **1** a person who mourns, especially at a funeral: *... a flock of mourners dispersing in a desolate cemetery* (Newsweek). **2** a sinner who repents and seeks salvation at a religious revival.

**mourners' bench**, a front bench for repenting sinners at an evangelical religious revival.

**mourn|ful** (môrn′fəl, mōrn′-), *adj.* **1** full of grief; sad; sorrowful: *a mournful voice. Tell me not, in mournful numbers, Life is but an empty dream!* (Longfellow). **SYN**: dolorous, melancholy, doleful. **2** causing or attended with sorrow or mourning: *a mournful death.* **3** gloomy; dreary; somber: *a mournful scene, the mournful howling of the wind.* **4** expressing or used in mourning for the dead: *No mournful bell shall ring her burial* (Shakespeare). *The busy heralds hang the sable scene With mournful 'scutcheons, and dim lamps between* (William Cowper). —**mourn′ful|ly**, *adv.* —**mourn′ful|ness**, *n.*

**mourn|ing** (môr′ning, mōr′-), *n., adj.* —***n.*** **1** the wearing of black or some other color (white in the Orient) to show sorrow for a person's death. **2** the action of draping buildings or flying flags at half-mast as an outward sign of sorrow for death. **3** clothes or decorations used to show sorrow for death: *The Houses to their Tops with Black were spread, And ev'n the Pavements were with Mourning hid* (John Dryden). **4** the act of a person who mourns; sorrowing; lamentation. **5** the period during which black or other display of sorrow is worn.
—***adj.*** of mourning; used in mourning: *mourning apparel.* —**mourn′ing|ly**, *adv.*

**mourning cloak**, a butterfly of Europe and America, having purplish-brown wings with a yellow border; Camberwell beauty.

**mourning dove**, a wild dove that has a low, mournful call. It is found from southern Canada through Mexico, and, in winter, in Panama.

**mourning warbler**, an American warbler with a yellow breast and gray head, and in the male, a black throat.

**mouse** (*n.* mous; *v.* mouz), *n., pl.* **mice**, *v.,* **moused, mous|ing.** —***n.*** **1** a small, gnawing rodent found throughout the world. Mice have soft fur, usually brown, gray, or white, a pointed snout, round, black eyes, rounded ears, and a thin tail. There are many kinds, such as the deer mouse, jumping mouse, and field mouse. Some kinds, such as the house mouse, are highly destructive to stored food. The house mouse is about 3 or 4 inches long and infests human dwellings. Field mice live in the grass of fields and meadows and eat grain and other seeds. **2** a shy, timid person: *Are you a man or a mouse?* **3** a term of affection for a woman or girl: *Let the king ... call you his mouse* (Shakespeare). **4a** a knot made in a rope, or a washer or knob of cord, or other device, fastened on a rope, to prevent it from slipping through an opening. **b** = mousing (def. 1). **5** *Slang.* a black eye.
—***v.i.*** **1** to hunt for mice; catch mice for food: *Cats and owls go mousing at night.* **2** to search as a cat does; move about as if searching; prowl.
—***v.t.*** **1** *U.S.* to hunt for by patient and careful search. **2a** to put a mouse on (a rope or stay). **b** to secure (a hook) with a mousing.
[Old English *mūs*]

**mouse|bird** (mous′bėrd′), *n.* = colie.

**mouse-col|or** (mous′kul′ər), *n.* a soft, dark, dull gray.

**mouse-col|ored** (mous′kul′ərd), *adj.* soft, dark, dull gray: *His forehead is high and narrow, his hair mouse-colored* (New Yorker).

**mouse deer**, = chevrotain.

**mouse-dun** (mous′dun′), *n.* a dark-gray color with a brownish tinge.

**mouse-ear** (mous′ir′), *n.* any one of several plants with small, soft, hairy leaves, such as the hawkweed and the forget-me-not: *Now I am quite content even to play croquet on a well-clipped surface of mouse-ears* (New Yorker).

**mouse-ear chickweed**, any one of a group of plants of the pink family of temperate regions.

**mouse|hole** (mous′hōl′), *n.* a hole through which mice pass, especially into their burrow.

**mouse lemur**, a gray lemur, about the size of a rat.

**mouse|like** (mous′līk′), *adj.* resembling a mouse in appearance, quietness, or timidity: *... remember her as a quiet, mouselike person off stage, with few intellectual interests* (Newsweek).

**mouse pox**, an infectious virus disease of mice characterized by gangrene and often the loss of a limb or limbs; ectromelia.

**mouse|proof** (mous′prüf′), *adj.* protected against mice.

**mous|er** (mou′zər), *n.* **1** an animal that catches mice, such as a cat or an owl. **2** a person who prowls about and pries into matters.

**mouse|tail** (mous′tāl′), *n.* any one of a group of plants of the crowfoot family, the flowers of which have a taillike torus.

**mouse|trap** (mous′trap′), *n., v.,* **-trapped, -trap|ping.** —***n.*** **1** a trap for catching mice. **2** *Football.* an attacking maneuver in which a defensive lineman is permitted to charge without initial opposition but blocked from the side while the ball carrier runs through the hole thus created: *Always they must beware the too-easy charge, the opposition that seems to fade away in front of them which warns of a mousetrap* (Time).
—***v.t.*** **1** *Football.* to lure (an opposing football player) into a mousetrap. **2** *Figurative.* to trick; wheedle: *... at night I'd mousetrap the doorman at the Empire to exult in Ethel Barrymore in Déclassée* (Tallulah Bankhead).

**mous|ey** (mou′sē), *adj.,* **mous|i|er, mous|i|est.** = mousy.

**mous|ie** (mou′sē), *n. Scottish.* little mouse, a pet name.

**mous|i|ly** (mou′sə lē), *adv.* in a mousy manner.

**mous|i|ness** (mou′sē nis), *n.* mousy character or condition.

**mous|ing** (mou′zing), *n.* **1** several turns of small rope or cord, uniting the shank and point of a hook, to keep a rope or an object from slipping off. **2** a knot formed on rope with yarn, rope, or cord; mouse.

**Mous|que|taire** (müs′kə tãr′), *n.* a member of the French royal household troops in the 1600's and 1700's, famous as dandies. [< French *mousquetaire* < *mousquet* musket]

**mous|que|taire** (müs′kə tãr′), *n., adj.* —***n.*** = musketeer.
—***adj.*** formal and colorful, in the style of the royal Mousquetaires: *Mousquetaire gloves are long closed gloves.*

**mous|sa|ka** (mü′sä kä′), *n.* a Greek baked dish consisting of layers of ground meat with eggplant or zucchini between them, olive oil, and a topping of cheese and dough. [< New Greek *mousaká* < Rumanian *musacá*]

**mousse** (müs), *n.* **1** a fancy food made with whipped cream, either frozen or stiffened with gelatin: *chocolate mousse, tomato mousse.* **2** a meat or fish purée lightened with gelatin or whipped cream or both. [< French *mousse* < Old French, froth, scum; perhaps same as *mousse* moss, apparently < Germanic (compare Old High German *mos* moss)]

**mousse|line** (müs lēn′), *n.* **1** fine muslin: *As simple as the jackets are the evening coats of ... beige wool mousseline* (New York Times). **2** a very thin glass used for fine wineglasses. [< French *mousseline;* see etym. under **muslin**]

**mousse|line de laine** (müs lēn′ də len′), a thin woolen fabric, often have a printed pattern; delaine. [< French *mousseline de laine* mousseline of wool]

**mousse|line de soie** (müs lēn′ də swä′), a thin, sheer, silk fabric, slightly stiffened. [< French *mousseline de soie* mousseline of silk]

**mous|tache** (mus′tash, mə stash′), *n.* = mustache.

**mous|ta|chio** (mə stä′shō), *n., pl.* **-chios.** *Especially British.* a mustache.

**Mous|te|ri|an** or **Mous|tie|ri|an** (müs tir′ē ən), *adj.* designating or having to do with a period of paleolithic culture marking the highest point of the Neanderthal race: *Prior to the Mousterian flints, there had been no evolution of flint-making* (Ogburn and Nimkoff). [< French *moustérien* < *Moustier,* a village in Dordogne, France, where cave remains were found]

**mous|y** (mou′sē), *adj.,* **mous|i|er, mous|i|est.** **1** resembling or suggesting a mouse in color, odor, or behavior: *a mousy little man afraid to stand up for his rights. She had mousy hair. In one bottle ... he found no poison, but testified he identified the mousy odor of conine* (Baltimore Sun). **2** as quiet as a mouse: *A man ought not to remain mousy* (Sporting Magazine). **3** overrun with mice: *... the roomy and mousy old closet beside the fireplace* (Mary E. Braddon). Also, **mousey**.

***mouth** (*n.* mouth; *v.* mouŦH), *n., pl.* **mouths** (mouŦHz), *v.* —***n.*** **1** the opening through which a person or an animal takes in food; space containing the tongue and teeth: *Several teeth were missing from the old man's mouth.* **2a** an opening suggesting a mouth: *the mouth of a cave, the mouth of a well, the mouth of a bottle.* **SYN**: entrance, inlet. **b** an opening out of which something shoots forth: *the mouth of a cannon, the mouth of a volcano.* **3** a part of a river or the like where its waters are emptied into the sea, another river, or some other body of water: *the mouth of the Ohio River.* **SYN**: estuary. **4** a grimace: *The foolish boy made mouths at us.* **5** the mouth as the structure for chewing, tasting, and, sometimes, swallowing. **6** a person or an animal requiring food and support: *He has seven mouths to feed in his family. The Lord never sends a mouth into the world without providing meat for it* (John Galt). **7a** the mouth as the source of spoken words: *And all ... wondered at the gracious words which proceeded out of his mouth* (Luke 4:22). *I was but the mouth of the rest, and spoke what they have dictated to me* (Samuel Pepys). **b** utterance of words; speech: *to get news by mouth, to give mouth to one's thoughts.* **c** a cry or bay of an animal: *My hounds are ... match'd in mouth like bells* (Shakespeare). **8** the fork between the open jaws of a vise, scissors, pincers, or the like. **9** *Music.* **a** the opening of an organ flue pipe by means of which the sound is produced. **b** an opening across which one blows, as in a flute.
—***v.t.*** **1** to utter (words) in an affected or pompous way: *I dislike actors who mouth their speeches. She mouthed her words in speaking; her voice was deep, its inflections very pompous* (Charlotte Brontë). **2** to rub, press, or mumble with the mouth or lips: *Psyche ... hugg'd ... and in her hunger mouth'd and mumbled it [a baby]* (Tennyson). **3** to put or take into the mouth; seize with the mouth or jaws. **4** to accustom (a horse) to the bit and bridle.
—***v.i.*** **1** to speak oratorically: *Stop mouthing and listen to what I have to say.* **2** to make grimaces. **SYN**: mow.
**down in the mouth**, *Informal.* in low spirits; discouraged: *"I'm not sure," the young man said, looking a bit down in the mouth* (New Yorker).
**foam at the mouth**, to be vehemently angry or enraged: *He ... foamed at the mouth, and was speechless* (Shakespeare).
**from the horse's mouth**. See under **horse**.
**laugh on the other side** (or **wrong side**) **of one's mouth**, *Informal.* to be annoyed; be made sorry: *You'll mayhap be making such a slip yourself someday; you'll laugh o' the other side of your mouth then* (George Eliot).
**make one's mouth water**, to arouse one's appetite or desire: *The display of exotic foods made his mouth water.*
**shoot off one's mouth**, or **shoot one's mouth off**, *U.S. Slang.* to talk freely and indiscreetly: *Don't you know better than to shoot your mouth off like that?* (George W. Cable).
[Old English *mūth*] —**mouth′like′**, *adj.*

***mouth**
definition 1

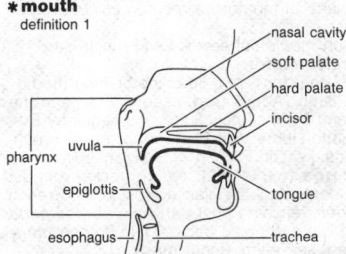

nasal cavity
soft palate
hard palate
incisor
uvula
pharynx
epiglottis
tongue
esophagus
trachea

**mouth|breed|er** (mouth′brē′dər), *n.* any one of various small fishes that hold their eggs and their

**Pronunciation Key:** hat, āge, cãre, fär; let, ēqual, tėrm; it, īce; hot, ōpen, ôrder; oil, out; cup, pu̇t, rüle; **ch**ild; lo**ng**; **th**in; **ŦH**en; **zh**, measure; **ə** represents **a** in about, **e** in taken, **i** in pencil, **o** in lemon, **u** in circus.

hatched young in their mouths.

**mouth brush**, the long hairs around the jaws of mosquito larvae which they use to sweep food into the mouth.

**mouthed** (mouᴛʜd, moutht), *adj.* having a mouth or mouths: *a mouthed shell* (Keats).

**-mouthed**, *combining form.* having a ___ mouth: *Open-mouthed = having an open mouth.*

**mouth|er** (mou′ᴛʜər), *n.* a person who mouths; long-winded talker.

**mouth|ful** (mouth′fu̇l), *n., pl.* **-fuls.** **1** the amount the mouth can easily hold: *The hikers stopped for a few mouthfuls of water and were soon on the trail again.* **2** what is taken into the mouth at one time: *His cheeks bulged with a huge mouthful of cake.* **3** a small amount: *I wanted only a mouthful of soup, not a whole bowl.* **4** *Informal.* a word or phrase that is very long or difficult to pronounce. **5** *Slang.* a statement notable for its truth or appropriateness: *You said a mouthful.*

**mouth|i|ly** (mou′ᴛʜə lē, -thə-), *adv.* in a mouthy manner.

**mouth|i|ness** (mou′ᴛʜē nis, -thē-), *n.* mouthy quality; talkativeness.

**mouth|ing** (mou′ᴛʜing), *n.* something which is uttered in a pompously oratorical style or with great distinctness of articulation, but often not with sincerity: *The pious mouthings of people like Mr. Sass are more exasperating than the rantings of ignorant fanatics* (Atlantic).

**mouth|less** (mouth′lis), *adj.* having no mouth or opening.

**mouth organ**, **1** = harmonica. **2** = Panpipe.

**mouth|parts** (mouth′pärts′), *n.pl. Biology.* the parts of the mouth, as of insects and crustaceans. The labrum, labium, mandible, and maxilla are mouthparts.

**mouth|piece** (mouth′pēs′), *n.* **1** the part of a musical instrument, such as a pipe, horn, or the like, or of a telephone or a tobacco pipe, that is placed in or against a person's mouth. **2a** the part of a bit or harness of a horse that is held in the mouth. **b** a rubber guard held in the mouth by a boxer to prevent chipped teeth or cut lips resulting from head blows: *I got to feel my right crashing on his jaw, see his mouthpiece flying off with the blood and the sweat* (New York Times). **3** a piece placed at or forming the opening of something: *the mouthpiece of a tube or a water pipe.* **4** a person, newspaper, or other medium that speaks for others; spokesman: *They fancied him the mouthpiece of Heaven's messages of wisdom, and rebuke, and love* (Hawthorne). **5** *Slang.* a lawyer, especially a criminal lawyer.

**mouth-to-mouth** (mouth′tə mouth′), *adj.* of or designating a method of artificial respiration in which air is breathed directly into the victim's mouth and nose to inflate the lungs, with intervals to allow the lungs to empty: *Christopher, 2, appeared lifeless, but firemen restored his breathing by mouth-to-mouth resuscitation* (New York Times).

**mouth|wash** (mouth′wosh′, -wôsh′), *n.* a mildly antiseptic liquid to cleanse the mouth and teeth.

**mouth-wa|ter|ing** (mouth′wôt′ər ing, -wot′-), *adj.* causing the mouth to water; appetizing; tempting: *... items laid out in a mouth-watering display of U.S. consumer goods* (Time).

**mouth|y** (mou′ᴛʜē, -thē), *adj.,* **mouth|i|er, mouth|i|est.** loud-mouthed; using many words to say little; ranting; bombastic: *He ... was prone to be mouthy and magniloquent* (Washington Irving).

**mou|ton**[1] (mü′ton), *n., adj.* —*n.* Also, **mouton lamb.** a fur made from a sheep's pelt by shearing it to medium length, processing, and dyeing it, commonly to resemble that of beaver: *The floor of the Directeur is covered with light-blue mouton* (New Yorker).

—*adj.* made of mouton: *a mouton collar, a mouton coat.*

[< French *mouton* sheep < Old French; see etym. under **mutton**]

**mou|ton**[2] (mü′ton), *n.* gold coins bearing the figure of a lamb (Agnus Dei), used in France in the 1300's and 1400's, including coins struck by Edward III and Henry V of England for their French dominions. [< Old French *mouton* sheep]

**mou|ton|née** (mü′tə nā′), *adj.* (of rocks) rounded like a sheep's back by glacial erosion. [< French *moutonnée,* feminine past participle of *moutonner* to round like a sheep's back < Old French *mouton* sheep; see etym. under **mutton**]

**mou|ton|néed** (mü′tə nād′), *adj.* = moutonnée.

**mov|a|bil|i|ty** (mü′və bil′ə tē), *n.* movable quality or condition. Also, **moveability.**

**mov|a|ble** (mü′və bəl), *adj., n.* —*adj.* **1** that can be moved; not fixed in one place or position: *Our fingers are movable.* **SYN**: mobile. **2** that can be carried from place to place as personal belongings can: *All movable articles including pictures and rugs were taken out of the apartment before the next tenants moved in.* **SYN**: portable, transportable. **3** changing from one date to another in different years: *Easter is a movable holy day. Thanksgiving is a movable holiday.*

—*n.* **1** a piece of furniture that is not a fixture but can be moved to another house or building: *The apartment ... was destitute of all movables save a broken armchair, and an old couch or sofa* (Dickens). **2** a thing that can be moved, removed, or set in motion. Also, **moveable.**

**movables**, *Law.* personal property: *Books of travel have familiarized every reader with the custom of burying a dead man's movables with him* (Herbert Spencer).

—**mov′a|ble|ness**, *n.*

**mov|a|bly** (mü′və blē), *adv.* in a movable manner; so as to be movable. Also, **moveably.**

**move** (müv), *v.,* **moved, mov|ing,** *n.* —*v.t.* **1** to change the place or position of: *Do not move your hand. Move your chair to the other side of the table. She moved her lips ... but could not speak* (Thomas Hardy). **SYN**: shift, remove, transfer. **2** to put or keep in motion; shake, stir, or disturb: *The wind moves the leaves.* **3** to impel; rouse; excite; prompt: *What moved you to do this? I have prepared such arguments as will not Fail to move them* (Byron). **4** to arouse (a person to laughter, anger, or pity): *The sad story moved her to tears.* **SYN**: influence. **5** (in games) to change the position of (a piece): *to move a pawn in chess.* **6** to bring forward formally; propose: *Mr. Chairman, I move that we adjourn.* **7** *Commerce.* to find buyers for; sell: *That store can move these dresses.* **8** to cause to act: *Castor oil moves the bowels.* **9** *Archaic.* to suggest; urge: *My mother refused to move it* [*a proposition*] *to my father* (Daniel Defoe). **10** *Obsolete.* **a** to exhort or urge to do something: *I ... begged him ... that he would move the Captains to take some pity on me* (Jonathan Swift). **b** to apply to for something: *The Florentine will move us For speedy aid* (Shakespeare).

—*v.i.* **1** to change place or position; pass from one place or position to another: *The child moved in his sleep. The earth moves around the sun.* **2** to change one's place of living: *We have moved from 96th Street to 110th Street.* **3** to be in motion; be stirred: *Then move the trees, the copses nod* (Tennyson). **4** to make progress; go; advance; proceed: *The train moved out slowly. Then the tale Shall move on soberly* (Keats). **SYN**: See syn. under **advance.** **5** to act: *God moves in a mysterious way, His wonders to perform* (William Cowper). *Had the city moved sooner ... there would have been no rising, no riot* (Cardinal Newman). **6a** to make a move in a game: *Move quickly, don't delay the game.* **b** to be moved in a game. **7** to make a formal request, application, or proposal: *to move for a new trial.* **8** *Commerce.* to change hands or be sold: *These pink dresses are moving slowly.* **9** to be active; exist: *to move in the best society, to move in artistic circles.* **10** to turn; swing; operate: *Most doors move on hinges.* **SYN**: work, revolve. **11** to carry oneself: *to move with dignity and grace.* **12** *Informal.* to start off; depart: *It's time to be moving. When the ambulance had left, the crowd moved on.* **13** (of the bowels) to be moved; act.

—*n.* **1** the act of moving; movement: *an impatient move of her head.* **2** *Figurative.* an action taken to bring about some result; step: *His next move was to earn some money. Our move to get a better place to play succeeded.* **3a** a player's turn to move in a game: *It is your move.* **b** the moving of a piece in chess and other games: *a good move.* **4** a change of a place to live.

**get a move on**, *Slang.* **a** to make haste; hurry up: *A correspondent from Rhodesia says, "Get cracking, or I will come over." We would say "get a move on!"* (Holiday). **b** to begin to move: *I remember with what excitement the Fleet received the signal: "Winston is back." Now we shall ... get a move on* (Lord Mountbatten).

**move in**, to move oneself, one's family, and one's belongings into a new place to live: *The new couple is moving in next week.*

**move in on**, *Informal.* **a** to attack: *The soldiers moved in on the well-defended old house from all sides.* **b** to take steps to dispossess (a person) of power or of control or ownership, as of a business or a property: *The bankers began talking of the "saturation point" in the auto market and moved in on him* (Time).

**move up**, to promote or be promoted: *Dr. Cabot was moved up from an associate to a full professorship.*

**on the move**, **a** moving about: *The action ... is nervy, always on the move* (Maclean's). **b** active: *The extremists in the Chinese leadership are on the move again* (Victor Zorza). **c** traveling: *He's been on the move from job to job for many years. ... a wandering people ... continually on the move* (Washington Irving).

[< Anglo-French *mover,* Old French *moveir* < Latin *movēre*]

—*Syn. v.t.* **3** **Move, actuate, prompt** mean to cause a person to act in a certain way. **Move,** the general word, does not suggest whether the cause is an outside force or influence or an inner urge or personal motive: *Something moved him to change his mind.* **Actuate,** a formal word, always implies a powerful inner force, like a strong feeling, desire, or principle: *He was actuated by desire for praise.* **Prompt** is used chiefly when the cause of action is thought of as comparatively minor: *My conversation with her prompted me to write you.*

**move|a|bil|i|ty** (mü′və bil′ə tē), *n.* = movability.

**move|a|ble** (mü′və bəl), *adj., n.* = movable.

—**move′a|ble|ness**, *n.*

**move|a|bles** (mü′və bəlz), *n.pl.* = movables. See under **movable.**

**move|a|bly** (mü′və blē), *adv.* = movably.

**move|less** (müv′lis), *adj.* without movement or motion; motionless; immovable: *His limbs were moveless in an exasperating and obstinate calm* (Arnold Bennett). —**move′less|ly**, *adv.* —**move′less|ness**, *n.*

**move|ment** (müv′mənt), *n.* **1** the act or fact of moving: *We run by movements of the legs. Sometimes he binds his limbs with rope so that reflex movements will not jar his hand* (Newsweek). **SYN**: move, action, stir. See syn. under **motion.** **2** a change in the placing of troops or ships, especially as part of a tactical maneuver. **3** the moving parts of a machine or mechanism; special group of parts that move on each other. The movement of a watch consists of many little wheels. **4** *Music.* **a** the kind of rhythm and speed a piece has: *The movement of a waltz is very different from the movement of a march.* **b** one division of a sonata, symphony, concerto, or other long selection. One movement is distinguished from the others by tempo and by melodic and rhythmical structure. **5** *Figurative.* rhythmical or accentual structure or character in poetry. **6** *Figurative.* the suggestion of action in a painting or sculpture. **7** abundance of incidents; action. **8** the efforts and results of a group of people working together to bring about some one thing: *the movement for a safe and sane Fourth of July.* **9** a notable change in the price of something. **10** activity in the market for some commodity, stock, or other security: *The movement in coffee is insignificant.* **11a** an emptying of the bowels. **b** the waste matter emptied from the bowels.

**mov|er** (mü′vər), *n.* **1** a person or thing that moves: *We* [*poets*] *are the movers and shakers of the World* (A. W. E. O'Shaughnessy). **2** a person or company whose occupation is moving furniture, office equipment, and the possessions in houses, stores, and offices, from one place to another: *When you plan ... a long distance move—you'll probably call several movers for quotations* (Maclean's).

**mov|ie** (mü′vē), *n., adj. Informal.* —*n.* **1** = motion picture. **SYN**: cinema. **2** a motion-picture theater: *a neighborhood movie.* **SYN**: cinema.

—*adj.* of or having to do with motion pictures: *a movie actress, a movie theater.*

**movies**, the motion-picture industry: *Movies are turning more toward producing for television.*

**the movies**, a showing of motion pictures: *We go once a week to the movies.*

[American English, short for *movi*(ng picture)]

**mov|ie|dom** (mü′vē dəm), *n.* = filmdom.

**mov|ie|go|er** (mü′vē gō′ər), *n.* cinemagoer; filmgoer: *They have been seen by millions of moviegoers in the nation's theaters* (Wall Street Journal).

**mov|ie|go|ing** (mü′vē gō′ing), *n., adj.* —*n.* the act or practice of a moviegoer; a going to the movies: *The experience of moviegoing ... gave us all a fantasy life in common* (Harper's).

—*adj.* that goes to the movies: *the moviegoing public.*

**movie house**, a motion-picture theater.

**mov|ie|mak|er** (mü′vē mā′kər), *n.* **1** a professional producer of motion pictures: *Moviemakers from thirty-five nations plan to show their wares at the Cannes Film Festival* (New York Times). **2** an individual who takes his own motion pictures: *... a brand-new camera, designed as the last word for amateur moviemakers* (Time).

**mov|ie|mak|ing** (mü′vē mā′king), *n., adj.* —*n.* **1** the production of a motion picture. **2** acting in or otherwise taking part in the production of a motion picture: *Power gave up fulltime moviemaking in 1952* (Time).

—*adj.* of, having to do with, or characteristic of moviemaking.

**mov|ie|o|la** (mü′vē ō′lə), *n.* a motion-picture projector used in film editing. It has a small viewing screen and allows control of the speed and direction of film movement.

**mov|ing** (mü′ving), *adj., v.* —*adj.* **1** that moves: *a moving car.* **2** causing or producing motion; having motion: *The more the moving force is distant*

*from the center of motion, so much the more force it shall have* (John Leak). **3** causing action; actuating: *He was the moving spirit in planning for the party.* **4** touching; pathetic: *a moving story. A decayed widow ... has laid her case of destitution before him in a very moving letter* (Hawthorne). SYN: affecting.
— *v.* present participle of **move**. —**mov′ing|ly,** *adv.* —**mov′ing|ness,** *n.*

**moving cluster,** a galactic cluster close enough to earth so that its relative motion can be easily measured. The Hyades form a moving cluster.

**moving picture,** = motion picture.

**moving-picture machine,** = motion-picture projector.

**moving platform** or **sidewalk,** a platform or sidewalk constructed on the principle of an endless belt and moving at a regular speed, for carrying along objects or persons.

**moving staircase** or **stairway,** a staircase constructed on the principle of an endless belt, that moves and carries people up or down; escalator.

**Mov|i|o|la** (mü′vē ō′lə), *n. Trademark.* a movieola.

**mow**[1] (mō), *v.,* **mowed, mowed** or **mown, mowing.** —*v.t.* **1** to cut down with a machine or a scythe: *to mow grass.* **2** to cut down the grass or grain from: *to mow a lawn, to mow a field.* **3** *Figurative.* to destroy at a sweep or in large numbers, as if by mowing: *The firing of the enemy mowed down our men like grass.*
—*v.i.* to cut down grass or grain: *The men are mowing today.*
[Old English *māwan*]

**mow**[2] (mou), *n.* **1** a place in a barn where hay or grain is piled or stored: *Littered the stalls, and from the mows Raked down the herd's-grass for the cows* (John Greenleaf Whittier). **2** a pile or stack of hay or grain in a barn. [Old English *mūga, mūwa*]

**mow**[3] or **mowe** (mō, mou), *v.,* **mowed, mowing,** *n.* —*v.i.* to grimace: *like apes that mow and chatter at me* (Shakespeare). SYN: mop.
—*n.* a grimace; derisive grimace: *that devil that ... made mows and mockery at his unsufferable tortures* (William Godwin). SYN: mop.
[Middle English *mouwe,* perhaps < Middle Dutch, or < Old French *moue* < Germanic (compare Middle High German *mouwe*)]

**mow|er** (mō′ər), *n.* **1** a person who mows grass, grain, or weeds. **2** a mowing machine or lawn mower.

**mow|ing** (mō′ing), *n.* **1** cutting down grass, grain, or weeds with a scythe or machine. **2** *U.S.* meadowland. **3** the amount of hay cut at one time.

**mowing machine, 1** a machine with cutting blades attached to a metal arm, used to cut down tall grass, standing hay, grain, or weeds. **2** any machine used to mow.

**mown** (mōn), *v.* mowed; a past participle of **mow**[1]: *New-mown hay is hay that has just been cut.*

**mox|a** (mok′sə), *n.* **1** a soft, downy substance prepared from dried leaves of a Chinese and Japanese wormwood. It is used in China and Japan to burn on the skin as a counterirritant or cauterizing agent. **2** the plant itself. **3** any substance similarly used. [< Japanese *mogusa*]

**mox|i|bus|tion** (mok′sə bus′chən), *n.* the use of moxa in medicine, especially as a cauterizing agent: *Next, the doctor resorted to another traditional Chinese treatment called moxibustion: he lit two pieces of an herb called ai or ngai (Artemisia vulgaris, or wormwood) and held the smoldering wads near Teston's abdomen* (Time). [< moxa + (com)*bustion*]

**mox|ie** (mok′sē), *n. U.S. Slang.* **1** courage; bravery; nerve: *But Miss Burnett has an ample supply of what might be called heart, or moxie, or even gall* (Ernest Havemann). **2** know-how; skill; experience. [< earlier *Moxie,* a trademark for a soft drink]

**moy|en âge** (mwȧ ye nȧzh′), *French.* the medieval period; Middle Ages: [*He*] *has set his novel of King Arthur in the Middle Ages—but his moyen âge is not the time of the chivalry-loving Sir Thomas* (New York Times).

**Moz|ar|ab** (mō zar′əb), *n.* one of a class of Spanish Christians who submitted to the domination of the Moors and were permitted to retain their own religion. [< Spanish *Mozárabe* < Arabic *musta′rib* (literally) a "would-be" Arab]

**Moz|ar|a|bic** (mō zar′ə bik), *adj.* **1** of or having to do with the Mozarabs. **2** having to do with the ancient Christian liturgy of Spain, a modified form of which is still used in certain Spanish chapels.

**Mozarabic chant,** the plain song of early Christian liturgy in Spain, fragments of which continue to be used in some Spanish churches though Gregorian chant has largely superseded it.

**Mo|zar|te|an** or **Mo|zar|ti|an** (mō tsär′tē ən, -zär′-), *adj.* of, having to do with, or characteristic of Wolfgang Amadeus Mozart (1756-1791) or his music: *the Mozartean touch.*

**moz|za|rel|la** (moz′ə rel′ə, mot′sə-), *n.* a soft, white, mild Italian cheese. [< Italian *mozzarella*]

**moz|zet|ta** or **mo|zet|ta** (mō zet′ə), *n.* a short, hooded cape worn by the pope, cardinals, bishops, and abbots. [< Italian *mozzetta* (diminutive) < *mozza* shortened]

**mp** (no periods), *Music.* mezzo piano.

**m.p.,** melting point.

**M.P.** or **MP** (no periods), an abbreviation for the following:
**1** Member of Parliament.
**2** Metropolitan Police (of London).
**3** Military Police.
**4** Mounted Police.

**MPA** (no periods) or **M.P.A.,** an abbreviation for the following:
**1** Magazine Publishers' Association.
**2** man-powered aircraft.
**3** Master of Public Administration.
**4** Motion Picture Association of America.

**MPC** (no periods), maximum permissible concentration (a measurement of radioactive fallout).

**M.P.C.,** military payment certificate.

**mpg** (no periods) or **m.p.g.,** miles per gallon.

**mph** (no periods) or **m.p.h.,** miles per hour.

**mpm** (no periods) or **m.p.m.,** meters per minute.

**M|pon|do** (em pon′dō), *n., pl.* **-dos** or **-do.** = Pondo.

**M.P.P.** or **MPP** (no periods), Member of the Provincial Parliament (of Canada).

**mr** (no period), **1** microroentgen. **2** milliroentgen.

**Mr.** or **Mr** (mis′tər), *pl.* **Messrs.** mister, a title put in front of a man's name or the name of his position: *Mr. Jackson, Mr. Chairman, Mr. President.* [(originally) abbreviation of *master*]
► **Mr.** is written out only when it represents informal usage and when it is used without a name: *"They're only two for five, mister."*

**MR** (no periods), milliroentgen.

**M.R.A.** or **MRA** (no periods), Moral Re-Armament.

**mrad** (no period), millirad.

**MRBM** (no periods), medium range ballistic missile; IRBM.

**Mr. Charlie** or **Mr. Charley,** = Mister Charlie.

**M.R.C.P.,** Member of the Royal College of Physicians (of England).

**M.R.C.S.,** Member of the Royal College of Surgeons (of England).

**M.R.E.,** Master of Religious Education.

**mrem** (no period), millirem.

**mri|dan|ga** (mrē däng′gə), *n.* an ancient drum of India with a long, conical shape and two heads, one larger than the other. [< Sanskrit *mṛdaṅga*]

**mRNA** (no periods), messenger RNA: *mRNA in DNA may also be the basis for the timing cycle that regulates cell activity* (Jacob Kastner).

**M-roof** (em′rüf′, -ru̇f′), *n.* a roof formed by the junction of two gable roofs with a valley between, so as in transverse section to resemble somewhat the letter M.

**MRP** (no periods) or **M.R.P.,** Mouvement Républicain Populaire (Popular Republican Movement, a French political party in the Fourth and Fifth Republics).

**Mrs.** or **Mrs** (mis′iz, miz′-; miz), *pl.* **Mmes.** mistress, a title put in front of a married woman's name: *Mrs. Jackson.* [abbreviation of *mistress*]
► **Mrs.** is written out only in representing informal usage and is then spelled *missis* (or *missus*): *Mrs. Dorothy M. Adams, Mrs. Smith. "Where's the missis?"*

**Mrs. Grundy,** = Grundy.

**MRV** (no periods), multiple reentry vehicle (a missile similar to the MIRV): *MRVs ... land in a preplanned pattern, but they cannot be steered to widely separated targets* (Time).

**ms** (no period), millisecond.

**m/s, 1** meters per second. **2** *Commerce.* months after sight.

**m.s.,** motorship.

**Ms.**[1], manuscript.

**Ms.**[2] (miz), *pl.* **Mses.** or **Ms.'s** (miz′ēz). an abbreviated title used instead of *Miss* or *Mrs.*: *The term Ms. itself, devised as a female honorific that, like Mr., does not reveal marital status, is winning wider acceptance* (Time).

**MS** (no periods), **1** Mississippi (with postal Zip Code). **2** multiple sclerosis.

**MS., Ms** (no period), or **ms.,** manuscript.

**M.S., 1** Master of Science. **2** motorship.

**MSA** (no periods), Mutual Security Agency.

**M.S.A., 1** Master of Science and Art. **2** Master of Science in Agriculture.

**MSC** (no periods), Manned Spacecraft Center.

**M.Sc.,** Master of Science.

**M.S.C.E.,** Master of Science in Civil Engineering.

**msec** (no period), millisecond.

**M.S.E.E.,** Master of Science in Electrical Engineering.

**MSG** (no periods), monosodium glutamate.

**Msgr., 1** Monseigneur. **2** Monsignor.

**M/Sgt** (no period) or **M.Sgt.,** master sergeant.

**MSH** (no periods), melanocyte-stimulating hormone; intermedin.

**MSI**[1] (no periods), medium-scale integration (a method of producing a number of integrated circuits on a single chip of silicon).

**MSI**[2] (no periods) or **M.S.I.,** Movimento Sociale Italiano (Italian Social Movement, a political party in Italy).

**m'sieur** (mə syœ′), *n.* = monsieur.

**m.s.l.,** mean sea level.

**MSO** (no periods), ocean minesweeper.

**MSR** (no periods), missile site radar (an electronic radar used at antiballistic missile sites).

**MSS., MSS** (no period), **Mss.,** or **mss.,** manuscripts.

**M.S.S., 1** Master of Social Science. **2** Master of Social Service.

**MST** (no periods), **M.S.T.,** or **m.s.t.,** Mountain Standard Time.

**MsTh** (no period), mesothorium.

**MSTS** (no periods) or **M.S.T.S.,** Military Sea Transportation Service.

**M.S.W.,** Master of Social Work.

**mt., 1** megaton. **2** mountain.

**m.t., 1** metric ton. **2** Mountain time.

**Mt.,** Mount: *Mt. Everest, Mt. Whitney.*

**MT** (no periods), **1** machine translation. **2** Montana (with postal Zip Code).

**M.T.,** an abbreviation for the following:
**1** Masoretic Text (of the Old Testament).
**2** metric ton.
**3** motor transport.
**4** Mountain Time.

**MTB** (no periods) or **M.T.B.,** motor torpedo boat.

**mtg., 1** meeting. **2** mortgage.

**mtgd.,** mortgaged.

**mtge.,** mortgage.

**MTI** (no periods), moving target indication (radar).

**mtn.,** mountain.

**MTO** (no periods), Mediterranean Theater of Operations (in World War II).

**Mt. Rev.,** Most Reverend.

**mts.,** mountains.

***mu** (myü), *n.* **1** the twelfth letter of the Greek alphabet. **2** = micron, a unit of length. **3** = mu-meson. [< Greek *mŷ*]

| ***mu** definition 1 | M capital letter | μ lower-case letter |
|---|---|---|

**Mu** (myü), *n.* a mythical lost continent, alleged to have sunk into the southwestern Pacific Ocean at about the same time Atlantis is alleged to have disappeared into the Atlantic.

**much** (much), *adj.,* **more, most,** *n., adv.,* **more, most,** *v.,* **muched, much|ing.** —*adj.* **1** in great amount or degree: *much rain, much pleasure, not much money. Too much cake will make you sick. A pale yellow sun ... showed the much dirt of the place* (Rudyard Kipling). **2** *Obsolete.* many; numerous: *Edom came out against him with much people* (Numbers 20:20).
—*n.* **1** a great deal or amount: *Much of this is not true. I did not hear much of the talk.* **2** a great, important, or notable thing or matter: *The rain did not amount to much. The house is not much to look at.*
—*adv.* **1** to a high degree; greatly: *much higher. I was much pleased with the toy.* **2** nearly; about: *This is much the same as the others. You have a son, much of his age* (Roger Ascham). SYN: approximately.
—*v.t. Dialect.* to make much of; pet; caress: *It is the mark of a good watchdog ... that he can't be muched by any passerby, but only by persons of rare talent* (Baltimore Sun).
**make much of,** to pay much attention to or do much for: *Young people usually don't make much of the customs of their parents.*
**much as, a** in the same way as: *Plants need food, much as animals do.* **b** though; although: *Much as he disagreed with the idea he was willing to go along with the majority.*
**much of a, a** nearly the same: *He and his brother are much of a size.* **b** in any great or special degree: *A job that keeps a worker in poverty is ... not much of a job* (Albert Shanker).
**so much, a** a small or limited amount: *You can only buy so much with five dollars.* **b** a great deal of; a lot: *This idea strikes me as so much nonsense.*
**too much, a** more than a match: *The big dog*

**Pronunciation Key:** hat, āge, cãre, fär; let, ēqual, tėrm; it, īce; hot, ōpen, ôrder; oil, out; cup, pu̇t, rüle; child; long; thin; ᴛʜen; zh, measure; ə represents **a** in about, **e** in taken, **i** in pencil, **o** in lemon, **u** in circus.

*was too much for him, and he couldn't hold him on the leash.* **b** *Slang.* very poor; terrible: *This actor is just too much!* **c** *Slang.* very funny or amusing: *Oh, you're too much!*
[Middle English *muche,* short for *muchel,* Old English *micel.* Compare etym. under **mickle.**]

**much|ly** (much′lē), *adv.* much; exceedingly: *Thanks muchly.*

**much|ness** (much′nis), *n.* greatness; magnitude.
**much of a muchness,** much alike; nearly equivalent: *much of a muchness—no better, and perhaps no worse* (Henry Kingsley).

**mu|cic acid** (myü′sik), a white, crystalline dibasic acid formed by oxidizing certain gums and lactose in the presence of nitric acid. *Formula:* $C_6H_{10}O_8$ [perhaps < French *mucique* < Latin *mūcus* slime, mucus]

**mu|cid** (myü′sid), *adj.* musty or slimy, as from decay; moldy. [< Latin *mūcidus* < *mūcus,* slime, mucus] —**mu′cid|ness,** *n.*

**mu|cif|er|ous** (myü sif′ər əs), *adj.* carrying or secreting mucus. [< Latin *mūcus* mucus + English *-ferous*]

**mu|cig|e|nous** (myü sij′ə nəs), *adj.* secreting mucus; muciparous. [< Latin *mūcus* mucus + English *-gen* + *-ous*]

**mu|cig|e|nous** (myü sij′ə nəs), *adj.* secreting mucus; muciparous. [< Latin *mūcus* mucus + English *-gen* + *-ous*]

**mu|ci|lage** (myü′sə lij), *n.* **1** a sticky, gummy substance used to make things stick together, especially a solution of gum or glue in water. **2** a secretion like glue or gelatin in plants such as seaweeds. [< Middle French *mucilage,* learned borrowing from Late Latin *mūcilāgo* musty juice < Latin *mūcus* mold[2], mucus]

**mu|ci|lag|i|nous** (myü′sə laj′ə nəs), *adj.* **1** like mucilage; sticky; gummy. **SYN:** glutinous, viscid. **2** containing or secreting mucilage. —**mu′ci|lag′i|nous|ly,** *adv.*

**mu|cin** (myü′sin), *n.* any one of various proteins forming the chief constituents of mucous secretions; mucoprotein: *Lysozyme ... interests bacteriologists because it dissolves the mucins with which the microbes are covered* (Sunday Times). [probably < French *mucine* < Latin *mūcus* mucus + French *-ine* -in]

**mu|cin|ous** (myü′sə nəs), *adj.* **1** of or having to do with mucin. **2** like mucin.

**mu|cip|a|rous** (myü sip′ər əs), *adj.* producing or secreting mucus: *muciparous glands.* [< Latin *mūcus* mucus + *parere* to give birth + English *-ous*]

**muck** (muk), *n., v.* —*n.* **1** dirt; filth; dirty slush: *The basement was covered with muck and slime after the flood.* **2** anything filthy, dirty, or disgusting. **3** moist farmyard manure, used as a fertilizer; dung. **4** *U.S.* **a** a heavy, moist, dark soil made up chiefly of decayed plants. **b** well-decomposed peat, used as a manure. **5** *Informal.* an untidy condition; mess: *a muck of sweat* (Oliver Goldsmith). **6** *Mining.* earth, rock, and other debris to be removed in getting at the mineral sought.
—*v.t.* **1** to soil or make dirty: *You can't touch pitch and not be mucked, lad* (Robert Louis Stevenson). **2** to put muck on.
**muck about** (or **around**), *Slang.* to waste time; putter; go about aimlessly: *Some players and spectators are fed up with the way they keep mucking about with the rules of the game* (Manchester Guardian Weekly).
**muck in,** *British Slang.* to mingle; associate (with); share quarters (with): *hurried back and forth among the confusion like a general mucking in with his troops on the eve of battle* (Manchester Guardian).
**muck out, a** to clean out (as a stable, mine, or tunnel): *After a couple of years getting up at dawn to work horses and muck out stables ...* (Time). **b** *British.* to clean up (anything): *... spoke of the trouble she would get into if she didn't get her employer's office properly mucked out* (Punch).
**muck up,** *Slang.* to spoil; foul up; make a mess of: *We mucked up two hundred quids' worth ... before getting it right, had to burn the lot* (Punch).
[< Scandinavian (compare Old Icelandic *myki, mykr* cow dung). See related etym. at **midden.**]

**muck car,** a vehicle used to carry away earth, rock, or detritus during mining or the excavation for a tunnel, foundation, or other construction.

**muck|er[1]** (muk′ər), *n. Slang.* a very vulgar, ill-bred person: *[Mucker] ... with the language and manners of the bargee and the longshoreman* (James Truslow Adams). **SYN:** cad. [probably < German *Mucker* sulky person]

**muck|er[2]** (muk′ər), *n.* a person who removes muck from a mine, tunnels, or other excavation: *The muckers work on ... pausing ... to pull Their boots out of suckholes where they slosh* (Carl Sandburg). [< *muck* + *-er*[1]]

**muck|le[1]** (muk′əl), *adj., adv., n. Dialect.* mickle; much. [dialectal variant of *mickle*]

**muck|le[2]** (muk′əl), *n. U.S. Dialect.* a club used to kill fish when they are caught and landed. [perhaps specialized noun use of *muckle*[1]]

**muck|le[3]** (muk′əl), *v.i.,* **-led, -ling.** *U.S. Dialect.*
**muckle through,** to make or work one's way through something despite obstacles; muddle through: *"We'll muckle through for old Mother Church in absolute confidence"* (New Yorker). [< *muck* + *-le*]

**muck|luck** (muk′luk), *n.* **1** a high, soft, waterproof, fur-lined sealskin boot worn by Eskimos and others in arctic regions. **2** a knitted wool sock, reaching the calf, to which a soft leather sole is stitched; slipper sock. Also, **mucluc, mukluk.** [American English < Eskimo *maklak* bearded seal; boot made of sealskin]

**muck|rake** (muk′rāk′), *v.,* **-raked, -rak|ing,** *n.* —*v.i.* to hunt for and expose corruption, especially in big business, government bureaus, or prominent individuals.
—*n.* a rake for scraping and piling muck or dung: *The men with the muckrakes are often indispensable to the well-being of society* (Theodore Roosevelt).

**muck|rak|er** (muk′rā′kər), *n.* a person, especially a journalist, who muckrakes. The name "muckrakers" was originally given to a group of American journalists and novelists of the early 1900's noted for exposing social and political evils. *Lincoln Steffens was a muckraker.* [American English (coined by Theodore Roosevelt) < "man with the *muckrake*" in John Bunyan's *Pilgrim's Progress*]

**muck|rak|ing** (muk′rā′king), *n.* the writings of muckrakers to expose social and political evils, especially in the early 1900's.

**muck-up** (muk′up′), *n. British Slang.* a mess or muddle; foul-up: *You cannot get away from the fact that Anzio was a bit of a muck-up* (Field Marshal Lord Montgomery).

**muck|worm** (muk′wėrm′), *n.* **1** a worm, larva, or grub living in muck or manure. **2** *Figurative.* a miser.

**muck|y** (muk′ē), *adj.,* **muck|i|er, muck|i|est. 1** of muck. **2** filthy; dirty.

**muc|luc** (muk′luk), *n.* = muckluck.

**mu|coid[1]** (myü′koid), *adj.* like mucus.

**mu|coid[2]** (myü′koid), *n.* any one of a group of glycoproteins resembling mucin. They occur in bone and connective tissue, and in the vitreous humor and cornea of the eye.

**mu|co|lyt|ic** (myü′kə lit′ik), *adj.* that dissolves mucus: *mucolytic agents, mucolytic enzymes.* [< Latin *mūcus* mucus + *-lyticus* loosening < Greek *lytikós* < *lýein* loosen]

**mu|co|pep|tide** (myü′kō pep′tīd), *n.* a complex protein in the cell wall of bacteria, whose synthesis is thought to be inhibited by the action of antibiotics: *The cell envelope, the outer portion of the bacterial cell, is a complex structure consisting of an inner plasma membrane and a rigid mucopeptide layer, the cell wall proper, that confers strength and shape* (Scientific American). [< Latin *mūcus* mucus + English *peptide*]

**mu|co|pol|y|sac|cha|ride** (myü′kō pol′ē sak′ə-rīd, -ər id), *n.* a carbohydrate compound, such as heparin, containing amino sugar and sugar acids, found mainly in the connective tissue but also present in mucous tissue and synovial fluid: *The blood group to which each of us belongs is determined by a presence ... of a mucopolysaccharide with specific antigenic qualities* (New Scientist). [< Latin *mūcus* mucus + English *polysaccharide*]

**mu|co|pro|tein** (myü′kō prō′tēn, -tē in), *n.* any one of various viscous protein compounds, such as mucin, containing a mucopolysaccharide in their molecular structure, and occurring in connective tissue and other body tissues.

**mu|cor** (myü′kər), *n.* any one of a group of molds that form small, downy, grayish-white tufts, as on bread, decaying fruit, and decaying mushrooms. [< Latin *mūcor* moldy]

**mu|co|sa** (myü kō′sə), *n., pl.* **-sae** (-sē). = mucous membrane. [< New Latin (*membrana*) *mucosa* mucous (membrane)]

**mu|co|sal** (myü kō′səl), *adj.* of, having to do with, or characteristic of a mucosa.

**mucosal disease,** any one of several, often fatal, diseases which affect cattle, striking at their mucosae and their respiratory and digestive tracts.

**mu|cos|i|ty** (myü kos′ə tē), *n.* mucous quality; sliminess.

**mu|cous** (myü′kəs), *adj.* **1** of mucus. **2** like mucus. **3** containing or secreting mucus. [< Latin *mūcōsus* slimy, like mucus < *mūcus* mucus]

**mucous membrane,** the lining of the nose, throat, anus, and other cavities of the body that are open to the air; tissue containing glands that secrete mucus; mucosa.

**mu|co|vis|ci|do|sis** (myü′kō vis′i dō′sis), *n.* = cystic fibrosis. [< *muco*(us) + *viscid* + *-osis*]

**mu|cro** (myü′krō), *n., pl.* **mu|cro|nes** (myü krō′-nēz). a sharp point; spinelike part: *the projecting mucro of a leaf.* [< Latin *mūcrō, -ōnis* point, sharp edge]

**mu|cro|nate** (myü′krə nit, -nāt), *adj.* having a sharp point: *a mucronate shell, feather, or leaf.* [< Latin *mūcrōnātus* < *mūcrō, -ōnis* point] —**mu′cro|nate|ly,** *adv.*

**mu|cro|nat|ed** (myü′krə nā′tid), *adj.* = mucronate.

**mu|cro|na|tion** (myü′krə nā′shən), *n.* **1** mucronate condition or form. **2** a mucronate process.

**mu|cron|u|late** (myü kron′yə lāt, -lit), *adj.* having a small mucro or abruptly projecting point, as a leaf. [< New Latin *mucronulatus* (diminutive) < Latin *mūcrō, -ōnis* point]

**mu|cus** (myü′kəs), *n.* a slimy substance that is secreted by and moistens and protects the mucous membranes of the body. A cold in the head causes a discharge of mucus. Mucus consists chiefly of mucin. [< Latin *mūcus* slime, mucus, mold[2], related to *ēmungere* sneeze out, blow one's nose]

**mud** (mud), *n., v.,* **mud|ded, mud|ding.** —*n.* **1** earth so wet that it is soft and sticky: *mud on the ground after rain, mud at the bottom of a pond.* **SYN:** mire, slime, ooze. **2** *Figurative.* slander; libel; defamation: *They were using not criticism but mud to maintain themselves in office* (Adlai E. Stevenson). **3** a mixture of water, clay, and certain chemicals used in well-drilling to lubricate the bit and carry debris loosened by the bit to the surface.
—*v.t.* **1** to muddy (a liquid): *The wolf Mudded the brook* (Tennyson). **2** to bury in mud: *I wish Myself were mudded in that oozy bed Where my son lies* (Shakespeare).
**sling** (or **fling** or **throw**) **mud at,** to make disgraceful remarks about (a person, his character, or his actions); slander: *A woman in my position must expect to have more mud thrown at her than a less important person* (Frederick Marryat).
[Middle English *mudde*]

**mu|dar** (mə där′), *n.* = madar.

**mud|bank** (mud′bangk′), *n.* a bank or shoal of mud beside or rising from the bed of a river, lake, or sea.

**mud bath,** a bath in mud mixed with certain medicines, as a remedy for rheumatism, gout, and other painful conditions of the body.

**mud|cat** (mud′kat′), *n.* (in the Mississippi Valley) a large catfish.

**mud dauber,** any one of various wasps, the females of which lay eggs in individual cells constructed of mud, and supply the larvae with insects or spiders for food.

**mud|der** (mud′ər), *n. Slang.* **1** a race horse that runs well on a wet, muddy track: *Experienced horsemen can distinguish a mudder simply by watching him gallop around the track* (Cincinnati Enquirer). **2** an athlete, such as a football player, who plays well on wet, muddy ground: *He had the most devastating weapon on the field; Navy's ... captain, Ned Oldham, a marvelous mudder* (Time).

**mud|di|ly** (mud′ə lē), *adv.* in a muddy manner.

**mud|di|ness** (mud′ē nis), *n.* **1** the quality or condition of being muddy: *the muddiness of a stream.* **2** *Figurative.* the state of being unclear or confused.

**mud|dle** (mud′əl), *v.,* **-dled, -dling,** *n.* —*v.t.* **1** to bring (things) into a mess; mix up: *to muddle a piece of work. Do you want to ... get things all muddled up?* (Mark Twain). **2** to make confused or stupid or slightly drunk: *The more you talk, the more you muddle me.* **3** to make (water or other liquid) muddy. **4** to waste or squander (money, time, or other assets) stupidly.
—*v.i.* to think or act in a confused, blundering way: *to muddle over a problem. He meddled, or rather muddled, with literature* (Washington Irving).
—*n.* a mess; disorder; confusion: *When Mother came home, she found the house in a muddle.*
**make a muddle of,** to bungle: *The present Government has made an immortal muddle of the whole business* (Saturday Review).
**muddle through,** to manage somehow; succeed in one's object in spite of lack of skill and foresight: *to muddle through a difficulty. Can it be that, faced with the serious business of self-immolation, we shall abandon the immemorial practice of muddling through, and discover logic and consistency at last?* (London Times).
[(originally) to mottle or obscure colors; to stir up sediment, perhaps < *mud.* Compare Middle Dutch *moddelen* to make water muddy.]

**mud|dle|head** (mud′əl hed′), *n.* a stupid or confused person; blockhead: *... unrepentant stubborn fanatics or smouldering muddleheads* (Manchester Guardian).

**mud|dle|head|ed** (mud′əl hed′id), *adj.* stupid; confused: *Can a country so impractical, so muddleheaded be trusted in a harsh material world?* (Harper's). —**mud′dle|head′ed|ness,** *n.*

**mud|dle|ment** (mud′əl mənt), *n.* muddled condition; confusion: *Many of the little muddlements that confront me in the morning are not susceptible to that kind of research* (New Yorker).

**mud|dler** (mud′lər), *n.* **1** a small rod of glass, plastic, wood, or metal for stirring a drink. **2** a person who muddles.

**mud|dy** (mud′ē), *adj.*, **-di|er, -di|est,** *v.*, **-died, -dy|ing.** — *adj.* **1** of or like mud: *muddy footprints on the floor.* **2** having much mud; covered with mud: *a muddy road, muddy shoes.* **3a** clouded with mud: *muddy water.* SYN: turbid, cloudy. **b** clouded with any sediment: *muddy coffee.* SYN: turbid, cloudy. **4** *Figurative.* not clear, pure, or bright; dull: *a muddy color, a muddy sound.* **5** *Figurative.* not clear in mind; confused; muddled: *muddy thinking.* **6** *Figurative.* obscure; vague: *Muddy writing is usually careless writing.* **7** living or growing in mud.
— *v.t.* **1** to make muddy; cover or soil with mud. **2** to make turbid or cloudy. **3** *Figurative.* to make confused or obscure: *Delivery difficulties and quick-changing models muddy the outlook for future sales* (Wall Street Journal).
— *v.i.* to become muddy.

**mud eel,** an eellike salamander of the southern United States, a kind of siren, found in swamps, bogs, and marshes.

**mud|fish** (mud′fish′), *n., pl.* **-fish|es** or (*collectively*) **-fish.** any one of certain fish that live in muddy water or burrow in mud, such as the bowfin or the killifish.

**mud|flat** (mud′flat′), *n.*, or **mud flat,** a stretch of muddy land left uncovered at low tide: *In twisting creeks and inlets, on bird-haunted mudflats, ... the sea anglers will soon forgather* (Sunday Times).

**mud|flow** (mud′flō′), *n.* **1** an eruption of mud from a volcano: *In Java dams have been built to divert volcanic mudflows away from villages and agricultural lands* (Scientific American). **2** a landslide of mud following spring thaws or heavy rain.

**mud|guard** (mud′gärd′), *n.* a guard or shield placed over or beside a wheel of a carriage, bicycle, or motor vehicle to prevent mud from splashing riders or passengers; fender.

**mud hen,** a water bird that looks like a duck and lives in marshes, such as a gallinule or coot.

**mu|dir** (mü dir′), *n.* a local administrator or governor in Egypt, Sudan, Turkey, or Zanzibar. [< Arabic *mudīr*]

**mud|lark** (mud′lärk′), *n.* **1** a person who dabbles, works, or lives in mud: *Illiterate mudlarks ... used to comb the flats around the London docks looking for pilgrim's badges, towards the end of the last century* (London Times). **2** a gamin; street urchin.

**mud|pack** (mud′pak′), *n.* a pack of mud applied on parts of the body for cosmetic or therapeutic purposes: *The American man has succumbed to cologne, hairnets, mudpacks for his wrinkles, and clothes cut to accent a handsome thigh or well-turned calf* (New York Times).

**mud pickerel,** a variety of pickerel found abundantly in the Mississippi Valley. It seldom grows more than a foot long.

**mud pie,** wet earth formed by children into the shape of a pie.

**mud puppy, 1** a large aquatic salamander of the Great Lakes, the Mississippi River, and the eastern United States as far south as Georgia, having bushy, external gills; water dog. **2** any one of various other salamanders, especially the hellbender.

**mu|dra** (mü drä′), *n.* one of a number of symbolic finger gestures used in the dances of India: *an Indian dancer who has in the mudras, in the subtle movement of his fingers, a rich vocabulary* (Sebastian de Grazia). [< Sanskrit *mudrā* seal]

**mud room,** a room in which muddy or wet shoes and clothes are put when entering a house.

**mud show,** *U.S. Slang.* **1** (formerly) a circus traveling with horses and wagons. **2** a small circus, especially one that travels in trucks rather than trains.

**mud|sill** (mud′sil′), *n.* the lowest sill of a wall, dam, or other structure, usually placed in or on the ground.

**mud|skip|per** (mud′skip′ər), *n.* a small fish, a variety of goby, with movable pectoral fins and a muscular tail, found in shallow coastal waters from western Africa to Polynesia; tree climber. It often moves about on mud flats, jumping and climbing roots after insects. *Of all living fish, the mudskippers ... demonstrate most clearly how terrestrial vertebrates with four legs could have evolved from primitive swimmers with no legs at all* (New Scientist).

**mud|sling|er** (mud′sling′ər), *n.* a person given to mudslinging.

**mud|sling|ing** (mud′sling′ing), *n.* the use of offensive charges and misleading or slanderous accusations against an opponent in a political campaign, public meeting, or the like: *Mudslinging for however good a cause seldom pays in the end* (Sunday Times).

**mud|stone** (mud′stōn′), *n.* a soft, sedimentary, clayey rock nearly uniform in texture, with little or no lamination.

**mud turtle, tortoise,** or **terrapin,** any one of a genus of freshwater turtles of North America.

**mud wasp,** a wasp that builds its nest of mud.

**Muen|ster** (mun′stər, mün′-), *n.*, or **Muenster cheese,** = Munster.

**mu|ez|zin** (myü ez′ən), *n.* the crier who, at dawn, noon, four o'clock in the afternoon, sunset, and nightfall calls Moslems to prayer: *There was a break in the proceedings at 5 p.m. in response to the symbolic muezzin's call* (London Times). [< Arabic *mu'adhdhin* the one who proclaims]

✱**muff** (muf), *n., v.* — *n.* **1** a covering, usually of fur, into which a woman or girl puts both hands, one at each end, to keep them warm. **2** a clumsy failure to catch a ball that comes into one's hands: *The catcher's muff allowed the runner to score.* **3** an awkward handling; bungling. **4a** a tuft or crest on the heads of certain birds. **b** a cluster of feathers on the side of the face, characteristic of the Houdan chicken. **5** *British Informal.* a clumsy, awkward person; bungler: *Pontifex was a young muff, a molly-coddle* (Samuel Butler).
— *v.t.* **1** to fail to catch (a ball) when it comes into one's hands: [*He*] ... *muffed a foul to help give the Redlegs three unearned runs* (New York Times). **2** to handle awkwardly; bungle: *He muffs his real job without a blush* (H. G. Wells).
— *v.i.* to muff a ball; bungle.
[< Dutch *mof* < French *moufle* mitten < Old French, thick glove, probably < a Germanic word]

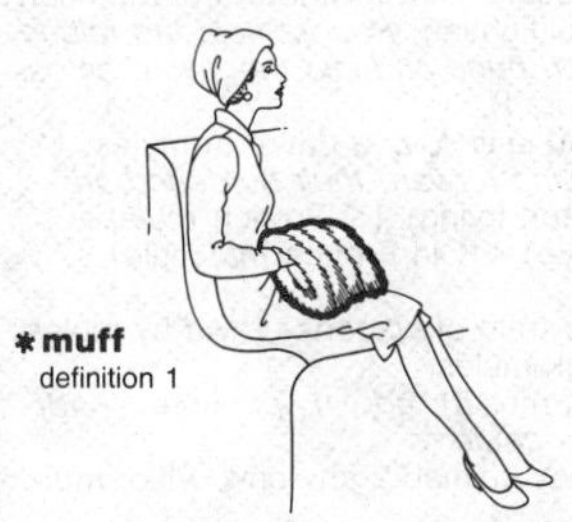

✱**muff**
definition 1

**muf|fin** (muf′ən), *n.* a small, round cake made of wheat flour, corn meal, or the like, often without sugar. Muffins are eaten with butter, and usually served hot. [origin uncertain; perhaps < French, Old French *moufflet* soft, as in *pain moufflet* soft bread]

**muf|fin|eer** (muf′ə nir′), *n.* **1** a utensil like a large saltshaker for sprinkling sugar, cinnamon, or other granular condiment, over muffins: *Silver and turquoise inlaid muffineers* (London Daily News). **2** a covered dish for keeping muffins, biscuits, and the like, hot.

**muffin tin,** a metal dish with cup-shaped holes for baking muffins and cupcakes.

**muf|fle¹** (muf′əl), *v.*, **-fled, -fling,** *n.* — *v.t.* **1** to wrap in something in order to soften or stop the sound: *to muffle oars, to muffle a drum. A bell can be muffled with cloth.* **2** to dull or deaden (a sound). *I heard voices, too, speaking with a hollow sound, and as if muffled by a rush of wind or water* (Charlotte Brontë). **3** to wrap or cover up in order to keep warm and dry: *She muffled her throat in a warm scarf.* **4** to wrap up the head of (a person) in order to keep him from speaking. **5** *Figurative.* to wrap or pull over so as to conceal: *to muffle one's face with a scarf. Alas, that love, whose view is muffled still Should, without eyes, see pathways to his will* (Shakespeare). **6** to dim (light): *through the dim length of the apartment, where crimson curtains muffled the glare of sunshine* (Hawthorne).
— *v.i.* to wrap oneself in garments or other covering.
— *n.* **1** a muffled sound. **2** a thing that muffles. **3** *Obsolete.* a boxing glove: *Just like a black eye in a recent scuffle* (*For sometimes we must box without a muffle*) (Byron). **4** *Scottish.* a mitten: *A muffle has only two divisions; one for the thumb and the other for the four fingers* (D. Nicholson).
[< Old French *mofler* to stuff < *moufle* thick glove, mitten. Compare etym. under **muff.**]

**muf|fle²** (muf′əl), *n.* the thick, bare part of the upper lip and nose of cows, moose, rabbits, and certain other animals. [< French *mufle;* origin unknown]

**muf|fle³** (muf′əl), *n.* **1** an oven or arched chamber in a furnace or kiln, used for heating substances without direct contact with the fire: *Pottery and porcelain are fired in a muffle.* **2** a furnace containing such a chamber. [< French *moufle,* probably a use of *moufle* mitten]

**muf|fler** (muf′lər), *n.* **1** anything used to deaden sound. An automobile muffler, attached to the end of the exhaust pipe, deadens the sound of the engine's exhaust. See picture under **exhaust pipe.** **2** a wrap or scarf worn around the neck for warmth. SYN: tippet. **3** any covering, such as a veil, used to conceal the face of a person. **4** a glove or mitten.

**muf|ti** (muf′tē), *n., pl.* **-tis. 1** ordinary clothes, not a uniform, especially when worn by someone who usually wears a uniform: *The retired general appeared in mufti.* **2** a Moslem official who assists a judge by formal exposition of the religious law. **3** the official head of the state religion in Turkey, or one of his deputies. [< Arabic *muftī* judge (apparently because of the informal costume traditional for the stage role of a *mufti*)]

**mug¹** (mug), *n., v.*, **mugged, mug|ging.** — *n.* **1** a heavy earthenware or metal drinking cup with a handle: *a coffee mug, a large mug of cider.* **2** the amount a mug holds: *to drink a mug of milk.* **3** *Slang.* **a** the face: *an ugly mug.* **b** the mouth: *Shut your mug!* **4** *Slang.* a grimace. **5** *U.S. Slang.* a ruffian; hoodlum; petty criminal: *Many a mug on the edge of the big time thinks there is a formula for dealing with newsmen: intimidate or bribe* (Time). **6** *Slang.* **a** a prize fighter, especially an inferior fighter: *People mostly figure once a fighter, always a mug* (New Yorker). **b** a fighter with a disfigured face. **7** *British Slang.* a fool; dupe; simpleton.
— *v.t. Slang.* **1** to attack (a person) from behind, usually to rob, and especially by locking the forearm around the neck and choking: *Even as the raid was going on, ... four youths mugged a 45-year-old woman* (Birmingham News). **2** to make a photograph of (a person's face) for police purposes. — *v.i. Slang.* to exaggerate one's facial expressions, as in acting: *Sutherland smirks and mugs through his dual role* (New Yorker).
**mug up,** *British Slang.* to study assiduously: *No longer do you have to mug up a set of dull figures* (Evening Standard).
[compare Norwegian *mugge,* Swedish *mugg;* definitions 3, 4 < the shape of early mugs]

**mug²** (mug), *n. Scottish.* a mist; drizzle; damp, gloomy state. [compare Old Icelandic *mugga*]

**mug|ful** (mug′fu̇l), *n., pl.* **-fuls.** enough to fill a mug: *a mugful of cocoa. Water is retailed by the bucket, and a potent brand of sherry by the mugful* (Daily Telegraph).

**mug|gar** (mug′ər), *n.* = mugger².

**mug|ger¹** (mug′ər), *n. Slang.* a person who mugs: *Other groups became counterfeiters, moonshiners, muggers* (Time).

**mug|ger²** (mug′ər), *n.* a large, freshwater crocodile of India, Pakistan, and Ceylon (Sri Lanka), having a broad snout and growing to about 12 feet in length. [< Hindi *magar* < Sanskrit *makara* sea monster]

**mug|gi|ly** (mug′ə lē), *adv.* in a muggy manner; damply.

**mug|gi|ness** (mug′ē nis), *n.* muggy condition.

**mug|gins** (mug′inz), *n.* **1** *Slang.* a simpleton. **2** a certain game played with dominoes. **3** any one of various simple card games. [origin uncertain]

**mug|gle** (mug′əl), *n. U.S. Slang.* a marijuana cigarette.

**mug|gur** (mug′ər), *n.* = mugger².

**mug|gy** (mug′ē), *adj.*, **-gi|er, -gi|est.** warm and humid; damp and close: *muggy weather, a muggy day.* SYN: sultry. [< *mug*² + *-y*¹]

**Mu|ghal** (mü′gul), *n. Especially British.* Mogul.

**mu|gho pine** (myü′gō, mü′-), a low, shrubby pine tree of the Swiss Alps, popular as a specimen plant. [< New Latin *mughus* < Italian *mugo*]

**mug-shoot** (mug′shüt′), *v.t.*, **-shot** (-shot′), **-shoot|ing.** *U.S.* to take a mug shot of; photograph for police purposes: *It was not until late in the afternoon that the wrongest man in Palo Alto was finally mug-shot, fingerprinted and given a summons to appear in court ... on a charge of "rioting"* (Time).

**mug shot,** a photograph of a person for police purposes: *Scotland Yard, the FBI and the Royal Canadian Mounted Police exchanged "mug shots" of some of their most wanted criminals* (New York Times).

**mug|wort** (mug′wėrt′), *n.* = wormwood.

**mug|wump** (mug′wump′), *n. U.S.* **1** a person who is independent in politics: *We cannot afford to modify our principles to secure the support of a limited number of mugwumps* (Newsweek). **2** a Republican who refused to support the party candidate, James G. Blaine, for President in 1884. [American English < Algonkian (Massachuset) *mugquomp* chief]

---

**Pronunciation Key:** hat, āge, cãre, fär; let, ēqual, tėrm; it, īce; hot, ōpen, ôrder; oil, out; cup, pu̇t, rüle; child; long; thin; ᴛʜen; zh, measure;
ə represents **a** in about, **e** in taken, **i** in pencil, **o** in lemon, **u** in circus.

**mug|wump|er|y** (mug′wum′pər ē), *n.* the principles or practice of mugwumps.

**mug|wump|ism** (mug′wum′piz əm), *n.* = mugwumpery.

**Mu|ham|mad|an** or **Mu|ham|med|an** (mù ham′ə dən), *adj., n.* = Mohammedan.

**Mu|ham|mad|an|ism** (mù ham′ə də niz′əm), *n.* = Mohammedanism.

**Mu|har|ram** (mù har′əm), *n.* **1** the first month of the Moslem year. It has 30 days. **2** an annual Moslem religious celebration held during this month: *The Shia sect was taking part in a Muharram procession when some people threw bricks* (London Times). Also, **Moharram**. [< Arabic *Muḥarram*]

**muis|hond** (mois′hônt′), *n. Afrikaans.* the zoril: *Tortoise eggs are much sought after by jackals ... and muishonds* (Cape Times).

**mu|jik** (mü zhik′, mü′zhik), *n.* = muzhik.

**mukh|tar** or **muh|tar** (mùk′tär, mùн′-), *n.* the elected headman of an Arab or Turkish town or village: *I was shown a red roof 500 yards away where the Turkish mukhtar was* (Manchester Guardian Weekly). [< Arabic *mukhtār* and Turkish *muhtar* (literally) chosen]

**muk|luk** (muk′luk), *n.* = muckluck.

**muk|tuk** (muk′tuk), *n.* the thin outer skin of the beluga or white whale, or of the narwhal, used as food by the Eskimos. [< Eskimo]

**mu|lat|to** (mə lat′ō, myù-), *n., pl.* **-toes**, *adj.* —*n.* **1** a person having one white and one Negro parent. **2** any person of mixed white and Negro descent.
—*adj.* of the color of a mulatto; tawny.
[< Spanish, Portuguese *mulato* < *mulo* mule < Latin *mūlus* (because of its hybrid origin)]

**mul|ber|ry** (mul′ber′ē, -bər-), *n., pl.* **-ries**. **1** a tree with small, berrylike fruit that can be eaten. The leaves of one kind are used for feeding silkworms. **2** its sweet, usually dark purple fruit. **3** a dark purplish red: *If ever there was a wolf in a mulberry suit that 'ere Job Trotter's him* (Dickens).
[Middle English *mulberie*, Old English *mōrberige* < Latin *mōrum* mulberry + Old English *berige* berry]

**mul|ber|ry-col|ored** (mul′ber ē kul′ərd, -bər-), *adj.* dark purplish-red.

*****mulberry family**, a group of dicotyledonous herbs, shrubs, and trees, found chiefly in tropical regions. The family includes the fig, breadfruit, Osage orange, rubber plant, and banyan.

***mulberry family**

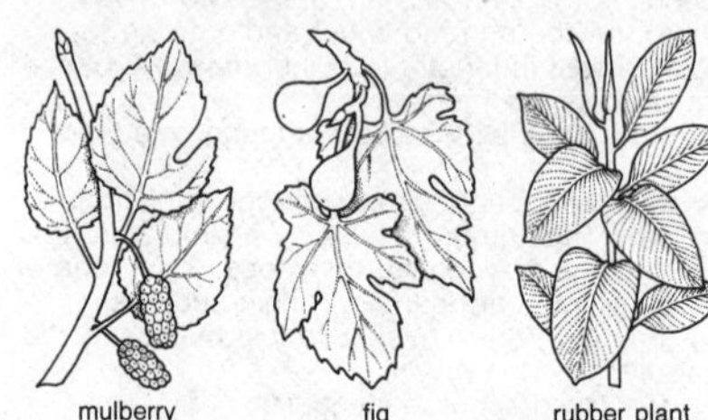


**mulch** (mulch), *n., v.* —*n.* straw, leaves, or loose earth spread on the ground around trees or plants. Mulch is used to protect the roots from cold or heat, to prevent evaporation of moisture from the soil, to check week growth, to decay and enrich the soil itself, or to keep the fruit clean.
—*v.t.* to cover (ground) with straw or leaves; spread mulch under or around (a tree or plant): *They complain that the plants need constant spraying against aphis, caterpillars, and diseases; that they need to be pruned ... and mulched* (London Times).
[probably Middle English *molsh* soft, Old English *melsc* mellow, sweet] —**mulch′er**, *n.*

**mulct** (mulkt), *v., n.* —*v.t.* **1** to deprive of something by cunning or deceit; defraud: *He was mulcted of his money by a shrewd trick.* **2** to punish (a person) by a fine: *Some [apostates] ... were again received into the Christian fold, after being severely mulcted* (Washington Irving).
—*n.* a fine; penalty.
[< Latin *mulctāre*, variant of *multāre* < *multa* a fine]

**mule**[1] (myül), *n.* **1** an animal which is half donkey and half horse, especially the offspring of a male donkey and a mare, the offspring of a female donkey and a stallion usually being distinguished as a *hinny.* A mule has the form and size of a horse, and the large ears, small hoofs, and tufted tail of a donkey, and is usually sterile. **2** *Informal, Figurative.* a stupid or stubborn person: *"Now don't be a young mule," said Good Mrs. Brown* (Dickens). **3** a kind of spinning machine which twists cotton, wool, or other fibers into yarn and winds it on spindles. **4** any hybrid animal, especially the sterile offspring of a canary and some related bird. **5** a tractor or small electric locomotive used to pull boats along a canal. [partly Old English *mūl* < Latin *mūlus;* partly < Old French *mule* < Latin *mūlus*]

**mule**[2] (myül), *n.* a loose slipper, covering only the toes and part of the instep, and leaving the rest of the foot and the heel uncovered. [< Middle French *mule* < Dutch *muil* < Latin (*calceus*) *mulleus* red leather (shoe)]

**mule|back** (myül′bak′), *n., adv.* —*n.* the back of a mule: *Sometimes they came on horse- or muleback but, more often, on foot* (Harper's).
—*adv.* on the back of a mule: *to ride muleback.*

**mule deer**, a deer of western North America having long ears, large, branching antlers, and a white tail with a black tip. It is related and similar to the white-tailed deer. A mule deer of the Pacific coast, the black-tailed deer, has a black tail with a white tip. See picture under **antler**.

**Mule-Foot** (myül′fùt′), *n.* a breed of hog that is bred for both lard and bacon. It has a solid hoof like that of a mule.

**mule|head|ed** (myül′hed′id), *adj.* stupidly obstinate or stubborn; pig-headed.

**mule killer**, = dragonfly.

**mule's foot**, a V-shaped tool used in leathercraft to cut and to decorate.

**mule skinner**, *Informal.* a man who drives or is in charge of mules: *He knew plenty of individuals who represented the types—mule skinners, cowboys, barkeeps* (Chicago Tribune).

**mu|le|ta** (mü lā′tä), *n. Spanish.* a small red cloth draped over a stick, used to attract the attention of the bull in bullfighting: *Paeota held the folded muleta in his left hand and laid the sword across it* (Barnaby Conrad).

**mu|le|teer** (myü′lə tir′), *n.* a driver of mules: *muleteers hurrying forward their burdened animals* (Washington Irving). [< French *muletier* < *mulet* (diminutive) < Old French *mul* mule[1] < Latin *mūlus*]

**mule train**, **1** a train of wagons drawn by mules. **2** a train of pack mules.

**mu|ley** (myü′lē, mùl′ē), *adj., n., pl.* **-leys**. —*adj.* hornless: *muley cattle.*
—*n.* **1** a hornless animal. **2** any cow. Also, **mulley**.
[variant of dialectal *moiley* hornless cow < Irish *maol*, Welsh *moel* bald]

**muley saw**, a saw for ripping timber, a long, stiff blade guided in a rapid reciprocating action by guide carriages at top and bottom. Also, **mully saw**.

**mul|ga** (mul′gə), *n.* any one of various small acacias of Australia, that yield a hard, durable wood much used for carving ornaments. [< an Australian native name]

**mu|li|eb|ri|ty** (myü′lē eb′rə tē), *n.* **1** womanly nature or qualities; femininity. **2** = womanhood. [< Latin *muliebritās* < *muliebris* of women < *mulier* woman]

**mul|ish** (myü′lish), *adj.* **1** like a mule; stubborn; obstinate: *... however mulish this makes them look in the eyes of world opinion* (Economist). **SYN**: intractable. **2** *Obsolete.* hybrid; sterile. —**mul′ish|ly**, *adv.* —**mul′ish|ness**, *n.*

**mull**[1] (mul), *v.t., v.i.* to think (about) without making much progress; ponder: *to mull over a problem. His subcommittee will mull the situation this fall and have a bill ready when Congress meets* (Wall Street Journal). **SYN**: ruminate. [American English; perhaps < *mull*[6]]

**mull**[2] (mul), *v.t.* to make (wine, beer, or cider) into a warm drink, adding sugar and spices. [origin uncertain] —**mull′er**, *n.*

**mull**[3] (mul), *n.* a thin, soft muslin. [earlier *mulmul* < Hindustani *malmal*]

**mull**[4] (mul), *n. Scottish.* a snuffbox: *Hendry once offered Mr. Dishart a snuff from his mull* (James M. Barrie). [variant of *mill*[1]]

**mull**[5] (mul), *n.* a moist, well-aerated humus which is conducive to plant growth. [< German *Mull.* Ultimately related to **mold**[3].]

**mull**[6] (mul), *v., n.* —*v.t.* **1** to grind to powder; crumble: *to mull bread.* **2** to soften or moisten (leather) by dipping it in water and hanging it in a moisture-filled chamber. **3** *British Slang.* **a** to bungle; botch: *to mull a pass in Rugby.* **b** to stupefy; muddle: *mulled with drink.*
—*n. British Slang.* a muddle; mess: *I nearly made a mull of the business* (E. E. Napier).
[Middle English *mullen* < *mul, mol* powder, dust, probably related to *meal*[2]]

**mul|lah** or **mul|la** (mul′ə, mùl′-), *n.* a title of respect in Moslem countries for a person who is learned in or teaches the sacred law: *He made Kim learn whole chapters of the Koran by heart, till he could deliver them with the very roll and cadence of a mullah* (Rudyard Kipling). [< Turkish *molla*, in Persian, Hindustani *mullā* < Arabic *mawlā*]

**mul|lein** or **mul|len** (mul′ən), *n.* **1** a weed with coarse, woolly leaves and spikes of yellow flowers. It belongs to the figwort family. There are various kinds, making up a genus of plants. **2** any one of various plants similar to this group of weeds. [< Anglo-French *moleine* < Old French *mol* soft < Latin *mollis*]

**mullein pink**, a white, woolly herb of the pink family, a native of southern Europe, with oval or oblong leaves and crimson flowers; rose campion.

**mull|er** (mul′ər), *n.* **1** an implement for grinding paints, powders, or other substances, on a slab. **2** a mechanical device for grinding or crushing. [< *mull*[6] + *-er*[1]]

**Mul|le|ri|an** or **Mül|le|ri|an duct** (myü lir′ē ən), the embryonic genital or reproductive tract of the female in vertebrate animals, corresponding to the mesonephric duct of the male. [< Johannes *Müller*, 1801-1858, a German anatomist + *-ian*]

**Mullerian** or **Müllerian mimicry**, protective mimicry in which the mimicking animal is as inedible or disagreeble to predators as the animal it mimics: *Mullerian mimicry ... gave all the species concerned an advantage in that fewer individuals would be sacrificed in the learning process whereby predators came to associate particular habits or colour patterns with distastefulness* (New Scientist). [< Fritz *Müller*, 1821-1897, a German naturalist + *-ian*]

**mul|let**[1] (mul′it), *n., pl.* **-lets** or (*collectively*) **-let**. a kind of fish that lives close to the shore in warm waters. It is good to eat. There are gray mullets and red mullets or surmullets. Mullets have small mouths and weak teeth. *Some say the mullet jump to shake off a parasite that annoys them* (New Yorker). [Middle English *molet* < Old French *mulet* < Latin *mullus* red mullet < Greek *mýllos*]

**mul|let**[2] (mul′it), *n. Heraldry.* a star-shaped figure, usually with five straight or regular points. See **estoile**. [< Old French *molette* rowel]

**mul|let-head|ed** (mul′it hed′id), *adj.* stupid; dull. [origin uncertain]

**mul|ley** (mùl′ē, mü′lē), *adj., n., pl.* **-leys**. = muley.

**mul|li|gan** (mul′ə gən), *n. U.S. Slang.* **1** Also, **mulligan stew**. a stew of meat, or sometimes fish, and vegetables: *Hoboes are traditionally makers of mulligan.* **2** *Golf.* a second drive, without penalty, off the first tee (when the first drive is bad). [American English; origin uncertain, perhaps from a proper name]

**mul|li|ga|taw|ny** (mul′ə gə tô′nē), *n.* a soup made from a chicken or meat stock flavored with curry, originally made in India. [< Tamil *milagutaṇṇi* pepper water]

**mul|li|grubs** (mul′i grubz), *n.pl. Slang.* **1** low spirits; the blues. **2** stomachache; colic: *Where spasms were ... afflicting him with mulligrubs* (George Colman). [a coined word]

**mul|lion** (mul′yən), *n., v.* —*n.* **1** a vertical bar between the panes of a window, the panels in the wall of a room, or used between other surfaces as decoration: *On the one side ran a range of windows lofty and large, divided by carved mullions of stones* (Scott). **2** a radiating bar in a round window.
—*v.t.* to divide or provide with mullions. Also, **munnion**.
[alteration of Middle English *muniall* or *monial* < Old French *moienel* in the middle < *meien* < Latin *mediānus* median < *medius* middle]

**mul|lioned** (mul′yənd), *adj.* having mullions: *mullioned windows.*

**mull|ite** (mul′īt), *n.* a mineral, a silicate of aluminum, that is similar to cyanite. It is rare as a mineral but common in artificial melting processes. *Formula:* $Al_6Si_2O_{13}$ [< *Mull*, an island in the Hebrides, Scotland + *-ite*[1]]

**mul|lock** (mul′ək), *n.* in Australia: **1** mining refuse. **2** ore or earth that does not contain gold. [Middle English *mullok* rubbish < obsolete *mull* rubbish + *-ok*, a diminutive suffix]

**mul|ly saw** (mul′ē), *U.S.* muley saw.

**mult-**, *combining form.* the form of **multi-** before some vowels, as in *multangular.*

**mul|ta do|cet fa|mes** (mul′tə dō′set fā′mēz), *Latin.* hunger teaches many things.

**mul|tan|gu|lar** (mul tang′gyə lər), *n., adj.* —*n.* either of two bones of the human wrist, the greater multangular (trapezium) at the base of the thumb, or the lesser multangular (trapezoid) at the base of the forefinger in the distal row of carpal bones.
—*adj.* **1** having many angles; polygonal. **2** of or having to do with one of the multangulars.

**mul|te|i|ty** (mul tē′ə tē), *n.* the quality of being many; manifoldness. [< Latin *multus* many + English *-ity*]

**multi-**, *combining form.* **1** many; having many or much: *Multiform = having many forms.* **2** many times: *Multimillionaire = a millionaire many times over.*

3 much; in many ways: *Multiradial = having radii along many lines.* Also, sometimes **mult-** before vowels.
[< Latin *multi-* < *multus,* much, many]

**mul|ti-ac|cess** (mul′ti ak′ses), *adj.* of or having to do with the sharing of one computer by two or more users simultaneously; multiple-access: *multi-access techniques.*

**mul|ti|ax|i|al** (mul′ti ak′sē əl), *adj.* having many or several axes.

**mul|ti|band** (mul′ti band′), *adj.* combining two or more wavelength exposures: ... *an enhanced multiband photograph* (Science Journal).

**mul|ti|cel|lu|lar** (mul′ti sel′yə lər), *adj.* having or consisting of many cells.

**mul|ti|cen|tric** (mul′ti sen′trik), *adj.* affecting or issuing from many centers: *the oral cavity with its well-known proclivity for multicentric and recurrent carcinoma* (London Times).

**mul|ti|chan|nel** (mul′ti chan′əl), *adj.* having or using several channels: *a multichannel cable, a multichannel tape recorder.*

**mul|ti|coil** (mul′ti koil), *adj.* having more than a single coil.

**mul|ti|col|or** (mul′ti kul′ər), *adj.* having or using many colors: *multicolor lacquers.*

**mul|ti|col|ored** (mul′ti kul′ərd), *adj.* having many colors. **SYN**: pied.

**mul|ti|com|pa|ny** (mul′ti kum′pə nē), *adj.* controlling or operating many different companies: *Litton ... prefers to be known as a multicompany company rather than a conglomerate* (New York Times).

**mul|ti|cos|tate** (mul′ti kos′tāt), *adj.* having many costae, ribs, or ridges.

**mul|ti|coun|ty** (mul′ti koun′tē), *adj.* serving many counties; regional: *a multicounty library.*

**mul|ti|cul|tur|al** (mul′ti kul′chər əl), *adj.* having or blending many distinct cultures: *a multicultural nation.*

**mul|ti|cul|tur|al|ism** (mul′ti kul′chər ə liz əm), *n.* the quality or state of being multicultural.

**mul|ti|den|tate** (mul′ti den′tāt), *adj.* having many teeth or toothlike processes.

**mul|ti|di|men|sion|al** (mul′ti də men′shə nəl), *adj.* having many dimensions or aspects: (*Figurative.*) *Intellectual resources are multidimensional* (Science News Letter).

**mul|ti|di|men|sion|al|i|ty** (mul′ti də men′shə nal′ə tē), *n.* multidimensional quality or character: ... *a new multidimensionality of art, music, and the spoken word* (Saturday Review).

**mul|ti|di|rec|tion|al** (mul′ti də rek′shə nəl, -dī-), *adj.* having more than one direction; moving in several directions: (*Figurative.*) *There is still a multidirectional market with the buying interest rotating between new issues and groups* (Wall Street Journal).

**mul|ti|dis|ci|pli|nar|y** (mul′ti dis′ə plə ner′ē), *adj.* involving many branches of learning: *a multidisciplinary research program.*

**mul|ti|en|gine** (mul′ti en′jin), *adj.* (of an aircraft or rocket) having a number of engines: *In a multiengine missile the malfunction of any one of the engines will cause the loss of the complete missile* (U.S. Air Force Report on the Ballistic Missile).

**mul|ti-eth|nic** (mul′ti eth′nik), *adj.* intended for or involving different groups: ... *to develop what educators and publishers call "multi-ethnic textbooks"—that is, classroom literature that depicts blacks and other minorities in a different and more equal perspective* (New York Times).

**mul|ti|fac|et|ed** (mul′ti fas′ə tid), *adj.* = many-faceted.

**mul|ti|fac|tor** (mul′ti fak′tər), *adj.* involving many factors or elements: ... *highly complex multifactor investigations* (New Scientist).

**mul|ti|fac|to|ri|al** (mul′ti fak tôr′ē əl, -tōr′-), *adj.* **1** involving many factors. **2** *Genetics.* of, having to do with, or caused by multiple factors.

**mul|ti|fam|i|ly** (mul′ti fam′ə lē, -fam′lē), *adj.* used by or intended for many families: *a multifamily residential development.*

**mul|ti|far|i|ous** (mul′tə fãr′ē əs), *adj.* **1** having many different parts, elements, or forms; having great variety: ... *the machinery of high politics—the incessant and multifarious business of a great State* (Lytton Strachey). **2** many and varied. **SYN**: manifold, diverse. **3** *Botany, Zoology.* arranged in many rows. [< Latin *multifārius* (with English *-ous*)] —**mul′ti|far′i|ous|ly**, *adv.* —**mul′ti|far′i|ous|ness**, *n.*

**mul|ti|fid** (mul′tə fid), *adj.* divided into many lobes or segments: *a multifid leaf.* [< Latin *multifidus* < *multus* many + *findere* to split, divide]

**mul|tif|i|dous** (mul tif′ə dəs), *adj.* = multifid.

**mul|ti|fil** (mul′tə fil), *n.* = multifilament.

**mul|ti|fil|a|ment** (mul′tə fil′ə mənt), *n.* yarn made up of many fine filaments.

**mul|ti|flo|ra rose** (mul′ti flôr′ə, -flōr′-), a climbing or trailing rose of Japan and Korea, having stout prickles and fragrant clusters of small flowers. [< New Latin *multiflora* multiflorous]

**mul|ti|flo|rous** (mul′ti flôr′əs, -flōr′-), *adj.* bearing many flowers. [< *multi-* + Latin *flōs, flōris* flower + English *-ous*]

**mul|ti|foil** (mul′ti foil), *adj., n. Architecture.* polyfoil.

**mul|ti|fold** (mul′tə fōld), *adj.* = manifold. **SYN**: multifarious.

**mul|ti|fo|li|ate** (mul′tə fō′lē it, -āt), *adj. Botany.* having many leaves or leaflets. [< *multi-* + *foliate*]

**mul|ti|font** (mul′ti font′), *adj.* having to do with a computer's ability to read many different fonts or type faces: *a multifont reading system, multifont character recognition.*

**mul|ti|form** (mul′tə fôrm), *adj.* having many different shapes, forms, or kinds: *It includes a model, drawings, and photographs of the multiform playhouse which the Questors Theatre ... hopes to build* (London Times). [< Middle French *multiforme,* learned borrowing from Latin *multiformis* < *multus* many + *forma* form]

**mul|ti|form|i|ty** (mul′tə fôr′mə tē), *n.* the character or condition of being multiform.

**mul|ti|fu|el** (mul′ti fyü′əl), *adj.* capable of running without adjustments on various types of fuels, such as gasoline, kerosene, or diesel oil: *a multifuel engine.*

**mul|ti|germ** (mul′ti jėrm′), *adj.* being or containing a seed cluster which develops into several plants: *Conventional sugar beet seed is of the multigerm variety.*

**mul|ti|grade** (mul′ti grād′), *adj.* combining the viscous properties of several grades: *multigrade oil.*

**Mul|ti|graph** (mul′tə graf, -gräf), *n. Trademark.* a machine for printing circulars, letters, or other matter, with type similar to that of a typewriter.

**mul|ti|graph** (mul′tə graf, -gräf), *v.t.* to make copies of by a Multigraph. —**mul′ti|graph|er**, *n.*

**mul|ti|hued** (mul′ti hyüd′), *adj.* = multicolored.

**mul|ti|hull** (mul′ti hul′), *n.* a sailing vessel having two or more hulls joined by a common deck, such as a catamaran.

**mul|ti-in|dus|try** (mul′ti in′də strē), *adj.* involved or operating in many different industries: *conglomerates—those multipurpose, multi-industry companies that specialize in hodgepodge acquisitions* (Times).

**mul|ti|jet** (mul′ti jet′), *adj.* (of aircraft) having a number of jet engines.

**mul|ti|lam|i|nate** (mul′ti lam′ə nāt, -nit), *adj.* having many laminae or layers.

**mul|ti|lane** (mul′ti lān′), *adj.* having more than two traffic lanes: *a multilane highway.*

**mul|ti|laned** (mul′ti lānd′), *adj.* = multilane.

**mul|ti|lat|er|al** (mul′ti lat′ər əl), *adj.* **1** having many sides; many-sided. **2** involving three or more nations: *a multilateral treaty.* —**mul′ti|lat′er|al|ly**, *adv.*

**mul|ti|lat|er|al|ism** (mul′ti lat′ər ə liz′əm), *n.* **1** a policy of reciprocity or freedom in trading with many nations (distinguished from *bilateralism*). **2** belief in or adoption of a multilateral policy, such as the joint control of nuclear weapons by the members of an alliance (distinguished from *unilateralism*).

**mul|ti|lat|er|al|ist** (mul′ti lat′ər ə list), *n., adj.* —*n.* an adherent of multilateralism.
—*adj.* of or having to do with multilateralism or multilateralists.

**mul|ti|lay|er** (mul′ti lā′ər), *adj., n.* —*adj.* **1** consisting of several layers: *a multilayer cake, multilayer wrappers.* **2** *Photography.* consisting of two or more layers of differently sensitized emulsions for producing differently colored images in each layer.
—*n. Chemistry.* a layer consisting of several monolayers.

**mul|ti|lay|ered** (mul′ti lā′ərd), *adj.* = multilayer.

**mul|ti|lev|el** (mul′ti lev′əl), *adj.* **1** having two or more planes or levels: *a multilevel roadway, a multilevel hospital complex.* **2** having many social or intellectual levels: *multilevel public services, a multilevel work of art.*

**mul|ti|lev|eled** (mul′ti lev′əld), *adj.* = multilevel.

**mul|ti|lin|e|al** (mul′ti lin′ē əl), *adj.* having many lines.

**mul|ti|lin|e|ar** (mul′ti lin′ē ər), *adj.* having many lines; multilineal: *a multilinear map, multilinear evolution.*

**mul|ti|lin|gual** (mul′ti ling′gwəl), *adj.* knowing or using many languages: *Another feature is a multilingual index giving English equivalents of mathematical terms in French, German, Russian and Spanish* (Scientific American). —**mul′ti|lin′gual|ly**, *adv.*

**mul|ti|lin|gual|ism** (mul′ti ling′gwə liz əm), *n.* the knowledge or use of many languages: *The discovery that multilingualism was cultivated as a way of life among certain South American Indians rendered the familiar concepts of society, tribe, and ethnic group elusive and difficult* (Ward H. Goodenough).

**Mul|ti|lith** (mul′ti lith), *n. Trademark.* a small offset press for printing office letters, circulars, and other matter.

**mul|ti|lith** (mul′ti lith), *v.t.* to make copies of by a Multilith.

**mul|ti|lo|bate** (mul′ti lō′bāt), *adj.* having many lobes: *a multilobate leaf.*

**mul|ti|lobed** (mul′ti lōbd′), *adj.* = multilobate.

**mul|ti|loc|u|lar** (mul′ti lok′yə lər), *adj.* having many chambers or cells.

**mul|til|o|quence** (mul til′ə kwəns), *n.* the use of many words; verbosity; loquacity. [< Late Latin *multiloquentia* < Latin *multus* much + *loquentia* fluency of speech]

**mul|til|o|quent** (mul til′ə kwənt), *adj.* speaking much; talkative; verbose.

**mul|ti|mar|ket** (mul′ti mär′kit), *adj.* involved or operating in many different markets: *a multimarket company.*

**mul|ti|me|di|a** (mul′ti mē′dē ə), *adj., n.* —*adj.* **1** using a combination of various media, such as tapes, film, phonograph records, photographs, and slides, to entertain, communicate, teach, and the like; mixed-media: *the multimedia rock musical Stomp* (London Times). **2** involving the use of different communications media in the same place: *These standards apply both to multimedia information centers with print and audiovisual materials and to schools with separate libraries and audiovisual centers* (Dan Bergen).
—*n.* the use of more than one medium of communication or entertainment at one time; mixed media: *Concerts and demonstrations of multimedia were given in schools, colleges, theatres, museums, warehouses, and barns, in a variety of musical, nonmusical, unmusical, and antimusical presentations* (Nicolas Slonimsky).

**mul|ti|meg|a|ton** (mul′ti meg′ə tun), *adj.* (of thermonuclear weapons) having a force of many megatons.

**mul|ti|mil|lion|aire** (mul′ti mil′yə nãr′), *n.* a person who owns property worth several millions (of dollars, pounds, francs, or other currency); millionaire many times over.

**mul|ti|mil|lions** (mul′ti mil′yənz), *n.pl.* millions of dollars, pounds, or other currency: *When he's finally made his multimillions, he finds all he can use them for is to buy better burglar alarms* (New Scientist).

**mul|ti|mo|tored** (mul′ti mō′tərd), *adj.* having a number of motors.

**mul|ti|na|tion|al** (mul′ti nash′ə nəl, -nash′nəl), *adj., n.* —*adj.* of or having to do with many nations: *a multinational economic organization. The United States was ready to contribute to a new fund to increase multinational projects in Latin America* (Manchester Guardian Weekly).
—*n.* a company having branches in several countries: *With so much economic power at their disposal the multinationals will be tough opponents for governments or unions* (New Scientist).

**mul|ti|no|mi|al** (mul′ti nō′mē əl), *adj., n.* = polynomial.

**mul|ti|nom|i|nal** (mul′ti nom′ə nəl), *adj.* having many names.

**mul|ti|nu|cle|ar** (mul′ti nü′klē ər, -nyü′-), *adj.* having more than one nucleus: *a multinuclear cell.*

**mul|ti|nu|cle|ate** (mul′ti nü′klē it, -nyü′-), *adj.* = multinuclear.

**mul|ti|nu|cle|at|ed** (mul′ti nü′klē ā′tid, -nyü′-), *adj.* = multinuclear.

**mul|ti|pack** (mul′ti pak′), *n.* a package containing two or more individually packaged products, sold as a unit.

**mul|tip|a|ra** (mul tip′ər ə), *n., pl.* **-a|rae** (-ə rē). a woman who has had more than one child. [< New Latin *multipara,* feminine of *multiparus* < Latin *multus* much + *parere* bring forth]

**mul|ti|par|i|ty** (mul′ti par′ə tē), *n.* plural birth; production of several at a birth. [< *multi-* + Latin *parere* bring forth + English *-ity*]

**mul|tip|a|rous** (mul tip′ər əs), *adj.* **1** producing many, or more than one, at a birth. **2** of or having to do with a woman who has borne more than one child. **3** *Botany.* (of a cyme) having many axes.

**mul|ti|par|tite** (mul′ti pär′tīt), *adj.* **1** divided into many parts; having many divisions. **2** = multilateral. [< Latin *multipartītus* < *multus* much + *partīre* to divide < *pars, partis* part]

**mul|ti|par|ty** (mul′ti pär′tē), *adj.* of or having to do with a number of political parties.

**mul|ti|ped** (mul′tə ped), *adj., n.* —*adj.* having many feet. —*n.* an animal with many feet. [< Latin *multipēs, -pedis* < *multus* many + *pēs, pedis* foot]

**Pronunciation Key:** hat, āge, cãre, fär; let, ēqual, tėrm; it, īce; hot, ōpen, ôrder; oil, out; cup, pu̇t, rüle; child; long; thin; ᴛʜen; zh, measure; ə represents **a** in about, **e** in taken, **i** in pencil, **o** in lemon, **u** in circus.

**mul|ti|pede** (mul′tə pēd), *adj., n.* = multiped.

**mul|ti|phase** (mul′ti fāz), *adj.* **1** having many phases. **2** *Electricity.* polyphase.

**mul|ti|pha|sic** (mul′ti fā′sik), *adj.* = multiphase.

**mul|ti|plane** (mul′ti plān), *n.* an airplane with several main lifting surfaces.

**mul|ti|ple** (mul′tə pəl), *adj., n.* —*adj.* **1** of, having, or involving many parts, elements, or relations; manifold: *Benjamin Franklin was a man of multiple interests.* **2** *Electricity.* **a** (of a circuit) having two or more conductors in parallel. **b** (of a group of terminals) giving access to a circuit at a number of points. **3** *British.* of or belonging to a chain of stores or shops: *a multiple grocer.*
—*n.* **1** a number which contains another number a certain number of times without a remainder: *20 is a multiple of 4.* **2** *Electricity.* a group of terminals arranged so as to give access to a circuit or group of circuits at a number of points. **3** *Especially British.* a multiple shop; chain store: *An individual store buyer is on a hopeless wicket in those sections where he has to meet competition from the multiples* (Sunday Times). **4** a mass-produced painting, sculpture, or other artistic work: *The artist who becomes interested in multiples takes the first step towards involving himself with the demands of technology* (London Times).
**in multiple**, *Electricity.* in parallel: *All the motors were connected in multiple and operated individually.*
[< French *multiple* < Late Latin *multiplus* manifold]

**mul|ti|ple-ac|cess** (mul′tə pəl ak′ses), *adj.* = multi-access.

**multiple alleles**, *Genetics.* a group of three or more allelomorphic genes, only two of which can be present at one time in the body cells of a diploid organism.

**mul|ti|ple-an|swer** (mul′tə pəl an′sər, -än′-), *adj.* = multiple-response (def. 2).

**mul|ti|ple-choice** (mul′tə pəl chois′), *adj.* containing two or more suggested answers from which the correct or best one must be chosen: *a multiple-choice test. In her two and a half years at Georgia, where even philosophy tests are usually made up of true-false and multiple-choice questions, Charlayne's grades fluctuated wildly* (New Yorker).

**multiple cropping**, growing two or more crops in one field in one year.

**multiple factors**, *Genetics.* combinations of two or more genes which act together to produce a trait, as size, yield, or skin pigmentation, or the variations in it.

**multiple fruit**, a fruit composed of a cluster of ripened ovaries produced by several flowers, as the mulberry; collective fruit; compound fruit.

**Multiple Independently Targeted Reentry Vehicle**, a guided missile with multiple nuclear warheads to be aimed at several targets at a time; MIRV.

**multiple myeloma**, a very painful cancer usually affecting a number of bones, originating in bone marrow, and causing lesions of the bone and of certain soft tissues such as the kidneys.

**multiple neuritis**, inflammation of several nerves at once.

**multiple personality**, a psychological condition in which a person, from time to time, exhibits the characteristics or behavior of two or more dissimilar personalities.

**mul|ti|ple-re|sponse** (mul′tə pəl ri spons′), *adj.* **1** *Psychology.* involving a great variety of responses to a new stimulus or situation before an organized response pattern is evolved: *multiple-response learning.* **2** *Education.* containing a group of suggested answers from which two or more correct answers must be chosen: *a multiple-response test.*

**multiple sclerosis**, a disorder of the nervous system, attacking the brain and the spinal cord, and characterized by the degeneration and scarring of patches of nerve tissue, followed by paralysis, muscle spasms, disorders of speech, and tremors of the hand. *Abbr:* MS (no periods).

**multiple shop** or **store**, *Especially British.* a chain store; multiple.

**multiple star**, a group of three or more stars comprising one gravitational system, and usually appearing to the naked eye as a single star.

**mul|ti|plet** (mul′tə plit), *n.* **1** *Physics.* two or more closely associated lines in a spectrum, exhibiting characteristic differences, as of frequency. **2** *Nuclear Physics.* two or more elementary particles exhibiting identical or similar characteristics: *The eightfold way puts nuclear particles into groups, or multiplets, and families of groups, or supermultiplets* (Science News Letter).

**mul|ti|ple-val|ued** (mul′tə pəl val′yüd), *adj.* = multivalued.

**multiple voting**, voting in more than one place at the same election. This was legally possible in Great Britain before 1918.

**mul|ti|plex** (mul′tə pleks), *adj., v.* —*adj.* **1** manifold; multiple. **2** *Telegraphy, Telephony.* of or designating a system for sending two or more messages in each direction over the same wire or circuit at the same time. **3** *Radio, Television.* of or designating the transmission of two or more signals on one carrier wave at the same time: *Center channel output and output for multiplex adaptor assure ... gratifying results* (Wall Street Journal).
—*v.t., v.i.* **1** *Telegraphy, Telephony.* to send (two or more messages) over the same wire at the same time. **2** *Radio, Television.* to send (two or more signals) on one carrier wave at the same time: *Multiplex your modulation into the intermediate frequency* (New York Times).
[< Latin *multiplex, -icis;* see etym. under **multiply**] —**mul′ti|plex′er**, *n.* —**mul′ti|plex′ly**, *adv.*

**mul|ti|pli|a|ble** (mul′tə plī′ə bəl), *adj.* that can be or will be multiplied, especially as the consequence of some action.

**mul|ti|pli|ca|ble** (mul′tə plə kə bəl), *adj.* = multipliable.

**mul|ti|pli|cand** (mul′tə plə kand′), *n.* a number or quantity to be multiplied by another: *In 5 times 497, the multiplicand is 497.* [< Latin *multiplicandus,* gerundive of *multiplicāre;* see etym. under **multiply**]

**mul|ti|pli|cate** (mul′tə plə kāt), *adj.* manifold; multifold; multiplex. [< Latin *multiplicātus,* past participle of *multiplicāre;* see etym. under **multiply**]

***mul|ti|pli|ca|tion** (mul′tə plə kā′shən), *n.* **1** the act or process of multiplying: *I fairly cowered down ... under this multiplication of hardships* (Herman Melville). **2** the condition of being multiplied: *One of the peculiarities which distinguish the present age is the multiplication of books* (Samuel Johnson). **3** the operation of multiplying one number or quantity by another; the operation of finding a product by adding a number or quantity (the multiplicand) as many times as there are units in another (the multiplier), or of calculating this addition briefly.

| | | |
|---|---|---|
| | 4 | multiplicand |
| ***multiplication** definition 3 | X 2 | multiplier |
| | 8 | product |

**mul|ti|pli|ca|tion|al** (mul′tə plə kā′shə nəl), *adj.* of or having to do with multiplication.

**multiplication fact**, a basic statement in multiplication, such as 6 X 3 = 18.

**multiplication sign**, either the symbol X or a centered dot, used to indicate the operation of multiplying. *Examples:* 3 X 4 = 12; 3 · 4 = 12

**multiplication table**, a table that lists the products of all the simple digits, from 1 times 1 to 12 times 12.

**mul|ti|pli|ca|tive** (mul′tə plə kā′tiv), *adj.* tending to multiply or increase; able to multiply. —**mul′ti|pli|ca′tive|ly**, *adv.*

**multiplicative inverse**, *Mathematics.* the reciprocal of a given number. *Example:* 2/3 is the multiplicative inverse of 3/2.

**mul|ti|pli|cious** (mul′tə plish′əs), *adj.* manifold; multiple.

**mul|ti|plic|i|ty** (mul′tə plis′ə tē), *n., pl.* **-ties.** **1** manifold variety; diversity: *the multiplicity of nature.* **2** a great many; great number: *a multiplicity of gifts, a multiplicity of interests.* [< Late Latin *multiplicitās* < Latin *multiplex, -icis;* see etym. under **multiply**]

**mul|ti|pli|er** (mul′tə plī′ər), *n.* **1** a number by which another number is to be multiplied: *In 5 times 83, the multiplier is 5.* **2** a person or thing that multiplies. **3** *Physics.* an instrument or device used for intensifying by repetition the intensity of a force, current, or other agent.

**multiplier onion**, a variety of the common onion that is raised from a bulb instead of a seed or a set and is used chiefly in salads.

**mul|ti|ply**[1] (mul′tə plī), *v.,* **-plied, -ply|ing.** —*v.t.* **1** to take (a number or quantity) a given number of times: *To multiply 16 by 3 means to take 16 three times, making 48.* **2** to increase the number or amount of: *Fear multiplies the difficulties of life.* **3** to increase by procreation: *that all creatures might be tempted to multiply their kind, and fill the world with inhabitants* (Joseph Addison). **4** to produce (animals or plants) by propagation.
—*v.i.* **1** to grow in number; increase: *As we climbed up the mountain the dangers and difficulties multiplied.* **2** to increase in number by natural generation or procreation: *Be fruitful, and multiply* (Genesis 1:22). **3** to perform the process of multiplication: *The little boy can add, subtract, and multiply, but he cannot divide.* [< Old French *multiplier* < Latin *multiplicāre* < *multiplex, -icis* < *multus* many + *-plex* -fold]

**mul|ti|ply**[2] (mul′tə plē), *adv.* in a multiple or manifold way; in the manner of a multiple.

**mul|ti|ply|ing gear** (mul′tə plī′ing), a gear larger than the one being turned by it. Multiplying gears are used to increase the speed of smaller gears.

**multiplying reel**, a fishing reel having a spool which turns several times for every revolution of its handle.

**mul|ti|po|lar** (mul′ti pō′lər), *adj.* having many poles.

**mul|ti|po|lar|i|ty** (mul′ti pō lar′ə tē), *n.* multipolar quality or condition: *the multipolarity of political power.*

**mul|tip|o|tent** (mul tip′ə tənt), *adj.* having much power; very powerful: *There are still undreamed-of possibilities in the multipotent clay that is his to mold* (Atlantic). [< *multi-* + Latin *pōtens, -entis* powerful]

**mul|ti|proc|ess|ing** (mul′ti pros′əs ing; *Especially British* mul′ti prō′səs ing), *n.* the use of two or more computer processors which have access to a common memory and can execute several programs simultaneously: *Multiprocessing, like multiprogramming, got off to a slow start because of the associated complexities in coordination and control, but a number of multiprocessing systems are now in operation and many more are planned* (I. Auerbach and J. R. Hillegass).

**mul|ti|proc|es|sor** (mul′ti pros′es ər; *Especially British* mul′ti prō′ses ər), *n.* a computer unit consisting of several processors, used in multiprocessing.

**mul|ti|pro|gram|ming** (mul′ti prō′gram ing, -grə-ming), *n.* the handling of several programs concurrently by a single computer.

**mul|ti|pur|pose** (mul′ti pėr′pəs), *adj.* having many purposes or functions; versatile: *a multipurpose building that can be used for machinery storage, for grain storage, and for housing cattle.*

**mul|ti|ra|cial** (mul′ti rā′shəl), *adj.* consisting of or having to do with a number of races: *the multiracial communities of the Caribbean.*

**mul|ti|ra|cial|ism** (mul′ti rā′shə liz əm), *n.* a political or social system in which all racial groups are accorded equal rights and opportunities: *The new federation* [*of Malaysia*] *is an experiment in multiracialism* (Manchester Guardian Weekly).

**mul|ti|re|sis|tant** (mul′ti ri zis′tənt), *adj.* resistant to various antibiotics: *In the right environment such as the intestinal tracts of cattle being fed a number of different antibiotics, multiresistant strains develop very rapidly* (Manchester Guardian Weekly).

**mul|ti|sen|so|ry** (mul′ti sen′sər ē), *adj.* having to do with or involving the use of various sensory organs: *multisensory learning; ... light, sound, and other elements to provide multisensory effects* (New York Times).

**mul|ti|spec|tral** (mul′ti spek′trəl), *adj.* capable of sensing emissions from several spectra, especially from parts of the visible, infrared, and microwave spectra: *All available evidence suggests an extensive scientific programme which includes placing the Earth under the most detailed observation with multispectral cameras and sensing equipment* (New Scientist and Science Journal).

**mul|ti|stage** (mul′ti stāj′), *adj.* **1** having a number of stages in going through a complete process: *multistage automatic washers or amplifiers, a multistage nuclear reaction.* **2** having two or more propulsive sections, each operating after the preceding stage has burned out and separated: *a multistage rocket.*

**mul|ti|state** (mul′ti stāt), *adj.* consisting of or serving many nations or states of a nation: *a multistate conference.*

**mul|ti|sto|rey** (mul′ti stôr′ē, -stōr′-), *adj. Especially British.* multistory.

**mul|ti|sto|ried** (mul′ti stôr′ēd, -stōr′-), *adj.* = multistory.

**mul|ti|sto|ry** (mul′ti stôr′ē, -stōr′-), *adj.* (of a building) have many stories.

**mul|ti|syl|lab|ic** (mul′ti sə lab′ik), *adj.* = polysyllabic.

**mul|ti|tude** (mul′tə tüd, -tyüd), *n.* **1** a great many: *a multitude of problems, a multitude of friends.* SYN: host, horde. **2** a large gathering of people; crowd: *An angry multitude collected in the street.* SYN: throng. **3** number: *Ye are this day as the stars of heaven for multitude* (Deuteronomy 1:10).
**the multitude**, the common people; the masses: *a play that appeals to the multitude.*
[< Latin *multitūdō, -inis* < *multus* much]

**mul|ti|tu|di|nism** (mul′tə tü′də niz əm, -tyü′-), *n.* the principle according to which the interests of multitudes are placed before those of individuals.

**mul|ti|tu|di|nous** (mul′tə tü′də nəs, -tyü′-), *adj.* **1** forming a multitude; very numerous; existing or occurring in great numbers: *Multitudinous echoes awoke and died in the distance* (Longfellow). **2** including many parts, elements, items, or features: *I heard again the multitudinous murmur of* *the city* (George W. Curtis). **3** crowded; thronged: *the multitudinous streets.* **4** *Obsolete.* of or having to do with the multitude: *Pluck out The multitudinous tongue; let them not lick The sweet which is their poison* (Shakespeare). —**mul'ti|tu'di|nous|ly,** *adv.* —**mul'ti|tu'di|nous|ness,** *n.*

**mul|ti|va|lence** (mul'ti vā'ləns, mul tiv'ə-), *n.* multivalent quality or property.

**mul|ti|va|lent** (mul'ti vā'lənt, mul tiv'ə-), *adj.* **1** having a valence of three or more. **2** having more than one valence.

**mul|ti|val|ued** (mul'ti val'yüd), *adj.* having many values: *a multivalued mathematical function.*

**mul|ti|valve** (mul'ti valv), *adj., n.* —*adj.* (of a shell) having many valves or ports.
—*n.* **1** a multivalve shell. **2** an animal having such a shell.

**mul|ti|val|vu|lar** (mul'ti val'vyə lər), *adj.* = multivalve.

**mul|ti|var|i|ate** (mul'ti vãr'ē āt), *adj.* having two or more variates.

**mul|ti|verse** (mul'ti vėrs), *n.* the universe regarded as lacking order or any single ruling or guiding power. [< *multi-* + (uni)*verse*]

**mul|ti|ver|si|ty** (mul'tə vėr'sə tē), *n., pl.* **-ties.** a large educational institution comprising several universities and their related colleges and professional schools; polyversity: *The Board of Governors, whether of a small liberal arts college or a multiversity, will need ... persuasiveness if our universities are to grow and change* (Saturday Night). [(coined by Clark Kerr, born 1911, former president of the University of California) < *multi-* + (uni)*versity*]

**mul|ti|vi|bra|tor** (mul'ti vī'brā tər), *n.* a type of oscillator having two stages, each of which utilizes the output voltage of the other as its input. Multivibrators are used especially in digital computers and electronic circuits.

**mul|ti|vi|ta|min** (mul'ti vī'tə min), *adj., n.* —*adj.* containing or combining various vitamins: *a multivitamin pill.*
—*n.* a drug or similar substance containing various vitamins.

**mul|tiv|o|cal** (mul tiv'ə kəl), *adj.* having many meanings; equivocal; ambiguous.

**mul|ti|vol|tine** (mul'ti vōl'tēn), *adj. Zoology.* that produces several broods in a single season: *a multivoltine moth or other insect.* [< *multi-* + Italian *volta* a turning, turn + English *-ine*[1]]

**mul|ti|vol|ume** (mul'ti vol'yəm), *adj.* **1** filling many volumes: *... the first multivolume history of Canada* (Maclean's). **2** containing many volumes: *a multivolume set, a multivolume library.*

**mul|ti|vol|umed** (mul'ti vol'yəmd), *adj.* = multivolume.

**mul|ti|wall bag** (mul'ti wôl), a large, heavy-duty paper bag consisting of a number of layers or sheets of kraft paper: *The cement industry has remained the top multiwall bag user* (Wall Street Journal).

**mul|toc|u|lar** (mul tok'yə lər), *adj.* having many eyes, or eyelike parts, as a fly or certain microscopes. [< *mult-* + *ocular*]

**mul|tum in par|vo** (mul'təm in pär'vō), *Latin.* much in little.

**mul|ture** (mul'chər), *n. Archaic.* **1** a fee consisting of a proportion of the grain, or of the flour, paid to the miller for grinding it. **2** the right to take this toll. [< Old French *molture,* learned borrowing from Medieval Latin *moltura,* for Late Latin *molitūra* < Latin *molere* to grind]

**mum**[1] (mum), *adj., interj.* —*adj.* saying nothing; silent: *Keep mum about this; tell no one. The company being otherwise rather mum and silent, my uncle told ... anecdotes* (Thackeray). **SYN:** mute, speechless, dumb.
—*interj.* be silent! say nothing! hush!
**mum's the word,** be silent; say nothing: *Don't forget! Mum's the word on plans for the surprise party.*
[perhaps imitative. Compare etym. under **mummer, mummery.**]

**mum**[2] (mum), *v.i.,* **mummed, mum|ming. 1** to go about as a mummer, as at Christmastime. **2** = masquerade. **3** *Archaic.* to act in dumb show. Also, **mumm.** [perhaps back formation < *mommyng* a disguising, mummer's play; origin uncertain. Compare etym. under **mummer.**]

**mum**[3] (mum), *n. Informal.* a chrysanthemum. [short for *chrysanthemum*]

**mum**[4] (mum), *n. Informal.* mother. [short for *mummy,* (originally) dialectal variant of *mammy,* or *mommy*]

**mum**[5] (mum), *n.* a strong ale or beer, popular in England in the 1600's and 1700's. [< German *Mumme,* or Dutch *mom*]

**mum|ble** (mum'bəl), *v.,* **-bled, -bling,** *n.* —*v.i.* **1** to speak indistinctly, as a person does when his lips are partly closed; speak in low tones; mutter: *She appeared as if she wanted to say something, and kept making signs ... and mumbling* (Charlotte Brontë). **SYN:** See syn. under **murmur. 2** to chew as a person does who has no teeth: *The old dog mumbled on a crust.* —*v.t.* **1** to say indistinctly, as a person does when his lips are partly closed: *to mumble one's words. He affirmed that we mumbled our speech with our lips and teeth, and ran the words together without pause or distinction* (Tobias Smollett). **SYN:** See syn. under **murmur. 2** to chew as a person does who has no teeth: *The old dog mumbled the crust.*
—*n.* the act or fact of mumbling; indistinct speech: *There was a mumble of protest from the team against the umpire's decision.*
[Middle English *momelen,* perhaps (frequentative) < *mum*[2]] —**mum'bler,** *n.* —**mum'bling|ly,** *adv.*

**mum|ble|ty-peg** (mum'bəl ti peg'), *n.* a game in which the players in turn flip a knife from various positions, trying to make it stick in the ground; the loser originally having to pull a peg out of the ground with his teeth. [earlier *mumble-the-peg*]

**Mum|bo Jum|bo** (mum'bō jum'bō), the guardian genius of a native African village in western Sudan, represented by a masked medicine man who fends off evil and keeps the women in subjection: *Mumbo Jumbo, God of the Congo ... will hoo-doo you* (Vachel Lindsay). [allegedly < a West African language; origin unknown]

**mumbo jumbo, 1** foolish or meaningless incantation; ritualistic or ceremonial nonsense: *You are lost if you preoccupy yourself with the old mumbo jumbo ... of an era that is done* (Harper's). **2** an object foolishly worshiped or feared; bugaboo; bogy. **SYN:** fetish.

**mum|chance** (mum'chans', -chäns'), *adj., adv. Especially British.* in silence; speechless; tongue-tied; mum: *The gunman ... had left with £7,500 while the smirking staff stood mumchance* (Punch). [< obsolete English *mumchance,* noun, a certain game of dice < Middle Low German *mummenschanze* < *mummen* to keep silence (probably < Old French *momer* mask oneself; see etym. under **mummer**) + *schanz* game of chance < Old French *cheance;* see etym. under **chance**]

**mu|me** (mü'mē), *n.* a small Japanese tree or shrub with fragrant, light-pink flowers and greenish inedible fruit, used in bonsai. It belongs to the rose family. [< Japanese *mume*]

**mu-mes|on** (myü'mes'on, -mē'son; -mez'on, -mē'zon), *n.,* or **mu meson,** a meson having a mass about 207 times that of the electron; muon. Mu-mesons are formed by the decay of pi-mesons and in turn decay to form high-energy electrons. [< Greek *mu,* arbitrary designation in a series + English *meson*]

**mumm** (mum), *v.i.* = mum[2].

**mum|mer** (mum'ər), *n.* **1** a person who wears a mask, fancy costume, or disguise for fun: *Six mummers acted in the play at Christmas.* **2** an actor. **3** an actor in one of the rural plays traditionally performed in England and elsewhere at Christmas: *The play was hastily rehearsed, whereupon the other mummers were delighted with the new knight* (Thomas Hardy). [< Old French *momeur* mummer < *momer* mask oneself < *momon* mask]

**mum|mer|y** (mum'ər ē), *n., pl.* **-mer|ies. 1** a performance of mummers. **2** any useless or silly show or ceremony: *Archbishop Grindal long hesitated about accepting a mitre from dislike of what he regarded as the mummery of consecration* (Macaulay). [< Middle French *mommerie* < Old French *momer* mask oneself; see etym. under **mummer**]

**mum|mi|chog** (mum'i chog), *n. U.S.* a killifish. [American English < Narraganset *moamitteaúg* (literally) they are many]

**mum|mi|fi|ca|tion** (mum'ə fə kā'shən), *n.* **1** the act or process of mummifying: *The thighbone of a dead African king, preserved for ritual uses, represents ... a diffusion of Egyptian mummification* (Melville J. Herskovitz). **2** the state of being mummified.

**mum|mi|fy** (mum'ə fī), *v.,* **-fied, -fy|ing.** —*v.t.* **1** to make (a dead body) into a mummy by embalming and drying. **2** *Figurative.* to make like a mummy; preserve.
—*v.i.* to shrivel up; dry up.

***mum|my**[1] (mum'ē), *n., pl.* **-mies,** *v.,* **-mied, -my|ing.** —*n.* **1** a dead body preserved from decay. Egyptian mummies have lasted more than 3,000 years. (*Figurative.*) *The old theological dogmas had become mere mummies* (Leslie Stephen). **2** a dead human or animal body dried and preserved by nature. **3** a withered or shrunken living being. **4a** a rich brown bituminous pigment. **b** a rich brown color. **5** *British Dialect.* a pulpy mass: *battering the warriors' faces into mummy by terrible yerks from their hinder hoofs* (Jonathan Swift). **6** *Obsolete.* dead flesh; a corpse. **7** *Obsolete.* bone or tissue matter from a mummy, formerly used as a medicine.
—*v.t., v.i.* = mummify.
[< Old French *mumie,* learned borrowing from Medieval Latin *mumia* < Arabic *mūmiyā* embalmed body < Persian *mūm* wax]

***mummy**[1] definition 1

***mummy case**

**mum|my**[2] (mum'ē), *n., pl.* **-mies.** *Informal.* mother.

***mummy case,** a case of wood or other material in which a mummy, wrapped in cloth, was enclosed. The case was rectangular or shaped to conform to the body, and often carved and painted to represent the dead person.

**mump** (mump), *Dialect.* —*v.i.* **1** to mumble; mutter. **2** to munch or chew. **3** to mope; sulk: *It is better to enjoy a novel than to mump* (Robert Louis Stevenson). **4** to grimace. **5** to sponge; beg.
—*v.t.* **1** to mumble; mutter: *Old men who mump their passion* (Oliver Goldsmith). **2** to munch or chew. **3** to beg. **4** to cheat.
[perhaps < Icelandic *mumpa* take into the mouth]

**mump|ish** (mum'pish), *adj.* sullenly angry; depressed in spirits. —**mump'ish|ly,** *adv.*

**mumps** (mumps), *n.pl.* a contagious disease that causes swelling of the glands in the neck and face, difficulty in swallowing, and sometimes inflammation of the testes or ovaries. It is caused by a virus. [plural of obsolete *mump* a grimace. See related etym. at **mump.**]
▶ **Mumps** is usually construed as singular: *Mumps is chiefly a children's disease.*

**mump|si|mus** (mump'sə məs), *n.* an error obstinately clung to, regardless of right or reason: *Al is a shrewd enough showman to know that this mumpsimus is excellent publicity* (Baltimore Sun). [< misreading of Latin *sumpsimus* we took (because the reader maintained repeatedly that *mumpsimus* was correct)]

**mu|mu**[1] (mü'mü'), *n.* = muumuu.

**mu|mu**[2] (mü'mü'), *n.* = filariasis. [perhaps < a Samoan word]

**mun** (mun), *auxiliary verb. Scottish.* must: *Poor folk mun get on as they can* (Charlotte Brontë). [< Scandinavian (compare Old Icelandic *mun* I shall)]

**mun.,** municipal.

**munch** (munch), *v., n.* —*v.t., v.i.* to chew vigorously and steadily; chew noisily: *The horse munched its oats. A sailor's wife had chestnuts in her lap, And munch'd, and munch'd, and munch'd* (Shakespeare).
—*n.* the act or sound of munching: ... *as crisp as the munch of a Baldwin apple* (New Yorker). [apparently imitative. Compare etym. under **crunch.**] —**munch'er,** *n.*

**Mun|chau|sen** (mun chô'zən), *adj.* of or having to do with exaggerated and boastful tales, such as those attributed to Baron Münchausen, and typical of Munchausenism.

**Mun|chau|sen|ism** (mun chô'zə niz əm), *n.* **1** the tendency to tell exaggerated stories. **2** an exaggerated story or statement. [< Baron *Münchausen,* 1720-1797, German cavalry officer, the supposed author of a book of incredible tales]

**Mun|da** (mủn'dä), *n.* an Austro-Asiatic group of languages spoken on the southern slopes of the Himalayas and in central India.

**mun|dane** (mun'dān), *adj.* **1** of this world, not of heaven; earthly: *mundane matters of business.* **2** of the universe; of the world; cosmic. [< Old French *mondain,* learned borrowing from Latin *mundānus* < *mundus* world] —**mun'dane|ly,** *adv.* —**mun'dane|ness,** *n.*

**mundane astrology,** = judicial astrology.

**mun|dan|i|ty** (mun dan'ə tē), *n.* mundane quality; worldliness; worldly feelings.

**Pronunciation Key:** hat, āge, cãre, fär; let, ēqual, tėrm; it, īce; hot, ōpen, ôrder; oil, out; cup, pủt, rüle; child; long; thin; ᴛʜen; zh, measure; ə represents **a** in about, **e** in taken, **i** in pencil, **o** in lemon, **u** in circus.

**mun|dic** (mun′dik), *n. British.* pyrites. [apparently < a Cornish word]

**mun|du** (mun′dü), *n.* a long cloth worn as a skirt especially in southern India, usually made of thin cotton: *Small dark boys with their mundus tucked up high beckon you toward their strange primitive boats* (Santha Rama Rau). [< a native name]

**mun|dun|gus** (mun dung′gəs), *n. Archaic.* bad-smelling tobacco. [alteration of Spanish *mondongo* tripe]

**mung bean** (mung), a bean grown in areas of tropical Asia, Iran, and eastern Africa, used as food and as a forage and cover crop. [< Hindi *mūng*]

**mun|go** (mung′gō), *n.* cloth of inferior quality, made of used wool. It is of better quality than shoddy. [origin unknown]

**mun|goos** or **mun|goose** (mung′güs), *n., pl.* **-goos|es.** = mongoose.

**Mu|nich** (myü′nik), *n.* an instance of appeasement which ultimately or immediately involves yielding to an aggressor at the expense of a principle or ally, and hence brings shame to the appeaser. [< the *Munich* Agreement, a noted instance of appeasement]

**Munich Agreement** or **Pact**, an agreement signed September 30, 1938, by Germany, France, Great Britain, and Italy, by which the Sudetenland, a part of Czechoslovakia, was given over to Germany.

**mu|nic|i|pal** (myü nis′ə pəl), *adj., n.* —*adj.* **1** of or having to do with the affairs of a city, town, or other municipality: *The state police assisted the municipal police.* **2** run by a city, town, or other municipality: *a municipal department store, a municipal hospital.* **3** having local self-government: *a municipal township.* **4** having to do with the internal affairs of a state, as distinguished from its foreign relations: *municipal or civil law.*
—*n.* **municipals**, bonds or other securities issued by a city, town, or other municipality: *The broker dealt chiefly in municipals.*
[< Latin *mūnicipālis* < *mūniceps, -ipis* a citizen; an inhabitant of a *mūnicipium* or free town < *mūnia* official duties + *capere* take, assume]

**mu|nic|i|pal|ise** (myü nis′ə pə līz), *v.t.,* **-ised, -is|ing.** *Especially British.* municipalize.

**mu|nic|i|pal|ism** (myü nis′ə pə liz′əm), *n.* **1** municipal government. **2** the policy of increasing the power of government in cities and towns.

**mu|nic|i|pal|ist** (myü nis′ə pə list), *n.* **1** a person who supports the policy of extending local self-government. **2** *British.* a person who is skilled or experienced in municipal administration: *It was odd to hear the son of the great municipalist attacking, in his father's presence, the municipalities for their heavy borrowing* (Daily Chronicle).

**mu|nic|i|pal|i|ty** (myü nis′ə pal′ə tē), *n., pl.* **-ties.** **1** a city, town, or other district having local self-government, especially an incorporated one: *Municipalities and cooperatives get preference over private utilities in the allocation of Federally-generated power* (Wall Street Journal). **2** a community under municipal jurisdiction. **3** the governing body of such a district or community. **4** an administrative subdivision of a province, somewhat like a county, and itself made up of still smaller communities.

**mu|nic|i|pal|i|za|tion** (myü nis′ə pə lə zā′shən), *n.* transference from private to municipal ownership: *Municipalization of the city's airport, as well as those of Edinburgh and Aberdeen, was first proposed in a White Paper* (London Times).

**mu|nic|i|pal|ize** (myü nis′ə pə līz), *v.t.,* **-ized, -iz|ing.** **1** to make into a municipality. **2** to bring under municipal ownership or control: *to municipalize subways.* —**mu|nic′i|pal|iz′er**, *n.*

**mu|nic|i|pal|ly** (myü nis′ə plē), *adv.* by a city or town; with regard to a city or town or to municipal affairs: *The whole idea of the new town was municipally conceived.*

**mu|nic|i|pals** (myü nis′ə pəlz), *n.pl.* See under **municipal**.

**mu|ni|ci|pi|o** (mü′nē sē′pē ō), *n., pl.* **-pi|os.** *Spanish.* a municipality; township: *Honduras is divided into 275 municipios.*

**mu|ni|cip|i|um** (myü nə sip′ē əm), *n., pl.* **-i|a** (-ē ə). **1** (in ancient times) an Italian town with local rights of self-government and some of the privileges of Roman citizenship. **2** (later) a town government similarly constituted wherever situated. [< Latin *municipium;* see etym. under **municipal**]

**mu|nif|i|cence** (myü nif′ə səns), *n.* **1** very great generosity: *My master's known munificence* (Robert Browning). *A scene which the munificence of nature had adorned with unrivalled beauties* (Charles Brockden Brown). **2** ample measure; bountiful quality: *the munificence of a gift.* [< Latin *mūnificentia* < *mūnificus* generous, ultimately < *mūnus, -eris* gift + *facere* make]

**mu|nif|i|cent** (myü nif′ə sənt), *adj.* **1** extremely generous: *My father gave me ten shillings and my mother five for pocket money and I thought them munificent* (Samuel Butler). **SYN:** bountiful, liberal. **2** characterized by great generosity: *a munificent reward.* **SYN:** bounteous, lavish. —**mu|nif′i|cent|ly**, *adv.*

**mu|ni|ment** (myü′nə mənt), *n.* a means of defense; protection: *We cannot spare the coarsest muniment of virtue* (Emerson). **SYN:** stronghold. **muniments**, *Law.* a document, such as a title deed or charter, by which rights or privileges are defended or maintained: *The privileges of London were recognized* [*in 1066*] *by a royal writ which still remains, the most venerable of its muniments, among the city's archives* (John R. Green).
[< Middle French, Anglo-French *muniment,* learned borrowing from Medieval Latin *munimentum* document, title deed < Latin *mūnīmentum* defense, fortification < *mūnīre* to fortify; see etym. under **munition**]

**mu|ni|tion** (myü nish′ən), *n., adj., v.* —*n.* Usually, **munitions. 1** material used in war. Munitions are military supplies such as guns, ammunition, and bombs. ... *to bring up reinforcements and supplies of military munition* (Scott). *Two thousand men, with seven fieldpieces, and many wagonloads of munitions* (John L. Motley). **2** material or equipment for carrying on any undertaking.
—*adj.* having to do with military supplies: *A munition plant is a factory for making munitions.*
—*v.t.* to provide with military supplies: *to munition a fort.*
[earlier, provision < Middle French *munition,* learned borrowing from Latin *mūnītiō, -ōnis* < *mūnīre* to fortify < *moenia* walls]

**mu|ni|tion|eer** (myü nish′ə nir′), *n.* **1** = munitioner. **2** a person who makes excessive profits in manufacturing or supplying munitions.

**mu|ni|tion|er** (myü nish′ə nər), *n.* a person who makes ammunition.

**mu|ni|tion|ment** (myü nish′ən mənt), *n.* a supply of munitions.

**mun|nion** (mun′yən), *n., v.t.* = mullion.

**Mun|see** (mun′sē), *n., pl.* **-see** or **-sees.** a member of a group of the Delaware Indians that formerly lived along the western bank of the Hudson River and around the headwaters of the Delaware River.

**Mün|ster** (mun′stər, mün′-), *n.,* or **Munster cheese**, a cheese of medium softness, made from whole cow's milk. Also, **Muenster.** [< the *Munster* Valley, in Alsace, where it was first made]

**mun|tin** (mun′tən), *n.* **1** a bar of wood or metal which holds the panes of glass in a window within the sash. **2** = mullion (def. 1). [alteration of French *montant,* present participle of *monter* to rise < Old French; see etym. under **mount**[1]]

**munt|jac** or **munt|jak** (munt′jak), *n.* any of certain small deer of southern and eastern Asia, Java, and the surrounding area. [< Malayan (compare Sundanese *minchek*)]

**Muntz metal** (munts), a brass containing 60 per cent copper and 40 per cent zinc, used for castings and rolled or stamped products. [< G. F. *Muntz,* an English metallurgist of the 1800's, who developed it]

**mu|on** (myü′on), *n.* = mu-meson.

**mu|on|ic** (myü on′ik), *adj.* of or producing mu-mesons: *Extensive studies of the sizes and shapes of nuclei have been made using muonic atoms* (New Scientist).

**mu|on|i|um** (myü on′ē əm), *n.* a short-lived particle consisting of a positively charged mu-meson bound to a single electron: *The positive muon has been observed to collect a negative electron when coming to rest in pure gases, and the resulting "atom," muonium, has been studied with great precision* (Leon M. Lederman). [< *muon* + *-ium,* as in *uranium*]

**mu|rae|na** (myu̇ rē′nə), *n.* = moray.

**mu|ral** (myu̇r′əl), *adj., n.* —*adj.* **1** on a wall: *A mural painting is painted for or on a wall of a building.* **2** of a wall; having to do with walls; like a wall: *Disburden'd heaven rejoiced, and soon repair'd her mural breach* (Milton).
—*n.* a picture painted on a wall.
[< Old French *muraille,* learned borrowing from Latin *mūrālis* of a wall < *mūrus* wall] —**mu′ral|ly**, *adv.*

**mural crown**, a golden crown formed with indentations to resemble a battlement, bestowed among the ancient Romans on the soldier who first mounted the wall of a besieged place and there lodged a standard.

**mu|ral|ist** (myu̇r′ə list), *n.* a painter or designer of murals: *Muralist Dean Cornwell captures the historic moment when Sir Walter Raleigh's men first landed on our shores* (New Yorker).

**mu|ram|ic acid** (myu̇ ram′ik), a lactic acid derivative of glucosamine, found in the cell walls of some bacteria and certain other microorganisms, such as the blue-green algae. *Formula:* $C_9H_{17}NO_7$ [< Latin *mūrus* wall + English (glucos)*am*(ide) + *-ic*]

**mur|der** (mėr′dər), *n., v.* —*n.* **1** the unlawful killing of one human being by another, especially when it is intentional. If a criminal commits a robbery and accidentally kills someone, he is guilty of murder. *The murder of Abraham Lincoln was one of the world's great tragedies.* **2** an instance of such a crime: *The detective solved the murder.* **3** *Slang, Figurative.* anything exceedingly difficult or unpleasant: *That job was murder.*
—*v.t.* **1** to kill (a human being) unlawfully and intentionally: *Cain murdered his brother. Hamilton murdered the old man in cold blood* (Macaulay). **SYN:** slay. See syn. under **kill**. **2** *Figurative.* to do (something) very badly; spoil or ruin: *to murder the king's English. She murdered the song every time she tried to sing it.* **SYN:** mangle, butcher. **3** to spend (time) unprofitably: *Their evenings they murder in private parties* (Tobias Smollett).
—*v.i.* to commit murder.
**get away with murder**, *Slang.* to do something objectionable with impunity: *They* [*cats*] *refuse to make the slightest concession to human communication, and in consequence they get away with murder* (Russell Baker).
**murder will out, a** murder cannot be hidden: *Murder will out, that see we day by day* (Chaucer). **b** any great wrong will be found out: *The robbery has not been discovered yet, but murder will out eventually.*
[Middle English *mordre,* variant of *murther,* Old English *morthor*]

**mur|der|ee** (mėr′də rē′), *n.* the victim of a murder: *One would never have thought that the most regretted of all Shakespeare's murderees was Polonius, with Julius Caesar, Romeo, and Juliet ... close behind* (Punch).

**mur|der|er** (mėr′dər ər), *n.* a person who murders somebody. **SYN:** slayer, killer.

**mur|der|ess** (mėr′dər is), *n.* a woman who murders somebody.

**mur|der|ous** (mėr′dər əs), *adj.* **1** able to inflict great harm or to kill: *The villain aimed a murderous blow at the hero's back.* (*Figurative.*) *murderous heat.* **2** ready to murder; guilty or capable of murder: *a murderous villain. Enforced to fly Thence into Egypt, till the murderous king Were dead, who sought his life* (Milton). **3** causing murder: *a murderous plot, a murderous hate.* **4** characterized by or involving murder, death, or bloodshed; bloody: *a murderous riot. A murderous deed* (Shakespeare). —**mur′der|ous|ly**, *adv.* —**mur′der|ous|ness**, *n.*

**mure** (myu̇r), *v.,* **mured, mur|ing,** *n.* —*v.t. Archaic.* to shut up; imprison; immure.
—*n. Obsolete.* a wall. [< Old French *murer* < Latin *mūrāre* < *mūrus* wall]

**mu|rex** (myu̇r′eks), *n., pl.* **mu|ri|ces** (myu̇r′ə sēz), **mu|rex|es.** any one of a group of marine gastropods with a rough, ridged, or spiny shell. The secretion from a gland in two species was the chief source of the famous purple dye of the ancient Phoenicians. [< Latin *mūrex*]

**mur|geon** (mėr′jən), *n., v. Scottish.* —*n.* a grimace.
—*v.t.* to make grimaces at (a person).
—*v.i.* **1** to grimace. **2** to mutter.
[origin unknown]

**mu|ri|ate** (myu̇r′ē āt), *n.* a chloride, especially potassium chloride, used as, or in making, fertilizer. [< French *muriate* < Latin *muria* brine]

**mu|ri|at|ed** (myu̇r′ē ā′tid), *adj.* **1** charged with or containing a chloride or chlorides: *muriated mineral water.* **2** salted; briny.

**muriate of potash**, = potassium chloride.

**mu|ri|at|ic acid** (myu̇r′ē at′ik), = hydrochloric acid. [< Latin *muriāticus* < *muria* brine (because obtained originally from sea salt)]

**mu|ri|cate** (myu̇r′ə kāt), *adj.* covered with many sharp points; prickly. [< Latin *mūricātus* < *mūrex, -icis* murex]

**mu|ri|cat|ed** (myu̇r′ə kā′tid), *adj.* = muricate.

**mu|rid** (myu̇r′id), *adj., n.* = murine. [< New Latin *Muridae* the murine family < Latin *mūs, mūris* mouse]

**mu|ri|form** (myu̇r′ə fôrm), *adj. Botany.* like or suggesting a wall made of bricks arranged in courses: *muriform cellular tissue.* [< Latin *mūrus* wall + English *-form*]

**mu|rine** (myu̇r′īn, -in), *adj., n.* —*adj.* **1** of or belonging to the family of rodents that includes many mice and rats. **2** of or like a mouse or rat.
—*n.* a rodent of this family.
[< Latin *mūrīnus* having to do with mice, mouse-like < *mūs, mūris* mouse]

**murine typhus**, a mild, endemic form of typhus spread among humans by fleas from rats, occurring in many parts of the world.

**murk** (mėrk), *n., adj.* —*n.* **1** darkness; gloom: *A light flashed through the murk of the night.* **2** thick or murky air or vapor.
—*adj.* dark; gloomy; murky. Also, **mirk.**
[perhaps < Scandinavian (compare Old Icelandic

*myrkr*). Compare Old English *mirce.*]

**murk|i|ly** (mėr′kə lē), *adv.* in a murky manner; darkly; gloomily.

**murk|i|ness** (mėr′kē nis), *n.* murky condition; darkness; gloominess; gloom: *As if within that murkiness of mind Work'd feelings fearful, and yet undefined* (Byron).

**murk|y** (mėr′kē), *adj.,* **murk|i|er, murk|i|est.** 1 very dark or gloomy: *a murky prison, a murky day, the murky blackness of the night.* **2** very thick and dark; misty; hazy: *a murky fog, a cloud of murky smoke.* **3** *Figurative.* hard to understand; obscure: *a murky argument.* Also, **mirky.**

**mur|mur** (mėr′mər), *n., v.* **—*n.* 1** a soft, low, indistinct sound that rises and falls a little and goes on without breaks: *the murmur of a stream, the murmur of little waves, the murmur of voices in another room. Faint murmurs from the meadows come* (Tennyson). **SYN:** hum, babble. **2** a sound in the heart or lungs, especially an abnormal sound caused by a leaky valve in the heart. **3** a softly spoken word or speech: *a murmur of thanks. The visitor made a grateful little murmur of acquiescence* (Hawthorne). **4** a complaint made under the breath, not aloud: *In the City of London, lately so turbulent, scarcely a murmur was heard* (Macaulay). **5** *Archaic.* a rumor: *There was a murmur ... that he possesses other sciences, now lost to the world* (Scott).

**—*v.i.* 1** to make a soft, low, indistinct sound. **2** to speak softly and indistinctly: *We saw the lights and heard The voices murmuring* (Tennyson). **3** to complain under the breath; grumble: *Many were murmuring against the leader they had chosen, and wished to depose him* (Francis Parkman).

**—*v.t.*** to utter in a murmur: *The shy girl murmured her thanks. The angry boy murmured a threat.*

[< Old French *murmure,* learned borrowing from Latin *murmur, -uris;* probably imitative] **—mur′mur|er,** *n.*

**—*Syn.*** *v.i.* **2,** *v.t.* **Murmur, mumble, mutter** mean to speak indistinctly. **Murmur** means to speak too softly to be clearly heard or plainly understood: *The children murmured as they memorized the poem.* **Mumble** means to speak with the lips partly closed, so that the sounds are not properly formed, either habitually or from embarrassment: *She mumbled an apology.* **Mutter** means to mumble in a low voice, as if not wanting to be heard, and especially suggests complaining or anger: *He muttered some rude remarks.*

**mur|mur|a|tion** (mėr′mə rā′shən), *n.* the action of murmuring: *General shoe shuffling and noncommittal murmuration* (Punch).

**mur|mur|ing** (mėr′mər ing), *n., adj.* **—*n.*** a continuous murmur; low, confused noise: *As when you hear the murmuring of a throng* (Michael Drayton).

**—*adj.* 1** having a low, continuous noise: *murmuring sound.* **2** grumbling; complaining: *the ... rock out of which Moses brought water to the murmuring Israelites* (John Evelyn). **—mur′mur|ing|ly,** *adv.*

**mur|mur|ous** (mėr′mər əs), *adj.* characterized by murmurs; murmuring: *There was a slight murmurous sound in the room, as of wind long pent up in many lungs suddenly exhaled* (W. H. Hudson). **—mur′mur|ous|ly,** *adv.*

**mur|phy** (mėr′fē), *n., pl.* **-phies.** *Slang.* **1** a white potato. **2** a Murphy game. [< *Murphy,* a common Irish surname]

**Murphy bed,** a bed that folds away on hinges into a closet; in-a-door bed.

**Murphy game,** a confidence game in which the confidence man exchanges an envelope with his victim's money in it for an identical one filled with paper scraps.

**Mur|phy's Law** (mėr′fēz), any one of various humorous rules of thumb: *Your reference to Murphy's Law touches on only part of that ancient Irish potentate's laws ... His set of the laws of life refer with circularity to nothing, everything and anything. They are: 1) nothing is as easy as it looks; 2) everything takes longer than you think it will; and 3) if anything can go wrong, it will* (Time). [see etym. under **murphy**]

**mur|ra** (mėr′ə), *n.* a substance, perhaps fluorite, porcelain, or agate, from which the ancient Romans made vases, wine cups, and other utensils. Also, **murrha.** [< Latin *murra*]

**mur|rain** (mėr′ən), *n.* **1** an infectious disease of cattle, such as anthrax or tick fever. **2** *Archaic.* a pestilence; plague: *A murrain on your monster!* (Shakespeare). [< Old French *morine* < Medieval Latin (England) *morina* plague < Latin *morī* die]

**murre** (mėr), *n.* **1** any one of a group of brown and white sea birds related to the guillemots, such as a common variety of the northern Atlantic. **2** = razor-billed auk. [origin uncertain]

**murre|let** (mėr′lit), *n.* any one of certain small auks of the North Pacific.

**mur|rey** (mėr′ē), *n., adj.* **—*n.*** a dark purplish-red color.

**—*adj.*** dark purplish-red.

[< Old French *more,* adjective and *moree,* noun < Medieval Latin *moratus* and *murretus* < Latin *mōrum* mulberry]

**mur|rha** (mėr′ə), *n.* = murra.

**mur|rhine** (mėr′in, -īn), *adj., n.* **—*adj.*** of or like murra.

**—*n.*** a murrhine vase.

[< Latin *murrhinus* < *murra* murra]

**murrhine glass, 1** glassware supposed to resemble the ancient Roman. **2** glassware in which gems, metals, or colored glass are embedded.

**mur|rine** (mėr′in, -īn), *adj., n.* = murrhine.

**mur|ther** (mėr′ᴛʜər), *n., v.t., v.i. Dialect.* murder. [Middle English *murther;* see etym. under **murder**]

**Mu|rut** (mü′rüt), *n.* a member of a Dyak people living in the hilly interior of Borneo and in Sarawak, a state in the Federation of Malaysia.

**mus., 1** museum. **2a** music. **b** musical. **3** musician.

**mu|sa|ceous** (myü zā′shəs), *adj.* belonging to the banana family of plants. [< New Latin *Musaceae* the family name (< *Musa* the typical genus < Arabic *mauza* the banana) + English *-ous*]

**mu|sang** (mü säng′, -sang′), *n.* **1** an East Indian palm cat or palm civet. **2** any one of various related or similar animals. [< Malay *mūsang*]

**Mus.B.** or **Mus.Bac.,** Bachelor of Music (Latin, *Musicae Baccalaureus*).

**Mus|ca** (mus′kə), *n., genitive* **Mus|cae.** a southern constellation near Crux, thought of as arranged in the shape of a fly. [< Latin *musca* fly]

**mus|ca|del** (mus′kə del′, mus′kə del), *n.* = muscatel.

**mus|ca|delle** (mus′kə del′), *n.* a kind of muscat grape grown especially in France. [< Old French *muscadel* muscatel]

**mus|ca|det** (mus′kə dā′), *n.* a light, dry, fresh white wine of the Loire valley: *Lacking the acidity which enables wine to last, muscadet tends to become flavourless if it is not drunk young* (London Times). [< the *Muscadet* vineyards, near Nantes, France]

**mus|ca|din** (mys kȧ daɴ′), *n.* **1** a member of a party of men of fashion or of privilege that held moderate or reactionary opinions during the French Revolution. **2** = dandy (def. 1). [< French *muscadin*]

**mus|ca|dine** (mus′kə din, -dīn), *n.* **1** a species of grape native to the southern United States, of which there are several varieties, such as the scuppernong. **2** *Obsolete.* muscatel (wine). [origin uncertain; perhaps < Middle French *muscade* (< Old Provençal, feminine of unrecorded *muscat*) + English *-ine*[1]]

**Mus|cae** (mus′sē), *n.* genitive of **Musca.**

**mus|cae vo|li|tan|tes** (mus′sē vol′ə tan′tēz), spots before the eyes. They may be caused by defects in the vitreous humor or in the lens. [< New Latin *muscae volitantes* (literally) flying flies]

**mus|ca|lure** (mus′kə lůr′), *n.* a synthetic form of the sex attractant of houseflies: *The potential usefulness of muscalure in reducing the need for insecticides was greatly enhanced by its ability to attract both males and females* (Marcella M. Memolo). [< Latin *musca* fly + English *lure*]

**mus|ca|rine** (mus′kə rēn, -kər in), *n.* a very poisonous alkaloid present in the fly agaric and other mushrooms, and in decaying fish. [< Latin *muscārius* of the flies (< *musca* a fly) + English *-ine*[1]]

**mus|cat** (mus′kat, -kət), *n.* **1** any one of several light-colored varieties of grape with the flavor or odor of musk. **2** = muscatel (def. 1). [< Old French *muscat* < unrecorded Old Provençal *muscat* with the fragrance of musk < *musc* musk < Late Latin *muscus*]

**mus|ca|tel** (mus′kə tel′, mus′kə tel), *n.* **1** a strong, sweet wine made from muscat grapes. **2** = muscat (def. 1). [earlier *muscadell* < Old French *muscatel,* and *muscadel* < *muscat;* see etym. under **muscat**]

**mus|cid** (mus′id), *adj., n.* **—*adj.*** of or belonging to a family of insects including the housefly and various other common flies.

**—*n.*** a muscid insect.

[< New Latin *Muscidae* the family name < Latin *musca* a fly]

**mus|ci|form**[1] (mus′ə fôrm), *adj.* resembling a fly. [< Latin *musca* a fly + English *-form*]

**mus|ci|form**[2] (mus′ə fôrm), *adj.* resembling moss. [< Latin *muscus* moss + English *-form*]

***mus|cle**[1] (mus′əl), *n., v.,* **-cled, -cling.** **—*n.* 1** the tissue in the body of people and animals that can be tightened or loosened to make the body move. Muscles contract in response to nerve stimuli. Muscle is composed of bundles of fibers and is of two general types, striated muscle and smooth muscle. *Muscles are sensitive to stretch and automatically (reflexly) adjust their activity to changes in tension or stretch* (Science News). **2** a special bundle of such tissue which moves some particular bone or part. The biceps muscle bends the arm. The heart muscle pumps blood. See picture below on the next page. **3** *Figurative.* strength: *a man of more muscle than brains.* **SYN:** brawn, sinew.

**—*v.t.*** *Informal.* to move or lift with effort: *Let's muscle this crate into that corner.*

**muscle in,** *Slang.* to force oneself into a situation where one is not wanted: *For months he has been trying to muscle in on the Pennsylvania machine* (Baltimore Sun).

**not move a muscle,** to keep perfectly still: *The injured man lay still, not moving a muscle.*

[< Old French *muscle,* learned borrowing from Latin *mūsculus* (diminutive) < *mūs, mūris* mouse (from the appearance of certain muscles)]

**mus|cle**[2] (mus′əl), *n. Obsolete.* mussel.

**mus|cle-bound** (mus′əl bound′), *adj.* having some of the muscles enlarged or tight, and lacking normal elasticity, usually as a result of too much exercise: *a muscle-bound fighter.*

**muscle car,** a medium-sized automobile with a powerful engine, designed for high speed and acceleration: *Muscle cars—equipped with huge engines, high rear-axle ratios, heavy duty suspensions, and oversized tires ...* (Jim Dunne).

**-muscled,** *combining form.* having ______ muscles: *A well-muscled athlete = an athlete having good muscles.*

**mus|cle|man** (mus′əl man′), *n., pl.* **-men, 1** *Informal.* a muscular man: *... another record and another reminder that U.S. musclemen will be hard to match in next fall's Olympics* (Time). **2** *Slang.* a strong-arm man; thug: *The syndicate's musclemen forced competitors to close their businesses and leave town.*

**muscle plasma,** the fluid contained in muscle tissue.

**muscle sense,** the sensations accompanying movements of parts of the body, caused by sense receptors located in the muscles, joints, and tendons.

**muscle spindle,** a sensory end organ that is attached to a muscle and is sensitive to stretching; stretch receptor: *Impulses from the muscle spindle ... excite the motoneuron, impulses from which cause contraction of the muscle* (Scientific American).

**mus|cly** (mus′lē), *adj.* = muscular.

**mus|coid** (mus′koid), *adj.* mosslike. [< Latin *muscus* moss + English *-oid*]

**mus|col|o|gist** (mus kol′ə jist), *n.* a person skilled in muscology; bryologist.

**mus|col|o|gy** (mus kol′ə jē), *n.* the branch of botany dealing with mosses; bryology. [< Latin *muscus* moss + English *-logy*]

**mus|cone** (mus′kōn), *n.* a thick, liquid, closed-ring ketone derived from musk or produced synthetically, used in making perfume. *Formula:* $C_{16}H_{30}O$ [< Late Latin *muscus* musk + English *-one*]

**mus|co|va|do** (mus′kə vā′dō), *n., adj.* **—*n.*** raw sugar, a sweet, dark-brown, crystalline substance derived from the juice of the sugar cane by evaporation and draining off the molasses.

**—*adj.*** of or having to do with raw sugar.

[alteration of Spanish *mascabado* (sugar) of lowest quality < *mascabar* to depreciate, for *menoscabar* to diminish < *menos* less (< Latin *minus;* see etym. under **minus**) + *cabo* head < Latin *caput*]

**mus|co|vite** (mus′kə vīt), *n.* a light-colored variety of mica. [< *Muscovy* (glass) + *ite*[1]]

**Mus|co|vite** (mus′kə vīt), *n., adj.* **—*n.* 1** a native or inhabitant of Moscow. **2** = Russian. **3** a native or inhabitant of the principality of Muscovy.

**—*adj.* 1** of or having to do with Moscow: *The Russian circus has had the most disarming effect on Paris of anything Muscovite since the October Revolution* (New Yorker). **2** = Russian. **3** of or having to do with the principality of Muscovy or its inhabitants.

[< Middle French *Muscovie* Muscovy, the principality of Moscow, often applied to Russia generally (ultimately < Russian *Moskva* Moscow) + *-ite*[1]]

**Mus|co|vit|ic** (mus′kə vit′ik), *adj.* = Muscovite.

**mus|co|vy** (mus′kə vē), *n., pl.* **-vies.** = Muscovy duck.

**Muscovy duck,** a large duck, originally native to tropical America, and now widely domesticated. [alteration of *musk duck;* influenced by *Muscovy*]

**mus|cu|lar** (mus′kyə lər), *adj.* **1** of the muscles;

---

**Pronunciation Key:** **h**a**t**, **ā**ge, **c**ã**re**, **f**ä**r**; **l**e**t**, **ē**qual, **t**ė**rm**; **i**t, **ī**ce; **h**o**t**, **ō**pen, **ô**rder; **oil**, **out**; **c**u**p**, **p**ů**t**, **r**ü**le**; **child**; **long**; **thin**; **ᴛʜ**en; **zh**, measure; **ə** represents **a** in about, **e** in taken, **i** in pencil, **o** in lemon, **u** in circus.

influencing the muscles: *a muscular strain, muscular structure, muscular contraction.* **2** having well-developed muscles; strong: *a muscular arm. His figure was short, fleshy, and enormously muscular* (Charles Lever). SYN: sinewy, brawny, powerful. **3** consisting of muscle: *muscular tissue.* **4** marked by forcefulness; powerful; virile: *The very language that Pratt used is muscular, tough and inspiring* (Canadian Saturday Night).
—**mus′cu|lar|ly**, *adv.*

**muscular dystrophy**, a disease in which the muscles gradually weaken and waste away.

**mus|cu|lar|i|ty** (mus′kyə lar′ə tē), *n.* muscular development or strength.

**mus|cu|la|tion** (mus′kyə lā′shən), *n.* = musculature.

**mus|cu|la|ture** (mus′kyə lə chůr, -chər), *n.* the system or arrangement of muscles. [< French *musculature* < Latin *mūsculus* muscle]

**mus|cu|lo|skel|e|tal** (mus′kyə lō skel′ə təl), *adj.* of muscles and bones; both muscular and skeletal: *the musculoskeletal system.*

**Mus.D., Mus.Doc.,** or **Mus.Dr.,** Doctor of Music (Latin, *Musicae Doctor*).

**muse** (myüz), *v.,* **mused, mus|ing,** *n.* —*v.i.* **1** to think in a dreamy way; think; meditate: *The Vicar sat musing before the fire in his study* (Henry Kingsley). SYN: reflect, ruminate, ponder. **2** to look thoughtfully: *For some time Rip lay musing on this scene* (Washington Irving). **3** *Archaic.* to wonder: *Do not muse at me, my most worthy friends* (Shakespeare).
—*v.t.* **1** to say thoughtfully. **2** *Archaic.* to ponder over; wonder; meditate on: *I muse what this young fox may mean* (Matthew Arnold).
—*n.* **1** *Archaic.* a fit of musing: *He would fall into a deep muse over our accounts, staring at the page or out of the window* (Robert Louis Stevenson). **2** *Obsolete.* wonder.
[< Old French *muser* ponder, loiter, apparently (originally) put one's nose in the air < *muse* muzzle. Compare etym. under **muzzle**.] —**mus′er**, *n.*

**Muse** (myüz), *n.* **1** *Greek Mythology.* one of the nine goddesses of the fine arts and sciences. They were Calliope (epic poetry), Clio (history), Erato (love poetry), Euterpe (lyric poetry), Melpomene (tragedy), Polyhymnia or Polymnia (sacred song), Terpsichore (dancing), Thalia (comedy and pastoral poetry), and Urania (astronomy). **2a** Sometimes, **muse.** a spirit that inspires a poet, composer, or writer; source of inspiration: *Fool, said my Muse to me, look in thy heart and write* (Philip Sidney). **b** a poet. [< Old French *Muse,* learned borrowing from Latin *Mūsa* < Greek *Moûsa*]

**muse|ful** (myüz′fəl), *adj.* deeply thoughtful: *museful planning.*

**mu|se|o|log|i|cal** (myü′zē ō loj′ə kəl), *adj.* of or having to do with museology: [*The museum's*] *whole attitude toward the museological enterprise places it under a moral and intellectual obligation* (New York Times).

**mu|se|ol|o|gist** (myü′zē ol′ə jist), *n.* a person skilled in museology.

**mu|se|ol|o|gy** (myü′zē ol′ə jē), *n.* the science of arranging, collecting for, and managing museums.

**mu|sette** (myü zet′), *n.* **1** a kind of bagpipe. **2a** a soft pastoral melody for, or imitating the sound of, the bagpipe. **b** a dance to such a melody. **3** = musette bag. [< Old French *musette* < *muse* bagpipe < *muser* play the musette]

**musette bag**, a small canvas or leather bag carried suspended from a shoulder, used by soldiers, hikers, and others to carry toilet articles, food, and small items.

**mu|se|um** (myü zē′əm), *n.* a building or room where a collection of objects illustrating science, art, history, or other subjects is kept and displayed: *A museum is where you seek the work inspired by the Muses* (New Yorker). *Abbr:* mus. [< Latin *mūsēum* < Greek *Mouseîon,* (originally) a seat or shrine of the *Muses* < *Moûsa* muse]

**museum beetle**, any beetle of two species that are often found in museums, where their larvae feed on the preserved or stuffed bodies of insects, birds, and other specimens.

**museum piece**, **1** an article fit to receive a place in a museum; a fine example of anything, especially of manufactured articles: ... *an elaborately carved Chippendale settee, a museum piece* (Horace A. Vachell). **2** an outdated or antiquated person or thing: *The chap outside was a museum piece—cavalry mustache, single eyeglass, gray cutaway* (New Yorker).

**mush¹** (mush), *n., v.* —*n.* **1** *U.S.* corn meal boiled in water or milk until thick. **2** a soft, thick, and pulpy mass: *After the heavy rain the old dirt road was a mush.* **3** *Informal, Figurative.* weak or maudlin sentiment; silly talk: *The play was full of mush and impossible situations.* **4** *Figurative.* anything lacking force, firmness, or dignity: *I hate, where I looked for ... at least a manly resistance, to find a mush of concession* (Emerson).
—*v.t., v.i. Dialect.* to reduce to mush or a mush; mash.
[variant of *mash¹*]

**mush²** (mush), *n., v., interj.* —*n.* a journey on foot through snow, driving a dog sled.
—*v.i., v.t.* to travel through snow; make (one's way) through snow: *Buses mushed along the uptown avenues, throwing up rich waves of slush* (New Yorker). *A resident of Campbellton had just mushed his way by dog team across the ice* (Maclean's).
—*interj.* a shout to a team of sled dogs to start or to speed up.
[American English, perhaps for interjection *mush on,* alteration of French *marchons!* let us advance] —**mush′er**, *n.*

**mush|i|ly** (mush′ə lē), *adv.* in a soft or mushy

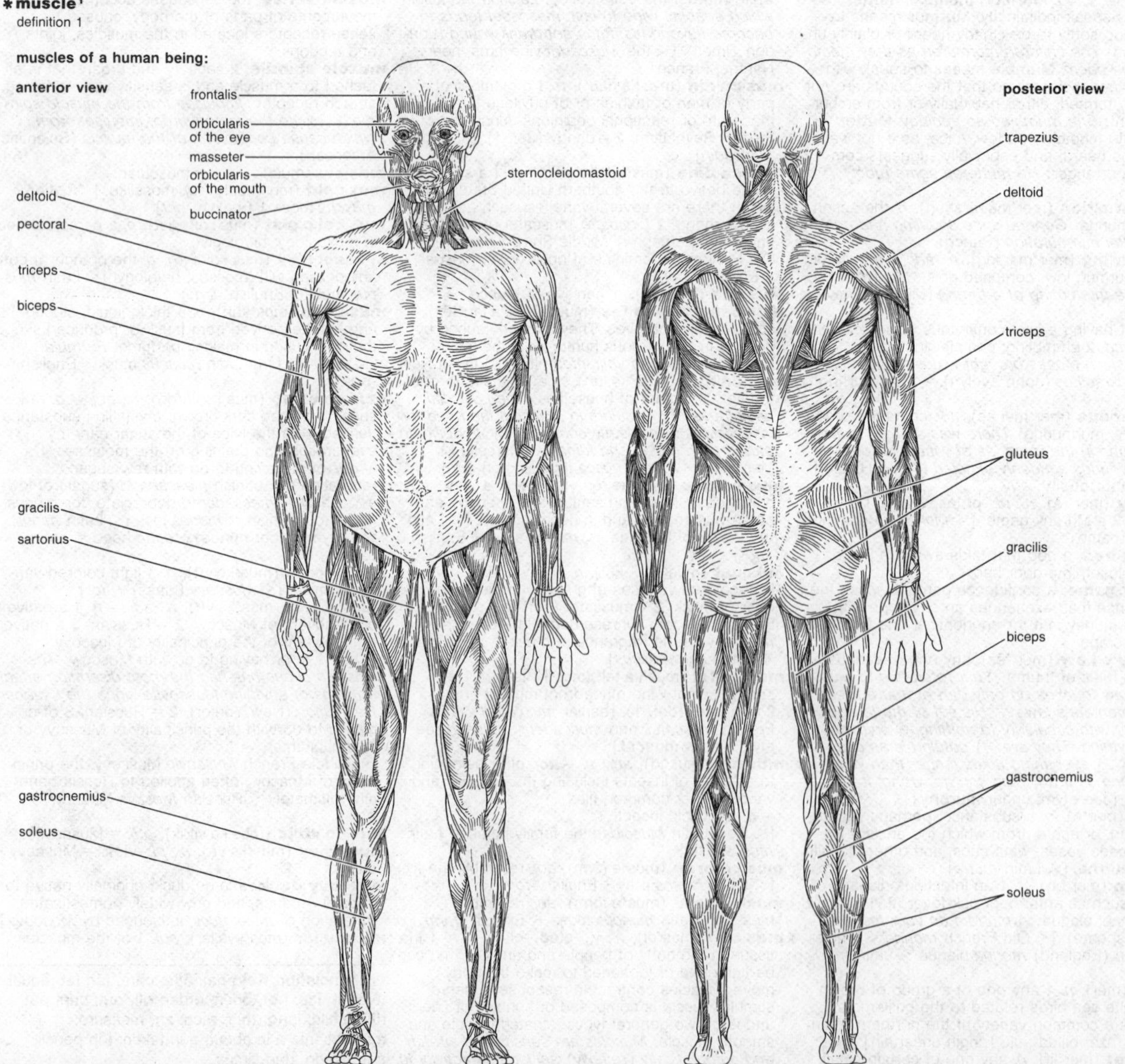

manner: *"A cool hundred," said Fuzzy thoughtfully and mushily* (O. Henry).

**mush|i|ness** (mush′ē nis), *n.* mushy quality; weak sentimentality; sloppiness.

**mush|romp** (mush′romp), *n. Obsolete.* a mushroom.

*** mush|room** (mush′rüm, -rům), *n., adj., v.* **—*n.*** **1a** a small fungus shaped like an umbrella, ball, or other thickened mass, that grows very fast. Some mushrooms are good to eat; some, such as toadstools, are poisonous. **b** an edible basidiomycetous fungus. **2** anything shaped or growing like a mushroom, such as the mushroom-shaped cloud of radioactive matter that rises from the explosion of a nuclear bomb: *The silent trembling of seismographs and the distant mushroom in the sky* (Punch). **3** *Archaic.* a bold and offensive newcomer; upstart: *Here is now a mushroom of opulence, who pays a cook seventy guineas a week for furnishing him with one meal a day* (Tobias Smollett).
**—*adj.*** **1** of or like a mushroom: *mushroom coral. The mushroom cloud of the A-bomb hung over the Nevada desert again* (Newsweek). **2** made of or with mushrooms: *a mushroom sauce, mushroom soup.* **3** *Figurative.* of very rapid growth: *a mushroom town.* **4** *Figurative.* of very recent growth; upstart: *mushroom fame.*
**—*v.i.*** **1** to grow very fast: *His business mushroomed when he opened the new store. The little town mushroomed into a city.* **2** to become flattened at one end: *A bullet sometimes mushrooms when it hits a very hard object.*
[alteration of Old French *mousseron,* or *moisseron,* perhaps < *mousse* moss] **—mush′room-like′**, *adj.*

*** mushroom**
definition 1a

puffball

umbrella

**mushroom anchor**, an anchor shaped like a bowl at the end of a shank.

**mushroom valve**, a poppet valve shaped like a mushroom.

**mush|room|y** (mush′rü mē, -rům ē), *adj.* of or like a mushroom: *Pine trees in a variety of mushroomy, distinctively Japanese shapes ...* (New Yorker).

**mush|y** (mush′ē), *adj.,* **mush|i|er, mush|i|est.** **1** like mush; pulpy: *Buck's feet sank into a white mushy something very like mud* (Jack London). **2** *Informal, Figurative.* weakly or foolishly sentimental: *mushy talk, a mushy scene.*

**mu|sic** (myü′zik), *n.* **1** the art of making sounds that are beautiful, and putting them together into beautiful, pleasing, or interesting arrangements. The study of music deals with the principles of melody, harmony, rhythm, tempo, and timbre. *Abbr:* mus. **2** beautiful, pleasing, or interesting arrangements of sounds, especially as produced by the voice or instruments: *Music, when soft voices die, Vibrates in the memory* (Shelley). **3** written or printed signs for tones; a score or scores: *Can you read music? Stacks of music lay in the corner.* **4** *Figurative.* any pleasant sound; something delightful to hear: *the music of a bubbling brook, the music of a thrush. We were made drowsy by the music of the wind blowing through the trees.* **5** appreciation of, or responsiveness to, musical sounds: *The man that hath no music in himself, Nor is moved with concord of sweet sounds, Is fit for treason, stratagems, and spoils* (Shakespeare). **6** a group of musicians: *He says many of the music are ready to starve, they being five years behind hand for their wages* (Samuel Pepys). **7** the cry of hounds on seeing the quarry, as in fox-hunting.
**face the music,** *Informal.* to meet trouble boldly or bravely: *Troops of less experience and hardihood would have flinched where these faced the music* (Frank Moore).
**set to music,** to provide (the words of a song, poem, or the like) with music: *... that nothing is capable of being well set to music that is not nonsense* (Joseph Addison).
[< Old French *musique,* learned borrowing from Latin *mūsica* < Greek *mousikē téchnē* art of the Muses < *Moûsa* Muse]

**mu|si|cal** (myü′zə kəl), *adj., n.* **—*adj.*** **1** of music: *a musical composer.* **2** sounding beautiful or pleasing; like music: *a musical voice. All little sounds made musical and clear* (William Morris). **SYN:** melodious, harmonious. **3** set to music or accompanied by music: *a musical performance.* **4** fond of music: *a musical family.* **5** skilled in music: *His playing shows that he is very musical. The English I confess, are not altogether so Musical as the French* (John Dryden).
**—*n.*** **1** = musical comedy: *Musicals are the unique contribution of the United States to world theater* (Lehman Engel). **2** *Informal.* a musicale.
**—mu′si|cal|ness,** *n.*

**musical box,** *Especially British.* a music box.

**musical chairs,** **1** a game in which players march to music around chairs numbering one less than the number of players, and try to sit down when the music stops, that player failing to reach a chair being eliminated: *We played blind man's buff ... and musical chairs* (Maclean's). **2** any switching or shifting about resembling this game: *Have you been playing musical chairs with your stocks—switching from one to another in the hope of coming out a winner?* (New Yorker).

**musical comedy,** a play or motion picture with songs, choruses, dances, incidental music, and a story spoken in dialogue form.

**mu|si|cale** (myü′zə kal′), *n.* a social gathering to enjoy music. [American English < French *musicale,* short for *soirée musicale* musical evening (party)]

**musical instrument,** **1** a piano, violin, or other instrument for producing music. Musical instruments are usually distinguished as stringed, wind, or percussion instruments. **2** an electronic instrument used to produce, not reproduce, musical sounds.

**mu|si|cal|i|ty** (myü′zə kal′ə tē), *n.* **1** = musicianship: *Badura-Skoda's musicality is best conveyed ... in his three cadenzas* (Saturday Review). **2** musical quality: (*Figurative.*) *This tendency, with its emphasis on the sensuous possibilities of language, on musicality and stylistic refinement, has not ceased to attract gifted writers to whom the realistic approach seemed inadequate* (Atlantic).

**mu|si|cal|i|za|tion** (myü′zə kə lə zā′shən), *n.* the act, fact, or process of musicalizing.

**mu|si|cal|ize** (myü′zə kə līz), *v.t.,* **-ized, -iz|ing.** to set to music; make into a musical composition: *to musicalize a poem or play. A line like "Be sure to take your bath, Gloria" is difficult to musicalize* (Arthur Miller).

**mu|si|cal|ly** (myü′zə klē), *adv.* **1** in a musical manner: *The bells on the door jingled musically as the guest came in.* **2** in music: *She is well educated musically.*

**musical saw,** a handsaw used as a musical instrument by bending it in various ways and at the same time stroking it with a violin bow or the like: *Apart from the saxophone and the musical saw—an instrument unjustly discredited—the music of the 20th century is made with the instruments of the 18th century* (François Baschet).

**mu|si|cas|sette** (myü′zə kə set′), *n.* a cassette of musical tape recordings.

**music box,** a box or case containing apparatus for producing music mechanically.

**music drama,** **1** an opera in which the music is the chief dramatic vehicle, typified by certain of the operas of Wagner. **2** any opera.

**music festival,** a series of musical programs usually recurring at regular intervals, as annually: *the summer music festival at Tanglewood, Massachusetts.*

**music hall,** **1** a hall for musical entertainments. **2** *Especially British.* a theater for vaudeville.

**mu|sic-hall** (myü′zik hôl′), *adj.* of or characteristic of a music hall; vaudeville.

**mu|si|cian** (myü zish′ən), *n.* **1** a person skilled in music: *The Scots are all musicians. Every man you meet plays on the flute, the violin or violoncello* (Tobias Smollett). **2** a person who sings or who plays on a musical instrument, especially as a profession or business: *An orchestra is composed of many musicians.* **3** a composer of music.

**mu|si|cian|er** (myü zish′ə nər), *n. Archaic or Dialect.* a musician: *The musicianers amused the retainers ... with a tune on the clarionet, fife, or trumpet* (Samuel Lover).

**mu|si|cian|ly** (myü zish′ən lē), *adj.* of or suited to a musician; showing the skill and taste of a good musician: *Mr. Cole's instincts appear to be intelligent and musicianly* (New York Times).

**mu|si|cian|ship** (myü zish′ən ship), *n.* skill in playing, conducting, or composing music; musical ability: *She was a great artist, remarkable not for the beauty of her voice, but for musicianship, dramatic power and general intelligence* (Sunday Times).

**mu|sic|less** (myü′zik lis), *adj.* **1** without music: *a musicless entertainment.* **2** unmusical; harsh in sound; discordant. **3** ignorant of music.

**mu|si|co-dra|mat|ic** (myü′zə kō drə mat′ik), *adj.* of or combining both music and the drama; musical and dramatic: *The librettist faithfully transmits the vivid bible pictures, but Milhaud fails to give them musico-dramatic reality* (New York Times).

**music of the spheres,** beautiful harmony or music, inaudible to human beings, supposedly produced, according to Pythagoras and certain other ancient mathematicians, by the movements of the planets and other heavenly bodies: *For there is music wherever there is harmony, order, or proportion; and thus far we may maintain the music of the spheres* (Sir Thomas Browne).

**mu|si|cog|ra|phy** (myü′zə kog′rə fē), *n.* the art of writing down music; musical notation.

**mu|si|co|log|ic|al** (myü′zə kə loj′ə kəl), *adj.* of or having to do with musicology.

**mu|si|col|o|gist** (myü′zə kol′ə jist), *n.* an expert in musicology: *The studies of musicologists have clearly shown that the music of all nonliterate peoples shows very definite patterns, and is not in the least random or chaotic* (Beals and Hoijer).

**mu|si|col|o|gy** (myü′zə kol′ə jē), *n.* the systematic study of music, especially of its literature, history, forms, methods, and principles.

**mu|si|co|ma|ni|a** (myü′zə kə mā′nē ə), *n.* an abnormal fondness of music; monomania for music.

**mu|si|co|pho|bi|a** (myü′zə kə fō′bē ə), *n.* an abnormal fear or dislike of music.

**mu|si|co|ther|a|py** (myü′zə kə ther′ə pē), *n.* the therapeutical use of music; listening to music as a means of promoting emotional growth and health.

**music room,** a room, as in a house, set apart or arranged for use in performing music: *When he was still an infant he would toddle into the music room and listen while his sisters were having their lessons* (New Yorker).

**music shell,** the shell of a marine gastropod, especially a volute of the Caribbean, having markings that suggest written music.

**mus|ing** (myü′zing), *adj., n.* **—*adj.*** dreamy; meditative. **SYN:** contemplative.
**—*n.*** = meditation. **—mus′ing|ly,** *adv.*

**mu|sique con|crète** (mʏ zēk′ kôɴ kret′), *French.* **1** a compilation of natural sounds recorded on tape and cut and spliced together to form a composition: *For 150 years the only new instruments to be invented are the saxophone, the musical saw, musique concrète and electronic devices* (Time). **2** such compositions collectively; electronic music.

**mus|jid** (mus′jid), *n.* = mosque.

**musk** (musk), *n.* **1a** a substance with a strong and lasting odor, used in making perfumes. Musk is found in a special gland in the skin of the abdomen of the male musk deer. **b** a similar substance found in the glands of other animals, such as the mink and muskrat. **2** an artificial imitation of this substance. **3** the odor of musk, or a similar odor: *The woodbine spices are wafted abroad, And the musk of the rose is blown* (Tennyson). **4** the musk deer or any animal like it, or one that has a musky smell. **5** any plant whose leaves or flowers smell like musk, such as the musk rose. [< Old French *musc,* learned borrowing from Late Latin *muscus* < Late Greek *móschos* < Persian *mushk* < Sanskrit *muṣka* testicle (diminutive) < *mūṣ* mouse]

**mus|kal|longe** (mus′kə lonj), *n., pl.* **-longe.** = muskellunge.

**musk ambrette,** a synthetic yellowish-white powder with the odor of amberseed, used as a fixative and diluting agent in perfumery. *Formula:* $C_{12}H_{16}N_2O_5$

**musk deer,** a small, hornless deer of central and northeastern Asia, the male of which has a gland containing musk.

**musk duck,** **1** = Muscovy duck. **2** an Australian duck, the male of which has a musky odor.

**mus|keg** (mus′keg), *n.* **1** a bog or marsh filled with sphagnum moss, chiefly in the tundra or forest regions of Canada, Alaska, and northern Europe: *Much of the Arctic land is muskeg, a swampy muck which will not support even a man, much less an airstrip* (Science News Letter). **2** any one of certain mosses. [< Algonkian (Cree) *maskik,* (Ojibwa) *maskeg* swamp, wet meadow]

**mus|kel|lunge** (mus′kə lunj), *n., pl.* **-lunge.** a very large North American pike. The muskellunge is valued as a food and game fish. It is a very hard fish to catch. Muskellunge occasionally grow to a length of about 5½ feet and a weight of about 70 pounds. Also, **maskalonge, maskanonge, muskallonge.** [American English < Canadian French *masquinongé* < Algonkian (Ojibwa) *mâskinonjē* (literally) big fish]

**mus|ket** (mus′kit), *n.* a gun introduced in the 1500's and widely used before the development of the rifle. [< Middle French *mousquet* < Italian *moschetto* (originally) a kind of hawk < *mosca* fly < Latin *musca*]

**mus|ket|eer** (mus′kə tir′), *n.* a soldier armed with a musket. [alteration (influenced by *musket*) of Middle French *mousquetaire* mousquetaire]

**mus|ket|ry** (mus′kə trē), *n., pl.* **-ries. 1** muskets: *The storming parties were assailed with cannon, with musketry, with pistols* (John L. Motley). **2** the art of shooting with muskets or rifles. **3** the fire of muskets, rifles, or other small arms; small-arms fire: *a sudden crackle of musketry.* **4** soldiers armed with muskets.

**musk hog,** = peccary.

**Mus|kho|ge|an** (mus kō′gē ən), *adj., n.* **—*adj.*** designating or having to do with a linguistic family of North American Indians originally from the southeastern United States, including Choctaw, Chickasaw, Creek, Seminole, Yazoo, and other tribes.
**—*n.*** this linguistic family.

**mus|kie** (mus′kē), *n. Informal.* a muskellunge. Also, **musky.**

**mus|ki|ness** (mus′kē nis), *n.* a musky quality or condition.

**musk|mal|low** (musk′mal′ō), *n.* a bushy plant of the mallow family grown in tropical and semitropical countries for its musky seeds, which are used in perfumes; abelmosk.

**musk|mel|on** (musk′mel′ən), *n.* **1** a small, sweet melon with a hard rind and a smell like that of musk. Muskmelons are round or oval, with juicy light-green or orange flesh and a rind with a smooth, ribbed, or netlike surface. The cantaloupe and honeydew melon are muskmelons. See picture under **gourd family. 2** the plant of the gourd family that it grows on.

**Mus|ko|ge|an** (mus kō′gē ən), *adj., n.* = Muskhogean.

**Mus|ko|gee** (mus kō′gē), *n., pl.* **-gee** or **-gees. 1** a member of a tribe of Indians of Georgia and Alabama that formed part of the Creek confederacy of Muskhogean tribes. **2** the language of this tribe.

***musk ox,** a large arctic mammal having a shaggy coat, stocky build, with a hump and dense, extremely long hair. The male gives off a strong smell like musk during its breeding season. The musk ox is found especially in the tundra regions of North America and Greenland. Musk oxen belong to the same family as the ox. *Musk oxen ... inhabit some of the most solitary, dreariest country on earth, where they have made a stubborn fight for survival* (Science News Letter).

***musk ox**

**musk plant,** a North American herb of the figwort family, having yellow flowers and musk-scented leaves.

**musk|rat** (musk′rat′), *n., pl.* **-rats** or (*collectively*) **-rat. 1** a water animal of North America somewhat like a rat, but larger; water rat. It has webbed hind feet, a glossy coat, and a musky smell. In swamps and ponds it builds small houses from reeds and other water plants, or, sometimes, makes a burrow in the bank, with the opening under water. See picture under **rat. 2** its dark-brown fur. Muskrat is valuable for garments. [American English, alteration of *musquash*]

**musk rose,** a rose with clusters of large, musky-smelling, white flowers, native to the Mediterranean region.

**musk thistle,** a thistle of the eastern United States, with nodding heads of musky-smelling flowers. It was introduced from Eurasia.

**musk turtle,** any one of a group of small turtles of eastern North America with a narrow plastron and glands capable of producing a strong musky odor.

**musk|y**[1] (mus′kē), *adj.,* **musk|i|er, musk|i|est.** of or like musk; like that of musk: *a musky odor.* [< *musk* + *-y*[1]]

**mus|ky**[2] (mus′kē), *n., pl.* **-kies.** *Informal.* a muskellunge.

**Mus|lem** (muz′ləm, mus′-), *n., adj.* = Moslem.

**Mus|lim** (muz′ləm, mus′-), *n., adj.* **—*n.* 1** = Black Muslim. **2** = Moslem.
**—*adj.*** = Moslem.

**mus|lin** (muz′lən), *n., adj.* **—*n.* 1** a thin, fine cotton cloth, used for dresses and curtains. **2** a heavier cotton cloth, used for sheets, undergarments, and the like. **3** *Nautical Slang.* sails; canvas: *They staggered out of the bay ... with a strong breeze and under all the "muslin" they could carry* (Herman Melville). **4** *British Slang.* womankind; femininity: *That was a pretty bit of muslin hanging on your arm—who was she?* (Thackeray).
**—*adj.*** made of muslin: *white muslin curtains.*
[< French *mousseline* < Italian *mussolina* < *Mussolo* Mosul, a city in Iraq]

**muslin delaine,** = mousseline de laine.

**mus|lined** (muz′lənd), *adj.* hung with or dressed in muslin.

**muslin kail,** *Scottish.* a broth of water, shelled barley, and greens. [< *muslin* + *kail,* variant of *kale* (perhaps because of the thinness of the broth)]

**Mus.M.,** Master of Music.

**mus|quash** (mus′kwosh), *n.* = muskrat. [< Algonkian (probably Powhatan) *muscascus* (literally) it is red (because of its red color)]

**muss** (mus), *v., n. Informal.* **—*v.t.* 1** to put into disorder; make untidy; rumple: *to muss up a room. The child's dress was mussed.* **2** to smear or soil; mess: *to muss up one's hands.*
**—*n.* 1** *Informal.* an untidy state; disorder; mess: *Straighten up your room at once; it's in a dreadful muss!* **SYN:** muddle. **2** a disturbance; row.
[variant of *mess* in sense of "disturbance, row"; probably influenced by *fuss*]

**mus|sel** (mus′əl), *n.* any one of several mollusks with two hinged parts to their shells. Mussels resemble clams and are found in both fresh and salt water. Sea mussels have dark-blue shells and can be eaten. The shells of freshwater mussels are an important source of mother-of-pearl, used in making buttons. See picture at **mollusk.** [Old English *muscle, musle* < Latin *mūsculus* mussel, muscle]

**muss|i|ly** (mus′ə lē), *adv. Informal.* in a mussy manner; messily.

**muss|i|ness** (mus′ē nis), *n. Informal.* mussy condition; messiness.

**Mus|sul|man** (mus′əl mən), *n., pl.* **-mans,** *adj.* = Moslem. [< Medieval Latin *Musulmani,* plural < Persian *musulmān* Mohammedan, adjective < *muslim* a Moslem < Arabic. See etym. of doublet **Moslem.**]

**muss|y** (mus′ē), *adj.,* **muss|i|er, muss|i|est.** *Informal.* untidy; messy; rumpled: *a mussy room.*

**must**[1] (must; *unstressed* məst), *auxiliary verb, past tense* **must,** *n., adj.* **—*aux.* v. 1** to be obliged to; be forced to: *All men must eat to live. When Duty whispers low, Thou must, The youth replies, I can* (Emerson). **2** ought to; should: *I must go home soon. I must keep my promise. You really must read this story.* **3** to be certain to (be, do, or appear): *I must seem very rude. The man must be crazy to talk so.* **4** to be supposed or expected to: *You must have that book. You must know he is a great writer* (Tobias Smollett). **5** *Must* is sometimes used with its verb omitted: *We must to horse. We must away.*
**—*n.*** something necessary; obligation: *This rule is a must.*
**—*adj.*** *Informal.* demanding attention or doing; necessary: *a must item, must legislation.*
[Old English *mōste,* past tense of *mōtan* mote[2]]
▶ **Must,** which is ordinarily an auxiliary verb, has recently become an adjective in informal English: *This is a must book for your reading.*

**must**[2] (must), *n.* the expressed, unfermented or partly unfermented juice of the grape or other fruit; new wine. [Old English *must* < Latin (*vīnum*) *mustum* fresh (wine)]

**must**[3] (must), *n., v.* **—*n.*** musty condition; mustiness; mold. **—*v.t., v.i.*** to make or become musty. [perhaps back formation < *musty*]

**must**[4] (must), *adj., n.* **—*adj.*** dangerously excited or irritable (used of male elephants or camels).
**—*n.* 1** dangerous excitement; frenzy. **2** a frenzied animal. Also, **musth.**
[< Hindi *mast* < Persian, (literally) intoxicated]

**must**[5] (must), *n., v. Scottish.* **—*n.* 1** musk. **2** a powder for the hair.
**—*v.t.*** to put powder on (the hair).
[< Old French *must,* variant of *musc* musk]

**MUST** (must), *n.* a manned underwater station, usually consisting of several buildings filled with compressed air or an oxygen-helium mixture and set up on the ocean floor: *Divers may live in a MUST for many weeks, going out each day to explore or work ... MUSTs have been tested at from about 30 to more than 400 feet below the surface* (James Dugan). [< *M*(anned) *U*(nderwater) *St*(ation)]

**mus|tache** (mus′tash, mə stash′), *n.* **1** Also, **mustaches.** hair growing on a man's upper lip: *a lofty, lordly kind of man ... with a meagre face, furnished with mustaches* (Washington Irving). **2** hairs or bristles growing near the mouth of an animal. Also, **moustache.** [< French *moustache* < Italian *mostaccio,* and *mostacchio* < Medieval Latin *mustacia* < Greek *mýstax, -akos* upper lip, mustache]

**mustache cup,** a man's drinking cup fitted with a special piece to drink through without wetting the mustache.

**mus|tached** (mus′tasht, mə stasht′), *adj.* having a mustache.

**mus|ta|chio** (mə stä′shō), *n., pl.* **-chios.** = mustache: *His face ... was more than half hidden by whisker and mustachio* (Edgar Allan Poe). [< Italian *mostacchio;* see etym. under **mustache**]

**mus|ta|chioed** (mə stä′shōd), *adj.* = mustached.

**mus|tang** (mus′tang), *n.* a small, wiry, wild or half-wild horse of the North American plains, descended from domesticated Spanish stock: *She [an Indian woman] was mounted on a mustang or half-wild horse* (Washington Irving). [American English < Spanish *mestengo* untamed, (literally) of the *mesta* association of graziers who divided strays or unclaimed animals < Latin *miscēre* to mix]

**mus|tard** (mus′tərd), *n.* **1** a yellow powder or paste made from seeds of the mustard plant. It is used as a seasoning to give a pungent taste to meats or other foods, or medicinally in a mustard plaster. **2** a plant whose seeds have a sharp, hot taste. **3** the flower of this plant. **4** a dark yellow color: *... satin-finished silk that is a mass of flowers in ... sapphire, and mustard* (New Yorker).
**cut the mustard,** *U.S. Slang.* to achieve a desirable end; succeed: *You can't cut the mustard at those prices* (Atlantic).
[< Old French *moustarde* < *moust* < Latin *mustum* must[2]]

**mus|tard-col|ored** (mus′tərd kul′ərd), *adj.* dull yellow with a tinge of green.

***mustard family,** a group of dicotyledonous herbs having cross-shaped, regular flowers, and bearing a two-valved capsule as the fruit. The family includes the mustard, sweet alyssum, cress, candytuft, and wallflower and such vegetables as the cabbage, cauliflower, and broccoli.

***mustard family**

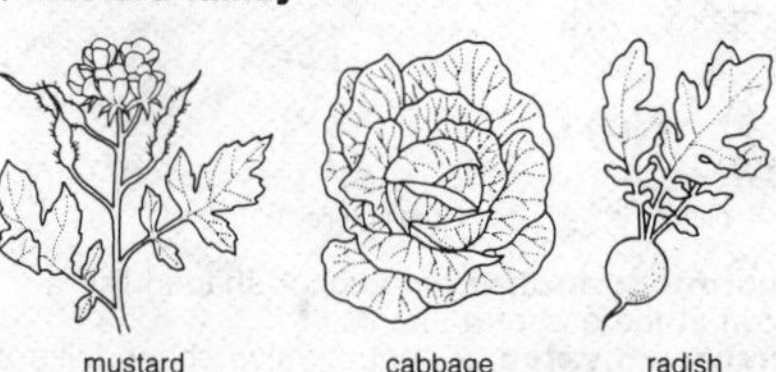


**mustard gas,** a colorless or brown oily liquid which evaporates slowly to a poison gas that causes burns, blindness, and death: *The main war gases available toward the end of the last war were phosgene, ... mustard gas, and lewisite* (James Phinney Baxter). *Formula:* $C_4H_8Cl_2S$

**mustard oil,** oil pressed from mustard seeds.

**mustard plaster,** a poultice made of mustard and water, or of mustard, flour, and water, used as a counterirritant.

**mustard seed,** the seed of the mustard plant: *The kingdom of heaven is like to a grain of mustard seed ... Which indeed is the least of all seeds* (Matthew 13:31-32).

**mus|tee** (mus tē′, mus′tē), *n.* **1** a child of a white person and a quadroon. **2** any half-breed. [< altered pronunciation of Spanish *mestizo* mestizo]

**mus|te|line** (mus′tə līn, -lin), *adj., n.* **—*adj.* 1** of or belonging to the family of mammals that includes the weasels, martens, skunks, sables, minks, badgers, and otters. **2** like a weasel; tawny.
**—*n.*** a musteline animal.
[< Latin *mūstēlīnus* < *mūstēla* weasel, perhaps < *mūs, mūris* mouse]

**mus|ter** (mus′tər), *v., n.* **—*v.t.* 1** to gather together; collect: *They could muster only a few dollars between them. Bring all the good players you can muster.* **SYN:** convene, marshal, array. **2** to assemble: *to muster soldiers. The starboard watch were mustered upon the quarterdeck* (Herman Melville). **3** *Figurative.* to summon: *Muster up your courage and fight.* **4** to number; comprise: *The garrison musters eighty men.* **5** (in Australia) to round up (cattle).
**—*v.i.* 1** to come together; gather; assemble: *The clouds were mustering in the sky. I see them muster in a gleaming row* (James Russell Lowell). *Why does my blood thus muster to my heart?* (Shakespeare). **SYN:** convene. **2** (in Australia) to round up cattle.
**—*n.* 1** an assembly; collection: *A large muster of admirers waited outside to congratulate the new champion.* **2** the act or fact of bringing together men or troops in formation for review or service: *There was a muster of all the guards.* **3** a list of those assembled; roll: *Call the muster.* **4** the number assembled: *Our present musters grow upon the file to five and twenty thousand men of choice* (Shakespeare). **5** *Commerce.* a pattern; specimen; sample.

**muster in**, to enlist; enroll: *Youths under eighteen cannot muster in.*
**muster out**, to discharge: *... mustered out of the service of the United States* (J. A. Wakefield).
**pass muster**, to be inspected and approved; come up to the required standards; get by: *Double-dealers may pass muster for a while, but all parties wash their hands of them in the conclusion* (Sir Roger L'Estrange).
[< Old French *mostrer* < Latin *mōnstrāre* to show < *mōnstrum* portent; see etym. under **monster**] — **mus'ter|er**, *n.*

**muster roll**, **1** an official roll or list, as of soldiers or sailors. **2** = roll call.

**musth** (must), *adj., n.* = must[4].

**mus|ti|ly** (mus'tə lē), *adv.* **1** in a musty manner; moldily; sourly. **2** *Obsolete.* dully; heavily.

**mus|ti|ness** (mus'tē nis), *n.* musty condition or quality; moldiness; damp foulness.

**must|n't** (mus'ənt), must not: *Father says we mustn't skate here.*

**mus|ty** (mus'tē), *adj.*, **-ti|er**, **-ti|est**, *n.* — ***adj.*** **1** having a smell or taste suggesting mold, damp, poor ventilation, or decay; moldy: *a musty room, musty crackers.* **SYN**: mildewy. **2** *Figurative.* out-of-date; stale: *musty laws about witches.* **3** *Figurative.* lacking vigor; dull: *a musty old fellow.*
— ***n.*** a variety of cheap, strong-smelling snuff, formerly sold in England.
[perhaps variant of *moisty*]

**mut** (mut), *n.* = mutt.

**mut.**, **1** mutilated. **2** mutual.

**Mut** (müt), *n.* an ancient Egyptian goddess of the sky, the wife of Amon-Re, and mother of the gods.

**mu|ta|bil|i|ty** (myü'tə bil'ə tē), *n.* **1** mutable condition or quality; tendency or ability to change: *Wherefore this lower world who can deny But to be subject still to Mutability?* (Edmund Spenser). **2** changeableness of mind, disposition, or will; fickleness: *The mayor's mutability in a political crisis made him a difficult man to predict.*

**mu|ta|ble** (myü'tə bəl), *adj.* **1** liable to change or capable of change: *mutable customs.* **SYN**: changeable, variable. **2** changing; inconstant; fickle: *a mutable person. Nature is a mutable cloud ... and never the same* (Emerson). [< Latin *mūtābilis* < *mūtāre* to change] — **mu'ta|ble|ness**, *n.*

**mu|ta|bly** (myü'tə blē), *adv.* in a mutable manner; changeably.

**mu|ta|gen** (myü'tə jən), *n.* an agent that induces or causes mutation in an organism: *Both chemical mutagens and radiations act in an unspecific, random way on chromosomes and genes* (Laurence H. Snyder). [< Latin *mūtāre* to change + English *-gen*]

**mu|ta|gen|e|sis** (myü'tə jen'ə sis), *n.* the developmental process leading to mutation in an organism. [< Latin *mūtāre* to change + English *genesis*]

**mu|ta|gen|ic** (myü'tə jen'ik), *adj.* of, having to do with, or characteristic of a mutagen: *mutagenic radiation, a mutagenic level, mutagenic action.* — **mu'ta|gen'i|cal|ly**, *adv.*

**mu|ta|gen|ic|i|ty** (myü'tə jə nis'ə tē), *n.* the inducement of mutations; the use of mutagens: *Chemical mutagenicity promises to become a boiling issue ... with controversies already having erupted over cyclamates, pesticides, LSD, and many other substances* (Science News).

**mu|ta|gen|ize** (myü'tə jə nīz), *v.t.*, **-ized**, **-iz|ing.** to induce mutation in: *Their approach was systematically to make individual tests on each of several hundreds of colonies from a heavily mutagenized stock of E. coli. This technique had already been successfully used to locate a mutant of E. coli lacking a ribonuclease activity* (Science Journal).

**mu|tant** (myü'tənt), *n., adj.* — ***n.*** a new genetic character or variety of animal or plant resulting from mutation: *Under these conditions the mutant may be expected eventually to replace the ancestral stock in ever widening areas* (Fred W. Emerson).
— ***adj.*** that is the result of mutation: *a mutant species.*
[< Latin *mūtāns, -antis,* present participle of Latin *mūtāre* to change]

**mu|ta|ro|ta|tion** (myü'tə rō tā'shən), *n. Chemistry.* a gradual change of optical rotation taking place in freshly prepared solutions of reducing sugars. [< Latin *mūtāre* to change + English *rotation*]

**mu|tase** (myü'tās), *n.* **1** an enzyme that is supposed to promote the simultaneous oxidation and reduction of a compound. **2** an enzyme that promotes the rearrangement of molecules in a substance. [< Latin *mūtāre* to change + English *-ase*]

**mu|tate** (myü'tāt), *v.t., v.i.*, **-tat|ed**, **-tat|ing.** **1** to change: *Sweet peas mutate from petal pink to coral* (New Yorker). **2** to undergo or produce mutation: *Farm animals will be mutated to produce more and better meats and dairy foods* (Science News Letter). **3** *Phonetics.* to change or be changed by umlaut. [< Latin *mūtāre* (with English *-ate*[1]) to change]

**mu|ta|tion** (myü tā'shən), *n.* **1** the act or process of changing; change; alteration: *The past is exempt from mutation* (Charles Brockden Brown). **2** a change within a gene or chromosome of animals or plants resulting in a new feature or character that appears suddenly and can be inherited: *Most mutations cause harmful effects, such as the reduction in the size of wings on a fly* (J. Herbert Taylor). *Many so-called gene mutations may actually be ultramicroscopic changes in chromosome structure* (The Effects of Atomic Weapons). **3** a new genetic character or new variety of plant or animal formed in this way; mutant: *It is claimed that the first of the small African violets came as mutations* (New York Times). **4** *Phonetics.* umlaut (def. 1): *Thus "man, men; woman, women;" ... show mutation, ... effected by an "i" or "j" in the succeeding syllable in Common Germanic* (Simeon Potter). [< Latin *mūtātiō, -ōnis* < *mūtāre* to change]

**mu|ta|tion|al** (myü tā'shə nəl), *adj.* of or having to do with biological mutation: *Through a number of mutational steps, ... it has been possible to obtain a thousand-fold increase in penicillin yield* (Bulletin of Atomic Scientists). — **mu|ta'tion|al|ly**, *adv.*

**mu|ta|tion|ist** (myü tā'shə nist), *n. Biology.* a person who emphasizes the importance of mutation as a factor in producing new and supposedly higher forms or species.

**mutation mink**, **1** a mink in captivity having fur of a color not found among wild minks, especially a shade from white to pale silver, arrived at by selective breeding. **2** the fur of such a mink.

**mu|ta|tis mu|tan|dis** (myü tā'tis myü tan'dis), *Latin.* with the necessary changes: *What would St. Francis have said to the beggar who ... wanted to get to the Assisian equivalent of Wall Street? Mutatis mutandis, what would Robert Owen have said? Or Lenin?* (Time).

**mu|ta|tive** (myü'tə tiv), *adj.* of or having to do with mutation; marked by change.

**mu|ta|to no|mi|ne** (myü tā'tō nom'ə nē), *Latin.* with the name changed.

**mutch** (much), *n. Scottish.* a cap or coif, usually of linen, worn by women and young children: *an old granny in a woolen mutch* (Robert Louis Stevenson). [< Middle Dutch *mutse,* perhaps short for *almutse* or < unrecorded Latin *almutius*]

**mutch|kin** (much'kin), *n.* a Scottish unit of liquid measure, equal to a little less than a U.S. legal pint. [perhaps < Middle Dutch *mudseken* (diminutive) < *mudde* a Dutch measure, ultimately < Latin *modius,* or (diminutive) < Middle Dutch *mutse* a measure]

**mute** (myüt), *adj., n., v.*, **mut|ed**, **mut|ing.** — ***adj.*** **1** not making any sound; silent: *The little girl stood mute with embarrassment. Mute did the minstrels stand To hear my story* (Longfellow). *Mute was the room—mute the house* (Charlotte Brontë). **SYN**: See syn. under **dumb**. **2** unable to speak; dumb. **SYN**: See syn. under **dumb**. **3** not pronounced; silent: *The "e" in "mute" is mute.* **4** *Phonetics.* articulated as a stop; produced by the complete momentary closure of the air passage: *The "p" in "hop" and "play" is a mute consonant.* **5** without speech or sound: *a mute refusal of an offer, mute astonishment.* **6** *Law.* (of a prisoner) making no response when arraigned: *to stand mute.*
— ***n.*** **1** a person who cannot speak, usually because of deafness or loss of or damage to the tongue or vocal cords. **2** a clip or pad put on a musical instrument to soften, deaden, or muffle sound. **3** a silent letter. **4** *Phonetics.* a stop; mute consonant. **5** an actor who plays pantomime. **6** *Law.* a prisoner who fails to plead to an indictment. **7** *Archaic.* a hired attendant at a funeral: *I saw the coffin, and the mutes, and the mourners* (John Galt).
— ***v.t.*** **1** to deaden or soften the sound of (a tone, voice, or musical instrument) with or as if with a mute: *He muted the strings of his violin.* **2** to soften or subdue (a color); tone down. **3** to keep silent; suppress: *He does not mute his own opinionatedness and egotism* (Punch).
[alteration (influenced by Latin) of Middle English *mewet* and *muet* < Old French *muet* < Latin *mūtus*] — **mute'ly**, *adv.* — **mute'ness**, *n.*

**mut|ed** (myü'tid), *adj.* **1** mute; silent: *They are frightened ... and prefer their politicians to be as bland and muted as possible* (New York Times). **2** (of musical instruments) played with a mute. — **mut'ed|ly**, *adv.*

**mute swan**, a common white swan of Europe and Asia that makes only hissing and snorting sounds. See picture under **swan**.

**mu|ti|cous** (myü'tə kəs), *adj. Biology.* without awns or spines; awnless; spineless. [< Latin *muticus* (with English *-ous*)]

**mu|ti|late** (myü'tə lāt), *v.*, **-lat|ed**, **-lat|ing**, *adj.* — ***v.t.*** **1** to cut, tear, or break off a limb or other important part of; injure seriously by cutting, tearing, or breaking off some part: *The victims of the accident were all mutilated.* **SYN**: maim, mangle, disfigure. **2** to make (a book, story, song, film, or the like) imperfect by removing a part or parts: *Lay authorities had "mutilated" the text of the pastoral letter he issued* (New York Times).
— ***adj.*** **1** *Biology.* without some organ or part, or having it only in an undeveloped or modified form. **2** *Poetic.* mutilated.
[< Latin *mutilāre* (with English *-ate*[1]) < *mutilus* maimed]

**mu|ti|la|tion** (myü'tə lā'shən), *n.* **1** the action of mutilating. **2** the condition of being mutilated: *Many ... were also sentenced to mutilation ... the hangman of Edinburgh cut off the ears of thirty-five prisoners* (Macaulay).

**mu|ti|la|tive** (myü'tə lā'tiv), *adj.* causing mutilation.

**mu|ti|la|tor** (myü'tə lā'tər), *n.* a person or thing that mutilates.

**mu|tine** (myü'tin), *n., v.*, **-tined**, **-tin|ing**, *adj. Obsolete.* — ***n.*** **1** a mutinous person; mutineer: *Methought I lay Worse than the mutines in the bilboes* (Shakespeare). **2** a mutiny.
— ***v.i.*** to rebel; mutiny.
— ***adj.*** rebellious; mutinous.
[< Old French *mutine, mutin;* see etym. under **mutiny**]

**mu|ti|neer** (myü'tə nir'), *n., v.* — ***n.*** a person who takes part in a mutiny: *Additional wireless messages received from the mutineers were accepted as indicating that they wished to bargain with the authorities* (Baltimore Sun).
— ***v.i.*** to take part in a mutiny; mutiny.
[< Middle French *mutinier* < *mutin* rebellious; see etym. under **mutiny**]

**mu|ti|nous** (myü'tə nəs), *adj.* **1** given to or engaged in mutiny; rebellious: *a mutinous crew. The men became mutinous and insubordinate* (Walter Besant). **SYN**: riotous, insubordinate, seditious. **2** like or involving mutiny; characterized by mutiny: *a mutinous look.* **3** *Figurative.* not controllable; unruly: *mutinous passions.* — **mu'ti|nous|ly**, *adv.* — **mu'ti|nous|ness**, *n.*

**mu|ti|ny** (myü'tə nē), *n., pl.* **-nies**, *v.*, **-nied**, **-ny|ing.** — ***n.*** **1** open rebellion against lawful authority, especially by sailors or soldiers against their officers: *The crew staged a mutiny against the brutal officers of the ship.* **SYN**: insurrection, revolt, uprising. **2** *Obsolete.* discord; strife: *A man ... whom right and wrong Have chose as umpire of their mutiny* (Shakespeare).
— ***v.i.*** to take part in a mutiny; rebel: *His troops, who had received no wages for a long time, had mutinied* (John L. Motley). **SYN**: revolt.
[< *mutine* to revolt < Old French *mutiner* < *mutin* rebellious < *meute* revolt, ultimately < Latin *movēre* to move]

**mut|ism** (myü'tiz əm), *n.* **1** the condition of being mute; muteness: *Paulina was awed by the savants, but not quite to mutism* (Charlotte Brontë). **2** *Psychoanalysis.* an emotional state in which the patient seems unable, or refuses, to speak.
[< obsolete French *mutisme* < Latin *mūtus* mute + French *-isme* -ism]

**mu|to|graph** (myü'tə graf, -gräf), *n.* an early form of motion-picture camera. [< Latin *mūtāre* to change + English *-graph*]

**mu|ton** (myü'ton), *n. Biology.* the smallest genetic unit capable of causing mutation: *The muton ... may be as small as ... a few nucleotide pairs of the chromosomal nucleic acid* (New Scientist). [< *mut*(ation) + *-on,* designating a unit]

**mu|to|scope** (myü'tə skōp), *n.* an early form of motion-picture projector. [< Latin *mūtāre* to change + English *-scope*]

**mutt** (mut), *n. Slang.* **1** a dog, especially a mongrel: *But the alley dogs, the homeliest mutts, the dogs that nobody wants, are moved in the cages to westward* (Baltimore Sun). **2** a stupid person. Also, **mut.** [American English; origin uncertain]

**mut|ter** (mut'ər), *v., n.* — ***v.t.*** to speak (words) low and indistinctly with lips partly closed; mumble: *The surgeon muttered his dissatisfaction* (James Fenimore Cooper). **SYN**: See syn. under **murmur**.
— ***v.i.*** **1** to speak indistinctly and in a low voice, with the lips partly closed; mumble: *He mutters of vengeance as he walks* (Lord Dunsany). **SYN**: See syn. under **murmur**. **2** to complain; grumble: *The new soldier muttered about the Army food.* **SYN**: See syn. under **murmur**. **3** to make a low

rumbling sound: *We heard thunder muttering; a storm was coming on* (Francis Parkman).
—*n.* **1** the act of muttering: *What started as a mutter rose to a shout as the hungry workers surged forward.* **2** muttered words: *We heard a mutter of discontent.*
[Middle English *muteren;* probably imitative. Compare dialectal German *muttern.*] —**mut′ter|er**, *n.* —**mut′ter|ing|ly**, *adv.*

**mut|ton** (mut′ən), *n.* **1** the meat of a sheep, especially of a mature sheep as distinguished from a lamb: *We had roast mutton for dinner.* **2** = sheep. [< Old French *mouton* < Medieval Latin *multo, -onis* a ram, perhaps < Celtic (compare Old Irish *mol*)]

**mut|ton-bird** (mut′ən bėrd′), *n.* a sea bird, one of the shearwaters, of the Atlantic and Pacific oceans: *The mutton-birds of the Pacific ... spend most of the year fishing, spread out ... from the equator to the Bering Strait* (Atlantic).

***mutton chop**, or **mut|ton|chop** (mut′ən chop′), *n.* **1** a small piece of mutton, usually with bone from the ribs or loin, for broiling or frying. **2** Also, **mutton chop** (or **muttonchop**) **whiskers**. a patch of whiskers on each side of the face shaped like a mutton chop, narrow at the temples and broad and rounded at the bottom, with the chin shaved both in front and beneath: *Baker wore mutton chop whiskers* (Newsweek).

***mutton chop**
definition 2

**mut|ton|fish** (mut′ən fish′), *n., pl.* **-fish|es** or (*collectively*) **-fish**. a snapper of the western Atlantic Ocean, valued as a food and game fish: *a delectable muttonfish for the pot* (Cyril Connolly).

**mut|ton|head** (mut′ən hed′), *n. Slang.* a slow, dull-witted person: *Tycho Brahe was the first to demonstrate what had already been conjectured by that strange combination of genius and muttonhead ...* (Scientific American).

**mut|ton-head|ed** (mut′ən hed′id), *adj. Slang.* dull; stupid.

**mutton snapper**, = muttonfish.

**mut|ton|y** (mut′ə nē), *adj.* like mutton; having the qualities of mutton.

**mu|tu|al** (myü′chü əl), *adj., n.* —*adj.* **1** done, said, or felt by each toward the other; given and received: *mutual promises, mutual dislike. A family has mutual affection when each person likes the others and is liked by them.* SYN: reciprocal. **2** each to the other: *mutual enemies.* **3** belonging to each respectively; respective; common. SYN: See syn. under **common**. **4** belonging to each of several: *We are happy to have him as our mutual friend.* **5** of or having to do with mutual insurance: *a mutual company.*
—*n.* **1** a mutual insurance company. **2** = mutual fund: *The mutuals seldom buy speculative stocks* (Maclean's).
[< Latin *mūtuus* reciprocal, related to *mūtāre* to change + English *-al*[1]]

**mutual fund**, a financial organization that pools the money of its members to invest it in a variety of securities. The fund does not have a fixed amount of capital stock but sells additional shares to investors as the demand requires. *Mutual funds ... were switching out of lower-yielding common stocks into fixed-income securities* (Wall Street Journal).

**mutual inductance**, *Physics.* a measure of the inductive effect of the magnetic fields produced by two circuits on each other.

**mutual insurance** or **plan**, a plan or method of insurance in which the persons who are insured jointly own and control the insurance society or company, protecting each other against loss by the payment of given amounts into a common fund, and dividing the profits as owners.

**mu|tu|al|ism** (myü′chü ə liz′əm), *n. Biology.* **1** a relationship of close interdependence between two species: *Between canine and human species the predator/prey relationship appears to have developed into a mutualism, which was bound to lead eventually to the one being domesticated by the other* (New Scientist). **2** = symbiosis.

**mu|tu|al|is|tic** (myü′chü ə lis′tik), *adj.* involved in or characterized by mutualism: *The mutualistic partners of insects are not limited to fungi; they include other microbial forms such as bacteria and protozoa* (Scientific American).

**mu|tu|al|i|ty** (myü′chü al′ə tē), *n.* the quality or condition of being mutual; reciprocity: *The need for a mutuality of understanding between the Joint Committee on Atomic Energy and the Atomic Energy Commission ... is of greater importance today than ever before* (Bulletin of Atomic Scientists).

**mu|tu|al|i|za|tion** (myü′chü ə lə zā′shən), *n.* the act or process of mutualizing: *The meeting had been called to vote on mutualization of the firm which has operated 49 years as a stock company* (Wall Street Journal).

**mu|tu|al|ize** (myü′chü ə līz), *v.t., v.i.,* **-ized, -iz|ing.** **1** to make or become mutual. **2** to sell much stock of (a corporation) to employees or customers.

**mu|tu|al|ly** (myü′chü ə lē), *adv.* each toward the other: *Those three girls have been mutually friendly for years.*

**mutual savings bank**, a savings bank with no capital, whose depositors share the profits: *Three New Jersey mutual savings banks announced plans to merge* (Wall Street Journal).

**mu|tu|el** (myü′chü əl), *n., adj.* —*n.* **1** = pari-mutuel. **2** the money paid on a minimum winning bet, usually a two-dollar ticket, on the pari-mutuel: *He won the Sheepshead Bay Handicap and paid an $81.80 mutuel* (New Yorker).
—*adj.* of or having to do with a mutuel: *mutuel tickets, mutuel windows.*

**mu|tule** (myü′tyül, myü′chül), *n. Architecture.* one of a series of projecting flat blocks under the corona of a Doric cornice. [< Latin *mūtulus* a modillion]

***mu|u|mu|u** (mü′mü′; *Hawaiian* mü′ü mü′ü), *n.* a long, loose-fitting cotton dress, like a Mother Hubbard, originally worn by Polynesian women, now common throughout the United States. [< Hawaiian *mu'u mu'u*]

***muumuu**

**Mu|zak** (myü′zak), *n. Trademark.* background music for offices, industry, and public areas, transmitted by either telephone or FM radio: *There's dinner music, too, for those who haven't been wired yet for Muzak* (New Yorker).

**mu|zhik** or **mu|zjik** (mü zhik′, mü′zhik), *n.* **1** a Russian peasant: *Until the end of ... the thirteenth century, the Russian muzhik ... was free* (Newsweek). **2** *U.S. Slang.* any Russian. Also, **moujik, mujik**. [< Russian *muzhik*]

**muzz** (muz), *Slang, Archaic.* —*v.t.* to make muzzy.
—*v.i.* **1** to study intently. **2** to loiter aimlessly. [origin uncertain]

**muz|zi|ly** (muz′ə lē), *adv. Informal.* in a muzzy manner; confusedly: *He would sit at home every night reading ..., brooding muzzily at last over his book* (Edmund Wilson).

**muz|zi|ness** (muz′ē nis), *n. Informal.* muzzy or befuddled character or appearance: *We lament the muzziness which seems inseparable from the process employed* (Athenæum).

**muz|zle** (muz′əl), *n., v.,* **-zled, -zling.** —*n.* **1** the nose, mouth, and jaws of a four-footed animal; snout: *the muzzle of a dog. The antler'd deer ... thrust his muzzle in the air* (Joaquin Miller). **2a** a cover or cage of straps or wires to put over an animal's head and mouth to keep it from biting or eating. **b** any one of various contrivances that resemble this, such as the respirator of a gas mask. **3** the open front end of the barrel of a gun: *Friday ... clapped the muzzle of his piece into his ear, and shot him dead as a stone* (Daniel Defoe).
—*v.t.* **1** to put a muzzle on. **2** *Figurative.* to compel (a person) to keep silent about something: *Fear that he might betray his friends muzzled him. The government muzzled the newspapers during the rebellion.* **3** to sniff at; poke the head into: *... a spaniel muzzling the wind* (Atlantic).
[Middle English *musell* < Old French *musel* < *muse* muzzle < Medieval Latin *musus* snout. Compare etym. under **muse**.] —**muz′zler**, *n.*

**muz|zle|load|er** (muz′əl lō′dər), *n.* a muzzleloading gun. See picture under **ramrod**.

**muz|zle|load|ing** (muz′əl lō′ding), *adj.* loaded by putting gunpowder or bullets in through the open front end of the barrel and ramming it down: *a muzzleloading gun.*

**muzzle velocity**, the velocity that a gun imparts to a projectile, measured as it leaves the muzzle in feet per second: *They produced an ingenious way of measuring the muzzle velocity of guns for battleships at sea* (New Scientist).

**muz|zy** (muz′ē), *adj.,* **-zi|er, -zi|est.** *Informal.* **1** befuddled; muddled; confused: *The whole company stared at me with a whimsical, muzzy look, like men whose senses were a little obfuscated by beer* (Washington Irving). **2** dull; gloomy; spiritless. [origin uncertain]

**mv** (no period), millivolt.

**m.v.**, an abbreviation for the following:
**1** market value.
**2** mean variation.
**3** medium voltage.
**4** motor vessel.
**5** softly (Italian, *mezza voce*).

**Mv** (no period), mendelevium (chemical element).

**M.V.** or **M/V** (no periods), motor vessel.

**MVA** (no periods), Missouri Valley Authority.

**MVD** (no periods) or **M.V.D.**, the Ministry of Internal Affairs of the Soviet Union, an official organization of police for conventional police protection and border police activity.

**M.V.O.**, Member of the Royal Victorian Order.

**MVP** (no periods), *U.S.* most valuable player: [*He*] *... was named the American League's MVP* (Bill Braddock).

**mvu|le** (vü′le), *n.* an African timber tree; iroko. [< a native name]

**mw** (no period), milliwatt.

**Mw** (no period), megawatt.

**MW** (no periods), *British.* megawatt.

**M.W.**, **1** Most Worshipful. **2** Most Worthy.

**M.W.A.**, Modern Woodmen of America.

**mwa|mi** (mwä′mē), *n.* the former title of the rulers of Burundi, in central Africa, and of the native rulers of Belgian East Africa. [< a Bantu word]

**M.W.G.M.**, Most Worthy or Worshipful Grand Master (of a Masonic order).

**my** (mī), *adj., interj.* —*adj.* a possessive form of **I**; of me; belonging to me; that I have, hold, or possess: *in my opinion. I learned my lesson. My house is around the corner.*
—*interj. Informal.* an exclamation of surprise: *My! How pleasant to see you!*
[Middle English *mī, mīn,* Old English *mīn*]

**my** (no periods), million years: *Previously, evidence for rocks older than about 3400-3500 my, has been sketchy, with an age for a Minnesota gneiss of 3550 my* (New Scientist and Science Journal).

**my-**, *combining form.* the form of **myo-** before vowels, as in *myoma.*

**mya.**, myriare.

**my|al|gi|a** (mī al′jē ə), *n.* muscular pain or rheumatism. [< New Latin *myalgia* < Greek *mŷs, myós* muscle + *álgos* pain]

**my|al|gic** (mī al′jik), *adj.* of or having to do with myalgia; affected with myalgia.

**my|all** (mī′ôl), *n.* (in Australia) an aborigine. [< a native name]

**my|as|the|ni|a** (mī′əs thē′nē ə), *n.* extreme muscular weakness. [< New Latin *myasthenia* < Greek *mŷs, myós* muscle + *astheneīā* weakness]

**myasthenia grav|is** (grav′is, gräv′-; grā′vis), a disease that causes extreme weakness of the muscles, because of an interruption of nerve impulses traveling to the muscles, and related in some way to the functioning of the thymus gland.

**my|as|then|ic** (mī′əs then′ik), *adj.* affected with myasthenia.

**my|ce|li|al** (mī sē′lē əl), *adj.* of or having to do with the mycelium.

**my|ce|li|an** (mī sē′lē ən), *adj.* = mycelial.

**my|ce|li|oid** (mī sē′lē oid), *adj.* of or like mycelium.

**my|ce|li|um** (mī sē′lē əm), *n., pl.* **-li|a** (-lē ə).
**1** the main part of a fungus, consisting of one or more white, interwoven fibers or hyphae, often not visible on the surface: *The umbrella growth, which most people call a mushroom, is really a stalk that grows up from the mycelium* (William F. Hanna). **2** a similar mass of fibers formed by some higher bacteria. [< New Latin *mycelium* < Greek *mýkēs, -ētos* mushroom, fungus]

**my|ce|loid** (mī′sə loid), *adj.* = mycelioid.

**My|ce|nae|an** (mī′sə nē′ən), *adj., n.* —*adj.* of or having to do with Mycenae, a very ancient city in southern Greece, or the civilization, culture, or art that flourished there from about 1500 B.C. to about 1100 B.C.: *The Late Bronze Age on the Greek mainland from 1580 to 1100 B.C. is often called the Mycenaean period* (Norman A. Doenges).
—*n.* a native or inhabitant of Mycenae: *During the 1100's B.C., the Dorians, who lived in northwestern Greece, conquered the Mycenaeans* (C. Scott Littleton).

**my|ce|to|ma** (mī′sə tō′mə), *n.* a fungous disease of the hands, feet, legs, and internal tissue, characterized by swelling, and the formation of nodules containing pus. It is most common in tropical areas and usually affects the foot, when it is called Madura foot. [< Greek *mýkēs, -ētos* fungus + English *-oma*]

**my|ce|to|zo|an** (mī sē′tə zō′ən), *n., adj.* —*n.* any

one of a group of primitive organisms, the slime molds, sometimes classified as animals and sometimes as plants; myxomycete.
—*adj.* of or designating the mycetozoans. [< New Latin *Mycetozoa* the group name (< Greek *mýkēs, -ētos* fungus + *zôion* animal) + English *-an*]

**my|co|bac|te|ri|al** (mī′kō bak tir′ē əl), *adj.* having to do with or caused by mycobacteria: *mycobacterial infections.*

**my|co|bac|te|ri|um** (mī′kō bak tir′ē əm), *n., pl.* **-te|ri|a** (-tir′ē ə). any one of a group of aerobic, acid-fast, rod-shaped bacteria. One species causes leprosy; certain other species cause tuberculosis in man, cattle, and fowl. [< New Latin *Mycobacterium* the genus name < Greek *mýkēs* fungus + New Latin *bacterium* bacterium]

**mycol.**, mycology.

**my|co|log|ic** (mī′kə loj′ik), *adj.* = mycological.

**my|co|log|i|cal** (mī′kə loj′ə kəl), *adj.* of or having to do with mycology. —**my′co|log′i|cal|ly**, *adv.*

**my|col|o|gist** (mī kol′ə jist), *n.* an expert in mycology.

**my|col|o|gy** (mī kol′ə jē), *n.* **1** the branch of botany that deals with fungi. **2** the fungi of a particular region or country. **3** facts about a particular fungus. [< Greek *mýkēs* fungus + English *-logy*]

**my|coph|a|gous** (mī kof′ə gəs), *adj.* that feed on fungi. [< Greek *mýkēs* fungus + *phageîn* eat + English *-ous*]

**my|coph|a|gy** (mī kof′ə jē), *n.* the practice or habit of eating fungi, especially mushrooms.

**my|co|phile** (mī′kə fīl), *n.* a person who is very fond of mushrooms: *"My wife and I are devout mycophiles"* (New Yorker). [< Greek *mýkēs* fungus + English *-phile*]

**my|co|plas|ma** (mī′kō plaz′mə), *n., pl.* **-mas, -ma|ta** (-mə tə). any one of a group of Gram-negative, filterable microorganisms that lack rigid cell walls and resemble both viruses and bacteria, including the Eaton agent and the causative agent of pleuropneumonia in cattle; pleuropneumonia-like organism. [< New Latin *Mycoplasma* the genus name < Greek *mýkēs* fungus + New Latin *plasma* plasma]

**my|cor|rhi|za** or **my|co|rhi|za** (mī′kə rī′zə), *n.* the symbiotic association of the mycelium of certain fungi with the roots of certain higher plants, living in close relationship with the surface cells: *It is possible with many, if not all, species of plant which normally form mycorrhizas in natural conditions to grow them in artificial surroundings without their appropriate fungi* (New Scientist). [< Greek *mýkēs* fungus + New Latin *-rrhiza* < Greek *rhíza* root]

**my|cor|rhi|zal** or **my|co|rhi|zal** (mī′kə rī′zəl), *adj.* of or having to do with mycorrhiza.

**my|cor|rhi|zic** or **my|co|rhi|zic** (mī′kə rī′zik), *adj.* = mycorrhizal.

**my|co|sis** (mī kō′sis), *n., pl.* **-ses** (sēz). **1** the presence of parasitic fungi in or on any part of the body. **2** a disease caused by such fungi. [< Greek *mýkēs* fungus + English *-osis*]

**My|co|stat|in** (mī′kə stat′in), *n. Trademark.* nystatin.

**my|cot|ic** (mī kot′ik), *adj.* of or having to do with mycosis.

**my|co|tox|in** (mī′kə tok′sən), *n.* a poison produced by a fungus: *the significance of aflatoxin and other mycotoxins* (New Scientist). [< Greek *mýkēs* fungus + English *toxin*]

**myc|to|phid** (mik′tə fid), *n.* = lantern fish. [< New Latin *Myctophidae* the family name < Greek *myktēr* nose + *óphis* serpent]

**my|dri|a|sis** (mi drī′ə sis, mī-), *n.* excessive dilation of the pupil of the eye, as the result of disease, drugs, or the like. [< Latin *mydriāsis* < Greek *mydríāsis*]

**myd|ri|at|ic** (mid′rē at′ik), *adj., n.* —*adj.* having to do with or causing mydriasis.
—*n.* a drug that produces mydriasis, such as atropine: *Ephedrine and its salts are used locally to shrink mucous membranes in colds and as a mydriatic* (Heber W. Youngken).

**my|e|len|ceph|a|lon** (mī′ə len sef′ə lon), *n.* **1** the posterior section of the hindbrain, which comprises the medulla oblongata; afterbrain. **2** the brain and spinal cord taken together and considered as a whole. [< Greek *myelós* marrow + English *encephalon*]

**my|e|lin** (mī′ə lin), *n.* a soft, whitish, fatty substance that forms a sheath about the core of certain nerve fibers: *The myelin sheath ... surrounds nerve fibers much as insulating material protects electric wire* (Science News Letter). [< German *Myelin* < Greek *myelós* marrow + German *-in* -in]

**my|e|lin|at|ed** (mī′ə lə nā′tid), *adj.* covered or surrounded by myelin: *myelinated nerve fibers.*

**my|e|lin|a|tion** (mī′ə lə nā′shən), *n.* the sheathing of nerve fibers; acquisition of a myelin sheath: *Myelination ... leads to lower levels of excitability and more mature function in the brain* (Science News Letter).

**my|e|line** (mī′ə lin, -lēn), *n.* = myelin.

**my|e|li|tis** (mī′ə lī′tis), *n.* inflammation of the spinal cord or of the bone marrow. [< Greek *myelós* marrow + English *-itis*]

**my|e|lo|blast** (mī′ə lə blast), *n.* a bone-marrow cell in its early stages; a rudimentary myelocyte. [< Greek *myelós* marrow + *blastós* sprout]

**my|e|lo|blas|tic** (mī′ə lə blas′tik), *adj.* having to do with myeloblasts.

**my|e|lo|cyte** (mī′ə lə sīt), *n.* an ameboid blood cell present in bone marrow and giving rise to leucocytes: *The marrow in early cases [of myeloid leukemia] shows an increase in ... myelocytes* (G. E. Beaumont and E. C. Dodds). [< Greek *myelós* marrow + English *-cyte*]

**my|e|lo|cyt|ic** (mī′ə lə sit′ik), *adj.* of or having to do with myelocytes.

**my|e|lo|cy|to|ma|to|sis** (mī′ə lō sī tō′mə tō′sis), *n.* a disease of poultry, a form of the avian leucosis complex, characterized by the formation of white tumors in the liver and along the sternum. [< *myelocyte* + Greek *-ōma, -ōmatos* a growth + *-ōsis* condition]

**my|e|lo|fi|bro|sis** (mī′ə lō fī brō′sis), *n.* fibrosis of the bone marrow. [< Greek *myelós* marrow + English *fibrosis*]

**my|e|lo|gen|ic** (mī′ə lə jen′ik), *adj.* originating or produced in the marrow. [< Greek *myelós* marrow + English *-gen* + *-ic*]

**my|e|log|e|nous** (mī′ə loj′ə nəs), *adj.* = myelogenic.

**myelogenous leukemia**, a form of leukemia characterized by an excess of myelogenic leucocytes in the blood.

**my|e|log|ra|phy** (mī′ə log′rə fē), *n.* a method of taking X-ray pictures of the space around the spinal cord by first injecting air or certain liquids into the space. [< Greek *myelós* marrow + English *-graphy*]

**my|e|loid** (mī′ə loid), *adj.* **1** of or having to do with the spinal cord. **2** having to do with or like marrow: *Myeloid leukemia ... involves the bone marrow and spleen primarily, the lymphoid tissue secondarily* (Science News Letter).

**my|e|lo|ma** (mī′ə lō′mə), *n., pl.* **-mas, -ma|ta** (-mə tə). a malignant tumor of the bone marrow. [< Greek *myelós* marrow + *-ōma* a growth]

**my|e|lo|ma|to|sis** (mī′ə lō mə tō′sis), *n., pl.* **-ses** (-sēz). any one of various cancers of the bone marrow characterized by multiple myelomas.

**my|e|lo|me|nin|go|cele** (mī′ə lō mə ning′gə sēl), *n.* a form of spina bifida with protrusion of a meningeal membrane and part of the spinal cord. [< Greek *myelós* marrow + *mêninx, -ingos* membrane + *koîlos* hollow]

**myg.**, myriagram.

**my|ia|sis** (mī′ə sis), *n., pl.* **-ses** (-sēz). a diseased condition of man or other animals due to the larvae of flies parasitic on or in the body. [< New Latin *myiasis* < Greek *myîa* fly + New Latin *-iasis* -iasis]

**myl.**, myrialiter.

**My|lar** (mī′lär), *n. Trademark.* a tough polyester film widely used in food packaging, recording tapes, and as an electrical insulator.

**My|le|ran** (mī′lə ran), *n. Trademark.* a drug used in the treatment of myelogenous leukemia. *Formula:* $C_6H_{14}O_6S_2$

**my|lo|don** (mī′lə don), *n.* an extinct giant ground sloth that lived in southern South America until recent times. [< Greek *mýlos* molar + *odoús, odóntos* tooth]

**my|lo|dont** (mī′lə dont), *adj., n.* —*adj.* of, having to do with, or like the mylodons.
—*n.* = mylodon.

**my|lo|nite** (mī′lə nīt, mil′ə-), *n.* a siliceous schist resulting from the crushing of quartzose rocks. [< Greek *mylṓn* mill[1] + English *-ite*[1]]

**mym.**, myriameter.

**my|na** or **my|nah** (mī′nə), *n.* any one of several birds related to the starlings that can mimic human speech, found in India and certain neighboring countries. Also, **mina**. [< Hindustani *mainā*]

**Myn|heer** (mīn hãr′), *n., pl.* **-heer|en** (-hãr′ən). *Dutch.* Sir; Mr.

**myn|heer** (mīn hãr′), *n.* a Dutchman.

**myo-**, *combining form.* muscle: *Myocardium = the muscular substance of the heart.* Also, **my-** before vowels. [< Greek *mŷs, myós* muscle; mouse; see etym. under **muscle**]

**my|o|blast** (mī′ə blast), *n.* a muscle cell in its early stages; a cell which develops into a myocyte. [< *myo-* + Greek *blastós* sprout]

**my|o|car|di|al** (mī′ə kär′dē əl), *adj.* of or having to do with the myocardium: *myocardial infarction, myocardial rupture.*

**my|o|car|di|o|graph** (mī′ə kär′dē ə graf, -gräf), *n.* an instrument that records heart action.

**my|o|car|di|tis** (mī′ō kär dī′tis), *n.* inflammation of the muscular part of the wall of the heart. [< *myocard*(ium) + *-itis*]

**my|o|car|di|um** (mī′ə kär′dē əm), *n.* the muscle tissue of the heart: *The coronary arteries bring oxygen and nutriment to the most important muscle in the body, the heart muscle or myocardium* (Paul Dudley White). [< New Latin *myocardium* < Greek *mŷs, myós* muscle + *kardíā* heart]

**my|o|cyte** (mī′ə sīt), *n.* **1** a muscle cell. **2** a contractile cell around the pores of sponges. [< *myo-* + *-cyte*]

**my|o|e|lec|tric** (mī′ō i lek′trik), *adj.* using electric currents produced by muscular contraction to actuate movement of an artificial limb, such as an arm or a hand: *Most other myoelectric controlled prostheses require two sets of electrodes, one for opening and another for closing* (Science). [< *myo-* + *electric*]

**my|o|e|lec|tri|cal|ly** (mī′ō i lek′trə klē), *adv.* by myoelectric means: *a myoelectrically controlled arm and hand unit.*

**my|o|fi|bril** (mī′ə fī′brəl), *n.* a striated fibril of a muscle fiber: *The striations [of the fiber] arise from a repeating variation in the density, i.e., the concentration of protein along the myofibrils* (Scientific American).

**my|o|gen|ic** (mī′ə jen′ik), *adj.* **1** arising from the muscles: *myogenic contractions.* **2** producing or forming muscle: *myogenic cells.*

**my|o|glo|bin** (mī′ə glō′bin), *n.* a protein similar to hemoglobin and present in muscle cells, that takes oxygen from the blood and stores it for future use: *Muscles contain myoglobin, a compound related to haemoglobin which takes up oxygen released by haemoglobin ... and stores it for use in time of oxygen shortage* (A. C. Allison). [< *myo-* + (hemo)*globin*]

**my|o|gram** (mī′ə gram), *n.* a record or tracing obtained by a myograph.

**my|o|graph** (mī′ə graf, -gräf), *n.* an instrument for recording muscular contractions and relaxations by means of tracings.

**my|oid** (mī′oid), *adj.* of or like muscle.

**my|ol|o|gist** (mī ol′ə jist), *n.* a person skilled in myology.

**my|ol|o|gy** (mī ol′ə jē), *n.* the scientific study of the structure, functions, and diseases of muscles. [< *myo-* + *-logy*]

**my|o|ma** (mī ō′mə), *n., pl.* **-mas, -ma|ta** (-mə tə). a tumor derived from muscular tissue. [< *my-* + *-oma*]

**my|om|a|tous** (mī om′ə təs, -ō′mə-), *adj.* of or characterized by myoma; affected with a myoma.

**my|o|neu|ral** (mī′ə nůr′əl, -nyůr′-), *adj.* having to do with both muscle and nerve, especially with nerve endings in muscle tissue: *The impulses activate myoneural junctions ... and cause the effector (muscle) cells to contract* (Elbert Tokay). [< *myo-* + *neural*]

**my|o|path|ic** (mī′ə path′ik), *adj.* of or having to do with myopathy.

**my|op|a|thy** (mī op′ə thē), *n.* disease of the muscles. [< *myo-* + *-pathy*]

**my|ope** (mī′ōp), *n.* a person having myopia; near-sighted person: *In general, myopes become aware of their abnormality because of the difficulty of distinguishing distant objects* (Hardy and Perrin). [back formation < *myopia*]

*****my|o|pi|a** (mī ō′pē ə), *n.* **1** near-sightedness; an abnormal condition of the eye in which only objects close to the eye produce distinct images because parallel rays of light are brought to a focus before they reach the retina. **2** *Figurative.* short-sightedness: *intellectual myopia.* [< New Latin *myopia* < Greek *myṓps* < *mŷein* to shut + *ôps* eye]

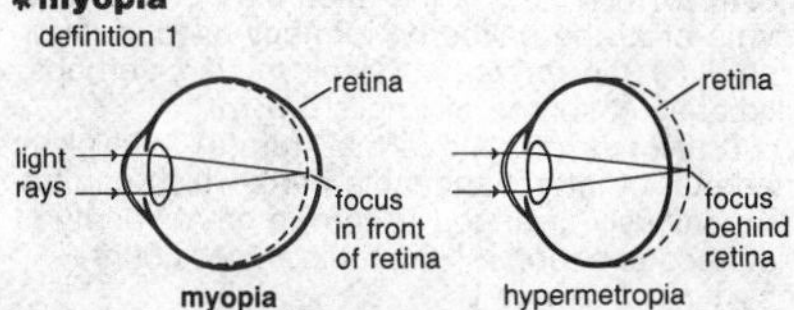


**my|op|ic** (mī op′ik), *adj.* near-sighted; of or affected with myopia: *Myopic children whose vision is deteriorating eat less food for every pound they increase in weight than do normally sighted children* (Science News Letter). —**my|op′i|cal|ly**, *adv.*

**my|o|py** (mī′ə pē), *n.* = myopia.

**my|o|scope** (mī′ə skōp), *n.* an instrument for observing muscular contraction.

**my|o|sin** (mī′ə sin), *n.* one of two protein components of muscle cells, important in the elasticity and contraction of muscles. The other is actin.

**my|o|sis** (mī ō′sis), *n.* = miosis[1].

**my|o|sote** (mī′ə sōt), *n.* = myosotis.

**Pronunciation Key:** hat, āge, cãre, fär; let, ēqual, tėrm; it, īce; hot, ōpen, ôrder; **oi**l, **ou**t; cup, pu̇t, rüle; **ch**ild; lo**ng**; **th**in; **ᴛʜ**en; **zh**, measure; **ə** represents **a** in about, **e** in taken, **i** in pencil, **o** in lemon, **u** in circus.

**my|o|so|tis** (mī′ə sō′tis), *n.* any one of a group of plants of the borage family, such as the forget-me-not. [earlier, hawkweed < Latin *myosōtis* < Greek *myosōtis* < *mŷs, myós* mouse + *oûs, ōtós* ear]

**my|ot|ic** (mī ot′ik), *adj., n.* —*adj.* producing miosis; miotic.
—*n.* a drug that causes miosis; a miotic.

**my|o|tis** (mī ō′tis), *n.* any small bat of a widely distributed group, including varieties commonly found about buildings and caves.

**my|o|tome** (mī′ə tōm), *n. Anatomy.* **1** the part of a metamere that differentiates into skeletal muscle. **2** a muscle supplied by a spinal nerve. [< *myo-* + Greek *tómos* cut, slice]

**my|o|to|ni|a** (mī′ə tō′nē ə), *n.* persistent muscular contraction; tonic spasm of the muscles. [< New Latin *myotonia* < *myo-* + Greek *tónos* tension]

**my|o|ton|ic** (mī′ə ton′ik), *adj.* characterized by persistent contraction of the muscles: *myotonic muscular dystrophy.*

**myr|i|ad** (mir′ē əd), *n., adj.* —*n.* **1** a very great number: *There are myriads of stars. The grove bloomed with myriads of wild roses* (Francis Parkman). **2** ten thousand.
—*adj.* **1** countless; innumerable: *the City's moonlit spires and myriad lamps* (Shelley). **2** ten thousand. **3** having innumerable aspects or phases: *the myriad mind of Shakespeare or Da Vinci.*
[< Late Latin *myrias, -adis* < Greek *mȳriás, -ados* ten thousand, countless]

**myr|i|ad|fold** (mir′ē əd fōld), *adj., n.* —*adj.* multiplied countless times; having innumerable aspects or features.
—*n.* an infinite amount.

**myr|i|a|gram** (mir′ē ə gram), *n.* 10 kilograms; 22.046 pounds. *Abbr:* myg. [< Greek *mȳriás* ten thousand + English *gram*]

**myr|i|a|gramme** (mir′ē ə gram), *n. Especially British.* myriagram.

**myr|i|a|li|ter** (mir′ē ə lē′tər), *n.* 10 kiloliters; 13.08 cubic yards U.S. dry measure; 2,641.7 gallons U.S. liquid measure. *Abbr:* myl. [< Greek *mȳriás* ten thousand + English *liter*]

**myr|i|a|li|tre** (mir′ē ə lē′tər), *n. Especially British.* myrialiter.

**myr|i|a|me|ter** (mir′ē ə mē′tər), *n.* 10,000 meters; 6.2137 miles. *Abbr:* mym. [< Greek *mȳriás* ten thousand + English *-meter*]

**myr|i|a|me|tre** (mir′ē ə mē′tər), *n. Especially British.* myriameter.

**myr|i|a|pod** (mir′ē ə pod), *n., adj.* —*n.* an arthropod having a wormlike body with many segments and many legs. Centipedes and millipedes are myriapods. The classification is obsolete, these arthropods being now considered to comprise four classes, of which the centipedes and millipedes are the two largest.
—*adj.* **1** of or belonging to the myriapods. **2** having many legs.
[< New Latin *Myriapoda* the class name < Greek *mȳriás* ten thousand + *poús, podós* foot]

**myr|i|ap|o|dal** (mir′ē ap′ə dəl), *adj.* of or having to do with the myriapods.

**myr|i|ap|o|dan** (mir′ē ap′ə dən), *n.* , *adj.* = myriapod.

**myr|i|ap|o|dous** (mir′ē ap′ə dəs), *adj.* = myriapod.

**my|ri|are** (mir′ē ãr), *n.* one square kilometer; about 247 acres. *Abbr:* mya. [< Greek *mȳriás* ten thousand + English *are*[2]]

**my|ri|ca** (mi rī′kə), *n.* the dried bark of the wax myrtle or of the bayberry, formerly used in medicine. [< Latin *myrīca* < Greek *myrīkē,* perhaps ultimately < source of English *myrrh*]

**myr|i|o|ra|ma** (mir′ē ə rä′mə, -ram′ə), *n.* a picture made up of interchangeable parts which can be harmoniously arranged to form a great variety of picturesque scenes. [< Greek *mȳ́rios* countless + *hórāma* view]

**my|ris|tic** (mi ris′tik, mī-), *adj.* of or derived from the nutmeg. [< Medieval Latin *myristica* nutmeg tree < Greek *myrízein* to anoint]

**my|ris|ti|ca|ceous** (mi ris′tə kā′shəs, mī-), *adj.* belonging to the family of trees and shrubs typified by the nutmeg.

**myristic acid,** an organic acid such as is found in oil of nutmeg or spermaceti, used especially in making soap and perfumes. *Formula:* $C_{14}H_{28}O_2$

**myr|me|co|log|i|cal** (mėr′mə kə loj′ə kəl), *adj.* of or having to do with ants.

**myr|me|col|o|gist** (mėr′mə kol′ə jist), *n.* an expert in myrmecology.

**myr|me|col|o|gy** (mėr′mə kol′ə jē), *n.* the scientific study of ants. [< Greek *mýrmēx, -ēkos* ant + English *-logy*]

**myr|me|coph|a|gous** (mėr′mə kof′ə gəs), *adj.* feeding on ants. [< Greek *mýrmēx, -ēkos* ant + *phageîn* to eat + English *-ous*]

**myr|me|co|phile** (mėr′mə kə fīl, -fil), *n.* a myrmecophilous insect.

**myr|me|coph|i|lous** (mėr′mə kof′ə ləs), *adj.* **1** fond of or living with ants. Myrmecophilous insects live in anthills. **2** benefited by ants, such as plants that are cross-fertilized by them. [< Greek *mýrmēx, -ēkos* ant + English *-phile* + *-ous*]

**Myr|mi|don** (mėr′mə don), *n., pl.* **Myr|mi|dons, Myr|mid|o|nes** (mėr mid′ə nēz). *Greek Legend.* a member of a warlike people of ancient Thessaly who, according to Homer, accompanied Achilles, their king, to the Trojan War.

**myr|mi|don** (mėr′mə don), *n.* **1** an obedient and unquestioning follower, especially one who unscrupulously carries out his master's orders: *No man could now be safe, when men like him* [*Egmont*] *were in the power of Alva and his myrmidons* (John L. Motley). **2** a policeman, bailiff, or deputy sheriff: *the justice and his myrmidons* (Tobias Smollett). [< *Myrmidon*]

**my|rob|a|lan** (mī rob′ə lən, mi-), *n.* the dried plumlike fruit of various tropical trees, used in dyeing, tanning, and making ink. [< Old French *myrobalon* < Latin *myrobalanum* < Greek *myrobálanos* fruit of a palm that yields balsam < *mýron* any balsam + *bálanos* acorn]

**myr|o|sin** (mir′ə sin, mī′rə-), *n.* an enzyme found in the seeds of the mustard and of various other plants of the mustard family. [< French *myrosyne* < Greek *mýron* unguent]

**myrrh** (mėr), *n.* a fragrant, gummy substance with a bitter taste, used in medicine as an astringent tonic, in perfumes, and in incense. It is obtained from certain shrubs of southern Arabia and eastern Africa. [Old English *myrre* < Latin *myrrha* < Greek *mýrrhā,* ultimately < Semitic, probably Akkadian *murrū*]

**myrrh|like** (mėr′līk′), *adj.* resembling myrrh.

**myrrh|y** (mėr′ē), *adj.* full of myrrh; fragrant with or as if with myrrh: *the myrrhy lands* (Robert Browning).

**myr|ta|ceous** (mėr tā′shəs), *adj.* **1** belonging to the myrtle family: *Myrtle, clove, allspice, guava, and eucalyptus are myrtaceous plants.* **2** of or like the myrtle. [< New Latin *Myrtaceae* the family name (< Latin *myrtāceus* < *myrtus* myrtle tree < Greek *mýrtos*) + English *-ous*]

**myr|tle** (mėr′təl), *n.* **1** a low, creeping evergreen vine of the dogbane family with blue flowers; periwinkle. **2** an evergreen shrub, especially of the southern part of Europe, with shiny leaves, fragrant, white flowers, and black, aromatic berries. It belongs to the myrtle family. The myrtle was held sacred to Venus (Aphrodite) and is used as an emblem of love. **3** a dark-green color. [earlier, fruit of the myrtle < Old French *mirtile,* probably < Medieval Latin *myrtilus* (diminutive) < Latin *myrtus* myrtle tree < Greek *mýrtos*]

**myr|tle|ber|ry** (mėr′təl ber′ē, -bər-), *n., pl.* **-ries.** the fruit of the myrtle (def. 2).

**myrtle bird,** = myrtle warbler.

**myrtle family,** a group of dicotyledonous woody plants, natives of warm climates, usually having a fragrant, volatile oil. The family includes plants valued for spices, such as the clove and allspice, for edible fruit, such as the guava, and for timber or gum, such as the eucalyptus.

**myrtle green,** a dark green with a bluish tinge; the color of myrtle leaves.

**myrtle warbler,** a North American warbler with yellow patches on the crown, the rump, and each side of the breast.

**myr|tle|wood** (mėr′təl wůd′), *n.* = Oregon laurel.

**myr|tol** (mėr′tol, -tōl), *n.* an oil obtained from the leaves of the common myrtle, used especially as an antiseptic and stimulant. [< Latin *myrt(us)* myrtle + English *-ol*[2]]

**my|self** (mī self′), *pron., pl.* **our|selves. 1** *Myself* is used to make a statement stronger. *I did it myself. I myself will go.* **2** *Myself* is used instead of *I* or *me* in cases like: *I hurt myself. I can cook for myself.* **3** my real self; my normal self: *I am not myself today.*
► In informal English, **myself** is sometimes substituted for *I* or *me* in a compound subject or object: *Mrs. Johnson and myself are both very grateful. He wrote to Richards and myself.* This use is not regarded as standard.

**My|so|line** (mī′sə lin, -lēn), *n. Trademark.* a drug used to control or prevent convulsions in some forms of epilepsy; primidone. *Formula:* $C_{12}H_{14}N_2O_2$

**my|sost** (mē′sost), *n.* a hard Norwegian cheese made from whey, similar to gjetost. [< Norwegian *mysost* < *myse* whey + *ost* cheese]

**mys|ta|gog|ic** (mis′tə goj′ik), *adj.* of or having to do with a mystagogue or mystagogy.

**mys|ta|gog|i|cal** (mis′tə goj′ə kəl), *adj.* = mystagogic.

**mys|ta|gogue** (mis′tə gôg, -gog), *n.* a person who initiates other persons into, or interprets, mysteries, especially religious mysteries. [< Latin *mystagōgus* < Greek *mystagōgós* < *mýstēs* one vowed to silence (< *mȳ́ein* close the lips or eyes) + *agōgós* leading < *ágein* to lead]

**mys|ta|go|gy** (mis′tə gō′jē), *n.* initiation into or interpretation of mysteries, especially religious mysteries.

**mys|te|ri|al** (mis tir′ē əl), *adj. Rare.* mysterious.

**mys|te|ri|ous** (mis tir′ē əs), *adj.* **1** full of mystery; hard to explain or understand; secret; hidden: *Electricity is mysterious.* **2** suggesting mystery; enigmatic: *the mysterious smile of the Mona Lisa. Why are you all so mysterious, so reserved in your communications?* (Cardinal Newman).
—**mys|te′ri|ous|ly,** *adv.* —**mys|te′ri|ous|ness,** *n.*
—*Syn.* **1 Mysterious, inscrutable** mean hard to explain or understand. **Mysterious** describes a person, thing, or situation about which there is something secret, hidden, or unknown that arouses curiosity, conjecture, or wonder: *She had a mysterious telephone call.* **Inscrutable** describes a thing that is so mysterious or such a riddle that it is impossible to make out its meaning, or a person who keeps his feelings, thoughts, and intentions completely hidden: *His mother began to cry, but his father's face was inscrutable.*
► See **mystical** for usage note.

**mys|te|ri|um** (mis tir′ē əm), *n.* a hydroxyl radical identified as emitter of a distinctive pattern of radio frequencies in several regions of the Milky Way: *In fact, one of the first groups to discover the hydroxyl line named it "mysterium" because they did not believe it could be hydroxyl emission* (Scientific American). [< Latin *mystērium* mystery]

**mys|ter|y**[1] (mis′tər ē, -trē), *n., pl.* **-ter|ies.** **1** something that is hidden or unknown; secret: *the mysteries of the universe, the mystery of love.* SYN: enigma. **2** secrecy; obscurity; condition or property of being secret or secretive: *an atmosphere of mystery, a man of mystery.* **3** something that is not explained or understood: *the mystery of the migration of birds. It is a mystery to me how he survived the accident.* **4** a novel, story, play, or motion picture about a mysterious event or events which are not explained until the end, so as to keep the reader or viewer in suspense: *a writer of mysteries. Let's watch a mystery on TV tonight.* **5** a religious conception or doctrine that human reason cannot understand: *Father Deacy preached on the mystery of the Trinity* (New York Times). **6** Often, **mysteries.** a secret religious rite to which only initiated persons are admitted. **7a** a sacramental rite of the Christian religion. **b** the Eucharist; Communion; Mass. **c** Often, **mysteries.** the elements of the Eucharist. **8** an incident in the life of Jesus or one of the saints, regarded as of special significance. **9** = mystery play. [< Latin *mystērium* < Greek *mystḗrion* < *mýstēs* an initiate < *mȳ́ein* close (the lips or eyes)]

**mys|ter|y**[2] (mis′tər ē, -trē), *n., pl.* **-ter|ies.** *Archaic.* **1** craft; trade: *It* [*a town*] *makes pretence at some kind of cloth mystery* (Walter Besant). **2** an association of craftsmen or merchants; guild: *Claus Hammerlein, president of the mysteries of the workers in iron* (Scott). [< Medieval Latin *misterium,* for Latin *ministerium* ministry; influenced by *mystery*[1]]

**mystery play,** a medieval religious play based on the Bible, often acted by the trade guilds. [< *mystery*[2]]

**mys|tic** (mis′tik), *adj., n.* —*adj.* **1** = mystical. **2** having to do with the ancient religious mysteries or other occult rites: *mystic arts.* **3** of or having to do with mystics or mysticism. **4** of hidden meaning or nature; enigmatic; mysterious: *To him all nature is instinct with mystic influence* (Francis Parkman).
—*n.* **1** a person who believes that truth or God can be known through spiritual insight independent of the mind: *Lady Julian of Norwich was one of the great English mystics* (Anya Seton). **2** a person who has the mental tendencies or habits of thought and feeling characteristic of a mystic. **3** a person initiated into mysteries.
[< Latin *mysticus* < Greek *mystikós* < *mýstēs* an initiate; see etym. under **mystery**[1]]

**mys|ti|cal** (mis′tə kəl), *adj.* **1** having some secret meaning; beyond human understanding; mysterious. **2** spiritually symbolic: *The lamb and the dove are mystical symbols of the Christian religion.* **3** of or concerned with mystics or mysticism. **4** of or having to do with secret rites open only to the initiated. **5** cryptic in speech or in style; enigmatic. —**mys′ti|cal|ly,** *adv.* —**mys′ti|cal|ness,** *n.*
► **Mystical** and **mysterious** are both used to describe experiences that are beyond human understanding. *Mystical* usually refers to an experience that fills a person with spiritual insight, enlightenment, or exaltation, while *mysterious* refers to an experience that fills a person with uncertainty and bewilderment: *As he prayed, he felt himself joined in a mystical union with God. She was puzzled by the mysterious appearance of an angel in her dream.*

**mys|ti|cism** (mis′tə siz əm), *n.* **1** the beliefs or mode of thought of mystics: *The Gospel of St.*

*John ... is the charter of Christian mysticism* (William R. Inge). **2** the doctrine that truth or God may be known through spiritual insight, independent of the mind: *Whatever it is, superstition or religion, mysticism in all its aspects is one of the most important parts of Indian life* (Santha Rama Rau). **3** vague or fuzzy thinking; dreamy speculation: *An acute and subtile perception was often clouded by mysticism and abstraction* (William H. Prescott).

**mys|tic|i|ty** (mis tis′ə tē), *n.* mystic quality.

**mys|ti|cize** (mis′tə sīz), *v.t.,* **-cized, -ciz|ing.** to make mystical; give a mystical character or meaning to.

**mys|ti|fi|ca|tion** (mis′tə fə kā′shən), *n.* **1** the action of mystifying or state of being mystified; bewilderment; perplexity. **2** something that mystifies or is designed to mystify; hoax.

**mys|ti|fi|ca|tor** (mis′tə fə kā′tər), *n.* a person who mystifies; mystifier.

**mys|ti|fi|ca|to|ry** (mis′tə fə kā′tər ē), *adj.* causing mystification; mystifying.

**mys|ti|fi|er** (mis′tə fī′ər), *n.* a person or thing that mystifies: *I am not a magician but a mystifier* (Harry Houdini).

**mys|ti|fy** (mis′tə fī), *v.t.,* **-fied, -fy|ing. 1** to bewilder purposely; perplex; puzzle: *The magician's tricks mystified the audience.* **SYN**: confuse, nonplus. **2** to make mysterious; involve in mystery; obscure: *the fabulous age, in which vulgar fact becomes mystified* (Washington Irving). [< French *mystifier* < *mystique* mystic + *-fier* -fy] **—mys′ti|fy′ing|ly,** *adv.*

**mys|tique** (mis tēk′), *n.* **1** an atmosphere of mystery about someone or something; mystic quality or air: *He dominated them by his reputation and his mystique, and when that was likely to fail he circumnavigated them* (Manchester Guardian). **2** a mystical or peculiar way of interpreting reality, especially one associated with a cult or doctrine and acting as a guide to action: *The mystique of Mammon has seldom found such passionate dialectics* (Time). **3** a mystic ritual: *Coloured chefs, suitably caparisoned, prepare the ducks with much devotion and mystique* (Sunday Times). [< French *mystique*]

**myth** (mith), *n., v.* **—*n.* 1a** a legend or story, usually one that attempts to account for something in nature. Most myths express a religious belief of a people and are of unknown origin. *The story of Proserpina is a famous myth that explains summer and winter.* **b** such stories collectively; mythology: *the realm of myth.* **2** any invented story: *Her sickness was a myth to cover up her dislike of the work.* **3** a made-up person or thing: *Her wealthy uncle was a myth invented to impress the other girls. "The rich farmer who spends his winters in Florida is a myth," says one agent* (Maclean's). **4** a belief, opinion, or theory that is not based on fact or reality: *He contends that he has dispelled the myth that whites will not move into a property already occupied by Negroes* (New York Times).

**—*v.t.*** to make mythical; turn into a myth: *A conservative Christianity, which hasn't mythed away God and angels, appeals to them* (Time).

[< New Latin *mythus* < Greek *mŷthos* word, story]

► See **legend** for usage note.

**myth.,** 1 mythological. 2 mythology.

**myth|ic** (mith′ik), *adj.* = mythical: *He sees his characters both as poor working people in Chicago and as mythic beings, descendants of the gods, larger than life* (Harper's).

**myth|i|cal** (mith′ə kəl), *adj.* **1** of myths: *mythical heroes.* **2** like a myth: *a mythical interpretation of nature.* **3** existing only in myths: *mythical monsters, mythical places.* **4** not real; made-up; imaginary: *Their wealth is merely mythical.* **SYN**: fictitious. **—myth′i|cal|ly,** *adv.*

**myth|i|cism** (mith′ə siz əm), *n.* **1** mythical treatment. **2** interpretation of myths.

**myth|i|cize** (mith′ə sīz), *v.t.,* **-cized, -ciz|ing.** to turn into a myth; treat or explain by myth.

**myth|i|co-his|tor|i|cal** (mith′ə kō his tôr′ə kəl, -tor′-), *adj.* both mythical and historical.

**myth|i|fi|ca|tion** (mith′ə fə kā′shən), *n.* **1** the act of mythifying. **2** the state of being mythified.

**myth|i|fy** (mith′ə fī), *v.t.,* **-fied, -fy|ing.** to make mythical; build a myth around (a person, place, thing, or event).

**myth|mak|er** (mith′mā′kər), *n.* **1** a maker of myths; fabricator: *The Communist mythmakers labored hard to destroy the myth they had once so laboriously mouthed ...* (Time). **2** a person who originates or preserves myths and legends: *He belonged perhaps to an older and simpler race of men, he belonged to the mythmakers* (Manchester Guardian).

**myth|mak|ing** (mith′mā′king), *n.* the making or construction of myths: *Frequently a respected patriarch or matriarch ... encouraged imaginative genealogy and mythmaking, so that ancestors ... became legendary heroes or beauties* (New Yorker).

**myth|o|gen|ic** (mith′ə jen′ik), *adj.* of or having to do with the forming of myths: *mythogenic forces, mythogenic processes.*

**my|thog|ra|pher** (mi thog′rə fər), *n.* a writer or narrator of myths: *Persephone is represented by most mythographers as the daughter of Zeus* (Punch).

**my|thog|ra|phy** (mi thog′rə fē), *n.* **1** descriptive mythology. **2** the representation of myths in graphic or plastic art. [< Greek *mŷthos* word, story]

**mythol.,** 1 mythological. 2 mythology.

**myth|o|log|ic** (mith′ə loj′ik), *adj.* = mythological.

**myth|o|log|i|cal** (mith′ə loj′ə kəl), *adj.* of mythology or myths; mythical: *The phoenix is a mythological bird.*

**myth|o|log|i|cal|ly** (mith′ə loj′ə klē), *adv.* according to mythology.

**my|thol|o|gise** (mi thol′ə jīz), *v.i., v.t.,* **-gised, -gis|ing.** *Especially British.* mythologize.

**my|thol|o|gist** (mi thol′ə jist), *n.* **1** a writer of myths. **2** a person who knows much about mythology.

**my|thol|o|gize** (mi thol′ə jīz), *v.,* **-gized, -giz|ing.** **—*v.i.* 1** to relate or explain myths. **2** to construct myths.

**—*v.t.*** to turn into a myth; mythicize. **—my|thol′o|giz′er,** *n.*

**my|thol|o|gy** (mi thol′ə jē), *n., pl.* **-gies. 1** a body of myths relating to a particular country or person: *Greek mythology. The tender and delicious mythology of Arthur* (Emerson). *The Pentagon has been frequently presented in ... anti-American mythology as the haunt of a bullheaded and aggressive militarism* (Punch). **2** myths collectively: *Mythology is an aspect of religion.* **3** the study of myths. **4** a book of myths; treatise on myths: *Cartari's book was the first popular mythology of the Renaissance* (New Yorker). [< Late Latin *mȳthologia* < Greek *mȳthologiā* < *mŷthos* word, story + *lógos* word, discourse]

**myth|o|ma|ni|a** (mith′ə mā′nē ə), *n.* an abnormal tendency to exaggerate and lie, especially in relating fantastic adventures as if they had really happened.

**myth|o|ma|ni|ac** (mith′ə mā′nē ak), *n.* a person subject to mythomania.

**myth|o|poe|ia** (mith′ə pē′ə), *n.* the making of myths: *Is myth an instinct or an artifice? ... Is mythopoeia chronologically prior to philosophy, or a parallel phenomenon?* (Theodor H. Gaster). [< Late Latin *mȳthopoēia* < Greek *mȳthopoiós* making myths < *mŷthos* myth + *poieîn* make, compose]

**myth|o|poe|ic** or **myth|o|pe|ic** (mith′ə pē′ik), *adj.* making myths; having to do with making myths.

**myth|o|poe|ism** or **myth|o|pe|ism** (mith′ə pē′iz əm), *n.* the making of myths.

**myth|o|poe|ist** or **myth|o|pe|ist** (mith′ə pē′ist), *n.* = mythmaker.

**myth|o|po|e|sis** (mith′ə pō ē′sis), *n.* = mythopoeia. [< New Latin *mythopoesis* < Greek *mȳthopoiēsis* < *mȳthopoiós;* see etym. under **mythopoeia**]

**myth|o|po|et|ic** (mith′ə pō et′ik), *adj.* = mythopoeic. **—myth′o|po|et′i|cal|ly,** *adv.*

**myth|o|po|et|ry** (mith′ə pō′ə trē), *n.* mythological poetry: *The English language is made for mythopoetry and epic, while the greatest poet of the language lived at the one time when the old British myths were popular in London* (Andrew Sinclair).

**my|thos** (mī′thos), *n.* myth; mythology. [< Greek *mŷthos*]

**myx|a|me|ba** or **myx|a|moe|ba** (mik′sə mē′bə), *n., pl.* **-bas, -bae** (-bē). a slime mold at the stage when it is an amebalike free-swimming swarm spore and before it fuses to form a plasmodium: *The myxamoebae ... now begin to congregate about a central point forming a mound of cells easily visible to the naked eye* (New Scientist). [< New Latin *myxamoeba* < Greek *mýxa* mucus + New Latin *amoeba*]

**myx|e|de|ma** or **myx|oe|de|ma** (mik′sə dē′mə), *n.* a disease characterized by thickening of the skin, blunting of the senses and intellect, and labored speech. It is associated with diminished functional activity of the thyroid gland: *Myxedema most frequently results from lack of iodine in food and drinking water* (Hyman S. Rubinstein). [< Greek *mýxa* mucus + *oidēma* edema]

**myx|e|dem|a|tous** or **myx|oe|dem|a|tous** (mik′sə dem′ə təs, -dē′mə-), *adj.* of or having to do with myxedema.

**myx|e|dem|ic** or **myx|oe|dem|ic** (mik′sə dem′ik), *adj.* = myxedematous.

**myx|o|bac|ter** (mik′sə bak′tər), *n.* any one of the myxobacteria: *Myxobacters live by dissolving and absorbing their victims* (N. R. Dreskin).

**myx|o|bac|te|ri|a** (mik′sə bak tir′ē ə), *n., pl. of* **myx|o|bac|te|ri|um** (mik′sə bak tir′ē əm). a group of saprophytic bacteria that secrete a slime over which they swarm to form extensive colonies: *The myxobacteria ... are widely distributed in the sea and in fresh water, and in cow-dung and similar places on land* (Listener). [< New Latin *Myxobacteria* < Greek *mýxa* mucus + New Latin *bacteria*]

**myx|o|ma** (mik sō′mə), *n., pl.* **-mas, -ma|ta** (-mə tə). a connective-tissue tumor in which the cells are separated by mucoid. [< Greek *mýxa* mucus + English *-oma*]

**myx|o|ma|to|sis** (mik sō′mə tō′sis), *n.* **1** the presence of numerous myxomas. **2** a fatal virus disease affecting only rabbits, introduced as a means of controlling them as pests. [< *myxomata* + *-osis*]

**myx|o|ma|tous** (mik sō′mə təs), *adj.* having to do with or resembling myxomas: *a myxomatous polyp.*

**myx|o|my|cete** (mik′sō mī sēt′), *n.* any one of the slime molds that grow on damp soil and decaying vegetable matter; mycetozoan. [< New Latin *Myxomycetes* the group name < Greek *mýxa* mucus, slime + *mýkēs, -ētos* fungus, mushroom]

**myx|o|my|ce|tous** (mik′sō mī sē′təs), *adj.* of or belonging to the slime molds.

**myx|o|phyte** (mik′sə fīt), *n.* a myxomycetous organism. [< Greek *mýxa* mucus + *phytón* plant]

**myx|o|vi|rus** (mik′sə vī′rəs), *n.* any one of a group of viruses that contain RNA and agglutinate red blood cells, including the viruses which cause influenza and mumps. [< Greek *mýxa* mucus + English *virus*]

***N[1]** or **n** (en), *n., pl.* **N's** or **Ns, n's** or **ns. 1** the 14th letter of the English alphabet. There are two *n's* in *cannot.* **2** any sound represented by this letter. **3** (used as a symbol for) the 14th, or more usually the 13th (of an actual or possible series either I or J being omitted): *row N in a theater.* **4** *Printing.* an en; half the width of an em.

**N[2]** (en), *n., pl.* **N's.** anything shaped like the letter N.

**n** (no period), an abbreviation for the following:
**1** *Algebra.* an indefinite number, usually a general positive integer.
**2** nano-.
**3** *Physics.* negative.
**4** *Physics.* neutron.

**n.**, an abbreviation for the following:
**1** born (Latin, *natus*).
**2** nail or nails.
**3** name.
**4** nephew.
**5** neuter.
**6** new.
**7** nominative.
**8** noon.
**9** normal (strength of a chemical solution).
**10a** north. **b** northern.
**11** not.
**12** note or notes.
**13** noun.
**14** number.

**N** (no period), **1** nitrogen (chemical element). **2a** North. **b** Northern.

**N.**, an abbreviation for the following:
**1** Navy.
**2** Noon.
**3** normal (strength of a chemical solution).
**4a** North. **b** Northern.
**5** November.

**na** (nä, nə), *adv., conj. Scottish.* **—adv. 1** no. **2** not (in compounds with *could, should,* etc.): *He canna sit still.*
**—conj.** *Obsolete.* nor.
[Old English *nā*]

**n.a.**, not available.

**n/a** (no periods), *Bookkeeping.* no account.

**Na** (no period), sodium (chemical element).

**NA** (no periods), **1** noradrenaline. **2** *Optics.* numerical aperture.

**N.A.**, **1a** National Academy. **b** National Academician. **2a** North Africa. **b** North African. **3a** North America. **b** North American.

**NAA** (no periods), **1** National Aeronautic Association. **2** neutron activation analysis: *NAA has already been used in the crime laboratory to detect counterfeit ancient Roman and Greek coins, which are a lucrative field for forgers* (Anthony Standen).

**NAACP** (no periods) or **N.A.A.C.P.**, National Association for the Advancement of Colored People.

**NAA|FI** (nä′fē), *n.* British armed forces post exchange. [< *N*(avy) + *A*(rmy) + (and) *A*(ir) + *F*(orce) + *I*(nstitutes)]

**Na|a|man** (nā′ə mən), *n.* the Syrian captain whom Elisha cured of leprosy by bathing in the Jordan (in the Bible, II Kings 5:10-14).

**naart|je** (När′chə), *n.* a small South African tangerine. [< Afrikaans *nartjie* < Malayan (compare Tamil *nartei*)]

**nab** (nab), *v.t.,* **nabbed, nab|bing.** *Slang.* **1** to catch or seize suddenly; grab. SYN: grasp. **2** to snatch away; steal. **3** to arrest: *The police soon nabbed the thief.* SYN: apprehend. [variant of *nap[4]*, probably < Scandinavian (compare Swedish *nappa,* Norwegian *nappe* catch, snatch)]

**NAB** (no periods), **1** National Alliance of Businessmen. **2** National Association of Broadcasters. **3** New American Bible.

**na|bam** (nā′bəm), *n.* a colorless, crystalline fungicide sprayed on the leaves of fruit trees and on vegetable and cereal grasses. [< *Na* (symbol for sodium) + (car)*bam*(ate)]

**Nab|a|tae|an** or **Nab|a|te|an** (nab′ə tē′ən), *n.* **1** a member of an ancient Arabian people whose kingdom extended from Syria in the west to the Persian Gulf in the east. **2** the language of the Nabataeans, an Aramaic dialect.

**nabe** (nāb), *n. U.S. Slang.* a neighborhood motion-picture theater.

**Na|bis** (nȧ bē′), *n.pl.* a group of French artists of the late 1800's, led by Pierre Bonnard and Aristide Maillol, who broke away from impressionism. They stressed purer and less fluid colors and lines in art and sculpture. [< French *nabis* (literally) prophets < Hebrew *nabi* prophet]

**na|bob** (nā′bob), *n.* **1** a native ruler in India under the Mogul empire; nawab. **2a** a very rich man, especially one who lives on a lavish scale: *The Colonel was one of the richest nabobs of his day* (New Yorker). SYN: tycoon. **b** any important person. SYN: mogul. **c** (in the 1700's and 1800's) a person who came home from India with a fortune acquired there: *Major Gilchrist, a nabob from India* (John Galt). [Anglo-Indian < Hindustani *nabāb,* variant of *navvāb* < Arabic *nuwwāb,* plural of *nā′ib* deputy]

**na|bob|er|y** (nā′bob ər ē, nā bob′ər-), *n., pl.* **-er|ies. 1** a place frequented by nabobs. **2** = nabobism.

**na|bob|ess** (nā′bob is), *n.* **1** a female nabob. **2** the wife of a nabob.

**na|bob|ism** (nā′bob iz əm), *n.* great wealth and luxury.

**Na|bo|kov|ian** (nä bô′kəf yən, -bə kôf′yən), *adj.* of or having to do with the writings or style of the Russian-born novelist and poet Vladimir Nabokov (born 1899): *Nabokovian comic anguish is the prevailing mood* (New Yorker).

**Na|both** (nā′both), *n.* the owner of a vineyard that King Ahab coveted and seized after Naboth was slain on the orders of Jezebel (in the Bible, I Kings 21:1-19).

**NACA** (no periods) or **N.A.C.A.**, National Advisory Committee for Aeronautics, superseded in 1958 by the National Aeronautics and Space Administration.

**na|celle** (nə sel′), *n.* **1a** the pod-shaped covering of an engine on the wing of an airplane or on an engine of an airship. **b** the part of the fuselage of a single-engine aircraft that contains the motor and compartment in which passengers are carried. **2a** the compartment in which the passengers are carried in airships and in airplanes with a twin tail boom, as the P-38 fighter plane of World War II. **b** the basket or car of a balloon. [< Old French *nacelle* < Late Latin *nāvicella* (diminutive) < Latin *nāvicula* (diminutive) < *nāvis* ship]

**na|cre** (nā′kər), *n.* **1** = mother-of-pearl. **2** any mollusk yielding mother-of-pearl. [< Middle French *nacre* < Italian *nacchera,* earlier *naccaro,* ultimately < Persian *nakára* pearl oyster]

**na|cre|ous** (nā′krē əs), *adj.* **1** of or containing nacre. **2** like nacre; iridescent.

**nacreous cloud**, an iridescent cloud, resembling a cirrus, seen only in northern latitudes some 15 to 20 miles above the earth; mother-of-pearl cloud.

**nacreous pigment**, = pearl essence.

**NACS** (no periods), National Association of College Stores.

**NAD** (no periods), nicotinamide adenine dinucleotide: *The availability of the hydrogen acceptor NAD is important for the dehydrogenation of alcohol to acetaldehyde* (New Scientist).

**N.A.D.**, National Academy of Design.

**na|da** (nä′də, -dä, -ᴛʜä), *n.* **1** nothingness: ... *listening to old ballads in glass-eyed rapport with nada* (John Malcolm Brinnin). **2** nothing: *"I was told that you are to become nothing, nada, you are nothing but a receptacle for Jesus"* (Richard Mann). [< Spanish *nada* nothing]

**Na-Dene** or **Na|dene** (nə dēn′), *n.* a group of American Indian languages, including the Athapascan family, and the languages named after the Tlingit and Haida.

**Na|der|ism** (nā′də riz əm), *n.* consumer protection, especially by exposing business practices detrimental to consumers; consumerism: *The emergence of a sort of British hybrid of Naderism is apparent in the way ... major United Kingdom companies are the target of increasingly strident criticism* (London Times). [< Ralph *Nader,* born 1934, an American lawyer engaged in consumer protection + *-ism*]

**Nadge** or **NADGE** (naj), *n.* Nato Air Defense Ground Environment.

**na|dir** (nā′dər), *n.* **1** the point in the heavens directly beneath the place where one stands; point opposite the zenith: *The two theories differed, as widely as the zenith from the nadir, in their main principles* (Hawthorne). **2** *Figurative.* the lowest point; time of greatest misfortune or adversity: *Efforts to achieve agreement reached their nadir.* [< Old French *nadir* < Arabic *naẓīr* opposite to (the zenith)]

**NADP** (no periods), nicotinamide adenine dinucleotide phosphate.

**nae** (nā), *adv., adj. Scottish.* **—adv. 1** no. **2** not.
**—adj.** no.

**NAE** (no periods), National Academy of Engineering.

**NAEB** (no periods), National Association of Educational Broadcasters.

**nae|thing** (nā′thing), *n., adv. Scottish.* nothing.

**nae|void** (nē′void), *adj.* = nevoid.

**nae|vus** (nē′vəs), *n., pl.* **-vi** (-vī). = nevus.

**N. Afr.**, **1** North Africa. **2** North African.

**nag[1]** (nag), *v.,* **nagged, nag|ging,** *n.* **—v.i.** to irritate or annoy by peevish complaints: *When she was sick she nagged at everybody.*
**—v.t.** to find fault with (a person) all the time; scold: *A tired mother sometimes nags her children.* SYN: torment.
**—n. 1** a person given to nagging: *She can be a terrible nag.* **2** the act of nagging.
[compare Danish *nage* vex, Icelandic *nagga* grumble] **—nag′ger,** *n.*

**nag[2]** (nag), *n.* **1** an old or inferior horse: *The ancient nag, Beauty, broke into her idea of a trot* (Atlantic). **2** *Informal.* a horse: *Bringing his nags up to the inn door in very pretty style, he gave the reins to his servant* (Charles J. Lever). **3** a small riding horse or pony: *My Ralph, whom I left training his little Galloway nag ... may one day attain thy years* (Scott). [Middle English *nagge* small horse, pony; origin unknown]

**na|ga** (nä′gə), *n.* a mythological water creature of India associated with serpents, and regarded as a spirit of peace and fertility. [< Sanskrit *nāga*]

**Na|ga** (nä′gə), *n.* **1** a member of a warlike Mongoloid tribe living in Assam, a state in northeastern India: *Naga terrorists kidnaped seven pro-government villagers in broad daylight* (Time). **2** a group of Indochinese languages, chiefly spoken in eastern Assam.

**na|gai|ka** (nä gī′kä), *n. Russian.* a whip.

**na|ga|na** (nə gä′nə), *n.* a serious disease of cattle, horses, camels, and other animals, common in Africa, and caused by a trypanosome transmitted by the tsetse fly. [< Zulu *nakane*]

**na|ge|wa|za** (nä′gə wä′zə), *n.* a form of judo which emphasizes the techniques of throwing an opponent instead of striking him or pinning and locking his body. [< Japanese *nagewaza* < *nage* a throw + *waza* skilled work]

**nag|ging** (nag′ing), *adj.* disturbing; bothersome; vexatious: *a vague, nagging suspicion. Canada's nagging problem of unemployment ...* (New York Times). **—nag′ging|ly,** *adv.*

**nag|gy** (nag′ē), *adj.,* **-gi|er, -gi|est. 1** inclined to nag; faultfinding. **2** *British Dialect.* ill-natured; bad-tempered.

**nag|maal** (naʜ′mäl′), *n. Afrikaans.* the service of the Lord's Supper, administered in the Dutch Reformed Churches.

**na|gor** (nā′gôr), *n.* an antelope of western Africa, having the horns curved forward.

**Nah.**, Nahum (a book of the Old Testament).

**Na|hal** (nä häl′), *n.* **1** a branch of the Israeli army: *The casualties were soldiers belonging to Nahal, an élite corps which combines military training with the establishment of agricultural settlements in exposed or remote areas* (London Times). **2** Also, **nahal.** a settlement established by Nahal. [< Modern Hebrew *nahal* < an acronym for "youth pioneers and fighters"]

**Na|hua** (nä′wə), *n., adj.* = Nahuatl.

**Na|hua|tl** (nä′wä təl), *n., adj.* **—n.** the language spoken by the Aztecs, Toltecs, and other American Indian tribes of central Mexico and parts of Central America.
**—adj.** of or having to do with this language.

**Na|hua|tlan** (nä′wä tlən), *adj., n.* = Nahuatl.

**Na|hum** (nā′əm, -həm), *n.* **1** a Hebrew prophet of about 600 B.C. **2** a book of the Old Testament

***N[1]**
definition 1

Script letters look like examples of fine penmanship. They appear in many formal uses, such as invitations to social functions.

Handwritten letters, both manuscript or printed (left) and cursive (right), are easy for children to read and to write.

Roman letters have *serifs* (finishing strokes) adapted from the way Roman stonecutters carved their letters. This is *Times Roman* type.

Sans-serif letters are often called *gothic.* They have lines of even width and no serifs. This type face is called *Helvetica.*

Between roman and gothic, some letters have thick and thin lines with slight flares that suggest serifs. This type face is *Optima.*

Computer letters can be sensed by machines either from their shapes or from the magnetic ink with which they are printed.

containing his prophecies. *Abbr:* Nah.

**N.A.I.A.**, National Association of Intercollegiate Athletics.

**nai|ad** (nā′ad, nī′-), *n., pl.* **-ads, -a|des** (-ə dēz). **1** Also, **Naiad.** *Greek and Roman Mythology.* one of a number of beautiful young nymphs guarding a stream or spring and giving life to it: *The Naiad 'mid her reeds Press'd her cold finger closer to her lips* (Keats). **2** a girl swimmer. **3** an immature insect in one of a series of aquatic stages of development characteristic of dragonflies and May flies. [< Latin *Nāias, -adis* < Greek *Naïás, -ados,* related to *nân* to flow]

**na|iant** (nā′ənt), *adj. Heraldry.* represented as swimming. [< Old French *naiant,* present participle of *naier* to swim < Latin *natāre;* see etym. under **natant**]

**na|ïf** or **na|if** (nä ēf′), *adj., n.* —*adj.* = naive. —*n.* a naive person; naive: *He was no naïf piping native wood notes wild* (Harper's).
[< French *naïf,* masculine of *naïve* naive]
► See **naive** for usage note.

**na|ik** (nä′ik), *n.* in India: **1a** a title of nobility or authority. **b** (formerly) a lord, prince, or governor. **2a** an army corporal. **b** (formerly) a military officer of native troops under the British. [< Hindustani *nāik* < Sanskrit *nāyaka* leader]

***nail** (nāl), *n., v.* —*n.* **1** a slender piece of metal having a point at one end and usually a flat or rounded head at the other end. Nails are hammered into or through wood to hold separate pieces together or to be used as pegs. **2** the hard layer of horn on the upper side of the end of a finger or toe in man or a claw or talon in other vertebrates. Nails are a modified form of epidermis. **3** an old measure of length for cloth, equal to 2¼ inches or 1⁄16 yard.
—*v.t.* **1** to fasten, close, or make secure with a nail or nails: *to nail shingles on a house, to nail a bracket to the wall, to nail a house together.* **2** to hold or keep fixed; make secure: *He kept his eyes nailed on the car in front of his.* **3** *Informal.* **a** to secure by prompt action; catch; seize: *He insisted on nailing me for dinner before he would leave me* (Thackeray). **b** to steal: *lubbers as couldn't keep what they got, and want to nail what is another's* (Robert Louis Stevenson). **4** *Informal.* to detect and expose (as a lie): *That lie—familiarity breeds contempt—needs nailing. Familiarity can breed love* (Manchester Guardian Weekly).
**hit the nail on the head,** to say or do something just right; guess or understand correctly: *Michael Harrington hit the nail on the head. There are a lot of Americans who aren't really living; they are just existing* (Clement Martin).
**nail down, a** to secure or hold firmly: *to nail down the lid of a box.* (*Figurative.*) *Nail him down to what he promised.* **b** to find out or settle definitely; make certain; settle finally: *With the historic rendezvous ... of the Gemini 6 and 7 capsules, the United States has nailed down its claim to be the first in space* (New York Times).
**nail in one's coffin,** something that helps to put one in his coffin or hasten his death: *Every minute he lies there is a nail in his coffin* (Scott).
**on the nail,** at once; immediately; without delay: *Why should a man be penalized for paying on the nail for his mistakes?* (Harper's).
[Old English *nægel*] —**nail′er,** *n.*

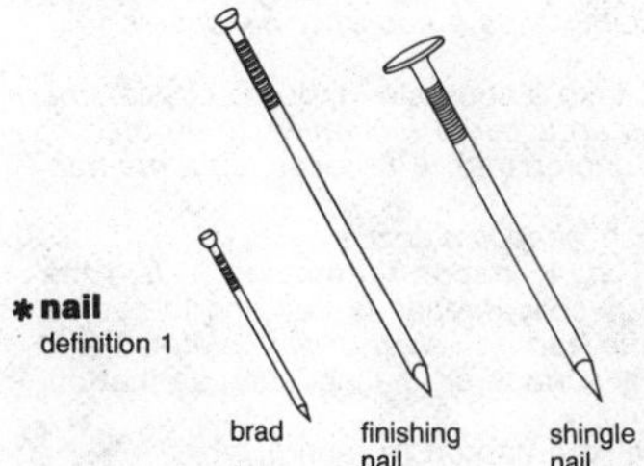


***nail** definition 1

**nail|a|ble** (nā′lə bəl), *adj.* that can be nailed: *nailable steel frames.*

**nail-bit|ing** (nāl′bī′ting), *n., adj.* —*n.* the habit of biting one's fingernails, especially when nervous, tense, or restless.
—*adj. Informal.* causing nervousness or anxiety: *It was a nail-biting finish* (London Times).

**nail bomb,** a bomb made with gelignite and filled with long nails, used especially against British troops in Ireland. —**nail bomber.**

**nail|brush** (nāl′brush′), *n.* a small, stiff-bristled brush for cleaning the fingernails.

**nail file,** a small, flat file used to file down, trim, and shape fingernails.

**nail|head** (nāl′hed′), *n.* **1** the head or enlarged end of a nail. **2** an ornament (usually one of a number) resembling the head of a nail driven in.

**nail mark,** the groove cut into the blade of a pocketknife so that the thumbnail can be used to open the knife.

**nail polish,** a kind of enamel, usually tinted, used by women or girls to smooth and give gloss to the fingernails or toenails.

**Nail|sea glass** (nāl′sē′), a clear glassware, often decorated with threads of colored glass, made in Nailsea, England, in the late 1700's and in the 1800's.

**nail|set** (nāl′set′), *n.* a tool for driving nails beneath the surface.

**nail-tailed wallaby** (nāl′tāld′), a small wallaby with a horny growth on the tip of the tail, found in semiarid parts of Australia.

**nain|sook** (nān′sůk, nan′-), *n.* a soft, fine white cotton cloth. It has a shiny finish, is sometimes dyed, and is used for underwear, dresses, and shirts. [< Hindustani *nainsukh* < *nain* eye + *sukh* pleasure]

**nai|ra** (nī′rə), *n., pl.* **-ra.** a unit of money of Nigeria, consisting of 100 kobo. [alteration of English *Nigeria*]

**nais|sance** (nā′səns), *n.* origin; birth: *Why then this sudden renaissance, or, more properly, naissance of an art?* (New York Times). [< French *naissance* birth; see etym. under **Renaissance**]

**na|ive** or **na|ïve** (nä ēv′), *adj., n.* —*adj.* **1** simple in nature; like a child; not sophisticated; artless: *... this naïve simple creature, with his straightforward and friendly eyes so eager to believe appearances* (Arnold Bennett). **SYN:** unaffected, natural, open, sincere. **2** not having or showing formal training or techniques in art; primitive: *"The United States possesses the oldest, the most original, and just about the most authentic naive painters," admitted Paris' Figaro Littéraire with an air of astonishment* (Time). **3** not previously subjected to a test, experiment, or examination; unconditioned: *The experiments just described have shown that fear of the dark, acquired by training, can be transferred to naïve animals by material extracted from the brain of trained donors* (Nature).
—*n.* a naive person: *Compared with the other partygoers, he was a complete naive.* Also, **naïf.**
[< French *naïve,* feminine of *naïf* (originally) native, natural < Latin *nātīvus.* See etym. of doublet **native.**] —**na|ive′ly** or **na|ïve′ly,** *adv.* —**na|ive′ness** or **na|ïve′ness,** *n.*
► **Naive,** although originally the feminine form of the French adjective, is used in English without reference to gender: *a naive girl, a naive boy.* The use of the masculine form *naïf* is now rare in English and somewhat affected.

**na|ive|té** or **na|ïve|té** (nä ēv′tā′), *n.* **1** the quality of being naive; unspoiled freshness; artlessness: *[She] was amused and pleased with his freshness and naïveté* (Edward G. Bulwer-Lytton). **2** a naive action or remark: *Applied with wide-eyed naivete in one instance, they may appear smartly sophisticated in another* (Saturday Review). [< Old French *naïvete* < Latin *nātīvitās* quality of being native. See etym. of doublet **nativity.**]

**na|ive|ty** or **na|ïve|ty** (nä ēv′tē), *n., pl.* **-ties.** *British.* naiveté: *They endured naivety and ignorance with almost saintly patience* (Manchester Guardian).

**na|ked** (nā′kid), *adj.* **1a** with no clothes on; bare: *naked shoulders. A barefoot boy has naked feet. And they were both naked ... and were not ashamed* (Genesis 2:25). **SYN:** nude, unclothed, undressed. See syn. under **bare. b** lacking adequate or sufficient clothing: *Poor naked wretches ... How shall ... Your loop'd and window'd raggedness, defend you From seasons such as these?* (Shakespeare). **2** not covered; stripped: *naked fields, a naked room.* **SYN:** uncovered. **3** *Figurative.* **a** not protected; exposed to attack, injury, or other harmful effect; defenseless: *... left me naked to mine enemies* (Shakespeare). **SYN:** unprotected. **b** exposed and ready for use; unsheathed: *a naked dagger.* **c** exposed to view; plainly revealed; uncovered: *a naked nerve, a naked threat.* **4** *Figurative.* without addition of anything else; unadorned; plain: *the naked truth, a naked outline of facts.* **SYN:** simple. **5** *Law.* not supported or confirmed: *a naked confession.* **6** *Botany.* **a** (of seeds) not enclosed in a case or ovary; having no pericarp, such as the seeds of a pine. **b** (of flowers) without a calyx or corolla. **c** (of stalks or branches) without leaves. **d** (of stalks or leaves) free from hairs; smooth; glabrous. **7** *Zoology.* lacking hair, feathers, shell, or other natural covering. [Old English *nacod*] —**na′ked|ly,** *adv.* —**na′ked|ness,** *n.*

**naked ape,** a human being: *The transient ambition of the adolescent naked ape ...* (New Scientist). [popularized by the British anthropologist Desmond Morris in his book *The Naked Ape* (1967)]

**naked diver,** a person engaged in naked diving as a sport or to search for pearls, sponges, and shells.

**naked diving,** underwater diving done without any equipment to aid breathing or sight. Some skin divers engage in naked diving wearing only a swimsuit and fins.

**naked eye,** the eye unaided by a glass, telescope, or microscope: *meteors visible to the naked eye.*

**na|ker** (nā′kər), *n. Archaic.* a kettledrum. [Middle English *naker* < Old French *nacre, naquere* < Arabic *nuqqārīya*]

**nal|i|dix|ic acid** (nal′ə dik′sik), an antibiotic effective against infections of the urinary tract caused by Gram-negative bacteria. *Formula:* $C_{12}H_{12}N_2O_3$ [a coined name]

**nal|or|phine** (nal ôr′fēn, -fin), *n.* a drug resembling morphine, used to test for narcotic addiction and in the treatment of morphine poisoning. *Formula:* $C_{19}H_{21}NO_3$ [< *Nal*(lylnorm)*orphine,* the chemical name]

**nal|ox|one** (nal ok′sōn), *n.* a drug used as an antidote for various narcotics. It works by blocking the paths of the narcotics to their active sites in the nervous system. *Formula:* $C_{19}H_{21}NO_4$ [< *N-al*(lyl) + (hydr)*ox*(y) + *-one*]

**N. Am.,** **1** North America. **2** North American.

**NAM** (no periods) or **N.A.M.,** National Association of Manufacturers.

**nam|a|ble** (nā′mə bəl), *adj.* **1** that can be named. **2** memorable. Also, **nameable.**

**Na|ma|qua** (nə mä′kwə), *n.* a Hottentot people of Namaqualand, South West Africa.

***na|mas|te** (nä mäs′te), *n.* a form of greeting used in India by pressing together the palms of one's hands. [< Hindi *namaste* < *namas* bow]

***namaste**

**nam|ay|cush** (nam′i kush, -ā-), *n.* a large trout of the lakes of the northern United States and Canada; lake trout. [< Algonkian (perhaps Ojibwa) *nameqos*]

**na|maz** (nə mäz′), *n.* the prescribed Moslem religious service or prayer, recited five times daily. [< Persian *namāz*]

**Nam|bi|cua|ra** (nam′bē kwä′rə), *n., pl.* **-ra** or **-ras. 1** a member of a South American Indian tribe of southwestern Brazil. **2** the language of this tribe.

**nam|by-pam|by** (nam′bē pam′bē), *adj., n., pl.* **-bies.** —*adj.* weakly simple, silly, or sentimental; lacking strength or firmness; insipid: *Valentines are often namby-pamby. She was a namby-pamby, milk-and-water, affected creature* (Thackeray).
—*n.* **1** a namby-pamby person. **2** namby-pamby talk or writing.
[rhyming alteration of *Ambrose* Philips, 1674-1749, a British poet, used by Alexander Pope to ridicule Philips' verses addressed to babies]

**nam|by-pam|by|ism** (nam′bē pam′bē iz əm), *n.* **1** weak or insipid sentimentality. **2** an instance of this: *... the namby-pambyisms of the "Book of Beauty"* (Tait's Magazine).

**name** (nām), *n., v.,* **named, nam|ing,** *adj.* —*n.* **1** the word or words by which a person, animal, place, or thing is spoken of or to: *Our dog's name is Butch. What's in a name? That which we call a rose By any other name would smell as sweet* (Shakespeare). **2** a word or words applied descriptively; appellation, title, or epithet: *"The Corn State" is a name for Iowa. Thus he bore without abuse The grand old name of gentleman* (Tennyson). **3** a title or term as distinguished from fact: *Liberty had become only a name. What is friendship but a name?* (Oliver Goldsmith). **4** persons grouped under one name; family; clan; tribe: *hostile to the name of Campbell.* **5a** reputation; fame: *to get a bad name. He made a name for himself as a writer. An honest man has a good name.* **SYN:** renown, note. **b** a famous or well-known person: *Sir William Osler was one of the great names in medicine.*
—*v.t.* **1** to give a name or names to: *They named the baby Mary. The Hudson river is named after the English explorer Henry Hudson.* **SYN:** denominate, entitle, call. **2** to call by name;

**Pronunciation Key:** hat, āge, cãre, fär; let, ēqual, tėrm; it, īce; hot, ōpen, ôrder; oil, out; cup, půt, rüle; child; long; thin; ᴛʜen; zh, measure; ə represents **a** in about, **e** in taken, **i** in pencil, **o** in lemon, **u** in circus.

mention by name: *Three persons were named in the report.* SYN: designate. **3** to give the right name for: *Can you name these flowers?* **4** to mention; speak of; state: *She named several reasons.* **5** to choose; settle on; specify; fix: *to name a price. The class named the day for its party.* **6** to choose for some duty or office; nominate; appoint: *He was named captain of the team.* SYN: select. **7** (of the Speaker of the British House of Commons or other parliamentary body) to indicate (a member) as guilty of disorderly conduct: *The Speaker "named" him, equivalent to ordering him to leave the House, but he continued to speak* (New York Times).
*—adj.* well-known: *a name brand, a name designer. There are scarcely a dozen name musicians in the U.S. who are both able and willing to play avant-garde music* (Time).
**by name, a** the name of: *She knows all her chickens by name.* **b** by hearing about but not actually having met: *We all know George Washington by name.* **c** by calling his or her name: *He mentioned the boy with red hair by name.*
**call names,** to call bad names; swear at; curse: *You can call me names, but I won't change my mind one bit.*
**in name only,** supposed to be, but not really so: *a king in name only.*
**in the name of, a** with appeal to the name of: *What in the name of common sense do you mean?* **b** acting for; with the authority or approval of: *He bought the car in the name of his employer.*
**name names,** to identify a person or persons by name, especially in incriminatory circumstances: *Six New York City teachers ... were suspended because they refused to "name names" in an investigation of Communist influence* (New York Times).
**one's name is legion.** See under **legion.**
**take a name in vain,** to use a name, properly God's name, and hence any other entitled to respect, lightly or irreverently: *Thou shalt not take the name of the Lord thy God in vain* (Exodus 20:7).
**the name of the game,** the essential thing; the thing that really counts: *The name of the game is trust; you've got to trust things* (James Dickey). *In the rough and tumble world of professional basketball, survival is often the name of the game* (Time).
**to one's name,** belonging to one: *not a dollar to his name.*
**you name it,** anything or anyone you can think of: *You name it—Fraser has written about it* (Maclean's).
[Old English *nama*]
*—Syn. n.* **2 Name, title** mean what someone or something is called. **Name** is used of any descriptive or characterizing term applied to a person or thing: *"Fun City" was a name intended to bring visitors to New York City.* **Title** is used of a descriptive or characterizing term given to a book, song, play, picture, or other work of art, or applied to a person as a sign of honor, rank, office, or occupation: *His title is Secretary.*
**name|a|ble** (nā′mə bəl), *adj.* = namable.
**name|board** (nām′bôrd′, -bōrd′), *n.* **1a** a board on which the name of a ship is painted. **b** in the absence of a board, the place on the hull where the name is painted. **2** any signboard with a name, such as of a station or shop.
**name-call|ing** (nām′kô′ling), *n.* the act of giving a bad name to; an attacking the name of; defamation: *Name-calling—giving an idea a bad label—is used to make us reject and condemn the idea without examining the evidence* (Ogburn and Nimkoff).
**name day, 1** the day sacred to the saint whose name a person bears: *The men were celebrating the Feast of St. Nicholas, the Czar's name day, with banquets and vodka* (New Yorker). **2** the day on which a child is named. —**name′-day′,** *adj.*
**name-drop** (nām′drop′), *v.i.,* **-dropped, -dropping.** to practice name-dropping. [back formation < *name-dropping*]
**name-drop|per** (nām′drop′ər), *n.* a person who practices name-dropping.
**name-drop|ping** (nām′drop′ing), *n.* the act of using a well-known person's name in conversation and implying acquaintance with him to make one seem important: *He mentioned associations with Russian leaders so numerous and so mighty in power as to expose himself to reproaches for name-dropping* (Harper's).
**name|less** (nām′lis), *adj.* **1** having no name; unnamed: *a nameless stranger.* **2** not marked with a name: *a nameless grave.* **3** that cannot be named or described: *a strange, nameless longing.* **4** not fit to be mentioned: *nameless crimes.* SYN: unmentionable. **5** not named: *a book by a nameless writer.* SYN: anonymous. **6** *Figurative.* unknown to fame; obscure: *Nameless in dark oblivion let them dwell* (Milton). SYN: inglorious. **7** having no legitimate name; not entitled to a father's name; illegitimate. —**name′less|ly,** *adv.* —**name′less|ness,** *n.*
**name|ly** (nām′lē), *adv.* that is to say; to wit: *This bridge connects two cities—namely, St. Paul and Minneapolis.*
**name part,** an important part in a play or motion picture, as that of the principal character, often having the same name as the title of the work: *He was asked to play the name part in Sherwood's "Abe Lincoln in Illinois."*
**name|plate** (nām′plāt′), *n.* a sign bearing the name of an occupant, contributor, manufacturer, or designer, and usually mounted on a door or in a lobby or other prominent part of a building: *They had painted the doors and put up brass nameplates.*
**nam|er** (nā′mər), *n.* **1** a person who gives a name to anything. **2** a person who calls by name.
**name|sake** (nām′sāk′), *n.* a person or thing having the same name as another, especially one named after another: *Theodore was proud to be the namesake of President Theodore Roosevelt.* [perhaps < phrase (*the*) *name*(*'s*) *sake*]
**name tape, 1** a cloth tape with a person's name woven or printed on it repeatedly, used for attaching each piece with a name on it on personal garments or other belongings for identification. **2** a piece cut off this tape for attachment to a garment.
**NAMH** (no periods), National Association for Mental Health.
**Na|mib|i|an** (nə mib′ē ən), *adj., n.* —*adj.* of or belonging to Namibia, the name by which African nationalists call the territory of South West Africa. —*n.* a native or inhabitant of Namibia. [< *Namib,* the coastal desert area of southwestern Africa + *-ian*]
**nan|a** (nan′ə), *n.* a woman employed to care for young children; nanny. [probably alteration of *nanny*]
**nance** (nans), *n. Slang.* an effeminate man; a sissy. [< *Nance,* short form of *Nancy,* a feminine name]
**nan|cy** (nan′sē), *n., pl.* **-cies.** = nance.
**Nan|di**[1] (nän′dē), *n., pl.* **-di** or **-dis. 1** a member of an East African people living in western Kenya. **2** the Nilo-Hamitic language of this people.
**Nan|di**[2] (nän′dē), *n. Hinduism.* a sacred bull whose image is placed before temples devoted to the worship of Siva. [< Sanskrit *nāndī*]
**Nandi bear,** a ferocious animal believed by the natives to roam the jungles of East Africa. It is generally thought to be the spotted hyena.
**nan|di|na** (nan dī′nə, -dē′-), *n.* an evergreen shrub of the barberry family, native to China and Japan. It reaches a height of about eight feet and is grown for its loose clusters of bright red berries and its thick foliage. [< New Latin *Nandina* the genus name < Japanese *nanten* < *nan* southern + *ten* sky]
**nan|dine** (nan′din), *n.* a small, spotted, ring-tailed, carnivorous animal closely related to the Asiatic palm cats. [< New Latin *Nandinia* the genus name < a native name]
**nan|du** (nan′dü), *n.* = rhea. [< Tupi-Guarani (Brazil) *ñandú*]
**ñan|du|ti** (nyän′də tē′), *n.* a fine lace of intricate design made in Paraguay. [< Guarani *ñandutí* spider web]
**nane** (nān), *pron., adv. Scottish.* none[1].
**na|nism** (nā′niz əm), *n.* (in animals and plants) abnormally small size or stature; dwarfishness. [< French *nanisme* < Latin *nānus* dwarf (< Greek *nânos*) + French *-isme* -ism]
**nan|keen** or **nan|kin** (nan kēn′), *n.* **1a** a firm, yellow or buff cloth originally made at Nanking, China, from a yellow variety of cotton. **b** a similar fabric made from ordinary cotton dyed that color. **2** a pale-buff color.
**nankeens,** trousers made of nankeen: *You had my nankeens on ..., and had fallen into a thicket of thistles* (Edward G. Bulwer-Lytton).
[< *Nankin,* early variant of *Nanking,* a city in China]
**Nan|keen** (nan kēn′), *n.* a fine Chinese porcelain, typically white with blue decorations.
**Nan|king** (nan king′), *n.* = Nankeen.
**Nan|nar** (nə när′), *n.* the moon god of Babylonian mythology; Sin.
**nan|no|fos|sil** (nā′nō fos′əl, nan′ō-), *n.* = nanofossil.
**nan|no|plank|ton** (nā′nō plang′tən, nan′ō-), *n.* = nanoplankton.
**nan|ny** (nan′ē), *n., pl.* **-nies,** *v.,* **-nied, -ny|ing.** *—n.* **1** *British.* a woman who takes care of the young children of a particular family; child's nurse: *Mistress Nellie cross-examined her on the subject of nannies* (H. Allen Smith). **2** *Informal.* a nanny goat.
*—v.t. British Informal.* to act like a nanny toward; treat as a child: *We don't want to nanny the firms taking part* (London Times).
[probably < *Nanny,* a feminine name]
**nanny goat,** a female goat. [< *Nanny,* a feminine name + *goat*]
**nan|ny|ish** (nan′ē ish), *adj.* **1** like a nanny. **2** old-fashioned; prudish.
**nano-,** *combining form.* **1** a billionth (used in subminiature units of measurement): *Nanosecond = a billionth of a second.* **2** very small; dwarf: *Nanoplankton = a very small plankton.*
[< Greek *nânos* dwarf]
**na|no|fos|sil** (nā′nō fos′əl, nan′ō-), *n.* a very small or microscopic fossil, such as that of a bacterial colony.
**na|no|hen|ry** (nā′nə hen′rē, nan′ə-), *n., pl.* **-ries** or **-rys.** a billionth of a henry.
**na|no|gram** (nā′nə gram, nan′ə-), *n.* a billionth of a gram: *a sample of fermium weighing 0.0005 nanograms.*
**na|no|me|ter** (nā′nə mē′tər, nan′ə-), *n.* a billionth of a meter.
**na|no|mole** (nā′nə mōl′, nan′ə-), *n.* a billionth of a mole.
**na|no|plank|ton** (nā′nō plangk′tən, nan′ō-), *n.* a very small plankton.
**na|no|sec|ond** (nā′nə sek′ənd, nan′ə-), *n.* a billionth of a second.
**na|no|sur|ger|y** (nā′nō sėr′jər ē, nan′ō-), *n.* surgery performed on microscopic parts of cells, tissues, etc., under an electron microscope.
**na|no|volt** (nā′nə vōlt′, nan′ə-), *n.* a billionth of a volt.
**na|no|watt** (nā′nə wot′, nan′ə-), *n.* a billionth of a watt.
**Nan|sen bottle** (nan′sən), a special container used in oceanography for taking samples of ocean water at different depths. [< Fridtjof *Nansen,* 1861-1930, a Norwegian polar explorer and pioneer oceanographer]
**Nansen cast,** a set of Nansen bottles lowered on the same wire rope and alternately closed at various depths by a sliding metal weight.
**Nansen passport,** a passport issued after World War I by an agency of the League of Nations to permit refugees to travel freely through different countries: *In the 1920's the young Nabokov, like other émigres, was really a stateless person traveling on a special Nansen passport* (Time). [< Fridtjof *Nansen*]
**Nantes** (nants; *French* näɴt), *n.* **Edict of,** an edict granting religious toleration to French Huguenots, signed in 1598 by Henry IV. It was revoked in 1685.
**Nan|tuck|et sleigh ride** (nan tuk′it), *U.S.* the towing, usually at great speed, of a whaleboat by a harpooned whale.
**nao** (nou), *n., pl.* **naos.** a sailing ship of former times, similar to but larger than a caravel and having a deck amidships. The flagship used by Columbus, the Santa Maria, was a nao. [< Spanish *nao* < Catalan *nau* < Latin *nāvis* ship]
**Na|o|mi** (nā ō′mē, nā′ō-), *n.* the mother-in-law of Ruth, a native of Judah, from whom Ruth refused to part (in the Bible, Ruth 1: 14-18).
**na|os** (nā′os), *n., pl.* **-oi** (-oi). **1** a temple. **2** the central chamber of an ancient Greek or Roman temple. [< Greek *nāós* temple]
**nap**[1] (nap), *n., v.,* **napped, nap|ping.** *—n.* a short sleep, especially one taken during the day; doze; snooze: *Baby takes a nap after his dinner.* [< verb]
*—v.i.* **1** to take a short sleep; doze: *Grandfather naps in his armchair.* **2** *Figurative.* to be off guard; be unprepared: *The test caught me napping.*
[Old English *hnappian* doze]
**nap**[2] (nap), *n., v.,* **napped, nap|ping.** *—n.* **1** the soft, short, woolly threads or hairs on the surface of cloth: *the nap on velvet or flannelette.* **2** a soft, downy surface or coating, such as that on some plants.
*—v.t.* to raise a nap on (a fabric).
[< Middle Dutch *noppe*] —**nap′less,** *adj.*
► See **pile**[3] for usage note.
**nap**[3] (nap), *n.,v.,* **napped, nap|ping.** *—n.* **1** = napoleon (def. 3). **2** = napoleon (def. 2). **3** *British.* a tip that a particular horse is certain to win a race.
*—v.t. British.* to recommend (a horse) as a certain winner.
**nap**[4] (nap), *v.t.,* **napped, nap|ping.** *Slang.* to seize; catch; nab; steal. [see etym. under **nab**]
**na|palm** (nā′päm, -pälm), *n., v.* *—n.* **1** a chemical substance that thickens gasoline. It is an aluminum soap of naphthenic, oleic, and palmitic acids. **2** the thickened or jellied gasoline, used for making incendiary bombs and in flame throwers.
*—v.t., v.i.* to attack with napalm.
[< *na*(phthenic) and *palm*(itic) acids (the salts of these acids are used in its manufacture)]

**napalm bomb**, an incendiary bomb containing napalm.
**NAPCA** (no periods), National Air Pollution Control Administration.
**nape** (nāp, nap), *n.* the back of the neck. [Middle English *nape;* origin uncertain]
▶ **Nape, scruff.** The terms differ in that *scruff,* unlike *nape,* may be used with reference to animals: *He seized the dog by the scruff of the neck.* Both words are followed by the redundant, but idiomatically necessary, phrase "of the neck."
**na|per|y** (nā′pər ē, nāp′rē), *n.* tablecloths, napkins, and doilies. [< Old French *naperie* < *nape;* see etym. under **napkin**]
**Naph|ta|li** (naf′tə lī), *n.* **1** the sixth of Jacob's twelve sons (in the Bible, Genesis 30: 7-8). **2** the tribe of Israel that claimed him as ancestor.
**naph|tha** (nap′thə, naf′-), *n.* **1** a liquid made by distillation from petroleum, coal tar, or natural gas, used chiefly as fuel and to take spots from clothing; petroleum naphtha. Naphthas, which are also used as solvents and in making varnishes, are highly inflammable, consisting of various mixtures of easily vaporized hydrocarbons. **2** *Obsolete.* petroleum. [< Latin *naphtha* < Greek *náphtha* (originally) an inflammable liquid issuing from the earth < Avestan *napta*]
**naph|tha|lene** or **naph|tha|line** (naf′thə lēn, nap′-), *n.* a white, crystalline hydrocarbon made by distillation from coal tar or petroleum, used in making moth balls, dyes, explosives, lubricants, and disinfectants. *Formula:* $C_{10}H_8$ [< *naphtha* + *al*(cohol) + *-ene, -ine*$^2$]
**naph|tha|len|ic** (naf′thə len′ik, nap′-), *adj.* of or derived from naphthalene.
**naph|thene** (naf′thēn, nap′-), *n.* any one of a group of saturated ring hydrocarbons having the general formula $C_nH_{2n}$, occurring in certain petroleums; cycloparaffin. [< *naphth*(a) + *-ene*]
**naph|the|nic acid** (naf thē′nik, -then′ik; nap-), any one of various oily liquids obtained from petroleum, used in certain soaps, paint driers, and fungicides.
**naph|thol** (naf′thōl, -thol; nap′-), *n.* **1** either of two isomeric crystalline substances occurring in coal tar, and derived from naphthalene by the substitution of a hydroxyl (-OH) radical for a hydrogen atom. Both are used in making dyes and as antiseptics. *Formula:* $C_{10}H_7OH$ **2** any one of several derivatives of naphthalene that contain a hydroxyl (-OH) radical. [< *naphth*(alene) + *-ol*$^2$]
**naph|thyl|a|mine** (naf thil′ə mēn, nap-), *n.* a highly toxic crystalline substance, with two white to reddish isomeric forms, used in dyes or as dye intermediates. *Formula:* $C_{10}H_9N$ [< *naphth*(alene) + *-yl* + *amine*]
**naph|tol** (naf′tōl, -tol; nap′-), *n.* = naphthol.
**Na|pier|i|an logarithms** (nə pir′ē ən), **1** natural logarithms. **2** an early system of logarithms which formed the basis for natural and common logarithms. [< John *Napier,* 1550-1617, a Scottish mathematician, who invented the system + *-ian*]
**Na|pier's bones** or **rods** (nā′pē ərz), a device for multiplying and dividing, consisting of narrow pieces of wood or other material which are separated into compartments marked with certain digits. It was invented by the Scottish mathematician John Napier and was used according to a method devised by him.
**na|pi|form** (nā′pə fôrm), *adj.* shaped like a turnip; large and round above and slender below: *a napiform root.* [< Latin *nāpus* turnip (< Greek *nâpy* mustard) + English *-form*]
**nap|kin** (nap′kin), *n.* **1** a piece of soft cloth or paper used at meals for protecting the clothing or for wiping the lips or fingers: *The boys left their dirty, unfolded napkins at the table.* SYN: serviette. **2** any similar piece, such as a small towel. **3** *British.* a baby's diaper. **4** *Archaic.* a handkerchief. [Middle English *napekyn* (diminutive) < Old French *nape* cloth < Latin *mappa* cloth]
**napkin ring**, a ring especially of silver, wood, or cloth, for holding a rolled-up table napkin.
**na|po|le|on** (nə pō′lē ən, -pōl′yən), *n.* **1** a pastry with a custard, cream, or jam filling, usually oblong with the filling in layers. **2** a former French gold coin, worth 20 francs, or about $3.86. **3a** a card game similar to euchre. **b** the highest bid in this game, proposing to win all five tricks of a hand. [< French *napoléon* < *Napoleon I,* Emperor of France, 1804-1815]
**Na|po|le|on|a|na** (nə pō′lē ə nä′nə, -nan′ə, -nā′nə), *n.pl.* writings, articles, personal belongings, and other physical effects, associated with Napoleon I of France; Napoleonic relics. [< *Napoleon* + *-ana*]
**Na|po|le|on|ic** (nə pō′lē on′ik), *adj.* of, having to do with, or resembling Napoleon I, or less often, Napoleon III: *Napoleonic legend.* —**Na|po′le|on′i|cal|ly,** *adv.*
**Napoleonic Code**, = Code Napoléon.
**Na|po|le|on|ism** (nə pō′lē ə niz′əm, -pōl′yə-), *n.* **1** the methods of government practiced by Napoleon I, especially the retention of unlimited power and its transmission to a dynasty. **2** any similar practice or policy: *The traditional Latin American leader's custom of renouncing ultimate power as soon as he had won it (for fear of accusations of "Napoleonism"), were less significant than the internal political and social divisions* (Sunday Times).
**nappe** (nap), *n.* either of the two equal parts of a conical surface which join at the vertex to form a cone. [< French *nappe* sheet]
**napped** (napt), *adj.* having a nap: *napped cloth.*
**nap|per$^1$** (nap′ər), *n.* a person who takes naps. [< *nap*$^1$ + *-er*$^1$]
**nap|per$^2$** (nap′ər), *n.* a person or machine that raises a nap on cloth. [< *nap*$^2$ + *-er*$^1$]
**nap|per$^3$** (nap′ər), *n.* a person who steals; thief. [< *nap*$^4$ + *-er*$^1$]
**nap|pie** (nap′ē), *n.* = nappy$^2$.
**nap|pi|ness** (nap′ē nis), *n.* the quality of having a nap, especially a thick nap, as on cloth.
**nap|py$^1$** (nap′ē), *adj.,* **-pi|er, -pi|est,** *n. Scottish.* —*adj.* **1** foaming. **2** heady; strong. **3** tipsy.
—*n.* ale; liquor.
[perhaps < *nappy*$^3$ in sense of "heady, foaming"]
**nap|py$^2$** (nap′ē), *n., pl.* **-pies.** *U.S.* a small, round, flat-bottomed dish, often of glass, with sloping sides. Also, **nappie.** [origin uncertain. Compare obsolete *nap* bowl, Old English *hnæpp.*]
**nap|py$^3$** (nap′ē), *adj.,* **-pi|er, -pi|est.** having a nap; downy; shaggy. [alteration (probably influenced by *nap*$^2$ + *-y*$^1$) of earlier *noppy,* perhaps < Middle Dutch *noppich*]
**nap|py$^4$** (nap′ē), *n., pl.* **-pies.** *British Informal.* diaper. [< *nap*(kin) + *-y*$^2$]
**nap|ra|path** (nap′rə path), *n.* a practitioner of naprapathy.
**na|prap|a|thy** (nə prap′ə thē), *n.* a method of treating disease by manipulating certain ligaments or connective tissues. [< Czech *napraviti* to correct + English *-pathy*]
**na|pu** (nä′pü), *n.* any one of various kinds of chevrotain. [< Malay *napū*]
**narc** (närk), *n. U.S. Slang.* a law-enforcement officer or agent in charge of preventing illegal trade in narcotic drugs; narcotics detective: *"I guess you know this town is on a bum trip—narcs everywhere and no good weed going unpunished"* (New Yorker). Also, **narco, nark.** [short for *narcotics agent*]
**nar|ce|ine** (när′sē ēn, -in), *n.* a bitter, white, crystalline alkaloid obtained from opium, formerly used as a substitute for morphine. *Formula:* $C_{23}H_{27}NO_8 \cdot 3H_2O$ [< French *narcéine* < Greek *nárkē* numbness + French *-ine* -ine$^2$]
**nar|cism** (när′siz əm), *n.* = narcissism.
**nar|cis|sism** (när sis′iz əm), *n.* **1** excessive love or admiration of oneself. **2** *Psychoanalysis.* gratification manifested in admiration and love of oneself, usually associated with infantile behavior and regarded as abnormally regressive in adults: *In my opinion, narcissism is the libidinal complement of egoism* (Sigmund Freud). [< German *Narzissmus* < *Narcissus*]
**nar|cis|sist** (när sis′ist), *n., adj.* —*n.* a person characterized by narcissism: *A narcissist, ... inspired by the homage paid to great painters, may become an art student* (B. Russell).
—*adj.* = narcissistic.
**nar|cis|sis|tic** (när′si sis′tik), *adj.* **1** of or having to do with narcissism: *I was just trying to make clear to a patient her excessive ambition, arising from narcissistic fixation* (Ernest Jones). **2** characterized by narcissism: *The child comes to admire himself, that is, becomes exhibitionistic and narcissistic* (Ogburn and Nimkoff). —**nar′cis|sis′ti|cal|ly,** *adv.*
**nar|cis|sus** (när sis′əs), *n., pl.* **-cis|sus|es, -cis|si** (-sis′ī). **1** a spring plant with yellow or white flowers and long, slender leaves. It grows from a bulb. The narcissus belongs to the amaryllis family. Jonquils and daffodils are narcissuses. See picture under **amaryllis family.** **2** its flower. [< Latin *narcissus* < Greek *nárkissos,* associated by folk etymology (from the sedative effect of the plant) with Greek *nárkē* numbness]
▶ In spoken English an unchanged plural, *narcissus,* is often used, presumably to avoid the excessive sibilance of *narcissuses.*
**Nar|cis|sus** (när sis′əs), *n. Greek Mythology.* a beautiful youth who caused Echo to die by failing to return her love. Nemesis then caused Narcissus to fall in love with his own reflection in a spring. He pined away and was changed into the flower narcissus.
**nar|cist** (när′sist), *n.* = narcissist.
**nar|co** (när′kō), *n., pl.* **-cos.** = narc.
**nar|co|a|nal|y|sis** (när′kō ə nal′ə sis), *n.* psychiatric analysis using narcosynthesis: *Narcoanalysis proved useful to physicians charged with the care of large numbers of emotional casualties in the armed forces of the U.S. during World War II and the Korean War* (Scientific American).
**nar|co|lep|sy** (när′kə lep′sē), *n.* **1** abnormal sleepiness. **2** a form of epilepsy accompanied by a brief unconsciousness; petit mal. [< Greek *nárkē* numbness + *lêpsis* a seizure]
**nar|co|lep|tic** (när′kə lep′tik), *adj., n.* —*adj.* affected by narcolepsy.
—*n.* a person affected by narcolepsy.
**nar|co|ma** (när kō′mə), *n., pl.* **-mas, -ma|ta** (-mə tə). stupor produced by narcotics: *Drugs such as marijuana and heroin can produce a deep and prolonged narcoma.* [< New Latin *narcoma*]
**nar|co|ma|ni|a** (när′kə mā′nē ə), *n.* a craving for a narcotic drug. [< *narco*(tic) + *mania*]
**nar|co|ma|ni|ac** (när′kə mā′nē ak), *n.* a person who craves for a narcotic drug.
**nar|co|sis** (när kō′sis), *n.* a condition of profound stupor and insensibility caused by the action or effect of narcotics or other chemicals. [< New Latin *narcosis* < Greek *nárkōsis* < *narkoûn* to benumb < *nárkē* numbness]
**nar|co|syn|the|sis** (när′kō sin′thə sis), *n.* the treatment of certain psychological disorders by guiding a person toward the resolution of emotional conflicts expressed while under the influence of a hypnotic drug: *... a short psychiatric exploration of the patient's unconscious mind by narcosynthesis* (Marguerite Clark). [< *narco*(tics) + *synthesis*]
**nar|cot|ic** (när kot′ik), *n., adj.* —*n.* **1a** any drug that produces dullness, drowsiness, sleep, or an insensible condition, and lessens pain by dulling the nerves. Opium and drugs made from it are powerful narcotics. Narcotics are used in medicine in controlled doses, but taken in excess cause systemic poisoning, delirium, paralysis, or even death. SYN: opiate, anodyne. **b** (as defined by U.S. narcotics laws) any drug that causes either physical or psychological addiction, such as marijuana, amphetamines, and LSD. **2** a person who has narcotism; drug addict. **3** *Figurative.* anything that numbs, soothes, or dulls: *The sad, mechanic exercise Like dull narcotics, numbing pain* (Tennyson).
—*adj.* **1** having the properties and effects of a narcotic; producing stupor or an insensible condition: *a narcotic drug.* (*Figurative.*) *He ... habitually fell asleep at that horrible council-board ... while the other murderers had found their work less narcotic* (John L. Motley). **2** of or having to do with narcotics or their use: *a narcotic addict, a narcotic squad.* **3** having to do with or intended for use in the treatment of drug addicts: *a narcotic substitute.*
[< Greek *narkōtikós* < *narkoûn* to benumb < *nárkē* numbness] —**nar|cot′i|cal|ly,** *adv.*
**nar|co|tine** (när′kə tēn, -tin), *n.* a crystalline alkaloid of opium, formerly thought to be a narcotic. It is used to relieve coughs. *Formula:* $C_{22}H_{23}NO_7$ [< *narcot*(ic) + *-ine*$^2$]
**nar|co|tism** (när′kə tiz əm), *n.* **1** addiction to the use of narcotics. **2** the effects produced by narcotics; narcosis. **3** abnormal sleepiness; narcolepsy. **4** anything having the influence of a narcotic.
**nar|co|tize** (när′kə tīz), *v.,* **-tized, -tiz|ing.** —*v.t.* **1** to subject to the action of a narcotic; stupefy. **2** to dull; deaden: *How much better is the restlessness of a noble ambition than the narcotized stupor of club life* (Oliver Wendell Holmes).
—*v.i.* to cause stupor; act as a narcotic: *Some drugs stimulate; others narcotize.* —**nar′co|ti|za′tion,** *n.*
**nard** (närd), *n.* **1** = spikenard. **2** the ointment which the ancients prepared from this plant. [< Old French *narde,* learned borrowing from Latin *nardus* < Greek *nárdos,* ultimately < Sanskrit *naladā*]
**nar|doo** (när dü′), *n.* an aquatic, cloverlike fern of Australia whose sporocarps are ground and eaten by the aborigines. [< the native name]
**nar|es** (năr′ēz), *n., pl.* of **naris.** the nostrils; nasal passages. [< Latin *nārēs,* plural of *nāris* a nostril]
**nar|ghi|le** or **nar|gi|le** (när′gə lē), *n.* an Oriental tobacco pipe in which the smoke is drawn through water; hookah. [< French *narghilé,* ultimately < Persian *nārgīleh* < *nārgīl* coconut (the original material of the tobacco holder)]
**nar|i|al** (năr′ē əl), *adj.* of or having to do with the nostrils (nares). [< Latin *nāris* nostril + English *-al*]
**nar|is** (năr′is), *n., pl.* **nar|es.** = nostril. [< Latin *nāris*]
**nark$^1$** (närk), *n., v. British Slang.* —*n.* a police spy; informer.
—*v.i.* to turn spy or informer.
[perhaps < Romany *nāk* nose < Sanskrit *nāsika*]

---

**Pronunciation Key:** hat, āge, cãre, fär; let, ēqual, tėrm; it, īce; hot, ōpen, ôrder; oil, out; cup, pu̇t, rüle; child; long; thin; ᴛʜen; zh, measure; ə represents **a** in about, **e** in taken, **i** in pencil, **o** in lemon, **u** in circus.

**nark**[2] (närk), *v., n.* —*v.t., v.i. British Slang.* to irritate or become irritated.
—*n. Especially Australian Slang.* a troublesome or irritating person.
[perhaps special use of *nark*[1]]

**nark**[3] (närk), *n.* = narc.

**nark|y** (när′kē), *adj.,* **nark|i|er, nark|i|est.** *British Slang.* narked; irritated.

**na|rod|nik** (nä rod′nik), *n., pl.* **-niks, -ni|ki** (-nē kē). a Russian populist of the 1800's, especially one belonging to a movement of middle-class students and intellectuals who went to live and work among the peasants to improve their condition. [< Russian *narodnik* < *narod* people, nation]

**Nar|ra|gan|set** or **Nar|ra|gan|sett**[1] (nar′ə gan′sit), *n., pl.* **-set** or **-sets, -sett** or **-setts. 1** a member of an American Indian tribe formerly living near Narragansett Bay, Rhode Island. They were of Algonkian stock, but are now extinct. **2** the language of this tribe. [American English < Algonkian (Narraganset) *naiagans* small point of land + *-et,* a locative suffix]

**Nar|ra|gan|sett**[2] (nar′ə gan′sit), *n.* a kind of medium-sized, American domestic turkey that has white markings and resembles the Bronze turkey.

**nar|rate** (na rāt′, nar′āt), *v.,* **-rat|ed, -rat|ing.**
—*v.t.* to tell the story of; relate: *In narrating interesting facts, his comments ... often fatigue by their plenitude* (Anna Seward). **SYN:** repeat, recount. See syn. under **describe.**
—*v.i.* to tell events or stories: *Most men ... speak only to narrate* (Thomas Carlyle).
[< Latin *nārrāre* relate (with English *-ate*[1])]

**nar|ra|tion** (na rā′shən), *n.* **1** the act of telling. **2** the form of composition that relates events or a story. Novels, short stories, histories, and biographies are forms of narration. [*Dante*] *the great master of laconic narration* (James Russell Lowell). **3** a story or account: *a long narration.* **SYN:** See syn. under **narrative. 4** the part of an oration in which the facts of the matter are stated.

**nar|ra|tion|al** (na rā′shə nəl), *adj.* of or having to do with narration; narrative: *a narrational style.*

**nar|ra|tive** (nar′ə tiv), *n., adj.* —*n.* **1** a story or account; tale: *pages of narrative broken by occasional descriptive passages. His trip through Asia made an interesting narrative.* **SYN:** anecdote. **2** the practice or act of telling stories; narration: *The path of narrative with care pursue, Still making probability your clue* (William Cowper). **SYN:** storytelling.
—*adj.* **1** that narrates or recounts: *"Hiawatha" and "Evangeline" are narrative poems.* **2** of or having the character of narration: *narrative conversation.* —**nar′ra|tive|ly,** *adv.*
**SYN:** *n.* **1 Narrative, narration** mean something told as a story or account. **Narrative** applies chiefly to what is told, emphasizing the events or experiences told like a story: *His experiences in the Near East made an interesting narrative.* **Narration** applies chiefly to the act of telling or to the way in which the story or account is put together and presented: *His narration of his trip was interesting.*

**nar|ra|tor** (na rā′tər, nar′ā-), *n.* a person who tells a story.

**nar|row** (nar′ō), *adj., n., v.* —*adj.* **1** not wide; having little width; less wide than usual for its kind. A path a foot wide is narrow. *You can return the board if it is too narrow.* **2** limited or small, as in extent, space, amount, range, scope, or opportunity: *He had only a narrow circle of friends.* **SYN:** confined, strait, restricted. **3** with a small margin; barely possible; barely accomplished; close: *a narrow escape, a narrow victory.* **4** *Figurative.* lacking breadth of view or sympathy; not liberal; prejudiced: *a narrow point of view. As often as a study is cultivated by narrow minds, they will draw from it narrow conclusions* (John Stuart Mill). **SYN:** illiberal, bigoted. **5** taking nothing for granted; close; careful; minute: *a narrow scrutiny.* **SYN:** detailed, scrupulous, strict, precise. **6** with barely enough to live on; very poor: *to live in narrow circumstances.* **SYN:** scanty, meager, impoverished. **7** *Dialect.* parsimonious; mean: *The chancellor's long robe ... was not so good as my own gown; but he is said to be a very narrow man* (John Galt). **8** *Phonetics.* pronounced with a narrow opening of the vocal organs; tense. **9** (of textile goods, such as braid or ribbon) woven less than 18 inches wide. **10** (of livestock diets, feed, and the like) containing proportionately more protein and fewer fats and carbohydrates than is usual.
—*n.* a narrow part, place, or thing.
—*v.t., v.i.* to make or become narrower; decrease in width or extent; restrict or constrict; limit: *The road narrows here.* (*Figurative.*) *The doctor narrowed his interest to diseases of the throat.*
**narrows,** the narrow part of a river, strait, sound, valley, or pass: *Through the narrows the tide bubbles, muddy like a river* (Robert Louis Stevenson).
[Old English *nearu*] —**nar′row|ly,** *adv.* —**nar′row|ness,** *n.*

**nar|row|band** (nar′ō band′), *adj.* operating on a narrow band of frequencies: *Broadband sounds, like those of jet aircraft, seem much louder than narrowband noise of the same sound pressure level* (Scientific American).

**nar|row|cast|ing** (nar′ō kas′ting, -käs′-), *n. U.S.* transmission of programs by cable television; cablecasting: *"The Big Giveaway," New York cable television's first game show, began live narrowcasting on public-leased Channel J from a Manhattan Cable TV studio* (New Yorker). [because of its limited range in contrast to *broadcasting*]

**narrow gauge,** a distance between the rails of a railroad less than the standard width of 56½ inches.

**nar|row-gauge** (nar′ō gāj′), *adj.* **1** having railroad tracks less than 56½ inches apart; less than standard gauge. **2** = narrow-minded.

**nar|row-leaf plantain** (nar′ō lēf′), a plantain having long, narrow leaves with prominent ribs and short, thick spikes; ribwort.

**nar|row-mind|ed** (nar′ō mīn′did), *adj.* lacking breadth of view or sympathy; prejudiced: *He is a narrow-minded man, that affects a triumph in any glorious study* (Ben Jonson). **SYN:** illiberal, intolerant, bigoted. —**nar′row-mind′ed|ly,** *adv.* —**nar′row-mind′ed|ness,** *n.*

**nar|rows** (nar′ōz), *n.pl.* See under **narrow.**

**narrow squeak,** *Informal.* a narrow escape.

**nar|thex** (när′theks), *n.* **1** a portico forming the entrance of some early Christian churches, usually at the western end. **2** a vestibule in a church that opens onto the nave. [< Greek *nárthēx, -ēkos* vestibule, casket, small receptable; (originally) a hollow-stalked plant, the giant fennel]

**nar|wal** (när′wəl), *n.* = narwhal.

***nar|whal** (när′hwəl, -wəl), *n.* a toothed whale of the arctic seas. The male narwhal has a long, slender, twisted tusk from 6 to 10 feet long, that extends forward, and develops from a tooth in the left upper jaw. Sometimes there are two such tusks. [< Danish or Swedish *narhval* < *nār* corpse + *hval* whale]

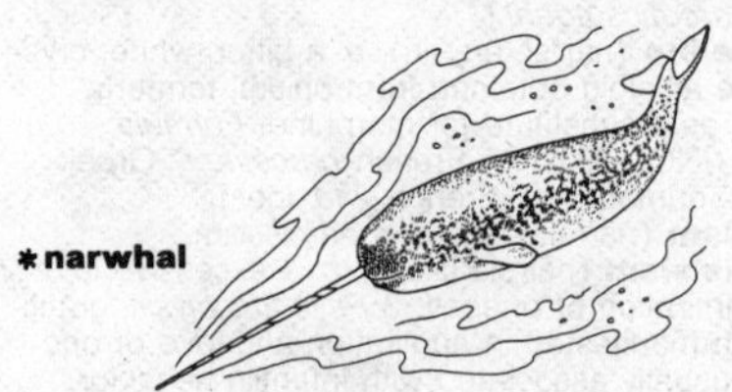
***narwhal**

**nar|whale** (när′hwāl), *n.* = narwhal.

**nar|y** (när′ē), *adj. Dialect.* **1** not: *nary a one.* **2** never a: *Three dozen steamboats and nary barge or raft* (Mark Twain). [< *ne'er a*]

**NAS** (no periods) or **N.A.S.,** National Academy of Sciences.

**NASA** (na′sə), *n.* National Aeronautics and Space Administration, an agency of the United States government established to direct and aid civilian research and development in aeronautics and aerospace technology.

**na|sal**[1] (nā′zəl), *adj., n.* —*adj.* **1** of, in, or from the nose: *nasal congestion, a nasal discharge, a nasal voice.* **2** of or having to do with the nasal bone. **3** *Phonetics.* requiring the nose passage to be open; spoken through the nose. *M, n,* and *ng* represent nasal sounds.
—*n.* **1** a nasal bone or part. **2** *Phonetics.* a nasal sound: *We call* [*m*] *a nasal because the escape of the sound through the nose gives it the characteristic resonance of the nasal passage* (Charles Kenneth Thomas).
[< Latin *nāsus* nose, related to *nāris* nostril + English *-al*[1]] —**na′sal|ly,** *adv.*

**na|sal**[2] (nā′zəl), *n.* a piece of armor on a helmet protecting the nose and adjacent parts of the face; nosepiece. [variant (influenced by Latin *nāsus* nose; see etym. under **nasal**[1]) of Middle English *nasel* < Old French < *nes* nose < Latin *nāsus*]

**nasal bone,** either of two flat oblong bones forming the bridge of the nose. See picture at **face.**

**nasal index, 1** the ratio of the greatest width (multiplied by 100) of the nasal opening in the skull to its height (the distance from the nasion to the lower edge of the nasal aperture), used in comparative anatomy. **2** the ratio of the base width (multiplied by 100) of the external nose to its height, used in comparative anthropology.

**na|sal|i|ty** (nā zal′ə tē), *n.* nasal quality.

**na|sal|ize** (nā′zə līz), *v.t., v.i.,* **-ized, -iz|ing.** to utter or speak with a nasal sound. —**na′sal|i|za′tion,** *n.*

**NASC** (no periods), **1** National Aeronautics and Space Council; a council of nine members headed by the President of the United States, concerned with developments in aeronautics and aerospace technology. **2** National Association of Student Councils.

**NASCAR** (no periods) or **N.A.S.C.A.R.,** National Association for Stock Car Auto Racing.

**nas|cence** (nas′əns, nā′səns), *n.* the quality of being nascent; birth; origin.

**nas|cen|cy** (nas′ən sē, nā′sən-), *n.* = nascence.

**nas|cent** (nas′ənt, nā′sənt), *adj.* **1** in the process of coming into existence; just beginning to exist, grow, or develop: *a nascent sense of right and wrong.* **SYN:** incipient, inchoate. **2** *Chemistry.* **a** having to do with the state or condition of an element at the instant it is set free from a combination. **b** (of an element) being in a free or uncombined state. [< Latin *nāscēns, -entis,* present participle of *nāscī* be born] —**nas′cent|ly,** *adv.*

**NASD** (no periods), National Association of Security Dealers, an organization that supervises the over-the-counter stock market in the United States.

**nase|ber|ry** (nāz′ber′ē, -bər-), *n., pl.* **-ries.** the sapodilla or its fruit. [< Spanish, or Portuguese *néspera* the medlar < earlier *niéspera* < *náspila* < Latin *mespila;* influenced by *berry*]

**Nash|ville warbler** (nash′vil), a North American warbler with a yellow throat and breast, olive back, gray head, and white ring around the eyes.

**na|si|al** (nā′zē əl), *adj.* of or having to do with the nasion.

**na|si|on** (nā′zē on), *n.* the midpoint of the region on the skull where the nasal bones and the frontal bone meet. [< New Latin *nasion* < Latin *nāsus* nose + Greek *-ion,* a diminutive suffix]

**Nas|ka|pi** (nas′kə pē), *n., pl.* **-pi** or **-pis. 1** a member of an Indian tribe of northern Quebec and the interior plateau of Labrador. **2** the Cree dialect of this tribe.

**na|sol|o|gist** (nā zol′ə jist), *n.* expert in nasology.

**na|sol|o|gy** (nā zol′ə jē), *n.* the study of the nose or of noses.

**na|so|pha|ryn|ge|al** (nā′zō fə rin′jē əl), *adj.* of or having to do with the part of the pharynx above the soft palate which is continuous with the nasal passages.

**na|so|phar|yn|gi|tis** (nā′zō far′ən jī′tis), *n.* inflammation of the nasopharynx.

**na|so|phar|ynx** (nā′zō far′ingks), *n.* the upper pharynx.

**Nas|sau system** (nas′ô), a system of scoring golf in which a point is given to the winner of each 9 holes, and an additional point for 18 holes. [< *Nassau,* capital of the Bahamas]

**Nas|ser|ism** (nas′ə riz əm), *n.* the policies and practices of Gamal Abdel Nasser (1918-1970), president of Egypt, especially his emphasis on Arab nationalism and independence.

**Nas|ser|ite** (nas′ə rīt), *n., adj.* —*n.* a supporter of Nasserism. —*adj.* of or supporting Nasserism.

**nas|tic** (nas′tik), *adj. Botany.* of or having to do with movement or growth of cellular tissue on one surface more than on another, as in the opening of petals or young leaves. [< Greek *nastós* pressed together (< *nássein* squeeze, press close) + English *-ic*]

**nas|ti|ly** (nas′tə lē, näs′-), *adv.* in a nasty manner.

**nas|ti|ness** (nas′tē nis, näs′-), *n.* **1** the quality or state of being nasty; extreme unpleasantness. **2** disgusting dirtiness; filth; dirt. **3** moral filth; vileness; obscenity.

**na|stur|tium** (nə stėr′shəm, nas tėr′-), *n.* **1** a plant grown in gardens for its showy yellow, orange, or red flowers. It has sharp-tasting seeds and leaves. The seeds can be pickled and used as a substitute for capers. **2** its flower. **3** any one of a group of plants of the mustard family, with a pungent flavor, such as the water cress. **4** a reddish orange. [< Latin *nāsturtium,* perhaps < *nāsus* nose + *torquēre* twist (from its pungent odor)]

**nas|ty**[1] (nas′tē, näs′-), *adj.,* **-ti|er, -ti|est,** *n., pl.* **-ties.** —*adj.* **1** disgustingly dirty; filthy: *a nasty room, a nasty person.* **SYN:** foul, squalid. **2** morally filthy; vile: *a nasty word, a nasty mind.* **SYN:** obscene, ribald, indecent. **3** offensive to smell or taste; nauseous: *a nasty medicine.* **SYN:** repulsive. **4a** very unpleasant: *cold, wet, nasty weather.* **b** obnoxious; objectionable: *He* [*Napoleon*] *was ... no longer the embodied spirit of a world reborn; he was just a new and nastier sort of autocrat* (H. G. Wells). **5** ill-natured; disagreeable (to another): *a nasty remark, a nasty temper.* **6** *Figurative.* rather serious; bad: *a nasty problem, a nasty accident.*
—*n.* a nasty person or thing: *They've always been around, the nasties—disguised as merely unpleasant people, as persons with hateful, mean, offensive characters* (Canadian Saturday Night).
[Middle English *nasty, nasky.* Compare Dutch

*nestig* dirty, dialectal Swedish *naskug*.]

**nas|ty²** (nas′tē, näs′-), *n., pl.* **-ties.** *Botany.* a tendency of a plant organ, such as a bud, petal, or leaf, to move in a direction determined especially by the nature and structure of the organ, rather than by external stimulus. [< Greek *nastós* pressed together (< *nássein* squeeze, press close) + English *-y³*]

**nat** (nät), *n.* (in Burma and Thailand) a demon; genie: *My gardener . . . opined that it must be some nat who was either jealous of the lawn or had an unconscionable appetite for grass* (London Times). [< Thai *nat*]

**nat.**, an abbreviation for the following:
1 national.
2 native.
3 natural.
4 naturalist.
5 naturalized.

**na|tal** (nā′təl), *adj.* **1** of or having to do with one's birth; dating from one's birth: *one's natal hour.* **2** = native. [< Latin *nātālis* < *nāscī* be born. See etym. of doublet **Noël**.]

**natal day**, = birthday.

**na|tal|i|ty** (nā tal′ə tē), *n.* **1** = birth rate: *The revival of religious ideas . . . might have some effect on natality* (Popular Science Monthly). **2** = birth. [< *natal* natal + *ity*. Compare French *natalité*.]

**na|tant** (nā′tənt), *adj.* **1** swimming; floating. **2** floating on the surface of water, as a lily pad. **3** *Heraldry.* represented as swimming, or horizontally, as a fish. [< Latin *natāns, -antis,* present participle of *natāre* to float, swim]

**na|ta|tion** (nā tā′shən), *n.* the act or art of swimming. [< Latin *natātiō, -ōnis* < *natāre* to float, swim]

**na|ta|tion|al** (nā tā′shə nəl), *adj.* having to do with swimming.

**na|ta|to|ri|al** (nā′tə tôr′ē əl, -tōr′-), *adj.* **1** having to do with swimming: *the natatorial powers of a champion swimmer.* **2** adapted for swimming: *Fins and flippers are natatorial organs.* **3** characterized by swimming: *Fishes are natatorial animals.* [< Late Latin *natātōriālis* < *natātōria,* or *-ium* bath, natatorium]

**na|ta|to|ri|um** (nā′tə tôr′ē əm, -tōr′-), *n., pl.* **-to|ri|ums, -to|ri|a** (-tôr′ē ə, -tōr′-). a swimming pool, especially one in a gymnasium or other building. [< Late Latin *natātōrium* < Latin *natātor, -ōris* swimmer < *natāre* to float, swim]

**natch** (nach), *adv. U.S. Slang.* naturally; of course.

**Natch|ez** (nach′iz), *n., pl.* **-ez. 1** an Indian of an extinct Muskhogean tribe that lived along the southern Mississippi River. **2** the language of this tribe.

**na|tes** (nā′tēz), *n.pl.* **1** = buttocks. **2** the anterior, larger pair of the optic lobes of the brain. [< Latin *natēs,* plural of *natis* rump, buttock]

**Na|than** (nā′thən), *n.* a prophet who rebuked King David for having Uriah killed (in the Bible, II Samuel 12:1-14).

**Na|than|a|el** (nə than′ē əl, -than′yəl), *n.* one of the followers of Jesus (in the Bible, John 1:45-51;21:2).

**nathe|less** (nāth′lis, nath′-), *adv., prep. Archaic.* —***adv.*** nevertheless: *The torrid clime Smote on him sore . . . Natheless he so endured* (Milton). —***prep.*** notwithstanding. [Old English *nā thȳ lǣs* never the less]

**nath|less** (nath′lis), *adv., prep. Archaic.* natheless.

**nat|i|ca** (nat′ə kə), *n., pl.* **-cas, -cae** (-sē). any one of a widespread group of predatory, carnivorous marine snails, having a globose shell with a flattened spire. [< New Latin *Natica* the genus name, perhaps < Medieval Latin *natica* buttock < Latin *natis*]

**na|tion** (nā′shən), *n.* **1a** the people occupying the same country, united under the same government, and usually speaking the same language: *The Americans, British, and French are nations. The President appealed to the nation to support his policy.* **SYN:** See syn. under **people**. **b** a sovereign state; country: *the nations of the West. The United States, Great Britain, and France are nations.* **2** a people, race, or tribe; those having the same descent, language, and history: *the Armenian nation, the Scottish nation.* **3** a tribe of North American Indians, especially one belonging to a confederacy: *the Sioux nation.* **4** *Archaic.* a great number; host: *What a nation of herbs he had procured* (Laurence Sterne).
**the nations, a** (in the Bible) the heathen nations, or Gentiles: *For all the gods of the nations are idols* (Psalms 96:5). **b** the peoples of the earth.
[< Old French *nation,* learned borrowing from Latin *nātiō, -ōnis* stock, race < *nāscī* be born]

**na|tion|al** (nash′ə nəl, nash′nəl), *adj., n.* —***adj.*** **1** of a nation; belonging to a whole nation: *national laws, a national language, a national disaster.* **2** strongly upholding one's own nation; patriotic. **3** extending throughout the nation; having chapters, branches, or members in every part of the nation: *the National Academy of Sciences. Abbr:* nat.
—***n.*** **1** a citizen of a nation: *Many nationals of Canada visit the United States.* **2a** a person who owes allegiance to a nation: *Before independence, Filipinos were U.S. nationals.* **b** a member of an ethnic group in the Soviet Union, Yugoslavia, or other Communist country: *Unlike other "nationals"— Ukrainians or Armenians or Uzbeks— the Jews don't have their own Soviet republic* (New York Times). **3** a fellow countryman; compatriot.

**national air**, a song which by national selection or consent is usually sung or played on certain public occasions.

**national anthem**, the official patriotic song or hymn of a nation, sung or played on certain public occasions, such as "God Save the Queen" in England, "The Star-Spangled Banner" in the United States, and the "Marseillaise" in France.

**National Assembly, 1** the lower house of the French legislature. **2** the two houses of the French parliament under the Third Republic. **3** the first legislature, from 1789 to 1791, during the French Revolution. **4** a title for the lower house of various national governments.

**national bank, 1** a bank that has a charter from the national government. In the United States, the national banks are members of the Federal Reserve System and at one time were permitted to issue notes acceptable as money. **2** a government-owned or controlled bank, usually closely associated with the financial structure of the country, such as the Bank of England.

**National Convention**, the legislature of France from 1792 to 1795, during the French Revolution.

**national debt**, the total amount that the government of a nation owes: *The small surplus in the budget achieved in the fiscal year just ended was used . . . to make a "modest" reduction in the national debt* (New York Times).

**national forest**, land and forest area set aside by the President of the United States to be protected and managed by the Federal government: *More than fifty million visitors are now using the National Forests alone each year* (Harper's).

**National Guard**, the reserve militia of each state of the United States, supported in part by the Federal government. Units of the National Guard meet to train periodically and are subject to call in time of emergency or war by a state or the Federal government. *Abbr:* N.G.

**National Heroes' Day**, November 30, a legal holiday in the Philippine Islands.

**national income**, the total net income of a country for a year, expressed in the currency of the country and computed as the total of money received as income or taxable revenue by individuals, business organizations, and publicly-owned undertakings in the country: *The national income of a nation bears a definite relation to that country's welfare* (Emory S. Bogardus).

**na|tion|al|ise** (nash′ə nə līz, nash′nə-), *v.t.,* **-ised, -is|ing.** *Especially British.* nationalize.

**na|tion|al|ism** (nash′ə nə liz′əm, nash′nə liz-), *n.* **1** patriotic feelings or efforts; devotion to the interests of one's own nation: *The spirit of nationalism is still far stronger than the spirit of world community* (Emory S. Bogardus). **2** extreme patriotism; chauvinism: *The experience of two wars . . . had shown . . . what too much nationalism could mean* (New York Times). **3** the desire and plans for national independence: *In an . . . appeal to the flammable nationalism of Africa's restive millions . . .* (Newsweek). **4** a form of socialism that advocates government ownership and control of all industries. **5** a word, phrase, trait, or custom viewed as peculiar to, and usually as an identifying sign of membership in, a given nation: *OK is probably the chief verbal nationalism of the United States.*

**na|tion|al|ist** (nash′ə nə list, nash′nə-), *n., adj.* —***n.*** an upholder of nationalism; person who believes in nationalism.
—***adj.*** **1** = nationalistic. **2 Nationalist,** of or having to do with Nationalist China: *a Nationalist garrison on Quemoy.*

**na|tion|al|is|tic** (nash′ə nə lis′tik, nash′nə-), *adj.* of nationalism or nationalists: *He has used the nationalistic instincts of the French more shrewdly than any politician of his generation* (Edmond Taylor). —**na′tion|al|is′ti|cal|ly,** *adv.*

**na|tion|al|i|ty** (nash′ə nal′ə tē), *n., pl.* **-ties. 1** a nation: *Several nationalities are represented in the line of ancestors of most Americans.* **2** the condition of belonging to a nation; status as a national, through birth or through naturalization. Citizens of the same country have the same nationality. *Strictly speaking, nationality is determined by legal residence* (Beals and Hoijer). **3** the condition of being an independent nation: *After the American Revolutionary War, the colonies attained nationality.* **4** national quality or character: *I have little faith in that quality in literature which is commonly called nationality* (James Russell Lowell).

**na|tion|al|i|za|tion** (nash′ə nə lə zā′shən, nash′nə-), *n.* **1** the act of nationalizing: *Control of industry, rather than outright nationalization, is the key to the new policy statement on public ownership by the Labor Party's national executive* (Atlantic). **2** the condition of being nationalized.

**na|tion|al|ize** (nash′ə nə līz, nash′nə-), *v.t.,* **-ized, -iz|ing. 1** to bring (industries, land, railroads, or other resources or enterprises) under the control or ownership of a nation, usually making the government responsible for their operation: *The United States nationalized the railroads in World War I.* **2** to make national: *The Mounties are the nationalized police of Canada.* **3** to make into a nation. —**na′tion|al|iz′er,** *n.*

**na|tion|al|ly** (nash′ə nə lē, nash′nə-), *adv.* **1** throughout the nation: *The President's speech was broadcast nationally.* **2** in a national manner; as a nation.

**national monument**, an area, especially in the United States, containing some noteworthy objects of nature or historical significance, such as Badlands, South Dakota, and Fort Sumter, South Carolina, usually maintained by a public agency.

**national park**, a relatively large area of land kept by a national government for its people to enjoy because of its natural beauty, historical or geological interest, or other remarkable feature: *Yellowstone National Park is in Wyoming. Mr. Kessel sets his story ["The Lion"] in Kenya, in a huge national park where every kind of wild animal roams free, protected from hunters and marauders by government law* (New Yorker).

**Na|ti|o|nal|rat** (nä′tsē ō näl′rät′), *n.* **1** the lower branch of the lawmaking body of Austria, whose members are elected for four-year terms. **2** the National Council of Switzerland, consisting of 200 members elected for four-year terms.

**National Service** or **national service**, *British.* the military service.

**National Socialism**, = Nazism.

**National Socialist**, = Nazi.

**National Socialist Party**, the fascist political party led by Adolf Hitler which ruled Germany from 1933 to 1945.

**National Weather Service**, a United States government agency that provides records and forecasts of the weather.

**na|tion|hood** (nā′shən hu̇d), *n.* **1** the condition or fact of being a nation: *But the great majority of former colonial people have now gained independence and nationhood* (Harper's). **2** = nationalism: *Often it was the struggle against the foreigner that brought the first strong feeling of nationhood* (Manchester Guardian).

**na|tion|ist** (nā′shə nist), *n., adj.* —***n.*** a person who favors nationalistic aspirations.
—***adj.*** favoring nationalistic aspirations.

**Nation of Islam**, the formal name of the Black Muslims.

**na|tions** (nā′shənz), *n.pl.* See under **nation**.

**na|tion-state** (nā′shən stāt′), *n.* a country whose citizens consider themselves of a single nationality because of common descent, language, history, or other cultural or physical attribute: *The Arab world is really a lot of little worlds— nation-states, kingdoms, sheikdoms . . .* (Time).

**na|tion|wide** (nā′shən wīd′), *adj.* extending throughout the nation; national: *a nationwide election, a nationwide tour.*

**na|tive** (nā′tiv), *n., adj.* —***n.*** **1** a person born in a certain place or country: *Many natives of the United States have moved to Israel to become citizens.* **2** a person who lives in a place, as opposed to visitors and foreigners: *Many natives of Florida have come from other states to live in their retirement.* **3** one of the people found in a place by its conquerors, settlers, or visitors: *The Spanish explorers were not so cruel to the American natives as were the Spanish conquerors.* **4** a member of a less civilized people, usually not white (now often used in an unfriendly way). **5** an animal or plant that originated in a place: *The zinnia plant is a native of Mexico.* **6** something grown or produced in nearby rather than remote or foreign regions. **7** (in Great Britain) an oyster. **8** *Astrology.* **a** a person born under the particular planet or sign mentioned. **b** the subject of a nativity or horoscope. [< Medieval

**Pronunciation Key:** hat, āge, cãre, fär; let, ēqual, tėrm; it, īce; hot, ōpen, ôrder; oil, out; cup, pu̇t, rüle; child; long; thin; ᴛʜen; zh, measure; ə represents **a** in about, **e** in taken, **i** in pencil, **o** in lemon, **u** in circus.

Latin *nativus;* see the adjective]
—*adj.* **1** born in a certain place or country: *native Texans. People born in New York are native sons and daughters of New York.* **2** belonging to a person because of his birth: *just and native rights of a human being. The United States is my native land; France is hers.* **3a** belonging to a person because of his country or the nation to which he belongs: *French is her native language.* **b** forming the source or origin of a person or thing; original: *Is this the way I must return to native dust?* (Milton). **4** born in a person; natural: *native ability, native courtesy.* **5a** of or having to do with the people found in a place by its conquerors, settlers, or visitors, especially those of a less civilized people: *native customs, native huts.* SYN: aboriginal. **b** ruled or inhabited by such people: *the native section of a city.* **6a** originating, grown, or produced in a certain place: *Tobacco is native to America.* SYN: indigenous. **b** grown or produced nearby. **7** found pure in nature: *native copper.* **8** found in nature; not produced: *Native salt is refined for use.* **9** in a natural state: *the native beauty of the hills.* **10** *Astrology.* born under the particular planet or sign mentioned.
**go native,** to live as the less civilized natives do: *The shipwrecked seamen, befriended by the friendly islanders, decided to go native.*
[< Old French *natif, -ive,* feminine, learned borrowing from Latin *nātīvus* innate (in Medieval Latin, a native) < *nāscī* be born, related to *gignere* beget, produce. See etym. of doublet **naive.**] —**na′tive|ly,** *adv.* —**na′tive|ness,** *n.*
—*Syn. adj.* **4 Native, natural** mean belonging to someone or something by birth or nature. **Native** emphasizes the idea of being born in a person, as contrasted with being acquired: *He has native artistic talent.* **Natural** emphasizes being part of the nature of a person, animal, or thing, belonging by birth or because of essential character: *Monkeys have natural agility.*

**Native American,** *U.S.* an American Indian.
► Many American Indians now prefer to use this term.

**na|tive-born** (nā′tiv bôrn′), *adj.* born in the place or country indicated: *a native-born New Yorker.*

**native cod,** a cod in or from the coastal waters of New England.

**native companion,** a brolga, in Australia.

**native sloth,** = koala.

**native son,** *U.S.* a native of one of the States of the United States.

**native trout,** = cutthroat trout.

**na|tiv|ism** (nā′tə viz əm), *n.* **1** a feeling or attitude of superiority shown by the natives of a country toward foreigners. **2** the policy of advancing the interests of native inhabitants rather than those of immigrants. **3** the philosophical doctrine of innate ideas. **4** a literary movement in Latin America emphasizing nature, national folklore, and the common man.

**na|tiv|ist** (nā′tə vist), *n., adj.* —*n.* **1** a person who supports or favors political nativism. **2** a person who maintains the philosophical doctrine of innate ideas. **3** a Latin-American writer supporting or advocating nativism.
—*adj.* = nativistic.

**na|tiv|is|tic** (nā′tə vis′tik), *adj.* of or having to do with nativism or nativists.

**na|tiv|i|ty** (nə tiv′ə tē, nā-), *n., pl.* **-ties. 1** a being born; birth: *I have served him from the hour of my nativity to this instant* (Shakespeare). **2** a person's horoscope at the time of his birth: *He ... proceeded to calculate the nativity of the young heir of Ellangowan* (Scott).
**the Nativity, a** the birth of Christ: *The cities have sobered down in their Christmas appearance. There are more models in the shop windows of the Nativity scene ...* (Alistair Cooke). **b** a picture of this, usually with the animals grouped about the manger. **c** Christmas; December 25: *The Nativity of our Lord Jesus Christ was now at hand* (Hamon L'Estrange).
[< Old French *nativite,* earlier *nativitet,* learned borrowing from Latin *nātīvitās* < *nātīvus;* see etym. under **native.** See etym. of doublet **naiveté.**]

**natl.,** national.

**NATO** or **Na|to** (nā′tō), *n.* North Atlantic Treaty Organization, an alliance of 14 non-Communist European and North American nations providing for joint military cooperation.

**na|tri|um** (nā′trē əm), *n.* = sodium. *Abbr.:* Na (no period). [< New Latin *natrium* < *natron* natron]

**nat|ro|lite** (nat′rə līt, nā′trə-), *n.* a mineral, a hydrous silicate of aluminum and sodium, usually occurring in white or colorless, often needle-shaped crystals. *Formula:* $Na_2Al_2Si_3O_{10}\cdot 2H_2O$ [< German *Natrolit* < *Natron* natron + *-lit* -lite]

**na|tron** (nā′tron), *n.* a mineral, a native sodium carbonate. *Formula:* $Na_2CO_3\cdot 10H_2O$ [< French *natron* < Spanish *natrón* < Arabic *naṭrūn* < Greek *nítron.* See etym. of doublet **niter.**]

**nat|ter** (nat′ər), *v., n.* —*v.i.* **1** to grumble; fret: *Their voices, like the voices of tired, nattering old women, retreated up the stairs* (New Yorker). **2** *Especially British.* to chatter; prate.
—*n.* idle chatter or prating, especially of a grumbling nature: *There is a minimum of natter in her chatter* (Time).
[earlier *gnatter;* origin uncertain]

**nat|ter|jack** (nat′ər jak), *n.,* or **natterjack toad,** a small European toad that runs rather than hops and has a yellow line down its back.

**nat|ty** (nat′ē), *adj.,* **-ti|er, -ti|est.** trim and tidy; neatly smart in dress or appearance; spruce: *a natty uniform, a natty young officer.* SYN: dapper. [origin uncertain] —**nat′ti|ly,** *adv.* —**nat′ti|ness,** *n.*

**Na|tu|fi|an** (nə tü′fē ən), *adj., n.* —*adj.* of or having to do with a microlithic culture of cave dwellers existing in the region of Palestine around 10,000 B.C.
—*n.* a prehistoric man belonging to this culture.
[< the valley of En-*Natuf,* in Palestine, where remains were found + *-ian*]

*__nat|u|ral__ (nach′ər əl, nach′rəl), *adj., n.* —*adj.* **1** produced by nature; based on some state of things in nature: *Scenery has natural beauty.* **2a** not man-made or artificial: *the natural color of hair. Coal and oil are natural products. The main reason for wanting to send a rocket to the Moon is to find out more about the Earth's natural satellite* (New Scientist). **b** (of plants) not introduced artificially. **3** belonging to the nature one is born with; not acquired or assumed; instinctive; inborn: *natural intelligence, natural ability. It is natural for ducks to swim.* SYN: innate, inherent. See syn. under **native. 4** coming or occurring in the ordinary course of events; normal: *natural feelings and actions, to die a natural death, a natural result.* SYN: regular, usual. **5** in accordance with the facts of some special case: *a natural conclusion, a natural response.* **6** instinctively felt to be right and fair, though not prescribed by any formal law or agreement: *natural law, natural rights.* **7** like nature; true to nature: *The picture looked natural.* **8** free from affectation or restraint; easy: *a natural manner.* SYN: simple, ingenuous, artless, unaffected. **9** of or about nature: *the natural sciences.* **10** concerned with natural science. **11** based on what is learned from nature by the light of human reason, rather than on supernatural revelation: *natural religion.* **12** having a real or physical existence, as opposed to what is spiritual, intellectual, fictitious, or the like: *Which is the natural man, And which the spirit?* (Shakespeare). **13** by birth merely, and not legally recognized; illegitimate: *a natural son.* **14** *Music.* **a** neither sharp nor flat; without sharps and flats. **b** not changed in pitch by a sharp or a flat: *C natural.* **c** having the pitch affected by the natural sign. **d** produced without the aid of valves or keys, as in brass instruments. **15** *Mathematics.* having 1 as the base of the system (applied to a function or number belonging or referred to such a system). Natural numbers are those that are positive integers, such as 1, 2, 3, and so on. Natural sines, cosines, tangents, and other functions are those taken in arcs whose radii are 1. They are not expressed as logarithms, but as the actual value of a ratio (of two sides of a right triangle) in which the hypotenuse of the triangle is taken as unity.
—*n.* **1** that which is natural: *This climbing business may be a natural for monkeys, but it doesn't fit a lion's life at all* (Punch). **2** *Music.* **a** a natural note or tone. **b** the sign used to cancel the effect of a preceding sharp or flat, and give a note its natural value; natural sign. **c** a white key on a piano. **3** a half-witted person: *She ... is not quite a natural, that is, not an absolute idiot* (Fanny Burney). **4** *Informal.* a person who is especially suited for something because of income talent or ability; an expert by nature: *He is a natural on the saxophone.* **5** *Informal.* a sure success.
[< Old French *naturel,* learned borrowing from Latin *nātūrālis* < *nātūra;* see etym. under **nature**] —**nat′u|ral|ness,** *n.*

***natural**
*n.,* definition 2b

**natural astrology,** astrology as used to make calendars and predict movement of the sun, moon, and planets. Natural astrology provided the basis for astronomy.

**nat|u|ral-born** (nach′ər əl bôrn′, nach′rəl-), *adj.* **1** that is so by nature; born so: *a natural-born boxer, a natural-born fool.* **2** native in a country; not alien: *a natural-born citizen or subject.*

**natural bridge,** a rock formation shaped like a bridge, especially one made by water working its way slowly through soft rock.

**natural childbirth,** the giving birth to a child without the use of anesthetics or pain-relieving drugs.

**natural frequency,** *Physics.* the frequency at which a body vibrates naturally, according to set wave patterns within itself.

**natural gas,** a combustible gas formed naturally in the earth, consisting primarily of methane, with hydrogen and other gases. It is used as a fuel.

**natural gasoline,** gasoline condensed from casinghead gas.

**natural harmonic,** one of the harmonics or overtones of an open string, produced on such stringed instruments as the viol, lute, or harp.

**natural history, 1** the study of animals, plants, minerals, and other things in nature: *Besides such common knowledge there are many items of natural history known to certain people, such as songs, habits, manner of nesting, and other details about birds or other conspicuous animals* (Tracy I. Storer). **2** a book dealing with this study.

**nat|u|ral|ise** (nach′ər ə līz, nach′rə-), *v.t., v.i.,* **-ised, -is|ing.** *Especially British.* naturalize.

**nat|u|ral|ism** (nach′ər ə liz′əm, nach′rə liz-), *n.* **1** close adherence to nature and reality in art and literature: *And with as little or as much as each artist needs of naturalism in his work, the essentials of the classics have always included expression and form as matters of the very first importance* (Atlantic). **2** the principles and methods of a group of writers of the late 1800's and early 1900's whose realism of description included all the details of an environment however repulsive and whose characters were molded by their environment. This group of writers included Émile Zola, George Moore, Stephen Crane, Frank Norris, and Theodore Dreiser. **3** action, thought, or belief based on natural instincts. **4** *Philosophy.* a view of the world that takes account only of natural elements and forces, excluding the supernatural or spiritual. **5** the doctrine that all religious truth is derived from the study of nature.

**nat|u|ral|ist** (nach′ər ə list, nach′rə-), *n.* **1** a person who makes a study of animals and plants, especially in their native habitats. Zoologists and botanists are naturalists. **2** a writer or artist who practices or advocates naturalism. **3** *Obsolete.* a physicist.

**nat|u|ral|is|tic** (nach′ər ə lis′tik, nach′rə-), *adj.* **1** of natural history or naturalists. **2** of naturalism, especially in art or literature: *The naturalistic painter ... deals ... with surface manifestations* (New Yorker). SYN: realistic. **3** of or in accordance with nature. —**nat′u|ral|is′ti|cal|ly,** *adv.*

**nat|u|ral|i|za|tion** (nach′ər ə lə zā′shən, nach′rə-), *n.* **1** the act of naturalizing: *Mr. P. G. Wodehouse ... filed a naturalization petition as a first step toward obtaining United States citizenship* (London Times). **2** the condition of being naturalized: *A suit to revoke his naturalization* (*which is the first step toward deportation since no U.S. citizen can be deported*) *was filed by the government* (Newsweek).

**nat|u|ral|ize** (nach′ər ə līz, nach′rə-), *v.,* **-ized, -iz|ing.** —*v.t.* **1** to admit (a foreigner) to citizenship. After living in the United States for a certain number of years, an immigrant can be naturalized if he passes a test. **2** to adopt (a foreign word or custom): *"Chauffeur" is a French word that has been naturalized in English.* **3a** to introduce and make at home (animals or plants) in another country: *The English oak has been naturalized in parts of Massachusetts.* **b** *Figurative.* to adapt or accustom to a place or to new surroundings: *I was now in my twenty-third year of residence ... and was ... naturalized to the place, and to the manner of living* (Daniel Defoe). SYN: acclimate, adjust. **4** to make natural; free from conventional characteristics. **5** to regard or explain as natural rather than supernatural: *to naturalize miracles.*
—*v.i.* **1** to become like a native. **2** to become a citizen of another country. **3** to be occupied with natural history.

**natural language,** any language that has evolved naturally over the ages, as distinguished from an artificially devised language: *It is a fallacy ... to suppose that the layman can be enabled to use a computer simply by designing a computer language to look like a natural language properly* (New Scientist).

**natural law, 1** law based upon nature or the natural tendency of human beings to exercise right reason in dealings with others. Natural law precedes and is regarded as the basis of common law. **2** a law or the laws of nature: *While it* *is apparent that natural laws are not infallible, nevertheless some of them hold within the limits of experimental accuracy* (Parks and Steinbach).

**natural logarithm**, a logarithm in which the base is the irrational number *e*, whose value is equal to 2.71828183+, used in analytical work.

**nat|u|ral|ly** (nach′ər ə lē, nach′rə-), *adv.* **1** in a natural way: *Speak naturally; don't try to imitate some actress.* **SYN**: unaffectedly. **2** by nature; without special teaching or training: *a naturally obedient child.* **3** as might be expected; of course: *She offered me some candy; naturally, I took it.*

**natural magnet**, a piece of magnetite; loadstone.

**natural number**, a positive integer; whole number. Natural numbers are 1, 2, 3, 4, and so on.

**natural philosopher**, **1** a student of natural philosophy. **2** = physicist.

**natural philosophy**, **1** = physics. **2** = natural science.

**natural resources**, materials supplied by nature that are useful or necessary for life. Minerals, timber, land, and water power are natural resources. *The effect of a diminution of natural resources is to lower the standard of living* (Ogburn and Nimkoff).

**natural rights**, rights instinctively felt to be right and fair, although not prescribed by any formal agreement.

**natural science**, **1** any science dealing with the facts of nature or the physical world. Zoology, botany, geology, chemistry, and physics are natural sciences as contrasted with such fields as pure mathematics, philosophy, or social science. **2** these sciences or branches of knowledge collectively.

**natural scientist**, a person who is trained or who works in the field of natural science.

**natural selection**, the process in nature by which animals and plants best adapted to their environment tend to survive; tendency of the environment to permit those members of its population to survive and breed who are best adapted to it by their genetic makeup: *In the formation of races and species, in man as in other animals, natural selection rarely takes place quickly* (Atlantic).

**natural sign**, the sign in music used to cancel the effect of a preceding sharp or flat; a natural.

**natural theology**, the study of theology pursued only by natural reason without the aid of supernatural revelation.

**natural uranium**, uranium as found in nature, or refined, with little or no fissionable material added.

**natural year**, = astronomical year.

**na|ture** (nā′chər), *n.* **1** the world; all things except those made by man: *the wonders of nature.* **SYN**: universe, cosmos. **2** the sum total of the forces at work throughout the universe: *the laws of nature.* **3** the regular ways in which people or things are and act; instincts or inherent tendencies directing conduct: *It is against nature for a mother to hurt her child. It is ... my nature, to believe the best of people* (George W. Curtis). **SYN**: temperament. **4** reality: *true to nature.* **5** life without artificial things; primitive, wild condition; condition of human beings before social organization: *The hermit lived in a state of nature.* **6** what a thing really is; quality; character: *It is the nature of robins to fly and to build nests.* **7** a particular sort; kind: *Books of a scientific nature do not interest her.* **SYN**: type. **8a** the basic functions of a living organism; physical being; vital powers: *food sufficient to sustain nature.* **b** a natural desire or function, such as that of sex or elimination: *the demands of nature.* **9** a person of a particular character: *She is a gentle nature.* **10** the moral state as unaffected by grace. **11** *Dialect.* natural feeling or affection.

**by nature**, because of the essential character of the person or thing: *Adeline was liberal by nature* (Byron).

**of** (or **in**) **the nature of**, having the nature of; being a kind of; being: *A Peace is of the nature of a Conquest* (Shakespeare).

[< Old French *nature*, learned borrowing from Latin *nātūra* birth, character < *nāscī* be born; see etym. under **native**]

**Na|ture** (nā′chər), *n.* the personification of all natural facts and forces: *Who can paint like Nature? Can imagination boast ... hues like hers?* (James Thomson).

**-natured**, *combining form.* having a ___ nature: *Good-natured = having a good nature.*

**na|ture morte** (nȧ tyr′ môrt′), *French.* a still life: *Of his small final natures mortes, one depicts a carafe and lemon, another a wineglass and egg* (New Yorker).

**nature strip**, *Australian.* a grassy area between a footpath and a road.

**nature study**, the study of animals, plants, and other things and events in nature.

**nature walk**, a walk through the countryside, a park, or similar area, for the purpose of observing or studying its plant or animal life.

**na|tur|ism** (nā′chə riz əm), *n. Especially British.* nudism.

**na|tur|ist** (nā′chər ist), *n., adj. Especially British.* —*n.* a nudist.
—*adj.* of or for nudists; nudist: *a naturist camp.*

**na|tur|o|path** (nā′chər ə path), *n.* a person who practices naturopathy.

**na|tur|o|path|ic** (nā′chər ə path′ik), *adj.* of or having to do with naturopathy.

**na|tur|op|a|thy** (nā′chə rop′ə thē), *n.* a system of therapy in which natural agencies, such as fresh air and exercise, are preferred to drugs or surgery. [< Latin *nātūra* (see etym. under **nature**) + English *-pathy*]

**Nau|ga|hyde** (nô′gə hīd), *n. U.S. Trademark.* a vinyl upholstery fabric resembling leather.

**naught** (nôt), *n., adv., adj.* —*n.* **1** nothing: *to ask naught for oneself. Away! all will be naught else* (Shakespeare). **SYN**: nil. **2** zero; 0: *Two naughts after a six make six hundred.* **SYN**: cipher. **3** a person or thing of no worth or importance; a mere nothing.
—*adv. Archaic.* in no way; not at all: *The trial hath ... Me naught advantaged* (Milton).
—*adj.* **1** good for nothing; worthless; useless: *It is naught, it is naught, saith the buyer: but when he is gone his way, then he boasteth* (Proverbs 20:14). **2** *Obsolete.* **a** (of things) bad in condition. **b** (of actions) injurious or wicked. Also, **nought**.

**set at naught**, to slight; disregard; disdain: *I am an aristocrat and it is my whim to set good manners at naught* (Punch).

[Old English *nāwiht* < *nā* no + *wiht* thing (wight)]

**naugh|ty** (nô′tē), *adj.*, **-ti|er**, **-ti|est**. **1** not obedient; bad: *The naughty child hit his baby sister.* **SYN**: mischievous. **2** somewhat improper; risqué: *a naughty joke.* **SYN**: racy. **3** *Archaic.* morally bad; wicked: *naughty persons, lewdly bent* (Shakespeare). [Middle English *naughty* having nothing; later, good for nothing < *naught* nothing] —**naugh′ti|ly**, *adv.* —**naugh′ti|ness**, *n.*

**nau|ma|chi|a** (nô mā′kē ə), *n., pl.* **-chi|ae** (-kē ē), **-chi|as**. **1** a mock sea fight staged by the ancient Romans as a spectacle. **2** a place for staging such spectacles. [< Latin *naumachia* < Greek *naumachiā* < *naûs* ship + *máchē* a fight]

**nau|pli|al** (nô′plē əl), *adj.* having the character of a nauplius.

**nau|pli|us** (nô′plē əs), *n., pl.* **-pli|i** (-plē ī). the first stage in development of certain crustaceans, such as the shrimp, after leaving the egg; a larval form with an unsegmented body, three pairs of appendages, and a single median eye. [< Latin *nauplius* a kind of shellfish < Greek *naúplios*]

**Na|u|ru|an** (nä ü′rə wən), *adj., n.* —*adj.* of or having to do with Nauru, a small island in the central Pacific Ocean, noted for its valuable deposits of high-grade phosphate.
—*n.* **1** a native or inhabitant of Nauru. **2** the language of Nauru.

**nau|sea** (nô′shə, -shē ə, -sē ə), *n.* **1** the feeling that one is about to vomit. **2** seasickness: *Most of the ship's passengers were seized with nausea during the storm at sea.* **3** *Figurative.* extreme disgust; loathing: *... sated to nausea as we have been with the doctrines of sentimentality* (Scott). **SYN**: repugnance. [< Latin *nausea* < Greek *nausiā* < *naûs* ship. See etym. of doublet **noise**.]

**nau|se|ant** (nô′shē ənt, -sē-), *adj.* inducing nausea or vomiting: *a nauseant drug.*

**nau|se|ate** (nô′shē āt, -sē-), *v.*, **-at|ed**, **-at|ing**.
—*v.t.* **1** to cause nausea in; make sick. **2** to reject (food) with loathing or a feeling of nausea: *Many dishes are commended in one age that are nauseated in another* (Sir Thomas Browne). **3** *Figurative.* to cause to feel loathing.
—*v.i.* to feel nausea; become sick: *the old-fashioned civility that presses food upon you until you nauseate* (Scott).
[< Latin *nauseāre* (with English *-ate*[1]) be seasick < *nausea* nausea] —**nau′se|at′ing|ly**, *adv.*
—**nau′se|a′tion**, *n.*

**nau|seous** (nô′shəs, -shē əs, -sē-), *adj.* **1** causing nausea; sickening: *a kind of slimy stuff ... of a most nauseous, odious smell* (Daniel Defoe). **2** *Figurative.* disgusting; loathsome: *The garbage dump was nauseous.* **3** feeling nausea; nauseated. [< Latin *nauseōsus* < *nausea* nausea]
—**nau′seous|ly**, *adv.* —**nau′seous|ness**, *n.*

**Nau|sic|a|ä** (nô sik′ā ə, -ē ə), *n. Greek Legend.* the maiden who, in the *Odyssey*, aided Odysseus (Ulysses) when he was shipwrecked.

**naut.**, nautical.

**nautch** (nôch), *n.* an entertainment consisting of dancing by professional dancing girls wearing light, filmy garments, originally in India but now imitated elsewhere. [< Hindustani *nāch* < Prakrit *nacca* < Sanskrit *nṛtya* dancing < *nṛit* to dance]

**nau|ti|cal** (nô′tə kəl), *adj.* having something to do with ships, sailors, or navigation: *nautical charts.* **SYN**: maritime. [< Latin *nauticus* (< Greek *nautikós* < *naûs* ship) + English *-al*[1]] —**nau′ti|cal|ly**, *adv.*

**nautical measure**, a system of linear measure used in navigation.

**nautical mile**, 6,076.11549 feet, the standard unit of distance in nautical measure; sea mile; international nautical mile.

**nau|ti|loid** (nô′tə loid), *adj., n.* —*adj.* resembling the nautilus in form: *nautiloid shells.*
—*n.* a nautiloid mollusk.

***nau|ti|lus** (nô′tə ləs), *n., pl.* **-lus|es**, **-li** (-lī). either of two small mollusks of warm seas. The pearly nautilus, or chambered nautilus, has a spiral shell with a pearly lining, divided into many compartments by septa. The paper nautilus has saillike arms and a very thin shell. It looks somewhat like an octopus. [< Latin *nautilus* < Greek *nautílos* (originally) sailor < *naûs* ship]

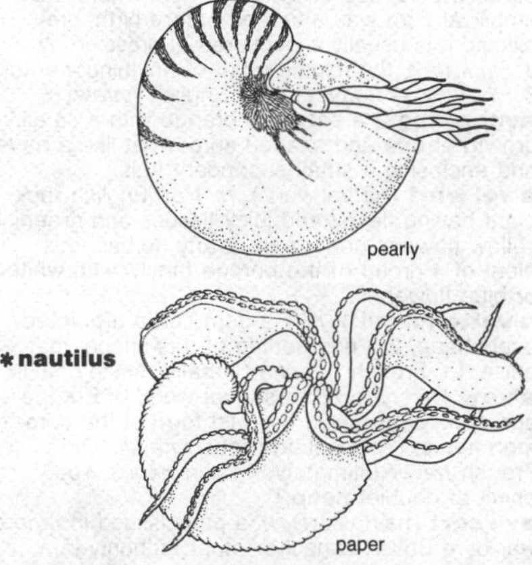

***nautilus**

**nav.**, **1** naval. **2** navigation.

**Nav|a|ho** (nav′ə hō), *n., pl.* **-ho**, **-hos**, or **-hoes**. **1** a member of a large tribe of American Indians of Athapascan stock living in New Mexico, Arizona, and Utah. The Navaho are noted for their skill in making turquoise and silver jewelry and in weaving blankets and rugs with bright patterns, usually of black, red and white color. **2** the language of this tribe. [American English < Mexican Spanish *Navajo* < Nahuatl *navajoa* place of the prickly pear cactus < *nava-* prickly pear cactus + *-joa* place of (from the abundance of this plant where the Navahos live)]

**nav|aid** (nav′ād′), *n.* a piece of electronic equipment designed to help in air navigation: *These "navaids" range from small location-marker beacons on the ground that light a bulb on the aircraft's instrument panel as it passes overhead to huge, long-range radar systems* (Time). [< *nav*(igation) *aid*]

**Nav|a|jo** (nav′ə hō), *n., pl.* **-jo**, **-jos**, or **-joes**. = Navaho.

**nav|a|jo|ite** (nav′ə hō′īt), *n.* a mineral of vanadium discovered in Arizona. [< *Navajo* + *-ite*[1] (because it was discovered on a Navajo reservation)]

**na|val** (nā′vəl), *adj.* **1** of the navy; for warships or the navy: *a naval officer, naval supplies, a naval squadron.* **2** having a navy: *the great naval powers.* **3** accomplished by means of ships or a navy: *naval strategy.* **4** nautical; maritime. [< Latin *nāvālis* < *nāvis* ship] —**na′val|ly**, *adv.*

**naval academy**, a school for training seamen. The United States Naval Academy is a school at Annapolis, Maryland, for training naval officers, founded in 1845.

**naval architect**, a person who designs ships.

**naval dockyard**, *British.* navy yard.

**naval holiday**, a period of cessation or reduction of naval activities, among nations not actually at war, by limitation of armaments and construction, usually to promote the interests of international peace.

**na|val|ism** (nā′və liz əm), *n.* the principle or policy of building up or maintaining a strong navy for a country.

**na|val|ist** (nā′və list), *n.* an advocate of navalism.

**naval stores**, rosin, turpentine, tar, pitch, and other materiel used in building and repairing wooden ships.

***nave**[1] (nāv), *n.* the main part of a church or cathedral between the side aisles. The nave ex-

**Pronunciation Key:** hat, āge, cãre, fär; let, ēqual, tėrm; it, īce; hot, ōpen, ôrder; oil, out; cup, pu̇t, rüle; child; long; thin; ᴛʜen; zh, measure; ə represents **a** in about, **e** in taken, **i** in pencil, **o** in lemon, **u** in circus.

tends from the main entrance to the transepts. [< Medieval Latin *navis* < Latin *nāvis* ship]

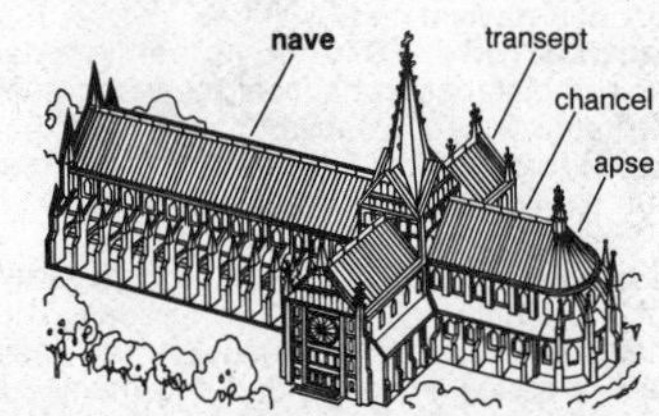

***nave[1]**

**nave[2]** (nāv), *n.* **1** the central part of a wheel, into which the axle is fitted; hub. **2** *Obsolete.* the navel. [Old English *nafu*]

**na|vel** (nā′vəl), *n.* **1** the mark or scar in the middle of the surface of the abdomen, where the umbilical cord was attached before birth; umbilicus. It is usually a puckered depression. **2** *Figurative.* the middle point of anything; center. **3** *Heraldry.* = nombril. [Old English *nafela*]

**navel orange**, a seedless orange with a small growth at one end shaped somewhat like a navel and enclosing a small secondary fruit.

**na|vel|wort** (nā′vəl wėrt′), *n.* **1** an English rock plant having fleshy and juicy tissues and greenish yellow flowers; pennywort. **2** any herbaceous plant of a group of the borage family, with white or blue flowers.

**na|vette** (nə vet′), *n.* **1** a gem cut to a pointed oval shape. **2** a ring setting of this shape; marquise. [< French *navette* (literally) small boat]

**na|vew** (nā′vyü), *n.* an annual weed of Europe and Asia, considered the wild form of the common turnip. [< obsolete French *naveu,* Old French *navel,* ultimately < Latin *nāpus.* See etym. of doublet **neep.**]

**nav|i|cert** (nav′ə sėrt), *n.* a pass issued in time of war by a British consul or other authority in a neutral country making goods exempt from seizure or search by naval vessels of Great Britain or its allies. [< *navi*(gation) *cert*(ificate)]

**na|vic|u|lar** (nə vik′yə lər), *adj., n.* —*adj.* resembling a boat in shape, as certain bones; scaphoid.
—*n.* **1a** a bone of the human foot between the talus and the metatarsals. See picture under **foot. b** a bone of the human wrist shaped like a comma. It is one of the eight short bones that make up this joint. **2** a small, oval bone in the foot of a horse.
[< Late Latin *nāviculāris* of a ship < Latin *nāvicula* (diminutive) < *nāvis* ship]

**na|vic|u|la|re** (nə vik′yə lãr′ē), *n.* = navicular.

**navig.**, navigation.

**nav|i|ga|bil|i|ty** (nav′ə gə bil′ə tē), *n.* the condition of being navigable.

**nav|i|ga|ble** (nav′ə gə bəl), *adj.* **1** that ships can travel on or through: *The Mississippi River is deep enough to be navigable.* **2** that can be sailed; seaworthy. **3** that can be steered: *Without a rudder the ship was not navigable.* SYN: steerable, dirigible. —**nav′i|ga|ble|ness,** *n.*

**nav|i|ga|bly** (nav′ə gə blē), *adv.* so as to be navigable.

**nav|i|gate** (nav′ə gāt), *v.,* **-gat|ed, -gat|ing.** —*v.t.* **1a** to sail, manage, or steer (a ship, aircraft, or rocket) on a course or to a destination: *If the captain died, the mate was in duty bound to navigate the ship to the nearest civilized port* (Herman Melville). **b** to direct (anything) on a course: *The President navigates the ship of state.* **2** to sail over or on (a sea or river). **3** to convey (goods) by water. **4** to fly through (the air) in or as if in an aircraft: *Stories of wizards and witches who navigated the upper air with the assistance of tubs and broomsticks* (C. L. M. Brown). **5** *Figurative.* to manage to get up, over, past, or through; negotiate: *to navigate the ramps in a garage, navigate a curving flight of stairs.* **6** *Figurative.* to guide, steer, or make (one's way).
—*v.i.* **1a** to travel by water; sail. **b** (of vessels) to sail the seas; ply. **2** to direct or manage the course of a ship or aircraft; be a navigator. **3** to move, walk, or swim about: *Turtles can navigate from one part of the ocean to another.* (*Figurative.*) *I can scarcely navigate today.* **4** *Figurative.* to guide, steer, or make one's way.
[< Latin *nāvigāre* (with English *-ate*) < *nāvis* ship + *agere* to drive]

**nav|i|ga|tion** (nav′ə gā′shən), *n.* **1** the act or process of navigating. **2** the art or science of figuring out the position and course of a ship, aircraft, or rocket. This may be done by making various calculations based on the triangle or the arc after making certain measurements of distance in relation to the position of a craft to heavenly bodies, radio beacons, landmarks, etc.

**nav|i|ga|tion|al** (nav′ə gā′shə nəl), *adj.* of, having to do with, or used in navigation.

**navigational satellite**, an artificial earth satellite that transmits astronomical and meteorological data to earth as an aid in navigation.

**navigation light**, one of the lights on an aircraft to make its size, position, and course visible at night.

**nav|i|ga|tor** (nav′ə gā′tər), *n.* **1** a person who has charge of the navigating of a ship or aircraft or who is skilled in navigating: *Navigators on ships and aircraft must work mathematical problems to find where they are in relation to landmarks and stars* (P. V. H. Weems). **2** a person who sails the seas: *The navigator set out on his long voyage.* **3** an explorer of the seas: *Columbus, Magellan, and other great navigators.* **4** *British.* a navvy. [< Latin *nāvigātor* < *nāvigāre;* see etym. under **navigate**]

**nav|vy** (nav′ē), *n., pl.* **-vies,** *v.,* **-vied, -vy|ing.** *Especially British.* —*n.* an unskilled laborer employed in the excavation and construction of canals, railways, roads, and other large undertakings: *O'Casey became a navvy and bricklayer when he grew up* (New Yorker).
—*v.i.* to work as a navvy: ... *Victoria Station, where he happened to be navvying at the time* (Punch).
—*v.t.* to excavate.
[short for *navigator*]

**na|vy** (nā′vē), *n., pl.* **-vies. 1** Often, **Navy.** all the ships of war of a country, with their officers and men and the department that manages them. Most navies now have aircraft and large land areas devoted to their task of protecting a nation. **2** the officers and men of the navy: *The parade included many of the navy.* **3** the ships and men of the British merchant fleet. **4** *Archaic.* a fleet of ships. **5** = navy blue. [< Old French *navie,* ultimately < Latin *nāvis* ship]

**navy bean**, a small, common white bean, dried for use as food, usually baked or in soup: *Commodore Perry coined the term "navy bean" while eating lunch one day out on Lake Erie during a British assault* (Philip Hamburger).

**navy blue**, a dark blue.

**Navy Cross**, a decoration awarded by the U.S. Navy for bravery in action.

**Navy Day**, October 27, a day formerly observed in honor of the U.S. Navy, now abolished in favor of Armed Forces Day.

**Navy Exchange** or **Navy exchange**, a general store at a naval base that sells cigarettes, candy, food, and personal items, to naval personnel.

**Navy Jack**, the union jack of the United States Navy.

**navy yard**, a government dockyard where naval vessels are built, repaired, and fitted out, and where naval stores and munitions of war are kept.

**Na|wab** (nə wôb′), *n.* a title given to important Moslems in India, giving princely status immediately below that of the Nizam of Hyderabad. [< variant of Arabic *nuwwāb;* see etym. under **nabob**]

**na|wab** (nə wôb′), *n.* **1** a native ruler in India under the Mogul empire; nabob. Nawabs were viceroys or direct deputies of the reigning head of the government. **2a** a very rich man; nabob. **b** any important or powerful person. [< *Nawab*]

**Nax|a|lite** (nak′sə līt), *n., adj.* —*n.* any one of a group of Communist revolutionaries, originally of West Bengal, engaged in terrorist activities in India.
—*adj.* of or belonging to the Naxalites: *Naxalite extremism.*
[< *Naxal*(bari), a district of West Bengal + *-ite*[1]]

**nay[1]** (nā), *adv., n.* —*adv.* **1** not only that, but also: *We are willing—nay, eager—to go. The daily work continued; nay, it actually increased* (Lytton Strachey). **2** *Archaic.* no: *He would not say her nay* (Sir Richard Steele).
—*n.* **1** a denial or refusal; no. **2** a vote or voter against something: *In response to a scattered voice vote, Speaker Rayburn ... facetiously remarked that the tally was three ayes and two nays, the ayes have it* (Wall Street Journal).
[< Scandinavian (compare Old Icelandic *nei* < *ne* not + *ei* ever)]

**nay[2]** (nā), *n.* an ancient Egyptian flute, usually with six holes and the mouth opening on the side. [< Arabic *nāy*]

**na|ya pai|sa** (nə yä′ pī sä′), *pl.* **na|ye pai|se** (nə yā′ pī sā′), a coin of India that replaced the pice in 1957, since 1964 called paisa, equal to 1/100 of a rupee. [< Hindi *nayā paisā* new pice]

**nay|say** (nā′sā′), *v., n.* —*v.t., v.i.* to say nay (to); deny; oppose; vote in the negative.
—*n. Archaic.* a denial or refusal. —**nay′say′er,** *n.*

**nay|word** (nā′wėrd′), *n. Especially British.* **1** a watchword. **2** a byword.

**Naz|a|rene** (naz′ə rēn′, naz′ə rēn), *n., adj.* —*n.* **1** a person born or living in Nazareth, a town in northern Palestine where Jesus lived during his boyhood. **2** an early Christian: *For we have found this man* [*Paul*] ... *a ringleader of the sect of the Nazarenes* (Acts 24:5). **3** a member of the Church of the Nazarene in the United States, a Protestant denomination following the early teachings of Methodism. **4** one of a group of German painters of the early 1800's, who tried to recapture the primitive religious intensity of medieval Christian art.
—*adj.* of or having to do with the Nazarenes or with Nazareth.
**the Nazarene**, Jesus Christ: *Some versions of the New Testament use the phrase "Jesus the Nazarene" instead of "Jesus of Nazareth."*
[< Late Latin *Nazarēnus* < Greek *Nazarēnós* < *Nazarét* Nazareth]

**Naz|a|rite** (naz′ə rīt), *n.* **1** (among the ancient Hebrews) a Jew who had taken certain strict religious vows (in the Bible, Numbers 6:1-27). **2** a native of Nazareth; Nazarene. Also, **Nazirite.** [< Late Latin *Nazaraeus* (< Greek *Nāzōraîos* dedicated one < Hebrew *nāzīr*) + English *-ite*[1]]

**Naz|ca** (näs′kə), *n.* a member of a people who lived in Peru around the time of Christ, noted for their pottery.

**Na|zi** (nät′sē, nat′-), *n., pl.* **-zis,** *adj.* —*n.* **1** a member or supporter of the National Socialist Party, a fascist political party in Germany, led by Adolf Hitler; advocate of Nazism. It came to power in Germany in 1933 and believed in state control of industry, denunciation of communism and Judaism, and the dominance of Germany as a world power. **2** Often, **nazi.** a believer in similar doctrines in any country; any fascist.
—*adj.* of or having to do with the Nazis or their doctrines.
[< German *Nazi,* short for *Nati*(*onalsozialist*) National Socialist]
► **Nazi** was a political nickname for the National Socialist Party in Germany and is capitalized like *Republican* or *Democrat.* The type of party represented by the Nazis is usually referred to as *fascist* or *totalitarian.*
► **Nazi.** A pronunciation somewhere between (nä′zē) and (naz′ē) never gained general acceptance in the United States or Great Britain, but deserves note for its use by Sir Winston Churchill, in whose mouth during World War II it was an utterance of remarkable eloquence, conveying unmistakably Churchill's loathing and contempt for Hitler and his works.

**Na|zi|dom** (nät′sē dom, nat′-), *n.* the Nazi realm or power.

**Na|zi|fi|ca|tion** or **na|zi|fi|ca|tion** (nät′sə fə kā′shən, nat′-), *n.* **1** the act of Nazifying. **2** the condition of being Nazified.

**Na|zi|fy** or **na|zi|fy** (nät′sə fī, nat′-), *v.t.,* **-fied, -fy|ing. 1** to place under the control of the Nazis: *With Germany nazified, he settled in Paris* (Atlantic). **2** to indoctrinate with Nazi views.

**Na|zi|ism** (nät′sē iz əm, nat′-), *n.* = Nazism.

**na|zir** (nä′zir), *n.* **1** the title of various officials in Moslem countries. **2** (formerly) a native official in the Anglo-Indian courts. [< Arabic *nāẓir*]

**Naz|i|rite** (naz′ə rīt), *n.* Nazarite.

**Na|zism** (nät′siz əm, nat′-), *n.* the doctrines and practices of the Nazis, including totalitarian government, state control of industry, anti-Semitism, and opposition to communism.

**Nb** (no period), niobium (chemical element).

**n.b.**, note well; observe carefully (Latin, *nota bene*).

**NB** (no periods), Nebraska (with postal Zip Code).

**N.B.**, **1** New Brunswick. **2** note well; observe carefully (Latin, *nota bene*).
► **N.B.** The abbreviation of the Latin *nota bene,* meaning note well, is occasionally found in formal announcements: *N.B. Members are to pay their dues not later than Monday, May 5.*

**NBA** (no periods) or **N.B.A.**, **1** National Bar Association. **2** National Basketball Association. **3** National Boxing Association.

**NBC** (no periods), National Broadcasting Company.

**N-bomb** (en′bom′), *n.* = neutron bomb.

**NBS** (no periods), National Bureau of Standards.

**n.c.**, nitrocellulose.

**NC** (no periods), an abbreviation for the following:
**1** Navy Cross.
**2** no comment.
**3** North Carolina (with postal Zip Code).
**4** numerical control.
**5** Nurse Corps.

**N.C.**, North Carolina.

**NCAA** (no periods) or **N.C.A.A.**, National Collegiate Athletic Association.

**NCC** (no periods) or **N.C.C.**, National Council of Churches.

**NCCJ** (no periods), National Conference of Christians and Jews.

**NCO** (no periods) or **N.C.O.**, noncommissioned officer.

**-nd**, a suffix added to the numeral 2 or any numeral ending with 2 (except 12) to indicate the

ordinal number: *42nd Street, November 22nd.*
**Nd** (no period), neodymium (chemical element).
**ND** (no periods), **1** national debt. **2** North Dakota (with postal Zip Code).
**n.d.**, no date; not dated.
**NDA** (no periods), new drug application: *an NDA submitted to the Food and Drug Administration.*
**N. Dak.** or **N.D.**, North Dakota.
**NDEA** (no periods), National Defense Education Act.
**né** (nā), *adj.* = born. [< French *né,* masculine past participle of *naître* be born; see etym. under **née**]
► **Né** is placed after a man's present name to show his original name: *Mark Stone* (*né Stein*) (Time).
**Ne** (no period), neon (chemical element).
**n.e.**, **1** northeast. **2** northeastern.
**NE** (no periods), **1** Nebraska (with postal Zip Code). **2** Northeast or northeast. **3** Northeastern or northeastern.
**N.E.**, **1** New England. **2a** Northeast or northeast. **b** Northeastern or northeastern.
**NEA** (no periods) or **N.E.A.**, National Education Association.
**Ne|an|der|tal** (nē an′dər tāl; *German* nā än′dər-täl), *adj.* = Neanderthal.
**Ne|an|der|tal|er** (nē an′dər tä′lər), *n.* = Neanderthaler.
**Neandertal man**, = Neanderthal man.
**Ne|an|der|thal** (nē an′dər thôl, -täl; *German* nā-än′dər täl), *adj., n.* —*adj.* **1** belonging to a group of prehistoric people who lived in caves in Europe, North Africa, and parts of Asia in the early Stone Age. **2** like the Neanderthal man. **3** *Figurative.* Often, **neanderthal**. reactionary, especially in politics: *the neanderthal wing of the party. Here was a good example of the type of excess we could expect ... especially on the more Neanderthal of the New York newspapers* (Atlantic).
—*n.* **1** a Neanderthal man: *Neanderthals buried their dead in carefully prepared graves, sometimes with offerings of food* (Bert Salwen).
**2** Often, **neanderthal**. a reactionary: *a political Neanderthal.*
[< *Neanderthal,* the Neander Gorge in West Germany, where the fossils of Neanderthal man were first found]
**Ne|an|der|thal|er** (nē an′dər thô′lər, -tä′-), *n.* = Neanderthal man.
**Neanderthal man**, an extinct species of man widespread in Europe, North Africa, and western and central Asia, in the early Stone Age, the first fossils of which were discovered in 1856 at the Neander Gorge near Düsseldorf, Germany. The Neanderthal man of Europe had a large, heavy skull and low forehead, a broad, flat nose, and a heavy lower jaw with teeth intermediate in shape between those of modern man and the apes. *We now reach the immediate forerunner of modern man, homo neanderthalensis, or Neanderthal man* (Melville J. Herskovits).
**Ne|an|der|thal|oid** (nē an′dər thô′loid, -tä′-), *adj.* of or like the Neanderthal man, his type of skull, or the race it is believed to represent.
**ne|an|throp|ic** (nē′an throp′ik), *adj.* of or belonging to the latest or modern period of the existence of man. [< *neo-* + *anthropic*]
**neap**[1] (nēp), *adj., n., v.* —*adj.* of or having to do with a neap tide or tides. —*n.* = neap tide.
—*v.i.* to become lower; tend towards the neap: *in time for a tide neaping to tomorrow night's full moon* (New Yorker).
[Old English *nēp*]
**neap**[2] (nēp), *n. U.S. Dialect.* the pole or tongue of a wagon intended to be drawn by two animals. [origin uncertain. Compare dialectal Norwegian *neip* forked pole, Old Icelandic *neip* the space between two fingers.]
**neaped** (nēpt), *adj.* grounded by neap tides and forced to wait for spring tides to get out.
**Ne|a|pol|i|tan** (nē′ə pol′ə tən), *adj., n.* —*adj.* of or having to do with Naples, a city in Italy.
—*n.* a person born or living in Naples.
[< Latin *Neāpolītānus* < *Neāpolis* Naples < Greek *Neápolis* < *néā,* feminine of *néos* new + *pólis* city]
**Neapolitan ice cream**, ice cream or sherbet made in layers of different colors and flavors.
**Neapolitan medlar**, = azarole.
**neap tide**, a tide that occurs when the difference in height between high and low tide is least; lowest level of high tide. Neap tide come twice a month, in the first and third quarters of the moon.
**near** (nir), *adv., adj., prep., v.* —*adv.* **1** to or at a short distance; not far; close: *The holiday season is drawing near. They searched near and far.*
**2** close in relation; closely: *tribes near allied.*
**3** close to something in resemblance; almost next (to): *Fool that's near To knave* (Robert Browning). **4** *Informal.* all but; almost; nearly: *The war lasted near a year.* **5** thriftily: *I had lived so near and so close that in a whole year I had not spent the 15s. which I had saved* (Daniel Defoe).
**6** *Nautical.* close to the direction of the wind.
—*adj.* **1** close by; not distant; less distant: *the near future. The post office is quite near.* SYN: close, nigh. **2** close in feeling; intimate; familiar: *a near friend.* **3** closely related: *a near relative.*
**4a** resembling closely: *near silk.* **b** approximating an original: *a near translation.* **5** on the left-hand side; left: *The near horse and the off horse make a team.* **6** short; direct: *Take the nearest route.*
**7** stingy: *Mr. Barkis was something of a miser, or as Peggotty dutifully expressed it, was "a little near"* (Dickens). **8** by a close margin; narrow: *a near escape.* **9** closely affecting or touching one: *War is a matter of great and near concern to all of us.*
—*prep.* close to in space, time, condition, or relation: *Our house is near the river. It is near five o'clock.*
—*v.t., v.i.* to come or draw near to; approach: *The ship neared the land. The vacation was nearing its end.*
**come near.** See under **come**.
[Old English *nēar* nearer, comparative of *nēah* nigh, near] —**near′ness**, *n.*
**near beer**, a beverage resembling beer but containing less than one half per cent alcohol.
**near|by** (nir′bī′), *adj., adv., prep.* —*adj., adv.* near; close by; close at hand: *a nearby house* (adj.). *They went nearby to visit* (adv.).
—*prep. Dialect.* close to (a place).
**Ne|arc|tic** (nē ärk′tik, -är′tik), *adj.* having to do with the region including temperate and arctic North America and Greenland, especially with reference to the distribution of animals. [< Greek *néos* new + English *arctic*]
**Near Eastern**, of or having to do with the Near East, the region comprising the countries of southwestern Asia, sometimes including the Balkan States, Sudan, and Egypt.
**near|ly** (nir′lē), *adv.* **1** almost: *It is nearly bedtime. I nearly missed the train.* **2** closely: *a matter that concerns you very nearly. It will cost too much, as nearly as I can figure it.*
**near-man** or **Near-Man** (nir′man′), *n., pl.* **-men** or **-Men**. an ape man.
**near-miss** (nir′mis′), *n.* **1a** the failure to make a direct hit on a target or other thing aimed at. **b** a rocket, guided missile, bomb, or the like that fails to make a direct hit upon a target: *With a thermonuclear warhead the attacker can be sure of inflicting great damage even with a near-miss* (Newsweek). **2** anything that does not fulfill but approaches very closely some standard of excellence: *The good near-misses scored by some of the first novelists* (Manchester Guardian). **3** a narrow escape from danger or an accident: *The near-miss left me slightly shaken* (Atlantic).
**near point**, *Optics.* the point nearest to the eye at which an image is clearly formed on the retina when there is maximum accommodation.
**near|side** (nir′sīd′), *n., adj.* —*n.* the side that is nearer or nearest, especially the left side: *We usually mount horses on the nearside.*
—*adj.* on or to the near or left side; near; left: *blue smoke arises from the nearside mudguard* (Punch). *Lalor on his best pony, Fifty, ... sent in Kishan to score with a good nearside shot* (London Times).
**near-sight** (nir′sīt′), *n.* = myopia.
**near-sight|ed** or **near|sight|ed** (nir′sī′tid), *adj.* not able to see far; seeing distinctly at a short distance only; myopic: *Near-sighted people usually wear glasses.* (*Figurative.*) *a near-sighted mind.* —**near′-sight′ed|ly, near′sight′ed|ly**, *adv.* —**near′-sight′ed|ness, near′sight′ed|ness**, *n.*
**near-term** (nir′tėrm′), *adj.* of or for a short period of time: *This has improved the market's near-term position* (Wall Street Journal).
**neat**[1] (nēt), *adj.* **1** clean and in order: *a neat desk, a neat room, a neat dress.* **2** able and willing to keep things in order: *a neat child.* **3** well-formed; in proportion: *a neat design.* **4** skillful; clever: *a neat trick, a neat turn of phrase.* SYN: deft, adroit. **5** without anything mixed in it; pure; straight: *He drinks his brandy neat. The gas is then enriched to the declared calorific value by the automatic addition of neat refinery gas* (London Times). SYN: undiluted, clear. **6** *Slang.* very pleasing; fine: *a neat party.* **7** clear; net: *a neat profit.* [< Anglo-French *neit,* Old French *net* < Latin *nitidus* gleaming < *nitēre* to shine] —**neat′ly**, *adv.* —**neat′ness**, *n.*
—*Syn.* **1 Neat, tidy, trim** mean in good order. **Neat** suggests cleanness and absence of disorder or litter: *Her clothes are always neat.* **Tidy** suggests orderliness: *She keeps her room tidy.* **Trim** suggests pleasing neatness and smartness or compactness, proportion, and clean lines: *That is a trim sailboat.*
**neat**[2] (nēt), *n., adj.* —*n. pl. or sing. Archaic.* **1** cattle; oxen. **2** an ox, cow, or heifer.
—*adj.* of the ox kind: *neat cattle.*
[Old English *nēat*]
**neat|en** (nē′tən), *v.t.* to put in order; clean; tidy up: *She ... began neatening the books in a low bookshelf* (New Yorker).
**neath** or **'neath** (nēth, nēᴛʜ), *prep. Archaic.* beneath: *'neath the silvery moon.*
**neat-hand|ed** (nēt′han′did), *adj.* neat or dexterous in the use of the hands; deft.
**neat|herd** (nēt′hėrd′), *n. Archaic.* cowherd.
**neat's-foot oil** (nēts′fu̇t′), a light-yellow oil obtained from the feet and shinbones of cattle by boiling. It is used to lubricate delicate machinery and to soften and preserve leather.
**neb** (neb), *n. Scottish.* **1** the bill or beak of a bird. **2** a person's mouth or nose. **3** an animal's snout. **4** the tip of anything; nib. **5** *Obsolete.* the face. [Old English *nebb*]
**NEB** (no periods) or **N.E.B.**, New English Bible.
**neb|bi|o|lo** (neb′bē ō′lō), *n.* a grape grown in Italy, used in most Italian red wines. [< Italian *nebbiolo*]
**neb|bish** (neb′ish), *n., adj. Slang.* —*n.* a pitifully clumsy or inept person.
—*adj.* pitifully clumsy or inept: *The central character is so nebbish he has not even a name* (Time).
[< Yiddish interjection *nebekh,* probably < German *nie bei euch* may it not happen to you]
**Ne|bi|im** (neb′ē ēm′; *Hebrew* nə vē′ēm′), *n.pl.* the books of the Prophets making up the second division of the Hebrew Old Testament canon. The first division is the Torah and the third division is the Kethubim. [< Hebrew *nəbi'im,* plural of *nābi* prophet]
**Ne|bo** (nā′bō), *n.* the god of wisdom in Babylonian mythology, who wrote down the judgments passed on the dead souls. He was the son of Marduk.
**Nebr.** or **Neb.**, Nebraska.
**Ne|bras|kan** (nə bras′kən), *adj., n.* —*adj.* **1** of or having to do with the state of Nebraska or its inhabitants. **2** of or having to do with the first period of glaciation in North America, beginning about 1,200,000 years ago, and lasting about 64,000 years.
—*n.* a native or inhabitant of Nebraska.
**neb|u|chad|nez|zar** (neb′yə kəd nez′ər, neb′ə-), *n.* a very large bottle for alcoholic liquor that holds about four gallons: *nebuchadnezzars of champagne* (New Yorker). [named in honor of *Nebuchadnezzar,* died 562 B.C., a famous king of Babylon (Daniel 1-4)]
**neb|u|la** (neb′yə lə), *n., pl.* **-lae** (-lē), **-las**. **1** a mass of dust particles and gases or a cloudlike cluster of stars which occurs in interstellar space, very far away from our sun and its planets. A nebula may be either luminous or dark in appearance. Galactic nebulae are clouds of luminous gas and dust particles within our galaxy and comparable in size with it. Extragalactic nebulae are clusters of stars outside our Milky Way. **2a** a cloudlike spot on the cornea of the eye. **b** cloudiness of the urine. [< Latin *nebula* mist, cloud]
**neb|u|lar** (neb′yə lər), *adj.* of or having to do with a nebula or nebulae.
**nebular hypothesis**, the theory that the solar system, and similar systems, developed from the cooling and contracting of a hot, rotating nebula to form rings of matter, and that in turn this matter formed planets. The theory was formulated by Pierre Simon de Laplace (1749-1827), a French astronomer and mathematician.
**neb|u|lé** (neb′yə lā), *adj. Heraldry.* having a wavy or serpentine form, like the edges of clouds. [< French *nébulé* < Latin *nebula* cloud]
**ne|bu|li|um** (nə byü′lē əm), *n.* a supposed chemical element to which certain green lines in the spectra of nebulae were once attributed, now known to be caused by oxygen, nitrogen, and other common gases. [< New Latin *nebulium* < Latin *nebula* mist, cloud + New Latin *-ium,* a suffix meaning "element"]
**neb|u|lize** (neb′yə līz), *v.t.,* **-lized, -liz|ing**. to reduce to fine mist or vapor; atomize. —**neb′u|li|za′tion**, *n.* —**neb′u|liz′er**, *n.*
**neb|u|lose** (neb′yə lōs), *adj.* = nebulous.
**neb|u|los|i|ty** (neb′yə los′ə tē), *n., pl.* **-ties**.
**1** cloudlike quality; nebulous state; mistiness.
**2** cloudlike matter; nebula: *His theory is the dust and gas have been cleaned out by frequent passage through nebulosities in the Milky Way* (Science News Letter).
**neb|u|lous** (neb′yə ləs), *adj.* **1** lacking form; hazy; vague; indistinct; confused: *a nebulous ambition. Prestige is a nebulous word, meaning many things to many people* (Wall Street Journal).

**Pronunciation Key:** hat, āge, cãre, fär; let, ēqual, tėrm; it, īce; hot, ōpen, ôrder; **oi**l, **ou**t; cup, pu̇t, rüle; **ch**ild; lo**ng**; **th**in; **ᴛʜ**en; **zh**, measure; **ə** represents **a** in about, **e** in taken, **i** in pencil, **o** in lemon, **u** in circus.

2 resembling a cloud or clouds; cloudlike. 3 of or like a nebula or nebulae. [< Latin *nebulōsus* < *nebula* mist] —**neb′u|lous|ly**, *adv.* —**neb′u|lousness**, *n.*

**n.e.c.**, not elsewhere classified.

**nec|es|sar|i|an** (nes′ə sãr′ē ən), *n., adj.* = necessitarian.

**nec|es|sar|i|an|ism** (nes′ə sãr′ē ə niz′əm), *n.* = necessitarianism.

**nec|es|sar|ies** (nes′ə ser′ēz), *n.pl.* See under **necessary**.

**nec|es|sar|i|ly** (nes′ə ser′ə lē, nes′ə sãr′-), *adv.* 1 because of necessity: *Leaves are not necessarily green.* 2 as a necessary result: *War necessarily causes misery and waste.* SYN: inevitably.

**nec|es|sar|i|ness** (nes′ə ser′ē nis), *n.* the state of being necessary.

**nec|es|sar|y** (nes′ə ser′ē), *adj., n., pl.* **-sar|ies.** —*adj.* 1 that must be had; that must be done; required; indispensable: *I prepared all things necessary for my journey.* SYN: essential. 2 that must be; inevitable: *Death is a necessary end.* 3 compelled by another or others; compulsory: *a necessary agent.* 4 *Logic.* **a** that cannot be denied because denial would entail contradiction of what has already been established: *a necessary truth.* **b** that cannot be avoided or escaped because based on a premise known to be true: *a necessary inference.* 5 *Archaic.* rendering certain essential services to a household or employer: *a necessary woman.*

—*n.* 1 a thing impossible to do without; requisite; essential; necessity: *Water and food, clothing, and shelter are necessaries of human life.* 2 *British Dialect.* a toilet.

**necessaries**, *Law.* the things, such as food, shelter, and clothing, required to support a dependent or incompetent and suitable to his station in life: *the obligation of parents to provide their offspring with necessaries.*

**the necessary**, money: *"Have you the necessary for such a long trip?"*

[< Latin *necessārius* < *necesse* unavoidable, probably < *ne-* not + *cēdere* withdraw]

—*Syn. adj.* 1 **Necessary, indispensable, essential** mean needed or required. **Necessary** applies to whatever is needed but not absolutely required: *Work is a necessary part of life.* **Indispensable** implies that, without it, the intended result or purpose cannot be achieved: *Studying is an indispensable part of education.* **Essential** implies that the existence or proper functioning of something depends upon it: *Food is essential to survival.*

**necessary evil**, something unpleasant that cannot be avoided: *He had profoundly disliked the Reform Bill, which he had only accepted at last as a necessary evil* (Lytton Strachey).

**ne|ces|si|tar|i|an** (nə ses′ə tãr′ē ən), *n., adj.* —*n.* a person who denies that the will is free, and maintains that all action is the necessary effect of prior causes.

—*adj.* having to do with necessitarians or necessitarianism.

**ne|ces|si|tar|i|an|ism** (nə ses′ə tãr′ē ə niz′əm), *n.* the doctrine of necessitarians, comprising a form of determinism.

**ne|ces|si|tate** (nə ses′ə tāt), *v.t.,* **-tat|ed, -tat|ing.** 1 to make necessary: *His broken leg necessitated an operation.* SYN: require, demand. 2 to compel, oblige, or force: *What necessitated you to take this action? I was necessitated to fight with an imaginary enemy* (Herman Melville). —**neces′si|ta′tion**, *n.*

**ne|ces|si|tous** (nə ses′ə təs), *adj.* very poor; needy: *a necessitous family.* SYN: indigent, destitute. —**ne|ces′si|tous|ly**, *adv.* —**ne|ces′si|tousness**, *n.*

**ne|ces|si|ty** (nə ses′ə tē), *n., pl.* **-ties.** 1 the fact of being necessary; extreme need; something that has to be: *We understand the necessity of eating.* SYN: exigency, indispensability. See syn. under **need**. 2 the quality or condition of being necessary; great urgency: *He flies only in cases of necessity. His orders lack necessity.* 3 that which cannot be done without; necessary thing: *Food and water are necessities.* SYN: essential, requisite. 4 that which forces one to act in a certain way: *Necessity often drives people to do disagreeable things.* 5 that which is inevitable, especially through the operation of a law of nature: *Night follows day as a necessity.* 6 need; poverty: *This poor family is in great necessity.* 7 *Philosophy.* **a** any form of compulsion, such as moral, legal, physical, or logical compulsion, that causes a person to do something against his will. **b** the inevitable connection between a cause and its effect; inevitability.

**of necessity**, because it must be: *. . . Marxism . . . in Russia, of necessity an outlawed movement . . . became, in its most effective form, narrow, concentrated, grim and cruel* (Edmund Wilson).

[< Old French *necessite,* learned borrowing from Latin *necessitās* (in Late Latin, poverty) < *necesse;* see etym. under **necessary**]

▶**Necessity**. The idiom is *necessity of* or *for* doing something (not *to* do something): *Most athletes can see the necessity of* (or *for*) *keeping training. There is no necessity for an immediate decision.*

**neck** (nek), *n., v.* —*n.* 1 the part of the body that connects the head with the shoulders. The neck contains vital passages for breathing, blood supply to the head, and ingestion of food, and includes the uppermost part of the spinal column. 2 the part of a garment that fits the neck: *the neck of a shirt.* 3 any narrow part like a neck: *The hammer broke off right at at the neck of the handle.* 4 a narrow strip of land; isthmus or peninsula: *a canal across a neck of land.* 5 a narrow strip of water. 6 the slender part of a bottle, flask, retort, or other container. 7 *Architecture.* the lowest part of the capital of a column, where it joins the shaft. 8 the long, slender part of a violin or similar instrument, extending from the body to the head; finger board. 9 the part of a tooth between the crown and the root. 10 a slender or constricted part of a bone or organ. 11 a long siphon occurring in certain mollusks: *the neck of a clam.* 12 *Printing.* the part of a type between the face and shoulder; beard. 13 the length of the neck of a horse or other animal as a measure in a race: *. . . Impasse was third, a neck behind Helianthus* (New York Times).

—*v.i. U.S. Slang.* to embrace; hug; kiss and caress.

—*v.t.* 1 to cut or snatch off the head of (a fowl). 2 *U.S. Slang.* to kiss and caress (a person).

**get (catch, take) it in the neck**, to be hard hit (by something); be severely reprimanded or punished: *Unfortunately, it is the public who is getting it in the neck* (New Yorker).

**neck and crop**, bodily; completely; altogether: *His application was indignantly opposed, sternly put to the vote, and thrown out neck and crop* (Manchester Guardian).

**neck and neck, a** abreast: *The race started with the horses nearly neck and neck.* **b** running equal or even in a race or contest: *Neck and neck with the Poujadiste gains were those of the hard-running Communists* (Newsweek).

**neck or nothing**, venturing all: *Cabs are all very well in cases of expedition, when it's a matter of neck or nothing* (Dickens).

**risk one's neck**, to put oneself in a dangerous position: *The rescuers risked their necks to save the lost mountain climbers.*

**stick one's neck out**, *Informal.* to put oneself in a dangerous or vulnerable position by foolish or zealous action: *He . . . has been fired for sticking his ignorant . . . neck out too far* (Sunday Times).

**talk through (the back of) one's neck**, *Especially British Slang.* to talk nonsense; blather: *That braggart is just talking through the back of his neck.*

**up to one's neck**, *Informal.* deeply taken up; thoroughly involved: *The host tends to look like a rather important civil servant up to his neck in an awkward piece of long-term diplomacy* (Manchester Guardian Weekly).

**win by a neck, a** to win a horse race by the length of a head and a neck: *Capeador . . . won by a neck from Social Outcast* (New Yorker). **b** to win by a close margin: *In his race for the city council, he won by a neck.*

[Old English *hnecca*] —**neck′er**, *n.* —**neck′less**, *adj.*

**neck|band** (nek′band′), *n.* 1 a band worn around the neck. 2 the part of a shirt to which the collar is attached.

**neck-break|ing** (nek′brā′king), *adj.* = breakneck.

**neck|cloth** (nek′klôth′, -kloth′), *n.* a cloth worn around the neck, especially by men; cravat.

**neck-deep** (nek′dēp′), *adj., adv.* 1 submerged up to the neck. 2 very much involved: *The United States was neck-deep in political intrigue* (New York Times).

**-necked**, *combining form.* having a ____neck: *Long-necked* = *having a long neck.*

**neck|er|chief** (nek′ər chif), *n.* a cloth worn around the neck. SYN: scarf. [< *neck* + *kerchief*]

**neck|ing** (nek′ing), *n.* 1**a** a molding or series of moldings separating the capital and shaft of a column. **b** the space between such moldings. 2 the part of a column between the capital and shaft; gorgerin. 3 *U.S. Slang.* the act of caressing and kissing; amorous play.

**neck|lace** (nek′lis), *n.* a string or chain of jewels, gold, silver, or beads, worn around the neck as an ornament.

**neck|line** (nek′līn′), *n.* the line around the neck where a garment ends.

**neck-or-noth|ing** (nek′ər nuth′ing), *adj.* headlong; reckless.

**neck|piece** (nek′pēs′), *n.* a fur scarf.

**neck-rest** (nek′rest′), *n.* a support for the neck in resting or sleeping, as used in China, Japan, and Africa.

**neck sweetbread**, the thymus gland, especially of a calf, used as food.

**neck|tie** (nek′tī′), *n.* 1 a narrow band or a tie worn around the neck, under the collar of a shirt, and tied in front; cravat. 2 any bow or the like, worn in front of the neck. 3 *Slang.* a hangman's rope.

**necktie party**, *U.S. Slang.* a lynching by hanging with a rope.

**neck verse**, a Latin verse printed in black-letter, usually Psalm 51:1, formerly set before an accused person claiming benefit of clergy, in order to test his ability to read; if he could read it, he was released, thus saving his neck.

**neck|wear** (nek′wãr′), *n.* collars, ties, and other articles worn around the neck.

**neck-yoke** (nek′yōk′), *n.* a bar, usually of wood, that is connected with the collars of a harness and from which the end of the tongue of a vehicle is suspended.

**nec|ro|gen|ic** (nek′rə jen′ik), *adj. Pathology.* produced or caused by dead bodies or dead animal matter. [< Greek *nekrós* corpse + English *-gen* + *-ic*]

**ne|crol|a|try** (ne krol′ə trē), *n.* worship of the dead. [< Greek *nekrós* dead body + *latreíā* worship]

**nec|ro|log|i|cal** (nek′rə loj′ə kəl), *adj.* having to do with necrology; giving an account of the dead or of deaths: (*Figurative.*) *The United States . . . is about to become a forum for political discussions of a predominantly clinical and necrological nature* (New Yorker). —**nec′ro|log′i|cal|ly**, *adv.*

**ne|crol|o|gist** (ne krol′ə jist), *n.* a person who writes or prepares obituaries.

**ne|crol|o|gy** (ne krol′ə jē), *n., pl.* **-gies.** 1 a list of persons who have died. 2 a notice of a person's death; obituary. [< Greek *nekrós* dead body + *lógos* count, reckoning]

**nec|ro|man|cer** (nek′rə man′sər), *n.* 1 a person who is supposed to foretell the future by communicating with the dead. 2 a magician; sorcerer; wizard.

**nec|ro|man|cy** (nek′rə man′sē), *n.* 1 a foretelling of the future by communicating with the dead: *By his skill in necromancy, he has a power of calling whom he pleases from the dead* (Jonathan Swift). 2 magic; sorcery; enchantment. [alteration of Old French *nygromancie,* learned borrowing from Medieval Latin *nigromantia* < Latin *necromantīa* < Greek *nekromanteiā* < *nekrós* dead body + *manteiā* divination; confusion with Latin *niger* "black" led to translation "black art"]

**nec|ro|man|tic** (nek′rə man′tik), *adj.* 1 having to do with necromancy: *old Merlin's necromantic spells* (Thomas Hood). 2 given to the practice of necromancy. —**nec′ro|man′ti|cal|ly**, *adv.*

**nec|ro|pha|gi|a** (nek′rə fā′jē ə), *n. Zoology.* the practice or habit of feeding on dead bodies or carrion. [< New Latin *necrophagia* < Greek *nekrós* dead body + *phageîn* eat]

**ne|croph|a|gous** (ne krof′ə gəs), *adj.* feeding on dead bodies or carrion: *necrophagous beasts.*

**ne|croph|a|gy** (ne krof′ə jē), *n.* = necrophagia.

**nec|ro|phile** (nek′rə fīl, -fil), *n.* a person who is affected with necrophily.

**nec|ro|phil|i|a** (nek′rə fil′ē ə), *n.* = necrophily.

**nec|ro|phil|i|ac** (nek′rə fil′ē ak), *n.* = necrophile.

**nec|ro|phil|ic** (nek′rə fil′ik), *adj.* of, having to do with, or characteristic of necrophily.

**ne|croph|i|lism** (ne krof′ə liz əm), *n.* = necrophily.

**ne|croph|i|lous** (ne krof′ə ləs), *adj.* = necrophilic.

**ne|croph|i|ly** (ne krof′ə lē), *n.* a morbid attraction to dead bodies. [< Greek *nekrós* dead body + *philía* affection]

**ne|crop|o|lis** (ne krop′ə lis), *n., pl.* **-lis|es, -leis** (-līs). 1 = cemetery. SYN: graveyard. 2 an ancient or prehistoric burying ground: *Hill and hillslope were the necropolis of a vanished race* (John R. Green). [< Greek *nekrópolis* < *nekrós* dead body + *pólis* city]

**nec|rop|sy** (nek′rop sē), *n., pl.* **-sies.** = autopsy; post-mortem examination. [< Greek *nekrós* dead body + *-opsiā* a viewing (< *optós* visible)]

**ne|crose** (ne krōs′, nek′rōs), *v.t., v.i.,* **-crosed, -cros|ing.** to affect or be affected with necrosis.

**ne|cro|sis** (ne krō′sis), *n., pl.* **-ses** (-sēz). 1 the death or decay of body tissues; mortification; gangrene. It may result from a degenerative disease, stoppage of the oxygen supply, infection, or destructive burning or freezing. 2 a disease of plants characterized by small black spots of decayed tissue. [< New Latin *necrosis* < Greek *nékrōsis,* ultimately < *nekrós* dead body]

**ne|crot|ic** (ne krot′ik), *adj.* of or showing necrosis: *a necrotic disease.*

**nec|ro|tize** (nek′rə tīz), *v.t., v.i.,* **-tized, -tiz|ing.** to affect or be affected with necrosis.

**ne|crot|o|my** (ne krot′ə mē), *n., pl.* **-mies.** 1 the cutting away and removal of necrosed bone.

2 the dissection of corpses. [< Greek *nekrós* dead body + *-tomiā* a cutting]

**nec|tar** (nek′tər), *n.* **1** *Greek and Roman Mythology.* **a** the drink of the gods: *But might I of Jove's nectar sup* (Ben Jonson). **b** the food of the gods. **2** any delicious drink. **3** a sweet liquid found in many flowers, which attracts insects and birds that carry out pollination. Bees gather nectar and make it into honey. [< Latin *nectar* < Greek *néktar*] —**nec′tar|like′**, *adj.*

**nec|tar|e|an** (nek tãr′ē ən), *adj.* = nectareous.

**nec|tared** (nek′tərd), *adj.* filled or flavored with or as if with nectar; delicious.

**nec|tar|e|ous** (nek tãr′ē əs), *adj.* of or like nectar; delicious; sweet.

**nec|tar|ine**[1] (nek′tə rēn′, nek′tə rēn), *n.* **1** a kind of peach with no down on its skin and a firm pulp. **2** the tree it grows on. [< *nectarine*[2]]

**nec|tar|ine**[2] (nek′tər in), *adj.* like nectar; delicious. [< *nectar* + *-ine*[1]]

**nec|tar|ous** (nek′tər əs), *adj.* = nectareous.

**nec|ta|ry** (nek′tər ē), *n., pl.* **-ries.** the gland of a flower or plant that secretes nectar.

**N.E.D.** or **NED** (no periods), New English Dictionary (Oxford English Dictionary). Also, **OED** (no periods).

**NEDC** (no periods), National Economic Development Council (of Great Britain).

**ned|dy** (ned′ē), *n., pl.* **-dies.** a donkey: *long-eared Neddies, giving themselves leonine airs* (Thackeray). [< *Neddy,* diminutive of *Ned,* a familiar nickname of *Edward*]

**Ned|dy** (ned′ē), *n., pl.* **-dies.** *British Slang.* **1** the National Economic Development Council of Great Britain. **2** any similar body for developing the national economy.

**nee** or **née** (nā), *adj.* = born. [< French *née,* feminine past participle of *naître* be born < Latin *nāscī*]

► **Nee** is placed after the name of a married woman to show her maiden name: *Mrs. Smith, nee Adams.* It is sometimes italicized.

**need** (nēd), *v., n.* —*v.t.* to be in want of; ought to have; be unable to do without; want; require: *He needs money. I need a new hat. Plants need water.* **SYN:** See syn. under **lack.**

—*v.i.* **1** to be in want: *Give to those that need.* **2** to be necessary: *The rope cuts his hands more than needs.* **3** to have to; ought to; must; should: *He need not go. Need she go?*

—*n.* **1** the lack of a useful or desired thing; want; lack: *For need of a nail, the shoe was lost. His writing showed need of grammar.* **2** a thing wanted or lacking; that for which a want is felt: *In the jungle their need was fresh water.* **3** something that has to be; necessity; requirement: *There is no need to hurry.* **4** a time of need; condition of need: *When I lacked money, my uncle was a friend in need.* **5** lack of money; being poor; extreme poverty: *The family's need was so great the children did not have shoes.* **SYN:** want, destitution, indigence.

**have need to,** must, should, have to, or ought to: *I have no need to go to town. The best of saints have need to be warned against the worst of sins* (Octavius Winslow).

**if need be,** if it has to be; if necessary: *They will fight to the bitter end, if need be.*

[Old English *nēd, nīed*] —**need′er,** *n.*

—*Syn. n.* **1 Need, necessity** mean lack of something required or desired. **Need** suggests pressing want, lack or absence of something required for one's welfare or of something useful or satisfying: *She is in need of a rest.* **Necessity** suggests an urgent need or imperative demand, but implies a more objective attitude and has less emotional appeal than *need* sometimes does: *She realizes the necessity of getting enough sleep.*

**need|fire** (nēd′fīr′), *n. Scottish.* **1** fire produced from dry wood by friction, formerly used to cure disease among cattle. **2** a beacon fire or bonfire.

**need|ful** (nēd′fəl), *adj., n.* —*adj.* **1** needed; necessary: *a needful change.* **SYN:** requisite, required, indispensable. **2** needy.

—*n.* a necessary thing.

**the needful, a** what is necessary or requisite: *His lawyer will do the needful in the event of the man's death.* **b** *Informal.* the necessary funds; money; cash: ... *to live, I must have what you call 'the needful,' which I can only get by working* (Charlotte Brontë). —**need′ful|ly,** *adv.* —**need′ful|ness,** *n.*

**need|i|ness** (nē′dē nis), *n.* the condition of being needy; poverty; want; indigence.

***nee|dle** (nē′dəl), *n., v.,* **-dled, -dling.** —*n.* **1** a very slender tool, sharp at one end and with a hole or eye to pass a thread through, used in sewing: *Mother sewed the button on my coat with needle and bright yellow thread.* **2** a slender rod used in knitting. **3** a rod with a hook at one end used in crocheting. **4** a thin steel pointer on a compass, electrical machinery, or some gauges, such as a speedometer or an altimeter: *The needle shot up above forty as we sped along in the car.* **5** a slender steel tube with a sharp point at one end. It is used at the end of a hypodermic syringe especially for injecting something below the skin or withdrawing blood or other body fluid. *The doctor jabbed the needle into my arm.* **6** *Informal.* an injection, as of a drug. **7** an instrument somewhat like a needle, used in engraving or etching. **8** = phonograph needle. **9** the thin pointed leaf of a fir tree or pine tree. **10** an object resembling a needle in sharpness: *needles of broken glass or ice.* **11** a slender rod that controls the opening of a valve. **12** a pillar; obelisk: *Cleopatra's Needle.* **13** *Mineralogy, Chemistry.* a crystal or spicule like a needle in shape: *One such isotope, in the form of germanium oxide needles, can be inserted in the body and left there* (New York Times). **14** *Geology.* a pinnacle of rock tapering to a point. **15** = dipole (def. 2b). **16** *Informal, Figurative.* **a** a spur, goad, or stimulus: *Without the constant needle of improving competition the men at the top will find it difficult to improve any further* (London Times). **b** a barbed or sarcastic remark.

—*v.t.* **1** *Informal.* to vex by sharp remarks; goad, incite, or annoy: *to needle someone into taking action. That ghoulish voice began needling me again* (S. J. Perelman). **2** to sew or pierce with a needle. **3** to add alcohol to (beer, ale, or the like): *The impact of the needled soft drink ... had been such as to make him ill* (New Yorker). **4** *Informal.* to give an injection, as of a drug, to.

—*v.i.* **1** to work with a needle. **2** *Mineralogy, Chemistry.* to form needle-shaped crystals.

**a needle in a** (or **the**) **haystack,** something extremely difficult or impossible to find or reach: *We are looking for a needle in the haystack—that one buyer in the hundreds of thousands who will see the ad* (Burnett Bear).

**give one the needle,** *Informal.* to urge to action or response; goad; incite; prod: *It's mostly a question of giving our personnel the needle to make them try a little harder* (Wall Street Journal).

**on the needle,** *U.S. Slang.* addicted to heroin: *"How she managed to protect her children is a mystery. None of us has been in prison. None has been on the needle"* (New York Times).

**thread the needle,** to accomplish a difficult task: *[He] expressed hope that the committee "can succeed in making the compromises and threading the needle" to get authorization for the central Arizona plan* (William M. Blair).

[Old English *nǣdl*] —**nee′dle|like′,** *adj.*

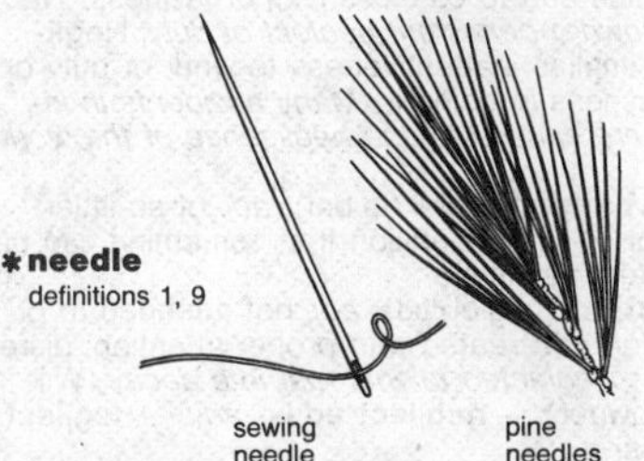


***needle**
definitions 1, 9

**needle bath,** a bath in which the water is forced against the body in needlelike jets.

**needle bug,** any one of the slender-bodied, long-legged hemipterous insects found in freshwater ponds, common in the United States.

**nee|dle|fish** (nē′dəl fish′), *n., pl.* **-fish|es** or (*collectively*) **-fish. 1** any one of a group of marine fishes comprising a family, similar to the freshwater garfish although not related to them; billfish; gar. **2** = pipefish.

**nee|dle|ful** (nē′dəl fu̇l), *n., pl.* **-fuls.** a suitable length of thread for using at one time with a needle.

**needle gun,** a breechloading rifle in which the charge is exploded by the impact of a needle or slender steel pin, used by the Prussian army in 1866 and 1870.

**needle ice,** slender bits of ice formed, as in wet soil or the bottom of a stream, during cold weather.

**nee|dle|leaf tree** (nē′dəl lēf′), any tree with narrow, pointed, needlelike or scalelike leaves, including most coniferous trees, such as firs, hemlocks, pines, cedars, and spruces.

**nee|dle-nosed** (nē′dəl nōzd′), *adj.* **1** having a tapered nose to reduce air resistance at high speeds: *The cramped cockpit of a needle-nosed, stub-winged plane* (Time). **2** having tapered ends for getting into small spaces or working with small objects: *needle-nosed pliers.*

**nee|dle|point** (nē′dəl point′), *n., adj.,* or **needle point.** —*n.* **1** embroidery made with colored yarns on a coarse, stiff canvas cloth and used to cover chairs and footstools, or to make wallhangings. Usually woolen yarns are used. **2** a lace made entirely with a needle instead of a bobbin, using a pattern of parchment or paper; point lace.

—*adj.* Also, **needle-point.** of or having to do with needlepoint.

**nee|dler** (nē′dlər), *n. Informal.* a person who incites or irritates others, usually by incessant nagging, heckling, reminding, or the like.

**nee|dle-shaped** (nē′dəl shāpt′), *adj.* long and slender, with one or both ends sharp.

**need|less** (nēd′lis), *adj.* not needed or wanted; unnecessary; useless: *It is silly to ask a needless question. Congress is taking a needless risk as long as it allows this important constitutional problem to remain clouded in doubt* (Newsweek). —**need′less|ly,** *adv.* —**need′less|ness,** *n.*

**nee|dle|stone** (nē′dəl stōn′), *n.* a mineral having needle-shaped crystals, such as natrolite.

**needle time,** *British.* the air time in radio broadcasting devoted to recorded music.

**needle trade** or **trades,** the trade or business of manufacturing clothing, including all of its members.

**needle valve,** a valve whose very small opening is controlled by a slender, needle-shaped rod projecting into it, used especially in carburetors and other devices requiring a precise adjustment of the flow of a liquid.

**nee|dle|wom|an** (nē′dəl wu̇m′ən), *n., pl.* **-women. 1** a woman who is a skillful sewer. **2** a woman who earns her living by sewing; seamstress.

**nee|dle|work** (nē′dəl wėrk′), *n.* **1** work done with a needle; sewing; embroidery. **2** the work or occupation of sewing with a needle.

**nee|dle|work|er** (nē′dəl wėr′kər), *n.* a person who does needlework.

**nee|dly** (nē′dlē), *adj.* like a needle or needles; full of needles: *a needly thorn, a needly bush.*

**need|ments** (nēd′mənts), *n.pl.* things needed; necessaries; requisites.

**need|n't** (nē′dənt), need not.

**needs** (nēdz), *adv.* because of necessity; necessarily: *A soldier needs must go where duty calls. You must needs be a stranger in this region ... else you would surely have heard of Mistress Hester Prynne* (Hawthorne). [Old English *nēdes,* (originally) genitive of *nēd* need]

**need|y** (nē′dē), *adj.,* **need|i|er, need|i|est.** not having enough to live on; characterized by poverty or need; very poor: *a needy family, to be in needy circumstances.* **SYN:** indigent, destitute, penniless.

**neem tree** (nēm), a meliaceous tree of India and Ceylon, sometimes 50 feet high, with broad, pinnate leaves; margosa. The natives chew its small twigs and use them as toothbrushes. [< Hindi *nīm*]

**neep** (nēp), *n. Scottish.* a turnip. [Old English *nǣp* < Latin *nāpus* turnip. See etym. of doublet **navew.**]

**ne'er** (nãr), *adv. Archaic.* never.

**ne'er-do-well** (nãr′dü wel′), *n., adj.* —*n.* a worthless fellow; good-for-nothing person: *The eldest son is a hard-drinking ne'er-do-well, with a bitter hostility toward his father* (Atlantic). **SYN:** scapegrace.

—*adj.* worthless; good-for-nothing: *one of those ne'er-do-well lads who seem to have a ... magnetic power for misfortunes* (Elizabeth Gaskell).

**neeze** (nēz), *v.i.,* **neezed, neez|ing.** *British.* to sneeze. [Middle English *nesen,* probably < Scandinavian (compare Old Icelandic *hnjōsa*)]

**ne|fan|dous** (ni fan′dəs), *adj.* unmentionable; abominable; impious. [< Latin *nefandus* (with English *-ous*) < *ne-* not + *fandus* to be spoken, gerundive of *fārī* to speak]

**ne|far|i|ous** (ni fãr′ē əs), *adj.* very wicked; villainous: *a nefarious scheme.* **SYN:** heinous, atrocious, infamous. [< Latin *nefārius* (with English *-ous*) < *nefās* < *ne-* not + *fās* right; (originally) divine decree < *fārī* speak] —**ne|far′i|ous|ly,** *adv.* —**ne|far′i|ous|ness,** *n.*

**neg.,** 1 negation. **2a** negative. **b** negatively.

**ne|gate** (ni gāt′, nē′gāt), *v.t.,* **-gat|ed, -gat|ing. 1** to destroy, nullify, or make ineffective: *If gravity can be understood scientifically and negated or neutralized in some relatively inexpensive manner* ... (New York Herald Tribune). **2** to declare not to exist; deny. [< Latin *negāre* (with English *-ate*[1]) say no, related to *nec* not]

**ne|gat|er** (ni gā′tər), *n.* = negator.

**ne|ga|tion** (ni gā′shən), *n.* **1** the act or fact of denying; denial: *Shaking the head is a sign of*

**Pronunciation Key:** hat, āge, cãre, fär; let, ēqual, tėrm; it, īce; hot, ōpen, ôrder; **oil, out;** cup, pu̇t, rüle; **ch**ild; lo**ng**; **th**in; **ᴛʜ**en; **zh,** measure; ə represents **a** in about, **e** in taken, **i** in pencil, **o** in lemon, **u** in circus.

*negation.* **2** the absence or opposite of some positive thing or quality: *Darkness is the negation of light. Death is nothing more than the negation of life* (Henry Fielding). **3** a negative statement, doctrine, or the like. **4** a thing or object of thought, consisting in the absence of something positive. [< Latin *negātiō, -ōnis* < *negāre* say no]

**ne|ga|tion|al** (ni gā′shə nəl), *adj.* using or involving negation; negative.

**ne|ga|tion|ist** (ni gā′shə nist), *n.* a person who denies or expresses negation, especially habitually.

**neg|a|tive** (neg′ə tiv), *adj., adv., n., v.,* **-tived, -tiv-ing.** —*adj.* **1a** saying no; stating that something is not so: *A shake of the head is negative. "I won't" is a negative expression.* **b** arguing against a question being debated: *the negative side.* **c** prohibitory, as a command or order. **2** not positive; consisting in the lack of the opposite: *Negative kindness means not being unkind. His negative suggestions are not helpful.* **3** *Mathematics.* **a** counting down from zero; minus: *Three below zero is a negative quantity. −5 is a negative number.* **b** lying on the side of a point, line, or plane opposite to that considered positive. **4a** of or having something to do with the kind of electricity produced on resin when it is rubbed with silk, or that is present in a charged body which has an excess of electrons: *Protons are positive; electrons are negative.* **b** having a tendency to gain electrons, and thus to become charged with negative electricity: *Oxygen and other nonmetals have a negative valence.* **c** measured or proceeding in the opposite direction to that considered as positive; of the part to which the current flows into the wire in an electric cell: *a negative electrode. Long ago, the direction of electric current flow was defined as being from positive to negative* (John R. Pierce). **5** *Photography.* showing the lights and shadows reversed: *the negative image on a photographic plate.* **6** showing the absence of a particular disease, condition, or germ. **7** *Biology.* moving or turning away from light, the earth, or any other stimulus: *If a plant organ reacts by turning ... away, the response is negative* (Fred W. Emerson). **8** *Logic.* (of a proposition) expressing denial of a predicate. **9** *Psychology.* resisting suggestions; very uncooperative. *Abbr:* neg.
—**adv.** *Informal.* no: *"Want to head home?" "Negative, Pop"* (John Updike).
—*n.* **1** a word or statement that says no or denies; negative reply or answer: *"I won't" is a negative. The positive and the negative are set before the mind for its choice* (Jonathan Edwards). **2** a negative quality or characteristic. **3** a negative number or quantity. **4** the negative element in an electric battery. **5** a photographic image in which the lights and shadows are reversed. Prints are made from it. **6** the right of veto.
—*v.t.* **1** to say no to; deny: *Father negatived our plan. The suggestion that it is a means of dealing with ectoparasites seems to be negatived by the following considerations* (New Scientist). **2** to vote against or veto. **3** to show to be false; disprove. **4** *Figurative.* to make useless; counteract; neutralize: *The method which both sides are using to negative the effects of atomic attack is the widest possible measure of dispersal* (London Times).
**in the negative, a** expressing disagreement by saying no; denying: *They unanimously answered in the negative* (Horace Walpole). **b** in favor of denying (a request, suggestion, or the like): *That should be determined in the negative* (Duke of Wellington).
**the negative,** the side that says no or denies in an argument especially in a formal debate.
[< Latin *negātīvus* < *negāre* say no] —**neg′a-tive|ly,** *adv.* —**neg′a|tive|ness,** *n.*

**negative acceleration,** a decrease in velocity.

**negative angle,** *Mathematics.* an angle formed by a line rotating in a clockwise direction. Compass directions in maritime navigation are given by means of negative angles.

**negative catalyst,** a substance that retards a chemical reaction without itself being permanently affected.

**negative electricity,** electricity in which the electron is the elementary unit.

**negative eugenics,** eugenics which attempts to increase the genetic transmission of favorable traits by encouraging persons who are below average mentally and physically to have fewer children.

**negative feedback,** feedback in which the output and input remain in a state of equilibrium; normal or stable feedback.

**negative income tax,** = guaranteed annual income. *Abbr:* NIT (no periods).

**negative lens,** = diverging lens.

**negative option,** the option of a person who received an unsolicited product or merchandise to return or refuse it within a given time or be charged for it by the seller: *The negative option ... used by Lloyds Bank, where the customer has 10 days to refuse the [credit] card, is banned in the US* (New Scientist).

**negative staining,** the immersing of small organisms, such as viruses and bacteria, in a stain which does not color them, so that their forms appear clearly defined against the colored background.

**neg|a|tiv|ism** (neg′ə tə viz′əm), *n.* **1** a tendency to say or do the opposite of what is suggested. **2** *Psychology.* a type of behavior marked by resistance to suggestion. Passive negativism is the kind in which the individual fails to do what is expected. Active negativism is the kind in which he does the opposite of what is expected. **3** *Philosophy.* **a** any doctrine of which doubt or denial is an essential characteristic, such as skepticism, agnosticism, or atheism. **b** any doctrine that rejects the validity of natural reality.

**neg|a|tiv|ist** (neg′ə tə vist), *n., adj.* —*n.* a negativistic person.
—*adj.* = negativistic.

**neg|a|tiv|is|tic** (neg′ə tə vis′tik), *adj.* given to or characterized by negativism.

**neg|a|tiv|i|ty** (neg′ə tiv′ə tē), *n.* negative quality or condition; negativeness.

**ne|ga|tor** (ni gā′tər), *n.* a person who denies. Also, **negater.**

**neg|a|to|ry** (neg′ə tôr′ē, -tōr′-), *adj.* denying; negative.

**neg|a|tron** (neg′ə tron), *n. Physics, Chemistry.* an electron with a negative charge, as contrasted with a positron or positively charged electron.

**neg|lect** (ni glekt′), *v., n.* —*v.t.* **1** to give too little care or attention to; slight: *to neglect one's children. Don't neglect your health.* SYN: See syn. under **slight. 2** to leave undone; not attend to: *The maid neglected her work.* SYN: disregard, ignore. **3** to omit; fail: *Don't neglect to water the plants before you leave.*
—*n.* **1** the act of neglecting; disregard: *His neglect of the truth is astonishing.* **2** a want of attention to what should be done: *That car has been ruined by neglect.* **3** the state of being neglected: *The children suffered from neglect. Rescue my poor remains from vile neglect* (Matthew Prior).
[< Latin *neglectus,* past participle of *negligere, neglegere,* variant of *neclegere* < *nec* not (< *ne-* not + *que* and) + *legere* pick up]
—*Syn. n.* **1 Neglect, negligence** mean lack of proper care or attention. **Neglect** implies habitual inattention due to carelessness or laziness: *He has shown a persistent neglect of duty.* **Negligence** implies inattentiveness to work or duty or carelessness in doing it: *Many accidents in industry are caused by the negligence of the workers.*

**neg|lect|a|ble** (ni glek′tə bəl), *adj.* of so little value or of such condition that something can be neglected; negligible.

**neg|lect|ed** (ni glek′tid), *adj.* not attended to or cared for; not treated with proper attention; disregarded: *Neglected talents rust into decay* (William Cowper). —**neg|lect′ed|ly,** *adv.* —**neg|lect′-ed|ness,** *n.*

**neg|lect|er** or **neg|lec|tor** (ni glek′tər), *n.* a person who neglects.

**neg|lect|ful** (ni glekt′fəl), *adj.* careless; negligent; heedless: *A man who does not vote is neglectful of his duty.* —**neg|lect′ful|ly,** *adv.* —**neg|lect′ful-ness,** *n.*

**né|gli|gé** (nā glē zhā′), *n. French.* negligee.

**neg|li|gee** (neg′lə zhā′, neg′lə zhā), *n.* **1** a woman's loose, usually decorative, dressing gown made of a light fabric. **2** any easy, informal dress or attire. [< French *négligée,* feminine past participle of *négliger* neglect, learned borrowing from Latin *negligere;* see etym. under **neglect**]

**neg|li|gence** (neg′lə jəns), *n.* **1a** lack of proper care or attention; neglect: *The ink was spilled on the rug through negligence.* SYN: remissness, inattention. See syn. under **neglect. b** *Law.* the failure to exercise reasonable care or the care required by the circumstances; lack of reasonable care in doing something or failing to do something: *A person is responsible in damages for the harm his negligence causes to another person* (Harry Kalven, Jr.). **2** careless conduct; indifference: *He dresses with easy negligence. Horace still charms with graceful negligence* (Alexander Pope). SYN: heedlessness, carelessness. **3** a careless or indifferent act.

**neg|li|gent** (neg′lə jənt), *adj.* **1** showing neglect; neglectful; given to neglect: *negligent officials. O, negligent and heedless discipline* (Shakespeare). SYN: remiss, derelict. **2** careless; indifferent. **3** in careless disorder: *All loose her negligent attire, All loose her golden hair* (Scott). [< Latin *negligēns, -entis,* present participle of *negligere;* see etym. under **neglect**] —**neg′li|gent|ly,** *adv.*

**neg|li|gi|bil|i|ty** (neg′lə jə bil′ə tē), *n.* the condition of being negligible.

**neg|li|gi|ble** (neg′lə jə bəl), *adj.* that can be disregarded: *In buying a suit, a difference of ten cents in price is negligible.* SYN: unimportant, insignificant. —**neg′li|gi|ble|ness,** *n.*

**neg|li|gi|bly** (neg′lə jə blē), *adv.* in a quantity or to a degree that can be disregarded.

**né|go|ciant** (nā gô syäɴ′), *n. French.* dealer; merchant.
► As used in English, the meaning of the word is close to being "a wine dealer," equivalent to French *négociant en vins.*

**ne|go|tia|bil|i|ty** (ni gō′shə bil′ə tē, -shē ə-), *n.* the condition of being negotiable.

**ne|go|tia|ble** (ni gō′shə bəl, -shē ə-), *adj.* **1** that can be talked over and settled: *negotiable terms, a negotiable demand.* **2** that can be negotiated or sold; whose ownership can be transferred, as bank drafts which are transferable by delivery, with or without endorsement: *negotiable securities. For accounting purposes, negotiable instruments are generally divided into two broad categories—notes receivable and notes payable* (Schmidt and Bergstrom). SYN: transferable. **3** that can be got past or over: *a negotiable path.* SYN: surmountable.

**ne|go|ti|ant** (ni gō′shē ənt, -shənt), *n.* a person who negotiates; agent.

**ne|go|ti|ate** (ni gō′shē āt), *v.,* **-at|ed, -at|ing.**
—*v.i.* to talk over and arrange terms: *The colonists negotiated for peace with the Indians. Negotiate, conciliate, arbitrate, try as hard as you can for agreement rather than stoppages, because strikes hurt everybody* (London Times). SYN: parley, confer, consult.
—*v.t.* **1** to arrange for, agree on, bring about, or get by negotiating: *They finally negotiated a peace treaty.* **2** *Informal.* **a** to get past or over: *The car negotiated the sharp curve by slowing down.* **b** to solve (a problem) or surmount (a difficulty) so as to be able to proceed toward something. **3a** to sell. **b** to circulate (as a bill of exchange) by transference and assignment of claim by endorsement. **c** to transfer or assign (a bill, stock, or other security) to another in return for some equivalent in value: *A broker negotiated the stocks and bonds for us.*
[< Latin *negōtiāre* (with English *-ate*) < *negōtium* business < *neg-* not (< *nec*) + *ōtium* ease, leisure, idleness]

**ne|go|ti|a|tion** (ni gō′shē ā′shən), *n.* the act of negotiating; arrangement of terms with others: *Negotiations for the new school are completed. ... the established channels of peaceable negotiation* (Duke of Wellington).

**ne|go|ti|a|tor** (ni gō′shē ā′tər), *n.* a person who negotiates.

**ne|go|ti|a|to|ry** (ni gō′shē ə tôr′ē, -tōr′-), *adj.* of or having to do with negotiation.

**Ne|gress** (nē′gris), *n.* a Negro woman or girl (often used in an unfriendly way).
► See **-ess** for a usage note.

**Ne|gri body** (nā′grē), a stainable structure found in the nerve cells of an animal infected with rabies. It is useful in arriving at the final diagnosis for the presence of this disease. [< Adelchi *Negri,* 1876-1912, an Italian physician]

**Ne|gril|lo** (ni gril′ō), *n., pl.* **-los.** a Pygmy of Africa. [< Spanish *negrillo* (diminutive) < *negro* Negro]

**Ne|grit|ic** (ni grit′ik), *adj.* of or having to do with Negroes or Negritos.

**ne|gri|to** (ni grē′to), *n., pl.* **-tos** or **-toes.** the ripened nut of the ivory palm.

**Ne|gri|to** (ni grē′tō), *n., pl.* **-tos** or **-toes,** *adj.* —*n.* a member of certain dwarfish Negroid peoples of southeastern Asia, especially of the Philippines and East Indies.
—*adj.* of or having to do with the Negritos.
[< Spanish *negrito* (diminutive) < *negro* Negro]

**Ne|gri|toid** (ni grē′toid), *adj.* resembling or related to the Negritos: *a Negritoid people.*

**ne|gri|tude** (nē′grə tüd, -tyüd; ne′grə-), *n.* **1** Often, **Negritude.** the distinctive qualities or characteristics of Negroes, especially African Negroes: *Black men ... have discovered the "African personality" and "negritude," and their attitude to blackness is not apologetic or resentful, but proud* (Punch). **2** pride in the cultural and artistic heritage of Negroes, especially African Negroes: *If any one idea has dominated the talk of Dakar's first World Festival of the Negro Arts, it is the controversy over "negritude," a word that is said to signify that the creative Negro artist is unique* (New York Times). [< French *négritude* (literally) the condition of being Negro < *nègre* Negro < Latin *niger* black. See etym. of doublet **nigritude.**]

**ne|gri|tu|di|nous** (nē′grə tü′də nəs, -tyü′-; neg′rə-), *adj.* Often, **Negritudinous.** characterized by or exhibiting negritude: *To continue to create works that will be Nigerian and African and negritudinous, I must respond to this call to say something, even as an artist* (Ben Enwonwu).

**Ne|gro** (nē′grō), *n., pl.* **-groes,** *adj.* —*n.* **1a** a person belonging to any of the black races of Africa, characterized by brown or black skin, coarse, woolly hair, and a broad, flat nose. The chief peoples of Africa south of the Sahara are Negroes. **b** a member of any other dark-skinned people. **2** a person having some black ancestors (subject to precise definition by law in certain states and countries).
—*adj.* **1** of or having to do with Negroes: *Negro melodies. The first Negro slaves were brought to Jamestown in Virginia in a Dutch ship as early as 1620* (H. G. Wells). **2** resembling Negroes.
[< Spanish, or Portuguese *negro* < Latin *niger* black]
▶ **Negro** and its derivations were formerly often written with a small *n,* but the regular practice today is to capitalize them. The pronunciations (nig′rō) and (nig′rə) occur, but are considered offensive by many, including most Negroes.
▶ See **black** for another usage note.

**Ne|groid** (nē′groid), *adj., n.* —*adj.* of, resembling, or related to the Negro race: *On the basis of the late appearance of the Negroes in Africa, and the distribution of the Oceanic Negro, some have suggested an Asiatic origin for the Negroid stock* (Beals and Hoijer).
—*n.* a person belonging to a Negroid race: *War, conquest, and the slave trade have permitted Negroids to appear in many ... areas* (Harbaugh and Goodrich).

**Ne|groi|dal** (ni groi′dəl), *adj.* = Negroid.

**Ne|gro|ness** (nē′grō nis, -grə-), *n.* the condition or quality of being Negro; blackness; negritude.

**Ne|gro|phil** (nē′grə fil), *n.* a person who favors the advancement of Negro interests or rights.

**Ne|gro|phile** (nē′grə fīl, -fil), *n.* = Negrophil.

**Ne|groph|i|lism** (ni grof′ə liz əm), *n.* a favoring the advancement of Negro interests or rights.

**Ne|groph|i|list** (ni grof′ə list), *n.* a person who favors the advancement of Negro interests and rights.

**Ne|gro|phobe** (nē′grə fōb), *n.* a person who has hatred or very great fear of Negroes.

**Ne|gro|pho|bi|a** (nē′grə fō′bē ə), *n.* hatred or very great fear of Negroes.

**ne|gus** (nē′gəs), *n.* a drink made of port or other wine, hot water, sugar, lemon, and nutmeg. [< Francis *Negus,* died 1732, a British army colonel, who concocted it]

**Ne|gus** (nē′gəs), *n.* the title of the sovereign of Ethiopia. [< Amharic *nəgus* king]

**Neh.,** Nehemiah.

**Ne|he|mi|ah** (nē′ə mī′ə), *n.* **1** a Hebrew leader of the 400's B.C. He returned from exile in Babylonia and rebuilt the walls of Jerusalem about 444 B.C. **2** the book of the Old Testament describing his achievements. *Abbr:* Neh.

**Ne|he|mi|as** (nē′ə mī′əs), *n.* Nehemiah, in the Douay Bible.

**Neh|ru** (nā′rü), *n.* = Nehru jacket.

*** Nehru jacket** or **coat,** a long narrow jacket or coat that buttons up the front, with a high collar; Mao jacket: *Those who feel that tuxedos are old-fashioned are trying out the long mandarin-collared ... Nehru coats* (Time). [< Jawaharlal *Nehru,* 1889-1964, prime minister of India]

*** Nehru jacket**

**Nehru suit,** a suit consisting of a Nehru jacket and tight pants.

**N.E.I.,** Netherlands East Indies.

**neigh** (nā), *n., v.* —*n.* the sound that a horse makes, long, high-pitched, and quavering. [< verb]
—*v.i.* to make the sound that a horse makes.
[Old English *hnǣgan*]

**neigh|bor** (nā′bər), *n., v., adj.* —*n.* **1** someone who lives in the next house or nearby: *I called him my neighbour, because his plantation lay next to mine* (Daniel Defoe). **2** a person or thing that is near or next to another: *The big tree brought down several of its smaller neighbors as it fell.* **3** a fellow human being: *Love thy neighbor.*
—*v.i.* **1** to live or be near (to): *a copse that neighbours by* (Shakespeare). *He seemed ... to suck in fresh vigour from the soil which he neighboured* (Charles Lamb). **2** to be friendly (with).
—*v.t.* **1** to touch or border upon; adjoin: *The United States neighbors Canada to the north and Mexico to the south.* **2** to place or bring near: *So neighbour'd to him, and yet so unseen, She stood* (Keats).
—*adj.* living or situated near to another; nearby: *two neighbor farms.*
[Old English *nēahgebūr* < *nēah* nigh, nearer + *gebūr* dweller, countryman]

**neigh|bor|hood** (nā′bər hu̇d), *n., adj.* —*n.* **1** the region near some place, thing, or person: *She lives in the neighborhood of the mill.* **SYN:** vicinity, environs. **2** a place; district: *Is North Street a good neighborhood?* **SYN:** locality. **3** people living near one another; people of a place: *The whole neighborhood came to the big party.* **4** neighborly feeling or conduct; neighborliness: *They live in love and good neighborhood with one another.* **5** nearness: *a large brindled cat ... kept back from its prey by our unwelcome neighbourhood* (Edward G. Bulwer-Lytton). **SYN:** proximity.
—*adj.* of or having to do with a neighborhood: *a neighborhood newspaper.*
**in the neighborhood of,** *Informal.* somewhere near; about: *The literacy rate in Thailand is in the neighborhood of 60 per cent.*

**neigh|bor|ing** (nā′bər ing, -bring), *adj.* living or being near; bordering; near; adjoining; adjacent: *We heard the bird calls from the neighboring woods.*

**neigh|bor|less** (nā′bər lis), *adj.* without neighbors.

**neigh|bor|li|ness** (nā′bər lē nis), *n.* neighborly disposition or quality.

**neigh|bor|ly** (nā′bər lē), *adj.* like or befitting a good neighbor; kindly, friendly, or sociable: *He hath a neighbourly charity in him* (Shakespeare).

**neigh|bour** (nā′bər), *n., v.i., v.t., adj. Especially British.* neighbor.

**neigh|bour|hood** (nā′bər hu̇d), *n., adj. Especially British.* neighborhood.

**nei|ther** (nē′ᴛʜər, nī′-), *conj., adj., pron., adv.*
—*conj.* **1** not either: *Neither you nor I will go.* **2** nor yet; nor: *They toil not, neither do they spin* (Matthew 6:28).
—*adj.* not the one or the other; not either: *Neither statement is true.*
—*pron.* not either: *Neither of the statements is true.*
—*adv. Dialect.* either: *nor the old lord neither* (George Meredith).
[Middle English *neyder,* earlier *naither,* alteration (influenced by *either*) of *nauther,* Old English *nāhwæther* < *nā* no + *hwæther* whether]
▶ The pronoun **neither** is regularly construed as a singular in formal English. In informal English, however, it is often treated as a plural, particulary if there is a dependent *of-* phrase with a plural object: *Neither of the men were at home.*

**nek** (nek), *n. Afrikaans.* a narrow ridge that connects two hills; saddle. [< Afrikaans *nek* < Dutch, neck]

**nek|ton** (nek′ton), *n.* the relatively large organisms, such as fish, that possess the power to swim freely in oceans and lakes, independent of water movements, in contrast to plankton that float or benthos that live on the ocean floor. [< German *Nekton* < Greek *nēktón,* neuter of *nēktós,* verbal adjective < *nēchein* to swim, related to *neîn* swim]

**nek|ton|ic** (nek ton′ik), *adj.* of or having to do with nekton.

**nel|lie**[1] (nel′ē), *adj. Slang.* feminine; effeminate. [< *Nellie,* nickname of *Helen*]

**nel|ly** or **nel|lie**[2] (nel′ē), *n.*
**not on your nelly** (or **nellie**), *British Slang.* emphatically no; absolutely not: *"Wear bell-bottoms? Not on your nelly," said a burly, 6 ft. 3 in. corporal* (Punch).
[shortened < *not on your Nelly Duff,* rhyming slang for *not on your puff,* "puff" meaning "(breath of) life"]

**nel|son** (nel′sən), *n. Wrestling.* a hold in which pressure is applied against an opponent's arm and neck: *a half nelson, a quarter nelson.* [apparently < *Nelson,* a proper name]

**ne|lum|bo** (ni lum′bō), *n., pl.* **-bos.** any one of a small group of aquatic plants of the water-lily family, as the sacred lotus of India and the water chinquapin. [variant of New Latin *Nelumbium* < Singhalese *neḷumbu*]

**nem|a|thel|minth** (nem′ə thel′minth), *n.* any one of a former grouping of worms, including the acanthocephalans, nematodes, and various other cylindrical worms. [< Greek *nêma, -atos* thread + English *helminth*]

**ne|mat|ic** (ni mat′ik), *adj.* (of liquid crystals) having the molecules arranged in loose parallel, vertical lines. [< Greek *nêma, -atos* thread + English *-ic*]

**nem|a|to|cide** (nem′ə tə sīd), *n.* a chemical, spray, or other substance used to kill nematodes.

**nem|a|to|cyst** (nem′ə tə sist), *n.* one of the cells of a coelenterate that contains a coiled thread-like stinging process, discharged to capture prey and for defense. [< Greek *nêma, -atos* thread + English *cyst*]

**nem|a|to|cyst|ic** (nem′ə tə sis′tik), *adj.* having to do with or having the characteristics of a nematocyst.

**Nem|a|to|da** (nem′ə tō′də), *n.pl.* the class or phylum of invertebrates comprising the nematodes.

**nem|a|tode** (nem′ə tōd), *n., adj.* —*n.* any one of a class or phylum of slender, unsegmented, cylindrical worms, often tapered near the ends; roundworm. Parasitic forms such as the hookworm, pinworm, and trichina belong to this phylum.
—*adj.* of or belonging to the nematodes.
[< New Latin *Nematoda* the class or phylum name, ultimately < Greek *nêma, -atos* thread < *neîn* spin]

**nem|a|toid** (nem′ə toid), *adj., n.* —*adj.* **1** thread-like. **2** belonging to the order containing the typical nematodes, or sometimes all the nematodes.
—*n.* a nematoid worm.

**nem|a|to|log|i|cal** (nem′ə tə loj′ə kəl), *adj.* of or having to do with nematology.

**nem|a|tol|o|gist** (nem′ə tol′ə jist), *n.* an expert in nematology.

**nem|a|tol|o|gy** (nem′ə tol′ə jē), *n.* the branch of parasitology that deals with nematodes. [< Greek *nêma, -atos* thread + English *-logy*]

**Nem|bu|tal** (nem′byə tôl, -tal), *n. Trademark.* pentobarbital sodium.

**Ne|me|an** (ni mē′ən, nē′mē-), *adj.* of or having to do with Nemea, a valley in Argolis, Greece.

**Nemean games,** a festival held at Nemea every two years by the ancient Greeks.

**Nemean lion,** *Greek Mythology.* a lion killed by Hercules at Nemea as the first of his twelve tasks: *As hardy as the Nemean lion's nerve* (Shakespeare).

**ne|mer|te|an** or **ne|mer|ti|an** (ni mėr′tē ən), *n., adj.* —*n.* any one of a phylum of chiefly marine worms, characterized by an elongated, flattened and unsegmented, contractile body, with a complete digestive system, mouth, and anus; ribbon worm. Nemerteans are brightly colored, sometimes growing up to 90 feet long and have a long extensible proboscis.
—*adj.* **1** belonging to the nemerteans. **2** of or having to do with the nemerteans.
[< New Latin *Nemertea* the phylum name (< Greek *Nēmertês,* a sea nymph) + English *-an, -ian*]

**ne|mer|tine** (ni mėr′tīn, -tin), *n., adj.* = nemertean.

**nem|er|tin|e|an** (nem′ər tin′ē ən), *n., adj.* = nemertean.

**ne|me|sia** (ni mē′zhə, -shē ə, -sē-), *n.* an annual or perennial plant of the figwort family, native to South Africa, often grown for decorative purposes because of its varicolored flowers. [< New Latin *Nemesia* the genus name < Greek *nḗmesis,* a related plant]

**Nem|e|sis** (nem′ə sis), *n. Greek Mythology.* the goddess of vengeance. [< Greek *Némesis* < *némein* give what is due]

**nem|e|sis** (nem′ə sis), *n., pl.* **-ses** (-sēz). **1** just punishment for evil deeds; retribution: *the inward suffering which is the worst form of nemesis* (George Eliot). **2** a person who punishes another for evil deeds; agent of retribution: *The courageous policeman was the bandit's nemesis.* **SYN:** avenger. [< *Nemesis*]

**ne|mo me im|pu|ne la|ces|sit** (nē′mō mē im-pyü′nē lə ses′it), *Latin.* nobody provokes me with impunity (the motto of Scotland).

**ne|moph|i|la** (ni mof′ə lə), *n.* an annual American plant of the waterleaf family, having showy blue flowers with a white center. [< New Latin *Nemophila* the genus name < Greek *némos* wooded pasture + *philos* loving]

**nem|o|ral** (nem′ər əl), *adj.* **1** of or having to do with a wood or grove. **2** inhabiting or frequenting woods, as animals. [< Latin *nemorālis* < *nemus, nemoris* grove]

**ne|ne** (nā′nā′), *n.* a very rare wild goose of Hawaii, grayish brown with black face and bill; Hawaiian goose. It is the state bird of Hawaii. [< Hawaiian *nēnē*]

**nen|u|phar** (nen′yə fär), *n.* a water lily, especially the common white or yellow variety. [< Medieval Latin *nenuphar* < Arabic *nīnūfar, nīlūfar,* ulti-

**Pronunciation Key: hat, āge, cãre, fär; let, ēqual, tėrm; it, īce; hot, ōpen, ôrder; oil, out; cup, pu̇t, rüle; child; long; thin; ᴛʜen; zh, measure; ə represents a in about, e in taken, i in pencil, o in lemon, u in circus.**

mately < Sanskrit *nīlotpala* blue lotus < *nīl* blue + *utpala* lotus]

**neo-**, *combining form.* **1** new; recent, as in *neocolonialism.*
**2** a new, modified form of: *Neoclassicism = a new, modified form of classicism.*
**3** most recent division of a geological period: *Neocene = the most recent part of the Tertiary period.*
[< Greek *néos* new]

**ne|o|ars|phen|a|min** (nē′ō ärs′fi nam′in), *n.* = neoarsphenamine.

**ne|o|ars|phen|a|mine** (nē′ō ärs′fen ə mēn′, -fi-nam′in), *n.* an organic arsenic compound, a yellow powder similar to arsphenamine but more readily soluble in water, used intravenously, before the development of antibiotics, in the treatment of syphilis and other bacterial infections. *Formula:* $C_{13}H_{13}As_2N_2NaO_4S$

**Ne|o|cene** (nē′ə sēn), *n., adj.* — *n.* **1** the later division of the Tertiary system of the Cenozoic era, comprising the Miocene and the Pliocene. **2** the rocks formed during this division.
— *adj.* of or having to do with this division or its rocks.
[< *neo-* + Greek *kainós* new]

**ne|o-Chris|ti|an|i|ty** (nē′ō kris chē an′ə tē), *n.* Christianity influenced or reshaped by a current philosophy, especially by rationalism.

**ne|o|clas|sic** (nē′ō klas′ik, -kläs′-), *adj.* of or having to do with the revival of classical principles or practices, especially in art, music, and literature: *Graceful neoclassic Corinthian columns in glazed white ceramic* (New Yorker).

**ne|o|clas|si|cal** (nē′ō klas′ə kəl, -kläs′-), *adj.* = neoclassic.

**ne|o|clas|si|cism** (nē′ō klas′ə siz əm, -kläs′-), *n.* **1** a movement in art and literature based on an interest in classical style and a desire to impose a form conceived of as embodying the formal principles of classical reason, restraint, order, and symmetry: **a** a movement in art of the late 1700's and early 1800's: *First came neoclassicism, during and shortly after the reign of Napoleon I. Its leaders ... opposed the luxurious ornamentation of the rococo period* (Thomas Munro). **b** a movement in literature of the late 1600's and the 1700's, based on the classics of ancient Greece and Rome. **2** *Music.* a movement, especially of the 1900's, based on an interest in and return to the style of the pre-Romantic composers, especially the classical style of Johann Sebastian Bach: *[Darius] Milhaud's musical idiom doggedly remains within the realm of neoclassicism* (New York Times). **3** neoclassic character in art or literature.

**ne|o|clas|si|cist** (nē′ō klas′ə sist, -kläs′-), *n.* a follower of neoclassicism in art, literature, or music.

**ne|o|co|lo|ni|al** (nē′ō kə lō′nē əl), *adj., n.* — *adj.* supporting or practicising neocolonialism: *a neocolonial power.*
— *n.* a person who supports or practices neocolonialism.

**ne|o|co|lo|ni|al|ism** (nē′ō kə lō′nē ə liz′əm), *n.* the supposed policy or practice of a large nation to dominate politically or economically smaller nations, especially former colonies; imperialism: *Indonesia and others ... use the notion of neocolonialism to attack the former colonial Powers* (Manchester Guardian Weekly).

**ne|o|co|lo|ni|al|ist** (nē′ō kə lō′nē ə list), *n., adj.* — *n.* an advocate or supporter of neocolonialism.
— *adj.* of or having to do with neocolonialism: *Thus African leaders who recognize that only the west can supply the resources they need to bring their people into twentieth-century economic life are still suspicious of western imperialist or "neocolonialist" aims* (London Times).

**ne|o|cor|tex** (nē′ō kôr′teks), *n, pl.* **-ti|ces** (-tə-sēz). the dorsal part of the cerebral cortex, which is specially large in higher mammals and is the most recent in development; neopallium: *Between the time of Australopithecus and Neanderthal man, the brain underwent rapid changes, gaining the large neocortex which was to provide the human species with its ability to manipulate symbols* (Science News).

**ne|o|cos|mic** (nē′ō koz′mik), *adj.* belonging to the modern period of the world, especially the races of mankind in historic times.

**ne|o-Da|da** (nē′ō dä′də), *n., adj.* — *n.* the revival of Dada in contemporary art; anti-art: *Abstraction, neo-Dada, and other up-to-date tendencies can be seen flourishing among "unofficial" works of the younger generation* (Hilton Kramer).
— *adj.* of or having to do with neo-Dada.

**ne|o-Da|da|ism** (nē′ō dä′də iz əm), *n.* = neo-Dada.

**ne|o-Da|da|ist** (nē′ō dä′də ist), *n.* a neo-Dada painter, sculptor, or decorator.

**Ne|o-Dar|win|i|an** (nē′ō där win′ē ən), *adj., n.*
— *adj.* having to do with Neo-Darwinism.
— *n.* an advocate of Neo-Darwinism.

**Ne|o-Dar|win|ism** (nē′ō där′wə niz əm), *n.* the theory, based on Darwinism, that the evolution of animals and plants depends upon the operation of natural selection and upon the variability caused by mutations within a population.

**Ne|o-Dar|win|ist** (nē′ō där′wə nist), *n., adj.* — *n.* an advocate of Neo-Darwinism.
— *adj.* of or having to do with Neo-Darwinism.

***ne|o|dym|i|um** (nē′ə dim′ē əm), *n.* a yellowish chemical element found in cerite and various other rare minerals. It is one of the rare-earth elements. The rose-colored salts of neodymium are used to color glass and in ceramic glazes. [< *neo-* + (di)*dymium*]

***neodymium**

| symbol | atomic number | atomic weight | oxidation state |
|---|---|---|---|
| Nd | 60 | 144.24 | 3 |

**ne|o-fas|cism** (nē′ō fash′iz əm), *n.* any movement to establish or restore the former principles and beliefs of fascism.

**ne|o-fas|cist** or **ne|o-Fas|cist** (nē′ō fash′ist), *n., adj.* — *n.* **1** a member of a political party favoring neo-fascism. **2** a person who favors or supports neo-fascism.
— *adj.* of or having to do with neo-fascism or neo-fascists.

**ne|o-Freud|i|an** (nē′ō froi′dē ən), *adj., n.* — *adj.* of or having to do with a group of psychoanalysts who follow Freud's major theories but emphasize social and other factors as part of the causes of individual neuroses: *the neo-Freudian systems of Erich Fromm and Karen Horney.*
— *n.* a person who believes in or uses neo-Freudian theories and methods: *He may learn from such neo-Freudians as Erik Erikson how the quest for personal identity may blend with broader social goals* (Saturday Review).

**Ne|o|gae|a** (nē′ə jē′ə), *n.* the Neotropical region, considered with reference to the geographical distribution of plants and animals. [< New Latin *Neogaea* < Greek *néos* new + *gaîa* earth]

**Ne|o|gae|an** (nē′ə jē′ən), *adj.* of or having to do with the Neogaea.

**Ne|o|gene** (nē′ə jēn), *n., adj.* — *n.* **1** the later of two divisions of the Cenozoic era (comprising the Miocene, Pliocene, Pleistocene, and Recent periods). **2** the rock strata formed during this division. **3** = Neocene.
— *adj.* of or having to do with these divisions or their rocks.
[< *neo-* + Greek *-genēs* born]

**ne|o|gen|e|sis** (nē′ō jen′ə sis), *n. Biology.* the formation of new tissue; regeneration.

**ne|o|ge|net|ic** (nē′ō jə net′ik), *adj. Biology.* of or having to do with neogenesis.

**ne|o|gla|cial** (nē′ō glā′shəl), *adj.* of or having to do with neoglaciation: *neoglacial moraines, neoglacial accumulations.*

**ne|o|gla|ci|a|tion** (nē′ō glā′shē ā′shən), *n.* the formation of new glaciers: *Historical records of the latest glacier fluctuations during neoglaciation are available from many Alpine regions* (Scientific American).

**ne|o-Goth|ic** (nē′ō goth′ik), *adj.* of or resembling the Gothic Revival: *Toronto was a small town—a murmurous place of horse troughs, ice wagons, [and] neo-Gothic churches* (Maclean's).

**ne|o|gram|mar|i|an** (nē′ō grə mãr′ē ən), *n., adj.* — *n.* any one of a group of linguists of the late 1800's who maintained that phonetic laws admit of no exceptions.
— *adj.* having to do with or resembling the neogrammarians: *Both authors are in line with the best neogrammarian tradition. Changes can only be regular; for apparent exceptions the cause(s) will be found sooner or later* (O. Szemerényi). [translation of German *Junggrammatiker* (literally) young grammarian]

**ne|o-Greek** (nē′ō grēk′), *adj.* belonging to or representing a revival of the ancient Greek style, as in architecture.

**Ne|o-He|bra|ic** (nē′ō hi brā′ik), *n., adj.* — *n.* Hebrew as written and spoken since the Diaspora, especially by scholars.
— *adj.* of or having to do with this form of Hebrew.

**ne|o|im|pe|ri|al** (nē′ō im pir′ē əl), *adj.* of or having to do with neoimperialism: *This analysis could embrace not just neoimperial China and neoimperial Russia* (C. L. Sulzberger).

**ne|o|im|pe|ri|al|ism** (nē′ō im pir′ē ə liz′əm), *n.* a revival or recurrence of imperialism.

**ne|o|im|pe|ri|al|ist** (nē′ō im pir′ē ə list), *n.* a person who supports neoimperialism: *I believe that, in fact, we are in danger of seeing the isolationists of the 1920s and 1930s replaced by the neoimperialists, who somehow imagine that the United States has a mandate to impose an American solution the world around* (George McGovern).

**ne|o|im|pres|sion|ism** (nē′ō im presh′ə niz əm), *n.* a theory and technique of painting, developed by Georges Seurat (1859-1891), consisting essentially in the adaptation of scientific methodology to impressionist principles through pointillism (the use of dots and squares of colors according to predetermined procedures).

**ne|o|im|pres|sion|ist** (nē′ō im presh′ə nist), *n.* an artist who uses neoimpressionism.

**ne|o|i|so|la|tion|ism** (nē′ō ī′sə lā′shə niz əm, -is′ə-), *n.* a revival or recurrence of isolationism.

**ne|o|i|so|la|tion|ist** (nē′ō ī′sə lā′shə nist, -is′ə-), *adj., n.* — *adj.* having to do with neoisolationism.
— *n.* a person who supports neoisolationism.

**ne|o-Kant|i|an** (nē′ō kan′tē ən), *adj., n.* — *adj.* of or having to do with the followers and successors of Immanuel Kant. — *n.* a follower of Kant and his philosophy.

**ne|o-Keynes|i|an** (nē′ō kān′zē ən), *adj., n.* — *adj.* having to do with or based upon the Keynesian concepts of government spending and fiscal programs as major factors in economic growth. — *n.* a supporter of a neo-Keynesian fiscal policy.

**Ne|o-La|marck|i|an** (nē′ō lə mär′kē ən), *adj., n.*
— *adj.* of or having to do with Neo-Lamarckism.
— *n.* = Neo-Lamarckist.

**Ne|o-La|marck|ism** (nē′ō lə mär′kiz əm), *n.* the revival in a modified form of Lamarck's theory of organic evolution that maintains that characteristics acquired by parents during their lifetime can be inherited by their offspring.

**Ne|o-La|marck|ist** (nē′ō lə mär′kist), *n.* an advocate of Neo-Lamarckism.

**ne|o-Lat|in** (nē′ō lat′ən), *n., adj.* — *n.* Latin written and used, especially in modern scientific literature, more or less as a living language; Modern Latin. — *adj.* of or having to do with such Latin.

**ne|o|lith** (nē′ə lith), *n.* a neolithic stone implement.

**ne|o|lith|ic** or **Ne|o|lith|ic** (nē′ə lith′ik), *adj., n.*
— *adj.* of the later Stone Age, marked by the beginning of agriculture and animal husbandry, and the use of polished stone weapons and tools: *Neolithic man witnessed profound social changes.* — *n.* the neolithic period.
[< *neo-* + Greek *líthos* stone + English *-ic*]

**ne|o|lo|gian** (nē′ə lō′jən), *adj., n.* — *adj.* given to neologism, as in views on religious subjects.
— *n.* a neologist, as on religious subjects.

**ne|o|log|i|cal** (nē′ə loj′ə kəl), *adj.* of, having to do with, or characterized by neology or neologism.
— **ne′o|log′i|cal|ly,** *adv.*

**ne|ol|o|gism** (nē ol′ə jiz əm), *n.* **1** the use of new words or old words with new meanings: *His particular grievance was neologisms ... even the newspaper, he complained, had got into the habit of using the adjective "off-colored"—properly applied only to certain diamonds—to describe the pigmentation of half-caste people* (New Yorker). **2** a new word or expression or a new meaning for an old word: *Such neologisms are clipped words like* lube *for* lubricating oil *and* co-ed *for* co-educational; *back-formations like* to televise *(1931) from* television ...; *blends like* cablegram *from* cable *and* telegram ...; *artificial or made-up formations like* carborundum, cellophane, *and* pianola (Simeon Potter). *The paradox is, therefore, that what may appear to the individual speaker as a neologism may be in the total overview of the language a long-established form* (Harold B. Allen). **3** the introduction of new views or doctrines, especially on religious subjects. [< French *néologisme* < Greek *néos* new + *lógos* word < *légein* speak]

**ne|ol|o|gist** (nē ol′ə jist), *n.* **1** a person who introduces or uses neologisms in language. **2** a person given to neologism in views, especially on religious subjects.

**ne|ol|o|gis|tic** (nē ol′ə jis′tik), *adj.* of or having to do with neologism or neologists.

**ne|ol|o|gize** (nē ol′ə jīz), *v.i.,* **-gized, -giz|ing.**
**1** to introduce or use neologisms in language.
**2** to introduce or adopt new views, especially on religious subjects.

**ne|ol|o|gy** (nē ol′ə jē), *n., pl.* **-gies.** = neologism.

**ne|o-Mal|thu|sian** (nē′ō mal thü′zhən, -zē ən), *adj., n.* — *adj.* of or having to do with the theory or view, based upon Malthusianism, which advocates selective birth control as a means of eliminating poverty and raising the standard of living.
— *n.* an advocate of this theory or view: *The neo-Malthusians of the 1900's urge planned parenthood* (H. W. Spiegel).

**ne|o-Mal|thu|sian|ism** (nē′ō mal thü′zhə niz əm, -zē ə-), *n.* the theories of the neo-Malthusians.

**Ne|o-Mel|a|ne|sian** (nē′ō mel′ə nē′zhən, -shən), *n.* the pidgin English of Melanesia; bêche-de-mer.

**ne|o|my|cin** (nē′ə mī′sin), *n.* an antibiotic substance similar to streptomycin and obtained from a related soil actinomycete. It is used in the treatment of tuberculosis and other bacterial diseases. [< *neo-* + (strepto)*mycin*]

***ne|on** (nē′on), *n., adj.* **— *n.*** **1** a rare chemical element that is a colorless, odorless, inert gas, forming a very small part of the air. Tubes containing neon are used in electric signs or lamps, giving off a fiery red glow. **2** = neon lamp. **3** a sign for advertising made up of neon lamps. **4** the light or glow of a neon lamp.
**— *adj.*** **1** composed of neon lamps: *a neon sign.* **2** like a neon lamp or light: ... *beneath the flickering neon sky* (Manchester Guardian Weekly). [< New Latin *neon* < Greek *neón,* neuter, new]

***neon**
definition 1

| symbol | atomic number | atomic weight |
|---|---|---|
| Ne | 10 | 20.183 |

**ne|o|na|tal** (nē′ō nā′təl), *adj.* of or having to do with newborn babies: *neonatal disease, neonatal mortality.* **—ne′o|na′tal|ly,** *adv.*
**ne|o|nate** (nē′ə nāt), *n.* a newborn baby. [< *neo-* + Latin *nātus* born, past participle of *nāscī* be born; see etym. under **native**]
**ne|o-Na|zi** (nē′ō nät′sē, -nat′-), *n., adj.* **— *n.*** **1** a member of a political party favoring neo-Nazism. **2** a person who favors or supports neo-Nazism.
**— *adj.*** of or having to do with neo-Nazism or neo-Nazis.
**ne|o-Na|zi|ism** (nē′ō nät′sē iz əm, -nat′siz-), *n.* = neo-Nazism.
**ne|o-Na|zism** (nē′ō nät′siz əm, -nat′-), *n.* any movement to restore the principles and beliefs of Nazism.
**neon lamp** or **light,** a glass tube filled with neon gas and containing two electrodes instead of a filament. When voltage is applied to the electrodes, an electric discharge occurs and the gas glows fiery red.
**neon tetra,** a small, bright red and blue fish of the upper Amazon region, commonly raised in aquariums.
**ne|o|or|tho|dox** (nē′ō ôr′thə doks), *adj.* of or characteristic of neoorthodoxy.
**ne|o|or|tho|dox|y** (nē′ō ôr′thə dok′sē), *n.* **1** a movement in Protestantism reverting to traditional Christian dogmas in reaction to liberalism: *In 1943 theological liberalism looked like an outworn creed beside the fashionable stringencies of* [*Reinhold*] *Niebuhr's neoorthodoxy* (Time). **2** any movement in other religions, such as Islam and Judaism, returning to an older form of religious beliefs and practices.
**ne|o|pa|gan** (nē′ō pā′gən), *adj.* of or characteristic of a revival of paganism.
**ne|o|pal|li|um** (nē′ō pal′ē əm), *n.* = neocortex.
**ne|o|phil|i|a** (nē′ō fil′ē ə), *n.* a love of novelty; great interest in anything new. [< New Latin *neophilia* < *neo-* + Greek *philiā* affection]
**ne|o|phil|i|ac** (nē′ō fil′ē ak), *n.* a person or animal characterized or affected by neophilia.
**ne|o|pho|bi|a** (nē′ō fō′bē ə), *n.* fear of anything new.
**ne|o|phyte** (nē′ə fīt), *n.* **1** a new convert; person recently admitted to a religious body. **2** a person who is new at something; beginner; novice: *The employer looked upon the new office boy as a hopeful young neophyte.* **SYN:** tyro. **3** in the Roman Catholic Church: **a** a newly ordained priest. **b** a novice of a religious order. **4** (in the early Christian Church) a person newly baptized. **5** *U.S.* (in fraternities) a person who has completed his pledging period, but has yet to be initiated into the fraternity. [< Latin *neophytus* < Greek *neóphytos* < *néos* new + *phýein* grow, produce]
**ne|o|pi|li|na** (nē′ō pi lī′nə), *n.* a primitive mollusk found at great depths in the Pacific Ocean. It is a living representative of an animal group which had previously been known to exist only as fossils 300 to 500 million years old. *The structure of neopilina shows it is much like the annelids, or segmented worms* (Science News Letter). [< New Latin *Neopilina* the genus name]
**ne|o|pla|sia** (nē′ə plā′zhə), *n.* the development of new tissue or of neoplasms.
**ne|o|plasm** (nē′ō plaz əm), *n.* a new, abnormal growth of tissue, such as a tumor: ... *organizations ... devoted to improving the control of those eroding growths of many types of body cells, neoplasms collectively known as cancer* (Perspectives in Cancer Research). [< *neo-* + Greek *plásma* something formed]
**ne|o|plas|tic** (nē′ə plas′tik), *adj.* having to do with a neoplasm.
**ne|o|plas|ti|cism** (nē′ō plas′tə siz əm), *n.* a movement in modern art led by the Dutch artist Piet Mondrian (1872-1944), emphasizing abstract and geometric designs and forms; De Stijl.
**ne|o|plas|ti|cist** (nē′ō plas′tə sist), *n.* a follower of neoplasticism.
**ne|o|plas|ty** (nē′ə plas′tē), *n., pl.* **-ties.** plastic surgery to repair or restore a part.
**Ne|o|pla|ton|ic** or **Ne|o-Pla|ton|ic** (nē′ō plə ton′ik), *adj.* having to do with the Neoplatonists or their doctrines.
**Ne|o|pla|to|nism** or **Ne|o-Pla|to|nism** (nē′ō plā′tə niz əm), *n.* **1** a philosophical and religious system composed chiefly of elements of Platonism, Oriental mysticism, and, in its later phases, Christianity, represented especially in the writings of Plotinus, Porphyry, Proclus, and Philo. It originated in Alexandria in the 200's A.D. **2** a later philosophy based upon this or upon Platonism.
**Ne|o|pla|to|nist** or **Ne|o-Pla|to|nist** (nē′ō plā′tə nist), *n.* a believer in the doctrines or principles of Neoplatonism.
**ne|o|prene** (nē′ə prēn), *n.* any one of a group of synthetic rubbers made from chloroprene, used in products where resistance to oil, heat, and weather is desirable. [< *neo-* + (chloro)*prene*]
**Ne|op|tol|e|mus** (nē′op tol′ə məs), *n.* = Pyrrhus.
**ne|o|re|al|ism** (nē′ō rē′ə liz əm), *n.* a contemporary form of realism in literature, art, and especially motion pictures, characterized by a strict adherence to physical or photographic detail, emphasis on earthy and realistic settings, and a preoccupation with social themes: *Italian neorealism ... the ... desire to search out life with the camera and throw it on the screen without apology or moral stricture* (Saturday Review).
**ne|o|re|al|ist** (nē′ō rē′ə list), *n., adj.* **— *n.*** a person who believes in or follows the principles of neorealism: *A story of love and squalor in equal measure, directed and written by two of Italy's most formidable neorealists* (Time).
**— *adj.*** of or having to do with neorealism: *A new Japanese film ... suggests that the use of the neorealist approach has been firmly adopted by the Japanese* (London Times).
**ne|o|re|al|is|tic** (nē′ō rē′ə lis′tik), *adj.* = neorealist.
**ne|o-Ro|man** (nē′ō rō′mən), *adj.* belonging to or representing a revival of the ancient Roman style, as in architecture.
**ne|o|ro|man|tic** (nē′ō rō man′tik), *adj., n.* **— *adj.*** of, having to do with, or characteristic of a revival of romantic style in literature, music, and art, especially in the 1900's: *His performances stress romantic and neoromantic music and emphasize fine string playing and rich orchestral tones* (Robert C. Marsh).
**— *n.*** a person who is a student of or believes in neoromanticism.
**ne|o|ro|man|ti|cism** (nē′ō rō man′tə siz əm), *n.* the revival of the romantic style or spirit in literature, music, and art; neoromantic tendency.
**Ne|o|sal|var|san** (nē′ō sal′vər san), *n. Trademark.* a preparation of neoarsphenamine.
**Ne|o-Scho|las|tic** (nē′ō skə las′tik), *adj., n.*
**— *adj.*** of or having to do with Neo-Scholasticism.
**— *n.*** a student or follower of Neo-Scholasticism.
**Ne|o-Scho|las|ti|cism** (nē′ō skə las′tə siz əm), *n.* a philosophical system or method consisting essentially in the application of scholasticism to modern problems, differing from medieval scholasticism especially in its acceptance of the findings and techniques of modern research.
**ne|o-Sta|lin|ism** (nē′ō stä′lə niz əm), *n.* resurgent Stalinism; Communism as was practiced by Joseph Stalin, especially in the 1930's: *He attacks the authoritarianism that hobbles Soviet intellectuals and artists, ... and the persistence of neo-Stalinism in Soviet political life* (Saturday Review).
**ne|o-Sta|lin|ist** (nē′ō stä′lə nist), *adj., n.* **— *adj.*** of or having to do with neo-Stalinism: *neo-Stalinist policies.*
**— *n.*** a person who supports or practices neo-Stalinism.
**ne|o|stig|mine** (nē′ō stig′mēn, -min), *n.* a drug for treating severe muscular debility and glaucoma, usually administered as a bromide or sulfate. [< *neo-* + (syn)*stigmin* (bromide) the chemical name]
**ne|o|style** (nē′ə stīl), *n., v.,* **-styled, -styl|ing.**
**— *n.*** a device used for making multiple copies of a document or the like; kind of cyclostyle.
**— *v.t.*** to duplicate (printed matter) with a neostyle.
**ne|o|tech|nic** (nē′ō tek′nik), *adj.* of, having to do with, or characteristic of the present-day development of technology: *Soon our neotechnic society will afford us six days of rest and one of toil* (Punch).
**ne|ot|e|nous** (nē ot′ə nəs), *adj. Zoology.* reproducing by neoteny.
**ne|ot|e|ny** (nē ot′ə nē), *n. Zoology.* the phenomenon of reaching sexual maturity and of reproducing while morphologically still in a youthful or larval stage, as in certain salamanders. [< New Latin *neotenia* < Greek *néos* new + *teínein* stretch, extend]
**ne|o|ter|ic** (nē′ə ter′ik), *adj., n.* **— *adj.*** recent; new; modern.
**— *n.*** a modern, especially a writer, thinker, or other person of modern times.
[< Late Latin *neōtericus* < Greek *neōterikós* < *neṓteros,* comparative of *néos* new]
**Ne|o|trop|ic** (nē′ə trop′ik), *adj.* = Neotropical.
**Ne|o|trop|i|cal** (nē′ə trop′ə kəl), *adj.* of or like the region that includes most of the Caribbean, tropical North America, and all of South America.
**ne|o|type** (nē′ō tīp′), *n. Biology.* a type specimen selected to replace a holotype: *If the type strain has been lost, an attempt is made to find a new strain that conforms to the original description. Such a strain may be designated as a neotype, which then represents the species* (W. E. Moore and L. V. Holdeman).
**ne|o|yt|ter|bi|um** (nē′ō i tėr′bē əm), *n.* = ytterbium.
**Ne|o|zo|ic** (nē′ə zō′ik), *n., adj.* **— *n.*** **1** the geologic period from the end of the Mesozoic to the present; Cenozoic. **2** the Mesozoic and Cenozoic (as a single era).
**— *adj.*** of or having to do with either of these geologic divisions.
[< *neo-* + Greek *zōē* life + English *-ic*]
► **Neozoic** was proposed, and gained occasional use, but was never widely accepted by professional geologists.
**NEP** or **Nep** (nep), *n.* the New Economic Policy of the government of the Soviet Union, in effect from 1921 to 1928, modifying some of the more extreme communistic policies put into effect by Lenin in 1921 and allowing some businesses to be privately owned. Its purpose was to stimulate an economy on the verge of collapse. *Under the NEP private marketing was restored* (Newsweek). [< Russian *nep,* abbreviation of *Novaja Ekonomičeskaja Politika* New Economic Policy]
**Nep.,** **1** Nepal. **2** Neptune.
**Nep|a|lese** (nep′ə lēz′, -lēs′), *n., pl.* **-lese,** *adj.*
**— *n.*** a native or inhabitant of Nepal, the Himalayan kingdom between Tibet and India.
**— *adj.*** of or having to do with Nepal or its people: *the Nepalese government.*
**Ne|pa|li** (ne pä′lē), *n., adj.* **— *n.*** **1** an Indic language used chiefly in Nepal; Gurkhali. **2** = Nepalese.
**— *adj.*** of or having to do with Nepal; Nepalese: *Half the valley had been resettled with 3,000 Nepali families* (Sunday Times).
**ne|pen|the** (ni pen′thē), *n.* **1a** a drink or drug supposed to bring forgetfulness of sorrow or trouble, according to old legend. Nepenthe is supposed to be of Egyptian origin and is mentioned in Homer's Odyssey. **b** the plant yielding this drug. **2** *Figurative.* anything that brings on easeful forgetfulness: *This western wind hath Lethean powers, Yon noonday cloud nepenthe showers* (John Greenleaf Whittier). [earlier *nepenthes* < Latin *nēpenthes* < Greek (*phármakon*) *nēpenthès* (drug) dispelling sorrow < *nē-* not + *pénthos* grief]
**ne|pen|the|an** (ni pen′thē ən), *adj.* of, having to do with, or induced by nepenthe.
**ne|pen|thes** (ni pen′thēz), *n.* **1** = nepenthe. **2** any one of a group of pitcher plants native chiefly to the East Indies, and cultivated also in hothouses. [< Latin *nēpenthes;* see etym. under **nepenthe**]
**neph|a|lism** (nef′ə liz əm), *n.* total abstinence from intoxicating drink.
**neph|a|list** (nef′ə list), *n.* a person who practices or advocates nephalism; teetotaler. [< Late Greek *nēphalismós* total abstinence (< *nēphálios* sober) + English *-ist*]
**neph|a|nal|y|sis** (nef′ə nal′ə sis), *n., pl.* **-ses** (-sēz). **1** analysis of the cloud formations over a large area, using weather charts drawn especially from photographs taken by weather satellites. **2** a chart of such cloud formations. [< Greek *néphos* cloud + English *analysis*]
**neph|e|line** (nef′ə lin), *n.* = nephelite. [< French *néphéline* < Greek *nephélē* cloud (< *néphos*) + French *-ine* -ine[2] (because it appears cloudy when fragments are put in nitric acid)]
**neph|e|lin|ic** (nef′ə lin′ik), *adj.* = nephelitic.
**neph|e|lin|ite** (nef′ə lə nīt), *n.* a heavy, dark-colored, volcanic rock, essentially a basalt containing nephelite and pyroxene but no feldspar and little or no olivine. [< *nephelin*(e) + *-ite*[1]]
**neph|e|lite** (nef′ə līt), *n.* a mineral, a silicate of aluminum, sodium, and sometimes potassium, occurring in various volcanic rocks: *Nephelite generally forms grains and shapeless lumps or masses resembling quartz* (Fenton and Fenton). [< *nephel*(ine) + *-ite*[1]]
**neph|e|lit|ic** (nef′ə lit′ik), *adj.* of or like nephelite.
**neph|e|loid layer** (nef′ə loid), a turbid layer of clay-sized mineral particles suspended in a

**Pronunciation Key:** hat, āge, cãre, fär; let, ēqual, tėrm; it, īce; hot, ōpen, ôrder; oil, out; cup, pu̇t, rüle; child; long; thin; ᴛʜen; zh, measure; ə represents **a** in about, **e** in taken, **i** in pencil, **o** in lemon, **u** in circus.

body of water. [< Greek *nephélē* cloud + English *-oid*]

**neph|e|lom|e|ter** (nef′ə lom′ə tər), *n.* **1** an instrument to measure the concentration of suspended matter in a liquid dispersion by measuring the amount of light transmitted or scattered by the dispersion. **2** a similar device consisting of a group of barium chloride standards, for estimating the number of bacteria in a suspension. **3** an instrument to measure the comparative cloudiness of the sky. [< Greek *nephélē* cloud (< *néphos*) + English *-meter*]

**neph|e|lo|met|ric** (nef′ə lə met′rik), *adj.* of or having to do with nephelometry.

**neph|e|lom|e|try** (nef′ə lom′ə trē), *n.* the measurement of the concentration of suspended matter in a liquid by means of a nephelometer.

**neph|ew** (nef′yü), *n.* **1** a son of one's brother or sister. See picture under **family tree**. **2** a son of one's brother-in-law or sister-in-law. **3** an illegitimate son of an ecclesiastic (used as a euphemism). **4** *Obsolete.* a grandson. **5** *Obsolete.* a descendant, especially a remote descendant. [< Old French *neveu* < Latin *nepōs, -ōtis*]

**Neph|ite** (nef′īt), *n.* (in the Book of Mormon) one of the two nations created by the division of the group of people led to the west coast of America in the 600's B.C. by the Hebrew prophet Lehi. The Nephites were destroyed by the Lamanites, the other nation.

**neph|o|gram** (nef′ə gram), *n.* a photograph of a cloud or clouds taken by a nephograph.

**neph|o|graph** (nef′ə graf, -gräf), *n.* an instrument for photographing clouds. [< Greek *néphos* cloud + English *-graph*]

**neph|o|log|i|cal** (nef′ə loj′ə kəl), *adj.* having to do with nephology; relating to clouds or cloudiness.

**ne|phol|o|gy** (ni fol′ə jē), *n.* the branch of meteorology that deals with clouds. [< Greek *néphos* cloud + English *-logy*]

**neph|o|scope** (nef′ə skōp), *n.* an instrument used to determine the altitude of clouds and the velocity and direction of their motion. [< Greek *néphos* cloud + English *-scope*]

**neph|o|scop|ic** (nef′ə skop′ik), *adj.* of or having to do with a nephoscope.

**ne|phral|gi|a** (ni fral′jē ə), *n.* pain in the kidneys; renal neuralgia. [< Greek *nephrós* kidney + *-algiā* < *álgos* pain]

**ne|phrec|to|my** (ni frek′tə mē), *n., pl.* **-mies.** the surgical removal of a kidney. [< Greek *nephrós* kidney + *ektomē* a cutting out]

**neph|ric** (nef′rik), *adj.* = renal. [< Greek *nephrós* kidney + English *-ic*]

**ne|phrid|i|al** (ni frid′ē əl), *adj.* of or having to do with the nephridium or nephridia.

**ne|phrid|i|um** (ni frid′ē əm), *n., pl.* **-i|a** (-ē ə). a primitive excretory organ in some invertebrates and lower vertebrates, such as mollusks, certain annelid worms, and brachiopods, analogous in function to the kidneys of higher animals, and in some cases serving also in reproduction. [< New Latin *nephridium* < Greek *nephrós* kidney + Latin *-idium* < Greek *-idion,* diminutive suffix]

**neph|rism** (nef′riz əm), *n.* a condition of poor health caused by chronic kidney disease. [< Greek *nephrós* kidney + English *-ism*]

**neph|rite** (nef′rīt), *n.* a kind of jade, a silicate of calcium and either magnesium or iron, varying in color from white to dark green, once supposed to protect the wearer against diseases of the kidneys; greenstone. [< German *Nephrit* < Greek *nephrós* kidney + German *-it* -ite[1]]

**ne|phrit|ic** (ni frit′ik), *adj.* **1** of, having to do with, or affected with kidney disease. **2** used against kidney disease. **3** = renal. [< Late Latin *nephrīticus* < Greek *nephrītikós* < *nephrîtis* nephritis]

**ne|phri|tis** (ni frī′tis), *n.* an inflammation of the kidneys, especially Bright's disease, characterized by the presence of albumin in the urine and swelling of the tissues. [< Late Latin *nephrītis* < Greek *nephrîtis* < *nephrós* kidney]

**neph|ro|gen|ic** (nef′rə jen′ik), *adj.* **1** produced in the kidney. **2** giving rise to kidney tissue. [< Greek *nephrós* kidney + English *-gen* + *-ic*]

**neph|ro|lith** (nef′rə lith), *n.* = kidney stone. [< Greek *nephrós* kidney + *líthos* stone]

**ne|phrol|o|gy** (ni frol′ə jē), *n.* the branch of medicine dealing with the kidneys. [< Greek *nephrós* kidney + English *-logy*]

***neph|ron** (nef′ron), *n.* any one of the numerous functional units of the kidney, serving to filter waste matter from the blood. A nephron consists of a Bowman's capsule, glomerulus, and tubule. *The rat kidney normally contains 32,000 nephrons, the human kidney contains about 1 million* (Richard J. Goss).

***nephron**

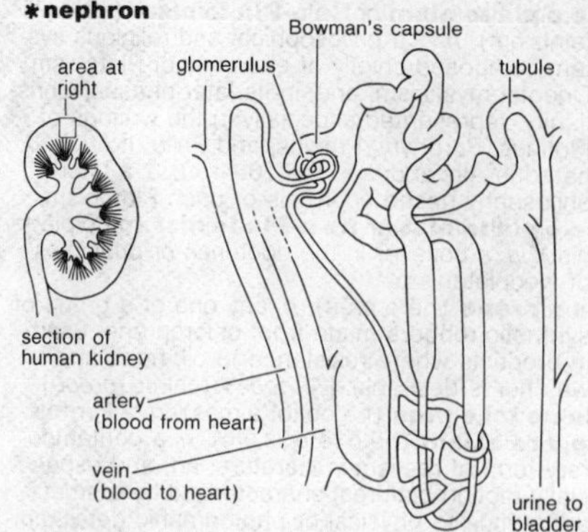


**ne|phrop|a|thy** (ni frop′ə thē), *n.* any disease of the kidneys, especially nephrosis. [< Greek *nephrós* + English *-pathy*]

**neph|ro|pex|i|a** (nef′rə pek′sē ə), *n.* the surgical fixation of a floating kidney. [< New Latin *nephropexia* < Greek *nephrós* kidney + *pêxis* a making fast]

**ne|phro|sis** (ni frō′sis), *n.* a degenerative disease of the kidneys, especially the renal tubules, marked by absence of inflammation: *Hospital reports also show that Meticorten has better results than cortisone in treating patients suffering from ... nephrosis* (Newsweek). [< Greek *nephrós* kidney + English *-osis*]

**neph|ro|stome** (nef′rə stōm), *n. Biology.* the ciliated funnel-shaped end of the nephridium in some invertebrates and lower vertebrates. [< Greek *nephrós* kidney + *stóma* mouth]

**ne|phrot|ic** (ni frot′ik), *adj.* **1** having to do with or affected by nephrosis. **2** having or resembling the symptoms of nephrosis.

**ne|phrot|o|my** (ni frot′ə mē), *n., pl.* **-mies.** surgical incision into the kidney. [< Greek *nephrós* kidney + *-tomiā* a cutting]

**Neph|ta|li** (nef′tə lī), *n.* Naphtali, in the Douay Bible.

**Neph|thys** (nef′this), *n.* an ancient Egyptian goddess of the dead, daughter of Geb and Nut, sister and wife of Set, and mother of Anubis.

**ne plus ul|tra** (nē′ plus ul′trə), the highest or furthest point attainable; height of excellence or achievement; culmination: *The people of Leinster ... do not vaunt Dublin as the ne plus ultra of cities* (The Nation). [< Latin *ne plus ultra* no more beyond]

**nep|man** (nep′mən), *n., pl.* **-men.** a person, especially a small tradesman or well-to-do peasant, allowed under the Nep to engage in private business in the Soviet Union during the early 1920's. [< Russian *nepman* < *nep* Nep + German *Mann* man]

**ne|pot|ic** (ni pot′ik), *adj.* = nepotistic.

**nep|o|tism** (nep′ə tiz əm), *n.* the showing of too much favor by one in power to his relatives, especially by giving them desirable appointments: *Nepotism sometimes occurs in political appointments. Such unsavory examples of corruption and nepotism in the highest circles of government have inevitably increased that inborn skepticism with which the Italians ... tend to treat politics and politicians* (Atlantic). [< French *népotisme* < Italian *nepotismo* < *nepote* nephew < Latin *nepōs, -ōtis* grandson, nephew + *-ismo* -ism]

**nep|o|tist** (nep′ə tist), *n.* a person who practices nepotism.

**nep|o|tis|tic** (nep′ə tis′tik), *adj.* = of or having to do with nepotism or nepotists.

**nep|ti|cu|lid** (nep tik′yə ləd), *n.* any one of a group of extremely small moths whose larvae are leaf miners, found throughout the world. [< New Latin *Nepticulidae* the family name < Late Latin *nepticula* (diminutive) < Latin *neptis* granddaughter]

***Neptune** definition 2 symbol

***Nep|tune** (nep′tün, -tyün), *n.* **1** *Roman Mythology.* the god of the sea. The Greeks called him Poseidon. **2** the fourth largest planet in the solar system, eighth in distance from the sun. It is so far from the earth that it cannot be seen without a telescope. Its orbit lies between those of Uranus and Pluto and takes 164.8 years to complete, at a mean distance from the sun of 2,794,-100,000 miles. See diagram under **solar system.** [< Latin *Neptūnus,* related to *nebula* cloud, mist]

**Nep|tu|ni|an** (nep tü′nē ən, -tyü′-), *adj.* **1** having to do with Neptune, the god of the sea, or the sea or ocean itself. **2** of the planet Neptune. **3** Also, **neptunian.** *Geology.* resulting from or produced by the action of water, particularly oceanic water.

**Neptunian theory,** *Geology.* an old theory that many rocks now known to be volcanic or plutonic were deposited by water.

**Nep|tun|ist** (nep′tü nist, -tyü-), *n. Geology.* an advocate of the Neptunian theory.

***nep|tu|ni|um** (nep tü′nē əm, -tyü′-), *n.* a radioactive, metallic chemical element produced artificially by bombardment of an isotope of uranium with neutrons. The less stable isotope of neptunium disintegrates rapidly to form an isotope of plutonium that can be used for nuclear fission. *Both neptunium and americium are artificially produced elements, heavier than uranium, not found in nature* (Science News Letter). [< *Neptune* + New Latin *-ium,* a suffix meaning "chemical element"]

***neptunium**

| symbol | atomic number | mass number | oxidation state |
|---|---|---|---|
| Np | 93 | 237 | 3, 4, 5, 6 |

**nerd** (nėrd), *n. U.S. Slang.* **1** a person without coordination or grace; a clumsy person. **2** a person who is not hip; square. [origin unknown]

**Ne|re|id** (nir′ē id), *n.* **1** *Greek Mythology.* any one of the fifty daughters of Nereus. The Nereids were sea nymphs who attended Poseidon (Neptune). **2** the smaller of the two moons of the planet Neptune.

**ne|re|id** (nir′ē id), *n.* any one of several polychaete worms with segmented bodies and distinct head parts, that live mostly along the seashore and reach a length of 5 feet or more. [< New Latin *Nereidae* < *Nereis* a Nereid]

**Ne|re|is** (nir′ē is), *n., pl.* **Ne|re|i|des** (ni rē′ə dēz). *Greek Mythology.* a Nereid.

**Ne|reus** (nir′üs), *n. Greek Mythology.* a sea god, who was the father of the Nereids; Old Man of the Sea.

**ne|ri|ne** (ni rī′nē), *n.* any South African plant of a group of the amaryllis family, with large scarlet, pink, or rose-colored flowers: *The nerine, with a head of sail, so to speak, on the top of a slender elastic stem, is forever more or less vibrating* (A. Handler Hamer). [< New Latin *Nerine* < Latin *Nērīnē,* a Nereid]

**ne|rit|ic** (ni rit′ik), *adj.* of or like that part of the ocean floor between the low tide mark and a depth of about 600 feet: *Life is most abundant in the shallower parts of the ocean or neritic region of the continental shelves* (Harbaugh and Goodrich). [< Latin *nērīta* a sea mussel + English *-ic* (because such life generally inhabit this depth)]

**ner|ka** (nėr′kə), *n.* an important salmon of the northern Pacific; blueback salmon; sockeye salmon. [apparently < a native name]

**ner|ol** (nir′ōl, -ol), *n.* a colorless liquid isomeric with geraniol, occurring in neroli and other essential oils and used in perfumes. *Formula:* $C_{10}H_{18}O$ [< *neroli*]

**ner|o|li** (ner′ə lē, nir′-), *n.* an essential oil distilled from various flowers or prepared synthetically, used chiefly in perfumes. [< French *néroli* < Italian *neroli* < Princess *Neroli,* who reputedly discovered it]

**neroli oil,** = neroli.

**Ne|ro|ni|an** (ni rō′nē ən), *adj.* of or having to do with the Roman emperor Nero, noted for his vices, cruelty, and tyranny.

**Ne|ron|ic** (ni ron′ik), *adj.* = Neronian.

**nerts** or **nertz** (nėrts), *interj. U.S. Slang.* an exclamation of disgust or contempt; nuts. [alteration of *nuts*]

**nerv|al** (nėr′vəl), *adj.* of or having to do with a nerve or nerves; neural.

**nerv|ate** (nėr′vāt), *adj.* having veins; veined: *nervate leaves.*

**ner|va|tion** (nėr vā′shən), *n.* the arrangement of the veins or ribs in a leaf or an insect's wings; venation.

**nerv|a|ture** (nėr′və chər), *n.* = nervation.

**nerve** (nėrv), *n., v.,* **nerved, nerv|ing.** — *n.* **1** a fiber or bundle of fibers connecting the brain or spinal cord with the eyes, ears, muscles, glands, and other parts of the body. Nerves are elements of the peripheral nervous system that carry impulses, especially of sensation and motion. The nerve fibers are enclosed within sheaths and are joined to each other with connective tissue. *The control of muscles is achieved via the nerves which pass from the central nervous system ... to the various muscles of the body* (Floyd and Silver). **2** *Figurative.* mental strength; courage: *to continue fighting on nerve alone, icy nerve, nerves of iron. It takes nerve to pilot an airplane. Prosperity had relaxed the nerves of discipline*

**Pronunciation Key:** hat, āge, cãre, fär; let, ēqual, tėrm; it, īce; hot, ōpen, ôrder; oil, out; cup, pu̇t, rüle; child; long; thin; ᴛʜen; zh, measure; ə represents **a** in about, **e** in taken, **i** in pencil, **o** in lemon, **u** in circus.

(Edward Gibbon). **3** *Figurative.* bodily strength; vigor; energy: *He led me on to mightiest deeds, Above the nerve of mortal arm* (Milton). **4** *Slang, Figurative.* rude boldness; impudence: *He claims he is a friend of mine? The nerve of the fellow!* **5a** a vein of a leaf. **b** a rib of an insects' wing; nervure. **6** the pulp of a tooth. **7** *Archaic.* sinew; tendon: *Before his tender joints with nerves are knit* (John Dryden).

—***v.t.*** to arouse strength or courage in: *The players nerved themselves for the championship game.*

**get on one's nerves**, to annoy or irritate one: *John Adams ... was honest, brave, and intelligent, but he just couldn't help getting on other people's nerves* (Gerald W. Johnson).

**nerves, a** nervousness: *He tried to soothe her nerves* (Graham Greene). **b** an attack of nervousness: *to suffer from nerves.*

**strain every nerve**, to exert oneself to the utmost: *Both horse and jockey were straining every nerve in the race.*

[< Latin *nervus* sinew, tendon; sense influenced by Greek *neûron,* meaning both "sinew" and "nerve"]

**nerve agent**, = nerve gas.

**nerve cell**, **1** a cell that conducts impulses; neuron: *The other part is in a special membrane of nerve cell material wrapped around the brain capillaries* (Science News Letter). **2** the cell body of a neuron, excluding its fibers.

**nerve center**, **1** a group of nerve cells closely connected with one another and acting together in the performance of some particular function or sense: *The physiological mechanism consists of a sense organ or set of sense organs, sensory nerves leading to a nerve center* (Science News). **2** *Figurative.* **a** any place that is the center of activity or a source of direction: *The village high street remains the nerve center of the whole community* (Manchester Guardian). **b** the person or persons who control such a place.

**nerved** (nėrvd), *adj.* **1** having nerves: *strong-nerved.* **2** *Botany.* nervate. **3** *Entomology.* having nervures.

**-nerved**, *combining form.* having _____ nerves: *Strong-nerved = having strong nerves.*

**nerve deafness**, deafness due to disorder of the acoustic nerve.

**nerve fiber**, any one of the long threadlike processes or fibers of a neuron; an axon or a dendrite: *In all the animals he examined ... he found a few nerve fibers that had narrow sensitivity curves with maxima in the red, green, or blue part of the spectrum* (Tansley and Weale).

**nerve gas**, any one of various poison gases containing phosphorus that may be absorbed through the skin, as well as by breathing, and that attack the central nervous system to cause extreme weakness or death. Various types have been developed for use in warfare such as tabun and sarin. *Poisons isolated from clams and from the puffer fish have been found to be several times more toxic than the most powerful nerve gases known* (Science News Letter).

**nerve|less** (nėrv′lis), *adj.* **1** without strength or vigor; feeble; weak: *The cup dropped from his nerveless hand.* **SYN**: flabby, flaccid. **2** without courage or firmness. **3** without nervousness; controlled; calm. **4** without nerves. —**nerve′less|ly**, *adv.* —**nerve′less|ness**, *n.*

**nerve net**, a network of nerve cells distributed throughout the tissues of coelenterates, echinoderms, and certain other lower forms, in which it makes up a primitive nervous system: *As might be expected from the dispersed arrangement of nerve cells, conduction in nerve nets is diffuse* (R. K. Josephson).

**nerve-rack|ing** or **nerve-wrack|ing** (nėrv′rak′-ing), *adj.* extremely irritating; causing great annoyance; very trying: *a nerve-racking day at the office. He felt cool and alert, ... and, the nerve-racking hours of waiting past, he listened for the starter's gun* (P. G. Wodehouse). —**nerve′-rack′ing|ly, nerve′-wrack′ing|ly**, *adv.*

**nerves** (nėrvz), *n.pl.* See under **nerve**.

**nerve trunk**, several nerve fibers bound together by a tough sheet of tissue.

**nerv|i|ly** (nėr′və lē), *adv.* in a nervy manner.

**ner|vine** (nėr′vēn, -vīn), *adj., n.* —***adj.*** **1** acting on or relieving disorders of the nerves; strengthening or soothing the nerves. **2** of or having to do with the nerves.

—***n.*** *Obsolete.* a nerve tonic.

[< New Latin *nervinus* < Late Latin *nervīnus* made of sinews < Latin *nervus;* see etym. under **nerve**]

**ner|vi|ness** (nėr′vē nis), *n.* nervy quality or condition.

**nerv|ing** (nėr′ving), *n. Veterinary Medicine.* the surgical removal of part of a bundle of nerve fibers.

**ner|vos|i|ty** (nėr vos′ə tē), *n.* nervous quality or condition; nervousness.

**nerv|ous** (nėr′vəs), *adj.* **1** of the nerves: *a nervous disorder.* **2** easily excited or upset: *a nervous driver, a nervous dog. A person who has been overworking is likely to become nervous.* **SYN**: high-strung, excitable, jumpy. **3** having or proceeding from nerves that are out of order: *a nervous patient, a nervous tapping of the fingers.* **4** deriving from a tense or quickened condition of the nerves: *nervous energy.* **5** restless or uneasy; timid: *She is nervous about staying alone at night.* **SYN**: apprehensive. **6** having nerves. **7** *Figurative.* strong; vigorous; powerful; spirited: *The artist painted with quick, nervous strokes. They were swept before the mettled horses and nervous arms of their antagonists like chaff before the wind* (James Fenimore Cooper). **SYN**: energetic. [< Latin *nervōsus* sinewy < *nervus*

***nervous system**

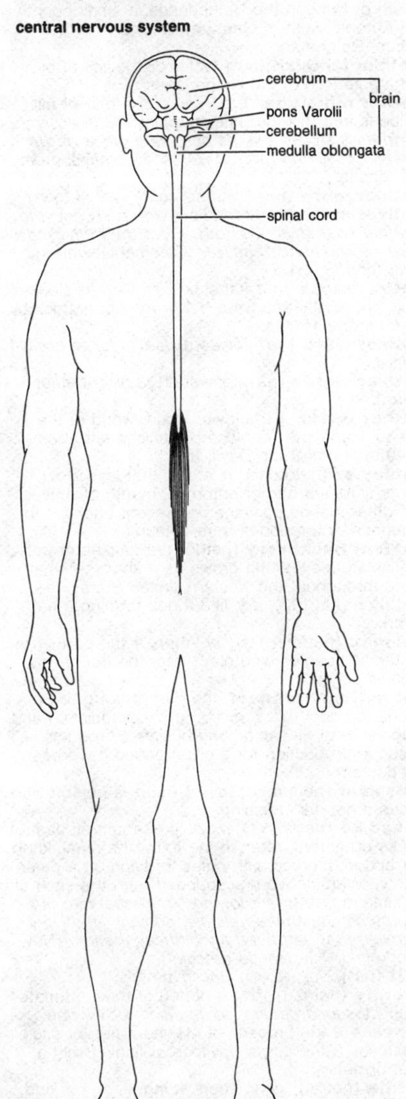


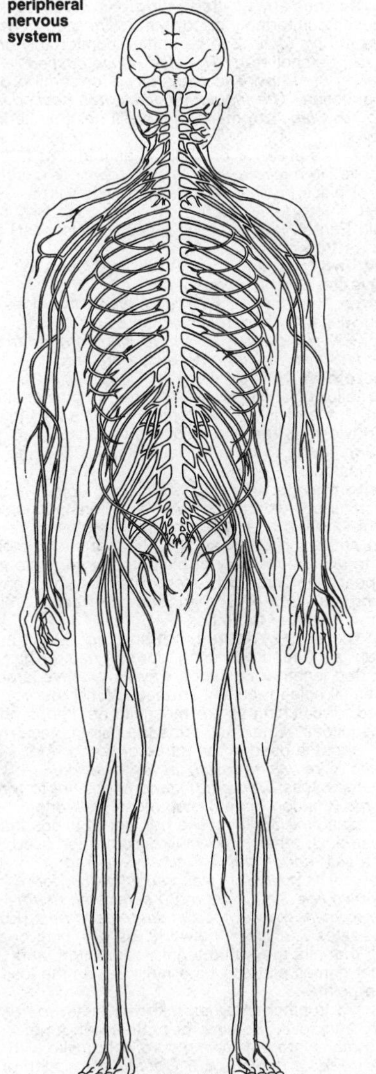

spinal nerves

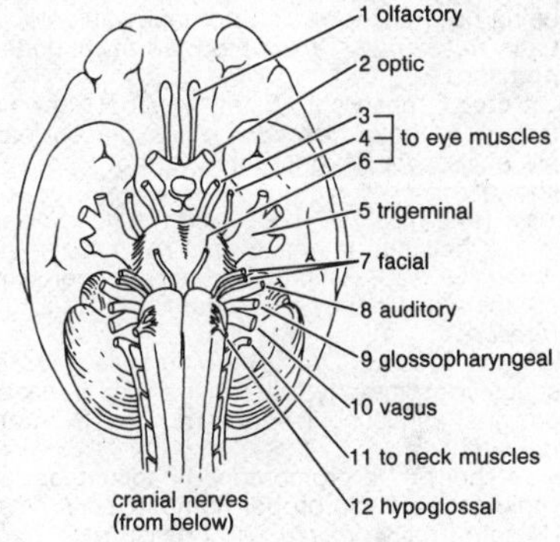

cranial nerves (from below)

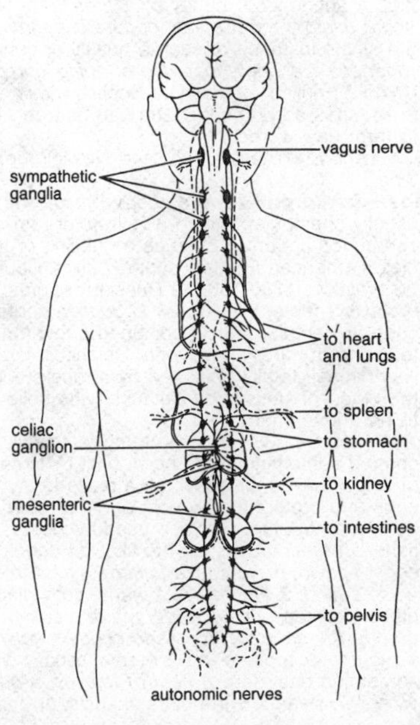

autonomic nerves

sinew; see etym. under **nerve**] —**nerv′ous|ly,** *adv.* —**nerv′ous|ness,** *n.*

**nervous breakdown,** any disabling mental disorder requiring treatment.

**nervous Nellie** or **Nelly,** *pl.* **nervous Nellies.** *Slang.* a nervous or easily excited person. [< *Nellie* or *Nelly,* a feminine name]

***nervous system,** the system of nerve fibers, nerve cells, and other nervous tissue in a person or animal by means of which impulses are received and interpreted. The human central nervous system and that of the other vertebrates consists of the brain and spinal cord, to and from which impulses are carried by the peripheral nervous system. The peripheral nervous system consists of the cranial nerves (12 pairs in man), the spinal nerves (31 pairs in man), and the autonomic nervous system (the ganglia and nerves that regulate the involuntary muscles, viscera, and glands). *The nervous system keeps us in contact with the world outside our bodies by receiving messages from the sense organs, such as the eyes and ears* (Herbert H. Jasper). See picture on the preceding page.

**ner|vure** (nėr′vyůr), *n.* **1** the principal vein of a leaf. **2** a rib of an insect's wing. [< Middle French *nervure* < *nerf* nerve < Latin *nervus;* see etym. under **nerve**]

**nerv|y** (nėr′vē), *adj.,* **nerv|i|er, nerv|i|est. 1** *Informal.* rude and bold; impudent: *It is a little "nervy" ... to walk into another man's house uninvited* (Elizabeth Robins). **2** *Figurative.* requiring courage or firmness: *a nervy undertaking.* **3** *Figurative.* strong; vigorous. **4** suffering from nervous tension; nervous: *Jaded, nervy, overworked men, who cannot sleep after taking ordinary coffee* (Punch).

**n.e.s.,** not elsewhere specified.

**nes|cience** (nesh′əns, -ē əns), *n.* **1** lack of knowledge; ignorance: *the ... involuntary nescience of men* (Jeremy Taylor). **2** the philosophical doctrine, implicit in many forms of agnosticism, that knowledge cannot rest on other than the phenomena of nature, God and the supernatural being both unknowable and unprovable. [< Late Latin *nescientia* < *nesciēns;* see etym. under **nescient**]

**nes|cient** (nesh′ənt, -ē ənt), *adj.* not knowing; ignorant. [< Latin *nesciēns, -entis,* present participle of *nescīre* be ignorant < *ne* not + *scīre* know]

**nesh** (nesh), *adj. Dialect.* **1** soft, tender, or succulent. **2** delicate or weakly: *the nesh hazels bending in the blast* (Robert Surtees). **3** poor-spirited; effeminate. **4** dainty or squeamish. [Old English *hnesce*]

**Nes|khi** (nes′kē), *n.* the flowing style of Arabic script or calligraphy, often used with arabesque designs, as distinguished from Kufic. [< Arabic *naskhī*]

**ness** (nes), *n.* a promontory, headland, or cape (now especially in proper names): *Loch Ness.* [Middle English *nasse,* Old English *næs, nes.* Compare Old Icelandic *nes.*]

**-ness,** *suffix added to adjectives to form nouns.* **1** quality or condition of being ___: *Blackness = the condition of being black. Kind-heartedness = the quality of being kind-hearted. Preparedness = the condition of being prepared.*
**2** ___ action; ___ behavior: *Carefulness* (*in some uses*) = *careful action; careful behavior.*
**3** a single instance of such a quality or condition: *Kindness = a single instance of being kind.*
[Middle English *-nesse,* Old English *-ness, -niss*]
▶ **-ness** is a living suffix and can be freely used to form new words.

**Nes|sel|rode** (nes′əl rōd), *n.* = Nesselrode pudding.

**Nesselrode pudding,** a custard made with nuts, usually chestnuts, fruits, fruit syrup, or rum, frozen as ice cream or used as a pudding or to fill pies. [American English, supposedly < Count *Nesselrode,* 1780-1862, a Russian diplomat]

**Nes|sus** (nes′əs), *n. Greek Legend.* a centaur shot by Hercules with a poisoned arrow for attempting to carry off his wife, Deianira. Hercules was himself fatally poisoned by a robe steeped in the blood of Nessus by Deianira, who believed it to be a love charm.

***nest** (nest), *n., v.* —*n.* **1** a structure, usually shaped something like a bowl, built by birds out of twigs, leaves, or straw, as a place to lay their eggs and protect their young ones: *a robin's nest.* **2** a structure or place used by insects, fishes, turtles, rabbits, or the like, for depositing eggs, spawn, or young: *a squirrel's nest, a wasp's nest.* **3** *Figurative.* a warm, cozy place; place to sleep: *The little girl made a cozy nest among the sofa cushions and cuddled down in it.* **4** *Figurative.* a place that swarms, usually with something bad; den: *a nest of thieves, a nest of vice.* SYN: swarm. **5** the birds, insects, or animals living in a nest. **6** a set or series, often from large to small, such that each fits within another: *a nest of drinking cups, bowls, or tables.* **7** *Informal.* a base for guided missiles.
—*v.i.* **1** to make and use a nest: *The bluebirds are nesting here again.* **2** to search for nests: *This is dull work for a bairn. Let's go nesting* (Robert Louis Stevenson).
—*v.t.* to settle or place in, or as if in, a nest; provide with a nest or place for nesting.
**feather one's nest,** to take advantage of chances to get rich: *His spouse ... was disposed to feather her own nest, at the expense of him and his heirs* (Tobias Smollett).
[Old English *nest*]

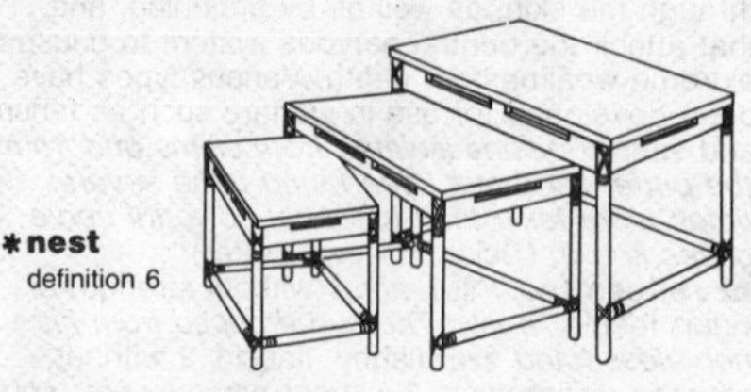
***nest** definition 6

**n'est-ce pas?** (nes pä′), *French.* isn't that so? don't you agree?

**nest egg, 1** something, usually a sum of money, saved up as the beginning of a fund or as a reserve: *She has a nice little nest egg put away for her retirement.* **2** a natural or artificial egg left in a nest to induce a hen or other bird to lay or continue laying eggs there.

**nest|er** (nes′tər), *n.* **1** *U.S.* a farmer, homesteader, or squatter seeking to settle on land used as a cattle range: *... as bitter as the Old West feud between ranchers and nesters for the one water hole in the sagebrush* (Harper's). **2** a bird or animal that makes or lives in a nest.

**nest|ing ground** or **site** (nes′ting), a place used by a bird to build its nest.

**nes|tle** (nes′əl), *v.,* **-tled, -tling.** —*v.i.* **1** to settle oneself comfortably or cozily: *She nestled down into the big chair.* **2** to be settled comfortably or cozily; be sheltered: *The little house nestled among the trees.* **3** to press close for comfort or in affection: *The frightened little kitten nestled in mother's lap.* **4** to make or have a nest; settle in a nest.
—*v.t.* **1** to press or hold close, as if in a nest; cuddle: *to nestle a baby in one's arms.* **2** to settle or place in or as in a nest; provide with a nest.
[Old English *nestlian* build a nest < *nest* nest]
—**nes′tler,** *n.*

**nest|ling** (nest′ling), *n.* **1** a bird too young to leave the nest. **2** a young child.

**Nes|tor** (nes′tər), *n.* **1** *Greek Legend.* the oldest and wisest of the Greeks at the siege of Troy. **2** any wise old man: *... an old man, in good truth the Nestor of his tribe* (Francis Parkman).

**Nes|to|ri|an** (nes tôr′ē ən, -tōr′-), *n., adj.* —*n.* **1** a follower of Nestorius; adherent of Nestorianism. **2** one of a modern remnant of this sect in northwestern Iran and adjoining regions.
—*adj.* having to do with Nestorius, his doctrine, or Nestorians.

**Nes|to|ri|an|ism** (nes tôr′ē ə niz′əm, -tōr′-), *n.* the doctrine of Nestorius, patriarch of Constantinople from 428 to 431. His teaching differentiated the two natures in Christ so sharply from each other as to disrupt the unity of his person and make it appear that Christ consisted of two persons, one being the Word of God and the other being a human indwelt by the other.

**net**[1] (net), *n., v.,* **net|ted, net|ting,** *adj.* —*n.* **1** an open fabric made of string, cord, thread, or hair, knotted together in such a way as to leave large or small holes regularly arranged. A fish net is used for catching fish. A mosquito net keeps off mosquitoes. A hair net holds the hair in place. A tennis net is used in the game of tennis. *Mrs. Fleitz ... remained mainly at the baseline, whereas Miss Breit often came to the net to win points* (London Times). SYN: mesh, network, reticulation. **2** anything like net; set of things that cross each other. **3** a lacelike cloth often used as a veil: *cotton net.* **4** *Figurative.* a trap or snare: *The guilty boy was caught in the net of his own lies. And I find more bitter than death the woman, whose heart is snares and nets* (Ecclesiastes 7:26). **5** = network. **6** a ball, bird, or ring that hits the net in tennis, badminton, and other games played with a net, causing the loss of a point.
—*v.t.* **1** to catch in a net; take with nets: *to net a fish.* **2** to cover, confine, or protect with a net. **3** to make into net: *to net cord.* **4** to make with net: *to net a hammock.* **5** *Figurative.* to catch or capture as if with a net: *Our patrol netted three prisoners.* **6** to hit (a ball, bird, or ring) into the net in tennis, badminton, and other games played with a net, thus losing a point.
—*adj.* **1** made of net: *a net dress.* **2** caught in a net or nets; netted.
[Old English *nett*] —**net′ter,** *n.*

**net**[2] (net), *adj., n., v.,* **net|ted, net|ting.** —*adj.* **1** remaining after deductions; free from deductions. A net gain or profit is the actual gain after all working expenses have been paid. The net weight of a glass jar of candy is the weight of the candy itself. The net price of a book is the real price from which no discount can be made. **2** sold at net prices: *a net book.*
—*n.* the net profit, price, or weight: *Final results for last year ... show a net of $430 million* (Newsweek).
—*v.t.* to gain or yield as clear profit: *The sale netted us a thousand dollars.*
[< French *net;* see etym. under **neat**[1]]

**NET** (no periods), National Educational Television: *NET ... has played a key role both in establishing more than 100 noncommercial television stations across the country and in supplying the local stations with programs of value and quality* (Saturday Review).

**net|ball** (net′bôl′), *n.* **1** *British.* a kind of basketball played by girls, usually on an outdoor court and with a less lively ball. **2** a net cord hit in tennis.

**net cord, 1** the top cord holding up the net in tennis, badminton, and other games played with a net. **2** a tennis ball which glances off the top of the net but continues in play: *A miraculous flick to kill a net cord on the volley saved Rosewall* (London Times).

**net|ful** (net′fůl), *n., pl.* **-fuls. 1** the amount that a net can hold. **2** the contents of a net.

**Neth.,** Netherlands.

**neth|er** (neᴛʜ′ər), *adj.* **1** lower; under: *The disappointed child's nether lip quivered.* **2** lying or conceived as lying beneath the earth's surface: *the nether regions.* [Old English *nithera*]

**Neth|er|land|er** (neᴛʜ′ər lən dər), *n.* a person born or living in the Netherlands, a small country in Europe, west of Germany and north of Belgium; Dutchman.

**Neth|er|land|ish** (neᴛʜ′ər lən dish), *adj.* of or characteristic of the Netherlands.

**nether millstone, 1** the lower of a pair of millstones in a mill for grinding grain: *His heart is as firm as a stone; yea, as hard as a piece of the nether millstone* (Job 41:24). **2** *Figurative.* great hardness.

**neth|er|more** (neᴛʜ′ər môr, -mōr), *adj.* = lower.

**neth|er|most** (neᴛʜ′ər mōst), *adj.* = lowest: *the nethermost abyss* (Milton). *From the nethermost fire ... Thy servant deliver* (Cardinal Newman). SYN: undermost.

**neth|er|stock** (neᴛʜ′ər stok′), *n.* a lower stocking, especially one worn below the upperstock by men in the 1500's.

**neth|er|ward** (neᴛʜ′ər wərd), *adv., adj.* = downward.

**neth|er|wards** (neᴛʜ′ər wərdz), *adv.* = netherward.

**nether world, 1** the lower world; world of the dead; Hades. **2** the place of punishment after death; realm of the Devil; hell.

**net|lay|er** (net′lā′ər), *n.* a ship that lays steel nets across a harbor entrance, mouth of a river, or other marine passage, to prevent enemy submarines or torpedoes from entering.

**net|leaf hackberry** (net′lēf′), a hackberry with reticulate leaves that grows as a shrub or small tree throughout the western United States.

**net|like** (net′līk′), *adj.* like a net; forming a network.

**net|man** (net′mən), *n., pl.* **-men. 1** the partner in a tennis doubles who plays near the net. **2** any tennis player.

**net national product,** the part of the gross national product that remains after depreciation and the value of all capital and business products used in production for a given period have been deducted.

**nets|man** (nets′mən), *n., pl.* **-men.** a person who uses a net, as in fishing.

**net|su|ke** (net′sü kā), *n., pl.* **-ke.** a carved Japanese ornament, often in the form of a small knob or button, pierced with holes for tying on a purse or other article worn suspended from the sash of a kimono: *He was showing Mr. Yashamoto our authentic Japanese netsuke, a lovely little ivory carving that had been my birthday present* (New Yorker). [< Japanese *netsuke*]

**nett** (net), *adj., n., v.t. British.* net[2].

**net|ting** (net′ing), *n.* **1** a netted or meshed material: *mosquito netting, wire netting for window screens.* **2** the process of making a net, or such material. **3** the act or privilege of fishing with a net or nets.

**net|tle** (net′əl), *n., v.,* **-tled, -tling.** —*n.* **1** a kind of plant having sharp bristles on the leaves and stems that sting the skin when touched. It is a

widely distributed, coarse herbaceous plant. *Young shoots of nettles can be cooked and eaten* (Arthur Cronquist). **2** any one of various related or similar plants. **3** *Figurative.* something vexing or nettlesome; irritation: *The Minister [the Irish Republic's Minister of External Affairs] said that someone had to deal with the nettle of the Orange Order* (London Times).
—***v.t.*** **1** to sting the mind of; irritate; provoke; vex: *His insulting remarks nettled me. I was very much nettled by their refusal to help.* **SYN:** exasperate, incense, pique. **2** to beat (a person or animal) with nettles. **3** to subject to the stinging of nettles.
**grasp the nettle**, to attack a difficulty boldly; deal promptly and firmly with a problem: *The Justices grasped the nettle on Monday and announced that they will rule on Mr. Powell's case* (New York Times).
[Old English *netele*] —**netʹtle|like′**, *adj.*

**net|tle-grasp|er** (netʹəl gras′pər, -gräs′-), *n.* a person who attacks a difficulty boldly.

**nettle rash**, = hives.

**net|tle|some** (netʹəl səm), *adj.* **1** easily nettled; irritable. **2** irritating: *A hot and nettlesome book and rather perplexing for a layman to handle* (Atlantic).

**nettle tree**, **1** a tree of Europe and Asia, belonging to the elm family, bearing a sweet, cherrylike fruit; lotus tree. **2** some allied species, as the hackberry. **3** an Australian tree closely related to the nettle, having stinging hairs and a bark which is used as a fiber.

**net ton**, a short ton; 2,000 pounds.

**net tonnage**, the cargo capacity of a ship, being its gross volume below decks less space allowed for fuel, engines, and crew and passenger accommodations, measured in units of 100 cubic feet or 2.83 cubic meters, called tons.

**net|ty** (netʹē), *adj.* of or like a net; netlike.

**net|work** (netʹwėrk′), *n., v.* —***n.*** **1** any system of lines that cross: *a network of vines, a network of railroads.* (*Figurative.*) *Their law is a network of fictions* (Emerson). **2** a group of radio or television stations that work together, so that what is broadcast by one may be broadcast by all: *Mr. Burgard mentioned two instances in which his corporation advised networks that it was withdrawing as a participating sponsor because of objections to scripts* (New York Times). **3** *Figurative.* anything that snares or catches, as a net does: *a police network.* **4** work or a piece of work having the texture of a net; netting; net: *The network of the spider web hung across the broken window full of flies and gnats.*
—***v.t.*** *Especially British.* to broadcast (a program) over a radio or television network: *Thirteen programmes on international economics ... will be networked nationally in January* (London Times).
[< *net*[1] + *work*]

**network analysis**, the mathematical or statistical study of networks and their connecting lines, points, and branches: *A modern society is to a large extent a system of networks for communication, transportation and the distribution of energy and goods. The complexity and cost of these networks demand that existing networks be effectively used and that new networks be rationally designed. To meet this demand there has evolved a new discipline called network analysis* (Scientific American).

**network analyst**, a person who studies network analysis.

**Neuf|châ|tel** (nœ shä telʹ), *n.,* or **Neufchâtel cheese**, a soft white cheese made from milk with or without the cream.

**neuk** (nyük), *n. Scottish.* nook (recess or corner).

**neu|mat|ic** (nü matʹik, nyü-), *adj.* = neumic.

**neume** or **neum** (nüm, nyüm), *n.* one of a set of signs used in the earliest plainsong notation to indicate the melody. [< Old French *neume* < Medieval Latin *neuma, neupma* a group of sounds sung in a single respiration < Greek *pneûma* breath]

**neu|mic** (nüʹmik, nyüʹ-), *adj.* of or like a neume: *a neumic curl intended to describe the interrogatory rise and fall in pitch* (Charles Dowsett).

**neur-**, *combining form.* the form of **neuro-** before vowels, as in *neural.*

**neu|ral** (nůrʹəl, nyůrʹ-), *adj.* **1** of or having to do with a nerve, neuron, or nervous system: *The [neural arch] encloses the neural canal which is occupied by the spinal cord* (A. Franklin Shull). **2** having to do with or situated in the region or side of the body containing the brain and spinal cord; dorsal: *The neural processes involved in learning a given operation, such as finding the way through a maze, occur in all or most parts of the cortex* (S. A. Barnett). [< *neur-* + *-al*[1]] —**neuʹral|ly**, *adv.*

**neural arch**, the arch on the dorsal side of a vertebra: *Each vertebra is made up of a spool-like centrum surmounted by a neural arch to house the nerve cord* (Tracy I. Storer).

**neural canal**, the canal formed by the vertebral foramina, enclosing and protecting the spinal cord.

**neu|ral|gia** (nů ralʹjə, nyů-), *n.* **1** a pain, usually sharp, along the course of a nerve. **2** a condition characterized by such pain: *facial neuralgia, sciatic neuralgia.* [< New Latin *neuralgia* < Greek *neûron* nerve + *álgos* pain]

**neu|ral|gic** (nů ralʹjik, nyů-), *adj.* of or having to do with neuralgia.

**neural spine**, a bony process on the dorsal side of a vertebra.

**neu|ra|min|ic acid** (nůr′ə minʹik, nyůr′-), a fatty acid found in the brain, shortage of which may be associated with schizophrenia. *Formula:* $C_9H_{17}NO_8$

**neur|a|min|i|dase** (nůr′ə minʹə dās, nyůr′-), *n.* an enzyme that hydrolyzes neuraminic acid and attacks mucous cells and substances.

**neu|ras|the|ni|a** (nůr′əs thēʹnē ə, nyůr′-), *n.* **1** a neurosis accompanied by varying aches and pains with no discernible organic cause, and characterized by extreme mental and physical fatigue and chronic depression: *I will tell you then that we distinguish three pure forms of actual neurosis: neurasthenia, anxiety-neurosis and hypochondria* (Sigmund Freud). **2** nervous exhaustion or weakness, as from overwork, vitamin deficiency, and disorder of the nervous system. [< New Latin *neurasthenia* < Greek *neûron* nerve + *asthéneia* weakness]

**neu|ras|then|ic** (nůr′əs thenʹik, nyůr′-), *adj., n.* —***adj.*** having to do with or suffering from neurasthenia.
—***n.*** a person who has neurasthenia. —**neu′ras-thenʹi|cal|ly**, *adv.*

**neu|ra|tion** (nů rāʹshən, nyů-), *n.* = nervation. [< *neur-* + *-ation*]

**neu|rec|to|my** (nů rekʹtə mē, nyů-), *n., pl.* **-mies.** the surgical removal of all or part of a nerve. [< *neur-* + Greek *ektomē* a cutting out]

**neu|ri|lem|ma** (nůr′ə lemʹə, nyůr′-), *n.* the delicate membranous outer sheath of peripheral nerve fibers. [< Greek *neûron* nerve + *eilēma* covering; the *-lemma* spelling from confusion with Greek *lémma* husk]

**neu|ril|i|ty** (nů rilʹə tē, nyů-), *n.* the properties which are characteristic of nerve tissue, such as the conducting of stimuli.

**neu|ris|tor** (nů risʹtər, nyů-), *n.* a very small live wire having properties similar to the nerve fiber or axon in a living organism, designed for use in microminiature electronic models of the human nervous system: *A first step toward making a completely artificial nerve cell was made with the development of the neuristor* (Science News Letter). [< Greek *neur(ôn)* nerve + English (trans)*istor*]

**neu|rite** (nůrʹīt, nyůrʹ-), *n. Obsolete.* an axon. [< *neur-* + *-ite*[1]]

**neu|rit|ic** (nů ritʹik, nyů-), *adj.* having to do with, characterized by, or affected with neuritis.

**neu|ri|tis** (nů rīʹtis, nyů-), *n.* inflammation of a nerve or nerves, causing pain, paralysis, disturbance of sensation, loss of the reflexes, and the wasting of muscles controlled by those nerves. [< New Latin *neuritis* < Greek *neûron* nerve + English *-itis*]

**neuro-**, *combining form.* nerve; nerve tissue; nervous system: *Neurology = study of the nervous system. Also,* **neur-** before vowels. [< Greek *neûron* nerve]

**neu|ro|an|a|tom|i|cal** (nůr′ō an′ə tomʹə kəl, nyůr′-), *adj.* of or having to do with neuroanatomy.

**neu|ro|a|nat|o|mist** (nůr′ō ə natʹə mist, nyůr′-), *n.* a person who studies neuroanatomy.

**neu|ro|a|nat|o|my** (nůr′ō ə natʹə mē, nyůr′-), *n.* the branch of anatomy that deals with the structure of the nervous system.

**neu|ro|bi|o|log|i|cal** (nůr′ō bī′ə lojʹə kəl, nyůr′-), *adj.* of or having to do with neurobiology.

**neu|ro|bi|ol|o|gist** (nůr′ō bī olʹə jist, nyůr′-), *n.* a person who studies neurobiology: *Neurobiologists ... uncovered a link between calcium and the establishment of the classic Pavlovian conditioned response ... by manipulating the cellular chemical in a living brain* (Science News).

**neu|ro|bi|ol|o|gy** (nůr′ō bī olʹə jē, nyůr′-), *n.* the branch of biology that deals with the nervous system.

**neu|ro|blast** (nůrʹə blast, nyůrʹ-), *n.* a cell in vertebrate embryos that develops into a nerve cell. [< *neuro-* + Greek *blastós* germ, sprout]

**neu|ro|blas|to|ma** (nůr′ə blas tōʹmə, nyůr′-), *n., pl.* **-mas, -ma|ta** (-mə tə). a malignant cancer of the sympathetic nervous system which attacks the neuroblasts of the embryo and is found usually in children. [< *neuroblast* + *-oma*]

**neu|ro|chem|i|cal** (nůr′ō kemʹə kəl, nyůr′-), *n., adj.* —***n.*** a chemical substance that affects the nervous system or some part of it: *Several neurochemicals, when applied to a specific area of the brain, appear to control killing behavior in laboratory rats* (Science News).
—***adj.*** of or having to do with neurochemistry: *neurochemical research.*

**neu|ro|chem|ist** (nůr′ō kemʹist, nyůr′-), *n.* a person who studies neurochemistry: *Probably one of the most baffling aspects of brain research concerns the nature of consciousness. Neurophysiologists and neurochemists have yet to find the exact seat of consciousness or to explain how it functions* (J. Edward Tether).

**neu|ro|chem|is|try** (nůr′ō kemʹə strē, nyůr′-), *n.* the branch of biochemistry that deals with the chemical makeup and effects of the nervous system: *Since mental health is the chief medical problem today, the study of neurochemistry assumes considerable importance* (Science News Letter).

**neu|ro|cir|cu|la|to|ry** (nůr′ō sėrʹkyə lə tôr′ē, -tōr′-; nyůr′-), *adj.* of or having to do with both the nervous and circulatory systems: *neurocirculatory disorders.*

**neu|ro|de|pres|sive** (nůr′ō di presʹiv, nyůr′-), *adj.* acting as a nerve depressant: *a neurodepressive drug.*

**neu|ro|der|ma|ti|tis** (nůr′ō dėr′mə tīʹtis, nyůr′-), *n.* a chronic skin disorder of nervous origin characterized by much itching and a leathery condition of the skin. It commonly affects the neck, armpits, and pubic area.

**neu|ro|en|do|crine** (nůr′ō enʹdə krin, nyůr′-), *adj.* of or having to do with the nervous system and the endocrine glands: *neuroendocrine activity.*

**neu|ro|en|do|cri|nol|o|gist** (nůr′ō en′dō kri nolʹə jist, -krī-; nyůr′-), *n.* a person who studies neuroendocrinology.

**neu|ro|en|do|cri|nol|o|gy** (nůr′ō en′dō kri nolʹə jē, -krī-; nyůr′-), *n.* the endocrinology of the nervous system: *Neuroendocrinology research was expected to establish the pathways in the brain that regulate the hypothalamic hormones and the role of the amines in the control of these pathways* (Albert Wolfson).

**neu|ro|fi|bro|ma** (nůr′ō fī brōʹmə, nyůr′-), *n., pl.* **-mas, -ma|ta** (-mə tə). a fibrous tumor, usually benign, arising from the outer sheath of peripheral nerve fibers. [< *neuro-* + *fibroma*]

**neu|ro|gen|ic** (nůr′ə jenʹik, nyůr′-), *adj.* originating in the nerves or nervous system. —**neu′ro|genʹi|cal|ly**, *adv.*

**neu|rog|li|a** (nů rogʹlē ə, nyů-), *n.* the delicate connective tissue forming a supporting network for the conducting elements of nervous tissue in the brain and the spinal cord. [< *neuro-* + Late Greek *gliā* glue]

**neu|rog|li|al** (nů rogʹlē əl, nyů-), *adj.* = neurogliar.

**neu|rog|li|ar** (nů rogʹlē ər, nyů-), *adj.* of or having to do with neuroglia: *the neurogliar cells.*

**neu|ro|he|mal organ** (nůr′ō hēʹməl, nyůr′-), an organ of the circulatory system having neurological importance. [< *neuro-* + *hemal*]

**neu|ro|hor|mo|nal** (nůr′ō hôr mōʹnəl, nyůr′-), *adj.* **1** of or having to do with neurohormones. **2** having to do with both nerves and hormones: *neurohormonal reaction.*

**neu|ro|hor|mone** (nůr′ō hôrʹmōn, nyůr′-), *n.* a hormone that stimulates nerve cells or the nervous system: *Serotonin, a neurohormone, acts as a sedative when given in large doses* (Scientific American).

**neu|ro|hu|mor** (nůr′ō hyüʹmər, nyůr′-), *n.* a chemical substance such as epinephrine, secreted by the endings of a nerve cell and capable of activating a muscle or another nerve cell.

**neu|ro|hu|mor|al** (nůr′ō hyüʹmər əl, nyůr′-), *adj.* of or having to do with a neurohumor or the response to it: *The nerve is accustomed to this ... because it is present on several natural neurohumoral agents such as adrenalin and histamine* (Science News Letter).

**neu|ro|hy|po|phys|e|al** or **neu|ro|hy|po|phys|i|al** (nůr′ō hī′pə fizʹē əl, nyůr′-), *adj.* of or having to do with the neurohypophysis: *a neurohypophyseal hormone.*

**neu|ro|hy|poph|y|sis** (nůr′ō hī pofʹə sis, -hi-; nyůr′-), *n., pl.* **-ses** (-sēz). the main portion of the posterior lobe of the pituitary gland. [< *neuro-* + *hypophysis*]

**neu|ro|ki|nin** (nůr′ə kīʹnən, nyůr′-), *n.* a protein substance that causes dilation of blood vessels and has an undetermined effect on nerves: *In 1960 a polypeptide, neurokinin, was isolated by Wolff and his colleagues in the USA, from the subcutaneous tissues near the temporal blood vessels in patients during an attack of migraine* (New Scientist).

---

**Pronunciation Key:** hat, āge, cãre, fär; let, ēqual, tėrm; it, īce; hot, ōpen, ôrder; **oi**l, **ou**t; cup, půt, rüle; **ch**ild; lo**ng**; **th**in; **ᴛʜ**en; **zh**, measure; **ə** represents **a** in about, **e** in taken, **i** in pencil, **o** in lemon, **u** in circus.

**neu|ro|lept** (nu̇r′ə lept, nyu̇r′-), *adj.* being or involving a neuroleptic or tranquilizer: *a neurolept drug, neurolept anesthesia. An innovation popular in Europe is the use of an anesthetic that combines a powerful analgesic and a neurolept agent* (Oliver H. French). [< *neuroleptic*]

**neu|ro|lep|tic** (nu̇r′ə lep′tik, nyu̇r′-), *n.* a tranquilizing drug: *Schizophrenics treated over long periods with neuroleptics have sometimes shown symptoms typical of endogenous depression* (New Scientist). [< *neuro-* + Greek *lêptikos* seizing (< *lêpsis* seizure)]

**neu|ro|log|i|cal** (nu̇r′ə loj′ə kəl, nyu̇r′-), *adj.* of or having to do with neurology: *neurological mechanisms.* —**neu′ro|log′i|cal|ly,** *adv.*

**neu|rol|o|gist** (nu̇ rol′ə jist, nyu̇-), *n.* a person who studies neurology, especially a specialist in organic diseases of the central nervous system: *It is a condition which is all too often missed by even experienced neurologists and psychiatrists* (Sunday Times).

**neu|rol|o|gy** (nu̇ rol′ə jē, nyu̇-), *n.* the study of the nervous system and its diseases. [< *neuro-* + *-logy*]

**neu|ro|ma** (nu̇ rō′mə, nyu̇-), *n., pl.* **-ma|ta** (-mə tə), **-mas.** a tumor growing upon a nerve or in nerve tissue. [< *neur-* + *-oma*]

**neu|ro|mast** (nu̇r′ə mast, nyu̇r′-), *n.* a specialized sensory organ beneath the lateral line of all fishes and aquatic amphibians, consisting of a cluster of sensory cells. [< Greek *neûron* nerve + *mastós* hillock]

**neu|ro|mus|cu|lar** (nu̇r′ō mus′kyə lər, nyu̇r′-), *adj.* of or having to do with the relationship of nerves to the muscles.

***neu|ron** (nu̇r′on, nyu̇r′-), *n.* one of the cells of which the brain, spinal cord, and nerves are composed; nerve cell. Neurons conduct impulses and consist of a cell body containing the nucleus, and usually several processes called dendrites, and a single long process called an axon. *To excite or "fire" a neuron, the nerve impulse has to cross the synapse, and it is probable that two or more impulses have to summate in space and time in order to "fire" a neuron* (George M. Wyburn). Also, **neurone.** [< New Latin *neuron* < Greek *neûron* sinew, nerve]

***neuron**

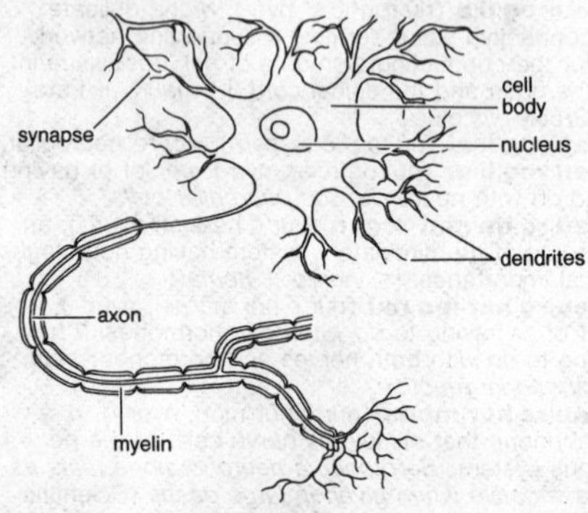


**neu|ron|al** (nu̇r′ə nəl, nyu̇r′-; nu̇ rō′-, nyu̇-), *adj.* of or having to do with a neuron: *Memory therefore, depends on an active neuronal mechanism which never rests* (New Scientist).

**neu|rone** (nu̇r′ōn, nyu̇r′-), *n.* = neuron.

**neu|ron|ic** (nu̇ ron′ik, nyu̇-), *adj.* of or having to do with a neuron.

**neu|ro|path** (nu̇r′ə path, nyu̇r′-), *n.* a person subject to or affected with nervous disorder, usually functional rather than organic.

**neu|ro|path|ic** (nu̇r′ə path′ik, nyu̇r′-), *adj.* relating to, caused by, or characterized by nervous disease. —**neu′ro|path′i|cal|ly,** *adv.*

**neu|ro|path|i|cal** (nu̇r′ə path′ə kəl, nyu̇r′-), *adj.* = neuropathic.

**neu|rop|a|thist** (nu̇ rop′ə thist, nyu̇-), *n.* a specialist in diseases of the nerves; neurologist.

**neu|ro|path|o|log|i|cal** (nu̇r′ō path′ə loj′ə kəl, nyu̇r′-), *adj.* of or having to do with neuropathology.

**neu|ro|pa|thol|o|gist** (nu̇r′ō pə thol′ə jist, nyu̇r′-), *n.* a person skilled in neuropathology.

**neu|ro|pa|thol|o|gy** (nu̇r′ō pə thol′ə jē, nyu̇r′-), *n.* the study of diseases of the nervous system.

**neu|rop|a|thy** (nu̇ rop′ə thē, nyu̇-), *n.* a disease of the nervous system.

**neu|ro|phar|ma|co|log|i|cal** (nu̇r′ō fär′mə kə loj′ə kəl, nyu̇r′-), *adj.* of or having to do with neuropharmacology: *neuropharmacological research.*

**neu|ro|phar|ma|col|o|gist** (nu̇r′ō fär′mə kol′ə jist, nyu̇r′-), *n.* a person who studies neuropharmacology.

**neu|ro|phar|ma|col|o|gy** (nu̇r′ō fär′mə kol′ə jē, nyu̇r′-), *n.* the study of the effects of drugs on the nervous system.

**neu|ro|phys|i|o|log|i|cal** (nu̇r′ō fiz′ē ə loj′ə kəl, nyu̇r′-), *adj.* of or having to do with the physiological functions of the nervous system: *The essential first step from the neurophysiological point of view is to find out more about how images are formed by the brain* (New Scientist). —**neu′ro|phys′i|o|log′i|cal|ly,** *adv.*

**neu|ro|phys|i|ol|o|gist** (nu̇r′ō fiz′ē ol′ə jist, nyu̇r′-), *n.* a person skilled in neurophysiology: *Electrical stimulation of certain areas in the brain ... evokes sensations of extreme pleasure which have recently attracted the attention of a number of neurophysiologists* (Scientific American).

**neu|ro|phys|i|ol|o|gy** (nu̇r′ō fiz′ē ol′ə jē, nyu̇r′-), *n.* the branch of physiology that deals with the nervous system: [*Galvani's*] *discovery that a muscle could be made to contract by an electrical current laid the foundation for the study of animal electricity, an important part of neurophysiology* (Caroline A. Chandler).

**neu|ro|plasm** (nu̇r′ə plaz′əm, nyu̇r′-), *n.* the protoplasm of the nerve cells and their fibrillae. [< Greek *neûron* nerve + *plásma* anything formed]

**neu|ro|psy|chi|at|ric** (nu̇r′ō sī′kē at′rik, nyu̇r′-), *adj.* of or having to do with neuropsychiatry: *neuropsychiatric hospitals.* —**neu′ro|psy′chi|at′ri|cal|ly,** *adv.*

**neu|ro|psy|chi|a|trist** (nu̇r′ō sī kī′ə trist, nyu̇r′-), *n.* a doctor of neuropsychiatry.

**neu|ro|psy|chi|a|try** (nu̇r′ō sī kī′ə trē, nyu̇r′-), *n.* a branch of medicine dealing with both the psychiatric and organic causes of mental disorders.

**neu|ro|psy|cho|log|i|cal** (nu̇r′ō sī′kə loj′ə kəl, nyu̇r′-), *adj.* of or having to do with neuropsychology.

**neu|ro|psy|chol|o|gist** (nu̇r′ō sī kol′ə jist, nyu̇r′-), *n.* a person who studies neuropsychology.

**neu|ro|psy|chol|o|gy** (nu̇r′ō sī kol′ə jē, nyu̇r′-), *n.* a branch of psychology dealing with the psychological functions of different parts of the nervous system.

**neu|ro|psy|cho|sis** (nu̇r′ō sī kō′sis, nyu̇r′-), *n., pl.* **-ses** (-sēz). **1** a mental disorder associated with or caused by organic disease of the nervous system. **2** = psychoneurosis.

**neu|rop|ter** (nu̇ rop′tər, nyu̇-), *n.* a neuropteran insect. [< New Latin *Neuroptera* the order name < Greek *neûron* nerve, sinew + *pterón* wing]

**neu|rop|ter|al** (nu̇ rop′tər əl, nyu̇-), *adj., n.* = neuropteran.

**neu|rop|ter|an** (nu̇ rop′tər ən, nyu̇-), *n., pl.* **-ter|a** (-tər ə), *adj.* —*n.* any one of an order of carnivorous insects having a complete metamorphosis, four large delicate wings, and mouthparts adapted for chewing. Lacewings and ant lions belong to this order.
—*adj.* of or belonging to the neuropterans.
[< New Latin *Neuroptera* the order name (< Greek *neûron* nerve, sinew + *pterón* wing) + English *-an*]

**neu|rop|ter|oid** (nu̇ rop′tə roid, nyu̇-), *adj.* resembling a neuropteran.

**neu|rop|ter|on** (nu̇ rop′tə ron, nyu̇-), *n.* a neuropteran insect.

**neu|rop|ter|ous** (nu̇ rop′tər əs, nyu̇-), *adj.* = neuropteran.

**neu|ro|sci|ence** (nu̇r′ō sī′əns, nyu̇r′-), *n.* any one of the sciences dealing with the nervous system, such as neurology and neurochemistry, or these sciences collectively.

**neu|ro|se|cre|tion** (nu̇r′ō si krē′shən, nyu̇r′-), *n.* **1** the secretion of substances, such as hormones, by nerve cells whose structures have temporarily become modified and taken on the function and appearance of gland cells: *This indication of the possibility of neurosecretion in crustaceans was soon confirmed and extended by other workers* (Sir Francis Knowles). **2** the substance secreted.

**neu|ro|se|cre|to|ry** (nu̇r′ō si krē′tər ē, nyu̇r′-), *adj.* of or having to do with neurosecretion: *the neurosecretory part of the brain.*

**neu|ro|sen|so|ry** (nu̇r′ō sen′sər ē, nyu̇r′-), *adj.* of or having to do with the sensory functions or activity of the nervous system: *The sudden emergence of preference in the chicks in their seventh week suggests ... that their neurosensory organization may be going through a critical period of maturation at that time* (Scientific American).

**neu|ro|sis** (nu̇ rō′sis, nyu̇-), *n., pl.* **-ses** (-sēz). **1** any one of various mental or emotional disorders, characterized by depression, anxiety, abnormal fears, and compulsive behavior. A neurosis is less severe than a psychosis. *A neurosis is an emotional problem that is solved in an irrational manner* (Marguerite Clark). **2** any action of nerve cells. [earlier, a functional disease < New Latin *neurosis* < Greek *neûron* nerve, sinew + *-ōsis* -osis]

**neu|ro|spo|ra** (nu̇r′ō spôr′ə, -spōr′-; nyu̇r′-), *n.* any fungus of a group that causes red and black mold in baked goods; bread mold. [< *neuro-* + Greek *sporá* seed]

**neu|ro|sur|geon** (nu̇r′ō sėr′jən, nyu̇r′-), *n.* a doctor who specializes in neurosurgery: *The neurosurgeon decides on the precise zone of destruction by the proton beam in the brain* (Frances Burns).

**neu|ro|sur|ge|ry** (nu̇r′ō sėr′jər ē, nyu̇r′-), *n.* surgery of the nervous system, especially of the brain.

**neu|ro|sur|gi|cal** (nu̇r′ō sėr′jə kəl, nyu̇r′-), *adj.* of or having to do with neurosurgery: *Drugs, conditioning, and neurosurgical procedures that modify drives, imagination, and personality have great value in treating some of the mentally ill* (Bulletin of Atomic Scientists).

**neu|rot|ic** (nu̇ rot′ik, nyu̇-), *adj., n.* —*adj.* **1a** having or suffering from emotional instability. **b** of or having to do with a neurosis or neuroses: *Neurotic symptoms, then, just like errors and dreams, have their meaning and, like these, are related to the life of the person in whom they appear* (Sigmund Freud). **2** *Informal.* too nervous. **3** acting upon or stimulating the nerves.
—*n.* **1** a person having or suffering from a neurosis: *The problem of the neurotic, then, is suffering, but of a particular kind, suffering due to guilt* (Sebastian de Grazia). **2** a drug or poison that acts on the nervous system. **3** *Obsolete.* a disease of the nerves. —**neu|rot′i|cal|ly,** *adv.*

**neu|rot|i|cism** (nu̇ rot′ə siz əm, nyu̇-), *n.* the state or condition of being neurotic: *Bartók's music is disturbing—possessed not only of a wild beauty but also of a neuroticism* (New Yorker).

**neu|rot|o|mist** (nu̇ rot′ə mist, nyu̇-), *n.* a person skilled in neurotomy.

**neu|rot|o|my** (nu̇ rot′ə mē, nyu̇-), *n., pl.* **-mies.** the surgical incision into a nerve to relieve a painful condition, as in neuralgia. [< Greek *neûron* nerve + *-tomiā* a cutting]

**neu|ro|tox|ic** (nu̇r′ō tok′sik, nyu̇r′-), *adj.* being or caused by a neurotoxin; toxic to nerve tissue: *... the neurotoxic action characteristic of the cobra poison* (New Scientist).

**neu|ro|tox|in** (nu̇r′ō tok′sin, nyu̇r′-), *n.* a toxin that can damage or destroy nerve tissue. The venom of the coral snake is a neurotoxin. *All of these neurotoxins in one way or another disrupt the microchemical mechanisms that transmit nerve impulses* (Scientific American).

**neu|ro|trans|mit|ter** (nu̇r′ō trans mit′ər, -tranz-; nyu̇r′-), *n.* a chemical substance that transmits impulses between nerve cells: *Norepinephrine is a neurotransmitter, a substance responsible for carrying a signal across the gap between two neurons. Neurons that use norepinephrine as a neurotransmitter have a role in the control of mood, learning, blood pressure, heart rate, blood sugar and glandular function* (Science News).

**neu|ro|trop|ic** (nu̇r′ō trop′ik, -trō′pik; nyu̇r′-), *adj.* drawn to or having an affinity for nervous tissue: *The virus of rabies is a neurotropic virus* (New Yorker). [< *neuro-* + Greek *tropḗ* a turning + English *-ic*]

**neus|ton** (nü′ston, nyü′-), *n.* minute organisms living on the surface film of a body of water: *Neuston ... inhabit the upper few centimetres of the water at night and live as deep as two thousand feet by day* (New Yorker). [< German *Neuston* < Greek *neustós* swimming < *neîn* to swim]

**neus|ton|ic** (nü ston′ik, nyü-), *adj.* of or having to do with neuston: *the neustonic zone of a pond.*

**Neus|tri|an** (nüs′trē ən, nyüs′-), *adj.* of or having to do with Neustria, the western kingdom of the Franks.

**neut.,** **1** neuter. **2** neutral.

**neu|ter** (nü′tər, nyü′-), *adj., n., v.* —*adj.* **1** *Grammar.* **a** neither masculine nor feminine: *"It" is a neuter pronoun.* **b** (of verbs) neither active nor passive; intransitive. *Abbr.:* neut. **2a** *Zoology.* without sex organs or with sex organs that are not fully developed: *Worker bees are neuter.* **b** *Botany.* having neither stamens nor pistils; functionally asexual. **3** being on neither side; neutral: *as to these matters I shall be impartial, though I cannot be neuter* (Sir Richard Steele).
—*n.* **1** *Grammar.* **a** a neuter word or form. **b** the neuter gender. **2** an animal, plant, or insect that is neuter. **3** a neutral: *which knows no neuter, owns but friends or foes* (Byron).
—*v.t.* **1** to castrate: *They had had the animal neutered some seven years back, and it had grown gross, sulky, and resentful* (New Yorker). **2** to counteract or make ineffective; neutralize: *A point of view that refused to neuter itself with a "nevertheless—" or a "but we must not overlook—"* (Sunday Times).
[< Latin *neuter* < *nē* not + *uter* either]

**neu|ter|cane** (nü′tər kān, nyü′-), *n.* a storm that draws its force from both tropical and cold-front disturbances in the atmosphere: *Weather satellites have been providing pictures of the progress* *and development of neutercanes* (Allan Yale Brooks). [< *neuter* + (hurri)*cane*]

**neu|tral** (nü′trəl, nyü′-), *adj., n.* —*adj.* **1** on neither side in a quarrel or a war: *a neutral attitude in an election. Switzerland was neutral in World War II.* **2** of or belonging to a neutral country or neutral zone: *a neutral vessel, a neutral port.* **3** neither one thing nor the other; indefinite. **4a** having little or no color; grayish: *a neutral sky.* **b** not tinted by mixture with any other color; pure: *a neutral yellow.* **5** neither acid nor base: *a neutral salt.* **6** *Electricity.* neither positive nor negative: *Recent experiments . . . have led to the discovery of . . . a neutral pion, that is a pion with practically the same mass as the charged pion but with no electric charge* (H. J. Bhaba). **7** *Biology.* not developed in sex; neuter.
—*n.* **1** a neutral person or country; one not taking part in a quarrel or war: *the rights of neutrals.* **2** a position of gears when they do not transmit motion from the engine to the wheels or other working parts. **3** the position of a gearshift lever when gears are in neutral. **4** a neutral color.
[< Latin *neutrālis* < *neuter* neuter] —**neu′tral|ly**, *adv.* —**neu′tral|ness**, *n.*

**neutral corner**, either of the two corners of a prize ring not occupied by the contestants between rounds.

**neutral current**, *Nuclear Physics.* a hypothetical flow of particles involving the weak interaction in which no electric charge is transferred; a stream of neutral W particles: *Evidence supporting the existence of neutral currents was obtained in experiments using a neutrino beam and a 12-ft. bubble chamber filled with liquid hydrogen* (Lawrence W. Jones).

**neu|tral|ise** (nü′trə līz, nyü′-), *v.t., v.i.,* **-ised, -is|ing.** *Especially British.* neutralize.

**neu|tral|ism** (nü′trə liz əm, nyü′-), *n.* the practice of maintaining a position as a neutral, especially in international affairs.

**neu|tral|ist** (nü′trə list, nyü′-), *n., adj.* —*n.* a person or government that practices or advocates neutrality, especially in international affairs.
—*adj.* practicing or advocating neutrality: *a neutralist country.* **SYN:** uncommitted, nonaligned.

**neu|tral|is|tic** (nü′trə lis′tik, nyü′-), *adj.* inclining toward neutrality. —**neu′tral|is′ti|cal|ly**, *adv.*

**neu|tral|i|ty** (nü tral′ə tē, nyü-), *n.* **1a** the condition of being neutral: *armed neutrality* (Woodrow Wilson). **SYN:** impartiality. **b** the attitude or policy of a nation that does not take part directly or indirectly in a war between other nations: *Neutrality is not equidistant from both sides. Neutrality is not considered to exclude membership of international organizations of a non-military character, still less does it imply any ideological restraint* (London Times). **SYN:** impartiality. **c** a neutral character or status, especially during a time of war: *Germany violated the neutrality of Belgium in World War I.* **SYN:** impartiality. **2** the condition of being neither acid nor alkaline: *Hemagglutination will occur . . . at a pH of 7, which of course is neutrality* (Scientific American).

**neu|tral|iz|a|ble** (nü′trə lī′zə bəl, nyü′-), *adj.* that can be neutralized.

**neu|tral|i|za|tion** (nü′trə lə zā′shən, nyü′-), *n.* **1** the act or process of neutralizing: *The process by which an acid and a base unite to form water and a salt is termed neutralization* (W. N. Jones). **2** the condition of being neutralized.

**neu|tral|ize** (nü′trə līz, nyü′-), *v.,* **-ized, -iz|ing.** —*v.t.* **1** to make neutral: *Bases neutralize acids.* **2** to keep war out of; keep neutral: *The city was neutralized so that peace talks could be held there. Switzerland was neutralized in 1815.* **3** to make of no effect by some opposite force; counterbalance: *She neutralized the bright colors in her room by using a tan rug. Some poisons neutralize each other.* **SYN:** counteract, offset.
—*v.i.* to become neutral or neutralized.

**neu|tral|iz|er** (nü′trə lī′zər, nyü′-), *n.* a person or thing that neutralizes.

**neutral spirits**, unaged ethyl alcohol used with aged whisky to make blended whiskies, with flavoring to make gin, or without blending as vodka.

**neutral vowel**, *Phonetics.* a central vowel; schwa.

**neu|tret|to** (nü tret′ō, nyü-), *n., pl.* **-tos.** any one of several elementary particles with a mass of or approximating zero, emitted in radioactive decay. [< *neutr*(on) + Italian *-etto,* a diminutive suffix]

**neu|tri|no** (nü trē′nō, nyü-), *n., pl.* **-nos.** a stable atomic particle having no electric charge and a mass too close to zero to be measured. A neutrino is emitted, with an electron, in beta rays. It is believed to play an important part in the decay of the fundamental particles which are unstable. [< *neutr*(on) + Italian *-ino,* a diminutive suffix]

**neu|tron** (nü′tron, nyü′-), *n.* a tiny particle that is neutral electrically and has about the same mass as a proton. Neutrons form a constituent of the nucleus of all atoms except that of the ordinary isotope of hydrogen, and are used to bombard the nuclei of various elements in the production of fission and other nuclear reactions. *Such an [atomic] explosion is triggered by the appearance of a neutron during the particular fraction of a microsecond when the chain reaction must be started* (Arthur H. Compton).
[< *neutr*(al) + *-on,* as in *electron, proton*]

**neutron activation analysis**, a method of analyzing the composition of a substance by radioactive bombardment with neutrons to identify the elements present by their characteristic radiation: *Neutron activation analysis offers a sensitive method for comparing bearing wear. The method can detect wear due to a few minutes' running, as well as abnormal wear* (New Scientist). *Abbr:* NAA (no periods).

**neutron bomb**, a hydrogen bomb set off with little heat or shock effect. It is designed to kill personnel by the release of highly lethal, short-lived neutrons or gamma rays.

**neutron capture**, the capture of a neutron by the nucleus of an atom.

**neutron flux**, **1** a flow of neutrons, as in a nuclear reactor. **2** a measure of this flow, expressed by the number of neutrons crossing a unit area in a unit time.

**neutron radiograph**, a picture produced by neutron radiography.

**neutron radiography**, a technique for producing an X-ray picture on photographic film by exposing an object to a stream of neutrons: *Neutron radiography gives promise of complementing X-ray radiography. X-rays emphasize the contrast between bone and soft tissue, while neutrons emphasize tissue differences and void spaces* (Frank B. Baranowski).

**neutron star**, a heavenly body that is the source of powerful X rays and consists of a mass of very densely packed neutrons probably formed by the collapsed atoms of a large star.

**neu|tro|phil** (nü′trə fil, nyü′-), *n.* a very abundant, phagocytic type of leucocyte that protects the body against infection, making up about 50 to 75 per cent of the total number of white blood cells.

**neu|tro|phile** (nü′trə fīl, -fil; nyü′-), *n. adj.* —*n.* = neutrophil. —*adj.* = neutrophilic. [< Latin *neuter* neuter + English *-phile*]

**neu|tro|phil|ic** (nü′trə fil′ik, nyü′-), *adj.* readily staining with either acidic or basic dyes: *neutrophilic granulocytes.*

**Nev.**, Nevada.

**Ne|vad|an** (nə vad′ən, -vä′dən), *adj., n.* —*adj.* of or having to do with the state of Nevada.
—*n.* a native or inhabitant of Nevada.

**né|vé** (nā vā′), *n.* **1** the crystalline or granular snow on the upper part of a glacier that has not yet been compressed into ice. **2** a field of such snow; firn. [< French *névé* < Swiss French, perhaps dialectal Savoy *névi* slope or mass of snow < Old French *neif* snow < Latin *nix, nivis snow*]

**nev|er** (nev′ər), *adv.* **1** not ever; at no time: *He never had to work for a living.* **2** in no case; not at all; to no extent or degree: *He will never be the wiser.*
**never ever**, *Informal.* never: *He was never ever late before.*
**never so, a** not even so: *He spoke never so much as a word.* **b** no matter how: *Let him be weighed never so scrupulously, . . . he will not be found . . . wanting* (C. J. Fox).
[Old English *nǣfre* < *ne* not + *ǣfre* ever]

**nev|er|mind** (nev′ər mīnd′), *n. U.S. Dialect.* **1** attention; heed: *Grandpa Murray is still paying the girl no more nevermind than if she was a vinegar gnat* (Jesse Hill Ford). **2** significant effect; difference: *"It don't make no real nevermind"* (Time).

**nev|er|more** (nev′ər môr′, -mōr′), *adv.* never again; never at any future time.

**nev|er-nev|er** (nev′ər nev′ər), *adj., n.* —*adj. Informal.* **1** unreal; imaginary: *a series of pictures about never-never monsters* (New Yorker). **2** not easily visualized or grasped and therefore seemingly unreal or imaginary; implausible: *It is a never-never world of protons, electrons, isotopic separation . . . and half-lives of the elements* (New York Times).
—*n.* **1** Also, **never never**. *British Slang.* installment plan. **2** *Australian Slang.* the remote, thinly settled region of northwest Queensland.

**never-never land**, an imaginary place or unrealistic condition: *the never-never land of "total" defense* (Wall Street Journal). *A never-never land of all play and no work* (New Yorker).

**nev|er-say-die** (nev′ər sā′dī′), *adj.* refusing to give up; die-hard: *those never-say-die purveyors of information— the press agents* (Newsweek).

**nev|er|the|less** (nev′ər ᴛʜə les′), *adv.* however; nonetheless; for all that; in spite of it: *She was very tired; nevertheless she kept on working.* **SYN:** but, still.

**ne|void** (nē′void), *adj.* like a nevus. Also, **naevoid.**

**ne|vus** (nē′vəs), *n., pl.* **-vi** (-vī). **1** a discolored or pigmented spot on the skin from birth, such as a mole; birthmark. **2** a tumor of the skin, usually congenital. Also, **naevus.** [< Latin *naevus* mole, wart]

**new** (nü, nyü), *adj., adv., n.* —*adj.* **1** never having been before; now first made, thought out, known or heard of, felt, or discovered: *a new invention. They own a new home.* **2** lately grown, come, or made; not old: *a new bud, a new make of car, new potatoes.* **3** now first used; not worn or used up: *a new path.* **SYN:** fresh, unused. **4** beginning again: *a new attempt. Sunrise makes a new day. The new moon is the moon when seen as a thin crescent.* **5** as if new; fresh: *to go on with new courage.* **6** different; changed; renewed: *to have a new teacher, to feel like a new person. The old order changeth, yielding place to new* (Tennyson). **7** not familiar; strange: *a new country to me.* **SYN:** unfamiliar. **8** not yet accustomed: *new to the work.* **9** later or latest; modern; recent: *new dances.* **10** just come; having just reached the position: *a new arrival, a new president, a new author.* **11** further; additional; more: *He sought new information on the subject.* **12** being the later or latest of two or more things of the same kind: *New England, the New Testament.* **13 New,** (of a language) in use in modern times, especially since the Middle Ages, usually contrasted with *Old* and *Medieval,* or *Middle: New Hebrew, New Latin.*
—*adv.* **1** recently or lately; newly; freshly: *new-fallen snow, a new-found friend.* **2** again; anew; afresh.
—*n.* that which is new; new thing: *I prefer the old to the new.*
[Old English *nīwe*] —**new′ness**, *n.*
—*Syn. adj.* **1 New, novel, modern** mean having only now or recently come into existence or knowledge. **New** describes something now existing, made, seen, or known for the first time: *They built a new house.* **Novel** adds and emphasizes the idea of being unusual, strikingly different, or strange, not of the ordinary kind: *The house has a novel dining room.* **Modern** describes people and things belonging to or characteristic of the present time, or recent times, and sometimes suggests being up-to-date, not old-fashioned: *The architecture is modern.*

**New American Bible**, an English translation of the Bible made by Roman Catholic scholars in the United States and published in 1970. *Abbr:* NAB (no periods).

**Ne|war** (ni wär′), *n., pl.* **-wars** or **-war.** a member of a Mongoloid ethnic group that ruled part of Nepal, a country between India and Tibet, before the Gurkha conquest in the late 1700's.

**Ne|wa|ri** (ni wä′rē), *n.* the language of the Newars, belonging to Tibeto-Burman.

**New Australian**, a recent immigrant to Australia.

**new blue**, **1** a blue pigment derived from an oxide of cobalt. **2** an artificial ultramarine; French blue. **3** = Prussian blue.

**new|born** (nü′bôrn′, nyü′-), *adj., n.* —*adj.* **1** recently or only just born: *a newborn baby.* **2** *Figurative.* ready to start a new life; born again. **SYN:** regenerated.
—*n.* a newborn baby.

**new broom**, a new person in charge who is very active at first.

**New|burg** (nü′bėrg, nyü′-), *adj.* prepared or served with a sauce of cream, butter, egg yolks, and wine: *lobster Newburg.* [< the proper name *Newburg* or *Newburgh*]

**New Canadian**, **1** an immigrant who has recently arrived in Canada. **2** a naturalized Canadian citizen.

**new candle**, a unit for measuring the strength or intensity of light, replacing the international candle; candela.

**New|cas|tle** (nü′kas′əl, -käs′-; nyü′-), *n.* **carry coals to Newcastle, a** to do something unnecessary; waste one's time, effort, resources, or talents: *At first sight it seems like carrying coals to Newcastle . . . when the impressive logic of senior . . . officials is applied to a process largely governed by the electronic logic of computers* (London Times). **b** to bring something to a place where it is unneeded (such as coal to Newcastle, England, where it is plentiful): *It sounds like carrying coals to Newcastle, but Lord & Taylor's cosmetics department is importing water* (New York Times).

**Newcastle cloak**, an inverted barrel with holes cut in it for the head and arms, and put upon a man as if it were a garment. It was a punishment formerly inflicted in England for drunkenness.

**Pronunciation Key:** hat, āge, cãre, fär; let, ēqual, tėrm; it, īce; hot, ōpen, ôrder; oil, out; cup, pu̇t, rüle; child; long; thin; ᴛʜen; zh, measure; ə represents **a** in about, **e** in taken, **i** in pencil, **o** in lemon, **u** in circus.

**Newcastle disease**, a disease of poultry, caused by a virus, forms of which attack the respiratory and nervous systems.

**new chum**, = New Australian.

**New Church**, the church of the Swedenborgians; New Jerusalem Church.

**new|come** (nü′kum′, nyü′-), *adj.* newly or lately come or arrived: *newcome settlers.*

**new|com|er** (nü′kum′ər, nyü′-), *n.* **1** a person who has just come or who came not long ago: *As the newcomers bought land and built houses, proved friendly neighbors and good credit risks, the tensions relaxed* (Newsweek). **2** a recent immigrant. **3** = novice.

**New Covenanters**, the members of the monastic community or sect who composed the Dead Sea Scrolls, so named because they believed that they were renewing God's covenant as set forth in the Old Testament; Qumran Community.

**new-cre|ate** (nü′krē āt′, nyü′-), *v.t.*, **-at|ed, -at-ing.** to create anew.

**New Critic**, a writer or practitioner of New Criticism.

**New Critical**, of, having to do with, or characteristic of New Criticism: *The commentary ... varied, if not in tone, at least in terms of critical standpoint, from New Critical to mimetic to contemporary eclectic* (Eliot Fremont-Smith).

**New Criticism**, a form of literary criticism that originated in the United States in the 1920's, characterized by close textual analysis, complex interpretations of poems, and use of the methods or principles of linguistics and other related disciplines.

**New Deal**, **1** the policies and measures advocated by President Franklin D. Roosevelt as a means of improving the economic and social welfare of the United States: *The country is now assimilating the New Deal, and adjusting to the mixed economy which has been developing ever since the turn of the century* (Harper's). **2** the administration of Franklin D. Roosevelt, 1933-1945.

**New Dealer**, a supporter or advocate of the New Deal.

**New Deal|ish** (dē′lish), characteristic of the New Deal; favoring the New Deal.

**New Deal|ism** (dē′liz əm), the principles and policies of the New Deal.

**New Democrat**, a member of the New Democratic Party of Canada, a political party founded in 1961.

**New Economic Policy**, = NEP.

**new economics**, the policy, based on Keynesian theory, of a flexible adjustment of money supply and government spending to influence or improve the economy; the policy of the neo-Keynesians: *The record boom seemed to have proved the validity of the "new economics"—that dexterous fiscal and monetary manipulation could assure prosperity* (Sylvia Porter).

**new economist**, a supporter of new economics; neo-Keynesian: *Even the new economists would favor either a tax increase or a cut in spending* (Tom Wicker).

**new|el** (nü′əl, nyü′-), *n.* **1** the post at the top or bottom of a stairway that supports the railing. **2** the central post of a winding stairway. [< Old French *nouel,* or *noiel* newel, kernel < Late Latin *nucālis* nutlike < Latin *nux, nucis* nut; probably inflenced by Old French *noel* bud, ultimately < Latin *nōdus* knot]

**New England aster**, a tall perennial aster, with purple flowers, native to northeastern North America.

**New Englander**, a person born or living in New England, the northeastern part of the United States.

**New English**, **1** = Modern English. **2** English as currently used, including especially new words, meanings, and expressions. **3** *U.S. Education.* English grammar taught with the concepts and methods of structural linguistics.

**New English Bible**, an English translation of the Bible and Apocrypha by British scholars, begun in 1949 and completed in 1970. The New Testament was separately published in 1961. *Abbr:* NEB (no periods).

**Newf.**, Newfoundland.

**new|fan|gle** (nü′fang′gəl, nyü′-), *adj., n., v.,* **-gled, -gling.** *Dialect.* —*adj.* = newfangled.
—*n.* a new thing or fashion; novelty: *A Pedlers packe of newefangles* (John Lyly).
—*v.t.* to make newfangled or fashionable; bring up to date: *... not hereby to control, and newfangle the Scripture* (Milton).

**new|fan|gled** (nü′fang′gəld, nyü′-), *adj.* **1** lately come into fashion; of a new kind: *the newfangled doctrine of utility* (John Galt). *Thousands of tradition-minded Londoners wanted no part of such ... newfangled devices as radio or TV* (Newsweek). **SYN**: novel, new-fashioned. **2** fond of novelty. [Middle English *newfangle* eager for novelty < *newe* new + *fangen* to take] —**new′fan′gled-ness**, *n.*

**new|fan|gle|ment** (nü′fang′gəl mənt, nyü′-), *n. Informal.* a novel or newfangled thing; novelty.

**new-fash|ioned** (nü′fash′ənd, nyü′-), *adj.* of a new fashion; lately come into style. **SYN**: modern.

**New Federalism**, a policy of Federal decentralization and revenue sharing advocated by President Richard M. Nixon.

**New Federalist**, a supporter or advocate of New Federalism.

**New|fie** (nü′fē, nyü′-), *n. Informal.* **1** *Canadian.* a Newfoundlander: *The Newfies aren't really very happy about being Canadians* (Maclean's). **2** a Newfoundland dog.

**new-found** (nü′found′, nyü′-), *adj.* recently found: *a new-found friend.*

**New|found|land** (nü found′lənd, nyü-; nü′fən-, -nyü′-), *n.* a shaggy, intelligent dog like a spaniel but much larger, usually having a black coat. The breed was developed in Newfoundland and originally used as working animals. The Newfoundland, a powerful swimmer, has become famous for its work in rescuing people from drowning.

**New|found|land|er** (nü found′lən dər, nyü-), *n.* a person born or living in Newfoundland.

**Newfoundland Standard Time**, the standard time in Newfoundland, one and a half hours ahead of Eastern Standard Time and constituting an independent time zone.

**New Frontier**, **1** the policies and programs advocated by President John F. Kennedy for the United States. **2** the administration of John F. Kennedy, 1961-1963.

**New Frontiersman**, **1** a supporter of the policies of the New Frontier. **2** a member of President Kennedy's administration.

**New|gate** (nü′gāt, nyü′-), *n.* a former prison in London, torn down in 1902.

**New Greek**, the Greek language as used in modern times, especially after 1500; Modern Greek.

**new|ground** (nü′ground′, nyü′-), *n.* land newly cleared.

**New Hampshire**, any one of an American breed of domestic chicken having reddish-brown feathers and yellow skin, raised for eggs and meat.

**New Hamp|shi|rite** (ham′shə rīt′, -shi-), a native or inhabitant of New Hampshire.

**New Hebrew**, = Modern Hebrew.

**new|ish** (nü′ish, nyü′-), *adj.* rather new.

**New Jer|sey|ite** (jėr′zē īt), a native or inhabitant of the state of New Jersey.

**New Jerusalem**, heaven; the City of God and the blessed (in the Bible, Revelation 21:2).

**New Jerusalem Church**, the church of the Swedenborgians; New Church.

**New Latin**, the Latin language after 1500; Modern Latin. It contains words formed from Greek and Latin elements.

**New Learning**, **1** the study of the Bible and Greek and Latin classical authors in the original tongues in England, in the 1500's. **2** the doctrines of the Reformation in England.

**New Left**, *U.S.* a diffuse political movement that began in the 1960's, made up chiefly of college and university students seeking radical changes in American foreign policy, civil rights, and the academic establishment: *What distinguishes the New Left is ... its unwillingness to define what it aims for after the revolution* (Arthur M. Schlesinger, Jr.).

**New Leftist**, a member of the New Left: *The New Leftists have a mystical faith in the purity and wisdom of the poor, "uncorrupted" by the Establishment—an idea that the New Right rejects as nonsense* (Time).

**New Lights**, *Ecclesiastical.* the members of any one of various parties adhering to new doctrines, or forming bodies separate from others with which they were formerly associated because of adherence to some new view of doctrine or duty.

**new look**, *Informal.* a striking change in appearance, policy, or performance.

**new|ly** (nü′lē, nyü′-), *adv.* **1** very lately; recently: *newly discovered, newly arrived, newly wedded.* **2** once again; freshly: *newly painted walls, a newly revived scandal.* **SYN**: afresh, anew. **3** in a new way. **SYN**: differently.

**new|ly|wed** (nü′lē wed′, nyü′-), *n.* a person who has recently become married.

**new-made** (nü′mād′, nyü′-), *adj.* **1** newly, recently, or freshly made: *a new-made peer, a new-made grave.* **2** made anew; remade.

**new|mar|ket** (nü′mär′kit, nyü′-), *n.* **1** Also, **New-market coat.** a long, close-fitting coat, worn by men and women outdoors about 1880. **2** a card game, a variety of stops, in which cards are played in sequence, the playing of certain cards winning bets placed on them; Michigan. [< *New-market,* a town in England]

**new math** or **new mathematics**, *U.S. Education.* mathematics designed to give the student an understanding of basic mathematical structures, concepts, and processes, with less emphasis on formal drills.

**New Mexican**, **1** of or having to do with the state of New Mexico: *a New Mexican town.* **2** a native or inhabitant of the state of New Mexico.

**new-mod|el** (nü′mod′əl, nyü′-), *v.t.*, **-eled, -el|ing** or (*especially British*) **-elled, -el|ling.** to model anew; remodel; give a new form to: *to new-model a house.*

**new moon**, **1** the moon when seen as a thin crescent with the hollow side on the left. **2** the moon when its dark side is toward the earth, appearing almost invisible: *At times of new moon, the moon is between us and the sun* (Hubert J. Bernhard).

**New Nationalism**, a political program of liberal social reform advocated by Theodore Roosevelt in 1910. The program called for checks on big business, conservation, and old-age and unemployment insurance.

**New Or|le|ans jazz** (ôr′lē ənz, ôr′lənz; ôr lēnz′), the jazz from which present-day jazz evolved, first played by Negro brass bands in parades and funeral processions in New Orleans during the late 1800's.

**new penny**, *pl.* **new pence.** the British penny in the decimal system established in 1971, equal to 1/100 of a pound and corresponding to 2.4 pence in the old system: *The minimum cost of a call would go down from 6d.—the equivalent of 2½ new pence—to 2 new pence with a compensating adjustment in the length of the call* (London Times). *Abbr:* np (no periods).

**New Politics** or **new politics**, a development in American politics, associated especially with Senators Eugene J. McCarthy, Robert F. Kennedy, and George S. McGovern, emphasizing intense participation of voters in the political processes rather than reliance on party machinery: *The "new politics" ... produced a new kind of candidate: an independent who minimizes party affiliation and stresses personality and policies* (Steven V. Roberts).

**new process**, the process by which corn meal is made from hulled corn kernels with the germ removed.

**New Realism**, **1** neorealism, especially in literature: *New Realism ... has been rated a "cult of squalidity" by some proper Britons* (Time). **2** any form of neorealistic (as opposed to abstract) art, especially pop art: *The "New Realism" ... takes as its subject matter the most banal objects and images of commerical culture* (New Yorker).

**New Realist**, **1** a follower of New Realism. **2** having to do with or characteristic of New Realism: *New Realist works.*

**new-rich** (nü′rich′, nyü′-), *n., adj.* —*n.* = nouveau riche.
—*adj.* **1** recently become rich. **2** vulgarly displaying wealth.

**New Right**, a political movement standing for conservatism and nationalism in response to both the New Left and the traditional or established conservatives.

**news** (nüz, nyüz), *n.* **1** something told as having just happened; information about something that has just happened or will soon happen: *The news that our teacher was leaving made us sad.* **SYN**: tidings, advices, intelligence, information. **2** a report of a current happening or happenings in a newspaper or on television or radio: *His chief interest was in the ways in which news is gathered* (Newsweek). **3** news important enought to report. **break the news**, to make something known; tell something: *There was much shouting and applause when the leaders broke the news that the strike was over.*
[Middle English *newes,* probably plural of *newe* (literally) that which is new, noun use of adjective; perhaps patterned on French *nouvelles*]
▶ **news.** Though plural in form, *news* is now invariably used as a singular: *The news from the various districts is sent to a central office.*

**news agency**, **1** a commercial agency that gathers and distributes news to newspapers, magazines, and radio and television stations subscribing to its service. **2** a similar government agency.

**news agent**, *British.* a newsdealer.

**news|board** (nüz′bôrd′, -bōrd′; nyüz′-), *n.* a coarse cardboard made from newspaper pulp.

**news|boy** (nüz′boi′, nyüz′-), *n.* a boy who sells or delivers newspapers; paperboy.

**news|cast** (nüz′kast′, -käst′; nyüz′-), *n., v.* —*n.* a radio or television program devoted to current events and news bulletins.
—*v.t., v.i.* to broadcast (news): *I'm afraid we have to face this—why women should not replace men in general newscasting and sportscasting* (Newsweek).

**news|cast|er** (nüz′kas′tər, -käs′-; nyüz′-), *n.* **1** a person who gives the news on a newscast: *Through open windows could be heard the cheerful voices of radio newscasters prophesying* *in air-conditioned studios a record [temperature] for the week end* (John Stephen Strange). **2** a commentator on the news.

**news|clip** (nüz′klip′, nyüz′-), *n.* a newspaper clipping: *I have before me a Los Angeles Times newsclip* (Atlantic).

**news conference**, a meeting at which newspaper reporters receive information from a person or group, especially in the form of answers to questions asked by the reporters; press conference: *The President would not hold a news conference this week* (New York Times).

**news|deal|er** (nüz′dē′lər, nyüz′-), *n.* a person who sells newspapers and magazines.

**news editor**, an editor on a newspaper, magazine, or radio or television station in charge of gathering, editing, and reporting the news.

**news|girl** (nüz′gėrl′, nyüz′-), *n.* a girl who sells newspapers.

**news|hawk** (nüz′hôk′, nyüz′-), *n. Informal.* a newspaper reporter or correspondent.

**news|hen** (nüz′hen′, nyüz′-), *n. Informal.* a woman journalist; newspaperwoman: *I found no newspaperwomen who liked being called newshens* (Time).

**news|hound** (nüz′hound′, nyüz′-), *n. Informal.* a newspaper reporter.

**news|let|ter** (nüz′let′ər, nyüz′-), *n.* **1** a letter or report giving informal or confidential news. Organizations often issue newsletters to members or subscribers. *One newsletter mentions glass lamps as leading sales of metal and ceramic-based types* (Wall Street Journal). **2** a forerunner of the modern newspaper, current in the 1600's and early 1700's, which presented news for general circulation.

**news magazine**, or **news|mag|a|zine** (nüz′-mag′ə zēn, nyüz′-), *n.* a magazine devoted to interpretive comment on news and current events, usually published weekly.

**news|mak|er** (nüz′mā′kər, nyüz′-), *n. U.S.* a newsworthy person or event.

**news|man** (nüz′man′, -mən; nyüz′-), *n., pl.* **-men.** **1** a man who sells or delivers newspapers and magazines. **2** a newspaperman or newscaster.

**news|mon|ger** (nüz′mung′gər, -mong′-; nyüz′-), *n.* a person who spreads news or gossip: *a knot of anxious newsmongers, each of whom departed ... to carry the story home to his family* (Washington Irving).

**news|pa|per** (nüz′pā′pər, nyüz′-), *n., v.* —*n.* **1** sheets of paper, usually printed every day or week, telling the news, carrying advertisements, and often having stories, pictures, feature articles, and useful information: *The newspaper, together with the telegraph, the telephone, and the radio, has created a special degree of social consciousness* (Emory S. Bogardus). **2** the paper used; newsprint.

—*v.i.* to work for a newspaper: *In Norway Willy supported himself by newspapering* (Time).

**news|pa|per|dom** (nüz′pā′pər dəm, nyüz′-), *n.* the world or sphere of newspapers.

**news|pa|per|ing** (nüz′pā′pər ing, nyüz′-), *n.* **1** the occupation of a newspaperman. **2** journalism: *Good newspapering arises from an inner conviction of what to do* (Harper's).

**news|pa|per|man** (nüz′pā′pər man′, nyüz′-), *n., pl.* **-men.** a reporter, editor, or other person who works for a newspaper.

**news|pa|per|wom|an** (nüz′pā′pər wům′ən, nyüz′-), *n., pl.* **-wom|en.** a woman who works on a newspaper as journalist, reporter, or editor.

**new|speak** (nü′spēk′, nyü′-), *n.* language in which the words are made to mean the opposite of their real meanings to conform to an ideology: *"Newspeak," in which "Big Brother" has become the ... word for "tyrant"* (Wall Street Journal). [coined by George Orwell, 1903-1950, an English novelist]

**news|print** (nüz′print′, nyüz′-), *n.* the soft, relatively coarse paper on which newspapers are usually printed. It is cheap paper made chiefly from wood pulp and unsized.

**news|read|er** (nüz′rē′dər, nyüz′-), *n.* **1** a person who reads the newspapers. **2** *British.* a news announcer.

**news|reel** (nüz′rēl′, nyüz′-), *n.* a motion picture showing current events or news.

**news|room** (nüz′rüm′, -rům′; nyüz′-), *n.,* or **news room**, the part of a newspaper office or radio or television station where news is prepared for publication or broadcasting.

**news service**, = news agency.

**news|sheet** (nüz′shēt′, nyüz′-), *n.* a printed sheet issued by clubs and business organizations reporting activities and events.

**news stall**, *British.* a newsstand.

**news|stand** (nüz′stand′, nyüz′-), *n.* a place where newspapers and magazines are sold: *The magazine is sold solely through subscriptions; it has no newsstand sales* (Wall Street Journal). SYN: kiosk.

**New|stead Abbey** (nü′sted, nyü′-), an ancient building in Nottinghamshire, England, founded in 1170 by Henry II, and later for a time the home of Lord Byron.

**New Stone Age**, the neolithic period of the Stone Age.

**New Style**, the method of reckoning time according to the Gregorian calendar, adopted in England, and generally throughout the English-speaking world, in 1752. *Abbr:* N.S.

**news|ven|dor** (nüz′ven′dər, nyüz′-), *n.* a seller of newspapers: *The ground floor ... is occupied by a small newsvendor's shop* (Wilkie Collins).

**news|week|ly** (nüz′wēk′lē, nyüz′-), *n., pl.* **-lies.** a weekly periodical reporting current events of general interest or of specialized interest.

**news|wom|an** (nüz′wům′ən, nyüz′-), *n., pl.* **-wom|en.** = newspaperwoman.

**news|wor|thy** (nüz′wėr′ŦHē, nyüz′-), *adj.,* **-thi|er, -thi|est.** having enough public interest to be printed in a newspaper: *Does a press photographer have the right to take a newsworthy picture even when the subject objects?* (Time). —**news′-wor′thi|ly,** *adv.* —**news′wor′thi|ness,** *n.*

**news|writ|ing** (nüz′rī′ting, nyüz′-), *n.* writing for a newspaper; journalism: *The audience may not be aware of bad newswriting, he says, but "they feel vaguely uncomfortable and turn away"* (Time).

**news|y**[1] (nü′zē, nyü′-), *adj.,* **news|i|er, news|i|est.** *Informal.* full of news: *a newsy letter.* [< *news* + *-y*[1]]

**news|y**[2] (nü′zē, nyü′-), *n., pl.* **news|ies.** *Slang.* a newsboy or newsman.

***newt** (nüt, nyüt), *n.* a small salamander that lives in water part of the time. There are various kinds of newts; all have lungs and lidded eyes, and are smooth-skinned as adults. [Middle English *neute,* misdivision of *an eut,* variant of *evet* eft]

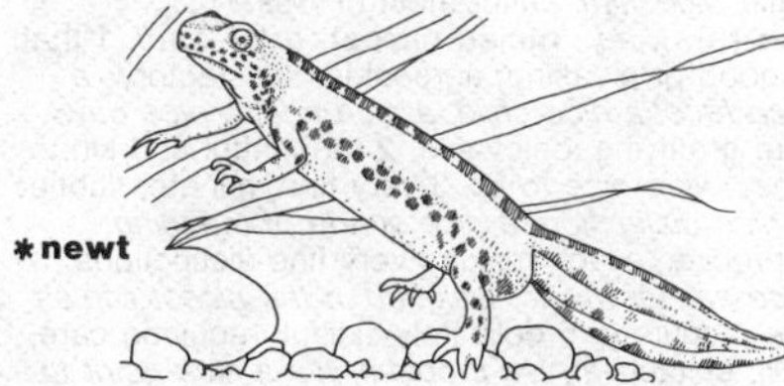
***newt**

**New Test.**, New Testament.

**New Testament**, **1** the part of the Bible which contains the life and teachings of Christ recorded by His followers, together with their own experiences and teachings. It is the second of the two principal divisions of the Christian Bible. *Abbr:* N.T. **2** the new covenant between God and mankind established by the birth, life, teachings, and death of Jesus Christ; the new or Christian dispensation, set forth especially in the writings of Paul and other apostles.

**new thing**, *Jazz Slang.* a form of experimental music based on jazz rhythms, developed in the 1960's: *... the heretic experiments of Milford Graves, the best of the "new thing" drummers* (Whitney Balliett).

**New Thought**, any one of several modern religious systems, not associated with Christian Science, maintaining that through good and proper ideas all bodily or mental ailments may be mastered.

**new|ton** (nü′tən, nyü′-), *n.* the unit of force in the meter-kilogram-second system, equal to 100,000 dynes. It is the force required to give an acceleration of one meter per second per second to a mass of one kilogram. [< Isaac *Newton,* 1642-1727, an English physicist]

**New|to|ni|an** (nü tō′nē ən, nyü-), *adj., n.* —*adj.* of or by Isaac Newton (1642-1727), the English mathematician, physicist, and philosopher: *The student of the history of ideas can render a service to science by showing the great influence exerted upon modern scientific thought by Newtonian physics* (John E. Owen).

—*n.* a follower of Isaac Newton.

**new|ton-me|ter** (nü′tən mē′tər, nyü′-), *n.* = joule.

**Newton's law of motion**, any one of the three fundamental statements on motion formulated by Isaac Newton: **a** a body at rest or moving uniformly in a straight line will remain so unless acted upon by some outside force. **b** a change in the motion of a body is proportional to and in the same direction as the force that produces it. **c** for every action there is an equal and opposite reaction.

**Newton's rings**, a series of alternately bright and dark circles seen when a slightly convex piece of glass is placed against a flat piece of glass, caused by interference between the light waves reflected from the top of the flat surface and those reflected from the bottom of the curved surface.

**new town**, a planned urban community where people can both live and work, designed especially to relieve the overcrowding of a nearby metropolis; satellite town: *A new town with an ultimate population of 60,000 is seen as a prime need for the area* (London Times). *There has grown up a strong if diffuse interest in ... providing green spaces, better planning, and coherent "new towns" rather than mere bedroom suburbs* (New York Times).

**new wave**, a movement in cinematography originating in France in the 1950's, characterized by extensive use of symbolism, sophisticated themes, and unconventional camerawork. [translation of French *nouvelle vague*]

**new-world** (nü′wėrld′, nyü′-), *adj.* of or having to do with the Western Hemisphere; not of the Old World: *new-world monkeys, new-world plants.* Also, **New-World.**

**New World**, the Western Hemisphere; North America and South America.

**new year**, the year approaching or newly begun.

**New Year** or **New Year's**, **1** the first day or days of the year. **2** = New Year's Day. **3 New Year,** = Rosh Hashanah.

**New Year's Day**, January 1, the first day of the year, usually observed as a legal holiday.

**New Year's Eve**, the night of December 31, often observed by celebrations welcoming the New Year.

**New York|er** (yôr′kər), a person born or living in New York City or New York State.

**New York|ese** (yôr kēz′, -kēs′), a type of English pronunciation heard in New York City: *Harvard accents, finishing school drawl, and plain New Yorkese mingled with the rock'n'roll racket in Greenwich Village* (New York Times).

**New Zea|land|er** (zē′lən dər), a native or inhabitant of New Zealand, a British dominion in the South Pacific.

**New Zea|land flax** or **hemp** (zē′lənd), **1** a tall plant of New Zealand, grown also in Europe and in California, with red, honey-laden blossoms. **2** the fiber made from the leaves of this plant, used for making ropes and fabrics.

**next** (nekst), *adj., adv., prep.* —*adj.* **1** nearest: *the next room.* **2** following at once: *the next train. The next day after Sunday is Monday.*

—*adv.* **1** the first time after this: *When you next come, bring it.* **2** in the place, time, or position that is nearest: *I am going to do my arithmetic problems next. Your name comes next.*

—*prep.* nearest to: *We live in the house next the church.*

**next to, a** nearest to: *Bobby is next to John in age.* **b** almost; nearly: *It was thought next to impossible* (William H. Ireland).

[Old English *nēhst* nearest, superlative of *nēah* near] —**next′ness,** *n.*

**next-door** (nekst′dôr′, -dōr′), *adj.* in or at the next house or apartment: *my next-door neighbor.*

**next door**, **1** in or at the next house or apartment: *He lives next door.* **2** *Figurative.* very close.

**next door to.** See under **door**.

**next friend**, *Law.* a person who, although not the legal guardian, acts for a child or other person who cannot legally act for himself, especially in a lawsuit.

**next of kin**, **1** the nearest blood relative or relatives. **2** *Law.* the relatives entitled to share in the estate of a person who has died intestate.

**nex|us** (nek′səs), *n., pl.* **-us** or **-us|es. 1** a connection; tie; link: *The cash nexus ... was ... a new role for the Grocer as cosmopolitan specialist* (Harper's). *Cash Payment ... the universal sole nexus of man to man* (Thomas Carlyle). **2** a connected series: *A man, to [John P.] Marquand, is a nexus of institutions* (Harper's). **3** *Grammar.* a predication or a construction akin to a predication. [< Latin *nexus, -ūs* < *nectere* to bind]

**Nez Per|cé** (nez′ pėrs′; *French* nā per sā′), *n., pl.* **Nez Per|cés** (nez′ pėr′siz; *French* nā per sā′). **1** a member of an American Indian tribe of Shahaptian stock, that formerly lived in Idaho, Oregon, and Washington. **2** the language of this tribe. **3** *Obsolete.* a member of any Indian tribe that was formerly believed to pierce the nasal septum in order to wear ornaments. [American English < French *nez percé* (literally) pierced nose (because of the alleged custom of the tribes to which it was first applied)]

**n.f.** or **N/F.**, *Banking.* no funds.

**N.F.**, an abbreviation for the following:
**1** National Formulary (a book containing stand-

**Pronunciation Key:** hat, āge, cãre, fär; let, ēqual, tėrm; it, īce; hot, ōpen, ôrder; oil, out; cup, pu̇t, rüle; child; long; thin; ŦHen; zh, measure; ə represents **a** in about, **e** in taken, **i** in pencil, **o** in lemon, **u** in circus.

ards for certain drugs, compiled by the American Pharmaceutical Association).
2 Newfoundland.
3 *Banking.* no funds.
4 Norman-French.

**NFC** (no periods) or **N.F.C.**, National Football Conference.

**NFL** (no periods) or **N.F.L.**, National Football League.

**Nfld.**, Newfoundland.

**N.F.O.** or **NFO** (no periods), National Farmers Organization.

**NFU** (no periods) or **N.F.U.**, National Farmers' Union (of Great Britain).

**ng** (no period), nanogram.

**n.g.**, no good.

**N.G.**, **1** National Guard. **2** no good.

**N galaxy**, a galaxy distinguished by a starlike central nucleus: *A program of photographic monitoring of quasars, N galaxies and Seyfert galaxies has been carried out ... at the University of Florida* (Science News). [*N* for *nuclear*]

**Ngo|ni** (eng gō′nē), *n., pl.* **-ni** or **-nis**. **1** a member of a large group of Bantu-speaking peoples of southern Africa. **2** their language.

**ngul|trum** (nul′trəm), *n.* a unit of money of Bhutan, introduced in 1975: *Ngultrums ... were at par with the Indian rupee* (Govindan Unny). [< the native name]

**Ngu|ni** (eng gü′nē), *n., pl.* **-ni** or **-nis**. = Ngoni.

**Ngu|ra** (eng gü′rə), *n., pl.* **-ra** or **-ras**. a member of a Bantu-speaking tribe of Malawi, in Africa.

**ngwee** (eng gwē′), *n., pl.* **ngwee**. a unit of money of Zambia, equal to 1/100 of a kwacha. [< the native name, meaning "bright"]

**Ngwe|nya|ma** (eng gwē′nyä′mə), *n.* the title of the hereditary ruler or king of Swaziland. [< Swazi *Ngwenyama*]

**NH** (no periods), New Hampshire (with postal Zip Code).

**N.H.**, New Hampshire.

**NHA** (no periods), **1** National Health Association. **2** National Housing Agency.

**N.H.I.**, (Great Britain) National Health Insurance.

**NHL** (no periods) or **N.H.L.**, National Hockey League.

**NHRA** (no periods), National Hot Rod Association.

**N.H.S.** or **NHS** (no periods), National Health Service.

**NHTSA** (no periods), National Highway Traffic Safety Administration.

**Ni** (no period), nickel (chemical element).

**N.I.**, Northern Ireland.

**NIA** (no periods), National Intelligence Authority.

**ni|a|cin** (nī′ə sin), *n.* = nicotinic acid. [earlier *Niacin* (trademark) < *ni*(cotinic) *ac*(id) + *-in*]

**ni|a|cin|a|mide** (nī′ə sin′ə mīd, -id), *n.* = nicotinamide.

**Ni|ag|a|ra** (nī ag′ər ə, -ag′rə), *n.* **1** a cataract; torrent; deluge: *a Niagara of tears. A Niagara of water rushed in* (Maclean's). **2** something resembling a cataract in amount and force: *a Niagara of lies and slander* (Newsweek). **3** a variety of sweet white grape grown especially in the eastern United States. [< *Niagara* (Falls) < an Iroquoian word]

**niaise|rie** (nyez rē′), *n. French.* **1** ignorant or stupid simplicity; foolishness; silliness. **2** an instance or example of silliness.

**ni|al|a|mide** (nī al′ə mīd), *n.* a monoamine-oxidase inhibitor, used as an antidepressant. *Formula:* $C_{16}H_{18}N_4O_2$ [< *ni*(cotinic acid) + (carb)*a*-(my)*l* + *amide*]

**nib**[1] (nib), *n., v.,* **nibbed, nib|bing.** —*n.* **1a** the point of a pen: *Ballpoint pens will be tested by the Post Office Department to replace the scratchy, ink-spilling nib pens* (Time). **b** either of its parts. **2** the point or tip of anything; peak; point; tip; prong. **3** the beak or bill of a bird. **4** *Dialect.* either of the two short projecting handles on the long shaft of a scythe.
—*v.t.* **1** to mend or replace the nib of (a pen); put a nib in or on. **2** to sharpen or trim the point of (a quill used as a pen); adapt for writing: *The lawyer nibbed his pen, spread out his paper, and prepared to write* (Washington Irving).
[Scottish variant of *neb*]

**nib**[2] (nib), *n.* = coffee bean.
**nibs**, the roasted and crushed seeds of the cacao; cocoa nibs.
[special use of *nib*[1]]

**nib|ble** (nib′əl), *v.,* **-bled, -bling,** *n.* —*v.t.* to eat away with quick, small bites, as a rabbit or a mouse does: *The boy was just nibbling his food.*
—*v.i.* **1** to bite gently or lightly: *The fish nibbled at the bait.* **2** to eat little or lightly: *to nibble at one's supper.* **3** *Figurative.* to take apart or attack, as if by taking small bites: *critics nibbling at a new play.*
—*n.* a nibbling; small bite: *He had only a nibble of cake because he was dieting.*
[origin uncertain. Compare Low German *knibbelen.*] —**nib′bler,** *n.* —**nib′bling|ly,** *adv.*

**Ni|be|lung** (nē′bə lůng), *n., pl.* **-lungs, -lung|en** (-lůng ən). *Germanic Legend.* **1** any one of a group of northern dwarfs, the children of the mist, who had a hoard of gold and a ring with magic powers. Siegfried and his followers captured their treasure. **2** any of Siegfried's followers, who captured this hoard and ring. **3** any of the Burgundian kings in the *Nibelungenlied.*

**Ni|be|lung|en|lied** (nē′bə lůng ən lēt′), *n.* a German epic based on the myths and legends found in the *Edda.* It was composed in its present poetic form by an unknown author in southern Germany during the first half of the 1200's. [< German *Nibelungenlied* lay of the Nibelungs]

**nib|lick** (nib′lik), *n.* a golf club with a heavy steel head having a sharply sloping face, used for high, short shots, as when the ball is in a sand trap. It is called a "9 iron." [origin uncertain]

**Ni|blung** (nē′blůng), *n.* = Nibelung.

**Nib|mar** or **NIBMAR** (nib′mär), *n.* no independence before majority African rule (a statement by Great Britain and members of the Commonwealth of Nations demanding proportional representation for the black population in white-ruled dependencies before granting independence).

**nibs**[1] (nibz), *n. Informal.* (with a possessive pronoun) a humorous title of respect for a person, as if in recognition of importance: *How is his nibs?* [origin uncertain]

**nibs**[2] (nibz), *n.pl.* See under **nib**[2].

**Ni|cae|an** (nī sē′ən), *adj.* = Nicene.

**Nic|a|ra|guan** (nik′ə rä′gwən), *adj., n.* —*adj.* of or having to do with Nicaragua. —*n.* a person born or living in Nicaragua.

**nic|co|lite** (nik′ə līt), *n.* a mineral, nickel arsenide, of a pale copper-red color and metallic luster. It usually occurs massive. *Formula:* NiAs [< New Latin *niccolum,* Latinization of *nickel*]

**nice** (nīs), *adj.,* **nic|er, nic|est,** *adv.* —*adj.* **1** that is good or pleasing; agreeable; satisfactory: *a nice face, a nice child, a nice ride, a nice day.* **SYN:** gratifying, enjoyable. **2** thoughtful and kind: *They were nice to us.* **3** very fine; minute; subtle: *a nice distinction, a nice shade of meaning.* **4** precise; exact; making very fine distinctions: *a nice ear for music, weighed in the nicest scales.* **SYN:** accurate. **5** delicately skillful; requiring care, skill, or tact: *a nice problem. It's a nice point to speak about ... and I'm afraid o' being wrong* (George Eliot). **6** particular; hard to please; fastidious; dainty: *nice in one's habits or dress.* **SYN:** exacting, delicate. **7** refined; cultured: *a nice accent.* **8** proper; suitable: *nice clothes for a party. It wasn't a nice song—for a parlor, anyway* (Mark Twain). **SYN:** fitting, seemly. **9** demanding a high standard of conduct; scrupulous: *too nice for a politician.* **10** *Archaic.* affectedly modest; coyly reserved: *We'll not be nice: take hands* (Shakespeare). **11** *Obsolete.* wanton; lascivious. **12** *Obsolete.* foolish; stupid.
—*adv. Archaic.* nicely.
[Middle English *nice* simple-minded < Old French, silly < Latin *nescius* ignorant < *ne-* not + *scīre* know] —**nice′ly,** *adv.* —**nice′ness,** *n.*

**Ni|cene** (nī sēn′, nī′sēn), *adj.* of or having to do with Nicaea, an ancient town in Asia Minor.

**Nicene Council**, either of two general ecclesiastical councils held at Nicaea, the first in A.D. 325 to deal with the Arian heresy, and the second in 787 to to consider the question of images.

**Nicene Creed**, **1** a formal statement of the chief tenets of Christian belief, adopted by the first Nicene Council, and generally accepted throughout western Christendom. **2** the creed of the first Nicene Council, expanded somewhat at a later date (probably at the Council of Constantinople in A.D. 381) and accepted by all orthodox Christians under the title of Nicene Creed.

**nice Nelly** or **Nellie**, *pl.* **nice Nellies.** *Slang.* a person who is overly modest or prudish: *By 1916, Dreiser was the hero of the avant-garde and the pet peeve of the nice Nellies, who denounced "The Genius" as literary sewage and got it banned by the censor* (Time). [< *Nelly* or *Nellie,* a feminine name] —**nice′-Nel′ly, nice′-Nel′lie,** *adj.*

**nice-Nel|ly|ism** (nīs′nel′ē iz əm), *n.* **1** extreme modesty or prudishness: *Nice-Nellyism seldom wins elections in this country* (Time). **2** circumlocution; euphemism: *Mr. Pyles attributes much of the nice-Nellyism that blighted polite speech and writing during the nineteenth century to Webster's Puritan prudishness* (New Yorker).

**Ni|ce|no-Con|stan|ti|no|pol|i|tan Creed** (nī sē′nō kon stan′tə nə pol′ə tən), = Nicene Creed (def. 2).

**ni|ce|ty** (nī′sə tē), *n., pl.* **-ties.** **1** the condition or quality of being precise; exactness; accuracy; delicacy: *Television sets require nicety of adjustment.* **2** a fine point; small distinction; detail: *the niceties of law. I play tennis but have not mastered its niceties.* **3** the quality of being very particular; daintiness; refinement: *This sense of the practical is the ballast for some of Mrs. Post's more airy niceties* (Newsweek). **4** something dainty or refined: *clean linen and other niceties.* **SYN:** amenity. **5** *Obsolete.* excessive refinement: *my own nicety and the nicety of my friends ... have made me ... an idle, helpless being* (Jane Austen). **6** *Obsolete.* coy prudishness or squeamishness.
**to a nicety**, just right: *cookies browned to a nicety.*
[< Old French *nicete* < *nice;* see etym. under **nice**]

**niche** (nich), *n., v.,* **niched, nich|ing.** —*n.* **1** a recess or hollow in a wall, as for a statue or vase. *Just over the grave, in a niche of the wall, is a bust of Shakespeare* (Washington Irving). **SYN:** nook, cavity. **2** *Figurative.* a suitable place or position; place for which a person is suited: *He will find his niche in the world. French planemakers see the possibility of carving a modest niche in the world's air markets* (Time). **3** *Ecology.* the function of an organism within a community.
—*v.t.* to place in a niche or similar recess.
[< Middle French *niche,* also *nique* < Old French *nichier* to nest, ultimately < Latin *nīdus* nest]

**Ni|chi|ren** (nē chē ren′), *n.* a militant and nationalistic Buddhist sect in Japan. [< *Nichiren,* a Japanese teacher of the 1200's, who founded it]

**Nich|o|las** (nik′ə ləs, nik′ləs), *n.* **Saint.** = Santa Claus.

**nicht wahr?** (niʜt vär′), *German.* isn't that right? isn't that so: *One doesn't shake hands with a man who is busy with both hands, nicht wahr?* (Harper's).

**nick** (nik), *n., v.* —*n.* **1** a place where a small bit has been cut or broken out; notch; groove: *She hit a saucer and made a nick in the edge of it. He cut nicks in a stick to keep count of his score.* **SYN:** dent, indentation. **2** *Printing.* a notch in the shank of a type, that serves as a guide in the identification of a font or the placing of the types. **3** the precise moment or time of some occurrence: *In the nick of being surprised, the lovers ... escape at a trap-door* (Sir Richard Steele). **4** *British Slang.* a jail; prison: *five years in the nick for larceny* (Punch). **5** *Australian and British.* condition; shape: *to be in good or bad nick. I have always refused to believe that every organ in my body wasn't in perfect nick* (Punch). **6** *Obsolete.* the exact point aimed at; mark.
—*v.t.* **1** to make a nick or nicks in; notch or chip: *to nick a stick or a cup.* **2** to cut into or through: *to nick a wire.* **3** to hit, guess, catch, or otherwise accomplish (something) exactly. **4a** to make an incision at the root of (a horse's tail) to cause him to hold it higher. **b** to cut (a horse) at the root of the tail. **5** to record or score: *to nick down an address or a point won.* **6** *Slang.* to cheat; defraud: *He nicked me out of everything I'd saved.* **7** *Slang.* to capture, especially by surprise; nab: *to nick a thief.* **8** *British Slang.* **a** to steal: *I nicked whatever I could lay my hands on* (Alan Sillitoe). **b** to put in prison; jail: *The answer was: "Take a cure in the nearest hospital, or I'll nick you"* (Sunday Times).
**in the nick of time**, just at the right moment: *The firemen arrived in the nick of time to save the building from burning down. He has learnt, thankfully, that atomic power is arriving in the nick of time to supplement not inexhaustible supplies of coal and oil* (London Times).
[origin uncertain]

**Nick** (nik), *n.* Usually, **Old Nick.** = the Devil. [probably short for *Nicholas.* Compare German *Nickel* goblin.]

***nick|el** (nik′əl), *n., v.,* **-eled, -el|ing** or (*especially British*) **-elled, -el|ling.** —*n.* **1** a metallic chemical element that looks like silver and is somewhat like iron. Nickel is hard and used as an alloy and in electroplating. It usually occurs in combination with arsenic or sulfur in igneous rocks, and is associated with cobalt. Nickel is malleable, ductile, and magnetic, but is not easily oxidized. **2** a coin, containing a mixture of nickel and copper, of the United States and Canada, worth five cents: *Hot-dog sellers, sandwich men, and jugglers peddled their offerings for nickels and dimes* (Newsweek).
—*v.t.* to cover or coat with nickel.
[< Swedish *nickel* < German *Kupfernickel* (literally) copper devil (the ore resembles copper but yields none)]

***nickel**
definition 1

| symbol | atomic number | atomic weight | oxidation state |
| --- | --- | --- | --- |
| Ni | 28 | 58.71 | 2, 3 |

**nick|el-cad|mi|um battery** (nik′əl kad′mē əm), a storage battery having a positive plate of nickel, a negative plate of cadmium, and an electrolyte of potassium hydroxide: *The nickel-cad-*

*mium battery ... can be recharged in an ordinary electric socket, can be made tiny enough to power a hearing aid, and is good for a total life of three or four thousand hours* (Time).

**nick|el|ic** (nik′ə lik, ni kel′ik), *adj.* **1** of nickel. **2** containing nickel, especially with a valence of three.

**nick|el|if|er|ous** (nik′ə lif′ər əs), *adj.* containing or yielding nickel.

**nickel iron**, an alloy of nickel and iron found in meteorites and small stones.

**nick|el|o|de|on** (nik′ə lō′dē ən), *n. U.S.* **1** (formerly) a place of amusement, such as a motion-picture theater or vaudeville, to which the price of admission was only five cents: *Loretta made her professional debut at thirteen in a Lynn, Massachusetts, nickelodeon* (Harper's). **2** = jukebox: *A nickelodeon at the end of the street emits a tinny piano tinkle* (Saturday Evening Post). [American English < *nickel* the coin + *odeon;* perhaps patterned on *melodeon*]

**nick|el|ous** (nik′ə ləs), *adj.* containing nickel, especially with a valence of two.

**nickel plate**, a thin coating of nickel deposited on a metal object by electroplating or other means, to prevent rust or improve the appearance.

**nick|el-plate** (nik′əl plāt′), *v.t.*, **-plat|ed, -plat|ing.** to coat with nickel by electroplating or other means.

**nickel silver**, a white alloy of copper, zinc, and nickel, used for ornaments, utensils, and wire; German silver.

**nickel steel**, an alloy of steel with high nickel content to make it strong, elastic, and rust resistant: *Nickel steel is used in armor plate, automobile axles, engine forgings, and various kinds of structural work* (Harrison Ashley Schmitt).

**nick|er**[1] (nik′ər), *n.* **1** a person or thing that nicks or cuts. **2** *British Slang.* (in horse racing) **a** one pound sterling. **b** pounds sterling. **3** a disorderly London youth in the 1700's, who nightly broke windows by throwing coins at them.

**nick|er**[2] (nik′ər), *v., n.* — *v.i., v.t.* **1** to neigh: *mounted on nags that nicker at the clash of the sword* (Scott). **2** to laugh loudly or shrilly.
— *n.* **1** = neigh. **2** a loud laugh.
[apparently imitative. Compare etym. under **neigh.**]

**nick|er**[3] (nik′ər), *n.*, or **nicker tree**, = bonduc. [probably < a native name]

**nick|nack** (nik′nak′), *n.* = knickknack.

**nick|name** (nik′nām′), *n., v.*, **-named, -nam|ing.**
— *n.* **1** a name added to a person's real name, or used instead of it: *"Ed" is a nickname for "Edward." Roy's nickname was "Buzz." As he* [*a doctor*] *wanted that deep magisterial voice which gives authority to a prescription ... he ... got the nickname of the Squeaking Doctor* (Sir Richard Steele). **SYN:** sobriquet. **2** such a name given to a place or thing: *Hawkeye State is a nickname for Iowa.*
— *v.t.* **1** to give a nickname to: *They nicknamed the tall boy "Shorty" as a joke.* **2** to misname: *With no great care for what is nicknamed glory* (Byron).
[Middle English *neke name* < misdivision of *an eke name* < *eke* an addition, Old English *eāca* + *name* name]

**Nic|ol** or **nic|ol** (nik′əl), *n.* = Nicol prism.

**Nic|o|la|i|tan** (nik′ə lā′ə tən), *n.* a member of an early religious sect that believed Christians could eat foods offered to idols and indulge in immoral practices (in the Bible, Revelation 2:6, 15). [< Greek *Nikolaïtēs* < *Nikólaos* Nicolas, the name of the sect's leader]

**Nicol** or **nicol prism**, *Optics.* **1** a prism made by cutting crystals of Iceland spar and cementing them together with Canada balsam, used to transform ordinary light into plane-polarized light. **2** any prism used for that purpose. [< John P. *Nicol,* 1804-1859, a British physicist, who invented it]

**ni|co|tian** (ni kō′shən), *n., adj.* — *n. Obsolete.* **1** a tobacco smoker: *It isn't for me to throw stones ... who have been a nicotian a good deal more than half my days* (Oliver Wendell Holmes). **2** the tobacco plant.
— *adj.* having to do with tobacco or smoking.

**ni|co|ti|a|na** (ni kō′shē ā′nə, -tē ä′-), *n.* any one of a group of plants of the nightshade family, such as the tobacco plant and certain varieties grown for their showy, fragrant, night-blooming flowers; flowering tobacco. [< New Latin *Nicotiana* < (*herba*) *nicotiana;* see etym. under **nicotine**]

**nic|o|tin** (nik′ə tin), *n.* = nicotine.

**nic|o|tin|a|mide** (nik′ə tin′ə mīd, -mid), *n.* the amide of nicotinic acid: *Anesthesia ... was effective for a longer time when nicotinamide was given* (Science News Letter). *Formula:* $C_6H_6N_2O$

**nicotinamide adenine dinucleotide**, = diphosphopyridine nucleotide. *Abbr:* NAD (no periods).

**nicotinamide adenine dinucleotide phosphate**, = triphosphopyridine nucleotide. *Abbr:* NADP (no periods).

**nic|o|tine** (nik′ə tēn), *n.* a poison contained in the leaves, roots, and seeds of tobacco, from which it is obtained as an oily, colorless, acrid liquid, used to kill insects and parasites. It is an alkaloid. *Formula:* $C_{10}H_{14}N_2$ [< French *nicotine* < *nicotiane* nicotiana < New Latin (*herba*) *nicotiana* < Jean *Nicot,* about 1530-1600, French ambassador to Portugal who introduced tobacco into France about 1560]

**nic|o|tine|less** (nik′ə tēn′lis), *adj.* without nicotine: *nicotineless smoking.*

**nic|o|tin|ic acid** (nik′ə tin′ik), one of a group of vitamins that is found in all cells and especially in lean meat, milk, eggs, yeast, liver, and wheat germ; niacin. It is a vitamin of the vitamin B complex and persons who lack this vitamin often suffer from pellagra. *Formula:* $C_6H_5NO_2$

**nic|o|tin|ism** (nik′ə tē niz′əm, -ti-), *n.* a poisoned condition due to excessive use of nicotine or tobacco.

**nic|tate** (nik′tāt), *v.i.*, **-tat|ed, -tat|ing.** = nictitate.

**nic|tat|ing membrane** (nik′tā ting), = nictitating membrane.

**nic|ta|tion** (nik tā′shən), *n.* = nictitation.

**nic|ti|tate** (nik′tə tāt), *v.i.*, **-tat|ed, -tat|ing.** = wink[1]. [< unrecorded Medieval Latin *nictitare* (with English *-ate*[1]) < Latin *nictāre* wink, blink]

**nic|ti|tat|ing membrane** (nik′tə tā′ting), a transparent inner eyelid present in birds and many reptiles that can draw over the eye to protect and moisten it.

**nic|ti|ta|tion** (nik′tə tā′shən), *n.* the act or habit of moving the eyelids; winking, especially with abnormal frequency.

**nid|a|men|tal** (nid′ə men′təl), *adj. Zoology.* **1** having to do with an egg or eggs. **2** forming a covering or protection for an egg or eggs. [< Latin *nīdāmentum* materials for a nest (< *nīdus* nest) + English *-al*[1]]

**ni|da|tion** (nī dā′shən), *n. Physiology.* the implantation of the fertilized egg in the lining (decidua) of the uterus: *Nidation ... in Man takes place about a week after fertilization* (New Scientist). [< Latin *nīdus* nest + English *-ation*]

**nid|der|ing** (nid′ər ing), *n., adj.* — *n.* a base coward.
— *adj.* base; cowardly; vile.
[(used by Sir Walter Scott in *Ivanhoe*) apparently < a misreading of Old English *nīthing* < Scandinavian (compare Old Icelandic *nīthingr*)]

**nide** (nīd), *n.* a brood, clutch, or nest of pheasants. [< Latin *nīdus* nest]

**nid|er|ing** (nid′ər ing), *n., adj.* = niddering.

**nidge** (nij), *v.t.*, **nidged, nidg|ing.** to dress (stone) with a sharp-pointed hammer instead of a chisel and mallet; nig. [origin uncertain]

**Nid|hoggr** (nēd′hôg′ər, -hôg), *n. Norse Mythology.* a giant serpent that continually gnawed at the root of the Yggdrasil to bring the tree down and the gods with it.

**ni|dic|o|lous** (nī dik′ə ləs), *adj.* that remains in the nest for some time after hatching; altricial: *Nidicolous species ... are born or hatched in a relatively helpless or dependent state* (Gilbert Gottlieb). [< Latin *nīdus* nest + *colere* inhabit + English *-ous*]

**nid|i|fi|cate** (nid′ə fə kāt), *v.i.*, **-cat|ed, -cat|ing.** to build a nest; nidify. [< Latin *nīdificāre* (with English *-ate*[1]) < *nīdus* nest + *facere* make]

**nid|i|fi|ca|tion** (nid′ə fə kā′shən), *n.* the process or the manner of building a nest.

**ni|dif|u|gous** (nī dif′yə gəs), *adj.* that leaves the nest a short time after hatching; precocial: *Birds ... may be divided into two main types, those having nidifugous or 'nest-quitting' young, and those having nidicolous or 'nest-dwelling' young* (A. L. Thomson). [< Latin *nīdus* nest + *fugere* take flight, flee + English *-ous*]

**nid|i|fy** (nid′ə fī), *v.i.*, **-fied, -fy|ing.** to build a nest or nests. [< Latin *nīdificāre;* see etym. under **nidificate**]

**nid|nod** (nid′nod′), *v.i., v.t.*, **-nod|ded, -nod|ding.** to nod repeatedly; keep nodding: *Lady K. nidnodded her head* (Thomas Hood). [reduplicative form of *nod*]

**nid|u|lant** (nij′ə lənt), *adj. Botany.* **1** lying free, or partially embedded, in a nestlike receptacle, as sporangia. **2** lying loose in a pulp, as seeds. [< Latin *nīdulāns, -antis,* present participle of *nīdulārī* build a nest < *nīdus* nest]

**ni|dus** (nī′dəs), *n., pl.* **-di** (-dī), **-dus|es.** **1** a nest in which insects, snails, and certain other small animals, deposit their eggs. **2** *Figurative.* a place or source of origin or development. [< Latin *nīdus* nest]

**niece** (nēs), *n.* **1** a daughter of one's brother or sister. See picture under **family tree.** **2** a daughter of one's brother-in-law or sister-in-law. **3** an illegitimate daughter of an ecclesiastic (used as a euphemism). [< Old French *niece* < Late Latin *neptia,* alteration of Latin *neptis* granddaughter; later, niece, feminine of *nepōs;* see etym. under **nephew**]

**ni|el|list** (nē el′ist), *n.* a worker in niello.

**ni|el|lo** (nē el′ō), *n., pl.* **-el|li** (-el′ē), **-el|los,** *v.*, **-el|loed, -el|lo|ing.** — *n.* **1** a black alloy of silver, lead, copper, and sulfur, with which engraved designs on silver or other metals are filled in, to produce an ornamental effect. **2** ornamental work done by the application of niello. **3** an example of this.
— *v.t.* to inlay with niello.
[< Italian *niello* < Latin *nigellus* (diminutive) < *niger* black]

**ni|el|lo|ware** (nē el′ō wãr′), *n.* articles inlaid or ornamented with niello.

**Nie|tzsche|an** (nē′chē ən), *adj., n.* — *adj.* of or having to do with the German philosopher Nietzsche or his doctrines: *The Nietzschean lady is very frank and not unjust* (New Age).
— *n.* a believer in or supporter of the philosophical doctrines of Nietzsche: *The writer ... is an enthusiastic Nietzschean* (Times Literary Supplement).

**Nie|tzsche|an|ism** (nē′chē ə niz′əm), *n.* = Nietzscheism.

**Nie|tzsche|ism** (nē′chē iz əm), *n.* the doctrines of Friedrich Wilhelm Nietzsche (1844-1900), German philosopher and writer, especially the doctrine that human beings could attain perfection only through ruthless self-assertion. From this doctrine stemmed the concept of a type of man, the superman, superior to all others, who was morally justified in using force to achieve his goals.

**nieve** (nēv), *n. Scottish.* a fist: *The cudgel in my nieve did shake* (Robert Burns). [Middle English *neve* < Scandinavian (compare Old Icelandic *nefi*)]

**Ni|fel|heim** (niv′əl hām), *n.* = Niflheim.

**nif|fer** (nif′ər), *v., n. Scottish.* — *v.t., v.i.* to exchange.
— *n.* an exchange.

**Ni|fl|heim** (niv′əl hām), *n. Norse Mythology.* the region of eternal cold, darkness, and fog in the extreme north. [< Old Icelandic *Niflheimr* Hades < *nifl* mist + *heimr* region]

**Ni|fl|heimr** (niv′əl hā′mər), *n.* = Niflheim.

**nif|ty** (nif′tē), *adj.*, **-ti|er, -ti|est,** *n., pl.* **-ties.** *Informal.* — *adj.* **1** attractive or stylish; smart: *Hetty ... looking so fresh and nifty and feminine* (H. L. Wilson). **2** fine; splendid.
— *n.* something nifty, such as a clever remark or act: *When the cops began throwing his complaints into their "crank" file, he came up with a real nifty* (Time).
[American English; origin uncertain]

**nig** (nig), *v.t.*, **nigged, nig|ging.** to dress (stone) with a sharp-pointed hammer instead of a chisel and mallet; nidge.

**ni|gel|la** (nī jel′ə), *n.* = fennelflower.

**Ni|ger-Con|go** (nī′jər kong′gō), *n.* the major language group in Africa, including the Bantu languages spoken in most of West Africa.

**Ni|ge|ri|an** (nī jir′ē ən), *adj., n.* — *adj.* of or having to do with Nigeria, a country in western Africa, or its people.
— *n.* a person born or living in Nigeria.
[< *Nigeri*(a), (< the river *Niger*) + English *-an*]

**Ni|ge|ri|an|ize** (nī jir′ē ə nīz), *v.t.*, **-ized, -iz|ing.** to make Nigerian; put under the control of the Nigerian government or Nigerian business interests. — **Ni|ge′ri|an|i|za′tion,** *n.*

**nig|gard** (nig′ərd), *n., adj.* — *n.* a stingy person; miser: *Little niggard! ... refusing me a pecuniary request* (Charlotte Brontë). **SYN:** skinflint.
— *adj.* stingy; miserly: *lands which a niggard nature had apparently condemned to perpetual poverty* (John L. Motley).
[Middle English *negarde,* perhaps < Scandinavian (compare Old Icelandic *knöggr* stingy)]

**nig|gard|ly** (nig′ərd lē), *adj., adv.* — *adj.* **1** stingy; miserly: *Let us not be niggardly; let the others have a share.* **SYN:** illiberal, stinting. **2** meanly small or scanty: *a niggardly gift.*
— *adv.* stingily; grudgingly: [*The story of his*] *life is niggardly doled to us in twelve short pages* (John Nettleship). — **nig′gard|li|ness,** *n.*

**nig|ger** (nig′ər), *n.* (used in an unfriendly way): **1** a Negro. **2** a member of any dark-skinned race. [< earlier *neger* < French *nègre* < Spanish *negro* black < Latin *niger*]

**nig|ger|fish** (nig′ər fish′), *n., pl.* **-fish|es** or (*collectively*) **-fish.** a red or yellowish grouper with bluish-black spots, of the Caribbean and the Flordia coast.

---

**Pronunciation Key:** hat, āge, cãre, fär; let, ēqual, tėrm; it, īce; hot, ōpen, ôrder; oil, out; cup, pu̇t, rüle; child; long; thin; ᴛʜen; zh, measure; ə represents **a** in about, **e** in taken, **i** in pencil, **o** in lemon, **u** in circus.

**nig|gle** (nig′əl), *v.*, **-gled, -gling,** *n.* —***v.i.*** **1** to do anything in a trifling way; work with too much care for petty details: *It was only to have been a sketch. And he has kept on niggling and niggling away at it* (William Black). **2** find fault; carp: *The nuclear consortia niggle at each other* (Sunday Times).
—***v.t.*** **1** to be trifling or petty with. **2** to find fault with; nag.
—***n.*** a petty or trifling complaint: *One minor niggle and this is to do with music* (Listener).
[apparently < Scandinavian (compare dialectal Norwegian *nigla*)] —**nig′gler,** *n.*

**nig|gling** (nig′ling), *adj., n.* —***adj.*** trifling; mean; petty: *Neither did I like the niggling way in which they dealt with me* (Robert Southey).
—***n.*** trifling work or activity; work with too much care for petty details: *Leadership has to be created, ... free from niggling or pettiness* (London Times). —**nig′gling|ly,** *adv.*

**nig|gly** (nig′lē), *adj.*, **-gli|er, -gli|est.** petty; niggling: *The only thing which has upset them—which shows how niggly, mean, and small they are—is that this is a person who has been on the left wing of the Labour movement* (London Times).

**nigh** (nī), *adv., adj.,* **nigh|er, nigh|est,** or **next,** *prep., v.* —***adv.*** **1** near: *So nigh is grandeur to our dust* (Emerson). **2** nearly; almost: *The wood is nigh as full of thieves as leaves* (Tennyson).
—***adj.*** **1** near; close. **2** direct. **3** (of one of a team of horses or a vehicle) left; near.
—***prep.*** close to; near.
—***v.t., v.i.*** *Archaic.* to draw near (to); approach.
**nigh upon** (or **on** or **about**), all but; close to: *He was nigh upon twenty miles from home* (Walter S. Landor).
[Old English *nēah.* Compare etym. under **near.**]

**nigh hand,** *Archaic.* **1** near at hand: *The shock made ... woods and mountains all nigh hand resound* (Edward Fairfax). **2** almost or nearly: *to nigh hand kill one o' my horses* (Samuel Lover).

**night** (nīt), *n., adj.* —***n.*** **1** the time between evening and morning; the time from sunset to sunrise, especially when it is dark. **2** the darkness of night; the dark: *to go out into the night.* **3** *Figurative.* **a** the darkness of ignorance, sin, sorrow, old age, death, or other condition or period: *Our share of night to bear, our share of morning* (Emily Dickinson). **b** concealment: *Robed in the long night of her deep hair* (Tennyson). **4** evening; nightfall: *the hour of night* (Milton). **5** a night as a particular time or during which something happens: *to travel three days and nights.*
—***adj.*** **1** of the night; seen at night: *night stars, night people.* **2** done or used at night: *night flying, a night safe.* **3** working at night: *a night clerk, the night staff.*
**make a night of it,** to celebrate until very late at night: *Friends and neighbors also made ... a night of it, in honor of the departed* (Scribner's Magazine).
**night after night,** every night: *Airplanes fly out of that airport night after night.*
**night and day,** all the time; continually; without stop: *Father worked night and day to earn enough money for the family.*
[Old English *niht*]

**night airglow,** = nightglow.

**night ape,** a small South American monkey; douroucouli.

**night-blind** (nīt′blīnd′), *adj.* affected with night blindness: *Americans are so used to electric lights they're practically night-blind* (Newsweek).

**night blindness,** a condition of the eyes in which the sight is normal in the day or in a strong light, but is abnormally poor or wholly gone at night or in a dim light; nyctalopia: *The condition known as night blindness is often corrected by eating foods rich in vitamin A* (Harbaugh and Goodrich).

**night-bloom|ing cereus** (nīt′blü′ming), any one of a genus of climbing American cactuses whose large, fragrant, white flowers open at night. One variety with flowers about one foot long is cultivated in the tropics as a hedge. See picture under **cactus family.**

**night|cap** (nīt′kap′), *n.* **1** a cap to be worn in bed. **2** *Informal.* a drink, especially an alcoholic drink, taken just before going to bed. **3** *Informal.* the last event in a sports program, especially the second baseball game of a double-header.

**night|capped** (nīt′kapt′), *adj.* wearing a nightcap: *a nightcapped head.*

**night clothes,** clothes to be worn in bed, as for sleeping.

**night|club** (nīt′klub′), *v.,* **-clubbed, -club|bing,** *n.* —***v.i.*** to go to or frequent night clubs: *She has put behind her memories of the gay young girl who nightclubbed until all hours* (Newsweek).
—***n.*** = night club. —**night′club′ber,** *n.*

**night club,** a place for dancing, eating, and entertainment, open only at night: *Bernardin opened a night club in the style of the wild and woolly West* (Time).

**night court,** *U.S.* a court of law in which cases are tried at night: *Like many of those who have been using night court in steadily increasing numbers to try to right what they consider wrongs, Mr. Spira was unlearned in the law* (New York Times).

**night crawler,** *U.S.* any large earthworm that comes to the surface of the ground at night; nightwalker.

**night|dress** (nīt′dres′), *n.* **1** = nightgown. **2** = night clothes.

**night|ed** (nī′tid), *adj. Archaic.* **1** made dark as night: *nighted colour* (Shakespeare). **2** overtaken by night; benighted: *Upon the nighted pilgrim's way* (Scott).

**night editor,** a newspaper editor who is on duty at night, especially the editor of the final makeup of a morning newspaper.

**night|er|y** (nī′tər ē), *n., pl.* **-er|ies.** *U.S. Informal.* a night club. Also, **nitery.**

**night|fall** (nīt′fôl′), *n.* the coming of night; dusk; evening: *He walked on, and I lost him in the nightfall—it was all I could do to grope my own way home then* (Christopher Rand).

**night fighter,** a fighter plane designed to operate at night.

**night fire,** = ignis fatuus.

**night|glow** (nīt′glō′), *n.* airglow occurring at night: *Nightglow is faintest at the zenith overhead and grows in intensity down the sky until it reaches a maximum about 10 degrees above the horizon* (Scientific American).

**night|gown** (nīt′goun′), *n.* **1** a loose gown worn by a woman or child in bed. SYN: nightdress. **2** = nightshirt.

**night|gowned** (nīt′gound′), *adj.* wearing a nightgown: *At this juncture I would be leaning forward upon one nightgowned elbow, in my fourposted bed* (New Yorker).

**night|hawk** (nīt′hôk′), *n.* **1** a bird, related to the whippoorwill, that flies about at dusk in search of insects, often over city roofs; bullbat; mosquito hawk. It is an American goatsucker, similar to the whippoorwill but with white wing patches. **2** the goatsucker or nightjar of Europe. **3** *Informal, Figurative.* **a** a person who stays up very late at night. **b** *U.S.* a cab which is operated at night: *One evening the driver of a horse-drawn hansom cab charged him $5 for a trip. "I got to brooding over this nighthawk," Mr. Allen said* (New York Times).

**night heron,** any one of various medium-sized herons that are active at dusk or at night, such as the black-crowned night heron or quabird.

**night|ie** (nī′tē), *n. Informal.* nighty.

**night|in|gale** (nī′tən gāl, -ting-), *n.* **1** a small, reddish-brown bird of Europe, related to the thrush. The male has a sweet song heard at night as well as in the daytime. *The solemn nightingale ... all night tuned her soft lays* (Milton). *The nightingale was anciently selected as the highest example of a perfect singer ... credited with all the best qualities of all the other singers* (W. H. Hudson). **2** *Figurative.* a person who sings or speaks with a melodious voice: *Her rich and warm coloratura voice ... won for her the title of the Swedish Nightingale from an adoring public* (Scott Goldthwaite). [Middle English *nightingale,* for earlier *nightgale,* Old English *nihtegale* < *niht* night + unrecorded *gale* singer, related to *galan* to sing]

**night|jar** (nīt′jär′), *n.* any one of a group of birds that fly and feed mostly at night; goatsucker. One kind sings in rapidly rising and falling sounds. [< *night* + *jar*[2] to make a harsh sound]

**night lamp,** a lamp for burning during the night, as in a bedroom or a sickroom.

**night latch,** a latch or lock unfastened by a key from the outside or by a knob from the inside.

**night|less** (nīt′lis), *adj.* being without night: *the nightless period in arctic regions.* —**night′less-ness,** *n.*

**night letter** or **lettergram,** *U.S.* a long telegram sent at night at a reduced rate and usually delivered the following morning.

**night life,** activity or entertainment at night, especially in night clubs and theaters.

**night lifer,** a devotee of night life.

**night light, 1** a small light to be kept burning all night: *The night light cast the shadow of his clenched fist on the sheet and it caught the child's eye* (Graham Greene). **2** the faint light that can be perceived during the night: *to appreciate the difference between daylight and nightlight* (A. Bruce).

**night|long** (nīt′lông′, -long′), *adj., adv.* —***adj.*** lasting all night: *Sleep ... thou hast forged ... A nightlong Present of the Past* (Tennyson).
—***adv.*** through the whole night: *Daylong and nightlong of the fourteenth and fifteenth, the undiminished flight went on* (Arthur H. Tasker).

**night|ly** (nīt′lē), *adj., adv.* —***adj.*** **1** done, happening, or appearing every night: *nightly attacks, nightly disorder.* **2** done, happening, or appearing at night: *nightly dew, a nightly visitor.* **3** of or belonging to night; characteristic of night: *the nightly skies, the nightly darkness.* **4** *Obsolete.* resembling night.
—***adv.*** **1** every night: *Performances are given nightly except on Sunday.* **2** at night; by night: *Many animals come out only nightly.*

**night|mare** (nīt′mãr′), *n., adj.* —***n.*** **1** a very distressing dream; dream causing fear or anxiety: *I would find myself plunged ... in some foul and ominous nightmare, from which I would awake strangling* (Robert Louis Stevenson). **2** *Figurative.* a very distressing experience: *The hurricane was a long nightmare.* **3** *Figurative.* a horrible fear or dread. **4** *Figurative.* a sight, object, or person such as might be seen in a nightmare: *What could have made so handsome a young man lend his arm to assist such a nightmare as Sister Ursula?* (Scott). **5** an evil spirit formerly supposed to oppress people while they are asleep: *King Arthur panted hard, Like one that feels a nightmare on his bed* (Tennyson).
—***adj.*** like a nightmare; nightmarish: *a nightmare voyage across the ocean. "For twelve hours I inhabited a nightmare world in which I experienced the torments of hell"* (Maclean's).
[Old English *niht* night + *mare* a monster oppressing men during sleep]

**night|mar|ish** (nīt′mãr′ish), *adj.* like a nightmare; causing fear or anxiety; very distressing; wild and strange; horrible: *nightmarish visions, the more terrible for their shapelessness and vagueness* (New York Times). —**night′mar′ish|ly,** *adv.*

**night owl, 1** *Informal.* a person who often stays up late. **2** an owl active only after dark.

**night raven,** a bird that calls in the night, such as a night heron or nightjar.

**night|rid|er** (nīt′rī′dər), *n. U.S.* one of a band of mounted men in the South who rode masked at night bent on mischief, intimidation, and violence.

**night robe,** = nightgown.

**nights** (nīts), *adv.* during the night; at night: *Some people work nights and sleep by day.*

**night school,** a school held in the evening, especially for persons who work during the day: *Traditionally, night schools ... emphasized elementary education, high-school completion, and citizenship training* (Leland P. Bradford).

**night|shade** (nīt′shād′), *n.* **1** any one of various plants somewhat like the potato and the tomato. There are many kinds, making up several genera of the nightshade family. The black nightshade has white flowers and black berries. Belladonna, or the deadly nightshade, has red flowers and black berries. **2** = henbane. [Old English *nihtscada* < *niht* night + unrecorded *-scada,* perhaps related to *sceatha* enemy (probably because of its narcotic or poisonous effects)]

* **nightshade family,** a group of dicotyledonous herbs, shrubs, or small trees, many of which contain narcotic or poisonous alkaloids. The family includes the potato, tobacco, belladonna, jimson weed, mandrake, tomato, bittersweet, and petunia.

**night shift, 1** a group of workers working all night: *At 11 o'clock in the forenoon the night shift ... was relieved by the day shift* (Andrew Ure). **2** the period of time during which they work: *Even when night shifts are not worked, many a factory will take the 24 hours' service of Muzak* (Punch).

**night|shirt** (nīt′shėrt′), *n.* a long, loose shirt, usually reaching the knees, worn in bed.

***nightshade family**

black nightshade petunia potato tobacco tomato

**night|side** (nīt′sīd′), *n.* **1** the side of a planet, moon, or other heavenly body, that faces away from the sun and is thus in darkness: *Temperatures on the nightside of the planet* [*Mars*] *were very low, dropping down to −85° F* (J. E. Tesar). **2** *Figurative.* the dark or unilluminated side of anything: [*Elias*] *Lönnrot awoke the nightside of the nineteenth-century professional and middle-class mind, represented by himself, and connected it with the prehistoric culture of subarctic medicine men* (Kenneth Rexroth).

**night-sight** (nīt′sīt′), *n.* a gunsight for use under adverse lighting conditions, especially at night.

**night soil**, contents of a privy or cesspool; human excrement: *In much of China, Korea, ... night soil is used to fertilize vegetables grown for human consumption* (R. S. J. Hawes). [because it is usually removed from privies or cesspools at night]

**night spot**, *U.S. Informal.* a night club: *Our jazz lives unhealthily ... in smoky dives, back rooms, night spots* (Harper's).

**night|stand** (nīt′stand′), *n.* = night table.

**night|stick** (nīt′stik′), *n. U.S.* a policeman's club.

**night sweat**, very heavy sweating occurring during the night, as in certain diseases.

**night table**, a small table, usually standing next to a bed, upon which certain objects necessary at night, such as a lamp and clock, are often placed.

**night|tide** (nīt′tīd′), *n.* = nighttime.

**night|time** (nīt′tīm′), *n., adj.* —*n.* the time between evening and morning; night: *In the nighttime once did Jason wake* (William Morris).
—*adj.* of the nighttime; occurring at night: *the nighttime hours, nighttime festivities, nighttime subway riders.*

**night|town** (nīt′toun′), *n.* a town at night, especially as a subject of a painting or as the scene of nightclub and cultural activity.

**night|view|er** (nīt′vyü′ər), *n.* a device which can provide daylight viewing conditions in the dark: *Information on nightviewers ... has been restricted because of their obvious military applications* (London Times).

**night|walk|er** (nīt′wô′kər), *n.* **1** a person who goes around at night, especially for a bad purpose. **2** = night crawler.

**night watch**, **1** a watch or guard kept during the night: *The wagon train posted a night watch of six men.* **2** the person or persons keeping such a watch: *The young night watch felt cold and sleepy.* **3** a period or division of the night: *When I ... meditate on thee in the night watches* (Psalms 63:6).

**night watchman**, **1** a man who works as watchman during the night. **2** *Cricket.* a second-rate batsman sent in to defend the wicket until the close of play, late in the day.

**night|wear** (nīt′wãr′), *n.* clothing to be worn in bed; night clothes.

**night|y** (nī′tē), *n., pl.* **night|ies**. *Informal.* a nightgown or nightshirt.

**ni|gres|cence** (nī gres′əns), *n.* **1** the process of becoming black. **2** = blackness.

**ni|gres|cent** (nī gres′ənt), *adj.* somewhat black; having a blackish color. [< Latin *nigrēscēns, -entis,* present participle of *nigrēscere* grow black < *niger* black]

**nig|ri|fy** (nig′rə fī), *v.t.,* **-fied, -fy|ing.** = blacken. [< Latin *nigrificāre* < *niger* black + *facere* make]

**Ni|gri|tian** (ni grish′ən), *adj., n.* —*adj.* **1** of or having to do with Nigritia or the Sudan, or its people. **2** of or having to do with the Negro race.
—*n.* a native or inhabitant of Nigritia; Sudanese.

**nig|ri|tude** (nig′rə tüd, -tyüd), *n.* **1** blackness; black color: *I like to meet a sweep ... one of those tender novices, blooming through their first nigritude* (Charles Lamb). **2** something black. [< Latin *nigritūdō* < *niger* black. See etym. of doublet **negritude**.]

**ni|gro|sin** (nī′grə sin), *n.* = nigrosine.

**ni|gro|sine** (nī′grə sēn, -sin), *n.* any one of various blue or black dyes obtained from aniline, used especially in dyeing textiles and leather: *The most effective repellent for sharks is a nigrosine dye that makes the water around a swimmer black and opaque* (Science News Letter). [< Latin *niger* black + English *-os*(e) + *-ine*²]

**ni|hil** (nī′hil, nē′-), *n.* **1** *Latin.* nothing. **2** a thing of no worth or value.

**ni|hil|ism** (nī′ə liz əm, nē′-), *n.* **1** entire rejection of established beliefs, as in religion, morals, government, and laws. **2** *Philosophy.* the denial of all existence; rejection of objective reality or of the possibility of an objective basis for morality: *His nihilism found a sympathetic audience among the young, and his death caused a great stir* (Atlantic). **3** the use of violent methods against a government; terrorism. **4** = Nihilism. [< Latin *nihil* nothing + English *-ism*]

**Ni|hil|ism** (nī′ə liz əm, nē′-), *n.* the beliefs and practices of a revolutionary party in Russia in the middle 1800's, which advocated destruction of the old order by violence and terrorism to make way for reform.

**ni|hil|ist** (nī′ə list, nē′-), *n., adj.* —*n.* **1** a person who believes in some form of nihilism. **2** a terrorist. **3** = Nihilist.
—*adj.* characterized by nihilism; nihilistic: *All of them were hostile to the routines of urbanization and industrialism as they found them and therefore, in terms of our society, nihilist* (Bulletin of Atomic Scientists).

**Ni|hil|ist** (nī′ə list, nē′-), *n.* a member of the Russian revolutionary party that advocated nihilism and was prominent from the 1860's to the 1880's.

**ni|hil|is|tic** (nī′ə lis′tik, nē′-), *adj.* of or having to do with nihilists or nihilism: *In between these two nihilistic strategies are a whole spectrum of possibilities* (Hanson Baldwin). —**ni′hil|is′ti|cal|ly,** *adv.*

**ni|hil|i|ty** (nī hil′ə tē, nē-), *n.* **1** nothingness; nonexistence: *Nor is there anyone who has not at some moments felt the nihility of all things* (Erasmus Darwin). **2** a mere nothing; nullity.

**ni|hil ob|stat** (nī′hil ob′stat, nē′-), **1** *Latin.* nothing hinders. **2** (in the Roman Catholic Church) a phrase on the title page of a book, preceding the name of the official censor and indicating his approval: *Milan's Roman Catholic Cardinal Montini withdrew the nihil obstat of the church* (Time). **3** official or authoritative approval: *The Foreign Office and the Colonial Office were duly consulted, and gave their nihil obstats* (Observer).

**-nik**, *suffix. Slang.* a person who is greatly interested in or enthusiastic about something; devotee of a cult, concept, or fad: *Jazznik = a person who is enthusiastic about jazz. Guitar-plunking protestniks ...* (Time). *The peaceniks ... had come to La Macaza ... to commit nonviolent civil disobedience* (Maclean's). [< Russian *-nik* (as in *sputnik*), a suffix meaning one that does, makes, or is connected with something; influenced by Yiddish *-nik* (as in *nudnik*) < Russian *-nik*]

***Ni|ke** (nī′kē, nē′kā), *n. Greek Mythology.* the goddess of victory, usually represented with wings.

***Nike**
Nike of Samothrace

**nil** (nil), *n., adj.* —*n.* **1** something of no worth or value; nothing: *The outcome of all these elaborate tests was nil* (Harper's). *As a conjurer her skill is nil* (New Yorker). **2** a score of zero: *They beat Manchester United by two goals to nil* (Listener).
—*adj.* none at all; zero: *nil profits. The Caravelle would ... land and take off in nil visibility* (London Times). *He regards his chances of nomination as nil* (Newsweek).
[< Latin *nīl,* earlier *nihil*]

**nil ad|mi|ra|ri** (nil ad′mi rãr′ī), *Latin.* to be astonished by nothing (an ideal of the ancient Stoics): *Sensations and excitements are now multiplying so fast in New York that ... they will result in infusing a little of the nil admirari spirit into the population* (New Yorker).

**nil de|spe|ran|dum** (nil des′pə ran′dəm), *Latin.* never despair; never give up.

**Nile blue** (nīl), a pale blue with a tinge of green. [< the river *Nile;* patterned on French *bleu de Nil*]

**Nile crocodile**, a large, vicious crocodile of Africa that was considered sacred by the ancient Egyptians. It may grow to be 20 feet long and will leave the water to attack.

**Nile green**, a pale bluish-green color.

**Nile monitor**, the amphibious monitor lizard of Africa, that climbs trees, burrows in the ground, and will lay its eggs in a termite nest.

**nil|gai** (nil′gī), *n., pl.* **-gais** or (*collectively*) **-gai**. a large grayish antelope of India: *The nilgai ... male has short horns, and long hair under its chin* (Victor H. Cahalane). Also, **nylghai, nylghau.** [< Hindi *nīlgāī* < *nīl* blue + *gāī* cow]

**nil|gau** (nil′gô), *n., pl.* **-gaus** or (*collectively*) **-gau.** = nilgai.

**nill** (nil), *v.t., v.i. Archaic.* to refuse; be unwilling: *Will you, nill you, I will marry you* (Shakespeare). [Old English *nyllan* < *ne* not + *willan* to will]

**nil ni|si bo|num** (nil nī′sī bō′nəm), *Latin.* nothing but good (abbreviated from *de mortuis nil nisi bonum,* of the dead say nothing but good).

**nil norm**, *British.* a standard of minimum wage and price increases set by the government; zero norm: *But for all the traditional wage demands some principle does need to be hammered out to establish who will be permitted to breach the nil norm* (Sunday Times).

**Ni|lo-Ham|it|ic** (nī′lō ha mit′ik, -hə-), *adj., n.* —*adj.* of or belonging to a group of East African tribes related especially by language and customs, including the Masai and the Nandi.
—*n.* a language group common to these tribes, forming the eastern division of Nilotic.

**Ni|lot|ic** (nī lot′ik), *adj., n.* —*adj.* of or having to do with the Nile or the inhabitants of the Nile Valley: *The tall Nilotic peoples are a modified Negro group of mixed origin who live near the headwaters of the Nile River* (George H. T. Kimble).
—*n.* **1** a language group of the Nile Valley and adjacent territories, having an eastern and a western division. **2** the western division of this group, including such languages as Dinka and Luo.
[< Latin *Nīlus* the Nile (< Greek *Neîlos*) + Greek *-otikós* having to do with]

**nil|po|tent** (nil′pō′tənt), *adj. Mathematics.* having a power equal to zero: *a nilpotent element.*

**nil si|ne nu|mi|ne** (nil sī′nē nü′mə nē), *Latin.* nothing except by the will of God (the motto of Colorado).

**nim¹** (nim), *v.t.,* **nam** or **nimmed, no|men** or **nome, nim|ming.** *Archaic.* **1** to take; seize. **2** to steal. [< Old English *niman*]

**nim²** (nim), *n.* any one of various games in which two players draw counters in turn from one or more piles, the object usually being to take the last counter, or to force the opponent to take the last counter: *Many mathematical recreations involve the binary system,* [*among them*] *the game of nim* (Scientific American). [origin unknown]

**nim|ble** (nim′bəl), *adj.,* **-bler, -blest. 1** quick-moving; active and sure-footed; light and quick; agile: *the nimble feet of a ballet dancer. Goats are nimble in climbing among the rocks.* **SYN:** lively, spry, brisk. **2** quick to understand and to reply; clever: *The boy had a nimble mind, and could come up with excuses as quickly as his mother could ask for them.* [Middle English *nymel, nemel,* Old English *numol,* quick to grasp, apparently related to *niman* take] —**nim′ble|ness,** *n.*

**nim|bly** (nim′blē), *adv.* in a nimble manner; quickly and lightly: *We saw a stag bound nimbly by* (Goldsmith).

**nim|bo|stra|tus** (nim′bō strā′təs), *n., pl.* **-ti** (-tī). a cloud formation consisting of a dark-gray layer of clouds and occurring usually at heights under 8,000 feet; nimbus. These clouds usually produce prolonged rain or snow. [< Latin *nimbus* + English *stratus*]

**nim|bus** (nim′bəs), *n., pl.* **-bus|es, -bi** (-bī). **1** a light disk or other radiance about the head of a divine or sacred person in a picture; halo: *One ... knows ... a saint by his nimbus* (John Ruskin). **2** a bright cloud surrounding a god, person, or thing; aura: *But on a deeper level ... there is a kind of nimbus about him at the end* (Time). **3** a low, dark layer of rain or snow clouds; nimbostratus. See picture under **cloud.** [< Latin *nimbus* cloud]

**NIMH** (no periods), National Institute of Mental Health.

**ni|mi|e|ty** (ni mī′ə tē), *n., pl.* **-ties. 1** excess; redundancy. **2** an instance of this. [< Latin *nimietās* < *nimius* excessive < *nimis* too much]

**nim|i|ny-pim|i|ny** (nim′ə nē pim′ə nē), *adj.* affectedly delicate or refined; mincing: *a niminy-piminy creature, afraid of a petticoat and a bottle* (Robert Louis Stevenson). [probably imitative rhyme]

**nim|i|ous** (nim′ē əs), *adj.* overmuch; excessive: *Nimious state interference is ... an evil thing* (Scotsman). [< Latin *nimius* (with English *-ous*); see etym. under **nimiety**]

**ni|mo|nic** (ni mō′nik), *adj. Metallurgy.* having to do with or designating any one of a group of nickel-chromium alloys with a very high tolerance of heat and stress due to varying and minute quantities of titanium, carbon, aluminum, or cobalt. [< *ni*(ckel) + *Mon*(el metal) + *-ic*]

**n'im|porte** (naɴ pôrt′), *French.* it does not matter; never mind.

**Nim|rod** (nim′rod), *n.* **1** a son of Cush, and a great hunter, king, and builder (in the Bible, Genesis 10:8-9). **2** a great hunter; hunter: *A tiger-hunting would not be the thing without some seasoned Nimrod to advise and direct us* (F. Marion Crawford).

---

**Pronunciation Key:** hat, āge, cãre, fär; let, ēqual, tėrm; it, īce; hot, ōpen, ôrder; oil, out; cup, pu̇t, rüle; child; long; thin; ᴛʜen; zh, measure; ə represents **a** in about, **e** in taken, **i** in pencil, **o** in lemon, **u** in circus.

**nin|com|poop** (nin′kəm püp), *n.* a fool; simpleton. [earlier *nicompoop*]

**nin|com|poop|er|y** (nin′kəm pü′pər ē), *n.* lack of good judgment and sense; foolishness: *the nincompoopery of customers who persist in buying cars they cannot afford* ... (Atlantic).

**nine** (nīn), *n., adj.* —*n.* **1** one more than eight; 9. Six and three make nine. **2a** a set of nine persons or things. **b** a team of nine players: *a baseball nine.* **c** a playing card, roll of dice, domino, billiard ball, or other part of a game with nine spots or "9" on it.
—*adj.* being one more than eight: *"Nine little, eight little, seven little Indians."*
**dressed to the nines,** elaborately dressed, as for a formal occasion: *When she's dressed up to the nines for some grand party* (Thomas Hardy).
**the Nine, a** the Muses: *For I, through grace of the Nine, Poet am also* (Charles S. C. Bowen). **b** *Especially British.* the countries comprising the European Economic Community since 1973; the nine nations of the Common Market: *The Nine are due to agree then on a new round of farm price increases* (Manchester Guardian Weekly).
[Old English *nigon*]

**nine ball,** *U.S.* a variety of pocket billards.

**nine-band|ed armadillo** (nīn′ban′did), the common variety of armadillo, having nine movable bands across its carapace, found from South America through Mexico, Texas, Florida, and neighboring areas; Texas armadillo; peba. It always gives birth to identical quadruplets.

**nine|bark** (nīn′bärk′), *n.* any shrub of an American and Asian group of the rose family, with alternate lobed leaves, clusters of white or pink flowers, and a bark that peels off in thin layers.

**nine days' wonder,** a subject of general surprise and interest for a short time.

**nine-eyes** (nīn′īz′), *n.* = sea lamprey.

**nine|fold** (nīn′fōld′), *adj., adv.* —*adj.* **1** nine times as much or as many. **2** having nine parts or members.
—*adv.* nine times as much or as many.

**nine|pence** (nīn′pəns), *n.* **1** nine British pennies. **2** a former British coin having this value.

**nine|pin** (nīn′pin′), *n.* one of the pins used in ninepins.

***nine|pins** (nīn′pinz′), *n.* a game in which nine large wooden pins are set up to be bowled over with a ball.

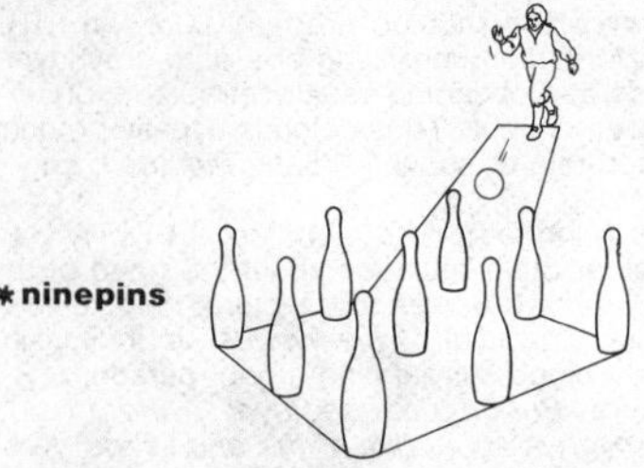

***ninepins**

**nine|teen** (nīn′tēn′), *n., adj.* nine more than ten; 19: *to score nineteen points* (adj). [Old English *nigontēne, nigontīene*]
**1984,** a date symbolizing a totalitarian society of the future in which truth and freedom are suppressed and people live in a totally regimented and dehumanized state: *Throughout the campaign, the political uses of television advertising and packaging of candidates were heralded ... by doomsayers as the ominous forerunner of 1984* (Time). [< *1984,* title of a novel by George Orwell, 1903-1950, which is set in such a society]

**nine|teenth** (nīn′tēnth′), *adj., n.* —*adj.* next after the 18th; last in a series of 19: *the nineteenth day in a row without rain.*
—*n.* **1** the next after the 18th; last in a series of 19: *That piece of gum will be your nineteenth.* **2** one of 19 equal parts: *There wasn't much to go round after we cut the birthday cake; each person had only a nineteenth.*

**nineteenth amendment,** an amendment to the Constitution of the United States granting women the right to vote, ratified in 1920.

**nineteenth hole,** *Informal.* **1** the time after a game when golfers relax, usually in the clubhouse. **2** the clubhouse or other place where they relax: *Women golfers, barred from the nineteenth hole at Clacton-on-Sea, England, are not taking it quietly* (Seattle Times).

**Pronunciation Key:** hat, āge, cãre, fär; let, ēqual, tėrm; it, īce; hot, ōpen, ôrder; oil, out; cup, pu̇t, rüle; child; long; thin; ᴛʜen; zh, measure; ə represents **a** in about, **e** in taken, **i** in pencil, **o** in lemon, **u** in circus.

**nine|ti|eth** (nīn′tē ith), *adj., n.* —*adj.* next after the 89th; last in a series of 90.
—*n.* **1** the next after the 89th; last in a series of 90: *That visitor was the ninetieth to enter the museum today.* **2** one of 90 equal parts: *The actress was paid a ninetieth of the earnings of the show.*

**nine-to-five** (nīn′tə fīv′), *n. Slang.* = nine-to-fiver.

**nine-to-fiv|er** (nīn′tə fī′vər), *n. Slang.* **1** a person who holds a routine office job with regular hours, usually nine in the morning to five in the evening. **2** an employee who carries out duties in a routine and often automatic way.

**nine|ty** (nīn′tē), *adj., n., pl.* **-ties.** —*adj.* nine times ten; 90. —*n.* nine times ten; 90. [Old English *nigontig*]

**nine|ty|ish** (nīn′tē ish), *adj.* of or characteristic of the 1890's; resembling or suggesting what was then current.

**nin|hy|drin** (nin hī′drin), *n.* **1** a chemical which produces a blue color in the presence of proteins and amino acids, used in chromatographic analysis, as a test for pregnancy, and in fingerprinting. *Formula:* $C_9H_6O_4$ **2 Ninhydrin.** a trademark for this chemical.

**nin|ny** (nin′ē), *n., pl.* **-nies.** a fool; simpleton. [perhaps misdivision of *an inno*(cent)]

**nin|ny|ham|mer** (nin′ē ham′ər), *n.* a simpleton; ninny. [< *ninny* + *hammer;* of uncertain origin]

**ni|non** (nē nôN′), *n. French.* a light-weight silk or rayon cloth with a plain weave, used especially for underwear, blouses, and curtains.

**ninth** (nīnth), *adj., n.* —*adj.* next after the eighth; last in a series of nine.
—*n.* **1** the next after the eighth; last in a series of nine: *I was ninth in line to look at the book.* **2** one of nine equal parts: *A ninth of the pie is mine.* **3** *Music.* **a** a tone distant from another by an octave and a second. **b** the interval between such tones. **c** the harmonic combination of such tones.

**ninth chord,** *Music.* a seventh chord with a superposed third.

**Ni|nus** (nī′nəs), *n.* the legendary founder of Nineveh, an ancient city in Assyria, and of the Assyrian Empire, husband of Semiramis.

**NIO** (no periods), National Institute of Oceanography.

**Ni|o|be** (nī′ō bē), *n.* **1** *Greek Mythology.* a mother whose fourteen beautiful children were slain by Apollo and Artemis because she boasted about them. Turned by Zeus into a stone fountain, she weeps forever for her children. She was the daughter of Tantalus. **2** *Figurative.* a weeping or inconsolable mother: *The Niobe of nations! there she* [*Rome*] *stands, Childless and crownless in her voiceless woe* (Byron).

**Ni|o|be|an** (nī′ō bē′ən), *adj.* of or like Niobe.

**ni|o|bic** (nī ō′bik), *adj.* **1** of niobium. **2** containing niobium, especially with a valence of five.

***ni|o|bi|um** (nī ō′bē əm), *n.* a white or steel-gray chemical element that is found in nature with tantalum. It is a lustrous, metallic substance that resembles tantalum in chemical properties and is used in making stainless steel and in other alloys. Formerly called **columbium.** [< New Latin *niobium* < Latin *Niobē* < Greek *Nióbē,* daughter of Tantalus (because it occurs with tantalum)]

***niobium**

| symbol | atomic number | atomic weight | oxidation state |
|---|---|---|---|
| Nb | 41 | 92.906 | 3, 5 |

**ni|o|bous** (nī ō′bəs), *adj.* containing niobium, especially with a valence of three.

**nip¹** (nip), *v.,* **nipped, nip|ping,** *n.* —*v.t.* **1** to squeeze tight and quickly; pinch; bite: *The crab nipped my toe.* **2** to take off by biting, pinching, or snipping: *to nip twigs from a bush.* **3** to hurt at the tips; spoil; injure: *Some of our tomato plants were nipped by frost.* SYN: blight. **4** to have a sharp, biting effect on: *A chill wind nipped our ears.* **5** *Slang.* to steal: *Now you get hold of all the doorkeys you can find, and I'll nip all of auntie's* (Mark Twain). **6** *Dialect.* to take suddenly or quickly; snatch: *She ... nipped up her petticoats, when she came out, as quick and sharp as ever I see* (Elizabeth C. Gaskell).
—*v.i. British Informal.* to move rapidly or nimbly: *I nipped in to see his mother today, and I couldn't look the old girl in the face* (Margery Allingham).
—*n.* **1** a tight squeeze; pinch; sudden bite: *The little puppy gave the child a playful nip.* **2** injury caused by frost: *So have I seen some tender slip, Sav'd with care from winter's nip* (Milton). **3** sharp cold; chill: *There is a nip in the air on a frosty morning.* **4** a small portion; bit. **5** a sharp flavor: *cheese with a real nip.* **6** a sharp or biting remark.
**nip and tuck,** *U.S. Informal.* so evenly matched in a race or contest that the result remains in doubt until the end: *So they had it, nip and tuck, for five miles or more* (Mark Twain).
[Middle English *nyppen.* Compare Middle Dutch, Middle Low German *nippen* to pinch.]

**nip²** (nip), *n., v.,* **nipped, nip|ping.** —*n.* a small drink, especially of alcoholic liquor.
—*v.i.* to take nips of alcoholic liquor.
—*v.t.* to drink in nips.
[origin uncertain]

**ni|pa** (nē′pə, nī′-), *n.* **1** a palm of the East Indies, the Philippines, and other areas of Australasia, with large feathery leaves that are used for thatching, mats, and the like. **2** the leaves of this palm. **3** a thatch of them. **4** liquor made from the juice of the nipa. [< Portuguese, or Spanish *nipa* the wine < Malay *nipah* palm tree; its wine]

**nip|cheese** (nip′chēz′), *n.* a person of cheese-paring habits; niggardly person; skinflint.

**nipped-in** (nipt′in′), *adj.* pinched in at the waist; made to fit very tightly: *a nipped-in jacket and full skirt.*

**nip|per** (nip′ər), *n.* **1** a person or thing that nips. **2** one of the large claws of a lobster or crab. **3** a cutting tooth of a horse. **4** *British.* a small boy; lad.
**nippers, a** pincers, forceps, pliers, or any tool that nips: *Its teeth are ... so arranged that the edges cut a hook like nippers* (David Livingstone). **b** *Slang.* (1) handcuffs: *The criminal was clapped in nippers.* (2) leg irons: *Nippers were used on the ancient galleys.*

**nip|ping** (nip′ing), *adj.* that nips; sharp; cutting: *a nipping wind, a nipping remark.* —**nip′ping|ly,** *adv.*

**nip|ple** (nip′əl), *n.* **1** the small projection on a breast or udder through which an infant or a baby animal gets its mother's milk; teat: *the nipple of a mother cat.* Nipples are common to all mammals. **2** the rubber cap or mouthpiece of a baby's bottle, through which the baby gets milk and other liquids. **3** anything shaped or used like a nipple, such as a device on a stopcock to regulate the flow of a liquid. **4a** a short piece of pipe threaded at each end for use as a coupling. **b** a threaded end of a pipe to which a faucet, hose, or other connecting part can be attached. [earlier *nible, neble;* origin uncertain, perhaps (diminutive) < *neb.* Compare etym. under **nib.**] —**nip′ple|like′,** *adj.*

**Nip|pon** (ni pon′, nip′on), *n.* Japan. [< Japanese *Nippon,* variant of *Nihon*]

**Nip|pon|ese** (nip′ə nēz′, -nēs′), *adj., n., pl.* **-ese.** = Japanese. [< *Nippon* + *-ese*]

**Nip|pon|i|za|tion** (ni pon′ə zā′shən, nip′on-), *n.* = Japanization.

**nip|py** (nip′ē), *adj.,* **-pi|er, -pi|est. 1** biting; sharp: *a nippy wind, nippy cheese.* **2** apt to nip: *a nippy dog.* **3** *Slang.* smart; stylish. **4** *British Informal.* quick; keen; active. **5** *Scottish.* stingy; grasping. —**nip′pi|ness,** *n.*

**nip|up** (nip′up′), *n.* **1** (in gymnastics) a sudden leap to the feet from a reclining position on one's back. **2** any sudden motion; jumping jerk: *My insides started to do nipups* (Tallulah Bankhead). **3** *Figurative.* a stunt; caper; clever performance: *Its moments of hilarity are a lot more rewarding than some of the nipups I've witnessed in farces of more recent vintage* (New Yorker). [< earlier slang *nip up* to move rapidly]

**nir|va|na** or **Nir|va|na** (nir vä′nə, -van′ə; nər-), *n.* **1** the Buddhist idea of heavenly peace; condition in which the soul is free from all desire and pain; perfect happiness reached by the complete absorption of oneself into the supreme universal spirit: *In the most final Heaven of the Buddhists ... the state of Nirvana, the soul loses its separate identity and is absorbed into the Great Soul of the World* (Norbert Wiener). **2** the Hindu idea of freedom of the soul; reunion with the world soul reached by the suppression of individual existence. **3** *Figurative.* any condition likened to either of these; blessed oblivion: *Jazz and fast cars, in that order, are Dean's ladder to nirvana* (Phoebe Adams). [< Sanskrit *nirvāna* extinction < *nis* out + *vā* to blow]

**Ni|san** (ni sän′, nis′ən), *n.* the seventh month of the civil year, and the first of the ecclesiastical year in the Jewish calendar, beginning late in March or early in April. [< Hebrew *nisān*]

**Ni|sei** or **ni|sei** (nē′sā′), *n., pl.* **-sei** or **-seis.** a native-born United States or Canadian citizen whose parents were Japanese immigrants. [American English < Japanese *nisei* second generation < *ni* two + *sei* generation]

**ni|si** (nī′sī), *conj.* unless, a term used in law, as after the words *decree* and *order,* to specify or suggest some contingency. A decree nisi will take effect at a specified time, unless cause is shown against it or it is altered for some other reason. [< Latin *nisī* unless]

**ni|sin** (nī′sən), *n.* any antibiotic of a group obtained from lactobacilli and streptococci, effective against mycobacteria and other Gram-positive organisms, and used especially to prevent spoilage caused by clostridia in dairy products. [a coined word]

**nisi pri|us** (prī′əs), *Law.* **1** unless before (applied to the trial of civil cases before a judge and jury). **2** *U.S.* designating the court in which trial is made before a jury, as distinguished from an appellate court. [< Anglo-French *nisi prius* < Medieval Latin, (literally) unless before (that time)]

**Nis|qual|ly** (niz′kwä lē), *n., pl.* **-ly** or **-lys. 1** a member of a Salishan tribe living in the region of Puget Sound, Washington. **2** the language of this tribe.

**Nis|sen hut** (nis′ən), a prefabricated shelter for soldiers, made of corrugated metal with a concrete floor; Quonset hut. [< Lieutenant Colonel Peter N. *Nissen,* 1871-1930, a British mining engineer, who designed it]

**ni|sus** (nī′səs), *n., pl.* **-sus.** effort; endeavor; impulse. [< Latin *nīsus, -ūs* a pressing on, exertion < *nītī* press upon, strive]

**nit**[1] (nit), *n.* **1** the egg of a louse or similar insect. **2** a very young louse or similar insect. [Old English *hnitu*]

**nit**[2] (nit), *n. Especially British Slang.* a nitwit: *a weak-willed nit* (Punch).

**nit**[3] (nit), *n.* a unit of luminance in the meter-kilogram-second system, equal to one candela per square meter. [< Latin *nit(ēre)* to shine]

**NIT** (no periods), **1** National Invitational Tournament. **2** negative income tax.

**ni|ter** (nī′tər), *n.* **1** potassium nitrate, especially when it occurs naturally as a white salt in the soil and encrusted on rocks; saltpeter. It is obtained from potash and is used in making gunpowder. *Formula:* $KNO_3$ **2** sodium nitrate, especially as it occurs in natural deposits; Chile saltpeter. It is used as a fertilizer. *Formula:* $NaNO_3$ Also, **nitre.** [< Old French *nitre,* learned borrowing from Latin *nitrum* < Greek *nítron* saltpeter; sodium carbonate < a Semitic word. See etym. of doublet **natron.**]

**nit|er|y** (nī′tər ē), *n., pl.* **-er|ies.** *U.S. Informal.* a night club. [variant of *nightery;* influenced by *nite,* slang variant of *night*]

**nit|id** (nit′id), *adj.* bright; shining; glossy. [< Latin *nitidus* < *nitēre* to shine]

**Nit|i|nol** (nit′ə nôl), *n.* a nonmagnetic alloy of titanium and nickel that has the property of regaining its original shape when reheated after having lost its shape through a melting and cooling process. [< *ni(ckel)* + *ti(tanium)* + *NOL* (abbreviation of *Naval Ordnance Laboratory,* where it was discovered)]

**ni|to** (nē′tō), *n., pl.* **-tos** (-tōz). a climbing fern of the Philippines, with glossy, wiry stems that are woven into hats and other articles. [< Spanish (Philippines) *nito*]

**ni|ton** (nī′ton), *n.* an early name of radon. *Symbol:* Nt [< New Latin *niton* < Latin *nitēre* to shine + English *-on,* as in *argon*]

**nit-pick** (nit′pik′), *Informal.* — ***v.t.*** to pick at (something) in a petty or niggling manner, as if removing a nit or louse; examine pedantically; search for petty faults: *To make a show of debate, delegates were allowed to nit-pick a few details* (Time).
— ***v.i.*** to pick at something nigglingly, especially with a view to finding faults; split hairs: *... nitpicking over who took whom to lunch* (Wall Street Journal). — **nit′-pick′er,** *n.*

**nitr-,** *combining form.* the form of **nitro-** before vowels, as in *nitryl.*

**ni|trate** (nī′trāt), *n., v.,* **-trat|ed, -trat|ing.** — ***n.*** **1** a salt or ester of nitric acid, containing the monovalent group $-NO_3$. **2** potassium nitrate or sodium nitrate when used as fertilizers.
— ***v.t.*** **1** to treat with nitric acid or a nitrate. **2** to change into a nitrate.
[< *nitr(ic)* + *-ate*[2]]

**nitrate bacteria,** = nitric bacteria.

**nitrate nitrogen,** a chemical substance produced by nitrification through bacteria located either in the nodules of leguminous plants or in the soil and necessary to the development of plants.

**ni|tra|tion** (nī trā′shən), *n.* the process of nitrating; introducing the radical $-NO_2$ into a compound.

**ni|tre** (nī′tər), *n.* = niter.

**ni|tric** (nī′trik), *adj.* **1** of or containing nitrogen, especially with a valence of five. **2** of or derived from niter. [< French *nitrique* < Old French *nitre;* see etym. under **niter**]

**nitric acid,** a clear, colorless, fuming liquid that eats into flesh, clothing, metal, and other substances. It has a pungent smell and is usually obtained by treating sodium nitrate with sulfuric acid. Nitric acid is used in making dyes, fertilizers, and explosives, and in etching and metallurgy. *Formula:* $HNO_3$

**nitric bacteria,** nitrobacteria that convert nitrites to nitrates by oxidation.

**nitric oxide,** a colorless, poisonous, gaseous compound, obtained by the oxidation of nitrogen or ammonia, or by treating copper with dilute nitric acid. *Formula:* NO

**ni|trid** (nī′trid), *n.* = nitride.

**ni|tride** (nī′trīd, -trid), *n., v.,* **-trid|ed, -trid|ing.** — ***n.*** a compound of nitrogen with a more electropositive element or radical, such as phosphorus, boron, or a metal.
— ***v.t.*** to transform into a nitride, as the surface of steel.
[< *nitr(ogen)* + *-ide*]

**ni|tri|fi|ca|tion** (nī′trə fə kā′shən), *n.* the act or process of nitrifying: *Ammonia may be oxidized to nitrous acid and the latter to nitric acid by bacteria in ... nitrification* (Harbaugh and Goodrich).

**ni|tri|fi|er** (nī′trə fī′ər), *n.* a thing that nitrifies: *Other organisms, called nitrifiers, convert this organic nitrogen into the mineral nitrates required by plants* (Scientific American).

**ni|tri|fy** (nī′trə fī), *v.t.,* **-fied, -fy|ing. 1** to oxidize (as ammonia compounds) to nitrites or nitrates, especially by bacterial action. **2** to impregnate (soil or the like) with nitrates. **3** to combine or treat with nitrogen or one of its compounds. [< French *nitrifier* < Old French *nitre* (see etym. under **niter**) + *-fier* -fy]

**ni|tri|fy|ing bacteria** (nī′trə fī′ing), = nitrobacteria.

**ni|tril** (nī′trəl), *n.* = nitrile.

**ni|trile** (nī′trəl, -trēl, -trīl), *n.* any one of a group of organic cyanides containing the univalent radical -CN. The nitriles form acids on hydrolysis, with the elimination of ammonia. [< *nitr(ogen)* + Latin *-ilis, -īlis* having to do with]

**nitrile rubber,** a synthetic rubber that is resistant to the dissolving effects of gasoline, grease, oil, wax, and solvents. It contains varying proportions of butadiene and acrylonitrile and is used in gasoline hoses, paper, leather products, and many types of cloth.

**ni|tril|o|tri|ac|e|tate** (nī tril′ō trī as′ə tāt), *n.* a salt or ester of nitrilotriacetic acid.

**ni|tril|o|tri|a|ce|tic acid** (nī tril′ō trī′ə sē′tik, -set′ik), a white, crystalline powder, used chiefly as a chelating agent: *In another attempt to curb marine pollution, nitrilotriacetic acid (NTA) was being considered as a replacement for phosphates in detergents* (Robert G. Eagon). *Formula:* $N(CH_2COOH)_3$

**ni|trite** (nī′trīt), *n.* a salt or ester of nitrous acid, containing the univalent $-NO_2$ radical.

**nitrite bacteria,** = nitrous bacteria.

**ni|tro**[1] (nī′trō), *adj.* **1** containing the univalent radical $-NO_2$. **2** containing niter. **3** = nitric.

**ni|tro**[2] (nī′trō), *n. Informal.* nitroglycerin.

**nitro-,** *combining form.* **1** formed by the action of nitric acid, as in *nitrobenzene.* **2** indicating the presence of the $-NO_2$ radical, as in *nitrocellulose.* **3** nitrification, as in *nitrobacteria.* Also, **nitr-** before vowels.
[< Greek *nítron* saltpeter]

**ni|tro|bac|te|ri|a** (nī′trō bak tir′ē ə), *n.pl.* any one of various bacteria living in soil that derive their energy from the oxidation of ammonium compounds. Members of one group convert ammonia to nitrites, and a second group then oxidizes the nitrite to nitrate which can be used as a source of nitrogen by higher plants.

**ni|tro|ben|zene** (nī′trō ben′zēn, -ben zēn′), *n.* a poisonous yellowish liquid that smells like oil of bitter almonds, obtained from benzene by the action of nitric acid, used in making aniline, in perfumery, and as a reagent. *Formula:* $C_6H_5NO_2$

**ni|tro|ben|zol** (nī′trō ben′zōl, -zol), *n.* = cellulose nitrate.

**ni|tro|cel|lu|lose** (nī′trō sel′yə lōs), *n.* = cellulose nitrate.

**ni|tro|cel|lu|lo|sic** (nī′trə sel′yə lō′sik), *adj.* of or containing cellulose nitrate.

**ni|tro|chalk** (nī′trə chôk′), *n.* an artificial fertilizer containing calcium carbonate and ammonium nitrate.

**ni|tro|cot|ton** (nī′trō kot′ən), *n.* = guncotton.

**ni|tro|fu|ran** (nī′trə fyůr′ən), *n.* any drug of a group derived from corncobs and oat husks, used against microbes and other germs.

**ni|tro|gel|a|tin** (nī′trō jel′ə tən), *n.* a jellylike explosive containing nitroglycerin, guncotton, and camphor.

***ni|tro|gen** (nī′trə jən), *n.* a gas without color, taste, or odor that forms about four-fifths of the air by volume. It is one of the most important chemical elements and is needed for the growth of all plants. Nitrogen is also a necessary part of all animal tissues. [< French *nitrogène* < Greek *nítron* niter + French *-gène* -gen]

***nitrogen**

| symbol | atomic number | atomic weight | oxidation state |
|---|---|---|---|
| N | 7 | 14.0067 | ±1, ±2, ±3, +4, +5 |

**ni|tro|gen|ase** (nī′trə jə nās), *n.* a natural enzyme that activates the conversion of nitrogen to ammonia by nitrogen-fixing bacteria.

***nitrogen cycle,** the circulation of nitrogen and its compounds by living organisms in nature. Nitrogen in the air passes into the soil, where it is oxidized to nitrate by bacteria and used by green plants and then in turn by animals. Decaying plants and animals, and animal waste products, are in turn acted on by bacteria and the nitrogen

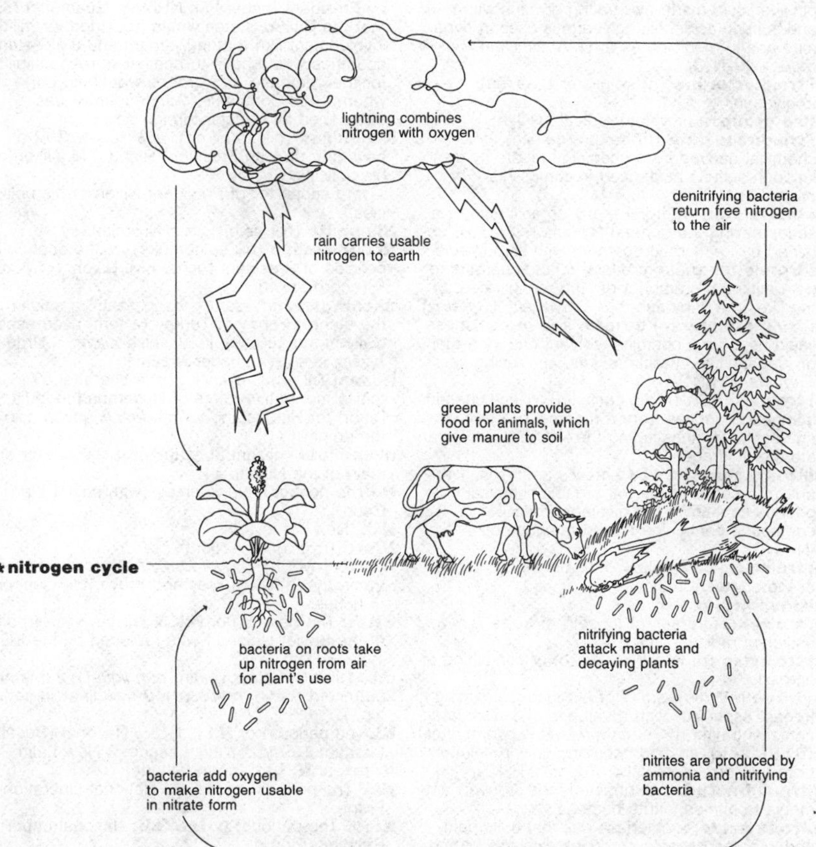
lightning combines nitrogen with oxygen
rain carries usable nitrogen to earth
denitrifying bacteria return free nitrogen to the air
green plants provide food for animals, which give manure to soil
bacteria on roots take up nitrogen from air for plant's use
nitrifying bacteria attack manure and decaying plants
bacteria add oxygen to make nitrogen usable in nitrate form
nitrites are produced by ammonia and nitrifying bacteria
***nitrogen cycle**

in them is again made available for circulation. See diagram below on the preceding page.

**nitrogen dioxide**, an extremely poisonous, brownish gas, used in producing nitric acid, as a catalyst, and as an oxidizer for liquid rocket propellants. *Formula:* $NO_2$

**nitrogen fixation**, **1** the conversion of atmospheric nitrogen into nitrates by certain blue-green algae and bacteria found in water and soil. Some of the algae or bacteria are free-living and some live symbiotically in nodules on the roots of mostly leguminous plants. Atmospheric nitrogen is thus brought into biological circulation and can be used in combined form by other organisms. *The number of bacteria found to be capable of nitrogen fixation steadily increases* (Scientific American). **2** the combination of free atmospheric nitrogen with other substances, as in making explosives and fertilizers.

**ni|tro|gen-fix|er** (nī′trə jən fik′sər), *n.* a nitrogen-fixing microorganism: *The free-living nitrogen-fixers are indirectly dependent on plants for their energy or ... obtain energy directly from sunlight* (Scientific American).

**ni|tro|gen-fix|ing** (nī′trə jən fik′sing), *adj.* causing atmospheric nitrogen to combine with elements in the soil to become nitrates: *nitrogen-fixing bacteria.*

**ni|tro|gen|i|za|tion** (nī′trə jə nə zā′shən), *n.* the process of nitrogenizing.

**ni|tro|gen|ize** (nī′trə jə nīz), *v.t.*, **-ized, -iz|ing.** to combine with nitrogen or one of its compounds.

**nitrogen mustard**, a substance similar to mustard gas but containing nitrogen instead of sulfur, used in medicine to treat Hodgkin's disease, leukemia, and similar malignant diseases.

**nitrogen narcosis**, a stupor caused by the presence of too much nitrogen in the blood and tissues of the body, occurring in divers and others working under high atmospheric pressure.

**ni|trog|e|nous** (nī troj′ə nəs), *adj.* of or containing nitrogen or a compound of nitrogen: [*In one*] *year, slightly more than two million tons of nitrogenous fertilizers were used by the nation's farmers* (Wall Street Journal).

**nitrogen oxide**, any one of the various oxides of nitrogen, often in the form of a colorless, poisonous gas such as nitric oxide: *Nitrogen oxides ... have been blamed for contributing to smog conditions in auto-packed Los Angeles* (Science News Letter).

**nitrogen tetroxide**, a poisonous compound existing in various states, used as a catalyst and oxidizing agent and considered a possible oxidizer for rocket fuels. *Formula:* $N_2O_4$

**ni|tro|glyc|er|in** (nī′trə glis′ər in), *n.* an oily, explosive liquid made by treating glycerin with nitric and sulfuric acids. Nitroglycerin is used in dynamite and in medicine as a heart stimulant. *Formula:* $C_3H_5N_3O_9$

**ni|tro|glyc|er|ine** (nī′trə glis′ər in, -ə rēn), *n.* = nitroglycerin.

**nitro group**, a univalent radical, $-NO_2$.

**ni|tro|gua|ni|dine** (nī′trə gwä′nə dēn), *n.* a chemical derived from guanidine nitrate by dissolution in sulfuric acid, used in explosives. *Formula:* $CH_4N_4O_2$

**ni|trol|ic acid** (nī trol′ik), any organic acid of a series having the general formula $RCN_2O_3H$, obtained by treating nitroparaffin with nitrous acid.

**ni|trom|e|ter** (nī trom′ə tər), *n.* an apparatus for determining the amount of nitrogen, nitrates, or the like, in a substance. [< *nitro*(gen) + *-meter*]

**ni|tro|meth|ane** (nī′trə meth′ān), *n.* a colorless liquid used as a chemical solvent and as a fuel or fuel additive in rockets, jets, and racing cars. *Formula:* $CH_3NO_2$

**ni|tro|par|af|fin** (nī′trə par′ə fin), *n.* any chemical compound derived from a member of the methane series by substituting the $-NO_2$ radical for an atom of hydrogen.

**ni|tros|a|mine** (nī′trōs ə mēn′, -am′in), *n.* **1** any one of a series of neutral organic chemical compounds containing the bivalent group -N.NO. **2** a compound containing the univalent group -NH.NO.

**ni|tro|so** (nī trō′sō), *adj.* indicating the presence of the univalent radical -NO.

**nitroso group**, = nitrosyl.

**ni|tro|syl** (nī trō′səl, nī′trə sēl′, nī′trə səl), *n.* a univalent radical, -NO.

**ni|tro|syl|ic** (nī′trə sil′ik), *adj.* of or containing a nitrosyl.

**ni|trous** (nī′trəs), *adj.* **1** of nitrogen; containing nitrogen, especially with a valence of 3. **2** of niter; containing niter. [< Latin *nitrōsus* < *nitrum* niter]

**nitrous acid**, an acid occurring only in solution or in the form of its salts. *Formula:* $HNO_2$

**nitrous bacteria**, nitrobacteria that convert ammonia to nitrites; nitrite bacteria.

**nitrous oxide**, a colorless gas that dulls pain, and in some patients produces exhilaration and occasionally uncontrollable laughter; laughing gas. It is used as an anesthetic in surgery and dentistry. *Formula:* $N_2O$

**ni|tryl** (nī′trəl), *n.* a univalent radical, $-NO_2$, containing nitrogen and oxygen.

**nit|ty-grit|ty** (nit′ē grit′ē), *n., pl.* **-ties**, *adj. Slang.* —*n.* the essential or fundamental part: *But they got bogged down in the nitty-gritties of negotiation* (Manchester Guardian Weekly). *How many meetings, finally at the nitty-gritty, are interrupted by your secretary asking if you want to take a call ...* (Harper's).
—*adj.* essential, fundamental, or detailed: *a nitty-gritty estimate of the situation, to deal with nitty-gritty problems.*
**get down to the nitty-gritty**, to get down to the fundamentals or details: *Dr. Swanson ... can really understand people in a gutsy way. And he's not afraid to get down to the nitty-gritty of unpleasant problems* (New York Times).
[origin uncertain]

**nit|wit** (nit′wit′), *n. Informal.* a very stupid person: *He's about the most complete nitwit I ever encountered—but useful ... and harmless* (Saturday Evening Post). [American English < *nit* nothing (probably < dialectal German *nit* < German *nichts* nothing) + *wit*]

**nit|wit|ted** (nit′wit′id), *adj.* very stupid.

**ni|val** (nī′vəl), *adj.* **1** of or having to do with snow. **2** (of plants) growing in or near snow. [< Latin *nivālis* < *nix, nivis* snow]

**niv|e|ous** (niv′ē əs), *adj.* snowy in color; snow-white. [< Latin *niveus* (with English *-ous*) < *nix, nivis* snow]

**Ni|vôse** (nē vōz′), *n.* the fourth month of the French Revolutionary calendar, extending from December 21 to January 19. [< French *nivôse*, learned borrowing from Latin *nivōsus* snowy < *nix, nivis* snow]

**nix[1]** (niks), *interj., n., v., adv. Slang.* —*interj.* **1** no! stop! **2** watch out!
—*n.* nothing; nobody.
—*v.t.* to refuse; deny.
—*adv.* no.
[probably < German *nix*, dialectal variant of *nichts* nothing, or < dialectal Dutch *nix*]

**nix[2]** (niks), *n., pl.* **nix|es.** *German Legend.* a water fairy. [< colloquial Dutch or German *Nix*. Compare etym. under **nixie[1]**.]

**nix|ie[1]** (nik′sē), *n. German Legend.* a female water fairy: *She who sits by haunted well, Is subject to the nixie's spell* (Scott). [< German *Nixe*, feminine, (originally) a legendary water creature]

**nix|ie[2]** or **nix|y** (nik′sē), *n., pl.* **nix|ies.** *U.S. Slang.* a letter or other mail that is not delivered because of an illegible or incorrect address. [< *nix*[1] + *ie, -y*[2]]

**Nix|on Doctrine** (nik′sən), a declaration made by President Richard M. Nixon in Guam in 1969, that the United States would avoid further military involvement like that in Vietnam and that Asian countries would have to bear main responsibility for their defense. U.S. troops would aid only when a non-Communist Asian country was threatened by a major foreign power.

**Nix|on|i|an** (nik sō′nē ən), *adj., n.* —*adj.* of or having to do with President Richard M. Nixon or his policies.
—*n.* a supporter of President Nixon or his policies.

**Nix|on|ite** (nik′sə nīt), *n.* = Nixonian.

**Nix|on|om|ics** (nik′sə nom′iks), *n.* the economic policies of President Richard M. Nixon. [< *Nixon* + (econ)*omics*]

**ni|zam** (ni zäm′, -zam′), *n., pl.* **-zam.** a soldier in the standing army of Turkey (a term used especially in the 1800's). [< Turkish *nizam* < Urdu *niẓām*; see etym. under **Nizam**]

**Ni|zam** (ni zäm′, -zam′), *n.* the title after 1713 of the former native rulers of Hyderabad in India. [short for Hindustani *niẓām-al-mulk* governor of the empire]

**ni|zam|ate** (ni zäm′āt, -zam′-), *n.* the rule or domain of the Nizam.

**NJ** (no periods), New Jersey (with postal Zip Code).

**N.J.**, New Jersey.

**Njord** (nyôrd), *n.* = Njorth.

**Njorth** (nyôrth), *n. Norse Mythology.* one of the Vanir, the father of Frey and Freya, the dispenser of riches.

**NKVD** (no periods) or **N.K.V.D.**, the secret police of the Soviet Union. It was replaced by the KGB in 1946.

**n.l.**, **1** it is not clear (Latin, *non liquet*). **2** it is not permitted (Latin, *non licet*). **3** new line (in setting type).

**NL** (no periods) or **N.L.**, **1** *U.S.* National (Baseball) League. **2** *British.* Navy League. **3** New Latin.

**N. lat.** or **N. Lat.**, north latitude.

**NLF** (no periods) or **N.L.F.**, National Liberation Front.

**NLRB** (no periods) or **N.L.R.B.** National Labor Relations Board.

**nm** (no period), nanometer.

**NM** (no periods), **1** nautical mile. **2** New Mexico (with postal Zip Code). **3** new moon.

**N.M.** or **N. Mex.**, New Mexico.

**NMA** (no periods), National Medical Association.

**NMB** (no periods), National Mediation Board.

**NME** (no periods), National Military Establishment.

**NMR** (no periods), nuclear magnetic resonance.

**N.M.U.**, National Maritime Union.

**NNE** (no periods) or **N.N.E.**, north-northeast.

**NNI** (no periods), Noise and Number Index: *The ... NNI is widely used to assess the nuisance level of airports to local residents* (New Scientist).

**NNW** (no periods) or **N.N.W.**, north-northwest.

**no[1]** (nō), *adv., adj., n., pl.* **noes.** —*adv.* **1** a word used to say that you can't or won't, or that something is wrong. "No" means the same as shaking your head from side to side. *Will you come? No. Can a cow fly? No.* **2** not in any degree; not at all: *He is no better.* **3** not, chiefly in phrases like *whether or no.*
—*adj.* **1** not any: *He has no friends. Dogs have no wings.* **2** not a: *He is certainly no athlete. Turnbull ... caught hold of her with no very gentle grasp* (Scott). [Middle English *no*, reduction of Old English *nān* none]
—*n.* **1** a word used to deny, refuse, or disagree. **2** a denial; refusal. **3** a vote against; person voting against: *The noes have it.*
[Old English *nā* < *ne* not + *ā* ever]
► See **yes** for usage note.

**no[2]** or **No** (nō), *n., pl.* **no** or **nos**, **No** or **Nos.** a type of Japanese classical drama with formalized dancing and chanting by actors wearing symbolic masks. [< Japanese *nō*]

**no.**, *pl.* **nos.** number (Latin, *numero*).
► See **No.** for usage note.

**No** (no period), nobelium (artificial chemical element).

**No.**, **1** north. **2** northern. **3** *pl.* **Nos.** number.
► **No.** The abbreviation *No.* for *number* (from the Latin *numero*, "by number") is usually written with a capital. It is used chiefly in business and technical English. In the United States *No.* is not written with street numbers.

**NOAA** (nō′ə), *n.* National Oceanic and Atmospheric Administration (of the United States): *Specifically, NOAA will be concerned with determining atmospheric conditions that make for pollution, the effects of pollution on weather, and contaminants in fish* (Science News).

**no-ac|count** (nō′ə kount′), *adj., n.* —*adj. U.S. Informal.* worthless; good-for-nothing: *A lazy, no-account, good-for-nothing thief* (David Cushman).
—*n.* a worthless person; good-for-nothing fellow: *dispensing wisdom to no-accounts like Billy Bigelow* (Wall Street Journal).

**No|a|chi|an** (nō ā′kē ən), *adj.* **1** of or having to do with Noah or his time: *the Noachian deluge.* **2** very ancient or old-fashioned.

**No|ah** (nō′ə), *n.* a man whom God told to make an ark to save himself, his family, and a pair of each kind of animal from the Flood (in the Bible, Genesis 6:9-22). Also, **Noe.**

**nob[1]** (nob), *n.* **1** *Slang.* the head: *a bald, shining nob.* **2** *Slang.* a knob; rounded part: *A man with a bottle nose—a nob of scarlet and blue on a yellow face* (Graham Greene). **3** *Cribbage.* the jack of the same suit as the card turned up, scoring one for the holder; his nobs. [perhaps a variant of *knob*]

**nob[2]** (nob), *n. Especially British Slang.* a person of wealth or social importance. [(originally) Scottish *knabb*; origin unknown]

**no-ball** (nō′bôl′), *n., v. Cricket.* —*n.* a ball illegally bowled: *The loping run, all arms and legs, and the no-ball were not forgotten* (London Times).
—*v.t.* to penalize (a player) for having delivered a no-ball: *He is one of five bowlers who have been no-balled for throwing this season* (Times of India).

**nob|ble** (nob′əl), *v.t.*, **-bled, -bling.** *British Slang.* **1** to tamper with (a horse) to prevent its winning a race, as by the use of drugs: *Tipsters whose dead certainties fail to win are often prone to complain that their favourites have been nobbled* (London Times). **2** to bring (a person) over to one's own side by bribery or other such means. **3** to obtain dishonestly; steal. **4** to swindle: *I don't know out of how much the reverend party has nobbled his poor old sister* (Thackeray). **5** to seize, catch, or capture. [origin uncertain]
—**nob′bler**, *n.*

**nob|bler** (nob′lər), *n. Australian.* a glass of beer or hard liquor.

**nob|by** (nob′ē), *adj.*, **-bi|er, -bi|est.** *Slang.* **1** smart; fashionable; elegant. **2** first-rate. [< *nob*[2] + *-y*[1]] —**nob′bi|ly**, *adv.*

**No|bel|ist** (nō bel′ist), *n.* a recipient of a Nobel prize: *Albert Einstein was the 1921 Nobelist in physics. The peace Nobelist for 1964 was Martin Luther King, Jr.*

***no|be|li|um** (nō bē′lē əm), *n.* a radioactive chemical element produced artificially by bombarding curium with carbon ions. [< New Latin *nobelium* < Alfred B. *Nobel,* who established the Nobel prizes]

***nobelium**

| symbol | atomic number | mass number |
|---|---|---|
| No | 102 | 254 |

**No|bel prize** (nō bel′), any one of six money prizes, averaging $150,000 each, established by Alfred B. Nobel (1833-1896) to be given annually to persons who have made valuable contributions to mankind in the fields of physics, chemistry, economics, medicine or physiology, literature, and in the promotion of international peace. Nobel prizes were first awarded in 1901.

**no|bil|i|ar|y** (nō bil′ē er′ē), *adj.* of or having to do with the nobility: *nobiliary rank.* [earlier, list of nobles < French *nobiliaire* of the nobility, learned borrowing from Latin *nōbilis* noble]

**no|bil|i|ty** (nō bil′ə tē), *n., pl.* **-ties. 1** people of noble rank, title, or birth; peerage. Earls, marquises, and counts belong to the nobility. *The United States does not have a nobility.* **2** noble birth; noble rank. **3** noble character: *What did they have that brought them so close to nobility, when most men would have cracked?* (Time). **SYN**: greatness. [< Old French *nobilite,* or *noblete,* learned borrowing from Latin *nōbilitās* < *nōbilis* noble]

**no|ble** (nō′bəl), *adj.,* **-bler, -blest,** *n.* **—*adj.* 1** high and great by birth, rank, or title: *a noble family, noble blood.* **SYN**: aristocratic, high-born, patrician. **2** high and great in character; showing greatness of mind; good: *a noble knight, a noble deed.* **SYN**: honorable, worthy. **3** excellent; fine; splendid; magnificent: *a noble poem, a noble animal; a cruciform hall of noble dimensions* (Nicholas P. S. Wiseman). *Niagara Falls is a noble sight.* **SYN**: imposing, stately. See syn. under **grand**. **4** not easily rusted or deteriorated; precious; valuable: *Gold and silver are noble metals.* **5** (in falconry) of the long-winged hawks, such as the falcons, that swoop down on the quarry: *The hawks have been classified as 'noble' or 'ignoble' according to the length and sharpness of their wings* (G. D. Campbell).
**—*n.* 1** a person high and great by birth, rank, or title: *[The Hittites] evolved a pioneering constitutional monarchy; their kings had to answer to a council of nobles* (Newsweek). **2** an English gold coin of the late Middle Ages, worth 6 shillings and 8 pence. **3** *Slang.* the leader of a group of strikebreakers.
[< Old French *noble,* learned borrowing from Latin *nōbilis, gnōbilis* noble, renowned, well known < *gnōscere* to know] **—no′ble|ness,** *n.*

**noble art,** *Especially British.* the art of boxing: *I was once a serious practitioner of the noble art* (Tommy Farr).

**noble gas,** any one of a group of gaseous elements that are relatively rare in nature and do not combine easily with other elements, including helium, neon, argon, krypton, xenon, and radon; inert gas.

**no|ble|man** (nō′bəl mən), *n., pl.* **-men. 1** a man of noble rank, title, or birth; peer: *noblemen of the royal court.* **2** a person of some specially favored or superior class: *The warrior, from the excellence of his physical proportions, might certainly have been regarded as one of nature's noblemen* (Herman Melville).

**noble rot,** a mold that forms on the skins of ripening grapes, concentrating the flavor within: *Noble rot ... gives sauternes and some Rhine wines their rich, almost oily, sweetness* (Atlantic). [translation of German *Edelfäule*]

**Noble Savage,** uncivilized man, viewed by European writers of earlier centuries as being good, brave, and uncorrupted by the evils of civilization: *The flattery ... was shot through with condescension implicit in the eighteenth-century adoration of the Noble Savage* (Harper's).

**no|blesse** (nō bles′), *n.* **1** noble birth or condition; nobility: *It roused her sense of noblesse and restored to her, brighter than before, her dream of living in style* (Jetta Carleton). **2** persons of noble rank; the nobility: *Of the garrulous noblesse we are confronted with, the most talkative is Louis XI ... and his vaporings make him quite a trial* (New Yorker). [< Old French *noblesse,* or *noblece* nobility, learned borrowing from Medieval Latin *nobilitia* < Latin *nōbilis* noble]

**no|blesse o|blige** (nō bles′ ō blēzh′), *French.* **1** persons of noble rank should behave nobly: *She taught her granddaughter that noblesse oblige was the greatest virtue and that aristocracy was the only proper order of society* (New York Times). **2** (literally) nobility obligates.

**no|ble|wom|an** (nō′bəl wu̇m′ən), *n., pl.* **-wom|en.** a woman of noble rank, title, or birth; peeress.

**no|bly** (nō′blē), *adv.* **1** in a noble manner; in a splendid way; as a noble person would do; gallantly: *a nobly fought battle.* **SYN**: splendidly. **2** of noble parentage: *nobly born.*

**no|bod|y** (nō′bod ē, -bə dē), *pron., n., pl.* **-bod|ies. —*pron.*** no one; no person.
**—*n.*** a person of no importance: *nobodies who think they are somebodies.*
**be nobody's fool,** to be hard to trick or deceive; be shrewder or cleverer than it may seem: *Miss Lesh is going to be nobody's fool on [the] courts* (London Times).
▶ **Nobody, nothing, nowhere** are written as single words. *Nobody* and *nothing* are singular, though *nobody* is informally treated as a collective: *Nothing is further from the truth. Nobody thinks that his own dog is a nuisance.* Informal: *Nobody thinks their own dog is a nuisance.*

**no|cent** (nō′sənt), *adj.* **1** hurtful; harmful; injurious. **2** guilty; criminal. [< Latin *nocēns, -entis,* present participle of *nocēre* to harm, related to *necāre* to kill]

**no|ci|as|so|ci|a|tion** (nō′sē ə sō′sē ā′shən, -sō′shē-), *n.* a loss of nervous energy as a result of traumatic injury or shock. [< Latin *nocēre* to harm + English *association.* Compare etym. under **anociassociation.**]

**no|ci|cep|tive reflex** (nō′si sep′tiv), a reflex caused by a painful stimulus. [< Latin *nocēre* to harm + English (re)*ceptive*]

**nock** (nok), *n., v.* **—*n.* 1** a notch on a bow or arrow for the bowstring. **2** *Nautical.* the forward upper corner of a sail set to a boom or of a staysail cut with a square tack. **3** *Obsolete.* the cleft in the buttocks.
**—*v.t.* 1** to furnish (a bow or arrow) with a nock. **2** to fit (an arrow) to the bowstring ready for shooting.
[Middle English *nocke* notch on a bow. Perhaps related to Dutch *nok* and Low German *nokk* point, tip.]

**nock|ing point** (nok′ing), the place on a bowstring where the nock of an arrow fits. Bowstrings usually have a protective nocking point.

**no-con|fi|dence** (nō′kon′fə dəns), *n., adj.* **—*n.*** a motion or vote by a legislative body expressing lack of confidence in the policies of a government or administration, especially in its basic policies. If such a motion is carried, the government is usually compelled to resign.
**—*adj.*** of or having to do with a vote of no-confidence: *He squeaked through a no-confidence vote ... intended to depose him as Premier* (Newsweek).

**no-count** (nō′kount′), *adj., n. U.S. Dialect.* no-account: *Ye miserable, mean-spirited, no-count critter!* (Helen Jackson).

**noc|tam|bu|la|tion** (nok tam′byə lā′shən), *n.* = sleepwalking. [< Latin *nox, noctis* night + *ambulātiō, -ōnis* a walking about < *ambulāre* to walk]

**noc|tam|bu|lism** (nok tam′byə liz əm), *n.* = noctambulation.

**noc|tam|bu|list** (nok tam′byə list), *n.* = sleepwalker.

**noc|ti|lu|ca** (nok′tə lü′kə), *n., pl.* **-cae** (-sē). any one of certain luminescent marine flagellates that gather together in great masses, often causing ocean waves to glow after nightfall. [earlier, a type of phosphorus < Latin *noctilūca* something shining at night < *nox, noctis* night + *lūcēre* to shine]

**noc|ti|lu|cence** (nok′tə lü′səns), *n.* noctilucent or phosphorescent quality.

**noc|ti|lu|cent** (nok′tə lü′sənt), *adj.* shining or luminous at night; phosphorescent: *The thin, noctilucent clouds, which can be observed only at twilight, suddenly change shape and move rapidly* (Science News Letter). [< Latin *nox, noctis* night + *lucēns, -entis,* present participle of *lūcēre* to shine]

**noc|to|graph** (nok′tə graf, -gräf), *n.* a frame with horizontal rows of wires to help blind people write without running lines together. [< Latin *nox, noctis* night + English *-graph*]

**noc|tu|id** (nok′chu̇ id), *adj., n.* **—*adj.*** of a very large group of usually dull-colored, nocturnal moths including most of those attracted to lights at night. Many of their larvae are injurious to crops, such as the cutworms, army worms, and cotton worms.
**—*n.*** a noctuid moth.
[< New Latin *Noctuidae* the family name < Latin *noctua* a night owl < *nox, noctis* night]

**noc|tule** (nok′chül), *n.* a large brown bat of Europe. [< French *noctule,* adaptation of Italian *nottola* bat, perhaps < Vulgar Latin *noctula* < Latin *nox, noctis* night]

**noc|turn** (nok′tėrn), *n.* a division of the service of matins in the Roman Catholic Church. [Middle English *nocturne* < Medieval Latin *nocturna* < Latin *nocturnus* nocturnal]

**noc|tur|nal** (nok tėr′nəl), *adj.* **1** of the night: *Stars are a nocturnal sight.* **2** in the night: *a nocturnal visitor.* **3** active in the night: *The owl is a nocturnal bird.* **4** closed by day, open by night: *a nocturnal flower.* [< Late Latin *nocturnālis* < Latin *nocturnus* < *nox, noctis* night. Compare etym. under **diurnal.**]

**nocturnal arc,** *Archaic.* the part of the diurnal circle of a heavenly body below the horizon.

**nocturnal emission,** = wet dream.

**noc|tur|nal|i|ty** (nok′tėr nal′ə tē), *n.* the quality, condition, or habit of being nocturnal.

**noc|tur|nal|ly** (nok tėr′nə lē), *adv.* **1** at night. **2** every night.

**noc|turne** (nok′tėrn), *n.* **1** a dreamy or pensive musical piece: *Nocturnes in G major and G minor are among Chopin's most beautiful compositions in this most Chopinesque genre* (C. Wierzynski). **2** a painting of a night scene. [< French, Middle French *nocturne,* learned borrowing from Latin *nocturnus* nocturnal]

**noc|u|ous** (nok′yu̇ əs), *adj.* noxious; hurtful; poisonous: *a nocuous gas.* [< Latin *nocuus* (with English *-ous*) < *nocēre* to harm] **—noc′u|ous|ly,** *adv.* **—noc′u|ous|ness,** *n.*

**nod** (nod), *v.,* **nod|ded, nod|ding,** *n.* **—*v.t.* 1** to bow (the head) slightly and raise it again quickly. **2** to express by bowing the head: *Father quietly nodded his consent.* **3** to invite, send, or bring by nodding the head: *He nodded me into the room. Cleopatra Hath nodded him to her* (Shakespeare). **4** to cause to bend or sway: *When the whale-boats ... nodded their slender masts at each other, and the dories pitched and tossed in the turf* (Hawthorne).
**—*v.i.* 1** to say yes by nodding. **2** to make a quick bow of the head, as in greeting, giving a command, or communicating a certain meaning: *He nods at us, as who should say, I'll be even with you* (Shakespeare). **3** to let the head fall forward and bob about when sleepy or falling asleep: *The sentinel ... began to nod at his post* (Washington Irving). **4** to be sleepy; become careless and dull: *Reason still keeps its throne, but it nods a little, that's all* (George Farquhar). **5** to droop, bend, or sway back and forth: *Trees nod in the wind. Or columbines, in purple dressed, Nod o'er the ground-bird's hidden nest* (William Cullen Bryant).
**—*n.* 1a** the action or fact of nodding the head: *He gave us a nod as he passed.* **b** a short sleep; nap. **2** a sign of approval: *With mute obeisance, grave and slow, Repaid by nod polite* (Oliver Wendell Holmes). **3** the act of bending or swaying.
**get** (or **give**) **the nod,** *Informal.* **a** to receive (or give) approval: *The merger must get the nod from stock-holders of both banks* (Wall Street Journal). **b** to receive (or give) a victory or decision: *The judges gave the nod to the winning challenger.*
**on the nod,** *British.* without formality; by tacit agreement or acknowledgment: *The agenda, usually the cause of great friction, was accepted "on the nod"* (Sunday Times).
[Middle English *nodden;* origin uncertain] **—nod′der,** *n.*

**Nod** (nod), *n.* the realm of sleep; sleep; land of nod. [< *Nod,* a Biblical place name (Genesis 4:16)]

**nod|al** (nō′dəl), *adj.* having to do with nodes; like a node. **—nod′al|ly,** *adv.*

**no|dal|i|ty** (nō dal′ə tē), *n.* nodal position or character: *Nodality is possessed by all points where the continuous flow of trade is broken, [such as] the terminal points of caravan routes crossing desert regions* (White and Renner).

**nod|ding** (nod′ing), *adj.* **1** that nods: *nodding plumes.* **2** *Botany.* bent or drooping downward, as a flower or bud. **—nod′ding|ly,** *adv.*

**nodding acquaintance, 1** a slight acquaintance with a person or persons, extending no further than recognition by a nod: *I have met with him at dinner, and have a nodding acquaintance with him* (Edmond Yates). **2** the person or persons with whom one has such an acquaintance. **3** a slight or superficial acquaintance with something: *Many English people have at least a nodding acquaintance with a wider range of wines than their French equivalents* (London Times).

**nodding cap,** a plant of the orchid family of eastern North America, with drooping purple flowers.

**nod|dle¹** (nod′əl), *n. Informal.* the head: *Slatternly girls, without an idea inside their noddles* (Anthony Trollope). [Middle English *nodel* or *nodul* the back of the head; origin uncertain]

**nod|dle²** (nod′əl), *v.t., v.i.,* **-dled, -dling.** to nod

**Pronunciation Key:** hat, āge, cãre, fär; let, ēqual, tėrm; it, īce; hot, ōpen, ôrder; **oi**l, **ou**t; cup, pu̇t, rüle; **ch**ild; lo**ng**; **th**in; **ŧh**en; **zh**, measure; **ə** represents **a** in about, **e** in taken, **i** in pencil, **o** in lemon, **u** in circus.

(the head) quickly or slightly. [perhaps frequentative of *nod*]

**nod|dled** (nod′əld), *adj. Informal.* having a noddle or head: *idle, empty-noddled boarders* (Arnold Bennett).

**nod|dy** (nod′ē), *n., pl.* **-dies. 1** a fool; simpleton: *To think that I should be such a noddy!* (Dickens). **2** a soot-colored, heavy-bodied tern with a rounded tail what breeds in the West Indies and Florida Keys. It has a habit of nodding its head to other noddies it meets, and is so fearless of man as to be easily caught. [compare etym. under **noddle**[1], **noddle**[2]]

***node** (nōd), *n.* **1** a knot, knob, or swelling. **2** any joint in a stem where leaves grow out. **3** *Physics.* a point, line, or plane in a vibrating body at which there is comparatively no vibration. **4** *Astronomy.* either of the two points at which the orbit of a heavenly body intersects the path of the sun or the orbit of another heavenly body. The plane may be the ecliptic in the case of a planet or the equatorial plane of a planet in the case of a planet's satellite. The ascending node is the node at which the body moves northward; the descending node is the node at which the body moves southward. **5** *Geometry.* a point at which a curve crosses itself, or a similar point on a surface. **6** *Figurative.* a central point in any system. **7** a small knotlike swelling or mass of specialized tissue on the body or an organ: *a lymph node.* **8** = lymph gland. **9** *Figurative.* a knot or complication in the plot or character development of a story, play, or the like: *There are characters which are continually creating collisions and nodes for themselves in dramas which nobody is prepared to act with them* (George Eliot). [earlier, complication, tumor < Latin *nōdus* knot]

***node**
definitions 2, 3

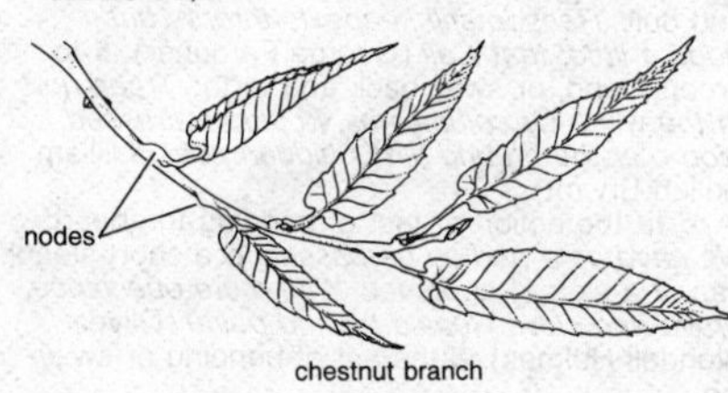


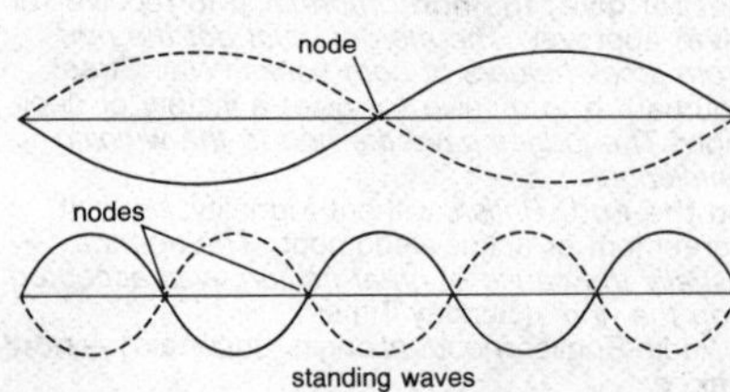


**node of Ran|vier** (rän vyā′), the site of a local constriction in the myelin and axon of a myelinated nerve cell: *The ion movements can occur only in the gaps in the myelin sheath ... called the nodes of Ranvier, and the nerve impulse has to jump from one node to the next* (New Scientist). [< L. A. *Ranvier,* 1835-1922, a French histologist]

**nod|i|cal** (nod′ə kəl, nō′də-), *adj. Astronomy.* of or having to do with nodes.

**no|dose** (nō′dōs, nō dōs′), *adj.* having nodes; knotty; knobbed. [< Latin *nōdōsus* knotty < *nōdus* node, knot]

**no|dos|i|ty** (nō dos′ə tē) *n., pl.* **-ties. 1** the quality or state of being nodose. **2** a knot; knob; knotty swelling: it has all the nodosities of the oak without its strength (Edmund Burke).

**no|dous** (nō′dəs), *adj.* full of knots; knotty.

**nod|u|lar** (noj′ə lər), *adj.* having nodules.

**nod|u|late** (noj′ə lāt), *v.t.,* **-lat|ed, -lat|ing.** to form nodular growths in: *Its surface is uneven and nodulated like that of a raspberry* (Robert B. Todd).

**nod|u|la|tion** (noj′ə lā′shən), *n.* the formation of nodular growths or nodules: *the nodulation of white clover.*

**nod|ule** (noj′ül), *n.* **1** a small knot, knob, or swelling. **2** a small, rounded mass or lump: *nodules of pure gold.* **3** *Botany.* a small swelling on the roots of certain plants, mostly legumes, that contains symbiotic nitrogen-fixing bacteria. [< Latin *nōdulus* (diminutive) < *nōdus* knot]

**nod|u|lose** (noj′ə lōs, noj′ə lōs′), *adj.* having little knots or knobs.

**no|dus** (nō′dəs), *n., pl.* **-di** (-dī). a difficulty or complication; knotty point or situation, as in a story or play: *The whole nodus may be more of a logical cobweb, than an actual material perplexity* (Thomas Carlyle). [< Latin *nōdus* knot]

**No|e** (nō′ə), *n.* = Noah.

**No|ël** or **No|el** (nō el′), *n.* = Christmas. [< French *Noël* < Latin *nātālis* natal (day, that is, specifically, of Christ) < *gnāscī* be born. See etym. of doublets **natal, nowel.**]

**no|ël** or **no|el** (nō el′), *n.* **1** a Christmas song; carol. **2** an expression of joy used in Christmas songs. [< *Noël*]

**no|e|sis** (nō ē′sis), *n.* **1** an act of pure intellect; a comprehending by the mind alone; reason. **2** *Psychology.* the property of yielding or being knowledge; cognition. [< Greek *nóēsis* < *noeîn* have mental perception < *nóos* mind, thought]

**no|et|ic** (nō et′ik), *adj.* **1** of or having to do with the mind or intellect. **2** originating or existing in the mind. **3** concerned with mental speculation.

**no-fault** (nō′fôlt′), *adj. U.S.* **1** of or having to do with a type of automobile insurance in which an accident victim is compensated for damages or expenses by his own insurance company, whether the accident was his fault or not: *The hearings were to focus on a modified no-fault bill ... designed to end much of the current reliance on litigation-oriented settlements for auto accidents* (New York Times). **2** having to do with any legal action in which fault is eliminated as a ground for finding against either party: *I take note of the rising pressures for no-fault divorce ... and what I would call no-fault medical malpractice* (Shana Alexander).

**no-frills** (nō′frilz′), *adj.* reduced to or providing only the essentials; without extras or embellishments: *a low-cost, no-frills flight. Home builders had unveiled the "no-frills house" as the answer to skyrocketing housing costs* (Fred M. Hechinger).

**nog**[1] (nog), *n.* eggnog or the like made with alcoholic liquor. [short for *eggnog*]

**nog**[2] (nog), *n. British.* a strong ale or beer.

**nog**[3] (nog), *n., v.,* **nogged, nog|ging.** *British.* —*n.* **1** a wooden peg, pin, or block used in shipbuilding, mining, and for other purposes. **2** a small block of wood set into a brick wall, for nails.
—*v.t.* **1** to secure or support by a nog or peg. **2** to build with or as nogging.
[origin uncertain; perhaps variant of *knag*]

**No|gai** (nō gī′), *n., pl.* **-gais. 1** a member of a Tartar people of northeastern Caucasia. **2** their Turkic language.

**no-ga|ku** (nō′gä′kü), *n.* a classical Japanese dramatic dance; no[2]. [< Japanese *nō-gaku*]

**nogg** (nog), *n.* = nog[1].

**nog|gin** (nog′in), *n.* **1** a small cup or mug. **2** a small drink, especially of an alcoholic liquor; ¼ pint: *Many a noggin of whiskey is here quaffed* (Hawthorne). **3** *Informal.* a person's head: *This thought kept chasing through our noggin* (New York Times).

**nog|ging** (nog′ing), *n. British.* bricks or brickwork set between crossed boards of a wooden frame.

**no-go** (nō′gō′), *adj.* **1** *Slang.* not in a favorable condition for proceeding: *In space jargon this was potentially a "no-go" situation: with no alternative open except to abort the mission* (Manchester Guardian Weekly). **2** *British.* not to be entered without special allowance; barred to designated persons or groups: *Is Liverpool to be a no-go area?* (London Daily Telegraph).

**no-good** (nō′gůd′), *n., adj. Informal.* —*n.* a worthless person; rogue: *The officer is plainly a no-good, but ... his wife is no domestic bargain* (John McCarten).
—*adj.* good-for-nothing; worthless: *Nor have we met more of a no-good scoundrel ... who ... suffers less for his knavery* (New York Times).

**no-good|nik** (nō′gůd′nik), *n. Slang.* a no-good person.

**noh** or **Noh** (nō), *n.* a classical Japanese dramatic dance; no[2]: *Noh, which is the oldest dramatic achievement of the Japanese originated with the Samurai class* (Atlantic). [< Japanese *nō*]

**no-hit** (nō′hit′), *adj. U.S.* being or consisting of a no-hitter.

**no-hit|ter** (nō′hit′ər), *n. U.S.* a baseball game in which a pitcher gives up no base hits to the opposing team in nine or more innings.

**no-holds-barred** (nō′hōldz′bärd′), *adj. Informal.* **1** unrestrained; uninhibited; violent: *a no-holds-barred fight.* **2** all-out; complete: *a no-holds-barred effort or attempt.*

**no-hop|er** (nō′hō′pər), *n.* **1** *Australian.* a worthless, lazy person. **2** *British Informal.* a person or thing that is certain to fail at something; loser: *Appeal to the no-hopers to pull out of the race* (Sunday Times).

**no|how** (nō′hou′), *adv. Informal or* (*with another negative*) *Dialect.* in no way; not at all: *That don't dovetail nohow* (Charles Reade).

**n.o.i.b.n.,** not otherwise indexed by name.

**noil** (noil), *n.* **1** a short fiber or knot of wool, cotton, or silk, separated from the long fiber in combing. **2** waste material composed of such pieces. [origin unknown]

**no-i|ron** (nō′ī′ərn), *adj. Informal.* that does not require ironing: *a drip-dry, no-iron shirt.*

**noise** (noiz), *n., v.,* **noised, nois|ing.** —*n.* **1** a sound that is not musical or pleasant; loud or harsh sound: *the noise of breaking dishes, the noise of machinery. The noise of thunder kept me awake.* **2** any sound: *the little noises in the woods at night, the noise of the rain on the roof; ... the reapers' rustling noise* (Robert Burns). **SYN:** See syn. under **sound**[1]. **3** a din of voices and movements; loud shouting; outcry; clamor: *The boys made too much noise at the movie and were asked to leave the theater. Whose noise is this that cries on murder?* (Shakespeare). **SYN:** babble, uproar, hubbub, tumult. **4a** any undesired or unintended disturbance in a radio or television signal. **b** *Physics.* a group of sound waves which are not periodic and which are produced by irregular vibrations; sound of no single fundamental frequency but many nonharmonic frequency components of varying amplitudes randomly placed. **c** any signal of disturbance: *As air in the first few feet of the atmosphere drifts past the sensing element of the instrument the pointer fluctuates constantly in response to 'temperature noise'* (Scientific American). **5** *Figurative.* public talk about some matter of interest or wonder: *The first* [*ballad*] *sold wonderfully, the event being recent, having made a great noise* (Benjamin Franklin). **6** *Archaic.* music or a sound of music: *Thus all Israel brought up the ark ... and with sound of the cornet, and with trumpets, and with cymbals, making a noise with psalteries and harps* (I Chronicles 15:28). **7** *Archaic, Figurative.* a rumor; report: *So grateful is the noise of noble deeds to noble hearts* (Tennyson). **8** *Obsolete.* a band of musicians: *see if thou cans't find out Sneak's noise* (Shakespeare).
—*v.t.* to spread the news of; report; tell: *It was noised about that the company was going out of business. All these saying were noised abroad* (Luke 1:65). *It is noised he hath a mass of treasure* (Shakespeare). —*v.i.* **1** to make a noise or outcry: *Noising loud And threatening high* (Milton). **2** to talk publicly or much.

**make a noise in the world,** to arouse public talk; make a public sensation: *It was pronounced ... the greatest poem of the age, and all anticipated the noise it would make in the great world* (Washington Irving).

**make noises,** to express or indicate (certain feelings, thoughts, or intentions) vocally: *General Electric and Alcoa, for example, are making noises about getting into city building* (New Scientist).

[< Old French *noise* uproar, brawl < Latin *nausea,* probably in Vulgar Latin, unpleasant condition (of various kinds). See etym. of doublet **nausea.**]

—*Syn. n.* **1 Noise, din, uproar** mean disagreeably loud, confused, or harsh and clashing sound. **Noise** applies to any disagreeably unmusical or loud sound made by one or more people or things: *The noise on the street kept me awake.* **Din** applies to prolonged and deafening confusion or clanging or piercing noises: *The din of machines and factory whistles hurt my ears.* **Uproar** applies especially to the tumult, shouting, and loud noises of a crowd and the wild excitement that causes such noise: *You should have heard the uproar when officials called back the touchdown.*

**noise|ful** (noiz′fəl), *adj.* = noisy.

**noise|less** (noiz′lis), *adj.* **1** making no noise; silent: *a noiseless step.* **2** making little noise; nearly quiet: *She owned a noiseless typewriter.* —**noise′less|ly,** *adv.* —**noise′less|ness,** *n.*

**noise|mak|er** (noiz′mā′kər), *n.* **1** a person who makes too much noise. **2** a thing that makes noise, especially a horn, rattle, or other device used to make noise at a party.

**noise|mak|ing** (noiz′mā′king), *n., adj.* —*n.* the making of noise, especially much noise: *Noise-making warns a bear of intruders and prevents what could be a perilous confrontation* (Robert A. Irwin). —*adj.* that makes noise.

**noise pollution,** a concentration of excessively loud sound or noise, as made by traffic, jet planes, and machinery; sound pollution: *Man is an adaptable animal. Without realizing it, he has become accustomed to excessive noise pollution in his environment* (Theodore Berland).

**noi|sette**[1] (nwä zet′, noi-), *n.* a variety of rose, supposedly a cross between a China rose and a musk rose. [< Philippe *Noisette,* a French horticulturist, who developed it]

**noi|sette**[2] (nwä zet′), *n.* a small, round piece of veal, lamb, mutton, or other lean meat, cooked and served with vegetables. [< French *noisette* a nut (diminutive) < *noix* < Latin *nux, nucis* (because of the resemblance in shape)]

**noi|some** (noi′səm), *adj.* **1** that disgusts; offensive; smelling bad: *a noisome odor, a noisome slum; ... kitchens and areas with noisome sewers*

(Charles Kingsley). SYN: foul, disgusting. **2** harmful; injurious: *a noisome pestilence; ... the noisome beast* (Ezekiel 14:21). SYN: noxious. [Middle English *noy,* variant of *annoy* + *-some*¹] —**noi′some|ly,** *adv.* —**noi′some|ness,** *n.*

**nois|y** (noi′zē), *adj.,* **nois|i|er, nois|i|est. 1** making much noise: *a noisy boy, a noisy crowd, a noisy little clock.* SYN: shouting, clamorous, brawling, blatant. See syn. under **loud. 2** full of noise: *a noisy street, the noisy city, a noisy house.* **3** having much noise with it: *a noisy quarrel, a noisy game, a noisy party.* —**nois′i|ly,** *adv.* —**nois′i|ness,** *n.*

**Nok** (nok), *adj., n.* —*adj.* of or having to do with a West African civilization that flourished from about 500 B.C. to about 200 A.D., noted especially for its terra-cotta sculpture and artifacts.
—*n.* the Nok civilization.
[< *Nok,* a village in Nigeria, where remains of the culture were discovered]

**no-knock** (nō′nok′), *adj. U.S.* involving or authorizing forcible entry into a suspect's quarters without having to give warning or identification: *The so-called no-knock provision authorizes searches under warrant in which a policeman may force his way into a building ... in cases in which evidence might be destroyed if warning were given* (Donald Goodman).

**no|lens vo|lens** (nō′lenz vō′lenz), *Latin.* whether willing or unwilling; willy-nilly: *Well, nolens volens, you must hold your tongue* (Scott).

**no|li-me-tan|ge|re** or **no|li me tan|ge|re** (nō′lī-mē tan′jə rē), *n., adj. Latin.* —*n.* **1** a notice that a person or thing must not be touched or interfered with: *I see it everywhere. In your work. In the way you stand, backed up against the wall. In your books. Noli me tangere* (New Yorker). **2** a picture portraying the appearance of Jesus to Mary Magdalene after the Resurrection (John 20:17). **3** = touch-me-not (def. 1). **4** *Medicine.* an open sore on the face or a lupus of the nose; rodent ulcer.
—*adj.* (literally) touch me not: *a sort of noli me tangere manner* (Thomas De Quincey).

**nol|le pros|e|qui** (nol′ē pros′ə kwī), *Law.* an entry made upon the records of a court by the plaintiff or prosecutor that he will proceed no further in a suit. [< Latin *nōlle prōsequī* be unwilling to pursue or prosecute]

**no-load** (nō′lōd′), *n., adj.* —*n.* a type of mutual fund in which shares are offered for sale without any sales charge and generally available through investment dealers: *The no-loads ... dispense not only with expensive salesmen but with the "load," or sales commission, that regular mutual funds charge* (Time).
—*adj.* of or designating such a mutual fund: *The so-called no-load funds ... sell their shares at net asset value with no sales or commission charge* (New York Times).

**no|lo con|ten|de|re** (nō′lō kən ten′də rē), *Law.* a defendant's plea that he will accept conviction but not admit his guilt: *The agencies pleaded nolo contendere to the criminal suit, and entered into a consent decree with respect to the civil* (Time). [< Latin *nōlō contendere* I do not wish to contend]

**nol|pros** (nol′pros′), *v.t.,* **-prossed, -pros|sing.** *Law.* to abandon (a lawsuit or indictment) by entering a nolle prosequi. [American English, short for Latin *nōlle prōsequī*]

**nol. pros.,** nolle prosequi.

**nom.,** nominative.

**no|ma** (nō′mə), *n.* a gangrenous open sore of the mouth and cheeks, occurring mainly in children weakened by disease. [< Latin *nomae,* plural, any "eating" ulcer < Greek *nomaí,* plural of *nomē* pasturage, a spreading, related to *némein* to feed, graze]

**no|mad** (nō′mad, nom′ad), *n., adj.* —*n.* **1** a member of a tribe that moves from place to place to find food or have pasture for its cattle: *Some Arabs are nomads.* **2** a wanderer. SYN: rover.
—*adj.* **1** wandering from place to place to find pasture. **2** wandering: *the nomad existence of the Gypsies.*
[< Latin *Nomas, -adis* a wandering tribe < Greek *nomás, -ados,* ultimately < *némein* to pasture]

**no|mad|ic** (nō mad′ik), *adj.* **1** of nomads or their life: *a nomadic custom. The geography of Asia and of Africa necessitated a nomadic life* (Emerson). **2** wandering; roving: *Most of the Indians of the North American plains were nomadic.* —**no·mad′i|cal|ly,** *adv.*

**no|mad|ism** (nō′mad iz əm), *n.* the way that nomads live.

**no man's land, 1** the land between opposing lines of trenches in a war. **2** a tract of land to which no one has a recognized or established claim. **3** *Figurative.* a scope of activity over which no jurisdiction or authority exists: *an ambiguous no man's land between Communism and democracy.*

**nom|arch** (nom′ärk), *n.* the governor of a nome or nomarchy. [earlier, a local governor < Greek *nomárchēs* < *nomós* nome + *árchein* to rule]

**nom|ar|chy** (nom′är kē), *n., pl.* **-chies.** one of the provinces into which modern Greece is divided for administrative purposes; nomos.

**nom|bril** (nom′brəl), *n. Heraldry.* the point in an escutcheon midway between the fess point and the middle base point; navel. [< French *nombril* navel]

**nom de guerre** (nom′ də ger′), an assumed name under which to pursue a profession, undertaking, or the like; pseudonym: *Malraux ... fought under a nom de guerre in the French Resistance* (New Yorker). [< French *nom de guerre* (literally) war name]

**nom de plume** (nom′ də plüm′), a name used by a writer instead of his real name; pen name; pseudonym: *Samuel L. Clemens used "Mark Twain" as his nom de plume.* [coined from French *nom* name, *de* of, *plume* pen]
► **Nom de plume** is an English usage coined from French words.

**nome**¹ (nōm), *n.* **1** a province of ancient Egypt. **2** an administrative department of modern Greece; nomos; nomarchy. [< Greek *nomós* any of the 36 divisions of Egypt < *némein* to divide, distribute; allot for grazing]

**nome**² (nōm), *v. Archaic.* a past participle of **nim.**

**no|men**¹ (nō′men), *n., pl.* **nom|i|na** (nom′ə nə). the name of one's clan or gens in ancient Rome. *Julius* in *Gaius Julius Caesar* is his *nomen,* indicating membership in the Julian gens. [< Latin *nōmen* (literally) name. See etym. of doublet **noun.**]

**no|men**² (nō′mən), *v. Archaic.* a past participle of **nim.**

**no|men|cla|tor** (nō′mən klā′tər), *n.* **1** a person who announces the names of persons or guests. **2** a person who gives or assigns names to objects that are scientifically classified. [< Latin *nōmenclātor* < *nōmen* name + *calāre* to call (out)]

**no|men|cla|to|ri|al** (nō men′klə tôr′ē əl, -tōr′-), *adj.* having to do with naming or nomenclature.

**no|men|cla|tur|al** (nō′mən klā′chər əl), *adj.* of or having to do with nomenclature: *nomenclatural rules, nomenclatural oddities.* —**no′men|cla′tur·al|ly,** *adv.*

**no|men|cla|ture** (nō′mən klā′chər, nō men′klə-), *n.* a set or system of names or terms in a particular science, art, or other subject: *the nomenclature of music. Another Ford venture into nomenclature, "Thunderbird," was a notable success* (New York Times). SYN: terminology. [< Latin *nōmenclātūra* < *nōmen* name + *calāre* to call (out)]

**no|men|cla|tur|ist** (nō′mən klā′chər ist), *n.* a person who devises a nomenclature.

**nom|i|na|ble** (nom′ə nə bəl), *adj.* = nominatable.

**nom|i|nal** (nom′ə nəl), *adj., n.* —*adj.* **1** existing in name only; not real: *a position with merely nominal duties. The president is the nominal head of the club, but the secretary is the one who really runs its affairs. A state of nominal peace existed between Spain, France, and England* (John L. Motley). **2** too small to be considered; unimportant compared with the real value: *We paid our friend a nominal rent for the cottage—$5 a month.* SYN: trivial, negligible. **3a** giving the name or names: *the nominal accounts of a business, a nominal list of the students in a class.* **b** mentioning specifically by name: *a nominal appeal.* **c** assigned to a person by name: *a nominal share of stock.* **4** *Grammar.* **a** of or having to do with a noun or nouns. *Day* is the nominal root of *daily, daybreak,* and *Sunday.* **b** (of a word or phrase) used or functioning as a noun or nouns. *Rich* and *poor* in the phrase *the rich and the poor* are nominal adjectives. **5** of or having to do with a name or names.
—*n.* a word or group of words functioning as a noun.
[< Latin *nōminālis* < *nōmen, -inis* name]

**nom|i|nal|ism** (nom′ə nə liz′əm), *n.* the philosophical doctrine that all abstract or general terms, such as *circle* or *man,* do not stand for real things, but exist for convenience in thought and are a necessary part of language.

**nom|i|nal|ist** (nom′ə nə list), *n., adj.* —*n.* a believer in nominalism.
—*adj.* = nominalistic.

**nom|i|nal|is|tic** (nom′ə nə lis′tik), *adj.* of or having to do with nominalists or nominalism.

**nom|i|nal|ly** (nom′ə nə lē), *adv.* **1** in name only; as a matter of form; in a nominal way only. **2** by name.

**nominal value,** an assigned value, such as the face or par value of a share of stock.

**nominal wages,** wages in terms simply of money, without regard to purchasing power.

**nom|i|nat|a|ble** (nom′ə nā′tə bəl), *adj.* that may be nominated: *a nominatable candidate.*

**nom|i|nate** (*v.* nom′ə nāt; *adj.* nom′ə nit, -nāt), *v.,* **-nat|ed, -nat|ing,** *adj.* —*v.t.* **1** to name as candidate for an office: *Three times the Democratic Party nominated William Jennings Bryan for President, but he was never elected.* SYN: designate. **2** to appoint or propose for an office, duty, or honor: *The President nominated him as Secretary of State. The magazine's readers nominated her Woman of the Year.* **3** to name; designate: *Parents will be allowed to nominate any two London secondary schools, although a child's profile will determine where he finally goes* (Time). SYN: entitle. **4** to fix; specify: *to nominate a figure for expenses. July 1 was nominated by the German National Union of Students for nationwide demonstrations* (L. R. Buckley). *Let the forfeit Be nominated for an equal pound Of your fair flesh* (Shakespeare).
—*adj.* **1** having or mentioning a particular name. **2** nominated, as to an office.
[< Latin *nōmināre* (with English *-ate*¹) < *nōmen, -inis* name]

**nom|i|na|tion** (nom′ə nā′shən), *n.* **1** the act or process of naming as a candidate for office: *The nominations for president of the club were written on the blackboard. In their nomination to office they will not appoint to the exercise of authority as to a pitiful job, but as to a holy function* (Edmund Burke). **2** selection for office or duty; appointment to office or duty. **3** the state of being nominated: *Her friends were pleased by her nomination.*

**nom|i|na|tive** (nom′ə nə tiv, -nā′-; nom′nə-), *adj., n.* —*adj.* **1** *Grammar.* showing the subject of a finite verb, the complement of a linking verb, or the words agreeing with the subject. The Modern English pronouns *I, he, she, we, they,* and *who* are in the nominative case. **2** appointed by nomination; nominated. **3** assigned to a person by name: *a nominative warrant, nominative shares of stock.*
—*n. Grammar.* **1** the nominative case. **2** a word in that case. *Who* and *I* are nominatives. *Abbr:* nom.
[< Latin *nōminātīvus* < *nōmināre;* see etym. under **nominate**]

**nominative absolute,** *Grammar.* a construction consisting of a substantive and its modifier (usually a participle) and not grammatically related to any other element in the sentence. *Example:* The day being warm, we took off our coats (*The day being warm* is a nominative absolute).

**nominative of address,** *Grammar.* a noun naming the person to whom one is speaking. *Example:* John, where is your coat? (*John* is the nominative of address).

**nom|i|na|tor** (nom′ə nā′tər), *n.* a person who nominates.

**nom|i|nee** (nom′ə nē′), *n.* a person who is nominated to or for an office or to be a candidate for election to an office. SYN: See syn. under **candidate.**

**no|mism** (nō′miz əm), *n.* the basing of religious conduct on moral law as derived from some sacred work. [< Greek *nómos* law + English *-ism*]

**no|mis|tic** (nō mis′tik), *adj.* of or founded on nomism.

**no|moc|ra|cy** (nō mok′rə sē), *n., pl.* **-cies.** government established and carried out in accordance with a code of laws. [< Greek *nomokratía* < *nómos* law + *krátos* rule]

***nom|o|gram** (nom′ə gram), *n.* **1** *Mathematics.* a chart from which one can determine by alignment of scales the value of a dependent variable for any given value of the independent variable. **2** any device which depicts numerical relations graphically. [< Greek *nómos* law + English *-gram*]

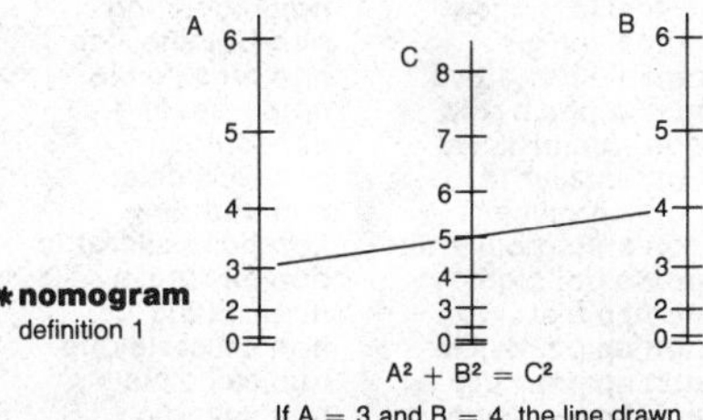


***nomogram** definition 1

$A^2 + B^2 = C^2$

If A = 3 and B = 4, the line drawn shows that C = 5.

**nom|o|graph** (nom′ə graf, -gräf), *n.* = nomogram.

**no|mog|ra|phy** (nō mog′rə fē), *n., pl.* **-phies. 1a** the art or process of drawing up laws. **b** a book on this subject. **2** the science of computation by

**Pronunciation Key:** hat, āge, cãre, fär; let, ēqual, tėrm; it, īce; hot, ōpen, ôrder; oil, out; cup, pu̇t, rüle; child; long; thin; ᴛʜen; zh, measure; ə represents **a** in about, **e** in taken, **i** in pencil, **o** in lemon, **u** in circus.

means of graphs. [< Greek *nomographiā* < *nómos* law + *gráphein* write, draw]

**nom|o|log|i|cal** (nom′ə loj′ə kəl), *adj.* of or having to do with nomology.

**no|mol|o|gy** (nō mol′ə jē), *n.* **1** the science of law. **2** the formulation of scientific laws. [< Greek *nómos* law + English *-logy*]

**no|mos** (nō′mos), *n., pl.* **-moi** (-moi). *Greek.* a nomarchy; nome.

**nom|o|thet|ic** (nom′ə thet′ik), *adj.* **1** lawgiving or lawmaking; legislative. **2** founded on law. **3** of or having to do with a science of general or universal laws. [< Greek *nomothetikós* < *nomothétēs* a lawgiver < *nómos* law + *thétēs* one who sets, gives, related to *tithénai* set, place]

**nom|o|thet|i|cal** (nom′ə thet′ə kəl), *adj.* = nomothetic.

**non** (nôn), *n., pl.* **nons** (nôɴ). *French.* no: *The most optimistic calculations showed the treaty would get 301 nons and only 287 ouis* (Newsweek).

**non-**, *prefix.* **1** not ___; not a ___; opposite of ___; lack of ___; failure of ___: *Nonbreakable = not breakable. Nonliving = not living. Noncompletion = lack of completion.*

**2** (prefixed to a noun) not real; sham; pretended: *nonart, nonbook, nonevent.*

[< Latin *nōn-* < *nōn* not, not a < Old Latin *noenum* < *ne-* not + unrecorded *oinom*, accusative of *oinos* one]

► If an adjective formed with *non-* is not defined in this dictionary, its meaning will be clear if *not* is put in the place of the *non,* as in *nonabsorbent, noncompetitive, nongenetic, nonparental.* If a noun formed with *non-* is not defined, its meaning will be clear if *not, not a, the opposite of,* or *the absence of* is put in place of the *non,* as in *nonadmission, noninfection, nonremission, nonsubscriber.*

*Non-* is a living prefix and may be used with any noun, adjective, or adverb; but if there is a commonly used word of the same meaning formed with *un-, in-,* or *dis-,* that word is usually preferable. Most of the words that have *non-* as the preferred usage, or as a respectable rival of *un-,* are listed below or as regular entries.

**non′a|bra′sive**
**non′ab|sorb′ent**
**non′ab|stain′er**
**non′ab|stract′**
**non′ac|a|dem′ic**
**non|ac′cent**
**non′ac|cred′it|ed**
**non|ac′id**
**non′a|cid′ic**
**non′a|cous′tic**
**non′ac|tin′ic**
**non|ac′tion**
**non|ac′tive**
**non|ac′tor**
**non′a|dap′tive**
**non′ad|her′ence**
**non′ad|he′sive**
**non|ad′ja|cent**
**non′ad|jec|ti′val**
**non′ad|just′a|ble**
**non′ad|min′is|tra′tive**
**non′ad|mis′sion**
**non′ad|van|ta′geous**
**non′ad|verb′i|al**
**non′aes|thet′ic**
**non-Af′ri|can**
**non′ag|gres′sive**
**non′a|gree′ment**
**non′ag|ri|cul′tur|al**
**non′al|le′giance**
**non′al|ler′gic**
**non′al|lit′er|a′tive**
**non′al|pha|bet′ic**
**non′-A|mer′i|can**
**non′an|a|lyt′ic**
**non-An′gli|can**
**non′an|tag′o|nis′tic**
**non′a|pol′o|get′ic**
**non′ap|o|stol′ic**
**non′ap|peal′a|ble**
**non′ap|pear′ing**
**non′ap|pre|hen′sion**
**non′ap|proach′**
**non′a|quat′ic**
**non|a′que|ous**
**non-Ar′ab**
**non-Ar′a|bic**
**non|ar′bi|trar′y**
**non′a|ris′to|crat′ic**
**non′ar|o|mat′ic**
**non′ar|tic′u|lat′ed**
**non-Ar′y|an**
**non′-A|si|at′ic**
**non|as′pi|rat′ed**
**non′as|ser′tive**
**non′as|sess′a|ble**
**non′as|sign′a|ble**
**non′as|sim′i|la|ble**
**non′as|sim′i|la′tion**
**non′as|so′cia|ble**
**non′as|so′ci|a′tion**
**non′as|so′ci|a′tive**
**non′ath|let′ic**
**non′at|mos|pher′ic**
**non′a|tom′ic**
**non′at|trib′ut|a|ble**
**non′at|trib′u|tive**
**non′au|ric′u|lar**
**non′au|thor′i|ta′tive**
**non′au|to|mat′ic**
**non′au|to|mo′tive**
**non′bac|te′ri|al**
**non′bal|lis′tic**
**non|ba′sic**
**non|be′ing**
**non′be|liev′er**
**non′be|liev′ing**
**non′bel|lig′er|ent**
**non|belt′ed**
**non′be|nev′o|lent**
**non-Bib′li|cal**
**non|bind′ing**
**non′bi|o|log′i|cal**
**non|bit′ing**
**non|bloom′ing**
**non-Bol′she|vist**
**non|break′a|ble**
**non|breed′ing**
**non-Brit′ish**
**non-Bud′dhist**
**non|bud′ding**
**non′bu|reau|crat′ic**
**non|busi′ness**
**non|cak′ing**
**non′cal|car′e|ous**
**non|call′a|ble**
**non′ca|lor′ic**
**non-Cal′vin|ist**
**non|can′cer|ous**
**non′ca|non′i|cal**
**non′cap|i|tal|is′tic**
**non′car|bo|hy′drate**
**non|car′bo|nat′ed**
**non′ca|reer′**
**non′car|niv′o|rous**
**non|cash′**
**non′cat|a|lyt′ic**
**non′cat|a|stroph′ic**
**non′cat|e|gor′i|cal**
**non-Cath′o|lic**
**non′-Cau|ca′sian**
**non|caus′a|tive**
**non′ce|les′tial**
**non|cel′lu|lar**
**non-Cel′tic**
**non|cen′tral**
**non|ce′re|al**
**non|cer′e|bral**
**non|cer′ti|fied**
**non|charge′a|ble**
**non|chem′i|cal**
**non′-Chi|nese′**
**non-Chris′tian**
**non|church′**
**non|church′go′er**
**non|cil′i|ate**
**non|cit′i|zen**
**non|civ′i|lized**
**non|clas′si|cal**
**non|clas′si|fi′a|ble**
**non|clas′si|fied**
**non|cler′i|cal**
**non|clin′i|cal**
**non|clot′ting**
**non′co|ag′u|la|ble**
**non′co|a|les′cing**
**non′co|er′cive**
**non|cog′ni|tive**
**non′co|her′ent**
**non′co|he′sive**
**non′col|lab′o|ra′tive**
**non′col|laps′i|ble**
**non′col|lect′a|ble**
**non′col|lect′i|ble**
**non|col′loid**
**non′co|lo′ni|al**
**non|col′or**
**non|com′bat**
**non′com|bin′ing**
**non′com|bus′ti|ble**
**non′com|mer′cial**
**non′com|mu′ni|ca|ble**
**non′com|mu′ni|cant**
**non′com|mu′ni|cat′ing**
**non′com|mu′ni|ca′tion**
**non|com′mu|nist**
**non-Com′mu|nist**
**non′com|mu′ta|tive**
**non|com′pen|sat′ing**
**non|com′pe|ten|cy**
**non′com|pet′ing**
**non′com|pet′i|tive**
**non′com|ple′tion**
**non′com|ply′ing**
**non′com|pre|hen′sion**
**non′com|press′i|ble**
**non′com|pres′sion**
**non′com|pul′sion**
**non′con|ceal′ment**
**non′con|cen|tra′tion**
**non′con|cil′i|at′ing**
**non′con|cil′i|a|to′ry**
**non′con|clu′sive**
**non′con|cord′ant**
**non′con|cur′rence**
**non′con|cur′ren|cy**
**non′con|cur′rent**
**non′con|den′sa|ble**
**non′con|di′tioned**
**non′con|du′cive**
**non′con|duc′ti|bil′i|ty**
**non′con|duc′tion**
**non′con|duc′tive**
**non′con|fer′ra|ble**
**non|con′fi|dence**
**non′con|fi|den′tial**
**non′con|fis′ca|ble**
**non′con|flict′ing**
**non′con|form′ing**
**non′con|geal′ing**
**non′con|gen′i|tal**
**non′con|ges′tion**
**non′-Con|gres′sion|al**
**non|con′gru|ent**
**non|con′ju|ga′tion**
**non′con|nec′tive**
**non′con|niv′ance**
**non|con′scious**
**non′con|sec′u|tive**
**non′con|sent′**
**non′con|sent′ing**
**non′con|ser|va′tion**
**non′con|serv′a|tive**
**non′con|sol′i|dat′ed**
**non′con|spir′ing**
**non′con|sti|tu′tion|al**
**non′con|struc′tive**
**non′con|sul′ta|tive**
**non′con|sum′a|ble**
**non′con|ta′gious**
**non′con|tem|pla′tive**
**non′con|tem′po|rar′y**
**non′con|ten′tious**
**non′con|tig′u|ous**
**non′con|ti|nen′tal**
**non′con|tin′u|ance**
**non′con|tin′u|ous**
**non|con′tra|band**
**non′con|trac′tile**
**non′con|trac′tu|al**
**non′con|tra|dic′to|ry**
**non′con|trib′ut|ing**
**non′con|trib′u|tor**
**non′con|trib′u|to′ry**
**non′con|trol′la|ble**
**non′con|trolled′**
**non′con|tro|ver′sial**
**non′con|ven′tion|al**
**non′con|ver′gent**
**non′con|ver′sant**
**non′con|ver′ti|ble**
**non′con|vic′tion**
**non′co|or′di|na′tion**
**non|cor′po|rate**
**non′cor|rec′tive**
**non′cor|res|pond′ence**
**non′cor|re|spond′ing**
**non′cor|rob′o|ra′tive**
**non′cor|rod′ing**
**non′cor|ro′sive**
**non|cos′mic**
**non′cre|a′tive**
**non|cred′i|ble**
**non|cred′i|tor**
**non|crim′i|nal**
**non|crit′i|cal**
**non|cru′cial**
**non|crys′tal|line**
**non|cul′pa|ble**
**non|cul′ti|vat′ed**
**non′cul|ti|va′tion**
**non′cu|mu|la′tive**
**non|cur′rent**
**non|cy′clic**
**non|cy′cli|cal**
**non-Czech′**
**non|dam′age|a|ble**
**non′-Dar|win′i|an**
**non′de|bate′**
**non′de|cay′ing**
**non′de|cep′tive**
**non′de|cid′u|ous**
**non′de|creas′ing**
**non′de|duc′ti|ble**
**non′de|fam′a|to′ry**
**non′de|fec′tive**
**non′de|fense′**
**non′de|fen′sive**
**non′de|fer′a|ble**
**non′def|er|en′tial**
**non′de|file′ment**
**non′de|fin′ing**
**non′de|gen′er|a′tion**
**non′de|his′cent**
**non|del′e|gate**
**non′de|lin′e|a′tion**
**non′de|lin′quent**
**non′de|lir′i|ous**
**non′de|liv′er|a|ble**
**non′de|mand′**
**non′dem|o|crat′ic**
**non′de|nom′i|na′tion|al**
**non′de|part|men′tal**
**non′de|par′ture**
**non′de|pend′ence**
**non′de|ple′tion**
**non′de|pos′i|tor**
**non′de|pre′ci|a′ting**
**non′de|riv′a|ble**
**non′de|riv′a|tive**
**non′de|rog′a|to′ry**
**non′des|pot′ic**
**non′de|tach′a|ble**
**non|det′o|nat′ing**
**non′de|vel′op|ment**
**non′de|vo′tion|al**
**non′di|a|bet′ic**
**non′di|a|lect′al**
**non′dic|ta|to′ri|al**
**non′di|dac′tic**
**non′dif|fer|en′ti|a′tion**
**non′dif|frac′tive**
**non′dif|fus′ing**
**non′dif|fu′sion**
**non′di|gest′i|ble**
**non′di|lat′a|ble**
**non′dip|lo|mat′ic**
**non|dir′i|gi|ble**
**non′dis|ap|pear′ing**
**non′dis|charg′ing**
**non|dis′ci|plin|ar′y**
**non′dis|clo′sure**
**non′dis|count|a|ble**
**non′dis|crim′i|na′tion**
**non′dis|crim′i|na|to′ry**
**non′dis|fran′chised**
**non′dis|par′ag|ing**
**non′dis|per′sion**
**non′dis|pos′a|ble**
**non′dis|pos′al**
**non′dis|qual′i|fy′ing**
**non′dis|rup′tive**
**non′dis|sem′i|na′tion**
**non′dis|tri|bu′tion**
**non′dis|trib′u|tive**
**non′di|ver′gent**
**non′-di|ver′si|fied**
**non′di|vid′ing**
**non′di|vis′i|ble**
**non′doc|tri|naire′**
**non|doc′tri|nal**
**non′doc|u|men′ta|ry**
**non′dog|mat′ic**
**non′do|mes′ti|cat′ed**
**non|dor′mant**
**non′dra|mat′ic**
**non|drink′ing**
**non|dry′ing**
**non|du′ti|a|ble**
**non′dy|nas′tic**
**non|earn′ing**
**non′ec|cle′si|as′tic**
**non′ec|cle′si|as′ti|cal**
**non′ec|lec′tic**
**non′ec|o|nom′ic**
**non|ed′i|ble**
**non|ed′i|to′ri|al**
**non|ed′u|ca|ble**
**non′ed|u|ca′tion|al**
**non′ef|fec′tive**
**non′ef|fer|ves′cent**
**non′ef|fi|ca′cious**
**non′ef|fi′cient**
**non′e|gal′i|tar′i|an**
**non′e|las′tic**
**non′e|lect′**
**non′e|lect′ed**
**non′e|lec′tion**
**non′e|lec′tive**
**non′e|lec′tric**
**non′e|lec′tri|cal**
**non′e|lec′tri|fied**
**non′e|lec|tron′ic**
**non′el|e|men′ta|ry**
**non|el′i|gi|ble**
**non′e|mer′gence**
**non′e|mo′tion|al**
**non′em|phat′ic**
**non′em|pir′i|cal**
**non′en|cy′clo|pe′dic**
**non′en|dem′ic**
**non′en|force′a|ble**
**non′en|force′ment**
**non-Eng′lish**
**non′en|tailed′**
**non′en|tan′gle|ment**
**non′en|vi′ron|men′tal**
**non′e|phem′er|al**
**non′e|pis′co|pal**
**non′-E|pis′co|pa′lian**
**non|e′qual**
**non′e|quiv′a|lent**
**non′e|quiv′o|cat′ing**
**non′e|rot′ic**
**non′e|rup′tive**
**non′es|tab′lish|ment**
**non′e|ter′nal**
**non|eth′i|cal**
**non′eth|no|log′i|cal**
**non′eu|gen′ic**
**non′-Eu|ro|pe′an**
**non′e|van|gel′i|cal**
**non′e|vic′tion**
**non′ev|o|lu′tion|ar′y**
**non′ex|change′a|ble**
**non′ex|clu′sive**
**non′ex|cus′a|ble**
**non′ex|e|cu′tion**
**non′ex|ec′u|tive**
**non′ex|empt′**
**non′ex|ist′ing**
**non′ex|ot′ic**
**non′ex|pan′si|ble**
**non′ex|pan′sive**
**non′ex|pend′a|ble**
**non′ex|pe′ri|enced**
**non′ex|per′i|men′tal**
**non|ex′pert**
**non′ex|ploi|ta′tion**
**non′ex|plo′sive**
**non′ex|port′a|ble**
**non′ex|por|ta′tion**
**non|ex′tant**
**non′ex|tend′ed**
**non′ex|ten′sile**
**non′ex|ten′sion**
**non′ex|ter′nal**
**non′ex|tra|dit′a|ble**
**non′ex|tra′ne|ous**
**non|ex′tro|vert**
**non|fac′tu|al**
**non|fad′ing**
**non|fam′i|ly**
**non′fa|nat′i|cal**
**non|fan′ci|ful**
**non|farm′**
**non-Fas′cist**
**non′fas|tid′i|ous**
**non|fat′**
**non|fa′tal**
**non′fa|tal|is′tic**
**non|fat′ten|ing**
**non|fed′er|al**
**non|fed′er|at′ed**
**non|feed′ing**
**non′fer|ment′a|ble**
**non|fer′tile**
**non|fes′tive**
**non|feu′dal**
**non′fi|du′ci|ar|y**
**non|fil′ter|a|ble**
**non′fi|nan′cial**
**non|fire′proof′**
**non|fis′cal**
**non|fis′sion|a|ble**
**non|flag′el|late**
**non|flow′er|ing**
**non|flow′ing**
**non|fluc′tu|at′ing**
**non|flu′ent**
**non′flu|id′ic**
**non′flu|o|res′cent**
**non|fo′cal**
**non|food′**
**non|for′feit|a|ble**
**non|for′feit|ing**
**non|for′fei|ture**
**non′for|tu′i|tous**
**non′fos|sil|if′er|ous**
**non|fran′gi|ble**
**non′fra|ter′nal**
**non|fraud′u|lent**
**non|freez′ing**
**non-French′**
**non|fric′a|tive**
**non|fric′tion**
**non|func′tion|al**
**non|func′tion|ing**
**non′fun|da|men′tal**
**non|gas′e|ous**
**non′ge|lat′i|nous**
**non|gen′er|a′tive**
**non′ge|ner′ic**
**non′ge|net′ic**
**non-Gen′tile**
**non-Ger′man**
**non′-Ger|man′ic**
**non|gla′cial**
**non|glan′du|lar**
**non-Goth′ic**
**non′gov|ern|men′tal**
**non|grad′u|ate**
**non|gran′u|lar**
**non′grav|i|ta′tion|al**
**non-Greek′**
**non′gre|gar′i|ous**
**non|hab′it|a|ble**
**non′ha|bit′u|al**
**non′har|mo′ni|ous**
**non|haz′ard|ous**
**non|hea′then**
**non′he|don|is′tic**
**non′-Hel|len′ic**
**non′he|red′i|tar′y**
**non|her′it|a|ble**
**non|her′i|tor**
**non|hi′ber|nat′ing**
**non|hi′ber|na′tor**
**non′-Hi|ber′ni|an**
**non′his|tor′ic**
**non′his|tor′i|cal**
**non′ho|mo|ge′ne|ous**
**non|hon′o|rar′y**
**non|hos′tile**
**non|hu′man**
**non|hu′mor|ous**
**non|hy′dro|gen|at′ed**
**non′hy|gro|scop′ic**
**non′i|de′a|lis′tic**
**non′i|den′ti|cal**
**non′i|den′ti|ty**
**non′i|de|o|log′i|cal**
**non′id|i|o|mat′ic**
**non′i|dol′a|trous**
**non′ig|nit′i|ble**
**non′i|mag′i|nar′y**
**non|im′i|ta′tive**
**non′im|mi|gra′tion**
**non′im|mune′**
**non′im|mu′ni|ty**
**non|im′mu|nized**
**non′im|peach′a|ble**
**non|im|per′a|tive**
**non′im|pe′ri|al**
**non′im|por|ta′tion**
**non′im|preg′nat|ed**

non′im|pres′sion|ist
non′im|pres|sion|is′tic
non′in|can|des′cent
non′in|clu′sive
non′in|de|pen′dent
non-In′di|an
non′in|dict′a|ble
non′in|dict′ment
non′in|dig′e|nous
non′in|di|vid′u|al
non′in|di|vid′u|al|is′tic
non-In′do-Eu′ro|pe′an
non′in|dus′tri|al
non′in|fal′li|ble
non′in|fect′ed
non′in|fec′tion
non′in|fec′tious
non|in′fi|nite
non′in|flam′ma|to′ry
non′in|fla′tion|ar′y
non′in|flect′ed
non′in|flec′tion|al
non′in|form′a|tive
non′in|her′it|a|ble
non′in|ju′ri|ous
non′in|sti|tu′tion|al
non′in|struc′tion|al
non′in|stru|men′tal
non|in′te|grat|ed
non′in|tel|lec′tu|al
non′in|tel′li|gent
non′in|ter|change′a|ble
non|in′ter|course
non′in|ter|fer′ence
non′in|ter|fer′ing
non′in|ter|mit′tent
non′in|ter|na′tion|al
non′in|ter|rupt′ed
non′in|ter|sect′ing
non′in|tox′i|cant
non′in|tox′i|cat′ing
non′in|tro|spec′tive
non|in′tro|vert
non′in|tu′i|tive
non′in|vert′ed
non′in|volve′ment
non|i′o|dized
non|i′o|nized
non-I′rish
non′ir|ra′di|at′ed
non|ir′ri|ga|ble
non|ir′ri|gat′ed
non′ir|ri|ga′tion
non|ir′ri|tant
non|ir′ri|tat′ing
non′-Is|lam′ic
non′-Is|rae′li
non-Is′ra|el|ite
non′is′sue
non′-I|tal′ian
non|it′er|a′tive
non′-Jap|a|nese′
non-Jew′
non-Jew′ish
non′judg|men′tal
non′ju|di′cial
non|jur′a|ble
non′ju|rid′i|cal
non′ju|ris′tic
non|ko′sher
non-Lat′in
non|le′gal
non|leg′is|la′tive
non|le′thal
non|lex′i|cal
non|lib′er|al
non|li′censed
non|lim′it|ing
non|liq′ue|fy′ing
non|liq′ui|dat′ing
non′liq|ui|da′tion
non|lit′er|ar′y
non′li|ti′gious
non′li|tur′gi|cal
non|lo′cal
non|log′i|cal
non′lu|mi|nes′cent
non|lu′mi|nous
non|lus′trous
non-Lu′ther|an
non-Mag′yar
non|main′te|nance
non-Ma′lay
non′ma|lig′nant
non|mal′le|a|ble
non′mam|ma′li|an
non′man|u|fac′tur|ing
non′ma|rine′
non|mar′i|tal
non|mar′i|time
non|mar′ket|a|ble
non|mar′riage|a|ble
non|mar′ry|ing
non|mar′tial
non|match′ing
non′ma|te′ri|al|is′tic
non′ma|ter′nal
non′math|e|mat′i|cal
non′ma|tric′u|lat′ed
non′me|chan′i|cal
non′mech|a|nis′tic
non′me|dic′i|nal
non|med′ul|lat′ed
non′me|lo′di|ous
non|melt′ing
non|mem′ber|ship
non|mer′can|tile
non′met|al|lif′er|ous
non′met|a|phys′i|cal
non′me|te|or′ic
non-Meth′o|dist
non|met′ri|cal
non′met|ro|pol′i|tan
non|mi′gra|to′ry
non|mil′i|tant
non|mil′i|tar′y
non′mi|met′ic
non|min′er|al
non′min|is|te′ri|al
non′mi|rac′u|lous
non′mis|chie|vous
non′mis′ci|ble
non|mo′bile
non′-Mo|ham′me|dan
non′mo|lec′u|lar
non|mon′e|tar′y
non′-Mon|go′li|an
non′mo|ral′i|ty
non-Mor′mon
non|mor′tal
non-Mos′lem
non|mo′tile
non|muf′fled
non′mu|nic′i|pal
non|mus′cu|lar
non|mu′si|cal
non′mu|si′cian
non|mys′ti|cal
non|myth′i|cal
non′nar|cot′ic
non|na′tion|al
non′na′tion|al|is′tic
non|na′tive
non|nat′u|ral
non|nat′u|ral|is′tic
non|nau′ti|cal
non|na′val
non|nav′i|ga|ble
non′ne|ces′si|ty
non|neg′a|tive
non-Ne′gro
non|neu′tral
non-Nor′dic
non-Nor′man
non-Norse′
non|nu′cle|at′ed
non′nu|tri′tious
non|nu′tri|tive
non′o|be′di|ence
non′o|blig′a|to′ry
non′ob|serv′ant
non′ob|serv′er
non′ob|struc′tion|ist
non′ob|struc′tive
non′oc|cu|pa′tion|al
non′oc|cur′rence
non|o′dor|ous
non′of|fi′cial
non|op′er|at′ing
non′op|er|a′tion
non′op|er|a′tion|al
non|op′er|a′tive
non|op′ti|cal
non|op′tion|al
non′or|gan′ic
non|or′i|en′tal
non|or′tho|dox
non|ox′i|diz′a|ble
non|ox′i|diz′ing
non|ox′y|gen|at′ed
non′pa|cif′ic
non|pac′i|fist
non|pa′gan
non|pal′a|tal
non′pal|a|tal|i|za′tion
non|pa′pal
non|pa′pist
non|par′
non|par′al|lel
non′par|a|lyt′ic
non′par|a|sit′ic
non|par′ent
non′pa|ren′tal
non′pa|rish′ion|er
non′par|lia|men′ta|ry
non′pa|ro′chi|al
non′par|tic′i|pant
non′par|tic′i|pa′tion
non|par′ty
non|pas′ser|ine
non′pa|ter′nal
non′pa|ter′nal|is′tic
non′path|o|gen′ic
non|pa′tient
non|pay′ing
non′pe|des′tri|an
non|pen′sion|a|ble
non′per|cep′tu|al
non|per′for|at′ed
non′per|form′er
non′per|form′ing
non′pe|ri|od′ic
non′pe|ri|od′i|cal
non|per′ish|a|ble
non|per′ish|ing
non|per′ma|nent
non|per′me|a|ble
non′per|mis′si|ble
non′per|pen|dic′u|lar
non′per|pet′u|al
non′per|se|cu′tion
non′per|sist′ence
non′per|sist′ent
non|per′son|al
non′phil|o|soph′i|cal
non′pho|net′ic
non|phys′i|cal
non′phys|i|o|log′i|cal
non|pig′ment|ed
non|plan′e|tar′y
non|plas′tic
non|plaus′i|ble
non|play′ing
non′po|et′ic
non|poi′son|ous
non′po′lar|iz′a|ble
non′po|lem′i|cal
non|pol′i|cy
non-Pol′ish
non′po|lit′i|cal
non|po′rous
non-Por′tu|guese′
non′pos|ses′so|ry
non|prac′tic|ing
non|pred′a|to′ry
non′pre|dict′a|ble
non′pref|er|en′tial
non|preg′nant
non′pre|hen′sile
non′prej|u|di′cial
non′pre|par′a|to′ry
non′prep|o|si′tion|al
non′-Pres|by|te′ri|an
non′pre|scrip′tion
non′pre|scrip′tive
non′pres|er|va′tion
non′pres|i|den′tial
non|pres′sur|ized
non|prev′a|lent
non|priest′ly
non|print′ing
non′pro|duc′er
non′pro|duc′ing
non′pro|duc′tion
non′pro|fes′sion|al
non′pro|fes|so′ri|al
non′pro|fi′cien|cy
non′pro|fi′cient
non′prof|it|eer′ing
non|prof′it|mak′ing
non′pro|gres′sive
non′pro|hib′i|tive
non′pro|lif′ic
non′pro|mis′cu|ous
non′pro|phet′ic
non′pro|por′tion|al
non′pro|pri′e|tar′y
non′pro|scrip′tive
non′pro|tec′tive
non-Prot′es|tant
non′pro|voc′a|tive
non-Prus′sian
non′psy|chi|at′ric
non|psy′chic
non′psy′cho|an′a|lyt′ic
non|pub′lic
non|punc′tur|a|ble
non|pun′ish|a|ble
non|pu′ni|tive
non|pur′u|lent
non|qual′i|fy′ing
non|qual′i|ta′tive
non|quan′ti|ta′tive
non|ra′cial
non|ra′di|at′ing
non|rad′i|cal
non′ra|di|o|ac′tive
non|ran′dom
non|rat′a|ble
non|ra′tion|al
non′re|ac′tive
non′read′ing
non′re|al|is′tic
non′re|al′i|ty
non′re|ceiv′ing
non′re|cip′ro|cal
non′re|cip′ro|cat′ing
non′rec|og|ni′tion
non|re′course
non′re|cur′rent
non′re|cur′ring
non′re|deem′a|ble
non′re|fill′a|ble
non′re|flect′ing
non′re|fu′el|ing
non′re|fund′a|ble
non′re|gen′er|at′ing
non′re|gen′er|a′tive
non|reg′i|ment′ed
non|reg′is|tered
non|reg′is|tra|ble
non|reg′u|lat′ed
non|reign′ing
non′re|lat′ed
non|rel′a|tive
non′rel|a|tiv|is′tic
non′re|li′gious
non′re|mis′sion
non′re|mu′ner|a′tive
non′re|new′a|ble
non′re|pay′a|ble
non′re|pent′ance
non′re|pet′i|tive
non′rep|re|hen′si|ble
non′rep|re|sen′ta|tive
non′re|pro|duc′tive
non′res|i|den′tial
non′re|sid′u|al
non′re|sist′ing
non′re|solv′a|ble
non|res′o|nant
non′re|strict′ed
non′res|ur|rec′tion
non′re|ten′tive
non′re|tir′ing
non′re|trace′a|ble
non′re|trac′tile
non′ret|ro|ac′tive
non′re|turn′
non′re|turn′a|ble
non′re|veal′ing
non′re|ver′sal
non′re|vers′i|ble
non′re|vert′i|ble
non′re|view′a|ble
non′re|volt′ing
non′rev|o|lu′tion|ar′y
non′re|volv′ing
non′rhe|tor′i|cal
non|rhym′ing
non|rhyth′mic
non′rit|u|al|is′tic
non|ri′val
non-Ro′man
non′ro|man′tic
non|ro′tat|ing
non|roy′al
non|roy′al|ist
non|ru′mi|nant
non|ru′ral
non-Rus′sian
non′sac|er|do′tal
non′sac|ra|men′tal
non|sa′cred
non′sac|ri|fi′cial
non|sal′a|ble
non|sal′a|ried
non|sal′u|tar′y
non|sat′u|rat′ed
non′-Scan|di|na′vi|an
non′schis|mat′ic
non|schol′ar
non′scho|las′tic
non|sci′ence
non′sci|en|tif′ic
non|scor′ing
non|sea′son|al
non|se′cret
non′se|cre′tive
non|se′cre|to|ry
non′sec|tar′i|an|ism
non|sec′tion|al
non|sec′u|lar
non|sed′en|tar′y
non′se|di′tious
non|seg′re|gat′ed
non′seg|re|ga′tion
non′se|lec′tive
non-Sem′ite
non′-Se|mit′ic
non|sen′si|tive
non|sen′si|tized
non|sen′so|ry
non|sen′tient
non|ser′ous
non|ser′vile
non′-Shake|spear′e|an
non|shar′ing
non|shat′ter
non|shrink′a|ble
non|sig′na|to′ry
non′sig|nif′i|cant
non|sil′ver
non|sink′a|ble
non|ski′er
non-Slav′ic
non|sleep′er
non|smok′er
non|smok′ing
non|so′cial
non|so′cial|ist
non′so|cial|is′tic
non|so′lar
non|sol′id
non|sol′vent
non|sov′er|eign
non-So′vi|et
non-Span′ish
non|spar′ing
non|spark′ing
non|spa′tial
non|speak′ing
non|spe′cial|ist
non|spe′cial|ized
non′spe|cif′ic
non′spec|tac′u|lar
non|spec′tral
non|spec′u|la′tive
non|spher′i|cal
non|spir′i|tu|al
non|spir′i|tu|ous
non′spon|ta′ne|ous
non|spot′ta|ble
non|stain′able
non|stain′ing
non|stand′ard|ized
non|start′er
non|start′ing
non|stat′ic
non|sta′tion|ar′y
non′sta|tis′ti|cal
non|stat′u|to′ry
non|stel′lar
non|ster′e|o
non|ster′oid
non|stra|te′gic
non|stretch′a|ble
non|strik′er
non|strik′ing
non|struc′tur|al
non|stu′dent
non′sub|mis′sive
non′sub|scrib′er
non′sub|scrib′ing
non|sub′si|dized
non′sub|stan′tial
non′suc|cess′
non′suc|cess′ful
non′suc|ces′sive
non′sup|port′er
non′sup|port′ing
non|sup′pu|ra′tive
non|sur′gi|cal
non|sus′pect
non′sus|tain′ing
non-Swed′ish
non|swim′mer
non|swim′ming
non-Swiss′
non′syl|lab′ic
non′sym|bi|ot′ic
non′sym|bol′ic
non′sym|met′ri|cal
non|sym′pa|thiz′er
non|sym|phon′ic
non′symp|to|mat′ic
non|syn′chro|nous
non′syn|tac′tic
non|syn′the|sized
non′sys|tem
non′sys|tem|at′ic
non′sys|tem′ic
non|tar′nish|a|ble
non|tax′a|ble
non|teach′a|ble
non|teach′ing
non|tech′ni|cal
non′tech|no|log′i|cal
non|ter′mi|na|ble
non|ter′mi|nal
non′ter|res′tri|al
non′ter|ri|to′ri|al
non′tes|ta|men′ta|ry
non′the|at′ri|cal
non′the|is′tic
non′the|o|log′i|cal
non′ther|a|peu′tic
non|ther′mal
non|think′ing
non|tit′u|lar
non|to′tal|i|tar′i|an
non′trans|fer′a|ble
non′tran|si′tion|al
non′trans|par′ent
non|trea′son|a|ble
non|trib′u|tar′y
non|triv′i|al
non|trop′i|cal
non|tru′ant
non|truth′
non-Turk′ish
non|typ′i|cal
non′ty|ran′ni|cal
non|ul′cer|ous
non′un|der|stand′a|ble
non|u′ni|form
non′u|ni|form′i|ty
non′-U|ni|tar′i|an
non′u|ni|ver′sal
non′u|ni|ver′si|ty
non|ur′ban
non|us′age
non|use′
non|us′er
non|u′ter|ine
non′u|til′i|tar′i|an
non|u′ti|lized
non|va′cant
non|val′id
non|var′i|a|ble
non|var′i|ant
non|vas′cu|lar
non|veg′e|ta′tive
non′ve|ne′re|al
non|ven′om|ous
non|ve′nous
non|ver′bal
non′ver|nac′u|lar
non|ver′ti|cal
non′ve|sic′u|lar
non|vet′er|an
non|vi′a|ble
non|vi′bra|to′ry
non′vi|car′i|ous
non′vi|o|la′tion
non|vir′u|lent
non|vis′cous
non|vis′it|ing
non|vis′u|al
non|vis′u|al|ized
non|vit′re|ous
non|vo′cal
non′vo|cal′ic
non′vo|ca′tion|al
non|vol′a|tile
non′vol|can′ic
non|vol′un|tar′y
non|vot′ing
non-West′ern
non|work′er
non|work′ing
non|yield′ing

**non|ab|sorb|a|ble** (non′ab sôr′bə bəl, -zôr′-), *adj.* not absorbable; that cannot be absorbed.

**non|ac|cept|ance** (non′ək sep′təns), *n.* failure or refusal to accept.

**non|ad|dict** (non′ad′ikt), *n.* a drug user who is not addicted to drugs.

**non|ad|dict|ing** (non′ə dik′ting), *adj.* = nonaddictive.

**non|ad|dic|tive** (non′ə dik′tiv), *adj.* not causing addiction: *a nonaddictive drug.*

**non|age** (non′ij, nō′nij), *n.* **1** the fact or condition

---

**Pronunciation Key:** hat, āge, cãre, fär; let, ēqual, tėrm; it, īce; hot, ōpen, ôrder; **oil**, **out**; cup, pu̇t, rüle; **ch**ild; lo**ng**; **th**in; ᴛʜen; **zh**, measure; ə represents **a** in about, **e** in taken, **i** in pencil, **o** in lemon, **u** in circus.

of being under the legal age of responsibility; minority: *Mr. Graziano recovered from a twisted nonage to become a first-class citizen* (New Yorker). **SYN**: infancy. **2** *Figurative.* an early stage; period before maturity. **SYN**: immaturity. [< Anglo-French *nonnage* < *non-* not (< Latin) + *age* age < Gallo-Romance *aetāticum* < Latin *aetās*]

**non|a|ge|nar|i|an** (non′ə jə nãr′ē ən; nō′nə-), *n., adj.* —*n.* a person who is 90 years old or between 90 and 100 years old.
—*adj.* 90 years old or between 90 and 100 years old.
[< Latin *nōnāgēnārius* containing ninety (< *nōnāgēni* ninety each, ultimately < *nōnus* ninth < *novem* nine) + English *-an*]

**non|ag|gres|sion** (non′ə gresh′ən), *n., adj.* —*n.* a refraining from aggression; lack of aggression: *A pact of nonaggression was signed by the two nations.*
—*adj.* of or having to do with the lack of aggression; specifying no aggressive action: *The idea of an East-West nonaggression pact ... is not new—and time has not made it any more sensible* (Wall Street Journal).

***non|a|gon** (non′ə gon), *n.* a plane figure having nine angles and nine sides. [< Latin *nōnus* ninth + Greek *gōniā* angle]

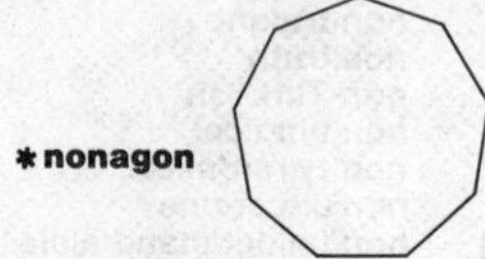
***nonagon**

**non|al|co|hol|ic** (non′al kə hôl′ik, -hol′-), *adj.* containing no alcohol.

**non|a|ligned** (non′ə līnd′), *adj., n.* —*adj.* not aligned politically; neutral: *In all its diplomatic dealings, Peking has persistently worked ... in subtle ways to align the nonaligned nations with the Communist orbit* (Atlantic). Also, **unaligned**.
—*n.* a nonaligned person or country: *The two groups in Indonesia opposing each other are the "nonaligneds" and the "interventionists"* (Manchester Guardian Weekly).

**non|a|lign|ment** (non′ə līn′mənt), *n.* the condition of being nonaligned; neutralism.

**non|al|lel|ic** (non′ə lē′lik), *adj.* not allelic.

**non|ap|pear|ance** (non′ə pir′əns), *n.* failure to appear, as in court. **SYN**: absence.

**non|ar|ith|met|ic** (non′ar ith met′ik), *adj.* = nonarithmetical.

**non|ar|ith|met|i|cal** (non′ar ith met′ə kəl), *adj.* **1** not arithmetical: *a nonarithmetical equation.* **2** not having to do with arithmetical work.

**non|art** (non′ärt′), *n.* **1** the negation of art: *He tends to look upon a good deal of Abstract Expressionism as nonart* (New Yorker). **2** a work that rejects or parodies conventional forms and techniques of art.

**non|ar|tic|u|late** (non′ar tik′yə lit), *adj.* **1** not made up of distinct parts, **2** not jointed, hinged, or segmented.

**no|na|ry** (nō′nər ē), *adj.* having nine for a base: *a nonary scale.*

**non|as|sent|ed** (non′ə sen′tid), *adj.* of stocks or bonds whose owners have not agreed to deposit them in exchange for new stocks or bonds during the reorganization after bankruptcy.

**non|as|tro|naut** (non as′trə nôt), *n.* a person not specifically trained for space flight: *The ability to fly nonastronauts on space missions will allow the research scientist ... to pursue the potential of his discipline as a space passenger without having to master the techniques of space flight* (Wernher von Braun).

**non|at|tend|ance** (non′ə ten′dəns), *n.* failure or neglect to be present: *My notice to appear arrived a good two weeks before the specified date and warned of penalties for nonattendance* (Maclean's). **SYN**: absence.

**non|bank** (non bangk′), *adj.* of or having to do with an individual or institution other than a bank.

**non|bi|o|de|grad|a|ble** (non′bī ō di grā′də bəl), *adj.* that is not susceptible to being decomposed by bacterial action: *Landfills should be limited to the minimum number and acreage necessary to dispose of the nonbiodegradable materials that have no resource value, such as broken concrete, earth materials, and similar rubble* (Percy H. McGauhey).

**non|black** (non blak′), *n.* a person who is not a Negro.

**non|board|ing** (non bôr′ding, -bōr′-), *adj.* **1** not living or eating in the place mentioned. **2** not for boarding.

**non|book** (non′bu̇k′), *n.* a printed work that uses various attention-getting devices in binding, inserts, and other mechanical features, and is put together in book form merely as a salable product: *This closely printed 896-page book is more like ... a nonbook than a disciplined treatment of a coherent theme* (Scientific American).

**non|can|di|da|cy** (non kan′də də sē), *n.* the status of a noncandidate.

**non|can|di|date** (non kan′də dāt, -dit), *n.* a person who has not announced or is unwilling to announce his candidacy for an office: *One of the most maddening candidates in a political race is the noncandidate. He is the fellow who is being talked for a race but who will just never admit his candidacy until the last minute* (Tuscaloosa News).

**non|cap|i|tal murder** (non kap′ə təl), (in Canadian law) murder that is not punishable by death but by life imprisonment: *The four original charges of noncapital murder ... were reduced to charges of manslaughter* (Canada Month).

**nonce** (nons), *n.* the one or particular occasion or purpose: *In a nonce they are sucked into adventure* (Alfred Wright).
**for the nonce**, for the present time or occasion: *We must compare the Marquis of Farintosh to a lamb for the nonce* (Thackeray).
[Middle English (*for the*) *nones,* misdivision of *for than ones* for the once, that is, for the one (time or thing)]

**non|cel|lu|lo|sic** (non′sel yə lō′sik), *n., adj.* —*n.* a synthetic fiber made from a base other than cellulose, such as nylon, Dacron, and Orlon.
—*adj.* of or characteristic of the noncellulosics: *noncellulosic fibers.*

**nonce word**, a word formed and used for a single occasion. *Examples: newspaporialist* = a journalist, *planeticose* = given to wandering, *observist* = a person who makes observation his business.

**non|cha|lance** (non′shə ləns, non′shə läns′), *n.* a cool unconcern; indifference: *She received the prize with pretended nonchalance.* **SYN**: impassivity. [< French *nonchalance* < Old French < *nonchalant* nonchalant]

**non|cha|lant** (non′shə lənt, non′shə länt′), *adj.* without enthusiasm; coolly unconcerned; indifferent: *a nonchalant manner, a nonchalant reply. She remained quite nonchalant during all the excitement.* **SYN**: apathetic. [< French *nonchalant* < Old French < *non-* not (< Latin) + *chaloir* have concern for, care for, be warm < Latin *calēre* be warm] —**non′cha|lant|ly**, *adv.*

**non|chro|mo|so|mal** (non′krō mə sō′məl), *adj.* transmitting hereditary characters without chromosomes; not chromosomal or Mendelian.

**non|col|lege** (non kol′ij), *adj.* **1** not attending or not having attended a college: *The data at hand indicate that the college man outstrips the noncollege man with astonishing ease in every measure of worldly success* (Harper's). **2** not suitable for college.

**non|col|le|giate** (non′kə lē′jit, -jē it), *adj.* **1** *British.* not belonging to a college; belonging to the body of students in a university not attached to any particular college or hall. **2** (of a university) not composed of separate colleges.

**non|com** (non′kom′), *n., adj. Informal.* —*n.* a noncommissioned officer: *To all appearances an impeccable soldier, he is a wizard at getting the better of noncoms* (Atlantic).
—*adj.* noncommissioned.

**noncom.**, noncommissioned officer.

**non|com|bat|ant** (non′kəm bat′ənt, non kom′bətənt), *n., adj.* —*n.* **1** a person in the armed forces who takes no part in combat. Surgeons, nurses, and chaplains are noncombatants even though with the army. **2** a person having civilian status in wartime.
—*adj.* not fighting; having civilian status in wartime: *noncombatant personnel.*

**non|com|mis|sioned** (non′kə mish′ənd), *adj.* without a commission; not put in commission: *a noncommissioned ship.*

**noncommissioned officer**, an officer in the armed forces who does not hold a commission or a warrant, especially an enlisted man with the rank of corporal, sergeant, petty officer, or airman first class.

**non|com|mit|ment** (non′kə mit′mənt), *n.* the state of being free of political alliance or other obligations or agreements: *Our politics are debilitated by the virus of cagey noncommitment* (Atlantic).

**non|com|mit|tal** (non′kə mit′əl), *adj.* not committing oneself; not saying yes or no: *"I will think it over" is a noncommittal answer.* —**non′com|mit′tal|ly**, *adv.*

**non|com|mit|ted** (non′kə mit′id), *adj.* not pledged to a particular political position; nonaligned.

**non|com|pli|ance** (non′kəm plī′əns), *n., adj.* —*n.* the fact of not complying; failure to comply: *They could not be punished for noncompliance with a court order* (New York Times).
—*adj. U.S.* grown in opposition to government acreage restrictions: *The Agriculture Department's announcement on price supports for noncompliance corn drew sharp protest* (Wall Street Journal).

**non|com|pli|ant** (non′kəm plī′ənt), *n.* a person who fails or refuses to comply.

**non com|pos men|tis** (non′ kom′pəs men′tis), *Latin.* mentally unable to manage one's affairs; not of sound mind: *My poor sister drank too much ... and most of the time she was non compos mentis* (New Yorker).

**non|con|duct|ing** (non′kən duk′ting), *adj.* not conducting; that is a nonconductor. Asbestos is a nonconducting material used in heat insulation.

**non|con|duc|tor** (non′kən duk′tər), *n.* a substance that does not readily conduct heat, electricity, or sound. Rubber is a nonconductor of electricity.

**non|con|form|ance** (non′kən fôr′məns), *n.* the fact of not conforming; failure to conform. **SYN**: nonconformity.

**non|con|form|er** (non′kən fôr′mər), *n.* = nonconformist.

**non|con|form|ism** or **Non|con|form|ism** (non′kən fôr′miz əm), *n.* the beliefs or practices of nonconformists or Nonconformists.

**non|con|form|ist** (non′kən fôr′mist), *n., adj.* —*n.* **1** a person who refuses to conform to the established conventions of the social group to which he belongs: *Whoso would be a man, must be a nonconformist* (Emerson). **SYN**: dissenter. **2** a person who refuses to conform to an established church.
—*adj.* **1** not conforming; failing or refusing to conform: *a nonconformist group.* **2** of or having to do with nonconformists: *nonconformist practices or beliefs.*

**Non|con|form|ist** (non′kən fôr′mist), *n.* a Protestant who is not a member of the Church of England.

**non|con|form|i|ty** (non′kən fôr′mə tē), *n., pl.* **-ties**. **1** lack of conformity; failure or refusal to conform. **2** failure or refusal to conform to an established church. **3** *Geology.* a break between rock strata in which the earlier rock formation is deformed and eroded before being overlaid with new strata.

**Non|con|form|i|ty** (non′kən fôr′mə tē), *n.* **1** the principles or practices of English Protestants who do not belong to the Church of England. **2** Nonconformists as a group.

**non|co|op|er|a|tion** (non′kō op′ə rā′shən), *n.* **1** failure or refusal to cooperate. **2** refusal to cooperate with a government for political reasons or as a political weapon. Civil disobedience as originally practiced by Mahatma Gandhi and his followers in India is a form of noncooperation.

**non|co|op|er|a|tion|ist** (non′kō op′ə rā′shə nist), *n.* an advocate of noncooperation.

**non|co|op|er|a|tive** (non′kō op′ə rā′tiv, -op′rə-), *adj.* **1** not cooperating. **2** of or having to do with noncooperation.

**non|co|op|er|a|tor** (non′kō op′ə rā′tər), *n.* **1** a person who refuses to cooperate. **2** an advocate of noncooperation.

**non|dair|y** (non′dãr′ē), *adj.* not made with milk, cream, butter, or cheese: *nondairy foods, nondairy ice cream, nondairy imitation milk.*

**non|de|grad|a|ble** (non′di grā′də bəl), *adj.* that does not decompose: *For centuries man's nondegradable waste materials have generally been hauled, along with the degradable wastes, for disposal in open gulleys or abandoned pits* (Richard B. Engdahl).

**non|de|liv|er|y** (non′di liv′ər ē, -liv′rē), *n., pl.* **-er|ies**. failure to deliver.

**non|de|script** (non′də skript), *adj., n.* —*adj.* not easily described; not of any one particular kind: *She has nondescript eyes, neither brown, blue, nor gray. A multitude of nondescript articles, indispensable on the prairies* (Francis Parkman). **SYN**: amorphous.
—*n.* a nondescript person or thing: *one of those originals and nondescripts, more frequent in German Universities than elsewhere* (Thomas Carlyle).
[earlier, not yet described (said of a species) < *non-* + Latin *dēscrīptus,* past participle of *dēscrībere* describe]

**non|de|struc|tive** (non′di struk′tiv), *adj.* not destructive or damaging; harmless. —**non′de|struc′tive|ly**, *adv.* —**non′de|struc′tive|ness**, *n.*

**non|di|rec|tion|al** (non′də rek′shə nəl, -dī-), *adj.* detecting sounds from any direction; omnidirectional: *a nondirectional microphone.*

**non|di|rec|tive** (non′də rek′tiv), *adj.* **1** not directive. **2** that does not attempt to guide or direct a patient, client, or informant toward any particular attitude or course of action: *Nondirective therapy is one of the nonpsychoanalytic schools of psychotherapy* (John L. Herma).

**non|dis|junc|tion** (non′dis jungk′shən), *n.* the failure of a pair of chromosomes to separate and go to different cells when the cell divides.

**non|dis|tinc|tive** (non′dis tingk′tiv), *adj.* **1** that fails to be or make distinctive. **2** *Phonetics.* that does not distinguish meanings; not phonemic: *Each phonetic symbol represents a distinctive English sound, though each may have several perceptible nondistinctive varieties* (John Kenyon).

**non|dol|lar** (non dol′ər), *adj.* of or having a currency unit other than the dollar.

**non|dom|i|nant** (non dom′ə nənt), *adj.* (of chords, especially seventh chords) standing on any step of the scale except the dominant.

**non|drink|er** (non dring′kər), *n.* a person who does not drink alcoholic liquor.

**non|dur|a|ble** (non dür′ə bəl, -dyür′-), *adj., n.*
—***adj.*** that will not last long; that can be used up or worn out quickly; perishable: *Tomatoes are nondurable.*
—***n.*** something that is nondurable: *Nondurables include foodstuffs, wearing apparel, and textiles generally* (New York Times).

**none**[1] (nun), *pron., adv., adj.* —***pron.*** **1** not any: *We have none of that paper left. That matter is none of our business.* **2** no one; not one: *None of these is a special case.* **3** no persons or things: *None have arrived. None come to the solemn feasts* (Lamentations 1:4). *I hear a voice, but none are there* (Tennyson). **4** no part; nothing: *The teacher said she would have none of our nonsense. He had none of the appearance of a man who sailed before the mast* (Robert Louis Stevenson).
—***adv.*** not at all; to no extent; in no way: *Our supply is none too great. Oh, our world is none the safer Now Great-Heart hath died!* (Rudyard Kipling).
—***adj.*** *Archaic.* not any; no: *I have none other disease, than a swelling in my leg* (Jonathan Swift).
**none the less.** See under **less**.
[Old English *nān* < *ne* not + *ān* one]
▶ **none, no one.** *None* is a single word, but *no one* is often used instead of *none* for emphasis. *None* may be either singular or plural, but *no one* is always singular: *As only ten jurors have been chosen so far, none of the witnesses were called* (or *was called*). *She tried on ten hats, but none of them were attractive. I read three books on the subject, no one of which was helpful.*

**none**[2] or **None** (nōn), *n.* singular of **nones**[2].

**non|ef|fec|tive** (non′i fek′tiv), *adj., n.* —***adj.*** not fit for duty or active service, as a soldier or sailor.
—***n.*** such a soldier or sailor.

**non|e|lec|tro|lyte** (non′i lek′trə līt), *n.* a substance which in water solution does not release ions and will therefore not conduct an electric current. Sugar is a nonelectrolyte; table salt is an electrolyte.

**non|en|ti|ty** (non en′tə tē), *n., pl.* **-ties. 1** a person or thing of little or no importance: *He was an atom, a nonentity, a very worm, and no man* (Edward G. Bulwer-Lytton). **2** something that does not exist, or that exists only in the imagination: *Mermaids do not exist: why speak of them as if they did? How can you find interest in speaking of a nonentity?* (Charlotte Brontë). **3** = nonexistence.

**nones**[1] (nōnz), *n.pl.* the ninth day before the ides in the ancient Roman calendar, counting both days, thus being the 7th of March, May, July, and October, and the 5th of the other months. [< Latin *nōnae,* (originally) feminine plural of *nōnus* ninth]

**nones**[2] or **Nones** (nōnz), *n.pl.* **1** the fifth of the seven canonical hours. **2** the service or services for this hour, following sext, originally fixed for the ninth hour after sunrise (about 3 P.M.) but generally recited earlier: *From noon till nones The brethren sate; and when the quire was done Renew'd their converse till the vesper bell* (Robert Southey). [Old English *nōn,* ninth hour < Latin *nōna* (*hōra*) ninth (hour) of daylight in Roman reckoning. See etym. of doublet **noon.**]

**non|es|sen|tial** (non′ə sen′shəl), *adj., n.* —***adj.*** not essential; not necessary: *Nonessential color is the result of an impurity in the mineral* (Frederick H. Pough). **SYN:** unnecessary.
—***n.*** a person or thing not essential.

**non est** (non est′), *Latin.* it is not; not there; absent.

**none|such** (nun′such′), *n.* **1** a person or thing without equal or parallel; paragon: *The uncanny ability of Fiorello La Guardia to get out the vote—on his side—made him a nonesuch in New York politics* (Atlantic). **SYN:** nonpareil. **2** *Botany.* the black medic. Also, **nonsuch.**

**no|net** (nō net′), *n.* **1** *Music.* a composition written for nine instruments or nine voices: *The small-group sides are the best, with the nonet in particular coming through as a sparkling unit* (Saturday Review). **2** a group of nine nuclear or subatomic particles. [< Italian *nonetto* < *nono* ninth]

**none|the|less** (nun′ᴛʜə les′), *adv.* none the less; nevertheless: *Everett, younger than any of these individuals, and correspondingly less of an individualist, was nonetheless a true member of the great generation* (Louis Auchincloss).

**non|eth|nic** (non eth′nik), *adj.* not belonging to a particular ethnic group.

**non-Eu|clid|e|an** (non′yü klid′ē ən), *adj.* of, based upon, or in accordance with certain postulates that differ from those of Euclid's geometry, such as the Euclidean postulate that through a given point not on a straight line, only one straight line may be drawn that is parallel to the given line: *Non-Euclidean geometry contributed much to the theory of relativity* (Howard W. Eves).

**non|e|vent** (non′i vent′), *n.* an event highly publicized as forthcoming but actually never taking place: *This nonevent was the great Red scare that was so confidently predicted in Europe* (Manchester Guardian).

**non|ex|ist|ence** (non′ig zis′təns), *n.* **1** the condition of not existing. **2** a thing that has no existence.

**non|ex|ist|ent** (non′ig zis′tənt), *adj.* having no existence.

**non|fea|sance** (non fē′zəns), *n. Law.* the failure to perform some act which ought to have been performed. [< *non-* + Anglo-French *fesance* < French *faire* do]

**non|fer|rous** (non fer′əs), *adj.* of or denoting metal that is not or contains no iron: *nonferrous metals.*

**non|fic|tion** (non fik′shən), *n.* writing that is not fiction; form of writing that deals with real people and events rather than imaginary ones. Biographies and histories are nonfiction.

**non|fic|tion|al** (non fik′shə nəl), *adj.* not fictional.

**nonfiction novel,** a factual account written in the form of a novel.

**non|fig|u|ra|tive** (non fig′yər ə tiv), *adj.* **1** (in art) using unrecognizable figures or symbols; not objective: *The recent emphasis on extreme abstraction—the nonobjective or nonfigurative art which has proved so controversial in the last few years* (New York Times). **2** not figurative, as of the usage of a word.

**non|fil|tered** (non fil′tərd), *adj.* having no filter: *nonfiltered cigarettes.*

**non|fis|sion|a|ble** (non fish′ə nə bəl), *adj.* not capable of nuclear fission.

**non|flam** (non flam′), *adj.* = nonflammable.

**non|flam|ma|ble** (non flam′ə bəl), *adj.* that will not catch fire.

**non|fly|ing** (non flī′ing), *adj.* that does not fly or is not capable of flying: *Before an airplane is built, a nonflying, full-scale model is made.*

**non|for|mal fallacy** (non fôr′məl), *Logic.* a type of fallacy that rests on false comparisons, wrong observations, and ambiguous terms.

**non|ful|fill|ment** (non′fu̇l fil′mənt), *n.* failure to fulfill; failure to be fulfilled.

**non|grad|ed** (non grā′did), *adj.* **1** without a proficiency rating: *Widdows, as the second highest nongraded driver, gains six points* (London Times). **2** *U.S. Education.* not divided into grades: *Nongraded classes, for example, permit a precocious five-year-old to take some classes with six-, seven-, and eight-year-olds, and the rest with youngsters his own age* (Saturday Review).

**non gra|ta** (non grā′tə, grä′-), *Latin.* not welcome: *He was accused of conspiring ... declared non grata and thrown out of the country* (Time).

**non|har|dy** (non här′dē), *adj.* that is not able to withstand the cold of winter in the open air; requiring a mild climate: *nonhardy alfalfa.*

**non|har|mon|ic** (non′här mon′ik), *adj.* not harmonic; without harmony: *When, as in the case of a drum or a bell,* [*overtones*] *are not integral multiples of the fundamental they are called nonharmonic* (Shortley and Williams).

**non|he|ro** (non′hir′ō), *n., pl.* **-roes.** = antihero.

**no|nil|lion** (nō nil′yən), *n., adj.* **1** (in the U.S., Canada, and France) an octillion multiplied by 1,000, equal to 1 followed by 30 zeros. **2** (in Great Britain and Germany) a million to the ninth power, equal to 1 followed by 54 zeros. [< Latin *nōnus* ninth (power) + French *million* million]

**no|nil|lionth** (nō nil′yənth), *adj., n.* **1** last in a series of a nonillion. **2** one of a nonillion equal parts.

**non|im|mi|grant** (non im′ə grənt), *n.* **1** a foreigner entering a country for a temporary stay only. **2** an alien reentering the country in which he lives after a short stay abroad.

**non|in|duc|tive** (non′in duk′tiv), *adj.* (of an electrical resistance) not inductive.

**non|in|flam|ma|ble** (non′in flam′ə bəl), *adj.* = nonflammable.

**non|in|for|ma|tion** (non′in fər mā′shən), *n.* knowledge or news that does not relate to a particular question, discussion, or other problem at hand.

**non|in|stall|ment** (non′in stôl′mənt), *adj.* payable all at once rather than in installments: *a noninstallment debt.*

**non|in|ter|ven|tion** (non′in tər ven′shən), *n.* **1** failure or refusal to intervene. **2** the systematic avoidance of any interference by a nation in the affairs of other nations or of its own states, provinces, or the like: *Nonintervention with "Popular Sovereignty" was the original and established Democratic doctrine with regard to Slavery in the Territories* (Horace Greeley). **SYN:** neutrality.

**non|in|ter|ven|tion|ist** (non′in tər ven′shə nist), *n., adj.* —***n.*** a person who favors or advocates nonintervention: *The Greek ecclesiastics are noninterventionists* (Saturday Review).
—***adj.*** that favors or advocates nonintervention: *The government's conservative opposition ... criticized Mexico's noninterventionist stand on Cuba* (Robert J. Shafer).

**non|i|on|ic** (non′ī on′ik), *adj.* that does not ionize in solution: *Nonionic substances combine with water because they remove internal pressure and thereby permit formation of a crystalline compound* (A. N. Buswell and W. H. Rodebush).

**non|i|ron** (non ī′ərn), *adj. Especially British.* no-iron.

**non|join|der** (non join′dər), *n. Law.* the failure of a person bringing a suit to include in it a party, person, or cause of action necessary to its determination.

**non|ju|ring** (non jür′ing), *adj.* refusing to take a required oath; being a nonjuror.

**non|ju|ror** (non jür′ər), *n.* a person who refuses to take a required oath.

**Non|ju|ror** (non jür′ər), *n.* **1** one of the clergymen of the Church of England who in 1689 refused to swear allegiance to William and Mary and who were deprived of their benefices. **2** a member of a separate communion founded by these clergymen. It survived until about 1800.

**non|ju|ry** (non jür′ē), *adj.* **1** held without a jury: *a nonjury trial, nonjury civil cases.* **2** imposed without a jury trial: *a nonjury sentence.*

**non|lead** (non led′), *adj.* = nonleaded.

**non|lead|ed** (non led′id), *adj.* containing no tetraethyl lead (an antiknock additive which is a contributor to air pollution); unleaded; lead-free: *nonleaded gasoline.*

**non|life** (non′līf), *n., adj.* —***n.*** absence or negation of life: *In the evolution from nonlife to life, atoms group themselves to form new combinations* (Science News Letter).
—***adj.*** of or having to do with insurance other than life insurance: *One bright feature of the companies' overseas activities—and some two-thirds of their nonlife business is conducted abroad—has been the low level of hurricane losses in the United States* (Economist).

**non|lin|e|ar** (non lin′ē ər), *adj.* **1** not linear: **a** not containing or contained in a line: *a nonlinear set of points.* **b** not proportional: *The ear is a very nonlinear instrument* (New Scientist). **2** *Electronics.* having an output not proportional to the input: *nonlinear electric circuits.*

**non|lin|e|ar|i|ty** (non′lin ē ar′ə tē), *n.* the condition of being nonlinear.

**non|lin|guis|tic** (non′ling gwis′tik), *adj.* **1** not consisting of or expressed in language: *Nonlinguistic communication has impact at least as profound as the spoken and printed word* (Saturday Review). **2** not having to do with linguistics.

**non|liq|uid** (non lik′wid), *adj.* **1a** without fluids: *a nonliquid diet.* **b** not in liquid form. **2** lacking liquidity: *nonliquid securities.*

**non|lit|er|ate** (non lit′ər it), *adj.* **1a** not able to read or write. **b** having no alphabet or other form of writing: *nonliterate peoples.* **2** having no knowledge of literature: *a nonliterate culture.*

**non|liv|ing** (non liv′ing), *adj.* not living: *Many of the common materials of the earth's crust may alternate between the living and the nonliving states* (Fred W. Emerson).

**non|mag|net|ic** (non′mag net′ik), *adj.* not having the properties of a magnet; that cannot be magnetized or attracted by a magnet.

**non|mas|ter** (non mas′tər, -mäs′-), *n.* a person who is not a master in contract bridge tournament play.

**non|ma|te|ri|al** (non′mə tir′ē əl), *adj.* having no material properties; not substantial: *The majority of people really long to experience that moment of pure, disinterested, nonmaterial satisfaction which causes them to ejaculate the word "beautiful"* (Kenneth Clark).

**non|med|i|cal** (non med′ə kəl), *adj.* having noth-

---

**Pronunciation Key:** hat, āge, cãre, fär; let, ēqual, tėrm; it, īce; hot, ōpen, ôrder; **oi**l, **ou**t; cup, pu̇t, rüle; **ch**ild; lo**ng**; **th**in; ᴛʜen; **zh**, measure; **ə** represents **a** in about, **e** in taken, **i** in pencil, **o** in lemon, **u** in circus.

ing to do with medicine, medical practice, or study.

**non|mem|ber** (non mem′bər), *n.* a person or thing that is not a member; one that does not belong.

**non|met|al** (non′met′əl), *n.* a chemical element, such as carbon or nitrogen, lacking the physical properties of a metal; nonmetallic element. A nonmetal forms acidic oxides and is electronegative in solution. ... *the halogen family—the family that begins with fluorine, the supreme example of a nonmetal* (J. Crowther).

**non|me|tal|lic** (non′mə tal′ik), *adj., n.* —***adj.*** not like a metal. Carbon, oxygen, sulfur, and nitrogen are nonmetallic chemical elements.
—***n.*** a nonmetallic substance: *In addition to its leading position in diamonds and lithium minerals, Africa produced important quantities of other nonmetallics* (Berenice B. Mitchell).

**non|mor|al** (non môr′əl, -mor′-), *adj.* having no relation to morality; neither moral nor immoral.

**non|ne|go|tia|ble** (non′ni gō′shə bəl, -shē ə-), *adj., n.* —***adj.*** that cannot be negotiated; not negotiable; unqualified; absolute: *a flat and nonnegotiable veto, nonnegotiable terms.*
—***n.*** a nonnegotiable point or item.

**non|ni|trog|e|nous** (non′nī troj′ə nəs), *adj.* not containing nitrogen.

**non|nu|cle|ar** (non nü′klē ər, -nyü′-), *adj., n.*
—***adj.*** not nuclear; not having to do with nuclear weapons or their use: *a nonnuclear power.*
—***n.*** a nonnuclear power; nation with an arsenal of only conventional weapons.

**no-no** (nō′nō′), *n., pl.* **-nos.** *U.S. Slang.* something one must not do, say, or use; something forbidden: *Some people ... have had a lifelong problem keeping their weight down. With some of these individuals, desserts are all-time "no-nos"* (Nancy Goldstein).

**✱non|ob|jec|tive** (non′əb jek′tiv), *adj.* **1a** not portraying or resembling natural objects, persons, or events. **b** of or having to do with a type of abstract art created from the interplay of forms, colors, and lines, without reference to other elements of the artist's experience: *The first ascertainable nonobjective painting was done by Kandinsky in about 1909* (New York Times). **2** lacking objectivity.

**✱nonobjective**
definition 1b

*Black and White* by Franz Kline
The Cleveland Museum of Art

**non|ob|jec|tiv|ism** (non′əb jek′tə viz əm), *n.* **1** nonobjective art: ... *the wide variety of American styles, from realism to nonobjectivism* (Newsweek). **2** = nonobjectivity (def. 2).

**non|ob|jec|tiv|ist** (non′əb jek′tə vist), *n.* an artist whose work follows the principles of nonobjectivism.

**non|ob|jec|tiv|i|ty** (non′ob jek tiv′ə tē), *n.* **1** a lack of objectivity: *His views were probably biased; he was, so to speak, objective about his nonobjectivity* (New Yorker). **2** the principles or practices of the nonobjective school of art.

**non|ob|serv|ance** (non′əb zėr′vəns), *n.* the act or fact of not observing laws or customs.

**no-non|sense** (nō′non′sens), *adj.* down-to-earth; practical; matter-of-fact: *It wasn't long before a stranger, a stout, no-nonsense type, suggested we find another vantage point* (New Yorker).

**non|op|er|at|ing** (non op′ə rā′ting), *adj.* of or having to do with railroad workers not directly concerned with the operation of trains, such as ticket agents or dispatchers: *a nonoperating union.*

**non|own|er** (non ō′nər), *n.* a person or group that is not an owner.

**non|pa|reil** (non′pə rel′), *adj., n.* —***adj.*** having no equal; peerless: *The literary salons have had a major part in making Paris the city nonpareil, for centuries the undisputed cultural centre of the world* (Canadian Forum).
—***n.*** **1** a person or thing having no equal: *Though you were crown'd The nonpareil of beauty* (Shakespeare). **2** a beautifully colored finch of the southern United States; painted bunting. **3** a kind of apple. **4** *Printing.* **a** a size of type; 6-point. **b** a slug 6 points high used between lines. **5** a small chocolate drop covered with tiny white pellets of sugar.
[< Middle French *nonpareil* < *non-* not (< Latin) + *pareil* equal < Vulgar Latin *pāriculus* (diminutive) < Latin *pār, paris* equal]

**non|par|tic|i|pat|ing** (non′pər tis′ə pā′ting), *adj.* **1** not participating: *The United States was a nonparticipating country in the League of Nations.* **2** *Insurance.* that does not give its owner the right to share in profits or surplus: *a nonparticipating policy.*

**non|par|ti|san** or **non|par|ti|zan** (non pär′tə zən), *adj., n.* —***adj.*** **1** not partisan: *a nonpartisan committee.* **SYN**: impartial. **2** not supporting, or controlled by, any of the regular political parties: *a nonpartisan voter.* **SYN**: independent.
—***n.*** a nonpartisan person: *Five of the fifteen candidates at-large would ... be nonpartisans* (New York Times).

**non|par|ti|san|ship** or **non|par|ti|zan|ship** (non pär′tə zən ship), *n.* nonpartisan quality or condition; impartiality.

**non|pay|ment** (non pā′mənt), *n.* failure to pay or the condition of not being paid: *The family had been evicted for nonpayment of rent* (New York Times). **SYN**: default.

**non|per|form|ance** (non′pər fôr′məns), *n.* the fact of not performing; failure to perform.

**non|per|son** (non′pėr′sən), *n.* **1** a nonexistent person: *An unborn child is regarded as a legal person in some areas of the law, and as a nonperson in others* (Maclean's). **2** a political nonentity; unperson.

**non pla|cet** (non plā′set), *Latin.* **1** a vote in the negative; veto. **2** (literally) it does not please.

**non|plus** (non plus′, non′plus), *v.,* **-plused, -plus|ing** or (*especially British*) **-plussed, -plus|sing,** *n.*
—***v.t.*** to puzzle completely; make unable to say or do anything: *We were nonplused to see two roads leading off to the left where we had expected only one. Right or wrong, he ne'er was nonplus't* (Samuel Butler). **SYN**: perplex, confound, confuse, mystify, embarrass.
—***n.*** a state of being nonplused: *Prophets are never at a nonplus, and never surprised by a question* (Augustus Jessopp). **SYN**: quandary, confusion, embarrassment.
[< Latin *nōn plūs* no more, no further]

**non|pol|lut|ing** (non′pə lü′ting), *adj.* that does not cause air or water pollution: *a nonpolluting gasoline.*

**non pos|su|mus** (non pos′yů məs), *Latin.* **1** a plea of being unable to consider, or act in, a matter. **2** (literally) we cannot.

**non|prin|ci|pled** (non prin′sə pəld), *adj.* rejecting moral principles; nonmoral.

**non|pro|duc|tive** (non′prə duk′tiv), *adj.* **1** not productive: *In early New England, laws were made to prohibit smoking because it was a nonproductive pastime* (Roy Flannagan). **2** not directly connected with production: *nonproductive charges or expenses. Clerks and supervisors are nonproductive workers.* —**non′pro|duc′tive|ness,** *n.*

**non|prof|it** (non prof′it), *adj.* not for profit; without profit: *The Salvation Army is a nonprofit organization.*

**non|pro|lif|er|a|tion** (non′prō lif′ə rā′shən), *n., adj.* —***n.*** the regulation of the spread of nuclear weapons among nations, especially by means of an agreement: *The Soviet Union would like the solution of nonproliferation to add dimensions and a sense of realism to the problems of outlawing nuclear weapons* (New York Times).
—***adj.*** of nonproliferation: *a nonproliferation treaty.*

**non|pros** (non′pros′), *v.t.,* **-prossed, -pros|sing.** *Law.* to enter a judgment of non prosequitur against (a plaintiff). [earlier, noun, abbreviation of *nōn prōsequitur*]

**non pros.,** non prosequitur.

**non pro|se|qui|tur** (non prō sek′wə tər), *Law.* a judgment entered against the plaintiff in a suit when he does not appear to prosecute it. [< Latin *nōn prōsequitur* he does not pursue (the suit)]

**non|pro|tein** (non prō′tēn, -tē in), *n., adj.* —***n.*** a substance that is not a protein or does not contain protein.
—***adj.*** having no protein or proteins: *a nonprotein molecule, a nonprotein diet.*

**non|quo|ta immigrant** (non kwō′tə), an immigrant whose national or other group is not subject to a quota set by immigration law: *Nonquota immigrants are not restricted numerically, although they must meet all other standards of health, morals, literacy, and economics established for all immigrants* (Joseph M. Strong).

**non|read|er** (non′rē′dər), *n.* **1** a child who cannot read: *Many boys are poor readers or nonreaders* (Maclean's). **2** a person who reads little: *The number of nonreaders will diminish if and when he can find more salesmen ... to sell books from door to door* (Time).

**non|re|cov|er|a|ble** (non′ri kuv′ər ə bəl, -kuv′rə), *adj.* **1** from which a person cannot recover: *A large part of the radiation injury is recovered from in time, but ... there is also a nonrecoverable fraction* (Bulletin of Atomic Scientists). **2** that cannot be recovered: *This will ... involve high expenses and nonrecoverable outlays* (Wall Street Journal).

**non|rep|re|sen|ta|tion|al** (non′rep ri zen tā′shə nəl), *adj.* not representing or resembling natural objects; nonobjective: *nonrepresentational art.*

**non|rep|re|sen|ta|tion|al|ism** (non′rep ri zen tā′shə nə liz′əm), *n.* nonrepresentational art; nonobjectivism.

**non|res|i|dence** (non rez′ə dəns), *n.* the state of being nonresident.

**non|res|i|den|cy** (non rez′ə dən sē), *n.* = nonresidence.

**non|res|i|dent** (non rez′ə dənt), *adj., n.* —***adj.*** **1** not living in a particular place; living elsewhere: *a nonresident voter.* **2** not living where official duties require one to live.
—***n.*** a nonresident person.

**non|re|sist|ance** (non′ri zis′təns), *n.* the fact or condition of not resisting; lack of resistance; passive obedience or submission to authority or force.

**non|re|sist|ant** (non′ri zis′tənt), *adj., n.* —***adj.*** not resisting; passively obedient or submissive to authority or force.
—***n.*** a person who does not resist authority or force; person who maintains that violence should never be resisted by force.

**non|re|straint** (non′ri strānt′), *n.* **1** absence of restraint. **2** the controlling of psychotic persons without strait jackets or other use of force, as by tranquilizing drugs or other placid means.

**non|re|stric|tive** (non′ri strik′tiv), *adj.* **1** *Grammar.* adding descriptive detail that is not an essential part of the sentence. Modifiers which do not limit the meaning of a noun but add a descriptive detail are nonrestrictive modifiers. **2** not restricting or limiting: *nonrestrictive legislation.*

**nonrestrictive clause,** *Grammar.* any clause which adds descriptive detail but is not an essential part of the sentence in which it appears. *Examples:* My bicycle, *which had a flat tire,* was stolen today. The President, *who just entered the room,* was smiling. (Contrast the same clause used in a restrictive sense: The man *who just entered the room* is the President.)

**non|rig|id** (non rij′id), *adj.* **1** not rigid. **2** having no supporting internal structure; given shape solely through inflation with a gas: *The initial flight of a new and larger class of nonrigid airships for airborne early warning "picket patrol" was made here* (Wall Street Journal).

**non sans droit** (non sanz droit′), not without right (an Old French motto on Shakespeare's coat of arms).

**non|sched|uled** (non skej′ůld), *adj.* **1** not operating or proceeding according to a regular schedule: *a nonscheduled flight.* **2** not according to a program or plan: *The train made a nonscheduled stop.*

**non|sci|en|tist** (non sī′ən tist), *n.* a person who is not trained in science: *Nonscientists have trouble understanding the scientific method and attitude* (Science News Letter).

**non|sec|tar|i|an** (non′sek târ′ē ən), *adj.* not connected with any religious denomination: *a nonsectarian college or hospital.*

**non-self-gov|ern|ing** (non self′guv′ər ning), *adj.* not having self-government; not autonomous: *non-self-governing territories.*

**non|sense** (non′sens), *n., adj.* —***n.*** **1** words, ideas, or acts without meaning; foolish talk or doings; a plan or suggestion that is foolish: *Father said "Nonsense!" and stalked out of the room when he heard my sister's foolish excuse. You are talking the greatest nonsense; and you know it* (George Bernard Shaw). **SYN**: foolishness, absurdity, humbug. **2** worthless stuff; junk: *a kitchen drawer full of useless gadgets and other nonsense.*
—***adj.*** **1** having no sense or meaning; senseless; nonsensical: *a nonsense word or phrase, nonsense stories.* **2** *Genetics.* **a** that does not specify a particular amino acid in the genetic code: *nonsense codons, nonsense triplets.* **b** that results from the presence of nonsense sequences in the genetic code: *a nonsense mutation, a nonsense protein.*
**take the nonsense out of,** to make (a person) behave or think rightly: *The instructor soon took the nonsense out of the students.*
[probably < *non-* + *sense.* Compare Old French *nonsens,* Latin *nonsensus.*]

**nonsense syllable,** a syllable formed by putting a vowel between any two consonants, used in various psychological and educational experiments, tests, and reading exercises: *Nonsense syllables, such as "fam" and "sil," are syllables in many longer words, such as "family" and "silly."*

**nonsense verse** or **poetry,** a type of humorous

verse or poetry, usually for children, dealing with illogical and silly characters and situations, and often including meaningless words and phrases coined for the occasion: *Two English authors of the 1800's, Lewis Carroll and Edward Lear, were masters of nonsense verse* (Zena Sutherland).

**non|sen|si|cal** (non sen′sə kəl), *adj.* foolish or absurd; ridiculous: *a nonsensical person.* **SYN:** senseless, silly, preposterous. —**non|sen′si|cal|ly,** *adv.* —**non|sen′si|cal|ness,** *n.*

**non seq.,** non sequitur.

**non se|qui|tur** (non sek′wə tər), **1** an inference or conclusion that does not follow from the premise: *"How does theatre and cooking mix?" the pamphlet inquired, mixing its syntax and laying the groundwork for a solid non sequitur* (New Yorker). **2** a remark that has no bearing on what the speaker is talking about or has just said: *It is ridiculous ... to mutilate the libretto so that the dialogue ... becomes a running non sequitur* (Harper's). [< Latin *non sequitur* it does not follow]

**non|sex|u|al** (non sek′shu̇ əl), *adj.* **1** having no sex; sexless; asexual. **2** done by or characteristic of sexless animals: *the nonsexual conjugation of protozoans.*

**non|sked** (non′sked′), *n. U.S. Informal.* a nonscheduled airline or aircraft.

**non|skid** (non′skid′), *adj.* made so as to prevent or reduce skidding: *nonskid tires, nonskid floor wax.*

**non|skid|ding** (non skid′ing), *adj.* = nonskid.

**non|slip** (non′slip′), *adj.* made so as to prevent or reduce slipping: *nonslip flooring, nonslip rope.*

**non|sport|ing** (non′spôr′ting, -spōr′-), *adj.* **1** not interested in or engaged in sports: *nonsporting circles.* **2** not used or suitable for hunting, especially in the manner of sporting dogs: *The Boston terrier is the only nonsporting breed developed in the United States* (Josephine Z. Rine).

**non|stand|ard** (non stan′dərd), *adj.* **1** not conforming, as to existing regulations or accepted specifications: *In the case of nonstandard items, the Government from now on will call for disclosure of proprietary information* (Wall Street Journal). **2** (of pronunciation, grammar, and vocabulary) not in the generally accepted pattern; not standard: *The social status of many nonstandard [language habits] is often different in different sections* (Harold B. Allen).

**nonstandard analysis,** the mathematical study of infinitely large and infinitely small numbers: *Nonstandard analysis, a revolutionary new approach to classical calculus, is deeply rooted in mathematical logic, the study of the reasoning process of mathematics itself* (Lynn A. Steen).

**non|ster|ling** (non stėr′ling), *adj.* of or having to do with countries outside the sterling area.

**non|stick** (non′stik′), *adj.* made to prevent sticking of unwanted material: *nonstick frying pans.*

**non|stop** (non′stop′), *adj., adv., n.* —*adj.* that travels between two places without stopping, or without scheduled stops for passengers: *We took a nonstop flight from New York to Rome.*
—*adv.* without stopping: *That plane flies nonstop from Los Angeles to Paris.*
—*n.* a nonstop airplane or flight.

**non|stri|at|ed** (non strī′ā tid), *adj.* not striped; smooth: *Nonstriated or smooth muscle consists of delicate spindle-shape cells* (Tracy I. Storer).

**non|such** (nun′such′), *n.* = nonesuch.

**non|sug|ar** (non shu̇g′ər), *n.* a substance that is not a sugar or does not contain sugar.

**non|suit** (non′süt′), *n., v.* —*n. Law.* a judgment terminating a lawsuit when the plaintiff neglects to prosecute, fails to show a legal case, or fails to bring sufficient evidence.
—*v.t.* to stop (a plaintiff) by a nonsuit.
[Middle English *noun suyt* < Anglo-French *noun sute* < *noun* non- + *sute* suit]

**non|sup|port** (non′sə pôrt′, -pōrt′), *n.* **1** lack of support. **2** *Law.* failure to provide for someone for whom one is legally responsible.

**non|tar|get** (non′tär′git), *adj.* **1** not intended as the subject of an experiment or of research: *a nontarget object or specimen.* **2** not intended for destruction: *Aldrin, dieldrin, endrin, and heptachlor are extremely toxic ... and have the capacity to inflict harm upon nontarget species* (Robert W. Risebrough).

**non|tel|e|vised** (non tel′ə vīzd), *adj.* **1** not shown on television: *a nontelevised boxing match.* **2** not exposed to television broadcasts: *Children exposed to this type of entertainment were 35 per cent less healthy than nontelevised children* (Birmingham News).

**non|tox|ic** (non tok′sik), *adj.* not toxic or poisonous: *Most paint used on children's toys is now required to be nontoxic.*

**non|tra|di|tion|al** (non′trə dish′ə nəl), not traditional or customary: *Charlotte Negroes have now begun to break into "nontraditional" jobs as store clerks, secretaries, bank tellers* (Harper's).

**non trop|po** (nōn trôp′pō), *Music.* not too much; moderately (as part of a direction). [< Italian *non troppo*]

**no|nu** (nō′nü), *n.* a tree of the madder family found in the East Indies and other Pacific islands, having a composite fruit full of seeds and a bark from which a dye is made. [< Samoan *nonu*]

**non-U** (non′yü′), *adj., n. Especially British Informal.* —*adj.* that is not generally acceptable in British upper class society; tending to be common or informal: *Such non-U usages as "met up with," "take in a show," "go steady," and "formal" used as a noun* (New Yorker).
—*n.* a person or thing that is non-U.
[< *non-u*(pper class)]

**non|un|ion** (non yün′yən), *adj., n.* —*adj.* **1** not belonging to a labor union: *a nonunion worker.* **2** not following labor-union rules: *nonunion working conditions.* **3** not recognizing or favoring labor unions: *a nonunion company.* **4** manufactured by other than union labor.
—*n.* **1** the condition of a broken bone in which the ends fail to unite. **2** failure to unite.

**non|un|ion|ism** (non yün′yə niz əm), *n.* the theories or practices of those opposed to labor unions: *Local trades councils should organize campaigns against nonunionism in their districts* (London Times).

**non|un|ion|ist** (non yün′yə nist), *n.* **1** a person who is opposed to labor unions. **2** a person who does not belong to a labor union.

**nonunion shop,** a business or industrial establishment in which the employer does not recognize and will not bargain with a labor union regarding wages, conditions of employment, or other employee or union demands.

**non|vi|o|lence** (non vī′ə ləns), *n.* **1** a political or philosophical belief based on peaceful methods to achieve any goal; opposition to any form of violence: *International nonviolence is no longer merely the fond hope of a few imaginative or saintly cranks* (Observer). **2** the absence of violence: *He believes that the world no longer has a choice between violence and nonviolence* (Manchester Guardian).

**non|vi|o|lent** (non vī′ə lənt), *adj.* not violent; opposing violence: *nonviolent protest.* —**non|vi′o|lent|ly,** *adv.*

**non|vot|er** (non vō′tər), *n.* a person who does not vote or is not eligible to vote: *It's believed that the nonvoters are more in the middle class than among the extremely poor and illiterate* (Wall Street Journal).

**non|white** (non hwīt′), *n., adj.* —*n.* **1** a person who is not a Caucasian. **2** (in South Africa) a person who is not of European origin: *Until now the Forest Town church has been the only Methodist one serving Johannesburg's nonwhites* (Cape Times).
—*adj.* **1** not Caucasian: *Moscow is representing itself as the champion of African colonial peoples ... and of the emergence of the nonwhite peoples everywhere* (Christian Science Monitor). **2** of or having to do with nonwhites: *a nonwhite association.*

**non|wo|ven** (non wō′vən), *n., adj.* —*n.* a fabric made by a method other than weaving.
—*adj.* **1** made by a method other than weaving: *a nonwoven fabric.* **2** made of a nonwoven fabric: *nonwoven raincoats.*

**non|ze|ro** (non zir′ō), *adj.* not having to do with or being equal to zero: *nonzero calculations, nonzero integers.*

**noo|dle¹** (nü′dəl), *n.* a mixture of flour and water, or flour and eggs, like macaroni, but made in flat strips. [< German *Nudel*]

**noo|dle²** (nü′dəl), *n., v.,* **-dled, -dling.** —*n.* **1** a very stupid or silly person; fool: *The fashionable left-wing stereotype of Lord Home as an effete upper-class noodle is ludicrously wide of the mark* (Spectator). **SYN:** simpleton. **2** *Slang.* the head.
—*v.i. Slang.* to play music in a casual, offhand manner: *A couple of easygoing ... dance bands noodle around in the Grill most of the evening* (New Yorker).
[origin uncertain. Compare etym. under **noddy.**]

**nook** (nu̇k), *n.* **1** a cozy little corner: *a nook facing the fire.* **SYN:** recess, niche. **2** a hidden or remote spot; sheltered place: *a shady nook. There is a wonderful nook in the woods behind our house.* **3** an interior angle formed by the meeting of two walls or partitions; corner: *The shades of twilight still hide themselves among the nooks of the adjacent buildings* (Hawthorne). **4** a corner or angular piece of land; small triangular field. **5** a piece at a corner or broken from a corner. [Middle English *noke*] —**nook′like′,** *adj.*

**nook|y** (nu̇k′ē), *adj.,* **nook|i|er, nook|i|est. 1** full of nooks. **2** = nooklike.

**noon** (nün), *n., adj., v.,* **nooned, noon|ing.** —*n.* **1** twelve o'clock in the daytime; middle of the day; midday: *Most people get hungry a few hours after breakfast and like to have some kind of meal around noon. Abbr:* m. or M. **2** *Figurative.* the highest, finest, or brightest point or part: *the noon of life. To behold the wandering moon Riding near the highest noon* (Milton). **3** the middle point of night; midnight: *at noon of night* (John Dryden).
—*adj.* of noon.
—*v.i. Dialect.* to halt for or take a noonday rest or meal: *We traveled six or seven miles farther, and 'nooned' near a brook* (Francis Parkman).
[Middle English *nōne* midday < Old English *nōn* the ninth hour < Latin *nōna* (*hōra*) ninth (hour of daylight by Roman reckoning), about 3 P.M.; the meaning shifted with a change in time of church service. See etym. of doublet **nones².**]

**noon|day** (nün′dā′), *n., adj.* = noon.

**no one,** or **no-one** (nō′wun′, -wən), *pron.* no person; nobody: *No one can leave the classroom without permission.*
▶ See **none** for usage note.

**noon|ing** (nü′ning), *n. Dialect.* **1** a rest or time for rest at noon: *She had said she would look at pictures all through the nooning [at school]* (Mark Twain). **2** a meal or snack taken at noon. **3** = noon.

**noon|tide** (nün′tīd′), *n., adj.* —*n.* **1** = noon. **2** *Figurative.* the highest, finest, or brightest point: *the noontide of your prosperity* (Charles Lamb).
—*adj.* = noon.

**noon|time** (nün′tīm′), *n., adj.* = noon.

**noose** (nüs), *n., v.,* **noosed, noos|ing.** —*n.* **1** a loop with a slip knot that tightens as the string or rope is pulled. Nooses are used especially in lassos and snares. **2** a similar loop used in execution by hanging. **3** *Figurative.* a snare or bond: *Many people today do not want to be caught in what they consider the noose of marriage.*
—*v.t.* **1** to make a noose with; tie a noose in. **2** to catch with a noose: *They run out, and with the lasso, dexterously noose him [a bear] by either leg* (Washington Irving). **3** *Figurative.* to snare or ensnare: *as dexterous a gipsy as ever ... noosed a hare* (George J. Whyte-Melville). **4** to put to death by hanging. **5** to marry.
**the noose,** death by hanging: *He was sentenced to the noose for his crimes.*
[Middle English *nose,* probably < Old French *nous,* perhaps < Old Provençal *nous* < Latin *nōdus* knot, node]

**no|o|sphere** (nō′əs fir), *n.* human thought and feeling conceived as a region above and surrounding the biosphere: *... the "noosphere" [is] the psychological habitat in which we live and on whose resources we must draw* (Sir Julian Huxley). [< Greek *nóos* mind + English (bio)*sphere*]

**Noot|ka** (nüt′kə), *n., pl.* **-ka** or **-kas. 1** a member of a Wakashan tribe of Indians living on Vancouver Island and in northwestern Washington. **2** the language of this tribe.

**n.o.p.,** not otherwise provided for.

**no|pal** (nō′pəl), *n.* **1** any one of various cactuses, especially a variety grown to nourish the cochineal insect. **2** = prickly pear. [< Mexican Spanish *nopal* < Nahuatl *nopalli*]

**no-par** (nō′pär′), *adj.* without any face value; issued without a par: *no-par stock.*

**nope** (nōp), *adv. U.S. Informal.* no: *"Will you help me win an argument?" ... "Nope. Slug it out."* (New Yorker).

**no|place** (nō′plās′), *adv., n. Informal.* —*adv.* nowhere: *"Don't seem to see her noplace," he said. "Might look around for her"* (Jesse Hill Ford).
—*n.* a place of no importance: *Several poems in this first collection are of ... nightmarish industrial noplaces* (New York Times).

**nor¹** (nôr; *unstressed* nər), *conj.* and not; or not; neither; and not either. *Nor* is used: **1** with a preceding *neither* or other negative: *There was neither stream nor spring in that desert. I have not gone there, nor will I ever go. He had neither food nor drink left.* **2** *Archaic.* with a preceding *neither* or *not* left out: *Great brother, thou nor I have made the world* (Tennyson). **3** *Archaic.* instead of *neither* as correlative to a following *nor: Nor silver nor gold can buy it. Nor bits nor bridles can his rage restrain* (John Dryden). *Drake nor devil nor Spaniard feared* (Henry Newboldt). [Middle English contraction of *nauther,* and *nother* neither, reduction of Old English *nāhwæther* < *ne* not + *āhwæther* either]

**nor²** (nôr), *conj. Dialect.* than: *Mighty small specimen ... Ain't bigger nor a derringer* (Bret Harte). [origin uncertain]

**nor³** (nôr), *adj., adv.* = north.

**Pronunciation Key:** hat, āge, cãre, fär; let, ēqual, tėrm; it, īce; hot, ōpen, ôrder; **oi**l, **ou**t; cup, pu̇t, rüle; **ch**ild; lo**ng**; **th**in; **ᴛʜ**en; **zh**, measure; **ə** represents **a** in about, **e** in taken, **i** in pencil, **o** in lemon, **u** in circus.

**Nor.**, an abbreviation for the following:
1 Norman.
2 North.
3 Norway.
4 Norwegian.

**NORAD** (nôr′ad, nor′-), *n.* North American Air Defense Command.

**nor|ad|ren|a|lin** (nôr′ə dren′ə lin), *n.* = norepinephrine.

**nor|ad|ren|a|line** (nôr′ə dren′ə lin, -lēn), *n.* = norepinephrine.

**Nord** (nôrd), *n.* a member of the Nordic race.

**Nor|dic** (nôr′dik), *adj., n.* —*adj.* **1** belonging to or characteristic of the Germanic people of northern Europe. Nordic people are typically tall and have blond hair, blue eyes, and long heads. *Among most Nordic types the skin is a light brown to a pinkish brown* (White and Renner). **2** of Scandinavia or its people; Scandinavian: *Nordic skiing, the Nordic climate. Denmark is a Nordic country.* **3** of or designating ski competition involving cross-country and ski-jumping events (distinguished from *Alpine*).
—*n.* **1** a northern European; member of the Nordic people. Scandinavians are Nordics. **2** any person of the Nordic type.
[< French *nordique* < *nord* north < Germanic (compare Old Icelandic *northr*)]

**nor′|east|er** (nôr′ēs′tər), *n.* = northeaster.

**nor|ep|i|neph|rine** (nôr′ep ə nef′rin), *n.* a hormone similar to epinephrine produced by the endings of the sympathetic nerves and found also in the adrenal medulla; noradrenalin. It stimulates the contraction of small blood vessels and is used in the treatment of hypotension and shock. *Formula:* $C_8H_{11}NO_3$ [< *nor*(mal) + *epinephrine*]

**nor|eth|y|no|drel** (nôr′eth i nō′drəl), *n.* = Enovid.

**Nor|folk Island pine** (nôr′fək), a tall pine tree native to Norfolk Island, near Australia, having tough, close-grained wood. It is a kind of araucaria, and is often raised dwarfed as a house plant.

***Norfolk jacket** or **coat**, a loose-fitting, single-breasted jacket with a belt and box pleats in front and back. [< *Norfolk*, England]

***Norfolk jacket**

**no|ri** (nôr′ē, nōr′-), *n.* a red, marine alga eaten in Japan especially in the form of a paste, with soy sauce. [< Japanese *nori*]

**no|ri|a** (nôr′ē ə, nōr′-), *n.* a device for raising water, used in Spain, North Africa, and Asia, consisting of a water wheel carrying buckets which fill as they pass through the water and empty on reaching the high point of the turning wheel. [< Spanish *noria* < Arabic *nā′ūra*]

**nor|ite** (nôr′īt), *n.* a granular igneous rock containing pyroxene in orthorhombic form, often associated with ore deposits. It is a variety of gabbro. [< *Nor*(way), where it is found + *-ite*[1]]

**nor|land** (nôr′lənd), *n. Poetic.* the north country; northland. [variant of *northland*]

**norm** (nôrm), *n.* **1** a standard for a certain group, type, model, or pattern: *to determine the norm for a test.* **2** an average; mean: *sales above the norm for the year. In arithmetic this class is above the norm for the eighth grade.* [< Latin *nōrma* rule, pattern]

**nor|mal** (nôr′məl), *adj., n.* —*adj.* **1** of the usual standard or type; regular; usual: *The normal temperature of the human body is 98.6 degrees. A normal day's work is eight hours.* **SYN:** natural, typical. **2** *Psychology.* **a** mentally healthy; not showing mental disorder; sane: *The borderline between the ... normal and abnormal states is indistinct* (Sigmund Freud). **b** of average intelligence or emotional stability. **3** well; healthy; not diseased; functioning normally: *In a group of normal children of the same age the difference between the tallest and the shortest may be very great* (Sidonie M. Gruenberg). **4** *Chemistry.* **a** (of an acidic or basic solution) containing the equivalent of one gram of hydrogen ions per liter. *Abbr:* N. **b** of or denoting an aliphatic hydrocarbon or hydrocarbon derivative consisting of a straight unbranched chain of carbon atoms, each carbon atom of which is united with no more than two other carbon atoms. **c** not found in association: *normal molecules.* **5** *Geometry.* **a** being at right angles; perpendicular. **b** of or like a normal line or plane. **6** *Electricity.* (of a galvanic cell) having a voltage that can be reproduced.
—*n.* **1** the usual state or level: *He is ten pounds above normal for his age.* **SYN:** average. **2** *Geometry.* **a** a line or plane that is at right angles to another. **b** the intercepted part of the line (on the normal line) between the curve and the x-axis. **3** a normal person in mental ability or adjustment. **4** *Psychology.* average intelligence or emotional stability. **5** *Optics.* a perpendicular to a mirror which strikes the mirror at the point of reflection.
[< Latin *nōrmālis* < *nōrma* a rule, pattern]
—**nor′mal|ness**, *n.*

**normal curve** or **distribution**, *Statistics.* a bell-shaped curve which represents theoretical frequency distribution, as of a series of chance happenings or occurrences of human characteristics; probability curve; Gaussian curve.

**nor|mal|cy** (nôr′məl sē), *n.* the quality of being normal; normal condition; normality: *back to normalcy. We must ... strive for normalcy* (Warren G. Harding).

**nor|mal|ise** (nôr′mə līz), *v.t.*, **-ised, -is|ing.** *Especially British.* normalize.

**nor|mal|i|ty** (nôr mal′ə tē), *n.* **1** normal condition; normalcy. **2** the normal concentration of a solution. It is expressed as the number of equivalents of a gram of hydrogen ions in a liter of solution.

**nor|mal|i|za|tion** (nôr′mə lə zā′shən), *n.* the act or process of making normal.

**nor|mal|ize** (nôr′mə līz), *v.t.*, **-ized, -iz|ing.** to make normal: *to normalize relations between two countries.* —**nor′mal|iz′er**, *n.*

**nor|mal|ly** (nôr′mə lē), *adv.* in the normal way; regularly; if things are normal: *to speak normally. A child normally begins to lose his first teeth when he is six or seven years old.* **SYN:** generally, ordinarily.

**normal pressure**, pressure equivalent to one atmosphere.

**normal salt**, a salt formed from an acid of which all of the hydrogen has been replaced.

**normal school**, a school where people, usually high school graduates, are trained to become teachers, especially a separate institution for teacher education offering a two-year course and a certificate. Normal schools were common in the United States during the early part of this century. [after French *école normale*]

**normal solution**, a solution containing one gram equivalent of a dissolved substance per liter.

**normal temperature**, zero degrees centigrade; 273 degrees absolute.

***Nor|man** (nôr′mən), *n., adj.* —*n.* **1** a person born or living in Normandy in France. **2** a member of the people descended from the Scandinavians who settled in Normandy in the 800's and 900's A.D. and from the French who lived there; Anglo-Norman. They conquered England in 1066. **3** one of the Scandinavian ancestors of these people; Norseman; Northman. **4** = Anglo-French.
—*adj.* **1** of or like the Normans or Normandy. **2** = Norman-French. **3** of or having to do with the architecture of Normandy, characterized by simplicity, massiveness, and use of the rounded arch. It is a variety of Romanesque developed there in the 900's and later introduced into England, southern Italy, and Sicily.
[< Old French *Normans*, plural of *Normant* < Germanic (compare Old High German *Northman*)]

***Norman**
definition 3

**Nor|mand** (nôr′mənd), *n.* = French Coach. [< French *Normand* Norman]

**Nor|man|esque** (nôr′mə nesk′), *adj.* after the Norman style, as of architecture.

**Nor|man-French** (nôr′mən french′), *n., adj.* —*n.* **1** a dialect of the French language spoken by the Normans who conquered England in 1066; Anglo-French. **2** a later form of this dialect, surviving in certain English legal phrases; law French.
—*adj.* of or having to do with this dialect or those who spoke it; Anglo-French; Anglo-Norman.

**Nor|man|ize** (nôr′mə nīz), *v.*, **-ized, -iz|ing.** —*v.i.* to adopt the Norman dialect or manners.
—*v.t.* to make Norman or like the Normans: *There is no wavering here—as there was none in the ruthless policy of William the Conqueror in subduing and Normanizing England* (Nikolaus Pevsner).

**nor|ma|tive** (nôr′mə tiv), *adj.* **1** establishing or setting up a norm or standard: *The normative judgments themselves are more clearly anchored in fact than in most other books dealing with this difficult topic* (Harold P. Green). **2** based on standards of usage: *normative grammar.* —**nor′ma|tive|ly**, *adv.* —**nor′ma|tive|ness**, *n.*

**normo-**, *combining form.* normal, as in *normocyte, normotensive.* [< Latin *nōrma* rule, pattern]

**nor|mo|cyte** (nôr′mə sīt), *n.* a red blood corpuscle of normal size, shape, and color.

**nor|mo|ten|sive** (nôr′mō ten′siv), *adj., n.* —*adj.* having normal blood pressure.
—*n.* a normotensive person.
[< *normo-* + *tensive*, as in *hypertensive*]

**nor|mo|ther|mic** (nôr′mō thėr′mik), *adj.* having normal body temperature: *normothermic mice.*

**nor|mo|typ|ic** (nôr′mō tip′ik), *adj.* of a normal type: *normotypic development.*

**Norn** (nôrn), *n. Norse Mythology.* any one of the three goddesses of fate, Urd, Verdande, and Skuld, to whose decrees the gods as well as men are subject. [< Old Icelandic *Norn*]

**Nor|roy** (nor′oi), *n.* the title of the third English King-of-Arms, ranking after Clarencieux. [< Anglo-French *nor-* north + *roy* king]

**Norse** (nôrs), *adj., n.* —*adj.* **1** of or having to do with ancient Scandinavia, its people, or their language. **2** of or having to do with Norway or its people: Norwegian.
—*n.* **1** the people of ancient Scandinavia; Norsemen; Northmen. **2a** the Norwegians. **b** the ancient Norwegians. **3** the language of the ancient Scandinavians, often called Old Norse. **4** the language of Norway; Norwegian.
[probably < Dutch *Noorsch* Norwegian]
▶ **Norse**, meaning the people of ancient Scandinavia and Norwegians, is singular in form and plural in use.

**Norse|man** (nôrs′mən), *n., pl.* **-men.** a member of a tall, blond people who used to live in the north of Europe, where Norway, Sweden, and Denmark now are; Northman. The Norsemen were great sailors and sea fighters. The Vikings were Norsemen.

**nor|te|a|me|ri|ca|no** (nôr′tā ä mä′rē kä′nō), *n., pl.* **-nos** (-nōs). *Spanish.* a citizen of the United States.

**north** (nôrth), *n., adj., adv.* —*n.* **1** the direction to which a compass needle points; direction to the right as one faces the setting sun. *Abbr:* N (no period). **2** Also, **North.** the part of any country toward the north, especially that part of Great Britain north of the Humber. **3** the north wind.
—*adj.* **1** toward the north: *the north side of town.* **2** coming from the north: *a north wind.* **3** in the north; facing the north: *the north windows of the house.* **4** in the northern part; northern.
—*adv.* toward the north; northward: *a train moving north. Drive north for the next mile.*
**north of**, further north than: *The city is north of us. Canada is north of the United States.*
[Old English *north*]

**North** (nôrth), *n., adj.* —*n.* **1** the northern part of the United States; the states north of Maryland, the Ohio River, and Missouri, making up most of the states that formed the Union side in the Civil War. **2** the north part of a country. **3** the player in the game of bridge sitting opposite and in partnership with South: *North responded by confirming interest in the slam and cue bidding the Ace of Diamonds* (London Times). **4** the developed or industrialized countries of the world: *During a four-day Conference on International Economic Cooperation ... held in Paris ... by 16 industrialized nations and 19 "poor ones" ..., the North made what it considered a generous offer ... The South grudgingly accepted the package* (Time).
—*adj.* in the northern part; northern.

**North African**, **1** of or having to do with North Africa or its people. **2** a native or inhabitant of North Africa.

**North American**, **1** of or having to do with North America or its people. **2** a person born or living in North America.

**North Atlantic Treaty**, the treaty of alliance signed by the 15 western nations that are members of NATO; Atlantic Pact.

**North Briton**, = Scot.

**north|bound** (nôrth′bound′), *adj.* going north; bound northward.

**north by east**, the point of the compass or the direction one point or 11 degrees 15 minutes to the east of north.

**north by west**, the point of the compass or the direction one point or 11 degrees 15 minutes to the west of north.

**North Carolinian**, **1** of or having to do with North Carolina or its people. **2** a native or inhab-

itant of North Carolina.
**north celestial pole**, the zenith of the northern end of the earth's axis from which every direction is south; North Pole. It is just over 1 degree from the North Star.
**North Da|ko|tan** (də kō′tən), **1** of or having to do with North Dakota or its people. **2** a native or inhabitant of North Dakota.
**north|east** (nôrth′ēst′; *Nautical* nôr′ēst′), *adj., n., adv.* —***adj.*** **1** halfway between north and east: *The compass had a northeast reading.* **2** coming from the northeast: *a northeast wind.* **3** lying toward or situated in the northeast: *a northeast district.* **4** directed toward the northeast.
—***n.*** **1** a direction midway between north and east. *Abbr:* NE (no periods). **2** a place that is in the northeast part or direction.
—***adv.*** **1** toward the northeast: *At this point the road turns northeast.* **2** from the northeast. **3** in the northeast.
**the Northeast**, New England and nearby states.
**northeast by east**, the point of the compass or the direction one point or 11 degrees 15 minutes to the east of northeast.
**northeast by north**, the point of the compass or the direction one point or 11 degrees 15 minutes to the north of northeast.
**north|east|er** (nôrth′ēs′tər), *n.* a wind or storm from the northeast: *The northeaster blew in fresh and cool.* Also, **nor'easter.**
**north|east|er|ly** (nôrth′ēs′tər lē), *adj., adv.* **1** toward the northeast. **2** from the northeast.
**north|east|ern** (nôrth′ēs′tərn; *Nautical* nôr′ēs′tərn), *adj.* **1** toward the northeast: *The northeastern sky is heavy with clouds.* **2** from the northeast: *a northeastern cold front.* **3** of the northeast; having to do with the northeast: *Northeastern winters are cold and damp.*
**North|east|ern** (nôrth′ēs′tərn), *adj.* of, having to do with, or in the Northeast.
**north|east|ern|er** (nôrth′ēs′tər nər), *n.* a person born or living in the northeast.
**North|east|ern|er** (nôrth′ēs′tər nər), *n.* a person born or living in the Northeast.
**north|east|ern|most** (nôrth′ēs′tərn mōst; *Nautical* nôr′ēs′tərn mōst), *adj.* farthest northeast: *New England forms the northeasternmost section of the United States.*
**north|east|ward** (nôrth′ēst′wərd; *Nautical* nôr′ēst′wərd), *adv., adj., n.* —***adv., adj.*** **1** toward the northeast. **2** = northeast.
—***n.*** = northeast.
**north|east|ward|ly** (nôrth′ēst′wərd lē; *Nautical* nôr′ēst′wərd lē), *adj., adv.* —***adj.*** **1** toward the northeast. **2** (of winds) from the northeast.
—***adv.*** toward the northeast.
**north|east|wards** (nôrth′ēst′wərdz; *Nautical* nôr′ēst′wərdz), *adv.* = northeastward.
**north|er** (nôr′ᴛʜər), *n.* **1** a wind or storm coming from the north. **2** *U.S.* a strong, intensely cold north wind which blows over Texas, the Gulf Coast, Florida, and the Gulf of Mexico during the autumn and winter months.
**north|er|ly** (nôr′ᴛʜər lē), *adj., adv., n.* —***adj.*** **1** toward the north; *the northerly window of the bedroom.* **2** from the north: *a northerly wind.* **3** of the north.
—***adv.*** **1** toward the north; northward: *The window faces northerly.* **2** from the north.
—***n.*** a northerly wind or storm. —**north′er|li|ness**, *n.*
**north|ern** (nôr′ᴛʜərn), *adj., n.* —***adj.*** **1** toward the north: *the northern side of a building.* **2** coming from the north: *a northern breeze.* **3** of or in the north: *He has traveled in northern countries.* **4** *Astronomy.* of or in the northern half of the celestial sphere: *the northern signs of the zodiac, a northern constellation.*
—***n.*** **1** Often, **Northern**, a person living in a northern region; northerner or Northerner. **2** a north wind; norther.
[Old English *northerne*]
**North|ern** (nôr′ᴛʜərn), *adj., n.* —***adj.*** of or in the northern part of the United States: *Boston is a Northern city.*
—***n.*** **1** a person living in a northern region. **2** the English dialect spoken in northern England, especially in the Middle English period; Northern English. **3** the dialect of American English spoken in the North of the United States.
**Northern Car**, *Astronomy.* Charles's Wain; Big Dipper.
**northern circle**, = tropic of Cancer.
**Northern Coalsack**, one of the large dark spaces in the Milky Way near Deneb.
**Northern Cross**, a cross of six stars in the northern constellation Cygnus.
**Northern Crown**, = Corona Borealis.
**northern eider**, a variety of eider duck of northeastern North America and Greenland, black and white in the male and brown in the female.
**Northern English**, the English language as spoken in the north of England.
**north|ern|er** (nôr′ᴛʜər nər), *n.* a person born or living in the north.
**North|ern|er** (nôr′ᴛʜər nər), *n.* a person born or living in the northern part of the United States.
**northern fur seal**, a fur seal found in the Bering Sea, a sea in the North Pacific.
**Northern Hemisphere**, the half of the earth that is north of the equator.
**northern lights**, streamers and bands of light appearing in the sky in northern regions; aurora borealis: *The northern lights seem to wax and wane in frequency with the rise and fall of the sunspot cycle* (Hubert J. Bernhard).
**northern mammoth**, a mammoth, formerly native to Europe and Northern Asia, remains of which have been found in Siberia; woolly mammoth.
**north|ern|most** (nôr′ᴛʜərn mōst), *adj.* farthest north: *A few of the northernmost stars in this constellation* (Science News Letter).
**northern pike**, a slender predatory food fish of the Northern Hemisphere reaching a length of over four feet and having spiny fins and a narrow, pointed head.
**northern prickly ash**, an aromatic species of prickly ash, having yellowish-green flowers, and found in rocky woods and along riverbanks.
**northern sea lion**, = Steller's sea lion.
**northern shrike**, = butcherbird.
**Northern Spy**, a tart, American winter apple, marked with yellow and red stripes.
**northern star**, = North Star.
**north geographic pole**, = North Pole.
**North Germanic**, the Scandinavian group of languages.
**north|ing** (nôr′thing, -ᴛʜing), *n.* **1** the distance of latitude reckoned northward from the last point of reckoning. **2** the distance northward covered by a ship on any northerly course. **3** *Astronomy.* declination measured northward.
**North Korean**, **1** of or having to do with North Korea or its people. **2** a native or inhabitant of North Korea.
**north|land** (nôrth′lənd), *n.* the land in the north; the northern part of a country. [Old English *northland*]
**North|land** (nôrth′lənd), *n.* **1** the northern regions of the world. **2** the peninsula containing Norway and Sweden: *I am the God Thor ... Here in my Northland ... Reign I forever!* (Longfellow).
**north|land|er** (nôrth′lən dər), *n.* an inhabitant of the northland.
**north magnetic pole**, the point on the earth's surface toward which a magnetic needle points; the pole of the earth's magnetic field. Its location varies slightly from year to year but is about 1,100 miles from the North Pole, near Bathurst Island. See picture under **aclinic line.**
**North|man** (nôrth′mən), *n., pl.* **-men. 1** = Norseman. **2** a native or inhabitant of northern Europe.
**north|most** (nôrth′mōst), *adj.* = northernmost.
**north-north|east** (nôrth′nôrth ēst′; *Nautical* nôr′nôr ēst′), *n., adj., adv.* —***n.*** the point of the compass or the direction midway between north and northeast, two points or 22 degrees 30 minutes to the east of north.
—***adj., adv.*** of, from, or toward the north-northeast.
**north-north|west** (nôrth′nôrth west′; *Nautical* nôr′nôr west′), *n., adj., adv.* —***n.*** the point of the compass or the direction midway between north and northwest, two points or 22 degrees 30 minutes to the west of north.
—***adj., adv.*** of, from, or toward the north-northwest.
**north pole**, the pole of a magnet that points north.

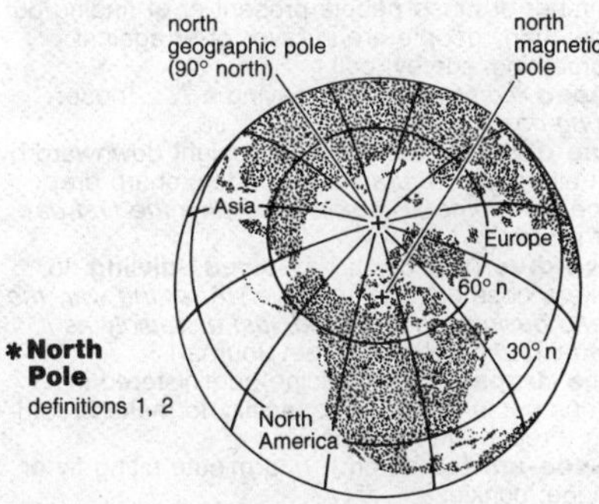

***North Pole** definitions 1, 2

***North Pole**, **1** the northern end of the earth's axis; that point on the earth's surface from which every direction is south: *The North Pole is surrounded by water and is at sea level* (Gabriele Rabel). **2** = north magnetic pole. **3** = north celestial pole.
**North Star**, the bright star almost directly above the North Pole; Polaris; polestar; lodestar. It was formerly much used as a guide by sailors. See picture under **constellation.**
**North|um|bri|an** (nôr thum′brē ən), *adj., n.* —***adj.*** **1** of or having to do with Northumbria, its people, or their dialect. **2** of or having to do with Northumberland, its people, or their dialect.
—***n.*** **1** a native or inhabitant of Northumbria, an ancient kingdom in northern England. **2** the dialect of Old English spoken in Northumbria. **3** a native or inhabitant of Northumberland. **4** the Northumberland dialect of Modern English.
**North Vietnamese**, **1** of or having to do with North Vietnam or its people. **2** a native or inhabitant of North Vietnam.
**north|ward** (nôrth′wərd; *Nautical* nôr′ᴛʜərd), *adv., adj., n.* —***adv.*** toward the north; in a northerly direction: *Rocks lay northward of the ship's course.*
—***adj.*** toward the north; north: *the northward slope of a hill.*
—***n.*** a northward part, direction, or point; north.
**north|ward|ly** (nôrth′wərd lē; *Nautical* nôr′ᴛʜərd-lē), *adj., adv.* —***adj.*** **1** toward the north. **2** (of winds) from the north.
—***adv.*** toward the north.
**north|wards** (nôrth′wərdz; *Nautical* nôr′ᴛʜərdz), *adv.* = northward.
**north|west** (nôrth′west′; *Nautical* nôr′west′), *adj., n., adv.* —***adj.*** **1** halfway between north and west: *a northwest course.* **2** coming from the northwest: *a northwest wind.* **3** lying toward or situated in the northwest: *a northwest landmark.* **4** directed toward the northwest: *a northwest window.*
—***n.*** **1** a direction midway between north and west. *Abbr:* NW (no periods). **2** a place that is in the northwest part or direction: *pasture to the northwest.*
—***adv.*** **1** toward the northwest: *The road from Chicago to Minneapolis runs northwest.* **2** from the northwest. **3** in the northwest.
**the Northwest**, Washington, Oregon, and Idaho.
**northwest by north**, the point of the compass or the direction one point or 11 degrees 15 minutes to the north of northwest.
**northwest by west**, the point of the compass or the direction one point or 11 degrees 15 minutes to the west of northwest.
**north|west|er** (nôrth′wes′tər; *Nautical* nôr′wes′tər), *n.* **1** a wind or storm from the northwest. **2** the strong wind which blows over Bengal, India, in March and April. Also, **nor'wester.**
**north|west|er|ly** (nôrth′wes′tər lē; *Nautical* nôr′wes′tər lē), *adj., adv.* **1** toward the northwest. **2** from the northwest.
**north|west|ern** (nôrth′wes′tərn; *Nautical* nôr′wes′tərn), *adj.* **1** toward the northwest: *the northwestern explorations of Lewis and Clark.* **2** from the northwest: *a northwestern approach.* **3** of or in the northwest; having to do with the northwest: *the team of a northwestern college.*
**North|west|ern** (nôrth′wes′tərn), *adj.* of, having to do with, or in the northwestern states of the United States.
**north|west|ern|er** (nôrth′wes′tər nər), *n.* a person born or living in the northwest.
**North|west|ern|er** (nôrth′wes′tər nər), *n.* a person born or living in the Northwest.
**north|west|ern|most** (nôrth′wes′tərn mōst; *Nautical* nôr′wes′tərn mōst), *adj.* farthest northwest.
**north|west|ward** (nôrth′west′wərd; *Nautical* nôr′west′wərd), *adv., adj., n.* —***adv., adj.*** **1** toward the northwest. **2** = northwest.
—***n.*** = northwest.
**north|west|ward|ly** (nôrth′west′wərd lē; *Nautical* nôr′west′wərd lē), *adj., adv.* —***adj.*** **1** toward the northwest. **2** (of winds) from the northwest.
—***adv.*** toward the northwest.
**north|west|wards** (nôrth′west′wərdz; *Nautical* nôr′west′wərdz), *adv.* = northwestward.
**Norw.**, **1** Norway. **2** Norwegian.
**nor|ward** (nôr′wərd), *adv., adj., n.* = northward.
**Nor|way haddock** (nôr′wā), = rosefish.
**Norway maple**, a large European maple with thick green leaves that turn pale-yellow in autumn, grown extensively in the United States as a shade tree.
**Norway pine** = red pine.
**Norway rat**, the common brown rat found about buildings, refuse, and other places frequented by man; brown rat.
**Norway spruce**, a tall spruce native to Europe and Asia, an important source of lumber and

**Pronunciation Key:** hat, āge, cãre, fär; let, ēqual, tėrm; it, īce; hot, ōpen, ôrder; oil, out; cup, pu̇t, rüle; child; long; thin; ᴛʜen; zh, measure; ə represents **a** in about, **e** in taken, **i** in pencil, **o** in lemon, **u** in circus.

wood pulp. Various dwarf varieties are grown for ornament.

**Nor|we|gian** (nôr wē′jən), *adj., n.* —*adj.* of Norway, a country in northern Europe, west and north of Sweden, its people, or their language: *Norwegian villages, a Norwegian costume.* —*n.* **1** a person born or living in Norway: *Many Norwegians immigrated to Minnesota in the 1800's.* **2** the Scandinavian language of Norway: *Danish, Swedish, and Norwegian are all related Germanic languages.*

**Norwegian elkhound**, any one of an ancient breed of Norwegian hunting dogs having a short body, gray coat, pointed ears, and a tail curled over the back, used for tracking elk and other game.

**Norwegian saltpeter**, = calcium nitrate.

**nor'west|er** (nôr wes′tər), *n.* **1** a heavy, waterproof oilskin hat or coat worn by seamen. **2** = northwester.

**Nor|wich terrier** (nôr′ij, -ich; nor′-), any one of a breed of small, short-legged terriers with a wiry, usually red coat, weighing from 10 to 15 pounds. It is used for hunting rabbits or kept as a house dog. [< *Norwich,* a city in England]

**n.o.s.**, not otherwise specified.

**Nos.** or **nos.**, numbers.

***nose** (nōz), *n., v.,* **nosed, nos|ing.** —*n.* **1** the part of the face or head just above the mouth. The nose has openings for breathing and smelling. *Savory odors greeted the nose.* **2** the sense of smell: *Most dogs have a good nose. A mouse has a good nose for cheese.* **3** *Figurative.* **a** faculty for perceiving or detecting: *A reporter must have a nose for news.* **4** a part that stands out, especially at the front of anything. The bow of a ship or airplane is often called the nose. *We saw the little steamer's nose poking around the cliff.* **5** odor. **6** *British Slang.* an informer.
—*v.t.* **1** to discover by smell; smell out; scent: *A dozen times, Perrault, nosing the way, broke through the ice bridges* (Jack London). **2** to examine with the nose; smell: *The dog nosed the bone before accepting it.* **3** to rub with the nose; nuzzle: *The cat nosed her kittens.* **4** to push with the nose or forward end: *The bulldozer nosed the rock off the road.*
—*v.i.* **1** to sniff (at): *The cat nosed at the toy mouse.* **2** to push forward or move, especially slowly, cautiously, or hesitantly: *The little boat nosed carefully between the rocks.* **3** *Figurative.* to search (for); pry (into): *Don't nose into my affairs.* **4** *British Slang.* to be an informer; serve as a police spy.
**count noses,** *Informal.* to find out how many people are present or in favor of or against something; make a nose count: *Some modern zealots appear to have no better knowledge of truth, nor better manner of judging it, than by counting noses* (Anthony Shaftesbury).
**cut off one's nose to spite one's face,** to be spiteful in such a way as to hurt oneself: *To threaten such a tragic thing as moving the Stock Exchange out of Lower Manhattan is ... cutting off one's nose to spite one's face* (New York Times).
**follow one's nose, a** to go straight ahead: *Adams asked him if he could direct him to an alehouse. The fellow ... bade him follow his nose* (Henry Fielding). **b** *Figurative.* to be guided by one's instinct: *All that follow their noses are led by their eyes, but blind men* (Shakespeare). **c** to be guided by one's sense of smell: *The hounds ran ahead, following their noses on the trail of the fox.*
**have** (or **keep** or **put**) **one's nose to the grindstone,** to work long and hard: *People whose heads are a little up in the world, have no occasion to keep their nose to the grindstone* (Lights and Shades).
**lead by the nose,** to have complete control over: *Seven-eighths of the town are led by the nose by this or that periodical work* (Frederick Marryat).
**look down one's nose at,** to treat with contempt or scorn: *People who prefer symphony concerts or chamber music tend to look down their noses at ... opera* (Winthrop Sargeant).
**nose around,** to look about quietly or secretly: *The detective was nosing around for clues.*
**nose out, a** to find out by looking around quietly or secretly: *to nose out the truth.* **b** to win (over someone) by a small margin; win by a nose: *The mayor nosed out his opponent by 4 votes in a very close election.*
**on the nose, a** exactly: *He was an instinctive showman, and he could hit it right on the nose* (New Yorker). **b** solidly: *He won the race on the nose.*
**pay through the nose,** to pay a great deal too much; charged exorbitantly: *The Russians have been making them pay through the nose for the war supplies they've received* (Wall Street Journal).
**poke one's nose into,** to pry into in a nosy way; meddle in: *A flourishing Evangelical, who poked his nose into everything* (Mark Pattison).
**put one's nose out of joint, a** to displace or supplant one: *The king is pleased enough with her: which, I fear, will put Madam Castlemaine's nose out of joint* (Samuel Pepys). **b** *Figurative.* to put in a bad humor; disconcert: *It puts his nose out of joint to see someone getting attention.*
**rub one's nose in (it), a** to make one experience closely (something unpleasant, especially as a punishment): [*The*] *vote against Carswell ... was also an attempt to rub the Senate's nose in the mess it had made* (New Yorker). **b** to keep on mentioning (something unpleasant): *I don't look back, unless someone rubs my nose in my past* (Brian St. Pierre).
**thumb one's nose at, a** to put one's thumb to one's nose in scorn of: *The boys thumbed their noses at each other.* **b** *Figurative.* to dismiss scornfully; disdain: *His film defiantly thumbs its nose at the fate all men fear* (Time).
**turn up one's nose at,** to treat with contempt or scorn: *What learning there was in those days ... turned up its nose at the strains of the native minstrels* (Bayard Taylor).
**under one's nose,** in plain sight; very easy to notice: *A wagon-load of valuable merchandise had been smuggled ashore ... directly beneath their unsuspicious noses* (Hawthorne).
**win by a nose, a** to win a horse race by no more than the length of a horse's nose: *Lucky Day won the race at Churchill Downs by a nose.* **b** *Figurative.* to win by a small margin: *With only 4 more votes than his opponent the mayor won reelection by a nose.*
[Old English *nosu*]

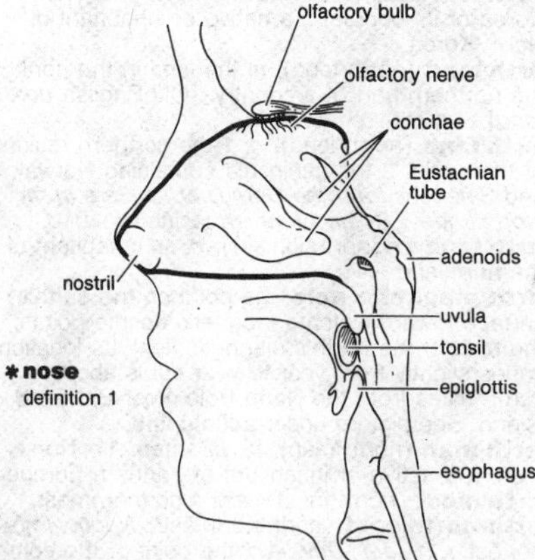

***nose**
definition 1

**nose bag,** a bag containing food, to be hung on a horse's head.

**nose|band** (nōz′band′), *n.* the part of a bridle that goes over the animal's nose.

**nose|bleed** (nōz′blēd′), *n.* a flow of blood from the nose; epistaxis.

**nose cone,** the cone-shaped front section of a missile or rocket made to carry a bomb to a target or to carry instruments or a man into space. The nose cone is made to withstand high temperatures from friction with air particles. It usually separates from the rest of the missile or rocket after the fuel runs out.

**nose count,** *Informal.* the act of determining the number of those people present or of finding out how many people are in favor of or against something; survey; poll.

**-nosed,** *combining form.* having a ____ nose: *Long-nosed = having a long nose.*

**nose dive, 1** a swift plunge straight downward by an aircraft. **2** *Figurative.* a sudden, sharp drop: *The thermometer took a nose dive the first day of winter.*

**nose-dive** (nōz′dīv′), *v.i.,* **-dived, -div|ing.** to take a nose dive: (*Figurative.*) *After the war, the seed business nose-dived, just as rapidly as it had expanded* (Wall Street Journal).

**nose drops,** liquid medicine administered in drops put in the nose especially to make breathing through the nose easier.

**no-see-um** (nō sē′əm), *n.* a minute biting fly or midge; punkie.

**nose flute,** a musical instrument blown with the nose, used in Thailand, in the Fiji and Society Islands, and elsewhere.

**nose|gay** (nōz′gā′), *n.* a bunch of flowers; bouquet: *a garden where I had ... gathered many a nosegay* (Samuel Butler). SYN: posy. [< *nose* + obsolete *gay* something gay or pretty]

**nose|piece** (nōz′pēs′), *n.* **1** the part of a helmet that covers and protects the nose. **2** the part of a microscope to which the objective is attached. **3** a noseband for an animal. **4** a piece of wood inserted to form the nose of a stuffed animal. **5** the nozzle of a hose or pipe. **6** the bridge of a pair of eyeglasses.

**nose ring, 1** a ring fixed in an animal's nose for leading it: *His bull had broken and dislodged its nose ring, which is, of course, the only means by which it is controlled* (Punch). **2** a ring worn in the nose for ornament by some peoples.

**nose|wheel** (nōz′hwēl′), *n.* a retractable landing wheel located at the nose of an airplane.

**nos|ey** (nō′zē), *adj.,* **nos|i|er, nos|i|est,** *n.* = nosy.

**Nosey Parker,** = Nosy Parker.

**nosh** (nosh), *n., v. Slang.* —*n.* **1** a meal or snack: *Evening nosh depended on what was going on at special prices* (Punch). *The company makes everything from "soup to nosh"* (New York Times). **2** *British.* food: *I've always found Chinese nosh both cheap and filling* (Colin Howard).
—*v.i.* to have a meal or snack: *He had called to see if my son would go out to nosh with him* (Punch).
—*v.t.* to nibble or eat: *The politician ... noshes his way along the campaign trail* (Time).
[probably < Yiddish *nosh, nash* < *nashen* to snack, nibble < German *naschen*] —**nosh′er,** *n.*

**no-show** (nō′shō′), *n. U.S.* a person who reserves a seat or other space, especially on an airplane, and fails either to cancel it or to use it. [< *no*[1] + *show* (up to claim or use)]

**no-side** (nō′sīd′), *n. British.* the conclusion of a game of Rugby.

**nos|i|ly** (nō′zə lē), *adv.* in a nosy way; inquisitively.

**nos|i|ness** (nō′zē nis), *n.* the quality or fact of being nosy: *More than indiscreet nosiness was involved* (Newsweek).

**nos|ing** (nō′zing), *n.* a horizontal edge that projects over a vertical surface, such as the edge of a stair tread.

**nos|o|co|mi|al** (nos′ə kō′mē əl), *adj.* of or having to do with a hospital. [< Late Latin *nosocomīum* hospital (< Greek *nosokomeîon* < *nósos* disease + *komeîn* take care of) + English *-al*[1]]

**nos|o|ge|og|ra|phy** (nos′ō jē og′rə fē), *n.* the study of disease in relation to geographical factors. [< Greek *nósos* disease + English *geography*]

**no|sog|ra|phy** (nō sog′rə fē), *n.* the systematic description of diseases. [< Greek *nósos* disease + English *-graphy*]

**nos|o|log|ic** (nos′ə loj′ik), *adj.* = nosological.

**nos|o|log|i|cal** (nos′ə loj′ə kəl), *adj.* having to do with nosology. —**nos′o|log′i|cal|ly,** *adv.*

**no|sol|o|gist** (nō sol′ə jist), *n.* an expert in nosology; classifier of diseases.

**no|sol|o|gy** (nō sol′ə jē), *n.* **1** the classification of diseases. **2** the branch of medicine dealing with the classification of diseases. **3** the special symptoms or characteristics of a disease, comprising the chief basis for diagnosis. [< Greek *nósos* disease + English *-logy*]

**nos|tal|gia** (nos tal′jə, -jē ə), *n.* **1** a painful or wistful yearning for one's home, country, or city; homesickness: *One who has to spend so much of his life in the East ... should not be hampered by ties and habits calculated ... to foster nostalgia* (Sidney J. Owen). **2** such a yearning for anything far removed in space or time: *a nostalgia for old movies. ... the nostalgia of the heathen past* (David H. Lawrence). [< New Latin *nostalgia* < Greek *nóstos* homecoming (< *neîsthai* come, go) + *-algiā* < *álgos* pain]

**nos|tal|gic** (nos tal′jik), *adj.* feeling or showing nostalgia; homesick: *Nostalgic Southerners ... speak of Jefferson Davis with respect but not with affection* (New York Times). —**nos|tal′gi|cal|ly,** *adv.*

**nos|toc** (nos′tok), *n.* any bluish-green alga of a group that lives in jellylike colonies in moist places, fresh water, or on plants. [< New Latin *Nostoc* (coined by Paracelsus)]

**nos|to|log|ic** (nos′tə loj′ik), *adj.* **1** characterized by extreme senility. **2** having to do with gerontology.

**nos|tol|o|gy** (nos tol′ə jē), *n.* = gerontology. [< Greek *nóstos* homecoming (see etym. under **nostalgia**) + English *-logy*]

**nos|to|ma|ni|a** (nos′tō mā′nē ə), *n.* obsessive nostalgia.

**Nos|tra|da|mus** (nos′trə dā′məs), *n.* a person who professes to foretell future events; prophet; seer. [< Latinization of Michel de *Notredame,* 1503-1566, a French physician and astrologer]

**nos|tril** (nos′trəl), *n.* either of the two openings in the nose. Air is breathed into the lungs, and smells come into the sensitive parts of the nose, through the nostrils. [Old English *nosthyrl* < *nosu* nose + *thyrel* hole]

**no-strings** (nō′stringz′), *adj. Informal.* free of conditions or obligations.

**nos|trum** (nos′trəm), *n., pl.* **-trums. 1** a medicine

for which great claims are made by the person who makes and sells it; quack remedy; patent medicine: *What drop or nostrum can this plague remove* (Alexander Pope). *The doctors and quack-salvers ... experimenting on his poor little body with every conceivable nostrum* (Thackeray). **2** a pet scheme for producing wonderful results; cure-all: *World government, his nostrum, is probably accepted by most thinking people today as a necessity at some time in the not too distant future* (Bulletin of Atomic Scientists). **SYN**: panacea. [< Latin *nostrum* (*remedium*) our (remedy) (because it is usually prepared by the person recommending it)]

**nos|y** (nō′zē), *adj.*, **nos|i|er, nos|i|est**, *n. Informal.* —*adj.* prying or inquisitive: *He said that those of his followers who had chased nosy tax collectors out of their shops ... were only fighting for their liberties* (New Yorker).
—*n.* **1** a person with a large or prominent nose. **2** = busybody. Also, **nosey**.

**Nosy Parker**, an offensively inquisitive person; one who is insatiably curious about things that are none of his business.

**not** (not), *adv.* a word that says "no"; a negative: *Cold is not hot. Six and two do not make ten. That is not true. Is it true or not? It is a fine day, is it not?* (used elliptically).
**whether or not** (or **no**), in any case; no matter what happens: *You may say that this is to degrade the state. Possibly. But whether or no, this is the principle already ... acted upon* (John Morley).
[unstressed variant of *nought*]

**no|ta be|ne** (nō′tə bē′nē), *Latin.* note well; observe what follows; take notice. *Abbr:* N.B., n.b.

**no|ta|bil|i|a** (nō′tə bil′ē ə), *n.pl.* things or events worth noting; notable things. [< Latin *notābilia*, neuter plural of *notābilis;* see etym. under **notable**]

**no|ta|bil|i|ty** (nō′tə bil′ə tē), *n., pl.* **-ties. 1** the quality of being notable; distinction. **SYN**: eminence. **2** a prominent person; notable.

**no|ta|ble** (nō′tə bəl; *also* not′ə bəl *for adj. 3*), *adj., n.* —*adj.* **1** worth noticing; striking; remarkable; important: *a notable event, a notable book, a notable painter.* **SYN**: memorable, conspicuous, famous. **2** that can be noted or perceived; perceptible; appreciable: *a notable quantity.* **3** capable; thrifty and industrious as a housewife: *His notable little wife, too, had enough to do to attend to her housekeeping* (Washington Irving).
—*n.* **1** a person who is notable: *Many notables came to the President's reception.* **2** Often, **Notable.** (in French history) one of a number of prominent men from the three estates, before the Revolution, called together by the king as a deliberative body in times of crisis.
[< Latin *notābilis* < *notāre* to note < *nota* a mark] —**no′ta|ble|ness**, *n.*

**no|ta|bly** (nō′tə blē), *adv.* in a notable manner; to a notable degree.

**no|taph|i|ly** (nō taf′ə lē), *n.* the collecting of bank notes as a hobby. [< Latin *nota* note + Greek *philia* fondness]

**no|tar|i|al** (nō tãr′ē əl), *adj.* **1** of or having to do with a notary public. **2** made or done by a notary public. —**no|tar′i|al|ly**, *adv.*

**no|ta|ri|za|tion** (nō′tə rə zā′shən), *n.* **1** the act of notarizing. **2** a certificate showing that a document has been notarized.

**no|ta|rize** (nō′tə rīz), *v.t.*, **-rized, -riz|ing.** to certify (a contract, deed, will, or other instrument), as a notary public does; give legal authenticity to: *Many documents must be notarized before they become legally effective. The purpose of notarizing a document is to protect those who use it from forgeries* (Erwin N. Griswold).

**no|ta|ry** (nō′tər ē), *n., pl.* **-ries.** = notary public. [< Latin *notārius* clerk, ultimately < *nota* a mark, note]

**notary public**, *pl.* **notaries public** or **notary publics.** a public officer authorized to certify deeds and contracts, to record the fact that a certain person swears that something is true, and to attend to other legal matters.

**no|tate** (nō′tāt), *v.t.*, **-tat|ed, -tat|ing.** to record or represent in notation: *Much of this music has been notated and preserved.*

**no|ta|tion** (nō tā′shən), *n.* **1** a set of signs or symbols used to represent numbers, quantities, or other values: *In arithmetic we use the Arabic notation* (*1, 2, 3, 4, and so on*) *or sometimes the Roman notation* (*I, II, III, IV, and so on*). **2** the representing of numbers, quantities, or other values by symbols or signs: *Music has a special system of notation, and so has chemistry.* **3** a note to assist the memory; record; jotting: *He made a notation in the margin of the paper.* **SYN**: memorandum. **4** the act of noting. [< Latin *notātiō, -ōnis* < *notāre* to note < *nota* a mark]

**no|ta|tion|al** (nō tā′shə nəl), *adj.* of or having to do with notation.

**notch** (noch), *n., v.* —*n.* **1** a nick or cut shaped like a V, made in an edge or on a curving surface, as for keeping a score or record: *a pole with notches for aid in climbing. The Indians cut notches on a stick to keep count of numbers.* **SYN**: dent, indentation. **2** *U.S.* a deep narrow pass or gap between mountains: *to smuggle goods by raft over a river that runs at the bottom of the notch.* **3** *Informal, Figurative.* a grade; step; degree: *In the hot weather many people set their air conditioners several notches higher.*
—*v.t.* **1** to make a notch or notches in. **2** to record by notches; score; tally: *British industry has already notched some impressive victories* (Punch).
[apparently earlier *a noch*, by misdivision of Middle English *an och* < French *oche* < Old French *oschier* to notch]

**notch|back** (noch′bak′), *n.* an automobile with a sloping or slanting roof and a pronounced rear bumper.

**✱note**
definition 7a

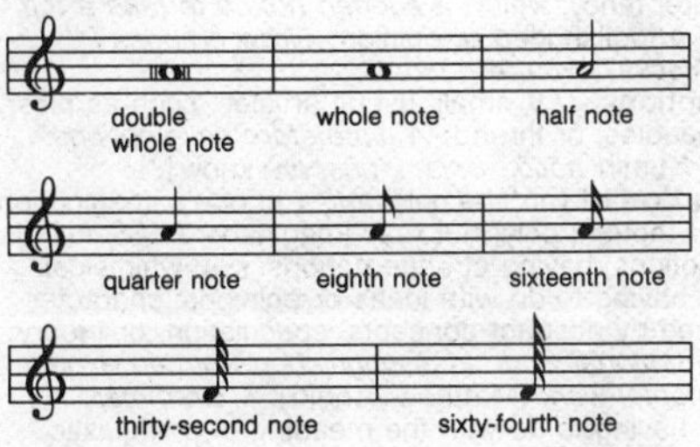

double whole note — whole note — half note
quarter note — eighth note — sixteenth note
thirty-second note — sixty-fourth note

**✱note** (nōt), *n., v.*, **not|ed, not|ing.** —*n.* **1** a short sentence, a phrase, or a single word written down to remind one of something, such as what was in a book, a speech, or an agreement: *Her notes helped her remember what the speaker said.* **2** notice; heed; observation: *Give careful note to his words. A streaming flight of wild geese ... gave note of the waning year* (Washington Irving). **3** a comment, remark, or piece of information added concerning a word, or a passage in a book, often to help pupils in studying a book: *A footnote is a note at the bottom of the page about something on the page. See the note below. Her chemistry book has many helpful notes at the back.* **4a** a very short letter: *a note of thanks. Drop me a note when you arrive.* **b** any short written instruction, list, or reminder: *a note to the milkman.* **5** a letter from one government to another; diplomatic or official communication in writing: *England sent a note of protest to France.* **6** a single musical sound: *a sudden shrill note from the clarinet. Sing this note for me.* **7** *Music.* **a** the written sign to show the pitch and length of a sound. Pitch is indicated by the position of a note on a staff and duration by its appearance. **b** a black or white key of a piano or other instrument: *to strike the wrong note.* **8** a song or call of a bird: *the robin's cheerful note.* **9** a song; melody; tune: *The pealing anthem swells the note of praise* (Thomas Gray). **10** *Figurative.* a significant tone, sound, or way of expression: *There was a note of anxiety in her voice.* **11** *Figurative.* a sign, token, or proof of genuineness; characteristic or distinguishing feature: *His writing displays the note of scholarship.* **SYN**: mark, symbol, character. **12** true importance; greatness; fame; distinction; consequence. **SYN**: repute, significance. **13** a written promise to pay a certain sum of money at a certain time; promissory note: *The note showed that his loan is due on March 15.* **14** a certificate of a government or bank passing current as money; piece of paper money; bank note. **15** a mark or sign, as of punctuation, used in writing or printing.
—*v.t.* **1** to write down as a thing to be remembered: *Our class notes the weather daily on a chart. Write it before them in a table, and note it in a book, that it may be for the time to come* (Isaiah 30:8). **SYN**: record. **2** to give attention to; observe; notice: *Now note what I do next. Note the sly smile on his face.* **SYN**: regard, perceive. **3** to mention especially; dwell on; emphasize. **4** to indicate; signify; denote. **5** to furnish with notes or annotations; annotate. **6** to set down in or furnish with musical notes.
**compare notes**, to exchange ideas or opinions: *Everybody put questions to everybody, and all compared notes* (Charles Reade).
**make a note of**, to write down as something to be remembered: *I must make a note of that. When found, make a note of* (Dickens).
**of note**, **a** that is important, great, or notable: *Washington is a person of note.* **b** of being noticed: *The manner in which these statutes were interpreted is worthy of note* (Law Quarterly Review).
**strike the right note**, to say or do something suitable: *The mediator struck the right note in his dealings with the union.*
**take note of**, to take notice of; give attention to; observe: *No one took any note of my leaving. What if thou withdraw in silence from the living and no friend take note of thy departure?* (William Cullen Bryant).
**take notes**, to write down things to be remembered: *Mr. L____ I was so kind as to accede to my desire that he would take notes of all that occurred* (Edgar Allan Poe).
[< Old French *note*, learned borrowing from Latin *nota* a mark, note] —**not′er**, *n.*

**note|book** (nōt′bu̇k′), *n.* **1** a book in which to write notes of things to be learned or remembered: *a loose-leaf notebook.* **2** a book for the registering of promissory notes.

**note-case** (nōt′kās′), *n. Especially British.* a billfold.

**not|ed** (nō′tid), *adj.* well-known; specially noticed; famous: *Samson was noted for his strength. Kipling is a noted author.* **SYN**: renowned, celebrated, distinguished, conspicuous. See syn. under **famous.** —**not′ed|ly**, *adv.* —**not′ed|ness**, *n.*

**note|hold|er** (nōt′hōl′dər), *n.* a holder of notes issued by a business company for temporary financing: *The fair's obligations to its noteholders might not be met in full* (Robert Alden).

**note|less** (nōt′lis), *adj.* **1** without note; undistinguished; unnoticed. **2** = unmusical. **3** = voiceless.

**note|let** (nōt′lit), *n.* a short note.

**note of hand**, = promissory note.

**note|pad** (nōt′pad′), *n.* a pad of paper for writing down notes.

**note paper**, paper used for writing letters.

**note shaver**, *U.S. Slang.* a promoter of bogus financial companies: *The wrinkled note shaver will have taken his railroad trip in vain* (Hawthorne).

**notes payable** (nōts), **1** current liabilities in the form of promissory notes given to creditors. **2** a record of this.

**notes receivable**, **1** current assets in the form of promissory notes presented by debtors. **2** a record of this.

**note ver|bale** (nôt′ ver bȧl′), *French.* **1** a diplomatic message written in the third person and sent unsigned. A note verbale is more formal than an aide-mémoire but less so than a note. **2** (literally) verbal note.

**note|wor|thy** (nōt′wėr′ᴛʜē), *adj.* worthy of notice; remarkable; notable: *The first flight across the Atlantic was a noteworthy achievement.* **SYN**: extraordinary. —**note′wor′thi|ly**, *adv.* —**note′wor′thi|ness**, *n.*

**noth|ing** (nuth′ing), *n., adv., adj.* —*n.* **1a** not anything; no thing: *He believes in nothing. Nothing arrived by mail.* **b** no part, share, or trace: *There is nothing of his father about him.* **2** a thing that does not exist: *to create a world out of nothing. Dead men rotting to nothing* (William Morris). **3** a thing or person of no value or importance: *People regard him as a nothing. Don't worry, it's nothing. Gratiano speaks an infinite deal of nothing* (Shakespeare). **4** zero; naught.
—*adv.* not at all; in no way: *She is nothing like her sister in looks. He was nothing wiser than before. We were nothing loath to go.*
—*adj. U.S. Slang.* worthless; no-account; insignificant: *a nothing job, a nothing young man. "There's a little nothing town up here, just past the high ground," Lewis said* (James Dickey).
**for nothing**, **a** without payment; free of charge: *to get something for nothing.* **b** with no results; in vain: *He did all that hard work for nothing.* **c** for no reason: *She is not liked and respected for nothing.*
**have nothing on**, **a** to be undressed or improperly dressed: *"I just got out of the shower; I have nothing on."* **b** to lack evidence of wrongdoing against: *The police have nothing on that suspect.* **c** to be unable to surpass: *That boxing match has nothing on the brutal one we saw today.*
**in nothing flat**, *Informal.* in no time at all; very quickly: *The conductor memorized the whole symphony score in nothing flat just two days before the concert.*
**make nothing of**, **a** to be unable to understand: *Bella could make nothing of it but that John was in the right* (Dickens). **b** to fail to use or do: *Tom made nothing of the opportunity afforded him.* **c** to consider as easy to do: *She makes nothing of leaping over a six-bar gate* (Joseph Addison). **d** to treat as unimportant or worthless: *The river*

---

**Pronunciation Key:** hat, āge, cãre, fär; let, ēqual, tėrm; it, īce; hot, ōpen, ôrder; **oi**l, **ou**t; cup, pu̇t, rüle; **ch**ild; lo**ng**; **th**in; ᴛʜen; **zh**, measure; **ə** represents **a** in about, **e** in taken, **i** in pencil, **o** in lemon, **u** in circus.

*makes nothing of washing away ... islands* (S. Parker).
**next to nothing**, very little: *He knows next to nothing about farming.*
**nothing but**, only: *Don't scold her; she's nothing but a child.*
**nothing doing**, *Informal.* **a** definitely not: *I wanted to make up with him, but he said "nothing doing."* **b** without success: *We looked all over for the lost dog, but nothing doing.* **c** no activity of interest: *There's nothing doing in this town.*
**nothing less than**, just the same as: *But yet, methinks, my father's execution was nothing less than bloody tyranny* (Shakespeare).
**nothing short of**, just the same as; nothing less then: *His ideas are nothing short of brilliant.*
**nothing to it**, *Informal.* no great effort is involved: *Nothing to it, I'll fix the leak in a jiffy.*
**not know from nothing**, *U.S. Dialect or Informal.* to know nothing: *"You're a girl," Sterling said ... "You don't know from nothing"* (Louise Meriwether).
**think nothing of**, **a** to consider as easy to do: *Harry thought nothing of swimming a mile.* **b** to treat as unimportant or worthless: *The executive thought nothing of his employee's advice.*
**to say nothing of**, not even considering; not to mention: *Almost everything in the house is new, to say nothing of the house itself.*
[Middle English *nothing* < Old English *nān* no + *thing* thing]
► See **nobody** for usage note.

**noth|ing|ness** (nuth′ing nis), *n.* **1** the state of being nothing; nonexistence: *A thing of beauty is a joy for ever ... it will never Pass into nothingness* (Keats). **2** the condition of being of no value; worthlessness; insignificance: *the vanity and nothingness of the things of time in comparison to those of eternity* (Scott). **3** an unimportant or worthless thing. **4** unconsciousness: *in the nothingness of sleep.*

**noth|o|saur** (noth′ə sôr), *n.* any marine reptile of an extinct group, common in the Triassic period, similar to the plesiosaurs but smaller. [< New Latin *Nothosaurus* the genus name < Greek *nóthos* bastard + *saûros* lizard]

**no|tice** (nō′tis), *n., v.,* **-ticed, -tic|ing.** —*n.* **1a** heed; attention; observation: *to escape one's notice. A sudden movement caught his notice.* **SYN**: awareness. **b** a polite ear; sympathetic attention; courteous heed: *I beg your notice of my needs.* **SYN**: regard, note. **2** information; announcement or warning: *The whistle blew to give notice that the boat was about to leave.* **SYN**: notification. **3** a written or printed sign; large sheet of paper giving information or directions: *We saw a notice of today's motion picture outside the theater.* **SYN**: bulletin, placard. **4** a warning that one will end an agreement with another at a certain time: *The marshal tried to deliver an eviction notice on the tenant who refused to pay his rent. It is customary to give a month's notice before leaving to take another job.* **5** a written or printed account in a newspaper about something, such as a review of a book or play: *The new book got a favorable notice. There is a notice in the paper describing the wedding.*
—*v.t.* **1** to take notice of; give attention to; see; observe; perceive: *I noticed a hole in my stocking. If you notice her so much she will be vain* (Harriet Beecher Stowe). **SYN**: mark, note, heed. **2** to mention; refer to; speak of: *to notice a matter in a speech or book.* **3** to serve with a notice; give notice to: *The attorneys have noticed us that they have withdrawn the suit* (Anthony Trollope). **4** to write a notice of (a book, play, performance, or motion picture); review.
**serve notice**, to give warning; inform; announce: *Before the blasting occurred, the builder served notice to the neighboring houses.*
**take notice (of)**, to give attention; observe; give attention to; see: *Take no notice of her. Taking no notice that she is so nigh* (Shakespeare).
[< Middle French *notice*, learned borrowing from Latin *nōtitia* cognizance (in Late Latin, list) < *nōscere* know]

**no|tice|a|ble** (nō′ti sə bəl), *adj.* **1** easily seen or noticed: *Our kitten is very noticeable because its fur is yellow.* **SYN**: discernible, observable, conspicuous. **2** worth noticing; deserving notice: *The class has made noticeable improvement.* —**no′tice|a|ble|ness**, *n.*

**no|tice|a|bly** (nō′ti sə blē), *adv.* to a noticeable degree: *It is noticeably cooler in the shade.*

**notice board**, *British.* a bulletin board.

**no|ti|fi|a|ble** (nō′tə fī′ə bəl), *adj. Especially British.* that must be reported to medical or other authorities.

**no|ti|fi|ca|tion** (nō′tə fə kā′shən), *n.* **1** the act or process of notifying or making known. **2** a notice, especially printed, written, or spoken.

**no|ti|fi|er** (nō′tə fī′ər), *n.* a person or thing that notifies.

**no|ti|fy** (nō′tə fī), *v.t.,* **-fied, -fy|ing. 1** to let know; give notice to; announce to; inform: *Our teacher notified us that there would be a test on Monday. We have a letter notifying us that he will visit us soon. I was notified of the unpaid bill.* **SYN**: apprise, acquaint. See syn. under **inform**. **2a** to make (something) known; proclaim. **b** to warn of. [< Old French *notifier*, learned borrowing from Latin *nōtificāre* < *nōscere* know + *facere* make]

**no|tion** (nō′shən), *n.* **1** an idea; understanding: *He has no notion of what I mean. Her notion of a joke is not very delicate* (Samuel Johnson). *He had no thoughts, no notion of its being me* (Daniel Defoe). *I considered that my notions of an advocate were false* (James Boswell). **SYN**: concept, impression. See syn. under **idea**. **2** an opinion; view; belief: *modern notions about raising children. One common notion is that red hair goes with a quick temper.* **3a** intention: *He has no notion of risking his money.* **b** an inclination or desire; fancy; whim: *a sudden notion to take a trip.* **4** a foolish idea or opinion: *Grow oranges in Alaska? What a notion!*
**notions**, *U.S.* small, useful articles, such as pins, needles, or thread: *A dime store sells notions.*
[< Latin *nōtiō, -ōnis* < *nōscere* know]

**no|tion|al** (nō′shə nəl), *adj.* **1** in one's imagination or thought only; not real; imaginary. **2** *U.S.* full of notions; having strange notions. **SYN**: whimsical. **3** having to do with ideas or opinions; characterized by abstract concepts, speculation, or theory: *a notional work as distinguished from an experimental work* (Matthew Arnold). **4** *Grammar.* **a** having to do with the meaning of a linguistic form. **b** (of meaning) lexical rather than syntactic. **5** *Semantics.* presentive. —**no′tion|al|ly**, *adv.*

**no|tion|ate** (nō′shə nāt, -nit), *adj. Informal.* **1** full of notions or fancies. **2** having a notion; opinionated.

**no|to|chord** (nō′tə kôrd), *n.* **1** a rodlike structure of cells, enclosed by a fibrous sheath running lengthwise in the back of many of the lowest vertebrates, such as the lancelet. It forms the main supporting structure of the body. **2** a similar structure in the embryos of higher vertebrates. It is considered to be the basis upon which the spinal column is laid down during development. [< Greek *nôton* the back + English *chord*[2]]

**no|to|chord|al** (nō′tə kôr′dəl), *adj.* **1** of or having to do with the notochord. **2** like a notochord.

**No|to|gae|a** (nō′tə jē′ə), *n.* a zoogeographic region of the earth's surface that includes Australia, New Zealand, South America, and tropical North America. [< Greek *nótos* south (wind) + *gaîa* earth, land]

**No|to|gae|an** (nō′tə jē′ən), *adj.* of or having to do with the Notogaea.

**no|to|ri|e|ty** (nō′tə rī′ə tē), *n., pl.* **-ties. 1** the fact or condition of being famous for something bad; ill fame: *A crime or scandal brings much notoriety to those involved in it.* **SYN**: notoriousness. **2** the fact or condition of being widely known: *The newspapers gave the plan notoriety overnight.* **3** a well-known person; celebrity: *They ... enjoy the vicarious pleasure of mixing with society notorieties* (New Statesman).

**no|to|ri|ous** (nō tôr′ē əs, -tōr′-), *adj.* **1** well known because of something bad; having a bad reputation: *The notorious thief was sent to prison for his many crimes.* **SYN**: infamous. **2** well-known; celebrated: *a notorious court case. Sir Winston Churchill's taste for cigars was notorious.* [< Medieval Latin *notorius* (with English *-ous*) < Latin *nōtus* known, past participle of *nōscere* know] —**no|to′ri|ous|ly**, *adv.* —**no|to′ri|ous|ness**, *n.*
► **Notorious** generally means well-known for unfavorable or unsavory reasons: *a notorious cheat.* **Famous** means well-known for accomplishments or excellence: *a famous writer.*

**no|tor|nis** (nō tôr′nis), *n.* any almost extinct flightless rail of a group that inhabits New Zealand. [< New Latin *Notornis* < Greek *nótos* south + *órnis* bird]

**no|tos|tra|can** (nō tos′trə kən), *n.* any of a group of branchiopods with sessile eyes and a low, oval carapace. [< New Latin *Notostraca* (< Greek *nôton* the back + *óstrakon* shell) + English *-an*]

**No|tre Dame** (nō′trə däm′), Our Lady, the Virgin Mary. [< French *notre dame*]

**no-trump** (nō′trump′), *adj., n.* —***adj.*** without any trumps, especially in bridge.
—*n.* **1** a declaration in bridge to play with no suit as trumps. **2** a hand in bridge that is, or is suitable to be, so played.

**no|tum** (nō′təm), *n., pl.* **-ta** (-tə). the dorsal part of an insect's thoracic segment. [< New Latin *notum* < Greek *nôton* the back]

**no|tun|gu|late** (nō tung′gyə lāt), *adj., n.* —***adj.*** of or belonging to a group of extinct herbivorous mammals abundant in South America during the Cenozoic era. —*n.* a notungulate animal. [< New Latin *Notungulata* the order name < Greek *nôton* the back + Latin *ungulātus* ungulate]

**not|with|stand|ing** (not′wiᴛʜ stan′ding, -with-), *prep., conj., adv.* —***prep.*** in spite of: *I bought it notwithstanding the high price.* **SYN**: despite.
—***conj.*** in spite of the fact that: *Notwithstanding there was need for haste, he still delayed.* **SYN**: although.
—***adv.*** **1** in spite of it; nevertheless: *It is raining; but I shall go, notwithstanding.* **2** in spite of anything; still; yet: *He is, notwithstanding, entitled to decent treatment.*

**nou|gat** (nü′gət, -gä), *n.* a kind of soft candy made chiefly from sugar and egg whites and containing nuts. [< French *nougat* < Provençal < Old Provençal *nogat* < Vulgar Latin *nucātus* made with nuts < Latin *nux, nucis* nut]

**nought** (nôt), *n., adv., adj.* = naught. [Old English *nōwiht*; see etym. under **naught**]

**noughts-and-cross|es** (nôts′ən krôs′iz, -kros′-), *n.* = tick-tack-toe.

**nou|me|na** (nü′mə nə, nou′-), *n.* plural of **noumenon**.

**nou|me|nal** (nü′mə nəl, nou′-), *adj.* **1** having to do with noumena. **2** consisting of noumena; understood only by intuition; not phenomenal. —**nou′me|nal|ly**, *adv.*

**nou|me|non** (nü′mə non, nou′-), *n., pl.* **-na** (-nə). **1** (in Kantian philosophy) something that seems real, but cannot be truly understood, although people have some intuitive idea of it, as God or the soul. **2** a thing-in-itself; something that remains of an object of thought after all the categories of understanding, such as space and time, have been removed from it. [< Greek *nooúmenon*, neuter passive present participle of *noeîn* apprehend]

**noun** (noun), *n., adj.* —*n.* **1** a word used as the name of a person, place, thing, quality, or event. Words like *John, table, school, kindness, skill,* and *party* are nouns. A noun can take a plural or possessive ending and is usually the subject or object in a sentence or phrase. **2** the part of speech or form class to which such words belong. **3** a word, phrase, or clause, functioning as a noun; nominal. *Abbr:* n.
—***adj.*** **1** of a noun. **2** like or used as a noun.
[< Anglo-French *noun*, variant of Old French *nom* < Latin *nōmen, -inis* name, noun. See etym. of doublet **nomen**[1].]
► **forms of English nouns.** *Nouns* may be single words or compound words written solid or as two words or hyphenated: *ceremony, bookcase, high school, go-getter.* Most nouns change their form to make the plural, usually adding *-s* or *-es: boys, kindnesses, manufacturers. Nouns* change their form for case only in the genitive or possessive, typically by adding *'s: boy's, Harriet's.* A few nouns may have different forms for male and female sex: *confidant-confidante, executor-executrix, actor-actress.*

**nour|ish** (nėr′ish), *v.t.* **1a** to make grow, or keep alive and well, with food; feed; nurture: *Milk is all we need to nourish our small baby. It's a' for the apple he'll nourish the tree* (Robert Burns). **b** to supply; sustain; support: *a river nourished by many small streams.* **2** *Figurative.* to encourage; support; maintain; foster: *to nourish a hope. I could find nothing to nourish my suspicion* (Daniel Defoe). [< Old French *noriss-*, stem of *norrir*, or *nurrir* < Latin *nūtrīre* feed] —**nour′ish|er**, *n.* —**nour′ish|ing|ly**, *adv.*

**nour|ish|ment** (nėr′ish mənt), *n.* **1** food; nutriment; sustenance: *Their nourishment consisted entirely of the vegetables of their garden, and the milk of one cow* (Mary W. Shelley). **2** the act or process of nourishing. **3** the condition of being nourished.

**nous** (nüs, nous), *n.* **1** the mind as the seat of reason; intellect. **2** *Informal.* common sense or gumption. [< Greek *noûs*, contraction of *nóos* mind]

**Nous** (nüs, nous), *n.* God (as the Supreme Intellect).

**nou|veau pau|vre** (nü vō pō′vrə), *pl.* **nou|veaux pau|vres** (nü vō pō′vrə). *French.* **1** a person who has recently become poor. **2** (literally) new poor. [patterned on *nouveau riche*]

**nou|veau riche** (nü vō rēsh′), *pl.* **nou|veaux riches** (nü vō rēsh′), *French.* **1a** a person who has recently become rich. **b** a person who makes a vulgar display of his wealth. **2** (literally) new rich.

**nou|veau ro|man** (nü vō′ rô män′), *pl.* **nou-veaux ro|mans** (nü vō′ rô män′), *French.* **1** a type of novel developed chiefly in France in the 1960's, characterized by lack of moral, social, or psychological comment and by precise descriptions that suggest the mental state of the person experiencing or seeing them; antinovel: *The detailed objectivity of the narration, giving every event movement by movement, the device of addressing the reader by the vocative ... and the* *drifting plotlessness of the book, are hallmarks of the nouveau roman* (London Times). **2** (literally) new novel.

**nou|veau|té** (nü vō tā′), *n., pl.* **-tés** (-tā′; *Anglicized* -tāz′), *French.* something new; novelty.

**nou|velle vague** (nü vel′ väg′), *French.* the new wave.

**Nov.,** November.

**nov.,** **1** novel. **2** novelist.

**no|va** (nō′və), *n., pl.* **-vae** (-vē), **-vas.** a star that suddenly becomes much brighter and then gradually fades, to its normal brightness, over a period of several weeks, months, or sometimes years: *[Stars] occasionally boil up to a state of instability that results in their exploding as a nova* (William A. Fowler). [< Latin *nova,* feminine singular of *novus* new]

**No|va|chord** (nō′və kôrd), *n. Trademark.* an electronic keyboard instrument somewhat like a spinet, capable of producing a variety of tones approximating the sounds of an organ, piano, stringed instrument, or woodwind, or a combination of these. [< Latin *nova* (see etym. under **nova**) + English *chord*[1]]

**no|vac|u|lite** (nō vak′yə līt), *n.* a very hard, dense, siliceous rock used especially for hones and for grinding wheels. [< Latin *novācula* razor + English *-ite*[1]]

**No|va Sco|tian** (nō′və skō′shən), **1** of or having to do with Nova Scotia, a province in southeastern Canada, or its inhabitants. **2** a native or inhabitant of Nova Scotia.

**no|vate** (nō′vāt, nō vāt′), *v.t.,* **-vat|ed, -vat|ing.** **1** to replace by something new. **2** *Law.* to replace by a new obligation or debt. [< Latin *novāre* (with English *-ate*[1]) < *novus* new]

**no|va|tion** (nō vā′shən), *n.* **1** *Law.* the substitution of a new obligation for an old one, as by replacing the old debtor or creditor with a new one or by altering the names. **2** a change; innovation. **3** *Obsolete.* alteration; renewal.

**nov|el**[1] (nov′əl), *adj.* of a new kind or nature; not known before; strange; new; unfamiliar: *Flying gives people a novel sensation. Red snow is a novel idea to us.* SYN: See syn. under **new.** [< Old French *novel,* learned borrowing from Latin *novellus* (diminutive) < *novus* new]

**nov|el**[2] (nov′əl), *n.* **1** a story with characters and a plot, long enough to fill one or more volumes. Novels are usually about people, scenes, and happenings such as might be met in real life. *It is absurd to ignore Cervantes, as many literary historians do ..., for the novel is there, complete and glorious, in "Don Quixote"* (J. B. Priestley). *Only a novel ... only some work in which the most thorough knowledge of human nature ... the liveliest effusions of wit and humour are conveyed in the best chosen language* (Jane Austen). **2** = novella.
**the novel,** the branch of literature represented by such stories: *The novel is about experience, and experience is always changing* (Newsweek).
[partly < Middle French *nouvelle* < Italian *novella,* partly < Italian < Latin, new things, neuter plural of *novellus* (see etym. under **novel**[1])]
—*Syn.* **Novel, romance** mean a long fictitious story. **Novel** applies particularly to a long work of prose fiction dealing with characters, situations, and scenes that represent those of real life and setting forth the action in the form of a plot. **Romance,** in its modern sense, applies particularly to a story, often a novel in form, presenting characters and situations not likely to be found in real life and emphasizing exciting or romantic adventures, usually set in distant or unfamiliar times or places: *W. H. Hudson's novel, "Green Mansions," is accurately subtitled, "A Romance of the Venezuelan Jungle."*

**nov|el**[3] (nov′əl), *n.* **1** (in Roman law) a new decree or constitution supplementary to a code. **2** (in civil law) a supplement to a law. [< Late Latin *novella* (*cōnstitūtiō*) new (constitution), feminine of *novellus* new, novel[1]]

**nov|el|ette** (nov′ə let′), *n.* a short novel or very long short story.

**nov|el|et|tish** (nov′ə let′ish), *adj.* **1** characteristic of a second-rate novelette. **2** *Especially British.* sentimental; trite: *an absurdly novelettish romance.* —**nov′el|et′tish|ness,** *n.*

**nov|el|ist** (nov′ə list), *n.* a writer of novels: *It is the duty of the novelist to make us believe in his people* (Atlantic).

**nov|el|is|tic** (nov′ə lis′tik), *adj.* of or like novels. —**nov′el|is′ti|cal|ly,** *adv.*

**nov|el|i|za|tion** (nov′ə lə zā′shən), *n.* **1** the process of novelizing; conversion into a novel. **2** the result of this process; a novelized work: *Turning a screenplay into a novel is generally fast work. Some authors bang out novelizations in as little as three weeks* (Wall Street Journal).

**nov|el|ize** (nov′ə līz), *v.t.,* **-ized, -iz|ing.** to put into the form of a novel; make a novel from: *to novelize history.*

**no|vel|la** (nō vel′ə; *Italian* nō vel′lä), *n., pl.* **no|vel|las,** *Italian* **no|vel|le** (nō vel′lā). **1** a short story or novelette with a simple plot: *The title novella depicts an unusual heroine who would be more at home in the medieval world of folk ballads than in the upper Mississippi valley town into which fate ... cast her* (Saturday Review). **2** a short prose tale, usually moral or satiric, such as one of those in Boccaccio's *Decameron.* [< Italian *novella;* see etym. under **novel**[2]]

**nov|el|ly** (nov′ə lē, -əl lē), *adv.* **1** in a novel manner; by a new method. **2** as in a novel.

**nov|el|ty** (nov′əl tē), *n., pl.* **-ties.** **1** novel character; newness: *After the novelty of washing dishes wore off, she did not want to do it any more.* SYN: recentness, freshness. **2** a new or unusual thing or occurrence; innovation: *Staying up late was a novelty to the children, and they enjoyed it.*
**novelties,** small, unusual articles, such as toys or cheap jewelry: *We bought some novelties on the boardwalk.*
[< Old French *novelte,* or *novelite* < Latin *novellitās* < *novellus;* see etym. under **novel**[1]]

**No|vem|ber** (nō vem′bər), *n.* **1** the eleventh month of the calendar year; month just before December. It has 30 days. *Abbr:* Nov. **2** *U.S.* a code name for the letter *n,* used in transmitting radio messages. [< Latin *November* < *novem* nine (because of its position in the early Roman calendar)]

**no|vem|de|cil|lion** (nō′vem də sil′yən), *n.* **1** (in the U.S., Canada, and France) 1 followed by 60 zeros. **2** (in Great Britain and Germany) 1 followed by 114 zeros. [< Latin *novemdecim* nineteen (< *novem* nine + *decem* ten) + English *-illion,* as in *million*]

**no|ve|na** (nō vē′nə), *n., pl.* **-nas, -nae** (-nē). (in the Roman Catholic Church) a devotion for some special purpose, consisting of prayers or services on nine successive days, or sometimes nine corresponding days in consecutive months: *a novena of nine first Fridays.* [< Medieval Latin *novena,* ultimately < Latin *novem* nine]

**no|ver|cal** (nō vėr′kəl), *adj.* **1** characteristic of or resembling a stepmother. **2** befitting a stepmother. [< Latin *novercālis* < *noverca* stepmother, related to *novus* new]

**No|vi|al** (nō′vē əl), *n.* an artificial language somewhat similar to Esperanto, devised by Otto Jespersen in 1928.

**nov|ice** (nov′is), *n.* **1** a person who is new to what he is doing; beginner: *Novices are likely to make some mistakes.* SYN: tyro, apprentice. **2** a person who is not yet a monk or a nun, but is in a period of trial and preparation: *After six months a postulant may receive the habit and white veil of a novice together with a new name* (Time). **3** a new member of the church. **4** a new convert to Christianity. [< Old French *novice, novisse,* learned borrowing from Latin *novīcius* < *novus* new]

**nov|ice|ship** (nov′is ship), *n.* = novitiate.

**no|vil|le|ro** (nō′vē lyā′rō), *n., pl.* **-ros.** *Spanish.* an apprentice bullfighter: *He had semi-flopped in his presentation as a novillero in Madrid nine years ago* (Barnaby Conrad).

**no|vi|ti|ate** or **no|vi|ci|ate** (nō vish′ē it, -āt), *n.* **1** the period of trial and preparation of a novice in a religious order. **2** = novice. **3** the house or rooms occupied by religious novices. **4** *Figurative.* the state or period of being a beginner in anything. [< Medieval Latin *novitiatus* or *noviciatus* < Latin *novīcius* < *novus* new]

**no|vo|bi|o|cin** (nō′və bī′ə sin), *n.* an antibiotic effective against Gram-positive bacteria, especially in infections where bacteria are resistant to other antibiotics. *Formula:* $C_{31}H_{36}N_2O_{11}$

**no|vo|caine** or **no|vo|cain** (nō′və kān), *n.* **1** an alkaloid compound, used as a local anesthetic; procaine hydrochloride. **2 Novocain,** a trademark for this compound. [< Latin *novus* new + English (co)*caine*]

**no|vus or|do se|clo|rum** (nō′vəs ôr′dō se klôr′əm, -klōr′-), *Latin.* a new order of the ages (the motto on the great seal of the United States, from Virgil, *Eclogues,* 4,5): *Novus Ordo Seclorum. When the Founding Fathers set these words—A New Order of the Ages—in the Great Seal of the United States, they had in mind a social order that would guarantee the individual political and personal freedom under law* (Time).

**now** (nou), *adv., n., conj., interj., adj.* —*adv.* **1** at the present time; at this moment: *He is here now. Most people do not believe in ghosts now.* SYN: currently. **2** by this time: *She must have reached the city now.* **3** at once: *Do it now!* SYN: immediately. **4** then; next: *If passed, the bill now goes to the President.* **5** at the time referred to: *The clock now struck three. Night was now approaching.* **6** a little while ago: *I just now saw what you're looking for.* **7** under the present circumstances; as things are; as it is: *I would believe almost anything now. Now I can never believe you again.* **8** *Now* is also used to introduce or emphasize, or where it makes very little difference in meaning: *Now what do you mean? Oh, come now! Now you knew that was wrong.*
—*n.* the present; this time: *by now, until now, from now on. An everlasting Now reigns in Nature* (Emerson).
—*conj.* since; inasmuch as; seeing that: *Now that you are older, you should know better. Now you mention it, I do remember.*
—*interj.* be careful! please!
—*adj.* **1** *Informal.* of or belonging to the immediate present; current; modern: *now styles, now clothes, now music.* **2** *Slang.* Also, **Now.** very fashionable or up-to-date; belonging to the Now Generation: *"This barbershop is Now. Everybody here is Now"* (New Yorker). *They pride themselves on being now people* (Harper's).
**now and again,** from time to time; once in a while: *I see my old neighbor now and again.*
**now and then,** from time to time; once in a while: *I see him now and then, but not often. These Gypsies now and then foretold very strange things* (Joseph Addison).
**now ... now,** at one time ... at another time: *like a stormy day, now wind, now rain* (Shakespeare).
[Old English *nū*]

**NOW** (nou), *n.,* or **N.O.W.,** National Organization for Women (a Women's Liberation organization founded in 1966).

**Now account** (nou), *U.S.* a savings account from which a depositor may withdraw money by check for payment to a third party as in a commercial checking account: *Now accounts, which are actually a check-like method of withdrawing from a savings account* (New York Times). [< *N*(egotiated) *O*(rder) of *W*(ithdrawal)]

**now|a|days** (nou′ə dāz′), *adv., n.* —*adv.* at the present day; in these times: *Nowadays people travel in automobiles rather than carriages.*
—*n.* the present day; these times: *the sports of nowadays.*

**no|way** (nō′wā), *adv.* = nowise.

**no|ways** (nō′wāz), *adv.* = nowise.

**now|el** or **now|ell** (nō el′, nō′el), *n. Archaic.* noël. [< Old French *nouel,* variant of *noël.* See etym. of doublets **Noël, natal.**]

**Now Generation** or **now generation,** the generation of young people of the 1960's and early 1970's, as characterized by their concern with current trends, fashions, and issues.

**no|where** (nō′hwãr), *adv., n., adj.* —*adv.* in no place; at no place; to no place; not anywhere: *a plant found nowhere else, to go nowhere.* (*Figurative.*) *The story goes nowhere special* (Oliver LaFarge).
—*n.* **1** a nonexistent or undefined place: *an imaginary nowhere. Airports are the great nowheres of this world* (Alistair Reid). **2** a remote or obscure place: *Some of the greatest leaders came out of nowhere.* **3** any place: *They live out in the country, miles from nowhere.*
—*adj. Slang.* **1** unimportant; worthless: *Suddenly, who shows up but a bunch of nowhere actors ...* (Bill Vaughan). **2** leading nowhere; pointless: *She sat there among them in the debris of a nowhere love affair* (New Yorker). **3** dull; square: *He's a nowhere man, woodenly proper* (Pauline Kael).
**get nowhere,** to accomplish nothing; be unsuccessful: *Evidence was accumulating that this drive was getting nowhere fast, and stronger medicine might be needed* (Wall Street Journal).
**nowhere near,** *Informal.* not nearly; not by a long way: *I have seen it [a play] three times and its treasures are nowhere near exhausted* (John Coleman).
[Old English *nāhwǣr* or *nōhwǣr*]
▶ See **nobody** for usage note.

**no|wheres** (nō′hwãrz), *adv., n. U.S. Dialect.* nowhere.

**no|whith|er** (nō′hwiᴛʜ′ər), *adv.* = nowhere.

**no|wise** (nō′wīz), *adv.* in no way; not at all.

**nowt**[1] (nout), *n. Scottish.* **1** cattle; oxen. **2** an ox; bullock. **3** a clumsy or stupid person. [< Scandinavian (compare Old Icelandic *naut* cattle)]

**nowt**[2] (nout, nōt), *n. English Dialect.* nothing; naught. [variant of *naught*]

**now|y** (nou′ē, nō′-), *adj. Heraldry.* **1** having a small semicircular projection at or near the middle, as a line or fess. **2** (of a cross) having a projection in each angle between the arms. [< Old French *noe,* past participle of *noer* to knot < Latin *nōdāre* < *nōdus* knot]

**Nox** (noks), *n.* the ancient Roman goddess of night, identified with the Greek Nyx.

---

**Pronunciation Key:** hat, āge, cãre, fär; let, ēqual, tėrm; it, īce; hot, ōpen, ôrder; oil, out; cup, pu̇t, rüle; child; long; thin; ᴛʜen; zh, measure; ə represents a in about, e in taken, i in pencil, o in lemon, u in circus.

**nox|ious** (nok′shəs), *adj.* **1** very harmful; poisonous; pernicious: *Fumes from the exhaust of an automobile are noxious. Poison ivy is a noxious plant; avoid touching its leaves.* **SYN:** unhealthful, deadly, unwholesome. **2** morally hurtful; corrupting: *an unjust and noxious tyranny* (Macaulay). **3** *Obsolete.* criminal. [< Latin *noxius* (with English *-ous*) < *noxa* a hurt < *nocēre* to hurt] **—nox′ious|ly,** *adv.* **—nox′ious|ness,** *n.*

**noy|ance** (noi′əns), *n. Obsolete.* annoyance.

**no|yau** (nwä yō′), *n.* a cordial or liqueur flavored with the kernels of peaches, cherries, or other fruit, or with some substitute. [< French *noyau* (literally) kernel]

**noz|zle** (noz′əl), *n.* **1** a tip put on a hose or pipe, forming an outlet: *He adjusted the nozzle so that the water came out in a fine spray.* **2** any duct through which a fluid is released in a stream: *the nozzle of a gas turbine, the nozzle of a rocket engine.* **3** a socket on a candlestick or sconce. **4** *Slang.* the nose: *His whole face was overshadowed by this tremendous nozzle* (Tobias Smollett). [diminutive of *nose*]

**np** (no periods), new pence.

**Np** (no period), neptunium (chemical element).

**NP** (no periods), an abbreviation for the following:
**1** neuropsychiatric.
**2** neuropsychiatrist.
**3** neuropsychiatry.
**4** proper name (Latin, *nomen proprium*) (used in prescriptions).

**N.P.**, **1** Nobel Prize. **2** notary public.

**NPC** (no periods), National Petroleum Council.

**N.P.D.**, **1** National Democratic Party (of West Germany): *Undoubtedly some members of the neo-Nazi . . . N.P.D. are genuine conservative nationalists* (New York Times). **2** North Polar Distance.

**NPT** (no periods), nonproliferation treaty.

**nr.**, near.

**NRA** (no periods) or **N.R.A.**, **1** National Recovery Administration (a United States government agency from 1933 to 1936, established to administer codes of fair competition for industry). **2** National Rifle Association.

**NRC** (no periods), **1** National Research Council. **2** Nuclear Regulatory Commission.

**NROTC** (no periods) or **N.R.O.T.C.**, Naval Reserve Officer Training Corps.

**NRR** (no periods), net reproductive rate: *This situation, defined by demographers as NRR = 1.0, would not lead to zero population growth (ZPG) at once.* (Paul R. Ehrlich, J. P. Holdren).

**N/S** or **n/s** (no periods), *Banking.* not sufficient (funds).

**n.s.**, not specified.

**Ns** (no period), nimbostratus.

**NS** (no periods), nuclear ship.

**N.S.**, an abbreviation for the following:
**1** National Society.
**2** New Series.
**3** New Style.
**4** Nova Scotia.

**N.S.A.**, or **NSA** (no periods), National Security Agency (the cryptologic organization of the United States government).

**NSC** (no periods), National Security Council (a board of advisers to the President of the United States on military, economic, and diplomatic affairs relating to the national security).

**nsec** (no period), nanosecond.

**NSF** (no periods), **1** Also, **N.S.F.** National Science Foundation. **2** *Banking.* not sufficient funds.

**NSM** (no periods), New Smoking Material (a tobacco substitute containing a cellulose base, added to cigarettes to reduce tar and nicotine content): *NSM also contains none of the irritants that cause bronchial ailments* (Frederick C. Price).

**N.S.P.C.A.**, National Society for the Prevention of Cruelty to Animals.

**N.S.P.C.C.**, National Society for the Prevention of Cruelty to Children.

**n.s.p.f.**, not specifically provided for.

**N.S.W.**, New South Wales.

**Nt** (no period), niton (the former name of radon, now replaced by the symbol Rn).

**N.T.**, **1** New Testament. **2** Northern Territory (in Australia).

**NTA** (no periods), nitrilotriacetic acid.

**N.T.A.**, National Tuberculosis Association.

**nth** (enth), *adj.* **1** last in the series 1,2,3,4, . . . n; being of the indefinitely large or small amount denoted by *n: the nth term in a series, the nth power of a number.* **2** *Informal, Figurative.* umpteenth: *I was reading Goldsworthy Lowes Dickinson's "A Modern Symposium" for the nth time the other day* (London Times).
**to the nth degree**, to the utmost: *He was dressed to the nth degree for the occasion. As the finale approached, the excitement rose to the nth degree.*
[< *n*(umber)]

**N.T.P.**, normal temperature and pressure; standard temperature and pressure.

**nt. wt.**, net weight.

**n-type** (en′tīp′), *adj.* of or having to do with semiconductor materials such as germanium and silicon, with electrical conducting properties that depend upon the presence of impurities such as phosphorus, antimony, and arsenic. The impurities have a density of free electrons greater than the density of holes (vacant spots not occupied by electrons). [< *n*(egative) *type*]

***nu** (nü, nyü), *n.* the 13th letter of the Greek alphabet. [< Greek *ny̆*]

***nu** — N (capital letter) ν (lower-case letter)

**nu|ance** (nü äns′, nyü-; nü′äns, nyü′-), *n.* **1** a shade of expression, meaning, feeling, or the like: *I heard the Brahms Sonata in E Minor, which he interpreted with a subtle feeling for nuance* (New Yorker). **2** a slight difference in the shade of a color or tone: *A single primary colour alone may have a surprisingly large number of nuances* (London Times). [< French *nuance* < *nuer* to shade < *nue* cloud < Vulgar Latin *nūba*, for Latin *nūbēs*]

**nu|anced** (nü änst′, nyü-; nü′änst, nyü′-), *adj.* marked by or exhibiting nuances.

**nub** (nub), *n.* **1** a knob or knotlike lump; protuberance. **2** a lump or small piece; nubbin. **3** *Informal.* the point or gist of anything: *The nub of this matter is that we must not fall into the egregious sin of lack of faith in . . . our youth* (Eugene Youngert). [apparently variant of obsolete *knub* knob]

**nub|bin** (nub′in), *n.* **1** a small or imperfect ear of corn. **2** an undeveloped fruit. **3** a small lump or piece: *a nubbin of wool on a sweater.* [American English, diminutive form of *nub*]

**nub|ble** (nub′əl), *n.* a nub or nubbin: *He was lying on a piece of dingy ticking full of lumps and nubbles* (Rudyard Kipling).

**nub|bly** (nub′lē), *adj.*, **-bli|er, -bli|est.** knobby or lumpy: . . . *nubbly daytime tweeds* (New Yorker).

**nub|by** (nub′ē), *adj.*, **-bi|er, -bi|est.** knobby or lumpy; nubbly.

**Nu|bi|an** (nü′bē ən, nyü′-), *adj., n.* **—*adj.*** of or having to do with Nubia, a region in northeastern Africa south of Egypt and bordering on the Red Sea, its inhabitants, or their language.
**—*n.*** **1** a member of the Negroid people inhabiting Nubia. **2** the language spoken by this people.

**Nubian goat**, any large, long-eared goat of a breed of northern Africa that gives rich milk.

**nu|bile** (nü′bəl, nyü′-), *adj.* (of a girl) old enough to be married; marriageable: *The moon's three phases of new, full, and old recalled the matriarch's three phases of maiden, nymph (nubile woman) and crone* (Robert Graves). [< Latin *nūbilis* < *nūbere* take a husband. Compare etym. under **nuptial**.]

**nu|bil|i|ty** (nü bil′ə tē, nyü-), *n.* the condition of being old enough to marry.

**nu|bi|lous** (nü′bə ləs, nyü′-), *adj.* **1** cloudy; foggy; misty. **2** *Figurative.* obscure; indefinite. [< Latin *nūbilōsus* < *nūbilus* cloudy < *nūbēs* cloud]

**nu body**, = nucleosome.

**nu|cel|lar** (nü sel′ər, nyü-), *adj.* **1** of or having to do with a nucellus. **2** like a nucellus.

**nu|cel|lus** (nü sel′əs, nyü-), *n., pl.* **-cel|li** (-sel′ī). *Botany.* the central mass of cells within the integument of the ovule containing the embryo sac; megasporangium. [< New Latin *nucellus* < Late Latin *nucella* hazelnut (diminutive) < *nucula* (diminutive) < *nux, nucis* nut]

**nu|cha** (nü′kə, nyü′-), *n., pl.* **-chae** (-kē). the nape of the neck. [< Medieval Latin *nucha* nape of the neck < Arabic *nukha'* spinal marrow]

**nu|chal** (nü′kəl, nyü′-), *adj.* **1** of or having to do with the nape of the neck: *the nuchal muscles.* **2** *Entomology.* situated on the thorax just behind the head, as certain markings on an insect larva.

**nu|cle|ar** (nü′klē ər, nyü′-), *adj., n.* **—*adj.*** **1a** of or having to do with atomic energy; atomic: *the nuclear age, nuclear processes.* **b** used in atomic energy; using atomic energy: *nuclear materials, a nuclear submarine.* **c** of or having to do with nuclear weapons or their use: *nuclear disarmament; . . . to see this crisis through even to a nuclear conclusion* (Observer). **2** of or having to do with a nucleus, as of a cell or an atom or the particles contained within the nucleus: *nuclear disintegration, a nuclear charge.* **3** having the character or position of a nucleus; like a nucleus. **4** forming a nucleus.
**—*n.*** **1** a nuclear weapon, especially a missile armed with an atomic warhead: *The West . . . is unlikely to initiate the use of nuclears* (London Times). **2** a nuclear power; nation with an arsenal of atomic weapons: *Negotiation between nuclears and non-nuclears has scarcely begun* (Listener).

**nuclear chemist**, an expert in nuclear chemistry.

**nuclear chemistry**, the branch of chemistry dealing with atoms and atomic nuclei, and their relation to chemical processes and reactions, especially reactions producing new elements.

**nuclear club**, the group of nations armed with nuclear weapons.

**nuclear energy**, = atomic energy.

**nuclear engineering**, the branch of engineering dealing with the design and production of nuclear reactors, particle accelerators, and the equipment and materials needed to produce or use nuclear energy.

**nuclear family**, the group consisting of a father, a mother, and their children: *The nuclear family is universal either as the sole prevailing form or as the basic unit form from which more complex familiar forms are compounded* (Clyde Kluckhohn).

**nuclear fission**, the splitting that occurs when the nucleus of an atom under bombardment absorbs a neutron and divides into two nearly equal parts; fission: *As a result of attempts to prepare isotopes of elements of atomic number greater than 92 [uranium] . . . nuclear fission was discovered* (W. N. Jones).

**nuclear fuel**, a fissionable substance which will sustain a chain reaction: *There was freedom also in discussing the relative roles of uranium and thorium as nuclear fuels* (A. W. Haslett).

**nuclear fusion**, the combining of two atomic nuclei to create a nucleus of greater mass; fusion.

**nu|cle|ar|ism** (nü′klē ər iz′əm, nyü′-), *n.* emphasis on nuclear weapons as a deterrent to war or as a means of attaining political and social goals.

**nu|cle|ar|ist** (nü′klē ər ist, nyü′-), *n.* a person who believes in or is an advocate of nuclearism.

**nu|cle|ar|i|za|tion** (nü′klē ər ə zā′shən, nyü′-), *n.* the act or process of nuclearizing.

**nu|cle|ar|ize** (nü′klē ə rīz, nyü′-), *v.t.*, **-ized, -iz|ing.** to furnish with nuclear weapons or nuclear power; convert to the use of nuclear weapons or power: *to nuclearize a country.*

**nuclear magnetic resonance**, the interaction of atomic nuclei with an external magnetic field when various radiation frequencies are applied to the nuclei, used especially in spectroscopic studies of the structure of molecules: *Nuclear magnetic resonance is being used to measure the rate of venous blood flow in the forearm* (Science News).

**nuclear medicine**, the use of radioactive isotopes in the diagnosis and treatment of diseases.

**nuclear particle**, a particle within, or emitted by, an atomic nucleus. Nuclear particles include neutrons, protons, deuterons, and alpha particles. *If the energy of the incident particle is high enough it can enter the target nucleus and cause it to break up with the emission of a number of nuclear particles* (P. E. Hodgson).

**nuclear physicist**, an expert in nuclear physics: *Between Copenhagen and Cambridge, there was a stream of travelers, all the nuclear physicists of the world* (C. P. Snow).

**nuclear physics**, the branch of physics dealing with atoms, their nuclear structure, and the behavior of nuclear particles: *In nuclear physics, the scientist is interested in the behavior within the nucleus of an atom* (W. P. Schenk).

**nu|cle|ar-pow|ered** (nü′klē ər pou′ərd, nyü′-), *adj.* operating on atomic power.

**nuclear reaction**, = reaction (def. 4).

**nuclear reactor**, = reactor.

**nuclear sap**, = karyolymph.

**nuclear test**, the experimental firing or exploding of a nuclear weapon.

**nuclear transmutation**, = transmutation (def. 3).

**nuclear warfare**, warfare using nuclear weapons.

**nuclear warhead**, a warhead containing fissionable or fusionable material as its explosive charge: *The world is instead putting its most concentrated imaginative efforts on the development of missiles with nuclear warheads* (Bulletin of Atomic Scientists).

**nuclear weapon**, a bomb, shell, rocket, guided missile, or other weapon carrying a nuclear warhead: *Fear of general annihilation may forestall indiscriminate use of nuclear weapons* (Newsweek).

**nu|cle|ar|y** (nü′klē er′ē, nyü′-; *especially British* nü′klē ər ē), *adj.* = nuclear.

**nu|cle|ase** (nü′klē ās, nyü′-), *n.* any one of a group of enzymes that hydrolyze nucleic acids.

**nu|cle|ate** (*v.* nü′klē āt, nyü′-; *adj.* nü′klē it, nyü′-; -āt), *v.*, **-at|ed, -at|ing,** *adj.* **—*v.t., v.i.*** to form into a nucleus or around a nucleus.
**—*adj.*** having a nucleus.
[< Late Latin *nucleāre* (with English *-ate*[1]) become full of kernels < Latin *nucleus* kernel

(diminutive) < *nux, nucis* nut]

**nu·cle·a·tion** (nü′klē ā′shən, nyü′-), *n.* the formation of nuclei: *Dust particles of the proper configuration . . . start the nucleation of snow crystals* (Scientific American).

**nu·cle·a·tor** (nü′klē ā′tər, nyü′-), *n.* a substance or agent that produces nuclei in gases or liquids.

**nu·cle·i** (nü′klē ī, nyü′-), *n.* a plural of **nucleus**.

**nu·cle·ic** (nü klē′ik, nyü-), *adj.* = nucleinic.

**nucleic acid,** a complex chemical compound found in all living cells. It occurs chiefly in combination with proteins. One form of nucleic acid, deoxyribonucleic acid or DNA, is partially responsible for the transmission of inherited characteristics. Nucleic acids consist of linked nucleotides. See also **deoxyribonucleic acid** and **ribonucleic acid.**

**nu·cle·in** (nü′klē in, nyü′-), *n.* any one of a class of substances present in the nuclei of cells, consisting chiefly of proteins, phosphoric acids, and nucleic acids.

**nu·cle·in·ic** (nü′klē in′ik, nyü′-), *adj.* **1** of or having to do with a nuclein or nucleins. **2** like a nuclein or nucleins.

**nucleo-,** *combining form.* **1** nucleus, as in *nucleophile, nucleosynthesis.*
**2** nucleic acid, as in *nucleocapsid, nucleotide.*
[< Latin *nucleus* kernel]

**nu·cle·o·cap·sid** (nü′klē ō kap′sid, nyü′-), *n.* the structure of a virus or virion, consisting of the capsid or protein coat and the nucleic acid which it encloses. [< *nucleo-* + *capsid*]

**nu·cle·o·gen·e·sis** (nü′klē ō jen′ə sis, nyü′-), *n.* the formation or production of atomic nuclei.

**nu·cle·o·his·tone** (nü′klē ō his′tōn, nyü′-), *n.* a basic protein of cell nuclei, influencing the structure and function of chromosomes.

**nu·cle·o·lar** (nü klē′ə lər, nyü-), *adj.* **1** of the nature of a nucleolus. **2** having to do with a nucleolus.

**nu·cle·o·late** (nü′klē ə lāt, nyü′-), *adj.* = nucleolated.

**nu·cle·o·lat·ed** (nü′klē ə lā′tid, nyü′-), *adj.* having a nucleolus or nucleoli.

**nu·cle·ole** (nü′klē ōl, nyü′-), *n.* = nucleolus.

**nu·cle·o·lus** (nü klē′ə ləs, nyü-), *n., pl.* **-li** (-lī). a small, usually round structure found within the nucleus of a cell. It contains a high concentration of ribonucleic acid. [< Late Latin *nucleolus* (diminutive) < Latin *nucleus* kernel (diminutive) < *nux, nucis* nut]

**nu·cle·on** (nü′klē on, nyü′-), *n.* one of the atomic particles that make up the nucleus of an atom, such as a proton or neutron. [< *nucle*(us) + *-on,* as in *electron*]

**nu·cle·on·ic** (nü′klē on′ik, nyü′-), *adj.* **1** of or having to do with nucleonics: *nucleonic equipment.* **2** of or having to do with an atomic nucleus: *nucleonic radiation.*

**nu·cle·on·ics** (nü′klē on′iks, nyü′-), *n.* the science of the behavior and characteristics of nucleons, or of nuclear phenomena.

**nu·cle·o·phile** (nü′klē ə fīl, nyü′-), *n.* a substance that is strongly attracted to atomic nuclei.

**nu·cle·o·phil·ic** (nü′klē ə fil′ik, nyü′-), *adj.* strongly attracted to the nuclei of atoms: *nucleophilic ions or molecules.*

**nu·cle·o·plasm** (nü′klē ə plaz′əm, nyü′-), *n.* the protoplasm found in the nucleus of a cell, not including the nucleoli; karyoplasm. [< *nucleus* + *-plasm,* as in *protoplasm*]

**nu·cle·o·plas·mic** (nü′klē ə plaz′mik, nyü′-), *adj.* **1** having to do with nucleoplasm. **2** like nucleoplasm.

**nu·cle·o·pro·tein** (nü′klē ō prō′tēn, -tē in; nyü′-), *n.* any one of a group of substances present in the nuclei of cells and viruses, consisting of proteins in combination with nucleic acids. On hydrolysis, nucleoproteins yield purine or pyrimidine bases, phosphoric acid, and a pentose sugar.

**nu·cle·o·side** (nü′klē ə sīd, -sid; nyü′-), *n.* any one of a group of compounds of a nitrogen base (purine or pyrimidine) and a sugar (pentose), similar to a nucleotide but lacking phosphoric acid. Adenosine is a nucleoside.

**nu·cle·o·som·al** (nü′klē ə sō′məl, nyü′-), *adj.* of or having to do with a nucleosome or nucleosomes.

**nu·cle·o·some** (nü′klē ə sōm, nyü′-), *n.* the basic structural unit of chromatin: *Each nucleosome is roughly spherical, about 100 A (10 nm) in diameter, and consists of 8 histone molecules and about 200 pairs of DNA* (Bruce A. J. Ponder). *The discovery of the nucleosome was a great advance in understanding chromosome structure* (Eugene R. Katz). [< *nucleo-* + *-some*[3]]

**nu·cle·o·syn·the·sis** (nü′klē ō sin′thə sis, nyü′-), *n.* the process by which chemical elements are created from the nuclei of hydrogen.

**nu·cle·o·tid·ase** (nü′klē ə tī′dās, nyü′-), *n.* an enzyme which splits phosphoric acid from a nucleotide, producing a nucleoside.

**nu·cle·o·tide** (nü′klē ə tīd, -tid; nyü′-), *n.* any one of a group of compounds of sugar, phosphoric acid, and a purine or pyrimidine base. Nucleotides are the principal constituents of nucleic acid and determine the structure of genes. *Inert molecules known as nucleotides and found in DNA were used as the starting material* (Science News Letter).

**nu·cle·us** (nü′klē əs, nyü′-), *n., pl.* **-cle·i** or **-cle·us·es.** **1** a central part or thing around which other parts or things are collected: *A very strange old gentleman, whose eccentricity had become the nucleus for a thousand fantastic stories* (Hawthorne). *The few hundred families, which formed the original nucleus of her citizenship* (Charles Merivale). SYN: center, core, heart. **2** *Figurative.* a beginning to which additions are to be made: *His five-dollar bill became the nucleus of a flourishing bank account. He had the nucleus of a good plan, but it required working out.* **3** a proton, or a group of protons and neutrons, or other nuclear particles, forming the central part of an atom. A nucleus has a positive charge of electricity. The nucleus forms the core around which the electrons orbit. It also contains most of the mass of the whole atom. *The exact ratio of protons to neutrons in a stable nucleus depends on the total number of particles it contains* (J. Little). See picture under **atom. 4** the fundamental, stable arrangement of atoms in a particular compound, to which other atoms may be joined in various ways. **5** *Biology.* a mass of specialized protoplasm found in most plant and animal cells, without which the cell cannot grow and divide. A nucleus is different in structure from the rest of the cell. It consists of complex arrangements of proteins, nucleic acids, and lipids surrounded by a delicate membrane, and typically containing such structures as chromosomes and nucleoli. The nucleus controls growth, cell division, and other activities, and contains DNA, a nucleic acid which passes on the genetic characteristics of the cell. *The hereditary endowment of a plant or animal is now known to be determined by a very special kind of material found primarily in the threadlike chromosomes that may be seen under the microscope in the nucleus of the cell* (Atlantic). See the diagram under **cell. 6** the relatively dense, central part of a galaxy or of a comet's head: *The astronomers tell us that some of these comets have no visible nucleuses* (James Fenimore Cooper). **7** one of a number of anatomically distinct masses of gray matter in the brain or spinal cord of vertebrates, consisting of the cell bodies of nerve cells, having special functions, and connected to one another by nerve fibers. **8** *Meteorology.* a speck of dust or other particle upon which water vapor condenses, as to form a drop; condensation nucleus. **9** the kernel of a seed. [< Latin *nucleus* kernel (diminutive) < *nux, nucis* nut]

**nu·clide** (nü′klīd, nyü′-), *n.* a particular type of atom having a characteristic nucleus and a measurable life span.

**nu·cule** (nü′kyül, nyü′-), *n. Botany.* a nutlet. [< Latin *nucula* (diminutive) < *nux, nucis* nut]

**nude** (nüd, nyüd), *adj., n.* **—*adj.*** **1** naked; bare; unclothed: *the nude trees of winter.* (*Figurative.*) *nude facts.* SYN: undraped, stripped. See syn. under **bare. 2** *Law.* not supported or confirmed; made without a consideration; not actionable, as an agreement.
**—*n.*** a naked human figure in painting, sculpture, or photography: *oldfashioned Rubenslike nudes* (New Yorker).
**the nude, a** the naked human figure: *Modern chalk drawings, studies from the nude* (Robert Browning). **b** a naked condition: *to swim in the nude. Stands sublimely in the nude, as chaste As Medicean Venus* (Elizabeth Barrett Browning).
[< Latin *nūdus*] **—nude′ly,** *adv.* **—nude′ness,** *n.*

**nudge** (nuj), *v.,* **nudged, nudg·ing,** *n.* **—*v.t.*** **1** to push slightly; jog with the elbow to attract attention: *His next neighbors nudged him* (Dickens). **2** *Figurative.* to prod; stimulate: *to nudge one's memory.*
**—*v.i.*** to give a nudge or slight push.
**—*n.*** a slight push or jog, as with the elbow.
[origin uncertain. Compare dialectal Norwegian *nyggja* to jostle.] **—nudg′er,** *n.*

**nu·di·branch** (nü′də brangk, nyü′-), *n., adj.* **—*n.*** any one of a group of marine gastropod mollusks that usually have external adaptive gills and no shell when adult.
**—*adj.*** of or belonging to this group.
[< New Latin *Nudibranchiata* the suborder name < French *nudibranche* < Latin *nūdus* naked + Greek *bránchia* gills]

**nu·di·bran·chi·ate** (nü′də brang′kē it, -āt; nyü′-), *n., adj.* = nudibranch.

**nu·die** (nü′dē, nyü′-), *n. Slang.* a motion picture, play, or magazine or other publication showing nude figures.

**nud·ism** (nü′diz əm, nyü′-), *n.* the practice of going naked for health or as a fad: *The meeting was presided over by state representative G. S. Sampsel, who had offered to sponsor legislation against nudism* (Harper's).

**nud·ist** (nü′dist, nyü′-), *n., adj.* **—*n.*** a person naked for health or as a fad: *The nudists of France are pursued by the police, by the clergy, by the wit of Parisian cartoonists* (John O'London's Weekly).
**—*adj.*** of nudism or nudists: *a nudist colony.*

**nu·di·ty** (nü′də tē, nyü′-), *n., pl.* **-ties. 1** a naked condition; nakedness. **2** something naked; a nude figure, especially as represented in painting or sculpture.

**nud·nik** or **nud·nick** (nu̇d′nik), *n. Slang.* a tiresome, annoying person; bore; pest; crank: *I have another nudnick here who wants a round table like King Arthur's* (S. J. Perelman). [< Yiddish *nudnik* < Russian *nudnyi* tedious + *-nik,* a personal suffix]

**nu·gae** (nyü′jē), *n.pl. Latin.* trifles; nonsense.

**nu·ga·to·ry** (nü′gə tôr′ē, -tōr′-; nyü′-), *adj.* **1** of no value or importance; trifling; worthless: *. . . sentimental interpretation of small part-songs of nugatory musical merit* (London Times). **2** ineffective; useless. SYN: futile. **3** of no force; invalid. [< Latin *nūgātōrius* < *nūgārī* to trifle < *nūgae* trifles]

**nug·gar** (nug′ər), *n.* a large, broad boat used on the Nile River for carrying cargo or troops. [< Arabic *nuqqār*]

**nug·get** (nug′it), *n.* **1** a lump: *Pea and lima bean nuggets can be ground into soup powders that reconstitute in hot water in a few minutes* (Wall Street Journal). *Stone Age man probably knew metals only as occasional nuggets of the precious metals* (J. Growther). **2** a lump of native gold. **3** anything valuable: *a nugget of wisdom.* **4** *Australian.* a short, thick-set person or beast.

**nug·get·y** (nug′ə tē), *adj.* **1** having the form of a nugget; occurring in nuggets or lumps. **2** *Australian.* short and sturdy.

**nui·sance** (nü′səns, nyü′-), *n.* **1** a thing or person that annoys, troubles, offends, or is disagreeable; annoyance: *Flies are a nuisance. The quartering of soldiers upon the colonists was a great nuisance* (H. G. Wells). SYN: plague, trouble, inconvenience. **2** *Law.* anything annoying, harmful, or offensive to a community, or a member of it, especially to a property owner, and always as defined by law. [Middle English *nusance* harm < Old French *nuisance* < *nuis-,* stem of *nuire* to harm < Latin *nocēre*]

**nuisance tax,** a tax that is annoying because it is collected in very small amounts from the consumer.

**nuke** (nük), *n., v.,* **nuked, nuk·ing.** *U.S. Slang.* **—*n.*** **1** an atomic nucleus: *Stage I involves the firing of an inner "nuke" . . . of U-235 or plutonium* (Bulletin of Atomic Scientists). **2** = nuclear weapon: *The enemy's temptation to . . . use "nukes" against Taiwan would be discouraged* (Atlantic). **3** a nuclear-powered electrical generating station: *According to the Hudson River Fishermen's Association, the nuke was directly responsible for the death of between 310,000 and 475,000 fish in a six-week period* (Time).
**—*v.t.*** to attack with nuclear weapons: *"If we felt hemmed in, we would have a right-wing government that . . . would say, 'We have to get ready to nuke 'em to kingdom come and stand guard'"* (New Yorker).

**N.U.L.,** National Urban League.

**null** (nul), *adj., n., v.* **—*adj.*** **1** not binding, especially under law; of no effect; as if not existing: *A promise obtained by force is legally null.* **2** of no value; unimportant; useless; meaningless; empty; valueless: *Here the principle of contribution . . . is reprobated as null, and destructive to equality* (Edmund Burke). SYN: nugatory. **3** not any; nothing; zero: *The effect was small or null.*
**—*n.*** **1** nothing; zero: *"Between my cradle and my tomb," he said not long before the end, "there is a great null"* (Time). **2** loss of a radio signal or an electric current; a condition of zero transmission or reception.
**—*v.t.*** to nullify; cancel: *to null an electronic signal.*
**null and void,** without force or effect, especially legally; not binding; worthless: *That all acts done by the authority of the usurper Harold were held to be null and void* (Edward A. Freeman).
[< Latin *nūllus* not any < *nē-* not + *ūllus* any (diminutive) < *ūnus* one]

**nul·lah** (nul′ə), *n.* a watercourse in India, especially one which is dry except after a heavy rain. [Anglo-Indian < Hindi *nālā*]

**nul·la-nul·la** (nul′ə nul′ə), *n.* a club used as a weapon by Australian aborigines.

---

**Pronunciation Key:** hat, āge, cãre, fär; let, ēqual, tėrm; it, īce; hot, ōpen, ôrder; oil, out; cup, pu̇t, rüle; child; long; thin; ᴛʜen; zh, measure; ə represents **a** in about, **e** in taken, **i** in pencil, **o** in lemon, **u** in circus.

**nul|li|fi|ca|tion** (nul′ə fə kā′shən), *n.* **1** the act or process of making null: *What labor really wants is nullification of right-to-work laws now in effect in eighteen states* (Newsweek). **2** the condition of being nullified: *the nullification of a treaty.* **3** Often, **Nullification.** *U.S.* an action taken by a state to nullify or declare unconstitutional a Federal law or judicial decision and prevent its enforcement within the state's boundaries.

**nul|li|fi|ca|tion|ist** or **Nul|li|fi|ca|tion|ist** (nul′ə-fə kā′shə nist), *n. U.S.* a supporter or advocate of the right of states to nullify Federal laws.

**nul|li|fi|er** (nul′ə fī′ər), *n.* **1** a person who nullifies. **2** *U.S.* a nullificationist.

**nul|li|fy** (nul′ə fī), *v.t.,* **-fied, -fy|ing. 1** to make not binding, especially legally; render void: *to nullify a treaty or a law.* **SYN:** annul, repeal. **2** to make of no effect; destroy; cancel; wipe out: *The difficulties of the plan nullify its advantages.* [< Latin *nūllificāre* < *nūllus* not any (see etym. under **null**) + *facere* make]

**nul|lip|a|ra** (nə lip′ər ə), *n., pl.* **-a|rae** (-ə rē). a woman who has never borne a child. [< New Latin *nullipara* < Latin *nūllus* not any + *parere* bear young]

**nul|lip|a|rous** (nə lip′ər əs), *adj.* having never borne a child: *a nulliparous woman.*

**nul|li|pen|nate** (nul′ə pen′āt), *adj.* having no light feathers, as the penguin. [< Latin *nūllus* not any + *penna* feather + English *-ate*[1]]

**nul|li|pore** (nul′ə pôr, -pōr), *n.* any of various marine red algae having the power of secreting lime, such as a coralline. [< Latin *nūllus* not any + English *pore*[2]]

**nul|li|ty** (nul′ə tē), *n., pl.* **-ties. 1** futility; nothingness. **2** the condition of being legally null and void; invalidity. **3** a mere nothing; nobody; nonentity: *The king's power in some European countries is practically a nullity.* **4** something that is null, such as a nullified law or agreement: *The Declaration was, in the eye of the law, a nullity* (Macaulay). [< Medieval Latin *nullitas* < Latin *nūllus* not any; see etym. under **null**]

**null set,** = empty set.

**num.,** **1** number or numbers. **2** numeral or numerals.

**Num.,** Numbers (book of the Old Testament).

**numb** (num), *adj., v.* **—*adj.*** having lost the power of feeling or moving: *My fingers are numb with cold.* **SYN:** deadened, insensible, benumbed.
**—*v.t.*** **1** to make numb: *arms and ankles, ... numbed and stiff with ... binding* (Daniel Defoe). **2** *Figurative.* to dull the feelings of: *The old lady was numbed with grief when her bird died.*
[Middle English *nome* < Old English *numen,* past participle of *niman* to take, seize] **—numb′ly,** *adv.* **—numb′ness,** *n.*

**num|bat** (num′bat), *n.* = banded anteater.

***num|ber** (num′bər), *n., v.* **—*n.*** **1** the amount of units; count or sum of a group of things or persons; total: *The number of your fingers is ten. The number of boys in our class is twenty.* **2a** a word that tells exactly how many. Two, fourteen, twenty-six are cardinal numbers; second, fourteenth, twenty-sixth are ordinal numbers. **b** a figure or mark that stands for a number; numeral. 2, 7, and 9 are numbers. *Abbr:* no. **3** a quantity, especially a rather large quantity: *a number of reasons. We saw a number of birds. A large number cannot read.* **4** a collection or company: *the number of saints. Two more are still required to make up the number.* **5** one of a numbered series, often a particular numeral identifying a person or thing: *an apartment number, a license number, a telephone number.* **6** a single part of a program. **7** a song or other piece of music: *She sings many old numbers.* **8a** a single issue of a magazine: *the latest number of the "Saturday Review." The May number has an unusually good story.* **b** a single part of a book published in parts. **9** *Informal.* any thing or person viewed apart or thought of as standing apart from a collection or company: *That dress is the most fashionable number in the store. He's a shrewd number, isn't he?* **10** *Grammar.* a word form or ending which shows one or more is meant. *Boy, ox,* and *this* are in the singular number; *boys, oxen,* and *these* are in the plural number. **11** regularity of beat or measure in verse or music; rhythm: *instrumental sounds in full harmonic number joined* (Milton).
**—*v.t.*** **1** to give a number to; mark with a number; distinguish with a number: *The pages of this book are numbered.* **2** to be able to show; have; contain: *This city numbers a million inhabitants.* **3** to be or amount to a given number; equal: *The states of the Union number 50. The candidate's plurality numbered 5,000 votes.* **SYN:** equal. **4** to reckon as one of a class or collection; classify: *I number you among my best friends.* **5** to fix the number of; limit: *That old man's years are numbered.* **6** to live or have lived (so many years): *The brave soldier had already numbered, nearly or quite, his threescore years and ten* (Hawthorne). **7a** to find out the number of; count: *The business of the poet ... is to examine, not the individual, but the species ... he does not number the streaks of the tulip* (Samuel Johnson). **SYN:** enumerate. **b** *Archaic.* to allot; apportion: *So teach us to number our days, that we may apply our hearts unto wisdom* (Psalm 90:12). **8** *Obsolete.* to levy (a number of, as soldiers).
**—*v.i.*** **1** to make a count: *Many of us can number automatically.* **2** to be numbered or included with: *Tho' thou numberest with the followers of one who cried "leave all and follow me"* (Tennyson).

**beyond number,** too many to count: *There were people beyond number at the circus.*

**do a number on,** *U.S. Slang.* **a** to make fun of; kid: *Fearless Johnny Carson ... did a number on his new boss, NBC president Fred Silverman ... with this line: "Freddy Silverman has just canceled his mother"* (New York Post). **b** to mislead; deceive: *The wife was shaken. "If I'm doing a number on the kid, I want to know about it," Mrs. Braun said* (Janet Malcolm).

**numbers, a** arithmetic: *He is very clever at numbers.* **b** many: *There were numbers who stayed out of school that day.* **c** being greater or more: *to win a battle by force of numbers.* **d** poetry; lines of verse: *I lisp'd in numbers, for the numbers came* (Alexander Pope). **e** groups of musical notes or measures: *Harp of the North! that ... down the fitful breeze thy numbers flung* (Scott). **f** *U.S.* = numbers game: *He hoped to make his fortune by playing the numbers.*

**one's number is up,** *Informal.* one is doomed: *When the bandits ambushed the stagecoach, the driver was sure that his number was up.*

**without number,** too many to be counted: *stars without number.*

[<Old French *nombre* <Latin *numerus*] **—num′ber|er,** *n.*

**—*Syn.*** *n.* **1 Number, sum** mean the total of two or more persons, things, or units taken together. **Number** applies to the total reached by counting the persons or things in a group or collection: *Only twelve came— a smaller number than usual.* **Sum** applies to the total reached by adding figures or things: *The sum of two and two is four.*

▶**Number** is a collective noun, requiring a singular or plural verb according as the total or the individual units are meant: *A number of tickets have already been sold. The number of tickets sold is astonishing.* See **amount** for another usage note.

▶**numbers.** In informal writing, figures are usually used for numbers over ten, words for smaller numbers. In formal writing, figures are usually used for numbers over 100 except when they can be written in two words: Informal: *four, ten, 15, 92, 114, 200.* Formal: *four, ten, fifteen, ninety-two, 114, two hundred.* But practice is not consistent.

$1, 2, 3, 4 \ldots$
natural numbers

$\sqrt{-1}, \sqrt{-2}, \sqrt{-3}, \sqrt{-4},$
imaginary numbers

$-3, -2, -1, 0, 1, 2, 3$
integers

***number**
definition 2b

$\sqrt{2}, \sqrt[3]{2}, \sqrt{5}, \pi$
irrational numbers

$2/2, 2/3, -3/4, 8/4$
rational numbers

**num|ber|less** (num′bər lis), *adj.* **1** very numerous; too many to count: *There are numberless fish in the sea.* **SYN:** countless, myriad, infinite. **2** without a number; not numbered.

**number line,** *Mathematics.* a line on which each point is associated with a real number in a one-to-one correspondence.

**number one, 1** *Informal.* oneself; one's own welfare. **2** the first or best of a group or series.

**num|ber-one** (num′bər wun′), *adj.* chief; leading; principal: *Television ... now seems to be firmly entrenched as the number-one medium for national advertising* (C. Jackson Shuttleworth).

**Number One,** *British.* the officer second in command of a naval vessel; first lieutenant or first mate.

**number plate,** *British.* a license plate.

**num|bers** (num′bərz), *n. pl.* See under **number.**

**Num|bers** (num′bərz), *n.* the fourth book of the Old Testament. It tells about the counting of the Israelites after they left Egypt. *Abbr:* Num.

**numbers game, racket,** or **pool,** *U.S.* an illegal daily lottery in which bets are made on the appearance of any three-digit numbers in a published statistic, such as the total amount bet at a race track or a stock market total; numbers.

**numbers runner** or **number runner,** *U.S.* a person who collects bets in a numbers game.

**number theory,** the study of integers and their relationships.

**number two,** *Slang.* second; not in the most important or powerful position: *It just does not pay to be number two* (Jonathan Steele).

**numb|ing** (num′ing), *adj.* that numbs or induces numbness: *numbing cold,* (*Figurative.*) *numbing grief.* **—numb′ing|ly,** *adv.*

**num|bles** (num′bəlz), *n. pl. Archaic.* the heart, liver, or certain other internal organs of an animal, especially of a deer, used as food. [< Old French *nombles,* or *numbles* a loin or fillet, apparently an alteration of unrecorded *lombles* < Latin *lumbulus* (diminutive) < *lumbus* loin]

**numb|skull** (num′skul′), *n.* = numskull.

**nu|men** (nü′mən, nyü′-), *n., pl.* **-mi|na** (-mə nə). *Roman Mythology.* a spirit presiding over the affairs of men; deity. [< Latin *nūmen* divine power; (originally) a nod, related to *nuere* nod]

**nu|mer|a|ble** (nü′mər ə bəl, nyü′-), *adj.* that can be counted. [< Latin *numerābilis* < *numerāre* to number, numerate]

**nu|mer|a|cy** (nü′mər ə sē, nyü′-), *n.* competence in mathematics; the quality of being numerate: *Literacy and numeracy* [*together*] *... cover whatever extensions of the three Rs are now required by the recharged meaning of "educated"* (London Times). [back formation < *innumeracy*]

**num|é|raire** (nʏ mā rãr′), *n. French.* a standard for currency exchange rates: *The Bretton Woods agreement ... established the dollar as the numeraire, or measuring rod, against which the value of other currencies was set* (New Yorker).

***nu|mer|al** (nü′mər əl, nyü′-), *n., adj.* **—*n.*** **1a** a figure, letter, or word standing for a number: *The numeral on the page was torn off; so I could not tell which page it was.* **b** a group of figures, letters, or words standing for a number. 1, 5, 10, 50, 100, and 1,000 are Arabic numerals; I, V, X, L, C, and M are Roman numerals. **2** one of the figures or symbols used to express a number; digit.
**—*adj.*** **1** of numbers; standing for a number: *a numeral word or adjective.* **2** belonging to or having to do with number.

**numerals,** big cloth numbers given by a school for excellence in some sport. They state the year in which the person who wins them will graduate. *He wore his varsity numerals with pride.*

[< Late Latin *numerālis* < Latin *numerus* number] **—nu′mer|al|ly,** *adv.*

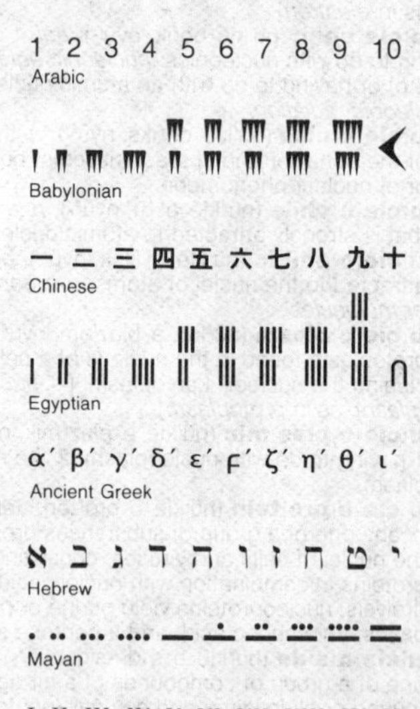

***numeral**
definition 1

**nu|mer|ar|y** (nü′mə rer′ē, nyü′-), *adj.* of or having to do with a number or numbers.

**nu|mer|ate**[1] (nü′mə rāt, nyü′-), *v.t.,* **-at|ed, -at|ing. 1** to number, count, or enumerate. **2** to read (an expression in numbers). [< Latin *numerāre* (with English *-ate*[1]) to number < *numerus* a number]

**nu|mer|ate**[2] (nü′mər it, nyü′-), *adj.* able to understand or use mathematics: *In the nineteenth century we recognized that to achieve commercial leadership we needed a literate population. We are now learning that technological leadership requires a numerate population* (New Scientist). [back formation < *innumerate*] **—nu′mer|ate|ly,** *adv.*

**nu|mer|a|tion** (nü′mə rā′shən, nyü′-), *n.* **1** the act or process of numbering, counting, or enumerating: *Numeration is but still the adding of one unit* *more* (John Locke). **2** the reading of numbers expressed in figures.

**numeration system**, any system of counting or naming numbers, such as the decimal system and the binary system.

**nu|mer|a|tor** (nü′mə rā′tər, nyü′-), *n.* **1** the number above the line in a fraction, which shows how many parts are taken: *In 3/8, 3 is the numerator and 8 the denominator.* **2** a person or thing that makes a count, takes a census, or the like. [< Late Latin *numerātor* counter < Latin *numerāre* numerate]

**nu|mer|ic** (nü mer′ik, nyü-), *adj.* = numerical.

**nu|mer|i|cal** (nü mer′ə kəl, nyü-), *adj.* **1** of a number; having something to do with numbers; in numbers; by numbers: *numerical order.* **2** shown by numbers, not by letters: *10 is a numerical quantity; bx is a literal or algebraic quantity.* **3** (of a mathematical quantity) designating the value in figures without considering the sign: *The numerical value of +4 is less than that of ‖7, though its algebraic value is more.*

**numerical analysis**, the study of mathematical methods for solving problems.

**numerical control**, a method of machine-tool automation using perforated tape carrying coded instructions: *Numerical control means a fully automatic control system which works from numerical information, of the kind found on an engineering drawing* (New Scientist). *Abbr:* NC (no periods).

**numerical forecasting**, a method of weather forecasting in which an electronic computer is fed numerical data on the current weather situation to compute the conditions likely to prevail in a short period of time. It then uses the resulting prediction as the basis for computing the weather at the end of the next period, and so on until a 24-hour forecast is obtained.

**nu|mer|i|cal|ly** (nü mer′ə klē, nyü-), *adv.* **1** by numbers; in a numerical manner: *to state one's findings numerically.* **2** in numerical respects; so far as numbers are concerned: *The size of our school is numerically larger than theirs.*

**nu|mer|i|cal|ly-con|trolled** (nü mer′ə klē kən trōld′, nyü-), *adj.* automated through numerical control.

**nu|mer|o|log|i|cal** (nü′mər ə loj′ə kəl, nyü′-), *adj.* of or having to do with numerology: *numerological analysis.*

**nu|mer|ol|o|gist** (nü′mə rol′ə jist, nyü′-), *n.* a person who practices numerology.

**nu|mer|ol|o|gy** (nü′mə rol′ə jē, nyü′-), *n.* the practice of foretelling the future by the study of supposedly meaningful numbers or combinations of numbers based on a date of birth, the letters of a name, and other personal factors; the occultism of numbers: *The supposed basis for numerology is that all numbers vibrate* (John Mulholland). [< Latin *numerus* number + English *-logy*]

**nu|mer|os|i|ty** (nü′mə ros′ə tē, nyü′-), *n., pl.* **-ties.** **1** large number; numerousness. **2** harmonious flow; poetical rhythm; harmony.

**nu|me|ro u|no** (nü′mə rō ü′nō), **1** *Informal.* the first or best of a group; number one: *Now along comes the 22-year-old Miss Evert, numero uno, a two-time defending champion* (New York Times). *Campaign jingoism can't cover up the fact that we're not Numero Uno* (Time). **2** = oneself. [< Spanish or Italian *numero uno* number one]

**nu|mer|ous** (nü′mər əs, nyü′-), *adj.* **1** very many; of great number: *The child asked numerous questions.* **syn**: manifold, several, innumerable. **2** in great numbers; consisting of many; plentiful: *He has a numerous acquaintance among politicians.* [< Latin *numerōsus* (with English *-ous*) < *numerus* number] —**nu′mer|ous|ly**, *adv.* —**nu′mer|ous|ness**, *n.*

**nu|me|rus clau|sus** (nü′mə rus klou′sus), **1** a quota formerly set in various European countries to restrict the admission of students of a particular race or creed to a school or university. **2** any system based on a quota for admission into an institution, profession, or the like. [< New Latin *numerus clausus* closed number]

**Nu|mid|i|an** (nü mid′ē ən, nyü-), *adj., n.* —*adj.* of or having to do with Numidia, an ancient country in northern Africa, its people, or their language. —*n.* **1** a native or inhabitant of Numidia. **2** the Hamitic language of ancient Numidia.

**Numidian crane**, = demoiselle.

**nu|mi|na** (nü′mə nə, nyü′-), *n.* plural of **numen.**

**nu|mi|nous** (nü′mə nəs), *adj.* **1** spiritual; holy; divine: *a numinous light. Certain human beings are publicly regarded as numinous* (W. H. Auden). **2** ethereal or nebulous; intangible: *everything for her was numinous—the butcher with his cleaver, the hunters in the woods* (New Yorker). [< Latin *nūmen, -inis* (see etym. under **numen**) + English *-ous*]

**nu|mis|mat|ic** (nü′miz mat′ik, nyü′-), *adj.* **1** of numismatics or numismatists. **2** of coins and medals. —**nu′mis|mat′i|cal|ly**, *adv.*

**nu|mis|mat|ics** (nü′miz mat′iks, nyü′-), *n.* the study or collecting of coins or paper currency, medals, tokens, and the like. [< French *numismatique* < Latin *numisma, -atis* coin, currency < Greek *nómisma, -atos* < *nomízein* have in use]

**nu|mis|ma|tist** (nü miz′mə tist, nyü-), *n.* an expert in numismatics: *A numismatist asked for a spot to spread coins* (Wall Street Journal).

**num|ma|ry** (num′ər ē), *adj.* of or having to do with coins or money; occupied with coins or money. [< Latin *nummārius* < *nummus* coin]

**num|mu|lar** (num′yə lər), *adj. Medicine.* somewhat flat and nearly round; shaped like a coin. [< Latin *nummulus* money (diminutive) < *nummus* a coin + English *-ar*]

**num|mu|lar|y** (num′yə ler′ē), *adj.* = nummary.

**num|mu|lat|ed** (num′yə lā′tid), *adj. Medicine.* nummular.

**num|mu|la|tion** (num′yə lā′shən), *n. Medicine.* the arrangement, like that of rolls of coins, assumed by red blood cells in freshly drawn blood. [< Latin *nummulus* money (see etym. under **nummular**) + English *-ation*]

**num|mu|lite** (num′yə līt), *n.* any foraminifer of an extinct group of the early Tertiary period, having a flat spiral shell. Their fossils are abundant in limestones of the Mediterranean area. [< Latin *nummulus* (diminutive) < *nummus* coin + *-ite*[1]]

**num|mu|lit|ic** (num′yə lit′ik), *adj.* **1** containing nummulites: *nummulitic limestone.* **2** characterized by nummulites.

**num|skull** (num′skul′), *n.* a stupid person; blockhead; dolt: *We considered them to be numskulls and little better than idiots* (Anthony Trollope). Also, **numbskull.**

**nun**[1] (nun), *n.* **1** a woman who gives up everything else for religion, and with other religious women lives a life of prayer and worship. Some nuns teach; others take care of the sick and the poor. **2** any one of various birds, such as the European blue titmouse, the smew, or a variety of domestic pigeon with a veillike crest. [Old English *nunne* < Late Latin *nonna,* feminine of *nonnus* monk (originally) a term of address] —**nun′like′**, *adj.*

**nun**[2] (nůn), *n.* the fourteenth letter of the Hebrew alphabet. [< Hebrew *nūn*]

**nu|na|tak** (nü′nə tak), *n.* the peak of a mountain or hill which projects above a surrounding glacier. [< an Eskimo word]

**nun|bird** (nun′bėrd′), *n.* any of the South American puffbirds, with dark feathers on the body, wings, and tail, and white on the head.

**nun buoy**, a buoy that is round in the middle and tapering toward each end. See picture under **buoy.**

**nunc di|mit|tis** (nungk′ di mit′is), *Latin.* permission to depart; departure; dismissal.

**Nunc Di|mit|tis** (nungk′ di mit′is), a canticle of Simeon, beginning "Lord, now lettest thou thy servant depart in peace," from the words of Simeon on recognizing the infant Jesus as the Christ (in the Bible, Luke 2:25-32). [< Latin *Nunc dimittis* now lettest thou depart]

**nun|cha|ku** (nun′chə kə), *n., pl.* **-kus.** a weapon of defense against frontal assault, used especially in karate, consisting of two wooden sticks connected by a rawhide or nylon cord. [< Japanese *nunchaku*]

**nun|cheon** (nun′chən), *n. British Informal or Dialect.* a light refreshment taken between meals. [reduction of Middle English *nonechenche* < Old English *nōn* noon + *scenc* drink]

**nun|ci|a|ture** (nun′shē ə chər), *n.* the office or term of service of a nuncio. [Latinization of Italian *nunziatura* < *nunzio* nuncio]

**nun|ci|o** (nun′shē ō), *n., pl.* **-ci|os.** an official representative or ambassador from the Pope to a government: *With the papal nuncio threatening, the Doge felt obliged to decline the gift* (New Yorker). **syn**: legate. [< Italian *nuncio,* or *nunzio* < Latin *nūntius* messenger]

**nun|cle** (nung′kəl), *n. Dialect.* uncle. [< misdivision of *an uncle*]

**nun|cu|pa|tive** (nung′kyə pā′tiv, nung kyü′pə-), *adj. Law.* not in writing; oral: *He left me a small legacy in a nuncupative will, as a token of his kindness for me* (Benjamin Franklin). [< Late Latin *nuncupātīvus* < *nuncupāre* to name, call by name < *nōmen* name + *capere* take]

**nun|di|nal** (nun′də nəl), *adj.* **1** having to do with a fair or market. **2** connected with the Roman nundines.

**nun|dine** (nun′dīn, -din), *n.* a periodical market day among the ancient Romans, being the ninth day as reckoned from the preceding market day taken as the first, or, as expressed in modern reckoning, occurring every eighth day. [< Latin *nundinae,* feminine plural of *nundinus* < *novem* nine + *diēs* day]

**nun moth**, a European moth, whose larva does great damage to forest trees.

**nun|na|tion** (nu nā′shən), *n.* the addition of a final *n* in the declension of nouns, as in Middle English and Arabic. [< New Latin *nunnatio, -onis* < Arabic *nūn* the letter "n"]

**nun|ner|y** (nun′ər ē), *n., pl.* **-ner|ies.** the building or buildings where nuns live; convent: *I shall take up my abode in a religious house, near Lisle—a nunnery, you would call it* (Charlotte Brontë).

**nun's veiling**, a thin, plain-woven woolen fabric, used mainly for women's dresses and sometimes for religious habits.

**nuoc mam** (nwôk′ mäm′), a thin, spicy Vietnamese fish sauce made from the liquor of decomposing fish. [< Vietnamese *nuóc mam*]

**Nu|pe** (nü′pā), *n., pl.* **-pe** or **-pes.** **1** a member of a people of central Nigeria, noted for their bronze sculptures and other art works. **2** the Kwa language of this people.

**nu|phar** (nü′fər, nyü′-), *n.* any perennial aquatic herb of a group of the water-lily family, with large floating or erect leaves and yellow or purplish flowers; yellow water lily; spatterdock. [< New Latin *nuphar* < Arabic, and Persian *nūfar,* reduction of *nīnūfar* nenuphar]

**nu|plex** (nü′pleks, nyü′), *n.* a nuclear-powered complex of industrial manufacturers. [< *nu*(clear) (com)*plex*]

**nup|tial** (nup′shəl), *adj., n.* —*adj.* **1** of marriage or weddings: *nuptial vows. I chose a Wife ... And in your City held my Nuptial Feast* (Milton). **2** of the mating or breeding season among animals: *nuptial display, nuptial territory.*
—*n.* **nuptials**, a wedding or the wedding ceremony: *a feast ... rich as for the nuptials of a king* (Tennyson).
[< Middle French *nuptial,* learned borrowing from Latin *nuptiālis* < *nuptiae, -ārum* wedding < *nūbere* take a husband]

**Nuptial Blessing**, (in the Roman Catholic Church) a special blessing bestowed upon the bride and groom at a Nuptial Mass.

**nup|ti|al|i|ty** (nup′shē al′ə tē), *n.* the rate or incidence of marriage.

**Nuptial Mass**, in the Roman Catholic and some other churches: **1** a Mass for the bride and groom incorporated into the wedding ceremony. **2** the wedding ceremony including this.

**nuptial plumage**, the colorful plumage of certain male birds at the beginning of the breeding season.

**nu|ra|ghe** (nů rä′gā), *n., pl.* **-ghi** (-gē). a towerlike structure of ancient date, of a kind peculiar to Sardinia. [< a dialectal Sardinian word]

**nurse** (nėrs), *n., v.,* **nursed, nurs|ing.** —*n.* **1** a person who takes care of the sick, the injured, or the old, especially under a doctor's supervision: *Hospitals employ many nurses.* **2** a woman who cares for and brings up the young children or babies of another person: *Mrs. Jones has hired a new nurse.* **3** = wet nurse. **4** *Figurative.* one who feeds and protects, or gives any sort of aid or comfort: *Gentle sleep, Nature's soft nurse* (Shakespeare). **5** a worker in a colony of bees or ants that cares for the young. **6** the act of controlling the balls for a series of shots in billiards.
—*v.i.* **1** to be a nurse; act as a nurse; work as a nurse. **2** to suck milk from the breast of a mother or nurse.
—*v.t.* **1** to act as a nurse for; wait on or try to cure (the sick); take care of (sick, injured, or old people). **2** to cure or try to cure by care: *She nursed a bad cold by going to bed.* **3** to take care of and bring up (another's baby or young child). **4** *Figurative.* to nourish; make grow; protect: *to nurse a plant, nurse a fire, nurse a hatred in one's heart. He nursed what property was yet left to him* (Scott). **5** to treat or use with special care: *He nursed his sore arm by using it very little.* **6** *Figurative.* to hold closely; clasp fondly: *Here I found my lord seated, nursing his cane* (Robert Louis Stevenson). **7** to give milk to (a baby). **8** to hit (billiard balls) softly so as to keep them close together for a series of shots. **9** *Informal.* to drink very slowly in sips: *to nurse a cocktail.*
[Middle English *nurice* < Old French *nurrice* < Latin *nūtrīcia* < *nūtrīre* to feed. Compare etym. under **nourish.**] —**nurs′er**, *n.*

**nurse balloon**, *Aeronautics.* a small portable balloon of heavy fabric, used for storing gas, as for replenishing the supply of gas of another balloon.

**nurse|ling** (nėrs′ling), *n.* = nursling.

**nurse|maid** (nėrs′mād′), *n., v.* —*n.* a girl or woman employed to care for children. —*v.t.* to take care of in the manner of a nursemaid; nurse; nurture: (*Figurative.*) *The families ... will*

---

**Pronunciation Key:** hat, āge, cãre, fär; let, ēqual, tėrm; it, īce; hot, ōpen, ôrder; **oi**l, **ou**t; cup, půt, rüle; **ch**ild; lo**ng**; **th**in; **ᵺ**en; **zh**, measure; **ə** represents **a** in about, **e** in taken, **i** in pencil, **o** in lemon, **u** in circus.

nursemaid *a llama for a year* (Atlantic).
**nurs|er|y** (nėrs′ər ē, nėrs′rē), *n., pl.* **-er|ies.** **1** a room set apart for the use of the small children and babies of the household: *What I should like best ... would be to go to the nursery, and see your dear little children* (Thackeray). **2** a piece of ground or place where young trees and plants are raised for transplanting or sale. **3** *Figurative.* a place or condition that helps something to grow and develop: *Slums are often nurseries of disease. Family life, the first and last nursery of the higher sympathies* (H. Drummond). **4** the brood or chambers in which larval, social insects attain maturity. **5** = nursery school. **6** *Obsolete.* upbringing.
**nurs|er|y|maid** (nėr′sər ē mād′, nėrs′rē-), *n.* = nursemaid: *A nurserymaid is not afraid of what you gentlemen call work* (William S. Gibert).
**nurs|er|y|man** (nėr′sər ē mən, nėrs′rē-), *n., pl.* **-men.** a man who grows or sells young trees and plants.
**nursery rhyme,** a short poem for children. "Sing a Song of Sixpence" is a famous nursery rhyme. *The origins of many nursery rhymes are shrouded in the fumes of taverns and mughouses* (Time).
**nursery school,** a school for children not old enough to go to kindergarten, especially children between the ages of three and five: *Nursery school gives young children space to play freely and actively* (Sidonie Gruenberg).
**nurse's aide,** a person who helps nurses in hospitals by performing tasks requiring little training, such as answering patients' calls and helping to feed and wash them.
**nurse shark,** any of various sharks that rest for a long time between movements, especially the gata-nosed shark.
**nurs|ing bottle** (nėr′sing), a bottle to which a rubber nipple is attached, for feeding infants.
**nursing home,** a private hospital, especially for convalescent patients.
**nurs|ling** (nėrs′ling), *n.* **1** a baby that is being nursed. **2** any person or thing that is receiving tender care: (*Figurative.*) *I am the daughter of Earth and Water, And the nursling of the sky* (Shelley). Also, **nurseling.**
**nur|tur|ance** (nėr′chə rəns), *n.* the action or process of nurturing; providing of sustenance and care.
**nur|tur|ant** (nėr′chə rənt), *adj.* providing sustenance and care: *Social scientists apply the term "nurturant" to typical female professions such as child care, teaching, nursing or social work* (Tom Alexander).
**nur|ture** (nėr′chər), *v.,* **-tured, -tur|ing,** *n.* — ***v.t.*** **1** to rear; bring up; care for; foster; train: *She nurtured the child as if he had been her own.* **2** to nourish; feed: *to nurture resentment.* [< noun]
— ***n.*** **1** the action of rearing; bringing up; training; education: *The two sisters had received very different nurture, one at home and the other at a convent.* **2** nourishment; food: (*Figurative.*) *Where ... from the heart we took our first and sweetest nurture* (Byron).
[< Old French *nourture,* or *norreture,* adaptation < Late Latin *nūtrītūra* a nursing, suckling < Latin *nūtrīre* to nurse, nourish. Compare etym. under **nutritious.**] — **nur′tur|er,** *n.*
***nut** (nut), *n., v.,* **nut|ted, nut|ting.** — ***n.*** **1** a dry fruit or seed with a hard, woody or leathery shell and a kernel inside which is often good to eat: *... two or three cents to buy candy, and nuts and raisins* (Hawthorne). **2a** the kernel of a nut; nutmeat. **b** *Botany.* a dry, one-seeded, indehiscent fruit similar to an achene, but larger and having a harder and thicker pericarp, such as an acorn, hazelnut, or beechnut. **c** *Figurative.* kernel; core; basic part: *The nut of Bray's argument ... is that the government's role in managing the economy would be more effective if the blanket approach were replaced by a new structure* (New Scientist). **3** a small, usually metal block having a threaded hole in the center, that screws on to a bolt to hold the bolt in place. **4a** a piece at the upper end of a violin, cello, or certain other stringed instruments, over which the strings pass. **b** a device at the lower end of the bow, by which the horsehair may be relaxed or tightened; frog. **5** *Slang.* **a** an odd or silly person: *The doctors had him on record as a nut* (Punch). **b** an overzealous person: *He answers the phone himself. He's a nut about keeping in touch* (Time). **c** an enthusiast; devotee; fan: *There's a darkroom for the camera nuts* (New Yorker). **6** *Slang.* the head: *He was about half off his nut* (Esquire). **7** *U.S. Slang.* the cost or expenses of an undertaking: *What often makes or breaks a show is its weekly operating cost—or "nut," as it's known in the business* (Wall Street Journal).
— ***v.i.*** to gather nuts: *The younger people, making holiday, with bag and sack and basket, great and small, went nutting to the hazels* (Tennyson).
— ***v.t.*** *British Slang.* to strike with the head: *While they [skinheads] favor the boot as a primary weapon, they also use their heads to "nut" or butt a victim* (Time).
**do one's (nut** or) **nuts,** *British Slang.* to act or work like one who is crazy: *Don't tell us, after the ... increased seat reservation fees, and another five shillings on sleepers, that they aren't doing their nuts to get themselves out of the red* (Punch).
**from soup to nuts.** See under **soup.**
**hard nut to crack,** *Informal.* a difficult question, problem, or undertaking: *Miss Lawrence, the Scottish champion, found Miss Cross too hard a nut to crack and for the second time in the day missed a holeable putt on the last green for a halved match* (London Times).
**nuts,** *Informal.* something especially enjoyable or delightful: *Tom had his store clothes on, and an audience—and that was always nuts for Tom Sawyer* (Mark Twain).
[Old English *hnutu*] — **nut′like′,** *adj.*

***nut**
definition 3

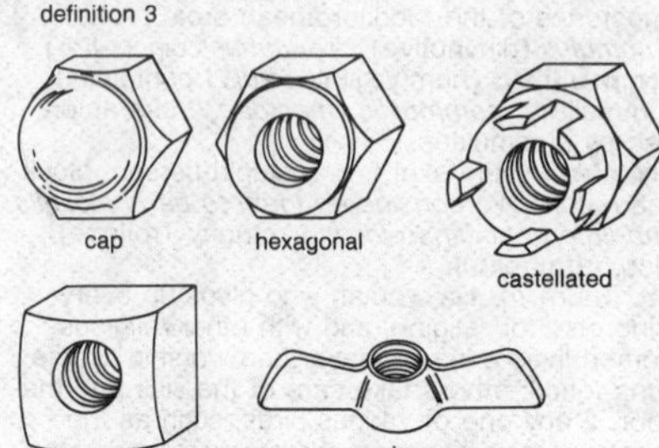


**Nut** (nut, nüt), *n.* the ancient Egyptian goddess of the sky, sister and wife of Geb, the god of the earth.
**NUT** (no periods) or **N.U.T.,** National Union of Teachers.
**nu|tant** (nü′tənt, nyü′-), *adj.* **1** *Botany.* drooping; nodding. **2** *Zoology.* **a** sloping in relation to the parts behind it or with the axis of the body: *a nutant head.* **b** bent or curved toward the anterior extremity of the body: *a nutant horn.* [< Latin *nutāns, -antis,* present participle of *nūtāre;* see etym. under **nutation**]
**nu|tate** (nü′tāt, nyü′-), *v.i.,* **-tat|ed, -tat|ing.** to undergo nutation; nod, twist, or oscillate: *If one boom is slow in erecting ... the satellite will be unbalanced and will nutate like a wobbling top* (New Scientist).
**nu|ta|tion** (nü tā′shən, nyü-), *n.* **1** the act of nodding the head. **2** an instance of nodding the head. **3** *Botany.* a twisting or rotation of the growing tip of a plant due to consecutive differences in growth rates of different sides: *Nutation is the spiral twisting of a stem as it grows* (Scientific American). **4** *Astronomy.* a slight oscillation of the earth's axis, which makes the motion of the precession of the equinoxes irregular. [< Latin *nūtātiō, -ōnis* < *nūtāre* to nod, sway (frequentative) < *nuere* to nod]
**nu|ta|tion|al** (nü tā′shə nəl, nyü-), *adj.* **1** of or having to do with nutation. **2** exhibiting nutation.
**nut-brown** (nut′broun′), *adj.* brown as a ripe nut: *spicy nut-brown ale* (Milton).
**nut cake,** **1** = doughnut. **2** a cake with nuts.
**nut|crack|er** (nut′krak′ər), *n.* **1** an instrument for cracking the shells of nuts. **2** a bird related to the crow, that feeds on nuts, especially on pine seeds, such as Clark's nutcracker, which lives in the mountains of western North America.
**Nutcracker Man,** = Zinjanthropus.
**nut|gall** (nut′gôl′), *n.* a lump or ball that swells up, especially on an oak tree, where the tree has been injured by an insect; any one of various galls resembling a nut.
**nut grass,** any sedge of a group having small tuberous roots.
**nut|hatch** (nut′hach′), *n.* a small, sharp-beaked, climbing bird that feeds on small nuts, seeds, and insects. The nuthatch has large feet and lives mostly in trees. There are several kinds, making up a family of birds. [Middle English *notehache* (literally) nut hacker. Compare etym. under **hack.**]
**nut|house** (nut′hous′), *n. Slang.* an insane asylum.
**nut|let** (nut′lit), *n.* **1** a small nut or nutlike fruit. **2** the stone of a drupe, especially a small drupe.
**nut|meat** (nut′mēt′), *n.* a kernel of a nut.
**nut|meg** (nut′meg), *n.* **1** a hard, spicy seed about as big as a marble, obtained from the fruit of a tree growing in the East Indies. The seed is grated and used for flavoring food. *Nutmeg and mace are the only two different spices harvested from the same fruit* (Science News Letter). **2** the evergreen tree it grows on. **3** the similar product of various related trees. [Middle English *notemuga,* half-translation of unrecorded Old French *nois mugue* nut smelling like musk < *nois* nut (< Latin *nux*) + *mugue* musk < Late Latin *muscus*]
**nutmeg melon,** a variety of small muskmelon with a netted rind.
**Nutmeg State,** a nickname of Connecticut.
**nut|pick** (nut′pik′), *n.* a pointed instrument to remove nuts from their shells.
**nut pine,** any one of several North American pines producing large edible seeds, especially a pine of the western United States.
**nu|tri|a** (nü′trē ə, nyü′-), *n.* **1** an aquatic rodent of South America resembling the muskrat; coypu. It has become established in parts of the southern and western United States. **2** its valuable dark, lustrous beaverlike fur. [< Spanish *nutria,* variant of *lutria* otter < Latin *lutra*]
**nu|tri|cul|ture** (nü′trə kul′chər, nyü′-), *n.* = hydroponics.
**nu|tri|ent** (nü′trē ənt, nyü′-), *adj., n.* — ***adj.*** nourishing.
— ***n.*** a nourishing substance, especially as an element or ingredient of a foodstuff: *a diet rich in nutrients.*
[< Latin *nūtriēns, -entis,* present participle of *nūtrīre* nourish]
**nu|tri|ment** (nü′trə mənt, nyü′-), *n.* **1** that which is required by an organism for life and growth; nourishment; food. **2** *Figurative.* something that maintains anything, or by which its development is made possible.
**nu|tri|men|tal** (nü′trə men′təl, nyü′-), *adj.* having the qualities of food; nutritious.
**nu|tri|tion** (nü trish′ən, nyü-), *n.* **1** the processes by which living things take in food and use it: *A balanced diet is important in nutrition.* **2** that which nourishes; nourishment; food: *Milk, meat, fruits, and vegetables provide good nutrition.* **3** the act of supplying or receiving nourishment: *the nutrition of plants.* **4** the study that deals with foods and the way the body uses them: *Nutrition is the part of medicine concerned with deficiency diseases and malnutrition.*
**nu|tri|tion|al** (nü trish′ə nəl, nyü-), *adj.* having to do with nutrition: *the good nutritional value of milk.* — **nu|tri′tion|al|ly,** *adv.*
**nu|tri|tion|ist** (nü trish′ə nist, nyü-), *n.* an expert in the study of nutrition.
**nu|tri|tious** (nü trish′əs, nyü-), *adj.* valuable as food; nourishing: *Oranges and bread are nutritious.* [< Latin *nūtrītius* or *nūtrīcius* < *nutrīx, -īcis* a nurse < *nūtrīre* nourish] — **nu|tri′tious|ly,** *adv.* — **nu|tri′tious|ness,** *n.*
**nu|tri|tive** (nü′trə tiv, nyü′-), *adj.* **1** having to do with foods and the use of foods. Digestion is part of the nutritive process. **2** giving nourishment; nutritious. — **nu′tri|tive|ly,** *adv.* — **nu′tri|tive|ness,** *n.*
**nuts**[1] (nuts), *adj., interj. U.S. Slang.* — ***adj.*** crazy: *"They're nuts if they think we'll go along with the plan ...," he said* (New York Times).
— ***interj.*** an exclamation of disgust, annoyance, contempt, or surprise: *Oh, nuts, I've lost the key! Nuts to you, wise guy!*
**be nuts about,** to be very fond of or delighted with (a person or thing): *My brother is nuts about detective stories. In Paris, they're all nuts about linen or linenlike fabrics* (Lois Long).
**nuts**[2] (nuts), *n.pl.* See under **nut.**
**nuts and bolts,** small but essential features, especially those that form an integral framework or make up practical details, as of a plan: *the busy executive who wants to see the underlying realities, the economic nuts and bolts, that are common to all business enterprises* (Sunday Times).
**nuts-and-bolts** (nuts′ən bōlts′), *adj.* basic; practical: *a nuts-and-bolts operation.*
**nut|shell** (nut′shel′), *n., v.* — ***n.*** **1** the shell of a nut; hard outside covering within which the kernel of a nut is enclosed. **2** someting extremely small or scanty.
— ***v.t.*** to put in a nutshell; summarize.
**in a nutshell,** in very brief form; in a few words: *You have my history in a nutshell* (Robert Browning).
**Nut|tall's woodpecker** (nut′ôlz), a black and white, barred woodpecker with a black crown and, in the male, red on the back of the head and neck, found in Oregon, California, and Baja California. [< Thomas *Nuttall,* 1786-1859, Anglo-American ornithologist]
**nut|ter** (nut′ər), *n.* **1** a person who gathers nuts. **2** *British Slang.* a crazy or eccentric person: *Much of this is born of ... affection for the shabby and odd, the nutters of the species* (Manchester Guardian Weekly).
**nut|ti|ness** (nut′ē nis), *n.* **1** the quality of being nutty. **2** nutty flavor.

**nut|ting** (nut′ing), *n.* the act of looking for nuts; gathering nuts.

**nut|ty** (nut′ē), *adj.*, **-ti|er**, **-ti|est**. **1** containing many nuts: *nutty cake.* **2** like nuts; tasting like nuts. **3** *Slang.* odd; silly. **4** *Slang.* very interested or enthusiastic. **5** full of zest or flavor; pleasant; rich: *the nutty Spanish ale* (John Masefield). **6** *Slang.* queer; crazy; nuts.

**nut weevil**, a weevil that feeds on the insides of nuts.

**nut|wood** (nut′wu̇d), *n.* **1** a tree bearing nuts, such as the hickory or walnut. **2** the wood of such a tree.

**nux vom|i|ca** (nuks vom′ə kə), **1** a bitter yellowish powder containing strychnine and made from the seed of a tree growing in southern Asia and Northern Australia. It is used as a stomachic and tonic. **2** the poisonous seed from which nux vomica is prepared. **3** the tree itself. [< New Latin *nux vomica* (literally) vomiting nut < Latin *nux* nut, *vomere* to vomit]

**nuz|zle**[1] (nuz′əl), *v.*, **-zled**, **-zling**. — ***v.t.*** **1** to poke or rub with the nose; press the nose against: *The calf nuzzles his mother.* **2** to burrow or dig (the snout) into, as a horse with grain or a hog with swill. — ***v.i.*** **1** to nestle; snuggle; cuddle. **2** to burrow or dig with the nose.
[< *nose* + *-le;* influenced by *nestle.* Compare etym. under **nozzle**.]

**nuz|zle**[2] (nuz′əl), *v.t.*, **-zled**, **-zling**. to cherish fondly; nurse. [perhaps related to **nuzzle**[1] and **nose**]

**NV** (no periods), Nevada (with postal Zip Code).

**NVA** (no periods), North Vietnamese Army.

**n.w.**, **1** net weight. **2a** northwest. **b** northwestern.

**NW** (no periods), **1** Northwest or northwest. **2** Northwestern or northwestern.

**N.W.**, **1** North Wales. **2** Northwest or northwest. **3** Northwestern or northwestern.

**N.W.T.**, Northwest Territories (in Canada).

**NY** (no periods), New York State (with postal Zip Code).

**N.Y.**, **1** New York State. **2** New York City.

**NYA** (no periods), National Youth Administration.

**ny|al|a** (nī al′ə), *n.* a South African antelope related to the bushbuck and having vertical stripes of a bluish-gray and faint white color. [< Bantu *inyala*]

**Ny|an|ja** (nē an′yə, nī-), *n., pl.* **-ja** or **-jas**. **1** a member of a Bantu-speaking tribe of Malawi in southern Africa. **2** the language of this tribe.

**ny|an|za** (nē an′zə, nī-), *n.* any relatively large body of water in the interior of Africa, especially a lake: *Albert Nyanza.* [< a native word appearing in several African languages]

**Ny|as|a** (nī as′ə, nē-), *adj., n.* = Nyasalander.

**Ny|as|a|land|er** (nī as′ə lan′dər, nē-), *adj., n.* — ***adj.*** of or having to do with Nyasaland (now Malawi), in southeastern Africa, or its people.
— ***n.*** a native or inhabitant of Nyasaland.

**N.Y.C.** or **NYC** (no periods), New York City.

**nyck|el|har|pa** (nik′əl här′pə), *n.* a stringed instrument of Sweden, similar to a hurdy-gurdy but played with a bow. [< Swedish *nyckelharpa* (literally) key harp]

**nyc|ta|gi|na|ceous** (nik′tə jə nā′shəs), *adj.* belonging to the four-o'clock family. [< New Latin *Nyctaginaceae* the family name (< *Nyctago, -inis* the former genus name < Greek *nýx, nýktos* night) + English *-ous*]

**nyc|ta|lo|pi|a** (nik′tə lō′pē ə), *n.* a visual defect characterized by poor adaptation of the eyes to darkness, associated with vitamin-A deficiency and xerophthalmia; night blindness; moon blindness. [< Late Latin *nyctalopia* < Greek *nyktálōps* (originally) night blindness < *nýx, nýktos* night + *alaós* blind + *ôps* eye]

**nyc|ta|lop|ic** (nik′tə lop′ik), *adj.* **1** having to do with nyctalopia. **2** like nyctalopia. **3** affected with nyctalopia.

**nyc|tit|ro|pism** (nik tit′rə piz əm), *n. Botany.* a tendency to assume at, or just before, nightfall, certain positions unlike those maintained during the day, as the leaves of certain plants. [< Greek *nýx, nýktos* night + English *tropism*]

**nyc|to|pho|bi|a** (nik′tə fō′bē ə), *n.* an abnormal fear of the dark and of night. [< Greek *nýx, nýktos* night + English *-phobia*]

**nyet** (nyet), *n., adj., adv. Russian.* no.

**nyl|ghai** (nil′gī), *n.* = nilgai.

**nyl|ghau** (nil′gô), *n.* = nilgai.

**ny|lon** (nī′lon), *n., adj.* — ***n.*** an extremely strong, elastic, and durable synthetic substance, used to make clothing, stockings, bristles, and other products. Nylon is made by polymerization of aliphatic dicarboxylic acids, such as adipic acid, and aliphatic diamines.
— ***adj.*** made of nylon: *Many toothbrushes have nylon bristles. Nylon rollers are often used to make drawers slide in and out smoothly.*
**nylons**, stockings made of nylon.
[< *Nylon*, a trademark]

**nymph** (nimf), *n.* **1** a lesser Greek and Roman goddess of nature, who lived in seas, rivers, springs, fountains, hills, woods, or trees. **2** a beautiful or graceful young woman: *Nymph, in thy orisons Be all my sins remember'd* (Shakespeare). **3** any one of certain insects in the stage of development between egg and adult. It resembles the adult but lacks fully developed wings. **4** any one of a fancy variety of goldfish. [< Old French *nymphe,* or *nimphe,* learned borrowing from Latin *nympha* < Greek *nýmphē*] — **nymph′like′**, *adj.*

**nym|pha** (nim′fə), *n., pl.* **-phae** (-fē). **1** *Anatomy.* either of the labia minora. **2** = nymph. [< New Latin *nympha* < Greek *nýmphē* the clitoris, probably as "source of water," transferred meaning from river goddess, nymph]

**nym|phae|a|ceous** (nim′fē ā′shəs), *adj.* belonging to the water-lily family of aquatic plants.

**nym|phal** (nim′fəl), *adj.* of or having to do with a nymph or nymphs.

**nym|pha|lid** (nim′fə lid), *n., adj.* — ***n.*** any one of a family of butterflies having the forelegs much reduced, including the admiral, mourning cloak, viceroy, and buckeye; brush-footed butterfly.
— ***adj.*** of or belonging to this family. [< New Latin *Nymphalis, -idis* the genus name < Latin *nympha* nymph]

**nym|phe|an** (nim fē′ən), *adj.* = nymphal.

**nym|phet** (nim fet′, nim′fit), *n.* a young girl, especially one in her teens, who attracts older men: *The novel* [*"Lolita"*] *by Vladimir Nabokov is about a man who has a passion for ... nymphets* (Manchester Guardian).

**nym|phic** (nim′fik), *adj.* = nymphal.

**nym|pho** (nim′fō), *adj., n. Informal.* nymphomaniac.

**nym|pho|lep|sy** (nim′fə lep′sē), *n.* **1** a state of rapture supposed to be inspired in men by nymphs. **2** a frenzy of emotion, especially that inspired by something unattainable. [< Greek *nymphólēptos* one bewitched by a nymph < *nýmphē* nymph + *lēptos,* stem of *lambánein* to seize; perhaps patterned on English *epilepsy*]

**nym|pho|lep|tic** (nim′fə lep′tik), *adj.* **1** of or belonging to nympholepsy. **2** possessed by nympholepsy; ecstatic; frenzied.

**nym|pho|ma|ni|a** (nim′fə mā′nē ə), *n.* **1** abnormal, uncontrollable sexual desire in a woman. **2** uncontrollable sexual desire in animals, especially in cattle. [< Greek *nýmphē* nymph, bride + English *mania*]

**nym|pho|ma|ni|ac** (nim′fə mā′nē ak), *n., adj.* — ***n.*** a woman who is affected with nymphomania.
— ***adj.*** = nymphomaniacal.

**nym|pho|ma|ni|a|cal** (nim′fə mə nī′ə kəl), *adj.* **1** characterized by nymphomania. **2** affected with nymphomania.

**Ny|norsk** (nү′nôrsk′, nü′-, nē′-), *n.* the newer form of standard literary Norwegian; Landsmål. [< Norwegian *Nynorsk* New Norwegian]

**NYSE** (no periods) or **N.Y.S.E.**, New York Stock Exchange.

**nys|tag|mic** (nis tag′mik), *adj.* of or like nystagmus.

**nys|tag|mus** (nis tag′məs), *n.* an involuntary movement of the eyeballs, frequently a symptom of disease. [< New Latin *nystagmus* < Greek *nystagmós* drowsiness; (literally) nodding < *nystázein* to nod, be sleepy]

**nys|tat|in** (nis tat′in), *n.* an antibiotic used to combat fungous diseases such as moniliasis, ringworm, and athlete's foot. *Formula:* $C_{46}H_{77}NO_{19}$

**Nyx** (niks), *n.* the ancient Greek goddess of night, identified with the Roman Nox.

**N.Z.** or **N.Zeal.**, New Zealand.

***O**[1] or **o** (ō), *n., pl.* **O's** or **Os, o's, os,** or **oes.** **1** the 15th letter of the English alphabet. There are two *o's* in *Ohio.* **2** any sound represented by this letter. **3** (used as a symbol) the 15th, or more usually the 14th, of a series (either I or J being omitted). **4** zero. **5** a mere nothing.

**O**[2] (ō), *n., pl.* **O's.** anything shaped like the letter O: *May we cram Within this wooden O [theater] the very casques That did affright the air at Agincourt?* (Shakespeare).

**O**[3] (ō), *interj., n., pl.* **O's.** —*interj.* = oh!: *O say, can you see, by the dawn's early light* (Francis Scott Key).
—*n.* an exclamation of oh: *O's of admiration* (Thackeray).
[Middle English *O*]

**O**[4] (ō), *n., pl.* **O's.** a person whose name begins with the prefix O'-: *Ireland her O's, her Macs let Scotland boast* (Henry Fielding).

**o'** (ə, ō), *prep.* **1** of: *man-o'-war, o'clock, will-o'-the-wisp.* **2** on: *Being knocked o' the head ...* (Richard Brinsley Sheridan).

**O'**, *prefix.* descendant, used as a prefix in Irish family names, as in *O'Connell, O'Connor, O'Neil.* [< Irish *ó* descendant]

**o-**, *prefix.* the form of **ob-** before *m,* as in *omit.*

**o** (no period), **1** ohm. **2** octavo.

**o.**, an abbreviation for the following:
**1** off.
**2** officer.
**3** order.
**4** *Baseball.* outs or putouts (in scoring).
**5** *Pharmacy.* pint (Latin, *octarius* or *octavus*).

**O** (no period), **1** oxygen (chemical element). **2** one of the four major blood types or groups widely used to determine blood compatibility in transfusions. A person with O type blood can receive blood of the O group only. **3** (in international flag code) man lost overboard.

**O.**, an abbreviation for the following:
**1** Ocean.
**2** Octavo.
**3** Ohio.
**4** Old.
**5** Ontario.

**O.A.**, Overeaters Anonymous.

**OAA** (no periods), Old Age Assistance.

**oaf** (ōf), *n., pl.* **oafs** or **oaves. 1** a very stupid child or man: *a great oaf, in wooden shoes and a blouse* (Charles Lever). **2** a clumsy person: *The oaf stumbled over the bucket, spilling all the water.* **3** a deformed child. **4** *Obsolete.* an elf's child; changeling. [earlier *auf,* or *aulf* < Scandinavian (compare Old Icelandic *ālfr* silly person, elf)]

**oaf|ish** (ō'fish), *adj.* very stupid or clumsy. **SYN:** lubberly. —**oaf'ish|ly,** *adv.* —**oaf'ish|ness,** *n.*

**oak** (ōk), *n., adj.* —*n.* **1** any one of a group of trees or shrubs found in most parts of the world, having nuts called acorns. The wood is very hard and strong. The oaks belong to the beech family. **2** the wood, used in building, for flooring, and in cabinetwork. **3** a tree or shrub resembling or suggesting an oak. **4** the leaves of an oak worn in a chaplet or garland. **5** *British Slang.* a door of oak or other wood.
—*adj.* **1** of an oak: *oak leaves.* **2** made of oak; oaken: *an oak table.*
**sport one's oak,** *British University Slang.* to shut one's outer door to show one is out or busy: *Your oak was sported and you were not at home to anybody* (Walter Besant).
[Old English *āc*] —**oak'like',** *adj.*

**oak apple,** an apple-shaped gall on an oak leaf or stem due to injury by a gall wasp.

**oak|en** (ō'kən), *adj.* **1** made of oak wood: *the old oaken bucket.* **2** *Figurative.* sturdy as an oak; solid: *... a splendidly oaken characterization* (Dan Sullivan). *... the family farmer—an oaken citizen* (John Kenneth Galbraith). **3** consisting of oak trees. **4** *Archaic.* of or having to do with the oak.

**Oa|kie** (ō'kē), *n.* = Okie.

**oak-leaf cluster** (ōk'lēf'), a cluster of bronze or silver oak leaves and acorns given as an honor to a person in the United States armed forces who has already earned the same award for an earlier act of valor.

**Oak|ley** (ōk'lē), *n. Slang.* Annie Oakley.

**oak|moss resin** (ōk'mōs', -mos'), an oleoresin obtained from lichens growing on oak trees, used in perfumery as a fixative.

**oak|tag** (ōk'tag'), *n.* a strong cardboard with some oak content, used for construction or to make charts in the early grades of elementary school.

**oa|kum** (ō'kəm), *n.* a loose fiber obtained by untwisting and picking apart old hemp ropes, used for stopping up the seams or cracks in ships and for packing joints in waste pipes. [Old English *ācumba* < *ā-* out + *cemban* to comb < *camb* a comb]

**oak wilt,** a serious fungous disease of oak trees that is spread by root grafts and insects. *Oak wilt is caused by ... a fungus that grows in the sapwood of oaks and stops the exchange of nutrients between roots and leaves* (Atomic Energy Commission Report).

**OAMS** (no periods), Orbital Attitude Maneuvering System (of a manned spacecraft).

**OAO** (no periods), Orbiting Astronomical Observatory (an unmanned satellite of NASA, designed for astronomical research from a circular orbit around the earth): *The OAO's ... study stars and nebulae in the ultraviolet region of the spectrum* (Jonathan Eberhart).

**OAP** (no periods) or **O.A.P.**, **1** old-age pension. **2** old-age pensioner.

**OAPEC** (no periods), Organization of Arab Petroleum Exporting Countries.

***oar** (ôr, ōr), *n., v.* —*n.* **1** a long pole with a flat end, used in rowing. Sometimes an oar is used to steer a boat. **2** a person who rows; oarsman: *He is the best oar in the crew.* **3** a paddle or pole for stirring.
—*v.t.* **1** to row (a boat). **2a** to travel across (a body of water). **b** to make (one's way) by or as if by rowing: *He ... oared himself with his good arms ... to the shore* (Shakespeare). **3** to move or use (an arm, hand, or some object) as an oar.
—*v.i.* to use an oar; row.
**put** (or **stick**) **one's oar in,** to meddle; interfere: *That prying man always sticks his oar in when my friends and I are talking privately.*
**rest on one's oars,** to stop working or trying and take a rest: *The managers of the usual autumn gathering of paintings ... will rest on their oars* (Athenaeum).
**ship oars,** to lift oars from the rowlocks and put them in the boat: *The sailors stopped rowing and shipped their oars.*
[Old English *ār*] —**oar'like',** *adj.*

***oar**
definition 1

blade
loom
handle

***oarfish**

**oar|age** (ôr'ij, ōr'-), *n.* **1** the use of oars; rowing: *the Viking ship, its rowers' oarage boiling up the sea.* **2** rowing apparatus.

**oared** (ôrd, ōrd), *adj.* furnished with oars; moved by oars.

***oar|fish** (ôr'fish', ōr'-), *n., pl.* **-fish|es** or (*collectively*) **-fish.** a deep-sea fish with a slender, tapelike body from 12 to 30 feet long. It has a long flat fin along the length of its body making it look somewhat like an oar, and was sometimes mistaken for a sea serpent. See picture below.

**oar|less** (ôr'lis, ōr'-), *adj.* **1** without oars: *an oarless boat.* **2** undisturbed by oars: *the ... oarless sea* (Tennyson).

**oar|lock** (ôr'lok', ōr'-), *n.* a notch or U-shaped support for holding the oar in place while rowing; rowlock. [Old English *ārloc* < *ār* oar + *loc* lock[1]]

**oars|man** (ôrz'mən, ōrz'-), *n., pl.* **-men. 1** a man who rows: *The British Foreign Office today cleared the way to give visas to nineteen Soviet oarsmen expected here for the Henley regatta* (New York Times). **2** a man who rows well.

**oars|man|ship** (ôrz'mən ship, ōrz'-), *n.* the art of rowing; skill as a rower.

**oar|weed** (ôr'wēd', ōr'-), *n.* a type of kelp, one of the brown algae. It has been used as a fertilizer in coastal areas of England and Scotland.

**oar|y** (ôr'ē, ōr'-), *adj.* **1** *Poetic.* shaped or used like an oar. **2** having oars; oared: *the oary trireme.*

**OAS** (no periods) or **O.A.S.**, Organization of American States (an organization of 25 American republics, founded in 1948 to succeed the Pan American Union).

**o|a|sis** (ō ā'sis, ō'ə-), *n., pl.* **-ses** (-sēz). **1** a fertile spot in the desert where there is water and usually trees and other vegetation: *a tiny oasis where there were camels, and a well ... and a patch of emerald-green barley* (Amelia B. Edwards). **2** *Figurative.* **a** any fertile spot in a barren land; any pleasant place in a desolate region. **b** a plot or spot refreshingly different from others around it: *a cultural oasis on the western frontier.* [< Latin *oasis* < Greek *Óasis,* name of various cities in the Libyan Desert, apparently of Egyptian origin]

**oast** (ōst), *n.* a kiln for drying hops, malt, or tobacco. [Old English *āst*]

**oat** (ōt), *n.* **1a** Often, **oats.** a plant whose grain is used in making oatmeal and other cereals and baked goods, and as food for horses and other livestock. It is a tall cereal grass. **b** = wild oats (def. 1). **c oats,** the seeds or grains of the oat plant. **2** a musical pipe made of an oat straw: *That strain I heard was of a higher mood: But now my oat proceeds* (Milton).
**feel one's oats,** *Informal.* **a** to be lively or frisky: *The youngster was feeling his oats as he bounced his ball against the side of the house.* **b** to feel pleased or important and show it: *American women are feeling their political oats* (Harper's).
**know one's oats,** *Informal.* to be well-informed; know one's stuff: *[He] really knows his oats where skiing is concerned* (Elizabeth Nicholas).
**sow one's oats,** to sow one's wild oats; indulge in youthful, carefree, uninhibited pleasures before settling down in life: *Alberto Sordi plays an Italian fur merchant testing some hopelessly romantic notions about sowing one's oats in Stockholm* (Time).
**sow one's wild oats.** See under **wild oats.**
[Old English *āte* grain of oats] —**oat'like',** *adj.*

**oat|cake** (ōt'kāk'), *n.* a thin cake of oatmeal.

**oat|en** (ō'tən), *adj.* **1** made of oats or oatmeal: *an oaten cake.* **2** made of oat straw: *his oaten pype* (Edmund Spenser). **3** of or having to do with the oat: *oaten straws* (Shakespeare).

**oat|er** (ō'tər), *n. U.S. Slang.* a motion picture or television show about the United States West; western.

**oat grass, 1** any one of various oatlike grasses. **2** any wild oat.

**oath** (ōth), *n., pl.* **oaths** (ōŦHz, ōths). **1a** a solemn promise: *The oath bound him to secrecy.* **SYN:** pledge. **b** a statement that something is true, which God or some holy person or thing is called on to witness; vow: *to repeat an oath on the Bible. He made an oath that he would tell the whole truth and nothing but the truth.* **c** the form of words in which such a statement or promise is made: *the President's oath of office, the Hippocratic oath.* **2** the name of God or some holy person or thing used as an exclamation to add force or to express anger. **3** a curse; word used in swearing: *The pirate cursed us with fearful oaths.*

***O**[1]
definition 1

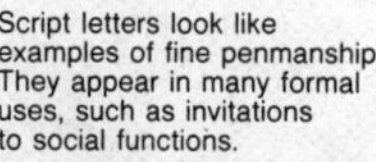

Script letters look like examples of fine penmanship. They appear in many formal uses, such as invitations to social functions.

Handwritten letters, both manuscript or printed (left) and cursive (right), are easy for children to read and to write.

Roman letters have *serifs* (finishing strokes) adapted from the way Roman stonecutters carved their letters. This is *Times Roman* type.

Sans-serif letters are often called *gothic.* They have lines of even width and no serifs. This type face is called *Helvetica.*

Between roman and gothic, some letters have thick and thin lines with slight flares that suggest serifs. This type face is *Optima.*

Computer letters can be sensed by machines either from their shapes or from the magnetic ink with which they are printed.

SYN: swearword, expletive.
**take oath**, to make an oath; promise or state solemnly: *He took oath to give up smoking.*
**under oath**, bound by an oath; sworn to tell the truth: *He had said under oath that his birthplace was Passaic, N.J.*
**upon one's oath**, sworn to tell the truth: *They cannot speak always as if they were upon their oath—but must be understood, speaking or writing, with some abatement* (Charles Lamb).
[Old English *āth*]

**oat|meal** (ōt′mēl′), *n., adj.* —*n.* **1** oats made into meal; ground or rolled oats: *The oatmeal spilled out of the box in the cupboard.* **2** a cooked cereal made from oatmeal: *We often have oatmeal with cream and sugar on cold wintry mornings.*
**3** a yellowish-gray color.
—*adj.* yellowish-gray: *an oatmeal tweed.*

**oat opera**, *U.S. Slang.* a horse opera: *California's High Sierra country fills the wide screen with some breathtaking acreage that no TV oat opera can duplicate* (Time).

**oats** (ōts), *n.pl.* See under **oat**.

**OAU** (no periods), Organization of African Unity (an association of 48 African nations, established in 1963).

**oaves** (ōvz), *n.* a plural of **oaf**.

**Oa|xa|can** (wä hä′kən, wə-), *adj.* of or having to do with Oaxaca, a state and city in southern Mexico, or its native Indian population and its culture: *Oaxacan art, Oaxacan costumes.*

**ob-**, *prefix.* **1** against; in the way; opposing; hindering, as in *obstruct.*
**2** inversely; contrary to the usual position, as in *oblate.*
**3** toward; to, as in *obvert.*
**4** on; over, as in *obscure.* Also: **o-** before *m;* **oc-** before *c;* **of-** before *f;* **op-** before *p;* **os-** in some cases before *c* and *t.*
[< Latin *ob-*, related to *ob* against]

**ob.**, **1** he, she, or it died (Latin, *obiit*). **2** in passing; incidentally (Latin, *obiter*). **3** oboe.

**OB** (no periods), **1** obstetrics. **2** off-Broadway.

**o|ba** (ô′bə), *n.* a traditional tribal ruler or king in Nigeria: *In western Nigeria the obas combine grass-roots machine politics with honorific tribal positions* (London Times). [< the native name]

**Obad.** or **Ob** (no period), Obadiah (a book of the Old Testament).

**O|ba|di|ah** (ō′bə dī′ə), *n.* **1** a Hebrew prophet.
**2** a book of the Old Testament containing his prophecies, placed among the Minor Prophets. *Abbr:* Obad.

**obb.**, obbligato.

**ob|bli|ga|to** (ob′lə gä′tō), *adj., n., pl.* **-tos, -ti** (-tē). *Music.* —*adj.* accompanying a solo, but having a distinct character and independent importance.
—*n.* an obbligato part or accompaniment, especially as instrumentation. Also, **obligato.**
[< Italian *obbligato* (literally) obliged]

**OBC** (no periods) or **O.B.C.**, Outboard Boating Club of America.

**ob|com|pressed** (ob′kəm prest′), *adj. Biology.* compressed or flattened in the opposite of the usual direction.

**ob|con|ic** (ob kon′ik), *adj. Botany.* conical, with the base upward or outward; inversely conical.
—**ob|con′i|cal|ly**, *adv.*

**ob|cor|date** (ob kôr′dāt), *adj.* heart-shaped, with the attachment at the pointed end; inversely cordate: *an obcordate leaf.* [< *ob-* + *cordate*]

**obdt.**, obedient.

**ob|du|ra|bil|i|ty** (ob′dər ə bil′ə tē, -dyər ə-), *n.* physical hardness and resistance: *Because of the apparent obdurability of bone it was supposed until very recently that once the skeleton of a vertebrate has been formed it ceases to partake of metabolism, or to have any appreciable breakdown* (Scientific American). [< *obdura*(te) + *-bility*, as in *durability*]

**ob|du|ra|cy** (ob′dər ə sē, -dyər ə-), *n.* the quality of being obdurate; hardness of heart; stubbornness.

**ob|du|rate** (ob′dər it, -dyər-), *adj.* **1** stubborn or unyielding; obstinate: *an obdurate refusal.* SYN: unbending, inexorable. **2** hardened in feelings or heart; unfeeling; pitiless; not repentant: *an obdurate criminal. Be ... obdurate, do not hear him plead* (Shakespeare). SYN: impenitent, callous.
**3** physically hard or resistant: *Well-tanned hides, obdurate and unyielding* (William Cowper). *These tough uniforms were made of ... obdurate material* (Sean O'Faolain). [< Latin *obdūrātus,* past participle of *obdūrāre* < *ob-* against + *dūrāre* harden < *dūrus* hard] —**ob′du|rate|ly**, *adv.*
—**ob′du|rate|ness**, *n.*

**O.B.E.** or **OBE** (no periods), Officer of the Order of the British Empire.

**o|be|ah** (ō′bē ə), *n.* **1** a kind of witchcraft practiced by certain Negroes in Africa, and formerly in the West Indies and the United States: *The same village recently held a trial for three women accused of practicing obeah* (New Yorker). **2** an amulet, charm, or fetish used in this witchcraft.
[American English; ultimately of West African origin]

**o|be|di|ence** (ō bē′dē əns), *n.* **1** the action of obeying; doing what one is told to do; submitting to authority or law: *Parents desire obedience from their children. Soldiers act in obedience to the orders of their officers.* SYN: compliance, subservience. **2** a sphere of authority, or a group of persons subject to some particular authority: *a church of the Roman Catholic obedience.* **3** *Archaic.* a bow or curtsy; obeisance: *to make one's obedience.*

**obedience trial**, a test given to dogs to determine their ability to follow commands, usually as a competitive exercise with a prize for the winner: *More than a thousand dog shows, field trials, and obedience trials were held* (New Yorker).

**o|be|di|ent** (ō bē′dē ənt), *adj.* doing what one is told to do; willing to obey; dutiful: *The obedient dog came at his master's whistle.* [< Latin *oboediēns, -entis,* present participle of *oboedīre* obey]
—**o|be′di|ent|ly**, *adv.*
—*Syn.* **Obedient**, **compliant**, **docile** mean acting as another asks or commands. **Obedient** emphasizes being willing to follow instructions and carry out orders of someone whose authority or control one acknowledges: *The obedient boy did his chores, though his friends wanted him to go swimming.* **Compliant** emphasizes bending easily, sometimes too easily, to another's will and being ready to do whatever he wishes or commands: *He is too compliant to make a good leader.* **Docile** emphasizes having a submissive disposition and no desire to rebel against authority or control: *She always rides a docile horse.*

**o|bei|sance** (ō bā′səns, -bē′-), *n.* **1** a movement of the body expressing deep respect or reverence; deep bow or curtsy: *The men made obeisance to the king. After three profound obeisances ... we were permitted to sit on three stools ... near his Highness's throne* (Jonathan Swift). **2** deference; homage: *acts of obeisance.* SYN: veneration. [< Old French *obeissance* obedience < *obeir* obey]

**o|bei|sant** (ō bā′sənt, -bē′-), *adj.* showing obeisance; deferential; subject. [< Old French *obeissant,* present participle of *obeir* obey]

∗**ob|e|lisk** (ob′ə lisk), *n.* **1** a tapering, four-sided shaft of stone with a top shaped like a pyramid: *The obelisk is of red, highly polished, and covered on all four sides with superb hieroglyphs* (Amelia B. Edwards). **2** something resembling such a shaft: *She strode like a grenadier, strong and upright like an obelisk* (Joseph Conrad).
**3** *Printing.* = dagger (def. 2). **4** = obelus. [< Latin *obeliscus* < Greek *obeliskos* (diminutive) < *obelós* pointed pillar]

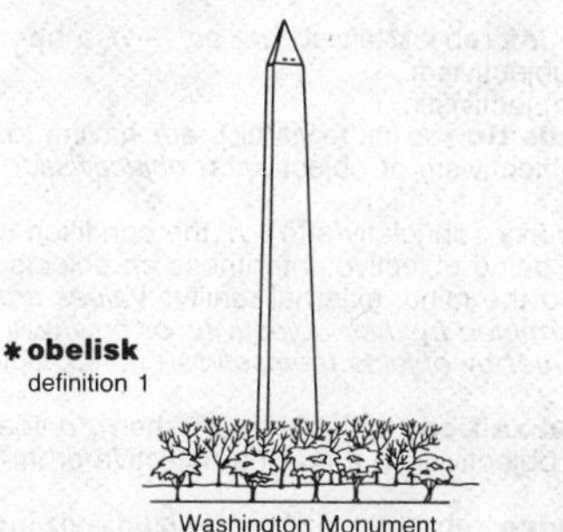

∗**obelisk** definition 1
Washington Monument

**ob|e|lize** (ob′ə līz), *v.t.,* **-lized, -liz|ing.** to mark (a word or passage) with an obelus; condemn as corrupt or not genuine.

**ob|e|lus** (ob′ə ləs), *n., pl.* **-li** (-lī). **1** a mark (often what is now used for a dash or sign of arithmetic divisions) used in old manuscripts to point out a word or passage that is corrupt, doubtful, or not genuine. **2** an obelisk in printing. [< Late Latin *obelus* < Greek *obelós* (literally) a spit]

**O|ber|bür|ger|meis|ter** (ō′bər byr′gər mīs′tər), *n. German.* lord mayor.

**o|be|rek** (ō′bə rek), *n.* a lively Polish folk dance: *Dances such as the mazurka and oberek resemble American square dances* (M. Kamil Dziewanowski). [< Polish *oberek*]

**O|ber|on** (ō′bə ron), *n.* **1** (in medieval folklore) the king of the fairies and husband of Titania. He is a main character in Shakespeare's *Midsummer Night's Dream.* **2** one of the five satellites of the planet Uranus.

**o|bese** (ō bēs′), *adj.* extremely fat; corpulent: *... a woman of robust frame ... though stout, not obese* (Charlotte Brontë). SYN: portly. [< Latin *obēsus,* past participle of *obedere* devour < *ob-* away + *edere* eat] —**o|bese′ly**, *adv.* —**o|bese′ness**, *n.*

**o|bes|i|ty** (ō bē′sə tē, -bes′ə-), *n.* extreme fatness; corpulence: *Obesity has become a national obsession* (Atlantic).

**o|bey** (ō bā′), *v.i.* to do what one is told: *The dog obeyed and went home.* —*v.t.* **1** to follow the orders of: *to obey a superior officer. We obey our father. He commandeth even the winds and water, and they obey him* (Luke 8:25). **2** to act in accordance with; comply with: *to obey the requirements of simple decency. A good citizen obeys the laws.* **3** to yield to the control of: *to obey one's conscience. A car obeys the driver. A horse obeys the rein.* (*Figurative.*) *A ship obeys the helm.* [< Old French *obeir* < Latin *oboedīre* < *ob-* to + *audīre* listen, give ear] —**o|bey′er**, *n.*
—**o|bey′ing|ly**, *adv.*

**ob|fus|cate** (ob fus′kāt, ob′fus-), *v.t.,* **-cat|ed, -cat|ing.** **1** to confuse; bewilder; stupefy: *A person's mind may be obfuscated by liquor or drugs.* SYN: perplex. **2** *Figurative.* to darken; obscure. SYN: becloud. Also, **offuscate.** [< Latin *obfuscāre* (with English *-ate*[1]) to darken < *ob-* against, in the way of + *fuscus* dark]

**ob|fus|ca|tion** (ob′fus kā′shən), *n.* **1** an obfuscating or being obfuscated: *In style they are admirably simple, direct, and uncluttered with medical obfuscation* (Harper's). **2** something that obfuscates.

**ob|fus|ca|tor** (ob fus′kā tər), *n.* a thing that obfuscates.

**ob|fus|ca|to|ry** (ob fus′kə tôr′ē, -tōr′-), *adj.* that obfuscates; confusing: *... hurried, well-meant but often obfuscatory explanations* (New York Times).

∗**o|bi** (ō′bē), *n.* a long, broad sash worn by Japanese people. It is worn around the waist of a kimono and tied at the back: *... geishas wearing their gaudy silks and brocaded obis* (Harper's). [< Japanese *obi*]

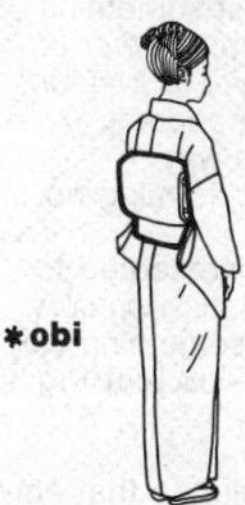

∗**obi**

**O|bie** (ō′bē), *n.* an annual award given by a newspaper for the best off-Broadway plays and performances presented in the American theater. [< the pronunciation of *OB,* abbreviation of *off-Broadway*]

**ob|i|it** (ob′ē it, ō′bē-), *Latin.* he, she, or it died. *Abbr:* ob.

**o|bis|po** (ō bis′pō), *n., pl.* **-poes.** a four-horned sheep of Bolivia and Peru. [< Spanish *obispo* (literally) bishop]

**o|bit** (ō′bit, ob′it), *n.* **1** *Informal.* an obituary. **2** a ceremony performed in memory of a dead person on the anniversary of his death. [< Old French *obit,* learned borrowing from Latin *obitus, -ūs* a departure, going down < *obīre* perish < *ob-* away, down + *īre* to go]

**ob|i|ter** (ob′ə tər), *adv.* by the way; in passing; incidentally: *His Lordship thought his observations, which were obiter, went too far* (London Times). [< Latin *obiter* < *ob-* to, against + *iter* route; journey]

**ob|i|ter dic|tum** (ob′ə tər dik′təm, ō′bə tər), *pl.* **ob|i|ter dic|ta** (ob′ə tər dik′tə, ō′bə tər). **1** an incidental statement; passing remark: *The Western world so excited about Soviet penetration and so affronted by Mr. Kruschchev's obiter dicta about the doom of capitalism ...* (Edward Crankshaw).
**2** an incidental opinion given by a judge on a rule of law not concerned with the case before him, and not binding: *... a few well-phrased obiter dicta on civil rights* (Time). [< Latin *obiter dictum* said by the way; *dictum* (a thing) said < *dīcere* to say]

**o|bit|u|ar|ese** (ō bich′ù e rēz′), *n.* the style, language, or content of obituaries: *Much orthodox obituarese only adds to the great corpus of bogus history enshrined in the printed word* (New Scientist).

**o|bit|u|ar|ist** (ō bich′ù er′ist), *n.* the writer of an obituary or obituaries.

**o|bit|u|ar|y** (ō bich′ù er′ē), *n., pl.* **-ar|ies,** *adj.* —*n.*

**Pronunciation Key:** hat, āge, cãre, fär; let, ēqual, tėrm; it, īce; hot, ōpen, ôrder; oil, out; cup, pu̇t, rüle; child; long; thin; ᴛʜen; zh, measure;
ə represents a in about, e in taken, i in pencil, o in lemon, u in circus.

a notice of death, often with a brief account of the person's life. **SYN**: necrology.
—*adj.* of a death; recording a death or deaths: *an obituary notice in a newspaper.*
[< Medieval Latin *obituarius* < Latin *obitus;* see etym. under **obit**]

**obj.**, 1 object. 2 objection. 3 objective.

**ob|ject** (*n.* ob′jikt, -jekt; *v.* əb jekt′), *n., v.* —*n.* 1 something that can be seen or touched; thing: *What is that object by the fence? A dark object moved between me and the door. The museum was full of interesting objects. Children, from their very birth, are daily growing acquainted with the objects about them* (Joseph Butler). **SYN**: article. 2 a person or thing toward which feeling, thought, or action is directed: *an object of study. The blind cripple was an object of charity. He was the object of his dog's affection.* 3 a person or thing that is absurd, funny, or foolish; sight; spectacle: *What an object you are with your hair pulled down over your face that way.* 4 a thing aimed at; end; purpose; goal: *My object in coming here was to get her address. Napoleon assumed that the objects of society were perpetual war and conquest, whereas its actual objects were production and consumption* (Edmund Wilson). **SYN**: aim. 5 *Grammar.* the word or group of words toward which the action of the verb is directed or to which a preposition expresses some relation. In "He threw the ball to his brother," *ball* is the object of *threw,* and *brother* is the object of *to.* 6a anything that can be presented to the mind: *objects of thought.* b a thing with reference to the impression it makes on the mind: *... objects of terror, pity, and of love* (Macaulay). 7 *Philosophy.* a thing that is or can be thought of.
—*v.i.* to make an objection or objections; be opposed; feel dislike: *Many people object to loud noise. Do you object to my going now?*
—*v.t.* 1 to give as a reason against something; bring forward in opposition; oppose: *Mother objected that the weather was too wet to play outdoors.* 2 *Archaic.* to bring forward; adduce. 3 *Archaic.* to throw or place in the way.
**no object**, not taken into account; forming no obstacle: *Price is no object.*
[< Medieval Latin *objectum* thing presented to the mind or thought < neuter of Latin *objectus,* past participle of *obicere* oppose something (to) < *ob-* against + *jacere* to throw] —**ob|ject′ing|ly,** *adv.*

**object.**, objective.

**object art**, a form of abstract sculpture that emphasizes the sculptured object by deliberately understating its shape, texture, and color: *The "object art" and "thingish" novel of the sixties are resurrections of the Cubist spirit* (Harold Rosenberg).

**object ball**, in billiards and pool: 1 the ball at which the player aims the cue ball. 2 any ball other than the cue ball.

**object glass**, a lens or combination of lenses that first receives light rays from the object and forms the image viewed through the eyepiece, as in a telescope or microscope; objective.

**ob|jec|ti|fi|ca|tion** (əb jek′tə fə kā′shən), *n.* the act or process of objectifying or of making objective: *Texts which have so far failed to show predictiveness when subjected to objectification and quantification may still provide a maximum of information* (Stone and Taylor).

**ob|jec|ti|fy** (əb jek′tə fī), *v.t.,* **-fied, -fy|ing.** to make objective; externalize: *Experiments in chemistry objectify the principles. Kind acts objectify kindness.* [< *object* + *-fy*]

**ob|jec|tion** (əb jek′shən), *n.* 1 something said or written in objecting; reason or argument against something: *One of his objections to the plan was that it would cost too much. Do I hear any objections?* 2 a feeling of disapproval or dislike: *A lazy person has an objection to working.* **SYN**: opposition. 3 the act of objecting: *What is the basis for your objection?* 4 a ground or cause of objecting: *It was his obesity that was the great objection to him* (Frederick Marryat).

**ob|jec|tion|a|ble** (əb jek′shə nə bəl), *adj.* 1 likely to be objected to: *an objectionable movie, objectionable scenes.* 2 unpleasant; disagreeable: *an objectionable odor or manner.* **SYN**: undesirable, offensive. —**ob|jec′tion|a|ble|ness,** *n.*

**ob|jec|tion|a|bly** (əb jek′shə nə blē), *adv.* in an objectionable manner; to an objectionable degree; so as to be objectionable.

**ob|jec|ti|vate** (əb jek′tə vāt), *v.t.,* **-vat|ed, -vat|ing.** to make objective; objectify.

**ob|jec|ti|va|tion** (əb jek′tə vā′shən), *n.* = objectification.

**ob|jec|tive** (əb jek′tiv), *n., adj.* —*n.* 1 something aimed at: *My objective this summer will be learning to play tennis better.* **SYN**: goal, object, aim. 2 something real and observable. 3 *Grammar.* a the objective case. b a word in the objective case. *Whom* and *me* are objectives. 4 lens or lenses nearest to the thing seen through a telescope or microscope; object glass: *The instrument is provided with a rotating nosepiece to which are permanently attached three objectives of different magnifications* (Sears and Zemansky). See diagram under **microscope**. 5 the goal or target of a military operation: *Paris was the real objective of the invading German army.*
—*adj.* 1 being the object of endeavor. 2 existing outside the mind as an actual object and not merely in the mind as an idea; real. Buildings and actions are objective; ideas are subjective. 3 about outward things, not about the thoughts and feelings of the speaker, writer, or painter; giving facts as they are without a bias toward either side; impersonal: *an objective analysis of a poem or painting. An "objective test" is often true and false or multiple choice. A scientist must be objective in his experiments. The policeman gave an objective report of the accident.* 4 *Grammar.* a showing the direct object of a verb or the object of a preposition. In "John hit me," *me* is in the objective case. b having to do with or being in this case. 5 perceptible to other persons as well as to the patient: *an objective symptom.* 6a (of a work of art) representing or resembling natural objects; not abstract. b (in perspective) that is, or belongs to, the object of which the delineation is required: *an objective point.*
[< Medieval Latin *objectivus* having to do with things as they are presented to the mind < *objectum;* see etym. under **object**] —**ob|jec′tive|ly,** *adv.* —**ob|jec′tive|ness,** *n.*

**objective complement**, *Grammar.* a word, such as a noun, pronoun, or adjective, used as a complement to a transitive verb to modify its direct object. In "I consider him smart," *smart* is the objective complement of *consider.*

**objective correlative**, 1 a situation, action, or image, that externalizes or objectifies an emotional or other subjective state in a story, novel, poem, or play: *The only way of expressing emotion in the form of art is by finding an "objective correlative"; in other words, a set of objects, a situation, a chain of events which shall be the formula of that particular situation* (T. S. Eliot). 2 any concrete or physical representation; personification: *[James] Stewart is more than just a good family man; he is the objective correlative of the Middle-American ideal* (Time).

**ob|jec|tiv|ism** (əb jek′tə viz əm), *n.* 1 any doctrine or philosophy that holds that external or objective elements of perception are the only real or worthwhile things: *It is the radical utilitarianism of our age, the fruit of our scientific objectivism, that speaks here* (Bulletin of Atomic Scientists). 2 the tendency to deal with objective things rather than thoughts or feelings, as in literature or art.

**ob|jec|tiv|ist** (əb jek′tə vist), *n., adj.* —*n.* a believer in objectivism.
—*adj.* = objectivistic.

**ob|jec|ti|vis|tic** (əb jek′tə vis′tik), *adj.* having to do with objectivism or objectivists: *objectivistic logic.*

**ob|jec|tiv|i|ty** (ob′jek tiv′ə tē), *n.* the condition or quality of being objective; intentness on objects external to the mind; external reality: *Values are also determined by their objectivity, or how well they are met by objects themselves* (James Collins).

**ob|jec|ti|vi|za|tion** (əb jek′tə və zā′shən), *n.* the action of objectivizing; a making objective or impersonal.

**ob|jec|ti|vize** (əb jek′tə vīz), *v.t.,* **-vized, -viz|ing.** to make objective or impersonal.

**object language**, 1 *Logic.* the language which is the object of an assertion, analysis, or discussion: *If we say, "In system S we can prove the formal sentence '1 + 1 = 2,'" we are making a statement in the metalanguage about "1 + 1 = 2," a statement in the object language* (Scientific American). 2 *Linguistics.* the language into which something is translated; target language. In a translation from Russian into English, Russian is the source language and English the object or target language. 3 *Education.* the language which is the object of instruction; foreign language.

**object lens**, the lens or lenses other than the eyepiece on an optical instrument; objective.

**ob|ject|less** (ob′jikt lis, -jekt-), *adj.* without an object or end in view; aimless; purposeless. —**ob′ject|less|ness,** *n.*

**object lesson**, 1 a practical illustration of a principle: *Many automobile accidents are object lessons in the dangers of speeding and carelessness.* 2 instructions conveyed by means of material objects.

**ob|jec|tor** (əb jek′tər), *n.* a person who objects.

**ob|jet d'art** (ôb zhe′ dår′), *pl.* **ob|jets d'art** (ôb zhe′ dår′), *French.* 1 a small picture, vase, or the like, of some artistic value: *The drawing-room was crowded with objets d'art* (London Times). 2 (literally) object of art.

**ob|jet de ver|tu** (ôb zhe′ də ver tʏ′), *pl.* **ob|jets de ver|tu** (ôb zhe′ də ver tʏ′). *French.* 1 an object of value because of its workmanship, antiquity, or rarity: *With other objets de vertu (small, precious ornaments), the cup was auctioned from the collection* (New York Times). 2 (literally) object of virtue.
► **Objet de vertu** is an English coinage made up of French words to Gallicize the phrase "object of virtu." The result is a misnomer, however, since the word *virtu* has no equivalent meaning in the French form *vertu.* The French word simply means "virtue."

**ob|jet trou|vé** (ôb zhe′ trü vā′), *pl.* **ob|jets trou|vés** (ôb zhe′ trü vā′). *French.* 1 any object found lying about, such as a piece of driftwood or shell, regarded as a work of art. 2 (literally) found object.

**ob|jur|gate** (ob′jər gāt, əb jėr′-), *v.t.,* **-gat|ed, -gat|ing.** to reproach vehemently; upbraid violently; berate: *Command all to do their duty. Command, but not objurgate* (Jeremy Taylor). **SYN**: vituperate, denounce, rebuke. [< Latin *objūrgāre* (with English *-ate*[1]) < *ob-* against + *jūrgāre* to scold, rebuke < *jūs, jūris* law + *agere* drive, lead]

**ob|jur|ga|tion** (ob′jər gā′shən), *n.* an objurgating; vehement reproach.

**ob|jur|ga|tor** (ob′jər gā′tər), *n.* a person who objurgates.

**ob|jur|ga|to|ry** (əb jėr′gə tôr′ē, -tōr′-), *adj.* vehemently reproachful; upbraiding; berating. **SYN**: vituperative.

**obl.**, 1 obligation. 2 oblique. 3 oblong.

**ob|lan|ce|o|late** (ob lan′sē ə lit, -lāt), *adj.* shaped like a lance head but with the tapering end at the base: *an oblanceolate leaf.*

**ob|last** (ob′ləst), *n., pl.* **-lasts, -las|ti** (-ləs tē). a regional subdivision of any of the constituent republics of the Soviet Union: *... pictures life in the Jewish autonomous oblast ... of the Soviet Union as busy, productive and growing* (New York Times). [< Russian *oblast′*]

**ob|late**[1] (ob′lāt, ob lāt′), *adj.* flattened at the poles: *The earth is an oblate spheroid.* [< New Latin *oblatus* < Latin *ob-* inversely + (*pro*)*lātus* prolate] —**ob′late|ly,** *adv.* —**ob′late|ness,** *n.*

**ob|late**[2] (ob′lāt, o blāt′), *n., adj.* —*n.* 1 a person devoted to the service of a monastery as a lay brother. 2 a member of any of various secular societies in the Roman Catholic Church devoted to religious work.
—*adj.* dedicated to religious work; consecrated.
[< Medieval Latin *oblatus,* noun use of past participle of Latin *offerre* offer]

**ob|la|tion** (ob lā′shən), *n.* 1 the act of offering to God or a god. 2a the offering of bread and wine in the Communion service: *a full, perfect and sufficient sacrifice, oblation and satisfaction* (Book of Common Prayer). b = Communion service. 3 something offered, now especially to God or a god: *Bring no more vain oblations; incense is an abomination unto me* (Isaiah 1:13). 4 any gift for religious or charitable uses: *We humbly beseech thee to accept our alms and oblations* (Book of Common Prayer). [< Old French *oblation,* learned borrowing from Late Latin *oblātiō, -ōnis* < *offerre* bring, offer. Compare etym. under **offertory**.]

**ob|li|ga|ble** (ob′lə gə bəl), *adj.* capable of being bound by an obligation.

**ob|li|gate** (*v.* ob′lə gāt; *adj.* ob′lə git, -gāt), *v.,* **-gat|ed, -gat|ing,** *adj.* —*v.t.* 1 to bind morally or legally; pledge: *A witness in court is obligated to tell the truth.* 2 to compel; oblige: *Don't feel obligated to answer.*
—*adj.* 1 *Biology.* able to exist under or restricted to only one set of environmental conditions, as a parasite is which can survive only by living in close association with its host: *Obligate parasites ... are completely dependent upon living hosts for their food* (Harbaugh and Goodrich). 2 obligated; bound.
[< Latin *obligāre* (with English *-ate*[1]) < *ob-* to + *ligāre* bind. See etym. of doublet **oblige**.]

**ob|li|gate|ly** (ob′lə git lē, -gāt-), *adv.* = obligatorily.

**ob|li|ga|tion** (ob′lə gā′shən), *n.* 1 a duty under the law; duty due to a promise or contract; duty on account of social relationship or kindness received: *an obligation to pay taxes. We have an obligation to our friends. Parents have obligations to their children. "The cultivation of the soil," we are told, is an obligation imposed by nature on mankind* (Washington Irving). **SYN**: responsibility. See syn. under **duty**. 2 binding power (of a law, promise, or sense of duty): *The one who did the damage is under obligation to pay for it. The painter is really under obligation to paint our house first.* 3a a binding legal agreement; bond; contract: *The firm was not able to meet its obligations.* b a bond containing such an agreement, with a condition or penalty attached. c a bond, note, bill, or certificate serving as security for payment of indebtedness, as of a government or corporation. **4** the condition of being in debt for a favor, service, or the like: *Every opportunity implies an obligation* (John D. Rockefeller, Jr.). *It was his obligation to return her favor.* **5** the act of binding oneself or state of being bound by oath, promise, or contract to do or not to do something. **6** a service; favor; benefit: *A self-reliant person likes to repay all obligations.*

**ob|li|ga|tion|al** (ob′lə gā′shə nəl), *adj.* = obligatory.

**obligational authority**, *U.S.* the authority given by Congress to an administrative agency in the Federal Government to spend a given amount of money in a given period: *The obligational authority, usually granted by Congress through appropriations, must precede all budget spending* (Wall Street Journal).

**ob|li|ga|tive** (ob′lə gā′tiv), *adj.* imposing or implying obligation. —**ob′li|ga′tive|ness**, *n.*

**ob|li|ga|to** (ob′lə gä′tō), *adj., n., pl.* **-tos, -ti** (-tē). *Music.* obbligato.

**ob|li|ga|tor** (ob′lə gā′tər), *n.* **1** *Law.* a person who binds himself or gives his bond to another; obligor. **2** a person who obliges another.

**ob|lig|a|to|ry** (ə blig′ə tôr′ē, -tōr′-; ob′lə gə-), *adj.* binding morally or legally; required; compulsory: *Attendance at elementary school is obligatory.* **SYN**: coercive, mandatory. [< Late Latin *obligātōrius* < Latin *obligāre;* see etym. under **obligate**] —**ob|lig′a|to′ri|ly**, *adv.* —**ob|lig′a|to′ri|ness**, *n.*

**o|blige** (ə blīj′), *v.,* **o|bliged, o|blig|ing.** —*v.t.* **1** to bind by a promise, contract, or duty; compel; force; require: *The law obliges parents to send their children to school. I am obliged to leave early to catch my train.* **SYN**: constrain. **2** to bind by a favor or service; do a favor to: *Kindly oblige me by closing the door. We are very much obliged for your kind offer.* **SYN**: accommodate.
—*v.i.* to do a favor: *She obliged graciously by singing another song.*
[< Old French *obliger,* learned borrowing from Latin *obligāre.* See etym. of doublet **obligate**.] —**o|blig′er**, *n.*

**ob|li|gee** (ob′lə jē′), *n.* **1** *Law.* a person to whom another is bound by contract; person to whom a bond is given. **2** a person under obligation to another.

**o|blig|ing** (ə blī′jing), *adj.* **1** willing to do favors; helpful; accommodating: *an obliging neighbor. Her obliging nature wins friends.* **2** = obligatory. —**o|blig′ing|ly**, *adv.* —**o|blig′ing|ness**, *n.*

**ob|li|gor** (ob′lə gôr′, ob′lə gôr), *n. Law.* a person who binds himself to another by contract; person who gives a bond.

**ob|lique** (ə blēk′, -blīk′), *adj., adv., v.,* **-liqued, -liqu|ing**, *n.* —*adj.* **1** not straight up and down; not straight across; slanting: *This terrace or garden ... took an oblique view of the open sea* (Thomas L. Peacock). *Upon others we can look but in oblique; only upon ourselves in direct* (John Donne). **2** *Figurative.* not straightforward; indirect: *She made an oblique reference to her illness, but did not mention it directly. All censure of a man's self is oblique praise* (Samuel Johnson). **3** *Figurative.* not upright and moral; underhanded: *oblique dealings.* **4** (of a solid figure) not having the axis perpendicular to the plane of the base. **5** *Grammar.* of or in an oblique case. **6** *Botany.* having unequal sides: *an oblique leaf.* **7** *Anatomy.* situated obliquely; not transverse or longitudinal: *oblique muscles, fibers, or ligaments.*
—*adv.* (in military use) by turning 45 degrees: *to march oblique to the left.*
—*v.i., v.t.* **1** to have or take an oblique direction; slant. **2** (in military use) to advance obliquely by turning 45 degrees to the right or left and marching in the new direction.
—*n.* **1** something oblique, such as a line or figure. **2** *Anatomy.* an oblique muscle: *The superior and inferior obliques roll the eyeball about the visual axis* (Scientific American).
[< Latin *oblīquus* < *ob-* against + a root *līc-* to bend, as in *licinus* bent upward] —**ob|lique′ly**, *adv.* —**ob|lique′ness**, *n.*

***oblique angle**, any angle that is not a right angle. Acute angles and obtuse angles are oblique angles.

***oblique angle**

acute angles: 90° obtuse angles:
60° 120° 30° 150° right angle 0° 180°

**oblique case**, any case of a noun or pronoun except the nominative and vocative, or sometimes except the nominative and objective.

***oblique motion**, *Music.* the motion of the parts of a composition in which one part repeats the same tone while the other rises or descends in pitch.

***oblique motion**

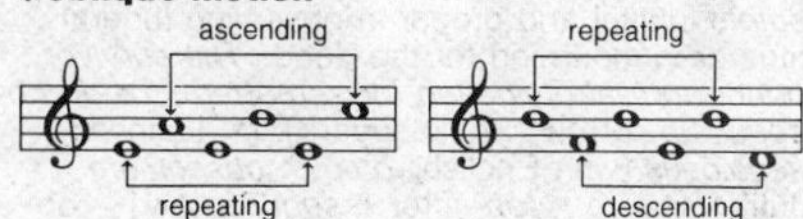


**ob|liq|ui|tous** (ə blik′wə təs), *adj.* exhibiting intellectual or moral obliquity.

**ob|liq|ui|ty** (ə blik′wə tē), *n., pl.* **-ties**. **1** indirectness or crookedness of thought or behavior, especially conduct that is not upright and moral: *a moral obliquity which grated very harshly against Ilbrahim's instinctive rectitude* (Hawthorne). **SYN**: deviation. **2** the fact or condition of being oblique. **3** inclination, or degree of inclination. **4** *Astronomy.* the angle (about 23 degrees 27 minutes) between the planes of the ecliptic and the equator.

**ob|lit|er|ate** (ə blit′ə rāt), *v.t.,* **-at|ed, -at|ing.** **1** to remove all traces of; wipe or blot out; destroy; efface: *The heavy rain obliterated all footprints.* (*Figurative.*) *By the destruction of that city,* [*they*] *obliterated the memory of their former disgrace* (Edward Gibbon). **SYN**: expunge, erase. **2** to blot out so as to leave no distinct traces; make unrecognizable. [< Latin *oblitterāre* (with English *-ate*[1]) < *ob litterās scrībere* to strike out, erase; (literally) draw across the letters]

**ob|lit|er|a|tion** (ə blit′ə rā′shən), *n.* the act or process of obliterating or state of being obliterated; effacement: *Mutual obliteration ... is "moral as well as practical nonsense"* (Bulletin of Atomic Scientists).

**ob|lit|er|a|tive** (ə blit′ə rā′tiv), *adj.* tending to obliterate: *Obliterative coloration* [*obscures*] *... the outlines of the animal, save when it moves* (Tracy I. Storer).

**ob|lit|er|a|tor** (ə blit′ə rā′tər), *n.* a person or thing that obliterates.

**ob|liv|i|on** (ə bliv′ē ən), *n.* **1** the condition of being entirely forgotten: *Many ancient cities have long since passed into oblivion. The very names of many plays have gone to oblivion* (Ashley Thorndike). **2** the fact of forgetting or having forgotten; forgetfulness: *The magic drink caused oblivion of all sorrows. Grandfather sat by the fire in peaceful oblivion. Oh, what would he have given for one five minutes of oblivion, of slumber, of relief from the burning thirst!* (Cardinal Newman). **3** intentional overlooking or disregard, especially of political offenses; pardon: *He* [*William III*] *expressed his hope that a bill of general pardon and oblivion would be ... presented for his sanction* (Macaulay). [< Latin *oblīviō, -ōnis* < *oblīvīscī* forget; (originally) even off, smooth out < *ob-* out + *lēvis* smooth]

**ob|liv|i|ous** (ə bliv′ē əs), *adj.* **1** not mindful; forgetful: *The book was so interesting that I was oblivious of my surroundings. She could hardly have been oblivious of Yuba Bill's adoration* (Bret Harte). **SYN**: unmindful. **2** bringing or causing forgetfulness: *an oblivious sleep.* **3** *Obsolete.* of or for forgotten things; forgotten. [< Latin *oblīviōsus* (with English *-ous*) < *oblīvium* forgetfulness < *oblīvīscī* forget; see etym. under **oblivion**] —**ob|liv′i|ous|ly**, *adv.* —**ob|liv′i|ous|ness**, *n.*

**Ob|lo|mov|ism** (ob lō′mə viz əm), *n.* extreme sluggishness; inertia; sloth. [< *Oblomov,* an extremely indolent Russian landowner who is the main character of a novel of the same name by Ivan Goncharov, 1812-1891]

**ob|long** (ob′lông, -long), *adj., n.* —*adj.* **1** longer than broad: *an oblong loaf of bread, an oblong leaf.* **2** *Geometry.* having the opposite sides parallel and the adjacent sides at right angles but not square.
—*n.* a rectangle that is not a square; something oblong in form.
[< Latin *oblongus* < *ob-* + *longus* long]

**ob|lo|quy** (ob′lə kwē), *n., pl.* **-quies**. **1** public reproach or condemnation; abuse; blame: *Was he not himself the mark of obloquy among the Reformers, because of his leniency to Catholics?* (John L. Motley). **SYN**: censure. **2** disgrace; shame: *his long public life, so singularly chequered with good and evil, with glory and obloquy* (Macaulay). **3** the act or fact of speaking evil against a person or thing; slander. **SYN**: calumny. **4** *Obsolete.* a cause of reproach. [< Late Latin *obloquium* abusive contradiction < Latin *ob-* against + *loquī* speak]

**ob|nox|ious** (əb nok′shəs), *adj.* **1** very disagreeable; offensive; hateful: *His disgusting manners at the table made him obnoxious to us. Persons obnoxious to the government were frequently imprisoned without any other authority than a royal order* (Macaulay). *It should be as easy to expel an obnoxious thought from your mind as shake a stone out of your shoe* (Edward Carpenter). **SYN**: objectionable. See syn. under **hateful**. **2** *Archaic.* exposed or liable to harm, injury, or evil: *Made hereby obnoxious more To all the miseries of life* (Milton). **3** *Obsolete.* **a** harmful; injurious. **b** liable to punishment or censure. [< Latin *obnoxiōsus* (with English *-ous*) ultimately < *ob-* against + *noxa* injury < *nocēre* to harm] —**ob|nox′ious|ly**, *adv.* —**ob|nox′ious|ness**, *n.*

**ob|nu|bi|late** (ob nü′bə lāt, -nyü′-), *v.t.,* **-lat|ed, -lat|ing.** to cloud over; darken or obscure; overcloud: *to obnubilate the sun;* (*Figurative.*) *to obnubilate the mind.* [< Latin *obnūbilāre* (with English *-ate*[1]) < *ob-* against + *nūbilus* cloudy < *nūbēs* cloud] —**ob|nu′bi|la′tion**, *n.*

***o|boe** (ō′bō), *n.* **1** a woodwind instrument in which the tone is produced by a double reed; hautboy. It is a slender instrument with a thin, high-pitched tone. **2** a reed stop in an organ that produces a penetrating tone like that of the oboe. **3** the oboist of an orchestra: *John Mack, the Cleveland Orchestra's principal oboe ...* (New Yorker). [< Italian *oboe* < French *hautbois* hautboy]

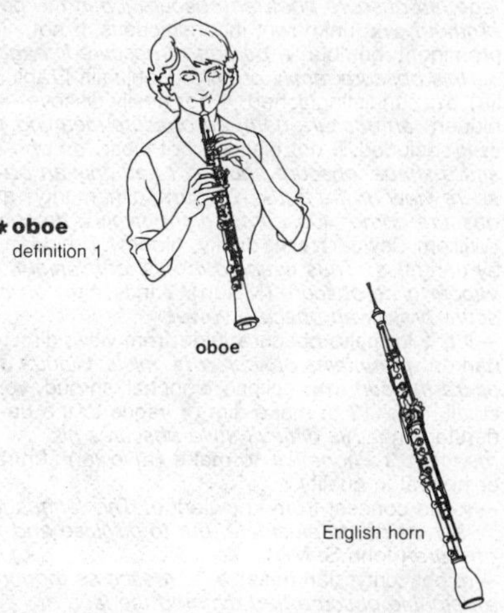

***oboe** definition 1

**o|bo|ist** (ō′bō ist), *n.* a person who plays the oboe.

**ob|ol** (ob′əl, ō′bəl), *n.* = obolus.

**ob|o|lus** (ob′ə ləs), *n., pl.* **-li** (-lī). an ancient Greek silver coin worth 1/6 of a drachma. [< Latin *obolus* < Greek *obolós,* variant of *obelós* nail (because nails were used for money)]

**O-Bon** or **O'Bon** (ō′bon′), *n.* a Buddhist festival celebrating the dead whose spirits are believed to return to the world of the living for the duration of the festival: *O'Bon has evolved from a strictly Buddhist to a national* [*Japanese*] *festival with all faiths participating* (New York Times). [compare Japanese *bon* Buddhist festival]

**ob|o|vate** (ob ō′vāt), *adj.* inversely ovate: *an obovate leaf.*

**ob|o|void** (ob ō′void), *adj.* inversely ovoid: *obovoid fruits.*

**obs.** or **Obs.**, **1** observation. **2** observatory. **3** obsolete; used formerly but not now.

**ob|scene** (əb sēn′), *adj.* **1** offending modesty or decency; impure; filthy; vile: *obscene language, books, or pictures, an obscene joke or dance.* **SYN**: indecent, gross, lewd, ribald. **2** *Archaic.* loathsome; disgusting; repulsive: *so heinous, black, obscene a deed* (Shakespeare). **3** *Obsolete.* ill-boding; ominous: *The boding bird ... Which ... beats about the tombs with nightly wings, Where songs obscene on sepulchers she sings* (John Dryden). [< Latin *obscēnus, obscaenus*] —**ob|scene′ly**, *adv.* —**ob|scene′ness**, *n.*

**ob|scen|i|ty** (əb sen′ə tē, -sē′nə-), *n., pl.* **-ties**. **1** obscene quality. **2** obscene language or behavior; an obscene word or act: *It is possible that the proposed new definition of literary obscenity ... may not entirely satisfy* (New Yorker).

**ob|scur|ant** (əb skyůr′ənt), *adj., n.* —*adj.* **1** that obscures or darkens. **2** = obscurantist.
—*n.* **1** = obscurantist. **2** a person that obscures.
[< German *Obskurant* < Latin *obscūrāns, -antis,* present participle of *obscūrāre* darken < *obscūrus* obscure]

**Pronunciation Key:** hat, āge, cãre, fär; let, ēqual, tėrm; it, īce; hot, ōpen, ôrder; oil, out; cup, pu̇t, rüle; child; long; thin; ᴛʜen; zh, measure; ə represents **a** in about, **e** in taken, **i** in pencil, **o** in lemon, **u** in circus.

**ob|scu|ran|tic** (ob'skyů ran'tik), *adj.* given to obscurantism; obscurant.

**ob|scur|ant|ism** (əb skyůr'ən tiz əm), *n.* **1** opposition to progress and the spread of knowledge. **2** the quality of being deliberately unclear or evasive: *the obscurantism of some modern poetry.* [probably < German *Obskurantismus* < *Obskurant,* noun, obscurant + *-ismus* -ism]

**ob|scur|ant|ist** (əb skyůr'ən tist), *n., adj.* —*n.* a person who is opposed to progress and the spread of knowledge; obscurant: *that ordinary, average man whose lack of spiritual life and resource ... the new obscurantists have been urging us to despise* (New Yorker).
—*adj.* of obscurantists or obscurantism: *the obscurantist technique of smothering the real issue with gobbledygook.*

**ob|scu|ra|tion** (ob'skyů rā'shən), *n.* **1** the act of obscuring. **2** the condition of being obscured.

**ob|scure** (əb skyůr'), *adj.,* **-scur|er, -scur|est,** *v.,* **-scured, -scur|ing,** *n.* —*adj.* **1** not clearly expressed; hard to understand: *an obscure passage in a book.* **2** not expressing meaning clearly: *an obscure style of writing. This obscure saying baffled him* (Arnold Bennett). **3a** not well known; attracting no notice: *an obscure little village, an obscure poet, an obscure job in the government.* SYN: unknown, inconspicuous. **b** not prominent; humble: *a person of obscure lineage; ... this obscure family of ours* (Benjamin Franklin). SYN: undistinguished. **4** not easily discovered; hidden: *an obscure path, an obscure meaning.* SYN: secluded. **5** not distinct; not clear: *an obscure shape, obscure sounds. I had only an obscure view of the battle.* **6a** dark; dim; murky: *an obscure corner. Obscurest night involv'd the sky* (William Cowper). SYN: dusky, gloomy. **b** hidden by darkness: *Thus wrapp'd in mist of midnight vapour glide obscure* (Milton). **7** indefinite: *an obscure brown, an obscure vowel.*
—*v.t.* **1** to make obscure; hide from view; dim; darken: *mountains obscured by mists. Clouds obscure the sun.* SYN: eclipse, conceal, shroud, veil, cloak, mask. **2** to make dim or vague to the understanding: *His difficult style obscures his meaning.* **3** *Phonetics.* to make (a vowel) central or neutral in quality.
—*v.i.* to conceal from knowledge: *This language ... serves not to elucidate, but to disguise and obscure* (John S. Mill).
—*n.* obscurity; darkness: *a ... feeling as though a palpable obscure had dimmed the face of things* (Charles Lamb).
[< Middle French *obscur* < Old French *oscur,* learned borrowing from Latin *obscūrus*] —**ob|scure'ly,** *adv.* —**ob|scure'ness,** *n.* —**ob|scur'er,** *n.*
—*Syn. adj.* **1 Obscure, vague, ambiguous, equivocal** mean not clearly expressed or understood. **Obscure** suggests that the meaning of something is hidden either because it is not plainly expressed or because the reader or hearer lacks the necessary knowledge to understand it: *To a layman much legal language is obscure.* **Vague** suggests that the meaning or statement is too general or not clearly and completely thought out: *No one can be sure what that vague statement means.* **Ambiguous** means so expressed that either of two meanings is possible: *"She kissed her when she left" is an ambiguous statement.* **Equivocal** suggests a conscious effort to confuse by allowing conflicting interpretations: *The candidate was a master of the equivocal statement which tended to satisfy everyone.*

**ob|scu|ri|ty** (əb skyůr'ə tē), *n., pl.* **-ties. 1** lack of clearness; difficulty in being understood: *The obscurity of the paragraph makes several interpretations possible. One of the most pernicious effects of haste is obscurity* (Samuel Johnson). SYN: ambiguity, vagueness. **2** something obscure; thing hard to understand; point or passage not clearly expressed; doubtful or vague meaning. **3** the condition of being unknown: *Lincoln rose from obscurity to fame.* **4** a little-known person or place. **5** lack of light; dimness: *The dog hid in the obscurity of the thick bushes.* SYN: darkness, shade.

**ob|se|crate** (ob'sə krāt), *v.t.,* **-crat|ed, -crat|ing. 1** to beg (a person or thing) solemnly; beseech. SYN: implore, supplicate. **2** to beg for (a thing). [< Latin *obsecrāre* (with English *-ate*[1]) entreat (in the name of something sacred) < *ob-* for + *sacer, sacris* sacred]

**ob|se|cra|tion** (ob'sə krā'shən), *n.* the act of obsecrating; entreaty; supplication: *Let us fly to God at all times with humble obsecrations* (Francis Bacon).

**ob|se|quies** (ob'sə kwēz), *n.pl.* funeral rites or ceremonies; stately funeral: *His funeral obsequies were celebrated with the utmost grandeur and solemnity* (Washington Irving). [< Medieval Latin *obsequiae,* plural, for Latin *exsequiae* funeral rites < *ex-* out + *sequī* follow]

**ob|se|qui|ous** (əb sē'kwē əs), *adj.* **1** polite or obedient from hope of gain or from fear; servile; fawning: *Obsequious courtiers greeted the king.* SYN: slavish. **2** properly obedient; dutiful. **3** *Obsolete.* dutiful and proper in observing funeral rites or in mourning for the dead: *The survivor bound In filial obligation for some term To do obsequious sorrow* (Shakespeare). [< Latin *obsequiōsus* (with English *-ous*) < *obsequium* dutiful service < *ob-* after + *sequī* follow] —**ob|se'qui|ous|ly,** *adv.* —**ob|se'qui|ous|ness,** *n.*

**ob|serv|a|ble** (əb zėr'və bəl), *adj., n.* —*adj.* **1** that can be or is noticed; noticeable; easily seen: *an observable loss of weight. That distant star is observable on a dark night.* **2** that can be followed or practiced; that can be or is observed: *This rule is not observable. Lent is observable by some churches.*
—*n.* something that can be observed or perceived by the senses: *No one denies that physical theories involving unobservables enable us to predict the behaviour of observables* (Bernard Mayo). —**ob|serv'a|ble|ness,** *n.*

**ob|serv|a|bly** (əb zėr'və blē), *adv.* so as to be observed; to an observable degree; remarkably; noticeably: *Most twins are observably different once you know them.*

**ob|serv|ance** (əb zėr'vəns), *n.* **1** the act of observing or keeping laws or customs: *the observance of traffic regulations, the observance of the Sabbath.* SYN: celebration. **2** an act performed as a sign of worship or respect; religious ceremony: *Our Sundays, at Blithedale, were not ordinarily kept with such rigid observance as might have befitted the descendants of the Pilgrims* (Hawthorne). SYN: rite. **3** a rule or custom to be observed: *strict observances.* **4** *Archaic.* respectful attention or service: *I have long loved her ... followed her with a doting observance* (Shakespeare). *He compass'd her with sweet observances and worship* (Tennyson). **5** observation; notice: *I passed, And pried, in every place, without observance* (Philip Massinger). **6a** the rules or laws of a Roman Catholic religious order or community. **b** an order or group following such rule or discipline.
▶ See **observation** for usage note.

**ob|serv|ant** (əb zėr'vənt), *adj., n.* —*adj.* **1** quick to notice; observing; watchful: *If you are observant in the fields and woods, you will find many flowers that others fail to notice. He was observant and thoughtful, and given to asking sagacious questions* (John Galt). SYN: heedful, regardful, attentive. **2** careful in observing (a law, rule, or custom); properly mindful: *A careful driver is observant of the traffic rules. No man ... could have been more observant of religious rites* (John L. Motley). SYN: aware, cognizant. [< noun]
—*n.* **1** a person who is strict in observing a law, rule, or custom. **2** an observer: *The nonparticipant observant remains aloof, and describes the [subjects'] behavior by time intervals* (Emory S. Bogardus). **3** *Obsolete.* a dutiful follower; obsequious attendant.
[< Latin *observāns, -antis,* present participle of *observāre* observe] —**ob|serv'ant|ly,** *adv.*

**ob|ser|va|tion** (ob'zər vā'shən), *n., adj.* —*n.* **1** the act, habit, or power of seeing and noting: *By his trained observation the doctor knew that the unconscious man was not dead.* **2** the fact or condition of being seen; notice: *The spy avoided observation.* **3** Often, **observations.** something seen and noted; data or information secured by observing: *The student of bird life kept a record of his observations.* **4** the act of watching for some special purpose; study: *The observation of nature is important in science.* **5** a remark; comment: *"Haste makes waste," was Father's observation when I spilled the ice cream.* **6** the process of measuring by a sextant or similar instrument the altitude of the sun or other heavenly body to determine the latitude and longitude of a ship or airplane. **7** *Obsolete.* observance.
—*adj.* **1** from which to observe: *an observation balloon. There were also observation towers which I was able to climb to look out across the forest and the mountains* (Manchester Guardian). **2** within which persons or animals can be watched and studied: *an observation cell or ward equipped with one-way glass.*
▶ **Observation, observance** are sometimes confused because both are related to the verb **observe. Observation,** connected with the meaning "watch closely," applies especially to the act or power of noticing things or watching closely, or to being watched or noticed: *An observatory is for the observation of the stars.* **Observance,** connected with the meaning "keep," applies to the act of keeping and following customs or duties, or to a rule or law, kept or celebrated: *You go to church for the observance of religious duties. Observation* is sometimes used in this sense, but this usage is now rare.

**ob|ser|va|tion|al** (ob'zər vā'shə nəl), *adj.* of or based on observation, especially as contrasted with experiment: *observational evidence.* —**ob'ser|va'tion|al|ly,** *adv.*

**observation balloon,** a captive balloon used for purposes of observation.

**observation car,** a railroad passenger car with a transparent dome, large windows, or an open platform at one end, so that passengers may view the scenery.

**observation station, 1** a place from which to observe and report what is happening nearby: *... to stop all nuclear tests, with compliance assured by a network of internationally manned observation stations* (David R. Inglis). **2** a building or camp equipped with instruments for making a scientific study over a period of time: *an observation station on a mountain for studying weather.*

**ob|serv|a|to|ri|al** (əb zėr'və tôr'ē əl, -tōr'-), *adj.* **1** of or belonging to a scientific observer. **2** like an observatory.

***ob|serv|a|to|ry** (əb zėr'və tôr'ē, -tōr'-), *n., pl.* **-ries. 1** a place or building with a telescope or other equipment for observing the stars and other heavenly bodies: *The Greek astronomer Hipparchus built an observatory on the island of Rhodes ... Early observatories also existed in the Orient, as shown by a stone tower built* A.D. *647 in Kyongju, Korea* (Helmut Abt). **2** a place or building for observing facts or happenings of nature: *a meteorological observatory.* **3** a high place or building giving a wide view: *I never knew of a ship sailing ... but I went up to the State House cupola or to the observatory on some friend's house ... and there watched the departure* (George W. Curtis). **4** an artificial satellite designed to gather information about the earth, sun, or other heavenly body: *Observatories are larger satellites, ... either carrying many (up to 30) small experiments or a few heavy (up to 1000 lb.) complex experiments. An observatory weighs from 1000 to 4000 lb.* (John E. Naugle).

***observatory**
definition 1

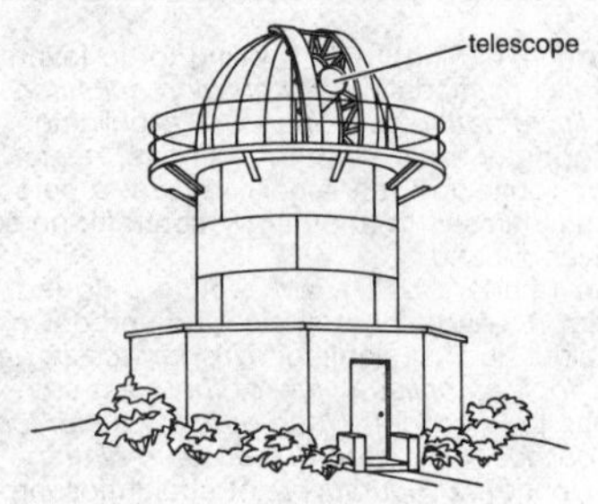


**ob|serve** (əb zėrv'), *v.,* **-served, -serv|ing,** *n.* —*v.t.* **1** to see and note; notice: *Did you observe anything strange in that boy's behavior? I saw the pots ... red-hot ... and observed that they did not crack at all* (Daniel Defoe). *... the distant radio sources observed by radio-astronomers* (Fred Hoyle). SYN: perceive. See syn. under **see. 2** to examine carefully; watch; study: *An astronomer observes the stars. The spy observed the enemy's military installations.* SYN: survey. **3** to remark; comment: *"Bad weather," the captain observed.* SYN: mention. **4** to follow in practice; keep: *We must observe silence in the classroom. Please observe the rule about not walking on the grass.* **5** to show regard for; celebrate: *to observe the Sabbath, to observe birthdays and anniversaries.* **6** *Obsolete.* to treat with respect or consideration.
—*v.i.* **1** to take notice. **2** to make observations. **3** to make a remark or observation; comment (on).
—*n. Scottish.* a remark; observation: *Thomas said he had not heard a mair sound observe for some time* (John Galt).
[< Latin *observāre* < *ob-* over + *servāre* to watch, keep] —**ob|serv'er,** *n.*

**observer force,** a group of military or civilian personnel sent to observe and report the social, military, or political situation of some area, and to perform certain administrative functions.

**ob|serv|ing** (əb zėr'ving), *adj.* quick to notice; observant. —**ob|serv'ing|ly,** *adv.*

**ob|sess** (əb ses'), *v.t.* **1** to fill the mind of; keep the attention of to an unreasonable or unhealthy extent; haunt: *Fear that someone might steal his money obsessed the old miser.* **2** (of an evil spirit) to beset or dominate (a person). [< Latin *obsessus,* past participle of *obsidēre* to sit at < *ob-* by, against + *sedēre* sit]

**ob|ses|sion** (əb sesh'ən), *n.* **1** the act of obsessing or state of being obsessed; influenced of a feeling, idea, or impulse that a person cannot escape. **2** the feeling, idea, or impulse itself. **3** *Psy-*

*chiatry.* a compelling or fixed idea or feeling, usually irrational, over which a person has little conscious control; compulsion. **4** domination by an evil spirit.

**ob|ses|sion|al** (əb sesh′ə nəl), *adj., n.* —***adj.*** = obsessive.
—***n.*** a person who has an obsessional neurosis: *treatment of psychotics and obsessionals* (Scientific American). —**ob|ses′sion|al|ly,** *adv.*

**obsessional neurosis,** a neurosis in which a person is obsessed with one idea or emotion, or compulsively repeats certain actions, as handwashing or looking in mirrors; compulsion neurosis.

**ob|ses|sive** (əb ses′iv), *adj., n.* —***adj.*** having to do with or causing obsession; obsessing: *an obsessive feeling or idea.*
—***n.*** a person having an obsession or obsessions: *There is, of course, a set of middle-class obsessives ... who live in a nightmarish world where they are threatened by juvenile delinquents, coloured immigrants, tax inspectors, trade union leaders, motorcyclists, and libertine publishers* (New Statesman). —**ob|ses′sive|ly,** *adv.* —**ob|ses′sive|ness,** *n.*

**ob|ses|sive-com|pul|sive** (əb ses′iv kəm pul′siv), *adj., n.* —***adj.*** of or having to do with an obsessional neurosis.
—***n.*** a person suffering from an obsessional neurosis: *Most gratifying was the success with victims of notoriously resistant types of illness —addicts and obsessive-compulsives* (Time).

**ob|sid|i|an** (ob sid′ē ən), *n.* a hard, dark, glassy rock that is formed when lava cools; volcanic glass: *Indians used obsidian to make arrowheads* (Richard M. Pearl). [< Latin *obsidiānus,* misreading of *obsiānus* (*lapis*) (stone) of *Obsius,* its alleged discoverer]

**ob|sid|i|o|nal** (ob sid′ē ə nəl), *adj.* of or having to do with a siege: *An obsidional crown was a crown or wreath conferred upon a Roman general who had delivered a besieged place.* [< Latin *obsidiōnālis* < *obsidiō, -ōnis* a siege < *obsidēre* sit at; see etym. under **obsess**]

**ob|sid|i|o|nar|y** (ob sid′ē ə ner′ē), *adj.* = obsidional.

**ob|so|lesce** (ob′sə les′), *v.i.,* **-lesced, -lesc|ing.** to be obsolescent; fall into disuse: *Service aircraft tend to obsolesce ... soon after leaving the drawing board* (Punch). [< Latin *obsolēscere;* see etym. under **obsolescent**]

**ob|so|les|cence** (ob′sə les′əns), *n.* **1** the act or fact of passing out of use; getting out of date; becoming obsolete: *Office buildings face obsolescence* (Wall Street Journal). **2** *Entomology.* an indistinct or blurred part, such as of a mark or stria: *a band with a central obsolescence.*

**ob|so|les|cent** (ob′sə les′ənt), *adj.* **1** passing out of use; tending to become out of date: *Horse carriages are obsolescent.* **2** *Biology.* gradually disappearing; imperfectly or slightly developed: *obsolescent organs.* [< Latin *obsolēscēns, -entis,* present participle of *obsolēscere* to fall into disuse, ultimately < *ob-* away + *solēre* be usual, be customary] —**ob′so|les′cent|ly,** *adv.*

**ob|so|lete** (ob′sə lēt), *adj., v.,* **-let|ed, -let|ing.**
—***adj.*** **1** no longer in use: *obsolete methods. Bowing to greet a lady is now an obsolete custom. Wooden warships are obsolete. Abbr:* obs. **SYN:** disused. **2** out-of-date: *We still use this machine though it is obsolete.* **SYN:** antiquated. **3** *Biology.* imperfectly developed and of little use; indistinct, especially in comparison with the corresponding character in other individuals or related species; vestigial.
—***v.t.*** to make obsolete; discard or disuse as being out of date: *We are about to obsolete the wheel, just as the wheel and axle invention obsoleted the skid, some ten thousand years ago* (Atlantic).
[< Latin *obsolētus,* past participle of *obsolēscere* become out-of-date; see etym. under **obsolescent**] —**ob′so|lete|ly,** *adv.* —**ob′so|lete|ness,** *n.*

**ob|so|let|ism** (ob′sə lēt′iz əm), *n.* **1** an obsolete custom, expression, word, or the like. **2** the condition of being obsolete.

**ob|sta|cle** (ob′stə kəl), *n.* something that stands in the way or stops progress: *... the grim obstacle of the mountain hidden in the storm* (Manchester Guardian). *He overcame the obstacle of blindness and became a musician.* [< Old French *obstacle,* learned borrowing from Latin *obstāculum* < *obstāre* to block, hinder < *ob-* in the way of + *stāre* to stand]
—***Syn.*** **Obstacle, obstruction, hindrance** mean something that gets in the way of action or progress. **Obstacle** applies to something that stands in the way and must be moved or overcome before one can continue toward a goal: *A fallen tree across the road was an obstacle to our car.* **Obstruction** applies especially to something that blocks a passage: *The enemy built obstructions in the road.* **Hindrance** applies to something that holds back or makes progress difficult: *Noise is a hindrance to studying.*

**obstacle course, 1** a military or athletic training area in which obstacles such as fences, ditches, and hurdles have to be climbed or crossed over in succession. **2** *Figurative.* any course filled with hurdles and difficulties: *New York has a fascinating obstacle course on Park Avenue where earth is being excavated for the foundation of a forty-four-story office building.*

**obstacle race,** a foot race in which various devices, such as walls, streams, and fences, have to be jumped or climbed over.

**obstet., 1a** obstetric. **b** obstetrical. **2** obstetrics.

**ob|stet|ric** (ob stet′rik), *adj.* having to do with the care of women before, in, and after childbirth.

**ob|stet|ri|cal** (ob stet′rə kəl), *adj.* = obstetric.
—**ob|stet′ri|cal|ly,** *adv.*

**obstetrical toad,** = midwife toad.

**ob|ste|tri|cian** (ob′stə trish′ən), *n.* a doctor who specializes in obstetrics.

**ob|stet|rics** (ob stet′riks), *n.* the branch of medicine and surgery concerned with treating women before, in, and after childbirth. [adaptation of Latin *obstetrīcia* midwifery (with English *-ics*) < *obstetrīx, -īcis* midwife < *ob-* by + *stāre* to stand]

**ob|sti|na|cy** (ob′stə nə sē), *n., pl.* **-cies. 1** stubborn nature or behavior: *Obstinacy drove the boy to repeat the statement even after he knew it was wrong.* **2** stubborn persistence; unyielding nature: *Obstinacy in a bad cause is but constancy in a good* (Thomas Browne). **3** an obstinate act: *rebuke for their pedantries and obstinacies* (Thomas Carlyle). [< Medieval Latin *obstinatia* < Latin *obstinātus,* past participle of *obstināre;* see etym. under **obstinate**]

**ob|sti|nate** (ob′stə nit), *adj.* **1** not giving in; stubborn: *The obstinate girl would go her own way, in spite of all warnings.* **2** hard to control or treat: *an obstinate cough.* **SYN:** persistent, intractable. [< Latin *obstinātus,* past participle of *obstināre* be determined, ultimately < *ob-* by + *stāre* to stand. Compare etym. under **destine.**] —**ob′stinate|ly,** *adv.* —**ob′sti|nate|ness,** *n.*
—***Syn.*** **1 Obstinate, stubborn** mean fixed in purpose or opinion. **Obstinate** suggests an unyielding persistence, often unreasonable or contrary: *The obstinate man refused to obey orders.* **Stubborn** suggests strong determination to withstand attempts to change one's way: *to fight one's enemies with stubborn courage.*

**ob|strep|er|ous** (əb strep′ər əs), *adj.* **1** loud or noisy; boisterous: *Most children are naturally obstreperous.* **SYN:** clamorous, vociferous. **2** unruly; disorderly: *It means reaching directly a pretty obstreperous sector of youth, some of them before they get into serious trouble* (New York Times). [< Latin *obstreperus* (with English *-ous*) < *ob-* against + *strepere* make a noise] —**ob|strep′er|ous|ly,** *adv.* —**ob|strep′er|ous|ness,** *n.*

**ob|struct** (əb strukt′), *v.t.* **1** to make hard to pass through; block or close up: *Fallen trees obstruct the road.* **SYN:** choke, clog. **2a** to be in the way of; block or close off: *Trees obstruct our view of the ocean.* **SYN:** impede. **b** *Figurative.* to oppose the course of; hinder: *to obstruct justice. A shortage of materials obstructed the work of the factory.* **SYN:** impede. [< Latin *obstrūctus,* past participle of *obstruere* < *ob-* in the way of + *struere* to pile]

**ob|struc|tion** (əb struk′shən), *n.* **1** a thing that obstructs; something in the way: *The soldiers had to get over such obstructions as ditches and barbed wire.* (*Figurative.*) *Ignorance is an obstruction to progress.* **SYN:** impediment, barrier, hindrance. See syn. under **obstacle. 2** the act or fact of blocking or hindering: (*Figurative.*) *the obstruction of progress by prejudice,* (*Figurative.*) *the obstruction of legislation by filibuster.*

**ob|struc|tion|ism** (əb struk′shə niz əm), *n.* the act or practice of hindering the progress of business as in a meeting or legislature.

**ob|struc|tion|ist** (əb struk′shə nist), *n., adj.* —***n.*** a person who hinders (progress, legislation, reform, or other change).
—***adj.*** of or having to do with obstructionism or obstructionists.

**ob|struc|tion|is|tic** (əb struk′shə nis′tik), *adj.* having to do with or characterized by obstructionism: *obstructionistic tactics.*

**ob|struc|tive** (əb struk′tiv), *adj., n.* —***adj.*** tending or serving to obstruct; blocking or hindering: *Academies may be said to be obstructive to energy and inventive genius* (Matthew Arnold).
—***n.*** a person or thing that obstructs. —**ob|struc′tive|ly,** *adv.* —**ob|struc′tive|ness,** *n.*

**ob|struc|tor** (əb struk′tər), *n.* a person or thing that obstructs.

**ob|stru|ent** (ob′strü ənt), *adj., n.* —***adj.*** obstructing natural openings or passages in the body.
—***n.*** **1** something that obstructs a natural opening or passage in the body. **2** *Phonetics.* a stop or fricative.
[< Latin *obstruēns, -entis,* present participle of *obstruere* obstruct]

**ob|tain** (əb tān′), *v.t.* **1** to get or procure through effort or diligence; come to have; acquire: *to obtain a job one applies for, to obtain a prize one has been working for, to obtain possession of a house one has rented, to obtain knowledge through study.* **SYN:** secure, gain. See syn. under **get. 2** *Archaic.* to attain; reach. **3** *Obsolete.* to hold; possess: *His mother then is mortal, but his Sire He who obtains the monarchy of Heaven* (Milton). —***v.i.*** **1** to be in use; be customary; prevail: *Different rules obtain in different schools.* **2** to get what is desired: *The simple heart, that freely asks In love, obtains* (John Greenleaf Whittier). **3** *Archaic.* to prevail; succeed: *This, though it failed at present, yet afterwards obtained* (Jonathan Swift). **4** *Obsolete.* to attain (to): *if a man cannot obtain to that judgment* (Francis Bacon). [< Middle English *obteynen* < Middle French *obtenir* < Latin *obtinēre* < *ob-* to + *tenēre* to hold] —**ob|tain′a|ble,** *adj.* —**ob|tain′er,** *n.* —**ob|tain′ment,** *n.*

**ob|tect** (ob tekt′), *adj.* = obtected.

**ob|tect|ed** (ob tek′tid), *adj.* having the appendages covered or protected by a hard shell or horny case, as the pupae of many insects, especially butterflies. [< Latin *obtēctus,* past participle of *obtegere* cover up, protect (< *ob-* against + *tegere* to cover) + English *-ed*[2]]

**ob|ten|tion** (əb ten′shən), *n.* the act of obtaining; obtainment.

**ob|test** (ob test′), *v.t.* **1** to call upon (God or something sacred) as witness; invoke. **2** to beg earnestly; beseech; entreat; implore. —***v.i.*** to make obtestation; make a solemn appeal or invocation. [< Latin *obtestārī* < *ob-* on account of + *testārī* bear witness]

**ob|tes|ta|tion** (ob′tes tā′shən), *n.* **1** entreaty; supplication: *Our humblest petitions and obtestations at his feet* (Milton). **2** a solemn confirmation or invocation: *They made oath and obtestation to stand faithfully by one another* (Thomas Carlyle).

**ob|trude** (əb trüd′), *v.,* **-trud|ed, -trud|ing.** —***v.t.*** **1** to put forward unasked and unwanted; force: *Don't obtrude your opinions on others. He wouldn't obtrude his assistance, if it were declined* (John L. Motley). **2** to push out; thrust forward: *A turtle obtrudes its head from its shell.* **SYN:** project, protrude.
—***v.i.*** to come unasked and unwanted; force oneself; intrude: *imagination ... that forward, delusive faculty, ever obtruding beyond its sphere* (Joseph Butler). *The remembrance that our poor captain was lying dead in the cabin was constantly obtruding* (Frederick Marryat).
[< Latin *obtrūdere* < *ob-* toward + *trūdere* to thrust] —**ob|trud′er,** *n.*

**ob|trun|cate** (ob trung′kāt), *v.t.,* **-cat|ed, -cat|ing.** to cut or lop off the head or top from: *obtruncated trees.* [< *ob-* + *truncate*]

**ob|tru|sion** (əb trü′zhən), *n.* **1** the action of obtruding. **2** something obtruded: *disturbed by the obtrusion of new ideas* (Samuel Johnson). [< Late Latin *obtrūsiō, -ōnis* < Latin *obtrūdere* obtrude]

**ob|tru|sive** (əb trü′siv), *adj.* **1** inclined to obtrude; putting oneself forward; intrusive: *What matters if you are considered obtrusive?* (Thackeray). **SYN:** meddlesome, officious, pushing, forward. **2** projecting; protruding. —**ob|tru′sive|ly,** *adv.* —**ob|tru′sive|ness,** *n.*

**ob|tund** (ob tund′), *v.t.* to blunt; dull; deaden. [< Latin *obtundere* to blunt, dull; see etym. under **obtuse**]

**ob|tund|ent** (ob tun′dənt), *adj., n.* —***adj.*** dulling sensibility, as of nerves.
—***n.*** an obtundent agent or anesthetic.

**ob|tu|rate** (ob′tyə rāt), *v.t.,* **-rat|ed, -rat|ing. 1** to stop up; close; obstruct. **2** to close (a hole, joint, or cavity in a gun breech) to prevent the escape of gas after firing. [< Latin *obtūrāre* (with English *-ate*[1]) to stop up] —**ob′tu|ra′tion,** *n.*

**ob|tu|ra|tor** (ob′tyə rā′tər), *n.* a thing that closes or stops up an entrance, cavity, or the like.

**ob|tuse** (əb tüs′, -tyüs′), *adj.* **1** not sharp or acute; blunt. **2** having an angle of more than 90 degrees but less than 180 degrees: *an obtuse triangle.* See diagram under **triangle. 3** *Figurative.* slow in understanding; stupid: *He was too obtuse to take the hint.* **4a** indistinctly felt or perceived: *an obtuse pain, an obtuse sound.* **b** *Figurative.* not sensitive; dull: *One's hearing often becomes obtuse in old age. a person ... obtuse in sensibility and unimaginative in temperament* (Harriet Beecher Stowe). **5** rounded at the top: *an obtuse leaf or petal.* [< Latin *obtūsus*

---

**Pronunciation Key:** hat, āge, cãre, fär; let, ēqual, tėrm; it, īce; hot, ōpen, ôrder; **oi**l, **ou**t; cup, pu̇t, rüle; **ch**ild; lo**ng**; **th**in; **ᴛʜ**en; **zh**, measure;
**ə** represents **a** in about, **e** in taken, **i** in pencil, **o** in lemon, **u** in circus.

blunt, dulled, past participle of *obtundere* < *ob-* on + *tundere* to beat] —**ob|tuse′ly**, *adv.* —**ob-tuse′ness**, *n.*

**obtuse angle**, an angle greater than a right angle but smaller than 180 degrees. See picture under **angle**[1].

**ob|tuse-an|gled** (əb tüs′ang′gəld, -tyüs′-), *adj.* having an obtuse angle.

**ob|tu|si|ty** (əb tü′sə tē, -tyü′-), *n., pl.* **-ties.** **1** insensibility; dullness: *obtusity of the ear.* **2** *Figurative.* folly; stupidity: [*His*] *purpose in parading this gallery of prophets is not to entertain us with the obtusities of our forebears but to save us from our own* (New Yorker).

**ob|verse** (*n.* ob′vėrs; *adj.* ob vėrs′, ob′vėrs), *n., adj.* —*n.* **1** the side of a coin, medal, seal, or the like, that has the principal design on it. **2** the face of anything that is meant to be turned toward the observer; front. **3** *Figurative.* a counterpart: *Alchemy is the medieval obverse of modern science.* **4** *Logic.* a proposition derived through obversion; the negative (or affirmative) counterpart of a given affirmative (or negative) proposition. [< adjective]
—*adj.* **1** turned toward the observer. **2** *Figurative.* being a counterpart to something else: ... *he was the malevolent obverse side of the rebel benefactor of man* (Edmund Wilson). **3** having the base narrower than the top or tip: *an obverse leaf.*
[< Latin *obversus,* past participle of *obvertere* < *ob-* toward + *vertere* to turn] —**ob|verse′ly**, *adv.*

**ob|ver|sion** (ob vėr′zhən, -shən), *n.* **1** the formation of an obverse or counterpart; an obverting. **2** *Logic.* inferring the negative or opposite of a proposition. By obversion the statement "All men are mortal" means also "No men are immortal."

**ob|vert** (ob vėrt′), *v.t.* **1** to turn (something) toward an object or in a contrary direction. **2** *Logic.* to change (a proposition) to the denial of its opposite. [< Latin *obvertere* to turn toward; see etym. under **obverse**]

**ob|vi|ate** (ob′vē āt), *v.t.,* **-at|ed, -at|ing.** to meet and dispose of; clear out of the way; remove: *to obviate a difficulty, to obviate danger, to obviate objections.* **SYN:** intercept, avert, preclude. [< Late Latin *obviāre* (with English *-ate*[1]) < Latin *obvius* in the way; see etym. under **obvious**]

**ob|vi|a|tion** (ob′vē ā′shən), *n.* **1** the act or fact of obviating. **2** the state of being obviated.

**ob|vi|a|tor** (ob′vē ā′tər), *n.* a person or thing that obviates.

**ob|vi|os|i|ty** (ob′vē os′ə tē), *n., pl.* **-ties.** something obvious: *Who says there's nothing charming about obviosities, clichés, and an 1890 style?* (Maclean's).

**ob|vi|ous** (ob′vē əs), *adj.* **1** easily seen or understood; clear to the eye or mind; not to be doubted; plain: *It is obvious that two and two make four. It is obvious that a blind man ought not to drive an automobile. The frail child was in obvious need of food and sunshine.* **2** *Obsolete.* being or standing in the way; fronting. **3** *Obsolete.* exposed or open (to): *The pedant is ... obvious to ridicule* (Sir Richard Steele). [< Latin *obvius* (with English *-ous*) < *obviam* in the way < *ob* across + *via* way] —**ob′vi|ous|ly**, *adv.* —**ob′-vi|ous|ness**, *n.*
—*Syn.* **1 Obvious, apparent, evident** mean plain to see, easy to understand. **Obvious** suggests standing out so prominently that the eye or mind cannot miss it: *His exhaustion was obvious when he fell asleep standing up.* **Apparent** means plainly to be seen as soon as one looks (with eye or mind) toward it: *A dent in the fender is apparent.* **Evident** means plainly to be seen because all the apparent facts point to it: *When he did not drive the car home, it was evident that he had had an accident.*

**ob|vo|lute** (ob′və lüt), *adj.* **1** = overlapping. **2** (of two leaves in a bud) folded together so that one half of each is exterior and the other interior, as in the poppy. [< Latin *obvolūtus,* past participle of *obvolvere* to wrap around < *ob-* against, over + *volvere* wind, roll]

**ob|vo|lu|tion** (ob′və lü′shən), *n.* **1** the wrapping or folding of a bandage around a limb. **2** *Obsolete.* a fold, twist, or turn.

**ob|vo|lu|tive** (ob′və lü′tiv), *adj.* = obvolute.

**oc-**, *prefix.* the form of **ob-** before *c,* as in *occasion.*

**o/c** (no periods), overcharge.

**o.c.**, in the work cited (Latin, *opere citato*).
► **op. cit.** is the abbreviation now more commonly used.



**Oc.** or **oc.**, ocean.

**OC** (no periods), oral contraceptive.

**O.C.**, **1** Officer Candidate. **2** *British.* Officer Commanding (*C.O.* in American use).

**o|ca** (ō′kə), *n.* **1** a wood sorrel of South America, with yellow flowers and a tuberous root. **2** the root, widely eaten in the Andes region of South America. [< Spanish *oca* < Quechua *okka*]

***oc|a|ri|na** (ok′ə rē′nə), *n.* a small wind instrument with holes as in a flute and a mouthpiece like a whistle. An ocarina is shaped something like a sweet potato and is usually made of terra cotta or plastic. It produces a soft sound. [< Italian *ocarina* (diminutive) < *oca* goose (because of its shape)]

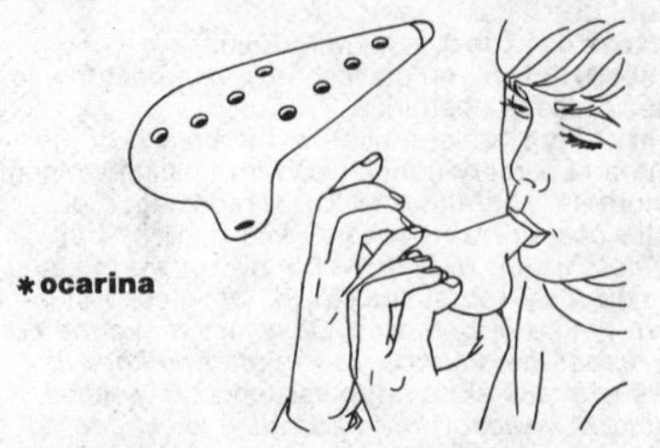

***ocarina**

**OCAS** (no periods), Organization of Central American States.

**O.C.B.**, Office of Collective Bargaining: *The O.C.B. provides for mediation and fact-finding procedures in bargaining impasses* (New York Times).

**Oc|cam's Razor** (ok′əmz), a principle devised by the English philosopher, William of Occam, which states that entities must not be multiplied beyond what is necessary; law of parsimony. In a scientific evaluation, Occam's Razor is the choice of the simplest theory from among the theories which fit the facts we know. In logic, Occam's Razor is the statement of an argument in its essential and simplest terms. Also, **Ockham's Razor**. [*Razor* refers to the idea in this principle of shaving an argument to its simplest terms]

**occas.**, **1** occasional. **2** occasionally.

**oc|ca|sion** (ə kā′zhən), *n., v.* —*n.* **1** a particular time: *We have met him on several occasions. He has said this on several occasions.* **2** a special event; important time: *The jewels were worn only on great occasions, such as a royal wedding or a coronation. A pair of gloves ... were to be worn on some great occasion of state* (Hawthorne). **3** a good chance; opportunity: *The trip we took together gave us an occasion to get better acquainted.* **4** a cause; reason; ground: *The dog that was the occasion of the quarrel had run away.* **SYN:** See syn. under **cause**. **5** need; necessity: *A simple cold is no occasion for alarm.* **6** *Scottish.* a religious function: *They should see about getting him* [*a minister*] *to help at the summer Occasion* (John Galt). **7** *Obsolete.* excuse; pretext: *Delay ... Whose manner was all passengers to stay And entertaine with her occasions sly* (Edmund Spenser). **8** *Obsolete.* occurrence.
—*v.t.* to cause; bring about: *to occasion an argument. His strange behavior occasioned a good deal of talk. I said nothing: I was afraid of occasioning some shock by declaring my identity* (Charlotte Brontë).
**improve the occasion**, to take advantage of an opportunity: *The friends improved the occasion of their meeting by celebrating it with a party.*
**occasions, a** affairs; business: *Such as pass on the seas upon their lawful occasions* (Book of Common Prayer). **b** *Archaic.* particular needs or requirements: *Martin ... could not supply his occasions any other way than by taking to the road* (Tobias Smollett).
**on occasion**, now and then; once in a while: [*Jenny Marx*] *had had herself on occasion to write begging letters to Engels* (Edmund Wilson).
**rise to the occasion**, to be equal to a situation requiring courage, discretion, or other decisive action; be able to handle a situation effectively: *By post time, he'll have had almost a fortnight in Maryland in which to recuperate, and I hope he'll rise to the occasion* (Audax Minor).
[< Latin *occāsiō, -ōnis* convenient time < *occāsus,* past participle of *occidere* to fall; see etym. under **occident**]

**oc|ca|sion|al** (ə kā′zhə nəl, -kāzh′nəl), *adj.* **1** happening or coming now and then, or once in a while: *occasional visits. We had fine weather all through July except for an occasional thunderstorm.* **SYN:** irregular, sporadic. **2** caused by or used for some special time or event: *occasional poetry. Occasional music was played at the graduation. The ruin of the ancient democracies was, that they ruled ... by occasional decrees* (Edmund Burke). **3** for use once in a while: *occasional chairs. Upon a little occasional table, was a tray with breakfast things* (H. G. Wells) **4** acting or serving for the occasion or on certain occasions: *The occasional soldier is no match for the professional soldier* (Macaulay).

**oc|ca|sion|al|ly** (ə kā′zhə nə lē, -kāzh′nə-), *adv.* now and then; once in a while; at times: *We have a shower occasionally on a summer day.*

**Oc|ci|dent** (ok′sə dənt), *n.* **1** the countries in Europe and America as distinguished from those in Asia; the West: *The Occident and the Orient have different ideals and customs.* **2** the Western Hemisphere. [< Latin *occidēns, -entis,* present participle of *occidere* fall down; go down < *ob-* down, away + *cadere* to fall (in reference to the setting sun)]

**oc|ci|dent** (ok′sə dənt), *n.* the west.

**Oc|ci|den|tal** (ok′sə den′təl), *adj., n.* —*adj.* Western; of the Occident.
—*n.* a native of the West. Europeans and Americans are Occidentals.
[< Latin *occidentālis* < *occidēns* Occident] —**Oc′-ci|den′tal|ly**, *adv.*

**oc|ci|den|tal** (ok′sə den′təl), *adj.* western. —**oc′-ci|den′tal|ly**, *adv.*

**Oc|ci|den|tal|ism** (ok′sə den′tə liz əm), *n.* the customs, characteristics, or institutions of the peoples and countries of the Occident.

**Oc|ci|den|tal|ist** (ok′sə den′tə list), *n., adj.* —*n.* a student or admirer of Occidental habits, customs, or institutions.
—*adj.* of or having to do with Occidentalism or Occidentalists.

**Oc|ci|den|tal|i|za|tion** (ok′sə den′tə lə zā′shən), *n.* a making Occidental, especially in habits, customs, or character.

**Oc|ci|den|tal|ize** (ok′sə den′tə līz), *v.t.,* **-ized, -iz|ing.** to make Occidental in habits, customs, or character.

**oc|cip|i|tal** (ok sip′ə təl), *adj., n.* —*adj.* of, belonging to, or situated in the back part of the head or skull: *occipital artery, occipital nerve, occipital condyle.*
—*n.* **1** = occipital bone. **2** any occipital part.
[< Medieval Latin *occipitalis* < Latin *occiput* occiput] —**oc|cip′i|tal|ly**, *adv.*

**occipital bone**, the compound bone forming the lower part of the skull.

**occipital lobe**, the posterior lobe of each cerebral hemisphere. See picture under **brain**.

**oc|ci|put** (ok′sə pət), *n., pl.* **oc|cip|i|ta** (ok sip′ə-tə). the back part of the head or skull. [< Latin *occiput, -cipitis* < *ob-* behind + *caput, capitis* head]

**oc|clude** (ə klüd′), *v.,* **-clud|ed, -clud|ing.** —*v.t.* **1** to stop up (as a passage or pores); close. **2** to shut in, out, or off: *The rain, in a grey occluding storm, thrashed the windows* (Eric Linklater). **3** *Chemistry.* to absorb and retain (gases and other substances): *Platinum occludes hydrogen.*
—*v.i. Dentistry.* to meet closely in proper positions: *The teeth in the upper jaw and those in the lower jaw should occlude.*
[< Latin *occlūdere* < *ob-* up + *claudere* to close]

**oc|clud|ed front** (ə klü′did), *Meteorology.* the front formed when a cold air mass overtakes a warm air mass and displaces it upward in a system of low barometric pressure: *Occluded fronts ... move more slowly than ordinary fronts and therefore bring persistent bad weather over the affected area* (Neuberger and Stephens).

**oc|clud|ent** (ə klü′dənt), *adj., n.* —*adj.* serving to shut up or close so as to prevent passage in or out.
—*n.* anything that closes.

**oc|clu|sal** (ə klü′səl), *adj. Dentistry.* of or for occlusion; used in biting or chewing.

**oc|clu|sion** (ə klü′zhən), *n.* **1** an occluding or being occluded. **2** *Medicine.* the blocking of a blood vessel, as by thrombosis, embolism, or gradual narrowing: *The President had suffered a mild cerebral occlusion* (Wall Street Journal). **3** *Dentistry.* the meeting of the teeth of the upper and lower jaws when closed. **4** *Phonetics.* the momentary cutting off of the stream of air in the articulation of a stop, produced as by pressing the lips together or the tongue against the upper teeth: *Nasal consonants are produced by the obstruction or occlusion of the buccal passage* (Simeon Potter). **5** *Meteorology.* **a** the process in which a cold air mass overtakes and forces upward a warm air mass in a cyclone, thereby meeting a second cold air mass originally in front of the warm air mass. Occlusion increases the intensity of a cyclone. **b** the contact between these two cold air masses. **6** *Chemistry.* the absorption and retention of a gas or other substance, as by a metal. [< Latin *occlūsus,* past participle of *occlūdere* occlude + English *-ion*]

**oc|clu|sive** (ə klü′siv), *adj.* serving to close; closing: *an occlusive dressing for a wound.*

**oc|cult** (ə kult′, ok′ult), *adj., v., n.* —*adj.* **1** beyond the bounds of ordinary knowledge; mysterious: *At*

*once the metaphysical panic turned into something physical—physical but at the same time occult* (Harper's). **SYN:** secret, hidden, mystic. **2a** outside the laws of the natural world. **b** of or having to do with laws or forces outside of the natural world; magical: *Astrology and alchemy are occult sciences.* **3** not disclosed; secret; revealed only to the initiated. **4** *Archaic.* hidden from sight; concealed: *We two will stand beside that shrine, Occult, withheld, untrod* (Dante Gabriel Rossetti).
— ***v.t., v.i.*** to cut off, or be cut off, from view by interposing some other body, as one heavenly body hiding another by passing in front of it; eclipse: *Because the corona-graph occults the photosphere it is difficult to observe the low- and high-altitude components of a flare simultaneously* (Harold Zirin).
— ***n.*** **the occult,** the occult sciences: *There were many students of the occult in northern Europe in the 1100's and 1200's.*
[< Latin *occultus* hidden, past participle of *occulere,* ultimately < *ob-* up + *cēlāre* conceal]
— **oc|cult′ly,** *adv.* — **oc|cult′ness,** *n.*

**oc|cul|ta|tion** (ok′ul tā′shən), *n.* **1** the action or fact of hiding the light of one heavenly body by another passing between it and the observer: *the occultation of a star by the moon.* **2** disappearance from view or notice; concealment; hiding.

**oc|cult|ism** (ə kul′tiz əm, ok′ul-), *n.* **1** belief in occult powers. **2** the study or use of occult sciences.

**oc|cult|ist** (ə kul′tist, ok′ul-), *n.* a person who believes or is skilled in occultism.

**oc|cu|pance** (ok′yə pəns), *n.* = occupancy.

**oc|cu|pan|cy** (ok′yə pən sē), *n.* **1** the act or fact of occupying; holding (land, houses, a pew, or other structure or area, or office) by being in possession: *The occupancy of the land by farmers was opposed by the cattlemen.* **SYN:** tenure. **2** *Law.* the act of taking possession of a thing belonging to no one in order to become its owner.

**oc|cu|pant** (ok′yə pənt), *n.* **1** a person who occupies: *The occupant of the shack stepped out as I approached.* **2** a person in actual possession of a house or other structure or area, or office: *The occupant will not pay rent and must be removed.* **3** *Law.* a person who becomes an owner by occupancy. [< Latin *occupāns, -antis,* present participle of *occupāre* occupy]

**oc|cu|pa|tion** (ok′yə pā′shən), *n.* **1** the work a person does regularly or to earn his living; business; employment; trade: *Caring for the sick is a nurse's occupation.* **2** the act of occupying or state of being occupied; possession: *the occupation of a house by a family, the occupation of a town by soldiers. Stooping down in complete occupation of the footpath* (Jane Austen). **3** something to do: *to be bored for lack of occupation.* [Middle English *occupacioun* < Anglo-French, Old French *occupation,* learned borrowing from Latin *occupātiō, -ōnis* < *occupāre* occupy]
— ***Syn.*** **1 Occupation, business, employment** mean work a person does regularly or to earn his living. **Occupation** means work of any kind one does regularly or for which he is trained, whether or not he is working at the moment or is paid: *By occupation she is a secretary.* **Business** means work done for profit, often for oneself, especially in commerce, banking, and merchandising: *My business is real estate.* **Employment** means work done for another, for which one is paid: *He has no employment at present.*

**oc|cu|pa|tion|al** (ok′yə pā′shə nəl, -pāsh′nəl), *adj.* of or having to do with a person's occupation, especially with trades, callings, and the like. An occupational hazard or disease is one that results from a person's particular work or occupation. *an occupational disease peculiar to beryllium workers.* — **oc′cu|pa′tion|al|ly,** *adv.*

**occupational therapist,** a specialist in occupational therapy.

**occupational therapy,** the treatment of persons having physical or mental disabilities, as through specific types of exercises or work, to promote recovery or rehabilitation.

**oc|cu|pi|er** (ok′yə pī′ər), *n.* one that occupies; occupant.

**oc|cu|py** (ok′yə pī), *v.,* **-pied, -py|ing.** — ***v.t.*** **1** to take up; fill: *The building occupies an entire block. The lessons occupy the morning.* **2** to keep busy; engage; employ: *Sports often occupy a boy's attention.* **SYN:** absorb. **3** to take possession of, as by invasion: *The enemy occupied our fort. The ... commanders ,.. descended upon Rhode Island, and occupied it without resistance* (William E. H. Lecky). **4** to keep possession of; hold; have: *A judge occupies an important position.* **SYN:** possess. **5** to live in: *The owner and his family occupy the house.* **6** *Obsolete.* to use: *new ropes that never were occupied* (Judges 16:11).
— ***v.i.*** **1** to take possession. **2** *Obsolete.* to trade; exchange: *And he called his ten servants, and then delivered them ten pounds, and said unto them, Occupy till I come* (Luke 19:13).
[< Old French *occupier,* learned borrowing from Latin *occupāre* seize < *ob-* onto + *capere* to grasp, seize]

**oc|cur** (ə kėr′), *v.i.,* **-curred, -cur|ring. 1** to take place; happen: *Storms often occur in winter. Delays are liable to occur.* **SYN:** See syn. under **happen. 2** to be found; exist; appear: *"E" occurs in print more often than any other letter.* **3** to come to mind; suggest itself: *Did it ever occur to you to close the windows? It never seems to occur to him to say "thanks."* [< Latin *occurrere* < *ob-* in the way (of) + *currere* to run]

**oc|cur|rence** (ə kėr′əns), *n.* **1** the act or fact of occurring: *The occurrence of storms delayed our trip.* **2** a happening; event: *an unexpected occurrence. Newspapers record the chief occurrences of the day.* **SYN:** incident. See syn. under **event.**

**oc|cur|rent** (ə kėr′ənt), *adj., n.* — ***adj.*** occurring; happening.
— ***n.*** *Obsolete.* an occurrence.
[< Latin *occurrēns, -entis,* present participle of *occurrere* occur]

**OCD** (no periods), Office of Civil Defense.

**✱o|cean** (ō′shən), *n.* **1** the great body of salt water that covers almost three fourths of the earth's surface; the sea: *Roll on, thou deep and dark blue ocean, roll* (Byron). **SYN:** main, deep. See picture below. **2** any of its four main divisions; the Atlantic, Pacific, Indian, and Arctic oceans. The waters around the Antarctic continent are considered by some to form a separate ocean. **3** *Figurative.* a vast expanse or quantity: *oceans of trouble. I turned and looked back over the undulating ocean of grass* (Francis Parkman). [< Old French *ocean,* learned borrowing from Latin *ōceanus* < Greek *Okeanós* Oceanus]

**o|cean|ar|i|um** (ō′shə nãr′ē əm), *n., pl.* **-i|ums, -i|a** (-ē ə). a very large saltwater aquarium built near an ocean to display living fish and other animals of the ocean: *Anyone who cares to will be able to get a ringside seat at the two new oceanariums* (Cape Times). [< *ocean* + (aqu)*arium*]

**o|cean|aut** (ō′shə nôt), *n.* an explorer of an ocean or sea; aquanaut: *French oceanauts last summer lived in a prefabricated village 36 feet below surface in the Red Sea* (Science News Letter). *Astronauts and oceanauts have to make special arrangements for their air supply and communications* (London Guardian).

**ocean bed,** the bottom of the ocean.

**ocean carrier,** any commercial ship crossing the ocean.

**o|cean|front** (ō′shən frunt′), *n., adj.* — ***n.*** the land along the ocean; seashore: *apartments on the oceanfront.*
— ***adj.*** having to do with or at the oceanfront: *oceanfront land.*

**o|cean-go|ing** (ō′shən gō′ing), *adj.* **1** going by sea: *a passenger ocean-going ship.* **2** fit to meet the dangers of sea travel: *ocean-going freighters.* **3** having to do with sea travel or commerce: *The success of the S.S. United States promises an enormous use for aluminum throughout the ocean-going world ...* (Newsweek).

**o|cean-gray** (ō′shən grā′), *n., adj.* — ***n.*** a light pearly or silvery gray.
— ***adj.*** light pearly- or silvery-gray.

**O|ce|an|i|an** (ō′shē an′ē ən), *adj., n.* — ***adj.*** of or having to do with Oceania, a division of the world which comprises Polynesia, Micronesia, and Melanesia, a group of islands in the southern Pacific, or its people.
— ***n.*** a native or inhabitant of Oceania.

**o|ce|an|ic** (ō′shē an′ik), *adj.* **1** of the ocean: *oceanic islands. In the deep sea ... the rocks over vast areas are covered with oceanic sediments which may be thousands of feet in thickness* (Gaskell and Hill). **2** living in or by the ocean: *oceanic fish.* **3** like the ocean; wide; vast: *A year ago the price supporters were burdened with an oceanic one billion pounds of* [*vegetable oil*] (Wall Street Journal). — **o′ce|an′i|cal|ly,** *adv.*

**O|ce|an|ic** (ō′shē an′ik), *adj.* of or having to do with Oceania, its inhabitants, or its culture; Oceanian: *The Baltimore Museum of Art acquired a rare collection of ... Oceanic art,* [*including*] *masks, figures, shields, jewelry* (Frederick A. Sweet).

**oceanic bonito,** = skipjack.

**o|ce|an|ics** (ō′shē an′iks), *n.* the group of sciences dealing with the exploration and study of the ocean.

**O|ce|a|nid** (ō sē′ə nid), *n. Greek Mythology.* a sea nymph, daughter of Oceanus. [< Greek *Okeanís, -ides* < *Okeanós* Oceanus]

**o|ce|an|i|ty** (ō′shē an′ə tē), *n.* **1** the condition of being oceanic. **2** *Meteorology.* the characteristics of an oceanic climate.

**o|cean|i|za|tion** (ō shē′ə nə zā′shən), *n.* a sinking of the land followed by a gradual changing of

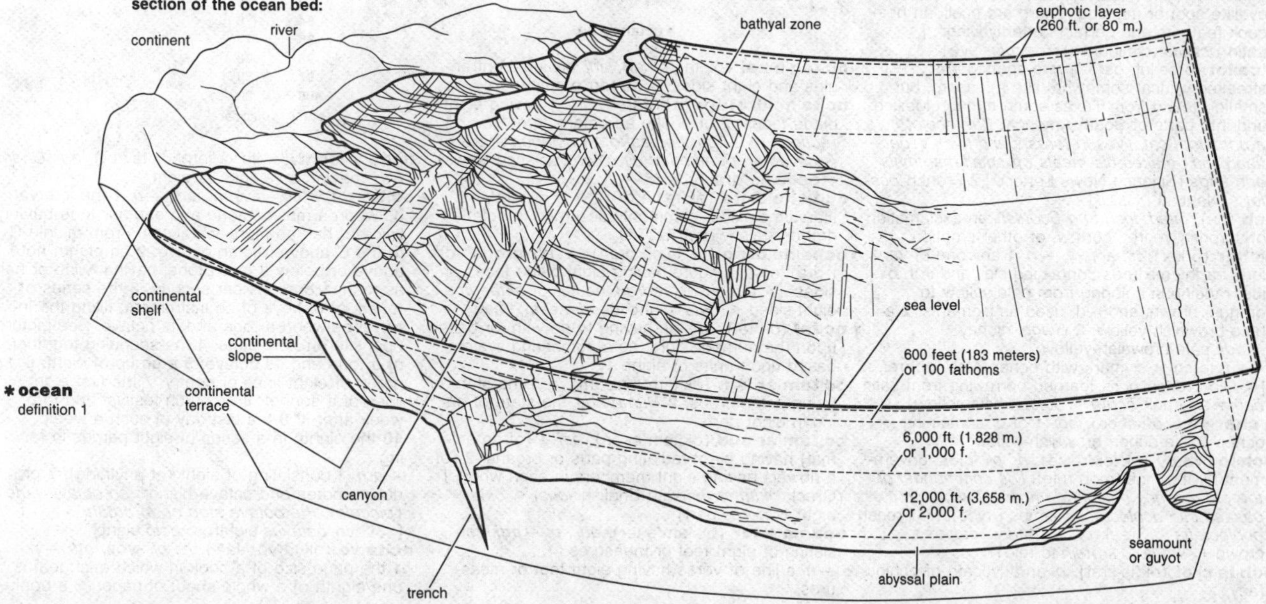


**✱ocean**
definition 1

the crust from the type normally composing continents to the type usually found on the ocean bed.

**ocean liner**, a ship used to carry passengers and some freight across the ocean, usually on regularly scheduled trips.

**o|cean|og|ra|pher** (ō′shə nog′rə fər), *n.* an expert in oceanography: *The oceanographer works on research ships that are equipped with special instruments to study the sea and everything in it* (Joel W. Hedgpeth).

**o|cean|o|graph|ic** (ō′shə nə graf′ik), *adj.* of or having to do with oceanography: *They will take samples of the marine life, and make gravitational, magnetic and oceanographic studies* (Science News Letter). —**o′cean|o|graph′i|cal|ly,** *adv.*

**o|cean|o|graph|i|cal** (ō′shə nə graf′ə kəl), *adj.* = oceanographic.

**o|cean|og|ra|phy** (ō′shə nog′rə fē), *n.* the branch of physical geography dealing with oceans, seas, and marine life: *Oceanography ... is not a single science but a composite of many basic sciences applied to the marine environment* (Edward Wenk).

**o|cean|o|log|i|cal** (ō′shə nə log′ə kəl), *adj.* of or having to do with oceanology: *oceanological research.*

**o|cean|ol|o|gist** (ō′shə nol′ə jist), *n.* = oceanographer.

**o|cean|ol|o|gy** (ō′shə nol′ə jē), *n.* the study of oceans; oceanography.

**ocean perch**, = rosefish.

**ocean race**, a race between ocean-going yachts.

**o|cean-race** (o′shən rās′), *v.i.*, **-raced, -rac|ing.** to take part in an ocean race or races: *[He] hopes that his son will one day ocean-race* (Muriel Bowen).

**ocean racer**, an ocean-racing yacht.

**ocean racing**, the sport of racing in yachts on the open ocean.

**o|cean-span|ning** (ō′shən span′ing), *adj.* that crosses or is able to cross the ocean: *The cigar-shaped Atlas [missile] is designed for ocean-spanning, H-bomb missions* (Newsweek).

**ocean sunfish**, a large marine fish with a compressed body, found in warm and temperate seas throughout the world; headfish; mola.

**O|ce|a|nus** (ō sē′ə nəs), *n. Greek Mythology.* **1** the god of the great stream that was supposed to surround all the land. **2** this stream.

**o|cean|ward** (ō′shən wərd), *adv.* toward the ocean.

**o|cean|wards** (ō′shən wərdz), *adv.* = oceanward.

**o|cel|lar** (ō sel′ər), *adj.* of or having to do with an ocellus or ocelli.

**oc|el|late** (os′ə lāt; ō sel′āt, -it), *adj.* = ocellated.

**oc|el|lat|ed** (os′ə lā′tid, ō sel′ā-), *adj.* **1** having ocelli or eyelike spots. **2** eyelike: *ocellated spots or markings.* [< Latin *ocellātus* having eye-spots (< *ocellus* ocellus) + English *-ed*²]

**oc|el|la|tion** (os′ə lā′shən), *n.* an eyelike spot or marking.

**o|cel|lus** (ō sel′əs), *n., pl.* **o|cel|li** (ō sel′ī). **1** a little eye; one of the rudimentary, single-lens eyes found in certain invertebrates, especially one of the simple eyes, usually three in number, situated between the compound eyes of insects: *Ocelli ... may function in increasing the irritability of the organism to light* (Harbaugh and Goodrich). **2** an eyelike spot or marking. There are ocelli on peacock feathers and certain butterfly wings. [< Latin *ocellus* (diminutive) < *oculus* eye]

**o|ce|lot** (ō′sə lot, os′ə-), *n.* a spotted and streaked wildcat somewhat like a leopard, but smaller, found from Texas south through Mexico and into parts of South America: *The ocelot, ... a nocturnal cat, lives in forests and thick vegetation [and] makes his meals off small mammals and birds* (Science News Letter). [< French *ocelot* < Nahuatl *ocelotl*]

**och** (ᴏʜ), *interj. Irish and Scottish.* an exclamation of surprise, regret, sorrow, or other emotion.

**o|cher** (ō′kər), *n., adj., v.* —*n.* **1** any one of various earthy mixtures containing clay and iron oxide, ranging in coloring from pale yellow to orange, brown, and red, used as pigments. **2** a pale brownish yellow. **3** *Slang.* money.
—***adj.*** pale brownish-yellow.
—***v.t.*** to color or mark with ocher. Also, **ochre.**
[< Old French *ocre,* learned borrowing from Latin *ōchra* < Greek *ôchra* < *ôchrós* pale yellow]

**o|cher|ous** (ō′kər əs), *adj.* **1** of or containing ocher. **2** like ocher; brownish-yellow.

**och|loc|ra|cy** (ok lok′rə sē), *n., pl.* **-cies.** government by the mob; mob rule: *The commonest of the old charges against democracy was that it passed into ochlocracy* (James Bryce). [< French *ochlocratie* < Greek *ochlokratiā* < *óchlos* a crowd + *-kratiā* < *kráteín* to rule]

**och|lo|crat** (ok′lə krat), *n.* an advocate of ochlocracy.

**och|lo|crat|ic** (ok′lə krat′ik), *adj.* of, having to do with, or having the form of ochlocracy. —**och′lo|crat′i|cal|ly,** *adv.*

**och|lo|crat|i|cal** (ok′lə krat′ə kəl), *adj.* = ochlocratic.

**och|one** (ᴏʜ ōn′), *interj. Scottish and Irish.* an exclamation of lamentation.

**o|chre** (ō′kər), *n., adj., v.t.,* **o|chred, o|chring.** = ocher.

**och|re|a** (ok′rē ə, ō′krē-), *n., pl.* **och|re|ae** (ok′rē-ē, ō′krē-). = ocrea.

**o|chre|ous** (ō′kər əs, -krē-), *adj.* = ocherous.

**o|chroid** (ō′kroid), *adj.* like ocher in color; brownish-yellow. [< Late Greek *ōchroeidês* pale-yellow colored < Greek *ôchra* ochre + *eîdos* form]

**-ock**, *suffix.* diminutive, as in *dunnock, hillock.* [Middle English *-ok,* Old English *-oc, -uc*]

**Ock|ham's Razor** (ok′əmz), = Occam's Razor.

**o'clock** (ə klok′), **1** of the clock; by the clock: *What o'clock is it? It is one o'clock.* **2** as if on the dial of a clock. 12 o'clock in an airplane is the horizontal direction straight ahead, or the vertical position straight overhead.

**o|co|til|lo** (ō′kə tēl′yō, -tē′yō), *n., pl.* **-los.** a spiny, scarlet-flowered shrub, a candlewood, growing in the southwestern United States and in Mexico. When the plants are not blooming, they look like dead sticks. [American English < Mexican Spanish *ocotillo* (diminutive) < *ocote* pine tree < Nahuatl *ocotl* a type of conifer]

**OCR** (no periods), optical character recognition (the ability of a computer unit to recognize printed characters or words and convert them into computer code without keyboard operation).

**oc|re|a** (ok′rē ə, ō′krē-), *n., pl.* **oc|re|ae** (ok′rē ē, ō′krē-). **1** a tubular stipule or stipules sheathing the stem above the node, as in buckwheat. **2** a similar part or growth on an animal, as on the legs of some birds. Also, **ochrea.** [< Latin *ocrea* legging]

**oc|re|ate** (ok′rē it, -āt), *adj.* having an ocrea or ocreae; sheathed.

**OCS** (no periods), *U.S.* Officer Candidate School.

**oct-**, *combining form.* the form of **octo-**, or **octa-**, before vowels, as in *octane.*

**oct.**, octavo.

**Oct.**, October.

**octa-**, *combining form.* a variant of **octo-**, as in *octachord.* [< Greek *okta-* < *oktô* eight]

**oc|ta|chord** (ok′tə kôrd), *n. Music.* **1** an instrument having eight strings. **2** a diatonic series of eight notes or tones.

**oc|ta|chord|al** (ok′tə kôr′dəl), *adj.* of the octachord.

**oc|tad** (ok′tad), *n.* **1** a group or series of eight. **2** *Chemistry.* an element, atom, or radical with a valence of eight. [< Greek *oktás, -ádos* eight]

**oc|tad|ic** (ok tad′ik), *adj.* of or having to do with an octad.

***oc|ta|gon** (ok′tə gon, -gən), *n.* a plane figure having eight angles and eight sides. [< Greek *oktágōnos* < *okta-* eight + *gōniā* angle]

***octagon**

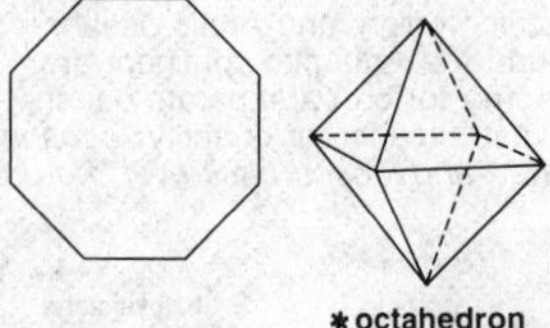

***octahedron**

**oc|tag|o|nal** (ok tag′ə nəl), *adj.* having eight angles and eight sides. —**oc|tag′o|nal|ly,** *adv.*

**oc|ta|he|dral** (ok′tə hē′drəl), *adj.* **1** having eight plane faces. **2** of or like an octahedron: *The direction ... at right angles to an octahedral plane is called an octahedral direction* (Science News). —**oc′ta|he′dral|ly,** *adv.*

**oc|ta|he|drite** (ok′tə hē′drīt), *n.* a mineral, titanium dioxide, commonly occurring in octahedral crystals. *Formula:* $TiO_2$

***oc|ta|he|dron** (ok′tə hē′drən), *n., pl.* **-drons, -dra** (-drə). a solid figure having eight plane faces or sides. [< Greek *oktáedron,* neuter of *oktáedros* eight-sided < *okta-* eight + *hédra* seat, base]

***oc|tal** (ok′təl), *adj.* of, having to do with, or based upon the number eight, as a numbering system based upon units of eight.

**oc|tam|er|ism** (ok tam′ə riz əm), *n.* **1** the state of being octamerous. **2** *Humorous.* the state of being in eight parts.

**oc|tam|er|ous** (ok tam′ər əs), *adj.* **1** (of an animal) having eight radiating parts or organs. **2** (of a flower) having eight members in each whorl. [< Greek *oktamerēs* (with English *-ous*) < *okta-* eight + *méros* part]

**oc|tam|e|ter** (ok tam′ə tər), *adj., n.* —***adj.*** consisting of eight feet or measures.
—***n.*** a line of verse having eight feet or measures.

[< Late Latin *octameter* < Greek *oktámetros* < *okta-* eight + *métron* measure]

**oc|tane** (ok′tān), *n.* a colorless, liquid hydrocarbon that occurs in petroleum and belongs to the methane series. High quality gasoline contains more octane than the lower grades. *Formula:* $C_8H_{18}$

**octane number** or **rating**, a number indicating the quality of a motor fuel, based on its anti-knock properties. The higher the compression ratio of an engine, the higher must be the octane number of its fuel to have satisfactory performance.

**oc|tan|gle** (ok′tang gəl), *n., adj.* —***n.*** = octagon.
—***adj.*** = octagonal.

**oc|tan|gu|lar** (ok tang′gyə lər), *adj.* having eight sides; octagonal. [< Latin *octangulus* eight-cornered < *octō* eight + *angulus* angle, corner]

**Oc|tans** (ok′tanz), *n., genitive* **Oc|tan|tis.** a southern constellation near the south celestial pole. [< New Latin *Octans* < Latin *octāns;* see etym. under **octant**]

**oc|tant** (ok′tənt), *n.* **1** one eighth of a circle; a 45-degree angle or arc. **2** one of the eight parts into which a space is divided by three planes intersecting at one point. **3a** an instrument having an arc of 45 degrees, used in navigation to measure the altitude of heavenly bodies in order to determine latitude and longitude. **b** an aircraft sextant by which angles up to 90 degrees may be measured against an artificial horizon of the bubble type. **4** *Astronomy.* the position of a planet, the moon, or other heavenly body when 45 degrees distant from another. [< Latin *octāns, -antis* < *octō* eight]

**Oc|tan|tis** (ok tan′tis), *n.* genitive of **Octans.**

**oc|ta|pep|tide** (ok′tə pep′tīd, -tid), *n.* a polypeptide chain made up of eight amino acids: *All the known actions of renin, including the principal ones of raising the arterial blood pressure ... are mediated through the octapeptide angiotension* (New Scientist).

**oc|tar|chy** (ok′tär kē), *n., pl.* **-chies. 1** government by eight persons. **2** a group of eight states, each under its own ruler. [< Greek *oktô* eight + *-archiā* empire (< *árchein* to rule) + English *-y*³]

**oc|ta|val** (ok tā′vəl, ok′tə-), *adj.* of or having to do with an octave or series of eight; numbered or proceeding by eights.

***octal**

| octal | decimal |
|---|---|
| 1 | 1 |
| 2 | 2 |
| 3 | 3 |
| 4 | 4 |
| 5 | 5 |
| 6 | 6 |
| 7 | 7 |
| 10 | 8 |
| 11 | 9 |
| 12 | 10 |
| 13 | 11 |
| 14 | 12 |
| 15 | 13 |
| 16 | 14 |
| 17 | 15 |
| 20 | 16 |
| 90 | 72 |
| 91 | 73 |
| 92 | 74 |
| 93 | 75 |
| 94 | 76 |
| 95 | 77 |
| 96 | 78 |
| 97 | 79 |
| 100 | 80 |

**oc|ta|va|lent** (ok′tə vā′lənt, ok tav′ə-), *adj. Chemistry.* having a valence of eight.

***oc|tave** (ok′tiv, -tāv), *n., adj.* —***n.*** **1** the interval between a musical tone and another tone having twice or half as many vibrations. From middle C to the C above it is an octave. **2** an eighth note above or below a given tone, having twice or half as many vibrations per second. **3** the series of tones, or of keys of an instrument, filling the interval between a tone and its octave. See picture opposite on next page. **4** the sounding together of a tone and its octave. **5** a group of eight. **6** a group of eight lines of poetry. **7** the first eight lines of a sonnet. **8** a church festival and the week after it. **9** the last day of such a week. **10** the eighth in a series of eight parries in fencing.
—***adj.*** **1** consisting of eight (of anything). **2** producing notes one octave higher: *an octave flute (piccolo), the octave stop of an organ.*
[< Latin *octāvus* eighth < *octō* eight]

**oc|ta|vo** (ok tā′vō, -tä′-), *n., pl.* **-vos,** *adj.* —***n.*** **1** the page size of a book in which each leaf is one eighth of a whole sheet of paper. **2** a book

having pages of this size, usually about 6 by 9 inches. *Abbr:* 8vo, 8º.
— ***adj.*** having this size.
[< Medieval Latin *in octavo* in an eighth]

**oc|ten|ni|al** (ok ten′ē əl), *adj.* **1** of or for eight years. **2** occurring every eight years. [< Late Latin *octennius* a period of eight years] —**oc|ten′ni|al|ly**, *adv.*

**oc|tet** or **oc|tette** (ok tet′), *n.* **1** a piece of music for eight instruments or voices. **2** a group of eight singers or players performing together. **3** a group of eight lines of verse; octave. **4** the first eight lines of a sonnet. **5** a group of eight electrons in the outer atomic shell. **6** any group of eight. [< *oct-* eight + *-et*, patterned on *duet*]

**oc|til|lion** (ok til′yən) *n., adj.* **1** (in the U.S., Canada, and France) 1 followed by 27 zeros. **2** (in Great Britain and Germany) 1 followed by 48 zeros. [< French *octillion* < Latin *octō* eight (in the sense "eighth power") + French *million* million]

**oc|til|lionth** (ok til′yənth), *n., adj.* **1** last in a series of an octillion. **2** one of an octillion equal parts.

**octo-**, *combining form.* eight: *Octosyllable = a verse of eight syllables.* Also, **oct-** before vowels, **octa-**. [< Latin *octō* and Greek *oktṓ*]

**Oc|to|ber** (ok tō′bər), *n.* **1** the tenth month of the calendar year. It has 31 days. *Abbr:* Oct. **2** *British.* ale brewed in October: *a bumper of October* (Tobias Smollett). [< Latin *Octōber* < *octō* eight (because of its place in the early Roman calendar)]

**oc|to|de|cil|lion** (ok′tō də sil′yən), *n.* **1** (in the U.S., Canada, and France) 1 followed by 57 zeros. **2** (in Great Britain and Germany) 1 followed by 108 zeros. [< Latin *octōdecim* eighteen + English *-illion*, as in *million*]

**oc|to|dec|i|mo** (ok′tə des′ə mō), *n., pl.* **-mos**, *adj.* —***n.*** **1** the page size of a book in which each leaf is one eighteenth of a whole sheet of paper; eighteenmo. **2** a book having pages of this size, usually about 4 by 6½ inches.
—***adj.*** in or of this size.
[< New Latin *in octodecimo; octodecimo,* ablative of Latin *octōdecimus* eighteen(th) < *octō* eight + *decimus* ten]

**oc|to|foil** (ok′tə foil′), *n.* **1** an ornamental figure consisting of eight leaves or lobes. **2** *Heraldry.* a bearing in the form of an octofoil, used as the mark of cadency of the ninth son. [< *octo-* + *-foil*, as in *trefoil*]

**oc|to|ge|nar|i|an** (ok′tə jə nãr′ē ən), *n., adj.* —***n.*** a person who is 80 years old or between 80 and 90 years old: *The dapper, athletic little octogenarian spoke from the assembly rostrum with vigour* (Clare Hollingworth).
—***adj.*** **1** 80 years old or between 80 and 90 years old. **2** of or belonging to such a person.
[< Latin *octōgēnārius* containing eighty (< *octōgēnī* eighty each, ultimately < *octō* eight) + English *-an*]

**oc|tog|e|nar|y** (ok toj′ə ner′ē), *n., pl.* **-nar|ies**, *adj.* = octogenarian.

**oc|to|nal** (ok′tə nəl), *adj.* based on the number eight, as a system of reckoning; octonary. [< Latin *octōnī* by eights (< *octō* eight) + English *-al*¹]

**oc|to|nar|y** (ok′tə ner′ē), *adj., n., pl.* **-nar|ies**.
—***adj.*** **1** having to do with the number eight; consisting of eight. **2** proceeding by eights; having eight as its base: *an octonary system of counting.*
—***n.*** **1** a group of eight; ogdoad. **2** an octave or octet.
[< Latin *octōnārius* containing eight < *octōnī* by eights < *octō* eight]

**oc|to|ploid** (ok′tə ploid), *adj., n. Biology.* —***adj.*** having a chromosome number that is eight times the haploid number: *C(eratophrys) ornata and C. dorsata* [*South American frogs*] *both are octoploid, each having 104 chromosomes which can be ordered into 13 groups of eight homologs each* (A. O. Wasserman).
—***n.*** an octoploid organism or cell.
[< *octo-* + *-ploid*, as in *haploid*]

**✱octave**
definition 3

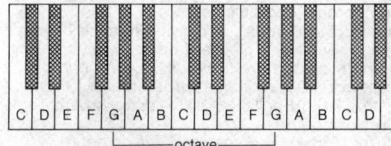

C D E F G A B C D E F G A B C D
octave

**oc|to|pod** (ok′tə pod), *n., adj.* —***n.*** any one of an order of two-gilled cephalopods having eight arms, such as the argonaut and the octopus.
—***adj.*** having eight feet or arms.
[< New Latin *Octopoda* the order name < Greek *oktṓpous, -podos* eight-footed; see etym. under **octopus**]

**oc|top|o|dous** (ok top′ə dəs), *adj.* = octopod.

**✱oc|to|pus** (ok′tə pəs), *n., pl.* **oc|to|pus|es, oc|to|pi** (ok′tə pī), **oc|top|o|des** (ok top′ə dēz). **1** a sea animal having a soft, stout body and eight arms with suckers on them; devilfish. It is a cephalopod mollusk. **2** *Figurative.* anything like an octopus. A powerful, grasping organization with far-reaching influence is often called an octopus. [< New Latin *octopus* < Greek *oktṓpous* eight-footed < *oktṓ* eight + *poús, podós* foot]

**✱octopus**
definition 1

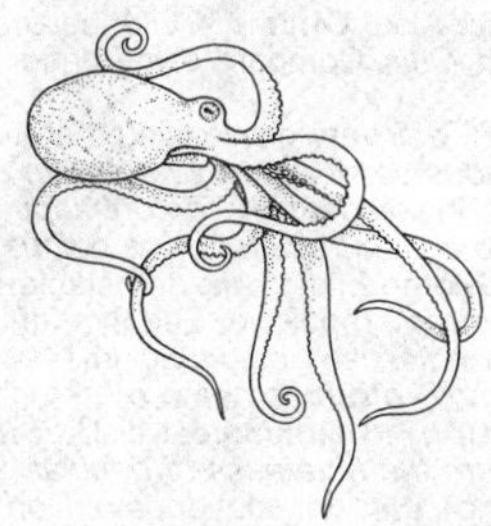

**oc|to|push** (ok′tə pu̇sh′), *n.* a form of hockey invented in Great Britain, played in a swimming pool: *Octopush is played by teams of six ... The object of the game is to propel or shovel the puck ... along the bottom of the pool and into the opponents' goal* (London Times). [blend of *octopus* and *push*]

**oc|to|roon** (ok′tə rün′), *n.* a person who is one-eighth Negro in ancestry. [American English < *octo-* + *-roon*, as in *quadroon*]

**oc|to|syl|lab|ic** (ok′tə sə lab′ik) *adj., n.* —***adj.*** having eight syllables: *the fatal facility of the octosyllabic verse* (Byron).
—***n.*** = octosyllable.

**oc|to|syl|la|ble** (ok′tə sil′ə bəl, ok′tə sil′-), *n., adj.* —***n.*** **1** a line of verse having eight syllables. **2** a word having eight syllables.
—***adj.*** = octosyllabic.

**oc|troi** (ok′troi; *French* ôk trwä′), *n., pl.* **-trois** (-troiz; *French* -trwä′). a local tax levied on certain articles on their admission into a town. [< French *octroi* < Middle French *octroyer* to grant, ultimately < Medieval Latin *auctorizare* to guarantee, authorize]

**oc|tu|ple** (ok′tu̇ pəl, -tyu̇-; ok tü′-, -tyü′-), *adj., n., v.,* **-pled, -pling.** —***adj.*** **1** consisting of eight parts; eightfold. **2** eight times as great.
—***n.*** a number or amount eight times as great as another.
—***v.t., v.i.*** to make or become eight times as great.
[< Latin *octuplus* < *octō* eight + *-plus*, as in *duplus* double]

**oc|tu|ply** (ok′tu̇ plē, -tyu̇-; ok tü′-, -tyü′-), *adv.* in an octuple manner; to an octuple degree.

**oc|u|lar** (ok′yə lər), *adj., n.* —***adj.*** **1** of or having to do with the eye: *an ocular muscle, ocular movements.* **2** like an eye; eyelike: *an ocular organ.* **3** received by actual sight; seen: *ocular proof.* SYN: visual.
—***n.*** the eyepiece of a telescope or microscope: *An ocular ... is a magnifier used for viewing an image formed by a lens or lenses preceding it in an optical system* (Sears and Zemansky).
[< Late Latin *oculāris* of the eyes < Latin *oculus* eye] —**oc′u|lar|ly**, *adv.*

**oc|u|list** (ok′yə list), *n.* a doctor who examines and treats defects and diseases of the eye; ophthalmologist. [< French *oculiste* < Latin *oculus* eye + French *-iste* -ist]

**oc|u|lo|mo|tor** (ok′yə lō mō′tər), *adj., n.* —***adj.*** of or having to do with the moving of the eyeball in its socket: *an oculomotor muscle, an oculomotor nerve.*
—***n.*** either of a pair of cranial nerves that supply most of the muscles moving the eyeball.
[< Latin *oculus* eye + *mōtor* that which moves < *movēre* move]

**oc|u|lus** (ok′yə ləs), *n., pl.* **-li** (-lī). **1** *Architecture.* **a** an opening at the summit of a dome. **b** a circular window, usually a small one without tracery or other special subdivision; oeil-de-boeuf. **2** *Anatomy.* an eye, especially a compound eye. [< Latin *oculus* eye]

**od** (od, ōd), *n.* an imaginary force formerly believed to pervade all nature and to manifest itself in magnetism, mesmerism, chemical action, and other effects. [< German *Od*, coined by Baron Karl von Reichenbach, 1788-1869, a German naturalist]

**OD** (ō′dē′), *n., pl.* **OD's** or **ODs**, *v.,* **OD'd, OD'ing.** *Slang.* —***n.*** **1** an overdose of a narcotic. **2** a person who has taken such an overdose: *"When I was shooting up ... I liked to hear about the ODs, and I'd think I was brave for taking it"* (Time).
—***v.i.*** to become sick or die from an overdose of a narcotic: *They were just about to start shooting a film called Zaccariah, a rock, shlock, cowboy musical ... when the drummer OD'd and had to be replaced* (Atlantic). Also, **oh-dee.**
[< *o*(ver)*d*(ose)]

**o/d** (no periods), *Banking.* **a** overdraft. **b** overdrawn.

**o.d.**, an abbreviation for the following:
**1** olive drab (uniform).
**2** on demand.
**3** on duty.
**4** outside diameter.
**5** outside dimension.

**O.D.** or **OD** (no periods), an abbreviation for the following:
**1** officer of the day.
**2** olive drab (uniform).
**3** ordinary seaman.
**4** *Banking.* **a** overdraft; **b** overdrawn.
**5** Doctor of Optometry.

**o|da|lisque** or **o|da|lisk** (ō′də lisk), *n.* a female slave in an Oriental harem, especially in that of a sultan of Turkey. [< French *odalisque*, also *odalique* < Turkish *odalik* < *oda* (originally) room in a harem + *-lik*, a noun suffix]

**odd** (od), *adj., n.* —***adj.*** **1** left over: *Here are seven plums for the three of us; you may have the odd one. Pay the bill with this money and keep the odd change.* SYN: extra. **2** being one of a pair or set of which the rest is missing: *There seems to be an odd stocking in the wash.* SYN: unmatched, unmated, single. **3** occasional; casual: *odd jobs, odd moments, odd numbers or volumes of a magazine.* **4** with some extra: *six hundred odd children in school, thirty odd dollars. Eighty odd years of sorrow have I seen* (Shakespeare). **5a** leaving a remainder of 1 when divided by 2: *Three, five, and seven are odd numbers.* **b** having an odd number: *the odd symphonies of Beethoven.* **6** strange; peculiar; queer: *a very odd fellow. It is odd that I cannot remember his name, because his face is surely familiar.* SYN: unusual, freakish, uncommon. See syn. under **strange.** **7** out-of-the-way; secluded: *from some odd corner of the brain* (Tennyson).
—***n.*** **1** an odd thing; oddity. **2** in golf: **a** a stroke more than the opponent, caused by hitting first during the playing of a hole. **b** *British.* a stroke taken from a player's total score before playing a hole to give him an advantage.
[< Scandinavian (compare Old Icelandic *odda-* odd, and *oddi* odd number)] —**odd′ness**, *n.*

**odd|ball** (od′bôl′), *n., adj. U.S. Slang.* —***n.*** a person or thing that differs from the usual or accepted standards in features, behavior, habits, or the like: *The platypus has been the oddball of the animal world* (New York Journal American). *The round, owl-eyed, oddball in horn-rimmed glasses ...* (Time).
—***adj.*** unusual for its type and often somewhat amusing; odd; eccentric: *a master of zany oddball humor* (New Yorker).

**odd-eyed** (od′īd′), *adj.* having eyes of two different colors, such as one yellow and one blue. Some white Persian and domestic shorthair cats are odd-eyed.

**Odd Fellow**, a member of the Independent Order of Odd Fellows, a secret social and benevolent society.

**odd fish**, *Informal.* an odd or singular person: *He was an odd fish; ignorant of common life, fond of rudely opposing received opinions, slovenly to extreme dirtiness, enthusiastic in some points of religion, and a little knavish withal* (Benjamin Franklin).

**odd|i|ty** (od′ə tē), *n., pl.* **-ties.** **1** strangeness; queerness; peculiarity: *the oddity of wearing a fur coat over a bathing suit. All people have their oddities* (Benjamin Disraeli). SYN: singularity. **2** a strange, queer, or peculiar person or thing: *Here is a strange, fantastical oddity ... who harangues every day in the pump room* (Tobias Smollett). SYN: freak, curiosity.

**odd-job|ber** (od′job′ər), *n. British.* an odd-job man.

**odd-job man** (od′job′), *British.* a man who does odd jobs; handyman.

**odd lot**, a quantity of goods or securities smaller than the normal or standard amount used in the trading: *On the New York Stock Exchange, the usual unit of trading is 100 shares, called a*

**Pronunciation Key:** hat, āge, cãre, fär; let, ēqual, tėrm; it, īce; hot, ōpen, ôrder; oil, out; cup, pu̇t, rüle; child; long; thin; ᴛʜen; zh, measure; ə represents **a** in about, **e** in taken, **i** in pencil, **o** in lemon, **u** in circus.

*"round lot." Smaller units are referred to as "odd lots"* (Wall Street Journal). —**odd′-lot′**, *adj.*

**odd-lot|ter** (od′lot′ər), *n.* one who buys shares in odd lots (less than 100 shares).

**odd|ly** (od′lē), *adv.* in an odd manner; queerly; strangely.

**odd-man-out** (od′man′out′), *n., adj.* —*n.* **1** a person or thing left out of a group; a person who does not fit or belong in a group: *He is an odd-man-out of his native world* (Harper's). **2a** the person singled out, as by tossing a coin or in some similar way, from among a number of people to perform some special act or service. **b** this way of selection.
—*adj.* left out or eliminated, especially for being different from the rest of the group.

**odd|ment** (od′mənt), *n.* a thing left over; extra bit; remnant.

**oddments, a** *Printing.* parts of a book other than the text, such as the title page, preface, and table of contents: *The oddments of this book are set in brevier and great primer.* **b** odds and ends: *oddments of furniture, including a desk* (Arnold Bennett).

**odd-num|bered** (od′num′bərd), *adj.* having a whole number which, when divided by 2, leaves a remainder of one: *May 19 is an odd-numbered day. 1939 is an odd-numbered year.*

**odd-pin|nate** (od′pin′āt, -it), *adj.* pinnate with an odd terminal leaflet; imparipinnate.

**odds** (odz), *n. pl. or sing.* **1** a difference in favor of one and against another; advantage. In betting, odds of 3 to 1 mean that 3 will be paid if the bet is lost for every 1 that is received if the bet is won. *The odds are in our favor and we should win. How can man die better Than facing fearful odds, For the ashes of his Fathers, And the temples of his Gods?* (Macaulay). **2** an extra allowance given to the weaker player or side in a game. **3** things that are odd, uneven, or unequal: *Yet death we fear, That makes these odds all even* (Shakespeare). **4** difference or the amount of difference: *It makes no odds to me when he goes.*
**at odds**, quarreling; disagreeing: *The two brothers were often at odds. Pity 'tis you lived at odds so long* (Shakespeare).
**by all odds**, by any reckoning; without doubt: *Herblock is by all odds one of the most ... useful commentators on the American scene. ... He can think, he can draw, and he can write* (New Yorker).
**odds and ends**, stray bits left over; scraps; remnants: *If there's ever a bit o' odds an' ends as nobody else 'ud eat, you're sure to pick it out* (George Eliot).
**the odds are**, the chances are; the probability is: *Since we are a better team, the odds are we will win. The odds are, that she has a thousand faults, at least* (Maria Edgeworth).
▶ **Odds** is sometimes construed as a singular, as in *What's the odds?* The plural, however, is usual: *The odds are against him.*

**odds board**, a large, usually illuminated board at a race track, on which are posted the betting odds on the horses entered in a given race.

**odds-mak|er** (odz′mā′kər), *n.* a person who makes a business of establishing the odds for betting, especially in a sporting event: *The professional odds-makers have established the slugging [prizefighter] a 13-5 favorite to retain his crown* (New York Times).

**odds-on** (odz′on′), *adj., n.* —*adj.* having the odds in one's favor; having a good chance to win in a contest: *[He] seems an odds-on favorite in the October 8 election* (Wall Street Journal).
—*n.* favorable odds; a good chance to win: *Silver Spoon started at odds-on ... and the best she could do was finish third* (New Yorker).

**odd trick**, (in contract bridge) a trick won by the declarer in excess of six.

**ode** (ōd), *n.* **1** a lyric poem full of noble or enthusiastic feeling expressed with dignity. It is often addressed to some person or thing. *Pindar, of ancient Greece, wrote odes in praise of athletic heroes* (Charles W. Cooper). **2** a poem intended to be sung. [< Middle French *ode,* learned borrowing from Latin *ōdē* < Greek *ōidê,* related to *aeídein* to sing]

**O|dels|ting** or **O|dels|thing** (ō′dəls ting), *n.* the larger of the two sections of the national legislature (Storting) of Norway. [< Norwegian *Odelsting* < *odel* land + *ting, thing* assembly, parliament]

**o|de|on** (ō dē′on), *n.* a theater or music hall; odeum: *Six years later ... [he] sought surcease in an odeon on the Champs Elysées* (Tallulah Bankhead). [< Greek *ōideîon;* see etym. under **odeum**]

**o|de|um** (ō dē′əm), *n., pl.* **o|de|a** (ō dē′ə). **1** a theater, hall, or other large enclosed area, used for musical or dramatic performances. **2** (in ancient Greece and Rome) a roofed building in which vocal and instrumental music was performed. [< Late Latin *ōdēum* < Greek *ōideîon* place for musical performances, related to *ōidê* song; see etym. under **ode**]

**od|ic** (ō′dik), *adj.* of or having to do with an ode. [< *od*(e) + *-ic*]

**o|dif|er|ous** (ō dif′ər əs), *adj.* = odoriferous: *We saw close-packed slum houses of crumbling cement—one- and two-room barracks fronting on streets of odiferous mud that served both as thoroughfare and plumbing* (Maclean's). [shortened form of *odoriferous*]

**O|din** (ō′din), *n. Norse Mythology.* the chief god. Odin was the god of wisdom, culture, war, and the dead. The Germans and Anglo-Saxons called him Woden. Also, **Othin.** [< Old Icelandic *Ōthinn,* or Danish *Odin.* Compare etym. under **Wotan.**]

**o|di|ous** (ō′dē əs), *adj.* very displeasing; hateful; offensive: *an odious smell. You told a lie, an odious damned lie* (Shakespeare). *The unhappy woman ... whose image became more odious to him every day* (George Eliot). SYN: detestable, abominable, abhorrent, repulsive. See syn. under **hateful.** [< Latin *odiōsus* < *odium* odium]
—**o′di|ous|ly**, *adv.* —**o′di|ous|ness**, *n.*

**o|di|um** (ō′dē əm), *n.* **1** hatred; great dislike: *It was his lot to taste the bitterness of popular odium* (Hawthorne). SYN: detestation, aversion, opprobrium. **2** reproach or blame: *to bear the odium of having betrayed one's friend. The West would surely be wise to let the Russians take on the odium of being the first to resume testing* (Manchester Guardian). SYN: disgrace, stigma, disfavor. [< Latin *odium*]

**odium the|o|log|i|cum** (thē′ə loj′ə kəm), rancor or acrimony characterizing or resembling theological dissensions. [< New Latin *odium theologicum* (literally) theological hatred]

**o|do|graph** (ō′də graf, -gräf), *n.* **1** an odometer that makes a record of what it measures. **2** = pedometer. [< Greek *hodós* way, course + English *-graph*]

**o|dom|e|ter** (ō dom′ə tər), *n.* a device for measuring distance traveled by a vehicle, by recording the number of revolutions of a wheel: *Odometers are as unreliable as speedometers because they operate from the same shaft that rotates the speedometer magnet* (New York Times). [American English < Greek *hodómetron* < *hodós* way + *métron* a measure; probably patterned on French *odomètre*]

**o|dom|e|try** (ō dom′ə trē), *n.* the measurement by some mechanical device of distances traveled.

**o|do|nate** (ō′də nāt), *adj., n.* —*adj.* of or belonging to an order of insects having chewing mouthparts, hind wings as large or larger than the forewings, and large compound eyes. Dragonflies and damsel flies belong to this order.
—*n.* an odonate insect.
[< New Latin *Odonata* the order name < Greek *odoús, odóntos* tooth]

**odont-**, *combining form.* the form of **odonto-** before vowels, as in *odontalgia.*

**o|don|tal|gi|a** (ō′don tal′jē ə), *n.* = toothache. [< New Latin *odontalgia* < Greek *odontalgiā* < *odoús, odóntos* tooth + *álgos* pain]

**o|don|tal|gic** (ō′don tal′jik), *adj., n.* —*adj.* of, having to do with, or suffering from toothache.
—*n.* a remedy for a toothache.

**odonto-**, *combining form.* tooth; teeth: *Odontology = the scientific study of the teeth.* Also, **odont-** before vowels. [< Greek *odoús, odóntos* tooth]

**o|don|to|blast** (ō don′tə blast), *n.* one of a layer of cells that produce dentine as a tooth develops. [< *odonto-* + Greek *blastós* germ, sprout]

**o|don|to|blas|tic** (ō don′tə blas′tik), *adj.* of or having to do with odontoblasts.

**o|don|to|glos|sum** (ō don′tə glos′əm), *n.* any epiphytic orchid of a group found in tropical American mountains, some of which are raised for their showy flowers. [< New Latin *Odontoglossum* the genus name < Greek *odoús, odóntos* tooth + *glôssa* tongue]

**o|don|to|graph** (ō don′tə graf, -gräf), *n.* **1** a kind of template for marking the outlines of teeth on a gear. **2** an instrument for showing the pattern of irregularity on the surface of tooth enamel.

**o|don|toid** (ō don′toid), *adj., n.* —*adj.* **1** of or having to do with a toothlike projection of the second cervical vertebra, upon which the first cervical vertebra rotates: *the odontoid process or peg.* **2** = toothlike.
—*n.* the odontoid process.
[< Greek *odontoeidēs* < *odoús, odóntos* tooth + *eîdos* form]

**o|don|to|lite** (ō don′tə līt), *n.* a mineral that resembles turquoise and is composed of fossil bone or tooth discolored by phosphate of iron; bone turquoise. [< *odonto-* + *-lite*]

**o|don|to|log|i|cal** (ō don′tə loj′ə kəl), *adj.* of or having to do with odontology. —**o|don′to|log′i|cal|ly**, *adv.*

**o|don|tol|o|gist** (ō′don tol′ə jist), *n.* a specialist in odontology.

**o|don|tol|o|gy** (ō don tol′ə jē), *n.* the branch of anatomy dealing with the structure, development, and diseases of the teeth; dentistry. [< *odonto-* + *-logy*]

**o|don|to|phore** (ō don′tə fôr, -fōr), *n.* a structure in the mouth of most mollusks (other than bivalve mollusks) over which the radula is drawn backward and forward in the process of breaking up food. [< Greek *odontophóros* < *odoús, odóntos* tooth + *-phóros* < *phérein* to bear]

**o|don|tor|nith|ic** (ō don′tôr nith′ik), *adj.* of or belonging to a group of extinct birds of the Mesozoic era, which had true teeth. [< New Latin *Odontornithes* the group name (< Greek *odoús, odóntos* tooth + *órnīs, -īthos* bird) + English *-ic*]

*****o|don|to|scope** (ō don′tə skōp), *n.* a small mirror with a long slender handle, for examining the teeth. [< *odonto-* + *-scope*]

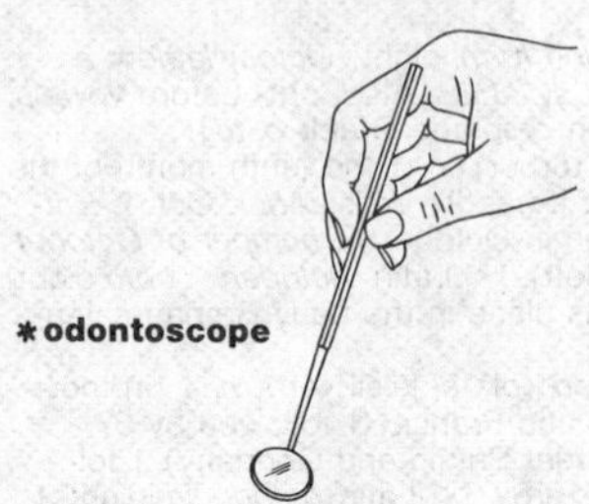

***odontoscope**

**o|do|phone** (ō′də fōn), *n.* a scale of odors or scents, used in grading perfumes. [< Latin *odor* odor + Greek *phōnē* sound (because of the analogy to the musical scale)]

**o|dor** (ō′dər), *n.* **1** smell: *the odor of roses, the odor of garbage, a gas without odor.* SYN: scent. See syn. under **smell. 2** *Figurative.* reputation; repute; standing. **3** fragrance; perfume. SYN: aroma. **4** *Figurative.* a taste or quality characteristic or suggestive of something: *There is no odor of impropriety about the case.* **5** *Archaic.* a fragrant substance, flower, or plant: *Through groves of myrrh, And flowering odors, cassia nard, and balm* (Milton). Also, *especially British,* **odour.**
**be in bad odor**, to have a bad reputation or inferior standing: *Those boys were in bad odor because they were suspected of stealing. These Sydney gentry ... are in excessively bad odor* (Herman Melville).
[< Old French *odor,* learned borrowing from Latin *odor*]

**o|dor|ant** (ō′dər ənt), *n., adj.* —*n.* anything that gives off or produces an odor: *Richfield Oil considers devising a synthetic skunk odorant to protect campers against rattlers; research shows the snakes flee from the smell of the natural skunk odor* (Wall Street Journal).
—*adj.* that emits a smell; odorous; fragrant.

**o|dored** (ō′dərd), *adj.* having an odor.

**o|dor|if|er|ous** (ō′də rif′ər əs), *adj.* **1** giving forth an odor, especially a pleasant odor; fragrant: *The rose is an odoriferous flower.* SYN: aromatic. **2** giving forth an unpleasant or foul odor: *an odoriferous slum; ... warehouses, ships, and smell of tar, and other odoriferous circumstances of fishery and the sea* (John Galt). SYN: malodorous. [< Latin *odōrifer* (< *odor, odōris* odor + *ferre* to bear) + English *-ous*] —**o′dor|if′er|ous|ly**, *adv.* —**o′dor|if′er|ous|ness**, *n.*

**o|dor|ize** (ō′də rīz), *v.t.,* **-ized, -iz|ing.** to give fragrance to; perfume: *The raw product would be dried ... for testing, odorizing, and onward transmission* (London Times).

**o|dor|less** (ō′dər lis), *adj.* without an odor; having no odor: *Pure water is odorless.*

**odor of sanctity**, **1** a sweet odor said to have been exhaled from the bodies of certain saints at death or on disinterment, and held to be evidence of their sanctity. **2** established reputation for sanctity or holiness: *... the odor of its sanctity —and golly how it stank* (G. K. Chesterton).

**o|dor|os|i|ty** (ō′də ros′ə tē), *n.* the quality of being odorous; odorousness.

**o|dor|ous** (ō′dər əs), *adj.* giving forth or having an odor, especially a pleasant odor; sweet-smelling; fragrant: *Spices are odorous. ... the odorous breath of morn* (Milton). SYN: aromatic. [< Latin *odorus* (with English *-ous*)] —**o′dor|ous|ly**, *adv.* —**o′dor|ous|ness**, *n.*

**o|dour** (ō′dər), *n. Especially British.* odor.

**Od|ys|se|an** (od′ə sē′ən), *adj.* of or like the Odyssey or its hero.

**O|dys|se|us** (ō dis′ē əs, -dis′yüs), *n.* the hero of Homer's *Odyssey,* a king of Ithaca, known for his wisdom and shrewd resourcefulness; Ulysses.

**Od|ys|sey** (od′ə sē), *n., pl.* **-seys. 1** a long Greek epic poem describing the adventures and wandering of Odysseus (Ulysses) during the ten years after the Trojan War and of his final return home to Ithaca. Homer is supposed to be its author. **2** Also, **odyssey**. *Figurative.* any long series of wanderings and adventures: *"The Grapes of Wrath" tells of the odyssey of migratory workers to California.* [< Latin *Odyssēa* < Greek *Odýsseia* < *Odysseús* Odysseus]

**oe** (oi), *n. Scottish.* oy.

**o.e.**, **1** omissions excepted. **2** original equipment.

**OE** (no periods), **1** Also, **O.E.**, Office of Education. **2** Also, **OE.**, Old English (Anglo-Saxon).

**OECD** (no periods), Organization for Economic Cooperation and Development (an organization established in 1961 to succeed the OEEC).

**oec|u|men|ic** (ek′yů men′ik), *adj.* = ecumenic.

**oec|u|men|i|cal** (ek′yů men′ə kəl), *adj.* = ecumenical.

**oec|u|men|i|cal|ism** ((ek′yů men′ə kə liz′əm), *n.* = ecumenicalism.

**oec|u|me|nic|i|ty** (ek′yů me nis′ə tē), *n.* = ecumenicity.

**OED** (no periods) or **O.E.D.**, Oxford English Dictionary. Also, **N.E.D.**

**oe|de|ma** (i dē′mə), *n. Especially British.* edema.

**oe|dem|a|tous** (i dem′ə təs), *adj. Especially British.* edematous.

**Oed|i|pal** or **oed|i|pal** (ed′ə pəl, ē′də-), *adj.* of, having to do with, or characteristic of Oedipus or the Oedipus complex: [*He*] *has succeeded in a most difficult biographical enterprise—to write of a famous father without ... indulging in Oedipal iconoclasm* (Time). **—Oed′i|pal|ly**, *adv.*

**Oed|i|pus** (ed′ə pəs, ē′də-), *n. Greek Legend.* a king of Thebes who unknowingly killed his father and married his mother. When he learned this, he blinded himself and passed the rest of his life wandering miserably.

**Oedipus complex**, *Psychoanalysis.* a strong childhood attachment, especially by a male child, for the parent of the opposite sex, based on early sexual desire and often accompanied by a feeling of rivalry, hostility, or fear toward the other parent. According to Freudian theory, it is a normal phase of personality development, but it is sometimes carried over into adulthood and then becomes a psychoneurotic tendency.

**OEEC** (no periods), Organization for European Economic Cooperation (an organization established in 1948 to administer the European Recovery Program, succeeded in 1961 by the OECD).

**oeil-de-boeuf** (œ′yə də bœf′), *n., pl.* **oeils-de-boeuf** (œ′yə də bœf′) *French.* **1** a small round or oval window, as in a frieze. **2** (literally) bull's-eye.

**oeil|lade** (œ yäd′), *n. French.* an amorous or flirtatious glance; ogle.

**oe|no|log|i|cal** (ē′nə loj′ə kəl), *adj.* of or having to do with oenology.

**oe|nol|o|gist** (ē nol′ə jist), *n.* a person skilled in oenology; wine connoisseur.

**oe|nol|o|gy** (ē nol′ə jē), *n.* the art of making wine; knowledge or study of wines. Also, **enology**. [< Greek *oînos* wine + English *-logy*]

**oe|no|mel** (ē′nə mel, en′ə-), *n.* **1** a drink made of wine and honey, drunk by the ancient Greeks. **2** *Figurative.* language or thought combining strength and sweetness. [< Late Latin *oenomelum*, variant of Latin *oenomeli* < Greek *oinómeli* < *oînos* wine + *méli* honey]

**Oe|no|ne** (ē nō′nē), *n. Greek Legend.* a nymph of Mt. Ida, who became the wife of Paris, but was deserted by him when he fell in love with Helen of Troy.

**oe|no|phile** (ē′nə fīl, -fil), *n.* = oenophilist.

**oe|noph|i|list** (ē nof′ə list), *n.* a lover of wine; an expert on wines.

**OEO** (no periods), Office of Economic Opportunity (an antipoverty agency of the U.S. government, established in 1964).

**o'er** (ôr, ōr), *prep., adv. Archaic.* over.

**Oer|li|kon** (ėr′lə kon), *n.* any one of certain 20-millimeter automatic aircraft or antiaircraft cannon which shoot greased ammunition. [< *Oerlikon*, Switzerland, where this type of cannon was developed]

**oer|sted** (ėr′sted), *n.* **1** the unit of magnetic intensity in the centimeter-gram-second system, equivalent to the intensity of the force of one dyne acting in a vacuum on a magnetic pole of unit strength at a distance of one centimeter. **2** a former unit of magnetic reluctance. [< Hans Christian *Oersted*, 1777-1851, a Danish physicist]

**OES** (no periods), Office of Economic Stabilization.

**oe|soph|a|gus** (ē sof′ə gəs), *n., pl.* **-gi** (-jī). = esophagus.

**oes|tra|di|ol** (es′trə dī′ōl, -ol), *n.* = estradiol.

**oes|trin** (es′trin, ēs′-), *n.* = estrin.

**oes|tri|ol** (es′trē ōl, -ol; ēs′-), *n.* = estriol.

**oes|tro|gen** (es′trə jən, ēs′-), *n.* = estrogen.

**oes|trone** (es′trōn), *n.* = estrone.

**oes|trous** (es′trəs, ēs′-), *adj.* = estrous.

**oes|trus** (es′trəs, ēs′-), *n.* = estrus.

**oeu|vre** (œ′vrə), *n., pl.* **oeu|vres** (œ′vrə). *French.* **1** a literary or artistic work; lifework of an artist. **2** (literally) work.

**of** (ov, uv; *unstressed* əv), *prep.* **1** belonging to: *the children of a family, a friend of his boyhood, the news of the day, the captain of a ship, the cause of the quarrel. One half of the fraction one fourth is one eighth.* **2** made from: *a house of bricks, castles of sand.* **3** that has; with; containing: *a house of six rooms.* **4** that has as a quality: *a look of pity, a word of encouragement, a woman of good judgment.* **5** that is; named: *the city of Chicago.* **6** away from; from: *north of Boston, to shoot wide of the mark, to take leave of a friend.* **7** having to do with; in regard to; concerning; about: *to think well of someone, to be fond of, to be fifteen years of age, to be hard of heart, hard of hearing, short of stature.* **8** that is used for or has as a purpose: *a house of prayer.* **9** by: *the writings of Shakespeare, Darwin, Freud, the symphonies of Beethoven.* **10** owing to; as a result of having or using; through: *to die of a disease, to expect much of a new medicine.* **11** out of: *She came of a noble family. His second marriage ... took place in 1922 and there was a son of the marriage* (London Times). **12** among: *a friend of mine, a mind of the finest. Two of us went and two of us stayed at home.* **13** during: *of late years.* **14** (in telling time) before: *ten minutes of six.* **15** *Of* connects nouns and adjectives having the meaning of a verb with the noun which would be the object of the verb; indicating the object or goal (especially of a verbal noun): *the eating of fruit, his drinking of milk, the love of truth, in search of a ball, a hall smelling of onions, a man sparing of words.* [Old English (unstressed) *of;* see etym. under **off**]

► **of, have**. In representations of nonstandard speech the form *of* is often written instead of *have,* since in unstressed position both are pronounced (əv): *You could of been a great athlete* (New Yorker). *I'd of chased them rascals myself* (Atlantic).

► **of, off**. A redundant *of* (as in *off of, inside of*) is sometimes used in informal English, but the usage is not regarded as standard: *He stepped off* (not *off of*) *the sidewalk.* See idiom under **off**.

**of-**, *prefix.* the form of **ob-** before *f,* as in *offer.*

**OF** (no periods), **O.F.**, or **OF.**, Old French.

**o|fay** (ō′fā, ō fā′), *n., adj. U.S. Slang.* (used in an unfriendly way). **—*n.*** a white person.

**—*adj.*** of or belonging to a white person; white. [origin uncertain]

**off** (ôf, of), *adv., prep., adj., interj., n., v.* **—*adv.*** **1** from the usual position or condition: *He took off his hat.* **2** away: *to go off on a journey.* **3** distant in time or space: *Christmas is only five weeks off. He stopped twenty yards off.* **4** so as to stop or lessen: *Turn the water off. The game was called off.* **5** without work: *an afternoon off.* **6** in full; wholly; entirely: *She cleared off her desk. They paid off the mortgage.* **7** on one's way: *The train started and we were off on our trip. Her friends saw her off at the station.*

**—*prep.*** **1a** from; away from; far from: *He pushed me off my seat. We are miles off the main road. He will be off duty at four o'clock.* **b** subtracted from: *25 per cent off the marked price.* **2** not in the usual or correct position on; not in the usual or correct condition of; not on: *A button is off your coat.* **3** below the usual or normal standard of performance: *to be off one's game.* **4** seaward from or straight out from: *The ship anchored off Maine. The boat anchored off the fort.* **5** leading out of: *an alley off 12th Street.* **6** *Informal.* from the possession of: *I bought it off a complete stranger.*

**—*adj.*** **1** not connected; not continued; stopped: *The electricity is off.* **2** no longer contemplated; canceled: *The game is off.* **3** not at work: *He pursues his hobby during off hours. It was with a team of those very horses* [*used for plowing, etc.*], *on an off day, that Miss Sharp was brought to the Hall* (Thackeray). **4** in a specified condition in regard to money, property, or the like: *How well off are the neighbors?* **5** not very good; not up to average: *Bad weather made last summer an off season for fruit. We all have our off days. All drivers have their off moments, which may be due to fatigue, frustration, worry, boredom or alcohol* (New Scientist). **6** possible but not likely: *There is an off chance of rain. I came on the off chance that I would find you.* **7** in error; wrong: *Your figures are way off.* **8** *Informal.* not normal or stable; abnormal: *Their personal lives ... are rather off and strange* (James Jones). **9** on the right-hand side: *The near horse and the off horse make a team.* **10** on one's way. **11** more distant; farther: *the off side of a wall.* **12** seaward: *Our men ... were at work ... on the off side* (Daniel Defoe). **13** *Cricket.* in, at, of, or directed toward that side of the wicket or ground which the batsman faces as he stands at bat.

**—*interj.*** go away! stay away!

**—*n.*** **1** the fact or state of being off: *The thermostat is set at "off."* **2** the side in cricket opposite to the batsman: *the young bowler is getting wild, and bowls a ball almost wide to the off* (Thomas Hughes).

**—*v.t.*** *U.S. Slang.* to kill.

**be off**. See under **be**.

**from the off**, *British.* from the beginning; from the start: *Heredity had thrust our roles on us from the off* (Catherine Drinkwater).

**off and on**, at some times and not at others; now and then: *He has lived in Europe off and on for ten years. It has been turning up off and on since at least 1757 in various collections of songs* (St. Louis Post-Dispatch).

**off of**, *Informal.* from: *"I ain't going to take no present off of you"* (Eudora Welty).

► See usage note under **of**.

**off with**, **a** take off: *Off with those wet clothes.* **b** away with!: *Off with the old and on with the new!*

[Middle English *off,* Old English *of,* in stressed position]

► See **of** for usage note.

**off.**, an abbreviation for the following:

**1** offered.

**2** office.

**3** officer.

**4** official.

**5** officinal.

**off-a|gain on-a|gain**, or **off-a|gain-on-a|gain** (ôf′ə gen′ on′ə gen′; of′-; -ôn′-), *adj.* wavering; inconclusive; unresolved. Also, **on-again off-again**.

**of|fal** (ôf′əl, of′-), *n.* **1** the waste parts of an animal, fish, or bird, that has been killed for food. **2** garbage; refuse; rubbish. **3** the waste produced by any of various industrial processes, such as chips in milling wood or scraps of leather in trimming hides. **4** dead or decaying flesh; carrion. [probably < *off* + *fall.* Compare Dutch *afval* refuse, shavings, German *Abfall* waste, garbage.]

**off-and-on** (ôf′ən on′, of′-; -ôn′), *adj.* occasional; interrupted; irregular; uncertain. Also, **on-and-off**.

**off-bal|ance** (ôf′bal′əns, of′-), *adj., adv.* **1** in an unsteady position: *Patterson, a little off-balance ... suddenly went to the floor in the second round* (Newsweek). **2** by surprise: [*He*] *was plainly caught off-balance at the first thrusts from his host on an occasion which ... called for informality, friendliness and courtesy* (Wall Street Journal).

**off|beat** (ôf′bēt′, of′-), *n., adj.* **—*n.*** a musical beat normally with little or no accent: *Gradually, the beat began to ricochet from the audience as more and more fans began to clap hands on the offbeats* (Time).

**—*adj.*** **1** out of the ordinary; unusual; not orthodox; unconventional: *an offbeat display, offbeat drama.* **2** *Music.* of or characterized by offbeats: *an offbeat rhythm, offbeat melody.*

**off-board** (ôf′bôrd′, of′-; -bōrd′), *adj., adv.* through a broker's office instead of a regular exchange; over-the-counter: *off-board trading* (adj.). *Exchange members were prohibited from going off-board* (London Times) (adv.).

**off break**, *Cricket.* a ball that travels away from a line between the bowler and batsman but breaks back toward the batsman upon hitting the ground.

**off-Broad|way** (ôf′brôd′wā′, of′-), *n., adj.* **—*n.*** the segment of the New York City professional theater outside of Broadway (the traditional theatrical center), noted for its introduction of experimental plays, often by unknown playwrights: *Theatre began to happen. Broadway was ... unwilling and unable to put on daring new works or revive the classics. Off-Broadway, basing itself in and around the* [*Greenwich*] *Village area, began to rock the American theatre with Albee's plays and the latest works from Europe* (Saturday Night).

**—*adj.*** **1** of or having to do with off-Broadway; being outside the main theater district in New York City: *an off-Broadway play or theater.* **2** close to, but not on, Broadway, in New York City: *an off-Broadway restaurant.*

**off|cast** (ôf′kast′, -käst′; of′-), *adj., n.* **—*adj.*** cast off; rejected.

**—*n.*** a thing that is cast off; person who is rejected.

**off-cen|ter** (ôf′sen′tər, of′-), *adj.* **1** not in the center; away from the center: *Some engines are off-center so that the drive shaft by-passes the driver and permits lower seating* (Newsweek).

**Pronunciation Key:** hat, āge, cãre, fär; let, ēqual, tėrm; it, īce; hot, ōpen, ôrder; **oi**l, **ou**t; cup, pu̇t, rüle; **ch**ild; lo**ng**; **th**in; ᴛʜen; **zh**, measure; ə represents **a** in about, **e** in taken, **i** in pencil, **o** in lemon, **u** in circus.

**2** *Figurative.* unconventional; strange; eccentric: *... an engaging parasite whose code is in part peculiarly off-center and in part gentlemanly to the point of being quixotic* (Atlantic).

**off-col|or** (ôf′kul′ər, of′-), *adj.* **1** not of the right or required color or shade; defective in color: *an off-color diamond.* **2** somewhat improper; objectionable: *an off-color joke.* **SYN**: risqué.

**off-col|ored** (ôf′kul′ərd, of′-), *adj.* = off-color.

**off-course** (ôf′kôrs′, of′-; -kōrs′), *adj.* **1** off-track: *If off-course betting does come, it will do racing no good* (New Yorker). **2** not on the right course; deviating: *a slightly off-course landing of a rocket.*

**off|cut** (ôf′kut′, of′-), *n.* **1** one of the pieces cut off in shaping a block of stone, a piece of lumber, or the like: *Timber has been used in the length in which it is imported, instead of having wasteful offcuts* (Manchester Guardian Weekly). **2** *Printing.* **a** a piece cut off from a sheet to reduce it to the proper size. **b** a part cut off the main sheet and folded separately, as in a sheet of duodecimo.

**off-drive** (ôf′drīv′, of′-), *n., v.,* **-drove, -driv|en, -driv|ing.** *Cricket.* **— *n.*** a drive to the left side of the field by a right-handed batsman or the right side by a left-handed batsman: *A slightly mistimed off-drive led to a fine catch by Knight, running around in front of the screen* (London Times).
**— *v.i., v.t.*** to hit an off-drive (of a bowler's delivery): *Webster gradually blossomed out into some handsome off-driving* (U. A. Titley).

**off-du|ty** (ôf′dü′tē, of′-; -dyü′-), *adj.* **1** not engaged or occupied with one's normal work: *an off-duty policeman.* **2** of or for a person who is not on duty: *off-duty entertainment, off-duty offense.*

**of|fence** (ə fens′), *n. Especially British and Canadian.* offense.

**of|fend** (ə fend′), *v.t.* **1** to hurt the feelings of; make angry, displease, or pain: *My friend was offended by my laughter. He offends first one side and then the other* (Manchester Guardian). *He often offended men who might have been useful friends* (John L. Motley). **SYN**: affront, provoke. **2** to affect in an unpleasant or disagreeable way: *the rankest compound of villainous smell that ever offended nostril* (Shakespeare). *Far voices, sudden loud, offend my ear* (William E. Henley). **3** *Obsolete.* to cause to sin: *And if thy right eye offend thee, pluck it out* (Matthew 5:29). **4** *Obsolete.* **a** to sin against; wrong (a person). **b** to violate; transgress (a law). **— *v.i.* 1** to sin or do wrong: *In what way have I offended? We have offended against thy holy laws* (Book of Common Prayer). **SYN**: transgress. **2** to give offense; cause displeasure. **3** *Archaic.* to act on the offensive: *the stroke and parry of two swords, offending on the one side and keeping the defensive on the other* (Scott). [< Old French *offendre* < Latin *offendere* < *ob-* against + *-fendere* to strike]

**of|fend|ed|ly** (ə fen′did lē), *adv.* in an offended manner.

**of|fend|er** (ə fen′dər), *n.* **1** a person who offends: *The noisy offender sat in the front row and demanded to speak on every point.* **2** a person who does wrong or breaks a law: *No smoking here; offenders will be fined $5.00.*

**of|fense** (ə fens′), *n.* **1a** the act of breaking the law; crime or sin: *a penal offense. The punishment for that offense is two years in prison. Murder is an offense against God and man.* **SYN**: misdemeanor, transgression. See syn. under **crime**. **b** *Law.* the act of breaking the law, less serious than a misdemeanor: *Disturbing the peace and breaking most traffic laws are offenses in this state.* **2** a cause of wrongdoing. **3** the condition of being offended; hurt feelings; anger or resentment: *Try not to cause offense.* **SYN**: displeasure. **4** the act of offending; hurting someone's feelings: *No offense was meant.* **5** something that offends or causes displeasure: *The offense was such a minor breach of manners everyone overlooked it.* **6** the act of attacking; being the one to attack rather than defend: *A gun is a weapon of offense. He drew his sword, and with a deliberate and prepared attitude of offence, moved slowly to the encounter* (Scott). **7** those who are attacking; attacking team or force: *On a professional football team, players on the offense seldom play defense.* **8** *Obsolete.* hurt; harm; injury: *So shall he waste his means, weary his soldiers, Doing himself offence* (Shakespeare). **9** *Obsolete.* stumbling: *And he shall be ... for a stone of stumbling and for a rock of offence to both the houses of Israel* (Isaiah 8:14). Also, *especially British and Canadian,* **offence.**
**give offense,** to offend: *I just did not see you and did not mean to give offense. Pleasing the most delicate reader, without giving offense to the most scrupulous* (Joseph Addison).
**take offense,** to be offended: *The players did not take offense when the coach criticized their basketball game. Unfortunately, offense is usually taken where offense is meant* (A. W. Ward).
[fusion of Middle English *offens* (< Old French *offense* < Latin *offensus* a striking upon, annoyance), and of *offense* (< Old French *offense* < Latin *offensa* an injury, affront); both Latin nouns < *offendere* offend]
► See **defense** for usage note.

**of|fense|less** (ə fens′lis), *adj.* **1** without offense; unable to attack. **2** not offending; inoffensive. **— of|fense′less|ly,** *adv.*

**of|fen|sive** (ə fen′siv), *adj., n.* **— *adj.* 1** giving offense; irritating; annoying; insulting: *"Shut up" is an offensive remark.* **2** unpleasant; disagreeable; disgusting: *Bad eggs have an offensive odor.* **SYN**: displeasing, distasteful. **3** ready to attack; attacking: *an offensive army.* **SYN**: aggressive. **4** used for attack; having something to do with attack: *offensive weapons, an offensive war for conquest.* **5** belonging to an attacking team or force: *offensive players.*
**— *n.* 1** a position or attitude of attack: *The army took the offensive. A boxer on the offensive hits hard and aggressively.* **2** an attack; assault: *Our planes bombed the enemy lines on the night before the offensive.* **— of|fen′sive|ly,** *adv.* **— of|fen′sive|ness,** *n.*

**of|fer** (ôf′ər, of′-), *v., n.* **— *v.t.* 1a** to hold out to be taken or refused; put forward; present: *to offer one's hand, to offer a gift. They offered us their help. Bets were freely offered and taken regarding the result* (Bret Harte). *Mr. Arbuton has offered himself to Kitty* (William Dean Howells). **b** to present for sale: *to offer suits at reduced prices.* **c** to bid as a price: *He offered twenty dollars for our old stove.* **2** to be willing if another approves: *They offered to help us. Shaw offered to accompany him* (Francis Parkman). **3** to bring forth for consideration; propose; suggest; advance: *She offered a few ideas to improve the plan.* **4** to present in worship or devotion: *to offer prayers, to offer sacrifices.* **5** to give; show: *The thieves offered no resistance to the policemen. That hath enrag'd him on, to offer strokes* (Shakespeare). **6** to show intention; attempt; try: *He did not offer to hit back. When they offered to depart he entreated their stay* (Samuel Johnson). **SYN**: endeavor. **7** to attempt to inflict, deal, or bring to bear (violence or injury of any kind). **8** to present to sight or notice: *The scene ... offered to his view* (James Fenimore Cooper).
**— *v.i.* 1** to present itself; occur: *I will come if the opportunity offers.* **2** to make an offer or proposal. **3** to make an offer of marriage: *Miss Pole had a cousin ... who had offered to Miss Matty long ago* (Elizabeth C. Gaskell). **4** to present a sacrifice or offering as an act of worship. **5** *Archaic.* to make an attempt (at).
**— *n.* 1** the act of offering: *an offer to sing, an offer of money, an offer of marriage, an offer of $25,000 for a house.* **2** a thing that is offered. **3** an attempt or show of intention: *He had no sooner spoke these words, but he made an offer of throwing himself into the water* (Sir Richard Steele). **4** *Law.* a proposal from one person to another which, if accepted, will become a contract.
[Old English *offrian* < Latin *offerre* < *ob-* to + *ferre* bring] **— of′fer|er,** *n.*
**— *Syn. v.t.* 1a Offer, proffer, tender** mean to hold out something to someone to be accepted. **Offer** is the common word: *She offered him coffee.* **Proffer** is a literary word, and usually suggests offering with warmth, courtesy, or earnest sincerity: *He refused the proffered hospitality.* **Tender** is a formal word, and usually applies to an obligation or politeness rather than to an object: *I tendered my apologies.*

**of|fer|ing** (ôf′ər ing, of′-; ôf′ring, of′-), *n.* **1** the act of giving something as an act of worship or devotion: *the slave's offering of obedience.* **SYN**: oblation. **2a** a contribution or gift, as to a church, for some special purpose: *Offerings from the congregation are small in hard times.* **SYN**: donation. **b** stocks, bonds, and other securites offered to the public for sale: *No big offerings came into the market last week* (Wall Street Journal). **3** the act of one that offers.

**of|fer|to|ri|al** (ôf′ər tôr′ē əl, -tōr′-; of′-), *adj.* **1** of or having to do with an offertory: *an offertorial hymn.* **2** used in sacrificial offerings.

**of|fer|to|ry** (ôf′ər tôr′ē, -tōr′-; of′-), *n., pl.* **-ries.** **1** a collection of offerings, as of money, at a religious service. **2** verses said or the music sung or played while the offering is received. **3** Sometimes, **Offertory. a** (in the Roman Catholic Church) the part of the Mass at which bread and wine are offered to God. **b** (in the Anglican Church) a similar offering of bread and wine to God. **c** the prayers said or sung at this time. [< Late Latin *offertōrium* place to which offerings were brought < Latin *offerre* to offer]

**off-fla|vor** (ôf′flā′vər, of′-), *n.* an undesirable or unnatural flavor: *The off-flavor from one egg can cause off-flavor to an entire case of eggs* (Seattle Times Magazine).

**off-glide** (ôf′glīd′, of′-), *n. Phonetics.* a transitional sound produced by the movement of the articulators away from the position first taken.

**off-grade** (ôf′grād′, of′-), *adj.* of average or less than average quality; intermediate between high-grade and low-grade: *off-grade steel, off-grade paper.*

**off|hand** (*adv.* ôf′hand′, of′-; *adj.* ôf′hand′, of′-), *adv., adj.* **— *adv.*** without previous thought or preparation; at once: *The carpenter could not tell offhand how much the work would cost. That question is too important to answer offhand.*
**— *adj.* 1** done or made offhand: *Her offhand remarks were sometimes very wise.* **SYN**: unpremeditated, unstudied, impromptu, extemporaneous. **2** free and easy; casual; informal: *The boy's offhand ways angered his father. He had gone about next day with his usual cool, offhand manner* (John Galsworthy). **SYN**: unceremonious.

**off|hand|ed** (ôf′han′did, of′-), *adj.* = offhand. **— off′hand′ed|ly,** *adv.* **— off′hand′ed|ness,** *n.*

**off-hour** (ôf′our′, of′-), *n., adj.* **— *n.* 1** a period of leisure time: *Clegg collects butterflies in his off-hours* (Time). **2** a period of lessened activity: *The tube trains are designed to handle express cargo ... during off-hours, providing ballast* (Scientific American).
**— *adj.* 1** of or for off-hours: *off-hour diversions.* **2** having off-hours: *The government [permits] private persons—chiefly off-hour craftsmen and the unemployed—to perform repairs* (Richard A. Pierce).

**offic.,** official.

**of|fice** (ôf′is, of′-), *n.* **1** a place in which the work of a position is done; room or rooms in which to do work: *a ticket office. The doctor's office is on the second floor. The post office is on Main Street.* **2** a position, especially a public position: *to accept or resign an office. The President holds the highest public office in the United States. Men too conversant with office are rarely minds of remarkable enlargement* (Edmund Burke). **SYN**: post, situation. **3** the duty of one's position; task; job; work: *It is my office to open the mail. His office is to decide on applications for aid. A teacher's office is teaching. It has been the office of art to educate the perception of beauty* (Emerson). **SYN**: function, charge. **4** a person or staff of persons carrying on work in an office: *Half the office is on vacation. Will the office approve such an expense?* **5** an administrative department of a governmental organization: *the Office of Civil and Defense Mobilization.* **6** an act of kindness or unkindness; attention; service: *Through the good offices of a friend, he was able to get a ticket.* **7** a religious ceremony or prayer: *the Communion office, last offices. There are seven daily offices in the Catholic Church.*
**offices,** the parts of a house devoted to household work, such as kitchen, pantry, or laundry, often also stables and buildings.
**the office,** *Slang.* a signal, usually a secret or special one; hint: *If the bloke you're working with is going too strong you give him what we call the office, you press his arm with finger and thumb, pincers like. That means take it a bit easy* (Manchester Guardian Weekly).
[< Old French *office,* learned borrowing from Latin *officium* service (in Medieval Latin, place for work) < *opus* work + *facere* do]

**office block,** *British.* an office building.

**of|fice-block ballot** (ôf′is blok′, of′-), *U.S.* a ballot that lists candidates according to the office they seek.

**office boy,** a boy whose work is doing odd jobs in an office.

**office building,** *U.S.* a building with offices for one or more businesses or professions.

**of|fice|hold|er** (ôf′is hōl′dər, of′-), *n.* a person who holds a public office; government official: *Already many Moslem officeholders appointed by the French have resigned from municipal and regional councils* (Newsweek).

**office hours,** the hours during the day when an office is open for work or business.

**of|fi|cer** (ôf′ə sər, of′-), *n., v.* **— *n.* 1** a person who commands others in the armed forces, such as a major, a general, a captain, or an admiral. An officer's authority is usually defined by his commission. **2** the captain of a merchant ship or any of his chief assistants, such as the first mate or the chief engineer. **3** a person who holds a public, church, or government office: *a health officer, a police officer.* **4** the president, vice-president, secretary, or treasurer of a club or society; person appointed or elected to an administrative position. **5** an executive in a corporation, company, or the like. **6** a member above the lowest

rank in some honorary societies. **7** *Obsolete.* an agent; minister: *slavish officers of vengeance* (Milton).
—***v.t.*** **1** to provide with officers: *They have ... officered the ships, and maintained the public utilities* (Newsweek). **2** to direct; conduct; manage: *The fire department was officered by brave and dedicated men. The Students' Union, the Zengakuren, is officered largely by Communists* (Atlantic).
[< Anglo-French *officer,* variant of Old French *officier,* learned borrowing from Medieval Latin *officiarius* < Latin *officium* service, office]

**of|fi|cer|less** (ôf′ə sər lis, of′-), *adj.* without officers.

**officer of arms**, *British.* a heraldic officer; herald.

**officer of the day**, a military officer who has charge, for any given day, of the guards, prisoners, barracks, etc. *Abbr:* O.D.

**officer of the guard**, an officer, under the officer of the day, who has charge of the guard detail on a military post, ship, or the like.

**officer of the watch**, an officer in charge of a ship during a watch at sea, usually the first, second, third, or fourth mate.

**of|fi|cer|ship** (ôf′ə sər ship, of′-), *n.* **1** the position, rank, or leadership of an officer: *Regiments of troops were abandoned or lost due to almost ridiculous officership* (Wall Street Journal). **2** a group of officers.

**of|fic|es** (ôf′is iz, of′-), *n.pl.* See under **office**.

**office seeker**, a person who tries to obtain a public office.

**of|fi|cial** (ə fish′əl), *n., adj.* —***n.*** **1** a person who holds a public position or who is in charge of some public work or duty: *The mayor is a government official. Postmasters are government officials.* **2** a person holding office; officer: *bank officials.*
—***adj.*** **1** of an office: *Policemen wear an official uniform. The official title is Superintendent of Playgrounds.* **2** having something to do with an office: *The policeman was on official business.* **3** authorized by government or other authority; having authority; authoritative: *An official record is kept of the proceedings of Congress.* **4** being an official: *Each state has its own official representatives in Congress. The unions ... refused to accept the intervention of an official mediator* (London Times). **5** suitable for a person in office: *the official dignity of a judge.* **6** holding office: *an official body.* **7** *Pharmacy.* authorized by the pharmacopoeia; officinal.
[< Old French *official,* learned borrowing from Latin *officiālis* < *officium* service] —**of|fi′cial|ly,** *adv.*

**of|fi|cial|dom** (ə fish′əl dəm), *n.* **1** the position or domain of officials. **2** officials or the official class. [< *official* + *-dom*]

**of|fi|cial|ese** (ə fish′ə lēz′, -lēs′), *n.* the language characteristic of officials or official documents, often formal and excessively wordy in style: *DP 32 ... is a certificate to be signed by a "medical practitioner"* (*officialese for a doctor, I suppose*) (Punch).

**of|fi|cial|ism** (ə fish′ə liz əm), *n.* **1** official methods of system. **2** excessive attention to official routine. **3** officials as a group.

**of|fi|cial|i|za|tion** (ə fish′ə lə zā′shən), *n.* the act or process of officializing: *The officialization of Hindi has long been fought by non-Hindi regions* (Time).

**of|fi|cial|ize** (ə fish′ə līz), *v.t.,* **-ized, -iz|ing.** to make official in character: *They have popularized, officialized, and standardized the modern vocabulary* (Atlantic).

**of|fi|ci|ant** (ə fish′ē ənt), *n.* a person who officiates at a religious service or ceremony. [< Medieval Latin *officians, -antis,* present participle of *officiare* officiate]

**of|fi|ci|ar|y** (ə fish′ē er′ē), *adj., n., pl.* **-ar|ies.**
—***adj.*** **1** (of a title) attached to or derived from an office. **2** (of a dignitary) having a title or rank derived from office.
—***n.*** **1** officials as a group. **2** an officer or official.

**of|fi|ci|ate** (ə fish′ē āt), *v.,* **-at|ed, -at|ing.** —***v.i.*** **1** to perform the duties of any office or position; act or serve in some official capacity: *The president officiates as chairman at all club meetings. The apothecary occasionally officiated as a barber* (William Godwin). **2** to perform the duties of a priest, minister, or rabbi: *The bishop officiated at the service in the cathedral.* **3** to do anything as a ritual or ceremony: *to officiate in carving the Thanksgiving turkey.*
—***v.t.*** *Obsolete.* to supply; minister: *Stars, that seem to roll Spaces incomprehensible ... merely to officiate light Round this opacous earth* (Milton). [< Medieval Latin *officiare* (with English *-ate*[1]) < Latin *officium* service, office]

**of|fi|ci|a|tion** (ə fish′ē ā′shən), *n.* the act of officiating; performance of a religious, ceremonial, or public duty.

**of|fi|ci|a|tor** (ə fish′ē ā′tər), *n.* a person who officiates.

**of|fic|i|nal** (ə fis′ə nəl), *adj., n.* —***adj.*** **1** kept in stock by druggists; not made by prescription: *officinal drugs or medicines.* **2** recognized by the pharmacopoeia; official. **3** of or having to do with a shop.
—***n.*** a drug or medicine that is kept in stock.
[< Medieval Latin *officinalis* of a monastery < Latin *officīna* shop, storeroom (in Medieval Latin, monastery) < *officium* service, office]

**of|fi|cious** (ə fish′əs), *adj.* **1** too ready to offer services or advice; minding other people's business; fond of meddling: *One of those officious, noisy little men who are always ready to give you unasked information* (Benjamin Disraeli). **SYN:** meddlesome; intrusive. **2** (in diplomacy) casual and friendly; unofficial; informal: *an officious exchange of views.* **3** *Obsolete.* eager to serve; obliging. [< Latin *officiōsus* dutiful < *officium* service, office] —**of|fi′cious|ly,** *adv.* —**of|fi′cious|ness,** *n.*

**off|ing** (ôf′ing, of′-), *n.* **1** the more distant part of the sea or other large body of water as seen from the shore. **2** a position at a distance from the shore.
**in the offing, a** just visible from the shore: *a schooner in the offing.* **b** within sight. **c** not far off; impending; in the making: *trouble in the offing. In sum ... an Arab-Israeli war was in the offing* (Atlantic).

**off|ish** (ôf′ish, of′-), *adj. Informal.* inclined to keep aloof; distant and reserved in manner; standoffish. —**off′ish|ness,** *n.*

**off-is|land** (ôf′ī′lənd, of′-), *n., adj., adv.* —***n.*** an offshore island: *The off-islands may seem to be just across the nautical street but the journey can still be an experience on a rough day* (Sunday Times).
—***adj.*** *U.S.* visiting or temporarily residing on an island; being an off-islander.
—***adv.*** away from an island: *One islander ... planned to go off-island* (New York Times).

**off-is|land|er** (ôf′ī′lən dər, of′-), *n. U.S.* a temporary or seasonal resident of an island.

**off-key** (ôf′kē′, of′-), *adj.* **1** not in the right musical key; not in harmony; discordant: *Her voice slightly off-key, was that of the Parisian street hawkers* (New Yorker). **2** somewhat improper; inconsistent; rash: *An irreverent, off-key assault on an assortment of sacred cows* (Time).

**off-li|cence** or **off-li|cense** (ôf′lī′səns, of′-), *n. British.* **1** a license for the sale by the bottle of alcoholic liquor for consumption off the premises: *A number of off-licences had been granted to Pakistanis in the city, but this was the first on-licence* (London Times). **2** an establishment with an off-licence; package store: *On the way home I called at the off-licence to collect six large tonics, a bottle of vodka, and a bottle of brandy* (Patrick Campbell).

**off-lim|its** (ôf′lim′its, of′-), *adj.* not to be entered; out of bounds: *... the entire control area would remain off-limits until official notices were published lifting restrictions* (New York Times).

**off-line** (ôf′līn′, of′-), *adj., adv.* —***adj.*** **1a** (of equipment associated with an electronic computer) operating outside of direct control by the central equipment: *The first of the three computers is an "off-line" machine that is used for production planning. It receives orders for specific sizes, amounts and types of steel, and groups them according to quantity and composition* (Fred Wheeler). **b** not operating in real-time. **2** (of a railroad operation or other service) being outside of the area served by the line.
—***adv.*** **1** outside the direct control of central equipment: *These tapes have to be coordinated and analyzed by a Mercury or Atlas computer working off-line* (New Scientist). **2** not in line with an actual process or operation; not in real-time.

**off-load** (ôf′lōd′, of′-), *v.t., v.i.* to unload or discharge a cargo: *Flight C wheeled away to off-load their bombs on the railway yards.*

**off-mike** (ôf′mīk′, of′-), *adj., adv.* **1** not heard clearly through the microphone: *Jane herself was distinctly off-mike some of the time* (*one turned up the volume control, only to have to turn it down lest Rochester blasted one's head off*) (Listener). **2** while not engaged in broadcasting; off the air: *... a B.B.C. radio actress who is famed as a kindly district nurse on the airwaves but is a sadistic, cigar-smoking old horror off-mike* (New Yorker).

**off-off-Broad|way** (ôf′ôf′brôd′wā′, of′of′-), *n., adj.* —***n.*** the segment of the New York City professional theater producing low-budget and often highly experimental plays that would not be presented in Broadway and off-Broadway theaters: *Off-off Broadway is completely outside the union because it never takes place in a "real" theatre; instead, off-off Broadway uses cafés, rooms, lofts, churches* (Manchester Guardian Weekly).
—***adj.*** of or having to do with off-off-Broadway; being outside the Broadway and off-Broadway theatrical centers in New York City.

**off-peak** (ôf′pēk′, of′-), *adj.* **1** less than what is usual or possible as a maximum: *off-peak production.* **2** characterized by reduced demand or output: *an off-peak season.*

**off|print** (ôf′print′, of′-), *n., v.* —***n.*** a separate reprint of an article, story, or other short segment, originally printed as a part of a magazine or book; printed excerpt: *... an offprint of a piece of his published in some journal I had never heard of* (Harper's).
—***v.t.*** to reprint separately or as an excerpt.

**off|put** (ôf′pu̇t′, of′-), *v.t.,* **-put, -put|ting.** *British Informal.* to disconcert; annoy. [back formation < *off-putting*]

**off-put|ting** (ôf′pu̇t′ing, of′-), *adj. British Informal.* disconcerting; annoying; discouraging: *Inspection is a bad word; it is politically off-putting* (London Guardian). —**off′-put′ting|ly,** *adv.*

**off-road** (ôf′rōd′, of′-), *adj.* **1** off or away from highways and paved roads: *off-road recreational driving.* **2** of or for off-road traveling: *the growing recreational use by off-road vehicle enthusiasts of the 17 million-ac. California Desert* (David A. Fredrickson).

**off|sad|dle** (ôf′sad′əl, of′-), *v.t., v.i.,* **-dled, -dling.** (in South Africa) to take the saddle off (a horse), as at a halt in a journey.

**off-sale** (ôf′sāl′, of′-), *n.* the sale of alcoholic liquor for consumption off the premises; take-home sale.

**off|scour|ings** (ôf′skour′ingz, of′-), *n.pl.* **1** low, contemptible, or depraved people. **2** *Figurative.* filth; refuse; rubbish.

**off|screen** (ôf′skrēn′, of′-), *adj., adv.* **1** not seen on the motion picture or television screen: *an off-screen voice or commentary.* **2** while not acting for motion pictures or television: *Japanese actors, offscreen, are less excitable than American actors* (New Yorker).

**off|scum** (ôf′skum′, of′-), *n.* something skimmed off; scum; refuse.

**off-sea|son** (ôf′sē′zən, of′-), *n., adj.* —***n.*** the period when something is out of season; the slack or inactive season, as of a business or sport.
—***adj.*** in or for the off-season: *off-season travel, off-season hotel rates.*

*__off|set__ (*v.* ôf′set′, of′-; *n., adj.* ôf′set′, of′-), *v.,* **-set, -set|ting,** *n., adj.* —***v.t.*** **1** to make up for; compensate for: *The better roads offset the greater distance.* **SYN:** counterbalance, neutralize. **2** to balance (one thing) by another as an equivalent: *We offset the greater distance by the better roads.* **3** to set off or balance: *I had offset a trip to the mountains against a summer job.* **4a** to make offsets or setoffs in (as a wall). **b** to furnish (a pipe or bar) with an offset or offsets. **5** *Printing.* to make an offset of.
—***v.i.*** to form or make an offset or offsets.
—***n.*** **1** something which makes up for something else; compensation: *In football, his speed and cleverness were an offset to his small size.* **2** a short side shoot from a main stem or root that starts a new plant, as in the houseleek or date palm. **3** any offshoot. **4** *Printing.* **a** a process in which the inked impression is first made on a rubber roller and then on the paper, instead of directly on the paper. See picture below on following page. **b** the impression thus made. **c** the transfer or blotting of an impression onto another sheet because the ink is still wet. **5** a short distance measured perpendicularly from the main line in surveying. **6** *Architecture.* a ledge formed on a wall by lessening its thickness above; setoff. **7** an abrupt bend in a pipe or bar to carry it past something in the way. **8** a minor branch of a mountain range; spur. **9** *Electricity.* a conductor going out from a principal conductor.
—***adj.*** of or having to do with offset: *The local printer makes offset plates directly from the film* (Time).

*__off|shoot__ (ôf′shüt′, of′-), *n.* **1** a shoot from the main stem of a plant; branch: *One of the offshoots of the trunk fell from high in the tree under the weight of the snow.* **2** *Figurative:* *an offshoot of a mountain range. The nation's annual spending for road construction ... is obviously a direct offshoot of the swelling auto population* (Newsweek).

**off|shore** (*adv., adj.* ôf′shôr′, -shōr′; of′-; *adj.* -shôr′), *adv., adj.* **1** off or away from the shore: *The wind was blowing offshore* (adv.). *We saw*

**Pronunciation Key:** hat, āge, cãre, fär; let, ēqual, tėrm; it, īce; hot, ōpen, ôrder; oil, out; cup, pu̇t, rüle; child; long; thin; ᴛʜen; zh, measure; ə represents **a** in about, **e** in taken, **i** in pencil, **o** in lemon, **u** in circus.

*offshore oil wells along the coast* (adj.). **2** *U.S.* outside the United States; foreign: *Offshore procurements are American purchases of airplanes, tanks, ammunition and other munitions in European countries* (Wall Street Journal).

**offshore bar**, = barrier beach.

**off|side** or **off-side** (ôf′sīd′, of′-), *adj., adv., n.* —*adj., adv.* not on the side permitted by the rules; illegally in advance of the ball, puck, or other playing piece.
—*n.* a play in football or other sport, that is offside.

**off|sid|er** (ôf′sī′dər, of′-), *n.* (in Australia) a person who assists another; helper.

**off-spin** (ôf′spin′, of′-), *n. Cricket.* a spin that results in an off break.

**off-spin|ner** (ôf′spin′ər, of′-), *n. Cricket.* **1** = off break. **2** a bowler who specializes in off breaks.

**off|spring** (ôf′spring′, of′-), *n.* **1** the young of a person, animal, or plant; what is born from or grows out of something; child or children; descendant: *Every one of his offspring had red hair just like his own.* **SYN:** progeny, issue. **2** *Figurative.* a result; effect: *He appeared to consider it* [*an assertion*] *as the offspring of delirium* (Mary W. Shelley). [Old English *ofspring*]

**off-stage** or **off|stage** (ôf′stāj′, of′-), *adj., adv.* **1** away from the part of the stage that the audience can see; behind the scenes: *He is about to start taking lessons so that the set of his lips and finger movements will correspond to the melody to be played off-stage by an expert musician* (New York Times). **2** while not acting for an audience.

**off-street** (ôf′strēt′, of′-), *adj.* away from the street, as for easing traffic or preventing congestion: *off-street parking.*

**off stump**, *Cricket.* the stump farthest from the batsman.

**off-tack|le** (ôf′tak′əl, of′-), *n. Football.* a running play in which the defensive end is blocked toward the sideline, and the defensive tackle is blocked inward, opening a hole for the runner.

**off|take** (ôf′tāk′, of′-), *n. British.* **1** the act of taking off, as when purchase of goods takes them off the market; consumption. **2** that which is taken off; a deduction. **3** a means of drawing off or away, as a pipe, tube, or course.

**off-the-cuff** (ôf′ᴛʜə kuf′, of′-), *adj., adv. U.S. Informal.* —*adj.* not prepared in advance; extemporaneous; impromptu: *Armed for his off-the-cuff speeches only with a list of candidates' names, he interweaves their names into his talk as if the speech had been built on that basis* (Wall Street Journal).
—*adv.* offhand; extemporaneously: *Only ... where he spoke completely off-the-cuff did he seem to be establishing any great rapport with his audience* (Alan Otten).

**off-the-face** (ôf′ᴛʜə fās′, of′-), *adj.* (of a woman's hat) being without a brim or with a narrow, usually upturned brim: *... an off-the-face turban of natural raffia* (New Yorker).

**off-the-job** (ôf′ᴛʜə job′, of′-), *adj.* **1** not on-the-job; done or happening away from, prior to, or in preparation for the job: *off-the-job study.* **2** being off one's job; laid off or unemployed: *an off-the-job worker.*

**off-the-peg** (ôf′ᴛʜə peg′, of′-), *adj. British.* ready-made: *An off-the-peg dress may cost £20 in a Geneva shop* (London Times). (*Figurative.*) *I sensed ... that personality was more important to a room than any amount of off-the-peg convention* (Punch)

**off-the-rack** (ôf′ᴛʜə rak′, of′-), *adj. U.S.* ready-made: *Rome's off-the-rack clothes are represented by Fabiani's culotte suit* (New York Times). (*Figurative.*) *Celebrities ..., custom-tailored and off-the-rack types, Ph.D's and blue-collar workers—all mingle in the elevators of the Terrace* (Ernest Dunbar).

**off-the-rec|ord** (ôf′ᴛʜə rek′ərd, of′-), *adj., adv.* —*adj.* not intended for publication; not to be repeated publicly or issued as news: *Two unions have held several off-the-record meetings here recently to discuss pending contract negotiations.* (Wall Street Journal).
—*adv.* not to be recorded or quoted; so as to be off-the-record: *Officials maintained a discreet public silence, but off-the-record they complained bitterly* (New York Times).

**off-the-shelf** (ôf′ᴛʜə shelf′, of′-), *adj., adv.* —*adj.* suitable for use without major or extensive modification.
—*adv.* without major modification: *Deliveries in practically all small items of construction equipment can be made off-the-shelf* (Wall Street Journal).

**off-the-wall** (ôf′ᴛʜə wôl′, of′-), *adj.,* or **off the wall**, *U.S. Informal.* not customary or usual; unconventional: *Brian knows how to startle the over-interviewed with off-the-wall questions that get surprising answers: Ever see a ghost? What makes you cry?* (National Review).

**off-track** (ôf′trak′, of′-), *adj.* **1** that is conducted away from the race track: *off-track betting on horse races.* **2** off the beaten track; out of the way: *... wanderings in the off-track Caribbean islands occupied by poor-white Frenchmen* (Punch). **3** that is not a usual function of railroading: *Southern Pacific ... has never had an eye for off-track business ventures* (New York Times).

**off-train** (ôf′trān′, of′-), *adj.* = nonoperating.

**off-white** (ôf′hwīt′, of′-), *n., adj.* —*n.* a very light shade of color, verging on white.
—*adj.* that is nearly white: *an off-white ceiling.*

**off-year** (ôf′yir′, of′-), *n., adj. U.S.* —*n.* **1** a year of unfavorable conditions or lower than average yield: *This one is an off-year for domestic exports.* **2** a year in which elections are held for offices other than the presidency, governorship, or mayoralty: *President Eisenhower hopped into the campaign more vigorously than any President ever had in an off-year* (New York Times).
—*adj.* of or taking place in an off-year: *off-year elections.*

**O.F.M.**, Order of Friars Minor; Franciscans (Latin, *Ordo Fratrum Minorum*).

**OFr** (no periods) or **OFr.**, Old French.

**O.F.S.** or **OFS** (no periods), Orange Free State.

**oft** (ôft, oft), *adv., adj.* —*adv. Archaic.* often; frequently: *Oft I talked with him apart* (Tennyson).
—*adj. Obsolete.* frequent [Old English *oft*]

**of|ten** (ôf′ən, of′-; -tən), *adv., adj.* —*adv.* in many cases or on many occasions; many times; frequently: *Blame is often directed toward the wrong person. We see our neighbors often. He comes here often.*
—*adj. Archaic.* frequent: *Use a little wine for ... thine often infirmities* (I Timothy 5:23).
[Middle English *often;* extension of *ofte* oft]
—*Syn. adv.* **Often, frequently** mean many times or in many instances, and are often interchangeable. But **often** suggests only that something happens or occurs a number of times or in a considerable proportion of the total number of instances: *We often see them.* **Frequently** emphasizes happening or occurring again and again, regularly or at short intervals. *We saw them frequently last week.*

**of|ten|times** (ôf′ən tīmz′, of′-; -tən-), *adv.* = often: *This song to myself did I oftentimes repeat* (Wordsworth).

**oft|time** (ôft′tīm′, oft′-), *adv., adj. Archaic.* —*adv.* often; ofttimes.
—*adj.* frequent.

**oft|times** (ôft′tīmz′, oft′-), *adv.* = often: *The fabled Haroun-al-Rashid ofttimes used to dress up in rags and mingle with his subjects in the bazaar* (New Yorker).

**O.G.**, an abbreviation for the following:
**1** officer of the guard.
**2** ogee (molding).
**3** Olympic Games.
**4** Also, **o.g.** *Philately.* original gum (a stamp in mint condition with the original mucilage).

**Og|a|la|la** (og′ə lä′lə), *n., pl.* **-las** or **-la.** = Oglala.

*** og|am** (og′əm, ōg′əm), *n.* **1** an alphabet of 20 characters used in ancient Britain and Ireland. **2** an inscription in such characters. **3** one of the characters. Also, **ogham.** [< Old Irish *ogam*]

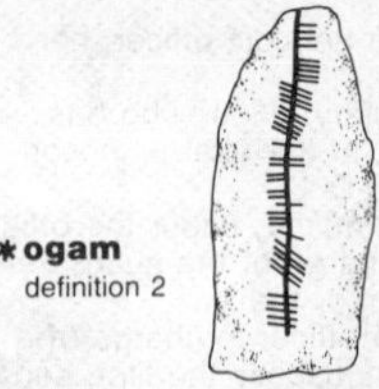
***ogam**
definition 2

**og|am|ic** (og′ə mik, ō gam′ik), *adj.* **1** of or having to do with the ogam. **2** consisting of ogams. Also, **oghamic, ogmic.**

**O gauge**, a gauge of model railroads in which the tracks are 1¼ inches wide.

**og|do|ad** (og′dō ad), *n.* **1** the number eight. **2** a group, set, or series of eight. [< Latin *ogdoas, -adis* < Greek *ogdoás, -ádos* < stem of *oktō̂* eight]

**o|gee** (ō jē′, ō′jē), *n.* **1** an S-shaped curve or line. **2** a molding with such a curve; cyma. **3** = ogee arch. **4** *Obsolete.* a diagonal rib or pointed arch; ogive. [variant of *ogive*]

*** ogee arch**, a form of pointed arch each side of which has the curve of an S-shape.

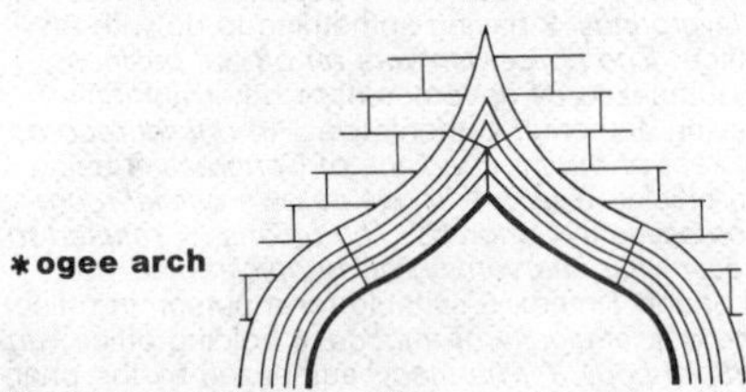
***ogee arch**

**og|ham** (og′əm, ōg′əm), *n.* = ogam.

**og|ham|ic** (og′ə mik, ō gam′ik), *adj.* = ogamic.

**o|gi|val** (ō jī′vəl), *adj. Architecture.* **1** of or like a diagonal rib or pointed arch in a building. **2** having pointed arches or diagonally ribbed vaulting: *Their ogival architecture was too foreign to impress the Renaissance world, except by the richness of its decoration* (New Yorker).

*** o|give** (ō′jīv, ō jīv′), *n.* **1** *Architecture.* **a** a diagonal rib of a vault. **b** a pointed arch. **2** *Statistics.* a distribution curve in which the frequencies are cumulative. In an ogive of wage levels in which 10 people earn less than $50, 60 people $50 to $100, and 40 people $100 to $150, the abscissas of the curve would be 50, 100, and 150 and the ordiantes 10, 70, 110. [< Middle French *ogive;* origin uncertain]

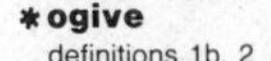
***ogive**
definitions 1b, 2

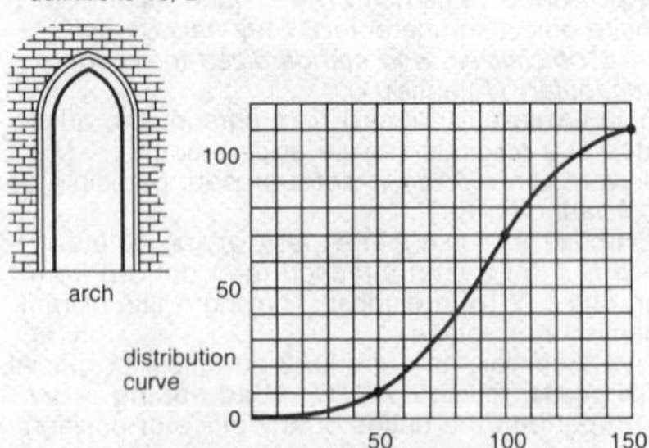


**Og|la|la** (og lä′lə), *n., pl.* **-las** or **-la.** **1** a member of a tribe of Sioux Indians of North and South Dakota. **2** the language of this tribe.

**o|gle** (og′əl, ō′gəl), *v.,* **o|gled, o|gling,** *n.* —*v.t.* **1** to look at with desire; make eyes at: *He ogled the ladies with an air of supreme satisfaction* (Herman Melville). **2** to look at; eye.
—*v.i.* to look with desire; make eyes: *She ogled, and nodded, and kissed her hands quite affectionately to Kew* (Thackeray).
—*n.* an ogling look: *Miss Brindle ... gave him two or three ogles* (Thomas L. Peacock).
[< Low German *oeglen* (frequentative) < *oegen* look at < *oege* eye] —**o′gler,** *n.*

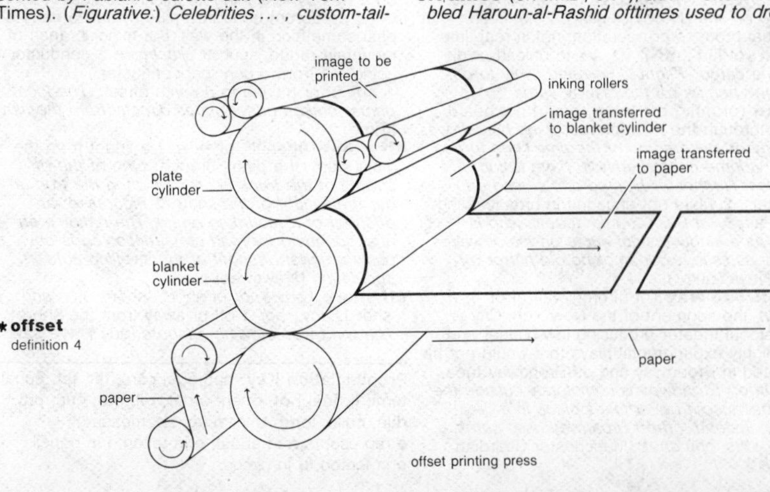

***offset**
definition 4

offset printing press

**OGO** (no periods), Orbiting Geophysical Observatory (an unmanned satellite of NASA, designed for gathering physical data about the earth): *The various OGO's and OSO's are ... making observations of direct importance to the space age* (Jonathan Eberhart).

**Og|pu** or **OGPU** (og′pü), *n.* the official organization of secret police and detectives in the Soviet Union from 1922 to 1935. It was named the NKVD in 1935, and, later, replaced by the MVD and KGB. [< Russian *O*(*b'edinennoe*) *G*(*osudarstvennoe*) *P*(*oliticheskoe*) *U*(*pravlenie*) "Unified State Political Administration"]

**o|gre** (ō′gər), *n.* **1** a hideous giant or monster in folklore and fairy tales that was supposed to eat people. **2** *Figurative: If those robber-barons were somewhat grim and drunken ogres, they had a certain grandeur of the wild beast in them* (George Eliot). [< French *ogre;* origin uncertain]

**o|gre|ish** (ō′gər ish), *adj.* of, having to do with, or like an ogre.

**o|gress**[1] (ō′gris), *n.* a female ogre.

**o|gress**[2] (ō′gris), *n. Heraldry.* a black, round spot on a shield, representing a cannon ball; roundel sable. [origin unknown]

**o|grish** (ō′grish), *adj.* = ogreish.

**oh** or **Oh** (ō), *interj., n., pl.* **oh's** or **ohs, Oh's** or **Ohs.** —*interj.* **1** a word used before a person's name in beginning to speak: *Oh Mary, look!* **2** a word used to express surprise, joy, grief, pain, and other feelings: *Oh, dear me! Oh! that hurt! Oh, what a pity!*
—*n.* the interjection of exclamation *Oh: You should have heard their Oh's and Ah's when they got the news.* Also, **O.**

**OH** (no periods), Ohio (with postal Zip Code).

**oh-dee** (ō′dē′), *n., v. Slang.* —*n.* = OD.
—*v.i.* = OD: (*Figurative.*) *"I'm worried that the commission* [*Commission on Campus Unrest*] *is close to oh-deeing"* (Time).

**OHE** (no periods) or **O.H.E., 1** *British.* Office of Health Economics: *The O.H.E. was set up in 1962 by the pharmaceutical industry to investigate the economics of medical care and other related matters* (London Times). **2** Office of the Housing Expediter.

**OHG** (no periods) or **O.H.G.,** Old High German.

**o|hi|a** (ō hē′ä), *n.,* or **ohia lehua,** the lehua of Hawaii. [< Hawaiian *'ōhi'a*]

**O|hi|an** (ō hī′ən), *n.* = Ohioan.

**O|hi|o|an** (ō hī′ō ən), *adj., n.* —*adj.* of or having to do with Ohio.
—*n.* a native or an inhabitant of Ohio.

**Ohio buckeye,** a kind of horse chestnut with white, soft, and spongy wood that grows in the Ohio and Mississippi valleys; fetid buckeye.

**ohm** (ōm), *n.* a measure of electrical resistance. A wire in which one volt produces a current of one ampere has a resistance of one ohm. [< Georg S. *Ohm,* 1787-1854, a German physicist]

**ohm|age** (ō′mij), *n.* the electrical resistance of a conductor, expressed in ohms.

**ohm|ic** (ō′mik), *adj.* **1** of or having to do with the ohm: *It is the ohmic resistance of the gas that generates the heat on passage of the current* (Lyman Spitzer, Jr.). **2** measured in ohms.

**ohm|me|ter** (ōm′mē′tər), *n.* an instrument for measuring in ohms the electrical resistance of a conductor.

**O.H.M.S.,** On His or Her Majesty's Service.

**Ohm's law** (ōmz), a law expressing the strength of an electric current, in which the current in amperes is directly proportional to the electromotive force in volts and inversely proportional to the resistance in ohms.

**o|ho** (ō hō′), *interj.* an exclamation expressing surprise, taunting, or exultation.

**o|hone** (ō hōn′), *interj. Scottish and Irish.* ochone.

**-oid,** *suffix forming adjectives and nouns.* **1** like ___; like that of a ___: *Ameboid = like an ameba.*
**2** a thing like a ___: *Spheroid = a thing like a sphere* (*in form*).
[< New Latin *-oides,* reduction of Greek *-oeidēs* in the form of < *eîdos* form]

**o|id|i|um** (ō id′ē əm), *n., pl.* **-i|a** (-ē ə). = arthrospore. [< New Latin *oidium* < Greek *ōión* egg]

**oil** (oil), *n., v., adj.* —*n.* **1** any one of several kinds of fatty or greasy liquids that are lighter than water, that burn easily, and that will not mix or dissolve in water but will dissolve in alcohol. Mineral oils, such as kerosene, are used for fuel; animal and vegetable oils, such as olive oil and peanut oil, are used in cooking and medicine and in many other ways. Essential or volatile oils, such as oil of peppermint, are distilled from plants, leaves, flowers, and other parts of plants, and are thin and evaporate very quickly. **2a** mineral oil; petroleum: *In the United States about half of each barrel of crude oil in the past has gone into gasoline* (New York Times). **b** = fuel oil. **3** = olive oil. **4** a substance that resembles oil in some respect. Sulfuric acid is called oil of vitriol. **5** = oil paint: *a landscape in oil.* **6** = oil painting: *The exhibition has more oils than water colors.*
—*v.t.* **1** to put oil on or in: *to oil the squeaky hinges of a door, to oil a tanker.* **SYN:** lubricate, grease. **2** *Informal, Figurative.* to bribe.
—*v.i.* to become oil: *Butter oils when heated.*
—*adj.* **1** of, having to do with, or for oil: *an oil filter, an oil pipeline.* **2** producing or supplying oil: *an oil company.* **3** containing or carrying oil: *an oil drum, an oil car.* **4** using oil as fuel: *an oil lamp.*

**burn the midnight oil,** to study or work late at night: *I cannot say that I burnt much midnight oil* (William Ballantine).

**pour oil on troubled waters,** to make things calm and peaceful: *The fight between the boys had become so fierce that the teacher had to come out to pour oil on troubled waters.*

**strike oil, a** to find oil by boring a hole in the earth: *He struck oil in Oklahoma.* **b** *Figurative.* to find something very profitable; succeed: *He has certainly struck oil in the ... loans* (Punch). *We are a nation which has struck oil* (James Russell Lowell).

[Middle English *olie, oyle* < Old North French *olie,* Old French *oille* < Latin *oleum* olive oil < Greek *élaion* oil]

**oil|bear|ing** (oil′bãr′ing), *adj.* containing or producing oil: *oilbearing rocks.*

**oil beetle,** a beetle that gives off an oily liquid when alarmed.

**oil|berg** (oil′bėrg′), *n.* an oil tanker with a capacity of 200,000 tons or more. [< *oil* + (ice)*berg*]

**oil|bird** (oil′bėrd′), *n.* = guacharo.

**oil|bug** (oil′bug′), *n.* = synura.

**oil burner,** a furnace, ship, manufacturer, or manufacturing plant or utility, that uses oil for fuel.

**oil cake,** a mass of cottonseed, linseed, coconut meat, or other residue, from which the oil has been pressed. Oil cakes are used as a food for cattle and sheep or as a fertilizer.

**oil can, 1** a can to hold oil. **2** a can with a narrow nozzle, used in lubricating machinery and moving parts.

**oil|cloth** (oil′klôth′, -kloth′), *n.* **1** a cloth made waterproof by coating it with paint or oil, used to cover tables, shelves, walls, or floors. **2** a piece of this cloth: *Mother bought a new oilcloth for the kitchen table.* **3** = oilskin.

**oil color, 1** a paint made by mixing pigment with oil; oil paint. **2** pigment that is ground in oil to make oil paint. **3** a painting done in such colors; oil painting.

**oil crop,** a crop, such as soybeans, cottonseed, peanuts, or coconuts, that supplies oil used in cooking and in making paints and other products.

**oil derrick,** a tall steel structure that holds the equipment used in drilling an oil well.

**oiled** (oild), *adj.* **1** saturated with oil so as to be waterproof: *oiled silk.* **2** *U.S. Slang.* drunk.

**oil|er** (oi′lər), *n.* **1** a person or thing that oils. **2** a can with a long spout used in oiling machinery; oil can. **3** *U.S. Informal.* an oilskin coat. **4** an oil tanker. **5** *U.S. Informal.* an oilman.

**oil field,** an area where significant deposits of petroleum have been found.

**oil-fired** (oil′fīrd′), *adj.* using oil as the fuel or source of heat.

**oil|fish** (oil′fish′), *n., pl.* **-fish|es** or (*collectively*) **-fish.** = escolar.

**oil gas,** any one of various hydrocarbon gases produced by heating oil vapor and steam: *The production of straight oil gas follows to some extent the process outlined for carbureted water gas* (H. Carl Wolf).

**oil gland, 1** = sebaceous gland. **2** = uropygial gland.

**oil|i|ly** (oi′lə lē), *adv.* in an oily manner.

**oil|i|ness** (oi′lē nis), *n.* oily quality or condition.

**oil lamp,** a lamp which uses kerosene or other oils as a fuel.

**oil|man** (oil′man′, -mən), *n., pl.* **-men.** an owner, administrator, worker, or other person engaged in the business of producing or selling oil: *U.S. oilmen are winning battles against imports, but can lose the war* (Wall Street Journal).

**oil nut, 1** any one of various nuts and seeds yielding oil, such as the buffalo nut, butternut, peanut, or castor bean. **2** any one of the plants producing them.

**oil of bergamot,** the greenish-yellow liquid with a strong, pleasant odor obtained from the rind of the bergamot, used in making perfumes.

**oil of cinnamon, 1** an oil used in perfumes and as a flavoring derived from the twigs and leaves of the cinnamon tree. **2** a somewhat similar oil derived from the twigs and leaves of the cassia tree; cassia oil.

**oil of ginger,** an aromatic oil of the ginger plant, used chiefly to season food and also as a medicine to relieve pain.

**oil of thuja,** an aromatic oil of an American species of thuja, used in medicine and in polishes.

**oil of turpentine,** a colorless, flammable, volatile oil made from turpentine, used in mixing paints.

**oil of vitriol,** = sulfuric acid.

**oil of wintergreen,** a heavy, volatile oil of the wintergreen plant, used in medicine and as a flavoring.

**oil paint,** paint made by grinding or mixing a pigment with oil.

**oil painting, 1** a picture painted with oil colors, usually on canvas. **2** the art or action of painting with oil colors.

**oil palm,** an African palm whose fruit and seeds yield palm oil.

**oil pan,** a detachable metal housing of an engine containing the lubricating oil.

**oil|pa|per** (oil′pā′pər), *n.* paper oiled to make it transparent and waterproof.

**oil pool,** a reservoir of accumulated petroleum in the pores of sedimentary rock.

**oil press,** an apparatus for expressing oil, as from fruits or seeds.

**oil|proof** (oil′prüf′), *adj., v.* —*adj.* resistant to oil: *A new treatment for cotton fabric made it ... waterproof, oilproof, and resistant to heat and rot* (Science News Letter).
—*v.t.* to make oilproof.

**oil sand,** any sandstone or rock that yields oil: *Oil may be obtained through underground nuclear explosions from two untapped sources, oil sands and tar sands* (Science News Letter).

**oil seal,** a device packed with material impermeable by oil, used to prevent leakage of oil, as in a machine.

**oil|seed** (oil′sēd′), *n.* any seed that yields oil, such as peanut, coconut, soybean, and cottonseed, especially the seed of an East Indian composite plant whose oil is used for lamps and as a condiment.

**oil shale,** shale containing kerogen, that yields oil upon distillation in the absence of air: *One of the largest potential reserves of oil in the world is that locked up in oil shale* (New Scientist).

***oil|skin** (oil′skin′), *n.* a cloth treated with oil to make it waterproof; oilcloth.
**oilskins,** a coat and trousers made of this cloth: *There were two men at the wheel in yellow oilskins* (Clark Russell).

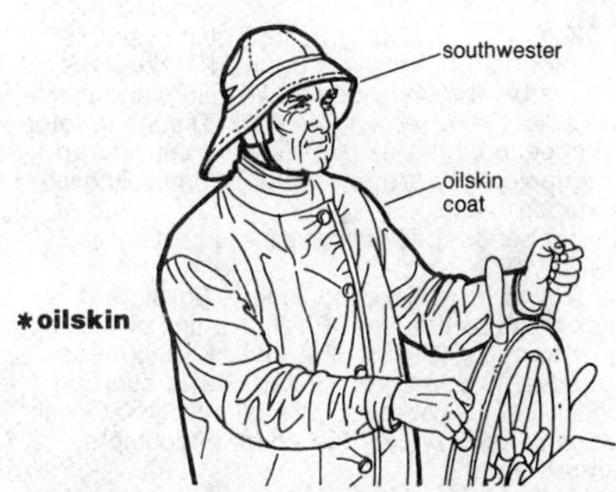

***oilskin**

**oil|skinned** (oil′skind′), *adj.* dressed in oilskins: *oilskinned men on the deck of a fishing schooner.*

**oil slick, 1** a smooth place on the surface of water caused by the presence of oil. **2** the oil covering such an area.

**oil|stone** (oil′stōn′), *n.* a fine-grained stone which is oiled and used for sharpening tools.

**oil stove,** a stove using kerosene, naphtha, or similar oil for fuel.

**oil switch,** an electric switch whose contacts move in oil to prevent sparking.

**oil tanker,** a ship with special tanks for transporting oil.

**oil well,** a well drilled in the earth to get oil.

**oil|y** (oi′lē), *adj.,* **oil|i|er, oil|i|est. 1** of oil: *an oily smell.* **2** containing oil: *an oily salad dressing.* **3** covered or soaked with oil: *oily rags. He mopped his oily pate* (Robert Browning). **4** like oil; smooth; slippery. **5** *Figurative.* too smooth; smooth in a suspicious or disagreeable way: *an oily smile. He has an oily manner.* **SYN:** unctuous.

**oink** (oingk), *n.,v.* —*n.* **1** the sound a hog makes. **2** a sound resembling or imitating this; grunt.
—*v.i.* to make the sound that a hog makes, or one resembling it.

**oi|noch|o|e** (oi nok′ō ē), *n.* a pitcherlike vessel with a three-lobed rim, used in ancient Greece for dipping wine from the crater or bowl and

**Pronunciation Key:** hat, āge, cãre, fär; let, ēqual, tėrm; it, īce; hot, ōpen, ôrder; **oil, out;** cup, pu̇t, rüle; **ch**ild; lo**ng**; **th**in; **ᴛʜ**en; **zh,** measure; ə represents **a** in about, **e** in taken, **i** in pencil, **o** in lemon, **u** in circus.

pouring it into the drinking cups. [< Greek *oino-chóē* < *oînos* wine + *chéin* pour]

**oint|ment** (oint′mənt), *n.* a substance made from oil or fat, often containing medicine, used on the skin to heal, soothe, or beautify, or to make it soft. Cold cream and salve are ointments. SYN: unguent, salve, balm. [Middle English *oignement* < Old French < *oindre* anoint < Latin *unguere;* influenced by English *anoint*]

**Oir|each|tas** (er′əᴴ thəs), *n.* the legislature of the Irish Republic. The lower house is called the Dail Eireann, and the upper house the Seanad Eireann. [< Irish *oireachtas* assembly]

**oi|ti|ci|ca** (oi′tə sē′kə), *n.* a South American tree of the rose family, whose seeds yield an oil used especially in paints and varnishes. [< a native word]

**o|jam** (ō′jəm), *n.* = galago.

**O|jib|wa** (ō jib′wā), *n., pl.* **-wa** or **-was. 1** a member of a large tribe of American Indians of Algonkian stock formerly living in the region of Lake Superior; Chippewa. **2** the language of these Indians. [American English < Algonkian (Ojibwa) *ojib* pucker up + *ub-way* roast (in reference to the puckered seam on their moccasins)]

**O|jib|way** (ō jib′wā), *n., pl.* **-way** or **-ways.** = Ojibwa.

**OJT** (no periods) or **O.J.T.**, on-the-job training.

**OK**[1] (no periods) or **O.K.** (ō′kā′), *adj., adv., interj., v.,* **OK'd, OK'ing** or **O.K.'d, O.K.'ing**; *n., pl.* **OK's** or **O.K.'s**. *Informal.* **—*adj.*** all right; correct; approved: *The new schedule was OK. Everyone agreed the seal was O.K.* (New York Times). *Rome ... is an O.K. city to work in* (Time). *Trouser-suited ladies are deemed OK* (Punch).
**—*adv.*** all right; well; fine: *The car turns over OK when cold* (Hot Rod).
**—*interj.*** all right: *OK, you can go if you come home before dark.*
**—*v.t.*** to put "OK" on to show that something is correct or has been approved; approve; endorse: *to OK a request for a loan. Barney grinned, "Pink has O.K.'d the article"* (John Stephen Strange).
**—*n.*** approval: *The foreman put his OK on the shipment. After she got Columbia's OK, they made the picture* (Saturday Evening Post).
[American English; apparently < the initial letters of "oll korrect," a phonetic respelling of *all correct*]
► **OK, O.K.** is generally accepted in business and informal English as a noun (*We need his OK*), verb (*Will you please OK this?*), and predicate adjective (*Her work is OK*). Though in informal speech all the uses of OK are considered acceptable, they are regarded in formal English as inappropriate.

**OK**[2] (no periods), Oklahoma (with postal Zip Code).

**o|ka** (ō′kə), *n.* in Greece, Turkey, Egypt, and other areas of the Near East: **1** a unit of weight, equal to about 2¾ lbs. **2** a unit of liquid measure, equal to about 1⅓ United States quarts. [< Turkish *okka* < Arabic *ūqiya*, ultimately < Greek *ounkiā* < Latin *uncia.* See etym. of doublets **ounce**[1], **inch**[1].]

**O|ka** (ō′kə), *n.* a cheese cured with brine and similar to Port du Salut, made by Trappist monks in Oka, a village in Quebec.

***o|ka|pi** (ō kä′pē), *n., pl.* **-pis** or **-pi.** an African mammal related to the giraffe and somewhat like it, but smaller, without spots, and with a much shorter neck. The okapi is a ruminant. [< a native word]

***okapi**

**o|kay, o|key,** or **o|keh** (ō′kā′), *adj., adv., interj., v.t., n. Informal.* = OK: *I muttered, "Okay," not feeling very sure that I could survive two hours of Devon* (Guy Endore). [American English; spelling for pronunciation of *O.K.*]

**oke** (ōk), *n.* = oka.

**o|key-doke** (ō′kē dōk′), *adj., adv., interj. Informal.* = OK: *"Okey-doke," he said indifferently. "It's your money, not mine"* (S. J. Perelman). [short for *okey-dokey*]

**o|key-do|key** (ō′kē dō kē), *adj., adv., interj. Informal.* = OK. [reduplication of *okeh*]

**O|kie** (ō′kē), *n.* **1** *U.S. Informal.* a migratory farmworker, originally one from Oklahoma, who wandered from place to place in search of work during the depression of the 1930's: *Okies—the owners hated them because the owners knew they were soft and the Okies strong, that they were fed and the Okies hungry* (John Steinbeck). **2** a person born or living in Oklahoma. Also, **Oakie.** [American English < *Ok*(lahoma) + *-ie*]

**O|ki|na|wan** (ō′kə nä′wən), *adj., n.* **—*adj.*** of or having to do with Okinawa, an island in the western Pacific, or its people.
**—*n.*** a native or inhabitant of Okinawa.

**Okla.,** Oklahoma.

**O|kla|ho|man** (ō′klə hō′mən), *adj., n.* **—*adj.*** of or having to do with Oklahoma.
**—*n.*** a native or inhabitant of Oklahoma.

**o|ko|le|hao** (ō′kə lā hou′), *n. Hawaiian.* an alcoholic liquor usually distilled from the root of the ti palm. Other ingredients sometimes used are rice, pineapple, and molasses. *Okolehao [is] a powerful spirit that resembles whisky in color and transparency* (New York Times).

**o|kou|mé** (ō′kə mā′), *n.* **1** a softwood used for veneer and plywood, produced in Gabon and the Congo. **2** the tree yielding this wood. [< French *okoumé* < a native name in Gabon]

**o|kra** (ō′krə), *n.* **1** a tall plant with sticky green pods, which are used in soups and as a vegetable; gumbo. Okra belongs to the mallow family and is grown especially in the southern United States. See picture under **mallow family. 2** the pods. **3** a stew or soup made with okra pods; gumbo. [< a West African word]

**o|kro** (ō′krō), *n. U.S. Dialect.* okra.

**O|kun's law** (ō′kənz), *U.S. Economics.* a formula that shows the correlation between the rate of unemployment and the gross national product. Okun's law indicates how much unemployment will rise for every $1-billion decline in the gross national product. [< Arthur M. *Okun,* born 1928, an American economist]

**-ol**[1], *suffix.* **1** containing, derived from, or like alcohol, as in *carbinol, phenol.*
**2** the phenols and phenol derivatives as in *thymol.* [< (alcoh)*ol*]

**-ol**[2], *suffix.* a variant of **-ole**, as in *terpinol.*

**OL** (no periods), **O.L.**, or **OL.**, Old Latin.

**old** (ōld), *adj.,* **old|er** or **eld|er, old|est** or **eld|est,** *n.* **—*adj.*** **1** not young; having been for some time; aged: *an old man. An old wall surrounds the castle. We are old friends.* **2** of age; in age: *The baby is one year old.* **3** not new; not recent: *an old debt, an old excuse, an old custom, an old family.* **4** belonging to the past; dating far back; ancient: *old countries, an old tomb.*
**5** much worn by age or use: *old clothes. Neither do men put new wine into old bottles; else the bottles break* (Matthew 9:17). *Your fooling grows old, and people dislike it* (Shakespeare). SYN: dilapidated, decayed, shabby, outworn. **6** that seems old; like an old person in some way; mature: *That child is old for her years.* **7** *Figurative.* having much experience: *to be old in wrongdoing* SYN: experienced, practiced. **8** former: *the old days before the war. An old student came back to visit his teacher.* **9 Old,** earlier or earliest: *Old English, the Old Testament.* **10** familiar; dear: *a good old fellow.* **11** *Informal.* good; fine; splendid: *We had a high old time at the party.* **12** (of topographical features) well advanced in the process of erosion to base level.
**—*n.*** the time long ago; earlier or ancient time; the past: *the heroes of old. Of old hast thou laid the foundation of the earth* (Psalms 102:25).
**the old,** old people: *a home for the old.*
[Old English *ald, eald*] **—old′ness,** *n.*
**—*Syn.*** *adj.* **1 Old, elderly, aged** mean having lived a long time. **Old** means advanced in years and near the end of life: *Grandmother is old, almost ninety, but she is hale and hearty.* **Elderly** means past middle age and getting old and frequently suggests a certain dignity and stateliness: *Elderly people have little interest in participating in vigorous sports.* **Aged** means very old and has a strong connotation of infirmity or even senility: *An aged woman sat mumbling by the fire.*
► See **elder** for usage note.

**old age,** the years of life from about 65 on in human beings. **—old′-age′,** *adj.*

**old-age pension** (ōld′āj′), a pension paid to retired employees or their beneficiaries, the cost of which is either shared by the pensioner and the administrator of the pension or financed entirely by the employer.

**Old Arabic,** the earliest form of Arabic, used from about the 100's A.D. to the 600's.

**old bean,** *British Slang.* old fellow; old man (as a familiar form of address): *The child of two and a half years ... addressed her learned parent as "old bean"* (Punch)..

**Old Believer,** a dissenter from the Russian Church; Raskolnik: *Old Believers ... split from the Russian Orthodox Church in the 17th century* (New York Times).

**old Bogy,** = the Devil.

**old boy, 1** old man. **2** Often, **Old Boy.** *Especially British Informal.* an alumnus, especially of a private boarding school for boys. **3** the Devil (a humorous use).

**old boy net,** *British.* old boy network: *The chairs are allocated on the old boy net years in advance* (New Scientist).

**old boy network,** *British.* a system of mutual exchange of favors, desirable positions, and the like, supposedly existing among the alumni of exclusive, class-oriented private schools, especially in Great Britain: *Nepotism and the old boy network still hamper progress toward meritocratic rule in the Civil Service, industry, commerce, and finance* (Punch).

**Old Bulgarian,** = Old Church Slavic.

**Old Catholics,** an independent church organization that developed from a party formed in the Roman Catholic Church in 1870 in opposition to the dogma of papal infallibility.

**old chum,** (in Australia) an old and experienced settler.

**Old Church Slavic** or **Slavonic,** a Slavic language preserved in Russian Orthodox religious texts of the 800's and 900's, and still used in the liturgy of some Orthodox Churches; Old Bulgarian.

**old-clothes-man** (ōld′klōz′man, -klōᴛʜz′-), *n., pl.* **-men.** a dealer in old or second-hand clothes.

**old country,** the country an immigrant comes from, especially a country of Europe.

**Old Dominion,** a nickname for Virginia.

**olde** (ōld), *adj.* = old.
► This archaic spelling is used for humorous, nostalgic, or eye-catching effect: ... *travelogue shots of Olde England* (Time).

**old|en**[1] (ōl′dən), *adj.* of old; old; ancient: *King Arthur lived in olden times of knights and armor. ... islands which the olden voyages had so glowingly described* (Herman Melville). SYN: bygone. [< *old* + *-en*[2]]

**old|en**[2] (ōl′dən), *v.i.* to grow old; age: *In six weeks he oldened more time than he had done for fifteen years before* (Thackeray).
**—*v.t.*** to cause to grow or appear old. [< *old* + *-en*[1]]

**Old English, 1** the period in the history of the English language and literature before A.D. 1100. **2** the language of this period; Anglo-Saxon. *Abbr:* OE (no periods). **3** *Printing.* a kind of black-letter type.

**Old English sheepdog,** any one of a breed of English working dogs having a long, shaggy, blue or gray coat, often with white markings, docked tail, and standing about 22 inches high.

**old|fan|gled** (ōld′fang′gəld), *adj.* = old-fashioned. [patterned on *newfangled*]

**old-fash|ioned** (ōld′fash′ənd), *adj.* **1** of an old fashion; out of fashion: *an old-fashioned dress. The writing was old-fashioned and rather uncertain, like that of an elderly lady* (Charlotte Brontë). SYN: out-of-date, fusty. **2** keeping to old ways or ideas: *an old-fashioned housekeeper.* **3** (of a child) old or mature in ways, thoughts, or speech: *"Oh! the old-fashioned little soul!" cried Mrs. Blimber* (Dickens). **—old′-fash′ioned|ly,** *adv.*

**old fashioned,** a cocktail made of whiskey, sugar, and bitters with a slice of orange and a cherry, mixed with soda and served cold.

**old fogy** or **fogey,** an old-fashioned or very conservative person.

**old-fo|gy** or **old-fo|gey** (ōld′fō′gē), *adj.* out-of-date; behind the times.

**old-fo|gy|ish** or **old-fo|gey|ish** (ōld′fō′gē ish), *adj.* = old-fogy.

**old-fo|gy|ism** or **old-fo|gey|ism** (ōld′fō′gē izəm), *n.* the ideas or behavior characteristic of old fogies; old-fashioned ways.

**old folks, 1** old or aged people. **2** persons of an older generation in a family, such as the parents: *The old folks encouraged me by continual invitations to supper, and by leaving us together* (Benjamin Franklin).

**Old French,** the French language from about 800 A.D. to about 1400. *Abbr:* OF (no periods).

**old gentleman,** = the Devil.

**Old Glory,** the flag of the United States; Stars and Stripes.

**old gold,** a dull-gold color; soft, rich yellow that is nearly brown.

**old-gold** (ōld′gōld′), *adj.* of the color old gold; dull-gold.

**Old Guard, 1** a very conservative section of the Republican Party of the United States: *The Republican National Committee ... remained an Old Guard stronghold even after Mr. Eisenhower's election* (Newsweek). **2** Also, **old guard.** the conservative members, as of a country, community, or organization. [translation of French *Vieille Garde* (of Napoleon I)]

**old hand**, **1** a very skilled or experienced person; expert: *an old hand at selling, an old hand at swimming.* **2** (in Australia) an ex-convict. —**old′-hand′**, *adj.*

**Old Harry**, = the Devil.

**old hat**, **1** out-of-date; old-fashioned. **2** familiar; well-known.

**Old High German**, the form of the German language used in southern Germany from about 800 A.D. to 1100. Modern standard German is descended from Old High German. *Abbr:* OHG (no periods).

**Old Icelandic**, the Icelandic language of the Middle Ages; Old Norse.

**old identity**, (in Australia) a well-known, long-time resident of a place.

**old|ie** (ōl′dē), *n. Informal.* something old and, often, well-known, as a motion picture or song. Also, **oldy**.

**Old Ionic**, the form of the Greek language spoken in the time of Homer. The *Iliad* and *Odyssey* were written in Old Ionic.

**Old Irish**, the Irish language before A.D. 1200.

**Old Ironsides**, the American frigate *Constitution,* famous for its exploits in the War of 1812; subject of Oliver Wendell Holmes' poem "Old Ironsides."

**old|ish** (ōl′dish), *adj.* somewhat old; no longer young: *I'm getting an oldish man* (Arnold Bennett).

**old lady**, **1** a familiar term for a mother or wife. **2** *Figurative.* a prim, fussy person.

**old lag**, *British.* a person who has been convicted more than once: ... *a semi-security centre for old lags regarded as past the escaping age* (Sunday Times).

**Old Latin**, the Latin language before the 100's B.C.

**Old Left**, the leftist movement, predominantly Marxist in ideology, that represented the radical element in politics before the emergence of the New Left: *The Old Left organized and proselyted, playing its part in bringing about the American welfare state.*

**Old Leftist**, a member of the Old Left.

**old-line** (ōld′līn′), *adj.* **1** keeping to old ideas and ways; conservative: *an old-line banker.* **2** having a long history; established: *an old-line company.* **3** of an old family or lineage. [American English, perhaps < the *Old-line* regiments, which Maryland contributed in the American Revolutionary War]

**old-lin|er** (ōld′lī′nər), *n.* an advocate of old or traditional ideas or policies; conservative: ... *the straight old-liners, some of them men of fossilized ideas* (Harper's).

**Old Line State**, a nickname for Maryland.

**Old Low German**, the form of the German language used in northern Germany and the Netherlands from about 800 A.D. to 1100. Modern Low German is descended from Old Low German.

**old maid**, **1** a woman who has not married and seems unlikely to. **SYN**: spinster. **2** *Figurative.* a prim, fussy person. **3** a simple card game for children in which players draw cards from each other's hands to make pairs. The player holding the extra queen at the end of the game loses.

**old-maid|ish** (ōld′mā′dish), *adj.* like, suggesting, or befitting an old maid; prim; fussy. **SYN**: spinsterish.

**old man**, **1** a familiar term of affection. **2** a familiar term for a father or husband: *His old man and his uncles also wore the "tools of ignorance"* (Time). **3** a familiar term for the man in charge of anything, such as a school principal, captain of a ship, or commander of a military unit.

**Old Man of the Sea**, **1** *Greek Mythology.* a name given to Nereus, father of the fifty Nereids. **2** (in *The Arabian Nights*) a horrible old man who clung to the back of Sinbad. **3** a person or thing that is hard to get rid of.

**old-man's-beard** (ōld′manz′bird′), *n.,* or **old-man's beard**. **1** = beard lichen. **2** = fringe tree. **3** *British.* a European clematis with fragrant, greenish-white flowers.

**old master**, **1** any great painter who lived before 1700: *About suffering they were never wrong, The Old Masters: how well they understood Its human position* (W. H. Auden). **2** a painting by such a painter.

**old moon**, the moon when seen as a thin crescent with the hollow side on the right.

**Old Nick**, = the Devil: *"Old Nick" (Niccolò Machiavelli) became in English a synonym for the Devil* (Mary McCarthy).

**Old Norse**, **1** the Scandinavian language from the Viking period to about 1300. **2** the Icelandic language in the Middle Ages; Old Icelandic. *Abbr:* ON (no periods).

**Old North French**, the dialects of northern France from the 800's A.D. to the 1500's, especially those of Normandy and Picardy.

**Old North State**, a nickname of North Carolina.

**Old One**, = the Devil.

**Ol|do|wan** (ol′də wən, ōl′-), *adj.* of or having to do with a pebble culture of eastern Africa that preceded the Abbevillean and Acheulian cultures, represented by tools discovered in Olduvai Gorge, Tanzania; Olduvai. Also, **Olduwan**.

**Old Persian**, an ancient Iranian language, recorded in cuneiform inscriptions.

**old process**, the process for making corn meal by grinding whole corn between rotating stones.

**Old Provençal**, the form of Provençal from about the 1000's A.D. to the 1500's.

**Old Prussian**, an extinct Baltic language preserved in records of the 1400's and 1500's.

**Old Regime**, = ancien régime.

**old rose**, a rose color with a purplish or grayish tinge.

**old-rose** (ōld′rōz′), *adj.* of the color old rose.

**old salt**, an old and experienced sailor.

**Old Saxon**, the form of Low German spoken by the Saxons in northwestern Germany from about 800 A.D. to about 1100.

**old school**, a group of people who have old-fashioned or conservative ideas: *a doctor of the old school, a lady of the old school.*

**old-school** (ōld′skül′), *adj.* old-fashioned or conservative: *old-school attitudes.*

**old school tie**, **1** loyalty among members of a group, especially among graduates of the same school or college. **2** a necktie worn by members of a group, as a sign of their association and loyalty.

**old-shoe** (ōld′shü′), *adj. U.S.* pleasantly casual; informal: *Buchwald's manner is so ingenuous and old-shoe that the subjects of his interviews are soon disarmed into chattering away like old friends* (Time).

**old sledge**, the card game seven-up.

**Old South**, *U.S.* the South or its ways of life before the Civil War: *The region south of Baltimore resembles the Old South* (Francis C. Haber).

**Old Spanish**, the Spanish language from the 1100's A.D. to the 1500's.

**old squaw**, a long-tailed sea duck of northern regions.

**old stager**, a person of long experience; veteran; old hand.

**old|ster** (ōld′stər), *n. Informal.* **1** an old or older person: *The discreet and sober conversation of the oldsters was much disturbed by the loud laughter of the younger folks* (Henry Kingsley). **2** (in the British Navy) a midshipman with four years in grade. [< *old* + *-ster,* as in *youngster*]

**Old Stone Age**, the Paleolithic.

**old story**, **1** a story long told or often repeated; something that has lost all its novelty: *Airplanes are an old story to them. You must find the trip quite an old story.* **2** a statement, excuse, complaint, or the like, that is repeatedly heard, or a thing that is repeatedly encountered.

**old stuff**, *Informal.* familiar; well-known: *To the sophisticated grade-schooler now happily on the verge of leaving classroom routine behind, returning to the fold next fall will be old stuff* (New York Times).

**old style**, a kind of type, such as Garamond or Caslon, characterized by slanting serifs and strokes of almost equal thickness.

**old-style** (ōld′stīl′), *adj.* of or in old style.

**Old Style**, the method of reckoning time according to the Julian calendar, replaced by the New Style in most European countries in 1582, when the date was moved ahead 10 days. In Great Britain the Old Style calendar was used until 1752, when all dates were moved ahead 11 days. It was used in Russia until 1918. *Abbr:* O.S.

**Old Test.**, Old Testament.

**Old Testament**, **1** the earlier and larger part of the Bible, which contains the religious and social laws of the Hebrews, a record of their history, their important literature, and writings of their prophets. *Abbr:* O.T. **2** the covenant between God and the Hebrew people established through Moses on Mount Sinai (in the Bible, Exodus 19:5).

**old thing**, *British Informal.* a familiar form of address used to a person: *By-bye, old thing* (Arnold Bennett).

**old-time** (ōld′tīm′), *adj.* of former times; like old times: *old-time religion.*

**old-tim|er** (ōld′tī′mər), *n. Informal.* **1** a person who has long been a resident, member, worker, or other associate, and whose experience goes back to an earlier day. **2** a person who favors old ideas and ways.

**old-times** (ōld′tīmz′), *adj.* = old-time.

**old-tim|ey** (ōld′tī′mē), *adj. Informal.* **1** old-time: *an old-timey looking dress.* **2** from the old days; veteran.

**old top**, *British Informal.* a familiar form of address used to a person.

**old tuberculin**, tuberculin prepared by heating, filtering, and concentrating a broth medium on which tubercle bacilli have been grown.

**Ol|du|vai** (ol′də vā, -wā; ōl′-), *adj.* = Oldowan.

**Ol|du|wan** (ol′də wən, ōl′-), *adj.* = Oldowan.

**Old Welsh**, the Welsh language before A.D. 1200.

**old|wife** (ōld′wīf′), *n., pl.* **-wives**, or **old wife**, **1** any one of various fishes, such as the alewife, menhaden, and certain triggerfish. **2** = old squaw. [(def. 1) probably variant of *alewife*]

**old wives' summer** or **Old Wives' Summer**, a warm period in autumn in Europe, similar to Indian summer. [translation of German *Altweibersommer*]

**old wives' tale**, a foolish story; silly or superstitious belief: *This [body of anthropological fact] came from travelers, missionaries, and soldiers, and formed a collection in which careful and precise description was often combined with folklore and old wives' tales* (Beals and Hoijer).

**old woman**, **1** a familiar term for a mother or wife. **2** *Figurative.* a fussy, worrisome person.

**old-wom|an|ish** (ōld′wům′ə nish), *adj.* suggesting or befitting an old woman; fussy.

**old-world** (ōld′wėrld′), *adj.* **1** Also, **Old-World.** of or having to do with the Eastern Hemisphere; not of the New World; not American: *old-world monkeys, old-world folk songs.* **2** belonging to or characteristic of a former period: *old-world courtesy.* **3** of or having to do with the ancient world: *The mammoth was an old-world elephant.* —**old′-world′ly**, *adv.*

**Old World**, Europe, Asia, Africa, and Australia; Eastern Hemisphere.

**old|y** (ōl′dē), *n., pl.* **old|ies**. = oldie.

**ole**[1] (ōl), *adj. U.S. Informal.* old (used to suggest a nonstandard, especially Southern, pronunciation): *He looks conservative—"just a good ole country boy," as one of his constituents described him* (John Fischer).

**o|lé** or **o|le**[2] (ō lā′, ō′lā), *interj. Spanish.* a cheer of enthusiasm or approval.

**-ole**, *suffix.* **1** containing a five-part ring, as in *pyrrole.*
**2** belonging to the ethers or aldehydes, as in *anethole.* Also, **-ol.**
[short for Latin *oleum* oil]

**o|le|a|ceous** (ō′lē ā′shəs), *adj.* belonging to the olive family of plants, including the ash and jasmine. [< New Latin *Oleaceae* the family (< Latin *olea* olive tree, alteration of *olīva* olive) + English *-ous*]

**o|le|ag|i|nous** (ō′lē aj′ə nəs), *adj.* **1** having the nature or properties of oil; oily; greasy: ... *the oleaginous scum that pollutes the surface of a city river* (Mary E. Braddon). **2** *Figurative.* unctuous: *an oleaginous hypocrite.* [< Latin *oleāginus* (with English *-ous*) of the olive < *olea* olive, alteration of *olīva* olive] —**o′le|ag′i|nous|ness**, *n.*

**o|le|ag|i|nous|ly** (ō′lē aj′ə nəs lē), *adv.* in an oleaginous manner: (*Figurative.*) *Anyone who tried to play Uriah Heep importantly would miss the essence of an oleaginously obsequious character* (Harper's).

**o|le|an|der** (ō′lē an′dər), *n.* a poisonous evergreen shrub with fragrant red, pink, white, or purple flowers. It belongs to the dogbane family. See picture under **dogbane family**. [< Medieval Latin *oleander,* origin uncertain]

**o|le|an|do|my|cin** (ō′lē an′də mī′sin), *n.* an antibiotic used in treating infections caused by bacteria, viruses, and other microorganisms, especially those immune to other antibiotics. *Formula:* $C_{35}H_{63}NO_{12}$

**o|le|as|ter** (ō′lē as′tər), *n.* **1** a shrub or small tree of southern Europe and western Asia, having fragrant yellow flowers and yellowish olivelike fruit. **2** the wild form of the olive. [< Latin *oleaster* < *olea* olive tree + *-aster,* a diminutive suffix]

**o|le|ate** (ō′lē āt), *n.* a salt or ester of oleic acid. [< *ole*(ic) + *-ate*[2]]

**o|lec|ra|non** (ō lek′rə non, ō′lə krā′-), *n.* a part of the ulna that forms the point of the elbow. [< Greek *ōlékrānon* point of the elbow, short for *ōlenókrānon* < *ōlénē* elbow + *krānion* head]

**o|le|fin** (ō′lə fin), *n.* one of a series of hydrocarbons homologous with ethylene, having the general formula $C_nH_{2n}$, which form with bromine and chlorine oily bromides and chlorides. [< French (*gaz*) *oléfiant* oil-forming (gas), ethylene + English *-in*]

**o|le|ic** (ō lē′ik, ō′lē-), *adj.* of or derived from oil.

**oleic acid**, an oily, unsaturated acid obtained by hydrolyzing various animal and vegetable oils and fats, much used in making soaps. *Formula:*

---

**Pronunciation Key:** hat, āge, cãre, fär; let, ēqual, tėrm; it, īce; hot, ōpen, ôrder; **oi**l, **ou**t; cup, pu̇t, rüle; **ch**ild; lo**ng**; **th**in; **ꟍ**en; **zh**, measure; **ə** represents **a** in about, **e** in taken, **i** in pencil, **o** in lemon, **u** in circus.

$C_{18}H_{34}O_2$ [< Latin *oleum* (olive) oil (< *olea* olive, alteration of *olīva*) + English *-ic*]

**o|le|in** (ō′lē in), *n.* **1** the ester of oleic acid and glycerin, one of the most abundant natural fats. Lard, olive oil, and cottonseed oil are mostly olein. *Formula:* $C_{57}H_{104}O_6$ **2a** the liquid or lower melting portions of any fat. **b** = oleic acid. [< Latin *oleum* (olive) oil + English *-in*]

**o|le|ine** (ō′lē in, -ēn), *n.* **1** the liquid part of any fat; olein. **2** = oleic acid.

**o|le|o** (ō′lē ō), *n.* **1** = oleomargarine. **2** = oleo oil. **3** = oleograph: ... *a painted Christ in a blue and pink oleo* (Time).

**o|le|o|graph** (ō′lē ə graf, -gräf), *n.* a chromolithograph made to look like an oil painting. [< Latin *oleum* oil + English *-graph*]

**o|le|o|graph|ic** (ō′lē ə graf′ik), *adj.* of or having to do with oleography. —**o′le|o|graph′i|cal|ly,** *adv.*

**o|le|og|ra|phy** (ō′lē og′rə fē), *n.* the art or process of preparing oleographs.

**o|le|o|mar|ga|rin** (ō′lē ō mär′jər in, -gər-), *n.* = oleomargarine.

**o|le|o|mar|ga|rine** (ō′lē ō mär′jər in, -jə rēn; -gər-in, -gə rēn), *n.* a substitute for butter made from animal fats and vegetable oils or from pure vegetable oils; margarine. [American English < French *oléo-margarine* < *oléine* olein + *margarine* margarine (the original substance was thought to be a compound of these two)]

**o|le|om|e|ter** (ō′lē om′ə tər), *n.* a hydrometer for testing the purity of an oil by means of its density. [< Latin *oleum* oil + English *-meter*]

**oleo oil,** *U.S.* oil obtained by pressing beef fat, used for making substitutes for butter.

**o|le|o|phil|ic** (ō′lē ō fil′ik), *adj.* attracting oil to itself: *Sawdust treated with appropriate silicones is water-repellent but strongly oleophilic and will soak up many times its weight of oil* (Science Journal).

**o|le|o|res|in** (ō′lē ō rez′ən), *n.* a natural or prepared mixture of resin in oil, such as that obtained from a plant by means of a volatile solvent. [< Latin *oleum* oil + English *resin*]

**o|le|o|res|in|ous** (ō′lē ō rez′ə nəs), *adj.* **1** of, like, or containing an oleoresin. **2** consisting of a mixture of resins and drying oils heated and dissolved in turpentine or petroleum products: *Spar varnish is an oleoresinous varnish.*

**ol|er|a|ceous** (ol′ə rā′shəs), *adj.* of or like a potherb or vegetable. [< Latin *holerāceus* (with English *-ous*) < *holus, -eris* potherb]

**ol|er|i|cul|ture** (ol′ər ə kul′chər), *n.* the raising of potherbs and vegetables. [< Latin *holus, -eris* potherb + *cultūra* culture]

**o|le|threu|tid** (ō′lə thrü′tid), *adj.* of or belonging to the family of moths that includes the peach moth and the codling moth. [< New Latin *Olethreutidae* the family name < Greek *olethreúein* to destroy < *ólethros* destruction]

**o|le|um** (ō′lē əm), *n.* a solution of sulfur trioxide and concentrated sulfuric acid, used in dyes and explosives and as an agent in chemical processes. [< New Latin *oleum* < Latin, oil]

**O level,** *British.* the ordinary level, lowest of three levels of examination given to secondary school students who wish to obtain a General Certificate of Education.

**ol|fac|tion** (ol fak′shən), *n.* **1** the act of smelling. **2** the sense of smell. [< obsolete verb *olfact* (< Latin *olfactus,* past participle *olfacere* smell out, detect < *olēre* emit a smell + *facere* make) + *-ion*]

**ol|fac|tive** (ol fak′tiv), *adj.* = olfactory.

**ol|fac|tom|e|ter** (ol′fak tom′ə tər), *n.* an instrument for measuring the acuteness of the sense of smell. [< *olfact*(ion) + *-meter*]

**ol|fac|to|ri|ly** (ol fak′tər ə lē, -trə lē), *adv.* with respect to smell; in an olfactory sense: *Colorful but olfactorily dull plants such as daffodils and tulips* ... (London Times).

**ol|fac|to|ry** (ol fak′tər ē, -trē), *adj., n., pl.* **-ries.** —*adj.* of smell; having to do with smelling. The nose is an olfactory organ. *Olfactory stimuli are important in regulating the social behavior of many fishes and mammals* (George W. Barlow). ... *holding a book in close contiguity to her nose, as if with the hope of gaining an olfactory acquaintance with its contents* (Hawthorne).
—*n.* **olfactories, a** an olfactory organ. **b** the ability to smell.
[< Latin *olfactōrius* < *olfacere;* see etym. under **olfaction**]

**olfactory bulb,** the enlarged distal end of the olfactory lobe. It is the point at which the olfactory nerve begins.

**olfactory lobe,** a lobe on the lower surface of the brain's frontal lobe, responsible for the sense of smell. The olfactory lobe is better developed in many animals than in man.

**olfactory nerve,** the first cranial nerve, a sensory nerve that carries the sensation of smell from the mucous membranes of the nose to the olfactory lobe of the brain.

**ol|fac|tron|ic** (ol′fak tron′ik), *adj.* of or having to do with olfactronics: *Another aspect of the olfactronic approach to detecting sources through their airborne signatures is the variety of possible ways in which this can be done* (New Scientist).

**ol|fac|tron|ics** (ol′fak tron′iks), *n.* the use of electronic instruments to detect and identify anything by its odor: *Eventually olfactronics may be used to guard bank vaults against burglars* (New York Times). [< *olfac*(tory) (elec)*tronics*]

**o|lib|a|num** (ō lib′ə nəm), *n.* = frankincense. [< Medieval Latin *olibanum,* alteration of Late Latin *libanus* frankincense < Greek *líbanos* fragrant gum, the gum-tree]

**olig-,** *combining form.* the form of **oligo-** before vowels, as in *oligarch.*

**ol|i|garch** (ol′ə gärk), *n.* one of the rulers in an oligarchy. [< Greek *oligárchēs* < *olígos* few + *árchein* to rule < *archós* leader]

**ol|i|gar|chic** (ol′ə gär′kik), *adj.* of an oligarchy or oligarchs; having to do with rule by few: *In autocratic or oligarchic societies* ... *the moral and intellectual flabbiness of only a few men in the seats of power will lead to the disintegration of great empires* (Harper's). —**ol′i|gar′chi|cal|ly,** *adv.*

**ol|i|gar|chi|cal** (ol′ə gär′kə kəl), *adj.* = oligarchic.

**ol|i|gar|chy** (ol′ə gär′kē), *n., pl.* **-chies. 1** a form of government in which a few people have the ruling power: *The Pilgrims at Plymouth Colony were governed by a Puritan oligarchy.* **2** a country or state having such a government: *Most ancient Greek city-states were classic examples of oligarchies* (William Ebenstein). **3** the ruling few. **4** any organization, such as a business or a church, having an administration controlled by a few people. [< Greek *oligarchíā,* ultimately < *olígos* few + *árchein* to rule < *archós* leader]

**oligo-,** *combining form.* small; little; few: *Oligochrome = a design in few colors.* Also, **olig-** before vowels. [< Greek *olígos* few]

**Ol|i|go|cene** (ol′ə gō sēn), *n., adj.* —*n.* **1** the third epoch of the Tertiary period of the Cenozoic era, after the Eocene and before the Miocene, during which the first apes appeared and modern mammals became dominant. **2** the series of rocks formed in this epoch.
—*adj.* of this epoch or these rocks.
[< *oligo-* + Greek *kainós* new, recent]

**ol|i|go|chaete** (ol′ə gō kēt), *n.* any one of a group of hermaphroditic annelid worms, such as the earthworms and various aquatic groups, having only a few setae projecting from each body segment, and lacking a distinct head. [< New Latin *Oligochaeta* < Greek *olígos* few + *chaítē* bristle]

**ol|i|go|chae|tous** (ol′ə gō kē′təs), *adj.* having the character of the oligochaetes.

**ol|i|go|chrome** (ol′ə gō krōm), *adj., n.* —*adj.* painted or done in few colors, as decorative work.
—*n.* a design in a few colors.

**ol|i|go|clase** (ol′ə gō klās), *n.* a feldspar containing sodium and calcium, occurring in light gray, yellow, or greenish crystals. [< *oligo-* + Greek *klásis* a breaking (because it was thought to be less perfect in cleavage than albite, another feldspar)]

**ol|i|go|cy|the|mi|a** or **ol|i|go|cy|thae|mi|a** (ol′ə-gō sī thē′mē ə), *n.* a form of anemia characterized by a deficiency of red cells in the blood. [< New Latin *oligocythaemia* < Greek *olígos* few + *kýtos* hollow + *haîma* blood]

**o|lig|o|mer** (ə lig′ə mər), *n.* a chemical compound with few molecular units, in contrast with a polymer or a monomer. [< *oligo-* + *-mer,* as in *polymer*]

**o|lig|o|mer|ic** (ə lig′ə mer′ik), *adj.* of or characteristic of an oligomer: *Most enzymes are* ... *composed of a small number of protein sub-units associated together. This oligomeric structure is useful in allowing certain control functions to operate* (New Scientist).

**ol|i|go|my|cin** (ol′ə gə mī′sin), *n.* either of three related antibiotics obtained from an actinomycete, used in treating various fungous diseases of animals and plants. [< *oligo-* + *mycin,* as in *streptomycin*]

**ol|ig|o|nu|cle|o|tide** (ol′ə gō nü′klē ō tīd, -nyü′-; -tid), *n.* a substance composed of a small number of nucleotides: *Since the sequence of nucleotides in many RNA molecules is known, specific oligonucleotides with three or four monomers may be designed to bind to a selected part of the molecule by complementary base pairing* (Science Journal).

**ol|i|goph|a|gous** (ol′ə gof′ə gəs), *adj.* eating few kinds of food; not polyphagous: *an oligophagous insect.* [< *oligo-* + Greek *phágeîn* to eat]

**ol|i|go|phre|ni|a** (ol′ə gō frē′nē ə, -frēn′yə), *n.* = mental deficiency.

**ol|i|go|phren|ic** (ol′ə gō fren′ik), *adj.* of, having to do with, or displaying mental deficiency.

**ol|i|gop|o|list** (ol′ə gop′ə list), *n.* a person or firm that creates or maintains an oligopoly: *The principal defect of present antitrust law is its inability to cope with market power created by jointly acting oligopolists—small groups of large companies that dominate an industry* (New York Times).

**ol|i|gop|o|lis|tic** (ol′ə gop′ə lis′tik), *adj.* of or having to do with oligopoly.

**ol|i|gop|o|ly** (ol′ə gop′ə lē), *n., pl.* **-lies.** a condition in a market in which so few producers supply a commodity or service that each of them can influence its price, with or without an agreement between them: *Ultimately, it is the oligopolies and not the State that set the economic priorities of our society* (Manchester Guardian). [< *oligo-* + *-poly,* as in *monopoly*]

**ol|i|gop|so|ny** (ol′ə gop′sə nē), *n.* a condition in which a few buyers have a strong influence on the demand for a commodity or service. [< *oligo-* + Greek *opsōnía* purchase of food]

**ol|i|go|sac|cha|ride** (ol′ə gō sak′ə rīd, -ər id), *n.* a carbohydrate that on hydrolysis yields a relatively small number (usually two to ten) of monosaccharides as compared to a polysaccharide.

**ol|i|go|troph|ic** (ol′ə gō trof′ik), *adj.* not providing nutrition, as a lake with scant vegetation.

**ol|i|got|ro|phy** (ol′ə got′rə fē), *n.* deficiency of nutrition. [< Greek *oligotrophíā* < *olígos* few, little + *tréphein* nourish]

**o|lim** (ō lēm′), *n.pl. Hebrew.* **1** Jewish immigrants to Israel: *Positively, the nation [Israel] feels refreshed by olim, the homecoming immigrants, justified in its deepest purpose, and strengthened to build a new life on its corner of the earth* (London Times). **2** (literally) those who ascend. See also **aliyah.**

**ol|in|go** (ol′ing gō), *n.* a mammal related to the raccoon, found from Ecuador to Nicaragua, having golden-brown fur and a bushy tail. [< a native name]

**o|li|o** (ō′lē ō), *n., pl.* **o|li|os. 1** any mixture; jumble; hodgepodge. **2a** a collection of artistic or literary pieces; miscellany: *Ben Jonson, in his "Sejanus and Catiline" has given us this olio of a play* (John Dryden). **b** a musical medley; potpourri. **3a** = olla-podrida (def. 1). **b** any dish made of many ingredients. [< Spanish *olla* pot, stew < Latin *ōlla* pot, jar. Compare etym. under **olla.**]

**ol|i|to|ry** (ol′ə tôr′ē, -tōr′-), *adj.* of or producing potherbs or vegetables. [< Latin *olitōrius* < *olitor* kitchen gardener]

**ol|i|va|ceous** (ol′ə vā′shəs), *adj.* olive; olive-green. [< Latin *olīva* olive (tree)]

**ol|i|var|y** (ol′ə ver′ē), *adj.* **1** shaped like an olive. **2** of or having to do with either of two olive-shaped bodies, one on each side of the anterior surface of the medulla oblongata. [< Latin *olīvārius* of olives < *olīva* olive]

**ol|ive** (ol′iv), *n., adj.* —*n.* **1** a kind of evergreen tree with gray-green leaves. The olive grows in the southern part of Europe and in other warm regions. It is grown for its fruit and also for its wood. **2** the fruit of this tree, with a hard stone and a bitter pulp. Olives are eaten green or ripe. *Olive oil is pressed from olives.* **3** the wood of the olive tree. **4** a wreath of olive leaves; olive branch: *I hold the olive in my hand; my words are as full of peace as matter* (Shakespeare). **5a** a yellowish green; olive green. **b** a yellowish brown; olive brown. **6** a gastropod mollusk with an elongated oval shell, found in tropical seas.
—*adj.* **1a** yellowish-green. **b** yellowish-brown. **2** of the olive.
[< Old French *olive,* learned borrowing from Latin *olīva* olive]

**ol|ive-backed thrush** (ol′iv bakt′), an American thrush with a grayish or olive-brown back, and a conspicuous eye ring, that breeds chiefly in the coniferous forests of Canada and the northern United States.

**olive branch, 1** a branch of the olive tree. **2** one or more such branches, used as an emblem or symbol of peace. **3** *Figurative.* anything offered as a sign of peace. **4** a child: *The wife and olive branches of one Mr. Kenwigs* (Dickens). SYN: scion.

**olive brown,** a yellowish-brown color.

**ol|ive-brown** (ol′iv broun′), *adj.* brown with a yellowish tinge.

**olive drab, 1** a dark greenish-yellow color. **2** a dark greenish-yellow woolen cloth, formerly used by the United States Army for uniforms.

**ol|ive-drab** (ol′iv drab′), *adj.* of or like olive drab.

* **olive family,** a group of dicotyledonous trees and shrubs, native to warm and temperate regions. The family includes the olive, ash, jasmine, lilac, forsythia, and fringe tree. See picture opposite on following page.

**olive green,** a dull, yellowish green; olive.

**ol|ive-green** (ol′iv grēn′), *adj.* dull yellowish-green.

**o|liv|en|ite** (ō liv′ə nīt, ol′ə və-), *n.* a mineral, an arsenate of copper, usually occurring in olive-green crystals or masses. *Formula:* $Cu_3As_2O_8$·

$Cu(OH)_2$ [< German *Olivenerz* olive ore + English *-ite*[1]]

**olive oil**, oil pressed from olives, used especially in cooking, in salad dressings, and in medicine.

**Ol·i·ver** (ol′ə vər), *n.* one of Charlemagne's heroic followers and a friend of Roland.

**olive sparrow**, an olive-green finch of southern Texas and Mexico, with yellow and reddish markings; Texas sparrow; greenfinch.

**olive warbler**, a grayish-and-white warbler of the southwestern United States, Mexico, and Central America, the male of which has a tawny head, neck, and breast.

**ol·ive·wood** (ol′iv wu̇d′), *n.* the hard, yellow wood of the olive tree, used in cabinet-making, for inlays, and other fine work, and canes.

**ol·i·vine** (ol′ə vēn, ol′ə vēn′), *n.* a chrysolite, especially when greenish or yellowish; silicate of iron and magnesium: *The rigid mantle of the earth is thought to consist largely of olivine, an insulator under normal conditions* (Science News Letter). [< *oliv*(e) + *-ine*[1]]

**ol·i·vin·ic** (ol′ə vin′ik), *adj.* having to do with or resembling olivine: *a silicate of the olivinic type.*

**ol·i·vin·it·ic** (ol′ə və nit′ik), *adj.* = olivinic.

**ol·la** (ol′ə), *n.* **1** an earthen water jar or cooking pot. **2** = olla-podrida (def. 1). [< Spanish *olla* < Latin *ōlla* pot, jar]

**ol·lamh** (ol′lä, -lō), *n.* one of a class of early poets and storytellers of Ireland, especially during the Middle Ages. [< Irish Gaelic *ollamh* (literally) sage, scholar, wizard]

**ol·la-po·dri·da** (ol′ə pə drē′də), *n.* **1** a stew made from fresh and smoked meats, chicken, chickpeas, onions, garlic, a variety of green vegetables, and seasonings. It is a Spanish national dish eaten throughout the Spanish-speaking world. **2** *Figurative.* a hodgepodge; olio: *And instead of making up an olla-podrida of Gothic and Renaissance . . . they were headstrong and imaginative enough to invent something for themselves* (Nikolaus Pevsner). [< Spanish *olla podrida* (literally) rotten pot < *olla* olla + *podrida* < Latin *putrida* putrid, rotten. Compare etym. under **potpourri**.]

**Ol·mec** (ōl′mek), *n., adj.* —*n.* a member of a highly civilized people who lived in southeastern Mexico before the Aztecs. Their culture flourished from about 1200 B.C. to 100 B.C. *The most ancient civilization of Mesoamerica is that of the Olmecs, who flourished in the sweltering Gulf Coast plain in the region of southern Veracruz and neighbouring Tabasco* (Listener).
—*adj.* of the Olmecs or their culture: *Olmec architecture.*

**ol·o·gist** (ol′ə jist), *n. Informal.* a specialist in any science or branch of knowledge: . . . *the enthronement of the intellectual and the ologist* (Atlantic).

**ol·o·gy** (ol′ə jē), *n., pl.* **-gies**. *Informal.* any science or branch of knowledge: *Etymology is an unpredictable ology* (New Yorker). [abstracted < words ending in *-ology*]

***olive family**

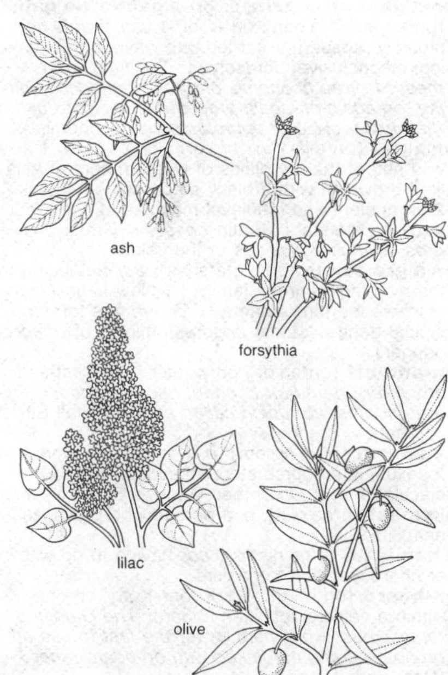


**o·lo·li·u·qui** (ō′lō lē ü′kē, -kwē), *n.* a narcotic drug made by Mexican Indians from the seeds of a plant of the morning-glory family. [< Nahuatl *ololiuqui* the name of the plant]

**O·lo·ro·so** or **o·lo·ro·so** (ō′lə rō′sō), *n., pl.* **-sos**. a sweet Spanish sherry. [< Spanish *oloroso* (literally) fragrant]

**ol·pe** (ol′pē), *n.* in ancient Greece: **1** a leather oil flask, used especially in the palestra. **2** a small pitcherlike vessel resembling an oinochoe but having a more slender body. [< Greek *ólpē*]

**O·lym·pi·ad** or **o·lym·pi·ad** (ō lim′pē ad), *n.* **1** a period of four years reckoned from one celebration of the Olympic Games to the next, by which the Greeks computed time from 776 B.C. **2** a celebration of the modern Olympic Games. **3** any international contest, especially one modeled on the Olympic Games: *the 22nd Chess Olympiad, the World Culinary Olympiad.* [probably < Middle French, Old French *olympiade*, learned borrowing from Latin *Olympias, -adis* < Greek *Olympiás, -ádos,* ultimately < *Ólympus* the village (where games were held), and the mountain]

**O·lym·pi·an** (ō lim′pē ən), *adj., n.* —*adj.* **1** having to do with Olympia in ancient Greece or with Mount Olympus; Olympic. **2** like a god; heavenly. **3** rather too gracious; superior: *Olympian calm. Olympian manners.* SYN: magnificent.
—*n.* **1** one of the major Greek gods, led by Zeus, that lived on Mount Olympus. **2** a contender in the Olympic Games.

**Olympian Games**, = Olympic Games.

**O·lym·pic** (ō lim′pik), *adj.* **1** of or having to do with Olympia in ancient Greece. **2** of or having to do with Mount Olympus. **3** of or having to do with the Olympic Games.

**Olympic Games**, **1** contests in athletics, poetry, and music, held every four years by the ancient Greeks in honor of Zeus. **2** modern athletic contests in the tradition of the athletic contests of these games. They are held once every four years in a different country, and athletes from many nations compete in them.

**O·lym·pics** (ō lim′piks), *n.pl.* **1** = Olympic Games. **2** = Olympiad (def. 3).

**O·lym·pus** (ō lim′pəs), *n.* heaven. [< Mount *Olympus*, in Greece, regarded as the home of the Greek deities]

**om** (ōm), *n.* a Hindu sacred word that symbolizes Brahma, used as a spell, spoken before reciting mantras, or mystically contemplated in its written or spoken form. [< Sanskrit *om*]

**O.M.**, *British.* Order of Merit.

**-oma**, *suffix, pl.* **-omas** or **-omata**. a growth, as a tumor or neoplasm, as in *adenoma, carcinoma.* [< Greek *-ōma, -ōmatos* a noun suffix]

**O·ma·gua** (ō mä′gwä), *n., pl.* **-gua** or **-guas**. **1** a member of a small tribe of South American Indians living on the upper Amazon River. The Omagua, who are of Tupi-Guarani stock, were very powerful at the time of the Spanish Conquest. **2** the language of this tribe.

**O·ma·ha** (ō′mə hô, -hä), *n., pl.* **-ha** or **-has**. **1** a member of an American Indian tribe of Siouan stock, now living in Nebraska. **2** the language of this tribe.

**O·ma·han** (ō′mə hôn, -hän), *n.* a native or inhabitant of Omaha, Nebraska.

**O·ma·ni** (ō mä′nē), *adj., n.* —*adj.* of or having to do with Oman, a country in southeastern Arabia.
—*n.* a native or inhabitant of Oman.

**o·ma·sum** (ō mā′səm), *n., pl.* **-sa** (-sə). the third stomach of a cow or other ruminant; manyplies. It receives the food when swallowed the second time, after having been chewed as a cud. [< Latin *omāsum* bullock's tripe]

**O·may·yad** (ō mī′ad), *n., pl.* **-yads, -ya·des** (-ə dēz). **1** a member of the dynasty of Moslem caliphs (A.D. 661-750) that preceded the Abbassids and had its seat at Damascus. **2** a member of a branch of this dynasty which founded the caliphate of Córdoba in Spain (A.D. 756). Also, **Ommiad, Umayyad.** [< *Omayya*, an ancestor of the first caliph of the dynasty + Greek *-ad*, a noun suffix]

**OMB** (no periods), Office of Management and Budget (a U.S. government agency that replaced the Bureau of the Budget in 1970).

**om·ber** (om′bər), *n.* **1** a card game, popular in the 1600's and 1700's, played by three persons with 40 cards, the eights, nines, and tens being left out. **2** the player who tries to win the pool in this game. [< Spanish *hombre* man (in this game, the challenger) < Latin *homō*]

**om·bre**[1] (om′bər), *n. Especially British.* omber.

**om·bré** or **om·bre**[2] (om brā′, om′brā; *French* ôN-brā′), *adj., n.* —*adj.* (of a fabric color) running gradually from light to darker shades to give a shaded or striped effect; shadowy; shaded.
—*n.* an ombré fabric. [< French *ombré* < *ombre* shadow < Latin *umbra*]

**om·bréd** or **om·bred** (om brād′, om′brād), *adj.* = ombré.

**om·bu** (om bü′), *n.* a rapidly growing, evergreen, dioecious shade tree of South America, having very dense foliage and a width of up to 15 feet at the base. The wood is very moist and spongy. [< American Spanish *ombú*]

**om·buds·man** (om′budz man′, -mən; om budz′-mən), *n., pl.* **-men**. **1** a government official appointed to receive and investigate grievances of citizens against the government. The office of ombudsman originated in the Scandinavian countries. *It would appoint Parliamentary Commissioners, or Ombudsmen, to redress the many cases of stark injustice that survive and defeat the best intentions of our legal and administrative systems* (C. H. Rolph). **2** any person who champions or defends individual rights: *How could one not know her, since she was everywhere, doing everything— columnist, lecturer, traveler constantly crisscrossing the country, ombudsman for every injustice, agitator for every cause that needed help, one-woman lobby?* (Max Lerner). [< Swedish *ombudsman* (literally) grievance man]

**om·buds·man·ship** (om′budz mən ship, om-budz′-), *n.* position or authority of ombudsman.

**om·buds·wom·an** (om′budz wu̇m′ən), *n., pl.* **-wom·en**. a female ombudsman.

***o·meg·a** (ō meg′ə; -mē′gə, -mā′-), *n.* **1** the 24th and last letter of the Greek alphabet, corresponding to English *O, o,* especially with the sound *ō*. **2** the last of any series; end. **3** *Nuclear Physics.* **a** omega meson. **b** = omega minus. [< Medieval Greek *o mega* large o (because of the length of the vowel)]

| ***omega** definition 1 | Ω capital letter | ω lower-case letter |
|---|---|---|

**omega meson**, a highly unstable and short-lived elementary particle with a mass 1540 times that of an electron.

**omega minus**, a negatively-charged elementary particle of extremely short life, produced in a nuclear accelerator after its existence and properties were predicted by the eightfold way.

**om·e·let** or **om·e·lette** (om′ə lit, om′lit), *n.* eggs beaten up with milk or water, fried or baked in a shallow pan, and folded over. An omelet is often filled with minced ham, tomato sauce, or cheese. [< Middle French *omelette,* alteration of *alemette,* alteration of *alemelle* < Latin *lāmella* (diminutive) < *lāmina* metal plate]

**o·men** (ō′mən), *n., v.* —*n.* **1** a sign of what is to happen; object or event that is believed to mean good or bad fortune: *Spilling salt is said to be an omen of misfortune.* SYN: augury, portent, presage. See syn. under **sign**. **2** prophetic meaning; foreboding: *A black cat is a creature of ill omen.*
—*v.t.* **1** to be a sign of; presage; forebode. **2** to predict as if from omens; divine.
[< Latin *ōmen*]

**o·mened** (ō′mənd), *adj.* preceded by or attended with omens.

**-omened**, *combining form.* containing a ____ omen: *Ill-omened = containing an ill omen*

**o·men·tal** (ō men′təl), *adj.* of or having to do with the omentum.

**o·men·tum** (ō men′təm), *n., pl.* **-ta** (-tə). a fold of the peritoneum connecting the stomach with certain of the other viscera. The great omentum is attached to the stomach and enfolds the transverse colon; the lesser omentum lies between the stomach and the liver. [< Latin *ōmentum*]

**o·mer** (ō′mər), *n.* **1** an ancient Hebrew unit of dry measure, equal to 1/10 of an ephah, about 3½ quarts. **2** the 49 days between Passover and Shabuoth during which weddings and other celebrations are prohibited to Orthodox Jews, except on the day of Lag Ba'Omer. [< Hebrew *'omer,* confused with *homer*[3]]

**o·mer·tà** or **o·mer·ta** (ō′mər tä′; *Italian* ō′mer-tä′), *n.* a Sicilian code of honor which forbids informing about crimes thought to be the private affairs of the persons involved. [< Italian (Naples) *omerta,* variant of *umilta* (literally) humility]

| ***omicron** | O capital letter | o lower-case letter |
|---|---|---|

***om·i·cron** (om′ə kron, ō′mə-), *n.* the 15th letter of the Greek alphabet. [< Greek *ò micrón* small o (because of the shorter length of the vowel)]

**om·i·nous** (om′ə nəs), *adj.* **1** of bad omen; unfa-

**Pronunciation Key:** hat, āge, cãre, fär; let, ēqual, tėrm; it, īce; hot, ōpen, ôrder; oil, out; cup, pu̇t, rüle; child; long; thin; ᴛʜen; zh, measure; ə represents a in about, e in taken, i in pencil, o in lemon, u in circus.

vorable; threatening: *a dull, ominous rumble* (Bret Harte). *Those clouds look ominous for our picnic.* SYN: inauspicious, foreboding. **2** of or like an omen; prophetic; portentous: *I feel a thousand fears Which are not ominous of right* (Byron). [< Latin *ōminōsus* (with English *-ous*) < *ōmen, -inis* omen] —**om'i|nous|ly,** *adv.* —**om'i|nous|ness,** *n.*

**o|mis|si|ble** (ō mis'ə bəl), *adj.* that can be omitted.

**o|mis|sion** (ō mish'ən), *n.* **1** the act or fact of omitting or state of being omitted: *the omission of a paragraph in copying a story.* SYN: exclusion. **2** a thing omitted: *His song was the only omission from the program.* [< Late Latin *omissiō, -ōnis* < Latin *omittere* omit]

**o|mis|sive** (ō mis'iv), *adj.* characterized by omission; omitting.

**o|mit** (ō mit'), *v.t.,* **o|mit|ted, o|mit|ting. 1** to leave out: *He made many mistakes in spelling by omitting letters. I must not omit that Sir Roger is a justice of the quorum* (Sir Richard Steele). **2** to fail to do; neglect: *to omit to say thanks. She omitted making her bed. He omitted to state his reasons.* SYN: overlook, ignore, skip. **3** *Obsolete.* to let go; lay aside: *Tempests themselves ... As having sense of beauty, do omit Their mortal natures, letting go safely by The divine Desdemona* (Shakespeare). [< Latin *omittere* < *ob-* by + *mittere* let go, send]

**om|ma|tid|i|al** (om'ə tid'ē əl), *adj.* of or having to do with the ommatidium.

**om|ma|tid|i|um** (om'ə tid'ē əm), *n., pl.* **-i|a** (-ē ə). one of the radial elements or segments that make up the compound eye, as of insects or crustaceans. [< New Latin *ommatidium* < Greek *ómma, -atos* eye + Latin *-idium,* a diminutive suffix]

**om|mat|o|phore** (ə mat'ə fôr, -fōr), *n.* a movable eyestalk, such as in certain snails. [< New Latin *ommatophorus* < Greek *ómma, -atos* eye + *-phóros* bearing *phérein* to bear]

**Om|mi|ad** (ō mī'ad), *n., pl.* **-ads, -a|des** (-ə dēz). = Omayyad.

**omni-,** *combining form.* all; completely: *Omnipotent = all powerful.* [< Latin *omnis* all]

**om|ni|a vin|cit a|mor** (om'nē ə vin'sit ā'môr), *Latin.* love conquers all.

**om|ni|bus** (om'nə bus), *n., pl.* **-bus|es,** *adj.* —*n.* **1** a large vehicle with seats inside and sometimes also on the roof; bus. An omnibus is used for carrying passengers between fixed stations along a route. **2** a volume of works by a single author or of similar works by several authors; anthology: *an omnibus of detective stories.*
—*adj.* covering many things at once: *an omnibus law.*
[< French (*voiture*) *omnibus* common (conveyance) < Latin *omnibus* for all, dative plural of *omnis* all. Compare etym. under **bus, autobus.**]

**om|ni|com|pe|tence** (om'nə kom'pə təns), *n.* complete or unlimited competence.

**om|ni|com|pe|tent** (om'nə kom'pə tənt), *adj.* competent in all matters; legally qualified in all cases: *The younger so-called Communist technocrats ... trained by an omnipotent but far from omnicompetent state ...* (Times Literary Supplement).

**om|ni|di|rec|tion|al** (om'nə də rek'shə nəl, -dī-), *adj.* transmitting or receiving signals in every direction: *an omnidirectional radio beacon, an omnidirectional microphone.*

**om|ni|fac|et|ed** (om'nə fas'ə tid), *adj.* covering all facets: [*His*] *omnifaceted study of the latest major societal breakdown in the U.S. seems remarkably relevant* (Time).

**om|ni|far|i|ous** (om'nə fãr'ē əs), *adj.* of all forms, varieties, or kinds: *omnifarious reading.* [< Late Latin *omnifārius* (with English *-ous*) < Latin *omnis* all + *fās, fāris* (originally) pronouncement of divine law < *fārī* speak] —**om'ni|far'i|ous|ness,** *n.*

**om|nif|ic** (om nif'ik), *adj.* creating all things: *Silence, ye troubled waves, and thou deep, peace, Said then the omnific Word* (Milton). [< Latin *omnis* all + *facere* make]

**om|nif|i|cent** (om nif'ə sənt), *adj.* = omnific. [< *omni-* + *-ficent,* as in *magnificent*]

**om|ni|fo|cal** (om'nə fō'kəl), *adj.* having continuously varying focal lengths: *Omnifocal lenses eliminate a typical sharp break between lens segments of bifocals* (Chicago Tribune).

**om|ni|form** (om'nə fôrm), *adj.* of all forms or shapes; taking any form or shape: *the omniform sea.* [< Latin *omniformis* < *omnis* all + *forma* form]

**om|ni|form|i|ty** (om'nə fôr'mə tē), *n.* omniform quality.

**om|nig|e|nous** (om nij'ə nəs), *adj.* of all kinds. [< Latin *omnigenus* (with English *-ous*) < *omnis* all + *genus* noun, kind]

**om|nip|o|tence** (om nip'ə təns), *n.* complete power; unlimited power: *the omnipotence of God, pursuing the guilty sinner* (William Godwin).

**Om|nip|o|tence** (om nip'ə təns), *n.* = God.

**om|nip|o|tent** (om nip'ə tənt), *adj., n.* —*adj.* **1** having all power; almighty: *Alleluia: for the Lord God omnipotent reigneth* (Revelation 19:6). **2** having very great power or influence: *The Senate was ... made omnipotent and irresponsible* (James A. Froude). **3** capable of anything; utter: *The most omnipotent villain that ever cried "Stand" to a true man* (Shakespeare).
—*n.* an omnipotent being.
[< Latin *omnipotēns, -potentis* < *omnis* all + *potēns,* present participle of *posse* be able] —**omnip'o|tent|ly,** *adv.*

**Om|nip|o|tent** (om nip'ə tənt), *n.* **the Omnipotent,** God: *Boasting I could subdue The Omnipotent* (Milton).

**om|ni|pres|ence** (om'nə prez'əns), *n.* presence everywhere at the same time: *God's omnipresence. His omnipresence fills Land, sea, and air* (Milton). SYN: ubiquity.

**om|ni|pres|ent** (om'nə prez'ənt), *adj.* **1** present everywhere at the same time; ubiquitous: *the omnipresent God* (William Godwin). **2** found everywhere: *the omnipresent Times newspaper* (Alexander W. Kinglake). [< Medieval Latin *omnipraesēns, -praesentis* < Latin *omnis* all + *praesēns* present, adjective]

**om|ni|range** (om'nə rānj'), *n.* a navigational system for aircraft, in which position is determined by picking up omnidirectional radio signals from a ground station.

**om|nis|cience** (om nish'əns), *n.* knowledge of everything; complete of infinite knowledge: *For many patients the notion that the doctor lacks omniscience or omnipotence in his domain is extremely disturbing* (Scientific American). *Science is his forte and omniscience his foible* (Sydney Smith). [< Medieval Latin *omniscientia* < Latin *omnis* all + *scientia* knowledge < *sciēns, -entis,* present participle of *scīre* to know]

**Om|nis|cience** (om nish'əns), *n.* = God: *the eye of Omniscience.*

**om|nis|cient** (om nish'ənt), *adj.* knowing everything; having complete or infinite knowledge: *By no means trust to your own judgment alone; for no man is omniscient* (Francis Bacon). —**om|nis'cient|ly,** *adv.*

**Om|nis|cient** (om nish'ənt), *n.* = God.

**om|ni|tude** (om'nə tüd, -tyüd), *n.* the state or fact of being or comprising all; universality. [< Latin *omnis* all + *-tude*]

**om|ni|um-gath|er|um** (om'nē əm gaᴛʜ'ər əm), *n.* a miscellaneous collection; confused mixture. SYN: medley. [< Latin *omnium* of all, genitive plural of *omnis* + *gatherum,* a Latinization coined from English *gather*]

**om|ni|vore** (om'nə vôr, -vōr), *n.* an omnivorous animal or person.

**om|niv|o|rous** (om niv'ər əs), *adj.* **1** eating every kind of food. **2** eating both animal and vegetable food: *Man is an omnivorous animal.* **3** *Figurative.* taking in everything; fond of all kinds : *An omnivorous reader reads all kinds of books.* [< Latin *omnivorus* (with English *-ous*) < *omnis* all + *vorāre* eat greedily] —**om|niv'o|rous|ly,** *adv.* —**omniv'o|rous|ness,** *n.*

**o|mo|pha|gi|a** (ō'mə fā'jē ə), *n.* the eating of raw flesh or raw food. [< New Latin *omophagia*]

**o|mo|phag|ic** (ō'mə faj'ik), *adj.* = omophagous.

**o|moph|a|gist** (ō mof'ə jist), *n.* an eater of raw flesh.

**o|moph|a|gous** (ō mof'ə gəs), *adj.* eating raw flesh or raw food. [< Greek *ōmophágos* < *ōmós* raw + *phágos* eating < *phageîn* eat]

**o|mo|plate** (ō'mə plāt), *n.* the shoulder blade or scapula. [< French *omoplate* < Greek *ōmoplátē* < *ômos* shoulder + *plátē* flat surface]

**Om|pha|le** (om'fə lē), *n. Greek Mythology.* a queen of Lydia whom Hercules had to serve for three years, dressed as a woman, to atone for a murder.

**om|pha|li|tis** (om'fə lī'tis), *n.* inflammation of the navel in young animals. [< Greek *omphalós* navel + English *-itis*]

**om|pha|los** (om'fə ləs), *n., pl.* **-li** (-lī). **1** = navel. **2** *Figurative.* a central point or part; center; hub. **3** a round or conical stone in the temple of Apollo at Delphi, believed by the ancient Greeks to mark the center of the earth. [< Greek *omphalós* navel, boss[2], hub]

**om|pha|lo|skep|sis** (om'fə lō skep'sis), *n.* the act of gazing steadily at one's navel in the process of mystical contemplation: *Omphaloskepsis, then, is no longer the métier of only the Buddhists* (Time). [< Greek *omphalós* navel + *sképsis* a looking at]

**O.M.S.,** output per man-shift.

**on** (on, ôn), *prep., adv., adj., n.* —*prep.* **1** above and supported by: *to stand on one foot, to ride on a train. The book is on the table.* **2** touching so as to cover or be around: *a blister on one's heel, shoes on one's feet, a ring on one's finger.* **3** close to; near: *a house on the shore, to border on absurdity.* **4** in the direction of; toward: *The invading soldiers marched on the Capitol.* **5** against; upon: *The picture is on the wall.* **6** by means of; by the use of: *to talk on the telephone. This news is on good authority.* **7** in the condition of; in the process of; in the way of: *on duty, on half pay, on fire, on purpose, on sale.* **8** at the time of; during: *They greeted us on our arrival.* **9** concerning; in relation to; in connection with: *a book on animals, a poem on winter.* **10** for the purpose of: *He went on an errand.* **11** in addition to: *Defeat on defeat discouraged them.* **12** among: *on a team. I am on the committee considering new members for our club.* **13** indicating risk or liability: *on pain of death.*
—*adv.* **1** on something or someone: *The walls are up, and the roof is on. Put on a clean shirt.* **2** to something: *Hold on, or you may fall.* **3** toward something: *Some played; the others looked on.* **4** farther: *March on.* **5** in or into a condition, process, manner, or action: *Turn the gas on.* **6** from a time; forward: *later on, from that day on.*
—*adj.* **1** taking place: *The race is on.* **2** near: *the on side.* **3** in operation; operating: *The radio is on. The brake is on.* **4** *Cricket.* of or on the side of the wicket or the field on which the batsman stands. **5** *British Slang.* **a** effective; working: *"So you see, old boy, that while I agree with you, denationalization just isn't on: Labour's made such a howling mess of these industries that no one in his senses would ever buy them back!"* (Punch). **b** knowing; aware: *Says Whiteley* [*a London painter*] *"Dylan is ... the most on person in America"* (Time).
—*n. Cricket.* the on side
**and so on.** See under **so**[1].
**have nothing on.** See under **have.**
**have on.** See under **have.**
**on and off,** at some times and not at others; now and then: *He looked out of the window on and off.*
**on and on,** without stopping: *The woman talked on and on throughout the whole afternoon.*
**on to,** *Slang.* aware of the truth about: *Some of the kids are sweet, though I have a feeling they're on to me* (Punch).
**put on.** See under **put**[1].
[Old English *on,* also *an* in, on, into. Compare etym. under **a-**[1].]

**-on,** *suffix.* **1** *Physics.* **a** a nuclear particle, as in *neutron, dyon, parton.* **b** any unit particle or quantum of energy, as in *photon, graviton, exciton.*
**2** *Genetics.* a unit of genetic material, as in *operon, cistron.*
**3** *Chemistry.* a variant of **-one,** used for a compound that is not a ketone, as in *diuron.*
[< *-on,* as in *ion, electron,* and *proton*]

**ON** (no periods), **O.N.,** or **ON.,** Old Norse.

**O|na** (ō'nə), *n., pl.* **-na** or **-nas.** a member of a tribe of American Indians formerly living on the island of Tierra del Fuego at the southernmost tip of South America: *The Ona hunted the guanaco, a small wild relative of the llama* (Charles Wagley).

**on-a|gain off-a|gain,** or **on-a|gain-off-a|gain** (on'ə gen' ôf'ə gen'; ôn'-; -of'-), *adj.* that is not steadily pursued or carried out; wavering; faltering; inconclusive; unresolved: *The fund was meant to free economic aid from the jerking, jolting, on-again-off-again procedures imposed by the annual cycle of appropriations* (Economist).

**on|a|ger** (on'ə jər), *n., pl.* **-gri** (-grī), **-gers. 1** a wild ass of the dry plains of western central Asia, light brownish with a black stripe along its back. **2** an ancient and medieval machine of war for throwing stones. [< Latin *onager* < Greek *ónagros* < *ónos ágrios* ass of the fields]

**on|a|gra|ceous** (on'ə grā'shəs), *adj.* belonging to the evening-primrose family. [< New Latin *Onagraceae* the family name < *Onagra* the former typical genus < Latin *onagra,* feminine of *onager* onager]

**on-and-off** (on'ən ôf', ôn'-; -of'), *adj.* = off-and-on: *After on-and-off contract negotiations for several months, the union called a strike* (Wall Street Journal).

**o|nan|ism** (ō'nə niz əm), *n.* **1** = masturbation. **2** sexual intercourse stopped suddenly before ejaculation. [< *Onan* (see Genesis 38:9) + *-ism*]

**o|nan|ist** (ō'nə nist), *n.* a person who practices onanism.

**o|nan|is|tic** (ō'nə nis'tik), *adj.* having to do with or characteristic of onanism.

**on-board** (on'bôrd', -bōrd'; ôn'-), *adj.* on or within a vehicle; installed aboard: *The Gemini 5 rendezvous experiment* [*was*] *the first to use an on-board computer linked with on-board radar* (New York Times).

**once** (wuns), *adv., n., conj., adj.* —*adv.* **1** one time: *Read it once more. He comes once a day. A man can die but once* (Shakespeare). **2** at some one time in the past; formerly: *a once pow-*

*erful nation. That big man was once a little baby.* **3** even a single time; ever: *if the facts once become known; once seen, never forgotten.* **4** *Archaic.* at some future time: *meditating that she must die once* (Shakespeare).
**—*n.*** a single occasion: *Once is enough. I think he might as well have favoured me this once* (Shelley).
**—*conj.*** if ever; whenever: *Most boys like to swim once they have learned how. Once you cross the river you are safe.*
**—*adj.*** former: *a once friend.* **SYN**: quondam.
**all at once,** suddenly: *All at once the sun disappeared and rain began to fall.*
**at once, a** immediately: *You must come at once.* **b** at one and the same time: *All three boys spoke at once.*
**for once,** for one time at least: *For once I wasn't thinking of you. I had other things in mind* (Graham Greene).
**once and again,** repeatedly: *That good woman would open the door once and again in the morning, and put her head through* (Mrs. Humphry Ward).
**once (and) for all.** See under **all.**
**once in a while.** See under **while.**
**once or twice,** a few times: *So the merchants ... lodged without Jerusalem once or twice* (Nehemiah 13:20)
**once upon a time.** See under **time.**
[Middle English *ones,* or *anes,* Old English *ānes, ǣnes* < *ān* one + adverbial genitive *-es*]

**once-o|ver** (wuns′ō′vər), *n. Informal.* a short, quick look, as for inspection or evaluation: *to give the new plans a quick once-over.*

**once-o|ver-light|ly** (wuns′ō′vər līt′lē), *n., adj.* **—*n.*** *Informal.* a light or superficial look, as for inspection or evaluation; a casual once-over: *The religious essays ... are a once-over-lightly in the principles of Catholicism* (Time).
**—*adj.*** superficial; casual: *once-over-lightly coverage of the news.*

**on|cho|cer|ci|a|sis** (ong′kō sėr sī′ə sis), *n.* a tropical disease that causes nodules under the skin and lesions of the eye which may result in blindness; river blindness. It is caused by a filarial worm whose carrier is a gnat. [< New Latin *Onchocera* genus of nematode that causes the disease (< Greek *ónkos* barb + *kérkos* tail) + English *-iasis*]

**on|cid|i|um** (on sid′ē əm), *n.* any one of a group of tropical American epiphytic orchids. Some kinds have flowers resembling butterflies. [< New Latin *oncidium* < Greek *ónkos* barb of an arrow (because of the shape of the corolla) + Latin *-idium,* a diminutive suffix]

**on|co|gen** (ong′kə jen), *n.* a tumor-producing virus or other agent; oncogenic substance or organism. [< Greek *ónkos* tumor; mass, bulk + English *-gen*]

**on|co|gene** (ong′kə jēn′), *n.* a tumor-producing gene: *The theory itself states that human cancer is viral in origin and is caused by a more or less hypothetical entity called the oncogene* (Harper's). [< Greek *ónkos* tumor; mass, bulk + English *gene*]

**on|co|gen|e|sis** (ong′kə jen′ə sis), *n.* the process of forming or producing tumors.

**on|co|gen|ic** (ong′kə jen′ik), *adj.* having to do with or producing tumors; tending to produce tumors.

**on|co|ge|nic|i|ty** (ong′kō jə nis′ə tē), *n.* the quality or condition of being oncogenic.

**on|co|log|ic** (ong′kə loj′ik), *adj.* = oncological.

**on|co|log|i|cal** (ong′kə loj′ə kəl), *adj.* of or having to do with oncology: *The U.S.S.R. has embarked on a nationwide specialist oncological service to deal with all growth disorders, benign and malignant* (London Times).

**on|col|o|gist** (ong kol′ə jist), *n.* a person who studies, or knows much about, oncology.

**on|col|o|gy** (ong kol′ə jē), *n.* the branch of medicine dealing with the study of tumors. [< Greek *ónkos* tumor; mass, bulk + English *-logy*]

**on|co|lyt|ic** (ong′kə lit′ik), *adj.* of or having to do with the destruction of cells comprising a tumor: *oncolytic properties.* [< Greek *ónkos* tumor; mass, bulk + English *lytic*]

**on|com|ing** (on′kum′ing, ôn′-), *adj., n.* **—*adj.*** approaching or advancing: *oncoming winter, the oncoming tide, oncoming traffic.*
**—*n.*** approach; advance: *the oncoming of the storm; the oncoming of numbness* (George Eliot).

**on|cor|na|vi|rus** (ong kôr′nə vī′rəs), *n.* any one of a group of viruses that produce tumors and contain ribonucleic acid: *Professor W. F. H. Jarrett ... spoke of the oncornaviruses particularly in fowls, mice and cats, in which they can lead to leukemia or sarcoma* (Nature). [< *onco*(genic) + *RNA* + *virus*]

**on|dé** (ON dā′), *adj. Heraldry.* wavy; undé. [< French *ondé* < Old French *onde, unde* wave < Latin *unda*]

**ondes Mar|te|not** (OND′ mär tə nō′), *pl.* **ondes Mar|te|not** (OND′ mär tə nō′). an electrophonic keyboard instrument. [< French *ondes Martenot* (literally) waves of Martenot, after the inventor, Maurice *Martenot,* a French musician]

**on-ding** (on′ding′), *n. Scottish.* a very heavy fall of rain or snow. [< *on* + Scottish *ding* rain heavily, probably < Scandinavian (compare Icelandic *dengya* to hammer, beat)]

**on dit** (ôN dē′), *French.* **1** they say; it is said. **2** a piece of gossip; report: *I thought it was a mere on dit* (Benjamin Disraeli).

**on|do|gram** (on′də gram), *n.* a record made by an ondograph.

**on|do|graph** (on′də graf, -gräf), *n.* an instrument for recording the oscillatory variations of electric currents, especially of alternating currents. [< French *onde* wave (< Latin *unda*) + *-graph*]

**on|dom|e|ter** (on dom′ə tər), *n.* a device for measuring the length of radio waves. [< French *onde* wave (< Latin *unda*) + English *-meter*]

**on-drive** (on′drīv′, ôn′-), *n., v.,* **-drove, -driv|en, -driv|ing.** *Cricket.* **—*n.*** a drive to the right side of the field when a right-handed batsman is batting or the left side when a left-handed batsman is batting. **—*v.i., v.t.*** to hit an on-drive (of a bowler's delivery).

**one** (wun), *n., adj., pron.* **—*n.*** **1** the first and lowest whole number; the number 1. **2** a single person or thing indicated: *I like the ones in that box. I gave him the one he wanted. Is this the one I gave you? Are you the one who is going to help?*
**—*adj.*** **1** being a single unit or individual: *one apple, one dollar. A person has one head and one neck.* **SYN**: a, any. **2** some: *One day he will be sorry.* **3** of a single kind, nature, or character; the same: *All face one way. They held one opinion. Graphite and diamond are chemically one substance.* **SYN**: identical. **4** joined together; united: *The class was one in its approval. They replied in one voice.* **SYN**: undivided. **5** a certain; particular: *A short speech was made by one John Smith.*
**—*pron.*** **1** some person or thing: *Two may go, but one must stay. One of Longfellow's poems was chosen for the new reader.* **2** any person standing for people in general: *One does not like to be left out. One must work hard to achieve success.* **3** the same person or thing: *In Robert Louis Stevenson's story, Doctor Jekyll and Mr. Hyde were one and the same.*
**all one, a** just the same: *'Twere all one That I should love a bright particular star, And think to wed it, he is so above me* (Shakespeare). **b** making no difference; of no consequence.
**at one,** in agreement or harmony: *The two judges were at one about the winner. Where Conservative and Labour critics of the Government's policy are at one is their common belief that the Prices and Incomes Bill will not achieve the restraints which the Government desires* (Manchester Guardian Weekly).
**make one, a** to form or be one of a number, assembly, or party: *I made one upon that winter's journey of which so many tales have gone abroad* (Robert Louis Stevenson). **b** to join together; unite in marriage: *The parson pronounced the words that made the couple one.*
**one and all,** everyone: *Towards this great end it behooves us one and all to work* (London Daily News).
**one by one,** one after another: *They came out the door one by one. As the teacher called out our names, we stepped up one by one to receive our report cards.*
**one or two,** a few: *The book was never popular and only one or two copies were sold in the larger bookstores.*
**one up on,** *Informal.* an advantage over: *Ever since the Russians put Sputnik I into orbit in 1957 the United States and Soviet Union have been trying to get one up on each other in the space race* (Observer).
[Old English *ān.* Compare etym. under **a**[2], **an**[1].]
► **one.** The use of the impersonal pronoun *one,* especially when repeated, is characteristically formal: *One can't be too careful, can one?*

**-one,** *suffix.* ketone, as in *acetone, progesterone.* [< Greek *-ōnē,* a feminine suffix]

**one-act|er** (wun′ak′tər), *n. Informal.* a one-act play or opera.

**one another,** one the other; each other: *They struck at one another. They were in one another's way.*
► **one another, each other.** As a reciprocal pronoun, *one another* is usually used with reference to more than two, *each other* with reference to two: *The members of the team support one another. The two hate each other.*

**one-arm bandit** (wun′ärm′), *U.S. Slang.* a gambling device having a lever at one side, operated by dropping a coin into a slot; slot machine.

**one-armed bandit** (wun′ärmd′), *U.S. Slang.* one-arm bandit.

**one-bag|ger** (wun′bag′ər), *n. Baseball Slang.* a one-base hit; single.

**one-base hit** (wun′bās′), *Baseball.* a hit that allows the batter to reach first base only; single.

**one-celled** (wun′seld′), *adj.* having only one cell: *one-celled protozoa.*

**one-class** (wun′klas′, -kläs′), *adj.* **1** providing the same accommodations for all passengers: *a one-class airline service.* **2** of or for one class of people only; exclusive: *a one-class school, a one-class club.*

**one-di|men|sion|al** (wun′də men′shə nəl), *adj.* **1** having no depth; of little scope; not profound; fanciful: *The one-dimensional world of bad men and good men.* **2** having only one dimension: *Time is one-dimensional.* **—one′-di|men′sion|al|ly,** *adv.*

**one-eyed** (wun′īd′), *adj.* **1** having only one eye. **2** blind in one eye.

**one|fold** (wun′fōld′), *adj.* consisting of but one; single; simple.

**one-for-one** (wun′fər wun′), *adj.* = one-to-one.

**one-hand|ed** (wun′han′did), *adj., adv.* **—*adj.*** **1** having or using only one hand: *a one-handed clock.* **2** used, worked, or performed with one hand: *... spectacular one-handed catches* (New Yorker).
**—*adv.*** with one hand: *He was caught ... finishing his stroke one-handed* (London Times).

**one-horse** (wun′hôrs′), *adj.* **1** drawn or worked by a single horse: *a little one-horse sleigh* (Harriet Beecher Stowe). **2** using or having only a single horse: *a one-horse farmer.* **3** *Informal, Figurative.* of little scope, capacity, or importance; minor: *a one-horse town.*

**O|nei|da** (ō nī′də), *n., pl.* **-da** or **-das. 1** a member of an American Indian tribe of Iroquoian stock formerly living in central New York State. **2** the language of this tribe. [American English < reduction of Iroquoian (Oneida) *tiionĕñ′iote′* "standing rock" (because such a rock was a landmark near one of their villages)]

**o|nei|ric** (ō nī′rik), *adj.* of or having to do with dreams.

**o|nei|ro|crit|i|cal** (ō nī′rə krit′ə kəl), *adj.* having to do with or practicing the interpretation of dreams. [< Greek *oneirokritikós* (< *óneiros* dream + *kritikós* critic, student (of) < *krítēs* a judge < *krīnein* to judge) + English *-al*[1]] **—o|nei′ro|crit′i|cal|ly,** *adv.*

**o|nei|rol|o|gy** (ō′nī rol′ə jē), *n.* the science or subject of dreams, or of their interpretation. [< Greek *óneiros* dream + English *-logy*]

**o|nei|ro|man|cy** (ō nī′rə man′sē), *n.* divination by dreams. [< Greek *óneiros* dream + *manteíā* divination < *mántis* seer]

**one-leg|ged** (wun′leg′id, -legd′), *adj.* **1** having only one leg: *... one-legged, pedestal-based chairs, dining tables and coffee tables that have all the weightless elegance of a stemmed wine glass* (Time). **2** *Figurative.* one-sided: *a one-legged argument.*

**one-lin|er** (wun′lī′nər), *n.* a snappy or pithy remark, usually of one sentence; wisecrack: *He even scored with an old one-liner about banks: "Never trust a place where they pull the shades down at three o'clock in the afternoon"* (Time).

**one-lung** (wun′lung′), *adj.* **1** having only one lung. **2** *Slang.* having only one cylinder: *The rice comes down to Bangkok ... in boats powered by one-lung motors* (Harper's).

**one-man** (wun′man′), *adj.* **1** consisting of only one person; exercised or managed by only one man: *a one-man rule or dictatorship, a one-man job.* **2** of or for a single person; designed to be carried, worn, or used by one man: *a one-man submarine.*

**one-man, one-vote** (wun′vōt′), *U.S. Politics.* of, having to do with, or designating the principle by which seats in a legislature are reapportioned according to the population of the area represented: *Under Federal Court mandate to draw new Congressional district lines that would meet the Supreme Court's one-man, one-vote doctrine, the Legislature ... ingeniously met the Court's stipulations but left untouched some of the worst gerrymanders in the state* (New York Times).

**one-man show,** an exhibition of the work of one man; display or performance of the skill of a particular man: *One-man shows of painting opening tomorrow include those of work by Picasso* (New York Times).

**one|ness** (wun′nis), *n.* **1** the quality of being one in number or the only one of its kind; singleness. **SYN**: individuality. **2** the quality of being the same in kind; sameness; identity: *the solidarity and*

---

**Pronunciation Key:** hat, āge, cãre, fär; let, ēqual, tėrm; it, īce; hot, ōpen, ôrder; **oil, out;** cup, pu̇t, rüle; **ch**ild; lo**ng**; **th**in; ᴛʜen; **zh,** measure; ə represents **a** in about, **e** in taken, **i** in pencil, **o** in lemon, **u** in circus.

*oneness of humanity* (John Greenleaf Whittier). **3** the fact of forming one whole; unity; union: *the oneness of marriage.* **4** agreement in mind, feeling, or purpose; harmony: *oneness of mind.*

**one-night|er** (wun′nī′tər), *n. U.S.* **1** a one-night stand: *A few units like ... the Modern Jazz Quartet are spending an increasing amount of their time playing one-nighters* (Nat Hentoff). **2** an actor or performer who plays one-night stands.

**one-night stand** (wun′nīt′), *U.S.* **1** a show for one night in a town by a touring company of actors or other performers. **2** the place where such a show is given.

**one-o-cat** or **one-o′-cat** (wun′ə kat′), *n.* a ball game in which there is one batter, three to six fielders, a pitcher, and one base in addition to home plate. It is a forerunner of baseball. *He spells me increasingly in romps and games of one-o-cat* (New Yorker).

**one-off** (wun′ôf′, -of′), *adj., n. British.* **—*adj.*** made or intended for only one time, occasion, or person: *These relationships involve money and are on a continuing basis rather than a one-off purchase* (London Times).
**—*n.*** anything made or intended for one time, occasion, or person; something special.

**one old cat,** = one-o-cat.

**one-on-one** (wun′on wun′), *adj.* (in basketball, football, and other team sport) of or characterized by each defensive player guarding only his opponent; man-to-man: *a one-on-one defense, a one-on-one drill or practice.*

**one-piece** (wun′pēs′), *adj.* of or in one piece; not having separate parts: *a one-piece garment.*

**one-piec|er** (wun′pē′sər), *n.* a one-piece garment.

**on|er** (wun′ər), *n.* **1** *Slang.* a person or thing of a unique or remarkable kind. **2** *Slang.* a person expert at or much addicted to something: *Miss Sally's such a oner for that* (Dickens). **3** *Informal.* something known by or in some way connected with the number one.

**one-reel|er** (wun′rē′lər), *n. U.S.* a short motion picture, such as a newsreel or cartoon, contained in a single reel of film that runs approximately twelve minutes.

**on|er|ous** (on′ər əs), *adj.* **1** hard to take or carry; burdensome; oppressive; troublesome: *Overtime work is well paid, but it is often onerous.* **SYN**: heavy, weighty, arduous. **2** *Law.* of the nature of a legal burden or obligation. [< Old French *onereus* (with English *-ous*), learned borrowing from Latin *onerōsus* < *onus, -eris* burden] **—on′er|ous|ly,** *adv.* **—on′er|ous|ness,** *n.*

**one|self** (wun self′, wunz-), *pron.* one's own self: *At the age of seven one ought to dress oneself. One should not praise oneself. To be pleased with oneself is the surest way of offending everybody else* (Edward G. Bulwer-Lytton).
**be oneself, a** to have full control of one's mind or body: *He was not himself after he heard the news that his son had been in a serious accident.* **b** to act naturally: *Be yourself and stop putting on airs.*
**by oneself, a** having no company; alone: *To sit down to dinner all by oneself!* (Anthony Trollope). **b** single-handed; unaided: *It was the first time that he did his homework by himself, without any help whatever.*
**come to oneself, a** to return to consciousness; come to: *When she came to herself she saw her mother at her bedside.* **b** to regain one's faculties or composure: *I was momentarily stunned by the news, but quickly came to myself and went on as if nothing happened.*
**fall over oneself,** to make every effort; show extreme eagerness: *Newspapers which virtually ignored the sport of sailing for years past, have recently been falling over themselves to glean the facts about* [*it*] (London Times).
**feel like oneself,** to feel fit; be in a sound or healthy condition: *He hasn't been feeling like himself since his operation.*
**find oneself.** See under **find.**
**speak for oneself, a** to represent only one's own opinion or ideas: *He speaks for himself, since none of us agrees with him.* **b** to be self-evident; show the facts or the whole truth: *The scores of the singles matches speak for themselves* (London Times).
**take it upon oneself,** to assume a task or responsibility: *One danger is that the junta leaders may take it upon themselves to force a showdown with the rebels* (New York Times).

**one-shot** (wun′shot′), *adj., n. U.S. Informal.* **—*adj.*** **1** intended for use on only one occasion, and sometimes as a quick, temporary measure: *The one-shot boycott was a low-pressure affair* (Wall Street Journal). **2** undertaken, issued, or occurring one time only; formed for a single project or venture: *a one-shot magazine. Solutions will not be easy, one-shot solutions* (Saturday Review).
**—*n.*** **1** a magazine or booklet, issued once, and usually devoted to a subject popular at the moment: *Sputnik's beep-beep already has signaled the start of a bunch of one-shots on space travel, satellites, moon missions* (Wall Street Journal). **2** a single subject or theme to the exclusion or neglect of others: *The western was the one-shot of last season's television.* **3** anything done or occurring only once: *His attempt to cross the English Channel was a one-shot, but he tried the Thames more than once.*

**one-sid|ed** (wun′sī′did), *adj.* **1** seeing only one side of a question; partial; unfair; prejudiced: *The umpire seemed one-sided in his decisions.* **2** uneven; unequal: *If one team is much better than the other, a game is one-sided.* **3** having but one side. **4** on only one side. **5** having one side larger or more developed than the other. **6** *Law.* involving but one side; unilateral: *a one-sided obligation.* **—one′-sid′ed|ly,** *adv.* **—one′-sid′ed|ness,** *n.*

**one's self,** = oneself.

**one-step** (wun′step′), *n., v.,* **-stepped, -stepping.** **—*n.*** **1** a ballroom dance much like a quick walk. Its original version, popular in the 1920's, was based on the turkey trot. **2** music for it, in two-quarter time.
**—*v.i.*** to dance the one-step.

**one-stop** (wun′stop′), *adj.* designed to eliminate making many stops; providing diverse services at a single location: *one-stop shopping, a one-stop department store.*

**one|time** or **one-time** (wun′tīm′), *adj.* **1** of the past; former: *a onetime millionaire; ... the onetime home of one of the nation's great amateur scientists* (Scientific American). **2** on only one instance; occurring only once: *Police who deal with homicide or other major crimes ... have onetime or rare contact with their customers* (Atlantic).

**one-to-one** (wun′tə wun′), *adj. Mathematics.* matching every element in a set with one and only one element in another set. *Examples:* {1, 2, 3, 4, 5} and {10, 20, 30, 40, 50} are two sets showing a one-to-one correspondence. The correspondence between a list of five boys' names and the five boys whose names are listed is one-to-one.

**one-track** (wun′trak′), *adj.* **1** having only one track: *a one-track railroad line.* **2** *Informal, Figurative.* understanding or doing only one thing at a time; narrow: *a one-track mind.*

**one-two** (wun′tü′), *n.* **1** (in boxing) two punches given in quick succession, usually one with the left hand followed by one with the right hand: *a lightning one-two on the jaw.* **2** *Slang, Figurative.* a quick retort: *He countered each question with a stunning one-two.*

**one-up** (wun′up′), *v.t.,* **-upped, -up|ping.** *Informal.* to gain one up on; outstrip; go one better: *Trying to be funny, he said to the salesgirl: "That horse is a fake." She one-upped him: "Yes, so was the original"* (Saturday Review). *The party's 46-year-old leader ... one-upped the socialists by endorsing the Saskatchewan plan* (Canada Month).

**one-up|man** (wun′up′mən), *v.t.,* **-manned, -manning.** *Informal.* to one-up; go one better. [back formation < *one-upmanship*]

**one-up|man|ship** (wun′up′mən ship), *n. Informal.* the skill of being able to gain the advantage over one's opponent. [< *one up* (*on*), idiom; patterned on *gamesmanship*]

**one-way** (wun′wā′), *adj.* **1** moving or allowing movement in only one direction: *a one-way street, a one-way ticket, one-way traffic.* **2** leading or developing in only one direction: *a one-way argument.* **3** that works in only one direction: *One-way glass looks like a mirror on one side but can be seen through on the other side.*

**one world** or **One World,** the idea that the world is a single unit in which, through international cooperation, ways must be found to keep it united and make it safe for different opinions.

**one-world|er** (wun′wėrl′dər), *n. U.S. Informal.* a person who favors internationalism.

**one-world|ism** (wun′wėrl′diz əm), *n. Informal.* internationalism.

**one-world|ness** (wun′wėrld′nis), *n. Informal.* the state or condition of having internationalism.

**on|fall** (on′fôl′, ôn′-), *n.* an onset; attack.

**on|flow** (on′flō′, ôn′-), *n.* an onward flow.

**on-glide** (on′glīd′, ôn′-), *n. Phonetics.* a transitional sound produced at the movement of the articulars to a position for a speech sound different from their first position.

**on|go|ing** (on′gō′ing, ôn′-), *adj., n.* **—*adj.*** continuous; uninterrupted.
**—*n.*** **ongoings,** goings on: *It breaks my heart to hear you upholding such ongoings* (Samuel R. Crockett).

***on|ion** (un′yən), *n.* **1** the bulb of a plant eaten raw or used in cooking. It has a sharp, strong smell and taste. The bulb is formed of concentric layers of modified leaves. *Indeed, the tears live in an onion that should water this sorrow* (Shakespeare). **2** the plant it grows on. It belongs to the amaryllis family. **3** any of various similar or related plants.
**know one's onions,** *Informal.* to have the knowledge and skill necessary for competence: *The author is a little pretentious ... but on the whole he does know his onions* (T. S. Eliot).
[< Old French *oignon* < Latin *uniō, -ōnis* onion] **—on′ion|like′,** *adj.*

***onion**
definitions 2, 3

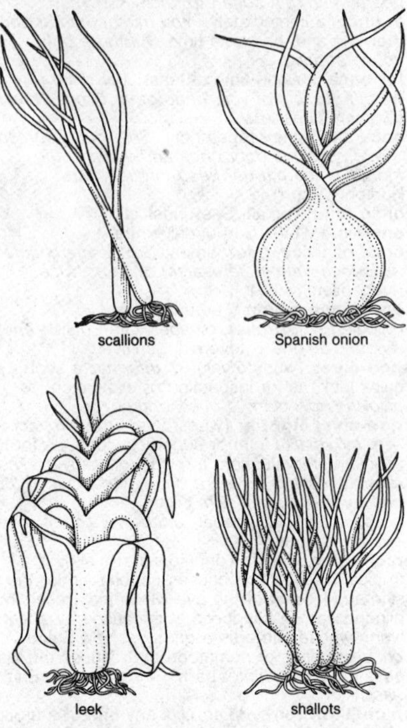


**onion fly,** a dipterous insect whose larva feeds underground on the onion.

**onion maggot,** the larva of an onion fly.

**on|ion|skin** (un′yən skin′), *n.* a very thin, translucent paper used especially for carbon copies of typewritten letters and bills.

**on|ion|y** (un′yə nē), *adj.* having the taste or smell of onions; onionlike: *Some bacterial cultures produce distinct fruity and oniony odors* (Science News Letter).

**on-is|land|er** (on′ī′lən dər, ôn′-), *n. U.S.* a permanent resident of an island.

**on-li|cence** or **on-li|cense** (on′lī′səns, ôn′-), *n. British.* a license for the sale of alcoholic liquor to be consumed on the premises.

**on|li|est** (ōn′lē ist), *adj., superlative of* **only.** *Informal.* best; finest: *I went there on the one and onliest trip I made on a tanker, when I was younger'n Davy* (New Yorker).

**on-line** (on′līn′, ôn′-), *adj., adv.* **—*adj.*** **1a** (of equipment associated with an electronic computer) operating under the direct control of the central equipment: *PSA* [*Pacific Southwest Airlines*] *has an on-line automated reservations system that helps make sure all its seats are filled with passengers and all its passengers have seats* (Scientific American). **b** operating in real-time. **2** (of a railroad or other transport operation or public service) being or taking place on the regular line.
**—*adv.*** **1** under the direct control of central equipment: [*The*] *computer is connected "on-line" to the plant* (London Daily Telegraph). **2** in line with an actual process or operation.

**on|look|er** (on′lu̇k′ər, ôn′-), *n.* a person who watches without taking part; spectator: *It is the onlooker that sees most of the game* (Macmillan's Magazine). **SYN**: bystander, looker-on.

**on|look|ing** (on′lu̇k′ing, ôn′-), *adj., n.* watching; seeing; noticing.

**on|ly** (ōn′lē), *adj., adv., conj.* **—*adj.*** **1** by itself or themselves; one and no more; sole or single: *an only son. Water is his only drink. This is the only road along the shore.* **SYN**: solitary, unique. See syn. under **single.** **2** best; finest: *She is the only woman for me. He is the only writer for my taste. He is the only man of Italy, Always excepted my dear Claudio* (Shakespeare).
**—*adv.*** **1** just; merely: *I sold only two.* **2** and no one else; and nothing more; and that is all: *Only he remained. I did it only through friendship.*
**—*conj.*** *Informal.* **1** except that; but: *I would have*

*started, only it rained.* **2** but then; it must be added that: *We had camped right beside a stream, only the water was not fit to drink.*
**if only,** I wish: *If you would only say yes. If only the sun would shine.*
**only too,** very: *She was only too glad to help us.* [Old English *ānlīc, ǣnlīc*]
► **Only** and several other limiting adverbs such as *scarcely* and *just* are often placed immediately before the verb even when they modify some other element in the sentence: *I only know this* (instead of *I know only this*); *I only see them when I go to New York* (instead of *only when I go to New York*); *I scarcely had enough time to finish* (instead of *scarcely enough time*). Although this construction has often been condemned as illogical and ambiguous, it has been firmly established for centuries, both in literary English and in ordinary speech. In actual fact, this word order is rarely ambiguous: in speaking, stress and intonation make clear which element is modified by the adverb; in writing, the context ordinarily excludes all meanings but the one intended.

**on|ly-be|got|ten** (ōn′lē bi got′ən), *adj.* begotten as an only child.

**ONO** (no periods) or **o.n.o.,** or the nearest offer (used of an advertised selling price especially in a classified advertisement).

**on|o|mas|tic** (on′ə mas′tik), *adj.* **1** of or connected with a name or names, or with the naming of something: *Naming a horse is not an easy matter ... The result was that for the seven years we had him the onomastic question remained pending* (New Yorker). **2** *Law.* designating the signature of a legal document the body of which is in the handwriting of another person. [< Greek *onomastikós* < *onomázein* to name < *ónoma* name]

**on|o|mas|ti|con** (on′ə mas′tə kon), *n.* a vocabulary of names, especially of persons, arranged in alphabetical or other order.

**on|o|mas|tics** (on′ə mas′tiks), *n.* the study of names: *Onomastics shows that a name like Puddifoot is not as hard to combat as, say, the stumpy foot that the name describes* (Manchester Guardian Weekly).

**on|o|ma|tol|o|gy** (on′ə mə tol′ə jē), *n.* = onomastics.

**on|o|mat|o|poe|ia** (on′ə mat′ə pē′ə), *n.* **1** the formation of a name or word by imitating the sound associated with the thing designated, as in *buzz, hum, cuckoo, hiss, slap, splash.* **2** a word or phrase so formed. **3** the adaptation of the sound to the sense for rhetorical effect. *Examples:* The tintinnabulation that so musically wells From the bells (Edgar Allan Poe). The double double double beat of the thundering drum (John Dryden). [< Latin *onomatopoeia* < Greek *onomatopoiiā* < *ónoma* word, name + *poieîn* make, do]

**on|o|mat|o|poe|ic** (on′ə mat′ə pē′ik), *adj.* having to do with or like onomatopoeia; imitative in sound; echoic. —**on′o|mat′o|poe′i|cal|ly,** *adv.*

**on|o|mat|o|po|e|sis** (on′ə mat′ə pō ē′sis), *n.* = onomatopoeia.

**on|o|mat|o|po|et|ic** (on′ə mat′ə pō et′ik), *adj.* = onomatopoeic. —**on′o|mat′o|po|et′i|cal|ly,** *adv.*

**On|on|da|ga** (on′ən dô′gə, -dä′-), *n., pl.* **-ga** or **-gas. 1** a member of a tribe of Iroquois Indians formerly living in central New York State. **2** the Iroquoian language of this tribe. [American English < Iroquoian (Onondaga) *Onontá'gé,* place name, (literally) on top of the hill]

**on|rush** (on′rush′, ôn′-), *n.* a violent forward rush: *He was knocked down by the onrush of water. ... the tremendous onrush and check of the German attack in the west that opened the great war* (H. G. Wells).

**on|rush|ing** (on′rush′ing, ôn′-), *adj.* that rushes on; moving forward rapidly: *the onrushing crowd at a bargain sale, onrushing vehicles; the onrushing advent of television* (Maclean's).

**on|screen** (on′skrēn′, ôn′-), *adj., adv.* **1** seen on the motion-picture or television screen: *an onscreen moderator.* **2** while acting for motion pictures or television: *onscreen showmanship.*

**on|set** (on′set′, ôn′-), *n.* **1** the beginning or start: *The onset of this disease is gradual.* **SYN:** commencement. **2** an attack: *The onset of the enemy took us by surprise.* **SYN:** assault, onslaught.

**on|shore** (on′shôr′, -shōr′; ôn′-), *adv., adj.* **1** toward the shore. **2** on the shore.

**on|side** (on′sīd′, ôn′-), *adj., adv.* in a position allowed by the rules of the game; not offside.

**on-site** (on′sīt′, ôn′-), *adj.* at the location of something; on the actual site where something takes place regularly: *on-site maintenance of aircraft. The working group of seismologists and physicists failed to agree on criteria for on-site inspection* (Bulletin of Atomic Scientists).

**on|slaught** (on′slôt′, ôn′-), *n.* a vigorous attack: *The Indians made an onslaught on the settlers' fort.* **SYN:** onset. [< Germanic (compare Middle Low German *anslach* attack)]

**on|stage** (on′stāj′, ôn′-), *adj., adv.* **1** on the part of the stage that the audience can see: *During the battle scene, a ship was sunk onstage.* **2** while acting for an audience: *The children begin their onstage Kabuki experience from the age of five* (Atlantic).

**on-stream** (on′strēm′, ôn′-), *adj., adv.* —*adj.* operating in a fluid manner; using a fluid method; of or by means of flow: *On-stream process control by fluorescent spectrometry has become established ... for control of the zinc coating of sheet metal* (G. L. Clark).
—*adv.* into fluid operation: *The plant ... is expected to come on-stream early next year* (New Scientist).

**on|sweep** (on′swēp′, ôn′-), *n.* the act or fact of sweeping onward: *the onsweep of our van* (Rudyard Kipling).

**Ont.,** Ontario.

**On|tar|i|an** (on tãr′ē ən), *adj., n.* —*adj.* of or having to do with Ontario, a province in Canada, north of the Great Lakes.
—*n.* a native or inhabitant of Ontario.

**on-the-cuff** (on′ᴛʜə kuf′, ôn′-), *adj., adv. U.S. Informal.* on credit: *And the proud symbol of the growing enthusiasm for on-the-cuff spending is the credit card* (Newsweek).

**on-the-job** (on′ᴛʜə job′, ôn′-), *adj.* during the actual performance of one's job or duties; not away from, prior to, or in preparation for a job: *on-the-job teaching, on-the-job experience. The boys would be put into on-the-job training situations throughout the conservation field* (Harper's).

**on-the-rec|ord** (on′ᴛʜə rek′ərd, ôn′-), *adj.* **1** for public consumption; not off-the-record: *In both on-the-record statements and private comments, leading officials portrayed* [*him*] *as a man of uncertain political purpose* (New York Times). **2** official: *Chiang's demand for an on-the-record commitment from Washington held up ... the planned evacuation* (New York Times).

**on-the-scene** (on′ᴛʜə sēn′, ôn′-), *adj.* = on-the-spot.

**on-the-spot** (on′ᴛʜə spot′, ôn′-), *adj. Informal.* **1** on the location of; at that very place: *on-the-spot news coverage. On-the-spot camerawork in Europe ...* (Maclean's). **2** that takes place immediately and usually without formality: *on-the-spot diagnoses of illnesses, an on-the-spot business deal.*

**on|tic** (on′tik), *adj. Philosophy.* of or having to do with being or actual existence: *ontic reality.* [< Greek *óntos* being + English *-ic*]

**on|to** (on′tü, ôn′-; *before consonants often* on′tə, ôn′-), *prep.* **1** on to; to a position on or upon: *to throw a ball onto the roof, to get onto a horse, a boat driven onto the rocks.* **2** *Informal.* familiar with; aware of; experienced in: *to get onto a new job. It doesn't take long to get onto him and his alibis.*
► **onto, on to.** When *on* is clearly an adverb and *to* a preposition, the two words should of course be separated: *The rest of us drove on to the city.* When the two words make a definite preposition, they are usually written solid: *The team trotted onto the floor. They looked out onto the park.*

**on|to|gen|e|sis** (on′tə jen′ə sis), *n.* = ontogeny.

**on|to|ge|net|ic** (on′tō jə net′ik), *adj.* of or having to do with ontogeny: *It is Gesell who has uniquely been the draftsman of the architecture of the developing mind—what he calls "the ontogenetic patterning of behavior"* (Harper's). —**on′to|ge|net′i|cal|ly,** *adv.*

**on|to|gen|ic** (on′tə jen′ik), *adj.* = ontogenetic.

**on|tog|e|nist** (on toj′ə nist), *n.* a person skilled in the study of ontogeny.

**on|tog|e|ny** (on toj′ə nē), *n. Biology.* the development of an individual organism, or the history of its development: *The development of any organism demonstrates the biological law that ontogeny repeats phylogeny* (New Yorker). [< Greek *ôn, óntos* being + *-geneia* origin < *-genēs* born, produced]

**on|to|log|i|cal** (on′tə loj′ə kəl), *adj.* of or having to do with ontology: *The root of every philosophy, says Tillich, is the ontological question. What is "being," what is "real," what is "ultimate reality beyond everything that seems to be real?"* (Time). —**on′to|log′i|cal|ly,** *adv.*

**ontological argument** or **proof,** the contention that since our idea of God is that of a perfect being and since existence is part of perfection, our idea of God is an idea of a necessarily existent being. This argument, used by Anselm and Descartes, is repeated by Thomas Aquinas.

**on|tol|o|gism** (on tol′ə jiz əm), *n.* the doctrine that human beings have an intuitive knowledge of God and that this knowledge is the basis of all other knowledge.

**on|tol|o|gist** (on tol′ə jist), *n.* a person skilled in ontology.

**on|tol|o|gy** (on tol′ə jē), *n.* the branch of philosophy that deals with the nature of reality. [< New Latin *ontologia* < Greek *ôn, óntos* being + *-logiā* -logy]

**o|nus** (ō′nəs), *n.* a burden; responsibility: *The onus of housekeeping fell upon the daughters. The onus of proving it was not right lay with those who disputed its being so* (Samuel Butler). **SYN:** duty, obligation. [< Latin *onus*]

**o|nus pro|ban|di** (ō′nəs prō ban′dī), *Latin.* the burden of proof.

**on|ward** (on′wərd, ôn′-), *adv., adj.* —*adv.* **1** toward the front; further on; on; forward: *The crowd around the store window began to move onward.* **SYN:** forth. See syn. under **forward. 2** *Archaic.* at a position in advance: *My grief lies onward and my joy behind* (Shakespeare).
—*adj.* on; further on; toward the front; forward: *An onward movement began. Resuming his onward course* (Washington Irving).
[Middle English *onward*]

**on|wards** (on′wərdz, ôn′-), *adv.* = onward.

**on|y|cha** (on′ə kə), *n.* an ingredient of the incense used in the Mosaic ritual, supposed to be the operculum of a marine gastropod. [< Late Latin *onycha* < Greek *ónycha,* accusative of *ónyx* a kind of aromatic substance]

**o|nych|i|a** (ō nik′ē ə), *n.* inflammation of the matrix of the nails or claws. [< New Latin *onychia* < Greek *ónyx, ónychos* claw]

**on|y|cho|my|co|sis** (on′ə kō mī kō′sis), *n.* a fungous disease of the nails characterized by thickened, brittle, white nails. [< Greek *ónyx, ónychos* claw + *mýkēs, -ētos* fungus + English *-osis*]

**on|yx** (on′iks), *n.* a variety of quartz with straight bands of different colors and shades. It is a semiprecious stone used in making cameos. [< Latin *onyx* < Greek *ónyx, ónychos* claw, fingernail (because of its color)]

**onyx marble,** a variety of calcite resembling true onyx, used for ornamental stonework; Mexican onyx; oriental alabaster. It is formed by water deposition, and is commonly found in caves.

**oo-,** *combining form.* egg or eggs; ovum: *Oology = the science of* (*birds'*) *eggs.* [< Greek *ōión* egg]

**oo** (ü), *interj., n., v.i.* = ooh.

**OO** (no periods), orbiting observatory.

**OOB** (no periods) or **O.O.B.,** off-off-Broadway.

**o|o|blast** (ō′ə blast), *n. Biology.* a primitive or formative ovum not yet developed into a true ovum. [< *oo-* + Greek *blastós* germ, sprout]

**o|o|cyst** (ō′ə sist), *n.* a cyst in sporozoans that contains developing sporozoites, present within a host organism. [< *oo-* + *cyst*]

**o|o|cyte** (ō′ə sīt), *n. Biology.* an ovum in the stage that precedes maturation.

**oo|dles** (ü′dəlz), *n.pl. Informal.* large or unlimited quantities; heaps; loads: *oodles of money. As for the den, we converted that into a Polynesian-style bar—oodles of rattan and hogsheads to roost on* (S. J. Perelman).

**oof** (üf), *n. British Slang.* cash; money. [earlier *ooftish* < Yiddish *auf tische* on the table (as "cash down")]

**oof-bird** (üf′bėrd′), *n. British Slang.* **1** the imaginary bird that produces oof. **2** a person from whom money is obtained.

**oof|y** (ü′fē), *adj.,* **oof|i|er, oof|i|est.** *British Slang.* rich; wealthy.

**o|og|a|mous** (ō og′ə məs), *adj. Biology.* heterogamous.

**o|og|a|my** (ō og′ə mē), *n. Biology.* the conjugation of two gametes of dissimilar form. [< *oo-* + *-gamy*]

**o|o|gen|e|sis** (ō′ə jen′ə sis), *n. Biology.* the origin and development of the ovum: *Different stages of spermatogenesis and oogenesis differ considerably in sensitivity* (C. Auerbach). [< *oo-* + *genesis*]

**o|o|ge|net|ic** (ō′ə jə net′ik), *adj.* of or having to do with oogenesis.

**o|o|go|ni|al** (ō′ə gō′nē əl), *adj.* of or having to do with an oogonium.

**o|o|go|ni|um** (ō′ə gō′nē əm), *n., pl.* **-ni|a** (-nē ə), **-ni|ums. 1** *Biology.* a primitive germ cell that divides and gives rise to the oocytes. **2** *Botany.* the female reproductive organ in various thallophytes, usually a rounded cell or sac containing one or more oospheres. [< New Latin *oogonium* < Greek *ōión* egg + *gónos* producing]

**ooh** (ü), *interj., n., v. Informal.* —*interj., n.* an exclamation of surprise, admiration, delight, fear, or other emotion or sensation: *The oohs and ahs of shoppers this week will not signal a rest for the display staff* (New York Times).
—*v.i.* to exclaim "ooh" in admiration, delight, or

**Pronunciation Key:** hat, āge, cãre, fär; let, ēqual, tėrm; it, īce; hot, ōpen, ôrder; oil, out; cup, pu̇t, rüle; child; long; thin; ᴛʜen; zh, measure; ə represents a in about, e in taken, i in pencil, o in lemon, u in circus.

other feeling of emotion or particular sensation: *Women oohed at the black-and-white sari worn by Madame Vijaya Lakshmi Pandit of India* (Newsweek). Also, **oo**.

**oo|la|kan** or **oo|la|chan** (ü′lə kən), *n.* the candlefish of the northwestern coast of America; eulachon. [< a native Chinook name]

**o|o|lite** (ō′ə līt), *n.* a rock, usually limestone, composed of rounded concretions of calcium carbonate resembling the roe of fish. [probably an adaptation of French *oölithe* < Greek *ōión* egg + *líthos* stone]

**o|o|lit|ic** (ō′ə lit′ik), *adj.* of or like oolite.

**o|o|log|i|cal** (ō′ə loj′ə kəl), *adj.* of or having to do with oology. **—o′o|log′i|cal|ly**, *adv.*

**o|ol|o|gist** (ō ol′ə jist), *n.* **1** a person skilled in oology. **2** a collector of birds' eggs.

**o|ol|o|gy** (ō ol′ə jē), *n.* the branch of ornithology that deals with the study of the eggs of birds.

**oo|long** (ü′lông, -long), *n.* a dark tea consisting of leaves that were partially fermented before they were dried. [< Chinese *wu-lung* black dragon]

**oom** (ōm), *n.* (in Dutch use) uncle, used affectionately before the name of an elderly man. [< Dutch *oom*]

**Oom** (ōm, üm, u̇m), *n. Afrikaans.* uncle.

**oo|mi|ak** or **oo|mi|ac** (ü′mē ak), *n.* = umiak.

**oo|ming|mack** (ü′ming mak), *n.* = musk ox. [< an Eskimo word]

**oom|pah** (üm′pä′), *n.* **1** the low, continuous, puffing sound of a large brass instrument, as the tuba: *The ubiquitous beer halls echo to the oompah of brass bands* (Newsweek). **2** *Slang.* a brassy, monotonous manner or style. [imitative]

**oomph** (u̇mf), *n. U.S. Slang.* **1** spirit; vigor; vitality; enthusiasm: *"Fellas, let's have all the oomph you can give these bass notes— just a little stronger"* (New York Times). **2** = sex appeal: *His clothes have oomph, said a buyer* (New York Times). [imitative]

**o|o|phore** (ō′ə fôr, -fōr), *n. Obsolete.* oophyte. [< *oo-* + *-phore*]

**o|o|pho|rec|to|my** (ō′ə fə rek′tə mē), *n., pl.* **-mies.** the surgical removal of one or both ovaries. [< New Latin *oophoron* ovary + Greek *ektomē* a cutting out]

**o|o|phor|ic** (ō′ə fôr′ik, -for′-), *adj. Obsolete.* of or having to do with the oophore.

**o|o|pho|ri|tis** (ō′ə fə rī′tis), *n.* inflammation of the ovary.

**o|o|phyte** (ō′ə fīt), *n.* the generation or form of a plant that bears the sexual organs in the alternation of generations, as in ferns, mosses, and liverworts.

**o|o|phyt|ic** (ō′ə fit′ik), *adj.* of or having to do with the oophyte.

**oops** (wups, üps, ups), *interj.* an exclamation of apology or dismay, as at a blunder: *Last week the court said oops, and ... withdrew both opinions* (Time). Also, **whoops**, **woops**. [origin unknown]

**oo|ra|li** (ü rä′lē), *n.* = curare. [< a Tupi word]

**oo|ri|al** (u̇r′ē əl), *n.* = urial.

**oo|rie** (u̇r′ē), *adj.* = ourie.

**Oort Cloud** (u̇rt, ōrt), a swarm of perhaps billions of comets surrounding the solar system in a zone extending from about 4 trillion to 13 trillion miles: *The comets in the Oort Cloud spend most of their time so far from the sun that they are easily perturbed by the gravitational influences of other stars* (Stephen P. Maran). [< Jan H. *Oort*, born 1900, Dutch astronomer, who first suggested its existence]

**o|o|sperm** (ō′ə spėrm), *n.* **1** *Zoology.* a fertilized ovum; zygote. **2** *Botany. Obsolete.* an oospore. [< *oo-* + Greek *spérma* seed]

**o|o|sphere** (ō′ə sfir), *n. Botany.* a female reproductive cell contained in an oogonium which when fertilized becomes an oospore.

**o|o|spore** (ō′ə spôr, -spōr), *n. Botany.* the fertilized female cell or oosphere within an oogonium which forms the cell of a future plant. [< *oo-* + Greek *spóros* seed, spore]

**o|o|spor|ic** (ō′ə spôr′ik, -spōr′-), *adj. Botany.* of or having to do with the oospore.

**o|os|po|rous** (ō os′pər əs; ō′ə spôr′-, -spōr′-), *adj.* = oosporic.

**o|o|the|ca** (ō′ə thē′kə), *n., pl.* **-cae** (-sē). an egg case or capsule of certain mollusks and insects, especially cockroaches and mantises. [< *oo-* + Greek *thēkē* receptacle]

**o|o|the|cal** (o′ə thē′kəl), *adj.* of or having to do with an ootheca or oothecae.

**ooze¹** (üz), *v.,* **oozed, ooz|ing,** *n.* **—*v.i.*** **1** to pass out slowly through small openings; leak out little by little, especially quietly: *Blood still oozed from the cut.* (*Figurative.*) *His courage oozed away as he waited.* **2** to give forth moisture little by little: *Swamp ground oozes when you step on it.*
**—*v.t.*** to give out slowly; make by oozing; exude: *The cut oozed blood. A scarcely perceptible creek, oozing its way through a wilderness of reeds and slime* (Edgar Allan Poe). [Middle English *wosen* < *wose;* see the noun]
**—*n.*** **1** a slow flow. **2** something that oozes. **3** a liquid used in tanning leather, obtained as an infusion especially from the bark of oak and sumac.
[alteration of Middle English *wose*, Old English *wōs* juice]

**ooze²** (üz), *n.* **1a** a soft mud or slime, especially at the bottom of a pond or river or on the ocean bottom: *Whereas the deep-sea bed elsewhere consisted of thick deposits of fine oozes and clays, here the bed was mainly composed ... of sand and silt* (Bruce C. Heezen). **b** *Figurative: Fishing a manuscript out of the ooze of oblivion* (James Russell Lowell). **2** white or gray finegrained matter, often calcareous, and largely composed of the shells and other remains of small organisms, covering large areas of the ocean floor. [probably earlier *wooze*, Middle English *wose*, Old English *wāse* mud, mire]

**ooze leather**, leather with a soft, velvety finish on the flesh side, made especially from calfskin.

**oo|zie** (ü′zē), *n.* (in Burma) the keeper and driver of an elephant; mahout. [< a native word]

**oo|zi|ly** (ü′zə lē), *adv.* in an oozy manner.

**oo|zi|ness** (ü′zē nis), *n.* oozy quality or condition.

**oo|zy¹** (ü′zē), *adj.* oozing. [< *ooz*(e)¹ + *-y*¹]

**oo|zy²** (ü′zē), *adj.,* **-zi|er, -zi|est.** containing ooze; muddy and soft; slimy: *a low oozy meadow* (Francis Parkman). [Middle English *wosie* < *wose* ooze²]

**op** or **Op** (op), *adj., n.* **—*adj.*** having to do with op art. **—*n.*** = op art. [< *op* art]

**op-**, *prefix.* the form of **ob-** before *p*, as in *oppress.*

**op.**, 1 opera. 2 operation. 3 opposite. 4 opus.

**o.p.** or **O.P.**, 1 out of print. 2 overprint (on a stamp). 3 overproof.

**OP** (no periods) or **O.P.**, observation post.

**O.P.**, (among Dominicans) Order of Preachers (Latin, *Ordo Praedicatorum*).

**OPA** (no periods), Office of Price Administration.

**o|pac|i|fi|ca|tion** (ō pas′ə fə kā′shən), *n.* **1** the act of opacifying. **2** the state of being opacified.

**o|pac|i|fy** (ō pas′ə fī), *v.t., v.i.,* **-fied, -fy|ing.** to make or become opaque.

**o|pac|i|ty** (ō pas′ə tē), *n., pl.* **-ties. 1** the quality or condition of being opaque; being impervious to light; darkness: *The small triangular area ... at the edge of the nebula is a dark cloud of very high opacity* (Scientific American). **2** the quality or condition of being impervious, as to heat or sound. **3** *Figurative.* obscurity of meaning. **4** something opaque. **5** *Figurative.* denseness or stupidity. [< Latin *opācitās* < *opācus* dark]

**o|pah** (ō′pə), *n.* a large, brilliantly colored deepsea fish, found especially in the warmer parts of the Atlantic Ocean. [< West African *úbà*]

**o|pal** (ō′pəl), *n., adj.* **—*n.*** a mineral, any of various forms of silica. Opals are somewhat like quartz. They are valued as gems and come in many varieties and colors. Certain opals reflect light with a peculiar rainbow play of color. Black opals show brilliant colored lights against a dark background; some are so dark as to seem almost black. Milk opals are milky white with rather pale lights. Fire opals are similar with more red and sometimes yellow flashes of color.
**—*adj.*** like an opal: *The opal murmuring sea* (Jean Ingelow).
[< Latin *opalus* < Greek *opállios* < Sanskrit *upala* gem]

**o|pal|es|cence** (ō′pə les′əns), *n.* a play of colors like that of an opal.

**o|pal|es|cent** (ō′pə les′ənt), *adj.* having a play of colors like that of an opal, especially the milk opal. [< *opal* + *-escent*]

**o|pal|esque** (ō′pə lesk′), *adj.* like an opal; opalescent.

**o|pal|eye** (ō′pə lī′), *n., pl.* **-eyes** or (*collectively*) **-eye.** a greenish, herbivorous fish found off the California coast, sometimes used for food; greenfish.

**opal glass**, a glass with a milky-white appearance caused by the addition of small colloidal particles which disperse the light passing through it; milk glass.

**o|pal|ine** (ō′pə lin, -līn), *adj., n.* **—*adj.*** of or like opal; opalescent. **—*n.*** = opal glass.

**o|paque** (ō pāk′), *adj., n.* **—*adj.*** **1a** not letting light through; not transparent: *A brick wall is opaque. The water is so charged with mud and sand that it is opaque* (Francis Parkman). **b** not conducting energy or radiation, as heat, sound, or electricity: *Even on the clearest day, the atmosphere is as opaque to many kinds of radiation as if it were an ocean of ink* (Time). **2** not shining; dark; dull: *an opaque star, an opaque light.* **3** *Figurative.* hard to understand; obscure: *The Critique of Political Economy ... had baffled even Marx's disciples by its relentless and opaque abstraction* (Edmund Wilson). **4** *Figurative.* stupid; dense.
**—*n.*** **1** something opaque. **2** *Photography.* a pigment used to shade parts of a negative.
[< Latin *opācus* dark, shady] **—o|paque′ly**, *adv.* **—o|paque′ness**, *n.*

***opaque projector**, a projector having a mirror and lens to throw the image of a drawing, book's page, or other opaque object on a screen.

***opaque projector**

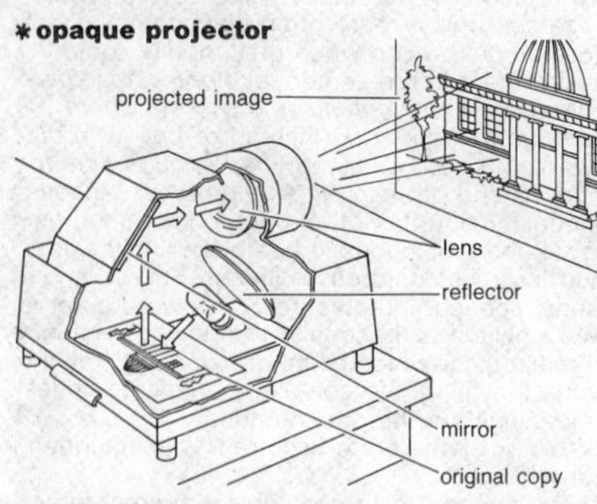


**op** or **Op art** (op), a form of abstract art in which unusual optical illusions and effects are produced by means of complex geometrical designs; optical art: *There is an obvious but superficial sense in which Op art ... can be called mathematical art. This aspect of Op is certainly not new. Hard-edge, rhythmic, decorative patterns are as ancient as art itself, and even the modern movement toward abstraction in painting began with the geometric forms of the cubists* (Scientific American). [< *op*(tical) *art*, on the analogy of *pop art*]

**op** or **Op artist**, a painter or sculptor who produces op art; optical artist: *The Op artists ... compose wavy lines of black and white, combinations and juxtaposition of color so abrupt that they deceive the optical sense* (Alistair Cooke).

**op. cit.**, in the work (previously) cited; in the book or article referred to (Latin, *opere citato*).

**ope** (ōp), *v.,* **oped, op|ing,** *adj. Archaic.* **—*v.t., v.i.*** to open: *Lord, ope their eyes that they may see!* (John Greenleaf Whittier).
**—*adj.*** open: *With both eyes wide ope* (Robert Browning).

**O|pec** or **OPEC** (ō′pek), *n.,* or **O.P.E.C.** Organization of Petroleum Exporting Countries.

**Op-Ed page**, or **Op-Ed** (op′ed′), *n. U.S.* a newspaper page featuring articles by columnists and other writers: *... the Op-Ed provides a variety of viewpoints in dozens of major metropolitan dailies* (Time). [< *Op*(posite) *Ed*(itorial) *page*]

**o|pen** (ō′pən), *adj., n., v.* **—*adj.*** **1** not shut; not closed; letting (anything or anyone) in or out: *an open drawer. The open windows let in the fresh air.* SYN: unclosed, ajar, unlocked. **2a** not having its door, gate, or lid closed; not shut up: *an open box, an open house.* **b** having no cover or roof: *an open car, an open boat.* **3** not closed in or confined: *the open sea, an open field.* **4** having spaces or holes: *open ranks, cloth of open texture. "Open air" is an open compound.* SYN: perforated, porous. **5** unfilled; not taken; available or accessible: *a position still open, to have an hour open, the only course still open. The invitation is still open to you.* SYN: unoccupied, free. **6a** that may be entered, used, shared, or competed for by all, or by a person or persons mentioned: *an open meeting. The race is open to boys under 15.* **b** ready for business or admission of the public: *The exhibition is now open.* **c** that may be entered by both professionals and amateurs: *an open lawn-tennis tournament.* **7** without prohibition or restriction: *an open society, open trade, open skies. The hunting season is open.* **8** *U.S. Informal.* allowing saloons, gambling, and the like: *an open town.* **9** not covered or protected; exposed: *an open fire, an open wound.* SYN: uncovered, unprotected. **10** *Figurative.* exposed to general view or knowledge; not hidden or secret: *open war, open disregard of rules.* SYN: public. **11** not obstructed: *an open view.* **12** *Figurative.* **a** not finally settled or determined; undecided: *an open question.* SYN: unsettled, debatable. **b** ready to listen to new ideas and judge them fairly; not prejudiced: *an open mind.* **c** not yet balanced or closed: *an open account.* **13** *Figurative.* unreserved, candid, or frank; sincere: *an open heart. Please be open with me.* SYN: straightforward. **14** that is spread out; unfolded; expanded: *an open flower, an open newspaper.* **15** *Figurative.* generous; liberal: *to give with an open hand.* **16a** free from frost: *an open winter.* **b** free from ice; not frozen: *open water on the lake, a river or harbor now open.* **c** *Nautical.* free of fog. **17** (of a city, town, or other inhabited area) unfortified; without strategic importance, or containing historic buildings and works of art of such value as to outweigh its military importance; protected from enemy attack under international law: *Rome was declared an open city in World War II.* 18 *Music.* **a** not closed at the upper end: *an open organ pipe.* **b** not stopped by the finger: *an open string.* **c** produced by such a pipe or string, or without aid of slide, key, or valve: *an open tone.* 19 *Phonetics.* **a** (of a vowel) uttered with a relatively wide opening above the tongue, as (ä) in *calm;* low. **b** (of a consonant) fricative; spirant. 20 not complete or closed: *an open electric circuit.* 21 *Printing.* **a** (of type) consisting of outlines; not solid black. **b** (of printed matter) widely spaced or leaded.

—*n.* 1 an open or clear space; opening. 2 an open competition or tournament: *to play in a golf open.*

—*v.t.* 1 to move or turn away from a shut or closed position to allow passage or give access: *to open a door, to open a bottle.* 2 to make open or more open; make accessible: *to open a path through the woods, to open a road.* **SYN**: clear. 3 to expand, extend, or spread out; make less compact: *to open a fan, open a book, open a letter, open a newspaper.* 4 to start or set up; establish: *to open an account. He opened a new store. The President opened his campaign for a second term.* 5 to begin: *to open a debate.* 6 *Law.* to make the first statement of (a case) to the court or jury. 7 to cut into: *to open a wound.* 8 *Figurative.* to lay bare; expose to view; uncover; disclose; reveal; divulge: *The spy opened our plans to the enemy. Herbs ... that sudden flower'd, Opening their various colours* (Milton). 9 *Figurative.* to make accessible to knowledge, sympathy, or public view; enlighten: *Then opened he their understanding, that they might understand the scriptures* (Luke 24:45). 10 to bring into view: *keeping a yellow warehouse on our starboard hand till we opened a white church to the larboard* (Herman Melville).

—*v.i.* 1 to have an opening or passage; afford access: *This door opens into the dining room.* 2a to become open or more open; become accessible. **b** *Figurative.* to become accessible to knowledge, sympathy, or public view; become enlightened. **c** *Figurative.* to become disclosed or revealed: *A new field of science opened to our view.* **d** to become more and more visible, especially as one approaches: *A large valley opened to our gaze.* 3 to move apart; become less compact: *The ranks opened.* 4a to begin; start: *Congress opens tomorrow. School opens soon.* **b** (of a theatrical company) to begin a season or tour: *They opened in Boston.* 5 to come apart or burst open, especially so as to allow passage or show the contents: *the wound opened, a crack where the earth had opened. The clouds opened and the sun shone through.* 6 (of hounds) to begin to bark when in pursuit on a scent. 7 (in poker) to begin the betting, as in a game requiring openers.

**lay oneself** (or **one**) **open**. See under **lay**[1].

**lay open**. See under **lay**[1].

**open to**, **a** ready to take; willing to consider: *open to suggestions.* **b** liable to; exposed to: *open to temptation. The service ... left me open to all injuries* (Shakespeare). **c** to be had or used by: *The old universities are open to all, without distinction of rank or creed* (The Speaker). **d** available to; within the discretion of: *It was open to Mr. Smith to sign an agreement covering all the issues providing for an immediate return to constitutional rule* (Manchester Guardian Weekly).

**open up**, **a** to make accessible: *By schemes such as this it is hoped to ... open up the almost undeveloped southeast* (London Times). **b** to become accessible: *Avenues of wealth opening up so readily* (David Livingstone). **c** *Figurative.* to bring to light: *The view of political economy which his [Ricardo's] genius was the first to open up* (John Stuart Mill). **d** to unfold; spread out: *to open up a folder.* **e** to begin; start: *to open up a new business.* **f** *Figurative.* to speak freely: *He was opening up because he knew that I was not making fun of him* (Atlantic).

**the open**, **a** an open or clear space; open country, air, or sea: *to sleep out in the open.* **b** public view or knowledge: *to act in the open. The secret is now out in the open.*

[Old English. See related etym. at **up**.] —**o′pen|able**, *adj.*

**open account**, 1 a course of business dealings still continuing between two parties. 2 an account not in balance.

**open admissions**, = open enrollment.

**open air**, the outdoors: *Children like to play in the open air.*

**o|pen-air** (ō′pən ãr′), *adj.* 1 = outdoor: *an open-air concert.* **SYN**: alfresco. 2 *Painting.* plein-air.

**o|pen-and-shut** (ō′pən ən shut′), *adj. Informal.* simple and direct; obvious; straightforward: *The prosecutor was sure he had an open-and-shut case against the suspect.*

**open|bill** (ō′pən bil′), *n.* any one of a group of small storks, with species in Africa and southern Asia, having a bill with mandibles separated by an interval before meeting at the tip.

**open book**, 1 something that is readily known or understood: *His life is an open book.* 2 a person who conceals nothing; one whose thoughts or actions are readily understood: *There's no mystery about me. I'm an open book* (P. G. Wodehouse).

**o|pen-cast** (ō′pən kast′, -käst′), *adj.* = open-pit.

**open chain**, *Chemistry.* atoms in an organic molecule represented in a structural formula by a chain with open ends rather than by a ring. —**o′pen-chain′**, *adj.*

**open champion**, the holder of an open championship in a sport or game.

**open championship**, a title in a sport or game that may be competed for by all.

**o|pen-cir|cuit** (o′pən sėr′kit), *adj.* 1 of or having to do with a television or radio program which is broadcast over the air to any viewers or listeners. 2 having to do with a device used in skin-diving that permits exhaled air to escape in a chain of fine bubbles.

**open-circuit cell**, an electric cell, as a dry-cell battery, having two poles connected by a flashlight switch or other device to make a closed circuit. Bubbles of hydrogen ions on the positive electrode finally stop the current, making open-circuit cells useful only for short periods.

**open classroom**, *U.S.* a classroom, especially at the elementary level, in which the activities are completely informal and the teacher's function is to guide or advise rather than to give formal instruction: *An open classroom means ... that learning is not dependent at every level on the presence of a teacher* (Ned O'Gorman). *Critics ... claim that the open classroom fails to equip children with basic skills and facts* (Linda Gail Lockwood).

**open cluster**, = galactic cluster.

**open corridor**, = open classroom.

**open couplet**, a couplet in which the second line does not complete a thought but depends on the line or lines that follow.

**open court**, 1 a court of law which has been formally convened to carry on its proper business. 2 a court of law which is open to the public: *The resolution added: "If the prosecution's case was made in open court that would, in our opinion, be the quickest way of clearing the air of rumour and speculation"* (London Times).

**o|pen-cut** (ō′pən kut′), *adj.* 1 = open-pit: *Soviet efforts to expand open-cut coal extraction, whose output is much cheaper than mined coal, have progressed slowly* (New York Times). 2 of or having to do with a subway, railroad line, road, or canal, which runs below ground level in an uncovered trench: *Brussels, Belgium, opened a 2-mile, 6-track, open-cut railway connection between its Nord and Midi Stations* (John W. Hazen).

**open dating**, the practice of stamping on packaged food the date when it was packaged or the limit of its shelf life: *Consumer groups campaigned for legislation demanding ... "open dating" practices at other stores* (Norman Thompson).

**open door**, the free and equal chance for all countries to do business in another country.

**o|pen-door** (ō′pən dôr′, -dōr′), *adj.* of or having to do with the doctrine of the open door: *The scientific and technological open-door policy which prevailed in east Asia* (Bulletin of Atomic Scientists).

**o|pen-doored** (ō′pən dôrd′, -dōrd′), *adj.* accessible; hospitable: *A house Once rich, now poor, but ever open-door'd* (Tennyson).

**o|pen-end** (ō′pən end′), *adj.* 1 of or having to do with investment trusts, such as mutual funds, that have no fixed capitalization and continually issue shares on request to old or new investors: *Open-end funds stand ready to repurchase shares at net asset value at all times* (Wall Street Journal). 2 that allows for adjusting or revising details later on: *an open-end contract, an open-end mortgage.* 3 (in poker) of a 4-card straight that can be filled at either end, such as 7,8,9,10.

**o|pen-end|ed** (ō′pən en′did), *adj.* 1 open to later consideration, revision, or adjustment: *an open-ended settlement.* 2 not closed at either end: *an open-ended stovepipe.* 3 not committed or predisposed; admitting many views or interpretations: *His exchanges between Mr. White and Mr. Black abounded in ambiguously open-ended clues to their real identity* (Time). 4 limitless, as in power, effect, or consequence: *The hydrogen bomb is an open-ended weapon. ... if you want to make it more powerful, you just shovel in more of the heavy-hydrogen mixture* (Saturday Evening Post). 5 having no single answer or response: *an open-ended question, an open-ended test.* 6 having no fixed time limit: *The Government was proposing to introduce "open-ended" drinking hours* (Manchester Guardian Weekly). —**o′pen-end′ed|ness**, *n.*

**open enrollment**, *U.S.* 1 the transfer of children from neighborhood public schools attended chiefly by one racial group into other neighborhood public schools in order to attain racial balance in the enrollments. 2 the policy of admitting any high school graduate to a college or university, regardless of his grades or academic standing.

**o|pen|er** (ō′pə nər), *n.* 1 a person or thing that opens. 2 the first better in a jackpot at poker. 3 the first game of a scheduled series. 4 the first part of anything; opening: *the opener of a speech.*

**for openers**, *Informal.* to begin with; as a starter: *For openers, just after he got back to New York, he won world-wide attention when his report ... became an issue in the 1960 presidential campaign* (Time).

**openers**, a pair of jacks, or better cards, in a jackpot at poker: *I didn't hold openers, an' yet if I didn't draw some cards an' see it out, I stood to lose entirely* (R. A. Wason).

**o|pen-eyed** (ō′pən īd′), *adj.* 1 having eyes wide open, as in wonder: *We saw him now, dumb with fear and astonishment, staring open-eyed at the emperor* (Sir Arthur Conan Doyle). 2 having the eyes open; watchful or vigilant; observant. **SYN**: alert. 3 done or experienced with the eyes open; frank and honest: *an open-eyed conspiracy* (William Dean Howells).

**o|pen-face** (ō′pən fās′), *adj.* made without a slice of bread or toast on top: *an open-face cheese sandwich.*

**o|pen-faced** (ō′pən fāst′), *adj.* 1 having the face uncovered. 2a having a frank and ingenuous face: *a blond, open-faced Scot* (Time). **b** done in a frank and honest way. 3 (of a watch) having no protective cover over the crystal. 4 = open-face.

**o|pen-field** (ō′pən fēld′), *adj.* 1 of or having to do with the division of the arable land of a community into unenclosed strips, each of which is owned or used by a person or family: *... walking along a dirt road, in high, open-field country like the farm* (New Yorker). 2 in the part of the playing field beyond the line of scrimmage, in football.

**open forum**, a forum or assembly for the discussion of questions of public interest, open to all who wish to take part.

**open fracture**, = compound fracture.

**o|pen-hand|ed** (ō′pən han′did), *adj.* generous; liberal. —**o′pen-hand′ed|ly**, *adv.* —**o′pen-hand′ed|ness**, *n.*

**o|pen-heart** (o′pən härt′), *adj.* with the pericardium opened for direct access to the heart. Open-heart surgery is performed within the heart to repair a damaged valve or a defective chamber wall while a heart-lung machine performs the circulatory function of the heart. *Direct vision or open-heart operations have become a reality* (Science News Letter).

**o|pen-heart|ed** (ō′pən här′tid), *adj.* 1 free in expressing one's real thoughts, opinions, and feelings; frank; candid; unreserved. 2 kindly; generous. —**o′pen-heart′ed|ly**, *adv.* —**o′pen-heart′ed|ness**, *n.*

*** o|pen-hearth** (ō′pən härth′), *adj., n.* —**adj.** 1a of or having an open hearth: *an open-hearth furnace.* **b** using a furnace with an open hearth. 2 made by the open-hearth process: *open-hearth steel.*

—*n.* an open-hearth furnace: *a steel-making open-hearth.* See diagram on following page.

**open-hearth process**, a process of making steel from pig iron in a furnace that reflects the heat from a low roof onto the raw material. The impurities become oxidized.

**open house**, 1 a party or other social event that is open to all who wish to come. 2 an occasion when a school, university, factory, or other institution or concern is opened for inspection by the public: *The High School open house is every other Friday evening.*

**keep open house**, to offer food, or food and lodging, to all visitors: *The Joneses are keeping open house this weekend.*

**open housing**, *U.S.* the sale or rental of a house, apartment, or other dwelling without discrimination against race, religion, or national origin; fair housing; open occupancy.

**o|pen|ing** (ō′pə ning, ōp′ning), *n., adj.* —*n.* 1 an open or clear space; gap, hole, or passage: *an*

**Pronunciation Key:** hat, āge, cãre, fär; let, ēqual, tėrm; it, īce; hot, ōpen, ôrder; oil, out; cup, pu̇t, rüle; child; long; thin; ᴛʜen; zh, measure; ə represents **a** in about, **e** in taken, **i** in pencil, **o** in lemon, **u** in circus.

*opening in a wall, an opening in the forest.* **SYN**: aperture, fissure, orifice. **2** the first part; beginning: *the opening of a lecture.* **SYN**: start, commencement, introduction. **3** a formal beginning; performance, display, or ceremony, that formally begins an undertaking and introduces it to the public, as the first performance of a play: *The opening will be at three o'clock tomorrow afternoon.* **4** a place or position that is open or vacant: *an opening for a teller in a bank, an opening for a teacher in a school.* **SYN**: vacancy. **5** a favorable chance or opportunity: *In talking with your mother, I made an opening to ask her about sending you to camp. As soon as I saw an opening, I got up quickly and left the room. Here is an opening which, if neglected by our government ... they will one day sorely repent* (Edmund Burke). **6** the act of making open or the fact of becoming open. **7** *Law.* the statement of the case made by the lawyer to the court or jury before adducing evidence. **8** *Chess.* **a** the beginning of a game, distinguished from the moves that follow. **b** a standard series of moves beginning a game, especially such a series adopted by a player to establish an attack or defense.
—***adj.*** first; beginning: *the opening words of a speech.*

**opening gun**, *Informal.* something that forms the beginning of a major event or proceeding.

**opening night**, the evening of the first formal performance of a new play, motion picture, broadcast series, or other type of entertainment. —**o′pen\|ing-night′**, *adj.*

**open letter**, a letter of protest, criticism, or appeal, addressed to a person or organization but published in a newspaper, magazine, or the like.

**open loop**, the path or flow of input in an automated system without feedback, as distinguished from a closed or feedback loop.

**o\|pen\|ly** (ō′pən lē), *adv.* without secrecy; frankly.

**open market**, **1** the general market; a market open to anyone, with no restrictions as to source of purchase or destination of sale; free market. **2** the buying and selling of government securities in a free market, especially as controlled or influenced by the activities of the Federal Reserve Bank. —**o′pen-mar′ket**, *adj.*

**open marriage**, a marriage based on the complete equality and freedom of both partners: *"Open marriage" covenants ... permit each party to form a variety of relationships—by no means just physical—with members of the opposite sex* (Newsweek).

**o\|pen-mind\|ed** (ō′pən mīn′did), *adj.* having or showing a mind open to new arguments or ideas: *The claim of scientific inquiry to be impartial and open-minded is erroneously associated with a definition of "open-mindedness" as a freedom from assumptions and presuppositions* (John E. Owen). **SYN**: unprejudiced. —**o′pen-mind′ed\|ly**, *adv.* —**o′pen-mind′ed\|ness**, *n.*

**o\|pen-mouthed** (ō′pən mouᴛʜd′, -moutht′), *adj.* **1** having the mouth open. **2** gaping with surprise or astonishment: *Countless men ... stared open-mouthed at the news* (H. G. Wells). **3** *Figurative.* greedy, ravenous, or rapacious. **4** *Figurative.* vociferous or clamorous: *open-mouthed hounds. Officers who are open-mouthed against the government* (Thomas Jefferson). **5** having a wide mouth: *an open-mouthed pitcher or jug.*

**o\|pen-necked** (ō′pən nekt′), *adj.* open at the neck: *an open-necked shirt.*

***open-hearth**

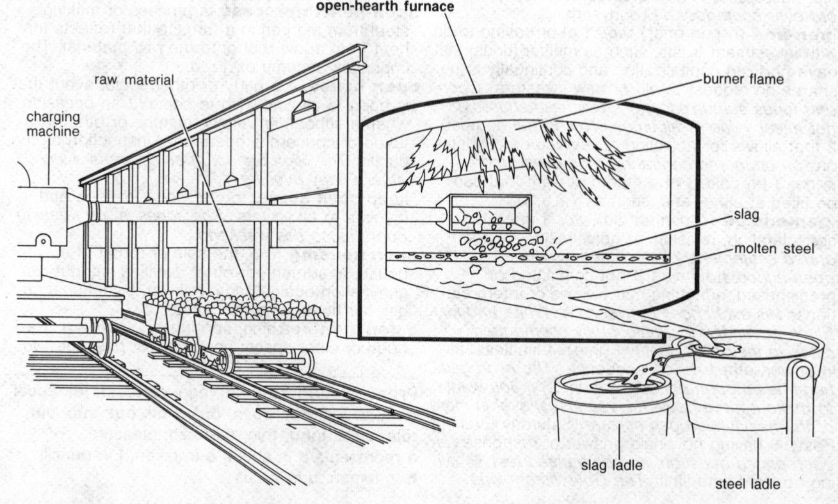


**o\|pen\|ness** (ō′pən nis), *n.* **1** the condition or quality of being open. **2** *Figurative.* lack of secrecy. **3** *Figurative.* frankness; candor: *I will answer him as clearly as I am able, and with great openness* (Edmund Burke). **4** *Figurative.* a willingness to consider new ideas or arguments. **SYN**: open-mindedness.

**open occupancy**, = open housing.

**open order**, an arrangement of military or naval units at a relatively great distance from each other, especially as a tactical device to offer a difficult target.

**o\|pen-pit** (ō′pən pit′), *adj.* exposed on the surface; worked on or slightly below the surface; not underground: *open-pit mining or a mine.*

**o\|pen-plan** (o′pən plan′), *adj.* (of an apartment, a house, or other living quarters) designed with an open, spacious interior; having the living or working parts divided into general areas instead of conventional rooms.

**open policy**, an insurance policy on varying amounts of goods, thus requiring a periodic, usually monthly, computation of premium charges.

**open primary**, *U.S.* a primary in which any registered voter of the state, city, or other electoral district, may vote, whether or not he is an enrolled member of a political party.

**open prison**, a prison designed to give inmates maximum freedom from custody and restraint.

**open question**, something undecided or uncertain: *Whether nations can settle their differences without war is an open question.*

**open sea**, **1** the part of the sea which is not enclosed by land. **2** the part of the sea which is outside the sphere of control of any nation.

**open season**, **1** any of various periods during which the hunting, trapping, or fishing of certain game is permitted. **2** *Figurative.* a time when complete freedom of action or expression prevails, especially in the nature of criticism, often without restraint: *A weak season on Broadway means open season on reviewers* (Walter Kerr).

**open secret**, a supposed secret that everyone knows about.

**open sentence**, *Mathematics.* a sentence that contains one or more variables and that is neither true nor false until a quantity is assigned to the variables.

**open sesame**, **1** the magic command that made the door of the robbers' cave fly open, in the tale of Ali Baba and the Forty Thieves, in the "Arabian Nights' Entertainments." **2** *Figurative.* anything that removes barriers to entering a restricted place or to reaching a certain goal: *Your note was an open sesame to the president's office.*

**o\|pen-shelf** (ō′pən shelf′), *adj.* of or having to do with a method of library organization under which patrons have access to the bookshelves.

**open shop**, a factory, shop, or other establishment that employs both members of labor unions and nonunion workers on equal terms. —**o′pen-shop′**, *adj.*

**open sight**, a rear sight on rifles, shotguns, and other weapons, consisting of a small metal plate with a V-shaped notch through which the front sight and target are brought into alignment.

**o\|pen-stack** (ō′pən stak′), *adj.* = open-shelf.

**open stock**, a stock or reserve of a particular item of merchandise which is carried at all times and from which a person can purchase in any desired quantity.

**open syllable**, a syllable that ends in a vowel or diphthong. *Example: clo- in clover.*

**open university**, *U.S.* a college or university without regular classroom instruction. Students receive instruction through mailed assignments, tape recordings, television, independent study, and periodic guidance and testing sessions at designated locations.

**o\|pen\|work** (ō′pən wėrk′), *n., adj.* —***n.*** ornamental work that shows openings. —***adj.*** resembling such ornamental work; of openwork.

**op\|er\|a**[1] (op′ər ə, op′rə), *n.* **1** a play that is mostly sung, with costumes, scenery, acting, and music to go with the singing: *Faust, Lohengrin, and Carmen are well-known operas.* **2** the branch of art represented by such plays: *the history of opera, to sing in opera. Opera is a blend of all the performing arts—song, instrumental music, dance and drama* (New York Times). **3** a performance of an opera. **4** a theater where operas are performed; opera house. **5** the libretto or the score for an opera. [< Italian *opera*, for *opera in musica* a (dramatic) work to music; *opera* < Latin *opera*, effort, (originally) neuter plural of *opus, -eris* a work]

**op\|er\|a**[2] (op′ər ə), *n.* a plural of **opus**.

**op\|er\|a\|bil\|i\|ty** (op′ər ə bil′ə tē), *n.* the quality or condition of being operable: *the operability of a policy or system, the operability of a patient.*

**op\|er\|a\|ble** (op′ər ə bəl, op′rə-), *adj.* **1** fit for a surgical operation; that can be operated on surgically. **2** that can be operated; in a condition to be used: *... how rapidly he can shift aircraft or salvaged equipment from an inoperable to an operable field* (Bulletin of Atomic Scientists). **3** that can or should be done; practicable. [< Latin *operārī* to operate + English *-able*]

**o\|pé\|ra bouffe** (op′ər ə büf′, op′rə; *French* ô pā rȧ büf′), **1** comic opera, especially of a farcical kind. **2** *Figurative.* an absurd situation; ridiculous arrangement: *The bureaucratic opéra bouffe which is more or less inseparable from the attempt to administer a gigantic philanthropic enterprise* (Atlantic). [< French *opéra bouffe* < Italian *opera buffa*]

**o\|pe\|ra buf\|fa** (op′ər ə bü′fə, op′rə; *Italian* ô′pe rä büf′fä), comic opera in which the dialogue is sung, not spoken: *Donizetti's opera buffa "Don Pasquale"* (New York Times).

**o\|pé\|ra co\|mique** (ô pā rȧ kô mēk′), *French.* comic opera: *Opéra comique is the French name for opera in which the dialogue is spoken instead of sung* (Konrad Neuger). [< Italian *opera buffa;* see etym. under **opera**; *buffa* buffoon]

**opera glasses** or **glass**, small binoculars for use at the opera and in theaters. Opera glasses are like field glasses, but smaller. **SYN**: lorgnette.

**op\|er\|a\|go\|er** (op′ər ə gō′ər, op′rə-), *n.* a person who regularly attends the opera.

**opera hat**, a tall collapsible hat worn by a man with formal clothes.

**opera house**, **1** a theater where operas are presented. **2** *U.S.* any theater, especially a rural one.

**op\|er\|and** (op′ə rand), *n.* **1** *Mathematics.* the quantity or expression that is to be subjected to a mathematical operation. **2** any one of the items of information involved in a computer operation: *Command language is oriented to the kinds of thing the user will require* [*the computer*] *to do; in computer jargon, its "operands" are files to be operated on, typical commands having the effect "use this program on these files to produce these resultant files"* (New Scientist). [< Latin *operandum*, neuter gerundive of *operārī;* see etym. under **operate**]

**op\|er\|ant** (op′ər ənt), *adj., n.* —***adj.*** **1** in operation; working: *No conscious courage was operant in me* (G. Macdonald). **2** of or having to do with operant conditioning: *operant learning.*
—***n.*** **1** a person or thing that operates. **2** *Rare.* a workman; operator.
[< Latin *operāns, -antis,* present participle of *operārī* work; see etym. under **operate**]

**operant conditioning**, *Psychology.* **1** a form of conditioning in which the subject's responses are reinforced to produce the desired pattern of responses; instrumental learning: *In operant conditioning, the response made by the individual is instrumental in obtaining a reward or reinforcement* (Austin E. Grigg). **2** = reinforcement therapy.

**opera pump**, a low-cut, untrimmed shoe for women.

**o\|pe\|ra se\|ri\|a** (ô′pe rä se′rē ä), *Italian.* serious or tragic opera.

**op\|er\|at\|a\|ble** (op′ə rā′tə bəl), *adj.* **1** that can be operated. **2** that can be operated on surgically.

**op\|er\|ate** (op′ə rāt), *v.,* **-at\|ed, -at\|ing.** —***v.i.*** **1** to be at work; run: *The machinery operates night and day.* **SYN**: perform, function. **2** to produce an effect; work; act: *Several causes operated to bring on the war.* **3** to produce a desired effect: *Some medicines operate more quickly than others.* **4** to do something to the body, usually with instruments, to improve or restore health; perform surgery: *The doctor operated on the injured*

*man, removing his damaged lung.* **5** to carry on military movements, duties, or functions. **6** to buy and sell stocks and bonds: *to operate in stocks.* —***v.t.*** **1** to keep at work; drive; run: *The boy operates the elevator.* **2** to direct the working of as owner or manager; manage: *That company operates three factories.* **3** to bring about; produce (some effect): *We admitted that the Book ... had even operated changes in our way of thought* (Thomas Carlyle).
[< Latin *operārī* (with English *-ate*[1]) < *opus, -eris* a work]

**op|er|at|ic** (op′ə rat′ik), *adj.* of or like the opera: *operatic music.* —**op′er|at′i|cal|ly,** *adv.*

**op|er|at|ing** (op′ə rā′ting), *adj.* **1** used in performing operations: *... the high operating speed of a computer* (Science News). **2** of or involving business operations: *operating costs.* **3** that operates: *an operating surgeon.*

**operating engineer,** an engineer who supervises the operation of machines, a plant, or a system of plants.

**operating room,** a room, usually in a hospital, that is specially equipped for surgical operations.

**operating table,** the table for a patient to lie on during a surgical operation.

**operating union,** a union of railroad workers who are directly involved in the operation of trains, such as engineers, conductors, and switchmen.

**op|er|a|tion** (op′ə rā′shən), *n.* **1** the act or process of operating; keeping something working: *The operation of a railroad needs many men. The operation of natural law is constant.* **2** the way a thing works; manner of working: *The operation of this machine is simple.* **3** the performance of something; doing; action; activity: *the operation of binding a book, the operation of brushing one's teeth.* **4** something done to the body, usually with instruments, to improve or restore health: *Taking out the tonsils is a common operation.* **5a** the movements of soldiers, ships, and supplies for war purposes: *The assembling of an invasion force is a major operation.* SYN: maneuver. **b** a particular military movement or undertaking, usually with a code name added. *Example:* Operation Overlord (the Allied invasion of Europe across the English Channel in June, 1944). **c** any plan, project, or undertaking designated by a code name: *Since 1953 the area has engaged in a strenuous "Operation Bootstrap" program of self-help* (Wall Street Journal).
**6a** something done to a number or quantity in mathematics according to specific rules. Addition, subtraction, multiplication, and division are the four commonest operations in arithmetic. **b** the act of making such a change. **7** a commercial transaction, especially one that is speculative and on a large scale: *operations in stocks or wheat.* **8** the power to operate or work; efficacy; force (now used chiefly of legal documents).
**in operation, a** running; working; in action: *The motor is now in operation.* **b** in use or effect: *The new law has been in operation since Monday.*

**op|er|a|tion|al** (op′ə rā′shə nəl), *adj.* **1** of or having to do with operations of any kind: *The problems uncovered by this report, and the present criticism by operational managers ... indicate that this emphasis has not been misplaced* (London Times Literary Supplement). **2** in condition to operate effectively: *The Hunter, which is comparable in performance with the Sabre Jet ... flies about 650 miles an hour in operational trim* (New York Times). **3** used in a military operation; trained or equipped to carry out a particular mission: *operational troops.* —**op′er|a′tion|al|ly,** *adv.*

**op|er|a|tion|al|ism** (op′ə rā′shə nə liz′əm), *n. Philosophy.* the doctrine that statements or ideas do not have meaning except for what they signify in actual practice. Only operation gives meaning.

**op|er|a|tion|al|ist** (op′ə rā′shə nə list), *n., adj.* —***n.*** a person who maintains the doctrine of operationalism. —***adj.*** of or having to do with operationalists or operationalism.

**operational research,** *British.* operations research.

**op|er|a|tion|ism** (op′ə rā′shə niz əm), *n.* = operationalism.

**op|er|a|tion|ist** (op′ə rā′shə nist), *n., adj.* = operationalist.

**operations analysis,** = systems analysis.

**operations research,** *U.S.* the use of scientific and mathematical methods in analyzing and solving problems dealing with the operation of any system or organization.

**op|er|a|tive** (op′ə rā′tiv, -ər ə tiv; op′rə-), *adj., n.* —***adj.*** **1** in operation; exerting force or influence; operating or in effect: *the laws operative in a community.* **2** producing the intended or proper effect; effective: *an operative medicine.* SYN: efficacious. **3** having to do with work or productiveness: *the operative sections of a factory.* **4** of, concerned with, or consisting of surgical operations: *Treatment of the disease requires operative measures.*
—***n.*** **1** a trained or experienced laborer; worker: *He is a skilled machine operative.* SYN: workman, hand. **2a** = detective. **b** a secret agent or spy.
—**op′er|a′tive|ly,** *adv.* —**op′er|a′tive|ness,** *n.*

**op|er|a|tize** (op′ər ə tīz), *v.t.,* **-tized, -tiz|ing.** to put (a play or story) into the form of an opera. [< *opera*[1] + *-tize,* as in *dramatize*]

**op|er|a|tor** (op′ə rā′tər), *n.* **1** a person who operates: *The operator of an automobile must have a license.* **2** a skilled worker who operates a machine, telephone switchboard, telegraph, or other device: *a telegraph or telephone operator. Operators taken off other machines say they "feel" the sensation of* [*the computer's*] *cosmic speed* (Newsweek). **3** a person who runs a factory, mine, or other establishment or concern: *The mine operators met with the striking workers.* **4** *U.S. Informal.* a shrewd individual who maneuvers people and events for his own purposes: *The musical stars Robert Preston, as a fast operator who is redeemed by contact with prairie honesty* (New Yorker). **5** a person who speculates in stocks or a commodity. **6** a doctor who performs surgical operations; surgeon. **7** *Mathematics.* a symbol indicating or expressing an operation to be carried out. **8** the part of the operon that activates and regulates the structural genes; operator gene: *According to a now classic hypothesis in genetics, there are two classes of genes. The first consists of structural genes that, through RNA, determine the sequence of the amino acids and thus the structure of protein. The second class of genes, called operators, control the first, turning them on and off to regulate gene expression. Working as a unit, a package of structural and operator genes is called an operon* (Science News).

**operator gene,** the gene which initiates and regulates the activity of the structural genes in an operon; regulatory gene.

**o|per|cu|lar** (ō pėr′kyə lər), *adj.* of or having to do with an operculum. —**o|per′cu|lar|ly,** *adv.*

**o|per|cu|late** (ō pėr′kyə lit, -lāt), *adj.* having an operculum.

**o|per|cu|lat|ed** (ō pėr′kyə lā′tid), *adj.* = operculate.

**o|per|cu|li|form** (ō pėr′kyə lə fôrm), *adj.* having the form of an operculum; lidlike.

**o|per|cu|lum** (ō pėr′kyə ləm), *n., pl.* **-la** (-lə), **-lums.** *Biology.* a lidlike part or organ; any flap covering an opening, such as the lid of the spore case in mosses, the plate of some gastropods that closes the opening of the shell, the gill cover of a fish, or the limb of the calyx on a species of eucalyptus. [< Latin *operculum* < *operīre* to cover]

**o|pe|re ci|ta|to** (op′ə rē sī tā′tō), *Latin.* in the work (previously) cited. *Abbr:* op. cit.

**op|er|et|ta** (op′ə ret′ə), *n., pl.* **-tas.** a short, amusing opera, with some spoken parts; light opera: *Whenever a production of Porgy really succeeds, you find that it's been changed into a sort of operetta* (Atlantic). [< Italian *operetta* (diminutive) < *opera* opera]

**op|er|ette** (op′ə ret′), *n.* = operetta. [< French *opérette* < Italian *operetta*]

**op|er|et|tist** (op′ə ret′ist), *n.* a composer of operettas.

**op|er|on** (op′ər on), *n.* the region of a chromosome which contains the operator gene and any structural genes involved in the production of messenger RNA for a given synthesis: *An operon is a chromosomal unit consisting of a group of adjacent structural genes, which are regulated together, and the operator, which coordinates their activities* (Clifford R. Noll, Jr.). [< *oper*(ator) + *-on*]

**op|er|ose** (op′ə rōs), *adj.* **1** involving much labor; laborious: *What an operose method! What a train of means to secure a little conversation!* (Emerson). **2** (of a person) industrious. [< Latin *operōsus* < *opus, -eris* work] —**op′er|ose′ly,** *adv.* —**op′er|ose′ness,** *n.*

**O|phel|ia** (ə fēl′yə), *n.* in Shakespeare's *Hamlet,* the daughter of Polonius who was driven to madness and suicide by Hamlet's capricious treatment of her.

**o|phid|i|an** (ō fid′ē ən), *n., adj.* —***n.*** a snake. —***adj.*** **1** like a snake: *the tremendous ophidian head ... with glistening scales and symmetrical markings* (W. H. Hudson). **2** of or having to do with snakes or serpents.
[< New Latin *Ophidia,* former name of an order of reptiles < Greek *óphis, ópheōs* serpent]

**o|phid|i|ar|i|um** (ō fid′ē ãr′ē əm), *n., pl.* **-i|ums, -i|a** (-ē ə). a place where snakes are kept in confinement, for exhibition or for other purposes. [< New Latin *ophidiarium* < *Ophidia;* see etym. under **ophidian**]

**oph|i|ol|a|try** (of′ē ol′ə trē, ō′fē-), *n.* the worship of serpents. [< Greek *óphis, ópheōs* snake + *latreîā* worship]

**oph|i|o|lite** (of′ē ə līt, ō′fē-), *n.* **1** any one of a group of igneous rocks ranging from basalt to gabbro and including those rich in serpentine. **2** = verd antique. **3** *Obsolete.* serpentine. [< Greek *óphis, ópheōs* snake + English *-lite*]

**oph|i|ol|o|gy** (of′ē ol′ə jē, ō′fē-), *n.* the branch of zoology dealing with snakes. [< Greek *óphis, ópheōs* snake + English *-logy*]

**oph|i|oph|a|gous** (of′ē of′ə gəs, ō′fē-), *adj.* feeding on snakes. [< Greek *óphis, ópheōs* serpent + *phageîn* to feed + English *-ous*]

**O|phir** (ō′fər), *n.* a place, probably in Arabia or Africa, from which Solomon obtained gold, precious stones, and wood for the Temple (in the Bible, I Kings 9:28; 10:11).

**oph|ite** (of′īt, ō′fīt), *n.* a greenish altered diabase, produced by the change of augite into uralite. [< Latin *ophītēs* < Greek *ophítēs líthos* serpentine[2] (stone), or a similar marble < *óphis* serpent]

**o|phit|ic** (ō fit′ik), *adj.* **1** of or like ophite. **2** of or having to do with certain rocks in which crystals of feldspar are embedded in a matrix of augite.

**Oph|i|u|chi** (of′ē yü′kī, ō′fē-), *n.* genitive of **Ophiuchus.**

**Oph|i|u|chus** (of′ē yü′kəs, ō′fē-), *n., genitive* **Oph|i|u|chi.** a constellation on the celestial equator, south of Hercules.

**oph|i|u|ran** (of′ē yůr′ən, ō′fē-), *n., adj.* —***n.*** any one of a class of echinoderms resembling the starfishes but having five slender arms, greatly elongated and flexible, that are sharply marked off from the central disk; brittle star.
—***adj.*** of or belonging to this order.
[< New Latin *Ophiura* the typical genus (< Greek *óphis* serpent + *ourá* tail) + English *-an*]

**oph|i|u|roid** (of′ē yůr′oid, ō′fē-), *n., adj.* = ophiuran.

**oph|thal|mi|a** (of thal′mē ə), *n.* an acute inflammation of the eye or the membrane around the eye, caused by infection or injury and sometimes causing blindness. [< Late Latin *ophthalmia* < Greek *ophthálmia* region of the eyes < *ophthalmós* eye]

**ophthalmia ne|o|na|to|rum** (nē′ō nə tôr′əm, -tōr′-), an acute inflammation of the eyes of newborn babies, often caused by gonorrheal infection.

**oph|thal|mic** (of thal′mik), *adj.* **1** of or having to do with the eye. SYN: ocular, optic. **2** having to do with or affected with ophthalmia.

**oph|thal|mi|tis** (of′thal mī′tis), *n.* = ophthalmia.

**oph|thal|mo|log|ic** (of thal′mə loj′ik), *adj.* = ophthalmological.

**oph|thal|mo|log|i|cal** (of thal′mə loj′ə kəl), *adj.* of or having to do with ophthalmology. —**oph|thal′mo|log′i|cal|ly,** *adv.*

**oph|thal|mol|o|gist** (of′thal mol′ə jist), *n.* a doctor who specializes in ophthalmology; oculist.

**oph|thal|mol|o|gy** (of′thal mol′ə jē), *n.* the branch of medicine dealing with the structure, functions, and diseases of the eye.

***oph|thal|mo|scope** (of thal′mə skōp), *n.* an instrument for examining the interior of the eye or the retina. It has a small mirror that reflects light into the eye and a hole in the middle of the mirror through which the eye can be examined. [< Greek *ophthalmós* eye + English *-scope*]

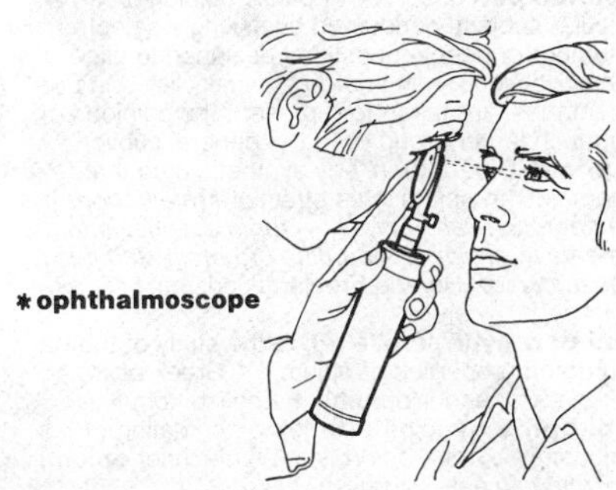

***ophthalmoscope**

**oph|thal|mo|scop|ic** (of thal′mə skop′ik), *adj.* **1** of or having to do with the ophthalmoscope or its use. **2** performed or obtained with an ophthalmoscope. —**oph|thal′mo|scop′i|cal|ly,** *adv.*

**oph|thal|mo|scop|i|cal** (of thal′mə skop′ə kəl), *adj.* = ophthalmoscopic.

**oph|thal|mos|co|py** (of′thal mos′kə pē), *n., pl.* **-pies.** the examination of the interior of the eye

**Pronunciation Key:** hat, āge, cãre, fär; let, ēqual, tėrm; it, īce; hot, ōpen, ôrder; oil, out; cup, pu̇t, rüle; child; long; thin; ᴛʜen; zh, measure; ə represents **a** in about, **e** in taken, **i** in pencil, **o** in lemon, **u** in circus.

with an ophthalmoscope. [< Greek *ophthalmós* eye + English *-scopy*]

**o|pi|ate** (*n., adj.* ō′pē it, -āt; *v.* ō′pē āt), *n., adj., v.,* **-at|ed, -at|ing.** —*n.* **1** a drug that contains opium and so dulls pain or brings sleep. **2** *Figurative.* anything that quiets: *opiates to grief. [She] found the opiate for her discontent in the exertion of her will about smaller things* (George Eliot).
—*adj.* **1** containing opium. **2** *Figurative.* bringing sleep or ease.
—*v.t.* to subject to an opiate.
[< Medieval Latin *opiatus* < Latin *opium* opium]

**o|pi|at|ic** (ō′pē at′ik), *adj.* of, having to do with, or caused by an opiate.

**o|pine** (ō pīn′), *v.t., v.i.,* **o|pined, o|pin|ing.** *Informal* (*now often humorous*). to hold or express an opinion; think: *Mr. Squeers yawned fearfully and opined that it was high time to go to bed* (Dickens). [< Middle French *opiner,* learned borrowing from Latin *opīnārī*] —**o|pin′er,** *n.*

**o|pin|i|a|tive** (ə pin′ē ā′tiv, -ə tiv), *adj.* = opinionative. —**o|pin′i|a′tive|ly,** *adv.* —**o|pin′i|a′tive-ness,** *n.*

**o|pin|ion** (ə pin′yən), *n.* **1** what one thinks; belief not so strong as knowledge; judgment: *I try to learn the facts and form my own opinions. Opinion in good men is but knowledge in the making* (Milton). **2** an impression; estimate: *What is your opinion of him as a candidate? Everyone has a poor opinion of a liar.* **3** a formal judgment by an expert; professional advice: *He wanted the doctor's opinion about the cause of his headaches.* **4** *Law.* a statement by a judge or jury of the reasons for the decision of the court. **5** *Obsolete.* self-esteem; self-conceit: *audacious without impudency, learned without opinion* (Shakespeare). **6** *Obsolete.* reputation; credit: *Thou hast redeem'd thy lost opinion* (Shakespeare).
**be of the opinion,** to hold the belief or view: *Most biologists are of the opinion that Darwin's theories of evolution were borrowed of Wallace.*
**have no opinion,** to have an indifferent or unfavorable estimate of someone: *Old Mr. Benjamin Bunny had no opinion of cats whatever* (Beatrix Potter).
[< Latin *opīniō, -ōnis*]
—*Syn.* **1 Opinion, view** mean what a person thinks about something. **Opinion** suggests a carefully thought out conclusion based on facts, but without the certainty of knowledge: *My opinion is based on wide reading about the subject.* **View** suggests an opinion affected by personal leanings or feelings: *His views are conservative.*

**o|pin|ion|at|ed** (ə pin′yə nā′tid), *adj.* obstinate or conceited with regard to one's opinions; dogmatic: *The general is too opinionated to listen to anyone else.* —**o|pin′ion|at′ed|ly,** *adv.* —**o|pin′-ion|at′ed|ness,** *n.*

**o|pin|ion|a|tion** (ə pin′yə nā′shən), *n.* obstinacy or conceit in one's opinions; dogmatism.

**o|pin|ion|a|tive** (ə pin′yə nā′tiv), *adj.* **1** = opinionated. **2** having to do with opinion or belief; doctrinal. —**o|pin′ion|a′tive|ly,** *adv.* —**o|pin′ion-a′tive|ness,** *n.*

**o|pin|ion|a|tor** (ə pin′yə nā′tər), *n.* an opinionated person.

**o|pin|ioned** (ə pin′yənd), *adj.* **1** having an opinion: *to be otherwise opinioned.* **2** = opinionated.

**opinion poll,** a survey of public opinion on a particular subject, conducted by asking a selected number of people questions designed to elicit their opinion. Their answers, usually listed in percentages, are taken to represent the opinions of a much larger group or of the general public.

**o|pi|oid** (ō′pē oid), *n.* any synthetic drug that resembles an opiate in its effects: *It [methadone] is a narcotic— an "opioid"— for in action it is fundamentally similar to morphine or heroin, and it is fully as addictive* (Horace Freeland Judson). [< *opi*(ate) + *-oid*]

**o|pi|ol|o|gy** (ō′pē ol′ə jē), *n.* the study of the nature and properties of opium. [< Greek *ópion* (see etym. under **opium**) + English *-logy*]

**o|pi|oph|a|gy** (ō′pē of′ə jē), *n.* the eating of opium. [< Greek *ópion* (see etym. under **opium**) + *phageîn* eat + English *-y*[3]]

**op|i|som|e|ter** (op′ə som′ə tər), *n.* an instrument for measuring curved lines, as on a map. [< Greek *opísō* backwards + English *-meter*]

**o|pis|tho|branch** (ə pis′thə brangk), *n., adj.* —*n.* any one of a group of marine gastropod mollusks having the gills behind the heart.
—*adj.* of or belonging to this group.
[< New Latin *Opisthobranchia* the order name < Greek *ópisthen* behind + *bránchia* gills]

**op|is|thog|na|thous** (op′is thog′nə thəs), *adj.* **1** having receding jaws. **2** (of a jaw) receding. [< Greek *ópisthen* behind + *gnáthos* jaw + *-ous*]

**o|pi|um** (ō′pē əm), *n., adj.* —*n.* **1** a powerful drug that causes sleep and eases pain. Opium is a narcotic made from the milky juice of the opium poppy and is a bitter substance, containing morphine and other alkaloids. Opium is valuable in medicine, but is dangerously habit-forming. **2** *Figurative.* anything having the properties or effects of opium: *There is no antidote against the opium of Time* (Sir Thomas Browne).
—*adj.* of or having to do with opium: *an opium dream, the opium traffic.*
[< Latin *opium* < Greek *ópion* poppy juice, poppy (diminutive) < *opós* vegetable juice]

**opium eater,** a person addicted to opium eating.

**opium eating,** the habitual eating or swallowing of opium in some form, as a narcotic.

**opium poppy,** a usually white poppy of Asia and Europe from which opium is derived. Its tiny seeds and oil are used as food.

**opium smoker,** a person addicted to opium smoking.

**opium smoking,** the practice or habit of smoking opium as a stimulant or intoxicant.

**opium tincture,** *Pharmacy.* laudanum.

**o|plat|ek** (ō plä′tek), *n., pl.* **-plat|ki** (-plät′kē). a thin wafer baked in a mold with figures of the Nativity, traditionally blessed by the priest in Polish churches and distributed during the Christmas season. [< Polish *opłatek*]

**o|pop|a|nax** (ō pop′ə naks), *n.* **1** a gum resin formerly used in medicine, obtained from the root of a southern European plant of the parsley family. **2** the plant itself. **3** a gum resin like myrrh, used in perfumery, obtained from an African tree. [< Latin *opopanax* < Greek *opopánax* < *opós* juice + *pánax* a kind of plant]

***o|pos|sum** (ə pos′əm), *n.* a small animal that carries its young in a pouch or on its back. The opossum is a mammal, feeds at night, and lives mostly in trees. There are several kinds, making up a family of animals. One kind, when caught or frightened, pretends to be dead. The opossum is common in the United States, Canada, and South America. Also, **possum.** [American English < Algonkian (Powhatan) *âpäsûm* white animal]

***opossum**

**opossum shrew,** = solenodon.

**opossum shrimp,** any one of a family of small crustaceans resembling shrimps, the females of which carry their eggs in a pouch on the underside of the body.

**op|o|ther|a|py** (op′ə ther′ə pē), *n.* the treatment of disease with extracts made from animal organs; organotherapy. [< Greek *opós* juice + English *therapy*]

**opp.,** 1 opposed. 2 opposite. 3 opposition.

**op|pi|dan** (op′ə dən), *adj., n.* —*adj.* of or having to do with a town; urban. —*n.* **1** an inhabitant of a town; townsman. **2** *British.* a student boarding in the town, such as at Eton College. [< Latin *oppidānus* of a town; urban < *oppidum* town]

**op|pi|dum** (op′ə dəm), *n., pl.* **-da** (-də). an ancient Roman provincial town. [< Latin *oppidum*]

**op|pi|late** (op′ə lāt), *v.t.,* **-lat|ed, -lat|ing.** to fill with obstructing matter; stop up; obstruct. [< Latin *oppīlāre* (with English *-ate*[1]) < *ob-* + *pīlāre* to ram down] —**op′pi|la′tion,** *n.*

**op|po** (op′ō), *n. British Slang.* opposite number; counterpart.

**op|po|nent** (ə pō′nənt), *n., adj.* —*n.* a person who is on the other side in a fight, game, or discussion; person fighting, struggling, or speaking against another: *He defeated his opponent in the election.* —*adj.* **1** being opposite; opposing. **2** of or having to do with opposable muscles, such as those of the hand by which the fingers and thumb may be placed against each other, so as to pick up or hold something. [< Latin *oppōnēns, -entis,* present participle of *oppōnere* set against < *ob-* against + *pōnere* place]
—*Syn. n.* **Opponent, antagonist, adversary** mean someone against a person or thing. **Opponent** applies to someone on the other side in an argument, game, or other contest, or against a plan, law, or other proposal, but does not suggest personal ill will: *The system has its zealous supporters and equally zealous opponents.* **Antagonist,** more formal, suggests active, personal, and unfriendly opposition, often in a fight for power or control: *Hamlet and his uncle were antagonists.* **Adversary** now usually means a hostile antagonist actively blocking or openly fighting another: *Gamblers found a formidable adversary in the new district attorney.*

**op|por|tune** (op′ər tün′, -tyün′), *adj.* fortunate or well-chosen; suitable; favorable: *You have come at a most opportune moment, for I need your advice. An opportune remark kept me from a disastrous investment.* SYN: See syn. under **timely.** [< Middle French *opportune,* learned borrowing from Latin *opportūnus* favorable < *ob portum* (*veniēns*) (going) toward a port[1] (said of the wind)] —**op′por|tune′ly,** *adv.* —**op′por|tune′-ness,** *n.*

**op|por|tun|ism** (op′ər tü′niz əm, -tyü′-), *n.* the policy or practice of using every opportunity to one's advantage without considering whether such an action is right or wrong in each particular circumstance: *[His] principles may keep him from this path to oblivion even if opportunism does not* (New Yorker). SYN: expediency.

**op|por|tun|ist** (op′ər tü′nist, -tyü′-), *n., adj.* —*n.* a person who uses every opportunity to his advantage, regardless of right or wrong: *He was surrounded by adventurers, slick opportunists, intriguers* (Atlantic).
—*adj.* = opportunistic.

**op|por|tun|is|tic** (op′ər tü nis′tik, -tyü-), *adj.* of or having to do with opportunism; characteristic of opportunists. —**op′por|tun|is′ti|cal|ly,** *adv.*

**op|por|tu|ni|ty** (op′ər tü′nə tē, -tyü′-), *n., pl.* **-ties.** **1** a good chance; favorable time; convenient occasion: *I had an opportunity to earn some money picking blueberries. I have had no opportunity to give him your message, because I have not seen him.* **2** a chance or prospect for advancing in position or attaining a goal: *good job opportunities.*

**op|pos|a|bil|i|ty** (ə pō′zə bil′ə tē), *n.* the state or property of being opposable: *the opposability of the jaws.*

**op|pos|a|ble** (ə pō′zə bəl), *adj.* **1** that can be opposed. **2** that can be placed opposite something else. The human thumb is opposable to the fingers.

**op|pose** (ə pōz′), *v.,* **-posed, -pos|ing.** —*v.t.* **1** to be against; be in the way of; act, fight, or struggle against; try to hinder; resist: *Many people opposed building a new highway because of the cost. A swamp opposed the advance of the army.* **2** to set up against; place in the way of: *Let us oppose good nature to anger, and smiles to cross words.* **3** to put in contrast: *Night is opposed to day. Love is opposed to hate.* **4** to put in front of; cause to face: *to oppose one's finger to one's thumb.*
—*v.i.* to be or act in opposition; create resistance: *to take arms against a sea of troubles And, by opposing, end them* (Shakespeare).
[< Old French *opposer* < *op-* against + *poser* put, pose[1]] —**op|pos′er,** *n.* —**op|pos′ing|ly,** *adv.*
—**Syn.** *v.t.* **1 Oppose, resist, withstand** mean to act or be against someone or something. **Oppose** implies setting oneself against a person or thing, especially an idea, plan, or other proposal, but does not suggest the nature, purpose, form, or effectiveness of the action or stand taken: *We opposed the plan because of the cost.* **Resist** implies making a stand and actively striving against an attack or force of some kind: *She resisted all our efforts to make her change her mind.* **Withstand** implies holding firm against attack: *The bridge withstood the flood.*

**op|pose|less** (ə pōz′lis), *adj.* not to be opposed; not resisting: *your great opposeless wills* (Shakespeare).

***op|po|site** (op′ə zit), *adj., n., prep., adv.* —*adj.* **1** placed against; as different in direction as can be; face to face or back to back: *The house straight across the street is opposite to ours.* **2** as different as can be; just contrary: *North and south are opposite directions. Sour is opposite to sweet.* **3** *Botany.* **a** situated in pairs on diametrically opposed sides of an axis; not alternate: *opposite leaves.* See picture above on next page. **b** in front of an organ, coming between it and its axis, as a stamen in front of a sepal or petal. **4** *Obsolete.* opposed in feeling or action; adverse; inimical: *a design of strengthening a party opposite to the public interest* (Jonathan Swift).
—*n.* **1** a thing or person as different as can be: *Black is the opposite of white. A brave person is the opposite of a coward.* **2** *Obsolete.* an antagonist; adversary; opponent: *By the law of arms thou wast not bound to answer An unknown opposite* (Shakespeare).
—*prep.* opposite to: *opposite the church. Wait for me in the building opposite the bank.*
—*adv.* in an opposite position or direction; on opposite sides: *to sit opposite.*
[< Latin *oppositus,* past participle of *oppōnere* < *ob-* against + *pōnere* place] —**op′po|site|ly,** *adv.* —**op′po|site|ness,** *n.*
—*Syn. adj.* **2 Opposite, contrary** mean completely different (from each other). **Opposite** particularly applies to two things so far apart in position, nature, meaning, or other characteristic, that they can never be made to agree: *"True"*

*and "false" have opposite meanings.* **Contrary** particularly applies to two things going in opposite directions, or set against each other, often in strong disagreement or conflict: *Your statement is contrary to the facts.*

***opposite**
definition 3a

**opposite number**, the person who has a similar or corresponding position, duty, or the like, to another; a person's counterpart.

**op|po|si|tion** (op′ə zish′ən), *n., adj.* —*n.* **1a** action against; resistance: *There was some opposition to the workers' request for higher wages. The mob offered opposition to the police.* **b** a being opposed or adverse: *Their opposition to the new law is surprising.* SYN: antagonism, hostility. **2** contrast: *high in opposition to low. His views are in opposition to mine. Between him and Darcy there was a very steady friendship, in spite of great opposition of character* (Jane Austen). SYN: antithesis. **3a** Also, **Opposition.** a political party opposed to the party that is in power: *On both occasions the Opposition managed to get themselves on the wrong foot* (Economist). **b** any party or body of opponents. **4** a placing opposite. **5** opposite direction or position: *Before mine eyes in opposition sits Grim Death* (Milton). **6** *Astronomy.* the position of two heavenly bodies when they are directly opposite each other and their longitude differs by 180 degrees, especially such a position of a heavenly body with respect to the sun. When Mars is on the opposite side of the earth from the sun, it is said to be in opposition. The moon is in opposition with the sun when it is a full moon. See picture under **aspect**. **7** *Logic.* **a** the relation between two propositions that have the same subject and predicate but differ in quantity or quality, or in both. **b** the relation between two propositions that differ in quantity and quality, so that from truth or falsity of one, truth or falsity of the other may be determined.
—*adj.* of or having to do with an opposition: *opposition forces, an opposition leader.*
[< Old French *opposicion,* learned borrowing from Latin *oppositiō, -ōnis* < *oppōnere;* see etym. under **opposite**]

**op|po|si|tion|al** (op′ə zish′ə nəl), *adj.* of or having to do with opposition or opponents.

**op|po|si|tion|ist** (op′ə zish′ə nist), *n.* a member of the opposition.

**op|pos|i|tive** (ə poz′ə tiv), *adj.* characterized by opposition; adversative.

**op|press** (ə pres′), *v.t.* **1** to govern harshly; keep down unjustly or by cruelty: *A good government will not oppress the people.* **2** to weigh down; lie heavily on; burden: *A sense of trouble ahead oppressed my spirits.* SYN: overburden, crush. **3** *Obsolete.* to press down by force; trample down. **4** *Obsolete.* to put down; suppress. [< Medieval Latin *oppressare* (frequentative) < Latin *opprimere* oppress < *ob-* against + *premere* press]

**op|pres|sion** (ə presh′ən), *n.* **1** the act or fact of oppressing; burdening: *The oppression of the people by the nobles caused the war.* **2** the state of being oppressed or burdened: *They fought against oppression.* **3** cruel or unjust treatment: *Oppression of the poor often leads to revolution. Our camp rules were so strict we considered them unnecessary oppression.* SYN: tyranny, persecution, despotism. **4** a heavy, weary feeling of the body or mind: *The very hot and humid weather caused a feeling of great oppression in us all.* SYN: weariness, lassitude, depression.

**op|pres|sive** (ə pres′iv), *adj.* **1** hard to bear; burdensome: *The great heat was oppressive. ... an oppressive modesty that found vent in endless apologies* (Elizabeth Gaskell). **2** harsh; severe; unjust: *Oppressive measures were taken to crush the rebellion.* SYN: tyrannical. —**op|pres′sive|ly,** *adv.* —**op|pres′sive|ness,** *n.*

**op|pres|sor** (ə pres′ər), *n.* a person who is cruel or unjust to people under him. SYN: despot, tyrant.

**op|pro|bri|ous** (ə prō′brē əs), *adj.* **1** expressing scorn, reproach, or abuse: *"Coward," "liar," and "thief" are opprobrious names.* SYN: vituperative, abusive. **2** disgraceful; shameful; infamous: *this dark opprobrious den of shame* (Milton). [< Late Latin *opprobriōsus;* see etym. under **opprobrium**] —**op|pro′bri|ous|ly,** *adv.* —**op|pro′bri|ous|ness,** *n.*

**op|pro|bri|um** (ə prō′brē əm), *n.* **1** the disgrace or reproach caused by shameful conduct; infamy; scorn; abuse: *Because I had turned against him ... I was loaded with general opprobrium* (Charlotte Brontë). *There might very well arise the ill-considered compromise such as made the mere words "Munich" and "Yalta" terms of opprobrium* (Wall Street Journal). SYN: odium, disrepute. **2** a cause or object of such reproach: *The village drunkard was the opprobrium of the community.* [< Latin *opprobrium* < *opprobrāre* to reproach, taunt < *ob-* at + *probrum* infamy, a shameful act]

**op|pugn** (ə pyün′), *v.t.* **1** to call in question (as rights, merits, or judgment). **2** to dispute (as a statement or belief): *When Law and Conscience ... seem to oppugn one another* (Thomas Hobbes). **3** *Obsolete.* to attack in fight or war. [< Latin *oppūgnāre* attack, besiege < *ob-* against + *pūgnāre* to fight < *pūgna* a fight] —**op|pugn′er,** *n.*

**op|pug|na|tion** (op′ug nā′shən), *n. Rare.* the act of oppugning; opposition.

**Ops** (ops), *n. Roman Mythology.* the wife of Saturn and goddess of plenty, identified by the Greeks with Rhea.

**op|si|math** (op′sə math), *n.* a person who begins to learn or study late in life: *He is what the Greeks called an opsimath; not ignorant, but a laggard in learning* (Saturday Review). [< Greek *opsimathḗs* late in learning < *opsé* late + *manthánein* learn]

**op|sin** (op′sin), *n.* a protein formed in the retina, one of the constituents of the visual pigments, such as rhodopsin. [< Greek *ōps, ōpós* eye + English *-in*]

**op|son|ic** (op son′ik), *adj.* of or having to do with opsonin.

**opsonic index**, the ratio of bacteria destroyed by the phagocytes in the blood serum of a given individual to the number destroyed in normal blood serum.

**op|son|i|fi|ca|tion** (op son′ə fə kā′shən), *n.* **1** the act of opsonifying. **2** the state of being opsonified.

**op|son|i|fy** (op son′ə fī), *v.t.,* **-fied, -fy|ing.** to make (bacteria) more susceptible to destruction by phagocytes by the action of opsonins.

**op|so|nin** (op′sə nin), *n.* a substance in blood serum that weakens bacteria and other foreign cells so that the phagocytes can destroy them more easily. [< Greek *ópson* a relish (as meat, fish) + English *-in*]

**op|so|nize** (op′sə nīz), *v.t.,* **-nized, -niz|ing.** **1** to increase the opsonins in, as by immunization. **2** to make (bacteria) more susceptible to destruction by leucocytes. —**op′so|ni|za′tion,** *n.*

**op|ster** (op′stər), *n. U.S. Informal.* an op artist. [< *op* + *-ster*]

**opt** (opt), *v.i.* to make a choice; choose or favor: *The class opted to go on a field trip. British legion women ... opted to ban knitting at all conferences on the ground that it stops concentration* (Punch).
**opt for,** to decide to choose; favor; choose: *Those colonies which choose to stay within the French community ... will have the chance to change their minds later and opt for independence* (Observer).
**opt out,** to choose to back out; withdraw; resign: *Union members pay a political levy, part of which goes to the party, unless they specifically opt out* (New York Times). *The children actually provide a useful excuse to opt out of tasks which ... she is usually expected to assume* (Manchester Guardian Weekly).
[< French *opter,* learned borrowing from Latin *optāre* choose, desire]

**opt.**, an abbreviation for the following:
**1** operation.
**2** optative.
**3a** optical. **b** optician. **c** optics.
**4** optional.
**5** best (Latin, *optimus*).

**op|ta|tive** (op′tə tiv), *adj., n. Grammar.* —*adj.* **1** expressing a wish. "Oh! that I had wings to fly!" is an optative expression. **2a** (in Greek and certain other languages) having to do with the verbal mood that expresses desire, wish, or the like. **b** having to do with distinctive verb forms with such meaning or function.
—*n.* **1** the optative mood. **2** a verb in the optative mood.
[< Latin *optātīvus* (*modus*) optative (mood) < *optāre* to wish, choose] —**op′ta|tive|ly,** *adv.*

**op|tic** (op′tik), *adj., n.* —*adj.* of the eye; of the sense of sight. See also **optic nerve**.
—*n. Informal.* the eye: *I concluded that, by the position of their optics, their sight was so directed downward, that they did not readily see objects that were above them* (Daniel Defoe).
[< Middle French *optique,* learned borrowing from Medieval Latin *opticus* < Greek *optikós* < *op-,* stem of *ópsomai,* future of *horân* see]

**op|ti|cal** (op′tə kəl), *adj.* **1** of the eye or the sense of sight; visual: *Being near-sighted is an optical defect. The strange optical illusion of that straight road seeming to grow narrower in the distance made it look as if two cars could not pass one another.* SYN: ocular. **2** made to assist sight: *Telescopes and microscopes are optical instruments.* **3** of vision and light in relation to each other. **4** having to do with optics. **5** of or having to do with op art: *Leaving aside the question of the contemporary fashion for "optical" painting, Vasarely's work shows—indeed it largely created—two important trends in abstract art today* (New Scientist). —**op′ti|cal|ly,** *adv.*

**optical activity**, *Chemistry.* the ability of a compound to turn the plane of vibration of polarized light.

**optical art**, = op art: *Optical art ... is neatly defined and geometrical in its pattern* (John Canaday).

**optical artist**, = op artist.

**optical astronomer**, a person who studies optical astronomy.

**optical astronomy**, the branch of astronomy that uses telescopes for direct observation of the heavens (as distinguished from radio astronomy and X-ray astronomy): *The first machine to automate completely one of the important processes of optical astronomy ... is used to locate and measure the star images on photographic plates from the Observatory's 400 mm Schmidt telescope* (Science Journal).

**optical bench**, an apparatus consisting of optical devices and instruments that can be moved or adjusted for accurate optical measurement and study.

**optical center**, a point in the axis of a lens so situated that all rays pass through the axis and the lens without being refracted.

**optical fiber**, one strand of fiber optics: *Optical fibers are a means of manipulating light that is rapidly finding use ... in chromatography, automatic titrations, and control of chemical reactions* (Morton Beroza).

**optical glass**, glass used for lenses and optical instruments, such as flint glass and crown glass.

**optical maser**, a device for amplifying and directing light waves; laser.

**optical pair**, a pair of stars that appear close together because they are in nearly the same direction in space. One such star may be much closer to earth than the other.

**optical scanner**, = scanner (def. 4).

**optical square**, a reflecting instrument used especially by surveyors to mark off right angles.

**optic axis**, the line in a double refracting crystal in the direction of which no double refraction occurs. Crystals having a single such line are uniaxial; crystals having two such lines are biaxial.

**optic chiasma** or **chiasm**, the structure forming the intersection or crossing of the optic nerve fibers at the base of the brain.

**optic disk**, the round spot on the retina where the optic nerve enters the eye; blind spot.

**op|ti|cian** (op tish′ən), *n.* a maker or seller of eyeglasses and other optical instruments: *An optician ... sells glasses prescribed for a patient* (Sidney Lerman). [< French *opticien* < Medieval Latin *optica* optics + French *-ien* -ian]

**optic nerve**, the nerve of sight, which goes from the brain to the eye. It terminates in the retina. See diagram under **eye**.

**op|tics** (op′tiks), *n.* the branch of physics that deals with light and vision; study of the properties and phenomena of those electromagnetic waves with wave lengths greater than X rays and smaller than microwaves. Optics includes the ultraviolet, visible, and infrared parts of the spectrum. [translation of Medieval Latin *optica* < Greek (*tà*) *optiká* (the) optics, neuter plural of *optikós* optic]

**optic thalamus**, = thalamus.

**Op|ti|ma** (op′tə mə), *n.* a style of sans-serif printing type.

**op|ti|mal** (op′tə məl), *adj.* most favorable; best; optimum. —**op′ti|mal|ly,** *adv.*

**op|ti|mal|i|ty** (op′tə mal′ə tē), *n.* the quality or condition of being optimal.

**op|ti|me** (op′tə mē), *n. British.* a candidate for honors in mathematics at Cambridge University. Those in the second grade of honors are called senior optimes; those in the third grade are called junior optimes. [apparently < New Latin *optime* (*disputasti*) (you have disputed) very well < Latin *optimē,* adverb < *optimus;* see etym. under **optimism**]

---

**Pronunciation Key:** hat, āge, cãre, fär; let, ēqual, tėrm; it, īce; hot, ōpen, ôrder; **oi**l, **ou**t; cup, pu̇t, rüle; **ch**ild; lo**ng**; **th**in; **ᴛʜ**en; **zh**, measure; **ə** represents **a** in about, **e** in taken, **i** in pencil, **o** in lemon, **u** in circus.

**op|ti|mi|sa|tion** (op′tə mə zā′shən), *n. Especially British.* optimization.

**op|ti|mise** (op′tə mīz), *v.t., v.i.,* **-mised, -mis|ing.** *Especially British.* optimize.

**op|ti|mism** (op′tə miz əm), *n.* **1** a tendency to look on the bright side of things. **2** the belief that everything will turn out for the best. **3a** the doctrine that the existing world is the best of all possible worlds. Optimism, as propounded by Leibniz, stated that any other doctrine would be inconsistent with the nature of God. **b** any doctrine that assumes that good will finally prevail over evil in the universe. [< French *optimisme* < New Latin *optimum* the greatest good (in Leibniz' philosophy); the best, neuter of Latin *optimus,* superlative of *bonus* good]

**op|ti|mist** (op′tə mist), *n.* **1** a person who looks on the bright side of things. **2** a person who believes that everything in life will turn out for the best. **3** a person who believes in or supports a doctrine of optimism.

**Op|ti|mist** (op′tə mist), *n., adj.* **—*n.*** a member of Optimist International, an organization of business and professional men devoted to civic improvement, friendship among all people, and service to youth, formed about 1919 in the United States.
**—*adj.*** of or having to do with Optimists or their organization: *Optimist clubs. The Optimist motto is "Friend of the Boy."*

**op|ti|mis|tic** (op′tə mis′tik), *adj.* **1** inclined to look on the bright side of things: *Many cheerful people are optimistic and refuse to worry about "what might happen."* **SYN:** sanguine. **2** hoping for the best: *I am optimistic about the chance of good weather this weekend.* **3** having to do with optimism: *an optimistic philosophy.* **—op′ti|mis′ti-cal|ly,** *adv.*

**op|ti|mis|ti|cal** (op′tə mis′tə kəl), *adj.* = optimistic.

**op|ti|mi|za|tion** (op′tə mə zā′shən), *n.* a making the best or most of anything.

**op|ti|mize** (op′tə mīz), *v.,* **-mized, -miz|ing.** **—*v.t.*** to make the best or most of; develop to the utmost: *One of the airlines wants to optimize the assignment of its maintenance help* (New Yorker). **—*v.i.*** **1** to make the best or most of a condition: *In many situations the criterion is probabilistic, and the engineer must optimize on the basis of probable behavior of the system* (John G. Truxal). **2** to hold or express optimistic views.
**—op′ti|miz′er,** *n.*

**op|ti|mum** (op′tə məm), *n., pl.* **-mums, -ma** (-mə), *adj.* **—*n.*** **1** the best or most favorable point, degree, or amount, for the purpose. **2** *Biology.* the degree or amount of heat, light, food, moisture, or other condition, most favorable for the reproduction or other vital process of an organism: *There is usually for each species a rather narrow range, the optimum, in which the organism lives most effectively* (Harbaugh and Goodrich).
**—*adj.*** best or most favorable: *An optimum population is one of a size and quality best fitted to achieve some social goal* (Emory S. Bogardus).
[< Latin *optimum,* neuter of *optimus;* see etym. under **optimism**]

**op|tion** (op′shən), *n., v.* **—*n.*** **1** the right or freedom of choice: *Each state has local option about daylight-saving time. Pupils in our school have the option of taking Spanish, French, or German.* **2a** the act of choosing; choice: *Where to travel should be left to each person's option.* **SYN:** See syn. under **choice. b** a thing that is or can be chosen. **SYN:** preference. **3** the right to buy or sell something at a certain price within a certain time: *We paid $500 for an option on the land.* **4** *Insurance.* the right of an insured person to decide how he shall receive the money due him on a policy. **5** *Football.* a play in which the quarterback has a choice of running or passing.
**—*v.t.*** to obtain or grant an option in reference to (something): *I've written five unproduced plays. One of them ... has been optioned so often I've made five thousand dollars out of it* (New Yorker).
[< Latin *optiō, -ōnis,* related to *optāre* to desire, choose]

**op|tion|al** (op′shə nəl), *adj.* left to one's choice; not required: *Attendance at the school picnic is optional.* **SYN:** elective. **—op′tion|al|ly,** *adv.*

**op|to|e|lec|tron|ic** (op′tō i lek′tron′ik, -ē′lek-), *adj.* **1** combing optical and electrical properties; using light and electricity to transmit signals: *an optoelectronic computer, an optoelectronic light switch.* **2** of or having to do with optoelectronics: *optoelectronic research, optoelectronic effects.* [< Greek *optós* seen + English *electronic*]

**op|to|e|lec|tron|ics** (op′tō i lek′tron′iks, -ē′lek-), *n.* the combined use of optical and electronic systems or devices: *Optoelectronics brings together optics, electronics, and precision mechanics. An optoelectronic system has an optical circuit (to replace the function of the human eye), a mechanical control circuit (to replace the hand), and an electronic circuit to link them* (New Scientist).

**op|to|ki|net|ic** (op′tō ki net′ik), *adj.,* of or having to do with movement of the eyes.

**op|tom|e|ter** (op tom′ə tər), *n.* any one of various instruments for testing or measuring the vision, especially the refractive power of the eye. [< Greek *optós* seen + English *-meter*]

**op|to|met|ric** (op′tə met′rik), *adj.* of or having to do with optometry. **—op′to|met′ri|cal|ly,** *adv.*

**op|to|met|ri|cal** (op′tə met′rə kəl), *adj.* = optometric.

**op|tom|e|trist** (op tom′ə trist), *n.* a person skilled in examining the eyes and prescribing eyeglasses. An optometrist diagnoses and treats conditions of the eye other than by the use of drugs or the practice of surgery. [American English < *optometr(y)* + *-ist*]

**op|tom|e|try** (op tom′ə trē), *n.* the measurement of powers of sight; practice or occupation of testing eyes in order to fit them with glasses. [< Greek *optós* seen + English *-metry*]

**op|to|phone** (op′tə fōn), *n.* an apparatus for converting optical effects into acoustic effects, especially a telephonic device for enabling the blind to read, the light effects peculiar to each printed letter being made to give rise to a characteristic sound. [< Greek *optós* seen + English *-phone*]

**op|u|lence** (op′yə ləns), *n.* **1** much money or property; wealth; riches: *The most meritorious public services have always been performed by persons in a condition of life removed from opulence* (C. J. Fox). **SYN:** affluence. **2** *Figurative.* abundance; plenty: *He has that opulence which furnishes, at every turn, the precise weapon he needs* (Emerson).

**op|u|len|cy** (op′yə lən sē), *n. Obsolete.* opulence.

**op|u|lent** (op′yə lənt), *adj.* **1a** having wealth; rich: *an opulent merchant.* **SYN:** affluent. **b** showing wealth; costly and luxurious: *an opulent home.* **2** *Figurative.* abundant; plentiful: *opulent sunshine.* **SYN:** profuse. [< Latin *opulentus* < *ops, opis* power, resources + *-lentus* abounding in] **—op′u|lent|ly,** *adv.*

**o|pun|ti|a** (ō pun′shē ə), *n.* **1** any cactus of a large group comprising fleshy herbs, shrubby plants, and sometimes trees; prickly pear. **2** the fruit of any one of these plants. [< New Latin *Opuntia* the genus name < Latin *opuntia* a kind of prickly pear, apparently < *Opus, -untis,* a city of Locris, Greece, where it grew]

**o|pus** (ō′pəs), *n., pl.* **op|er|a** or **o|pus|es.** a work or composition: *The violinist played his own opus, No. 16.* **SYN:** creation, production. [< Latin *opus, -eris* a work]
▶Because the Latin plural is identical with *opera* "musical drama," it is now generally replaced, except in learned use, by *opuses.*

**o|pus|cule** (ō pus′kyül), *n.* a small work, especially a literary or musical work of small size or limited scope: *In this opuscule he points out that Modern Society is passing through a great crisis* (John Morley). [< Latin *opusculum* (diminutive) < *opus, -eris* a work]

**o|pus|cu|lum** (ō pus′kyə ləm), *n., pl.* **-la** (-lə). = opuscule. [< Latin *opusculum;* see etym. under **opuscule**]

**O|pus De|i** (ō′pəs dā′ē), an international religious organization of Roman Catholic laymen and priests, founded in Spain. [< Latin *Opus Dei* Work of God]

**o|quas|sa** (ō kwas′ə), *n.* a small, bluish trout, found especially in the lakes of central Maine. [American English, apparently < *Oquassa* Lake, Maine]

**or**[1] (ôr; *unstressed* ər), *conj.* **1** a word used to express a choice or a difference, or to connect words or groups of words of equal importance in the sentence: *You may go or stay. Is it sweet or sour?* **2** and if not; otherwise: *Either eat this or go hungry. Hurry, or you will be late.* **3** that is; being the same as: *an igloo or Eskimo snow house. This is the end or last part.* [Middle English *or,* reduction of *other,* perhaps fusion of Old English *oththe* or, and *āther* either]

**or**[2] (ôr), *prep., conj. Archaic.* before; ere: *I'll be there long or that* (Robert Louis Stevenson). [Old English *ǣr* early, confused in sense with *ǣr* ere]

**or**[3] (ôr), *n. Heraldry.* the gold or yellow in coats of arms. [< French *or* < Old French < Latin *aurum* gold]

**-or,** *suffix added to verbs to form nouns.* **1** person or thing that ___s: *Actor = a person who acts. Accelerator = a thing that accelerates.*
**2** act, state, condition, quality, or characteristic, especially in words from Latin, as in *error, horror, labor, terror.*
[< Middle French *-our* < Old French < Latin *-or*]
▶**-or, -our.** American spelling prefers *-or* in such words as *color, governor, honor.* When referring to Jesus Christ, *Saviour* is frequently spelled with the *u,* but in other senses without it. *Glamour* still survives, but the *u* is rapidly being dropped from this word. British usage prefers *-our* spellings, but not in certain derivatives. Thus words like *honorific, honorary,* and *humorous* are so spelled on both sides of the Atlantic.

**OR** (no periods), **1** operating room. **2** operations research. **3** Oregon (with postal Zip Code).

**o|ra** (ôr′ə, or′-), *n. Latin.* plural of **os**[2].

**or|ach** or **or|ache** (ôr′ək, or′-), *n.* any plant of a group of the goosefoot family, especially a tall annual whose leaves can be eaten like spinach. [Middle English *orage, arage* < Old French (Picard) *arrache,* ultimately < Latin *atriplex, -icis* < Greek *atráphaxys*]

**or|a|cle** (ôr′ə kəl, or′-), *n.* **1** in ancient Greece and Rome: **a** an answer to some question believed to be given by a god through a priest or priestess. It often had a hidden meaning that was hard to understand. **b** a place where the god was believed to give such answers. A famous oracle was at Delphi. **c** the priest, priestess, or other means by which the god's answer was believed to be given. **2** *Figurative.* a very wise person: *Under the instructions of these political oracles the good people ... became exceedingly enlightened* (Washington Irving). **SYN:** sage.
**3** *Figurative.* something regarded as a reliable or sure guide, such as a compass or a watch.
**4** *Figurative.* a very wise answer. **5** divine revelation; a message from God. **6** = prophet.
**7** the holy of holies in the ancient Jewish Temple.
**oracles,** the Bible: *... unto them were committed the oracles of God* (Romans 3:2).
**work the oracle, a** to scheme; pull strings: *Every reader will be able to form his own judgment of the methods which [certain publishers] adopt to work the oracle in their favour* (Pall Mall Gazette). **b** *Slang.* to raise money: *With ... big local loan mongers to work the oracle* (John Newman).
[< Old French *oracle,* learned borrowing from Latin *ōrāculum* < *ōrāre* (originally) recite solemnly]

**oracle bone,** a bone used for divination by the ancient Chinese, especially during the Shang dynasty. Questions about the future would be written on the bone, which would then be heated and the answers divined from the changes appearing on the bone.

**o|rac|u|lar** (ô rak′yə lər, ō-), *adj.* **1** of or like an oracle: (*Figurative.*) *That irrepressibly oracular figure, Dr. Samuel Johnson* (Atlantic). **2** *Figurative.* with a hidden meaning that is difficult to make out. **3** *Figurative.* very wise: *an oracular statement or manner. They referred to each other as oracular sources of wisdom and good taste* (Arnold Bennett). **SYN:** sagacious. [< Latin *ōrāculum* oracle + English *-ar*] **—o|rac′u|lar|ly,** *adv.*

**o|rac|u|lar|i|ty** (ô rak′yə lar′ə tē, ō-), *n.* the quality or character of being oracular.

**o|ral** (ôr′əl, ōr′-), *adj., n.* **—*adj.*** **1** using speech; spoken: *an oral command. An oral agreement is not enough; we must have a written promise.*
**2** of the mouth: *oral hygiene. The oral opening in an earthworm is small.* **3** through or by the mouth: *an oral dose of antibiotic.* **4** *Phonetics.* articulated with the breath stream passing out entirely through the mouth: *Most sounds are, in fact, oral, or better perhaps, buccal* (Simeon Potter). **5** of or having to do with instruction of the deaf and dumb by or in lip reading. **6** *Psychoanalysis.* of or having to do with a pattern of personality traits supposed to have developed from the stage where the child's interest was focused on suckling, eating, and biting. An oral character is supposed to be manifested by excessive optimism, dependence on others, and aggressiveness.
**—*n.*** an oral examination.
**orals,** a series of oral examinations taken by a candidate for a degree: *He handed in his doctoral thesis in March, and passed his orals four months later.*
[< Latin *ōs, ōris* mouth + English *-al*[1]]
▶**oral, verbal.** Strictly, *oral* means spoken, as distinguished from written: *She gave an oral report. Verbal* means in words, as distinguished from other means of expression: *This written report contains both a verbal description and a sketch of the building.*

**oral contraceptive,** any one of various drugs containing a combination of sex hormones that prevent ovulation, taken orally, usually in the form of pills, on a regular schedule: *Although "the pill," or oral contraceptive, has received a bad press in recent years, it probably ranks second only to sterilization as a birth control method* (Kenneth N. Anderson).

**oral history,** the recollections and opinions of important contemporary persons concerning historical events in which they participated, usually in the form of tape-recorded or typewritten interviews.

**o|ral|i|ty** (ô ral′ə tē, ō-), *n.* **1** the quality of being oral. **2** *Psychology.* the derivation of sexual

pleasure from stimulation of the mouth.
**oral law**, a body of laws handed down by word of mouth from generation to generation.
**Oral Law**, the Mishnah.
**o|ral|ly** (ôr′ə lē, ōr′-), *adv.* **1** by spoken words: *He gave his report orally.* **2** by the mouth: *medicine given orally.*
**oral moniliasis**, moniliasis of the mouth and throat; thrush.
**or|a|mon** (ôr′ə mən, or′-), *n.* a hybrid fruit produced by crossing the orange and the lemon.
**o|rang** (ō rang′), *n.* = orangutan.
**or|ange** (ôr′inj, or′-), *n., adj.* — *n.* **1** a round, reddish-yellow, juicy citrus fruit that is good to eat. Oranges grow in warm climates. The pulp is sweetish or slightly acid and is enclosed in a soft rind. **2** the tree it grows on. The orange is an evergreen which belongs to the rue family and has fragrant white blossoms and oval or elliptical leaves. Its blossom is the floral emblem of Florida. **3** a fruit or tree that suggests an orange, such as the Osage orange and a hardy Japanese tree grown chiefly for hedges in the United States. **4** a reddish yellow.
— *adj.* **1** of or like an orange: *a drink with orange flavor.* **2** reddish-yellow: *an orange sky at sunset.*
[< Old French *pomme d'orenge* < Spanish *naranja* < Arabic *nāranj* < Persian *nārang;* influenced in Old French by *or* gold, and the *n* was lost by misdivision of the article *un*] — **or′ange-like′**, *adj.*
**Or|ange** (ôr′inj, or′-), *n., adj.* — *n.* a princely family of Europe that ruled the former principality of Orange, in western Europe (now a part of France). William III of England was of this family, and so is the present royal family of the Netherlands.
— *adj.* of or having to do with Orangemen or Orangeism: *the Orange leadership, Orange protest marches.*
**or|ange|ade** (ôr′inj ād′, or′-), *n.* a drink made of orange juice, sugar, and water.
**orange blossom**, the fragrant white flower of the orange, much worn by brides in wreaths, or carried in bridal bouquets.
**or|ange-crowned warbler** (ôr′inj kround′, or′-), a North American warbler with dull greenish plumage and an inconspicuous tawny patch on the crown.
**or|ange|cup lily** (ôr′inj kup′, or′-), a lily of the eastern United States that bears a cup-shaped orange flower with purple spots.
**Orange Day**, July 12, set aside by Protestants in Northern Ireland as a celebration to commemorate William of Orange's victory at the Battle of the Boyne in 1690.
**orange hawkweed**, a European variety of hawkweed with orange-red clusters of flowers, that has become naturalized in eastern North America; devil's paintbrush.
**Or|ange|ism** (ôr′in jiz əm, or′-), *n.* the principles and practices of the Orangemen; the principle of Protestant political supremacy in Ireland. — **Or′ange|ist**, *n.*
**Or|ange|man** (ôr′inj mən, or′-), *n., pl.* **-men. 1** a member of a secret society formed in the north of Ireland in 1795, to uphold the Protestant religion and Protestant control in Ireland: *The very objective for which the Orangemen say they stand* [*is*] *the maintenance of Ulster's present Constitution* (Manchester Guardian Weekly). **2** any Irish Protestant, especially one living in Northern Ireland. [< William III, the Prince of *Orange* + *-man*]
**orange pekoe**, a black tea that comes from Ceylon or India. It is usually made from the youngest leaves at the tips of the branches.
**or|ange|root** (ôr′inj rüt′, or′-; -rut′), *n.* = goldenseal.
**or|ange|ry** (ôr′inj rē, or′-), *n., pl.* **-ries.** a place, usually a greenhouse, for growing orange trees in cool climates. Orangeries were formerly common to the formal gardens of great estates. [< French *orangerie* < *orange* orange]
**oranges and lemons**, a children's singing game in which the players take sides according to their answer to the question, "Which will you have, oranges or lemons?": *The brother and sister, deciding which side to elect, seem to be playing oranges and lemons* (London Times).
**orange squash**, *Especially British.* orangeade.
**orange stick**, a small stick used in manicuring, originally of orangewood, and pointed at one end and with the other end broad and tapered.
**or|ange|wood** (ôr′inj wu̇d′, or′-), *n., adj.* — *n.* the hard, fine-grained wood of the orange tree, used as a cabinet-wood, for small dental tools, and for manicuring the nails. — *adj.* of this wood.
**or|ange|y** (ôr′in jē, or′-), *adj.* like an orange, especially in color or taste.
**o|rang-ou|tang** (ō rang′u̇ tang′), *n.* = orangutan.
**o|rang|u|tan** or **o|rang-u|tan** (ō rang′u̇ tan′), *n.* a large ape of the forests of Borneo and Sumatra, having long, reddish-brown hair and very long arms. The orangutan is an anthropoid ape that lives mostly in trees and eats fruits and leaves. Also, **ourang-outang**. See picture under **ape**. [ultimately < Malay *orangutan* wild man < *orang* man + *utan* of the woods]
**or|ang|y** (ôr′in jē, or′-), *adj.* = orangey.
**o|rant** (ôr′ənt, ōr′-), *n.* = orante. [< Latin *ōrāns, -āntis;* see etym. under **orante**]
**o|ran|te** (ô ran′tē, ō-), *n.* (in early Christian art) a figure, usually female, standing with arms outspread or raised in prayer. [< Italian *orante* < Latin *ōrāns, -āntis,* present participle of *ōrāre* recite, pray]
**o|ra pro no|bis** (ôr′ə prō nō′bis, ōr′-), *Latin.* **1** pray for us. **2** (in the Roman Catholic liturgy) the refrain of a litany to the Virgin Mary.
**o|rate** (ô rāt′, ō-; ôr′āt, ōr′-), *v.,* **o|rat|ed, o|rat|ing.** *Informal.* — *v.i.* to make an oration; talk in a grand manner. — *v.t.* = harangue.
[apparently back formation < *oration*]
**o|ra|tion** (ô rā′shən, ō-), *n.* **1** a formal public speech delivered on a special occasion: *the orations of Cicero.* SYN: address. See syn. under **speech. 2** a speech given in an overly formal or affected style. [< Latin *ōrātiō, -ōnis* < *ōrāre* recite. See etym. of doublet **orison.**]
**o|ra|ti|o o|bli|qua** (ô rā′shē ō ə blē′kwə, ō-; -shō), *Latin.* **1** indirect use of language. **2** (literally) oblique oration.
**or|a|tor** (ôr′ə tər, or′-), *n.* **1** a person who makes an oration: *Lincoln was one of the orators at the ceremonies dedicating the military cemetery at Gettysburg.* **2** a person who can speak very well in public and often with great eloquence: *I come not, friends, to steal away your hearts: I am no orator, as Brutus is* (Shakespeare). **3** *Law, Obsolete.* the plaintiff in a suit of chancery. [< Latin *ōrātor* speaker < *ōrāre;* see etym. under **oration**]
**or|a|to|ri|al** (ôr′ə tôr′ē əl, -tōr′-; or′-), *adj.* **1** of, having to do with, or befitting an orator. **2** of or having to do with an oratorio. — **or′a|to′ri|al|ly**, *adv.*
**Or|a|to|ri|an** (ôr′ə tôr′ē ən, -tōr′-; or′-), *adj., n.* — *adj.* of or having to do with an Oratory.
— *n.* a member of an Oratory.
**or|a|tor|i|cal** (ôr′ə tôr′ə kəl, or′ə tor′-), *adj.* **1** of oratory; having to do with orators or oratory: *an oratorical contest.* SYN: declamatory. **2** characteristic of orators or oratory: *He has an oratorical manner even in conversation.* SYN: eloquent.
— **or′a|tor′i|cal|ly**, *adv.*
**or|a|to|ri|o** (ôr′ə tôr′ē ō, -tōr′-; or′-), *n., pl.* **-ri|os.** a musical composition, usually based on a religious theme, for solo voices, chorus, and orchestra. It is dramatic in character, but performed without action, costumes, or scenery. [< Italian *oratorio* (originally) place of prayer < Late Latin *ōrātōrium.* See etym. of doublet **oratory**².]
**or|a|tor|ize** (ôr′ə tə rīz, or′-), *v.i.,* **-ized, -iz|ing.** to play the orator; orate.
**or|a|to|ry**¹ (ôr′ə tôr′ē, -tōr′-; or′-), *n.* **1** skill in public speaking; fine speaking: *Their leader's rabble-rousing oratory had parlayed the seething resentments* (Newsweek). SYN: eloquence. **2** the art of public speaking, especially according to definite rules. SYN: declamation. [< Latin (*ars*) *ōrātōria* oratorical (art), feminine adjective < *ōrāre* plead, speak formally]
**or|a|to|ry**² (ôr′ə tôr′ē, -tōr′-; or′-), *n., pl.* **-ries.** a small chapel; room set apart for prayer. [< Late Latin *ōrātōrium,* noun use of adjective < Latin *ōrāre* pray, recite formally. See etym. of doublet **oratorio.**]
**Or|a|to|ry** (ôr′ə tôr′ē, -tōr′-; or′-), *n., pl.* **-ries. 1** any one of certain religious societies of the Roman Catholic Church, especially one composed of secular priests, not bound by vows, devoted to simple and familiar preaching. **2** a local branch or house of an Oratory society.

***orb**
definition 4

***orb** (ôrb), *n., v.* — *n.* **1** anything round like a ball; sphere; globe: *What a hell of witchcraft lies In the small orb of one particular tear!* (Shakespeare). SYN: ball. **2a** the sun, the moon, a planet, or a star: *the orb of day, the sun; the orb of night, the moon.* **b** the earth; the world. **3** the eyeball or eye: *His eyelids heavily closed over their orbs* (Washington Irving). **4** Also, **Orb.** a globe surmounted by a cross, symbolizing royal sovereignty. **5** an organized or collective whole. **6** *Astrology.* the space within which the influence of a planet, star, or house is supposed to act. **7** *Obsolete.* anything of circular form.
— *v.t.* **1** to form into a circle, disk, or sphere; make round. **2** *Archaic.* to encircle; enclose.
— *v.i.* **1** to form itself into an orb. **2** to move in an orbit.
[< Old French *orbe,* learned borrowing from Latin *orbis* circle]
**or|bic|u|lar** (ôr bik′yə lər), *adj.* **1** like a circle or sphere; rounded. SYN: circular, spherical. **2** *Botany.* having the shape of a flat body with a nearly circular outline: *an orbicular leaf.* [< Late Latin *orbiculāris* < Latin *orbiculus* < *orbis* circle]
— **or|bic′u|lar|ly**, *adv.* — **or|bic′u|lar|ness**, *n.*
**or|bi|cu|lar|is** (ôr bik′yə lãr′is, -lär′-), *n. Anatomy.* a muscle surrounding an opening of the body, such as that of the mouth or the eye; sphincter. [< New Latin *orbicularis* < Late Latin *orbiculāris* orbicular]
**or|bic|u|lar|i|ty** (ôr bik′yə lar′ə tē), *n., pl.* **-ties.** an orbicular quality or form.
**or|bic|u|late** (ôr bik′yə lit, -lāt), *adj.* = orbicular. [< Latin *orbiculātus* < *orbiculus;* see etym. under **orbicular**] — **or|bic′u|late|ly**, *adv.*
**or|bic|u|lat|ed** (ôr bik′yə lā′tid), *adj.* = orbicular.
***or|bit** (ôr′bit), *n., v.* — *n.* **1** the path of the earth or any one of the planets about the sun: *the orbit of Mars.* **2** the path of any heavenly body about another heavenly body: *the moon's orbit about the earth.* **3** the path of a man-made satellite about any heavenly body: *to put a weather satellite into orbit about the earth.* **4** the curved path of an electron about the nucleus of an atom. **5** *Figurative.* the regular course of life or experience; sphere of knowledge or activity: *a problem not in his orbit. They knew each other by sight, but their orbits did not touch* (Arnold Bennett). SYN: field. **6** *Figurative.* the sphere of influence of a country, as in politics or trade: *The U.S.S.R. makes constant efforts to woo Asian neutrals into the Communist orbit.* **7a** the bony cavity or socket in which the eyeball is set. **b** the eye; eyeball.
— *v.t.* **1** to travel in an orbit around (the earth or some other heavenly body): *Some artificial satellites can orbit the earth in less than an hour.* **2** to put into an orbit: *to orbit a satellite.*
— *v.i.* **1** to travel in an orbit: *The satellite itself will orbit around the earth for a period of days* (New York Times). **2** (of a satellite or space station) to arrive in its orbit; achieve orbital velocity. [< Latin *orbita* wheel track < *orbis* circle, wheel]

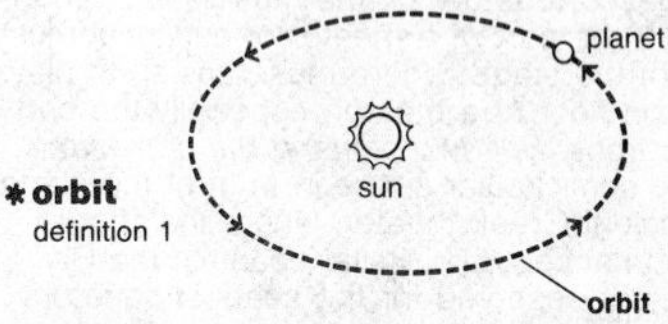


***orbit**
definition 1

**or|bi|tal** (ôr′bə təl), *adj., n.* — *adj.* **1** of an orbit: *A Discoverer IX satellite rocket ... failed to reach orbital speed and burned up while falling back into the earth's atmosphere* (Wall Street Journal). **2** of or having to do with the orbit of the eye.
— *n.* **1** *Physics.* the wave function of an electron moving in a molecule or atom, corresponding to the orbit or path of an electron in earlier theory. **2** *British.* a highway going around the suburbs of a city: *First priority for roads, after the orbitals outside Greater London, is Ringway 2* (*North and South Circular Roads*) (London Times).
**orbital index**, the ratio of length to height of the orbit of the eye.
**orbital steering**, *Biochemistry.* a process by which enzymes are thought to facilitate chemical reactions by guiding the atoms in the reacting compounds at precise angles to enable them to join together: *They call this process "orbital steering," since the electron orbitals of the reacting atoms are manoeuvred into the proper juxtaposition* (New Scientist).
**orbital velocity**, **1** the velocity at which a body, as a satellite, revolves about another body: *Orbital velocity is 18,000 miles per hour* (*24,200 feet per second*) *for a circular orbit at 300 miles altitude* (United States Air Force Report on the Ballistic Missile). **2** the velocity a body must achieve and maintain to go into or remain in orbit; circular velocity.
**or|bit|er** (ôr′bit ər), *n.* something that orbits, especially an artificial satellite.
**orb weaver**, any one of a group of strong-jawed spiders that spin nearly circular webs, anchored at various points around the circumference.
**orb web**, the web spun by an orb weaver: ... *the*

**Pronunciation Key:** hat, āge, cãre, fär; let, ēqual, tėrm; it, īce; hot, ōpen, ôrder; oil, out; cup, pu̇t, rüle; child; long; thin; ᴛʜen; zh, measure;
ə represents **a** in about, **e** in taken, **i** in pencil, **o** in lemon, **u** in circus.

*orb webs of the nearly blind cave spiders* (Scientific American).

**orc** (ôrk), *n.* any one of various marine mammals, such as the grampus or killer whale: *The haunt of seals, and orcs, and sea-mews' clang* (Milton). Also, **ork**. [< Latin *orca* a kind of whale]

**ORC** (no periods) or **O.R.C.**, **1** Officers' Reserve Corps. **2** Organized Reserve Corps (of the U.S. Army).

**Or|ca|di|an** (ôr kā′dē ən), *adj., n.* —***adj.*** of or having to do with the Orkney Islands, north of Scotland.
—***n.*** a native or inhabitant of the Orkney Islands.
[< Latin *Orcadēs* the Orkney Islands + English *-ian*]

**or|ce|in** (ôr′sē in), *n.* a reddish or purplish nitrogenous dye obtained from orcinol by the action of ammonia and oxygen, or from the dye orchil. It is used in microscopic stains and as a reagent. *Formula:* $C_{28}H_{24}O_7N_2$ [< French *orcein,* alteration of earlier English *orcin;* see etym. under **orcinol**]

**orch.**, orchestra.

**or|chal** (ôr′kəl), *n.* = orchil.

**or|chard** (ôr′chərd), *n.* **1** a piece of ground on which fruit trees are grown: *We walked over the orchard's soggy ground.* **2** the trees in an orchard: *The orchard should bear a good crop this year.* [Old English *orcgeard,* and *ortgeard,* perhaps < Latin *hortus* garden. Compare Old English *geard* yard[1].]

**orchard grass**, a perennial grass, valuable for hay and pasture; cocksfoot.

**or|chard|ist** (ôr′chər dist), *n.* a person who grows or cares for an orchard.

**or|chard|man** (ôr′chərd mən), *n., pl.* **-men.** = orchardist.

**orchard oriole**, an oriole of the eastern and central United States and Mexico, similar to the Baltimore oriole but having chestnut instead of orange feathers on its body. It suspends its nest from the branches of fruit and shade trees.

***or|ches|tra** (ôr′kə strə), *n., adj.* —***n.*** **1** a group of musicians playing together, as at a concert, an opera, or a play. An orchestra is usually distinguished from a band by the use of violins and other stringed instruments. *a symphony orchestra, a dance orchestra.* See picture below. **2** the violins, cellos, clarinets, horns, and other instruments played together by the musicians in an orchestra. **3** the part of a theater or auditorium just in front of the stage, where musicians sit to play. **4** the main floor of a theater, especially the part near the front: *Buy two seats in the orchestra.* **5** a large semicircular space in front of the stage of an ancient Greek theater, where the chorus sang and danced. **6** a similar space in the Roman theater, reserved for the seats of senators and other persons of distinction.
—***adj.*** of or having to do with an orchestra: *the orchestra pit, orchestra seats.*
[< Latin *orchēstra* < Greek *orchēstra* the space where the chorus of dancers performed, ultimately < *orcheîsthai* to dance]

**orchestra bells**, = glockenspiel (def. 1).

**or|ches|tral** (ôr kes′trəl), *adj.* of an orchestra; composed for or performed by an orchestra.
—**or|ches′tral|ly**, *adv.*

**or|ches|trate** (ôr′kə strāt), *v.t., v.i.,* **-trat|ed, -trat|ing.** **1** to compose or arrange (music) for performance by an orchestra. **2** *Figurative.* to combine or arrange harmoniously: *These flashbacks are so orchestrated that changes in location and pace ... have a cumulative effect* (Listener).

**or|ches|tra|tion** (ôr′kə strā′shən), *n.* **1** the arrangement of music for an orchestra: *The orchestration is so thick that the tunes can't emerge as buoyantly as they should* (New Yorker). **2** *Figurative.* any harmonious arrangement: *... a wonderful orchestration of deep and pale colours* (Manchester Guardian Weekly).

**or|ches|tra|tor** (ôr′kə strā′tər), *n.* a person who composes or arranges music for performance by an orchestra.

**or|ches|tri|na** (ôr′kə strē′nə), *n.* a reed organ that can imitate instruments such as the flute, clarinet, oboe, bassoon, and French horn by varying the form of the reeds or wind channels.

**or|ches|tri|on** (ôr kes′trē ən), *n.* a mechanical musical instrument, resembling a barrel organ, for producing the effect of an orchestra. [< German *Orchestrion* < Greek *orchêstra;* see etym. under **orchestra**]

***or|chid** (ôr′kid), *n., adj.* —***n.*** **1** the flower of the orchid plant. An orchid has three petallike sepals and three petals, one petal being much longer than the other two and of special color and shape. **2** a plant bearing these beautiful flowers. There are many kinds, making up a family of plants. Orchids are either terrestrial or epiphytic. **3** a light purple.
—***adj.*** **1** light-purple. **2** having orchids; composed of orchids: *an orchid lei.*
[< New Latin *orchid-,* erroneous stem of Latin *orchis* a kind of orchid < Greek *órchis* an orchid; (originally) testicle (because of the shape of its root)]

***orchid**
definition 1

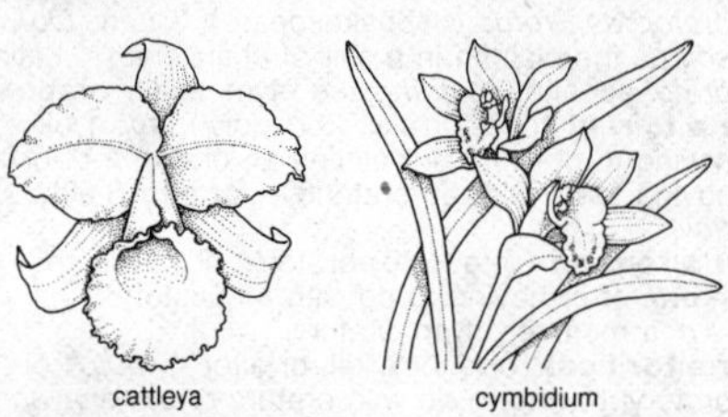


**or|chi|da|ceous** (ôr′kə dā′shəs), *adj.* belonging to the orchid family of plants.

**orchid family**, any plant of a family of terrestrial and epiphytic monocotyledonous herbs, widely distributed in temperate and tropical regions. Orchid flowers have their style, stigma, and stamens united into a central body (the column). The orchid family includes the lady's-slipper, arethusa, rattlesnake plantain, twayblade, showy orchis, and lady's-tresses.

**or|chid|ol|o|gy** (ôr′kə dol′ə jē), *n.* the branch of botany, or of horticulture, that deals with orchids.

**or|chil** (ôr′kəl, -chəl), *n.* **1** a red or violet coloring matter obtained from certain lichens. **2** any lichen that yields it. Also, **archil, orchal**. [Middle English *orchell* < Old French *orcheil*]

**or|chis** (ôr′kis), *n.* **1** = orchid. **2** any one of a genus of terrestrial orchids of temperate regions. The showy orchis, a common North American kind, has a spike of pink-purple flowers with a white lip. **3** any related orchid, such as the fringed orchis. [< Latin *orchis* < Greek *órchis* (originally) testicle; see etym. under **orchid**]

**or|cin|ol** (ôr′sə nōl, -nol), *n.* a white crystalline substance, a phenol, obtained from various lichens or prepared artificially. It is used chiefly as a reagent and also as an antiseptic. *Formula:* $C_7H_8O_2 \cdot H_2O$ [< *orcin* ultimately < New Latin *Variolaria orcina* orchil (because it was originally prepared from this lichen) + *-ol*[2]]

**Or|cus** (ôr′kəs), *n. Roman Mythology.* **1** the abode of the dead; Hades. **2** the god of the abode of the dead; Pluto.

**ord.**, an abbreviation for the following:
1 ordained.
2 order.
3 ordinal.
4 ordinance.
5 ordinary.
6 ordnance.

**or|dain** (ôr dān′), *v.t.* **1** to pass as a law; order; decide; fix; appoint: *In some places the law ordains that convicted criminals shall go to prison. The eternal rules of order and right, which Heaven itself has ordained* (Time). **SYN**: decree, prescribe. **2** to officially appoint or consecrate as a minister in a Christian church. **3** to appoint (a person) to a charge, duty, or office. **4** to appoint as part of the order of the universe or of nature; destine. —***v.i.*** to command. [< Anglo-French *ordeigner,* Old French *ordener,* learned borrowing from Latin *ōrdināre* arrange (in Medieval Latin, consecrate; take holy orders) < *ōrdō, -inis* order]
—**or|dain′er**, *n.* —**or|dain′ment**, *n.*

**or|deal** (ôr dēl′, ôr′dēl), *n.* **1** a severe test or experience: *He dreaded the ordeal of a visit to the dentist. She wondered how he, and how she, would comport themselves in the ordeal of adieu* (Arnold Bennett). **SYN**: trial. **2** (in early times) an effort to decide the guilt or innocence of an accused person by making him do something dangerous like holding fire or taking poison. It was supposed that God would not let an innocent person be harmed by such danger. [Old English *ordāl, ordēl* judgment; influenced by *deal*]

***or|der** (ôr′dər), *n., v.* —***n.*** **1** the way one thing follows another: *in order of size, in alphabetical order. Copy the words in order. This is a printed form of the order of business at the next meeting.* **SYN**: sequence, succession. **2a** the condition in which every part or piece is in its right place: *to put a room in order.* **b** a regular, methodical, or harmonious arrangement: *the order of a fleet of ships.* **3** condition; state: *a machine in good working order. My affairs are in good order.* **4** the way the world works; way things happen: *the order of nature.* **5** the state or condition of things in which the law is obeyed and there is no trouble; rule of law: *to keep order. Order was established after the riot.* **6** the principles and rules by which a meeting is run: *to rise to a point of order.* **7** the action of telling what to do; command: *On a ship the orders of the captain must be obeyed.* **8** a direction of a court or judge, especially one made in writing and not included in a judgment. **9a** a paper saying that money is to be given or paid, or something handed over: *a postal money order.* **b** the account of someone; someone's disposition of money: *He received a note for $1,000 payable to his order after one year.* **10a** a spoken or written request for goods that one wants to buy or receive: *Mother gave the grocer an order for two dozen eggs, a loaf of bread, and two cans of tomatoes.* **b** the goods so requested: *Mother asked when they would deliver our order.* **11** a kind or sort: *He had ability of a high order.* **12** *Biology.* a group in the classifying of plants and animals that is below or smaller than a class, but larger than a family. The rose family, the pea family, and several others belong to one order. **13** a social rank, grade, or class: *all orders of society. He had found, in general, the lower orders debased; the superior immersed in sordid pursuits* (Benjamin Disraeli). **14** a rank or position in the church: *the order of bishops.* **15** Usually, **orders. a** ordination to the ministry of a church. **b** the rite of ordination; holy orders. **16a** a brotherhood of monks, friars, or knights: *the order of Saint Francis, the Benedictine Order.* **b** a sisterhood of nuns. **17** a society to which one is admitted as an honor: *the Order of the Golden Fleece, the Order of the Garter.* **18** a modern fraternal organization: *the Order of Masons.* **19** the badge worn by those belonging to an honorary order. **20a** any one of several styles of columns and architecture, having differences in proportion and decoration: *the Doric, Ionic, and Corinthian orders of Greek architecture.* See picture opposite on next page. **b** a style of building. **21** a regular form of worship for a given occasion. **22** a portion or serving of food in a restaurant, or other place that prepares food for sale. **23** *Mathematics.* the degree (of complexity). **24** the arrangement of the constituents in a linguistic expression. **25** *Military.* the command or position of order arms. **26** any of the nine ranks or grades of angels in medieval angelology. **27** *Especially British.* a pass for admission, without payment or at a reduced price, as to a theater or museum.
—***v.t.*** **1** to put in order; arrange: *to order one's affairs. I had to order my life methodically* (Joseph Conrad). **SYN**: regulate. **2** to tell what to do; give an order to; command; bid: *to order a per-*

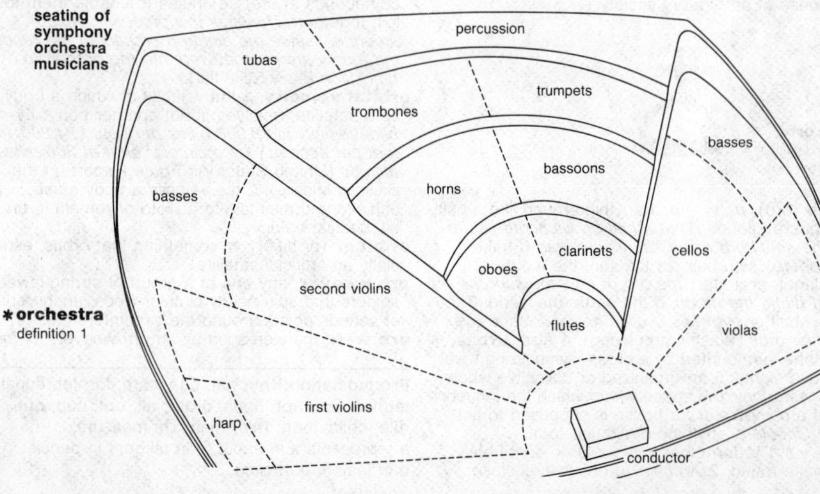


***orchestra**
definition 1

*son to leave. The policeman ordered that the prisoners be handcuffed.* **SYN**: direct, instruct. See syn. under **command**. **3** to prescribe as medicine: *to order a tonic for a patient.* **4** to give (a store, waitress, milkman, or the like) an order for; direct (a thing) to be made or furnished: *to order dinner, to order a cab. Mother ordered milk, eggs, and butter from the grocer.* **5** to decide; will; determine: *The authorities ordered it otherwise.* **6** *Ecclesiastical.* to invest with clerical rank and authority. **7** *Archaic.* to draw up in order of battle.

—***v.i.*** to give orders or direction: *Please order for me.*

**by order**, according to an order given by the proper person: *The bank was closed by order of the governor.*

**call to order**, **a** to open (a convention, meeting or other gathering) for formal proceedings: *The annual town meeting of the town of Seekonk was called to order Monday by Town Clerk Hill* (Providence Journal). **b** to ask to be quiet and start work: *The teacher called the class to order.*

**in order**, **a** in the right arrangement: *Take the lowest first, then without stop the rest in order to the top.* **b** in proper condition; working right: *Having set all things in order for that voyage ...* (Miles Coverdale). **c** in obedience to authority: *One of the chief duties of these societies is to keep the women in order* (Mary Kingsley). **d** allowed by the rules of a meeting or other gathering: *The motion is in order.* **e** likely to be done; natural; logical: *A visit to the place seemed in order.* **f** current, in fashion; appropriate: *A quotation from Professor James on any subject which his brilliant pen has touched is always in order* (H. H. Horne).

**in orders**, being a clergyman: *A master of arts, in full orders, is desirous of a curacy* (Harriet Martineau).

**in order that**, so that; with the aim that: *Come early in order that you may see him.*

**in order to**, as a means to; with a view to; for the purpose of: *She worked hard in order to win the prize. He ran in order to catch the train.*

**in short order**, without delay; quickly: *They got the broken windows replaced in short order.*

**on order**, having been ordered but not yet received: *The furniture store has several tables on order, but until they arrive we must wait to buy one.*

**on** (or **of**) **the order of**, somewhat like; similar to: *a house on the order of ours. The next day the photographer arrived, a nice tall thin man of the order of Mel Ferrer* (Punch).

**order about** (or **around**), to send here and there; tell to do this and that: *He was exasperated by the thought that he was ordered about and overruled by Russell* (Macaulay).

**out of order**, **a** in the wrong arrangement: *He listed the states alphabetically but California was out of order.* **b** not in proper condition; not working right: *The watch is out of order.* **c** against the rules of a meeting or other gathering: *Senator W. Kerr Scott ... ruled the motion out of order on grounds that a quorum was not present* (New York Times). **d** indisposed; sick: *His ... Majesty being out of order, by reason of a cold* (London Gazette). **e** in confusion or disorder: *The boy's room was out of order.* **f** inappropriate; uncalled-for: *It was out of order to make such a tactless remark.*

**take (holy) orders**. See under **holy orders**.

**to order**, according to the buyer's wishes or requirements: *a coat made to order.*

[earlier, class, division < Old French *ordre* < *ordene,* learned borrowing from Latin *ōrdō, -inis* row, series, regular arrangement] —**or′der|er**, *n.*

***order**
definition 20a

Doric Ionic Corinthian

**order arms**, **1** the command to bring a weapon to a prescribed position, especially to bring a rifle to an erect position at the side with the butt on the ground while one is standing at attention. **2** the position in the manual of arms in which a weapon is thus held.

**or|dered pair** (ôr′dərd), *Mathematics.* any two numbers written in a meaningful order, so that one can be considered as the first and the other as the second of the pair.

**order in council** or **Order in Council**, *British.* an order by the sovereign with the advice of the privy council. Such an order generally has previously been authorized by Parliament. *In 1807, Great Britain issued Orders in Council in answer to Napoleon's threat to blockade the island empire* (Basil D. Henning).

**or|der|less** (ôr′dər lis), *adj.* without order, arrangement, method, or regularity; disorderly: *The orderless lives of society's castoffs and stepchildren.*

**or|der|li|ness** (ôr′dər lē nis), *n.* **1** orderly condition or character. **2** orderly manner or behavior: *He bears testimony to the orderliness of the crowd* (Hawthorne).

**or|der|ly** (ôr′dər lē), *adj., n., pl.* **-lies**, *adv.* —***adj.*** **1** in order; with regular arrangement, method, or system: *an orderly arrangement of dishes on shelves, an orderly mind.* **2** keeping order; well-behaved or regulated: *an orderly class.* **3** concerned with carrying out orders; being on duty.

—***n.*** **1** a hospital attendant who keeps things clean and in order and often helps with patients in certain ways. **2** a noncommissioned officer or private soldier who attends a superior officer to carry orders and to help him in other ways: *The general's orderly delivered the message.*

—***adv.*** in or with due order; methodically: *We'll do this orderly* (Time).

—***Syn.*** *adj.* **1 Orderly, methodical, systematic** mean following a plan of arrangement or action. **Orderly** suggests lack of confusion and careful arrangement of details or things in proper relation to each other according to some rule or scheme: *The chairs are in orderly rows.* **Methodical** suggests following step by step a plan carefully worked out in advance or regularly followed: *The bookkeeper made a methodical check of the accounts for the error.* **Systematic** adds to *methodical* and emphasizes the idea of thoroughness and completeness: *The commission made a systematic investigation of the problem of air pollution.*

**orderly officer**, *British.* the officer of the day.

**orderly room**, the office of the commanding officer of an infantry company or equivalent military unit, in which the first sergeant and company clerk are also situated.

**order of battle**, an arrangement or disposition of the different parts of an army or fleet, especially for the purpose of engaging in battle or to be reviewed.

**order of the day**, **1** the business to be considered on a particular day, especially by a legislature. **2** specific commands or notices issued by a commanding officer to his troops. **3** *Figurative.* the prevailing rule or custom: *In Wall Street, ... giant money maneuvers are the order of the day* (New York Times).

**order paper**, a paper or form used in the British House of Commons (or other legislative assembly of the Commonwealth) for recording questions or other business set down for future debate.

**or|di|naire** (ôr dē ner′), *n. French.* an inexpensive wine; vin ordinaire.

**or|di|nal** (ôr′də nəl), *adj., n.* —***adj.*** **1** showing order or position in a series. **2** having to do with an order of animals or plants.

—***n.*** **1** = ordinal number. **2** Also, **Ordinal**. a book of special forms of certain church ceremonies, such as the conferring of holy orders in the Church of England or the conducting of the daily office in the Roman Catholic Church.

[< Late Latin *ōrdinālis* < Latin *ōrdō, -inis* row, series] —**or′di|nal|ly**, *adv.*

**or|di|nal|i|ty** (ôr də nal′ə tē), *n.* the condition or property of being expressible in order.

**ordinal number** or **numeral**, a number that shows order or position in a series. First, second, third, fourth, and so on are ordinal numbers; one, two, three, four, and so on are cardinal numbers. ▶ See **cardinal number** for usage note.

**or|di|nance** (ôr′də nəns), *n.* **1** a rule or law made by authority, especially one adopted and enforced by a municipal or other local authority; decree: *a traffic ordinance. Some cities have ordinances forbidding the use of soft coal. Freedom of religious worship was guaranteed to all settlers in the Northwest Territory by the Ordinance of 1787* (Ray Allen Billington). **SYN**: regulation, canon. **2** an established religious ceremony, especially the sacrament of Holy Communion. **3** what is ordained or decreed by God or by fate. **4** *Archaic.* direction or management. [Middle English *ordynaunce* < Old French *ordenance* < Latin *ōrdināre* arrange, regulate; see etym. under **ordain**]

**or|di|nand** (ôr′də nand), *n.* a person about to be ordained or to receive holy orders. [< Latin *ō rdinandus,* gerundive of *ōrdināre* ordain]

**or|di|nant** (ôr′də nənt), *adj., n.* —***adj.*** ordering; directing; ordaining: *Why, even in that was heaven ordinant* (Shakespeare).

—***n.*** a person who ordains or confers holy orders.

[< Latin *ōrdināns, -antis,* present participle of *ōrdināre* ordain]

**or|di|nar|i|ly** (ôr′də ner′ə lē, ôr′də nãr′-), *adv.* **1** commonly; usually; normally; regularly: *We ordinarily go to the movies on Saturday.* **2** to the usual extent.

**or|di|nar|i|ness** (ôr′də ner′ē nis), *n.* ordinary quality or condition; commonness: *The ordinariness of these stories makes them boring.*

**or|di|nar|y** (ôr′də ner′ē), *adj., n., pl.* **-nar|ies**.

—***adj.*** **1** usual; common; normal; regular; according to habit or custom: *an ordinary day's work. His ordinary lunch consists of soup, a sandwich, and milk. In ordinary life we use a great many words with a total disregard of logical precision* (William S. Jevons). **SYN**: customary, habitual, wonted. See syn. under **common**. **2** not special; common; everyday; average: *an ordinary situation.* **3** somewhat below the average: *The speaker was ordinary and tiresome.* **SYN**: mediocre, inferior. **4a** having authority in his own right, by virtue of office: *a judge or bishop ordinary.* **b** immediate or original, not delegated: *jurisdiction ordinary.*

—***n.*** **1** a meal served at a fixed price: *A board hung out of a window signifying, "An excellent Ordinary on Saturdays and Sundays"* (Henry Mackenzie). **2** *British.* **a** an inn. **b** the dining room of an inn. **3** a person who has authority in his own right, such as a bishop or a judge, especially a judge of a probate court. **4** Also, **Ordinary**. **a** the usual or unchangeable parts of the Mass; common. **b** the form for saying Mass. **c** a book containing this form. **5** *Heraldry.* a bearing of the earliest, simplest, and commonest kind, usually bounded by straight lines. **6** an early kind of bicycle having a high wheel in front with the seat on top, and a small wheel behind; high wheeler. **7** *Obsolete.* a clergyman appointed to prepare condemned criminals for death.

**in ordinary**, in regular service: *a physician in ordinary to the king.*

**out of the ordinary**, not regular or customary; unusual; extraordinary: *Such a long delay is out of the ordinary.*

[< Latin *ōrdinārius* < *ōrdō, -inis* row, rank; see etym. under **order**]

**ordinary seaman**, a sailor having some experience, but not yet an able seaman. *Abbr:* O.S.

**ordinary share** or **stock**, *British.* a share of common stock.

**or|di|nate** (ôr′də nit, -nāt), *n.* the distance of a point on a graph above or below the horizontal axis, measured along a line parallel to the vertical axis. The ordinate and the abscissa together are coordinates of the point. [< Latin *ōrdinātus,* past participle of *ōrdināre* arrange; see etym. under **ordain**]

**or|di|na|tion** (ôr′də nā′shən), *n.* **1** the act or ceremony of ordaining a person to the ministry of a church. **2** the condition of being ordained as a minister in a church: *His ordination gives him the right to conduct a marriage or a funeral.* **3** arrangement; disposition. [< Latin *ōrdinātiō, -ōnis* < *ōrdināre;* see etym under **ordain**]

**ordn.**, ordnance.

**ord|nance** (ôrd′nəns), *n.* **1** cannon or artillery: *heavy ordnance.* **2** military weapons of all kinds, such as guns, combat vehicles, and ammunition, together with the tools for repairing and maintaining them. **SYN**: arms, armament. [reduction of *ordinance*]

**or|do** (ôr′dō), *n., pl.* **or|di|nes** (ôr′də nēz). the schedule of offices, services, and festivals for every day of the year in the Roman Catholic Church. [< Latin *ōrdō, -inis* row, rank, series, regular order]

**or|don|nance** (ôr′də nəns; *French* ôr dô näns′), *n.* **1** the arrangement or disposition of parts, as of a building, a picture, or a literary composition. **2** a decree or law. [< Middle French *ordonnance,* alteration of Old French *ordenance;* see etym. under **ordinance**]

**Or|do|vi|cian** (ôr′də vish′ən), *n., adj.* —***n.*** **1** a geological period, the second in the Paleozoic era, after the Cambrian and before the Silurian. The Ordovician is characterized by the first appearance of vertebrates and the development of many trilobites, brachiopods, and other invertebrates. **2** the rocks formed in this period.

**Pronunciation Key:** hat, āge, cãre, fär; let, ēqual, tėrm; it, īce; hot, ōpen, ôrder; **oi**l, **ou**t; cup, pu̇t, rüle; **ch**ild; lo**ng**; **th**in; **ᴛʜ**en; **zh**, measure; ə represents **a** in about, **e** in taken, **i** in pencil, **o** in lemon, **u** in circus.

—*adj.* of the Ordovician or its rocks.
[< Latin *Ordovicēs* ancient Celtic tribe in Wales + English *-ian*]

**or|dure** (ôr′jər, -dyůr), *n.* **1** filth; dung; excrement. **2** *Figurative.* anything morally filthy or defiling, especially vile language: *Those let me curse; what vengeance will they urge, Whose ordures neither plague nor fire can purge?* (John Dryden). [< Old French *ordure* < *ord* filthy < Latin *horridus* repulsive, horrid]

**ore** (ôr, ōr), *n.* **1** a mineral or rock containing enough of a metal or metals to make mining it profitable. The ore may be found in its natural state or chemically combined with other substances. *Gold ore was discovered in California in 1848.* **2** a natural substance yielding a nonmetallic material, such as sulfur. [Middle English *ure, ore,* fusion of Old English *ōra* ore, unworked metal, and of *ār* brass]

**ö|re** (œ′rə), *n.* **1** a unit of money equal to 1/100 of a Danish or Norwegian krone or of a Swedish krona. **2** a bronze, aluminum, or zinc coin having this value. [< Danish, Norwegian *øre,* Swedish *öre*]

**Ore.**, Oregon.

**O|re|ad** or **o|re|ad** (ôr′ē ad, ōr′-), *n. Greek Mythology.* a mountain nymph. [< Latin *Orēas, -adis* < Greek *Oreiás, -ádos* < *óros, óreos* mountain]

**ore|bod|y** (ôr′bod′ē, ōr′-), *n., pl.* **-bod|ies**. a bed or vein of ore.

**ore bridge**, a gantry crane used to pick up ore.

**ore carrier**, a ship that carries ore.

**ore dressing**, the act or process of obtaining the valuable minerals contained in an ore by means involving physical changes only, as by crushing or washing.

**Oreg.**, Oregon.

**o|reg|a|no** or **o|ré|ga|no** (ə reg′ə nō, -rig′-; ôr′ə-gä′-), *n.* an aromatic herb, a species of marjoram. Oregano belongs to the mint family. The leaves are used for seasoning food. [< Spanish *orégano* < Latin *orīganum;* see etym. at **origan**]

**Or|e|gon grape** (ôr′ə gon, -gən; or′-), **1** an evergreen shrub of the barberry family, growing in the western United States and bearing clusters of yellow flowers and small blue-black berries. The blossom is the state flower of Oregon. **2** the berry.

**Or|e|go|ni|an** (ôr′ə gō′nē ən, or′-), *adj., n.* —*adj.* of or having to do with Oregon or its people.
—*n.* a native or inhabitant of Oregon.

**Oregon jay**, a jay of the northwestern United States similar in appearance and habits to the Canada jay but with different coloring.

**Oregon larch**, = western larch.

**Oregon laurel**, an evergreen tree of the laurel family, growing in Oregon and California; spice tree; myrtlewood.

**Oregon maple**, a maple tree of the Pacific Coast, with large leaves and a valuable hardwood.

**Oregon pine** or **fir**, = Douglas fir.

**Oregon towhee**, a towhee of the Pacific coast region of the United States and Canada.

**o|ren|da** (ō ren′də), *n.* a supernatural or magic power believed by the Iroquois Indians to be contained in every object and being. [< Wyandot *orenda*]

**O|re|o** (ôr′ē ō, ō′rē-), *n. U.S. Slang.* a black man who thinks and acts like a white man (used in an unfriendly way): *"Trouble is Negroes been programmed by white folks to believe their products are inferior. We've developed into a generation of Oreos—black on the outside, white on the inside"* (Harper's). [< *Oreo,* a trademark for a chocolate cookie with a vanilla cream filling]

**Or|e|o|pith|e|cus** (ôr′ē ō pith′ə kəs), *n.* a humanoid that lived between ten and twelve million years ago, whose remains have been found in coal beds in Italy. Opinion varies as to whether or not it is a true ancestor of man. [< New Latin *Oreopithecus* < Greek *óros, óreos* mountain + *pithekōs* ape]

**o|re ro|tun|do** (ôr′ē rō tun′dō, ōr′-), *Latin.* **1** clearly and distinctly. **2** (literally) with round mouth.

**ore shoot**, a concentration of mineral ore within an orebody: *In veins and dikes ore generally is concentrated into irregularly shaped bodies called ore shoots* (Fenton and Fenton).

**O|res|tes** (ô res′tēz, ō-), *n. Greek Legend.* the son of Agamemnon and Clytemnestra, who killed his mother because she had murdered his father. He was pursued by the Furies for this crime.

**o|rex|is** (ô rek′sis, ō-), *n.* appetite; desire. [< Latin *orexis* < Greek *órexis* < *orégein* to desire]

**org.**, an abbreviation for the following:
**1** organ.
**2** organic.
**3** organist.
**4** organization.
**5** organized.

***or|gan** (ôr′gən), *n.* **1a** a musical instrument made of pipes of different lengths, which are sounded by compressed air blown by a bellows, and played by keys arranged in one or more keyboards, pipe organ. Organs are used especially in church, and the modern organ is the most comprehensive of all musical instruments. **b** any one of certain smaller instruments somewhat like the pipe organ but sounded by electronic devices. **2** any one of various other musical instruments: **a** a street organ or hand organ. **b** a parlor organ or reed organ. **c** a mouth organ or harmonica. **d** (in the Bible) any wind instrument. **3** any part of an animal or plant that is composed of various tissues organized to do certain things in life. The eyes, stomach, heart, and lungs are organs of the body. Stamens, pistils, and roots are organs of plants. *In most complex organisms, some organs become specialized to perform only a portion of a process* (Harbaugh and Goodrich). **4** *Figurative.* a means of action; instrument: *A court is an organ of government.* SYN: agency. **5** *Figurative.* a means of giving information or expressing opinions; newspaper, magazine, or the like, that speaks for and gives the views of a political party or some other organization.
[< Latin *organum* < Greek *órganon* instrument, body organ, related to *érgon* work. Compare etym. under **erg**.]

***organ**
definition 1a

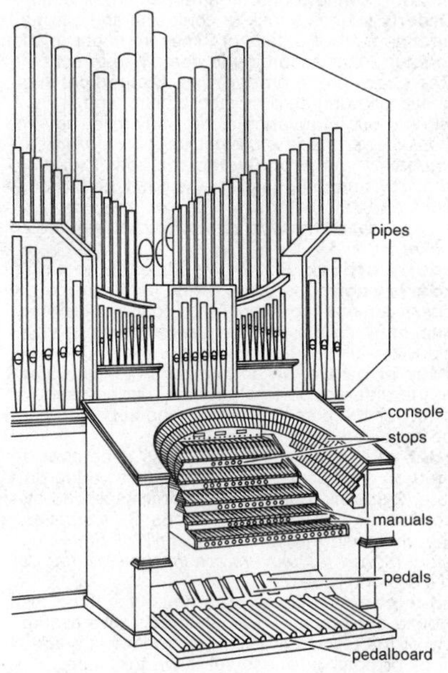


**or|ga|na** (ôr′gə nə), *n.* a plural of **organum** and a plural of **organon**.

**or|gan|dy** or **or|gan|die** (ôr′gən dē), *n., pl.* **-dies**. a fine, thin, stiff, transparent muslin, used especially for dresses, curtains, and trimming. [< French *organdi;* origin uncertain]

**or|gan|elle** (ôr′gə nel′), *n. Biology.* a minute specialized part of a cell, such as a vacuole in protozoans, analogous in function to an organ of higher animals.

***organ grinder**, a person, especially a wandering street musician, who plays a hand organ by turning a crank.

***organ grinder**

**or|gan|ic** (ôr gan′ik), *adj., n.* —*adj.* **1** of the bodily organs; vital; affecting the structure of an organ: *an organic disease, an organic process.* **2** produced by animal or plant activities: *organic fertilizer.* **3** *Chemistry.* of or having to do with compounds containing carbon. Starch is an organic compound. **4** having organs, or an organized physical structure, as plants and animals have; not of the mineral kingdom. **5** made up of related parts, but being a unit; coordinated: *The United States is an organic whole made up of 50 states.* SYN: organized. **6** that is part of the structure or constitution of a person or thing; fundamental: *The Constitution is the organic law of the United States.* SYN: inherent, innate, constitutional. **7a** grown or prepared with natural fertilizers or without the use of insecticides and other chemicals: *organic food.* **b** having to do with or using natural fertilizers; not involving the use of chemicals: *organic farming. Going organic ... will mean that the Thanksgiving turkey must be imported from an organic farm* (Time).
—*n.* any organic substance, such as a fertilizer of animal or vegetable origin.
[< Latin *organicus* < Greek *organikós* < *órganon* instrument; see etym. under **organ**]

**organic acid**, any carbon compound that displays typical acidic properties, especially one containing the carboxyl radical—COOH.

**or|gan|i|cal** (ôr gan′ə kəl), *adj.* = organic.

**or|gan|i|cal|ly** (ôr gan′ə klē), *adv.* **1** in an organic manner. **2** by or with animal or plant organs. **3** in organization. **4** as part of an organization. **5** with natural fertilizers and without the use of insecticides and other chemicals: *to grow fruits and vegetables organically, organically prepared food.*

**organic chemistry**, the branch of chemistry that deals with compounds of carbon; chemistry of organic compounds, such as foods and fuels.

**or|gan|ic-cooled** (ôr gan′ik küld′), *adj.* cooled by an organic compound: *an organic-cooled nuclear reactor.*

**or|gan|i|cism** (ôr gan′ə siz əm), *n.* **1a** the doctrine that everything in nature has an organic basis or explanation. **b** the medical theory that all symptoms of disease can be traced back to an organic lesion or defect. **2** the doctrine that organic structure is merely the result of an inherent property in matter to adapt itself to circumstances.

**or|gan|i|cist** (ôr gan′ə sist), *n.* **1** a person who believes that all symptoms of disease have an organic cause. **2** a person who favors or advocates a doctrine of organicism.

**or|gan|ic|i|ty** (ôr′gə nis′ə tē), *n.* organic quality.

**or|gan|ic-mod|er|at|ed** (ôr gan′ik mod′ə rā′tid), *adj.* = organic-cooled.

**or|gan|ise** (ôr′gə nīz), *v.t., v.i.,* **-ised, -is|ing**. *Especially British.* organize.

**or|gan|ism** (ôr′gə niz əm), *n.* **1** a living body having organs that work together to carry on the processes of life; individual animal or plant: *It is almost impossible to keep any space in the habitable parts of the earth's surface free from organisms* (Fred W. Emerson). **2** a very tiny animal or plant; microorganism. **3** a whole made up of related parts that work together. Human society, or any community, may be spoken of as a social organism.

**or|gan|is|mal** (ôr′gə niz′məl), *adj.* of or produced by living organisms.

**or|gan|is|mic** (ôr′gə niz′mik), *adj.* = organismal.

**or|gan|ist** (ôr′gə nist), *n.* a person who plays an organ: *a church organist.*

**or|gan|is|tic** (ôr′gə nis′tik), *adj.* **1** of, having to do with, or characteristic of the organ or organ music: *These pieces both are rather "organistic," but so was the aim of the record, which is achieved gloriously* (John M. Conly). **2** of or having to do with animal or plant organs: *Until quite recently, the theories proposed for anesthesia have been based on gross and organistic concepts rather than upon concepts arising out of actions at the molecular level* (Raymond C. Ingraham).

**or|gan|iz|a|bil|i|ty** (ôr′gə nī′zə bil′ə tē), *n.* **1** capability for organization or for being turned into living tissue: *the organizability of fibrin.* **2** the quality of being organizable.

**or|gan|iz|a|ble** (ôr′gə nī′zə bəl), *adj.* **1** that can be organized. **2** *Biology.* that can be converted into living tissue.

**or|gan|i|za|tion** (ôr′gə nə zā′shən), *n.* **1** a group of persons united for some purpose. Churches, clubs, and political parties are organizations. SYN: association. **2** a grouping and arranging of parts to form a whole; organizing: *The organization of a big picnic takes time and thought.* SYN: arrangement. **3** the way in which a thing's parts are arranged to work together: *The organization of the human body is very complicated.* SYN: constitution. **4** a thing made up of related parts, each having a special duty; organism: *A tree is an organization of roots, trunk, branches, leaves, and fruit.* **5** the people who manage an organization, as in a political party or business; management: *Politics is a business ... you got to have organization* (Newsweek).

**or|gan|i|za|tion|al** (ôr′gə nə zā′shə nəl), *adj.* of or

having to do with organization: *This results in a vote-getting free-for-all and minimizes party loyalty and organizational possibilities* (New York Times). **— or′gan|i|za′tion|al|ly**, *adv.*

**organization chart**, a chart showing the structure of an organization: *Although there are many kinds of organizations, the same type of organization chart is used to decribe them all. This is the familiar pyramid of lines and boxes arranged in ascending order of importance* (Harper's).

**organization man**, an employee of a large corporation, generally an executive, who has absorbed its philosophy and has merged his personality, habits, and activities into it to the extent that he has lost his identity as an individual. [suggested and popularized by *The Organization Man,* a book that deals with this concept, by William H. Whyte, born in 1917, an American writer]

**or|gan|ize** (ôr′gə nīz), *v.,* **-ized, -iz|ing.** **— *v.t.*** **1** to put into working order; get together and arrange: *The explorer organized an expedition to the North Pole.* **SYN**: form, systematize. **2** to bring together into a labor union (the workers of a particular industry): *to organize the truckers, to organize the steel industry.* **3** to furnish with organs; provide with an organic structure; make organic. **4** *Slang.* to steal; talk someone out of (something): *We tracked the group down in a butcher shop, where they were busy organizing some sausage from the reluctant proprietor* (New Yorker). **— *v.i.*** **1** to combine in a company, political party, labor union, or other group; form an organization: *The employees organized in an effort to form a union.* **2** to assume organic structure; become living tissue. [< Late Latin *organizāre* to play on the organ (in Medieval Latin, organize) < Latin *organum* < Greek *órganon* organ]

**or|gan|ized** (ôr′gə nīzd), *adj.* **1** combined in an organization, such as a company, party, or labor union: *... the leader of organized crime in the U.S., won court review of the narcotic conviction that sent him to prison* (Wall Street Journal). **2** put into working order; systematically arranged: *An assembly governs each organized borough. ... The state legislature governs all unorganized boroughs* (Lyman E. Allen). **3** having organs or organic structure: *A rose is a highly organized plant.*

**organized labor**, **1** the workers who belong to labor unions. **2** labor unions as a group.

**organized ferment**, a living organism, such as yeast or other fungi, which is used to cause fermentation.

**or|gan|iz|er** (ôr′gə nī′zər), *n.* **1** a person who organizes or brings elements or parts together; one who brings into being or action. **2** *Biology.* an inductor.

**organo-**, *combining form.* **1** organ, as in *organography, organotherapy.*
**2** organic, as in *organochlorine, organophosphate.*
[< Greek *órganon* organ]

**or|ga|no|chlo|rine** (ôr′gə nō klôr′ēn, -in; -klōr′-), *n.* **1** an organic compound containing chlorine, such as methyl chloride. **2** a chlorinated hydrocarbon, such as DDT, chlordane, and aldrin. Organochlorines are among the most persistent pesticides.

**organ of Cor|ti** (kôr′tē), a part of the structure of the inner ear that lies along the basilar membrane of the cochlea. It contains over 15,000 hair cells which transmit sound vibrations to the nerve fibers. [< Alfonso *Corti,* 1822-1888, an Italian anatomist]

**or|ga|no|gen|e|sis** (ôr′gə nō jen′ə sis), *n. Biology.* the origin or development of the organs of an animal or plant.

**or|ga|no|ge|net|ic** (ôr′gə nō jə net′ik), *adj.* having to do with organogenesis. **— or′ga|no|ge|net′i|cal|ly**, *adv.*

**or|ga|nog|en|y** (ôr′gə noj′ə nē), *n.* = organogenesis.

**or|ga|nog|ra|phy** (ôr′gə nog′rə fē), *n.* the description of the organs of living beings; descriptive organology.

**or|ga|no|lep|tic** (ôr′gə nō lep′tik), *adj.* using various sense organs to determine flavor, texture, or other quality. [< *organo-* + Greek *leptós* fine, delicate + English *-ic*] **— or′ga|no|lep′ti|cal|ly**, *adv.*

**or|ga|no|log|ic** (ôr′gə nə loj′ik), *adj.* = organological.

**or|ga|no|log|i|cal** (ôr′gə nə loj′ə kəl), *adj.* of or having to do with organology.

**or|ga|nol|o|gy** (ôr′gə nol′ə jē), *n.* **1** the branch of biology that deals with the structure and function of animal and plant organs. **2** = phrenology.

**or|ga|no|mer|cu|ri|al** (ôr′gə nō mər kyůr′ē əl), *n., adj.* **— *n.*** any one of various highly toxic organic compounds that contain mercury.
**— *adj.*** having to do with or containing organomercurials: *organomercurial seed dressings.*

**or|ga|no|mer|cu|ry** (ôr′gə nō mėr′kyər ē), *n., adj.* = organomercurial.

**or|ga|no|me|tal|lic** (ôr′gə nō mə tal′ik), *adj., n.* **— *adj.*** consisting of an atom of a metal in combination with one or more alkyl radicals.
**— *n.*** an organometallic compound.

**or|ga|non** (ôr′gə non), *n., pl.* **-na** or **-nons. 1** an instrument of thought or knowledge; means by which some process, such as reasoning or discovery, is carried on: *Language has been called "the supreme organon of the mind's self-ordering growth." It is the means by which we not only communicate our thoughts to others but interpret our thoughts to ourselves* (Wall Street Journal). **2** a system of rules or principles for investigation of a field of knowledge. [< Greek *órganon*]

**or|ga|no|phos|phate** (ôr′gə nō fos′fāt), *n.* an organophosphorous compound: *Organophosphates in drinking water ... can indicate the presence of toxic pesticides* (Science News).

**or|ga|no|phos|pho|rous** (ôr′gə nō fos′fər əs; -fos fôr′-, -fōr′-), *adj.* having to do with or containing organophosphorus: *organophosphorous nerve gases, organophosphorous insecticides.*

**or|ga|no|phos|pho|rus** (ôr′gə nō fos′fər əs), *n.* a chemical compound consisting of an atom of phosphorus combined with an atom of carbon and one or more alkyl radicals, used especially as a pesticide. Malathion is an organophosphorus. Organophosphorus acts by inhibiting the enzyme cholinesterase.

**or|gan|o|sol** (ôr gan′ə sol), *n.* **1** any organic liquid containing a colloidal suspension. **2** = plastisol.

**or|ga|no|ther|a|py** (ôr′gə nō ther′ə pē), *n.* therapy using preparations from the organs of animals, such as the thyroid gland, the pancreas, and suprarenal bodies.

**organ pipe**, one of the pipes of a pipe organ.

**or|gan-pipe cactus** (ôr′gən pīp′), a large columnar cactus of Mexico and Arizona, having ribbed stems up to 25 feet high and 6 inches in diameter.

**organ point**, *Music.* a pedal point.

**or|ga|nule** (ôr′gə nyül), *n.* = molechism. [< *organ-*(ism) + (molec)*ule*]

**or|ga|num** (ôr′gə nəm), *n., pl.* **-na** or **-nums.** in medieval music: **1** the addition of a part below or above a melody, usually at the interval of a fourth, fifth, or octave. **2** the singing of such a part. [< Latin *organum* < Greek *órganon* organ]

**or|gan|za** (ôr gan′zə), *n.* a sheer cloth, as of rayon or silk, resembling organdy, used especially for dresses. [origin uncertain]

**or|gan|zine** (ôr′gən zēn), *n.* a very fine quality of silk thread made of several single threads twisted together, used for the warp in weaving. [< French *organsin* < Italian *organzino,* perhaps < *Organzi,* medieval form of *Urganj,* a silk center in Turkestan]

**or|gasm** (ôr′gaz əm), *n.* **1** the highest point of sexual excitement, accompanied by a release of sexual tension, and in the male by ejaculation of semen; climax. **2** *Figurative.* a paroxysm of excitement; rage; fury: *the periodic orgasm of war.* [< Greek *orgasmós* < *orgân* be in heat, become ripe for; (literally) to swell]

**or|gas|mic** (ôr gaz′mik), *adj.* of, characteristic of, or like an orgasm.

**or|gas|tic** (ôr gas′tik), *adj.* characterized by or exhibiting orgasm.

**or|geat** (ôr′zhat; *French* ôr zhȧ′), *n.* a syrup flavored with almonds (formerly, barley) and water in which orange flowers have been steeped. [< Middle French *orgeat* < Provençal *ourjat* < Old French *orge* (in Old Provençal, *ordi*) barley < Latin *hordeum*]

**or|gi|ac** (ôr′jē ak), *adj.* having to do with orgies; orgiastic.

**or|gi|ast** (ôr′jē ast), *n.* one who celebrates orgies.

**or|gi|as|tic** (ôr′jē as′tik), *adj.* of, having to do with, or of the nature of orgies; wild; frenzied: *an orgiastic carnival, gross in all its manifestations of joy* (Arnold Bennett). [< Greek *orgiastikós* < *orgiázein* celebrate < *orgiā* secret rites < *érgon* act, deed] **— or′gi|as′ti|cal|ly**, *adv.*

**org-man** (ôrg′man′), *n., pl.* **-men.** *U.S. Slang.* an organization man: *They [white Anglo-Saxon Protestants] ... shaped the institutions and organizations. Then they drew the institutions around themselves, moved to the suburbs, and became org-men* (Peter Schrag).

**or|gone** (ôr′gōn), *n., adj.* **— *n.*** energy found in nature, according to the theories of Wilhelm Reich (1897-1957), an Austrian psychoanalyst.
**— *adj.*** of or having to do with orgone: *orgone energy, an orgone accumulator box.*
[probably < *org*(asm) + *-one,* as in *ozone*]

**or|gu|lous** (ôr′gyə ləs), *adj. Archaic.* proud; haughty. [< Old French *orguillus* (with English *-ous*) < *orguil* pride; origin uncertain]

**or|gy** (ôr′jē), *n., pl.* **-gies. 1** a wild, drunken revel. **2a** a period or activity of uncontrolled indulgence: *an orgy of eating.* **b** *Figurative.* any activity in which controls are lacking or ineffective: *an orgy of bloodshed or crime. The worship of the beautiful always ends in an orgy* (Benjamin Disraeli).

**orgies**, secret rites or ceremonies in the worship of certain Greek and Roman gods, especially Dionysus, the god of wine, celebrated by drinking, wild dancing, and singing: *The orgies of Bacchus ... were famed through all the Ages of Antiquity* (John Brown).
[originally, plural < Middle French *orgies,* learned borrowing from Latin *orgia,* plural < Greek *orgiā* secret rites; see etym. under **orgiastic**]

**o|rib|a|tid** (ō rib′ə tid), *n., adj.* **— *n.*** any one of a group of small mites that feed on fungi.
**— *adj.*** of or belonging to this group.
[< New Latin *Oribatidae* the family name < Greek *oribatēs* mountain-going < *óros* mountain + *-batos* going]

**or|i|bi** (ôr′ə bē, or′-), *n., pl.* **-bis** or (*collectively*) **-bi.** any one of several small, brownish African antelopes with short, straight horns in the male. [< Afrikaans *oribi,* apparently < a Hottentot word]

**o|ri|el** (ôr′ē əl, ōr′-) *n.* a bay window projecting from the outer face of a wall, often supported by a bracket of stone or wood. [< Old French *oriol* porch, corridor, gallery; origin uncertain]

**o|ri|ent** (*v.* ôr′ē ent, ōr′-; *n., adj.* ôr′ē ənt, ōr′-), *v., n., adj.* **— *v.t.*** **1** to place in the right position; bring into the right relationship with surroundings or with the facts or principles; adjust; correct: *These men will ask for nothing specific in return although they will help to orient and determine the general course of party policies* (Paul H. Douglas). **2** to find the direction or position of; determine the compass bearings of. **3** to place so that it faces in any indicated direction: *The building is oriented north and south.* **4** to put so as to face the east, as a church built with the chief altar to the east. **5** *Surveying.* to place (a map) so that a north and south line on the map is pointed to the north and south direction on the earth.
**— *v.i.*** **1** to turn toward any specified direction. **2** to turn toward the east.
**— *n.*** **1** = east. **2a** the soft, glowing luster or sheen of a pearl of excellent quality: (*Figurative.*) *In every nobler mood We feel the orient of their spirit glow* (James Russell Lowell). **b** a natural pearl having such a luster: *a very Sea of Thought ... wherein the toughest pearl-diver may dive ... and return ... with true orients* (Thomas Carlyle).
**— *adj.*** **1** = eastern: *Now morning from her orient chamber came* (Keats). **SYN**: oriental. **2** bright; shining: (*Figurative.*) *Ten thousand banners ... With orient colours waving* (Milton). **SYN**: radiant, effulgent. **3** of the best or very fine quality; brilliant or lustrous: *an orient pearl.* **4** *Archaic.* rising: *the orient sun. ... the orient moon of Islam* (Shelley).
**orient oneself**, to get in the right relations to the things or persons about one: *to orient oneself on coming to a new city, to orient oneself in the group of people one is to work with. The new student had to orient himself to new teachers and different courses of study.*
[< Old French *orient,* learned borrowing from Latin *oriēns, -entis* the East; the Orient; (literally) the rising sun, properly, present participle of *orīrī* to rise] **— o′ri|ent|er**, *n.*

**O|ri|ent** (ôr′ē ənt, ōr′-), *n., adj.* **— *n.*** the countries in Asia, as distinguished from those in Europe and America; the East. China and Japan are important nations of the Orient. The Orient usually includes Asia and countries east and southeast of the Mediterranean.
**— *adj.*** of the Orient; Oriental.

**o|ri|en|tal** (ôr′ē en′təl, ōr′-), *adj.* = eastern. **— o′ri|en′tal|ly**, *adv.*

**O|ri|en|tal** (ôr′ē en′təl, ōr′-), *adj., n.* **— *adj.*** **1** Eastern; of the Orient: *The Oriental way of life is quite different from the European way of life.* **2** Also, **oriental.** belonging to the region that includes Asia south of the Himalayas, the Philippines, and the East Indies. **3a** (of a gem, especially a saphire) that resembles in color a gem of the type indicated. An Oriental topaz is actually a yellow sapphire. **b** Also, **oriental.** (of a gem) of the best or very fine quality; orient.
**— *n.*** **1a** a native of the East. Turks, Arabs, Iranians, Indians, Japanese, and Chinese are Orientals. **b** an Asian (now often used in an unfriendly way). **2** a person who is trained in or adopts any of the cultures of Asia.
[< Old French *oriental,* learned borrowing from Latin *orientālis* < *oriēns;* see etym. under **orient**]

**Pronunciation Key:** **h**a**t**, **ā**ge, **c**ã**re**, **f**ä**r**; **l**e**t**, **ē**qual, **t**ė**rm**; **i**t, **ī**ce; **h**o**t**, **ō**pen, **ô**rder; **oi**l, **ou**t; **c**u**p**, **p**ů**t**, **r**ü**le**; **ch**ild; **lo**ng; **th**in; **ᴛʜ**en; **zh**, measure;
**ə** represents **a** in about, **e** in taken, **i** in pencil, **o** in lemon, **u** in circus.

**oriental alabaster,** = onyx marble.
**oriental amethyst,** = amethyst (def. 2).
**oriental arbor vitae,** a low, bushy species of arbor vitae found in China and Korea and commonly used as an ornamental tree. It has a reddish-brown, scaly bark and often branches near the base.
**Oriental carpet,** = Oriental rug.
**oriental cockroach,** a black or dark-brown cockroach, originally from Asia but found throughout the world, usually on the lower level of houses and buildings.
**oriental emerald,** = emerald (def. 2).
**Oriental fruit fly,** a fruit fly common in Hawaii, Indonesia, and the Philippines.
**Oriental fruit moth,** = peach moth.
**O·ri·en·ta·li·a** (ôr′ē ən tā′lē ə, ōr′-; -tāl′-yə), *n.pl.* **1** a collection of books, documents, facts, or other material about the Orient. **2** a collection of objects of or from the Orient.
**O·ri·en·tal·ism** or **o·ri·en·tal·ism** (ôr′ē ən′tə liz-əm, ōr′-), *n.* **1a** Oriental character or characteristics: *To Eastern ears this may seem about as exotic as Rimsky-Korsakov's orientalism is to our own* (Harper's). **b** an Oriental mode of thought or expression. **2** the knowledge or study of Oriental languages, literature, and culture.
**O·ri·en·tal·ist** or **o·ri·en·tal·ist** (ôr′ē en′tə list, ōr′-), *n.* an expert in Oriental languages, literature, history, and culture.
**O·ri·en·tal·ize** (ôr′ē en′tə līz, ōr′-), *v.t., v.i.,* **-ized, -iz·ing.** to make or become Oriental.
**oriental persimmon,** = Japanese persimmon.
**Oriental poppy,** a perennial poppy of Asia, having showy red, orange, white, or salmon flowers, often with blackish-purple centers, much cultivated as an ornamental.
**Oriental rug,** a handmade rug in one piece with a distinctive pattern, made especially in the Middle East.
**Oriental sore,** a type of leishmaniasis characterized by ulcerous infections of the skin, occurring chiefly in central Asia and the Mediterranean region; Aleppo boil.
**o·ri·en·tate** (ôr′ē en tāt, ōr′-), *v.t., v.i.,* **-tat·ed, -tat·ing.** = orient. [< *orient* + *ate*[1]]
**o·ri·en·ta·tion** (ôr′ē en tā′shən, ōr′-), *n.* **1** the act or process of orienting. **2** the state of being oriented. **3** the direction that any process, movement, or development follows: *The present orientation of Soviet policy* (Bulletin of Atomic Scientists). **4** the act or process of finding out the actual facts and conditions and putting oneself in the right relation to them. **SYN:** adjustment, adaptation. **5** the ability of many birds and other animals to find their way back to their usual habitat after going to another point distant from it. **6** a general point of view toward a topic or object. **7** *Chemistry.* **a** the relative position of atoms or radicals in complex molecules. **b** the determination of the position of atoms and radicals to be substituted in a substance.
**o·ri·en·ta·tion·al** (ôr′ē en tā′shə nəl, ōr′-), *adj.* having to do with or characterized by orientation. **—o′ri·en·ta′tion·al·ly,** *adv.*
**o·ri·en·teer** (ôr′ē en tir′, ōr′-), *v., n.* **—*v.i.*** to engage in orienteering.
**—*n.*** a person who engages in orienteering.
**o·ri·en·teer·ing** (ôr′ē en tir′ing, ōr′-), *n.* a sport, developed in Sweden as a combination of map-reading and cross-country running, in which participants race to get first through an unknown area with the use of a compass and topographical map: *Orienteering combines vigorous exercise with the development and use of compass and map reading skills* (Science News).
**or·i·fice** (ôr′ə fis, or′-), *n.* a mouth; opening or hole: *the orifice of a tube, pipe, or furnace.* **SYN:** aperture, vent. [< Middle French *orifice,* learned borrowing from Latin *ōrificium* < *ōs, ōris* mouth + *facere* make]
**or·i·fi·cial** (ôr′ə fish′əl, or′-), *adj.* of or having to do with an orifice.
**or·i·flamme** (ôr′ə flam, or′-), *n.* **1** the red banner of Saint Denis carried as a military ensign by the early kings of France from the time of the Crusades until the early Renaissance. It was split at one end to form pointed streamers suggesting flames. **2** any banner used as an ensign or standard. **3** *Figurative.* anything that serves as a rallying point in a struggle: *And be your oriflamme today the helmet of Navarre* (Macaulay). **4** *Figurative.* anything that is bright, colorful, or showy: *the oriflamme of day* (John Greenleaf Whittier). [< Old French *orie flambe; orie,* learned borrowing from Latin *aureus* golden, and *flambe,* ultimately < Latin *flamma* flame]
**orig.,** **1** origin. **2a** original. **b** originally. **3** originated.
***or·i·ga·mi** (ôr′ə gä′mē), *n., pl.* **-mis** or **-mi. 1** the Japanese art of folding paper to make decorative objects, such as figures of birds and flowers. **2** an object thus made. [< Japanese *origami* < *ori* fold + *kami* paper]

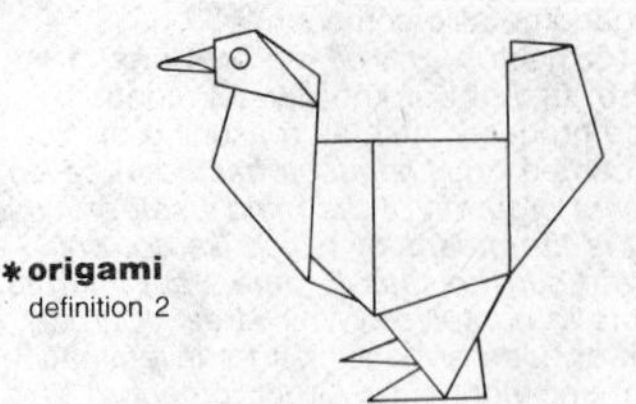

***origami**
definition 2

**or·i·gan** (ôr′ə gən, or′-), *n.* **1** = oregano. **2** = marjoram (def. 1). [< Old French *origane,* learned borrowing from Latin *orīganum* < Greek *orīganon* wild marjoram]
**or·i·gin** (ôr′ə jin, or′-), *n.* **1** the thing from which anything comes; beginning; starting point; source: *the origin of a quarrel, the origin of a disease. Ancient Greece has been called the origin of Western civilization.* **SYN:** root. **2** parentage, ancestry, or birth: *Abraham Lincoln was a man of humble origin.* **3** the fact of rising or springing from a particular source; derivation: *to trace the origin of a word, these and other reports of like origin.* **SYN:** rise. **4** *Anatomy.* the main or more fixed attachment of a muscle, which does not change position during the muscle's contraction. **5** *Mathematics.* the intersection of the horizontal axis and the vertical axis in a coordinate system. [< Latin *orīgō, -īginis* < *orīrī* to rise]
**o·rig·i·nal** (ə rij′ə nəl), *adj., n.* **—*adj.*** **1** belonging to the beginning; first; earliest: *The Dutch were the original settlers of New York. The hat has been marked down from its original price. Which is the original error?* **SYN:** initial. **2** new; fresh; novel: *It is hard to plan original games for a party.* **3** able to do, make, or think something new; inventive: *a very original writer. Edison had an original mind.* **4** not copied, imitated, or translated from something else; firsthand: *She wrote an original poem.*
**—*n.*** **1** a thing from which another is copied, imitated, or translated: *The original of this painting is in Rome.* **2** a new written work, picture, or sculpture that is not a copy or imitation. **3** the language in which a book was first written: *Our minister can read the Bible in the original.* **SYN:** creative, ingenious. **4** *Figurative.* an unusual person; odd person: *Teufelsdröckh passed . . . as one of those originals and nondescripts, more frequent in German universities than elsewhere* (Thomas Carlyle). **5** a person who acts or thinks in an original way. **6** *Archaic.* origin; source.
**—o·rig′i·nal·ness,** *n.*
**o·rig·i·nal·i·ty** (ə rij′ə nal′ə tē), *n.* **1** the ability to do, make, or think up something new: *Originality is the seeing nature differently from others, yet as it is in itself* (William Hazlitt). **SYN:** inventiveness, imagination. **2** freshness; novelty: *The originality of his humor made everyone laugh.* **3** a being original.
**o·rig·i·nal·ly** (ə rij′ə nə lē), *adv.* **1** by origin; indigenously: *a plant originally African.* **2a** at first; in the first place: *a house originally small.* **SYN:** initially. **b** from the beginning; from the first: *Originally conceived as an emergency measure, it has taken on the look of a long-range policy* (Time). **3** in an original manner: *We want this room decorated originally.*
**original sin,** **1** *Theology.* a depravity, or tendency to sin or do evil, held to be innate in mankind and transmitted from Adam to the race of man in consequence of his sin. **2** (in Roman Catholic theology) the privation of sanctifying grace in consequence of Adam's sin.
**o·rig·i·nate** (ə rij′ə nāt), *v.,* **-nat·ed, -nat·ing. —*v.t.*** to cause to be; invent: *to originate a new style of painting.* **—*v.i.*** to come into being; begin; arise: *Where did that story originate?* **SYN:** commence. [< *origin* + *-ate*[1]]
**o·rig·i·na·tion** (ə rij′ə nā′shən), *n.* **1** the action or fact of originating. **2** = origin.
**o·rig·i·na·tive** (ə rij′ə nā′tiv), *adj.* **1** having originality; inventive; creative. **2** = productive. **—o·rig′i·na′tive·ly,** *adv.*
**o·rig·i·na·tor** (ə rij′ə nā′tər), *n.* a person who originates; inventor: *Next to the originator of a good sentence is the first quoter of it* (Emerson).
**o·ri·na·sal** (ôr′i nā′zəl, ōr′-), *adj., n. Phonetics.* **—*adj.*** articulated with the breath stream passing out through both nose and mouth, as the French nasal vowels.
**—*n.*** an orinasal sound.
[< Latin *ōs, ōris* mouth + English *nasal*]
**O ring,** a rubber ring similar to a washer or gasket, used especially in hydraulic equipment.
**o·ri·ole** (ôr′ē ōl, ōr′-), *n.* **1** any one of several American songbirds that build hanging nests and usually have orange- or yellow-and-black feathers. Orioles belong to the same family as the blackbirds, meadow larks, grackles, and bobolinks. **2** any one of several birds of Europe, Asia, Africa, and Australia that build hanging nests and have rich yellow-and-black feathers, such as the golden oriole. [< New Latin *oriolus* < Old French *oriol* < Latin *aureolus* (diminutive) < *aureus* golden < *aurum* gold]
**O·ri·on** (ô rī′ən, ō-), *n., genitive* (def. 1) **O·ri·on·is.** **1** a constellation near the celestial equator, that contains the extremely bright stars Betelgeuse and Rigel; Great Hunter. To the ancients it suggested a man wearing a belt and a sword, and holding a shield and a club. **2** *Greek Mythology.* a giant hunter of great strength, who was slain by Artemis. After his death Orion was supposedly placed in the heavens with his belt and sword.
**O·ri·on·is** (ô rī′ə nis, ō-; or′ē ō′nis), *n.* genitive of **Orion** (the constellation).
**or·i·son** (ôr′ə zən, or′-), *n. Archaic.* a prayer: *Nymph, in thy orisons be all my sins remembered* (Shakespeare). [< Old French *oreisoun,* learned borrowing from Late Latin *ōrātiō, -ōnis* prayer < *ōrāre* pray, speak formally. See etym. of doublet **oration.**]
**O·ri·ya** (ō rē′yä), *n.* an Indo-European language spoken in India, mainly in the state of Orissa and adjoining areas.
**ork** (ôrk), *n.* = orc.
**Or·lan·do** (ôr lan′dō), *n., pl.* **-dos.** a variety of tangelo grown in the United States.
**orle** (ôrl), *n. Heraldry.* a narrow band of half the width of the bordure (an outside bearing), following the outside, but not reaching the edge, of the shield. [< Old French *ourle* border < Vulgar Latin *ōrulus* (diminutive) < Latin *ōra* edge, boundary]
**Or·le·an·ist** (ôr′lē ə nist), *n.* an adherent of the house of Orléans in French politics.
**Or·lé·ans** (ôr′lē ənz; *French* ôr lā äɴ′), *n.* a French royal family whose members claimed the throne as descendants of a younger brother of Louis XIV. The last French king, Louis Philippe, belonged to the house of Orléans.
**Or·lon** (ôr′lon), *n. Trademark.* a lightweight synthetic fiber that resists sun, rain, and acids. It is an acrylic used for sportswear, outdoor clothing, sails, awnings, and the like.
**or·lop** (ôr′lop), *n.,* or **orlop deck,** the lowest deck of a ship, especially of a warship, laid over the beams of the hold. [reduction of Scottish *ouerlop, overloppe,* probably < Middle Low German *overlōp* < *overlopen* run over]
**Or·mazd** (ôr′məzd), *n.* the principle of good, light, and law in the Zoroastrian religion; Ahura Mazda. It is in ceaseless conflict with Ahriman, the spirit of evil. Also, **Ormuzd.** [< Persian *Ormazd* < Avestan *Ahura Mazda* wise lord]
**or·mo·lu** (ôr′mə lü), *n.* an alloy of copper, zinc, and tin, used to imitate gold. Ormolu is used in decoration, especially of furniture, clocks, and the like: *an eighteenth-century Chinese . . . vase, with ormolu mounts* (London Times). [< French *or moulu* (literally) ground gold < *or* gold + *moulu* ground up, past participle of *moudre* to grind < Latin *molere* < *mola* millstone]
**Or·muzd** (ôr′məzd), *n.* = Ormazd.
**or·na·ment** (*n.* ôr′nə mənt; *v.* ôr′nə ment), *n., v.* **—*n.*** **1** something pretty; something to add beauty: *ornaments for a Christmas tree. Lace, jewels, vases, and statues are ornaments.* **SYN:** adornment, decoration, embellishment. **2** the use of ornaments: *Loveliness Needs not the foreign aid of ornament* (James Thomson). **3** the condition of having an ornament or ornaments. **4** *Figurative.* a person or act that adds beauty, grace, or honor: *That charming girl would be an ornament to any society. But let it be the hidden man of the heart, in that which is not corruptible, even the ornament of a meek and quiet spirit, which is in the sight of God of great price* (I Peter 3:4). **5** *Music.* an additional note or notes introduced as an embellishment but not essential to the harmony or melody: *His ornaments are correct . . . and his tempi are relatively strict* (Edward Tatnall Canby). **6** the things used in church services, such as the organ, bells, and silver plate.
**—*v.t.*** to add beauty to; make more pleasing or attractive; decorate; adorn: *A man, formed to ornament, to enlighten, and to defend his country* (Scott). **SYN:** deck, beautify, embellish. See syn. under **decorate.**
[alteration of Old French *ornement,* learned borrowing from Latin *ōrnāmentum* < *ōrnāre* adorn]
**or·na·men·tal** (ôr′nə men′təl), *adj., n.* **—*adj.*** **1** of or having to do with ornament: *ornamental purposes.* **2** for ornament; used as an ornament: *ornamental plants.* **3** decorative: *ornamental designs in wallpaper, ornamental vases.*
**—*n.*** something ornamental, especially a plant cultivated for decorative purposes: *No doubt the Russian olive came West as a workhorse tree, not as an ornamental* (Sunset). **—or′na·men′tal·ly,** *adv.* **—or′na·men′tal·ness,** *n.*
**or·na·men·tal·ism** (ôr′nə men′tə liz əm), *n.* **1** the character of being ornamental. **2** ornamental

style, as in art or literature.
**or|na|men|ta|tion** (ôr′nə men tā′shən), *n.* **1** the action or fact of ornamenting or the state of being ornamented. **2** decorations; ornaments: *She was dressed simply, with no ornamentation. The Quaker meeting house in our city has no ornamentation.*
**or|nate** (ôr nāt′), *adj.* **1** much adorned; much ornamented: *She likes ornate furniture.* **SYN**: elaborate, showy, sumptuous. **2** characterized by the use of elaborate figures of speech, flowery language, and the like: *an ornate style of writing. In diction, Virgil is ornate and Homer simple* (William Ewart Gladstone). **3** *Archaic.* adorned; ornamented (with). [< Latin *ōrnātus,* past participle of *ōrnāre* adorn] — **or|nate′ly,** *adv.* — **or|nate′ness,** *n.*
**or|ner|i|ness** (ôr′nər ē nis), *n. Informal.* the fact or condition of being ornery: *They ... let loose their deviltries just for pure orneriness* (Booth Tarkington).
**or|ner|y** (ôr′nər ē), *adj.,* **-ner|i|er, -ner|i|est.** *Informal.* **1a** mean or irritable in disposition: *an ornery horse.* **SYN**: contrary. **b** of a mean kind: *an ornery remark.* **2** inferior. **3** homely. **4** low; vile. **SYN**: contemptible. [American English; reduction of *ordinary,* in the sense of "mean, vile"]
**or|nis** (ôr′nis), *n.* the birds or bird life of a region or country; avifauna. [< German *Ornis* < Greek *órnīs* bird]
**ornith.,** 1 ornithological. 2 ornithology.
**or|nith|ic** (ôr nith′ik), *adj.* of or characteristic of birds. [< Greek *ornīthikós* < *órnīs, -īthos* bird]
**or|ni|thine** (ôr′nə thin), *n.* an amino acid formed by hydrolyzing arginine. *Formula:* $C_5H_{12}O_2N_2$ [< Greek *órnīs, -īthos* bird (because it is found in their excrement) + English *-ine*]
**or|ni|this|chi|an** (ôr′nə this′kē ən), *n., adj.* — *n.* any one of an order of dinosaurs that lived during the Jurassic and Cretaceous periods and had a hip structure similar to that of modern birds, including the stegosaurus.
— *adj.* of or belonging to this order.
[< Greek *órnīs, -īthos* bird + *ischíon* hip + English *-ian*]
**or|ni|thoid** (ôr′nə thoid), *adj.* having a certain structural resemblance to a bird: *an ornithoid lizard.* [< Greek *órnīs, -īthos* bird + English *-oid*]
**ornithol.,** 1 ornithological. 2 ornithology.
**or|nith|o|lite** (ôr nith′ə līt), *n.* the fossilized remains of a bird. [< Greek *órnīs, -īthos* bird + English *-lite*]
**or|ni|tho|log|ic** (ôr′nə thə loj′ik), *adj.* = ornithological.
**or|ni|tho|log|i|cal** (ôr′nə thə loj′ə kəl), *adj.* of or having to do with birds. — **or′ni|tho|log′i|cal|ly,** *adv.*
**or|ni|thol|o|gist** (ôr′nə thol′ə jist), *n.* an expert in the study of birds and their habits.
**or|ni|thol|o|gy** (ôr′nə thol′ə jē), *n.* **1** the branch of zoology dealing with the study of birds. **2** a book on this subject. [< New Latin *ornithologia* < Greek *órnīs, -īthos* bird + *-logiā* -logy]
**or|ni|tho|pod** (ôr′nə thə pod, ôr nī′-), *adj., n.*
— *adj.* belonging to or having to do with a group of extinct saurians, containing herbivorous dinosaurs, whose hind feet resembled those of birds and left similar tracks.
— *n.* a member of this group.
[< New Latin *Ornithopoda* the group name < Greek *órnīs, -īthos* bird + *poús, podós* foot]
*__or|ni|thop|ter__ (ôr′nə thop′tər), *n.* a machine designed to fly by flapping its wings. Examples are cited from ancient times until the present. *Observing the flight of birds,* [*Leonardo da Vinci*] *invented the ornithopter* (Atlantic). Also, **orthopter.** [< Greek *órnīs, -īthos* bird + *pterón* wing]

***ornithopter**

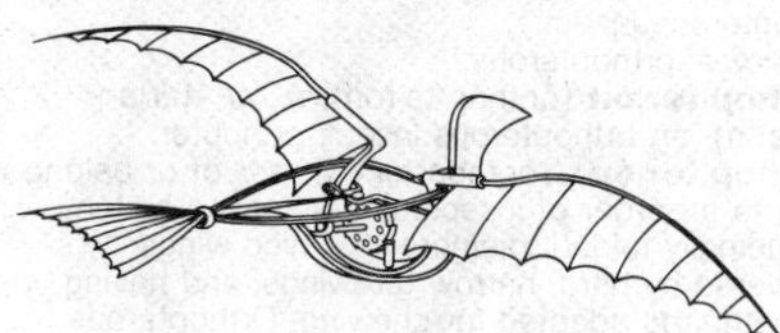

**or|ni|tho|rhyn|chus** (ôr′nə thə ring′kəs, ôr nī′-), *n.* = duckbill. [< Greek *órnīs, -īthos* bird + *rhýnchos* bill, beak]
**or|ni|thos|co|pist** (ôr′nə thos′kə pist), *n.* a bird watcher. [< Greek *órnīs, -īthos* bird + *skopeîn* look at + English *-ist*]
**or|ni|tho|sis** (ôr′nə thō′sis), *n.* a contagious virus disease of birds other than parrots, such as pigeons, chickens, and other fowl. It is communicable to man. The similar disease occurring in parrots and related birds is called psittacosis. [< Greek *órnīs, -īthos* bird + English *-osis*]
**or|o|gen** (ôr′ə jən, or′-), *n.* a mountain formation: *Orogens can be examined for signs of the descent of the lithosphere into a trench* (Science). [< Greek *óros* mountain + English *-gen*]
**or|o|gen|e|sis** (ôr′ə jen′ə sis, or′-), *n.* = orogeny.
**or|o|ge|net|ic** (ôr′ə jə net′ik, or′-), *adj.* = orogenic.
**or|o|gen|ic** (ôr′ə jen′ik, or′-), *adj.* having to do with the formation of mountains: *We believe that the whole sedimentary and structural framework of orogenic* (*deformational mountain*) *belts is related to the expansion and contraction of ocean basins* (Science News).
**o|ro|gen|ics** (ôr′ə jen′iks, or′-), *n.* the process of mountain formation; orogeny: *Because the book is primarily concerned with the effects of the Caledonian, Hercynian, and Alpine orogenics in Europe, no detailed stratigraphy is given* (Science Journal).
**o|rog|e|ny** (ô roj′ə nē, ō-), *n., pl.* **-nies.** the formation of mountains, especially by the folding of the earth's crust: *The deposits comprise mostly shale and sandstone which represent rock materials eroded from adjacent mountain areas formed in the Nevadan orogeny* (Raymond Cecil Moore). [< Greek *óros* mountain + English *-gen* + *-y*[3]]
**or|o|graph|ic** (ôr′ə graf′ik, or′-), *adj.* **1** of or having to do with orography. **2** *Meteorology.* produced by the forced ascent of warm air into cooler regions because of a mountain range lying in its path: *orographic rainfall.* — **or′o|graph′i|cal|ly,** *adv.*
**or|o|graph|i|cal** (ôr′ə graf′ə kəl, or′-), *adj.* = orographic.
**o|rog|ra|phy** (ô rog′rə fē, ō-), *n.* the branch of physical geography that deals with the formation and features of mountains. [< Greek *óros* mountain + English *-graphy*]
**or|o|ide** (ôr′ō īd, -id; ōr′-), *n.* an alloy consisting chiefly of copper and tin or zinc, resembling gold in appearance, used in making inexpensive jewelry. [American English < French *or* gold + *oïde* -oid]
**o|rom|e|ter** (ô rom′ə tər, ō-), *n.* an aneroid barometer with a scale giving elevations above sea level, used for measuring the altitudes of mountains. [< Greek *óros* mountain + English *-meter*]
**or|o|met|ric** (ôr′ə met′rik, or′-), *adj.* of or having to do with the measurement of mountains.
**o|rom|e|try** (ô rom′ə trē, ō-), *n.* the measurement of mountains.
**o|ro|tund** (ôr′ə tund, ōr′-), *adj.* **1** strong, full, rich, and clear in voice or speech. **SYN**: resonant. **2** wordy and pompous in speech or writing; bombastic: *The actors have fallen into the classical cliches—strutting figures in flowing costumes, orotund, expressionless voices* (New York Times). [alteration of Latin *ōre rotundō* in well-rounded phrases; (literally) with round mouth] — **o′ro|tund′ly,** *adv.*
**o|ro|tun|di|ty** (ôr′ə tun′də tē, ōr′-), *n., pl.* **-ties.** **1** the quality of being orotund: *Max's voice boomed into orotundity again* (New Yorker). **2** pompousness and ornateness of style: *Despite the orotundity of Mr. Levy's lines the actors do remarkably well* (Wall Street Journal). **3** an orotund expression or writing: *Wordsworthians were there to discover the hallmark of genius on his most insignificant orotundities* (J. M. Murry).
**O|roy|a fever** (ō rō′yə), an infectious disease prevalent in South America, caused by a germ carried by sand flies and characterized by fever, anemia, headaches and, often, wartlike spots on the skin. [< *Oroya,* Peru, where the disease was first discovered]
**o|ro y pla|ta** (ō′rō ē plä′tä), *Spanish.* gold and silver (the motto of Montana).
**or|phan** (ôr′fən), *n., adj., v.* — *n.* **1a** a child whose parents are dead: *The child was made an orphan when both parents died in an airplane crash.* **b** a child whose father or mother is dead. **2** an infant animal whose mother is dead. **3** *Figurative: Prospective customers got cold feet at the thought they might be purchasing an orphan if they bought one of our cars* (Jerry M. Flint). *Children are known to harbor a variety of viruses known as "orphans," so called because they are not known to cause specific diseases* (Frederick G. Hofmann).
— *adj.* **1** of or for orphans: *an orphan asylum.* **2** without a mother or father: *The orphan boy was brought up by pirates.* **3** *Figurative: an orphan church.*
— *v.t.* to make an orphan of: *The war orphaned her at an early age.*
[< Latin *orphanus* < Greek *orphanós* bereaved]
**or|phan|age** (ôr′fə nij), *n.* **1** a home for orphans: *A boy's orphanage near Palermo, Sicily, which the I.L.G.W.U. has supported* (Time). **2** the condition of being an orphan. **3** orphans as a group.
**or|phan|hood** (ôr′fən hu̇d), *n.* the condition of being an orphan.
**Or|phe|an** (ôr fē′ən), *adj.* **1** of or having to do with Orpheus: *the Orphean lyre* (Milton). **2** like the music of Orpheus.
**Or|phe|us** (ôr′fē əs, -fyüs), *n. Greek Legend.* a Thracian musician, son of Calliope and Apollo, who played his lyre so sweetly that animals and even trees and rocks followed him.
**Or|phic** (ôr′fik), *adj.* **1** of or having to do with Orpheus. **2** having to do with religious or philosophical cults ascribed to Orpheus as founder. **3** Also, **orphic.** having a hidden meaning; mystic; oracular. **4** like the music or verses of Orpheus; melodious; entrancing.
**Or|phism** (ôr′fiz əm), *n.* **1** a religion or philosophical system based on the mysteries and verses attributed to Orpheus. **2** a style of abstract painting current in France in the early 1900's, characterized by the use of geometric forms painted in rich, glowing colors to produce prismatic effects.
**Or|phist** (ôr′fist), *n.* an artist who follows the style of Orphism.
**or|phrey** (ôr′frē), *n., pl.* **-phreys.** **1** an ornamental border or band, often embroidered, on an ecclesiastical vestment. **2** *Archaic.* gold embroidery or any similarly rich embroidery. [Middle English *orfreis,* singular < Old French *orfreis,* probably ultimately < Latin *aurum* gold + *phrygium* of Phrygia (because the region was noted for its gold embroidery)]
**or|pi|ment** (ôr′pə mənt), *n.* a bright-yellow mineral, arsenic trisulfide, found in soft, foliated masses or prepared synthetically as a yellow powder, used as a pigment. *Formula:* $As_2S_3$ [< Old French *orpiment,* also *or pigment,* learned borrowing from Latin *auripigmentum* < *aurum* gold + *pigmentum* pigment]
**or|pine** or **or|pin** (ôr′pin), *n.* a succulent herb of the Old World, a variety of stonecrop, with smooth, fleshy leaves and clusters (corymbs) of purple flowers. It was formerly used as a remedy for wounds. [< Old French *orpin,* (originally) reduction of *orpiment*]
**orpine family,** a widely distributed group of dicotyledonous, succulent herbs or low shrubs, commonly grown in rock gardens or greenhouses. The family includes the orpine, houseleek, kalanchoe, and live-forever.
**Or|ping|ton** (ôr′ping tən), *n.* any large sturdy chicken of a breed originally from England, raised for the production of both meat and eggs. The skin is white and the eggs are brown. [< *Orpington,* a town in Kent, England]
**or|ra** (ôr′ə), *adj. Scottish.* not one of a pair; left over; odd; extra. [origin unknown]
*__or|rer|y__ (ôr′ər ē, or′-), *n., pl.* **-rer|ies.** **1** a device with balls representing various planets that are moved by clockwork to illustrate motions of the solar system. **2** a planetarium or similar device. [< Charles Boyle, Earl of *Orrery,* 1676-1731, who first had such a device made]

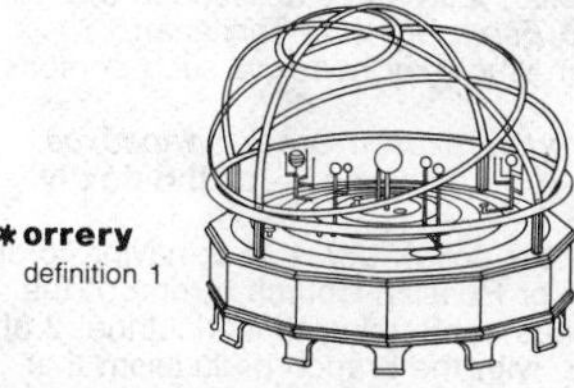

***orrery**
definition 1

**or|ris** (ôr′is, or′-), *n.* **1** any one of certain kinds of iris of Europe with a fragrant rootstock. **2** its rootstock; orrisroot. [apparently alteration of *iris*]
**or|ris|root** (ôr′is rüt′, -ru̇t′; or′-), *n.* the fragrant rootstock of orris, a variety of iris, used in making perfume and formerly used in cosmetic powders and toothpaste.
**or|seille** (ôr sā′, -säl′, -sel′), *n.* = orchil. [< French *orseille* < Old French *orseil, orcheil*]
**ort** (ôrt), *n.* See under **orts.**
**ORT** (no periods) or **O.R.T.,** Organization for Rehabilitation through Training (an international organization for the vocational and technical training of Jews in underdeveloped countries).
**or|thi|con** (ôr′thə kon), *n.* a television camera tube, similar to the iconoscope but using a low-velocity electron beam. [< *orth*(o)- + *icon*-(oscope)]
**or|tho** (ôr′thō), *adj.* (of a salt or acid) having the highest number of water molecules within a series. [< *ortho-*]
**ortho-,** *combining form.* **1** straight; upright: *Orthoclase = straight cleavage.* **2** correct; proper: *Orthography = correct spelling.* **3** ortho, as in *orthophosphoric acid.* [< Greek *orthós* straight]

**Pronunciation Key:** hat, āge, cãre, fär; let, ēqual, tėrm; it, īce; hot, ōpen, ôrder; **oi**l, **ou**t; cup, pu̇t, rüle; **ch**ild; lo**ng**; **th**in; **ᴛʜ**en; **zh**, measure; ə represents **a** in about, **e** in taken, **i** in pencil, **o** in lemon, **u** in circus.

**or|tho|bo|ric acid** (ôr′thō bô′rik, -bō′-), = boric acid.
**or|tho|cen|ter** (ôr′thə sen′tər), *n.* the point at which the altitudes of a triangle intersect. [< *ortho-* + *center*]
**or|tho|ce|phal|ic** (ôr′thə sə fal′ik), *adj.* having a skull that is of medium height for its breadth or length; intermediate between brachycephalic and dolichocephalic. [< *ortho-* + Greek *kephalḗ* head + English *-ic*]
**or|tho|ceph|a|ly** (ôr′thə sef′ə lē), *n.* orthocephalic character or structure.
**or|tho|chro|mat|ic** (ôr′thə krə mat′ik), *adj. Photography.* **1** of, having to do with, or reproducing the tones of light and shade as they appear in nature. **2** (of film) sensitive to all colors except red. [< *ortho-* + Greek *chrōmatikós* chromatic]
**or|tho|clase** (ôr′thə klās, -klāz), *n.* common or potash feldspar, a silicate of aluminum and potassium, occurring in crystals of right-angular cleavage and in various colors, often in granite. Orthoclase is used in making glass, ceramics, and abrasives. *Formula:* $KAlSi_3O_8$ [< *ortho-* + Greek *klásis* cleavage (because of the way it breaks)]
**or|tho|clas|tic** (ôr′thə klas′tik), *adj. Mineralogy.* having cleavages at right angles to each other, as certain feldspars, especially orthoclase.
**or|tho-cous|in** (ôr′thə kuz′ən), *n.* = parallel cousin.
**or|tho|cy|mene** (ôr′thə sī′mēn), *n.* one of three isomeric forms of cymene.
**or|tho|don|tia** (ôr′thə don′shə, -shē ə), *n.* the branch of dentistry that deals with straightening and adjusting teeth. [< New Latin *orthodontia* < Greek *orthós* straight + *odoús, odóntos* tooth]
**or|tho|don|tic** (ôr′thə don′tik), *adj.* of or having to do with orthodontia: *The condition can usually be corrected by orthodontic treatments, during which the teeth are moved gently and gradually to acceptable positions* (Peter J. Brekhus).
**or|tho|don|tics** (ôr′thə don′tiks), *n.* the science or practice of orthodontia.
**or|tho|don|tist** (ôr′thə don′tist), *n.* a dentist who specializes in orthodontia.
**or|tho|dox** (ôr′thə doks), *adj., n.* —*adj.* **1** generally accepted, especially in religion: *orthodox beliefs. And prove their doctrines orthodox By apostolic blows and knocks* (Samuel Butler). **SYN:** canonical. **2** having generally accepted views or opinions, especially in religion; adhering to established customs and traditions: *an orthodox Methodist, a very orthodox young man.* **3** approved by convention; usual; customary: *The orthodox Thanksgiving dinner includes turkey and pumpkin pie.* **SYN:** conventional, standard. **4a** conforming to the basic Christian faith as established in the early creeds. **b** *Especially U.S.* Trinitarian.
—*n.* **1** a person who is orthodox. **2** such persons as a group.
[< Late Latin *orthodoxus* < Greek *orthodóxos* < *orthós* correct + *dóxa* opinion] —**or′tho|dox′ly,** *adv.*
**Or|tho|dox** (ôr′thə doks), *adj.* **1** of or having to do with the Greek or Russian Church or one of the national churches conforming to its doctrine. **2** of or having to do with the branch of Judaism that adheres most closely to the ancient ritual, customs, and traditions: *The Orthodox and Conservative branches* [*of Judaism*] *emphasize the binding authority of that law* (New York Times). **3** of or having to do with the body of Quakers that adheres most closely to the austere manner of worship and life originally associated with members of the Society of Friends.
**Orthodox Church,** the group of Christian churches in eastern Europe, western Asia, and Egypt, that do not recognize the pope as the supreme head of the Catholic Church; Eastern Church; Greek Orthodox Church.
**orthodox sleep,** the dreamless part of sleep, during which the body undergoes no marked changes: *There are two basic kinds of sleep: 'orthodox' sleep and 'paradoxical' sleep. During orthodox sleep there are no dreams and measurements of brain waves show a slow 'alpha' rhythm* (Science Journal).
**or|tho|dox|y** (ôr′thə dok′sē), *n., pl.* **-dox|ies.** the holding of correct or generally accepted beliefs; orthodox practice, especially in religion; being orthodox: *All the royal children were brought up in complete orthodoxy* (Lytton Strachey). *It is the theorist ... who is more likely to see the dangers of a scientific orthodoxy* (John E. Owen).
**or|tho|ep|ic** (ôr′thō ep′ik), *adj.* of or having to do with orthoepy: *It is often impossible to suggest any explanation of orthoepic mutations* (G. P. Marsh). —**or′tho|ep′i|cal|ly,** *adv.*
**or|tho|ep|i|cal** (ôr′thō ep′ə kəl), *adj.* = orthoepic.
**or|tho|e|pist** (ôr thō′ə pist, ôr′thō-), *n.* an expert in the pronunciation of words.
**or|tho|e|py** (ôr thō′ə pē, ôr′thō-), *n.* **1** correct, accepted, or customary pronunciation. **2** the part of grammar that deals with pronunciation; phonology. [< Greek *orthoépeia* < *orthós* correct + *épos* utterance, word]
**or|tho|fer|rite** (ôr′thō fer′īt), *n.* any one of a class of crystalline materials in which magnetic bubbles can be formed by the application of electric current, used especially in computers to store and transmit data. Orthoferrites are compounds of iron oxides and rare-earth elements having the general formula $RFeO_3$, where R is any one of the rare earths. *An 8-by-50 millimeter single-crystal orthoferrite capable of storing up to several million digital data bits has been developed* (Science News).
**or|tho|gen|e|sis** (ôr′thə jen′ə sis), *n.* **1** *Biology.* the theory that evolution of new species proceeds along lines predetermined by inherent tendencies and uninfluenced by external forces or natural selection. **2** *Anthropology.* the theory that social patterns follow an identical, predictable course in every culture, regardless of external pressures, conditions, or other factors.
**or|tho|ge|net|ic** (ôr′thə jə net′ik), *adj.* of, having to do with, or exhibiting orthogenesis.
**or|tho|gen|ic** (ôr′thə jen′ik), *adj.* of, having to do with, or providing care and training for children who are mentally retarded or emotionally disturbed: *an orthogenic center or institution.* [< *ortho-* + *-gen* + *-ic*]
**or|thog|nath|ic** (ôr′thog nath′ik), *adj.* = orthognathous.
**or|thog|na|thism** (ôr thog′nə thiz əm), *n.* the character of being orthognathous.
**or|thog|na|thous** (ôr thog′nə thəs), *adj. Anthropology.* straight-jawed; not having the jaws projecting beyond the vertical line drawn from the forehead. [< *ortho-* + Greek *gnáthos* jaw + English *-ous*]
**or|thog|na|thy** (ôr thog′nə thē), *n.* = orthognathism.
**or|tho|gon** (ôr′thə gon), *n.* a rectangular figure. [< Latin *orthogōnium,* neuter of Latin *orthogōnius;* see etym. under **orthogonal**]
**or|thog|o|nal** (ôr thog′ə nəl), *adj., n.* —*adj.* **1** *Mathematics.* **a** having to do with or involving right angles; rectangular. **SYN:** right-angled. **b** (of certain functions) having an integral that is equal to zero or to one. **c** (of vectors) having a dot product equal to zero. **d** consisting of orthogonal elements. **2** *Crystallography.* orthorhombic.
—*n.* an orthogonal line or plane: *... reading in both directions along all orthogonals and main diagonals* (Scientific American).
[< Latin *orthogōnius* right-angled (< Greek *orthogṓnios* < *orthós* right + *gōníā* angle) + English *-al*[1]] —**or|thog′o|nal|ly,** *adv.*
**or|thog|o|nal|i|ty** (ôr′thog ə nal′ə tē), *n.* orthogonal quality or state.
**or|thog|o|nal|ize** (ôr thog′ə nə līz), *v.t.,* **-ized, -iz|ing.** to make orthogonal.
**or|thog|ra|pher** (ôr thog′rə fər), *n.* **1** a person skilled in orthography. **2** a person who spells correctly.
**or|tho|graph|ic** (ôr′thə graf′ik), *adj.* **1** having to do with orthography: *an orthographic mistake.* **2** correct in spelling: *For the sake of simplicity only the orthographic spellings are here given* (Simeon Potter). **3** *Geometry.* orthogonal.
**or|tho|graph|i|cal|ly** (ôr′thə graf′ə klē), *adv.* in an orthographic manner; according to the rules of proper spelling.
***orthographic projection,** a projection on a plane by lines perpendicular to the plane.

***orthographic projection**

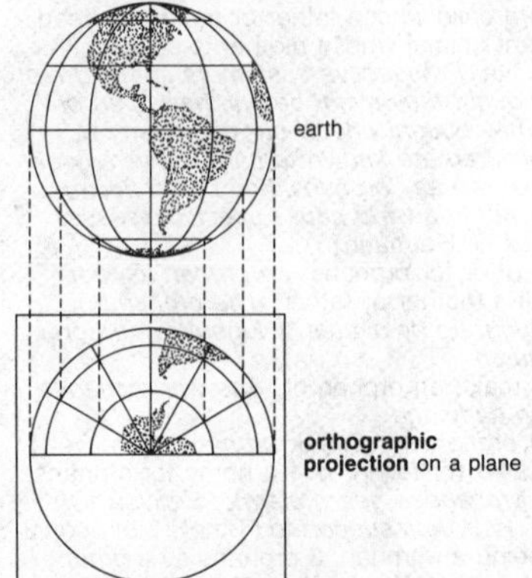


**or|thog|ra|phy** (ôr thog′rə fē), *n., pl.* **-phies.** **1a** correct spelling considered as right or wrong according to accepted usage. **b** any system of spelling: *The function of orthography is to identify the phonemes, or distinctive vowels and consonants, of a language* (Harold B. Allen). **2** the art of spelling; study of spelling. **3** a drawing in which the object is projected on a plane by lines perpendicular to the plane. [< Latin *orthographia* < Greek *orthographíā* < *orthós* correct + *gráphein* write]
**or|tho-hy|dro|gen** (ôr′thō hī′drə jən), *n.* a form of hydrogen consisting of molecules whose pairs of nuclei have spins in the same direction: *Three quarters of hydrogen gas is ortho-hydrogen* (Monroe M. Offner).
**or|tho|ker|a|tol|o|gy** (ôr′thō ker′ə tol′ə jē), *n.* a method of correcting or improving the eyesight by altering the cornea through the periodical application of new contact lenses. [< *ortho-* + *kerato-* + *-logy*]
**or|tho|mo|lec|u|lar** (ôr′thō mə lek′yə lər), *adj.* of or based upon a theory according to which disease may be caused by deficient molecular concentrations of essential substances in the body, so that cures may be effected by combining medical treatment with dietary and vitamin therapy to overcome the molecular deficiency: *Another way in which the disease* [*diabetes*] *can be kept under control, if it is not serious, is by adjusting the diet, regulating the intake of sugar, in such a way as to keep the glucose concentration in the blood within the normal limits. This procedure also represents an example of orthomolecular medicine* (Linus Pauling).
**or|tho|nor|mal** (ôr′thə nôr′məl), *adj. Mathematics.* having to do with or consisting of normal orthogonal elements.
**or|tho|pae|dic** (ôr′thə pē′dik), *adj.* orthopedic.
**or|tho|pe|dic** (ôr′thə pē′dik), *adj.* of or having to do with orthopedics: *an orthopedic surgeon.* —**or′tho|pe′di|cal|ly,** *adv.*
**or|tho|pe|dics** (ôr′thə pē′diks), *n.* the branch of surgery that deals with the deformities and diseases of bones and joints, especially in children. [< French *orthopédique* < *orthopédie* < New Latin *orthopaedia* < Greek *orthós* straight + *paideíā* rearing of children < *país, paidós* child]
**or|tho|pe|dist** (ôr′thə pē′dist), *n.* a surgeon who specializes in orthopedics: *The big Cornell athletic clinic, headed by a crack team of orthopedists and physiotherapists, is equipped to handle everything from mild Charley horses to severe skull fractures* (Newsweek).
**or|tho|pe|dy** (ôr′thə pē′dē), *n.* = orthopedics.
**or|tho|phos|phate** (ôr′thō fos′fāt), *n.* a salt or ester of phosphoric acid.
**or|tho|phos|phor|ic acid** (ôr′thō fos fôr′ik, -for′-), = phosphoric acid.
**or|thop|ne|a** (ôr thop′nē ə), *n.* a condition, associated with asthma and certain heart ailments, in which satisfactory breathing can take place only when one is in an erect position. [< Latin *orthopnoea* < Greek *orthópnoia* < *orthós* straight + *pneîn* blow, breathe]
**or|tho|prax|y** (ôr′thə prak′sē), *n.* **1** correctness of practice, action, or procedure. **2** corrective treatment of deformities; orthopedics. [< *ortho-* + Greek *prâxis* a doing, acting]
**or|tho|psy|chi|at|ric** (ôr′thō sī′kē at′rik), *adj.* of or having to do with orthopsychiatry. —**or′tho-psy′chi|at′ri|cal|ly,** *adv.*
**or|tho|psy|chi|a|trist** (ôr′thō sī kī′ə trist), *n.* a person who practices orthopsychiatry.
**or|tho|psy|chi|a|try** (ôr′thō sī kī′ə trē), *n.* the branch of psychiatry dealing with the prevention or early correction of mental disorders, as personality and behavior problems, especially in young people. [< *ortho-* + *psychiatry*]
**or|thop|ter** (ôr thop′tər), *n.* **1** = ornithopter. **2** an orthopterous insect. [< French *orthoptère* < Greek *orthós* straight + *pterón* wing]
**or|thop|ter|an** (ôr thop′tər ən), *n., adj.* —*n.* an orthopterous insect.
—*adj.* = orthopterous.
**or|thop|ter|on** (ôr thop′tə ron), *n., pl.* **-ter|a** (-tər ə). an orthopterous insect; orthopter.
**or|thop|ter|ous** (ôr thop′tər əs), *adj.* of or belonging to an order of insects characterized by longitudinally folded, membranous hind wings covered by hard, narrow forewings, and having mouthparts adapted for chewing. Orthopterous insects have an incomplete metamorphosis. The order includes crickets, grasshoppers, locusts, and cockroaches.
**or|thop|tic** (ôr thop′tik), *adj.* of, having to do with, or producing normal binocular vision. [< *ortho-* + *optic*]
**orthoptic exercises,** a method of exercising the muscles of the eye, especially to correct cross-eye or muscular weaknesses.
**or|thop|tics** (ôr thop′tiks), *n.* the treatment of certain visual defects by exercising and training the eye muscles. [< *ortho-* + *optics*]
**or|tho|rhom|bic** (ôr′thə rom′bik), *adj.* of or having to do with a system of crystallization in which the three unequal axes intersect at right angles; rhombic: *an orthorhombic crystal.* See picture un-

der **crystal**. [< *ortho-* + *rhombic*]

**or|tho|scop|ic** (ôr′thə skop′ik), *adj.* having to do with or producing correct or normal vision: *orthoscopic glasses, an orthoscopic eyepiece on a telescope.* [< *ortho-* + *scop*(e) + *-ic*]

**or|tho|stat|ic** (ôr′thə stat′ik), *adj. Medicine.* caused by standing up, especially for long periods of time; affecting the body in a vertical position: *orthostatic hypotension, orthostatic albuminuria.* [< *ortho-* + *static*]

**or|thot|ic** (ôr thot′ik), *adj., n.* —*adj.* of or having to do with orthotics: *Nickel and his colleagues devised an electrically operated orthotic system to provide patients having severe paralysis of the upper limbs with mobility and voluntary hand movements* (Richard G. Burwell). —*n.* a device providing artificial support for an impaired joint or muscle of the leg or foot.

**or|thot|ics** (ôr thot′iks), *n.* the rehabilitation of injured or impaired joints or muscles through artificial support. [< *ortho-* + *-tics,* as in *prosthetics*]

**or|tho|tone** (ôr′thə tōn), *adj., n.* —*adj.* **1** having an accent, as a word. **2** acquiring an accent, as from position, though not ordinarily accented.
—*n.* an orthotone word. The English articles, usually proclitics. are orthotones when emphasized. *Example:* "I did not say *a* man, I said *the* man."
[< Greek *orthótonos* having the right accent < *orthós* right, correct + *tónos* tone]

**or|tho|trop|ic** (ôr′thə trop′ik), *adj.* **1** *Botany.* of, having to do with, or exhibiting orthotropism; growing vertically upward or downward, as a stem or root. **2** having to do with or using a type of bridge design in which steel plates, strengthened by longitudinal ribs, serve both as roadway and structural support: *an orthotropic bridge or girder. The orthotropic deck, a European innovation, was used for the first time in the United States in two bridges completed in 1967* (William H. Quirk). —**or′tho|trop′i|cal|ly,** *adv.*

**or|thot|ro|pism** (ôr thot′rə piz əm), *n. Botany.* a tendency to grow in a vertical direction, upward or downward.

**or|thot|ro|pous** (ôr thot′rə pəs), *adj. Botany.* (of an ovule) having the nucellus straight, or not inverted, so that the chalaza is at the evident base and the micropyle at the opposite end. [< New Latin *orthotropus* (with English *-ous*) < Greek *orthós* straight + *-tropos* turned]

**or|thot|ro|py** (ôr thot′rə pē), *n. Botany.* orthotropous condition.

**or|tho|wa|ter** (ôr′thə wôt′ər, -wot′-), *n.* = polywater.

**or|tho|xy|lene** (ôr′thə zī′lēn), *n.* one of three isomeric forms of xylene.

**or|to|lan** (ôr′tə lən), *n.* **1** a small bunting of Europe, northern Africa, and western Asia, the meat of which is regarded as a delicacy: *Let me die eating ortolans to the sound of soft music* (Benjamin Disraeli). **2** any one of various small wild birds of North America, such as the bobolink and the sora. [< French *ortolan* (literally) gardener < Provençal < Latin *hortulānus* of gardens < *hortulus* (diminutive) < *hortus* garden]

**orts** (ôrts), *n.pl.* leftover fragments of food or fodder; scraps; leavings: *The poor thought the rich were entirely in the right of it to lead a jolly life; besides, their feasting caused a multiplication of orts, which were the heirlooms of the poor* (George Eliot). (*Figurative.*) *There, in the shadow of a mountain of yesterday's orts ... in a yard outside the Department of Sanitation's mighty destructor plant, was the car pound* (Newsweek). [Middle English *ort.* Compare Middle Dutch *orte,* and Low German *ort.*]

**Or|well|i|an** (ôr wel′ē ən), *adj., n.* —*adj.* **1** of, having to do with, or in the style of George Orwell (1903-1950): *The American Dream becomes more dreamlike, and in order to comprehend it one must exercise the difficult Orwellian technique of doublethink* (Patrick Skene Catling).
**2** characteristic of the regimented and dehumanized society described in George Orwell's novel *1984.*
—*n.* a student or follower of Orwell or his ideas.

**Or|well|ism** (ôr′wel iz əm), *n.* the manipulation or distortion of facts for propaganda purposes. [so called in allusion to the society of the future described in George Orwell's novel *1984*]

**-ory,** *suffix forming adjectives and nouns.* **1** ____ing: *Contradictory = contradicting.*
**2** of or having to do with ____; of or having to do with ____ion: *Illusory = of or having to do with illusion.*
**3** characterized by ____ion: *Compulsory = characterized by compulsion.*
**4** serving to ____: *Preparatory = serving to prepare.*
**5** tending to ____; inclined to ____: *Conciliatory = inclined to conciliate.*
**6** place for ____ing; establishment for ____ing: *Depository = a place for depositing.*
**7** other meanings, as in *conservatory.*
[< Old North French *-ory, -orie,* Old French *-oir, -oire* < Latin *-ōrius, -ōria, -ōrium* < *-or, -ōris* -or + *-ius* -y[3]]

**o|ryx** (ôr′iks, ōr′-), *n., pl.* **o|ryx|es** or (*collectively*) 103 **o|ryx.** an African antelope with long, nearly straight horns in the adult of both sexes. One kind of oryx, the gemsbok, has the longest horns. A rare species of oryx exists in the deserts of Arabia. *In Arabia Talbot found that the oryx, a handsome black-and-white antelope, is almost extinct* (Time). [< Latin *oryx* < Greek *óryx, -ygos* an antelope (in Biblical Latin and Greek, wild ox)]

**os**[1] (os), *n., pl.* **os|sa** (os′ə). *Latin.* a bone.

**os**[2] (os), *n., pl.* **o|ra** (ôr′ə, ōr′-). *Latin.* a mouth; opening.

**os**[3] (ōs), *n., pl.* **o|sar.** *Geology.* an esker. [< Swedish *ås* ridge (of a hill or roof); *åsar,* plural]

**os-,** *prefix.* the form of **ob-** in some cases before *c* and *t,* as in *oscine, ostensible.*

**o.s.** or **o/s** (no periods), out of stock.

**Os** (no periods), osmium (chemical element).

**OS** (no periods) or **O.S.,** Old Saxon.

**O.S.,** **1** Old Style. **2** ordinary seaman.

**O.S.A.,** Order of Saint Augustine; Augustinians (Latin, *Ordinis Sancti Augustini*) .

**O|sage** (ō′sāj, ō sāj′), *n.* **1** a member of a tribe of American Indians, originally inhabiting the region of the Arkansas River and the Missouri River. **2** their Siouan language. [American English < Siouan (Osage) *Wazhazhe* "war people," originally applied to one of the three Osage bands]

**Osage orange,** **1** an ornamental, spreading tree of the mulberry family, with glossy leaves and hard, bright-orange wood; yellowwood. It was originally native to Arkansas and surrounding regions. **2** its inedible, greenish fruit that looks somewhat like an orange.

**o|sar** (ō′sär), *n.* plural of **os**[3].

**O.S.B.,** Order of Saint Benedict; Benedictines (Latin, *Ordinis Sancti Benedicti*).

**os cal|cis** (os kal′sis), the bone of the heel; calcaneus. [< New Latin *os calcis*]

**Os|can** (os′kən), *n.* **1** one of the ancient inhabitants of Campania, a region in southern Italy. **2** the ancient Italic dialect of Campania, closely related to Umbrian.

***Os|car**[1] or **os|car** (os′kər), *n.* **1** a golden statuette awarded annually by the Academy of Motion Picture Arts and Sciences for the best performances, production, photography, or other achievement during the year. **2** a prize. [American English; supposedly from the remark, "He reminds me of my Uncle Oscar," made by the secretary of the Academy when he saw one of the statuettes]

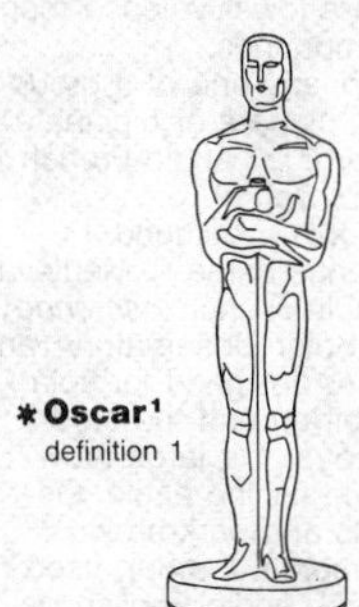

***Oscar**[1]
definition 1

**Os|car**[2] (os′kər), *n. U.S.* a code name for the letter *o,* used in transmitting radio messages.

**os|cil|late** (os′ə lāt), *v.,* **-lat|ed, -lat|ing.** —*v.i.* **1** to swing to and fro like a pendulum; move to and fro between two points. **2** to vary or waver, as between opinions, purposes, or courses of action: *Human nature oscillates between good and evil* (Benjamin Jowett). SYN: vacillate. **3** *Physics.* **a** to have or produce oscillations. **b** to swing from one limit to another.
—*v.t.* **1** to cause to swing to and fro. **2** to cause (an electric current) to alternate at a high frequency. [< Latin *ōscillāre* (with English *-ate*[1]) to swing, rock < *ōscillum* a swing]

**os|cil|la|tion** (os′ə lā′shən), *n.* **1** the fact or process of swinging to and fro like a pendulum. **2** a single swing of a vibrating body: *Each oscillation of the pendulum takes one second.* **3** *Physics.* **a** the variation of a quantity from one limit to another, such as the voltage of an alternating current: *Oscillations may be sustained in a circuit if some provision is made for returning energy at the same rate as it is removed* (Sears and Zemansky). **b** a single swing from one limit to another. **c** an electric wave.

**os|cil|la|tor** (os′ə lā′tər), *n.* **1** a person or thing that oscillates. **2** a device which converts direct current into alternating current of a particular frequency. The oscillator in a radio transmitting apparatus is a vacuum tube which produces the carrier wave for a radio signal. *It is also proposed to use a number of electrical oscillators to provide acceleration* (A. W. Haslett).

**os|cil|la|to|ry** (os′ə lə tôr′ē, -tōr′-), *adj.* oscillating: *The small oscillatory movements of a fixating eye have been observed.*

**os|cil|lo|gram** (os′ə lə gram, ə sil′ə-), *n.* a record made by an oscillograph: *An oscillogram ... pictures the slightest flaw that anxious eyes and modern microscopes can see* (New Yorker). [< Latin *ōscillāre* to swing + English *-gram*]

**os|cil|lo|graph** (os′ə lə graf, -gräf; ə sil′ə-), *n.* an instrument for recording electric oscillations, as of currents and voltages: *The electrical potentials can be ... then recorded either photographically or by an ink-writing oscillograph* (Floyd and Silver). [< French *oscillographe* < Latin *ōscillāre* to swing + French *-graphe* -graph]

**os|cil|lo|graph|ic** (os′ə lə graf′ik), *adj.* of or produced by an oscillograph. —**os′cil|lo|graph′i|cal|ly,** *adv.*

**os|cil|log|ra|phy** (os′ə log′rə fē), *n.* the recording of electric oscillations with an oscillograph.

**os|cil|lo|scope** (ə sil′ə skōp), *n. Electricity.* an instrument for representing the oscillations of a varying voltage or current on the fluorescent screen of a cathode-ray tube. [< Latin *ōscillāre* to swing + English *-scope*]

**os|cil|lo|scop|ic** (ə sil′ə skop′ik), *adj.* of or produced by an oscilloscope. —**os|cil′lo|scop′i|cal|ly,** *adv.*

**os|cine** (os′in, -īn), *n., adj.* —*n.* any one of a large suborder of perching birds that have well-developed vocal organs and usually sing.
—*adj.* of or belonging to this group of birds.
[< New Latin *Oscines* the suborder name < Latin *oscinēs,* plural of *oscen, -inis* bird with a voice (usable in augury) < *ob-* to + *canere* sing]

**os|ci|tan|cy** (os′ə tən sē), *n.* **1** a gaping or yawning; drowsiness. **2** *Figurative.* negligence; inattention; dullness.

**os|ci|tant** (os′ə tənt), *adj.* **1** gaping; yawning; drowsy. **2** *Figurative.* inattentive; negligent; dull. [< Latin *ōscitāns, -antis,* present participle of *ōscitāre* yawn, gape, probably < *ōs* mouth + *citāre* move, agitate]

**os|ci|ta|tion** (os′ə tā′shən), *n.* **1** the act of gaping or yawning; drowsiness. **2** *Figurative.* inattention.

**Os|co-Um|bri|an** (os′kō um′brē ən), *adj., n.* —*adj.* of or having to do with the group of Italic dialects comprising Oscan and Umbrian.
—*n.* this group of dialects.

**os|cu|la** (os′kyə lə), *n.* plural of **osculum.**

**os|cu|lant** (os′kyə lənt), *adj.* **1** *Biology.* intermediate between two or more groups (applied as to genera or families, that connect or link others together). **2** *Zoology.* adhering closely; embracing. [< Latin *ōsculāns, -antis,* present participle of *ōsculārī* to kiss; see etym. under **osculate**]

**os|cu|lar** (os′kyə lər), *adj.* **1** *Zoology.* of or having to do with the osculum of a sponge or the like. **2** of or having to do with the mouth or with kissing.

**os|cu|late** (os′kyə lāt), *v.,* **-lat|ed, -lat|ing.** —*v.t.* **1** *Humorous.* to kiss. **2** to come into close contact with. **3** *Geometry.* to have three or more points coincident with: *A plane or a circle is said to osculate a curve when it has three coincident points in common with the curve.*
—*v.i.* **1** *Humorous.* to kiss. **2** *Geometry.* (of two curves, surfaces, etc.) to osculate each other. **3** *Biology.* to share the characters of two or more groups; be intermediate. [< Latin *ōsculārī* (with English *-ate*[1]) to kiss < *ōsculum* kiss (literally) little mouth (diminutive) < *ōs, -ōris* mouth]

**os|cu|lat|ing circle** (os′kyə lā′ting), *Geometry.* circle of curvature.

**os|cu|la|tion** (os′kyə lā′shən), *n.* **1** *Humorous.* the act of kissing. **2** *Humorous.* a kiss: *And here, I suppose, follow osculations between the sisters* (Thackeray). **3** *Geometry.* a contact, as between two curves or surfaces, at three or more common points.

**os|cu|la|to|ry** (os′kyə lə tôr′ē, -tōr′-), *adj., n., pl.* **-ries.** —*adj.* **1** *Humorous.* of or having to do with kissing. **2** coming into close contact. **3** *Geometry.* osculating. [< Latin *ōsculātus,* past participle of *ōsculārī* (see etym. under **osculate**) + English *-ory*]
—*n.* (in the Roman Catholic Church) a small tablet in former times kissed by priest and congregation in the Mass.
[< Medieval Latin *osculatorium* < Latin *ōsculārī* to kiss]

**os|cu|lum** (os′kyə ləm), *n., pl.* **-la.** *Zoology.* a

**Pronunciation Key:** hat, āge, cãre, fär; let, ēqual, tėrm; it, īce; hot, ōpen, ôrder; oil, out; cup, pu̇t, rüle; child; long; thin; ᴛʜen; zh, measure; ə represents **a** in about, **e** in taken, **i** in pencil, **o** in lemon, **u** in circus.

mouth or mouthlike opening, as of a sponge or tapeworm. [< Latin *ōsculum;* see etym. under **osculate**]

**O.S.D.**, Order of Saint Dominic; Dominicans (Latin, *Ordinis Sancti Dominici*).

**-ose**[1], *suffix forming adjectives.* **1** full of; having much or many: *Verbose = having many words.*
**2** inclined to; fond of: *Jocose = fond of jest.*
**3** like: *Schistose = like schist.*
[< Latin *-ōsus*]

**-ose**[2], *suffix forming chemical terms.* **1** type of sugar or other carbohydrate, as in *fructose, lactose.*
**2** a primary protein derivative, as in *proteose.*
[< French *-ose,* in *glucose* glucose]

**O|see** (ō′zē, -sē), *n.* Hosea, in the Douay Bible.

**O|se|tian** (o sē′shən), *adj., n.* = Ossetian.

**O|set|ic** (o set′ik), *n., adj.* = Ossetic.

**O.S.F.**, Order of Saint Francis; Franciscans (Latin, *Ordinis Sancti Francisci*).

**OSHA** (ō′shə), *n.* Occupational Safety and Health Administration (of the U.S. Department of Labor): *OSHA's permanent standards for worker exposure to vinyl chloride monomer—a cancer-causing material—went into effect in April* (Edward Abrams).

**o|sier** (ō′zhər), *n., adj.* —*n.* **1a** a kind of willow with tough, flexible branches or shoots. **b** one of these branches, used in weaving baskets or other wickerwork. SYN: withe. **2** any one of various shrubby dogwoods of North America.
—*adj.* made of osiers.
[< French *osier* < Old French *osiere,* perhaps related to Medieval Latin *auseria*]

**O|si|ris** (ō sī′ris), *n.* one of the chief gods of ancient Egypt, brother and husband of Isis, ruler of the lower world, and judge of the dead. He represented good and productivity and is identified with the Nile.

**-osis**, *pl.* **-oses.** *suffix.* **1** act or process of ____, or state or condition of ____, as in *osmosis, cyanosis.*
**2** an abnormal condition, as in *mononucleosis, neurosis, trichinosis, thrombosis.*
[< Latin *-osis* < Greek *-ōsis*]

**Os|man|li** (oz man′lē, os-), *n., pl.* **-lis**, *adj.* —*n.* **1** = Ottoman. **2** the language of the Ottoman Turks. —*adj.* = Ottoman.
[< Turkish *Osmanlı* belonging to *Osman,* 1259-1326, founder of the Ottoman Empire. Compare etym. under **Ottoman**.]

**os|mat|ic** (oz mat′ik, os-), *adj.* of, having to do with, or possessing the sense of smell. [< Greek *osmḗ* smell + English *-ate*[1] + *-ic*]

**os|me|te|ri|um** (oz′mə tir′ē əm, os′-), *n., pl.* **-te|ri|a** (-tir′ē ə). a forked process of the first thoracic segment of certain butterfly larvae, noted for the disagreeable odor it emits. [< New Latin *osmeterium* < Greek *osmḗ* smell]

**os|mic** (oz′mik, os′-), *adj. Chemistry.* **1** of osmium. **2** containing osmium, especially with a valence of four.

**osmic acid**, = osmium tetroxide.

**os|mics** (oz′miks, os′-), *n.* the science that deals with the sense of smell. [< Greek *osmḗ* smell, odor + English *-ics*]

**os|mi|ous** (oz′mē əs, os′-), *adj. Chemistry.* **1** of osmium. **2** containing osmium, especially with a valence of three.

**os|mi|rid|i|um** (oz′mə rid′ē əm, os′-), *n.* = iridosmine.

***os|mi|um** (oz′mē əm, os′-), *n.* a hard, bluish-white chemical element which occurs with platinum and iridium. Osmium is a metal and the heaviest known element. It is used for electric-light filaments and phonograph needles. [New Latin *osmium* < Greek *osmḗ* smell, odor (from the odor of one of the osmium oxides)]

***osmium**

| symbol | atomic number | atomic weight | oxidation state |
|---|---|---|---|
| Os | 76 | 190.2 | 3, 4 |

**osmium tetroxide**, an oxide of osmium used in electron microscopy to stain and fix biological material, especially animal tissues. *Formula:* $OsO_4$

**os|mol** (oz′mōl′, os′-), *n.* a unit of osmotic pressure. [< *os*(mosis) + *mol*]

**os|mo|lal** (oz mō′lal, os-), *adj.* of or having to do with the osmol.

**os|mo|lal|i|ty** (oz′mə lal′ə tē, os′-), *n.* the degree of the pressure operative in osmosis.

**os|mo|lar** (oz mō′lər, os-), *adj.* of or having to do with osmosis.

**os|mo|lar|i|ty** (oz′mə lar′ə tē, os′-), *n.* the quality or tendency characteristic of osmosis: *The most important functions of the kidney are to keep constant the volume, osmolarity, and composition of the fluid which surrounds the cells of the body* (New Scientist).

**os|mom|e|ter** (oz mom′ə tər, os-), *n.* a device for measuring osmotic pressure. [< Greek *ōsmós* a thrust + English *-meter*]

**os|mo|met|ric** (oz′mə met′rik, os′-), *adj.* of or having to do with osmometry or an osmometer. —**os′mo|met′ri|cal|ly**, *adv.*

**os|mom|e|try** (oz mom′ə trē, os-), *n.* the measurement of osmotic pressure.

**os|mo|reg|u|la|tion** (oz′mō reg′yə lā′shən, os′-), *n.* the process by which the osmotic activity of a living cell is increased or decreased by the organism in order to maintain the most favorable conditions for the vital processes of the cell and the organism.

**os|mo|reg|u|la|to|ry mechanism** (oz′mō reg′yə lə tôr′ē, -tōr′-; os′-), a biological device or chemical reaction by which an organism carries out osmoregulation.

**os|mose** (oz mōs′, os-), *v.,* **-mosed, -mos|ing,** *n.* —*v.t.* to subject to osmosis. —*v.i.* to pass by osmosis.
—*n.* = osmosis.

**os|mo|sis** (oz mō′sis, os-), *n.* **1** the tendency of two fluids of different strengths that are separated by something porous to go through it and become mixed. Osmosis is the chief means by which the body absorbs food and by which fluid in the tissues moves into the blood vessels. Osmosis is specifically the tendency of a fluid of lower concentration to pass through a semipermeable membrane into a solution of higher concentration. **2** *Chemistry.* the diffusion or spreading of fluids through a membrane or partition till they are mixed. **3** *Figurative.* a gradual, often unconscious, absorbing or understanding of facts, theories, ideas, and the like: *to learn French by osmosis. A hilarious round of sport and pleasure which could only be described as the broadest education by osmosis* (Harper's). [Grecized variant (as in *endosmosis*) of *osmose* < French < Greek *ōsmós* a thrust]

**os|mot|ic** (oz mot′ik, os-), *adj.* of or having to do with osmosis.

**os|mot|i|cal|ly** (oz mot′ə klē, os-), *adv.* by osmosis; diffusively: *"Concentration" for this purpose means the total concentration of osmotically active particles* (G. R. Hervey).

**osmotic pressure**, the force acting upon a semipermeable membrane placed between a solution and a pure solvent, such as water, caused by the flow of solute molecules through the membrane toward the pure solvent: *One cell contains a solution of high osmotic pressure, such as a solution of sugar* (Susann and Orlin Biddulph).

**os|mous** (oz′məs, os′-), *adj. Chemistry.* containing osmium, especially with a lower valence than that contained in osmic compounds.

**os|mund** (oz′mund, os′-), *n.* any one of a group of ferns, with large, upright, pinnate or bipinnate fronds, such as the royal fern. [< Anglo-French *osmunde,* Old French *osmonde*]

**os|mun|da** (oz mun′də, os-), *n.* = osmund. [< New Latin *Osmunda* the genus name < Medieval Latin *osmunda* osmund < Old French *osmonde*]

**OSO** (no periods), Orbiting Solar Observatory (an unmanned satellite of NASA, designed for solar research from a circular orbit around the earth).

**os|prey** (os′prē), *n., pl.* **-preys. 1** a large hawk that feeds on fish; fish hawk; fishing eagle. Ospreys have white underparts and dark-brown back and wings. **2** an ornamental feather, used especially for trimming hats. [Middle English *ospray,* apparently < Latin *ossifraga;* see etym. under **ossifrage**]

**OSS** (no periods) or **O.S.S.**, Office of Strategic Services (an agency of the United States government during World War II).

**os|sa** (os′ə), *n. Latin.* plural of **os**[1].

**os|se|in** (os′ē in), *n.* the organic basis of bone tissue, remaining after the mineral matter has been removed; ostein. [< Latin *osseus* bony, osseous + English *-in*]

**os|se|let** (os′ə lit), *n.* **1** a hard substance growing on the inside of a horse's leg above the knee.
**2** a small, bonelike part; ossicle. [< Old French *osselet* a little bone < Latin *os, ossis* bone]

**os|se|ous** (os′ē əs), *adj.* **1** bony: *True bone or osseous tissue occurs only in the skeletons of bony fishes and land vertebrates* (Tracy I. Storer). **2** containing bones. [< Latin *osseus* (with *-ous*) < *os, ossis* bone] —**os′se|ous|ly**, *adv.*

**Os|set** (os′et), *n.* a native or inhabitant of Ossetia, in the southern Soviet Union.

**Os|se|tian** (o sē′shən), *adj., n.* —*adj.* = Ossetic.
—*n.* = Osset. Also, **Osetian**.

**Os|set|ic** (o set′ik), *n., adj.* —*n.* the Iranian language spoken by the Ossets.
—*adj.* of or having to do with the Ossets or their language. Also, **Osetic**.

**Os|si|an|ic** (osh′ē an′ik, os′-), *adj.* **1** of or having to do with the style of poetry or rhythmic prose used by James Macpherson in *Poems of Ossian* (1762) and *Temora* (1763), purporting to be translations of works by Ossian. **2** grandiloquent; bombastic. **3** of or having to do with Ossian, a legendary Gaelic poet and hero of the 200's A.D.

**os|si|cle** (os′ə kəl), *n.* **1** a small bone, especially of the ear: *As vibrations strike against this drum they set in motion the chain of bones or ossicles of the middle ear* (Simeon Potter). **2** a small bony or bonelike part: *The individual portions of the skeleton of a starfish, sea urchin, or sea cucumber are termed ossicles* (Harbaugh and Goodrich). [< Latin *ossiculum* little bone (diminutive) < *os, ossis* bone]

**os|si|cu|lar** (o sik′yə lər), *adj.* of or having to do with an ossicle or ossicles.

**ossicular chain**, a series of three small bones, the malleus, incus, and stapes, located in the middle ear of mammals and connecting the tympanic membrane with the vestibule.

**os|sic|u|late** (o sik′yə lit), *adj.* = ossicular.

**os|sif|er|ous** (o sif′ər əs), *adj.* containing or yielding bones, as a cave or a geological deposit. [< Latin *os, ossis* bone + English *-ferous*]

**os|sif|ic** (o sif′ik), *adj.* making or forming bone; ossifying.

**os|si|fi|ca|tion** (os′ə fə kā′shən), *n.* **1** the process of changing into bone. **2** the state of being changed into bone. **3** a part that is ossified; bony formation. **4** *Figurative.* the state of being or becoming fixed, hardened, or very conservative: ... *to prevent the ossification that can easily overtake state theatrical enterprises* (London Times).

**os|si|frage** (os′ə frij), *n.* = lammergeier. [< Latin *ossifragus,* or *ossifraga* sea eagle, osprey < *os, ossis* bone + *-fragus* breaker < *frangere* to break]

**os|si|fy** (os′ə fī), *v.t., v.i.,* **-fied, -fy|ing. 1** to change into bone; become bone: *The soft parts of a baby's skull ossify as he grows older.*
**2** *Figurative.* to harden like bone; make or become fixed, hardened, or very conservative: *Long-continued doubt ... must in the end ossify the higher parts of the mind* (R. H. Hutton). [< Latin *os, ossis* bone + English *-fy*]

**os|su|ar|i|um** (os′yů ãr′ē əm, osh′-), *n., pl.* **-i|a** (-ē ə). = ossuary. [< Late Latin *ossuārium;* see etym. under **ossuary**]

**os|su|ar|y** (os′yů er′ē, osh′-), *n., pl.* **-ar|ies.** a vault, urn, or the like for the bones of the dead: *In addition to the crematory jar, there was an ossuary under the daislike steps before the altar* (Science News Letter). [< Late Latin *ossuārium,* neuter of *ossuārius* of bones < Latin *os, ossis* bone]

**os|te|al** (os′tē əl), *adj.* bony; osseous. [< Greek *ostéon* bone + English *-al*[1]]

**os|te|ich|thy|an** (os′tē ik′thē ən), *n.* any one of a class of fishes having a bony skeleton, gills, scales, and fins. Perch, carp, and trout belong to this class. [< Greek *ostéon* bone + *ichthŷs* fish]

**Os|te|ich|thy|es** (os′tē ik′thē ēz), *n.pl.* the class of fishes comprising the osteichthyans.

**os|te|in** (os′tē ən), *n.* = ossein.

**os|te|it|ic** (os′tē it′ik), *adj.* having to do with or affected with osteitis. Also, **ostitic**.

**os|te|i|tis** (os′tē ī′tis), *n.* inflammation of the substance of bone. [< Greek *ostéon* bone + English *-itis*]

**os|ten|si|ble** (os ten′sə bəl), *adj.* according to appearances; declared as genuine; apparent; pretended; professed: *Her ostensible purpose was to borrow sugar, but she really wanted to see her neighbor's new furniture.* SYN: seeming.
[< French *ostensible* < Latin *ostēnsus,* past participle of *ostendere* to show < *ob-* toward + *tendere* stretch]

**os|ten|si|bly** (os ten′sə blē), *adv.* on the face of it; as openly stated or shown; apparently: *Though ostensibly studying his history, he was really drawing pictures behind the big book.*

**os|ten|sive** (os ten′siv), *adj.* **1a** manifestly or directly demonstrative: *It has been manifested ... by ostensive proof from Scriptures* (Thomas Jackson). **b** (of a definition) giving meaning to a word by referring to examples coming after it. **2** = ostensible. —**os|ten′sive|ly**, *adv.*

**os|ten|so|ri|um** (os′ten sôr′ē əm, -sōr′-), *n., pl.* **-so|ri|a** (-sôr′ē ə, -sōr′-). = monstrance: *The priest ... walked under the canopy, and held the ostensorium up in an imposing manner as high as his head* (Harper's Magazine). [< Medieval Latin *ostensorium* < Latin *ostendere;* see etym. under **ostensible**]

**os|ten|so|ry** (os ten′sər ē), *n., pl.* **-ries.** = ostensorium.

**os|tent** (os tent′), *n. Archaic.* **1a** the act of showing; a show or display: *fair ostents of love* (Shakespeare). **b** ostentatious display. **2** a sign, portent, or prodigy: *Latinus, frighted with this dire ostent, For counsel to his father Faunus went* (John Dryden). [< Latin *ostentum,* noun use of neuter past participle of *ostendere;* see etym. under **ostensible**]

**os|ten|ta|tion** (os′ten tā′shən), *n.* **1** the act of showing off; display intended to impress others: *the ostentation of a rich, vain man.* SYN: parade, pomp. **2** *Archaic.* a show, exhibition, or display of something: *to hide the distress and danger ... under an ostentation of festivity* (Hawthorne). [< Latin *ostentātiō, -ōnis* < *ostentāre* to display (frequentative) < *ostendere* to show; see etym. under **ostensible**]

**os|ten|ta|tious** (os′ten tā′shəs), *adj.* **1** done for display; intended to attract notice: *He rode his new bicycle up and down in front of our house in an ostentatious way. His religion was sincere, not ostentatious* (Joseph Addison). **SYN:** showy, spectacular, pretentious, gaudy. **2** showing off; liking to attract notice: *Were I to detail the books which I have consulted ... I should probably be thought ridiculously ostentatious* (James Boswell). — **os′ten|ta′tious|ly,** *adv.* — **os′ten|ta′tious-ness,** *n.*

**osteo-,** *combining form.* bone: *Osteogenesis = the development or formation of bone.* [< Greek *ostéon*]

**os|te|o|ar|thrit|ic** (os′tē ō är thrit′ik), *adj.* affected by or having osteoarthritis: *an osteoarthritic hip joint.*

**os|te|o|ar|thri|tis** (os′tē ō är thrī′tis), *n.* arthritis caused by degeneration of the cartilage of the joints, especially in older people.

**os|te|o|ar|thro|sis** (os′tē ō är thrō′sis), *n.* = osteoarthritis.

**os|te|o|blast** (os′tē ə blast), *n.* a bone-forming cell; bone cell. [< German *Osteoblast* < Greek *ostéon* bone + *blastós* germ, sprout]

**os|te|o|blas|tic** (os′tē ə blas′tik), *adj.* forming bone; osteogenetic.

**os|te|o|chon|dri|tis** (os′tē ō kon drī′tis), *n.* inflammation of the bone and cartilage. [< *osteo-* + *chondr-* + *-itis*]

**os|te|o|chon|dro|sis** (os′tē ō kon drō′sis), *n.* an abnormal condition of bone and cartilage formation involving temporary degeneration of tissue due to inadequate blood supply. [< *osteo-* + *chrondr-* + *-osis*]

**os|te|oc|la|sis** (os′tē ok′lə sis), *n.* **1** the breaking down or absorption of bone tissue. **2** the surgical breaking of a bone to correct deformity. [< *osteo-* + Greek *klásis* fracture < *klân* to break]

**os|te|o|clast** (os′tē ə klast), *n.* **1** one of the large multinuclear cells found in growing bone which absorb bony tissue, as when canals and cavities are formed. **2** a surgical instrument for performing an osteoclasis. [< German *Osteoklast* < Greek *ostéon* bone + *klastós* broken]

**os|te|o|clas|tic** (os′tē ə klas′tik), *adj.* of or having to do with osteoclasts.

**os|te|o|cyte** (os′tē ə sīt), *n.* one of the branched cells that lie in the lacunae of bone tissue. [< *osteo-* + *-cyte*]

**os|te|o|gen|e|sis** (os′tē ə jen′ə sis), *n.* the formation or growth of bone.

**os|te|o|ge|net|ic** (os′tē ō jə net′ik), *adj.* of or having to do with osteogenesis; ossific.

**osteogenetic cell,** = osteoblast.

**os|te|o|gen|ic** (os′tē ə jen′ik), *adj.* = osteogenetic.

**os|te|oid** (os′tē oid), *adj.* bonelike; bony. [< *oste*(o)- + *-oid*]

**os|te|o|log|i|cal** (os′tē ə loj′ə kəl), *adj.* of or having to do with osteology. — **os′te|o|log′i|cal|ly,** *adv.*

**os|te|ol|o|gist** (os′tē ol′ə jist), *n.* a person skilled in osteology.

**os|te|ol|o|gy** (os′tē ol′ə jē), *n., pl.* **-gies. 1** the branch of anatomy that deals with bones. **2** the bony structure or system of bones of an animal or of a major part of an animal, such as the head or trunk. [< New Latin *osteologia* < Greek *ostéon* bone + *-logiā* -logy]

**os|te|o|ma** (os′tē ō′mə), *n., pl.* **-mas, -ma|ta** (-mə tə). a tumor composed of bony tissue, usually benign. [< New Latin *osteoma* < Greek *ostéon* bone + *-ōma* -oma]

**os|te|o|ma|la|cia** (os′tē ō mə lā′shə), *n.* a softening of the bones, usually in adults, caused by the gradual disappearance of calcium salts. [< *osteo-* + Greek *malakía* softness < *malakós* soft]

**os|te|o|ma|lac|ic** (os′tē ō mə las′ik), *adj.* of or affected with osteomalacia.

**os|te|o|my|e|li|tis** (os′tē ō mī′ə lī′tis), *n.* an inflammation of the bone and bone marrow, caused by infection with certain pus-forming microorganisms. [< *osteo-* + Greek *myelós* marrow + English *-itis*]

**os|te|on** (os′tē on), *n.* = Haversian system. [< Greek *ostéon* bone]

**os|te|o|path** (os′tē ə path), *n.* a person who specializes in osteopathy. [American English < *osteopathy*]

**os|te|o|path|ic** (os′tē ə path′ik), *adj.* of osteopathy or osteopaths: *osteopathic medicine.* — **os′te|o|path′i|cal|ly,** *adv.*

**os|te|op|a|thist** (os′tē op′ə thist), *n.* = osteopath.

**os|te|op|a|thy** (os′tē op′ə thē), *n.* the treatment of disease chiefly by manipulation of the bones and muscles. Osteopathy also includes all types of medical and physical therapy. Osteopathy is based on the concept that the structure and functions of a body and its organs are interdependent and any structural deformity may lead to functional breakdown. [American English < *osteo-* + *-pathy*]

**os|te|o|pe|tro|sis** (os′tē ō pə trō′sis), *n.* a form of osteosclerosis occurring mostly in children, in which a chalky tissue replaces the bone marrow, resulting in severe anemia; marble bones. [< *osteo-* + *petro-* + *-osis*]

**os|te|o|phyte** (os′tē ə fīt), *n.* a bony outgrowth. [< *osteo-* + Greek *phytón* plant]

**os|te|o|phyt|ic** (os′tē ə fit′ik), *adj.* of or like an osteophyte.

**os|te|o|plas|tic** (os′tē ə plas′tik), *adj.* **1** of or having to do with osteoplasty. **2** of or having to do with the formation of bone.

**os|te|o|plas|ty** (os′tē ə plas′tē), *n., pl.* **-ties.** the surgical transplanting or inserting of bone to supply a defect or loss. [< *osteo-* + *-plasty*]

**os|te|o|po|ro|sis** (os′tē ō pə rō′sis), *n.* a disease in which the bone spaces or Haversian canals become enlarged and the bones become weak and brittle. It occurs especially among old people, causing the bones to break easily and heal slowly. *Horses stabled indoors may go lame because they get so little sunlight that they get a mild form of the porous bone disease, osteoporosis* (Science News Letter).

**os|te|o|scle|ro|sis** (os′tē ō skli rō′sis), *n.* an abnormal hardening and increased density of bone, especially at the ends or outer surface, often caused by an infection or a tumor.

**os|te|o|tome** (os′tē ə tōm), *n.* a surgical instrument for cutting or dividing bone. [< *osteo-* + Greek *-tomos* that cuts]

**os|te|ri|a** (os′tə rē′ə), *n.* a hostelry; inn; tavern; restaurant: *Austrians or Germans as well as British and Scandinavians throng the wine shops and osterias below the Brenner to sample wines inferior to their own* (Cyril Connolly). [< Italian *osteria* < Medieval Latin *hospitale* inn; see etym. under **hospital**]

**os|ti|ar|y** (os′tē er′ē), *n., pl.* **-ar|ies. 1** a doorkeeper, especially of a church. **2** in the Roman Catholic Church: **a** the lowest of the four minor orders. **b** a person ordained in this order. [< Latin *ōstiārius* < *ōstium* door, opening, related to *ōs* mouth]

**os|ti|na|to** (os′tə nä′tō), *n., pl.* **-tos.** *Music.* a constantly repeated melody, usually in the bass, but occasionally in other voices. [< Italian *ostinato* (literally) obstinate < Latin *obstinātus*]

**os|ti|o|lar** (os′tē ə lər, os tī′-), *adj.* of or having to do with any ostiole.

**os|ti|ole** (os′tē ōl), *n.* a very small orifice or opening, such as those in certain algae and fungi through which the spores are discharged. [< Latin *ōstiolum* (diminutive) < *ōstium* door, opening]

**os|tit|ic** (os tit′ik), *adj.* = osteitic.

**os|ti|um** (os′tē əm), *n., pl.* **-ti|a** (-tē ə). an opening or mouthlike hole, as in the heart of an arthropod. [< Latin *ōstium*]

**ost|ler** (os′lər), *n.* = hostler.

▶ **Ostler, hostler.** In British use, *ostler* was generally preferred in Shakespeare's day, yielding to *hostler* in the 1700's, and regaining favor in the 1800's (although agreement was and remains far from unanimous; one finds *ostler* in George Eliot, *hostler* in Dickens). American usage has always favored *hostler.*

**ost|mark** (ôst′märk′), *n.* a unit of money in East Germany. [< German *Ostmark* < *Ost* east + *Mark*]

**os|to|sis** (os tō′sis), *n.* the formation of bone. [< Greek *osto-* < *ostéon* bone + English *-osis*]

**os|to|the|ca** (os′tə thē′kə), *n., pl.* **-cae** (-sē). a receptacle for the bones of the dead in ancient Greece. [< New Latin *ostotheca* < Greek *ostothḗkē* < *ostéon* bone + *thḗkē* case, box]

**Ost|po|li|tik** (ôst′pō′li tēk′), *n.* **1** a policy of the West German government to establish normal diplomatic and trade relations with the Communist countries of eastern Europe. **2** a similar policy of any Western nation. [< German *Ostpolitik* Eastern policy]

**os|tra|cise** (os′trə sīz), *v.t.,* **-cised, -cis|ing.** *Especially British.* ostracize.

**os|tra|cism** (os′trə siz əm), *n.* **1** banishment from one's native country. **2** *Figurative.* the fact or condition of being shut out from society, from favor, from privileges, or from association with one's fellows: *His continued rudeness led finally to ostracism.* **3** a method of temporary banishment practiced in Athens and other cities of ancient Greece, determined by popular vote with ballots consisting of potsherd or tile.

**os|tra|ci|za|tion** (os′trə sə zā′shən), *n.* **1** the act of ostracizing. **2** the fact or condition of being ostracized; ostracism: (*Figurative.*) *Social ostracization, particularly in small communities, can just as effectively silence the religious dissenter as can a powerful government* (Clayton and Heinz).

**os|tra|cize** (os′trə sīz), *v.t.,* **-cized, -ciz|ing. 1** to condemn to leave a country; banish. The ancient Greeks ostracized a dangerous or unpopular citizen by public vote on ballots consisting of potsherds or tiles. **2** *Figurative.* to shut out from society, from favor, from privileges, or from association with one's fellows: *A boy who boasts too much or tries to show off in a new school is sometimes ostracized until he learns how to get on with his new schoolmates.* [< Greek *ostrakízein* < *óstrakon* tile, potsherd, related to *ostéon* bone] — **os′tra|ciz′er,** *n.*

**os|tra|cod** (os′trə kod), *n.* any one of a subclass of very small, free-swimming, bivalve crustaceans living in fresh or salt water, and found in fossil form in all geologic strata since the early Paleozoic. [< New Latin *Ostracoda* < Greek *ostrakṓdēs* like a shell < *óstrakon;* see etym. under **ostracize**]

**os|tra|code** (os′trə kōd), *n.* = ostracod.

**os|tra|co|derm** (os′trə kō dėrm), *n.* any one of a large group of jawless, bony-plated vertebrates of the Ordovician, Silurian, and Devonian periods. [< New Latin *ostracodermi* name of the group < Greek *ostrakódermos* having a shell < *óstrakon* shell, tile + *dérma* skin]

**os|tra|kon** (os′trə kon), *n., pl.* **-ka** (-kə), **-kons. 1** a potsherd or tile used in ancient Greece as a ballot on which the name of a citizen to be ostracized was inscribed. **2** *Archaeology.* a fragment of pottery or limestone on which an inscription is written: *Nearly 200 ostrakons* (*ink descriptions on pottery*) *have been found* (Scotsman). [< Greek *óstrakon;* see etym. under **ostracize**]

**os|tre|i|cul|ture** (os′trē ə kul′chər), *n.* the artificial breeding and cultivation of oysters. [< Latin *ostrea* oyster + *cultūra* culture]

***os|trich** (ôs′trich, os′-), *n., adj.* — *n.* **1** a large bird of Africa that can run fast but cannot fly. Ostriches have two toes and are the largest of existing birds. They have large feathers or plumes which were much used as ornaments. In former times it was believed that an ostrich buried its head in the sand to avoid oncoming dangers. **2** = rhea. **3** *Figurative.* a person who refuses to face reality or an approaching danger: *Over the last decade Ministers had acted like economic ostriches* (London Times).

— *adj.* = ostrichlike: (*Figurative.*) *These ostrich attitudes are like the frivolity of those who deny the reality of* [*evil*] *by refusing to think about it* (Time).

[< Old French *ostrusce* < Vulgar Latin *avis strūthiō* < Latin *avis* bird + Late Latin *strūthiō, -ōnis* ostrich < Late Greek *strouthíōn* < Greek *strouthós* (*mégas*) (great) sparrow]

***ostrich**
definition 1

resembling an ostrich:

**os|trich|ism** (ôs′tri chiz əm, os′-), *n.* refusal to face reality or an approaching danger: *It is stupid ostrichism ... to pretend that history will never, under any circumstances, be invited to repeat itself* (Bernard Hollowood).

**os|trich|like** (ôs′trich līk′, os′-), *adj.* like an ostrich: (*Figurative.*) *He was "unwilling to accept the ostrichlike materialistic viewpoint that such a problem does not exist"* (Science News Letter).

**Os|tro|goth** (os′trə goth), *n.* a member of the eastern division of Goths that overran the Roman Empire and controlled Italy from A.D. 493 to 555. [< Late Latin *Ostrogothi,* earlier *Austrogothi* < Germanic; perhaps earlier taken as "the splendid Goths," but later taken as "the eastern Goths"]

**Pronunciation Key:** hat, āge, cãre, fär; let, ēqual, tėrm; it, īce; hot, ōpen, ôrder; oil, out; cup, pu̇t, rüle; child; long; thin; ᴛʜen; zh, measure; ə represents a in about, e in taken, i in pencil, o in lemon, u in circus.

**Os|tro|goth|ic** (os′trə goth′ik), *adj.* of or having to do with the Ostrogoths.

**Os|ty|ak** (os′tē ak), *n.* an Ugric language spoken in western Siberia, in the northern Soviet Union.

**Os|we|go tea** (os wē′gō), a North American plant of the mint family, with small, showy, bright-red flowers; bee balm. A tea can be brewed from its leaves, and its flowers attract hummingbirds. [< the *Oswego* River, in central New York State]

**OT** (no periods), old tuberculin.

**O.T.**, Old Testament.

**o|tal|gi|a** (ō tal′jē ə), *n.* = earache. [< New Latin *otalgia* < Greek *ōtalgíā* < *oûs, ōtós* ear + *álgos* pain]

**o|tal|gic** (ō tal′jik), *adj., n.* —*adj.* having to do with earache.
—*n.* a remedy for earache.

**o|ta|rine** (ō′tə rīn, -tər in), *adj.* having to do with otaries or eared seals.

**o|ta|ry** (ō′tər ē), *n., pl.* **-ries**. any one of the eared seals, such as the sea lions and fur seals. [< New Latin *Otaria* the typical genus < Greek *oûs, ōtós* ear]

**OTB** (no periods), off-track betting (a state-licensed system in the United States for placing bets on race horses away from the race track): *Seems that the OTB computers that are linked with those at the race track developed a colic or something, and wagers at the fourteen shops around town had to be recorded manually* (New Yorker).

**OTC** (no periods) or **O.T.C.**, 1 *British.* Officer Training Corps (correlative with the American OCS). 2 Organization for Trade Cooperation. 3 over-the-counter: *The O.T.C. market deals in thousands of tightly held and rarely traded stocks such as Upjohn Co.* (Wall Street Journal).

**O tem|po|ra! O mo|res!** (ō tem′pər ə ō môr′ēz, mōr′-), *Latin.* Oh the times! Oh the manners! (from the first of Cicero's orations against Catiline).

**O|thel|lo** (ə thel′ō), *n.* 1 a play by Shakespeare, first printed in 1622. 2 the principal character in this play, a brave but jealous Moor who kills his wife after being falsely persuaded that she is not true to him. Later he kills himself when he discovers her innocence.

**oth|er** (uᴛʜ′ər), *adj., pron., adv.* —*adj.* 1 remaining: *He is here, but the other boys are at school.* 2 additional or further: *I have no other place to go.* 3 not the same as one or more already mentioned: *Come some other day.* 4 different: *I would not have him other than he is.*
—*pron.* 1 the other one; not the same ones: *Each praises the other.* 2 another person or thing: *She helps others. There are others to be considered.*
—*adv.* in a different way; otherwise: *I could not do other than I did. I can't do other than to go.*
**every other.** See under **every**.
**of all others**, more than all others: *Of tame beasts ... the most gross and indocile of all others, namely an ass* (Philemon Holland).
**the other day** (**night**, etc.), recently: *What did you do the other night? I bought this dress the other day.*
[Old English *ōther* the second; other]

**oth|er-di|rect|ed** (uᴛʜ′ər də rek′tid, -dī-), *adj., n.* —*adj.* conforming to the practices, ideas, or expectations of one's group or society rather than following personal convictions; practicing conformity: *Your intransigence in this other-directed world we live in is a delightful curiosity* (New Yorker).
—*n.* a person who is other-directed. —**oth′er-di|rect′ed|ness**, *n.*

**oth|er-di|rec|tion** (uᴛʜ′ər də rek′shən, -dī-), *n.* the tendency to be other-directed; other-directedness; conformity.

**oth|er|gates** (uᴛʜ′ər gāts′), *adv., adj. British Dialect.* —*adv.* in another manner; differently; otherwise.
—*adj.* of another, different kind.
[< *other* + *gate*[3] + adverbial genitive *-s*]

**oth|er|guess** (uᴛʜ′ər ges′), *adj., adv. Archaic.* —*adj.* of another kind or sort: *It was otherguess work with Bellamy* (Pall Mall Gazette).
—*adv.* otherwise.
[variant of *othergates*]

**oth|er|ness** (uᴛʜ′ər nis), *n.* 1 the quality of being other; difference; diversity. 2 the fact of being other.

**oth|er|where** (uᴛʜ′ər hwãr′), *adv. Archaic.* in another place; somewhere else; elsewhere.

**oth|er|wheres** (uᴛʜ′ər hwãrz′), *adv. Archaic.* otherwhere.

**oth|er|while** (uᴛʜ′ər hwīl′), *adv. Archaic.* 1 at another time or times. 2 sometimes.

**oth|er|whiles** (uᴛʜ′ər hwīlz′), *adv. Archaic.* otherwhile. [< *otherwhile* + adverbial genitive *-s*]

**oth|er|wise** (uᴛʜ′ər wīz′), *adv., adj., conj.* —*adv.* 1 in a different way; differently: *I could not do otherwise.* 2 in other ways: *an otherwise satisfactory piece of work. He is noisy, but otherwise a very nice boy.* 3 under other circumstances; in a different condition: *You reminded me of what I would otherwise have forgotten.*
—*adj.* different: *It might have been otherwise.*
—*conj.* or else; if not: *Come at once; otherwise you will be too late.*
[< Old English *on ōthre wīsan* in another way]

**oth|er|world** (uᴛʜ′ər wėrld′), *n.,* or **other world**, the life to come; life after death.

**oth|er|world|li|ness** (uᴛʜ′ər wėrld′lē nis), *n.* the quality of being otherworldly.

**oth|er|world|ly** (uᴛʜ′ər wėrld′lē), *adj.* 1 devoted to the world to come; preoccupied with life after death. 2 devoted to the world of mind or imagination: *The strange world of the Byzantine Empire had an art type all its own—intellectualized, otherworldly* (Newsweek). 3 of or having to do with a world or realm other than that of actual life; supernatural; weird: *The sound above is rather otherworldly* (New Yorker).

**O|thin** (ō′ᴛʜin), *n.* = Odin.

**o|tic** (ō′tik, ot′ik), *adj.* of or having to do with the ear. [< Greek *ōtikós* < *oûs, ōtós* ear + *-ikós* -ic]

**o|ti|ose** (ō′shē ōs, ō′tē-), *adj.* 1 at leisure or rest; lazy; idle; inactive: *Our policy in Turkey has now dwindled into an otiose support of the Government* (Saturday Review). 2 of no value; trifling; nugatory: *Such stories ... require ... nothing more than an otiose assent* (William Paley). 3 having no practical function; superfluous; useless: *An alphabet which ... possesses otiose and needless letters* (Nature). [< Latin *ōtiōsus* unemployed < *ōtium* leisure] —**o′ti|ose|ly**, *adv.* —**o′ti|ose|ness**, *n.*

**o|ti|os|i|ty** (ō′shē os′ə tē, ō′tē-), *n.* 1 laziness; idleness: *Joseph Sedley then led a life of dignified otiosity, such as became a person of his eminence* (Thackeray). 2 worthlessness. 3 uselessness.

**o|ti|tis** (ō tī′tis), *n.* inflammation of the ear. [< New Latin *otitis* < Greek *oûs, ōtós* ear + *-ītis* -itis]

**o|ti|um cum dig|ni|ta|te** (ō′shē əm kum dig′nə tā′tē), *Latin.* leisure with dignity; dignified ease: *Intending there to lead my future life in the otium cum dignitate of half-pay and annuity* (Scott).

**o|to|cyst** (ō′tə sist), *n.* an organ in many invertebrates, probably of sense of direction and balance, containing fluid and otoliths, once supposed to be an organ of hearing. [< Greek *oûs, ōtós* ear + English *cyst*]

**o|to|cys|tic** (ō′tə sis′tik), *adj.* of or having to do with an otocyst or otocysts.

**o|to|la|ryn|go|log|ic** (ō′tə lə ring′gə loj′ik), *adj.* 1 of or having to do with otolaryngology. 2 of or having to do with the nose, throat, and ear: *serious otolaryngologic diseases.*

**o|to|la|ryn|go|log|i|cal** (ō′tə lə ring′gə loj′ə kəl), *adj.* = otolaryngologic.

**o|to|lar|yn|gol|o|gist** (ō′tə lar′ing gol′ə jist), *n.* a doctor who specializes in otolaryngology.

**o|to|lar|yn|gol|o|gy** (ō′tə lar′ing gol′ə jē), *n.* the branch of medicine that deals with diseases of the ear, nose, and throat and their treatment. [< Greek *oûs, ōtós* ear + English *laryngology*]

**o|to|lith** (ō′tə lith), *n.* one of the calcareous bodies in the inner ear of lower vertebrates and some invertebrates, often very large in fishes. It helps maintain equilibrium. [< French *otolithe* < Greek *oûs, ōtós* ear + *líthos* stone]

**o|to|lith|ic** (ō′tə lith′ik), *adj.* of or having to do with an otolith or otoliths.

**o|to|log|ic** (ō′tə loj′ik), *adj.* = otological.

**o|to|log|i|cal** (ō′tə loj′ə kəl), *adj.* of or having to do with otology.

**o|tol|o|gist** (ō tol′ə jist), *n.* a doctor who specializes in otology.

**o|tol|o|gy** (ō tol′ə jē), *n.* the branch of medicine that deals with the ear and the diagnosis and treatment of its diseases. [American English < Greek *oûs, ōtós* ear + *-logíā* -logy]

**o|to|rhi|no|lar|yn|gol|o|gy** (ō′tə rī′nō lar′ing gol′ə jē), *n.* = otolaryngology.

**o|to|scle|ro|sis** (ō′tə skli rō′sis), *n.* a disorder of the ear, in which the base of the stapes becomes immobile because of bony growths in the inner ear. It results in deafness. *The two principal types of deafness are those caused by destruction of the auditory nerves and by otosclerosis* (Scientific American). [< Greek *oûs, ōtós* ear + English *sclerosis*]

**o|to|scle|rot|ic** (ō′tə skli rot′ik), *adj.* of or having to do with otosclerosis.

***o|to|scope** (ō′tə skōp), *n.* 1 an instrument for examining the ear, especially the eardrum. See the picture above. 2 a modification of the stethoscope for listening in the ear. [< Greek *oûs, ōtós* ear + English *-scope*]

**o|to|spon|gi|o|sis** (ō′tə spun′jē ō′sis), *n.* = otosclerosis. [< New Latin *otospongiosis* < Greek *oûs, ōtós* ear + *spongiā* sponge + *-ōsis* -osis]

**OTS** (no periods), Officer Training School (of the United States Air Force).

**ot|tar** (ot′ər), *n.* = attar.

**ot|ta|va** (ōt tä′vä), *n., pl.* **-ve** (-vā). *Music.* an octave.

**ot|ta|va ri|ma** (ə tä′və rē′mə; *Italian* ōt tä′vä rē′mä), a stanza of eight lines with the lines according to the rhyme scheme *a b a b a b c c*. In Italian each line normally has eleven syllables; in English ten. [< Italian *ottava rima* (literally) octave rhyme]

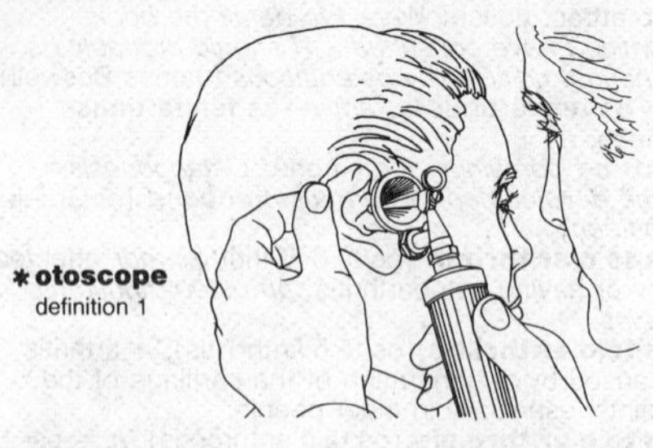

***otoscope**
definition 1

**Ot|ta|wa** (ot′ə wə, -wä), *n., pl.* **-wa** or **-was**. a member of a tribe of Algonkian Indians who lived near Lake Superior and Lake Huron. [American English < Canadian French *Otaua* < Algonkian (probably Cree) *atàwáyoo* trader]

**Ot|ta|wan** (ot′ə wən), *n.* a native or inhabitant of Ottawa, the capital of Canada.

***ot|ter** (ot′ər), *n., pl.* **-ters** or (*collectively*) **-ter**. 1 a water animal that eats fish and is related to the minks and weasels. The otter is a mammal and a good swimmer with webbed toes and with claws. It has a thick tapered tail and is hunted for its fur. 2 its short, thick, glossy fur. Otter is somewhat like seal or beaver. 3a a kind of tackle with float, line, and hooks, used in freshwater fishing. b a kind of gear used in deep-sea trawling. 4 a device towed by a ship for cutting the mooring cables of mines; paravane. 5 the larva of a moth that is very destructive to hop vines. [Old English *oter*]

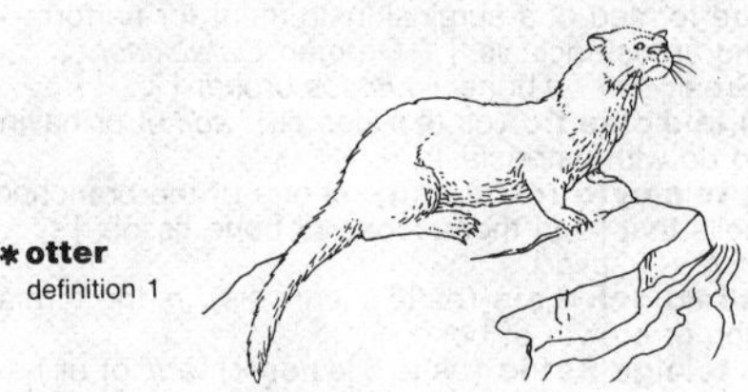

***otter**
definition 1

**otter gear**, 1 a kind of tackle used in trawling; otter. 2 = paravane.

**otter hound**, any sturdy dog of a breed developed in Great Britain for hunting otter. It has a thick, oily coat and slightly webbed feet and is an excellent swimmer.

**otter trawl**, a trawl net with two large boards, one at either side of the mouth. Pressure of water against the boards while trawling holds the net open.

**ot|to** (ot′ō), *n.* = attar.

**ot|to|man** (ot′ə mən), *n.* 1a a low, cushioned seat without back or arms. b a cushioned footstool. 2 a cushioned, armless sofa, with or without a back. 3 a heavy, corded fabric of silk or rayon, often with a cotton woof, used for coats and trimming.
[< French *ottomane* (literally) Ottoman (to suggest the Oriental style of the seat)]

***ottoman**
definition 1b

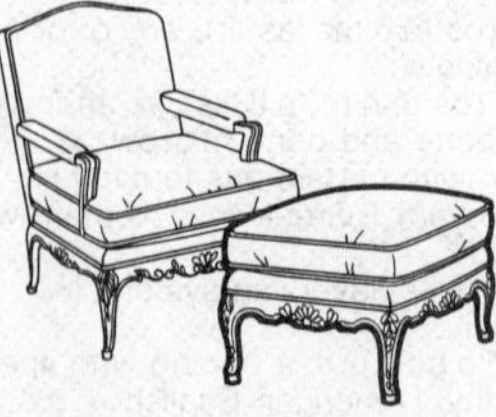

***Ot|to|man** (ot′ə mən), *n., pl.* **-mans**, *adj.* —*n.* 1 = Turk. 2 a Turk descended from or belonging to the tribe of Osman, the founder of the Ottoman Empire; Osmanli.
—*adj.* 1 = Turkish. 2 of or having to do with the Turkish dynasty founded by Osman I about 1300 or the Ottoman Empire.
[< Middle French *Ottoman* < Italian *Ottomano* < Arabic *'uthmānī* belonging to *'uthmān* < Turkish

*Osman;* see etym. under **Osmanli**]

**Ottoman Empire**, a former empire of the Turks which occupied Asia Minor and, at various times between the 1400's and the 1900's, parts of northern Africa, southeastern Europe, and southwestern Asia.

**oua|ba|in** (wä bä′in), *n.* a poisonous glucoside obtained from the seeds of various African plants of the dogbane family, used as an arrow poison and as a substitute for digitalis. *Formula:* $C_{29}H_{44}O_{12}\cdot 8H_2O$ [< earlier *ouabaio* the plant name; its juice (< French < Somali *wabāyo*) + *-in*]

**oua|ka|ri** (wä kä′rē), *n., pl.* **-ris.** a South American monkey having a short tail, and long, light-colored hair, part of which it loses upon reaching adulthood. Also, **uakari.** [< Tupi *uakari*]

**oua|na|niche** (wä′nä nēsh′), *n., pl.* **-niche.** a freshwater salmon of eastern Canada. [< Canadian French *Ouananiche* < Algonkian (Cree), diminutive form of *wanans* salmon]

**ou|bli|ette** (ü′blē et′), *n.* **1** a secret dungeon with an opening only at the top. **2** a deep pit in the floor of a dungeon. [< French, Middle French *oubliette* < Old French *oublier* forget < Vulgar Latin *oblītāre* (frequentative) < Latin *oblīvīscī* forget]

**ouch**[1] (ouch), *interj.* an exclamation expressing sudden pain. [probably < Pennsylvania German *autsch*]

**ouch**[2] (ouch), *n., v. Obsolete.* **—*n.*** **1** a brooch or buckle worn as an ornament. **2** the setting of a precious stone, usually part of a brooch or buckle: *onyx stones inclosed in ouches of gold* (Exodus 39:6). **3** a glittering jewel; precious ornament; gem.

**—*v.t.*** to adorn with or as if with gems: *A lamplit bridge ouching the troubled sky* (William E. Henley).

[Middle English *ouche,* by misdivision < *a nouche* < Anglo-French, Old French *nouche* < Late Latin *nusca* < Germanic (compare Old High German *nusche*)]

**oud** (üd), *n.* an Arabian lute, usually having seven pairs of strings. It was the prototype of the medieval European lute. *The oud, a large Egyptian stringed instrument ... resembles a gourd sliced in half and ... emits an urgent nasal, tingling sound* (New Yorker). [< Arabic *'ud* (literally) wood]

**oud|ist** (ü′dist), *n.* a person who plays the oud.

**oued** (wed), *n.* = wadi: *The Romans had worked out means of harnessing the oueds—seasonal watercourses which are to be found all over the area* (London Times).

**ough** (üн, ùн), *interj.* an exclamation expressing disgust.

**ought**[1] (ôt), *v., n.* **—*auxiliary verb.*** **1** to have a duty; be obliged: *You ought to obey your parents.* **SYN**: must, should. **2** to be right or suitable: *A trip to the museum ought to be allowed.* **3** to be wise: *I ought to go before it rains.* **4** to be expected: *At your age you ought to know better.* **5** to be very likely: *It ought to be a fine day tomorrow. The defending champion ought to win the race.*

**—*n.*** a duty; obligation: *the moral oughts to which a person is bound.*

[Old English *āhte,* past tense of *āgan* owe; own]

▶ **ought.** Originally a past tense, *ought* now has present or future meaning. The past sense is expressed by a dependent perfect infinitive: *He ought to have answered* (not *had ought to answer,* which is substandard).

**ought**[2] (ôt), *n., adv.* aught; anything. [variant of *aught*]

**ought**[3] (ôt), *n. Informal.* naught; zero; 0. [earlier *an ought,* apparently misdivision of *a nought;* perhaps influenced by *aught*]

**ought|n't** (ôt′ənt), ought not.

**ou|gui|ya** (wä gē′yə), *n.* the unit of money of Mauritania, introduced in 1973 and replacing the franc. [< French *ouguiya* < Arabic *wagīya*]

**oui** (wē), *adv., n., pl.* **ouis** (wē). *French.* yes.

**✱Ouija**

**✱Oui|ja** (wē′jə, -jē′), *n. Trademark.* a device that consists of a small board on legs that rests on a larger board marked with words, letters of the alphabet, or other characters. The person wishing an answer to questions rests his fingers lightly on the small board which may then move and touch letters or words. Ouijas are sometimes used at spiritualistic meetings and as games. [American English, supposedly < French *oui* yes + German *ja* yes]

**ouis|ti|ti** (wis tē′tē), *n.* = wistiti.

**ounce**[1] (ouns), *n.* **1** a unit of weight: **a** 1/16 of a pound in avoirdupois or 28.3495 grams. *Abbr:* oz. **b** 1/12 of a pound in troy weight or 31.1035 grams. *Abbr:* oz.t. **2** a measure for liquids; fluid ounce or about .0295 liter. 16 ounces = 1 pint in the United States. *Abbr:* oz. **3** *Figurative.* a little bit; very small amount: *An ounce of prevention is worth a pound of cure.*

[< Old French *unce* < Latin *uncia* twelfth part (of various measures). See etym. of doublets **inch, oka.**]

**ounce**[2] (ouns), *n.* **1** a large, carnivorous catlike mammal having thick, heavy, whitish or brownish hair with irregular dark spots resembling those of a leopard; snow leopard. It is found in the mountains of central Asia. **2** *Obsolete.* a lynx. [< Old French *once,* for *lonce* < Vulgar Latin *lyncea* < Latin *lynx* lynx < Greek *lýnx, lynkós*]

**ouph** or **ouphe** (ouf, üf), *n. Archaic.* an elf, sprite, or goblin: *We'll dress like urchins, ouphes, and fairies, green and white* (Shakespeare). [variant of *oaf,* earlier *oaph*]

**our** (our, är), *adj.* a possessive form of **we. 1** of us; belonging to us: *We need our coats now.* **2** of me (an imperial or royal use, instead of *my*). [Old English *ūre* of us, genitive plural of *ic* I]

**ou|rang-ou|tang** (ù rang′ù tang′), *n.* = orangutan.

**ou|ra|nog|ra|phy** (ùr′ə nog′rə fē), *n.* = uranography.

**ou|ra|ri** (ü rä′rē), *n.* = curare.

**Our Father**, the Lord's Prayer: ... *the click of the beads of a rosary on which he was numbering numberless Our Fathers and Hail Marys* (Theodore Dreiser).

**ou|rie** (ùr′ē), *adj. Scottish.* poor in appearance; shabby; dingy; dreary. [origin uncertain. Compare Old Icelandic *ūrig* wet.]

**Our Lady**, = Virgin Mary.

**ourn** (ourn), *pron. Dialect.* ours.

**ou|rol|o|gy** (ù rol′ə jē), *n.* = urology.

**ou|ros|co|py** (ù ros′kə pē), *n.* = uroscopy.

**ours** (ourz, ärz), *pron. Possessive form of* **we. 1** of us; belonging to us: *This garden is ours.* **2** the one or ones belonging to us: *Ours is a large house. I like ours better than yours.*

**our|self** (our self′, är-), *pron.* myself: *Ourself behind ourself* (Emily Dickinson).

▶ **Ourself** is used by an author, king, judge, etc.: *"We will ourself reward the victor," said the queen.*

**our|selves** (our selvz′, är-), *pron.pl.* **1** the form of **we** or **us** used to make a statement stronger: *We ourselves will do the work. We did it ourselves.* **2** the form used instead of **we** or **us** in cases like: *We help ourselves. We cook for ourselves. We cannot see ourselves as others see us.* **3** our real or true selves: *We weren't ourselves when we said that.*

**-ous**, *suffix added to nouns to form adjectives.*
**1** having ___; having much ___; full of ___: *Famous = having much fame. Joyous = full of joy.*
**2** characterized by ___: *Zealous = characterized by zeal.*
**3** having the nature of ___: *Murderous = having the nature of murder. Idolatrous = having the nature of an idolater.*
**4** of or having to do with ___: *Monogamous = having to do with monogamy.*
**5** like ___: *Thunderous = like thunder.*
**6** committing or practicing ___: *Bigamous = practicing bigamy.*
**7** inclined to ___: *Blasphemous = inclined to blasphemy.*
**8** *Chemistry.* indicating the presence in a compound of the designated element in a lower valence than indicated by the suffix *-ic. Stannous* means containing tin in larger proportions than a corresponding *stannic* compound.
[< Old French *-os, -us* < Latin *-ōsus. -ous* is often used to represent the Latin adjective ending, *-us,* as in Latin *omnivorus* omnivorous, or the Greek adjective ending, *-os,* as in Greek *anōnymos* anonymous]

**ou|sel** (ü′zəl), *n.* = ouzel.

**oust** (oust), *v.t.* **1** to force out; drive out: *The sparrows have ousted the bluebirds from the birdhouse. The war problem ... ousted for a time all other intellectual interests* (H. G. Wells). **SYN**: eject, expel. **2** *Law.* to deprive (a person) of the possession of something; dispossess. **SYN**: evict. [< Anglo-French *ouster,* Old French *oster,* perhaps < Latin *obstāre* to block, hinder < *ob-* in the way of + *stāre* stand. Compare etym. under **obstacle.**]

**oust|er** (ous′tər), *n.* **1** an ousting, especially an illegal forcing of a person out of his property. **2** a person who ousts.

**out** (out), *adv., adj., n., prep., interj., v.* **—*adv.*** **1** away; forth: *The water will rush out. Spread the rug out.* **2** not in or at a position or state: *That style went out of fashion. The miners are going out on strike.* **3a** not at home, away from one's office or work: *My mother went out just now.* **b** into the open air: *Let's go out before it rains.* **4** to or at an end: *to play a game out. Let them fight it out.* **5** from the usual place, condition, position, etc.: *Put the light out. The boy turned his pockets out.* **6** completely; effectively: *to fit out a boat.* **7** so as to project or extend: *to stand out, to stick out one's hand.* **8** into the open; made public; made known; into being; so as to be seen: *You have let the secret out now. His new book is about to come out. A rash broke out on his chest. Flowers came out.* **9** aloud; loudly; plainly: *Speak out so that we can hear.* **10** to others: *to let out rooms. Give out the books.* **11** from among others; from a number, stock, store, source, cause, or material: *Pick out an apple for me. She picked out a new coat.* **12** from a state of composure, satisfaction, or harmony: *to feel put out, to fall out with a friend.* **13** not in play; no longer at bat or on base; so as to be retired from offensive play: *The outfielder caught the fly and put the batter out. He flied out.* **14** into society: *She came out last year.*

**—*adj.*** **1** not in possession or control: *the Republicans are out, the Democrats in.* **2** not in use, action, fashion, or existence: *The fire is out. Full skirts are out this season.* **3** not correct; in the wrong: *He was out in his figuring.* **4** at a money loss: *to be out ten dollars.* **5** external; exterior; outer; outlying: *an out island.* **6** for that which is outgoing; outgoing: *an out basket for mail. I took an out flight.* **8** no longer at bat or on base in baseball: *the out side. The batter was out at third.* **7** not usual or normal: *an out size.* **9** *Slang.* not up-to-date or fashionable; not in: *Fantasy, we keep being told, is "out"; but those of us who are not "in" can keep right on enjoying fantasy* (Punch).

**—*n.*** **1 outs,** people not in office; political party not in power: *An internal struggle is now taking place that is more than an effort by the outs to get in* (Time). **2** something wrong. **3** that which is omitted. **4** the fact of being out or putting out in baseball: *An inning lasts until three outs are made.* **5** a defense or excuse: *to have an out for stealing.* **6** an answer or solution: *The other possible "out" for bondholders is a proposed bill pending before Congress* (Wall Street Journal). **7** a serve or return that lands outside the lines in tennis. **8** *Dialect.* an excursion; outing: *Us London lawyers don't often get an out* (Dickens).

**—*prep.*** **1** from out; forth from: *He went out the door.* **2** *Informal.* out along: *Drive out Main Street.*

**—*interj.*** *Archaic.* an exclamation of indignation or reproach: *Out upon you!*

**—*v.i.*** to go or come out; be disclosed: *Murder will out.*

**—*v.t.*** to put out: *Please out the fire.*

**at** (or **on the**) **outs,** quarreling; disagreeing: *to be on the outs with a friend.*

**out and away,** beyond all others; by far: *This is out and away the warmest day we have had this summer. He is out and away the best player.*

**out for,** looking for; trying to get: *He is out for the best deal he can get.*

**out of, a** from within: *She took a piece of candy out of the box. I sipped some soup out of the bowl.* **b** so as to have left; no longer in: *He is out of the house. In another year he will be out of the army.* **c** not within: *He is out of town.* **d** away from; outside of: *forty miles out of San Francisco.* **e** beyond the reach of: *The jet plane was soon out of sight. He moved out of hearing.* **f** not having; without: *We are out of coffee.* **g** so as to take away: *She was cheated out of her money.* **h** from: *a house made out of brick. My dress is made out of silk.* **i** from among; from the group of: *We picked our puppy out of that litter.* **j** because of; by reason of: *I went only out of curiosity.* **k** from the proceeds of; by the pursuit of: *Few of them managed to make a good living out of their art alone, without running a sideline such as a brewery or an insurance office* (Ellis Waterhouse). **l** born of: *a colt out of a good dam.*

**out of it,** *Informal.* left out of what is going on; lacking a sense of being part of the proceedings: *The Bishop had never felt so out of it as he did late in July, at the dedication of the new cathedral* (New Yorker).

---

**Pronunciation Key:** hat, āge, cãre, fär; let, ēqual, tėrm; it, īce; hot, ōpen, ôrder; oil, out; cup, pu̇t, rüle; child; long; thin; ᴛʜen; zh, measure; ə represents **a** in about, **e** in taken, **i** in pencil, **o** in lemon, **u** in circus.

**out to**, eagerly or determinedly trying to: *to be out to show him up.*
[Old English *ūt*]
▶ **Out** is used both adverbially and, following the verb *be* in some form, as a predicate adjective in many of the same senses: *That dress is out of fashion. Mother is out today. The secret is out. His new book is out. The outfielder caught the fly and the batter was out.*

**out-**, *prefix.* **1** outward; forth; away: *Outburst* = *a bursting forth. Outbound* = *outward bound.* Other examples are:

| | |
|---|---|
| **out\|beam′** | **out\|length′en** |
| **out′bent** | **out′lipped** |
| **out′blow′ing** | **out\|pass′** |
| **out′bowed** | **out′path** |
| **out′branch′ing** | **out\|ring′** |
| **out\|breathe′** | **out\|shape′** |
| **out\|bulge′** | **out\|slide′** |
| **out′drawn** | **out\|spew′** |
| **out′flight** | **out\|spill′** |
| **out′flood** | **out′spring** |
| **out\|flung′** | **out′spurt** |
| **out\|fly′** | **out\|strain′** |
| **out′gleam** | **out\|stream′** |
| **out\|is′sue** | **out′throw** |
| **out′jet** | **out′thrust** |
| **out′jut** | **out′voy′age** |
| **out\|launch′** | **out\|weep′** |
| **out\|leaf′** | **out\|wrench′** |

**2** outside, in literal or figurative positions; at a distance; living or acting outside boundaries (opposed to those within): *Outlying* = *lying outside.* Other examples are:

| | |
|---|---|
| **out′cit′y** | **out′of′fice** |
| **out′clerk′** | **out′pick′et** |
| **out′coun′try** | **out′port′** |
| **out′dis′trict** | **out′pu′pil** |
| **out′dwell′er** | **out′quar′ters** |
| **out′dwell′ing** | **out′serv′ant** |
| **out′gate′** | **out′set′tle\|ment** |
| **out′kit′chen** | **out′set′tler** |
| **out′lodg′ing** | **out′vil′lage** |
| **out′mer′chant** | **out′world′** |

**3** more than or longer than: *Outlive* = *live longer than.* Other examples are:

| | |
|---|---|
| **out′ar\|tic′u\|late** | **out\|ring′** |
| **out\|bar′gain** | **out\|scold′** |
| **out\|bawl′** | **out\|scream′** |
| **out\|bluff′** | **out\|serve′** |
| **out\|blus′ter** | **out\|shout′** |
| **out\|brag′** | **out\|shriek′** |
| **out\|bra′zen** | **out\|snore′** |
| **out\|bribe′** | **out\|speed′** |
| **out\|chat′ter** | **out\|strain′** |
| **out\|chide′** | **out\|stride′** |
| **out\|dance′** | **out\|strike′** |
| **out\|drink′** | **out\|sulk′** |
| **out\|eat′** | **out\|swag′ger** |
| **out\|glare′** | **out\|thun′der** |
| **out\|gross′** | **out\|wait′** |
| **out\|howl′** | **out\|waltz′** |
| **out\|laugh′** | **out\|weep′** |
| **out\|reign′** | |

**4** better than: *Outdo* = *do better than.* Other examples are:

| | |
|---|---|
| **out\|bowl′** | **out\|plot′** |
| **out\|box′** | **out\|preach′** |
| **out\|curse′** | **out\|pro\|duce′** |
| **out\|daz′zle** | **out\|prom′ise** |
| **out\|dress′** | **out\|race′** |
| **out\|fly′** | **out\|rate′** |
| **out\|gain′** | **out\|rea′son** |
| **out\|gal′lop** | **out\|score′** |
| **out\|gam′ble** | **out\|sprint′** |
| **out\|glit′ter** | **out\|spy′** |
| **out\|jest′** | **out\|strive′** |
| **out\|jump′** | **out\|swim′** |
| **out\|kill′** | **out\|swin′dle** |
| **out\|la′bor** | **out\|think′** |
| **out\|love′** | **out\|trade′** |
| **out\|meas′ure** | **out\|trick′** |
| **out\|pass′** | **out\|trot′** |
| **out\|plan′** | **out\|wres′tle** |

**out\|a\|chieve** (out′ə chēv′), *v.t.*, **-chieved, -chiev\|ing.** to surpass in achievements; do better than: *America has almost begged for trouble by expecting children to outachieve their parents, yet wanting them still to look up to them* (Time).

**out\|act** (out akt′), *v.t.* to surpass in acting.

**out\|age** (ou′tij), *n.* **1** a period of interrupted service; time during which the providing of something, as electric power, gas, or water, is halted. **2** the condition of being interrupted.

**out-and-out** (out′ən out′), *adj.* thorough; complete; unqualified: *an out-and-out lie.*

**out-and-out\|er** (out′ən ou′tər), *n.* a thoroughgoing person or thing; perfect example of the kind.

**out\|ar\|gue** (out är′gyü), *v.t.*, **-gued, -gu\|ing.** to outdo or defeat in arguing.

**out\|a\|site** or **out\|a\|sight** (out′ə sīt′), *adj. U.S. Slang.* **1** very advanced or unconventional; far-out. **2** out of this world; incomparable; wonderful. [< *out of sight*]

**out\|back** (out′bak′), *n., adj.* —*n.* **1** the Australian hinterland or back country. **2** the hinterland of any country: *the Canadian outback.*
—*adj.* of, belonging to, or located in the outback: *In the outback country he found a shifting population of aborigines* (Time).

**out\|back\|er** (out′bak′ər), *n.* a person who lives or settles in the back country of Australia.

**out\|bal\|ance** (out bal′əns), *v.t.*, **-anced, -anc\|ing.** **1** to weigh more than. **2** *Figurative.* to exceed, as in value, importance, or influence.

**out-bas\|ket** (out′bas′kit, -bäs′-), *n.* a shallow container with a low rim, used to hold completed or outgoing work, mail, or memorandums; out-tray.

**out\|bid** (out bid′), *v.t.*, **-bid, -bid** or **-bid\|den, -bid\|ding.** **1** to bid higher than (someone else), as in a card game. **2** to underbid: *Three firms from the United States ... outbid British and Belgian companies for Government contracts* (London Times).

**out\|bloom** (out blüm′), *v.t.* to surpass in bloom.

**out\|board** (out′bôrd′, -bōrd′), *adj., adv., n.* —*adj., adv.* **1** outside of the hull of a ship or boat. **2** away from the middle of a ship, boat, or aircraft. **3** outside of or away from the middle of an aircraft or spacecraft: *an outboard aerial.* **4** (in machinery) outside; outer.
—*n.* **1** a small boat with an outboard motor. **2** = outboard motor.

**outboard bearing**, the bearing farthest from the crank or other driving part.

**out\|board\|ing** (out′bôr′ding, -bōr′-), *n.* riding in a boat that has an outboard motor.

**outboard motor**, a portable gasoline or electric motor attached to the outside of the stern of a boat or canoe. It usually has a vertical drive shaft connected to a propeller.

**out\|bound** (out′bound′), *adj.* outward bound: *an outbound ship, outbound flights.*

**out\|brave** (out brāv′), *v.t.*, **-braved, -brav\|ing.** **1** to face bravely, especially with a show of defiance. **2** to be braver than; surpass in daring or courage: *I would ... Outbrave the heart most daring on earth ... To win thee, lady* (Shakespeare). **3** to outdo or excel, as in beauty, splendor, or finery.

**out\|break** (*n.* out′brāk′; *v.* out brāk′), *n., v.*, **-broke, -bro\|ken, -break\|ing.** —*n.* **1** a breaking out: *outbreaks of anger.* SYN: outburst. **2** a public disturbance; riot: *The outbreak was mastered by the police in two hours.*
—*v.i. Archaic.* to break out; burst forth: *The blare of horns outbroke* (William Morris).

**out\|breed** (out brēd′), *v.t.*, **-bred, -breed\|ing.** to breed from individuals or stocks that are not closely related.

**out\|breed\|ing** (out′brē′ding), *n.* a breeding from individuals or stocks that are not closely related.

**out\|build** (out bild′), *v.t.*, **-built, -build\|ing.** to build more or better than.

**out\|build\|ing** (out′bil′ding), *n.* a shed or building built against or near a main building: *Barns are outbuildings on a farm.*

**out\|burn** (out bėrn′), *v.*, **-burned** or **-burnt, -burn\|ing.** —*v.i.* to burn out, or until consumed: *She burn'd out love, as soon as straw outburneth* (Shakespeare).
—*v.t.* to surpass in burning; burn brighter than: *We lit Lamps which outburn'd Canopus* (Tennyson).

**out\|burst** (out′bėrst′), *n.* **1** the act of bursting forth: *an outburst of laughter, an outburst of anger, an outburst of smoke.* **2** a sunspot or stellar explosion. **3** an outbreak; violent disorder; riot: *racial outbursts.*

**out\|bye** or **out\|by** (out′bī′), *adv. Scottish.* out a little way; outside: *Step outbye to the door a minute* (Robert Louis Stevenson).

**out\|cast¹** (*n., adj.* out′kast′, -käst′; *v.* out kast′, -käst′), *n., adj., v.*, **-cast, -cast\|ing.** —*n.* **1** a person or animal cast out from home and friends: *Criminals are outcasts of society. That kitten was just a little outcast when we found it. Pearl was a born outcast of the infantile world* (Hawthorne). **2a** refuse; offal. **b** a plant thrown out from a garden.
—*adj.* **1** being an outcast; homeless; friendless. **2** (of things) rejected; discarded.
—*v.t.* to cast out; reject; banish: *The patient was outcast by society, left on a barren island* (Philip Hope-Wallace).
[< *out* + *cast,* verb]

**out\|cast²** (out′kast′, -käst′), *n. Scottish.* a falling out; quarrel. [< *out-* to the end + dialectal *cast* disagree]

**out\|caste** (out′kast′, -käst′), *n.* in India: **1** a Hindu who has lost or is put out of his caste. **2** a person not of one of the four principal castes, such as a Pariah; person without caste or of so low a caste as to be for all practical purposes without caste; an untouchable. Such persons were formerly denied virtually all ordinary social privileges. This is now forbidden by law under the constitution of the Republic of India.

**out\|class** (out klas′, -kläs′), *v.t.* to be of higher class than; be much better than: *... and found themselves outclassed financially and socially by the flashy ringside crew* (Harper's).

**out\|climb** (out klīm′), *v.t.*, **-climbed** or (*Archaic*) **-clomb, -climb\|ing.** to surpass in climbing: *This ... truck can outspeed, outclimb, outdo any other VW Truck on the road today* (New York Times).

**out\|come** (out′kum′), *n.* a result; consequence: *the outcome of a race.* SYN: upshot, issue.

**out\|crop** (*n.* out′krop′; *v.* out krop′), *n., v.*, **-cropped, -crop\|ping.** —*n.* **1** the state or fact of a rock, stratum, or the like, coming to the surface of the earth: *the outcrop of a vein of coal.* **2** a part that comes to the surface; such rock exposed at the surface or covered only by soil: *The outcrop that we found proved to be very rich in gold.*
—*v.i.* to come to the surface; appear: *a field outcropped with many boulders.*

**out\|crop\|ping** (out′krop′ing), *n.* **1** the act or fact of cropping out. **2** a part that crops out.

**out\|cross** (*v.* out krôs′, -kros′; *n.* out′krôs′, -kros′), *v., n.* —*v.t.* **1** to subject to outcrossing. **2** to cross with an unrelated breed or race; outbreed.
—*n.* the offspring resulting from outcrossing.

**out\|cross\|ing** (out′krôs′ing, -kros′-), *n.* the mating of livestock of different strains but the same breed.

**out\|cry** (out′krī′), *n., pl.* **-cries,** *v.*, **-cried, -cry\|ing.** —*n.* **1** a crying out; sudden cry or scream. SYN: shout. **2** a great noise or clamor: (*Figurative.*) *an outcry of disgust by the students and teachers.* SYN: uproar. **3** *Archaic.* an auction.
—*v.t.* to outdo in clamor; shout down.

**out\|curve** (out′kėrv′), *n.* a baseball pitch that curves away from the batter.

**out\|dare** (out dãr′), *v.t.*, **-dared** or **-durst, -dared, -dar\|ing.** **1** to dare or meet defiantly; outbrave: *And boldly did outdare The dangers of the time* (Shakespeare). **2** to surpass in daring.

**out\|date** (out dāt′), *v.t.*, **-dat\|ed, -dat\|ing.** to make out of date or obsolete: *Constantly improving communications are steadily outdating many of the old reasons for divided authority* (Roderick Haig-Brown).

**out\|dat\|ed** (out dā′tid), *adj.* out-of-date; old-fashioned: *Some outdated dances, such as the Charleston, are still danced sometimes for fun. Good manners can never become outdated.* SYN: obsolete.

**out\|did** (out did′), *v.* the past tense of **outdo**: *The girls outdid the boys in neatness.*

**out\|dis\|tance** (out dis′təns), *v.t.*, **-tanced, -tanc\|ing.** to leave behind; outstrip: *The winner outdistanced all the other runners in the race.* (*Figurative.*) *The Bolsheviks brought out a paper called Pravda* (*Truth*) *in April, and its circulation outdistanced the Menshevik paper* (Edmund Wilson).

**out\|do** (out dü′), *v.t.*, **-did, -done, -do\|ing.** to do more or better than; surpass: *Men will outdo boys in most things.* SYN: exceed, beat. See syn. under **excel.** —**out\|do′er,** *n.*

**out\|done** (out dun′), *v.* the past participle of **outdo**: *The girls were outdone by the boys in baseball.*

**out\|door** (out′dôr′, -dōr′), *adj.* **1** done, used, or living outdoors: *outdoor games, an outdoor meal.* **2** designed for the outdoors; open-air: *an outdoor theater.* **3** outside a hospital, poorhouse, or other institution, as a person supported by public or private charity, but not living in an institution: *outdoor relief.*

**out\|doors** (out′dôrz′, -dōrz′), *adv., n., adj.* —*adv.* out in the open air; not indoors or in the house: *to sleep outdoors.*
—*n.* the world outside of houses; the open air: *We must protect the wildlife of the great outdoors.*
—*adj.* outdoor; outdoorsy: *outdoors clothing, outdoors sports.*

**out\|doors\|man** (out′dôrz′mən, -dōrz′-; -man′), *n., pl.* **-men.** a man, such as a hunter, fisherman, or camper, who spends much time outdoors for pleasure.

**out\|door\|sy** (out′dôr′zē, -dōr′-), *adj.* characteristic of or suitable for the outdoors or for outdoorsmen: *outdoorsy clothing.*

**out\|draw** (out drô′), *v.t., v.i.*, **-drew, -drawn, -draw\|ing.** **1** to attract more people or attention than (something else): *The football games out-*

*drew all the other college sports combined.* **2** to pull out a pistol, sword, or other weapon faster than (an opponent).

**out|drive** (out drīv′), *v.t.*, **-drove, -driv|en, -driv|ing.** **1** to drive a vehicle faster or more skillfully than (someone else). **2** to drive a golf ball farther than (someone else).

**out|en** (ou′tən), *prep. Dialect.* out; out of; out from. [Middle English *outen, uten,* Old English *ūtan* from without]

**out|er** (ou′tər), *adj.* **1** on the outside; external: *an outer garment. Shingles are used as an outer covering for many roofs.* **SYN**: exterior. **2** farther out from a center: *the sun's outer corona.* **SYN**: outward. [< *out* + *-er*[3]]

**outer city,** *U.S.* the outskirts of a city; suburbs.

**out|er|coat** (ou′tər kōt′), *n.* a coat worn over the regular clothing, such as a topcoat or overcoat, but usually not a raincoat.

**outer core,** the third of the four layers of the earth, lying between the mantle and the inner core. See picture under **core**[1].

**out|er-di|rec|ted** (out′ər də rek′tid, -dī-), *adj.* outgoing; sociable; extroverted: *... almost 28 per cent feel that a minister should be an "outer-directed person" or "radiant personality"* (Time).

**outer ear,** = external ear.

**out|er|most** (ou′tər mōst′), *adj., adv.* —*adj.* farthest out; most outward: *an atom which has only one electron in its outermost electron shell* (W. H. Haslett).
—*adv.* in the most outward position.

**outer product,** *Mathematics.* = cross product.

**outer shell,** the first of the four layers of the earth, lying above the mantle; crust.

**outer space,** **1** space beyond the earth's atmosphere: *The moon is in outer space. Far up in outer space, U.S. satellites derive their radio voices from the transistor* (New Yorker). **2** space beyond the solar system: *There are other suns in outer space.* —**out′er-space′,** *adj.*

**outer table,** the side of a backgammon board opposite the inner table.

**out|er|wear** (ou′tər wãr′), *n.* clothing worn over underwear or other clothing: *shirts, slacks, jackets and other outerwear* (Wall Street Journal).

**out|face** (out fās′), *v.t.*, **-faced, -fac|ing.** **1** to face boldly; defy: *The world's hostility, steadily increasing, was confronted and outfaced by ... Victoria* (Lytton Strachey). **SYN**: brave. **2a** to stare at (a person) until he stops staring back. **SYN**: abash. **b** to bully; frighten into doing something by overbearing looks or words. **SYN**: browbeat.

**out|fall** (out′fôl′), *n.* the outlet or mouth of a river, drain, sewer, or other effluent source.

**out|field** (out′fēld′), *n.* **1a** the part of a baseball field beyond the diamond or infield. **b** the three players in the outfield. **2** the part of a cricket field farthest from the batsman. **3** *Scottish.* the outlying land of a farm, that is not enclosed and seldom tilled.

**out|field|er** (out′fēl′dər), *n.* a baseball player stationed in the outfield.

**out|fight** (out fīt′), *v.t.*, **-fought, -fight|ing.** to fight better than; surpass in a fight.

**out|fit** (out′fit), *n., v.*, **-fit|ted, -fit|ting.** —*n.* **1** all the articles necessary for any undertaking or purpose: *a sailor's outfit, an outfit for a camping trip, a bride's outfit.* **SYN**: equipment, gear. **2** *U.S.* **a** a group working together, such as a group of soldiers, or a group of cowboys from a particular ranch: *His father and mine were in the same outfit during the war. A television outfit went there to shoot the story* (New Yorker). **b** *Informal.* an industrial company or business organization. **3a** a fitting out, as for an expedition. **b** the expense of fitting out.
—*v.t.* to furnish with everything necessary for any purpose; equip: *He outfitted himself for camp.*
—*v.i.* to secure an outfit or equipment: *We will outfit two days before sailing.*

**out|fit|ter** (out′fit′ər), *n.* **1** a person who outfits, especially a dealer in outfits as for traveling or athletic sports. **2** a person who sells clothing at retail, especially men's clothing.

**out|flank** (out flangk′), *v.t.* **1** to go around or extend beyond the flank of (an opposing army or other hostile force); turn the flank of: *The city was perilously outflanked, and* [*George*] *Washington had to pull back* (New Yorker). **2** *Figurative.* to get the better of; circumvent. —**out-flank′er,** *n.*

**out|flow** (out′flō′), *n.* **1** a flowing out: *the outflow from a water pipe, an outflow of sympathy.* **2** that which flows out.

**out|foot** (out fůt′), *v.t.* **1** (of a boat, especially a sailboat) to go faster than (another). **2** to surpass as in walking or running.

**out|fox** (out foks′), *v.t.* = outsmart: *Since I couldn't outrun him I had to outfox him* (New York Times).

**out|frown** (out froun′), *v.t.* to outdo in frowning; frown down.

**out|game** (out gām′), *v.t.*, **-gamed, -gam|ing.** to surpass in gaminess or mettle.

**out|gas** (out gas′), *v.t.*, **-gassed, -gas|sing.** to drive out or free gases from: *to outgas a metal or a vessel.*

**out|gate** (out′gāt′), *n.* **1** a way to go out; exit. **2** a passage or way out; outlet.

**out|gen|er|al** (out jen′ər əl, -jen′rəl), *v.t.*, **-aled, -al|ing** or (*especially British*) **-alled, -al|ling.** to be a better general than; get the better of by superior strategy.

**out|giv|ing** (out′giv′ing), *n., adj.* —*n.* **1** the act of giving out something. **2** that which is given out. **3** an utterance or statement.
—*adj.* very friendly; outgoing: *They are outgiving, they apparently like to have fun, they appreciate a joke* (Wall Street Journal).
**outgivings,** money spent; outgoings: *... the outgivings and disbursements to traders* (Robert Blair).

**out|go** (out′gō′), *n., pl.* **-goes,** *v.*, **-went, -gone, -go|ing.** —*n.* **1** what goes out, especially what is paid out; amount that is spent; outlay; expenditure: *Damage to their economy through these restrictions is costing the Mexican Government more than it loses in dollar outgo* (New York Times). **2** the fact of going out. **3** a going out; outflow; efflux.
—*v.t.* **1** to exceed or surpass; excel; outstrip; outdo: *In worth and excellence he shall outgo them* (Milton). **2** *Archaic.* to pass; outdistance.

**out|go|ing** (out′gō′ing), *adj., n.* —*adj.* **1a** outward bound; going out; departing: *an outgoing ship, the outgoing tide.* **b** retiring or defeated: *an outgoing legislator.* **2** inclined to offer one's time, ideas, energy, or the like, without much urging; very friendly and helpful to others; sociable; outgiving: *a very outgoing person.*
—*n.* **1** the act or fact of going out. **2** that which goes out.
**outgoings,** an amount of money spent: *... causing the Chairman's eyebrows to lift when he looks at the outgoings for stationery on the Balance Sheet* (Observer).

**out|go|ing|ness** (out′gō′ing nis), *n.* the quality of being outgoing; sociability; friendliness: *so extreme in his expansiveness and outgoingness* (Harper's).

**out|grew** (out grü′), *v.* the past tense of **outgrow**: (*Figurative.*) *He used to stutter but he outgrew it.*

**out-group** (out′grüp′), *n. Sociology.* everyone outside the group of which one is a member.

**out|grow** (out grō′), *v.*, **-grew, -grown, -grow|ing.** —*v.t.* **1** to grow too large for: *to outgrow one's clothes.* **2** *Figurative.* to grow beyond or away from; get rid of by growing older: *to outgrow boyhood friends, to outgrow a babyish habit.* **3** to grow faster, or taller, or bigger than: *This variety of pole bean will outgrow the dwarf kind. By the time he was ten he had outgrown his elder brother.*
—*v.i.* to grow out; project; protrude.

**out|grown** (out grōn′), *v.* the past participle of **outgrow**: *My last year's clothes are now outgrown.*

**out|growth** (out′grōth′), *n.* **1** something that has grown out; offshoot: *A corn is an outgrowth on a toe. A twig is an outgrowth on a branch.* **2** *Figurative.* a natural development, product, or result: *This big store is the outgrowth of the little shop started ten years ago. Many American cities are the outgrowths of small frontier settlements.* **3** the process of growing out or forth: *the outgrowth of new leaves in the spring.*

**out|guard** (out′gärd′), *n.* a guard at a distance from the main body of an army; advance guard; outpost.

**out|guess** (out ges′), *v.t.* to be too clever for; get the better of; outwit.

**out|gun** (out gun′), *v.t.*, **-gunned, -gun|ning.** **1** to have more weapons than (the opposition): *Admittedly the Reds ... outgunned U.N. artillery by 2 to 1* (Newsweek). **2** to outshoot: *Viewers will not be surprised that Cooper outfoxes and outguns every one of that old gang of his* (Time). **3** *Figurative.* to defeat: *Columbia outgunned Yale in the second half today* (New York Times).

**out|gush** (*v.* out gush′; *n.* out′gush), *v., n.* —*v.i.* to gush out or forth.
—*n.* the act or fact of gushing out; sudden outflow.

**out|haul** (out′hôl′), *n. Nautical.* a rope by which a sail is hauled out to the end of a boom, yard, or spar.

**out-Her|od** (out her′əd), *v.t.* to surpass (anyone) in evil or extravagance.
**out-Herod Herod, a** to outdo Herod (represented in the old mystery plays as a blustering tyrant) in violence: *I could have such a fellow whipt for overdoing Termagant: it out-Herods Herod* (Shakespeare). **b** to outdo in any excess of evil or extravagance: *The figure in question had out-Heroded Herod, and gone beyond the bounds of even the prince's indefinite decorum* (Edgar Allan Poe).

**out|hit** (out hit′), *v.t.*, **-hit, -hit|ting.** to surpass in hitting skill or number of hits: *Williams, 39, but still pulling the ball sharply, outhit Mickey Mantle, 25, by some 21 points* (Newsweek).

**out|house** (out′hous′), *n.* **1** an enclosed outdoor toilet; privy. **2** a separate building used in connection with a main building; outbuilding: *Near the farmhouse were sheds and other outhouses.*

**out|ing** (ou′ting), *n., adj.* —*n.* **1a** a short pleasure trip or excursion; walk or drive: *On Sunday the family went on an outing to the beach.* **b** a holiday spent outdoors away from home: *a weekend outing on the sea.* **2** the part of the sea out from the shore; offing.
—*adj.* of or for an outing: *an outing dress.*

**outing flannel** or **cloth,** a soft cotton cloth with a short nap, woven to look like flannel.

**out-is|land** (out′ī′lənd), *n.* an outlying island: *I would rather make for an out-island like Eleuthera, which is well-spoken of, or remote Inagua with its flamingoes and spoonbills* (Cyril Connolly).

**out-is|land|er** (out′ī′lən dər), *n.* a native or inhabitant of an out-island.

**out|jock|ey** (out jok′ē), *v.t.*, **-eyed, -ey|ing.** to get the better of by adroitness or trickery; outwit; overreach.

**out|laid** (out lād′), *v.* the past tense and past participle of **outlay.**

**out|lain** (out lān′), *v.* the past participle of **outlie**[1].

**out|land** (out′land′), *adj., n.* —*adj.* **1** outlying: *outland districts.* **2** *Archaic.* foreign; alien: *outland merchants* (William Morris).
—*n.* **1** outlying land: *the outland of an estate.* **2** *Archaic.* a foreign land.
[Old English *ūtland* < *ūt* out + *land* land]

**out|land|er** (out′lan′dər), *n.* **1** *Informal.* an outsider; stranger. **2** a foreigner; alien.

**out|land|ish** (out lan′dish), *adj.* **1** not familiar; strange or ridiculous; queer: *an outlandish hat. What outlandish manners!* **SYN**: odd, bizarre. **2** looking or sounding as if it belonged to a foreign country: *an outlandish custom or dialect.* **3** far removed from civilization; out-of-the-way; remote: *Alaska was once regarded as an outlandish place.* **4** *Archaic.* foreign: *outlandish women* (Nehemiah 13:26). —**out|land′ish|ly,** *adv.* —**out|land′ish|ness,** *n.*

**out|last** (out last′, -läst′), *v.t.* **1** to last longer than: *a work to outlast immortal Rome* (Alexander Pope). **2** to outlive; survive.

**out|law** (out′lô′), *n., v.* —*n.* **1** a lawless person; criminal. **SYN**: bandit, highwayman, desperado. **2** a person outside the protection of the law; exile; outcast. **3** an untamed or untamable horse or other animal.
—*v.t.* **1** to make or declare unlawful: *A group of nations agreed to outlaw war.* **SYN**: proscribe. **2** to deprive of legal force. An outlawed debt is one that cannot be collected because it has been due too long. **3** to make or declare (a person) an outlaw.
[Old English *ūtlaga,* noun, *ūtlah,* adjective < Scandinavian (compare Old Icelandic *ūtlagi,* noun, *ūtlaga,* adjective)]

**out|law|ry** (out′lô′rē), *n., pl.* **-ries.** **1** the condition of being condemned as an outlaw. Outlawry was formerly used as a punishment in England. Before the 1200's outlawry meant forfeiture of all possessions to the Crown, and liability to be killed with impunity. **2** the condition of being an outlaw. **3** the act of making or declaring illegal; outlawing: *the outlawry of war.*

**out|lay** (*n.* out′lā′; *v.* out lā′), *n., v.*, **-laid, -lay|ing.** —*n.* **1** the action of spending or laying out money; expense: *a large outlay for clothing.* **2** the amount spent; expenditure: *The outlay to acquire the business exceeded several million dollars.*
—*v.t.* to lay out; spend; expend: *to outlay money in improvements.*

**out|leap** (out lēp′), *v.*, **-leaped** or **-leapt, -leap|ing.** —*v.i.* to leap out or forth.
—*v.t.* **1** to leap over or beyond. **2** to surpass in leaping: *Rabbits outleap frogs in distance but not in number of hops.*

**out|let** (out′let), *n.* **1a** a means or place of letting out or getting out; way out; opening; exit: *an outlet of an express highway,* (*Figurative.*) *an outlet for one's energies.* **SYN**: vent. **b** a stream that drains or flows out of a lake or other body of water. **2a** a market for a product: *Discount houses are a growing and virtually indispensable outlet*

---

*for goods* (Newsweek). **b** a store selling the products of a particular manufacturer: *The shoe manufacturer had several outlets.* **3a** a place in a wall for inserting an electric plug. **b** = outlet box.

**outlet box**, a metal box containing the wires to connect lamps, fixtures, and other devices to a system of electric wiring.

**out|lie¹** (out lī′), *v.*, **-lay, -lain, -ly|ing.** *— v.i.* **1** to lie outside. **2** to camp out.
*— v.t.* to lie outside of or beyond.

**out|lie²** (out lī′), *v.t.*, **-lied, -ly|ing.** to outdo in telling lies.

**out|li|er** (out′lī′ər), *n.* **1** an outlying part of anything, detached from the main mass, body, or system to which it belongs. **2** a part of a geological formation left detached through the removal of surrounding parts by denudation: *An outlier is surrounded by rocks older than itself.* **3** a person who lives away from the place with which he is connected by business or otherwise.

***out|line** (out′līn′), *n., v.*, **-lined, -lin|ing.** *— n.* **1** a line that shows the shape of an object; line that bounds a figure: *We saw the outlines of the mountains against the evening sky. The outline of Italy suggests a boot.* **2** a drawing or style of drawing that gives only outer lines without shading: *Make an outline of the scene before you paint.* **3** *Figurative.* a general plan, sketch, account, or report, giving only the main features; rough draft: *Make an outline before trying to write a composition. The teacher gave a brief outline of the work planned for the term.*
*— v.t.* **1** to draw or trace the outer line of; draw in outline: *Outline a map of North America.* **2** to indicate or define the outline of: *hills outlined against the sky. Each rib and every bone in his [a dog's] frame were outlined cleanly through the loose hide* (Jack London). **3** *Figurative.* to give a plan of; describe in general terms; sketch out: *She outlined her plans for a trip abroad.*
**in outline, a** with only the outline shown: *The shore was dimly seen only in outline.* **b** *Figurative.* with only the main features: *He presented his idea in outline before preparing a detailed plan.*
**outlines**, the main features or leading characteristics of any subject; general principles: *the outlines of science.*
**— out′lin′er**, *n.*
*— Syn. n.* **1 Outline, contour, profile** mean the line or lines showing the shape of something. **Outline** applies to the line marking the outer limits or edge of an object, figure, or shape: *We could see the outline of a man.* **Contour** emphasizes the shape shown by the outline: *The contours of his face are rugged.* **Profile** applies to the side view of something in outline, especially the face in a side view, seen against a background: *a sketch of the model's head in profile. You would stand up straight if you could see your profile when you slouch.*

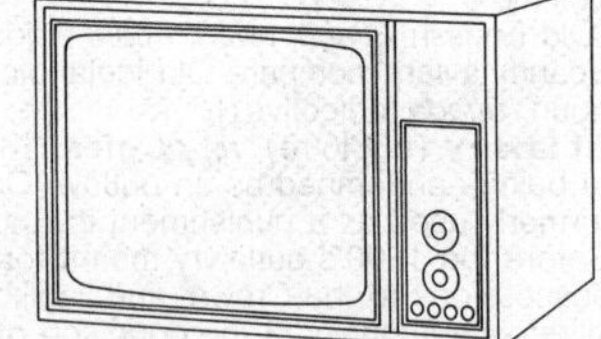
***outline** definition 2

**outline stitch**, = stem stitch.

**out|live** (out liv′), *v.t.*, **-lived, -liv|ing.** to live or last longer than; survive; outlast. *She outlived her older sister. The idea was good once, but it has outlived its usefulness.*

**out|look** (*n.* out′lu̇k′; *v.* out lu̇k′), *n., v. — n.* **1** what one sees on looking out; view: *The room has a pleasant outlook.* **SYN**: scene. **2** what seems likely to happen; prospect: *the outlook for better times. The outlook for our picnic is not very good; it looks as if it will rain.* **3** *Figurative.* a way of thinking about things; attitude of mind; point of view: *a cheerful outlook on life.* **4** a lookout; tower or other place to watch from. **5** a vigilant watching.
*— v.t.* **1** to outdo in looks or appearance: *He tells the King he's going to outlook him* (Calvin Trillin). **2** to disconcert by looking; stare down.
*— v.i.* to look out or forth: *I saw those three wan shapes outlooking from the greenness of the woods* (R. Buchanan).

**out|ly|ing** (out′lī′ing), *adj.* **1** lying outside the boundary; far from the center; remote: *outlying suburbs, the lonely outlying houses of a settlement.* **SYN**: distant, isolated, out-of-the-way. **2** lying or situated outside certain limits: *a few outlying shoals, well beyond the marked channel.*

**out|man¹** (out man′), *v.t.*, **-manned, -man|ning.** **1** to surpass in manpower, or number of men: *Outmanned and outgunned, they still fought on bravely.* **2** to surpass in manly qualities or achievements.

**out|man²** (out′mən), *n., pl.* **-men.** an outsider.

**out|ma|neu|ver** (out′mə nü′vər), *v.t.*, **-vered, -ver|ing.** to outdo in maneuvering; get the better of by maneuvering: *Southerners were grateful for the help—and sore at the Republicans for outmaneuvering them* (Time).

**out|ma|noeu|vre** (out′mə nü′vər), *v.t.*, **-vred, -vring.** *Especially British.* outmaneuver.

**out|march** (out märch′), *v.t.* to outstrip or outdo in marching.

**out|match** (out mach′), *v.t.* to overmatch; surpass; outdo.

**out-mi|grant** (out′mī′grənt), *n.* a person who out-migrates.

**out-mi|grate** (out′mī′grāt), *v.i.*, **-grat|ed, -grat|ing.** to take part in an out-migration; move out of a community or area to live somewhere else.

**out-mi|gra|tion** (out′mī grā′shən), *n.* the act or process of moving out of an area, community, or locality to settle elsewhere.

**out|mode** (out mōd′), *v.t.*, **-mod|ed, -mod|ing.** to make out of fashion or out-of-date: *The arrival of the ... shorter skirts, outmoding the extreme chemise* (New York Times).

**out|mod|ed** (out mō′did), *adj.* no longer in fashion; not in present use; out-of-date: *an outmoded custom, outmoded machinery.* **SYN**: outdated.

**out|most** (out′mōst), *adj.* farthest out from the inside or center; outermost.

**out|ness** (out′nis), *n.* the state of being out or external; externality.

**out|num|ber** (out num′bər), *v.t.* to be more than; exceed in number: *They outnumbered us three to one.*

**out-of-bounds** (out′əv boundz′), *adj., adv.* **1** outside the established limits or boundaries; not to be crossed, entered, or used: *Some of its offices and workshops are completely out-of-bounds to everyone except an authorized handful of research men* (Johns Hopkins Magazine). (*Figurative.*) *We consider bad manners out-of-bounds here.* **2** beyond the expected limits; surpassing expectations: *Our cars are having a formidable out-of-bounds sale this year.* **3** outside the boundary line; out of play: *an out-of-bounds ball* (adj.). *He kicked the ball out-of-bounds* (adv.).

**out-of-court settlement** (out′əv kôrt′, -kōrt′), the settlement of a litigation between parties without the aid or sponsorship of the court. Such a settlement is not binding upon the court, but the court usually permits withdrawal of the suit. *The out-of-court settlement terminates a legal battle among shareholders* (Wall Street Journal).

**out-of-date** (out′əv dāt′), *adj.* not in present use; old-fashioned: *A horse and buggy is an out-of-date means of traveling.* **SYN**: outmoded. **— out′-of-date′ness**, *n.*
▶ **Out-of-date** is always hyphenated when used attributively: *He has an out-of-date model.* In a predicate position it is usually not hyphenated: *His model plane is out of date.*

**out-of-door** (out′əv dôr′, -dōr′), *adj.* = outdoor.

**out-of-doors** (out′əv dôrz′, -dōrz′), *adj., n., adv.* *— adj.* = outdoor.
*— n., adv.* = outdoors.
▶ **Out-of-doors** is always hyphenated when used as an attributive adjective or as a noun: *She likes to wear out-of-doors clothes. We enjoy the out-of-doors.* In a predicate position it is usually not hyphenated: *The storm prevented us from going out of doors.*

**out-of-phase** (out′əv fāz′), *adj.* (of electric currents) of different phases: *The resulting interference of the out-of-phase waves reduces the strength of the signal* (Scientific American).

**out-of-pock|et** (out′əv pok′it), *adj.* requiring or incurred through direct cash payment: *The government's actual out-of-pocket expenditures will not exceed the total revenue taken in* (Wall Street Journal).

**out-of-print** (out′əv print′), *adj., n. — adj.* no longer in type or being reprinted and therefore not actively being sold by the publisher: *He loaned us out-of-print books* (Kathryn Hulme).
*— n.* an out-of-print book.

**out-of-the-way** (out′əv ᴛʜə wā′), *adj.* **1** seldom visited; remote; unfrequented; secluded: *an out-of-the-way cottage.* **2** seldom met with; unusual: *out-of-the-way bits of information.*

**out-of-town** (out′əv toun′), *adj.* living or situated in, coming from, or having to do with territory outside the limits of a town or city specified or understood: *We're treating all rehearsals ... as if they were out-of-town tryouts* (Saturday Review).

**out-of-town|er** (out′əv tou′nər), *n. Informal.* a person who lives outside the limits of a town or city.

**out-of-work** (out′əv wėrk′), *n., adj. — n.* a person who is unemployed: *Lord Rowton started the first hostels in 1892 to meet the urgent need for clean, cheap accommodation for ... the out-of-work* (Manchester Guardian Weekly).
*— adj.* = unemployed.

**out|pace** (out pās′), *v.t.*, **-paced, -pac|ing.** **1** to outstrip; outdo; surpass: *As state spending has continued to outpace revenues, the states have been running more deeply into debt* (Wall Street Journal). **2** to run faster than: *... outpacing two other defenders, he cut in* (London Times).

**out|par|ish** (out′par′ish), *n. British.* an outlying or rural parish; a parish lying outside the boundaries of a city or town, with which it is in some way connected.

**out-par|ty** (out′pär′tē), *n., pl.* **-ties.** a political party not in power: *For a minority out-party, any position except "me too" almost inevitably is going to become simple opposition* (Tom Wicker).

**out|pa|tient** (out′pā′shənt), *n.* a patient receiving treatment at a hospital but not staying there: *A psychiatrist concluded that [she] needed more treatment than he could give her as an outpatient, but not enough to require admission to the full-time inpatient hospital* (Time).

**out|pay|ment** (out′pā′mənt), *n.* **1** the act or fact of paying out. **2** an amount paid out: *One way to help the balance of payments problem would be to cut down on the Government's own huge outpayments of dollars* (Wall Street Journal).

**out|pen|sion** (out′pen′shən), *n., v. — n.* a pension granted to one not required to reside in a particular charitable institution.
*— v.t.* to grant an outpension to.

**out|pen|sion|er** (out′pen′shə nər), *n.* a person who receives an outpension; nonresident pensioner.

**out|per|form** (out′pər fôrm′), *v.t.* to outdo; surpass.

**out|place** (out plās′), *v.t.*, **-placed, -plac|ing.** *U.S.* to place in a new job before actual discharge from a company; help secure new employment.

**out|place|ment** (out′plās′mənt), *n.* the act or process of outplacing: *The outplacement firms have their critics. Some industrial psychologists feel that an executive who has been fired needs the determination to reassess his abilities and find a job on his own* (Time).

**out|play** (out′plā′), *v.t.*, **-played, -play|ing.** to play better than; beat or surpass in playing.

**out|pock|et|ing** (out′pok′ə ting), *n.* an evagination: *The lateral appendages or parapodia are formed by outpocketings of the lateral body walls* (Hegner and Stiles).

**out|point** (out point′), *v.t.* **1** to score more points than in a game or contest. **2** to sail closer to the wind than; move on a tack nearer the direction of the wind than (another sailing vessel).

**out|poll** (out pōl′), *v.t.* to receive more votes than: *in Glasgow, Aberdeen, and Stirling, they outpolled major parties to win the balance of political power* (Time).

**out|port** (out′pôrt′, -pōrt′), *n.* **1** an outlying port: *The union itself is expected to put pressure on the outports* (New York Times). **2** (in Canada) an isolated fishing village, especially in Newfoundland.

**out|port|er** (out′pôr′tər, -pōr′-), *n.* a native or inhabitant of an outport: *Smallwood interspersed the yarns with friendly greetings and messages to outporters* (Ian Sclanders).

**out|post** (out′pōst′), *n.* **1a** a guard, or small number of soldiers, placed at some distance from an army or camp to prevent a surprise attack. **b** the place where they are stationed. **2** *Figurative.* anything thought of as an outpost or advance guard, especially a settlement in an outlying place: *a frontier outpost. Missionaries and traders have been outposts of civilization.*

**out|pour** (*n.* out′pôr′, -pōr′; *v.* out pôr′, -pōr′), *n., v. — n.* **1** the action of pouring out. **2** that which is poured out; overflow.
*— v.t., v.i.* to pour out.

**out|pour|ing** (out′pôr′ing, -pōr′-), *n.* **1** anything that is poured out; outflow: *The outpouring from the factory has mounted in startling style* (Wall Street Journal). **2** a pouring out. **3** an uncontrolled expression of thoughts or feelings: *an outpouring of grief.*

**out|pull** (out pu̇l′), *v.t.* to outdo; outdraw.

**out|put** (*n.* out′pu̇t′; *v.* out′pu̇t′, out pu̇t′), *n., v.*, **-put, -put|ting.** *— n.* **1** the amount produced; product or yield: *the daily output of automobiles.* **2** the act of putting forth; production: *With a sudden output of effort he moved the rock.* **3** the power or energy produced as by a machine: *The power output of a transformer is necessarily less than the power input because of the unavoidable loss in the form of heat* (Sears and Zemansky). **4** information supplied by the storage unit of a computer.
*— v.t.* to put out or deliver from the storage unit: *The computer, though it may hoard a large quantity of information, will output only a very small quantity: the replies to specific questions that are put to it* (Tom Margerison).

**out|rage** (out′rāj), *n., v.,* **-raged, -rag|ing.** *—n.* **1a** an act showing no regard for the rights or feelings of others; a very offensive act; offense; insult: *His request is an outrage.* **SYN**: affront, indignity. **b** the action of overturning the rights of others by force or the threat of force; shameful act of violence: *Setting the house on fire was an outrage.* **2** *Archaic.* violent behavior, or violence of language; fury: *I fear some outrage, and I'll follow her* (Shakespeare).

*—v.t.* **1** to offend greatly; do violence to; insult: *The cattlemen outraged the farmers by driving the herds over their crops.* **SYN**: injure. **2** to break (the law or a rule of morality) openly; treat as nothing at all: *to outrage good taste. He outraged all rules of a good host by making fun of those present who did not agree with him.* **3** = rape.

[< Old French *outrage* < *outre* < Latin *ultrā* beyond]

**out|ra|geous** (out rā′jəs), *adj.* **1** very bad or insulting; shocking: *outrageous behavior in public, outrageous language.* **SYN**: atrocious, flagrant. **2** of or involving gross injury or wrong: *outrageous injustice.* **SYN**: villainous, heinous. **3a** unrestrained in action; violent; furious: *At these words the squire grew still more outrageous than before* (Henry Fielding). **b** *Obsolete.* excessively bold or fierce. *—* **out|ra′geous|ly,** *adv.* *—* **out|ra′geous|ness,** *n.*

**out|ran** (out ran′), *v.* the past tense of **outrun**: *He outran me easily.*

**ou|trance** (ü träns′), *n. French.* the last extremity; the end: *To fight the owner to extremity or outrance* (Tobias Smollett).

**out|range** (out rānj′), *v.t.,* **-ranged, -rang|ing.** **1** to have a greater range or firing power than, as a military weapon, craft, etc. **2** to be able to fly, cruise, or otherwise go, farther than.

**out|rank** (out rangk′), *v.t.* to rank higher than: *A captain outranks a lieutenant.*

**ou|tré** (ü trā′), *adj.* passing the bounds of what is usual and considered proper; eccentric; bizarre: *Ernest was always so outré and strange; there was never any knowing what he would do next* (Samuel Butler). [< French *outré,* past participle of *outrer* exaggerate, push to excess < Old French *outre* beyond < Latin *ultrā*]

**out|reach** (*v.* out rēch′; *n.* out′rēch′), *v., n.* *—v.t.* **1** to reach beyond; surpass: *He outreached his own ambitions by his spectacular success.* **2** to reach out; stretch out; extend.

*—v.i.* **1** to reach too far. **2** to stretch; exceed.

*—n.* the act of reaching out.

**ou|tre|cui|dance** (ü′tėr kwē′dəns; *French* ü trə-kwē däns′), *n.* excessive self-confidence; overweening conceit. [< Old French *outrecuidance* < *outre* (< Latin *ultrā* beyond) + *cuider* < Latin *cogitāre* think]

**ou|tre|mer** (ü trə mer′), *n., adv. French.* *—n.* **1** the lands beyond the sea; foreign countries. **2** ultramarine.

*—adv.* beyond the sea.

**out|ride** (*v.* out rīd′; *n.* out′rīd′), *v.,* **-rode, -rid-den, -rid|ing,** *n.* *—v.t.* **1** to ride faster, better, or farther than: *like a tempest that outrides the wind* (John Dryden). **2** (of ships) to last through (a storm); ride out (a gale or hurricane).

*—n.* **1a** the act of riding out; excursion. **b** a place for riding. **2** *Prosody.* one to three unaccented syllables added to a foot, especially in sprung rhythm.

**out|rid|er** (out′rī′dər), *n.* **1** a servant or attendant riding on a horse before or beside a carriage, wagon, or the like. **2** a person who rides out or forth.

**out|rigged** (out′rigd′), *adj.* fitted with outriggers.

***outrigger**
definition 1

***out|rig|ger** (out′rig′ər), *n.* **1** a framework ending in a float, extending outward from the side of a light boat or canoe to keep it from turning over: *With the outrigger not only was danger of capsizing reduced ... but the craft could tack, that is, sail into the wind at an angle* (Beals and Hoijer). **2a** a boat equipped with brackets extending outward from either side to hold oarlocks. **b** such a bracket. **3** a spar projecting outward from the rail of a ship on which a sail may be set. **4** a projecting frame or spar connecting extended parts of an aircraft, such as the tail unit, with the main structure: *Tubular outriggers give the launcher good stability with maximum weight conservation* (Scientific American).

**out|rig|gered** (out′rig′ərd), *adj.* fitted with an outrigger.

**out|right** (out′rīt′), *adv., adj.* *—adv.* **1** not gradually; altogether; entirely: *to sell a thing outright. We paid for our car outright.* **2** without restraint, reserve, or concealment; openly: *I laughed outright.* **3** at once; on the spot: *She fainted outright.* **4** directly onward; straight ahead: *I never travelled in this journey above two miles outright in a day* (Daniel Defoe).

*—adj.* **1** complete; thorough: *He would have to be an outright thief to do that. The gift outright* (Robert Frost). **2** downright; straightforward; direct: *an outright refusal.* **3** entire; total. **4** directed or going straight on: *The river ... glided seaward with an even, outright, but imperceptible speed* (Robert Louis Stevenson). *—* **out′right′ly,** *adv.* *—* **out′right′ness,** *n.*

**out|ri|val** (out rī′vəl), *v.t.,* **-valed, -val|ing;** (*especially British*) **-valled, -val|ling.** to outdo as a rival; surpass in competition: *Having tried to outrival one another upon that subject* (Joseph Addison).

**out|road** (out′rōd′), *n. Archaic.* a hostile or predatory excursion; raid.

**out|roar** (out rôr′, -rōr′), *v.t.* to outdo in roaring; roar louder than: *This animal—miscalled "howler" ... would outroar the mightiest lion that ever woke the echoes of an African wilderness* (W. H. Hudson).

**out|rode** (out rōd′), *v.* the past tense of **outride.**

**out|root** (out rüt′, -ru̇t′), *v.t.* to root out; eradicate; exterminate.

**out|row** (out rō′), *v.t.* to outdo in rowing.

**out|run** (out run′), *v.t.,* **-ran, -run, -run|ning.** **1** to run faster than: *He can outrun his older sister.* **2** *Figurative.* to leave behind; run beyond; pass the limits of: *His story was interesting but it had outrun the facts and we could not believe it all.*

**out|run|ner** (out′run′ər), *n.* **1** an attendant who runs in advance of or beside a carriage. **2** the lead dog of a team pulling a sledge. **3** *Figurative.* a forerunner.

**out|rush** (out′rush′), *n., v.* *—n.* the act or process of rushing out; violent overflow: *Ow! he shouted, with a tremendous outrush of scandalised breath* (Manchester Guardian).

*—v.i.* to rush out or forth.

**out|sail** (out sāl′), *v.t.* to outdo in sailing: *We were several times chased in our passage, but outsailed everything* (Benjamin Franklin).

**out|scorn** (out skôrn′), *v.t.* to overcome or defeat by scorn.

**out|seg** (out seg′), *v.t.,* **-segged, -seg|ging.** *U.S. Slang.* to be more segregationist than; surpass as a segregationist: *Wallace is supposed to have said that never again would he allow anyone to outseg him* (Tuscaloosa News).

**out|sell** (out sel′), *v.t.,* **-sold, -sell|ing.** **1** to outdo in selling; sell more than: *He outsold every salesman in the company last year. Financially, it outsold by far previous French loans for the same period of subscription* (Wall Street Journal). **2** to be sold in greater quantity than: *This brand outsells all other brands on the market.* **3** to sell for more than.

**out|sen|try** (out′sen′trē), *n., pl.* **-tries.** a sentry placed considerably in advance; picket.

**out|sert** (out′sėrt′), *n.* a section printed and arranged so that it can be folded around another section in a magazine, book, or other publication. [< *out-,* patterned on *insert*]

**out|set** (out′set′), *n.* a setting out; start; a beginning: *At the outset, it looked like a nice day.*

**out|shine** (out shīn′), *v.,* **-shone, -shin|ing.** *—v.t.* **1** to shine more brightly than. **2** *Figurative.* to be more brilliant or excellent than; surpass: *Russia far outshone any of her satellites by building at a rate ... a little better than the European-wide average* (Time). **SYN**: excel.

*—v.i.* to shine forth or out: *From the east faint yellow light outshone* (William Morris).

**out|shoot** (*v.* out shüt′; *n.* out′shüt′), *v.,* **-shot, -shoot|ing,** *n.* *—v.t., v.i.* **1** to shoot better or farther than: *they outshot Robin Hood* (Philip Sidney). **2** to shoot beyond. **3** to shoot or send forth.

*—n.* **1** = projection. **2** = offshoot. **3** the act or fact of shooting or thrusting out. **4** = outcurve (in baseball).

**out|side** (out′sīd′; *prep. also* out′side′), *n., adj., adv., prep.* *—n.* **1** the side or surface that is out; outer part: *to polish the outside of a car, to paint the outside of a house.* **SYN**: exterior. **2** external appearance: *O, what a goodly outside falsehood hath!* (Shakespeare). **3** the space or position that is beyond or not inside: *Wait on the outside.* **4** *Figurative.* a person or group not a member, employee, or officer who makes up part of a company, management, government, or other organization: *The new president of the company came from the outside.* **5** *Informal, Figurative.* those who are not in a position to know about something or not in a position of authority.

*—adj.* **1** on the outside; of or nearer the outside: *the outside leaves.* **2** *Figurative.* not belonging to or included in a certain group, set, district, discipline of study, or organization: *Outside people tried to get control of the business.* **3** being, acting, done, or originating without or beyond a wall, boundary, or other limit: *the outside world. Outside noises disturbed the class.* **4** *Figurative.* reaching the utmost limit; highest or largest: *an outside estimate of the cost.* **SYN**: maximum. **5** *Figurative.* barely possible; very slight: *The team has an outside chance to win.* **6** covering the greater distance in making a turn or following a circular course: *The right-hand wheels are the outside wheels in a turn to the left.* **7** *Baseball.* (of a pitch) missing the strike zone on the side of the plate opposite the batter. **8** *Obsolete.* superficial.

*—adv.* **1** on or to the outside: *Please step outside and wait to be called into the office.* **2** out in the open air; outdoors: *Run outside and play.*

*—prep.* **1** *Informal.* with the exception of: *Outside him, none of us liked the play.* **2** out of; beyond the limits of: *Stay outside the house. That is outside my plans.* (*Figurative.*) *Both had lost faith ... in the liberal politics of the period and both stood outside its conventional culture* (Edmund Wilson).

**at the outside,** at the utmost limit: *I can do it in a week, at the outside.*

**outside in,** so that what would ordinarily be outside is inside; with the outside not showing: *He did not know that a keeper is only a poacher turned outside in, and a poacher a keeper turned inside out* (Charles Kingsley).

**outside of,** *Informal.* **a** with the exception of: *Outside of tennis, she had no interest in sports.* **b** beyond the limits of: *to act outside of the law. The relatives waited outside of the chapel.*

**outside half,** *Rugby Football.* a stand-off half-back.

**out|side|ness** (out′sīd′nis), *n.* the state or quality of being outside; externality.

**out|sid|er** (out′sī′dər), *n.* **1** a person not belonging to a particular group, set, company, party, or district: *What good did an outsider ever get by meddling in a love affair?* (Mrs. Humphry Ward). **2** a person unconnected or unacquainted with the matter in question. **3** a person who is outside. **4** a horse, contestant, or team, not favored to win.

**out|sight** (out′sīt′), *n.* the act or process of viewing the outside or external parts (of something) with understanding: *One who wants to prepare a "repository of information" takes as his models Baedeker, encyclopedias, and almanacs. ... He relies on outsight, not on insight* (Milton R. Konvitz).

**out|sing** (out sing′), *v.,* **-sang** or **-sung, -sung, -sing|ing.** *—v.t.* **1** to surpass or excel in singing; sing better than: *Each appeared to be trying to outsing the other* (The Athenaeum). **2** to sing louder than: *She would sing over the washing tub ... outsinging Martha's scolding* (Mary Russell Mitford).

*—v.i.* to sing out: *When once more ... The meadow-lark outsang* (John Greenleaf Whittier).

**out sister,** a nun, especially of a secluded order, working outside a convent.

**out|sit** (out sit′), *v.t.,* **-sat, -sit|ting.** **1** to sit beyond the time of: *to outsit the twilight.* **2** to sit longer than.

**out|size** (out′sīz′), *adj., n.* *—adj.* larger than the usual size: *An outsize nylon umbrella, as big as a doorman's* (New Yorker).

*—n.* an article, especially of clothing, larger than the usual size.

**out|sized** (out′sīzd′), *adj.* = outsize.

**out|skirts** (out′skėrts′), *n.pl.* the outer parts or edges of a town or district, or of a subject of discussion; outlying parts: *He has a farm on the outskirts of town.*

**out|sleep** (out slēp′), *v.t.,* **-slept, -sleep|ing.** **1** to sleep beyond; oversleep. **2** to sleep longer than (another). **3** to sleep to the end of: *he has outslept the winter* (William Cowper).

**out|slick** (out slik′), *v.t. Slang.* outslicker.

**out|slick|er** (out slik′ər), *v.t. Slang.* to outdo in slickering; outwit; outsmart: [*He*] *frankly admitted he had been grossly outslickered* (New York Times).

**out|smart** (out smärt′), *v.t.* to outdo in cleverness; outwit: *This was demagogy outsmarting itself* (Newsweek).

**Pronunciation Key:** hat, āge, cãre, fär; let, ēqual, tėrm; it, īce; hot, ōpen, ôrder; oil, out; cup, pu̇t, rüle; child; long; thin; ᴛʜen; zh, measure; ə represents **a** in about, **e** in taken, **i** in pencil, **o** in lemon, **u** in circus.

**out|soar** (out sôr′, -sōr′), *v.t.* to soar above or beyond; exceed in height of flight: (*Figurative.*) *He has outsoared the shadow of our night* (Shelley).

**out|sold** (out sōld′), *v.* the past tense and past participle of **outsell**.

**out|sole** (out′sōl′), *n.* the outer sole of a shoe or boot: *The postmen's walking experiments showed that after original outsoles and two resoles were worn through ...* (Science News Letter).

**out|span** (out span′), *v.,* **-spanned, -span|ning,** *n.* in South Africa: **—*v.t., v.i.*** **1** to unyoke or unharness (horses or other beast of burden) from a wagon: *They very frequently unyoke, or outspan ... at Salt River* (W. J. Burchell). **2** to encamp: *They outspan and picnic just outside the town* (Beatrice M. Hicks).
**—*n.*** **1** the act of outspanning. **2** the time or place of outspanning; encampment.
[< Afrikaans *uitspannen* unharness < Dutch < *uit* out + *spannen* to hitch, harness, span[2]. Compare etym. under **inspan.**]

**out|spar|kle** (out spär′kəl), *v.t.,* **-kled, -kling.** to surpass in sparkling.

**out|speak** (out spēk′), *v.,* **-spoke, -spo|ken, -speak|ing. —*v.t.*** **1** to outdo or excel in speaking. **2** to speak (something) out; utter frankly or boldly.
**—*v.i.*** to speak out.

**out|spend** (out spend′), *v.t.,* **-spent, -spend|ing.** to exceed or surpass in spending.

**out|spent** (out spent′), *adj., v.* **—*adj.*** completely spent; exhausted.
**—*v.*** the past tense and past participle of **outspend.**

**out|spo|ken** (out′spō′kən), *adj.* frank; not reserved: *an outspoken person, an outspoken criticism. Your own family is likely to be outspoken in its remarks about you.* **SYN:** blunt. See syn. under **frank. —out′spo′ken|ly,** *adv.* **—out′spo′ken-ness,** *n.*

**out|spread** (*adj., n.* out′spred′; *v.* out spred′), *adj., v.,* **-spread, -spread|ing,** *n.* **—*adj.*** spread out; extended: *an eagle with outspread wings, the outspread stars above.*
**—*v.t.*** **1** to spread out; stretch out; expand; extend. **2** *Obsolete.* to exceed in expanse.
**—*n.*** **1** a spreading out. **2** an expanse or expansion.

**out|stand** (out stand′), *v.,* **-stood, -stand|ing.**
**—*v.i.*** **1** to stand out distinctly or prominently. **2** to sail away from land; move from the shore: *Many a keel shall seaward turn, And many a sail outstand* (John Greenleaf Whittier).
**—*v.t.*** *Dialect.* to stand or hold out against.

**out|stand|ing** (out stan′ding), *adj.* **1** standing out from others; well-known; important: *an outstanding work of fiction, an outstanding statesman. He is an outstanding baseball pitcher because of his control.* **SYN:** prominent, eminent. **2** unsettled or unpaid: *outstanding bills, an outstanding claim.* **3** projecting: *outstanding ears.* **—out|stand′ing-ly,** *adv.*

**out|stare** (out stãr′), *v.t.,* **-stared, -star|ing.** to outdo in staring.

**out|state** (out′stāt′), *n., adj. U.S.* **—*n.*** the area away from metropolitan or industrial centers in any of certain States, especially Michigan and Wisconsin.
**—*adj.*** **1** in, of, or toward outstate. **2** coming from or living in another state: *an outstate visitor, an outstate shipment.*

**out|sta|tion** (out′stā′shən), *n., adj. Especially British.* **—*n.*** an outlying military post, trading post, or the like, in a sparsely settled region, such as in parts of Australia, or a place in which Europeans are relatively few, as in parts of Africa.
**—*adj.*** of or having to do with such a place: *outstation life.*

**out|stay** (out stā′), *v.t.,* **1** to stay longer than: *to outstay the other guests at a party.* **2** to stay beyond the limit of; overstay: *to outstay one's welcome.* **3** = outlast.

**out|stood** (out stůd′), *v.* the past tense and past participle of **outstand.**

**out|stretch** (out strech′), *v.t.* **1** to stretch out or forth. **2** to extend in area or content; expand.

**out|stretched** (out′strecht′), *adj.* stretched out; extended: *He welcomed his old friend with outstretched arms.*

**out|strip** (out strip′), *v.t.,* **-stripped, -strip|ping.** **1** to go faster than; leave behind in a race: *A horse can outstrip a man.* **2** *Figurative.* to do better than; excel: *He can outstrip most boys in both sports and studies.* **3** *Obsolete.* to pass beyond (a place).

**out|stroke** (out′strōk′), *n.* a stroke directed outward, especially the stroke of a piston in an engine during which the piston moves toward the crankshaft.

**out|swear** (out swãr′), *v.t.,* **-swore, -sworn, -swear|ing.** **1** to outdo in swearing. **2** to overcome by swearing.

**out|swing|er** (out′swing′ər), *n. Cricket.* a bowl which curves to the outside of the wicket.

**out|take** (out′tāk′), *n.* a portion of film, videotape, or the like, that has been edited out of the final program of a telecast or broadcast: *All the networks had made available without subpoena their outtakes ... on the riots* (Harper's).

**out|talk** (out tôk′), *v.t.* to talk better, faster, longer, or louder than; get the better of by talking.

**out|tell** (out tel′), *v.t.,* **-told, -tell|ing.** **1** to declare. **2** to tell to the end; tell completely. **3** to tell better than; outtalk.

**out|tongue** (out tung′), *v.t.,* **-tongued, -tongu|ing.** **1** to excel in speaking. **2** to speak louder than; drown the sound of.

**out|top** (out top′), *v.t.,* **-topped, -top|ping.** to rise above; surpass.

**out-tray** (out′trā′), *n. Especially British.* out-basket.

**out|trump** (out trump′), *v.t.* **1** to lay down a higher trump at cards than. **2** *Figurative.* to get the better of.

**out|turn** (out′tėrn′), *n.* the quantity turned out or yielded; produce; output.

**out|val|ue** (out val′yü), *v.t.,* **-ued, -u|ing.** to exceed in value.

**out|vie** (out vī′), *v.t.,* **-vied, -vy|ing.** to outdo in competition or rivalry: *... he outvied them all by the reach and freshness of his imagination and the variety and inventiveness of his resource* (London Times).

**out|vote** (out vōt′), *v.t.,* **-vot|ed, -vot|ing.** to defeat in voting; cast more votes than.

**out|walk** (out wôk′), *v.t.* to walk faster or farther than.

**out|wall** (out′wôl′), *n.* **1** the outer wall. **2** the exterior.

**out|ward** (out′wərd), *adj., adv., n.* **—*adj.*** **1** going toward the outside; turned toward the outside: *an outward motion. She gave one outward glance.* **2** outer: *to all outward appearances.* **SYN:** external, exterior, superficial. **3** that can be seen; plain to see: *outward behavior. He [John Bunyan] must have still been a very young man when that outward reformation took place* (Robert Southey). **4** on the surface; seeming: *the outward man, an outward and misleading air of kindness.* **5** *Obsolete.* lying outside some sphere of work, duty, or interest; external. **6** *Obsolete.* done or situated outside; outdoor.
**—*adv.*** **1** toward the outside; away: *Porches extended outward from the house.* **2** away from the dock, station, or other starting point: *That ship is bound outward.* **3** on the outside; without: *He turned the coat with the lining outward.* **4** *Obsolete.* in outward appearance as opposed to inner reality; outwardly; externally.
**—*n.*** **1** outward appearance; the outside; exterior. **2** that which is outside the mind; external or material world. **3** *Obsolete.* an outer part of anything.
**outwards,** outward things; externals: *Nature ... makes us all equal; we are differenc'd but by accident and outwards* (Owen Feltham).
[Old English *ūtweard* < *ūt* out (ward) + *-weard* -ward]

**out|ward-bound** (out′wərd bound′), *adj.* going out to sea; leaving port: *an outward-bound steamer.*

**out|ward-look|ing** (out′wərd lůk′ing), *adj.* interested in places and things outside one's own country or region; cosmopolitan: *With the wool of Australia, the tobacco of Indonesia, the rice of Burma, and the tropical woods of South America ... in its huge warehouses, such a city could never be other than outward-looking* (London Times).

**out|ward|ly** (out′wərd lē), *adv.* **1** on the outside or outer surface; externally. **2** toward the outside. **3** in appearance or outward manifestation: *Though frightened, the boy remained outwardly calm.*

**out|ward|ness** (out′wərd nis), *n.* **1** the state of being outward; outward existence; externality. **2** occupation with outward things.

**out|wards** (out′wərdz), *adv.* = outward.

**out|wash** (out′wôsh′, -wosh′), *n. Geology.* glacial debris, such as rock fragments, deposited beyond a glacier by streams of water from the melting ice: *There was, however, a sufficient supply of debris, lake deposits ... sandy and gravelly outwash to fill the basin completely so that in the end the lake consisted only of a thin skin of water* (G. H. Drury).

**out|watch** (out woch′, -wôch′), *v.t.* **1** to watch longer or more carefully than. **2** to watch until the disappearance or end of.

**out|wear** (out wãr′), *v.t.,* **-wore, -worn, -wear|ing.** **1** to wear longer than; be useful or serviceable for a greater time than: *Some plastics can outwear leather. I have made a Calender for every yeare, That steele in strength, and time in durance, shall outweare* (Edmund Spenser). **2a** to wear out or to an end: *to outwear someone's patience.* **b** to exhaust in strength or endurance. **3** *Figurative.* to outlive; outgrow: *to outwear sorrow.*

**out|wear|y** (out wir′ē), *v.t.,* **-wear|ied, -wear|y-ing.** to weary to exhaustion; tire out.

**out|weigh** (out wā′), *v.t.* **1** to weigh more than: *He outweighs me by ten pounds.* **2** to exceed in value, importance, or influence: *The advantages of the plan outweigh its disadvantages.*

**out|well** (out wel′), *v.i.* to well or gush out.

**out|went** (out′went′), *v.* the past tense of **outgo.**

**out|wind** (out wind′), *v.t.,* **-wind|ed, -wind|ing.** to put out of wind or breath.

**out|wit** (out wit′), *v.t.,* **-wit|ted, -wit|ting.** **1** to get the better of by being more intelligent; be too clever for: *The prisoner outwitted his guards and escaped.* **2** *Archaic.* to surpass in wisdom or knowledge.

**out|woo** (out wü′), *v.t.* to woo or court better than.

**out|work** (*n.* out′wėrk′; *v.* out wėrk′), *n., v.,* **-worked** or **-wrought, -work|ing. —*n.*** **1** the part of the fortifications of a place lying outside the main ones; a less important defense: *the outworks of a castle.* **2** work upon the outside or exterior of anything.
**—*v.t.*** **1** to surpass in working; work harder, longer, or faster than. **2** to work out to a conclusion; complete.

**out|work|er** (out′wėr′kər), *n.* a person who works outside, as outdoors or outside a factory.

**out|worn** (*adj.* out′wôrn′, -wōrn′; *v.* out wôrn′, -wōrn′), *adj., v.* **—*adj.*** **1** worn-out: *outworn clothes.* **2** *Figurative.* out-of-date: *outworn opinions.* **3** *Figurative.* outgrown: *outworn habits.*
**—*v.*** the past participle of **outwear:** *He has outworn the coat he bought last year.*

**out|write** (out rīt′), *v.t.,* **-wrote, -writ|ten, -writ-ing.** to surpass or excel in writing; write better than.

**out|wrought** (out rôt′), *v.* outworked; a past tense and a past participle of **outwork.**

**out|yield** (out yēld′), *v.t.* to yield more than: *... late sown spring wheats have outyielded winter varieties locally* (London Times).

**ou|zel** (ü′zəl), *n.* **1** any one of certain European birds of the thrush family, such as the blackbird and the ring ouzel, black with a white ring or bar on the breast. **2** the water ouzel or dipper that often wades into deep water: *The ouzel alone of all birds dares to enter a white torrent* (John Muir). Also, **ousel.** [Old English *ōsle* blackbird, merle]

**ou|zo** (ü′zō), *n.* a licorice-flavored apéritif derived from resinated Greek wine. [< New Greek *ouzôn*]

**o|va** (ō′və), *n.* plural of **ovum.**

**o|val** (ō′vəl), *adj., n.* **—*adj.*** **1** shaped like an egg: *The oval eggplant is named for its shape.* **2** shaped like an ellipse; ellipsoidal: *the oval path of the earth around the sun.*
**—*n.*** **1** something having an oval shape, such as some athletic fields, a track, or a plane figure. **2** *U.S. Informal.* a football.
[< New Latin *ovalis* < Latin *ōvum* egg] **—o′val-ness,** *n.*

**ov|al|bu|min** (ōv′al byü′mən), *n.* the albumin of egg white.

**o|val|i|ty** (ō val′ə tē), *n.* **1** the condition of being oval: *... charmingly oval-faced (that ovality coincided with the idea of feminine beauty in the eighteen-nineties)* (Vladimir Nabokov). **2** the fact or condition of being ovalized: *... vibration-induced engine ovality* (New Scientist).

**o|val|ize** (ō′və līz), *v.,* **-ized, -iz|ing. —*v.t.*** to make oval: *to ovalize a round neckline.*
**—*v.i.*** to become oval; stretch out of true circular shape: *The Boeing 747 ... engines were modified to correct a tendency to "ovalize"* (John B. Bentley).

**o|val|ly** (ō′vəl lē), *adv.* in an oval form.

**Oval Office,** the office of the President of the United States: *There are few men on the Hill who have got this appealing picture of the man in the Oval Office* (Time).

**o|val|oid** (ō′və loid), *adj.* resembling an oval; ovoid.

**oval window,** a membrane in the ears of mammals and other vertebrates connecting the middle ear with the inner ear. See picture under **ear**[1].

**O|vam|bo** (ō väm′bō), *n., pl.* **-bo** or **-bos,** *adj.* **—*n.*** a member of a Bantu tribe living in northern South West Africa.
**—*adj.*** of or having to do with the Ovambo.

**o|var|i|an** (ō vãr′ē ən), *adj.* of or having to do with an ovary.

**o|var|i|ec|to|mize** (ō vãr′ē ek′tə mīz), *v.t.,* **-mized, -miz|ing.** to remove (an ovary) by surgery.

**o|var|i|ec|to|my** (ō vãr′ē ek′tə mē), *n., pl.* **-mies.** = ovariotomy.

**o|var|i|ot|o|my** (ō vãr′ē ot′ə mē), *n., pl.* **-mies.** surgical incision into or removal of an ovary. [< New Latin *ovarium* ovary + Greek *-tomiā* a cutting]

**o|va|ri|tis** (ō′və rī′tis), *n.* inflammation of an ovary.

***o|va|ry** (ō′vər ē), *n., pl.* **-ries. 1** the organ of a female animal in which eggs and sex hormones are produced. **2** the part of a flowering plant enclosing the young seeds. It is the enlarged lower part of the pistil. See diagram under **flower**. **3** the core or pit of a fleshy fruit. [< New Latin *ovarium* < Latin *ōvum* egg + *-ārium* -ary]

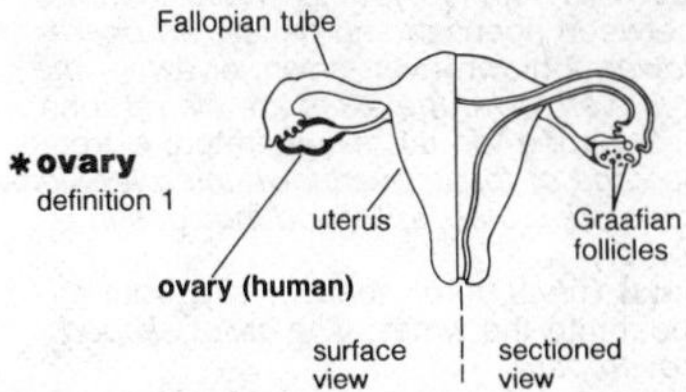


***o|vate**[1] (ō′vāt), *adj.* egg-shaped: *an ovate leaf.* [< Latin *ōvātus* < *ōvum* egg] **—o′vate|ly**, *adv.*

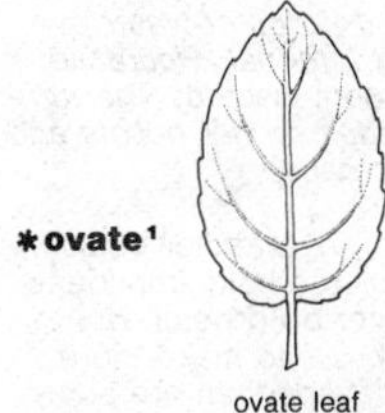


**o|vate**[2] (ō′vāt), *n.* a person awarded the third degree of achievement in poetry and music at an eisteddfod: *... the green robes of the ovates and the barbs' blue ones* (Punch). [< Greek *ouateis*, probably < Gaulish]

**o|va|tion** (ō vā′shən), *n.* **1** an enthusiastic public welcome; burst of loud clapping or cheering: *The President received a great ovation.* **2** a lesser celebration than a triumph, given to a victorious commander in ancient Rome. [< Latin *ovātiō, -ōnis* < *ovāre* rejoice]

**ov|en** (uv′ən), *n.* **1** an enclosed space, usually in a stove or near a fireplace, for baking food. **2** a small furnace for heating or drying pottery; kiln. [Old English *ofen*] **—ov′en|like′**, *adj.*

**ov|en|bird** (uv′ən bėrd′), *n.* any one of various birds that build nests with dome-shaped roofs something like a primitive oven. The ovenbird of North America is a wood warbler that has an olive-brown back, black-streaked white breast, and orange crown. It nests on the ground.

**ov|en|proof** (uv′ən prüf′), *adj.* made of material that can withstand the heat of an oven without cracking.

**ov|en-read|y** (uv′ən red′ē), *adj.* prepared for immediate baking: *oven-ready chickens or ducklings.*

**ov|en|ware** (uv′ən wãr′), *n.* a dish or dishes for baking that can withstand the heat of an oven.

**o|ver** (ō′vər), *prep., adv., adj., n., v.* **—*prep.* 1** above in place or position: *the roof over one's head.* **2** above, as in authority or power: *We have a captain over us.* **3** above and to the other side of; from side to side of; across: *to leap over a wall, to fly over the ocean, to cross over the road, to walk over a bridge.* **4** on the other side of: *lands over the sea.* **5** out and down from; down from the edge of: *The ball rolled over the edge of the cliff.* **6** on; upon: *a coat over one's shoulders, a blanket lying over a bed.* **7** at all or various places on: *A smile came over her face. Farms were scattered over the valley.* **8** here and there on or in; throughout: *We shall travel over the United States on our summer vacation.* **9** through every part of; all through: *The student went over his notes before the test. He went over everything in his pockets, looking for the letter.* **10** from end to end of; along: *We drove over the new thruway.* **11** during: *payments lasting over a period of years. He wrote that book over many years.* **12** more than; beyond: *over sixty miles. It costs over ten dollars. He likes golf over all other sports.* **13** in reference to; about; concerning: *He is worried over his health.* **14** while engaged in or concerned with: *to talk over dinner. Don't go to sleep over your work.* **15** until the end of: *to stay over the weekend.* **16** by means of: *to talk over the telephone.*

**—*adv.* 1** above; on high: *to hang over.* **2** from side to side; across a space or distance: *Go over to the store for me.* **3** from one to another: *Hand the money over. He willed the house over to his son.* **4** over and above the top of something: *The soup boiled over. Climb over into the garden.* **5** down; out and down (from an edge or from an upright position): *The ball rolled too near the edge and went over.* **6** above or upon; so as to cover the surface, or affect the whole surface: *to paint a wall over. Cover the tar over with sand until it has hardened.* **7** on the other side; at some distance: *over in Europe, over by the hill.* **8** from beginning to end; at some length: *to talk a matter over, to read a newspaper over.* **9** in excess or addition; more; besides: *to receive the full sum and something over.* **10** so as to bring the upper side or end down or under; upside down: *to turn over a page. Roll over.* **11** through a region, area, or other place: *to travel all over.* **12** again; once more; in repetition: *He did that problem three times over, before he got the right answer.* **13** too; excessively (often used in compounds): *to be overcareful. I am not over well.* **14** throughout or beyond a period of time: *Please stay over until Monday.*

**—*adj.* 1** at an end; done; past: *The play is over; let's go home.* **2** higher in authority or station (used chiefly in compounds): *an overlord.* **3** extra; surplus: *to pay for overtime. There was a copy of the bylaws for each club member and three copies over.* **4** upper; higher up: *the over eyelid.* **5** serving to cover something; outer: *an over drapery.* **6** too much; too great; excessive (used chiefly in compounds): *an overuse of drugs.*

**—*n.* 1** an amount in excess; extra. **2** *Military.* a shot which strikes beyond the target, especially while firing to adjust the range. **3** *Cricket.* **a** the number of balls (usually six) delivered between successive changes of bowlers. **b** the part of the game between such changes.

**—*v.t.*** *Archaic.* to leap or jump over; clear.

**—*v.i.*** *Archaic.* to go over; pass over.

**all over.** See under **all**.

**over again**, once more: *Let's do that problem over again.*

**over against, a** opposite to; in front of: *a house over against the park.* **b** so as to bring out a difference: *to consider one book over against another.*

**over and above**, in addition to; besides: *He had some repairs to pay for over and above the cost of the car.*

**over and over**, again and again; repeatedly: *I have told them over and over; they should know what to do. Play the piece over and over until you do it right.*

**over one's head.** See under **head**.

**over there**, *U.S. Informal.* in Europe at the scene of World War I: *The Yanks are coming ... and we won't be back till it's over over there* (George M. Cohan).

**over with**, *Informal.* done; finished: *Let's hurry and get the job over with.*

**put (one) over on.** See under **put**[1].

[Old English *ofer*]

**—*Syn.*** *prep.* **1, 2 Over, above** express a relation in which one thing is thought of as being higher than another. **Over**, the opposite of *under*, suggests being directly higher or in the position or space immediately higher up: *Carry the umbrella over your head. A sergeant is over a corporal.* **Above**, opposed to *below* and *beneath*, suggests being on or at or rising to a higher level, but seldom suggests being straight up or in a direct connection: *The plane flew above the clouds. An admiral is above a sergeant.*

▶ **Over with** is used in informal speech and writing to mean over or finished. Spoken: *I'd like to get this over with today.* More formal: *I'd like to get this finished today.*

**over-**, *prefix.* **1** above: *Overhead* = *above the head.*
**2** higher in rank; superior: *Overlord* = *superior lord.*
**3** across: *Overseas* = *across the seas.*
**4** too; too much; too long: *Overcrowded* = *too crowded. Overburden* = *burden too much.*
**5** above normal; extra: *Oversize* = *above normal size. Overtime* = *extra time.*
**6** being above; worn as an outer covering: *Overcoat* = *coat worn as an outer covering.*
[< *over*]

**If an adjective beginning with** *over-* **is not specially defined in this dictionary, its meaning may be learned by putting** *too* **in place of** *over.* **Some such words are:**

**o′ver|ab|ste′mi|ous**
**o′ver|a|cute′**
**o′ver|ag|gres′sive**
**o′ver|am|bi′tious**
**o′ver|ap′pre|hen′sive**
**o′ver|apt′**
**o′ver|at|ten′tive**
**o′ver|bash′ful**
**o′ver|big′**
**o′ver|bit′ter**
**o′ver|boun′te|ous**
**o′ver|bred′**
**o′over|bright′**
**o′ver|ca′pa|ble**
**o′ver|cap′tious**
**o′ver|care′less**
**o′ver|cas′u|al**
**o′ver|char′i|ta|ble**
**o′ver|child′ish**
**o′ver|cir′cum|spect**
**o′ver|civ′il**
**o′ver|civ′il|ized**
**o′ver|clean′**
**o′ver|cold′**
**o′ver|com′mon**
**o′ver|com|pet′i|tive**
**o′ver|com|pla′cent**
**o′ver|com′plex**
**o′ver|con′sci|en′tious**
**o′ver|con′scious**
**o′ver|con|serv′a|tive**
**o′ver|con|sid′er|ate**
**o′ver|cor|rect′**
**o′ver|cor|rupt′**
**o′ver|cost′ly**
**o′ver|cour′te|ous**
**o′ver|cov′e|tous**
**o′ver|cred′u|lous**
**o′ver|cun′ning**
**o′ver|dain′ty**
**o′ver|dear′**
**o′ver|de|lib′er|ate**
**o′ver|del′i|cate**
**o′ver|de|sir′ous**
**o′ver|de|tailed′**
**o′ver|dig′ni|fied**
**o′ver|dis′ci|plined**
**o′ver|dra|mat′ic**
**o′ver|ear′ly**
**o′ver|ear′nest**
**o′ver|eas′y**
**o′ver|e|lab′o|rate**
**o′ver|e|mo′tion|al**
**o′ver|em|phat′ic**
**o′ver|en|thu′si|as′tic**
**o′ver|ex|act′**
**o′ver|ex|cit′a|ble**
**o′ver|ex|plic′it**
**o′ver|ex|u′ber|ant**
**o′ver|fa|mil′iar**
**o′ver|far′**
**o′ver|fast′**
**o′ver|fas|tid′i|ous**
**o′ver|fat′**
**o′ver|fear′ful**
**o′ver|flu′ent**
**o′ver|fool′ish**
**o′ver|for′mal**
**o′ver|for′ward**
**o′ver|frail′**
**o′ver|fre′quent**
**o′ver|fruit′ful**
**o′ver|gen′er|ous**
**o′ver|gen′ial**
**o′ver|gen′tle**
**o′ver|glad′**
**o′ver|grate′ful**
**o′ver|greas′y**
**o′ver|greed′y**
**o′ver|hap′py**
**o′ver|har′dy**
**o′ver|harsh′**
**o′ver|haugh′ty**
**o′ver|i|mag′i|na|tive**
**o′ver|im|pul′sive**
**o′ver|in′tel|lec′tu|al**
**o′ver|ir′ri|ta|ble**
**o′ver|jeal′ous**
**o′ver|joy′ful**
**o′ver|joy′ous**
**o′ver|ju|di′cious**
**o′ver|keen′**
**o′ver|kind′**
**o′ver|late′**
**o′ver|lav′ish**
**o′ver|lean′**
**o′ver|lib′er|al**
**o′ver|lit′tle**
**o′ver|live′ly**
**o′ver|log′i|cal**
**o′ver|lov′ing**
**o′ver|lus′cious**
**o′ver|lust′y**
**o′ver|lux|u′ri|ant**
**o′ver|man′y**
**o′ver|mas′ter|ful**
**o′ver|ma|ture′**
**o′ver|meek′**
**o′ver|mel′low**
**o′ver|mer′ci|ful**
**o′ver|mer′ry**
**o′ver|mild′**
**o′ver|mod′est**
**o′ver|moist′**
**o′ver|mourn′ful**
**o′ver|neat′**
**o′ver|neg′li|gent**
**o′ver|nerv′ous**
**o′ver|nu′mer|ous**
**o′ver|o|be′di|ent**
**o′ver|ob|se′qui|ous**
**o′ver|of|fi′cious**
**o′ver|of′ten**
**o′ver|op′ti|mist′ic**
**o′ver|par′tial**
**o′ver|par|tic′u|lar**
**o′ver|pas′sion|ate**
**o′ver|per|emp′to|ry**
**o′ver|plau′si|ble**
**o′ver|plen′ti|ful**
**o′ver|plump′**
**o′ver|pop′u|lar**
**o′ver|pop′u|lous**
**o′ver|pos′i|tive**
**o′ver|pow′er|ful**
**o′ver|pre|cise′**
**o′ver|pre|sump′tu|ous**
**o′ver|priv′i|leged**
**o′ver|prompt′**
**o′ver|pub′li|cized**
**o′ver|quick′**
**o′ver|rash′**
**o′ver|read′y**
**o′ver|re|fined′**
**o′ver|re|li′gious**
**o′ver|rep|re|sent′ed**
**o′ver|res′o|lute**
**o′ver|rich′**
**o′ver|rife′**
**o′ver|right′eous**
**o′ver|rig′id**
**o′ver|rig′or|ous**
**o′ver|rude′**
**o′ver|sad′**
**o′ver|san′guine**
**o′ver|sau′cy**
**o′ver|scent′ed**
**o′ver|scru′pu|lous**
**o′ver|sea′soned**
**o′ver|sen′si|ble**
**o′ver|sen′si|tive**
**o′ver|sen′ti|men′tal**
**o′ver|se′ri|ous**
**o′ver|ser′vile**
**o′ver|se|vere′**
**o′ver|sharp′**
**o′ver|short′**
**o′ver|si′lent**
**o′ver|sim′ple**
**o′ver|skep′ti|cal**
**o′ver|slow′**
**o′ver|small′**
**o′ver|soft′**
**o′ver|sol′emn**
**o′ver|so|lic′i|tous**
**o′ver|soon′**
**o′ver|squeam′ish**
**o′ver|stiff′**
**o′ver|strong′**
**o′ver|stu′di|ous**
**o′ver|suf|fi′cient**
**o′ver|su′per|sti′tious**
**o′ver|sure′**
**o′ver|sus|cep′ti|ble**
**o′ver|sus|pi′cious**
**o′ver|sweet′**
**o′ver|talk′a|tive**
**o′ver|tame′**
**o′ver|tech′ni|cal**
**o′ver|te′di|ous**
**o′ver|ten′der**
**o′ver|thick′**
**o′ver|thought′ful**
**o′ver|thrif′ty**
**o′ver|tight′**
**o′ver|tim′or|ous**
**o′ver|trim′**
**o′ver|truth′ful**
**o′ver|ven′ture|some**
**o′ver|vig′or|ous**
**o′ver|vit′ri|fied**
**o′ver|weak′**
**o′ver|well′**
**o′ver|wet′**
**o′ver|word′y**
**o′ver|zeal′ous**

**Pronunciation Key:** hat, āge, cãre, fär; let, ēqual, tėrm; it, īce; hot, ōpen, ôrder; oil, out; cup, pu̇t, rüle; child; long; thin; ᴛʜen; zh, measure; ə represents **a** in about, **e** in taken, **i** in pencil, **o** in lemon, **u** in circus.

**If a noun beginning with *over* is not specially defined in this dictionary, its meaning may be learned by putting *too much* or *excessive* in place of *over*. Some such words are:**

**o'ver|a|nal'y|sis**
**o'ver|at|ten'tion**
**o'ver|cau'tious|ness**
**o'ver|civ'i|li|za'tion**
**o'ver|clas'si|fi|ca'tion**
**o'ver|com'pli|ca'tion**
**o'ver|con'cen|tra'tion**
**o'ver|con|cern'**
**o'ver|con|ges'tion**
**o'ver|con|sump'tion**
**o'ver|cre|du'li|ty**
**o'ver|cul'ti|va'tion**
**o'ver|cut'**
**o'ver|de|mand'**
**o'ver|de|pend'ence**
**o'ver|de|sign'**
**o'ver|dil'i|gence**
**o'ver|dos'age**
**o'ver|e|lab'o|ra'tion**
**o'ver|em|ploy'ment**
**o'ver|en|thu'si|asm**
**o'ver|ex'er|cise**
**o'ver|ex|pan'sion**
**o'ver|fer'ti|li|za'tion**
**o'ver|fre'quen|cy**
**o'ver|gen'er|al|i|za'tion**
**o'ver|in|fla'tion**
**o'ver|in|sist'ence**
**o'ver|in|ten'si|ty**
**o'ver|in|ter'pre|ta'tion**
**o'ver|loud'ness**
**o'ver|neg'li|gence**
**o'ver|op'ti|mism**
**o'ver|or'gan|i|za'tion**
**o'ver|pro|vi'sion**
**o'ver|reg'u|la'tion**
**o'ver|re|li'ance**
**o'ver|rep're|sen|ta'tion**
**o'ver|se|ver'i|ty**
**o'ver|sim|plic'i|ty**
**o'ver|spec'u|la'tion**
**o'ver|stim'u|la'tion**
**o'ver|stud'y**
**o'ver|u'ti|li|za'tion**
**o'ver|wor'ry**
**o'ver|zeal'ous|ness**

**If a verb beginning with *over* is not specially defined in this dictionary, its meaning may be learned by putting ___ *too much* in place of *over*___. Some such words are:**

**o'ver|as|sess'**
**o'ver|bake'**
**o'ver|boil'**
**o'ver|bor'row**
**o'ver|breed'**
**o'ver|broil'**
**o'ver|com'pli|cate**
**o'ver|con|trol'**
**o'ver|cook'**
**o'ver|cor|rect'**
**o'ver|cor|rupt'**
**o'ver|cul'ti|vate**
**o'ver|cut'**
**o'ver|dec'o|rate**
**o'ver|de|mand'**
**o'ver|de|sign'**
**o'ver|ed'it**
**o'ver|e|lab'o|rate**
**o'ver|es|teem'**
**o'ver|ex'er|cise**
**o'ver|ex|pand'**
**o'ver|fer'ti|lize**
**o'ver|gen'er|al|ize**
**o'ver|glo'ri|fy**
**o'ver|gov'ern**
**o'ver|grat'i|fy**
**o'ver|hard'en**
**o'ver|im|press'**
**o'ver|in|crease'**
**o'ver|in|flate'**
**o'ver|in'tel|lec'tu|al|ize**
**o'ver|in|ter'pret**
**o'ver|lean'**
**o'ver|learn'**
**o'ver|light'**
**o'ver|lin'ger**
**o'ver|meas'ure**
**o'ver|mech'a|nize**
**o'ver|mix'**
**o'ver|mort'gage**
**o'ver|mourn'**
**o'ver|mul'ti|ply**
**o'ver|nour'ish**
**o'ver|pam'per**
**o'ver|plant'**
**o'ver|press'**
**o'ver|pro|mote'**
**o'ver|pro|tect'**
**o'ver|prove'**
**o'ver|pro|vide'**
**o'ver|pro|voke'**
**o'ver|pun'ish**
**o'ver|pur'chase**
**o'ver|rank'**
**o'ver|reg'u|late**
**o'ver|rip'en**
**o'ver|salt'**
**o'ver|sen'ti|men'tal|ize**
**o'ver|short'en**
**o'ver|sim'pli|fy**
**o'ver|spe'cial|ize**
**o'ver|spec'u|late**
**o'ver|staff'**
**o'ver|stim'u|late**
**o'ver|store'**
**o'ver|stud'y**
**o'ver|tar'ry**
**o'ver|trim'**
**o'ver|trust'**
**o'ver|u'ti|lize**
**o'ver|wor'ry**

**o|ver|a|bound** (ō'vər ə bound'), *v.i.* to abound to excess.

**o|ver|a|bun|dance** (ō'ver ə bun'dəns), *n.* excessive abundance; too abundant a supply.

**o|ver|a|bun|dant** (ō'vər ə bun'dənt), *adj.* too abundant; superabundant. — **o'ver|a|bun'dant|ly**, *adv.*

**o|ver|a|chieve** (ō'vər ə chēv'), *v.t., v.i.*, **-chieved, -chiev|ing.** to do or perform better than expected: *This succinct yet passionate ballet overachieves its immediate purpose ... with a series of brilliantly visualized cinematic-style vignettes* (New York Times).

**o|ver|a|chieve|ment** (ō'vər ə chēv'ment), *n.* achievement above expectations, especially in schoolwork.

**o|ver|a|chiev|er** (ō'vər ə chēv'ər), *n.* a pupil whose work is better than might be expected from his intelligence tests.

**o|ver|a|cid|i|ty** (ō'vər ə sid'ə tē), *n.* excessive acidity; hyperacidity.

**o|ver|act** (ō'vər akt'), *v.t., v.i.* to act to excess; overdo in acting; act (a part) in an exaggerated manner.

**o|ver|ac|tion** (ō'vər ak'shən), *n.* action carried to excess.

**o|ver|ac|tive** (ō'vər ak'tiv), *adj.* too active; active to excess: *Most of the 108 children in the study were overactive, overirritable ... and doing poorly scholastically* (Science News Letter). **SYN:** hyperactive. — **o'ver|ac'tive|ly**, *adv.*

**o|ver|ac|tiv|i|ty** (ō'vər ak tiv'ə tē), *n.* excessive activity.

**o|ver|age¹** (ō'vər āj'), *adj.* past a certain age; past the age of greatest use, eligibility, or other terminable characteristic. [< *over-* + *-age*]

**o|ver|age²** (ō'vər ij), *n.* **1** a surplus of any commodity. **2a** the value of surplus goods not included in records of stock. **b** surplus money not accounted for in records of sales. [< *over* + *age*]

**o|ver|all** (ō'vər ôl'), *adj., adv., n.* — *adj.* **1** from one end to the other: *an overall length of 10 feet.* **2** including everything: *the overall estimate.*
— *adv.* **1** from one end to the other: *The room's length was ten feet overall.* **2** for the most part; in general: *Overall, he seems to be suitable for the job.*
— *n. British.* an outer garment, such as a smock, worn over clothing to protect against wet, dirt, or other damaging agent.

***o|ver|alls** (ō'vər ôlz'), *n.pl.* **1** loose trousers worn over clothes to keep them clean. Overalls are often made of denim, usually have a part that covers the chest, and may be worn instead of pants. **2** *British.* long leather or waterproof leggings reaching to the thigh.

***overalls**
definition 1

**o|ver-and-un|der** (ō'vər ən un'dər), *n.* a double-barreled shotgun in which the barrels are placed one above the other rather than side by side.

**o|ver|anx|i|e|ty** (ō'vər ang zī'ə tē), *n.* excessive anxiety.

**o|ver|anx|ious** (ō'vər angk'shəs, -ang'-), *adj.* too anxious; unnecessarily anxious. — **o'ver|anx'ious|ly**, *adv.*

**o|ver|arch** (ō'vər ärch'), *v.t.* **1** to arch over; span with or like an arch: *The street was overarched by elm trees.* **2** to curve like an arch.

**o|ver|arch|ing** (ō'vər är'ching), *adj.* **1** that arches over; forming an arch overhead: *the overarching sky, an overarching bower.* **2** *Figurative.* covering or including all; all-embracing: *All the tribes were held together within the overarching structure of the British government* (Listener).

**o|ver|arm** (ō'vər ärm'), *adj.* with the arm raised above the shoulder; overhand: *an overarm pitch.*

**o|ver|as|sess|ment** (ō'vər ə ses'mənt), *n.* an assessment that is too high or higher than usual.

**o|ver|ate** (o'vər āt'), *v.* past tense of **overeat**: *I have a stomachache because I overate. He and I overate, overdrank, overslept, just generally overdid things* (New Yorker).

**o|ver|awe** (ō'vər ô'), *v.t.*, **-awed, -aw|ing.** to overcome or restrain with awe: *Eclipses of the sun overawed primitive man.* **SYN:** intimidate, cow.

**o|ver|bal|ance** (ō'vər bal'əns), *v., -anced, -anc|ing, n.* — *v.t.* **1** to be greater than, as in weight, importance, or value; outweigh: *The gains overbalanced the losses.* **SYN:** overpower, subdue. **2** to cause to lose balance: *As he leaned over the side, his weight overbalanced the canoe and it upset.* **SYN:** upset.
— *n.* an excess of weight, value, or amount: *There is an overbalance of chemistry courses in your program.*

**o|ver|bear** (ō'vər bãr'), *v.*, **-bore, -borne** or **-born, -bear|ing.** — *v.t.* **1** to overcome by weight or force; oppress; master: *My father bore all my objections.* **SYN:** overpower, subdue. **2** to bear down by weight or force; overthrow; upset: *As a wild wave ... overbears the bark ... so they overbore Sir Lancelot and his charger* (Tennyson). **3** to overbalance; outweigh.
— *v.i.* to bear or produce too much or too many.

**o|ver|bear|ing** (ō'vər bãr'ing), *adj.* inclined to dictate; forcing others to one's own will; masterful; domineering: *We found it hard to like the new boy because of his overbearing manners. That old man is a very overbearing person.* **SYN:** dictatorial, imperious, arrogant. See syn. under **proud.** — **o'ver|bear'ing|ly**, *adv.* — **o'ver|bear'ing|ness**, *n.*

**o|ver|be|lief** (ō'vər bi lēf'), *n.* belief in more than is warranted by the evidence or in that which cannot be verified.

**o|ver|bid** (ō'vər bid'), *v.*, **-bid, -bid** or **-bid|den, -bid|ding**, *n.* — *v.t.* **1** to bid more than the value of (a thing). **2** to bid higher than (a person); outbid.
— *v.i.* to bid too high.
— *n.* the act or fact of overbidding.

**o|ver|bite** (ō'vər bīt'), *n.* the overlapping by the upper incisors of the lower incisors when the mouth is closed.

**o|ver|blouse** (ō'vər blous'), *n.* a blouse that is worn outside a skirt, shorts, or slacks, rather than being tucked in.

**o|ver|blow** (ō'vər blō'), *v.*, **-blew, -blown, -blow|ing.** — *v.t.* **1** to blow over or away. **2** to blow down; overthrow by blowing. **3** to cover by blowing over, as wind, sand, or snow.
— *v.i.* to blow hard or with too much violence: *Finding it was likely to overblow, we took in our spritsail* (Jonathan Swift).

**o|ver|blown** (ō'vər blōn'), *adj.* **1** more than full-blown; between ripeness and decay: *an overblown flower.* **2** blown over, down, or away: *the tempest is o'erblown, the skies are clear* (John Dryden). **3** carried too far; exaggerated; extreme; overdone: *one of those overblown interpretations of Biblical stories that Hollywood indulges in* (New Yorker).

**o|ver|board** (ō'vər bôrd', -bōrd'), *adv.* from a ship or boat into the water: *The sailor slipped and fell overboard.*
**go overboard**, *Informal.* to go too far in an effort, especially because of extreme enthusiasm: *She went overboard and bought three new hats at once.*
**throw overboard**, **a** to throw into the water: *The Pearl ... had thrown about 14 tons of water overboard* (Pascoe Thomas). **b** *Informal, Figurative.* to get rid of; give up; abandon; discard: *The turncoats threw overboard all their former beliefs and abjectly joined the enemy's cause.*
[< Old English *ofer bord*]

**o|ver|bod|ice** (ō'vər bod'is), *n.* an outer bodice.

**o|ver|bold** (ō'vər bōld'), *adj.* too bold; impudent. — **o'ver|bold'ly**, *adv.* — **o'ver|bold'ness**, *n.*

**o|ver|book** (ō'vər bůk'), *v.t., v.i.* to make more reservations for accommodations than are actually available (as in an airplane, ship, or hotel): *A senior official told them the aircraft was overbooked and that they had been taken off the flight on his orders* (London Times). *I know people overbook and then fail to show up* (John Ciardi).

**o|ver|bore** (ō'vər bôr', -bōr'), *v.* the past tense of **overbear.**

**o|ver|born** (ō'vər bôrn'), *v.* a past participle of **overbear.**

**o|ver|borne** (ō'vər bôrn', -bōrn'), *v.* a past participle of **overbear.**

**o|ver|bought** (ō'vər bôt'), *v.* the past tense and past participle of **overbuy.**

**o|ver|bowed** (ō'vər bōd'), *adj.* (in archery) equipped with too strong a bow.

**o|ver|bridge** (ō'vər brij'), *n.* = overpass.

**o|ver|bril|liant** (ō'vər bril'yənt), *adj.* too brilliant; overly splendid or ornate.

**o|ver|brim** (ō'vər brim'), *v.*, **-brimmed, -brim|ming.** — *v.i.* to brim over; overflow at the brim: *If the pitcher shall overbrim with water* (Scott).
— *v.t.* to flow over the brim of: *The liquor that o'erbrims the cup* (Robert Browning).

**o|ver|build** (ō'vər bild'), *v.*, **-built, -build|ing.**
— *v.t.* **1** to build too much or too elaborately: *The administrative structure was overbuilt.* **2** to build over or upon: (*Figurative.*) *aquiline his nose, and overbuilt with most impending brows* (William Cowper). **3** to build too much upon: *A city which has been overbuilt, which has 'superfluous' houses and flats by the block and mile* (Chicago Advance).
— *v.i.* to build too much; build too many houses on a site or in an area: *The recent zoning controversy ... has roused New Yorkers to a wider understanding of zoning with the threatened possibility of overbuilding* (New York Times).

**o|ver|bur|den** (*v.* ō'vər bėr'dən; *n.* ō'vər bėr'dən), *v., n.* — *v.t.* to load with too great a burden: (*Figurative.*) *A catalogue of the absurdities in which we have indulged under the influence of fear would overburden this document* (Bulletin of Atomic Scientists).
— *n.* **1** too great a burden. **2** *Mining.* clay, rock, or other matter, which has to be removed to get at a deposit of ore.

**o|ver|bur|den|some** (ō'vər bėr'dən səm), *adj.* excessively burdensome: *Too many tasks become overburdensome.*

**o|ver|burn** (ō'vər bėrn'), *v.*, **-burned, -burnt, -burn|ing.** — *v.i.* **1** to burn too much. **2** *Figurative.* to be overzealous: *overburning with ambition.* **3** to be excessive.
— *v.t.* to burn too much.

**o|ver|bur|then** (ō'vər bėr'ᴛʜən), *v.t. Archaic.* overburden.

**o|ver|bus|y** (ō'vər biz'ē), *adj.* **1** too busy. **2** obtrusively officious.

**o|ver|buy** (ō'vər bī'), *v.*, **-bought, -buy|ing.** — *v.t.* to buy on margin more (stock or other securities) than one can support if prices drop.
— *v.i.* to buy too much or beyond one's means.

**o|ver|by** (ō′vər bī′), *adv.* a little way over or across.

**o|ver|call** (*v.* ō′vər kôl′; *n.* ō′vər kôl′), *v., n.* —*v.t.* to outbid at cards.
—*v.i.* **1** to bid higher than a previous bid. **2** to make an overcall in cards: *Opponents will hardly suspect you of being strong in their suit if you choose to overcall instead of remaining silent* (Manchester Guardian Weekly).
—*n.* a higher bid at cards, especially one made with minimal values over an opponent's bid when one's partner has passed or not bid: ... *to make shutout calls when partner has opened the bidding and an opponent has made a simple overcall* (Observer).

**o|ver|came** (ō′vər kām′), *v.* the past tense of **overcome**: *She finally overcame her shyness.*

**o|ver|can|o|py** (ō′vər kan′ə pē), *v.t.*, **-pied, -py|ing.** to cover over with or as if with a canopy.

**o|ver|ca|pac|i|ty** (ō′vər kə pas′ə tē), *n., pl.* **-ties.** productive capacity above what is required or profitable.

**o|ver|cap|i|tal|ize** (ō′vər kap′ə tə līz), *v.t.*, **-ized, -iz|ing.** to fix or estimate the capital of (a company or other enterprise) at too high an amount.
—**o′ver|cap′i|tal|i|za′tion,** *n.*

**o|ver|care** (ō′vər kãr′), *n.* excessive care or anxiety.

**o|ver|care|ful** (ō′vər kãr′fəl), *adj.* too careful.
—**o′ver|care′ful|ly,** *adv.* —**o′ver|care′ful|ness,** *n.*

**o|ver|cast** (ō′vər kast′, -käst′), *adj., v.,* **-cast, -cast|ing,** *n.* —*adj.* **1** cloudy or dark; gloomy: *The sky was overcast before the storm.* (*Figurative.*) *an overcast quality of depression.* **SYN**: obscure, becloud. **2** sewed with overcast stitches.
—*v.t.* **1** to cover (the sky or sun) with clouds or darkness; make gloomy: *The distress spreads as wintry gray overcasts a sky* (George W. Cable). **2** to sew over and through (the edges of a seam) with long stitches to prevent raveling.
—*v.i.* to become dark or cloudy; become gloomy: (*Figurative.*) *to overcast with dire predictions.*
—*n.* **1** a sky covered with clouds: ... *straight up into the grey overcast* (Time). **2** the clouds covering the sky: *The sun was obscured by a cloudy overcast.* **3** *Figurative.* gloom: *There was a dark overcast to the depressed forecast of the future.*

**o|ver|cast|ing** (ō′vər kas′ting, -käs′-), *n.* **1** the act or process of coating a brick or stone surface with a layer of plaster or other material. **2** the use of overcast stitching to edge a fabric.

**o|ver|cau|tion** (ō′vər kô′shən), *n.* excessive caution.

**o|ver|cau|tious** (ō′vər kô′shəs), *adj.* too cautious: *an overcautious estimate.*

**o|ver|cen|tral|i|za|tion** (ō′vər sen′trə lə zā′shən), *n.* **1** the act or process of overcentralizing: *overcentralization of government.* **2** the condition of being overcentralized: *an industry marked by overcentralization.*

**o|ver|cen|tral|ize** (ō′vər sen′trə līz), *v.t.*, **-ized, -iz|ing.** to centralize in excess of what is necessary, profitable, or desirable: *We are one of the largest countries in the world* (*in numbers, I mean, not geographical size*) *ruled by a unitary centralized system, and in my opinion, at least, we are ... overcentralized* (London Times).

**o|ver|cer|ti|fi|ca|tion** (ō′vər sėr′tə fə kā′shən), *n.* **1** the action of overcertifying. **2** the condition of being overcertified.

**o|ver|cer|ti|fy** (ō′vər sėr′tə fī), *v.t.*, **-fied, -fy|ing.** to certify (a check) drawn for an amount greater than the balance in the drawer's account.

**o|ver|charge** (*v.* ō′vər chärj′; *n.* ō′vər chärj′), *v.,* **-charged, -charg|ing,** *n.* —*v.t.* **1** to charge too high a price: *The grocer overcharged you for the eggs.* **2** to load too heavily; fill too full: *The overcharged old musket burst.* **3** *Figurative.* to exaggerate.
—*v.i.* to charge too much.
—*n.* **1** a charge that is too great. **2** too heavy or too full a load.

**o|ver|check[1]** (ō′vər chek′), *n.* an overcheck rein or bridle.

**o|ver|check[2]** (ō′vər chek′), *n.* a checked pattern in one color or design superimposed on a different pattern of checks on a fabric: *A huge-patterned gray-and-black plaid covers the cotton, and the red overcheck on it matches the jersey sash* (New Yorker).

**overcheck bridle,** a bridle fitted with an overcheck rein.

**overcheck rein,** a kind of checkrein passing over a horse's head between the ears.

**o|ver|choice** (ō′vər chois′), *n.* too many choices: *He describes the explosive growth of choice in the field of consumer goods, education, art and music ... Indeed it is the problem of overchoice, as he sees it, that helps to explain the identity crisis about which so much has already been written* (Listener).

**o|ver|climb** (ō′vər klīm′), *v.t.*, **-climbed** or (*Archaic*) **-clomb, -climb|ing.** to climb over.

**o|ver|clothes** (ō′vər klōz′, -klōᴛʜz′), *n.pl.* outer garments.

**o|ver|cloud** (ō′vər kloud′), *v.t., v.i.* **1** to cloud over or become clouded over; darken. **2** *Figurative.* to make or become gloomy.

**o|ver|coat** (ō′vər kōt′), *n.* **1** a heavy coat worn over the regular clothing for warmth in cold weather: *the only argument available with an east wind is to put on your overcoat* (Lowell). **2** an outer coating or covering: *Photomicrographs show the emptied protein overcoat that encloses a virus* (Scientific American).

**o|ver|coat|ing** (ō′vər kō′ting), *n.* the stuff or material from which overcoats are made.

**o|ver|col|lar** (ō′vər kol′ər), *n.* a collar on a coat that is made of a different fabric or color than the coat itself: *An overcollar of black Russian sable or chinchilla can be snapped in* (New Yorker).

**o|ver|col|or** (ō′vər kul′ər), *v.t.* **1** to color too highly. **2** *Figurative.* to exaggerate.

**o|ver|col|ored** (ō′vər kul′ərd), *adj.* brightly colored, so as to be in bad taste: *The overlarge and overcolored automobile* (Alfred Kazin).

**o|ver|com|a|ble** (ō′vər kum′ə bəl), *adj.* that can be overcome.

**o|ver|come** (ō′vər kum′), *v.,* **-came, -come, -com|ing.** —*v.t.* **1** to get the better of; win the victory over; conquer; defeat: *We can overcome difficulties, enemies, and our own faults. Rage overcame her and she burst into angry tears.* **SYN**: overpower, vanquish, master. See syn. under **defeat. 2** to make weak or helpless; overwhelm: *The child was overcome by weariness and slept deeply.* **3** *Archaic.* to spread over; overrun: *Trees .... o'ercome with moss and baleful mistletoe* (Shakespeare).
—*v.i.* to gain the victory; conquer: *To him that overcometh will I grant to sit with me in my throne* (Revelation 3:21). [Old English *ofercuman*]

**o|ver|com|er** (ō′vər kum′ər), *n.* a person who overcomes, vanquishes, or surmounts.

**o|ver|com|mer|cial|ism** (ō′vər kə mėr′shə lizəm), *n.* excessive or undue commercialism: *overcommercialism of research.*

**o|ver|com|mer|cial|i|za|tion** (ō′vər kə mėr′shə lə zā′shən), *n.* excessive or undue commercialization: *Advertisers howl at any suggestion of a tax on commercials, yet a tax may be the only way to curb the overcommercialization of television and radio* (Vance Packard).

**o|ver|com|mit** (ō′vər kə mit′), *v.t.*, **-mit|ted, -mit|ting.** to commit, involve, or pledge beyond what is required or expected: *But we simply cannot do it all at once—and we are already close to being dangerously overcommitted at all levels of government* (Sidney Schanberg).

**o|ver|com|mit|ment** (ō′vər kə mit′mənt), *n.* a commitment beyond what is required or expected: *Perhaps it is time ... to investigate the drives and compulsions that have led to our overcommitment to technology* (Lewis Mumford).

**o|ver|com|pen|sate** (ō′vər kom′pən sāt), *v.i.*, **-sat|ed, -sat|ing. 1** *Psychology.* to make up for a shortcoming in one's personality by overcompensation: ... *the basic Oedipal situation of a son overcompensating by hero-worshipping his father* (Punch). **2** to make up for any deficiency in an excessive manner: *The circulatory system evidently cannot adjust quickly to the lack of gravity and overcompensates by pumping too much blood to the head* (Manchester Guardian Weekly).

**o|ver|com|pen|sa|tion** (ō′vər kom′pən sā′shən), *n.* **1** *Psychology.* an excessive effort or exaggerated attempt to make up for a shortcoming in one's personality, as by overemphasizing a particular ability or concealing one's inadequacy with a display of overconfidence: *The little man who talks too loudly and too much, who is always itching to fight a bigger fellow ... illustrates overcompensation to a feeling of inferiority* (Floyd L. Ruch). **2** an excessive compensation for any deficiency: *In order to progress from here, Notting Hill needs overcompensation. There should be a really solid increase in the staff of the social services ...* (Nesta Roberts).

**o|ver|con|fi|dence** (ō′vər kon′fə dəns), *n.* the quality or condition of being overconfident; too much confidence.

**o|ver|con|fi|dent** (ō′vər kon′fə dənt), *adj.* too confident. —**o′ver|con′fi|dent|ly,** *adv.*

**o|ver|con|tain** (ō′vər kən tān′), *v.t.* to contain or check to excess: *If a Negro writer ... overcontains his emotions, he becomes a white Negro writer* (Atlantic).

**o|ver|cooked** (ō′vər kůkt′), *adj.* cooked too much or too long.

**o|ver|cool** (ō′vər kül′), *v.t.* to cool below the temperature of fusion without bringing about solidification. It is possible, under certain conditions, to cool water to a temperature several degrees below its freezing point, without converting it into ice.

**o|ver|cor|rec|tion** (ō′vər kə rek′shən), *n.* **1** correction beyond the normal or necessary degree: *Tax increases contain certain risks—above all, of the sort of overcorrection which initiates a recession instead of checking an inflation* (Atlantic). **2** the conversion of one defect of vision into its opposite by means of a too powerful lens. **3** the surgical correction of a deformity beyond the usual degree to allow for later modification of the correction.

**o|ver|count** (ō′vər kount′), *v.t.* **1** = overestimate. **2** = outnumber.

**o|ver|cov|er** (ō′vər kuv′ər), *v.t.* to cover over; cover completely.

**o|ver|crit|i|cal** (ō′vər krit′ə kəl), *adj.* too critical; hypercritical.

**o|ver|crop** (ō′vər krop′), *v.t.*, **-cropped, -crop|ping.** to exhaust the fertility of (soil) by uninterrupted planting and harvesting.

**o|ver|crow** (ō′vər krō′), *v.t.* **1** to crow or exult over. **2** to triumph over; overcome.

**o|ver|crowd** (ō′vər kroud′), *v.t., v.i.* to crowd too much; put in too much or too many: *These people overcrowd into the already overcrowded smaller properties that lie around* (London Daily News).

**o|ver|cul|ture** (ō′vər kul′chər), *n.* a dominant culture: *In America, where the melting pot and conflict of cultures and life-styles replace a strong overculture, we lack rituals and strong agreed-upon traditions* (Harper's).

**o|ver|cup oak** (ō′vər kup′), any one of various oaks, such as the bur oak, whose acorns are covered by large cups.

**o|ver|cu|ri|ous** (ō′vər kyůr′ē əs), *adj.* curious to excess.

**o|ver|cur|tain** (ō′vər kėr′tən), *v.t.* to cover; shadow; obscure.

**o|ver|dare** (ō′vər dãr′), *v.,* **-dared, -dar|ing.** —*v.i.* to exceed in daring; dare too much or rashly; be too daring.
—*v.t.* to dishearten; discourage; daunt.

**o|ver|date** (ō′vər dāt′), *v.t.*, **-dat|ed, -dat|ing. 1** to date beyond the proper period. **2** to cause to continue beyond the proper date.

**o|ver|de|stroy** (ō′vər di stroi′), *v.i.* (of bombs) to develop more energy at the explosion center than is necessary for total destruction, thereby wasting considerable energy.
—*v.t.* to destroy in this way: *The high-pressure region of a bomb burst on or close to the ground would overdestroy the target in the near vicinity of the bomb* (The Effects of Atomic Weapons).

**o|ver|de|struc|tion** (ō′vər di struk′shən), *n.* **1** the process of overdestroying. **2** an instance of this.

**o|ver|de|ter|mined** (ō′vər di tėr′mənd), *adj. Psychoanalysis.* that results from the convergence of several distinct influences: *Freud suggested that we act as a result of a combination of forces; that what we do is, as he puts it, overdetermined* (Listener).

**o|ver|de|vel|op** (ō′vər di vel′əp), *v.t.* to develop too much or too long. If a photograph is overdeveloped, it is too dark. ... *overdeveloped curiosity, overdeveloped muscles.*

**o|ver|de|vel|op|ment** (ō′vər di vel′əp mənt), *n.* development carried too far or continued too long: *Weight lifters show overdevelopment.*

**o|ver|did** (ō′vər did′), *v.* the past tense of **overdo.**

**o|ver|dil|i|gent** (ō′vər dil′ə jənt), *adj.* diligent to excess.

**o|ver|dis|charge** (ō′vər dis chärj′), *n. Electricity.* the discharge of an accumulator or storage battery beyond the usual limit.

**o|ver|do** (ō′vər dü′), *v.,* **-did, -done, -do|ing.** —*v.t.* **1** to do too much or attempt to do too much: carry to excess: *She overdoes exercise.* **SYN**: overwork. **2** to make too much of; exaggerate: *The funny scenes in the play were overdone.* **3** to cook too much: *to overdo a roast. The vegetables were overdone.* **4** to overtax the strength of; exhaust; tire: *It might be that she was a little overdone with work and anxiety* (George Eliot). **SYN**: fatigue.
—*v.i.* to do or attempt to do too much: *She overdid and became tired.* **SYN**: overwork. [Old English *oferdōn*]

**o|ver|do|er** (ō′vər dü′ər), *n.* a person who does more than is necessary or expedient.

**o|ver|dog** (ō′vər dôg′, -dog′), *n.* the person or group that is dominant or successful in a struggle; top dog: *When I was first here, we had the advantages of the underdog. Now we have the disadvantages of the overdog* (Abba Eban).

**o|ver|done** (ō′vər dun′), *adj., v.* —*adj.* **1** carried to excess: *The wonderfully overdone upperclass*

**Pronunciation Key:** hat, āge, cãre, fär; let, ēqual, tėrm; it, īce; hot, ōpen, ôrder; **oi**l, **ou**t; cup, půt, rüle; **ch**ild; lo**ng**; **th**in; ᴛʜen; **zh**, measure; ə represents **a** in about, **e** in taken, **i** in pencil, **o** in lemon, **u** in circus.

*interiors ... are photographed ... [so] that moviegoers ... will recognize [them]* (Time). 2 overcooked: *overdone vegetables.*
—*v.* past participle of **overdo**: *Yet the harshness can be and has been overdone* (Observer).

**o|ver|door** (ō′vər dôr′, -dōr′), *adj., n.* —***adj.*** placed, or to be placed, over a door, as a decorative piece.
—***n.*** a piece of decorative work over a door.

**o|ver|dose** (*n.* ō′vər dōs′; *v.* ō′vər dōs′), *n., v.,* **-dosed, -dos|ing.** —***n.*** too big a dose; more than is needed or wanted: *an overdose of sleeping pills, an overdose of criticism.*
—***v.i.*** to take an overdose, especially of a narcotic: *to overdose on heroin.*
—***v.t.*** to give an overdose to: *to be overdosed with medication. Abbr:* OD (no periods).

**o|ver|draft** (ō′vər draft′, -dräft′), *n.* **1a** the act or fact of overdrawing an account, especially a bank account: *Mr. Orrin also told the witness that he (the witness) was improvident and had an overdraft* (London Times). **b** the amount of the excess. **2** a draft passing over a fire, such as in a furnace, or downward through a kiln.

**o|ver|dram|a|tise** (ō′vər dram′ə tīz, -drä′mə-), *v.t.,* **-tised, -tis|ing.** *Especially British.* overdramatize.

**o|ver|dram|a|tize** (ō′vər dram′ə tīz, -drä′mə-), *v.t.,* **-tized, -tiz|ing.** to present in a melodramatic way; overstate so as to impress: *A political aspirant who constantly overstates or overdramatizes his case to create shock effect* (Saturday Review).

**o|ver|draught** (ō′vər draft′, -dräft′), *n.* = overdraft.

**o|ver|draw** (ō′vər drô′), *v.,* **-drew, -drawn, -draw|ing.** —***v.t.*** **1** to draw from (a bank account, allowance, or other fund) more than the amount one has to his credit or at his disposal: *The careless man overdrew his bank account.* **2** *Figurative.* to exaggerate: *The characters in the book were greatly overdrawn.* **3** to draw or strain too much.
—***v.i.*** **1** to make an overdraft. **2** *Figurative.* to exaggerate.

**o|ver|dress** (*v.* ō′vər dres′; *n.* ō′vər dres′), *v., n.*
—***v.t., v.i.*** to dress too elaborately.
—***n.*** a dress worn over the main dress.

**o|ver|drink** (ō′vər dringk′), *v.i.,* **-drank, -drunk|en, -drink|ing.** to drink to excess: *They overeat and overdrink, and they try to forget what they really want* (J. O. Hobbes).

***o|ver|drive¹** (ō′vər drīv′), *n.* an arrangement of gears in an automobile that produces greater speed, while using less power, than when the car is in high gear: *Overdrive permits the drive shaft to turn four times for every three revolutions of the engine crankshaft* (Franklin M. Reck).

***overdrive¹**

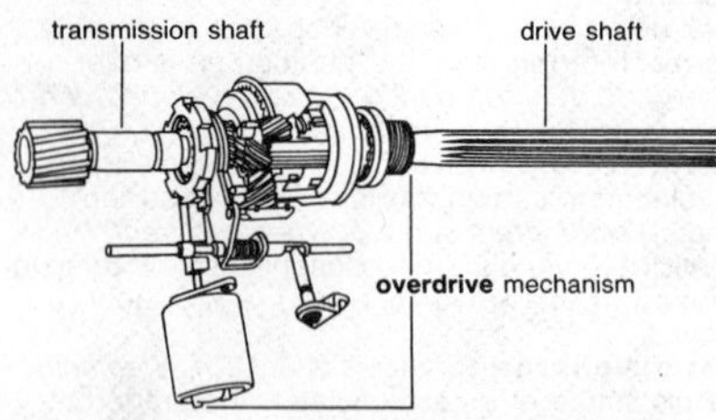


**o|ver|drive²** (ō′vər drīv′), *v.t.,* **-drove, -driv|en, -driv|ing.** **1** to drive too hard: *If men should overdrive them one day, all the flock will die* (Genesis 33:13). **2** *Figurative.* to push or carry to excess; overwork: *You must not fancy I am sick, only overdriven and under the weather* (Robert Louis Stevenson). **3** to hit a golf ball beyond.

**o|ver|drop** (ō′vər drop′), *v.t.,* **-dropped, -drop|ping.** to drop over; overhang; overshadow.

**o|ver|dry** (ō′vər drī′), *v.t.,* **-dried, -dry|ing.** to make too dry.

**o|ver|dub** (ō′vər dub′), *v.t.,* **-dubbed, -dub|bing.** to add (one or more vocal or instrumental parts) to a recording: *She also prefers to use her own voice, overdubbed several times, as a backing choir* (London Times).

**o|ver|due** (ō′vər dü′, -dyü′), *adj.* more than due; due some time ago but not yet arrived or paid: *The train is overdue. This bill is overdue.* **SYN:** belated, tardy.

**o|ver|dye** (ō′vər dī′), *v.t.,* **-dyed, -dye|ing.** **1** to dye (cloth, fabric, or yarn) with a second color over the first. **2** to dye (cloth or yarn) too long or with too dark a color.

**o|ver|ea|ger** (ō′vər ē′gər), *adj.* too eager; overanxious. —**o′ver|ea′ger|ly,** *adv.* —**o′ver|ea′ger|ness,** *n.*

**o|ver|eat** (ō′vər ēt′), *v.,* **-ate, -eat|en, -eat|ing.**
—***v.i.*** to eat too much.
—***v.t.*** to eat more than is good for (oneself): *Without doubt, the most of mankind grossly overeat themselves* (Robert Louis Stevenson).

**o|ver|eat|en** (ō′vər ē′tən), *v.* the past participle of **overeat**: *Nearly everyone has overeaten at the picnic.*

**o|ver|ed|u|cate** (ō′vər ej′ù kāt), *v.t.,* **-cat|ed, -cat|ing.** to provide with more education than is required for a job: *Finally critics contend that new students are being "overeducated" for nonexistent jobs, and would do better at technical training institutes* (Time).

**o|ver|e|lec|tri|fi|ca|tion** (ō′vər i lek′trə fə kā′shən), *n.* **1** the act or process of overelectrifying. **2** the state of being overelectrified.

**o|ver|e|lec|tri|fy** (ō′vər i lek′trə fī), *v.t.,* **-fied, -fy|ing.** to electrify too much or beyond necessary or desirable limits.

**o|ver|em|pha|sis** (ō′vər em′fə sis), *n.* **1** too much force; undue stress; unjustified importance, often resulting in an undesirable outcome: *... the slightest overemphasis can transmute its simplicity into banality* (New Yorker). **2** too much force given to a particular syllable, word, or phrase.

**o|ver|em|pha|size** (ō′vər em′fə sīz), *v.t.,* **-sized, -siz|ing.** **1** to give too much force or emphasis to; stress too much: *He overemphasized the details and ruined the story.* **2** to call too much attention to: *Because the scenery was overemphasized with loud colors, nobody paid any attention to the actors.*

**o|ver|en|dowed** (ō′vər en doud′), *adj.* having an abundance of; being well supplied with: *The villages ... are overendowed with supermarkets* (Maclean's).

**o|ver|en|treat** (ō′vər en trēt′), *v.t.* to persuade or gain over by entreaty.

**o|ver|es|ti|mate** (*v.* ō′vər es′tə māt; *n.* ō′vər es′tə mit), *v.,* **-mat|ed, -mat|ing,** *n.* —***v.t., v.i.*** to estimate at too high a value, amount, or rate: *Men often overestimate their capacity for evil* (Hawthorne). **SYN:** overrate.
—***n.*** an estimate that is too high. **SYN:** overvaluation.

**o|ver|es|ti|ma|tion** (ō′vər es′tə mā′shən), *n.* **1** the act of overestimating. **2** the condition of being overestimated.

**o|ver|ex|cite** (ō′vər ik sīt′), *v.t.,* **-cit|ed, -cit|ing.** to excite too much.

**o|ver|ex|cite|ment** (ō′vər ik sīt′mənt), *n.* **1** the state of being overexcited. **2** too much excitement.

**o|ver|ex|ert** (ō′vər ig zėrt′), *v.t.* to exert too much.

**o|ver|ex|er|tion** (ō′vər ig zėr′shən), *n.* too much exertion.

**o|ver|ex|ploit** (ō′vər ek sploit′), *v.t.* to exploit too much: *If we fail to control our economic system, we overexploit our resources* (Julian Huxley)

**o|ver|ex|ploi|ta|tion** (ō′vər eks′ploi tā′shən), *n.* too much exploitation, especially of a natural resource.

**o|ver|ex|pose** (ō′vər ik spōz′), *v.t.,* **-posed, -pos|ing.** **1** to expose too much. **2** *Photography.* to expose (a film or negative) too long to light.

**o|ver|ex|po|sure** (ō′vər ik spō′zhər), *n.* too much or too long an exposure: *Underexposing the negative results in loss of detail in the shadows, whereas overexposure results in loss of detail in the high lights* (Hardy and Perrin).

**o|ver|ex|qui|site** (ō′vər ek′skwi zit, -ik skwiz′it), *adj.* excessively or unduly exquisite or exact; too nice; too careful or anxious.

**o|ver|ex|tend** (ō′vər ik stend′), *v.t.* **1** to spread (something) out too far; to expand over too large an area: *[He] ... said Russia had overextended herself in her drive for world domination* (New York Times). **2** *Figurative.* to overdo or belabor (something) to the point of fatique or unwarranted excess: *to overextend one's visit. However much Miss West overextends her material, her turn of phrase is a delight* (Charles J. Rolo). **3** *Finance.* to take on financial obligations to the point where there are too few assets to cover them and bankruptcy is imminent: *Typically, the small businessman stretches his limited capital too far, overextends his credit in order to get customers* (George S. Odiorne).

**o|ver|ex|tend|ed** (ō′vər ik sten′did), *adj.* having greater liabilities than assets: *The American family, buying hard goods on the newly discovered installment plan, was equally exposed to the hazard of overextended credit* (Bulletin of Atomic Scientists).

**o|ver|ex|ten|sion** (ō′vər ik sten′shən), *n.* **1** the act or process of overextending. **2** something overextended: (*Figurative.*) *The play had been little more than "an overextension of a quite small idea"* (Time).

**o|ver|fall** (ō′vər fôl′), *n.* **1a** a turbulent stretch of water caused by the meeting of currents or by a strong current running over a submerged ridge or shoal. **b** such a ridge or shoal. **2** a sudden drop in the sea-bottom. **3** a place for the overflow of water, as from a canal.

**o|ver|fa|mil|iar|i|ty** (ō′vər fə mil′yar′ə tē), *n.* too much familiarity.

**o|ver|fa|tigue** (ō′vər fə tēg′), *n.* fatigue beyond the normal limits of recovery.

**o|ver|feed** (ō′vər fēd′), *v.t., v.i.,* **-fed, -feed|ing.** to feed too much; feed to excess.

**o|ver|fill** (ō′vər fil′), *v.t., v.i.* to fill too full; fill so as to cause overflowing.

**o|ver|fine** (ō′vər fīn′), *adj.* too fine. —**o′ver|fine′ness,** *n.*

**o|ver|fired** (ō′vər fīrd′), *adj.* exposed to too great a heat in firing, resulting in the running together of the colors, or the melting of the enamel or the ceramic work itself.

**o|ver|fish** (ō′vər fish′), *v.i.* to catch fish faster than they can reproduce, thereby gradually depleting the fisheries. —***v.t.*** to deplete (a fishery or a kind of fish) by excessive fishing: *Many of the area's salmon fisheries [are] overfished* (Science News Letter).

**o|ver|flight** (ō′vər flīt′), *n.* the act of flying over the territory of a country: *Israel was about to ban the overflights of U.S. and British planes across Israeli territory* (Time).

**o|ver|flood** (ō′vər flud′), *v.t.* to pour over in or as if in a flood: *The rising river overflooded the dike onto the fields.*

**o|ver|flow** (*v.* ō′vər flō′; *n., adj.* ō′vər flō′), *v.,* **-flowed, -flown, -flow|ing,** *n., adj.* —***v.i.*** **1** to flow over the bounds: *Rivers often overflow in the spring.* **2** to have the contents flowing over: *My cup is overflowing.* **3** to pass from one part to another because of lack of room: *The crowd overflowed from the auditorium into the hall.* **4** *Figurative.* to be very abundant: *an overflowing harvest, overflowing kindness; ... to make the coming hour o'erflow with joy* (Shakespeare).
—***v.t.*** **1** to cover or flood: *The river overflowed my garden. Behold, waters rise up ... and shall overflow the land, and all that is therein* (Jeremiah 47:2). **SYN:** inundate, overrun. **2a** to flow over the top of: *Stop pouring! The milk is overflowing the cup.* **b** to fill to the point of overflowing: (*Figurative.*) *So they overflowed his house, smoked his cigars and drank his health* (Rudyard Kipling). **3** to extend out beyond; be too many for: *The crowd overflowed the little room and filled the hall.*
—***n.*** **1** an overflowing; excess: *the annual overflow of the Nile. The overflow from the glass ran onto the table.* **2** something that flows or runs over: *an overflow of people from the cities, to carry off the overflow from a fountain.* **3** an outlet or container for overflowing liquid.
—***adj.*** superabundant; overflowing: *In theaters and student hostels from White Russia to Central Asia, overflow crowds listen to poets with almost religious fervor* (Time).
[Old English *oferflōwan*] —**o′ver|flow′ing|ly,** *adv.*

**o|ver|fly** (ō′vər flī′), *v.t.,* **-flew, -flown, -fly|ing.** **1** to fly over (the territory of a country): *The U-2 has been overflying Russia* (Time). **2** to fly over or past without stopping; fly without landing for a scheduled stop: *If no passengers are to be dropped or picked up ... stops are overflown* (Newsweek). **3** to fly faster, farther, or higher than.

**o|ver|fond** (ō′vər fond′), *adj.* too fond. —**o′ver|fond′ly,** *adv.* —**o′ver|fond′ness,** *n.*

**o|ver|fraught** (ō′vər frôt′), *adj.* fraught or laden too heavily; overladen.

**o|ver|free** (ō′vər frē′), *adj.* too free. —**o′ver|free′ly,** *adv.*

**o|ver|ful|fill** or **o|ver|ful|fil** (ō′vər fu̇l fil′), *v.t.,* **-filled, -fill|ing.** to go beyond a required duty, quota, or norm; do more than is expected.

**o|ver|ful|fill|ment** or **o|ver|ful|fil|ment** (ō′vər fu̇l fil′mənt), *n.* a state of being overfulfilled: *overfulfillment of a quota.*

**o|ver|full** (ō′vər fu̇l′), *adj.* too full: *There has been excess demand and overfull employment* (Economist). —**o′ver|full′ness,** *n.*

**o|ver|gar|ment** (ō′vər gär′mənt), *n.* an outer garment: *The cloth used for overgarments ... was completely windproof* (Scientific American).

**o|ver|gild** (ō′vər gild′), *v.t.,* **-gild|ed** or **-gilt, -gild|ing.** **1** to cover with gilding. **2** *Figurative.* to tinge with a golden color.

**o|ver|glaze** (*n.* ō′vər glāz′; *v.* ō′vər glāz′), *n., v.,* **-glazed, -glaz|ing.** —***n.*** a glaze applied over another glaze on pottery.
—***v.t.*** to apply an overglaze to.

**o|ver|go** (ō′vər gō′), *v.,* **-went, -gone, -go|ing.** *Archaic.* —***v.t.*** **1** to pass over or through. **2** *Figurative.* to go beyond; exceed; surpass. **3** to overcome. **4** to overwhelm; weigh down.
—***v.i.*** **1** to go by; pass away; disappear. **2** to go to excess.

**o|ver|gorge** (ō′vər gôrj′), *v.t., v.i.,* **-gorged, -gorg|ing.** to gorge too much.

**o|ver|graze** (ō′vər grāz′), *v.t., v.i.,* **-grazed, -graz|ing.** to graze or allow to graze so long and uninterruptedly as to reduce seriously the grass cover and destroy pastureland: *Most of the range in the West has been or is being overgrazed* (Bernard De Voto).

**o|ver|great** (ō′vər grāt′), *adj.* too great.

**o|ver|grew** (ō′vər grü′), *v.* the past tense of **overgrow**: *Vines overgrew the wall.*

**o|ver|ground** (ō′vər ground′), *adj.* above the ground.

**o|ver|grow** (ō′vər grō′), *v.*, **-grew, -grown, -grow·ing.** —*v.t.* **1** to grow over: *The wall is overgrown with vines.* **2** to grow out of or beyond; outgrow: *The rosebush has overgrown its support.* **3** to outdo in growing; choke or replace by a more profuse growth: *seeds of a new and rampant quality, which were destined to overgrow them all* (Harriet Beecher Stowe).
—*v.i.* to grow too fast; become too big.

**o|ver|grown** (ō′vər grōn′), *adj., v.* —*adj.* **1** grown too big: *an overgrown boy.* **2** grown over, as with vegetation or weeds.
—*v.* the past participle of **overgrow**: *The vines have overgrown the wall.*

**o|ver|growth** (ō′vər grōth′), *n.* **1** too great or too rapid growth. **2** a growth overspreading or covering something: (*Figurative.*) *the selective overgrowth of the culture by a few individuals that are able to multiply in its presence* (Evelyn M. Witkin).

**o|ver|hand** (ō′vər hand′), *adj., adv., n., v.* —*adj., adv.* **1** with the hand raised above the shoulder and the arm swung downward; overarm: *an overhand throw* (adj.), *to pitch overhand* (adv.). **2** with the knuckles upward. **3** over and over; with stitches passing successively over an edge: *an overhand stitch.*
—*n.* an overhand throw or stroke; performance, or style of performance, in making overhand plays, as in tennis: *He has a strong overhand.*
—*v.t.* to sew with overhand stitches.

**o|ver|hand|ed** (ō′vər han′did), *adj.* **1** = overhand. **2** supplied with too many workers.

**overhand knot** or **loop**, a simple knot, used in beginning other knots; thumb knot. See picture under **knot**[1].

**o|ver|hang** (*v.* ō′vər hang′; *n.* ō′vər hang′), *v.*, **-hung, -hang|ing,** *n.* —*v.t.* **1** to hang over; project over: *Trees overhang the street to form an arch of branches.* **2** *Figurative.* to hang over so as to darken, sadden, or threaten: *The threat of war overhangs mankind.* **3** to drape or decorate with hangings.
—*v.i.* to hang over; jut out over something below: *The granite walls, overhanging, bend forward above to meet one another, almost forming an arch* (Henry Kingsley).
—*n.* **1** something that projects: *The overhang of the roof shaded the flower bed beneath. The overhang of the stern or bow of a ship is between the water line and the deck.* **2** the act or fact of hanging over. **3** amount of projecting: *Frames generally will be stretched to reduce front and rear overhang* (Wall Street Journal). **4** the distance the tip of the upper wing of a biplane extends beyond the tip of the lower wing.

**o|ver|hard** (ō′vər härd′), *adj.* too hard.

**o|ver|hast|i|ly** (ō′vər hās′tə lē), *adv.* in an overhasty manner; with too much haste.

**o|ver|hast|i|ness** (ō′vər hās′tē nis), *n.* a being overhasty; too much haste: *failure because of dilatoriness or overhastiness.*

**o|ver|hast|y** (ō′vər hās′tē), *adj.* too hasty.

**o|ver|haul** (*v.* ō′vər hôl′; *n.* ō′vər hôl′), *v., n.* —*v.t.* **1** to examine completely so as to make any repairs or changes that are needed: *to overhaul an automobile, to overhaul a government department. Once a year we overhaul our boats.* **2** to gain upon; overtake: *An automobile can overhaul any horse. Our horse overhauled the favorite to win by a head.* **3** *Nautical.* **a** to slacken (a rope) by hauling in the opposite direction to that in which it was drawn taut. **b** to release the blocks of (a tackle).
—*n.* the act or process of overhauling: *The repair bill ... was $411.92 for two transmission overhauls* (Time).

**o|ver|haul|ing** (ō′vər hô′ling), *n.* a thorough examination to find and make any needed repairs or changes.

**o|ver|head**[1] (*adv.* ō′vər hed′; *adj., n.* ō′vər hed′), *adv., adj., n.* —*adv.* **1** over the head; on high; far above: *the stars overhead, the flag overhead, birds flying overhead. Overhead was a gray expanse of cloud* (Hawthorne). SYN: aloft. **2** on the floor above; just above: *the family overhead, people dancing overhead.*
—*adj.* placed above; placed high up; being, working, or passing overhead: *overhead wires.*
—*n.* **1** a tennis stroke made with an overhand motion downward from above the head: *She never went to the net voluntarily, though she won with her overhead when drawn in* (New York Times). **2** = overhead projector.

**o|ver|head**[2] (ō′vər hed′), *n., adj.* —*n.* general expenses including rent, lighting, heating, taxes, and repairs. Overhead is the charges of a business which cannot be charged against a particular operation.
—*adj.* of or having to do with overhead in business: *overhead charges or expenses.*

**o|ver|head**[3] (ō′vər hed′), *adj. Especially British.* applying to one and all; general: *an overhead tax.* [Middle English *overheved,* Old English *ofer hēafod,* in the earlier sense of "taking everything together"]

**overhead projector**, a projector for showing pictures, especially of instructional material, on a screen and allowing the operator to point at features of the projected material lying on a flat bed over the projector light. The image is cast at right angle on a wall through a mirror and focusing device about 12 inches above the projection bed.

**overhead railway**, *British.* an elevated railroad.

**overhead valve**, a valve in the cylinder head, above the piston in certain internal-combustion engines.

**o|ver|hear** (ō′vər hir′), *v.t.*, **-heard, -hear|ing.** to hear when one is not meant to hear: *They spoke so loud that I could not help overhearing what they said.* [Old English *oferhēran*] —**o′ver|hear′er,** *n.*

**o|ver|heard** (ō′vər hėrd′), *v.* the past tense and past participle of **overhear**: *I overheard what you told them.*

**o|ver|heat** (*v.* ō′vər hēt′; *n.* ō′vər hēt′), *v., n.* —*v.t., v.i.* **1** to heat too much: *Running for home through the snowstorm, he got overheated and later got a chill. It may be found that the rocket overheats in spite of this cooling* (D. Hurden). **2** *Economics.* to cause to be, or to become, excessively stimulated, as by government spending or increased investment: *The pressure of demand is rising and we shall soon encounter the familiar danger of overheating the economy* (Manchester Guardian). *When our economy overheats—because of too many stimulants or some overwhelming development such as the war in Vietnam—it is imperative to ... restrain the rate of growth* (Sylvia Porter).
—*n.* too much heat.

**o|ver|high** (ō′vər hī′), *adj., adv.* too high.

**o|ver|hit** (ō′vər hit′), *v.i., v.t.*, **-hit, -hit|ting.** to hit too hard or too far: *Miss Wade overhit too often in the first set but settled down to outclass Miss Krantzcke in the second* (London Times).

**o|ver|hours** (ō′vər ourz′), *n.pl.* **1** extra hours of work; overtime. **2** spare or odd hours: *I only worked at it in overhours—often late at night* (George Eliot).

**o|ver-housed** (ō′vər houzd′), *adj.* having more space than necessary in which to live: *In 1965 they found themselves over-housed and decided to sublet the fourth floor* (London Times).

**o|ver|hung** (*adj.* ō′vər hung′; *v.* ō′vər hung′), *adj., v.* —*adj.* **1** hung from above: *an overhung door.* **2** (of the upper jaw) projecting beyond the lower jaw.
—*v.* the past tense and past participle of **overhang**: *A big awning overhung the sidewalk.*

**o|ver|in|dulge** (ō′vər in dulj′), *v.t., v.i.*, **-dulged, -dulg|ing.** to indulge too much.

**o|ver|in|dul|gence** (ō′vər in dul′jəns), *n.* excessive or too much indulgence: *Overindulgence is as bad for children as overstrictness* (Sidonie M. Gruenberg).

**o|ver|in|dul|gent** (ō′vər in dul′jənt), *adj.* too indulgent.

**o|ver|in|flat|ed** (ō′vər in flā′tid), *adj.* too large; oversized: *... opening up the ranks to younger officers presently stymied by the overinflated bureaucracy* (Time).

**o|ver|in|spi|ra|tion|al** (ō′vər in′spə rā′shə nəl), *adj.* excessively or self-consciously inspirational: *It is in some ways what one might term a small film, not overinspirational* (Manchester Guardian Weekly).

**o|ver|in|sure** (ō′vər in shu̇r′), *v.t.*, **-sured, -sur·ing.** to insure for more than the real value.

**o|ver|is|sue** (ō′vər ish′ü; *especially British,* ō′vər-is′yü), *n., v.*, **-sued, -su|ing.** —*n.* an issue of stocks, bonds, or other securities in excess of what is authorized or needed.
—*v.t.* to issue (notes or securities) in excess of a proper or authorized amount.

**o|ver|joy** (ō′vər joi′), *v.t.* to make very joyful: *My sister ... was overjoyed at the intelligence of my safe return* (Frederick Marryat). SYN: delight.

**o|ver|jump** (ō′vər jump′), *v.t., v.i.* **1** to jump over. **2** to jump too far over. **3** *Figurative.* to transcend; pass over.

**o|ver|kill** (*v.* ō′vər kil′; *n.* ō′vər kil′), *v., n.* —*v.i., v.t.* to destroy with greater force or damage than necessary: *A missile with a single enormous warhead is a lousy weapon. It overkills at the center* (Stewart Alsop).
—*n.* **1** the act or process of overkilling. **2** the capacity of a force or weapon to cause greater destruction than necessary: *What does being ahead mean when possessing more or less overkill cannot be translated into anything that is militarily or humanly meaningful?* (New York Times). **3** *Figurative: The nation's fiscal and monetary authorities, in their desire to correct inflation, might pursue restrictive policies too long, leading to economic overkill* (Clifton H. Kreps, Jr.).

**o|ver|la|bor** (ō′vər lā′bər), *v.t.* **1** to overwork. **2** to labor too much over; elaborate too much.

**o|ver|lad|en** (ō′vər lā′dən), *adj.* overloaded.

**o|ver|laid** (ō′vər lād′), *v.* the past tense and past participle of **overlay**[1]: *The workmen overlaid the dome with gold. The iron had become overlaid with rust.*

**o|ver|lain** (ō′vər lān′), *v.* the past participle of **overlie**: *In most oceanic areas, however, the crust seems to be overlain with half a mile of sediment* (Willard Bascom).

**o|ver|land** (ō′vər land′, -lənd), *adv., adj., v.* —*adv., adj.* on land; across land: *We traveled overland from New York to Florida* (adv.). *He followed an overland route* (adj.).
—*v.t.* (in Australia) to drive overland, especially for long distances: *to overland a herd of cattle.*
—*v.i.* (in Australia) to travel overland driving livestock. —**o′ver|land′er,** *n.*

**overland stage**, *U.S.* a sturdy stagecoach that carried passengers and mail in the West before the railroads, in the mid-1800's.

**o|ver|lap** (*v.* ō′vər lap′; *n.* ō′vər lap′), *v.*, **-lapped, -lap|ping,** *n.* —*v.t.* **1** to lap over; cover and extend beyond: *Shingles are laid so that they overlap each other.* **2** to coincide partly with. Overlapping sets in mathematics have some members in common. (*Figurative.*) *Though his cousin came to their grandfather's farm a week later, the vacation of the two boys overlapped each other for the time that they were there together.*
—*v.i.* to overlap another thing or each other: *The shingles overlap.* (*Figurative.*) *Our arguments seem to overlap.*
—*n.* **1** the act or fact of lapping over: *Overlaps do not matter and thin spots can be touched up at any time* (New York Times). **2** the amount by which one thing laps over another. **3** a part that overlaps.

**o|ver|large** (ō′vər lärj′), *adj.* too large; oversized.

**o|ver|lay**[1] (*v.* ō′vər lā′; *n.* ō′vər lā′), *v.*, **-laid, -lay·ing,** *n.* —*v.t.* **1** to lay or place (one thing) over or upon another. SYN: superimpose. **2a** to cover, overspread, or surmount with something. **b** to put a coating over the surface of; finish with a layer or applied decoration of something: *The dome is overlaid with gold. ... bright ivory overlaid with sapphires* (Canticles 5:14). **3** *Figurative.* to weigh down: *to be overlaid with responsibilities.* SYN: encumber, overburden. **4** *Printing.* to place an overlay on. **5** to conceal or obscure as if by covering. **6** = overlie.
—*n.* **1a** something laid over something else; covering: *The tablecloth was used as an overlay for the beautiful, old wooden table.* **b** an ornamental layer; layer or decoration of something applied: *an overlay of fine wood, an overlay of gold.* **2** a sheet of some transparent substance by means of which special geographical or other information, such as the various organs of an animal's body, may be located when it is placed over the surrounding organs and outline of the body to which it is keyed. **3** *Printing.* a piece of paper, or a sheet with pieces pasted on it, laid on the press cylinder as part of make-ready to compensate for low spots in the form. **4** *Scottish.* a necktie.

**o|ver|lay**[2] (ō′vər lā′), *v.* the past tense of **overlie**.

**overlay glass**, glassware consisting of layers of glass of contrasting colors. Overlay glass was first made in Europe and the United States during the 1800's.

**o|ver|leaf** (ō′vər lēf′), *adv., adj.* on the reverse side of a piece of paper.

**o|ver|leap** (ō′vər lēp′), *v.t.* **1** to leap over or across; pass beyond: *Her joy overleaped all bounds.* **2** *Figurative.* to overreach (oneself) by leaping too far: *Vaulting ambition, which o'erleaps itself* (Shakespeare). **3** *Figurative.* to pass over; omit; skip. **4** to leap farther than; outleap.

**o|ver|lie** (ō′vər lī′), *v.t.*, **-lay, -lain, -ly|ing.** **1** to lie over; lie upon. **2** to smother by lying on; overlay.

**o|ver|ling** (ō′vər ling), *n.* a person who is over others in position or authority (used in an unfriendly way).

**o|ver|live** (ō′vər liv′), *v.*, **-lived, -liv|ing.** —*v.t.* to

---

**Pronunciation Key:** hat, āge, cãre, fär; let, ēqual, tėrm; it, īce; hot, ōpen, ôrder; oil, out; cup, pu̇t, rüle; child; long; thin; ᴛʜen; zh, measure; ə represents a in about, e in taken, i in pencil, o in lemon, u in circus.

live longer than or beyond; outlast; outlive: *The mighty Pyramids ... have overlived the feeble generations of mankind* (Robert Southey).
— ***v.i.*** to continue to live; survive: *Why do I overlive? Why am I mocked with death, and lengthen'd out To deathless pain?* (Milton).

**o|ver|load** (*v.* ō'vər lōd'; *n.* ō'vər lōd'), *v., n.*
— ***v.t.*** **1** to load too heavily; overburden: *to overload a boat, to overload an electric circuit.* **2** to overcharge (a gun).
— ***n.*** too great a load or charge: *The overload of electric current blew the fuse. One of the most familiar dissatisfactions in the Doing Period of thirty-five to fifty is work overload, especially for teachers* (Harper's).

**o|ver|long** (ō'vər long'), *adj., adv.* too long.

**o|ver|look** (*v.* ō'vər lu̇k'; *n.* ō'vər lu̇k'), *v., n.* — ***v.t.*** **1** to fail to see; neglect: *Here are the letters you overlooked.* **SYN**: disregard, ignore. See syn. under **slight**. **2** to pay no attention to; excuse: *I will overlook your bad behavior this time.* **SYN**: forgive, condone. **3** to have a view of from above; be higher than: *This high window overlooks half the city.* **4** to look over; watch: *She did not know that she was being overlooked by the woman next door.* **SYN**: survey, scrutinize. **5** to look after and direct; manage. **SYN**: oversee, superintend. **6** *Figurative.* to look over the top of; rise above; overtop. **7** to look upon with the evil eye; bewitch: *I tell you she has overlooked me; and all this doctor's stuff is no use, unless you can say a charm as will undo her devil's work* (Henry Kingsley).
— ***n.*** a lookout: *The overlook is a short hike from the road's end. The view down has a smashing impact* (New York Times). — **o'ver|look'er**, *n.*

**o|ver|lord** (ō'vər lôrd'), *n.* **1** a person who is lord over another lord or other lords: *The duke was the overlord of barons and knights who held land from him.* **2** any person, group, or government having comparable status or authority.

**o|ver|lord|ship** (ō'vər lôrd'ship), *n.* the position, rank, or authority of an overlord: *... the last Jewish revolt against Roman overlordship* (New York Times).

**o|ver|ly** (ō'vər lē), *adv.* excessively; too; overmuch: *The trip by bus was not overly long. He is overly shy with strangers.*

**o|ver|ly|ing** (ō'vər lī'ing), *v.* the present participle of **overlie**.

**o|ver|man** (*n.* *1 and 2* ō'vər mən; *3* ō'vər man'; *v.* ō'vər man'), *n., pl.* **-men**, *v.*, **-manned**, **-manning**. — ***n.*** **1** *Especially British.* a foreman or overseer, especially in a coal mine: *This sparking had been observed by workmen, deputies, and the overman* (London Times). **2** *Especially British.* an arbiter; arbitrator; umpire. **3** = superman.
— ***v.t.*** to supply with too many workers: *The union-owned Vulcan Foundries, Ltd., decided it was overmanned and dismissed some union members* (Wall Street Journal).

**o|ver|man|tel** (ō'vər man'təl), *n.* a piece of decorative work placed above a mantelpiece, often a piece of ornamental cabinet-work with or without a mirror.

**o|ver|mark** (ō'vər märk'), *v.t.* to mark or grade too generously.

**o|ver|mas|ter** (ō'vər mas'tər, -mäs'-), *v.t.* to overcome; overpower. **SYN**: defeat, surmount.
— **o'ver|mas'ter|ing|ly**, *adv.*

**o|ver|match** (ō'vər mach'), *v., n.* — ***v.t.*** to be more than a match for; surpass; outdo.
— ***n.*** a person or thing that is more than a match.

**o|ver|much** (ō'vər much'), *adj., adv., n.* too much.

**o|ver|nice** (ō'vər nīs'), *adj.* too fastidious. **SYN**: finical.

**o|ver|night** (*adv., v.* ō'vər nīt'; *adj., n.* ō'vər nīt'), *adv., adj., n., v.* — ***adv.*** **1** during the night; through the night: *to stay overnight with a friend.* **2** on the night before: *Preparations were made overnight for an early start the next morning.* **3** at once; immediately; in a very short time: *Change will not come overnight.*
— ***adj.*** **1** done or occurring during the night: *an overnight stop, overnight hospitality.* **2** for the night: *overnight guests. An overnight bag contains articles needed for one night's stay.* **3** of or having to do with the night before.
— ***n.*** the previous evening.
— ***v.i.*** to stay overnight: *to overnight at a hotel.*

**o|ver|num|ber** (ō'vər num'bər), *v.t.* = outnumber.

**o|ver|nu|tri|tion** (ō'vər nü trish'ən, -nyü-), *n.* ingestion of too much or unnecessary food, especially in an unbalanced diet of more fat, calcium, or other food substance than the body can effectively use: *The neglect of this branch of science is little short of a tragedy, because enormous problems of malnutrition and overnutrition remain unsolved and untackled* (New Scientist and Science Journal).

**o|ver|oc|cu|pied** (ō'vər ok'yə pīd), *adj.* too crowded; not providing sufficient space: *Its street scenes ... have an impressive shabbiness—that stained and damaged identity of overoccupied housing and underoccupied people* (Manchester Guardian Weekly).

**o|ver|or|gan|ize** (ō'vər ôr'gə nīz), *v.t., v.i.*, **-ized**, **-iz|ing**. to subject to excessive organization; organize too much.

**o|ver|paid** (ō'vər pād'), *v.* the past tense and past participle of **overpay**.

**o|ver|paint** (ō'vər pānt'), *v.t.* **1** to paint (as one picture or layer) over or upon another: *Icons were heavily overpainted and smudged by centuries of candle smoke* (Time). **2** to overemphasize; exaggerate.

**o|ver|part|ed** (ō'vər pär'tid), *adj.* having too difficult a part, or too many parts, to play: *to be overparted in a play.*

**o|ver|pass** (*n.* ō'vər pas', -päs'; *v.* ō'vər pas', -päs'), *n., v.*, **-passed** or **-past**, **-pass|ing**. — ***n.*** a bridge over a road, railroad, or canal: *Drive several miles down the turnpike, around the cloverleaf, under an overpass* (Atlantic).
— ***v.t.*** **1** to pass over (as a region or bounds): *The next few miles would be no light thing for the whale-boats to overpass* (Rudyard Kipling). **2** *Figurative.* to go beyond; exceed; surpass: *Men Who overpass their kind* (Robert Browning). **3** *Figurative.* to pass without notice; overlook; disregard: *All the beauties of the East He slightly view'd, and slightly overpass'd* (Milton).
— ***v.i.*** **1** to pass over or across something. **2** to pass by or away: *I view her ... As a sweet sunset almost overpast* (William E. Henley). **3** *Figurative.* to remain unnoticed.

**o|ver|pay** (ō'vər pā'), *v.t.*, **-paid**, **-pay|ing**. **1** to pay too much: *This high official ... Is grossly overpaid* (A. P. Herbert). **2** to pay more than (an amount due).

**o|ver|pay|ment** (ō'vər pā'mənt), *n.* too great a payment.

**o|ver|peo|ple** (ō'vər pē'pəl), *v.t.*, **-pled**, **-pling**. to fill with too many people; overpopulate.

**o|ver|per|form** (ō'vər pər fôrm'), *v.t.* to perform with interpretation not justified in the score or script: *Monteverdi's late four-part Mass also seemed slightly overperformed for what is basically a fairly austere work: a lot of detail was pressed to our notice, and the character of some movements was almost parodied* (London Times).

**o|ver|per|suade** (ō'vər pər swād'), *v.t.*, **-suad|ed**, **-suad|ing**. to bring over by persuasion, especially against one's inclination or intention: *I should have left you before now, if Mrs. Jakeman had not overpersuaded me* (William Godwin).

**o|ver|per|sua|sion** (ō'vər pər swā'zhən), *n.* **1** the act of overpersuading. **2** the state of being overpersuaded.

**o|ver|plaid** (ō'vər plad'), *n.* **1** a plaid pattern appearing over another pattern on woven fabrics. **2** cloth with such a combination of patterns.

**o|ver|plant** (ō'vər plant', -plänt'), *v.t., v.i.* to plant in excess or beyond what is required: *A drought in one area of the country encourages farmers in another area to overplant their crops in the hope of making a better profit.*

**o|ver|play** (ō'vər plā'), *v.t.* **1** to play (as a part) in an exaggerated manner; overact. **2** *Figurative.* to count too heavily on the power or advantage of: *The diplomat was careful not to overplay his hand during the negotiations.* **3** to play better than; surpass; defeat. **4** to hit (a golf ball) past the green.

**o|ver|please** (ō'vər plēz'), *v.t.*, **-pleased**, **-pleasing**. to please too much: *He was not overpleased with your reply.*

**o|ver|plus** (ō'vər plus'), *n.* **1** an amount left over; surplus. **2** too great an amount; excess: (*Figurative.*) *He was ruined, morally, by an overplus of the very same ingredient* [*purpose*] (Hawthorne).

**o|ver|pop|u|late** (ō'vər pop'yə lāt), *v.t.*, **-lat|ed**, **-lat|ing**. = overpeople.

**o|ver|pop|u|la|tion** (ō'vər pop'yə lā'shən), *n.* too great a population: *Overpopulation ... affects a great many other needs of mankind besides bread* (Julian Huxley).

**o|ver|pow|er** (ō'vər pou'ər), *v.t.* **1** to overcome or conquer; master; overwhelm: *He overpowered all his enemies. He overpowered his assailant. The thought of one man owning all those books overpowered him* (Winston Churchill). **SYN**: vanquish, defeat, overthrow. **2** to be much greater or stronger than: *The wind brought a terrible smell which overpowered all others. Anger overpowered every other feeling.* **3** to provide with an excess of power: *to overpower an automobile.*
— **o'ver|pow'er|ing|ly**, *adv.*

**o|ver|praise** (*v.* ō'vər prāz'; *n.* ō'vər-), *v.*, **-praised**, **-prais|ing**, *n.* — ***v.t.*** to praise too much or too highly.
— ***n.*** too much or too high praise.

**o|ver|pre|scribe** (ō'vər pri skrīb'), *v.i., v.t.*, **-scribed**, **-scrib|ing**. to prescribe drugs, especially narcotics, in excess of the patient's actual need: *When a doctor seems to be regularly overprescribing, he gets two warnings* (Time). *I cannot tolerate the overprescribing of unnecessary and expensive drugs* (H. P. Bower).

**o|ver|pre|scrip|tion** (ō'vər pri skrip'shən), *n.* the act or practice of overprescribing; unnecessary or excessive prescription of medicines.

**o|ver|pres|sure** (ō'vər presh'ər), *n.* **1** excessive pressure; a pressing or being pressed too hard, especially with study or intellectual work: *The intellectual overpressure of children in the schools* (Popular Science Monthly). **2** pressure over and above the normal atmospheric pressure, such as that generated by explosions: *Any target within this radius and vulnerable to the specified overpressure will be destroyed* (United States Air Force Report on the Ballistic Missile).

**o|ver|price** (ō'vər prīs'), *v.t.*, **-priced**, **-pric|ing**. to put or set at too high a price; price higher than the real value: *an overpriced gadget.*

**o|ver|print** (*v.* ō'vər print'; *n.* ō'vər print'), *v., n.*
— ***v.t.*** **1** to print or stamp over with additional marks or matter, as in making revisions, or in color work. **2** *Photography.* to print (a positive) darker than intended.
— ***n.*** **1** any mark, design, or writing printed across a stamp to change its use or value. **2** a postage stamp printed with such a mark.

**o|ver|prize** (ō'vər prīz'), *v.t.*, **-prized**, **-priz|ing**. to prize or value too highly; overrate.

**o|ver|pro|duce** (ō'vər prə düs', -dyüs'), *v.t., v.i.*, **-duced**, **-duc|ing**. **1** to produce more than is needed. **2** to produce more than can be sold, or more than can be sold at a profit: *Pig iron has been overproduced ... in recent years* (London Daily News).

**o|ver|pro|duc|tion** (ō'vər prə duk'shən), *n.* **1** the production of more than is needed: *Problems of surplus must be met ... by adjusting price supports to remove incentives for overproduction* (Time). **2** the production of more than can be sold at a profit.

**o|ver|proof** (ō'vər prüf'), *adj.* containing a greater proportion of alcohol than proof spirit contains; higher than 100 proof. In the United States, overproof liquor contains more than 50 per cent alcohol by volume.

**o|ver|pro|por|tion** (ō'vər prə pôr'shən, -pōr'-), *n., v.* — ***n.*** excess of one thing in proportion to another.
— ***v.t.*** to make or estimate in excess of the true or proper proportion.

**o|ver|pro|por|tion|ate** (ō'vər prə pôr'shə nit, -pōr'-), *adj.* in excess of the true or proper proportion; disproportionate. — **o'ver|pro|por'tion|ate|ly**, *adv.*

**o|ver|pro|por|tioned** (ō'vər prə pôr'shənd, -pōr'-), *adj.* = overproportionate.

**o|ver|pro|tec|tive** (ō'vər prə tek'tiv), *adj.* excessively protective. — **o'ver|pro|tec'tive|ness**, *n.*

**o|ver|proud** (ō'vər proud'), *adj.* too proud.

**o|ver|qual|i|fied** (ō'vər kwol'ə fīd), *adj.* having too much education, knowledge, or experience for a particular job or position; being more qualified than is necessary or expected: *The belief that a higher education level is beneficial to society under any circumstances has meant that many industrial establishments here now have an overqualified staff* (London Times).

**o|ver|ran** (o'vər ran'), *v.* the past tense of **overrun**.

**o|ver|rate** (ō'vər rāt'), *v.t.*, **-rat|ed**, **-rat|ing**. **1** to rate or estimate too highly: *He overrated his strength and soon had to ask for help. His fortune has been greatly overrated.* **SYN**: overvalue, overestimate. **2** *British.* to assess too highly for purposes of taxing.

**o|ver|reach** (ō'vər rēch'), *v.t.* **1** to reach over or beyond. **2** to get the better of by cunning: *to overreach someone in a bargain.* **SYN**: outwit. **3** to get the better of by trickery or fraud; cheat. **SYN**: defraud, swindle, dupe. **4** *Archaic.* **a** to overtake. **b** to overcome. — ***v.i.*** **1** to reach too far. **2** to cheat. **3** (of a horse) to bring a hind foot against a forefoot and injure it in walking or running.
**overreach oneself, a** to fail or miss by trying for too much: *A common error when working to windward in a race ... is for a boat to overreach herself* (Edward F. Qualtrough). **b** to fail by being too crafty or tricky: *The cat overreached itself falling into the pool while pretending to sleep on a branch near the bird's nest.* **c** to be too anxious; try for too much: *Rudeness is another matter, and any interviewer who overreaches himself should be nailed in his place* (Punch).
— **o'ver|reach'er**, *n.*

**o|ver|re|act** (ō'vər ri akt'), *v.i.* to react with greater force, intensity or emotion than is necessary or expected.

**o|ver|re|ac|tion** (ō'vər ri ak'shən), *n.* a reaction of greater force, intensity, or emotion than is necessary or expected: *Americans so long ignored their Latin neighbors to the South that an* *overreaction probably was inevitable once they woke up to the trouble south of the border* (Atlantic).

**o|ver|re|fine** (ō′vər ri fīn′), *v.t., v.i.,* **-fined, -fin-ing.** to refine too much.

**o|ver|re|fine|ment** (ō′vər ri fīn′mənt), *n.* too much refinement: *If Twain suffered from a certain crudity of sensibility, James's defect was overrefinement* (Time).

**o|ver|rep|re|sent** (ō′vər rep′ri zent′), *v.t.* to represent by more than a proper proportion: *... whether the state actually intended to overrepresent certain groups or merely let this happen by failure to reapportion while cities grew* (Wall Street Journal).

**o|ver|ride** (ō′vər rīd′), *v.,* **-rode, -rid|den, -rid|ing,** *n.* — ***v.t.*** **1** to act in spite of: *to override advice or objections.* **2** *Figurative.* **a** to prevail over; set aside: *The new rule overrides all previous ones. The chairman's veto was overridden by the committee.* **b** to ride over; trample on: *overriding another's happiness in pursuit of your own* (George W. Cable). **3** to ride over or across (as a region or place). **4** to tire out (a horse) by riding; ride too much. **5** to pass or extend over; overlap, as the pieces of a fractured bone or ice floes forced against each other.
— ***n.*** a commission paid to a sales manager, in addition to his basic wage, based on the total sales in his territory.
[Old English *oferrīdan*] — **o′ver|rid′ing|ly,** *adv.*

**o|ver|rid|er** (ō′vər rī′dər), *n. British.* a protective metal guard on an automobile bumper.

**o|ver|ripe** (ō′vər rīp′), *adj.* too ripe; more than ripe: *The time is overripe for a new translation of the American theme—freedom through order* (Time). — **o′ver|ripe′ness,** *n.*

**o|ver|roast** (ō′vər rōst′), *v.t.* to roast too much.

**o|ver|roof** (ō′vər rüf′, -rụ̇f′), *v.t.* to cover over with or as if with a roof.

**o|ver|ruff** (*v.* ō′vər ruf′; *n.* ō′vər ruf′), *v., n.* — ***v.t., v.i.*** to trump with a card higher than that with which a previous player has already trumped: *If the diamonds do not break favourably there is a chance that West will overruff* (Manchester Guardian Weekly).
— ***n.*** an act or instance of overruffing: *It was East's overruff that set the contract.*

**o|ver|rule** (ō′vər rül′), *v.t.,* **-ruled, -rul|ing. 1** to rule or decide against (a plea, argument, or objection); set aside: *The president overruled my plan.* **SYN:** override, reject, annul, disallow. **2** to prevail over; be stronger than: *I was overruled by the majority.* — **o′ver|rul′ing|ly,** *adv.*

**o|ver|run** (*v.* ō′vər run′; *n.* ō′vər run′), *v.,* **-ran, -run, -run|ning,** *n.* — ***v.t.*** **1** to spread over and spoil or harm in some way: *Weeds had overrun the old garden. The conquering army overran the village.* **SYN:** invade, ravage, infest. **2** to spread over: *Vines overran the wall.* **3** *Figurative.* to run or go beyond; exceed: *He overran third base and was tagged out. The speaker overran the time set for him.* **4** *Printing.* **a** to carry over (words or lines of type) into another line or page to provide for addition or removal of other matter. **b** to remake (columns or pages) by carrying over words, lines, or pictures. **5** to run over; crush: *Like a gallant horse fall'n ... O'errun and trampled on* (Shakespeare). **6** *Archaic.* to outrun; surpass: *Atalanta ... overran A white high-crested bull* (William Morris).
— ***v.i.*** to run over; overflow; extend beyond the proper or desired limit.
— ***n.*** **1** an amount overrunning or carried over, such as a balance or surplus; an excess: *The principal problem ... has been the overrun in the capital expenditure of the uranium mines* (Economist). **2** the act or process of overrunning.
— **o′ver|run′ner,** *n.*

**o|ver|sang** (ō′vər sang′), *v.* the past tense of **oversing.**

**o|ver|saw** (ō′vər sô′), *v.* the past tense of **oversee.**

**o|ver|score** (*n.* ō′vər skôr′, -skōr′; *v.* ō′vər skôr′, -skōr′), *n., v.,* **-scored, -scor|ing.** — ***n.*** one or more tricks over the contract in the game of contract bridge.
— ***v.i.*** to make more tricks than bid for in contract bridge.
— ***v.t.*** to make strokes or lines over: *to overscore a word or sentence.*

**o|ver|sea** (*adv.* ō′vər sē′; *adj.* ō′vər sē′), *adv., adj.* = overseas.

**o|ver|seam** (*n.* ō′vər sēm′; *v.* ō′vər sēm′), *n., v.* — ***n.*** a seam made by oversewing edges: *The overseam is finished with a thread holding the seam together, with the threads going over the edge of the seam* (Bernice G. Chambers).
— ***v.t., v.i.*** to sew with an overseam.

**o|ver|seas** (*adv.* ō′vər sēz′; *adj.* ō′vər sēz′), *adv., adj.* — ***adv.*** across the sea; beyond the sea; abroad: *to travel overseas. While the presses are still rolling in the U.S., negatives of each page are on their way overseas* (Newsweek).
— ***adj.*** **1** done, used, or serving overseas: *overseas military service, overseas equipment.* **2** of or in countries across the sea; foreign: *overseas trade, overseas investments.*

**overseas cap,** *U.S. Military.* a small, soft hat without a visor; garrison cap.

**o|ver|see** (ō′vər sē′), *v.t.,* **-saw, -seen, -see|ing. 1** to look after and direct (work or workers); superintend; manage: *to oversee a factory. None but a grandmother should ever oversee a child. Mothers are only fit for bearing* (Rudyard Kipling). **SYN:** supervise. **2** to overlook, as from a higher position; survey. **3** *Archaic.* to examine. [Old English *ofersēon*]

**o|ver|seen** (ō′vər sēn′), *v.* the past participle of **oversee.**

**o|ver|se|er** (ō′vər sē′ər), *n.* a person who oversees others or their work.

**overseer of the poor,** an officer of parish administration in England.

**o|ver|se|er|ship** (ō′vər sē′ər ship), *n.* the position, rank, or authority of an overseer.

**o|ver|sell** (*v.* ō′vər sel′; *n.* ō′vər sel′), *v.,* **-sold, -sell|ing,** *n.* — ***v.t.*** **1** to sell to excess: *At La-Guardia it turned out that the flight she was booked on was oversold* (New Yorker). **2** to sell too much of: **a** to sell more of (a commodity, stock, or other security) than can be delivered: *We are badly oversold beyond our production capacity* (Wall Street Journal). **b** to sell more of (a commodity, stock, or other security) than one can support if prices rise. **3** *U.S. Informal.* to urge (a person) to buy something too aggressively or too long, often at the risk of losing a sale.
— ***v.i.*** to sell more of something than can be delivered: *Overselling is the second greatest complaint received by the board* (New York Times).
— ***n.*** excessive or overly aggressive selling: *Out of this swam intercontinental hordes of ... agents, PRO's, dealers, copywriters and columnists, all feverishly dedicated to the oversell* (Punch).

**o|ver|set** (*v.* ō′vər set′; *n.* ō′vər set′), *v.,* **-set, -set|ting,** *n.* — ***v.t.*** **1** to upset; overturn: *The boat was overset by a sudden flurry from the north* (Jonathan Swift). **2** to overthrow. **3** to disturb mentally or physically: *So overset was she by the dramatic surprise of his challenging remark ... that her manner changed in an instant* (Arnold Bennett). **4** *Printing.* to set too much type for: *to overset a page by three lines.*
— ***v.i.*** **1** to become upset or overturned: *This raft ... overset, and threw me ... into the water* (Daniel Defoe). **2** *Printing.* to set too much type.
— ***n.*** **1** an upset; overturn. **2** = overthrow. **3** *Printing.* matter set in type in excess of available space.

**o|ver|sew** (ō′vər sō′, ō′vər sō′), *v.t.,* **-sewed, -sewed** or **-sewn, -sew|ing.** to sew over (an edge or edges of material) with many close stitches.

**o|ver|sexed** (ō′vər sekst′), *adj.* having an excessive interest in or capacity for sexual activity.

**o|ver|shade** (ō′vər shād′), *v.t.,* **-shad|ed, -shad-ing.** = overshadow.

**o|ver|shad|ow** (ō′vər shad′ō), *v.t.* **1** to be more important than: *The older boy overshadows his brother in school. Mr. Gamaliel Ives ... would have been the first citizen if that other first citizen had not ... so completely overshadowed him* (Winston Churchill). **SYN:** outrival, surpass. **2** to cast a shadow over; make dark or gloomy: (*Figurative.*) *Those misfortunes which were soon to overshadow her* (James A. Froude). **SYN:** darken. **3** *Archaic.* to shelter; protect: *The power of the Highest shall overshadow thee* (Luke 1:35).

**o|ver|shine** (ō′vər shīn′), *v.t.,* **-shone, -shin|ing. 1** to shine over or upon; illumine. **2** *Figurative.* to surpass; outshine.

**o|ver|shoe** (ō′vər shü′), *n.* a waterproof shoe or boot, often made of rubber, worn over another shoe to keep the foot dry and warm; galosh. [American English; compare Dutch *overschoe,* German *Überschuh*]

**o|ver|shoot** (ō′vər shüt′), *v.,* **-shot, -shoot|ing,** *n.,* — ***v.t.*** **1** to shoot over, higher than, or beyond: *to overshoot a target.* **2** to go over, higher than, or beyond. **3** *Figurative.* to force or drive beyond the proper limit.
— ***v.i.*** to go, run, or shoot too far.
— ***n.*** **1** the act of overshooting. **2** *Figurative.* a failure resulting from aiming too high or trying for too much: *He sees the market economy as a system with high gain and strong feedback, possessing self-regulation, but troubled by overshoots* (New Scientist).

**overshoot oneself,** to go too far in any course or matter; overreach oneself: *He was the first, in a manner, that put his hand to write Commentaries ... and therefore no marvel, if he overshot himself many times* (Translators' Preface to the King James Version).

**o|ver|shot** (*adj.* ō′vər shot′; *v.* ō′vər shot′), *adj., v.* — ***adj.*** **1** having the upper jaw projecting beyond the lower: *The mouths of some collies are slightly overshot.* **2** driven by water flowing over from above: *an overshot water wheel.*
— ***v.*** the past tense and the past participle of **overshoot.**

**o|ver|side** (*adv.* ō′vər sīd′; *adj., n.* ō′vər sīd′), *adv., adj., n.* — ***adv.*** over the side, as of a ship.
— ***adj.*** **1** done over the side of a ship: *an overside delivery of coal.* **2** unloading or unloaded over the side.
— ***n.*** the second or reverse side: *The folksongs, on the overside of the record, are authoritative* (Atlantic).

**o|ver|sight** (ō′vər sīt′), *n.* **1** failure to notice or think of something: *By an oversight, the kitten got no supper last night.* **SYN:** overlooking, inadvertence, omission, slip. **2** watchful care: *While children are at school, they are under their teacher's oversight and direction.* **SYN:** supervision, superintendence, charge.

**o|ver|sim|pli|fi|ca|tion** (ō′vər sim′plə fə kā′shən), *n.* excessive or undue simplification of something complicated, leading to distortion or misrepresentation.

**o|ver|sing** (ō′vər sing′), *v.i.,* **-sang, -sung, -sing-ing.** to sing more loudly or with more interpretation than is justified.

**o|ver|size** (ō′vər sīz′), *adj., n.* — ***adj.*** too big; larger than the proper or usual size; very large.
— ***n.*** **1** a size larger than the proper or usual size. **2** something larger than is necessary.

**o|ver|sized** (ō′vər sīzd′), *adj.* over the usual size; very large; oversize.

**o|ver|skirt** (ō′vər skėrt′), *n.* **1** an outer skirt. **2** a separate skirt over the upper part of the main skirt or slacks.

**o|ver|slaugh** (ō′vər slô′), *v., n.* — ***v.t.*** **1** *U.S.* to pass over in favor of another, as in a promotion or appointment to an office. **2** *British.* **a** to excuse from (military duty). **b** to excuse (a soldier or other military personnel) from one duty in order to perform some other duty. **3** = ignore. **4** to hinder; obstruct.
— ***n.*** **1** *British.* an excusing or exemption from duty. **2** *U.S.* a sandbank or bar obstructing navigation in a river.
[< Dutch *overslaan.* Compare German *überschlagen.*]

**o|ver|sleep** (ō′vər slēp′), *v.,* **-slept, -sleep|ing.**
— ***v.i.*** to sleep too long: *If you oversleep you'll miss the bus.*
— ***v.t.*** to sleep beyond (a certain hour).

**o|ver|slept** (ō′vər slept′), *v.* the past tense and past participle of **oversleep**: *I overslept and missed the bus to school. I have overslept three days in a row.*

**o|ver|slip** (ō′vər slip′), *v.t.,* **-slipped, -slip|ping. 1** to slip past or beyond, especially in secret. **2** *Figurative.* to pass by; omit; miss.

**o|ver|snow** (ō′vər snō′), *adj.* **1** done or taking place on or across snow-covered ground or ice: *The results of United States IGY oversnow traverses reveal the nature of a large portion of ice-covered Antarctica* (Science). **2** of or for use in traveling over such ground or ice: *oversnow equipment.*

**o|ver|sold** (ō′vər sōld′), *v.* the past tense and past participle of **oversell.**

**o|ver|so|phis|ti|cate** (ō′vər sə fis′tə kāt, -kit), *n.* an excessively sophisticated person.

**O|ver|soul** or **o|ver|soul** (ō′vər sōl′), *n.* the Deity as the spiritual unity of all being in the philosophy of Emerson and other transcendentalists: *that Unity, that Oversoul, within which every man's particular being is contained and made one with all other* (Emerson).

**o|ver|spe|cial|i|za|tion** (ō′vər spesh′ə lə zā′shən), *n.* excessive or undue specialization: *Both must somehow steer a course between superficiality and overspecialization* (Scientific American).

**o|ver|speed** (*v.* ō′vər spēd′; *n.* ō′vər spēd′), *v.,* **-sped** or **-speed|ed, -speed|ing,** *n.* — ***v.t.*** to operate (a motor, vehicle, boat, or other device) at excessive speeds.
— ***v.i.*** to run at too high a speed: *Then an indicator showed that one of the six engines was overspeeding* (Time).
— ***n.*** speed that is more than normal: *An audible speed warning system which conveys ... the degree of overspeed* (New Scientist).

**o|ver|spend** (ō′vər spend′), *v.,* **-spent, -spend-ing.** — ***v.i.*** to spend more than one can afford.
— ***v.t.*** **1** to spend more than (a specified amount).

**Pronunciation Key:** hat, āge, cãre, fär; let, ēqual, tėrm; it, īce; hot, ōpen, ôrder; oil, out; cup, pụ̇t, rüle; child; long; thin; ᴛʜen; zh, measure; ə represents **a** in about, **e** in taken, **i** in pencil, **o** in lemon, **u** in circus.

2 to spend more than is necessary. 3 *Archaic.* to wear out; exhaust. — **o′ver|spend′er,** *n.*

**o|ver|spill** (*n., adj.* ō′vər spil′; *v.* ō′vər spil′), *n., v.,* **-spilled** or **-spilt, -spill|ing,** *adj.* — ***n.*** *Especially British.* **1** the act of spilling over: *There should be such an overspill of compressed air outwards ...* (New Scientist). **2** something which has spilled over; an excess: (*Figurative.*) *Even to pass along the street outside is difficult because of the overspill of customers* (Punch).
— ***v.i.*** to spill over; overflow: *Something, it seems, has overspilled, And trickled half the way to Hants* (Punch).
— ***adj.*** spilling over; overflowing: *overspill population.*

**o|ver|spin** (ō′vər spin′), *n.* **1** a forward rolling motion given a ball in the direction of flight: *The ball ... carried overspin which gave it the necessary impetus* (London Times). **2** a ball with overspin: *Playing faultlessly, he got off smashes, drop shots, overspins ... and cannonball serves* (Time).

**o|ver|spray** (*n.* ō′vər sprā′; *v.* ō′vər sprā′), *n., v.* — ***n.*** **1** a spray that does not adhere to a surface: *Overspray dries as it falls—turns to a harmless dust easily wiped or swept away* (Wall Street Journal). **2** a spraying beyond the intended area.
— ***v.t.*** to spray over, as one color or layer on another: *The design ... is built up by overspraying the base coat with contrasting colors of the same material* (New Scientist).

**o|ver|spread** (ō′vər spred′), *v.,* **-spread, -spread|ing.** — ***v.t.*** to spread over: *A smile overspread his broad face. The hot lava overspread the mountainside.* **SYN:** cover.
— ***v.i.*** to be spread over.

**o|ver|sta|bil|i|ty** (ō′vər stə bil′ə tē), *n.* great or excessive stability; resistance to change or fluctuation: *No segment of modern man's environment and organization as yet shows any signs of fixation or overstability* (Lewis Mumford).

**o|ver|stand** (ō′vər stand′), *v.t., v.i.,* **-stood, -stand|ing.** *Nautical.* to go beyond (a mark), especially in making way by tacking against the wind.

**o|ver|state** (ō′vər stāt′), *v.t.,* **-stat|ed, -stat|ing.** to state too strongly; exaggerate: *She was ... anxious to overstate ... her real social status* (H. G. Wells).

**o|ver|state|ment** (ō′vər stāt′mənt), *n.* too strong a statement; exaggeration.

**o|ver|stay** (ō′vər stā′), *v.t.* **1** to stay beyond the time of: *to overstay one's welcome.* **SYN:** outstay. **2** *Commerce, Informal.* to hold a stock, commodity, or other security, beyond the most profitable time to sell. — ***v.i.*** to stay too long.

**o|ver|steer** (*v.* ō′vər stir′; *n.* ō′vər stir′), *v., n.* — ***v.i.*** to have an automobile turn sharper on a curve than intended by the driver: *Almost all claim that the car's rear axle* (*since redesigned*) *gave* [*it*] *an inherent instability and a tendency to oversteer, resulting sometimes in fatal accidents* (Time).
— ***n.*** **1** an act or instance of oversteering: *The wider track of the rear wheels has reduced the tendency towards oversteer, but has not eliminated it* (Sunday Times). **2** a tendency to oversteer.

**o|ver|step** (ō′vər step′), *v.t., v.i.,* **-stepped, -step|ping.** to go beyond; exceed: (*Figurative.*) *to overstep the limits of good manners.*

**o|ver|stock** (*v.* ō′vər stok′; *n.* ō′vər stok′), *v., n.* — ***v.t.*** to supply with more than is needed.
— ***n.*** too great a stock or supply.

**o|ver|stor|age** (ō′vər stôr′ij, -stōr′-), *n.* excessive storage; the storing of more goods, supplies, or the like, than is needed.

**o|ver|sto|ry** (ō′vər stôr′ē, -stōr′-), *n., pl.* **-ries.** the topmast layer of plants in a forest: *Fires ... are most often located at ground level beneath dense forest overstories* (S. N. Hirsch).

**o|ver|strain** (*v.* ō′vər strān′; *n.* ō′vər strān′), *v., n.* — ***v.t., v.i.*** to strain too much.
— ***n.*** excessive strain: (*Figurative.*) *The economy is entering ... a period of overstrain* (New York Times).

**o|ver|stress** (ō′vər stres′), *v.t.* to give excessive or undue stress to: *It is impossible to overstress the importance of this remarkable assemblage of soil organisms* (New Scientist).

**o|ver|stretch** (*v.* ō′vər strech′; *n.* ō′vər strech′), *v., n.* — ***v.t.*** to stretch beyond the proper length, amount, or degree: (*Figurative.*) *The amount of capital which this country can provide without overstretching itself is something of a puzzle* (Manchester Guardian).
— ***n.*** the action or fact of overstretching resources; overextension: (*Figurative.*) *By concentrating Britain's role in the European defence theatres the Navy was increasingly able to match commitments and meet the problem of overstretch* (London Times).

**o|ver|strict** (ō′vər strikt′), *adj.* too strict. — **o′ver|strict′ness,** *n.*

**o|ver|stride** (ō′vər strīd′), *v.t.,* **-strode, -strid|den, -strid|ing.** **1** to stride over or across. **2** (*Figurative.*) to stride or go beyond; surpass. **3** to bestride.

**o|ver|struc|tured** (ō′vər struk′chərd), *adj.* too elaborately planned or arranged; overorganized: *In the fifties, one was expected to play the game and then lie about the results. I suppose the undergraduates of today would consider our game "overstructured"* (Calvin Trillin).

**o|ver|strung** (ō′vər strung′), *adj.* too highly strung; too nervous or sensitive: *overstrung nerves.*

**o|ver|stuff** (ō′vər stuf′), *v.t.* **1** to stuff too full. **2** to make (upholstered furniture) soft and comfortable by thick padding: *an overstuffed chair.*

**o|ver|sub|scribe** (ō′vər səb skrīb′), *v.t., v.i.,* **-scribed, -scrib|ing.** to subscribe for in excess of what is available or required: *The concert series was oversubscribed and many people could not buy tickets.*

**o|ver|sub|scrip|tion** (ō′vər səb skrip′shən), *n.* **1** the act or fact of oversubscribing. **2** an amount subscribed for in excess.

**o|ver|sub|tle** (ō′vər sut′əl), *adj.* too subtle.

**o|ver|sub|tle|ty** (ō′vər sut′əl tē), *n., pl.* **-ties.** too great subtlety.

**o|ver|sung** (ō′vər sung′), *v.* the past tense and past participle of **oversing.**

**o|ver|sup|ply** (*v.* ō′vər sə plī′; *n.* ō′vər sə plī′), *v.,* **-plied, -ply|ing,** *n., pl.* **-plies.** — ***v.t.*** to supply with more than is needed: *to oversupply buyers with oil, to oversupply oil.*
— ***n.*** too great a supply; excessive supply: *It is futile economically ... to give governmental authorities the right ... to ration the oversupply* (Newsweek).

**o|ver|swarm** (ō′vər swôrm′), *v.t.* **1** to swarm over; spread over in swarms. **2** to swarm in excess of.

**o|ver|sway** (ō′vər swā′), *v.t.* **1** to sway over, or cause to incline to one side or fall over. **2** *Obsolete.* to persuade, as to some course of action: *If he be so resolved, I can o'ersway him* (Shakespeare).

**o|ver|sweep** (ō′vər swēp′), *v.t.,* **-swept, -sweep|ing.** to sweep over.

**o|ver|swell** (ō′vər swel′), *v.,* **-swelled, -swelled** or **-swol|len, -swell|ing.** — ***v.t.*** to swell so as to pass over or beyond; overflow.
— ***v.i.*** to swell beyond the bounds or limits.

**o|ver|swing** (ō′vər swing′), *v.i.,* **-swung, -swing|ing.** to swing too hard and with too much follow-through: *When he is up against a long course like the Augusta National,* [*he*] *has a tendency to overswing in search of added yardage, and as a result, he is far off balance more than occasionally at the finish of a full shot* (New Yorker).

**o|vert** (ō′vėrt, ō vėrt′), *adj.* **1** open or public; evident; not hidden: *Hitting someone is an overt act. I know only his overt reasons for refusing; he may have others.* **SYN:** plain, manifest, apparent. **2** *Heraldry,* (of a bearing) having an open figure; outspread, as the wings of a bird in flight. [< Old French *overt* < Vulgar Latin *ōpertus,* alteration of Latin *apertus,* past participle of *aperīre* open] — **o′vert|ly,** *adv.* — **o′vert|ness,** *n.*

**overt act,** *Law.* an open or outward act from which criminal intent is inferred.

**o|ver|take** (ō′vər tāk′), *v.,* **-took, -tak|en, -tak|ing.** — ***v.t.*** **1** to come up with; catch up to: *The blue car overtook ours.* **2** to catch up with and pass: *They soon overtook us and were at the picnic grounds before we arrived.* **3** to come upon suddenly or unexpectedly: *A storm overtook the children. Fearful was the fate that ... overtook some of the members of that party* (Francis Parkman). **SYN:** surprise. **4** *Scottish.* to get through when pressed for time, or within the time: *It's a job you could doubtless overtake with the other* (Robert Louis Stevenson). **5** *Dialect.* to overcome the mind or senses of; intoxicate: *I don't appear to carry drink the way I used to ... I get overtaken* (Robert Louis Stevenson).
— ***v.i.*** *British.* to pass a motor vehicle: *At peak hour in English cities English drivers mount the pavement, overtake on the wrong side, and weave in and out like lunatic drivers in a ballet* (Listener).

**o|ver|tak|en** (ō′vər tā′kən), *v.* the past participle of **overtake.**

**o|ver|talk** (ō′vər tôk′), *n.* excessive talkativeness: *Perhaps the only thing that could seriously hurt his chances now is his ... penchant for overtalk* (Time).

**o|ver|task** (ō′vər task′, -täsk′), *v.t.* to give too long or too hard tasks to: *In those days children's brains were not overtasked, as they are now* (Samuel Butler).

**o|ver|tax** (ō′vər taks′), *v.t.* **1** to tax too heavily; overburden or oppress with taxes. **2** to put too heavy a burden on; make too great demands on: *I had overtaxed my strength and was exhausted.*

**o|ver|tax|a|tion** (ō′vər tak sā′shən), *n.* **1** the act or practice of overtaxing: *Overtaxation in the middle and higher brackets produces only 17% ... of total income tax revenues* (Wall Street Journal). **2** the condition of being overtaxed: *... attributed his death to a general prostration of the system from overtaxation of its powers* (New Yorker).

**o|ver|tech|nol|o|gize** (ō′vər tek nol′ə jīz), *v.t.,* **-gized, -giz|ing.** to make excessively technological: *to overtechnologize a government bureau.*

**o|ver|teem** (ō′vər tēm′), *v.i.* to teem, breed, or produce too much. — ***v.t.*** to wear out or exhaust with too much breeding or production.

**o|ver-the-count|er** (ō′vər ᴛʜə koun′tər), *adj.* **1** not bought or sold through a regular exchange; not listed on a stock exchange: *over-the-counter securities.* **2** that may be dispensed without a doctor's prescription: *over-the-counter drugs.*

**o|ver-the-ho|ri|zon** (ō′vər ᴛʜə hə rī′zən), *adj.* of or having to do with a system of communication using ultrahigh-frequency radio waves transmitted beyond the curvature of the earth by reflection off the troposphere.

**o|ver-the-road** (ō′vər ᴛʜə rōd′), *adj.* of or having to do with long-distance transportation by road.

**o|ver-the-shoul|der** (ō′vər ᴛʜə shōl′dər), *adj.* **1** worn or carried over the shoulder: *an over-the-shoulder bag.* **2** obtained by or as if by watching over someone's shoulder as he works: *... to learn what can be learned only by over-the-shoulder training* (United States Air Force Report on the Ballistic Missile).

**over-the-shoulder bombing,** = loft-bombing.

**o|ver|threw** (ō′vər thrü′), *v.* the past tense of **overthrow.**

**o|ver|throw** (*v.* ō′vər thrō′; *n.* ō′vər thrō′), *v.,* **-threw, -thrown, -throw|ing,** *n.* — ***v.t.*** **1** to take away the power of; defeat: *The nobles overthrew the king. A fierce, bloody, and confused action succeeded, in which the patriots were completely overthrown* (John L. Motley). **SYN:** rout, conquer, vanquish, overcome. **2** to put an end to; destroy; ruin: *to overthrow slavery. Much of the city was overthrown by the earthquake and a great fire. O, what a noble mind is here o'erthrown* (Shakespeare). **3** to overturn; upset; knock down: *The cart and fruit were overthrown as a speeding car swerved into them.* **4** to throw (a ball) past the place for which it is intended.
— ***n.*** **1** the act of overthrowing or state of being overthrown; defeat; upset: *The overthrow of his plans discouraged him. The overthrow of the party in power left the country in a turmoil.* **SYN:** destruction. **2** a ball thrown past the place for which it is intended: *... helped by indiscriminate throwing, which led to many overthrows* (London Times). — **o′ver|throw′er,** *n.*

**o|ver|thrown** (ō′vər thrōn′), *v.* the past participle of **overthrow.**

**o|ver|thrust** (ō′vər thrust′), *n., adj.* — ***n.*** a geological fault in which the earth's surface has cracked and been forced upward by internal pressure, pushing rocks of an earlier formation horizontally over those of later formation.
— ***adj.*** of or like an overthrust: *an overthrust fault.*

**o|ver|thwart** (*adv., prep.* ō′vər thwôrt′; *adj.* ō′vər-thwôrt′), *adv., prep., adj. Dialect.* — ***adv., prep.*** across; athwart.
— ***adj.*** **1** lying across; situated across or opposite. **2** *Figurative.* contrary; perverse; cross.

**o|ver|time** (*n., adv., adj.* ō′vər tīm′; *v.* ō′vər tīm′), *n., adv., adj., v.,* **-timed, -tim|ing.** — ***n.*** **1** extra time; time beyond the regular hours: *He was paid for the overtime he worked.* **2** wages for this period: *to pay overtime.* **3** the time added to the normal length of an athletic contest to break a tie in the score: *The Gophers lagged for much of the first overtime, but tied it up ... with 40 seconds remaining* (New York Times).
— ***adv.*** beyond the regular hours; during overtime: *After the office closed he worked overtime.*
— ***adj.*** **1** of or for overtime: *overtime work, overtime pay.* **2** beyond the allotted or permitted time: *overtime parking.*
— ***v.t.*** to give too much time to: *to overtime a camera exposure.*

**o|ver|tire** (ō′vər tīr′), *v.t.,* **-tired, -tir|ing.** to tire too much.

**o|ver|tone** (ō′vər tōn′), *n.* **1** a fainter and higher musical tone heard along with the main or fundamental tone; harmonic: *It is the overtones which give a musical tone its characteristic timbre or quality* (New York Times). **2** the color of the light reflected from a painted or glazed surface or the like. **3** *Figurative.* a hint or suggestion of something felt, believed, or perceived: *an overtone of anger.*

**overtone series,** *Music.* the entire range of overtones having frequencies that are integral multiples of the fundamental tone; harmonic series.

**o|ver|took** (ō′vər tu̇k′), *v.* the past tense of **overtake.**

**o|ver|top** (ō′vər top′), *v.t.,* **-topped, -top|ping.** **1** to rise above; be higher than: *The new building will overtop all the others.* **SYN:** surmount. **2** *Figurative.* to surpass; excel: *In them the man somehow overtops the author* (James Russell Lowell). *She overtops now her previous appearances on the screen* (London Times).

**o|ver|trade** (ō′vər trād′), *v.i.,* **-trad|ed, -trad|ing.** to purchase goods or lay in stock beyond the limit of one's capital or the requirements of the market.

**o|ver|train** (ō′vər trān′), *v.t., v.i.* to subject to or undergo so much athletic training that the condition is injured rather than improved; train to excess, going stale as a result.

**o|ver|trick** (ō′vər trik′), *n.* (in card games) a trick more than the number bid for or needed for game.

**o|ver|trump** (ō′vər trump′), *v.i.* to play a higher trump than one played earlier in a card game: *East did not overtrump on the third spade* (New York Times). **—*v.t.*** to play a higher trump than: *to overtrump a trump.* (*Figurative.*) *There is widespread opinion that he has overtrumped the Protectionists* (Manchester Examiner).

**o|ver|ture** (ō′vər chu̇r, -chər), *n., v.,* **-tured, -tur|ing.** **—*n.*** **1** a proposal or offer: *The enemy is making overtures for peace.* **SYN:** proposition. **2** a musical composition played by the orchestra as an introduction to an opera, oratorio, or other long musical composition: *Once the musicians were seated. Rapee ... raised his baton and the band swung into its booming overture* (New Yorker). **SYN:** prelude. **3** an introductory part, as of a poem. **4** in Presbyterian churches: **a** the sending of a proposal or question to the highest court or to the presbyteries. **b** the proposal or question itself.
**—*v.t.*** **1** to bring or put forward as an overture. **2** to introduce with a musical overture.
[earlier, an opening, aperture < Old French *overture,* alteration of Latin *apertūra* opening. Compare etym. under **overt.** See etym. of doublet **aperture.**]

**o|ver|turn** (*v.* ō′vər tėrn′; *n.* ō′vər tėrn′), *v., n.* **—*v.t.*** **1** to turn upside down; upset: *The cat overturned the vase of flowers.* **SYN:** invert. **2** *Figurative.* to make fall down; overthrow; destroy the power of; defeat: *The rebels overturned the government.*
**—*v.i.*** to fall down, turn over, or upset: *The boat overturned.* **SYN:** capsize. See syn. under **upset.**
**—*n.*** **1** the act or process of overturning. **2** a turnover in business or industry. **3** *Ecology.* the reversal or mixture of different temperature layers in a lake, occurring in the spring and fall. **—o′ver-turn′er,** *n.*

**o|ver-un|der** (ō′vər un′dər), *n.* = over-and-under.

**o|ver|use** (*v.* ō′vər yüz′; *n.* ō′vər yüs′), *v.,* **-used, -us|ing,** *n.* **—*v.t.*** **1** to use too much. **2** to use too hard or too often.
**—*n.*** too much or too hard use: *The easy overuse of "pretty" and "little" exacerbated his uneasy mind* (James Thurber).

**o|ver|val|u|a|tion** (ō′vər val′yu̇ ā′shən), *n.* too high valuation; overestimate.

**o|ver|val|ue** (ō′vər val′yü), *v.t.,* **-ued, -u|ing.** to value too highly; put too high a value on.

**o|ver|view** (ō′vər vyü′), *n.* a broad view; survey; inspection; examination: *An overview of the published studies of this year reveals some gaps and some significant trends* (Stone and Taylor).

**o|ver|volt|age** (ō′vər vōl′tij), *n.* the difference between the theoretical voltage and the actual required voltage of an electrode in an electrolytic process.

**o|ver|warm** (ō′vər wôrm′), *adj.* too warm or solicitous: *Her voice was as overwarm as if she were coaxing a shy child* (New Yorker).

**o|ver|watch** (ō′vər woch′, -wôch′), *v.t.* **1** to watch over. **2** to make weary by watching.

**o|ver|wa|ter** (ō′vər wôt′ər, -wot′-), *adj., v.* **—*adj.*** above or across water: *overwater travel, an overwater flight.*
**—*v.t.*** to water too much: *... it would be easy to overwater it, and this would rot the roots* (Sunset).

**o|ver|wear** (ō′vər wãr′), *v.t.,* **-wore, -worn, -wear|ing.** **1** to wear out; exhaust. **2** to outwear; outgrow.

**o|ver|wea|ry** (ō′vər wir′ē), *adj., v.,* **-ried, -ry|ing.** **—*adj.*** very weary; tired out.
**—*v.t.*** to weary to excess.

**o|ver|weath|er** (ō′vər weᴛʜ′ər), *adj.* of or at altitudes high enough to avoid unfavorable weather conditions: *an overweather flight.*

**o|ver|ween** (ō′vər wēn′), *v.i.* to have too high an opinion of oneself; be conceited or arrogant; presume.

**o|ver|ween|ing** (ō′vər wē′ning), *adj., n.* **—*adj.*** **1** thinking too much of oneself; conceited; self-confident; presumptuous: *overweening confidence in his own powers* (William H. Prescott). **2** excessive; exaggerated: *overweening ambition, an overweening desire.*
**—*n.*** excessive esteem; overestimation.
[present participle of Middle English *overween* < *over-* + *ween* expect] **—o′ver|ween′ing|ly,** *adv.* **—o′ver|ween′ing|ness,** *n.*

**o|ver|weigh** (ō′vər wā′), *v.t.* **1** to be greater than in weight, importance, etc.; outweigh: *My duty is imperative, and must overweigh my private feelings* (Nicholas P. S. Wiseman). **SYN:** overbalance. **2** to weigh down; oppress.

**o|ver|weight** (*adj., n.* ō′vər wāt′; *v.* ō′vər wāt′), *adj., n., v.* **—*adj.*** having too much weight: *The boy is overweight for his age and height.*
**—*n.*** **1** too much weight: *an overweight of people on a floor, an overweight of care on the mind.* **2** extra weight: *The butcher gave us overweight on this roast.*
**—*v.t.*** **1** to overburden: *a small child overweighted with heavy schoolbooks.* **2** *Figurative.* to weigh too heavily; attach too much importance to; overstress: *Our efforts ... may leave the impression that we are overweighing the Arab side* (Wall Street Journal).

**o|ver|went** (ō′vər went′), *v.* the past tense of **overgo.**

**o|ver|whelm** (ō′vər hwelm′), *v.t.* **1** to overcome completely; crush: *She was overwhelmed with grief.* **2** to cover completely, as a flood would: *A great wave overwhelmed the boat.* **SYN:** submerge. **3** to heap, treat, or address with an excessive amount of anything: *He ... overwhelmed her with a profusion of compliment* (Tobias Smollett). [< *over-* + *whelm* roll, submerge]

**o|ver|whelm|ing** (ō′vər hwel′ming), *adj.* too many, too great, or too much to be resisted; overpowering: *an overwhelming majority of votes.* **—o′ver|whelm′ing|ly,** *adv.*

**o|ver|wind** (ō′vər wīnd′), *v.t.,* **-wound, -wind|ing.** to wind beyond the proper limit; wind too far: *to overwind a watch.*

**o|ver|win|ter** (ō′vər win′tər), *v.i.* to stay through the winter enduring cold and snow: *Dahlia tubers can overwinter right in the ground ...* (Sunset).

**o|ver|wise** (ō′vər wīz′), *adj.* too wise. **—o′ver-wise′ly,** *adv.*

**o|ver|word** (ō′vər wėrd′), *n. Scottish.* a word or phrase repeated, such as the refrain of a song.

**o|ver|wore** (ō′vər wôr′, -wōr′), *v.* the past tense of **overwear.**

**o|ver|work** (*n.* ō′vər wėrk′; *v.* ō′vər wėrk′), *n., v.,* **-worked** or **-wrought, -work|ing.** **—*n.*** **1** too much or too hard work: *exhausted from overwork.* **2** extra work.
**—*v.i.*** to work too hard or too much.
**—*v.t.*** **1** to cause to work too hard or too long: *I know how busy you are; you mustn't overwork yourself* (G. K. Chesterton). **2** to use to excess: *to overwork a pose of childlike innocence.* **3** to fill too full with work. **4** to work too much upon (as a book or speech); elaborate too much. **5** *Figurative.* to stir up or excite too much. **6** to figure or decorate the surface of.

**o|ver|world** (ō′vər wėrld′), *n.* **1** the respectable section of society: *They lapse in time into what sociologists call a subculture, an underworld of mores subtly opposed to those of the overworld* (Maclean's). **2** a section of society seeking privileges because of wealth or position: *As if the underworld weren't enough of a problem, Dist. Atty. McKesson has come up with something new to worry about, the overworld* (Tuscaloosa News). **3** a world above or higher than this; heaven: *They* [*primitive men*] *believed there was an overworld where God resided in space, and an underworld where all departed spirits were gathered together* (Edmund Hamilton Sears).

**o|ver|worn** (ō′vər wôrn′, -wōrn′), *v.* the past participle of **overwear.**

**o|ver|wound** (ō′vər wound′), *v.* the past tense and past participle of **overwind:** *The clock broke when it was overwound.*

**o|ver|wrap** (ō′vər rap′), *n.* a material, usually transparent such as cellophane, often used as a second, outside wrapping for cigarettes, bread, and other items that have to be kept fresh.

**o|ver|write** (ō′vər rīt′), *v.t., v.i.,* **-wrote, -writ|ten, -writ|ing.** **1** to write too much (about a subject). **2** to write ornately or pretentiously: *Why should books about the Arab world be ... grossly overwritten?* (Manchester Guardian Weekly). **3** to write on or over (other writing).

**o|ver|wrought** (*adj.* o′vər rôt′; *v.* ō′vər rôt′), *adj., v.* **—*adj.*** **1** wearied or exhausted by too much work or excitement: *overwrought nerves.* **2** worked up to too high a pitch; too excited. **3** decorated all over: *an overwrought platter. Of Gothic structure was the Northern side, O'erwrought with ornaments of barbarous pride* (Alexander Pope). **4** too elaborate. **SYN:** overdone.
**—*v.*** a past tense and a past participle of **overwork.**

**o|vi|bos** (ō′və bos), *n.* = musk ox. [< New Latin *ovibos* < Latin *ovis* sheep + *bōs* ox]

**o|vi|cid|al** (ō′və sī′dəl), *adj.* that destroys the eggs of insects: *an ovicidal insecticide.*

**o|vi|cide** (ō′və sīd), *n.* a chemical substance for destroying the eggs of insects: *This fungicide ... has the added advantage of being a mite ovicide* (New Scientist). [< Latin *ōvum* egg + English *-cide*[1]]

**O|vid|i|an** (ō vid′ē ən), *adj.* of or having to do with the Roman poet Ovid, 43 B.C.-A.D. 17? or his poetry: *... a series of Ovidian allusions* (London Times).

**o|vi|duct** (ō′və dukt), *n.* the tube through which the ovum or egg passes from the ovary. In human beings the oviduct connects with the uterus and is called the Fallopian tube. [< New Latin *oviductus* < Latin *ōvum* egg + *ductus,* past participle of *dūcere* to lead]

**o|vi|duc|tal** (ō′və duk′təl), *adj.* of or having to do with the oviduct.

**o|vif|er|ous** (ō vif′ər əs), *adj.* producing or bearing eggs. [< Latin *ōvum* egg + English *-ferous*]

**o|vi|form** (ō′və fôrm), *adj.* egg-shaped. [< Latin *ōvum* egg + English *-form*]

**o|vine** (ō′vīn, -vin), *adj.* of, having to do with, or like sheep. [< Latin *ovīnus* < *ovis* sheep]

**o|vip|a|ra** (ō vip′ər ə), *n.pl.* egg-laying animals as a formerly recognized group. [< New Latin *Ovipara*]

**o|vi|par|i|ty** (ō′və par′ə tē), *n.* condition of being oviparous; the laying of eggs to be hatched outside the body.

**o|vip|a|rous** (ō vip′ər əs), *adj.* producing eggs that hatch after leaving the body. Birds, and most reptiles, fishes, and insects are oviparous. [< Latin *ōviparus* (with English *-ous*) < *ōvum* egg + *parere* bring forth] **—o|vip′a|rous|ly,** *adv.* **—o|vip′a|rous|ness,** *n.*

**o|vi|pos|it** (ō′və poz′it), *v.i.* to deposit or lay eggs, especially by means of an ovipositor, as an insect. [< Latin *ōvum* egg + *positus,* past participle of *pōnere* to place, put]

**o|vi|po|si|tion** (ō′və pə zish′ən), *n.* the laying of eggs by means of an ovipositor.

**o|vi|pos|i|tor** (ō′və poz′ə tər), *n.* an organ or set of organs at the end of the abdomen in certain female insects, by which eggs are deposited. [< Latin *ōvum* egg + *positor* builder; (literally) one who places < *pōnere* to place]

**o|vi|sac** (ō′və sak), *n.* **1** a sac, cell, or capsule containing an ovum or ova. **2** = Graafian follicle.

**o|vism** (ō′viz əm), *n. Biology.* the old doctrine that the egg contains all the organs of the future animal.

**o|vis po|li** (ō′vis pō′lī, -lē), *n., pl.* **-lis.** = Marco Polo sheep. [< New Latin *Ovis poli* the genus and species name; (literally) sheep of Polo (in reference to Marco Polo, about 1254-1324, the Venetian traveler, who described it in his book)]

**o|vist** (ō′vist), *n.* an adherent of the doctrine of ovism.

**o|vo|gen|e|sis** (ō′və jen′ə sis), *n.* = oogenesis.

**o|vo|ge|net|ic** (ō′və jə net′ik), *adj.* = oogenetic.

**o|void** (ō′void), *adj., n.* **—*adj.*** **1** oval with one end more pointed than the other; egg-shaped; ovate. **2** of this form with the broader end at the base, as a pear or avocado is.
**—*n.*** an egg-shaped object.

**o|voi|dal** (ō voi′dəl), *adj.* = ovoid.

**o|vo|lo** (ō′və lō), *n., pl.* **-li** (-lē). *Architecture.* a convex molding whose cross section is approximately a quarter of a circle or an ellipse. [< Italian *ovolo* (diminutive) < *ovo* < Latin *ōvum* egg. Compare etym. under **ovule.**]

**O|von|ic** or **o|von|ic** (ō von′ik), *adj.* of or based upon the property shown by certain glasses of switching from a state of high electrical resistance to one of low resistance upon the application of a particular voltage to the glass: *Ovonic devices, Ovonic switches.*
[< Stanford R. *Ov*(shinsky), born 1923, an American inventor, who discovered the Ovonic property + (electr)*onic*]

**O|von|ics** or **o|von|ics** (ō von′iks), *n.* the use or application of Ovonic devices.

**o|vo|tes|tis** (ō′və tes′tis), *n., pl.* **-tes** (-tēz). a combined male and female reproductive organ, as in the snail. [< New Latin *ovotestis* < Latin *ōvum* egg + *testis* testis]

**o|vo|vi|tel|lin** (ō′vō vī tel′in, -vi-), *n.* a protein contained in the yolk of eggs. [< Latin *ōvum* egg + *vitellin*]

**o|vo|vi|vip|a|rous** (ō′vō vī vip′ər əs), *adj.* producing eggs that are hatched within the body of the parent, so that young are born alive but without placental attachment. Certain reptiles and fishes and many invertebrate animals are ovoviviparous. [< Latin *ōvum* egg + *viviparous*] —**o'vo|vi|vip'a-rous|ly**, *adv.* —**o'vo|vi|vip'a|rous|ness**, *n.*

**Ov|shin|sky effect** (ov shin'skē), Ovonic property: *To achieve "the Ovshinsky effect" the voltage must be matched precisely to fit each combination of chemicals in the glass; the voltage must also be varied with the thickness of the glass* (Saturday Review). [< Stanford R. *Ovshinsky;* see etym. under **Ovonic**]

**o|vu|lar** (ō'vyə lər), *adj.* of an ovule; being an ovule.

**o|vu|lar|y** (ō'vyə ler ē), *adj.* = ovular.

**o|vu|late** (ō'vyə lāt), *v.i.,* **-lat|ed, -lat|ing. 1** to produce ova, oocytes, or ovules. **2** to discharge ova or oocytes from the ovary. [< New Latin *ovulum* ovule + English *-ate*[1]]

**o|vu|la|tion** (ō'vyə lā'shən), *n.* **1** the formation or production of ova or ovules: *In 1936 F. H. A. Marshall and E. B. Verney found that strong electrical stimulation of the nervous system of the rabbit caused ovulation* (Science News). **2** the discharge of an ovum from the ovary.

**o|vu|la|to|ry** (ō'vyə lə tôr'ē, -tōr'-), *adj.* of or having to do with ovulation: *A ... gynecologist recently announced a new concept of ovulatory timing* (Wall Street Journal).

**o|vule** (ō'vyül), *n.* **1** a small ovum, especially when immature or unfertilized; the ovum before its release from the ovarian follicle. **2a** the part of a plant that develops into a seed. In higher plants, the ovule contains the female germ cell or egg, which after fertilization develops into an embryo. **b** a young seed. [< New Latin *ovulum* (diminutive) < Latin *ōvum* egg]

**o|vu|lif|er|ous** (ō'vyə lif'ər əs), *adj.* producing ovules.

**o|vum** (ō'vəm), *n., pl.* **o|va. 1** the germ cell produced in the ovary of the female; egg. After the ovum is fertilized, a new organism or embryo develops. **2** *Architecture.* an egg-shaped ornament. [< Latin *ōvum* egg]

**owe** (ō), *v.,* **owed, ow|ing.** —***v.t.* 1** to have to pay; be in debt for: *I owe the grocer a dollar. He owes not any man* (Longfellow). **2** *Figurative.* to be obliged or indebted for: *We owe a great deal to our parents. Never in the field of human conflict was so much owed by so many to so few* (Sir Winston Churchill). **3** to bear toward another: *to owe a grudge.* **4** *Obsolete.* to own; possess.
—***v.i.*** to be in debt: *He is always owing for something.*
[Old English *āgan* to own, have an obligation to]

**O|wen|ism** (ō'ə niz əm), *n.* the theory or system of Robert Owen (1771-1858), a British social reformer who advocated the reorganization of society into a system of communistic cooperation, which he tried to put into practice in several experimental communities: *Owenism remained the creed of a substantial body of followers, who turned back to the attempt to establish villages of cooperation* (G. D. H. Cole).

**O|wen|ite** (ō'ə nīt), *n.* a follower of Robert Owen; believer in Owenism: *A community of Owenites, early Utopian socialists, set up a short-lived colony ... in 1826* (New York Times).

**OWI** (no periods), Office of War Information.

**ow|ing** (ō'ing), *adj.* **1** due; owed: *to pay what is owing.* **SYN**: outstanding. **2** that owes. **3** *Archaic, Figurative.* indebted; beholden: *I am greatly owing to your Lordship for your last favour* (Samuel Pepys).

**owing to**, on account of; because of; due to; as a result of: *Owing to a serious illness, she was absent from school for over a month. I could not see many yards ahead owing to the bushes* (W. H. Hudson).

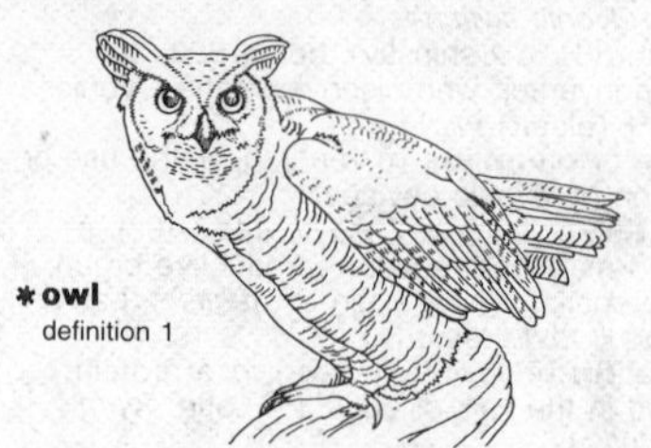

***owl**
definition 1

great horned owl

***owl** (oul), *n.* **1** a bird with a big head, big eyes, and a short hooked beak. Owls have very soft feathers that enable them to fly noiselessly. Some kinds have tufts of feathers on their heads called "horns" or "ears." Most owls hunt at night and live on mice, small birds, and reptiles. There are a number of kinds, making up an order of birds. **2** any one of various domestic pigeons that look like owls. **3** *Figurative.* a person who stays up late at night. **4** *Figurative.* a person who looks solemn and wise, as an owl is supposed to be. [Old English *ūle*] —**owl'like'**, *adj.*

**owl|et** (ou'lit), *n.* **1** a young owl. **2** a small owl.

**owlet moth**, a noctuid moth.

**owl-eyed** (oul'īd'), *adj.* **1** having eyes like those of an owl; seeing best in the dark. **2** *Figurative.* looking somewhat strange or staring, and having a wide-eyed appearance: *The round, owl-eyed, oddball in horn-rimmed glasses* (Time).

**owl|ish** (ou'lish), *adj.* **1** like an owl; like an owl's: *owlish eyes.* **2** trying to look wise: *an owlish air of wisdom.* —**owl'ish|ly**, *adv.* —**owl'ish|ness**, *n.*

**owl|light** (oul'līt'), *n.* twilight; dusk.

**owl's-clo|ver** (oulz'klō'vər), *n.* any herb of a group of the figwort family, growing especially in California.

**owl train**, *U.S.* a railroad train that makes its trip late at night.

**owl|wise**[1] (oul'wīz'), *adj.* as wise as an owl. [< *owl* + *wise*[1]]

**owl|wise**[2] (oul'wīz'), *adv.* in the manner of an owl. [< *owl* + *-wise*]

**own** (ōn), *v., adj., n.* —***v.t.* 1** to have; possess: *I own many books. Enjoy the land but own it not* (Henry David Thoreau). **SYN**: hold. See syn. under **have. 2** to admit; confess; acknowledge: *He owned his guilt. I own you are right.* **SYN**: concede, grant. **3** to admit that one owns or is the parent of: *His father will not own him.*
—***v.i.*** to confess: *She owns to many faults. I own to being afraid.*
—***adj.* 1** of oneself or itself; belonging to oneself or itself: *This is my own book. She makes her own dresses. We have our own troubles.* **2** in closest relationship: *Own brothers have the same parents.*
—***n.*** the one or ones belonging to oneself or itself: *The cup ... from which our Lord Drank at the last sad supper with his own* (Tennyson).
**come into one's own, a** to get what belongs to one: *His inheritance was held in trust; not until he was twenty-one would he come into his own.* **b** to get the success or credit that one deserves: *It was when the primitive vigor of his carving united with the human sensuality of his life drawing, at the end of the twenties, that he* [*Henry Moore*] *came into his own as a sculptor.* (Donald Hall).
**hold one's own, a** to keep one's position against opposition; not be forced back; stand one's ground; make no concessions: *Strange superstitions still hold their own in many parts of the world.* **b** to maintain one's strength or state of health; lose no ground: *The doctor assured us that grandfather was holding his own, despite the new complications.*
**of one's own**, belonging to oneself: *You have a good mind of your own.*
**on one's own**, not ruled or directed by someone else; on one's own account, responsibility, or resources: *When he was a young man, he traveled about the world on his own.*
**own up**, to confess fully: *The boy owned up to his part in the Hallowe'en prank.*
[Old English *āgen*]

**own-brand** (ōn'brand'), *adj.* bearing the name or brand of the store which sells it instead of the manufacturer's name: *The principles of own-brand groceries date back to the turn of the century when stores such as Lipton and Home & Colonial did much of their own packaging* (London Times).

**own|er** (ō'nər), *n.* a person who owns: *The owner of the dog brought him a collar.* **SYN**: possessor, proprietor.

**own|er|less** (ō'nər lis), *adj.* having no owner: *an ownerless dog.*

**own|er-oc|cu|pa|tion** (ō'nər ok'yə pā'shən), *n. British.* occupation of a house by its owner: *The truth is that less homes have been built for owner-occupation in the last six months than in the same period a year ago* (Listener).

**own|er-oc|cu|pied** (ō'nər ok'yə pīd), *adj. British.* lived in by the owner: *Gains on owner-occupied houses are not subject to tax* (Sunday Times).

**own|er-oc|cu|pi|er** (ō'nər ok'yə pī'ər), *n. British.* a person who owns the house he lives in; homeowner: *Nobody could tell whether 200,000 houses for sale each year would be the right number ... but he was certain that at least three-fifths of the population would want to be owner-occupiers* (London Times).

**own|er|ship** (ō'nər ship), *n.* ther state of being an owner; the possessing (of something); right of possession: *He claimed ownership of a boat he found drifting down the river.*

**owse** (ous), *n., pl.* **ow|sen, ows|sen** (ou'sən, -zən), *Scottish.* ox.

**owt** (out, ōt), *n. English Dialect.* anything; aught: *... the old Yorkshire saying that you can't get owt for nowt* (London Times). [variant of *aught*]

**ox** (oks), *n., pl.* **ox|en. 1** the full-grown male of domestic cattle, that has been castrated and is used as a draft animal or for beef. An ox is slow but very strong. **2** any one of a group of mammals with horns and cloven hoofs, to which domestic cattle, buffaloes, and bison belong; bovine animal. Oxen are ruminants. [Old English *oxa,* singular of *oxan*] —**ox'like'**, *adj.*

**ox|a|cil|lin** (ok'sə sil'in), *n.* a semisynthetic form of penicillin that is resistant to neutralizing by penicillinase: *Oxacillin ... cured nearly two-thirds of 124 patients who had acquired severe staphylococcal infections* (Science News Letter). [< *ox*(ygen) + *a*(zole) + (peni)*cillin*]

**ox|al|ac|e|tate** (ok'sə las'ə tāt), *n.* = oxaloacetate.

**ox|al|a|cet|ic acid** (ok'sə lə sē'tik, -set'ik), = oxaloacetic acid.

**ox|a|late** (ok'sə lāt), *n.* a salt or ester of oxalic acid. [< *oxal*(ic) + *-ate*[2]]

**ox|al|ic** (ok sal'ik), *adj.* **1** of or derived from oxalis. **2** of oxalic acid.

**oxalic acid**, a colorless, crystalline, poisonous organic acid found in many vegetables and other plants, such as wood sorrel, spinach, rhubarb, tomatoes, grapes, and sweet potatoes. It is also produced in the body, and is prepared commercially by heating sodium formate with sodium hydroxide. *Industry uses oxalic acid in processing textiles, bleaching straw hats, and removing paint and varnish* (John E. Leffler). *Formula:* $C_2H_2O_4 \cdot 2H_2O$ [< French *acide oxalique* < Latin *oxalis;* see etym. under **oxalis**]

**ox|al|i|da|ceous** (ok sal'ə dā'shəs), *adj.* belonging to the family of plants typified by the wood sorrel. [< New Latin *Oxalidaceae* the family name (< *Oxalis* the typical genus) < Latin (see etym. under **oxalis**) + *-aceous*]

**ox|a|lis** (ok'sə lis), *n.* any one of a group of plants with acid juice, usually having leaves composed of three heart-shaped leaflets, and delicate white, yellow, or pink flowers; wood sorrel. [< Latin *oxalis* sorrel[2] < Greek *oxalís* < *oxýs* sour, sharp]

**ox|a|lo|ac|e|tate** (ok'sə lō as'ə tāt), *n.* a salt or ester of oxaloacetic acid.

**ox|a|lo|a|cet|ic acid** (ok'sə lō ə sē'tik, -set'ik), a colorless, crystalline, unstable acid that combines with acetic acid at the beginning and end of the Krebs cycle. *Formula:* $C_4H_4O_5$ [< *oxalic* + *acetic acid*]

**ox|a|zin** (ok'sə zin), *n.* = oxazine.

**ox|a|zine** (ok'sə zēn, -zin), *n.* one of a series of isomeric chemical compounds consisting of one oxygen, one nitrogen, and four carbon atoms arranged in a ring. *Formula:* $C_4H_5ON$ [< *ox*(ygen) + *azine*]

**ox|blood** (oks'blud'), *n.* a deep red color.

**ox|bow** (oks'bō'), *n.* **1** a piece of wood shaped like a U that is placed under and around the neck of an ox, with the upper ends inserted in the bar of the yoke. **2** a bend in a river shaped like a U. **3** the land contained within it.

**oxbow lake**, a small lake or pond formed by a river that has straightened its meandering bed, so that a former oxbow becomes separated from the river.

**Ox|bridge** (oks'brij'), *adj., n. British.* —***adj.*** of or having to do with Oxford and Cambridge Universities, together contrasted with redbrick universities.
—***n.*** a student or graduate of Oxford or Cambridge.

**Ox|bridg|e|an** or **Ox|bridg|i|an** (oks brij'ē ən), *adj., n. British.* Oxbridge.

**ox|cart** (oks'kärt'), *n.* a cart drawn by an ox or oxen.

**ox|en** (ok'sən), *n.* plural of **ox.**

**ox|er** (ok'sər), *n. British Slang.* **1** a fence to keep oxen from straying. **2** (in fox-hunting) a fence consisting of a wide ditch bordered by a strong hedge, beyond which is a railing: *The fence ... was an oxer, about seven feet high, and impervious to a bird* (G. J. Whyte-Melville).

**ox|eye** (oks'ī'), *n.* **1** the common American daisy; oxeye daisy. **2** any one of several other composite plants like it. **3** any one of various shore birds, such as the semipalmated sandpiper and the black-bellied plover of North America.

**ox-eyed** (oks'īd'), *adj.* having large, full eyes like those of an ox.

**oxeye daisy**, the common American daisy, having flower heads with a yellow disk and white rays; oxeye.

**Ox|fam** or **OXFAM** (oks'fam), *n.* a British voluntary organization for the relief of poverty and disease, especially in underdeveloped countries, founded in 1942 and headquartered at Oxford. [< *Ox*(ford Committee for) *Fam*(ine Relief)]

**ox|fly** (oks'flī'), *n., pl.* **-flies.** a fly troublesome to cattle.

***ox|ford** or **Ox|ford** (oks'fərd), *n.* **1** a kind of low shoe, laced over the instep, usually with three or more eyelets. **2** a kind of cotton or synthetic cloth used for men's shirts, women's blouses, and other garments. It has a basket weave. **3** a very dark gray. **4** *British Slang.* five shillings. [< *Oxford,* a city in England]

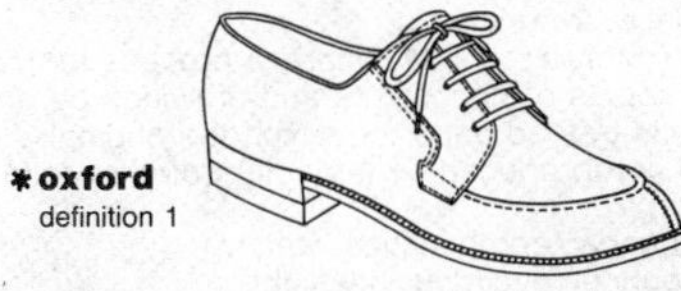

***oxford**
definition 1

**Oxford bags**, a style of trousers very wide at the ankles, worn especially in the 1920's.
**Oxford corners**, *Printing.* ruled borderlines around the print, as of a book, that cross and extend beyond the corners.
**Oxford Down**, any one of an English breed of hornless sheep.
**Oxford gray**, a very dark gray.
**Oxford Group** or **Oxford Group movement**, = Buchmanism.
**Ox|for|di|an** (oks fôr′dē ən), *n.* a supporter of the theory that the Earl of Oxford was the author of Shakespeare's plays: *What can the Oxfordians say about the fact that the Earl of Oxford died in 1604 and the author of the plays was writing until 1613?* (New Yorker).
**Oxford movement**, **1** a movement in the Church of England favoring High-Church principles, which originated at Oxford University about 1833. **2** = Buchmanism.
**Oxford shoe**, a kind of low shoe; oxford.
**Oxford theory**, the theory that the Earl of Oxford was the author of Shakespeare's plays.
**Oxford tie**, a kind of low shoe; oxford.
**Oxford University**, a famous university at Oxford, England, founded in the 1200's.
**ox|heart** (oks′härt′), *n.* a large, heart-shaped, sweet cherry.
**ox|hide** (oks′hīd′), *n.* **1** the hide of an ox. **2** leather made from it: *It was an exhilarating feeling to be hauled up on a length of oxhide tied around the waist* (London Times).
**ox|id** (ok′sid), *n.* = oxide.
**ox|i|dant** (ok′sə dənt), *n.* an oxidizer, such as liquid oxygen, used for burning the fuel of missiles and rockets.
**ox|i|dase** (ok′sə dās, -dāz), *n.* any one of a group of enzymes that cause or promote oxidation.
**ox|i|da|sic** (ok′sə dā′sik, -zik), *adj.* of or having to do with oxidase.
**ox|i|date** (ok′sə dāt), *v.t., v.i.,* **-dat|ed, -dat|ing.** = oxidize.
**ox|i|da|tion** (ok′sə dā′shən), *n.* **1** the act or process of oxidizing. Burning is one kind of oxidation. **2** the condition of being oxidized. Also, **oxydation.**
**oxidation enzyme**, = oxidase: *Oxidation enzymes are required in all living matter to help cells burn oxygen* (Wall Street Journal).
**oxidation potential**, *Chemistry, Physics.* a measure, in volts, of an element's tendency to oxidize or lose electrons, used to predict how the element will react with another substance. The oxidation potential of hydrogen is arbitrarily assigned as zero. The standard oxidation potential of potassium is +2.92, and of gold, −1.42.
**ox|i|da|tion-re|duc|tion** (ok′sə dā′shən ri duk′shən), *n.,* or **oxidation-reduction reaction**, a chemical reaction involving the transfer of electrons from one atom or ion to another atom or ion by the processes of oxidation and reduction; redox.
**oxidation-reduction potential**, the electromotive force resulting from oxidation-reduction, usually measured relative to a standard hydrogen electrode: *Electron-donor and electron-acceptor molecules can be characterized by the quantity called oxidation-reduction potential, which can be positive or negative and is usually expressed in volts* (Scientific American).
**oxidation state**, *Chemistry.* the state of an element or atom in a compound with respect to the number of electrons it has lost or gained, expressed as a positive or negative number indicating the ionic charge of the atom and equal to its valence. In most of their compounds, the oxidation state of oxygen is −2 and that of hydrogen is +1.
**ox|i|da|tive** (ok′sə dā′tiv), *adj.* having the property of oxidizing: *The metabolic significance of porphyrins in cellular oxidative processes is well known to biochemists* (B. Nickerson). **—ox′i|da′tive|ly,** *adv.*
**oxidative phosphorylation**, the process in cell metabolism by which mitochondria oxidize organic molecules and store the energy by converting adenosine diphosphate (ADP) to adenosine triphosphate (ATP): *The final stage of the breakdown of carbohydrates and fats ... is one which consumes oxygen, and is normally linked intimately with the production of ATP in the process known as oxidative phosphorylation* (New Scientist).
**ox|ide** (ok′sīd, -sid), *n.* a compound of oxygen with another element or radical. The oxides of sulfur and nitrogen can be used to form sulfuric and nitric acids. [< earlier French *oxide* < *ox(ygène)* oxygen + *(ac)ide* acid]
**ox|id|ic** (ok sid′ik), *adj.* of or involving an oxide or oxides.
**ox|i|dim|e|try** (ok′sə dim′ə trē), *n. Chemistry.* an analytical method using oxidizing agents for titrations.
**ox|i|dise** (ok′sə dīz), *v.t., v.i.,* **-dised, -dis|ing.** *Especially British.* oxidize.
**ox|i|diz|a|ble** (ok′sə dī′zə bəl), *adj.* that can be oxidized: *The iron atom is in its "reduced," or oxidizable form* (Martin D. Kamen).
**ox|i|di|za|tion** (ok′sə də zā′shən), *n.* = oxidation.
**ox|i|dize** (ok′sə dīz), *v.,* **-dized, -diz|ing.** **—*v.t.*** **1** to combine with oxygen; make into an oxide. When a substance burns or rusts, it is oxidized. *Water oxidizes some metals, producing rust. The normal liver of the rat utilized acetic acid to synthesize fatty acids and oxidized (burned) it to carbon dioxide and water* (New York Times). **2** to cause to rust. **3** to cause to lose hydrogen by the action of oxygen; dehydrogenate. **4** to change (the atoms or ions) to a higher positive valence by loss of electrons.
**—*v.i.*** to become oxidized: *Fuel oxidizes rapidly, producing heat. Iron oxidizes in water.* Also, *especially British,* **oxidise.**
**ox|i|diz|er** (ok′sə dī′zər), *n.* **1** something that oxidizes; oxidizing agent. **2** *Aerospace.* a substance that supports the combustion of a fuel.
**ox|i|do-re|duc|ing** (ok′sə dō ri dü′sing, -dyü′-), *adj.* of, having to do with, or causing oxidation-reduction; redox: *an oxido-reducing reaction, an oxido-reducing enzyme.*
**ox|i|do|re|duc|tase** (ok′sə dō ri duk′tās), *n.* an enzyme that catalyzes a reaction in which one molecule of a compound is oxidized and the other reduced; an oxido-reducing enzyme.
**ox|im** (ok′sim), *n.* = oxime.
**ox|ime** (ok′sēm, -sim), *n.* any one of a group of chemical compounds having the general formula RC:NOH, where R is an alkyl group or hydrogen. Oximes are formed by treating aldehydes or ketones with hydroxylamine.
**ox|im|e|ter** (ok sim′ə tər), *n.* a device for measuring the oxygen saturation of hemoglobin, operating on the basis of photoelectricity: *Oxygen tension in the blood flowing through the skin can be measured ... by means of an oximeter* (New Scientist).
**ox|lip** (oks′lip′), *n.* **1** a primrose that has clusters of pale-yellow flowers. **2** a natural hybrid between the cowslip and other varieties of primrose; polyanthus. [Old English *oxanslyppe* < *oxan* ox's + *slyppe* slime. Compare etym. under **cowslip.**]
**Oxon.**, **1** of Oxford (Latin, *Oxoniensis*). **2** Oxford (Latin, *Oxonia*). **3** Oxfordshire.
**Ox|o|ni|an** (ok sō′nē ən), *adj., n.* **—*adj.*** of or having to do with Oxford University or Oxford, a city in southern England.
**—*n.*** **1** a member or graduate of Oxford University. **2** a native or inhabitant of Oxford. [< Medieval Latin *Oxonia* Oxford + English *-an*]
**ox|o|ni|um compound** (ok sō′nē əm), a chemical compound formed when an organic compound containing a basic atom of oxygen reacts with a strong acid. [< *ox*(ygen) + (amm)*onium*]
**ox|peck|er** (oks′pek′ər), *n.* a small African starling that feeds on external parasites that infest the hides of cattle and other animals; tickbird.
**ox|tail** (oks′tāl′), *n.* the skinned tail of a steer, ox, or cow, used in making soup.
**ox|ter** (oks′tər), *n., v. Scottish.* **—*n.*** the armpit: *Wi' his sleeves up tae his oxters* (Ian Maclaren).
**—*v.t.*** to support or lift by the arm or armpit. [apparently Old English *ōxta.* See related etym. at **axle.**]
**ox|tongue** (oks′tung′), *n.* **1** the tongue of an ox. **2** a composite plant with yellow flowers and prickly leaves, growing on clayey soil. **3** any one of various plants with rough tongue-shaped leaves, such as the bugloss.
**ox|y**[1] (ok′sē), *adj.* of or like an ox; oxlike: *Tell that to the oxy chap downstairs* (New Yorker). [< *ox* + *-y*[1]]
**ox|y**[2] (ok′sē), *adj.* of or containing oxygen: *the oxy form of hemoglobin.* [< *oxy-*]
**oxy-**, *combining form.* **1** of or containing oxygen, as in *oxyacetylene, oxyhydrogen, oxysalt.*
**2** of acid, as in *oxyphilic.*
**3** containing hydroxyl, as in *oxytetracycline.* [< *oxy*(gen)]
**ox|y|a|cet|y|lene** (ok′sē ə set′ə lēn, -lin), *adj.* of or using a mixture of oxygen and acetylene.
**oxyacetylene torch**, a tool producing a very hot flame for welding or cutting metals; acetylene torch. It burns a mixture of oxygen and acetylene.
**ox|y|ac|id** (ok′sē as′id), *n.* **1** an acid that contains oxygen, such as sulfuric acid; oxygen acid. **2** any organic acid containing both a carboxyl and a hydroxyl group.
**ox|y|cal|ci|um** (ok′sē kal′sē əm), *adj.* of or using oxygen and calcium.
**oxycalcium light**, = limelight.
**ox|y|chlo|ride** (ok′sē klôr′īd, -klōr′-; -id), *n.* **1** a combination of oxygen and chlorine with another element. **2** a compound of a metallic chloride with the oxide of the same metal.
**ox|y|da|tion** (ok′sə dā′shən), *n.* = oxidation.
***ox|y|gen** (ok′sə jən), *n.* a gas without color, odor, or taste that forms about one fifth of the air. Animals and plants cannot live without oxygen. Fire will not burn without oxygen. Oxygen is a chemical element present in a combined form in water, carbon dioxide, iron ore, and many other substances. [< French *oxygène,* intended as "acidifying (principle)" < Greek *oxýs* sharp + *-genēs* born, ultimately < *gígnesthai* be born]

***oxygen**

| symbol | atomic number | atomic weight | oxidation state |
|---|---|---|---|
| O | 8 | 15.9994 | −2 |

**oxygen acid**, = oxyacid.
**ox|y|gen|ate** (ok′sə jə nāt), *v.t.,* **-at|ed, -at|ing.** **1** to treat or combine with oxygen. **2** = oxidize.
**ox|y|gen|at|ed water** (ok′sə jə nā′tid), **1** water that has been treated or combined with oxygen. **2** = hydrogen peroxide.
**ox|y|gen|a|tion** (ok′sə jə nā′shən), *n.* **1** the act or process of oxygenating: *He assists in work on physiochemical problems associated with the oxygenation of the blood* (Science News). **2** = oxidation.
**ox|y|gen|a|tor** (ok′sə jə nā′tər), *n.* a device for oxygenating blood as it passes through the heart-lung machine that maintains circulation during open-heart operations: *The all-glass dispersion oxygenator introduces the oxygen as fine bubbles freed from extra gas by a siliconed surface* (Science News Letter).
**oxygen debt**, depletion of oxygen stored in the tissues and red blood cells due to a burst of exercise. Oxygen is restored after the exercise is completed. *Although the other tissues can accumulate an oxygen debt, it is essential for the brain to maintain its oxygen supply* (New Scientist).
**ox|y|gen|ic** (ok′sə jen′ik), *adj.* having to do with or containing oxygen; oxygenous.
**ox|y|gen|ic|i|ty** (ok′sə jə nis′ə tē), *n.* the quality or degree of being oxygenic.
**ox|y|gen|ise** (ok′sə jə nīz), *v.t.,* **-ised, -is|ing.** *Especially British.* oxygenize.
**ox|y|gen|iz|a|ble** (ok′sə jə nī′zə bəl), *adj.* that can be oxygenized.
**ox|y|gen|ize** (ok′sə jə nīz), *v.t.,* **-ized, -iz|ing.** to treat with oxygen; combine with oxygen; oxygenate.
**ox|y|gen|ize|ment** (ok′sə jə nīz′mənt), *n.* = oxidation.
**ox|y|gen|iz|er** (ok′sə jə nī′zər), *n.* thing that oxidates or converts into an oxide.
**ox|y|gen|less** (ok′sə jən lis), *adj.* having no oxygen: *Sea creatures never before known may lurk in deep, nearly oxygenless basins beneath the Gulf of California* (Science News).

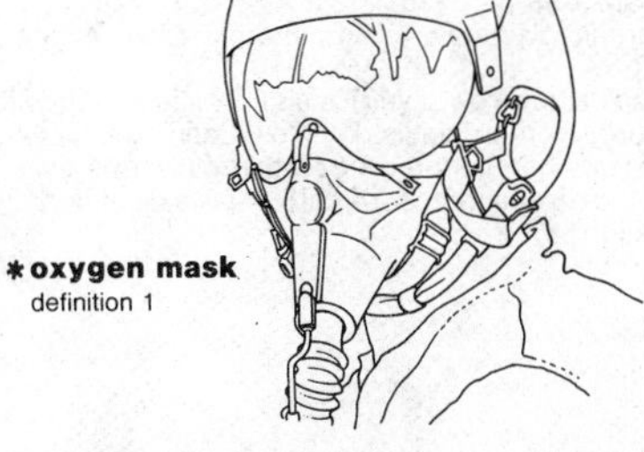

***oxygen mask**
definition 1

***oxygen mask**, **1** a device worn over the nose and mouth through which oxygen is supplied from an attached container. Oxygen masks are used by aviators at high altitudes, by submarine crews, and by people suffering respiratory emergencies. **2** a mask for a device that supplies air for breathing.
**ox|yg|e|nous** (ok sij′ə nəs), *adj.* consisting of or

---

**Pronunciation Key:** hat, āge, cãre, fär; let, ēqual, tėrm; it, īce; hot, ōpen, ôrder; oil, out; cup, pu̇t, rüle; child; long; thin; ᴛʜen; zh, measure; ə represents **a** in about, **e** in taken, **i** in pencil, **o** in lemon, **u** in circus.

containing oxygen; oxygenic.

**oxygen tent**, a small tent that can be filled with a mixture of oxygen and air, used in treating pneumonia and other diseases. An oxygen tent is usually transparent and placed over the head and shoulders of a patient who has difficulty breathing.

**ox|y|he|mo|glo|bin** or **ox|y|hae|mo|glo|bin** (ok′si hē′mə glō′bin, -hem′ə-), *n.* the combination of hemoglobin and oxygen in arterial blood. Oxyhemoglobin gives arterial blood its bright red color.

**ox|y|hy|dro|gen** (ok′si hī′drə jən), *adj.* of, having to do with, or using a mixture of oxygen and hydrogen: *By 1875 ... limelight—created by directing an oxyhydrogen flame against a block of lime enclosed in a lamp with a powerful lens—had made its appearance* (New Yorker).

**oxyhydrogen torch**, a tool with a very hot flame for welding or cutting through metals. It uses a mixture of oxygen and hydrogen.

**ox|y|mel** (ok′si mel), *n.* a mixture of acetic acid or vinegar and honey, formerly used in medicines: *The patient took a draught made with oxymel of squills* (Tobias Smollett). [< Latin *oxymeli* < Greek *oxýmeli* < *oxýs* sharp, acid + *méli* honey]

**ox|y|mo|ron** (ok′si môr′on, -mōr′-), *n., pl.* **-mo|ra** (-môr′ə, -mōr′-). a figure of speech in which words of opposite meaning or suggestion are used together. Examples: *a wise fool, cruel kindness, to make haste slowly. Perhaps it is an oxymoron ... to say that the President was both resolute and restrained* (Richard B. Russell). [< Greek *oxýmōron*, noun use of neuter of *oxýmōros*, adjective, pointedly foolish < *oxýs* sharp + *mōrós* stupid]

**ox|y|mor|phone** (ok′sē môr′fōn), *n.* a semisynthetic narcotic used as an analgesic. *Formula:* $C_{17}H_{19}NO_4 \cdot HCl$ [< *oxy-* + *morph*(ine) + *-one*]

**ox|y|mu|ri|at|ic acid gas** (ok′sē myůr′ē at′ik), the name given to chlorine before its recognition as an element.

**ox|y|phil** (ok′sə fil), *n.* = acidophil.

**ox|y|phil|ic** (ok′sə fil′ik), *adj.* = acidophilic.

**ox|y|salt** (ok′si sôlt′), *n.* a salt containing oxygen in place in other electronegative radicals, BiOCl.

**ox|y|sul|fid** or **ox|y|sul|phid** (ok′si sul′fid), *n.* = oxysulfide.

**ox|y|sul|fide** or **ox|y|sul|phide** (ok′si sul′fīd, -fid), *n.* a sulfide compound in which one part of the sulfur is replaced by oxygen.

**ox|y|tet|ra|cy|cline** (ox′si tet′rə sī′klin), *n.* an antibiotic obtained from a soil microorganism, which is effective against a wide range of disease organisms, including bacteria, viruses, and protozoa; Terramycin: *Injecting livestock ... with ... oxytetracycline permits the high temperature aging of meat, without spoilage* (Science News Letter). *Formula:* $C_{22}H_{24}N_2O_9 \cdot 2H_2O$

**ox|y|to|cia** (ok′si tō′shə), *n.* rapid childbirth. [< New Latin *oxytocia* < Greek *oxytokiā* < *oxýs* sharp + *tókos* birth < *tiktein* give birth to]

**ox|y|to|cic** (ok′si tō′sik, -tos′ik), *adj., n.* —*adj.* hastening childbirth, especially by stimulating the contraction of the uterine muscles.
—*n.* an oxytocic drug or medicine.

**ox|y|to|cin** (ok′si tō′sin, -tos′in), *n.* a hormone of the pituitary gland effecting contraction of the uterus in childbirth and stimulating lactation. *Formula:* $C_{43}H_{66}N_{12}O_{12}S_2$

**ox|y|tone** (ok′si tōn), *adj., n.* —*adj.* having an acute accent on the last syllable.
—*n.* an oxytone word.
[< Greek *oxýtonos* < *oxýs* sharp + *tónos* accent, tone]

**ox|y|u|ri|a|sis** (ok′si yů rī′ə sis), *n.* infestation with pinworms; enterobiasis. [< New Latin *oxyuriasis* < *Oxyuris* genus name of certain pinworms (< Greek *oxýs* sharp + *ourá* tail) + *-iasis* diseased condition]

**oy** or **oye** (oi), *n. Scottish.* a grandchild. Also, **oe.** [< Gaelic *ogha.* Compare Irish *úa.*]

**o|yer** (ō′yər, oi′ər), *n. Law.* **1** a hearing; criminal trial (abbreviation of *oyer and terminer*). **2a** the hearing in court of some document demanded by one party, which the other is compelled to produce (make profert of). **b** such a demand. [< Anglo-French *oyer,* noun, variant of Old French *oïr,* to hear < Latin *audīre*]

**oyer and terminer**, *Law.* a hearing and determining; a trial. It is used in England of a writ directing the holding of a court or commission of assize to try indictable offenses, and in the United States of various higher criminal courts. [< *oyer,* and Old French *terminer* terminate < Latin *termināre*]

**o|yez** or **o|yes** (ō′yes, -yez), *interj., n.* "hear! attend!" a cry uttered, usually three times, by a public or court crier to command silence and attention before a proclamation is made. [< Anglo-French *oyez* hear ye, imperative of *oyer* to hear; see etym. under **oyer**]

***oys|ter** (ois′tər), *n.* **1** a kind of mollusk much used as food, having a rough, irregular shell in two halves. Oysters are found in shallow water along seacoasts. There are several kinds. Some kinds yield pearls. **2** an oyster-shaped bit of dark meat found on either side of the back of a fowl. **3** *Informal. Figurative.* a very reserved or uncommunicative person: *Secret, and self-contained, and solitary as an oyster* (Dickens). **4** *Figurative.* something from which to take or derive advantage: *The world's mine oyster, Which I with sword will open* (Shakespeare). [< Old French *oistre* < Latin *ostrea* < Greek *óstreon,* related to *osteón* bone]

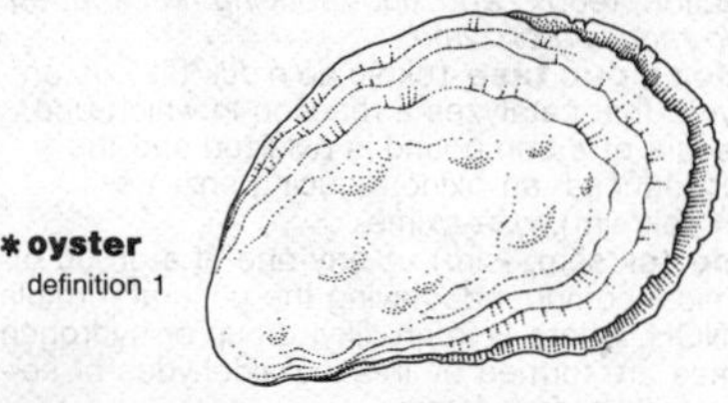
***oyster** definition 1

**oys|ter|age** (ois′tər ij), *n.* = oyster bed.

**oyster bed**, a place where oysters breed or are cultivated.

**oyster catcher**, any one of various wading birds of world-wide distribution that are black and white, have red, wedge-shaped bills for opening shellfish, and grow to about 20 inches long.

**oyster crab**, a small crab that lives harmlessly within the shell of a live oyster. Related kinds live similarly in mussels and scallops.

**oyster cracker**, a small, round or hexagonal, salted cracker eaten with oysters, soup, an appetizer, or the like.

**oyster farm**, a place where oysters are raised for the market.

**oyster gray**, a slightly dark, silvery color.

**oys|ter|ing** (oi′stər ing), *adj., n.* —*adj.* having to do with taking or cultivating oysters: *...near the oystering grounds of Louisiana ...* (Atlantic).
—*n.* the business of taking oysters: *Oystering was his livelihood.*

**oyster leaf**, = sea lungwort.

**oys|ter|man** (ois′tər mən), *n., pl.* **-men. 1** a man who gathers, sells, or raises oysters. **2** a boat or ship used to gather oysters.

**oyster mushroom**, an edible mushroom with white gills and one-sided stalks that grows in clusters on stumps or partly decayed trees.

**oyster plant**, **1** = salsify. **2** = sea lungwort.

**oyster rake**, a rake with a long handle and long, curved teeth, used for gathering oysters from oyster beds.

**oyster rock**, an oyster bed, often containing masses of old shells.

**oys|ter|root** (ois′tər rüt′, -růt′), *n.* = salsify.

**oyster tongs**, an implement for dredging up oysters.

**oyster white**, white with a greenish-gray or yellowish-gray tinge.

**oz.**, **1** ounce. **2** ounces.

**Oz|a|lid** (oz′ə lid), *n. Trademark.* a process for making copies of documents and drawings on a chemically treated paper on which the original material is reproduced by the action of ultraviolet light.

**oz. ap.**, ounce (apothecaries' weight).

**oz. av.**, ounce (avoirdupois weight).

**o|zo|ce|rite** (ō zō′kə rīt, -sə rīt; ō′zō sir′īt), *n.* a mineral, a waxlike fossil resin of brownish-yellow color and aromatic odor, consisting of a mixture of natural hydrocarbons, and sometimes occurring in sandstones; mineral wax. It is used in making candles and for insulating electrical conductors. [< German *Ozokerit* < Greek *ózein* to smell (because it is aromatic) + *kērós* bees wax + German *-it* -ite[1]]

**o|zo|ke|rite** (ō zō′kə rīt), *n.* = ozocerite.

**o|zone** (ō′zōn), *n.* **1** a form of oxygen produced by electricity and present in the air, especially after a thunderstorm. Ozone has a sharp, pungent odor like that of weak chlorine. It is a strong oxidizing agent and is produced commercially for use in bleaching and in sterilizing water. *Formula:* $O_3$ **2** *Informal, Figurative.* pure air that is refreshing. [< French *ozone* < Greek *ózein* to smell (because of its odor)]

**ozone layer**, = ozonosphere.

**o|zon|er** (ō′zō nər), *n. U.S. Slang.* a drive-in motion-picture theater: *In the movie trade, drive-ins or ozoners ... are "passion pits with pix"* (New York Times).

**o|zone|sonde** (ō′zōn sond), *n.* a radiosonde designed to measure the distribution of ozone above the earth and transmit the data back to earth.

**o|zon|ic** (ō zon′ik, -zō′nik), *adj.* of, having to do with, or containing ozone.

**ozonic ether**, a solution of hydrogen peroxide in ether.

**o|zo|nid** (ō′zə nid), *n.* = ozonide.

**o|zo|nide** (ō′zə nīd), *n.* any one of a group of organic compounds formed when ozone is added to an unsaturated hydrocarbon.

**o|zo|nif|er|ous** (ō′zə nif′ər əs), *adj.* containing ozone. [< *ozon*(e) + *-ferous*]

**o|zo|nise** (ō′zə nīz), *v.t.,* **-nised, -nis|ing.** *Especially British.* ozonize.

**o|zo|ni|za|tion** (ō′zə nə zā′shən), *n.* **1** the act or process of ozonizing. **2** the state or condition of being ozonized.

**o|zo|nize** (ō′zə nīz), *v.t.,* **-nized, -niz|ing. 1** to charge or treat with ozone. **2** to convert (oxygen) into ozone. [< *ozon*(e) + *-ize*]

**o|zo|niz|er** (ō′zə nī′zər), *n.* an apparatus for producing ozone.

**o|zo|nol|y|sis** (ō′zə nol′ə sis), *n.* **1** the process of treating a hydrocarbon with ozone followed by hydrolysis. **2** decomposition following treatment with ozone. [< *ozon*(e) + Greek *lýsis* a loosening]

**o|zo|nom|e|ter** (ō′zə nom′ə tər), *n.* a device for determining the amount of ozone present, as in air. [< *ozone* + *-meter*]

**o|zo|nom|e|try** (ō′zə nom′ə trē), *n.* the method or process of measuring the amount of ozone in the atmosphere.

**o|zon|o|sphere** (ō zon′ə sfir), *n.* a region of concentrated ozone in the outer stratosphere and the mesosphere, located about 20 to 40 miles above the earth's surface. It shields the earth from excessive ultraviolet radiation.

**o|zo|nous** (ō′zə nəs), *adj.* of or like ozone. [< *ozon*(e) + *-ous*]

**o|zos|to|mi|a** (ō′zos tō′mē ə), *n.* an offensive breath. [< New Latin *ozostomia* < Greek *ózein* to smell + *stóma* mouth]

**ozs.**, ounces.

**oz. t.**, ounce (troy weight).

# Pp

***P**[1] or **p** (pē), *n., pl.* **P's** or **Ps, p's** or **ps. 1** the 16th letter of the English alphabet. There are three *p's* in *pepper.* **2** any sound represented by this letter. **3** (used as a symbol for) the 16th, or more usually the 15th (of an actual or possible series either *I* or *J* being omitted). **4** *Genetics.* (as a symbol) parental generation (used with a subscript number, as $P_1$ or the parents, $P_2$, the grandparents, and so forth).
**mind one's p's and q's,** to be careful or particular about what one says or does: *Even the cleverest must mind their p's and q's with such a lady* (Arnold Bennett).

**P**[2] (pē), *n., pl.* **P's.** anything shaped like the letter P.

**p-,** *prefix.* para-[1].

**p** (no period), a symbol or abbreviation for the following:
1 *Chess.* pawn.
2 penny or pence (in the British decimal system established in 1971): *4p, 53 ½p.*
3 pico-.
4 *Physics.* positive.
5 *Physics.* proton.
6 *Music.* **a** soft. **b** softly (Italian, *piano*).

**p.,** an abbreviation for the following:
1 after (Latin, *post*).
2 father (Latin, *pater;* French, *père*).
3 first (Latin, *primus*).
4 for (Latin, *pro*).
5 in part (Latin, *partim*).
6 page.
7 part.
8 participle.
9 *Meteorology.* passing (showers).
10 past.
11 perch (unit of measure).
12 perishable.
13 peseta.
14 peso.
15 piaster.
16 pint.
17 pipe.
18 *Baseball.* pitcher.
19 *Music.* poco.
20 pole (unit of measure).
21 population.
22 pressure.

**P** (no period), **1** phosphorus (chemical element).
**2** *Physics.* **a** parity. **b** pressure.

**P.,** an abbreviation for the following:
1 Father (Latin, *Pater;* French, *Père*).
2 Pastor.
3 Pope.
4 post.
5 President.
6 Priest.
7 Prince.
8 Progressive.
9 Province.

**pa**[1] (pä, pô), *n. Informal.* papa; father.

**pa**[2] (pä), *n. Maori.* a village.

**p.a.,** **1** participial adjective. **2** per annum. **3** public address (system).

**Pa** (no period), protactinium (chemical element).

**Pa.,** Pennsylvania.

**PA** (no periods), **1** Pennsylvania (with postal Zip Code). **2** public address (system).

**P/A** (no periods), power of attorney.

**P.A.,** an abbreviation for the following:
1 Passenger Agent.
2 personal appearance.
3 physician's assistant.
4 Post Adjutant.
5 power of attorney.
6 Press Agent.
7 Press Association.
8 public address (system).
9 Purchasing Agent.

**pa'an|ga** (pä äng'gə), *n.* the unit of money of Tonga, equal to 100 seniti. [< Tongan *pa'anga* coin-shaped seed; money]

**PABA** (no periods), para-aminobenzoic acid.

**pab|lum** (pab'ləm), *n.* **1** a source of sustenance; pabulum: (*Figurative.*) *The Presidential Commission on Campus Unrest ... he said, had produced a report which 'was sure to be taken as more pablum for the permissivists'* (Listener). **2** something intellectually watered down or insipid; pap: *You can go to Hollywood as a second assistant unit manager for ten years, make the long, stultifying climb, and finally turn out predigested pablum* (New Yorker). [< *Pablum,* a trademark of a bland cereal for infants, with meaning (especially of def. 1) influenced by *pabulum*]

**pa|bouche** (pä büsh'), *n.* = babouche.

**pab|u|lum** (pab'yə ləm), *n.* **1** food; anything taken in by an animal or plant to maintain life and growth. SYN: aliment, nutriment. **2** = fuel. **3** *Figurative.* intellectual or spiritual nourishment; food for the mind: *The idea that it is "progressive" to hold that "democracy" consists of giving the same educational pabulum to everybody ... is weakening* (Wall Street Journal). **4** *Figurative.* intellectual pap; pablum: *... screening an almost unvaried nightly pabulum of light-interest-sex and predictable melodrama* (Manchester Guardian Weekly). [< Latin *pābulum* fodder, related to *pāscere* to feed]

**Pac.,** Pacific.

**PAC** (no periods) or **P.A.C.,** Political Action Committee (of the Congress of Industrial Organizations).

**pa|ca** (pä'kə, pak'ə), *n.* any one of a group of large rodents of Central and South America, related to the agouti; spotted cavy. [< Spanish and Portuguese *paca* < Tupi *páca,* or perhaps < Quechua *paco* reddish]

**Pac|chi|o|ni|an bodies** or **glands** (pak'ē ō'neən), small villi, not glandular in character, found in clusters on the membranes enveloping the brain. Cerebrospinal fluid passes through them into the veins. [< Antonio *Pacchioni,* 1665-1726, an Italian anatomist + *-an*]

**pace**[1] (pās), *n., v.,* **paced, pac|ing.** *—n.* **1** a step: *He took three paces into the room. Behind her Death following pace for pace* (Milton). **2** the length of a normal adult step in walking, sometimes used as a rough unit of measure; about 2½ feet: *There were perhaps ten paces between me and the bear.* **3** a way of stepping; gait. The walk, trot, and gallop are some of the paces of a horse. **4** a particular gait of some horses in which the feet on the same side are lifted and put down together. See picture under **gait. 5** rate of movement; speed: *He sets a fast pace in walking. I like the deliberate pace of a Haydn symphony.*
*—v.i.* **1** to walk with slow or regular steps: *The tiger paced back and forth in his cage.* **2** to move at a pace: *Some horses are trained to pace.*
*—v.t.* **1** to walk over with slow or regular steps: *to pace the floor. Then, pale and worn, he paced his deck* (Joaquin Miller). **2** to measure by pacing or in paces: *We paced off the distance and found it to be 69 paces.* **3** to set the pace for: *A motorboat will pace the boys training for the canoe race.* **4** to train (a horse) to a certain step, especially to lift and put down the feet on the same side together.
**go through one's paces,** to show what one can do; prove one's skill: *One has the impression of actors going through their paces* (New York Times).
**keep pace (with), a** to go as fast as: *He walked so fast that we could hardly keep pace with him.* **b** *Figurative: A lot of things are changing, and the ... Bank must surely try to keep pace* (Punch).
**put through one's** (or **the**) **paces,** to try one out; find out what one can do: *The captain ordered the Nautilus put through her paces* (Time).
**set the pace, a** to set a rate of speed for others to keep up with: *The champion set a rapid pace for the other racers.* **b** *Figurative.* to be an example or model for others to follow: *Right up with the pace set by this is Trigère's ensemble of heavy wool in black, chestnut, and white* (New Yorker).
[< Old French *pas* < Latin *passus, -ūs* a step < *pandere* to stretch. See etym. of doublet **pass**[1], noun]

**pa|ce**[2] (pā'sē), *prep., adv. Latin.* with the indulgence of; by the leave of; with regrets for differing from: *But it is not (pace the 618 scientists who wrote to Mr. Macmillan) radioactivity that really matters in stopping the tests* (Economist).

**pace car** (pās), a car used in automobile racing to lead the racing cars off at the start of a race.

**paced** (pāst), *adj.* **1** having a pace: *slow-paced.* **2** traversed or measured by pacing. **3** having the speed in racing set by a pacemaker or run at a set speed.

**pace egg** (pās), *British Dialect.* Easter egg. [*pace* < earlier *pase* < Middle French *pasche* < Old French *pasche, pasque;* see etym. under **Pasch**]

**pace|mak|er** (pās'mā'kər), *n.* **1a** a person, animal, or thing that sets the pace: *These enzyme proteins in turn act as catalyzers or pacemakers of the chemical reactions that take place in the cell* (Scientific American). **b** *Figurative.* leader; pacesetter. **2** an area of specialized tissue in the heart, near the top of the wall of the right auricle, that sends out the rhythmic impulses which regulate the contractions of the heart muscles; sinoatrial node: *Normally the ventricles ... beat regularly in rhythmic response to the heart's pacemaker* (Paul Dudley White). **3** an electronic device implanted near the heart when the natural pacemaker does not function, to maintain or restore the normal rhythm of the heartbeat: *The solution to this condition would be to supply the heart with an artificial pacemaker* (New Scientist).

**pace|mak|ing** (pās'mā'king), *n., adj. —n.* the act of setting the pace.
*—adj.* setting the pace; acting as a pacemaker: *an electronic pacemaking device.*

**pac|er** (pā'sər), *n.* **1** a person or thing that paces, especially one bred or trained for racing. **2** a horse that lifts and puts down the feet on the same side together, whether natural or taught. **3** = pacemaker.

**pace|set|ter** (pās'set'ər), *n.* a person, animal, or thing that sets the pace; pacemaker: (*Figurative.*) *The auto industry is regarded as a pacesetter* (Wall Street Journal).

**pace|set|ting** (pās'set'ing), *adj.* setting the pace; pacemaking.

**pac|ey** (pā'sē), *adj. British Informal.* **1** fast; speedy: *a pacey fullback, a pacey bowler.* **2** lively; racy: *His style is the pacey modern one of ... relentless recruitment of random facts* (London Times). Also, **pacy.**

**pa|cha** (pə shä', pash'ə, pä'shə), *n.* = pasha.

**pa|cha|lic** (pə shä'lik), *n.* = pashalik.

**pa|chan|ga** (pə chang'gə), *n.* a fast, hopping dance of Cuban origin. [< Cuban Spanish *pachanga*]

**pa|chin|ko** (pä'chin kō'), *n.* a pinball game played in Japan. [< Japanese *pachinko*]

**pa|chi|si** (pə chē'zē), *n.* **1** a game somewhat resembling backgammon, originally from India, played on a cross-shaped board. **2** = parcheesi. [< Hindustani *pachīsī* (literally), adjective < *pachīs* twenty-five (the highest throw on the dice)]

**pach|ou|li** (pach'ů lē, pə chü'-), *n.* = patchouli.

**pa|chu|co** (pə chü'kō), *n., pl.* **-cos.** *U.S.* a flashily dressed young tough of Mexico or of Mexican descent. [< Mexican Spanish *pachuco*]

**pach|y|derm** (pak'ə dėrm), *n.* **1** any one of certain thick-skinned mammals with hoofs. The elephant, hippopotamus, and rhinoceros are pachyderms. **2** *Figurative.* a person who is not sensitive to criticism or ridicule; thick-skinned person. [< French *pachyderme* < Greek *pachýdermos* thick-skinned < *pachýs* thick + *dérma* skin]

**pach|y|der|ma|tous** (pak'ə dėr'mə təs), *adj.* **1** of or like the pachyderms; characteristic of pachyderms. **2** *Figurative.* insensitive to criticism or rebuff; thick-skinned: *A distinct impression of pachydermatous personality emerges* (Observer).

**pach|y|der|mous** (pak'ə dėr'məs), *adj.* = pachydermatous. **—pach'y|der'mous|ly,** *adv.*

**pach|y|os|te|o|morph** (pak'ē os'tē ə môrf), *n.* an evolutionary level characterized by heavy bone structure. [< Greek *pachýs* thick + *ostéon* bone + *morphḗ* form]

**pach|y|san|dra** (pak'ə san'drə), *n.* any one of a group of trailing, usually evergreen plants of the box family, commonly planted for ground cover. [< New Latin *Pachysandra* the genus name < Greek *pachýs* thick + New Latin *-andrus* man, male]

**pach|y|tene** (pak'ə tēn), *n. Biology.* the state of the prophase of meiosis in which the paired chromosomes attain a thick, stable form. [<

***P**[1]
definition 1

Script letters look like examples of fine penmanship. They appear in many formal uses, such as invitations to social functions.

Pp *Pp*

Handwritten letters, both manuscript or printed (left) and cursive (right), are easy for children to read and to write.

Pp *Pp*

Roman letters have *serifs* (finishing strokes) adapted from the way Roman stonecutters carved their letters. This is *Times Roman* type.

**Pp *Pp***

Sans-serif letters are often called *gothic.* They have lines of even width and no serifs. This type face is called *Helvetica.*

Pp *Pp*

Between roman and gothic, some letters have thick and thin lines with slight flares that suggest serifs. This type face is *Optima.*

P

Computer letters can be sensed by machines either from their shapes or from the magnetic ink with which they are printed.

Greek *pachýs* thick + *tainíā* band]

**Pacif.**, Pacific.

**pa|cif|ar|in** (pə sif′ər ən), *n.* a bacterial substance that prevents certain germs from causing disease while permitting them to survive within the organism they have invaded. [< *pacif*(ier) + *-arin,* as in *heparin*]

**pac|i|fi|a|ble** (pas′ə fī′ə bəl), *adj.* that can be pacified or appeased.

**pa|cif|ic** (pə sif′ik), *adj.* **1** tending to make peace; making peace: *The traders made pacific advances toward the Indians. The policy of the Prince was pacific and temporizing* (John L. Motley). **SYN**: peaceable, conciliatory. **2** loving peace; not warlike: *a pacific nature. The Quakers are a pacific people.* **3** peaceful; calm; quiet: *pacific weather. Mr. Britling ... marked the steady conversion of the old pacific countryside into an armed camp* (H. G. Wells). **SYN**: placid, tranquil. [< Middle French *pacifique,* learned borrowing from Latin *pācificus* < *pāx, pācis* peace + *facere* make] —**pa|cif′i|cal|ly**, *adv.*

**Pa|cif|ic** (pə sif′ik), *adj.* **1** of the Pacific Ocean: *Pacific fish.* **2** on, in, over, or near the Pacific Ocean: *a Pacific storm, Pacific air routes.* **3** of or on the Pacific coast of the United States: *California is one of the Pacific states.*

**pa|cif|i|cal** (pə sif′ə kəl), *adj.* = pacific.

**pa|cif|i|cate** (pə sif′ə kāt), *v.t.,* **-cat|ed, -cat|ing.** to bring into a state of peace; pacify: *The remaining dominions ... will doubtless by degrees be conquered and pacificated* (Thomas Carlyle). [< Latin *pācificāre* (with English *-ate*[1]) < *pācificus* pacific]

**pac|i|fi|ca|tion** (pas′ə fə kā′shən), *n.* **1** the act of pacifying; making peaceful: *French forces are engaged, so the official thesis goes, in an effort at "pacification"* (Wall Street Journal). **2** the condition of being pacified: *"I ... offer my retirement if that will be a guarantee of pacification," Peron declared* (Wall Street Journal). **3** a compact or treaty establishing peace: *The pacification had just been signed at Ghent* (John L. Motley). **4** the elimination of insurgent activity in an area: *It [the book] draws critical distinctions between true peacekeeping ... and the sort of "pacification" the British Army considers itself expert in: no more than heavy-handed police operations in support of the civil government* (Manchester Guardian Weekly).

**pa|cif|i|ca|tor** (pə sif′ə kā′tər), *n.* a person who pacifies; peacemaker.

**pa|cif|i|ca|to|ry** (pə sif′ə kə tôr′ē, -tōr′-), *adj.* tending to make peace; conciliatory.

**Pacific barracuda**, a harmless silver-colored barracuda found along the west coast of the Americas.

**pacific blockade**, a blockade imposed in peacetime to halt shipments into a country, especially to force it to follow some course of action.

**pa|cif|i|cism** (pə sif′ə siz əm), *n.* = pacifism.

**pa|cif|i|cist** (pə sif′ə sist), *n., adj.* = pacifist.

**Pacific loon**, a loon of the Pacific coast, smaller than the common loon and having a purple-black throat.

**Pacific Standard Time**, the standard time in the westernmost parts of the continental United States and Canada, a belt centered on the 120th meridian, and excluding most of Alaska. Pacific Standard Time is eight hours behind Greenwich Time. *Abbr:* P.S.T.

**Pacific time**, = Pacific Standard Time. *Abbr:* P.t.

**Pacific yew**, a species of yew grown on the Pacific coast of North America; western yew. The wood of this tree is used in cabinetwork and in making canoe paddles.

**pac|i|fi|er** (pas′ə fī′ər), *n.* **1** a person or thing that pacifies. **2** a rubber or plastic nipple or ring given to a baby to suck: *But certainly a pacifier should not be offered to a child who shows no need for it* (Sidonie M. Gruenberg).

**pac|i|fism** (pas′ə fiz əm), *n.* the principle or policy of universal peace; settlement of all differences between nations by peaceful means; opposition to war. [< *pacif*(ic) + *-ism;* probably patterned on French *pacifisme*]

**pac|i|fist** (pas′ə fist), *n., adj.* —*n.* a person who is opposed to war and favors settling all disputes between nations by peaceful means: *This is to confuse pacifism with appeasement. The pacifist is definitely not a passivist* (Bulletin of Atomic Scientists).
—*adj.* belonging to or like pacifists: *He has often publicly praised the pacifist provision of the new Japanese Constitution, renouncing war and the use of armed force* (Wall Street Journal).

**pac|i|fis|tic** (pas′ə fis′tik), *adj.* **1** of pacifism or pacifists. **2** favoring pacifism: *Opinion polls showed the people very pacifistic, and this attitude was reflected in the smallness of Britain's army and air force, in comparison with the much superior numbers of Germany and Italy* (Ogburn and Nimkoff). —**pac′i|fis′ti|cal|ly**, *adv.*

**pac|i|fy** (pas′ə fī), *v.t.,* **-fied, -fy|ing. 1** to make calm; quiet down; give peace to: *Can't you pacify that screaming baby? We tried to pacify the man we bumped into.* **SYN**: See syn. under **appease**. **2** to bring peace to: *Soldiers were sent to pacify the country.* [< Middle French *pacifier,* Old French, make peace, learned borrowing from Latin *pācificāre* < *pācificus* pacific]

**Pa|cin|i|an body** or **corpuscle** (pə sin′ē ən), one of the numerous oval, seedlike bodies attached to nerve endings, especially in the subcutaneous tissue of the hand and foot. [< Filippo *Pacini,* 1812-1883, an Italian anatomist + *-an*]

**pack**[1] (pak), *n., v.* —*n.* **1a** a bundle of things wrapped up or tied together for carrying: *a pack of gum, a pack of letters.* **SYN**: parcel, bale, package, packet. **b** = packsack: *The hikers carried packs on their backs.* **2** the amount packed; the total quantity of any natural product, especially a food, canned, frozen, or otherwise preserved in one year or season: *This year's pack of fish is larger than last year's.* **3** a set; lot; a number together: *a pack of thieves, a pack of nonsense. Would you rather that I should write you a pack of lies?* (Thomas Jefferson). *It's a wicked, thieving, lying, scheming lot you are—the pack of you* (John M. Synge). **4a** a number of animals of the same kind hunting or living together: *Wolves often hunt in packs; lions usually hunt alone.* **b** a group of dogs kept together for hunting: *The pack of hounds soon treed a possum.* **5** a complete set of playing cards, usually 52; deck: *The pack of cards fell all over the floor as he tried to shuffle it.* **6** a large area of floating pieces of ice pushed together; ice pack: *A ship forced its way through the pack.* **7a** something put on the body or skin as a treatment. A cloth soaked in hot or cold water is often used as a pack. **b** the cloth, sheet, blanket, ice, or other application so used. **c** a small, absorbent cotton pad that is applied to open wounds or body cavities in order to check the flow of blood; tampon: *Tapes were regarded by many surgeons ... as a help towards finding packs and ensuring their removal after operation* (London Times). **8** several groups of Cub Scouts or Brownies joined together and led by an adult: *A feature of the evening was the presentation of group flags to the 61st Boy Scout Troop and the 61st Cub Pack* (Ottawa Citizen). **9** *U.S.* the practice of raising the price of an automobile to offer a larger discount: *Price packs and overallowances fret auto finance men* (Wall Street Journal). **10** *British.* **a** the players on a Rugby team who are in the front line; all of the forwards together: *Both sides played excellent rugby, with two well-matched packs concentrating on getting the ball back* (London Times). **b** = scrummage. **11** *Archaic.* a worthless person: *a naughty pack.* **12** *Obsolete.* a plot; conspiracy.
—*v.t.* **1** to put together in a bundle, bale, bag, box, or other container: *Pack your books in this box. We pack onions in bags.* **2** to fill with things; put one's things into: *Pack your suitcase. Pack the car for a trip.* **3** *Figurative.* to press or crowd closely together: *A hundred people were packed into one small room.* **SYN**: cram. **4** to press together; make firm: *The heavy trucks packed the snow on the highway.* **5** to fill (a space) with all that it will hold: *to pack a small theater with a large audience. The air became stifling, for now the front of the gallery was packed* (Winston Churchill). **6** to put into a container to be sold or stored: *Meat, fish, and vegetables are often packed in cans.* **7** to make tight with something that water, steam, or air cannot leak through: *The plumber packed the joint of the pipe with string and a special compound.* **8** to load (an animal) with a pack; burden. **9** *Informal.* to carry: *Be careful! He packs a gun.* **10** *U.S.* to carry in a pack: *to pack supplies up a mountain.* **11** *Informal.* **a** to possess as a characteristic or power: *That mule packs a knockout punch in its hind feet.* **b** to be capable of administering. **12** to cover, surround, or protect with closely applied materials; treat with a therapeutic pack: *The dentist packed my gum after he extracted my tooth.* **13** *U.S.* to raise (the price of an automobile) to offer a larger discount: *Some dealers pack their prices from $50 to $500, depending on the strength of competition.* **14** to form (hounds) into a pack. **15** to put (cards) together in a pack. **16** to drive (floating ice) into a pack.
—*v.i.* **1** to put things together in a bundle, bale, bag, box, or other container: *Are you ready to pack?* **2** to fit together closely; admit of storing and shipping: *These small cans will pack well.* **3** to become or be packed; crowd together: *The whole group packed into one small room.* **4** to become relatively compact: *The Navaho Indians found that mud will pack easily to make bricks.* **5** to gather into a pack or packs, as certain animals do. **6** to be off; take oneself off: *Seek shelter! Pack!* (Shakespeare).

**pack in**, *Informal.* to stop working; fail: *If your kidney happened to pack in when you were thirty but the rest of you was going to last you until you were seventy, then obviously there would be a good case for replacing your kidney* (Listener).

**pack it in**, *Informal.* to give up, abandon, or leave something or someplace: *Southampton, too ... would suffer similarly should Melia decide to pack it in* (Listener).

**pack off** (or **away**), **a** to send away: *The child was packed off to bed.* **b** to go away suddenly; depart: *to pack off at dawn.*

**pack out**, to sell out: *We're packed out, and again chiefly [to] young people. Godot has become a box-office draw* (London Times).

**pack up**, *Informal.* **a** to stop working; cease operating; fail: *One of the aircraft's engines packed up.* **b** to die: *The old dog quietly packed up in his sleep.*

**send packing**. See under **send**.

[probably < Middle Dutch *pac*] —**pack′a|ble**, *adj.*

**pack**[2] (pak), *v.t.* **1** to arrange unfairly. To pack a jury, court, legislature, or convention is to fill it unfairly with those who will favor one side. *They packed the convention with bought delegates.* **2** *Archaic.* to shuffle (playing cards) so as to cheat. [origin uncertain; perhaps influenced by *pack*[1]]

**pack**[3] (pak), *adj., adv. Scottish.* —*adj.* **1** (of persons) intimate; friendly. **2** (of animals) tame.
—*adv.* intimately.
[origin uncertain]

**pack|a|bil|i|ty** (pak′ə bil′ə tē), *n.* the condition or quality of being easily packed: *the packability of clothes.*

**pack|age** (pak′ij), *n., adj., v.,* **-aged, -ag|ing.** —*n.* **1** a bundle of things packed or wrapped together; box with things packed in it; parcel: *a package of books, a package of laundry.* **SYN**: packet, bale. **2a** a box, can, bottle, jar, case, or other receptacle for packing goods, especially one designed for a particular commodity and printed with matter intended both to identify it and to attract buyers: *We need the best package we can get for this new breakfast food.* **b** such a package with its contents, as offered for sale: *a package of soap, a package of frozen peas.* **3** a group of related things, such as goods, services, laws, or articles of agreement in a negotiation, offered as a unit: *A television package is a complete program, including script, cast, and music, which is sold as a unit either to a sponsor or a network. Our Florida package includes transportation, hotel, and meals for a week. The guaranteed wage, pension and welfare clauses of the auto package* (New York Times). **4** a compact assembly of various units or elements: *Its substitute on Apollo 11 was a package of three experiments—a passive seismometer, laser reflector, and solar wind sensor* (Science Journal).
—*adj.* **1** including a number of elements or items provided or offered as a unit: *a package summer vacation, a package wage increase. The company ... handles package tours to over 30 destinations in the Mediterranean and east Africa* (London Times). **2** of or having to do with a package deal: *NBC hoped to encourage non-network package producers to use the talents of its comedy unit writers* (Saturday Review).
—*v.t.* **1** to put in a package or packages; box, can, bottle, bag, or bale, in order to sell: *to package meat.* **SYN**: pack. **2** to make a package or packages out of: *to wrap and package Christmas presents.* —**pack′age|a|ble**, *adj.* —**pack′ag|er**, *n.*

**package deal**, an offer or transaction involving a number of things grouped as a unit: *The proposal was presented as a final, take-it-or-leave-it package deal.*

**package store**, *U.S.* a store selling alcoholic beverages in sealed containers which must be removed from the premises for consumption.

**pack|ag|ing** (pak′i jing), *n.* **1** the act of putting in a package: *the packaging of glassware.* **2** the preparation of goods for distribution and sale in bottles, boxes, cans, and other containers, including the design and testing of containers and container materials. **3** a package: *The best packaging for this new cereal is one which will attract attention.*

**pack animal**, a horse, mule, donkey, or other animal used for carrying loads or packs.

**pack|board** (pak′bôrd′, -bōrd′), *n.* a backpack consisting of a rigid frame and shoulder straps, sometimes having a bottom shelf that bends out to the rear.

**pack drill**, a military punishment in which the offender must walk up and down for a certain amount of time in full uniform and gear.

**pack|er** (pak′ər), *n.* **1** a person or thing that packs, especially a person or company that packs merchandise, such as meat, fruit, or vegetables, to be sold at wholesale or to wholesalers: *a meat packer.* **2** *U.S., Canada, and Australia.* a person who transports goods by means of pack animals: *The peaks were heavy with wet snow and the pass so treacherous that the experienced packers flatly refused to climb it* (Maclean's).

**pack|er|y** (pak′ər ē), *n., pl.* **-er|ies.** = packing house.

**pack|et** (pak′it), *n., v.* —*n.* **1** a small package; parcel: *a packet of letters, a packet of seeds, a packet of pins.* **2** = packet boat.
—*v.t.* to make into or wrap in a packet; package.
**cost a packet,** *British Slang.* to cost a large sum of money: *Well, it cost him a packet but it cured his indigestion* (Cape Times).
[earlier *pacquet,* perhaps < an Anglo-French diminutive form of Middle English *pakke* pack[1]]

**packet boat** or **ship,** a boat or ship that carries mail, passengers, and goods regularly on a fixed route, usually along a river or the coast.

**pack horse,** or **pack|horse** (pak′hôrs′), *n.* a horse used to carry loads or packs of goods.

**pack|house** (pak′hous′), *n.* = warehouse.

**pack ice,** the ice forming a pack, often squeezed or piled into fantastic formations: *the desolate mountains and pack ice next to the Arctic Circle* (Wall Street Journal).

**pack|ing** (pak′ing), *n.* **1** material used to pack or to keep water, steam, or other liquid or gas, from leaking through: *the packing around the valves of a radiator.* **SYN:** stuffing. **2** material placed around goods to protect them from damage in shipment, storage, or handling. **3** the business of preparing and packaging meat, fish, fruit, vegetables, and other produce to be sold: *This spring, packing companies will be shifting summer sausage production to the new culture* (Wall Street Journal). **4** *Printing.* the cloth, cardboard, or other part of a tympan that is added to equalize the impression.

**packing box** or **case,** a box or case for packing goods in.

**packing effect,** *Physics.* mass defect.

**packing house** or **plant,** a place where meat, fruit, vegetables, and other produce are prepared and packed to be sold.

**pack load,** the weight or amount that can be put or carried in a pack: *The pack load for a mule is about 300 pounds; for a burro, about 150 pounds.*

**pack|man** (pak′mən), *n., pl.* **-men.** = peddler.

**pack mule,** a mule used for carrying loads: *They met 60 allies leading pack mules and horses and headed into the trackless jungle* (Time).

**pack rat, 1** a large North American rat with a hairy tail, that carries away bits of food, clothing, small tools, and other articles and hides them in its nest, often leaving something else, as if in exchange; wood rat. **2** *Figurative.* a person who hoards unneeded articles: *"There has been a pack rat in every generation of Harleys ... I can't throw anything out, and I've been busy dividing the loot between my ... 12 grandchildren"* (New York Times).

**pack|sack** (pak′sak′), *n.* a bag of strong material to hold equipment, carried on the back when traveling: *Climbers carry packsacks loaded with first-aid supplies, food, and extra clothing for sudden changes in weather* (Paul W. Wiseman).

**pack|sad|dle** (pak′sad′əl), *n., v.,* **-dled, -dling.**
—*n.* a saddle specially adapted for supporting the load on a pack animal.
—*v.t.* to convey on a packsaddle; transport by a pack animal.

**packsaddle roof,** = saddle roof.

**pack|thread** (pak′thred′), *n.* a strong thread or twine for sewing or tying up packages.

**pack train,** or **pack|train** (pak′trān′), *n.* a line or group of animals carrying loads: *a pack train of 50 mules and 100 men.*

**pact** (pakt), *n.* an agreement; compact: *The three nations signed a peace pact.* **SYN:** covenant, treaty. [< Latin *pactum,* (originally) neuter past participle of *pacīscī* to covenant, agree]

**pac|tion** (pak′shən), *n.* **1** = agreement. **2** an agreement, compact, or pact.

**pac|tion|al** (pak′shə nəl), *adj.* of the nature of a pact.

**Pac|to|li|an** (pak tō′lē ən), *adj.* **1** of or having to do with the river Pactolus in ancient Lydia, Asia Minor, famed for the gold obtained from the sands. **2** = golden.

**pac|y** (pā′sē), *adj. British Informal.* pacey.

**pad**[1] (pad), *n., v.,* **pad|ded, pad|ding.** —*n.* **1** a soft mass used for comfort, protection, or stuffing; cushion: *to put a pad on a bench or under a rug, to wear pads on one's knees in hockey, to put a pad under a hot plate. The baby's carriage has a pad.* **2** a soft, stuffed saddle. **3** a cushionlike part on the bottom side of the feet of dogs, foxes, camels, and some other animals. The pad is a fleshy and elastic part forming the sole. **4a** the foot of a fox, dog, wolf, rabbit, or other animal: *The rabbit's pad was caught in a trap.* **b** the footprint of such an animal. **5** a tarsal cushion of an insect's foot; pulvillus. **6** any cushionlike part of an animal body. **7** the large floating leaf of the water lily; lily pad: *Several small frogs sat sunning on a pad.* **8** a number of sheets of paper fastened tightly together along one edge; tablet: *to jot a note on the pad by the telephone.* **9** a cushionlike piece of cloth soaked with ink to use with a rubber stamp: *The clerk inked the stamp on the pad.* **10** = launching pad: *Gravity is what makes it so hard for rockets to hop off their pads and hit the moon* (New Yorker). **11** the socket of a brace, in which the bit is inserted. **12** a tool handle for various sizes or kinds of tools. **13** *Obsolete.* a bundle of straw or the like to lie on. **14** *U.S. Slang.* a place where a person sleeps, such as a room, house, or apartment. **15** *U.S. Slang.* **a** graft shared among various members of a police precinct or department: *When a cop was transferred to a new post, the pad from his old station kept up for another two months* (Time). **b** a secret pad or notebook on which the names of those receiving graft are listed.
—*v.t.* **1** to fill with something soft; stuff: *to pad a chair, to pad a suit for football.* **2** *Figurative.* to add words to, just to fill space; expand or lengthen (a story, written paper, or speech) by including unnecessary material: *to pad a short story with anecdotes. Mr. Killmayer never padded a song beyond what it was worth* (New York Times). **3** *Figurative.* to increase the amount of (a bill, expense account, or other statement) by false entries.
**on the pad,** *U.S. Slang.* sharing in graft or dishonest money collected by policemen of a precinct or department: *For years ... it was as if the whole town was on the pad, as if a sidewalk couldn't be cleaned without grease, as if the garbage could not be carted without paying grease* (New York Post).
[origin uncertain]

**pad**[2] (pad), *v.,* **pad|ded, pad|ding,** *n.* —*v.t.* **1** to walk along (a path or road); tramp; trudge: *to pad the same path every day.* **2** to beat down by treading.
—*v.i.* **1** to travel on foot; tramp or trudge along. **2** to walk or trot steadily and softly: *a wolf padding through the forest. He put on his slippers and padded out to the kitchen.*
—*n.* **1** a dull sound, as of footsteps on the ground: *'Tis the regular pad of the wolves in pursuit of the life in the sledge* (Robert Browning). **2** a slow horse for riding on a road, as for journeying: *an abbot on an ambling pad* (Tennyson). **3** *British.* a path or track: *It is a curious fact that wild animals do not seem to notice anything above the pad* (Observer). **4** *Obsolete.* a highway robber; highwayman; footpad: *Four pads in ambush lay* (Byron).
[probably < earlier Dutch or Low German *pad* path. Compare Low German *padden* to tread.]

**pa|dauk** (pə douk′), *n.* **1** any one of various Indian and Malaysian trees of the pea family that yield a useful wood, such as a redwood grown in the Andaman Islands and Amboina wood. **2** the wood of any of these trees, often used in place of mahogany and teak. Also, **padouk.** [< the Burmese name]

**pad|ded cell** (pad′id), a room in an insane asylum or prison, having the walls padded to prevent the person confined in it from injuring himself.

**pad|ding** (pad′ing), *n.* **1** material used to pad with, such as cotton, felt, straw, or hair. **SYN:** wadding. **2** unnecessary words used just to fill space in making a speech or a written paper longer: *His letters were usually all common form and padding* (Samuel Butler). **3** the act of a person or thing that pads.

**pad|dle**[1] (pad′əl), *n., v.,* **-dled, -dling.** —*n.* **1** a short oar with a broad blade at one end or both ends, used without an oarlock. Paddles are used especially to propel canoes and kayaks. **2** the act of paddling; turn at the paddle: *Each man had a paddle for an hour and then a rest.* **3a** one of the broad boards fixed around a water wheel or a paddle wheel to push, or be pushed by, the water: *Some tugs on rivers still have paddles.* **b** = paddle wheel. **4** a paddle-shaped piece of wood used for stirring or for mixing: *The butter churn had two paddles to whip the cream.* **5** an instrument or tool of this shape, used in various trades or industries, especially for stirring and mixing. **6** a flipper or similar limb, such as that of a turtle, whale, or penguin. **7** a small, flat wooden racket, faced with sandpaper or rubber, used to hit the ball in table or paddle tennis; racket. **8** the signaling arm of a semaphore. **9** Also, **pettle.** *British.* a small, long-handled, spadelike tool used for cleaning a plowshare, digging up thistles, etc.
—*v.t.* **1** to move (a canoe or boat) with a paddle or paddles: *The explorers paddled their canoe cautiously upstream.* **2** to transport or convey, as in a canoe, by paddling: *She would herself paddle me off to the ship* (Herman Melville). **3** to beat with a paddle; spank.
—*v.i.* **1** to use a paddle to move a canoe or boat through water: *Being fatigued with rowing, or paddling, as it is called* (Daniel Defoe). **2** to row gently, so as barely to move through the water or simply to hold a boat steady against the current: *a rainbow shell That paddles in a halcyon sea* (Christina G. Rossetti). —**pad′dler,** *n.* —**pad′dle-like′,** *adj.*

**pad|dle**[2] (pad′əl), *v.i.,* **-dled, -dling. 1** to move the hands or feet about in water; dabble or play in shallow water: *the children paddling in the mud puddle. Children love to paddle at the beach.* **2** to toy with the fingers. **3** to walk with short, unsteady steps, like those of a young child; toddle. [apparently related to **pad**[2]. Compare Low German *paddlen* tramp about < *padden* to tread, pad[2].] —**pad′dler,** *n.*

**pad|dle|ball** (pad′əl bôl′), *n.* a game in which two opposing sides alternate in hitting a tennis ball with a wooden paddle against a single wall or the walls of a court.

**pad|dle|boat** (pad′əl bōt′), *n.* a steamboat equipped with a paddle wheel on each side or one at the stern; paddlesteamer.

**pad|dle|board** (pad′əl bôrd′, -bōrd′), *n.* a surfboard shaped somewhat like the blade of a paddle.

**paddle box,** the guard or casing covering the upper part of a paddle wheel.

**paddle court,** a level, rectangular area, half the size of a tennis court, prepared and marked out for playing paddle tennis.

**paddle doll,** an ancient Egyptian figurine carved in the shape of a canoe paddle, with lines painted or carved on it to look like clothes, and hair made of short strings of beads.

**pad|dle|fish** (pad′əl fish′), *n., pl.* **-fish|es** or (*collectively*) **-fish.** a large, scaleless fish with sharklike fins and an oarlike snout which is a sense organ probably used in locating food; spoonbill. The paddlefish lives in the rivers of the Mississippi Valley and the Great Lakes and is usually about four feet long. It is related to the sturgeon.

**paddle foot,** *Slang.* an infantry soldier.

**pad|dle|steam|er** (pad′əl stē′mər), *n.* = paddleboat.

**paddle tennis,** a game of tennis played with wooden paddles on a court half the size of a tennis court and using a lower net than that of a tennis court.

**paddle wheel,** a wheel with paddles fixed around it for propelling a ship over the water.

***pad|dle|wheel|er** (pad′əl hwē′lər), *n.* a boat or ship equipped with paddle wheels or a paddle wheel.

***paddlewheeler**

side-wheeler

stern-wheeler

**pad|dock**[1] (pad′ək), *n., v.* —*n.* **1** a small, enclosed field near a stable or house, used for exercising animals or as a pasture, especially for horses: *Ten cows were grazed in each break and moved into a new paddock every morning* (John Hancock). **2** a pen at a race track, where horses are saddled before a race. **3** (in Australia and New Zealand) any field or piece of tillable or grass-covered land enclosed by a fence, often used as a sheep and cattle pasture.

**Pronunciation Key:** hat, āge, cãre, fär; let, ēqual, tėrm; it, īce; hot, ōpen, ôrder; **oil, out;** cup, pu̇t, rüle; **ch**ild; lo**ng**; **th**in; **ᵺ**en; **zh,** measure; **ə** represents **a** in about, **e** in taken, **i** in pencil, **o** in lemon, **u** in circus.

— ***v.t.*** **1** to put or keep in or as if in a paddock: *Shakespeare himself would have been commonplace had he been paddocked in a thinly-shaven vocabulary* (James Russell Lowell). **2** (in Australia) to fence in (land).
[variant of *parrock,* Old English *pearroc* enclosed space; fence. Compare etym. under **park.**]

**pad|dock²** (pad′ək), *n. Dialect.* **1** a frog. **2** a toad: *Paddock calls* (Shakespeare). [Middle English *paddoke* < *pade* toad, frog + *-ok* diminutive suffix]

**pad|dy¹** (pad′ē), *n., pl.* **-dies. 1** a field of rice; paddyfield: *From 4,300 acres of paddy the family's holding dropped to 10 acres* (London Times). **2** rice in the husk, uncut or gathered. Also, **padi.** [< Malay *padi* rice in the husk]

**pad|dy²** (pad′ē), *n., pl.* **-dies.** *British Informal.* a tantrum; paddywhack.

**Pad|dy** (pad′ē), *n., pl.* **-dies.** *Slang.* a nickname for an Irishman. [< nickname for Irish *Pādraig* Patrick]

**pad|dy|bird** (pad′ē bėrd′), *n.* any one of various birds that frequent rice fields, such as the Java sparrow.

**pad|dy|field** (pad′ē fēld′), *n.* a water-covered field in which rice is grown; paddy: *The dry season drains the swamps and paddyfields, making fighting easier* (Time).

**pad|dy|mel|on** (pad′ē mel′ən), *n.* = pademelon.

**paddy wagon,** *U.S. Slang.* a patrol wagon: *Three paddy wagons shuttled back and forth ... hauling 276 men and three women to headquarters for questioning* (Time).

**pad|dy|whack** (pad′ē hwak′), *n.* **1** *U.S. Informal.* a spanking or beating. **2** *British Informal.* a rage; passion; temper. [apparently < *Paddy*]

**pad|e|mel|on** (pad′ē mel′ən), *n.* a small Australian kangaroo. [< a native name]

**pad foot,** a flattened ornamental foot at the end of a cabriole leg: *A Queen Anne table with ... cabriole legs and pad feet has come through unscathed* (New York Times).

**pad|i** (pad′ē), *n., pl.* **pad|is.** = paddy¹.

**pa|di|shah** or **Pa|di|shah** (pä′di shä), *n.* great king; emperor (a title applied especially to the Shah of Iran and, formerly, to the Sultan of Turkey or to the British sovereign as emperor of India). [< Persian *pādshah*]

**pad|lock** (pad′lok′), *n., v.* — ***n.*** a lock that can be put on and removed. A padlock is used to keep a hasp closed or on a chain, locker, or gate. A bicycle padlock has a long shackle to fit through a wheel.
— ***v.t.*** to fasten with a padlock: *At other schools the playgrounds were left open for afterhours recreation, but at Quincy Adams the playground gates were padlocked as soon as school was out* (Atlantic).
[< pad, perhaps variant of *pod*³ + *lock*¹]

**pad|nag** (pad′nag′), *n.* a horse with an easy gait; pad. [< *pad*² + *nag*²]

**pa|douk** (pə douk′), *n.* = padauk.

**pa|dre** (pä′drā), *n.* **1** father. It is used as a name for a priest, especially in regions where Spanish, Portuguese, or Italian is spoken. **2** *Informal.* a chaplain in the armed forces: *To some villages a padre has come from the services who has faced the grimmest realities* (J. W. R. Scott). [< Italian, Spanish, and Portuguese *padre* < Latin *pater, patris* father]

**pa|dro|ne** (pä drō′nā *for 1;* pə drō′nē *for 2*), *n., pl.* **pa|dro|ni** (pä drō′nē), *for 1;* **pa|dro|nes** (pə drō′nēz) *for 2.* **1** *Italian.* **a** a master; boss. **b** an innkeeper. **c** the master of a small coastal vessel. **2** a man who controls and supplies Italian laborers on contract with an employer, as in America. Originally he was paid by the employer, and his force of recent immigrant laborers was given a nominal wage by the padrone. [< Italian *padrone* < Latin *patrōnus.* See etym. of doublet **patron, patroon.**]

**pa|dro|nism** (pə drō′niz əm), *n.* boss control of Italian laborers.

**Pad|u|an** (paj′ù ən, pad′yù ən), *adj., n.* — ***adj.*** of or having to do with Padua, a city in northeastern Italy, or its people.
— ***n.*** a native or inhabitant of Padua.

**pad|u|a|soy** (paj′ù ə soi), *n., adj.* — ***n.*** **1** a smooth, strong, heavy, rich fabric of corded silk, much worn by both men and women in the 1700's. **2** a garment of this fabric: *The paduasoy ... was being made into a christening cloak for the baby* (Elizabeth Gaskell).
— ***adj.*** made of this fabric.
[< French *pou-de-soie;* origin uncertain; spelling influenced by earlier English *padou* (or *Padua*) *say* (literally) silk serge of Padua]

**pae|an** (pē′ən), *n.* **1** a song of praise, thanksgiving, joy, or triumph: *Loud paeans chanted through the valley announced the approach of the victors* (Herman Melville). *He ended with a fervent paean to the country he had served so long* (Newsweek). **SYN:** hallelujah. **2** (in ancient Greece) a hymn or chant of triumph or thanksgiving to a deity, especially to Apollo or Artemis. Also, **pean.** [< Latin *paean* < Greek *paiân, -ânos* hymn to Apollo]

**pae|di|a|tri|cian** (pē′dē ə trish′ən, ped′ē-), *n. Especially British.* pediatrician.

**pae|do|gen|e|sis** (pē′dō jen′ə sis), *n.* = pedogenesis.

**pae|do|mor|phism** (pē′dō môr′fiz əm), *n.* = pedomorphism.

**pa|el|la** (pä el′ə), *n.* a spicy dish consisting of seasoned rice, cooked in oil with saffron, and of lobster or shrimp, scraps of chicken, or of beef and pork, and fresh vegetables. [< Spanish *paella* < Catalan, a frying pan, ultimately < Latin *patella* a small pan]

**pae|on** (pē′ən), *n.* (in Greek and Latin verse) a foot of four syllables, one long and three short. The long syllable may come anywhere in the foot. [< Latin *paeon* < Greek *peiōn, paiân* paean]

**pae|o|ny** (pē′ə nē), *n., pl.* **-nies.** *Especially British.* peony.

**pa|gan** (pā′gən), *n., adj.* — ***n.*** **1** a person who is not a Christian, Jew, or Moslem; person who worships many gods or no god; heathen. The ancient Greeks and most of the Romans were pagans because they did not know or believe in the God worshiped by the Christians and Jews, and later, the Moslems. *I'd rather be a pagan, suckled in a creed outworn* (Wordsworth). **SYN:** See syn. under **heathen. 2** a person who has no religion.
— ***adj.*** **1** having something to do with pagans; not Christian, Jewish, or Moslem; heathen: *pagan customs.* **2** not religious.
[< Latin *pāgānus* rustic (in Late Latin, heathen) (at a time when Christianity was accepted by urban populations) < *pāgus* village]

**pa|gan|dom** (pā′gən dəm), *n.* = heathendom.

**pa|gan|i|ca** (pə gan′ə kə), *n.* an ancient Roman game played in the open countryside with a bent stick and a leather ball stuffed with feathers. [< Latin (*pila*) *pāgānica* rustic (ball)]

**pa|gan|ish** (pā′gə nish), *adj.* having to do with or characteristic of pagans; heathenish.

**pa|gan|ism** (pā′gə niz əm), *n.* **1** a pagan attitude toward religion or morality. **2** the beliefs and practices of pagans. **3** the condition of being pagan: *The rising paganism of the western world will make our civilization as cold as interstellar spaces* (Time).

**pa|gan|ize** (pā′gə nīz), *v.t., v.i.,* **-ized, -iz|ing.** to make or become pagan: *In spite of the commercializing—even the paganizing—of a religious festival, people are forcibly aware of it* (Newsweek). — **pa′gan|i|za′tion,** *n.* — **pa′gan|iz′er,** *n.*

**page¹** (pāj), *n., v.,* **paged, pag|ing.** — ***n.*** **1** one side of a leaf or sheet of paper: *a page in this book. Abbr:* p. **2a** the print or writing on one side of a leaf. **b** *Printing.* the type set and made up to be printed as a page. **3** *Figurative.* **a** a record: *the pages of history.* **b** a happening or time considered as part of history: *The settling of the West is an exciting page in the history of the United States.*
— ***v.t.*** to number the pages of; folio; paginate.
[< French *page* < Old French *pagene,* learned borrowing from Latin *pāgina,* related to *pangere* to fasten]

**page²** (pāj), *n., v.,* **paged, pag|ing.** — ***n.*** **1a** a boy or manservant; person who carries parcels, delivers messages, and runs errands; errand boy; bellboy. The pages at hotels usually wear uniforms. **b** a boy or girl, usually of high-school age, who is employed by a legislature as a messenger. Congressional pages carry messages between the Capitol and the Senate and House office buildings, and run errands for the senators and congressmen. **2** a very small boy, usually elaborately dressed, who is a nominal attendant of the bride in a wedding ceremony. **3a** a youth who attends a person of high rank. **b** a youth who was preparing to be a knight, and who was attached to the household of a lord or knight whom he followed in the course of training for knighthood. **4** *Obsolete.* a boy; youth; lad.
— ***v.t.*** **1a** to try to find (a person) at a hotel or club by having his name called out. **b** (of a page or bellhop) to try to find (a person) by calling out his name: *The bellhop is paging you in the lobby.* **2** to wait on, attend, or follow like a page.
— ***v.i.*** to act as page; be a page.
[< Old French *page,* perhaps < Medieval Latin *pagius* rustic < Latin *pāgus* country district]

**pag|eant** (paj′ənt), *n., v.* — ***n.*** **1** an elaborate spectacle; procession in costume; pomp; display; show: *The coronation of the new king was a splendid pageant.* **2a** a public entertainment that represents scenes from history, legends, or the like: *Our school gave a pageant of the coming of the Pilgrims to America.* **b** a drama or series of scenes played outdoors by local actors: *a children's Christmas pageant.* **3** *Figurative.* an empty show, not reality: *Once in a while one meets with a single soul greater than all the living pageant which passes before it* (Oliver Wendell Holmes). *These our actors, As I foretold you, were all spirits and Are melted into air, into thin air ... And like this insubstantial pageant faded, Leave not a rack behind* (Shakespeare). **4a** *Archaic.* a stage or platform, usually moving on wheels, on which scenes from medieval mystery plays were presented. **b** a similar stage bearing any kind of spectacle. **5** *Archaic.* any dramatic piece or play: *This wide and universal theatre Presents more woeful pageants than the scene Wherein we play in* (Shakespeare). **6** *Archaic, Figurative.* anything viewed as a drama within which one has a part, such as a course of duty or the course of a life.
— ***v.t.*** to honor with a pageant; celebrate with pageantry: *He pageants us* (Shakespeare).
[Middle English *pagent, pagen;* origin uncertain; probably < Late Latin *pāgina* scaffold, stage; plank < Latin, page¹]

**pag|eant|ry** (paj′ən trē), *n., pl.* **-ries. 1** a splendid show; gorgeous display; pomp: *The large Stratford company of some 90-odd players manages swordplay and panoplied pageantry with great facility* (Newsweek). **SYN:** spectacle. **2** *Figurative.* mere show; empty display. **SYN:** ostentation, pretension. **3** a pageant, or pageants collectively.

**pageant wagon,** a wagon used for the performance of plays in medieval England. It carried the setting of a play and was drawn through a city to places where audiences gathered. The actors probably performed on a platform alongside the wagon.

***page boy,** or **page|boy** (pāj′boi′), *n.* **1** a person, usually a boy, who works as a page. **2** a shoulder-length hairstyle for women in which the hair in the back and on the sides is turned under at the ends in a soft roll.

***page boy**
definition 2

**page proof,** *Printing.* a proof taken after type has been made up into a page.

**Pag|et's disease** (paj′its), **1** a severe disorder of the bones, characterized by their enlargement, weakening, and deformation. **2** cancer of the breast involving the nipple and associated ducts. [< Sir James *Paget,* 1814-1899, an English surgeon]

**pag|i|nal** (paj′ə nəl), *adj.* **1** of, having to do with, or consisting of a page or pages. **2** page for page: *a paginal reprint.* [< Latin *pāginālis* < *pāgina* page¹]

**pag|i|nar|y** (paj′ə ner′ē), *adj.* = paginal.

**pag|i|nate** (paj′ə nāt), *v.t.,* **-nat|ed, -nat|ing.** to mark the number of pages of; page; folio.

**pag|i|na|tion** (paj′ə nā′shən), *n.* **1** the act or process of numbering the pages of books, manuscript, or other written work. **2** the figures with which pages are numbered; numbering of pages. **3** the number of pages or (now rarely) leaves in a book or other printed matter.

**pag|ing** (pā′jing), *n.* = pagination.

***pa|go|da** (pə gō′də), *n.* **1** a temple or other sacred building with many stories forming a tower. Each story of a pagoda has a roof curving upward. There are many pagodas in China, Japan, and parts of India and southeastern Asia. **2** a gold or silver coin formerly current in India. [< Portuguese *pagode,* perhaps < Tamil *pagavadi* < Sanskrit *bhagavatī* goddess]

***pagoda**
definition 1

**pagoda tree, 1** any one of several trees so called from their resemblance to or their association with pagodas, such as the banyan of India.

**2** a mythical East Indian tree fabled to let fall pagodas (the coins) when shaken.

**pa|go|dite** (pə gōʹdīt), *n.* = agalmatolite.

**pa|gu|ri|an** (pə gyůrʹē ən), *adj., n.* —***adj.*** of or belonging to a family of crustaceans comprising the hermit crabs. —***n.*** = hermit crab. [< New Latin *Pagurus* the genus name (< Latin *pagūrus* a kind of crab < Greek *págouros*) + English *-ian*]

**pah** (pä), *interj.* an exclamation of disgust.

**pah|la|vi** (päʹlə vē), *n.* a gold coin of Iran, worth 20 rials. [< Persian *pahlavi* < Reza Khan *Pahlavi,* the Shah of Iran (Persia)]

**Pah|la|vi** (päʹlə vē), *n.* **1** the principal language of Persia from the 200's to the 800's, an Iranian language using a Semitic script. **2** the Semitic script of Pahlavi. Also, **Pehlevi**. [< Persian *Pahlavi* Parthian < Old Persian *Parthava* Parthia]

**pa|ho|e|ho|e** (pä hōʹē hōʹē), *n.* lava that has hardened into a smooth, shiny surface. [< Hawaiian *pāhoehoe*]

**paid** (pād), *v., adj.* —***v.*** the past tense and past participle of **pay**[1]: *I have paid my bills. These bills are all paid.*
—***adj.*** **1** receiving money; hired: *a paid worker, a paid informer.* **2** no longer owed; settled: *a paid mortgage. Abbr.:* pd. **3** cashed: *a paid check.*
**put paid to,** *British Informal.* to dispose of; finish off; settle: *We became fast friends after we decided to put paid to our quarrel once and for all.*
► **paid, payed.** *Paid* is the spelling of the past tense and past participle of pay[1] (*He paid his bills*) in all senses except "let out" (*They payed out the rope*), and occasionally in that sense also.

**pai|dei|a** (pī dāʹə), *n.* the classical ideal of education; broad intellectual training and experience: *Paideia, that famous, ambiguous word which meant both education and culture … "acquired the value of an absolute and became in a way an end in itself"* (James R. Newman). [< Greek *paideía* training, education, culture, ultimately < *paîs, paidós* child]

**paid-in surplus** (pādʹinʹ), capital surplus obtained by selling shares of stock above their face value.

**paid-up** (pādʹupʹ), *adj.* that has paid in full; not in arrears: *a paid-up member.*

**pai-hua** (pīʹhwäʹ), *n.* an informal or vernacular style of Chinese writing and literature, popularized in China after 1917. [< Chinese (Peking) *pai* plain + *hua* talk, speech]

**paik** (pāk), *British Dialect. n., v.* —***n.*** a hard blow, especially against the body.
—***v.t.*** to beat; pummel; thrash.
[origin unknown]

**pail** (pāl), *n.* **1** a round container with a handle, used for carrying liquids, sand, or the like; bucket: *a milk pail.* **2** the amount a pail holds; pailful. [Old English *pægel* wine vessel; gill, and < Old French *paielle* warming pan, both < Medieval Latin *pagella* a measure (diminutive) < Latin *pāgina* (originally) something fixed]

**pail|ful** (pālʹfu̇l), *n., pl.* **-fuls.** the amount that fills a pail: *The rain was falling by pailfuls* (Macaulay).

**pail|lasse** (pal yasʹ, palʹyas), *n.* a mattress or under mattress filled with straw or some similarly simple, inexpensive material. Also, **palliasse.** [< Old French *paillasse* < *paille* straw < Latin *palea* chaff, straw]

**pail|lette** (pal yetʹ), *n.* **1** = spangle. **2** a piece of bright metal or thin metal foil used in enamel painting. [< Middle French *paillette* (diminutive) < *paille* chaff < Latin *palea*]

**pail|let|ted** (pal yetʹid), *adj.* spangled.

**pail|lon** (pä yôɴʹ), *n., pl.* **-lons** (-yôɴʹ). *French.* thin metal foil, used in gilding or for other decorations.

**pai|lou** (pīʹlōʹ), *n.* (in China) an elaborate structure forming or resembling a gateway, erected as a memorial. [< Chinese (Peking) *p'ai lou*]

**pain** (pān), *n., v.* —***n.*** **1** a feeling of being hurt; suffering: *A cut gives pain.* **2** a single or localized feeling of hurt: *a sharp pain in one's back. A toothache is a pain.* **3** mental suffering; grief; sorrow: *The death of one we love gives pain.* **4** *Obsolete.* labor; effort; work: *'Tis most strange Nature should be so conversant with pain* (Shakespeare). **5** *Obsolete.* punishment; penalty: *liable to the pains and penalties of high treason* (Jonathan Swift).
—***v.t.*** to cause to suffer; give pain to: *Does your tooth pain you?* **SYN:** hurt, afflict, torture.
—***v.i.*** to cause suffering; give pain: *a natural desire to pain* (Rudyard Kipling).
**feel no pain,** to be intoxicated: *Having come down out of the woods to Berlin, Jack was feeling no pain* (Atlantic).
**on** (or **under**) **pain of,** with the punishment or penalty of, unless a certain thing is done: *The traitor was ordered to leave the country on pain of death.*
**pain in the neck,** *Slang.* a very troublesome or irritating thing or person: *O'Malley is tall and gentle, and has a wife who is a pain in the neck* (Frank O'Connor).
**pains,** a trouble to do something; effort; care: *She took pains to be neat. Great … pains have been taken to inflame our minds* (Edmund Burke). *You … are like to have nothing but your travel for your pains* (John Bunyan). **b** the sufferings of childbirth: *labor pains.*
[< Old French *peine* < Latin *poena* penalty < Greek *poinḗ*]
—*Syn. n.* **1, 2 Pain, ache** mean a feeling of being hurt. **Pain** particularly suggests a sharp hurt, but of any degree from a sudden jab in one spot to a very severe and sometimes long-lasting hurt of the whole body: *I have a pain in my side.* **Ache** suggests a steady and usually dull hurt: *I have a headache from reading too long. I have a stomachache.*

**pained** (pānd), *adj.* **1** hurt, distressed, or grieved: *I am greatly pained to learn of your refusal.* **2** expressing or showing pain: *a pained look.*

**pain|ful** (pānʹfəl), *adj.* **1** hurting; causing pain; unpleasant: *a painful illness, a painful duty, a painful back.* **2** difficult; involving much trouble or labor: *a painful ascent of a mountain by its steepest face.* **SYN:** toilsome. **3** *Archaic.* painstaking; careful: *The painful chronicle of honest John Stowe* (Robert Southey). —**painʹful|ly,** *adv.*
—**painʹful|ness,** *n.*

**pain|kill|er** (pānʹkilʹər), *n.* **1** any drug or remedy for getting rid of or alleviating pain, such as morphine, novocaine, and aspirin: *A new painkiller, propoxyphene hydrochloride, is as effective as codeine* (Newsweek). **2** anything that serves to relieve pain: *Some dental patients have found stereophonic sound to be an effective painkiller* (Science News Letter).

**pain|kill|ing** (pānʹkilʹing), *adj.* relieving pain: *a painkilling drug.*

**pain|less** (pānʹlis), *adj.* without pain; causing no pain: *painless childbirth.* —**painʹless|ly,** *adv.*
—**painʹless|ness,** *n.*

**pains|tak|ing** (pānzʹtāʹking), *adj., n.* —***adj.*** **1** very careful; particular; scrupulous: *a painstaking writer.* **SYN:** assiduous. **2** marked or characterized by attentive care; carefully done: *a painstaking reproduction.*
—***n.*** the taking of pains; careful effort in doing anything: *I afterwards, with a little painstaking, acquired as much of the Spanish as to read their books* (Benjamin Franklin). —**painsʹtakʹing|ly,** *adv.*

**paint**[1] (pānt), *n., v.* —***n.*** **1a** a solid coloring matter mixed with a liquid, that can be spread on a surface to make a layer or film of white, black, or colored matter. **b** the solid coloring matter alone; pigment: *a box of paints.* **2** the layer or film created by applying paint to a surface. **3** coloring matter put on the face or part of the body. **4** the act or fact of painting or coloring. [< verb]
—***v.t.*** **1** to cover or decorate with paint: *to paint a house or a room.* **2** to represent (an object, person, or scene) in colors, usually on a prepared surface: *The artist painted fairies and angels. Paint me a cavernous waste shore* (T. S. Eliot). **3** *Figurative.* to show as if by painting: *A lively surprise … was painted on his countenance* (Mary W. Shelley). **4** *Figurative.* to picture vividly in words: *I shall … paint to you … something like the true form of the whale as he actually appears to the eye of the whaleman* (Herman Melville). **5a** to put on like paint: *The doctor painted iodine on the cut.* **b** to treat (a wound or any part) in this way. **6** to put color on (the face or other part) in order to beautify it artificially: *to paint one's fingernails.*
—***v.i.*** **1** to use paint in covering, decorating, or coloring. **2** to practice the art of painting; make pictures. **3** *Obsolete.* to apply, as rouge: *Nor could it sure be such a sin to paint* (Alexander Pope).
[< Old French *peint,* past participle of *peindre* to paint < Latin *pingere*] —**paintʹa|ble,** *adj.*

**paint**[2] (pānt), *n. U.S. Dialect.* a piebald or particolored horse: *I ride an old paint …* (American cowboy song). [< Spanish *pinto*]

**paint|box** (pāntʹboksʹ), *n.* a box used by artists for holding cakes or tubes of pigment.

**paint|brush** (pāntʹbrushʹ), *n.* **1** a brush for putting on paint. **2** = Indian paintbrush.

**paint cards,** *U.S. Slang.* the picture cards (king, queen, jack) in a deck of cards.

**paint|ed** (pānʹtid), *adj.* **1** depicted or executed in colors; coated or decorated with paint: *Painted Bulletins, the next most popular form of outdoor advertising, are usually larger than posters, and are often illuminated* (Marion Harper, Jr.). **2** of bright or variegated coloring, as certain animals. **3** *Archaic, Figurative.* feigned, artificial, or insincere.

**painted bunting,** **1** a small bright-colored finch of the southern United States, the male of which has a purple head, red breast, and green back; nonpareil. **2** a longspur of the Arctic and central North America.

**painted cup,** any one of a group of plants of the figwort family, having bright-colored bracts about the flowers, especially the Indian paintbrush.

**painted daisy,** = pyrethrum (def. 1).

**painted lady,** **1** a very common, handsome butterfly of an orange-red color spotted with black and white, found in temperate regions throughout the world. **2** a gladiolus with pink splashes upon its flowers. **3** = pyrethrum (def. 1).

**painted redstart,** a warbler of southwestern North America, black with red and white markings.

**painted tongue,** = salpiglossis.

**painted trillium,** a North American trillium with white flowers having deep pink or purple stripes. It grows from Quebec to Georgia and west as far as Wisconsin and Missouri.

**painted turtle,** a common freshwater turtle of North America, having a slate-colored carapace and yellow underside, with red and yellow markings on the head, legs, and shell.

**painted wake-robin,** = painted trillium.

**paint|er**[1] (pānʹtər), *n.* **1** a person who paints pictures; artist: *Bonnard may not have been the most profound of modern painters, but he was one of the most charming* (London Times). **2** a person who puts on paint as a protective coating or decoration for walls of buildings and houses, or woodwork, or any other surface: *a house painter, a sign painter.* [< Anglo-French *painter,* Old French *peinteur* < Vulgar Latin *pinctor,* for Latin *pictor* < *pingere* to paint]

**paint|er**[2] (pānʹtər), *n.* a rope, usually fastened to the bow of a boat, for tying it, as to a ship or pier. [probably < Old French *pentoir,* and *pentour* cordage for hanging, ultimately < Latin *pendēre* to hang]

**paint|er**[3] (pānʹtər), *n.* the American panther or mountain lion; cougar (so called especially by early settlers in the eastern United States); puma: *The painters (panthers) used to come round their log cabin at night* (Harriet Beecher Stowe). [American English, variant of earlier English *panter* panther]

**paint|er|ish** (pānʹtər ish), *adj.* = painterly.

**paint|er|ly** (pānʹtər lē), *adj., adv.* —***adj.*** of, suitable to, or characteristic of a painter; artistic: *four pictures which are sensitive, workmanlike and painterly* (Manchester Guardian).
—***adv.*** in a way proper to a painter; artistically.
—**paintʹer|li|ness,** *n.*

**painter's colic,** severe and continuing abdominal pain resulting from chronic lead poisoning; lead colic.

**paint-in** (pāntʹinʹ), *n.* the action of painting or decorating the exterior of buildings by a group of people to improve, or show the need to improve, the appearance of a run-down area.

**paint|ing** (pānʹting), *n.* **1** something painted; picture: *a very lifelike painting.* **2** the act or process of a person who paints: *You must clean the walls before painting.* **3** the art of representation, decoration, and creating beauty with paints: *She studied painting at the Academy of Design.*

**paint|less** (pāntʹlis), *adj.* without paint.

**paint|pot** (pāntʹpotʹ), *n.* **1** a container for holding paint: *We sat, with our brushes and paintpots by us* (Richard Henry Dana). **2** *Geology.* a type of hot spring containing brightly colored boiling mud.

**paint|ress** (pānʹtris), *n.* a woman painter.

**paint|work** (pāntʹwėrkʹ), *n.* **1** paint spread and dried on a surface: *A raised strip of chromium protects the paintwork.* **2** the manner or quality of work in applying paint: *Only the most painstaking paintwork could produce such a satiny finish.*

**paint|y** (pānʹtē), *adj.* of, having to do with, or containing too much paint: *a painty odor.*

**pair** (pãr), *n., pl.* **pairs** or (*sometimes after a numeral*) **pair,** *v.* —***n.*** **1** a set of two; two that go together: *a pair of shoes, a pair of eyes, a pair of horses, a pair of pistols.* **2** a single thing consisting of two parts that cannot be used separately: *a pair of scissors, a pair of trousers.* **3** a man and woman who are married or are engaged to be married: *Among the members of the household of Claremont, near Esher, where the royal pair were established* (Lytton Strachey). **4** two partners in a dance. **5** two animals that are mated: *In many cases one or a few pairs of a species are entirely inadequate for the establishment or for the preservation of an animal species* (Science News Letter). **6a** two members on opposite sides in a legislative body who arrange not to vote on a certain question or for a certain time, especially so that their absence may not af-

**Pronunciation Key:** hat, āge, cãre, fär; let, ēqual, tėrm; it, īce; hot, ōpen, ôrder; oil, out; cup, pu̇t, rüle; child; long; thin; ᴛʜen; zh, measure; ə represents **a** in about, **e** in taken, **i** in pencil, **o** in lemon, **u** in circus.

fect the voting. **b** the arrangement thus made. **7a** two cards of the same value in different suits, viewed as a unit in one's hand: *a pair of sixes, a pair of jacks.* **b** two identical cards in games using a multiple deck. **c** a team of two who remain partners through the several rounds of a match, as in duplicate bridge. **8** *Mechanics.* a set of two parts (elements) so connected as to act mutually to constrain relative motion. **9** *Dialect.* a set, not limited to two: *a pair of beads.*
—*v.t.* **1** to arrange in pairs: *to pair socks. Her gloves were neatly paired in a drawer.* **2** *U.S.* to arrange with (another legislator) that both will abstain from voting on a certain question: *At the time the vote to "censure" McCarthy was taken, Kennedy was ill. He did not vote, nor was he paired* (Newsweek).
—*v.i.* **1** to be arranged in pairs; match: *The children in the class paired up as partners for a trip to the zoo.* **2** to join in love and marriage. **3** to mate; couple: *Birds pair and build nests in spring.*
**pair off,** to arrange in pairs; form into pairs: *Suppose the three hundred heroes at Thermopylae had paired off with three hundred Persians* (Emerson).
[< Old French *paire* < Latin *paria* equals, neuter plural of *pār, paris* part, share]
—*Syn. n.* **1 Pair, couple** mean two of the same kind. **Pair** applies to two things that belong together because they match or complement each other: *I bought a new pair of gloves.* **Couple** usually applies to any two of the same kind: *I bought a couple of shirts.*
▶**pair.** The plural form *pair* is used only after a numeral or *many, several, few,* or other such adjective of number: *I bought six pair* (or *pairs*).

**pair bond,** a monogamous bond or union between a male and female pair of a species: *Ritual "Dance" of the wandering albatross is actually the agonistic responses of an unmated male and female that are not familiar with each other . . . until eventually the birds are at ease in each other's presence and a pair bond is established* (Scientific American).

**pair bonding,** the act or condition of forming a pair bond.

**pair-oar** (pãr′ôr′, -ōr′), *n., adj.* —*n.* a shell or boat rowed by two oarsmen, one seated behind the other, each pulling one oar in unison with the other.
—*adj.* of or having to do with a pair-oar.

**pair-oared** (pãr′ôrd′, -ōrd′), *adj.* = pair-oar.

**pair of compasses,** a drawing compass.

**pair production,** *Physics.* the simultaneous formation of an electron and a positron from a photon passing through a strong electric field.

**pair|wise** (pãr′wīz′), *adv., adj.* —*adv.* in pairs: *There are two-electron oxidations in biochemistry that proceed pairwise and do not involve radicals as intermediates* (Scientific American).
—*adj.* occurring in pairs: *pairwise genetic crosses* (Science).

**pai|sa** (pī sä′, pī′sä), *n., pl.* **pai|se** (pī sā′, pī′sā), **pai|sa,** or **pai|sas.** **1** a coin of India, Pakistan, Bhutan, and Nepal, equal to 1/100 of a rupee. **2** a coin of Bangladesh worth 1/100 of a taka. [< Hindustani *paisā* pice]

**pai|sa|no** (pī sä′nō), *n., pl.* **-nos.** *Spanish.* countryman.

***pais|ley** or **Pais|ley** (pāz′lē), *n., pl.* **-leys,** *adj.* —*n.* **1** a soft woolen cloth with a very elaborate and colorful pattern. **2** something made of paisley: *[The] lovely blouses are available in breathtaking array of traditional paisleys, gay stripes, charming moderns* (New Yorker).
—*adj.* made of paisley; having a pattern and colors like paisley: *Old Paisley shawls have been collected from Scotland, Persia, and India* (New Yorker).
[< *Paisley,* a city in Scotland]

***paisley**
definition 1

**Pais|ley|ism** (pāz′lē iz′əm), *n.* separatism between Catholics and Protestants in Northern Ireland. [< Ian *Paisley,* born 1926, head of the Free Presbyterian Church of Ulster + *-ism*]

**Pais|ley|ite** (pāz′lē īt), *n., adj.* —*n.* a follower of Ian Paisley; supporter of Paisleyism.
—*adj.* of or having to do with Paisleyites or Paisleyism.

**Pai|ute** (pī yüt′), *n., pl.* **-ute** or **-utes.** **1** a member of a small tribe of Indians of Shoshone stock living in Utah, Nevada, California, and Arizona. **2** the Uto-Aztecan language of this tribe.

**pa|ja|maed** (pə jä′mid, -jam′id), *adj.* wearing pajamas.

**pa|ja|ma party** (pə jä′mə, -jam′ə), = slumber party.

**pa|ja|mas** (pə jä′məz, -jam′əz), *n.pl.* **1** garments to sleep in, usually consisting of a jacket and loose trousers fastened at the waist: *In the . . . showrooms, models and salesmen show pajamas to a buyer* (Newsweek). **2** loose trousers worn especially in Iran and parts of India and southeast Asia. Also, *especially British,* **pyjamas.** [< Hindustani *pājāmā,* or *paijāmā* < Persian *pāē-jamah* < *pāī* leg + *jāmah* clothing]

**pa|ke|ha** (pä′kə hä), *n., pl.* **-has** or **-ha.** (in New Zealand) a white man, especially a New Zealander of European ancestry. [< Maori *pakeha*]

**Pakh|tun** (päk tün′), *n.* = Pathan.

**Pak|i** (pak′ē, päk′-), *n., pl.* **Pak|is.** *British. Slang.* a Pakistani.

**Pak|i|stan|i** (pak′ə stan′ē, pä′kə stä′nē), *n., pl.* **-stan|i** or **-stan|is,** *adj.* —*n.* a person born or living in Pakistan.
—*adj.* of or having to do with Pakistan: *Pakistani women are demonstrating against proposals to revive polygamy* (Punch).

**pak|tong** (pak′tong), *n.* a Chinese alloy having the same ingredients as German silver. [< dialectal variant of Chinese *pai t'ung* (literally) white copper]

**pal** (pal), *n., v.,* **palled, pal|ling.** *Informal.* —*n.* a close friend; playmate or comrade; chum: *I miss you— I've no pal now* (Leonard Merrick). **SYN:** buddy, partner.
—*v.i.* to associate as pals: *The two older boys pal around together on most of their school holidays.*
[< Gypsy (England) *pal* brother, mate, variant of *pral,* or *plal,* perhaps < Sanskrit *bhrātr* brother]

**Pal.,** Palestine.

**PAL** (no periods), Phase Alternation Line (a system of color television adopted by many European countries).

**P.A.L.,** Police Athletic League (an organization set up by a police department to provide sports, camping, and other activities for youth).

**pa|la|bra** (pä lä′brä), *n. Spanish.* **1** a word. **2** profuse talk; palaver.

**pal|ace** (pal′is), *n.* **1a** a grand house for a king, queen, bishop, or other exalted personage to live in: *As Her Serene Highness . . . she is expected to live in the great 200-room, yellow-stone palace overlooking the Mediterranean* (Newsweek). **SYN:** castle. **b** *British.* the official residence of an archbishop or bishop within his cathedral city: *Lambeth Palace.* **2** a very fine house or building: *The palaces of the rich dot the coastline.* **3** a more or less imposing or pretentious place of entertainment: *an old movie palace.* **4** an official building, especially one of imposing size (often by extension from use as in French and Italian): *the palace of justice.* [< Old French *palais* < Latin *Palātium* (originally) the Palatine Hill in Rome, site of the emperor's palace]

**palace car,** a luxuriously equipped passenger car on a railroad.

**palace revolution,** a revolution plotted and carried out by a group of insiders: *A cabal of Appalachian district directors will undertake a palace revolution* (Atlantic).

**pal|a|din** (pal′ə din), *n.* **1** one of the twelve knights who comprised, according to legend, the bodyguard and closest companions of Charlemagne. **2** *Figurative.* a knightly defender: *Let others sing of knights and paladins* (Samuel Daniel). *No longer a Kremlin paladin destined to carry the Red banner of Communism westward into Europe . . .* (New York Times). **SYN:** champion. [< Middle French *paladin* < Italian *paladino,* learned borrowing from Latin *Palātīnus;* see etym. under **palatine**[1]]

**pa|lae|arc|tic** or **Pa|lae|arc|tic** (pā′lē ärk′tik, pal′ē-), *adj.* = palearctic.

**palaeo-,** *combining form. Especially British.* a variant form of **paleo-.**

**pa|lae|o|an|throp|ic** (pā′lē ō an throp′ik, pal′ē-), *adj. Especially British.* paleoanthropic.

**pa|lae|o|arc|tic** or **Pa|lae|o|arc|tic** (pā′lē ō ärk′tik, pal′ē-), *adj.* = palearctic.

**pa|lae|o|bot|a|ny** (pā′lē ō bot′ə nē, pal′ē-), *n. Especially British.* paleobotany.

**pa|lae|o|cli|ma|tol|o|gy** (pā′lē ō klī′mə tol′ə jē, pal′ē-), *n. Especially British.* paleoclimatology.

**pa|lae|o|mag|net|ic** (pā′lē ō mag net′ik, pal′ē-), *adj. Especially British.* paleomagnetic.

**pa|lae|o|mag|net|ism** (pā′lē ō mag′nə tiz əm, pal′ē-), *n. Especially British.* paleomagnetism.

**Pa|lae|o|si|be|ri|an** (pā′lē ō sī bir′ē ən, pal′ē-), *n., adj.* = Paleosiberian.

**pa|laes|tra** (pə les′trə), *n., pl.* **-tras, -trae** (-trē). **1** a public place for physical exercise and training in ancient Greece. **2a** a wrestling school. **b** any gymnasium. Also, **palestra.** [< Latin *palaestra* < Greek *palaistra* < *palaiein* to wrestle]

**pal|a|fitte** (pal′ə fit), *n.* a prehistoric lake dwelling, supported on piles, especially one in Switzerland or northern Italy. [< French *palafitte* < Italian *palafitta* pile fence]

**pa|lais de danse** (pá lā′də däɴs′), *French.* dance hall.

**Pal|a|me|des** (pal′ə mē′dēz), *n. Greek Legend.* a hero of the Trojan war whom Odysseus hated for having forced him through cunning to go to war. After the Greeks reached Troy, Odysseus caused them to put Palamedes to death.

***pal|an|quin** or **pal|an|keen** (pal′ən kēn′), *n., v.* —*n.* a covered couch carried by poles resting on men's shoulders, formerly used in the Orient. It was enclosed by shutters or heavy curtains. . . . *a procession of highly decorated lacquer palanquins bearing the ladies* (Atlantic). **SYN:** litter.
—*v.i.* to travel in a palanquin: *the land of slaves and palankeening* (Thomas Hood).
[< Portuguese *palanquim,* or Italian *palanchino;* of Indian origin. Compare Malay *palangki,* Sanskrit *palyanka, paryanka* couch.]

***palanquin**

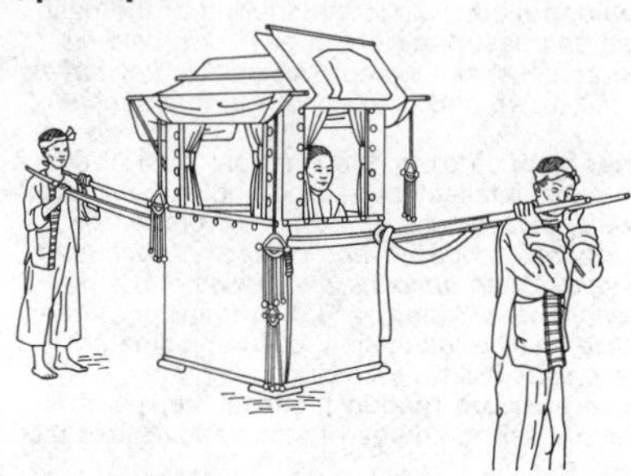

**pa|las** (pa läs′), *n.* = dhak. [< Hindi *palās*]

**pal|at|a|bil|i|ty** (pal′ə tə bil′ə tē), *n.* palatable quality or condition: *The palatability of eggs is associated with their size rather than with their coloring* (Scientific American).

**pal|at|a|ble** (pal′ə tə bəl), *adj.* **1** agreeable to the taste; pleasing: *That was a most palatable lunch.* **SYN:** savory. **2** *Figurative.* agreeable to the mind or feelings; acceptable: *His eloquence was distinguished by a bold, uncompromising, truth-telling spirit, whether the words might prove palatable or bitter to his audience* (John L. Motley). —**pal′at|a|ble|ness,** *n.* —**pal′at|a|bly,** *adv.*

**pal|a|tal** (pal′ə təl), *adj., n.* —*adj.* **1** of or having to do with the palate. **2** *Phonetics.* (of speech sounds) made with the front or middle of the tongue near or touching the hard palate. The *y* in *yet* is a palatal sound. *The palatal nasal, or "n" mouillé, occurs frequently in French* (Simeon Potter). —*n. Phonetics.* a palatal sound. [< French *palatal* < Latin *palātum* palate] —**pal′a|tal|ly,** *adv.*

**pal|a|tal|i|za|tion** (pal′ə tə lə zā′shən), *n.* **1** the act of palatalizing: *The introduction of a "y" sound before a vowel is called palatalization, because in pronouncing "y" the tongue is humped up toward the palate* (Scientific American). **2** the state of being palatalized.

**pal|a|tal|ize** (pal′ə tə līz), *v.t.,* **-ized, -iz|ing.** *Phonetics.* to make palatal; change into a palatal sound.

**pal|ate** (pal′it), *n.* **1a** the roof of the mouth. The bony part in front is the hard palate, formed by parts of the maxillary and palatine bones, and the fleshy part in back is the soft palate, formed by several muscles. **b** = hard palate. **2** the sense of taste (from the belief, once generally held, that the palate is the organ of taste): *The new flavor pleased his palate.* **3** *Figurative.* a liking: *The lazy girl had no palate for washing dishes. Any subject that was not to their palate they condemned* (Milton). **SYN:** relish. [< Latin *palātum*]

**pa|la|tial** (pə lā′shəl), *adj.* like a palace; fit for a palace; magnificent: *a palatial apartment.* **SYN:** splendid. [< Latin *palātium* palace + English *-al*[1]] —**pa|la′tial|ly,** *adv.* —**pa|la′tial|ness,** *n.*

**pa|lat|i|nate** (pə lat′ə nāt, -nit), *n.* the region under the rule of a count palatine.

**Pa|lat|i|nate** (pə lat′ə nāt, -nit), *n., adj.* = Palatine.

**pal|a|tine**[1] (pal′ə tīn, -tin), *adj., n.* —*adj.* **1** having royal rights in one's own territory. A count palatine was subject only to the emperor or king, especially the Holy Roman Emperor. **2** of a lord who has royal rights in his own territory. **3** = palatial.
—*n.* **1** a lord having royal rights in his own territory; palatine lord. **2** an officer of an imperial palace, originally the chamberlain of a palace. **3** a

fur scarf, cape, or the like, formerly worn by women over the shoulders.
[< Latin *Palātīnus* of the *Palātium* or Palatine Hill (palace); a palace official, a chamberlain (in Late Latin, an imperial representative)]

**pal|a|tine**[2] (pal′ə tīn, -tin), *adj., n.* —**adj.** **1** of, having to do with, or in the region of the palate: *In human beings, a palatine tonsil can be seen on each side of the back of the mouth just above the throat and below the roof of the mouth* (William V. Mayer). **2** designating or having to do with either of the two bones (palatine bones) forming the hard palate.
—**n.** a palatine bone.
[< French *palatine* < Latin *palātum* palate + French *-ine* -ine[1]]

**Pal|a|tine** (pal′ə tīn, -tin), *adj., n.* —**adj.** of or having to do with the Palatinate, a region in West Germany west of the Rhine.
—**n.** a native or inhabitant of the Palatinate.

**Palatine Guards** or **Guard**, the militia of the Pope, on duty at Vatican City. [< *palatine*[1]]

**Pal|a|ti|no** (pal′ə tē′nō), *n.* a style of modern printing type. [< Italian *palatino* palatine]

**Pa|lau|an** (pä lou′ən), *adj., n.* —**adj.** of or having to do with the Palau Islands in the western Pacific, its people, or their language.
—**n. 1** a native or inhabitant of the Palau Islands. **2** the Austronesian language of the Palauans.

**pa|lav|er** (pə lav′ər, -läv′ər), *n., v.* —**n. 1** a parley or conference, especially between European traders or travelers and people of other cultures, whose customs required the formal exchange of compliments, gifts, and other ritual, before the bringing up of any matter of business. **SYN**: colloquy. **2** unnecessary or idle words; mere talk: *After years of futile palaver, Latin America's coffee-producing nations are finally getting together in a hard-boiled cartel to hold up the price of coffee* (Time). **3** smooth, persuading talk; fluent talk; flattery: *smooth-tongued palaver.* **SYN**: cajolery.
—**v.i. 1** to talk, especially to talk profusely or unnecessarily: *Don't stand there palavering all day* (Mark Twain). **2** to talk fluently or flatteringly, especially so as to persuade or cajole. **3** to engage in a palaver; parley.
—**v.t.** to treat to palaver; flatter, wheedle, or cajole: *Dodd never spoke to his officers like a ruffian, nor yet palavered them* (Charles Reade).
[< Portuguese *palavra* < Latin *parabola* comparison, story, parable. See etym. of doublets **parable**, **parabola**, **parabole**, **parole**.] —**pa|lav′er|er**, *n.*

**pa|lay** (pä′lī), *n.* (in the Philippines) rice in the husk. [< Tagalog *palay.* See related etym. at **paddy**[1].]

**pa|laz|zo** (pä lät′sō), *n., pl.* **-zi** (-sē). *Italian.* **1** a palace: *She lives in ... Palazzo Altieri, in old Rome—a fairy-story palazzo with many courtyards, entrances and exits, porches, and monumental stairways* (Harper's). **2** a large, substantial mansion in a city, especially in Italy: *What he was called upon to do was almost exclusively the designing of town and country houses, "palazzi" and "ville"* (Nikolaus Pevsner).

**palazzo pajamas**, a woman's garment for lounging or semiformal wear, consisting of loose, wide-legged trousers and a matching jacket or blouse.

**pale**[1] (pāl), *adj.,* **pal|er, pal|est,** *v.,* **paled, pal|ing.** —**adj. 1** without much color; lacking natural color; whitish: *When you have been ill, your face is sometimes pale. Dry sherry is usually pale.* **2** not bright; dim: *a pale blue, a pale glow from the windows. The bright stars are surrounded by hundreds of pale ones.* **SYN**: faint, indistinct. **3** *Figurative.* lacking vigor; feeble; faint: *a pale policy.*
—**v.i.** to turn pale; lose color or brilliancy: *Her face paled at the bad news.*
—**v.t.** to cause to become pale; dim: *The glow-worm ... 'gins to pale his uneffectual fire* (Shakespeare).
[< Old French *pale* < Latin *pallidus* < *pallēre* be pale. See etym. of doublet **pallid**.] —**pale′ly**, *adv.* —**pale′ness**, *n.*
—*Syn. adj.* **1 Pale, pallid, wan** mean with little or no color. **Pale**, describing the face of a person, means without much natural or healthy color, and describing things, without much brilliance or depth: *She is pale and tired-looking. The walls are pale green.* **Pallid**, chiefly describing the face, suggests having all color drained away, as by sickness or weakness: *Her pallid face shows her suffering.* **Wan** emphasizes the faintness and whiteness coming from a weakened or unhealthy condition: *The starved refugees were wan.*

**pale**[2] (pāl), *n., v.,* **paled, pal|ing.** —**n. 1** a long, narrow board, pointed at the top, used for fences; picket: *stakes ... stuck in one by another like pales* (Daniel Defoe). **2** *Figurative.* boundary; restriction: *Murderers are outside the pale of civilized society. The exercise of foreign jurisdiction, within the pale of their own laws* (Thomas Jefferson). **SYN**: limit. **3** an enclosed place; enclosure: *I brought all my goods into this pale* (Daniel Defoe). **4** a district or territory within fixed bounds or subject to a particular jurisdiction. **5** *Archaic.* a fence; barrier: *It is as if a pale had been built round the British Isles* (London Times). **6** *Heraldry.* a broad vertical stripe in the middle of a shield, usually occupying one third of its breadth.
—**v.t.** to enclose with pales or a fence; fence (in).
**beyond** (or **outside**) **the pale**, overstepping the bounds; socially unacceptable; improper: *His rude behavior at the party was beyond the pale.*
**per pale**, *Heraldry.* (of the shield) divided by a vertical line through the middle: *an ordinary per pale invecked.*
[< Old French *pal,* learned borrowing from Latin *pālus* stake. See etym. of doublets **peel**[3], **pole**[1].]

**pale-**, *combining form.* the form of **paleo-** usually used before vowels, as in *paleethnology.*

**pa|le|a** (pā′lē ə), *n., pl.* **-le|ae** (-lē ē). *Botany.* **1** one of the inner, scalelike, usually membranous bracts enclosing the stamens and pistil in the flower of grasses. **2** one of the bracts at the base of the individual florets in many composite plants. **3** the scales on the stems of certain ferns. [< Latin *palea* chaff]

**pa|le|a|ceous** (pā′lē ā′shəs), *adj. Botany.* **1** furnished or covered with paleae. **2** of the nature or consistency of chaff; chaffy.

**pa|le|arc|tic** or **Pa|le|arc|tic** (pā′lē ärk′tik, pal′ē-), *adj.* belonging to the northern division of the Old World (Europe, Africa north of the tropic of Cancer, and Asia north of the Himalayas). [< *pale-* + *arctic*]

**pa|le|eth|nol|o|gy** (pā′lē eth nol′ə jē, pal′ē-), *n.* the branch of ethnology that treats of the earliest or most primitive races of men. [< *pale-* + *ethnology*]

**pale|face** (pāl′fās′), *n.* a white person. The North American Indians are said to have called white people palefaces. *Where a Paleface comes, a Red man cannot stay* (James Fenimore Cooper).

**pa|le|ich|thy|ol|o|gy** (pā′lē ik′thē ol′ə jē, pal′ē-), *n.* = paleoichthyology.

**paleo-**, *combining form.* **1** old; ancient; prehistoric: *Paleography = ancient writing.* **2** early or earliest: *Paleocene = the earliest epoch of the Tertiary period.* Also, **pale-** before certain vowels. Also, **palaeo-**.
[< Greek *palaio-* < *palaiós* ancient]

**pa|le|o|an|throp|ic** (pā′lē ō an throp′ik, pal′ē-), *adj.* of or belonging to the geological period intermediate between protoanthropic and neanthropic.

**pa|le|o|an|thro|pol|o|gist** (pā′lē ō an′thrə pol′ə-jist, pal′ē-), *n.* an expert in paleoanthropology: *By utilizing the logic of structure and the logic of evolutionary development, it has been possible for paleoanthropologists to achieve what seems to the uninitiated almost miracles in reconstructing the characteristics of the earlier, extinct forms of mankind* (Melville J. Herskovits).

**pa|le|o|an|thro|pol|o|gy** (pā′lē ō an′thrə pol′ə jē, pal′ē-), *n.* the study of the early types of human beings, as represented by their fossils and remains of their cultures.

**pa|le|o|arc|tic** or **Pa|le|o|arc|tic** (pā′lē ō ärk′tik, pal′ē-), *adj.* = palearctic.

**pa|le|o|bi|o|chem|is|try** (pā′lē ō bī′ō kem′ə strē, pal′ē-), *n.* a branch of paleontology that deals with the biochemical constituents of fossil animals and plants: *In one of the first applications of paleobiochemistry it has been found that hydrocarbon compounds in rocks 3 billion years old may be composed of fossilized chlorophyll* (Franklin J. Tobey, Jr.).

**pa|le|o|bo|tan|ic** (pā′lē ō bə tan′ik, pal′ē-), *adj.* = paleobotanical.

**pa|le|o|bo|tan|i|cal** (pā′lē ō bə tan′ə kəl, pal′ē-), *adj.* of or having to do with paleobotany.

**pa|le|o|bot|a|nist** (pā′lē ō bot′ə nist, pal′ē-), *n.* a person skilled in paleobotany: *Fossil plants have suffered much alteration and the paleobotanist ... is from the first concerned with the details of preservation and the use of unpromising material* (Tom. M. Harris).

**pa|le|o|bot|a|ny** (pā′lē ō bot′ə nē, pal′ē-), *n.* the branch of paleontology dealing with fossil plants: *This science [paleontology] in turn is divided into paleozoology, for animals, and paleobotany, for plants* (William C. Beaver). [< *paleo-* + *botany*]

**Pa|le|o|cene** (pā′lē ə sēn, pal′ē-), *n., adj.* —**n. 1** a geological epoch, the earliest of the Tertiary period of the Cenozoic era, before the Eocene, during which shallow inland seas drained and the first primates appeared: *Both in Europe and in North America, the Tertiary System is recognized as containing main divisions that in upward order are named "Paleocene," "Eocene," "Oligocene," "Miocene," and "Pilocene"* (Raymond Cecil Moore). **2** the rocks formed during this epoch.
—**adj.** of this epoch or its rocks.
[< *paleo-* + Greek *kainós* new]

**pa|le|o|chro|nol|o|gy** (pā′lē ō krə nol′ə jē, pal′ē-), *n.* the dating of fossil animals and plants, as by counting the ridges on fossil shells and corals.

**pa|le|o|cli|mate** (pā′lē ō klī′mit, pal′ē-), *n.* a prehistoric climate: *A new independent method has been developed to study paleoclimates based on deep ice cores from the ice sheets in Antarctica and Greenland* (W. Dansgaard).

**pa|le|o|cli|ma|tol|o|gy** (pā′lē ō klī′mə tol′ə jē, pal′ē-), *n.* the study of the climate of prehistoric times.

**pa|le|o|cor|tex** (pā′lē ō kôr′teks, pal′ē-), *n.* the older portion of the cortex of the human brain, having to do with the sense of smell.

**pa|le|o|crys|tic** (pā′lē ō kris′tik, pal′ē-), *adj.* consisting of or containing ice supposed to have remained frozen since early ages. [< *paleo-* + Greek *krýstallos* ice + English *-ic*]

**pa|le|o|ec|o|log|i|cal** (pā′lē ō ek′ə loj′ə kəl, -ē′kə-; pal′ē-), *adj.* of or having to do with paleoecology.

**pa|le|o|e|col|o|gist** (pā′lē ō ē kol′ə jist, pal′ē-), *n.* an expert in paleoecology.

**pa|le|o|e|col|o|gy** (pā′lē ō ē kol′ə jē, pal′ē-), *n.* the study of the relationship of living things to environment and each other in prehistoric times; the ecology of prehistoric life.

**pa|le|o|fau|na** (pā′lē ō fô′nə, pal′ē-), *n., pl.* **-nas, -nae** (-nē). the fossil fauna of a geological formation or period. [< *paleo-* + *fauna*]

**pa|le|o|flo|ra** (pā′lē ō flôr′ə, -flōr′-; pal′ē-), *n., pl.* **-flo|ras, -flo|rae** (-flôr′ē, -flōr′-). the fossil flora of a geological formation or period. [< *paleo-* + *flora*]

**paleog.**, paleography.

**Pa|le|o|gene** (pā′lē ə jēn, pal′ē-), *n., adj.* —**n.** the lower division of the Tertiary period; Eogene.
—**adj.** or of having to do with this division or its rocks. [< *paleo-* + Greek *-genês* -gen]

**pa|le|o|ge|net|ics** (pā′lē ō jə net′iks, pal′ē-), *n.* the study of the genetics of fossil animals and plants.

**pa|le|o|ge|o|graph|ic** (pā′lē ō jē ə graf′ik, pal′ē-), *adj.* = paleogeographical.

**pa|le|o|ge|o|graph|i|cal** (pā′lē ō jē ə graf′ə kəl, pal′ē-), *adj.* of or having to do with paleogeography. —**pa′le|o|ge|o|graph′i|cal|ly**, *adv.*

**pa|le|o|ge|og|raph|y** (pā′lē ō jē og′rə fē, pal′ē-), *n.* the geography of former geological time. [< *paleo-* + *geography*]

**pa|le|o|ge|o|phys|i|cal** (pā′lē ō jē′ō fiz′ə kəl, pal′ē-), *adj.* of or having to do with paleogeophysics.

**pa|le|o|ge|o|phys|ics** (pā′lē ō jē′ō fiz′iks, pal′ē-), *n.* the study of the physical phenomena within or upon the earth in geological times. [< *paleo-* + *geophysics*]

**pa|le|og|ra|pher** (pā′lē og′rə fər, pal′ē-), *n.* an expert in paleography: *Archaeologists, paleographers, Old and New Testament scholars and language experts had combined forces on deciphering the leather scrolls* (Science News Letter).

**pa|le|o|graph|ic** (pā′lē ə graf′ik, pal′ē-), *adj.* of or having to do with paleography. —**pa′le|o|graph′i|cal|ly**, *adv.*

**pa|le|o|graph|i|cal** (pā′lē ə graf′ə kəl, pal′ē-), *adj.* = paleographic.

**pa|le|og|ra|phy** (pā′lē og′rə fē, pal′ē-), *n.* **1** ancient writing or ancient forms of writing. **2** the study of ancient writings to determine the dates, origins, meanings, etc. [< *paleo-* + *-graphy*]

**pa|le|o|ich|thy|ol|o|gist** (pā′lē ō ik′thē ol′ə jist, pal′ē-), *n.* an expert in paleoichthyology.

**pa|le|o|ich|thy|ol|o|gy** (pā′lē ō ik′thē ol′ə jē, pal′ē-), *n.* the branch of ichthyology that deals with fossil fishes. Also, **paleichthyology.**

**Pa|le|o-In|di|an** (pā′lē ō in′dē ən, pal′ē-), *n., adj.* —**n.** one of a prehistoric group of people believed to have migrated from Asia to the Americas during the late Ice Age: *Paleo-Indians ... were big game hunters and preyed on bison and mammoths* (Science News Letter).
—**adj.** of or having to do with Paleo-Indians: *Paleo-Indian artifacts, Paleo-Indian culture.*

**pa|le|o|lim|nol|o|gist** (pā′lē ō lim nol′ə jist, pal′ē-), *n.* an expert in paleolimnology: *Paleolimnologists aspire to interpret past conditions and processes in lakes by comparison with the present and thereby also to gain a better understanding of the present by knowing its genesis* (Science).

**pa|le|o|lim|nol|o|gy** (pā′lē ō lim nol′ə jē, pal′ē-), *n.* the study of the condition of lakes, ponds, and other enclosed bodies of water, in geological times.

---

**Pronunciation Key:** hat, āge, cãre, fär; let, ēqual, tėrm; it, īce; hot, ōpen, ôrder; **oi**l, **ou**t; cup, pu̇t, rüle; **ch**ild; lo**ng**; **th**in; **ᴛʜ**en; **zh**, measure; **ə** represents **a** in about, **e** in taken, **i** in pencil, **o** in lemon, **u** in circus.

**pa|le|o|lith** (pā′lē ə lith, pal′ē-), *n.* an artifact of paleolithic man; paleolithic tool. [< *paleo-* + Greek *líthos* stone]

**pa|le|o|lith|ic** or **Pa|le|o|lith|ic** (pā′lē ə lith′ik, pal′ē-), *adj., n.* —*adj.* of or having to do with the earliest part of the Stone Age. Paleolithic tools were crudely chipped out of stone. *In the Paleolithic period, no animals seem to have been domesticated, and fire was probably unknown* (Emory S. Bogardus).
—*n.* this period.

**paleolithic man,** *Anthropology.* any of the men of the early Stone Age, including, in addition to Homo sapiens, various species now extinct.

**pa|le|ol|o|gist** (pā′lē ol′ə jist, pal′ē-), *n.* a person skilled in paleology; a student or a writer on antiquity.

**pa|le|ol|o|gy** (pā′lē ol′ə jē, pal′ē-), *n.* the science of antiquities; archaeology. [< *paleo-* + *-logy*]

**pa|le|o|mag|net|ic** (pā′lē ō mag net′ik, pal′ē-), *adj.* of or having to do with paleomagnetism.

**pa|le|o|mag|net|ism** (pā′lē ō mag′nə tiz əm, pal′ē-), *n.* the study of the direction of the residual magnetism in ancient rocks to determine the movement of the magnetic poles or of the rocks: *Recent studies of paleomagnetism* (*the determination of the location of the earth's magnetic poles in past eras*) *have brought renewed interest in the theory of continental drift* (George R. Tilton).

**pa|le|o|mag|net|ist** (pā′lē ō mag′nə tist, pal′ē-), *n.* an expert in paleomagnetism.

**pa|le|on|to|graph|ic** (pā′lē on′tə graf′ik, pal′ē-), *adj.* = paleontographical.

**pa|le|on|to|graph|i|cal** (pā′lē on′tə graf′ə kəl, pal′ē-), *adj.* of or having to do with paleontography.

**pa|le|on|tog|ra|phy** (pā′lē on tog′rə fē, pal′ē-), *n.* the description of fossil remains. [< *paleo-* + Greek *ṓn, óntos* a being + English *-graphy*]

**paleontol.,** paleontology.

**pa|le|on|to|log|ic** (pā′lē on′tə loj′ik, pal′ē-), *adj.* = paleontological.

**pa|le|on|to|log|i|cal** (pā′lē on′tə loj′ə kəl, pal′ē-), *adj.* of or having to do with paleontology. —**pa′le|on′to|log′i|cal|ly,** *adv.*

**pa|le|on|tol|o|gist** (pā′lē on tol′ə jist, pal′ē-), *n.* an expert in paleontology: *The paleontologist is interested in a fossil for hints as to the nature of the organism which caused it* (Science News Letter).

**pa|le|on|tol|o|gy** (pā′lē on tol′ə jē, pal′ē-), *n.* the science of the forms of life existing in prehistoric times, as represented by fossil animals and plants: *Paleontology, the study of indications of prehistoric life, contributes much critical information to the biological sciences even as they, in turn, contribute to paleontology* (Harbaugh and Goodrich).
[< *paleo-* + Greek *ṓn, óntos* a being + English *-logy*]

**pa|le|o|pa|thol|o|gy** (pā′lē ō pə thol′ə jē, pal′ē-), *n.* the study of the diseases of historic and prehistoric times.

**pa|le|o|pe|dol|o|gy** (pā′lē ō pi dol′ə jē, pal′ē-), *n.* the branch of geology dealing with the soils of former geological time. [< *paleo-* + Greek *pédon* earth + English *-logy*]

**pa|le|o|phy|tol|o|gy** (pā′lē ō fī tol′ə jē, pal′ē-), *n.* = paleobotany.

**pa|le|or|ni|thol|o|gy** (pā′lē ôr′nə thol′ə jē, pal′ē-), *n.* the branch of ornithology that deals with fossil birds. [< *pale-* + *ornithology*]

**Pa|le|o|si|be|ri|an** (pā′lē ō sī bir′ē ən), *n., adj.* —*n.* **1** any one of a number of aboriginal peoples of northeastern Siberia speaking languages that do not belong to any of the large language families. **2** the group of languages spoken by these peoples.
—*adj.* of or having to do with the Paleosiberians or their languages. Also, **Palaeosiberian.** [< *paleo-* + *Siberian*]

**pa|le|o|tech|nic** (pā′lē ō tek′nik, pal′ē-), *adj.* having to do with the earlier historical phase of the development of modern industrial machinery, characterized by the use of coal, iron, and the steam engine. The term has become familiar to students of technological history through the writings of Patrick Geddes and Lewis Mumford.

**pa|le|o|tem|per|a|ture** (pā′lē ō tem′pər ə chər, -chůr; -prə-; pal′ē-), *n.* the temperature of oceans and seas in geological times, obtained by measuring or analyzing the chemical components of fossil sediments: *the paleotemperatures of the Mesozoic Era.*

**Pa|le|o|trop|i|cal** (pā′lē ō trop′ə kəl, pal′ē-), *adj.* belonging to the tropical (and subtropical) regions of the Old World or Eastern Hemisphere. [< *paleo-* + *tropical*]

**Pa|le|o|zo|ic** (pā′lē ə zō′ik, pal′ē-), *n., adj.* —*n.* **1** an early geological era whose fossils represent early forms of life. It was characterized by the development of the first fishes, land plants, amphibians, reptiles, insects, and forests of fernlike trees and came after the Proterozoic and before the Mesozoic. *Beginning about 505 million years ago, the Paleozoic is divided into six periods: Cambrian, Ordovician, Silurian, Devonian, Carboniferous, and Permian* (Beals and Hoijer). **2** the rocks formed in this era.
—*adj.* of this era or its rocks: *The Paleozoic rocks are the oldest that contain abundant evidence of life* (Raymond Cecil Moore).
[< *paleo-* + Greek *zōḗ* life + English *-ic*]

**pa|le|o|zo|o|log|i|cal** (pā′lē ō zō′ə loj′ə kəl, pal′ē-), *adj.* of or having to do with paleozoology.

**pa|le|o|zo|ol|o|gist** (pā′lē ō zō ol′ə jist, pal′ē-), *n.* a person skilled in paleozoology.

**pa|le|o|zo|ol|o|gy** (pā′lē ō zō ol′ə jē, pal′ē-), *n.* the branch of paleontology dealing with fossil animals: *This science* [*paleontology*] *in turn is divided into paleozoology, for animals, and paleobotany, for plants* (William C. Beaver). [< *paleo-* + *zoology*]

**Pa|ler|mi|tan** (pə lėr′mə tən, -lär′-), *adj., n.* —*adj.* of or having to do with Palermo, the capital of Sicily.
—*n.* a native or inhabitant of Palermo.
[< Italian *palermitano*]

**Pal|es|tin|i|an** (pal′ə stin′ē ən), *adj., n.* —*adj.* of or having to do with Palestine, or the Holy Land, a region in southwestern Asia: *On the Arab side of the fence the basic difficulty lies in the Palestinian refugees and their state of mind* (Atlantic).
—*n.* a native or inhabitant of Palestine: *The problem of the 213,000 former Palestinians in the Gaza strip was unsolved* (New York Times).

**pa|les|tra** (pə les′trə), *n., pl.* **-tras, -trae** (-trē). = palaestra.

**pa|let** (pā′lit, pal′it), *n. Botany.* a palea. [< *pal*(ea) + *-et*]

**pal|e|tot** (pal′ə tō, pal′tō), *n.* a loose outer garment, such as a coat or cloak, for men or women. [< French *paletot* < Middle French *palletot,* earlier *palletocq,* apparently < Middle English *paltock* a sleeved jacket; origin uncertain]

**pal|ette** (pal′it), *n.* **1** a thin board, usually oval or oblong with a thumb hole at one end, used by an artist to lay and mix his colors on. **2** a set of colors on this board. **3** the selection of colors used by a particular artist: *to use a wide palette.*
**4** Also, **pallette.** a small rounded plate protecting the armpit on a suit of armor. [< French *palette* < Old French (diminutive) < *pale* shovel, oar blade < Latin *pāla* spade, shoulder blade]

**palette knife,** a thin flexible blade of steel rounded at one end and set in a handle, used for mixing colors on a palette and to scrape the paint off the canvas before putting on another layer.

**pale|wise** (pāl′wīz′), *adv. Heraldry.* in the manner or direction of a pale; vertically.

**pal|frey** (pôl′frē), *n., pl.* **-freys.** *Archaic.* a gentle riding horse, especially one used by ladies: *He ... shook his drowsy squire awake, and cried, "My charger and her palfrey"* (Tennyson). [< Old French *palefreyd* < Late Latin *palafrēdus,* variant of *paraverēdus* a horse for outlying districts < Greek *para-* beside, secondary + Latin *verēdus* light horse < a Celtic word]

**Pa|li** (pä′lē), *n.* the Middle Indic language, a later form of Sanskrit, used in the sacred writings of the Buddhists and still existing as a literary language in Ceylon (Sri Lanka), Burma, and Thailand. [< Pali *pāli-bhāsā* language of the canonical texts < Sanskrit *pāli* line, canon + *bhāsā* language]

**pa|li|kar** (pal′i kär), *n.* a Greek or Albanian militiaman in the war of independence, 1821-1828, against Turkey. Also, **pellekar.** [< New Greek *palikári,* or *pallēkári* < Late Greek *pallikárion* a page (diminutive) < Greek *pállēx, pállēkos* a youth]

**pal|imp|sest** (pal′imp sest), *n.* **1** parchment or other writing material from which one or more previous writings have been erased to make room for another. **2** a manuscript with one text written over another. **3** an oil painting that has lost its original intent by overpainting by another artist. [< Latin *palimpsestus* < Greek *palímpsēstos* (literally) scraped again < *pálin* again + *psēs-,* stem of *psên* to rub smooth]

**pal|in|drome** (pal′in drōm), *n.* a word, verse, sentence, or numeral which reads the same backward or forward. The sentence "Madam, I'm Adam" is a palindrome that contains (in its first word) another palindrome. The numerals 1111 and 7557 are palindromes. *In Classical Latin 'the wolf' was simply* lupus, *in Vulgar Latin* ille lupus *or* lupus ille, *and today the former has become* le loup *in French,* el lobo *in Spanish and* il lupo *in Italian, whereas the latter has produced the palindrome* lupul *in Rumanian* (Simeon Potter).
[< Greek *palíndromos* a recurrence; (literally) a running back < *pálin* again, back + *drómos* a running, related to *drameîn* run]

**pal|in|drom|ic** (pal′in drom′ik), *adj.* having to do with or of the nature of a palindrome.

**pal|in|drom|ist** (pal′in drom′ist), *n.* a person who makes up palindromes.

**pal|ing** (pā′ling), *n.* **1** a fence of pales: *I had seen ... a gap in the paling—one stake broken down* (Charlotte Brontë). **2** pales collectively, as fencing material: *The fence was only of split paling, but I got my trousers caught on the points* (Geoffrey Household). **3** a pale in a fence: *The palings round the little gardens were broken and ruinous* (Mrs. Humphry Ward). **SYN:** picket. **4** the act of making a fence, or of enclosing a place, with pales; fencing.

**pal|in|gen|e|sis** (pal′in jen′ə sis), *n.* **1** rebirth, regeneration, or reincarnation. **2** the reproduction of ancestral features without change. [< Greek *pálin* again + *génesis* birth, genesis]
► See **cenogenesis** for usage note.

**pal|in|ge|net|ic** (pal′in jə net′ik), *adj.* of, having to do with, or based on palingenesis: *palingenetic processes of evolution.* —**pal′in|ge|net′i|cal|ly,** *adv.*

**pal|i|node** (pal′ə nōd), *n.* **1** a poem or song, especially an ode, in which the author retracts something said in a former poem. **2** (in Scottish Law) a formal retracting; recantation. [< Latin *palinōdia* < Greek *palinōidiā* recantation, retraction < *pálin* again + *ōidḗ* song, ode]

**pal|i|sade** (pal′ə sād′), *n., v.,* **-sad|ed, -sad|ing.** —*n.* **1** a long, strong wooden stake pointed at the top end. **SYN:** pale. **2** a fence of stakes set firmly in the ground to enclose or defend. **3** = palisade layer.
—*v.t.* to furnish or surround with a palisade: *The Mississippians were also an agricultural people who lived in a palisaded town containing specialized buildings* (Science News Letter). *Our carpenters ... palisaded our camp quite round with long stakes* (Daniel Defoe).
**palisades,** a line of high, steep cliffs: *the Palisades of the Hudson River.* See picture under **plain**[1].
[< Middle French *palissade* < Provençal *palissada* < Latin *pālus* stake]

**palisade cell,** any one of the long, slender cells with many chloroplasts that lie just beneath the epidermis of leaves. Palisade cells are useful in making food for the plant.

**palisade layer,** a layer of palisade cells; palisade.

**palisade mesophyll** or **parenchyma,** the tissue formed by a layer of palisade cells.

**pal|i|sa|do** (pal′ə sā′dō), *n., pl.* **-does.** palisade. [< Spanish *palizada;* influenced by words ending in *-ado*]

**pal|i|san|der** (pal′ə san′dər), *n., adj.* —*n.* = rosewood.
—*adj.* made of rosewood: *a Louis XV inlaid palisander table.*
[< French *palissandre,* earlier *palixandre* < a native Guiana name]

**pal|ish** (pā′lish), *adj.* somewhat pale; rather pale.

**pall**[1] (pôl), *n., v.* —*n.* **1** a heavy cloth of black, purple, or white velvet spread over a coffin, a hearse, or a tomb. **2** *Figurative.* **a** a dark, gloomy covering: *A thick pall of smoke shut out the sun from the city.* **b** anything thought of as resembling this in effect: *His anger cast a pall over our merriment.* **3** *Ecclesiastical.* **a** a linen cloth, or now usually a square piece of cardboard covered with linen, used to cover the chalice. **b** *Archaic.* an altar cloth, especially a corporal. **c** = pallium (def. 2a). **4** *Heraldry.* a bearing representing the front half of an ecclesiastical robe, consisting of three bands in the form of a Y, charged with crosses. **5** *Archaic.* a robe, cloak, or mantle, especially of rich stuff: *My velvet pall and silken gear* (Child's Ballads). **6** *Archaic.* a rich cloth spread upon or over something.
—*v.t.* to cover with or as if with a pall: *The Holy Grail, All pall'd in crimson samite* (Tennyson).
[Old English *pæll* rich cloth; a cloak; an altar cloth < Latin *pallium* cloak; covering < *palla* robe, cloak; shroud]

**pall**[2] (pôl), *v.i.* **1** to become distasteful or very tiresome because there has been too much of it: *Even the most tasty food palls if it is served every day.* **2** to become satiated or cloyed (with): *If thy stomach palls with it, discontinue it from time to time* (Laurence Sterne). —*v.t.* **1** to render distasteful or very tiresome; make stale. **2** to cloy (as the appetite or senses); satiate.
[fusion of short form of *appall,* and Middle English *pallen* become vapid, lose spirit, ultimately < Latin *pallēscere*]

**pal|la** (pal′ə), *n., pl.* **pal|lae** (pal′ē). **1** a full outer robe or wrap worn out of doors by women in ancient Rome. **2** *Ecclesiastical.* **a** an altar cloth; corporal. **b** a pall for the chalice. [< Latin *palla*]

***Pal|la|di|an**[1] (pə lā′dē ən), *adj.* of, belonging to, or according to the school of Andrea Palladio (1508-1580), an Italian architect, or his adaptation of ancient Roman architecture: *I supposed* *that all authors who did not live in garrets must live in splendid Palladian mansions* (Punch).

***Palladian¹**

**Pal|la|di|an²** (pə lā′dē ən), *adj.* **1** of or having to do with Athena (Pallas Athena), the goddess of wisdom. **2** having to do with wisdom, knowledge, or study. [< Latin *palladius* of Pallas (Athena) + *-an*]

**Pal|la|di|an|ism** (pə lā′dē ə niz′əm), *n.* the system, style, taste, or method of Andrea Palladio and his followers.

**pal|lad|ic** (pə lad′ik, -lā′dik), *adj. Chemistry.* **1** of palladium. **2** containing palladium, especially with a valence of four.

**pal|la|di|ous** (pə lā′dē əs), *adj. Chemistry.* palladous.

***pal|la|di|um¹** (pə lā′dē əm), *n.* a light, silver-white chemical element which occurs with platinum. Palladium is a ductile and malleable metal, harder than platinum but lighter and more readily fused. It is used in making scientific instruments, in alloys with precious metals such as gold and silver, and as a catalyst. *Powdered palladium can absorb 800 times its own volume of hydrogen gas* (Monroe M. Offner). [< New Latin *palladium* < the asteroid *Pallas* < *Pallas* (Athena)]

***palladium¹**

| symbol | atomic number | atomic weight | oxidation state |
|---|---|---|---|
| Pd | 46 | 106.4 | 2, 4 |

**pal|la|di|um²** (pə lā′dē əm), *n., pl.* **-di|a** (-dē ə). anything regarded as an important safeguard: *Trial by jury ... is looked upon by all as the Palladium of our liberties* (Benjamin Disraeli). SYN: shield. [< Latin *Palladium* < Greek *Pallādion* sacred image of *Pallas* (Athena) upon which depended the safety of Troy]

**palladium black**, a finely divided precipitate obtained from a solution of palladium salts, used as a catalyst in hydrogenation. [< *palladium¹*]

**pal|la|dous** (pə lā′dəs, pal′ə-), *adj. Chemistry.* **1** of palladium. **2** containing palladium, especially with a valence of two.

**Pal|las** (pal′əs), *n.* **1** *Greek Mythology.* **a** a name of Athena. **b** a winged giant whom Athena killed, sometimes said to be her father. **2** *Astronomy.* one of the asteroids.

**Pallas Athena**, = Athena.

**pall|bear|er** (pôl′bãr′ər), *n.* one of the men who walks with or carries the coffin at a funeral, so called from the old custom of holding up the corners or edges of the pall carried over the coffin.

**pal|let¹** (pal′it), *n.* a bed of straw, or any other small or poor bed: *a humble pallet. A pallet of mats* (Washington Irving). [< Old French *paillet* < *paille* straw < Latin *palea* straw, chaff]

**pal|let²** (pal′it), *n.* **1** a flat blade used by potters and others for shaping their work. **2** an artist's palette. **3a** a projection on a pawl, that engages with a ratchet wheel. **b** any one of the projections in the escapement of a watch, clock, or other mechanism, that alternately catch and release the notches of the wheels. **4** a low, portable platform on which loads are stacked to keep them off the ground in storage and to make the entire stack, including the pallet, easy to pick up, as by a fork lift, for handling. **5** a flat brush for taking up gold leaf. [earlier variant of *palette*]

**pal|let|ize** (pal′ə tīz), *v.t.*, **-ized, -iz|ing. 1** to put (a load) on a pallet: *Palletize shipments for easier warehouse handling, storage, and shipment* (Wall Street Journal). **2** to equip with pallets: *to palletize machines.* —**pal′let|i|za′tion**, *n.* —**pal′let|iz′er**, *n.*

**pal|lette** (pal′it), *n.* = palette.

**pal|li|al** (pal′ē əl), *adj. Zoology.* having to do with a pallium, especially of a mollusk.

**pal|liasse** (pal yas′, pal′yas), *n. Especially British.* paillasse.

**pal|li|ate** (pal′ē āt), *v.t.*, **-at|ed, -at|ing. 1** to lessen without curing; mitigate: *to palliate a disease.* SYN: ease. **2** to make appear less serious; excuse: *to palliate a fault. The culprit ... had not striven to deny or palliate his offence* (Rudyard Kipling). SYN: extenuate. **3** *Archaic.* to hide; conceal; disguise. **4** *Obsolete.* to cloak; clothe; shelter. [< Late Latin *palliāre* (with English *-ate¹*) to cover with a cloak < Latin *pallium* cloak]

**pal|li|a|tion** (pal′ē ā′shən), *n.* **1** the act or process of palliating: *In patients with advanced ovarian cancer and extensive spread, only palliation can be achieved* (Science News Letter). SYN: alleviation. **2** something that palliates. SYN: palliative.

**pal|li|a|tive** (pal′ē ā′tiv), *adj., n.* —*adj.* **1** useful to lessen or soften; mitigating: *Treatment turns out to be only palliative at best; the truth is they are schizos, whose psychic split is too wide ever to be healed* (Harper's). **2** tending or seeking to palliate; excusing; extenuating: *palliative remarks.*
—*n.* **1** something that lessens or softens pain or disease: *Drug firms have palliatives, but no promising cure for coronary thrombosis* (Wall Street Journal). **2** something that mitigates or excuses: *It is, therefore, necessary in the present world climate to examine less drastic palliatives* (Bulletin of Atomic Scientists). —**pal′li|a′tive|ly**, *adv.*

**pal|li|a|tor** (pal′ē ā′tər), *n.* a person who palliates; extenuator.

**pal|lid** (pal′id), *adj.* lacking color; pale; wan: *a pallid complexion, a pallid imitation.* SYN: See syn. under **pale¹**. [< Latin *pallidus.* See etym. of doublet **pale¹**.] —**pal′lid|ly**, *adv.* —**pal′lid|ness**, *n.*

**pal|li|da Mors** (pal′ə də môrz′), *Latin.* the pallid (specter of) death; Death.

**pal|li|um** (pal′ē əm), *n., pl.* **-li|ums, -li|a** (-lē ə). **1** a large rectangular mantle worn by men, especially philosophers and scholars in ancient Greece and Rome (so called in Latin; in Greek called a *himation*). **2a** (in the Roman Catholic Church) a woolen vestment of the Pope, conferred by him on cardinals and certain other high dignitaries as a symbol of investiture, consisting, in its present form, of a narrow circular band of wool, worn on the shoulders, with two short vertical strips falling on the breast and back. **b** an altar cloth. **3** the cortex of the brain. **4** *Zoology.* **a** the mantle of mollusks and brachiopods, an outgrowth of the dorsal body wall. **b** the back and folded wings of a bird taken together, when in any way distinguished from other parts, as by color as on a gull or tern; mantle; stragulum. [< Latin *pallium* a cover; pall¹]

**pall-mall** (pel′mel′), *n.* **1** a game formerly played in which players tried to hit a ball of boxwood through a ring at the end of an alley. **2** an alley in which this game was played. [< Middle French *pallemaille* < Italian *palla-maglio* < *palla,* variant of *balla* ball¹ + *maglio* (< Latin *malleus*) mallet]

**pal|lor** (pal′ər), *n.* lack of color from fear, illness, or death; paleness: *Pallor suggested a marked reduction in the flow of blood in shock* (Harper's). SYN: wanness. [< Latin *pallor* < *pallēre* become pale]

**pal|ly** (pal′ē), *adj.*, **-li|er, -li|est.** *Informal.* like a pal; companionable; chummy: *The girls are sweet, the chaps are pally* (Punch).

**palm¹** (päm, pälm), *n., v.* —*n.* **1** the inside of the hand between the wrist and fingers: *It had now been established that no two human beings had the same palm prints* (London Times). **2** a similar part of the forefoot of a four-footed animal. **3a** the width of a hand as a rough unit of measure; three to four inches. SYN: handbreadth. **b** the length of a hand as a rough unit of measure; seven to ten inches. **4** the part of a glove covering the palm. **5** any relatively flat, widened part at the end of an armlike projection, such as the blade of an oar or paddle or the inner side of the fluke of an anchor. **6** the flat widened part of the antler of certain members of the deer family, especially of the moose. **7** a leather pad worn over the palm and having a small metal plate in the center, used somewhat like a thimble in sewing sails.
—*v.t.* **1** to conceal in the hand, especially in the palm with the hand down: *The magician palmed the nickel. Do you see that gambler over there at the table, palming the ace of clubs?* (Newsweek). **2** to pass or get accepted (something not good): *Thinking you could palm such stuff on me* (John Gay). **3** to touch or stroke with the palm or hand; handle: *The muscular man with the hard eyes palms the phone* (Time). **4** to shake hands with.
**grease** (or **oil**) **the palm of**, to bribe: *He avoided jail by greasing the palm of several corrupt police officials.*
**have an itching palm**, to be greedy for money: *Cassius, you yourself Are much condemn'd to have an itching palm* (Shakespeare).
**in the palm of one's hand**, under one's complete control: *The young American soprano, making her stadium debut, held the audience in the palm of her hand* (New York Times).
**palm off**, to pass off or get accepted by tricks, fraud, or false representation: *to palm off spurious things as genuine.*
[< Old French *paume* < Latin *palma*]

**palm²** (päm, pälm), *n.* **1a** any one of many kinds of trees and shrubs growing widely in warm climates, chiefly in the tropics. Most palms have tall trunks, no branches, and a bunch of leaves at the top, which are either fan-shaped or pinnate. Palms belong to the palm family. The coconut palm has large seeds and is well-known for the white meat and cloudy oil the coconut contains. **b** any one of several similar trees or shrubs. **2** a leaf or stalk of leaves of a palm tree as a symbol of victory or triumph: *A great multitude ... stood before the throne ... clothed with white robes, and palms in their hands* (Revelation 7:9). **3** *Figurative.* victory; triumph: *But the palm must rightly be given to the Italian historians speaking in their own fields, particularly Ancient History, Roman Law, and the history of medieval religion* (London Times). **4** something that looks like a small palm leaf or branch, as on a decoration of honor, or as an addition of honor to a military decoration: *There are ... many true stories of splendid acts ... The V.C.'s and the palms do but indicate samples* (H. G. Wells).
**bear** (or **carry**) **off the palm**, to be the victor; win: *He bore off the palm in both tennis and swimming.*
**yield the palm to**, to admit defeat by; defer to: *He cannot make a speech—in this he yields the palm to Protagoras* (Benjamin Jowett).
[Old English *pælm, palma* < Latin *palma* palm tree (perhaps because of the shape of the leaves); palm¹] —**palm′like′**, *adj.*

**pal|ma|ceous** (pal mā′shəs), *adj.* belonging to the palm family of plants; phoenicaceous.

**pal|mar** (pal′mər), *adj., n.* —*adj.* of or having to do with the palm of the hand or the corresponding part of the forefoot of an animal.
—*n.* a palmar muscle, nerve, or other structure. [< Latin *palmāris* < *palma* palm¹]

**pal|ma|ry** (pal′mər ē), *adj.* deserving the palm; preeminent; chief: *a palmary example, palmary proof.* [< Latin *palmārius* < *palma* palm¹]

***pal|mate** (pal′māt), *adj.* **1** shaped somewhat like a hand with the fingers spread out, especially: **a** having divisions or leaflets which are all attached at one point at the end of the petiole, as the clover does: *a palmate compound leaf.* **b** having several large veins radiating from one point at the end of the petiole, as the maple leaf does: *A leaf which has several large veins of approximately equal size radiating from its base out into the lamina is said to possess palmate venation* (Heber W. Youngken). **2** *Zoology.* having the front toes joined by a web; web-footed. [< Latin *palmātus,* past participle of *palmāre* to make the print of one's hand < *palma* palm¹] —**pal′mate|ly**, *adv.*

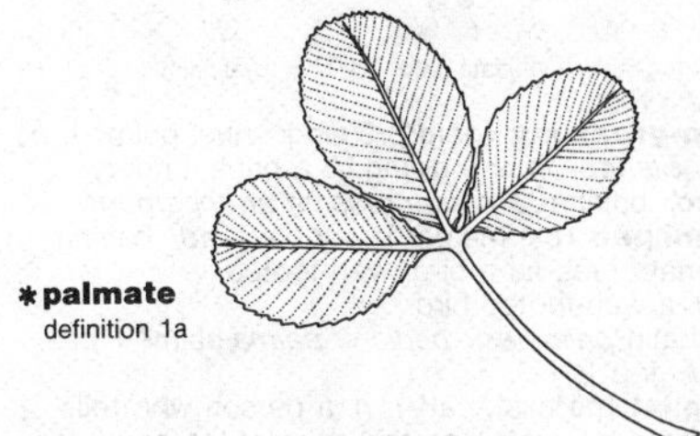

***palmate**
definition 1a

**pal|mat|ed** (pal′mā tid), *adj.* = palmate.

**pal|mat|i|fid** (pal mat′ə fid), *adj. Botany.* cleft in a palmate manner, with the divisions extending halfway down to the base, or somewhat further, and the sinuses or lobes narrow or acute, as a leaf. [< Latin *palmātus* palmate + *findere* to split, cleft]

**pal|ma|tion** (pal mā′shən), *n.* **1** palmate formation or structure. **2** one division of a palmate structure.

**Palm Beach cloth**, *Trademark.* a lightweight mohair and cotton fabric used for summer apparel.

**palm branch**, a palm leaf with its stalk, used as an emblem of triumph or victory or a decoration.

**palm cabbage**, **1** = cabbage palm. **2** = cabbage.

**palm civet** or **cat**, any one of certain long-tailed civets, that live mainly in trees, are found in Asia and Africa, and are about the size of the domestic cat with spotted or striped fur and a long tail; paradoxure.

**palm crab**, = coconut crab.

**palm|er¹** (pä′mər, päl′-), *n., v.* —*n.* **1** a pilgrim re-

**Pronunciation Key:** hat, āge, cãre, fär; let, ēqual, tėrm; it, īce; hot, ōpen, ôrder; oil, out; cup, pu̇t, rüle; child; long; thin; ᴛʜen; zh, measure; ə represents **a** in about, **e** in taken, **i** in pencil, **o** in lemon, **u** in circus.

turning from the Holy Land, bringing a palm branch as a token: *Here is a holy Palmer come, From Salem first, and last from Rome* (Scott). **2** any pilgrim: *The escalloped shell ... was adopted as the universal badge of the palmer* (William H. Prescott).
**—*v.i.*** *Scottish.* to wander about like a palmer; be a vagrant.
[< Anglo-French *palmer,* Old French *palmier,* learned borrowing from Medieval Latin *palmarius* carrying palms < Latin *palma* palm[2]]

**palm|er**[2] (pä′mər, päl′-), *n.* a person who palms or conceals something. [< *palm*[1] + *-er*[1]]

**Pal|mer|sto|ni|an** (pä′mər stō′nē ən, päl′-), *adj.* having to do with or characteristic of the English statesman and prime minister, Viscount Palmerston (1784-1865) or his political views.

**palmer worm,** any one of various caterpillars that appear in large numbers and are destructive to fruit trees, such as the larva of an American moth that feeds on apple leaves. [earlier *palmer* < *palmer*[1] (from its wandering habits)]

**pal|mette** (pal met′), *n. Archaeology.* an ornament, sculptured or painted, more or less resembling a palm leaf. [< French *palmette* (diminutive) < *palme* palm[2]]

**pal|met|to** (pal met′ō), *n., pl.* **-tos** or **-toes. 1** any one of several kinds of palms with fan-shaped leaves, such as the saw palmetto and the cabbage palm. See picture under **fan palm. 2** the leaves, used in making baskets. [< Spanish *palmito* (diminutive) < *palma* palm[2]]

**Palmetto State,** a nickname for South Carolina.

*** palm family,** a large family of woody monocotyledonous plants growing chiefly in the tropics and made up of the palms. Palms are usually unbranched trees or shrubs having large pinnate or fan-shaped leaves at the top. In different species the fruit, seed, and leaves are used for food, the wood for building, and the leaves for thatching or making paper and baskets.

***palm family**

**palm-greas|ing** (päm′grē′sing, -zing; pälm′-), *n., adj. Slang.* **—*n.*** the giving of a bribe; bribery.
**—*adj.*** bribing: *a palm-greasing arrangement.*

**pal|mi|ped** (pal′mə ped), *adj., n.* **—*adj.*** having palmate feet, as a bird; web-footed.
**—*n.*** a web-footed bird.
[< Latin *palmipes, -pedis* < *palma* palm[2] + *pēs, pedis* foot]

**palm|ist** (pä′mist, päl′-), *n.* a person who tells fortunes by examining the palm of the hand; chiromancer.

**palm|ist|er** (pä′mə stər, päl′-), *n.* = palmist.

**palm|is|try** (pä′mə strē, päl′-), *n.* the supposed art, or its practice, of telling a person's fortune, or of describing his character, from the lines and marks in the palm of his hand; chiromancy. [Middle English *palmestrie* < *palme* palm[1]]

**pal|mi|tate** (pal′mə tāt), *n.* a salt or ester of palmitic acid.

**pal|mit|ic acid** (pal mit′ik), a white crystalline acid, solid at ordinary temperatures, contained as a glyceride in palm oil and in most solid fats. *Formula:* $C_{16}H_{32}O_2$ [< French *palmitique* < Latin *palma* palm[2], or < French *palmite* palm-tree pith]

**pal|mi|tin** (pal′mə tin), *n.* a colorless crystalline solid, a glyceride of palmitic acid, present in palm oil and, in association with stearin and olein, in solid animal fats. It is used in making soap. *Formula:* $C_{51}H_{98}O_6$ [< French *palmitine* < *palmitique* palmitic + *-ine* -in]

**palm kernel oil,** a white to yellowish fat from the seeds of the palm tree, used in making margarine.

**palm leaf,** a leaf of a palm tree, used for making hats, baskets, fans, and thatching. **—palm′-leaf′,** *adj.*

**palm oil, 1** a yellowish or orange-colored, butter-like fat from the fruit of the oil palm, used in cosmetics and to make soap and candles. **2** *British Slang.* money given as a bribe.

**palm|print** (päm′print′, pälm′-), *n.* a mark or impression made by the palm of the hand.

**palm sugar,** a sugar obtained from the sap of certain palm trees; jaggery.

**Palm Sunday,** the Sunday before Easter Sunday, celebrated in memory of the triumphal entry of Christ into Jerusalem, when palm branches were strewn before Him.

**palm warbler,** a warbler of eastern North America with a yellow and white breast and chestnut crown, noted for its habit of wagging its tail up and down.

**palm wax,** a waxy substance secreted by certain palm trees.

**palm wine,** wine made from the sap of certain palm trees; toddy.

**palm|y** (pä′mē, päl′-), *adj.,* **palm|i|er, palm|i|est. 1** abounding in palms or shaded by palms: *palmy islands; fairer than Rachel by the palmy well* (Tennyson). **2** like, having to do with, or derived from palms. **3** flourishing; prosperous; glorious: *palmy days of peace; in the most high and palmy state of Rome* (Shakespeare). **SYN:** fortunate, thriving.

**pal|my|ra** (pal mī′rə), *n.,* or **palmyra palm** or **tree,** a tropical Asian palm with large, fan-shaped leaves, important for its great variety of uses, such as the wood for timber, the leaves for thatch, baskets, and paper, the sap for a kind of sugar, and the fruit and young roots for food; borassus palm: *The ancient Hindu scholars used strips from the leaves of the palmyra and talipot palms for writing material* (Ivan Murray Johnston). [< Portuguese *palmeira* < Latin *palma* palm[2]; spelling perhaps influenced by *Palmyra,* proper name]

**pa|lo blan|co** (pa′lō blang′kō, pä′-; bläng′-), any one of several trees or shrubs of the elm family growing in the southwestern United States, having a white wood or bark. [< Spanish *palo blanco* (literally) white wood]

**pa|lo|lo** (pə lō′lō), *n.* any one of several marine worms that burrow in coral reefs of tropical seas, the posterior parts of which, when mature, separate from the anterior parts and rise in swarms to the surface to spawn. One species is found in West Indian waters, another in the south Pacific, where it is gathered for food by the natives. [< the native name in Samoa]

**pal|o|mi|no** (pal′ə mē′nō), *n., pl.* **-nos.** a cream-colored or golden-tan horse of Arabian stock. Its mane and tail are usually light colored and its build slender and graceful. ... *a parade led by a pretty teen-ager riding a palomino* (Newsweek). [American English < Spanish *palomino* a young stock dove < Latin *palumbīnus* (diminutive) < *palumba* ringdove, wood pigeon (because of the color)]

**pa|loo|ka** (pə lü′kə), *n. Slang.* **1** a mediocre or inferior boxer or player of any sport or game: *In rubber bridge, a pair of utter palookas could conceivably outscore two experts for an evening simply by holding better cards* (Maclean's). **2** a stupid, awkward, though frequently muscular lout or hoodlum. [origin uncertain]

**pa|lo|ver|de** (pä′lō vär′dā), *n.* any one of various shrubs or trees of the pea family, found in the arid regions of the southwestern United States and northern Mexico. [< Spanish *paloverde* < *palo* stick, wood (< Latin *pālus* pale[2]) + *verde* green < Latin *viridis*]

**palp** (palp), *n.* = palpus. [< French *palpe,* learned borrowing from Latin *palpus*]

**pal|pa|bil|i|ty** (pal′pə bil′ə tē), *n.* the quality of being palpable.

**pal|pa|ble** (pal′pə bəl), *adj.* **1** readily seen or heard and recognized; obvious: *a palpable error. For shore it was, and high ... and palpable to view* (Byron). **SYN:** perceptible, plain, evident, manifest. **2** that can be touched or felt; tangible: *A hit, a very palpable hit* (Shakespeare). **3** *Medicine.* perceptible by palpation. [< Late Latin *palpābilis* < Latin *palpāre* to feel, stroke, pat] **—pal′pa|ble|ness,** *n.* **—pal′pa|bly,** *adv.*

**pal|pal** (pal′pəl), *adj. Zoology.* having to do with or of the nature of a palpus.

**pal|pate**[1] (pal′pāt), *v.t.,* **-pat|ed, -pat|ing. 1** to examine by the sense of touch. **2** to examine (as a bodily organ or growth) by touching or manipulating with the hands, especially as a preliminary to or in order to confirm a medical diagnosis. [< Latin *palpāre* (with English *-ate*[1]) touch gently, stroke, feel, pat]

**pal|pate**[2] (pal′pāt), *adj. Zoology.* having a palpus or palpi. [< New Latin *palpus* palpus + English *-ate*[1]]

**pal|pa|tion** (pal pā′shən), *n.* **1** the act of touching. **2** *Medicine.* examination by touch or feeling, as with the hand: *Palpation may disclose the pulse to be fast or slow, regular or irregular, strong or weak, and hard or soft* (Harbaugh and Goodrich).

**pal|pe|bra** (pal′pə brə), *n., pl.* **-brae** (-brē). *Anatomy.* an eyelid. [< Latin *palpebrae* eyelids, related to *palpāre* pat gently]

**pal|pe|bral** (pal′pə brəl), *adj.* of or having to do with an eyelid or the eyelids.

**pal|pi** (pal′pī), *n.* plural of **palpus.**

**pal|pi|tant** (pal′pə tənt), *adj.* palpitating. [< Latin *palpitāns, -antis,* present participle of *palpitāre* palpitate]

**pal|pi|tate** (pal′pə tāt), *v.i.,* **-tat|ed, -tat|ing. 1** to beat very rapidly, irregularly, or strongly: *Your heart palpitates when you are excited.* **SYN:** throb. **2** to quiver; tremble; flutter: *His body palpitated with terror. ... fountains palpitating in the heat* (Tennyson). [< Latin *palpitāre* (with English *-ate*[1]) to throb, flutter (frequentative) < *palpāre* to pat, touch lightly] **—pal′pi|tat′ing|ly,** *adv.*

**pal|pi|ta|tion** (pal′pə tā′shən), *n.* **1** a very rapid beating of the heart; throb. **2** a quivering; trembling: *I was seized with such a palpitation and trembling that I could not stand* (Tobias Smollett).

**pal|pus** (pal′pəs), *n., pl.* **-pi.** one of the jointed feelers attached to the mouth of insects, spiders, lobsters, and other arthropods; palp. Palpi are organs of touch or taste. [< New Latin *palpus* < Latin, soft palm[1]]

**pals|grave** (pôlz′grāv, palz′-), *n. Historical.* a German count palatine. [< earlier Dutch *paltsgrave,* adaptation of Middle High German *pfalzgrāve* < Old High German *pfalenzgrâvo* < *pfalenza* palace, palatine[1] + *grâvo* count]

**pals|gra|vine** (pôlz′grə vēn, palz′-), *n.* the wife or widow of a palsgrave.

**pal|ship** (pal′ship), *n. U.S. Informal.* the state of being pals; comradeship.

**pal|sied** (pôl′zid), *adj.* **1** having the palsy; paralyzed. **2** *Figurative.* shaking; trembling: *old palsied houses* (Robert Louis Stevenson).

**pal|stave** (pôl′stāv), *n., pl.* **-staves.** *Archaeology.* a form of celt that resembles a chisel, having a tongue that fits directly into a handle. [< Danish *paalstav* < Old Icelandic *pālstafr* < *pāll* hoe + *stafr* stave]

**pal|sy** (pôl′zē), *n., pl.* **-sies,** *v.,* **-sied, -sy|ing.**
**—*n.*** paralysis; lessening or loss of power to feel, to move, or to control motion in some part of the body. Palsy occurs especially with Parkinson's disease. *The man had palsy in his arm.*
**—*v.t.*** **1** to afflict with palsy; paralyze. **2** *Figurative.* to make powerless or inert: *Disappointment palsied her heart* (Jane Porter).
[Middle English *palesie, parlesie* < Old French *paralysie,* learned borrowing from unrecorded Medieval Latin *paralysia,* alteration of Latin *paralysis.* See etym. of doublet **paralysis.**]

**pal|sy wal|sy** (pal′zē wal′zē), *Slang.* like pals; friendly; closely associated: ... *in view of the palsy walsy relationship between Roll and Bill* (Newsweek).

**pal|ter** (pôl′tər), *v.i.* **1** to talk or act insincerely; trifle deceitfully: *Do not palter with the truth. Man crouches and blushes ... he palters and steals* (Emerson). **SYN:** equivocate. **2** to act carelessly; trifle: *Do not palter with a decision involving life and death. A hunger for music is one of our noblest appetites, and nothing to be paltered with* (Atlantic). **3** to deal crookedly; use tricks and dodges in bargaining; haggle: *Who never sold the truth to serve the hour, Nor palter'd with Eternal God for power* (Tennyson). [origin unknown] **—pal′ter|er,** *n.*

**pal|tri|ly** (pôl′trə lē), *adv.* in a paltry manner; despicably; meanly.

**pal|tri|ness** (pôl′trē nis), *n.* the condition of being paltry; very slight value; meanness.

**pal|try** (pôl′trē), *adj.,* **-tri|er, -tri|est. 1** almost worthless; trifling; petty; mean: *The thief stole a paltry sum of money from the child. He ... considered the prize too paltry for the lives it must cost* (John L. Motley). **SYN:** insignificant. **2** of no worth; despicable; contemptible: *a paltry trick, a paltry crowd. Pay no attention to paltry gossip. He is a paltry, imitating pedant* (Jonathan Swift). [perhaps < dialectal *palt,* or *pelt* trash, dirty rag, waste. Compare Low German *paltrig* ragged, torn; Frisian *palt* rag, torn piece.]

**pa|lu|dal** (pə lü′dəl, pal′yə-), *adj.* **1** of or having to do with a marsh or fen; marshy. **2** caused by or arising from a marsh; malarial. [< Latin *palūs, -ūdis* marsh + English *-al*[1]]

**pa|lu|da|ment** (pə lü′də mənt), *n.* a kind of cloak or mantle worn in war by a general in ancient Rome, but later reserved exclusively for the emperor as head of the army. [< Latin *palūdāmentum*]

**pa|lu|da|men|tum** (pə lü′də men′təm), *n.* = paludament.

**pa|lu|dic** (pə lü′dik), *adj.* = paludal.

**pa|lu|di|cole** (pə lü′də kōl), *adj.* inhabiting or frequenting marshes: *paludicole birds.* [< Latin *palūs, -ūdis* marsh + *colere* inhabit]

**pal|u|dic|o|line** (pal′yə dik′ə lin), *adj.* = paludicole.

**pal|u|dic|o|lous** (pal′yə dik′ə ləs), *adj.* = paludicole.

**pal|u|dine** (pal′yə din, -dīn), *adj.* = paludal.

**pal|u|dism** (pal′yə diz əm), *n. Medicine.* malaria.

[< Latin *palūs, -ūdis* marsh + English *-ism*]

**pal|u|dose** (pal′yə dōs), *adj.* living or growing in marshes, as animals or plants. [< Latin *palūdōsus* < *palūs, -ūdis* marsh]

**Pal|u|drine** (pal′yə drēn, -drin), *n. Trademark.* a colorless, synthetic antimalarial drug. *Formula:* $C_{11}H_{16}ClN_5$

**pa|lus|tral** (pə lus′trəl), *adj.* of or having to do with marshes; found in or inhabiting marshes; paludal: *In these palustral homes we only croak and wither* (Manchester Guardian). [< Latin *paluster, -tris* (< *pālus* marsh) + English *-al*[1]]

**pa|lus|trine** (pə lus′trin), *adj.* = paludal.

**pal|y**[1] (pā′lē), *adj.,* **pal|i|er, pal|i|est.** *Archaic.* somewhat pale: *paly locks of gold* (John Greenleaf Whittier).

**pal|y**[2] (pā′lē), *adj. Heraldry.* (of a shield or a bearing) divided palewise (vertically) into four or more (usually) equal parts of alternate tinctures. [< Old French *palé,* apparently < *pal* a pale[2], stake]

**pal|y|no|log|ic** (pal′ə nə loj′ik), *adj.* = palynological.

**pal|y|no|log|i|cal** (pal′ə nə loj′ə kəl), *adj.* of or having to do with palynology. **–pal′y|no|log′i|cal|ly,** *adv.*

**pal|y|nol|o|gist** (pal′ə nol′ə jist), *n.* a person who studies or is skilled in palynology.

**pal|y|nol|o|gy** (pal′ə nol′ə jē), *n.* the study of plant spores and pollen, especially in fossil form. [< Greek *palýnein* to strew + English *-logy*]

**pal|y|tox|in** (pal′ə tok′sən), *n.* a highly poisonous substance discharged by polyps, especially as protection against octopuses. [probably < Greek *palýnein* to strew + English *toxin*]

**pam** (pam), *n.* **1** the jack of clubs in one variety of the game of loo. **2** the variety of loo in which it is the best trump. [apparently abbreviation of French *pamphile* the knave of clubs in loo < Greek *pámphilos* loved by all]

**pam.,** pamphlet.

**pa|ma|quine** (pä′mə kwīn), *n.* a yellowish, odorless synthetic drug effective in the treatment of malaria but often toxic to humans. *Formula:* $C_{42}H_{45}N_3O_7$ [< *p*(entane) + *a*(mino) + *m*(ethyl) + *-aquine,* as in *primaquine*]

**Pa|mir sheep** (pä mir′), = Marco Polo sheep. [< the *Pamirs,* a mountain range in Central Asia]

**pam|pa** (pam′pə), *n.* singular of **pampas**: *Stoneless, soft, immensely fertile, the Argentine pampa stretches sea-flat to the horizon* (Economist).

**pam|pas** (pam′pəz), *n.pl.* the vast, grassy plains of South America, without trees. The pampas are south of the forest-covered belt of the Amazon Basin, especially in Argentina. *... across the grassy pampas, where wild gauchos tend their restless herds* (New York Times). [< Spanish *pampas,* plural < Quechua (Peru) *pampa* a plain]

**pampas deer,** a small, reddish or yellowish brown deer with simple antlers that lives on the South American pampas. The pampas deer is able to jump over eight- to ten-foot grass clumps.

**pampas grass,** an ornamental grass, native in South America but widely cultivated, having large, thick, feathery panicles of a silvery white, borne on stems which sometimes reach a height of 12 feet.

**pam|pe|an** (pam pē′ən, pam′pē-), *adj., n.* **–*adj.*** of or having to do with the pampas.
**–*n.*** an Indian living on or in the region of the pampas.

**pam|per** (pam′pər), *v.t.* **1** to indulge too much; allow too many privileges to: *to pamper a child, to pamper a sick person, to pamper one's appetite.* **SYN:** spoil, humor. **2** *Obsolete.* to cram or glut with food, especially rich food; feed luxuriously. [Middle English *pamperen,* perhaps (frequentative) < obsolete *pampen* to pamper, cram] **–pam′per|er,** *n.*

**pam|pe|ro** (päm pãr′ō; *Spanish* päm pã′rō), *n., pl.* **-pe|ros** (-pãr′ōz; *Spanish* -pã′rōs). a piercing cold wind that blows from the Andes across the pampas of South America to the Atlantic. [American English < Spanish *pampero* < *pampa;* see etym. under **pampas**]

**pamph.,** pamphlet.

**pam|phlet** (pam′flit), *n.* **1** a booklet in paper covers. A pamphlet often deals with a question of current interest. *In Europe, the pamphlet is a short piece of writing essentially polemic in nature, concerned with a problem of the moment* (Harper's). **SYN:** tract, brochure. **2** any printed booklet with few pages. [< Medieval Latin (England) *panfletus,* for Old French *Pamphilet,* popular name for a Latin poem of the 1100's "Pamphilus, seu de Amore" < Greek *pámphilos* loved by all < *pan-* (see etym. under **pan-**) + *philos* loved (one), lover < *philein* to love]

**pam|phlet|ar|y** (pam′flə ter′ē), *adj.* of, like, or having to do with a pamphlet or pamphleteering.

**pam|phlet|eer** (pam′flə tir′), *n., v.* **–*n.*** a person who writes pamphlets, especially on controversial subjects: *As a pamphleteer Thomas Paine is without his equal in American literature* (Jones and Leisy).
**–*v.i.*** to write and issue pamphlets.

**pam|poo|tie** (pam pü′tē), *n.* a simple shoe consisting of a piece of hide held to the foot by leather cords, worn by the island fishermen of western Ireland. [perhaps alteration of *papoosh*]

**pam|pro|dac|ty|lous** (pam′prō dak′tə ləs), *n. Ornithology.* having all four toes turned forward, as in the coly. [< Greek *pam-* pan- + *pró* before + *dáktylos* finger or toe + English *-ous*]

**pan**[1] (pan), *n., v.,* **panned, pan|ning.** **–*n.*** **1** a dish for cooking and other household uses, usually broad, shallow, and often with no cover: *pots and pans.* **2** anything like this. Gold and other metals are sometimes obtained by washing ore in pans. The dishes on a pair of scales are called pans. **3a** a relatively broad, shallow vessel, usually of cast iron, in which ores, especially of silver, were formerly ground and amalgamated. **b** a shallow vessel used for evaporating water from any of various liquid substances, so as to obtain a desired substance, such as salt from brine or maple syrup from maple sap. **4** the contents of a pan; amount that a pan will hold. **5** the hollow part of the lock in old-fashioned guns, used to hold a little gunpowder to set off the gun. **6** hard subsoil; hardpan. **7** a hollow or depression in the ground, especially one in which water stands: *A dry pan, or waterhole, which ... was densely covered with weeds* (H. Rider Haggard). **8** a natural or artificial basin in which salt is obtained by evaporating seawater. **9** = pan ice. **10** *Informal.* severe criticism: *The reviews usually said I gave an adequate or good performance. I never got raves, but neither did I get pans* (Robert Taylor). **11** *Slang.* a face: *Francis ... has a genial, happy pan* (New York Times).
**–*v.t.*** **1** to cook in a pan. **2a** to wash in a pan: *to pan gold.* **b** to wash (gravel, sand, etc.) in a pan to separate the gold. **3** *Informal.* to criticize severely: *The drama critic panned the new play.*
**–*v.i.*** **1** to wash gold-bearing gravel, sand, etc., in a pan in order to separate the gold: *Panning consists merely of segregating by gravity and water the earthy material from the metal in the pan* (White and Renner). **2** to yield gold when washed in a pan.
**pan out,** *Informal.* to turn out or work out: *The signs revealed that the experiment wasn't panning out* (Harper's).
[Old English *panne,* apparently < Medieval Latin *panna* < Latin *patina*]

**pan**[2] (pän), *n.* **1** the betel leaf. **2** a combination, as of betel leaf, areca nut, and lime, used for chewing like gum in various parts of Asia. [< Hindi *pān* < Sanskrit *parṇa* leaf, feather, betel leaf]

**pan**[3] (pan), *v.,* **panned, pan|ning,** *n.* **–*v.i.*** to move a motion picture or television camera either vertically or horizontally, so as to take in a larger scene or to follow a moving object: *The camera panned from the speaker to the audience. The TV camera panned over a crowded room* (Punch).
**–*v.t.*** to move (a camera) in this way.
**–*n.*** **1** the act or process of panning: *Compressed into a film, too, the scene-transitions* [*were*] *made by smooth dissolves or pans* (Richard Mallett). **2** a panning motion: *All of the cameras have ... pan* (Science News). *He ... took in the lobby with one pan of his leonine head* (Maclean's).
[short for *panorama*]

**Pan** (pan), *n. Greek Mythology.* the god of forests, pastures, flocks, hunters, and shepherds. Pan is described as a man with legs, horns, and ears of a goat, who wandered through the woods playing on musical pipes. The Romans called him Faunus.

**pan-,** *combining form.* all; of all; entirely: *Pan-American* = *of all Americans. Panacea* = *a remedy for all diseases. Panchromatic* = *entirely chromatic.* [< Greek *pân,* neuter of *pâs* all]

**pan.,** panchromatic.

**Pan.,** Panama.

**PAN** (no periods), **1** peroxyacetyl nitrate. **2** polyacrylonitrile.

**pan|a|ce|a** (pan′ə sē′ə), *n.* **1** a remedy for all diseases or ills; cure-all: *For my panacea ... let me have a draught of undiluted morning air* (Thoreau). **2** *Figurative.* anything that resembles such a remedy or medicine in the range of virtues claimed for it, such as an economic program or a political reform: *There are no panaceas in education. The first panacea for a mis-managed nation is inflation of the currency* (Ernest Hemingway). [< Latin *panacēa* an all-healing herb; also, the goddess of healing < Greek *panákeia* panacea < *panakês* all-healing < *pan-* all + *ákos* cure]

**pan|a|ce|an** (pan′ə sē′ən), *adj.* of the nature of a panacea.

**pa|nache** (pə nash′, -näsh′), *n.* **1** a tuft or plume of feathers used ornamentally, especially on a helmet: *With him came a gallant train ... decorated with rich surcoats and panaches of feathers* (Washington Irving). **2** *Figurative.* a flamboyant manner or style; swagger; dash: *With the poise and panache most debs would envy, Catrina Colston wears palest blue organdie* (Sunday Times). [< French *panache,* Middle French *pennache* < Italian *pennaccio,* variant of *pennacchio* < *penna* feather < Latin]

**pa|na|da** (pə nä′də), *n.* a dish made of bread or crackers boiled in water or milk to a pulp and variously seasoned or flavored. [< Spanish, Portuguese *panada* < Italian *panata* < *pane* bread < Latin *pānis*]

**Pan-Af|ri|can** (pan af′rə kən), *adj.* **1** of or for all African peoples: *a Pan-African union.* **2** of Pan-Africanism: *a Pan-African policy.*

**Pan-Af|ri|can|ism** (pan af′rə kə niz′əm), *n.* **1** a movement or policy seeking the political union of all African peoples. **2** belief in or support of this movement or policy.

**Pan-Af|ri|can|ist** (pan af′rə kə nist), *n., adj.* **–*n.*** a person who believes in or supports Pan-Africanism.
**–*adj.*** of or having to do with Pan-Africanism.

**pan|a|ma** (pan′ə mä, -mô), *n.* **1a** a fine hat woven from the young leaves of a palmlike plant of Central and South America, especially the jipijapa plant. **b** any hat made in imitation of this: *Worsted flannels ... and cotton and tropical panamas* (Sunday Times). **2** the leaves or straw from which the hat is made. [< *Panama,* where they were formerly shipped from]

**Panama disease,** a common disease of the banana plant, caused by a fungus that attacks the roots and grows on the plant, finally withering it.

**Panama hat,** = panama (def. 1).

**Pan|a|man** (pan′ə män′), *adj., n.* = Panamanian.

**Pan|a|ma|ni|an** (pan′ə mā′nē ən), *adj., n.* **–*adj.*** of or having to do with Panama.
**–*n.*** a person born or living in Panama: *Most Panamanians are of mixed white, Indian, and Negro ancestry* (John and Mavis Biesanz).

**Pan-A|mer|i|can** (pan′ə mer′ə kən), *adj.* **1** of all the people of North, Central, and South America. **2** including all the countries of North, Central, and South America.

**Pan American Day,** April 14, a day observed by more than 20 American republics to commemorate the date of founding of the Pan American Union in 1890: *Pan American Day serves as a reminder of the independence of the American nations and of their cooperation with one another* (Elizabeth Hough Sechrist).

**Pan American Games,** a series of athletic contests, patterned after the Olympic Games and held in one of the countries of the Western Hemisphere once every four years, usually during the summer before the Olympic Games.

**Pan-A|mer|i|can|ism** (pan′ə mer′ə kə niz′əm), *n.* **1** the principle or policy that all the countries in North, Central, and South America should cooperate to promote cultural, commercial, and social progress: *Pan-Americanism rests upon the conviction that there are primary and mutual interests which are peculiar to the republics of this hemisphere and that these can best be conserved by taking counsel together* (Nelson A. Rockefeller). **2** the advocacy of a political alliance of these countries.

**Pan American Union,** an organization of 21 American republics, formed in 1890 to promote mutual cooperation and peace. It created the Organization of American States in 1948.

**Pan-An|gli|can** (pan ang′glə kən), *adj.* of, having to do with, or including all the churches or church members of the Anglican Communion.

**Pan-Ar|ab** (pan ar′əb), *adj., n.* **–*adj.*** of or for all Arab peoples: *a Pan-Arab empire, a Pan-Arab labor federation.*
**–*n.*** a person who believes in or supports Pan-Arabism.

**Pan-Ar|a|bic** (pan ar′ə bik), *adj.* = Pan-Arab.

**Pan-Ar|ab|ism** (pan ar′ə biz əm), *n.* **1** a movement or policy seeking the political union of all Arab peoples. **2** belief in or support of this movement or policy.

**Pan-A|sian** (pan ā′zhən, -shən), *adj.* **1** of or for all Asian peoples: *a Pan-Asian federation.* **2** of Pan-Asianism: *a Pan-Asian doctrine.*

**Pan-A|sian|ism** (pan ā′zhə niz əm, -shə-), *n.* **1** a movement or policy seeking the political union of all Asian nations. **2** belief in or support of this movement or policy.

**Pan-A|sian|ist** (pan ā′zhə nist, -shə-), *n.* a person who believes in or supports Pan-Asianism.

**pan|a|tel|a** (pan′ə tel′ə), *n.* = panetela.

---

**Pronunciation Key:** hat, āge, cãre, fär; let, ēqual, tėrm; it, īce; hot, ōpen, ôrder; oil, out; cup, pu̇t, rüle; child; long; thin; ᴛʜen; zh, measure; ə represents **a** in about, **e** in taken, **i** in pencil, **o** in lemon, **u** in circus.

**Pan|ath|e|nae|a** (pan′ath ə nē′ə), *n.pl.* the chief national festival of ancient Athens, held annually in honor of Athena, the patroness of the city. The celebration every four years was known, from its special solemnity and magnificence, as the greater Panathenaea. [< New Latin *Panathenaea* < Greek *Panathēnaia* < *pan-* all + *Athênaia* games in honor of *Athena*]

**Pan|ath|e|nae|an** (pan′ath ə nē′ən), *adj.* = Panathenaic.

**Pan|ath|e|na|ic** (pan′ath ə nā′ik), *adj.* of or having to do with the Panathenaea.

**Pan-Bri|tan|nic** (pan′bri tan′ik), *adj.* of, having to do with, or including all the British dominions.

**pan|broil** or **pan-broil** (pan′broil′), *v.t.* to cook quickly over a very hot fire in a pan with little or no fat: *to panbroil fish in a skillet.*

**pan|cake** (pan′kāk′), *n., v.,* **-caked, -cak|ing.**
—*n.* **1** a thin, flat cake made of batter and fried or baked in a pan or on a griddle: *To his lips he raised the buckwheat pancakes, dripping with molasses* (Maurice Thompson). **2** a quick, almost flat landing made by an aircraft, as a result of its leveling off and stalling several feet above the ground. **3a** a facial makeup in the form of a cake, applied as a base for face powder. **b Pan-Cake,** a trademark for this makeup.
—*v.i.* **1** (of an aircraft) to flatten out several feet above the landing surface, stall, and make a quick, almost flat landing. **2** to spread out flat: *The very abnormal weather conditions ... produced bands of warm air pancaked on top of very cold air at temperatures wavering just either side of freezing point* (Sunday Times).
—*v.t.* to cause (an aircraft) to pancake: *The pilot pancaked his damaged plane onto an open field.*
► **Pancake, griddlecake,** though often used as synonyms, are usually differentiated in cookbooks. *Pancake* applies particularly to a relatively light and thin cake, often resembling the *crêpes* of French cookery. *Griddlecake* applies to a somewhat thicker and heavier cake.

**Pancake Day** or **Pancake Tuesday,** Shrove Tuesday, on which it was formerly customary to eat pancakes.

**pan|cha|ma** (pun′chə mə), *n.* a member of the Scheduled Caste in India; an untouchable: *Panchamas ... did the most menial work* (Scientific American). [< Hindi *panchama* < *pañcama* fifth < *pañca* five]

**pan|cha|yat** (pun chä′yət), *n.* a village council in India and Nepal, usually consisting of five elders who manage the affairs of the village and represent it before the state government. [< Hindi *panchayat* < *panch* five < Sanskrit *pañca*]

**Pan|chen Lama** (pän′chən), one of the two principal lamas of Tibetan Buddhism (the Dalai Lama is the other one). He is doctrinally preeminent in spiritual matters. *They brought back the Panchen Lama, who had been exiled for years in China, to share nominal political power and spiritual rule with the Dalai Lama* (Theodore Hsi-En Chen). [compare Tibetan *Panchen-rin-bochi* magnificent, (literally) large-jewel pundit]

**pan|chres|ton** (pan kres′tən), *n.* an explanation designed to cover or to fit all possible cases equally well; catch-all explanation or proposition. [< Greek *panchrēston* good for everything < *pan-* all, everything + *chrēstós* useful, good]

**pan|chro|mat|ic** (pan′krō mat′ik), *adj.* sensitive to light of all colors: *a panchromatic photographic film.*

**pan|chro|ma|tism** (pan krō′mə tiz əm), *n.* panchromatic quality; panchromatic work.

**pan|crat|ic** (pan krat′ik), *adj.* having to do with the pancratium.

**pan|cra|ti|um** (pan krā′shē əm), *n., pl.* **-ti|a** (-shē ə). an athletic contest in ancient Greece, combining wrestling and boxing. [< Latin *pancratium* < Greek *pankrátion* an exercise of all skills < *pan-* all + *krátos* mastery, strength]

**pan|cre|as** (pan′krē əs, pang′-), *n.* a gland near the stomach that helps digestion. The pancreas secretes insulin into the blood and pancreatic juice, which contains various enzymes, into the small intestine. The insulin is produced in the islets of Langerhans. The pancreas of a young animal, especially a calf, when used for food, is called the sweetbread. *The pancreas is interesting because it is both a duct and a ductless gland at the same time* (A. M. Winchester). See picture under **digestion.** [< New Latin *pancreas* < Greek *pánkreas, -atos* sweetbread < *pan-* all + *kréas, -atos* flesh]

**pan|cre|a|tec|to|mize** (pan′krē ə tek′tə mīz, pang′-), *v.t.,* **-mized, -miz|ing.** to perform a pancreatectomy on.

**pan|cre|a|tec|to|my** (pan′krē ə tek′tə mē, pang′-), *n., pl.* **-mies.** the surgical removal of the pancreas. [< *pancreat*(ic) + *-ectomy*]

**pan|cre|at|ic** (pan′krē at′ik, pang′-), *adj.* of the pancreas: *The pancreatic juice contains chemicals that help dissolve all three classes of food—fats, carbohydrates, and proteins.*

**pan|cre|a|tin** (pan′krē ə tin, pang′-), *n.* **1** a mixture of the enzymes anylopsin, trypsin, and steapsin, obtained from the fresh pancreas of hogs and oxen. It is used in medicine in the form of a cream-colored powder. **2** a preparation extracted from the pancreas of animals, used to aid digestion. [< *pancreat*(ic) + *-in*]

**pan|cre|a|ti|tis** (pan′krē ə tī′tis, pang′-), *n.* inflammation of the pancreas.

**pan|cre|a|tize** (pan′krē ə tīz, pang′-), *v.t.,* **-tized, -tiz|ing.** to treat with pancreatin.

**pan|cre|a|tot|o|my** (pan′krē ə tot′ə mē, pang′-), *n., pl.* **-mies.** surgical incision into the pancreas.

**pan|cre|o|zy|min** (pan′krē ō zī′min, pang′-), *n.* an intestinal hormone that stimulates secretion of enzymes by the pancreas. [< *pancreas* + *zymin*]

**pan|cy|to|pe|ni|a** (pan′sī tə pē′nē ə), *n.* = aplastic anemia. [< *pan-* + *cyto-* + Greek *peniā* poverty]

***pan|da** (pan′də), *n.* **1** a bearlike mammal of Tibet and parts of southern and southwestern China, mostly white with black legs and shoulders; giant panda. The panda is related to the raccoon. **2** a slender, reddish-brown mammal somewhat like a raccoon, that lives in the Himalayas; lesser panda. The lesser panda is also related to the raccoon. [origin uncertain; probably < the native name in Nepal]

***panda** definition 1

**panda car,** *British.* a prowl car. [< *panda* (because of the black and white color of the cars)]

**pan|dal** (pan′dəl), *n.* (in India) a shed or arbor constructed for temporary use. [< Tamil *pendal*]

**pan|da|na|ceous** (pan′də nā′shəs), *adj.* belonging to a family of tropical monocotyledonous trees and shrubs, typified by the screw pines. [< New Latin *Pandanaceae* (< Malay *pandan* screw pine) + English *-ous*]

**pan|da|nus** (pan dā′nəs), *n.* any one of a genus of tropical trees and shrubs, especially of the islands of the Malay Archipelago and the Indian and the Pacific oceans; screw pine. A pandanus usually has a palmlike or branched stem, long, narrow leaves, and strong aerial roots that support the stem or the whole plant. Its edible fruit grows into large heads. *There are, for example, the exotic tales of Mr. Maugham, who can deal with blood, thunder, spices and pandanus leaves as well as anybody in the business* (John P. Marquand). [< New Latin *Pandanus* the typical genus < Malay *pandan* screw pine]

**Pan|da|rus** (pan′dər əs), *n.* a Lycian hero, on the Trojan side in the Trojan War, portrayed by Homer as a great archer and valiant soldier. In medieval romance and by Boccaccio, Chaucer, and Shakespeare, he is portrayed as the go-between in the love affair of Troilus and Cressida.

**Pan|de|an** (pan dē′ən), *adj.* of or having to do with the god Pan.

**Pandean pipes,** = Panpipe.

**pan|dect** (pan′dekt), *n.* **1** a complete body or code of laws. **2** a comprehensive digest. **SYN:** compendium. [< *Pandects*]

**Pan|dects** (pan′dekts), *n.pl.* a digest of Roman civil law in 50 books, made by order of Justinian in the 500's, systematizing the decisions and opinions of jurists; Digest. [< Latin *pandectes* < Greek *pandéktēs* encyclopedic book (in plural, the Justinian Code); (literally) all-receiver < *pan-* all + *déchesthai* receive]

**pan|dem|ic** (pan dem′ik), *adj., n.* —*adj.* **1** spread over an entire country or continent, or the whole world. An epidemic disease may be endemic or pandemic. *Two specifically human diseases usually associated with high mortality rates are pandemic influenza and cholera* (Fenner and Day). **2** of or having to do with all living people; general; universal.
—*n.* a pandemic disease: *The most recent great pandemic of bubonic plague in the world began somewhere in China at the end of the last century* (J. L. Cloudsley-Thompson).
[< Greek *pándēmos* pertaining to all the people (< *pan-* all + *dêmos* the populace) + English *-ic*]

**pan|de|mo|ni|ac** (pan′də mō′nē ak), *adj.* of, having to do with, or characteristic of pandemonium.

**pan|de|mon|ic** (pan′də mon′ik), *adj.* = pandemoniac.

**Pan|de|mo|ni|um** (pan′də mō′nē əm), *n.* **1** the abode of all the demons; hell. **2** hell's capital. In Milton's *Paradise Lost,* it is the palace built by Satan as the central part of hell. [< New Latin *Pandemonium* (coined by Milton in *Paradise Lost*) < Greek *pan-* all + *daímōn* demon]

**pan|de|mo|ni|um** (pan′də mō′nē əm), *n.* **1** a place of wild disorder or lawless confusion: *What kind of a pandemonium that vessel was, I cannot describe, but she was commanded by a lunatic, and might be called a floating Bedlam* (Robert Louis Stevenson). **2** wild uproar or lawlessness: *McArdle was the only man there who had not been affected by the pandemonium of the factory* (Harper's).
[< *Pandemonium*]

**pan|der** (pan′dər), *n., v.* —*n.* **1** a person who helps other people indulge low desires, passions, or vices. **2** a man who procures prostitutes for others; male bawd; pimp; procurer. **3** a go-between in illicit amours.
—*v.i.* to act as a pander; supply material or opportunity for vices: *The newspaper pandered to people's liking for sensational stories. In his quest for popular support he panders to the least responsible elements in the community* (London Times).
—*v.t.* to act as a pander to.
[alteration of earlier *pandar* < Middle English *Pandare* Pandarus; influenced by *-er*[1]] —**pan′der|er,** *n.*

**pan|der|ess** (pan′dər is), *n.* a female pander; procuress.

**pan|der|ly** (pan′dər lē), *adj.* of the nature of or suitable for a pander.

**pan|di|a|ton|ic** (pan dī′ə ton′ik), *adj.* completely diatonic.

**pan|dic|u|la|tion** (pan dik′yə lā′shən), *n.* an instinctive stretching, as on awakening from sleep or while yawning. [< French *pandiculation* < Latin *pandiculāri* stretch oneself < *pandere* to stretch]

**pan|dit** (pan′dit, pun′-), *n.* a Hindu scholar or learned man; pundit: *They consulted the family pandit, who ... recited a few mantras and told them not to worry* (Maurice deCunha). [< Hindi *paṇḍit;* see etym. under **pundit**]

**Pan|dit** (pan′dit, pun′-), *n.* a title of respect used in India for a pundit: *Pandit Mountbatten was an unqualified success. The Indians showed their affection for him ... plainly* (New York Times). [see **pandit**]

**P. and L.,** profit and loss.

**pan|door** (pan′dùr), *n.* = pandour.

**pan|do|ra** (pan dôr′ə, -dōr′-), *n.* an old musical instrument resembling a guitar or lute, with three, four, or six strings; bandore. [< Italian *pandora* < Latin *pandūra* < Greek *pandoûrā* three-stringed lute. Compare etym. under **bandore, mandolin.**]

**Pan|do|ra** (pan dôr′ə, -dōr′-), *n. Greek Mythology.* the first woman, created by the gods to punish mankind for having learned the use of fire. Curiosity led her to open a box and thus let out all sorts of ills into the world. Only Hope remained at the bottom. [< Latin *Pandōra* < Greek *Pandôrā* < *pan-* all + *dôra,* plural of *dôron* gift (because of the gifts that the gods gave her at her creation)]

**Pandora's box, 1** *Greek Mythology.* the box containing all human ills. Zeus gave it to Pandora who opened it and let escape all the human ills which mankind now suffers from. **2** *Figurative.* a source of many troubles: *In 1957 the FCC opened up a skimpy slice of wavelengths for what it projected as "Citizens Radio Service". ... In so doing, the FCC also opened a Pandora's box for itself* (Atlantic).

**pan|dore** (pan dôr′, -dōr′), *n.* = bandore.

**pan|dour** (pan′dùr), *n.* **1** one of a force of notoriously brutal and rapacious soldiers organized in Croatia in the 1700's, and later incorporated as a regiment in the Austrian Army. **2** any brutal, plundering soldiers. [< French *pandour* < German *Pandur* < Serbo-Croatian *pàndūr,* earlier *bàndūr* constable, mounted guard, probably < Italian (Venetian) *bandiore* < Medieval Latin *banderius* one who guards; perhaps follower of a *bandum* banner]

**pan|dow|dy** (pan dou′dē), *n., pl.* **-dies.** *U.S.* a deep-dish apple pie or pudding with a crust on top only, often sweetened with brown sugar or molasses. [American English, perhaps related to obsolete dialectal English *pandoulde* custard < *dowl* mix dough in a hurry]

**pan|du|rate** (pan′dyə rāt), *adj.* fiddle-shaped, as a leaf. [< Latin *pandūra* pandora, lute + English *-ate*[1]]

**pan|dy** (pan′dē), *n., pl.* **-dies,** *v.,* **-died, -dy|ing.** *Especially Scottish.* —*n.* a stroke on the extended palm with a rod or leather strap, given as a punishment to schoolboys.
—*v.t.* to inflict a pandy or pandies on, as a punishment.
[supposedly < Latin *pande palmam* hold out

(your) hand (the order preceding punishment); *pande,* imperative of *pandere* extend, *palmam,* accusative of *palma* hand]

**pane** (pān), *n.* **1** a single sheet of glass in a division of a window, a door, or a sash: *Big hailstones and sudden gusts of wind broke several panes of glass.* **2** a panel, as of a wainscot, ceiling, or door. **3** *Philately.* **a** a portion of a full sheet containing a unit of stamps as distributed to post offices. **b** a page from a booklet of stamps as sold by post offices. **4** one of the sides of a nut or of the head of a bolt. **5** one of the sides of the upper surface (table) of a diamond cut as a brilliant. **6** a piece, portion, or side of anything. **7** *Obsolete.* a counterpane. [< Old French *pan* < Latin *pannus* piece of cloth (because, earlier, a window was a hole in a wall, covered by flimsy material)]

**-paned,** *combining form.* having ___ panes: *Diamond-paned = having diamond panes.*

**pan|e|gyr|ic** (pan′ə jir′ik), *n.* **1** a speech or writing in praise of a person or thing; formal eulogy: *I profess to write, not his [Johnson's] panegyric ... but his Life* (James Boswell). **2** enthusiastic or extravagant praise; eulogy. **SYN**: acclaim. [< Latin *panēgyricus* < Greek *panēgyrikós* < *panēgyris* public assembly < *pan-* all + *ágyris* assembly < *ageírein* gather together]

**pan|e|gyr|i|cal** (pan′ə jir′ə kəl), *adj.* of the nature of a panegyric; eulogistic; highly laudatory: *She filled a whole page of her diary with panegyrical regrets* (Lytton Strachey). —**pan′e|gyr′i|cal|ly,** *adv.*

**pan|e|gyr|ist** (pan′ə jir′ist, pan′ə jir′-), *n.* a person who praises enthusiastically or extravagantly; eulogist.

**pan|e|gy|rize** (pan′ə jə rīz), *v.,* **-rized, -riz|ing.** —***v.t.*** = eulogize. —***v.i.*** to compose or utter panegyrics.

**pan|el** (pan′əl), *n., v.,* **-eled, -el|ing** or (*especially British*) **-elled, -el|ling.** —***n.*** **1** a strip or surface that is different in some way from what is around it. A panel is often sunk below or raised above the rest, and used for a decoration. Panels may be in a door or other woodwork, or on large pieces of furniture, or made as parts of a dress. **SYN**: section. **2** a group formed for discussion: *A panel of experts gave its opinion on ways to solve the traffic problem.* **3a** a list of persons called as jurors. **b** the members of a jury. **4a** one section of a switchboard. **b** the whole, or a section of, an instrument board containing the controls and indicators used in operating an automobile, aircraft, computer, or other mechanism. **5** = panel truck. **6a** a picture, photograph, or design much longer than wide. **b** the frame of a cartoon or one of the frames of a comic strip. **7a** a thin wooden board used as a surface for oil painting, sometimes made of several pieces fastened together. **b** a painting on such a board. **8** the space in a framework between two posts or struts, such as the space in a fence or rail between two posts. **9** the space between raised bands on the back of a book. **10** a compartment or division of a coal mine separated from the rest by thick masses of coal. **11** a rectangular section of the hull of a rigid airship between two transverse and two longitudinal girders in the frame. **12** a list of physicians in Great Britain available for the treatment of persons paying for health insurance. **13a** a pad or cushion used as a saddle. **b** the pad or stuffed lining of a saddle.
—***v.t.*** **1** to furnish or decorate with panels; arrange in panels: *The walls of the dining room were paneled halfway to the ceiling with oak.* **2** to fit or place as a panel in its frame. **3** to list for jury duty; select (a jury).
[< Old French *panel* piece < Vulgar Latin *pannellus* (diminutive) < Latin *pannus* piece of cloth. Compare etym. under **pane.**]

**pan|el|beat|er** (pan′əl bē′tər), *n. Especially British.* a person who hammers metal panels into shape or does bodywork.

**pan|el|board** (pan′əl bôrd′, -bōrd′), *n.* **1** a metal box attached to or set in a wall and containing switches, fuses, and sometimes circuit breakers for a number of electric circuits: *Wilson produces power and lighting distribution panelboards* (Wall Street Journal). **2** a heavy, hard fiberboard used especially in making luggage and parts of vehicles: *Hardboard is made by tearing pieces of wood into its basic fibres, then compressing them into panelboards* (Wall Street Journal).

**panel discussion,** the discussion of a particular issue by a selected group of people, usually before an audience: *A panel discussion on "Radiotelescopes, present and future" will be a feature of the program* (Science).

**panel heating,** = radiant heating.

**pan|el|ing** (pan′ə ling), *n.* **1** panels collectively. **2** the material, such as milled lumber, used for panels.

**pan|el|ist** (pan′ə list), *n.* **1** a person who takes part in a panel discussion: *Many of the panelists, however, volunteered their own ideas on what to do about the farm problem* (Wall Street Journal). **2** a member of a panel on a television panel show: *Panelists on "Face the Nation" need not be recognized by the moderator before they put their queries* (Newsweek).

**pan|el|ling** (pan′ə ling), *n. Especially British.* paneling.

**panel show,** a television show featuring a group of people, usually celebrities, who take part in a quiz, game, or discussion: *For some, the panel show, in which premeditated questions must be answered spontaneously, is a stiffer test than a prepared speech* (John Lardner).

**panel truck,** a small, fully enclosed truck, used especially for delivering and by servicemen, such as plumbers and electricians.

**pan|en|do|scope** (pan en′də skōp), *n.* a cystoscope which gives a wide view of the urinary bladder. [< *pan-* + *endoscope*]

**pan|e|tel|a** or **pan|e|tel|la** (pan′ə tel′ə), *n.* a long, slender cigar pointed at the closed end. Also, **panatela.** See picture under **cigar.** [American English < Spanish *panetela* long, thin cigar, shaped like a thin loaf of bread < *pan* bread < Latin *pānis*]

**pan|et|to|ne** (pan′ə tō′nē; *Italian* pä′net tô′ne), *n., pl.* **-ni** (-nē). a Milanese holiday cake made with raisins, candied fruit peels, and almonds. [< Italian *panettone* < *panetto* small loaf < *pane* bread < Latin *pānis*]

**Pan-Eu|ro|pe|an** (pan′yůr ə pē′ən), *adj.* of or having to do with the political union of all Europeans or European countries.

**Pan-Eu|ro|pe|an|ism** (pan′yůr ə pē′ə niz əm), *n.* the concept of a political union of all Europeans or European countries.

**pan fish, 1** an edible fish of a size that permits frying whole, such as a perch or sunfish. **2** = king crab.

**pan|ful** (pan′fůl), *n., pl.* **-fuls.** a quantity sufficient to fill a pan.

**pang** (pang), *n., v.* —***n.*** **1** a sudden, short, sharp pain: *the pangs of a toothache.* **SYN**: throe. **2** *Figurative.* a sudden feeling: *A pang of pity moved her heart.*
—***v.t.*** to cause to suffer pangs.
[origin uncertain]

**pan|ga** (päng′gə), *n.* a long, broad-bladed, and sometimes hooked knife resembling a machete, used in Africa. [< a native name]

**Pan|gae|a** (pan jē′ə), *n.* a hypothetical continent that included all the land masses of the earth before the Triassic period, when continental drift began with the breaking away of the northern group (Laurasia) from the southern group (Gondwana). [(coined in the 1920's by Alfred L. Wegener, a German geologist) < Greek *pan-* all + *gaîa* land]

**Pan|gae|an** (pan jē′ən), *adj.* of or having to do with Pangaea.

**pan|gen** (pan′jen), *n. Biology.* one of the hypothetical primary constituent units of germ plasm. [< *pan-* + *-gen*]

**pan|gen|e|sis** (pan jen′ə sis), *n.* the theory, now discredited, advanced by Charles Darwin to explain the phenomena of heredity, that every separate unit or cell of an organism reproduces itself by contributing its share to the germ or bud of the offspring. [< *pan-* + *genesis*]

**pan|ge|net|ic** (pan′jə net′ik), *adj.* of or having to do with pangenesis.

**Pan-Ger|man** (pan jėr′mən), *adj., n.* —***adj.*** having to do with all Germans or Pan-Germanism.
—***n.*** an advocate of Pan-Germanism.

**Pan-Ger|man|ic** (pan′jėr man′ik), *adj.* = Pan-German.

**Pan-Ger|man|ism** (pan jėr′mə niz əm), *n.* **1** the idea or principle of a political or cultural union of all German peoples. **2** belief in or support of this principle.

**Pan|glos|si|an** (pan glos′ē ən), *adj., n.* —***adj.*** characteristic of Doctor Pangloss, a philosopher in Voltaire's satire *Candide,* who maintained that everything is for the best in this best of possible worlds; given to stubborn and undue optimism: *This is not an area in which Panglossian complacency should flourish amid a general hum of self-approval* (London Times).
—***n.*** a person given to undue optimism: *The Panglossians ... point out that three of the four U.S. recessions since World War II were due to special causes* (Time).

**pan|go|lin** (pang gō′lən), *n.* any one of a genus of scaly, toothless mammals of tropical Asia and Africa that roll themselves into a ball when in danger; scaly anteater. [apparently < Malay *pĕng-giling* roller on which tiller-ropes of Malay boats turn, perhaps < *pĕng-* one who + *giling* to roll (because the animal rolls up into a ball when attacked)]

**pan|gram** (pan′gram), *n.* a sentence made up to include all the letters of the alphabet. [< *pan-* + *-gram* letter, as in *anagram*]

**pan|gram|mat|ic** (pan′grə mat′ik), *adj.* of or having to do with a pangram.

***pan|han|dle**[1] (pan′han′dəl), *n.* **1** the handle of a pan. **2** a narrow strip of land projecting like a handle, such as a state or territory extending between two others: *the Texas panhandle.* [< *pan* dish for cooking + *handle*]

***panhandle**[1] definition 2

**pan|han|dle**[2] (pan′han′dəl), *v.i., v.t.,* **-dled, -dling.** *Informal.* to beg, especially in the streets: *He prides himself on the fact that he has never panhandled, never visited a soup kitchen, or taken a night's lodging in one of the various hostels maintained by charitable agencies in the city* (Harper's). [American English, probably back formation < *panhandler* < *pan* receptacle used for collecting money + *handler*]

**pan|han|dler** (pan′han′dlər), *n.* a person who begs, especially in the streets: *A panhandler approached them, and Tony gave him a dollar* (New Yorker).

**Pan|hel|len|ic** or **pan|hel|len|ic** (pan′hə len′ik), *adj.* **1** of or having to do with all Greek people or all Greece. **2** of or having to do with all college fraternities and sororities.

**Pan|hel|len|ism** (pan hel′ə niz əm), *n.* **1** the idea or principle of a political union of all Greeks. **2** belief in or support of this principle. —**Pan|hel′len|ist,** *n.*

**pan|hu|man** (pan hyü′mən), *adj.* affecting all human beings: ... *malnutrition can also be regarded as a panhuman genetic defect* (Joshua Lederberg).

**pan|ic**[1] (pan′ik), *n., adj., v.,* **-icked, -ick|ing.** —***n.*** **1** a fear affecting an individual or spreading through a whole group of persons or animals so that they lose control of themselves; unreasoning fear: *When the theater caught fire there was panic in the audience.* **2** an outbreak of widespread alarm, as in a community, over financial or commercial matters, which tends to demoralize judgment and lead to hasty, ill-advised measures to avoid loss: *When four banks failed in one day, there was a panic among businessmen.* **3** *Slang.* a very amusing person or thing: *His costume is a panic.*
—***adj.*** caused by panic; showing panic; unreasoning: *panic terror, panic fear.* **SYN**: panicky, frantic.
—***v.i.*** to be affected with panic: *The audience panicked when fire broke out in the theater.*
—***v.t.*** **1** to affect with panic: *Orson Welles, who panicked his fellow Americans with the great Martian invasion broadcast in 1938, has returned to his native heath for good, after nearly ten years abroad* (Newsweek). **2** *Slang.* to make (an audience) laugh; amuse greatly: *His jokes simply panic me.*
[< Middle French *panique* < Greek *Pānikós* of Pan (because he was said to cause contagious fear in herds and crowds)]

**pan|ic**[2] (pan′ik), *n.* **1** foxtail millet, cultivated in southern Europe for its edible grain. **2** = panic grass. [< Latin *pānīcum* foxtail millet < *pānus* ear of millet; (originally) thread. Compare etym. under **panicle.**]

**Pan|ic** (pan′ik), *adj.* of or having to do with Pan or the terror supposed to be caused by him.

**panic button,** *U.S. Informal.* a control button or switch, as in an aircraft, for use in an emergency: *They are not in real danger and can push the panic button and halt the experiment if they really need to* (New York Times).
**hit the panic button** (or **switch**), *Slang.* to become prematurely or overly excited in the face of a supposed emergency: *Pull yourself together; there's no need to hit the panic button.*

**pan ice,** *Geology.* blocks or pieces of ice formed

along the shore, and afterwards loosened and driven by winds or currents.

**panic grass**, **1** any of a group of grasses, many species of which produce edible grain. **2** the grain of any such grass.

**pan|ick|y** (pan′ə kē), *adj.*, **-ick|i|er, -ick|i|est.** **1** caused by panic: *panicky haste.* **2** showing panic: *panicky actions.* **3** like panic: *panicky feelings.* **4** liable to lose self-control and have a panic: *a panicky market.*

***pan|i|cle** (pan′ə kəl), *n. Botany.* **1** a loose, diversely branching flower cluster. A panicle is produced when a raceme becomes irregularly compound and is one kind of indeterminate inflorescence: *a panicle of oats.* **2** any loose, diversely branching cluster in which the flowers are borne on pedicels. [< Latin *pānicula* (diminutive) < *pānus* a swelling; thread wound on a bobbin; ear of millet]

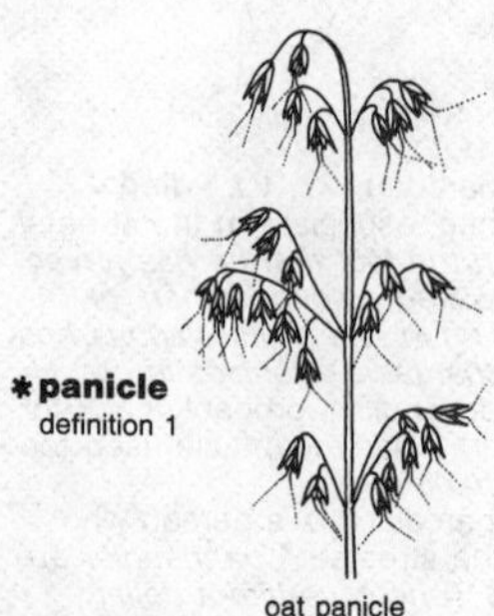

***panicle**
definition 1

oat panicle

**pan|i|cled** (pan′ə kəld), *adj.* having or forming panicles.

**pan|ic-strick|en** (pan′ik strik′ən), *adj.* frightened out of one's wits; demoralized by fear: *The Moors, confused and ... panic-stricken, vainly seek to escape* (Robert Southey). *Owen and I looked at one another in panic-stricken silence* (W. Wilkie Collins).

**pan|ic-struck** (pan′ik struk′), *adj.* = panic-stricken.

**pa-nic|u|late** (pə nik′yə lāt, -lit), *adj. Botany.* growing in a panicle; arranged in panicles. [< Latin *pānicula* panicle + English *-ate*[1]] —**pa|nic′u|late′ly**, *adv.*

**pa|nic|u|lat|ed** (pə nik′yə lā′tid), *adj.* = paniculate.

**pan|i|er** (pan′ē ər), *n.* = pannier.

**pa|ni|o|lo** (pä′nē ō′lō), *n., pl.* **-los.** (in Hawaii) a cowboy: *The saddle base is patterned after those brought to Hawaii by the paniolos, originally Mexican vaqueros who taught Hawaiians to ride, rope, and work with leather* (New York Times). [< Hawaiian *paniolo* < Spanish *español* Spaniard]

**Pan-I|ran|ist** (pan′i ran′ist, -ī-), *n., adj.* —*n.* an advocate or supporter of the political union of all Iranians, especially the union of Bahrain with Iran.
—*adj.* of or having to do with the Pan-Iranists or their policies: *the Pan-Iranist Party.*

**Pan-Is|lam|ic** (pan′is lam′ik, -lä′mik), *adj.* having to do with all Islam or with a union of all Moslem nations.

**Pan-Is|lam|ism** (pan is′lə miz əm), *n.* **1** the idea or principle of a political union of all Moslem states. **2** belief in or support of this principle.

**Pan|ja|bi** (pun jä′bē), *n., pl.* **-bis. 1** = Punjabi. **2** an Indic language of the Punjab, a region in northwestern India, related to Hindi; Punjabi.

**pan|jan|drum** (pan jan′drəm), *n.* **1** a mock title for an imaginary personage of great power or importance: *So he died and she very imprudently married the barber and there were present the Picninnies, and the Joblillies ... and the grand Panjandrum himself with the little round button at top* (Samuel Foote). **2** any pretentious personage or official: *There is not space here to describe methods by which the budget officer has become the grand panjandrum of public administration* (New York Times). [(coined by Samuel Foote, 1720-1777, an English dramatist) probably < Greek *pan-* all + *-jandrum,* a pseudo-Latin ending]

**pan|leu|co|pe|ni|a** (pan lü′kə pē′nē ə), *n.* = feline enteritis. [< *pan-* + *leucopenia*]

**pan|mix|i|a** (pan mik′sē ə), *n.* indiscriminate crossing of breeds without selection. [< New Latin *panmixia* < Greek *pan-* all + *mîxis* a mixing]

**pan|nage** (pan′ij), *n.* **1** the act of feeding of swine in a forest or wood: *... herding swine in the forests, in the time of pannage, when acorns and beechmast were on the floor* (Punch). **2** the right of pasturing swine in a forest. **3** the payment made to the owner of the forest for this right. [< Old French *panage, pasnage* < Medieval Latin *pasnaticum,* ultimately < Latin *pāscere* to feed]

**panne** (pan), *n.* a soft, highly lustrous cloth with a long nap, resembling velvet: *We see her in a dress of grey panne* (Westminster Gazette). [< French *panne* downy fabric, fur; Old French, feather, down < Latin *penna* feather]

***pan|ni|er** (pan′ē ər), *n.* **1** a basket, especially one of a pair of considerable size to be slung across the shoulders or across the back of a beast of burden: *panniers slung on sturdy horses* (Wordsworth). **2** a frame formerly used for stretching out the skirt of a woman's dress at the hips. **3** a puffed drapery about the hips on a woman's skirt. Also, **panier.** [< Old French *panier* < Latin *pānārium* bread basket < *pānis* bread]

***pannier**
definitions 1, 3

definition 1 definition 3

**pan|ni|ered** (pan′ē ərd), *adj.* having, or laden with, a pannier or panniers: *panniered skirts.*

**pan|ni|kin** (pan′ə kin), *n.* **1** a small pan. **2** a metal cup or mug, usually shallow.

**pan|ning** (pan′ing), *n. Slang.* a severe criticism or reprimand: *They were afraid the film would get the same sort of panning as "Peeping Tom" got* (Punch).

**pan|nose** (pan′ōs), *adj. Botany.* having the appearance or texture of felt or woolen cloth. —**pan′nose|ly**, *adv.*

**Pa|no** (pä′nō), *n., pl.* **-nos** or **-no.** a member of a group of South American Indian tribes occupying the forest regions of Peru, Bolivia, and Brazil.

**Pa|no|an** (pä nō′ən, pä′nə wən), *adj., n.* —*adj.* of or having to do with the Panos or their languages.
—*n.* the languages of the Panos, constituting a family.

**pa|no|cha** (pə nō′chə), *n.* **1** a coarse grade of dark sugar made in Mexico. **2** candy made from brown sugar, butter, milk, and nuts. Also, **penuche, penuchi.** [American English < Mexican Spanish *panocha* < Latin *pānucula,* and *pānicula* panicle]

**pa|no|che** (pə nō′chē), *n.* = panocha.

**pan|o|plied** (pan′ə plid), *adj.* completely armed, equipped, covered, or arrayed: *The large Stratford company manage swordplay and panoplied pageantry with great facility* (Newsweek).

**pan|o|ply** (pan′ə plē), *n., pl.* **-plies,** *v.,* **-plied, -plying.** —*n.* **1** a complete suit of armor: *In arms they stood Of golden panoply, refulgent host* (Milton). **2** *Figurative.* **a** complete equipment or covering: *an Indian in panoply of paint and feathers. The panoply swells with new weapons which complement the old* (Bulletin of Atomic Scientists). **b** any splendid array: *That night, the Faery, usually so homely in her attire, appeared in a glittering panoply of enormous uncut jewels* (Lytton Strachey).
—*v.t.* to furnish with a panoply: (*Figurative.*) *A rhymed commentary panoplied by snatches or entire choruses of some thirty Irving Berlin songs* (New Yorker).
[< Greek *panopliā* the full armor of a hoplite < *pan-* all + *hópla* arms, neuter plural of *hóplon* tool, implement]

**pan|op|tic** (pan op′tik), *adj.* commanding a full view; seeing everything at once: *... his panoptic survey of the American scene called "America as a Civilization"* (Atlantic).

**pan|o|ram|a** (pan′ə ram′ə, -rä′mə), *n.* **1** a wide, unbroken view of a surrounding region: *a panorama of beach and sea. At Rio de Janeiro, Sugar Loaf* [*Mountain*] *is the centerpiece of a breathtaking panorama* (Newsweek). **SYN:** prospect. **2** *Figurative.* a complete survey of some subject: *a panorama of history.* **3a** a picture of a landscape or other scene, often shown as if seen from a central point. **b** such a picture unrolled a part at a time and made to pass continuously before the spectators. **4** *Figurative.* a continuously passing or changing scene: *the panorama of city life.* [< *pan-* + Greek *hórāma* a view < *horân* to see]

**pan|o|ram|ic** (pan′ə ram′ik, -rä′mik), *adj.* of or like a panorama: *a panoramic view.* —**pan′o|ram′i|cal|ly**, *adv.*

**panoramic camera**, any one of various forms of photographic camera for taking panoramic views, especially such a camera fitted with a wide-angle lens.

**panoramic sight**, a periscopic gunsight, usually fitted with a telescopic lens, by which a wide view can be obtained and which may be manipulated to sight in any direction.

**pan|o|ram|ist** (pan′ə ram′ist, -rä′mist), *n.* a painter of panoramas.

**pa|nou|chi** (pə nü′chē), *n.* = panocha.

**Pan|pipe** or **pan|pipe** (pan′pīp′), *n.* an early musical instrument made of reeds or tubes of different lengths, fastened together side by side, in order of their length. The reeds or tubes were closed at one end, and the player blew across their open tops. [< *Pan* + *pipe* (because he played such an instrument)]

**pan|psy|chism** (pan sī′kiz əm), *n.* the doctrine that the entire universe, or any least particle of it, has a psychic or mental as well as physical side or aspect. [< *pan-* + Greek *psȳchê* soul, mind + English *-ism*]

**pan|psy|chist** (pan sī′kist), *n.* a believer in panpsychism.

**pan|sex|u|al** (pan sek′shü əl), *adj.* of or having to do with pansexualism.

**pan|sex|u|al|ism** (pan sek′shü ə liz′əm), *n.* the view that the sexual instinct plays a role in all human thought and activity.

**pan|sex|u|al|i|ty** (pan sek′shü al′ə tē), *n.* = pansexualism.

**Pan-Slav** (pan släv′, -slav′), *adj.* **1** of or having to do with all the Slavic races. **2** of or having to do with Pan-Slavism.

**Pan-Slav|ic** (pan slä′vik, -slav′ik), *adj.* = Pan-Slav.

**Pan-Slav|ism** (pan′slä′viz əm, -slav′iz-), *n.* **1** the idea or principle of a political union of all Slavic peoples. **2** belief in or support of this principle.

**Pan-Slav|ist** (pan slä′vist, -slav′ist), *n.* an adherent or promoter of Pan-Slavism.

**pan|soph|ic** (pan sof′ik), *adj.* **1** having or pretending to have universal knowledge. **2** relating to universal wisdom or knowledge.

**pan|soph|i|cal** (pan sof′ə kəl), *adj.* = pansophic.

**pan|so|phism** (pan′sə fiz əm), *n.* the professed possession of universal knowledge.

**pan|so|phist** (pan′sə fist), *n.* a claimant or pretender to universal knowledge.

**pan|so|phy** (pan′sə fē), *n.* **1** universal knowledge; all-embracing wisdom. **2** the claim or pretension to universal knowledge. [< New Latin *pansophia* < Greek *pánsophos* < *pan-* all + *sophós* clever, wise]

**pan|sper|ma|tism** (pan spėr′mə tiz əm), *n.* the doctrine that the atmosphere is full of invisible germs ready for development under favorable conditions. [< *pan-* + Greek *spérma, -atos* seed + English *-ism*]

**pan|sper|mi|a** (pan spėr′mē ə), *n.* = panspermatism. [< New Latin *panspermia*]

**pan|sper|my** (pan spėr′mē), *n.* = panspermatism. [< New Latin *panspermia*]

**Pan's pipes**, = Panpipe.

**pan|sy** (pan′zē), *n., pl.* **-sies,** *adj.* —*n.* **1a** a flower somewhat like a violet but much larger and having flat, velvety petals, usually of several colors; heartsease. **b** the plant it grows on. **2** *Slang, used in an unfriendly way.* **a** a homosexual man or boy. **b** an effeminate man or boy.
—*adj. Slang.* **1** homosexual. **2** effeminate: *The Egyptians do not need these fine varieties of ... cotton for themselves. The fellas ... don't wear such pansy varieties* (Punch).
[earlier, *pensy,* and *pensee* < French *pensée* pansy; (literally) thought < Old French *penser* to think; see etym. under **pensive**]

**pant**[1] (pant), *v., n.* —*v.i.* **1** to breathe hard and quickly, as one does when out of breath: *to pant from the long, steep climb. He is panting from playing tennis.* **SYN:** gasp, puff. **2** to speak with short, quick breaths: *He panted excitedly giving us the news as he had just heard it.* **3** *Figurative.* to long eagerly; yearn: *Readers ... were panting to hear more about him* (Punch). **4** (of the heart or breast) to throb violently; palpitate; pulsate; beat. **5** to emit steam or the like in loud puffs: *ships moving, tugs panting, hawsers taut* (H. G. Wells).
—*v.t.* to breathe or utter gaspingly: *"Come quick. Come quick," he panted. He has come, I panted* (Robert Louis Stevenson).
—*n.* **1** a short, quick breath; catching of the breath; gasp: *He heard the pants of the wolf running close behind him.* **2** a puff or cough of an engine. **3** a throb or heave of the breast.
[perhaps short for Old French *pantoisier,* or *pantiser,* probably < Vulgar Latin *phantasiāre* be oppressed with a nightmare; < Latin *phantasia.* Compare etym. under **fantasy.**] —**pant′er**, *n.*

**pant**[2] (pant), *n., adj.* —*n.* a pair of pants.
—*adj.* of or belonging to pants: *pant cuffs, pant legs.*

**Pan|tag|ru|el** (pan tag′rü el; *French* päɴ tȧ grү-el′), *n.* (in Rabelais' *Gargantua and Pantagruel*) the last of the giants, son of Gargantua, represented as a coarse and extravagant humorist, dealing satirically with serious subjects.

**Pan|ta|gru|el|i|an** (pan′tə grü el′ē ən), *adj., n.* —***adj.*** of, having to do with, characteristic of, or appropriate to Pantagruel.
—***n.*** = Pantagruelist.

**Pan|ta|gru|el|ism** (pan′tə grü′ə liz əm, pan tag′-rü-), *n.* Pantagruelian spirit, principles, or practice; coarse humor with satirical intent, often applied to serious subjects.

**Pan|ta|gru|el|ist** (pan′tə grü′ə list, pan tag′rü-), *n.* an imitator, admirer, or student of Pantagruel or Rabelais.

**pan|ta|lets** or **pan|ta|lettes** (pan′tə lets′), *n.pl.* **1** long, loose drawers with a frill or the like at the bottom of each leg, extending to the ankles and showing beneath the skirt, formerly worn by women and girls. **2** a pair of trimmed pieces, frills, or the like for attaching to the legs of drawers.

***pan|ta|loon** (pan′tə lün′), *n.* **1** a clown. **SYN:** buffoon. **2** Also, **Pantaloon. a** a lean and foolish old man wearing spectacles, tight-fitting trousers, and slippers, who is a comic character in old Italian comedies: *the lean and slipper'd pantaloon* (Shakespeare). **b** (in modern pantomime) a foolish old man, the butt and abettor of the clown.
**pantaloons,** *Archaic.* tight-fitting trousers with bands that fastened under the insteps: *Sure to goodness he's wearing rings outside his gloves ... and—poppy red pantaloons* (Doris Leslie).
[< French *pantalon* < Italian *Pantalone,* a character in early Italian comedies who wore tight breeches; (originally) a Venetian < *Pantaleone,* a patron saint of Venice]

***pantaloon**

**pan|ta|looned** (pan′tə lünd′), *adj.* wearing pantaloons.

**pant|dress** (pant′dres′), *n.* a dress with a skirt divided and sewed like trousers; dress with culottes.

**pan|tech|ni|con** (pan tek′nə kon), *n. British.* **1** a moving van. **2** a furniture warehouse. [< name of a building in London, (originally) housing a bazaar of varied craftwork < *pan-* + *technikón,* neuter of Greek *technikós* of the arts < *téchnē* art, skill]

**pan|tel|e|graph** (pan tel′ə graf, -gräf), *n.* an early form of telegraph for transmitting facsimile messages and pictures.

**pan|te|leg|ra|phy** (pan′tə leg′rə fē), *n.* facsimile telegraphy.

**pan|ter|er** (pan′tər ər), *n.* = pantler. [< earlier *panter* (see etym. under **pantler**) + *-er*²]

**Pan|tha|las|sa** (pan′thə las′ə), *n.* the universal ocean surrounding Pangaea. [< *pan-* + Greek *thálassa* sea]

**pan|the|ism** (pan′thē iz əm), *n.* **1** the belief that God and the universe are the same; doctrine that God is an expression of the physical forces of nature: *The author, whose philosophy seems to be a crude but genuinely mystical pantheism, succeeds in communicating the wonder and terror of being alone on a storm-tossed raft in the middle of the world's widest ocean* (New Yorker). **2** the worship of all the gods.

**pan|the|ist** (pan′thē ist), *n.* a believer in pantheism. [< *pan-* + Greek *theós* god + English *-ist*]

**pan|the|is|tic** (pan′thē is′tik), *adj.* of or having to do with pantheists or pantheism. —**pan′the|is′ti|cal|ly,** *adv.*

**pan|the|is|ti|cal** (pan′thē is′tə kəl), *adj.* = pantheistic.

**Pan|the|on** (pan′thē on, pan thē′ən), *n.* **1** a temple for all the gods, built at Rome about 27 B.C. It was rebuilt by Hadrian about A.D. 125 and used as a Christian church between the early 600's and 1885. **2** a building resembling or compared to the Pantheon at Rome, especially a large public building in Paris containing tombs or memorials of famous French people. [< Latin *Pantheon* < Greek *Pántheion* < *pan-* all + *theós* god + *-ion* place for]

**pan|the|on** (pan′thē on, pan thē′ən), *n.* **1** a temple dedicated to all the gods. **2** a public building containing tombs or memorials of the illustrious dead of a nation. **3** all the deities of a people, country, or culture: *the ancient Greek pantheon.* **4** *Figurative.* any group of exalted persons or things: *His disciples have already enshrined "the great helmsman"* [*Mao Tse-tung*] *in much the same way that Lenin lives in the Soviet pantheon* (Seymour Topping). *The teeming pantheon of guided missiles* (Time). [< Pantheon]

**pan|the|on|ic** (pan′thē on′ik), *adj.* of the nature of or resembling a pantheon.

**pan|ther** (pan′thər), *n., pl.* **-thers** or (*collectively*) **-ther. 1** a puma; cougar; mountain lion. **2** a leopard, especially the black leopard. **3** = jaguar. [spelling alteration of Middle English *panter* < Old French *pantere,* learned borrowing from Latin *panthēra* < Greek *pánthēr*] —**pan′ther|like′,** *adj.*

**Pan|ther** (pan′thər), *n.* = Black Panther.

**pan|ther|ess** (pan′thər is), *n.* **1** a female panther. **2** a woman thought of as resembling a female panther in manner or temperament.

**pan|ther|ine** (pan′thər in, -thə rīn), *adj.* **1** like a panther. **2** like that of a panther: *Her pantherine leaps and rapid turns were breathtaking* (New York Times).

**pan|ther|ish** (pan′thər ish), *adj.* **1** like a panther. **2** like that of a panther: *Tosca is a jealous lover, and Callas played the part with pantherish intensity* (Time). —**pan′ther|ish|ly,** *adv.*

**Pan|ther|ism** (pan′thər iz əm), *n.* the beliefs and practices of the Black Panthers.

**pan|tie** (pan′tē), *n., pl.* **-ties.** = panty.

**pan|ti|hose** (pan′tē hōz′), *n.* = pantyhose.

**pan|tile** (pan′tīl′), *n.* **1** a roofing tile made in an S-curve, laid with the concave surface of one overlapped by the concave surface of the next. **2** a roof tile made with a single curve, laid edge to edge with the next, the junction of two edges being covered by another tile laid with its concave side downward.

**pan|tiled** (pan′tīld′), *adj.* covered with pantiles: *... shimmerings of summer sun upon the pantiled roofs* (Elizabeth Nicholas).

**pan|til|ing** (pan′tī′ling), *n.* **1** the covering of a roof with pantiles. **2** pantiles collectively.

**pan|tin** (pan′tin), *n.* a pasteboard doll resembling a jumping jack, popular in France in the 1700's. Pantins were played with by pulling strings to make them dance and act. [< French *pantin* (earlier *pantine*)]

**pan|tine** (pan′tīn), *n.* = pantin.

**pan|ti|soc|ra|cy** (pan′tə sok′rə sē), *n., pl.* **-cies. 1** a scheme of social organization in which all are equal in rank and social position. **2** a utopian community in which all the members are equal and all rule. [< Greek *pant-* all + English *isocracy*]

**pan|ti|so|crat|ic** (pan′tə sō krat′ik), *adj.* having to do with, involving, or upholding pantisocracy.

**pant|ler** (pan′tlər), *n.* (formerly) an officer in a great household who supplied the bread and had charge of the pantry: *A' would have made a good pantler, a' would ha' chipped bread well* (Shakespeare). [alteration of earlier *panter* < Old French *panetier* < Latin *pānis* bread; perhaps influenced by *butler*]

**pan|to** (pan′tō), *n. British Informal.* pantomime.

**Pan|toc|ra|tor** (pan tok′rə tər), *n.* the omnipotent ruler (said of Christ): *The range* [*of artistic themes*] *was later expanded to include Jesus Christ in his role as Pantocrator* (Harper's). [< Greek *pantokrátōr* < *panto-* all + *krátōr* ruler]

**pan|to|fle** or **pan|tof|fle** (pan′tə fəl; pan tof′əl, -tü′fəl), *n.* a slipper: *White pantofles with red heels* (Thackeray). [< Middle French *pantoufle;* origin unknown]

***pantograph**
definition 1

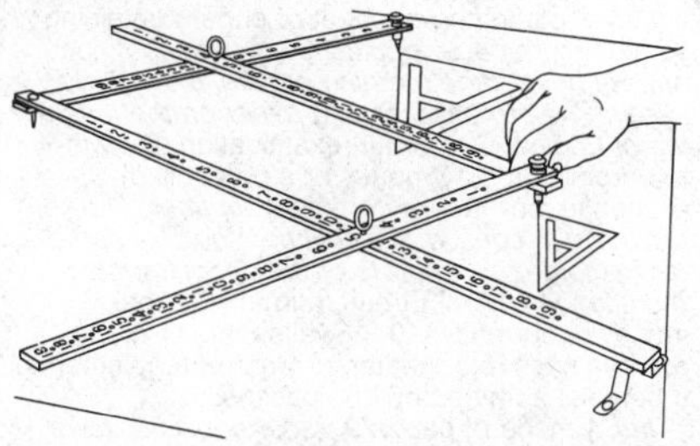

***pan|to|graph** (pan′tə graf, -gräf), *n.* **1** an instrument for the mechanical copying of plans, drawings, etc., on any scale desired. It consists of a framework of slender, jointed metal rods which simultaneously reproduce a line or circle drawn by the operator. **2** an insulated, jointed framework on certain electric locomotives and some other vehicles, for conveying electric current from overhead wires to the motors. [< French *pantographe* < Greek *panto-* all + *graphikē* art of drawing or writing]

**pan|to|graph|ic** (pan′tə graf′ik), *adj.* of, having to do with, or produced by a pantograph. —**pan′to-graph′i|cal|ly,** *adv.*

**pan|tog|ra|phy** (pan tog′rə fē), *n.* **1** a general description; entire view of an object. **2** the process of copying by means of the pantograph.

**pan|tol|o|gist** (pan tol′ə jist), *n.* a person who studies or is versed in universal knowledge.

**pan|tol|o|gy** (pan tol′ə jē), *n.* a systematic view of all branches of human knowledge; universal knowledge. [< Greek *panto-* all + English *-logy*]

**pan|to|mime** (pan′tə mīm), *n., v.,* **-mimed, -miming.** —***n.*** **1** a play without words, in which the actors express themselves by gestures. **2** gestures without words; dumb show: *As ... he could not speak a word of French ... he was obliged to convey this sentiment into pantomime* (Leslie Stephen). **3** a dramatized tale with broad comedy, music, and dancing, common in England during the Christmas season. **4** a mime or mimic, especially in the ancient Roman theater: *In come troops of dancers from Lydia, or pantomimes from Alexandria* (Cardinal Newman).
—***v.t.*** to express by gestures; represent by dumb show: *Thomas pantomimed infinite perplexity* (H. G. Wells).
—***v.i.*** to express oneself by dumb show.
[< Latin *pantomīmus* a mime; also, dancer < Greek *pantómīmos* < *panto-* all + *mîmos* mime, mimic]

**pan|to|mim|ic** (pan′tə mim′ik), *adj.* of, in, or like pantomime: *pantomimic gestures which ... are substituted for intelligible words* (Macaulay). —**pan′to|mim′i|cal|ly,** *adv.*

**pan|to|mim|ist** (pan′tə mī′mist), *n.* **1** an actor in a pantomime. **2** a person who writes or composes pantomimes.

**pan|to|then|ic acid** (pan′tə then′ik), a yellow, oily hydroxy acid, a constituent of the vitamin B complex, which promotes growth, found in plant and animal tissues, especially liver, yeast, bran, and molasses: *The B vitamin they found useful for this detoxifying purpose is pantothenic acid* (Science News Letter). *Formula:* $C_9H_{17}NO_5$ [< Greek *pántothen* from every side (< *panto-* all + *the-,* root of *tithénai* to place, set) + English *-ic*]

**pan|toum** (pan tüm′), *n.* a French and English adaptation of the Malay pantun, consisting of a series of stanzas of four lines rhyming *abab, bcbc, cdcd,* and so forth, the last rhyme being *a.* [< French *pantoum* < Malay *pantun*]

**pan|trop|ic** (pan′trop′ik, -trō′pik), *adj.* drawn to or having an affinity for many kinds of tissues: *a pantropic virus.* [< *pan-* + Greek *tropē* a turning + English *-ic*]

**pan|try** (pan′trē), *n., pl.* **-tries. 1** a small room in which food, dishes, silverware, or table linen are kept: *A pantry adjoins the kitchen.* **SYN:** buttery. **2** = butler's pantry. [Middle English *panetrie* < Anglo-French *panetrie,* variant of Old French *paneterie* bread room < Medieval Latin *panetaria* < Latin *pānis* bread]

**pan|try|man** (pan′trē mən), *n., pl.* **-men.** a man employed in a pantry.

**pants** (pants), *n.pl.* **1** trousers: *He tore his pants putting his hands in his pockets all the time. I let him have a charge of No. 5 shot in the seat of the pants* (Geoffrey Household). **2** drawers, especially women's; underpants.
**beat the pants off,** *Slang.* to beat soundly or completely: *All told, the BBC beat the pants off ITV* (Sunday Times).
**bore the pants off,** *Slang.* to bore completely: [*He*] *is oblivious to the comedy of the situation, to the element of farce in the picture of Her Majesty boring the pants off himself and his fellow-guests* (Listener).
**catch with one's pants down,** *Slang.* to catch off one's guard or unprepared: *We have realigned our whole sales operations toward the German civilian market so as not to be caught with our pants down in the event of a military pullout* (Wall Street Journal).
**scare the pants off,** to scare thoroughly: *In the case of the Angry Brigade, whose real aims are undeclared* (*unless it is to scare the pants off authority*), *I can appreciate why they reject the ballot box* (Manchester Guardian Weekly).
**wear the pants,** *Slang.* to play the dominant or masculine role: *Over 90% of the West's nuclear power will remain in American hands, anyway. "Uncle Sam will still wear the pants," stresses a high official* (William Beecher).

---

**Pronunciation Key:** hat, āge, cãre, fär; let, ēqual, tėrm; it, īce; hot, ōpen, ôrder; **oi**l, **ou**t; cup, pu̇t, rüle; **ch**ild; lo**ng**; **th**in; **ᴛʜ**en; **zh,** measure; ə represents **a** in about, **e** in taken, **i** in pencil, **o** in lemon, **u** in circus.

[American English, short for *pantaloons*]
▶**Pants, trousers**. In formal usage the word for men's breeches is *trousers;* on other levels the word is *pants.*

**pant|shoes** (pant′shüz′), *n.pl.* shoes designed to be worn with flaring or bell-bottomed trousers.

**pant|skirt** (pant′skėrt′), *n.* a divided skirt resembling trousers; culottes.

**pants suit**, a woman's or girl's suit consisting of matching jacket and trousers.

**pant|suit** (pant′süt′), *n.* = pants suit.

**pan|tun** (pan tün′), *n.* a Malay verse form, usually of four lines in which the first and third, and the second and fourth, rhyme. [< Malay *pantun*]

**pan|ty** (pan′tē), *n., pl.* **-ties**. Usually, **panties**. a kind of undergarment with short legs, worn by women and children. It fits around the waist and the lower torso. Also, **pantie**.

**panty girdle**, a girdle with short legs, worn as a panty: *If worn tightly, the doctors say, panty girdles . . . may act like tourniquets* (Time).

**pan|ty|hose** (pan′tē hōz′), *n.,* or **panty hose**, an undergarment that combines panty and hose. Also, **pantihose**.

**panty raid**, *U.S.* a raid made as a prank by male college students on a women's dormitory to steal their undergarments.

**pan|ty|waist** (pan′tē wāst′), *n., adj.* **—*n.*** **1** an undergarment in two pieces with short pants buttoning to the shirt at the waist, worn especially by children. **2** *U.S. Slang.* a somewhat effeminate man or boy; sissy: *That pantywaist . . . doesn't even like beer* (Time).
—***adj.*** *U.S. Slang.* of, having to do with, or like a somewhat effeminate man or boy.

**pa|nung** (pä′nung), *n.* a piece of colorful cloth worn like a sarong by men and women in Thailand. [< Thai *panung*]

**Pan|urge** (pan′ėrj; *French* pá nyrzh′), *n.* (in Rabelais' *Gargantua and Pantagruel*) a clever, likeable rogue, boon companion of Pantagruel.

**pan|zer** or **Pan|zer** (pan′zər; *German* pän′tsər), *adj., n.* **—*adj.*** armored, or mechanized and armored. A panzer division consists largely of tanks.
—***n.*** a mechanized and armored force: *On May 26, 1940, Gort's army was in full retreat from Hitler's Panzers toward the Channel ports* (Time).
[< German *Panzer* tank, (literally) armor < Italian *panciera* < *pancia* belly < Latin *pantex*]

**pap¹** (pap), *n., v.,* **papped, pap|ping.** **—*n.*** **1** very soft food for infants or invalids. **2** money or other favors from a government official; political patronage. **3** *Figurative.* ideas or facts watered down to a characterless consistency to make them palatable, considered as innocuous and as unsuitable for adults as baby food: *He loathed the pseudoscientific pap which is fed to judges in patent cases and never concocted any of it himself* (Harper's).
—***v.t.*** to feed with pap.
[compare Low German, Middle German *pappe*]

**pap²** (pap), *n. Dialect.* **1** a teat or nipple. **2** something resembling a teat or nipple in form. [Middle English *pappe,* probably < Scandinavian (compare Swedish *pappe*)]

**pa|pa¹** (pä′pə, pə pä′), *n.* father; daddy. [< French *papa* < Late Latin *pāpa*]

**pa|pa²** (pä′pä), *n.* **1** *Greek Orthodox Church.* **a** a parish priest. **b** the patriarch of Alexandria. **2** *Rare.* a pope. [< Medieval Latin *papa* pope < Late Latin *pāpa* bishop; (originally) father]

**Pa|pa** (pä′pə), *n. U.S.* a code name for the letter *p,* used in transmitting radio messages.

**pa|pa|bi|le** (pä pä′bē lā), *adj., n., pl.* **-li** (-lē). *Italian.* **—*adj.*** of papal quality or caliber; capable of being elected pope: *The cardinals who are "papabile" . . . are well known to the other cardinals* (Xavier Rynne).
—***n.*** a cardinal regarded as a possible successor to a pope.

**pa|pa|cy** (pā′pə sē), *n., pl.* **-cies**. **1** the position, rank, or authority of a pope. **2** the time during which a pope rules. **3** all the popes. **4** government by a pope. [< Medieval Latin *papatia,* alteration of *papatus* < Late Latin *pāpa* pope]

**Pa|pa|ga|yo** (pä′pə gī′ō), *n., pl.* **-yos**. a violent northeast wind with tornadic whirls that descends during October to May from the mountains into the Gulf of Papagayo, at the northwest corner of Costa Rica and the southwest corner of Nicaragua.

**Pa|pa|go** (pä′pə gō), *n., pl.* **-gos** or **-go**. **1** a member of an American Indian people of southwestern North America. **2** the Piman language of this people.

**pa|pa|in** (pə pā′ən, -pī′ən), *n.* **1** a proteolytic enzyme obtained from the half-ripe fruit of the papaya, resembling both pepsin and trypsin in its action. **2** a preparation of this in the form of a grayish powder, used medicinally to assist digestion.

**pa|pal** (pā′pəl), *adj.* **1** of or having to do with a pope: *a papal letter.* SYN: pontifical. **2** of the papacy. **3** of the Roman Catholic Church: *papal ritual.* [< Medieval Latin *papalis* < Late Latin *pāpa* pope] —**pa′pal|ly**, *adv.*

**papal bull**, a formal announcement or official order from a pope.

**papal cross**, a cross with three transoms; triple cross. See diagram under **cross**.

**papal crown**, = tiara.

**papal infallibility**, the Roman Catholic doctrine, proclaimed by the first Vatican Council in 1870, that the Pope can commit no error when he speaks as the head of the church to define, in matters of faith and morals, what is to be accepted by all Roman Catholics as the teaching laid down by Jesus Christ and the Apostles.

**pa|pal|ism** (pā′pə liz əm), *n.* the papal system.

**pa|pal|ist** (pā′pə list), *n.* an adherent of the papal system or the papacy.

**pa|pal|ize** (pā′pə līz), *v.i., v.t.,* **-ized, -iz|ing**. to become or make papal.

**Pa|pa|ni|co|laou test** or **smear** (pä′pə nē′kə-lou, pap′ə nik′ə-), = Pap test.

**pa|pa|raz|zo** (pä′pə rät′sō), *n., pl.* **-zi** (-sē). *Italian.* an aggressive photographer or reporter who pursues celebrities wherever they go: *In Italy . . . actors and actresses are woefully harassed by paparazzi everywhere from Via Veneto to Fiumicino airport* (Saturday Review).

**pa|pas** (pä′päs), *n.* a parish priest of the Greek Church; papa: *The papas is a prominent figure . . . because of his long black gown, his tall steeple hat* (Scribner's Magazine). [< Greek *pápas* father]

**pa|pav|er|a|ceous** (pə pav′ə rā′shəs), *adj.* belonging to the poppy family of plants. [< New Latin *Papaveraceae* the family name (< Latin *papāver* poppy) + English *-ous*]

**pa|pav|er|in** (pə pav′ər in, -pā′vər-), *n.* = papaverine.

**pa|pav|er|ine** (pə pav′ə rēn, -ər in; -pā′və rēn, -vər in), *n.* a crystalline alkaloid obtained from opium or made synthetically, used especially in its hydrochloride form. *Formula:* $C_{20}H_{21}NO_4$ [< Latin *papāver* poppy + English *-ine²*]

**papaverine hydrochloride**, a white, slightly bitter powder, a non-habit-forming narcotic, used to relax smooth muscles. *Formula:* $C_{20}H_{21}NO_4 \cdot HCl$

**pa|paw** (pô′pô), *n.* **1** a small North American tree having oblong, yellowish fruit with many beanlike seeds; fetid shrub. It belongs to the custard apple family. **2** its fruit, which is good to eat. **3** = papaya. Also, **pawpaw**. [American English, apparently the same word as *papaya*]

**pa|pa|ya** (pə pī′ə, -pä′yə), *n.* **1** a tropical American tree that looks like a palm tree with a tuft of large leaves at the top and a fruit with yellowish pulp that looks like a melon. **2** its fruit, which is good to eat. Also, **pawpaw**. [< Spanish *papaya,* probably < Arawak (West Indies) *papaya*]

**pap|a|ya|ceous** (pap′ə yā′shəs), *adj.* belonging to the family of tropical and subtropical trees typified by the papaya.

**pap boat**, a boat-shaped, shallow vessel for holding pap to feed infants and invalids: *Still with this infant* (*or another*) *in mind, you might have a look at half dozen or so eighteenth-century pap boats* (New Yorker).

**pa|per** (pā′pər), *n., adj., v.* **—*n.*** **1a** a material used for writing, printing, drawing, wrapping packages, and covering walls. Paper is made in thin sheets from wood pulp, rags, or straw. **b** a material like paper, such as papyrus. **c** a material made from paper pulp, such as papier-mâché. **2** a piece or sheet of paper: *his mind was in its original state of white paper* (Charles Lamb). **3** a piece or sheet of paper with writing or printing on it; document: *Important papers were stolen.* **4** a wrapper, container, or sheet of paper containing something: *a paper of pins.* **5** a newspaper; journal: *He bought the morning papers.* **6** an article; essay: *The professor read a paper on the teaching of English.* **7** a written examination. **8** a written promise to pay money or a note, bill of exchange, or the like: *commercial paper. The rapid rise in consumer installment debt— particularly auto paper— is one of the danger spots in the economy* (Wall Street Journal). **9** paper money or currency. **10** = wallpaper. **11** *Slang.* **a** a free pass to a theater or other entertainment. **b** persons admitted by free passes.
—***adj.*** **1** made of paper: *a paper napkin or towel.* **2** *Figurative.* like paper; thin or flimsy: *almonds with paper shells, paper walls.* SYN: frail. **3** existing only on paper; planned but not carried out: *a paper blockade. The Western allies are not concerned with any paper arrangement the Soviets may wish to make with a regime of their own creation* (John F. Kennedy). *The proposed . . . Oroville Dam . . . is still a paper dream* (Time). See also **paper profits**. **4** having to do with or used for paper: *a paper holder.* **5** *Figurative.* of, consisting of, or carried on by means of letters to newspapers, pamphlets, or books: *paper warfare.*
—***v.t.*** **1** to cover with wallpaper: *to paper a room.* **2** to enclose in or cover with paper. **3** to supply with or furnish with paper. **4** to smooth with sandpaper. **5** to write or set down on paper. **6** to write about; describe in writing. **7** *Slang.* to fill (a place of entertainment) with an audience admitted mostly by free passes: *To get a crowd at the concert, they had to paper the house.*
—***v.i.*** to put up wallpaper; wallpaper.
**commit to paper**, to write down: *He memorized the message and as soon as he got home committed it to paper.*
**on paper, a** in writing or print: *I like your idea. Let's get it down on paper.* **b** in theory: *The form of their constitution, as it is on paper, admits not of coercion. But necessity introduced it in practice* (American Museum).
**paper over**, to smooth over or cover up (a quarrel, disagreement, or the like): *The talks were called originally to try to paper over the ideological differences between Peking and Moscow* (New York Times).
**papers, a** documents telling who or what one is: *My former husband's papers are in the safe.* **b** a ship's papers (the documents of a ship showing where it is registered, who owns it, and other particulars): *A fine ship named the Redbridge . . . Her papers had been made out for Alicant* (Macaulay).
[< Old French *papier,* learned borrowing from Latin *papȳrus* a paper rush; writing material made from it < Greek *pápȳros* a paper rush. See etym. of doublet **papyrus**.] —**pa′per|er**, *n.* —**pa′per-like′**, *adj.*

**pa|per|back** (pā′pər bak′), *n., adj.* **—*n.*** a book with a binding of heavy paper, especially one that is sold at a low price and to a mass market: *The print is doing for painting what the paperback did for literature* (Time). *Paperbacks are not only cheaper than the hard-cover books but to the students they seem . . . easier to read* (New York Times).
—***adj.*** **1** bound in heavy paper: *A two-volume paperback reissue of a famous work* (Scientific American). **2** of or having to do with paperback books: *the paperback market.*

**pa|per|backed** (pā′pər bakt′), *adj.* = paperback.

**pa|per|bark** (pā′pər bärk′), *n.* any one of various Australian trees, the bark of which peels off in layers.

**paper birch**, a large North American birch, having a tough, durable white bark used by the Indians in making canoes and tents, and yielding a valuable timber; canoe birch; white birch.

**pa|per|board** (pā′pər bôrd′, -bōrd′), *n., adj.* pasteboard; cardboard: *Old newspapers, an important ingredient in paperboard* (Wall Street Journal).

**pa|per|book** (pa′pər bu̇k′), *n.* = paperback.

**pa|per|bound** (pā′pər bound′), *n., adj.* = paperback.

**pa|per|boy** (pā′pər boi′), *n.* a boy who delivers or sells newspapers; newsboy.

**paper chase**, the game of hare and hounds when paper is used for the "scent."

**paper chromatography**, the separation of mixtures of chemical compounds by the use of filter paper as the adsorbing material.

**paper clay**, a fine variety of clay used to give paper a smooth, shiny surface.

**paper clip**, a flat, looped piece of wire forming a clip for holding papers together.

**paper curtain**, *U.S.* an obstacle consisting of red tape and bureaucratic indirection, especially one set up by a governmental body to restrict or prevent the free flow of information and maintain secrecy: *a paper curtain hampering the issue of visitors' permits.*

**paper cutter**, **1** a machine or device equipped with one or more heavy knifelike blades for cutting, or for trimming the edges of, paper, especially in bulk. **2** = paper knife.

**paper doll**, the figure of a person cut out of a sheet of paper or cardboard for use as a child's doll.

**paper electrophoresis**, a form of paper chromatography in which the mixture to be separated is moved across the filter paper by passing an electric current through the paper.

**paper factor**, a terpene of the balsam fir which is a naturally occurring insect juvenile hormone: *Paper factor is highly effective in killing the cotton stainer bug, which destroys up to half the cotton crop in Asia, Africa and South America each year* (New York Times). [so called for the fact that it was first discovered in newsprint]

**paper gold**, a monetary reserve of the International Monetary Fund; Special Drawing Rights: *Paper gold . . . has been designed to provide managed money on an international scale, to provide steady additions to the supply of money reserves unrelated to the vagaries of gold mining* (New York Times).

**paper hanger**, or **pa|per|hang|er** (pā′pər hang′ər), *n.* a person whose business is to cover walls with wallpaper.

**paper hanging**, the work or business of a paper hanger.

**paper hangings**, = wallpaper.

**pa|per|i|ness** (pā′pər ē nis), *n.* papery quality; flimsiness.

**pa|per|ing** (pā′pər ing), *n.* **1** the act of one who papers, especially the work of a paper hanger. **2** = wallpaper: *a room ... with such large-figured papering on the walls as inn rooms have* (Charlotte Brontë).

**paper knife**, **1** a knife with a blade of metal, wood, ivory, plastic, or other material, used to cut open letters and the pages of books. **2** = paper cutter.

**pa|per|less** (pā′pər lis), *adj.* transferring information or data without the use of paper: *An experimental paperless service in San Francisco already provides computer transfer of funds from the accounts of industrial corporations to those of their employees* (New Scientist and Science Journal).

**paper loss**, a loss existing on paper, but not yet realized. A decrease in the market value of a security is a paper loss until the security is actually sold at a loss.

**paper machine**, a machine for making paper, consisting of rolls which spread paper pulp into a uniform layer and press it into the final product.

**pa|per|mak|er** (pā′pər mā′kər), *n.* a person who makes or manufactures paper: *The book is beautifully printed with over eighty illustrations covering Mason's own work and the methods used by primitive papermakers in the Far East* (New Science).

**pa|per|mak|ing** (pā′pər mā′king), *n.* the science, process, or business of producing paper: *In timber-starved South Africa the eucalyptus is a prime source of pulp for papermaking* (Harper's).

**paper mill**, a mill in which paper is made: *The paper mill at Hahnemuehle started a monthly delivery of 20,000 sheets of the specially made linen bank note paper* (Harper's).

**paper money**, **1** money made of paper, not metal, which by law represents money. Paper money bears no interest. A dollar bill is paper money. *The words now appear on coins but not on paper money* (New York Times). **2** negotiable instruments used instead of money, such as checks, notes, or drafts.

**paper mulberry**, a tree of the mulberry family, native to eastern Asia, whose soft inner bark is used in the Far East for making paper and tapa cloth.

**paper nautilus**, any one of a group of eight-armed sea mollusks somewhat like an octopus; argonaut. The female has a very thin, delicate shell in which the young develop. See picture under **nautilus**.

**paper profit**, a profit existing on paper, but not yet realized. An increase in the market value of a security is a paper profit until the security is actually sold at a profit.

**paper pulp**, a mass of fibrous material prepared to be made into paper, an intermediate product in the manufacture of paper.

**paper rush**, = papyrus.

**pa|pers** (pā′pərz), *n.pl.* See under **paper**.

**pa|per|shell** (pā′pər shel′), *n.* a thin-shelled variety of pecan, popular because its fragile shell can be cracked between the fingers.

**Pa|per|tex** (pā′pər teks), *n. Trademark.* a strong, synthetic paper made chiefly of nylon. It is highly resistant to tearing and fire, and is used as a fabric in upholstery, garments, and tents, or as paper for documents requiring long preservation.

**pa|per-thin** (pā′pər thin′), *adj.* thin as paper; extremely slender, flimsy, or meager: *a paper-thin blade, paper-thin walls, a paper-thin victory.*

**paper tiger**, a person or thing that appears to be strong or threatening but is really weak, ineffectual, or cowardly: *Those who call imperialism a paper tiger should reflect that the tiger has nuclear teeth* (Manchester Guardian).

**paper wasp**, any one of the social wasps that builds its nest of a papery substance made from dry wood moistened into a paste.

**pa|per|weight** (pā′pər wāt′), *n.* a small, heavy object put on papers to keep them from being blown away or scattered. It is often ornamental.

**paper white**, a kind of narcissus that can be grown indoors, bearing clusters of small, heavily scented, pure white flowers; polyanthus.

**pa|per|work** (pā′pər wėrk′), *n.* **1a** work done on paper; writing: *There's five hours' paperwork a night for any minister* (Atlantic). **b** office or clerical work, such as the writing, checking, and sorting of letters, and reports: *In the rear echelon of the corps headquarters, there was only paperwork* (Ralph Ingersoll). **c** the written work of a student; classroom work; homework: *A four-to-seven-year-old does as much paperwork as any bureaucrat* (New Yorker). **2** planning and theoretical work rather than practical application, such as mechanical drawing or drafting. **3** work in paper; work or a structure made of paper.

**pa|per|work|er** (pā′pər wėr′kər), *n.* = papermaker.

**pa|per|works** (pā′pər wėrks′), *n.pl. or sing.* an establishment where paper is made.

**pa|per|y** (pā′pər ē), *adj.* like paper; thin or flimsy.

**pap|e|terie** (pap′ə trē; *French* pȧp trē′), *n.* a case or box, usually ornamental, for paper and other writing materials. [< French *papeterie* stationery case; the paper trade < Middle French *papetier* papermaker, or dealer < Old French *papier* paper]

**Pa|phi|an** (pā′fē ən), *adj., n.* —*adj.* **1** of, having to do with, or belonging to Paphos, an ancient city of Cyprus sacred to Aphrodite or Venus, and containing one of her most celebrated temples. **2a** having to do with love, especially illicit love or sexual indulgence. **b** of prostitutes; being a prostitute: *the Paphian sisterhood.*
—*n.* a prostitute.

**Pa|pi|a|men|to** (pä′pē ə men′tō), *n.* a lingua franca spoken in the Netherlands Antilles, consisting chiefly of a mixture of Dutch, English, and Spanish. [< Papiamento *Papiamento* < *papia* to speak]

**pa|pier col|lé** (pȧ pyā′ kô lā′), *pl.* **pa|piers col|lés** (pȧ pyā′ kô lā′). *French.* (in cubism) a collection of pieces of paper or other material arranged to form a design and pasted on a flat surface: *They began stimulating reality by pasting it on their pictures in what became known as papiers collés, or collages, collé being the French word for paste* (New Yorker).

**pa|pier-mâ|ché** (pā′pər mə shā′), *n., adj.* —*n.* a paper pulp mixed with some stiffener such as glue and molded while moist. It becomes hard and strong when dry and is used chiefly for decorative objects and for stage properties. *Enormous pieces of group statuary in painted papier-mâché [are] put up by various guilds and other organizations in many parts of the city* (New York Times).
—*adj.* made of papier-mâché: *Parents and 5-to-12-year-olds will learn how to make papier-mâché puppets and costumes* (New York Times). *The well-known papier-mâché bedstead in the Victoria and Albert Museum is a metal bedstead with papier-mâché head and foot panels* (London Times).
[< French *papier* paper, and *mâché* compressed, mashed < *mâcher* (literally) to chew < Late Latin *masticāre* masticate]

**pa|pil|i|o|na|ceous** (pə pil′ē ə nā′shəs), *adj.* **1** *Botany.* **a** having a zygomorphic corolla somewhat like a butterfly in shape, as most leguminous plants. A papilionaceous flower consists of a large upper petal (vexillum), two lateral petals (alae), and two narrow lower petals below these, forming the carina or keel. **b** belonging to the pea family of plants; fabaceous. **2** having to do with or resembling a butterfly. [< Latin *pāpiliō, -ōnis* butterfly + English *-aceous*]

**pa|pil|la** (pə pil′ə), *n., pl.* **-pil|lae** (-pil′ē). **1** a small, nipplelike projection. **2** a small vascular process at the root of a hair or feather. See picture under **hair**. **3** one of certain small protuberances concerned with the senses of touch, taste, or smell: *the papillae on the tongue.* **4** a papule, pimple, or pustule. [< New Latin *papilla* the nipple < Latin *papilla* nipple of the breast, diminutive < *papula* swelling, pimple; see etym. under **papule**]

**pap|il|lar|y** (pap′ə ler′ē), *adj.* **1** of or like a papilla. **2** having papillae.

**pap|il|late** (pap′ə lāt), *adj.* covered with papillae.

**pap|il|le|de|ma** (pap′ə lə dē′mə), *n.* a swelling or inflammation of the optic nerve due to edema.

**pap|il|lo|e|de|ma** (pap′ə lō ə dē′mə), *n.* = papilledema.

**pap|il|lo|ma** (pap′ə lō′mə), *n., pl.* **-mas**, **-ma|ta** (-mə tə). a benign tumor of the skin or mucous membrane, formed by overgrown papillae and usually covered by a layer of thickened epidermis or epithelium, such as a wart or corn: *By condensing the smoke of burning cigarettes and painting the brown gummy condensates or "tar" on the backs of mice, [they] produced papillomas—benign tumors regarded as precancerous —in 59 per cent of them, and these tumors progressed to true cancer in 44 per cent* (Atlantic). [< New Latin *papilloma* < *papilla* papilla + *-oma* -oma]

**pap|il|lo|ma|tous** (pap′ə lō′mə təs), *adj.* of or characterized by a papilloma or papillomas.

**pap|il|lon** (pap′ə lon), *n.* any toy spaniel of a European breed developed from the dwarf spaniels of the 1500's, standing about 11 inches high and having a silky coat of varying color marked with black, red, or tan. [< French, Old French *papillon* (literally) butterfly, learned borrowing from Latin *pāpiliō, -ōnis* because of their large, curved ears). See etym. of doublet **pavilion**.]

**pap|il|lose** (pap′ə lōs), *adj.* having many papillae. [< *papill*(a) + *-ose*[1]]

**pap|il|los|i|ty** (pap′ə los′ə tē), *n.* papillose condition.

**pap|il|lote** (pap′ə lōt), *n.* **1** = curlpaper. **2** a ring of paper fringed at one end, put on chops, cutlets, and the like for decoration. [< French, Middle French *papillote* butterfly-like paillette or ornament < Old French *papillon;* see etym. under **papillon**]

**pa|pish** (pā′pish), *adj., n. Dialect.* —*adj.* popish.
—*n.* a papist.

**pa|pism** (pā′piz əm), *n.* Roman Catholicism (used in an unfriendly way).

**pa|pist** (pā′pist), *n., adj.* Roman Catholic (used in an unfriendly way). [< New Latin *papista* < Late Latin *pāpa* pope]

**pa|pis|tic** (pā pis′tik, pə-), *adj.* = papistical.

**pa|pis|ti|cal** (pā pis′tə kəl, pə-), *adj.* of or having to do with the Pope or the papal system; resembling Roman Catholic usages (used in an unfriendly way). —**pa|pis′ti|cal|ly**, *adv.*

**pa|pis|try** (pā′pə strē), *n.* the system, doctrines, or usages of the Roman Catholic Church (used in an unfriendly way).

**pap|meat** (pap′mēt′), *n.* pap or soft food, as for infants or invalids. [< *pap*[1] + *meat*]

**pa|poose** or **pap|poose** (pa püs′), *n.* a North American Indian baby. [American English < Algonkian (Narragansett) *papoos* child]

**pa|poosh** (pə püsh′), *n.* = babouche. [< Persian *pāpūsh*]

**pa|po|va|vi|rus** (pə pō′və vī′rəs), *n.* any one of a group of viruses containing DNA, associated with or causing cancerous tumors and other growths, such as warts, including the polyoma virus. [< *pa*(pilloma) + *po*(lyoma) + *v*(erruc)*a* + *virus*]

**pap|pi** (pap′ī), *n.* plural of **pappus**.

**pap|pose** (pap′ōs), *adj. Botany.* **1** having a pappus. **2** = downy. [< New Latin *papposus* < Latin *pappus* pappus]

**pap|pous** (pap′əs), *adj.* = pappose.

**pap|pus** (pap′əs), *n., pl.* **pap|pi**. *Botany.* an appendage to a seed, often made of down or bristles, which aids in the seed's dispersal by the wind. Dandelion and thistle seeds have pappi. [< Latin *pappus* down[2] on seeds; (originally) old man, grandfather < Greek *páppos*]

**pap|py**[1] (pap′ē), *adj.,* **-pi|er**, **-pi|est**. like pap; watered down: *The demand for pap—pappy plays, pappy views about life, death, and a pappy hereafter—is very much greater than the demand for what requires more energy and guts* (Tyrone Guthrie). [< *pap*[1] + *-y*[1]]

**pap|py**[2] (pap′ē), *n., pl.* **-pies**. *Dialect.* papa; father.

**pap|ri|ka** or **pa|pri|ca** (pa prē′kə, pap′rə-), *n.* **1** the ground, dried fruit of certain mild red peppers, used as seasoning in food. It is much milder than ordinary red pepper. **2** the plant that produces the fruit from which this is made, grown especially in Hungary and Spain. [< Hungarian *paprika* < Serbo-Croatian < New Greek *pipéri* pepper]

**Pap test** or **smear** (pap), a test used to diagnose certain cancers, in which exfoliated cells of organs, such as the cervix, stomach, or uterus, are obtained, smeared on a glass slide, and stained for microscopic examination: *The "Pap smear" is effective in spotting potential cancers of the cervix* (Harper's). [< George N. *Pap*(*anicolaou*), 1883-1962, a Greek-born American physician, who developed it]

**Pap|u|an** (pap′yu̇ ən), *adj., n.* —*adj.* of or having to do with Papua, part of a large island north of Australia, or with the native Negroid race living in Papua.
—*n.* **1** a native or inhabitant of Papua or a person belonging to the racial type that is found there. **2** any one of the native languages or dialects spoken in New Guinea and adjacent islands.
[< *Papua,* the island < Malay *papuah* frizzled; because of the appearance of the hair of the inhabitants]

**pap|u|lar** (pap′yə lər), *adj.* of, having to do with, or covered with papillae or pimples.

**pap|ule** (pap′yül), *n.* a pimple that does not form pus. [< Latin *papula* a swelling, pimple]

**pap|y|ra|ceous** (pap′ə rā′shəs), *adj.* of the consistency or thinness of paper; papery; paperlike. [< *papyr*(us) + *-aceous*]

**pa|py|ro|graph** (pə pī′rə graf, -gräf), *n.* any one of various devices for producing copies of a writ-

---

**Pronunciation Key:** hat, āge, cãre, fär; let, ēqual, tėrm; it, īce; hot, ōpen, ôrder; oil, out; cup, pu̇t, rüle; child; long; thin; ᴛʜen; zh, measure; ə represents **a** in about, **e** in taken, **i** in pencil, **o** in lemon, **u** in circus.

ing or the like, especially by a paper stencil. [< Greek *pápȳros* (see etym. under **papyrus**) + English *-graph*]

**pap|y|rol|o|gist** (pap′ə rol′ə jist), *n.* a person who studies or is an expert in papyrology: *Papyrologists* [*are*] *... devoted to the care and interpretation of ancient papyri* (New Yorker).

**pap|y|rol|o|gy** (pap′ə rol′ə jē), *n.* the study of papyri. [< Greek *pápȳros* + English *-logy*]

**pa|py|rus** (pə pī′rəs), *n., pl.* **-ri** (-rī). **1** a tall water plant from which the ancient Egyptians, Greeks, and Romans made a kind of paper to write on. It belongs to the sedge family. Papyrus has stems three to to ten feet high, and though it is comparatively rare today, it is still found in Egypt, Ethiopia, Syria, and Sicily. Papyrus is the bulrush of the Bible. See picture under **bulrush**. **2** a writing material made from the pith of the papyrus plant, by laying thin slices or strips of it side by side, the whole being then soaked, pressed, and dried: *Letters, written on papyrus in the hieratic character* (Amelia B. Edwards). **3** an ancient record written on papyrus: *According to papyri found in one of the ancient Negev cities, Nisana, their desert farming produced barley, wheat, legumes, grapes, figs, and dates* (Scientific American). [< Latin *papȳrus* the paper rush; writing material made from it < Greek *pápȳros* any plant of the paper rush genus. See etym. of doublet **paper**. Compare etym. under **Bible**.]

**par** (pär), *n., adj., v.,* **parred, par|ring.** —*n.* **1** equality; equal level: *The gains and losses are about on a par. He is quite on a par with his brother in intelligence.* **2** an average or normal amount, degree, or condition: *A sick person feels below par.* **3** the value of a bond, a note, a share of stock, or other security, that is printed on it; face value: *That stock is selling above par.* **4** the established normal value of the money of one country in terms of the money of another country. **5** a score in golf which is used as a standard for a particular hole or course and which represents the number of strokes that will be taken if the hole or course is played well. Par is based on the length and difficulty of the hole or course. On many golf courses 72 is par. *He had hammered out a 5-under par 65 in the second round* (New York Times).
—*adj.* **1** average; normal. **2** of or at par.
—*v.t. Golf.* to score par on (a hole): *Palmer went over par on only six holes, he birdied eighteen holes, and he parred the rest* (New Yorker).
**par for the course,** *Informal.* nothing unusual; the expected thing: *Mr. Spivak said it was "par for the course" to tell a participant on his show the identity of the panelists if the participant asked* (New York Times).
**up to par,** up to the average, normal, or usual amount, degree, or condition, or quality: *Her work is not up to par today because she has a headache.*
[< Latin *pār, paris,* adjective, equal; noun, a counterpart. See etym. of doublet **peer**[1].]

**par-,** *prefix.* the form of **para-**[1] before vowels and *h,* as in *parenthesis, parhelion.*

**par.,** an abbreviation for the following:
**1** paragraph.
**2** parallel.
**3** parenthesis.
**4** parish.

**PAR** (no periods), perimeter acquisition radar (a radar forming the outermost part of an antiballistic missile system).

**pa|ra**[1] (pä rä′), *n., pl.* **-ras** or **-ra. 1** 1/40 of a Turkish piaster. **2** 1/100 of a Yugoslavian dinar. **3** either of the two coins having these values. [< Turkish *para*]

**par|a**[2] (par′ə), *n., pl.* **par|as.** *Informal.* a paratrooper: *The Belgian paras sustained only seven casualties in rescuing the hostages* (Time).

**Pa|rá** (pä rä′), *n.* = Pará rubber.

**para-**[1], *prefix.* **1** beside; near, as in *parathyroid.*
**2** beyond, as in *parapsychology, paramagnetism.*
**3** related to but not quite; supplementary to; subordinate to, as in *paramilitary, paramedical, paraprofessional.*
**4** disordered condition, as in *paranoia, paraplegia.*
**5** (in chemical terms) a modification of; an isomer of; a substance related to, as in *para-aminobenzoic.* Also, **par-** before vowels and *h.*
[< Greek *pará* beside; near; from]

**para-**[2], *combining form.* **1** a defense against; protection from: *Parachute = a device that protects from falls. Parasol = a device that protects from the sun.*
**2** that uses a parachute: *Paratrooper = a soldier that uses a parachute.*
**3** that is like or serves as a parachute: *Parawing = a parachutelike wing. Paraglider = a parachutelike glider.*
[< French *para-* < Italian < *para,* imperative of *parare* ward off, defend against < Latin *parāre* prepare against]

**para.,** paragraph.

**Para.,** Paraguay.

**par|a-a|mi|no|ben|zo|ic acid** (par′ə ə mē′nō-ben zō′ik, -am′ə nō-), a yellow, crystalline acid, a constituent of the vitamin B complex, present in yeast and in bran. It is used in the manufacture of local anesthetics and in the treatment of rheumatic fever and various skin conditions. *Formula:* $C_7H_7NO_2$ *Abbr:* PABA (no periods). [< *para-*[1] + *aminobenzoic acid*]

**par|a-a|mi|no|sal|i|cyl|ic acid** (par′ə ə mē′nō-sal′ə sil′ik, -am′ə nō-), a synthetic drug used widely in the treatment of tuberculosis, usually in combination with other drugs such as isoniazid and streptomycin. *Formula:* $C_7H_7NO_3$ *Abbr:* PAS (no periods).

**par|a|bal|loon** (par′ə bə lün′), *n.* a mobile radar antenna consisting principally of two paraboloids made of fabric, in part coated thinly with metal, which can be inflated and raised, or lowered and deflated for transportation: *The cameras are mounted in capsules which are equipped with a paraballoon, a combination of a parachute and balloon* (Birmingham Post-Herald).

**pa|rab|a|sis** (pə rab′ə sis), *n., pl.* **-ses** (-sēz). the chief of the choral parts in ancient Greek comedy, sung by the chorus during an intermission in the action, and consisting of an address from the poet to the audience. [< Greek *parábasis* < *parabaínein* < *pará-* beside + *baínein* to go]

**par|a|bi|o|sis** (par′ə bī ō′sis), *n.* the natural or surgical union of two animals in such a way that there is an exchange of blood. [< *para-*[1] + *-biosis,* as in *anabiosis*]

**par|a|bi|ot|ic** (par′ə bī ot′ik), *adj.* of or having to do with parabiosis. —**par′a|bi|ot′i|cal|ly,** *adv.*

**par|a|blast** (par′ə blast), *n. Embryology.* the nutritive yolk of an ovum or egg. [< *para-*[1] + Greek *blastós* germ, sprout]

**par|a|blas|tic** (par′ə blas′tik), *adj.* of, having to do with, or derived from the parablast.

**par|a|ble** (par′ə bəl), *n.* **1** a brief story used to teach some moral lesson or truth: *Jesus taught in parables. If the story-tellers could ha' got decency and good morals from true stories, who'd have troubled to invent parables?* (Thomas Hardy). **SYN:** apologue. **2** *Archaic.* a comparison or enigmatic saying. [< Old French *parable,* learned borrowing from Latin *parabola* comparison (in Late Latin, allegory, parable) < Greek *parabolē* analogy, comparison; a parabola < *para-* alongside + *bolē* a throwing, casting. See etym. of doublets **palaver, parabola, parabole, parole.**]
▶ See **allegory** for usage note.

***pa|rab|o|la** (pə rab′ə lə), *n., pl.* **-las. 1** a plane curve formed by the intersection of a cone with a plane parallel to a side of the cone. **2** a curve like this: *When we throw a ball, it rises for a while and then begins to fall downward; the curve it follows is called a parabola* (John R. Pierce). [< Greek *parabolē* parabola; comparison; (literally) putting side by side; see etym. under **parable**. See etym. of doublets **palaver, parable, parabole, parole.**]

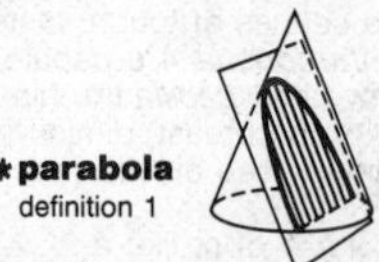

***parabola**
definition 1

**pa|rab|o|le** (pə rab′ə lē), *n. Rhetoric.* **1** a comparison. **2** a metaphor. [< Greek *parabolē.* See etym. of doublets **palaver, parable, parabola, parole.**]

**par|a|bol|ic**[1] (par′ə bol′ik), *adj. Geometry.* **1** having the form of a parabola: *a parabolic orbit. He compelled the frothy liquor ... to spout forth from one glass and descend into the other, in a great parabolic curve* (Hawthorne). **2** having to do with or resembling a parabola: *a parabolic area.*
—**par′a|bol′i|cal|ly,** *adv.*

**par|a|bol|ic**[2] (par′ə bol′ik), *adj.* of, having to do with, or expressed in a parable. [< *parable* + *-ic*]
—**par′a|bol′i|cal|ly,** *adv.*

**par|a|bol|i|cal**[1] (par′ə bol′ə kəl), *adj.* = parabolic[1].

**par|a|bol|i|cal**[2] (par′ə bol′ə kəl), *adj.* = parabolic[2].

**parabolic mirror** or **reflector,** a concave mirror the reflecting surface of which has the shape of a paraboloid, capable of focusing rays parallel to its axis to a point without spherical aberration: *Parabolic mirrors or reflectors are used in certain telescopes, automobile headlights, searchlights, etc.*

**pa|rab|o|lize**[1] (pə rab′ə līz), *v.t.,* **-lized, -liz|ing.** to give the form of a parabola or paraboloid to.

**pa|rab|o|lize**[2] (pə rab′ə līz), *v.t.,* **-lized, -liz|ing.** **1** to represent in a parable. **2** to treat as a parable.

**pa|rab|o|loid** (pə rab′ə loid), *n. Geometry.* **1** Also **paraboloid of revolution.** a solid or surface generated by the revolution of a parabola about its axis. **2** a conoid of which sections made by planes parallel to a given line are parabolas. [< Greek *paraboloeidês* showing comparison < *parabolē* juxtaposition + *eîdos* form]

**pa|rab|o|loi|dal** (pə rab′ə loi′dəl), *adj.* having to do with or resembling a paraboloid.

**paraboloid of revolution,** = paraboloid (def. 1).

**par|a|ca|sein** (par′ə kā′sēn, -sē in), *n.* casein obtained from milk by the action of rennet. [< *para*[1]- + *casein*]

**Par|a|cel|si|an** (par′ə sel′sē ən), *adj., n.* —*adj.* of or having to do with Paracelsus (1493?-1541), a Swiss-German physician and alchemist, or his theories: *We are still close to alchemy, medieval travellers' tales, the Paracelsian twilight zone which lies between magic and science* (Observer).
—*n.* a follower or adherent of Paracelsus.

**par|a|ce|ta|mol** (par′ə sē′tə môl), *n.* a drug used to relieve headaches and reduce fever. [< *para-*[1] + *acetam*(ide) + *-ol*[1]]

***par|a|chute** (par′ə shüt), *n, v.,* **-chut|ed, -chut|ing.** —*n.* **1** an apparatus somewhat like an umbrella, made of silk or nylon and used in descending safely through the air from a great height, as from an aircraft: *There are huge parachutes used in guided missile tests, chutes to stabilize torpedoes dropped from airplanes ... and a parachute that is intended to yank an airplane out of a spin if anything goes wrong in test flights* (Wall Street Journal). **2** the expansible fold of skin of a flying mammal or reptile, such as the flying squirrel. **3** any contrivance, natural or artificial, serving to check a fall through the air.
—*v.i.* to come down by, or as if by, a parachute: *The men in the burning plane parachuted safely to the ground.*
—*v.t.* to convey by a parachute.
[< French *parachute* < *para-* para-[2] + *chute* a fall] —**par′a|chute|like′,** *adj.*

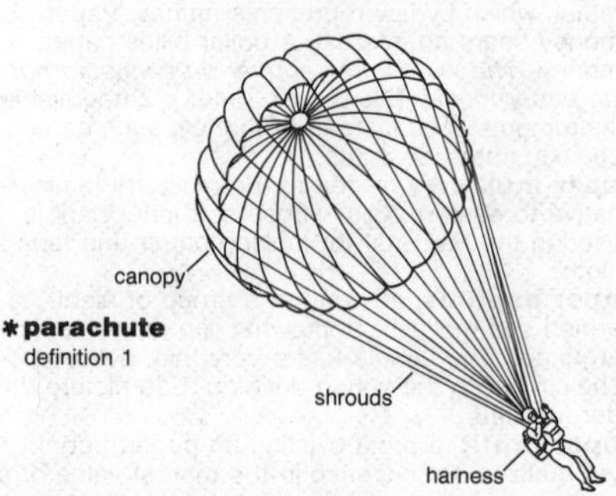


***parachute**
definition 1

**parachute spinnaker,** a type of very large spinnaker used on racing yachts.

**par|a|chut|ist** (par′ə shü′tist), *n.* **1** a person who uses a parachute or is skilled in making descents with a parachute: *Parachutists will be dropped to prepare a field for light aircraft* (Science News Letter). **2** = paratrooper.

**Par|a|clete** (par′ə klēt), *n.* the Holy Ghost; the Comforter: *It was approaching the third hour, the hour at which the Paraclete originally descended upon the Apostles* (Cardinal Newman). [< Old French *paraclet,* learned borrowing from Latin *paraclētus* < Greek *paráklētos* advocate; (literally) one called to aid < *parakaleîn* to call (in) < *para-* beside + *kaleîn* to call; to comfort, console]

**par|a|clete** (par′ə klēt), *n.* a friend, advocate, or comforter. [< *Paraclete*]

**par|a|com|man|do** (par′ə kə man′dō, -män′-), *n., pl.* **-dos** or **-does.** a commando moved by air and landed by parachute in a battle area or behind enemy lines: *The mutiny was put down after Gen. Joseph D. Mobutu, the army commander, led paracommandos into the main police barracks* (New York Times). [< *para-*[2] + *commando*]

**par|a|con|scious** (par′ə kon′shəs), *adj. Psychology.* in a secondary consciousness; coconscious.

**par|a|crys|tal|line** (par′ə kris′tə lin, -līn), *adj. Chemistry.* having the molecular grouping of a substance just prior to crystallization; resembling the crystalline state. [< *para-*[1] + *crystalline*]

**pa|ra|cy|mene** (par′ə sī′mēn), *n. Chemistry.* one of three isomeric forms of cymene.

**pa|rade** (pə rād′), *n., v.,* **-rad|ed, -rad|ing.** —*n.* **1** a march for display; procession: *Thanksgiving Day parade, the Columbus Day parade.* **2** a group of people walking for display or pleasure: *the Easter parade on Fifth Avenue after church services.* **3** *British.* a place where people walk for display or pleasure; public promenade. **4** a great

show or display: *A modest man will not make a parade of his wealth.* **5** a military display or review of troops: *A parade of troops passed in review.* **6a** a place used for the regular parade of troops: *The soldiers stood at attention on the parade.* **b** the level, open space within the walls of a fortification. **7** *Fencing.* a parry: *He was an admirable swordsman. His parade and riposte were as quick as lightning* (Sir Arthur Conan Doyle).
– ***v.t.*** **1** to march through in procession or with display: *The circus performers and animals paraded the streets.* **2** *Figurative.* to make a show or display of: *to parade one's wealth.* **SYN**: display, flaunt. **3** to assemble (troops) for review, ceremony, or inspection. **4** to march (a person) up and down or through the streets either for show or to expose him to contempt.
– ***v.i.*** **1** to march in procession; walk proudly as if in a parade: *The haughty lady paraded by, looking neither to the right nor the left.* **2** to come together in military order for review, ceremony, or inspection: *Photographs of the latest Soviet planes were taken when they "paraded" over Moscow* (New York Times).
[< French *parade* (originally) checking (a horse) in maneuvers < Spanish *parada* < *parar* to check; dispose in position < Latin *parāre* prepare; influenced by French *parer* arrange, deck elegantly]

**parade ground**, **1** an extent of open, level ground, usually within or adjacent to a fort, where soldiers are accustomed to parade. **2** *Figurative.* a place for making a great show or display of something.

**pa|rad|er** (pə rā′dər), *n.* a person who parades.

**parade rest**, *Military.* a position of rest, especially at parade, in which the soldier stands silent and motionless. It is more relaxed than attention and more controlled than at ease.

**par|a|di|chlor|ben|zene** (par′ə dī′klôr ben′zēn, -klōr-; -ben zēn′), *n.* = paradichlorobenzene.

**par|a|di|chlo|ro|ben|zene** (par′ə dī klôr′ō ben′zēn, -klōr′-; -ben zēn′), *n.* a colorless or white, crystalline substance, one of three isomers. used as an insecticide, fumigant, etc. *Formula:* $C_6H_4Cl_2$

**par|a|did|dle** (par′ə did′əl), *n. Jazz Slang.* a basic drum roll on the snare drum. [imitative]

**par|a|digm** (par′ə dim, -dīm), *n.* **1** a pattern; example: *Sir John is impeccable, a paradigm of the gentleman soldier* (Harper's). **2** *Grammar.* **a** an example, such as of a noun, verb, or pronoun, in all its inflections. **b** the set of inflectional forms for a word or class of words: *The final step in morphology is the establishment of paradigms, which can be viewed as sets of grammatical suffixes* (Harold B. Allen). [< Latin *paradigma* < Greek *parádeigma, -matos* pattern, ultimately < *para-* side by side + *deiknýnai* to show, point out]

**par|a|dig|mat|ic** (par′ə dig mat′ik), *adj.* **1** of, having to do with, or consisting of a paradigm. **2** inflectional, as an affix. – **par′a|dig|mat′i|cal|ly**, *adv.*

**par|a|dig|mat|i|cal** (par′ə dig mat′ə kəl), *adj.* = paradigmatic.

**par|a|di|sa|ic** (par′ə di sā′ik), *adj.* = paradisiacal. – **par′a|di|sa′i|cal|ly**, *adv.*

**par|a|di|sa|i|cal** (par′ə di sā′ə kəl), *adj.* = paradisiacal: *paradisaical ecstasy.*

**par|a|di|sal** (par′ə dī′səl), *adj.* of or having to do with paradise: *... Rio de Janeiro, where thousands of Negroes live in conditions of infernal poverty among scenes of paradisal beauty* (Time).

**par|a|dise** (par′ə dīs), *n.* **1a** the abode of God, the angles, and the righteous; heaven. **b** an intermediate place spoken of by some theologians, where the souls of the righteous await the Last Judgment. **c** the Moslem heaven, especially when thought of as a place of hedonistic delight: *The Moors imagined the paradise of their prophet to be situated in that part of the heaven which overhung the kingdom of Granada* (Washington Irving). **2** *Figurative.* a place or condition of great happiness: *The summer camp was a paradise for him. This state of things should have been to me a paradise of peace* (Charlotte Brontë). *This sunny island off the Spanish coast has been a smuggler's paradise since time immemorial* (New York Times). **3** a place of great beauty. **4** Also, **Paradise**. the Garden of Eden. [partly Old English *paradīs*, partly < Old French *paradis*, learned borrowing from Latin *paradīsus* < Greek *parádeisos* < Iranian (compare Avestan *pairidaēza* enclosed park < *pairi-* around + *daēza* wall)]

**par|a|di|se|an** (par′ə dī′sē ən, par′ə di sē′ən), *adj.* **1** like that of paradise; paradisiacal: *After that I see the caravan, ... winding among hills of a paradisean green shade* (Vladimir Nabokov). **2** of or belonging to the birds of paradise.

**paradise fish**, a brilliantly colored East Indian fish, remarkable for the extension of its fins, sometimes kept in aquariums.

**paradise nut**, = sapucaia nut.

**par|a|dis|i|ac** (par′ə dis′ī ak), *adj.* = paradisiacal.

**par|a|di|si|a|cal** (par′ə di sī′ə kəl), *adj.* of, having to do with, or belonging to paradise; like that of paradise: *The Balinese themselves are fully aware of its [Bali's] paradisiacal nature* (New Yorker). [< Late Latin *paradīsiacus* < Greek *paradeisiakós* (originally) like a park < *parádeisos* (see etym. under **paradise**) + English *-al*[1]] – **par′a|di|si′a|cal|ly**, *adv.*

**pa|ra|dor** (pä′rä ᴛʜôr′), *n., pl.* **-do|res** (-ᴛʜō′rās). *Spanish.* an inn in Spain, operated by the government: *Paradores are usually in out-of-the-way, scenic spots, and frequently are remodeled parts of ancient castles and monasteries* (Walter C. Langsam).

**par|a|dos** (par′ə dos), *n.* a mound of earth thrown up behind a trench to prevent its occupants from being silhouetted against the skyline when standing on the firing step and to protect them from shells and bombs that explode in the rear. [< French *parados* < *para-* para-[2] + *dos* back[1]]

**par|a|dox** (par′ə doks), *n.* **1** a statement that may be true but seems to say two opposite things. "More haste, less speed," and "The child is father to the man" are paradoxes. **2** a statement that is false because it says two opposite things: *There is that glorious epicurean paradox ... : "give us the luxuries of life, and we will dispense with its necessaries"* (Oliver Wendell Holmes). **3** a person or thing that seems to be full of contradictions: *Man is an embodied paradox, a bundle of contradictions* (Charles Caleb Colton). **4** a statement contrary to received opinion or belief. **5** any inconsistent or contradictory fact, action, or condition: *The Western Allies celebrated the World War II victory over Germany today with the paradox of embracing their old enemy as a new ally* (New York Times). [< Latin *paradoxum* < Greek *parádoxon*, neuter of *parádoxos*, adjective, contrary; noun, paradox < *para-* contrary to, aside + *dóxa* opinion < *dokeîn* to seem]
▶ See **epigram** for usage note.

**par|a|dox|i|al** (par′ə dok′sē əl), *adj.* = paradoxical.

**par|a|dox|i|cal** (par′ə dok′sə kəl), *adj.* **1** of paradoxes; having to do with a paradox: *Comedians, paradoxical as it may seem, may be too natural* (Charles Lamb). **2** having the habit of using paradoxes: *He was an eternal talker—brilliant, various, paradoxical, florid* (Edward G. Bulwer-Lytton). – **par′a|dox′i|cal|ly**, *adv.* – **par′a|dox′i|cal|ness**, *n.*

**paradoxical sleep**, any one of about five periods in a night's sleep, each period lasting about ten minutes, during which dreams occur and the body undergoes marked changes, including rapid eye movement, loss of reflexes, and increased brain activity; REM sleep: *After about an hour of this orthodox sleep phase, a change occurs and paradoxical sleep begins and lasts about 10 minutes before orthodox sleep is resumed ... In paradoxical sleep, unlike orthodox sleep, the blood flow through the brain is increased far above waking levels* (New Scientist).

**par|a|dox|ist** (par′ə dok′sist), *n.* a person given to paradoxes.

**par|a|dox|ure** (par′ə doks′yər), *n.* = palm civet. [< New Latin *Paradoxurus* the typical genus < Greek *parádoxos* incredible + *ourá* tail (because of its appearance)]

**par|a|drop** (par′ə drop′), *n., v.,* **-dropped, -dropping.** – ***n.*** an airdrop by means of a parachute: *Carrier crews recently dropped 400 tons of construction vehicles in the first mass paradrop of heavy engineering equipment* (Science News Letter).
– ***v.t.*** to drop (something) by parachute.

**par|aes|the|sia** (par′əs thē′zhə), *n.* = paresthesia.

**par|aes|thet|ic** (par′əs thet′ik), *adj.* = paresthetic.

**par|af|fin** (par′ə fin), *n., v.* – ***n.*** **1a** a colorless or white, almost tasteless substance, like wax, used for making candles and for sealing jars of jelly or jam; paraffin wax. Paraffin has no odor and is a solid at ordinary temperatures. It is obtained chiefly from crude petroleum, being chemically a mixture of hydrocarbons. **b** any of various other mixtures of hydrocarbons. **2** *Chemistry.* **a** any member of the methane series. Ethane, propane, and butane are paraffins. *Formula:* $C_nH_{2n+2}$ **b** one of the solid (higher) members of this series, that boils at temperatures over 300 degrees centigrade (Celsius). Commercial paraffin is made up largely of these hydrocarbons. **3** = paraffin oil.
– ***v.t.*** to cover or treat with paraffin.
[< German *Paraffin* < Latin *parum* not very, too little (< *parvus* small) + *affīnis* associated with, related (because of its low affinity for other substances). Compare etym. under **affined**.]

**par|af|fine** (par′ə fin, -fēn), *n., v.t.,* **-fined, -fining.** = paraffin.

**par|af|fin|ic** (par′ə fin′ik), *adj.* derived from, related to, or like the paraffins: *The microorganisms are capable of consuming certain paraffinic hydrocarbons found in petroleum* (Scientific American).

**paraffin oil**, **1** any one of various oils associated with paraffin, such as oils distilled from bituminous shale, oils obtained from petroleum (especially, heavy or lubricating oils), and oils from which paraffin may be made. **2** *British.* kerosene.

**paraffin series**, *Chemistry.* methane series.

**paraffin test**, a measurement of the amount of gunpowder nitrates contained in a paraffin mold of a person's hand. It is used in criminology to determine whether or not a suspect has recently fired a gun. *Evidence has long been accumulating which shows that the standard "paraffin test" ... is unreliable* (New Scientist).

**paraffin wax**, solid paraffin, as distinct from paraffin oil.

**par|a|foil** (par′ə foil′), *n.* a combination of parachute and airfoil; parawing: *The parafoil would enable pilots bailing out over enemy territory to glide like birds until they reached safety* (New York Times).

**par|a|form|al|de|hyde** (par′ə fôr mal′də hīd), *n.* a colorless powder obtained by the polymerization of formaldehyde, used as an antiseptic. *Formula:* $(CH_2O)_n$ [< *para-*[1] + *formaldehyde*]

**par|a|ge|ne|si|a** (par′ə jə nē′sē ə), *n.* = paragenesis.

**par|a|gen|e|sis** (par′ə jen′ə sis), *n.* the formation of minerals in close contact, so that the development of individual crystals is interfered with, resulting in an interlocked crystalline mass.

**par|a|ge|net|ic** (par′ə jə net′ik), *adj.* of, having to do with, or originating by paragenesis. – **par′a|ge|net′i|cal|ly**, *adv.*

***par|a|glid|er** (par′ə glī′dər), *n.* a kitelike device with flexible wings, designed to slow down the descent of a space vehicle or serve as an independent reentry vehicle. [< *para-*[2] + *glider*]

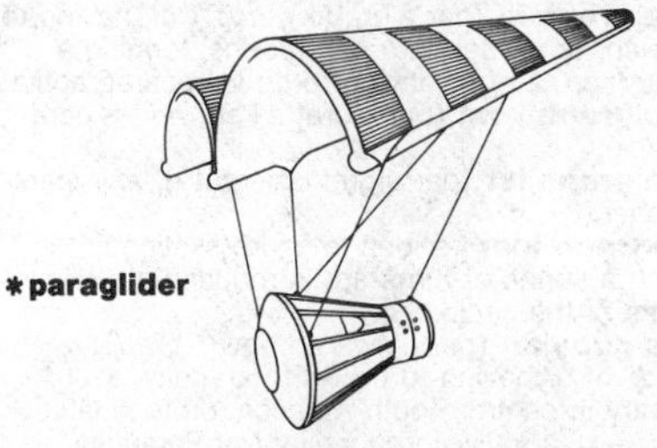

***paraglider**

**par|a|go|ge** (par′ə gō′jē), *n.* the addition of a letter, sound, or syllable at the end of a word, often for ease in pronunciation, without changing the meaning of the word. *Examples:* among-*st*, height-*th* (substandard). [< Late Latin *paragōgē* < Greek *paragōgē* (literally) a leading by < *para* beside, beyond + *agōgē* a leading < *ágein* to lead]

**par|a|gog|ic** (par′ə goj′ik), *adj.* having to do with or of the nature of paragoge.

**par|a|gon** (par′ə gon), *n., adj., v.,* **-goned, -goning.** – ***n.*** **1** a model of excellence or perfection: *a paragon of beauty. Winter, the paragon of art, that kills all forms of life ... save what is pure and will survive* (Roy Campbell). **2** a flawless diamond weighing 100 carats or more. **3** a size of printing type (20 points) twice as large as long primer.
– ***adj.*** of surpassing excellence: *Those jewels were paragon, without flaw, hair, ice or cloud* (Sir Thomas Browne).
– ***v.t.*** **1** *Archaic.* to parallel; compare. **2** *Archaic.* to match; mate: *Pass to join your peers, paragon charm with charm* (Robert Browning). **3** *Obsolete.* to excel; surpass: *A maid that paragons description* (Shakespeare). **4** *Obsolete.* to set forth as a perfect model. **5** *Obsolete.* to typify; exemplify.
[< Middle French *paragon* comparison; criterion < Italian *parangone* (originally) touchstone < Medieval Greek *parakone* whetstone < Greek *parakonân* to whet, ultimately < *para-* on the side + *akónē* whetstone < *ákaina* point, barb]

**pa|rag|o|nite** (pə rag′ə nīt), *n.* a kind of mica analogous to muscovite but containing sodium instead of potassium. [< Greek *paragōn*, present participle of *parágein* mislead (because it contains sodium, not potassium) + English *-ite*[1]]

***par|a|graph** (par′ə graf, -gräf), *n., v.* – ***n.*** **1** a

**Pronunciation Key:** hat, āge, cãre, fär; let, ēqual, tėrm; it, īce; hot, ōpen, ôrder; oil, out; cup, pu̇t, rüle; child; long; thin; ᴛʜen; zh, measure; ə represents **a** in about, **e** in taken, **i** in pencil, **o** in lemon, **u** in circus.

group of sentences that belong together; distinct part of a chapter, letter, or composition. A paragraph usually has some unifying elements, such as meaning or subject, that are not shared with the sentences that come before or follow. Paragraphs usually begin on a new line which is indented, except in some business letters. **2** a separate note or item of news in a newspaper: *She had been irritated by newspaper paragraphs —nobody could ever find out who wrote them* (H. G. Wells). **3a** a sign used to show where a paragraph begins or should begin, used mostly in correcting written or printed work. **b** such a sign used to indicate a note or footnote.
*—v.t.* **1** to divide into paragraphs: *to paragraph an essay.* **2** to write paragraphs about.
*—v.i.* to write paragraphs.
[< Medieval Latin *paragraphus* < Greek *parágraphos* line (in the margin) marking a break in the continuity of thought < *para-* beside + *gráphein* to write. See etym. of doublet **paraph.**]

***paragraph**
definition 3a

**par|a|graph|er** (par′ə graf′ər, -gräf′-), *n.* a person who writes paragraphs, as for a newspaper: *A gossip paragrapher in the evening newspaper said darkly that the situation had become "intolerable"* (Maclean's).
**par|a|graph|i|a** (par′ə graf′ē ə), *n.* the writing of words and letters other than those intended, an aphasia associated with certain disorders caused by injury to the brain. [< New Latin *paragraphia* < Greek *para-* beyond + *-graphīā* a writing < *gráphein* to write, draw]
**par|a|graph|ic** (par′ə graf′ik), *adj.* **1** of, having to do with, or divided into paragraphs; forming a paragraph. **2** of or having to do with paragraphia.
**par|a|graph|i|cal** (par′ə graf′ə kəl), *adj.* = paragraphic.
**par|a|graph|ist** (par′ə graf′ist, -gräf′-), *n.* = paragrapher.
**paragraph loop**, a loop in figure skating in which a series of turns are introduced at various points of the circle.
**Par|a|guay|an** (par′ə gwā′ən, -gwī′-), *adj., n.* *—adj.* of or having to do with Paraguay, a country in central South America, or its inhabitants. *—n.* a native or inhabitant of Paraguay.
**Paraguayan cat**, a South American domestic cat smaller than most domestic cats that has been bred for over 300 years.
**Par|a|guay tea** (par′ə gwā, -gwī), = maté.
**par|a-hy|dro|gen** (par′ə hī′drə jən), *n.* a form of hydrogen consisting of molecules whose pairs of nuclei have spins in opposite directions.
**par|a|in|flu|en|za** (par′ə in flü en′zə), *n.* a respiratory illness similar to influenza, caused by any of various viruses that are associated with the common cold and various other respiratory diseases.
**par|a|jour|nal|ism** (par′ə jėr′nə liz əm), *n.* newspaper and magazine writing that avoids the methods and practices of standard journalism; unconventional journalism: *... the current fad for first person parajournalism, where the reporter —me, say—looks into his own heart for information about politics, war, or suffering, and tells what he finds there in long loping sentences all stuffed with literary allusion* (Herbert Gold).
**par|a|jour|nal|ist** (par′ə jėr′nə list), *n.* a practitioner of parajournalism: *Also working for the parajournalist is the tendency of the misinformed ... to accept as truth whatever is boldly asserted as such* (Dwight Macdonald).
**par|a|jour|nal|is|tic** (par′ə jėr′nə lis′tik), *adj.* of or having to do with parajournalism or parajournalists.
**par|a|keet** (par′ə kēt), *n.* any one of various small, brightly colored parrots, most of which have slender bodies and long tails. Also, **paraquet, paroquet, parrakeet, parroket, parroquet.** [< Middle French, Old French *paroquet,* apparently alteration of *perrot* parrot < *Perrot* (diminutive) < *Pierre* Peter]
**par|a|ker|a|to|sis** (par′ə ker′ə tō′sis), *n.* a relatively mild disease of pigs, marked by dry, scaly, crusted skin.
**par|a|kite** (par′ə kīt), *n.* a number of kites connected in series and flying tandem, used for sending up meteorological instruments.
**par|a|kit|ing** (par′ə kī′ting), *n.* the act or sport of soaring in a parachute while being towed by a motorboat, car, or other fast vehicle: *In parakiting, the water skier becomes airborne when his trailing parachute pops open* (Time).

**par|a|lan|guage** (par′ə lang′gwij), *n.* the paralinguistic parts of language.
**par|al|de|hyde** (pə ral′də hīd), *n.* a colorless liquid, obtained by the action of sulfuric acid on ordinary acetaldehyde, used as a hypnotic and sedative and as a solvent, in the manufacture of organic compounds. *Formula:* $C_6H_{12}O_3$
**par|a|le|gal** (par′ə lē′gəl), *adj.* of or having to do with law in an auxiliary capacity: *Greater use can be made of paralegal aides—nonlawyers who are specially trained to do minutiae that require an inefficiently large amount of an attorney's time* (Time). [< *para-*[1] + *legal*]
**par|a|leip|sis** (par′ə līp′sis), *n., pl.* **-ses** (-sēz). = paralipsis.
**par|a|lep|sis** (par′ə lep′sis), *n., pl.* **-ses** (-sēz). = paralipsis.
**par|a|lin|guis|tic** (par′ə ling gwis′tik), *adj.* of or having to do with factors connected with but not essentially part of language, such as tone of voice, tempo of speech, gestures, and facial expressions: *Wolfram ... rejects the possibility of distinguishing 'careful' and 'casual' speech, as Labov had done, on the grounds that interpretation of paralinguistic cues is open to subjective bias* (Language).
**par|a|lin|guis|tics** (par′ə ling gwis′tiks), *n.* the study of paralinguistic phenomena.
**Par|a|li|pom|e|non** (par′ə li pom′ə non, -lī-), *n.* either of the books in the Douay Bible known as "Chronicles" in the Protestant Old Testament. [< Latin *paralīpomena* < Greek *paraleipómena* (literally) things omitted, ultimately < *paraleípein* omit < *para-* beside + *leípein* to leave (because it contains details omitted in I, II Kings)]
**par|a|lip|sis** (par′ə lip′sis), *n., pl.* **-ses** (-sēz). a rhetorical device by which a speaker or writer emphasizes something by pretending to ignore it. *Examples:* "disregarding his other faults," "not to mention his heroism," "to say nothing of his virtues." [< Greek *paráleipsis* omission, passing over < *paraleípein* pass by, leave to the side < *para-* beside + *leípein* leave]
**par|al|lac|tic** (par′ə lak′tik), *adj.* of or having to do with a parallax: *parallactic angle.*

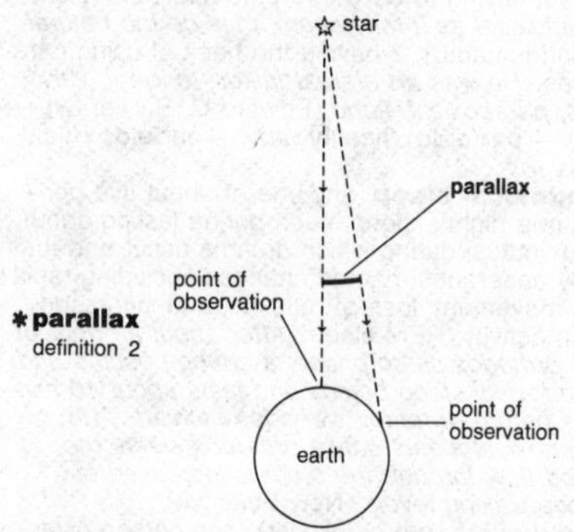


***parallax**
definition 2

***par|al|lax** (par′ə laks), *n.* **1** the apparent change in the position of an object when it is seen or photographed from two different points which are not on a direct line with the object. Parallax is used in surveying to determine distances of objects. **2** *Astronomy.* the angle between the straight lines that join a heavenly body to two different points of observation, equal to the difference in the directions in which the body is seen from the two points. See also **annual parallax, diurnal parallax. 3** *Photography.* the difference between what the viewfinder shows and what the lens records on a film. **4** an apparent shifting of the cross hairs of a telescope, caused by imperfect focusing. [< Greek *parállaxis* change, alternation, < *parallássein* to alter < *para-* beside + *allássein* to change < *állos* other]
***par|al|lel** (par′ə lel), *adj., n., v.,* **-leled, -lel|ing** or (*especially British*) **-lelled, -lel|ling.** *—adj.* **1** at or being the same distance apart everywhere like the two rails of a railroad track. In geometry, parallel lines or planes extend alongside one another, always equidistant and (in Euclidean geometry) never meeting however far extended, or (in projective geometry) meeting at infinity. *The Appalachian ridge-and-valley region is the most notable example in the world of parallel ridges and valleys* (Finch and Trewartha).
**2** *Figurative.* similar; corresponding: *parallel customs in different countries, parallel points in the characters of different men.* **SYN:** analogous, like.
**3** *Music.* **a** (of parts) moving so that the interval between them remains the same: *parallel thirds, fifths, etc.* **b** having to do with major and minor keys having the same tonic, such as C major and C minor. **4** having to do with things, especially mechanisms, of which some essential parts are parallel, or which are used to produce parallelism of movement: *a parallel digital computer.* **5** *Electronics.* having all positive poles joined to one conductor, and all negative ones to the other: *a parallel circuit.*

**music:**

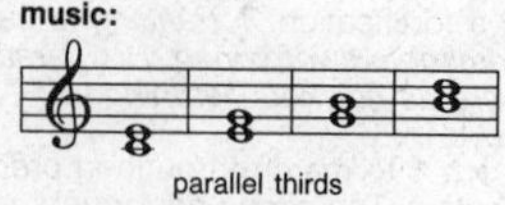

parallel thirds

***parallel**
definitions 3a, 2a

**earth:**

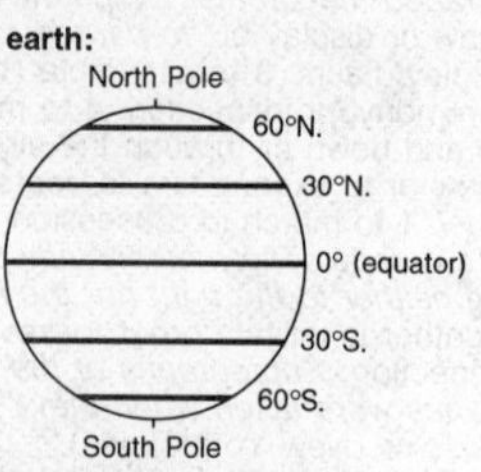


**parallels (lines of latitude)**

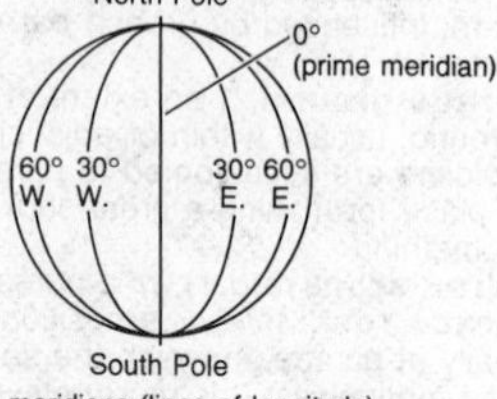


meridians (lines of longitude)

*—n.* **1** a parallel line or surface: *the parallels seem to come together in the distance.* **2** in geography: **a** any of the imaginary circles around the earth parallel to the equator, marking degrees of latitude: *The 49th parallel marks much of the boundary between Canada and the United States.* **b** the markings on a map or globe that represent these circles. **3** *Figurative.* a person or thing like or similar to another: *His experience was an interesting parallel to ours. We have to go to other centuries to find a parallel to his career* (William Osler). **SYN:** counterpart, match.
**4** *Figurative.* a comparison to show likeness: *Draw a parallel between this winter and last winter. There is no sort of parallel between the cases* (Joseph Butler). **5** the condition or relation of being parallel; parallelism: (*Figurative.*) *Niles-Bement-Pond and Bell "would work in parallel" if the transaction is completed* (Wall Street Journal). **6** an arrangement of the wiring of batteries, lights, or other electrical devices in which all the positive poles or terminals are joined to one conductor, and all the negative to the other: *When several devices are connected "in parallel," you can turn on one light or one toaster without having everything else going* (Beauchamp, Mayfield, West). **7** trench dug parallel to the defenses of a fort by an attacking force for its own protection.
*—v.t.* **1** to be at the same distance from throughout the length: *The street parallels the railroad. He had then ... crossed over a ridge that paralleled their rear* (Rudyard Kipling). **2** to cause to be or run parallel to. **3** *Figurative.* to find a case that is similar or parallel to; furnish a match for: *Can you parallel that for friendliness?* **4** *Figurative.* to be like; be similar to; correspond or be equivalent to: *Your story closely parallels what he told me.* **5** *Figurative.* to compare in order to show likeness; bring into comparison; liken.
**6** *Obsolete.* to bring into conformity.
**parallels,** *Printing.* a reference mark consisting of a pair of vertical parallel lines: *parallels inserted on the margin.*
[< Latin *parallēlus* < Greek *parállēlos* < *pará allêlois* beside one another]

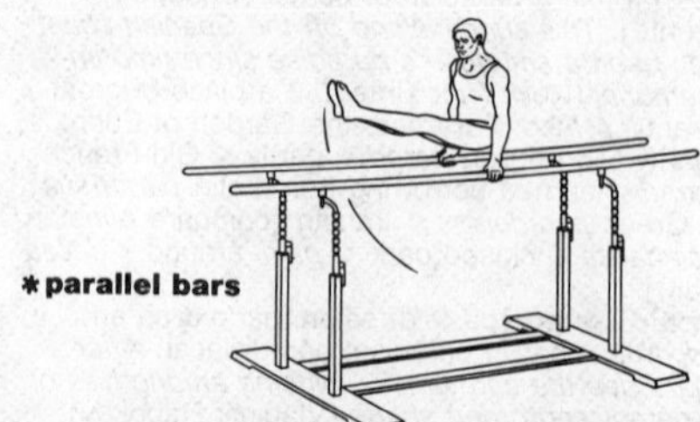

***parallel bars**

***parallel bars**, a pair of raised bars horizontal to the ground, used in gymnastics to develop the muscles, especially of the arms and chest.

**parallel cousin**, *Anthropology.* one of two cousins whose parents include two brothers or two sisters; ortho-cousin.

***par|al|lel|e|pi|ped** (par′ə lel′ə pī′pid, -pip′id), *n. Geometry.* a solid with three pairs of opposite, parallel faces which are parallelograms. [< Late Latin *parallēlepipedon* < Greek *parallēlepípedon* body with parallel surfaces < *parállēlos* parallel + *epípedon* a plane surface < *epi-* upon + *pédon* ground[1]]

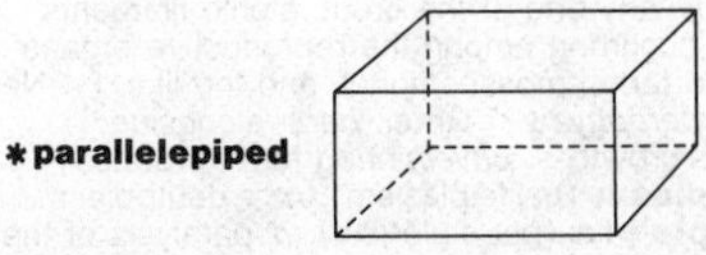
***parallelepiped**

**par|al|lel|e|pip|e|don** (par′ə lel′ə pip′ə don), *n.* = parallelepiped.

**parallel file**, a file of uniform section without taper from tang to point.

**parallel forces**, *Mechanics.* forces that act in parallel lines.

**par|al|lel|ism** (par′ə lel′iz əm), *n.* **1** a being parallel. **2** *Figurative.* likeness; similarity; correspondence; agreement: *For the first 14 years of life, the schooling of a girl is virtually the same as for a boy. But in high school ... parallelism is likely to end* (Science News Letter). **3** parallel statements in writing, expressed in the same grammatical form. *Example:* "He was advised to rise early, to work hard, and to eat heartily." **4** *Metaphysics.* the doctrine that mental and bodily processes are concomitant, each varying with variation of the other, but that there is no causal relation of interaction between the two series of changes. **5** *Obsolete.* a simile.

**par|al|lel|ist** (par′ə lel′ist), *n.* **1** a person who draws a parallel or comparison. **2** an advocate of the metaphysical doctrine of parallelism.

**par|al|lel|is|tic** (par′ə le lis′tik), *adj.* of the nature of or involving parallelism: (*Figurative.*) *This parallelistic development of corbeling differs from that of the true arch, which seems everywhere to be derived from a single original source* (Alfred L. Kroeber).

**par|al|lel|i|ty** (par′ə lel′ə tē), *n.* parallel arrangement, condition, or character.

**par|al|lel|ize** (par′ə le līz), *v.t.*, **-ized, -iz|ing. 1** to make parallel; place so as to be parallel, especially for comparison; bring into comparison; compare. **2** to furnish a parallel for, or form a parallel to; match. —**par′al|lel|i|za′tion**, *n.*

**par|al|lel|ly** (par′ə lel′lē), *adv.* in a parallel manner.

**parallel motion**, **1** *Music.* motion involving two parts or voices sounded together and moving in the same direction at the same intervals, usually parallel thirds or sixths. **2** a mechanism by which the end of a piston rod is caused to move in a straight line in spite of deflecting effort.

**parallel of declination**, *Astronomy.* any imaginary circle whose plane is parallel to the celestial equator.

**parallel of latitude**, any imaginary circle on the earth's surface, parallel to the equator, by which degrees of latitude are represented: *Parallels of latitude ... decrease in size with increasing distance from the equator* (Robert H. Baker).

***par|al|lel|o|gram** (par′ə lel′ə gram), *n.* **1** a four-sided plane figure whose opposite sides are parallel and equal, such as a rectangle or diamond. **2** a thing shaped like this. [< Latin *parallēlogrammus* < Greek *parallēlógrammos* < *parállēlos* parallel + *grammḗ* line[1]]

***parallelogram**
definition 1
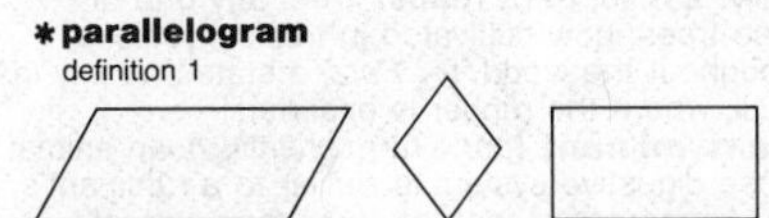

**par|al|lel|o|pi|ped** (par′ə lel′ə pī′pid, -pip′id), *n.* = parallelepiped.

**parallel parking**, parking with the length of the car parallel to the curb.

**par|al|lels** (par′ə lelz), *n.pl.* See under **parallel**.

**parallel sailing**, sailing due east or west, as along a parallel of latitude.

**par|a|lo|gi|a** (par′ə lō′jē ə), *n. Psychology.* a mental disorder characterized by difficulty in expressing ideas or illogicalness and irrelevance in speech. [< New Latin *paralogia* < *para-*[1] + *-logia* -logy]

**pa|ral|o|gism** (pə ral′ə jiz əm), *n. Logic.* **1** a piece of false or erroneous reasoning, especially one of which the reasoner himself is unconscious. **2** reasoning of this kind. [< Late Latin *paralogismus* < Greek *paralogismós* < *paralogízesthai* to reason falsely < *para-* beside + *logízesthai* to reason, argue < *lógos* speech, systematic logic]

**pa|ral|o|gist** (pə ral′ə jist), *n.* a person who uses paralogisms; a false reasoner.

**pa|ral|o|gis|tic** (pə ral′ə jis′tik), *adj.* characterized by paralogism or incorrect reasoning; illogical.

**pa|ral|o|gize** (pə ral′ə jīz), *v.i.*, **-gized, -giz|ing.** to commit a paralogism.

**Par|a|lym|pic** (par′ə lim′pik), *adj.* of or having to do with the Paralympics: *the world Paralympic record in archery.*

**Par|a|lym|pics** (par′ə lim′piks), *n.pl.* a series of international sports contests in which the participants are paraplegics. [< *Para*(plegic) (O)*lympics*]

**par|a|lyse** (par′ə līz), *v.t.*, **-lysed, -lys|ing.** *Especially British.* paralyze.

**pa|ral|y|sis** (pə ral′ə sis), *n., pl.* **-ses** (-sēz). **1a** a lessening or loss of the power of motion or sensation in any part of the body: *The accident left him with paralysis of the legs. To the public "paralysis" means a serious crippling, whereas it may actually be only a barely perceptible and transient loss of muscular control* (New York Times). **b** a disease characterized by this. **2** *Figurative.* a condition of helpless lack of activity; state of being helpless; crippling: *The war caused a paralysis of trade.* [< Latin *paralysis* < Greek *parálysis* palsy, disablement; (literally) loosening < *paralýein* loosen from beside < *para-* beside + *lýein* loosen. See etym. of doublet **palsy**.]

**paralysis ag|i|tans** (aj′ə tanz), = Parkinson's disease. [< New Latin *paralysis agitans* shaking palsy]

**par|a|lyt|ic** (par′ə lit′ik), *adj., n.* —*adj.* paralysis; having paralysis: *Latest reports showed that there were only forty-nine cases of paralytic polio and two cases of nonparalytic* (New York Times). —*n.* **1** a person who has paralysis. **2** a stroke of paralysis.

**par|a|ly|za|tion** (par′ə lə zā′shən), *n.* **1** the act of paralyzing. **2** the state of being paralyzed; paralysis.

**par|a|lyze** (par′ə līz), *v.t.*, **-lyzed, -lyz|ing. 1** to affect with a lessening or loss of the power of motion or feeling; palsy: *His left arm was paralyzed.* **2** *Figurative.* to make powerless or helplessly inactive; make ineffective; cripple; stun; deaden: *Fear paralyzed my mind. I overcame the extreme shyness that had formerly paralyzed me in her presence* (Washington Irving). **SYN:** benumb, stupefy. —**par′a|lyz′er**, *n.* —**par′a|lyz′ing|ly**, *adv.*

**par|a|mag|net** (par′ə mag′nit), *n.* a paramagnetic body or substance.

**par|a|mag|net|ic** (par′ə mag net′ik), *adj., n.* —*adj.* having to do with a class of substances, such as liquid oxygen, whose capability of being magnetized is slightly greater than that of a vacuum or unity, though much less than that of iron. The magnetization of such a substance is parallel to the lines of force in a magnetic field and proportional to the intensity of the magnetic field.
—*n.* a paramagnetic substance.
[< *para-*[1] + *magnetic*] —**par′a|mag|net′i|cal|ly**, *adv.*

**par|a|mag|net|ism** (par′ə mag′nə tiz əm), *n.* the phenomena exhibited by paramagnetic substances.

**par|a|mat|ta** (par′ə mat′ə), *n.* a light-weight cloth with a cotton (formerly, silk) warp and a merino wool filling, used for dresses. Also, **parramatta**. [< *Paramatta*, a city in Australia]

***par|a|me|ci|um** (par′ə mē′shē əm, -sē-), *n., pl.* **-ci|a** (-shē ə, -sē ə). an extremely small, one-celled animal shaped like a slender slipper, covered with cilia, and having a groove along one side leading into an open mouth. Paramecia live in almost all fresh water. *One strain of paramecium—the 'killer' strain—can produce a toxin which destroys another strain—the 'sensitive' strain* (G. M. Wyburn).
[< New Latin *Paramecium* the typical genus < Greek *paramḗkēs* oblong < *para-* on one side, against + *mêkos* length]

***paramecium**
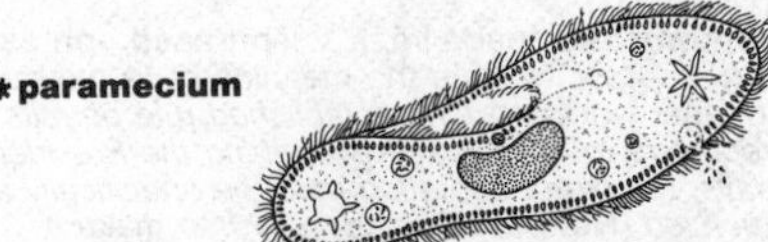

**par|a|med|ic**[1] (par′ə med′ik), *n.* a medical corpsman who parachutes from an aircraft: *the rescue plane with paramedics aboard* (Chicago Tribune). [< *para-*[2] + *medic*[1]]

**par|a|med|ic**[2] (par′ə med′ik), *n., adj.* —*n.* a medical technician or other auxiliary worker in medicine.
—*adj.* = paramedical.
[back formation < *paramedical*]

**par|a|med|i|cal** (par′ə med′ə kəl), *adj.* having to do with medicine in an auxiliary capacity; involving services or studies that are related to but not part of the medical profession: *The complexity of health problems has given rise to many paramedical callings, from the university physiologist to the hospital aide* (Harper's). [< *para-*[1] + *medical*]

**par|a|men|stru|al** (par′ə men′strů əl), *adj.* of or having to do with the paramenstruum.

**par|a|men|stru|um** (par′ə men′strů əm), *n.* a period of eight days comprising the four days preceding menstruation and the first four days of menstruation: *Recent studies have shown that in women half of all medical and surgical admissions to hospital occur during the paramenstruum ... At this time women appear to have a lowered pain threshold, lowered resistance to infection, and an increased tendency to fever and allergy* (London Times). [< *para-*[1] + New Latin *menstruum* < Latin *mēnstruus* menstrual]

**par|a|ment** (par′ə mənt), *n.* a decorative ecclesiastical vestment. [< Medieval Latin *parāmentum* < Latin *parāre* to prepare + *-mentum* -ment]

**pa|ram|e|ter** (pə ram′ə tər), *n.* **1** *Mathematics.* a constant in a particular calculation or case that varies in other cases, especially a constant occurring in the equation of a curve or surface, by the variation of which the equation is made to represent a family of such curves or surfaces. **2** a measurable factor which helps with other such factors to define a system: *Various individual experiments have climbed past various obstacles to reach positions close to the break-even level. In fact, in some instances two of the three essential parameters (density, temperature and confinement time) have already been achieved* (Scientific American). **3** any defining or characteristic factor: *the mind with all its parameters and limits ingrained through years of constant failure to aim beyond the "feasible" and "allowable," the "probable"* (Atlantic). [< New Latin *parametrum* < Greek *para-* beside + *métron* meter]

**par|a|met|ric** (par′ə met′rik), *adj.* of, having to do with, or in the form of a parameter. —**par′a|met′ri|cal|ly**, *adv.*

**parametric amplifier**, a high-frequency amplifier of very low noise that amplifies a signal by varying the capacitance or inductance.

**parametric conversion**, a process for changing a beam of light of one frequency into two beams of different frequencies: *the parametric conversion of X rays.*

**pa|ram|e|trize** (pə ram′ə trīz), *v.t.*, **-trized, -triz|ing.** to determine the parameters of: *The nuclear charge distribution ... can be parametrized directly using a suitable mathematical form which does not necessarily have fundamental significance* (New Scientist). —**pa|ram′e|tri|za′tion**, *n.*

**par|a|mil|i|tar|ism** (par′ə mil′ə tə riz′əm), *n.* paramilitary principles and practices.

**par|a|mil|i|tar|y** (par′ə mil′ə ter′ē), *adj.* **1** organized militarily, but not part of or in cooperation with the official armed forces of a country. **2** of or having to do with a military force so organized and its tactics: *In the paramilitary arenas of subversion, intimidation, and insurrection, an open and peaceful society is again at a disadvantage* (John F. Kennedy). [< *para-*[1] + *military*]

**par|am|ne|sia** (par′am nē′zhə, -zē ə), *n.* **1** a perversion of the memory characterized by the illusory impression of having previously experienced, seen, heard, or otherwise sensed that with or in which one is involved at a given moment and for the first time. **2** a condition, technically a form of aphasia, in which the correct use of words cannot be recalled. [< *par-* + *amnesia*]

**par|am|ne|sic** (par′am nē′sik, -zik), *adj.* of, causing, or resembling paramnesia: *The whole place took on a paramnesic air of unreality* (Time).

**par|a|mo** (par′ə mō; *Spanish* pä′rä mō), *n., pl.* **-mos** (-mōz; *Spanish* -mōs). a high plateau region in tropical South America, especially in the Andes, often bare of all vegetation except mosses, lichens, and the like, and swept constantly by strong, cold winds. [< Spanish *páramo;* origin unknown]

**par|a|morph** (par′ə môrf), *n. Mineralogy.* a pseudomorph formed by a change in molecular structure without a change in chemical composition. [< *para-*[1] + Greek *morphḗ* form]

**par|a|mor|phic** (par′ə môr′fik), *adj.* of, having to do with, or resembling a paramorph.

**Pronunciation Key:** hat, āge, cãre, fär; let, ēqual, tėrm; it, īce; hot, ōpen, ôrder; oil, out; cup, pu̇t, rüle; child; long; thin; ᴛʜen; zh, measure; ə represents **a** in about, **e** in taken, **i** in pencil, **o** in lemon, **u** in circus.

**par|a|mor|phism** (par′ə môr′fiz əm), *n.* the change of one mineral to another having the same chemical composition but a different molecular structure.

**par|a|mount** (par′ə mount), *adj., n.* —*adj.* chief in importance; above others; supreme: *Truth is of paramount importance. ... to make Britain the paramount power in India* (Macaulay). SYN: See syn. under **dominant**.
—*n.* an overlord; supreme ruler.
[< Anglo-French *paramont* above < *par-* by + *amont* up < Latin *ad montem* to the mountain]
—**par′a|mount|ly**, *adv.*

**par|a|mount|cy** (par′ə mount′sē), *n.* the condition or status of being paramount; supremacy: *We have a duty to them, the duty of recognising the paramountcy of business interests* (Punch).

**par|a|mount|ship** (par′ə mount′ship), *n.* = paramountcy.

**par|a|mour** (par′ə mu̇r), *n.* **1** a person who takes the place of a husband or wife illegally. **2** *Archaic.* a lover. [< Old French *paramour* < *par amour* by (or for) love < Latin *per amorem*]

**par|am|y|lum** (par am′ə ləm), *n.* a starchlike food reserve found in certain one-celled organisms, such as euglena. [< *par-* + *amylum*]

**par|a|my|o|sin** (par′ə mī′ə sin), *n.* a fibrous form of myosin that freezes muscle tension: *Many mollusks have special muscles, usually containing a high proportion of paramyosin, which can maintain powerful contractions over long periods with a low energy expenditure* (Graham Hoyle). [< *para-*[1] + *myosin*]

**par|a|myx|o|vi|rus** (par′ə mik′sə vī′rəs), *n.* any one of a group of viruses that includes the viruses causing mumps and various respiratory diseases. [< *para-*[1] + *myxovirus*]

**pa|ra|na pine** (par′ə nä′), **1** an araucaria of Brazil, grown for its lumber. **2** the wood of this tree, used in building and construction. [< *Paraná*, a river in Brazil]

**par|a|nee** (par′ə nē′), *n.* the object of a paranoiac's delusions: *Every paranoiac has ... paranees who just can't wait to confirm his delusions of grandeur and even feed on them* (Harper's). [< *paran*(oia) + *-ee*]

**par|a|neph|ric** (par′ə nef′rik), *adj.* of or having to do with a paranephros.

**par|a|neph|ros** (par′ə nef′ros), *n.* = adrenal gland. [< New Latin *paranephros* < Greek *para* beside + *nephrós* kidney]

**pa|rang** (pä′rang), *n.* a large, heavy knife, somewhat like a machete, used by the Malayans and others as a tool or weapon: *One of Lingard's seamen at once retaliated by striking at the ... savage with his parang—three such choppers brought for the purpose of clearing the bush* (Joseph Conrad). [< Malay *parang*]

**par|a|noe|a** (par′ə nē′ə), *n.* = paranoia.

**par|a|noe|ac** (par′ə nē′ak), *n., adj.* = paranoiac.

**par|a|noi|a** (par′ə noi′ə), *n.* **1** a form of psychosis in which a person imagines that he is being persecuted or that he is very great or important. People suffering from paranoia maintain their intelligence, although paranoia is a chronic disorder whose symptoms approach schizophrenia the closer the consciousness comes to realizing the conflicts of personality. *The "Napoleonic complex" disease, paranoia may take the form either of belief that one has unique ability or that all the world is plotting against one* (New York Times). **2** an irrational distrust of others; complex of persecution. [< New Latin *paranoea* < Greek *paránoia* < *paránoös* distracted < *para-* beside, beyond + *nóos, noûs* mind]

**par|a|noi|ac** (par′ə noi′ak), *n., adj.* —*n.* a person afflicted with paranoia.
—*adj.* **1** of or like paranoia. **2** afflicted with paranoia. —**par′a|noi′a|cal|ly**, *adv.*

**par|a|noic** (par′ə noik′), *adj.* of or characterized by paranoia; paranoid. —**par′a|noi′cal|ly**, *adv.*

**par|a|noid** (par′ə noid), *adj., n.* —*adj.* **1** resembling or tending toward paranoia (used especially of symptoms occurring in many psychoses): *Pure paranoia is rare, but many ill persons exhibit traces of paranoid thinking* (New York Times). **2** having the characteristics of paranoia: *A patient with paranoid psychosis carries to extremes the normal methods of maintaining self-esteem* (Merck Manual).
—*n.* a paranoid person: ... *the prancing paranoid who planned to rule the world from Berlin* (Time).

**paranoid schizophrenia**, *Psychiatry.* a mental disease resembling paranoia but also characterized by autistic behavior, hallucinations, and gradual deterioration of the personality.

**par|a|nor|mal** (par′ə nôr′məl), *adj.* outside normal perception or knowledge; psychic: *paranormal communication.* —**par′a|nor′mal|ly**, *adv.*

**Par|an|thro|pus** (par′an thrō′pəs, pə ran′thrə-), *n.* any manlike ape of an extinct genus characterized by massive jaws and teeth, fossils of which have been discovered in South Africa. [< *par-* + Greek *ánthrōpos* man]

**par|a|nu|cle|in** (par′ə nü′klē in, -nyü′-), *n. Chemistry.* any amorphous substance of a group that, unlike true nucleins, does not yield nitrogenous bases on decomposition; pseudonuclein.

**pa|ra**, or **Pa|rá nut** (pä rä′), = Brazil nut. [< *Pará*, a state and city in Brazil]

**par|a|nymph** (par′ə nimf), *n.* **1** in ancient Greece: **a** a friend who went with the bridegroom to bring home the bride. **b** the bridesmaid who escorted the bride to the bridegroom. **2** *Poetic.* **a** a bridesmaid. **b** a best man. [< Late Latin *paranymphus, paránymphos*, masculine, and *paranýmphē*, feminine < *para-* beside + *nýmphē* bride]

***par|a|pet** (par′ə pet, -pit), *n.* **1** a low wall or mound of stone or earth to protect soldiers, in front of a walk or platform at the top of a fort, trench, or other fortification. SYN: rampart. **2** a low wall or barrier at the edge of a balcony, roof, bridge, or the like: *the parapet of the great dam* (H. G. Wells). [< Middle French *parapet* < Italian *parapetto* < *para* defend! (see etym. under **para-**[2]) + *petto* breast < Latin *pectus*]

***parapet** definition 2

**par|a|pet|ed** (par′ə pet′id), *adj.* having a parapet or parapets: *a parapeted terrace.*

**par|aph** (par′əf), *n., v.* —*n.* a flourish made after a signature such as in a document, originally as a precaution against forgery and therefore very elaborate.
—*v.t.* **1** to add a paraph to. **2** to sign, especially with one's initials.
[< Middle French *paraphe*, learned borrowing from Medieval Latin *parraffus*, perhaps short for *paragraphum* paragraph mark. See etym. of doublet **paragraph**.]

**par|a|pher|nal|ia** (par′ə fər nāl′yə), *n.pl.* **1** personal belongings: *Trunks containing ... personal property—their sole chattels and paraphernalia on earth* (Arnold Bennett). **2** equipment; outfit: *the paraphernalia for a chemical experiment. Mountain climbing paraphernalia include ropes, straps, and climbing shoes. The ample fireplace ... garnished with a crane having various hooks and other paraphernalia* (Harriet Beecher Stowe). *The existence of constructed theories implies deductions, inductions, assumptions and all the paraphernalia of methodology which constitute the philosophy of science* (F. H. George). **3** *Law.* the articles of personal property which the law formerly allowed a woman to keep during her marriage. [< Medieval Latin *paraphernalia* < Late Latin *parapherna* < Greek *parápherna* a woman's personal property besides her dowry < *para-* besides + *phernê* dowry, related to *phérein* to bear]

▶ **Paraphernalia** meaning personal belongings is plural in form and use: *My paraphernalia are ready to be shipped.* When the meaning is equipment, *paraphernalia* is sometimes singular in use: *Camping paraphernalia includes tents, sleeping bags, and cooking equipment.*

▶ See **data, insignia** for related usage notes.

**par|a|phil|i|a** (par′ə fil′ē ə), *n. Psychology.* anomalous or deviant sexuality. [< New Latin *paraphilia* < *para-*[1] + *-philia*]

**par|a|phras|a|ble** (par′ə frā′zə bəl), *adj.* that can be paraphrased: *Some sort of paraphrasable meaning could be extracted from every poem* (Listener).

**par|a|phrase** (par′ə frāz), *v.,* **-phrased, -phrasing,** *n.* —*v.t.* to state the meaning of (a passage) in other words: *A long-established rule permits reporters to paraphrase everything the President says, but direct quotation must be specifically authorized* (New York Times). —*v.i.* to make a paraphrase. [< noun]
—*n.* **1** an expression of the meaning of a passage in other words: *I have here given my own paraphrase of this document, which has inspired so much controversy and commentary* (Edmund Wilson). **2** paraphrasing as a manner of literary treatment or educational technique.
[< Middle French *paraphrase*, learned borrowing from Latin *paraphrasis* < Greek *paráphrasis* < *para-* alongside of + *phrázein* to say] —**par′a-phras′er**, *n.*

**par|a|phrast** (par′ə frast), *n.* a person who paraphrases; paraphraser.

**par|a|phras|tic** (par′ə fras′tik), *adj.* **1** of, having to do with, or of the nature of paraphrase. **2** given to the use of paraphrase. —**par′a|phras′ti|cal|ly**, *adv.*

**par|a|phre|ni|a** (par′ə frē′nē ə), *n. Psychiatry.* any paranoid disorder or disease. [< New Latin *paraphrenia* < *para*(*noea*) + Greek *phrḗn, phrenós* mind]

**pa|raph|y|sis** (pə raf′ə sis), *n., pl.* **-ses** (-sēz). *Botany.* any one of the erect, sterile filaments often occurring among the reproductive organs in certain ferns, mosses, fungi, and the like. [< New Latin *paraphysis* < Greek *para-* alongside + *phýsis* growth < *phýein* bring forth, produce]

**par|a|plasm** (par′ə plaz əm), *n.* = deutoplasm.

**par|a|ple|gi|a** (par′ə plē′jē ə), *n.* paralysis of the legs and the lower part of the trunk; paralysis from the waist downward. [< New Latin *paraplegia* < Greek *paraplēgíē* paralysis < *paraplḗssein* to strike at the side; to be paralyzed < *para-* beside + *plḗssein* to strike]

**par|a|ple|gic** (par′ə plej′ik, -plē′jik), *n., adj.* —*n.* a person afflicted with paraplegia: *Then there are the paraplegics (both sides paralyzed from the waist down) who can be taught to crutch-walk and wait on themselves* (Marguerite Clark).
—*adj.* having to do with, or afflicted with, paraplegia.

**par|a|po|di|um** (par′ə pō′dē əm), *n., pl.* **-di|a** (-dē ə). one of the paired, jointless metameric processes or rudimentary limbs of certain annelids, that serve as organs of locomotion and sometimes of sensation or respiration. [< New Latin *parapodium* < Greek *para-* subsidiary + *poús, podós* foot]

**par|a|pro|fes|sion|al** (par′ə prə fesh′ə nəl, -fesh′nəl), *n., adj.* —*n.* a person who assists a teacher, nurse, social worker, or other professional; aide or assistant in a professional field who does not have full professional training; subprofessional: *Classes were proceeding, with regular teachers and "paraprofessionals," mostly mothers, to help out with classes in reading and in English, which is taught by modern adult methods of language instruction* (New Yorker).
—*adj.* of, having to do with, or acting as a paraprofessional: *There is some talk now of using paraprofessional help, trained on the job like interns* (Maclean's).

**par|a|psy|chi|cal** (par′ə sī′kə kəl), *adj.* = parapsychological.

**par|a|psy|cho|log|i|cal** (par′ə sī′kə loj′ə kəl), *adj.* of or having to do with parapsychology: *Critics often complain about the lack of repeatability of parapsychological experiments* (Harper's).

**par|a|psy|chol|o|gist** (par′ə sī kol′ə jist), *n.* a person who studies and records parapsychological phenomena.

**par|a|psy|chol|o|gy** (par′ə sī kol′ə jē), *n.* the branch of psychology dealing with the study of psychic phenomena, such as extrasensory perception, telepathy, and clairvoyance; psychical research: *Parapsychology, which is the serious study of ... occult matters by intelligent and unhysterical people, has become a recognized science* (Wall Street Journal). [< *para-*[1] beyond + *psychology*]

**par|a|quat** (par′ə kwot), *n.* a herbicide activated by photosynthesis upon contact with weeds. [< *para-*[1] + *quat*(ernary), part of the formula]

**par|a|quet** (par′ə ket), *n.* = parakeet.

**par|a|res|cue** (par′ə res′kyü), *n.* a rescue by parachutists. [< *para-*[2] + *rescue*]

**Pará rubber**, **1** rubber obtained from any of various tropical South American trees of the spurge family. **2** Also, **Pará rubber tree.** any one of these trees, now cultivated in tropical regions throughout the world. [< *Pará*, a state and city in Brazil, where the rubber is exported]

**par|a|ru|mi|nant** (par′ə rü′mə nənt), *n.* an animal whose digestive system is similar to a ruminant's: *Red kangaroos ... do not chew their cud, although they have a complex stomach structure that harbors a rich microbial community; they are pararuminants* (Scientific American). [< *para-*[1] + *ruminant*]

**par|a|sail** (par′ə sāl′), *n.* = parawing.

**par|a|sang** (par′ə sang), *n.* an ancient Persian measure of length, equal to about 3¼ miles as used by Herodotus and Xenophon, but ranging, according to Pliny and Strabo, to as much as 6½ miles. [< Latin *parasanga* < Greek *parasángēs*]

**par|a|se|le|ne** (par′ə sə lē′nē), *n., pl.* **-nae** (-nē). a bright moonlike spot on a lunar halo; mock moon: *And all in a moment, reading the very first words of her [Edith Sitwell's] "English Eccentrics," we are plunged into moonlight (albeit paraselene), mummies, hocus-pocus itself* (New York Times).
[< New Latin *paraselene* < Greek *para-* alongside, subsidiary + *selḗnē* moon < *sélas, -aos* brightness, light]

**par|a|se|len|ic** (par'ə sə len'ik), *adj.* of or having to do with a paraselene.

**par|a|shah** (par'ə shä), *n., pl.* **par|a|shoth** (par'ə-shōth), **par|a|shi|oth** (par'ə shē'ōth). *Judaism.* **1** a portion of the Torah (Law) appointed to be read in synagogue services every Sabbath and festival; lesson or reading. **2** one of the sections into which these lessons are divided. [< Hebrew *pārāshāh* division < *pārash* be separated]

**par|a|site** (par'ə sīt), *n.* **1** an animal or plant that lives on or in another from which it gets its food, always at the expense of the host. It may or may not injure the host, but it is usually unable to exist independently. Lice and tapeworms are parasites on animals. Mistletoe is a parasite on oak trees. **2** *Figurative.* a person who lives on others without making any useful and fitting return; hanger-on: *The lazy man was a parasite on his family. Nine people out of ten looked on him as something of a parasite, with no real work in the world* (John Galsworthy). **3** = parasite plane. **4** in ancient Greece: **a** a person who ate at the table or at the expense of another, earning meals by flattery or wit. **b** a priest's assistant who was admitted with the priests to the feast after a sacrifice. [< Latin *parasītus* < Greek *parásītos,* adjective, feeding beside < *para-* alongside of + *sîtos* food]

**parasite drag**, the drag caused by skin friction and the shape of those surfaces of an aircraft which do not contribute lift, such as the fuselage, nacelles, and ducts.

**par|a|sit|e|mi|a** (par'ə sī tē'mē ə), *n. Medicine.* the presence of parasites in the blood.

**parasite plane**, an aircraft designed to be carried aloft by another aircraft and launched in flight.

**par|a|sit|ic** (par'ə sit'ik), *adj.* **1** of or like a parasite; living on others: *The white blood cells constitute a gendearmery which is always ready to repeal parasitic invasion by engulfing the microscopic invaders and then digesting them* (Scientific American). **2** caused by parasites: *a parasitic disease.* —**par'a|sit'i|cal|ly**, *adv.*

**par|a|sit|i|cal** (par'ə sit'ə kəl), *adj.* = parasitic.

**par|a|sit|i|cide** (par'ə sit'ə sīd), *adj., n.* —*adj.* that kills parasites.
—*n.* a substance, such as a chemical compound or other agent, that kills parasites.
[< *parasit*(e) + *-cide*[1]]

**parasitic jaeger**, the commonest variety of jaeger, a hawklike sea bird of arctic regions with two pointed central tail feathers; arctic skua.

**parasitic stomatitis**, a form of stomatitis caused by a parasitic fungus; thrush.

**par|a|sit|ism** (par'ə sī'tiz əm), *n.* **1a** the relationship between two organisms in which one obtains benefits at the expense of the other, often injuring it: *Parasitism even goes so far as to destroy the cells of the life form that gives a home to the parasite* (Emory S. Bogardus). **b** parasitic infestation. **c** a disease caused by parasites. **2** *Figurative.* the practice of living as a human parasite.

**par|a|sit|ize** (par'ə sī'tīz), *v.t.,* **-ized, -iz|ing.** to infest as a parasite; be parasitic upon: *Certain bee flies parasitize velvet ants, and robber flies have been observed to capture bee flies* (Scientific American).

**par|a|sit|oid** (par'ə sī'toid), *n., adj.* —*n.* any one of various insects, especially wasps, that feed as larvae on other insects, causing their death when they complete their own development.
—*adj.* having to do with or characteristic of parasitoids: *a parasitoid wasp, parasitoid predators.*

**par|a|si|to|log|i|cal** (par'ə sī'tə loj'ə kəl), *adj.* having to do with parasitology.

**par|a|si|tol|o|gist** (par'ə sī tol'ə jist), *n.* an expert in parasitology.

**par|a|si|tol|o|gy** (par'ə sī tol'ə jē), *n.* the branch of biology or of medicine dealing with parasites and parasitism. [< Greek *parásītos* parasite + English *-logy*]

**par|a|sit|o|sis** (par'ə sī tō'sis), *n.* any parasitic condition or disease; parasitism. [< *parasit*(e) + *-osis*]

**par|a|ske|ni|a** (par'ə skē'nē ə), *n.pl.* the side wings of an ancient Greek theater, projecting from the stage toward the audience. [< Greek *paraskēnion,* singular < *para-* aside + *skēnē* stage]

**par|a|sol** (par'ə sôl, -sol), *n.* a light umbrella used especially as a protection against the sun; sunshade. It is often brightly colored. *The ladies sat protecting their complexions under large beach umbrellas and small ruffled parasols* (New Yorker). [< French *parasol* < Italian *parasole* < *para-* (see etym. under **para-**[2]) + *sole* sun < Latin *sōl, sōlis*]

**parasol ant**, = leaf-cutter ant.

**parasol mushroom**, a tall, white or light-tan, edible mushroom that resembles a parasol, growing usually in the fall.

**par|a|sta|tal** (par'ə stā'təl), *adj., n.* —*adj.* serving the state or government indirectly or in an auxiliary capacity; working with the state though not officially a part of it: *The* [*Uganda*] *Government monopoly of importing is to be exercised through parastatal bodies, such as the National Trading Corporation, and the Uganda Development Corporation* (London Times).
—*n.* a parastatal group.

**pa|ras|ti|chy** (pə ras'tə kē), *n., pl.* **-chies.** *Botany.* a spiral arrangement of lateral members, such as leaves or scales, where the internodes are short and the members closely crowded, as in the houseleek and pine cone. [< *para-*[1] + Greek *-stichia* < *stíchos* row[1], rank[1] < *steíchein* walk]

**par|a|sym|pa|thet|ic** (par'ə sim'pə thet'ik), *adj., n.* —*adj.* of or having to do with the part of the autonomic nervous system that produces such involuntary responses as dilating blood vessels, increasing the activity of digestive and reproductive organs and glands, contracting the pupils of the eyes, slowing down the heartbeat, and others, opposed to the action of the sympathetic nervous system.
—*n.* a nerve of the parasympathetic nervous system.

**par|a|syn|ap|sis** (par'ə si nap'sis), *n.* the side-by-side union of chromosomes during synapsis. [< New Latin *parasynapsis* < Greek *para-* para-[1] + *sýnapsis* union. Compare etym. under **synapse.**]

**par|a|syn|the|sis** (par'ə sin'thə sis), *n.* the formation of words by adding prefixes or suffixes to a compound or phrase. *Examples: free trade + -er = free-trader; great heart + -ed = great-hearted.* [< New Latin *parasynthesis* < Greek *para-* alongside + *sýnthesis* composition, synthesis]

**par|a|syn|thet|ic** (par'ə sin thet'ik), *adj.* having to do with parasynthesis: *Parasynthetic compounds of this same type are dressmaker, innkeeper, ... and woodpecker* (Simeon Potter).

**par|a|tac|tic** (par'ə tak'tik), *adj.* of, having to do with, or characterized by parataxis. —**par'a|tac'ti|cal|ly**, *adv.*

**par|a|tac|ti|cal** (par'ə tak'tə kəl), *adj.* = paratactic.

**par|a|tax|is** (par'ə tak'sis), *n. Grammar.* the arranging of clauses one after the other without connectives showing the relation between them. *Example:* The rain fell; the river flooded; the house was washed away. [< Greek *parátaxis* placement side by side < *para-* alongside + *táxis* arrangement]

**par|a|thi|on** (par'ə thī'on), *n.* a yellow or brown liquid, highly toxic to man, that is used to kill mites, aphids, and other insect pests. *Formula:* $C_{10}H_{14}NO_5PS$ [< *para-*[1] + *thi-* + *-on*]

**par|a|thor|mone** (par'ə thôr'mōn), *n.* the hormone produced by the parathyroid glands, which regulates the way the body uses calcium and phosphorus. [< *parath*(yroid) + (h)*ormone*]

**par|a|thy|roid** (par'ə thī'roid), *adj., n.* —*adj.* **1** near the thyroid gland. **2** of, having to do with, or obtained from the parathyroid glands: *Parathyroid extract can increase survival following irradiation by more than 50%* (Science News Letter). *Parathyroid hormone ... directs the removal of calcium from bone and its release into the blood* (Time).
—*n.* one of the parathyroid glands.

**par|a|thy|roid|ec|to|mize** (par'ə thī'roi dek'tə-mīz), *v.t.,* **-mized, -miz|ing.** to perform a parathyroidectomy on.

**par|a|thy|roid|ec|to|my** (par'ə thī'roi dek'tə mē), *n., pl.* **-mies.** the surgical removal of a parathyroid gland or glands. [< *parathyroid* + *-ectomy*]

**parathyroid glands**, small endocrine glands in or near the thyroid gland. Their secretion, which enables the body to use calcium and phosphorus, is necessary for life. There are usually four parathyroid glands. See picture under **endocrine gland.**

**par|a-trans|it** (par'ə tran'sit, -zit), *n.* transportation for carrying people from one place to another intermediate between conventional private and public forms of transportation: *Para-transit covered a multitude of services, including shared taxis, jitney buses, dial-a-ride, and car pools* (Richard Casement).

**par|a|troop** (par'ə trüp'), *adj.* of or having to do with paratroops: *a paratroop division.*

**par|a|troop|er** (par'ə trü'pər), *n.* a soldier trained to use a parachute for descent from an aircraft into a battle area or behind enemy lines. [< *para-*[2] + *trooper*]

**par|a|troops** (par'ə trüps'), *n.pl.* troops trained to use parachutes for descent from an aircraft into a battle area or behind enemy lines.

**par|a|tu|ber|cu|lo|sis** (par'ə tü bėr'kyə lō'sis, -tyü-), *n.* a usually fatal, bacterial disease of cattle, sheep, and goats characterized by intestinal infection; Johne's disease.

**par|a|ty|phoid** (par'ə tī'foid), *adj., n.* —*adj.* of the nature of or having to do with paratyphoid fever. —*n.* = paratyphoid fever.

**paratyphoid fever**, a bacterial disease resembling typhoid fever but usually milder, caused by salmonella organisms. It occurs in different varieties and with different effects in man, domestic fowl, and other animals.

**par a|vance** (pȧr ȧ väns'), *French.* in advance.

**par|a|vane** (par'ə vān), *n.* **1** a device shaped somewhat like a torpedo, with sawlike teeth at the front end and sides, towed usually as one of a pair at an angle outward from the stern of a minesweeper or destroyer so as to cut the mooring cables of mines, causing them to rise to the surface of the water at a safe distance from the ship, where they are exploded or sunk by gunfire. **2** a somewhat similar device loaded with a heavy explosive charge and linked to the vessel by a cable through which it may be exploded electrically, used against submarines. [< *para-*[1] + *vane*]

**par a|vi|on** (pȧr ȧ vyôN'), *French.* by airplane (a label for letters and packages to be sent by air mail).

**par|a|wing** (par'ə wing'), *n.* a sail-shaped, parachutelike device that unfurls to act like a wing during descent; combination of parachute and wing; parasail: *The parawings being tested by the Army are about 400 feet in area, and can be folded, packed, and deployed like a parachute* (Science News).

**par|a|xy|lene** (par'ə zī'lēn), *n.* one of three isomeric forms of xylene: *Paraxylene is used in the manufacture of polyester fiber and film* (Wall Street Journal).

**par|boil** (pär'boil'), *v.t.* **1** to boil till partly cooked: *Mother always parboils the beans before baking them.* **2** to overheat.
—*v.i.* to become overheated: (*Figurative.*) *to parboil in the hot sun.*
[< Old French *parboillir* < Late Latin *perbullīre* < *per-* thoroughly + *bullīre* to boil[2]; *par-* later taken as *part*]

**par|buck|le** (pär'buk'əl), *n., v.,* **-led, -ling.** —*n.* **1** a device for raising or lowering a heavy object (especially a cylindrical object such as a barrel or naval gun) vertically or in an inclined plane, consisting of a rope the middle of which is looped around a post at the height to which the object is to be raised, with its two ends passed around the object, and pulled in or let out from above, the object serving as a pulley. **2** a kind of double sling formed by passing the two ends of a rope, around the object, as a cask, to be raised or lowered.
—*v.t.* to raise or lower (something) by means of a parbuckle.
[alteration (perhaps influenced by *buckle*) of earlier *parbunkel;* origin unknown]

**Par|cae** (pär'sē), *n.pl. Roman Mythology.* the Fates.

**par|cel** (pär'səl), *n., v.,* **-celed, -cel|ing** or (*especially British*) **-celled, -cel|ling,** *adj., adv.* —*n.* **1** a bundle of things wrapped or packed together; package: *Her arms were filled with gift parcels.* **SYN:** See syn. under **bundle. 2** a box with things packed in it: *Put your shirts in this parcel.* **3** a piece; tract: *a parcel of land, a two-acre parcel fronting on the road.* **4** a lot; group of indefinite size; pack: *The peddler had a whole parcel of odds and ends in his sack.* (*Figurative.*) *a parcel of liars.* **5** *Commerce.* a quantity (sometimes definite) of a commodity dealt with in one transaction, especially in the wholesale market. **6** *Archaic.* a constituent or component part; item; fragment: *I sent your grace The parcels and particulars of our grief* (Shakespeare).
—*v.t.* **1** to make into a parcel; put up in parcels. **2** to wrap strips of canvas around (a rope) for protection.
—*adj., adv.* in part; partly; partially: *He was a jester and a parcel poet* (Scott) (adj.). *My grandame ... is parcel blind with age* (Scott) (adv.).
**parcel out**, to divide into portions or distribute in portions: *The two big nations parceled out the little country between them. When I asked why I could not be served by the only other competing distributor ... I was told that the two companies had parcelled out London between them* (London Times).
[< Old French *parcelle* < Vulgar Latin *particella* (diminutive) < Latin *particula* particle]

**par|cel-gilt** (pär'səl gilt'), *adj.* partly gilded: *a parcel-gilt cup, parcel-gilt silver.*

**par|cel|ing** (pär'sə ling), *n.* **1** *Nautical.* **a** the act or process of wrapping strips of canvas, usually tarred, around a rope. **b** strips of canvas

---

wrapped around a rope for its protection. **2** a division into parcels or portions; partition.

**par|cel|ling** (pär′sə ling), *n. Especially British.* parceling.

**parcel post**, the branch of the postal service that carries parcels.

**par|ce|nar|y** (pär′sə ner′ē), *n. Law.* joint heirship.

**par|ce|ner** (pär′sə nər), *n. Law.* a joint heir; coheir. [earlier, a partaker < Anglo-French *parcener,* Old French *parçonier,* perhaps < *parçon* partition, or < Medieval Latin *partionarius* < Latin *partītiō, -ōnis* partition]

**parch** (pärch), *v.t.* **1** to dry by heating; heat to evaporate the water, especially to store without spoiling; roast slightly: *The Indians parched corn.* **SYN**: scorch, sear, singe, char. **2** to make hot and dry or thirsty: *The fever parched him.* **3** to dry, shrivel, or wither with cold. —***v.i.*** to become hot and dry, or thirsty: *I am parching with the heat. There is a fresh sweet growth of grass in the Spring, but it ... parches up in the course of the summer* (Washington Irving).
[Middle English *parchen,* and *perchen;* origin uncertain]

**parched** (pärcht), *adj.* **1** dried by heat; roasted. **2** dried up; scorched. **3** dry or thirsty, as from heat.

**parch|ed|ness** (pär′chid nis), *n.* parched condition or quality.

***par|chee|si** or **par|che|si** (pär chē′zē), *n.* **1** a game somewhat like backgammon, played by moving pieces according to throws of dice. **2 Parcheesi,** a trademark for this game. **3** = pachisi. [see etym. under **pachisi**]

***Parcheesi**
definition 2

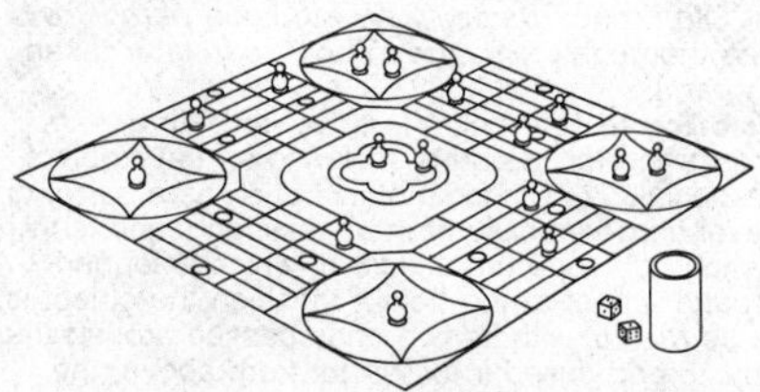

**parch|ment** (pärch′mənt), *n.* **1** the skin of sheep, goats or other animals, prepared for use as a writing material. **2** a manuscript or document written on parchment: *a parchment with the seal of Caesar* (Shakespeare). **3** paper that looks like parchment, especially parchment paper. [< Old French *parchemin* (influenced by *parche* bookcover < Latin *parthica* (*pellis*) Parthian leather) < Vulgar Latin *pergamīnum* < Late Greek *pergamēnón* (*mémbrānon*) Pergamene (skin), neuter of Greek *Pergamēnós* of *Pérgamon* Pergamum, the city of its origin] —**parch′ment|like′**, *adj.*

**parchment paper**, a tough, translucent, glossy paper that looks like parchment, made by soaking ordinary unsized paper in dilute sulfuric acid, then washing and drying it under pressure; vegetable parchment.

**parch|ment|y** (pärch′mən tē), *adj.* like parchment: *The lees of the strand traversed, with its trash, parchmenty paper, bottles, bags, and beer tins* (New Yorker).

**pard**[1] (pärd), *n. Archaic.* a leopard or panther: *a soldier, Full of strange oaths and bearded like the pard* (Shakespeare). *Freckled like a pard* (Keats). [< Old French *parde,* learned borrowing from Latin *pardus* < Greek *párdos* male panther]

**pard**[2] (pärd), *n. Dialect.* partner; friend; companion: *Thanks, pard, and them's big hopes to live up to* (Alaska Highway News). [short for *pardner,* variant of *partner*]

**par|di, par|die,** or **par|dy** (pär dē′), *adv., interj. Archaic.* a form of oath formerly much used for emphasis, meaning verily, certainly, or assuredly. Also, **perdie.** [Middle English *pardee,* also *perde* < *par deu* < Old French *par de* by God! < Latin *per* by through, *deus* god]

**pard|ner** (pärd′nər), *n. Dialect.* partner.

**par|don** (pär′dən), *n., v.* —***n.*** **1** forgiveness; passing over an offense without punishment: *Pardon for his hasty remark was all the boy asked.* **SYN**: absolution, amnesty. **2** excuse or toleration: *I beg your pardon, but I didn't hear you.* **3a** a setting free from punishment: *The judge's pardon meant the arrested man would be free if he stayed out of trouble.* **b** a legal document setting a person free from punishment. **4** a papal indulgence. [< Old French *pardon* < *pardoner;* see the verb]
—***v.t.*** **1** to forgive; pass over without punishment or blame: *Grandmother pardons us when we misbehave.* **SYN**: acquit, absolve. See syn. under **excuse.** **2** to excuse: *Pardon my impatience, but I have a train to catch.* **3** to set free from punishment; give a legal pardon to: *The governor pardoned the thief.* **4** *Obsolete.* to remit (as an obligation or debt).
[< Old French *pardoner,* and *perduner* < Medieval Latin *perdonare* < Latin *per-* thoroughly + *dōnāre* to give < *dōnum* gift]
► See **excuse** for a usage note.

**par|don|a|ble** (pär′də nə bəl), *adj.* that can be pardoned; excusable: *It gives me a feeling of pardonable importance* (George W. Curtis). *I dare say your daughter is pardonable* (Jane Porter). —**par′don|a|ble|ness**, *n.*

**par|don|a|bly** (pär′də nə blē), *adv.* in a manner admitting of pardon.

**par|don|er** (pär′də nər, pärd′nər), *n.* **1** a person who pardons or forgives. **2** a church official charged with the granting of indulgences in the Middle Ages, in return for offerings made to the church.

**pare** (pãr), *v.t.,* **pared, par|ing.** **1** to cut, trim, or shave off the outer part of; peel: *to pare an apple.* **SYN**: skin. **2** to cut away (an outer part or layer): *to pare one's nails.* **3** *Figurative.* to cut away little by little: *to pare down expenses.* [< Old French *parer* arrange, dispose < Latin *parāre* make ready, prepare. See etym. of doublet **parry.**]

**pa|re|cious** (pə rē′shəs), *adj. Botany.* paroecious.

**par|e|gor|ic** (par′ə gôr′ik, -gor′-), *n., adj.* —***n.*** a soothing medicine containing camphor, benzoic acid, and glycerin, and a very little opium. It is used especially to check an upset stomach or to relieve pain.
—***adj.*** soothing.
[< Late Latin *parēgoricus* < Greek *parēgorikós* soothing < *parēgoreîn* speak soothingly to < *para-* at the side of + *agoreýein* speak in public < *agorá* market place, assembly]

**pa|rei|a|sau|ri|an** (pə rī′ə sôr′ē ən), *adj., n.* —***adj.*** belonging to or having to do with an order or group of extinct, heavily built reptiles, known by fossil remains found in South Africa and elsewhere.
—***n.*** a pareiasaurian reptile. Also, **pariasaurian.**
[< New Latin *Pareiasauria* the order name (< Greek *pareiá* cheek + *saûros* lizard) + English *-an*]

**pa|rei|ra** (pə rãr′ə), *n.* = pareira brava.

**pareira bra|va** (brä′və, brā′-), the root of a South American vine related to the moonseed, formerly used especially in treating disorders of the urinary passages. [< Portuguese *pareira brava* (literarlly) wild vine]

**paren.**, parenthesis.

**pa|ren|chy|ma** (pə reng′kə mə, par′ən kī′-), *n.* **1** the fundamental tissue in higher plants, composed of living, unspecialized cells from which all other cells are formed. Most of the tissue in the softer parts of leaves, the pulp of fruits, and the cortex pith of young stems is parenchyma. **2** the tissue of an animal organ or part special or essential to it, as distinguished from its connective or supporting tissue. **3a** the soft, undifferentiated tissue composing the general substance of the body in some invertebrates, such as sponges and flatworms. **b** the undifferentiated cell substance or endoplasm of a protozoan. [< Greek *parénchyma* anything poured in < *para-* beside + *énchyma* infusion < *en-* in + *chýma* what is poured < *cheîn* to pour]

**par|en|chy|mal** (pə reng′kə məl, par′ən kī′-), *adj.* = parenchymatous.

**par|en|chym|a|tous** (par′eng kim′ə təs, par′ən-kī′mə-), *adj.* having to do with or of the nature of parenchyma. —**par′en|chym′a|tous|ly**, *adv.*

**parens.**, parentheses.

**pa|rens pa|tri|ae** (pãr′enz pā′trē ē), *n. Latin.* **1** *Law.* the sovereign power of guardianship over minors and insane or incompetent people as vested in the state or in the monarch: *The Crown, as parens patriae, took under its protection every infant child who was ordinarily resident within the realm* (London Times). **2** (literally) parent of the country.

**par|ent** (pãr′ənt), *n., adj.* —***n.*** **1a** a father or mother: *A positive means of prompt baby identification brings peace of mind to parents and hospital administrators alike* (Newsweek). **b** a person who has not produced the offspring but has the legal status of a father or mother, as by adoption. **2** any animal or plant that produces offspring: *The mother fox was a parent for the first time and became very nervous when the father would come to inspect his new family.* **3** *Figurative.* source; cause; origin: *Too much leisure is often the parent of mischief.* **4** = parent company: *American Cable asserted it was prepared, "backed by the full resources of its parent," [International Telephone and Telegraph Corp.] to establish and operate an overseas cable system* (Wall Street Journal).
—***adj.*** = parental.
[< Old French *parent* < Latin *parēns, -entis,* earlier present participle of *parere* to bring forth]

**par|ent|age** (pãr′ən tij), *n.* **1** descent from parents; family line; ancestry: *His parentage was Italian ancestry, of a grandfather and grandmother who came from Italy many years ago.* **SYN**: birth. **2** the condition or fact of being a parent; parenthood.

**pa|ren|tal** (pə ren′təl), *adj.* **1** of or having to do with a parent or parents; like a parent's: *parental advice, parental feelings.* **2** *Genetics.* of the generation in which hybrids are produced by crossbreeding. *Symbol:* P. —**pa|ren′tal|ly**, *adv.*

**Par|en|ta|li|a** (par′ən tā′lē ə), *n.pl.* an ancient Roman annual festival in honor of deceased parents and relatives, held from the 13th to the 21st of February, marked by the closing of the temples, the visiting of tombs, and the offering of oblations to the shades of the dead. [< Latin *Parentālia,* neuter plural of *parentālis* parental]

**parent company**, a business firm which controls one or more subsidiary firms: *A clause in its contract ... gives the parent company the right to buy up (at cost) and sell back to the distributor any product that he sells outside his area or to an unauthorized dealer* (Time).

**parent element**, *Physics.* an element that yields an isotope or daughter element through radioactive decay or nuclear bombardment.

**par|en|ter|al** (pə ren′tər əl), *adj. Physiology.* not entering by means of or passing through the alimentary canal; not intestinal. An intravenous injection provides parenteral nourishment. [< *par-* + *enter*(on) + *-al*[1]] —**par|en′ter|al|ly**, *adv.*

**pa|ren|the|ses** (pə ren′thə sēz), *n.* plural of **parenthesis.**

***pa|ren|the|sis** (pə ren′thə sis), *n., pl.* **-ses.** **1a** either or both of two curved lines used to set off a word, phrase, or sentence that explains or qualifies something within a sentence. **b** a word, phrase, or sentence inserted within a sentence to explain or qualify something. **2** an interval or digression; interlude; hiatus: *During the parenthesis of bad government and national tumult which filled the years between the death of Aldfrith ... and the renewed peace and order under Ceolwulf* (S. A. Brooke). [< Medieval Latin *parenthesis,* Late Latin, addition of a letter (or syllable) in a word < Greek *parénthesis* < *parentithénai* put in beside < *para-* beside + *en-* in + *tithénai* put, place]

***parenthesis**
definition 1a

...a hiatus (gap) in the action.

**pa|ren|the|size** (pə ren′thə sīz), *v.t.,* **-sized, -siz|ing.** **1** to insert as or in a parenthesis. **2** to put between the marks of parenthesis. **3** to put many parentheses in.

**par|en|thet|ic** (par′ən thet′ik), *adj.* **1** serving or helping to explain; qualifying; explanatory. **2** enclosed in parentheses. **3** using parentheses. **4** *Figurative.* occurring in the course of something else. —**par′en|thet′i|cal|ly**, *adv.*

**par|en|thet|i|cal** (par′ən thet′ə kəl), *adj.* = parenthetic.

**par|ent|hood** (pãr′ənt hůd), *n.* the condition of being a parent; fatherhood or motherhood: *Parenthood begins "officially" with the birth or adoption of an infant, but every girl or boy develops a certain background for motherhood or fatherhood during the years leading to maturity and marriage* (Sidonie M. Gruenberg).

**par|ent|ing** (pãr′ən ting), *n.* the process of caring for and raising offspring: *[He] turns to research on the history of parenting from primates to man ... and concludes, ... Parenting is mostly learned from identification with models* (New Republic).

**par|ent-in-law** (pãr′ənt in lô′), *n., pl.* **par|ents-in-law.** a father-in-law or mother-in-law: *All is well at the end for everybody but the interfering parents-in-law* (Punch).

**par|ent|less** (pãr′ənt lis), *adj.* **1** without parents: *He was my own uncle ... he had taken me when a parentless infant to his house* (Charlotte Brontë). **2** *Figurative.* without known parents, author, or source.

**Par|ent-Teach|er Association** (pãr′ənt tē′-chər). See **P.T.A.**

**par|er** (pãr′ər), *n.* **1** a person who pares. **2** an instrument for paring: *an apple parer.*

**par|er|gon** (pa rėr′gon), *n., pl.* **-ga** (-gə). subordinate or secondary work; by-work: *He and his orchestra played a suite of Symphonic Dances from West Side Story, a parergon of the musical show, and a very distinguished one* (London Times).

**pa|re|sis** (pə rē′sis, par′ə-), *n.* **1** a partial or incomplete paralysis. Paresis affects the ability to move, but does not affect the ability to feel. **2** a progressive disease of the brain caused by syphilis that gradually causes general paralysis: *General paresis (the result of long-standing syphilitic infection) has yielded spectacularly to treatment with reserpine* (Time). [< New Latin *paresis* < Greek *páresis* loss of strength, paralysis; (literally) a letting go < *pariénai* let pass, fall < *para-* by + *hiénai* let go]

**par|es|the|sia** (par′əs thē′zhə), *n.* an abnormal sensation of prickling, tingling, or itching of the skin. Also, **paraesthesia**. [< *par-* + *-esthesia* sensation, as in *anesthesia*]

**par|es|thet|ic** (par′əs thet′ik), *adj.* of, characterized by, or affected with paresthesia. Also, **paraesthetic**.

**pa|ret|ic** (pə ret′ik, -rē′tik), *adj., n.* —*adj.* of or having to do with paresis; caused by paresis.
—*n.* a person who has paresis.

**pa|re|u** (pä′rā ü), *n.* a rectangular piece of printed cotton cloth worn as a skirt or loincloth by the Polynesians. [< Tahitian *pareu*]

**pa|re|ve** (pär′ə və), *n.* = parve.

**par ex|cel|lence** (pȧr ek sə läns′; *Anglicized* pär ek′sə läns), *French.* beyond comparison; above all others of the same sort: *Michelangelo on the other hand is always in quest of new motifs, and in this sense he is par excellence the modern artist* (Atlantic).

**par ex|em|ple** (pȧr eg zäɴ′plə), *French.* for example.

**par|fait** (pär fā′, pär′fā), *n.* **1** ice cream with syrup or crushed fruit and whipped cream, served in a tall glass. **2** a rich ice cream containing eggs and whipped cream frozen unstirred. [< French, Old French *parfait* perfect]

**par|fi|lage** (pȧr fē lȧzh′), *n. French.* the unraveling of textile fabrics, galloons, or lace, especially those containing gold or silver threads, in vogue as a pastime in France and elsewhere in the latter part of the 1700's.

**par|fleche** (pär′flesh, pär flesh′), *n.* **1** a kind of very tough rawhide made (originally) by removing the hair from the skin of a buffalo by steeping it in a strong solution of wood ashes (or lye) and water and then drying it in the sun. **2** an article made of this rawhide: *The Plains Indian parfleche, a large envelope of hide used to store and carry personal possessions, sacred objects, foods, and other objects* (Beals and Hoijer). [American English < Canadian French *parflèche*, apparently < French *parer* to parry, ward off + *flèche* arrow (because it was used as a shield)]

**par|get** (pär′jit), *n., v.,* **-get|ed, -get|ing** or **-get|ted, -get|ting.** —*n.* **1** gypsum or other stone for making plaster. **2** a type of rough plaster consisting of lime, animal hair, and cow dung, formerly used in chimney flues. **3** plasterwork of an ornamental kind. **4** = whitewash.
—*v.t.* **1** to coat or plaster with parget. **2** to plaster with ornamental designs.
[< Old French *pargeter,* and *parjeter* to cast over a surface < *par-* through + *jeter* to throw]

**par|get|ing** or **par|get|ting** (pär′jə ting), *n.* **1** the act or process of applying parget or plastering ornamentally. **2** ornamental plaster or plasterwork.

**par|he|li|a|cal** (pär′hē lī′ə kəl), *adj.* = parhelic.

**par|he|lic** (pär hē′lik), *adj.* having to do with or resembling a parhelion.

**parhelic circle** or **ring**, a horizontal halo or circle of light that appears to pass through the sun.

**par|he|li|on** (pär hē′lē ən, -hēl′yən), *n., pl.* **-he|li|a** (-hē′lē ə, -hēl′yə). a bright circular spot of light, often showing the colors of the spectrum, that is sometimes seen on either side of the sun and level with it on a solar halo; mock sun; sundog. Parhelia are caused by the refraction of sunlight through ice crystals suspended in the atmosphere. [< Latin *parēlion* < Greek *parēlion* < *para-* beside + *hēlios* sun]

**Pa|ri|ah** (pə rī′ə, pä′rē-, par′ē-), *n.* a member of a low caste in southern India and Burma. [< Tamil *paṛaiyar,* plural of *paṛaiyan* drummer (the caste's hereditary duty at festivals) < *paṛai* large festival drum]

**pa|ri|ah** (pə rī′ə, pä′rē-, par′ē-), *n.* any person or animal generally despised; outcast: *the juvenile pariah of the village, Huckleberry Finn, son of the town drunkard* (Mark Twain). [< *Pariah*]

**pa|ri|ah|dom** (pə rī′ə dəm, pä′rē ə-, par′ē-), *n.* the quality or condition of being a pariah; degraded position.

**Par|i|an** (pãr′ē ən), *adj., n.* —*adj.* **1** of Paros, an island in the Aegean Sea: *Parian marble.* **2** having to do with or made of a type of fine white porcelain resembling Parian marble: *Parian statuary.*
—*n.* **1** a native or inhabitant of Paros. **2** Parian porcelain. **3** articles made of Parian porcelain; Parian ware.
[< Latin *Parius* of Paros (< Greek *Páros,* proper name) + English *-an*]

**Parian ware**, **1** a variety of unglazed, vitrified porcelain with a smooth, white surface, first made in the 1840's, and used especially for busts and figures. **2** busts, figures, and other articles made from this porcelain.

**pa|ri|a|sau|ri|an** (pə rī′ə sôr′ē ən), *adj., n.* = pareiasaurian.

**par|i|dig|i|tate** (par′ə dij′ə tāt), *adj.* having the same number of toes on each foot. [< Latin *pār, paris* + English *digitate*]

**pa|ri|es** (pãr′ē ēz), *n., pl.* **pa|ri|e|tes.** a wall or structure enclosing, or forming the boundary of, a cavity in an animal or plant body. [< Latin *pariēs, -etis* wall, partition]

**pa|ri|e|tal** (pə rī′ə təl), *adj., n.* —*adj.* **1** *Anatomy.* **a** of the wall of the body or of one of its cavities. **b** of or having to do with a parietal bone. **2** *Botany.* belonging to, connected with, or attached to the wall of a hollow organ or structure, especially of the ovary or of a cell (used especially of ovules). **3** *U.S.* having to do with or having authority over the residents in the buildings of a college: *a parietal committee.*
—*n.* **1** either of two bones that form part of the sides and top of the skull. **2** *U.S.* Usually, **parietals.** visitation rules in a dormitory for members of the opposite sex: ... *for liberalized "parietals" —campus term for women's visiting hours in male dormitories, or vice versa* (New York Times).
[< Late Latin *parietālis* < Latin *pariēs, -etis* wall]

**parietal cell**, a cell of the mucous membrane of the stomach that secretes hydrochloric acid.

**parietal lobe**, the middle lobe of each cerebral hemisphere. See picture under **brain**.

**pa|ri|e|tes** (pə rī′ə tēz), *n.* plural of **paries**.

**pa|ril|lin** (pə ril′in), *n. Chemistry.* a bitter white crystalline principle obtained from the root of sarsaparilla, used as a flavoring agent. *Formula:* $C_{45}H_{74}O_{17}$ [< (sarsa) *parilla* + *-in*]

**par|i-mu|tu|el** or **par|i|mu|tu|el** (par′i myü′chü əl), *n., adj.* —*n.* **1** the system of betting on a race, such as a horse race or dog race, in which those who have bet on the winners divide all the money bet, except for a part withheld by the management for costs, profits, taxes, and other expenses. **2** a machine for recording such bets; totalizator.
—*adj.* of or having to do with this system or machine: *Revenues from pari-mutuel taxes in recent years have been accounting for about 1.5% of the states' total annual tax take* (Wall Street Journal).
[< French *parimutuel* mutual wager; *pari* < *parier* to bet < Latin *pariāre* make equal; *mutuel* < Latin *mūtuus* borrowed]

**par|i mu|tu|el** (par′i myü′chü əl; *French* pȧ rē′-mʏ tʏ el′), *pl.* **par|is mu|tu|els.** pari-mutuel, a system of betting on races.

**par|ing** (pãr′ing), *n.* **1** a part pared off; skin; rind: *apple parings.* **2** the act of paring.

**paring knife**, a small knife used for paring.

**pa|ri pas|su** (pãr′ī pas′yü; par′ē pas′ü), *Latin.* at an equal pace or rate; in equal proportion: *The over-all productivity of labor has risen pari passu with this investment* (Atlantic). *Any method which would prevent hemolytic streptococcus infection would, pari passu, prevent further bouts of rheumatic fever* (David Seegal).

**par|i|pin|nate** (par′i pin′āt), *adj.* (of a leaf) pinnate with an even number of leaflets; pinnate without an odd terminal leaflet. [< Latin *pār, paris* equal + English *pinnate*]

**Par|is** (par′is), *n. Greek Legend.* a son of Priam, king of Troy. The carrying off of Helen, the wife of King Menelaus of Sparta, by Paris was the cause of the Trojan War.

**Paris** or **paris green**, a poisonous, emerald-green powder used as a pigment and in making sprays for killing insects. It is a compound of copper, arsenic, and acetic acid. [< *Paris,* France, where it was formerly made]

**par|ish** (par′ish), *n., adj.* —*n.* **1** a district that has its own church and clergyman: *The minister worked very hard to make the rounds of his parish and visit the homes of the sick.* **2** the people of a parish: *I look upon all the world as my parish* (John Wesley). **3** the congregation of a particular church. **4** a county in Louisiana. **5** a civil district in Great Britain, Northern Ireland, and some other parts of the Commonwealth.
—*adj.* of or having to do with a parish: *The large and lovely parish church of a country town has now been without a vicar for five months* (Manchester Guardian Weekly).
[< Old French *paroisse,* learned borrowing from Late Latin *parochia,* alteration of *paroecia* < Late Greek *paroikīā* ultimately < Greek *para-* near + *oîkos* a dwelling]

**parish house**, **1** any building maintained by a parish for its nonreligious functions. **2** the house of a clergyman.

**par|ish|ion|er** (pə rish′ə nər, -rish′nər), *n.* an inhabitant or member of a parish. [< Old French *paroissien* < *paroisse* parish]

**par|ish-pump** (par′ish pump′), *adj. Especially British.* of local interest or importance; limited in scope or outlook: *Resistance from parish-pump politics is clearly being encountered* (London Times).

**parish pump**, *Especially British.* local interests; parochial matters: *A regrettable feature of the new policies is a retreat from internationalism towards the parish pump* (Sunday Times).

**Pa|ri|sian** (pə rizh′ən, -rē′zhən), *adj., n.* —*adj.* of or having to do with Paris, the capital of France, or with its people.
—*n.* a person born or living in Paris.

**Pa|ri|si|enne** (pə rē′zē en′; *French* pȧ rē zyen′), *n., adj.* —*n.* a Parisian woman.
—*adj.* Parisian (feminine).

**par|is mu|tu|els** (par′i myü′chü əlz; *French* pȧ rē′ mʏ tʏ el′), plural of **pari mutuel**.

**par|i|syl|lab|ic** (par′i sə lab′ik), *adj.* (of Greek and Latin nouns) having the same number of syllables in the oblique cases as in the nominative case. [< Latin *pār, paris* equal + English *syllabic*]

**par|i|ty**[1] (par′ə tē), *n., pl.* **-ties.** **1** similarity or close correspondence with regard to state, position, condition, value, quality, or degree; equality: *To try to achieve parity in conventional weapons would mean such a regimentation of our industry and manpower* (Bulletin of Atomic Scientists). **2** *U.S.* a balance between the market prices for a farmer's commodities and his own gross expenditures. Parity is calculated to maintain the price of the farmer's product at a level equal in purchasing power to that of a base period, as from 1910 to 1914, or a later ten-year period. *If the index number of prices received equals the index number of prices paid, prices are at parity* (John H. Frederick). **3** *Finance.* **a** equivalence in value in the currency of a foreign country. **b** equivalence in value at a fixed ratio between moneys of different metals. **4** (in quantum mechanics) the behavior of a wave function in an atomic or other physical system when it is reflected to form its mirror image. If the sign of the function remains unchanged, parity is even; if the sign is changed, parity is odd. [< Latin *paritās* < *pār, paris* equal]

**par|i|ty**[2] (par′ə tē), *n. Medicine.* the condition of being parous; fact of having borne children. [< Latin *parere* to give birth + English *-ity*]

**parity index**, *U.S.* the average prices received by the farmer for his products and the average prices he paid for goods and services in a particular year, each expressed in terms of the equivalent prices during the base period used. It is used to establish the parity ratio.

**parity ratio**, *U.S.* the ratio between the index of prices received by the farmer and the index of prices he paid in a particular year, used in measuring his purchasing power in that year.

**park** (pärk), *n., v.* —*n.* **1** land set apart for the pleasure of the public: *Many cities have beautiful parks. Hyde Park is in London. A park may be only a tiny bit of green in a large city, with a few flowers, trees, and benches, or it may be a natural wilderness larger than some states* (Philip L. Seman). **2** land set apart for wild animals: *a game park.* **3** *British.* a place to leave an automobile or other vehicle, such as a baby carriage, for a time: *Motorists with time on their hands have hunted through parks of two and three hundred cars* (Punch). **4a** a space where army vehicles, supplies, artillery, and other such equipment are put when an army camps: *A torch gleamed momentarily in the transport park across the road* (Graham Greene). **b** the group so assembled. **5** the grounds around a fine house: *the turrets of an ancient chateau rising out of the trees of its walled park* (Washington Irving). **6** *U.S.* a high plateaulike valley among mountains. **7** an open space in a forest or wood. **8** (in English law) an enclosed tract of land held by royal grant for keeping game. **9** a place set aside for oyster breeding: *Oysters are obtained chiefly from cultivated parks in Chesapeake Bay* (White and Renner).
—*v.t.* **1a** to leave (an automobile, truck, or other vehicle) for a time in a certain place: *Park your car here.* **b** to place (a space vehicle) in orbit temporarily: *The satellite was parked about the earth before being transferred to a lunar orbit.* **2** to assemble and arrange (army vehicles, artillery, or other such equipment) in a park. **3** *Informal, Figurative.* to place, put, or leave: *to park oneself or one's coat on a chair.* **4** to enclose in, as if in, or as a park.
—*v.i.* to park an automobile, truck, or other vehi-

---

**Pronunciation Key:** hat, āge, cãre, fär; let, ēqual, tėrm; it, īce; hot, ōpen, ôrder; oil, out; cup, pu̇t, rüle; child; long; thin; ᴛʜen; zh, measure; ə represents **a** in about, **e** in taken, **i** in pencil, **o** in lemon, **u** in circus.

cle: *He parked near the library.* [< Old French *parc* < Medieval Latin *parricus* enclosure, probably < Germanic (compare Old English *pearroc* enclosure, paddock)] —**park′er**, *n.* —**park′like′**, *adj.*

***par|ka** (pär′kə), *n.* **1** a fur jacket with a hood, worn in Alaska and in northeastern Asia: *The icicles hang down like tusks under the parka hood* (Robert W. Service). **2** a long woolen or fabric shirt or jacket with a hood. [apparently ultimately < Samoyed (Siberia) *parka* outer garment made of skins]

***parka** definition 1

**Park Avenue**, a thoroughfare in New York City along part of which there are very fine, large, expensive office and residential buildings.

**park hack**, a horse trained and hired for riding in a public park: ... *park hacks and splendid high-stepping carriage horses* (Thackeray).

**par|kin** (pär′kin), *n.* a gingerbread cake made with oatmeal and molasses in and near Scotland. [perhaps < the name *Perkin* or *Parkin*]

**park|ing** (pär′king), *n.* **1** the act of a person who parks, especially of leaving an automobile, truck, or other vehicle for a time, especially in a public place: *They ... rely on better control of the traffic ... and much firmer restrictions on parking* (New Scientist). **2** parking space: *Some businessmen also help by providing free parking for their customers* (Matthew C. Sielski). **3** ground for or like a park. **4** turf, with or without trees, in the middle or along the side of a street.

**parking light**, either of two small lights at the front of a motor vehicle, used in combination with the tail lights for parking at night on a thoroughfare and for driving when visibility is partially obscured.

**parking lot**, *U.S.* an open area used for parking automobiles and other vehicles, often for a fee. In Great Britain it is called *car park.*

**parking meter**, *U.S.* a device containing a clock mechanism that is operated by the insertion of coins. It allows an automobile a specified amount of time in a parking area for each coin.

**parking orbit**, a temporary orbit in which a space vehicle is placed until an increase in its velocity sends it out into space: *The United States has used parking orbits on its Ranger shots to the Moon. Under this technique, the probe and a booster rocket are "parked" in orbit around the earth. At the appropriate point in the orbit, the booster is re-ignited, sending the vehicle toward its goal* (New York Times).

**parking space**, *U.S.* a space in which an automobile or other vehicle may be parked: ... *U.S. motorists, whose lot it is to dodge potholes, fight traffic jams, and search for nonexistent parking spaces* (Time).

**Par|kin|so|ni|an** (pär′kin sō′nē ən), *adj.* **1** of, having to do with, or like Parkinson's disease: *Parkinsonian tremors.* **2** of, having to do with, or suggesting Parkinson's Law: *The impact of the computer may to some extent be offset by Parkinsonian growth in staffs* (New Scientist).

**Par|kin|son|ism** (pär′kin sə niz′əm), *n.* = Parkinson's disease.

**Par|kin|son's disease** (pär′kin sənz), a chronic nervous disease, usually occurring late in life, characterized by muscular tremors and weakness, a tendency to walk peculiarly, and a fixity in facial expression: *Antihistamines have been used with moderate success in the treatment of Parkinson's disease* (Beaumont and Dodds). [< James *Parkinson,* 1755-1824, an English physician, who first described it]

**Parkinson's Law**, any one of various humorous tenets satirizing bureaucratic assumptions and practices, propounded by C. Northcote Parkinson (born 1909), a British historian: *Alone among the great institutions in Washington, the Court seems to have escaped Parkinson's Law, which holds that the number of employees in any office increases constantly and that the work expands to occupy the new hands* (Anthony Lewis). *Parkinson's Second Law is that Government expenditure rises to meet revenue* (Edwin L. Dale, Jr.).

**park-keep|er** (pärk′kē′pər), *n. British.* an official charged with maintaining and guarding a public park: *London's parks have ... tidy-minded park-keepers* (New Scientist).

**park|land** (pärk′land′), *n.* **1** a grassland area, especially in the temperate zone, with trees in small groups or isolated rather than in forests. **2** land set aside for use by the public: ... *New York State's aggressive program to convert the seaway border areas into parkland* (Toronto Daily Star).

**park|way** (pärk′wā′), *n.* **1** a broad road with spaces planted with grass, trees, and other plants, usually restricted to use by cars: *Parkways ... are great screened corridors, cut off by banks and trees from the sight of urban sprawl and rural mess* (Observer). **2** a strip along a road planted with grass, shrubs, and other plants.

**park|y** (pär′kē), *n., pl.* **park|ies.** *British Informal.* a park-keeper.

**parl** (pärl), *v.i., v.t., n.* = parle.

**parl.**, parliamentary.

**Parl.**, 1 Parliament. 2 Parliamentary.

**par|lance** (pär′ləns), *n.* **1** way of speaking; talk; language: *common parlance, legal parlance. "I'm satisfied where we be, Sir," said Mrs. Lapham, recurring to the parlance of her youth* (William Dean Howells). SYN: idiom. **2** *Archaic.* speech, especially debate; parleying. [< Anglo-French, Old French *parlance* < *parler* to speak; see etym. under **parley**]

**par|lan|do** (pär län′dō), *adj. Music.* **1** with great freedom (an instrumental direction). **2** in a speechlike manner (a vocal direction): [*She*] *sang ... too slowly and with too much tone—this is a parlando song* (London Times). [< Italian *parlando,* gerund of *parlare* speak]

**par|lan|te** (pär län′tā), *adj. Music.* parlando.

**par|lay** (pär′lā, -lē), *v., n. U.S.* —*v.t.* **1** to risk (an original bet and its winnings) on another bet. **2** to build up (a small business, talent, investment, or other enterprise) very successfully or profitably (into): *Since 1933, he has parlayed the proceeds of a small pipe company into a $200 million industrial empire* (New York Times).
—*v.i.* to wager an original bet with its winnings on a new race, game, or other events of uncertain outcome.
—*n.* such a wager or a series of such wagers. [American English < French *paroli* < Italian, the grand cast at dice < *paro* equal < Latin *pār, paris*]

**parle** (pärl), *v.,* **parled, parl|ing,** *n. Archaic.* —*v.i.* to discuss terms; parley.
—*v.t.* to parley with.
—*n.* a parley; talk; discussion.
[< Old French *parler;* see etym. under **parley**]

**par|le|ment** (pär′lə mənt), *n.* **1** (in France before the Revolution of 1789) the name given to a certain number of supreme courts of justice, in which also the edicts, declarations, and ordinances of the king were registered. **2** *Obsolete.* parliament. [< Old French *parlement* (literally) speaking; see etym. under **parliament**]

**par|ley** (pär′lē), *n., pl.* **-leys,** *v.,* **-leyed, -ley|ing.** —*n.* **1** a conference or talk to discuss terms or matters in dispute: *The Administration's position is that a conference of the Big Four foreign ministers should precede any parley "at the summit"* (New York Times). **2** an informal discussion with an enemy during a truce, as about terms of surrender, exchange of prisoners, supplies, or medical care: *The general held a parley with the enemy about exchanging prisoners.*
—*v.i.* **1** to discuss terms, especially with an enemy: *We arm to parley* (Sir Winston Churchill). **2** *Archaic.* to speak; talk: *The housemaids parley at the gate, The scullions on the stair* (Oliver Wendell Holmes).
[< Old French *parlee* < feminine past participle of *parler* to speak < Late Latin *parabolāre* < Latin *parabola* parable]

**par|lia|ment** (pär′lə mənt), *n.* **1** a council or congress that is the highest lawmaking body in some countries. **2** a high court of justice in France before the French Revolution; parlement. **3** the lawmaking body of France, Switzerland, or Italy, or that of Scotland until 1707 or Ireland until 1800, and of certain other countries. **4** the highest lawmaking body of any political unit: *The illusion has grown up that a "parliament of man" can be assembled under the UN roof* (Wall Street Journal). **5** *Obsolete.* a formal conference or council for the discussion of some matter or matters of general importance. [< Old French *parlement* < *parler* to speak; see etym. under **parley**]

**Par|lia|ment** (pär′lə mənt), *n.* **1** the national lawmaking body of Great Britain and Northern Ireland. It consists of the House of Lords and the House of Commons. *Only then will Parliament be in a position to prescribe for these industries attainable targets* (London Times). **2** the national lawmaking body of Canada, consisting of the Senate and the House of Commons. **3** the lawmaking body of a country or colony having the British system of government: *In British Columbia we elected the only Indian legislator to sit in a provincial Parliament* (Vancouver Native Voice).

**par|lia|men|tar|i|an** (pär′lə men tãr′ē ən), *n.* **1** a person skilled in parliamentary procedure or debate. **2** a member of a parliament: *A lunch was given ... for a party of Cabinet Ministers and parliamentarians* (Cape Times).

**Par|lia|men|tar|i|an** (pär′lə men tãr′ē ən), *n.* a person who supported Parliament against Charles I of England.

**par|lia|men|tar|i|an|ism** (pär′lə men tãr′ē ə niz′əm), *n.* the parliamentary system of government: *It is necessary to make a distinction between ... the constant weaknesses of French parliamentarianism and ... the causes of the present crisis* (Manchester Guardian).

**par|lia|men|tar|i|ly** (pär′lə men′tə rə lē, -trə lē), *adv.* in a parliamentary manner.

**par|lia|men|ta|ri|za|tion** (pär′lə men′tər ə zā′shən), *n.* **1** the act of parliamentarizing. **2** the state of being parliamentarized.

**par|lia|men|ta|rize** (pär′lə men′tə rīz), *v.t.,* **-rized, -riz|ing.** to make (a government) parliamentary; subject to the control of a parliament.

**par|lia|men|ta|ry** (pär′lə men′tər ē, -trē), *adj.* **1** of a parliament: *parliamentary authority.* **2** done by a parliament: *parliamentary statutes.* **3** according to the rules and customs of a parliament or other lawmaking body: *The United States Congress functions in accordance with the rules of parliamentary procedure.* **4** having a parliament: *a parliamentary form of government.*

**parliamentary government**, = cabinet government.

**parliamentary law**, a body of rules recognized for preserving order and regulating debate and procedure in legislative or deliberative bodies; rules of order.

**Parliament Hill**, **1** the hill in Ottawa, capital of Canada, on which the buildings of the Canadian Parliament stand. **2** the Parliament of Canada: *Old hands on Parliament Hill were shaken to hear the government criticized* (Maclean's).

**par|lor** (pär′lər), *n., adj.* —*n.* **1** a room for receiving or entertaining guests; sitting room; living room: *In what was called the parlor ... there was a sofa, an uncomfortable couch, ... our show-piece, much admired* (Arthur H. Tasker). **2** a decorated room or suite of rooms used as a shop or for various other commercial purposes: *a funeral parlor, a beauty parlor.* **3a** *British.* a room in an inn more private than the taproom. **b** a separate and somewhat similar room in a hotel, club, or other public building.
—*adj.* **1** used in or suitable for a parlor: *parlor furniture.* **2** advocating views as if from the safe remoteness of the parlor rather than from a practical contact with the matters involved: *a parlor radical.* Also, *especially British,* **parlour.**
[< Anglo-French *parlur,* Old French *parleor* < *parler* to speak; see etym. under **parley**]

**parlor boarder**, *British.* a pupil in a boarding school who lives with the principal's family and has privileges not granted to the ordinary pupils.

**parlor car**, a railroad passenger car for day travel, more luxurious than a coach and for which a higher fare is charged; Pullman car.

**parlor game**, a game played indoors, usually by a group of people in polite society. Quizzes and charades are parlor games.

**par|lor|maid** (pär′lər mād′), *n.* a maidservant who waits on table, answers the door, and performs other duties.

**parlor match**, a friction match containing little or no sulfur.

**parlor organ**, = harmonium.

**parlor pew**, *British.* a family pew in a church, furnished like a small parlor, sometimes occupied by the lord of the manor or squire with his household.

**par|lour** (pär′lər), *n., adj. Especially British.* parlor.

**par|lous** (pär′ləs), *adj., adv. Archaic.* —*adj.* **1** full of peril; dangerous: *the parlous state of the European coal industry* (London Times). *Thou art in a parlous state, shepherd* (Shakespeare). SYN: perilous. **2** very clever; shrewd: *A parlous boy: go to, you are too shrewd* (Shakespeare).
—*adv.* extremely; excessively: *You look parlous handsome when you smile* (George J. Whyte-Melville).
[short for *perilous*] —**par′lous|ly,** *adv.*

**par|ma** (pär′mə), *n.* a medium or deep shade of violet. [< *Parma,* a city in Italy]

**Par|me|san** (pär′mə zan, pär′mə zan′), *n., adj.* —*n.* Also, **Parmesan cheese.** a hard, dry Italian cheese made from skim milk: *To go with this, there is some of the finest Parmesan we have come across* (New Yorker).
—*adj.* **1** of or belonging to the city, the province,

or the former duchy of Parma in northern Italy. **2** prepared with Parmesan (cheese): *veal Parmesan.*
[probably < Middle French *parmesan,* adaptation of Italian *parmigiano* of *Parma,* a region in Italy]

**par|mi|gia|na** (pär'mə jä'nə), *adj.* prepared with Parmesan cheese: *veal parmigiana, eggplant parmigiana.* [< Italian *parmigiana,* feminine of *parmigiano* Parmesan]

**Par|nas|si|an** (pär nas'ē ən), *adj., n.* —*adj.* **1** of or having to do with Mount Parnassus, in southern Greece. **2** of or having to do with a school of French poetry of the latter half of the 1800's, that emphasized metrical form and repression of emotion.
—*n.* a French poet of the Parnassian school.

**Par|nas|si|an|ism** (pär nas'ē ən iz'əm), *n.* the Parnassian style in French poetry.

**par|nas|si|us** (pär nas'ē əs), *n.* a white, tailless butterfly with thin wings and short antennae, found in high or mountainous regions from Europe across Asia and North America to New Mexico. [< New Latin *parnassius* (literally) of Parnassus]

**Par|nas|sus** (pär nas'əs), *n.* **1a** the fabled mountain of poets, whose summit is their goal. **b** any gathering place for poets. **2** a collection of poems, belles-lettres, or the like.
**try** (or **strive**) **to climb Parnassus,** to try to write poetry: *There is Lowell, who's striving Parnassus to climb With a whole bale of isms tied together with rhyme* (James Russell Lowell).
[< Mount *Parnassus,* in central Greece, in ancient times sacred to Apollo and the Muses]

**pa|ro|chi|aid** (pə rō'kē ād'), *n. U.S.* governmental aid to parochial schools. [< *parochi*(al) *aid*]

**pa|ro|chi|al** (pə rō'kē əl), *adj.* **1** of or in a parish: *a parochial church, parochial calls, parochial relief of the poor.* **2** *Figurative.* very limited; narrow: *His viewpoint was too parochial. Some pride or ambition, big or small, imperial or parochial* (Alexander Kinglake). [< Old French *parochial* < Late Latin *parochiālis* < *parochia;* see etym. under **parish**] —**pa|ro'chi|al|ly,** *adv.*

**pa|ro|chi|al|ism** (pə rō'kē ə liz'əm), *n.* parochial character, spirit, or tendency; narrowness of interests or views: *In a journal such as Science News, there is a pressure toward parochialism in the choice of authors which is hard to resist* (Science News).

**pa|ro|chi|al|ize** (pə rō'kē ə līz), *v.,* **-ized, -iz|ing.**
—*v.t.* to make parochial.
—*v.i.* to do parish work.

**parochial school,** a private school maintained by a religious group: *Catholic parochial schools charge tuition.*

**par|o|di|a|ble** (par'ə dē ə bəl), *adj.* that can be parodied: *Why is it that nobody has been able to write a successful parody of one who is presumably so supremely parodiable?* (New York Times).

**pa|rod|ic** (pə rod'ik), *adj.* having to do with or of the nature of a parody: *I am reasonably certain that the author's intentions are not essentially parodic* (Atlantic).

**pa|rod|i|cal** (pə rod'ə kəl), *adj.* = parodic.

**par|o|dist** (par'ə dist), *n.* a writer of parodies: *... Charlotte Rae, a parodist whose target is songbirds that even the Audubon Society wouldn't want to save* (New Yorker).

**par|o|dis|tic** (par'ə dis'tik), *adj.* of the nature of a parody; that parodies: *"The Hollow Men" is in every way a better poem than "The Waste Land," though the parodistic style again enforces a poverty of statement and language* (Saturday Review).

**par|o|don|tal** (par'ə don'təl), *adj.* = periodontal.

**pa|ro|dos** (par'ə dos), *n.* in ancient Greek drama: **1** the entrance of the chorus into the orchestra. **2** the song they sang while entering. **3** the passage by which they entered. [< Greek *párodos*]

**par|o|dy** (par'ə dē), *n., pl.* **-dies,** *v.,* **-died, -dy|ing.**
—*n.* **1** a humorous imitation of a serious writing. A parody follows the form of the original, but often changes its sense to nonsense, thus making fun of the writer's characteristics. *Parodies and caricatures are the most penetrating of criticisms* (Aldous Huxley). *[Phyllis] McGinley does not disdain a single trick of the trade: parody, puns ... persiflage ... and epigrams* (Atlantic). **2** *Figurative.* a poor imitation; travesty: *its old pavillion, a little wooden parody of the temple of Vesta at Tibur* (H. G. Wells). **3** a musical composition making fun of another: *The songs are parodies, or parody-medleys if you're really lucky* (Manchester Guardian Weekly).
—*v.t.* **1** to make fun of by imitating; make a parody on: *All these peculiarities [of Johnson's style] have been imitated by his admirers and parodied by his assailants* (Macaulay). **2** *Figurative.* to imitate poorly: *Behind him ... the creature's shadow repeated and parodied his swift gesticulations* (Robert Louis Stevenson).
[< Latin *parōdia* < Greek *parōidiā* < *para-* beside, parallel to + *ōidē* song]

**parody Mass,** (in medieval music) a Mass in which parts of some other composer's chanson or motet were interwoven and alternated with freely invented sections.

**pa|roe|cious** (pə rē'shəs), *adj. Botany.* having the male and female reproductive organs beside or near each other, as certain mosses; paroicous; parecious. [< Greek *pároikos* (with English *-ous*) dwelling side by side < *para* beside + *oîkos* house. Compare etym. under **parish.**]

**pa|roe|mi|og|ra|pher** (pə rē'mē og'rə fər), *n.* a writer or compiler of proverbs.

**pa|roe|mi|og|ra|phy** (pə rē'mē og'rə fē), *n., pl.* **-phies. 1** the writing of proverbs. **2** a collection of proverbs. [< Greek *paroimiā* proverb + English *-graphy*]

**par of exchange,** the established normal value of the money of one country in terms of the money of another country using the same metal as a standard of value.

**pa|roi|cous** (pə roi'kəs), *adj.* = paroecious.

**pa|rol** (pə rōl', par'əl), *n., adj. Law.* —*n.* **1** word of mouth; oral statement. **2** the pleadings in a suit.
—*adj.* **1** presented by word of mouth; oral: *parol evidence.* **2** not under seal.
[earlier *parole;* see etym. under **parole**]

**pa|role** (pə rōl'), *n., v.,* **-roled, -rol|ing,** *adj.* —*n.* **1a** a conditional release from prison or jail before the full term is served. **b** the state of being paroled or the period of a parole. **2** conditional freedom allowed in place of imprisonment. **3** word of honor, especially the promise of a prisoner of war not to escape if permitted a degree of freedom by his captors or not to take up arms against them if released. **4** a password given only to officers of the guard and the officer of the day to give them admittance to places otherwise forbidden. **5** *Law.* parol. **6** *Linguistics.* language as spoken and understood by people; individual speech (contrasted with *langue*).
—*v.t.* to give a conditional release from jail or prison before the full term is served: *The prisoner was paroled after serving two years of his three-year sentence. The judge paroled the boys on condition that they report to him every three months.*
—*adj.* of or having to do with paroles: *a parole officer.*
[< French, Old French *parole* word, speech < Vulgar Latin *parabla* < Latin *parabola* parable; (in Late Latin) a speech, saying. See etym. of doublets **parable, parabola, parabole, palaver.**]

**parole board,** a group of persons having the authority to parole a prisoner before his sentence has expired, supervise the parolee after his release, and revoke the parole under certain conditions: *Some years ago I had occasion to dedicate a book to the real underdog of the whole prison system: the parole board* (Erle Stanley Gardner).

**pa|rol|ee** (pə rō'lē'), *n.* a person released on parole.

**par|o|no|ma|sia** (par'ə nə mā'zhə), *n.* the act or fact of playing on words that sound alike; punning; pun. [< Latin *paronomasia* < Greek *paronomasiā* < *paronomázein* to alter slightly in naming < *para-* aside + *onomázein* to name < *ónoma* name]

**par|o|no|mas|tic** (par'ə nə mas'tik), *adj.* having to do with or of the nature of paronomasia; punning. —**par'o|no|mas'ti|cal|ly,** *adv.*

**par|o|nych|i|a** (par'ə nik'ē ə), *n. Medicine.* an inflammation about the nail; whitlow. [< Latin *parōnychia* < Greek *parōnychiā* < *para-* beside + *ónyx, ónychos* nail]

**par|o|nych|i|al** (par'ə nik'ē əl), *adj.* having to do with or of the nature of a paronychia.

**par|o|nym** (par'ə nim), *n.* a paronymous word.

**pa|ron|y|mous** (pə ron'ə məs), *adj.* **1** (of words) derived from the same root; cognate. **2** derived from a word in another language with little or no change in form, as English *canal* for Latin *canalis.* **3** having the same sound but different spelling and meaning, as *feat* and *feet;* homophonic. [< Greek *parṓnymos* (with English *-ous*) a derivative formed by a slight change < *parōnymeîn* (literally) to alter in naming < *para-* aside, amiss + dialectal *ónyma* name]

**pa|ron|y|my** (pə ron'ə mē), *n.* **1** paronymous character. **2** the transference of a word from one language to another with little or no change in form.

**par|o|quet** (par'ə ket), *n.* = parakeet.

**par|o|rex|i|a** (par'ə rek'sē ə), *n. Medicine.* perversion of the appetite; a craving to eat articles not suitable for food. [< New Latin *parorexia* < Greek *para-* aside + *órexis* appetite]

**pa|ros|mi|a** (pə ros'mē ə, -roz'-), *n. Medicine.* disease or perversion of the sense of smell. [< New Latin *parosmia* < Greek *para-* aside + *osmḗ* smell]

**pa|rot|ic** (pə rot'ik), *adj.* in the region of the ear; parotid.

**pa|rot|id** (pə rot'id), *adj., n.* —*adj.* **1** near the ear. **2** of the parotid glands, one in front of each ear, that supply saliva to the mouth through the parotid ducts.
—*n.* either parotid gland.
[< Latin *parōtis, -idis* < Greek *parōtís, -ídos* tumor of the parotid gland < *para-* beside + *oûs, ōtós* ear]

**pa|rot|i|di|tis** (pə rot'ə dī'tis), *n.* = parotitis.

**par|o|tit|ic** (par'ə tit'ik), *adj.* affected with parotitis.

**par|o|ti|tis** (par'ə tī'tis), *n.* inflammation of the parotid gland, especially as in mumps. [< Latin *parōtis* (see etym. under **parotid**)]

**pa|ro|toid** (pə rō'toid), *adj., n.* —*adj.* resembling a parotid gland, especially applied to certain cutaneous glands forming the bulge above the eardrum of frogs and toads.
—*n.* a parotoid gland.

**par|ous** (par'əs), *adj.* having borne children. [< Latin *parere* to give birth]

**Par|ou|si|a** (pär'ü sē'ə, pə rü'zē ə), *n.* **1** the second coming of Christ; Second Advent: *For the first believers ... this hope of an imminent Parousia was at the furthest possible remove from the medieval memento mori. It was something they longed for, not something that they dreaded* (Bishop F. R. Barry). **2** *Figurative.* Usually, **parousia.** an expected return or revival: *Robert Flaherty's longed-for parousia ... has not yet arrived* (Saturday Review). [< Greek *parousía* presence]

**par|ox|ysm** (par'ək siz əm), *n.* **1a** a severe, sudden attack: *a paroxysm of coughing.* **b** a sudden, severe attack of the symptoms of a disease, usually recurring periodically: *a malarial paroxysm.* **2** a sudden outburst of emotion or activity: *a paroxysm of rage.* [< Middle French *paroxysme* < Medieval Latin *paroxysmus* < Greek *paroxysmós* < *paroxýnein* to exasperate, goad < *para-* beyond + *oxýnein* render acute; goad < *oxýs* sharp, pointed]

**par|ox|ys|mal** (par'ək siz'məl), *adj.* of, like, or having paroxysms: *a paroxysmal frenzy of contending passions* (Shelley). —**par'ox|ys'mal|ly,** *adv.*

**par|ox|y|tone** (pa rok'sə tōn), *adj., n. Greek Grammar.* —*adj.* having an acute accent on the next to the last syllable (penult).
—*n.* a word so accented.
[< Greek *paroxýtonos* < *para-* beside, next to + *oxýtonos* oxytone]

**par|quet** (pär kā', -ket'), *n., v.,* **-queted** (-kād', -ket'id), **-quet|ing** (-kā'ing, -ket'ing) or (*especially British*) **-quet|ted** (-ket'id), **-quet|ting** (-ket'ing).
—*n.* **1** an inlaid wooden flooring composed especially of small blocks of wood. **2a** the main floor of a theater; orchestra. **b** the part of the main floor of a theater from the orchestra pit to the part under the balcony. The British term is *stalls.*
—*v.t.* to make or put down (an inlaid wooden floor).
[< Middle French *parquet,* and *parchet* wooden flooring, compartment; an enclosed portion of a park; (literally) diminutive of *parc* park]

**parquet circle,** the part of the main floor of a theater that is under the balcony.

**par|quet|ry** (pär'kə trē), *n., pl.* **-ries.** a mosaic of wood used especially for floors, wainscoting, and paneling; parquet. [< French *parqueterie* < *parquet* parquet]

**parr** (pär), *n., pl.* **parrs** or (*collectively*) **parr. 1** a young salmon before it is old enough to go to sea, identifiable by dark bands on its sides. **2** the young of any of various other fishes, such as the coalfish. [origin unknown]

**par|rain** (pə rān'), *n.* the person who knighted a squire in medieval times. [< Middle French *parrin* (literally) godfather < Vulgar Latin *patrinus* < Latin *pater, patris* father]

**par|ra|keet** (par'ə kēt), *n.* = parakeet.

**par|ra|mat|ta** (par'ə mat'ə), *n.* = paramatta.

**par|rel** or **par|ral** (par'əl), *n.* a sliding ring or collar of rope or iron by which a yard, boom, or spar is attached to a mast and can move up and down on it. [apparently variant of Middle English *parail* equipment, short for *apparail* apparel. Compare Old French *parail* rigging.]

**par|ri|cid|al** (par'ə sī'dəl), *adj.* of or having to do with parricide.

**par|ri|cide**[1] (par'ə sīd), *n.* the crime of killing one's parent or parents, or any person for whom one is supposed to have respect or reverence comparable to that traditionally considered owing to a parent: *Oedipus was guilty of parricide.* [< Latin *parricīdium,* earlier *pāricīdium* < unrecorded *pārus* relative + *-cīdium* -cide[2]]

---

**Pronunciation Key:** hat, āge, cãre, fär; let, ēqual, tėrm; it, īce; hot, ōpen, ôrder; oil, out; cup, pu̇t, rüle; child; long; thin; ᴛʜen; zh, measure; ə represents **a** in about, **e** in taken, **i** in pencil, **o** in lemon, **u** in circus.

**par|ri|cide²** (par′ə sīd), *n.* a person who kills his parent or parents: *Oedipus was a parricide.* [< Latin *parricīda,* earlier *pāricīda* < unrecorded *pārus* relative + *-cīda* -cide¹]

**par|ridge** (pär′ij), *n.* = porridge.

**par|ritch** (pär′ich), *n. Scottish.* porridge.

**par|rock** (par′ək), *n. Scottish.* a small field or enclosure; paddock. [Old English *pearroc* inclosure, paddock; see etym. under **park**]

**par|ro|ket** or **par|ro|quet** (par′ə ket), *n.* = parakeet.

**par|rot** (par′ət), *n., v.* —*n.* **1** a bird with a stout, hooked bill, and often with bright-colored feathers. There are many kinds, comprising an order of birds. Parakeets, cockatoos, lovebirds, macaws, and lories are parrots. Some parrots, such as the gray parrot of West Africa, have fleshy tongues and can be taught to imitate sounds and to repeat words and sentences.
**2** *Figurative.* a person who repeats words or acts without understanding them.
—*v.t.* to repeat without understanding or sense: *On the whole, the students seemed serious and hard-working, but they confined themselves to parroting textbooks* (Atlantic).
[perhaps < French *Perrot* (diminutive) < *Pierre* Peter] —**par′rot|like′,** *adj.*

**par|rot-cry** (par′ət krī′), *n., pl.* **-cries.** a slogan, catch phrase, or other expression parroted or repeated over and over without understanding or sense: *The economic writings of today are filled with parrot-cries of "laissez-faire is dead"* (Canada Month).

**parrot fever** or **disease,** = psittacosis.

**parrot fish,** any one of various, mainly tropical, marine fishes having brilliant coloring or a strong hard mouth resembling the bill of a parrot.

**par|rot|let** (par′ət let), *n.* any one of various small, tropical, South American parrots, with green and yellow heads.

**par|ry** (par′ē), *v.,* **-ried, -ry|ing,** *n., pl.* **-ries.** —*v.t.* to ward off; turn aside; evade (as a thrust, stroke, or weapon): *He parried the sword with his dagger.* (*Figurative.*) *She parried our question by asking us one.*
—*v.i.* to ward off or turn aside a thrust, blow, or weapon.
—*n.* the act of parrying.
[< French *parez,* imperative of *parer* ward off < Italian *parare* ward off, make ready < Latin *parāre* prepare. See etym. of doublet **pare.**]

**parse** (pärs), *v.,* **parsed, pars|ing.** —*v.t.* **1** to analyze (a sentence) grammatically, telling its parts of speech and their uses in the sentence: *Their small world consists in parsing a sentence* (Time).
**2** to describe (a word) grammatically, telling what part of speech it is, its form, and its use in a sentence.
—*v.i.* **1** to analyze a sentence grammatically.
**2** to describe a word grammatically. **3** to be grammatically or syntactically acceptable: *She is in London ... wearing exquisite clothes and speaking sentences that parse* (New Yorker).
[perhaps Middle English *pars* parts of speech < Old French *pars* < Latin *pars* (*ōrātiōnis*) part (of speech)] —**pars′er,** *n.*

**par|sec** (pär′sek), *n.* a unit of distance, used in computing the distances of stars, equal to the distance of a star whose annual parallax is one second of arc, or about 206,265 times the mean distance of the earth from the sun or 3.26 light-years, or 19.2 trillion miles. Also, **secpar.** [< *par*(allax of one) *sec*(ond)]

**Par|si** or **Par|see** (pär′sē, pär sē′), *n.* a member of a Zoroastrian sect in India, descended from the Persians who settled there in the early part of the A.D. 700's. The sect is located chiefly in western India near Bombay. *Parsis, religious exiles from Persia hundreds of years ago, are still Zoroastrians* (Santha Rama Rau). [< Hindustani and Persian *Pārsī* a Persian < *Pārs* Persia]

**Par|si|fal** (pär′sə fəl, -fäl), *n. German Legend.* a knight corresponding to the Percival of Arthurian legend. Also, **Parzival.**

**Par|si|ism** or **Par|see|ism** (pär′sē iz əm, pär-sē′-), *n.* the religion and customs of the Parsis.

**par|si|mo|ni|ous** (pär′sə mō′nē əs), *adj.* **1** too economical; stingy: *parsimonious housekeeping.* **SYN:** frugal, stinting, miserly. **2** *Figurative.* (of things) poor; mean. —**par′si|mo′ni|ous|ly,** *adv.* —**par′si|mo′ni|ous|ness,** *n.*

**par|si|mo|ny** (pär′sə mō′nē), *n.* **1** extreme economy; stinginess: *There is no need to dwell on the other limitations of his character, his jealousy, his parsimony* (Atlantic). **SYN:** niggardliness.
**2** sparingness in the use or expenditure of means: (*Figurative.*) *This is the grand overriding law of the parsimony of nature: every action within a system is executed with the least possible expenditure of energy* (Scientific American).
[< Latin *parsimōnia,* ultimately < *parcere* spare]

**pars|ley** (pärs′lē), *n., pl.* **-leys. 1** a garden plant with finely divided, often curled, fragrant leaves used to flavor food and to trim platters of meat or fish. Parsley is a biennial herb native to the Mediterranean region. It belongs to the parsley family. **2** any one of certain similar or related plants. [fusion of Old English *petersilie,* and of Middle English *percil* (< Old French *peresil*); both < Vulgar Latin *petrosilium* < Latin *petroselīnum* < Greek *petrosélīnon* < *pétros* rock + *sélīnon* parsley]

∗**parsley family,** a group of dicotyledonous plants, chiefly herbs, having alternate, usually compound, and aromatic leaves and small flowers borne in umbels, and bearing a dry fruit consisting of two carpels that split at the base when mature. The family includes the parsley, carrot, celery, caraway, anise, poison hemlock, and angelica. See picture below.

**pars|nip** (pärs′nip), *n.* **1** a plant having compound leaves, yellow flowers, and a long, tapering whitish root that in the cultivated variety is fleshy, sweet, and nutritious. It is a biennial plant which belongs to the parsley family and is native to Europe and parts of Asia. **2** its root, which is eaten as a vegetable. **3** any one of certain allied or similar plants. [alteration of Middle English *passenep* < Old French *pasnaie* < Latin *pastināca;* influenced by Middle English *nep* turnip, neep] —**pars′nip|like′,** *adj.*

**par|son** (pär′sən), *n.* **1** a minister in charge of a parish: *But all the instruction he got ... was ... on Sundays, from a parson who taught little effectively* (J. W. R. Scott). **2** *Informal.* any clergyman; minister; rector. [< Medieval Latin *parsona,* and *persona* parson < Latin *persōna* person, character; actor's mask. See etym. of doublet **person.**]

**par|son|age** (pär′sə nij), *n.* **1** the house provided for a minister by a church: *The country parsonage may now be the most popular literary symbol of England's religious life* (Newsweek). **2** the benefice of a parson (now used only in ecclesiastical law). [< *parson* + *-age*]

**parson bird,** = tui.

**par|son|ess** (pär′sə nis), *n. Informal.* the wife of a parson.

**par|son|ic** (pär son′ik), *adj.* of, like, or characteristic of a parson: *Others can hardly imagine him as anything else—Broad Church, clean, uplift stuff indeed—no court flunkey he—but every inch of him parsonic* (Punch). —**par|son′i|cal|ly,** *adv.*

**par|son|i|cal** (pär son′ə kəl), *adj.* = parsonic.

**part** (pärt), *n., v., adj., adv.* —*n.* **1** something less than the whole; not all: *He ate part of an apple. Cowboys live in the western part of the country.* **2** each of several equal quantities into which a whole may be divided; fraction: *A dime is a tenth part of a dollar.* **3** a thing that helps to make up a whole: *A radio has many parts.* **4** a portion of an organism; member, limb, or organ. Stamens and pistils are floral parts. **5** a replacement, as for a worn or otherwise defective component of a machine or tool: *spare parts.* **6** a share: *Everyone must do his part. He had no part in the mischief.* **7** *Figurative.* a side in a dispute or contest: *He always takes his brother's part.* **8a** a character in a play or motion picture; role: *He played the part of Hamlet.* **b** the words spoken by a character in a play: *to study one's part. She spoke the part of the heroine in our play.* **9** *Figurative.* a role played by a person in real life: *All the world's a stage ... And one man in his time plays many parts* (Shakespeare). **10** a dividing line left in combing one's hair. **11a** one of the voices or instruments in music: *the violin part. The four parts in singing are soprano, alto, tenor, and bass.* **b** the music for it. *Abbr:* pt. [< Old French *part* < Latin *pars, partis*]
—*v.t.* **1a** to divide into two or more pieces: *He parted the old stump with one mighty blow of the ax.* **SYN:** sever, sunder. **b** *Nautical.* to cause (a rope or cable) to break. **2** to force apart; divide: *The policeman on horseback parted the crowd.* **3** to keep apart; form a boundary between. **4** to separate by a chemical or other technical process. **5** to brush or comb (the hair) away from a dividing line. **6** to dissolve or terminate (as a connection) by separation of the parties concerned: *to part company.* **7** *Archaic.* to divide among a number of persons; distribute as shares; apportion: *They part my garments among them, and cast lots upon my vesture* (Psalms 22:18).
—*v.i.* **1** to go apart; separate: *The friends parted in anger. We met to part no more* (Tennyson). **2** to be divided into parts; come or go in pieces; break up; break. **3** *Archaic.* **a** to die. **b** to go away; depart.
—*adj.* less than the whole: *part time.*
—*adv.* in some measure or degree; partly: *He spoke in words part heard* (Tennyson).
**bear a part, a** to take or sustain a part in a play or in part singing: *He bore a part in the school cantata.* **b** to have a share in any action, transaction, or other proceeding: *The king himself ... bore a part in it* (Joseph Priestley).
**for one's (own) part,** as far as one is concerned: *For my own part, I was indifferent which it might be* (Sir Arthur Conan Doyle).
**for the most part,** mostly; mainly; usually: *The attempts were for the most part unsuccessful.*
**in good part,** in a friendly or gracious way: *I am sure he will take it in good part* (Anthony Trollope).
**in ill** (or **bad**) **part,** with displeasure or offense: *"People treat us very familiarly," said the Frenchman, "and they do it so innocently that we should be very hard to get on with if we took it in bad part"* (Catherine Drinker Bowen).
**in part,** in some measure or degree; to some extent; partly: *For we know in part, and we prophesy in part* (I Corinthians 13:9).
**on the part of one** or **on one's part, a** as far as one is concerned: *He was friendly enough on his part.* **b** by one: *No objection on my part, I said* (Benjamin Jowett).
**part and parcel,** a necessary part: *It is part and parcel of their whole tradition of duplicity, sham, and subversion* (Wall Street Journal).
**part from,** to go away from; leave: *Our poor boy Thornie parted from us today* (George Eliot).
**parts, a** ability; talent: *He had a strong face, twinkling bright-blue eyes, and a sand-yellow beard, and he seemed a man of parts* (New Yorker). **b** regions; districts; places: *He has traveled much in foreign parts.*
**part with,** to give up; let go: *The miser hated to part with his gold.*
**take part,** to take or have a share; participate or be involved: *She took no part in the discussion.*
[< Old French *partir* divide into parts; depart < Latin *partīre* < *pars, partis* part, noun]
—***Syn.*** *n.* **1 Part, portion, piece** mean something less than the whole. **Part** is the general word meaning an element or member of the whole, considered apart from the rest: *Save part of the roast for tomorrow night.* **Portion** means a part thought of less in relation to the whole than as an amount or quantity making up a section or share: *Give a portion of each day to recreation.* **Piece** means a separate part, often thought of as complete in itself: *He ate a big piece of cake.*
▶ **On the part of** is often a rather long substitute for *by, among, for,* and the like: *In recent years there has been a noticeable feeling on the part of* (among) *students that education is all-important.*

**part., 1a** participial. **b** participle. **2** particular.

**part. adj.,** participial adjective.

**par|take** (pär tāk′), *v.,* **-took, -tak|en, -tak|ing.** —*v.i.* **1** to eat or drink some; take some: *We are eating lunch; will you partake?* **2** to take or have a share; participate: *Thou hast provided all things: but with me I see not who partakes ... who can enjoy alone?* (Milton). **SYN:** See syn. under **share.**
—*v.t.* to take a part in; share in: *The soul partakes The season's youth* (James Russell Lowell).
**partake of, a** to take some; have a share in: *Will you partake of this cake?* **b** to have to some extent the nature or character of: *Her graciousness partakes of condescension.*
[back formation < earlier *partaker,* or *partaking,*

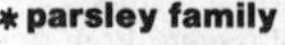
∗ **parsley family**

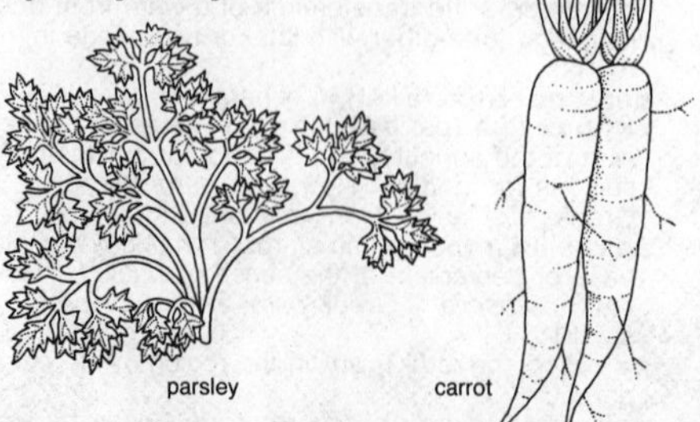

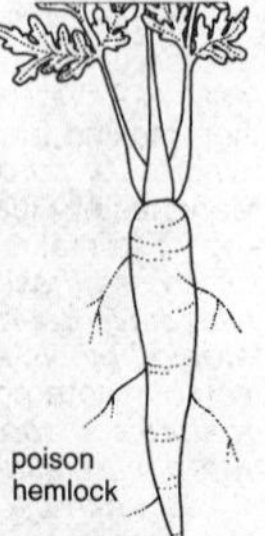

for *part-taker,* or *part-taking*]

**par|tak|en** (pär tā′kən), *v.* the past participle of **partake.**

**par|tak|er** (pär tā′kər), *n.* a person who partakes.

**par|tan** (pär′tən), *n. Scottish.* a crab. [< Gaelic *partan*]

**part|ed** (pär′tid), *adj.* **1** divided into parts; severed; cloven. **2** divided by a parting: *neatly parted hair.* **3** placed or standing apart; separated. **4** *Botany.* divided into distinct lobes by depressions extending from the margin nearly to the midrib or to the base: *a parted leaf.* **5** *Heraldry.* party, as a shield. **6** *Archaic.* deceased.

**par|terre** (pär tãr′), *n.* **1** *U.S.* the part of the main floor of a theater under the balcony. The British term is the *pit.* **2** an ornamental arrangement of flower beds: *They [gardens of Damascus] are not the formal parterres which you might expect from the Oriental taste* (Alexander Kinglake). [< Middle French *parterre* garden space, noun use of *par terre* on the ground[1] < Latin *per* on, *terra* ground]

**parterre boxes,** a series of boxes in a theater, located just above the back of the main floor: *the parterre boxes of the old Metropolitan Opera House.*

**par|the|no|car|pic** (pär′thə nō kär′pik), *adj.* produced without fertilization: *Of course, such parthenocarpic fruits contain no viable seed* (P. W. Brian). **—par′the|no|car′pi|cal|ly,** *adv.*

**par|the|no|car|py** (pär′thə nō kär′pē), *n. Botany.* the development of fruit without seeds or fertilization: *Seedless fruits such as the banana and the navel orange are produced by parthenocarpy.* [< Greek *parthénos* virgin + *karpós* fruit + English *-y*[3]]

**par|the|no|gen|e|sis** (pär′thə nō jen′ə sis), *n.* **1** *Biology.* reproduction without any male element, as the development of eggs in certain insects from virgin females without fertilization by union with one of the opposite sex: *Parthenogenesis, or virgin birth, is common among insects but rare among higher forms of life* (Scientific American). **2** *Botany.* the development of one of the sexual cells of a plant, such as an alga or fungus, without previous fusion with a cell of the opposite sex. [< Greek *parthénos* virgin + English *genesis*]

**par|the|no|ge|net|ic** (par′thə nō jə net′ik), *adj.* having to do with or exhibiting the phenomenon of parthenogenesis: *Parthenogenetic development has been induced in the eggs of a number of animals which ordinarily require fertilization* (A. Franklin Shull). **—par′the|no|ge|net′i|cal|ly,** *adv.*

**par|the|nog|e|none** (pär′thə noj′ə nōn), *n.* an organism born through parthenogenesis, especially the offspring of a gynandromorph: *The human population, by virtue of its enormous size, could indeed contain a few parthenogenones. These would be very difficult to distinguish from normal individuals: they would of course be female and they would resemble their mothers very closely but otherwise they need show no distinctive features* (Science Journal). [< *parthenogenesis*]

**par|the|nog|e|ny** (pär′thə noj′ə nē), *n.* = parthenogenesis.

**Par|the|non** (pär′thə non), *n.* the temple of Athena on the Acropolis at Athens, built about 447-438 B.C., regarded as the finest example of Doric architecture. It is equally famous for its decorative sculpture. *The Parthenon with its architectural purity and impressive monumentality* (Atlantic). [< Latin *Parthenōn* < Greek *Parthenṓn* < *hē Parthénos* the virgin goddess (Athena)]

**Par|then|o|pe** (pär then′ə pē), *n. Greek Legend.* a siren who drowned herself because she failed to lure Odysseus (Ulysses) with her singing.

**Par|the|nos** (pär′thə nos), *n.* a virgin (a name applied especially to Athena). [< Greek *hē Parthénos* the virgin goddess]

**Par|thi|an** (pär′thē ən), *adj., n.* **—*adj.*** having to do with Parthia, an ancient kingdom of southwestern Asia, southeast of the Caspian Sea, or its inhabitants; of a kind attributed to or associated with the Parthians: *The Moors kept up a Parthian retreat; several times they turned to make battle* (Washington Irving).
**—*n.*** a native or inhabitant of Parthia: *or like the Parthians I shall flying fight* (Shakespeare).

**Parthian shot,** a sharp parting remark or the like (from the traditional tactic of the mounted archers of ancient Parthia, which was to shoot arrows back at an adversary as they fled or pretended to flee).

**par|ti** (pär tē′), *n.* a person considered as a matrimonial match: *A girl in our society accepts the best parti which offers itself* (Thackeray). [< French *parti* party, match[2] < Old French, past participle of *partir* to leave]

**par|tial** (pär′shəl), *adj., n.* **—*adj.*** **1** not complete; not total: *a partial eclipse. Father has made a partial payment on our new car.* **SYN:** incomplete, imperfect. **2** inclined to favor one side more than another; favoring unfairly: *A parent should not be partial to any one of his children.* **SYN:** biased, prejudiced, one-sided. **3** having a liking for; favorably inclined: *He is partial to sports.* **4** *Mathematics.* (of a function of two or more variables) relative to only one of the variables involved, the rest being for the time supposed constant: *Partial product is the result of multiplying a number by one digit of the multiplier* (Richard Madden).
**—*n.*** **1** *Music.* partial tone: *The audibility of partials is not only limited by the threshold of frequency sensitivity* (F. A. Kuttner). **2** *Informal.* partial denture.
[< Old French *parcial,* learned borrowing from Late Latin *partiālis* < Latin *pars, partis* part]
**—par′tial|ness,** *n.*

**partial denture,** an artificial replacement of only one or several teeth. A partial denture may be fixed or removable.

**partial fraction,** *Algebra.* one of the fractions into which a given fraction can be resolved, the sum of such simpler fractions being equal to the given fraction.

**par|ti|al|i|ty** (pär′shē al′ə tē, -shal′-), *n., pl.* **-ties.** **1** a favoring of one more than another or others; favorable prejudice; being partial: *Either I am blinded by the partiality of a parent, or he is a boy of very amiable character* (Tobias Smollett). **SYN:** bias, favoritism. **2** a particular liking; fondness; preference; bent: *Children and adults alike often have a partiality for candy.*

**par|tial|ly** (pär′shə lē), *adv.* **1** in part; not generally or totally; partly: *a school for blind and partially blind children. When stars high in the sky are being studied, the partially closed shutter will serve as a windscreen* (Science News Letter). **SYN:** See syn. under **partly.** **2** in a partial manner; with undue bias.

**partial tone,** *Music.* one of the higher or lower tones which sound together with the fundamental tone and form a resulting compound tone. Upper partial tones are also called harmonics on stringed instruments or open tones on wind instruments.

**par|ti|bil|i|ty** (pär′tə bil′ə tē), *n.* the quality of being partible: *the partibility of an inheritance.*

**par|ti|ble** (pär′tə bəl), *adj.* that can be divided or distributed among a number; divisible; separable.

**par|ti|ceps cri|mi|nis** (pär′tə seps krim′ə nis), *Latin.* a person who shares in a crime; accomplice.

**par|tic|i|pance** (pär tis′ə pəns), *n.* the fact or quality of participating.

**par|tic|i|pan|cy** (pär tis′ə pən sē), *n.* = participance.

**par|tic|i|pant** (pär tis′ə pənt), *n., adj.* **—*n.*** a person who shares or participates; sharer; participator: *Each correct answer gives the audience participant a right to take [an item] from the girl in the spotlight* (Time).
**—*adj.*** participating; sharing.
[< Latin *participāns, -antis,* present participle of *participāre* participate]

**par|tic|i|pate** (pär tis′ə pāt), *v.,* **-pat|ed, -pat|ing.** **—*v.i.*** to have a share; take part; share in an undertaking: *The teacher participated in the children's games.* **SYN:** See syn. under **share.**
**—*v.t.*** to possess or enjoy in common with others; share; partake: *When I am glowing with the enthusiasm of success, there will be none to participate my joy* (Mary W. Shelley).
[< Latin *participāre* (with English *-ate*[1]) < *particeps, -cipis* (one) partaking < *pars, partis* part + *capere* to take]

**par|tic|i|pat|ing insurance** (pär tis′ə pā′ting), a form of insurance in which the policyholder receives a share or dividend from the insurance company's surplus earnings.

**par|tic|i|pa|tion** (pär tis′ə pā′shən), *n.* the act or fact of taking part; participating: *They wanted more direct participation in the solution of steel production problems* (Newsweek).

**par|tic|i|pa|tion|al** (pär tis′ə pā′shə nəl), *adj.* involving the participation of spectators or an audience.

**par|tic|i|pa|tive** (pär tis′ə pā′tiv), *adj.* characterized by participation; participating. **—par|tic′i|pa′tive|ly,** *adv.*

**par|tic|i|pa|tor** (pär tis′ə pā′tər), *n.* a person who participates: *participators in our misfortune.*

**par|tic|i|pa|to|ry** (pär tis′ə pə tôr′ē, -tōr′-), *adj.* = participative.

**participatory democracy,** active participation by citizens in politics, especially by public campaigning, demonstration, or protest: *Participatory democracy calls for each person to have a voice in all the decisions affecting his life* (Bonnie B. Stretch). *"Participatory democracy" increasingly means minority action without the benefit of open debate* (Fred M. Hechinger).

**participatory theater,** a form of theater in which the plays include participation or physical involvement by the audience.

**par|ti|cip|i|al** (pär′tə sip′ē əl), *adj., n. Grammar.* **—*adj.*** of or having to do with a participle. *Examples:* a *masked* man, a *becoming* dress (participial adjectives), the *cutting* of ice, the fatigue of *marching* (participial nouns).
**—*n.*** a verbal derivative of the nature of, or akin to, a participle.
[< Latin *participiālis* < *participium* participle]

**par|ti|cip|i|al|ly** (pär′tə sip′ē ə lē), *adv.* as a participle. In "the girl singing sweetly," *singing* is used participially.

**par|ti|ci|ple** (pär′tə sip′əl), *n.* a form of a verb used as an adjective or noun. *Abbr:* part. [< Old French *participle,* variant of *participe,* learned borrowing from Latin *participium* (literally) sharing, partaking < *particeps;* see etym. under **participate**]
▶A **participle** retains the attributes of a verb, such as tense, voice, power to take an object, and modification by adverbs. *Examples:* the girl *writing* sentences at the blackboard, the recently *stolen* silver, the boy *having missed* the boat. In these phrases, *writing* is a present participle; *stolen* is a past participle; *having missed* is a perfect participle. See also **dangling participle.**

**par|ti|cle** (pär′tə kəl), *n.* **1** a very little bit: *I got a particle of dust in my eye.* **2a** any one of the extremely small units of which all matter is composed, such as the molecule, atom, electron, photon, neutrino, or meson; elementary particle: *[The theory of photons] involves the basic dualism between the continuous and the discontinuous, between wave and particle* (I. Bernard Cohen). **b** a minute mass of matter that while still having inertia and attraction is treated as a point without length, breadth, or thickness. **3a** a derivational prefix or suffix, such as *un-, -ment, -ly, -ness.* **b** a word that cannot be inflected, such as a preposition, conjunction, article, or interjection. *In, if, an,* and *ah* are particles. **c** the term sometimes applied to all such words collectively when classed together as a single part of speech or form class. **4** in the Roman Catholic Church: **a** a fragment of the Eucharistic Host. **b** the wafer given to each lay communicant. [< Latin *particula* (diminutive) < *pars, partis* part]

**particle accelerator,** any one of several machines, such as the betatron or cyclotron, that greatly increase the speed and energy of protons, electrons, and other atomic particles and direct them in a steady stream at a target; accelerator. The accelerated particles are used to bombard the nuclei of atoms, causing the nuclei to release new particles and energy. *The monoenergetic neutrons produced by particle accelerators have energies above the displacement threshold* (Science).

**particle beam, 1** a concentrated flow of charged nuclear particles: *Particle beams have been essential research tools for [studying] the structure of the atom and its constituent particles* (New York Times). **2** a directed, high-energy stream of such particles, used as a weapon; death ray: *Particle beams fired from the ground or space at close to the speed of light . . . have been suggested as a means of stopping enemy nuclear missiles* (New York Post).

**particle board,** an inexpensive type of fiberboard, made from wood chips and shavings by a gluing and pressing process, and used in construction and as a base for furniture.

**particle physicist,** a person who studies particle physics.

**particle physics,** a branch of physics dealing with elementary particles: *One of the basic hypotheses of particle physics is that nature should be symmetrical with regard to three basic characteristics of particle interaction: electric charge, parity (right or left handedness), and direction of motion in time* (Science News).

**par|ti-col|or** (pär′tē kul′ər), *adj., n.* **—*adj.*** = parti-colored.
**—*n.*** **1** a mixture or combination of colors. **2** a dog with a parti-colored coat: *Solid-black cocker spaniels are often preferred to parti-colors.*

**par|ti-col|ored** (pär′tē kul′ərd), *adj.* **1** colored differently in different parts; variegated in color: *a parti-colored dress.* **2** *Figurative.* diversified; varied: *a parti-colored story.* Also, **party-colored.** [< French *parti* divided, past participle of *partir* to part + English *colored*]

**par|tic|u|lar** (pər tik′yə lər), *adj., n.* **—*adj.*** **1** considered apart from others; taken separately; single: *That particular chair is already sold.* **SYN:** See syn. under **special.** **2** belonging to some one person, thing, group, or occasion: *His particular task is to care for the dog. A particular characteristic*

**Pronunciation Key:** hat, āge, cãre, fär; let, ēqual, tėrm; it, īce; hot, ōpen, ôrder; oil, out; cup, pu̇t, rüle; child; long; thin; ᴛʜen; zh, measure; ə represents **a** in about, **e** in taken, **i** in pencil, **o** in lemon, **u** in circus.

*of a skunk is its smell.* **SYN**: individual, distinctive. **3** different from others; unusual; special: *This vacation was of particular importance to her, for she was going to Europe. He is a particular friend of mine.* **4** hard to please; wanting everything to be just right; very careful; exact: *She is very particular; nothing but the best will do.* **SYN**: precise, exacting, fastidious. **5** giving details; full of details: *a particular account of the game.* **SYN**: detailed, minute. **6** *Law.* **a** having to do with an estate granted to one person for a number of years or for life but ultimately to be the property of someone else. **b** having to do with the tenant of such an estate. **7** *Logic.* not referring to the whole extent of a class, but only to some individual or individuals in it; not general: *a particular proposition.* **8** *Obsolete.* private; personal: *These domestic and particular broils* (Shakespeare).

—***n.*** **1** an individual part; item; point: *All the particulars of the accident are now known. The work is complete in every particular.* **SYN**: See syn. under **item**. **2** *Logic.* **a** an individual thing in relation to or contrast to the whole class. **b** a particular proposition.

**in particular**, especially: *We strolled around, not going anywhere in particular.*

[< Middle French *particuler,* learned borrowing from Latin *particulāris* < *particula* particle]

**par|tic|u|lar|ism** (pər tik′yə lə riz′əm), *n.* **1** exclusive attention or devotion to one's particular party, sect, nation, or other group: *Patriotism and the sense of political unity are not at the root of local particularism, they merely grow out of it and crown it* (Atlantic). **2** the principle of letting each state of a federation keep its own laws and promote its own interests. **3** *Theology.* the doctrine, especially in Calvinism, that only those who have been individually predestined to it may achieve salvation.

**par|tic|u|lar|ist** (pər tik′yə lər ist), *n.* an advocate or adherent of particularism.

**par|tic|u|lar|is|tic** (pər tik′yə lə ris′tik), *adj.* having to do with, characterized by, or upholding particularism: *Boas and his school do not so much refute evolution as avoid it in favor of particularistic historical researches* (Beals and Hoijer).

**par|tic|u|lar|i|ty** (pər tik′yə lar′ə tē), *n., pl.* **-ties.** **1** detailed quality; minuteness: *[The characters in the play] are not given that kind of particularity or interior life* (Arthur Miller). **2** special carefulness. **3** attentiveness to details: *She had from time to time remarked the Chichester, but never with any particularity* (Arnold Bennett). **4** a particular feature or trait: *He had a great many other particularities in his character which I will not mention* (Henry Fielding). **5** the quality of being hard to please. **6** the quality or fact of being particular. **7** *Obsolete.* a detail.

**par|tic|u|lar|i|za|tion** (pər tik′yə lər ə zā′shən), *n.* the act of particularizing.

**par|tic|u|lar|ize** (pər tik′yə lə rīz), *v.,* **-ized, -iz|ing.** —***v.t.*** to mention particularly or individually; treat in detail; specify: *In his family portraits ... the autobiography becomes particularized and memorable* (Harper's).

—***v.i.*** to mention individuals; give details: *Stans is more analyst than stylist: "Let me particularize," he is fond of saying* (Time). —**par|tic′u|lar|iz′er,** *n.*

**par|tic|u|lar|ly** (pər tik′yə lər lē), *adv.* **1** in a high degree; especially: *The teacher praised her particularly. I am particularly fond of her.* **SYN**: principally, mainly. See syn. under **especially**. **2** in a particular manner: *The teacher particularly mentioned each assignment.* **3** in detail; in all of its parts; minutely: *The inspector examined the machine particularly.*

**par|tic|u|lar|ness** (pər tik′yə lər nis), *n.* **1** the character of being particular; particularity; individuality. **2** close attention to detail; fastidiousness; fussiness: *You're getting to be your aunt's own niece, I see, for particularness* (George Eliot).

**par|tic|u|late** (pär tik′yə lit, -lāt), *adj., n.* —***adj.*** of, having to do with, or consisting of small, separate particles: *Some filters ... effectively remove particulate matter from gases* (Science News Letter).

—***n.*** a very small, separate particle, such as a particle of dust or fiber: *The major source of atmospheric particulates include combustion of coal, gasoline, and fuel oil; cement production; lime kiln operation; incineration; and agricultural burning* (Francis A. Wood).

[< Latin *particula* particle]

**par|tie car|rée** (pår tē′ kå rā′), *French.* a party of four: *Parties carrées with the Soviet representative and his wife were a nightmare that was to pursue them to liberated Paris* (Punch).

**part|ing** (pär′ting), *n., adj.* —***n.*** **1** the action or fact of departing; going away; taking leave: *The friends were sad at parting.* **SYN**: departure. **2** a division; separation. **3** a place of division or separation: *to reach the parting of the roads. Her hair is arranged with a side parting.* **4** something that parts or separates two things, such as a layer of rock or clay lying between two beds of different formations. **5** *Archaic.* decease; death.

—***adj.*** **1** given, taken, or done, at parting: *a parting request, a parting shot.* **2a** going away; departing: *The curfew tolls the knell of parting day* (Thomas Gray). **b** *Figurative.* dying. **3** dividing; separating.

**parting cup**, a drinking cup having two handles, used by two people in taking a draft of liquor at parting.

**parting strip**, the strip in each side of a window frame to keep the upper and lower sashes apart.

**par|ti pris** (pår tē′ prē′), *French.* a decision or opinion formed in advance: *They said Nocero had deserved to win, but I think they had a parti pris* (New Yorker).

**par|ti|san**[1] (pär′tə zən), *n., adj.* —***n.*** **1** a strong supporter of a person, party, or cause; one whose support is based on feeling rather than on reasoning: *He was a passionate partisan of these people and had organized a Workers' Union* (Edmund Wilson). **SYN**: follower, adherent, disciple. **2** a member of light, irregular troops or armed civilians; guerrilla.

—***adj.*** of or like a partisan: *There are often partisan favors in politics. Leadership is either partisan or scientific. Partisan leadership takes sides* (Emory S. Bogardus). Also, **partizan.**

[< Middle French *partisan,* adaptation of dialectal Italian *partezan,* variant of *partigiano* < *parte* part < Latin *pars, partis* part]

**par|ti|san**[2] (pär′tə zən), *n.* a weapon with a broad blade like a halberd and a long shaft like a pike, carried by foot soldiers in the 1500's and on ceremonial occasions by the bodyguards of a great personage. Also, **partizan.** [< Middle French *partizane* < Italian *partesana,* or *partigiana* < Medieval Latin (Spain) *partesana.* Compare Old High German *parta* halberd.]

**par|ti|san|ship** (pär′tə zən ship), *n.* **1** strong loyalty to a party or cause: *Regardless of partisanship, however, one could select in the day-to-day happenings of the past year in Japan many symptoms of the poor health of the body politic* (Atlantic). **2** the act or fact of taking sides: *They wanted a President who would stand above petty partisanship* (Newsweek).

**par|ti|ta** (pär tē′tə), *n.* a series of dance tunes in the same or related keys for one or more instruments. [< Italian *partita* (originally) feminine past participle of *partire* divide < Latin *partīre;* see etym. under **partite**]

**par|tite** (pär′tīt), *adj.* **1** divided into parts or portions. **2** *Botany.* parted. **3** *Entomology.* divided to the base, as a wing. [< Latin *partītus,* past participle of *partīre* to divide < *pars, partis* part]

**par|ti|tion** (pär tish′ən), *n., v.* —***n.*** **1** a division into parts: *the partition of a man's wealth when he dies.* **SYN**: apportionment. **2** a portion; part; section. **3** something that separates, such as a wall between rooms or a septum or other separating membrane in a plant or animal body. **4** *Mathematics.* a way of expressing a number as a sum of positive whole numbers. **5** *Logic.* analysis by separation of the integral parts.

—***v.t.*** **1** to divide into parts: *to partition an empire among three brothers, to partition a building into apartments.* **2** to separate by a partition. **3** *Law.* to divide (property) to separate the individual interests.

[Middle English *particion* < Old French *particion,* learned borrowing from Latin *partītiō, -ōnis* < *partīre* to part] —**par|ti′tion|er,** *n.*

**partition chromatography**, the separation of chemical mixtures by passing solutions of them through two separate solvents, one of which is stationary, the other mobile. Partition chromatography is used in separating carbohydrates, amino acids, and other compounds from a mixture of substances.

**par|ti|tion|ist** (pär tish′ə nist), *n.* a person who supports or advocates the partition of a country or territory.

**par|ti|tion|ment** (pär tish′ən mənt), *n.* the act of dividing; partition.

**par|ti|tive** (pär′tə tiv), *n., adj.* —***n.*** a word or phrase meaning a part of a collective whole. *Some, few,* and *any* are partitives.

—***adj.*** expressing a part of a collective whole: *a partitive adjective.* —**par′ti|tive|ly,** *adv.*

**par|ti|zan**[1] (pär′tə zən), *n., adj.* = partisan[1].

**par|ti|zan**[2] (pär′tə zən), *n.* = partisan[2].

**par|ti|zan|ship** (pär′tə zən ship), *n.* = partisanship.

**part|let**[1] (pärt′lit), *n.* a kind of garment worn around the neck and upper part of the chest, especially by women during the 1500's. [apparently variant of earlier *patelet* < Old French *patelette* band of stuff, diminutive of *patte* flap, paw]

**part|let**[2] or **Part|let** (pärt′lit), *n.* a hen (especially as a proper name, often in *Dame Partlet*). [< Old French *Pertelote,* a woman's name (from its use as the name of a hen in Chaucer's *Nun's Priest's Tale*)]

**part|ly** (pärt′lē), *adv.* in part; in some measure or degree: *He is partly to blame.*

—***Syn.*** **Partly, partially** mean in part or to a certain extent, not wholly or totally. **Partly** means not wholly or entirely what is described or stated, with all parts included or in all ways or respects, but only in part or in some measure or degree: *He is partly right.* **Partially** means not totally or generally, with no exceptions and nothing held back, but affecting only one part or to only a limited extent: *He is partially paralyzed.*

**part music**, music for two or more parts, especially vocal music.

**part|ner** (pärt′nər; *see note below*), *n., v.* —***n.*** **1** one who shares: *Members of a family are all partners in life.* **SYN**: sharer, partaker. **2** a member of a company or firm who shares the risks and profits of the business: *The three partners in the store each made enough money to live on.* **3** a wife or husband: *The wife mourned for her partner lost in the shipwreck.* **4** a companion in a dance: *The partners all joined hands and danced in a big circle.* **5** a player on the same team or side in a game: *The two old partners in tennis beat the younger men in a surprising match.*

—***v.t.*** **1** to associate as partners. **2** to be the partner of: *David Blair ... bears with grace the burden of partnering Miss Fonteyn* (Saturday Review).

—***v.i.*** to be a partner: *Mr. Adams partnered well and acted with a forthright manner* (London Times).

**partners**, a framework of timber fitted around a hole in a ship's deck: *Our mainmast breaking in the partners of the upper deck, disabled both our pumps* (Alexander Hamilton).

[Middle English variant of *parcener;* influenced by *part*]

► The variant **pardner** (pärd′nər) is more common in literature than spoken dialect, although it was recorded in the 1700's as common in cockney English.

**part|ner|ship** (pärt′nər ship), *n.* **1** the condition of being a partner or partners; joint interest; association: *a business partnership, the partnership of marriage.* **2a** a company or firm with two or more members who share the risks and profits of the business: *a law partnership.* **b** the contract that creates such a relation.

**part of speech**, any one of the classes into which words are divided according to their use or function in sentences. The traditional parts of speech are the noun, pronoun, adjective, verb, adverb, preposition, conjunction, and interjection.

► **parts of speech**. One of the fundamental facts of English grammar is that a word may function as more than one part of speech: In "Iron rusts if left in the rain," *rust* is a verb; in "Remove the rust with a wire brush," *rust* is a noun; in "She wore a rust dress and brown shoes," *rust* is an adjective. This shows that the part of speech to which a word belongs cannot be definitely decided by looking at the word by itself; we need to know how it is used.

**par|ton** (pär′ton), *n.* any one of certain concentrated charges into which a proton or neutron may break up under nuclear bombardment: *It takes very high energy even to get evidence of the individuality of partons, let alone to pull them apart* (Science News). [< *part*(icle) + *-on,* as in *proton*]

**par|took** (pär tu̇k′), *v.* the past tense of **partake**: *He partook of food and drink.*

**par|tridge** (pär′trij), *n., pl.* **-tridg|es** or (*collectively*) **-tridge,** *adj.* —***n.*** **1** any one of several kinds of game birds of Europe, Asia, and Africa, belonging to the same family as the quail, pheasant, and peacock. **2** any one of several birds in the United States and Canada, that nest on the ground and fly only short distances, such as the ruffed grouse and the quail or bobwhite. **3** any one of several tinamous of South America.

—***adj.*** having a color pattern like that of a partridge, as certain chickens do.

[Middle English *partrich* < Old French *perdriz* < Latin *perdix* < Greek *pérdix* partridge < *pérdesthai* to break wind (from the whirring noise of its wings)]

**par|tridge|ber|ry** (pär′trij ber′ē), *n., pl.* **-ries.** **1** a North American trailing plant of the madder family, having evergeen leaves, fragrant white flowers, and scarlet berries; checkerberry. **2** the berry, which is edible but insipid.

**partridge pea**, a wild plant of the eastern and central United States and of Mexico, bearing seeds in pods and having leaves made up of many small leaflets, which are somewhat sensitive to touch; sensitive pea.

**partridge wood**, the hard, beautifully marked,

reddish wood of a tropical American tree of the pea family.

**parts** (pärts), *n.pl.* See under **part**.

**part song**, a song with parts in simple harmony for two or more voices, especially one to be sung without an accompaniment.

**part-time** (pärt′tīm′), *adj., adv.* for part of the usual or required time: *a part-time job* (adj.). *High school students leave school to work part-time* (New York Times) (adv.).

**part-tim|er** (pärt′tī′mər), *n.* a part-time employee or worker: *The part-timer, once the auxiliary, has become the regular— and many part-timers have more than one job* (New York Times).

**par|tu|ri|en|cy** (pär tůr′ē ən sē, -tyůr′-), *n.* the state of being parturient.

**par|tu|ri|ent** (pär tůr′ē ənt, -tyůr′-), *adj.* **1** bringing forth young; about to give birth to young. **2** having to do with childbirth. **3** *Figurative.* ready to bring forth or produce a discovery, idea, principle, or other new thing.

**par|tu|ri|fa|cient** (pär tůr′ə fā′shənt, -tyůr′-), *n., adj.* **—*n.*** something that hastens childbirth. **—*adj.*** hastening childbirth. [< Latin *parturīre* be in labor + *faciēns, -entis,* present participle of *facere* to make, do]

**par|tu|ri|tion** (pär′tů rish′ən, -tyů-, -chů-), *n.* the act of giving birth to young; childbirth. **SYN:** delivery. [< Latin *parturītiō, -ōnis* < *parturīre* be in labor < *parere* to bear]

**part|way** (pärt′wā′), *adv.* part of the way; partially; partly: *Mr. Kennedy, going partway back to a proposal he made eight days ago, said . . .* (New York Times).

**part|work** (pärt′wėrk′), *n.* a book or set of books published one part or fascicle at a time: *Purnell's three most successful partworks [were] The History of the Second World War (launched in October 1966 and extended from 96 to 120 parts), The History of the Twentieth Century (launched in 1968), and The History of the First World War (launched in 1969)* (William A. Katz).

**par|ty** (pär′tē), *n., pl.* **-ties,** *adj., v.,* **-tied, -ty|ing.** **—*n.*** **1** a group of people gathered to have a good time together: *a busy round of Christmas parties. On her birthday she gave a party and invited her friends.* **2** a group of people doing something together: *a sewing party, a dinner party, a scouting party of three soldiers.* **SYN:** band. See syn. under **company**. **3** a group of people wanting the same kind of government or action: *the Democratic Party.* **4** a person who takes part in, aids, or knows about: *He was a party to our secret.* **5** each of the persons or sides as in a contract or lawsuit. **6** *Informal.* a person: *The party you are telephoning is out.* **7** *Obsolete.* a part.
**—*adj.*** **1** of or having to do with a party of people: *a party feeling.* **2** of or belonging to a political party: *Bulganin was a party man put in charge of the army* (Wall Street Journal). **3** *Heraldry.* (of a shield) divided into parts.
**—*v.i.*** *Informal.* to give, go to, or take part in a party or parties: *Newsmen . . . keep vigil over the Princess and Townsend partying nearby* (Newsweek).
[< Old French *partie,* (originally) feminine past participle of *partir* to divide < Latin *partīre* < *pars, partis* part]
▶See **person** for usage note.

**par|ty-col|ored** (pär′tē kul′ərd), *adj.* = parti-colored.

**party-col|oured** (pär′tē kul′ərd), *adj. Especially British.* parti-colored.

**party girl**, **1** *U.S.* a prostitute. **2** a girl who enjoys socializing and spending time going to parties.

**par|ty|go|er** (pär′tē gō′ər), *n.* a person who goes to parties.

**par|ty|go|ing** (pär′tē gō′ing), *n.* the activities of a partygoer; partying.

**party line**, **1** a telephone line by which two or more subscribers are connected with the exchange by one circuit. **2** a boundary line between adjoining premises. **3** the officially adopted policies of a political party: *the Administration is insisting on a military party line* (New York Times). **4** the policies advocated and followed by the Communist Party: *The target was anything in books or pictures that didn't carry the party line* (Newsweek).

**party liner**, **1** a person who follows the policies of a political party. **2** a person who follows the policies of the Communist Party.

**party man**, **1** a man belonging to a party. **2** a man who adheres to his party, regardless of any individual opinion.

**party poop|er** (pü′pər), *U.S. Slang.* a killjoy; spoilsport; wet blanket.

**party wall**, *Law.* a wall dividing adjoining properties. Each owner has certain rights in it.

**par|u|la** (par′ə lə), *n.* an eastern North American warbler of blue, golden-brown, yellow, and white. [< New Latin *Parula* (diminutive) < Latin *pārus* titmouse]

**pa|rure** (pə rür′), *n.* a set of jewels or other ornaments to be worn together. [< French *parure* < *parer* to arrange < Latin *parāre* to prepare]

**par value**, the value of a stock, bond, note, or other commercial paper, printed on it; face value.

**par|ve** (pär′və), *adj.* (in Jewish dietary law) neither meat nor dairy; neutral, as fish, eggs, and all fruits and vegetables: *a parve cake, a parve meal.* Also, **pareve**. [< Yiddish *parev, pareve*]

**par|ve|nu** (pär′və nü, -nyü), *n., adj.* **—*n.*** **1** a person who has risen above his class, especially one who has risen as through the acquisition of wealth or political power. **2** a person who has risen to a higher place than he is fit for; upstart.
**—*adj.*** of or like a parvenu.
[< French *parvenu,* past participle of *parvenir* to arrive < Latin *pervenīre* < *per-* through + *venīre* to come]

**par|ve|nue** (pär′və nü, -nyü), *n.* a woman parvenu: *She has often been dismissed as an amoral parvenue, but there is much in her to admire* (Punch). [< French *parvenue,* feminine of *parvenu*]

**par|vis** (pär′vis), *n.* **1** the enclosed area in front of a building, especially a cathedral, sometimes surrounded with colonnades: *In the recent production here, the audience sat in stands erected on the parvis in front of Notre Dame* (New Yorker). **2** a single portico or colonnade in front of a church. **3** a room over a church porch. [< Old French *parevis,* alteration of *pareïs* paradise < Latin *paradīsus* paradise, (in Medieval Latin, the name given to the atrium of St. Peter's in Rome and to similar courts of churches)]

**par|vo|lin** (pär′və lin), *n.* = parvoline.

**par|vo|line** (pär′və lēn, -lin), *n.* an oily liquid obtained from certain shales and bituminous coals, or as a ptomaine from decaying mackerel and horseflesh. *Formula:* $C_9H_{13}N$ [< Latin *parvus* little]

**par|y|lene** (par′ə lēn), *n.* a plastic derived from an isomer of xylene (paraxylene) by polymerization: *We developed parylene to protect things like bees— fragile, complex things so intricate in shape they are next to impossible to coat* (Scientific American). [< *par*(ax)*ylene*]

**Par|zi|val** (pär′tsi fäl), *n.* = Parsifal.

**pas** (pä), *n. French.* **1** a step or movement in dancing. **2** a kind of dance.

**PAS** (no periods), para-aminosalicylic acid.

**Pas|ca|gou|la** (pas′kə gü′lə), *n., pl.* **-la** or **-las.** a member of an American Indian tribe that formerly inhabited part of the Gulf Coast of Mississippi.

**pas|cal** (pas kal′, pas′kəl), *n.* the unit of pressure in the meter-kilogram-second system. It is equal to the pressure resulting from the force of 1 newton exerted over 1 square meter. [< Blaise *Pascal;* see etym. under **Pascal's law**]

**pas|cal celery** (pas′kəl, -kal; pas kal′), celery marketed without bleaching. [probably < the name *Pascal*]

**Pas|cal's law** (pas kalz′, pas′kəlz), *Physics.* the principle in hydrostatics that in a fluid at rest the pressure is the same in all directions and that, except for the differences of pressure produced by the action of gravity, pressure applied to a confined fluid is transmitted equally in all directions. [< Blaise *Pascal,* 1623-1662, a French physicist and philosopher, who formulated it]

**Pascal's triangle**, a triangular arrangement of numbers in which each number is the sum of the two numbers to the right and the left of it in the row above. [< Blaise *Pascal,* who devised it; see etym. under **Pascal's law**]

**Pasch** (pask), *n. Archaic.* **1** the Jewish feast of the Passover; Pesah. **2** the Christian feast of Easter. [< Old French *pasque,* learned borrowing from Late Latin *pascua,* alteration of Latin *pascha* < Greek *páscha* the Passover < Hebrew *pesaḥ*]

**pas|chal** (pas′kəl), *adj.* **1** of or having to do with the Passover. **2** of or having to do with Easter; used in Easter celebrations.

**paschal candle** or **taper** a large wax candle placed in Roman Catholic churches at the gospel side of the altar on Holy Saturday, there to remain until Ascension Day.

**paschal lamb**, the lamb killed and eaten at Passover, commemorated at the modern Seder by a bone kept on the table with other symbolic foods (in the Bible, Exodus 12:3-14).

**Paschal Lamb**, Christ or any representation of Him.

**paschal moon**, the first full moon on or after the vernal equinox. The Roman Catholic Church dates Easter as the first Sunday after the paschal moon.

**pas|cu|al** (pas′kyů əl), *adj.* growing in pastures. [< Latin *pascuum* pasture]

**pas d'ac|tion** (pä′ dák syôɴ′), *French.* a dance used in ballet as a narrative.

**pas de bour|rée** (pä′ də bü rā′), *French.* a light, rapid ballet movement of one foot in front of or behind the other.

**pas de chat** (pä′ də shä′), *French.* a springing ballet movement in which one foot jumps over the other while moving diagonally across the stage.

**pas de deux** (pä′ də dœ′), *French.* a dance or figure in ballet for two persons.

**pas de qua|tre** (pä′ də ká′trə), *French.* a dance or figure in ballet for four persons.

**pas de trois** (pä′ də trwá′), *French.* a dance or figure in ballet for three persons.

**pas du tout** (pä′ dʏ tü′), *French.* not at all; not in the least.

**pa|se** (pä′sā), *n.* the maneuver in bullfighting in which the matador attracts the bull with his cape and guides its attack. [< Spanish *pase* a pass]

**pa|se|ar** (pä′sā är′), *n. Southwestern U.S. Slang.* a walk; promenade; airing. [< Spanish *pasear* to promenade]

**pa|se|o** (pä sā′ō), *n., pl.* **-se|os** (-sā′ōs). **1** a place to walk; promenade: *The crowds stroll on the paseo, chattering, laughing, joking* (Atlantic). **2** a stroll. [< Spanish *paseo*]

**pash**[1] (pash), *v., n. Dialect.* **—*v.t.*** **1** to smash; shatter. **2** to strike with a smashing or violent blow.
**—*v.i.*** to dash or strike violently, as waves or rain.
**—*n.*** **1** a smashing blow. **2** a crashing fall.

**pash**[2] (pash), *n. Dialect.* the head.

**pa|sha** (pə shä′, pash′ə, pä′shə), *n.* **1** a former title used after the name of Turkish civil or military officials of high rank. **2** a person having this title. Also, **pacha**. [< Turkish *paşa,* variant of *başa* < *baş* head]

**pa|sha|lik** or **pa|sha|lic** (pə shä′lik), *n.* the jurisdiction of a pasha. [< Turkish *paşalık* < *paşa* (see etym. under **pasha)** + *-lik* -ship]

**Pash|to** (push′tō), *n., pl.* **-tos.** **1** the Iranian language of Afghanistan and of the Pathan tribes of Pakistan; Afghan: *speaking a language that only a few non-Pathans, usually British, ever learned — Pashto* (New York Times). **2** = Pathan. Also, **Pushtu**. [< Persian *pashtō* Afghan]

**pa|sig|ra|phy** (pə sig′rə fē), *n.* any one of various systems of writing with characters representing ideas instead of words, that may be understood and used by all nations. [< Greek *pási* for all, dative plural of *pâs* all + *gráphein* write]

**Pa|siph|a|ë** (pə sif′ə ē), *n. Greek Legend.* the daughter of Helios, wife of Minos (of Crete), and mother of Ariadne and the Minotaur.

**pa|so do|ble** (pa′sə dō′blā, pä′sō), *n.* **1** a brisk march in a quick 2/4 rhythm, frequently played at bullfights. **2** a one-step dance done to this rhythm. [< Spanish *pasodoble* (literally) double step]

**Pasque** (pask), *n.* = Pasch.

**pasque|flow|er** (pask′flou′ər), *n.* any one of several anemones with purple or white flowers that bloom early in the spring; wild anemone; wild crocus. [< *pasque* (variant of *Pasch*) + *fleur* flower < Old French *flour*]

**pas|quil** (pas′kwəl), *n.* = pasquinade.

**pas|quin|ade** (pas′kwə nād′), *n., v.,* **-ad|ed, -ad|ing.** **—*n.*** a publicly posted satirical writing; lampoon.
**—*v.t.*** to attack by lampoons.
[< French *pasquinade* < Italian *pasquinata* < *Pasquino,* name of a statue where lampoons were posted] **—pas′quin|ad′er,** *n.*

**pass**[1] (pas, päs), *v.,* **passed, passed** or **past, pass|ing,** *n.* **—*v.t.*** **1** to go by; move past; leave behind: *We passed the big truck. They pass our house every day on the way to school.* **2** to cause to go from one to another; hand around: *Please pass the butter. The old coin was passed around for everyone to see. The owner passed the business to his partner.* **3** to get through or by: *The ship passed the channel. We passed the dangerous section of the road successfully.* **4** to go across or over: *The horse passed the stream.* **5** to move; make (a thing) go in a specific manner or direction; direct: *He passed a rope around his waist for support. Pass your hand over the velvet and feel how soft it is.* **6** to cause to go, move onward, or proceed: *to pass troops in review, to pass dishes under running water.* **7** to discharge from the body. **8a** to be successful in (an examination or a course): *I passed Latin.* **b** to allow to go through an examination or a course successfully: *to pass a student.* **9** *Figurative.* to cause or allow to go through something; cause to be accepted or received; approve: *to pass accounts as correct. The inspector passed the item after examining it.* **10** to ratify or enact: *to pass a bill or law.* **SYN:** confirm. **11** to be ap-

**Pronunciation Key:** hat, āge, cãre, fär; let, ēqual, tėrm; it, īce; hot, ōpen, ôrder; oil, out; cup, pùt, rüle; child; long; thin; ᴛʜen; zh, measure; ə represents a in about, e in taken, i in pencil, o in lemon, u in circus.

proved by (as a lawmaking body): *The bill passed Congress. The new law passed the city council.* **12** *Figurative.* to go beyond; exceed; surpass: *Such a strange story passes belief.* **SYN**: transcend. **13** to use or spend: *We passed the days happily.* **14** to cause to go about; circulate: *to pass a counterfeit bill.* **15** to express; pronounce: *A judge passes sentence on guilty persons. The reviewer passed heavy criticism on the book.* **16** *Figurative.* to let go without action or notice; leave unmentioned: *to pass an insult.* **17** to leave out; omit, especially payment of (a dividend or financial commitment). **18a** to transfer to another player (the ball, puck, or other playing piece) in basketball, football, hockey, and other games. **b** to pitch four balls to (a batter in baseball), allowing him to walk to first base. **19** to refuse (as a hand or chance to bid) while playing cards. **20** to promise: *to pass one's word.* **21** to thrust.

—***v.i.*** **1** to go on; move on; make one's way: *The parade passed. The salesman passed from house to house.* **SYN**: proceed, advance. **2** to go from person to person: *The property passed from father to son.* **3** to go away; depart: *The days pass quickly. The time for action has passed.* **SYN**: disappear, vanish. **4** to be successful in an examination or a course. **5** to be discharged as waste matter from the body. **6** to be approved, as by a court or lawmaking body; be ratified: *The bill passed.* **7** to come to an end; die: *King Arthur passed in peace. Dynasties pass.* **8a** to change: *Water passes from a liquid to a solid state when it freezes.* **b** to be interchanged or transacted: *Hot words passed when the men quarreled. Friendly words passed between them.* **9** to take place; happen: *Tell me all that has passed.* **10** to be handed about; be in circulation: *Money passes from person to person.* **11** *Figurative.* to be accepted (for or as): *She could pass for twenty. Use silk or a material that will pass for silk. Mr. Crook moved to another city where he passed by the name of Mr. Smith.* **12** to give a judgment or opinion: *The judges passed on each contestant.* **13** *Figurative.* to go without notice: *He was rude, but let that pass.* **14** to throw a football or basketball or shoot a hockey puck from one player to another. **15** to refrain from bidding or playing a hand in playing cards. **16** to make a thrust in fencing.

—***n.*** **1** the act of passing; passage: *With this arrangement we have a 90 per cent chance of intercepting every pass of a satellite which is higher than 300 miles* (Scientific American). **2** success in an examination, test, or the like; passing an examination but without a distinctive grade or honors: *If ... after the dropping of a pass in Latin as an entrance qualification, Latin would continue to be taught ... there need be no fears* (New Scientist). **3** a written note, permission, or license to do something: *No one can get into the fort without a pass. The soldier was home on a pass. The officer had a safe-conduct pass through the enemy lines to negotiate the release of U.N. prisoners.* **4** a free ticket: *a pass to the circus.* **5** a state; condition: *Things have come to a strange pass when children give orders to their parents.* **6** a motion of the hand or hands, as by a hypnotist: *Alexis, after a few passes from Dr. Elliotson, despises pain, reads with the back of his head, sees miles off* (Thackeray). **7** a sleight-of-hand motion; manipulation; trick: *The magician made passes in the air.* **8** a throw or transfer of a ball or puck to another player, as in basketball, football, or hockey. **9** *Baseball.* the pitching of four balls to a batter, allowing him to walk to first base; walk: *The passes were bad enough but there was no excuse for the wild pitch* (New York Times). **10** a thrust in fencing. **11** the action of refraining from bidding or playing a hand in playing cards. **12** *Informal.* **a** an attempt to kiss or flirt. **b** a sexual overture. **13** *Archaic.* accomplishment; completion. **14** *Obsolete.* a sally of wit.

**bring to pass**, to cause to be; accomplish: *to bring a miracle to pass.*

**come to pass**, to take place; happen: *The prophecy came to pass.*

**make passes at**, to attempt to kiss or otherwise flirt with: *Men seldom make passes At girls who wear glasses* (Dorothy Parker).

**pass away**, **a** to die: *Mr. Richard Williams ... passed away ... at the great age of ninety years* (Law Times). **b** to come to an end: *Thus passed the winter away so rapidly* (Frederick Marryat). **c** to while away: *One day is passed away here very like its defunct predecessor* (Thackeray).

**pass by**, **a** to go or proceed past: *The countrymen ... would all look up When she pass'd by* (Robert Southey). **b** *Figurative.* to fail to notice; overlook; disregard; ignore: *to pass by a mistake or an offense.* **c** *Figurative.* to fail to have an effect on: *The ordinary tourist is seen in all his ordinariness in these circumstances. The Romantic Revolution has passed him by* (London Times).

**pass muster**. See under **muster**.

**pass off**, **a** to go away; disappear gradually: *The smell of the paint will pass off in a few days.* **b** to take place; be done: *In every sense the festival passed off as its promoters must have desired* (London Times). **c** *Figurative.* to get accepted; pretend to be: *He passed himself off as a wealthy man.* **d** *Figurative.* to palm off; impose: *The applicants pass off their goods for those of the Baron de Geer* (Law Times). **e** *Figurative.* to parry: *The young man passed off lightly all such reference* (Algernon Gissing).

**pass on**, **a** to proceed; advance: *Pass on, weak heart, and leave me where I lie* (Tennyson). **b** to send or hand to the next member of a series: *Please read this and pass it on.* **c** *Figurative.* to die: *Well, how long is it since Fletch passed on?* (John O'Hara). **d** to pass judgment on; express approval or disapproval of: *"I never bought a dress he didn't pass on," she added* (New York Times).

**pass out**, **a** to hand out or distribute: *Please pass out this test to the members of the class. Librarians ... are willing to pass out catalogs that have won their confidence* (Publishers' Weekly). **b** *Slang.* to faint; lose consciousness: *We carried him home after he passed out.* **c** *Slang, Figurative.* to die. **d** *British.* to undergo (a course of instruction) successfully: *At last, I was able to "pass out," and found myself ... a second lieutenant in the King's Royal Rifle Corps* (Harold Macmillan).

**pass over**, **a** to fail to notice; overlook; disregard: *to pass over a mistake. It is his glory to pass over a transgression* (Proverbs 19:11). **b** *Figurative.* to die: *to pass over early in life.* **c** to ignore the claims of (a person) to promotion, a post, honor, or other recognition: *He was passed over by the Army Promotion Board.* **d** *Informal.* (of Negroes) to be accepted as white: *... numerous persons with only a few Negroid traits annually "pass over" and are absorbed into the dominant Caucasoid population* (Beals and Hoijer). **e** to hand over to another; transfer: *Geology here passes over the continuation of the history of man to Archeology* (James Dwight Dana).

**pass the buck**. See under **buck**[5].

**pass the hat**. See under **hat**.

**pass up**, to fail to take advantage of; give up; renounce; refuse: *to pass up the chance to go to college, to pass up dessert at dinner.*

[< Old French *passer* < Vulgar Latin *passāre* < Latin *passus, -ūs* a step; see etym. under **pace**[1]]

▶ **passed, past.** The past tense and past participle of *pass* are *passed* (He *passed* the first post. He had *passed*), though *past* is fairly common as the participle. *Past* is the adjective (*past* favors), preposition (*past* the crisis), and adverb (*past* due. They went *past*).

**pass**[2] (pas, päs), *n.* **1** a narrow road, path, way, or channel, especially through mountains: *A pass crosses the mountains. Many passes have become great roads of history.* See picture under **mountain**. **2** a navigable channel, such as at the mouth or in the delta of a river. [< Old French *pas* step, pace, track < Latin *passus, -ūs.* See etym. of doublet **pace**[1].]

**pass.**, **1** here and there (in a work cited; Latin, *passim*). **2** passenger. **3** passive.

**pass|a|ble** (pas′ə bəl, päs′-), *adj.* **1** fairly good; moderate: *a passable knowledge of geography.* **SYN**: tolerable, mediocre, middling. **2** that can be passed: *a passable river. The ford was not passable.* **3** that may be circulated; current; valid: *passable coin.* **4** that may be enacted: *a passable bill.* [< Old French *passable* < *passer* to pass] —**pass′a|ble|ness**, *n.*

**pass|a|bly** (pas′ə blē, päs′-) *adv.* fairly; moderately: *a passably good job.*

**pas|sa|ca|glia** (pä′sə käl′yə), *n.* **1** an old form of dance tune of Spanish origin, constructed on a recurring theme, usually a ground bass, in slow triple rhythm. **2** the dance performed to this. [< Italian *passacaglia* < Spanish *pasacalle* < *pasar* pass + *calle* street]

**pas|sa|caille** (pȧ sȧ kä′yə), *n. French.* passacaglia.

**pas|sade** (pə sād′), *n.* **1** a turn or course of a horse backward or forward on the same ground. **2** = passado. [< Middle French *passade* (originally) action of passing < Italian *passata* < *passare* to pass < Vulgar Latin *passāre*]

**pas|sa|do** (pə sä′dō), *n., pl.* **-dos** or **-does.** a forward thrust with the sword in fencing, one foot being advanced at the same time. [alteration of Middle French *passade*, or Spanish *pasada* < Italian *passata;* see etym. under **passade**]

**pas|sage**[1] (pas′ij), *n., v.,* **-saged, -sag|ing.** —***n.*** **1** a hall or way through a building; passageway: *And face with an undaunted tread the long black passage up to bed* (Robert Louis Stevenson). **SYN**: corridor. **2** a means of passing; way through: *The police opened a passage through the crowd for the governor.* **SYN**: road, path, route. **3** the right, liberty, or leave to pass: *The guard refused us passage.* **4** *Figurative.* **a** the act of passing; going or moving onward: *the passage of time.* **b** the act of passing from one place or state to another: *the passage from sleep to wakefulness.* **5** a piece from a speech or writing: *a passage from the Bible.* **6** a phrase or other division of a piece of music. **7** the act of going across; voyage: *We had a stormy passage across the Atlantic.* **8** a ticket that entitles the holder to transportation, especially by boat: *to obtain passage for Europe.* **9** the act of making into law by a favoring vote of a legislature: *The passage of the bill by both houses of Congress was forecast by the political reporter.* **10** *Figurative.* what passes between persons. **11** *Archaic.* an occurrence, incident, or event: *It is no act of common passage* (Shakespeare). **12** *Figurative.* **a** an exchange of blows or a dispute: *a passage of arms.* **b** an amorous encounter. **13** a movement of the bowels. **14** *Obsolete.* death.

—***v.i.*** **1** to make a passage, as in a ship; move across; pass; cross. **2** to carry on a passage or dispute.

[< Old French *passage* < *passer* to pass]

**pas|sage**[2] (pas′ij), *v.,* **-saged, -sag|ing,** *n.* —***v.i.*** **1** (of a horse) to move sideways, in obedience to pressure of the rider's leg on the opposite side. **2** (of a rider) to cause a horse to do this.

—***v.t.*** to cause (a horse) to passage.

—***n.*** a movement of a horse sideways: *She guided Jubilee through ... such dressage movements as ... passage* (Newsweek).

[< French *passager,* alteration of *passéger* to promenade < Italian *passeggiare* < Latin *passus;* see etym. under **pace**[1]]

**pas|sage|way** (pas′ij wā′), *n.* a way along which one can pass; passage. Halls and alleys are passageways. **SYN**: corridor.

**pas|sage|work** (pas′ij wėrk′), *n.* a musical passage consisting for the most part of flourishes, such as arpeggios and double octaves, intended for virtuoso display.

**pas|sa|lid beetle** (pas′ə lid), a large, shiny beetle that lives in well-rotted wood, widespread in tropical countries and east of the Rocky Mountains in the United States. [< New Latin *Passalidae* the family name < Greek *pássalos* a peg]

**Pas|sa|ma|quod|dy** (pas′ə mə kwod′ē), *n., pl.* **-dy** or **-dies.** **1** a member of a tribe of American Indians living in the Passamaquoddy Bay region, between Maine and New Brunswick, Canada. **2** the Algonkian language of this tribe.

**pas|sant** (pas′ənt), *adj. Heraldry.* walking and looking to the right side: *a lion passant.* [< Old French *passant* walking, present participle of *passer* to pass]

**pass|back** (pas′bak′, päs′-), *n.* = snapback (def. 2).

**pass|band** (pas′band′, päs′-), *n. Electronics.* the band of frequencies that will pass through a circuit, filter, or other device without much attenuation.

**pass|book** (pas′bu̇k′, päs′-), *n.* **1** a small book in which a bank keeps an account of what a person deposits and withdraws; bankbook. In the United States passbooks are now used chiefly for savings accounts. **2** a customer's book in which a merchant makes entries of goods sold on credit. **3** identity papers required of nonwhites by the South African government.

**pass degree**, *Especially British.* a degree without honors from a college, university, or school.

**pas|sé** (pa sā′, pas′ā), *adj.* **1** past its usefulness; out-of-date: *Cloak-and-dagger techniques and mass employment of low-level agents are passé* (Newsweek). **SYN**: outmoded, antiquated. **2** past. [< French *passé,* past participle of *passer* to pass]

**passed** (past, päst), *adj.* **1** that has passed or has been passed. **2** having passed an examination. **3** qualified for promotion by examination but waiting for a vacancy in the higher grade: *a passed assistant surgeon in the navy.* **4** (of a dividend) not paid at the proper time.

**passed ball**, *Baseball.* a pitched ball, not touched by the bat, on which a runner or runners advance to the next base or bases because of the catcher's failure to stop the ball.

**pas|sel** (pas′əl), *n.* a group of indeterminate number; parcel: *a passel of birds, a passel of TV commercials. A whole passel of people kissed the bride* (Atlantic). [variant of *parcel*]

**passe|ment** (pas′mənt), *n., v. Archaic.* —***n.*** lace (as of gold or silver), braid, or gimp for trimming. —***v.t.*** to trim with passement. [< Middle French *passement* < Old French *passer* to pass]

**passe|men|terie** (pas men′trē; *French* pȧs mäN trē′), *n.* trimming made of beads, braid, cord, gimp, or the like, used for dressmaking and millinery. [< French *passementerie* < Middle French *passementer*, verb < *passement;* see etym. under *passement*]

**pas|sen|ger** (pas′ən jər), *n.* **1** a traveler in a train, bus, boat, airplane, or car, usually one that pays a fare: *The airplane had many passengers going to London.* **2** *Archaic.* **a** a passer-by. **b** a traveler; wayfarer: *a foot passenger. And the passengers that pass through the land ...* (Ezekiel 39:15). [alteration of Middle English *passager* < Old French *passagier* < *passage* passage]

**pas|sen|ger-mile** (pas′ən jər mīl′), *n.* the transportation of one passenger for one mile.

**passenger pigeon,** a kind of wild pigeon of North America, with a long, narrow tail, able to fly for long periods at a time, usually in very large flocks. It was a fairly common item of food in the central United States in the 1800's. The passenger pigeon is now extinct.

**passe partout,** or **passe-par|tout** (pas′ pär tü′, päs′-), *n.* **1a** a frame for a picture consisting of strips of gummed paper that fasten the glass to the backing. **b** the paper prepared for this purpose. **2** that which passes everywhere, or by means of which one can pass everywhere, such as a master key. [< French *passe-partout* pass everywhere; *passe,* imperative of *passer* to pass; *partout* (literally) through all < *par* (< Latin *per*) + *tout* (< Latin *tōtus*)]

**passe|pied** (pås pyā′), *n. French.* **1** a lively French dance of the 1600's and 1700's which originated in Brittany and later became a formal and court dance. **2** the music for this dance.

**pass|er** (pas′ər, päs′-), *n.* **1** = passer-by. **2** a player in sports who passes.

**pass|er-by** (pas′ər bī′, päs′-), *n., pl.* **pass|ers-by.** a person who passes by: *That cry is so common ... that the passers-by never turned their heads* (Rudyard Kipling).

**pas|ser|ine** (pas′ər in, -ə rīn), *adj., n.* —*adj.* belonging to or having to do with the very large order of perching birds, including more than half of all birds, such as the warblers, sparrows, chickadees, wrens, thrushes, and swallows: *Among passerine birds the raven has the widest range* (Alfred R. Wallace).
—*n.* a perching bird.
[< Latin *passerīnus* < *passer, -eris* sparrow]

**pas seul** (pä sœl′), *French.* a dance movement or dance for one performer; solo dance.

**pass-fail** (pas′fāl′, päs′-), *adj.* of or having to do with a system of crediting academic work in which a student either passes or fails but otherwise is not graded: *a pass-fail basis, without any indication of the actual quality of the work performed* (Fred M. Hechinger).

**pas|si|bil|i|ty** (pas′ə bil′ə tē), *n.* the quality of being passible.

**pas|si|ble** (pas′ə bəl), *adj.* capable of suffering or feeling; susceptible of sensation or of emotion. [< Old French *passible,* learned borrowing from Latin *passibilis* < *passus,* past participle of *patī* to suffer]

**pas|si|flo|ra|ceous** (pas′i flô rā′shəs, -flō-), *adj.* belonging to the family of plants typified by the passionflower. [< New Latin *Passifloraceae* the family name < *Passiflore* the genus name]

**pas|sim** (pas′im), *adv. Latin.* here and there; in various places.
▶**Passim** is used in footnotes in referring to material found in several places in some book or books: "Jespersen, *Language, passim.*"

**pass|ing** (pas′ing, päs′-), *adj., n., adv.* —*adj.* **1** that goes by or passes. **2** done or given in passing; transient; fleeting: *a passing smile.* **SYN:** transitory. **3** *Figurative.* cursory; incidental: *passing mention, a passing fancy.* **4** that is now happening: *the passing scene.* **5a** allowing a person to pass an examination, test, or course: *75 will be a passing mark.* **b** in charge of testing and passing candidates; examining. **6** *Archaic.* surpassing; preeminent: *'Tis a passing shame* (Shakespeare).
—*n.* **1** the act of one that passes; going by; departure. **2** a means or place of passing: *A river Runs in three loops around her livingplace; And o'er it are three passings* (Tennyson). **3** *Figurative.* death: *The passing of Einstein was a great blow to science.*
—*adv.* surpassingly; very: *Our love was passing fair and wove a wondrous spell* (Harper's).
**in passing,** by the way; incidentally; in that connection: *It may be remarked, in passing, that ...* (Charlotte Brontë). *The translation, to note this in passing, is not without faults* (Nikolaus Pevsner).
—**pass′ing|ly,** *adv.*

**passing bell, 1** a bell tolled to announce that a death has just occurred or that a funeral is taking place. **2** *Figurative.* a portent or sign of the passing away of anything: *... the passing bell of tyranny* (Shelley).

**passing note,** = passing tone.

**passing shot,** a tennis ball hit to the side and beyond the reach of an opponent near the net.

**passing tone,** a musical tone not essential to the harmony, introduced between two successive notes in order to produce a melodic transition.

**pas|sion** (pash′ən), *n.* **1** a very strong feeling; emotion: *Hate and fear are passions. The opera star sang with great passion.* **SYN:** See syn. under **feeling. 2** Often, **passions.** strong feelings or emotions as an obstacle to civilized conduct or rational behavior: *Passions have their root in that which is crippled, blemished, or insecure within us* (Harper's). **3** a fit or mood of some emotion, especially violent anger; rage: *He flew into a passion, shouting insults at us. She broke into a passion of tears* (Dickens). **4a** a very strong love or desire between a man and a woman: *I love thee so, that ... Nor wit nor reason can my passion hide* (Shakespeare). **b** a person who is the object of such love or desire. **5** *Figurative.* **a** a very strong liking: *She has a passion for music. Her passion for caraway seeds, for instance, was uncontrollable* (Lytton Strachey). **b** a thing for which a strong liking is felt: *Music is her passion.* **6** *Archaic.* suffering. **7** Often, **the Passion. a** the sufferings of Jesus on the Cross or after the Last Supper. **b** the story of these sufferings in the Bible. **c** a musical setting of this story: *Bach's Passion According to Saint Matthew.* **d** a representation in art of the sufferings of Christ. **8a** the fact or condition of being affected by external force: *The word passion signifies the receiving any action, in a large philosophical sense* (Isaac Watts). **b** an effect produced by action from without. [< Old French *passiun,* and *passion,* learned borrowing from Latin *passiō, -ōnis* < *patī* to suffer]

**pas|sion|al** (pash′ə nəl), *adj., n.* —*adj.* of or having to do with passion or the passions: *passional crimes.* —*n.* a book containing accounts of the sufferings (passions) of saints and martyrs, for reading on their festival days.

**pas|sion|ar|y** (pash′ə ner′ē), *n., pl.* **-ar|ies.** = passional.

**pas|sion|ate** (pash′ə nit), *adj.* **1** having or showing strong feelings: *The fathers of our country were passionate believers in freedom.* **2** easily moved to strong feelings, especially to violent anger: *My brother was passionate, and had often beaten me, which I took extremely amiss* (Benjamin Franklin). **SYN:** quick-tempered, irascible, fiery. **3** resulting from strong feeling: *He made a passionate speech against surrender.* **4** having or showing a very strong love or desire, as of a man for a woman: *a passionate lover.* [< Medieval Latin *passionatus* < Latin *passiō* passion]
—**pas′sion|ate|ly,** *adv.* —**pas′sion|ate|ness,** *n.*

**pas|sion|flow|er** (pash′ən flou′ər), *n.* **1** any one of a genus of mostly American climbing plants with flowers supposed to suggest the crown of thorns, the nails, and the Cross of Christ's crucifixion. Passionflowers are grown for their edible, yellowish or purple fruits and their large, showy flowers. **2** the flower of any one of these plants. [translation of New Latin *flos passionis* flower of the Passion (from the imagined likeness of parts of the flower to the instruments of Christ's passion)]

**pas|sion|fruit** (pash′ən früt′), *n.* the fruit of a passionflower, when edible, such as the maypop.

**pas|sion|ful** (pash′ən fəl), *adj.* = passionate.

**Pas|sion|ist** (pash′ə nist), *n.* a member of the Congregation of Discalced (barefooted) Clerks of the Most Holy Cross and Passion of Our Lord Jesus Christ, a Roman Catholic order founded by St. Paul of the Cross, in Italy, in 1720. The members are pledged to the utmost zeal in keeping fresh the memory of Christ's passion.

**pas|sion|less** (pash′ən lis), *adj.* without passion; calm. —**pas′sion|less|ly,** *adv.* —**pas′sion|less|ness,** *n.*

**passion music,** dramatic vocal music that tells the Gospel story of the sufferings and death of Christ. Passion music is usually sung during Holy Week.

**Passion Play** or **passion play,** a play representing the sufferings and death of Christ. One is given every ten years at Oberammergau, Germany.

**Passion Sunday,** the second Sunday before Easter Sunday. It is the fifth Sunday in Lent.

**Pas|sion|tide** (pash′ən tīd′), *n.* the last two weeks of Lent.

**passion vine,** = passionflower.

**Passion Week, 1** the second week before Easter; fifth week in Lent, between Passion Sunday and Palm Sunday. **2** (in some Eastern Orthodox churches) the week before Easter; Holy Week.

**pas|si|vate** (pas′ə vāt), *v.t.,* **-vat|ed, -vat|ing.** to make chemically passive —**pas′si|va′tion,** *n.*

**pas|sive** (pas′iv), *adj., n.* —*adj.* **1** not acting in return; being acted on without itself acting: *a passive mind, a passive disposition.* **SYN:** impassive. **2** not resisting; yielding or submitting to the will of another: *The slaves gave passive obedience to their master. It would not be a passive condition, but eminently constructive* (London Times). **SYN:** submissive, unresisting, patient. **3** *Grammar.* **a** showing the subject as acted upon. In "The window was broken by John," *was broken* is in the passive voice. **b** having to do with the passive voice. **4** not readily entering into chemical combination; inert; inactive. **5** used to reflect but not amplify energy pulses: *a passive radar, a passive lunar seismograph.* **6** of or having to do with an infection or other abnormal condition of the body, as of an organ in the body, that causes reduced vitality and imperfect muscular reaction. **7** (of a note, bond, share of stock, or the like) not bearing interest, but entitling the holder to some future benefit or claim.
—*n.* **1** = passive voice. *Abbr:* pass. **2** a verb form or verbal construction in the passive voice. **3** a person or thing that is passive.
[< Latin *passīvus* < *patī* to suffer] —**pas′sive|ly,** *adv.* —**pas′sive|ness,** *n.*

**passive defense,** military or civil defense designed to cope with the effects of an attack, such as bomb shelters do.

**passive euthanasia,** the act or fact of causing the death of a person who is incurably ill or injured by withholding artificial measures or extreme treatment necessary to prolong his life.

**passive immunity,** immunity conferred by injecting into one organism antibodies of a serum obtained from another organism.

**passive resistance,** peaceful refusal to comply with a law, injunction, or rule, especially as a form of resistance to a government or other authority: *Many of the Civil Rights protests have been carried out in passive resistance.*

**passive restraint,** a device, such as an airbag, in an automobile that automatically protects the occupants from dangerous injury in the event of an accident.

**passive satellite,** a communications satellite that reflects a signal but does not receive it and transmit it again.

**passive smoker,** a person who is subjected to passive smoking.

**passive smoking,** the inhaling of smoke from other people's cigarettes, cigars, and pipes: *Passive smoking can injure the health of ... people with chronic heart and lung diseases and allergies to tobacco smoke* (Jane E. Brody).

**passive voice,** a form of transitive verbs used to represent the subject as acted upon, not acting. In "A letter was written by me," *was written* is in the passive voice.

**pas|siv|ism** (pas′ə viz əm), *n.* **1** the quality of being passive. **2a** passive resistance, as a concept. **b** the practice of passive resistance.

**pas|siv|ist** (pas′ə vist), *n.* a person who favors or advocates passivism.

**pas|siv|i|ty** (pa siv′ə tē), *n.* the quality or condition of being passive; lack of action or resistance: *But basic passivity kept him from those heights and depths which the really good writer now and again reaches* (Newsweek).

**pass|key** (pas′kē′, päs′-), *n., pl.* **-keys. 1** a key for opening several locks, especially all the locks of a particular set or in a given building; master key. **2** a private key.

**pass|less** (pas′lis, päs′-), *adj.* **1** = impassable. **2** without a pass, or license to pass.

**pass|o|ver** (pas′ō′vər, päs′-), *n.* **1** the paschal lamb, the sacrifice formerly offered in the Temple at Passover (in the Bible, II Chronicles 30:15). **2** *Figurative.* Christ, the Paschal Lamb: *Christ our passover is sacrificed for us* (I Corinthians 5:7).

**Pass|o|ver** (pas′ō′vər, päs′-), *n.* an eight-day, annual Jewish holiday in memory of the escape of the Hebrews from Egypt, where they had been slaves; Feast of Unleavened Bread; Pesah. It begins on the eve of the 15th of Nisan (March-April) and is marked by the celebration of the Seder service and the eating of matzoth, or unleavened bread. [< verbal phrase *pass over,* translation of Hebrew *pesaḥ* (in reference to the Biblical account, in Exodus 12, of a destroying angel "passing over" houses of the Hebrews in Egypt when it killed the first-born children of the Egyptians). Compare etym. under **Pasch.**]

**pass|port** (pas′pôrt, -pōrt; päs′-), *n., v.* —*n.* **1a** a paper or book giving a citizen official permission to travel in a foreign country, under the protection of his own government and giving him the right to leave and reenter his own country: *Every American citizen carrying an American passport is entitled to, at the very least, the diplomatic*

---

**Pronunciation Key:** hat, āge, cãre, fär; let, ēqual, tėrm; it, īce; hot, ōpen, ôrder; oil, out; cup, pu̇t, rüle; child; long; thin; ᴛʜen; zh, measure; ə represents **a** in about, **e** in taken, **i** in pencil, **o** in lemon, **u** in circus.

*protection of the U.S. Government* (New York Times). **b** a document granted in the 1920's and 1930's by an authority of the League of Nations to various persons who had no national identity, by means of which travel through or residence in certain countries was made possible; Nansen passport. **2** *Figurative.* anything that gives one admission or acceptance: *An interest in gardening was a passport to my aunt's favor.* **3** a document granting a ship, especially a neutral merchant ship in time of war, permission to enter certain waters freely, or requesting such permission for it. **4** *Archaic.* a safe-conduct, especially one permitting an enemy to leave or pass through a given country or territory.
—*v.t.* to supply or provide with a passport.
[< Middle French *passeport* < *passe,* imperative of Old French *passer* to pass[1] + *port* harbor, port[1]] —**pass′port′less,** *adj.*

**pass-through** (pas′thrü′, päs′-), *n.* **1** a rectangular opening in the wall between two rooms, as between a kitchen and a dining room or pantry, to permit dishes and food to be passed through upon a shelf or counter space provided there. **2** the complete transfer of an increase in the cost of a raw material to the ultimate consumer through proportional price increases by the intermediate processors, manufacturers, and dealers.

**pas|sus** (pas′əs), *n., pl.* **-sus** or **-sus|es.** a section or division of a story, poem, or other written work; canto. [< Medieval Latin *passus* < Latin *passus, -ūs* a step; see etym. under **pace**[1]]

**pass|word** (pas′wėrd′, päs′-), *n.* a secret word that allows a person speaking it to pass a guard.

**past** (past, päst), *adj., n., prep., adv., v.* —*adj.* **1** gone by; ended; over; *Summer is past. Our troubles are past.* **2** just gone by: *The past year was full of trouble. For some time past she has been ill.* SYN: bygone, preceding, foregoing. **3** having served a term or terms in office but not now in office: *a past president.* **4** indicating time gone by, or former action or state: *the past tense, a past participle. The past forms of "eat" and "smile" are "ate" and "smiled."*
—*n.* **1a** the time gone by; time before: *Life began far back in the past.* **b** what has happened in the time gone by: *to forget the past. History is a study of the past.* **2** a past life or history: *Our country has a glorious past.* **3** a person's past life, especially if hidden or unknown: *He cannot change his past.* **4** the past tense or a verb form in it. The past of *do* is *did.* *Abbr.:* p.
—*prep.* **1** farther on than; beyond: *to run past the house. The arrow went past the mark.* **2** later than; after: *half past two. It is past noon.* **3** beyond in number, amount, age, or degree; more than: *a boy past twelve.* **4** beyond the ability, range, scope, or the like, of: *absurd fancies that are past belief.* **5** no longer capable of: *I was almost past making any exertion* (W. H. Hudson).
—*adv.* so as to pass by or beyond; by: *The bus goes past once an hour.*
—*v.* passed; a past participle of **pass**[1].
▶ See **pass**[1] for usage note.

***pas|ta** (päs′tä), *n.* any one of various foods, such as macaroni or spaghetti, made of flour, water, salt, and sometimes milk or eggs, shaped in tubular or other forms and dried. See picture below. [< Italian *pasta* < Late Latin *pasta;* see etym. under **paste**[1]]

**past absolute,** the simple past tense or preterit.

**past-due** (past′dü′, -dyü′), *adj.* due some time ago; past maturity: *past-due accounts.*

**paste**[1] (pāst), *n., v.,* **past|ed, past|ing.** —*n.* **1** a mixture, such as flour and water boiled together, that will stick paper together and stick it to a wall or to a box: *The clerk used thick paste to put the label on the package.* **2a** dough for pastry, made with butter, lard, or other shortening. **b** noodles, spaghetti, macaroni, or the like; pasta. **c** any dough. **3** a soft, doughlike mixture or plastic mass: **a** a preparation of fish, tomatoes, ground nuts, or some other article of food reduced to a smooth, soft mass: *liver paste, shrimp paste, almond paste.* **b** a mixture of clay and water to make earthenware or porcelain. **c** any one of various cleaning materials in the form of a soft mass: *silver-polishing paste.* **4a** a hard, glassy material made of powdered rock crystal, red lead, and dry potassium carbonate, used in making imitations of precious stones; strass: *shoe buckles of the best paste, sparkling like real diamonds* (Harriet Beecher Stowe). **b** an artificial gem made of this. **5** any one of various soft, jellylike confections: *fig paste.*
—*v.t.* **1** to stick with paste: *to paste a label on a box.* **2** to cover by pasting: *to paste a door over with notices.*
[< Old French *paste* < Late Latin *pasta* pastry, cake < Greek *pastá* (barley) porridge < *pássein* to sprinkle. Compare etym. under **pasty**[2].]

**paste**[2] (pāst), *v.,* **past|ed, past|ing,** *n. Slang.* —*v.t.* **1** to hit with a hard, sharp blow. **2** to beat; thrash.
—*n.* a hard, sharp blow.
[probably special use of *paste*[1]]

**paste|board** (pāst′bôrd′, -bōrd′), *n., adj.* —*n.* **1** a stiff material made of sheets of paper pasted together or of paper pulp pressed and dried. **2** *Slang.* **a** a playing card. **b** a business card or visiting card. **c** a railway ticket. **d** a ticket of admission to a game, play, circus, or other event.
—*adj.* **1** made of pasteboard. **2** *Figurative.* unsubstantial; counterfeit; sham.
**pasteboards,** *Slang.* a deck of playing cards: *I'm that neat with the pasteboards. I can shuffle 'em any way I want* (Benjamin L. Farjeon).

**paste|board|y** (pāst′bôr′dē, -bōr′-), *adj.* **1** like pasteboard. **2** *Figurative.* unsubstantial; hollow: *The characters are pasteboardy and the dialogue improbable* (Punch).

**paste|down** (pāst′doun′), *n.* one of the outer blank leaves of a book that are pasted down on the cover.

**paste job,** something made up of collected bits and pieces; pastiche: *Your story "The Malpractice Mess"... wasn't your usual incisive approach but rather a superficial paste job* (Charles Kramer).

**pas|tel**[1] (pas tel′, pas′tel), *n., adj.* —*n.* **1a** a kind of chalklike crayon used in drawing, made of a dry paste of ground pigments compounded with resin or gum: *He drew the dancer in soft pastel that crumbled in his grip.* **b** this paste. **2** a drawing made with such crayons: *The artist drew a beautiful pastel.* **3** the art of drawing with pastels. **4** a soft, pale shade of some color. **5** a short and slight prose sketch.
—*adj.* soft and pale: *pastel pink, pastel shades.*
[< French *pastel* < Italian *pastello* (literally) material reduced to a paste < Late Latin *pastellus* a seal or its impression; woad < *pasta* paste[1]]

**pas|tel**[2] (pas′tel), *n.* **1** = woad. **2** the blue dye made from woad. [< Middle French *pastel* < Provençal < Late Latin *pastellus;* see etym. under **pastel**[1]]

**pas|tel|ist** or **pas|tel|list** (pas tel′ist, pas′tel ist), *n.* an artist who draws with pastels or colored crayons.

**paste|pot** (pāst′pot′), *n., adj.* —*n.* a pot or vessel for holding paste.
—*adj. Informal.* hastily or carelessly put together, as if with paste: [*He*] *called the report "a pastepot job" and "pretty sloppy work"* (New York Times).

**past|er** (pās′tər), *n.* **1** a slip to paste on or over something. **2** a person or thing that pastes.

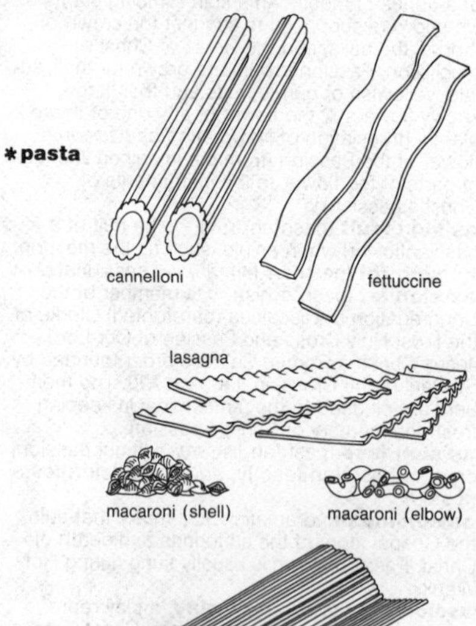

***pasta**

**pas|tern** (pas′tərn), *n.* **1** the part of a horse's foot between the fetlock and the hoof. See picture at **horse.** **2** the corresponding part in related animals, such as a donkey, mule, or cow. **3** either of two bones of this part, the upper or great pastern bone and the lower or small pastern bone, connected at a joint, the pastern joint. [Middle English *pastron* < Old French *pasturon* (diminutive) < *pasture* pastern; shackle; pasture]

**paste-up** (pāst′up′), *n.* an item which is a composition of parts of other things pasted together or in position on a background material. It may be an art collage, a printer's dummy, or offset copy ready for photographing.

**Pas|teur effect** (pas tėr′), *Biology.* the shift of primitive organisms from fermentation to respiration in the presence of certain amounts of oxygen. [< Louis *Pasteur;* see etym. under **pasteurize**]

**pas|teur|ism** (pas′tə riz əm), *n.* the theories and techniques of Louis Pasteur, the French chemist and bacteriologist, especially the technique of treating or preventing certain diseases, such as rabies (hydrophobia), by inoculation with a virus of gradually increasing strength.

**pas|teur|i|za|tion** (pas′chər ə zā′shən, -tər-), *n.* **1** the process of pasteurizing: *The pasteurization of milk is required by law.* **2** the fact or condition of being pasteurized.

**pas|teur|ize** (pas′chə rīz, -tə-), *v.t.,* **-ized, -iz|ing.** **1** to heat (milk, wine, beer, or other liquid) hot enough and long enough to kill harmful bacteria and to prevent or stop fermentation. Pasteurizing milk to at least 145 degrees Fahrenheit (63 degrees centigrade) for about 30 minutes, and then chilling it quickly to 50 degrees Fahrenheit (10 degrees centigrade) or less, kills the bacteria of undulant fever and bovine tuberculosis. **2** *Obsolete.* to treat or prevent (rabies) by Pasteur's technique of virus inoculation. [< Louis *Pasteur,* 1822-1895, a French chemist, who invented the process]

**pas|teur|iz|er** (pas′chə rī′zər, -tə-), *n.* an apparatus for pasteurizing milk, wine, beer, or other liquid.

**pas|tic|cio** (päs tēt′chō), *n., pl.* **-ci** (-chē). pastiche; hodgepodge: *What a pasticcio of gauzes, pins, and ribbons go to compound that multifarious thing—a well-dressed woman* (Richard Cumberland). [< Italian *pasticcio;* see etym. under **pastiche**]

**pas|tiche** (pas tēsh′, päs-), *n., v.,* **-tiched, -tich|ing.** —*n.* **1** an artistic, musical, or literary work made up of portions of various works; medley, hodgepodge, or potpourri: *The surprise was that they looked like pleasant pastiches of Corot, Pissarro, and Cézanne* (New Yorker). **2** something done in imitation or ridicule of another artist's style.
—*v.t.* to combine (as various works, styles, or materials) into a mixture or hodgepodge: *the unfortunate Victorian habit of "reviving," that is, pastiching, the Renaissance, the Baroque, and just about every style of the past* (London Times).
[< French *pastiche* < Italian *pasticcio* < Vulgar Latin *pastīcium* composed of paste < Late Latin *pasta* pastry; see etym. under **paste**[1]]

**pas|ti|cheur** (pas′tē shėr′, päs′-), *n.* a composer of pastiches. [< French *pasticheur* < *pastiche*]

**past|ies** (pā′stēz), *n.pl.* a pair of small adhesive coverings on the breasts.

**pas|til** (pas′təl), *n.* = pastille.

**pas|till|age** (pas′til ij), *n.* **1** confectionary work made of sugar paste and formed in imitation of various objects: *The cake is decorated with 46 lb. of marzipan and 25 lb. of royal icing and pastillage* (London Times). **2** ornamentation in ceramics by means of a surface application, as of scrolls or flowers, modeled separately in clay. [< French *pastillage* imitation in sugar paste < *pastille;* see etym. under **pastille**]

**pas|tille** (pas tēl′), *n.* **1** a flavored or medicated lozenge; troche: *The ancient Egyptians chewed aromatic pastilles* (New Yorker). **2** a small roll or cone of aromatic paste, burned especially as a disinfectant or incense. **3** pastel for crayons. **4** a crayon made from pastel. [< French *pastille* < Spanish *pastilla* perfume pellet < Latin *pastillus* roll, aromatic lozenge (diminutive) < *pānis, -is* bread]

**pas|time** (pas′tīm′, päs′-), *n.* a pleasant way of passing time; amusement; recreation, as a game or sport: *Baseball has been called America's national pastime. She also finds time for ... such normal pastimes as knitting a sweater* (Newsweek). SYN: diversion. [< *pass*[1] + *time;* perhaps translation of Middle French *passe-temps*]

**past|i|ness** (pās′tē nis), *n.* pasty quality, condition, or consistency.

**past|ing** (pās′ting), *n. Slang.* a violent and damaging attack; beating: *The Hawks beat the Canadiens 7-1, the worst pasting the Stanley Cup champions took all season* (Maclean's).

**pas|tis** (pas tēs′), *n.* a strong liqueur with a flavor like absinthe. [< French *pastis*]

**past master, 1** a person who has much experience in any profession, art, or other enterprise. SYN: adept, expert. **2** a person who has filled the office of master in a society, lodge, or other similar organization.

**past mistress,** a woman well skilled in some accomplishment or study.

**past|ness** (past′nis, päst′-), *n.* the quality or state of being past: *Although they may seem archaic, their pastness isn't so very past* (New Yorker).

**pas|tor** (pas′tər, päs′-), *n.* **1** a minister in charge of a church or congregation; spiritual guide: *A*

*Moses or a David, pastors of their people* (Francis Bacon). **2a** a starling of Asia and Europe, whose plumage is partly rose-colored. **b** any bird of the same group. **3** *Archaic.* a herdsman or shepherd. [< Anglo-French *pastour,* Old French *pasteur,* < Latin *pāstor* shepherd < *pāscere* to feed]

**pas|tor|age** (pas′tər ij, päs′-), *n.* = parsonage.

**pas|tor|al** (pas′tər əl, päs′-), *adj., n.* —*adj.* **1** of shepherds or country life: *a pastoral occupation, a pastoral poem. The pastoral tribes of the mountains graze their sheep on the hillside.* **SYN:** rustic, country, bucolic. See syn. under **rural**. **2** simple or naturally beautiful like the country: *a pastoral landscape.* **3** of a pastor, his office, or his duties: *a pastoral visit.*
—*n.* **1a** a play, poem, or novel dealing with shepherds or country life. **b** such works as a type or class: *There are some things of an established nature in pastoral, which are essential to it, such as a country scene, innocence, simplicity* (Sir Richard Steele). **2** a picture or scene depicting shepherds or country life. **3** = pastoral letter. **4** = crosier (def. 1). **5** = pastorale.
[< Latin *pāstōrālis* < *pāstor;* see etym. under **pastor**] —**pas′tor|al|ly**, *adv.*

**pas|to|ra|le** (pas′tə rä′lē, päs′-; pas′tə ral′; *Italian* päs′tô rä′lā), *n., pl.* **-ra|li** (-rä′lē), **-ra|les** (-rä′lēz, -ralz′). *Music.* **1** an opera, cantata, or other vocal work with a pastoral subject. **2** an instrumental composition in pastoral or rustic style, usually in 6/8, 9/8, or 12/8 time. [< Italian *pastorale* (originally) pastoral < Latin *pāstōrālis* < *pāstor;* see etym. under **pastor**]

**Pastoral Epistle**, one of the Epistles to Timothy or Titus in the New Testament, dealing especially with a pastor's work.

**pas|to|ral|ism** (pas′tər ə liz′əm, päs′-), *n.* pastoral quality or character.

**pas|to|ral|ist** (pas′tər ə list, päs′-), *n.* **1** a keeper of flocks or herds. **2** a writer of pastorals.

**pas|tor|al|ize** (pas′tər ə līz, päs′-), *v.t.,* **-ized, -iz|ing.** **1** to make pastoral or rural: *The* [*Morgenthau*] *plan proposed to destroy all German industry and pastoralize the nation* (Time). **2** to make the subject or theme of a pastoral; celebrate in a pastoral poem.

**pastoral staff**, = crosier (def. 1).

**pas|tor|ate** (pas′tər it, päs′-), *n.* **1** the position or duties of a pastor. **2** the term of service of a pastor. **3** pastors as a group. **4** a pastor's residence; parsonage.

**pas|to|ri|um** (pas tôr′ē əm, päs-; -tōr′-), *n., pl.* **-to|ri|ums, -to|ri|a** (-tôr′ē ə, -tōr′-). *Southern U.S.* a parsonage. [American English < *pastor* + *-orium,* as in *emporium*]

**pas|tor|ship** (pas′tər ship, päs′-), *n.* the position or duties of a pastor; pastorate.

**past participle**, the participle that indicates time gone by, or a former action or condition. *Played* and *thrown* are past participles in "She has played all day," and "The ball should have been thrown to me." The past participle is used in forming the English passive (*is stolen*) and perfect (*has stolen*) constructions and as an adjective (*stolen* money). For most verbs the past participle has the same form whether used as an adjective or in a verb phrase; for a few it differs (clean-*shaven* man, had *shaved*). *Abbr:* pp.
► See **participle** for usage note.

**past perfect**, **1** the verb tense used to show that an event was completed before a given past time. In "He had learned to read before he went to school," *had learned* is the past perfect of *learn. Past perfect* and *pluperfect* mean the same. **2** a verb form or verbal phrase in such a tense.

**past progressive**, the verbal tense or tense form that expresses progress, recurrence, or habitual action in the past, as *were running* in the sentence *They were running away from the place.*

**pas|tra|mi** (pə strä′mē), *n.* a smoked and well-seasoned cut of beef, especially a shoulder cut. [< Yiddish *pastrami* < Rumanian *pastrámă,* ultimately < Turkish *basdirma* dried meat < *basmak* to press]

**pas|try** (pās′trē), *n., pl.* **-tries.** **1** pies, tarts, and other foods wholly or partly made of rich flour paste. **2** any food made of baked flour paste, made rich with lard, butter, or a vegetable shortening. [< *paste;* probably influenced by Old French *pastaierie* < *pastaier* pasty cook < *paste* paste[1]]

**pastry bag**, a bag of heavy cloth, rubber, or plastic, tapering to a small opening to which nozzles of various shapes can be attached. It is used to decorate cakes and pastries by squeezing frosting, whipped cream, or filling, through a nozzle.

**pastry cook**, a person who makes pastry or whose business is making or selling pastry.

**pastry tube**, a small tube serving the same function as a pastry bag, equipped with a plunger to force out the decorative material.

**past tense**, **1** the verbal tense expressing time gone by, or a former action or condition. The past tense is used either without reference to the duration of action (called the *simple past* or *preterit* or *past absolute: He ran a mile yesterday*) or as being in progress, recurring, or habitual (called *past progressive* or *imperfect: He was running a mile when he fell*). **2** a verb form or verbal phrase in this tense.

**pas|tur|a|bil|i|ty** (pas′chər ə bil′ə tē, päs′-), *n.* the capability of affording pasture.

**pas|tur|a|ble** (pas′chər ə bəl, päs′-), *adj.* fit for use as pasture; affording pasture.

**pas|tur|age** (pas′chər ij, päs′-), *n.* **1** growing grass and other plants for cattle, sheep, or horses to feed on: *Most livestock thrive on fresh spring pasturage.* **2** = pastureland. **3** the act or right of pasturing cattle, sheep, or other grazing animals; pasturing. [< Old French *pasturage* < *pasturer,* verb < *pasture* pasture, noun]

**pas|tur|al** (pas′chər əl, päs′-), *adj.* of or having to do with pasture: *Our most common pastural ornaments, the daisy, buttercup, and primrose* (Pall Mall Gazette).

**pas|tu|ral|ist** (pas′chər ə list, päs′-), *n.* a keeper of flocks or herds; shepherd: *The tribe were pasturalists, unlikely to surrender their nomadic ways* (Manchester Guardian Weekly). [variant of *pastoralist*]

**pas|ture** (pas′chər, päs′-), *n., v.,* **-tured, -tur|ing.** —*n.* **1** a grassy field or hillside; grasslands on which cattle, sheep, horses, or other grazing animals can feed: *To-morrow to fresh woods and pastures new* (Milton). **2** the grass and other plants growing in a field or on a hillside: *These lands afford good pasture.* **3** any area which serves as a source of food for something: *Drifting plankton pastures are as necessary for good fish nutrition as grasses and vegetation are for land animals* (Science News Letter).
—*v.t.* **1** to put (cattle, sheep, horses, or other grazing animals) out to pasture. **2** (of cattle, sheep, or other grazing animals) to feed on (grass or other growing plants). **3** (of land) to supply pasturage for.
—*v.i.* **1** (of cattle, sheep, horses, or goats) to graze: *There were smooth areas where sheep had pastured* (W. H. Hudson). **2** *Obsolete.* to afford pasture.
[< Old French *pasture* < Late Latin *pāstūra* < Latin *pāstus, -ūs* pasture, fodder < *pāscere* to feed] —**pas′tur|er**, *n.*

**pas|ture|land** (pas′chər land′, päs′-), *n.* grassland used or suitable for the grazing of cattle, sheep, or horses; pasturage.

**pasture thistle**, a biennial species of thistle of North America, with a purple flower.

**past|y**[1] (pās′tē), *adj.,* **past|i|er, past|i|est.** **1** like paste, especially in texture: *a pasty mixture.* **2** pale; sallow: *A little pasty woman with a pinched yellowish face* (John Galsworthy). **3** *Figurative.* flabby. [< *paste*[1] + *-y*[1]]

**pas|ty**[2] (pas′tē; *see note below*), *n., pl.* **-ties.** a pie filled with meat, game, fish, or the like: *a venison pasty. "Stary-gazy" is the Cornish word for fish pie or pasty* (Punch). [Middle English *pastei* < Old French *paste* paste, dough < Late Latin *pasta* **paste**[1]. See etym. of doublet **patty**.]
► In Great Britain **pasty** is pronounced (pas′tē) or (päs′tē). In the United States the word is read in English literature as (pās′tē), although (pas′tē) is heard in parts of Pennsylvania, Minnesota, and other areas, where Cornish miners settled in the 1800's.

**past|y-faced** (pās′tē fāst′), *adj.* having a pale, sallow complexion: *pasty-faced stay-at-homes* (Punch).

**P.A. system**, public-address system.

**pat**[1] (pat), *v.,* **pat|ted, pat|ting,** *n.* —*v.t.* **1** to strike or tap lightly with something flat or with the fingers or hand, especially so as to flatten or smooth: *his foot patting the ground* (Robert Louis Stevenson). *She patted the dough into a flat cake.* **2** to tap with the hand as a sign of sympathy, approval, or affection: *to pat a dog.*
—*v.i.* **1** to walk or run with a patting sound. **2** to strike lightly or gently.
—*n.* **1** a light stroke or tap with the hand or with something flat: *a fatherly pat o' the cheek* (Robert Browning). **2** the sound made by patting: *the pat, pat of rain dripping from the eaves.* **3** a small mass, especially of butter: *a pat of butter melting on a hot potato.*
**pat on the back, a** to praise; compliment: *"We have a mission to wake up the country," preaches the bushy-browed editor. "Instead of patting it on the back, we're kicking it"* (Wall Street Journal). **b** a word of praise; compliment: *Congress gets an awful kicking around. ... I just wanted to give them a pat on the back* (Hubert H. Humphrey).
[perhaps imitative]

**pat**[2] (pat), *adj., adv.* —*adj.* to the point; suitable; apt: *a pat reply. When a Keats or an Alexander the Great is the subject, the explanation of his achievement is both too pat and too unenlightening; it is simply genius* (Harper's). **SYN:** appropriate, pertinent, relevant.
—*adv.* aptly; exactly; suitably.
**have (down) pat** or **know pat**, *Informal.* to have perfectly; know thoroughly: *He ... had the whole story pat enough* (Mrs. J. H. Riddell).
**stand pat, a** *Informal.* to hold to things as they are and refuse to change: *We can't just stand pat on this important issue.* **b** to refuse the opportunity to draw cards in poker; play the cards dealt: *Holding a flush, I stood pat.*
[perhaps special use of *pat*[1]] —**pat′ly**, *adv.* —**pat′ness**, *n.*

**Pat** (pat), *n.* a nickname for an Irishman.

**pat.**, **1** patent. **2** patented.

**PAT** (no periods), point after touchdown (in football).

**pa|ta|ca** (pə tä′kə), *n.* **1** a unit of Portuguese money worth 5.5 escudos, used as local currency in Macao. **2** a coin having this value. [< Portuguese *pataca*]

**pat-a-cake** (pat′ə kāk′), *n.* a children's game played by patting the hands together to a nursery rhyme. Also, **patty-cake**.

**pa|ta|gi|al** (pə tā′jē əl), *adj.* of or having to do with a patagium.

**pa|ta|gi|um** (pə tā′jē əm), *n., pl.* **-gi|a** (-jē ə). **1** a wing membrane, such as of a bat. **2** a fold of skin extending along the side of the body of certain gliding mammals and reptiles, as the flying squirrel. **3** the fold of skin between the upper arm and forearm of birds. **4** a small, flat sclerite above the wing base of many insects. [< New Latin *patagium* < Latin, gold border of a Roman lady's tunic]

**Pat|a|go|ni|an** (pat′ə gō′nē ən), *adj., n.* —*adj.* of or having to do with Patagonia, a region in the extreme south of South America, or its people.
—*n.* a native or inhabitant of Patagonia.

**Patagonian cavy** or **hare**, = mara.

**pat|a|mar** (pat′ə mär), *n.* a lateen-rigged vessel with an upward-curving keel and considerable overhang of stern and especially stem, used in the coasting trade of western India. [< Portuguese *patamar* < Marathi *patēmāri* < *patta* tidings + *-māri* a carrier]

**pat|a|phys|ics** (pat′ə fiz′iks), *n.* an imaginary science satirizing scientific and scholarly thought and writing: *Pataphysics was defined ... as a science that will 'examine the laws governing exceptions,' and describe 'a universe which can be—and perhaps should be—envisaged in the place of the traditional one'* (Listener). [partial translation of French *pataphysique,* coined by Alfred Jarry, 1873-1907, a French writer, probably after *métaphysique* metaphysics]

**pa|tas** (pə tä′), *n.* a large, red, terrestrial monkey of western Africa. [< French *patas* < a native word in Senegal]

**pat-ball** (pat′bôl′), *n.* the game of rounders.

**patch** (pach), *n., v.* —*n.* **1** a piece put on to mend a hole or a tear or to strengthen a weak place: *Many a patch of brown and grey variegated the faded scarlet of our uniform* (Charles J. Lever). **2** a piece of cloth put over a wound or a sore: *a gauze patch held over a skinned elbow.* **3** a pad over a hurt eye to protect it: *The man with the patch over his eye turned out to be a musicologist and composer* (New Yorker). **4** a small bit of black cloth that ladies used to wear on their faces, especially in the 1600's and 1700's, to show off their fair skin. **5** a small, uneven spot: *a patch of brown on the skin.* **6** a piece of ground: *a garden patch, a cabbage patch.* **7** a scrap or bit of cloth left over: *The quilt was made of colorful patches.* **8** a hookup for connecting a telephone line to a short-wave radio transmitter. **9** = shoulder patch. **10** *Informal.* a dolt; booby. **11** *U.S. Slang.* a lawyer.
—*v.t.* **1** to protect or adorn with a patch or patches; put patches on; mend: *to patch clothes.* **SYN:** See syn. under **mend**. **2** to serve for mending: *O, that that earth ... Should patch a wall to expel the winter's flaw* (Shakespeare). **3** to make by joining patches or pieces together: *to patch a quilt; a miscellaneous old gentleman ... patched together, too, of different epochs, an epitome of times and fashions* (Hawthorne). **4** to piece together; make hastily.
—*v.i.* to mend clothes with patches.
**not a patch on**, in no way comparable with; nowhere near: *But what had happened wasn't a*

**Pronunciation Key:** hat, āge, cãre, fär; let, ēqual, tėrm; it, īce; hot, ōpen, ôrder; oil, out; cup, pu̇t, rüle; child; long; thin; ᴛʜen; zh, measure; ə represents **a** in about, **e** in taken, **i** in pencil, **o** in lemon, **u** in circus.

*patch on what might happen* (Punch).
**patch up, a** to put an end to; settle: *to patch up a quarrel.* **b** to make right hastily or for a time: *to patch up a leaking faucet. They bought the aircraft in Australia, patched it up, and flew it to Britain, where it has had a complete overhaul* (London Times). **c** to put together hastily or poorly: *to patch up a costume for a play.* **d** to revise; amend: *The first decision that had to be made was whether the existing penal law could be satisfactorily patched up or whether a more basic change in its structure was needed* (New York Times).
[Middle English *pacche;* origin uncertain] —**patch′er,** *n.*

**patch|board** (pach′bôrd′, -bōrd′), *n.* a removable panel in a computer or other electronic equipment having multiple electric terminals into which wires may be plugged in various ways according to the operation desired; patch panel; plugboard.

**patch box,** a small box for holding patches for the face, used especially in the 1600's and 1700's.

**patch|cord** (pach′kôrd′), *n.* an electrical cord with plugs or clips at both ends, used to connect different parts of a sound system, or two different systems. Patchcords are used to connect the terminals of a patchboard.

**patch|er|y** (pach′ər ē), *n., pl.* **-er|ies. 1** the act of patching; rough mending; hasty or clumsy patching together; botchery. **2** something made by patching parts together.

**patch|i|ly** (pach′ə lē), *adv.* in a patchy manner; irregularly; spasmodically.

**patch|i|ness** (pach′ē nis), *n.* the condition of being patchy.

**patch|ing** (pach′ing), *n.* **1** the act of mending with a patch or patches. **2** a patch, or patches collectively. **3** wadding for a rifle.

**patch|ou|li** or **patch|ou|ly** (pach′u̇ lē, pə chü′-), *n.* **1** a penetrating perfume derived from an East Indian plant. **2** an East Indian plant of the mint family having an essential oil from which the perfume is obtained. [probably < Hindustani *pacholi,* the trade name. Compare Tamil *pachai-* green, and *ilai* leaf.]

**patch panel,** = patchboard.

**patch pocket,** a flat pocket made by sewing a piece of material, usually one of which the garment is made, on the outside of a garment.

**patch test,** a test for allergy to a particular substance, made by applying the substance to a small area of unbroken skin, usually by means of pads.

**patch-up** (pach′up′), *adj.* **1** makeshift: *Usually this is a patch-up kind of job* (Atlantic). **2** restorative; remedial: *The Administration is now looking to the Senate for some major patch-up work on its housing program* (Wall Street Journal).

**patch|work** (pach′wėrk′), *n.* **1** pieces of cloth of various colors or shapes sewed together by the edges: *She made a cover of patchwork for the cushion.* **2** anything like this: *From the airplane we saw a patchwork of fields and woods.*
**3** *Figurative.* anything made of fragments; jumble: *His memoirs were an amateurishly arranged patchwork of reminiscences.*

**patch|y** (pach′ē), *adj.,* **patch|i|er, patch|i|est.**
**1** abounding in or characterized by patches: *land patchy with rock.* **2** occurring in, forming, or resembling patches: *a patchy growth of corn.*
**3** *Figurative.* **a** made up of fragments, usually put together hurriedly: *a patchy excuse or story.*
**b** uneven; spotty: *As a critic, Professor Ray is patchy and rather incurious* (Manchester Guardian).

**patd.,** patented.

**pate**[1] (pāt), *n.* **1a** the head: *Let him to the Tower, And chop away that factious pate of his* (Shakespeare). **b** the top of the head: *a bald pate.* SYN: crown. **2** *Figurative.* brains: *a notion fit for an idiot's pate.* **3** *Figurative.* a person with brains: *a shallow pate.* [Middle English *pate;* origin uncertain]

**pa|te**[2] (pä tā′), *n.* = pâté.

**pâte** (pät), *n. French.* **1** paste[1]. **2** pottery or porcelain paste used in ceramics.

**pâ|té** (pä tā′), *n. French.* **1** a paste of finely chopped meat, liver, or the like, with spices and herbs, often served chilled and sliced: *A superb pâté made of saddle of hare, a chicken, a duck, two red partridges ... and a score of other ingredients* (New York Times). **2** a case or form of pastry filled with chicken, sweetbreads, oysters, etc.; patty.

**-pated,** *combining form.* having a ___pate: *Empty-pated = having an empty pate.*

**pâ|té de foie gras** (pä tā′ də fwä grä′), *French.* a patty or paste made with livers of specially fattened geese and usually finely chopped truffles: *It was worth its weight in pâté de foie gras* (New York Times).

**pa|tel|la** (pə tel′ə), *n., pl.* **-tel|las, -tel|lae** (-tel′ē). **1** = kneecap. **2** a small pan or shallow vessel. **3** *Biology.* a structure in the form of a shallow pan or cup, such as the spore-bearing structure of certain lichens. [< Latin *patella* (diminutive) < *patina* pan; see etym. under **paten**]

**pa|tel|lar** (pə tel′ər), *adj.* having to do with the kneecap: *The knee jerk is a patellar reflex.*

**pa|tel|late** (pə tel′āt, -it), *adj.* **1** having a patella. **2** = patelliform.

**pa|tel|li|form** (pə tel′ə fôrm), *adj.* having the form of a patella; shaped like a shallow pan, kneecap, or limpet shell. [< Latin *patella* kneecap, shallow pan (see etym. under **patella**) + English *-form*]

**pâ|té mai|son** (pä tā′ me zôɴ′), *French.* the patty or paste that is the specialty of a particular restaurant.

**pat|en** (pat′ən), *n.* **1** the plate on which the bread is placed at the celebration of the Eucharist, or Mass. **2** a plate or flat piece of metal. Also, **pat-in, patina, patine.** [< Latin *patena,* or *patina* pan, dish < Greek *patánē* flat dish. See etym. of doublet **patina**[2].]

**pa|ten|cy** (pā′tən sē, pat′ən-), *n.* **1** the state of being patent; obviousness. **2** *Medicine.* (of a passage) the condition of being open or unobstructed. **3** *Phonetics.* openness in varying degrees of the breath passage, characteristic of all sounds but stops.

**pat|ent** (*n., adj. 1, 4, 6, v.* pat′ənt; *adj. 2, 3, 5* pā′tent, pat′ənt; *especially British* pā′tənt), *n., adj., v.* —*n.* **1** a government grant which gives a person or company sole rights to make, use, or sell a new invention for a certain number of years: *Patents ... are not issued for an idea, but for a specific device, process, or machine that is presumably workable* (Alfred L. Kroeber). **2** an invention that is given a patent: *The telephone was finally established as Bell's patent.* **3** an official document from a government giving a right, privilege, or office; letters patent: *Alva ... received an especial patent ... by which Philip empowered him to proceed against all persons implicated in the troubles* (John L. Motley).
**4** *Figurative.* a sign or token indicating a right to something; leave to possess something. **5a** the instrument by which public land is granted to a person. **b** the land so granted: *the 'Patent'... the district ... originally granted to old Major Effingham by the 'king's letters patent'* (James Fenimore Cooper). **6** a local, minor civil division in Maine.
—*adj.* **1a** given or protected by a patent: *a patent stove. A patent right is an exclusive right to an invention.* **b** of or having to do with patents: *patent law.* **2** open to view or knowledge; evident; plain: *It is patent that cats dislike dogs.* SYN: obvious, manifest, palpable. **3a** open, as a door, tube, or the passage through which the breath flows. **b** open to general use; public. **4** appointed to a right, privilege, or office, by a patent. **5** *Biology.* spreading; expanded, as a plant's petals. **6** (of flour) of high quality; superior: *Millers blend straight flour from ... patent, or best-quality flour, and first and second clear flours* (W. B. Dohoney).
—*v.t.* **1a** to get a patent for: *Edison patented many inventions.* **b** to grant a patent to. **2** *U.S.* to obtain a patent right to (land).
[< Latin *patēns, -entis,* present participle of *patēre* lie open] —**pat′ent|a|ble,** *adj.*

**pat|ent|a|bil|i|ty** (pat′ən tə bil′ə tē), *n.* the capability of being patented.

**pa|tente** (pȧ täɴt′), *n. French.* a license or tax that all business or professional persons in France must pay in order to operate legally.

**pat|ent|ee** (pat′ən tē′), *n.* **1** a person to whom a patent is granted: *Each Patentee shall be obliged, within three years after the Date of his Patent, to clear and work three acres* (Ontario Bureau of Archives Report). **2** a person licensed to use another's patent: *a small price to pay for what A.T. and T. spent on teaching its patentees the know-how to use the patents* (Wall Street Journal).

**patent insides,** newspaper sheets printed on the inside only, and thus sold to publishers of small newspapers, who fill the unprinted side with matter of their own selection.

**patent leather,** a leather with a very glossy, smooth surface, usually black, made by a process formerly patented. Some shoes are made of patent leather.

**patent log,** one of a variety of patented instruments for recording the speed and distance run by a ship.

**pa|tent|ly** (pā′tənt lē, pat′ənt-), *adv.* **1** plainly; clearly; obviously. SYN: manifestly. **2** openly.

**patent medicine, 1** any medicine that may be purchased without a doctor's prescription. **2** a medicine sold by a company which has a patent on its composition or manufacture; a proprietary medicine.

**Patent Office,** the government office that issues patents and registers trademarks: *If the Patent Office believes a proposed device to be unworkable, it refuses the patent* (Alfred L. Kroeber).

**pat|en|tor** (pat′ən tər), *n.* **1** a person who grants a patent. **2** = patentee.

**patent outsides,** newspaper sheets printed on the outside only, sold to publishers and filled up by them like patent insides.

**patent pool,** an agreement between individuals or companies to share the exclusive rights to certain patents, often as a means of limiting the market or preventing normal competition.

**pa|ter** (pā′tər), *n.* **1** *British Informal.* father. **2** the paternoster (being the first word of the Lord's Prayer in Latin). [< Latin *pater* father; (definition 2) short for *paternoster*]

**pat|er|a** (pat′ər ə), *n., pl.* **-er|ae** (-ər ē). **1** a broad, shallow, saucerlike dish, used especially in making libations in ancient Rome. **2** *Architecture.* an ornament in bas-relief resembling a round, shallow dish, or having a generally round form. [< Latin *patera* < *patēre* to be open]

**pa|ter|fa|mil|i|as** (pā′tər fə mil′ē əs), *n., pl.* **pa-tres|fa|mil|i|as** (pā′trēz fə mil′ē əs). **1** a father or head of a family: *According to this account, he was a tender, grousing, home-loving paterfamilias who liked to be with his children when they were young, play with them, and tell them bedtime stories* (New Yorker). **2** a male citizen who was the head of a family under Roman law. [< Latin *paterfamiliās* < *pater, patris* father + Old Latin *familiās,* genitive singular of *familia* a family]

**pa|ter|nal** (pə tėr′nəl), *adj.* **1** of or like a father; fatherly: *paternal authority. My position being paternal and protective* (Hawthorne). **2** related on the father's side of the family: *Everyone has two paternal grandparents and two maternal grandparents.* **3** received or inherited from one's father: *Her blue eyes were a paternal inheritance.* [< Late Latin *paternālis* < Latin *paternus* of a father < *pater, patris* father] —**pa|ter′nal|ly,** *adv.*

**pa|ter|nal|ism** (pə tėr′nə liz əm), *n.* the principle or practice of managing the affairs of a country or group of employees as a father manages the affairs of his children.

**pa|ter|nal|ist** (pə tėr′nə list), *n., adj.* —*n.* a person who believes in or practices paternalism: *... paternalists who believe that the human estate is one of perennial childhood* (Saturday Review).
—*adj.* = paternalistic: *paternalist aspirations.*

**pa|ter|nal|is|tic** (pə tėr′nə lis′tik), *adj.* having to do with or characterized by paternalism. —**pa-ter′nal|is′ti|cal|ly,** *adv.*

**pa|ter|nal|ize** (pə tėr′nə līz), *v.t.,* **-ized, -iz|ing. 1** to make paternalistic. **2** to treat in a paternalistic manner.

**pa|ter|ni|ty** (pə tėr′nə tē), *n.* **1** the condition of being a father; fatherhood. **2** paternal origin or descent: *King Arthur's paternity was unknown.* (*Figurative.*) *Many of the historical proverbs have a doubtful paternity* (Emerson). [< Late Latin *paternitās* < Latin *paternus* of a father < *pater, patris* father]

**pat|er|nos|ter** or **Pat|er|nos|ter** (pat′ər nos′tər, pā′tər-), *n., v.* —*n.* **1** the Lord's Prayer, especially in Latin. **2a** one of the beads of a rosary on which the Lord's Prayer is said. **b** the whole rosary. **3** an object resembling or strung together like a rosary, especially a fishing line to which hooks and beaded sinkers are attached at regular intervals.
—*v.i.* to fish with a paternoster: *Mr. Such-and-Such of Nuneaton paternostered with a half herring four inches above the river bed ... and landed a 31 lb. 8 oz. pike* (Punch).
[< Latin *pater noster* our father (from the first two words of the Lord's Prayer)]

**Pa|ter Pa|tri|ae** (pā′tər pā′trē ē), *Latin.* father of his country (applied originally as an epithet to Cicero after his suppression in 63 B.C. of the conspiracy of Catiline against the republic).

**pâte-sur-pâte** (pät′sər pät′), *n. Ceramics.* decoration by means of slip applied in successive layers to a previously prepared surface so as to produce a very low relief. [< French (literally) paste on paste]

**path** (path, päth), *n., pl.* **paths** (paᴛʜz, päᴛʜz). **1** a way made by people or animals walking. It is usually too narrow for automobiles or wagons. *He left the barren-beaten thoroughfare, Chose the green path that show'd the rarer foot* (Tennyson). SYN: walk, trail, lane. **2a** a way made to walk upon: *a garden path.* **b** a way made to ride horses or bicycles on. **c** *British.* a track for bicycle or foot racing. **3** the line along which a person or thing moves; route; track: *The moon has a regular path through the sky.* SYN: course. **4** *Figurative.* a way of acting or behaving; way of life: *Some choose paths of glory; some choose paths of ease.*

**beat a path to,** to hurry to as with great enthusiasm or zeal: *The reporters beat a path to the new candidate's hotel suite for an interview as soon as his nomination was announced.*

**cross one's path, a** to be met by one; be encountered: *He gave a friendly greeting to everyone who crossed his path.* **b** *Figurative.* to stand in one's way; thwart, oppose, or hinder one's interest, purpose, or designs: *Yet such was his [Cromwell's] genius and resolution that he was able to overpower and crush everything crossing his path* (Macaulay).
[Old English *pæth*]

**path.**, 1 pathological. 2 pathology.

**Pa|than** (pə tän′, pət hän′), *n., adj.* —*n.* **1** a member of a major tribal group of Afghanistan and of colonies in India and Pakistan. **2** = Afghan (in Afghan use, especially as an ethnic designation).
—*adj.* of or having to do with Pathans.
[< Hindustani *Paṭhān* < Afghan *Pĕṣtāna* Afghans]

**path|break|ing** (path′brā′king), *adj.* that prepares or shows the way; innovating: (*Figurative.*) *the pathbreaking education bill now on the floor* (Wall Street Journal).

**pa|thet|ic** (pə thet′ik), *adj.* **1** arousing pity; pitiful: *A lost child is pathetic.* SYN: pitiable, moving, touching, affecting. **2** of the emotions; that affects the emotions. **3** arousing passion or other powerful emotions; stirring: *Thee too, enamour'd of the life I lov'd, Pathetic in its praise ... Ingenious Cowley* (William Cowper). [< Late Latin *pathēticus* < Greek *pathētikós* < *pathētós* liable to suffer < *path-*, stem of *páschein* to suffer]
—**pa|thet′i|cal|ly**, *adv.*

**pa|thet|i|cal** (pə thet′ə kəl), *adj.* = pathetic.

**pathetic fallacy**, the attributing of human emotions and characteristics to nature: *The leonine old illustrator never let his pupils fall for the pathetic fallacy, that empty barrels are lonely* (Time).

**Pa|thet La|o** (pä′thət lä′ō), the communist-supported government and forces in Laos, a country in southeastern Asia.

**path|find|er** (path′fīn′dər, päth′-), *n.* one who finds a path or way, as through a wilderness or other unexplored area: (*Figurative.*) *A hundred years ago science was not yet conceived to be the pathfinder of the practical arts* (Atlantic).

**path|find|ing** (path′fīn′ding), *n., adj.* —*n.* the act or process of discovering a path or way; pioneering: *The 593, the first civil engine designed for supersonic flight ... will benefit from three years of pathfinding by TSR-2 before the first prototype ... takes to the air* (London Times).
—*adj.* pathbreaking; trailblazing: *... a pathfinding study which opens up new perspectives in the comparative analysis of Soviet and American political institutions* (Merle Fainsod).

**path|ic** (path′ik), *n., adj.* —*n.* **1** a person who suffers or undergoes something: *... a mere pathic to thy devilish art* (Philip Massinger). **2** = catamite.
—*adj.* **1** undergoing something; passive: *... the pathic attitude of captive animals towards man* (New Scientist). **2** having to do with suffering or disease; morbid.
[< Latin *pathicus* < Greek *path-* (stem of *páschein* to suffer) + Latin *-icus* -ic]

**path|less** (path′lis, päth′-), *adj.* having no path through or across it; untrodden; trackless: *a pathless mountain.* —**path′less|ness**, *n.*

**path|o|gen** (path′ə jən), *n.* any agent capable of producing disease, especially a living microorganism or virus. [< Greek *páthos* suffering + English *-gen*]

**path|o|gene** (path′ə jēn), *n.* = pathogen.

**path|o|gen|e|sis** (path′ə jen′ə sis), *n.* the production or development of disease.

**path|o|ge|net|ic** (path′ə jə net′ik), *adj.* = pathogenic.

**path|o|gen|ic** (path′ə jen′ik), *adj.* producing disease; having to do with pathogenesis: *pathogenic germs.*

**path|o|ge|nic|i|ty** (path′ə jə nis′ə tē), *n.* the state or quality of being pathogenic.

**pa|thog|e|ny** (pə thoj′ə nē), *n.* the production of disease; pathogenesis.

**pa|thog|no|mon|ic** (pə thog′nə mon′ik), *adj.* indicative or characteristic of a particular disease: *an oblique pathognomonic reference to homosexuality* (Punch). [< Greek *pathognōmonikós* skilled in diagnosis of diseases, ultimately < *páthos* disease + *gnōmōn* judge]

**pa|thog|no|my** (pə thog′nə mē), *n.* **1** the study of the emotions or the indications of emotions. **2** the science of the signs or symptoms indicating particular diseases.

**pathol.**, 1 pathological. 2 pathology.

**path|o|log|ic** (path′ə loj′ik), *adj.* = pathological.

**path|o|log|i|cal** (path′ə loj′ə kəl), *adj.* **1** of pathology; dealing with diseases or concerned with diseases: *pathological studies.* **2** due to disease or accompanying disease: *a pathological condition of the blood cells.* SYN: morbid. —**path′o|log′i|cal|ly**, *adv.*

**pa|thol|o|gist** (pə thol′ə jist), *n.* an expert in pathology.

**pa|thol|o|gy** (pə thol′ə jē), *n., pl.* **-gies. 1** the study of the causes and nature of diseases, especially the structural and functional changes brought about by diseases. Human pathology is a branch of medicine. *Abbr:* path. **2** the unhealthy conditions and processes caused by a disease, especially changes in the tissues and organs of the body. [probably < French *pathologie* < New Latin *pathologia* < Greek *páthos* disease, suffering, emotion + *-logiā* -logy]

**path|o|phys|i|o|log|i|cal** (path′ə fiz′ē ə loj′ə kəl), *adj.* of or having to do with pathophysiology.

**path|o|phys|i|ol|o|gist** (path′ə fiz′ē ol′ə jist), *n.* a person skilled in pathophysiology.

**path|o|phys|i|ol|o|gy** (path′ə fiz′ē ol′ə jē), *n.* the science dealing with the abnormal functions of organisms and their parts: *Pathophysiology is a comparatively novel course, combining various approaches to the study of disease and its effect on the body* (London Times). [< Greek *páthos* disease + English *physiology*]

**pa|thos** (pā′thos), *n.* **1** the quality in speech, writing, music, events, or a scene that arouses a feeling of pity or sadness; power of evoking tender or melancholy emotion: *She pleaded for mercy with a touching pathos.* **2** a pathetic expression or utterance: *As for pathos, I am as provocative of tears as an onion* (Hawthorne). **3** *Obsolete.* suffering. [< Greek *páthos* suffering; feeling, emotion < *pénthos* grief, sorrow]

**path|o|type** (path′ə tīp′), *n.* a pathogenic organism.

**path|way** (path′wā′, päth′-), *n.* = path.

**-pathy**, *combining form.* **1** feeling; emotion: *Antipathy = a hostile feeling.*
**2** disease: *Psychopathy = mental disease.*
**3** treatment of disease in___, or by___: *Osteopathy = treatment of disease in bones. Hydropathy = treatment of disease by the use of water.*
[< Greek *-pátheia* act or quality of suffering; feeling < *páthos;* see etym. under **pathos**]

**pa|tience** (pā′shəns), *n.* **1** willingness to put up with waiting, pain, or anything that annoys, troubles, or hurts; calm endurance without complaining or losing self-control: *The cat watched the mouse hole with great patience. The boy needed patience when he was having his teeth filled.*
**2** long, hard work; steady effort: *to labor with patience.* **3** a card game played by one person; solitaire. **4** *Obsolete.* sufferance; indulgence; leave; permission: *I can go no further, sir ... By your patience, I needs must rest me* (Shakespeare). [< Old French *pacience,* learned borrowing from Latin *patientia* < *patiēns* patient]
—*Syn.* **1, 2 Patience, forbearance, fortitude** mean power to endure, without complaining, something unpleasant or painful. **Patience** implies calmness and self-control and applies whether one is enduring something unpleasant, or merely waiting, or doing something requiring steady effort: *Teachers need patience.* **Forbearance** implies uncommon self-control when greatly tried or provoked: *He endured the many attacks of his political opponents with admirable forbearance.* **Fortitude** implies strength of character and calm courage in facing danger or enduring suffering: *With fortitude, the disabled veteran learned a new trade.*

**pa|tient** (pā′shənt), *adj., n.* —*adj.* **1** willing to put up with waiting, pain, or anything that annoys, troubles, or hurts; enduring calmly without complaining or losing self-control: *patient suffering, patient expectation. Beware the fury of a patient man* (John Dryden). SYN: forbearing. **2** with steady effort or long, hard work; persistent; constant; diligent: *patient research, patient labor.* SYN: persevering. **3** *Archaic.* undergoing the action of another; passive.
—*n.* **1** a person who is being treated by a doctor: *A physician ... may cure the disease and kill the patient* (Francis Bacon). **2** a person or thing that undergoes some action; recipient: *He that is not free is not an Agent but a Patient* (John Wesley). *Every creature is man's agent or patient* (Emerson). **3** *Obsolete.* a person who endures or suffers patiently.
**patient of, a** able to bear or tolerate: *patient of cold or hunger. Patient of constitutional control, he bears it with meek manliness of soul* (William Cowper). **b** susceptible to (a particular interpretation): *A way open for them to despise the law which was made patient of such a weak evasion* (Jeremy Taylor).
[< Old French *pacient,* learned borrowing from Latin *patiēns, -entis,* present participle of *patī* to suffer, endure] —**pa′tient|ly**, *adv.*

**pa|tient|hood** (pā′shənt hu̇d), *n.* the condition of being a patient.

**pat|in** (pat′ən), *n.* = paten.

**pat|i|na**[1] (pat′ə nə), *n.* **1** a film or incrustation, usually green, on the surface of old bronze or copper, formed by oxidation. A patina is often regarded as ornamental on a statue or other object of art. **2** a film or coloring produced in the course of time on wood or other substance. **3** a surface appearance added to or assumed by anything: *the patina of soft, supple leather,* (*Figurative.*) *the patina of success.* [< Italian *patina,* perhaps < Latin *patina* pan, patina[2] (because of the incrustation on ancient dishes)]

**pat|i|na**[2] (pat′ə nə), *n., pl.* **-nae** (-nē). **1** a broad, shallow dish or pan used by the ancient Romans. **2** = paten. [< Latin *patina* shallow pan, dish. See etym. of doublet **paten.**]

**pat|i|nate** (pat′ə nāt), *v.t.,* **-nat|ed, -nat|ing.** to coat with a patina: *It had taken two thousand years to patinate the urn so beautifully.* —**pat′i|na′tion**, *n.*

**pat|ine**[1] (pat′ən), *n.* = paten.

**pa|tine**[2] (pə tēn′), *n., v.,* **-tined, -tin|ing.** —*n.* = patina[1].
—*v.t.* to coat with a patina; patinate: *Its foundation was once ivory satin, now patined to a rich oyster colour* (London Times).
[< French *patine* < Latin *patina*]

**pat|i|nize** (pat′ə nīz), *v.t.,* **-nized, -niz|ing.** = patinate.

**pat|i|o** (pat′ē ō, pä′tē-), *n., pl.* **-i|os. 1** an inner court or yard open to the sky. Patios are found especially in relatively large dwellings of Spanish or Spanish-American design. **2** a terrace for outdoor eating or lounging, made usually of cement or flat stones: *sitting out on the patio swatting bugs.* [American English < Spanish *patio,* ultimately < Latin *patēre* to lie open]

**pâ|tis|se|rie** (pə tis′ər ē; *French* pä tēs rē′), *n.* **1** pastry: *Tante Marie School of Cookery, Pâtisserie and Refresher Courses* (Sunday Times). **2** a shop that sells pastries: *Lovers have at last the choice between the trees of the park and Danish pâtisseries as a setting for romance* (Manchester Guardian). [< French *pâtisserie* < *pâtissier* pastry cook < Vulgar Latin *pasticium* pasty < Late Latin *pasta;* see etym. under **paste**[1]]

**pa|to** (pä′tō), *n.* a game popular in Argentina played with a ball having six leather handles, and by players mounted on horses. It combines features of polo and basketball. [< Spanish *pato* duck[1]]

**Pat. Off.**, Patent Office.

**pat|ois** (pat′wä), *n., pl.* **pat|ois** (pat′wäz). **1** a dialect spoken by the common people of a particular district: *the patois of the French Canadians.* **2** the cant or jargon of a particular group. SYN: argot. **3** *British.* a provincial dialect or form of speech (sometimes used in an unfriendly way).
[< French *patois* < Old French *patoier* handle clumsily < *pate* paw < a Germanic word]

**Pa|tres con|scrip|ti** (pä′trēz kən skrip′tī), *Latin.* **1** the senators of ancient Rome, collectively; the conscript fathers. **2** a senate, as that of Venice in the late Middle Ages and Renaissance.

**pa|tri|al** (pā′trē əl), *adj., n.* —*adj.* **1** of or having to do with one's native country. **2** (of nouns and adjectives or their suffixes) indicating nationality or local extraction: *"Rumanian" is a patrial noun and adjective.*
—*n. British.* a native or naturalized citizen of a country: *Patrials are defined as "all people who are citizens of Britain by being born there, or become citizens by adoption, registration, or naturalisation in the UK, or who have a parent or grandparent who was born here or acquired citizenship by adoption, registration, or naturalisation"* (Manchester Guardian Weekly).
[< Old French *patrial* < Latin *patria* fatherland]

**pa|tri|al|i|ty** (pā′trē al′ə tē), *n. British.* the condition of being a native or naturalized citizen of a country.

**pa|tri|a po|tes|tas** (pā′trē ə pō tes′tas), **1** the authority or control of a father. **2** the authority, in Roman law, of a male citizen who was the head of a family (paterfamilias), by which technically he controlled the activities and owned the property of his wife and of his children and grandchildren in the male line. [< Latin *patria potestas* (literally) fatherly power]

**pa|tri|arch** (pā′trē ärk), *n.* **1** the father and ruler of a family or tribe, especially one of the ancestral figures in the Bible, such as: **a** Abraham, Isaac, or Jacob, as the founders of Israel. **b** any one of the twelve sons of Jacob, supposed to be ancestors of the twelve Israelite tribes. **c** one of the tribal or family heads living before Noah and the Flood. **2** *Figurative.* a person thought of as the father or founder of something. **3** *Figurative.* **a** a venerable old man, especially the oldest man of a village or the oldest member of a profession,

---

**Pronunciation Key:** hat, āge, cãre, fär; let, ēqual, tėrm; it, īce; hot, ōpen, ôrder; oil, out; cup, pu̇t, rüle; child; long; thin; ᴛʜen; zh, measure; ə represents **a** in about, **e** in taken, **i** in pencil, **o** in lemon, **u** in circus.

company, or the like: *He ... was reverenced as one of the patriarchs of the village* (Washington Irving). **b** the head of a flock, herd, or other group: *a goat, the patriarch of the flock* (Scott); *the monarch oak, the patriarch of the trees* (John Dryden). **4** a bishop of the highest rank in the early Christian Church, especially the bishop of Antioch, Alexandria, Rome, Constantinople, or Jerusalem. **5** a bishop of the highest rank in the Eastern Church or the Roman Catholic Church. **6** = pope. **7** one of the highest dignitaries in the Mormon Church, who pronounces the blessing of the church; Evangelist. [< Latin *patriarcha* < Greek *patriárchēs* < *patriā* family, clan + *archós* leader]

**pa|tri|ar|chal** (pā′trē är′kəl), *adj.* **1** suitable to a patriarch; having to do with a patriarch: *The governor ... gave a short but truly patriarchal address to his citizens* (Washington Irving). **2** under the rule of a patriarch: *patriarchal life, a patriarchal church.* **3** like a patriarch; venerable: *The Selectmen of Boston, plain, patriarchal fathers of the people* (Hawthorne). —**pa′tri|ar′chal|ly,** *adv.*

**patriarchal cross,** a cross with two transverse pieces, the upper being the shorter, an emblem of the patriarchs of the Greek Church. See diagram under **cross**.

**pa|tri|ar|chal|ism** (pā′trē är′kə liz əm), *n.* a patriarchal form of society or government.

**pa|tri|ar|chate** (pā′trē är′kit), *n.* **1** the position, dignity, or authority of a church patriarch. **2** the church district under a patriarch's authority. **3** the residence of a patriarch. **4** = patriarchy.

**pa|tri|ar|chic** (pā′trē är′kik), *adj.* = patriarchal.

**pa|tri|ar|chy** (pā′trē är′kē), *n., pl.* **-chies.** **1** a form of social organization in which the father is head of the family and in which descent is reckoned in the male line, the children belonging to the father's clan. The joint family of the Hindus and the Roman family are examples. **2** a family, community, or tribe having this form of organization governed by a patriarch or eldest male.

**pa|tri|a|tion** (pā′trē ā′shən), *n. Canadian.* the process of putting under Federal control the amending of Canada's constitution (embodied in the act of the British Parliament that created the Dominion of Canada and serves as Canada's constitution): *The maintenance of the legitimate and historical powers of the provinces may be at stake if patriation is carried forward unilaterally* (Peter Longheed). [< (re)*patriation*]

**pat|ri|cen|tric** (pat′rə sen′trik), *adj.* having or recognizing the father as the center of the family.

**pa|tri|cian** (pə trish′ən), *n., adj.* —*n.* **1** a person of noble birth; noble; aristocrat: *The Prince of Orange, Count Egmont, and many of the leading patricians of the Netherlands* (John L. Motley). **2** a member of the nobility of ancient Rome or the later Roman Empire and the Byzantine Empire. The ancient Roman nobility was composed of the families descended from the original body of Roman citizens. **3** a hereditary noble of a medieval Italian republic, such as Venice, or citizen of high rank in a German free city.

—*adj.* **1** of high social rank; aristocratic. **2** characteristic of an aristocrat: *a patrician air, patrician aloofness.* **3** of the patricians.

[< Latin *patricius* belonging to the *patrēs* senators; (literally) fathers (at Rome) + English *-an*] —**pa|tri′cian|ly,** *adv.*

**pa|tri|cian|ism** (pə trish′ə niz əm), *n.* patrician rank or spirit.

**pa|tri|ci|ate** (pə trish′ē āt), *n.* **1** the position, dignity, or rank of a patrician. **2** a patrician order or class; aristocracy.

**pat|ri|ci|dal** (pat′rə sī′dəl), *adj.* of or having to do with patricide.

**pat|ri|cide¹** (pat′rə sīd), *n.* the crime of killing one's father. [< Late Latin *patricīdium* < Latin *pater* father + *-cīdium* act of killing, -cide²]

**pat|ri|cide²** (pat′rə sīd), *n.* a person who kills his father. [< Medieval Latin *patricida* < Latin *pater* father + *-cīda* killer, -cide¹]

**pat|ri|lat|er|al** (pat′rə lat′ər əl), *adj.* = paternal.

**pat|ri|lin|e|age** (pat′rə lin′ē ij), *n.* descent through the male line, as of a family, clan, or tribe.

**pat|ri|lin|e|al** (pat′rə lin′ē əl), *adj.* **1** traced through male links only: *"Patrilineal" descent (father to son) was the rule in ancient Rome, China and Israel, and occurs in many primitive societies* (Scientific American). **2** descending or heritable through male links only: *patrilineal rights.* [< Latin *pater, patris* father + English *lineal*]

**pat|ri|lo|cal** (pat′rə lō′kəl), *adj.* having its focus in the home of the husband's family: *When the wife comes to live at her husband's home, this is called patrilocal residence* (Melville Herskovits).

**pat|ri|lo|cal|i|ty** (pat′rə lō kal′ə tē), *n.* residence in or near the home of the husband's family.

**pat|ri|mo|ni|al** (pat′rə mō′nē əl), *adj.* having to do with a patrimony; inherited from one's father or ancestors. —**pat′ri|mo′ni|al|ly,** *adv.*

**patrimonial waters,** the waters off the coastline of a state, usually extending up to 200 miles out to sea, within which the state may exercise jurisdiction over natural resources but may not restrict the freedom of navigation of other states: *"Patrimonial" waters is the term they use, as opposed to "territorial" waters, where full sovereignty is exercised* (Peter Tonge).

**pat|ri|mo|ny** (pat′rə mō′nē), *n., pl.* **-nies.** **1** property inherited from one's father or ancestors: *Like a man devouring the patrimony of his sons, we have piled up our debts to buy prosperity on credit* (Wall Street Journal). SYN: inheritance. **2** property belonging to a church, monastery, or convent. **3** *Figurative.* any heritage: *The patrimony of a poor man lies in the strength and dexterity of his hands* (Adam Smith). SYN: legacy. [< Old French *patremoine* < Latin *patrimōnium* < *pater, patris* father]

**pat|rin** (pat′rin), *n.* leaves, grass, stones, or twigs placed as a mark by Gypsies to indicate the course taken. Also, **patteran.** [< Romany *patrin*]

**pa|tri|ot** (pā′trē ət; *especially British* pat′rē ət), *n.* a person who loves his country and gives it loyal support. [< Late Latin *patriōta* < Greek *patriṓtēs* (fellow) countryman < *patrís, -idos* fatherland < *patḗr, patrós* father]

**pa|tri|ot|eer** (pā′trē ə tir′; *especially British* pat′rē ə tir′), *n., v.* —*n.* a person who makes a parade of his patriotic spirit or service, especially in doing what is for his own profit: *They are quick to detect the phony and they can distinguish a patriot from a patrioteer* (Birmingham News).

—*v.i.* to act as a patrioteer; parade as patriotic what is done for one's own profit.

**pa|tri|ot|ic** (pā′trē ot′ik; *especially British* pat′rē ot′ik), *adj.* **1** loving one's country: *a patriotic soldier.* **2** showing love and loyal support of one's country: *A patriotic mind anxious to be proud of its country even in little things* (H. G. Wells). —**pa′tri|ot′i|cal|ly,** *adv.*

**pa|tri|ot|ism** (pā′trē ə tiz′əm; *especially British* pat′rē ə tiz′əm), *n.* love and loyal support of one's country: *Patriotism is absolutely essential to national welfare* (Emory S. Bogardus).

**Patriots' Day,** *U.S.* April 19, the anniversary of the initial skirmishes in the Revolutionary War, at Lexington and Concord, Massachusetts. It is observed on the third Monday in April as a legal holiday in Maine and Massachusetts.

**pa|tris|tic** (pə tris′tik), *adj.* having to do with the early leaders, or fathers, of the Christian Church, or with their writings. [< Latin *pater, patris* father + English *-ist* + *-ic*] —**pa|tris′ti|cal|ly,** *adv.*

**pa|tris|ti|cal** (pə tris′tə kəl), *adj.* = patristic.

**pa|tris|tics** (pə tris′tiks), *n.* the study of the doctrines, writings, and lives of the fathers of the Christian Church.

**Pa|tro|clus** (pə trō′kləs), *n. Greek Legend.* a friend of Achilles, slain in battle in Achilles' armor by Hector while Achilles sulked in his tent.

**pa|trol** (pə trōl′), *v.,* **-trolled, -trol|ling,** *n.* —*v.i.* **1** to go the rounds as a watchman or a policeman does watching, guarding, and checking irregularity or disorder so as to protect life and property: *Police patrol at night guarding the town.* **2** to go on patrol; reconnoiter as a patrol.

—*v.t.* **1** to go around (an area, district, camp or building) to watch or guard: *The camp was carefully patrolled.* **2** to make a patrol of; reconnoiter.

—*n.* **1** the act of going the rounds to watch or guard. **2** a person or persons who patrol: *a police patrol. The patrol was changed at midnight.* **3** a small group of soldiers, ships, or airplanes, sent to find out all they can about the enemy, to engage in a raid, or to warn and protect the main body. **4** a unit of usually eight boy scouts or girl scouts.

[< French *patrouiller* paddle in mud < Old French *patouiller,* probably < *patte* paw] —**pa|trol′ler,** *n.*

**patrol car,** an automobile used by policemen to patrol an area.

**pa|trol|man** (pə trōl′mən), *n., pl.* **-men.** **1** a man who patrols. **2** a policeman who patrols a certain district.

**pat|ro|log|ic** (pat′rə loj′ik), *adj.* belonging to patrology.

**pat|ro|log|i|cal** (pat′rə loj′ə kəl), *adj.* = patrologic.

**pa|trol|o|gist** ((pə trol′ə jist), *n.* a person skilled in patrology.

**pa|trol|o|gy** (pə trol′ə jē), *n., pl.* **-gies.** **1a** the study of the writings of the fathers of the Christian Church; patristics. **b** a treatise on these writings. **2** a collection of the writings of the fathers and other early ecclesiastical writers. [< Greek *patḗr, patrós* father + *-logiā* -logy]

**patrol wagon,** **1** a closed wagon or truck used by the police for carrying prisoners. **2** a light vehicle used by an underwriters' group in reaching fires in order to protect insured goods.

**pa|tron¹** (pā′trən), *n., adj.* —*n.* **1** a person who buys regularly at a given store or goes regularly to a certain hotel or restaurant: *The enormous demand for military boots was rendering it ... difficult for him to give to old patrons that ... attention which he would desire to give* (Arnold Bennett). **2** a person who gives his approval and support to some person, art, cause, or undertaking: *a patron of artists; a renowned patron of learning* (Jonathan Swift). *Books ... ought to have no patrons but truth and reason* (Francis Bacon). SYN: sponsor, benefactor. **3** a guardian saint; patron saint: *St. Crispin, the patron of shoemakers.* **4** (in ancient Rome) an influential man who took certain persons under his protection, or a master who had freed a slave but retained some claims upon him. **5** a person who holds the right to present a clergyman to a benefice. **6** *Obsolete.* a founder of a religious order.

—*adj.* guarding; protecting: *a patron saint.*

[< Old French *patroun,* learned borrowing from Latin *patrōnus* patron advocate, protector; person to be respected < *pater, patris* father. See etym. of doublets **padrone, patroon¹, pattern.**]

**pa|tron²** (pȧ trôɴ′), *n. French.* a proprietor.

**pa|tron|age** (pā′trə nij, pat′rə-), *n.* **1** regular business given to a store, hotel, or restaurant by customers: *to give one's patronage to a local store.* **2** favor, encouragement, or support given by a patron: *Aided by their patronage and his own abilities, he had arrived at distinguished posts* (John L. Motley). **3** condescending favor: *an air of patronage.* **4** the power to give jobs or favors, especially by naming people to hold government jobs and by awarding business contracts: *the patronage of a governor, mayor, or congressman.* **5** political jobs or favors. **6** the right of presentation to an ecclesiastical benefice; advowson.

**pa|tron|al** (pā′trə nəl), *adj.* acting the part of a patron; protecting; favoring.

**pa|tron|ess** (pā′trə nis, pat′rə-), *n.* a woman patron: *the patroness of a fine dress shop. Saint Rose of Lima ... is the patroness of South America* (Fulton J. Sheen).

**pa|tron|ise** (pā′trə nīz, pat′rə-), *v.t.,* **-ised, -is|ing.** *Especially British.* patronize.

**pat|ron|ite** (pat′rə nīt), *n.* one of the chief ores of vanadium, containing sulfur also. [< A. Rizo-*Patrona,* a Peruvian mineralogist of the 1900's]

**pa|tron|ize** (pā′trə nīz, pat′rə-), *v.t.,* **-ized, -iz|ing.** **1** to be a regular customer of; give regular business to: *We patronize our neighborhood stores.* **2** to act as a patron toward; support or protect: *to patronize the ballet.* **3** to treat in a condescending way: *We dislike to have anyone patronize us.* —**pa′tron|i|za′tion,** *n.* —**pa′tron|iz′er,** *n.* —**pa′tron|iz′ing|ly,** *adv.*

**pa|tronne** (pȧ trôn′), *n. French.* a proprietress.

**patron saint,** **1** a saint regarded as the special guardian, as of a person, church, city, nation, or trade: *St. Christopher is the patron saint of travelers.* **2** *Figurative: The late John Maynard Keynes ... is the patron saint of many of the Administration's economists* (New York Times).

**pat|ro|nym** (pat′rə nim), *n.* = patronymic.

**pat|ro|nym|ic** (pat′rə nim′ik), *n., adj.* —*n.* a name derived from the name of a father or paternal ancestor, especially by the addition of a prefix or suffix: *Williamson meaning "son of William," and MacDonald meaning "descendant of Donald" are patronymics.*

—*adj.* **1** (of a family name) derived from the name of a father or ancestor. **2** of or having to do with a suffix or prefix showing such derivation.

[< Late Latin *patrōnymicus* < Greek *patrōnymikós,* ultimately < *patḗr, patrós* father + dialectal *ónyma* name]

**pa|troon¹** (pə trün′), *n.* a landowner who had certain privileges under the former Dutch governments of New York and New Jersey. A patroon usually owned a large amount of land. [American English < Dutch *patroon* < Latin *patrōnus.* See etym. of doublets **padrone, patron¹, pattern.**]

**pa|troon²** (pə trün′), *n. Obsolete.* patron¹.

**pa|troon|ship** (pə trün′ship), *n.* **1** the position of a patroon. **2** the position of a patroon. **2** the land granted a patroon.

**pat|sy** (pat′sē), *n., pl.* **-sies.** *Slang.* **1** an easy mark; victim: *The Cards stopped being the patsies of the league and zoomed to the championship* (New York Times). **2** a person to be given the blame for what someone else has done; fall guy: *O'Malley had already picked out his patsy* (Time). SYN: scapegoat. [origin uncertain]

**pat|tée** or **pat|té** (pa tā′, pat′ē), *adj. Heraldry.* (of a cross) having nearly triangular arms that narrow where they meet and widen toward the extremities. Also, **paty.** [< Old French *patte* pawed < earlier *pate* paw]

**pat|ten** (pat′ən), *n.* **1** a wooden overshoe with a thick sole; clog. **2** wooden sandal or overshoe mounted on an iron ring, to raise the foot above wet ground. [< Old French *patin* < *pate* paw]

**pat|tened** (pat′ənd), *adj.* wearing pattens: *Wherever they went, some pattened girl stopped to courtesy* (Jane Austen).

**pat|ter¹** (pat′ər), *v., n.* —*v.i.* **1** to make rapid

taps: *The rain patters on a windowpane. Bare feet pattered along the hard floor.* **2** to move with a rapid tapping sound: *to patter across the room.*
—***v.t.*** to make rapid taps on or against; fall on with a rapid tapping: *The trees would patter me all over with big drops from the rain of the afternoon* (Robert Louis Stevenson).
—***n.*** a series of quick taps or the sound they make: *the patter of sleet, the patter of little feet.*
[frequentative form < *pat*[1]]

**pat|ter**[2] (pat′ər), *n., v.* —***n.*** **1** rapid and easy talk: *a magician's patter, a salesman's patter.* **2** the special vocabulary of a class or group: *I have more respect for conjurer's patter than for doctor's patter. They are both meant to stupefy* (G. K. Chesterton). **SYN**: jargon, lingo. **3** rapid speech, usually for comic effect, introduced into a new song.
—***v.i.*** **1** to talk rapidly, fluently, or glibly: *We take the name of God in vain when we patter through prayers in our worship* (London Times). **2** *Slang.* to speak or talk some jargon.
—***v.t.*** to talk or say rapidly and easily, without much thought: *to patter a prayer.*
[apparently variant of Middle English *pater,* as in *paternoster*] —**pat′ter|er,** *n.*

**pat|ter|an** (pat′ər ən), *n.* = patrin.

**pat|tern** (pat′ərn), *n., v.* —***n.*** **1** an arrangement of forms and colors; design: *the patterns of wallpaper, rugs, cloth, and jewelry; a pattern of polka dots.* **SYN**: motif. **2** a model or guide for something to be made: *Mother used a paper pattern in cutting out her new dress.* **SYN**: See syn. under **model.** **3** a fine example; model to be followed: *Washington was a pattern of manliness.* **SYN**: ideal, exemplar. **4** form; shape; configuration: *a large, deep cup with a bowllike pattern.* **5** the structure or design in a work as of literature or music: *a novelistic pattern, the regular, easily recognized pattern of a Haydn symphony.* **6** any arrangement; the configuration of qualities or traits characterizing a person or group: *a speech pattern, cultural patterns, patterns of thought. Ways of behaving abstracted directly from observation of behavior in a given society are called patterns* (Beals and Hoijer). **7a** a typical specimen; sample. **b** something formed after a prototype; copy; likeness. **8** a model in wood or metal from which a mold is made for casting. **9** the distribution of shot or shrapnel over or on a target from a shell, bomb, or the like. **10** *Irish.* the festival of a patron saint or the festivities with which it is celebrated: *the occasion of a fair, or a pattern, or market day* (Samuel Lover).
—***v.t.*** **1** to make according to a pattern: *She patterned herself after her mother.* **2** to work or decorate with a pattern: *The German anti-aircraft guns ... begin to pattern the sky about them with little balls of black smoke* (H. G. Wells). **3** *Archaic.* to match, parallel, or equal. **4a** *Rare.* to imitate; copy. **b** *Obsolete.* to be a pattern for; prefigure or foreshadow: *Pattern'd by thy fault, foul sin may say, He learn'd to sin, and thou didst teach the way* (Shakespeare).
[variant of Middle English *patron* < Old French *patron* patron; pattern (from a client's copying his patron) < Latin *patrōnus.* See etym. of doublets **padrone, patron, patroon**[1].]

**pat|terned** (pat′ərnd), *adj.* having a pattern or patterns; decorated or worked with a pattern or design: *patterned tiles, a fancy-patterned sofa.*

**pattern glass,** glassware which has been pressed with decorative patterns.

**pat|tern|ing** (pat′ər ning), *n.* **1** the formation or arrangement of patterns, as in an artistic work. **2** physical therapy guiding brain-damaged or retarded children through creeping, crawling, walking, and other movements, to develop patterns of function which the brain failed to develop.

**pat|tern|less** (pat′ərn lis), *adj.* without a pattern: *a patternless assortment of numbers.*

**pat|tern|mak|er** (pat′ərn mā′kər), *n.* a person who makes patterns, as for castings or clothing.

**pat|tern|mak|ing** (pat′ərn mā′king), *n.* the act or process of making patterns; the work of a patternmaker.

**patter song,** a humorous song in which a large number of words are fitted to a few notes and sung rapidly.

**pat|ty** (pat′ē), *n., pl.* **-ties.** **1** a hollow form of pastry filled with meat, fish, or poultry; pâté. **2** a small, round, flat piece of food or candy. [< French *pâté* < Old French *paste.* See etym. of doublet **pasty**[2].]

**pat|ty-cake** (pat′ē kāk′), *n.* = pat-a-cake.

**pat|ty|pan** (pat′ē pan′), *n.,* or **patty pan, 1** a small pan for baking little cakes, patties, and the like. **2** a variety of summer squash shaped somewhat like a small pan.

**patty shell,** a pastry case for an individual serving as of creamed meat.

**pat|u|lous** (pach′ə ləs), *adj.* **1** opening rather widely; expanded. **2** slightly spreading, as the boughs of a tree. **3** *Botany.* **a** spreading slightly, as a calyx. **b** bearing the flowers loose or dispersed, as a peduncle. [< Latin *patulus* (with English *-ous*) open < *patēre* lie open] —**pat′u|lous|ly,** *adv.* —**pat′u|lous|ness,** *n.*

**pat|y** (pat′ē), *adj. Heraldry.* pattée.

**patz|er** (pats′ər, pots′-), *n. Slang.* an amateur chess player, especially one who plays the game without skill or style: *He played as though Petrosian were a patzer, and nobody can take that kind of liberty with so great a player* (Harold C. Schonberg). [probably < German (dialectal) *Patzer* spoiler < *patzen* to spoil, botch]

**pau** (pou), *adj. Hawaiian.* finished; completed; done.

**P.A.U.** or **PAU** (no periods), Pan American Union.

**pau|cis ver|bis** (pô′sis vėr′bis), *Latin.* in few words; with brevity.

**pau|ci|ty** (pô′sə tē), *n.* **1** a small number; fewness: *the paucity of the troops* (John L. Motley). **2** a small amount; scarcity; lack: *Because of the paucity of coonskins, he's using Australian rabbit, skunk, and even American silver fox* (Wall Street Journal). **SYN**: dearth, scantiness. [< Latin *paucitās* < *paucus* few]

**paugh|ty** (pô′tē), *adj.,* **-ti|er, -ti|est.** *Scottish.* **1** haughty; proud. **2** saucy; impertinent. [origin unknown]

**Paul** (pôl), *n.* **Saint,** died A.D. 67?, an early Christian missionary who started Christian communities in many countries and wrote most of the epistles in the New Testament. He was known as the "Apostle to the Gentiles."

**Paul-Bun|nell test** (pôl′bun′əl), a blood test for infectious mononucleosis. [< J. R. *Paul,* 1893-1971, and W. W. *Bunnell,* born 1902, American physicians]

**Paul Bunyan.** See under **Bunyan.**

**paul|dron** (pôl′drən), *n.* a piece of armor for the shoulder. [earlier *pouldron,* alteration of Old French *espauleron* < *espaule* shoulder]

**Pau|li exclusion principle** (pou′lē), = Pauli's principle.

**Paul|ine** (pô′līn, -lēn), *adj.* **1** of, having to do with, or written by the Apostle Paul. **2** of his doctrines or writings, especially the epistles attributed to him in the New Testament.

**Pau|li's principle** (pou′lēz), *Physics.* the exclusion principle. [< Wolfgang *Pauli,* 1900-1958, an Austrian physicist, who suggested the principle]

**Paul|ist** (pô′list), *n., adj.* —***n.*** **1** a member of the Congregation of the Missionary Priests of Saint Paul the Apostle, a Roman Catholic society of priests founded at New York in 1858: *The Paulists preach missions, especially to non-Catholics* (Fulton J. Sheen). **2** *Obsolete.* (in India) a Jesuit.
—***adj.*** of or belonging to the Congregation of the Missionary Priests of Saint Paul the Apostle: *a Paulist priest. The Paulist Fathers* [*were*] *the first religious society of Catholic priests to be founded in the United States* (New York Times).

**Paul|is|ta** (pô lis′tə), *n.* an inhabitant of São Paulo, Brazil. [< Brazilian Portuguese *Paulista* < São *Paulo*]

**pau|low|ni|a** (pô lō′nē ə), *n.* any Chinese tree of a group of the figwort family, such as a species bearing clusters of purplish, trumpet-shaped flowers that bloom in early spring, widely cultivated for ornament. [< New Latin *Paulownia* < Anna *Pavlovna,* daughter of Czar Paul I of Russia]

**paunch** (pônch, pänch), *n.* **1** a large, protruding belly: *a short, rosy-cheeked, apoplectic-looking subject, with ... a paunch like an alderman's* (Charles J. Lever). **SYN**: pot-belly. **2** the belly; stomach. **SYN**: abdomen. **3** the first and largest stomach of a cud-chewing animal. [< Old French *panche* < Latin *pantex*]

**paunch|i|ness** (pôn′chē nis, pän′-), *n.* a paunchy condition.

**paunch|y** (pôn′chē, pän′-), *adj.,* **paunch|i|er, paunch|i|est.** having a big paunch: *Now, a little paunchier, a little shorter of wind, they are still successful, but in business, not ball handling* (Newsweek).

**pau|per** (pô′pər), *n., adj.* —***n.*** **1** a very poor person: *On pauper's rations she has made the museum outstanding* (Time). **2** a person supported by charity or public welfare: *The pauper lives better than the free laborer; the thief better than the pauper* (Emerson).
—***adj.*** of, relating to, or intended for a pauper or paupers.
[< Latin *pauper* poor, related to *paucus* few. See etym. of doublet **poor.**]

**pau|per|ism** (pô′pə riz əm), *n.* **1** the condition of being very poor; poverty. **SYN**: indigence, destitution. **2** paupers as a group.

**pau|per|ize** (pô′pə rīz), *v.t.,* **-ized, -iz|ing.** to make a pauper of: *In their search for financial security, they may unwittingly pauperize themselves* (New Yorker). —**pau′per|i|za′tion,** *n.* —**pau′per|iz′er,** *n.*

***pause** (pôz), *v.,* **paused, paus|ing,** *n.* —***v.i.*** **1** to stop for a time; wait: *to pause for lunch. The dog paused when he heard me.* **SYN**: See syn. under **stop.** **2** to dwell; linger: *to pause upon a word.* [partly < the noun; partly < Late Latin *pausāre* < Latin *pausa;* see the noun]
—***n.*** **1** a brief stop or rest: *After a pause for lunch the men returned to work. It had continued to rain almost without pause all day* (London Times). **2a** a brief stop in speaking or reading: *He made a short pause and then went on reading.* **b** a punctuation mark indicating such a stop. **3** *Music.* **a** a sign above or below a note or rest, meaning that it is to be held for a longer time; fermata. **b** = rest. **4** *Prosody.* an interval in a line of verse; caesura.
**give pause,** to cause to stop or hesitate: *The hazards of the move gave them pause.*
[< Middle French *pause,* learned borrowing from Latin *pausa* < Greek *paûsis* < *paúein* to stop, cease] —**paus′er,** *n.* —**paus′ing|ly,** *adv.*

***pause**
definition 3a

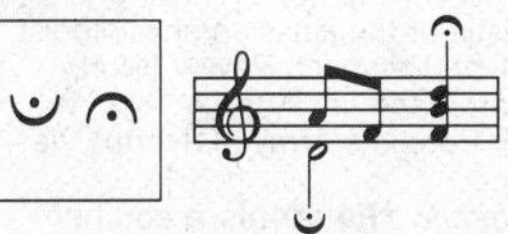

**pause|less** (pôz′lis), *adj.* without pause; ceaseless. —**pause′less|ly,** *adv.*

**pa|uw** (pä′ü, pou), *n.* = paauw.

**pav|an** (pav′ən), *n.* **1** a slow, stately dance in duple time, introduced into England in the 1500's, performed by couples. **2** music for it. Also, **pavin.** [< Middle French *pavane* < Spanish *pavana* < Italian, feminine of *pavano,* variant of *padovano* having to do with Padua, a city in Italy]

**pav|ane** (pav′ən; *French* pà vàn′), *n.* = pavan.

**pave** (pāv), *v.t.,* **paved, pav|ing.** **1** to cover (a street, sidewalk, or driveway) with a pavement: *to pave a road with concrete.* **2** *Figurative.* to overlay as if with a pavement; cover in a mass or compactly. **3** *Figurative.* to make smooth or easy; prepare: *He paved the way for me by doing careful work. The discovery of electricity paved the way for many inventions.* **SYN**: facilitate. [< Old French *paver,* ultimately < Latin *pavīre* to beat, tread down] —**pav′er,** *n.*

**pa|vé** (pə vā′), *n., adj.* —***n.*** a setting in which jewels are placed close together to show no metal.
—***adj.*** set in a pavé; placed close together to show no metal: *Cover-the-ear tree earring, ... available in precious metal or pavé jewels* (New York Times). [< French *pavé* (literally) pavement < *paver* pave]

**pa|véd** (pə vād′), *adj.* **1** = pavé. **2** having jewels or jewellike decorations set close together to show no metal: *Dresses completely pavéd with gold or silver beads twinkled and gleamed* (Bernardine Morris).

**pave|ment** (pāv′mənt), *n.* **1** a covering or surface for streets, sidewalks, or driveways, made of such material as concrete, asphalt, gravel, stones, bricks, or wood: *Traffic loads like this are far more than the pavement was designed to bear* (Newsweek). **2** a paved street, sidewalk, or driveway. **3** the material used for paving. [< Old French *pavement* < *paver* to pave, patterned on Latin *pavīmentum* a beaten-down floor < *pavīre* beat, tread down]

**pavement artist, 1** a person who works in the street sketching and selling his drawings, especially portraits of passers-by. **2** a person who draws figures or scenes on the pavement in order to get money from passers-by.

**pav|id** (pav′id), *adj.* frightened; fearful; timid: *The pavid matron within the one vehicle ... shrieked and trembled* (Thackeray). [< Latin *pavidus* fearful, trembling < *pavēre* tremble with fear]

**pa|vil|ion** (pə vil′yən), *n., v.* —***n.*** **1** a light building, usually one somewhat open, used for shelter or pleasure: *a dance pavilion, a bathing pavilion.* **2** a large tent raised on posts, and usually with a peaked top. **3** any building that houses an exhibition at a fair. **4** a part of a building higher and more decorated than the rest. **5** one of a group of buildings forming a hospital. **6** the lower part of a gem cut as a brilliant, especially the sloping surfaces between the girdle and the culet, or base. **7** *Anatomy.* the auricle of the ear. **8** *Obsolete.* a covering or canopy.
—***v.t.*** **1** to enclose or shelter in a pavilion. **2** to furnish with a pavilion.

---

**Pronunciation Key:** hat, āge, cãre, fär; let, ēqual, tėrm; it, īce; hot, ōpen, ôrder; oil, out; cup, pu̇t, rüle; child; long; thin; ᴛʜen; zh, measure; ə represents **a** in about, **e** in taken, **i** in pencil, **o** in lemon, **u** in circus.

[ < Old French *pavillon* < Latin *pāpiliō, -ōnis* tent; (originally) butterfly. See etym. of doublet **papillon.**]

**pav|in** (pav′ən), *n.* = pavan.

**pav|ing** (pā′ving), *n.* **1** material for pavement: *The truck dumped a load of paving.* **2** a pavement: *She fell on the paving and skinned her knee.* **3** the act or work of a person or thing that paves.

**pav|ior** (pāv′yər), *n.* a person who lays pavements.

**pav|iour** (pāv′yər), *n. Especially British.* pavior.

**pav|is** or **pav|ise** (pav′is), *n.* a large shield used in the Middle Ages, covering the whole body. [< Old French *pavais* < Italian *pavese,* apparently < *Pavia,* a city in Italy, where they were first made]

**pav|is|er** or **pav|i|sor** (pav′ə sər), *n.* a soldier armed with or carrying a pavis.

**Pav|lo|va** or **pav|lo|va** (pav lō′və), *n.* a cake eaten especially in Australia, made of meringue with a filling of whipped cream and fruit. [after Anna *Pavlova,* 1885-1931, a Russian ballerina]

**Pav|lov|i|an** (päv lō′vē ən), *adj.* of, having to do with, or characteristic of the Russian physiologist and psychologist Ivan Petrovich Pavlov (1849-1936), or his research and findings.

**PAVN** (no periods), People's Army of (North) Vietnam.

**Pa|vo** (pā′vō), *n., genitive* **Pa|vo|nis.** a southern constellation; the Peacock.

**pav|o|nine** (pav′ə nīn, -nin), *adj.* **1** of, having to do with, or like a peacock. **2** resembling the plumage of the neck or tail of the peacock in coloring; having an iridescent greenish-blue color. [< Latin *pāvōnīnus* < *pāvō, -ōnis* peacock]

**Pa|vo|nis** (pə vō′nis), *n.* genitive of **Pavo.**

**paw** (pô), *n., v.* **—*n.*** **1** the foot of an animal having claws or nails. Cats, dogs, monkeys, and bears have paws. **2** *Informal.* the hand, especially when it is clumsy, or awkwardly used.
**—*v.t.*** **1** to strike or scrape with the paws or feet: *The cat pawed the mouse she had caught. The horse pawed the ground, eager to be going again.* **2** *Informal.* to handle awkwardly, roughly, or in too familiar a manner: *The young father pawed the baby's clothes in a helpless way.*
**—*v.i.*** **1** to strike or scrape with the paws or feet: *Neighing steeds, tied to swinging limbs ... pawed, wheeled, and gazed after their vanished riders* (George Washington Cable). **2** to use the hands awkwardly, roughly, or in too familiar a manner: *Upstairs the hall was dark, but I found the duke's room and started to paw around it* (Mark Twain).
[< Old French *powe, poue,* or *poe,* perhaps < a Germanic word] **—paw′er,** *n.*

**pawk** (pôk), *n. British.* a trick or wile. [origin unknown]

**pawk|y** (pô′kē), *adj.,* **pawk|i|er, pawk|i|est.** *British.* **1** tricky; sly; cunning; crafty: *Benjamin Franklin at the court of Louis XVI, with his long hair, his plain clothes, and his pawky manner* (H. G. Wells). **2a** saucy. **b** squeamish. **c** proud. [< *pawk* + *-y*[1]] **—pawk′i|ly,** *adv.* **—pawk′i|ness,** *n.*

***pawl** (pôl), *n.* a pivoted bar arranged to catch in the teeth of a ratchet wheel or the like so as to prevent movement backward or to impart motion. [perhaps < Dutch *pal,* or < Middle French *pal* stake]

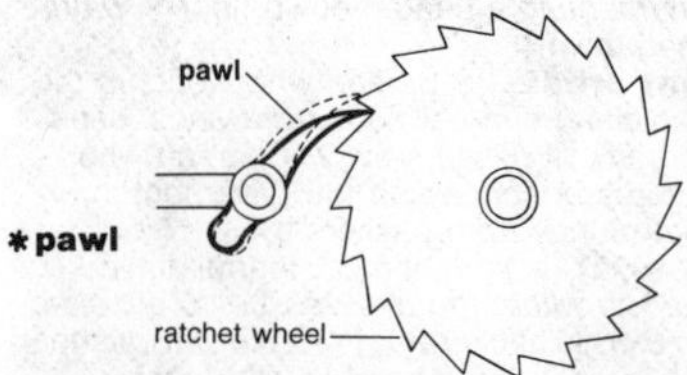

***pawl**

**pawn**[1] (pôn), *v., n.* **—*v.t.*** **1** to leave (something) with another person as security that borrowed money will be repaid: *He pawned his watch to buy food until he could get work.* **2** *Figurative.* to pledge or stake; wager: *Thereon I pawn my credit and mine honour* (Shakespeare). [< noun]
**—*n.*** **1a** something left as security. **b** a hostage: *He must leave behind, for pawns, His mother, wife and son* (John Dryden). **2** *Figurative.* a pledge. **3** the act of pawning.
**in pawn,** in another's possession as security: *His television set is in pawn to pay his room rent.*
[< Old French *pan,* and *pant* piece; pledge, that is, something taken away] **—pawn′a|ble,** *adj.*

**pawn**[2] (pôn), *n.* **1** one of the sixteen pieces of lowest value in the game of chess that are often given up to gain some advantage. A pawn moves a square forward at a time, except on its first move, with the option of moving two squares. When capturing it moves diagonally. On reaching the last rank of the board, the pawn acquires the value of any piece its player may desire, except a king. See picture under **chess**[1]. **2** *Figurative.* an unimportant person or thing used by someone to gain some advantage: *We have got the poor pawn but the hand which plays the game is still out of our reach* (Sir Arthur Conan Doyle). [< Anglo-French *poun,* Old French *paon,* or *peon* (originally) foot soldier < Late Latin *pedō, -ōnis* splay-footed < Latin *pēs, pedis* foot. See etym. of doublet **peon.**]

**pawn|age** (pô′nij), *n.* the action or object of pawning.

**pawn|bro|ker** (pôn′brō′kər), *n.* a person who lends money at interest on articles that are left with him as security for the loan.

**pawn|bro|king** (pôn′brō′king), *n., adj.* **—*n.*** the business of a pawnbroker.
**—*adj.*** that carries on the business of a pawnbroker.

**pawn|ee** (pô nē′), *n.* the person with whom something is deposited as a pawn or security.

**Paw|nee** (pô nē′), *n., pl.* **-nee** or **-nees,** *adj.* **—*n.*** **1** a member of an American Indian tribe that lived near the forks of the Platte River in Nebraska and Kansas and belonged to the confederacy of Caddoan linguistic stock. The Pawnee now live mainly in Oklahoma. **2** their language.
**—*adj.*** of or having to do with this tribe or confederacy.
[American English < Caddoan (Pawnee) *parīsu'* hunters]

**pawn|er** (pô′nər), *n.* the owner of an article or articles in pawn as security.

**pawn|or** (pô′nər, pô nôr′), *n. Law.* pawner.

**pawn|shop** (pôn′shop′), *n.* a pawnbroker's shop: *Pawnshops, so often the fences for concealing stolen goods, abound most in the precincts infamous for poverty and crime* (Harper's).

**paw|paw** (pô′pô), *n.* **1** = papaw. **2** = papaya. [American English, variant of *papaw*]

**pax** (paks), *n.* in the Roman Catholic Church: **1** a kiss of peace given by the celebrant at a Mass. **2** a small tablet, bearing a representation of the Crucifixion or some other sacred subject, used, especially during the Middle Ages, as a means of giving the kiss of peace at Mass, being kissed by the celebrant, the clergy, and the congregation. [< Late Latin *pāx, pācis* the kiss of peace < Latin, peace]

**Pax** (paks), *n.* the Roman goddess of peace, equivalent to the Greek goddess Irene. [< Latin *Pāx*]

**Pax A|mer|i|ca|na** (paks′ ə mer′ə kä′nə, -kan′ə), peace imposed or enforced by American power: *Mr. Steel's final advice to America ... is that Pax Americana should model itself on Pax Britannica which although often "insufferably smug and hypocritical" reserved its power for situations it could hope to control and which were directly related to the national interest* (Punch). [< New Latin *Pax Americana* (literally) American peace]

**Pax Bri|tan|ni|ca** (paks′bri tan′ə kə), the peace imposed or enforced by British power, especially in the 1800's. [< New Latin *Pax Britannica* (literally) British peace]

**pax in bel|lo** (paks′in bel′ō), *Latin.* peace in war.

**Pax Ro|ma|na** (paks′ rō mä′nə), a period of approximately 200 years (27 B.C.-A.D. 180) which began with the reign of Augustus Caesar, during which there was comparative peace in the then-known civilized world, a peace enforced by the might of Rome: *The barbaric realities of 6th century Britain, with its ... sheltered relics of the Pax Romana* (Time). [< Latin *pāx Rōmāna* (literally) Roman peace]

**Pax So|vi|et|i|ca** (paks′ sō′vē et′ə kə, sov′ē-), peace imposed or enforced by Soviet power. [< New Latin *Pax Sovietica* (literally) Soviet peace]

**pax vo|bis|cum** (paks′ vō bis′kəm), *Latin.* peace (be) with you.

**pax|wax** (paks′waks′), *n.* the tough, elastic ligament, composed of yellow, fibrous tissue, at the back of the neck of various quadruped mammals, by which the head is supported. [apparently variant of Middle English *faxwax,* probably < Old English *feax* hair of the head + *weaxan* to grow]

**pay**[1] (pā), *v.,* **paid** or (*Obsolete except for def. 10*) **payed, pay|ing,** *n., adj.* **—*v.t.*** **1** to give money to for things or work: *He paid the doctor.* **2** to give (money) that is due: *to pay $50 for a coat.* **3** to give money for: *Pay your fare.* **4** to hand over (money owed); hand over the amount of: *to pay a debt, to pay taxes.* **5** to give or offer; make: *to pay attention, pay compliments, pay a visit.* **6** to give a profit; be worth while to: *It paid him to be polite. It wouldn't pay me to take that job.* **7** *Figurative.* to yield as a return: *That stock pays me four per cent. The will to establish a society in which the superior development of some is not paid for by the exploitation, that is, by the deliberate degradation of others* (Edmund Wilson). **8** *Figurative.* to give for favors or hurts; reward or punish; recompense or requite: *He paid them for their insults by causing them trouble.* **9** *Figurative.* to suffer; undergo: *The one who does wrong must pay the penalty.* **10** to let out (a rope or cable) by slackening: *As they paid out the chain, we swung clear of them* (Richard Henry Dana).
**—*v.i.*** **1** to give money; give what is owed: *He owes it and must pay.* **2** *Figurative.* to be profitable or advantageous: *It pays to be polite.*
**—*n.*** **1a** money given for things or work; wages; salary: *He gets his pay every Friday.* SYN: compensation, remuneration. **b** *Figurative.* return for favors or hurts: *Dislike is the pay for being mean.* **2** a source of payment. **3** the act of paying. **4** payment, especially of wages: *rate of pay.* **5** the condition of being paid, or receiving wages: *workers in a person's pay or employment.* **6** a person's ability to pay his bills or his record in discharging his debts.
**—*adj.*** **1** containing a device for receiving money for use: *a pay telephone.* **2** containing enough of something, such as metal or oil, to be worth mining or drilling: *a pay lode.* **3** limited to paying subscribers: *pay television.*
**in the pay of,** paid by and working for: *Policemen and firemen are in the pay of the city. Unless we should suppose that the murderers were in the pay of Sparta* (Connop Thirlwall).
**pay back, a** to return borrowed money: *He paid back the money he borrowed.* **b** *Figurative.* to give the same treatment as received: *I'll pay her back for her hospitality by inviting her to dinner.* **c** *Figurative.* to take revenge on: *I'll pay you back yet!*
**pay in, a** to make payment of: *He had paid in all the money* (Daniel Defoe). **b** to make contributions (to a fund): *Men must pay in to the trade society to which they transfer their labor* (Parliamentary Commission Report).
**pay off, a** to give all the money that is owed; pay in full: *To enable the directors to pay off pressing liabilities* (Law Reports). **b** *Figurative.* to get even with; get revenge on: *... to pay off some grudge* (Julian Hawthorne). **c** to cause (a ship) to turn leeward: *The Captain paid his vessel off before the wind.* **d** (of a ship) to fall off to leeward after facing into the wind: *The little vessel 'paid off' from the wind* (Richard Henry Dana). **e** *Informal.* to pay money for so-called protection, but actually as a tribute to racketeers or other thugs: *I got a phone call from an underworld person ... who warned me I had to pay off* (Wall Street Journal). **f** *Figurative.* to be profitable or advantageous: *It takes time ... before overseas processing pays off* (Wall Street Journal).
**pay out,** to make payment of; spend: *I could hardly expect him to pay out a large sum of money for a drawing he knew nothing about* (Listener).
**pay up,** to pay in full; pay: *The loan has been paid up.*
[< Old French *paier* < Vulgar Latin *pācāre* pay, satisfy a creditor < Latin, pacify < *pāx, pācis* peace]
**—*Syn.*** *v.t.* **1 Pay, compensate, remunerate** mean to give money or its equivalent in return for something. **Pay** is the common word meaning to give someone money due for goods, work, or services: *I paid the grocer for the things I bought.* **Compensate** suggests making up for time spent, things lost, service given, or the like: *We'll compensate him for his work as consultant.* **Remunerate** suggests giving a reward in return for services, trouble, or favors, and is used especially, as *compensate* also is, as more polite than *pay* and not suggesting crudely that money is expected or due: *The club remunerated the lecturer.*
▶See **paid** for usage note.

**pay**[2] (pā), *v.t.,* **payed, pay|ing.** to cover (as a ship's bottom, seams, rope, or hatches) with tar, pitch, or another waterproof substance. [< Old North French *peier,* Old French *poier* < Latin *picāre* < *pix, picis* pitch]

**pay|a|bil|i|ty** (pā′ə bil′ə tē), *n.* capability of being profitably worked, as a mine: *Ore of high payability containing a relatively large proportion of high values* (Cape Times).

**pay|a|ble** (pā′ə bəl), *adj.* **1** required to be paid; falling due; due: *He must spend $100 soon on bills payable.* SYN: unpaid, owing. **2** that may be paid. **3** *Law.* (of a debt) capable of being discharged by delivering the value in money or goods. **4** capable of yielding profit; commercially profitable: *payable ore deposits.*

**pay-as-you-earn** (pā′əz yü ėrn′), *n. British.* the withholding of income tax at the time wages or salaries are paid.

**pay-as-you-go** (pā′əz yü gō′), *n., adj. U.S.* **—*n.*** **1** the payment or discharge of obligations as they are incurred: *His major emphasis in taking office was to achieve pay-as-you-go* (New York Times). **2** the withholding of income tax at the

time wages or salaries are paid.
—*adj.* of or having to do with pay-as-you-go: *The proposal to put California taxes on a pay-as-you-go basis is sure to touch off a controversy in the legislature* (Wall Street Journal).

**pay board**, *U.S.* a board or council responsible for setting standards for wage and salary increases, especially to curb or control inflation: *The 90-day freeze . . . was succeeded by an indefinite period of control exercised by a tripartite pay board, composed of five representatives of labor, five of management, and five of the public* (James Bishop).

**pay|box** (pā′boks′), *n. British.* a cashier's booth.

**pay|check** (pā′chek′), *n.*, or **pay check**, a check given in payment of wages or salary: *I took my first paycheck and went out and bought myself what I thought was a genuine Savile Row wardrobe* (New Yorker).

**pay claim**, **1** a claim for money owed or desired: *These managers voted fat bonuses for themselves before considering the pay claims of the workers* (Wall Street Journal). **2** a claim for unemployment insurance: *Jobless pay claims dipped for the fifth straight week* (Newsweek).

**pay|day** (pā′dā′), *n.* the day on which wages are paid: *The following payday Bok found an increase in his weekly envelope* (Edward W. Bok).

**pay dirt**, **1** *U.S.* earth, ore, or the like containing enough metal to be worth mining: *Two of her officers staked an Indian to search pay dirt* (Maclean's). **2** *Informal, Figurative.* something that yields a profit or beneficial result: *Mayor Lee has struck political pay dirt in an unpromising issue* (Harper's).

**PAYE** (no periods) or **P.A.Y.E.**, **1** *British.* pay-as-you-earn: *It has many features comparable to the British income tax system, including P.A.Y.E.* (Manchester Guardian). **2** pay as you enter.

**pay|ee** (pā ē′), *n.* a person to whom money is paid or is to be paid, especially a person to whom a bill or check is made payable.

**pay envelope**, an envelope in which a person's salary or wages are delivered either in cash or by check: *Already this year such clauses have meant fatter pay envelopes for a lot of workers* (Wall Street Journal).

**pay|er** (pā′ər), *n.* a person who pays, person who is to pay a bill or note.

**pay|ing** (pā′ing), *adj.* **1** that pays; giving money or compensation for what is received: *a paying guest.* **2** yielding a return or profit; remunerative: *a paying business.*

**pay|load** (pā′lōd′), *n.* **1** the load carried by an aircraft, train, truck, or other vehicle, which is capable of producing a revenue. Passengers and freight are the payload of a train or airplane. **2** the cargo of a rocket, including passengers and instruments: *The Lunik series perfected and proved Russia's ability to propel heavy payloads through and beyond the restraining gravity of earth* (Joseph L. Zygielbaum). **3** the warhead of a missile.

**pay|load|er** (pā′lō′dər), *n.* a tractor on wheels with a large scoop attached somewhat like a bulldozer.

**pay|mas|ter** (pā′mas′tər, -mäs′-), *n.* a person whose job is to pay wages.

**paymaster general**, the officer at the head of the pay department of an army, navy, or air force.

**pay|ment** (pā′mənt), *n.* **1** the act of paying: *payment of debts.* SYN: compensation, remuneration, settlement. **2a** the amount paid: *a monthly payment of $10.* **b** money or other thing paid as wages or a price; pay: *What will he accept as payment?* **3** *Figurative.* reward or punishment: *Baby's good health is payment enough for me.*
**suspend payments**, to declare inability to pay one's debts; become bankrupt; fail: *Because of lagging sales and mounting costs, the corporation had to suspend payments.*

**pay|mis|tress** (pā′mis′tris), *n.* a woman charged with the payment of wages.

**pay|nim** or **Pay|nim** (pā′nim), *n., adj. Archaic.* —*n.* **1** a pagan; heathen. **2** a Moslem; Saracen: *. . . the crusader, who had sunk thirty thousand paynims at a blow* (John L. Motley). **3** pagandom; heathendom.
—*adj.* **1** pagan; heathen: *A people . . . a remnant that were left Paynim amid their circles, and the stones They pitch up straight to heaven* (Tennyson). **2** Moslem; Saracen: *Paynim sons of swarthy Spain* (Scott).
[< Old French *paienimme,* earlier *paienisme* < Late Latin *pāgānismus* the religion of the pagans < Latin *pāgānus* rustic; see etym. under **pagan**]

**pay|off** (pā′ôf′, -of′), *n., adj.* —*n.* **1** the act of paying wages. **2** the time of such payment. **3a** the returns, as from an enterprise or specific action; result: *You will see the payoff immediately . . . without need for specially trained operators* (Wall Street Journal). . . . *venturing from sixpence up in the football pools — and dreaming of payoffs as high as 300,000 pounds for predicting results* (Maclean's). **b** *Informal.* the act of dividing the returns from some undertaking among those having an interest in it: *the investigation of alleged payoffs by big Government contractors to officials* (New York Times). **c** *Slang.* anything given or received in reward or punishment. **4** *Slang.* the climax (as of a story or situation): *Brother, I've heard some dillies in my day, but that's the payoff* (New Yorker). SYN: culmination.
—*adj.* of or having to do with making payment.

**pay|o|la** (pā ō′lə), *n. Slang.* undercover payments or graft, made or given in return for favors, such as the promotion of a product. [< *pay*(off) + *-ola,* as in *victrola, pianola*]

**pay|out** (pā′out′), *n.* money paid out; expense.

**pay packet**, *British.* a pay envelope.

**pay pause**, *British.* wage freeze: *Because of the pay pause, Service men are to receive only half the increase this year (on April 1), and the rest in a year's time* (Manchester Guardian).

**pay|roll** (pā′rōl′), *n.*, or **pay roll**, **1** a list of persons to be paid and the amounts that each one is to receive: *He never had to meet a payroll. Payrolls tend to grow and resist pruning and frequently politics substitutes for economics* (Bulletin of Atomic Scientists). **2** the total amount to be paid to them: *a payroll of $10,000 a month.*

**payroll tax**, a tax levied on business payrolls, and paid either by the employer or the employee, or both, especially to provide for unemployment insurance.

**pay|sage** (pā ē zäzh′), *n. French.* a painting or drawing of a rural scene; landscape.

**pay scale**, range of salaries or wages: *These, then, the highest paid scholars in the land, attain a place on the pay scale equivalent to that of a colonel, at the bottom rank of the military noblesse* (Atlantic).

**pay|sheet** (pā′shēt′), *n. British.* a list of persons receiving wages with the amounts due to them.

**pay station**, a public pay telephone.

**payt.**, payment.

**pay television**, = pay-TV.

**pay-TV** (pā′tē′vē′), *n.* a system of subscription television in which the user's set is connected directly to the broadcast studio and he pays a monthly charge for an agreed number of special programs: *To theater owners and others, pay-TV was no longer a remote possibility but a distinct threat* (Newsweek).

**pa|zazz** (pə zaz′), *n.* = pizazz.

**Pb** (no period), lead (chemical element).

**P.B.**, **1** British Pharmacopoeia (Latin *Pharmacopoeia Britannica*) . **2** Prayer Book.

**PBA** (no periods), Public Buildings Administration.

**P.B.A.**, Patrolmen's Benevolent Association.

**PBB** (no periods), polybrominated biphenyl.

**PBX** (no periods), private branch (telephone) exchange.

**pc.**, **1** piece. **2** prices.

**p.c.**, **1** per cent. **2** post card.

**PC** (no periods), **1** a patrol craft of the U.S. Navy or Coast Guard, a class of fast, small, lightly armed boats used especially for antisubmarine patrolling and reconnaissance. **2** Peace Corps.

**P.C.**, an abbreviation for the following:
**1** Past Commander.
**2** Philippine Constabulary.
**3** *British.* Police Constable.
**4** *British.* **a** Privy Council. **b** Privy Councilor.
**5** *U.S.* Professional Corporation: *A doctor whose medical practice has been incorporated for tax purposes must use the initials "P.C."* (New York Times).
**6** *Canadian.* Progressive Conservative.

**p/c** (no periods) or **P/C** (no periods), **1** petty cash. **2** price or prices current.

**PCA** (no periods), **1** Production Code Administration. **2** Progressive Citizens of America.

**PCB** (no periods), polychlorinated biphenyl.

**pcl.**, parcel.

**PCM** (no periods) or **pcm** (no periods), pulse-code modulation.

**PCP** (no periods), phencyclidine.

**PCPA** (no periods), para-chlorophenylalanine (a drug which reduces the level of serotonin in the blood, used in clinical research to treat a variety of conditions, including intestinal tumors and schizophrenia).

**pct.**, **1** per cent. **2** precinct.

**PCV** (no periods), Peace Corps Volunteer.

**pd.**, paid.

**p.d.**, **1** per diem. **2** potential difference.

**Pd** (no period), palladium (chemical element).

**P.D.**, **1** per diem. **2** Police Department. **3** Postal District. **4** Public Defender.

**Pd.B.**, Bachelor of Pedagogy (Latin, *Pedagogiae Baccalaureus*).

**Pd.D.**, Doctor of Pedagogy.

**Pd.M.**, Master of Pedagogy.

**PDQ** (no periods) or **p.d.q.**, *Slang.* quickly; immediately: *When he gives an order he wants you to carry it out PDQ!* [< *p*(retty) *d*(amn *q*(uick)]

**PDT** (no periods), Pacific Daylight Time.

**pe** (pā), *n.* = peh.

**p.e.**, *Statistics.* probable error.

**PE** (no periods), **1** polyethylene. **2** price-earnings (ratio).

**P.E.**, **1** Presiding Elder. **2** *Statistics.* probable error. **3** professional engineer. **4** Protestant Episcopal.

**pea** (pē), *n., pl.* **peas**, *Archaic* or *British Dialect* **pease**, *adj.* —*n.* **1** one of several round seeds in the pod of a plant used as vegetable. Peas are either smooth or wrinkled. **2** the plant itself, a vine having pinnate leaves, white flowers, and long dehiscent pods. It is an annual, leguminous plant that belongs to the pea family. **3** any one of various similar or related plants or seeds, especially when used for food, such as the cowpea and chickpea. **4** something small and round like a pea, such as the roe of certain fish. **5** a fragment of iron pyrites from ⅛ to ½ inch in diameter, used in the manufacture of sulfuric acid.
—*adj.* of the size of a pea: *pea coal.*
**as like as two peas (in a pod)**, exactly alike: *It has become fashionable among sophisticated European intellectuals, and among some Americans of the same type, to subscribe to the theory that the United States and the Soviet Union are almost as like as two peas in a pod* (Wall Street Journal).
**row of peas**, something of little value; even a very little bit: *That old compass he traded his knife for isn't worth a row of peas.*
[new singular < *pease*[1], taken as a plural]
—**pea′like′**, *adj.*

**pea bean**, a small, white, nutritious variety of the kidney bean, much used for baking.

**pea|ber|ry** (pē′ber′ē, -bər-), *n., pl.* **-ries**. a coffee berry with one of its two seeds aborted, the developed seed being round and pealike, not flattened on one side like the ordinary seed.

**Pea|bod|y** or **pea|bod|y** (pē′bod′ē, -bə dē), *n., v.,* **-bod|ied, -bod|y|ing.** —*n.* a dance similar to the fox trot but with quick, running steps, popular especially in the 1920's.
—*v.i.* to dance the Peabody.
[< the proper name *Peabody*]

**peabody bird**, = white-throated sparrow. [probably imitative of its song]

**peace** (pēs), *n., interj., v.,* **peaced, peac|ing.** —*n.* **1** freedom from strife of any kind: *peace in the family.* SYN: harmony, concord, amity. **2** public quiet, order, and security. **3** freedom from war: *to work for world peace.* **4** an agreement between enemies to end war: *to sign the peace.* **5** quiet; calm; stillness: *peace of mind. We enjoy the peace of the country.* SYN: tranquillity, serenity. **6** *Obsolete.* a person who imposes or maintains peace.
—*interj.* keep still! stay quiet! be silent!
—*v.i. Archaic.* to be or become silent: *When the thunder would not peace at my bidding* (Shakespeare).
**at peace**, **a** not in a state of war: *The United States is at peace with her neighbors.* **b** not quarreling; not at strife or at variance: *He is at peace with this world and the next* (John W. Warter). **c** in a state of quietness; quiet; peaceful: *All was at peace in the dead of the night.*
**hold (or keep) one's peace**, to keep still; remain quiet: *Do not speak when you should hold your peace.*
**keep the peace**, to refrain, or prevent others, from disturbing the (public) peace; maintain public order: *Dragoons . . . stationed near Berwick, for the purpose of keeping the peace* (Macaulay).
**make one's peace**, to effect reconciliation for oneself or for someone else: *to make one's peace with an enemy. I will make your peace with him, if I can* (Shakespeare).
**make peace**, **a** to effect a reconciliation between persons or parties at variance: *to make peace between union and management.* **b** to conclude peace with a nation at the close of war: *They of Gibeon had made peace with Israel* (Miles Coverdale).
[< Old French *pais* < Latin *pāx, pācis,* related to *pangere* to agree upon]

**peace|a|ble** (pē′sə bəl), *adj.* **1** liking peace; keeping peace: *Peaceable people keep out of quarrels.* SYN: pacific, amicable, friendly. **2** peaceful: *a peaceable reign.* SYN: See syn. under **peaceful**. —**peace′a|ble|ness**, *n.* —**peace′a|bly**, *adv.*

**Peace Corps**, an agency of the U.S. government, established in 1961, which sends trained

**Pronunciation Key:** hat, āge, cãre, fär; let, ēqual, tėrm; it, īce; hot, ōpen, ôrder; oil, out; cup, pu̇t, rüle; child; long; thin; ᴛʜen; zh, measure; ə represents **a** in about, **e** in taken, **i** in pencil, **o** in lemon, **u** in circus.

volunteers and people with technical skill to help improve conditions in underdeveloped countries: *For the Peace Corps to succeed ... its volunteers must have some ideal of life to which they are dedicated* (Saturday Review). *Abbr:* PC (no periods).

**Peace Corpsman**, a member of the Peace Corps.

**Peace Democrat**, *U.S.* a northern Democrat who favored compromise with the Confederate States to end the Civil War.

**peace|ful** (pēs′fəl), *adj.* **1** full of peace; quiet; calm: *It was peaceful in the mountains.* **2** liking peace; keeping peace; peaceable: *a peaceful disposition.* **3** of or having to do with peace: *to settle a dispute by peaceful means.* —**peace′ful|ly**, *adv.* —**peace′ful|ness**, *n.*

—***Syn.* 1 Peaceful, peaceable, placid, serene** mean quiet and calm. **Peaceful** suggests a state of inner quiet, free from disturbance or strife: *She felt peaceful and contented after a hard day's work.* **Peaceable** usually suggests a disposition that avoids strife and seeks to maintain peace and order: *We have friendly, peaceable neighbors.* (In informal usage these two words are often interchangeable.) **Placid** suggests a disposition that stays undisturbed and undistracted: *Placid cows grazed beside the highway.* **Serene** suggests a disposition that remains quietly and graciously composed even in the midst of confusion: *She is always cool, gracious, and serene.*

**peace|keep|er** (pēs′kē′pər), *n.* a person or group that arranges the cessation of hostilities between belligerent countries.

**peace|keep|ing** (pēs′kē′ping), *adj., n.* —***adj.*** maintaining, enforcing, or intervening to achieve a cessation of hostilities between opposing armies, countries, or other groups: *a peacekeeping force.*

—***n.*** the action or function of a peacekeeper or a peacekeeping force: *the U.N.'s role in peacekeeping.*

**peace|less** (pēs′lis), *adj.* without peace; unquiet. —**peace′less|ness**, *n.*

**peace|mak|er** (pēs′mā′kər), *n.* a person who makes peace. **SYN**: mediator.

**peace|mak|ing** (pēs′mā′king), *n., adj.* —***n.*** the act of making or bringing about peace: *a programme of positive peacemaking* (London Times).

—***adj.*** that makes or brings about peace: *a peacemaking mission.*

**peace marcher**, a person who takes part in a march to a government seat, an embassy, or the like, to demonstrate for peace: *A group of "peace marchers" ... will leave Delhi tomorrow on a walk to Peking of some 3,500-4,000 miles* (London Times).

**peace|mon|ger** (pēs′mung′gər -mong′-), *n.* a person who persistently advocates peace (used in an unfriendly way): *The peacemongers were ready to have sacrificed the honor of England* (Robert Southey).

**peace|nik** (pēs′nik), *n. U.S. Slang.* a person who engages in peace demonstrations; an active opponent of war: *What is the real offense of a long-haired peacenik who holds his fingers in a V as the hardhats come marching by?* (Harper's). [< *peace* + *-nik*]

**peace offensive**, a determined attempt or campaign by a country to end a state of hostility or to ease strained relations between itself and another country.

**peace offering**, **1** an offering made to obtain peace, such as a gift or favor. **2** (in old Jewish custom) an offering of thanksgiving to God, as prescribed in the Levitical law. Leviticus 3:1-17.

**peace officer**, a policeman, sheriff, constable, or other civil officer in charge of preserving and enforcing the public peace.

**peace pipe**, a pipe smoked by certain North American Indian tribes as a token or pledge of peace; calumet. It was used ceremonially by adult males. *The Professor and Red Cloud ... were photographed with clasped hands and the peace pipe between them* (J. H. Cook).

**peace sign**, **1** a V-shaped sign made with the forefinger and middle finger held up and the palm facing outward. **2** = peace symbol.

**peace symbol**, a sign in the form of a bisected circle enclosing an upside-down V, used as a symbol of peace: *The familiar peace symbol ... was devised in Britian for the first Ban-the-Bomb Aldermaston march in 1958. The lines inside the circle stand for "nuclear disarmament." They are a stylized combination of the semaphore signal for N (flags in an upside-down V) and D (flags held vertically, one above the signaler's head and the other at his feet)* (Time). See picture under **symbol**.

**peace|time** (pēs′tīm′), *n., adj.* —***n.*** a time of peace: *some of the toughest controls ever imposed on Canadian business in peacetime* (Time).

—***adj.*** of or having to do with a time of peace: *the peacetime uses of atomic energy.*

**peach[1]** (pēch), *n., adj.* —***n.* 1** a juicy, nearly round fruit of a yellowish-pink color, with downy skin, a sweet pulp, and a rough stone or pit. It is good to eat. Peaches are grown in temperate climates in many varieties. Peaches are called clingstones if the pulp sticks to the stone, or freestones if it separates from the stone easily. **2** the tree that this fruit grows on. It belongs to the rose family. **3** = peach blossom. **4** any of various similar trees or fruits. **5** a yellowish pink. **6** *Slang.* a person or thing especially admired or liked: *Produce dealers here were getting a peach of a price for peaches today* (New York Times).

—***adj.*** yellowish-pink.

[< Old French *peche*, earlier *pesche* < Late Latin *persica* < Latin *Persica,* plural of *Persicum* (*mālum*) (literally) Persian apple < Greek *Persikón* (*mâlon*)] —**peach′like′**, *adj.*

**peach[2]** (pēch), *v.i. Slang.* to give secret information; turn informer: *No good was to be got by peaching on him* (Henry Kingsley).

—***v.t.*** *Obsolete.* to impeach or indict. [short for Middle English *apechen* appeach < Anglo-French *apecher,* Old French *empechier* hinder, impeach < Late Latin *impedicāre*]

**peach bloom glass**, = Burmese glass.

**peach blossom**, the pink flower that blooms on the peach tree just before the leaves in the spring. It is the floral emblem of Delaware.

**peach|blow** (pēch′blō′), *n.* **1** a delicate purplish-pink color, like that of a peach blossom. **2** a ceramic glaze of this color, an identifying feature of some Chinese porcelain.

**peach blow glass**, = Burmese glass.

**peaches and cream**, *Slang.* splendid; fine; wonderful: *It would be unfair to maintain that all was peaches and cream ... or to suggest that all city neighborhoods are as filled with goods and services within any walking distance as our own* (Atlantic).

**peach|i|ness** (pē′chē nis), *n.* the quality of being peachy.

**peach leaf curl**, a fungous disease of peach trees that causes the leaves to curl.

**peach Melba**, a dessert of ice cream and peaches, usually flavored with raspberry syrup. [< earlier French *pêche* + Nellie *Melba,* 1861-1931, an Australian opera star]

**peach moth**, a small, mottled brown moth whose larvae burrow into peaches and other fruits; Oriental fruit moth.

**Peach State**, a nickname for Georgia.

**peach twig borer**, a moth larva that bores into the trunk and branches of peach trees.

**peach|y** (pē′chē), *adj.,* **peach|i|er, peach|i|est.** **1** like a peach; like that of a peach. **2** *Slang.* fine; wonderful: *Mrs. Stimson came over and said everything looked just peachy* (New Yorker).

**peach yellows**, a virus disease of some fruit, especially peaches, that causes leaves to become dwarfed and shrivel and the fruit to ripen prematurely.

**pea coat**, = pea jacket.

**pea|cock** (pē′kok′), *n., pl.* **-cocks** or (*collectively*) **-cock**, *v.* —***n.* 1** a large bird with beautiful green, blue, and gold feathers and a splendid train. The tail coverts of the male have spots like eyes on them and can be spread out and held upright like a fan. The peacock lives in Asia and Africa, nests on the ground, and can fly only short distances. **2** any male peacock, especially as contrasted with the *peahen.* **3** *Figurative.* a person who is vain and fond of showing off.

—***v.i.*** to strut like a peacock; make a conceited display; pose.

—***v.t.* 1** to cause to strut or pose like a peacock; make vain. **2** *Australian Slang.* to pick out the choicest piece of land, so that the adjoining land loses its value to anyone else.

[Middle English *pekok,* also *pakock* < Old English *pēa, pāwa* a peafowl of either sex (< Latin *pāvō, -ōnis*) + *cocc* cock[1]] —**pea′cock′like**, *adj.*

**Pea|cock** (pē′kok′), *n.* the constellation Pavo.

**peacock blue**, a greenish blue. —**pea′cock-blue′**, *adj.*

**pea|cock|ish** (pē′kok′ish), *adj.* like a peacock or that of a peacock: *An ardent, almost peacockish vanity* (Spectator).

**peacock ore**, an iridescent copper ore; bornite.

**peacock pheasant**, any one of various Asiatic pheasants notable for their handsome plumage with eyelike spots and the spurred legs of the male.

**pea|cock|y** (pȧ′kok′ē), *adj.* peacocklike; showy; vainglorious.

**pea comb**, a type of comb on certain breeds of chickens, such as the brahmas, made up of three short rows of low serrations.

**pea crab**, any one of certain small crabs that live in the mantle cavities of certain mollusks.

***pea family**, one of the largest of all plant families, containing dicotyledonous plants of great variety and wide distribution, characterized by having a legume as the fruit; the legumes. The family includes ornamentals such as the lupine and wisteria, and many plants of great economic importance such as the pea, peanut, bean, indigo, clover, and licorice.

***pea family**

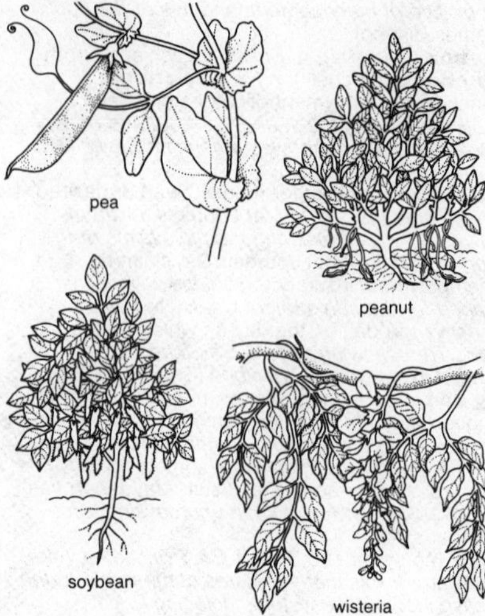


**pea|fowl** (pē′foul′), *n.* a peacock or peahen. There are several kinds of peafowl, belonging to the same family as the pheasant and found in India, Ceylon (Sri Lanka), southeast Asia, the East Indies, and Africa.

**peag** or **peage** (pēg), *n.* = wampum. [American English; short for *wampunipeag*]

**pea green**, a light green. —**pea′-green′**, *adj.*

**pea|hen** (pē′hen′), *n.* the female of the peacock. It is smaller and less showy than the male peacock.

**pea jacket**, a short, double-breasted, usually dark-blue coat of thick woolen cloth, worn especially by sailors. [American English, perhaps < Frisian *pijekkat*]

**peak[1]** (pēk), *n., v., adj.* —***n.* 1** the pointed top of a mountain or hill: *snowy peaks.* **2** a mountain or hill that stands alone: *Pike's Peak.* **3** any pointed end or top: *the peak of a roof, the peak of a beard.* **4** *Figurative.* the highest point: *to reach the peak of one's profession.* **SYN**: summit, pinnacle. **5** the front part of the brim of a cap that stands out. **6** the narrow part of a ship's hold at the bow or at the stern. **7** the upper rear corner of a sail that is extended by a gaff, such as a spanker. **8** the outer end of a gaff: *a full-rigged brig, with the Yankee ensign at her peak* (Richard Henry Dana). **9** a promontory or point of land; headland. **10** an advancing or retreating point formed by the hair on the forehead. **11** *Physics.* **a** the greatest frequency or highest value of a varying quantity during a given period. **b** the greatest amount of power used or generated by a unit or group of units during a given period. **12** *Obsolete.* a beak or bill.

—***v.t.* 1** to raise straight up; tilt up. **2** to raise the end of (as a yard or gaff) so that it is as nearly vertical as possible. **3** *Figurative.* to bring to a peak or head.

—***v.i.*** to reach the highest point; come to a peak: *Winds peaked at 140 miles an hour* (New York Times). *Operations peaked at 84.5% of capacity in late May* (Wall Street Journal). *Unemployment peaked at 6.2%* (Time). *It may develop a typical pattern with appropriations peaking in the first quarter* (Newsweek).

—***adj.*** reaching the highest point (as of capacity, activity, or production): *a peak output. Trains are now able to make extra runs during the peak hours* (Harper's). *A peak load is the maximum demand* [*for electricity*] *encountered in a given period* (Peter Van Note). **SYN**: highest, maximum.

**peak out**, to level off at a peak; come to the end of a rise: *Economists said that the cost of a home mortgage had probably already peaked out, and should start to decline soon* (New York Times). *It traces the rise, the peaking out, and the decline of Ernest Hemingway as stylist* (Time).

**peak[2]** (pēk), *v.i.* to droop in health and spirits; waste away: *peaking and pining over what people think of him* (Charles Kingsley). [origin uncertain]

**peaked[1]** (pēkt, pē′kid), *adj.* having a peak;

pointed: *a peaked hat.* [< *peak*[1] + *-ed*[2]]
—**peaked′ness**, *n.*

**peak|ed**[2] (pē′kid), *adj.* sickly in appearance; wan; thin: *He really looked quite peaked and rundown* (John Stephen Strange). [< *peak*[2] + *-ed*[2]]

**peak-hour** (pēk′our′), *adj.* of or having to do with the hour or period of time when something is at its peak: *The Post Office says even peak-hour mail could be speeded up if more of it were properly prepared* (Wall Street Journal).

**peak|y** (pē′kē), *adj.,* **peak|i|er, peak|i|est.** **1** peaked or pointed; peaklike. **2** abounding in peaks.

**peal**[1] (pēl), *n., v.* —*n.* **1** a loud, long sound: *a peal of thunder, peals of laughter.* SYN: roar. **2** the loud ringing of bells. **3a** a set of bells tuned to each other, especially a set of seven tuned to the tones of the major scale for use in ringing changes; chimes. **b** a series of changes rung on a set of bells.
—*v.t.* **1** to sound out in a peal; ring. *The bells pealed forth their message of Christmas joy.* **2** *Obsolete.* to overwhelm with noise; assail (the ears or a person) as with a loud noise or clamor.
—*v.i.* to sound forth in a peal or peals; resound: *an outcry that went pealing through the night* (Hawthorne).
[Middle English *pele;* origin uncertain]

**peal**[2] (pēl), *n. Obsolete.* appeal. [Middle English *pele,* short for *appeal,* noun]

**pe|an** (pē′ən), *n.* = paean.

**pea|nut** (pē′nut′), *n.* **1** the nutlike seed of a plant of the pea family. Peanuts are roasted and used for food or are pressed to obtain their oil for use in cooking. **2** the plant it grows on. It is probably native to South America. It is an annual, low-growing herb with small, yellow flowers, widely cultivated in warm climates. See picture under **pea family**. **3** a pod of this plant, ripening underground and usually containing two large seeds. **4** *Slang.* a small or unimportant person.
**peanuts,** *Informal.* **a** something of little or no value. **b** a relatively small amount of money: *In terms of cash outlay, the sum is peanuts for an outfit like Krupps* (Montreal Star).
[American English < *pea* + *nut*]

**peanut brittle,** a candy of carmelized sugar and peanuts.

**peanut butter,** a food made of roasted peanuts ground until soft and smooth. It is spread on bread or crackers.

**peanut gallery,** *Slang.* the uppermost balcony of a theater or public hall.

**peanut oil,** oil pressed from peanuts, used especially in cookery and as an ingredient of oleomargarine, cosmetics, and medicine: *Peanut oil more closely resembles olive oil than any of the other vegetable oils* (Leone R. Carroll).

**pear** (pãr), *n.* **1** a sweet, juicy fruit rounded at one end and smaller toward the stem end. It is good to eat. Pears are pomes and are grown in temperate climates. **2** the tree that this fruit grows on. It belongs to the rose family. **3** any one of various similar trees or fruits, such as the avocado or the prickly pear. [Old English *pere* < Vulgar Latin *pira,* or *pēra* feminine singular < neuter plural of Latin *pirum*]

**pear blight,** = fire blight.

**pear drop, 1** a pear-shaped candy, usually flavored with essence of jargonelle. **2** a pear-shaped jewel used as a pendant.

**pearl**[1] (pėrl), *n., adj., v.* —*n.* **1** a hard, smooth, white or nearly white gem that has a soft shine like satin. Pearls are formed inside the shell of a kind of oyster, or in other similar shellfish. The secretions of calcium carbonate with layers of animal membrane around a grain of sand, parasitic worm, or other foreign matter in the shell produce a pearl. **2** a thing that looks like a pearl, such as a dewdrop or a tear. **3** *Figurative.* a very fine one of its kind: *She is a pearl among women.* **4** a very pale, clear, bluish gray; pearl blue. **5** = mother-of-pearl. SYN: nacre. **6** a size of printing type (5 point).
—*adj.* **1** of, like, or made of pearls: *pearl beads.* **2** like mother-of-pearl; nacreous. **3** very pale, clear bluish-gray. **4** made up of small, round pieces: *pearl tapioca, pearl onions.*
—*v.i.* to hunt or dive for pearls: *We've pearled on half-shares in the Bay* (Rudyard Kipling).
—*v.t.* **1** to adorn or set with or as if with pearls, or with mother-of-pearl. **2** to make pearly in color or luster. **3** to make like pearls in form; convert or reduce to small round pieces, as in making pearl tapioca from the ground root of the cassava.
**cast pearls before swine,** to give something very fine to a person who cannot appreciate it: *Oh I do a thankless thing, and cast pearls before swine!* (Dickens).
[< Old French *perle* < Vulgar Latin *perla;* origin uncertain] —**pearl′like′**, *adj.*

**pearl**[2] (pėrl), *v.t., v.i., n.* = purl[2].

**pearl|ash** (pėrl′ash′), *n.* potassium carbonate, usually made by refining potash.

**pearl barley,** barley reduced by polishing to small rounded grains, used in soups.

**pearl blue,** a very pale, clear bluish gray; pearl.

**pearl bush,** a tall bush of the rose family, native to Asia but cultivated in the western United States as a garden plant, bearing white flowers.

**pearl diver,** a person who dives to the ocean bottom to bring up pearl oysters.

**pear-leaf blister mite** (pãr′lēf′), a mite that produces brownish blisters on the undersides of leaves of the pear tree and causes the fruit to grow small and to fall early.

**pearl|er** (pėr′lər), *n.* **1** a person who fishes for pearls, especially by diving for, or dredging, and opening, oysters. **2** a boat used in the pearl fishing industry.

**pearl|es|cent** (pėr les′ənt), *adj.* having a high luster of many colors like a pearl: *We are also told that our swanlike necks should be swathed in pearlescent beads* (New Yorker).

**pearl essence,** a shiny, creamy liquid extracted from the silvery scales of herring and some other fishes, used for coating glass beads to make artificial pearls and as an ingredient in plastics; nacreous pigment; essence d'orient.

**pearl farming,** the act or business of cultivating pearl oysters.

**pearl|fish** (pėrl′fish′), *n., pl.* **-fish|es** or (*collectively*) **-fish. 1** any one of the small fishes that live in the shells of mollusks and in large holothurians. **2** any one of certain fishes, such as a minoow, whose scales are used in the manufacture of artificial pearls.

**pearl gray,** a soft, pale, bluish gray. —**pearl′-gray′**, *adj.*

**pearl|i|ness** (pėr′lē nis), *n.* the state of being pearly.

**pearl|ing** (pėr′ling), *n.* the act or industry of hunting for pearls.

**pearl|ite** (pėr′līt), *n.* **1** a mixture formed by carbon steels cooling slowly from a high temperature, normally made up of ferrite and cementite in alternate layers. Pearlite contains approximately 0.83 per cent carbon. **2** = perlite.

**pearl|ize** (pėr′līz), *v.t.,* **-ized, -iz|ing.** to give a pearly luster to; make pearlescent: *pearlizing of eye shadows and lipsticks* (London Times). *Hats ... of white pearlized straw* (New Yorker).

**pearl millet,** a tall grass grown in the southern United States for forage and in India, Africa, and elsewhere for its edible seeds.

**pearl oyster,** a pearl-bearing oyster.

**pearl spar,** a dolomite containing crystals of the purest variety.

**pearl tapioca,** tapioca in the form of small, round grains.

**pearl|wort** (pėrl′wėrt′), *n.* any one of a group of small matted or tufted herbs with threadlike or awl-shaped leaves and minute flowers.

**pearl|y** (pėr′lē), *adj.,* **pearl|i|er, pearl|i|est,** *n., pl.* **-lies.** —*adj.* **1** like a pearl; having the color or luster of pearls: *pearly teeth.* **2** like mother-of-pearl, especially in color and luster; nacreous. **3** adorned with or containing many pearls: *She is wearing a charcoal-gray suit, black pumps, no stockings, a small string of pearls, and square pearly earrings* (New Yorker).
—*n. British.* **1** clothing covered with many pearl buttons, worn on festive occasions by costermongers. **2** a costermonger who wears such clothing. **3** one of the pearl buttons worn on such clothing.

**pearly everlasting,** a small leafy herb of the composite family, having pearly white bracts about the flowers. It can be dried and kept for winter bouquets.

**pearly nautilus,** any of several sea mollusks that are somewhat like squids, but have a shell that has a pearly lining and is coiled in a flat spiral composed of a series of chambers. See picture under **nautilus**.

**pear|main** (pãr′mān), *n.* any one of various different varieties of apple. [originally, a type of pear < Old French *permain, parmain,* perhaps < unrecorded Medieval Latin *parmanus* of *Parma,* Italy]

**pear psylla,** a dark reddish-brown insect that attacks pear trees, causing leaves and fruit to fall and the fruit to be of poor quality.

**pear-shaped** (pãr′shāpt′), *adj.* **1** in the shape of a pear: *a pear-shaped lamp.* **2** *Figurative.* mellow; resonant; ringing, as if sung with the mouth held open in the shape of a pear: *A handsome man in his mid-forties, who can speak, sing, and write in pear-shaped tones* (New York Times).

**peart** (pirt, pėrt), *adj. Dialect.* pert. —**peart′ly**, *adv.*

**pear|wood** (pãr′wu̇d′), *n.* the wood of the pear tree.

**peas|ant** (pez′ənt), *n., adj.* —*n.* **1** a farmer of the working class in Europe: *Just before sunset the peasants quit laboring in their fields.* **2** any farm laborer of low social status: *A European farmer would hire many peasants to tend the crops in his fields.* **3** an uneducated, uncouth, or boorish person: *Those drunkards are a bunch of peasants, rude and full of foul language.*
—*adj.* of peasants: *peasant labor.*
[< Anglo-French *paisant,* Old French *paysant,* earlier *païsenc* < *pays* country < Late Latin *pāgensis* living in a rural district; the territory of a distirct < Latin *pāgus* rural district]

**peas|ant|ry** (pez′ən trē), *n.* **1** peasants as a group: *the British peasantry* (Charlotte Brontë). **2** the condition of being a peasant. **3** the conduct or quality of a peasant; rusticity.

**pease**[1] (pēz), *n., pl.* **peas|es, peas|en, pease.** *Archaic.* a pea. [< Old English *pise* < Late Latin *pisa,* variant of Latin *pīsum* < Greek *píson*]

**pease**[2] (pēz), *n. Archaic.* a plural of **pea.**

**pease|cod** or **peas|cod** (pēz′kod′), *n.* the pod of a pea.

**pease|cod-bel|lied** (pēz′kod′bel′ēd), *adj.* (of a doublet) having the lower front part so shaped and quilted as to project from the body, in a fashion in vogue toward the end of the 1500's.

**pease meal,** a meal made by grinding peas.

**peas|en** (pē′zən), *n. Archaic.* a plural of **pease**[1].

**pea|shoot|er** (pē′shü′tər), *n.* a toy weapon, consisting of a tube, through which one blows peas or similar small objects.

**pea-soup|er** (pē′sü′pər), *n. Informal.* a pea-soup fog: *The London pea-souper made her homesick for her house in Hollywood* (This Week).

**pea-soup fog** (pē′süp′), *Informal.* a very thick and heavy fog: *The term "pea-soup" has no standing among weathermen, but then most pea-soup fogs—the ones in London, for instance —aren't simply fogs but combinations of fog and smog* (E. B. White).

**pea|stick** (pē′stik′), *n.* a stake upon which a pea plant is trained: *A generous growth of chickweed et al. around the stems of peas gives support before their tendrils have obtained a firm hold on peasticks* (Punch).

**peat**[1] (pēt), *n.* **1** a kind of heavy turf made of partly rotted moss and other plants, especially sphagnum moss. It is used as a fertilizer or especially as fuel in Ireland, Great Britain, and other parts of the world where there are many peat bogs. *Climatic changes may be detected in shifts in the kinds of trees and plants surrounding a bog as reflected in changing pollens in the levels of peat* (Harper's). **2** a piece of this, usually cut in the shape of a brick, and dried for use as fuel: *The fireplace ... was fed in winter with sticks and peats brought by the scholars* (Ian Maclaren).
[Middle English *pete* < Medieval Latin (England) *peta,* apparently < Scottish; origin uncertain]
—**peat′like′**, *adj.*

**peat**[2] (pēt), *n. Archaic.* a pet or darling (used of a woman or girl). [probable variant of *pet*]

**peat bog,** an accumulation of peat or peaty matter: *By the Middle Ages ... peat bogs were supplying the principal fuel needs of many large towns* (New Scientist).

**peat|er|y** (pē′tər ē), *n., pl.* **-er|ies.** a place from which peat is dug.

**peat hag,** broken ground from which peats have been dug: *As the heathery hill rose, it broke into peat hags* (London Times).

**peat|land** (pēt′land′), *n.* a stretch of land abounding in peat.

**peat moor,** = peat bog.

**peat moss, 1** a kind of moss, such as sphagnum, from which peat has formed or may be formed. It is dried and added to garden and potting soil to keep it loose and retain moisture. **2** = peat bog.

**peat|y** (pē′tē), *adj.,* **peat|i|er, peat|i|est.** of, like, or abounding in peat: *A thin seam of peaty matter ... along the bottom of a bed of clay* (James Croll).

**peau** (pō), *n.* **1** *French.* skin. **2** any one of various fabrics resembling skin: *Gelaperm acetate gives brilliant iridescence to this peau, makes its color last longer* (New Yorker).

**peau d'ange** (pō däNzh′), a smooth, lustrous crepe or satin fabric much used for wedding gowns; angelskin. [< French *peau d'ange* (literally) angel skin]

**peau-de-cygne** (pō′də sē′nyə), *n.* a soft, lustrous, satin-faced silk fabric. [< French *peau-de-cygne* (literally) swan skin]

**peau de soie** or **peau-de-soie** (pō′də swä′), *n.* a soft, silk fabric with little luster, having a satin finish on one or both sides. [< French *peau de soie* (literally) silk *skin*]

***pea|vey** (pē′vē), *n., pl.* **-veys.** a strong stick that is tipped with an iron or steel point and has a hinged hook near the end. Lumbermen use peaveys in managing logs. [American English, apparently < J. *Peavey,* who invented it]

***peavey**

**pea|vy** (pē′vē), *n., pl.* **-vies.** = peavey.

**pe|ba** (pē′bə), *n.* = nine-banded armadillo. [apparently < a Tupi word]

**peb|ble** (peb′əl), *n., v.,* **-bled, -bling.** —*n.* **1** a small stone, usually worn smooth and rounded, especially by being rolled about by water or by glacial action: *to wake a person by throwing pebbles at his window. So wears the paving pebble in the street* (John Dryden). **2** a rough, uneven surface on leather, paper, or other material. **3** a substance, especially leather, with a rough, uneven surface. **4a** a colorless transparent kind of rock crystal sometimes used instead of glass in spectacles. **b** a lens made of this.
—*v.t.* **1** to pave with pebbles: *to pebble a walk.* **2** to prepare (leather) so that it has a grained surface. **3** to pelt with pebbles: *The peasants ... betook themselves to stones, and ... pebbled the priest* (Scott).
[Old English *papolstānas* pebblestones] —**peb′ble|like′,** *adj.*

**pebble culture,** a stage in the very early culture of prehistoric man in which he used tools crudely fashioned from pebbles.

**peb|bled** (peb′əld), *adj.* abounding in pebbles; pebbly: *the pebbled shore* (Shakespeare).

**peb|ble|dash** (peb′əl dash′), *n.* mortar with pebbles incorporated into it, used for surfacing or finishing walls or buildings; stucco.

**pebble mill,** a ball mill used in ceramic work.

**pebble tool,** a crude tool made by early man by chipping away one side of a pebble to form a rough cutting edge.

**peb|bly** (peb′lē), *adj.,* **-bli|er, -bli|est. 1** having many pebbles; covered with pebbles: *The pebbly beach hurt our bare feet.* **2** *Figurative.* rough; scratchy: *a pebbly voice.*

**pé|brine** (pā brēn′), *n.* an epidemic protozoan disease of silkworms, in which small black spots appear. [< French *pébrine* < Provençal *pebrino* < *pebre* pepper < Latin *piper*]

***pe|can** (pi kän′, -kan′; pē′kan), *n.* **1** a nut that is shaped like an olive and has a smooth, thin shell, used for food. **2** the tree that it grows on. It is a kind of hickory tree that belongs to the walnut family. Pecans grow in the central and southern United States and in California. [American English < Algonkian (compare Cree *pakan* hard-shelled nut)]

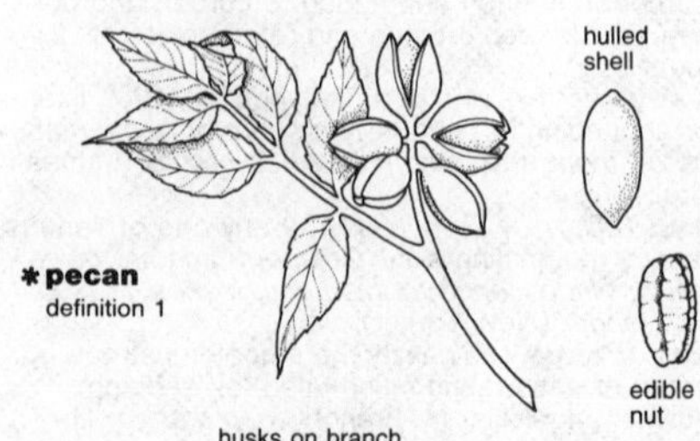

***pecan** definition 1

**pec|ca|bil|i|ty** (pek′ə bil′ə tē), *n.* capability of sinning.

**pec|ca|ble** (pek′ə bəl), *adj.* liable to sin or err: *We hold all mankind to be peccable ... and errable* (George Berkeley). [< earlier French *peccable* < Latin *peccāre* to sin]

**pec|ca|dil|lo** (pek′ə dil′ō), *n., pl.* **-loes** or **-los.** a slight sin or fault: *My sins were all peccadilloes* (Henry James). *The artful old man who hides his major offences behind a frank admission of peccadilloes* (London Times). [< Spanish *pecadillo* (diminutive) < *pecado* sin < Latin *peccātum* < *peccāre* to sin]

**pec|can|cy** (pek′ən sē), *n.* the state or quality of being peccant: *Sins of commission have more of peccancy in them than sins of omission* (Thomas Goodwin).

**pec|cant** (pek′ənt), *adj.* **1** guilty of a sin or moral offense; sinning: *a peccant soul* (Milton). **2** violating some rule or accepted principle, as of behavior; not correct: *The peccant officials ... fell on their knees* (Thomas Carlyle). **3** *Obsolete.* inducing or that may induce disease; unhealthy. [< Latin *peccāns, -antis,* present participle of *peccāre* to sin] —**pec′cant|ly,** *adv.*

**pec|ca|ry** (pek′ər ē), *n., pl.* **-ries** or (*collectively*) **-ry.** a kind of wild pig, found in South and Central America and north into Texas, New Mexico and Arizona; javelina; musk hog. The collared peccary and the white-lipped peccary are two kinds. Peccaries usually live and travel in groups in forests. *Once we found a peccary which, though tame, did not take readily to transport in a canoe and nearly tipped us into the river* (London Times). [< Carib (Guiana or Venezuela) *pakira*]

**pec|ca|vi** (pe kā′vī, -kä′vē), *n., pl.* **-vis.** an acknowledgment or confession of guilt. [< Latin *peccāvī* I have sinned]

**pech** (peʜ), *n., v. Scottish.* —*n.* a short, labored breath; pant.
—*v.i.* to breathe hard from exertion; pant. [apparently imitative]

**pech|an** (peʜ′ən), *n. Scottish.* the stomach.

**pêche Mel|ba** (pesh′ mel′bə), = peach Melba.

**peck**[1] (pek), *n.* **1** a measure of capacity for grain, fruit, vegetables, and other dry things equal to eight quarts or one fourth of a bushel or 8.8096 liters: *a peck of beans, a peck of tomatoes. Abbr:* pk. **2** a container holding just a peck, to measure with. **3** *Figurative.* a great deal: *a peck of trouble.* **SYN**: heap. [Middle English *pek;* origin uncertain]

**peck**[2] (pek), *v., n.* —*v.t.* **1** to strike at and pick up with the beak: *A hen pecks corn.* **2** to make by striking with the beak or a pointed tool: *Woodpeckers peck holes in trees.* **3** to strike and pick with the beak or a pointed tool. **4** *Informal.* to eat only a little, bit by bit.
—*v.i.* **1** to strike with or use the beak. **2** to make a pecking motion; aim with the beak. **3** to take food with the beak. **4** *Informal.* to eat very lightly and daintily. **5** *Figurative.* to find fault.
—*n.* **1** a stroke made with the beak: *The hen gave me a peck.* **2** a hole or mark made by pecking. **3** *Informal.* a stiff, unwilling kiss: *a peck on the cheek.* **4** *British Slang.* food.
**peck at, a** *Informal.* to eat only a little, bit by bit: *Because she is not feeling well, she just pecks at her food.* **b** to try to peck: *It was ... the greatest of triumphs when the birds ... pecked at the grapes in a picture* (Leslie Stephen). **c** *Figurative.* to keep criticizing: *Miss Watson ... kept pecking at me, and it got tiresome* (Mark Twain).
**peck out, a** to pluck out by or as if by pecking: *She flieth ... about his eyes and face, and pecketh ... out his eyes* (John Maplet). **b** to type on a typewriter with one's forefinger or forefingers only, slowly and laboriously: *The next step was pecking out stories* (Harper's).
[apparently dialectal variant of *pick*[1]]

**peck|er** (pek′ər), *n.* **1** a person or thing that pecks. **2** = woodpecker. **3** *British Slang.* courage.

**peck|er|wood** (pek′ər wůd′), *n. U.S. Dialect.* **1** a woodpecker. **2** a poor white; cracker.

**peck horn,** = althorn.

**peck|ing order** (pek′ing), **1** an order of dominance, originally noted among chickens, prescribing which bird can peck another and which bird or birds can, in turn, peck it. The pecking order never changes once it is established at an early age among a flock. **2** a hierarchy of precedence among any group: *In any modern hospital a pecking order, similar to that seen in bird flocks, may be observed* (Atlantic).

**peck|ish** (pek′ish), *adj.* **1** somewhat hungry; disposed to peck or eat: *At forty, admittedly, I rarely feel even peckish* (New Yorker). **2** *Figurative.* impatient; irritable: *I am hungry, thirsty, peckish* (Manchester Guardian). —**peck′ish|ly,** *adv.*

**peck order,** = pecking order.

**Peck's Bad Boy** (peks), *U.S. and Canada.* a person who behaves recklessly or indiscreetly; enfant terrible: *The book is an earnest effort ... to buttress his reputation as the Peck's Bad Boy of advertising* (Time). [*He*] *is the Peck's Bad Boy of the parliamentary Labor Party* (Maclean's). [< *Peck's Bad Boy* (*and His Pa*), a collection of stories about the pranks played by a mischievous boy on his father, written by George Wilbur *Peck,* 1840-1916, an American writer]

**Peck|snif|fi|an** (pek snif′ē ən), *adj.* like Pecksniff; unctuously hypocritical. [< *Pecksniff,* a hypocritical pretender to righteousness in Dickens' *Martin Chuzzlewit*]

**peck|y** (pek′ē), *adj.* having pecks, or marks made by or as if by pecking: *The rooms are paneled in pecky cypress* (Time).

**Pe|co|ri|no** (pā′kə rē′nō), *n.* a sharp-flavored Italian cheese. [< Italian *pecorino* sheeplike]

**Pe|cos Bill** (pā′kōs), *U.S.* an imaginary hero of the wild West who invented roping and other cowboy skills.

**pec|tase** (pek′tās), *n.* an enzyme found in various fruits that has the property of changing pectin into pectic acid and methyl alcohol: *Pectase hydrolyzes the methyl alcohol from soluble pectin to produce pectic acid* (Heber W. Youngken). [< *pect*(in) + *-ase*]

**pec|tate** (pek′tāt), *n.* a salt or ester of pectic acid.

**pec|ten** (pek′tən), *n., pl.* **-ti|nes. 1** a comblike part, especially a membrane in the eyes of most birds and some reptiles and fishes that projects from the choroid coat into the vitreous humor and has parallel folds that suggest the teeth of a comb. **2** any of a common genus of scallops. [< Latin *pecten, -inis* a comb, rake < *pectere* to comb]

**pec|tic** (pek′tik), *adj.* of, having to do with, or derived from pectin: *Pectic enzymes from fruits can be made less active if phenolic substances are present* (New Scientist). [< Greek *pēktikós* curdling, congealing < *pektós* < *pēgnýnai* make stiff]

**pectic acid,** a transparent gelatinous acid, insoluble in water, formed by the hydrolysis of certain esters of pectin. *Formula:* $C_{17}H_{24}O_{16}$

**pec|tin** (pek′tən), *n.* a substance that occurs in most fruits and certain vegetables, especially apples and currants. Pectin is soluble in water and, as the solution evaporates, makes fruit jelly stiff. *Pectin tends to take up water and become gelatinous under certain conditions* (Fred W. Emerson). [< *pect*(ic) (acid) + *-in*]

**pec|ti|na|ceous** (pek′tə nā′shəs), *adj.* of the nature of or containing pectin.

**pec|ti|nate** (pek′tə nāt), *adj.* formed like a comb; having straight, narrow, closely set projections or divisions like the teeth of a comb. [< Latin *pectinātus* < *pecten, -inis* a comb]

**pec|ti|nat|ed** (pek′tə nā′tid), *adj.* = pectinate.

**pec|ti|na|tion** (pek′tə nā′shən), *n.* **1** the state or condition of being pectinate. **2** a comblike structure; pecten.

**pec|tin|e|al** (pek tin′ē əl), *adj.* **1** of or connected to the pubic bone: *a pectineal ligament.* **2** = pectinate. [< New Latin *pectineus* (< Latin *pecten, -inis* a comb) + English *-al*[1]]

**pec|ti|nes** (pek′tə nēz), *n.* plural of **pecten.**

**pec|tin|ic** (pek tin′ik), *adj.* = pectic.

**pec|to|ral** (pek′tər əl), *adj., n.* —*adj.* **1** of, in, or on the breast or chest; thoracic: *the pectoral muscles.* **2** used in treating diseases of the lungs: *a pectoral medicine.* **3** worn on the breast: *the pectoral cross of a bishop.* **4** *Figurative.* proceeding from the heart or inner consciousness; subjective. **5** (of a vocal quality) having a full resonance, as if coming from the chest.
—*n.* **1** a medicine for the lungs. **2** something worn on the breast for ornament or protection, such as a breastplate or a pectoral cross. **3** = pectoral fin.
[< Latin *pectorālis* < *pectus, -oris* chest] —**pec′to|ral|ly,** *adv.*

**pectoral arch** or **girdle,** the bony or cartilaginous arch supporting the forelimbs of vertebrates, formed in man by the scapulae and clavicles: *In the coelacanth, the pectoral girdle, which in normal teleost fish is a hooplike ring of bones embracing the shoulder blades and so on, has no skeletal connections whatever with the head* (New Scientist).

**pectoral fin,** either of a pair of fins in fishes that are attached to the body, usually just behind and in line with the gills, and correspond to the forelimbs of higher vertebrates. See picture under **fin**[1].

**pectoral sandpiper,** a reddish-brown sandpiper with a dark biblike marking on the breast, that breeds in the arctic regions of North America and eastern Siberia and winters in South America. The male inflates the throat and breast at mating time.

**pec|tose** (pek′tōs), *n.* a substance that is contained in the pulp of unripe fleshy fruit, and is readily converted into pectin. [< *pect*(ic) + *-ose*[2]]

**pec|u|late** (pek′yə lāt), *v.t., v.i.,* **-lat|ed, -lat|ing.** to steal (money or goods entrusted to one); embezzle. [< Latin *pecūlārī* (with English *-ate*[1]) embezzle < *pecūlium* (private) property < *pecū* money; cattle]

**pec|u|la|tion** (pek′yə lā′shən), *n.* the act of peculating; embezzlement.

**pec|u|la|tor** (pek′yə lā′tər), *n.* a person who peculates; embezzler.

**pe|cul|iar** (pi kyül′yər), *adj., n.* —*adj.* **1** out of the ordinary; strange; odd; unusual: *A woman's hat on a man's head looks peculiar. What a peculiar thing to say. It was peculiar that the fish market had no fish last Friday.* **SYN**: eccentric, queer, singular. See syn. under **strange. 2** belonging to

one person, thing, or group and not to another; special: *This book has a peculiar value; it belonged to George Washington. The Amish people wear a dress peculiar to themselves.* SYN: particular, distinctive.
—*n.* **1** a property or privilege that is exclusively one's own. **2** (in English ecclesiastical law) a parish or church exempted from the jurisdiction of the ordinary or bishop in whose diocese it lies.
[< Latin *pecūliāris* of one's own (property) < *pecūlium;* see etym. under **peculate**] —**pe|cul'iar|ly**, *adv.*

**peculiar galaxy**, any one of a group of galaxies having highly unusual shapes: *Many of the peculiar galaxies look as though they were normal in shape at one time, but were subsequently distorted in appearance by some unusual event ... either a collision with another galaxy, or a gigantic explosion within the galaxy that literally blew it apart* (Robert Jastrow and Malcolm H. Thompson).

**pe|cu|li|ar|i|ty** (pi kyü'lē ar'ə tē), *n., pl.* **-ties.**
**1** the condition of being peculiar; strange or unusual quality; oddness: *We noticed the peculiarity of his manner at once.* SYN: strangeness, unusualness, eccentricity, singularity.
**2** some little thing or feature that is strange or odd: *One of his peculiarities is that his two eyes are not the same color.* **3** a peculiar or characteristic quality. SYN: idiosyncrasy. **4** a distinguishing quality or feature.

**pe|cul|iar|ize** (pi kyül'yə rīz), *v.t.,* **-ized, -iz|ing.** to make peculiar; set apart.

**peculiar people**, **1** God's own chosen people, the Jews (in the Bible, Deuteronomy 14:2). **2** a term applied to themselves by a number of Christian sects.

**pe|cu|li|um** (pi kyü'lē əm), *n., pl.* **-li|a** (-lē ə).
**1** *Roman Law.* property that a father allowed his wife, child, or other descendant relation, or a master allowed his slave, to have for his own.
**2** a private possession or appurtenance; private property. [< Latin *pecūlium* (private) property < *pecū* money; cattle]

**pe|cu|ni|ar|y** (pi kyü'nē er'ē), *adj.* **1** of or having to do with money: *I pass my whole life, miss, in turning an immense pecuniary mangle* (Dickens).
**2** in the form of money: *pecuniary assistance, a pecuniary gift.* [< Latin *pecūniārius* < *pecūnia* money < *pecū* money; cattle] —**pe|cu'ni|ar'i|ly**, *adv.*

**pe|cu|ni|os|i|ty** (pi kyü'nē os'ə tē), *n.* the state or fact of being supplied with money: *A Frenchman, whose beringed fingers ... betokened a certain amount of pecuniosity* (G. A. MacDonnell).

**pe|cu|ni|ous** (pi kyü'nē əs), *adj.* having much money; wealthy: *But in very truth money is as dirt among those phenomenally pecunious New Yorkers* (Archibald Forbes).

**ped.**, **1** pedal. **2** pedestal.

**ped|a|gese** (ped'ə gēz', -gēs'), *n. U.S. Informal.* the jargon of pedagogues; academese: *With what relief the pedagogues subside into pedagese!* (Time). Also, **pedaguese**.

**ped|a|gog** (ped'ə gog, -gôg), *n.* = pedagogue.

**ped|a|gog|ic** (ped'ə goj'ik, -gō'jik), *adj.* of teachers or teaching; of pedagogy: *pedagogic ability, pedagogic methods.* —**ped'a|gog'i|cal|ly**, *adv.*

**ped|a|gog|i|cal** (ped'ə goj'ə kəl, -gō'jə-), *adj.* = pedagogic.

**ped|a|gog|ics** (ped'ə goj'iks, -gō'jiks), *n.* the science, art, or principles of teaching or education; pedagogy.

**ped|a|gog|ism** or **ped|a|gogu|ism** (ped'ə gog'iz əm, -gôg'-), *n.* the occupation, character, or ways of a pedagogue; system of pedagogy.

**ped|a|gog|ist** (ped'ə goj'ist, -gō'jist), *n.* an expert in pedagogy or pedagogics.

**ped|a|gogue** (ped'ə gog, -gôg), *n.* **1** a teacher of children; schoolmaster: *The master, a dryish Scotsman whose reputation as a pedagogue derived from a book he had written* (Scientific American). SYN: instructor. **2** a dull, narrow-minded teacher; pedant. [< Old French *pedagoge,* learned borrowing from Latin *paedagōgus* < Greek *paidagōgós* < *paîs, paidós* boy + *agōgós* leader < *ágein* to lead]

**ped|a|gogu|ish** (ped'ə gog'ish, -gôg'-), *adj.* characteristic of a pedagogue; pedantic.

**ped|a|go|gy** (ped'ə gō'jē, -goj'ē), *n.* **1** the act or practice of teaching. **2** the art or science of teaching: *The PEA* [*Progressive Education Association*] *was formed in 1919 as a protest against the humdrum, the cut and dried, the rote and recitation methods of pedagogy* (Newsweek).

**ped|a|guese** (ped'ə gēz', -gēs'), *n.* = pedagese.

**ped|al** (ped'əl; pē'dəl *for adj. 1*), *n., v.,* **-aled, -al|ing** or (*especially British*) **-alled, -al|ling,** *adj.* —*n.*
**1** a lever worked by the foot; the part on which the foot is placed to move any kind of machinery. Organs and pianos have pedals for changing the tone. The two pedals of a bicycle, pushed down one after the other, make it go. The brake pedal in an automobile is pushed toward the floor to apply the brakes. *As you ride* [*a bicycle*] *you push down on the pedals ... that act like spokes of the wheel* (Beauchamp, Mayfield, and West). *Bach had a harpsichord with two rows of keys and pedals* (A. J. Hipkins). See pictures under **bicycle** and **organ**. **2** = pedal point.
—*v.t.* to work or use the pedals of; move by pedals: *He pedaled his bicycle slowly up the hill.*
—*v.i.* to work pedals.
[< Middle French *pedale* foot, trick with the feet < Italian, a footstool < Latin *pedāle* (thing) of the foot, neuter of *pedālis;* see the adjective]
—*adj.* **1** of or having to do with a pedal or pedals; consisting of pedals. **2** of or having to do with the foot or feet: ... *reverse himself laterally some 180 degrees so that his pedal extremities are towards the offending overflow* (New Scientist).
[< Latin *pedālis* of the foot (in size, shape) < *pēs, pedis* foot]

**ped|al|board** (ped'əl bôrd', -bōrd'), *n.* the keyboard or set of levers of an organ, played by the feet, and consisting of black and white keys similar in form and arrangement to the manuals, only on a larger scale: *The organ has two full 44-note keyboards and a 13-note pedalboard* (Wall Street Journal).

**ped|al|er** (ped'ə lər), *n. Informal.* a bicycle rider: *Oregon's biennial budget will include about $2.6 million for pedalers and pedestrians* (Time).

**pe|dal|fer** (pə dal'fər), *n.* a type of soil characteristic of humid regions, which has built up under a cover of forest or high grass. It is low in calcium and humus content, rich in iron and aluminum salts. [< Greek *pédon* soil + English *al*(uminum salts) + Latin *ferrum* iron]

**ped|al|fer|ic** (ped'al fer'ik), *adj.* of, having to do with, or characteristic of pedalfers.

**pedal harp**, a harp with seven pedals which can make each note of the scale in each octave a half note higher.

**ped|a|lier** (ped'ə lir'), *n.* **1** a pedal keyboard, as of an organ. **2** a piano equipped with a pedal keyboard, for playing the bass with the feet. [< French *pédalier* < *pédale* pedal]

**ped|al|ist** (ped'ə list), *n.* a person skilled in the use of the pedals, as of an organ or a bicycle.

**ped|al|ler** (ped'ə lər), *n. Especially British.* pedaler.

**ped|a|lo** (ped'ə lō), *n., pl.* **-los.** a kind of raft often built of two pieces separated by a paddle wheel. Pedalos are operated by pedals and used especially as a sports or pleasure craft. [alteration of *pedal*]

**pedal point**, *Music.* **1** a tone (usually either tonic or dominant) sustained in one part (usually the bass) through various harmonies, often independent, in the other parts. **2** the part of a piece containing this.

***pedal pushers**, a pair of close-fitting calf-length pants for women, originally for bicycle riding, but later in general use as sportswear.

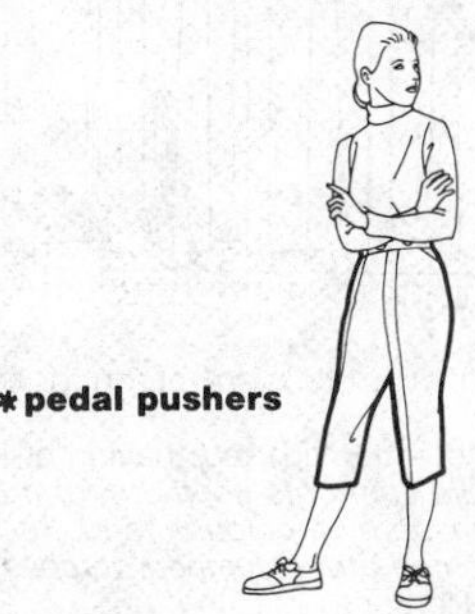
***pedal pushers**

**ped|ant** (ped'ənt), *n.* **1** a person who displays his knowledge in an unnecessary or tiresome way or who puts great stress on minor points of learning. A pedant may make a show of knowledge without knowing how to use it well. *A man who has been brought up among books, and is able to talk of nothing else, is ... what we call a pedant* (Joseph Addison). **2** a dull, narrow-minded teacher or scholar: *He* [*James I*] *had the temper of a pedant; and with it a pedant's love of theories, and a pedant's inability to bring his theories into any relation with actual facts* (Richard H. Green). **3** *Obsolete.* a schoolmaster; teacher. [< Italian *pedante,* perhaps ultimately < Greek *paideúein* educate < *paîs, paidós* boy]

**pe|dan|tic** (pi dan'tik), *adj.* **1** displaying one's knowledge more than is necessary: [*He*] *is learned, but neither stuffy nor pedantic* (Scientific American). **2** tediously learned; scholarly in a dull and narrow way: *He does not ... sacrifice sense and spirit to pedantic refinements* (Macaulay). —**pe|dan'ti|cal|ly**, *adv.*

**pe|dan|ti|cal** (pi dan'tə kəl), *adj.* = pedantic.

**pe|dan|ti|cism** (pi dan'tə siz əm), *n.* a pedantic notion or expression; piece of pedantry.

**ped|ant|ism** (ped'ən tiz əm), *n.* **1** = pedantry. **2** = pedanticism.

**ped|ant|ize** (ped'ən tīz), *v.i.,* **-ized, -iz|ing.** to play the pedant, display pedantry: *To vegetate and pedantize on the classics ...* (Saturday Review).

**ped|an|toc|ra|cy** (ped'ən tok'rə sē), *n., pl.* **-cies.** government by pedants or a pedant; system of government founded on mere book learning. [< *pedant* + *-ocracy,* as in *democracy*]

**pe|dan|to|crat** (pi dan'tə krat), *n.* a ruler who governs on pedantic principles.

**pe|dan|to|crat|ic** (pi dan'tə krat'ik), *adj.* characterized by pedantocracy.

**ped|ant|ry** (ped'ən trē), *n., pl.* **-ries.** **1** an unnecessary or tiresome display of knowledge: *At the risk of seeming to be pedantic about an art whose most despised enemy is pedantry, let's look briefly at some of the attributes of graphic humor* (Harper's). **2** overemphasis on rules, details, and other fine points, especially in learning: *Pedantry proceeds from much Reading and little Understanding* (Sir Richard Steele). **3** a pedantic form or expression: *Vanderbilt tends to be impatient with legal pedantries and artificialities* (Harper's).

**ped|ate** (ped'āt), *adj.* **1a** having a foot or feet. **b** having tubular, somewhat footlike organs, as many echinoderms do. **2** footlike. **3** having divisions like toes; divided in a palmate manner with the two lateral lobes divided into smaller segments: *a pedate leaf.* [< Latin *pedātus,* past participle of *pedāre* to furnish with feet < *pēs, pedis* foot] —**ped'ate|ly**, *adv.*

**Ped. D.**, Doctor of Pedagogy.

**ped|der** (ped'ər), *n. Scottish.* a peddler.

**ped|dle** (ped'əl), *v.,* **-dled, -dling.** —*v.t.* **1** to carry from place to place and sell: *The farmer peddled his fruit from house to house.* [*He*] *had emigrated from Britain to Canada in 1908, made a fortune peddling clothes and real estate in the Chinatowns of the Far West* (Newsweek).
**2** *Figurative.* to offer or deal out in small quantities: *to peddle candy, to peddle a new idea, to peddle gossip.*
—*v.i.* **1** to travel about with things to sell.
**2** *Figurative.* to occupy oneself with trifles; piddle: *Coteries ... peddling with the idlest of all literary problems* (John A. Symonds).
[apparently < *peddler*]

**ped|dler** (ped'lər), *n.* a person who travels about selling things that he carries in a pack or in a truck, wagon, or cart. SYN: hawker, huckster. Also, **pedlar, pedler.** [perhaps variant of Middle English *pedder,* apparently < *ped* basket, pannier]

**ped|dler|y** (ped'lər ē), *n., pl.* **-dler|ies.** **1** the business of a peddler. **2** peddlers' wares. **3** trumpery; trash.

**ped|dling** (ped'ling), *adj.* **1** engaged in the trade of a peddler. **2** *Figurative.* piddling; trifling; paltry.

**ped|er|ast** (ped'ə rast, pē'də-), *n.* a person who engages in pederasty.

**ped|er|as|tic** (ped'ə ras'tik), *adj.* of or having to do with pederasty. —**ped'er|as'ti|cal|ly**, *adv.*

**ped|er|as|ty** (ped'ə ras'tē, pē'də-), *n.* the unnatural sexual union of males with males, especially of a man with a boy. [< Greek *paiderastiā* < *paiderastēs* a pederast < *paîs, paidós* boy, child + *erân* to love]

**pe|des** (pē'dēz, ped'ēz), *n.* plural of **pes**.

**ped|es|tal** (ped'ə stəl), *n., v.,* **-taled, -tal|ing** or (*especially British*) **-talled, -tal|ling.** —*n.* **1** the base on which a column or statue stands. **2** the base of a tall vase or lamp. **3** any base; support; foundation: *Respect for others is the pedestal of society.* **4** *Figurative.* a place or position of importance, especially one of idolization: *In his eyes, she was always on a pedestal.*
—*v.t.* to set on or supply with a pedestal.
[< Middle French *piédestall* < Italian *piedestallo* < *piè* foot (< Latin *pēs, pedis*) + *di* of + *stallo* stall[1]]

**pe|des|tri|an** (pə des'trē ən), *n., adj.* —*n.* a person who goes on foot; walker: *Pedestrians have to watch out for automobiles turning corners.*
—*adj.* **1** going on foot; walking. **2** for or used by pedestrians: *The pedestrian windows* [*at the bank*] *are proving highly popular with housewives who find it hard to push their baby buggies through a revolving door, or don't feel they are dressed well enough to go into the bank* (Birmingham News). **3** *Figurative.* without imagination; dull; slow: *a pedestrian style in writing. The*

*circumstances and events of his life were anything but pedestrian* (Scientific American). **SYN**: commonplace, uninspired, prosaic.
[< Latin *pedester, -tris* on foot; (of writing) commonplace, prosaic (< *pēs, pedis* foot) + English *-ian*]

**pe|des|tri|an|ism** (pə des′trē ə niz′əm), *n.* **1** the practice of traveling on foot; walking: *a large, cheerful street, in which ... a great deal of pedestrianism went forward* (Henry James). **2** *Figurative.* a commonplace quality or style.

**pe|des|tri|an|ize** (pə des′trē ə nīz), *v.t.,* **-ized, -iz|ing.** to convert (a road, street, alley, or bridle path) to use by pedestrians; make free of vehicular traffic: *Eventually it intends to pedestrianize Low Street and turn the whole centre into a traffic-free area* (Sunday Times). —**pe|des′tri|an|i|za′tion,** *n.*

**pe|di|ar|chy** (pē′dē är′kē), *n., pl.* **-chies.** a society or culture dominated or ruled by children. [< Greek *paîs, paidós* child + *árchein* rule]

**pe|di|at|ric** (pē′dē at′rik, ped′ē-), *adj.* of or having to do with pediatrics. Also, **paediatric.** [< Greek *paîs, paidós* child + English *iatric*]

**pe|di|a|tri|cian** (pē′dē ə trish′ən, ped′ē-), *n.* a doctor who specializes in pediatrics. Also, **paediatrician.**

**pe|di|at|rics** (pē′dē at′riks, ped′ē-), *n.* the branch of medicine dealing with children's diseases and the care of babies and children. Also, **paediatrics.** [< *pediatr*(ic) + *-ics*]

**pe|di|at|rist** (pē′dē at′rist, ped′ē-), *n.* = pediatrician.

**pe|di|at|ry** (pē′dē at′rē, ped′ē-), *n.* = pediatrics.

***ped|i|cab** (ped′ə cab′), *n.* a three-wheeled vehicle with a hooded cab for one or two passengers, operated by pedals. It is used especially in the Orient. [< Latin *pēs, pedis* foot + English (taxi)*cab*]

***pedicab**

**ped|i|cel** (ped′ə səl), *n.* **1** a small stalk or stalklike part; an ultimate division of a common peduncle, supporting one flower only. The main flower stalk when small, a secondary stalk that bears flowers, or each of the secondary or subordinate stalks that immediately bear the flowers in a branched inflorescence is a pedicel. *All those parts—calyx, corolla, stamens, and carpels—are attached to the receptacle, the somewhat specialized summit of the pedicel* (Fred W. Emerson). **2** any small stalklike structure in an animal. [< New Latin *pedicellus* (diminutive) < Latin *pedīculus* pedicle]

**ped|i|cel|lar** (ped′ə sel′ər), *adj.* having to do with or of the nature of a pedicel.

**ped|i|cel|lar|i|a** (ped′ə sə lãr′ē ə), *n., pl.* **-i|ae** (-ē ē). any one of many small pincers which project from the base of the spines of echinoderms and have the functions of warding off foreign matter and seizing food. [< New Latin *pedicellaria* < *pedicellus;* see etym. under **pedicel**]

**ped|i|cel|late** (ped′ə sə lit, -lāt), *adj.* having a pedicel or pedicels.

**ped|i|cel|lat|ed** (ped′ə sə lā′tid), *adj.* = pedicellate.

**ped|i|cel|la|tion** (ped′ə sə lā′shən), *n.* pedicellate condition.

**ped|i|cle** (ped′ə kəl), *n.* a small stalk; pedicel or peduncle: *A vertebra has a body, and above this a pedicle on either side* (A. Brazier Howell). [< Latin *pedīculus* footstalk (diminutive) < *pēs, pedis* foot]

**pe|dic|u|lar** (pi dik′yə lər), *adj.* of or having to do with a louse or lice; lousy. [< Latin *pēdiculāris* < *pēdiculus* louse (diminutive) < *pēdis* louse]

**pe|dic|u|late** (pi dik′yə lāt, -lit), *adj., n.* —*adj.* of or belonging to an order of teleost deep-sea fishes characterized by the elongated rays of the dorsal fin, the front one having a bulb on the tip which serves to lure smaller fish.
—*n.* a pediculate fish.
[< New Latin *Pediculati* the group name < Latin *pedīculus;* see etym. under **pedicle**]

**ped|i|cule** (ped′ə kyül), *n.* = pedicle. [< French *pédicule* < Latin *pedīculus;* see etym. under **pedicle**]

**pe|dic|u|lo|sis** (pi dik′yə lō′sis), *n.* the condition of being infested with lice; lousiness; phthiriasis. [< New Latin *pediculosis* < Latin *pēdiculus* louse + New Latin *-osis* -osis]

**pe|dic|u|lous** (pi dik′yə ləs), *adj.* infested with lice; lousy: *Like a ... pediculous vermin thou hast but one suit to thy back* (Thomas Dekker).

**ped|i|cure** (ped′ə kyůr), *n.* **1** treatment of the feet and toenails, including removal of corns, massage, and the trimming of nails. **2** a person who cares for the feet and toenails, such as a podiatrist or chiropodist. [< French *pédicure* < Latin *pēs, pedis* foot + *cūrāre* take care of < *cūra* care]

**ped|i|cur|ist** (ped′ə kyůr′ist), *n.* a podiatrist or chiropodist.

**ped|i|form** (ped′ə fôrm), *adj.* shaped like a foot. [< Latin *pēs, pedis* foot]

**ped|i|gree** (ped′ə grē), *n., v.,* **-greed, -gree|ing.** —*n.* **1** a list of ancestors of a person, animal, or plant; family tree: *That champion dog has a very fine pedigree. Pedigrees of plants ... are usually made for groups rather than individual plants* (J. Herbert Taylor). **2** line of descent; ancestors; ancestry: *I can look but a very little way into my pedigree* (Daniel Defoe). *Virtue lieth not in pedigree* (Thomas Hobbes). **SYN**: lineage. **3** derivation, as from a source: *the pedigree of a word.* **4** distinguished or noble descent: *a man of pedigree.*
—*v.t.* **1** to breed (animals) so as to establish a pedigree. **2** to obtain a pedigree for (an animal), especially by formal registry of it as the offspring of parents with a pedigree.
[apparently < Old French *pied de grue* foot of a crane (because of the clawlike, three-branched mark used in genealogies to show succession) < Latin *pēs, pedis* foot, *dē* of, and Vulgar Latin *grua,* for Latin *grus* crane]

**ped|i|greed** (ped′ə grēd), *adj.* having a known pedigree. Horses, cows, dogs, and other animals of known and recorded ancestry are called pedigreed stock. *Her dog is pedigreed.*

***ped|i|ment** (ped′ə mənt), *n.* **1** the low triangular part on the front of buildings in the Greek style. A pediment is like a gable. **2** any similar decorative part on a building, door, bookcase, or other facade. **3** a base; foundation. **4** *Geology.* a gradual slope at the base of a mountainous region in desert or semiarid areas. It consists of a bedrock foundation covered by a veneer of gravel eroded from the hills. See picture under **plain**[1]. [earlier *periment* and *peremint,* perhaps alteration of *pyramid*]

***pediment**
definition 1

pediment
portico

**ped|i|men|tal** (ped′ə men′təl), *adj.* of, on, or like a pediment.

**ped|i|ment|ed** (ped′ə men′tid), *adj.* having or like a pediment: *The pile confronts us in the form of a large rectangle made by a colonnade of Roman Doric; pedimented and columned porches set off the wings* (Harper's).

**ped|i|palp** (ped′ə palp), *n., pl.* **ped|i|pal|pi** (ped′ə pal′pī). **1** one of a pair of short, leglike appendages near the mouth and fangs of spiders, used as aids in feeding and as copulatory organs. **2** any of an order of arachnids, including the whip scorpions, distinguished by large pedipalpi. [< New Latin *pedipalpus* < Latin *pēs, pedis* foot + New Latin *palpus* palp]

**ped|i|pal|pate** (ped′ə pal′pāt), *adj.* having pedipalpi.

**ped|i|pal|pus** (ped′ə pal′pəs), *n., pl.* **-pi** (-pī). = pedipalp (def. 1).

**ped|lar** or **ped|ler** (ped′lər), *n.* = peddler.

**ped|lar|y** or **ped|ler|y** (ped′lər ē), *n., pl.* **-lar|ies** or **-ler|ies.** = peddlery.

**pedo-,** *combining form.* child; children: *Pedodontics = dentistry for children.* [< Greek *paîs, paidós* child]

**pe|do|bap|tism** (pē′dō bap′tiz əm), *n.* infant baptism.

**pe|do|bap|tist** (pē′dō bap′tist), *n.* an advocate of the baptism of infants.

**ped|o|cal** (ped′ə kal), *n.* a type of soil characteristic of arid or semiarid regions, which has built up under short grass or sparse vegetation. High in calcium and low in iron content, a pedocal is an alkaline soil. [< Greek *pédon* soil + English *cal*(cium)]

**ped|o|cal|ic** (ped′ə kal′ik), *adj.* of, having to do with, or characteristic of pedocals: *Pedocalic soils evolve in an arid, semiarid or sub-humid climate* (White and Renner).

**pe|do|don|tics** (pē′də don′tiks), *n.* the branch of dentistry dealing with the prevention of disease in children's teeth and their special care.

**pe|do|don|tist** (pē′də don′tist), *n.* a dentist who specially practices pedodontics.

**pe|do|gen|e|sis** (pē′dō jen′ə sis), *n.* reproduction by animals in the larval state: *In this type of reproduction, known as pedogenesis, the young of certain species are produced from non-fertilized eggs while in other species the young are produced only from fertilized eggs* (Harbaugh and Goodrich). Also, **paedogenesis.**

**pe|do|ge|net|ic** (pē′dō jə net′ik), *adj.* having to do with or characterized by pedogenesis.

**pe|do|gen|ic** (pē′dō jen′ik), *adj.* = pedogenetic.

**pe|do|log|i|cal**[1] (pē′də loj′ə kəl), *adj.* of or having to do with the scientific study of soils: *The soil scientists would study pedological topics and the physical properties of soils in relation to civil engineering demands* (London Times).

**pe|do|log|i|cal**[2] (pē′də loj′ə kəl), *adj.* of or having to do with the scientific study of the nature of children: *They [children] need to be individually studied by every pedological method, physical and psychic* (Granville Stanley Hall).

**pe|dol|o|gist**[1] (pi dol′ə jist), *n.* a student of, or expert in, the scientific study of soils.

**pe|dol|o|gist**[2] (pi dol′ə jist), *n.* a student of, or expert in, the scientific study of the nature of children.

**pe|dol|o|gy**[1] (pi dol′ə jē), *n.* the scientific study of the origin, classification, and utilization of soils. [< Greek *pédon* soil + English *-logy*]

**pe|dol|o|gy**[2] (pi dol′ə jē), *n.* the scientific study of the nature of children. [< Greek *paîs, paidós* child + English *-logy*]

**pe|dom|e|ter** (pi dom′ə tər), *n.* an instrument for recording the number of steps taken by the person who carries it and thus measuring the distance traveled. [< French *pédomètre* < Latin *pēs, pedis* foot + Greek *métron* measure]

**pe|do|mor|phic** (pē′dō môr′fik), *adj.* having to do with or characterized by pedomorphism.

**pe|do|mor|phism** (pē′dō môr′fiz əm), *n.* the retention by an adult organism of infantile or juvenile characteristics. Also, **paedomorphism.**

**pe|do|phile** (pē′də fīl, -fil), *n.* an adult who is sexually attracted to children.

**pe|do|phil|i|a** (pē′də fil′ē ə), *n.* sexual attraction in an adult toward children.

**pe|do|phil|ic** (pē′də fil′ik), *adj.* of, having to do with, or characterized by pedophilia.

**ped|rail** (ped′rāl), *n.* **1** a series of flat, round, footlike treads or supporting surfaces fastened around the wheels of a tractor or similar vehicle to enable it to travel over very rough ground. **2** a tractor or other vehicle fitted with such supports. [< Latin *pēs, pedis* foot + English *rail*]

**pe|dre|gal** (pā′drə gäl′, ped′rə gəl), *n.* (in Mexico and the southwestern United States) a rough and rocky tract, especially in a volcanic region; an old lava field. [< Spanish *pedregal* < *piedra* stone < Latin *petra*]

**pe|dro** (pē′drō), *n., pl.* **-dros. 1** the five of trumps in cinch and other card games resembling seven-up. **2** one of several card games resembling seven-up in which five points are scored for winning the five of trumps in a trick. [American English < Spanish *Sancho-pedro* and *Pedro,* names of card games; trump cards in them < *Pedro,* proper name < Latin *Petrus* Peter]

**pe|dun|cle** (pi dung′kəl), *n.* a stalk; stem; stalklike part (of a flower, fruit, cluster, or animal body), such as a stalk that bears the fructification in some fungi, the stalk of a lobster's eye, or a white bundle of nerve fibers connecting various parts of the brain.
[< New Latin *pedunculus* (diminutive) < Latin *pēs, pedis* foot]

**pe|dun|cled** (pi dung′kəld), *adj.* = pedunculate.

**pe|dun|cu|lar** (pi dung′kyə lər), *adj.* of or having to do with a peduncle.

**pe|dun|cu|late** (pi dung′kyə lit, -lāt), *adj.* **1** having a peduncle. **2** growing on a peduncle.

**pe|dun|cu|lat|ed** (pi dung′kyə lā′tid), *adj.* = pedunculate.

**peek** (pēk), *v., n.* —*v.i.* to look quickly and slyly; peep: *You must not peek while you are counting in such games as hide-and-seek.*
—*n.* a quick, sly look.
[Middle English *piken;* origin uncertain]

**peek|a|boo** or **peek-a-boo** (pē′kə bü), *n., adj., interj.* —*n.* a young child's game in which a person's face or body is alternately hidden and revealed to the call of "boo" or "peekaboo"; bopeep: *When they play peek-a-boo, a father*

and his baby are sharing an activity (Sidonie M. Gruenberg).
— *adj.* *Informal.* characterized by a partial revealing, sometimes of a startling nature: *Her peekaboo sheath dress is high-necked forward and slit to the waist astern* (New Yorker).
— *interj.* an exclamation, usually used toward a child, intended to startle him.

**peel**[1] (pēl), *n., v.* — *n.* the outer covering or rind of certain fruits, especially citrus fruits: *the long, floppy, yellow peel of a banana.* **SYN**: skin, bark, husk. [< verb]
— *v.t.* **1** to strip skin, rind, or bark from: *to peel an orange, to peel a potato.* **2** to strip: *The Indians peeled the bark from trees to make canoes.* **3** *Informal.* to remove (clothing): *to peel off a heavy sweater.*
— *v.i.* **1** to come off: *When I was sunburned, my skin peeled. The paint on the shed is peeling.* **2** *Informal.* to remove clothing, entirely or in part; strip. **3** to loosen rind, bark, skin, or other covering. **4** *Informal.* to remove or detach oneself from a group: *Wiltshire peeled from the lineout for a try after five minutes of incessant pressure* (London Times). **5** *Archaic.* to plunder; despoil: *Is thy land peeled, thy realm marauded?* (Emerson).
**peel off, a** (of an aircraft) to move at an angle, sharply and suddenly away from a group, especially to dive or land: *They swept the field twice in a tight line of four and then peeled off to land at 5:40* (New York Times). **b** to remove or detach oneself from a group: *The rest of us would follow and we'd rattle along for a mile or so in a rinky-dink parade of Pied Piper trucks, before each of us in turn ... peeled off and headed out alone for his own territory* (New Yorker).
**peel out,** *U.S. Slang.* to accelerate sharply in an automobile, often so that the tires leave rubber marks on the pavement: *As an adolescent man he is freer to drive a car carefully rather than "peel out" and display the "horsepower" of his car—a vicarious display of his own power* (New York Times).
[variant of *pill*[2], apparently < Old English *pilian* < Latin *pilāre* to strip of hair < *pilus* body hair]

**peel**[2] (pēl), *n.* a long-handled shovel used to put bread, pies, or the like, into an oven or take them out. [< Old French *pele* < Latin *pāla* spade, shovel, baker's peel. Compare etym. under **palette.**]

**peel**[3] (pēl), *n.* **1** a small fortified tower or dwelling common in the border counties of England and Scotland in the 1500's, typically having the ground floor vaulted and used as a shelter for cattle, with access to the upper part by a door considerably raised above the ground and reached by a movable stair or the like. **2** *Obsolete.* **a** stockade. **b** a stake. [< Old French *pel*, or *piel* < Latin *pālus* or *pālum* stake. See etym. of doublet **pale**[2], **pole**[1].]

**peel|a|ble** (pē′lə bəl), *adj.* that can be peeled.

**peeled** (pēld), *adj.* stripped of skin, bark, rind, or other outer covering.
**keep one's eyes peeled.** *U.S. Informal.* to be on the alert: *I kept my eyes peeled, but I didn't see her in the afternoon crowd* (Munsey's Magazine).

**peel|er**[1] (pē′lər), *n.* **1** a person or thing that peels, strips, or pares. **2** a log of softwood, such as Douglas fir, from which veneer can be taken by cutting around the log. **3** *U.S. Slang.* a striptease dancer.

**peel|er**[2] or **Peel|er** (pē′lər), *n. Archaic. British Slang.* originally, a member of the Irish constabulary and, later, any British policeman; bobby: *He's gone for a peeler and a search warrant* (Charles Kingsley). [< Sir Robert *Peel,* 1788-1850, a British statesman, who reorganized the London police force]

**peel|ing** (pē′ling), *n.* a part peeled off or pared off: *a potato peeling.* **SYN**: paring.

**Peel|ite** (pē′līt), *n.* (in English history) one of a party of Conservatives who sided with Sir Robert Peel after the repeal of the Corn Laws in 1846. They continued for some years to form a group intermediate between the protectionist Tories and the Liberals, and finally joined the Liberal Party.

**peen** (pēn), *n., v.* — *n.* the part of the head of a hammer or sledge, opposite to the face, when rounded, edged, or otherwise shaped for a special use: *The claw hammer for woodworking and pulling nails is not suitable for metal work which requires a peen on the hammer that will not cut through or mark metal.*
— *v.t.* to shape, bend, or make less thick by striking regularly all over with the peen of a hammer: *They divided the heads [of oil drums] into pie-shaped segments, peened them until each segment gave out a separate musical note when struck with padded sticks* (Time). Also, **pein.**
[compare dialectal Norwegian *pen* or *pænn* back end of a hammer head, Old Swedish *pæna* beat iron thin with the hammer]

**peep**[1] (pēp), *v., n.* — *v.i.* **1** to look through a small or narrow hole or crack: *I shall be upstairs in my room peeping through the window-blinds* (William Dean Howells) **SYN**: peer, peek. **2** to look when no one knows it; look furtively, slyly, or pryingly: *In the corn opposite to her a rabbit stole along, crouched, and peeped* (John Galsworthy). **3** *Figurative.* to look out as if peeping; come partly out: *Violets peeped among the leaves.*
— *v.t.* to cause to stick out a little; show slightly.
— *n.* **1** a look through a hole or crack; little look; peek: *to take a peep into the pantry.* **2** a secret look. **3** *Figurative.* the first looking or coming out: *at the peep of day.* **4** a small hole or crack to look through; peephole.
[perhaps variant of *peek*]

**peep**[2] (pēp), *n., v.* — *n.* **1** a cry of a young bird or chicken or of certain other animals that make a high-pitched noise, such as various frogs; sound like a chirp or a squeak; cheep: *the peep of baby chicks scratching for corn.* **2** *Figurative.* a slight word or sound, often of complaint: *without a peep out of anyone.* **3** any one of various small sandpipers or other shore birds. **4** = jeep.
— *v.i.* **1** to make a short, sharp sound; chirp: *The bird peeped.* **2** *Figurative.* to speak in a thin, weak voice.
[probably imitative. Compare Danish *pibe,* Swedish *pipa*]

**peep|er**[1] (pē′pər), *n.* **1** a person who peeps, especially a Peeping Tom. **2** *Informal.* **a** a mirror. **b** a spyglass.
**peepers,** *Informal.* **a** a pair of spectacles. **b** the eyes: *A secret ... invisible ... to the stupid peepers of that young whiskered prig, Lieutenant Osborne* (Thackeray).
[< *peep*[1] + *-er*[1]]

**peep|er**[2] (pē′pər), *n.* **1** a person or thing that peeps or cheeps. **2** any one of certain frogs that make peeping noises. [< *peep*[2] + *-er*[1]]

**peep|hole** (pēp′hōl′), *n.* a hole through which one may peep.

**Peep|ing Tom** (pē′ping), **1** Also, **peeping tom.** a prying observer, especially a man, who gets pleasure from watching the occupants of a house, room, or other private place without himself being observed. **2** the tailor who was the only person to look at Lady Godiva as she rode naked through Coventry, for which, according to the legend, he was struck blind.

**peep show,** an exhibition of objects or pictures viewed through a small opening, usually fitted with a magnifying glass.

**peep sight,** a rear sight for a gun consisting of a small flat piece of metal, with a tiny hole in the center through which the front sight is aligned with the target.

**pee|pul** (pē′pəl), *n.* = pipal.

**peer**[1] (pir), *n., v.* — *n.* **1a** a person of the same rank, ability, or qualities as another; equal: *a jury of one's peers. He is so fine a man that it would be hard to find his peer. And drunk delight of battle with my peers* (Tennyson). **b** anything equal to something else in quality: *a book without a peer.* **2** a man who has a title; man who is high and great by birth or rank. A duke, marquis, earl, count, viscount, or baron is a peer.
— *v.t.* **1** to rank with; equal. **2** *Informal.* to raise to the peerage; ennoble.
[< Old French *per* < Latin *pār, paris* equal. See etym. of doublet **par.**]

**peer**[2] (pir), *v.i.* **1** to look closely to see clearly, as a near-sighted person does: *to peer into the night. She peered at the tag to read the price.* **2** *Figurative.* to come out slightly; peep out; appear: *The sun was peering from behind a cloud. When daffodils begin to peer* (Shakespeare).
[probably related to Middle English *piren* < Flemish; influenced by *pear,* variant of *appear*]

**peer|age** (pir′ij), *n.* **1** the rank or dignity of a peer: *Five ministers who lost their jobs were consoled with the customary peerages* (Time). **2** the peers of a country. **SYN**: nobility. **3** a book giving a list of the peers of a country and their family histories.

**peer|ess** (pir′is), *n.* **1** the wife or widow of a peer: *The invitations will be restricted to peeresses whose husbands are members of the House of Lords at present* (London Times). **2** a woman having the rank of a peer in her own right.

**peer group,** **1** a group of people of about the same age; age group: *... the happy, easy comfortable adaptation of a child to his peer group* (Max Rafferty). **2** a group of people of the same background, class, social status, or occupation.

**peer|less** (pir′lis), *adj.* without an equal; matchless: *His peerless performance won him a prize.* **SYN**: unequaled. — **peer′less|ly,** *adv.* — **peer′less|ness,** *n.*

**peer of the realm** or **of the United Kingdom,** a peer entitled as a matter of hereditary right to sit in the House of Lords.

**pee|sash** (pē säsh′), *n.* a hot, dry, dust-laden desert wind of India. [< Hindustani *pisachi*]

**peet|weet** (pēt′wēt), *n.* = spotted sandpiper.

[American English; imitative of its cry]

**peeve** (pēv), *v.,* **peeved, peev|ing,** *n. Informal.*
— *v.t., v.i.* to make peevish. — *n.* **1** an annoyance. **2** a peevish mood or disposition. [American English; back formation < *peevish*]

**peeved** (pēvd), *adj.* annoyed; irritated: *They are peeved about the late trains.*

**pee|vish** (pē′vish), *adj.* **1** cross; fretful; complaining: *A peevish child is unhappy and makes others unhappy.* **SYN**: petulant, pettish, irritable, querulous. **2** showing annoyance or irritation. **3** *Obsolete.* obstinate. [Middle English *pevysh,* and *pevyeshe;* origin unknown] — **pee′vish|ly,** *adv.* — **pee′vish|ness,** *n.*

**pee|wee** (pē′wē), *n., adj.* — *n.* **1** a very small person or thing. **2a** = pewee. **b** *Australian.* magpie lark.
— *adj.* **1** small; undersized: *a peewee fighter.* **2** of, having to do with, or characteristic of younger and smaller players in some sport: *a peewee hockey game, a peewee football league.*

**pee|wit** (pē′wit), *n.* = pewit.

**peg** (peg), *n., v.,* **pegged, peg|ging.** — *n.* **1** a pin or small bolt of wood or metal, used to fasten parts together, to hang things on, to stop a hole, to make fast a rope or string, or to mark the score in a game: *Hang your coat on the peg in the wall. The head [of a violin] contains pegs, or pins, which are used to tighten or loosen the strings* (R. G. Pauly). **2** a step; degree: *His work is several pegs above yours.* **3** *Informal.* a hard throw of a ball, especially in baseball: *Willie Mays saved the Giants a run in the second inning with one of his amazing pegs* (New York Times). **4** *Informal.* **a** a wooden leg; peg leg: *The hardest thing about the role was keeping Ahab's wooden peg away from him* (Newsweek). **b** a leg: *You'll hear about the cannonball That carried off his pegs* (Oliver Wendell Holmes). **5** *British.* a small drink of alcoholic liquor: *I suspected the old fellow was going to cool his wrath with a 'peg'* (F. M. Crawford). **6** *Dialect.* a tooth, especially a child's tooth. **7** an implement furnished with a pin, claw, or hook, used for tearing, harpooning, and other work where it is necessary to catch on to an object. **8** the price at which a commodity, stock, or other security is pegged.
— *v.t.* **1** to fasten or hold with pegs: *We must peg down our tent.* **2** to mark with pegs. **3** to keep the price of (a commodity, stock, or other security) from going up or down: *to peg wheat at $1.56 a bushel.* **4** *Figurative.* to attach; make dependent on: *The Algerian franc is pegged to the French franc.* **5** *Informal.* to mark; tag; identify: *He was pegged as a jolly, jowly journeyman closing out a career* (Maclean's). *The two titles, in fact, most precisely peg the tone and content of each feature* (New York Times). **6** *Informal.* to throw hard: *The left fielder pegged the ball to the shortstop.* **7** to strike or pierce with a peg.
— *v.i.* **1** *Informal.* to work hard; keep on energetically and patiently: *He pegged away at his studies so that he would get high marks.* **2** to keep score by moving pegs, as in cribbage. **3** to hit a croquet peg with the ball.
**a peg to hang** (something) **on,** an occasion, pretext, or excuse for: *The chief use of a fact is as a peg to hang a thought on* (Lancet).
**off the peg,** ready-made: *Clothes made in his workrooms are sold off the peg* (Punch).
**peg out, a** to peg or pitch one's tent: *We are pegging out in a very comfortless spot* (Harper's). **b** to die: *A fierce little piece bought to console the children after the dog pegged out* (Punch). **c** to mark the boundary of (a mining claim or other piece of ground) with pegs: *I ... pegged out eight square feet, paid the licence fee, and returned to my mates* (W. H. Hall).
**take down a peg (or two),** to lower the pride of; humble: *She took that proud girl down a peg or two.*
[apparently < Middle Dutch *pegge*] — **peg′like′,** *adj.*

**Peg|a|si** (peg′ə sī), *n.* genitive of **Pegasus** (the constellation).

*** Peg|a|sus** (peg′ə səs), *n., genitive* (def. 3) **Peg|a|si. 1** *Greek Mythology.* a horse with wings, the steed of the Muses. **2** poetic genius; the means by which poets soar in the realms of poetry. **3** a constellation in the northern sky near Andromeda: *Standing high in the eastern sky, just below Cygnus, we find Pegasus, the winged horse, which contains no stars of the first magnitude although it does have a characteristic figure called the "great square"* (Science News Letter).

---

**Pronunciation Key:** hat, āge, cãre, fär; let, ēqual, tėrm; it, īce; hot, ōpen, ôrder; **oi**l, **ou**t; cup, pu̇t, rüle; **ch**ild; lo**ng**; **th**in; **ᴛʜ**en; **zh**, measure; **ə** represents **a** in about, **e** in taken, **i** in pencil, **o** in lemon, **u** in circus.

**mount (one's) Pegasus**, to begin writing a poem: *Then he mounted the ... vulture-winged Pegasus of passion* (Christina Stead).

***Pegasus** definition 1

**peg|board** (peg′bôrd′, -bōrd′), *n.* **1** a board containing evenly spaced holes for pegs, used for scoring games, such as cribbage. **2** a larger board, attached to a wall, having holes in which pegs or hooks are inserted to hold tools, utensils, displays, memorandums, etc.

**peg|box** (peg′boks′), *n.* the head of a stringed instrument containing the pegs to which the strings are attached for tuning.

**pegged pants** (pegd), pants wide at the hips and gradually narrowing to the ankles; peg tops.

**peg|ger** (peg′ər), *n.* **1** a person or thing that pegs. **2** a machine for driving pegs in shoemaking.

**peg leg**, **1** a wooden leg. **2** *Informal.* a person who has a wooden leg.

**peg-leg|ged** (peg′leg′id, -legd′), *adj.* having a wooden leg.

**peg|ma|tite** (peg′mə tīt), *n.* **1** a coarsely crystallized kind of granite occurring in veins and dikes, and usually containing crystals of the common minerals found in granite, but sometimes containing rare minerals rich in such elements as lithium, uranium, and tantalum. **2** granite with a graphic texture. [< Greek *pêgma, pêgmatos* something joined together or congealed (< *pegnýnai* to fix in, join, make solid) + English *-ite*[1]]

**peg|ma|tit|ic** (peg′mə tit′ik), *adj.* consisting of, characteristic of, or resembling pegmatite: *pegmatitic deposits in Norway.*

**peg|ma|ti|za|tion** (peg′mə tə zā′shən), *n.* the filling of a rock with veins of pegmatite.

**peg tankard**, a tankard with pegs inserted at regular intervals, formerly used to mark the quantity each person was to drink.

**peg top**, a wooden top with a metal peg on which it spins when a string wound around the top is rapidly uncoiled.

**peg-top** (peg′top′), *adj.* shaped like a peg top.

**peg tops**, trousers wide at the hips and gradually narrowing to the ankles.

**peg-top trousers** or **peg trousers**, = peg tops.

**peh** (pā), *n.* the seventeenth letter of the Hebrew alphabet. Also, **pe.** [< Hebrew *peh* (literally) mouth]

**Peh|le|vi** (pā′lə vē), *n.* = Pahlavi.

**P.E.I.**, Prince Edward Island.

**peign|oir** (pān wär′, pān′wär), *n.* **1** a loose or very full dressing gown for women, originally worn while the hair was being combed: *[She] padded about the palace kitchen in her silken peignoir, serving endless cups of coffee* (Time). **2** any negligee. [< French *peignoir* < earlier *peignouoir* < *peigner* to comb < Latin *pectināre* < *pecten, -inis* a comb]

**pein** (pēn), *n., v.t.* = peen.

**peine forte et dure** (pen fôr′ tā dyr′), *French.* **1** very severe and harsh punishment. **2** a former method of punishment or torture inflicted on a prisoner who refused to plead. It consisted of placing heavy weights on the body of the prisoner until he pleaded or died.

**peise** (pāz, pēz), *v.t.*, **peised, peis|ing.** *Dialect.* **1** to weigh or measure the weight of, as in a balance. **2** *Figurative.* to weigh in the mind; consider; ponder. **3** to weigh down; oppress; burden. [Middle English *peise* < Old French *peser* < Latin *pensāre* to weigh (frequentative) < *pendere*]

**pe|jo|rate** (pē′jə rāt), *v.*, **-rat|ed, -rat|ing.** — ***v.t.*** to make worse; cause to deteriorate; disparage. — ***v.i.*** to become worse.
[< Latin *pejorāre* (with English *-ate*[1]) make worse < *pejor* worse]

**pe|jo|ra|tive** (pē′jə rā′tiv; pi jôr′ə-, -jor′-), *adj., n.* — ***adj.*** **1** tending to make worse; disparaging; depreciatory: *Throughout all the changes of religion, social and political constitution, and rulers, the real mistress of the Greeks has been sophism—sometimes, but not always, in the pejorative sense of the word* (Atlantic). **2** of or having to do with various disparaging or depreciatory derivative words formed by the addition of a suffix to a root word of neutral or favorable connotations.
— ***n.*** a pejorative word, suffix, or phrase: *What it [ingratiatingly] actually means is something like 'cringingly anxious to please.' It is a pejorative, and it should be used only as such* (New Yorker).
[< *pejorate* + *-ive*] — **pe′jo|ra′tive|ly**, *adv.*

**pek|an** (pek′ən), *n.* = fisher (def. 1a). [American English < Canadian French *pécan* < Algonkian (perhaps Abnaki) *pékané*]

**Peke** (pēk), *n.* a Pekingese dog: *The breed standard issued by the Kennel Club decrees ... that the Peke be leonine in shape with massive skull* (Cape Times).

**pe|kin** (pē kin′), *n.* a silk fabric, originally made only in China, often patterned with broad stripes or figures. [< French *Pékin,* spelling of Chinese *Pei-ching* Peking, capital of the Chinese People's Republic]

**Pe|kin** (pē kin′), *n.*, or **Pekin duck**, any one of a breed of large white ducks, originally of China, raised primarily for the production of meat: *Pekin ducks, which weigh about 8 pounds, are the most common commercially raised ducks in the United States* (William H. Drury).

**Pe|kin|ese** (pē′kə nēz′, -nēs′), *n., pl.* **-ese**, *adj.* = Pekingese.

**Pe|king** (pē king′), *n.*, or **Peking duck**, = Pekin.

**Pe|king|ese** (pē′king ēz′, -ēs′), *n., pl.* **-ese**, *adj.* — ***n.*** **1** a very small dog originally of China, with long silky hair and a pug nose. **2** a native or inhabitant of Peking, China: *Most Pekingese, men and women alike, now wear a baleful blue dungaree uniform that gives them, and the city streets, a monotonous look* (Time). **3** the form of Chinese used in Peking, the standard form of Mandarin.
— ***adj.*** of or having to do with Peking or its people.

**Peking man**, a prehistoric man of the Pleistocene, identified from fossil bones found in caves near Peking in 1929; Sinanthropus pekinensis: *Peking man, Java man, the Neanderthal—none dates farther back than 600,000 years* (Newsweek).

**Pe|king|ol|o|gist** (pē′king ol′ə jist), *n.* a student or observer of the policies and practices of the government of the Chinese People's Republic: *Professional China watchers—often called Pekingologists, ... are constantly sifting through the raw material that Hong Kong provides them with* (New Yorker).

**Pe|king|ol|o|gy** (pē′king ol′ə jē), *n.* the study of the policies and practices of the government of the Chinese People's Republic.

**Pe|kin|ol|o|gist** (pē′kin ol′ə jist), *n.* = Pekingologist.

**Pe|kin|ol|o|gy** (pē′kin ol′ə jē), *n.* = Pekingology.

**pekin stripes**, **1** lengthwise stripes, especially of uniform width, in textile fabrics. **2** fabrics with such stripes.

**pe|koe** (pē′kō; *especially British* pek′ō), *n.* a kind of black tea from Ceylon (Sri Lanka) or India, made from leaves picked while very young. [< Chinese (Amoy dialect) *pek-ho* (literally) white down (because the leaves are picked young with the "down" still on them)]

**pel|age** (pel′ij), *n.* the hair, fur, wool, or other soft covering of a four-footed mammal. [< French *pelage* the covering of a mammal < Old French *peil,* or *pel* hair < Latin *pilus*]

**Pe|la|gi|an** (pə lā′jē ən), *n., adj.* — ***n.*** a follower of Pelagianism.
— ***adj.*** of or having to do with Pelagius or Pelagianism.

**Pe|la|gi|an|ism** (pə lā′jē ə niz′əm), *n.* the doctrines of Pelagius, a British monk who died about 420 A.D., which denied original sin and maintained that the human will is of itself capable of good without the assistance of divine grace.

**pe|lag|ic** (pə laj′ik), *adj.* **1** of the ocean or the open sea; oceanic: *In the open parts of the ocean, the pelagic region, plants and animals differ considerably from those along the seashore* (Harbaugh and Goodrich). **2** living on or near the surface of the open sea or ocean, at some distance from land, as certain animals and plants do. **3** of or having to do with a person who hunts seals, or the operation of hunting seals, as a commercial venture on the high seas, using rifles, harpoons, and other equipment: *pelagic fishery investigations.* [< Latin *pelagicus* < Greek *pelagikós* < *pélagos* sea] — **pe|lag′i|cal|ly**, *adv.*

**pe|lar|go|nate** (pə lär′gə nāt), *n.* a salt of pelargonic acid.

**pel|ar|gon|ic acid** (pel′är gon′ik, -gō′nik), a colorless or yellowish oily acid, present as an ester in an oil in geranium leaves and produced synthetically. *Formula:* $C_9H_{18}O_2$

**pel|ar|go|ni|um** (pel′är gō′nē əm), *n.* any one of a genus of plants of the geranium family, chiefly natives of South Africa, having fragrant leaves and large clusters of showy flowers; stork's-bill; geranium. The plants are often grown in pots and window boxes. *The plant that most gardeners in the West—and elsewhere—refer to as a geranium is botanically a pelargonium* (New York Times). [< New Latin *Pelargonium* the genus name < Greek *pelārgós* stork]

**Pe|las|gi** (pə laz′jī), *n.pl.* the Pelasgians, as a people. [< Latin *Pelasgi* < Greek *Pelasgoí*]

**Pe|las|gi|an** (pə laz′jē ən), *n., adj.* — ***n.*** one of an ancient people (the Pelasgi) of doubtful ethnological affinities, widely spread over the coasts and islands of the eastern Mediterranean and Aegean, and believed to have occupied Greece in prehistoric times.
— ***adj.*** of, having to do with, or characteristic of the Pelasgians: *The Tosks live south of the river, and descend from European Pelasgian tribes* (S. Skendi).

**Pe|las|gic** (pə laz′jik), *adj.* = Pelasgian.

**pe|lec|y|pod** (pə les′ə pod), *n., adj.* — ***n.*** any one of a class of mollusks having a headless body enclosed in a hinged, two-part shell and a hatchet-shaped foot; lamellibranch. Oysters, clams, and scallops belong to this class.
— ***adj.*** **1** having a hatchet-shaped foot: *a pelecypod mollusk.* **2** of or having to do with such a mollusk.
[< Greek *pélekys* hatchet + *poús, podós* foot]

**Pe|lée|an** (pə lā′ən, -lē′-), *adj.* having to do with or designating a kind of volcano characterized by violent eruptions which create a circular hill of lava around the vent. [< Mount *Pelée,* a volcano in Martinique]

**pel|er|ine** (pel′ə rēn′), *n.* a kind of cape or mantle worn by women, especially a long narrow silk or lace piece, with ends coming down to a point in the front. [< French *pèlerine,* feminine of *pèlerin* pilgrim < Medieval Latin *pelegrinus*]

**Pe|le's hair** (pē′lēz, pā′lāz), volcanic glass occurring in fine hairlike threads, as in Hawaii, commonly supposed to have been formed from drops of lava by the wind. [< *Pele,* the Hawaiian goddess of Mount Kilauea, a Hawaiian volcano]

**Pe|leus** (pē′lyüs, -lē əs), *n. Greek Legend.* a king of the Myrmidons, father of Achilles.

**pelf** (pelf), *n.* **1** money or riches, thought of as bad or degrading: *The scholar whom the love of pelf Tempts from his books and from his nobler self* (Longfellow). **SYN:** lucre, mammon. **2** *Archaic.* spoil; booty. [< Old French *pelfre* booty, spoils; origin uncertain]

**Pel|ham** (pel′əm), *n.* a horse's bit combining the snaffle and the curb in one. [< the surname *Pelham*]

**Pe|li|as** (pē′lē əs, pel′ē-), *n. Greek Legend.* the uncle of Jason, who set as his condition for yielding the throne of Iolcus, in Thessaly, to Jason (its heir) the obtaining of the Golden Fleece, hoping that the quest for this would lead to Jason's death.

**pel|i|can** (pel′ə kən), *n.* a very large fish-eating water bird having a huge bill and a pouch on the bottom side of the bill for scooping up fish. There are several kinds. In fable, the pelican was said to feed her young with her own blood. *What, would'st Thou have me turn Pelican and feed thee out of my own vitals* (William Congreve). *Pelicans are large grotesque birds with comical faces and a remarkable talent for fishing* (Science News Letter). [< Late Latin *pelicānus* < Greek *pelekân, -ânos,* perhaps ultimately < *pélekys, -eos* ax (because of the shape of its bill)]

**pelican flower**, a tropical vine with a wide flower made up of a large greenish-yellow tube that starts downward, then bends up and out.

**Pelican State**, a nickname for Louisiana.

**Pe|li|des** (pē lī′dēz), *n. Greek Legend.* **1** Achilles (as the son of Peleus). **2** any descendant in the male line of Peleus.

**pe|lisse** (pə lēs′), *n.* **1** a long cloak or coat lined or trimmed with fur. **2** a long cloak, as of silk or velvet, with armholes or sleeves, worn by women. [< French *pelisse* < Old French *pelice* < Late Latin *pellīcia* < Latin *pellīcius* of fur < *pellis* skin]

**pe|lite** (pē′līt), *n.* a rock composed especially of particles of mud or clay. [< Greek *pēlós* potter's clay, earth + English *-ite*[1]]

**pel|lag|ra** (pə lag′rə, -lā′grə), *n.* a disease marked by eruption on the skin, digestive disturbances, a nervous condition, and sometimes insanity. It is caused by improper diet, especially one lacking sufficient nicotinic acid (niacin). *Pellagra is a deficiency disease prevalent in districts where maize is one of the staple foodstuffs* (Beaumont and Dodds). [< Italian *pellagra,* apparently < *pelle* (< Latin *pellis* skin) + *agro* rough < Latin *ager;* influenced by *podagra* gout in the feet, podagra]

**pel|lag|rin** (pə lag′rin, -lā′grin), *n.* a person affected with pellagra.

**pel|lag|rous** (pə lag′rəs, -lā′grəs), *adj.* of, having to do with, or affected with pellagra.

**pel|le|kar** (pel′ə kär), *n.* = palikar.

**Pel|les** (pel′ēz), *n.* **Sir**, *Arthurian Legend.* the father of Elaine and grandfather of Galahad,

Elaine's son by Lancelot.

**pel|let** (pel′it), *n., v.* —*n.* **1** a little ball, as of mud, paper, hail, snow, or medicine; pill: *The pet rabbits ate little green pellets of dried grass, meal, and powdered milk.* **2** a bullet, especially a spherical bullet intended to be fired by a shotgun or other gun without a rifled barrel: *a pellet of birdshot.* **3** a ball, usually of stone, used as a missile in the 1300's and 1400's. **4** the undigested and indigestible matter, such as bones, feathers, and fur, ejected from the crop by a hawk or other bird of prey.
—*v.t.* **1** to hit with pellets. **2** to form into pellets: *Researchers are experimenting with a pelleted cattle feed made from newsprint, vitamins, and minerals* (Wall Street Journal).
[< Old French *pelote* < Vulgar Latin *pilotta* (diminutive) < Latin *pila* ball] —**pel′let|er,** *n.*

**pellet bomb,** = fragmentation bomb.

**pel|le|tier|ine** (pel′ə tir′ēn), *n.* a light-yellow, astringent powder consisting of a mixture of several alkaloids, used in the treatment of tapeworm infections. [< Pierre J. *Pelletier,* 1782-1842, a French chemist + *-ine*]

**pel|let|ize** (pel′ə tīz), *v.t.,* **-ized, -iz|ing.** to form into pellets: *to pelletize ore.* —**pel′let|i|za′tion,** *n.*

**pel|li|cle** (pel′ə kəl), *n.* a very thin skin; external membrane: *The outer covering of Paramecium is called the pellicle, which is a tough, yet flexible material that enables the animal to maintain its definite shape* (A. M. Winchester). [< Latin *pellicula* (diminutive) < *pellis* skin]

**pel|lic|u|lar** (pə lik′yə lər), *adj.* having the character or quality of a pellicle.

**pel|li|to|ry** (pel′ə tôr′ē, -tōr′-), *n., pl.* **-ries. 1** Also, **pellitory of Spain.** a composite plant growing chiefly in Algeria. Its pungent root is used in medicine as a local irritant and sedative. **2** any one of a group of herbs related to the nettle, such as the wall pellitory. **3** any one of several similar plants, such as the yarrow and feverfew. [fusion of earlier *pelytory,* Middle English *pelestre* < Anglo-French, Old French *piretre,* ultimately < Greek *pyretós* fever, and of earlier *pelletorie,* alteration of Middle English *paritarie* < Anglo-French < Late Latin *parietāria* (*herba*) wall (plant) < *pariēs, -etis* wall]

**pell-mell** or **pell|mell** (pel′mel′), *adv., adj., n.* —*adv.* **1** in a rushing, tumbling mass or crowd: *The children dashed pell-mell down to the beach and into the waves.* **2** in headlong haste: *She had made her escape that way, and down after her they rushed, pell-mell* (W. H. Hudson).
—*adj.* headlong; tumultuous: *The pell-mell rush of industrial activity has started the railroads clicking faster, too* (Newsweek).
—*n.* a violent disorder or confusion: *It is the men who are the casualties of this pell-mell* (New Yorker).
[< French *pêle-mêle* < Old French *pesle mesle;* latter element apparently < *mesler* mix. Compare etym. under **melee, medley.**]

**pel|lu|cid** (pə lü′sid), *adj.* **1** transparent; clear: *the pellucid water of a mountain lake, a pellucid sky.* **2** *Figurative.* clearly expressed; easy to understand: *pellucid language, a pellucid style.* [< Latin *pellūcidus* < *perlūcēre* < *per-* through + *lūcēre* to shine. Compare etym. under **lucid.**] —**pel|lu′cid|ly,** *adv.* —**pel|lu′cid|ness,** *n.*

**pel|lu|cid|i|ty** (pel′yə sid′ə tē), *n.* pellucid quality; pellucidness.

**Pel|man|ism** (pel′mə niz əm), *n.* the training system of the Pelman Institute, a British educational organization concerned with the learning and memorizing processes.

**pel|met** (pel′mit), *n.* a valance or similar covering over a door or window to conceal a curtain rod.

**Pel|o|pon|ne|sian** (pel′ə pə nē′shən, -zhən), *adj., n.* —*adj.* of or having to do with the Peloponnesus, a peninsula in Greece, or its people.
—*n.* a person born or living in the Peloponnesus.

**Pe|lops** (pē′lops), *n. Greek Mythology.* a son of Tantalus, and father of Atreus and Thyestes, served to the gods as food, but later restored to life by them.

**pe|lo|ri|a** (pə lôr′ē ə, -lōr′-), *n. Botany.* regularity or symmetry of structure occurring abnormally in flowers normally irregular or unsymmetrical. [< New Latin *peloria* < Greek *pélōros* monstrous < *pélōr* a prodigy]

**pe|lor|ic** (pə lôr′ik, -lor′-), *adj.* characterized by peloria.

**pel|o|rize** (pel′ə rīz), *v.t.,* **-rized, -riz|ing.** to affect with peloria: *The most perfectly pelorized examples had six petals, each marked with black striae like those on the standard petal* (Charles Darwin). —**pel′o|ri|za′tion,** *n.*

**pel|o|ro|vis** (pel′ə rō′vis), *n.* an extinct prehistoric giant sheep with a horn spread of twelve feet. [< New Latin *Pelorovis* the genus name < Greek *pélōr* prodigy + Latin *ovis* sheep]

***pe|lo|rus** (pə lôr′əs, -lōr′-), *n.* a device used on ships for taking bearings, consisting typically of a circular metal plate set in gimbals and having mounted on its surface a compass card and alidade, each of which may be revolved independently of the other. [< *Pelorus,* supposedly Hannibal's navigator on his return from Italy]

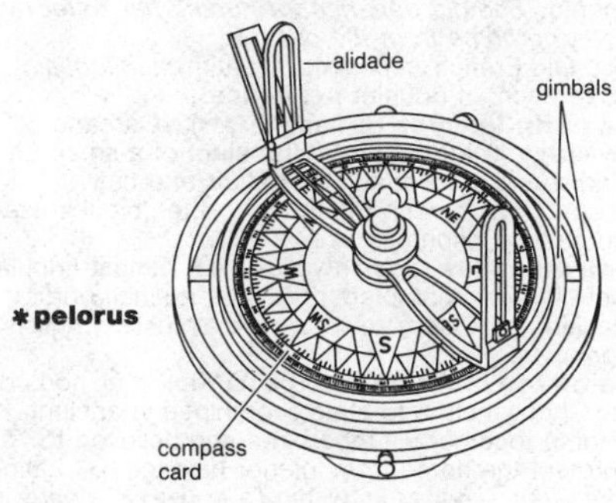

***pelorus**

**pe|lo|ta** (pe lō′tə; *Spanish* pā lō′tä), *n.* **1a** a game of Basque or Spanish origin played on a walled court with a hard rubber ball. **b** the ball, caught and slung back with a curved wicker racket strapped over the hand and lower arm: *After the pelota, a rubber-cored ball, is smacked against the wall, an opposition player must catch it and fire it back before it has bounced more than once* (Time). **2** the game of jai alai, or the ball used in this game. [< Spanish *pelota* < *pella* ball < Latin *pila*]

**pelt**[1] (pelt), *v., n.* —*v.t.* **1** to throw things at; assail: *The children were pelting each other with snowballs.* (*Figurative.*) *The attorney pelted the witness with angry questions.* **2** to beat heavily or continuously upon: *Hail pelted the roof.* **3** to throw; hurl: *The clouds pelted rain upon us.*
—*v.i.* **1** to beat heavily or continuously: *The rain came pelting down.* **2** to throw. **3** to go rapidly; hurry.
—*n.* **1** a pelting. **2** speed: *The horse is coming at full pelt.*
[earlier, to strike repeatedly, perhaps variant of Middle English *pilt, pult* thrust; influenced by *pellet*] —**pelt′er,** *n.*

**pelt**[2] (pelt), *n.* **1** the skin of a sheep, goat, or small fur-bearing animal, before it is tanned. SYN: See syn. under **skin. 2** the raw skin of a sheep, goat, or other animal stripped of its wool or fur and ready for tanning. **3** something likened to the pelt of an animal: *his powerful arms folded on the grizzled pelt of his bare breast* (Joseph Conrad). **4a** a skin of an animal worn as a garment. **b** a garment made of a skin. [probably back formation < *peltry*]

**pel|ta** (pel′tə), *n., pl.* **-tae** (-tē). a kind of light, small, leather shield used especially by the ancient Greeks. [< Latin *pelta* < Greek *péltē* small leather shield]

**pel|tast** (pel′tast), *n.* an ancient Greek soldier armed with a pelta. [< Latin *peltasta* < Greek *peltastês* < *péltē* small leather shield]

**pel|tate** (pel′tāt), *adj. Botany.* shield-shaped: **a** (of a leaf) having the petiole attached to the lower surface of the blade at or near the middle (instead of at the base or end). **b** (of stalked parts) having a similar attachment. [< Latin *pelta* shield (< Greek *péltē*) + English *-ate*[1]] —**pel′tate|ly,** *adv.*

**Pel|tier effect** (pel tyā′), a heating or cooling effect produced by the passage of an electric current through the junction of two dissimilar metals, the heating or cooling depending on the direction of the current. [< Jean *Peltier,* 1785-1845, a French physicist, who discovered it]

**pelt|ing** (pel′ting), *adj. Archaic.* paltry; petty; mean. [probably related to dialectal *palt* or *pelt* thrash; see etym. under **paltry**]

**Pel|ton wheel** (pel′tən), a form of water wheel or turbine having cup-shaped buckets arranged around its circumference, which are struck at a tangent by one or more jets of water moving at a high velocity. [< Lester A. *Pelton,* an American engineer of the 1800's, who invented it]

**pelt|ry** (pel′trē), *n., pl.* **-ries. 1** pelts; skins; furs. **2** a pelt: *The traders Touching at times on the coast, to barter and chaffer for peltries* (Longfellow). [< Anglo-French *pelterie,* Old French *peleterie* < *peletier* furrier < *pel* skin < Latin *pellis*]

**pe|lure** (pə lůr′, -lyůr′), *n.* a crisp, hard, very thin paper. [< French *pelure* < Old French *peleüre* < *peler* to peel]

**pel|vic** (pel′vik), *adj., n.* —*adj.* of, having to do with, or in the region of the pelvis.
—*n.* = pelvic fin.

**pelvic arch** or **girdle,** the bony or cartilaginous arch supporting the hindlimbs of vertebrates, in man formed by the innominate bones and the sacrum: *Each side of the pelvic girdle consists of an ilium, ischium, and pubis* (A. Franklin Shull).

**pelvic fin,** either of a pair of fins in fishes situated on the fore part of the lower surface of the body, and corresponding to the hindlimbs of higher vertebrates; ventral fin. See picture under **fin**[1].

**pel|vi|met|ric** (pel′və met′rik), *adj.* of or having to do with pelvimetry: *pelvimetric X rays.*

**pel|vim|et|ry** (pel vim′ə trē), *n.* the measurement of the size of the pelvis, especially of the female, manually, by instrument, or by X rays.

***pel|vis** (pel′vis), *n., pl.* **-ves** (-vēz). **1** the basin-shaped cavity in human beings formed by the hipbones and the end of the backbone. **2** the corresponding cavity of any vertebrate. **3** the bones forming this cavity: *At the hips is the hip girdle, or pelvis, to which the leg bones are attached* (Beauchamp, Mayfield and West). **4** the expanded upper end of the ureter, forming a basinlike cavity in the kidney, which collects urine before its passage into the ureter. [< Latin *pelvis* basin < Greek *pellís, -idos* basin, pelvis]

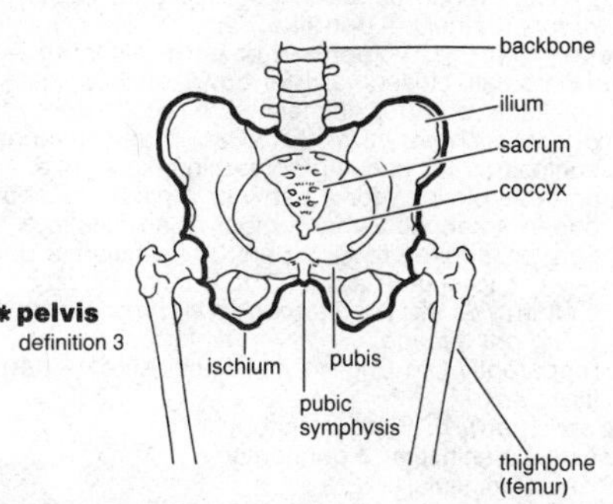

***pelvis**
definition 3

**pel|y|co|saur** (pel′ə kō sôr), *n.* a prehistoric carnivorous reptile, sometimes more than eight feet in length, which had a tall spiny fin along its back and a few early mammalian characteristics: *Pelycosaurs were ancestors of the mammal-like reptiles called therapsids, and both belong to groups that form links between mammals and reptiles* (Science News Letter). [< New Latin *Pelycosauria* the division name < Greek *pélyx, -ykos* bowl (taken as "pelvis") + *saûros* lizard]

**Pem|a|quid** (pem′ə kwid), *n., pl.* **-quids** or **-quid.** a member of an Algonkian tribe of North American Indians friendly to the Pilgrim settlers of Plymouth Colony.

**Pem|broke** (pem′brůk, -brōk), *n.* one of the two varieties of the Welsh corgi breed of dogs, characterized by a relatively short tail. [< *Pembroke,* a town in Wales]

**Pembroke table,** a kind of drop-leaf table.

**pem|mi|can** or **pem|i|can** (pem′ə kən), *n.* **1** dried, lean meat pounded into a paste with melted fat and pressed into cakes. It was an important food among certain tribes of North American Indians. **2** a somewhat similar preparation, usually of beef, with sugar, currants, and other flavoring food: *A Cree Indian word for the conglomerate mixture of dried, shredded, and pounded meats, berries, roots, seeds, and whatever good or bad extraneous object may become trapped in the kneading, pemmican was—and is to this day—the "bread of life" of cold-country explorers* (Wall Street Journal). [American English < Algonkian (Cree) *pimikan* < *pimikew* he makes grease < *pimiy* grease]

**pem|o|line** (pem′ə lēn), *n.* **1** a synthetic drug used as a stimulant or to relieve depression: *Pemoline has been known sometime to be a mild brain stimulant, midway in strength between amphetamine and coffee* (Sunday Times). *Formula:* $C_9H_8N_2O_2$. **2** = magnesium pemoline. [perhaps < its chemical components *p*(h)*e*(nyli)*m*(ino-oxaz)-*oli*(dino)*ne*]

**pem|phi|goid** (pem′fə goid, pem fī′-), *adj.* like or of the nature of pemphigus.

**pem|phi|gus** (pem′fə gəs, pem fī′-), *n.* a disease of the skin and mucous membranes characterized by eruption of large bubble-like blisters. [< New Latin *pemphigus* < Greek *pémphix, -īgos* pustule, blister; drop of liquid; blast of air]

**pen**[1] (pen), *n., v.,* **penned, pen|ning.** —*n.* **1a** an instrument with a point to use in writing or drawing with ink, such as a ballpoint pen, a fountain pen, or a quill. Some pens hold their own ink; others must be dipped into ink. **b** such a tool fixed to a recording device to make a written record of measurements on a graph. **2a** = penpoint.

**Pronunciation Key:** hat, āge, cãre, fär; let, ēqual, tėrm; it, īce; hot, ōpen, ôrder; oil, out; cup, pu̇t, rüle; child; long; thin; ᴛʜen; zh, measure; ə represents **a** in about, **e** in taken, **i** in pencil, **o** in lemon, **u** in circus.

**b** a penpoint and holder together. **3** *Figurative.* a style of writing; writing: *to use a bitter and ironic pen. The pen is mightier than the sword* (Edward G. Bulwer-Lytton). **b** a writer; author: [*A book*] *wherein a second Pen had a good share* (Ben Jonson). **4** = pinfeather. **5** *Zoology.* the internal, somewhat feather-shaped shell of various cephalopods, such as the squids. **6** a female swan: *The male swan is called a cob, and the female a pen* (R. Meyer de Schauensee). **7** *Archaic.* a feather or quill. **8** *Dialect.* anything similar to or suggesting a feather, such as the midrib of a leaf.
—***v.t.*** **1** to put into writing; write: *I penned a few words to father today.* **2** to draw up (a document).
**dip one's pen in gall,** to write with hatred and spite: *Swift dipped his pen in gall when he described the stupidities and vices of mankind in "Gulliver's Travels."*
[< Old French *penne* pinion, quill pen < Latin *penna* feather] —**pen′like′**, *adj.*

**pen²** (pen), *n., v.,* **penned** or **pent, pen|ning.** —***n.*** **1a** a small, closed yard for cows, sheep, pigs, chickens, or other animals: *The rabbits were in a pen of stiff wire in the backyard.* **b** any of various enclosures for keeping something, such as a portable playpen for a baby, or a place to keep a dog in a kennel. **2** the number of animals in a pen, or required to fill a pen. **3** = submarine pen.
—***v.t.*** **1** to shut in a pen. **2** to confine closely; shut in: *He had me penned in a corner where I could not escape.*
[apparently Old English *penn* enclosure] —**pen′like′**, *adj.*

**pen³** (pen), *n. Slang.* penitentiary.

**pen.,** **1** peninsula. **2** penitentiary.

**Pen.,** Peninsula.

**P.E.N.,** International Association of Poets, Playwrights, Editors, Essayists, and Novelists.

**pe|nal** (pē′nəl), *adj.* **1** of, having to do with, or given as punishment: *penal laws, penal labor.* **2** liable to be punished: *Robbery is a penal offense.* **3** used as a place of punishment: *a penal colony.* [< Latin *poenālis* < *poena* punishment < Greek *poinē* penalty] —**pe′nal|ly**, *adv.*

**penal code,** a code of laws dealing with crime and its punishment.

**pe|nal|ise** (pē′nə līz, pen′ə-), *v.t.,* **-ised, -is|ing.** *Especially British.* penalize.

**pe|nal|i|za|tion** (pē′nə lə zā′shən), *n.* the act of penalizing: *There must be an incentive to invest capital and no penalization of enterprise and risk-taking* (Wall Street Journal).

**pe|nal|ize** (pē′nə līz, pen′ə-), *v.t.,* **-ized, -iz|ing.** **1** to declare punishable by law or by rule; set a penalty for: *Speeding on city streets is penalized. Fouls are penalized in many games.* **2** to inflict a penalty on; punish: *Our football team was penalized five yards for being offside.* **3** *Figurative: His deafness penalizes him in public life.* —**pe′nal|iz′er**, *n.*

**pen|al|ty** (pen′əl tē), *n., pl.* **-ties.** **1** a punishment: *The penalty for speeding is a fine of fifteen dollars.* **2** a disadvantage placed on a side or player for breaking the rules of some game or contest. **3** *Figurative: the penalties of old age.* **SYN:** disadvantage. **4** something forfeited by a person if an obligation is not fulfilled. **5** = handicap. [alteration of earlier *penality* < Medieval Latin *poenalitas* < Latin *poenālis* having to do with punishment; see etym. under **penal**]

**penalty box,** an enclosure alongside an ice hockey rink where penalized players must stay during the period in which they are barred from play: *The Vees lost a man to the penalty box at 8:10 when McAvoy made a body check against the boards* (Penticton, British Columbia, Herald).

**penalty goal,** a goal scored upon a penalty kick in either Rugby or soccer: *In the 16th minute of the first half T. E. Davies kicked a fine penalty goal for Wales from 35 yards, and wide out* (Sunday Times).

**penalty kick,** (in soccer and Rugby) a free kick, without interference, trying for a goal, awarded to a team because of a major infraction of the rules by their opponents.

**pen|ance** (pen′əns), *n., v.,* **-anced, -anc|ing.** —***n.*** **1** a punishment borne to show sorrow for sin, to make up for a wrong done, and to obtain pardon for sin: *When the scourge Inexorably, and the torturing hour Calls us to penance* (Milton). **2** a sacrament of the Roman Catholic, Greek, and other churches, that includes repentance, intention to amend, full confession of sin to a priest, submission to penalty, and absolution.
—***v.t.*** to impose penance on; punish or discipline by requiring a penance.
**do penance,** to perform some act, or undergo some penalty, to show that one is sorry or repents: *She did penance for hurting her sister by staying home from the circus.*
[< Old French *peneance* < Latin *paenitentia.* See etym. of doublet **penitence.**]

**Pronunciation Key:** hat, āge, cãre, fär; let, ēqual, tėrm; it, īce; hot, ōpen, ôrder; oil, out; cup, pu̇t, rüle; child; long; thin; ᴛʜen; zh, measure; ə represents **a** in about, **e** in taken, **i** in pencil, **o** in lemon, **u** in circus.

**pe|nang-law|yer** (pi nang′lô′yər), *n.* a cane or walking stick made from the stem of a small East Indian palm. [probably alteration of a native name; *lawyer,* with reference to the object's use in settling disputes]

**pen|an|nu|lar** (pe nan′yə lər), *adj.* almost annular; forming an incomplete ring (with a small portion lacking). [< Latin *pēne, paene* almost + English *annular*]

**pe|na|tes** or **Pe|na|tes** (pə nā′tēz), *n.pl.* gods of the household and state, worshiped in ancient Rome together with the lares and believed to protect the home from interior damage. [< Latin *Penātēs* < *penes* in, within (a house) < *penus* inner room (sanctuary of a temple); provisions]

**pence** (pens), *n.* more than one English penny: *Tobacco and paint shares closed a few pence dearer among the industrial shares* (London Times). *Abbr:* (in the old system) d (no period); (in the new decimal system) p (no period).

**pen|cel** (pen′səl), *n.* **1** *Archaic.* a small streamer, especially one carried as a banner on a lance. **2** *Obsolete.* a lady's favor worn or carried by a knight. Also, **pennoncel, pennoncelle, penoncel, pensil, pensile.** [< Anglo-French *pensil,* Old French *penoncel* (diminutive) < *penon,* or *pannon* pennon]

**pen|chant** (pen′chənt), *n.* a strong taste or liking; inclination: *a penchant for taking long walks.* **SYN:** bent. [< French *penchant,* (literally) present participle of Old French *pencher* to incline < Vulgar Latin *pendicāre* < Latin *pendēre* to hang]

**pen|cil** (pen′səl), *n., v.,* **-ciled, -cil|ing** or (*especially British*) **-cilled, -cil|ling.** —***n.*** **1** a pointed instrument to write or draw with, usually with a slender rod of graphite encased in wood or in a metal tube. **2** any object of like shape: *a styptic pencil.* **3** a stick of coloring matter: *an eyebrow pencil.* **4** *Figurative.* the skill or style of an artist. **5** *Archaic.* an artist's paintbrush: *Take your pallet ... choose your most delicate camel-hair pencils* (Charlotte Brontë). **6** a set of lines, light rays, or the like, coming to a point or extending in different directions from a point: *The light used for all practical purposes comes from sources of finite area, every point of which emits a pencil* (Hardy and Perrin).
—***v.t.*** **1** to mark or write with a pencil: *to pencil corrections in the margin of a book, to pencil a note.* **2** to draw or sketch with a pencil: *to pencil an outline of a house.*
**pencil in,** to include, list, or schedule, especially in haste: *to pencil in an increase in the budget. An unknown actor was penciled in to play the leading role.*
[< Old French *pincel,* ultimately < Latin *pēnicillus* painter's brush, pencil (diminutive) < *pēnis* (originally) tail] —**pen′cil|er** or (*especially British*) **pen′cil|ler**, *n.* —**pen′cil|like′**, *adj.*

**pencil beam,** a narrow, conical radar beam, used for homing in on a target with maximum accuracy.

**pen|ciled** (pen′səld), *adj.* **1** marked with or as with a pencil: *her soft, penciled eyebrows* (Harriet Beecher Stowe). **2** executed, drawn, or written with or as with a pencil: *penciled lines, a penciled note.* **3** formed into a pencil or pencils, as rays; radiated.

**pen|cil|i|form** (pen sil′ə fôrm), *adj.* having the form or appearance of a pencil, as of rays.

**pen|cil|ing** (pen′sə ling), *n.* **1** the act of one who pencils. **2** fine coloring or delicate drawing, as may be done with a pencil.

**pencil pusher,** *Slang.* an office worker; person who works at a desk.

**pencil sharpener,** a device for sharpening a wooden pencil by shaving it with a blade or series of rotating blades.

**pen|craft** (pen′kraft′, -kräft′), *n.* writing; penmanship; authorship.

**pend¹** (pend), *v.i.* **1** to remain undecided or unsettled. **2** *Dialect.* to depend. [back formation < *pending*]

**pend²** (pend), *n. Scottish.* a pendant.

**pend|ant** (pen′dənt), *n., adj.* —***n.*** **1** a hanging ornament, such as a locket. **2** an ornament hanging down from an arch, ceiling, or roof. **3** *Figurative.* a person or thing forming a parallel or match to another; match; companion piece. **4** an additional statement, consideration, or the like, that completes or complements another. **5** an attachment by which something is suspended, such as the ring and stem of a pocket watch. **6** *British, Nautical.* pennant: *I hoisted my pendant on the Irresistible* (Horatio Nelson).
—***adj.*** = pendent.
[< Old French *pendant,* (originally) present participle *pendre* to hang < Vulgar Latin *pendere* < Latin *pendēre*]

**pende|loque** (pänd lôk′), *n. French.* a pear-shaped pendant, as a diamond cut in this form. See picture under **gem.**

**pend|en|cy** (pen′dən sē), *n., pl.* **-cies.** the state or condition of being pending or continuing undecided or awaiting settlement: *The mere pendency of such charges impairs my further service on the commission* (Newsweek).

**pend|ent** (pen′dənt), *adj., n.* —***adj.*** **1** hanging: *the pendent branches of a willow.* **SYN:** suspended. **2** overhanging: *a pendent cliff.* **3** *Figurative.* = pending.
—***n.*** = pendant.
[< Latin *pendēns, -entis,* present participle of *pendēre* to hang] —**pend′ent|ly**, *adv.*

**pen|den|te li|te** (pen den′tē lī′tē), *Latin.* during litigation; while a lawsuit is pending.

**pen|den|tive** (pen den′tiv), *n. Architecture.* **1** the concave, triangular segment of the lower part of a hemispherical dome, between two adjacent penetrating arches: *Builders achieved the transition from a square space to a circular dome by inserting pendentives* (*spherical triangles*) *over the four corners* (Cyril Mango). **2** a similar segment of a groined vault that springs from a single support. [< earlier French *pendentif* < Latin *pendēns;* see etym. under **pendent**]

**pen|di|cle** (pen′də kəl), *n. Scottish.* **1** a pendant. **2** an adjunct or appendage. **3** a small piece of land, a cottage, or the like, attached to an estate. [diminutive form of Latin *pendēre* to hang]

**pend|ing** (pen′ding), *adj., prep.* —***adj.*** **1** waiting to be decided or settled: *while the agreement was pending.* **2** likely to happen soon; threatening; about to occur. **3** overhanging.
—***prep.*** **1** while waiting for; until: *Pending his return, let us get everything ready.* **2** during: *pending the investigation.*

**pen|drag|on** or **Pen|drag|on** (pen drag′ən), *n.* chief leader, ruler, or king, a title of ancient British chiefs: *the dread Pendragon, Britain's King of kings* (Tennyson). [< Welsh *pendragon* < *pen* chief + *dragon* war leader; dragon standard < Latin *dracō, -ōnis* the dragon emblem of a cohort]

**pen|drag|on|ship** or **Pen|drag|on|ship** (pen-drag′ən ship), *n.* the state, condition, or power of a pendragon.

**pen|du|lar** (pen′jə lər, -dyə-), *adj.* **1** of or having to do with a pendulum. **2** resembling the movement of a pendulum; oscillating: (*Figurative.*) *History may suggest pendular swings, but history has never before seen the breadth of communication and the speed of change* (*some of it progress*) *that we have today* (Maclean's).

**pen|du|lous** (pen′jə ləs, -dyə-), *adj.* **1** hanging loosely: *The oriole builds a pendulous nest.* **2** swinging like a pendulum: *pendulous jowls.* [< Latin *pendulus* (with English *-ous*) < *pendēre* hang] —**pen′du|lous|ly**, *adv.* —**pen′du|lous|ness**, *n.*

**pen|du|lous-eared cat** (pen′jə ləs ird′, -dyə-), a breed of cat native to China, having long, droopy ears; lop-eared cat.

**pen|du|lum** (pen′jə ləm, -dyə-), *n.* a weight so hung from a fixed point that it is free to swing to and fro. It moves through a regular arc under the influence of gravity. The movement of the works of a tall clock is often timed by a pendulum. *The utility of the pendulum as a timekeeper is based on the fact that the period is practically independent of the amplitude* (Sears and Zemansky). [< New Latin *pendulum,* (literally) neuter of Latin *pendulus* pendulous]

**Pe|nel|o|pe** (pə nel′ə pē), *n. Greek Legend.* the faithful wife of Odysseus. She waited twenty years for his return in spite of the entreaties of her many suitors.

*** pe|ne|plain** (pē′nə plān′), *n., v.* —***n.*** a formerly mountainous or hilly area reduced nearly to a plain by erosion: *There is evidence of several peneplains during Cenozoic time in the Appalachians, indicating crustal uplift, renewed uplift, erosion, etc.* (Robert M. Garrels). See picture opposite on next page.
—***v.t.*** to make a peneplain of, as by erosion.
[American English < Latin *pēne,* or *paene* almost + English *plain*]

**pe|ne|pla|na|tion** (pē′nə plə nā′shən), *n.* the forming of a peneplain by erosion: *Peneplanation, especially in a region of much disturbed hard rocks, is judged to demand very prolonged work of erosive processes during time when the land surface was neither raised nor lowered appreciably by earth deformation* (Raymond Cecil Moore).

**pe|ne|plane** (pē′nə plān), *n., v.t.,* **-planed, -plan|ing.** = peneplain.

**pen|e|tra|bil|i|ty** (pen′ə trə bil′ə tē), *n.* capability of being penetrated.

**pen|e|tra|ble** (pen′ə trə bəl), *adj.* that can be

penetrated: *It is not penetrable by the eye of man* (Edward Topsell). [< Latin *penetrābilis* < *penetrāre* to penetrate] —**pen′e|tra|ble|ness**, *n.*

**pen|e|tra|bly** (pen′ə trə blē), *adv.* so as to be penetrable: ... *to make their prayers more penetrably enforcing* (Thomas Nashe).

**pen|e|tra|li|a** (pen′ə trā′lē ə), *n. pl.* **1** the innermost parts or recesses of a building, especially the sanctuary or inmost shrine of a temple: *Mr. Campbell ... is fain to ... retire into the penetralia of his habitation, in order to avoid this diurnal annoyance* (Tobias Smollett). **2** innermost parts; secret or hidden recesses: *to disclose the very penetralia of my heart* (Charles J. Lever). [< Latin *penetrālia,* neuter plural of *penetrālis* interior, inmost < *penetrāre* to penetrate]

**pen|e|tra|li|um** (pen′ə trā′lē əm), *n.* the most secret or hidden part: *The novice ... may be found unworthy of acceptance in the inner penetralium and be rejected* (George Steiner). [< *penetralia*]

**pen|e|trance** (pen′ə trəns), *n.* **1** the action of penetrating; penetration. **2** *Genetics.* the measurement, expressed in percentages, of the ability of a gene to manifest itself or its effects: *Penetrance refers to the regularity with which a gene produces a detectable effect* (Hegner and Stiles).

**pen|e|trant** (pen′ə trənt), *adj., n.* —***adj.*** = penetrating.
—***n.*** a person or thing that penetrates; penetrator.

**pen|e|trate** (pen′ə trāt), *v.,* **-trat|ed, -trat|ing.**
—***v.t.*** **1** to get into or through: *A bullet can penetrate this wall, or two inches into that wall.* **2** to pierce through: *Our eyes could not penetrate the darkness.* **3** to soak through; spread through: *The aroma of fresh bread penetrated the whole house. The rain penetrated our clothes.* **SYN**: pervade, permeate. **4** *Figurative.* to see into or through; understand: *I could not penetrate the mystery.* **SYN**: discern, comprehend. **5** *Figurative.* to affect or impress very much.
—***v.i.*** **1** to pass through; make a way: *Even where the trees were thickest, the sunshine penetrated.* **2** *Figurative.* to affect the feelings: *I advised him to give her music o′ mornings; they say it will penetrate* (Shakespeare).
[< Latin *penetrāre* (with English *-ate*[1]) < *penitus* deep within, related to *penes* within; see etym. under **penates**]
—***Syn.*** *v.t.* **1 Penetrate, pierce** mean to go into or through something. **Penetrate** implies going deeply into something and suggests both a driving force and resistance to it: *The arrow penetrated the board.* **Pierce** implies stabbing through the surface, or passing right through, with a sharp-pointed object or something sharp and cutting, such as a knife: *She had the lobes of her ears pierced for earrings.*

**pen|e|trat|ing** (pen′ə trā′ting), *adj.* **1** sharp; piercing: *a penetrating sound, a penetrating odor.* **2** *Figurative.* having or showing insight; understanding thoroughly; acute; discerning: *a penetrating mind, penetrating criticism. Nature herself seems ... to write for him with her own bare, sheer, penetrating power* (Matthew Arnold).
—**pen′e|trat′ing|ly,** *adv.*

**pen|e|tra|tion** (pen′ə trā′shən), *n.* **1** the act or power of penetrating: *Only a drill will make penetration of that wall possible.* **2** the act of entering a country and gaining influence there: *economic penetration.* **3** *Figurative.* sharpness of intellect; insight: *You can pretend to be a man of penetration* (Sir Richard Steele). **SYN**: acumen, acuteness, shrewdness, discernment. See syn. under **insight. 4** the depth to which a projectile will enter a material at a given range. **5a** the power in a telescope of making distant objects visible or distinct, considered in relation to their distance. **b** the power in the objective of a microscope to give distinct vision for some distance both beyond and within its exact focus.

**pen|e|tra|tive** (pen′ə trā′tiv), *adj.* penetrating; piercing: (*Figurative.*) *the penetrative character of temptations* (Richard C. Trench). *Perhaps one can distinguish between the great scientist and the researcher who is a mere technician largely on the basis of the penetrative logic of the former* (John E. Owen). **SYN**: acute, keen. —**pen′e|tra′tive|ly,** *adv.* —**pen′e|tra′tive|ness,** *n.*

**pen|e|tra|tor** (pen′ə trā′tər), *n.* a person or thing that penetrates: (*Figurative.*) *He is the perfect penetrator into human vices* (Edward G. Bulwer-Lytton).

**pen|e|trom|e|ter** (pen′ə trom′ə tər), *n.* an instrument designed to measure the density, compactness, or penetrability of a substance. A marine penetrometer records the firmness of the sediment at the bottom of the ocean. *The penetrometer was designed for use in marine geological and biological research* (Science News Letter).

**pen|friend** or **pen-friend** (pen′frend′), *n. Especially British.* a pen pal: *The teacher asked if I would correspond with one of the islanders who wanted a pen-friend* (Cape Times).

**P.Eng.,** Professional Engineer.

**peng|hu|lu** (peng hü′lü), *n.* (in the area of the Malay Peninsula and Borneo) a village or tribal chief: *The elderly penghulu, or headman, of an Iban tribe of Sea Dayaks invited* [*us*] *to spend a night at his long house before we sailed* (London Times). [< Indonesian *penghulu*]

**pen|gö** (peng′gœ), *n., pl.* **-gö, -gös** (-gœz). **1** the standard unit of money of Hungary from 1925 to 1946, superseded by the forint. **2** a silver coin or a bank note, representing this unit. [< Hungarian *pengö* (literally) present participle of *peng* to sound, ring; imitative]

***penguin** definition 1

***pen|guin** (pen′gwin, peng′-), *n.* **1** a sea bird with flippers for diving and swimming in place of wings for flying. Penguins live chiefly in Antarctica and other cold areas of the Southern Hemisphere. They are short-legged with webbed feet, and have black and white plumage. There are several kinds, making up an order of birds. *Lady penguins lay only one egg a year and guard it well* (New York Times). **2** an apparatus for training airplane pilots, having stubby wings, a tail, motor, and controls, but capable of being maneuvered only on the ground. **3** any one of a class of racing dinghies with one mast set far forward. **4** *Slang.* an aviator who does not fly; administrative officer in the air force. **5** *Obsolete.* the great auk. [supposedly < Welsh *pen* head + *gwyn* white]

**penguin suit,** *Slang.* an astronaut's space suit.

**pen|hold|er** (pen′hōl′dər), *n.* **1** the handle by which a pen is held in writing. **2** a rack for pens.

**pen|i|cil** (pen′ə sil), *n.* a small bundle or tuft of slightly diverging hairs, resembling a paintbrush, such as those on a caterpillar. [< Latin *pēnicillus;* see etym. under **pencil**]

**pen|i|cil|la|mine** (pen′ə sil′ə mēn), *n.* an amino acid derived from penicillin, used as a chelating agent. *Formula:* $C_5H_{11}NO_2S$

**pen|i|cil|late** (pen′ə sil′it, -āt), *adj.* having or forming a small tuft or tufts of hairs, scales, or feathers; furnished with a penicil or penicils. [< Latin *pēnicillus* (see etym. under **pencil**) + English *-ate*[1]] —**pen′i|cil′late|ly,** *adv.*

**pen|i|cil|la|tion** (pen′ə sə lā′shən), *n.* a growth of hairs, scales, etc., in the form of a penicil.

**pen|i|cil|lin** (pen′ə sil′in), *n.* a very powerful drug for destroying bacteria. It is made from a fungus or penicillium mold. Penicillin is effective against various harmful bacteria, such as some strains of staphylococci, gonococci, and pneumococci. *Although penicillin is the least poisonous antibiotic available, a few persons become sensitive, or allergic, to it* (Howard W. Florey). *Formula:* $C_{16}H_{17}N_2O_4SNa$ [< *penicill*(ium) + *-in*]

**pen|i|cil|lin|ase** (pen′ə sil′ə nās), *n.* an enzyme that destroys penicillin, produced by many forms of bacteria and used to neutralize allergic reactions to penicillin: *If a person is known to be penicillin sensitive, either a penicillin-free vaccine should be administered or an injection of penicillinase given before the vaccine shot* (Science News Letter).

**pen|i|cil|li|um** (pen′ə sil′ē əm), *n., pl.* **-cil|li|ums, -cil|li|a** (-sil′ē ə). any one of a group of fungi, including several of the common molds, such as two kinds used in ripening cheese, and a kind that forms crusts on jellies and jams. It is a green or bluish-green ascomycetous fungus. The group also includes species used in the production of penicillin and certain other antibiotic drugs. [< New Latin *Penicillium* the genus name < Latin *pēnicillus* small brush or tail; see etym. under **pencil**]

**pen|i|cil|lo|ic acid** (pen′ə sə lō′ik), the resultant product, no longer antigenic, after the neutralization and breakdown of penicillin by penicillinase: *It acts by rapidly breaking down penicillin to penicilloic acid, which has no antibiotic activity and which does not create sensitivity* (Observer).

**pe|nile** (pē′nīl), *adj.* of the penis: *penile tumor.*

**pe|nill** (pə nil′), *n., pl.* **-nil|lion** (-nil′yən). **1** a form of improvised verse adapted to an air played on the harp, and sung by the Welsh at an eisteddfod and on other occasions. **2** a stanza of such verse: *The bards ... struck up a sort of consecutive chorus in a series of penillion or stanzas in praise of Maelgon and his heirship* (Thomas Love Peacock). [< Welsh *pennill* verse, stanza (plural

**formation of a peneplain:**

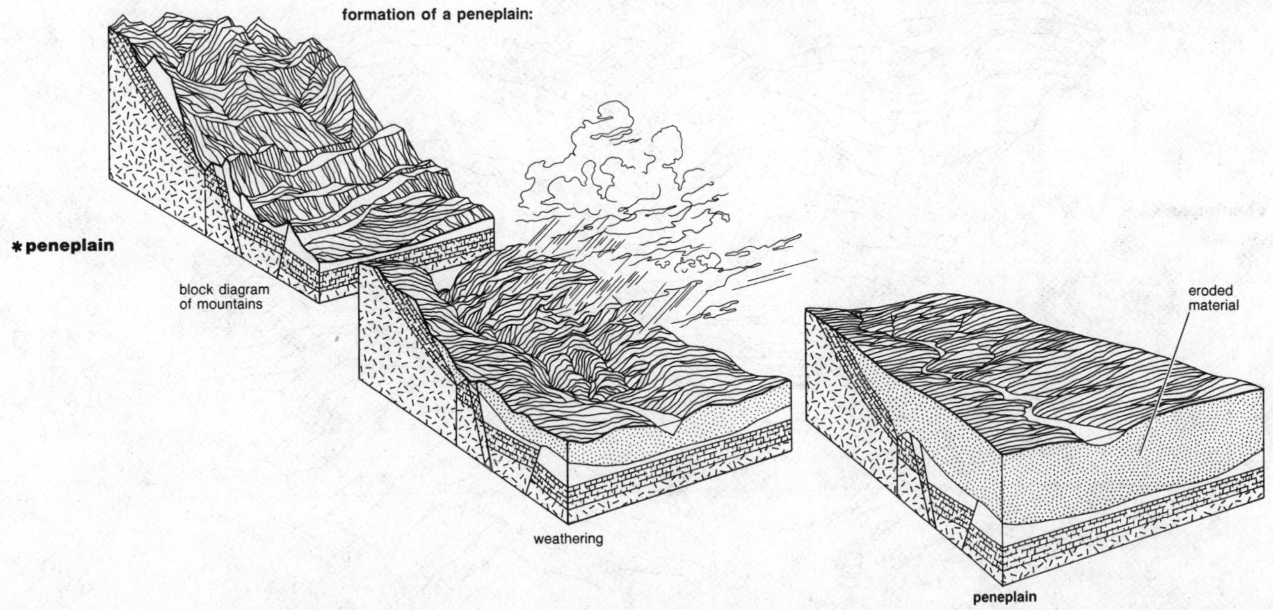

*pennillion, penillion*) < *penn* head]

***pen\|in\|su\|la** (pə nin′sə lə, -syə-), *n.* a piece of land almost surrounded by water, or extending far out into the water. Florida is a peninsula. See picture below. [< Latin *paeninsula* < *paene* almost + *īnsula* island]

**pen\|in\|su\|lar** (pə nin′sə lər, -syə-), *adj., n.* —*adj.* **1** like a peninsula. **2** in or of a peninsula.
—*n.* an inhabitant of a peninsula: *The Arabs traded with the far-off peninsulars* (Nation).

**pen\|in\|su\|lar\|i\|ty** (pə nin′sə lar′ə tē, -syə-), *n.* **1** the state of being a peninsula. **2** *Figurative.* the character or habit of mind attributed to those living in a peninsula and having little contact with other people; narrowness of mind; provincialism: *But a tour through Italy at election time ... conveys the tang of a potent peninsularity* (Manchester Guardian).

**Peninsula State**, a nickname for Florida.

**pen\|in\|su\|late** (pə nin′sə lāt, -syə-), *v.t.,* **-lat\|ed, -lat\|ing.** to form into a peninsula or peninsulas: *There are six considerable rivers which, with their numerous branches, peninsulate the whole state* (Jedidiah Morse). [< *peninsul*(a) + *-ate*[1]]

**pe\|nis** (pē′nis), *n., pl.* **-nis\|es, -nes** (-nēz). the male organ of copulation. Urine leaves the body of male mammals through the penis. [< Latin *pēnis* penis; (originally) tail]

**pen\|i\|tence** (pen′ə təns), *n.* sorrow for sinning or doing wrong; repentance. [< Old French *penitence,* learned borrowing from Latin *paenitentia* < *paenitēns, -entis,* present participle of *paenitēre* repent. See etym. of doublet **penance.**]

**pen\|i\|tent** (pen′ə tənt), *adj., n.* —*adj.* **1** sorry for sinning or doing wrong; repenting: *The penitent boy promised never to cheat again.* **SYN:** repentant, contrite, remorseful. **2** expressing repentance: *a low, penitent voice.*
—*n.* **1** a person who is sorry for sin or wrongdoing. **2** a person who confesses and does penance for his sins under the direction of the church. —**pen′i\|tent\|ly,** *adv.*

**Pen\|i\|ten\|te** (pen′ə ten′tā, -tē), *n.* a member of a religious order of flagellants among certain Spanish-American natives of New Mexico and southern Colorado, who practice flagellantism especially during Holy Week. [< American Spanish *Penitente* (literally) penitent, short for *Hermanos Penitentes* Penitent Brothers (the name of the order)]

**pen\|i\|ten\|tial** (pen′ə ten′shəl), *adj., n.* —*adj.* **1** of, showing, or having to do with penitence: *The penitential psalms express remorse for sin. Mr. Benson, on penitential knee, bent to recover her scattered property* (John Stephen Strange). **2** of or having to do with penance.
—*n.* **1** a person performing or undergoing penance; penitent. **2** a book or code of the church canons on penance and its imposition. —**pen′i\|ten′tial\|ly,** *adv.*

**pen\|i\|ten\|tia\|ry** (pen′ə ten′shər ē), *n., pl.* **-ries,** *adj.* —*n.* **1** a prison for criminals, especially a state or federal prison: *He had worked as a $600-a-month assistant warden at the Huntsville, Texas, state penitentiary, until a convict spotted his picture in an old crime stories magazine* (Newsweek). **2** in the Roman Catholic Church: **a** a diocesan officer empowered to rule on cases of conscience beyond the scope of the parish priest. **b** a congregation of the Papal Curia, presided over by a cardinal, that decides questions of penance.
—*adj.* **1** making one liable to punishment in a prison: *a penitentiary offense.* **2** used for punishment, discipline, and reformation: *penitentiary measures.* **3** of penance; penitential.
[(definition 1) < Medieval Latin *poenitentiaria;* (definition 2) < Medieval Latin *poenitentiarius,* both noun uses of adjective < Latin *paenitentia* penitence]

**pen\|knife** (pen′nīf′), *n., pl.* **-knives.** a small pocketknife.

**pen\|light** or **pen\|lite** (pen′līt′), *n., adj.* —*n.* a small flashlight roughly the size of a fountain pen.
—*adj.* of or having to do with a penlight: *penlight batteries.*

**pen\|lop** (pen′lop), *n.* a powerful territorial lord in Bhutan. [< the native name in Bhutan]

**pen\|man** (pen′mən), *n., pl.* **-men. 1** a writer; author: *the penman of a good mystery story.* **2** a person who has good handwriting: *Before the typewriter many people were fine penmen.* **3** *British.* a person whose work is to copy documents.

**pen\|man\|ship** (pen′mən ship), *n.* **1** writing with pen or pencil; handwriting; calligraphy: *He was criticized for sloppy penmanship.* **2** the manner or style of composing a written work; literary composition.

**Penn.**, Pennsylvania.

**pen\|na** (pen′ə), *n., pl.* **pen\|nae** (pen′ē). a contour feather of a bird, as distinguished from a down feather or plume. [< Latin *penna* feather]

**Penna.**, Pennsylvania.

**pen\|na\|ceous** (pə nā′shəs), *adj.* of or like a penna or pennae. [< New Latin *pennaceus* < Latin *penna* feather]

**pen name**, a name used by a writer instead of his real name; nom de plume; pseudonym: *Voltaire was the pen name of François Marie Arouet, a French author and philosopher* (Otis Fellows). *As a way of sloughing off one personality and acquiring a new one, the pen name is not a new idea, nor historically limited to the arts* (Harper's).

**pen\|nant** (pen′ənt), *n.* **1** a flag, usually long and tapering, used on ships for signaling or identification, or as a school banner. **2** a flag taken as an

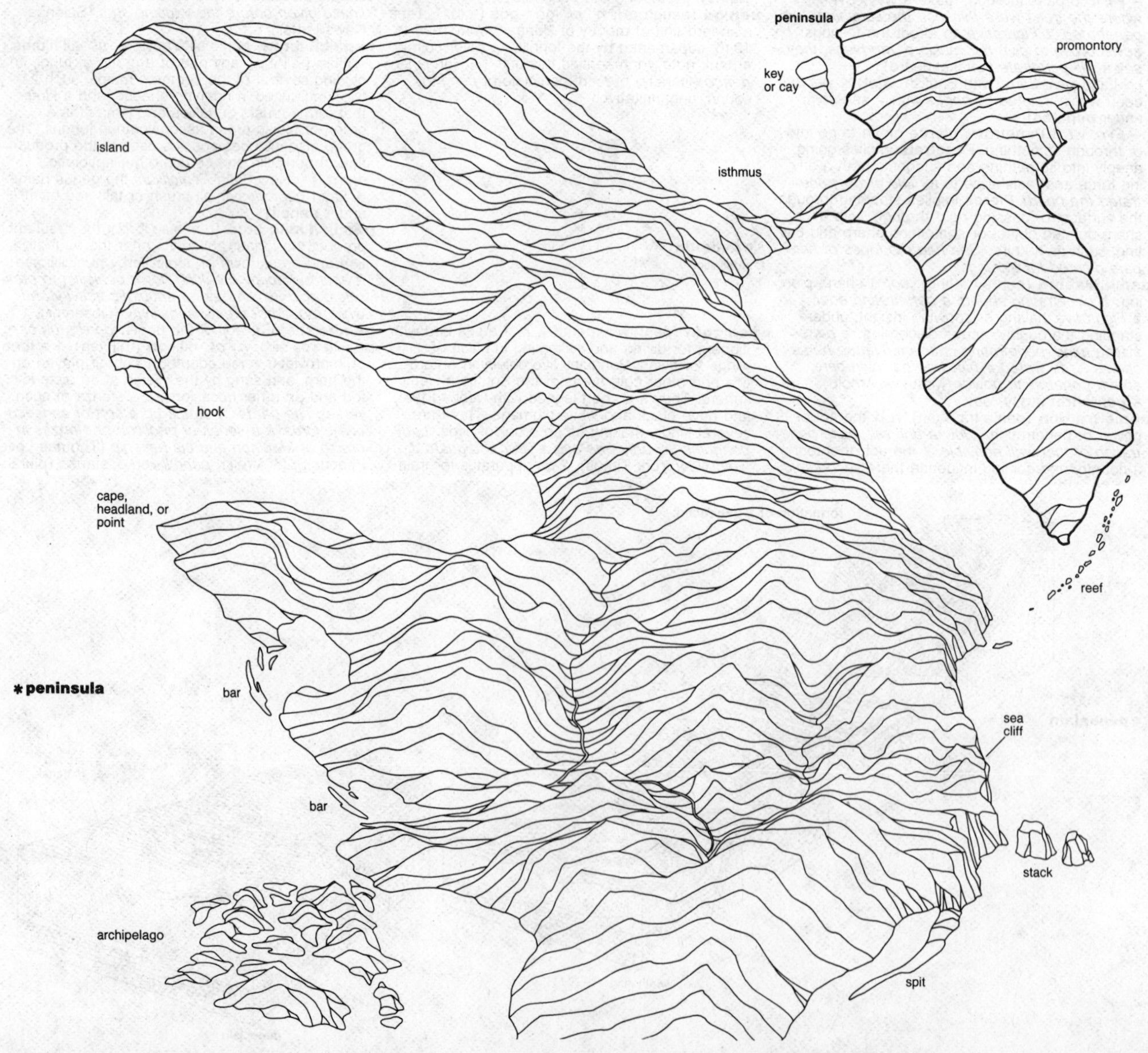

***peninsula**

emblem of superiority or success, especially in an athletic contest: *The mad pace of the Dodgers has most folks believing that [these] hotshots have virtually clinched the pennant* (New York Times). **3** a line at the end of the stem of certain musical notes; hook. [apparently blend of *pendant* ship's rope of various kinds, and of *pennon*]

**pen|nate** (pen′āt), *adj.* **1** having wings; having feathers. **2** *Botany, Obsolete.* pinnate. [< Latin *pennātus* < *penna* feather, wing]

**pen|nat|ed** (pen′ā tid), *adj.* = pennate.

**pen|nat|u|la** (pə nat′yə lə), *n., pl.* **-las, -lae** (-lē). = sea pen. [< New Latin *Pennatula* the typical genus, feminine of Late Latin *pennatulus* (diminutive) < Latin *pennātus* winged; see etym. under **pennate**]

**pen|ni** (pen′ē), *n., pl.* **pen|ni|a** (pen′ē ə), **pen|nis.** **1** a Finnish unit of money, 1/100 of a markka, now used especially as a money of account. **2** a coin representing this unit. [< Finnish *penni* < Old Swedish *penninger*]

**pen|nied** (pen′ēd), *adj.* having a penny or pennies; not penniless: ... *while you dispensed the fragile chocolate to pennied youngsters* (Westminster Gazette).

**pen|ni|less** (pen′ē lis), *adj.* without a cent of money; very poor: *The thief snatched my purse and left me penniless in the big city.* **SYN:** destitute, indigent. See syn. under **poor.** — **pen′ni|less|ly,** *adv.* — **pen′ni|less|ness,** *n.*

**pen|non** (pen′ən), *n.* **1** a long, usually triangular or swallow-tailed flag originally carried on the lance of a knight. **2** any flag or banner. **3** *Nautical.* a pennant. **4** a wing; pinion: *Fluttering his pennons vain, plumb down he drops Ten thousand fathom deep* (Milton). [< Old French *penon* < *penne* feather < Latin *penna*]

**pen|non|cel** or **pen|non|celle** (pen′ən sel), *n.* = pencel.

**pen|noned** (pen′ənd), *adj.* bearing a pennon: *Behind this line we get a glimpse of plumed helmets and pennoned lances of some of the cavalry* (Westminster Gazette).

**penn'orth** (pen′ərth), *n. British Dialect.* pennyworth.

***Penn|syl|va|ni|a Dutch** or **German** (pen′səl vā′nē ə, -vān′yə), **1** the descendants of immigrants of the 1600's and 1700's to southeastern Pennsylvania from southern Germany and Switzerland. **2** a dialect of High German with English intermixed, spoken by them. **3** a style of architecture, furniture, or design characteristic of or derived from the Pennsylvania Dutch.
▶ See **Dutch** for a usage note.

***Pennsylvania Dutch**
definition 3

**Penn|syl|va|ni|an** (pen′səl vā′nē ən, -vān′yən), *n., adj.* — *n.* **1** a native or inhabitant of Pennsylvania. **2** *Geology.* the second period of the Carboniferous period, after the Mississippian and before the Permian, characterized by coal-, oil-, and gas-bearing deposits; Upper Carboniferous (the name used outside of North America). **3** the rocks formed during this period.
— *adj.* **1** of or having to do with Pennsylvania. **2** *Geology.* of or having to do with the Pennsylvanian or its rocks: *The Mississippian and the next following Pennsylvanian Period are the only widely recognized major geologic time divisions that are "made in America"* (Raymond Cecil Moore).

**Pennsylvania rifle,** = Kentucky rifle.

**pen|ny** (pen′ē), *n., pl.* **pen|nies** or *British (collectively for 2)* **pence,** *adj.* — *n.* **1** a copper coin of the United States and Canada; cent. 100 pennies = 1 dollar. **2a** a bronze coin used in Great Britain, formerly equal to 1/12 of a shilling and since 1971 equal to 1/100 of a pound. **b** a coin of similar value in Australia and New Zealand. *Abbr:* p (no period). **3** a sum of money; money. **4** a unit of measurement of the length of nails, as in *eightpenny* nail (about 2½ inches) or *twelvepenny* nail (about 3¼ inches) originally referring to the price for 100 of each size nail.
— *adj.* **1** costing one penny. **2** cheap.
**turn an honest penny,** to earn money honestly: *He turns an honest penny by horse hire* (Augustus Jessopp).
**two a penny,** *British Informal.* very plentiful or common and therefore not valued; a dime a dozen: *Foreign theologians, two a penny in Oxford or in Boston, are curiosities in Sofia* (London Times).
[Old English *pending,* later *penig*]

**pen|ny-a-line** (pen′ē ə līn′), *adj.* **1a** paid at the rate of a penny a printed line (as many journalists and writers of popular fiction formerly were). **b** paid at a low rate and on the basis of space filled (as some writers still are). **2** carelessly written and with little or no literary merit.

**pen|ny-a-lin|er** (pen′ē ə lī′nər), *n.* a person who writes, as for a newspaper, at a penny a line or some low rate; hack writer.

**penny ante,** any variety of poker in which, by agreement between the players, the ante for each hand is set at one cent or some other trifling sum: *Swede spent many an hour at the Belle Springs Creamery playing penny ante poker with Night Foreman Eisenhower during the long, lonely night shift* (Time).

**pen|ny-an|te** (pen′ē an′tē), *adj.* indicating something of little value or importance; cheap: *a penny-ante salary.*

**penny arcade,** a place of cheap amusements where the games of chance, pinball machines, and the like, originally cost a penny a play.

**penny bank, 1** a savings bank at which a sum as low as a penny may be deposited: *A penny bank, for savings of amounts too small to be received at the ordinary savings banks, was opened in Jersey on the 1st of January, 1862* (David T. Ansted). **2** a small metal, plastic, or ceramic container for saving pennies or small coins: *"I've got the patent on a penny bank—it's a plastic reproduction of an old iron bank"* (New Yorker).

**pen|ny|cress** (pen′ē kres′), *n.* a cruciferous herb with flat, round pods, found throughout Europe and temperate Asia: *I found a plant of pennycress in a piece of waste ground* (G. Travers).

**penny dreadful,** *British.* a piece of cheap, sensational fiction, especially a novel or novelette in magazine form or paperback, characterized by violent episodes and maudlin sentiment: *The country was also flooded with an unprecedented quantity of shilling shockers, penny dreadfuls, and popular magazines* (New Yorker).

**pen|ny-far|thing** (pen′ē fär′ᴛʜing), *n.* an early form of bicycle having a large front wheel and a small rear one.

**penny fee,** *Scottish.* small wages paid in money.

**penny gaff,** *British Slang.* a cheap theater or music hall.

**penny paper,** a newspaper of the 1800's that sold for a penny.

**penny pincher,** or **pen|ny-pinch|er** (pen′ē pin′chər), *n. Informal.* a stingy person; person who does not spend or use money freely: *Like so many other men of means, he was a penny pincher* (New Yorker). **SYN:** miser, skinflint.

**pen|ny-pinch|ing** (pen′ē pin′ching), *n., adj. Informal.* — *n.* an exercising of care in the spending of money; being stingy: *Penny-pinching is fine as far as it goes, but it is the whole inflated balloon of Government that really needs to be pinched* (Wall Street Journal). **SYN:** stinginess.
— *adj.* niggardly with money; tight; stingy: *a penny-pinching state legislature.*

**pen|ny-plain** (pen′ē plān′), *adj.* plain and unpretentious: *"The Wanting Seed" is far less disastrous, but in its penny-plain style, it ... can be ranked with ... Orwell and Huxley* (Time).

**penny post,** the postal system, called such in the days when mail traveled for a penny.

**penny press,** newspapers produced in the 1800's for the general public rather than for select or literary readers and selling for a penny each: *The penny press dogged the Princess' footsteps, struggling to make significant gossip of every transient expression* (Time).

**pen|ny|roy|al** (pen′ē roi′əl), *n.* **1** any one of various plants of the mint family, especially: **a** a perennial European herb having small aromatic leaves. **b** a similar American herb that yields a pungent oil formerly much used as a mosquito repellent and medicinally; fleamint. **2** a fragrant oil made from either plant. [earlier *penneryal,* apparently alteration of *pulyole riall* < Anglo-French *puliol real* < Old French *pouliol,* earlier *pulioel* thyme (ultimately < Latin *pūlejum* pennyroyal), *real* royal]

**penny stock,** stock offered for sale for less than a dollar per share, often for only a few cents: *In a move to eliminate racketeers in penny stocks, the SEC will tighten its small securities regulations* (Time).

**pen|ny|weight** (pen′ē wāt′), *n.* 24 grains or 1/20 of an ounce in troy weight. *Abbr:* dwt.

**penny wheep,** (hwēp), *Scottish.* small beer (formerly sold at a penny a bottle).

**pen|ny|whis|tle** (pen′ē hwis′əl), *n., adj.* — *n.* a toy whistle such as children use: *The noise that emerges from some organs of British publicity abroad is more like the peep of a pennywhistle than a fanfare* (Manchester Guardian).
— *adj.* of poor quality; inferior: *Since 1949, a million ex-Nazis have been re-enfranchised. A dozen pennywhistle Führers are after their votes* (Time).

**pen|ny-wise** (pen′ē wīz′), *adj.* saving in regard to small sums: *Franklin was far from being a foxy grandpa benignly counseling homely virtues over the rims of his bifocals or a penny-wise mouther of platitudes* (Wall Street Journal).
**penny-wise and pound-foolish,** saving in small expenses and wasteful in big ones: *He asserted that dribbling out funds as we are presently doing is penny-wise and pound-foolish* (New York Times).

**pen|ny|wort** (pen′ē wėrt′), *n.* any one of various plants having roundish leaves, such as the wall pennywort or navelwort.

**pen|ny|worth** (pen′ē wėrth′), *n.* **1** as much as can be bought for a penny. **2** *Figurative.* a small amount: *Give me a pennyworth of advice.* **3** *Figurative.* a bargain (good, bad, fair, cheap, or otherwise): *Many have been ruined by buying good pennyworths* (Benjamin Franklin). **4** *Figurative.* a good bargain.

**Pe|nob|scot** (pə nob′skot), *n., pl.* **-scots** or **-scot.** **1** a member of an American Indian tribe of Algonkian stock formerly living near the Penobscot River, Maine. **2** their language.

**pe|no|log|i|cal** (pē′nə loj′ə kəl), *adj.* of or having to do with penology: *For eight years I did time in just such a penitentiary, under administrations representing opposite extremes of penological thought* (Atlantic). — **pe′no|log′i|cal|ly,** *adv.*

**pe|nol|o|gist** (pē nol′ə jist), *n.* an expert in penology: *The Senate committee was listening to doctors, penologists, and policemen disagree on how to control drug distribution and handle addicts* (Newsweek).

**pe|nol|o|gy** (pē nol′ə jē), *n.* the science of the punishment and rehabilitation of criminals and the management of prisons. [< Latin *poena* punishment + *-logy*]

**pen|on|cel** (pen′ən sel), *n.* = pencel.

**pen pal,** a person with whom one corresponds regularly, often in another country and without ever having met: *Ellen Roberts, a California teenager, was snowed under by an avalanche of Italian pen pals last fall* (Harper's).

**pen picture** or **portrait, 1** a picture drawn with a pen. **2** a brief written description, such as of a person or event: *Time [magazine] writers were as flattering with their pen pictures ... as Australia's Dobell was awry with his brushwork* (Time).

**pen|point** (pen′point′), *n.* **1** a small metal instrument with a split point, used with a holder for writing in ink; nib. **2** a point used for writing on any pen, such as the ball at the end of a ballpoint pen.

**pen-push|er** (pen′pu̇sh′ər), *n. Slang.* an office worker; person who works at a desk: *"I take on the paperwork," he said, ... "I'm a pen-pusher"* (New Yorker).

**pen|sée** (päɴ sā′), *n., pl.* **pen|sées** (päɴ sā′). *French.* a thought or reflection put in literary form: *He expressed this knowledge in a typical Churchillian pensée, under date of April 8, 1945* (Atlantic).

**pen|sile**[1] (pen′səl), *adj.* **1** hanging down; pendent. **2** building a hanging nest: *a pensile bird.* [< Latin *pēnsilis* < *pendēre* to hang]

**pen|sile**[2] or **pen|sil** (pen′səl), *n.* = pencel.

**pen|sion**[1] (pen′shən), *n., v., adj.* — *n.* **1** a regular payment to a person of a specified sum of money which is not wages. Pensions are often paid because of long service, special merit, or injuries received: *A man or woman who makes the armed forces a career may retire with a pension after serving the required time* (Robert J. Myers). **2** a regular payment made to a person not an employee to retain his good will, assistance when needed, or other service; subsidy; fixed allowance. **3** = pension[2].
— *v.t.* to give a pension to: *The Army pensioned the soldier for his years of loyal service.*
— *adj.* of or having to do with a pension: *a pension plan, pension rolls.*
**pension off,** to retire from service with a pension: *You have taken it into your head that I mean to pension you off* (Dickens).

---

**Pronunciation Key:** hat, āge, cãre, fär; let, ēqual, tėrm; it, īce; hot, ōpen, ôrder; oil, out; cup, pu̇t, rüle; child; long; thin; ᴛʜen; zh, measure; ə represents **a** in about, **e** in taken, **i** in pencil, **o** in lemon, **u** in circus.

[< Old French *pension,* learned borrowing from Latin *pēnsiō, -ōnis* payment, rent < *pendere* to pay, weigh]

**pen|sion[2]** (päɴ syôɴ′), *n. French.* **1** a boarding house or boarding school in France and other parts of Continental Europe: *In the tiny village of Trisenberg, high up on the mountainside, I very much liked a small homely pension run by a friendly, jolly woman, who does all the cooking* (Observer). **2** payment, such as for board and lodging or for the board and education of a child: *A full day's pension, if one has a room with bath, will cost about £3* (Atlantic).

**pen|sion|a|ble** (pen′shə nə bəl), *adj. Especially British.* **1** qualified for or entitled to a pension. **2** entitling to a pension: *The Civil Service is to offer pensionable jobs to men and women aged between 40 and 60* (London Times).

**pen|sion|ar|y** (pen′shə ner′ē), *n., pl.* **-ar|ies,** *adj.* — ***n.*** **1** = pensioner. **2** (formerly, in the Netherlands) the chief magistrate of a city: *Jean Sersanders, the pensionary of Ghent* (J. F. Kirk). — ***adj.*** **1** consisting or of the nature of a pension. **2** receiving a pension. **3** mercenary; hireling; venal.

**pen|sio|ne** (pen syō′nā), *n., pl.* **-ni** (-nē). *Italian.* a boarding house, or pension, in Italy: *"Take it or leave it" is the attitude of the pensione keeper of the better sort when showing a room. As for the inferior pensioni, they have a practice of shanghaiing tourists* (Mary McCarthy).

**pen|sion|er** (pen′shə nər), *n.* **1** a person who receives a pension: *In a country that is slowly growing old, there is the overriding problem of the old-age pensioners* (Atlantic). **2** a hireling; dependent. **3** a student who pays all his expenses, such as for food and lodging, (commons) at Cambridge University, England, and is not supported by any foundation. **4** *Obsolete.* **a** *British.* a gentleman-at-arms. **b** a member of a bodyguard; attendant; retainer.

**pension fund,** a fund set up on an actuarial basis to provide pensions for a group at a later date: *This man earned £17 a week, had looked after his money, and contributed about £1 a week to a pension fund that would give him £6 10s a week when he retired at 65* (Manchester Guardian). — **pen′sion-fund′,** *adj.*

**pen|sion|less** (pen′shən lis), *adj.* receiving no pension.

**pen|sion|naire** (päɴ syô ner′), *n. French.* a person who boards in a pension: *On the fifth floor were the salon, the dining room and kitchen, and some of the rooms occupied by the pensionnaires* (New Yorker).

**pension plan,** a plan, usually set up on an actuarial basis by an employer alone or by an employer jointly with a union, to provide pensions for retired or disabled employees.

**pen|sive** (pen′siv), *adj.* **1** thoughtful in a serious or sad way: *She was in a pensive mood, and sat staring out the window.* **SYN:** meditative, reflective. **2** melancholy: ... *the pensive shade of the Italian ruins* (George W. Curtis). **SYN:** sober, grave, sad. [< Old French *pensif* < *penser* to think < Latin *pensāre* weigh, consider (frequentative) < *pendere* to pay, weigh] — **pen′sive|ly,** *adv.* — **pen′sive|ness,** *n.*

**pen-stab** (pen′stab′), *n.* an article for a writing desk, commonly a small vessel containing a brush with the bristles turned upward, for thrusting a pen into after using.

**pen-stab|ber** (pen′stab′ər), *n.* = pen-stab.

**pen|ste|mon** (pen stē′mən), *n.* any chiefly North American herb of a group of the figwort family, cultivated for their showy clustered flowers that are usually tubular and two-lipped and of various colors; beardtongue. Also, **pentstemon.** [American English < New Latin *Penstemon* the genus name < Greek *penta-* five + *stēmōn* thread, but taken as "stamen"]

**pen|ster** (pen′stər), *n.* a petty writer.

**pen|stock** (pen′stok′), *n.* **1a** a channel for carrying water to a water wheel. **b** a pipe for carrying water to a turbine: *Water to drive the turbines drops sixteen times the height of Niagara Falls, through a penstock bored into the mountain and connecting with a huge ten-mile-long tunnel from Tahtsa Lake to the east* (New York Times). **2** a sluice or floodgate for restraining or regulating the flow from a head of water formed by a weir, dam, or other obstruction: *Apart from the associated damage to penstocks and valves, the large-scale flooding might cause great damage to industrial facilities downstream* (The Effects of Atomic Weapons). [< *pen*[2] + *stock,* in the obsolete sense "trough"]

**pent[1]** (pent), *adj., v.* — ***adj.*** closely confined; penned; shut: *pent in the house all winter.* — ***v.*** a past tense and a past participle of **pen**[2]: *as if he had in prison long been pent* (Edmund Spenser).

**pent[2]** (pent), *n.* a sloping roof or covering; penthouse.

**pent-,** *combining form.* the form of **penta-** before vowels, as in *pentacid.*

**penta-,** *combining form.* **1** five: *Pentameter = poetry having five metrical feet to the line.* **2** having five atoms of a specified substance: *Pentabasic = having five atoms of replaceable hydrogen.* Also, **pent-** before vowels. [< Greek *penta-* < *pénte* five]

**pen|ta|ba|sic** (pen′tə bā′sik), *adj. Chemistry.* having five atoms of hydrogen replaceable by basic atoms or radicals: *a pentabasic acid.*

**pen|ta|car|pel|lar|y** (pen′tə kär′pə ler′ē), *adj. Botany.* having five carpels.

**pen|ta|chlor|o|phe|nol** (pen′tə klôr′ə fē′nōl, -nol; -klōr′-), *n.* a chemical used as a wood preservative and fungicide: *Pentachlorophenol is sometimes used in swabbing decks of U.S. Navy vessels because it is a wood preservative* (Science News Letter). *Formula:* $C_6Cl_5OH$

**pen|ta|chord** (pen′tə kôrd), *n. Music.* **1** an instrument with five strings. **2** a diatonic series of five tones.

**pen|tac|id** (pen tas′id), *adj. Chemistry.* capable of combining with five molecules of a monobasic acid. [< *pent-* + *acid*]

**pen|ta|cle** (pen′tə kəl), *n.* **1** a five-pointed star-shaped figure used as a magic or mystic symbol; pentagram: *He was tracing circles and pentacles in the grass and talking the language of the elves* (G. K. Chesterton). **2** any one of certain other more or less star-shaped figures similarly used, such as a hexagram formed by overlapping triangles. [< earlier French *pentacle* or < Medieval Latin *pentaculum,* apparently < Latin *penta-* five + *-culum,* noun suffix]

**pen|tad** (pen′tad), *n.* **1** a period of five years. **2** an element, atom, or radical with a valence of five. **3** a group or series of five. [< Greek *pentás, -ádos* group of five < *pénte* five]

**pen|ta|dac|tyl** (pen′tə dak′təl), *adj.* having five toes or fingers: *The limbs are almost typically pentadactyl* (Hegner and Stiles). [< *penta-* + Greek *dáktylos* toe, finger]

**pen|ta|e|ryth|ri|tol** (pen′tə i rith′rə tōl, -tol), *n.* a white, crystalline compound used for making synthetic lubricants, resins, and paints.

**pentaerythritol te|tra|ni|trate** (tet′rə nī′trāt), a white, crystalline substance derived from the esterification of pentaerythritol with nitric acid, used as an explosive and in treating certain heart disorders. *Formula:* $C(CH_2ONO_2)_4$ *Abbr:* PETN (no periods).

***pen|ta|gon** (pen′tə gon), *n.* a plane figure having five angles and five sides. [< Late Latin *pentagōnum* < Greek *pentágōnon* (literally) neuter of *pentágōnos* five-angled < *pénte* five + *gōniā* angle]

***pentagon**
***pentagram**
definition 1
***pentahedron**

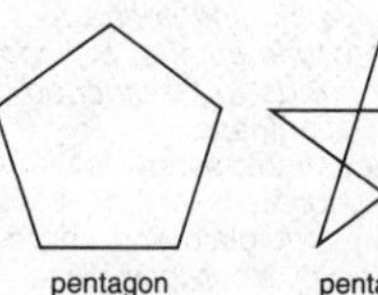
pentagon

pentagram

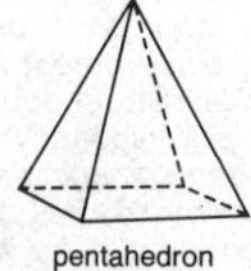
pentahedron

**Pen|ta|gon** (pen′tə gon), *n.* **1** a five-sided building that is the headquarters of the U.S. Department of Defense. It is in Arlington, Virginia. **2** the Department of Defense.

**pen|tag|o|nal** (pen tag′ə nəl), *adj.* having five sides and five angles. — **pen|tag′o|nal|ly,** *adv.*

**Pen|ta|gon|ese** (pen′tə gə nēz′, -nēs′), *n. U.S. Informal.* military jargon, especially as written or spoken in the Pentagon: *He has been highly successful in translating from the Pentagonese for other members of the Senate* (Time).

**Pen|ta|go|ni|an** (pen′tə gō′nē ən), *n., adj. U.S.* — ***n.*** a person who works in the Pentagon: *The season's dinner parties are invariably dimpled with a dizzying variety of ambassadors, Cabinet members, agency heads, socialites, Pentagonians, and sometimes the President himself* (Time). — ***adj.*** of or having to do with the Pentagon: *Pentagonian military strategy.*

***pen|ta|gram** (pen′tə gram), *n.* **1** a five-pointed star-shaped figure made by extending the sides of a regular pentagon until they meet, used as a mystic or magic symbol; pentacle, pentalpha, or pentangle. **2** *Mathematics.* a figure of five lines connecting five points. [< Greek *pentágrammon* (literally) a figure of five lines < *pénte* five + *grámma* -gram[1]]

**pen|ta|gram|mat|ic** (pen′tə grə mat′ik), *adj.* having the figure of a pentagram.

**pen|ta|he|dral** (pen′tə hē′drəl), *adj.* having five faces.

***pen|ta|he|dron** (pen′tə hē′drən), *n., pl.* **-drons, -dra** (-drə). a solid figure having five faces. See picture below. [< *penta-* + Greek *-hedron,* neuter of *-hedros* having bases < *hédra* base[1]]

**pen|tail** (pen′tāl′), *n.* a variety of tree shrew, a small, squirrellike, insectivorous animal of Borneo, Sumatra, and other islands in Southeast Asia, having a long tail naked toward the base, but with the terminal portion fringed on opposite sides with long hairs, so as to look somewhat like a quill pen.

**pen|tal|o|gy** (pen tal′ə jē), *n., pl.* **-gies.** a combination of five mutually connected parts; pentad: *The story ... forms part of Heinlein's "History of the Future" pentalogy* (Punch).

**pen|tal|pha** (pen tal′fə), *n.* = pentagram. [< Greek *pentálpha* < *pénte* five + *alpha* alpha (because the figure resembles five Greek *alphas* (A) combined)]

**pen|ta|mer** (pen′tə mər), *n.* a polymer consisting of five molecules.

**pen|ta|mer|ic** (pen′tə mer′ik), *adj.* consisting of five parts: *A pentameric pattern is the one pattern that is never found in naturally occurring crystals* (New Scientist). [< *penta-* + Greek *méros* part]

**pen|tam|er|ous** (pen tam′ər əs), *adj.* **1** *Zoology.* composed or consisting of five parts or organs or five sets of similar parts. **2** (of a flower) having five members in each whorl (generally written *5-merous*). [< Greek *pentamerês* (with English *-ous*) < *pénte* five + *méros* part]

**pen|tam|e|ter** (pen tam′ə tər), *n., adj.* — ***n.*** **1a** poetry having five metrical feet or measures in each line. *Example:* "A lít/tle léarn/ing ís/ a dań/g'rous thíng." **b** = iambic pentameter (the measure of *heroic verse,* rhymed or unrhymed, and the *heroic couplet* in English literature). **2** a line in ancient Greek and Latin verse consisting of two feet (either dactyls or spondees), a long syllable, two more dactyls, and another long syllable. When this line is alternated with a hexameter line the resulting form is an elegiac. — ***adj.*** consisting of five metrical feet or measures. [< Latin *pentameter,* noun < Greek *pentámetros* having five metrical feet < *pénte* five + *métron* measure]

**pen|tane** (pen′tān), *n.* any one of three colorless, flammable, isomeric hydrocarbons of the methane series, derived from petroleum and used as a solvent, as an anesthetic, and for filling thermometers: *The light liquids usually used in bubble chambers—liquid hydrogen or pentane—are almost transparent to gamma rays* (Scientific American). *Formula:* $C_5H_{12}$ [< *pent-* + *-ane*]

**pen|tan|gle** (pen′tang′gəl), *n.* **1** = pentagram. **2** = pentagon.

**pen|tan|gu|lar** (pen tang′gyə lər), *adj.* having five angles.

**pen|ta|pep|tide** (pen′tə pep′tīd, -tid), *n.* a polypeptide composed of five amino acids.

**pen|tap|o|dy** (pen tap′ə dē), *n., pl.* **-dies.** *Prosody.* a measure or series of five feet in a verse. [< Greek *pentápous, -podos* of five feet (< *pénte* five + *poús, podós* foot) + English *-y*[3]]

**pen|ta|quine** (pen′tə kwēn, -kwin), *n.* a yellowish, crystalline, synthetic drug, used in the treatment of malaria, often in combination with quinine. *Formula:* $C_{18}H_{27}N_3O$

**pen|tar|chy** (pen′tär kē), *n., pl.* **-chies.** **1** a government by five persons. **2** a governing body composed of five persons. **3** a group of five states, each under its own ruler. [< Greek *pentarchíā* rule of five < *pénte* five + *árchein* to rule]

**pen|ta|stich** (pen′tə stik), *n.* a group of five lines of verse that form a stanza, strophe, or poem. [< Greek *pentástichos* of five lines < *pénte* five + *stíchos* line of verse < *steíchein* to walk, go]

**pen|ta|style** (pen′tə stīl), *adj., n.* — ***adj.*** having five columns in front, as a temple or a portico. — ***n.*** a pentastyle structure. [< *penta-* + Greek *stŷlos* pillar, column]

**pen|ta|syl|lab|ic** (pen′tə sə lab′ik), *adj.* having five syllables: *Stress may be measured by instruments precisely, and it is not difficult to perceive the alternating degrees of stress here indicated by numbers in such diverse English pentasyllabic forms as equanimity* (Simeon Potter).

**pen|ta|syl|la|ble** (pen′tə sil′ə bəl), *n.* a word of five syllables.

**Pen|ta|teuch** (pen′tə tük, -tyük), *n.* the first five books of the Old Testament: Genesis, Exodus, Leviticus, Numbers, and Deuteronomy: *He dons the traditional black-and-white prayer shawl and straps phylacteries* (*small leather cases containing texts from the Pentateuch*) *to his left arm and his forehead* (Time). [< Latin *Pentateuchus* < Greek *pentáteuchos* < *pénte* five + *teûchos* book; (originally) the case for the scrolls < *teúchein* to produce, make]

**Pen|ta|teuch|al** (pen′tə tü′kəl, -tyü′-), *adj.* of or

having to do with the Pentateuch: *I have long regretted that I ... used the Pentateuchal term of "creation"* (Charles Darwin).

**pen|tath|lete** (pen tath′lēt), *n.* a contestant in a pentathlon. [blend of *pentathlon* and *athlete*]

**pen|tath|lon** (pen tath′lon), *n.* **1** an athletic contest consisting of five different events, usually the broad jump, discus throw, javelin throw, 200-meter sprint, and 1,500-meter run. The person having the highest total score wins. **2** = modern pentathlon. [< Greek *péntathlon* < *pénte* five + *âthlon* exercise of skill]

**pen|ta|tom|ic** (pen′tə tom′ik), *adj. Chemistry.* **1** having five atoms in the molecule. **2** containing five replaceable atoms or groups. [< *pent-* + *atomic*]

***pen|ta|ton|ic** (pen′tə ton′ik), *adj. Music.* having five tones: *Melodies are built on varieties of pentatonic and heptatonic scales, and every African society specialized in one of these scales* (Atlantic).

**pen|ta|ton|i|cism** (pen′tə ton′ə siz′əm), *n.* pentatonic quality or character: *Bantock, who arranged many Scottish and Hebridean folk tunes ..., was influenced by their basic pentatonicism* (Listener).

**pen|ta|ton|ism** (pen′tə ton′iz əm), *n.* = pentatonicism.

**pen|ta|va|lent** (pen′tə vā′lənt, pen tav′ə-), *adj. Chemistry.* having a valence of five; quinquevalent: *pentavalent antimony compounds.*

**pen|taz|o|cine** (pen taz′ə sin, -sēn), *n.* a synthetic narcotic used in medicine as a substitute for morphine to relieve pain. *Formula:* $C_{19}H_{27}NO$

**Pen|te|cost** (pen′tə kôst, -kost), *n.* **1** the seventh Sunday after Easter; Whitsunday. Pentecost is a Christian festival in memory of the descent of the Holy Ghost upon the Apostles (in the Bible, Acts 2). **2** a Jewish religious holiday, observed about seven weeks after Passover; Shabuoth. [< Latin *pentēcostē* < Greek *pentēkostē* (*hēméra*) fiftieth (day)]

**Pen|te|cos|tal** or **pen|te|cos|tal** (pen′tə kôs′təl, -kos′-; pen′tə kôs′-, -kos′-), *adj., n.* —*adj.* **1** of or having to do with Pentecost. **2** of or having to do with any of various American Protestant religious groups that stress divine inspiration and believe in such manifestations of the Holy Ghost as divine healing, speaking in tongues (glossolalia), and visions. Most Pentecostal groups are fundamentalist.
—*n.* = Pentecostalist.

**Pen|te|cos|tal|ism** (pen′tə kôs′tə liz′əm, -kos′-), *n.* the beliefs and practices of the Pentecostalists: *Pentecostalism asserts as its basic tenet the need for baptism by the Holy Spirit, the supreme manifestation of which is glossolalia, or speaking in tongues* (Time).

**Pen|te|cos|tal|ist** (pen′tə kôs′tə list, -kos′-), *n.* a member of a Pentecostal sect or church.

**Pen|tel|ic** (pen tel′ik), *adj.* of or from Mount Pentelicus, north of Athens, Greece, especially with reference to the famous marble quarried there.

**Pentelic marble**, a fine-grained white marble much used in ancient Greek sculpture and architecture.

**pent|house** (pent′hous′), *n.* **1** an apartment or house built on the top of a building. **2** a small roofed structure over an elevator shaft, in which the motor, pulley wheels, and other mechanisms, are housed. **3** a sloping roof projecting from a building, as to shelter a door. **4** a shed with a sloping roof, attached to a building. **5** any one of various structures like a sloping roof, such as a shed for the protection of besiegers or a covering formed of soldiers' shields held over their heads. [alteration of Middle English *pentis*, apparently short for Old French *apentis* lean-to (influenced by *pente* slope), learned borrowing from Medieval Latin *appendicium* an attached building < Latin *appendere* to append]

**pen|tice** or **pen|tise** (pen′tis), *n. Obsolete.* penthouse.

**pen|ti|men|to** (pen′tə men′tō), *n., pl.* **-ti** (-tē). **1** the emergence of an earlier form in a painting that has been altered and painted over. **2** such a form before or after its emergence: *Radiographs confirm that the bars cover pentimenti* (New York Times). [< Italian *pentimento* (literally) penitence, reparation]

**pen|tjak** (pen tyäk′), *n.* a formal system of self-defense practiced in Indonesia. [< Indonesian *pentjak*]

**pent|land|ite** (pent′lən dīt), *n.* a mineral found in Ontario, Canada, the chief ore of nickel. It is a combination of nickel, sulfur, and iron. [< a proper name + *-ite*[1]]

**pen|to|bar|bi|tal** (pen′tə bar′bə tôl, -tal), *n.* a white granular barbiturate used in the preparation of certain medicines, such as pentobarbital sodium. *Formula:* $C_{11}H_{18}O_3N_2$ [< *pent-* (because sodium is attached to the fifth radical of the chain) + *barbital*]

**pentobarbital sodium**, a white, slightly bitter, soluble crystalline powder used as a sedative and hypnotic; Nembutal. *Formula:* $C_{11}H_{17}N_2O_3Na$

**pent|ode** (pen′tōd), *n.* **1** the vacuum tube formerly most commonly used for amplification in radio and television sets, so called because it has five electrodes: *Three-grid tubes, or pentodes, are capable of greater amplification than triodes* (Roy F. Allison). **2** a high-power transistor used for the same purpose, having four wires: *The new transistors ... are equivalent to more complex vacuum tubes called tetrodes and pentodes ... The pentode transistor, now being perfected, has four cat whiskers and can replace three triode transistors for some applications* (Newsweek). [< *pent-* + (electr)*ode*]

**pen|to|lin|i|um tartrate** (pen′tə lin′ē əm), a crystalline drug used in the treatment of high blood pressure. *Formula:* $C_{23}H_{42}N_2O_{12}$

**pen|to|lite** (pen′tə līt), *n.* a high explosive composed of pentaerythritol tetranitrate and TNT.

**pen|tom|ic** (pen tom′ik), *adj.* of, having to do with, or designating an army division organized into five highly mobile, self-supporting battle groups trained in the use of atomic weapons: *a pentomic infantry or airborne division, a pentomic army.* [< *pent-* five + (at)*omic*]

**pen|tom|i|no** (pen tom′ə nō), *n., pl.* **-noes** or **-nos.** a polyomino made to cover five squares on a game board: *The reader may enjoy experimenting with the 12 pentominoes (all patterns of five rookwise-connected counters) to see what happens to each* (Scientific American). [< *pent-* five + (d)*omino*]

**pen|to|san** (pen′tə san), *n.* any one of a group of complex carbohydrates (polysaccharides) that yield pentoses when hydrolyzed. Pentosans occur in most plants and in humus: *Xylose, an example of such a sugar, is found in plants only as a constituent of such complex carbohydrates as pentosans, gums, and hemicelluloses* (Harbaugh and Goodrich).

**pen|to|sane** (pen′tə sān), *n.* = pentosan.

**pen|tose** (pen′tōs), *n.* any one of a class of simple sugars (monosaccharides) that contain five atoms of carbon in each molecule, are constituents of ribonucleic acid, and are not fermented by yeast. Pentoses are produced in animal tissues, and are obtained from pentosans by hydrolysis. Deoxyribose and ribose are pentoses. *The nucleus of all cells contains a considerable amount of nucleic acid, a complex molecule containing a pentose sugar, phosphoric acid and a series of organic bases* (John E. Harris). [< *pent-* + *-ose*[2]]

**Pen|to|thal Sodium** (pen′tə thôl, -thol), *Trademark.* thiopental sodium.

**pent|ox|id** (pen tok′sid), *n.* = pentoxide.

**pent|ox|ide** (pen tok′sīd, -sid), *n.* a compound containing five atoms of oxygen combined with another element or radical.

**pent roof**, a roof sloping in one direction only; shed roof.

**pent|ste|mon** (pent stē′mən), *n.* = penstemon. [American English, alteration of New Latin *Penstemon* the genus name; see etym. under **penstemon.**]

**pent-up** (pent′up′), *adj.* shut up; closely confined: *Her pent-up feelings could no longer be restrained, and she burst into tears.*

**pen|tyl** (pen′təl), *n.* a univalent radical derived from pentane; amyl. *Formula:* $-C_5H_{11}$ [< *pent*(ane) + *-yl*]

**pen|tyl|ene|tet|ra|zol** (pen′tə lēn tet′rə zōl, -zol), *n.* a bitter, white, crystalline substance used as a stimulant of the central nervous system, especially in narcotic depression, barbiturate poisoning, and the treatment of senile patients; Metrazol. *Formula:* $C_6H_{10}N_4$ [< *pent-* + (meth)*ylene* + *tetr-* + *az-* + *-ol*[2]]

**pe|nu|che** (pə nü′chē), *n.* = panocha.

**pe|nu|chi** (pə nü′chē), *n.* = panocha.

**pe|nuch|le** or **pe|nuck|le** (pē′nuk′əl), *n.* = pinochle.

**pe|nult** (pē′nult, pi nult′), *n., adj.* —*n.* the next to the last syllable in a word.
—*adj.* = penultimate.
[(originally) abbreviation of earlier *penultima* < Latin *paenultima*, feminine adjective, next-to-last < *paene* almost + *ultimus* last]

**pe|nul|ti|ma** (pi nul′tə mə), *n.* = penult.

**pe|nul|ti|mate** (pi nul′tə mit), *adj., n.* —*adj.* **1** next to the last: *the penultimate number in a series, the penultimate day of the month. This is the penultimate link in the chain of evidence ... that there has been a conscious, deliberate effort to obstruct justice* (John B. Anderson). **2** of or having to do with the penult.
—*n.* = penult. —**pe|nul′ti|mate|ly**, *adv.*

**pe|nul|ti|ma|tum** (pi nul′tə mā′təm), *n.* a declaration, demand, or the like, that immediately precedes an ultimatum, or is all but an ultimatum.

***pe|num|bra** (pi num′brə), *n., pl.* **-brae** (-brē), **-bras. 1** the partial shadow outside of the complete shadow formed by the sun or moon during an eclipse: *An observer within the umbra cannot see any part of the source; one within the penumbra can see a portion of the source, while from points outside the penumbra the entire source can be seen* (Sears and Zamansky). **2** the grayish outer part of a sunspot: *A complete and fully formed spot shows a dark central portion, known as the umbra, surrounded by a not-so-dark area called the penumbra* (Wasley S. Krogdahl). **3** *Figurative.* a partial shade or shadow: *One of the handicaps of poetry is that penumbra of holiness, the legacy of the nineteenth century, which still surrounds it* (Atlantic). [< New Latin *penumbra* < Latin *paene* almost + *umbra* shadow]

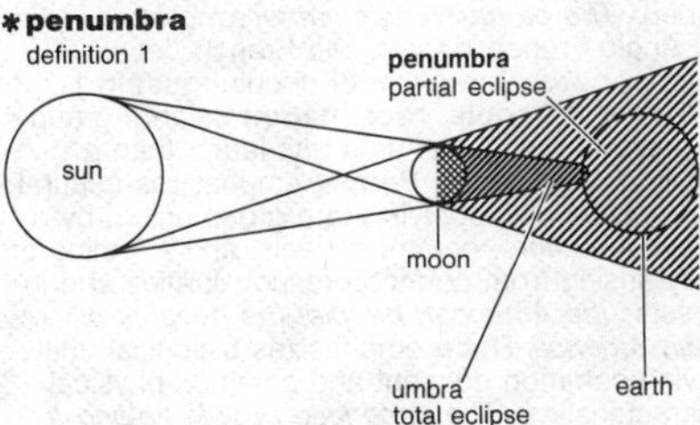


**pe|num|bral** (pi num′brəl), *adj.* having to do with or like a penumbra: *This penumbral region of faint partial shadow can scarcely be detected near the beginning of eclipse* (Bernhard, Bennett, and Rice).

**pe|nu|ri|ous** (pi nür′ē əs, -nyür′-), *adj.* **1** mean about spending or giving money; stingy: *a penurious, accumulating curmudgeon* (Washington Irving). *He lived in the most penurious manner and denied himself every luxury* (William Godwin). **SYN:** niggardly. **2** in a condition of penury; indigent; poverty-stricken. **3** *Obsolete.* **a** scanty. **b** not rich or fertile; barren. [probably < Middle French *penurieux* (with English *-ous*), learned borrowing from Medieval Latin *penuriosus* < Latin *pēnūria* penury] —**pe|nu′ri|ous|ly**, *adv.* —**pe|nu′ri|ous|ness**, *n.*

**pen|u|ry** (pen′yər ē), *n.* very great poverty; extreme want; destitution; indigence: *My scanty purse was exhausted, and ... I experienced the sordid distress of penury* (Washington Irving). [< Latin *pēnūria* want, need, related to *paene* almost]

**Pe|nu|ti|an** (pə nü′tē ən, -shən), *n., adj.* —*n.* a grouping of North American Indian languages of the western United States.
—*adj.* of or belonging to this grouping: *Maidu is a Penutian language.*
[< Maidu *pen* two + Costanoan *uti* two + English *-an*]

**pe|on** (pē′on, -ən), *n.* **1a** a person doing work that requires little skill; unskilled worker. **b** an impoverished Indian laborer in Latin America. **2** (formerly in the southwestern United States and Mexico) a worker held for service to work off a debt. **3** formerly, in India: **a** a native foot soldier. **b** a native constable. **c** a native attendant or orderly. [(definition 1, 2) American English < Mexican Spanish *peón;* (definition 3) < Portuguese *peão* foot soldier; both < Late Latin *pedō, -ōnis* splay-footed. See etym. of doublet **pawn**[2].]

**pe|on|age** (pē′ə nij), *n.* **1** the condition or service of a peon. **2** the practice of holding persons to work off debts. **3** the practice of leasing convict labor on contract to work on farms, in lumber camps, or at other jobs usually of heavy manual labor.

**pe|on|ism** (pē′ə niz əm), *n.* = peonage.

**pe|o|ny** (pē′ə nē), *n., pl.* **-nies. 1** a garden plant with large, showy flowers of various shades of red and white, often becoming double under cultivation. There are several kinds, comprising a genus of the crowfoot family. Peonies are perennials. **2** its flower. Also, **paeony.** [< Old French *peoine*, learned borrowing from Latin *paeōnia* < Greek *paiōniā* < *Paiōn* physician of the gods (supposedly because of its use in medicine)]

**peo|ple** (pē′pəl), *n., pl.* **-ple** or (*for def. 2*) **-ples,**

*v.,* **-pled, -pling.** —*n.* **1** men, women, and children; human beings; persons: *a street emptied of people. There were ten people present.* **2** a body of persons composing a tribe, race, or nation: *the French people, the peoples of Asia.* **3** persons in general; the public: *to seek the support of the people, music that appeals to the people. A democracy is a government of the people.* **SYN**: population. **4** persons of a place, class, or group: *city people, Southern people, the people here.* **5** the common people; lower classes: *The French nobles oppressed the people.* **6** persons in relation to a superior: *a pastor and his people. A king rules over his people.* **7** family; relatives: *He spends his holidays with his people.* **8** ancestors: *Our people were Dutch.* **9** a species or other group of animals: *the monkey people.*
—*v.t.* **1a** to fill with people; populate: *Europe largely peopled America.* **b** *Figurative.* to fill (especially with animals or inanimate objects); stock: *pools peopled with fish.* **2** to constitute the population of (a country or other area); inhabit.
**be gathered to one's people,** to die and be buried: *The patriarch was gathered to his people.*
[< Anglo-French *people,* Old French *peuple* < Latin *populus.* See etym. of doublet **pueblo.**]
—*Syn. n.* **2 People, race, nation** mean a group of persons thought of as a unit larger than a family or community. **People** emphasizes cultural and social unity, applying to a group united by a common culture, common ideals, and a feeling of unity arising from common responsibilities and interests: *the American people, the peoples of Latin America.* **Race** emphasizes biological unity, having common descent and common physical characteristics: *The Japanese people belong to the Mongolian race.* **Nation** emphasizes political unity, applying to a group united under one government: *Americans are a people and a nation, not a race.*

**peo|ple|hood** (pē′pəl hu̇d), *n.* the state or fact of being a people, with special emphasis on cultural and social unity, as opposed to political unity: *"These people," says Lodge, "have always had a strong sense of peoplehood. What we are now trying to give them is a strong sense of nationhood"* (Time).

**peo|ple|less** (pē′pəl lis), *adj.* having no people or population; uninhabited: *a desolate and peopleless island.*

**people mover,** any one of various devices for transporting people quickly between two fixed points: *They will enable commuters ... to change from subway to a noiseless pedestrian conveyor called a people mover* (New York Times).

**peo|pler** (pē′plər), *n.* a person who peoples; inhabitant; colonizer.

**people's front,** = popular front.

**people sniffer,** a portable chemical and electronic apparatus that can detect the presence of hidden persons: *United States troops refer to the gadget as the "people sniffer." It leads American officers ... to enemy hideouts by "sniffing out" the kind of ammonia odors given off by the human body* (New York Times).

**people's park,** *U.S.* a park for the use of people as they see fit, without regulatory or other impositions on its use by government officials.

**People's Party,** a political organization formed in the United States in 1891, and active until 1896, that advocated increase of currency, state control of railroads, restrictions upon the ownership of land, and an income tax; Populist Party.

**People's Republic,** any one of the Communist states of Europe and Asia: *the Polish People's Republic, the People's Republic of China.*

**Pe|o|ri|a** (pē ôr′ē ə, -ōr′-), *n., pl.* **-ri|a** or **-ri|as.** **1** a member of a woodland tribe of North American Indians, part of the Illinois confederacy, who lived in northeastern Iowa and later in central Illinois. **2** their Algonkian language, a dialect of Illinois.

**pep**[1] (pep), *n., v.,* **pepped, pep|ping.** —*n.* spirit; energy; vim.
—*v.t.* **pep up,** to fill or inspire with energy; put new life into: *A brisk walk after dinner will pep you up. Besides, Will and I had stuck at home so much that I couldn't help feeling kind of pepped up at the idea of going to any party again* (Frannie Kilbourne).
[American English, short for *pepper*]

**pep**[2] (pep), *n.* the pip or central part of an artificial flower. [variant of *pip*[3]]

**P.E.P.,** *British.* Political and Economic Planning Organization.

**pe|pi|no** (pe pē′nō), *n., pl.* **-nos.** **1** an evergreen shrub of the lily family, a native of the extreme southern part of South America, bearing showy red flowers. **2** a tropical American plant of the nightshade family, bearing an edible melonlike fruit. [< Spanish *pepino* (diminutive) < Latin *pepō, -ōnis* melon, pumpkin; see etym. under **pepo**]

**pep|los** or **pep|lus** (pep′ləs), *n.* a peplum worn by women in ancient Greece. [< Greek *péplos*]

***pep|lum** (pep′ləm), *n., pl.* **-lums, -la** (-lə). **1** a kind of short overskirt attached about the waist, usually reaching around the hips, such as one on a dress or coat. **2** a full garment worn by women in ancient Greece. [< Latin *peplum,* neuter of *peplus* < Greek *péplos*]

***peplum**
definitions 1, 2

definition 1 definition 2

**pep|lumed** (pep′ləmd), *adj.* **1** having a peplum: *a peplumed blouse.* **2** having the form of a peplum: *peplumed lace.*

**pe|po** (pē′pō), *n., pl.* **-pos.** the characteristic fruit of plants of the gourd family, a berry having a fleshy interior with numerous seeds covered by a hard or firm rind that is not easily separated, such as the melon, cucumber, and squash. [< New Latin *pepo* < Latin *pepō, -ōnis* pumpkin < Greek *pépōn* (*síkyos*) gourd ripe for eating < *pépōn* ripened, (literally) cooked by the sun < *péptein* to cook]

***pep|per** (pep′ər), *n., v.* —*n.* **1** a seasoning with a hot, spicy taste used for soups, meats, vegetables, and other foods. Pepper is made by grinding the berries of a shrub. Black pepper is made from whole berries; white pepper is made from husked berries. Pepper has been used from ancient times for flavoring and acts as a digestive stimulant and carminative. **2** the plant bearing berries from which pepper is made. It is a climbing shrub of the pepper family and is native to the East Indies. Pepper has alternate stalked leaves, with green spikes of hanging flowers, and small berries turning red when ripe. **3a** a hollow, green, red, or yellow vegetable that is eaten raw, cooked, or pickled, or dried and ground and used as seasoning. Paprika is made from a variety of pepper. **b** a low American herb or shrub bearing such a fruit, such as the sweet pepper, bird pepper, and chili. Peppers belong to the nightshade family. **4** a container for pepper: *silver salts and peppers.* **5** *Figurative.* pungent, biting or energetic quality: *There was plenty of pepper left in the old man.* **SYN**: vigor, energy, pungency.
—*v.t.* **1** to season with pepper; sprinkle with pepper. **2** *Figurative.* to sprinkle thickly; dot: *His face is peppered with freckles.* **3** to hit with, or as if with, small objects, sent thick and fast: *We peppered the enemy's lines with our shot.* (*Figurative.*) *Members of council peppered him with questions about details of his plan* (Maclean's). **4** to beat severely; trounce. **5** *Figurative.* to enliven: *Pretty soon he was ... peppering their restrained, unvarying arrangements with exuberant improvisations on his trumpet* (New Yorker).
[Old English *pipor* < Latin *piper* < Greek *píperi,* variant of *péperi.* Compare Sanskrit *pippalī* the long pepper.]

***pepper**
definitions 2, 3b

black pepper sweet pepper

**pep|per-and-salt** (pep′ər ən sôlt′), *adj.* **1** black and white finely mixed: *pepper-and-salt hair.* **2** woven of alternate threads of black and white cotton, wool, or other yarn, so as to have a grayish appearance at a slight distance: *a pepper-and-salt suit.*

**pep|per|box** (pep′ər boks′), *n.* **1** a container with holes in the top for sprinkling ground pepper on food. **2** *Informal, Figurative.* a hot-tempered person; pepperer.

**pep|per|corn** (pep′ər kôrn′), *n.* **1** one of the dried berries or fruits that are ground up to make pepper. **2a** such a berry or fruit paid as a nominal rent: *Manhattan's first art museum building ... was a neoclassic, circular structure, a few steps from City Hall, on ground rented from the city for one peppercorn a year* (Time). **b** *Figurative.* a small tribute or nominal token. **3** a small, tight knob of curled hair, characteristic of Bushmen and Hottentots. [Old English *piporcorn* < *pipor* pepper + *corn* corn, in sense of "seed, fruit"]

**pep|pered moth** (pep′ərd), a European moth with light-colored, speckled wings, which has evolved black or melanic varieties in industrially polluted areas.

**pep|per|er** (pep′ər ər), *n.* **1** a dealer in pepper and spices. **2** something that peppers. **3** *Figurative.* a hot-tempered person.

**pepper family,** a group of dicotyledonous aromatic or pungent herbs and shrubs found chiefly in tropical regions. The family includes the pepper and cubeb.

**Pepper Fog,** *Trademark.* = pepper gas.

**pepper game,** *Baseball.* a practicing of quick throws and bunts by a team just before a game as a warm-up.

**pepper gas,** a riot-control gas that forms a thick haze and causes irritation of the throat and nasal passages.

**pep|per|grass** (pep′ər gras′, -gräs′), *n.* a common weed of the mustard family, with a peppery taste, such as garden cress, used in salads: *"One of the characteristics of peppergrass," the wild-flower book said, "is that its seed pods are as hot as pepper when chewed"* (New Yorker).

**pep|per|idge** (pep′ər ij), *n.* = black gum. [American English; origin unknown]

**pep|per|i|ness** (pep′ər ē nis), *n.* peppery quality.

**pepper mill,** a device for grinding peppercorns.

**pep|per|mint** (pep′ər mint), *n.* **1** an herb grown for its aromatic, pungent essential oil that is used in medicine and in candy. It belongs to the mint family and is native to Europe. **2** this oil, or a preparation of it. **3** a candy flavored with oil of peppermint.

**peppermint stick,** a stick of peppermint-flavored hard candy, usually made in alternating straight or spiral stripes of red and white.

**pep|per|mint-stick** (pep′ər mint stik′), *adj.* colored like a peppermint stick in red and white stripes: *peppermint-stick toothpaste.*

**pepper pot, 1a** a West Indian stew of meat, fish, or game and vegetables, made with cassareep, cayenne pepper, and other spices. **b** any one of various somewhat similar highly seasoned stews. **2** a highly seasoned, rather thick soup made of tripe and vegetables; Philadelphia pepper pot. **3** *Archaic.* pepperbox.

**pepper shaker,** a container of metal, glass, or plastic, usually with a perforated top, from which ground pepper may be shaken on food.

**pepper tree** or **shrub,** an evergreen tree or shrub of the cashew family, native to tropical America, much grown for its ornamental pinnate leaves, clusters of white flowers, and bunches of small reddish fruit (drupes). One kind is widely grown in California. *When as a child in South Africa the train would pass a wayside station, and I would see a native sitting quietly under a pepper tree, it symbolized permanency to me* (Cape Times).

**pepper upper,** *Slang.* something that produces pep.

**pepper vine,** an upright, scarcely twining shrub of the grape family, of the southern United States, with bipinnate leaves and small purplish-black berries.

**pep|per|wort** (pep′ər wėrt′), *n.* = peppergrass.

**pep|per|y** (pep′ər ē), *adj.* **1** full of pepper; like pepper: (*Figurative.*) *Some good, strong, peppery doctrine* (Dickens). **2** hot; sharp. **3** *Figurative.* **a** having a hot temper; easily made angry: *Pettingil, whose peppery temper was well known among the boys* (Thomas Bailey Aldrich). **b** angry and sharp: *peppery words.*

**pep pill,** *Informal.* a stimulating drug, such as amphetamine, put up in pill form and used as a means of combating fatigue and inducing greater effort: *I began to step up my output, using pep pills and so on to maintain my metabolic rate* (Punch).

**pep|pi|ly** (pep′ə lē), *adv. Informal.* in a peppy manner: *They all walked off, the Doctor conversing peppily* (New Yorker).

**pep|pi|ness** (pep′ē nis), *n. Informal.* the quality or state of being peppy: *The old lady had peppiness and determination in spite of her years.*

**pep|py** (pep′ē), *adj.*, **-pi|er, -pi|est.** *Informal.* full of pep; energetic; lively: *Scotch terriers are peppy dogs.* [American English, perhaps < *pep*[1] + *-y*[1]]

**pep rally,** *Informal.* a meeting designed to arouse enthusiasm for a team, political campaign, or the like.

**pep|sin** or **pep|sine** (pep′sin), *n.* **1** an enzyme in the gastric juice of the stomach that helps to digest meat, eggs, cheese, and other proteins: *Pepsin is a digestive enzyme contained in the stomach juices that can bore into tissues and cause ulcers* (Science News Letter). **2** a medicine to help digestion, containing this enzyme. It is usually obtained from the stomach lining of pigs. [< obsolete German *Pepsine* < Greek *pépsis* digestion; (originally) ripening < *péptein* to cook]

**pep|sin|ate** (pep′sə nāt), *v.t.*, **-at|ed, -at|ing.** to treat, prepare, or mix with pepsin.

**pep|sin|o|gen** (pep sin′ə jən), *n.* the substance present in the gastric glands from which pepsin is formed during digestion: *Pepsin as it comes from the gastric glands is in an inactive state in which it is called pepsinogen* (A. Franklin Shull). [< *pepsin* + (zym)*ogen*]

**pep talk,** *Informal.* a speech or short talk designed to fill or inspire, as with energy or enthusiasm; exhortation: *Its language is deliberately that of a sales manager giving a pep talk to the boys* (Saturday Review).

**pep-talk** (pep′tôk′), *v.t. Informal.* to exhort; give a pep talk (to).

**pep|tic** (pep′tik), *adj., n.* —***adj.*** **1** having to do with or promoting digestion; digestive. **2** able to digest. **3** of, having to do with, or secreting pepsin.
—***n.*** a substance promoting digestion.
[< Latin *pepticus* < Greek *peptikós* < *peptós* cooked, digested < *péptein* to cook]

**peptic ulcer,** an ulcer of the mucous membrane of the stomach or of the duodenum, caused entirely or in part by the digestive action of gastric juice: *From their own experience with 32 cases of peptic ulcer in children up to age 15, they conclude that chronic peptic ulcer in children occurs in boys more frequently than girls* (Science News Letter).

**pep|tid** (pep′tid), *n.* = peptide.

**pep|ti|dase** (pep′ti dās), *n.* an enzyme that breaks down peptides or peptones into amino acids.

**pep|tide** (pep′tīd, -tid), *n.* any combination of two or more amino acids in which the carboxyl group of one acid is joined with the amino group of another: *The protein of the virus can be broken down by moderate chemical treatment into subunits, each of which is a single peptide chain containing about 150 amino acids* (Scientific American). [< *pept*(one) + *-ide*]

**peptide bond,** a chemical bond formed by the removal of water from two adjacent molecules of amino acid. The amino acids of proteins are linked by peptide bonds in protein synthesis.

**pep|ti|za|tion** (pep′tə zā′shən), *n.* the process of peptizing or converting into colloidal form.

**pep|tize** (pep′tīz), *v.t.*, **-tized, -tiz|ing.** to change (as a gel) into a colloidal solution or form: *Materials called protective colloids, or peptizing agents, are added to the mixture; and they apparently coat the suspended particles and so prevent their coalescing* (Monroe M. Offner). [< Greek *péptein* to cook + English *-ize*] —**pep′tiz|er,** *n.*

**pep|to|gen** (pep′tə jən), *n.* a substance or preparation that facilitates peptic digestion. [< *pepto*(ne) + *-gen*]

**pep|tone** (pep′tōn), *n.* any one of a class of diffusible and water-soluble substances into which meat, eggs, cheese, and other proteins are changed by pepsin or trypsin: *A continuation of the process results in the formation of a still more complex peptid called a peptone. Peptones in turn may combine to form proteins* (Harbaugh and Goodrich). [< German *Pepton* < Greek *peptós* cooked, digested (see etym. under **peptic**) + German *-on* -one]

**pep|ton|ic** (pep ton′ik), *adj.* having to do with or containing peptones.

**pep|ton|i|za|tion** (pep′tə nə zā′shən), *n.* the process of peptonizing or converting into peptones.

**pep|to|nize** (pep′tə nīz), *v.t.*, **-nized, -niz|ing.** **1** to convert into a peptone. **2** to subject (food) to an artificial partial digestion by means of pepsin or pancreatic extract, as an aid to digestion. —**pep′to|niz′er,** *n.*

**Pepys|i|an** (pēp′sē ən), *adj.* of, written by, or characteristic of Samuel Pepys (1633-1703), English diarist: *The book as published is not a diary in any spontaneous Pepysian sense* (Atlantic).

**Pe|quot** (pē′kwot), *n., pl.* **-quots** or **-quot.** **1** a member of a tribe of American Indians of Algonkian stock formerly living in southern New England. **2** the language of this tribe. [American English, apparently < Algonkian (some eastern North American language) *Pequatoog* destroyers < *paquatoog* they destroy]

**per** (pər; *stressed* pėr), *prep.* **1** for each; for every: *a pint of milk per child, ten cents per pound.* **2** by; by means of; through: *I send this per my son.* **3** according to: *per invoice.* [< Latin *per* through, on account of]
▶ **Per** is used chiefly in business or technical English: *per capita, per cent, $50 per week, revolutions per minute.* In general English it is usually avoided: *$50 a week, eight hours a day.*

**per-,** *prefix.* **1** throughout; thoroughly; utterly; very: *Perfervid = very fervid. Peruse = use* (i.e., read) *thoroughly.*
**2** *Chemistry.* **a** the maximum or a large amount of, as in *peroxide.* **b** having the indicated element in its highest or a high valence, as in *perchloric acid.*
[< Latin *per-* < *per*]

**per.,** **1** period. **2** person.

**per|a|ce|tic acid** (pėr′ə sē′tik, -set′ik), a colorless, pungent liquid, related to acetic acid as a peracid, and used as a bleaching agent in textiles and paper, and as a bactericide and fungicide. *Formula:* $CH_3COOOH$

**per|ac|id** (pėr as′id), *n.* an acid containing a greater proportion of oxygen than others made up of the same elements. *Example:* perchloric acid ($HClO_4$) is a peracid in its relation to chloric acid ($HClO_3$).

**per|ad|ven|ture** (pėr′əd ven′chər), *n., adv.* —***n.*** uncertainty; doubt; chance; question: *It was affirmed—and the truth was certainly beyond peradventure—that religious liberty was dead* (John L. Motley). [< adverb]
—***adv.*** *Archaic.* maybe; perhaps: *Peradventure I may be an hour later* (Henry Fielding). **SYN:** possibly.
[Middle English alteration of *per-,* or *parauntre,* reduction of *par aventure* < Old French *par aventure* < *par* by + *aventure* chance, adventure; influenced by Latin *adventura*]

**per|am|bu|late** (pə ram′byə lāt), *v.*, **-lat|ed, -lat|ing.** —***v.t.*** **1** to walk through: *Burgomaster Van der Werf ... ordered the city musicians to perambulate the streets, playing lively melodies and martial airs* (John L. Motley). **2** to walk through and examine.
—***v.i.*** to walk or travel about; stroll.
[< Latin *perambulāre* (with English *-ate*[1]) < *per-* through + *ambulāre* to walk] —**per|am′bu|la′tion,** *n.*

***per|am|bu|la|tor** (pə ram′byə lā′tər), *n.* **1** *British.* a small carriage in which a baby is pushed about; pram. **2** a person who perambulates. **3** instrument for measuring distances by clocking the number of revolutions of a wheel rolled over the ground, formerly used in surveying.

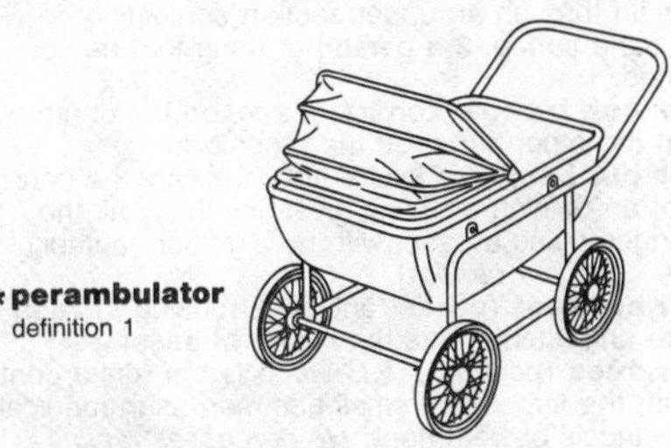

***perambulator** definition 1

**per|am|bu|la|to|ry** (pə ram′byə lə tôr′ē, -tōr′-), *adj.* of perambulating; traveling.

**per an.** or **per ann.,** per annum.

**per an|num** (pər an′əm), per year; yearly; for each year: *Her salary was $10,000 per annum.* [< Medieval Latin *per* for every (< Latin, through), and Latin *annum,* accusative of *annus* year]

**per|bo|rate** (pėr bôr′āt, -bōr′-), *n.* a salt of perboric acid, having either the univalent radical $-BO_3$ or the bivalent radical $-B_4O_8$, as perborax (sodium perborate).

**per|bo|rax** (pėr bôr′aks, -bōr′-), *n.* a crystalline powder, a salt of perboric acid, used in bleaching, as an oxidizing agent, and as an antiseptic; sodium perborate. *Formula:* $NaBO_3 \cdot 4H_2O$

**per|bo|ric acid** (pėr bôr′ik, -bōr′-), an acid occurring only in solution or in the form of its salts; peroxyboric acid. *Formula:* $HBO_3$

**per|bro|mate** (pər brō′māt), *n.* a salt of perbromic acid.

**per|bro|mic acid** (pər brō′mik), a compound of bromine in its highest oxidation state. It lies between the analogous perchloric and periodic acids. *Formula:* $HBrO_4$

**per|cale** (pər kāl′, -kal′), *n.* a closely woven cotton cloth with a smooth finish, used especially for dresses and sheets. [< French *percale* < Persian *pergāl*]

**per|ca|line** (pėr′kə lēn′), *n.* a fine, usually glossy, cotton cloth, often dyed a solid color, and used for linings and covering books. [< French *percaline* (diminutive) < *percale*]

**per cap.,** per capita.

**per cap|i|ta** (pər kap′ə tə), **1** for each person: *$40 for eight men is $5 per capita.* **2** *Law.* divided among a number of individuals in equal shares, as an inheritance or estate. [< Medieval Latin *per* by, according to, and Latin *capita,* neuter plural of *caput, -itis* head]

**per ca|put** (pər kā′pət, kap′ət), = per capita. [< Medieval Latin *per* by, according to + Latin *caput* head]

**per|ceiv|a|ble** (pər sē′və bəl), *adj.* that can be perceived; perceptible. **SYN:** intelligible, appreciable. —**per|ceiv′a|bly,** *adv.*

**per|ceive** (pər sēv′), *v.*, **-ceived, -ceiv|ing.** —***v.t.*** **1** to be aware of through the senses; see, hear, taste, smell, or feel: *Did you perceive the colors of that bird? We perceived a little girl coming toward us* (Frederick Marryat). **SYN:** See syn. under **see.** **2** to take in with the mind; observe: *I soon perceived that I could not make him change his mind. I plainly perceive some objections remain* (Edmund Burke). **SYN:** understand, comprehend. See syn. under **see.**
—***v.i.*** to grasp or take in something with the senses or mind.
[< Old North French *perceivre* < Latin *percipere* < *per-* thoroughly + *capere* to grasp] —**per|ceiv′er,** *n.*

**per|ceived noise decibel** (pər sēvd′), a standard unit for measuring noise as perceived by people, based on the type of sound and its intensity: *Airplane noise is measured in perceived noise decibels* (New York Times). *Abbr:* PNdB or PNdb (no periods).

***per cent,** or **per|cent** (pər sent′), *n., adj.* —***n.*** **1** hundredths; parts in each hundred. Five per cent is 5 of each 100, or 5/100 of the whole. Five per cent of 40 is 2. The use of *per cent* is a convenient way to express many proportions: *shrinkage of less than one per cent. Ten per cent of the children were absent because of illness. Abbr:* pct. *Symbol:* % **2** *Informal.* percentage: *A large per cent of the state's apple crop was ruined.*
—***adj.*** by the hundred; for, in, or to every hundred (used with a preceding numeral to express a proportion): *a 50 per cent chance to win, a 10 percent deduction, a two percent sales tax.*
**per cents** or **percents, a** (with preceding numeral) securities, especially public ones, bearing the designated rate of interest: *to invest in the three per cents.* **b** (without preceding numeral) percentages: *The tread of the businessmen who must count their per cents by the paces they take* (Elizabeth Barrett Browning).
[(originally) *per cent.,* abbreviation of Medieval Latin *per centum* by the hundred(s)]
▶ **Per cent** may be written as either two words or one and in U.S. usage is not followed by a period.

***per cent** definition 1

% ...a 3% rise in enrollment.

symbol

**per|cent|age** (pər sen′tij), *n.* **1** a rate or proportion of each hundred; part of each hundred: *What percentage of children were absent? The French were ... suffering a lower percentage of casualties than the British* (H. G. Wells). **2** a part or proportion: *A large percentage of schoolbooks now have pictures. Television attracts a large percentage of the people.* **3** an allowance, commission, discount, rate of interest, or other share, figured by per cent. **4** *Informal.* advantage or profit.

**per|cent|age|wise** (pər sen′tij wīz), *adv.* from the standpoint of percentage or percentages: *He estimated sales probably would be off a little more percentagewise for the six months as a whole than the 2 per cent drop suffered in the first quarter* (Wall Street Journal).

**per|cen|tile** (pər sen′tīl, -təl), *n., adj.* —***n.*** **1** any value in a series of points on a scale arrived at by dividing a group into a hundred equal parts in order of magnitude. **2** one of these parts: *A student in the ninetieth percentile of his class on a*

**Pronunciation Key:** hat, āge, cãre, fär; let, ēqual, tėrm; it, īce; hot, ōpen, ôrder; oil, out; cup, pu̇t, rüle; child; long; thin; ᴛʜen; zh, measure;
ə represents **a** in about, **e** in taken, **i** in pencil, **o** in lemon, **u** in circus.

*particular test is in the top ten per cent.*
—***adj.*** of or having to do with percentiles; being or expressed as a percentage: *a percentile rating.*
[apparently < *per cent,* patterned on *quartile, sextile*]

**per cen|tum** (pər sen′təm), **1** by the hundred. **2** for or in every hundred: [*The*] *senate bill ... would require all organizations that lend money or give credit to disclose to the customer his cost in interest per centum per annum* (Maclean's).

**per|cept** (pėr′sept), *n.* **1** that which is perceived. **2** the understanding that is the result of perceiving. [< Latin *perceptum* (thing) perceived, neuter past participle of *percipere* to perceive]

**per|cep|ti|bil|i|ty** (pər sep′tə bil′ə tē), *n.* the fact, quality, or state of being perceptible.

**per|cep|ti|ble** (pər sep′tə bəl), *adj.* that can be perceived; observable; appreciable: *a perceptible improvement, a perceptible time. The other ship was barely perceptible in the fog.* **SYN**: palpable, cognizable. —**per|cep′ti|ble|ness,** *n.* —**per|cep′ti|bly,** *adv.*

**per|cep|tion** (pər sep′shən), *n.* **1** the act of perceiving: *His perception of the change came in a flash.* **SYN**: insight, apprehension, discernment, comprehension. **2** the power of perceiving: *a keen perception. Defect in manners is usually the defect of fine perceptions* (Emerson). **3** understanding that is the result of perceiving; percept: *He had a clear perception of what was wrong, and soon fixed it.* **4** *Psychology.* the study of the complex process by which patterns of environmental energies become known as objects, events, people, and other aspects of the world. [< Latin *perceptiō, -ōnis* < *percipere* perceive]

**per|cep|tion|al** (pər sep′shə nəl), *adj.* of or having to do with perception.

**per|cep|tive** (pər sep′tiv), *adj.* **1** having to do with perception. **2** having the power of perceiving; intelligent: *a perceptive reader of poetry, a perceptive audience.* **SYN**: discerning. —**per|cep′tive|ly,** *adv.* —**per|cep′tive|ness,** *n.*

**per|cep|tiv|i|ty** (pėr′sep tiv′ə tē), *n.* perceptive quality; power of perception or thinking.

**per|cep|tu|al** (pər sep′chů əl), *adj.* of or having to do with perception. —**per|cep′tu|al|ly,** *adv.*

**Per|ce|val** (pėr′sə vəl), *n.* = Percival.

**perch**[1] (pėrch), *n., v.* —*n.* **1** a bar, branch, or anything else on which a bird can come to rest: *The bird kept away from the cat on a perch high in the tree.* **2** a rather high place or position: *From my perch on the crosstrees, I had nothing below me but the surface of the bay* (Robert Louis Stevenson). (*Figurative.*) *Not making his high place the lawless perch Of wing'd ambitions* (Tennyson). **3** a measure of length equal to 5½ yards or 5.0292 meters; rod. *Abbr:* p. **4** a measure of area equal to 30¼ square yards or 25.293 square meters; square rod. **5** a measure of volume in masonry; 24¾ cubic feet or .7004 cubic meter. **6** a pole connecting the front and rear running parts in a wagon.
—***v.i.*** **1** to alight and rest; sit: *A robin perched on our porch railing.* **2** to sit rather high: *He perched on a stool.* (*Figurative.*) *The little village perches high among the hills* (H. G. Wells).
—***v.t.*** to place high up: *Little birds perch themselves on the cows' backs to eat ticks and mites.*
[< Old French *perche* < Latin *pertica* pole, measuring rod]

**perch**[2] (pėrch), *n., pl.* **perch|es** or (*collectively*) **perch. 1** a small, freshwater fish with a spiny fin, used for food, especially the yellow perch of North America. **2** any one of various related freshwater or saltwater fishes, such as the white perch. [< Old French *perche* < Latin *perca* < Greek *pérkē,* related to *perknós* dark-colored]

**per|chance** (pər chans′, -chäns′), *adv.* **1** perhaps; it may be; by chance: *To sleep: perchance to dream* (Shakespeare). *The climax would be interesting, if perchance uncomfortable* (Winston Churchill). **SYN**: peradventure. **2** by any chance; accidentally: *I counsel thee to stand aloof ... lest perchance He smite thee with his spear* (William Cullen Bryant). [< Anglo-French *par chance* < Old French *par* by + *cheance* chance]

**perch|er** (pėr′chər), *n.* **1** a person or thing that perches. **2** a bird with feet adapted for perching.

**Per|che|ron** (pėr′chə ron, -shə-), *n.* one of a breed of large and strong draft horses originally raised in Perche, France. [< French *Percheron* < Le *Perche,* a district in France]

**per|chlo|rate** (pėr klôr′āt, -klōr′-), *n.* a salt of perchloric acid.

**per|chlor|eth|yl|ene** (pėr′klôr eth′ə lēn, -klōr-), *n.* = perchloroethylene.

**per|chlo|ric acid** (pėr klôr′ik, -klōr′-), a colorless, syrupy liquid used as an oxidizing agent, for plating metals, and in explosives. It is stable when diluted, but its concentrated form is highly explosive when in contact with oxidizable substances. *Formula:* $HClO_4$

**per|chlo|ride** (pėr klôr′īd, -id; -klōr′-), *n.* a compound of chlorine with another element or radical, containing the maximum proportion of chlorine.

**per|chlo|rin|ate** (pėr klôr′ə nāt, -klōr′-), *v.t.,* **-at|ed, -at|ing.** to combine or charge with the maximum proportion of chlorine. —**per|chlo′rin|a′tion,** *n.*

**per|chlo|ro|eth|yl|ene** (pėr′klôr ō eth′ə lēn, -klōr-), *n.* a colorless, nonflammable liquid, used as a dry-cleaning fluid, degreaser, and solvent, and medically as an anthelmintic agent; tetrachloroethylene. *Formula:* $Cl_2C{:}CCl_2$

**per|chro|mate** (pėr krō′māt), *n.* a salt of perchromic acid.

**per|chro|mic acid** (pėr krō′mik), an unstable, deep-blue crystalline acid. *Possible formula:* $H_3CrO_8 \cdot 2H_2O$

**per|cip|i|ence** (pər sip′ē əns), *n.* the act, condition, or power of perceiving; perception; discernment; cognizance.

**per|cip|i|en|cy** (pər sip′ē ən sē), *n., pl.* **-cies.** = percipience.

**per|cip|i|ent** (pər sip′ē ənt), *adj., n.* —***adj.*** **1** that perceives or is capable of perceiving; conscious. **2** having keen perception; discerning.
—*n.* a person or thing that perceives.
[< Latin *percipiēns, -entis,* present participle of *percipere* perceive] —**per|cip′i|ent|ly,** *adv.*

**Per|ci|val** or **Per|ci|vale** (pėr′sə vəl), *n.* one of King Arthur's knights in the Arthurian legends, who sought and finally saw the Holy Grail.

**per|coid** (pėr′koid), *adj., n.* —***adj.*** **1** resembling a perch. **2** of or belonging to a large suborder of spiny-finned teleost fishes, including the freshwater perches, basses, and sunfishes, and certain saltwater fishes, such as the mackerels and tunas.
—*n.* a percoid fish.
[< New Latin *Percoidea* the perch family < Latin *perca* (< Greek *pérkē* perch) + Greek *eîdos* form]

**per|coi|de|an** (pər koi′dē ən), *adj.* = percoid.

**per|co|late** (pėr′kə lāt), *v.,* **-lat|ed, -lat|ing,** *n.*
—***v.i.*** **1** to drip or drain through small holes or spaces: *Let the coffee percolate for seven minutes.* **2** *Slang, Figurative.* to act efficiently. —***v.t.*** **1** to filter through; permeate: *Water percolates sand.* (*Figurative.*) *relief payments percolate the economy.* **SYN**: filter, ooze, trickle. **2** to cause (a liquid or particles) to pass through; filter; sift. **3** to make (coffee) in a percolator.
—*n.* a liquid that has been percolated.
[< Latin *percōlāre* (with English *-ate*[1]) < *per-* through + *cōlāre* to filter through < *cōlum* strainer]

**per|co|la|tion** (pėr′kə lā′shən), *n.* the act or process of percolating.

**per|co|la|tor** (pėr′kə lā′tər), *n.* **1** a kind of coffeepot in which boiling water drains over and over again through an upper section containing ground coffee. **2** a person or thing that percolates.

**per con|tra** (pər kon′trə), *Latin.* on the contrary; on the other hand; on the other side.

**per cur|i|am** (pėr kyůr′ē am), *Law.* by the court (of an opinion or ruling given jointly by all the judges trying a case, with no signatory author). [< Latin *per curiām*]

**per|cur|rent** (pər kėr′ənt), *adj.* running through the entire length, as the midrib of a leaf.

**per|cuss** (pər kus′), *v.t., v.i.* to tap or strike gently with the finger or a small hammer, as in medical diagnosis or treatment: *He percusses rapidly over a nerve when the pain is dull or grinding, and percusses slowly when the pain is acute* (T. L. Brunton). [< Latin *percussus,* past participle of *percutere* < *per-* (intensive) + *quatere* strike, beat]

**per|cus|sion** (pər kush′ən), *n.* **1** the striking of one body against another with force; stroke; blow: *The tremendous percussion of the waterfall sent up a deafening roar.* **SYN**: impact. **2** the striking of a percussion cap or other similar device to set off the charge in a firearm. **3** the shock made by the striking of one body against another with force; impact: *Every part however small which turned over as the result of percussion would suddenly cause another balance to fall* (Science News). **4** *Medicine.* the tapping of a part of the body to determine by the quality of the sound the condition of the organs underneath. **5** *Music.* **a** the striking of percussion instruments to produce tones: [*She*] *plays piano with miraculous precision and tremendous percussion* (New Yorker). **b** the percussion instruments of an orchestra. **c** their players. **6** the striking of sound upon the ear. [< Latin *percussiō, -ōnis* < *percussus;* see etym. under **percuss**]

**percussion cap,** a small cap containing powder. When struck by the hammer of a gun, it explodes and sets off a larger charge.

**percussion instrument,** a musical instrument played by striking it, such as a drum, cymbal, piano, tambourine, castanets, or chimes.

**per|cus|sion|ist** (pər kush′ə nist), *n.* a person who plays a percussion instrument or instruments, especially in an orchestra.

**percussion lock,** a type of gunlock that strikes and fires a percussion cap.

**per|cus|sive** (pər kus′iv), *adj., n.* —***adj.*** of, having to do with, or characterized by percussion: *His piano Bach is in the approved lighter, percussive, and staccato style* (Edward Tatnall Canby).
—*n.* = percussion instrument. —**per|cus′sive|ly,** *adv.* —**per|cus′sive|ness,** *n.*

**per|cu|ta|ne|ous** (pėr′kyü tā′nē əs), *adj.* made, done, or effected through the skin: *percutaneous absorption.* —**per′cu|ta′ne|ous|ly,** *adv.*

**per|die** (pər dē′), *adv., interj.* = pardi.

**per di|em** (pər dī′əm, dē′əm), **1** per day; for each day: *Rental of the boat per diem was $5. Petitioner was compensated at a specified per diem rate* (New York Times). **2** an allowance of so much every day for living expenses, usually while traveling in connection with work: *a rate ... sufficient to cover costs ... including crew per diem* (Newsweek). [< Medieval Latin *per* to, for every; and Latin *diem,* accusative of *diēs* day]

**per|di|tion** (pər dish′ən), *n.* **1** the loss of one's soul or of the joys of heaven; final spiritual ruin; damnation. **2** hell: *Would you send A soul straight to perdition?* (Robert Browning). **3** utter loss or destruction; complete ruin: *the Arabian invaders had sealed the perdition of Spain* (Washington Irving). **4** *Obsolete.* diminution; loss. [< Latin *perditiō, -ōnis* < *perdere* to destroy < *per-* (pejorative) + *dare* give]

**per|du** (pər dü′, -dyü′), *adj., n.* —***adj.*** hidden away; out of sight; concealed: *James ... was lying perdu in the lobby* (Scott).
—*n.* *Obsolete.* a soldier in a position of special danger, and hence considered as virtually lost.
[< Middle French *perdu,* past participle of *perdre* to lose < Latin *perdere* destroy; see etym. under **perdition**]

**per|due** (pər dü′, -dyü′), *adj.* the feminine of **perdu.**

**per|du|ra|bil|i|ty** (pər důr′ə bil′ə tē, -dyůr′-), *n.* perdurable quality or state.

**per|du|ra|ble** (pər důr′ə bəl, -dyůr′-), *adj.* everlasting; imperishable; permanent: *cables of perdurable toughness* (Shakespeare); *leaving a name perdurable on earth* (Robert Southey). [< Old French *pardurable* < Late Latin *perdūrābilis* < *perdūrāre* to endure; see etym. under **perdure**]

**per|du|ra|bly** (pər důr′ə blē, -dyůr′-), *adv.* in a perdurable manner; permanently.

**per|dure** (pər důr′, -dyůr′), *v.i.,* **-dured, -dur|ing.** to endure or continue long or forever. [< Late Latin *perdūrāre* < Latin *per-* (intensive) + *dūrāre* endure, harden < *dūrus* hard]

**père** (per), *n. French.* father; senior, often used after proper names to distinguish a father from his son (*fils*): *Dumas père.*

**Père** (per), *n. French.* Father, used before the name of a priest: *Père Marquette.*

**Père David's deer,** a large, grayish-brown deer of northern China. [< *Père* (Armand) *David,* 1826-1900, a French missionary and naturalist]

**per|e|gri|nate** (per′ə grə nāt), *v.,* **-nat|ed, -nat|ing.** —***v.i.*** to travel around; journey.
—***v.t.*** to travel over; traverse.
[< Latin *peregrīnārī* (with English *-ate*[1]) *peregrīnus* peregrine]

**per|e|gri|na|tion** (per′ə grə nā′shən), *n.* **1** the act or fact of peregrinating; journeying: *The pursuit of the trade meant ... a regular camping out from month to month, a peregrination among farms which could be counted by the hundred* (Thomas Hardy). **2** a journey; travel: *The gray-haired veteran retired, after a long peregrination, to his native town* (George Borrow).
**peregrinations, a** travels: *It describes the finding and perilous peregrinations of the Scrolls* (James R. Newman). **b** a narrative of travels: *to write peregrinations.*

**per|e|gri|na|tor** (per′ə grə nā′tər), *n.* a person who peregrinates.

**per|e|grine** (per′ə grin, -grīn, -grēn), *n., adj.* —***n.*** **1** a large, swift, powerful falcon, the species preferred for falconry. The American variety is the duck hawk. *Out of the reeds, like an arrow, shot the peregrine* (Charles Kingsley). **2** a foreign visitor in a country; resident who is not a citizen.
—***adj.*** **1** not native; foreign. **2** outlandish; strange. **3** being upon a pilgrimage; traveling abroad: *the passage now presents no hindrance To the spirit unappeased and peregrine Between two worlds* (T. S. Eliot). **4** *Astrology.* (of a planet) so situated in the zodiac that it has none of its essential dignities.
[< Latin *peregrīnus* from foreign parts < *peregrē,* adverb, abroad, or *perager,* noun, one who has gone through (lands) < *per-* outside + *ager* (*Romanus*) the (Roman) territory. See etym. of doublet **pilgrim.**]

**peregrine falcon,** = peregrine (def. 1).

**pe|reir|a bark**, or **pe|reir|a** (pə rār′ə), *n.* **1** the bark of a South American tree of the dogbane family, used in medicine as a source of pereirine. **2** the tree itself. [< Jonathan *Pereira,* 1804-1853, an English pharmacologist]

**pe|rei|rin** (pə rār′in), *n.* = pereirine.

**pe|rei|rine** (pə rār′ēn, -in), *n.* an alkaloid obtained as a brown powder from pereira bark, formerly used as a substitute for quinine and in tonics. *Formula:* $C_{20}H_{26}N_2O$

**per|emp|to|ry** (pə remp′tər ē; per′əmp tôr′ē, -tōr′-), *adj., n., pl.* **-ries.** —*adj.* **1** leaving no choice; decisive; final; absolute; conclusive: *a peremptory decree. It is a peremptory point of virtue that a man's independence be secured* (Emerson). **SYN**: definite. **2** allowing no denial or refusal: *A peremptory command would have compelled obedience* (Samuel Johnson). **3** imperious; positive; dictatorial: *a peremptory teacher. He spoke in a loud and peremptory voice, using the tone of one in authority* (Booth Tarkington). **SYN**: arbitrary, dogmatic.
—*n. Law.* = peremptory challenge.
[< Latin *perēmptōrius* decisive, deadly; that ends < *perēmptor, -ōris* destroyer < *perimere* destroy < *per-* completely + *emere* (originally) take, buy]
—**per|emp′to|ri|ly**, *adv.* —**per|emp′to|ri|ness**, *n.*

**peremptory challenge**, *Law.* the right to challenge the selection of a juror without showing cause.

**per|en|nate** (per′ə nāt, pə ren′āt), *v.i.,* **-nat|ed, -nat|ing.** to last through a number of years, as a perennial plant. [< Latin *perennāre* (with English *-ate*[1]) < *perennis* perennial] —**per′en|na′tion**, *n.*

**per|en|ni|al** (pə ren′ē əl), *adj., n.* —*adj.* **1** lasting through the whole year: *a perennial stream.* **2** lasting for a very long time; enduring: *the perennial beauty of the hills.* **SYN**: abiding, continual, permanent, perpetual, everlasting, eternal. **3** having underground parts that live more than two years: *perennial garden plants.*
—*n.* a perennial plant. Roses are perennials.
[< Latin *perennis* lasting through the year(s) (< *per-* through + *annus* year) + English *-al*[1]] —**per|en′ni|al|ly**, *adv.*

**perennial ragweed**, a kind of ragweed that grows from long, spreading roots and has fruit with blunt tubercles instead of spines.

**perf.**, an abbreviation for the following:
**1** perfect.
**2** perforated (of stamps).
**3** performance.
**4** performed.

**per|fect** (*adj., n.* pėr′fikt; *v.* pər fekt′), *adj., v., n.* —*adj.* **1** having no faults; not spoiled at any point; without defect: *a perfect spelling paper, a perfect apple, a perfect life. Perfect work shows great care.* **SYN**: faultless, impeccable. **2a** completely skilled; expert: *a perfect golfer. Our battle is more full of names than yours, Our men more perfect in the use of arms* (Shakespeare). **SYN**: accomplished. **b** thoroughly learned or acquired: *The lesson is but plain, And once made perfect, never lost again* (Shakespeare). **3** having all its parts there; whole; complete: *The set was perfect; nothing was missing or broken.* **SYN**: intact. **4** exact: *a perfect copy, a perfect circle.* **SYN**: precise. **5** entire; utter; total: *perfect quiet. He was a perfect stranger to us.* **6** pure; unmixed; unalloyed: *perfect blue.* **7** *Grammar.* **a** showing an action or event completed at the time of speaking or at the time spoken of. **b** designating a verb form or verb phrase with such a meaning. Three perfect tenses in English are: present perfect (*I have done*), past perfect (*I had done*), and future perfect (*I will have done*). **8** *Botany.* having both stamens and pistils: *a perfect flower.* **9** *Music.* having to do with the intervals or original consonances of unison, a fourth, fifth, and octave, as contrasted with the major intervals of a third and sixth. **10** *Mathematics.* (of a whole number) equal to the sum of its divisors. **11** *Obsolete.* assured; certain: *Thou art perfect then, our ship hath touch'd upon The deserts of Bohemia?* (Shakespeare). **12** *Obsolete.* satisfied; contented: *Might we but have that happiness ... we should think ourselves forever perfect* (Shakespeare).
—*v.t.* **1** to make perfect; remove all faults from; add the finishing touches to; improve: *to perfect an invention. The artist is perfecting his picture.* **2** to carry through; complete; finish: *to perfect a plan; ... the system of religious persecution commenced by Charles, and perfected by Philip* (John L. Motley). **3** to make fully skilled: *to perfect oneself in an art.*
—*n. Grammar.* **1** the perfect tense. **2** a verb form or verb phrase in the perfect tense. *Have eaten* is the perfect of *eat. Abbr:* perf.
[alteration (influenced by Latin) of Middle English *parfite* < Old French *parfit* < Latin *perfectus* completed, past participle of *perficere* < *per-* thoroughly + *facere* make, do] —**per|fect′er**, *n.* —**per′fect|ness**, *n.*

**per|fec|ta** (pər fek′tə), *n., pl.* **-tas.** = exacta. [< American Spanish *perfecta,* short for *quiniela perfecta* perfect quiniela]

**per|fect|a|bil|i|ty** (pər fek′tə bil′ə tē), *n., pl.* **-ties.** = perfectibility.

**perfect binding**, a method of binding books, pads of paper, and the like, in which glue is applied to each cut sheet of paper on the binding edge, and a paper cover is put on or a stiff backing is attached. Perfect binding is used for most inexpensive paperback books.

**per|fect-bound** (pėr′fikt bound′), *adj.* (of a book) bound by perfect binding.

**perfect cadence**, *Music.* a cadence in which the closing chord is the tonic.

**perfect game**, **1** a baseball game in which the pitcher does not allow any member of the opposing team to reach first base and in which there are no base hits, no walks, and no runs in nine or more innings. **2** a bowling game of twelve consecutive strikes.

**per|fect|i|bil|i|ty** (pər fek′tə bil′ə tē), *n., pl.* **-ties.** capability of becoming, or being made, perfect: *Patience, he derives from the innermost faith in the perfectibility of man* (Bulletin of Atomic Scientists).

**per|fect|i|ble** (pər fek′tə bəl), *adj.* capable of becoming, or being made, perfect; able to attain perfection: *Man, he thought, was perfectible, and a little calm argument would make him perfect* (Leslie Stephen).

**per|fec|tion** (pər fek′shən), *n.* **1** perfect condition; faultless quality; highest excellence. **SYN**: faultlessness. **2** a perfect person or thing: *His work was always perfection. The Empire coach was the perfection of fast travelling* (Charles Lever). **3** the act or process of making complete or perfect: *Perfection of our plans will take another week.* **SYN**: fulfillment. **4** a quality, trait, or accomplishment, of a high degree of excellence. **5** the highest or most perfect degree of a quality or trait: *the perfection of goodness.*
**to perfection**, perfectly: *He played the difficult violin concerto to perfection.*
[< Latin *perfectiō, -ōnis* < *perfectus* completed; see etym. under **perfect**]

**per|fec|tion|ism** (pər fek′shə niz əm), *n.* **1** any one of various doctrines maintaining that religious, moral, social, or political perfection is attainable: *An anxious perfectionism can ... destroy those real underpinnings of existence, found in faith, modesty, humor* (Atlantic). **2** the beliefs or practices of a perfectionist: *Often she has tried to moderate his irritable perfectionism, which can result in his berating other actors* (Time).

**per|fec|tion|ist** (pər fek′shə nist), *n., adj.* —*n.* **1** a person who is not content with anything that is not perfect or nearly perfect: *It is hard to keep house for a perfectionist.* **2** a person who believes that it is possible to lead a sinless life.
—*adj.* of or having to do with perfectionists or perfectionism.

**per|fec|tion|is|tic** (pər fek′shə nis′tik), *adj.* seeking or demanding perfection, especially to an impractical degree; being a perfectionist.

**per|fec|tive** (pər fek′tiv), *adj., n.* —*adj.* **1** tending to make perfect or complete. **2** *Grammar.* (in some languages) designating or having to do with an aspect of the verb that expresses completion of action.
—*n. Grammar.* **1** the perfective aspect. **2** a verb form or verb phrase in the perfective aspect
—**per|fec′tive|ly**, *adv.* —**per|fec′tive|ness**, *n.*

**per|fect|ly** (pėr′fikt lē), *adv.* in a perfect manner or degree; fully or faultlessly; completely or thoroughly; with utmost exactness; entirely: *perfectly new, perfectly clear, to do a job perfectly. I am perfectly able to do it myself. I understand the difficulty perfectly, mother* (George Eliot).

**perfect number**, a positive integer which is equal to the sum of its factors (other than itself). Six, being the sum of its factors 1, 2, and 3, is a perfect number, as is 28 (1, 2, 4, 7, and 14).

**per|fec|to** (pər fek′tō), *n., pl.* **-tos.** a thick cigar that tapers nearly to a point at both ends. See picture under **cigar**. [American English < Spanish *perfecto* perfect < Latin *perfectus;* see etym. under **perfect**]

**perfect participle**, a participle expressing action completed before the time of speaking or acting. In "Having written the letter, she mailed it," *having written* is a perfect participle.
► See **participle** for usage note.

**perfect pitch**, the sense of pitch that enables a person to identify a tone heard and name it as a note on a musical scale; absolute pitch.

**perfect ream**, a package or pile of 516 uniform sheets of printing paper; 21½ quires.

**perfect rhyme**, **1** rhyme between two words having the same pronunciation but different meanings; rich rhyme. Examples: *bear* (animal), *bear* (carry), *bare* (naked); *sale, sail.* **2** rhyme between two words having the same stress but different sounds preceding the stressed vowels, as in *frightening* and *tightening* or *June* and *moon.*

**perfect year**, = abundant year.

**per|fer|vid** (pėr fėr′vid), *adj.* very fervid; very ardent: *She was moved by this perfervid letter ... Its effect—the effect of its passionate flattery—was to lift her nobly to an eminence* (Maurice Hewlett). —**per|fer′vid|ly**, *adv.* —**per|fer′vid|ness**, *n.*

**per|fer|vor** (pėr fėr′vər), *n.* perfervid quality.

**per|fid|i|ous** (pər fid′ē əs), *adj.* deliberately faithless; treacherous: *Compelled to parley, Bossu resorted to a perfidious stratagem* (John L. Motley). **SYN**: false, traitorous, unfaithful. [< Latin *perfidiōsus* (with English *-ous*) < *perfidia* perfidy] —**per|fid′i|ous|ly**, *adv.* —**per|fid′i|ous|ness**, *n.*

**per|fi|dy** (pėr′fə dē), *n., pl.* **-dies.** a breaking faith; base treachery; being false to a trust: *a forsaken lady ... bewailing the perfidy of her lover* (Charlotte Brontë). **SYN**: faithlessness, betrayal, disloyalty. [< Latin *perfidia* < *perfidus* faithless < *per-* (pejorative) + *fidēs, -ēī* faith]

**per|fo|li|ate** (pər fō′lē it, -āt), *adj.* having the stem apparently passing through the blade: *a perfoliate leaf.* [< New Latin *perfoliatus* < Latin *per-* through + *folium* leaf]

**per|fo|li|a|tion** (pər fō′lē ā′shən), *n.* perfoliate condition.

**per|fo|rate** (*v.* pėr′fə rāt; *adj.* pėr′fər it, -fə rāt), *v.,* **-rat|ed, -rat|ing,** *adj.* —*v.t.* **1a** to make a hole or holes through; bore or punch through, as with a sharp instrument; pierce: *The target was perforated by bullets.* **SYN**: puncture. **b** to make a hole or holes into; bore into: *trees perforated by woodpeckers. The well was perforated from 9,082 to 9,092 feet* (Wall Street Journal). **2** to make a row or rows of holes through: *Sheets of postage stamps are perforated.* —*v.i.* to make its way into or through something; make a perforation.
—*adj.* pierced; *perforate corals.*
[< Latin *perforāre* (with English *-ate*[1]) < *per-* through + *forāre* to bore[1]] —**per′fo|ra′tor**, *n.*

**per|fo|rat|ed** (pėr′fə rā′tid), *adj.* **1** pierced with rows of small holes: *a perforated sheet of stamps or coupons.* **2** full of holes.

**per|fo|ra|tion** (pėr′fə rā′shən), *n.* **1** a hole bored or punched through or into something: *the perforations in the top of a saltshaker. Detach the check at the line of perforations.* **2** the act of perforating. **3** the condition of being perforated.

**per|force** (pər fôrs′, -fōrs′), *adv., n.* —*adv.* **1** by necessity; necessarily: *The wind was foul and boisterous, so perforce There must they bide* (William Morris). **2** *Obsolete.* by force: *to take't again perforce!* (Shakespeare).
—*n.* necessity.
[< Old French *par force* by force]

**per|form** (pər fôrm′), *v.t.* **1** to do; go through and finish; accomplish: *Perform your duties well. It takes training to perform a swan dive.* **SYN**: See syn. under **do**. **2** to put into effect; carry out; fulfill: *Perform your promise.* **3** to go through; render: *to perform the marriage ceremony, to perform a piece of music, to perform the part of Hamlet.* **4** *Obsolete.* to construct; produce; complete.
—*v.i.* **1** to act, play, sing, or do tricks in public: *The performing dog danced on its hind legs.* **2** to act; work; behave: *to perform well in a test.* **3** to carry out a command, promise, or undertaking: *Wise to resolve, and patient to perform* (Alexander Pope).
[< Anglo-French *parfourmer,* variant of Old French *parfournir* accomplish, achieve < *par-* completely + *fournir* to furnish, finish]
—*Syn. v.t.* **2 Perform, execute, discharge** mean to carry out or put into effect. **Perform** suggests carrying out a process that is long or that requires effort, attention, or skill: *The surgeon performed an operation.* **Execute** suggests carrying out a plan or an order: *The nurse executed the doctor's orders.* **Discharge** suggests carrying out an obligation or duty: *She gave a large party to discharge all her social obligations.*

**per|form|a|ble** (pər fôr′mə bəl), *adj.* that can be performed.

**per|form|ance** (pər fôr′məns), *n.* **1** the act of carrying out; doing; performing: *in the performance of one's regular duties, the efficient performance of an automobile.* **SYN**: execution, accomplishment, achievement. **2** a thing performed; act; deed: *The child's kicks and screams made a disgraceful performance.* **3** the act or manner of performing on a musical instrument, in a play, or otherwise before an audience. **4** the act of giving a play, concert, circus, or other show: *The evening performance is at 8 o'clock.* **5** the power or ability to perform: *a machine's performance.*

**performance contracting**, the practice of contracting a private business to manage a school or to take charge of an instructional program, being paid according to pupil performance as shown in achievement tests.

**performance test**, *Psychology.* a test in which overt motor reactions are substituted for verbal reactions, used in measuring the intelligence of deaf children, very young children, children speaking only a foreign language, or children that have some other communicative block.

**per|form|a|tive** (pər fôr′mə tiv), *adj. Grammar, Philosophy.* stating or asserting the actual performance of a wish, command, or plan.

**per|form|a|to|ry** (pər fôr′mə tôr′ē, -tōr′-), *adj.* of or having to do with performance.

**per|form|er** (pər fôr′mər), *n.* a person who performs, especially one who performs for the entertainment of others: *a talented performer.*

**per|form|ing arts** (pər fôr′ming), drama, music, and the dance: *Crucial to the projected cultural center is a school of performing arts* (New York Times).

**per|fume** (*n.* pėr′fyüm, pər fyüm′; *v.* pər fyüm′), *n., v.,* **-fumed, -fum|ing.** —*n.* **1** a liquid having the sweet smell of flowers, fragrant wood, or the like, made from natural or synthetic oils: *All the perfumes of Arabia will not sweeten this little hand* (Shakespeare). **2** a sweet smell: *We enjoyed the perfume of the flowers.* **SYN**: fragrance, scent. **3** *Figurative.* reputation or character. [< Middle French *parfum* < *parfumer* to scent; see the verb]
—*v.t.* **1** to give a sweet smell to; fill with sweet odor: *Flowers perfumed the air.* **2** to put a sweet-smelling liquid on: *to perfume one's hair.*
[< Middle French *parfumer* < earlier Italian *perfumare* < Latin *per-* through + *fūmāre* to smoke < *fūmus* smoke]

**per|fum|er** (pər fyü′mər), *n.* **1** a maker or seller of perfumes. **2** a person or thing that perfumes.

**per|fum|er|y** (pər fyü′mər ē, -fyüm′rē), *n., pl.* **-er|ies.** **1** a perfume. **2** perfumes as a group. **3** the business of making or selling perfumes. **4** a perfumer's place of business.

**per|func|to|ry** (pər fungk′tər ē), *adj.* **1** done merely for the sake of getting rid of the duty; done from force of habit; mechanical; indifferent: *a perfunctory smile. The little boy gave his face a perfunctory washing. He saw her ... and raised his hat, but in a perfunctory, preoccupied manner* (Arnold Bennett). **SYN**: careless, superficial. **2** acting in a perfunctory way, merely to get rid of a duty or matter: *The new nurse was perfunctory; she did not really care about her work.* [< Latin *perfūnctōrius* (literally) like one who wishes to get through a thing < *perfungī* perform < *per-* completely, or badly + *fungī* execute] —**per|func′to|ri|ly,** *adv.* —**per|func′to|ri|ness,** *n.*

**per|fus|ate** (pər fyü′zāt), *n.* a substance that is perfused: *The soil perfusate is adequately mixed and aerated and the perfusion is intermittent* (J. H. Quasel).

**per|fuse** (pər fyüz′), *v.t.,* **-fused, -fus|ing.** **1** to pass a substance through (an organ or other part of the body), especially by way of the bloodstream: *to perfuse the heart with a muscle stimulant.* **2** to overspread, as with color or moisture; suffuse. **3** to cause to flow or spread through or over; diffuse. [< Latin *perfūsus,* past participle of *perfundere* pour out < *per-* (intensive) + *fundere* pour]

**per|fu|sion** (pər fyü′zhən), *n.* **1** the action of perfusing: *The gland might be kept alive by perfusion, and supplied with suitable synthetic substances which it could convert to cortisone* (A. J. Birch). **2** the condition of being perfused.

**per|fu|sive** (pər fyü′siv), *adj.* adapted to perfusion; easily perfused.

**Per|ga|mene** (pėr′gə mēn), *adj.* of or having to do with the ancient city of Pergamum, in Asia Minor, or its famous school of sculpture that flourished in the 100's and 200's B.C.

**per|go|la** (pėr′gə lə), *n.* an arbor made of a trellis supported by posts, for training vines or other plants. [< Italian *pergola* < Latin *pergula* lean-to (roof), arbor (diminutive) < unrecorded *perga* timber work]

**perh.,** perhaps.

**per|haps** (pər haps′, -aps′), *adv.* it may be; maybe; possibly: *Perhaps a letter will come to you today. You may think, perhaps, that this work is unnecessary.* [Middle English *per happes* by chances]

**pe|ri** (pir′ē), *n., pl.* **-ris.** **1** *Persian Mythology.* a beautiful fairy descended from fallen angels who is shut out from paradise until penance is accomplished. **2** a very beautiful or fairylike being. [< Persian *perī*]

**peri-**, *prefix.* **1** around; surrounding, as in *perimeter, periscope, peripheral.* **2** near, as in *perihelion.* [< Greek *peri-* < *perí* around]

**per|i|anth** (per′ē anth), *n.* the envelope of a flower, including the calyx and the corolla. [< French *périanthe* < Greek *peri-* around + *ánthos* flower]

**per|i|apt** (per′ē apt), *n.* a charm; amulet. [< French *périapte* < Greek *periapton* < *periáptein* < *peri-* about + *háptein* to fasten]

**per|i|ar|ter|i|tis no|do|sa** (per′ē är′tə rī′təs nə-dō′sə), = polyarteritis.

**per|i|as|tron** (per′ē as′tron), *n., pl.* **-tra** (-trə). the point in their orbits at which the two components of a double star come closest to each other. [< *peri-* + Greek *ástron* star]

**per|i|blast** (per′ə blast), *n.* the protoplasm surrounding the nucleus of a cell or ovum; cytoplasm. [< *peri-* + *blastós* germ, sprout]

**per|i|blem** (per′ə blem), *n.* the layer of meristem in the growing ends of stems and roots of plants from which the cortex develops. [< German *Periblem* < Greek *periblēma* garment; (literally) thing thrown around < *peribállein* throw around, cover with < *peri-* around + *bállein* to throw]

**per|i|car|di|ac** (per′ə kär′dē ak), *adj.* = pericardial.

**per|i|car|di|al** (per′ə kär′dē əl), *adj.* **1** around the heart. **2** of or having to do with the pericardium: *Blood is taken into the heart from the surrounding pericardial sinus through three pairs of openings in the heart, the ostia* (A. M. Winchester).

**per|i|car|di|tis** (per′ə kär dī′tis), *n.* inflammation of the pericardium.

**per|i|car|di|um** (per′ə kär′dē əm), *n., pl.* **-di|a** (-dē ə). the membranous sac enclosing the heart. [< Greek *perikárdion,* neuter of adjective *perikárdios* < *peri-* around + *kardíā* heart]

**per|i|carp** (per′ə kärp), *n.* **1** the walls of a ripened ovary or fruit of a flowering plant, sometimes consisting of three layers, the epicarp, mesocarp, and endocarp; seed vessel. See picture under **fruit.** **2** a part that holds the spores in certain algae, such as one surrounding the cystocarp of red algae. [< New Latin *pericarpium* < Greek *perikárpion* pod, husk < *peri-* around + *karpós* fruit]

**per|i|car|pi|al** (per′ə kär′pē əl), *adj.* of or having to do with a pericarp.

**per|i|chon|dri|al** (per′ə kon′drē əl), *adj.* of or having to do with the perichondrium.

**per|i|chon|dri|um** (per′ə kon′drē əm), *n., pl.* **-dri|a** (-drē ə). a membrane of fibrous connective tissue covering the surface of cartilages except at the joints. [< New Latin *perichondrium* < Greek *peri-* around + *chóndros* cartilage]

**Per|i|cle|an** (per′ə klē′ən), *adj.* of or having to do with Pericles (about 490-429 B.C.), Athenian statesman and military commander, or the period of his leadership, during which ancient Athens reached its peak of culture, power, and prosperity.

**per|i|cline** (per′ə klīn), *n.* a variety of albite found in large, white, opaque crystals. [< Greek *periklinēs* sloping on all sides < *peri-* around + *klīnein* to slope]

**per|i|cón** (per ə kôn′), *n., pl.* **-co|nes** (-kō′nās). a folk dance of Argentina in which several couples dance in a circle. [< American Spanish *pericón*]

**pe|ric|o|pe** (pə rik′ə pē), *n., pl.* **-pes, -pae** (-pē). **1** an extract or selection from a book. **2** = lection (def. 2). [< Late Latin *pericopē* < Greek *perikopê* < *perí* around + *kóptein* to cut]

**per|i|cra|ni|al** (per′ə krā′nē əl), *adj.* of or having to do with the pericranium.

**per|i|cra|ni|um** (per′ə krā′nē əm), *n., pl.* **-ni|a** (-nē ə). the membrane covering the bones of the skull; external periosteum of the cranium. [< New Latin *pericranium* < Greek *perikrānion,* neuter of *perikrānios* < *peri-* around + *krānion* skull]

**per|i|cy|cle** (per′ə sī′kəl), *n.* the outer portion of the stele of a plant, lying between the vascular tissues internally and the innermost layer of the cortex externally, and consisting mainly of parenchyma cells. [< Greek *perikyklos* all around, encircling < *peri-* around + *kýklos* a circle]

**per|i|cy|clic** (per′ə sī′klik, -sik′lik), *adj.* of or having to do with the pericycle.

**per|i|cyn|thi|on** (per′ə sin′thē ən), *n.* = perilune. [< *peri-* near + *Cynthia* goddess of the moon]

**per|i|den|tal** (per′ə den′təl), *adj.* = periodontal.

**per|i|derm** (per′ə dėrm), *n.* the cork-producing tissue of stems, together with the cork layers and other tissues derived from it. [< German *Peridermis* < Greek *peri-* + *dérma* skin]

**per|i|der|mal** (per′ə dėr′məl), *adj.* of or having to do with the periderm.

**pe|rid|i|al** (pə rid′ē əl), *adj.* of or having to do with a peridium.

**per|i|din|i|an** (per′ə din′ē ən), *n.* any single-celled plant that forms one of the three main groups of plankton (the other two being the diatoms and the coccospheres). [< New Latin *peridinium* (< Greek *perídinēs* circular) + English *-an*]

**pe|rid|i|um** (pə rid′ē əm), *n., pl.* **-i|a** (-ē ə). the outer coat or envelope enclosing the sporophore of certain fungi. [< New Latin *peridium* < Greek *pērídion* (diminutive) < *pērā* leather bag]

**per|i|dot** (per′ə dot), *n.* a yellowish-green variety of chrysolite, used as a gem; olivine. [< Old French *peritot,* French *péridot;* origin uncertain]

**per|i|dot|ic** (per′ə dot′ik), *adj.* of or containing peridot; like peridot.

**per|i|do|tite** (per′ə dō′tīt), *n.* any coarse-grained igneous rock of a group consisting of olivine with an admixture of various other minerals, such as pyroxene, or sometimes mica, chromite, and spinel. [< *peridot* + *-ite*[1]]

**per|i|do|tit|ic** (per′ə də tit′ik), *adj.* having to do with or consisting of peridotite; like peridotite.

**per|i|ge|al** (per′ə jē′əl), *adj.* of or having to do with perigee.

**per|i|ge|an** (per′ə jē′ən), *adj.* = perigeal.

**per|i|gee** (per′ə jē), *n.* **1** the point closest to the earth in the orbit of the moon or any other earth satellite: *The speed is greatest at perigee, when the moon is nearest the earth* (Robert H. Baker). See picture under **apogee.** **2** *Figurative.* the closest point; lowest point. [< French *périgée* < New Latin *perigeum* < Greek *perígeion* < *peri-* near + *gê* earth]

**per|i|gla|cial** (per′ə glā′shəl), *adj.* **1** bordering a glacier or glaciers: *a periglacial region.* **2** of or characteristic of a periglacial region: *periglacial deposits.*

**Per|i|gor|di|an** (per′ə gôr′dē ən), *adj.* of or having to do with the upper paleolithic culture of southern France. [< *Périgord,* region in southern France where remains of this culture were found + *-ian*]

**pe|rig|y|nous** (pə rij′ə nəs), *adj.* **1** situated around the pistil on the edge of a cuplike receptacle, as stamens, sepals, and petals. **2** (of a flower) having its parts so arranged, as the cherry. [< New Latin *perigynus* (with English *-ous*) < Greek *peri-* around + *gynê* female, wife]

**pe|rig|y|ny** (pə rij′ə nē), *n.* perigynous condition.

**per|i|he|li|on** (per′ə hē′lē ən, -hēl′yən), *n., pl.* **-he|li|a** (-hē′lē ə, -hēl′yə). **1** the point closest to the sun in the orbit of a planet, comet or other heavenly body. See picture under **aphelion.** **2** *Figurative.* highest point; zenith: *Receiving a Nobel prize was the perihelion of his distinguished career.* [Grecized form of New Latin *perihelium* < Greek *peri-* near + *hêlios* sun]

**per|i|kar|y|on** (per′ə kar′ē on), *n.* the part of a nerve cell containing the nucleus; cell body of a neuron. [< *peri-* + Greek *káryon* kernel]

**per|il** (per′əl), *n., v.,* **-iled, -il|ing** or (*especially British*) **-illed, -il|ling.** —*n.* **1** the chance of harm, loss, or destruction; danger: *a time of great peril. The peril of war grew as the negotiations for a settlement of the dispute broke down.* **SYN**: jeopardy. See syn. under **danger.** **2** a cause of peril or danger: *Hidden rocks are a peril to ships.* **SYN**: hazard.
—*v.t.* to put in danger; imperil: *It threatened to encroach upon our anchorage, and peril the safety of the vessel* (Elisha Kane).
**at one's peril,** taking the risk or responsibility of the consequences: *This bridge is not safe; cross it at your peril.*
**perils,** a case or cause of perils; risks; dangers: *the perils of the sea. To smile at scapes and perils overblown* (Shakespeare).
[< Old French *peril,* learned borrowing from Latin *perīculum* trial, risk < unrecorded root *peri-* try]

**pe|ril|la** (pə ril′ə), *n.* any one of a group of Asiatic herbs of the mint family whose seeds yield a yellow oil that is used in making varnish and printing ink, and in the Orient for cooking. Some kinds are grown in gardens for their colorful leaves. [< New Latin *Perilla;* origin unknown]

**per|il|ous** (per′ə ləs), *adj.* full of peril; dangerous: *a perilous journey. It is always perilous to adopt expediency as a guide* (Benjamin Disraeli). **SYN**: hazardous, risky, unsafe. [< Anglo-French *perillous* < Latin *perīculōsus* (with English *-ous*) < *perīculum;* see etym. under **peril**] —**per′il|ous|ly,** *adv.* —**per′il|ous|ness,** *n.*

**peril point,** *Commerce.* the rate of duty on an imported product or commodity at or below which the quantity imported from abroad does or probably would do serious damage to the domestic industry producing similar goods: *The bill would provide peril points of 17 cents a pound for lead and 14½ cents for zinc* (Wall Street Journal).

**per|i|lune** (per′ə lün), *n.* that point in the orbit of a spacecraft where it comes closest to the moon; pericynthion. [< *peri-* near + French *lune* moon (< Latin *luna*)]

**per|i|lymph** (per′ə limf′), *n.* a fluid between the bony and the membranous labyrinths of the inner ear.

**per|i|lym|phat|ic** (per′ə lim fat′ik), *adj.* of or having to do with perilymph.

**pe|rim|e|ter** (pə rim′ə tər), *n.* **1** the outer boundary of a figure or area: *the perimeter of a circle, the perimeter of a garden.* **SYN:** periphery. **2** the distance around such a boundary. The perimeter of a square equals four times the length of one side. **3** the outer line or edge of an area or object. **4** the outermost line of observation posts, entrenchments, or the like, around a military position: *His audacious delaying tactics before the Pusan perimeter meant the difference between maintaining a foothold on the peninsula and retreat to Japan* (Newsweek). **5** an instrument for measuring the field of vision and determining visual power at different points on the retina. [< Latin *perimetros* < Greek *perímetros* < *peri-* around + *métron* measure]

**per|i|met|ric** (per′ə met′ric), *adj.* of or having to do with the perimeter: *perimetric measurements.* —**per′i|met′ri|cal|ly,** *adv.*

**per|i|morph** (per′ə môrf), *n.* a mineral enclosing another mineral (contrasted with *endomorph*). [< *peri-* + Greek *morphē* form]

**per|i|mor|phic** (per′ə môr′fik), *adj.* of, having to do with, or like perimorph.

**per|i|my|si|um** (per′ə mizh′ē əm, -miz′-), *n., pl.* **-my|si|a** (-mizh′ē ə, -miz′-). *Anatomy.* the thin connective tissue which surrounds a muscle and also divides its fibers into bundles. [< New Latin *perimysium* < Greek *peri-* around + *mŷs, myós* muscle]

**per|i|na|tal** (per′ə nā′təl), *adj.* of or having to do with the period of a child's life including the five months preceding birth and the first month after. [< Greek *peri-* around + English *natal*]

**per|i|ne|al** (per′ə nē′əl), *adj.* of or having to do with the perineum.

**per|i|neph|ri|um** (per′ə nef′rē əm), *n., pl.* **-ri|a** (-rē ə). the capsule of connective and fatty tissue surrounding a kidney. [< New Latin *perinephrium* < Greek *peri-* around + *nephrós* kidney]

**per|i|ne|um** (per′ə nē′əm), *n., pl.* **-ne|a** (-nē′ə). **1** the region of the body between the thighs, especially between the anus and the genitals. **2** the region included in the opening of the pelvis, containing the roots of the genitals, the anal canal, and the urethra. [< Late Latin *perinēum* < Greek *perínaion*]

**per|i|neu|ri|tis** (per′ə nů rī′tis, -nyů-), *n.* inflammation of the perineurium.

**per|i|neu|ri|um** (per′ə nůr′ē əm, -nyůr′-), *n., pl.* **-neu|ri|a** (-nůr′ē ə, -nyůr′-). the sheath of connective tissue surrounding a bundle of nerve fibers. [< New Latin *perineurium* < Greek *peri-* around + *neûron* nerve, sinew]

✱**pe|ri|od** (pir′ē əd), *n., adj., interj.* —*n.* **1** a portion of time having certain features or conditions: *They visited us for a short period.* **SYN:** term, interval. **2** a portion of time marked off by events that happen again and again; time after which the same things begin to happen again: *A month, from new moon to new moon, is a period. The seventh satellite revolves in an eccentric orbit with a period of some 200 days* (Scientific American). **3** a certain series of years: *the period of the Civil War.* **4** a portion of a game during which there is actual play: *The game was won in the third period.* **5** one of the portions of time into which a school day is divided. **6** the time needed for a disease to run its course. **7** an end; termination; final stage: *When some well-contested and decisive victory had put a period to the war* (Hawthorne). **8** the dot marking the end of most sentences or showing an abbreviation. *Examples:* Mr. or Dec. or U.S. **9** the pause at the end of a sentence. **10** a complete sentence: *The orator spoke in stately periods.* **11** = periodic sentence. **12** one of the subdivisions of a geological era. A period is divided into epochs. **13** the time of menstruating; menstruation. **14** *Physics.* the interval of time between the recurrence of like phases in a vibration or other periodic motion or phenomenon. **15** *Chemistry.* a horizontal row of elements having consecutive atomic numbers in the periodic table. **16** *Mathematics.* **a** a digit or a group of digits set off by commas. *Example:* In 6,527,308 there are three periods, 6 being the millions period and 527 the thousands period. **b** the smallest interval of the independent variable required for a function to begin to repeat itself. **17** a musical passage, usually a group of eight or sixteen measures divided into two or more complementary or contrasting phrases ending with a cadence. **18** *Obsolete.* a goal: *This is the period of my ambition* (Shakespeare). **19** *Greek Prosody.* a metrical group of two or more cola.
—*adj.* characteristic of a certain period of time, especially an earlier period: *period furniture, a period novel.*
—*interj. Informal.* that's it! that's final! *He said that the bank did not like to lend money for so short a time, and I said the bank didn't like to lend money, period* (Maclean's).
[< Latin *periodus* < Greek *períodos* cycle, circuit; (literally) a going around < *peri-* around + *hodós* a going, a way]
▶ **period.** Whether it logically belongs there or not, a period is generally placed inside the final quotation marks: *"The longer you put it off," he said, "the harder it's going to be."*

✱**period** definition 8 — Dr. Dooley left the U.S. by air.

**per|i|o|date** (pėr ī′ə dāt), *n.* a salt of periodic acid. [< *period*(ic acid) + *-ate*[2]]

**pe|ri|od|ic** (pir′ē od′ik), *adj.* **1** occurring, appearing, or done again and again at regular intervals: *periodic attacks of malaria.* **2** happening every now and then: *a periodic fit of clearing up one's desk.* **3** of or having to do with a period: *The coming of the new moon is a periodic occurrence.* **4** expressed in formal or complete sentences: *periodic writing, a periodic style.* [< Latin *periodicus* < Greek *periodikós* recurring at stated intervals < *períodos* period]

**per|i|od|ic acid** (pėr′ī od′ik), a colorless crystalline acid containing iodine with a valence of 7, its highest valence. *Formula:* $H_5IO_6$ [< *per-* + *iodic*]

**pe|ri|od|i|cal** (pir′ē od′ə kəl), *n., adj.* —*n.* a magazine that appears regularly, but less often than daily: *The quarterly magazine is a periodical published every three months.*
—*adj.* **1** of or having to do with periodicals. **2** published at regular intervals, less often than daily: *Periodical publications are usually bought by subscription through the mail.* **3** happening at regular intervals; periodic: *The periodical crises of the system [were becoming] less serious instead of more so* (Edmund Wilson).

**periodical cicada,** = seventeen-year locust.

**pe|ri|od|i|cal|ism** (pir′ē od′ə kə liz′əm), *n.* the work of writing for or publishing periodicals. —**pe′ri|od′i|cal|ist,** *n.*

**pe|ri|od|i|cal|ly** (pir′ē od′ə klē), *adv.* **1** at regular intervals: *Sections of the track were periodically removed so that ... hurdlers would have a clear lane to their finish line* (Time). **2** every now and then: *It rains periodically during the summer.* **SYN:** occasionally.

**periodic chart,** = periodic table.

**pe|ri|o|dic|i|ty** (pir′ē ə dis′ə tē), *n., pl.* **-ties.** **1** periodic character; tendency to happen at regular intervals: *He would interest himself in the periodicity of the attacks, timing them by his watch* (Arnold Bennett). **2** *Electricity.* frequency of alternation. **3** the tendency of elements having similar positions in the periodic table to have similar properties: *The Periodic Classification is universally attributed to Mendeléeff, yet the fundamental discovery of periodicity was made by Newlands* (Science News).

**periodic kiln,** a kiln heated and cooled at intervals.

**periodic law,** the law that the properties of chemical elements vary at regular intervals when the elements are arranged in the order of their atomic numbers.

**periodic sentence,** a sentence not complete in meaning or grammatical structure without the final words. *Example:* Delighted with the invitation to visit the farm, we prepared to go.

**periodic system,** a classification of chemical elements based on the periodic law.

**periodic table,** a table in which the chemical elements, arranged in the order of their atomic numbers, are shown in related groups: *The chemists' periodic table first was proposed by Dmitri Mendeleev in 1869* (Robert H. March). *The position of an element in the periodic table determines the complexity of its atom* (Hardy, Perrin).

**per|i|o|dide** (pėr ī′ə dīd, -did), *n.* an iodide with the maximum proportion of iodine.

**pe|ri|od|ize** (pir′ē ə dīz), *v.t., v.i.,* **-ized, -iz|ing.** to divide (painting, music, literature, or other art) into historical periods: *For a long time, musical historians ... tended to "periodize" music* (Winthrop Sargeant). —**pe′ri|od|i|za′tion,** *n.*

**per|i|o|don|tal** (per′ē ə don′təl), *adj.* **1** encasing or surrounding a tooth; peridental: *a periodontal membrane.* **2** having to do with or affecting the tissue surrounding a tooth or the teeth: *periodontal disease.* **3** of or having to do with periodontics. [< *peri-* around + Greek *odoús, odóntos* tooth + English *-al*[1]]

**per|i|o|don|tia** (per′ē ə don′shə, -shē ə), *n.* = periodontics. [< New Latin *periodontia*]

**per|i|o|don|tics** (per′ē ə don′tiks), *n.* the branch of dentistry concerned with the supporting tissues of the teeth.

**per|i|o|don|tist** (per′ē ə don′tist), *n.* a dentist who specializes in periodontics.

**per|i|o|don|ti|tis** (per′ē ō don tī′tis), *n.* inflammation of the supporting tissues of the teeth. [< *periodont*(al) + *-itis*]

**period piece,** an object that belongs to a particular period of the past; a painting, music, literature, or other form of art, having an antique, archaic, or dated quality: *Perhaps it appealed to her for its Spartan, Victorian qualities or simply as a period piece* (Manchester Guardian Weekly).

**Per|i|oe|ci** (per′ē ē′sī), *n.pl.* a class of persons in ancient Sparta who had no political rights, but enjoyed personal freedom and were protected by law. [< Medieval Latin *perioecī* < Greek *períoikoi* neighboring inhabitants < *períoikos* dwelling around < *peri-* around + *oîkos* house]

**per|i|os|te|al** (per′ē os′tē əl), *adj.* of, having to do with, or connected with the periosteum.

**per|i|os|te|um** (per′ē os′tē əm), *n., pl.* **-te|a** (-tē ə). the dense fibrous membrane covering the surface of bones except at the joints. New bone tissue is produced from the inner layer. [< New Latin *periosteum* < Late Latin *periosteon* < Greek *periósteon* < *peri-* around + *ostéon* bone]

**per|i|os|ti|tis** (per′ē os tī′tis), *n.* inflammation of the periosteum.

**per|i|os|tra|cum** (per′ē os′trə kəm), *n.* the hard outer layer of the shell of most mollusks. [< New Latin *periostracum* < Greek *peri-* around + *óstrakon* shell]

**per|i|o|tic** (per′ē ō′tik, -ot′ik), *adj.* **1** surrounding the ear. **2** of or having to do with certain bones or bony elements of the skull that form a protective capsule for the internal ear. [< Greek *peri-* around + *oûs, ōtós* ear + English *-ic*]

**Per|i|pa|tet|ic** (per′ə pə tet′ik), *adj., n.* —*adj.* having to do with the philosophy of Aristotle, Greek philosopher, who taught while walking; Aristotelian.
—*n.* one of Aristotle's disciples.
[< Latin *peripatēticus* < Greek *peripatētikós,* ultimately < *peri-* around + *pateîn* to walk]

**per|i|pa|tet|ic** (per′ə pə tet′ik), *adj., n.* —*adj.* walking about; traveling from place to place; itinerant: *a peripatetic scissors grinder.* **SYN:** ambulatory.
—*n.* a person who wanders or travels about from place to place: *The peripatetic who walked before her was a watchman in that neighbourhood* (Sir Richard Steele).
[< *Peripatetic*] —**per′i|pa|tet′i|cal|ly,** *adv.*

**per|i|pa|tet|i|cism** (per′ə pə tet′ə siz əm), *n.* **1** the habit or practice of walking about or traveling from place to place. **2** peripatetic action, exercise, or behavior. **3** Usually, **Peripateticism.** the Peripatetic system of philosophy.

**pe|rip|a|tus** (pə rip′ə təs), *n.* any one of certain primitive, invertebrate, wormlike animals, found in widely separated tropical regions, and having some characteristics of annelid worms and some of arthropods. [< New Latin *Peripatus* the genus name < Greek *peripátos* walking about < *peri-* around + *pateîn* to walk]

**per|i|pe|te|ia** (per′ə pə tē′ə), *n.* a sudden change in circumstances or fortune, as in a play or novel. [< Greek *peripéteia* < *peri-* around + *píptein* fall]

**pe|riph|er|al** (pə rif′ər əl), *adj., n.* —*adj.* **1** having to do with, situated in, or forming an outside boundary: *More houses and parks were to be seen in the peripheral areas of the city.* **2a** of the surface or outer part of a body; external. **b** perceived or perceiving near the outer edges of the retina: *peripheral vision.* **3** of or having to do with the peripheral nervous system: *peripheral neurons.* **4** of or having to do with computer peripherals: *It is likely that Poland will produce small central processors, tape readers, line printers and other components; East Germany will probably supply peripheral equipment* (Scientific American).
—*n.* any part of the electromechanical equipment of a computer, such as magnetic tape, high-speed printers, keyboards, and display units.
—**pe|riph′er|al|ly,** *adv.*

**peripheral nervous system,** the part of the nervous system of vertebrates that branches from the central nervous system, especially the cranial and spinal nerves, and the nerves of the autonomic nervous system. See diagram under **nervous system.**

**pe|riph|er|y** (pə rif′ər ē), *n., pl.* **-er|ies.** **1** an outside boundary. **2** *Geometry.* **a** the circumference of a circle or other closed curve. **b** the sum of the sides of a polygon. **c** the length of, or the boundary line of, any closed plane figure. **d** the surface of a solid figure. **3** *Anatomy.* the region in which nerves end. [< Late Latin *peripherīa* < Greek *periphéreiā* < *peri-* around + *phérein* to carry (off)]

**Pronunciation Key:** hat, āge, cãre, fär; let, ēqual, tėrm; it, īce; hot, ōpen, ôrder; oil, out; cup, pu̇t, rüle; child; long; thin; ᴛʜen; zh, measure; ə represents **a** in about, **e** in taken, **i** in pencil, **o** in lemon, **u** in circus.

**per|i|phon|ic** (per′ə fon′ik), *adj.* of or having to do with an omnidirectional sound system.

**pe|riph|ra|sis** (pə rif′rə sis), *n., pl.* **-ses** (-sēz). a roundabout way of speaking or writing; circumlocution: *"The wife of your father's brother" is a periphrasis for "your aunt."* [< Latin *periphrasis* < Greek *períphrasis* < *periphrázein* speak in roundabout way < *peri-* around + *phrázein* speak]

**per|i|phras|tic** (per′ə fras′tik), *adj.* **1** expressed in a roundabout way: *A periphrastic study in a worn-out poetical fashion* (T. S. Eliot). **2** *Grammar.* formed by using auxiliaries or particles rather than inflection. *Examples: of John* (periphrastic genitive) rather than *John's; did run* (periphrastic conjugation) rather than *ran.* —**per′i|phras′ti|cal|ly,** *adv.*

**per|i|phy|ton** (per′ə fī′ton), *n.* a complex colony of microscopic algae, insect larvae, small crustaceans, and other organisms that form a thick layer, as on the bottom of swamps and marshes, covering the stems of plants. The periphyton is a dominant biological complex in the Florida Everglades. [< *peri-* around + *phyton*]

**per|i|plast** (per′ə plast), *n. Biology.* a cell wall or cell membrane. [< *peri-* + *-plast*]

**per|i|proct** (per′ə prokt), *n.* the part of the body of various invertebrates which surrounds the anus: *the periproct of an echinoderm.* [< *peri-* + Greek *prōktós* anus]

**pe|rip|ter|al** (pə rip′tər əl), *adj.* surrounded by a single row of columns, as a temple. [< French *périptère* (see etym. under **periptery**) + English *-al*[1]]

**pe|rip|ter|y** (pə rip′ter ē), *n., pl.* **-ter|ies. 1** the air immediately surrounding a flying or falling object, such as a bird, aircraft, or bomb, containing cyclic or vertical air disturbances. **2** a peripteral building. [< French *périptère* (ultimately < Greek *peri-* around + *pterón* wing) + English *-y*[3]]

**pe|rique** (pə rēk′), *n.* a strongly flavored, dark tobacco grown in Louisiana: *Perique, prized because of its rich flavor, is cured by putting the leaves under great pressure* (Roy Flannagan). [American English < Creole French *périque*]

**per|i|sarc** (per′ə särk), *n.* the external horny or chitinous covering of certain hydrozoans. [< Greek *peri-* around + *sárx, sarkós* flesh]

***per|i|scope** (per′ə skōp), *n.* **1** an instrument that allows those in a submarine or trench to see a view of the surface. It is a tube with an arrangement of prisms or mirrors that reflect light rays down a vertical tube. The periscope works on the principle that the angle of reflection equals the angle of incidence. **2** a periscopic lens. [< Greek *peri-* around + *-scope*] —**per′i|scope|like′,** *adj.*

light
prism
lens system
standard
seal
eyepiece
prisms

***periscope**
definition 1

**per|i|scop|ic** (per′ə skop′ik), *adj.* **1** giving distinct vision obliquely as well as in a direct line: *a periscopic lens.* **2** of or having to do with periscopes.

**per|i|se|le|ni|um** (per′ə si lē′nē əm), *n.* the point in an elliptical orbit around the moon that is closest to the moon. [< *peri-* near + New Latin *selenium* < Greek *selḗnē* moon]

**per|ish** (per′ish), *v.i.* **1** to be destroyed; die: *Buildings perish in flames. Soldiers perish in battle. Flowers perish when frost comes. I felt ready to perish with cold.* **SYN:** See syn. under **die. 2** to come to ruin morally or spiritually; come to an end: *Except ye repent, ye shall all likewise perish* (Luke 13:3).
—*v.t.* **1** *Dialect.* to injure severely. **2** *Archaic.* to put an end to; destroy; kill: *We charm man's life and do not perish it* (Thomas Hood).
[< Old French *periss-,* stem of *perir* < Latin *perīre* < *per-* (pejorative) + *īre* go]

**per|ish|a|bil|i|ty** (per′i shə bil′ə tē), *n.* perishable quality.

**per|ish|a|ble** (per′i shə bəl), *adj., n.* —*adj.* **1** liable to spoil or decay: *Fruit is perishable.* **2** liable to perish; that perishes: *the perishable enthusiasm of youth.*
—*n.* Usually, **perishables,** something perishable, especially food, flowers, or the like. —**per′ish|a|ble|ness,** *n.*

**per|ish|er** (per′ish ər), *n. British Slang.* annoying fellow; rascal.

**per|ish|ing** (per′ish ing), *adj., adv.* —*adj.* **1** that perishes. **2** = deadly. **3** *British Informal.* beastly; darned: *Hold this perishing split pin* (Punch).
—*adv.* excessively; extremely: *a perishing cold morning.* —**per′ish|ing|ly,** *adv.*

**per|i|spore** (per′ə spôr, -spōr), *n.* the outer membrane or covering of a spore.

**pe|ris|sad** (pə ris′ad), *n., adj.* —*n.* an atom or element whose valence is expressed by an odd number.
—*adj.* having the valence expressed by an odd number.
[< Greek *perissós* odd, uneven]

**pe|ris|so|dac|tyl** or **pe|ris|so|dac|tyle** (pə ris′ə-dak′təl), *n., adj. Zoology.* —*n.* any one of a large order of quadruped mammals having an odd number of hoofed toes on each foot, the third being the largest and sometimes the only functional one. Horses, tapirs, and rhinoceroses belong to this order.
—*adj.* having an uneven number of toes.
[< New Latin *Perissodactyla* the order name < Greek *perissós* uneven + *dáktylos* a toe]

**per|i|stal|sis** (per′ə stal′sis), *n., pl.* **-ses** (-sēz). a movement in the wall of a hollow organ by which its contents are moved onward, such as the wavelike, circular contractions of the alimentary canal. [< New Latin *peristalsis* < Greek *peristaltikós;* see etym. under **peristaltic**]

**per|i|stal|tic** (per′ə stal′tik), *adj.* of or having to do with peristalsis: *peristaltic contractions.* [< Greek *peristaltikós* contracting around < *peristéllein* to compress; (originally) wrap around < *peri-* around + *stéllein* to wrap, bind, compress] —**per′i|stal′ti|cal|ly,** *adv.*

**per|i|stome** (per′ə stōm), *n.* **1** *Botany.* the one or two rings or fringes of toothlike appendages around the mouth of the capsule or theca in mosses. **2** *Zoology.* any special structure or set of parts around the mouth or oral opening in various invertebrates. [< New Latin *peristoma* < Greek *peristómion* the region around the mouth (of anything); epiglottis < *peri-* around + *stóma* mouth]

**per|i|sto|mi|al** (per′ə stō′mē əl), *adj.* of or having to do with a peristome.

**per|i|sty|lar** (per′ə stī′lər), *adj.* of, having to do with, or like a peristyle.

***per|i|style** (per′ə stīl), *n.* **1** a row of columns surrounding a building, court, or the like. **SYN:** colonnade. **2** a space or court so enclosed. [< French *péristyle,* learned borrowing from Latin *peristylum* < Greek *peristȳlon* < *peri-* around + *stȳlos* pillar]

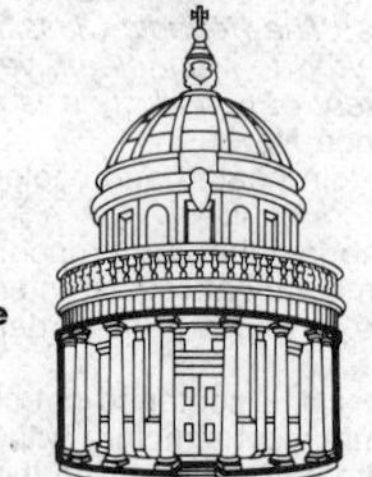

***peristyle**
definition 1

**per|i|styl|i|um** (per′ə stī′lē əm, -stil′ē-), *n., pl.* **-styl|i|a** (-stī′lē ə, -stil′ē ə). the peristyle of an ancient Roman dwelling. [< Latin *peristylium,* variant of *peristylum;* see etym. under **peristyle**]

**per|i|tec|tic** (per′ə tek′tik), *adj.* neither solid nor liquid; being intermediate between the solid and liquid phases of a melt: *a peritectic compound.* [< *peri-* + Greek *tēktikós* able to melt]

**per|i|the|ci|al** (per′ə thē′shē əl, -thē′sē-), *adj.* of or having to do with the perithecium.

**per|i|the|ci|um** (per′ə thē′shē əm, -thē′sē-), *n., pl.* **-ci|a** (-sē ə). the fruit of certain fungi, usually a rounded or flask-shaped receptacle with a narrow opening, enclosing the asci or spore sacs. [< New Latin *perithecium* < Greek *peri-* around + *thḗkē* case, receptacle]

**per|i|to|ne|al** (per′ə tə nē′əl), *adj.* of the peritoneum.

**per|i|to|ne|um** (per′ə tə nē′əm), *n., pl.* **-ne|a** (-nē′ə). the thin membrane that lines the walls of the abdomen and covers the organs in it. The peritoneum is a thin, transparent structure with many folds, such as the omentum and mesentery. [< Late Latin *peritonaeum* < Greek *peritónaion* stretched over < *peri-* around + *teínein* to stretch]

**per|i|to|ni|tis** (per′ə tə nī′tis), *n.* inflammation of the peritoneum.

**per|i|ton|sil|lar abscess** (per′ə ton′sə lər), = quinsy.

**pe|rit|ri|cha** (pə rit′rə kə), *n.pl.* bacteria with the cilia (organs of locomotion) around the entire body. [< New Latin *Peritricha* the order name < Greek *peri-* around + *thríx, trichós* the hair]

**pe|rit|ri|chous** (pə rit′rə kəs), *adj.* **1** having a band of cilia around the body. **2** of or having to do with peritricha. —**pe|rit′ri|chous|ly,** *adv.*

**pe|ri|tus** (pe rē′tůs), *n., pl.* **-ti** (-tē). a theological advisor or consultant in the Roman Catholic Church. [< New Latin *peritus* < Latin, skilled]

**per|i|vas|cu|lar** (per′ə vas′kyə lər), *adj.* surrounding a blood vessel: *perivascular areas of the heart.*

**per|i|vis|ce|ral** (per′ə vis′ər əl), *adj.* surrounding and containing viscera. The perivisceral cavity is the general body cavity containing the alimentary canal and its appendages.

**per|i|wig** (per′ə wig), *n.* = peruke. [< earlier *perewyke* < French *perruque;* influenced by *wig.* See etym. of doublet **peruke.**]

**per|i|wigged** (per′ə wigd), *adj.* wearing a periwig.

**per|i|win|kle**[1] (per′ə wing′kəl), *n.* **1** a low, trailing evergreen plant with blue, white, or purplish flowers. There are several kinds, making up a genus of the dogbane family. The American periwinkle is called myrtle. See picture under **dogbane family. 2** a light-blue color. [alteration of Middle English *perwynke,* Old English *pervince* < Latin *pervinca* < *pervincīre* fasten around < *peri-* around + *vincīre* bind; influenced by *periwinkle*[2]]

**per|i|win|kle**[2] (per′ə wing′kəl), *n.* **1a** a sea snail with a thick, cone-shaped, spiral shell, used for food in Europe. There are several kinds, making up a genus of mollusks. **b** the shell of this snail or of certain other marine univalve mollusks. **2** any one of certain other relatively large marine snails used for food; winkle. **3** a kind of freshwater snail of the southern United States. [origin uncertain. Compare Old English *pīnewincle* < Latin *pīna* mussel < Greek *pīnē.*]

**per|jure** (pėr′jər), *v.t.,* **-jured, -jur|ing.** to make (oneself) guilty of perjury.
**perjure oneself,** to swear falsely; lie under oath; swear that something is true which one knows to be false: *The witness perjured himself by lying about what he did on the night of the crime.*
[Middle English *parjuren* < Old French *parjurer,* learned borrowing from Latin *perjūrāre* < *per-* (pejorative) + *jūrāre* to swear < *jūs, jūris* right, justice]

**per|jured** (pėr′jərd), *adj.* **1** guilty of perjury: *a perjured witness.* **SYN:** forsworn. **2** characterized by or involving perjury: *perjured evidence.*

**per|jur|er** (pėr′jər ər), *n.* a person who commits or is guilty of perjury.

**per|ju|ri|ous** (pər jůr′ē əs), *adj.* = perjured. —**per|ju′ri|ous|ly,** *adv.*

**per|ju|ry** (pėr′jər ē), *n., pl.* **-ries. 1** the act or crime of swearing that something is true which one knows to be false, or of withholding testimony while under oath. **2** a violation of a promise made on oath to do or not to do something: *If thou swear'st, Thou mayst prove false; at lovers' perjuries, They say, Jove laughs* (Shakespeare). [< Anglo-French *perjurie* < Latin *perjūrium* < *perjūrāre* perjure]

**perk**[1] (pėrk), *v., adj.* —*v.t.* to raise smartly or briskly: *The dog perked his ears when he heard his master.* —*v.i.* **1** to move, lift the head, or act briskly or saucily: *... their round, little-eyed meek faces perking sidewise* (William Hone). **2** to put oneself forward briskly or assertively. **3** *British.* to preen, as before a mirror: *You'd be perking at the glass the next minute* (George Eliot).
—*adj.* **1** saucy; pert; cocky. **2** in good spirits. **3** spruce; smart.
**perk out,** to make trim or smart: *She is all perked out in her Sunday clothes.*
**perk up, a** liven or brighten up; become lively and vigorous: *The sick girl perked up when she received the flowers. Demand for lead has perked up amid reports that the price might move up again* (Wall Street Journal). **b** to make trim or smart: *You are not quite a woman yourself—though you perk yourself up so daintily* (J. P. Kennedy).
[Middle English *perken;* origin uncertain]

**perk**[2] (pėrk), *v.t., v.i. Informal.* to percolate (coffee).

**perk**[3] (pėrk), *n. Informal.* perquisite: *The list of such "perks" recommended for taxation ranges from company jets, and cars for personal use to day-care centers for children of employees* (New York Times).

**perk|y** (pėr′kē), *adj.,* **perk|i|er, perk|i|est.** smart; brisk; saucy; pert: *a perky squirrel. The suits include a perky one of gray flannel with a nipped-in jacket* (New Yorker). **SYN:** jaunty. —**perk′i|ly,** *adv.* —**perk′i|ness,** *n.*

**per|lite** (pėr′līt), *n.* a form of obsidian or other vitreous rock broken up by minute spherical cracks; pearlite. [< French *perlite* < German *Perlit* < *Perle* pearl + *-it* -ite[1]]

**per|lit|ic** (pėr lit′ik), *adj.* of or having to do with perlite.

**perm** (pėrm), *n., v. British Informal.* —*n.* a permanent wave. —*v.t.* to give a permanent wave to.

**perm.**, permanent.

**perm|a|frost** (pėr′mə frôst′, -frost′), *n.* a layer of permanently frozen soil and other deposits, sometimes reaching a depth of a thousand feet or more, found near the surface throughout most of the arctic regions. [apparently < *perma*(nent) + *frost*]

**Perm|al|loy** (pėr′mə loi), *n. Trademark.* any alloy of a group consisting of iron and nickel with small amounts of various other metals, noted for high magnetic permeability.

**per|ma|nence** (pėr′mə nəns), *n.* the condition of being permanent; lasting quality or condition: *the permanence of the sun.* **SYN**: durability.

**per|ma|nen|cy** (pėr′mə nən sē), *n., pl.* **-cies. 1** = permanence. **2** a permanent person, thing, or position.

**per|ma|nent** (pėr′mə nənt), *adj., n.* — ***adj.* 1** lasting; intended to last; not for a short time only: *a permanent filling in a tooth. After doing odd jobs for a week, he got a permanent position as a helper in a store.* **SYN**: abiding, enduring. See syn. under **lasting**. **2** *Botany.* persistent.
— ***n.*** *Informal.* a permanent wave.
[< Latin *permanēns, -entis* staying to the end, present participle of *permanēre* < *per-* through + *manēre* to stay] — **per′ma|nent|ly**, *adv.* — **per′ma|nent|ness**, *n.*

**permanent magnet**, a magnet that retains its magnetism after the magnetizing current or force has been removed: *Permanent magnets are used in thermostats, television sets, and guided missiles* (Wall Street Journal).

**permanent magnetism**, magnetism which continues after the magnetizing influence has been withdrawn.

**per|ma|nent-mold casting** (pėr′mə nənt mōld′), a cast-iron cavity used to mold aluminum castings that have a stronger and better surface finish than sand-casting.

**permanent press**, = durable press.

**permanent tooth**, *pl.* **permanent teeth.** one of the set of teeth that replace the milk teeth and become permanent in adults. Human beings have 32 permanent teeth.

**permanent wave**, a wave put in the hair by a special process so as to last several months.

**permanent way**, *British.* the roadbed and track of a railroad.

**per|man|ga|nate** (pər mang′gə nāt), *n.* a salt of an acid containing manganese. A solution of potassium permanganate is used as an antiseptic.

**per|man|gan|ic acid** (pėr′man gan′ik), an acid that is unstable except in dilute solutions. Its aqueous solution is used as an oxidizing agent. *Formula:* $HMnO_4$

**per|me|a|bil|i|ty** (pėr′mē ə bil′ə tē), *n.* **1** the condition of being permeable: *The damage may be in the form of changing the permeability of cell walls* (Science News Letter). **2** *Physics.* the ratio of magnetic induction to the intensity of the magnetic field: *The permeability depends on the past history (magnetically speaking) of the iron* (Sears and Zemansky). **3** the amount of gas diffused through the fabric of an airship in a given period of time.

**per|me|a|ble** (pėr′mē ə bəl), *adj.* that can be permeated; allowing the passage or diffusion of liquids or gases through it: *permeable cell walls. A sponge is permeable by water.* **SYN**: pervious. [< Latin *permeābilis* < *permeāre;* see etym. under **permeate**] — **per′me|a|ble|ness**, *n.* — **per′me|a|bly**, *adv.*

**per|me|ance** (pėr′mē əns), *n.* **1** the act or fact of permeating. **2** *Physics.* the reciprocal of the reluctance of a magnetic circuit.

**per|me|ase** (pėr′mē ās), *n.* an enzyme that helps to effect the transport and concentration of certain sugars in cells. [< *perme*(ate) + *-ase*]

**per|me|ate** (pėr′mē āt), *v.,* **-at|ed, -at|ing.** — ***v.t.* 1** to spread through the whole of; pass through: *The odor of smoke permeated the house.* (*Figurative.*) *The effects of technology have permeated the lives of every human being alive today.* **SYN**: pervade. **2** to penetrate through pores or openings; soak through: *Water will easily permeate a cotton dress.* **SYN**: saturate.
— ***v.i.*** to diffuse itself.
[< Latin *permeāre* (with English *-ate*[1]) < *per-* through + *meāre* to pass]

**per|me|a|tion** (pėr′mē ā′shən), *n.* the act or fact of permeating; penetration; diffusion through; saturation.

**per|me|a|tive** (pėr′mē ā′tiv), *adj.* tending to permeate.

**per men|sem** (pər men′səm), *Latin.* by the month.

**Per|mi|an** (pėr′mē ən), *n., adj.* — ***n.* 1** a geological period, the last of the Paleozoic, after the Pennsylvanian and before the Triassic. It was characterized by the end of the trilobites, the spread of the reptiles, and the occurrence of ice-sheet glaciation in Australia, India, and South Africa. **2** the rocks formed in this period.
— ***adj.*** of this period or these rocks.
[< *Perm,* a former province in Russia, where such strata are found + *-ian*]

**per mill** or **per mil** (pər mil′), by the thousand; in thousands.

**per|mil|lage** (pər mil′ij), *n.* rate per thousand.

**per|min|er|al|i|za|tion** (pər min′ər ə lə zā′shən), *n.* a process of fossil petrifaction in which minerals fill in the small air spaces in the fossil bones or shells without changing the original shape of the fossil.

**per|mis|si|bil|i|ty** (pər mis′ə bil′ə tē), *n.* the quality of being permissible; allowableness.

**per|mis|si|ble** (pər mis′ə bəl), *adj.* that can be permitted; allowable. **SYN**: admissible. — **per|mis′si|ble|ness**, *n.* — **per|mis′si|bly**, *adv.*

**per|mis|sion** (pər mish′ən), *n.* a permitting; consent; leave: *I asked the teacher's permission to go home early. Father gave me his permission to use his camera.* **SYN**: sufferance, authorization, sanction. [< Latin *permissiō, -ōnis* < *permittere* to permit]

**per|mis|sive** (pər mis′iv), *adj., n.* — ***adj.* 1** not forbidding; tending to permit; allowing: *a permissive attitude, permissive parents. Not a positive, but a permissive command* (Henry More). *A discussion of pragmatism was naturally related to their own anxieties about permissive education* (Harper's). **2** that may or may not be done; permitted; allowed; optional: *[He] emphasized that the legislation was "permissive" and not binding upon the city* (New York Times).
— ***n.*** = permissivist. — **per|mis′sive|ly**, *adv.* — **per-mis′sive|ness**, *n.*

**per|mis|siv|ism** (pər mis′ə viz əm), *n.* the beliefs and attitudes of permissivists.

**per|mis|siv|ist** (pər mis′ə vist), *n.* a person who is excessively indulgent toward unacceptable behavior or attitudes.

**per|mit**[1] (*v.* pər mit′; *n.* pėr′mit, pər mit′), *v.,* **-mit|ted, -mit|ting,** *n.* — ***v.t.* 1a** to allow (a person) to do something; give leave to: *Most parents will not permit their young children to stay up late. Permit me to explain. The farmer permitted us to swim in his pond.* **b** to provide opportunity for; allow: *vents permitting the escape of gases, conditions permitting no delay.* **2** to let (something) be done or occur; authorize: *The law does not permit smoking in this store. It is not permitted unto them to speak* (I Corinthians 14:34). **3** *Obsolete.* to hand over or give up.
— ***v.i.*** to give leave or opportunity; allow: *I will go on Monday, if the weather permits.*
— ***n.* 1** a formal written order giving permission to do something: *Have you a permit to fish in this lake?* **2** = permission.
**permit of**, to admit of: *rules that permit of no exceptions.*
[< Latin *permittere* to allow < *per-* through + *mittere* send]
— ***Syn.*** *v.t.* **1a, b Permit, allow** mean to let someone or something do something. **Permit** implies willingness or consent: *His parents permitted him to enlist when he was seventeen.* **Allow** implies letting something happen without necessarily giving permission or approval: *That teacher allows too much noise in the room.*

**per|mit**[2] (pėr′mit, pər mit′), *n.* a large pompano, about three feet long, found in the sea from Florida to the West Indies; great pompano. [alteration of Spanish *palometa* small dove]

**per|mit|ter** (pər mit′ər), *n.* a person who permits.

**per|mit|tiv|i|ty** (pėr′mə tiv′ə tē), *n. Electricity.* dielectric constant or coefficient.

**per|mut|a|ble** (pər myü′tə bəl), *adj.* **1** = interchangeable. **2** liable to change; changeable.

**per|mu|tate** (pėr′myə tāt, pər myü′-), *v.t.,* **-tat|ed, -tat|ing. 1** to change; alter. **2** to exchange; change the order of. [< Latin *permūtātus,* past participle of *permūtāre* permute]

**per|mu|ta|tion** (pėr′myə tā′shən), *n.* **1** a change from one state, position, order, or form, to another; alteration: *A good deal of the score ... is based on various permutations of the simple interval of a fifth* (New Yorker). *After trying hundreds of permutations of nutrient media we hit on several which suited the microorganisms* (Hutner and McLaughlin). **SYN**: mutation, modification. **2** *Mathematics.* **a** a changing of the order of a set of things; arranging in different orders. **b** such an arrangement or group. The permutations of *a, b,* and *c* are *abc, acb, bac, bca, cab, cba.* [< Latin *permūtātiō, -ōnis* < *permūtāre* permute]

**per|mu|ta|tion|al** (pėr′myə tā′shə nəl), *adj.* of or having to do with permutation or permutations.

**per|mute** (pər myüt′), *v.t.,* **-mut|ed, -mut|ing. 1** to change; alter. **2** *Mathematics.* to change the order of (numbers, letters, or other symbols); subject to permutation. [< Latin *permūtāre* < *per-* throughout + *mūtāre* to change] — **per|mut′er**, *n.*

**pern** (pėrn), *n.* any one of various Old World hawks of moderate size that eat chiefly insects. [< New Latin *Pernis* the genus name, adaptation of Greek *ptérnis* a kind of hawk]

**Per|nam|bu|co wood** (pėr′nəm bü′kō), = brazilwood. [< *Pernambuco,* a seaport in Brazil]

**per|ni|cious** (pər nish′əs), *adj.* **1** that will destroy or ruin; causing great harm or damage; injurious: *Most doctors agree that smoking is a pernicious habit.* **SYN**: noxious. **2** fatal; deadly. **3** wicked; villainous: *O most pernicious woman!* (Shakespeare). [< Middle French *pernicieux* (with English *-ous*) destructive, learned borrowing from Latin *perniciōsus* < *perniciēs* destruction < *per-* completely + *necāre* to kill < *nex, necis* death]
— **per|ni′cious|ly**, *adv.* — **per|ni′cious|ness**, *n.*

**pernicious anemia**, a very severe form of anemia in which the number of red corpuscles in the blood decreases. It is accompanied by paleness, fatigue, and digestive and nervous disturbances.

**per|nick|e|ti|ness** (pər nik′ə tē nis), *n. Informal.* fastidiousness; fussiness.

**per|nick|e|ty** (pər nik′ə tē), *adj. Informal.* **1** overly fastidious; fussy: *It is clear that the planning, no matter how grandiose, is also much too pernickety* (London Times). **2** requiring precise and careful handling; ticklish. Also, **persnickety.** [extension of Scottish *pernicky;* origin uncertain]

**Per|nod** or **per|nod** (per nō′), *n.* a yellowish-green, anise-flavored apéritif, similar to absinthe, made in France.

**per|o|ne|al** (per′ə nē′əl), *adj. Anatomy.* **1** of or having to do with the fibula. **2** in the region of the fibula. [< New Latin *perone* fibula (< Greek *perónē*) + English *-al*[1]]

**Pe|ron|ism** (pə rō′niz əm), *n.* the beliefs, policies, and government of, or typical of, Juan Perón (1895-1974), former president of Argentina.

**Pe|ro|nis|mo** (pe′rō nēz′mō), *n. Spanish.* Peronism.

**Pe|ron|ist** (pə rō′nist), *adj., n.* = Peronista.

**Pe|ro|nis|ta** (pe′rō nēs′tä), *adj., n. Spanish.* — ***adj.*** of or having to do with Juan Perón or Peronism: *the Peronista Party, Peronista leaders.*
— ***n.*** a supporter of Peronism.

**per|o|rate** (per′ə rāt), *v.i.,* **-rat|ed, -rat|ing. 1** to make a formal conclusion to a speech. **2** to speak at length; make a speech; harangue. **SYN**: descant, expatiate. [< Latin *perōrāre* (with English *-ate*[1]) < *per-* completely + *ōrāre* speak formally]

**per|o|ra|tion** (per′ə rā′shən), *n.* **1** the last part of an oration or discussion. It sums up what has been said and is usually delivered with considerable force. **2** a rhetorical speech or passage: *a fiery peroration.* **3** = discourse.

**per|o|ra|tion|al** (per′ə rā′shə nəl), *adj.* of or having to do with a peroration.

**per|ox|i|dase** (pə rok′sə dās, -dāz), *n.* an enzyme found in many plants, leucocytes, and bacteria, which catalyzes the transfer of oxygen from organic peroxides to another substance which is able to receive it.

**per|ox|ide** (pə rok′sīd), *n., v.,* **-id|ed, -id|ing.** — ***n.*** **1** an oxide of a given element or radical that contains the greatest possible, or an unusual, amount of oxygen, especially one containing an oxygen atom joined to another oxygen atom. **2** = hydrogen peroxide.
— ***v.t.*** to bleach (hair) by applying hydrogen peroxide.
[< *per-* + *oxide*]

**peroxide of hydrogen**, = hydrogen peroxide.

**per|ox|i|so|mal** (pə rok′sə sō′məl), *adj.* of or having to do with the peroxisome.

**per|ox|i|some** (pə rok′sə sōm), *n.* an organelle thought to protect cells from oxygen. Peroxisomes contain enzymes that catalyze the direct reduction of oxygen molecules through the oxidation of metabolites, such as amino acids and other organic acids. [< *peroxide* + *-some*[3]]

**per|ox|y|ac|e|tyl nitrate** (pə rok′sē as′ə təl, -ə sē′-), a highly toxic compound that is the principal constituent of smog.

**per|ox|y|ac|id** (pə rok′sē as′id), *n.* an acid in which the -OH group has been replaced by the -OOH group.

**per|ox|y|bo|rate** (pə rok′sē bôr′āt, -bōr′-), *n.* a salt of peroxyboric acid; perborate.

**per|ox|y|bo|ric acid** (pə rok′sē bôr′ik, -bōr′-), = perboric acid.

**per|pend** (pər pend′), *Archaic.* — ***v.t.*** to weigh mentally; ponder; consider: *Perpend my words* (Shakespeare).
— ***v.i.*** to ponder; reflect: *Therefore perpend, my princess, and give ear* (Shakespeare). [< Latin *perpendere* < *per-* thoroughly + *pendere* ponder;

---

**Pronunciation Key:** hat, āge, cãre, fär; let, ēqual, tėrm; it, īce; hot, ōpen, ôrder; oil, out; cup, pu̇t, rüle; child; long; thin; ᴛʜen; zh, measure; ə represents **a** in about, **e** in taken, **i** in pencil, **o** in lemon, **u** in circus.

(literally) to weigh. Compare etym. under **pensive.**]

**per|pen|dic|u|lar** (pėr′pən dik′yə lər), *adj., n.* —*adj.* **1** standing straight up; upright: *The tree was leaning against the house and no longer perpendicular.* **SYN**: vertical, erect. **2** very steep; precipitous: *a perpendicular cliff.* **3** at right angles. One line is perpendicular to another when it makes a square corner with another. The floor of a room is perpendicular to the side and parallel to the ceiling. **4** Often, **Perpendicular.** of or having to do with a type of English Gothic architecture of the 1400's and 1500's, characterized by emphasis on vertical lines, especially in window tracery.
—*n.* **1** a perpendicular line or plane: *The sagging walls of the old barn were no longer on the perpendicular.* **2a** an upright or erect position: *Springing to her accustomed perpendicular like a bowed sapling* (Thomas Hardy). **b** a steep or precipitous slope. **3** *Figurative.* moral uprightness; rectitude. **4** an instrument or appliance for indicating the vertical line from any point, such as a plumb rule.
[< Old French *perpendiculer,* learned borrowing from Latin *perpendiculāris* < *perpendiculum* plumb line, ultimately < *per-* through + *pendēre* to hang] —**per′pen|dic′u|lar|ly,** *adv.*

**per|pen|dic|u|lar|i|ty** (pėr′pən dik′yə lar′ə tē), *n.* the position or direction at right angles to a given line, surface, or plane; vertical or upright attitude or position. **SYN**: verticality.

**per|pe|trate** (pėr′pə trāt), *v.,* **-trat|ed, -trat|ing,** *adj.* —*v.t.* **1** to do or commit (a crime, fraud, trick, or anything bad or foolish): *The two thieves perpetrated the robbery of the jewelry store.* **2** *Informal.* to do or make (something implied to be bad or atrocious): *to perpetrate a pun. Sir Philip induced two of his sisters to perpetrate a duet* (Charlotte Brontë). —*adj. Obsolete.* perpetrated.
[< Latin *perpetrāre* (with English *-ate*[1]) < *per-* (intensive) + *patrāre* perform, accomplish]
—**per′pe|tra′tion,** *n.* —**per′pe|tra′tor,** *n.*

**per|pet|u|al** (pər pech′ů əl), *adj., n.* —*adj.* **1** lasting forever; eternal: *the perpetual hills.* **SYN**: permanent, enduring, everlasting. **2** lasting throughout life; ceasing only at death: *a perpetual income.* **3** never ceasing; continuous: *a perpetual stream of visitors. He moved in an atmosphere of perpetual ambush* (Rudyard Kipling). **SYN**: constant. **4** *Horticulture.* being in bloom more or less continuously throughout the year or the season.
—*n.* **1** any one of several continuously-blooming hybrid varieties of rose. **2** = perennial.
[< Old French *perpetuel,* learned borrowing from Latin *perpetuālis* < *perpetuus* continuous < *perpes, -etis* lasting < *per-* through + root of *petere* seek] —**per|pet′u|al|ly,** *adv.* —**per|pet′u|al|ness,** *n.*

**perpetual calendar,** a calendar to show the day of the week on which a date will fall in any given year.

**perpetual check,** *Chess.* a check repeated over and over again, allowing the player who makes it to claim a draw.

**perpetual motion,** the motion of a hypothetical machine which being once set in motion should go on forever by creating its own energy, unless it were stopped by some external force or the wearing out of the machine.

**per|pet|u|ate** (*v.* pər pech′ů āt; *adj.* pər pech′ů it), *v.,* **-at|ed, -at|ing,** *adj.* —*v.t.* to make perpetual; keep from being forgotten: *The Washington Monument was built to perpetuate the memory of a great man.*
—*adj.* made perpetual.
[< Latin *perpetuāre* (with English *-ate*[1]) < *perpetuus;* see etym. under **perpetual**] —**per|pet′u|a|tor,** *n.*

**per|pet|u|a|tion** (pər pech′ů ā′shən), *n.* **1** the act of perpetuating: *perpetuation of the species.* **2** the condition of being perpetuated.

**per|pe|tu|i|ty** (pėr′pə tü′ə tē, -tyü′-), *n., pl.* **-ties.** **1** the condition of being perpetual; existence forever: *A third attribute of the king's majesty is his perpetuity ... The king never dies* (William Blackstone). **SYN**: endlessness, eternity. **2** a perpetual possession, tenure, or position. **3** *Law.* **a** (of an estate) the quality or condition of being inalienable perpetually or longer than the legal time limit. **b** the estate so restricted: *A perpetuity can spend only the income from its assets* (Joseph C. Kiger). **4** a perpetual annuity.
**in perpetuity,** forever: *The idea was not for the United States to subsidize their armed forces in perpetuity* (Wall Street Journal).
[< Old French *perpetuite,* learned borrowing from Latin *perpetuitās* < *perpetuus;* see etym. under **perpetual**]

**per|pe|tu|um mo|bi|le** (pər pet′yů əm mob′ə lē), **1** perpetual motion. **2** a piece of music that proceeds from beginning to end with the same rapid motion. [< New Latin *perpetuum mobile*]

**per|plex** (pər pleks′), *v.t.* **1** to trouble with doubt; puzzle; bewilder: *This problem even perplexed the teacher.* **SYN**: mystify, nonplus. See syn. under **puzzle.** **2** to make difficult to understand or settle; confuse: *difficulties that must have perplexed the engagement and retarded the marriage* (Jane Austen). **SYN**: complicate, muddle. [originally, adjective < Latin *perplexus* confused, involved < *per-* completely + *plexus* entangled, past participle of *plectere* to intertwine]

**per|plexed** (pər plekst′), *adj.* **1** bewildered; puzzled. **2** intricate; involved; complicated.

**per|plex|ed|ly** (pər plek′sid lē), *adv.* in a perplexed manner.

**per|plex|ing** (pər plek′sing), *adj.* that perplexes; causing perplexity. —**per|plex′ing|ly,** *adv.*

**per|plex|i|ty** (pər plek′sə tē), *n., pl.* **-ties.** **1** a perplexed condition; confusion; being puzzled; not knowing what to do or how to act: *His perplexity was so great that he asked many persons for advice.* **SYN**: bewilderment, distraction. **2** an entangled or confused state. **3** something that perplexes: *There are many perplexities in such a complicated job.* [< Late Latin *perplexitās* < Latin *perplexus* perplex]

**per|qui|site** (pėr′kwə zit), *n.* **1** something advantageous specially belonging: *perquisites of trade. Undergraduate elections are important events ... and the winners enjoy many lucrative perquisites* (New Yorker). **2a** anything received for work besides the regular pay: *The maid had the old dresses of her mistress as a perquisite. The minister had a parsonage as a perquisite.* **SYN**: bonus. **b** a tip expected as a matter of course for doing one's job. **3** the income from any job, office, or other position; pay; wages. **4** casual profits that come to the lord of a manor, in addition to his regular annual revenue. **5** *Obsolete.* an adjunct. [< Medieval Latin *perquisitum* a thing gained; profit < Latin *perquīsītum* a thing sought after, neuter past participle of *perquīrere* to seek, ask for < *per-* (intensive) + *quaerere* to seek]

**per|ron** (per′ən), *n. Architecture.* **1** a flight of steps ascending to a platform, such as at an entrance, or to a terrace. **2** a platform at the entrance of a large building, with steps to the ground. **3** a large block of stone used as a platform. [< Old French *perron,* perhaps < Vulgar Latin *petrō, -onis* (augmentative) < Latin *petra* rock < Greek *pétrā* stone]

**per|ru|quier** (pe ry kyā′; *Anglicized* pə rü′kē ər), *n. French.* a wigmaker.

**per|ry** (per′ē), *n., pl.* **-ries.** *British.* a beverage somewhat resembling hard cider, made from fermented pear juice. [Middle English *pereye* < Old French *pere,* ultimately Latin *pirum* pear]

**pers.,** **1** person. **2** personal.

**Pers.,** **1** Persia. **2** Persian.

**per|salt** (pėr′sôlt′), *n. Chemistry.* a salt formed by the combination of an acid with the peroxide of a metal; salt of a peracid.

**perse** (pėrs), *adj., n.* **1** dark blue; purplish-black. **2** *Archaic.* blue; bluish; blue-gray. [< Old French *perse,* perhaps < Late Latin *persus* blue]

**per se** (pėr sā′, sē′), *Latin.* by itself; in itself; intrinsically: *Disarmament, per se, will not prevent war* (Bertrand Russell).

**per second per second,** during one second, of a series of seconds (in connection with a constant acceleration measured in intervals of one second each). *Example:* the acceleration of gravity is about 32 feet per second per second, which means that the velocity of a freely falling body increases by 32 feet per second during each successive second of fall.

**per|se|cute** (pėr′sə kyüt), *v.t.,* **-cut|ed, -cut|ing.** **1** to treat badly; do harm to again and again; oppress: *The cruel boy persecuted the kitten by throwing stones at it whenever it came near.* **SYN**: wrong, torment. **2** to treat badly because of one's principles or beliefs: *Christians were persecuted in ancient Rome. Blessed are they which are persecuted for righteousness' sake* (Matthew 5:10). **3** to annoy; harass: *persecuted by silly questions. We sat in the shade ... persecuted by small stinging flies* (W. H. Hudson). **SYN**: worry, vex. [< Middle French *persécuter,* back formation < Old French *persecuteur,* learned borrowing from Latin *persecūtor* < *persequī;* see etym. under **pursue**]

**per|se|cu|tion** (pėr′sə kyü′shən), *n.* **1** the act of persecuting: *The boy's persecution of the kitten was cruel.* **2** the state of being persecuted: *The kitten's persecution by the boy made it run away.* **3** a course or period of systematic punishment or oppression. **4** *Obsolete.* prosecution. [< Latin *persecūtiō, -ōnis* < *persequī;* see etym. under **pursue**]

**per|se|cu|tive** (pėr′sə kyü′tiv), *adj.* of a persecuting character; tending or addicted to persecution.

**per|se|cu|tor** (pėr′sə kyü′tər), *n.* a person who persecutes.

**per|se|cu|to|ry** (pėr′sə kyü′tər ē, pėr′sə kyü′-), *adj.* = persecutive.

**Per|se|i** (pėr′sē ī), *n.* genitive of **Perseus** (the constellation).

**Per|se|id** (pėr′sē id), *n.* one of a shower of meteors occurring about August 12. The Perseids seem to radiate from the constellation Perseus. [< New Latin *Perseïdes,* plural of *Perseïs* daughter of Perseus < *Perseus*]

**Per|seph|o|ne** (pər sef′ə nē), *n. Greek Mythology.* the daughter of Zeus and Demeter, who was carried off by Pluto, the king of the lower world, and made his queen. She was allowed to spend part of each year on the earth. The Romans called her Proserpina.

**Per|se|us** (pėr′sē əs, -syüs), *n., genitive* (def. 2) **Per|se|i.** **1** *Greek Mythology.* a hero, the son of Zeus and Danaë, who slew Medusa and rescued Andromeda from a sea monster. **2** a northern constellation near Cassiopeia. It contains the famous variable star, Algol.

**per|se|ver|ance** (pėr′sə vir′əns), *n.* **1** the act or fact of sticking to a purpose or an aim; never giving up what one has set out to do: *By perseverance the crippled boy learned how to swim. 'Tis known by the name of perseverance in a good cause—and of obstinacy in a bad one* (Laurence Sterne). **SYN**: tenacity, diligence. See syn. under **persistence.** **2** *Theology.* continuance in a state of grace leading finally to eternal salvation.

**per|se|ver|ant** (pėr′sə vir′ənt), *adj.* = persevering.

**per|sev|er|ate** (pər sev′ə rāt), *v.i.,* **-at|ed, -at|ing.** *Psychology, Education.* to continue or repeat an action after the stimulus or need for it has passed: *The neural processes initiated in learning perseverate through time and become more firmly fixed because of this persisting activity* (Charles E. Osgood).

**per|sev|er|a|tion** (pər sev′ə rā′shən), *n.* **1** *Psychology, Education.* **a** the tendency to perseverate. **b** the act or process of perseverating. **2** *Obsolete.* a persevering.

**per|se|vere** (pėr′sə vir′), *v.i.,* **-vered, -ver|ing.** to continue steadily in doing something hard; persist: *in our opposed paths to persevere* (Coventry Patmore). [< Old French *perseverer,* learned borrowing from Latin *persevērāre* < *persevērus,* adjective < *per-* very + *sevērus* strict]

**per|se|ver|ing** (pėr′sə vir′ing), *adj.* that perseveres; stubbornly persistent. —**per′se|ver′ing|ly,** *adv.*

**Per|sian** (pėr′zhən; *especially British* pėr′shən), *adj., n.* —*adj.* of or having to do with ancient Persia or modern Iran, its people, or their language. —*n.* **1** a native or inhabitant of ancient Persia or modern Iran. **2** the Iranian language of Persia; Farsi. **3** = Pahlavi. **4** a thin, soft silk fabric, formerly used for linings.
**Persians,** = Persian blinds.

**Persian apple,** = citron.

**Persian blinds,** window shutters made with adjustable slats like Venetian blinds, but hung outside rather than inside.

**Persian carpet,** = Persian rug.

**Persian cat,** a long-haired domestic cat, originally from Persia (Iran) and Afghanistan.

**Persian lamb,** **1** a very curly fur from karakul lambs of Persia (Iran) and some parts of central Asia. **2** a lamb having this fur.

**Persian lynx,** = caracal.

**Persian rug,** an Oriental rug or carpet made in Persia (Iran).

**Persian walnut,** = English walnut.

**per|si|ennes** (pėr′zē enz′; *French* per syen′), *n.pl.* = Persian blinds. [< French *persiennes*]

**per|si|flage** (pėr′sə fläzh), *n.* light, joking talk or writing: *She could see, behind the screen of persiflage, that John was worried* (New Yorker). **SYN**: banter, raillery. [< French *persiflage* < *persifler* to banter, apparently < *per-* through + Old French *siffler* to whistle, hiss < Latin *sīfilāre,* variant of *sībilāre.* Compare etym. under **sibilant.**]

**per|sim|mon** (pər sim′ən), *n.* **1** a North American tree with a yellowish-orange, plumlike fruit containing one to ten seeds. A Japanese and Chinese species bears a large red fruit. **2** the fruit of the North American tree, very bitter when green, but sweet and good to eat when very ripe. [American English < Algonkian (Powhatan) *pasimenan* fruit dried artificially < *pasimeneu* he dries fruit]

**per|sist** (pər sist′, -zist′), *v.i.* **1** to stick to it; continue firmly; refuse to stop or be changed: *She persisted in reading the newspaper at the dinner table.* **SYN**: persevere. **2** to remain in existence; last; stay; endure: *On the tops of some very high mountains, snow persists throughout the year.* **3** to say again and again; maintain: *He persisted that he was innocent of the crime.* **4** *Archaic.* to continue to be; remain: *They persisted deaf ...* (Milton). [< Latin *persistere* < *per-* thoroughly + *sistere* to stand] —**per|sist′er,** *n.*

**per|sist|ence** (pər sis′təns, -zis′-), *n.* **1** the act or fact of persisting. **2** the condition of being persistent; doggedness: *the persistence of a fly buzzing around one's head.* **3** a continuing exist-

ence: *the stubborn persistence of a cough.*
—***Syn.*** **1 Persistence, perseverance** mean a holding fast to a purpose or course of action. **Persistence**, having a good or bad sense according to one's attitude toward what is done, emphasizes holding stubbornly or obstinately to one's purpose and continuing firmly and often annoyingly against disapproval, opposition, advice, or attempts at persuasion: *By persistence many people won religious freedom.* **Perseverance**, always in a good sense, emphasizes refusing to be discouraged by obstacles or difficulties, but continuing steadily with courage and patience: *Perseverance led to his success.*

**per|sist|en|cy** (pər sis′tən sē, -zis′-), *n.* = persistence.

**per|sist|ent** (pər sis′tənt, -zis′-), *adj.* **1** having lasting qualities, especially in the face of disapproval, dislike, or difficulties; persisting; not giving up: *a persistent worker, a persistent beggar.* **SYN:** persevering, untiring, insistent. **2** going on; continuing; lasting: *a persistent headache that lasted all day.* **3** constantly repeated; recurring. **4** *Botany.* continuing without withering, as a calyx which remains after the corolla has withered; permanent. **5** *Zoology.* permanent; not lost or altered during development: *persistent horns.* **6** (of toxic chemicals, especially insecticides) hard to decompose; chemically stable and therefore degradable only over a long period of time. —**per|sist′ent|ly**, *adv.*

**per|snick|e|ty** (pər snik′ə tē), *adj.* = pernickety.

**per|son** (pėr′sən), *n.* **1** a man, woman, or child; human being: *Any person who wishes may come to the fair. If that person calls again, tell him I refuse to see him.* **2** the human body, distinct from the mind or soul: *The person of the king was well guarded. Beelzebub arose, With care his sweet person adorning* (Shelley). **3** bodily appearance: *He kept his person neat and trim. He has a fine person.* **4** *Grammar.* **a** a change in pronouns or verbs used to show the person speaking (first person), the person spoken to (second person), or the person or thing spoken of (third person). *I* and *we* are used for the first person; *thou* and *you,* for the second person; *he, she, it,* and *they,* for the third person. **b** a form of pronouns or verbs giving such indication. *Comes* is the third person singular of *come. Abbr:* pers. **5** *Theology.* any of the three modes of being in the Trinity (Father, Son, and Holy Ghost). **6** a character assumed in a drama or in actual life viewed as a drama; part played: *I must take upon me the person of a philosopher, and make them a present of my advice* (Sir Richard Steele). **7** *Law.* a human being, or an entity such as a corporation, a partnership, or occasionally a collection of property, such as the estate of a dead person, recognized by the law as capable of having legal rights and duties. A corporation is sometimes called an artificial person. **8** *Obsolete.* a mask anciently worn by actors; disguise.
**in person, a** with or by one's own action or presence; personally: *Come in person; do not write or phone. Charlemagne excused the bishops from serving in person* (Joseph Priestley). **b** on the stage, as opposed to a motion picture or television: *The star will be featured in person in the forthcoming production.*
**in the person of**, in the character or guise of: *... persecuting Horace and Virgil in the persons of their successors* (John Dryden).
[Middle English *persone* < Old French < Latin *persōna* person, personality; (originally) character in a drama; actor; mask worn by an actor. See etym. of doublet **parson.**]
▶**Person** is the ordinary word for referring to a human being: *She is a nice person. Individual* has the same meaning (though it is applied to single objects and animals as well) but emphasizes the person's singleness, aloneness, and is slightly heavy or pretentious unless that emphasis is needed: *I speak as an individual.* Unless *party* means one who takes part (*a party to the conspiracy*), it is restricted to legal or informal use: *the party of the first part. Who is the party that called?*

**Per|son** (pėr′sən), *n. Theology.* person.

**-person**, *combining form.* ____man or ____woman (used chiefly to eliminate the reference to the subject's sex), as in *newsperson; an effective spokesperson for higher education* (Science). *The report shuns the word "freshman" in favor of, yes, "freshperson"* (National Review).

**per|so|na** (pər sō′nə), *n., pl.* **-nae, -nas. 1** the public impression of a person; outward appearance; facade; image: *... the glamourized career-girl's difficulties with her new persona* (Punch). *A clown dons his make-up like a mask to create a persona* (Listener). **2** the voice of the author or the author's creation in a literary work: *Reilly seems to be partly a persona of the poet* (Manchester Guardian Weekly). **3** = person. [< Latin *persōna* person]

**per|son|a|ble** (pėr′sə nə bəl), *adj.* having a pleasing appearance; good-looking; attractive: *Miss Ingamells ... a personable if somewhat heavy creature of twenty-eight* (Arnold Bennett). **SYN:** comely, presentable. —**per′son|a|ble|ness**, *n.*

**per|so|nae** (pər sō′nē), *n.pl.* persons or characters in a book, play, or other literary or artistic work: *The plot has, so far as personae are concerned, just about everything* (Saturday Review). [< Latin *persōnae,* plural of *persōna* person]

**per|son|age** (pėr′sə nij), *n.* **1** a person of importance, distinction, or high rank: *Who am I indeed? Perhaps a personage in disguise* (Charlotte Brontë). **2** a person: *a grandfatherly sort of personage* (Hawthorne). **3** a character in a book or play or in history: *The hero is the chief personage in that mystery story.* **4** the impersonation of such a character; part: *to assume the personage of Caesar or Hamlet.* **5** *Archaic.* the body; bodily frame. [< Old French *personage* < *persone* person + *-age* -age. See etym. of doublet **parsonage.**]

**per|so|na gra|ta** (pər sō′nə grā′tə), *pl.* **per|so|nae gra|tae** (pər sō′nē grā′tē). *Latin.* **1** an acceptable person: *If it were published, he would no longer be persona grata at Stanbrook* (Atlantic). **2** a diplomatic representative personally acceptable to the government to which he is accredited.

**per|son|al** (pėr′sə nəl, pėrs′nəl), *adj., n.* —***adj.*** **1** belonging to a person; individual; private: *a personal letter, a personal matter, a personal call.* **2** done in person; directly by oneself, not through others or by letter: *a personal visit.* **3** of the body or bodily appearance: *personal cleanliness, personal beauty or charms.* **SYN:** physical, corporeal. **4** about or against a person or persons: *personal remarks, personal abuse, a personal question.* **5** inclined to make remarks or ask questions about the private affairs of others: *Don't be too personal.* **6** *Grammar.* showing person. *I, we, thou, you, he, she, it* and *they* are personal pronouns. **7** *Law.* **a** of or having to do with property that can be moved, such as furniture and clothing, as contrasted with real property, such as land and buildings. **b** of or having to do with persons rather than things: *a personal action.* **8** having the nature of a person; that is a person, not a thing or abstraction.
—***n.*** *U.S.* **1** a short paragraph in a newspaper about a particular person or persons: *Put a personal in the Baltimore Sun* (Mark Twain). **2** *Sports, Informal.* a personal foul.
[< Latin *persōnālis* < *persōna* person]

**personal effects**, the belongings that an individual wears or carries on his person; private or intimate articles.

**personal equation**, an individual tendency for which allowance should be made.

**personal flotation device**, *U.S.* any device to keep a person afloat in the water; life preserver: *Personal flotation devices...must be bought in the proper size— and not necessarily "the bigger the better"* (Popular Mechanics).

**personal foul**, *Sports.* a foul that occurs when a player makes an illegal physical contact with an opposing player, as by holding or pushing him in basketball or by kicking or striking him in football.

**per|son|a|li|a** (pėr′sə nā′lē ə, -nāl′yə), *n.pl.* personal items, anecdotes, letters, and the like. [< New Latin *personalia,* neuter plural of Latin *persōnālis* personal]

**per|son|al|ism** (pėr′sə nə liz′əm, pėrs′nə liz-), *n.* **1** the quality or character of being personal: *In Texas ... personalism is the curse of politics* (Harper's). **2** any doctrine or system in which personal feelings and relationships rather than impersonal or universal standards or axioms are stressed.

**per|son|al|ist** (pėr′sə nə list, pėrs′nə-), *adj., n.* —***adj.*** of, having to do with, or characteristic of personalism. —***n.*** a believer in personalism.

**per|son|al|is|tic** (pėr′sə nə lis′tik), *adj.* = personalist.

**per|son|al|i|ty** (pėr′sə nal′ə tē), *n., pl.* **-ties. 1** the personal or individual quality that makes one person be different and act differently from another. In psychology, personality is the total physical, intellectual, and emotional structure of an individual, including abilities, interests, and attitudes. *A baby two weeks old does not have much personality. Many psychologists are inclined to attribute the formation of personality entirely to the operation of the cultural and physical environment* (Beals and Hoijer). **SYN:** See syn. under **character. 2** pleasing or attractive qualities of a person; distinctive personal character: *That boy may be smart, but he has no personality.* **3** a person, especially a person of distinction; personage: *personalities of stage and screen.* **4** the quality of being a person, not a thing. **5** *Law.* personal estate or property; personalty.
**personalities**, remarks made about or against one particular person: *Personalities are not in good taste in general conversation.*

**personality cult**, = cult of personality.

**personality test**, a test intended to measure or reveal the characteristics of an individual's personality.

**per|son|al|ize** (pėr′sə nə līz, pėrs′nə-), *v.t.,* **-ized, -iz|ing. 1** to make personal; cause to be distinctly one's own: *to personalize stationery.* **2** to personify. **3** to take as personal. —**per′son|al|i|za′tion**, *n.*

**per|son|al|ly** (pėr′sə nə lē, pėrs′nə-), *adv.* **1** in person; not by the aid of others: *to deal personally with one's customers. The hostess personally saw to the comforts of her guests.* **SYN:** individually. **2** as far as oneself is concerned: *Personally, I like apples better than oranges.* **SYN:** subjectively. **3** as a person: *We like him personally, but dislike his way of earning a living.* **4** as being meant for oneself: *Do not take criticism of your writing personally.*

**personal property**, property that is not land, buildings, mines, or forests; possessions that can be moved.

**personal realism**, *Philosophy.* a form of personalism that stresses the importance of personality in the natural world.

**personal shopper**, an employee in a store who selects merchandise ordered by mail or telephone or who assists customers in suggesting appropriate purchases.

**per|son|al|ty** (pėr′sə nəl tē), *n., pl.* **-ties.** *Law.* personal property.

**per|so|na non gra|ta** (pər sō′nə non grā′tə), *pl.* **per|so|nae non gra|tae** (pər sō′nēnon grā′tē). *Latin.* **1** a person who is not acceptable: *Some men, would-be customers but apparently personae non gratae, never got in the café* (New Yorker). **2** a diplomatic representative who is not acceptable to the government to which he is accredited.

**per|son|ate**[1] (pėr′sə nāt), *v.,* **-at|ed, -at|ing.** —***v.t.*** **1** to act the part of (a character in a play or in history); impersonate. **2** to represent as a person in literature or art; personify. **3** *Law.* to pretend to be (someone else), usually for purposes of fraud. —***v.i.*** to act; play a part.
[< Late Latin *persōnāre* (with English *-ate*[1]) represent < Latin *persōna,* see etym. under **person**] —**per′son|a′tion**, *n.* —**per′son|a′tor**, *n.*

**per|son|ate**[2] (pėr′sə nit, -nāt), *adj. Botany.* (of a labiate corolla) having the lower lip pushed upward so as to close the opening between the lips, as in the snapdragon; masked. [< Latin *persōnātus* masked < *persōna* mask; see etym. under **person**]

**per|son|a|tive** (pėr′sə nā′tiv), *adj.* having the quality of personating.

**per|son-day** (pėr′sən dā′), *n.* a unit of time designating one day of an average person's normal activities.

**per|son|hood** (pėr′sən hůd), *n.* the distinctive personal quality of a human being; individuality.

**per|son|i|fi|ca|tion** (pər son′ə fə kā′shən), *n.* **1** a striking example; embodiment; type: *A miser is the personification of greed.* **SYN:** exemplification. **2** the act or fact of representing as a person, such as speaking of the sun as *he* and the moon as *she.* In John Bunyan's *Pilgrim's Progress,* Mr. Worldly-Wiseman and Mr. Good-will are personifications. **3** a person or creature imagined as representing a thing or idea: *Satan is the personification of evil.* **4** a figure of speech in which a lifeless thing or quality is spoken of as if alive. *Examples:* The music sobbed. Duty calls us. There Honour comes, a pilgrim grey (William Collins).

**per|son|i|fy** (pər son′ə fī), *v.t.,* **-fied, -fy|ing. 1** to be a type of; embody: *Satan personifies evil.* **SYN:** exemplify. **2** to regard or represent as a person. We often personify the sun and moon, referring to the sun as *he* and the moon as *she.* We personify time and nature when we refer to *Father Time* and *Mother Nature. Greek philosophy has a tendency to personify ideas* (Benjamin Jowett). [probably patterned on French *personnifier* < *personne* person + *-fier* -fy] —**per|son′i|fi′er**, *n.*

**per|son|nel** (pėr′sə nel′), *n., adj.* —***n.*** the persons employed in any work, business, or service: *to issue an order to all personnel, the personnel of a hospital.*
—***adj.*** **1** of or having to do with personnel. **2** used by personnel. **3** in charge of personnel: *a personnel manager, a military personnel officer.* [< French *personnel,* adjective, personal]

---

**Pronunciation Key:** hat, āge, cãre, fär; let, ēqual, tėrm; it, īce; hot, ōpen, ôrder; **oi**l, **ou**t; cup, pu̇t, rüle; **ch**ild; lo**ng**; **th**in; **ŦH**en; **zh**, measure; **ə** represents **a** in about, **e** in taken, **i** in pencil, **o** in lemon, **u** in circus.

**personnel administration** or **management**, the branch of management concerned with the effective and efficient use of employees.

**per|son-to-per|son** (pėr′sən tə pėr′sən), *adj.* between persons; between individuals; personal: *a person-to-person telephone call. The Yurok had a good many person-to-person quarrels and enmities, but few class or communal clashes* (Alfred L. Kroeber).

*** per|spec|tive** (pər spek′tiv), *n., adj.* **—*n.* 1a** the art of picturing objects on a flat surface so as to give the appearance of distance or depth: [*Fauvism*] *had discarded perspective, the sublime technical triumph of the Renaissance* (New Yorker). See picture below. **b** a drawing or picture in perspective. **2** the effect of distance on the appearance of objects: *Railroad tracks seem to meet at the horizon because of perspective.* **3** *Figurative.* the effect of the distance of events upon the mind: *Perspective makes happenings of last year seem less important.* **4** a view of things or facts in which they are in the right relations: *a lack of perspective. We have endeavoured ... to observe a kind of perspective, that one part may cast light upon another* (Francis Bacon). **5** a view in front; distant view: *a perspective of lakes and hills.* **SYN**: vista. **6** *Figurative.* a mental view, outlook, or prospect: *Sleeping or waking, I beheld the same black perspective of approaching ruin* (Robert Louis Stevenson). **7** *Obsolete.* an optical glass, such as a magnifying glass. [< Medieval Latin *perspectiva* (*ars*) (science) of optics, feminine of *perspectivus;* see the adjective]
**—*adj.* 1** of perspective. **2** drawn so as to show the proper perspective: *a perspective drawing.* **3** *Obsolete.* **a** optical. **b** assisting the sight, as an optical instrument does: *a perspective glass.*
**in perspective, a** drawn or viewed in accordance with the rules or principles of perspective: *The engraver said he must ... "put it in proper perspective"* (London Daily Chronicle). **b** *Figurative.* from a particular mental point of view: *to examine an issue in perspective.*
[< Medieval Latin *perspectivus* < Latin *perspicere* look through; inspect < *per-* through + *specere* to look] **—per|spec′tive|ly,** *adv.*

**per|spec|tiv|ism** (pər spek′tə viz əm), *n.* **1** *Philosophy.* the theory or view that everything is seen or known only from particular perspectives. **2** the use of perspective in art or literature. **—per|spec′tiv|ist,** *adj., n.*

**per|spi|ca|cious** (pėr′spə kā′shəs), *adj.* **1** keen in observing and understanding; discerning: *perspicacious wit.* **SYN**: shrewd, acute. **2** *Archaic.* clear-sighted. [< Latin *perspicāx, -ācis* (with English *-ous*) sharp-sighted < *perspicere* to see through < *per-* through + *specere* to look] **—per′spi|ca′cious|ly,** *adv.*
▶ **Perspicacious** and **perspicuous** are not synonymous; the former means "discerning," the latter "lucid": *a perspicacious critic, a perspicuous argument.*

**per|spi|cac|i|ty** (pėr′spə kas′ə tē), *n.* **1** wisdom and understanding in dealing with people or with facts; keen perception; discernment: *Unbelievable artistic perspicacity and integrity mingle with childlike humor and credulity* (Wall Street Journal). **SYN**: penetration. **2** *Archaic.* keenness of eyesight.

*** perspective**
definition 1a

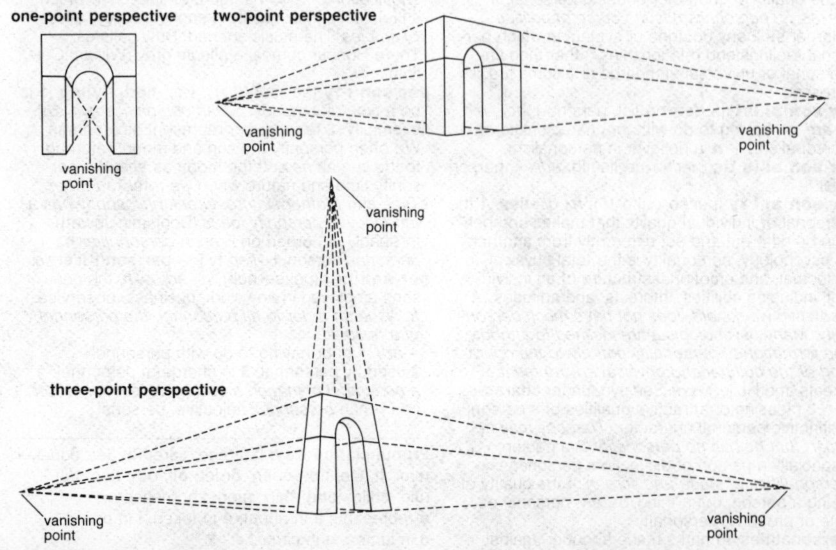


**per|spi|cu|i|ty** (pėr′spə kyü′ə tē), *n.* clearness in expression; ease in being understood: *There is nothing more desirable in composition than perspicuity; and in perspicuity precision is included* (Robert Southey). **SYN**: plainness, lucidity.

**per|spic|u|ous** (pər spik′yü əs), *adj.* easily understood; clear; lucid: *His manner of telling a story, or explaining his thoughts, was forcible, perspicuous and original* (William Godwin). **SYN**: intelligible. [< Latin *perspicuus* (with English *-ous*) transparent, clear < *perspicere* < *per-* through + *specere* to look] **—per|spic′u|ous|ly,** *adv.* **—per|spic′u|ous|ness,** *n.*
▶ See **perspicacious** for usage note.

**per|spi|ra|tion** (pėr′spə rā′shən), *n.* **1** sweat: *The runner's forehead was damp with perspiration.* **SYN**: See syn. under **sweat. 2** sweating: (*Figurative.*) *Genius is one per cent inspiration and ninety nine per cent perspiration* (Thomas A. Edison).

**per|spir|a|to|ry** (pər spīr′ə tôr′ē, -tōr′-), *adj.* **1** of sweat. **2** causing sweat.

**per|spire** (pər spīr′), *v.i., v.t.,* **-spired, -spir|ing.** to sweat: *The lumberman perspired as he cut the trees down under the blazing sun.* [< Latin *perspīrāre* to blow or breathe constantly (said of the wind) < *per-* through + *spīrāre* to breathe, blow] **—per|spir′a|ble,** *adj.* **—per|spir′ing|ly,** *adv.*

**per stir|pes** (pər stėr′pēz), *Law.* by stocks or families (used of succession to property in which the descendants of one heir share the portion which would have come to that heir if living): *to divide an estate per stirpes.* [< Medieval Latin *per* by, according to, and Latin *stirpes,* plural of *stirps, stirpis* stock; family; (originally) stem, stalk]

**per|suad|a|ble** (pər swā′də bəl), *adj.* that can be persuaded; easy to persuade.

**per|suade** (pər swād′), *v.t.,* **-suad|ed, -suad|ing. 1** to win over to do or believe; make willing or sure by urging or arguing; convince: *I knew I should study, but he persuaded me to go to the movies. We persuaded him that he was wrong.* **2** *Archaic.* to urge, plead with, or counsel strongly: *Hadst thou thy wits, and didst persuade revenge, It could not move thus* (Shakespeare). [< Latin *persuādēre* < *per-* (intensive) + *suādēre* to urge, related to *suāvis* sweet, agreeable] **—per|suad′er,** *n.*
**—*Syn.* 1 Persuade, convince** mean to get someone to do or believe something. **Persuade** emphasizes winning a person over to a desired belief or action by strong urging, arguing, advising, and appealing to his feelings as well as to his mind: *She wanted to buy the orange dress, but we persuaded her that the blue one was more becoming.* **Convince** emphasizes overcoming a person's objections or disbelief by proof or arguments appealing to his reason and understanding: *I have convinced her that she needs a vacation, but cannot persuade her to take one.*

**per|sua|si|bil|i|ty** (pər swā′sə bil′ə tē), *n.* the quality of being persuasible; capability of being, or readiness to be, persuaded.

**per|sua|si|ble** (pər swā′sə bəl), *adj.* open to persuasion; persuadable.

**per|sua|sion** (pər swā′zhən), *n.* **1** the act of persuading: *All our attempts at persuasion were useless; she would not come.* **2** the power of persuading: *He is a poor salesman because he lacks persuasion. Is't possible that my deserts to you can lack persuasion?* (Shakespeare). **3** a firm belief; conviction: *different political persuasions. He had a strong persuasion that Likeman was wrong* (H. G. Wells). **SYN**: assurance, conviction. **4a** a religious belief; creed: *All Christians are not of the same persuasion.* **b** a body of persons holding a particular religious belief; sect; denomination: *The Quakers have been called the "friendly persuasion."* **5** *Humorous.* kind; sort; description: *a house filled with pets of every persuasion.*
**persuasions,** beliefs: *to cling tenaciously to old persuasions.*
[< Latin *persuāsiō, -ōnis* < *persuādēre* persuade]

**per|sua|sive** (pər swā′siv, -ziv), *adj., n.* **—*adj.*** able to persuade; fitted to persuade: *a persuasive argument, a persuasive smile. The salesman had a very persuasive way of talking.* **SYN**: moving, winning.
**—*n.*** something adapted or intended to persuade. **—per|sua′sive|ly,** *adv.* **—per|sua′sive|ness,** *n.*

**per|sul|fate** (pėr sul′fāt), *n.* a salt of persulfuric acid.

**per|sul|fu|ric acid** (pėr′sul fyůr′ik), **1** a highly unstable, crystalline acid used as an oxidizing agent. *Formula:* $H_2SO_5$ **2** a crystalline acid containing a high proportion of sulfur and oxygen, used as an oxidizing agent. *Formula:* $H_2S_2O_8$

**pert** (pėrt), *adj.* **1** too forward or free in speech or action; saucy; bold: *a pert girl, a pert reply. The boy was very pert.* **SYN**: impudent, impertinent. **2** stylish; jaunty: *a pert outfit for casual wear.* **3** *Informal.* in good health or spirits; lively: *a very pert old woman.* **4** *Obsolete.* **a** expert; skilled. **b** sharp; adroit; clever. [short for Middle English *apert* open, frank < Old French *apert* < Latin *apertus,* past participle of *aperīre* to open] **—pert′ly,** *adv.* **—pert′ness,** *n.*

**PERT** (pėrt), *n.* Program Evaluation and Review Technique (a computerized management system for handling complex programs, such as the production of missile systems).

**pert.,** pertaining.

**per|tain** (pər tān′), *v.i.* **1** to belong or be connected as a part or possession: *We own the house and the land pertaining to it.* **2** to have to do with; be related; refer: *documents pertaining to the case.* **3** to be appropriate: *We had a turkey and everything else that pertains to Thanksgiving Day.* **4** *Archaic.* to belong as one's care or concern. [Middle English *perteynen* < Old French *partenir* < Latin *pertinēre* to reach, concern < *per-* (intensive) + *tenēre* to hold]

**per|ti|na|cious** (pėr′tə nā′shəs), *adj.* **1** holding firmly to a purpose, action, or opinion; very persistent; resolute: *a pertinacious beggar. A bulldog is a pertinacious fighter.* **SYN**: determined, dogged, stubborn. **2** stubborn to excess; obstinate. **3** obstinately or persistently continuing; not yielding to treatment: *a pertinacious cough.* [< Latin *pertināx, -ācis* firm (with English *-ous*) < *per-* (intensive) + *tenāx, -ācis* tenacious] **—per′ti|na′cious|ly,** *adv.* **—per′ti|na′cious|ness,** *n.*

**per|ti|nac|i|ty** (pėr′tə nas′ə tē), *n.* great persistence; holding firmly to a purpose, action, or opinion: *Again and again ... with the inexorable pertinacity of a child intent upon some object important to itself, did he renew his efforts* (Hawthorne). **SYN**: tenacity.

**per|ti|nence** (pėr′tə nəns), *n.* the quality of being to the point; fitness; relevance: *The pertinence of the boy's replies showed that he was alert and intelligent.*

**per|ti|nen|cy** (pėr′tə nən sē), *n.* = pertinence.

**per|ti|nent** (pėr′tə nənt), *adj.* having to do with what is being considered; relating to the matter in hand; to the point; relevant: *If your question is pertinent, I will answer it.* [< Latin *pertinēns, -entis,* present participle of *pertinēre;* see etym. under **pertain**] **—per′ti|nent|ly,** *adv.*
**—*Syn.* Pertinent, relevant** mean relating to the matter in hand. **Pertinent** means directly to the point of the matter, belonging properly and fitting to what is being considered and helping to explain or clarify it: *A summary of the events leading up to this situation would be pertinent information.* **Relevant** means having some bearing on the problem or enough connection with it to have some meaning or importance: *Even incidents seeming unimportant in themselves might be relevant.*

**per|turb** (pər tėrb′), *v.t.* **1** to disturb greatly; make uneasy or troubled; upset: *Teachers are always perturbed by low grades. Highly perturbed, he wondered what was coming next* (Arnold Bennett). **SYN**: excite, trouble, distress. **2** to cause disorder or irregularity in; agitate: *perturbed waters.* **3** *Astronomy.* to cause perturbation in. [< Latin *perturbāre* < *per-* thoroughly + *turbāre* to confuse < *turba* turmoil, disorder] **—per|turb′a|ble,** *adj.* **—per|turb′er,** *n.*

**per|turb|a|bil|i|ty** (pər tėr′bə bil′ə tē), *n.* the quality of being perturbable; capability of being, or readiness to be, perturbed.

**per|tur|ba|tion** (pėr′tər bā′shən), *n.* **1** the act or fact of perturbing. **2** a perturbed condition: *Though the violence of her perturbations gradually subsided, her cheerfulness did not return* (Lytton Strachey). **3** a thing, act, or event that causes disturbance or agitation: *The crown ... O polish'd perturbation! golden care!* (Shakespeare). **4** *Astronomy.* a disturbance in the motion of a planet or other heavenly body in orbit caused by the attraction of a body or bodies other than its primary: *Perturbations, or disturbances in the motions, of the planets Neptune and Uranus first led ... astronomers to hunt for a distant planet beyond Neptune* (Science News Letter).

**per|tur|ba|tion|al** (pėr′tər bā′shə nəl), *adj.* = perturbative.

**per|tur|ba|tive** (pər tėr′bə tiv), *adj.* **1** causing perturbation; disturbing. **2** *Astronomy.* of or having to do with perturbations.

**per|tur|ba|tor** (pėr′tər bā′tər), *n.* a person who perturbs; disturber.

**per|tus|sal** (pər tus′əl), *adj.* of or having to do with whooping cough.

**per|tus|sis** (pər tus′is), *n.* = whooping cough. [< New Latin *pertussis* < Latin *per-* (intensive) + *tussis* a cough]

**Pe|ru balsam** (pə rü′), = balsam of Peru.

**Peru Current,** a cool ocean current of the Pacific which flows northward along the west coast of South America; Humboldt Current.

***pe|ruke** (pə rük′), *n.* a wig, especially of the kind worn by men in the 1600's and 1700's; periwig. [< Middle French *perruque* (originally) head of hair, hairdress < Italian *perrucca;* origin uncertain. See etym. of doublet **periwig.**]

***peruke**

**pe|ruked** (pə rükt′), *adj.* wearing a peruke: *a peruked barrister in trailing robes* (Time).

**pe|ru|sal** (pə rü′zəl), *n.* the act of perusing, especially a reading through or over: *I have just finished the perusal of your letter.*

**pe|ruse** (pə rüz′), *v.t.,* **-rused, -rus|ing. 1** to read through carefully: *I will show you what to turn over unread and what to peruse* (Sir Richard Steele). *She perused "Middlemarch"; she was disappointed* (Lytton Strachey). **2** to read, now often hastily or more or less casually: *to peruse the paper at breakfast.* **3** to examine, inspect, or consider in detail: *The Stranger ... with a curious eye Perused the Arab youth* (Robert Southey). [earlier, use up < *per-* completely + *use,* verb] — **pe|rus′a|ble,** *adj.* — **pe|rus′er,** *n.*

**Peruv.,** Peruvian.

**Pe|ru|vi|an** (pə rü′vē ən), *adj., n.* — ***adj.*** of or having to do with Peru, a country on the west coast of South America, or its people.
— ***n.*** a person born or living in Peru.

**Peruvian bark,** bark from which quinine is obtained; cinchona.

**per|vade** (pər vād′), *v.t.,* **-vad|ed, -vad|ing. 1** to go or spread throughout; be throughout: *The odor of pines pervades the air. He worked so hard that weariness pervaded his whole body.* **SYN:** penetrate, permeate, impregnate. **2** to be found throughout (something, such as a literary work, a talk, or a life style, so as to characterize, flavor unmistakably, or otherwise mark: *a broad generosity pervaded his life* (Baron Charnwood). **3** to pass through; traverse. [< Latin *pervādere* < *per-* through + *vādere* to go] — **per|vad′er,** *n.*

**per|va|sion** (pər vā′zhən), *n.* **1** the act of pervading. **2** the state of being pervaded.

**per|va|sive** (pər vā′siv), *adj.* **1** tending to pervade. **2** having power to pervade. — **per|va′sive|ly,** *adv.* — **per|va′sive|ness,** *n.*

**per|verse** (pər vėrs′), *adj.* **1a** contrary and willful; obstinately opposing what is wanted, reasonable, or required; stubborn: *The perverse child did just what we told him not to do.* **SYN:** wayward, obstinate. **b** that is is contrary to what is wanted, reasonable, or required: *perverse weather.* **2** persistent in wrong: *What is more likely, considering our perverse nature, than that we should neglect the duties, while we wish to retain the privileges, of our Christian profession?* (Cardinal Newman). **3** turned away from what is right or good; wicked; morally bad: *blameless ... in the midst of a crooked and perverse nation* (Philippians 2:15). **SYN:** perverted, depraved. **4** not correct; wrong: *perverse reasoning.* [< Latin *perversus* turned away, past participle of *pervertere* pervert] — **perverse′ly,** *adv.* — **per|verse′ness,** *n.*

**per|ver|sion** (pər vėr′zhən, -shən), *n.* **1** the act of turning or condition of being turned to what is wrong; change to what is unnatural, abnormal, or wrong: *A tendency to eat sand is a perversion of appetite.* **2** a perverted form. **3** deviation or abnormality in sexual behavior.

**per|ver|si|ty** (pər vėr′sə tē), *n., pl.* **-ties. 1** the quality of being perverse. **2** perverse character or conduct. **3** a perverse act.

**per|ver|sive** (pər vėr′siv), *adj.* that perverts or tends to pervert.

**per|vert** (*v.* pər vert′; *n.* pėr′vėrt), *v., n.* — ***v.t.* 1** to lead or turn from the right way or from the truth; lead astray: *Reading silly stories perverted their taste for good books.* **SYN:** corrupt, debase, deprave. **2** to give a wrong meaning to; misconstrue: *His enemies perverted his friendly remark and made it into an insult. Ye have perverted the words of the living God* (Jeremiah 23:36). **SYN:** misinterpret, distort, falsify. **3** to use for wrong purposes or in a wrong way; misapply: *A clever criminal perverts his talents.* **4** to change from what is natural or normal, now especially what is generally accepted or defined by law as natural or normal in sexual behavior.
— ***n.*** a perverted person, now especially one who practices sexual perversion.
[< Latin *pervertere* < *per-* (pejorative) + *vertere* to turn] — **per|vert′er,** *n.*

**per|vert|ed** (pər vėr′tid), *adj.* **1** turned from the right or usual way; misguided; misapplied: *a perverted enthusiasm for coarse and vulgar literature.* **2** distorted: *a perverted meaning.* **3** vicious by nature or habit; wicked. **4** being a sexual pervert. — **per|vert′ed|ly,** *adv.* — **per|vert′ed|ness,** *n.*

**per|vert|i|ble** (pər vėr′tə bəl), *adj.* that can be perverted.

**per|vi|ous** (pėr′vē əs), *adj.* **1** giving passage or entrance; permeable: *Sand is easily pervious to water.* **2** *Figurative.* open to influence or argument. **3** having the quality of penetrating or permeating; pervasive. [< Latin *pervius* (with English *-ous*) < *per-* through + *via* way] — **per′vi|ous|ness,** *n.*

**pes** (pēz), *n., pl.* **pe|des. 1** *Anatomy.* the terminal segment of the hindlimb of a vertebrate animal, corresponding to the human foot. **2** *Botany.* a footlike part or organ; base of support. [< Latin *pēs, pedis* foot]

**Pe|sah** or **Pe|sach** (pā′säн), *n.* the Passover festival. [< Hebrew *pasaḥ* a passing over; see etym. under **Pasch**]

**pe|se|ta** (pə sā′tə), *n.* **1** the unit of money of Spain, equal to 100 centimos. **2** a coin or bank note equal to one peseta. [< Spanish *peseta* (diminutive) < *pesa* weight; see etym. under **peso**]

**pe|se|wa** (pə sā′wə), *n.* a unit of money in Ghana, equal to 1/100 of a cedi. The pesewa replaced and is equivalent to the British penny. [< Fanti *pesawa*]

**Pe|shi|to** or **Pe|shit|to** (pə shē′tō), *n.* = Peshitta.

**Pe|shit|ta** (pə shēt′tä), *n.* the chief Syriac version of the Bible. [< Syriac *pshiṭto* simple]

**pes|ky** (pes′kē), *adj.,* **-ki|er, -ki|est.** *U.S. Informal.* troublesome; annoying: *a pesky cold, pesky mosquitoes.* [alteration of *pesty* < *pest*] — **pes′ki|ly,** *adv.* — **pes′ki|ness,** *n.*

**pe|so** (pā′sō), *n., pl.* **-sos. 1** the unit of money in various countries of Latin America and in the Philippines, usually equal to 100 centavos. **2** a coin or piece of paper money equal to a peso in any of these countries. 100 centavos make a peso. **3** a former gold or silver coin used in Spain and in the Spanish colonies, worth eight reals; a piece of eight. **4** *U.S. Slang.* an American dollar. [< Spanish *peso* a coin of a certain weight; weight < Latin *pēnsum,* past participle of *pendere* to weigh. Compare etym. under **poise**[1].]

**peso boliviano,** the unit of money of Bolivia, equal to 100 centavos; peso. It replaced the boliviano in 1963.

**pes|sa|ry** (pes′ər ē), *n., pl.* **-ries.** *Medicine.* **1** a device worn in the vagina to prevent or remedy various displacements of the uterus. **2** a device worn in the vagina or cervical canal to prevent conception. **3** a vaginal suppository. [< Late Latin *pessārium* < *pessum* or *-us* pessary, medicated tampon of wool or lint < Greek *pessós* oval stone]

**pes|si|mism** (pes′ə miz əm), *n.* **1** the tendency to look on the dark side of things or to see difficulties and disadvantages: *Pessimism, when you get used to it, is just as agreeable as optimism* (Arnold Bennett). **2a** the belief that things naturally tend to evil, or that life is not worth while. **b** the belief or doctrine that the evil in life outweighs the good. [< Latin *pessimus,* superlative of *malus* bad, worst + English *-ism;* patterned on *optimism*]

**pes|si|mist** (pes′ə mist), *n.* **1** a person inclined to look on the dark side of things or to see all the difficulties and disadvantages: *The optimist proclaims that we live in the best of all possible worlds; and the pessimist fears this is true* (James Branch Cabell). **2** a person who believes that things naturally tend to evil. **3** a believer in the doctrine of pessimism.

**pes|si|mis|tic** (pes′ə mis′tik), *adj.* **1** having a tendency to look on the dark side of things or to see all the difficulties and disadvantages. **SYN:** See syn. under **cynical. 2** expecting the worst: *The lame man was pessimistic about his chances of passing the test for postman.* **3** having to do with or characterized by pessimism; believing that life holds more evil than good, and so is not worth while. — **pes′si|mis′ti|cal|ly,** *adv.*

**pes|si|mum** (pes′ə məm), *n., pl.* **-mums, -ma** (-mə). — ***n.* 1** the least favorable or worst point, degree, amount, or condition for the purpose. **2** *Biology.* the degree or amount of heat, light, food, moisture, or other factor, least favorable for the reproduction or other vital processes of an organism. [< Latin *pessimum,* neuter of *pessimus;* see etym. under **pessimism**]

**pest** (pest), *n.* **1** any person or thing that causes trouble, injuries, or destruction; nuisance: *garden pests. Flies and mosquitoes are pests. Whining children are pests. I was a nuisance, an incumbrance, and a pest* (Dickens). **SYN:** annoyance. **2** *Archaic.* a pestilence, especially an outbreak of the plague. [< Latin *pestis* plague]

**pes|ter** (pes′tər), *v.t.* **1** to trouble persistently; annoy; vex: *Flies pester us. Don't pester me with foolish questions.* **SYN:** See syn. under **tease. 2** *Obsolete.* to crowd to excess; overcrowd. [apparently short for obsolete *empester* encumber < Old French *empestrer* to hobble an animal at pasture; influenced by *pest*] — **pes′ter|er,** *n.* — **pes′ter|ing|ly,** *adv.*

**pest|hole** (pest′hōl′), *n.* a place that breeds or is likely to have epidemic disease.

**pest|house** (pest′hous′), *n.* a hospital for persons ill with very contagious diseases.

**pes|ti|cide** (pes′tə sīd), *n.* any one of various substances used to kill harmful insects (insecticide), fungi (fungicide), vermin, or other living organisms that destroy or inhibit plant growth, carry disease, or are otherwise harmful. [< Latin *pestis* plague, pest + English *-cide*[1]]

**pes|tif|er|ous** (pes tif′ər əs), *adj.* **1** bringing disease or infection; pestilential: *Rats are pestiferous.* **2** *Figurative.* bringing moral evil; pernicious: *the pestiferous influence of a bad example.* **3** *Informal.* troublesome; annoying. **4** *Archaic.* stricken with a dangerous, very contagious disease, especially the plague. [< Latin *pestiferus* (with English *-ous*) < *pestis* plague + *ferre* bring] — **pes|tif′er|ous|ly,** *adv.* — **pes|tif′er|ous|ness,** *n.*

**pes|ti|lence** (pes′tə ləns), *n.* **1** any disease that spreads rapidly causing many deaths. Smallpox, yellow fever, and the plague are pestilences. **SYN:** epidemic, pest. **2** *Figurative.* something morally pestilent; wickedness: *Corruption is a pestilence of bureaucracy.*

**pes|ti|lent** (pes′tə lənt), *adj.* **1** often causing death: *Smallpox is a pestilent disease.* **2** *Figurative.* very harmful to morals; destroying peace; noxious; pernicious: *a pestilent den of vice, the pestilent effects of war.* **3** troublesome; annoying: *a few pestilent agitators* (Gaspard D. Coligny). **4** having to do with a pestilence. [< Latin *pestilēns, -entis* pestilent < *pestis* plague] — **pes′ti|lent|ly,** *adv.*

**pes|ti|len|tial** (pes′tə len′shəl), *adj.* **1** like a pestilence; having to do with pestilences. **2** causing or likely to cause pestilence; carrying infection: *pestilential vapors* (Longfellow). **3** *Figurative.* harmful; dangerous; pernicious: *So pestilential, so infectious a thing is sin* (Jeremy Taylor). — **pes′ti|len′tial|ly,** *adv.*

**pes|tle** (pes′əl, -təl), *n., v.,* **-tled, -tling.** — ***n.* 1** a tool, usually club-shaped, for pounding or crushing something into a powder in a mortar. See picture under **mortar**[2]. **2** any one of various mechanical appliances for pounding, stamping, or pressing, such as a vertically moving or pounding part in a machine.
— ***v.t., v.i.*** to pound or crush with a pestle.
[< Old French *pestel,* learned borrowing from Medieval Latin *pestillum,* variant of Latin *pistillum* < *pīnsere* to pound. See etym. of doublet **pistil.**]

**pest|y** (pes′tē), *adj.,* **pest|i|er, pest|i|est. 1** like a pest; pestiferous: *Ants were particularly pesty*

**Pronunciation Key:** hat, āge, cãre, fär; let, ēqual, tėrm; it, īce; hot, ōpen, ôrder; oil, out; cup, pu̇t, rüle; child; long; thin; ᴛʜen; zh, measure; ə represents **a** in about, **e** in taken, **i** in pencil, **o** in lemon, **u** in circus.

*last year* (New York Times). **2** full of pests.

**pet**[1] (pet), *n., adj., v.,* **pet|ted, pet|ting.** *—n.* **1** any animal kept as a favorite and treated with affection: *The farmer told his daughter she could bring the little lamb into the house as a pet.* **2** any person who is treated with special kindness or favor; a darling or favorite: *teacher's pet; ... the spoiled pet of a wealthy family* (Charlotte Brontë).
*—adj.* **1** treated or kept as a pet: *a pet rabbit.* **2** especially cherished; darling or favorite: *a pet chair.* **3** showing affection; expressing fondness: *a pet name.* **4** *Informal.* particular; special: *a pet aversion, a pet theory, a pet phrase.*
*—v.t.* **1** to treat as a pet; stroke or pat; touch lovingly and gently: *She is petting the kitten.* **SYN**: coddle, pamper. **2** to yield to the wishes of; indulge: *She enjoyed being fêted and petted as much as a cat enjoys being stroked* (Harriet Beecher Stowe). **SYN**: coddle, pamper.
*—v.i. U.S. Informal.* to make love by caressing and fondling.
[< Scottish Gaelic *peata*]

**pet**[2] (pet), *n., v.,* **pet|ted, pet|ting.** *—n.* a fit of being cross or peevish; fretful discontent: *When he didn't get his way, he jumped on his bicycle and rode off in a pet.* **SYN**: peevishness.
*—v.i.* to be in a pet; sulk.
[origin uncertain; perhaps influenced by *petulant*]

**Pet.,** Peter (2 books of the New Testament).

**pet|al** (pet′əl), *n.* one of the parts of a flower that are usually colored; one of the leaves of a corolla: *A rose has many petals.* See picture under **calyx.** [< New Latin *petalum* (in Latin, metal plate) < Greek *pétalon* leaf, thin plate < *petannýnai* to spread open] **—pet′al|like′,** *adj.*

**pet|aled** (pet′əld), *adj.* having petals: *six-petaled.*

**pet|al|if|er|ous** (pet′ə lif′ər əs), *adj.* bearing petals. [< *petal* + *-ferous*]

**pet|al|ine** (pet′ə lin, -līn), *adj.* **1** having to do with a petal. **2** attached to a petal. **3** resembling a petal. [< *petal* + *-ine*[1]]

**pet|al|ite** (pet′ə līt), *n.* a mineral composed of a silicate of aluminum and lithium, occurring in white masses, often tinged with gray, red, or green. [< Greek *pétalon* leaf + English *-ite*[1]]

**pet|alled** (pet′əld), *adj.* = petaled.

**pet|a|lo|dy** (pet′ə lō′dē), *n.* a condition in flowers in which other organs assume the appearance of petals, as the stamens in most double flowers. [< Greek *petalṓdēs* leaflike (< *pétalon* petal) + English *-y*[3]]

**pet|al|oid** (pet′ə loid), *adj.* having the form of a petal; resembling petals in texture and color, as certain bracts.

**pet|al|ous** (pet′ə ləs), *adj.* having petals.

**pé|tanque** (pā täNk′), *n. French.* a game somewhat resembling bowls.

**pe|tard** (pi tärd′), *n.* **1** an explosive device formerly used in warfare to break doors or gates or to breach a wall. **2** *Especially British.* a kind of firecracker.
**hoist with** (or **on**) **one's own petard,** injured or destroyed by one's own scheme or device for the ruin of others: *Almost every British proposal for self-government to date has been similarly hoist on its own petard* (Harper's).
[< Middle French *pétard* < *péter* break wind < Old French *pet* a breaking of wind, ultimately < Latin *pēdere* to break wind]

**pet|a|sus** or **pet|a|sos** (pet′ə səs), *n.* **1** a low-crowned, broad-brimmed hat worn by the ancient Greeks. **2** the winged hat worn by Hermes (Mercury). [< Greek *pétasos* < root of *petannýnai* to spread out]

**pe|ta|te** (pā tä′tā), *n.* a mat made of dried palm leaves or straw, used as a bed in parts of South America and the Philippines. [< American Spanish *petate*]

**pe|tau|rist** (pə tôr′ist), *n.* = flying phalanger. [< Latin *petaurista* < Greek *petauristḗs* leaper < *pétauron* springboard]

**pet|cock** (pet′kok′), *n.* a small faucet or valve inserted in a pipe or cylinder for draining liquids or testing or reducing pressure. [< *pet,* in an uncertain sense + *cock*[1] faucet]

**pe|tech|i|a** (pə tek′ē ə, -tē′kē-), *n., pl.* **-tech|i|ae** (-tek′ē ē-, -tē′kē-). a small reddish or purplish spot occurring on the skin or on mucous or serous membranes, caused by minute hemorrhages in connection with certain infectious diseases, asphyxia, or radiation sickness. [< New Latin *petechiae* < Italian *petecchia,* singular, speck]

**pe|tech|i|al** (pə tek′ē əl, -tē′kē-), *adj.* having to do with or accompanied by petechiae.

**petechial fever, 1** = typhus. **2** = cerebrospinal meningitis.

**pe|tech|i|ate** (pə tek′ē āt, -it; -tē′kē-), *adj.* having petechiae.

**pe|ter**[1] (pē′tər), *v.i. U.S. Informal.*
**peter out,** to come gradually to an end; give out; fail: *The worst blizzard since 1949 lashed the upper Midwest, then petered out in Canada* (Wall Street Journal).
[American English; origin unknown]

**pe|ter**[2] (pē′tər), *n.* = blue peter.

**Pe|ter** (pē′tər), *n.* **1 Saint,** died A.D. 67?, a fisherman who was one of Christ's twelve apostles. He was also called Simon or Simon Peter and assumed the leadership of the disciples after Christ's death. **2** either of two books in the New Testament that bear his name. *Abbr:* Pet.
**rob Peter to pay Paul,** to take something away from one to pay, satisfy, or advance another: *... those that rob Peter, as we say, to pay Paul, and take the bread out of their masters' mouths to give it to strangers* (Roger L'Estrange).

**Peter Pan, 1** a play by Sir James Barrie, produced in 1904. **2** the hero of this play and of several stories by Barrie, a little boy who refused to grow up.

**Peter Pan collar,** a small, round collar which can close at the front.

**Peter Principle,** a humorous rule of bureaucracy formulated by the American educator Laurence Peter, which holds that employees advance until they are promoted to their level of incompetence: *Much blame must attach to the administrative system, which has not only set out to prove Parkinson's Law, but which religiously follows the Peter Principle of promoting mediocrities* (Manchester Guardian Weekly).

**pe|ter|sham** (pē′tər shəm), *n.* **1** a heavy, rough woolen fabric. **2** a garment made of this, especially a type of overcoat or breeches fashionable in the early 1800's. [< Viscount *Petersham,* 1780-1851, a famous dandy]

**Peter's pence** or **Peter pence, 1** a tax of one penny from every householder in England (and certain countries of Europe) having land of a certain value, paid annually before the Reformation to the papal see. **2** a voluntary contribution to the papal treasury, made since 1849 by Roman Catholics of various countries. [< St. *Peter,* traditionally, the first bishop of Rome]

**peth|i|dine** (peth′ə dēn, -din), *n.* = meperidine hydrochloride.

**pet|i|o|lar** (pet′ē ə lər), *adj.* **1** of or having to do with a petiole. **2** proceeding from a petiole; supported by a petiole.

**pet|i|o|late** (pet′ē ə lāt), *adj.* having a petiole: *a petiolate leaf, a petiolate insect.*

**pet|i|o|lat|ed** (pet′ē ə lā′tid), *adj.* = petiolate.

**pet|i|ole** (pet′ē ōl), *n.* **1** *Botany.* the slender stalk by which a leaf is attached to the stem; leafstalk. See picture under **leaf. 2** *Zoology.* a stalklike part, such as that connecting the abdomen and thorax in wasps or the eyestalk in lobsters. [< New Latin *petiole* < Latin *petiolus* stalk; (literally, diminutive) < *pēs, pedis* foot]

**pet|i|o|lule** (pet′ē ə lül, pet′ē ol′yül), *n. Botany.* a small or partial petiole, such as belongs to the leaflets of compound leaves. [< New Latin *petiolulus* (diminutive) < *petiolus* petiole]

**pet|it** (pet′ē; *French* pə tē′), *adj. Law.* minor; small; petty; trivial: *petit larceny.* [< Old French *petit,* ultimately < Late Latin *pitinnus* very small (child). See etym. of doublet **petty.**]

**pe|tit bour|geois** (pə tē′ bür zhwä′), *pl.* **pe|tits bour|geois** (pə tē′ bür zhwä′). *French.* **1** a member of the petite bourgeoisie, or lower middle class: *This mass of essentially conservative petit bourgeois* (New York Times). **2** the petite bourgeoisie, or lower middle class: *French peasants and the petit bourgeois have hoarded more than 15 times as much gold as there is in the Bank of France* (Time).

**pe|tit-bour|geois** (pə tē′bür zhwä′), *adj. French.* of, having to do with, characteristic of the lower middle class or a member of it: *There was something shabby, something petit-bourgeois, about taking meals in the stuffy cubicle in which you were also to sleep* (New Yorker). Also, **petty-bourgeois.**

**pe|tite** (pə tēt′), *adj., n. —adj.* **1** of small size; little; tiny: *a petite woman or girl. The Balinese dancers are extraordinarily delicate and petite* (Saturday Review). **2** of or designating a size of clothing for short women or girls: *the petite figure, petite patterns.*
*—n.* the petite size of clothing.
[< Old French *petite,* feminine of *petit* little] **—pe|tite′ness,** *n.*

**pe|tite bour|geoise** (pə tēt′ bür zhwäz′), *pl.* **pe|tites bour|geoises** (pə tēt′ bür zhwäz′). *French.* the feminine of **petit bourgeois:** *petite bourgeoise housewives ... very bustling and gossipy, good mothers and housekeepers* (Katherine Gauss Jackson).

**pe|tite bour|geoi|sie** (pə tēt′ bür zhwä zē′), *French.* the class of small businessmen and white-collar workers, in general belonging to the lower middle class.

**pet|it four** (pet′ē fôr′, fōr′; *French* pə tē für′), *pl.* **pet|its fours** (pet′ē fôrz′, fōrz′; *French* pə tē-für′), a small fancy cake or cooky with decorative frosting. [< French *petit four* little oven; *four* < Latin *furnus.* Compare etym. under **furnace.**]

**pet|it|grain oil** (pet′ē grān′), a yellowish oil from the leaves, twigs, and fruit of the sour orange tree, used in the manufacture of perfumes and marmalade. [< French *petit grain* little seed]

**pe|ti|tion** (pə tish′ən), *n., v. —n.* **1a** a formal request to someone in authority for some privilege, right, or benefit: *The right of petition is one of the fundamental privileges of a free people* (Thomas A. Cowan). **SYN**: suit, entreaty, supplication. **b** the document containing such a request, and usually the signatures of the persons making it: *The people on our street signed a petition asking the city council for a new sidewalk.* **2** *Law.* a written application for an order of court or for some action by a judge: *Mr. P. G. Wodehouse ... filed a naturalization petition as a first step towards obtaining United States citizenship* (London Times). **3a** a prayer. **b** one of the clauses of a prayer, such as of the Lord's Prayer. **4** that which is requested or prayed for: *... if it please the king to grant my petition, and to perform my request* (Esther 5:8). **5** the act of formally asking or humbly requesting. **6** *English History.* the form in which Parliament formerly presented a measure to be granted by the king (now represented by the passing of a bill for the royal assent).
*—v.t., v.i.* **1** to ask earnestly; make a formal request to: *They petitioned the mayor to use his influence with the city council.* **2** to pray.
**make** (**a**) **petition,** to ask; supplicate: *to make petition for clemency.*
[< Old French *peticion,* learned borrowing from Latin *petītiō, -ōnis* < *petere* to seek] **—pe|ti′tion|er,** *n.*

**pe|ti|tion|ar|y** (pə tish′ə ner′ē), *adj.* **1** of a petition. **2** containing a petition. **3** *Archaic.* suppliant; entreating: *To say no to a poor petitionary rogue* (Charles Lamb).

**pe|ti|ti|o prin|ci|pi|i** (pə tish′ē ō prin sip′ē ī), *Logic.* **1** a fallacy of reasoning in which what is to be proved is assumed to be true in the premise; begging the question. **2** a fallacy of reasoning arising from the assumption of a premise which no opponent will admit to be true. *Example:* Since all students are of the same faith, therefore religion ought to be taught in the public schools. This begs the question as to whether all students are, in fact, of the same faith. [< Latin *petītiō principiī* (literally) a begging of the beginning (or first premise)]

**pet|it juror** (pet′ē), a juror on a petit jury.

**pet|it jury** (pet′ē), a jury consisting of 6 or 12 persons, chosen to decide a case in court; trial jury. Also, **petty jury.**

**pet|it larceny** (pet′ē), = petty larceny.

**pe|tit-maî|tre** (pə tē me′trə), *n., pl.* **pe|tits-maî|tres** (pə tē me′trə). *French.* a fop; dandy: *Every clerk, apprentice, and even waiter ... assumes the air and apparel of a petit-maître* (Tobias Smollett).

**pe|tit mal** (pə tē mȧl′), a mild form of epilepsy characterized especially by short lapses of consciousness without warning and without violent convulsions and with slight muscular tremors. [< French *petit mal* (literally) small sickness]

**pe|tit point** (pet′ē point′), embroidery made on canvas by short, slanting parallel stitches suggesting tents; tent stitch. [< French *petit* small, *point* stitch]

**pe|tits pois** (pə tē pwä′), *French.* very small green peas.

**PETN** (no periods), pentaerythritol tetranitrate.

**pet|nap|per** (pet′nap ər), *n.* a person who practices petnapping.

**pet|nap|ping** (pet′nap ing), *n.* the act or practice of stealing pet animals, especially to sell them to animal dealers and research laboratories.
► Though *petnapping* and *petnapper* are formed on analogy with *kidnaping* and *kidnaper,* the traditional American forms *-naping* and *-naper* have been supplanted by the spellings *-napping* and *-napper,* which are more usual in Britain.

**pe|to** (pā′tō), *n.* any one of various large marine food and game fishes of warm waters; wahoo[3]. [< American Spanish *peto* < Spanish, breastplate]

**Pe|trar|chan sonnet** (pi trär′kən), the Italian sonnet, composed of an octave and a sestet. [< *Petrarch* (Francesco Petrarca), 1304-1374, an Italian sonneteer]

**pet|rel** (pet′rəl), *n.* a small black-and-white sea bird with long, pointed wings. Petrels breed especially on oceanic islands and fly far out to sea, often following ships. There are various kinds. The smaller kinds are also called Mother Carey's chickens. [supposedly a diminutive of Saint *Peter,* from his walking on the sea]

***Pe|tri** or **pe|tri dish** (pē′trē, pā′-), a shallow, circular glass dish with a loose cover, used in the preparation of bacteriological cultures. [< Julius *Petri,* 1852-1922, a German bacteriologist, who invented it]

***Petri dish**

**pet|ri|fac|tion** (pet′rə fak′shən), *n.* **1** a petrifying or being petrified. **2** something petrified.

**pet|ri|fac|tive** (pet′rə fak′tiv), *adj.* causing petrifaction.

**pet|ri|fi|ca|tion** (pet′rə fə kā′shən), *n.* = petrifaction.

**pet|ri|fied lightning** (pet′rə fīd), = fulgurite.

**pet|ri|fy** (pet′rə fī), *v.,* **-fied, -fy|ing.** *— v.t.* **1** to turn into stone; change (plant or animal matter) into a substance like stone: *There is a petrified forest in Arizona.* **2** *Figurative: I don't learn much from our senators ... Policy seems to petrify their minds* (George Meredith). **SYN:** deaden. **3** *Figurative.* to paralyze with fear, horror, or surprise; stupefy: *The bird was petrified as the snake came near.* *— v.i.* **1** to become stone or a substance like stone: *Cement like that of the Ancients, which petrified* (Alexander Gordon). **2** *Figurative: Like Niobe we marble grow, and petrify with grief* (John Dryden). **SYN:** harden.
[< French *pétrifier* < Latin *petra* stone (< Greek *pétra*) + French *-fier* -fy]

**Pe|trine** (pē′trīn, -trin), *adj.* of or having to do with the apostle Peter or the two New Testament Epistles bearing his name.

**petro-,** *combining form.* **1** rock; rocks: *Petrology = the science of rocks.*
**2** petroleum: *Petrochemical = (a chemical) derived from petroleum.*
[< Greek *pétra* rock]

**pet|ro|chem|i|cal** (pet′rō kem′ə kəl), *n., adj.* *— n.* a chemical made or derived from petroleum or natural gas: *One important petrochemical is ammonia, which ... finds its chief use in commercial fertilizers* (Richard C. McCurdy).
*— adj.* of or having to do with petrochemicals or petrochemistry: *[Their] record growth ... is an indication of their success in cutting investment costs of petroleum and petrochemical units* (Economist).

**pet|ro|chem|is|try** (pet′rō kem′ə strē), *n.* **1** the study or science of the chemical properties and derivatives of petroleum; the chemistry of petroleum. **2** the manufacture of chemicals from petroleum and natural gas. [< *petro-* + *chemistry*]

**pet|ro|dol|lars** (pet′rō dol′ərz), *n.pl.* surplus U.S. dollars obtained by oil-rich countries from increased oil revenues and usually spent by investing heavily in foreign, especially large industrial, countries: *The Arabs, using excess dollars (the so-called petrodollars) from the quadrupling of crude oil prices, ... invested close to $11 billion in the U.S. in 1974* (New York Sunday News).

**pet|ro|drome** (pet′rə drōm), *n.* an East African elephant shrew having hind feet with only four toes, and frequenting rocky hills. [< New Latin *Petrodomus* the genus name < Greek *pétra* rock + *drómos* course, related to *dramein* to run]

**petrog.,** petrography.

**pet|ro|gen|e|sis** (pet′rə jen′ə sis), *n.* the genesis or origin of rocks, especially as a subject of scientific study.

**pet|ro|ge|net|ic** (pet′rō jə net′ik), *adj.* of or having to do with petrogenesis.

**pet|ro|gen|ic** (pet′rə jen′ik), *adj.* = petrogenetic.

**pe|trog|e|ny** (pi troj′ə nē), *n.* = petrogenesis.

**pet|ro|glyph** (pet′rə glif), *n.* a rock carving (usually prehistoric), especially a pictograph or the like incised or carved in rock: *The crescent is not a common figure among petroglyphs and pictographs of northern Arizona* (Science News Letter). [< French *pétroglyphe* < Greek *pétra* rock + *-glyphê* a carving, glyph]

**pet|ro|glyph|ic** (pet′rə glif′ik), *adj.* **1** belonging to a petroglyph. **2** like a petroglyph.

**pe|trog|ly|phy** (pi trog′lə fē), *n.* the art or process of carving upon rocks.

**pet|ro|gram** (pet′rə gram), *n.* a drawing or painting on stone, usually found in prehistoric caves.

**pe|trog|ra|pher** (pi trog′rə fər), *n.* a person who studies, or is expert in, petrography.

**pet|ro|graph|ic** (pet′rə graf′ik), *adj.* of or having to do with petrography. *—* **pet′ro|graph′i|cal|ly,** *adv.*

**pet|ro|graph|i|cal** (pet′rə graf′ə kəl), *adj.* = petrographic.

**petrographic microscope,** a microscope equipped with two Nicol prisms for polarizing light, used for studying and identifying rocks and minerals.

**pe|trog|ra|phy** (pi trog′rə fē), *n.* the branch of geology that deals with the scientific description and classification of rocks.

**pet|rol** (pet′rəl), *n.* **1** *British.* gasoline: *a petrol filling station* (London Times). **2** *Obsolete.* petroleum. [< Old French *petrole,* learned borrowing from Medieval Latin *petroleum* mineral oil. See etym. of doublet **petroleum.**]

**petrol.,** petrology.

**pet|ro|la|tum** (pet′rə lā′təm), *n.* **1** a colorless to light-yellow salve or ointment made from petroleum. **2** = mineral oil (def. 2). [American English < New Latin *petrolatum* < English *petrol* + New Latin *-atum* -ate[1]]

**petrol bomb,** *British.* Molotov cocktail.

**pe|tro|le|ous** (pə trō′lē əs), *adj.* containing petroleum: *In the sweltering reaches of the petroleous Persian Gulf* (Time).

**pe|tro|le|um** (pə trō′lē əm), *n.* an oily, dark-colored, flammable liquid found in the earth, consisting mainly of a mixture of various hydrocarbons. Gasoline, kerosene, fuel oil, paraffin, and lubricants are made from petroleum. *Petroleum ... is nature's composite of the hydrocarbon-remains of many forms of marine life* (P. V. Smith).
[< Medieval Latin *petroleum* < Greek *pétra* rock + Latin *oleum* oil. See etym. of doublet **petrol.**]

**petroleum coke,** a substance composed of almost pure carbon, derived as a by-product of the distillation of heavy crude oil. Petroleum coke is used in electrodes, in the refining of certain metals such as aluminum, and for other purposes.

**petroleum ether,** = ligroin.

**petroleum fly,** a fly found near pools of crude petroleum in which it breeds.

**petroleum geologist,** an expert in or a student of the branch of geology dealing with petroleum deposits in the earth.

**petroleum jelly,** = petrolatum (def. 1).

**petroleum naphtha,** = naphtha.

**pe|trol|ic** (pə trol′ik), *adj.* **1** of petroleum. **2** like petroleum. **3** obtained from petroleum.

**pet|rol|i|za|tion** (pet′rə lə zā′shən), *n.* the act or process of petrolizing.

**pet|rol|ize** (pet′rə līz), *v.t.,* **-ized, -iz|ing. 1** to treat with petroleum; spread petroleum on (water) to destroy mosquito larvae. **2** to set on fire by means of petroleum.

**pet|ro|log|ic** (pet′rə loj′ik), *adj.* having to do with or relating to petrology. *—* **pet′ro|log′i|cal|ly,** *adv.*

**pet|ro|log|i|cal** (pet′rə loj′ə kəl), *adj.* = petrologic.

**pe|trol|o|gist** (pi trol′ə jist), *n.* a person who studies, or is expert in, petrology.

**pe|trol|o|gy** (pi trol′ə jē), *n.* the branch of geology that deals with rocks, including their origin, structure, and changes.

**pet|ro|nel** (pet′rə nəl), *n.* a large pistol or carbine fired with the butt held against the chest, used in the 1500's and the 1600's, especially by cavalry. [< Middle French *petrinal,* dialectal variant of *poitrinal* < *poitrine* breast, chest < Vulgar Latin *pectorīna* < Latin *pectus, pectoris*]

**pe|tro|sal** (pi trō′səl), *adj., n.* *— adj.* = petrous. *— n.* a petrous bone or part. [< Latin *petrōsus* + English *-al*]

**pet|rous** (pet′rəs, pē′trəs), *adj.* **1** *Anatomy.* designating or having to do with the very dense, hard portion of the temporal bone (or, in certain animals, an analogous separate bone) which forms a protective case for the internal ear. **2** of the nature of stone; stony; rocky. [< Latin *petrōsus* (with English *-ous*) < *petra* rock, stone < Greek *pétra*]

**pet|ta|ble** (pet′ə bəl), *adj.* that can be petted: *... as pettable as a kitten* (Atlantic).

***pet|ti|coat** (pet′ē kōt), *n., adj.* *— n.* **1** a skirt worn beneath the dress or outer skirt by women or girls. It hangs from the waist or from the shoulders. **2** a skirt, trimmed and sometimes stiffened. **3** *Informal.* a woman or girl: *There was nobody knew better how to make his way among the petticoats than my grandfather* (Washington Irving). **4** a dressing-table cover reaching down to the floor. **5** a sheeting hung around a yacht while being launched, to hide its outlines. **6a** a skirt or flared part of a petticoat insulator. **b** = petticoat insulator.
*— adj.* **1** of a woman; female or feminine: *A kind of petticoat council was forthwith held ... at which the governor's lady presided* (Washington Irving). **2** womanish (used often in an unfriendly way): *petticoat gossip.*
**petticoats, a** women (used in an unfriendly way): *There was ... brutality in his [Bismarck's] exclamation that the Emperor Frederick's death would put an end to the rule of 'petticoats in politics'* (London Daily News). **b** *Archaic.* skirts worn typically by women or children collectively.
[Middle English *pety coote* little coat; see etym. under **petty**]

***petticoat**
definition 1

***petticoat breeches**

petticoat

petticoat breeches

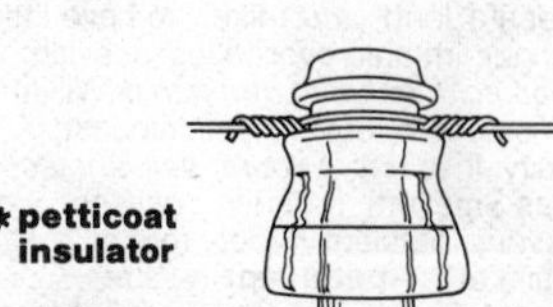

***petticoat insulator**

***petticoat breeches,** a kind of loose breeches not gathered at the bottom of each leg but hanging somewhat like petticoats, worn by men in the middle 1600's.

**pet|ti|coat|ed** (pet′ē kō′tid), *adj.* wearing petticoats.

**petticoat government,** the rule or predominance of women in the home or in politics (used in an unfriendly way).

***petticoat insulator,** an inverted cup-shaped insulator as for supporting a telegraph or telephone wire, having one or more flared parts suggesting skirts.

**pet|ti|fog** (pet′ē fog, -fôg), *v.i.,* **-fogged, -fog|ging. 1** to plead or conduct a petty case in a minor court of law. **2** to use petty, mean, or cheating methods in law. **3** to wrangle or quibble about small petty points. [back formation < *pettifogger*]

**pet|ti|fog|ger** (pet′ē fog′ər, -fôg′-), *n.* **1** an inferior lawyer who uses petty, mean, cheating methods: *He carried home with him all the knavish chicanery of the lowest pettifogger* (Tobias Smollett). **2** any inferior person who habitually uses such methods: *appointing as ambassador some political pettifogger skilled in delays, sophisms, and misapprehensions* (Washington Irving). [apparently < *petty* + *fogger,* probably < the *Fugger* family, German merchants in the 1400's and 1500's]

**pet|ti|fog|ger|y** (pet′ē fog′ər ē, -fôg′-), *n., pl.* **-ger|ies. 1** the practice of a pettifogger; trickery; chicanery. **2** an act characteristic of a pettifogger.

**pet|ti|fog|ging** (pet′ē fog′ing, -fôg′-), *adj., n.* *— adj.* shifty, tricky, or quibbling: *Some men ... retain through life ... a pettifogging and disputatious spirit* (London Times).
*— n.* trickery; chicanery.

**pet|ti|ly** (pet′ə lē), *adv.* in a petty manner.

**pet|ti|ness** (pet′ē nis), *n.* **1** smallness; meanness; petty nature or behavior; triviality; insignificance. **2** an instance of this; petty trait.

**pet|ting** (pet′ing), *n. U.S. Informal.* hugging, kissing, and other amorous play.

**pet|tish** (pet′ish), *adj.* peevish; cross; petulant: *a pettish reply.* [< *pet*[2] + *-ish*] *—* **pet′tish|ly,** *adv.* *—* **pet′tish|ness,** *n.*

**pet|ti|toes** (pet′ē tōz′), *n.pl.* **1** the feet of a pig, especially when used as food: *a present of pigs' pettitoes* (George Eliot). **2** the feet or toes of a human being, especially of a child. [apparently < *petty* + *toes*]

**pet|tle**[1] (pet′əl), *v.t.,* **-tled, -tling.** *Scottish.* to pet; fondle; indulge. [(frequentative) < *pet*[1]]

**pet|tle**[2] (pet′əl), *n. British.* paddle[1] (def. 9).

**pet|ty** (pet′ē), *adj.,* **-ti|er, -ti|est. 1a** having little importance or value; small: *She insisted on telling me all her petty troubles.* **SYN:** trifling, slight, paltry, trivial, insignificant. **b** on a small scale: *a petty shopkeeper, petty theft, petty animosities.* **2** mean; narrow-minded: *A gossip has a petty mind.* **3** of lower rank or importance; subordinate: *a petty official.* **SYN:** minor. **4** *Obsolete.* small in

**Pronunciation Key:** hat, āge, cāre, fär; let, ēqual, tėrm; it, īce; hot, ōpen, ôrder; oil, out; cup, pu̇t, rüle; child; long; thin; ᴛʜen; zh, measure;
ə represents **a** in about, **e** in taken, **i** in pencil, **o** in lemon, **u** in circus.

size or stature. [spelling variant of *petit* < later English pronunciation of Old French *petit.* See etym. of doublet **petit**.]

**pet|ty-bour|geois** (pet′ē bůr zhwä′), *adj.* = petit-bourgeois.

**petty cash**, **1** small sums of money spent or received. **2** a sum of money kept on hand to pay small expenses.

**petty juror**, = petit juror.

**petty jury**, = petit jury.

**petty larceny**, theft in which the value of the property taken is less than a certain amount.

**petty officer**, a noncommissioned officer in the United States, Canadian, or British navy or in the United States Coast Guard; an enlisted man of any of the four grades or classes above seaman.

**petty sessions**, *British.* a court with summary jurisdiction over minor offenses in a given district.

**pet|u|lance** (pech′ə ləns), *n.* **1** bad humor; condition of being irritated by trifles; being peevish. **SYN:** peevishness. **2** *Obsolete.* **a** immodesty. **b** sauciness; rudeness.

**pet|u|lan|cy** (pech′ə lən sē), *n.* = petulance.

**pet|u|lant** (pech′ə lənt), *adj.* **1** likely to have little fits of bad temper; irritable over trifles; peevish: *His temper was acid, petulant and harsh* (William Godwin). **2** *Obsolete.* **a** forward or immodest; wanton. **b** saucy; insolent: *a young petulant jackanapes* (Tobias Smollett). [< Latin *petulāns, -antis* mischievous, petulant < *pet-*, root of *petere* seek, aim at] **—pet′u|lant|ly**, *adv.*

**pe|tu|ni|a** (pə tü′nē ə, -tyü′-; -tün′yə, -tyün′-), *n.* **1** a common garden plant that has white, pink, or purple flowers shaped like funnels. The petunia was originally native to South America and is a member of the nightshade family. There are several kinds, comprising a genus of plants. **2** the flower of any one of these plants. **3** a dark violet or purple. [< New Latin *Petunia* the genus name < French *petun* tobacco < Guarani (Paraguay) *petȳ* (the *ȳ* is a nasal sound)]

**pe|tun|se** (pe tůn′se), *n.* = petuntse.

**pe|tun|tse** or **pe|tun|tze** (pe tůn′tse; *Chinese* bī′důn′dzə), *n.* a white earth made by pulverizing partially decomposed granite, used especially in China in the manufacture of porcelain; China stone. Petuntse holds the nonfusible china clay, or kaolin, together. [< Chinese *pai* white + *tuntzŭ* briquettes (because the pulverized granite is transported in this form)]

**peu à peu** (pœ′ à pœ′), *French.* little by little; a little or few at a time.

**peu de chose** (pœd′ shōz′), *French.* a small thing; trivial matter.

**Peul** or **Peuhl** (pyül, pül), *n.* a Fulani, especially one living in Guinea, Senegal, or Chad.

**pew** (pyü), *n.* a bench in a church for people to sit on, fastened to the floor and provided with a back. In some churches the pews are separated by partitions and are set apart for the use of certain worshipers, such as the members of a family. *One of the senior boys ushered them into a pew at the rear of the chapel* (New Yorker). [Middle English *puwe* pew, pulpit < Old French *puie,* or *puy* balcony, < Latin *podia,* plural of *podium* balcony (in Medieval Latin, raised lectern or pulpit)]

**pew|age** (pyü′ij), *n.* **1** the pews in a church collectively. **2** the arrangement of pews. **3** the rent paid for pews.

**pe|wee** (pē′wē), *n.* a small American bird with an olive-colored or gray back, such as the wood pewee, phoebe, or certain other American flycatchers. Its call sounds somewhat like its name. [American English, variant of *pewit*]

**pew|hold|er** (pyü′hōl′dər), *n.* a person who owns or rents a pew.

**pe|wit** (pē′wit, pyü′it), *n.* **1** = lapwing. **2** a European black-headed gull. **3** = pewee. [imitative. Compare Flemish *piewit-voghel* pewit bird.]

**pew|ter** (pyü′tər), *n., adj.* **—*n.*** **1** an alloy, formerly of tin with lead, copper, or other metals, and now, usually of tin with antimony and copper: *the soft clank of dishes made of pewter.* **2** dishes or other utensils made of this alloy: *She polishes the pewter.*
**—*adj.*** made of pewter: *a pewter mug.*
[< Old French *peaultre,* perhaps < Italian *peltro,* perhaps < Latin *peltrum*]

**pew|ter|er** (pyü′tər ər), *n.* a worker in pewter; person who makes pewter utensils.

**pe|yo|te** (pā ō′tē; *Spanish* pā yō′tā), *n.* **1** the mescal or any one of several other cacti. **2** a stimulating drug contained in the small buttonlike tops of the mescal, used by Indians in Mexico and the southwest United States; mescaline. It induces hallucinations and reactions associated with psychoses. *That's what's so bad about peyote. It can make sick people well, and that's how it gets converts* (New Yorker). [American English < Mexican Spanish *peyote* < Nahuatl *peyotl*]

**pe|yo|tism** (pā ō′tiz əm), *n.* **1** use of or addiction to peyote: *The peyotism of the Mescaleros spread to the Comanches and Kiowas* (Scientific American). **2** Also, **Peyotism.** the form of religion of an American Indian sect which combines Christian beliefs with native rituals that include the ceremonial use of peyote.

**pe|yo|tl** (pā ō′təl), *n.* = peyote.

**pey|tral** or **pey|trel** (pā′trəl), *n.* = poitrel.

**pf** (no periods), *Music.* a little louder (as a direction; Italian, *più forte)*.

**pf.**, **1** pfennig. **2** preferred.

**pF** (no periods), picofarad.

**PF** (no periods), **1** popular forces. **2** productivity factor.

**Pfc.** or **Pfc** (no period), private first class.

**pfd.**, preferred.

**PFD** (no periods), personal flotation device.

**PFDA** (no periods), Pure Food and Drug Administration (officially, FDA).

**Pfeif|fer's bacillus** (fī′fėrz), a bacillus found in the respiratory tract and thought to cause influenzal meningitis and conjunctivitis. [< Richard *Pfeiffer,* 1858-1945, a German bacteriologist]

**pfen|nig** (pfen′ig), *n., pl.* **pfen|nigs, pfen|ni|ge** (pfen′i gə). a unit of money in East and West Germany, a coin equal to 1/100 of a Deutsche mark. [< German *Pfennig.* See related etym. at **penny**.]

**pfg.**, pfennig.

**PFLP** (no periods), Popular Front for the Liberation of Palestine.

**pfu|i** (pfü′ē), *interj. German.* an exclamation of disgust or impatience.

**Pg.**, **1** Portugal. **2** Portuguese.

**p.g.**, paying guest.

**PG** (no periods), **1** Parental Guidance (a symbol used in the United States for motion pictures recommended to the general audiences, with parental guidance advised). **2** prostaglandin.

**P.G.**, **1** Past Grand (Master). **2** paying guest. **3** postgraduate.

**PGA** (no periods) or **P.G.A.**, Professional Golfers' Association.

**PGE** (no periods), one of two groups of prostaglandins (the other being PGF).

**PGF** (no periods), one of two groups of prostaglandins (the other being PGE).

***pH**, a symbol used (with a number) to indicate acidity or alkalinity in testing soils for suitability to specific crops, in analyzing body secretions, and in various industrial applications. It represents the relative concentration of hydrogen ions (in gram atoms per liter) in a given solution, usually determined by the use of a substance (indicator) known to change color at a certain concentration. The *p*H scale in common use ranges from 0 to 14, *p*H7 (the hydrogen-ion concentration, $10^{-7}$ or .0000001, in pure water) being taken as neutral, 6 to 0 increasingly acid, and 8 to 14 increasingly alkaline. Most soils are in the range between *p*H3 and *p*H10. *The soil with its pH6.5, the most preferable for growing roses, is ideal* (New York Times).

***pH**

**common pH values:**

| | common substances | pH | concentration of $H^+$ ions in moles per liter at 25°C | |
|---|---|---|---|---|
| | | 0 | | |
| acid solution | | 1 | 0.1 | $(10^{-1})$ |
| | lemons | 2 | .01 | $(10^{-2})$ |
| | apples | 3 | .001 | $(10^{-3})$ |
| | tomatoes | 4 | .0001 | $(10^{-4})$ |
| | bread | 5 | .00001 | $(10^{-5})$ |
| neutral solution | cow's milk | 6 | .000001 | $(10^{-6})$ |
| | blood plasma | 7 | .0000001 | $(10^{-7})$ |
| | seawater | 8 | .00000001 | $(10^{-8})$ |
| basic solution | | 9 | .000000001 | $(10^{-9})$ |
| | milk of magnesia | 10 | .0000000001 | $(10^{-10})$ |
| | | 11 | .00000000001 | $(10^{-11})$ |
| | | 12 | .000000000001 | $(10^{-12})$ |
| | | 13 | .0000000000001 | $(10^{-13})$ |
| | | 14 | .00000000000001 | $(10^{-14})$ |

**ph.**, **1** phase. **2** phone. **3** phosphor.

**Ph** (no period), *Chemistry.* phenyl.

**P.H.**, Purple Heart.

**PHA** (no periods) or **P.H.A.**, Public Housing Administration.

**Phae|dra** (fē′drə), *n. Greek Legend.* the daughter of Minos and Pasiphaë, and wife of Theseus, king of Athens. She loved her stepson Hippolytus, but caused his death by falsely accusing him.

**phae|no|gam** (fē′nə gam), *n.* = phanerogam.

**phae|nog|a|mous** (fi nog′ə məs), *adj.* = phanerogamous.

**Pha|ë|thon** (fā′ə thon), *n. Greek and Roman Mythology.* the son of Helios and Clymene, who tried for one day to drive the sun, his father's chariot. He so nearly set the earth on fire that Zeus had to strike him dead with a thunderbolt. [< Latin *Phaëthon* < Greek *Phaethōn* (literally) shining, related to *phaínein* show forth, shine]

**pha|e|ton** (fā′ə tən), *n.* **1** a lightweight, four-wheeled carriage with or without a top. It is pulled by one or two horses, and has one or two seats. **2** an open automobile similar to a touring car. **3** the body of such an automobile. [< French *phaéton* < *Phaëton* Phaëthon]

**phage** (fāj), *n.* = bacteriophage.

**-phage**, *combining form.* that eats or devours: *Bacteriophage = that devours bacteria.* [< Greek *phageîn* eat]

**phag|e|de|na** or **phag|e|dae|na** (faj′ə dē′nə), *n. Medicine.* **1** an ulcer or ulceration that spreads rapidly and destroys the surrounding parts. **2** = gangrene. [< Latin *phagedaena* < Greek *phagédaina* an "eating" sore or ulcer < *phageîn* eat]

**phag|e|den|ic** or **phag|e|daen|ic** (faj′ə den′ik, -dē′nik), *adj. Medicine.* **1** like phagedena. **2** characterized by phagedena. **3** affected with phagedena.

**phag|o|cyte** (fag′ə sīt), *n.* a cell, such as a white blood cell, capable of absorbing and destroying waste or harmful material, such as disease-producing bacteria. Phagocytes occur in body fluids and tissues. *All through [Fleming's] life he never abandoned the search for a substance which would kill the microbes without weakening the phagocytes* (André Maurois). [< German *Phagocyten,* plural < Greek *phageîn* eat + *kýtos* hollow vessel; body]

**phag|o|cyt|ic** (fag′ə sit′ik), *adj.* **1** having to do with a phagocyte or phagocytes. **2** having the nature of function of a phagocyte.

**phagocytic index**, the average number of bacteria destroyed by each phagocyte during an incubation of phagocytes, bacteria, and serum.

**phag|o|cyt|ize** (fag′ə sī′tīz), *v.t.,* **-ized, -iz|ing.** (of phagocytes) to absorb or destroy (foreign matter or bacteria).

**phag|o|cy|to|sis** (fag′ə sī tō′sis), *n.* the absorption or destruction of foreign matter or bacteria by a phagocyte or phagocytes.

**phag|o|cy|tot|ic** (fag′ə sī tot′ik), *adj.* of or having to do with phagocytosis.

**pha|gol|y|sis** (fə gol′ə sis), *n.* the dissolution or destruction of phagocytes. [< Greek *phageîn* eat + *lýsis* a loosening]

**phag|o|some** (fag′ə səm), *n.* a pouchlike structure formed by a cell membrane to hold bacteria and other foreign substances which the cell has ingested: *Lysosome and invader, now packaged in a phagosome, are drawn together and fuse* (Time). [< *phago-* (< Greek *phageîn* eat)]

**pha|i|no|pep|la** (fā ī′nō pep′lə, fā′ə-), *n.* a bird of the southwestern United States and Mexico, related to the waxwings. It has shiny black plumage and a pointed crest. [< New Latin *Phainopepla* the genus name < Greek *phaínein* to shine + *péplos* robe]

**phal|ae|nop|sis** (fal′ə nop′sis), *n.* any one of a group of orchids native to India, Malaya, and the Philippines, used in bridal bouquets and for other decorative purposes. [< New Latin *Phalaenopsis* the genus name < Greek *phálaina* moth + *ópsis* appearance]

**pha|lan|gal** (fə lang′gəl), *adj.* = phalangeal.

**phal|ange** (fal′ənj, fə lanj′), *n.* **1** *Anatomy.* any bone of the fingers or toes; phalanx. See pictures under **foot** and **hand**. **2** *Botany.* a bundle of stamens united by their filaments; phalanx. [< Old French *phalange,* learned borrowing from Latin *phalanx;* see etym. under **phalanx**]

**pha|lan|ge|al** (fə lan′jē əl), *adj. Anatomy.* **1** of or having to do with a phalanx or phalanges. **2** like a phalanx or phalanges.

**pha|lan|ger** (fə lan′jər), *n.* any one of several genera of comparatively small, tree-climbing mammals of Australia and New Guinea. They hunt chiefly at night, carry their young in a pouch, and have long tails. [< New Latin *phalanger* < Greek *phalángion* venomous spider < *phálanx, -angos;* see etym. under **phalanx** (because the phalanger has webbed hind toes)]

**pha|lan|ges** (fə lan′jēz), *n.* a plural of **phalanx**.

**pha|lan|gid** (phə lan′jid), *n.* = daddy longlegs. [< New Latin *Phalangium* the genus name < Greek *phalángion* venomous spider; see etym. under **phalanger**]

**Pha|lan|gist** (fə lan′jist), *n., adj.* **—*n.*** a member of a right-wing Christian political and military group in Lebanon, modeled after the Spanish Falangists: *Rightist forces in the capital, composed mostly of Phalangists, . . . attacked two Moslem slum areas* (Time). **—*adj.*** of or belonging to this group. [see **Falangist** for etym.]

**phal|an|ste|ri|an** (fal′ən stir′ē ən), *adj., n.* **—*adj.*** **1** of or having to do with a phalanstery. **2** of or having to do with phalansterianism.
**—*n.*** **1** a member of a phalanstery. **2** a supporter of phalansterianism; Fourierist.

**phal|an|ste|ri|an|ism** (fal′ən stir′ē ə niz′əm), *n.* the system of phalansteries; Fourierism.

**phal|an|ster|ism** (fal′ən stə riz′əm), *n.* = phalansterianism.

**phal|an|ster|y** (fal′ən ster′ē), *n., pl.* **-ster|ies.** **1** in Fourierism: **a** the building or set of buildings occupied by a phalanx. **b** a socialistic community; phalanx. **2a** any similar association of persons. **b** the building or buildings occupied by them. [< French *phalanstère* (coined by Fourier) < *phalange* a community in Fourier's system (< Greek *phálanx, -angos;* see etym. under **phalanx**), with ending < *monastère* monastery]

***pha|lanx** (fā′langks, fal′angks), *n., pl.* **-lanx|es** or **-lan|ges.** **1a** (in ancient Greece), a special battle formation of infantry fighting in close ranks with their shields joined and long spears overlapping each other. **b** any body of troops in close array: *Anon they* [*the demons*] *move in perfect phalanx* (Milton). **2** a compact or closely massed body of persons, animals, or things: *A phalanx of sheep blocked the road.* **3** *Figurative.* a number of persons united for a common purpose. **4** *Anatomy.* any bone in the fingers or toes. **5** *Botany.* a bundle of stamens united by their filaments in plants with two or more groups of stamens. **6** (in Fourierism) a community of about 1,600 persons living in a phalanstery as one family, with property held in common.
**in phalanx**, in combination; unitedly; solidly: *On this occasion, the crown lawyers opposed in phalanx* (James Mill).
[< Latin *phalanx, -angis* < Greek *phálanx, -angos* line of battle; finger bone; (originally) round bar or leg]

***phalanx**
definition 1a

**phal|a|rope** (fal′ə rōp), *n.* any one of three species of small swimming and wading birds that breed in the Northern Hemisphere, resembling the sandpipers but with lobate toes. The females are larger and more brightly colored than the males, which brood the eggs. [< French *phalarope* < New Latin *Phalaropus* < Greek *phalārís* coot (< *phálāros* white-spotted, bald white head) + *poús, podós* foot]

**phal|lic** (fal′ik), *adj.* of or having to do with a phallus or phallicism; symbolic of male generative power. [< Greek *phallikós* < *phallós* penis, phallus] —**phal′li|cal|ly,** *adv.*

**phal|li|cism** (fal′ə siz əm), *n.* worship of the phallus or of the organs of sex as symbols of the generative power in nature.

**phal|lo|crat** (fal′ə krat), *n.* a believer in the superiority of the male sex; male chauvinist. [< French *phallocrate*] —**phal′lo|crat′ic,** *adj.*

**phal|lus** (fal′əs), *n., pl.* **phal|li** (fal′ī). **1** *Anatomy.* **a** the penis or clitoris. **b** the embryonic structure from which either develops. **2** an image or model of the penis, symbolizing the generative power of nature, venerated and carried in solemn processions in Bacchic and other ceremonies, and commonly worn as part of his costume by any actor in the Old Comedy, in ancient Greece. [< Latin *phallus* < Greek *phallós* penis, phallus]

**Pha|nar|i|ot** (fə nar′ē ət), *n.* one of a class of Greeks of Constantinople who, after the Turkish conquest, held important official positions under the Turks. [< New Greek *phanariōtês* < Turkish *Fanar* a district of Constantinople in which Greeks lived]

**phan|er|o|gam** (fan′ər ə gam), *n. Botany.* an old term for plants that produce seeds. They are now called spermatophytes. [< French *phanérogame* < Greek *phanerós* visible (< *phaínein* to show, appear) + *gámos* marriage]

**phan|er|o|gam|ic** (fan′ər ə gam′ik), *adj.* of or having to do with the phanerogams; resembling phanerogams.

**phan|er|og|a|mous** (fan′ə rog′ə məs), *adj.* = phanerogamic.

**phan|er|o|phyte** (fan′ər ə fīt), *n.* a perennial plant whose buds are high enough above the ground to project freely into the air. [< Greek *phanerós* visible + *phytón* plant]

**Phan|er|o|zo|ic** (fan′ər ə zō′ik), *adj., n.* —*adj.* of or having to do with the geological eon comprising the Paleozoic, Mesozoic, and Cenozoic eras. —*n.* the Phanerozoic eon: *At most times during the Phanerozoic, the sea covered much more of the continents than it does at present* (New Scientist).
[< Greek *phanerós* visible (see etym. under **phanerogam**) + *zōē* life + English *-ic*]

**phan|ta|scope** (fan′tə skōp), *n.* the first film projector of life-size motion pictures, developed between 1891 and 1894.

**phan|tasm** (fan′taz əm), *n.* **1** a thing seen only in one's imagination; unreal fancy, such as a ghost: *the plantasms of a dream.* **2** a supposed appearance of an absent person, living or dead. **3** a deceiving likeness (of something): *a phantasm of hope.* **4** *Philosophy.* a mental image or representation of a real object. **5** *Archaic.* deceptive appearance; illusion: *'Tis all phantasm* (Emerson).
[< Old French *fantasme,* learned borrowing from Latin *phantasma* < Greek *phántasma* image < *phantázein* make visible, ultimately < *phaínein* to show. See etym. of doublets **phantasma, phantom.**]

**phan|tas|ma** (fan taz′mə), *n., pl.* **-ma|ta.** **1** an illusion; vision; dream: *Like a phantasma or a hideous dream* (Shakespeare). **2** an apparition; specter. [< Latin *phantasma.* See etym. of doublets **phantasm, phantom.**]

**phan|tas|ma|go|ri|a** (fan taz′mə gôr′ē ə, -gōr′-), *n.* **1** a shifting scene of real things, illusions, imaginary fancies, deceptions, and the like: *the phantasmagoria of a dream. Instead of a turreted town crammed with phantasmagoria, it now appeared before him as a plain, ordinary, workaday city* (Harper's). **2** a show of optical illusions in which figures increase or decrease in size, fade away, and pass into each other. [coined < Greek *phántasma* image, perhaps + *agorā* assembly]

**phan|tas|ma|go|ri|al** (fan taz′mə gôr′ē əl, -gōr′-), *adj.* = phantasmagoric.

**phan|tas|ma|gor|ic** (fan taz′mə gôr′ik, -gor′-), *adj.* of or like a phantasmagoria; phantasmal: *The lanterns gave a phantasmagoric quality to the funeral procession* (Jorge Amado).

**phan|tas|ma|gor|i|cal** (fan taz′mə gôr′ə kəl, -gor′-), *adj.* = phantasmagoric.

**phan|tas|ma|go|rist** (fan taz′mə gôr′ist, -gōr′-), *n.* a person who exhibits or produces a phantasmagoria.

**phan|tas|ma|go|ry** (fan taz′mə gôr′ē, -gōr′-), *n., pl.* **-ries.** = phantasmagoria.

**phan|tas|mal** (fan taz′məl), *adj.* of a phantasm; unreal; imaginary. —**phan|tas′mal|ly,** *adv.*

**phan|tas|ma|ta** (fan taz′mə tə), *n.* plural of **phantasma.**

**phan|tas|mic** (fan taz′mik), *adj.* = phantasmal.

**phan|ta|sy** (fan′tə sē, -zē), *n., pl.* **-sies.** **1** = fantasy. **2** *Music.* fantasia.

**phan|tom** (fan′təm), *n., adj.* —*n.* **1** an image of the mind that seems to be real: *the phantoms of a dream. His fevered brain filled the room with phantoms from the past. She was a phantom of delight When first she gleamed upon my sight* (Wordsworth). **2** a thought or apprehension of anything that haunts the imagination: *The phantom of starvation drove him to theft.* **3** a vague, dim, or shadowy appearance; ghost: *The forms Of which these are the phantoms* (Shelley). **3 SYN:** apparition, specter. **4** *Figurative.* a mere show; appearance with no substance: *a phantom of a government, the phantom of a once flourishing town.* **5** *Obsolete.* **a** unreality; deception. **b** an instance of this; a delusion or deception.
—*adj.* like a ghost; unreal; merely apparent: *a phantom ship;* (*Figurative.*) *phantom prosperity.*
[< Old French *fantosme* < Vulgar Latin *phantagma,* variant of Latin *phantasma.* See etym. of doublets **phantasm, phantasma.**] —**phan′tom-like′,** *adj.*

**phantom freight**, a charge for shipping from a distant plant a product, such as an automobile, actually delivered from a plant close by.

**phan|tom|ic** (fan tom′ik), *adj.* phantomlike; unreal.

**phantom larva**, the aquatic larva of a variety of nonbiting gnat. Phantom larvae commonly live in mud on lake bottoms.

**phantom limb pain**, pain felt in a limb that has been amputated.

**phantom order**, a standing order for materials, especially weapons, airplanes, and other armament, placed by the United States government with a firm, but not acted upon until an official signal for proceeding is given.

**Phar.** or **phar.**, **1** pharmaceutic. **2** pharmacopoeia. **3** pharmacy.

**Phar|aoh** or **phar|aoh** (fãr′ō, fer′ō), *n.* the title given to the kings of ancient Egypt. [Old English *Pharaon* < Late Latin *Pharaō, -ōnis* < Greek *Pharaō* < Hebrew *par'oh* < an Egyptian word meaning literally "great house"]

**Pharaoh's ant**, a very tiny reddish or pale ant. It is a common house pest that is attracted by greasy food.

**Pharaoh's hen** or **chicken**, a vulture of the Mediterranean region and southern Asia, about two feet long, with mostly white plumage; Egyptian vulture. It is frequently represented in ancient Egyptian art.

**Pharaoh's rat**, = ichneumon (def. 1).

**Phar|a|on|ic** (fãr′ē on′ik), *adj.* **1** of or having to do with a Pharaoh or the Pharaohs. **2** like or characteristic of a Pharaoh or the Pharaohs.

**Phar.B.**, *U.S.* Bachelor of Pharmacy.

**Phar.D.**, *U.S.* Doctor of Pharmacy.

**phare** (fãr), *n.* = pharos.

**Phar|i|sa|ic** (far′ə sā′ik), *adj.* of or having to do with the Pharisees. [< Late Latin *Pharisaicus* < Greek *pharisaïkós*]

**phar|i|sa|ic** (far′ə sā′ik), *adj.* **1** making an outward show of religion or morality without the real spirit. **2** thinking oneself more moral than others; hypocritical or self-righteous: *smug and pharisaic fools* (John Galsworthy). [< *Pharisaic*] —**phar′i-sa′i|cal|ly,** *adv.* —**phar′i|sa′i|cal|ness,** *n.*

**phar|i|sa|i|cal** (far′ə sā′ə kəl), *adj.* = pharisaic.

**Phar|i|sa|ism** (far′ə sā iz′əm), *n.* the doctrine and practice of the Pharisees.

**phar|i|sa|ism** (far′ə sā iz′əm), *n.* **1** rigid observance of the external forms of religion without genuine piety. **2** self-righteousness or hypocrisy.

**Phar|i|see** (far′ə sē), *n.* a member of a Jewish sect at the time of Christ that was very strict in keeping to tradition and the laws of its religion.
[< Old French *pharise,* and Old English *fariseōs,* plural, both learned borrowings from Latin *pharisaeus* < Greek *pharīsaîos* < Aramaic *pərishayyā*]

**phar|i|see** (far′ə sē), *n.* **1** a person who makes a show of religion rather than following its spirit; formalist; hypocrite. **2** a person who considers himself much better than other persons. [< *Pharisee*]

**Phar|i|see|ism** (far′ə sē iz′əm), *n.* = Pharisaism.

**phar|i|see|ism** (far′ə sē iz′əm), *n.* = pharisaism.

**Pharm.** or **pharm.**, **1** pharmaceutic. **2** pharmacopoeia. **3** pharmacy.

**Phar.M.**, *U.S.* Master of Pharmacy.

**phar|ma|cal** (fär′mə kəl), *adj.* = pharmaceutic.

**phar|ma|ceu|tic** (fär′mə sü′tik), *adj., n.* —*adj.* **1** having to do with pharmacy. **2** engaged in pharmacy. —*n.* a pharmaceutic preparation; medicinal drug. [< Late Latin *pharmaceuticus* < Greek *pharmakeutikós* < *pharmakân* be in need of drugs < *phármakon* drug, poison] —**phar′ma|ceu′ti|cal|ly,** *adv.*

**phar|ma|ceu|ti|cal** (fär′mə sü′tə kəl), *adj., n.* —*adj.* = pharmaceutic. —*n.* a medicinal drug.

**phar|ma|ceu|tics** (fär′mə sü′tiks), *n.* = pharmacy (def. 2).

**phar|ma|ceu|tist** (fär′mə sü′tist), *n.* = pharmacist.

**phar|ma|cist** (fär′mə sist), *n.* a person licensed to fill prescriptions; druggist.

**phar|ma|co|dy|nam|ic** (fär′mə kō dī nam′ik), *adj.* having to do with the powers or effects of drugs.

**phar|ma|co|dy|nam|i|cal** (fär′mə kō dī nam′ə-kəl), *adj.* = pharmacodynamic.

**phar|ma|co|dy|nam|ics** (fär′mə kō dī nam′iks), *n.* the branch of pharmacology dealing with the powers or effects of drugs in an organism. [< Greek *phármakon* drug, poison]

**phar|ma|co|ge|net|ic** (fär′mə kō jə net′ik), *adj.* of or having to do with pharmacogenetics.

**phar|ma|co|ge|net|i|cist** (fär′mə kō jə net′ə sist), *n.* a person skilled in pharmacogenetics.

**phar|ma|co|ge|net|ics** (fär′mə kō jə net′iks), *n.* the study of the interaction of genetics and drugs: *A body of knowledge, called pharmacogenetics, was accumulating that showed that the fate of a drug in the body, or even the nature and extent of its therapeutic effect, depends in certain cases upon a discrete genetic trait* (Sumner M. Kalman).

**phar|ma|cog|no|sist** (fär′mə kog′nə sist), *n.* a person skilled in pharmacognosy.

**phar|ma|cog|nos|tic** (fär′mə kog nos′tik), *adj.* having to do with pharmacognosy.

**phar|ma|cog|no|sy** (fär′mə kog′nə sē), *n.* the branch of pharmacy dealing with medicinal substances in their natural or unprepared state; the knowledge of drugs. [< Greek *phármakon* drug, poison + *gnôsis* knowledge (< *gignṓskein* to know) + English *-y*[3]]

**phar|ma|co|ki|net|ics** (fär′mə kō ki net′iks), *n.* the study of the way the body takes up, distributes, and eliminates drugs.

**pharmacol.**, pharmacology.

**phar|ma|co|log|ic** (fär′mə kə loj′ik), *adj.* = pharmacological.

**phar|ma|co|log|i|cal** (fär′mə kə loj′ə kəl), *adj.* of or having to do with pharmacology. —**phar′ma-co|log′i|cal|ly,** *adv.*

**phar|ma|col|o|gist** (fär′mə kol′ə jist), *n.* a person skilled in the science of drugs.

---

**Pronunciation Key:** hat, āge, cãre, fär; let, ēqual, tėrm; it, īce; hot, ōpen, ôrder; **oi**l, **ou**t; cup, pu̇t, rüle; **ch**ild; lo**ng**; **th**in; **ᴛʜ**en; **zh**, measure;
ə represents **a** in about, **e** in taken, **i** in pencil, **o** in lemon, **u** in circus.

**phar|ma|col|o|gy** (fär′mə kol′ə jē), *n.* the science of drugs, their properties, preparation, uses, and effects. [< New Latin *pharmacologia* < Greek *phármakon* drug, poison + *-logiā* -logy]

**phar|ma|co|poe|ia** or **phar|ma|co|pe|ia** (fär′mə kə pē′ə), *n., pl.* **-ias. 1** a book containing an official list and description of drugs and medicines. **2** a stock or collection of drugs, chemicals, medicines, or remedies. [< New Latin *pharmacopoeia* < Greek *pharmakopoiīā* < *pharmakopoiós*, adjective, preparing drugs < *phármakon* drug, poison + *poieîn* to make]

**phar|ma|co|poe|ial** or **phar|ma|co|pe|ial** (fär′mə kə pē′əl), *adj.* **1** having to do with a pharmacopoeia. **2** recognized in, or prepared and administered according to the directions of the official pharmacopoeia.

**phar|ma|co|poe|ist** or **phar|ma|co|pe|ist** (fär′mə kə pē′ist), *n.* a compiler of a pharmacopoeia.

**phar|ma|co|ther|a|peu|tic** (fär′mə kō ther′ə pyü′tik), *adj.* of or having to do with pharmacotherapeutics.

**phar|ma|co|ther|a|peu|tics** (fär′mə kō ther′ə pyü′tiks), *n.* the scientific study of the treatment of disease by means of drugs.

**phar|ma|co|ther|a|py** (fär′mə kō ther′ə pē), *n.* treatment of disease by means of drugs.

**phar|ma|cy** (fär′mə sē), *n., pl.* **-cies. 1** a place where drugs and medicines are prepared or sold; drugstore. **2** the preparation and dispensing of drugs and medicines; business of a druggist; pharmaceutics. **3** = pharmacopoeia (def. 2). [Middle English *fermocie* a medicine; the use of medicines < Old French *farmacie*, learned borrowing from Medieval Latin *pharmacia* < Greek *pharmakeíā* < *pharmakeús* preparer of drugs < *phármakon* drug, poison]

**Pharm.D.**, *U.S.* Doctor of Pharmacy.

**phar|mic** (fär′mik), *adj.* of or having to do with pharmacy or drugs.

**Pharm.M.**, *U.S.* Master of Pharmacy.

**phar|os** (får′os), *n.* a lighthouse, beacon, or other guiding light: *a steep ... mount, on the top of which ... had been a pharos or lighthouse* (Washington Irving). [< Latin *pharos* < Greek *pháros* lighthouse < *Pháros* Pharos (of Alexandria)]

**Phar|os of Al|ex|an|dri|a** (får′os əv al′ig zan′drē ə), one of the seven wonders of the ancient world, a celebrated lighthouse on the island of Pharos, now a small peninsula in Northern Egypt.

**pha|ryn|gal** (fə ring′gəl), *adj.* **1** *Phonetics.* articulated in the pharynx. **2** = pharyngeal.

**pha|ryn|ge|al** (fə rin′jē əl, far′in jē′-), *adj.* **1** having to do with the pharynx. **2** connected with the pharynx.

**pharyngeal tonsil**, a mass of lymphoid glandular tissue at the back of the upper part of the pharynx, especially in children, the abnormal enlargement of which is called adenoids.

**phar|yn|gec|to|my** (far′in jek′tə mē), *n., pl.* **-mies.** the removal of part or all of the pharynx.

**pha|ryn|ges** (fə rin′jēz), *n.* a plural of **pharynx.**

**phar|yn|gi|tis** (far′in jī′tis), *n.* inflammation of the mucous membrane of the pharynx.

**phar|yn|gol|o|gy** (far′ing gol′ə jē), *n.* the branch of medicine dealing with the structure, functions, and diseases of the pharynx.

**pha|ryn|go|na|sal** (fə ring′gō nā′zəl), *adj.* having to do with the pharynx and nose.

**pha|ryn|go|scope** (fə ring′gə skōp), *n.* an instrument for examining the pharynx.

**phar|yn|gos|co|py** (far′ing gos′kə pē), *n.* inspection of the pharynx.

**phar|yn|got|o|my** (far′ing got′ə mē), *n., pl.* **-mies.** surgical incision into the pharynx.

***phar|ynx** (far′ingks), *n., pl.* **phar|ynx|es** or **pha|ryn|ges.** the cavity at the back of the mouth where the passages to the nose, lungs, and stomach begin: *The length of the pharynx varies slightly as the larynx is raised or lowered in speech* (C. K. Thomas). [< New Latin *pharynx* < Greek *phárynx, -yngos* pharynx, windpipe, throat]

***pharynx**

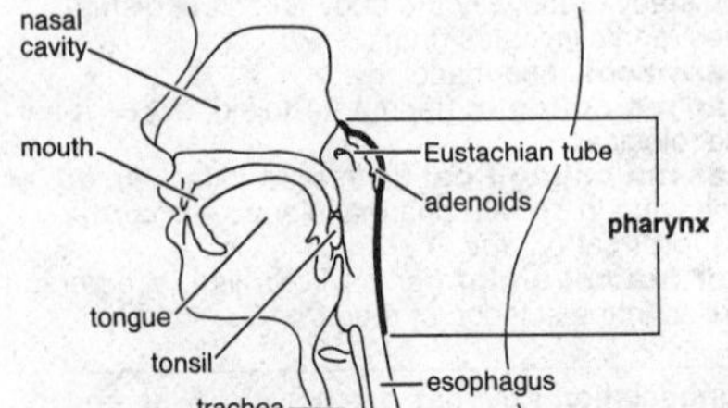


**phase** (fāz), *n., v.,* **phased, phas|ing.** —*n.* **1** one of the changing states or stages of development of a person or thing: *At present his voice is changing; that is a phase all boys go through. A phase of my life was closing tonight, a new one opening tomorrow* (Charlotte Brontë). *The aim of Phase II was to allow some flexibility in the rigid economic controls of Phase I without bringing on a resurgence of rampant inflation* (Norman S. Thompson). **2** one side, part, or view (of a subject): *What phase of arithmetic are you studying now?* **3** the shape of the moon or of a planet as it is seen at a particular time. The new moon, first quarter, full moon, and last quarter are four phases of the moon. **4** *Physics.* a particular stage or point in a recurring sequence of movements or changes, considered in relation to a starting point of normal position (used especially with reference to circular motion, simple harmonic motion, or an alternating current, sound vibration, or vibration of atomic particles): *The current in all parts of a series circuit is in the same phase.* **5** one of the states, especially of coloration, of fur or plumage, characteristic of certain animals at certain seasons or ages; color phase: *Ermine is the fur of a weasel in its winter phase.* **6** *Physical Chemistry.* a homogeneous part of a heterogeneous system, separated from other parts by definite boundaries, such as ice in water. **7** *Biology.* one of the distinct stages in meiosis or mitosis. *Abbr:* ph.

—*v.t.* **1** to carry out or adjust (an action, operation, or program) by stages: *to phase an army's withdrawal.* **2** to bring or put (something) into an operation, program, or action, as a phase or in phases.

**in phase, a** *Physics.* in the same phase: *They are in phase with each other, both reaching maximum values at the same instant* (J. A. Ratcliffe). **b** *Figurative.* in harmony or agreement: *There was much cheering as the candidate's remarks were very much in phase with the feelings of his audience.*

**out of phase, a** *Physics.* in a different phase, or in different phases: *voltages that are out of phase.* **b** *Figurative.* out of step: *He was childlike and foolish, totally out of phase with all other Dominicans, a stranger in a foreign land* (Atlantic).

**phase down,** to reduce gradually; reduce by phases: *The secretary said that the programme to phase down American air operations in Indo-China ... "is solidly based and progressing"* (London Times).

**phase in,** to develop or integrate as a phase or in phases: *It is hoped that seven to nine additional units will be "phased in" yearly until the planned total is reached* (New York Times).

**phase out,** to discontinue or eliminate as a phase or in phases: *During the last few years the service has been phasing out its aircraft of World War II vintage* (New York Times).

[probably back formation < *phases*, plural of *phasis*]

**phase angle, 1** *Astronomy.* the angle formed by the earth and the sun as seen from a planet: *The phase angle is greatest when the planet is near quadrature* (Robert H. Baker). **2** *Physics.* an angle representing two quantities which show differences in phase: *The current is said to lag behind the voltage by ... a phase angle of 60 electrical degrees* (Shortley and Williams).

**phase-con|trast microscope** (fāz′kon′trast), a microscope which uses the differences in phase of light passing through or reflected by the object under examination, to form distinct and contrastive images of different parts of the object: *The phase-contrast microscope ... has made it possible to observe in living cells structures which previously could be seen only if the cells were killed and stained* (Scientific American).

**phased-ar|ray** (fāzd′ə rā′), *adj.* having or based on a complex of electronically steerable radiating elements in place of a mechanically rotated antenna: *These phased-array radars, with computer complexes, could sight incoming missiles more than 1,000 miles away* (Heather M. David).

**phase|down** (fāz′doun′), *n.* the act or process of phasing down; gradual reduction.

**phase-locked** (fāz′lokt′), *adj.* operating in precise synchronization; locked in phase: *Bursts of action potentials, phase-locked with the oscillations, took place in the prodded finger as they do in normal tremor* (Scientific American).

**phase modulation,** a means of electronic modulation in which the phase of the carrier wave is varied in order to transmit the amplitude and pitch of the signal.

**phase-out** (fāz′out′), *n.* the discontinuation of an operation, production, program, or action, by stages: *The British government would plan a gradual phase-out of the British strategic nuclear forces* (Harper's).

**phase rule,** *Physical Chemistry.* $F = C - P + 2$, where F represents the freedom of a substance, C its components, and P its phases.

**pha|sis** (fā′sis), *n., pl.* **-ses** (-sēz). phase, especially: **a** any one aspect of a thing of varying appearances. **b** a state or stage of change or development. [< New Latin *phasis* < Greek *phásis* phase, appearance < *phaínein* to show, appear]

**phas|mid** (faz′mid), *n.* = walking stick (def. 2). [< New Latin *Phasma* the genus name < Greek *phásma* apparition < *phaínein* to appear]

**phat|ic** (fat′ik), *adj.* of or having to do with communication of friendly feeling or sociableness by words or gestures instead of communication of ideas: *We normally use words to express purpose or to persuade (much less for that "phatic" purpose of making and maintaining human contact for its own sake)* (Anthony Burgess). [< Greek *phatós* spoken < *phanai* to speak]

**Ph.B.**, *U.S.* Bachelor of Philosophy (Latin, *Philosophiae Baccalaureus*).

**Ph.C.**, Pharmaceutical Chemist.

**Ph.D.**, Doctor of Philosophy (Latin, *Philosophiae Doctor*).

**pheas|ant** (fez′ənt), *n., pl.* **-ants** or (*collectively*) **-ant. 1** a large game bird with brilliant feathers in the male, and long pointed tail feathers, that nests on the ground and flies only short distances. There are various kinds, related to the domestic fowl and the peacock. Pheasants are native to Asia but are now established in many parts of Europe and America. **2** any one of various similar birds, such as the ruffed grouse. [< Anglo-French *fesant*, Old French *fesan*, learned borrowing from Latin *phāsiānus* < Greek *phāsiānós* (literally) Phasian (bird) < *Phâsis*, the river Phasis in Colchis]

**pheas|ant|ry** (fez′ən trē), *n., pl.* **-ries.** a place where pheasants are bred and kept.

**pheas|ant's-eye** (fez′ənts ī′), *n.* any one of certain plants, such as an herb of the crowfoot family grown for its scarlet or crimson flowers, or a variety of common garden pink.

**phe|be** (fē′bē), *n.* = phoebe.

**phel|lem** (fel′əm), *n. Botany.* cork. [< Greek *phellós* cork + English *-em,* as in *phloem*]

**phel|lo|derm** (fel′ə dėrm), *n. Botany.* a layer of parenchymatous cells often containing chlorophyll, formed in the stems and roots of some plants from the inner cells of the phellogen. [< Greek *phellós* cork + *dérma* skin]

**phel|lo|der|mal** (fel′ə dėr′məl), *adj.* of or having to do with the phelloderm.

**phel|lo|gen** (fel′ə jən), *n.* a layer of cellular tissue or secondary meristem forming cork cells toward the outside and phelloderm toward the inside of the stem and root of many plants; cork cambium. [< Greek *phellós* cork + English *-gen*]

**phel|lo|ge|net|ic** (fel′ə jə net′ik), *adj.* **1** producing cork. **2** like phellogen.

**phel|lo|gen|ic** (fel′ə jen′ik), *adj.* **1** like phellogen. **2** having to do with phellogen.

**phen-**, *combining form.* a benzene derivative, as in *phenol, phenyl.* Also, **pheno-** before consonants. [< French *phén-* < Greek *phaínein* show forth (because such early substances were by-products from the making of illuminating gas)]

**phe|na|caine hydrochloride,** or **phe|na|caine** (fē′nə kān, fen′ə-), *n.* a white, soluble crystalline powder used as a local anesthetic, especially for the eye; Holocaine hydrochloride. *Formula:* $C_{18}H_{22}N_2O_2 \cdot HCl \cdot H_2O$

**phe|nac|e|tin** or **phe|nac|e|tine** (fə nas′ə tin), *n.* a white, soluble crystalline powder, used to relieve fever and pain; acetophenetidin. *Formula:* $C_{10}H_{13}NO_2$

**phen|a|cite** (fen′ə sīt), *n.* a mineral, a colorless, yellow, or brown silicate of beryllium, sometimes used as a gem, occurring in quartzlike transparent or translucent crystals. *Formula:* $Be_2SiO_4$ Also, **phenakite.** [< Greek *phénāx, -ākos* a cheat + English *-ite*[1] (because it was mistaken for quartz)]

**phe|nac|o|mys** (fə nak′ə mis), *n.* any one of a group of small voles or mice with, usually, long, silky fur, found in Canada, Alaska, and mountains of the western United States. [< New Latin *Phenacomys* the genus name < Greek *phénāx, -akos* deceiver + New Latin *-mys* mouse]

**phen|a|kis|to|scope** (fen′ə kis′tə skōp), *n.* a scientific toy consisting of a disk with figures upon it arranged radially, representing a moving object in successive positions. When the disk is turned around rapidly and the viewer sees the figures through a fixed slit (or their reflections in a mirror through radial slits in the disk itself) in quick succession the eye receives the impression of actual motion. [< Greek *phenakistês* cheater + English *-scope* (because the viewer sees only a representation of motion)]

**phen|a|kite** (fen′ə kīt), *n.* = phenacite.

**phe|nan|threne** (fə nan′thrēn), *n.* a colorless hydrocarbon crystallizing in shining scales, found in association with anthracene (with which it is isometric) and used in making dyes, drugs, and explosives. *Formula:* $C_{14}H_{10}$

**phen|a|zin** (fen′ə zin), *n.* = phenazine.

**phen|a|zine** (fen′ə zēn, -zin), *n.* a basic chemical compound crystallizing in long yellowish needles. It is a source of many important dyes. *Formula:* $C_{12}H_8N_2$

**phe|naz|o|cine** (fə naz′ə sēn, -sin), *n.* a synthetic pain reliever more powerful than morphine and thought to be less addictive. *Formula:* $C_{22}H_{27}NO$

**phe|na|zone** (fē′nə zōn), *n.* **1** = antipyrine. **2** a yellowish, crystalline compound isomeric with phenazine.

**phen|cyc|li|dine** (fen′sik lə dēn), *n.* a depressant drug with powerful hallucinatory side effects in humans, now used legally only as a tranquilizer for monkeys and elephants. *Abbr:* PCP *Formula:* $C_{17}H_{25}N$

**phen|el|zine** (fen′əl zēn), *n.* a synthetic drug that helps to relieve mental depression. It is a monoamine-oxidase inhibitor. *Formula:* $C_8H_{12}N_2$

**Phen|er|gan** (fen′ər gan), *n. Trademark.* a tranquilizing drug used in treating allergies and motion sickness and as a light anesthetic; promethazine. *Formula:* $C_{17}H_{20}N_2S$

**phe|net|ic** (fē net′ik), *adj.* of or having to do with a system of classification of organisms based on overall or relative degrees of observable similarity among the organisms to be classified. [< *phen-* (< Greek *phaínein* show forth) + *-etic,* as in *phyletic*] —**phe|net′i|cal|ly,** *adv.*

**phe|net|i|cist** (fē net′ə sist), *n.* a person who uses or favors phenetic classification.

**phe|net|ics** (fē net′iks), *n.* the phenetic system of classification.

**phe|net|i|din** (fə net′ə din), *n.* = phenetidine.

**phe|net|i|dine** (fə net′ə dēn, -din), *n.* a colorless liquid base found in three isomeric forms. It is derived from phenetole, and is used in making phenacetin and dyes. *Formula:* $C_8H_{11}ON$

**phen|e|tol** (fen′ə tol), *n.* = phenetole.

**phen|e|tole** (fen′ə tōl, -tol), *n.* a colorless volatile, aromatic liquid. *Formula:* $C_8H_{10}O$ [< *phen*(o)- + *et*(hyl) + *-ol*[1]]

**phen|for|min** (fen′fər min), *n.* a drug used against diabetes; DBI.

**Phe|ni|cian** (fə nish′ən, -nē′shən), *adj., n.* = Phoenician.

**phe|nix** (fē′niks), *n.* = phoenix.

**phen|met|ra|zine** (fen met′rə zēn), *n.* a sympathomimetic drug used as an appetite depressant. *Formula:* $C_{11}H_{15}NO$

**pheno-,** *combining form.* the form of **phen-** before consonants, as in *phenobarbital.*

**phe|no|bar|bi|tal** (fē′nō bär′bə tôl, -tal; fen′ə-), *n.* a white, crystalline powder, used chiefly in the form of phenobarbital sodium as a hypnotic or sedative. Phenobarbital is a barbiturate. *Formula:* $C_{12}H_{12}N_2O_3$

**phenobarbital sodium,** a bitter, white soluble powder, used as a hypnotic or sedative. *Formula:* $C_{12}H_{11}N_2O_3Na$

**phe|no|bar|bi|tone** (fē′nō bär′bə tōn), *n. Especially British.* phenobarbital.

**phe|no|cop|y** (fē′nə kop′ē), *n., pl.* **-cop|ies.** a phenotype that stimulates the traits characteristic of another genotype.

**phe|no|cryst** (fē′nə krist, fen′ə-), *n.* any one of the large or conspicuous crystals in a porphyritic rock. [< French *phénocryste* < Greek *phaínein* to show, appear + *krýstallos* crystal]

**phe|no|gam** (fē′nə gam), *n.* = phanerogam.

**phe|no|gam|ic** (fē′nə gam′ik), *adj.* = phanerogamic.

**phe|nog|a|mous** (fi nog′ə məs), *adj.* = phanerogamous.

**phe|nol** (fē′nol, -nōl), *n.* **1** = carbolic acid. **2** any one of a series of aromatic hydroxyl derivatives of benzene, of which carbolic acid is the first member.

**phe|no|late** (fē′nə lāt), *n.* a salt of phenol; phenoxide.

**phe|no|lic** (fi nō′lik, -nol′ik), *adj., n.* —*adj.* **1** of the nature of phenol. **2** belonging to phenol.
—*n.* any one of a group of thermosetting synthetic resins, obtained chiefly by the reaction of a phenol with an aldehyde, used for molding and in varnishes.

**phenolic resin,** = phenolic.

**phe|no|lize** (fē′nə līz), *v.t.,* **-lized, -liz|ing.** to treat with phenol: *Phenolized vaccine gives better protection than the alcoholized type* (Science News Letter).

**phe|no|log|i|cal** (fē′nə log′ə kəl), *adj.* of or having to do with phenology or the objects of its study. —**phe′no|log′i|cal|ly,** *adv.*

**phe|nol|o|gist** (fi nol′ə jist), *n.* a person who studies phenology.

**phe|nol|o|gy** (fi nol′ə jē), *n.* the study of periodic occurrences in nature, such as the migration of birds and the ripening of fruit, and their relation to climate.

**phe|nol|phthal|ein** (fē′nōl thal′ēn, -fthal′-), *n.* a white or pale-yellow powder used in testing acidity, making dyes, and as a laxative. Its solution is red when basic, colorless when acid. *Formula:* $C_{20}H_{14}O_4$

**phenol red,** a bright- to dark-red crystalline powder, used in testing acidity and in the diagnosis of kidney malfunction. *Formula:* $C_{19}H_{14}O_5S$

**phe|nom** (fə nom′), *n. U.S. Informal.* a phenomenon: *Even if the young phenom does choose baseball, he no longer enjoys the same lengthy apprenticeship* (New Yorker).

**phe|nom|e|na** (fə nom′ə nə), *n.* a plural of **phenomenon**: *It is expected to obtain data on solar radiation, sky brightness and other important phenomena* (New York Times).
► **Phenomena** is sometimes taken to be a singular and so used, but this construction is not current in standard English.

**phe|nom|e|nal** (fə nom′ə nəl), *adj., n.* —*adj.* **1** very notable or remarkable; extraordinary; exceptional: *a phenomenal memory.* **2** of or having to do with a phenomenon or phenomena. **3** having the nature of a phenomenon; apparent; sensible; perceptible: *Seen in the light of thought, the world always is phenomenal* (Emerson). **4** based on or dealing entirely in terms of things that are or have been observed; not using or containing hypotheses: *phenomenal geology.*
—*n.* **the phenomenal,** things that are known by the senses: *The ideal is the subjective, the phenomenal the objective* (John Grote).
—**phe|nom′e|nal|ly,** *adv.*

**Phe|nom|e|nal** (fə nom′ə nəl), *n.* a form of loganberry grown in southern California that has a more raspberrylike fruit than the common loganberry.

**phe|nom|e|nal|ism** (fə nom′ə nə liz′əm), *n.* **1** any one of various theories that knowledge is attainable only through careful observation of phenomena; doctrine that knowledge consists solely in the accumulation and manipulation of observed data. **2** *Philosophy.* the doctrine that phenomena are the realities and therefore the only possible objects of knowledge; absolute externalism.

**phe|nom|e|nal|ist** (fə nom′ə nə list), *n.* a supporter of phenomenalism.

**phe|nom|e|nal|is|tic** (fə nom′ə nə lis′tik), *adj.* of or having to do with phenomenalism. —**phe-nom′e|nal|is′ti|cal|ly,** *adv.*

**phe|nom|e|nal|i|ty** (fə nom′ə nal′ə tē), *n., pl.* **-ties.** **1** the quality or state of being phenomenal. **2** a phenomenal act, feat, or occurrence.

**phe|nom|e|no|log|i|cal** (fə nom′ə nə loj′ə kəl), *adj.* of or having to do with phenomenology.
—**phe|nom′e|no|log′i|cal|ly,** *adv.*

**phe|nom|e|nol|o|gist** (fə nom′ə nol′ə jist), *n.* a person engaged in phenomenology.

**phe|nom|e|nol|o|gy** (fə nom′ə nol′ə jē), *n.* **1** the science of phenomena, as distinct from ontology or the science of being. **2** that division of any science which describes and classifies its phenomena.

**phe|nom|e|non** (fə nom′ə non), *n., pl.* **-na** or (*especially for def. 4*) **-nons.** **1** a fact, event, or circumstance that can be observed: *Lightning is an electrical phenomenon.* **2** any sign, symptom, or manifestation: *Fever and inflammation are phenomena of disease.* **3** any exceptional fact or occurrence: *historical phenomena.* **4** something or someone extraordinary or remarkable: *The Grand Canyon is a phenomenon of nature. The fond grandparents think their daughter's little son is a phenomenon.* **5** *Philosophy.* something that the senses or the mind directly takes note of; an immediate object of perception, as distinguished from a thing-in-itself. [< Late Latin *phaenomenon* appearance < Greek *phainómenon,* ultimately < *phaínein* show forth]

**phe|no|thi|a|zine** (fē′nō thī′ə zēn, -zin), *n.* a yellowish crystalline substance used in making dyes, as an insecticide, and as a vermifuge for cattle, sheep, and other livestock. *Formula:* $C_{12}H_9NS$

**phe|no|type** (fē′nə tīp), *n. Biology.* **1** a character or individual organism defined by its appearance and not by its genetic constitution or hereditary potentialities. **2** a group of animals or plants having one or more such characters in common. **3** the visible result of the interaction between a genotype and its environment. [< German *Phänotypus* < Greek *phaínein* show forth + *týpos* type]

**phe|no|typ|ic** (fē′nə tip′ik), *adj.* of or having to do with phenotypes: *Flowering is an apparent or phenotypic response of the genotype to its environment* (Science News Letter). —**phe′no|typ′i-cal|ly,** *adv.*

**phe|no|typ|i|cal** (fē′nə tip′ə kəl), *adj.* = phenotypic.

**phe|nox|ide** (fi nok′sīd), *n.* = phenolate.

**phen|yl** (fen′əl, fē′nəl), *n.* a univalent radical (-$C_6H_5$) occurring in benzene, phenol, and an extensive series of aromatic compounds, formed by removing one hydrogen atom from a benzene molecule. *Abbr:* Ph (no period). [< French *phényle* < *phène* benzene + *-yle* -yl]

**phen|yl|al|a|nine** (fen′ə lal′ə nēn, fē′nə-), *n.* an amino acid which results from the hydrolysis of protein and is normally converted to tyrosine in the body. When, as a result of a hereditary defect, the conversion does not take place properly, phenylketonuria results. *Formula:* $C_9H_{11}NO_2$

**phen|yl|a|mine** (fen′ə lə mēn′, fē′nə lam′in), *n.* the systematic name for aniline.

**phen|yl|bu|ta|zone** (fen′əl byü′tə zōn, fē′nəl-), *n.* a synthetic drug derived from coal tar, used as an analgesic to treat rheumatism and arthritis; Butazolidin. *Formula:* $C_{19}H_{20}N_2O_2$

**phen|yl|ene** (fen′ə lēn, fē′nə-), *n.* a bivalent radical (-$C_6H_4$-) formed by removing two hydrogen atoms from a benzene molecule.

**phen|yl|eph|rine** (fen′əl ef′rin, fē′nəl; -rēn), *n.* a sympathomimetic drug used to constrict blood vessels. *Formula:* $C_9H_{13}NO_2$ [< *phenyl* + (epin)*ephrine*]

**phen|yl|gly|cine** (fen′əl glī′sēn, fē′nəl-; -glī-sēn′), *n.* a crystalline compound forming an intermediate in the production of indigo dyes, often prepared by condensation of aniline and chloroacetic acid. *Formula:* $C_8H_9NO_2$

**phe|nyl|ic** (fi nil′ik), *adj.* **1** of phenyl. **2** derived from phenyl.

**phen|yl|ke|to|nu|ri|a** (fen′əl kē′tə nyu̇r′ē ə, fē′nəl-; -nu̇r′-), *n.* a hereditary disease caused by an inability to metabolize phenylalanine properly in the body, resulting in mental deficiency and poor physical development: *A special diet permits normal brain development in children born with the defect called phenylketonuria* (New York Times). *Abbr:* PKU (no periods). [< *phenyl*(alanine) + *ketonuria*]

**phen|yl|ke|to|nu|ric** (fen′əl kē′tə nyu̇r′ik, fē′nəl-; -nu̇r′-), *adj., n.* —*adj.* of, having to do with, or affected with phenylketonuria: *It will be possible to perform experiments with these animals that cannot be performed with phenylketonuric children* (Science News Letter).
—*n.* a person affected with phenylketonuria: *The mental defect of phenylketonurics is graded, and a few of them are stupid but not sufficiently so to be classed as feeble-minded* (J. B. S. Haldane).

**phen|yl|thi|o|car|bam|ide** (fen′əl thī′ō kär bam′-īd, -id; fē′nəl-), *n.* = phenylthiourea.

**phen|yl|thi|o|u|re|a** (fen′əl thī′ō yu̇ rē′ə, -yu̇r′ē-; fē′nəl-), *n.* a crystalline substance that is either bitter, slightly sweet, or tasteless, depending on the heredity of the taster, used in various genetic tests. *Formula:* $C_7H_8N_2S$

**phe|o|chro|mo|cy|to|ma** (fē′ō krō′mō sī tō′mə), *n.* a tumor of the sympathetic nervous system made up of chromaffin cells. [< Greek *phaiós* gray + English *chromo-* + *-cyte* + *-oma*]

**phe|on** (fē′on), *n.* **1** *Heraldry.* the barbed head of an arrow or spear, with the point directed downward. **2** a barbed javelin formerly carried by a royal sergeant at arms. [origin unknown]

**Pher|e|cra|te|an** (fer′ə krə tē′ən), *adj., n. Ancient Prosody.* —*adj.* noting or having to do with a logaoedic tripody, catalectic or acatalectic, whose first or second foot is a dactyl, the others being trochees.
—*n.* a Pherecratean tripody or verse.
[< *Pherecrates,* a Greek comic poet of the 400's B.C. + *-an*]

**Pher|e|crat|ic** (fer′ə krat′ik), *adj., n.* = Pherecratean.

**pher|o|mo|nal** (fer′ə mō′nəl), *adj.* of or having to do with pheromones: *Of all the likely influences, a pheromonal communication, by subliminal odour, seemed biologically the most likely* (Alex Comfort).

**pher|o|mone** (fer′ə mōn), *n.* a substance secreted externally by certain animal species, especially insects, to affect the behavior or development of other members of the species: *The queen substance of honeybees, which inhibits ovary development ... in workers, is a pheromone* (New Scientist). [< Greek *phero-* (< Greek *phérein* carry) + (hor)*mone*]

**phew** (fyü, pfyü), *interj.* an exclamation of disgust, impatience, surprise, or the like. [imitative of blowing outward with the lips. Compare etym. under **poof.**]

**Ph.G.,** *U.S.* Graduate in Pharmacy.

***phi** definition 1

| Φ | φ |
|---|---|
| capital letter | lower-case letter |

***phi** (fī, fē), *n.* **1** the 21st letter of the Greek alphabet corresponding phonetically to English *f,*

**Pronunciation Key:** hat, āge, cãre, fär; let, ēqual, tėrm; it, īce; hot, ōpen, ôrder; oil, out; cup, pu̇t, rüle; child; long; thin; ᴛʜen; zh, measure; ə represents **a** in about, **e** in taken, **i** in pencil, **o** in lemon, **u** in circus.

but usually transliterated by *ph.* **2** = phi meson. [< Greek *phí*]

**phi|al** (fī′əl), *n.* a small bottle; vial. [Middle English *fiole* < Old French *fiole,* apparently learned borrowing from Medieval Latin *phiola,* variant of Latin *phiala* < Greek *phiálē* broad, flat drinking vessel]

**Phi Be|ta Kap|pa** (fī′ bā′tə kap′ə, bē′tə), **1** an honorary society composed of American college students and graduates in liberal arts and science who have ranked high in scholarship: *[She] was graduated summa cum laude in 1947 from Barnard College, where she was elected to Phi Beta Kappa* (New York Times). **2** a member of this society. [< the initial letters of the Greek phrase *ph(ilosophiā) b(íou) k(ybernêtēs)* philosophy the guide of life]

**Phi Bete** (fī′bāt′), *U.S. Informal.* a member of Phi Beta Kappa.

**Phid|i|an** (fid′ē ən), *adj.* **1** of or having to do with the sculpture of Phidias. **2** like the work of Phidias. [< *Phidias,* about 490-420 B.C., a Greek sculptor + English *-an*]

**phil-**, *combining form.* the form of **philo-** before vowels, as in *philanthropy.*

**-phil**, *combining form.* variant of **-phile**, as in *eosinophil.*

**phil.**, philosophy.

**Phil.**, an abbreviation for the following:
**1** Philemon (book of the New Testament)
**2** Philip.
**3** Philippians (book of the New Testament).
**4a** Philippine. **b** Philippines.

**Phila.**, Philadelphia.

**phil|a|beg** (fil′ə beg), *n.* = filibeg.

**Phil|a|del|phi|a lawyer** (fil′ə del′fē ə, -fyə), *U.S.* **1** a very shrewd, able lawyer (as many in Philadelphia, Pennsylvania, were, and all were popularly believed to be, during the 1700's). **2** a very shrewd lawyer of dubious scruples, enormously skilled in the niceties and technicalities of legal language and tactics (as many in Philadelphia were popularly believed to be during the 1800's).

**phil|a|del|phi|an** (fil′ə del′fē ən, -fyən), *adj., n.* —*adj.* having or showing brotherly love, especially for one's fellow beings.
—*n.* a person imbued with brotherly love, especially for his fellow beings.
[< Greek *philadelphiā* (< *philádelphos* having brotherly love < *phílos* loving + *adelphós* brother) + English *-an*]

**Phil|a|del|phi|an** (fil′ə del′fē ən, -fyən), *adj., n.* —*adj.* of or having to do with Philadelphia, Pennsylvania.
—*n.* a native or inhabitant of Philadelphia.

**Philadelphia pepper pot**, = pepper pot.

**Philadelphia vireo**, a North American vireo with a light yellowish breast.

**phil|a|del|phus** (fil′ə del′fəs), *n., pl.* **-phus|es.** = syringa.

**Phi|lan|der** (fə lan′dər), *n.* a name given to a lover in old romance and poetry. [< Greek *phílandros,* adjective < *phílos* loving, fond of + *anḗr, andrós* man]

**phi|lan|der** (fə lan′dər), *v.i.* to make love to a woman without serious intentions; flirt. [< *Philander*] —**phi|lan′der|er**, *n.*

**phil|an|thrope** (fil′ən thrōp), *n.* = philanthropist. [< French *philanthrope* < Greek *philánthrōpos* loving mankind < *phílos* loving + *ánthrōpos* mankind]

**phil|an|throp|ic** (fil′ən throp′ik), *adj.* **1a** having to do with or characterized by philanthropy. **b** engaged in philanthropy: *a philanthropic foundation.* **2** charitable; benevolent; kindly: *a philanthropic nature.* —**phil′an|throp′i|cal|ly**, *adv.*

**phil|an|throp|i|cal** (fil′ən throp′ə kəl), *adj.* = philanthropic.

**phi|lan|thro|pist** (fə lan′thrə pist), *n.* a person who loves mankind and works for its welfare, especially by giving sizable donations of money to worthy causes.

**phi|lan|thro|pize** (fə lan′thrə pīz), *v.t.,* **-pized, -piz|ing.** to treat philanthropically.

**phi|lan|thro|py** (fə lan′thrə pē), *n., pl.* **-pies.**
**1** love of mankind shown by practical kindness and helpfulness to humanity: *The Red Cross appeals to philanthropy.* SYN: benevolence, charity.
**2** a thing that benefits humanity; philanthropic agency, enterprise, gift, or act: *A hospital is a useful philanthropy.* [< Late Latin *philanthrōpia* < Greek *philanthrōpiā* < *philánthrōpos;* see etym. under **philanthrope**]

**phil|a|tel|ic** (fil′ə tel′ik), *adj.* of or having to do with philately. —**phil′a|tel′i|cal|ly**, *adv.*

**phil|a|tel|i|cal** (fil′ə tel′ə kəl), *adj.* = philatelic.

**phi|lat|e|list** (fə lat′ə list), *n.* a collector of postage stamps, postmarks, and envelopes sent through the mail.

**phi|lat|e|ly** (fə lat′ə lē), *n.* the collecting, arranging, and study of postage stamps, postmarks, stamped envelopes, and post cards. [< French *philatélie,* ultimately < Greek *phílos* loving + *atéleia* exemption from public assessments (since a postage stamp shows prepayment of postal tax)]

**Phi|la|the|a** (fə lā′thē ə), *n.* an international, interdenominational organization of Bible classes for young women. [< Greek *phílos* loving + *theós* god]

**-phile**, *combining form.* **1** a lover or admirer of ___; person or animal that is fond of ___: *Bibliophile = a lover of books. Sarcophile = an animal that loves flesh.*
**2** a thing having an affinity for ___; substance strongly attracted to ___: *Electrophile = a substance strongly attracted to electrons.* Also, **-phil**.
[< French *-phile,* ultimately < Greek *phílos* loving]

**Philem.**, Philemon (book of New Testament).

**Phi|le|mon** (fə lē′mən), *n.* **1** one of the shortest books of the New Testament. It is a letter from Paul to a convert of his who lived in Colossae. *Abbr:* Philem. **2** *Greek Mythology.* a poor man who, with his wife Baucis, showed hospitality to Zeus and Hermes in disguise.

**phi|le|nor** (fə lē′nər), *n.* a handsome North American swallow-tailed butterfly, having black forewings and steel-blue hind wings, all with greenish reflections. [< New Latin *philenor* < Greek *philḗnōr* loving one's husband < *phílos* loving + *anḗr* man]

**phil|har|mon|ic** (fil′här mon′ik, fil′ər-), *adj., n.* —*adj.* **1** devoted to music; loving music. A musical club is often called a philharmonic society. **2** given by a philharmonic society: *a philharmonic concert.*
—*n.* a philharmonic society or concert.
[< French *philharmonique* < Italian *filarmonico* < Greek *phílos* loving + *tà harmoniká* the (theory of) music. Compare etym. under **harmonic.**]

**Phil|har|mon|ic** (fil′här mon′ik, fil′ər-), *n.* a particular symphony orchestra: *the Vienna Philharmonic, New York Philharmonic.*

**phil|hel|lene** (fil hel′ēn), *n.* a friend or supporter of the Greeks, especially in their struggle against the Turks for independence. [< Greek *philéllēn* loving the Greeks < *phílos* loving + *Héllēn* Greek, Hellene]

**phil|hel|len|ic** (fil′hə len′ik, -lē′nik), *adj.* loving, friendly to, or supporting the cause of Greece or the Greeks, especially relating to national independence.

**phil|hel|len|ism** (fil hel′ə niz əm), *n.* philhellene spirit or principles.

**phil|hel|len|ist** (fil hel′ə nist, fil′hə lē′-), *n.* = philhellene.

**Phil. I.** or **Phil. Is.**, Philippine Islands.

**-philia**, *combining form.* a fondness, craving, or affinity for ___: *Aelurophilia = a fondness for cats.* [< Greek *philía* affection < *phílos* loving]

**phil|i|beg** (fil′ə beg), *n.* = filibeg.

**Phil|ip** (fil′əp), *n.* **1** one of Christ's twelve apostles (in the Bible, John 1:43-4). **2** one of the seven overseers of charitable works at Jerusalem, and afterwards a missionary; Philip the Evangelist (in the Bible, Acts 6:5; 8:5-40; 21:8-9).

**Phi|lip|pi|an** (fə lip′ē ən), *adj., n.* —*adj.* of or having to do with Philippi, a city of ancient Macedonia.
—*n.* a native or inhabitant of Philippi.

**Phi|lip|pi|ans** (fə lip′ē ənz), *n.pl.* (*singular in use*) one of the books of the New Testament, a letter from Paul to the early Christians of Philippi. *Abbr:* Phil.

**Phi|lip|pic** (fə lip′ik), *n.* **1** any one of several orations by Demosthenes denouncing King Philip II of Macedonia and attempting to arouse the Athenians to resist Philip's growing power. **2** any one of several orations by Cicero denouncing Mark Antony. [< Latin *Philippicus* < Greek *Philippikós* having to do with *Phíllipos* Philip (here, Philip of Macedonia)]

**phi|lip|pic** (fə lip′ik), *n.* a bitter attack in words: *With what satisfaction did I remember all Miss Debby Kittery's philippics against Ellery Davenport* (Harriet Beecher Stowe).

**Phil|ip|pine** (fil′ə pēn), *adj.* of or having something to do with the Philippines, a country of islands in the western Pacific, or its inhabitants. Also, **Filipine, Filipino.**

**Philippine mahogany**, **1** any one of several kinds of hardwood trees of the Philippines that are not true mahoganies, belonging to the same family as the gurjun. **2** the wood of any one of these trees, resembling and used in place of mahogany.

**Philippine Spanish**, the dialect of Spanish spoken by Spanish speakers in the Philippines.

**Philip the Evangelist**, = Philip (def. 2).

**Phi|lis|ti|a** (fə lis′tē ə), *n.* **1** a place where uncultured, commonplace people live. **2** the land of the ancient Philistines. [< Medieval Latin *Philistia;* see etym. under **Philistine**]

**Phi|lis|tine** (fə lis′tin; fil′ə stēn, -stīn), *n., adj.* —*n.* **1** (in the Bible) one of the warlike people in southwestern Palestine who attacked the Israelites many times: *He shall begin to deliver Israel out of the hand of the Philistines* (Judges 13:5). **2** Also, **philistine.** *Figurative.* a person who is commonplace in ideas and tastes; one who is indifferent to or contemptuous of poetry, music, the fine arts, and the like: *You are a Philistine, Henry: you have no romance in you* (George Bernard Shaw).
—*adj.* **1** of the Philistines: *Goliath, the Philistine champion.* **2** Also, **philistine.** *Figurative.* lacking culture; commonplace: *Byron ... had in him a cross of the true Philistine breed* (Algernon Charles Swinburne).
[(definition 1) < Late Latin *Philistīnī,* plural < Greek *Philistînoi* < Hebrew *pəlishtim;* (definition 2) < German *Philister,* adapted by Matthew Arnold]

**Phi|lis|tin|ism** or **phi|lis|tin|ism** (fə lis′tə niz əm, fil′ə stə niz′-), *n.* the character or views of uncultured, commonplace persons: *Philistinism! We have not the expression in English ... perhaps ... because we have so much of the thing* (Matthew Arnold).

**Phil|lips curve** (fil′əps), a curve showing a correlation between rates of unemployment and rates of inflation: *The Phillips curve ... lays it down that the rate at which wages rise is inversely proportional to the level of unemployment—that is, that the greater the pressure on the labour market (and hence the lower the level of unemployment), the faster the price of labour will rise* (Manchester Guardian Weekly). [< A.W.H. *Phillips,* born 1914, a British economist]

**Phillips screw**, a screw with two beveled slots in the head crossing each other at right angles to take greater pressure in driving. A Phillips screw is usually self-tapping.

**Phillips screwdriver**, a screwdriver with crossed beveled blades for driving a Phillips screw.

**Phil|lis** (fil′is), *n.* = Phyllis.

**phil|lu|men|ist** (fi lü′mə nist, fī-), *n.* a collector of matchbox labels. [< *phil-* + Latin *lūmen* light + English *-ist*]

**phil|lu|me|ny** (fi lü′mə nē, fī-), *n.* the hobby of a phillumenist.

**philo-**, *combining form.* loving; having an affection for: *Philoprogenitive = loving one's progeny.* Also, **phil-** before vowels. [< Greek *philo-* < *phílos* loving]

**phil|o|bib|lic** (fil′ə bib′lik), *adj.* fond of books; bibliophilous. [< Greek *philóbiblos* (< *phílos* loving + *biblos* book) + English *-ic*]

**phil|o|bib|list** (fil′ə bib′list), *n.* a lover of books; bibliophile.

**Phil|oc|te|tes** (fil′ok tē′tēz), *n. Greek Legend.* a Greek archer, hero in the Trojan War. He inherited the bow and arrow of Hercules from his father; only by means of this could Paris be shot and Troy destroyed. Bitten by a serpent on the way to the war, and obnoxious to his companions because of his wound, he was for some years abandoned on the uninhabited island of Lemnos, but later brought to Troy.

**phil|o|den|dron** (fil′ə den′drən), *n.* **1** a climbing evergreen plant with smooth (but tough), shiny leaves, often grown as a house plant. It is a tropical American plant that belongs to the arum family. There are several kinds of philodendron, comprising a genus of plants. See picture under **arum family.** **2** any one of certain related or similar plants. [< New Latin *Philodendron* the genus name < Greek *philódendron,* neuter of *philódendros* < *phílos* fond of + *déndron* tree (because it clings to trees)]

**phi|log|y|nist** (fə loj′ə nist), *n.* a lover or admirer of women.

**phi|log|y|nous** (fə loj′ə nəs), *adj.* loving women.

**phi|log|y|ny** (fə loj′ə nē), *n.* love of women. [< Greek *philogyniā* < *philogýnēs* loving women < *phílos* loving + *gynḗ* woman]

**philol.**, philology.

**phi|lol|o|ger** (fə lol′ə jər), *n. Archaic.* a philologist.

**phil|o|lo|gi|an** (fil′ə lō′jē ən), *n.* = philologist.

**phil|o|log|ic** (fil′ə loj′ik), *adj.* having to do with philology; concerned with the study of language. —**phil′o|log′i|cal|ly**, *adv.*

**phil|o|log|i|cal** (fil′ə loj′ə kəl), *adj.* = philologic.

**phi|lol|o|gist** (fə lol′ə jist), *n.* a person who studies philology: *The philologists of the nineteenth century succeeded in promoting the autonomy of linguistics as an independent discipline* (Simeon Potter).

**phil|o|logue** (fil′ə log, -lôg), *n.* = philologist.

**phi|lol|o|gy** (fə lol′ə jē), *n.* **1** an older name for linguistics; the science of language. **2** the study of literary and other records. **3** (formerly) literary or classical scholarship; the study of literature, including grammar, criticism, and etymology. [< Latin *philologia* < Greek *philologiā* < *philólogos* fond of words or discourse < *phílos* loving + *lógos* word, speech]

**phil|o|math** (fil′ə math), *n.* **1a** a lover of learning.

**b** a student, especially of mathematics or science. **2** *Obsolete.* an astrologer. [< Greek *philomathēs* fond of learning < *phílos* loving + *manthánein* learn]

**phil|o|math|ic** (fil′ə math′ik), *adj.* **1** devoted to learning. **2** *Obsolete.* astrological.

**phi|lom|a|thy** (fə lom′ə thē), *n.* love of learning.

**phil|o|mel** or **Phil|o|mel** (fil′ə mel), *n. Archaic.* the nightingale: *All night long sweet Philomel pours forth her ravishing, delightful song* (Tobias Smollett). [< Latin *philomela* < Greek *Philomêla* Philomela; nightingale < *phílos* loving + *mêlon* apple, fruit]

**Phil|o|me|la** (fil′ə mē′lə), *n.* **1** *Greek Mythology.* a princess who was turned into a nightingale and as a bird continued to lament the tragedy of her life. **2** *Poetic.* the nightingale.

**phil|o|pe|na** (fil′ə pē′nə), *n.* **1** a game involving the sharing of a nut with two kernels between two people, with the agreement that the one failing to keep some stated condition shall pay a forfeit. **2** the nut. **3** the forfeit. [American English < French, or Dutch *Philippine,* half-translation of *Philippchen,* mispronunciation of German *Vielliebchen* (literally) very dear one]

**phil|o|pro|ge|ne|i|ty** (fil′ə prō′jə nē′ə tē), *n.* love of one's offspring; philoprogenitiveness.

**phil|o|pro|gen|i|tive** (fil′ō prō jen′ə tiv), *adj.* **1** loving one's offspring; having to do with love of offspring. **2** inclined to produce many offspring; prolific. [< *philo-* + Latin *progenitus,* past participle of *progignere* to beget + English *-ive*] —**phil′o|pro|gen′i|tive|ness,** *n.*

**philos.,** philosophy.

**phil|o|sophe** (fil′ə zof′), *n.* **1** one of a group of French rationalist, humanistic, deistic, and often revolutionary philosophers of the 1700's, typified by Denis Diderot: *The intellectual life of Paris centered on ... the philosophes, who were presently to compile a great encyclopedia of human knowledge* (Atlantic). **2** a philosopher: *Madison was the last of the Virginia philosophes, the ultimate innocent who could seriously consult the Cabbala for the principles of good government* (Manchester Guardian). [< Old French *philosophe;* see etym. under **philosopher**]

**phi|los|o|pher** (fə los′ə fər), *n.* **1** a lover of wisdom; person who studies philosophy a great deal: *Our philosophers have not been slow to go beyond the ... dogma that all utterances other than statements of fact ... are literally meaningless* (London Times). **2** a person who has a system of philosophy: *Plato, the great Greek philosopher wrote of many of his theories of government in "The Republic."* **3a** a person who is calm and reasonable under hard conditions, accepting life and making the best of it: *There was never yet philosopher That could endure the toothache patiently* (Shakespeare). **b** a person who is guided in his life by principles which relate to man as a rational and social being: *To be a philosopher is not merely to have subtle thoughts, nor even to found a school, but so to love wisdom, as to live according to its dictates, a life of simplicity, independence, magnanimity, and trust* (Thoreau). **4** *Obsolete.* **a** an alchemist. **b** an expert in some other occult science. [< Anglo-French *philosofre,* Old French *philosophe,* learned borrowing from Latin *philosophus* < Greek *philósophos* lover of wisdom < *phílos* loving + *sophós* wise]

**philosophers' stone,** a substance believed by alchemists to have the power to change baser metals into gold or silver. It had, according to some, the power of prolonging life indefinitely and of curing all wounds and diseases.

**phil|o|soph|ic** (fil′ə sof′ik), *adj.* **1** of philosophy or philosophers: *Some scientian prejudices need superseding when applied without discrimination to problems essentially philosophic* (A. T. Macqueen). **2** knowing much about philosophy. **3** devoted to philosophy. **4** wise, calm, and reasonable: *to be philosophic in defeat. They were mostly scholarly, quiet men, of calm and philosophic temperament* (Harriet Beecher Stowe). —**phil′o|soph′i|cal|ly,** *adv.*

**phil|o|soph|i|cal** (fil′ə sof′ə kəl), *adj.* philosophic; like a philosopher.

**philosophical analysis,** = linguistic analysis.

**phi|los|o|phise** (fə los′ə fīz), *v.i., v.t.,* **-phised, -phis|ing.** *Especially British.* philosophize.

**phi|los|o|phism** (fə los′ə fiz əm), *n.* **1** the affectation of philosophy, especially sophistry. **2** a sophism.

**phi|los|o|phist** (fə los′ə fist), *n.* a person who philosophizes or speculates erroneously.

**phi|los|o|phize** (fə los′ə fīz), *v.,* **-phized, -phiz|ing.** —*v.i.* to think or reason as a philosopher does; try to understand and explain things: *to philosophize about life, death, mind, matter, and God.*
—*v.t.* to explain or treat philosophically. —**phi|los′o|phiz′er,** *n.*

**phi|los|o|phy** (fə los′ə fē), *n., pl.* **-phies. 1** the study of the truth or principles of all real knowledge; study of the most general causes and principles of the universe: *I regard philosophy then ... as the study which takes all knowledge for its province* (Henry Sidgwick). **2** an explanation or theory of the universe, especially the particular explanation or system of a philosopher: *the philosophy of Plato.* **3** a system for guiding life, such as a body of principles of conduct, religious beliefs, or traditions: *the philosophy of a New England Puritan.* **4** the broad general principles of a particular subject or field of activity: *the philosophy of history, the army's military philosophy, a design philosophy for aircraft.* **5** a calm and reasonable attitude; accepting things as they are and making the best of them; calmness: *That teacher has a good philosophy about children and so never gets upset.* **6** (originally) the love or pursuit of wisdom, in its broadest sense. [< Latin *philosophia* < Greek *philosophiā* love of wisdom < *philósophos* philosopher]

**Phil. Soc.,** **1** Philological Society (of London). **2** Philosophical Society (of America).

**phil|ter** or **phil|tre** (fil′tər), *n.* **1** a drug or magic potion which is supposed to make a person fall in love; love potion: *He is a veritable necromancer, equipped with philters and elixirs of wondrous potency* (Harper's). **2** a drug or potion to produce some magical effect: *Tell me now, fairy ... can't you give me a charm, or a philtre, or something of that sort, to make me a handsome man?* (Charlotte Brontë). [< French *philtre,* learned borrowing from Latin *philtrum* < Greek *phíltron* love charm < *phileîn* to love]

**Phil. Trans.,** Philosophical Transactions (of the Royal Society of London).

**phi meson,** a highly unstable and short-lived elementary particle with a large mass and zero charge.

**Phin|e|us** (fin′ē əs, fī′nüs), *n. Greek Legend.* the blind king of Thrace who guided the Argonauts through the dangerous clashing rocks by sending a dove before them.

**phi phenomenon,** *Psychology.* **1a** the perception of movement in a moving object. **b** the movement perceived in such an object. **2** the apparent movement perceived when several pictures or other stationary visual stimuli are presented successively at very brief intervals.

**phiz** (fiz), *n., pl.* **phiz|es.** *Slang.* face; countenance: *There was no mistaking that tanned, genial phiz of his* (Thomas Bailey Aldrich). [short for *physiognomy*]

**phle|bi|tis** (fli bī′tis), *n.* inflammation of a vein. [< Greek *phléps, phlebós* vein + English *-itis*]

**phle|bol|o|gist** (fli bol′ə jist), *n.* a person skilled in phlebology.

**phle|bol|o|gy** (fli bol′ə jē), *n.* the study of veins. [< Greek *phléps, phlebós* vein + English *-logy*]

**phleb|o|scle|ro|sis** (fleb′ō skli rō′sis), *n.* a thickening and hardening of the wall of a vein. [< Greek *phléps, phlebós* vein + English *sclerosis*]

**phleb|o|scle|rot|ic** (fleb′ō skli rot′ik), *adj.* having to do with phlebosclerosis.

**phle|bot|o|mist** (fli bot′ə mist), *n.* **1** a person who treats patients by phlebotomy. **2** a technician who is in charge of blood transfusion or collection at a hospital or blood bank.

**phle|bot|o|mize** (fli bot′ə mīz), *v.t., v.i.,* **-mized, -miz|ing.** to practice phlebotomy; bleed.

**phle|bot|o|my** (fli bot′ə mē), *n., pl.* **-mies. 1** the opening of a vein to let blood; bleeding as a therapeutic device; venesection. **2** the transfusion or collection of blood, as at a blood bank. [< Late Latin *phlebotomia* < Greek *phlebotomiā,* ultimately < *phléps, phlebós* blood vessel + *témnein* to cut]

**Phleg|e|thon** (fleg′ə thon, flej′-), *n. Greek Mythology.* the river of fire, one of the five rivers of Hades. [< Latin *Phlegethon* < Greek *Phlegéthōn,* present participle of *phlegéthein* to burn, blaze]

**phlegm** (flem), *n.* **1** the thick mucous discharge from the nose and throat that accompanies a cold or other respiratory disease. It is often an abnormally heavy discharge and is composed of mucus secreted by the mucous membranes of the respiratory passages. **2** sluggish disposition or temperament; indifference: *Michael Redgrave as the air marshal is just the right mixture of phlegm and haw* (Time). **3** coolness; calmness: *The French government's only sustainers of phlegm and order appear to be the Foreign Legion* (New Yorker). *The patience of the people was creditable to their phlegm* (George Meredith). **4** one of the four humors, supposedly a somewhat cold, viscous substance in the body, thought in ancient and medieval times to cause sluggishness. [< Old French *fleugme,* learned borrowing from Late Latin *phlegma* < Greek *phlégma* moist humor (resulting from heat) < *phlégein* to burn]

**phleg|mat|ic** (fleg mat′ik), *adj.* **1** sluggish; indifferent; not easily aroused to feeling or action; apathetic. **2** not easily excited; cool; calm: *He is phlegmatic; he never seems to get excited about anything.* **3** *Obsolete.* **a** of the nature of phlegm considered as one of the four humors. **b** abounding in phlegm. **c** producing phlegm. [< Late Latin *phlegmaticus* < Greek *phlegmatikós* full of phlegm < *phlégma* phlegm] —**phleg|mat′i|cal|ly,** *adv.*

**phleg|mat|i|cal** (fleg mat′ə kəl), *adj.* = phlegmatic.

**phleg|ma|tism** (fleg′mə tiz əm), *n.* phlegmatic character; apathy.

**phleg|mon** (fleg′mon), *n. Medicine.* inflammation of the connective tissue, especially the subcutaneous connective tissue. [< Latin *phlegmon* < Greek *phlegmonê* inflammation < *phlégein* to burn]

**phleg|mo|nous** (fleg′mə nəs), *adj.* **1** having to do with a phlegmon. **2** like a phlegmon.

**phlegm|y** (flem′ē), *adj.* **1** like phlegm. **2** characterized by phlegm. **3** = phlegmatic.

**phlob|a|phene** (flob′ə fēn), *n. Chemistry.* any one of various reddish-brown substances found in the bark of the oak or in other material containing tannin. [< Greek *phlóos* bark + *baphê* dyeing, dye + English *-ene*]

**phlo|em** or **phlo|ëm** (flō′em), *n.* the tissue in a plant or tree through which the sap containing dissolved food materials passes downward to the stems and roots; bast: *The phloem carries away the sugars and proteins which are synthesized there* (Fred W. Emerson). See picture under **bark**[1]. [< German *Phloem* < Greek *phlóos* bark, (human) skin; (originally) a swelling, growth < *phleîn* be full of, abound (in)]

**phloem necrosis,** a disease of elm trees in which the phloem is destroyed and the leaves turn yellow and fall, caused by a virus carried by the leaf hopper.

**phloem ray,** a ray or plate of phloem between two medullary rays.

**phlo|gis|tic** (flō jis′tik), *adj.* **1** *Medicine.* inflammatory. **2** *Old Chemistry.* having to do with or relating to phlogiston. **3** *Obsolete.* **a** burning; fiery. **b** expressive of passionate anger; very heated.

**phlo|gis|ton** (flō jis′tən; *British, also* flō gis′tən), *n.* a supposed element causing inflammability, once thought to exist in all things that burn. [< New Latin *phlogiston,* adjective < Greek *phlogistón,* neuter of *phlogistós* inflammable, ultimately < *phlóx, phlogós* flame]

**phlog|o|pite** (flog′ə pīt), *n. Mineralogy.* a magnesium mica, usually of a brownish-yellow or brownish-red color. [< German *Phlogopit* < Greek *phlogōpós* fiery (< *phlóx, phlogós* flame + *ôps, ōpós* face, look) + German *-it* -ite[1]]

**phlo|go|sis** (flə gō′sis), *n. Medicine.* inflammation, especially of external parts of the body. [< New Latin *phlogosis* < Greek *phlógōsis* < *phlóx, phlogós* flame]

**phlo|rhi|zin** (flə rē′zin), *n.* = phlorizin.

**phlo|rid|zin** (flə rid′zin), *n.* = phlorizin.

**phlor|i|zin** (flôr′ə zin, flor′-; flə rī′-), *n.* a bitter glucoside crystallizing in silky white needles, obtained from the bark of the root of the apple, pear, plum, and cherry, formerly used medicinally as a tonic and antimalarial. *Formula:* $C_{21}H_{24}O_{10}$ [< Greek *phlóos* bark (see etym. under **phloem**) + *rhíza* root + English *-in*]

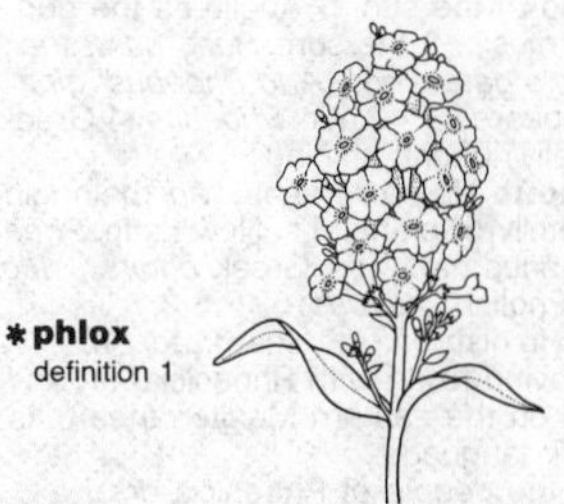

*** phlox**
definition 1

*** phlox** (floks), *n.* **1** a common garden plant that has showy flower clusters of various colors. It is one of several North American herbs that comprise a genus of plants. Phlox either spreads by creeping or stands erect to a height of up to five feet. *By and large, however, phlox is one of the most satisfactory garden plants* (New York Times). **2** the flower of any of these plants. [< New Latin *Phlox* the genus name < Latin *phlox* < Greek *phlóx* a kind of plant; (literally) flame]

**phlox|in** (flok′sin), *n.* a purple coal-tar dye,

**Pronunciation Key:** hat, āge, cãre, fär; let, ēqual, tėrm; it, īce; hot, ōpen, ôrder; oil, out; cup, pu̇t, rüle; child; long; thin; ᴛʜen; zh, measure; ə represents **a** in about, **e** in taken, **i** in pencil, **o** in lemon, **u** in circus.

resembling eosin. [< Greek *phlóx* flame + English *-in*]

**phlyc|te|na** or **phlyc|tae|na** (flik tē′nə), *n., pl.* **-nae** (-nē). *Medicine.* a small vesicle or blister. [< New Latin *phlyctaena* < Greek *phlýktaina* blister < *phlýein* to swell]

**phlyc|te|nule** (flik′tə nyül, flik ten′yül), *n. Medicine.* a minute vesicle or blister, especially upon the conjunctiva or cornea of the eye. [< New Latin *phlyctaenula* (diminutive) < *phlyctaena*]

**Ph.M.**, Master of Philosophy.

**-phobe**, *combining form.* a person who has fear, aversion, or hatred toward ____: *Anglophobe = a person who fears or hates England or the English.* [< French *-phobe,* learned borrowing from Latin *-phobus* < Greek *-phóbos* fearing < *phóbos* panic, fear]

**pho|bi|a** (fō′bē ə), *n.* a persistent, abnormal, or irrational fear of a certain thing or group of things: *a phobia of water. She has a phobia about snakes. Sigmund Freud, the founder of psychoanalysis, thought that in phobia the thing feared served as a symbol for some other fear* (George A. Ulett). [< *-phobia*]

**-phobia**, *combining form.* fear, hatred, or dread of ____: *Francophobia = fear of the French or France. Claustrophobia = fear of enclosed rooms or narrow places.* [< Greek *-phobiā* < *phóbos* panic, fear]

**pho|bic** (fō′bik), *adj.* **1** having or characterized by a morbid or insane fear. **2** of or having to do with a morbid or insane fear.

**Pho|bos** (fō′bəs, fob′əs), *n.* the inner satellite of Mars, about eleven miles in diameter from pole to pole. It is the only satellite yet discovered that revolves around its planet faster than the planet rotates. [< New Latin *Phobos* < Greek *Phóbos* a son of Mars < *phóbos* fear]

**Pho|cian** (fō′shən), *adj., n.* **—*adj.*** of or having to do with Phocis, a region in central Greece. **—*n.*** a native or inhabitant of Phocis.

**pho|cine** (fō′sīn, -sin), *adj.* **1** of or having to do with seals. **2** of or belonging to the subfamily comprising the typical seals. [< New Latin *Phocinae* the subfamily name < Latin *phōca* < Greek *phṓkē* seal]

**pho|co|me|li|a** (fō′kə mē′lē ə), *n.* a congenital absence or incomplete development of the arms or legs, the hands or feet being attached close to the body; seal limb. [< Greek *phōkē* seal + *mélos* limb]

**Phoe|be** (fē′bē), *n.* **1** *Greek Mythology.* the goddess of the moon. Phoebe was also called Artemis by the Greeks and Diana by the Romans. **2** the moon. [< Latin *Phoebe* < Greek *Phoíbē,* feminine of *Phoîbos* Phoebus]

**phoe|be** (fē′bē), *n.* a small American bird with a grayish-brown back, a yellowish-white breast, and a low crest on the head. Phoebes are flycatchers, found especially in eastern North America. There are several kinds. [American English; earlier, *phebe,* imitative of the bird's song; spelling later adapted to *Phoebe,* proper name]

**Phoe|be|an** (fi bē′ən), *adj.* **1** of or having to do with Phoebus or Apollo as the god of poetry. **2** characteristic of Phoebus or Apollo as the god of poetry.

**phoebe bird**, = phoebe.

**Phoe|bus** (fē′bəs), *n.* **1** *Greek Mythology.* **a** Apollo, the god of the sun. **b** Apollo as the god of poetry and music. **2** the sun: *Hark, hark! the lark at heaven's gate sings, And Phoebus' gins arise* (Shakespeare). [< Latin *Phoebus* < Greek *Phoîbos* (literally) bright, shining]

**phoe|ni|ca|ceous** (fē′nə kā′shəs), *adj.* belonging to the palm family of plants. [< New Latin *Phoenix, -icis* the genus name (< Greek *phoînix, -īkos* date-palm) + English *-aceous*]

**Phoe|ni|cian** (fə nish′ən, -nē′shən), *adj., n.* **—*adj.*** of or having to do with Phoenicia, an ancient kingdom on the eastern Mediterranean, its people, or their language.
**—*n.*** **1** one of the people of Phoenicia or of a Phoenician colony: *The invention of the alphabet by the Phoenicians more than three thousand years ago was one of the greatest single contributions to the cultural development of mankind* (New York Times). **2** the extinct Semitic language of Phoenicia.

**Phoe|ni|cis** (fi nī′sis), *n.* genitive of **Phoenix**.

**phoe|nix** (fē′niks), *n.* **1** a mythical bird, the only one of its kind, said to live 500 or many thousands of years, to burn itself on a funeral pyre of herbs and to rise again from a small worm in the ashes, fresh and beautiful, for another long life. It is often used as a symbol of immortality. **2** *Figurative.* that which rises from the ashes of its predecessor. Also, **phenix**. [Old English *fenix* < unrecorded Medieval Latin *phenix,* variant of Latin *phoenix, -īcis* < Greek *phoînix, -īkos*]

**Phoe|nix** (fē′niks), *n., genitive* **Phoe|ni|cis**. a southern constellation.

**phon** (fon), *n.* the unit for measuring the level of loudness of sound, especially of complex sound: *A 60-decibel sound with a frequency of 1,000 vibrations a second has a loudness of 60 phons* (Robert T. Beyer). [< Greek *phōnḗ* a sound]

**phon-**, *combining form.* the form of **phono-** before vowels, as in *phonic.*

**phon.**, phonetics.

**pho|nas|the|ni|a** (fō′nəs thē′nē ə), *n.* weakness of the voice from fatigue.

**pho|nate** (fō′nāt), *v.t., v.i.,* **-nat|ed, -nat|ing.** to utter (speech sounds); sound vocally.

**pho|na|tion** (fō nā′shən), *n.* **1** the production or utterance of vocal sound, usually as distinguished from articulation. **2** vocal utterance; voice production.

**phon|au|to|graph** (fōn ô′tə graf, -gräf), *n.* an early automatic apparatus for indicating the vibrations of sound graphically, having a membrane set in vibration by sound waves and having a stylus attached which makes a tracing on a revolving cylinder.

**phon|au|to|graph|ic** (fōn ô′tə graf′ik), *adj.* of or having to do with a phonautograph.

**phone**[1] (fōn), *n., v.t., v.i.,* **phoned, phon|ing.** *Informal.* telephone. [American English; short for *telephone*]

**phone**[2] (fōn), *n. Phonetics.* a speech sound: ... [*the linguistic scientist*] *begins by breaking up the flow of speech into minimum sound-units, or phones* (W. Nelson Francis). [< Greek *phōnḗ* voice, sound]

**-phone**, *combining form.* sound, as in *megaphone, microphone, saxophone, xylophone.* [< Greek *phōnḗ* a sound]

**phone-in** (fōn′in′), *n.* a radio or television program centered around people who call the studio by telephone to ask questions or air opinions.

**pho|ne|mat|ic** (fō′nə mat′ik), *adj.* = phonemic.

**pho|ne|mat|ics** (fō′nə mat′iks), *n.* = phonemics.

**pho|neme** (fō′nēm), *n.* **1** *Linguistics.* one of a group of distinctive sounds that make up the words of a language; the smallest significant unit of speech in a language. The words *cat* and *bat* are distinguished by their initial phonemes /k/ and /b/. A phoneme comprises several slightly different sounds (allophones) the differences between which are not meaningful. The *p* in *pit* and the *p* in *ship,* though differing slightly in pronunciation, belong to the one phoneme /p/. *And one contrast anywhere in the language is enough to establish separate phonemes elsewhere in the language* (George P. Faust). **2** *Obsolete.* phone[2]. [< French *phonème* < Greek *phṓnēma* a sound < *phōneîn* to sound < *phōnḗ* a sound]

**pho|ne|mic** (fō nē′mik, fə-), *adj.* **1** of or having to do with phonemics: *a phonemic analysis of speech sounds.* **2** having to do with or involving phonemes: *The difference between "p" and "b" is phonemic in English.* **—pho|ne′mi|cal|ly,** *adv.*

**pho|ne|mics** (fō nē′miks, fə-), *n.* the branch of linguistics dealing with phonemes: ... *phonemics is phonetics systematized* (Simeon Potter).

**phone phreak** (frēk), *Informal.* a person who tampers illegally with the telephone to make free calls: *Thirty million telephone calls were monitored ... to trap US phone phreaks* (New Scientist).

**phonet.**, phonetics.

**pho|net|ic** (fō net′ik, fə-), *adj.* **1** of or having to do with sounds made with the voice. Phonetic exercises are drills in pronunciation. **2a** representing sounds made with the voice; indicating pronunciation. Phonetic symbols are used to show pronunciation. We use ō as the phonetic symbol of *o* in *photo.* **b** of or having to do with phonetics; having each sound represented by one letter and each letter represent one sound. [< New Latin *phoneticus* < Greek *phōnētikós* vocal < *phōnētós* utterable < *phōneîn* to speak < *phōnḗ* a sound]

**pho|net|i|cal** (fō net′ə kəl, fə-), *adj.* = phonetic.

**pho|net|i|cal|ly** (fō net′ə klē, fə-), *adv.* in a phonetic manner; as regards the sound and not the spelling of words.

**phonetic alphabet**, a set of characters or symbols for transcribing speech sounds, in which each character or symbol represents one distinct sound.

**pho|ne|ti|cian** (fō′nə tish′ən), *n.* an expert in phonetics.

**pho|net|i|cist** (fō net′ə sist), *n.* = phonetician.

**pho|net|i|cize** (fō net′ə sīz), *v.t.,* **-cized, -ciz|ing.** to represent or spell phonetically: [*He*] *had made a pleasant speech to the company carefully phoneticized in Russian* (London Times).

**pho|net|ics** (fō net′iks, fə-), *n.* **1** the science dealing with sounds made in speech and the art of pronunciation. Phonetics is a branch of linguistics. Phonetics is concerned with the production of these speech sounds by the articulating organs of the speaker, the sound waves in which they result, and the auditory effect they produce on the hearer. **2** the body of speech sounds of any one language, their manner of articulation, and their relation to one another. **3** the application of the science of speech sounds to the learning of languages.

**pho|ne|tism** (fō′nə tiz əm), *n.* the use of a phonetic system of writing or spelling.

**pho|ne|tist** (fō′nə tist), *n.* **1** = phonetician. **2** a supporter or user of phonetic spelling.

**pho|ney** (fō′nē), *adj.,* **-ni|er, -ni|est,** *n., pl.* **-neys,** *v.t.,* **-neyed, -ney|ing.** = phony.

**pho|ney|ness** (fō′nē nis), *n.* = phoniness.

**phon|gyi** (pōn′jē, pun′-), *n.* = pongyi.

**pho|ni|at|rics** (fō′nē at′riks), *n.* the treatment of speech defects.

**phon|ic** (fon′ik, fō′nik), *adj.* **1** of or having to do with sound. **2** of sounds made in speech; phonetic: *The phonic system of the language he speaks is quite different from the system ... which the reading primers use* (Harper's). **3** = voiced. [< Greek *phōnikós,* for *phōnētikós* vocal, ultimately < *phōnḗ* a sound]

**phon|ics** (fon′iks, fō′niks), *n.* **1** a method of teaching reading by the association of letters and combinations of letters with their appropriate speech sounds; simplified phonetics for teaching reading. **2** the science of sound; acoustics. **3** *Obsolete.* phonetics. [< Greek *phōnḗ* a sound]

**pho|ni|ly** (fō′nə lē), *adv. Informal.* in a phony manner; falsely.

**pho|ni|ness** (fō′nē nis), *n. Informal.* phony quality or character; sham.

**phono-**, *combining form.* sound; sounds: *Phonology = the system of sounds* (*used in a language*). Also, **phon-** before vowels. [< Greek *phōnḗ* sound]

**pho|no|an|gi|og|ra|phy** (fō′nō an′jē og′rə fē), *n.* examination of blood vessels by monitoring the sound made by the bloodstream: *The sound of blood flowing through the vessels is picked up by a sensitive microphone, recorded on magnetic tape, and analyzed by phonoangiography—a new method of locating and estimating size of arterial obstructions* (Michael E. DeBakey). [< *phono-* + *angiography*]

**pho|no|car|di|o|gram** (fō′nō kär′dē ə gram), *n.* the record made by a phonocardiograph.

**pho|no|car|di|o|graph** (fō′nō kär′dē ə graf, -gräf), *n.* a device that graphically represents on a photographic film the sounds of the heart: *Working with the electrocardiograph, ... the phonocardiograph is of particular value in detecting types of heart disease curable by surgery* (Family Weekly).

**pho|no|car|di|og|ra|phy** (fō′nō kär′dē og′rə fē), *n.* the graphic recording of the sounds of the heart by means of a phonocardiograph: *His problem was to find a way of quietening pregnant women so that the technique of phonocardiography could be used to record the heart-beats of the unborn child* (New Scientist).

**pho|no|disc** (phō′nə disk), *n.* a phonograph record.

**Pho|no|film** (fō′nə film′), *n. Trademark.* an early form of sound track invented by Lee De Forest, an American inventor.

**pho|no|gram** (fō′nə gram), *n.* **1** a character or symbol representing a single speech sound, syllable, or word. **2** *Obsolete.* a phonograph record.

**pho|no|gram|ic** or **pho|no|gram|mic** (fō′nə-gram′ik), *adj.* **1** like a phonogram. **2** *Obsolete.* consisting of phonograph records.

**pho|no|graph** (fō′nə graf, -gräf), *n.* **1** an instrument that reproduces the sounds from records; record player. As the record turns, a special needle picks up its sounds, which are heard on a loudspeaker. **2** *Obsolete.* an instrument that records and reproduces sounds, usually on a wax cylinder or disk. [American English < *phono-* + *graph*]

**pho|nog|ra|pher** (fō nog′rə fər), *n.* **1** a person who uses phonography; a shorthand writer (in Pitman's system). **2** = phonetist.

**pho|no|graph|ic** (fō′nə graf′ik), *adj.* **1** of a phonograph. **2** produced by a phonograph. **3** of phonography. **4** of phonograms. **—pho′no-graph′i|cal|ly,** *adv.*

**phonograph needle**, the small, pointed piece of metal, sapphire, diamond, or other material in a phonograph which receives and transmits the vibrations from the record.

**phonograph record**, a thin disk, now usually of vinyl or other plastic, on the surface of which sound is transcribed in narrow grooves. The pitch of the sound picked up by the needle is controlled by microscopic variations in the grooves.

**pho|nog|ra|phy** (fō nog′rə fē), *n.* **1** the art of writing according to sound; phonetic spelling. **2** phonetic shorthand, especially the phonetic shorthand devised by Sir Isaac Pitman in 1837. **3** *Obsolete.* the study of speech sounds and their phonetic transcription.

**pho|no|lite** (fō′nə līt), *n.* any one of various volcanic rocks which ring when struck, composed of orthoclase, nephelite, and certain other minerals; clinkstone.

**pho|no|lit|ic** (fō′nə lit′ik), *adj.* **1** having to do with phonolite. **2** consisting of phonolite.

**pho|no|log|ic** (fō′nə loj′ik), *adj.* of, having to do with, or relating to phonology. —**pho′no|log′i|cal|ly,** *adv.*

**pho|no|log|i|cal** (fō′nə loj′ə kəl), *adj.* = phonologic.

**pho|nol|o|gist** (fō nol′ə jist), *n.* an expert in phonology: *The phonologist will begin his task by making numerous phonetic transcriptions ... before attempting to construct his phonemic pattern* (Simeon Potter).

**pho|nol|o|gy** (fō nol′ə jē), *n.* **1** the system of sounds used in a language: *A linguist examining the phonology of a language can identify the points at which divergences of interpretation can be expected* (H. A. Gleason, Jr.). **2** the study of sounds of a language, their history and changes: *Phonology deals with the phonemes and sequences of phonemes* (H. A. Gleason, Jr.).

**phon|o|ma|ni|a** (fon′ə mā′nē ə), *n.* a mania for murder or killing. [< New Latin *phonomania* < Greek *phónos* murder, slaughter + English *mania*]

**pho|nom|e|ter** (fō nom′ə tər), *n.* an instrument for measuring the pitch (frequency) or volume (intensity) of sound.

**pho|no|met|ric** (fō′nə met′rik), *adj.* **1** having to do with a phonometer. **2** having to do with the measurement of sound.

**pho|nom|e|try** (fō nom′ə trē), *n.* the measurement of sound with a phonometer.

**pho|non** (fō′non), *n.* a particle or quantum of thermal energy in the form of sound or vibration in a crystal lattice, analogous to the photon: *When electrons penetrate a crystal they set up units of vibrations called phonons* (Herbert Kondo). [< *phon-* + *-on*]

**pho|no|phore** (fō′nə fôr, -fōr), *n.* **1** an apparatus which permits telephoning over a telegraph wire without interfering with the current by which telegraph messages are simultaneously transmitted. **2** a system using such an apparatus.

**pho|no|pore** (fō′nə pôr, -pōr), *n.* = phonophore.

**pho|no|re|cep|tion** (fō′nō ri sep′shən), *n.* the reception of sound by a sense organ.

**pho|no|re|cep|tor** (fō′nō ri sep′tər), *n.* a sense organ which is sensitive to sound.

**pho|no|rec|ord** (fō′nə rek′ərd), *n.* = phonodisc.

**pho|no|scope** (fō′nə skōp), *n.* **1** an instrument for indicating or representing sound vibrations in a visible form. **2** an instrument for testing the quality of musical strings.

**pho|no|type** (fō′nə tīp), *n.* **1** a character or letter of a phonetic alphabet adapted for printing. **2** phonetic print or type.

**pho|no|typ|ic** (fō′nə tip′ik), *adj.* having to do with or relating to phonotype or phonotypy. —**pho′no|typ′i|cal|ly,** *adv.*

**pho|no|typ|i|cal** (fō′nə tip′ə kəl), *adj.* = phonotypic.

**pho|no|typ|ist** (fō′nə tī′pist), *n.* an advocate or user of phonotypy.

**pho|no|ty|py** (fō′nə tī′pē), *n.* a system of phonetic shorthand, devised by Sir Isaac Pitman; phonography.

**pho|ny** (fō′nē), *adj.*, **-ni|er, -ni|est,** *n., pl.* **-nies,** *v.,* **-nied, -ny|ing.** *Informal.* —*adj.* not genuine; counterfeit; fake: *I ... gave the sucker my name and address* (*both phony of course*) *and promised to send two hundred dollars as soon as I got home* (Saturday Evening Post). **SYN:** sham, false, bogus, spurious.
—*n.* a fake; pretender: *He says he is a very important man but he is nothing but a phony. The twenty-dollar bill was a phony.*
—*v.t.* to make phony; counterfeit; fake; pretend: *But when they talk like McCarthy,* [*they*] *do not merely exaggerate their case, they phony it* (Life).
Also, **phoney.**
[American English; apparently, earlier *fawney* a gilt brass ring used by swindlers, perhaps < Irish *fáinne* ring]

**pho|ny|ness** (fō′nē nis), *n.* = phoniness.

**phoo|ey** (fü′ē), *interj. U.S. Slang.* an exclamation of scorn or contempt; bah; pfui: *Ruben and I are pals. All those stories about a fight—phooey* (New York Times).

**pho|rate** (fôr′āt, fōr′-), *n.* a highly toxic organophosphorous compound used as a systemic insecticide: *Systemic insecticides such as phorate ... while killing pests at the same time often harm the seeds and reduce the proportion which germinate* (New Scientist). *Formula:* $C_7H_{17}O_2PS_3$ [< *ph*(osph)*or*(odithio)*ate,* a part of its chemical name]

**-phore,** *combining form.* a thing that bears, or carries ___: *Oophore = a structure that bears eggs. Semaphore = an apparatus that carries signaling devices.* [< Greek *-phóros* < *phérein* to bear, carry]

**phor|e|sy** (fôr′ə sē), *n. Zoology.* the nonparasitic transportation of one species by another, especially among arthropods: *This mode of travel, known as phoresy, seems to be a response to specific conditions of the environment* (Scientific American). [< New Latin *phoresia* < Greek *phórēsis* a carrying < *phérein* to carry]

**phos|gene** (fos′jēn), *n.* a colorless, poisonous liquid or gas with a suffocating odor, formed by the reaction of carbon monoxide and chlorine, and used in chemical warfare and also in organic synthesis; carbonyl chloride: *The main war gases available toward the end of the last war were phosgene, mustard gas, and lewisite* (James P. Baxter). *Formula:* $COCl_2$ [< Greek *phôs, phōtós* light[1] + *-genēs* -gen (because originally obtained by action of sunlight on chlorine and carbonic oxide)]

**phos|ge|nite** (fos′jə nīt), *n.* a mineral, a chloride and carbonate of lead, occurring in white or yellowish tetragonal crystals, and playing a role in bone formation. *Formula:* $Pb_2Cl_2CO_3$

**phos|pha|gen** (fos′fə jən), *n.* = phosphocreatine.

**phos|pha|tase** (fos′fə tās), *n.* an enzyme which splits carbohydrate and phosphate compounds.

**phos|phate** (fos′fāt), *n.* **1** a salt or ester of phosphoric acid. It is present in rocks and in plant and animal remains. Phosphates are necessary to the growth of plants and animals and have extensive use as fertilizers. Bread contains phosphates. **2** a fertilizer containing such salts. **3** a drink of carbonated water flavored with fruit syrup, and containing a little phosphoric acid. [< French *phosphate* < *phosph*(*ore*) phosphorus + *-ate* -ate[2]]

**phosphate rock,** a sedimentary rock that contains calcium phosphate. It is, when crushed, a primary source of phosphorus in agriculture.

**phos|phat|ic** (fos fat′ik), *adj.* **1** of or containing phosphoric acid or phosphates. **2** characterized by phosphoric acid or phosphates.

**phos|pha|tide** (fos′fə tīd, -tid), *n.* any fatty substance of a group present in cellular tissue and consisting of esters of phosphoric acid; phospholipid.

**phos|pha|tid|ic** (fos′fə tid′ik), *adj.* of, having to do with, or formed from phosphatides: *phosphatidic acid.*

**phos|pha|ti|za|tion** (fos′fə tə zā′shən), *n.* **1** the act of phosphatizing. **2** the fact or condition of being phosphatized.

**phos|pha|tize** (fos′fə tīz), *v.t.*, **-tized, -tiz|ing.** **1** to treat with phosphates. **2** to reduce to the form of a phosphate or phosphates.

**phos|pha|tu|ri|a** (fos′fə tůr′ē ə, -tyůr′-), *n. Medicine.* an abnormal condition indicated by an excess of phosphates in the urine.

**phos|pha|tu|ric** (fos′fə tůr′ik, -tyůr′-), *adj. Medicine.* of or having to do with phosphaturia.

**phos|phene** (fos′fēn), *n.* a luminous image, as of rings of light, produced by mechanical excitation of the retina, as by pressing the eyeball when the lid is closed. [< French *phosphène* < Greek *phôs, phōtós* light[1] + *phaínein* to shine, make appear]

**phos|phid** (fos′fid), *n.* = phosphide.

**phos|phide** (fos′fīd, -fid), *n.* a compound of phosphorus with a basic element or radical.

**phos|phin** (fos′fin), *n.* = phosphine.

**phos|phine** (fos′fēn, -fin), *n.* **1** a colorless, extremely poisonous gas, a phosphorus hydride, with an odor like that of garlic or decaying fish. It is spontaneously inflammable in air. *Formula:* $PH_3$ **2** any one of various organic compounds derived from this gas. **3** an acridine dye.

**phos|phin|ic** (fos fin′ik), *adj.* **1** of or having to do with phosphine. **2** derived from phosphine.

**phos|phite** (fos′fīt), *n.* a salt or ester of phosphorous acid. [< *phosph*(orus) + *-ite*]

**phos|pho|cre|a|tin** (fos′fō krē′ə tin), *n.* = phosphocreatine.

**phos|pho|cre|a|tine** (fos′fō krē′ə tēn, -tin), *n.* an energy-giving substance in muscle tissue, consisting of creatine and phosphoric acid. *Formula:* $C_4H_{10}N_3O_5P$

**phos|pho|gly|cer|ic acid** (fos′fō gli ser′ik, -glis′ər-), a phosphate of glyceric acid in two isomeric forms, that is an intermediate compound in carbohydrate metabolism.

**phos|pho|lip|id** (fos′fō lip′id, -lī′pid), *n.* = phosphatide.

**phos|pho|ni|um** (fos fō′nē əm), *n.* a univalent radical ($PH_4$-), analogous to ammonium.

**phos|pho|pro|tein** (fos′fō prō′tēn, -tē in), *n.* any one of a group of proteins, as caseinogen, consisting of a simple protein combined with some phosphorus compound other than nucleic acid or lecithin.

**phos|pho|py|ru|vic acid** (fos′fō pī rü′vik, -pi-), a phosphate of pyruvic acid that is an intermediate compound in the reversible conversion of glycogen to lactic acid.

**phos|phor** (fos′fər), *n., adj.* —*n.* **1** a substance which gives off light when exposed to certain types of energy, such as ultraviolet rays or X rays. Phosphor is widely used in fluorescent lamps and television tubes. **2** *Obsolete.* phosphorus.
—*adj. Obsolete.* phosphorescent.
[< New Latin *phosphorus* phosphorus]

**Phos|phor** (fos′fər), *n.* the morning star; Venus (when appearing at or just before sunrise). [< Latin *phōsphorus;* see etym. under **phosphorus**]

**phos|pho|rate** (fos′fə rāt), *v.t.*, **-rat|ed, -rat|ing.** to combine or impregnate with phosphorus.

**phosphor bronze,** a hard, tough bronze containing less than one per cent of phosphorus, used especially in marine propellers and fittings.

**phos|pho|resce** (fos′fə res′), *v.i.*, **-resced, -resc|ing.** to be luminous without noticeable heat.

**phos|pho|res|cence** (fos′fə res′əns), *n.* **1** the act or process of giving out light without burning or by very slow burning that seems not to give out heat: *The phosphoresence of fireflies is also called bioluminescence.* **2** the light given out in this way. **3** the property of a substance that causes this. **4** *Physics.* light given out by a substance as a result of the absorption of certain rays, such as X rays or ultraviolet rays, and continuing for a period of time after the substance has ceased to be exposed to these rays.

**phos|pho|res|cent** (fos′fə res′ənt), *adj.* showing phosphorescence: *A phosphorescent jewel gives off its glow and color in the dark and loses its beauty in the light of day* (Atlantic). —**phos′pho|res′cent|ly,** *adv.*

**phos|pho|ret|ed** or **phos|pho|ret|ted** (fos′fə ret′id), *adj.* = phosphureted.

**phos|phor|ic** (fos fôr′ik, -for′-), *adj.* having to do with or containing phosphorus, especially with a valence of five.

**phosphoric acid, 1** a colorless, odorless acid containing phosphorus, obtained chiefly by the decomposition of phosphates, and used in making fertilizers, and as a reagent; orthophosphoric acid. *Formula:* $H_3PO_4$ **2** = metaphosphoric acid. **3** = pyrophosphoric acid.

**phos|pho|rism** (fos′fə riz əm), *n.* chronic phosphorus poisoning.

**phos|pho|rite** (fos′fə rīt), *n.* **1** a mineral, a noncrystallized variety of apatite. **2** any variety of phosphate rock.

**phos|pho|rit|ic** (fos′fə rit′ik), *adj.* of or having to do with phosphorite.

**phos|pho|rol|y|sis** (fos′fə rol′ə sis), *n.* chemical decomposition in which the elements of phosphoric acid are taken up by a compound. [< *phosphor*(ic acid) + *-olysis,* as in *hydrolysis*]

**phos|pho|ro|lyt|ic** (fos′fə rə lit′ik), *adj.* of or producing phosphorolysis.

**phos|phor|o|scope** (fos fôr′ə skōp, -for′-), *n.* an apparatus for observing and measuring the duration of phosphorescence caused by rays of light or other energy.

**phos|pho|rous** (fos′fər əs; fos fôr′-, -fōr′-), *adj.* **1** having to do with or containing phosphorus, especially with a valence of three. **2** = phosphorescent.

**phosphorous acid,** a colorless, unstable, crystalline acid obtained from phosphorus by oxidation and by other methods. Its salts are phosphites. *Formula:* $H_3PO_3$

***phos|pho|rus** (fos′fər əs), *n.* **1** a solid nonmetallic chemical element which exists in several forms different in physical and chemical properties but not in kind of atoms. The most common form is a yellow, poisonous, waxy substance, which burns slowly at ordinary temperatures and glows in the dark. Another common form is a reddish-brown powder, nonluminous, nonpoisonous, and less flammable. *No animal or plant can exist without phosphorus, and of all the substances necessary for plant growth, compounds containing available phosphorus are the most likely to be deficient* (W. R. Jones). **2** a phosphorescent substance. [< New Latin *phosphorus* < Latin *phōsphorus* morning star < Greek *phōsphóros* morning star, torchbearer < *phôs, phōtós* light[1] + *-phóros* -phore < *phérein* to bear]

***phosphorus**
definition 1

| symbol | atomic number | atomic weight | oxidation state |
|---|---|---|---|
| P | 15 | 30.9738 | ±3, +5 |

**phosphorus 32,** a radioisotope of phosphorus used in biological research and medical therapy. It has been applied to the study of bone metabolism, employed as a radioactive tracer to measure the distribution and absorption of phosphorus in plant growth, and used in the diagnosis and

treatment of cancer. [its mass number is 32]
**phos|phor|y|lase** (fos fôr′ə lās, -fōr′-), *n.* an enzyme which assists in the formation of glucose (in the form of a phosphate) from glycogen and a phosphate.
**phos|pho|ryl|ate** (fos′fər ə lāt), *v.t.*, **-at|ed, -at|ing.** to convert into a phosphorus compound.
**phos|pho|ryl|a|tion** (fos′fər ə lā′shən), *n.* conversion into a phosphorus compound: *The mitochondria are the site of oxidative phosphorylation, which is the main mechanism by which the energy of respiration is stored* (Scientific American).
**phos|phu|ret|ed** or **phos|phu|ret|ted** (fos′fyə-ret′id), *adj.* combined with phosphorus. [< earlier *phosphuret* phosphide, alteration of earlier *phosphur* < French *phosphure*]
**phosphureted hydrogen,** = phosphine.
**phos|sy jaw** (fos′ē), necrosis of the jawbone or teeth, caused by continued inhalation of phosphorus vapors.
**phos|vi|tin** (fos′vī′tən), *n.* a phosphoprotein contained in the yolk of eggs. [< *phos*(phorus) + Latin *vit*(*ellus*) egg yolk + English *-in*]
**phot** (fōt, fot), *n.* a centimeter-gram-second unit of illumination, equivalent to one lumen to a square centimeter. [< Greek *phôs, phōtós* light[1]]
**phot.,** 1 photograph. 2 photography.
**pho|tic** (fō′tik), *adj.* 1 of or having to do with light. 2 relating to the production of light by organisms, or to their stimulation under the influence of light. [< Greek *phôs, phōtós* light[1] + English *-ic*]
**pho|tics** (fō′tiks), *n.* the science of light and its intrinsic properties (sometimes used instead of *optics,* when optics is restricted to the science of light as affecting vision).
**pho|to** (fō′tō), *n., pl.* **-tos,** *v.t., v.i. Informal.* photograph.
**photo-,** *combining form.* 1 light: *Photometer = an instrument that measures light.*
2 photographic or photograph: *Photoengraving = photographic engraving.*
[< Greek *phōto-* < *phôs, phōtós* light[1]]
**pho|to|ac|tin|ic** (fō′tō ak tin′ik), *adj.* giving off rays which produce chemical changes in the objects irradiated, especially blue light or ultraviolet rays.
**pho|to|ac|ti|vate** (fō′tō ak′tə vāt), *v.t.*, **-vat|ed, -vat|ing.** to activate by photocatalysis.
**pho|to|ac|ti|va|tion** (fō′tō ak′tə vā′shən), *n.* activation through photocatalysis.
**pho|to|au|to|troph** (fō′tō ô′tə trof), *n.* an autotroph that obtains its nourishment and energy from light: *The majority of blue-green algae are aerobic photoautotrophs: their life processes require only oxygen, light, and inorganic substances* (Scientific American).
**pho|to|au|to|troph|ic** (fō′tō ô′tə trof′ik), *adj.* providing its own nourishment and obtaining energy from light: *With the exception of the colorless forms, most algae are photoautotrophic* (Osmund Holm-Hansen). [< *photo-* + *autotrophic*]
**pho|to|bi|o|log|i|cal** (fō′tō bī′ə loj′ə kəl), *adj.* of or having to do with photobiology or biological processes, such as photosynthesis, using radiant energy. —**pho′to|bi′o|log′i|cal|ly,** *adv.*
**pho|to|bi|ol|o|gy** (fō′tō bī ol′ə jē), *n.* the branch of biology dealing with the relation of light or radiant energy to biological processes, such as photosynthesis.
**pho|to|bi|ot|ic** (fō′tō bī ot′ik), *adj.* (of an organism) needing light, especially sunlight, to live or thrive.
**pho|to|bot|a|ny** (fō′tō bot′ə nē), *n.* the branch of botany that studies the effects of light on plants.
**pho|to|ca|tal|y|sis** (fō′tō kə tal′ə sis), *n.* catalysis depending upon radiant energy.
**pho|to|cat|a|lyst** (fō′tō kat′ə list), *n.* a catalyst activated by radiant energy.
**pho|to|cath|ode** (fō′tō kath′ōd), *n.* a cathode which emits electrons when stimulated by radiant energy.
**pho|to|cell** (fō′tə sel′), *n.* = photoelectric cell.
**pho|to|chem|i|cal** (fō′tō kem′ə kəl), *adj., n.* —*adj.* of or having to do with the chemical action of light: *Night sky glow not caused by moonlight and starlight is due to photochemical reactions in the upper air* (Science News Letter).
—*n.* a chemical produced by the action of light on a substance. —**pho′to|chem′i|cal|ly,** *adv.*
**photochemical glass,** a composition of photosensitive glass which can be cut by acid.
**pho|to|chem|ist** (fō′tō kem′ist), *n.* a person who studies or is skilled in photochemistry.
**pho|to|chem|is|try** (fō′tō kem′ə strē), *n.* the branch of chemistry dealing with the chemical action of light, as in photography.
**pho|to|chrome** (fō′tə krōm), *n.* a photograph in colors; a colored picture produced by color photography.
**pho|to|chro|mic** (fō′tə krō′mik), *adj.* 1 changing colors when exposed to light: *A reversible photochromic glass—one that darkens on exposure to light and clears again when the light fades—has been invented* (Scientific American). 2 having to do with photochromes.
**pho|to|chro|mism** (fō′tō krō′miz əm), *n.* the quality or property of being photochromic.
**pho|to|chro|my** (fō′tə krō′mē), *n. Obsolete.* color photography.
**pho|to|chron|o|graph** (fō′tō kron′ə graf, -gräf), *n.* 1 a device for photographing a moving object at regular, brief intervals. 2 a photograph so taken. 3 an instrument for photographing the transit of a star. 4 a device for measuring and recording small time intervals.
**pho|to|co|ag|u|lat|ing** (fō′tō kō ag′yə lā ting), *adj.* inducing photocoagulation: *a photocoagulating laser pulse.*
**pho|to|co|ag|u|la|tion** (fō′tō kō ag′yə lā′shən), *n.* coagulation induced by laser beams: *In ... photocoagulation, for example, one of the problems has been that the red light of the ruby is not well absorbed by the red color of hemoglobin, thus limiting its effectiveness in treating blood vessel diseases of the retina* (Scientific American).
**pho|to|co|ag|u|la|tor** (fō′tō kō ag′yə lā′tər), *n.* a laser device used in photocoagulation.
**pho|to|com|pose** (fō′tō kəm pōz′), *v.t.*, **-posed, -pos|ing.** to prepare (printing plates) by photocomposition; compose on a photocomposing machine. —**pho′to|com|pos′er,** *n.*
**pho|to|com|pos|ing** (fō′tō kəm pō′zing), *adj.* of or having to do with photocomposition.
**pho|to|com|po|si|tion** (fō′tō kom′pə zish′ən), *n.* a method of typesetting in which negatives and positives of type are made on film or photosensitive paper and then transferred to metal printing plates.
**pho|to|con|duct|ance** (fō′tō kən duk′təns), *n. Electricity.* conductance varying with illumination.
**pho|to|con|duct|ing** (fō′tō kən duk′ting), *adj.* conducting electricity only upon exposure to light: *photoconducting materials.*
**pho|to|con|duc|tion** or **pho|to-con|duc|tion** (fō′tō kən duk′shən), *n.* the ability of an electrical conductor to conduct electricity upon exposure to light.
**pho|to|con|duc|tive** (fō′tō kən duk′tiv), *adj.* of or having to do with photoconduction; photoconducting: *photoconductive detectors, photoconductive properties.*
**pho|to|con|duc|tiv|i|ty** (fō′tō kon′duk tiv′ə tē), *n. Electricity.* conductivity varying with illumination.
**pho|to|con|duc|tor** (fō′tō kən duk′tər), *n.* a conductor whose ability to conduct electricity improves notably upon exposure to light.
**pho|to|cop|i|er** (fō′tō kop′ē ər), *n.* a device or machine that produces photocopies.
**pho|to|cop|y** (fō′tō kop′ē), *n., pl.* **-cop|ies,** *v.,* **-cop|ied, -cop|y|ing.** —*n.* a photographic copy of a document or print, reproduced by a device which photographs and automatically develops images of the original.
—*v.t.* to produce a photocopy of.
**pho|to|cube** (fō′tō kyüb′), *n.* a transparent plastic cube usually filled with a piece of spongy material to hold a photograph up against the inside of each surface so that it may be displayed.
**pho|to|cur|rent** (fō′tō kėr′ənt), *n. Physics.* the electric current produced by the movement of a stream of electrons given off by certain substances, usually in a photoelectric cell, when exposed to light or certain other radiations.
**pho|to|de|com|po|si|tion** (fō′tō dē′kom pə zish′-ən), *n.* = photolysis.
**pho|to|de|tec|tor** (fō′tō di tek′tər), *n.* a semiconductor device that detects radiant energy, especially infrared radiation, by photoconductive or photovoltaic action, used especially in electronic equipment to detect changes in temperature, in solar telescopes.
**pho|to|dis|in|te|gra|tion** (fō′tō dis in′tə grā′shən), *n. Physics.* the breaking down of the nucleus of an atom caused by bombardment with high-energy gamma rays.
**pho|to|dis|so|ci|a|tion** (fō′tō di sō′sē ā′shən, -shē-), *n.* dissociation of a chemical compound by the absorption of radiant energy, such as light and ultraviolet rays.
**pho|to|dra|ma** (fō′tə drä′mə, -dram′ə), *n.* a motion picture; photoplay.
**pho|to|dra|mat|ic** (fō′tə drə mat′ik), *adj.* 1 of or having to do with a photodrama. 2 like a photodrama.
**pho|to|dram|a|tist** (fō′tə drä′mə tist, -dram′ə-), *n.* a writer of photodramas.
**pho|to|du|pli|ca|tion** (fō′tō dü′plə kā′shən, -dyü′-), *n.* the act or process of making photocopies.
**pho|to|dy|nam|ic** (fō′tō dī nam′ik, -di-), *adj.* having to do with the energy of light.
**pho|to|dy|nam|ics** (fō′tō dī nam′iks, -di-), *n.* the science dealing with the energy of light, especially in relation to growth or movement in plants.
**pho|to|e|las|tic** (fō′tō i las′tik), *adj.* of or having to do with photoelasticity.
**pho|to|e|las|tic|i|ty** (fō′tō i las′tis′ə tē, -ē′las-), *n. Physics.* optical changes in a transparent dielectric, such as glass, due to compression or other stresses.
**pho|to|e|lec|tric** (fō′tō i lek′trik), *adj.* 1 having to do with the electricity or the electrical effects produced by the action of light or other radiation: *The photoelectric measurement of starlight has become ... a major instrument for studying the universe* (New Astronomy). 2 of or having to do with an apparatus for taking photographs by electric light. —**pho′to|e|lec′tri|cal|ly,** *adv.*
**pho|to|e|lec|tri|cal** (fō′tō i lek′trə kəl), *adj.* = photoelectric.
***photoelectric cell,** 1 any cell or vacuum tube, used for the detection and measurement of light, that varies the flow of electric current according to the amount of light falling upon its sensitive element; electric eye; photocell. Variations or interruptions of the light can be used to trigger mechanisms to open doors at the approach of a person or car, set off alarms, measure light intensity by electric meter, and perform other tasks of simple monitoring. Photoconducting cells, phototubes, and solar cells are all photoelectric cells. *This light falls on a photoelectric cell which produces an electric current corresponding to the intensity of the light* (John Pierce). 2 = phototube.

***photoelectric cell**
definition 1

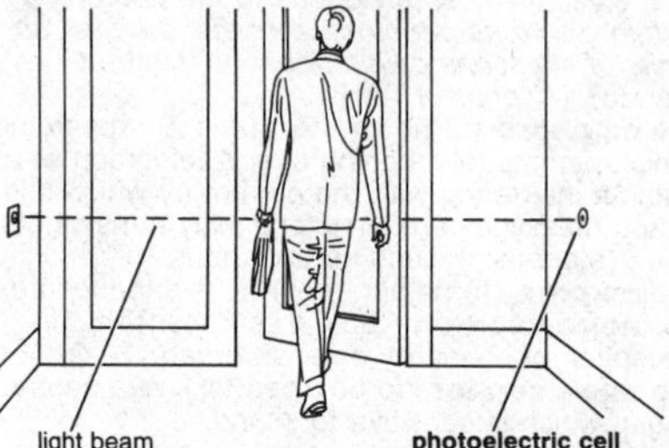


**photoelectric effect,** the transfer of the kinetic energy of a photon in light or gamma radiation to an electron of a metal it strikes, causing the emission or escape of the electron.
**photoelectric exposure meter,** *Photography.* a type of exposure meter in which the amount of light on a subject is measured by a photoelectric cell.
**pho|to|e|lec|tric|i|ty** (fō′tō i lek′tris′ə tē, -ē′lek-), *n.* 1 electricity produced or affected by light. 2 the science dealing with electricity or electrical effects produced by light.
**pho|to|e|lec|tron** (fō′tō i lek′tron), *n.* an electron emitted from a surface exposed to light.
**pho|to|e|lec|tron|ic** (fō′tō i lek′tron′ik, -ē′lek-), *adj.* of or having to do with the relationships between electricity and light.
**pho|to|e|lec|tron|ics** (fō′tō i lek′tron′iks, -ē′lek-), *n.* the study and application of the effects of electricity and light upon each other.
**pho|to|e|lec|tro|type** (fō′tō i lek′trə tīp), *n.* an electrotype made by photography.
**pho|to|e|mis|sion** (fō′tō i mish′ən), *n.* the emission of electrons from a metal subjected to the action of light or other suitable radiation.
**pho|to|e|mis|sive** (fō′tō i mis′iv), *adj.* giving out, or capable of giving out, electrons when subjected to the action of light or other suitable radiation: *photoemissive metals.*
**pho|to|e|mit|ter** (fō′tō i mit′ər), *n.* a photoemissive substance.
**pho|to|e|mit|ting** (fō′tō i mit′ing), *adj.* = photoemissive.
**pho|to|en|grave** (fō′tō en grāv′), *v.t.*, **-graved, -grav|ing.** to make a photoengraving of. —**pho′to|en|grav′er,** *n.*
**pho|to|en|grav|ing** (fō′tō en grā′ving), *n.* 1 a process by which plates to print from are produced with the aid of photography. 2 the plate so produced. 3 a picture printed from it.
**pho|to|etch** (fō′tō ech′), *v.t.* to etch with the aid of photography; make a photoetching of.
**pho|to|etch|ing** (fō′tō ech′ing), *n.* 1 any process of photoengraving in which the plate is etched, as by acid. 2 a plate or print so produced.
**pho|to|fab|ri|ca|tion** (fō′tō fab′rə kā′shən), *n.* the use of photography in the manufacture of integrated circuits by photoetching semiconductor surfaces on a small silicon wafer or chip.
**photo finish,** 1 a finish in racing so close that a photograph is required to decide the winner. 2 *Figurative: While the verdict went against him, it was very much a photo finish with no clear vote of confidence for the* [*victor*] *either* (Sunday Times).

**pho|to|fin|ish|er** (fō′tō fin′i shər), *n.* **1** a person who does photofinishing: *One major photofinisher went so far as to import qualified help from abroad* (Jacob Deschin). **2** one of two or more contestants in a photo finish: *He was third, three-quarters of a length back of the photofinishers* (New York Times).

**pho|to|fin|ish|ing** (fō′tō fin′i shing), *n.* the developing, printing, and enlarging of exposed photographic films or plates, especially by a commercial establishment.

**pho|to|flash bomb** (fō′tə flash′), a bomblike device dropped from an aircraft at night to emit a high-intensity light so that aerial photographs may be taken of the ground below.

**photoflash lamp**, *Photography.* a flashbulb.

**photoflash photography**, photography with the aid of flashbulbs.

**pho|to|flood lamp** (fō′tə flud′), an electric lamp of high wattage that gives very bright, sustained light for taking photographs.

**photog.**, **1** photographic. **2** photography.

**pho|to|gel|a|tin** (fō′tō jel′ə tin), *adj.* **1** designating or having to do with a photographic process using gelatin. **2** made by a photographic process using gelatin.

**pho|to|gen** (fō′tə jen), *n.* **1** a substance, organ, or organism that emits light, as the firefly. **2** *Obsolete.* kerosene.

**pho|to|gene** (fō′tə jēn), *n.* **1** a visual afterimage. **2** *Obsolete.* a photograph.

**pho|to|gen|ic** (fō′tə jen′ik), *adj.* **1** having characteristics that photograph very well, especially in motion pictures: *a photogenic face.* **2** *Biology.* phosphorescent; luminescent. Certain bacteria are photogenic. **3** produced or caused by light. [< *photo-* + Greek *-gen* producing, produced (by) + *-ic*] —**pho′to|gen′i|cal|ly**, *adv.*

**pho|to|ge|o|log|ic** (fō′tō jē′ə loj′ik), *adj.* = photogeological.

**pho|to|ge|o|log|i|cal** (fō′tō jē′ə loj′kəl), *adj.* of or having to do with photogeology: *SOEKOR has also carried out seven photogeological surveys covering about 120,000 square miles* (Sunday Times). —**pho′to|ge′o|log′i|cal|ly**, *adv.*

**pho|to|ge|ol|o|gy** (fō′tō jē ol′ə jē), *n.* the study of aerial photographs to identify and map geological formations.

**pho|to|gram** (fō′tə gram), *n.* a shadowy photograph made by exposing to light an object placed on sensitized paper.

**pho|to|gram|met|ric** (fō′tō grə met′rik), *adj.* of or having to do with photogrammetry.

**pho|to|gram|me|trist** (fō′tō gram′ə trist), *n.* a person skilled in photogrammetry.

**pho|to|gram|me|try** (fō′tō gram′ə trē), *n.* the art or science of making surveys or maps with the help of photographs, especially aerial photographs. [< *photogram,* obsolete variant of *photograph* + *-metry;* probably influenced by German *Photogrammetrie*]

**pho|to|graph** (fō′tə graf, -gräf), *n., v.* —*n.* a picture made with a camera. A photograph is made by the action of the light rays from the thing pictured coming through the lens of the camera onto a film or plate.
—*v.t.* to take a photograph of: *to photograph a meeting of the President.*
—*v.i.* **1** to take photographs. **2** to look (as clear or unnatural) in a photograph: *She does not photograph well.*

**pho|to|graph|a|ble** (fō′tə graf′ə bəl), *adj.* that can be photographed: *The most distant photographable galaxies are so faint that they are not visible to the eye through the telescope* (Scientific American).

**pho|tog|ra|pher** (fə tog′rə fər), *n.* **1** a person who takes photographs: *All the tourists who were photographers trained their cameras on the Statue of Liberty.* **2** a person whose business is taking photographs: *The new driver went to a photographer to have his picture taken for his license.*

**pho|to|graph|ic** (fō′tə graf′ik), *adj.* **1** of or like photography: *photographic accuracy.* **2** used in or produced by photography: *photographic plates, a photographic process, a photographic record of a trip.* **3** reproducing images accurately; minutely accurate: *a photographic painting.* —**pho′to|graph′i|cal|ly**, *adv.*

**pho|to|graph|i|cal** (fō′tə graf′ə kəl), *adj.* = photographic.

**pho|tog|ra|phy** (fə tog′rə fē), *n.* the taking of photographs: *Photography is the marvelous, anonymous folk-art of our time* (New York Times). *Photography is, above all, reporting* (Helmut Gernsheim).

**pho|to|gra|vure** (fō′tə grə vyůr′, -grā′vyər), *n.* **1** = photoengraving. **2** a picture printed from a metal plate on which a photograph has been engraved. [< French *photogravure* < *photo(graphie)* (ultimately < English *photograph*) + *gravure* process or art of engraving]

**pho|to|he|li|o|graph** (fō′tə hē′lē ə graf, -gräf), *n.* a telescope adapted for making photographs of the sun.

**photo interpretation**, the study of photographs to describe or identify the things contained in them, used especially in military intelligence.

**pho|to|i|on|i|za|tion** (fō′tō ī′ə nə zā′shən), *n.* ionization by the action or energy supplied by light or other radiation: *Because an atom which has lost an electron is called an ion, the process is known as photoionization* (Harrie Massey).

**pho|to|jour|nal|ism** (fō′tō jėr′nə liz əm), *n.* journalism which uses photographic rather than written material as the basis of a story: *Photojournalism has a powerful immediate impact upon millions of people, for the impact of the visual image is far greater than that of words* (Harper's).

**pho|to|jour|nal|ist** (fō′tō jėr′nə list), *n.* a photographer who specializes in photojournalistic work.

**pho|to|jour|nal|is|tic** (fō′tō jėr′nə lis′tik), *adj.* of or having to do with photojournalism: *He* [*Brady*] *pioneered the full-scale photojournalistic reporting of war, setting the ground rules for photography in the field from his day on* (Saturday Review).

**pho|to|ki|ne|sis** (fō′tə ki nē′sis, -kī-), *n. Physiology.* movement caused by light. [< *photo-* + Greek *kī́nēsis* motion, a setting in motion < *kīneîn* to set in motion, move]

**pho|to|ki|net|ic** (fō′tə ki net′ik, -kī-), *adj.* of or having to do with photokinesis.

**pho|to|lith** (fō′tə lith), *adj.* = photolithographic.

**pho|to|lith|o** (fō′tə lith′ō), *n., pl.* **-lith|os.** = photolithograph.

**pho|to|lith|o|graph** (fō′tə lith′ə graf, -gräf), *n., v.* —*n.* a print produced by photolithography.
—*v.t.* to produce or copy by photolithography.

**pho|to|li|thog|ra|pher** (fō′tə li thog′rə fər), *n.* a person who makes photolithographs.

**pho|to|lith|o|graph|ic** (fō′tə lith′ə graf′ik), *adj.* **1** having to do with photolithography. **2** produced by photolithography.

**pho|to|li|thog|ra|phy** (fō′tə li thog′rə fē), *n.* a process of producing, by photography, designs upon lithographic stone or metal plates, from which prints may be taken as in ordinary lithography or by offset.

**pho|to|log|i|cal** (fō′tə loj′ə kəl), *adj.* having to do with photology; optical. —**pho′to|log′i|cal|ly**, *adv.*

**pho|tol|o|gist** (fō tol′ə jist), *n.* an expert in photology.

**pho|tol|o|gy** (fō tol′ə jē), *n.* the science of light.

**pho|to|lu|mi|nes|cence** (fō′tō lü′mə nes′əns), *n.* luminescence caused by the absorption of radiant energy in the form of visible or nonvisible light.

**pho|tol|y|sis** (fō tol′ə sis), *n.* chemical decomposition of a substance resulting from the action of light: *Further tests with the dye-reducing extracts showed that they caused photolysis, producing oxygen* (Science News Letter). *In photolysis the energy necessary to perform the split comes from light through the mediation of chlorophyll* (H. Lees). [< *photo-* + Greek *lýsis* a loosening]

**pho|to|lyt|ic** (fō′tə lit′ik), *adj.* having to do with or producing photolysis: *The intense photolytic flash is replaced by a pulse of microwave energy* (New Scientist).

**pho|to|lyze** (fō′tə līz), *v.t., v.i.,* **-lyzed, -lyz|ing.** to break down by the action of light; cause to undergo photolysis: *to photolyze ozone into oxygen atoms.*

**photom.**, photometry.

**pho|to|mac|ro|graph** (fō′tō mak′rə graf, -gräf), *n.* a macrograph made by photography; macrophotograph: *A photograph of a coin at twice life-size is a photomacrograph* (Kodak Handbook News).

**pho|to|ma|crog|ra|phy** (fō′tō mə krog′rə fē), *n.* = macrophotography.

**pho|to|mag|net|ic** (fō′tō mag net′ik), *adj.* designating certain rays of the spectrum having, or supposed to have, a magnetic influence.

**pho|to|mag|net|ism** (fō′tō mag′nə tiz əm), *n.* the science dealing with the relation of magnetism to light.

**pho|to|map** (fō′tō map′), *n., v.,* **-mapped, -map|ping.** —*n.* **1** a map made from an aerial photograph or photographs, now usually one in which a number of photographs made from a given altitude are matched and given, by means of an overlay, such conventional characteristics of a map as a grid and lines of contour: *a photomap of Tokyo.* **2** a star map prepared by means of a phototelescope: *When the atlas is completed . . . it will include 1,758 . . . "photomaps"* (London Times).
—*v.t.* to prepare a photomap or photomaps of: *to photomap the skies by using a telescopic camera. The project . . . may lead to photomapping of nearly every square inch of land in the Western hemisphere* (Science News Letter).

**pho|to|me|chan|i|cal** (fō′tō mə kan′ə kəl), *adj.* having to do with or designating any method of printing in which the plate or other printing surface is prepared by means of a photographic and a mechanical process, as photoengraving, photogravure, or photo-offset. —**pho′to|me|chan′i|cal|ly**, *adv.*

**pho|tom|e|ter** (fō tom′ə tər), *n.* any one of various instruments for measuring light, such as the intensity of light, light distribution, illumination, or luminous flux: *The photometer is used to measure, simultaneously, the luminosities and diameters of galaxies lying beyond those in our own neighborhood of the universe* (Science News Letter).

**pho|to|met|ric** (fō′tō met′rik), *adj.* having to do with photometry or a photometer. —**pho′to|met′ri|cal|ly**, *adv.*

**pho|to|met|ri|cal** (fō′tō met′rə kəl), *adj.* = photometric.

**pho|tom|e|trist** (fō tom′ə trist), *n.* a person who studies or is skilled in photometry.

**pho|tom|e|try** (fō tom′ə trē), *n.* **1** the branch of physics dealing with measurements of the intensity of light, light distribution, illumination, and luminous flux. **2** the measurement of light, especially with the aid of the photometer.

**pho|to|mi|cro|graph** (fō′tō mī′krə graf, -gräf), *n.* an enlarged photograph of a microscopic object, taken through a microscope; microphotograph; micrograph.

**pho|to|mi|cro|graph|ic** (fō′tō mī′krə graf′ik), *adj.* **1** of, having to do with, or used in photomicrography: *photomicrographic apparatus.* **2** obtained or made by photomicrography.

**pho|to|mi|crog|ra|phy** (fō′tō mī krog′rə fē), *n.* the art of obtaining photographs of microscopic objects on a magnified scale by replacing the eyepiece of a microscope with a camera.

**pho|to|mi|cro|scope** (fō′tō mī′krə skōp), *n.* an apparatus consisting of a microscope, a camera, and a light source, all mounted on a stable base, and used to photograph microscopic objects.

**pho|to|mon|tage** (fō′tō mon täzh′, -môn-), *n.* **1** the process of combining several photographs, or parts of them, into a single picture. **2** the resulting picture.

**pho|to|mo|sa|ic** (fō′tō mō zā′ik), *n.* a group of aerial photographs put together to form a continuous photograph of an area.

**pho|to|mul|ti|pli|er** (fō′tō mul′tə plī′ər), *n.* or **photomultiplier tube**, a vacuum tube having a series of supplementary electrodes between the photocathode and the anode. When light strikes the photoemissive cathode a cascade of electrons is emitted and amplified at each supplementary electrode.

**pho|to|mu|ral** (fō′tō myůr′əl), *n.* a mural consisting of a greatly enlarged photograph or group of matched photographs.

**pho|ton** (fō′ton), *n.* a unit particle of light, an element of radiant energy, according to the quantum theory; a light quantum. It has a momentum equal to its energy divided by the velocity of light, and moves as a unit with the velocity of light. It is considered to be one of the elementary particles. [*Einstein*] *said that light, in spite of its wave nature, must be composed of energy particles, or photons* (Harvey E. White). *When you see different colors your eyes are being hit by streams of photons which differ in their rates of vibration* (Ralph E. Lapp). [< *photo-* + *-on*]

**pho|to|nas|ty** (fō′tō nas′tē), *n. Biology.* response to diffuse light or to variations in the intensity of light, as in the growth of a plant organ.

**pho|to|neg|a|tive** (fō′tō neg′ə tiv), *adj.* showing avoidance of light; photophobic: *Normally the beetles are photonegative, tending to stay in the dark half of the chamber* (New Scientist).

**pho|to|nov|el** (fō′tō nov′əl), *n.* a novel depicted in photographs and legends, with dialogue usually enclosed in a circled or boxed space in the style of a comic strip: *Photonovels are . . . equipped with the plots of soap operas, models as characters, the color of the finest slick magazines, and comic book-style formats* (New York Daily News). [< Spanish *fotonovela*]

**pho|to|nu|cle|ar** (fō′tō nü′klē ər, -nyü′-), *adj.* of or having to do with the action or effect of photons upon atomic nuclei.

**pho|to-off|set** (fō′tō ôf′set, -of′-), *n., v.,* **-set, -set|ting.** —*n.* a process of printing in which a page of type, a picture, or other matter is photographed and the image then transferred to a specially sensitized lithographic plate and printed by offset; offset lithography.
—*v.t.* to print or reproduce by photo-offset.

**pho|to|ox|i|da|tion** (fō′tō ok′sə dā′shən), *n.* oxi-

**Pronunciation Key:** hat, āge, cãre, fär; let, ēqual, tėrm; it, īce; hot, ōpen, ôrder; **oil**, **out**; cup, půt, rüle; **child**; long; **thin**; ᴛʜen; **zh**, measure; ə represents **a** in about, **e** in taken, **i** in pencil, **o** in lemon, **u** in circus.

dation induced by the chemical action of light: *Cellulose is a prey to all four of the major museum enemies: photooxidation, humidity change, air pollution, and biological attack* (New Scientist).

**pho|to|pe|ri|od** (fō′tō pir′ē əd), *n.* the length of time during which a plant or animal is exposed to light each day, considered especially with reference to the effect of the light on growth and development.

**pho|to|pe|ri|od|ic** (fō′tō pir′ē od′ik), *adj.* of or having to do with a photoperiod or photoperiodism: *photoperiodic behavior.* —**pho′to|pe′ri|od′i|cal|ly,** *adv.*

**pho|to|pe|ri|od|i|cal** (fō′tō pir′ē od′ə kəl), *adj.* = photoperiodic: *There is some kind of photoperiodical response in every higher plant* (Science News Letter).

**pho|to|pe|ri|od|ism** (fō′tō pir′ē ə diz′əm), *n. Physiology.* the response of a plant or animal to the length of its daily exposure to light, especially as shown by changes in vital processes: *Photoperiodism ... is largely responsible for the separation of many wild flowers into spring, summer, and fall blooming classes* (Science News Letter).

**pho|toph|i|lous** (fō tof′ə ləs), *adj.* (of an organism) flourishing in strong light, especially sunlight; light-loving.

**pho|toph|i|ly** (fō tof′ə lē), *n.* the quality or condition of living or flourishing in light.

**pho|to|pho|bi|a** (fō′tō fō′bē ə), *n.* **1** an abnormal dread of, or shrinking from, light. **2** extreme sensitivity to light: *Paralysis of these muscles [of the iris] puts the iris at rest and decreases the pain and photophobia* (Sidney Lerman).

**pho|to|pho|bic** (fō′tō fō′bik), *adj.* showing photophobia; shrinking from light; photonegative: *The mole is photophobic* (James Neylon).

**pho|to|phone** (fō′tō fōn), *n.* a telephone in which sound vibrations are conveyed by means of a beam of reflected light. [American English < *photo-* + (tele)*phone*]

**pho|to|phore** (fō′tō fôr, -fōr), *n.* a luminous, cup-shaped organ on the bellies of certain deep-sea crustaceans and fishes.

**pho|to|pho|re|sis** (fō′tō fə rē′sis), *n.* the unidirectional movement of small particles, suspended in gas or falling in a vacuum, produced by a beam of light. [< *photo-* + Greek *phórēsis* a carrying < *phérein* carry]

**pho|to|phos|pho|ryl|a|tion** (fō′tō fos′fər ə lā′shən), *n.* phosphorylation induced by the presence of radiant energy in the form of visible or nonvisible light: *Cyclic photophosphorylation ... provides a mechanism for the utilization of light energy without the consumption of water* (Science).

**pho|to|pi|a** (fō tō′pē ə), *n.* the ability to see in light, especially sunlight, of a sufficient intensity to permit color differentiation. [< New Latin *photopia* < Greek *phôs, phōtós* light[1] + *ōps* eye]

**pho|top|ic** (fō top′ik, -tō′pik), *adj.* able to see in light of a sufficient intensity to permit color differentiation.

**pho|to|pig|ment** (fō′tō pig′mənt), *n.* a pigment whose characteristics are changed by the action of light: *The photochemist cannot study the photopigments of a single receptor in living animals and the finest microelectrode is gross in size when compared with the diameter of some of the processes which we assume to carry electric potentials in the nerve net* (Science Journal).

**pho|to|play** (fō′tə plā′), *n.* a motion-picture story or scenario: *It is a good deal better than either the photoplay or the novel which were its cause* (Atlantic).

**pho|to|po|la|rim|e|ter** (fō′tō pō′lə rim′ə tər), *n.* an instrument combining telescopic, photographic, and polarimetric apparatus for producing detailed images of planetary features.

**pho|to|pol|y|mer** (fō′tō pol′i mər), *n.* a plastic made by photopolymerization, used especially to make printing plates.

**pho|to|pol|y|mer|i|za|tion** (fō′tō pol′i mər ə zā′shen, -pə lim′ər ə-), *n.* polymerization induced by the action of light.

**pho|to|pos|i|tive** (fō′tō poz′ə tiv), *adj.* attracted to light; photophilous; phototactic.

**pho|to|print** (fō′tə print′), *n.* a print produced by a photomechanical process.

**pho|to|re|ac|tion** (fō′tō rē ak′shən), *n.* any chemical reaction induced by the presence of light.

**Pho|to-Re|al|ism** (fō′tō rē′ə liz əm), *n.* a form of painting based on and often imitating still photographs: *Photo-Realism is photographic (many of the Photo-Realist painters simply copy blown-up photographs they have projected onto their enormous canvases) and cruelly noticing of things as they are* (New Yorker). —**Pho′to-Re′al|ist,** *adj., n.*

**pho|to|rec|ce** (fō′tō rik′ē), *n. U.S. Informal.* = photoreconnaissance.

**pho|to|re|cep|tion** (fō′tō ri sep′shən), *n.* the reception of and response to light by plant or animal cells having pigments sensitive to radiant energy. Photoreception is essential to photosynthesis and phototropism in plants, and to vision in animals. *The collective evidence in favor of photoreception by some form of riboflavin conjugate is also sufficiently impressive* (Scientific American).

**pho|to|re|cep|tive** (fō′tō ri sep′tiv), *adj.* of or having to do with photoreception.

**pho|to|re|cep|tor** (fō′tō ri sep′tər), *n.* a nerve ending which is sensitive to light: *Rod photoreceptors of the eye are responsible for colourless vision of low intensities* (New Scientist).

**pho|to|re|con|nais|sance** (fō′tō ri kon′ə səns), *n.* aerial reconnaissance during which information is gathered by taking aerial photographs: *Photoreconnaissance indicated that the enemy had installed a hundred or more sites for launching flying bombs and perhaps half a dozen sites for a larger type of rocket* (James Phinney Baxter).

**pho|to|re|sist** (fō′tō ri zist′), *n.* a plastic material that hardens to varying degrees depending on the intensity of the light to which it is exposed, used especially as a protective coating on the surface of silicon wafers or chips in the manufacture of integrated circuits.

**pho|to|res|pi|ra|tion** (fō′tō res′pə rā′shən), *n. Botany.* respiration induced or stimulated by the presence of light.

**pho|to|scan|ner** (fō′tō skan′ər), *n.* a device that reproduces on X-ray film the distribution of a radioactive isotope injected in the body for diagnostic purposes: *The gamma rays coming from the abnormal portions of bone are detected by a photoscanner that is passed externally over the body. Any portion of bone that gives off gamma rays is considered diseased* (Science News).

**pho|to|scan|ning** (fō′tō skan′ing), *n.* the use of a photoscanner: *Photoscanning using radioactive isotopes can tell us if cancer is present in such organs as the thyroid gland, the liver, and the brain* (London Times).

**pho|to|sen|si|tive** (fō′tō sen′sə tiv), *adj.* readily stimulated to action by light or other radiant energy.

**photosensitive glass,** a special glass which, upon exposure to a photographic negative, develops a print when heated. It is used for making ornaments, permanent records, etc.

**pho|to|sen|si|tiv|i|ty** (fō′tō sen′sə tiv′ə tē), *n.* the quality of being readily stimulated to action by light or other radiant energy.

**pho|to|sen|si|ti|za|tion** (fō′tō sen′sə tə zā′shən), *n.* the act or process of photosensitizing.

**pho|to|sen|si|tize** (fō′tō sen′sə tīz), *v.t.,* **-tized, -tiz|ing.** to make sensitive to the action of light; make photosensitive.

**pho|to|sen|sor** (fō′tō sen′sər, -sor), *n.* a device that is sensitive to light: *In a study of commonly used type fonts, for instance, it has been found that 24 rows of photosensors are necessary to recognise unambiguously a typical character* (New Scientist).

**pho|to|spec|tro|scope** (fō′tō spek′trə skōp), *n.* a spectroscope with an attached camera, used for photographing and recording spectra.

**pho|to|spec|tro|scop|ic** (fō′tō spek′trə skop′ik), *adj.* having to do with photographing and recording spectra with a spectroscope.

**pho|to|sphere** (fō′tə sfir), *n.* **1** the brilliant gaseous layer surrounding the sun or other stars: *While the particles in the corona move at a far higher speed than those in the photosphere, they are so much more thinly dispersed that radiating collisions are relatively infrequent* (Fred Hoyle). **2** *Figurative.* a sphere of light, radiance, or glory: *Her hopes mingled with the sunshine in an ideal photosphere* (Thomas Hardy).

**pho|to|spher|ic** (fō′tə sfer′ik), *adj.* **1** of or having to do with the photosphere or a photosphere. **2** characteristic of the photosphere or a photosphere.

**pho|to|stat** (fō′tə stat), *n., v.,* **-stat|ed, -stat|ing** or **-stat|ted, -stat|ting.** —*n.* **1** a photograph made with a special camera for making photocopies of documents, maps, drawings, pages of books, and other printed material, directly on specially prepared paper. **2 Photostat,** *Trademark.* a name for a camera of this kind. —*v.t.* to make a photostat of. —**pho′to|stat′er,** *n.*

**pho|to|stat|ic** (fō′tə stat′ik), *adj.* **1** of or having to do with a photostat. **2** produced by a photostat.

**pho|to|sur|face** (fō′tō sėr′fis), *n.* a photographic surface: *Every time an exposed photographic plate is removed, the air destroys the highly reactive photosurface* (Scientific American).

**pho|to|syn|the|sis** (fō′tə sin′thə sis), *n.* **1** the process by which plant cells make carbohydrates from carbon dioxide and water in the presence of chlorophyll and light, and release oxygen as a by-product: *Photosynthesis, called by some the most important chemical reaction occurring in nature, takes place only in plants containing certain pigments, principally chlorophyll* (Harbaugh and Goodrich). **2** the process by which chemical compounds are synthesized by means of light or other forms of radiant energy.

**pho|to|syn|the|size** (fō′tə sin′thə sīz), *v.,* **-sized, -siz|ing.** —*v.i.* to carry on photosynethesis: *A red alga is best adapted to photosynthesize in the bluish-green light of deep water* (G. E. Fogg). —*v.t.* to produce by photosynethesis: *Plants photosynthesize protein as well as carbohydrates directly under light* (Time).

**pho|to|syn|thet|ic** (fō′tə sin thet′ik), *adj.* **1** of or having to do with photosynthesis: *The crux of the whole photosynthetic process was the conversion of light energy into chemical energy* (Harper's). **2** promoting photosynthesis: *The photosynthetic function is accomplished by the green stems* (Fred W. Emerson). —**pho′to|syn|thet′i|cal|ly,** *adv.*

**pho|to|tac|tic** (fō′tō tak′tik), *adj.* of, having to do with, or characterized by phototaxis: *A phototropic or phototactic response might become dependent on the oxygen supplied by photosynthesis* (Scientific American).

**pho|to|tax|is** (fō′tō tak′sis), *n.* the tendency of an organism to move in response to light: *Several workers have found negative phototaxis (movement away from light) in a number of species* (E. B. Edney). [< German *Phototaxis* < Greek *phôs, phōtós* light[1] + *táxis* arrangement]

**pho|to|tax|y** (fō′tō tak′sē), *n.* = phototaxis.

**pho|to|tel|e|graph** (fō′tō tel′ə graf, -gräf), *v., n.* —*v.t., v.i.* to send by phototelegraphy. —*n.* a picture, message, or other printed matter, thus sent.

**pho|to|tel|e|graph|ic** (fō′tō tel′ə graf′ik), *adj.* of or having to do with phototelegraphy. —**pho′to-tel′e|graph′i|cal|ly,** *adv.*

**pho|to|tel|e|graph|i|cal** (fō′tō tel′ə graf′ə kəl), *adj.* = phototelegraphic.

**pho|to|te|leg|ra|phy** (fō′tō tə leg′rə fē), *n.* **1** telegraphy by means of light, as with a heliograph. **2** the electric transmission of facsimiles of photographs; telephotography.

**pho|to|tel|e|scope** (fō′tō tel′ə skōp), *n.* a telescope with a photographic apparatus, used for photographing heavenly bodies.

**pho|to|tel|e|scop|ic** (fō′tō tel′ə skop′ik), *adj.* of or having to do with a phototelescope.

**pho|to|the|od|o|lite** (fō′tō thē od′ə līt), *n.* a camera with the movability of a theodolite, used for tracking space vehicles or for photographing very large objects.

**pho|to|ther|a|peu|tic** (fō′tō ther′ə pyü′tik), *adj.* having to do with phototherapy.

**pho|to|ther|a|peu|tics** (fō′tō ther′ə pyü′tiks), *n.* = phototherapy.

**pho|to|ther|a|py** (fō′tō ther′ə pē), *n.* therapy in which light rays are used, as in treating certain skin diseases.

**pho|to|ther|mic** (fō′tō thėr′mik), *adj.* **1** having to do with the heating effects of light. **2** of or relating to both light and heat.

**pho|to|ton|ic** (fō′tō ton′ik), *adj.* exhibiting phototonus in the normal way; sensitive to light.

**pho|tot|o|nus** (fō tot′ə nəs), *n.* **1** the normal condition of sensitiveness to light, as in leaves, maintained by regular exposure to light, as opposed to the rigidity induced by long exposure to darkness. **2** the irritability exhibited by protoplasm when exposed to light of a certain intensity. [< New Latin *phototonus* < Greek *phôs, phōtós* light[1] + *tónos* tension]

**pho|to|top|o|graph|ic** (fō′tō top′ə graf′ik), *adj.* = photogrammetric.

**pho|to|to|pog|ra|phy** (fō′tō tə pog′rə fē), *n.* = photogrammetry.

**pho|to|tran|sis|tor** (fō′tō tran zis′tər), *n.* a semiconductor device that is sensitive to light, usually consisting of a small disk of germanium which generates photoelectric currents when light is focused upon it: *The principle is similar to the light-sensitive effect used in phototransistors, and has been known for some time* (New Scientist).

**pho|to|troph** (fō′tō trof), *n. Biology.* an organism that uses light to break down carbon dioxide for its metabolism. [< *photo-* + Greek *trophḗ* nourishment]

**pho|to|troph|ic** (fō′tō trof′ik), *adj. Biology.* using light to break down carbon dioxide for its metabolism: *phototrophic bacteria.*

**pho|to|trop|ic** (fō′tō trop′ik), *adj.* **1** *Botany.* bending or turning in response to light: *Most plants are phototropic.* **2** sensitive to changes in amount of radiation: *phototropic glass.* —**pho′to|trop′i|cal|ly,** *adv.*

**pho|tot|ro|pism** (fō tot′rə piz əm, fō′tō trō′piz-əm), *n.* **1** a tendency of plants to turn in response to light. **2** growth in a certain direction in response to light.

**pho|to|tube** (fō′tō tüb′, -tyüb′), *n.* a vacuum tube in which electrons are emitted as a direct result of light or other radiation falling on the cathode: *The currents obtainable with vacuum phototubes are extremely small ...* (Sears and Zemansky).

**pho|to|type** (fō′tə tīp), *n.* **1** a block on which a photograph is reproduced so that it can be printed. **2** the process used in making such a block. **3** a picture printed from such a block.

**pho|to|type|set|ter** (fō′tō tīp′set′ər), *n.* a machine that does phototypesetting: *a computer-driven phototypesetter.*

**pho|to|type|set|ting** (fō′tō tīp′set′ing), *n.* any one of several typesetting processes in which negatives of type are produced on photographic film and made into metal printing plates.

**pho|to|typ|ic** (fō′tō tip′ik), *adj.* **1** of or like a phototype. **2** produced by phototypy.

**pho|to|ty|po|graph|ic** (fō′tō tī′pə graf′ik), *adj.* **1** of or having to do with phototypography. **2** like phototypography.

**pho|to|ty|pog|ra|phy** (fō′tō tī pog′rə fē), *n.* any one of various methods of making printing surfaces by a photographic or photomechanical process.

**pho|to|ty|py** (fō′tō tī′pē, fō tot′ə-), *n.* the art or process of making phototypes.

**pho|to|vol|ta|ic** (fō′tō vol tā′ik), *adj.* **1** generating an electric current when acted on by light or a similar form of radiant energy, as a photoelectric cell is: *The photovoltaic cell is even more sluggish than selenium, and it therefore does not lend itself to use with rapidly varying light sources* (Hardy and Perrin). **2** = photoelectric.

**phr.**, phrase.

**phrag|mo|cone** (frag′mə kōn), *n.* the conical, chambered or septate, internal skeleton of a belemnite (a fossil). [< Greek *phragmós* fence + *kônos* cone]

**phrag|mo|plast** (frag′mə plast), *n.* the cytoplasmic mechanism in cell division responsible for the formation of the cell plate. [< Greek *phragmós* fence + English *-plast*]

**phras|al** (frā′zəl), *adj.* consisting of or like a phrase or phrases.

**phrase** (frāz), *n., v.,* **phrased, phras|ing.** **—*n.*** **1** a combination of words: *He spoke in simple phrases so that the children understood him.* **2** an expression often used: *"Call up" is the common phrase for "make a telephone call to." In the old phrase, it is six of the one and half a dozen of the other* (Robert Louis Stevenson). **3** a short, striking expression. *Examples:* A Fair Deal. A war to end wars. Liberty or death. **4** *Grammar.* a group of words not containing a subject and verb and used as a single word within a sentence. *In the house, coming by the church,* and *to eat too fast* are phrases. **5** a division of a piece of music, usually several measures in length, ending with a cadence. It is either independent or forms part of a period. *To establish the mood of a phrase, ... to convey what we believe to be the precise meaning the composer wishes to express, is one of the greatest problems facing a pianist* (Ruth Slenczynska). **6** a series of movements that make up a dance pattern. **7** manner or style of expression; diction; phraseology; language: *the lady who was, in chivalrous phrase, empress of his thoughts and commander of his actions* (Scott). **8** a group of words spoken as a unit and separated by pauses: *His short phrases made his speech sound jerky.*
**—*v.t.*** **1** to express in a particular way; find expression for: *She phrased her excuse in polite words.* **2** to mark off or bring out the phrases of (a piece of music).
**—*v.i.*** **1** to use a phrase or phrases. **2** to indicate or make phrases, as in music.
[< Latin *phrasis* < Greek *phrásis* speech, way of speaking < *phrázein* to express, tell]

**phrase|book** (frāz′bu̇k′), *n.* a book containing a collection of idiomatic phrases used in a language, with their explanations or translations: *I started mugging up my handy phrasebook, which tells you in six languages how to cope with the emergencies that arise* (Manchester Guardian).

**phrase|mak|er** (frāz′mā′kər), *n.* person skilled in making up unusual or striking phrases: *Above all, there is Churchill the phrasemaker, who could beat even Bernard Shaw to the verbal draw* (Time).

**phrase|mak|ing** (frāz′mā′king), *n.* skill in making up unusual or striking phrases: *In his outline of radio's fiscal woes, Minow again showed his penchant for colorful phrasemaking, which a year ago had pinned the "vast wasteland" tag on television* (Sam Chase).

**phrase marker**, *Linguistics.* a marker or signal representing one of the phrasal components of a construction: *Now, the fundamental idea of transformational grammar is that the bracketed and labelled representation of a sentence is its surface structure, and associated with each sentence is a long sequence of more and more abstract representations of the sentence—we transformationalists call them phrase markers—of which surface structure is only the first* (Noam Chomsky).

**phrase|mon|ger** (frāz′mung′gər, -mong′-), *n.* a person who deals in phrases; person given to fine but often empty phrases: *If Robespierre had been a statesman instead of a phrasemonger ...* (John Morley).

**phrase|mon|ger|ing** (frāz′mung′gər ing, -mong′-), *n.* the action or practice of a phrasemonger.

**phra|se|o|gram** (frā′zē ə gram), *n.* a written symbol representing a phrase, especially in shorthand.

**phra|se|o|graph** (frā′zē ə graf, -gräf), *n.* **1** a phrase represented by a phraseogram. **2** = phraseogram.

**phra|se|o|graph|ic** (frā′zē ə graf′ik), *adj.* **1** of phraseograms; like a phraseogram. **2** written in phraseograms.

**phra|se|og|ra|phy** (frā′zē og′rə fē), *n.* **1** the representation of phrases or sentences by abbreviated, written characters or symbols, especially in shorthand; the use of phraseograms. **2** written phraseology.

**phra|se|o|log|i|cal** (frā′zē ə loj′ə kəl), *adj.* **1** of or having to do with phraseology: *He was at every moment in complete command ... of every phraseological subtlety* (New Yorker). **2** characterized by a particular phraseology, or by the use of phrases or peculiar expressions. **—phra′se|o|log′i|cal|ly,** *adv.*

**phra|se|ol|o|gist** (frā′zē ol′ə jist), *n.* **1** a person who deals with phraseology. **2** a skillful inventor or user of phrases; phrasemaker: *All that could come out of any new conference is what cold-war phraseologists term an "easing of tensions"* (Newsweek).

**phra|se|ol|o|gy** (frā′zē ol′ə jē), *n., pl.* **-gies.** the selection and arrangement of words; particular way in which thoughts are expressed in language: *scientific phraseology, the phraseology of the Bible, the phraseology of the sports page in a newspaper.* **SYN:** See syn. under **diction.**

**phras|er** (frā′zər), *n.* **1** a person who uses or makes phrases. **2** a person given to fine phrases; phrasemonger.

**phrase-struc|ture grammar** (frāz′struk′chər), *Linguistics.* a grammar consisting of phrase-structure rules: *Considerable progress has been made ... in using computers to manipulate languages, both vernaculars and programming languages. Grammars called phrase-structure grammars and transformational grammars supply the theoretical backdrop for this activity* (Scientific American).

**phrase-structure rule**, *Linguistics.* one of the rules governing the construction of the phrasal constituents of a sentence: *It has become clear that phrase-structure rules and transformations provide a grossly inadequate characterization of the notion 'rule of grammar'. The problem is this: phrase-structure rules and transformations are local: they define well-formedness conditions on individual phrase-markers and on pairs of successive phrase-markers* (Language).

**phras|ing** (frā′zing), *n.* **1a** the manner or style of verbal expression; phraseology; wording: *Milton ... mixes the extremest vernacular with the most exquisite and scholarly phrasing* (George Saintsbury). **b** the grouping of spoken words by pauses. **2** *Music.* **a** a marking off or dividing into phrases. **b** the playing of phrases. **c** the manner in which a composition is phrased.

**phra|tric** (frā′trik), *adj.* **1** of or having to do with a phratry or clan. **2** consisting of phratries.

**phra|try** (frā′trē), *n., pl.* **-tries.** **1** each of the larger subdivisions of a tribe in ancient Athens. Members of a phratry regarded one another as "brothers." **2** a similar tribal unit, usually comprising two or more clans: *... the head woman then notifies the chief of all the clans in her phratry* (Beals and Hoijer). [< Greek *phrātriā* < *phrātēr* fellow clansman. Compare etym. under **fraternity.**]

**phre|at|ic** (frē at′ik), *adj.* **1** of or having to do with a well or wells. **2** having to do with or characteristic of water in the saturated area just below the water table. [< Greek *phréat-, phréar* well + English *-ic*]

**phre|at|o|phyte** (frē at′ə fīt), *n.* any plant that obtains water by the deep penetration of its roots into the water table: *It is almost impossible to get rid of phreatophytes by any means other than denying them water* (Roscoe Fleming). [< Greek *phréat-, phréar* well + English *-phyte*]

**phren.**, phrenology.

**phre|net|ic** (fri net′ik), *adj., n.* **—*adj.*** **1** excessively excited; frenzied; frantic: *He would ... make them even more phrenetic than they had been originally* (New Yorker). **2** = insane.
**—*n.*** = madman. Also, **frenetic.**
[< Old French *frenetique*, learned borrowing from Latin *phrenēticus.* See etym. of doublet **frantic.**]
**—phre|net′i|cal|ly,** *adv.*

**phre|net|i|cal** (fri net′ə kəl), *adj.* = phrenetic.

**phren|ic** (fren′ik), *adj.* **1** *Anatomy.* of or having to do with the diaphragm: *The lung may be put to rest by cutting the phrenic nerve* (Marguerite Clark). **2** *Obsolete.* of or having to do with the mind, especially as distinguished from the soul. [< New Latin *phrenicus* < Greek *phrēn* the diaphragm, midriff; also, mind, spirit]

**phre|nit|ic** (fri nit′ik), *adj.* affected with or suffering from phrenitis; subject to fits of delirium or madness.

**phre|ni|tis** (fri nī′tis), *n. Obsolete.* **1** inflammation of the diaphragm. **2** inflammation of the brain; encephalitis. **3** delirium. [< Greek *phrenîtis* inflammation of the brain. Compare etym. under **frantic.**]

**phrenol.**, phrenology.

**phren|o|log|ic** (fren′ə loj′ik), *adj.* = phrenological.

**phren|o|log|i|cal** (fren′ə loj′ə kəl), *adj.* of or having to do with phrenology. **—phren′o|log′i|cal|ly,** *adv.*

**phre|nol|o|gist** (fri nol′ə jist), *n.* a person who professes to tell a person's character from the shape of his skull.

**phre|nol|o|gy** (fri nol′ə jē), *n.* **1** the theory that the shape of the skull shows what sort of mind and character a person has. **2** the practice of reading character from the shape of the skull. [American English < Greek *phrēn, phrēnos* (see etym. under **phrenic**) + English *-logy*]

**phren|sy** (fren′zē), *n., pl.* **-sies,** *v.t.,* **-sied, -sy|ing.** = frenzy.

**Phrix|us** (frik′səs), *n. Greek Legend.* the son of a Boeotian king who escaped on the ram with the Golden Fleece.

**Phryg|i|an** (frij′ē ən), *adj., n.* **—*adj.*** of or having to do with Phrygia, an ancient country in central and northwestern Asia Minor, its people, or their language.
**—*n.*** **1** a native or inhabitant of Phrygia. **2** the Indo-European language of the ancient Phrygians.

***Phrygian cap**, a conical cap with its apex turned over toward the front, worn by the ancient Phrygians and in modern times adopted as a symbol of liberty; liberty cap.

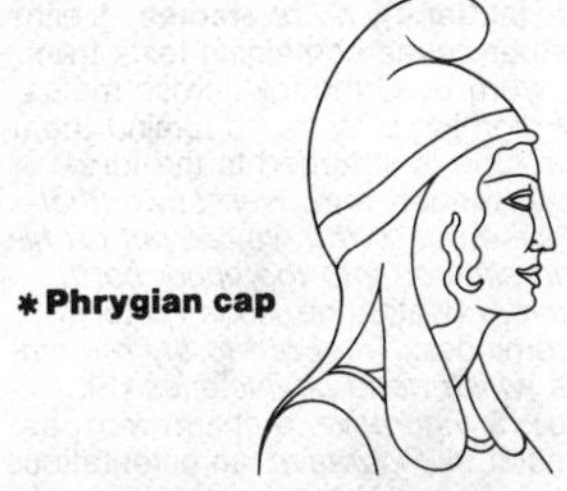
***Phrygian cap**

**PHS** (no periods), Public Health Service.

**phthal|ate** (thal′āt, fthal′-), *n.* a salt of phthalic acid.

**phthal|ein** (thal′ēn, -ē in; fthal′-), *n.* any one of a series of organic dyes, as eosin, produced by combining phthalic anhydride with phenols.

**phthal|ic acid** (thal′ik, fthal′-), one of three isomeric acids formed from certain benzene derivatives, especially a colorless crystalline substance prepared from naphthalene and used in making dyes and various synthetics. *Formula:* $C_8H_6O_4$ [short for *naphthalic* < *naphthal*(ene) + *-ic*]

**phthalic anhydride**, a white crystalline substance prepared from naphthalene, used in making various resins, dyes, and insecticides: *The new fireproof plastic is made from phthalic anhydride by addition of four chorine atoms* (Science News Letter). *Formula:* $C_8H_4O_3$

**phthal|in** (thal′in, fthal′-), *n.* any one of a series of colorless chemical compounds produced by the reduction of phthaleins.

**phthal|o|cy|a|nine** (thal′ə sī′ə nēn, -nin; fthal′-), *n.* **1** a blue-green crystalline compound derived from phthalic anhydride. *Formula:* $C_{32}H_{18}N_8$ **2** any one of various blue or green pigments derived by the reaction of this compound with a metal. [< *phthal*(ic) + *cyanine*]

**phthal|yl|sul|fa|thi|a|zole** (thal′il sul′fə thī′ə zōl, -zol; fthal′-), *n.* a sulfa drug used in treating infections in the intestinal tract. *Formula:* $C_{17}H_{13}N_3O_5S_2$

**phthi|o|col** (thī′ə kōl, -kol), *n. Biochemistry.* a yellow pigment having certain properties of vitamin K. *Formula:* $C_{11}H_8O_3$

**Pronunciation Key:** hat, āge, cãre, fär; let, ēqual, tėrm; it, īce; hot, ōpen, ôrder; oil, out; cup, pu̇t, rüle; child; long; thin; ᴛʜen; zh, measure; ə represents **a** in about, **e** in taken, **i** in pencil, **o** in lemon, **u** in circus.

**phthi|ri|a|sis** (thi rī′ə sis, fthi-), *n. Medicine.* the state of being infested with lice, with the resulting irritation or other effects; pediculosis. [< Latin *phthīriasis* < Greek *phtheirίasis* < *phtheiriân* be full of lice < *phtheír* louse]

**phthis|ic** (tiz′ik), *n., adj. Archaic.* — ***n.*** phthisis. — ***adj.*** phthisical. [< Latin *phthisica,* feminine of *phthisicus* < Greek *phthisikós,* adjective, consumptive < *phthísis* phthisis]

**phthis|i|cal** (tiz′ə kəl), *adj.* having to do with, like, or affected with phthisis.

**phthis|ick|y** (tiz′ə kē), *adj. Archaic.* **1** tubercular. **2** asthmatic.

**phthi|sis** (thī′sis), *n.* any progressive, wasting disease of the body or of some part of the body, especially tuberculosis of the lungs. [< Latin *phthisis* < Greek *phthísis* any wasting disease < *phthíein* to waste away]

**phy|co|cy|a|nin** (fī′kō sī′ə nin), *n.* a blue pigment found in association with chlorophyll, especially in the cells of the blue-green algae: *Phycocyanin was found to be the key to why plants blossom in accordance with the length of daylight and darkness* (Science News Letter). [< Greek *phŷkos* seaweed + *kýanos* blue + English *-in*]

**phy|co|e|ryth|rin** (fī′kō ə rith′rin), *n.* a red pigment found in the red algae and, in association with phycocyanin, in the blue-green algae. [< Greek *phŷkos* seaweed + *erythrós* red + English *-in*]

**phy|col|o|gist** (fī kol′ə jist), *n.* person who studies phycology; algologist.

**phy|col|o|gy** (fī kol′ə jē), *n.* the branch of botany dealing with seaweeds or algae; algology. [< Greek *phŷkos* seaweed + English *-logy*]

**phy|co|my|cete** (fī′kō mī sēt′), *n.* a phycomycetous fungus.

**phy|co|my|ce|tous** (fī′kō mī sē′təs), *adj.* of or belonging to the lowest class or group of fungi, whose members live as parasites or saprophytes and resemble algae. [< New Latin *Phycomyceteae* a division of fungi (< Greek *phŷkos* seaweed + *mýkēs, -ētos* fungus, mushroom) + English *-ous*]

**phy|la** (fī′lə), *n.* **1** plural of **phylum**. **2** plural of **phylon.**

***phy|lac|ter|y** (fə lak′tər ē), *n., pl.* **-ter|ies. 1** either of two small leather cases containing texts from the Jewish law, worn by Orthodox Jewish males during weekday morning prayers, to remind them to keep the Law. One is strapped to the forehead, the other to the left arm. *Herr Löwenthal put his sample case out of the way ... put on his phylacteries, and climbed into the upper berth and said his prayers* (Katherine Anne Porter). **2** *Figurative.* a reminder: *Trust not to thy remembrance in things which need phylacteries* (Sir Thomas Browne). **3** *Figurative.* a charm worn as a protection; amulet. **4** *Figurative.* an ostentatious or hypocritical display of righteousness; mark of pharisaism.
[< Late Latin *phylactērium* < Greek *phylaktḗrion* safeguard; guardpost < *phylaktḗr* guard, watchman]

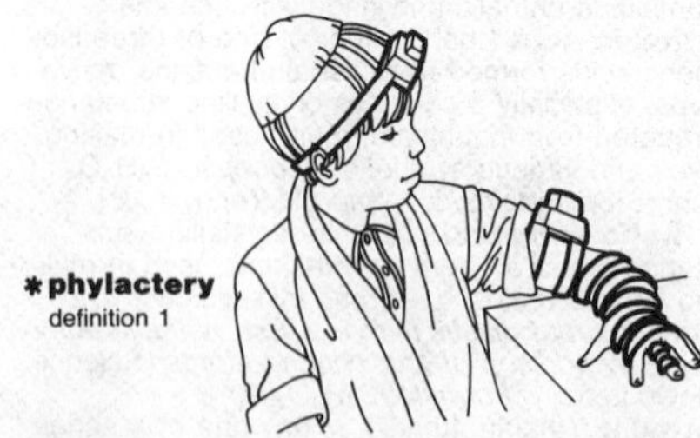

***phylactery**
definition 1

**phy|le** (fī′lē), *n., pl.* **-lae** (-lē). **1** (in ancient Greece) a tribe or clan, based on supposed kinship. **2** (in Attica) a political, administrative, and military subdivision, made chiefly on a geographical basis. [< Greek *phȳlḗ* tribe, clan, related to *phýein* beget]

**phy|let|ic** (fī let′ik), *adj.* of or having to do with a biological phylum, or a line of descent: *... a special terminology arising from the experimental and natural observation of animals at their own phyletic level* (new Scientist). [< Greek *phȳletikós* tribal < *phȳlétēs* tribesman < *phȳlḗ* tribe; with meaning from English *phylum*] — **phy|let′i|cal|ly,** *adv.*

**Phyl|lis** (fil′is), *n.* a name in pastoral poetry for a comely rustic maiden or sweetheart. Also, **Phillis.** [< Latin *Phyllis,* a girl's name in Virgil and Horace < Greek *Phyllís* (literally) foliage < *phýllon* leaf]

**phyl|lite** (fil′īt), *n.* a rock consisting of an argillaceous schist or slate, containing scales or flakes of mica. [< Greek *phýllon* leaf + English *-ite*[1]]

**phyl|lo|clad** (fil′ə klad), *n.* = phylloclade.

**phyl|lo|clade** (fil′ə klād), *n.* **1** a flattened or enlarged stem or branch, resembling or performing the function of a leaf, as in the cactus. **2** = cladophyll. [< New Latin *phyllocladium* < Greek *phýllon* leaf + *kládos* branch, sprout]

***phyl|lode** (fil′ōd), *n.* an expanded and, usually, flattened petiole resembling and having the functions of a leaf, the true leaf blade being absent or much reduced in size, as in many acacias. [< French *phyllode* < New Latin *phyllodium* < Greek *phyllṓdēs* leaflike < *phýllon* leaf + *eîdos* form]

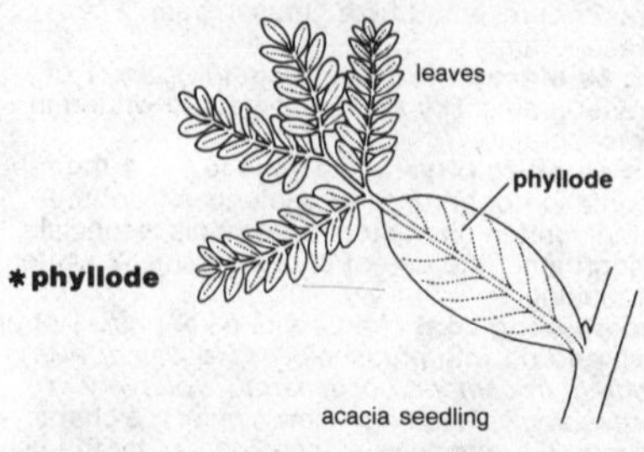


***phyllode**

**phyl|lo|dy** (fil′ə dē), *n.* **1** the condition in which parts of a flower are transformed into ordinary leaves. **2** the condition in which a leafstalk is changed into a phyllode. [< *phyllode* + *-y*[3]]

**phyl|loid** (fil′oid), *adj.* resembling a leaf.

**phyl|lome** (fil′ōm), *n.* **1** a leaf of a plant or any organ homologous with a leaf, or regarded as a modified leaf, such as a sepal, petal, or stamen. **2** all the leaves of a plant, taken as a whole; foliage. [< German *Phyllome* < New Latin *phylloma* < Greek *phýllōma* foliage < *phýllon* leaf]

**phyl|lom|ic** (fə lom′ik, -lō′mik), *adj.* of or like a phyllome.

**phyl|loph|a|gous** (fə lof′ə gəs), *adj.* leaf-eating, as certain beetles and chafers. [< Greek *phýllon* leaf + *phageîn* eat + English *-ous*]

**phyl|lo|phore** (fil′ə fôr, -fōr), *n. Botany.* the terminal leaf-producing bud or growing point of a stem (used especially with reference to palms). [< Greek *phýllon* leaf + English *-phore*]

**phyl|lo|pod** (fil′ə pod), *adj., n.* — ***adj.*** of or belonging to a group of small crustaceans with four or more pairs of leaflike appendages which function as both swimming feet and gills.
— ***n.*** a phyllopod crustacean.
[< New Latin *Phyllopoda* the group name < Greek *phýllon* leaf + *poús, podós* foot]

**phyl|lop|o|dan** (fə lop′ə dən), *adj., n.* = phyllopod.

**phyl|lo|tac|tic** (fil′ə tak′tik), *adj.* of or having to do with phyllotaxis: *the phyllotactic spiral of leaves.*

**phyl|lo|tax|is** (fil′ə tak′sis), *n.* **1** the distribution or arrangement of leaves on a stem. **2** the laws collectively which govern such distribution. [< New Latin *phyllotaxis* < Greek *phýllon* leaf + *táxis* arrangement]

**phyl|lo|tax|y** (fil′ə tak′sē), *n.* = phyllotaxis.

**phyl|lox|e|ra** (fil′ok sir′ə, fə lok′sər-), *n., pl.* **phyl|lox|e|rae** (fil′ok sir′ē, fə lok′sə rē). any one of a group of plant lice. The grape phylloxera destroys grapevines by infesting the leaves and roots. [< New Latin *Phylloxera* the genus name < Greek *phýllon* leaf + *xērós* dry (because the lice "dry up the foliage")]

**phyl|lox|e|ral** (fə lok′sər əl), *adj.* of or having to do with the phylloxera.

**phyl|lox|e|rat|ed** (fə lok′sə rā′tid), *adj.* infested with phylloxerae.

**phyl|lox|er|ic** (fil′ok ser′ik), *adj.* = phylloxeral.

**phyl|lox|e|rized** (fə lok′sə rīzd), *adj.* = phylloxerated.

**phy|lo|gen|e|sis** (fī′lə jen′ə sis), *n.* = phylogeny.

**phy|lo|ge|net|ic** (fī′lə jə net′ik), *adj.* of or having to do with phylogeny. — **phy′lo|ge|net′i|cal|ly,** *adv.*

**phy|lo|gen|ic** (fī′lə jen′ik), *adj.* = phylogenetic.

**phy|log|e|nist** (fī loj′ə nist), *n.* a person who studies phylogeny: *As phylogenists, Whitman and Heinroth both sought to develop in detail the relationship between families and species of birds* (Scientific American).

**phy|log|e|ny** (fī loj′ə nē), *n., pl.* **-nies.** the origin and development of a species or higher grouping of animal or plant, or the history of its development: *Ontogeny recapitulates phylogeny* (Henry E. Crampton). [< German *Phylogenie* < Greek *phȳlon* race[2] + *-geneia* origin]

**phy|lon** (fī′lon), *n., pl.* **-la.** *Biology.* a tribe; a genetically related subdivision; phylum. [< Greek *phŷlon* race[2]]

**phy|lum** (fī′ləm), *n., pl.* **-la. 1** *Biology.* a primary division of the animal or plant kingdom, consisting of one or more classes, usually equivalent to a subkingdom, such as the thallophytes, Protozoa, or Arthropoda. The animals or plants in a phylum are thought to be related by descent from a common ancestral form. *Since all animal phyla with the exception of the vertebrates are present in early Cambrian rocks, it is evident that much of the evolutionary sequence has not yet been examined* (Willard Bascom). **2** a group of languages that includes two or more linguistic families or stocks: *... Haida and Tlingit, apparently related to the Athabascan family, with which they form the Na-Dené phylum, are immediately adjacent* (H. A. Gleason, Jr.). [< New Latin *phylum* < Greek *phŷlon* race[2], stock]

**phys.,** **1** physical. **2** physician. **3** physics.

**phys. ed.,** physical education.

**phys|i|at|rics** (fiz′ē at′riks), *n.* = physical medicine.

**phys|i|at|rist** (fiz′ē at′rist), *n.* a person skilled in physiatrics.

**phys|ic** (fiz′ik), *n., v.,* **-icked, -ick|ing.** — ***n.*** **1** a medicine, especially one that acts as a laxative; cathartic. **2** *Archaic.* the art of healing; science and practice of medicine: *Throw physic to the dogs; I'll none of it* (Shakespeare). **3** *Archaic.* natural science.
— ***v.t.*** **1** to give a laxative to. **2** *Figurative.* to give medicine to; dose; treat. **3** to act like a medicine on; cure: *The labor we delight in physics pain* (Shakespeare). **SYN:** relieve, alleviate.
[< Latin *physica* < Greek *physikḗ* (*epistḗmē*) (knowledge) of nature < *phýsis* nature < *phýein* to produce]

**phys|i|cal** (fiz′ə kəl), *adj., n.* — ***adj.*** **1** of the body: *physical exercise, physical strength, a physical disability.* **SYN:** bodily. **2** of matter; material: *The tide is a physical force.* **3** according to the laws of nature: *It is a physical impossibility for the sun to rise in the west.* **4** of the science of physics.
— ***n.*** *Informal.* a physical examination. — **phys′i|cal|ness,** *n.*

**physical anthropologist,** a person who studies physical anthropology: *The physical anthropologist is, in one sense, a biologist who concentrates his attention on man* (Beals and Hoijer).

**physical anthropology,** the branch of anthropology that deals with the development of man's personal characteristics, including his bodily formation and mental traits.

**physical change,** *Chemistry.* a change in the size or form of a substance without any alteration in the composition of its molecules or without its producing or becoming a new substance.

**physical chemistry,** the branch of chemistry that deals with the basic laws of the properties of substances as formulated by physics and their relations to chemical composition and changes.

**physical culture,** the development of the body by appropriate exercise.

**physical education,** instruction in how to exercise and take care of the body, especially as a course at a school or college.

**physical examination,** an examination of the various parts of a person's body to determine the state of health, especially as made by a physician.

**physical geography,** the branch of geography that deals with the natural features of the earth's surface; physiography. Physical geography teaches about the earth's formation, climate, clouds, winds, ocean currents, and all other physical features of the earth.

**physical inventory,** an inventory made by a count of stock or equipment instead of by checking books of account.

**phys|i|cal|ism** (fiz′ə kə liz′əm), *n.* the doctrine that physical properties, functions, and processes are the only valid subject of scientific study and experimentation: *There is no necessary border to battle between physicalism and mentalism* (Noam Chomsky).

**phys|i|cal|ist** (fiz′ə kə list), *n.* a person who believes in physicalism.

**phys|i|cal|i|ty** (fiz′ə kal′ə tē), *n.* physical quality or condition.

**phys|i|cal|ly** (fiz′ək lē), *adv.* in a physical manner; in physical respects; as regards the body: *After his vacation he was in fine condition both physically and mentally.*

**physical medicine,** the branch of medicine that deals with curing disease and improving health by physical means, especially physical therapy or physiotherapy.

**physical metallurgy,** the science and technology of the production and compounding of metals and alloys; alloy metallurgy: *Physical metallurgy is the branch of metallurgy which adapts metals to human use* (A. E. Adami).

**physical production,** production measured by quantities of goods produced, rather than by money values. An index of physical production reflects changes in output, not changes in price.

**physical restoration,** occupational therapy that involves rehabilitation of the muscles and joints, as after paralysis or an accident, or during a period of adjustment to an artificial limb; functional therapy.

**physical science**, 1 physics. 2 physics, chemistry, geology, astronomy, and other sciences dealing with inanimate matter.

**physical scientist**, a person who studies or is skilled in one of the physical sciences.

**physical therapist**, a person skilled in physical therapy.

**physical therapy**, the treatment of diseases and physical defects of the body by remedies such as massage or electricity, rather than by drugs; physiotherapy.

**phy|si|cian** (fə zish′ən), *n.* **1** a doctor of medicine: *The physician gave his sick patient some strong medicine.* **2** any practitioner of the healing art: *More needs she the divine than the physician* (Shakespeare). **3** a person who cures any one of various maladies or infirmities, as of the soul; healer. [Middle English *fisicien* < Old French, learned borrowing from Medieval Latin *physicus* doctor, or *physica* medical science (in Latin, natural science); see etym. under **physic**]
► **Physician**, in the sense of def. 1, is subject to strict definition under law throughout most of the world today. The usual prerequisites are a successfully completed course of study in an accredited school of medicine, normally followed by a period of internship and oftentimes further examination by some governmental or other official authority preliminary to the granting of a license to engage in the practice of medicine. In Great Britain, the physician is one who practices medicine as distinguished from one who practices surgery (a surgeon). Today, all surgeons in the United States hold degrees as doctors of medicine, although one who specializes in surgery is usually referred to as a "surgeon," just as one who specializes in gynecology is referred to as a "gynecologist," one who specializes in psychiatry is referred to as a "psychiatrist," and so on.

**phys|i|cist** (fiz′ə sist), *n.* **1** a person who studies or is skilled in physics: *In studying these phenomena, the classical aerodynamicist must learn from the physicist who has some knowledge of spectroscopy* (Louis N. Ridenour). **2** *Archaic.* a natural philosopher.

**phys|i|co|chem|i|cal** (fiz′i kō kem′ə kəl), *adj.* **1** of or having to do with the physical and chemical properties of substances: *physicochemical research.* **2** having to do with physical chemistry. —**phys′i|co|chem′i|cal|ly**, *adv.*

**phys|ics** (fiz′iks), *n.* **1** the science that deals with matter and energy, and the action of different forms of energy, excluding chemical and biological change. Physics studies force, motion, heat, light, sound, electricity, magnetism, radiation, and atomic structure. *The aim of theoretical physics must be to find a complete set of mutually consistent postulates or axioms from which the properties of nature ... can be deduced in the form of a number of theorems* (H. J. Bhaba). **2** a textbook or treatise on physics. **3** *Archaic.* natural science. [< Latin *physica,* or Greek *tà physiká* the natural things. Compare etym. under **metaphysics.**]

**physio-**, *combining form.* physical, as in *physiology, physiography.*

**phys|i|o|chem|i|cal** (fiz′ē ō kem′ə kəl), *adj.* of or having to do with the chemistry of living animals and plants.

**phys|i|oc|ra|cy** (fiz′ē ok′rə sē), *n., pl.* **-cies. 1** the economic doctrines and system advocated by the physiocrats. **2** government by, or in accordance with, nature.

**phys|i|o|crat** (fiz′ē ə krat), *n.* a follower of the school of economic thought founded by the French economist François Quesnay, in the 1700's, who believed that land was the only real source of wealth and the only proper source of taxation, maintained that society should be governed by an inherent natural order, and advocated free trade. [< French *physiocrate* < *physiocratie* physiocracy < Greek *phýsis* nature + *krátos* rule]

**phys|i|o|crat|ic** (fiz′ē ə krat′ik), *adj.* **1** of or having to do with government according to nature. **2** of or having to do with the physiocrats or their doctrines.

**phys|i|og|nom|ic** (fiz′ē og nom′ik, -ə nom′-), *adj.* of or having to do with physiognomy. —**phys′i|og|nom′i|cal|ly**, *adv.*

**phys|i|og|nom|i|cal** (fiz′ē og nom′ə kəl, -ə nom′-), *adj.* = physiognomic.

**phys|i|og|no|mist** (fiz′ē og′nə mist, -on′ə-), *n.* a person skilled in physiognomy.

**phys|i|og|no|my** (fiz′ē og′nə mē, -on′ə-), *n., pl.* **-mies. 1** the kind of features or type of face one has; one's face. *a ruddy physiognomy, a kindly physiognomy. His physiognomy indicated the inanity of character which pervaded his life* (Scott). SYN: countenance. **2** the art of estimating character from the features of the face or the form of the body. **3** the general aspect or looks of something, such as the countryside or a situation: *the rugged physiognomy of northern Scotland.* [< Late Latin *physiognōmia* < a variant of Greek *physiognōmoníā* < *phýsis* nature + *gnṓmōn, -onos* a judge]

**phys|i|og|ra|pher** (fiz′ē og′rə fər), *n.* an expert in physiography.

**phys|i|o|graph|ic** (fiz′ē ə graf′ik), *adj.* of or having to do with physiography.

**phys|i|o|graph|i|cal** (fiz′ē ə graf′ə kəl), *adj.* = physiographic.

**physiographic climax**, *Ecology.* a climax that is determined mainly by the physical features or topography of the area, for example whether it has grass, woods, or hills.

**phys|i|og|ra|phy** (fiz′ē og′rə fē), *n.* **1** = physical geography. **2** = geomorphology. **3** (formerly) the science of nature or of natural phenomena in general. [< Greek *phýsis* nature + English *-graphy*]

**physiol.**, 1 physiological. 2 physiologist. 3 physiology.

**phys|i|ol|a|ter** (fiz′ē ol′ə tər), *n.* a person who worships nature.

**phys|i|ol|a|try** (fiz′ē ol′ə trē), *n.* the worship of nature. [< Greek *phýsis* nature + *latreíā* worship]

**phys|i|o|log|ic** (fiz′ē ə loj′ik), *adj.* = physiological.

**phys|i|o|log|i|cal** (fiz′ē ə loj′ə kəl), *adj.* **1** having to do with physiology: *Digestion is a physiological process.* **2** having to do with the normal or healthy functioning of an organism: *Food and sleep are physiological needs.* —**phys′i|o|log′i|cal|ly**, *adv.*

**physiological chemistry**, = biochemistry.

**physiological psychologist**, a person skilled in physiological psychology.

**physiological psychology**, the study of the effects of physiological functions and processes on the behavior of people and animals.

**phys|i|ol|o|gist** (fiz′ē ol′ə jist), *n.* a person who studies or is skilled in physiology.

**phys|i|ol|o|gy** (fiz′ē ol′ə jē), *n., pl.* **-gies. 1** the science dealing with the normal functions of living things or their parts: *animal physiology, plant physiology, the physiology of the blood.* **2** a textbook or treatise on this science. **3** all the functions and activities of a living thing or of one of its parts. [< Latin *physiologia* < Greek *physiologíā* natural science < *physiólogos* one discoursing on nature < *phýsis* nature + *-lógos* treating of < *légein* speak]

**phys|i|o|pa|thol|o|gy** (fiz′ē ō pə thol′ə jē), *n.* the science dealing with the physiological aspects of disease.

**phys|i|o|sorp|tion** (fiz′ē ō sôrp′shən, -zôrp′-), *n.* adsorption in which one or more layers of molecules are held weakly to a surface by physical forces. [< Greek *phýsis* nature + English (ad)*sorption*]

**phys|i|o|ther|a|peu|tic** (fiz′ē ō ther′ə pyü′tik), *adj.* of or having to do with physiotherapy.

**phys|i|o|ther|a|pist** (fiz′ē ō ther′ə pist), *n.* = physical therapist.

**phys|i|o|ther|a|py** (fiz′ē ō ther′ə pē), *n.* = physical therapy. [< Greek *phýsis* nature + English *therapy*]

**phy|sique** (fə zēk′), *n.* bodily structure, organization, or development; physical appearance; body: *Samson was a man of strong physique.* [< French *physique,* noun use of adjective, physical < Old French *fusique* a physic < Latin *physicus* < Greek *physikós;* see etym. under **physic**]

**phy|so|clis|tous** (fī′sō klis′təs), *adj.* (of fishes) having no duct joining the air bladder with the alimentary canal, as perches. [< Greek *phŷsa* bladder + *-kleistos* (with English *-ous*) closed, shut]

**phy|so|stig|min** (fī′sō stig′min), *n.* = physostigmine.

**phy|so|stig|mine** (fī′sō stig′mēn, -min), *n.* a highly potent, crystalline alkaloid, constituting the active principle of the Calabar bean; eserine. It has various uses in medicine, such as to stimulate the parasympathetic nerves, to contract the pupil of the eye, and to treat myasthenia gravis. *Formula:* $C_{15}H_{21}N_3O_2$ [< German *Physostigmin* < New Latin *Physostigma* the Calabar bean genus (< Greek *phŷsa* bladder, bellows + New Latin *stigma* stigma, part of a pistil of a plant) + German *-in* -ine[2]]

**phy|sos|to|mous** (fī sos′tə məs), *adj.* (of fishes) having the air bladder connected with the alimentary canal by an air duct. [< New Latin *Physostomi* the group name (< Greek *phŷsa* bladder + *stóma* mouth)]

**phyt-**, *combining form.* the form of **phyto-** before vowels, as in *phytin.*

**phy|tane** (fī′tān), *n.* a complex hydrocarbon, a product of the breakdown of chlorophyll, the presence of which in oilbearing rocks is thought to be evidence of the existence of living matter 3 billion years ago. *Formula:* $C_{20}H_{42}$ [< Greek *phytón* plant + *-ane* (chemical suffix)]

**-phyte**, *combining form.* a growth or plant, as in *epiphyte.* [< Greek *phytón* a plant, shoot < *phýein* grow, beget]

**phy|tic acid** (fī′tik), an acid found in cereal seeds. It is a constituent of Phytin and other salts, and is used as a rust inhibitor, metal cleaner, etc. *Formula:* $C_6H_{18}O_{24}P_6$

**Phy|tin** (fī′tin), *n. Trademark.* a calcium and magnesium salt containing phosphorus, present as a reserve material in seeds, tubers, and rhizomes. Phytin is used as a dietary supplement, providing calcium, organic phosphorus, and inositol. [< *phyt-* + *-in*]

**phyto-**, *combining form.* a plant; plants: *Phytotoxic = toxic to plants.* Also, **phyt-** before vowels. [< Greek *phytón* plant]

**phy|to|a|lex|in** (fī′tō ə lek′sin), *n.* any substance produced by a plant to counteract disease. [< *phyto-* + *alexin*]

**phy|to|bi|ol|o|gy** (fī tō bī ol′ə jē), *n.* the branch of biology which deals with plants.

**phy|to|chem|i|cal** (fī′tō kem′ə kəl), *adj.* of or having to do with phytochemistry.

**phy|to|chem|is|try** (fī′tō kem′ə strē), *n.* the chemistry of plants.

**phy|to|chrome** (fī′tə krōm), *n.* a bluish, light-sensitive pigment in plants which absorbs red or infrared rays and acts as an enzyme in controlling growth and other photoperiodic responses: *Phytochrome molecules regulate such processes as germination, growth, and flowering, turning these functions on and off in response to the length of days and nights* (James A. Pearre).

**phy|to|cid|al** (fī′tō sī′dəl), *adj.* able to kill plants. [< *phyto-* + *-cid*(e)[2] + *-al*[1]]

**phy|to|gen|e|sis** (fī′tō jen′ə sis), *n.* the development or evolution of plants.

**phy|to|ge|net|ic** (fī′tō jə net′ik), *adj.* **1** of or having to do with phytogenesis. **2** of vegetable or plant origin. —**phy′to|ge|net′i|cal|ly**, *adv.*

**phy|to|ge|net|i|cal** (fī′tō jə net′ə kəl), *adj.* = phytogenetic.

**phy|to|gen|ic** (fī′tō jen′ik), *adj.* = phytogenetic.

**phy|tog|e|nous** (fī toj′ə nəs), *adj.* = phytogenetic.

**phy|tog|e|ny** (fī toj′ə nē), *n.* = phytogenesis.

**phy|to|ge|o|graph|i|cal** (fī′tō jē ə graf′ə kəl), *adj.* of or having to do with phytogeography: *Botanists have always regarded the British Isles as a phytogeographical whole* (New Scientist). —**phy′to|ge′o|graph′i|cal|ly**, *adv.*

**phy|to|ge|og|ra|phy** (fī′tō jē og′rə fē), *n.* the science that deals with the geographical distribution of plants: *What bearing had the phytogeography of the past on the evolution and dispersal of major groups like the flowering plants?* (London Times).

**phy|tog|ra|phy** (fī tog′rə fē), *n.* the branch of botany that deals with the description, naming, and classifying of plants; descriptive botany; plant taxonomy. [< New Latin *phytographia* < Greek *phytón* plant + English *-graphy*]

**phy|to|he|mag|glu|ti|nin** (fī′tō hē′mə glü′tə nin, -hem′ə-), *n.* any one of various protein substances extracted from plants that cause blood cells to change in shape, divide, or clump together. [< *photo-* + *hemagglutinin*]

**phy|to|hor|mone** (fī′tō hôr′mōn), *n. Botany, Chemistry.* plant hormone.

**phy|toid** (fī′toid), *adj.* of or like a plant.

**phy|tol** (fī′tōl, -tol), *n.* a colorless, oily, unsaturated alcohol, derived from chlorophyll, used in making vitamins E and K. *Formula:* $C_{20}H_{40}O$

**phy|to|lac|ca|ceous** (fī′tō la kā′shəs), *adj.* belonging to a family of chiefly tropical dicotyledonous trees, shrubs, and herbs, typified by the pokeweed. [< New Latin *Phytolacca* the genus name (< Greek *phytón* plant + New Latin *lacca* lake[2]) + English *-aceous* (because of the red juice of the berries]

**phy|to|log|ic** (fī′tə loj′ik), *adj.* of or having to do with phytology; botanical.

**phy|to|log|i|cal** (fī′tə loj′ə kəl), *adj.* = phytologic.

**phy|tol|o|gist** (fī tol′ə jist), *n.* a person skilled in phytology; botanist.

**phy|tol|o|gy** (fī tol′ə jē), *n.* the science of plants; botany.

**phy|ton** (fī′ton), *n.* the smallest part of a plant; plant unit.

**phy|to|pa|le|on|tol|o|gy** (fī′tō pā′lē on tol′ə jē), *n.* = geologic botany.

**phy|to|path|o|gen|ic** (fī′tō path′ə jen′ik), *adj.* causing plant disease, especially by parasitic destruction of the host: *mixed populations of nonparasitic and phytopathogenic organisms* (Science News).

**Pronunciation Key:** hat, āge, cãre, fär; let, ēqual, tėrm; it, īce; hot, ōpen, ôrder; oil, out; cup, pu̇t, rüle; child; long; thin; ᴛʜen; zh, measure; ə represents **a** in about, **e** in taken, **i** in pencil, **o** in lemon, **u** in circus.

**phy|to|pa|thol|o|gist** (fī′tō pə thol′ə jist), *n.* a person skilled in phytopathology; mycologist.

**phy|to|pa|thol|o|gy** (fī′tō pə thol′ə jē), *n.* **1** the science that deals with the diseases of plants: *The control of banana leaf disease probably represents one of the greatest achievements in the history of phytopathology* (C. W. Wardlaw). **2** *Medicine.* the study of diseases as caused by plant parasites and fungi; mycology.

**phy|toph|a|gous** (fī tof′ə gəs), *adj.* feeding on plants; herbivorous: *A wide variety of animals, including most carnivorous and phytophagous vertebrates and invertebrates, might be classed as predators* (Harbaugh and Goodrich). [< *phyto-* + Greek *phageîn* eat + English *-ous*]

**phy|to|plank|ton** (fī′tō plangk′tən), *n.* the part of the plankton of any body of water which consists of plants, usually algae: *The phytoplankton serves as food for tiny sea animals ... which in turn are eaten by fish, birds or other sea-going animals* (Science News Letter).

**phy|to|so|ci|ol|o|gy** (fī′tō sō′sē ol′ə jē, -sō′shē-), *n.* the branch of plant ecology dealing with the interrelations among the plants of various areas. [< *phyto-* + *sociology*]

**phy|tos|ter|ol** (fī tos′tə rōl, -rol), *n.* any one of several plant alcohols, such as ergosterol, that have the properties of sterols.

**phy|to|tox|ic** (fī′tō tok′sik), *adj.* toxic or injurious to plants: *A fungicide must have no damaging effect on the plant, that is, it should not be phytotoxic* (R. L. Wain).

**phy|to|tox|i|cant** (fī′tō tok′sə kənt), *n.* any substance toxic to plants.

**phy|to tox|ic|i|ty** (fī′tō tok sis′ə tē), *n.* a toxic or poisonous quality injurious to plants: *There are available a number of excellent protective fungicides which, although not entirely free from phytotoxicity, are playing an important part in controlling plant diseases* (New Scientist).

**phy|to|tron** (fī′tə tron), *n.* a structure or laboratory apparatus in which climatic conditions are simulated for the study of plants in a controlled environment. [< *phyto-* + *-tron*]

***pi¹** (pī), *n., pl.* **pis. 1** the ratio of the circumference of any circle to its diameter, usually written as *π* and equal to 3.14159+. **2** the 16th letter of the Greek alphabet, equivalent to English *P, p.* [(definition 1) < name of Greek letter *π*, used as abbreviation of Greek *periphéreia* periphery]

***pi¹**
definitions 1, 2

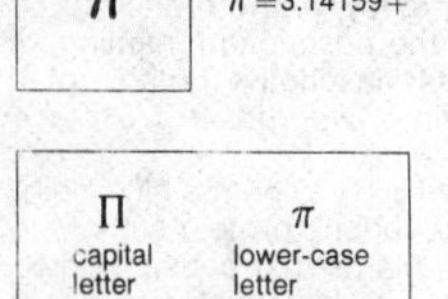


**pi²** (pī), *n., pl.* **pis,** *v.,* **pied, pi|ing.** *— n.* **1** printing types all mixed up. **2** any confused mixture.
*— v.t.* to mix up (type). Also, **pie.**
[origin uncertain; perhaps < *pie¹* (because of its miscellaneous contents)]

**pi³** (pī), *adj. British Informal.* pious: *God's grace (and I don't mean to sound pi) is what England seems to lack at the moment* (Listener).

**pi.,** piaster.

**PI** (no periods), **1** photo interpretation. **2** programed instruction.

**P.I.,** Philippine Islands.

**pi|a¹** (pī′ə), *n.* = pia mater.

**pi|a²** (pē′ə), *n.* a perennial herb of Polynesia, the East Indies, and the surrounding areas, with a tuberous root that yields a nutritious starch, the so-called South Sea arrowroot. [< the Polynesian name]

**pi|ac|u|lar** (pī ak′yə lər), *adj.* **1** making expiation; expiatory. **2** needing expiation; sinful; wicked. [< Latin *piāculāris* expiatory < *piāculum* expiation < *piāre* to appease < *pīus* devout]

**pi|ac|u|la|tive** (pī ak′yə lə tiv), *adj.* = piacular.

**piaffe** (pyaf), *v.i.,* **piaffed, piaf|fing.** in horsemanship: **1** to move the diagonally opposite legs, as in the trot, but without going forward, backward, or sideways. **2** to move at a very slow trotting pace forward, backward, or sideways. [< French *piaffer* to strut; see etym. under **piaffer**]

**piaf|fer** (pyaf′ər), *n.* the act of piaffing. [< French *piaffer,* noun use of infinitive, to strut < obsolete *piaffe* outward show, parade; origin uncertain]

**Pi|a|get|ian** (pē ə zhā′ən), *adj., n. — adj.* of or having to do with the Swiss psychologist Jean Piaget (born 1896) or his theories of child development: [*In*] *articles representative of the theoretical and empirical research derived from Piagetian theory, focus is on intellectual development of the young elementary school child* (Science News).
*— n.* an advocate or supporter of Jean Piaget and his theories: *Quite possibly, Piagetians sometimes speculate, adolescents' fascination with their ability to visualize alternatives is what makes them so eager to test new life-styles and utopian ideals* (Time).

**pi|al** (pī′əl), *adj.* of or having to do with the pia mater: *the pial surface.*

**pi|a ma|ter** (pī′ə mā′tər), *Anatomy.* the delicate, vascular membrane which is the innermost of three membranes enveloping the brain and spinal cord. [< Medieval Latin *pia mater* pious mother, mistranslation of Arabic *'umm raqīqah* thin (or tender) mother]

**pi|a|nette** (pē′ə net′), *n. British.* **1** a small upright piano. **2** a street piano. [< *pian*(o) + *-ette*]

**pi|an|ism** (pē an′iz əm, pē′ə niz-), *n.* performance on the piano; technique or skill in playing the piano: *His pianism has refined, and he achieved beautiful tone coloring in the fourth poetical variation of the slow movement* (New York Times).

***pi|a|nis|si|mo** (pē′ə nis′ə mō), *adj., adv., n., pl.* **-mos, -mi** (-mē). *Music. — adj.* very soft (used as a direction).
*— adv.* very softly: *We simply paid closer attention to the score. When it said pianissimo, we played pianissimo* (Time).
*— n.* a very soft passage or movement: *I especially admired the orchestra's dry, understated pianissimos* (New Yorker).
[< Italian *pianissimo,* superlative of *piano;* see etym. under **piano²**]

***pianissimo**

**pi|an|ist** (pē an′ist, pē′ə nist), *n.* a person who plays the piano: *a concert pianist.*

**pia|niste** (pyȧ nēst′), *n. French.* a pianist.

**pi|a|nis|tic** (pē′ə nis′tik), *adj.* of, having to do with, or characteristic of, a pianist: *pianistic artistry.* — **pi′a|nis′ti|cal|ly,** *adv.*

**Pi|an|ka|shaw** (pī an′kə shô), *n., pl.* **-shaw** or **-shaws.** a member of a North American Indian tribe within the Miami, formerly occupying the Wabash River valley in Indiana and Illinois.

***pi|an|o¹** (pē an′ō), *n., pl.* **-os.** a large musical instrument whose tones come from many wires and range over several octaves. The wires are sounded by felt-covered hammers that are worked by striking keys on a keyboard. *Although the piano is the only true solo instrument among our standard concert instruments, it is the exception, rather than the rule, to find it unaccompanied in modern jazz* (New Yorker). See picture below. [< Italian *piano,* short for *pianoforte*]

***pi|a|no²** (pē ä′nō), *adj., adv., n., pl.* **-nos.** *Music. — adj.* soft; low (used as a direction): *In piano singing her tone remains pure* (London Times).
*— adv.* softly.
*— n.* a soft passage or movement.
[< Italian *piano* < Latin *plānus* plain, flat (in Late Latin, smooth, graceful). See etym. of doublets **plain¹, plane¹, plan.**]

***piano²**

**pi|an|o|for|te** (pē an′ə fôr′tē, -fōr′-; -an′ə fôrt, -fōrt), *n.* = piano¹. [< Italian *pianoforte* < *piano* soft (see etym. under **piano²**) + *forte* loud < Latin *fortis* strong (because of its greater capability of gradation in dynamics)]

**pi|a|no|la** (pē′ə nō′lə), *n.* **1** a piano played by machinery; player piano. **2 Pianola,** a trademark for a player piano.

**pia|no no|bi|le** (pyä′nō nô′bē lā), *n., pl.* **pia|ni no|bi|li** (pyä′nē nô′bē lē). *Italian.* the main floor of a palazzo: *The first floor of her palace on the Tiber had been converted into shops, and she lived on the piano nobile* (John Cheever).

**pi|as|sa|ba** or **pi|a|sa|ba** (pē′ə sä′bə), *n.* = piassava.

**pi|as|sa|va** or **pi|a|sa|va** (pē′ə sä′və), *n.* **1** a stout woody fiber obtained from the leafstalks of two Brazilian palms, one of which also yields the coquilla nut, used in making coarse brooms, brushes, and ropes. **2** a stiff, coarse fiber obtained from an African palm. **3** one of these palms. [< Portuguese *piassaba,* also *piassava* < Tupi (Brazil) *piaçába*]

**pi|as|ter** or **pi|as|tre** (pē as′tər), *n.* **1** any of the various coins worth 1/100 of a pound, used in Egypt, Lebanon, Libya, Sudan, Syria, and Turkey. **2** the unit of money in former South Vietnam. **3** a former Spanish silver coin worth about a dollar; peso. [< French *piastre* < Italian *piastra* (literally) metal plate < Medieval Latin *plastra* < Latin *emplastra* plaster, salve. See etym. of doublet **plaster.**]

**pi|az|za** (pē az′ə; *Italian* pyät′tsä), *n., pl.* **-zas,** *Italian* **-ze** (-tsā). **1** a large porch along one or more sides of a house; veranda: *the low projecting eaves forming a piazza along the front, capable of being closed up in bad weather* (Washington Irving). **2** an open public square in Italian cities and towns: *Rome's Il Tempo suggests that "statues be built to him and piazzas named in his honor"* (Time). **3** *British.* an exterior covered walk with columns. [< Italian *piazza* < Vulgar Latin *plattia,* for Latin *platēa* courtyard, broad street. See etym. of doublets **place¹, plaza.**]

**PIB** (no periods) or **P.I.B.,** Prices and Incomes Board (of Great Britain).

**pi|broch** (pē′brok), *n.* a kind of musical piece performed on the bagpipe. It is usually warlike or sad. *Some pipe of war Sends the bold pibroch from afar* (Scott). [< Scottish Gaelic *piobaireachd* art of pipe-playing < *piobair* piper < *piob* pipe, probably ultimately < Latin *pīpa*]

**pic¹** (pik), *n. Informal.* **1** a picture; photograph. **2** a motion picture: *the latest pics.*

**pic²** (pik), *n.* the lance used by a picador. [< Spanish *pica* pike¹]

***pi|ca¹** (pī′kə), *n.* **1a** a size of type (12 point). **b** this size used as a unit of linear measure; about 1/6 inch. **2** a size of typewriter type, larger than elite, having 10 characters to the inch (the equivalent of 12-point printing type). [< Medieval Latin (England) *pica* name of a book of rules for determining dates of holy days, supposed to have been printed in pica]

***pica¹**
definition 2 abcdefghij

**pi|ca²** (pī′kə), *n.* a craving for substances unfit for food, such as chalk or clay. It is a form of geophagy, sometimes occurring during pregnancy. [< Medieval Latin *pica* < Latin *pīca* magpie (because the bird appears to be omnivorous)]

**pic|a|dor** (pik′ə dôr), *n.* **1** one of the horsemen who open a bullfight by lancing the bull to weaken the neck muscles so that it will charge with lowered head. **2** *Figurative.* an agile debater; witty person. [< Spanish *picador* (literally) one who pricks < *picar* to pierce < *pica* pike¹]

**Pic|ard** (pik′ərd), *n.* the dialect of French spoken in Picardy.

**Pic|ar|dy third** (pik′ər dē), *Music.* **1** the major third in the final chord of a passage composed in the minor key. **2** the effect that it produces. [translation of French *tierce de Picardie* < *Picardie* Picardy, France, where it is used in church compositions]

**pic|a|resque** (pik′ə resk′), *adj., n. — adj.* dealing

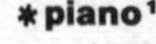
***piano¹**

grand piano

upright piano

spinet

with rogues and their adventures: *"Gil Blas," "Moll Flanders,"* and *"Anthony Adverse" are picaresque works.*
—***n.*** a picaresque work of fiction: *The more lasting and important kind of novel of the open road in England and America is the modern picaresque, such as Kingsley Amis's "Lucky Jim" and Saul Bellow's "Adventures of Augie March"* (Harper's).
[< Spanish *picaresco* < *pícaro* rogue; see etym. under **picaro**] —**pic'a|resque'ly**, *adv.*

**pic|a|ro** (pik'ə rō), *n., pl.* **-ros.** a rogue; knave. [< Spanish *pícaro* a rogue, roguelike; origin uncertain; perhaps < *picar* to prick < *pica* pike[1]]

**pic|a|roon** (pik'ə rün'), *n., v.* —***n.*** **1** a rogue, thief, or brigand: *I see in thy countenance something of the pedlar—something of the picaroon* (Scott). **2** a pirate: *He was somewhat of a trader, something more of a smuggler, with a considerable dash of the picaroon* (Washington Irving). **3** a piratical or privateering ship: *Kennelled in the picaroon a weary band were we* (Rudyard Kipling).
—***v.i.*** to act or cruise as a brigand or pirate.
[< Spanish *picarón* (augmentative) < *pícaro* rogue; see etym. under **picaro**]

**pic|a|yune** (pik'ə yün'), *adj., n.* —***adj.*** small; petty; mean; paltry: *picayune criticism. My accent was excellent, but my vocabulary picayune* (Atlantic).
—***n.*** **1** an insignificant person or thing; trifle. **2** any coin of small value, especially the 5-cent piece. **3** the Spanish half real (formerly used in Florida, Louisiana, and Texas).
[American English, apparently < Creole *picaillon* coin worth 5 cents < Provençal *picaioun* a coin, perhaps related to *picar* to sound, clink]

**pic|a|yun|ish** (pik'ə yü'nish), *adj.* = picayune.

**Pic|ca|dil|ly** (pik'ə dil'ē), *n.* one of the main business streets in London.

**Piccadilly Circus,** an open space formed by the convergence of several streets in western London.

**pic|ca|lil|li** (pik'ə lil'ē), *n., pl.* **-lis.** a relish of East Indian origin made of chopped pickles, onions, tomatoes, etc., with hot spices. [origin uncertain; perhaps a fanciful derivative of *pickle*]

**pic|ca|nin|ny** (pik'ə nin'ē), *n., pl.* **-nies.** = pickaninny.

**pic|co|lo** (pik'ə lō), *n., pl.* **-los,** *adj.* —***n.*** a small, shrill flute sounding an octave higher than the ordinary flute: *The best suspense music is supplied by muted brasses, and combinations like the piccolo, harp and xylophone* (Time). See picture under **flute.**
—***adj.*** of or like a piccolo, especially by comparison in size or sound: *a piccolo trumpet.*
[< Italian *piccolo* < (*flauto*) *piccolo* small (flute). Compare Italian *picca* point.]

**pic|co|lo|ist** (pik'ə lō'ist), *n.* a player on the piccolo.

**pice** (pīs), *n., pl.* **pice.** a former bronze coin of India and Pakistan equal to ¼ of an anna, replaced in India in 1957 and in Pakistan in 1961 by the paisa. [< Hindi *paisā* a copper coin, perhaps < *pāī* < Sanskrit *pad, pāda* one quarter; (originally) foot]

**pic|e|ous** (pis'ē əs, pī'sē-), *adj.* of, having to do with, or resembling pitch: **a** inflammable; combustible. **b** *Zoology.* of the color of pitch; pitch-black. [< Latin *piceus* (with English *-ous*) < *pix, picis* pitch[2]]

**pi|ces|cent** (pi ses'ənt), *adj.* nearly piceous or pitch-black in color. [< *pice*(ous) + *-escent*]

**pich|i|ci|a|go** (pich'ə sē ä'gō, -ā'gō), *n., pl.* **-gos** or (*collectively*) **-go.** a small armadillo of South America, about 5 inches long, with a pinkish shell covering its back. [< Spanish *pichiciego* < *pichey* the little armadillo, perhaps from a native name + Spanish *ciego* blind (< Latin *caecus*)]

**pich|u|rim** (pich'ər im, pish'-), *n.* a South American tree of the laurel family, with seeds having thick aromatic cotyledons (pichurim beans) that are used medicinally and as a substitute for nutmegs. [apparently < a native word]

**pi|cine** (pī'sīn, -sin), *adj.* of or having to do with woodpeckers. [< Latin *pīcus* woodpecker + English *-ine*[1]]

**pick**[1] (pik), *v., n.* —***v.t.*** **1** to choose out of a number or quantity; select: *to pick the right words. I picked a winning horse at the races.* **SYN:** See syn. under **choose. 2** to pull away, as if with the fingers or beak; gather; pluck: *to pick a caterpillar from a leaf. We pick fruit and flowers.* **3** to pierce, dig into, or break up with some pointed tool: *to pick ground, to pick rocks.* **4** to use something pointed to remove things from: *to pick one's teeth, to pick a bone.* **5a** to open with a pointed instrument or wire, or by manipulation of the mechanism: *The burglar picked the lock on the garage.* **b** to steal the contents of: *Someone picked his pocket.* **6** to prepare for use by removing feathers or waste parts: *to pick a chicken.* **7** to pull apart: *to pick rags. The hair in the pillow needs to be picked, as it has matted.* **8** *U.S.* **a** to use the fingers on (the strings of a musical instrument) with a plucking motion: *to play a banjo by picking its strings.* **b** to play thus; pluck at: *He could pick the banjo in a way no one has ever heard it picked since.* **9** *Figurative.* to seek and find occasion for; seek and find: *He picked a quarrel with her. He picks flaws in every offer I make.* **10a** to take up (seeds or other small pieces of food) with the bill or teeth, as a bird or squirrel does. **b** to eat (food) in small pieces, slowly, or without appetite: *I picked a meal in fear and trembling* (Robert Louis Stevenson).
—***v.i.*** **1** to use or work with a pick, pickax, or other such tool. **2** to eat with small bites, slowly, or without appetite. **3** to make a careful choice or selection. **4** to gather fruit or other growing produce. **5** = pilfer: *to pick and steal.*
—***n.*** the act of choosing; choice or selection: *He let me have the first pick.* **2** a person or thing selected from among others: *This red rose is my pick. That book is my first pick.* **3** *Figurative.* the best or most desirable part: *We got a high price for the pick of our peaches.* **4** the total amount of a crop gathered at one time. **5** = plectrum.

**pick and choose,** to select with great care; be very particular in choosing: *As matters stand, the army is an employer that can pick and choose* (Maclean's).

**pick at, a** to pull, as with the fingers or beak: *The sick man picked at the blankets.* **b** to eat only a little at a time: *The bird picked at the bread. She just picked at her food because she did not like it.* **c** *Informal, Figurative.* to find fault with; nag: *I'm always being picked at. I wish I was dead* (Cosmopolitan).

**pick in,** to work in or fill in in a painting or drawing: *Then the shadows are "picked in" by assistants* (George A. Sala).

**pick off, a** to shoot one at a time; bring down one by one, by or as if by shooting: *to pick off a few disorganized opponents. The hunter picked off a goose from the flock flying overhead.* **b** to catch (a runner in baseball) off base and put him out with a sudden throw: *The catcher handles bunts and pop-ups, picks off runners who stray from base* (Atlantic).

**pick on, a** *Informal.* to find fault with; nag at: *Why pick on me? The teacher picked on him for always being late.* **b** *Informal.* to annoy; tease: *The bigger boys picked on him during recess.* **c** to choose; select: *Why did he pick on you first?*

**pick out, a** to choose with care; select: *Pick out a dress you will like to wear. He picked out for this purpose a Pole whom he believed to be a genuine revolutionary* (Edmund Wilson). **b** to distinguish (a thing) from its surroundings: *Can you pick me out in this group picture?* **c** to make out (the sense or meaning): *Goethe ... did not know Greek well and had to pick out its meaning by the help of a Latin translation* (Matthew Arnold). **d** to select the notes of (a tune) one by one, especially laboriously, as on a keyboard, and so play it: *She picked it out upon the keyboard, and ... enriched the same with well-sounding chords* (Robert Louis Stevenson). **e** to embellish, especially by lines or spots of contrasting color following outlines: *The ceiling ... was richly gilt and picked out in violet* (Benjamin Disraeli). **f** to remove or extract by picking: *to pick mussels out of the shells, to pick out loose threads from a hem.*

**pick over, a** to look over carefully: *to pick over vegetables before buying.* **b** to prepare for use: *Pick over and hull the strawberries.*

**pick up, a** to take up: *The boy picked up a stone. The bird picked up a worm.* **b** to summon or recover (as courage or hope): *to pick up one's spirits.* **c** *Informal.* to recover; improve: *He seemed to pick up quickly after his fever went down. Unless demand picks up, mill men fear the cutbacks may spread throughout synthetics* (Wall Street Journal). **d** to give (a person) fresh energy, courage, hope, or the like: *A good dinner will pick you up.* **e** to get by chance: *The woman picked up a bargain at the dress sale.* **f** to learn without being taught; acquire or attain (a skill or knowledge) by chance or opportunity: *He picks up games easily.* **g** to pay for: *The London casino offered to pick up the $35,000 bill for a charter flight from New York* (New York Times). **h** to take into a vehicle or ship: *The bus picks up passengers at every other corner.* **i** to take along with one: *to pick up a coat at the cleaner's.* **j** *Figurative.* to find again; regain: *Here we picked up the trail.* **k** to succeed in seeing or hearing: *to pick up four of Jupiter's moons with a telescope. He picked up a radio broadcast from Paris.* **l** to go faster; increase in speed: *Other rivers picked up speed, boiled out of gorges* (Time). **m** to pack; prepare to move out: *What will happen when we pick up and leave in a year or so?* (New Yorker). **n** to arrest: *Many colleges have long intervened with police when their students had been picked up for such apolitical offenses as brawling or disturbing the peace* (Saturday Review). **o** *Informal.* to become acquainted with without being introduced: *The only girls I knew were the ones I picked up* (New Yorker). **p** *U.S.* to tidy up; put in order: *to pick up a room or one's desk.* **q** *Golf.* to pick up one's ball: *He [Bobby Jones] "picked up" during the 1921 British Open in a fit of pique* (New Yorker).
[Middle English *picken,* perhaps < Scandinavian (compare Old Icelandic *pikka* pick, peck)]

**pick**[2] (pik), *n.* **1** a tool with a heavy, sharp-pointed iron or steel bar, attached through an eye in the center to a wooden handle, used for breaking and prying up earth, rock, and other compacted or heavy material; pickax. **2** a sharp-pointed tool or instrument. Ice is broken into pieces with a pick. [Middle English *pik,* variant of *pike* pike[2], Old English *pīc.* Probably related to **pick**[1].]

**pick**[3] (pik), *v., n.* —***v.t.*** **1** to throw (the shuttle) across the loom. **2** *British Dialect.* **a** to throw; hurl. **b** to pitch (as hay or grain).
—***n.*** **1** a cast or throw of the shuttle in weaving. **2** a single thread of the woof in cloth, especially as a measure of its fineness: *20 picks per inch.* **3** *British Dialect.* a pitch; throw.
[variant of *pitch*[1]]

**pick|a|back** (pik'ə bak'), *adv., adj.* = piggyback. [origin uncertain]

**pick|a|nin|ny** (pik'ə nin'ē), *n., pl.* **-nies. 1** a small Negro child (now usually used in an unfriendly way in the United States). **2** any small child. [perhaps American English, ultimately < Portuguese *pequenino* very small or perhaps < Spanish *pequeñín* < *pequeño* small + *niño* boy]
► **Pickaninny.** In the United States and the West Indies, this word is normally applied only to a Negro child; in Australia (where the preferred spelling is *piccaninny*), it is applied to a child belonging to any one of the various dark-skinned aboriginal tribes. In some areas, as in parts of Africa, the term has become part of a native dialect, or the lingua franca of the region, and is used, without any implication of contempt, simply to mean "a small child."

**pick|a|pack** (pik'ə pak'), *adv., adj.* = pickaback.

**pick|ax** or **pick|axe** (pik'aks'), *n., v.,* **-axed, -axing.** —***n.*** a tool with a heavy metal bar, pointed at one or both ends, attached through the center to a wooden handle; pick. It is used for breaking and prying up earth, rocks, and other compacted or heavy material.
—***v.t.*** to break, clear, or pry up with a pickax.
—***v.i.*** to work with or use a pickax.
[alteration of Middle English *picois,* and *pikeis* < Old French *picois,* related to *pic,* or *pik* pick[2]; influenced by English *ax*]

**picked**[1] (pikt), *adj.* **1** specially selected for merit: *The crew of the lugger ... all of whom were picked men, remarkable for their strength and activity* (Frederick Marryat). **SYN:** choice, excellent. **2** with waste parts removed and ready for use: *a freshly picked chicken.* **SYN:** plucked. **3** with fruit, grain, or other produce removed; stripped: *a clean picked field.* [< *pick*[1] + *-ed*[2]]

**picked**[2] (pikt), *adj.* **1** having a sharp point; pointed; spiked. **2** covered with sharp points; prickly. [< *pick*[2] + *-ed*[2]]

**pick|eer** (pi kir'), *v.i. Archaic.* to reconnoiter; scout. [apparently < French *picorer* maraud, steal cattle, ultimately < Latin *pecus* cattle]

**pick|er**[1] (pik'ər), *n.* **1** a person who gathers, picks, or collects: *an apple picker, a ragpicker.* **2** a tool or machine for picking anything: *Mr. Alleman showed ... the corn picker with which he can pick twenty acres of corn in a ten-hour day* (New York Times). **3a** a machine for separating and cleaning the fibers of cotton, wool, and the like. **b** a person who runs such a machine.

**pick|er**[2] (pik'ər), *n.* the small piece in a loom, usually of leather, that drives the shuttle back and forth through the warp.

**pick|er|el** (pik'ər əl, pik'rəl), *n., pl.* **-els** or (*collectively*) **-el. 1** any one of various smaller kinds of pike, used for food. **2** *British.* a pike not yet full grown, but of a size large enough to catch. **3** = pike perch. [Middle English *pykerel* (diminutive) < *pike*[3]]

**pickerel frog,** a common, spotted, green or brown frog of eastern North America; green frog.

**pick|er|el|weed** (pik'ər əl wēd', pik'rəl-), *n.* any of a genus of North American herbs with spikes of blue flowers and heart-shaped leaves, growing in shallow, usually quiet, water.

**pick|er-up** (pik'ər up), *n., pl.* **pick|ers-up.** a per-

**Pronunciation Key:** hat, āge, cãre, fär; let, ēqual, tėrm; it, īce; hot, ōpen, ôrder; oil, out; cup, pu̇t, rüle; child; long; thin; ᴛʜen; zh, measure; ə represents **a** in about, **e** in taken, **i** in pencil, **o** in lemon, **u** in circus.

son who picks up: *a picker-up of words, a picker-up of trifles.*

**pick|et** (pik′it), *n., v.* —*n.* **1** a pointed stake or peg driven into the ground to make a fence or to tie a horse to: *The dogs were afraid to jump the pickets of the fence.* **2** a small body of troops, or a single man, posted at some place to watch for the enemy and guard against surprise attacks: *Pickets were posted on all sides of the camp.* **SYN:** sentry, sentinel. **3** a person stationed by a labor union near a factory or store where there is a strike. Pickets try to prevent employees from working or customers from buying. *Pickets had been removed and workers had returned to their jobs at twelve different plants where they had been on strike* (New York Times). **4** a person who takes part in a public demonstration or boycott to support a cause; demonstrator: *500 pickets marched around City Hall … protesting the treatment of Negroes in Birmingham* (Wall Street Journal).
—***v.t.*** **1** to enclose with pickets; fence: *to picket a yard.* **2** to tie to a picket: *Picket your horse here.* **3** to station as a picket; guard with or as if with pickets: *to picket soldiers around a camp.* **4** to station pickets at or near: *to picket a factory during a strike.*
—***v.i.*** to act as a picket. Also, *British,* **picquet.**
[< French *piquet* (diminutive) < *pic* pick[2]; see etym. under **pike**[1]] —**pick′et|er,** *n.*

**picket boat,** an armed naval boat that patrols an area, especially at night.

**picket fence,** a fence made of pickets.

**picket line, 1** a line of persons acting as pickets at or near a factory, store, or other establishment: *When the skeleton crew showed up for work … they were met by a sullen, hostile picket line of several hundred strikers* (Newsweek). **2** a military position held by an advance guard of men stationed at intervals: *The picket line of Minitrack stations across their expected path is strung out in a north-south line* (Scientific American).

**picket pin,** a long iron pin with a swivel link at the top, to which a picket rope is tied.

**picket ship,** a ship used to watch for and warn against an enemy approach, now especially a radar picket.

**pick|i|ly** (pik′ə lē), *adv. Informal.* in a picky manner; choosily.

**pick|i|ness** (pik′ē nis), *n. Informal.* picky quality or condition; choosiness.

**pick|ing** (pik′ing), *n.* the act of a person or thing that picks.
**pickings, a** amount picked: *The final pickings may bring the crop closer to 15 million bales* (Wall Street Journal). **b** things left over; scraps: *The vultures had then but small pickings* (Milton). **c** *Figurative.* profits; returns: *The time was 1930 and interior designers in that lean year were having slim pickings indeed* (New York Times). **d** things stolen or received dishonestly: *It must be confessed that the pickings of the office* [*of Paymaster General*] *were enormous* (W. P. Courtney).

**pick|le**[1] (pik′əl), *n., v.,* **-led, -ling.** —*n.* **1a** a cucumber preserved in salt water (brine), vinegar, or other liquid: *a dill pickle.* **b** any other vegetable preserved in such a way. **2** salt water (brine), vinegar, or other liquid in which meats, fish, and vegetables can be preserved: *to put ham in pickle before smoking it.* **3** *Informal, Figurative.* trouble; difficulty: *I got in a bad pickle today.* **SYN:** plight, predicament. **4** an acid bath or other chemical preparation, used for removing oxides or other corrosion from metals.
—***v.t.*** **1** to preserve in pickle: *Grandmother pickled several quarts of beets.* **2** to clean with an acid bath or other chemical preparation: *The cold-rolling firms take steel from the rerollers and "pickle" it to clean off scale* (London Times).
**in pickle,** kept prepared for use: *to have a rod in pickle to punish a naughty child.*
[< Middle Dutch *pekel*] —**pick′ler,** *n.*

**pick|le**[2] (pik′əl), *n. Scottish.* **1** a grain of wheat, barley, or oats; kernel. **2** a very small quantity; trifle. [origin unknown]

**pick|led** (pik′əld), *adj.* **1** preserved in or treated with a pickle. **2** *U.S. Slang.* intoxicated; drunk.

**pick|le|worm** (pik′əl wėrm′), *n.* the larva of a pyralid moth of North and South America that lays its eggs on young cucumbers and other plants of the gourd family, the larva boring into the fruit and spoiling it.

**pick|lock** (pik′lok′), *n.* **1** a person who picks locks, especially to steal; thief; burglar. **2** an instrument for picking locks.

**pick-me-up** (pik′mē up′), *n. Informal.* a stimulating or bracing drink, food, or medicine: *When his spirits flag, he takes an egg as a pick-me-up* (New Yorker).

**pick|off** (pik′ôf′, -of′), *n.* **1** a baseball play in which a runner is caught off base by a sudden throw from the pitcher or catcher: *They proved that a perfect pickoff at first could be foozled not once but again* (New York Times). **2** an offensive play in basketball in which one player blocks a defensive man in order to free another player, guarded by that man, for a pass. **3** an electronic device that detects geometric changes in a pattern and responds to them with a signal. Pickoffs are used especially in automation.

**pick|pock|et** (pik′pok′it), *n.* a person who steals from people's pockets: *Pickpockets often work in crowds of people.*

**pick|proof** (pik′prüf′), *adj.* very hard or impossible to break open: *This lock is practically pickproof.*

**pick|purse** (pik′pėrs′), *n.* a person who steals purses or their contents.

**pick|some** (pik′səm), *adj.* given to picking and choosing; fastidious; particular. —**pick′someness,** *n.*

**pick|thank** (pik′thangk′), *n.* a flatterer; toady: *He takes to sulking at home and dining a crew of worthless pickthanks who … tell him what he wants to hear* (Time). [< phrase *pick a thank* to curry favor]

**pick|up** (pik′up′), *n., adj.* —*n.* **1** the act of picking up: *the daily pickup of mail.* **2** *Informal.* the act or fact of getting better; improvement: *a pickup in his health, a pickup in business.* **3** the act or fact of going faster; increase in speed; acceleration: *People who must drive a lot know the big difference a gasoline can make in pickup, economy and all around smooth operation* (Maclean's). **4** *Informal.* **a** an acquaintance made without an introduction, especially an acquaintance of the opposite sex. **b** a person who is picked up by a vehicle, such as a passenger or hitchhiker: *The school bus has a dozen pickups every morning.* **5** something obtained or secured when or as chance offers, such as a bargain or a hurried meal: *While we were having our pickup … the children came down and settled around the table* (New Yorker). **6** *Sports.* a catching (or sometimes hitting) of a ball very soon after it has bounced on the ground: *Two snappy double-plays, the first that started with a dazzling pickup by Sam Dente, helped the youngster* (New York Times). **7** *Radio.* **a** the reception of sound waves in the transmitter and their conversion into electrical waves for broadcasting: *The short-wave pickups … lost a good deal of their value when nobody had anything very special to say* (New York Times). **b** the apparatus for such reception. **c** the place from which a broadcast is transmitted: *The network said the program would originate at thirteen pickup points from the Atlantic to the Pacific* (New York Times). **d** the electrical system for connecting a program originating outside the studio to the broadcasting station. **8** *Television.* **a** the reception of images in the transmitter and their conversion into electrical waves for broadcasting: *A new measuring circuit … simplifies range changing and reduces stray pickup* (Scientific American). **b** the apparatus that does this. **9** a device that transforms into electric current the vibrations set up in a phonograph needle by variations in the grooves of a phonograph record, the current being typically very weak, capable in itself only of serving as a signal to the amplifier: *a stereo pickup.* **10** = pickup truck.
—***adj.*** of or having to do with an informal game or group that is assembled on the spot or for one time only: *Small groups of correspondents—seldom more than enough for a pickup baseball game* (A. J. Liebling).

**pickup arm,** = tone arm.

**pickup man,** a man on horseback who lifts a rodeo rider off a bronco or off the ground if an animal is charging.

**pickup truck,** a small, light truck with an open back, used for light hauling.

**pickup tube,** an electron beam tube for conversion of an optical image into an electric signal; camera tube.

**Pick|wick|i|an** (pik wik′ē ən), *adj.* **1** of, having to do with, or characteristic of Samuel Pickwick, the chief character of Charles Dickens' novel *The Pickwick Papers,* or the club which he founded. **2** given a special meaning for the occasion, regardless of the real meaning: *words used in a Pickwickian sense.*

**pick|y** (pik′ē), *adj.,* **pick|i|er, pick|i|est.** *U.S. Informal.* **1** choosy; particular: *People are very picky this year in buying new cars.* **2** finding fault about trifles; nagging: *If I hear one more picky, cavilling, unconstructive word out of you … you and I are finished* (New Yorker).

**pi|clor|am** (pī klôr′əm, -klōr′-), *n.* a highly active and persistent herbicide, used as a defoliant and crop-destroying agent, especially in warfare. *Formula:* $C_6H_3Cl_3N_2O_2$ [< *pic*(oline) + (ch) *lor-* + *am*(ine)]

**pic|nic** (pik′nik), *n., v.,* **-nicked, -nick|ing,** *adj.* —*n.* **1a** a pleasure trip or party with a meal in the open air: *We had a picnic at the beach.* **b** any outdoor meal: *to have a picnic in one's yard.* **2** *Slang.* a pleasant time or experience; very easy job: *He tells you about some new stratagem he's planning, and there's no question he's having a picnic in this new limelight* (Maclean's). **3** = picnic ham.
—***v.i.*** **1** to go on or take part in a picnic: *Our family often picnics at the beach.* **2** to eat in picnic style.
—***adj.*** for or at a picnic: *a picnic lunch.*
[< French *piquenique,* perhaps a rhyming reduplication of French *pique*]

**picnic ham,** a smoked shoulder of pork, cut to look like a ham; picnic.

**pic|nick|er** (pik′nik ər), *n.* a person who picnics.

**pic|nick|y** (pik′nik ē), *adj.* of or like a picnic: *a picnicky dinner.*

**pico-,** *combining form.* **1** one trillionth of a ____: *Picofarad = one trillionth of a farad.* **2** very small, as in *picornavirus.*
[< Spanish *pico* small number, peak]

**pi|co|cu|rie** (pī′kō kyůr′ē, pē′-), *n.* one trillionth of a curie; micromicrocurie.

**pi|co|far|ad** (pī′kō far′ed, -ad; pē′-), *n.* one trillionth of a farad; micromicrofarad.

**pi|co|gram** (pī′kō gram, pē′-), *n.* one trillionth of a gram.

**pic|o|line** (pik′ə lēn, -lin), *n.* a colorless liquid obtained in three isomeric forms by the distillation of bones and coal, used especially as a solvent for waterproofing fabrics. *Formula:* $C_6H_7N$ [< Latin *pix, picis* pitch[2]]

**pic|o|lin|ic** (pik′ə lin′ik), *adj.* of or derived from picoline: *picolinic acid.*

**pi|cor|na|vi|rus** (pi kôr′nə vī′rəs), *n.* any one of a group of viruses containing ribonucleic acid, including the poliovirus, rhinovirus, and similar viruses. [< *pico-* + *RNA* + *virus*]

**pi|co|sec|ond** (pī′kō sek′ənd, pē′-), *n.* one thousand billionth ($10^{-12}$) of a second; a trillionth part of a second: *Laser pulses lasting about … one picosecond, can now be measured accurately for the first time, making it possible to measure picosecond events in atoms and molecules* (Science News).

**pi|cot** (pē′kō), *n., pl.* **-cots** (-kōz), *v.,* **-coted** (-kōd), **-cot|ing** (-kō ing). —*n.* one of a number of fancy loops, as in embroidery and tatting, or along the edge of lace or ribbon: *A hard-twisted yarn is used to add to the beauty of the small picots* (H. M. Calaway).
—***v.t., v.i.*** to trim with picots.
[< French *picot* (diminutive) *pic* a point, pick[2]; see etym. under **pike**[1]]

**pic|o|tee** (pik′ə tē′), *n.* a variety of carnation having white or yellow petals edged with a darker color, usually red. [< French *picotée,* past participle of *picoter* mark with pricks or points < Old French *picot* little peak; see etym. under **picot**]

**pic|quet**[1] (pik′it), *n., v.t., v.i. British.* picket.

**pic|quet**[2] (pi ket′), *n.* = piquet.

**pic|rate** (pik′rāt), *n.* a salt or ester of picric acid. [< *picr*(ic acid) + *-ate*[2]]

**pic|ric acid** (pik′rik), a very poisonous, yellow, crystalline, intensely bitter acid, used in explosives, in dyeing, and in medicine. *Formula:* $C_6H_3N_3O_7$ [< Greek *pikrós* bitter, sharp + English *-ic*]

**pic|rite** (pik′rīt), *n.* any one of a group of igneous rocks of granular texture, composed chiefly of olivine and augite. [< Greek *pikrós* bitter + English *-ite*[1] (because of the bitter taste of the magnesium it contains)]

**pic|rol** (pik′rōl, -rol), *n.* a bitter, odorless, colorless, crystalline antiseptic, used as a substitute for iodoform. [< *picr*(ic acid) + *-ol*[1]]

**pic|ro|tox|ic** (pik′rō tok′sik), *adj.* of or derived from picrotoxin.

**pic|ro|tox|in** (pik′rō tok′sin), *n.* a bitter, very poisonous, crystalline, chemical compound obtained from the seeds of several plants, similar to strychnine in action. *Formula:* $C_{30}H_{34}O_{13}$ [< Greek *pikrós* bitter, sharp + English *toxin*]

**Pict** (pikt), *n.* a member of an ancient people who formerly lived in the northern part of Great Britain, especially northern Scotland, between the 200's and 900's A.D. The ethnic origin of the Picts is uncertain. [< Late Latin *Pictī,* plural]

**Pict|ish** (pik′tish), *adj., n.* —***adj.*** of or having to do with the Picts. —*n.* the language of the Picts.

**pic|to|gram** (pik′tə gram), *n.* = pictograph.

**pic|to|graph** (pik′tə graf, -gräf), *n.* **1** a picture used as a sign or symbol, especially in a system of picture writing. **2** a writing or record in such symbols: *Discovery was made of pictographs in Arizona indicating that the brilliant supernova of July 4, 1054, was observed and recorded by prehistoric American Indians* (Science News Letter). **3** a diagram or chart presenting statistical data by using pictures of different colors, sizes, or numbers. See picture under **graph**[1]. [< Latin *pictus,* past participle of *pingere* to paint + English *-graph*]

**pic|to|graph|ic** (pik′tə graf′ik), *adj.* **1** like, of the nature of, or consisting of pictographs. **2** of or having to do with pictography.

**pic|tog|ra|phy** (pik tog′rə fē), *n.* the use of pictographs; picture writing.

**Pic|tor** (pik′tər), *n., genitive* **Pic|to|ris.** a southern constellation near the star Canopus.

**pic|to|ri|al** (pik tôr′ē əl, -tōr′-), *adj., n.* —*adj.* **1** having something to do with pictures; expressed in pictures: *pictorial writing or symbols.* **2** *Figurative.* making a picture for the mind; vivid: *pictorial phrases.* SYN: graphic. **3** illustrated by pictures: *a pictorial history, a pictorial magazine.* **4** of, belonging to, or produced by a painter; having to do with painting or drawing: *pictorial skill.*
—*n.* a magazine or part of a newspaper in which pictures are an important part.
[< Latin *pictōrius* (< *pictor, -ōris* painter < *pingere* to make pictures, paint, color) + English *-al*$^1$] —**pic|to′ri|al|ly,** *adv.*

**pic|to|ri|al|ism** (pik tôr′ē ə liz′əm, -tōr′-), *n.* the use of a pictorial style; art of a pictorialist.

**pic|to|ri|al|ist** (pik tôr′ē ə list, -tōr′-), *n.* a person who uses a pictorial style, especially a photographer whose purpose is artistic rather than commercial or documentary.

**pic|to|ri|al|ize** (pik tôr′ē ə līz, -tōr′-), *v.t.,* **-ized, -iz|ing.** to make pictorial; show or illustrate with pictures: *to pictorialize a series of events.* —**pic|to′ri|al|i|za′tion,** *n.*

**Pic|to|ris** (pik tôr′is, -tōr′-), *n.* genitive of **Pictor.**

**pic|tur|al** (pik′chər əl), *adj.* = pictorial.

**pic|ture** (pik′chər), *n., v.,* **-tured, -tur|ing.** —*n.* **1** a drawing, painting, portrait, or photograph, or a print of any of these: *This book contains a good picture of a tiger.* **2** a scene: *The trees and brook make a lovely picture.* **3** *Figurative.* something beautiful: *She was a picture in her new dress.* **4** an exact likeness; image: *He is the picture of his father.* **5** an example; embodiment: *She was the picture of happiness. Old Balthus van Tassel was a perfect picture of a thriving, contented, liberal-hearted farmer* (Washington Irving). **6** *Figurative.* a mental image; visualized conception; idea: *to have a clear picture of the problem.* **7** *Figurative.* a vivid description or account: *Gibbon's picture of the latter days of ancient Rome.* **8** a motion picture: *It is more often the director, not the star, who makes a picture great, or even good* (Newsweek). **9** a visible image of something formed by physical means, as by a lens: *a picture on a television screen.* **10** a tableau, as in the theater. **11** *Informal.* state of affairs; condition; situation: *The employment picture is much brighter than it was a year ago* (New York Times).
—*v.t.* **1a** to draw or paint; make into a picture: *The artist pictured the saints.* **b** to reflect, as a mirror does. **2** to form a picture of in the mind; imagine: *It is hard to picture life a hundred years ago. He was older than she had pictured him.* **3** *Figurative.* to show by words; describe graphically and vividly: *The speaker pictured the suffering of the poor. I think this last sentence pictures him exactly* (Madame D'Arblay).
**pictures,** *Informal.* **a** motion pictures; movies: *During his very successful career in pictures he has appeared in some ... thrilling productions* (Kinematograph and Lantern Weekly). **b** a motion-picture theater: *Charlotte is coming to the Zoo with me this afternoon. Alone. And later on to the pictures* (P. G. Wodehouse).
**put** (or **keep**) **in the picture,** *Informal.* to keep informed: *Were the press able to see the film, ... they would be in a position to put the public in the picture* (London Times).
[< Latin *pictūra* < *pingere* to make pictures, paint] —**pic′tur|a|ble,** *adj.*

**picture book,** a book consisting largely or wholly of pictures, especially for children: *a colorful picture book of animals.*

**picture hat,** a woman's wide-brimmed hat, originally often black and trimmed with ostrich feathers.

**picture molding,** a molded strip of wood high on a wall, as to hang pictures from by means of hooks which fit over one of the members of the molding.

**Pic|ture|phone** (pik′chər fōn′) *n. Trademark.* a videophone.

**picture postcard,** a postcard with a picture on one side and space to write a message on the other.

**picture rail** or **rod,** = picture molding.

**pic|tures** (pik′chərz), *n.pl.* See under **picture.**

**picture show,** *U.S. Informal.* **1** a motion picture. **2** a motion-picture theater.

**pic|tur|esque** (pik′chə resk′), *adj., n.* —*adj.* **1** quaint or interesting enough to be used as the subject of a picture: *a picturesque old mill. An experienced, industrious, ambitious, and often quite picturesque liar* (Mark Twain). **2** making a picture for the mind; vivid: *picturesque language.* SYN: graphic, pictorial.
—*n.* **the picturesque,** something picturesque; the picturesque principle, element, or quality in art, nature, or language: *a study of the picturesque in literature, a love of the picturesque.*
[< *pictur*(e) + *-esque,* perhaps patterned on French *pittoresque* < Italian *pittoresco* pictorial < *pittore* painter (< Latin *pictor, -ōris*) + *-esco* -esque] —**pic′tur|esque′ly,** *adv.* —**pic′tur|esque′ness,** *n.*

**picture telephone,** = videophone.

**picture tube,** a cathode-ray tube which reproduces a transmitted picture on the screen of a television set; kinescope.

**picture window,** a large window in a house or apartment, designed to frame a wide view of the outside: *Will that architectural pet the "picture" window succumb to the rising desire for personal privacy?* (Sunday Times).

**picture writing, 1** the recording of events or expressing of ideas by pictures or drawings that literally or figuratively represent things and actions; pictography. **2** the pictures so used: *All the various receipts and disbursements were set down in the picture writing of the country* (William H. Prescott).

**pic|tur|ize** (pik′chə rīz), *v.t.,* **-ized, -iz|ing. 1** to represent in a picture or pictures. **2** to put (a novel, drama, or other written work or an event) into the form of a motion picture. —**pic′tur|i|za′tion,** *n.*

**pic|ul** (pik′əl), *n., pl.* **-ul** or **-uls.** a unit of weight equal to 100 catties, or about 135 pounds, long used in commerce in various parts of southern and southeastern Asia. [< Malay, or Javanese *pikul* a man's load]

**pic|u|let** (pik′yə lit), *n.* any one of a group of small, soft-tailed birds of tropical regions, related to and resembling the woodpeckers. [< obsolete *picule* (< Latin *pīcus* woodpecker) + *-et*]

**pid|dle** (pid′əl), *v.i.,* **-dled, -dling. 1** to do anything in a trifling or ineffective way. SYN: dabble. **2** to pick at one's food. **3** *Slang.* to urinate. [origin uncertain] —**pid′dler,** *n.*

**pid|dling** (pid′ling), *adj.* trifling; petty: *It's too piddling, she thought, to worry about curling your eyelashes* (New Yorker).

**pid|dock** (pid′ək), *n.* any one of a group of bivalve mollusks with a long egg-shaped shell, that burrow, as into clay, wood, or soft rock. [origin uncertain; perhaps Old English *puduc* wart]

**pidg|in** (pij′ən), *n.* **1** pidgin English: *Hawaiian pidgin.* **2** any language spoken with a reduced grammar and vocabulary as a trade or communications jargon: *a French pidgin. The men keep calling to the team in a sort of pidgin Eskimo language* (New Yorker). **3** *Chinese pidgin English.* business. Also, **pigeon.** [alteration of pronunciation of *business*]
► **pidgin, pigeon.** The latter form, sometimes occurring in popular use but without currency among linguists, derives from the more familiar homonym. In British slang, *pigeon* is the common form used for the meaning "business" or "affair."

**pidgin** or **Pidgin English,** one of several forms of English, with simplified grammatical structure and often a mixed vocabulary, used in western Africa, Australia, Melanesia, and formerly in China, as a language of trade or communication between natives and foreigners: *A good deal of amusement, too, was to be had in the exchanges of pidgin English* (London Times).

**pidg|in|ize** (pij′ə nīz), *v.t.,* **-ized, -iz|ing.** to form or develop into pidgin or any mixture of languages such as pidgin: *Pidginized varieties of French are found in North Africa and New Caledonia* (Robert A. Hall, Jr.).

**pi-dog** (pī′dôg′, -dog′), *n.* = pye-dog.

**pie$^1$** (pī), *n.* **1** fruit, meat, vegetables, or other ingredients enclosed in pastry and baked in a round, flat dish or pan: *apple pie, chicken pie.* **2** a round layer cake with a filling, as of cream, custard, or jelly: *Boston cream pie.* **3** *U.S.* the sum total of income, costs, or other figure, with reference to the portions into which it may be divided, such as on a pie chart: *Transportation is that slice of the cost pie often overlooked by management when it wants to cut costs* (Wall Street Journal). **4** *U.S. Slang.* something quite easy or desirable: *easy as pie.* [Middle English *pye,* origin uncertain] —**pie′like′,** *adj.*

**pie$^2$** (pī), *n.* = magpie. [< Old French *pie* < Latin *pīca*]

**pie$^3$** (pī), *n., v.t.,* **pied, pie|ing.** = pi$^2$.

**pie$^4$** (pī), *n.* a book of rules for finding the particulars of the service for the day, as used in England before the Reformation. Also, **pye.** [Middle English *pye,* perhaps abbreviation of Medieval Latin *pica* pica$^1$]

**pie$^5$** (pī), *n.* a bronze coin of India, equal to 1/12 of an anna. [Anglo-Indian < Hindi and Marathi *pāī* < Sanskrit *padī,* or *pad* quarter]

**pie|bald** (pī′bôld′), *adj., n.* —*adj.* **1** spotted in two colors, especially white and black or another dark color: *a piebald horse.* **2** *Figurative.* mixed or mongrel: *Here we are, a society and a nation ... a vast and piebald congregation* (Maurice Hewlett).
—*n.* a piebald animal, especially a horse.
[apparently < *pie*$^2$ + *bald,* with the meanings "spotted," or "white" (because of the magpie's pied plumage)]

**piece** (pēs), *n., v.,* **pieced, piec|ing,** *adj.* —*n.* **1** one of the parts into which a thing is divided or broken; bit: *a piece of wood, to fall or cut to pieces. The cup broke into pieces.* SYN: scrap, fragment. **2** a limited part: *a piece of land containing two acres.* SYN: See syn. under **part. 3** a small quantity; portion; part: *a piece of bread, a piece of paper.* SYN: See syn. under **part. 4** a single thing of a set or class: *a piece of furniture, a piece of luggage. This set of china has 144 pieces.* **5** a single composition in an art: *a new piece at a theater, a piece of music, a piece of poetry, to recite a piece. His pieces went over so well that he was offered sixty rubles a month to become a regular contributor* (Edmund Wilson). **6** a coin: *pieces of eight. A nickel is a five-cent piece.* **7** an example or instance of an action, function, or quality: *a piece of luck, a piece of news. Sleeping with the light on in the room is a piece of nonsense.* **8** a quantity in which goods are put up for the market: *cloth, ribbon, or lace sold only by the piece.* **9** the amount of work done or to be done at any one time: *to work by the piece, to be paid by the piece.* **10a** a gun; cannon: *a fowling piece. Clean the piece after firing.* **b** *U.S. Slang.* a firearm, usually a pistol: *"Just having a piece doesn't cut the mustard," he continued* (New York Times). **11a** any one of the disks, cubes, figures, or stones, used in playing checkers, chess, and other games; man. **b** a superior man in chess, as distinguished from a pawn; a king, queen, bishop, knight, or rook. **12** *U.S. Slang.* a woman or girl, especially thought of as a sex partner or sex object. **13** *Dialect.* **a** a short period of time; while: *to sit and rest for a piece.* **b** a short distance: *down the road a piece.* **14** *Obsolete.* an individual; person.
—*v.t.* **1** to make or repair by adding or joining pieces; patch: *to piece a dress. Mother pieced a quilt yesterday.* **2** to join the pieces of; unite or put together in one piece: (*Figurative.*) *to piece together a story.*
—*adj.* **1** composed of pieces. **2** having to do with piecework.
**go to pieces, a** to break into fragments; break up: *Another ship had gone to pieces on the rocks.* **b** to break down physically or mentally; collapse: *When his business failed, he went completely to pieces.* **c** to become disorganized or confused; fall apart: *Where the book goes to pieces is in its economic, social, and political history* (New Scientist).
**of a piece,** of the same kind; in keeping; uniform: *That plan is of a piece with the rest of his silly suggestions. His rusty and worn suit ... was of a piece with his uncarpeted room* (Charles Reade). *His face and body look all of a piece like some fabulous Humpty Dumpty* (Harper's).
**piece of one's mind,** *Informal.* **a** a scolding: *His mother gave him a piece of her mind for coming late again.* **b** a candid opinion: *He gave them a piece of his mind on the subject.*
**pick up the pieces,** *Informal.* to restore order or normalcy; bring about a recovery: *After ... a revolt shattered the constitution he'd helped construct, he was being urged to step in again to help pick up the pieces* (Maclean's).
**speak one's piece,** to voice one's opinions: *I feel better after speaking my piece.*
**to pieces, a** to bits or fragments: *to break a dish to pieces.* **b** to a state of separation of the constituent parts, or apart: *to take a clock to pieces. Given these facts, his argument falls to pieces.*
[< Old French *piece* < Vulgar Latin *pettia* fragment, probably < Celtic, or Gaulish (compare Welsh *peth,* Breton *pez*)]

**pièce de ré|sis|tance** (pyes də rā zēs täɴs′), *French.* **1** the chief dish of a meal. **2** *Figurative.* the most important or outstanding item, in any collection, group, or series: *A table service for a party of four in the nursery is made of pliable, unbreakable plastic, and includes, as the pièce de résistance, a Lazy Susan* (New Yorker).

**pièce d'oc|ca|sion** (pyes dô kà zyôɴ′), *French.* **1** a piece or work for a special occasion: *The work ... is certainly a pièce d'occasion for this orchestra, who played it with tremendous verve and finish* (London Times). **2** a bargain.

**Pronunciation Key:** hat, āge, cãre, fär; let, ēqual, tėrm; it, īce; hot, ōpen, ôrder; oil, out; cup, pu̇t, rüle; child; long; thin; ᴛʜen; zh, measure; ə represents **a** in about, **e** in taken, **i** in pencil, **o** in lemon, **u** in circus.

**piece-dyed** (pēsʹdīdʹ), *adj.* (of cloth) dyed in the piece, or after it is woven or knitted.

**piece goods**, cloth cut to measure and sold by the yard from bolts; yard goods: *Quietly steady conditions prevailed in the cotton piece goods market last week* (Times of India).

**piece|meal** (pēsʹmēlʹ), *adv., adj., v.* —*adv.* **1** piece by piece; a little at a time: *work done piecemeal. In reality he has treated such problems piecemeal in various segments of the book* (Bulletin of Atomic Scientists). **2** piece from piece; to pieces; into fragments: *The lamb was torn piecemeal by the wolves.*
—*adj.* done piece by piece; fragmentary.
—*v.t.* to divide piecemeal; dismember: *They moved in slowly and gave the* [*enemy*] *a chance to piecemeal them* (Time).
[Middle English *pece mele* < *pece* piece + *-mele,* obsolete suffix meaning "by small measures"]

**piece of cake**, *Especially British Slang.* something sure and easy; a cinch: *"We don't pretend this is going to be a piece of cake for us, but I think we can do it," he said* (London Times).

**piece of eight**, a former Spanish peso, worth 8 reals. It corresponded to the United States dollar.

**piec|er** (pēʹsər), *n.* a person who pieces or patches, especially one who joins broken threads together in a spinning mill.

**piece rate**, the rate of payment for piecework; payment by the amount or piece of work done, not by the time worked.

**piece|work** (pēsʹwėrkʹ), *n.* work paid for by the amount or piece of work done, not by the time it takes.

**piece|work|er** (pēsʹwėrʹkər), *n.* a person who does piecework.

**pie chart**, a graph in the form of a circle divided into sectors that resemble pieces of a pie, drawn to show the percentages into which any total sum is divided; circle graph: *The Company provided a pie chart in the report, showing how it spent the $7,627,000,000 total income* (Wall Street Journal).

**pie crust**, pastry used for the bottom or top of a pie.

**pie crust table**, a table having an ornamental edge suggesting the crust of a pie.

**pied** (pīd), *adj.* **1** having patches of two or more colors; many-colored; parti-colored. **2** spotted: *Daisies pied and violets blue* (Shakespeare). **SYN:** dappled. **3** wearing a costume of two or more colors: *The Pied Piper.* [< *pie*[2] + *-ed*[2] (because of the variegation in a magpie's plumage)]

**pied-à-terre** (pyā tà terʹ), *n., pl.* **pieds-à-terre** (pyā tà terʹ), *French.* **1** a temporary lodging: *In England most of the noblemen and nearly all the squires still regarded their London houses only as pieds-à-terre, and looked on their seats in the country as their real homes* (Nikolaus Pevsner). **2** a foothold. **3** (literally) foot on the ground.

**pied-billed grebe** (pīdʹbildʹ), a small North American grebe with a rounded bill, that lives in ponds and swamps.

**pied|fort** (pē āʹfôr, pyāʹ-), *n.* a coin struck on a blank of unusual thickness. [< French *piedfort* < *pied* foot + *fort* strong]

**pied|mont** (pēdʹmont), *n., adj.* —*n.* a district lying along or near the foot of a mountain range.
—*adj.* lying along or near the foot of a mountain range: *a piedmont plain, a piedmont glacier.*
[American English < *Piedmont,* a region in Italy, (literally) foot of the mountain]

**Pied|mon|tese** (pēdʹmon tēzʹ, -tēsʹ), *adj., n., pl.* **-tese.** —*adj.* of or having to do with Piedmont, a region in northwestern Italy, or its people.
—*n.* a native or inhabitant of Piedmont.

**pied noir** (pyā nwärʹ), *pl.* **pieds noirs** (pyā nwärʹ). *French.* **1** a North African, especially an Algerian, of European descent (used in an unfriendly way). **2** (literally) black foot.

**Pied Piper**, **1** (in medieval legend) a magician who freed the town of Hamelin in Prussia from a plague of rats by playing on his pipe. When refused his promised reward, he led its children away. **2** Also, **pied piper.** *Figurative.* a person who entices or misleads others.

**pie-eyed** (pīʹīdʹ), *adj. Slang.* **1** drunk. **2** visionary; impractical: *pie-eyed theories.*

**pie-faced** (pīʹfāstʹ), *adj.* having a round, expressionless face; moonfaced.

**pie|fort** (pē āʹfôr, pyāʹ-), *n.* = piedfort.

**Pie|gan** (pē ganʹ), *n., pl.* **-gan** or **-gans. 1** a member of a tribe of Blackfoot Indians formerly inhabiting Alberta, Canada, and central Montana. **2** the language of this tribe.

**pie in the sky**, something pleasant but unattainable; impractical ideal: *Talk of economic growth to support a higher budget seems like pie in the sky to this Administration* (Atlantic).

**pie|plant** (pīʹplantʹ, -plänt), *n. U.S.* the common garden rhubarb, so called from its use in pies.

**pie|pou|dre** or **pie|pow|der** (pīʹpouʹdər), *n.* a traveling merchant or trader during the Middle Ages. In England a so-called Court of Piepoudre (or Piepowder) was held at fairs and markets to settle disputes among peddlers and local merchants. [< Anglo-French *piepoudrous* (literally) dusty foot]

***pier** (pir), *n.* **1** a structure built out over the water, supported on columns or piles, and used as a walk or a landing place for ships: *The Chelsea* [*a ferry boat*] *was found nosed against a pier a block away from where she was supposed to be* (Newsweek). **2** = breakwater. **3** one of the solid supports on which the arches of a bridge rest. **4a** the solid part of a wall between windows or doors. See picture below. **b** any solid support, especially of masonry, that bears pressure or thrust from above, such as the pillar or portion of wall from which an arch springs, or a buttress. **c** a support larger than a column, especially (in medieval vaulting) a member resembling a cluster of columns, or a square pillar. **d** the support on which a door, gate, or the like is hung. [Middle English *per* < Medieval Latin *pera,* perhaps Latinization of Old North French *pire, piere* a breakwater, related to Old French *pierre* stone < Latin *petra*]

**pierce** (pirs), *v.,* **pierced, pierc|ing.** —*v.t.* **1** to make a hole in; bore into or through: *to pierce leather with an awl. A nail pierced the tire of our car.* **SYN:** prick, perforate. **2** to go into; go through: *A tunnel pierces the mountain.* **SYN:** See syn. under **penetrate. 3** to force a way through or into; force a way: *to pierce a line of defense.* (*Figurative.*) *The cold wind pierced our clothes.* (*Figurative.*) *A sharp cry pierced the air.* **4** *Figurative.* to make a way through with the eye or the mind: *to pierce a disguise, to pierce a mystery.* **5** *Figurative.* to affect sharply with some feeling: *Her heart was pierced with grief. Can no prayers pierce thee?* (Shakespeare).
—*v.i.* to force or make a way into or through something: (*Figurative.*) *a chill that pierced into the marrow* (Robert Louis Stevenson). **SYN:** penetrate.
[Middle English *percen* < Old French *percier* < Vulgar Latin *pertūsiāre* to bore, or press through < Latin *pertundere* < *per-* through + *tundere* to beat] —**piercʹer,** *n.*

**pierce|a|ble** (pirʹsə bəl), *adj.* that can be pierced.

**pierced ear** (pirst), an earlobe punctured to insert an earring or similar ornament.

**pierced earring**, an earring made for insertion in a pierced ear.

**pierc|ing** (pirʹsing), *adj.* that pierces; penetrating: (*Figurative.*) *piercing cold, a piercing look;* (*Figurative.*) *eyes, blue and piercing, truly eagle-like ... perhaps staring into his own fierce spirit* (Edmund Wilson). **SYN:** sharp, keen. —**piercʹing|ly,** *adv.* —**piercʹing|ness,** *n.*

***pier glass**, a tall mirror, originally one designed to fill the pier or space between two windows. See picture below.

**pier|head** (pirʹhedʹ), *n.* the outward or seaward end of a pier.

**Pi|e|ri|an** (pī irʹē ən), *adj.* **1** of or having to do with the Muses or with poetry. **2** of or having to do with Pieria, a district in ancient Thessaly, the fabled home of the Muses.

**Pierian spring**, the fountain of knowledge and poetic inspiration: *A little learning is a dangerous thing; Drink deep, or taste not the Pierian spring* (Alexander Pope).

**pi|er|id** (pī erʹəd), *adj., n.* —*adj.* = pieridine.
—*n.* a pieridine butterfly.

**pi|er|i|dine** (pī erʹə dīn, -din), *adj.* of or belonging to a family of butterflies that includes the cabbage white and the sulphurs. [< New Latin *Pieris, -idis* the genus name < Greek *Pīerides* the Muses; (literally) ones inhabiting Pieria]

**Pier|rette** (pi retʹ; *French* pye retʹ), *n.* a female character corresponding to Pierrot. [< French *Pierrette,* (feminine) < *Pierrot*]

**Pi|er|rot** (pēʹə rō; *French* pye rōʹ), *n.* a clown who is a frequent character in French pantomime, derived from the traditional Italian comedy. He has his face whitened and wears loose white pantaloons and usually a white jacket, with big buttons and a ruff. [< French, Old French *Pierrot* (diminutive) < *Pierre* Peter]

**pier|side** (pirʹsīdʹ), *n., adj.* —*n.* the area on or near a pier or piers: *At pierside, nine ships waited to load* (Time).
—*adj.* on or near a pier or piers: *a pierside warehouse.*

***pier table**, a table or low bracket intended to occupy the pier or space between two windows, often used under a pier glass. See picture below.

**pi|e|tà** or **Pi|e|tà** (pē ā täʹ, pyā täʹ), *n.* a representation in painting or sculpture of the Virgin Mary seated and holding the body of the dead Christ on her lap or in her arms. [< Italian *pietà* piety, pity < Latin *pietās* pietas]

**pi|e|tas** (pēʹā täs, pyā täsʹ), *n.* dutiful or tender feeling; compassion: *The anthology ... does reveal a writer of rare genius and rarer virtues, who had a Romantic love of order, ceremony, and pietas* (Time). [< Latin *pīetās*]

**Pi|e|tism** (pīʹə tiz əm), *n.* **1** a movement, beginning in the late 1600's in Germany, to revive personal piety in the Lutheran Church. **2** the principles and practices of the Pietists. [< German *Pietismus* < Latin *pīetās* piety + German *-ismus* -ism]

**pi|e|tism** (pīʹə tiz əm), *n.* **1** deep piety. **2** exaggerated or pretended piety. [< *Pietism*]

**Pi|e|tist** (pīʹə tist), *n.* an adherent of Pietism.

**pi|e|tist** (pīʹə tist), *n.* a person conspicuous for pietism. **SYN:** devotee.

**Pi|e|tis|tic** (pīʹə tisʹtik), *adj.* of or having to do with Pietism or the Pietists.

**pi|e|tis|tic** (pīʹə tisʹtik), *adj.* **1** conspicuous for pietism; very pious. **2** too pious; pious with exaggeration or affectation: *... within the framework of pietistic moralism* (Time). —**piʹe|tisʹti|cal|ly,** *adv.*

**pi|e|ty** (pīʹə tē), *n., pl.* **-ties. 1** the quality or character of being pious; reverence for God (or the gods); religious character or conduct; devotion to religion; holiness; goodness: *True piety is cheerful as the day* (William Cowper). **SYN:** godliness, devoutness. **2** a pious act, remark, or belief: *the small pieties with which they larded their discourse* (Samuel Butler). **3** dutiful regard for one's parents. **4** *Obsolete.* pity. [Middle English *piete* pity < Old French *piete,* learned borrowing from Latin *pīetās, -ātis* piety < *pīus* pious. See etym. of doublet **pity.**]

**piezo-**, *combining form.* pressure, as in *piezochemistry, piezometer.* [< Greek *piézein* to press, squeeze]

**pi|e|zo|chem|is|try** (pē āʹzō kemʹə strē, pī ēʹ-), *n.* chemistry that deals with the effects of pressure on chemical processes and materials.

**pi|e|zo|e|lec|tric** (pē āʹzō i lekʹtrik, pī ēʹ-), *adj., n.* —*adj.* of, having to do with, or affected by piezoelectricity: *A piezoelectric material produces electricity when subjected to stress or strain* (Science Journal).
—*n.* a piezoelectric material: *... the inherent advantage of surface acoustic waves in piezoelectrics* (New Scientist). —**pi|eʹzo|e|lecʹtri|cal|ly,** *adv.*

**pi|e|zo|e|lec|tric|i|ty** (pē āʹzō i lek trisʹə tē, -ēʹ-lek-; pī ēʹ-), *n.* electricity or polarity induced by pressure, as in certain crystals, such as quartz, vibrating in an alternating electrical field.

**pi|e|zo|mag|net|ic** (pē āʹzō mag netʹik, pī ēʹ-), *adj.* of, having to do with, or affected by changes of magnetization induced by pressure.

**pi|e|zom|e|ter** (pēʹə zomʹə tər, pīʹ-), *n.* any one of several instruments for measuring pressure, or something connected with pressure, such as one for showing the compressibility of water or other liquids under varying pressures.

**pi|e|zo|met|ric** (pē āʹzə metʹrik, pī ēʹ-), *adj.* of, having to do with, or done by piezometry.

**pi|e|zo|met|ri|cal** (pē āʹzə metʹrə kəl, pī ēʹ-), *adj.* = piezometric.

**pi|e|zom|e|try** (pēʹə zomʹə trē, pīʹ-), *n.* the measurement of pressure or something connected with pressure; use of the piezometer.

***pier** definition 4a

***pier glass**

***pier table**

**pif|fle** (pif′əl), *n., v.,* **-fled, -fling.** *Informal.* —*n.* silly talk or behavior; nonsense.
—*v.i.* to talk or act in a weakly foolish, trifling, or ineffective manner: *They piddled and piffled with iron. I'd given my orders for steel!* (Rudyard Kipling).
[probably imitative] —**pif′fler,** *n.*

*****pig**[1] (pig), *n., v.,* **pigged, pig|ging.** —*n.* **1a** a swine or hog, a four-footed domestic animal with a stout, heavy body, cloven hoofs, and a broad snout, raised for its meat. **b** any similar animal. See picture below. **2** a young pig. **3** pork (used humorously, except in reference to young or suckling pigs). **4** *Informal, Figurative.* a person who seems or acts like a pig; one who is greedy, dirty, dull, sullen, or stubborn. **5a** an oblong mass of iron, lead, or other metal that has been poured into a mold, usually of sand, while molten so that it is of a size and shape convenient for storage: *The first actual tap of the metal for casting into pigs occurred yesterday* (Wall Street Journal). **b** a mold or channel in a pig bed. **c** metal in such masses; pig iron or pig lead. **6** *Slang.* a derogatory term for a police officer.
—*v.i., v.t.* **1** to bring forth pigs; farrow. **2** to herd, lodge, or sleep together like pigs, especially in filth: *a dozen felons, pigging together on bare bricks in a hole fifteen feet square* (Macaulay).
**in a pig's eye,** *Slang.* certainly not; never: *"I should apologize to them? In a pig's eye!"*
**in pig,** (of a sow) pregnant: *The September pig sample on farms in England and Wales shows a slight increase in the breeding herd compared with July, but little difference between the numbers of sows and gilts in pig* (London Times).
**pig it,** to herd, lodge, or sleep together like pigs: *You'd have to pig it with the goats and the cattle* (Grant Allen).
[Middle English *pigge,* perhaps unrecorded Old English *picga,* implied in *pic-bred* acorn, mast; (literally) pig-bread] —**pig′like′,** *adj., adv.*

**pig**[2] (pig), *n. Scottish.* an earthenware container, such as a pot, pitcher, or jar; crock. [origin unknown]

**pig bed,** the bed or series of sand molds in which pigs of iron are cast.

**pig board,** *Surfing.* a surfboard shaped like a wedge of pie; tear drop.

**pig|boat** (pig′bōt′), *n. U.S. Navy Slang.* a submarine.

**pi|geon**[1] (pij′ən), *n., pl.* **-geons** or (*collectively*) **-geon. 1** any one of a group of birds with a plump body, short tail, and short legs. The rock pigeon, the passenger pigeon (now extinct), and the white-crowned pigeon are three kinds. Pigeons are found throughout the world. There are numerous species, making up a family of birds. The smaller kinds are usually called doves. **2** *Slang.* a person who is, or lets himself be, easily tricked, especially in gambling: *This living and moving Moggs is a pigeon for the plucking if ever there was one* (Punch). *He was a famous pigeon for the play-men; they lived upon him* (Thackeray). **SYN:** simpleton, dupe, gull. [Middle English *pejoun* < Old French *pijon* young dove < Vulgar Latin *pībiō, -ōnis* squab, a young piping bird. Compare Latin *pīpiāre,* or *pīpīre* to cheep.]

**pi|geon**[2] (pij′ən), *n.* **1** = pidgin. **2** *British Slang.* business, concern, or affair: *I don't suppose airport acoustics are really your pigeon* (Punch). [alteration (influenced by the pronunciation) of *pidgin*]
▶ See **pidgin** for usage note.

**pi|geon|ber|ry** (pij′ən ber′ē), *n., pl.* **-ries.** = pokeberry.

**pigeon blood,** = pigeon's-blood.

**pigeon breast,** = chicken breast.

**pi|geon-breast|ed** (pij′ən bres′tid), *adj.* = chicken-breasted. —**pi′geon-breast′ed|ness,** *n.*

**pigeon guillemot,** = sea pigeon.

**pigeon hawk,** a pigeon-sized falcon which breeds in northern North America; merlin.

**pi|geon-heart|ed** (pij′ən här′tid), *adj.* very timid or cowardly; fainthearted.

**pi|geon|hole** (pij′ən hōl′), *n., v.,* **-holed, -hol|ing.** —*n.* **1a** a small place built, usually as one of a series, for domestic pigeons to nest in. **b** a small hole in a wall for pigeons to pass in and out. **2** one of a set of boxlike compartments for holding papers and other articles, as in a desk or a cabinet, or standing by itself: *A frivolous little Chinese pagoda at each side of a compartment of pigeonholes* (New Yorker). **3** *Figurative.* a category or class; classification: *Another notable performance also defied pigeonholes* (Harper's). *There's nothing they like better than gathering up ... miscellaneous Americans and jamming them all into the same upper-class pigeonholes* (New Yorker).
—*v.t.* **1** to put in a pigeonhole or compartment. **2** *Figurative.* **a** to classify and lay aside in memory where one can refer to it: *to pigeonhole a witty remark.* **b** to put aside, especially with the idea of dismissing, forgetting, or neglecting: *The plan was pigeonholed and never heard of again.* **c** to put into a category or class; categorize: *Commentators found it difficult to pigeonhole the President as either a "liberal" or "conservative"* (Richard Harwood). **3** to furnish with pigeonholes. —**pi′geon|hol′er,** *n.*

**pi|geon|ite** (pij′ə nīt), *n. Mineralogy.* a variety of pyroxene similar to diopside, occurring in basalt, gabbro, and other rocks. [< *Pigeon* Point, Minnesota + *-ite*[1]]

**pi|geon-liv|ered** (pij′ən liv′ərd), *adj. Archaic.* meek; gentle: *But I am pigeon-livered, and lack gall To make oppression bitter* (Shakespeare).

**pigeon milk,** = pigeon's milk.

**pigeon pea, 1** the small, nutritious seed of an East Indian shrub of the pea family, now widely cultivated in tropical areas. **2** the plant itself.

**pigeon post,** the conveyance of letters or dispatches by pigeon: *The Caliphs made the pigeon post a regular institution in the Nile delta* (London Daily News).

**pigeon pox,** an infectious, viral disease of pigeons, marked chiefly by the breaking out of small yellow nodules on the head.

**pi|geon's-blood** (pij′ənz blud′), *n.,* or **pigeon's blood,** a deep-red color, the color most esteemed in the ruby.

**pigeon's milk,** a whitish liquid containing solid, cheeselike bits, which is formed in the crop of the adult pigeon and regurgitated to feed its young.

**pi|geon-toe** (pij′ən tō′), *v.t., v.i.,* **-toed, -toe|ing.** to walk with the toes turned inward: *He pigeon-toed his way across the rug* (Harper's).

**pi|geon-toed** (pij′ən tōd′), *adj.* having the toes or feet turned inward.

**pi|geon|wing** (pij′ən wing′), *n. U.S.* **1** a figure in skating, in which the skater makes the outline of a bird's wing. **2** a dance step performed by jumping and hitting the heels together in the air.

**pig|fish** (pig′fish′), *n., pl.* **-fish|es** or (*collectively*) **-fish.** any one of certain fishes, such as a grunt of the Atlantic coast of North America, or the sailor's-choice.

**pig|ger|y** (pig′ər ē), *n., pl.* **-ger|ies.** *Especially British.* **1** a place where pigs are kept or raised. **2** pigs as a group; swine.

**pig|gie** (pig′ē), *n., pl.* **-gies.** = piggy.

**pig|gin** (pig′in), *n. Especially Dialect.* a small wooden pail with one stave longer than the rest and serving as a handle; pipkin. [perhaps related to **pig**[2]]

**pig|gish** (pig′ish), *adj.* **1** of, having to do with, or like a pig. **2** *Figurative.* very selfish; greedy. **3** *Figurative.* dirty; filthy. —**pig′gish|ly,** *adv.* —**pig′gish|ness,** *n.*

**pig|gy** (pig′ē), *n., pl.* **-gies,** *adj.,* **-gi|er, -gi|est.** —*n.* a little pig.
—*adj.* like a pig; piggish: *Henry VIII ... is even piggier* (Punch).

**pig|gy|back** (pig′ē bak′), *adv., adj., n., v.* —*adv.* on the back or shoulders: *a father carrying a baby piggyback. Flatcars often take trucks piggyback from one place to another.*
—*adj.* **1** of or having to do with the transporting of loaded truck trailers on flatcars: *Piggyback traffic, hauling loaded trucks to the terminal nearest their destination, went up ... to more than 250,000 carloads during the year* (Austin C. Wehrwein). **2** on top of or supplementary to the main load: *The 50-pound package of needles will be carried into orbit as a piggyback payload on an Air Force satellite* (New York Times).
—*n.* the transporting of loaded truck trailers on flatcars to the point nearest the place where the freight is to be delivered: *Trucks often offer lower rates, too; rails fight back with piggyback* (Wall Street Journal).
—*v.t., v.i.* to carry or move by piggyback: *The New Haven Railroad has been piggybacking trucks for several years on a limited basis in New England* (Wall Street Journal).
[variant of *pickaback*]

**piggy bank, 1** a small container in the shape of a pig, with a slot in the top for coins: *Taxes and inflation have cracked more of their piggy banks than wild spending* (Harper's). **2** any coin bank.

**pig-head|ed** (pig′hed′id), *adj.* stupidly obstinate or stubborn. —**pig′-head′ed|ly,** *adv.* —**pig′-head′ed|ness,** *n.*

**pig in a poke,** something that a person buys or accepts without seeing it or knowing its value: *What price do you put on a pig in a poke?* (Punch).

**pig iron,** crude iron as it first comes from the blast furnace or smelter. It was formerly usually cast into oblong masses called pigs, but is now often transferred in molten form to the next process. Pig iron is used to make steel, cast iron, and wrought iron.

**pig Latin,** a children's slang consisting of English pronounced with the initial consonant of each word placed at the end and with a nonsense syllable (usually "ay") added. *Example:* Oodgay orningmay = Good morning.

**pig lead** (led), lead in the form of pigs.

**pig|let** (pig′lit), *n.* a little pig.

**pig|ling** (pig′ling), *n.* = piglet.

**pig|ment** (pig′mənt), *n., v.* —*n.* **1** a coloring matter, especially a powder or some easily pulverized dry substance. Paint and dyes are made by mixing pigments with oil, water, or some other liquid. *A remarkably white pigment, titanium dioxide, makes possible the sparkling beauty of your refrigerator, the enduring whiteness of your home, the pastel shades for your car* (Newsweek). **2** the natural substance occurring in and coloring the tissues of an animal or plant. The color of a person's hair, skin, and eyes is due to pigment.
—*v.t.* to color with or as if with pigment.
[< Latin *pigmentum* < root of *pingere* to paint, color. See etym. of doublet **pimento.**]

**pig|men|tar|y** (pig′mən ter′ē), *adj.* **1** of, having to do with, containing, or consisting of pigment. **2** *Biology.* characterized by the formation or presence of pigment.

**pig|men|ta|tion** (pig′mən tā′shən), *n.* **1** the deposit of pigment in the tissue of a living animal or plant, causing coloration or discoloration. **2** the coloration of an animal or plant.

**pig|my** (pig′mē), *n., pl.* **-mies,** *adj.* = pygmy.

**Pig|my** (pig′mē), *n., pl.* **-mies,** *adj.* = Pygmy.

**pigmy sperm whale,** a rare black and grayish whale of warm seas, 9 to 13 feet long with a small dorsal fin.

**pi|gno|lia nut** (pi nōl′yə, pig-), = pine nut. [*pignolia,* alteration of Italian *pignolo,* ultimately < Latin *pīnea* pine cone < *pīnus* pine tree]

**pig|nus** (pig′nəs), *n., pl.* **-no|ra** (-nər ə). *Roman and Civil Law.* **1** property pledged or pawned. **2** a contract for pawning property. [< Latin *pignus, -eris* pledge]

**pig|nut** (pig′nut′), *n.* **1a** a thin-shelled, oily, bitterish nut of any one of several species of hickory of North America. **b** any one of the trees that bear these nuts. **2a** the tuber of a European earthnut. **b** the plant itself. Also, **hognut.** [< *pig*[1] + *nut*]

**pig|pen** (pig′pen′), *n.* **1** a pen where pigs are

*****pig**[1]
definitions 1a, 1b

domestic hog

bush pig

wart hog

wild boar

**Pronunciation Key:** hat, āge, cãre, fär; let, ēqual, tėrm; it, īce; hot, ōpen, ôrder; oil, out; cup, pu̇t, rüle; child; long; thin; ᴛʜen; zh, measure; ə represents a in about, e in taken, i in pencil, o in lemon, u in circus.

kept: *loud squealings from the pigpen.* **2** *Figurative.* a filthy place: *The bed unmade, clothes everywhere, the room was a pigpen.*

**pigs in blankets**, **1** small frankfurters or sausages baked or broiled in a casing of dough. **2** broiled or sautéed oysters, chicken livers, or other delicacies wrapped in slices of bacon.

**pig|skin** (pig′skin′), *n.* **1** the skin or hide of a pig. **2** leather made from it. **3** *Informal.* a football. **4** *Informal.* a saddle.

**pig|stick** (pig′stik′), *v.i.,* **-stuck, -stick|ing.** to hunt wild boar on horseback, with a spear.

**pig|stick|er** (pig′stik′ər), *n.* **1** a person who hunts wild boar. **2** *Informal.* a large pocketknife.

**pig|sty** (pig′stī′), *n., pl.* **-sties.** = pigpen.

**pig|tail** (pig′tāl′), *n.* **1** a braid of hair hanging from the back of the head.: *Her abundant hair hung over her shoulder in two tight pigtails* (Arnold Bennett). **2** tobacco in a thin, twisted roll or rope.

**pig|tailed** (pig′tāld′), *adj.* **1** wearing a pigtail or pigtails. **2** having a tail like a pig's.

**pigtailed macaque** or **monkey**, a macaque of the East Indies that grows to a length of about 20 inches and has a short, nearly hairless tail which it can curl up like a pig's.

**pigtail macaque** or **monkey**, = pigtailed macaque.

**pig|weed** (pig′wēd′), *n.* **1** any one of a genus of goosefoots, especially the white pigweed, a coarse weed with narrow, notched leaves sometimes used as a potherb and in salad; lamb's-quarters. See picture under **goosefoot family**. **2** any one of certain weedy amaranths, especially the redroot.

**pi|ka** (pī′kə), *n.* any one of certain small mammals, related to the rabbit but having short ears, and inhabiting rocky mountain slopes in the Northern Hemisphere; cony; calling hare; rock rabbit. [< Tungus (Siberia) *piika,* probably imitative of its cry]

**pi|ka|ke** (pē′kä ke), *n.* a jasmine of Hawaii, introduced from the East Indies, with round, dark-green leaves and small, white, very fragrant flowers that are used to make leis. [< Hawaiian *pīkake* (originally) peafowl, probably alteration of English *peacock*]

**pike[1]** (pīk), *n., v.,* **piked, pik|ing.** —*n.* a spear with a long wooden handle, which foot soldiers used to carry before the invention of the bayonet; spear. Pikes had an iron or steel head. *He wanted pikes to set before his archers* (Shakespeare).
—*v.t.* to pierce, wound, or kill with or as if with a pike.
[< French *pique* < *piquer* pierce < *pic* pick[2], probably through Vulgar Latin *piccus,* ultimately < Germanic (compare Old English *pīc*)]

**pike[2]** (pīk), *n.* a sharp point or spike, such as the head of an arrow or spear or the spike in the center of a buckler. [Old English *pīc* pick[2]; probably influenced by French *pique* pike[1]]

**pike[3]** (pīk), *n., pl.* **pikes** or (*collectively*) **pike**. **1** a large, slender, freshwater fish of the Northern Hemisphere, having spiny fins and a long narrow, pointed head. The muskellunge and pickerel are pikes. *And pikes, the tyrants of the watery plains* (Alexander Pope). **2** any one of certain similar fishes, such as the garfish and the pike perch. [apparently short for *pikefish* < *pike*[2] + *fish* (because of the shape of its snout)]

**pike[4]** (pīk), *n.* **1** = turnpike. **2** any main highway, especially one on which toll is paid. **3** the toll paid at a turnpike gate. **4** a railroad or model railroad.

**come down the pike**, *U.S. Informal.* to make an appearance; show up; come along: *The same Board ... has a tendency to reject—on preposterously formal, checklist grounds—some of the most interesting teachers who come down the pike* (Harper's). *"I don't fall for all the propaganda that comes down the pike* (New Yorker).
[short for *turnpike*]

**pike[5]** (pīk), *n.* in Northern England: **1** a pointed summit. **2** a mountain or hill with a pointed summit (widely used in the names of mountains and hills, especially in Cumberland, Westmorland, and Lancashire). [perhaps extended use of *pike*[2] (compare Old English *hornpīc* pinnacle), or < dialectal Norwegian *pîk* peaked mountain]

**pike[6]** (pīk), *v.i.,* **piked, pik|ing.** *Informal.* **1** to depart. **2** to die. [Middle English *pyken* (perhaps originally) to furnish oneself with a walking stick (see etym. under **pike**[2]); origin uncertain]

**pike[7]** (pīk), *v.i.,* **piked, pik|ing.** to gamble or do anything in a small, cautious way; be a piker. [origin uncertain; perhaps back formation < *piker*]

**pike[8]** (pīk), *n.* a diving position in which the diver bends his body forward from the hips and keeps his legs straight at the knees with his toes pointed. Usually the diver touches his toes or puts his hands on his legs or knees in performing the pike. [probably special use of **pike**[3]]

**piked** (pīkt), *adj.* pointed; spiked; peaked.

**piked dogfish**, = spiny dogfish.

**piked whale**, a small baleen whale with a gray and white band across the flipper.

**pike|man** (pīk′mən), *n., pl.* **-men.** a soldier armed with a pike.

**pike perch**, any one of several large varieties of North American perches, such as the walleyed pike and the sauger, that resemble a pike, especially in the shape of the head.

**pike pole**, a pole eight to sixteen feet long with a metal hook, used by firemen in pushing, pulling, or prying materials that are hard to reach.

**pik|er** (pī′kər), *n. Slang.* **1** a person who does things in a small or cheap way. **2** a stingy or niggardly person. **3** a cautious or timid gambler who makes only small bets. [American English < *Pike* a migrant to California, (originally) from Pike County, Missouri. Compare English *piker* a tramp.]

**pike|staff** (pīk′staf′, -stäf′), *n., pl.* **-staves** (-stāvz′). **1** the wooden staff or shaft of a pike or spear. **2** *Scottish.* a staff or walking stick with a metal point or spike at the lower end like an alpenstock. [< *pike*[1] + *staff*]

**pi|laf** or **pi|laff** (pi läf′), *n.* = pilau.

**pi|lar** (pī′lər), *adj.* having to do with the hair. [< Latin *pilus* hair + English *-ar*]

**pi|la|ry** (pī′lər ē), *adj.* = pilar.

**pi|las|ter** (pə las′tər), *n.* a flat, rectangular pillar, especially when not standing alone, but supporting or decorating part of a wall from which it projects somewhat. [< Middle French *pilastre* < Italian *pilastro* < *pila* pilaster, pillar < Latin *pīla* pillar]

**pi|las|tered** (pə las′tərd), *adj.* furnished with pilasters.

**pil|as|trade** (pil′ə strād′), *n.* a row of pilasters. [< Italian *pilastrata* < *pila* pilaster + *strata* row[1]]

**pi|lau** or **pi|law** (pi lô′), *n.* an Oriental dish consisting of rice or cracked wheat boiled with mutton, fowl, or fish, and flavored, as with spices and raisins. [< Persian *pilāw,* or Turkish *pilâv*]

**pil|chard** (pil′chərd), *n.* **1** a small European marine food fish, related to the herring, but smaller and rounder. A sardine is a young pilchard. **2** any one of certain similar fishes, such as a variety found off the California coast: *In the Mediterranean and off California considerably larger "sardines" are caught, more correctly called pilchards* (Wall Street Journal). [alteration of earlier *pilcher;* origin uncertain]

**pile[1]** (pīl), *n., v.,* **piled, pil|ing.** —*n.* **1** many things lying one upon another in a more or less orderly way: *a pile of stones, a pile of wood.* **SYN**: stack, heap. **2** a mass like a hill or mound: *a pile of dirt, snow, or sand.* **3** *Figurative.* a large structure or mass of buildings; massive edifice: *The cathedral is a huge, gloomy pile* (Tobias Smollett). **4** Also, **piles.** *Informal, Figurative.* a large amount: *I have a pile of work to do. We took piles of pictures.* **5** *Informal, Figurative.* a very large amount of money; fortune: *to make one's pile.* **6** a heap of wood on which a dead body or sacrifice is burned; funeral pile. **7** *Nuclear Physics.* the former name of a reactor: *Fissionable material to fuel the pile will be obtained from the AEC on an extended loan basis* (Science News Letter). **8** *Electricity.* **a** a series of plates of different metals, arranged alternately with cloth or paper wet with acid between them, for producing an electric current; galvanic pile. **b** any similar apparatus for producing an electric current; battery. **9** = fagot (def. 1).
—*v.t.* **1a** to make into a pile; heap evenly; heap up; stack: *The boys piled the blankets in the corner.* **b** *Figurative.* to amass; accumulate: *to pile up a fortune.* **2** to cover with large amounts: *to pile a plate with food.* **3** to place (an object) above something else.
—*v.i.* **1** to gather or rise in piles: *Snow piled against the fences. No doubt, at slightly lower artificial price props, surpluses may pile up at a less appalling rate than otherwise; but they will pile up* (Newsweek). **2** to go in a confused, rushing crowd: *to pile out into the street.* **3** to join together in a group to attack someone.
[< Middle French, Old French *pile* < Latin *pīla* pillar] —**pil′er,** *n.*

**pile[2]** (pīl), *n., v.,* **piled, pil|ing.** —*n.* **1** a large, heavy beam driven upright into the ground or the bed of a river to help support a bridge, wharf, or building: *He could see on the shore ... bamboo huts perched upon piles* (Joseph Conrad). **2** the heavy javelin used in the ancient Roman army by foot soldiers. **3** a pointed blade of grass. **4** the pointed head of an arrow, usually made of metal. **5** a wedge-shaped heraldic bearing, usually extending from the top or upper third (chief) of the escutcheon, with point downward.
—*v.t.* to furnish, strengthen, or support with piles; drive piles into.
[Old English *pīl* stake[1], shaft < Latin *pīlum* heavy javelin]

**pile[3]** (pīl), *n.* **1** the nap of a fabric, especially a soft, thick nap on velvet, plush, and many carpets: *The pile of that Chinese rug is almost half an inch long.* **2** one of the projecting threads or loops of such a nap. **3** a soft fine hair or down, such as the fine short hair of cattle and the wool of sheep. [< Latin *pilus* hair]
► **Pile** in the sense of def. 1 is commonly thought of as a special kind of *nap,* but in strict technical use *nap* is limited to the short fibers of certain yarns, raised as by brushing, and forming a less dense and regular surface, as on wool or flannel. *Shag,* originally any long, rough nap, is now used chiefly of woven loops, cut or uncut, that are longer and coarser than *pile,* as on certain kinds of rugs.

**pi|le|a** (pī′lē ə, pil′ē-), *n.* plural of **pileum.**

**pi|le|ate** (pī′lē it, -āt; pil′ē-), *adj.* **1** *Botany.* having a pileus or cap, as certain fungi do. **2** = pileated. [< Latin *pīleātus,* variant of *pilleātus* having a *pilleus* a felt skullcap, related to *pilus* hair]

**pi|le|at|ed** (pī′lē ā′tid, pil′ē-), *adj.* **1** having the feathers on the top of the head conspicuous; crested. **2** *Botany.* pileate.

**pileated woodpecker**, a very large woodpecker of North America, black with white markings on face, neck, and wings, and a prominent bright-red crest.

**piled** (pīld), *adj.* having a soft, thick nap, as velvet and similar woven fabrics do.

***pile driver**, or **pile|driv|er** (pīl′drī′vər), *n.* **1** a machine for driving piles or stakes into the ground, usually a tall framework in which a heavy weight is raised and then allowed to fall upon the pile; pile engine. **2** *Figurative.* a person who hits or strikes with great power or impact: *Hill, a 6-ft. 3-in. 212-lb. pile driver, rewarded them by leading the league in rushing* (Time). **3** (in wrestling) a slamming downward of an opponent so that the top of his head hits the canvas.

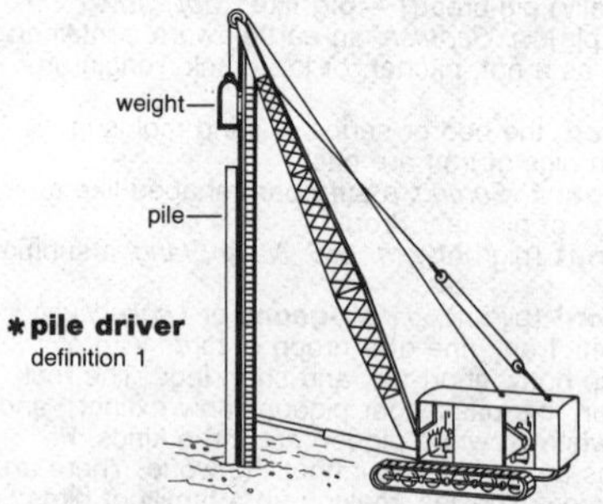

***pile driver**
definition 1

**pile dwelling**, a lake dwelling; palafitte.

**pile engine**, = pile driver (def. 1).

**pi|le|ous** (pī′lē əs, pil′ē-), *adj.* of or having to do with hair; pilose; hairy.

**piles** (pīlz), *n.pl.* a swelling of blood vessels at the anus, often painful; hemorrhoids. [Middle English *pyles;* origin uncertain. Compare Latin *pila* ball[1].]

**pi|le|um** (pī′lē əm, pil′ē-), *n., pl.* **pi|le|a** (pī′lē ə, pil′ē-). the top of a bird's head between the bill and the nape; the forehead and crown. [< New Latin *pileum* < Latin *pīleum,* neuter of *pīleus* skullcap]

**pile-up** or **pile|up** (pīl′up′), *n.* **1** the act or fact of piling up; accumulation: *a pile-up of airplanes waiting to land, a pile-up of boxes at the bottom of the stairs.* **2** a massive collision, especially of vehicles: *a pile-up of cars, the twisted wreckage of a freight-train pile-up.*

**pi|le|us** (pī′lē əs, pil′ē-), *n., pl.* **pi|le|i** (pī′lē ī, pil′ē-). **1** *Botany.* the broad umbrellalike fruiting structure forming the top of certain fungi, such as mushrooms; cap. It is supported by a stalk or stem (the stipe) and bears radiating plates (gills) on the under side. **2** a kind of felt skullcap worn by the ancient Romans and Greeks. [< New Latin *pileus* a fungus cap; < Latin *pīleus, pilleus* skullcap]

**pile|wort** (pīl′wėrt′), *n.* **1** a European herb of the crowfoot family, with bright-yellow, starry flowers and tuberous roots, formerly used in poultices; celandine; lesser celandine. **2** = fireweed. **3** = prince's-feather.

**pil|fer** (pil′fər), *v.i., v.t.* to steal in small quantities: *to pilfer from a cash box, to pilfer stamps. The tramp pilfered some apples from the barrel.* (*Figurative.*) *And not a year but pilfers as he goes Some youthful grace that age would gladly keep* (William Cowper). **SYN**: filch. See syn. under **steal.** [< Old French *pelfrer* to rob, or < Middle English *pilfre* booty, both from Old French *pelfre* booty, pelf] —**pil′fer|er,** *n.*

**pil|fer|age** (pil′fər ij), *n.* **1** the act or practice of pilfering; petty theft. **2** that which is pilfered; stolen goods.

**pil|fer|ing** (pil′fər ing), *n.* = pilferage.

**pil|gar|lic** (pil gär′lik), *n. Dialect.* **1** a poor creature; wretch: *And so poor pilgarlic came home alone* (Jonathan Swift). **2a** a bald head. **b** a bald-headed man.

**pil|grim** (pil′grəm), *n.* **1** a person who goes on a journey to a sacred or holy place, especially a distant shrine, as an act of religious devotion. In the Middle Ages, many people used to go as pilgrims to Jerusalem and to holy places in Europe. *Pilgrimes were they alle That toward Canterbury wolden ryde* (Chaucer). (*Figurative.*) *Pilgrims from the fifty states going through the tribal ritual of posing for snapshots on the steps of the Lincoln Memorial* (Ian Sclanders). **2** a person on a journey; traveler; wanderer: *Like pilgrims to th' appointed place we tend; The world's an inn and death the journey's end* (John Dryden). **SYN**: wayfarer, sojourner. [< unrecorded Anglo-French *pelegrin,* Old French *pelerin* < Medieval Latin *peregrinus* pilgrim < Latin *peregrīnus* foreigner. See etym. of doublets **peregrine, pelerine.**]

**Pil|grim** (pil′grəm), *n.* any one of the Pilgrim Fathers, or early settlers of New England.

**pil|grim|age** (pil′grə mij), *n., v.,* **-aged, -ag|ing.** —*n.* **1** a pilgrim's journey; journey to some sacred place as an act of religious devotion: *Give me my scallopshell ... My staff of faith ... My scrip of joy ... and thus I'll take my pilgrimage* (Sir Walter Raleigh). **2** a journey, especially a long one. **SYN**: peregrination, wayfaring. **3** *Figurative.* life thought of as a journey: *My sword I give to him that shall succeed me in my pilgrimage, and my courage and skill to him that can get it* (John Bunyan).
—*v.i.* to make a pilgrimage; go on a pilgrimage: *They pilgrimaged to the Holy Land.*
[< unrecorded Anglo-French *pelgrimage,* Old French *pelrimage* < *pelegriner* go as a pilgrim < *pelerin* pilgrim]

**pilgrim bottle,** = costrel.

**Pilgrim Fathers,** the early settlers of New England, especially the English separatist leaders of the first group to come in the *Mayflower,* who founded the first colony in New England, at Plymouth, Massachusetts, in 1620.

**pi|li** (pē lē′), *n.* **1** the edible nut or seed of a Philippine tree; pili nut. **2** the tree itself. [< Tagalog *pili*]

**pi|lif|er|ous** (pī lif′ər əs), *adj.* bearing or having hair, hairs, or hairlike processes. [< Latin *pilus* hair + English *-ferous*]

**pil|i|form** (pil′ə fôrm), *adj.* having the form of a hair; hairlike. [< Latin *pilus* hair + English *-form*]

**pi|lig|er|ous** (pī lij′ər əs), *adj.* bearing hair. [< Latin *pilus* hair + *gerere* to bear + English *-ous*]

**pi|li|ki|a** (pē lē kē′ä), *n. Hawaiian.* trouble; bother.

**pil|ing** (pī′ling), *n.* **1** piles or heavy beams driven into the ground, often under water. **2** a structure made of piles. **3** the placing and driving of piles into position.

**pili nut,** = pili.

**Pil|i|pi|no** (pil′ə pē′nō), *n.* the official language of the Philippines, based on Tagalog. [< Tagalog *pilipino* < Spanish *Filipino* Philippine]

**pill**[1] (pil), *n., v.* —*n.* **1** medicine made up into a small, solid mass to be swallowed whole, now usually round and flattened or in capsule form: *The pill stuck in his throat but an extra drink of water washed it down.* **2** *Figurative.* something disagreeable that has to be endured: *This is a bitter pill for him to swallow.* **3** a very small ball or mass of anything; pellet. **4** *Slang.* a ball, especially a golf ball or baseball. **5** *Slang.* an unpleasant, disagreeable, or boring person. **6** *Slang.* a cigarette.
—*v.t.* **1** to treat or dose with pills. **2** *Slang.* to reject by ballot; blackball.
—*v.i.* to form small fuzzy balls of fibers on certain knitted fabrics, especially fabrics made from spun nylon yarn or wool: *a sweater that pills.*
**pills,** *British Slang.* billiards: *We can play pills then till lunch, you know* (Westminster Gazette).
**sugar** (or **sweeten**) **the pill,** to cause the unpleasant to seem more agreeable: *Although the decision may be a disappointment, the pill is sweetened by the forecast of a higher dividend for next year* (London Times).
**the pill,** an oral contraceptive for women: *85 per cent of all the patients had shifted to using the two most effective family planning methods—the pill and the intrauterine device* (New York Times).
[Middle English *pille* < Middle Dutch, or Middle Low German *pille,* ultimately < Latin *pilula* (diminutive) < *pila* ball[1]]

**pill**[2] (pil), *v.t.* **1** *Archaic.* to rob, plunder, or pillage (a person or country). **2** *Archaic or Dialect.* to peel. **3** *Obsolete.* **a** to remove the hair from; make bald. **b** to remove (hair). —*v.i. Obsolete.* to pillage; rob; plunder. [Middle English *pilien,* Old English *pilian* to peel off; to pluck, probably < Latin *pilāre* take off hair (and hide[2]) < *pilus* hair]

**pil|lage** (pil′ij), *v.,* **-laged, -lag|ing,** *n.* —*v.t.* **1** to rob with violence; plunder: *Pirates pillaged the towns along the coast.* **SYN**: sack, strip, rifle. **2** to take possession of or carry off as booty.
—*v.i.* to take booty; plunder: *The soldiers were allowed to pillage.*
—*n.* **1** the act of plundering or taking as spoil; plunder, especially that practiced in war; robbery: *The deserted village was a scene of pillage after the victorious troops had moved in.* **SYN**: spoliation. **2** goods forcibly taken from another, especially from an enemy in war; booty.
[< Old French *pillage* < *piller* to plunder; origin uncertain] —**pil′lag|er,** *n.*

**pil|lar** (pil′ər), *n., v.* —*n.* **1** a strong, slender, upright structure; column. Pillars are usually made of stone, wood, or metal, and used as supports or ornaments for a building. Sometimes a pillar stands alone as a monument or is one of several columns, as in a mine shaft. **2** any upright support of a structure, such as a bedpost, one of the posts in a framed truss in a roof, or the single central support or pedestal of a table or a machine. **3** *Figurative.* anything slender and upright; column: *a pillar of smoke. The Lord went before them by day in a pillar of a cloud ... and by night in a pillar of fire* (Exodus 13:21). **4** *Figurative.* an important support or supporter, as of a state, institution, or principle: *a pillar of society. He is a pillar of the church.* **SYN**: mainstay. **5** the upright post of a harp, farthest from the player.
—*v.t.* to provide with or as if with a pillar or pillars for support or ornament; buttress; strengthen.
**from pillar to post,** from one thing or place to another without any definite purpose: *He seems to have dragged his family from pillar to post in Tennessee, Alabama, and Georgia* (New Yorker).
[< Old French *piler,* noun < Vulgar Latin *pīlāre* (in Medieval Latin, *pīlārius* pillar) < Latin *pīla* pillar, pile[1]]

**pillar box,** *British.* a hollow pillar about five feet high, containing a receptacle for posting letters; mailbox.

**pil|lared** (pil′ərd), *adj.* **1** having pillars: *a pillared gateway.* **2** formed into pillars.

**pillar of society,** a person of strong character or important position.

**pillar post,** *British.* pillar box.

**Pil|lars of Hercules** (pil′ərz), the two high points of land at the eastern end of the Strait of Gibraltar, one on either side of the strait. The one on the European side is the Rock of Gibraltar; the one on the African side is Jebel Musa. According to Greek legend, they were placed there by Hercules.

**pill|box** (pil′boks′), *n.* **1** a small box, usually shallow and often round, for holding pills. **2** a small, low fortress, especially one with thick, strong walls and roof of reinforced concrete, equipped with machine guns and other weapons. **3** a woman's brimless hat fashioned like a shallow cylinder.

**pill bug,** a small, terrestrial, isopod crustacean similar to the sow bug, that rolls into a ball when disturbed.

**pill|head** (pil′hed′), *n. Slang.* a person addicted to taking pills, such as tranquilizers, barbiturates, and amphetamines.

**pil|lion** (pil′yən), *n., adv.* —*n.* **1** a pad attached behind a saddle, especially for a person to sit on: *I proposed that Jack ... should ride on my Aunt Gainor's horse, with Miss Peniston on the pillion behind him* (Weir Mitchell). **2** a seat behind the ordinary saddle on a motorcycle, on which a second person may ride. **3** *Obsolete.* a kind of saddle, especially a woman's light saddle.
—*adv.* on a pillion: *to ride pillion on a motorcycle.*
[< Scottish Gaelic *pillin,* or *pillean* (diminutive) < *pell* cushion < Latin *pellis* skin]

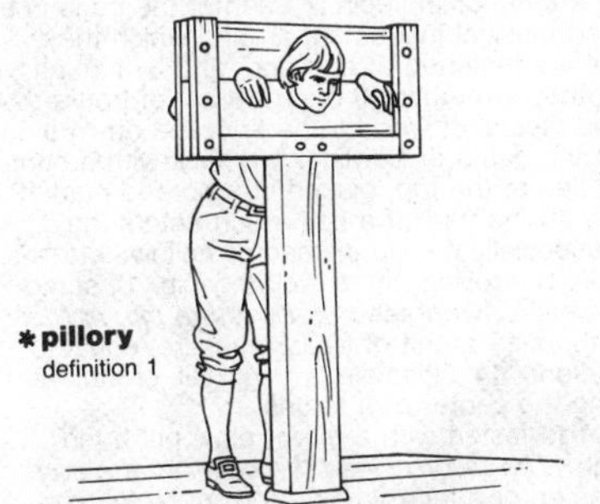

***pillory**
definition 1

***pil|lo|ry** (pil′ər ē), *n., pl.* **-ries,** *v.,* **-ried, -ry|ing.** —*n.* **1** a frame of wood erected on a post, with holes through which a person's head and hands were put. The pillory was formerly used as a punishment, being set up in a public place where the crowd could make fun of the offender. **2** *Figurative.* any means or instance of exposing something, such as a person, some act, condition, or experiment, to public ridicule, contempt, or abuse.
—*v.t.* **1** to put (a person) in the pillory; punish by exposure in a pillory. **2** *Figurative.* to expose to public ridicule, contempt, or abuse: *The newspapers pilloried the unpopular mayor.*
[< Old French *pellori;* origin uncertain]

**pil|low** (pil′ō), *n., v.* —*n.* **1a** a bag or case filled with feathers, down, foam rubber, or other soft material, used to support the head (or, sometimes, other parts) when resting or sleeping. **b** any object improvised for the same purpose: *to use one's coat for a pillow.* **2** = pillion. **3** a pad on which bobbin (or pillow) lace is made. **4** a supporting piece or part, such as the block on which the inner end of a bowsprit rests.
—*v.t.* **1** to rest or place on or as if on a pillow: *to pillow a child on one's lap.* **2** to be a pillow for: *He lay with his arm pillowing his head.*
—*v.i.* to rest the head on or as if on a pillow: *Thou shalt pillow on my breast* (Joseph Rodman Drake).
[Old English *pyle,* and *pilu,* ultimately < Latin *pulvīnus* cushion] —**pil′low|like′,** *adj.*

**pillow block,** a block or cradle, similar to a bearing, that supports a shaft or roller.

**pil|low|case** (pil′ō kās′), *n.* a cotton or linen cover pulled over a pillow.

**pillow lace,** = bobbin lace.

**pillow lava,** lava, usually of a basaltic kind, found in the form of round, closely packed masses.

**pillow sham,** a decorative covering, separate from but often matching the bedspread, laid over the pillow of a bed.

**pil|low|slip** (pil′ō slip′), *n.* = pillowcase.

**pil|low|y** (pil′ō ē), *adj.* pillowlike; soft; yielding.

**pill pusher,** *Slang.* **1** a doctor. **2** a druggist.

**pills** (pilz), *n.pl.* See under **pill.**

**pi|lo|car|pine** (pī′lō kär′pēn, -pin; pil′ō-), *n.* an alkaloid obtained from the leaves of the jaborandi. It is used to stimulate perspiration and the secretion of urine, as an antidote for atropine poisoning, and as a myotic. *Formula:* $C_{11}H_{16}N_2O_2$ [< New Latin *Pilocarpus* the jaborandi genus (< Greek *pîlos* hair; ball + *karpós* fruit) + English *-ine*[2] (the fruit is ball-shaped)]

**pi|lo|ni|dal cyst** or **sinus** (pī′lə nī′dəl), a cyst of cogenital origin which has an opening at the base of the spine, and usually contains a wad of hair. [< Latin *pilus* hair + *nīdus* nest + English *-al*[1]]

**pi|lose** (pī′lōs), *adj.* covered with hair, especially with fine soft hair; hairy; pilous. **SYN**: villous. [< Latin *pilōsus* < *pilus* hair. See etym. of doublet **pilous.**]

**pi|los|i|ty** (pī los′ə tē), *n.* the state of being pilose or pilous; hairiness.

**pi|lot** (pī′lət), *n., v., adj.* —*n.* **1** a person who steers a ship or boat; steersman; helmsman. **2** a person whose business it is to steer ships in or out of a harbor or through dangerous waters. A ship takes on a pilot before coming into a large harbor or proceeding up a dangerous river. **3** a person who operates the controls of an aircraft in flight, especially one qualified and licensed to do this. **4** *Figurative.* a guide; leader. **5** a device in a machine or motor that guides or activates a larger or more complex part. **6** *U.S.* the cowcatcher, as of a locomotive or streetcar. **7** a pilot film, study, or the like: *A pilot is now being filmed* (New York Times).
—*v.t.* **1** to act as the pilot of; steer or navigate: *The aviator pilots his airplane.* (*Figurative.*) *The Finance Minister was obviously unhappy while piloting the Bill* (London Times). **2** *Figurative.* to guide; lead: *The manager piloted us through the big factory.*
—*adj.* **1** of or having to do with a pilot or pilots: *a pilot launch.* **2** that acts as a pilot or in any way as a guide: *a pilot star.* **3a** that serves as an advance, preliminary, or experimental version of some action or operation to be carried out on a larger or more elaborate scale: *a pilot study, a pilot film for a new television series.* **b** that guides, controls, or activates the operation of another, usually a larger and more complex, part: *a pilot switch.*
[< Middle French *pilot* < Italian *piloto,* alteration of unrecorded Late Greek *pēdótēs* < Greek *pēdón* steering oar] —**pi′lot|less,** *adj.*

**pi|lot|age** (pī′lə tij), *n.* **1** the act or practice of piloting. **2** the art or duties of a pilot. **3** the fee paid for the service of a pilot.

**Pronunciation Key:** hat, āge, cãre, fär; let, ēqual, tėrm; it, īce; hot, ōpen, ôrder; oil, out; cup, pu̇t, rüle; child; long; thin; ᴛʜen; zh, measure; ə represents **a** in about, **e** in taken, **i** in pencil, **o** in lemon, **u** in circus.

**pilot balloon**, a small, free balloon sent aloft to indicate the direction and speed of winds or air currents to observers on the ground.

**pilot biscuit** or **bread**, a large, flat cracker; ship biscuit; hardtack.

**pilot boat**, a boat in which pilots cruise offshore in order to meet incoming ships.

**pilot burner**, = pilot light.

**pilot cloth**, a heavy, woolen cloth used especially for pea jackets.

**pilot coat**, = pea jacket.

**pilot engine**, a locomotive sent on ahead of a railroad train to see that the way is clear.

**pilot film**, one of a projected series of filmed television programs, used by the producer as a sample in selling the series to a network or sponsor.

**pilot fish**, a small fish, bluish with dark vertical bars, found in warm seas, often accompanying sharks.

**pilot flag**, a flag flown from a ship that is ready to take on a pilot when entering port.

**pilot house**, or **pi|lot|house** (pī′lət hous′), *n.* an enclosed place on the upper deck of a ship, sheltering the steering wheel and other instruments used by the helmsman; wheelhouse.

**pi|lot|ing** (pī′lə ting), *n.* **1** the work or profession of a pilot; pilotage. **2** air or marine navigation by reference to known landmarks, such as mountain peaks, railroad tracks, or beacons, often with the aid of a map or chart.

**pi|lo|tis** (pē lô tē′), *n.pl.* a row of massive, wedge-shaped stilts of concrete used as the foundation of a building. [< French]

**pilot jack**, = pilot flag.

**pilot lamp**, a small electric light on many machines and appliances, often mounted behind red glass, lighting up when the electric or other power is turned on, or burning continuously to show the location of a switch or the like.

**pilot light**, **1** a small light kept burning all the time and used to light a main light whenever desired. Gas stoves and gas water heaters have pilot lights. **2** = pilot lamp.

**pilot plant**, the equipment necessary to carry out on a small scale for test purposes a process for which full-scale operations are planned.

**pilot snake**, **1** = copperhead. **2** a harmless black snake or rat snake of the eastern United States.

**pilot study**, a preliminary study to determine factors requiring analysis, as a tentative analysis, often of sociological data.

**pilot truck**, an assembly of two or four wheels on a locomotive, forward of the driving wheels.

**pi|lot|weed** (pī′lət wēd′), *n.* a coarse plant of the midwestern United States that reaches a height of ten feet and is covered with short, rough hairs.

**pilot whale**, any one of several dolphinlike, black whales with a white streak down the middle of the underside, found in warm seas; blackfish. The pilot whale grows from 14 to 21 feet long.

**pi|lous** (pī′ləs), *adj.* **1** pilose; hairy. **2** consisting of hair; hairlike. [< Latin *pilōsus* (with English *-ous*). See etym. of doublet **pilose**.]

**pil|pul** (pil′pül), *n.* subtle or searching debate on a Talmudic subject among Jewish scholars; scholarly and often hairsplitting argumentation: *One is reminded ... of the technique of Jewish pilpul, that purely intellectual exercise which consists in explaining some passage from Scripture in a fantastically far-fetched way* (Edmund Wilson). [< Aramaic *pilpūl* discussion, controversy]

**pil|pul|ist** (pil′pü list), *n.* a person who is skilled in pilpul or pilpulistic debate.

**pil|pul|is|tic** (pil′pü lis′tik), *adj.* having to do with or of the nature of pilpul: *pilpulistic arguments.*

**Pil|sen|er** (pil′zə nər, -sə-; -znər, -snər), *n.* **1** a pale lager beer made in or near Pilsen. **2** any superior lager beer. **3** Usually, **Pilsener glass.** a tall, cone-shaped glass used for serving beer. [< German *Pilsener* < *Pilsen,* a city in Czechoslovakia]

**Pil|sner** (pil′znər, -snər), *n.* = Pilsener.

**Pilt|down man** (pilt′doun′), an alleged prehistoric man identified from bones found at Piltdown, Sussex, England, in 1911, but proved in 1953 to be a hoax.

**pil|u|lar** (pil′yə lər), *adj.* of, having to do with, or like a pill: *medicine in pilular form.* [< Latin *pilula* pilule + English *-ar*]

**pil|ule** (pil′yül), *n.* a pill, especially a small pill. [< Middle French *pilule,* learned borrowing from Latin *pilula* pill]

**pil|u|lous** (pil′yə ləs), *adj.* = pilular.

**pi|lum** (pī′ləm), *n., pl.* **-la** (-lə ). a short heavy spear used by the ancient Roman foot soldiers. [< Latin *pīlum*]

**pi|lus** (pī′ləs), *n., pl.* **-li** (-lī). a hairlike part or structure, especially on the surface of a cell or microorganism. [< Latin *pilus* hair]

**Pi|ma¹** (pē′mə), *n.,* or **Pima cotton**, **1** a cotton, originally raised in Arizona by crossing native and Egyptian cotton, used in rainwear, tires, and shirt and other fine fabrics. **2** a strong, smooth fabric made of this cotton. [< *Pima,* a county in Arizona]

**Pi|ma²** (pē′mə), *n., pl.* **-ma** or **-mas**. **1** a member of an agricultural tribe of Pimans living in southern Arizona and northwestern Mexico. **2** their Piman language.

**Pi|mai** (pē′mī′), *n.* the Laotian New Year, marked by water-throwing ceremonies.

**Pi|man** (pē′mən), *n., pl.* **-mans** or **-man**, *adj.* — ***n.*** **1** an American Indian linguistic family of southern Arizona and northwestern Mexico, a branch of Uto-Aztecan. **2** a member of a tribe speaking a language of this family.
— ***adj.*** of or having to do with this linguistic family or the tribes that speak a language of this family.

**pi|men|to** (pə men′tō), *n., pl.* **-tos**. **1** (in popular use) a kind of sweet red pepper, used as a vegetable, a relish, and a stuffing for green olives; pimiento. **2** = allspice. **3** the tropical American tree that bears berries from which allspice is made. It belongs to the myrtle family. [< Spanish *pimienta* black pepper, or *pimiento* green or red pepper, capsicum < Medieval Latin *pigmentum* spice < Late Latin, vegetable juice; a drug < Latin, pigment. See etym. of doublet **pigment**.]

**pimento cheese**, a processed cheese, used sliced or as a spread, made by mixing chopped pimentos (sweet red peppers) with a smooth cheese, especially Neufchatel.

**pi-mes|on** (pī′mes′on, -mē′son; -mez′on, -mē′-zon), *n.,* or **pi meson**, a meson having a mass from 264 to 273 times that of an electron; pion. Charged pi-mesons decay into neutrinos and mumesons; neutral pi-mesons decay into quanta of light or radiation.

**pi|mien|to** (pi myen′tō), *n., pl.* **-tos**. (in technical use) = pimento (def. 1). [< Spanish *pimiento* pimento]

**pi|mo|la** (pi mō′lə), *n.* an olive stuffed with pimento (sweet red pepper). [perhaps < *pim*(ento) + Latin *olea* olive]

**pimp** (pimp), *n., v.i., v.t.* = pander. [origin uncertain]

**pim|per|nel** (pim′pər nel), *n.* **1** a plant with small, bright scarlet, purple, white, or blue flowers that close in cloudy or rainy weather. It is a small herb belonging to the primrose family. There are several kinds, comprising a genus of plants. **2** the flower. [< Old French *pimprenele,* learned borrowing from Medieval Latin *pimpinella* perhaps related to Latin *piper* pepper]

**pimp|er|y** (pim′pər ē), *n., pl.* **-er|ies**. the act or occupation of a pimp.

**pimp|ing** (pim′ping), *adj. Informal.* **1** trifling; paltry; petty. **2** weak; sickly. [origin uncertain]

**pim|ple** (pim′pəl), *n.* a small, inflamed swelling on the skin; papule or pustule. It may or may not contain pus. [origin uncertain. Compare Old English *piplian* to grow pimply.] — **pim′ple|like′**, *adj.*

**pim|pled** (pim′pəld), *adj.* having pimples: *a pimpled adolescent.*

**pim|ply** (pim′plē), *adj.,* **-pli|er**, **-pli|est**. = pimpled.

**pin** (pin), *n., v.,* **pinned**, **pin|ning**. — ***n.*** **1** a short, slender piece of wire with a point at one end and a head at the other, for fastening things together: *The tailor used straight pins to hold the cloth together for sewing.* **2** anything that fastens, consisting essentially or in part of a pointed penetrating bar, such as a hairpin or safety pin: *She took the pins out of her hair.* **3** a badge with a pin or clasp, usually concealed at the back, to fasten it to the clothing: *She wore her class pin.* **4** an ornament that has a pin or clasp; brooch: *a beautiful gold pin with diamonds.* **5** a peg made of wood, metal, or plastic, used to fasten things or parts together, hold something, or hang things on: *By dropping the pin through the hole in the axle the wheel was fastened on.* **6a** = belaying pin. **b** a thole or tholepin. **7** each of the pegs in a stringed musical instrument around which the strings are fastened at one end, and by turning which they are tuned. **8** one of a set of bottle-shaped pieces of wood to be knocked down by a ball in the game of bowling. **9** a stick with a numbered flag at the top, placed in a hole to mark it in golf. **10** the part of a key which enters the lock, especially if solid instead of hollow. **11a** = linchpin. **b** = rolling pin. **c** = clothespin. **12** something small or worthless: *not worth a pin, not to care a pin.* **13** a unit of liquid measure, equal to 4½ gallons. **14** *Obsolete.* a peg, nail, or stud marking the center of a target.
— ***v.t.*** **1** to fasten with a pin or pins; put a pin through: *The tailor pinned the collar to the coat.* **2** to fasten or attach firmly to or on; tack: (*Figurative.*) *A couple of professed wits, who ... had thought to pin themselves upon a gentleman* (Tatler). **3** *Figurative.* to hold fast in one position: *When the tree fell, it pinned him to the ground.* **4** to cause (an opponent in wrestling) to have a fall and to hold both his shoulders on the ground: *The Penn State wrestler pinned his man, the first bout of the day to end with a fall* (New York Times). **5** *Slang.* to give a fraternity pin to, as an indication of interest in becoming engaged.
**on pins and needles**, very anxious or uneasy: *It does mean that a particular American industry is on pins and needles for many months and that the manufacturers can't make many plans ahead* (Wall Street Journal).
**pin down**, **a** to hold or bind to an undertaking or pledge: *one of those pestilent fellows that pin a man down to facts* (Washington Irving). **b** to fix firmly; determine with accuracy; establish: *We have pinned down the important principle* (New York Times).
**pin on**, **a** to fix (as blame or responsibility) on: *The police could not pin the crime on him.* **b** to place (as one's trust or hope) entirely on: *I now pin my hopes on a meeting at Dieppe* (Harriet Granville).
**pins**, *Informal.* legs: *Who ventures this road need be firm on his pins* (Richard H. Barham).
[Old English *pinn* peg, perhaps ultimately < Latin *pinna* wing, pinion] — **pin′like′**, *adj.*

**pi|ña** (pē′nyä), *n., pl.* **-ñas**. *Spanish.* **1** the pineapple. **2** a beverage flavored with pineapple.

**pi|na|ceous** (pī nā′shəs), *adj.* of or belonging to the pine family of trees and shrubs. [< New Latin *Pinaceae* the pine family (< Latin *pīnus* pine tree) + English *-ous*]

**piña cloth**, a fine, sheer fabric made in the Philippines and elsewhere from the fibers of the leaves of the pineapple plant.

**pin|a|coid** (pin′ə koid), *n.* a form of crystal consisting of two parallel faces. [< Greek *pínax, -akos* slab + English *-oid*]

**pin|a|co|the|ca** (pin′ə kō thē′kə), *n.* a picture gallery; art gallery. [< Latin *pinacothēca* < Greek *pinakothēkē* < *pínax, -akos* slab, tablet + *thēkē* chest, repository]

**pin|a|fore** (pin′ə fôr, -fōr), *n.* **1** a child's apron that covers most of the dress. **2** a light dress without sleeves. [< *pin,* verb + *afore* (because it was originally pinned to the dress front)]

**pin|a|fored** (pin′ə fôrd, -fōrd), *adj.* wearing a pinafore.

**pi|nas|ter** (pī nas′tər, pə-), *n.* a pine of southern Europe, having stout leaves set in dense whorls and cones arranged around the branches in radiating clusters of from four to eight; maritime pine. [< Latin *pīnāster* wild pine < *pīnus* pine tree]

**pi|ña|ta** (pē nyä′tä), *n., pl.* **-tas**. *Spanish.* a papier-mâche or clay pot shaped especially like a person or animal, and filled with candy, fruit, and toys, which is hung above the heads of children at Christmastime in Mexico and other Latin-American countries. The children are blindfolded and given chances to break the piñata with a stick to obtain its contents.

**pin|ball** (pin′bôl′), *n.* a game played on a slanted board in which a ball or marble is hit with a hammer on a spring so that it rolls up a groove, then down the board, striking bumpers, pins, or pegs, or rolling into numbered compartments or through alleys to score points.

**pinball machine**, a mechanical device on which pinball is played.

**pin|board** (pin′bôrd′, -bōrd′), *n.* a board, usually mounted on the wall, on which pins or pegs are fixed for holding small articles, such as bobbins and keys.

**pin borer**, any one of various small beetles of Europe and North America that make minute holes through the bark of infested trees.

**pin boy**, a boy or man who sets up the pins in a bowling alley; pinsetter.

***pince-nez** (pans′nā′, pins′-), *n.* a pair of eyeglasses kept in place by a spring that clips onto the bridge of the nose. [< French *pince-nez* (literally) pinch-nose]

***pince-nez**

**pin|cer** (pin′sər), *adj., n.* — ***adj.*** of or like pincers or their actions.
— ***n.*** = pincers. — **pin′cer|like′**, *adj.*

**pin|cers** (pin′sərz), *n., pl.* **-cers**. **1** a tool for gripping and holding tight, made like scissors but with jaws instead of blades: *They also tried a piece of rubber tubing and a pair of pincers, but ... they had trouble with high-velocity jets of gas* (Alban Charnley). **2** Also, **pincer**. the large claw with which crabs, lobsters, and crayfish grip and hold their prey. **3** a military operation in which the enemy is surrounded and crushed by the meeting of columns driven around each side of him. [Middle English *pynceours,* apparently < Anglo-French < Old French *pincier* to pinch]

**pinch** (pinch), *v., n.* — ***v.t.*** **1** to squeeze between the thumb and forefinger, with the teeth or claws, or with any instrument having two jaws or parts between which something may be grasped: *Father pinched the baby's cheek playfully.* **SYN:** nip, tweak. **2** to press so as to hurt; squeeze: *He pinched his finger in the door. These shoes pinch my feet.* **3** *Figurative.* to cause sharp discomfort or distress to, as cold, hunger, or want does. **4** *Figurative.* to cause to shrink or become thin: *a face pinched by hunger.* **5** to cause (a plant) to shrivel or wither up, as by frost. **6** *Figurative.* to bring into difficulty or trouble; afflict: *The king finding his affairs pinch him at home* (Daniel Defoe). **7** *Figurative.* **a** to limit closely; stint: *to be pinched for space or time. With earnings pinched by disappointing demand, the oil companies would like to cut their reliance on domestic oil* (Wall Street Journal). **b** to limit or restrict closely the supply of (anything); be stingy with: *The miser pinched pennies on food to the point of near starvation.* **8** to put in or add by pinches or small quantities: *The cook pinched more salt into the soup each time she sampled it.* **9** *Slang.* to arrest. **10** *Slang.* to steal; purloin: *His father caught him pinching apples.* **11** to sail (a vessel) close to the wind to such a degree that the sails shake. **12** to move (something heavy) by a succession of small heaves with a pinch bar.
— ***v.i.*** **1** to exert a squeezing pressure or force; compress: *Where does that shoe pinch?* **2** *Figurative.* to cause discomfort or distress: *Here's the pang that pinches* (Shakespeare). **3** to be stingy; stint oneself: *Her father and sister were obliged to pinch, in order to allow her the small luxuries* (Elizabeth Gaskell). **4** (of a vein or deposit of ore) to become narrower or smaller; give out altogether.
— ***n.*** **1** the act of pinching; a squeeze between two hard edges; nip. **2** a sharp pressure that hurts; squeeze: *the pinch of tight shoes.* **3a** as much as can be taken up with the tip of the finger and thumb: *a pinch of salt or snuff.* **b** *Figurative.* a very small quantity. **SYN:** bit. **4** *Figurative.* sharp discomfort or distress: *the pinch of poverty, the pinch of hunger.* **5** a time of special need; emergency: *I will help you in a pinch.* **SYN:** hardship, strait. **6** *Slang.* an arrest. **7** *Slang.* a stealing. **8** = pinch bar.
**with a pinch of salt,** with some reservation or allowance: *It was necessary to take all his statistics with a pinch of salt* (Peter Ustinov).
[perhaps < Old North French *pinchier,* variant of Old French *pincier;* origin uncertain. Compare Vulgar Latin *pīccāre* to pierce, Flemish *pinssen.*]
— **pinch′er,** *n.*

**pinch bar,** a kind of crowbar or lever with a projection that serves as a fulcrum, used for moving heavy objects or loosening coal; wrecking bar.

**pinch|beck** (pinch′bek), *n., adj.* — ***n.*** **1** an alloy of zinc and copper, used in imitation of gold and in cheap jewelry. **2** *Figurative.* something not genuine; imitation.
— ***adj.*** **1** made of pinchbeck. **2** *Figurative.* not genuine; sham: *pinchbeck patriotism, pinchbeck heroism.* **SYN:** spurious.
[< Christopher *Pinchbeck,* about 1670-1732, an English watchmaker, inventor of the alloy]

**pinch|bot|tle** (pinch′bot′əl), *n.* a bottle with pinched or concave sides.

**pinch|cock** (pinch′kok′), *n.* a clamp used to compress a flexible or elastic tube so as to regulate or stop the flow of a liquid. [< *pinch* + *cock*[1] faucet]

**pin|check** (pin′chek′), *n.* **1** a fine check smaller than a shepherd's check, used as part of a regular pattern in certain worsteds, rayons, and other fabrics. **2** a garment or fabric having such checks.

**pinched** (pincht), *adj.* **1** compressed, as between the finger and thumb. **2** *Figurative.* contracted, as if by pinching; shrunken, or thin and drawn, as the face or features: *In the biting easterly wind her face looked small and pinched, and cold* (John Galsworthy). **3** *Figurative.* distressed; straitened: *Apparently not too badly pinched, the smallest producer is not, however, turning out cars at anything like its pace of a year earlier* (Wall Street Journal).

**pinch|ed|ness** (pin′chid nis), *n.* the state of being pinched.

**pinch effect,** *Nuclear Physics.* the constriction of plasma by the magnetic field of an electric current, used in controlling thermonuclear fusion.

**pin cherry,** a wild cherry that has light-red, sour fruit.

**pinch|ers** (pin′chərz), *n., pl.* **-ers.** = pincers.

**pinch-hit** (pinch′hit′), *v.,* **-hit, -hit|ting.** — ***v.i.*** **1** *Baseball.* to bat as a substitute for the officially listed batter, especially when a hit is badly needed. **2** *Figurative.* to take another's place in an emergency: *Wild signals of distress from the Chief Whip called on some back-bencher to rise and pinch-hit until the Prime Minister was ready* (Punch).
— ***v.t.*** *Baseball.* to score by pinch-hitting: *He pinch-hit a triple in the last game of the season* (New York Times).
[American English, back formation < *pinch hitter*]

**pinch hit,** *Baseball.* a hit made by a pinch hitter.

**pinch hitter,** a person who pinch-hits for another.

**pinch homer,** *Baseball.* a home run made by a pinch hitter.

**pinch|ing** (pin′ching), *adj.* **1** that pinches; nipping; sharp. **2** *Figurative.* distressing; causing straits. **3** *Figurative.* sparing, parsimonious, or niggardly.
— **pinch′ing|ly,** *adv.*

**pinching bug,** a variety of stag beetle of the eastern United States that flies by night.

**pinch|pen|ny** (pinch′pen′ē), *adj., n., pl.* **-nies.** *Informal.* — ***adj.*** too economical; frugal; miserly: *a pinchpenny management.*
— ***n.*** a niggardly person; skinflint; miser.

**pinch roller,** a soft roller, usually made of rubber, that presses the tape against the capstan in a tape recorder.

**pinch runner,** *Baseball.* a player who is substituted for a base runner: *Casey then took Hook out for a pinch runner, Rod Kanehl* (New York Times).

**pin curl,** a curl of hair kept in place by a bobby pin or clip.

**pin-curl** (pin′kėrl′), *v.t.* to curl (hair) by keeping the locks in place with bobby pins.

**pin|cush|ion** (pin′kůsh′ən), *n.* a small cushion to stick pins (and sometimes needles) in until needed.

***pincushion distortion,** *Optics.* a distortion produced by a lens causing the sides of a square to curve inwards, suggesting the shape of a pincushion.

***pincushion distortion**

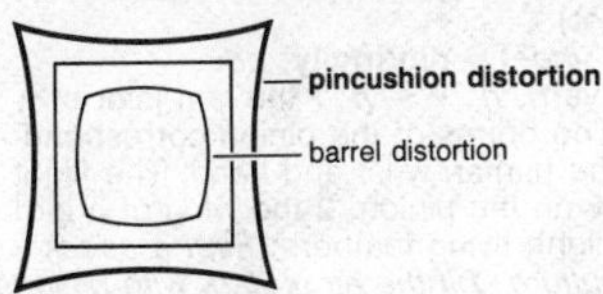


**pincushion flower,** **1** = guelder-rose. **2** = scabious.

**pin|da** (pin′də), *n. Southern U.S.* the peanut. Also, **pinder.** [< Kongo *mpinda*]

**Pin|dar|ic** (pin dar′ik), *adj., n.* — ***adj.*** **1** of, having to do with, or in the style of Pindar, a Greek lyric poet: *The Rector of Exeter in my day was a Pindaric scholar* (New Yorker). **2** of elaborate or irregular metrical structure.
— ***n.*** an ode in irregular or constantly changing meter.
[< *Pindar,* about 522?-443 B.C., a Greek lyric poet + *-ic*]

**Pindaric ode,** an ode or other form of verse with an elaborate or irregular metrical structure.

**Pin|dar|ics** (pin dar′iks), *n.pl.* = Pindaric ode.

**pin|der** (pin′dər), *n.* = pinda.

**pin|dling** (pin′dling), *adj. U.S. Informal.* puny; sickly; delicate. [origin uncertain; perhaps variant of *piddling*]

**pine**[1] (pīn), *n.* **1a** a tree bearing woody cones and clusters of evergreen leaves shaped like needles that grow out from temporary scalelike leaves. The various kinds of pine make up a genus of the pine family. Many kinds are valuable for lumber, turpentine, resin, and tar. *It is usually easy to distinguish the pines from other evergreen conifers by the arrangement of their leaves (needles) in groups of two, three, or five* (Fred W. Emerson). **b** any one of various coniferous trees resembling pines, especially in areas where true pines do not occur. **2** the wood of any one of these trees much used in construction. **3** *Informal.* the pineapple. [Old English *pīn* < Latin *pīnus, -ūs*] — **pine′like′,** *adj.*

**pine**[2] (pīn), *v.,* **pined, pin|ing,** *n.* — ***v.i.*** **1** to long eagerly; yearn: *to pine for home. The mother was pining to see her son.* **2** to waste away with pain, hunger, grief, or desire: *to pine with homesickness, to pine away with longing.* **SYN:** languish.
— ***v.t.*** *Archaic.* to repine at; lament; mourn.
— ***n.*** **1** *Archaic or Scottish.* pain, suffering, or misery: *heavy-dragg'd wi' pine an' grievin'* (Robert Burns). **2** *Obsolete.* effort; pains.
[Old English *pīnian* cause to suffer; later, suffer < *pīn* torture, punishment < Vulgar Latin *pēna,* variant of Latin *poena* penalty < Greek *poinē.* Compare etym. under **pain.**]

**pin|e|al** (pin′ē əl), *adj.* **1** having to do with a pine cone or resembling it in shape. **2** of or having to do with the pineal body. [< French *pinéal* < Latin *pīnea* pine cone < *pīnus* pine tree]

**pineal body** or **gland,** a small, somewhat conical structure in the brain of all vertebrates that have a cranium. It secretes various chemical substances, such as melatonin, and appears to function in various animals as a light-sensing organ, as a biological clock, or as a ductless gland whose secretions regulate the activity of sex glands. See picture under **endocrine gland.**

**pineal eye,** the projection of the pineal gland on the head of some reptiles, that resembles an eye in structure.

**pine|ap|ple** (pī′nap′əl), *n.* **1** a large, juicy fruit that looks somewhat like a large pine cone and is good to eat. It is a seedless, multiple fruit developed from a conical spike of flowers and surmounted by a crown of small leaves. **2** the plant that it grows on. Pineapple is widely cultivated in tropical regions. It has a short stem and bears a dense cluster of small flowers, rising from a cluster of slender, stiff leaves which are edged with spines. **3** some other plant of the same family, such as the wild pineapple. **4** *Slang.* a hand grenade or bomb (so called from the crisscross pattern on some kinds). [Middle English *pīnappel* pine cone]

**pineapple cloth,** = piña cloth.

***pineapple family,** a large group of monocotyledonous tropical American herbs, mostly epiphytic plants with stiff leaves. The family includes the pineapple, Spanish or black moss, and billbergia.

***pineapple family**

**pine barren,** *Especially U.S.* a level, sandy tract covered sparsely with pine trees: *the Georgia pine barrens.*

***pine cone,** the cone or fruit (strobile) of a pine tree. The cone of the white pine with a tassel of needles is the emblem of Maine.

***pine cone**

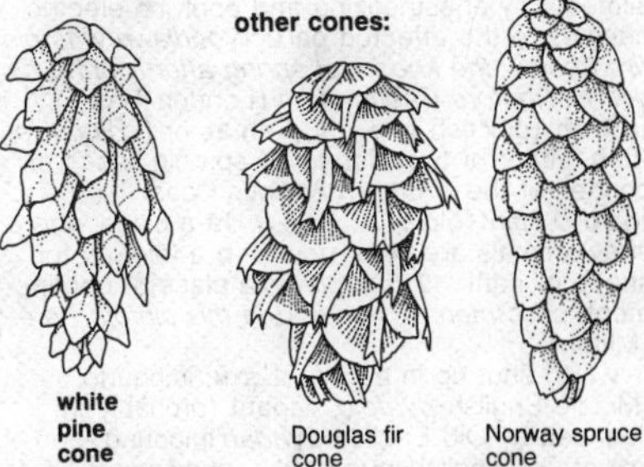


**pine|drops** (pīn′drops′), *n., pl.* **-drops.** **1** a slender, purplish, leafless, North American plant related to the Indian pipe, with nodding white to red flowers. It is parasitic on the roots of pine trees. **2** = beechdrops.

**pine family,** a large group of coniferous, mostly evergreen trees and shrubs that have needle-shaped leaves and resinous sap, including the pine, fir, spruce, hemlock, larch, and cedar of Lebanon.

**pine finch,** = pine siskin.

**pine grosbeak,** a finch about the size of a robin, living in the northern and mountainous regions of Europe and North America. The male has rosy plumage.

**pine linnet,** = pine siskin.

**pine marten,** **1** a marten of the forests of Europe, closely related to the American marten. **2** the American marten.

**pi|nene** (pī′nēn), *n.* a terpene found in oil of turpentine and other essential oils, occurring in two isomeric forms, and used in making resins, and

**Pronunciation Key:** hat, āge, cãre, fär; let, ēqual, tėrm; it, īce; hot, ōpen, ôrder; oil, out; cup, pu̇t, rüle; child; long; thin; ŧʜen; zh, measure; ə represents **a** in about, **e** in taken, **i** in pencil, **o** in lemon, **u** in circus.

as a solvent. *Formula:* $C_{10}H_{16}$ [< *pin*(e)[1] + *-ene*]

**pine needle**, the very slender leaf of a pine tree. It is shaped like a needle.

**pine nut**, 1 the edible seed or kernel found in the cone of any one of various pines, such as the piñon; pignolia nut. 2 a pine cone, especially one containing edible seeds.

**pin|er|y** (pī′nər ē), *n., pl.* **-er|ies.** 1 a forest or plantation of pine trees. 2 a place where pineapples are grown.

**pine|sap** (pīn′sap′), *n.* a leafless, yellowish or reddish plant of the Northern Hemisphere, similar and related to the Indian pipe, and parasitic on pine roots or growing in decaying organic matter.

**pine siskin**, a small, streaked, brownish North American finch, that has yellow patches on the wings and tail.

**pine snake**, a harmless, burrowing, bull snake of the eastern United States.

**pine tar**, tar obtained by destructive distillation of pine wood, used in making certain soaps and paints and in medicine for the treatment of certain skin diseases and as an expectorant.

**pine tree shilling**, a silver coin bearing the figure of a pine tree, minted by the Massachusetts Bay Colony in the 1600's, and having the legal value of an English shilling but a slightly smaller silver content.

**Pine Tree State**, a nickname for Maine.

**pi|ne|tum** (pī nē′təm), *n., pl.* **-tums, -ta** (-tə). 1 a plantation or collection of growing pine trees of various species, especially for scientific or ornamental purposes. 2 a treatise on pines. [< Latin *pīnētum* pine grove < *pīnus* pine tree]

**pine warbler**, a grayish-green, yellow-breasted warbler, inhabiting the pine forests of eastern North America.

**pine|wood** (pīn′wu̇d′), *n.* 1 the wood of the pine tree. 2 a wood or forest of pines.

**pine woods sparrow**, a brownish sparrow with a buff breast, found in the southern United States and Mexico, especially in pine woods.

**pine|y** (pī′nē), *adj.,* **pin|i|er, pin|i|est.** = piny.

**pin|feath|er** (pin′feᴛʜ′ər), *n.* an undeveloped feather, especially one just breaking through the skin, that looks like a small stub: *Remove all the pinfeathers from the chicken before cooking it.*

**pin-fire** (pin′fīr′), *adj., n., v.,* **-fired, -fir|ing.** —*adj.* 1 having to do with an early type of cartridge fitted with a pin which, when struck by the hammer of the firearm, is driven into and explodes a percussion cap in the cartridge. 2 having to do with a firearm using such a cartridge. —*n.* 1 a pin-fire cartridge. 2 a firearm using a pin-fire cartridge. —*v.t.* to treat (a horse) for splints and other leg ailments by anesthetizing and applying electric needles to the affected part: *Woodlawn was pinfired below the knee last spring after injuring himself just before Cheltenham* (London Times).

**pin|fish** (pin′fish′), *n., pl.* **-fish|es** or (*collectively*) **-fish.** either of two elongated sparoid fishes or porgies of the southern Atlantic Coast.

**pin|fold** (pin′fōld′), *n., v.* —*n.* **1a** a place where stray animals are kept; pound. **b** a fold, as for sheep or cattle. 2 *Figurative.* a place of confinement; pen: *men ... pester'd in this pinfold here* (Milton). —*v.t.* to shut up in a pinfold. **SYN:** impound. [Middle English *pynfold,* variant (probably influenced by Old English *pyndan* impound, pen up) of Old English *pundfald* < *pund* pound[3] + *fald* fold[2]]

**ping** (ping), *n., v.* —*n.* a sound like that of a rifle bullet whistling through the air or striking an object. —*v.i.* to make such a sound; produce a ping: *After her marriage, she installed a range in the cellar of her own city house and spent hours pinging away at the target* (New Yorker). —*v.t.* to strike with such a sound; cause to ping. [imitative]

**ping|er** (ping′ər), *n.* an electronic device, such as an echo sounder, that transmits sound under water, used especially for tracking objects or tracing surfaces under water: *Pingers, for locating instruments near the bottom, were ... used* (New Scientist). [< *ping* + *-er*[1]]

**pin|go** (ping′gō), *n., pl.* **-gos** or **-goes.** an arctic mound or hill shaped like a volcano, consisting of an outer layer of soil covering a core of solid ice: *The Mackenzie flows away from everything useful, away from civilization itself into a region where pingos pop out of the permafrost and builders drill holes through glare ice with steam hoses* (Maclean's). [< an Eskimo word]

**ping-pong** (ping′pong′, -pông′), *n., v.* —*n.* 1 a game somewhat like tennis played on a large table with small wooden paddles and a light, hollow celluloid ball; table tennis. 2 **Ping-Pong.** a trademark for the equipment used in this game. 3 *Informal, Figurative.* the act or fact of tossing or bouncing back and forth: *Important moves are repeatedly delayed or stymied by ... legislative ping-pong between City Hall and Albany* (New York Times). —*v.t., v.i. Informal, Figurative.* 1 to toss or bounce back and forth: *Soon space satellites will be ping-ponging video news from every point of the earth to every other point* (Punch). 2 to refer a patient for a variety of unneeded tests and treatments: *Exposés of the costly abuses that threaten to disable the nation's Medicaid system often include ... needless Medicaid-reimbursed tests and treatments ... known to the trade as "ping-ponging"* (New Yorker).

**pin|guid** (ping′gwid), *adj.* 1 unctuous; greasy; oily. 2 (of soil) rich; fertile. [< Latin *pinguis* fat + English *-id,* as in *liquid*]

**pin|guid|i|ty** (ping gwid′ə tē), *n.* fatness; fatty matter.

**pin|head** (pin′hed′), *n.* 1 the head of a pin. 2 *Figurative.* something very small or worthless. 3 a small minnow. 4 *Slang, Figurative.* a person of little intelligence; nitwit.

**pin|head|ed** (pin′hed′id), *adj.* 1 having a head like that of a pin. 2 *Slang, Figurative.* having little intelligence; stupid.

**pin|hold|er** (pin′hōl′dər), *n.* a device for holding cut flowers, consisting of a mounting or base studded with pins.

**pin|hole** (pin′hōl′), *n.* 1 a small hole made by or as if by a pin. 2 a hole for a pin or peg to go in.

**pinhole camera**, a simple camera, such as a box camera, having a small opening in place of a lens, through which light enters when uncovered. At any normal distance, it renders a sharp image of the photographed objects, but it requires very bright light and long exposure time.

**pin|ing** (pī′ning), *adj., n.* —*adj.* that pines; languishing; wasting; failing with grief or longing. —*n.* a disease of progressive weakness and emaciation in sheep or cattle, resulting from a cobalt deficiency in the diet: *Pining is most common where the underlying bedrock is granite* (New Scientist). [< *pin*(e)[2] + *-ing*[2]] —**pin′ing|ly,** *adv.*

**pin|ion**[1] (pin′yən), *n., v.* —*n.* 1 the last joint of a bird's wing. The bones of the pinion correspond to those of the human wrist and hand. The flight feathers grow on the pinion. 2 the wing of a bird, as used for flight; flying feathers: *First a speck, and then a vulture, Till the air is dark with pinions* (Longfellow). 3 any one of the stiff flying feathers of a bird's wing; quill: *He is pluck'd, when hither He sends so poor a pinion of his wing* (Shakespeare). 4 the anterior border of an insect's wing, especially in reference to its color or markings. —*v.t.* **1a** to cut off or tie the pinions of (a bird) to prevent it from flying. **b** to cut or bind (a wing) thus. **2a** to bind the arms of (a person) so as to deprive him of their use: *Finding us all prostrate upon our faces ... they pinioned us with strong ropes* (Jonathan Swift). **b** to bind (the arms) to something: *The captive's arms were pinioned to his sides.* [< Middle French *pignon* < Old French *pennon* < *penne* < Latin *penna* feather, also *pinna* wing]

**pin|ion**[2] (pin′yən), *n.* 1 a small gear with teeth that fit into those of a larger gear or rack; planetary gear; bevel gear or spur gear. 2 a spindle, arbor, or axle having teeth that engage with the teeth of a wheel. [< Middle French *pignon* < Old French, crenelation, battlement < Vulgar Latin *pinniō, -ōnis* < Latin *pinna* pinnacle, battlement; (originally) pinion[1], feather]

**pin|ioned** (pin′yənd), *adj.* having pinions; winged.

**pin|ite**[1] (pin′īt, pī′nīt), *n.* a mineral consisting essentially of a silicate of aluminum and potassium. [< German *Pinit* < *Pini,* a mine at Aue, East Germany, where it is found + *-it* -ite[1]]

**pi|nite**[2] (pī′nīt, pin′īt), *n.* a sweetish, white, crystalline substance obtained from the resin of a species of pine, and from certain other plants. *Formula:* $C_7H_{14}O_6$ [< French *pinite* < Latin *pīnus* pine tree + French *-ite* -ite[1]]

**pi|ni|tol** (pī′nə tōl, pin′ə tol), *n.* = pinite[2]. [< *pinit*(e)[2] + *-ol*[2]]

**pink**[1] (pingk), *n., adj., v.* —*n.* 1 a color obtained by mixing red with white; a light or pale red, often with a slight purple tinge. **2a** *Figurative.* the highest degree or condition; height: *By exercising every day he kept himself in the pink of health. Even near the soft spots, the economy seems to be in the pink of condition* (Time). **b** the highest type or example of excellence: *He is the pink of courtesy. My fellow motorists were the pink of consideration* (News Chronicle). 3 a garden plant with spicy-smelling flowers of various colors, mostly white, pink, and red. Pinks are herbs, widely grown for their showy flowers. The sweet william and the clove pink or carnation are kinds of pinks. 4 the flower of the pink. 5 scarlet cloth, as worn by foxhunters: *an English country gentleman, hunting in pink* (Francis M. Crawford). 6 = foxhunter. 7 Also, **Pink.** *Informal.* a person with somewhat radical political opinions: *He can hardly be called a pink, much less a Red* (Time). 8 *Obsolete.* a fop or dandy. —*adj.* 1 light-red or pale-red, often with a slight purple tinge: *a pink carnation, pink ribbon, pink cheeks.* 2 *Informal.* somewhat radical: *Many of them speak ... in the mildly indulgent tone ... used when speaking of a son at college whose politics were faintly pink* (New Yorker). 3 *Informal.* over-refined; exquisite; smart: *a pink tea.* —*v.i. Informal.* to turn pink; flush; blush. [origin uncertain] —**pink′ly,** *adv.* —**pink′ness,** *n.*

**pink**[2] (pingk), *v.t.* 1 to prick or pierce with a sword, spear, or dagger: *The épée wielder can score by pinking his opponent anywhere on the body* (Time). 2 to cut the edge of (cloth) in small scallops or notches, to prevent the edge from raveling or to make a decorative finish. 3 to ornament (cloth, leather, or the like) with small, round holes, often in order to show a material or color beneath. 4 *British Dialect.* to adorn; beautify; deck. [Middle English *pynken,* perhaps Old English *pyngan* to prick. Compare Old English *pynca* point.]

**pink**[3] (pingk), *n.* any one of various sailing vessels or boats with a narrow stern. [apparently < Middle Dutch *pincke* small ship, fishing boat]

**pink**[4] (pingk), *v., adj. Dialect.* —*v.i.* 1 (of the eyes) to be half shut; blink. 2 to look or peer with contracted eyes: *A hungry fox lay winking and pinking as if he had sore eyes* (Sir Roger L'Estrange). —*adj.* (especially of the eye) contracted or winking; half-shut.

**pink in,** *Dialect.* (of daylight or early morning or evening) to diminish: *I'll be with ye as soon as daylight begins to pink in* (Thomas Hardy). [probably < Middle Dutch *pincken* to blink, glimmer; origin unknown]

**pink bollworm**, a small, pinkish moth larva which feeds on seeds of the cotton plant and on cotton bolls. It is a serious pest of cotton throughout the world.

**pink cockatoo**, = Leadbeater's cockatoo.

**pink disease**, 1 = acrodynia. 2 a fungous disease that attacks the bark of trees and is characterized by a pink growth on their branches.

**pink elephants**, visions or hallucinations caused by prolonged and excessive drinking of alcoholic liquor.

**pink|en** (ping′kən), *v.i.* to become pink: *The sky pinkened* (New Yorker).

**pink|er** (ping′kər), *n.* 1 a person or thing that pinks. 2 = pinking iron.

**Pin|ker|ton** (ping′kər tən), *n. U.S. Slang.* a private detective, especially one employed by the company founded by Allan Pinkerton (1819-1884), an American detective born in Scotland.

**pink|eye** (pingk′ī′), *n.* 1 a contagious disease that causes inflammation and soreness of the membrane that lines the eyelids and covers the eyeball. It is an acute form of conjunctivitis. 2 any form of conjunctivitis. [American English, taken as < *pink*[1]. Compare earlier *pink-yied,* and *pinkenye* small eyed < *pink*[4] to blink.]

**pink family**, a group of dicotyledonous herbs found chiefly in temperate and subarctic regions. The family includes the pink, campion, lychnis, babies'-breath, and chickweed.

**pink gin**, an alcoholic drink consisting of gin and Angostura Bitters, often with water or ice added.

**pink|ie**[1] (ping′kē), *n.* the smallest finger of the human hand; little finger: *She keeps her pinkie raised when holding a teacup* (Time). Also, **pinky.** [origin uncertain; probably < Dutch *pink* little finger]

**pink|ie**[2] (ping′kē), *n. U.S.* a type of fishing boat with a very narrow stern, used along the Atlantic coast. Also, **pinky.** [perhaps American English < *pink*[3] + *-ie*]

**pink|ing iron** (ping′king), a tool of iron or steel with a specially shaped end for pinking cloth. It is driven through the material by blows of a hammer on the other end.

**pinking shears**, shears for pinking cloth.

**pink|ish** (ping′kish), *adj.* somewhat pink. **SYN:** rosy. —**pink′ish|ness,** *n.*

**Pink Lady,** *U.S.* a cocktail made with gin and brandy, mixed with fruit juices, grenadine, and egg white.

**pink|o** (ping′kō), *n., pl.* **pink|os** or **pink|oes,** *adj. U.S. Slang.* —*n.* a suspected Communist sympathizer; leftist. —*adj.* suspected of sympathizing with the Communists; leftist; radical. [< *pink*[1], as close to *Red*]

**pink rhododendron**, a rhododendron of the western United States, with pink flowers; California rosebay.

**pink|root** (pingk′rüt′, -ru̇t′), *n.* 1 the root of any of a group of herbs, especially a variety of the southern United States with showy red and yellow, funnel-shaped flowers, used as a vermifuge. 2 any one of these plants.

**pink salmon**, = humpback salmon.

**pink slip**, *U.S. Slang.* a notification to an employee that he has been discharged.

**pink spot**, a chemical substance closely related to mescaline, discovered in the urine of certain types of schizophrenics and held to be a biochemical indication of schizophrenia: *There are strong arguments against the pink spot being due to diet, drugs, or institution life* (New Scientist). [from the pink spot on the porous chromatographic paper used in the urine analysis]

**Pink|ster** (pingk′stər), *n. U.S. Dialect, now Archaic.* Whitsuntide. Also, **Pinxter**. [American English < Dutch *Pinkster* Pentecost. Compare Old Saxon *pincostôn*.]

**pinkster flower**, = pinxter flower.

**pink|y**[1] (ping′kē), *adj.* somewhat pink; pinkish. [< *pink*[1] + *-y*[1]]

**pink|y**[2] (ping′kē), *n., pl.* **pink|ies**. = pinkie[1].

**pink|y**[3] (ping′kē), *n., pl.* **pink|ies**. a fishing boat of the Atlantic coast; pinkie. [< *pink*[3] + *-y*[2]]

**pin-lev|er watch** or **clock** (pin′lev′ər, -lē′vər), a timepiece having all or most of its holes fitted with metals in place of jewels. Pin-lever watches and clocks are less reliable and durable and less costly than jeweled timepieces.

**pin mark**, a small depression in the shank of a printing type, sometimes containing an identifying number or symbol.

**pin money**, **1** an allowance of money made by a man to his wife or daughter for her own use. **2** a small amount of money used to buy extra things for one's own use and often earned through part-time activities.

**pin|na** (pin′ə), *n., pl.* **pin|nae** (pin′ē), **pin|nas**. **1** *Zoology.* **a** a feather, wing, or winglike part. **b** a fin, flipper, or similar part. **2** *Anatomy.* the auricle of the ear. **3** *Botany.* one of the primary divisions of a pinnate leaf, especially in ferns; leaflet. [< Latin *pinna* feather, wing]

**pin|nace** (pin′is) *n.* **1** a ship's boat: *He used ... to take the ship's pinnace and go out into the road a-fishing* (Daniel Defoe). **2** any light sailing vessel: *The winged pinnace shot along the sea* (Alexander Pope). [< Middle French *pinace* < Italian *pinaccia*, or Spanish *pinaza* < Spanish *pina* pine[1] < Latin *pīnus* pine tree]

**pin|na|cle** (pin′ə kəl), *n., v.,* **-cled, -cling.** *—n.* **1** a high peak or point of rock: *Far off, three mountaintops, Three silent pinnacles of aged snow, Stood sunset-flush'd* (Tennyson). **2** *Figurative.* the highest point: *at the pinnacle of one's fame.* **SYN:** apex, top, zenith, acme. **3** a slender turret or spire. A pinnacle is usually ornamental, and terminates in a pyramid or cone, crowns a buttress, or rises above the roof or coping of a building.
*—v.t.* **1** to put on or as if on a pinnacle. **2** to furnish with a pinnacle or pinnacles. **3** to form the pinnacle of; crown.
[< Old French *pinacle*, learned borrowing from Latin *pinnāculum* (diminutive) < *pinna* peak, point; pinion[1]]

**pin|nal** (pin′əl), *adj.* having to do with the pinna of the ear.

***pin|nate** (pin′āt, -it), *adj.* **1** like a feather; having lateral parts or branches arranged on each side of a common axis, like the vanes of a feather. **2** (of a compound leaf) having a series of leaflets arranged on each side of a common stalk. The leaflets are usually opposite, sometimes alternate. Also, **pennate**. [< Latin *pinnātus* (with English *-ate*[1]) < *pinna* point, pinion, feather]
**—pin′nate|ly**, *adv.*

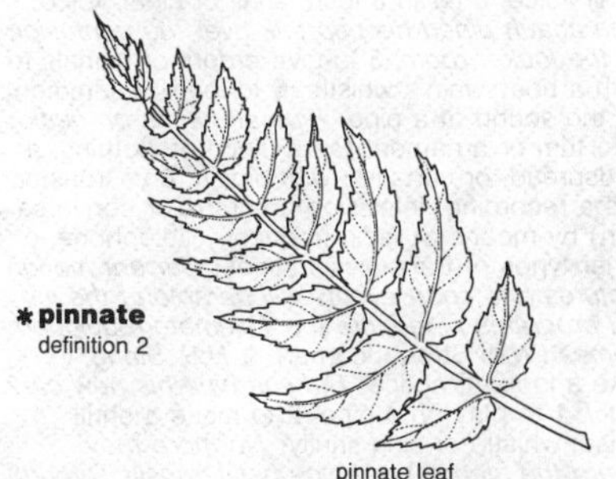

***pinnate**
definition 2

**pin|nat|ed** (pin′ā tid), *adj.* = pinnate.

**pin|nat|i|fid** (pi nat′ə fid), *adj. Botany.* divided or cleft in a pinnate manner, with the divisions extending halfway down to the midrib, or somewhat further, and the divisions or lobes narrow or acute: *a pinnatifid leaf.* [< New Latin *pinnatifidus* < Latin *pinnātus* winged, feathered + a root of *findere* to cleave, divide]

**pin|nat|i|lo|bate** (pi nat′ə lō′bāt), *adj. Botany.* lobed in a pinnate manner: *a pinnatilobate leaf.* [< Latin *pinnātus* pinnate + *lobate*]

**pin|nat|i|lobed** (pi nat′ə lōbd), *adj.* = pinnatilobate.

**pin|na|tion** (pi nā′shən), *n. Botany.* a pinnate condition or formation.

**pin|nat|i|par|tite** (pi nat′ə pär′tīt), *adj. Botany.* parted in a pinnate manner: *a pinnatipartite leaf.*

**pin|nat|i|ped** (pi nat′ə ped), *adj.* having lobate toes: *a pinnatiped bird.* [< Latin *pinnātus* pinnate + *pēs, pedis* foot]

**pin|nat|i|sect** (pi nat′ə sekt), *adj. Botany.* divided in a pinnate manner; cut down to the midrib, but with the divisions not articulated so as to form separate leaflets: *a pinnatisect leaf.* [< Latin *pinnātus* pinnate + *secāre* to cut]

**pin|ner** (pin′ər), *n.* **1** a person or thing that pins. **2** Also, **pinners**. a kind of headdress with two long flaps, pinned on and hanging down, one on each side, worn especially by noblewomen in the 1600's and 1700's.

**pin|ni|grade** (pin′ə grād), *adj., n. —adj.* moving on land by means of finlike parts or flippers, as seals and walruses.
*—n.* a pinnigrade animal.
[< Latin *pinna* feather, wing + *gradus, -ūs* step < *gradī* to walk]

**pin|ni|ped** (pin′ə ped), *adj., n. —adj.* **1** of or belonging to a suborder (or, in some classifications, an order) of carnivorous mammals that includes seals and walruses. **2** having finlike feet.
*—n.* a pinniped animal.
[< New Latin *Pinnipedia* the suborder name; (literally) fin-footed ones < *penna*, or Latin *pinna* wing, fin + *pēs, pedis* foot]

**pin|ni|pe|di|an** (pin′ə pē′dē ən), *adj., n.* = pinniped.

**pin|nu|la** (pin′yə lə), *n., pl.* **-lae** (-lē). **1** = pinnule. **2** a barb of a feather. [< Latin *pinnula* (diminutive) < *pinna* pinna]

**pin|nu|lar** (pin′yə lər), *adj.* of or having to do with a pinnule.

**pin|nu|late** (pin′yə lāt), *adj.* having pinnules.

**pin|nu|lat|ed** (pin′yə lā′tid), *adj.* = pinnulate.

**pin|nule** (pin′yül), *n.* **1** *Zoology.* a part or organ resembling a small wing or fin, or a barb of a feather: **a** a small, finlike appendage or short, detached fin ray in certain fishes, as the mackerel. **b** each of the lateral branches of the arms in crinoids. **2** *Botany.* one of the secondary or ultimate divisions of a pinnate leaf, especially in ferns; a subdivision of a pinna. [< Latin *pinnula* pinnula]

**pin|ny** (pin′ē), *n., pl.* **-nies**. *Informal.* a pinafore.

**pin oak**, an oak native to the eastern United States but widely distributed, whose dead branches resemble pins driven into the trunk; swamp oak.

**pi|noch|le** or **pi|noc|le** (pē′nuk′əl, -nok′-), *n.* **1** a card game played with a double deck of all cards from the nine through the ace, totaling 48. The object is to score points according to the value of certain combinations of cards. **2** a combination of the jack of diamonds and the queen of spades in this game. [American English; origin uncertain]

**pi|no|cy|to|sis** (pi′nō sī tō′sis, pī′-), *n.* a process by which cells take in fluids, in which the cell membrane folds back into itself to engulf the fluid and then closes up to become a vesicle: *Glucose, which amoebae normally absorb only in trace amounts, enters freely by means of pinocytosis* (Scientific American). [< Greek *pinein* to drink + English *cyt-* + *-osis*]

**pi|no|cy|tot|ic** (pi′nō sī tot′ik, pī′-), *adj.* of or having to do with pinocytosis: *pinocytotic vesicles.*

**pi|no|le** (pi nō′lā), *n.* a coarse meal made from parched corn (or, occasionally, wheat), usually slightly sweetened with the flour of mesquite beans, used as a foodstuff in the southwestern United States. [American English < Mexican Spanish *pinole* < Nahuatl *pinolli*]

**pi|ñon** (pin′yən, pēn′yōn), *n.* **1** a low pine, especially of the southern Rocky Mountain region, southwestern United States, and Mexico, producing large, nutlike seeds which are good to eat. **2** its seed. See picture under **gymnosperm**. Also, **pinyon**. [American English < Spanish *piñón* pine nut; a pine bearing edible seed < *piña* pine cone < Latin *pīnea* < *pīnus* pine tree]

**pin|point** (pin′point′), *n., v., adj. —n.* **1** the point of a pin. **2** something extremely small: *What diamonds you'll see are mostly tiny things, used to add a pinpoint of a sparkle to a watch face* (New Yorker). **3** the exact location of something, such as a target that has been pinpointed: *The bombs hit the pinpoints at which they were aimed.*
*—v.t.* **1** to mark the exact geographical position of, by sticking a pin or similar pointer into the spot on a map where coordinates intersect: *to pinpoint a field on a military map, to pinpoint a topographical feature.* **2** to ascertain the exact nature or extent of: *A Midwest machine tool maker foresees industry entering a period of uncertainty until it can better pinpoint the consequences of a Democratic victory* (Wall Street Journal). **3** to determine precisely: *His refusal to help simply pinpoints his cowardice.* **4** to aim at accurately; seek not to hit anything other than what is specified, as in dropping bombs or firing missiles, or artillery: *They were Israeli planes, picking off objectives pinpointed by ground-to-air radio* (Newsweek).
*—adj.* **1** extremely accurate or precise: *pinpoint bombing.* **2** of the size of a pinpoint; very small; minute: *pinpoint perforations, pinpoint particles.*

**pin|prick** (pin′prik′), *n., v. —n.* **1** the prick of a pin; a minute puncture such as that made by the point of a pin: *Its destination was a pinprick in the map* (Harper's). **2** *Figurative.* a petty annoyance; minute irritation: *The action was viewed in Allied circles as another pinprick in the "cold blockade" of the city* (New York Times).
*—v.t., v.i. Figurative.* to cause petty annoyance or irritation: *If [his] ego were all that big, he wouldn't shout quite so loud when pinpricked* (Harper's).

**pins** (pinz), *n.pl.* See under **pin**.

**PINS** (pinz), *n. U.S.* a runaway, truant, or other nondelinquent boy or girl placed in the custody of a juvenile court: *The girl was "a person in need of supervision"—or, in the jargon of the courts, a "PINS"* (New York Times). [< *P*(erson) *I*(n) *N*(eed of) *S*(upervision)]

**pin|scher** (pin′shər), *n.* = Doberman pinscher. [< German *Pinscher*, a kind of rough-haired terrier, earlier *Pinsch*, apparently < English *pinch* (because its ears are usually clipped)]

**pin|seal** (pin′sēl′), *n.* **1** sealskin tanned into high-grade leather, as for making wallets and shoes. **2** the skin of the fur seal.

**pin|set|ter** (pin′set′ər), *n. U.S.* **1** pinspotter. **2** a pin boy.

**pin|spot|ter** (pin′spot′ər), *n. U.S.* **1** a machine that automatically sets up the pins in a bowling alley, removes downed pins, and returns the ball to the bowler. **2** **Pinspotter**, the trademark for this machine.

**pin|stripe** (pin′strīp′), *n.* **1** a fine stripe. **2** a garment made of cloth having fine stripes.

**pin|striped** (pin′strīpt′), *adj.* having pinstripes; marked with fine stripes.

***pint** (pīnt), *n.* **1** a unit of measure equal to half a quart or one-eighth of a gallon; two cups. In liquid measure, a pint is equal to 16 fluid ounces or 0.4732 liter; in United States dry measure, a pint is equal to 33.6 cubic inches or 0.5506 liter. *Abbr:* pt. **2a** a container holding a pint. **b** such a container with its contents: *a pint of milk, a pint of strawberries.* **c** the contents: *to drink two pints of milk.* [< Old French *pinte*, perhaps < Middle Dutch *pinte* (originally) a plug]

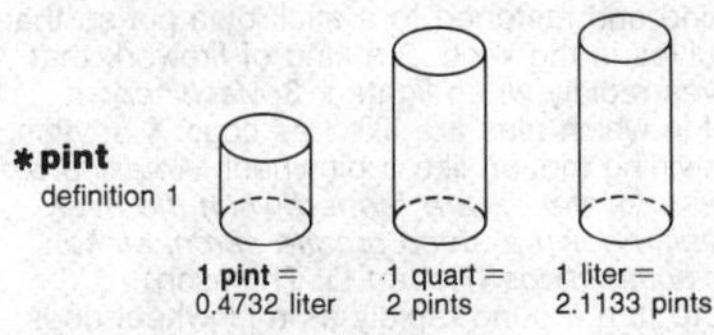

***pint**
definition 1

**pin|ta**[1] (pin′tə), *n.* a skin disease prevalent especially in tropical America and parts of the Caribbean, characterized by roughness, blotches, and ulceration of the skin. It is caused by a spirochete which appears to be identical to the one causing syphilis. [< Spanish *pinta* (literally) colored spot < Vulgar Latin *pincta*, for Latin *picta* < *pingere* to paint]

**pin|ta**[2] (pīn′tə), *n. British Informal.* a pint of a beverage, especially milk. [< the advertising slogan "drinka *pinta* milka day" introduced by the National Dairy Council of Great Britain in 1958]

**pin table**, *British.* a pinball machine.

**pin|ta|do** (pin tä′dō), *n., pl.* **-dos, -does**, or (*collectively*) **-do**. a food and game fish found along the Atlantic coast of America; cero. [< Spanish *pintado* (literally) painted, past participle of *pintar* to paint]

**pin|tail** (pin′tāl′), *n., pl.* **-tails** or (*collectively*) **-tail**. any one of various birds that have long feathers in the center of the tail, such as: **a** the pintail duck. **b** the ruddy duck. **c** the sharp-tailed grouse. **d** the pin-tailed sand grouse.

**pintail duck**, a freshwater duck of the Northern Hemisphere, with a pointed tail, the two middle feathers being longer than the rest; pintail.

**pin-tailed sand grouse** (pin′tāld′), a sand grouse of Asia, Africa, and southern Europe, having its central tail feathers elongated.

**pin|ta|no** (pin tä′nō), *n., pl.* **-nos** or (*collectively*) **-no**. a small tropical American fish, green with

**Pronunciation Key:** hat, āge, cãre, fär; let, ēqual, tėrm; it, īce; hot, ōpen, ôrder; oil, out; cup, pu̇t, rüle; child; long; thin; ᴛʜen; zh, measure; ə represents **a** in about, **e** in taken, **i** in pencil, **o** in lemon, **u** in circus.

dark stripes, found especially in the relatively shallow water over or near coral reefs; sergeant major. [origin uncertain; compare Spanish *pinta* spot]

**Pin|ter|esque** (pin′tə resk′), *adj.* characteristic of the plays or style of the English playwright Harold Pinter (born 1930), noted especially for their blend of humor, realism, and sinister atmosphere: *... a Pinteresque amalgam of the incongruous and the comic* (Time).

**pin|tle** (pin′təl), *n.* **1** a pin or bolt, especially one on which something turns, as in a hinge. **2** a sturdy metal pin on the back of a powered towing vehicle by which it is attached to a towed vehicle. [Old English *pintel* penis]

**pin|tle-hook** (pin′təl hůk′), *n.* the hook of a gun limber by which the eye of the gun carriage is engaged; pintle.

**pin|to** (pin′tō), *adj., n., pl.* **-tos.** — ***adj.*** spotted in two or more colors; pied; piebald.
— ***n.*** **1** a pinto horse or pony. **2** = pinto bean. [American English < Spanish *pinto* painted]

**pinto bean**, *Western U.S.* a field or shell variety of the common bean, whose edible seeds are spotted or mottled.

**Pintsch gas** (pinch), an illuminating gas obtained by distilling oil, formerly much used in railroad passenger cars, and still used in certain types of buoys. [< Richard *Pintsch,* 1840-1919, a German inventor]

**pint-size** (pīnt′sīz′), *adj. Informal.* pint-sized.

**pint-sized** (pīnt′sīzd′), *adj. Informal.* relatively small in size; smaller than the standard size of its kind; small: *a pint-sized tractor. They also developed a pint-sized gas turbine delivering 5 to 10 horsepower* (M. Mildred Wyatt).

**pin tuck**, a very narrow tuck, as made in cloth by sewing.

**pin|up** or **pin-up** (pin′up′), *n., adj. Informal.* — ***n.*** **1** a picture of a very attractive or famous person, pinned up on a wall, as in a barracks, usually by admirers who have not met the subject. **2** a very attractive girl, especially one considered attractive enough to be the subject of such a picture.
— ***adj.*** **1** designed for hanging on a wall: *a pinup lamp.* **2** very attractive: *a pinup girl.* **3** of or consisting of pinups: *pinup art, a pinup calendar.*

**pin|wale corduroy** (pin′wāl′), a corduroy with very fine, narrow ridges.

**pin|weed** (pin′wēd′), *n.* **1** any one of a group of low North American herbs related to the rockrose, with slender stems and leaves. **2** = alfileria.

**pin|wheel** (pin′hwēl′), *n., v.* — ***n.*** **1** a toy made of a wheel of paper, twisted into vanes that catch the wind and fastened to a stick by a pin so that it revolves in the wind. **2** a kind of firework that revolves rapidly when lighted. **3** *Machinery.* a wheel in which pins are fixed as cogs. **4** anything with swirling motion like a pinwheel: *Amazing pinwheels of water ... are formed when the river, cascading down a steep granite apron, strikes rocky obstructions* (Robert D. Thomson).
— ***v.i.*** to turn around rapidly as a pinwheel does: *While Woodhouse was hauling frantically on the reins, the saddle slipped, and the jockey went pinwheeling into the dirt* (New York Times).

**pin|work** (pin′wėrk′), *n.* the small, fine, raised parts of a design in needlepoint lace.

**pin|worm** (pin′wėrm′), *n.* a small, threadlike, nematode worm infesting the large intestine and rectum, especially of children.

**pin wrench**, a wrench that has a pin or pins to fit into holes in nuts to be turned.

**pinx.**, pinxit.

**pinx|it** (pingk′sit), *Latin.* he (or she) painted (it or this). It is inscribed on some paintings after the name of the painter.

**Pinx|ter** (pingk′stər), *n.* = Pinkster.

**pinxter flower**, a wild azalea common in swamps and woods from Canada to Texas, having pink or whitish flowers. Also, **pinkster flower**. [< Dutch *Pinkster* Pinkster, Pentecost]

**pin|y** (pī′nē), *adj.,* **pin|i|er, pin|i|est. 1** abounding in, covered with, or consisting of pine trees: *piny mountains.* **2** having to do with or suggesting pine trees: *a piny odor.* Also, **piney**.

**pin|yon** (pin′yən, pēn′yōn), *n.* = piñon.

**pinyon jay**, a grayish-blue jay, having no crest, found especially in the Rocky Mountains or their foothills.

**PIO** (no periods), **1** public information office. **2** public information officer.

**piob|aireachd** (pē′brok), *n.* = pibroch.

**pi|on** (pī′on), *n.* = pi-meson. [< *pi-*(mes)*on*]

**pi|o|neer** (pī′ə nir′), *n., v., adj.* — ***n.*** **1** a person who settles in a part of the country that has not been occupied before except by primitive tribes: *The pioneers of the American West included trappers, woodsmen, farmers, and explorers.* **2** *Figurative.* a person who goes first, or does something first, and so prepares a way for others: *Florence Nightingale was a pioneer in hospital reform.* **3** *Especially British.* one of a group of soldiers in a unit, especially of military engineers, who make roads, build bridges, dig trenches, and carry out other construction necessary to troop movement. **4** *Obsolete.* a person who digs a trench, pit, or the like; digger; miner.
— ***v.t.*** **1** to prepare or open up (a way, road, or area): *I will pioneer a new way, explore unknown powers* (Mary Shelley). **2** *Figurative.* to prepare the way for: *It was the first airline to use X rays for inspecting equipment, and pioneered "package" summer vacations in cooperation with Miami hotels* (Newsweek). — ***v.i.*** to act as pioneer; open or prepare the way: (*Figurative.*) *Astronauts are pioneering in exploring space.*
— ***adj.*** **1** that is a pioneer: *a pioneer settler.* **2** *Figurative.* that goes ahead so that others may follow; exploratory: *pioneer research.*
[< Middle French *pionnier* Old French *paonier* < *peon* foot soldier < Medieval Latin *pedo, -onis* < Latin *pēs, pedis* foot. See related etym. at **pawn²**, **peon**.]

**pi|on|ic** (pī on′ik), *adj.* of or having to do with pimesons: *pionic atoms.* [< *pion* + *-ic*]

**pi|on|i|um** (pī on′ē əm), *n.* a short-lived neutral particle consisting of a combined pi-meson and mu-meson, produced in the decay of a heavy meson: *Some light may be shed on the nature of the muon by studies of a new kind of quasiatom, called pionium, ... discovered at Brookhaven National Laboratory* (New Scientist). [< *pion* + *-ium,* as in *muonium*]

**pi|ous** (pī′əs), *adj.* **1** having or showing reverence for God; active in worship or prayer; religious: *The pious old woman made every effort to go to worship each time she could.* **2** done or used under pretense of religion: *a pious fraud, a pious deception.* **3** *Archaic.* dutiful to parents. **4** sacred, as distinguished from secular. [< Latin *pīus* (with English *-ous*) dutiful] — **pi′ous|ly**, *adv.* — **pi′ousness**, *n.*
— ***Syn.*** **1 Pious, devout** mean religious. **Pious** emphasizes showing religion or reverence for God by carefully observing religious duties and practices, such as going to church, and sometimes suggests that more religion is shown than felt: *She is a pious woman who goes to church every morning.* **Devout** emphasizes feeling true reverence that usually is expressed in prayer or devotion to religious observances, but may not be shown at all: *He is a charitable, humble, and devout Christian and a good man.*

**pip¹** (pip), *n.* **1** the seed of an apple, orange, or other fleshy fruit. **2** *Slang.* a person or thing that is very attractive, admirable, or extraordinary; pippin: *Wait till you meet her—she's really a pip!* [apparently short for *pippin*]

**pip²** (pip), *n.* **1a** a contagious disease of poultry and other birds, characterized by the secretion of thick mucus in the mouth and throat and sometimes by white scale on the tongue. **b** the scale itself. **2** *Informal.* a slight illness (used in a humorous way). [apparently < Middle Dutch *pippe* < Vulgar Latin *pippīta,* and *pīpīta,* ultimately < Latin *pītuīta* (literally) phlegm]

**pip³** (pip), *n.* **1** one of the spots or symbols on playing cards, dominoes, or dice: *The object is to draw cards to get a higher number of pips ... than the dealer without going over 21* (Scientific American). **2** the starlike shoulder insigne worn by second lieutenants (one pip), lieutenants (two pips), and captains (three pips) in the British Army, or the armies of any of the countries in the Commonwealth. **3a** the individual rhizome of the lily of the valley. **b** the dormant rhizome or root of any of several other plants, such as the peony and anemone. **4** one of the diamond-shaped segments of the surface of a pineapple. **5** central part of an artificial flower; pep. [origin uncertain]

**pip⁴** (pip), *v.,* **pipped, pip|ping,** *n.* — ***v.i.*** to peep; chirp. — ***v.t.*** (of a young bird) to break through (the shell) when hatching.
— ***n.*** a brief, high-pitched sound, as in radio transmission. [probably variant of *peep²*]

**pip⁵** (pip), *n.* a luminous spot or irregularity on a radar screen; blip: *These pulses were recorded as pips on a cathode ray screen* (Scientific American). [perhaps < *pip³*]

**pip⁶** (pip), *v.t.,* **pipped, pip|ping.** *British Slang.* **1** to defeat; beat: *Scotland required to win the last four singles to pip England by half a point* (London). **2** to blackball: *If Buckle were pipped [at the club election], they would do the same for every clergyman put up* (A. H. Huth). [special use of *pip³*]

**pi-pa** (pē′pä′), *n.* an ancient lutelike instrument, popular in China. [< Chinese *p'i p'a*]

**pip|age** (pī′pij), *n.* **1** the conveyance of water, gas, petroleum, or other fluid, by means of pipes. **2** the charge made for this. **3** a system or network of such pipes. [< *pip*(e) + *-age*]

**pi|pal** (pē′pəl), *n.,* or **pipal tree**, a fig tree of India, resembling the banyan but lacking prop roots; bo tree. Also, **peepul, pipul**. [< Hindi *pīpal* < Sanskrit *pippala*]

***pipe** (pīp), *n., v.,* **piped, pip|ing.** — ***n.*** **1** a tube through which a liquid or gas flows: *A stove or furnace must have a pipe and a chimney to carry away the gases and smoke.* **SYN**: conduit, duct. **2a** a tube of clay, wood, or other material with a bowl at one end, for smoking: *The smell of tobacco filled the room as clouds of smoke rose from his pipe.* **b** the quantity of tobacco, opium, or other substance a pipe will hold: *Sir Jeoffrey ... gave me a pipe of his own tobacco* (Sir Richard Steele). **3** a musical wind instrument with a single tube of reed, straw, or especially wood, into which a player blows. A flute, oboe, or clarinet is a pipe. **4** any tube by which the sounds are produced in a musical instrument, especially each of the wooden or metal tubes in an organ; flue pipe or reed pipe: *An organ pipe sounds only one note, and the larger the pipe the lower its pitch* (New Yorker). **5** a small kind of flute, formerly played with one hand while the other hand beat a drum or tabor. **6** a shrill sound, voice, or song: *the pipe of a lark.* **7a** a boatswain's whistle. **b** the signal or call made by blowing it. **8a** a cask, varying in size, especially for wine. **b** as much as such a cask holds, now usually reckoned as four barrels or 126 (wine) gallons. **c** such a cask with its contents. **9** any one of various tubular or cylindrical objects, contrivances, or parts. **10a** any one of various tubular or cylindrical natural formations, such as the stem of a plant. **b** a tubular organ, passage, canal, or vessel in an animal body. **11a** a vein of ore of a more or less cylindrical form. **b** a mass, more or less cylindrical and often extending far into the ground, of bluish, volcanic rock within which diamonds are embedded, found especially in parts of South Africa. **12** *U.S. Slang.* something sure and easy; a cinch: *Despite its informality, Sach's course was no pipe* (Time). **13** *Surfing.* the fastest part of a wave, where it rolls over and down.

***pipe** definition 2a

— ***v.t.*** **1** to carry by means of a pipe or pipes: *to pipe oil into storage tanks from ships anchored offshore.* **2** to supply with pipes: *Our street is being piped for gas.* **3** to play (a tune, music) on a pipe: *to pipe some country music.* **4** to sing in a shrill voice; utter in a loud, shrill or clear voice: *The coach piped his pep talk over the confusion of the locker room.* **5** to give orders or signals to with a boatswain's whistle. **6** to lead or summon by the sound of a pipe: *Pipe all hands on deck.* **7** to trim or ornament (as a piece of clothing, a bedspread, or curtains) with piping. **8** to transmit (as a recording, television program, or conversation) by means of radio-frequency, telephone, or other types of transmission lines: *Current motion pictures and sport events will be among the initial programs piped into the Telemeter-equipped homes* (Wall Street Journal). **9** *U.S. Slang.* to take a look at; notice: *Did you pipe his new car?*
— ***v.i.*** **1** to play on a pipe. **2** to make a shrill noise; whistle or sing shrilly: *No more they ... heard the steady wind pipe boisterously Through the strained rigging* (William Morris). **3** to speak or talk loudly and shrilly. **4** to give orders or signals with or as if with a boatswain's whistle. **5** *Metallurgy.* to form cylindrical cavities, as steel ingots or castings when solidifying. **6** *Mining.* to carve so as to form a cylindrical hole.

**pipe down**, *Slang.* to be quiet; shut up: *Listen, if you don't pipe down about TV and programming and keep quiet, you won't be able to sell a show in Sheboygan* (New Yorker).

**pipe one's** (or **the**) **eye**. See under **eye**.

**pipes, a** a set of musical tubes or pipes; syrinx: *the pipes of Pan.* **b** a bagpipe: *The pipes resumed their clamorous strain* (Scott). **c** *Slang.*

the vocal apparatus, especially of a singer: *A strange orator straining his pipes, to persuade strange people* (Richard Mulcaster). **d** *Informal.* the respiratory passages: *Depth of girth he [the horse] must have, or his pipes and heart have no room to play* (Joseph Addison)
**pipe up, a** to begin to play or sing (music); strike up: *Once he piped up to a different air, a kind of country love song* (Robert Louis Stevenson). **b** *Slang.* to speak: *As the guard laid a hand upon me, she piped up* (Mark Twain). **c** to rise or increase: *The wind is heading me and piping up, so I shall be lucky if I don't start losing some of my advantage now* (Observer).
[Old English *pīpe* < Vulgar Latin *pīppa,* for Latin *pīpa* < *pīpāre* to chirp; probably (originally) imitative] —**pipe′less,** *adj.* —**pipe′like′,** *adj.*

**pipe band,** a group of musicians all of whom play on bagpipes.

**pipe bomb,** a homemade bomb encased in an iron or steel pipe.

**pipe clay,** a fine white kind of clay, that forms a ductile paste with water, originally used for making tobacco pipes and whitening shoes.

**pipe-clay** (pīp′klā′), *v.t.* to whiten with pipe clay.

**pipe cleaner,** a short piece of wire covered with tufted material, run through the stem of a tobacco pipe to catch the dirt and moisture.

**pipe dream,** *Informal.* **1** an impractical, groundless, or fantastic idea or scheme. **2** a dream produced by smoking opium.

***pipe|fish** (pīp′fish′), *n., pl.* **-fish|es** or (*collectively*) **-fish.** any one of a group of marine fishes commonly having a long snout and a long, slender, angular body covered with armorlike plates.

***pipefish**

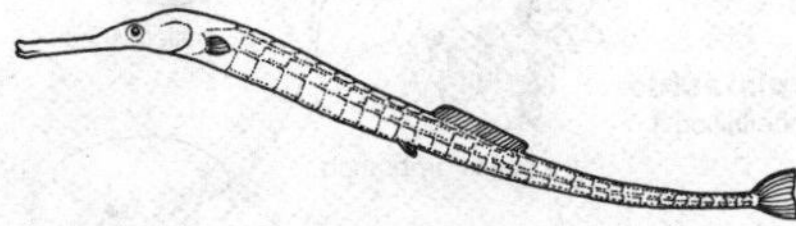

**pipe fitter,** a person specially trained or experienced in the installing and repairing of pipes.

**pipe fitting, 1** the work of a pipe fitter. **2** an appliance, such as an elbow, bushing, or tee, used in pipe fitting.

**pipe|ful** (pīp′fu̇l), *n., pl.* **-fuls.** a quantity of tobacco sufficient to fill the bowl of a pipe.

**pipe|lay|er** (pīp′lā′ər), *n.* **1** a person who lays pipes for the conveyance of water, gas, oil, or other liquid. **2** *Figurative.* a person, especially a politician, who lays plans for the promotion of some scheme or purpose.

**pipe|lay|ing** (pīp′lā′ing), *n.* **1** the act of laying down pipes for gas, water, and other purposes. **2** *Figurative.* a laying of plans for the accomplishment of some scheme or purpose, especially a political one.

**pipe|line** (pīp′līn′), *n., v.,* **-lined, -lin|ing.** —*n.* **1** a line of pipes for carrying oil, natural gas, water, or other fluid, now usually over a considerable distance. There are often (especially in the case of oil) pumps at intervals to maintain the rate of flow. *The pipeline is the low-cost, efficient transporter of fuel for any distance* (Harper's). **2** *Informal, Figurative.* a source of information, usually secret: *a pipeline into the White House. His pipeline this time was a seat next to a Dutch diplomat at a luncheon* (Newsweek). **3** *Figurative.* a flow of materials through a series of productive processes: *How fast civilian pipelines fill up ... depends on government rationing of the output of steel mills* (Newsweek).
—*v.t.* **1** to carry by a pipeline. **2** to provide with a pipeline.
**in the pipeline,** *Informal.* in progress; in the works; underway: *There are plans in the pipeline for converting more forest land to parkland* (Manchester Guardian Weekly).

**pipe major,** the leader of a band of bagpipers.

**pipe of peace,** peace pipe; calumet.

**pipe organ,** an organ with pipes of different lengths sounded by air blown through them, as distinguished from a reed or electronic organ.

**pipe pilot,** *Slang.* a jet airplane pilot.

**pip|er** (pī′pər), *n.* a person who plays on a pipe or bagpipe, especially one who goes about the country playing at different places.
**pay the piper, a** to pay for one's pleasure; bear the consequences: *One who is always late or absent must finally pay the piper and quit or make up the time.* **b** to defray the cost: *In the commercial theatre the cheerfully amoral majority pays the piper—and calls the tune* (London Times).

**pip|er|a|ceous** (pip′ə rā′shəs), *adj.* belonging to the pepper family of plants. [< Latin *piper, -eris* pepper + English *-aceous*]

**pi|per|a|zin** (pi per′ə zin), *n.* = piperazine.

**pi|per|a|zine** (pi per′ə zin, -zēn), *n.* a basic, crystalline compound, used medicinally in treating roundworm infestation, and, formerly, rheumatism. *Formula:* $C_4H_{10}N_2$ [< Latin *piper* pepper + English *azine*]

**pi|per|i|dine** (pi per′ə din, -dēn), *n.* a volatile liquid base, having a pepperlike odor, obtained from pyridine or piperine. It is a vasodilator. *Formula:* $C_5H_{22}N$ [< *piper*(ine) + *-ide* + *-ine*[2]]

**pip|er|in** (pip′ər in), *n.* = piperine.

**pip|er|ine** (pip′ər in, -ə rēn), *n.* a white, crystalline alkaloid, obtained from a species of pepper or prepared synthetically, used as an antipyretic and insecticide. *Formula:* $C_{17}H_{19}NO_3$ [< Latin *piper* pepper + English *-ine*[2]]

**pip|er|o|nal** (pip′ər ə nal), *n.* a white, crystalline aldehyde, a benzene derivative, with an odor like that of heliotrope, used especially in making perfumes and suntan lotions. *Formula:* $C_8H_6O_3$ [< *piper*(ine) + *-on*(e) + *-al*[1]]

**pipes** (pīps), *n.pl.* See under **pipe.**

**pipe|stem** (pīp′stem′), *n.* **1** the rigid tube (stem) of a tobacco pipe, through which the smoke is drawn from the bowl by sucking. **2** *Figurative.* something thin, such as a leg or arm. **3** Usually, **pipestems.** = pipestem trousers.

**pipestem trousers** or **pants,** narrow trousers that taper at the bottom.

**pipe|stone** (pīp′stōn′), *n.* a hard red clay or soft stone used by the North American Indians for peace pipes.

**pipe tomahawk,** a tomahawk used by North American Indians especially as a tobacco pipe, containing a tobacco bowl on the blunt side of the hatchet and a hollow handle as the stem.

**pi|pette** or **pi|pet** (pī pet′, pi-), *n., v.,* **-pet|ted, -pet|ting.** —*n.* a slender pipe or tube used for transferring or measuring small quantities of liquids or gases. The most common type is a small glass tube that widens into a bulb at the middle, into which liquid may be sucked, and in which it may be retained by closing the top end with a stopper or finger. *The buret and the pipet are both calibrated to deliver a certain volume rather than to contain a certain volume* (W. N. Jones).
—*v.t.* to pour, transfer, or draw off or out by means of a pipette: *With a medicine dropper he catches the animal in a drop of water, pipettes the drop on a glass slide and places the slide under his microscope* (Scientific American).
[< French *pipette* (diminutive) < Old French *pipe* pipe]

**pipe|work** (pīp′wėrk′), *n.* pipes; piping: *Fuels affected by heat may give rise to deposits which foul the pipework* (New Scientist).

**pipe|wort** (pīp′wėrt′), *n.* any one of a family of chiefly tropical aquatic or marsh herbs, stemless or nearly so, with fibrous roots, linear leaves, and naked scapes bearing dense heads of minute flowers.

**pipe wrench,** a wrench used for turning or gripping pipes, such as the Stillson wrench.

**pi|pi** (pē′pē), *n.* any one of various kinds of bivalve shellfish, used in Australia as food and bait, especially one commonly found on the coast of New South Wales. [< Maori *pipi*]

**pip|ing** (pī′ping), *n., adj.* —*n.* **1** a shrill sound: *the piping of frogs in the spring.* **2** pipes: *a house equipped with copper piping.* **3** material for pipes; pipe: *three feet of piping.* **4** the music of pipes. **5** a narrow band of material, sometimes containing a cord, used for trimming along edges and seams: *A two-piece dress of black-and-taupe striped wool jersey has piping of black leather on the collar* (New Yorker). **6** ornamental lines of icing, frosting, or meringue.
—*adj.* **1** sounding shrilly; shrill: *a high, piping voice.* **2** *Archaic.* **a** characterized by or appropriate to the music of the pastoral pipe: *In this weak piping time of Peace* (Shakespeare). **b** that plays a musical pipe: *Lowing herds, and piping swains* (Jonathan Swift).
**piping hot,** so as to hiss; very hot; boiling: *The coffee is piping hot.*

**piping crow,** any one of various birds related to the shrikes and found in and around Australia and New Guinea, such as a species with black and white plumage, that is often domesticated and can be taught to speak words.

**piping plover,** a small white and sand-colored plover of eastern North America.

**pip|is|trel** or **pip|is|trelle** (pip′ə strel′), *n.* any one of a group of small brown or grayish bats, especially one found in the eastern United States and Mexico. [< French *pipistrelle* < Italian *pipistrello,* variant of *vespertilio* < Latin *vespertīliō;* see etym. under **vespertilionine**]

**pip|it** (pip′it), *n.* a small, brownish bird, somewhat like a lark, that sings while flying; titlark. There are various kinds. [imitative. Compare French *pitpit.*]

**pip|kin** (pip′kin), *n.* **1** *British.* a small earthenware or metal pot, used chiefly in cookery. **2** *Dialect.* a piggin. [perhaps < *pip*(e) + *-kin*]

**pip|less** (pip′lis), *adj.* without pips or seeds, as an orange.

**pip|per** (pip′ər), *n.* a small hole in the reticle of an optical sight or computing sight. [< *pip*[3] + *-er*[1]]

**pip|pin** (pip′in), *n.* **1** any one of several kinds of apple. Pippins ripen in the fall, are roundish in form and yellowish-green in color, and have firm flesh of excellent flavor. *I will make an end of my dinner, there's pippins and cheese to come* (Shakespeare). **2** *Obsolete or Dialect.* the seed (pip) of a fruit. **3** *Slang.* someone or something especially attractive. [< Old French *pepin;* origin uncertain]

**pip|ra|dol** (pip′rə dol), *n.* a drug used to stimulate the central nervous system in cases of emotional depression or fatigue; Meratran. *Formula:* $C_{18}H_{21}NO$ [irregular < *piperid*(ine) + (methan)*ol*]

**pip|sis|se|wa** (pip sis′ə wə), *n.* any one of a genus of low, creeping evergreen plants related to the shinleaf, especially a kind whose leaves are used in medicine as a tonic, astringent, and diuretic; wintergreen. [American English < Algonkian (Cree) name < *pipisisikweu* it reduces (stone in the bladder) to fine particles]

**pip|squeak** (pip′skwēk′), *n. Slang.* **1** an insignificant person; petty object: *Her notion is that he could be a big wheel on Madison Avenue instead of a publicity pipsqueak in a charitable foundation if he would just show a little get-up-and-go* (New Yorker). **2** a small type of high-velocity shell distinguished by the sound of its flight. It was used during World War I.

**pi|pul** (pē′pəl), *n.* = pipal.

**pip|y** (pī′pē), *adj.,* **pip|i|er, pip|i|est. 1** pipelike; tubular. **2** piping; shrill.

**pi|quan|cy** (pē′kən sē), *n.* **1** the quality of exciting the mind pleasantly: *To his piquancy and richness of characterization he was able to add the deepest spiritual dimensions* (Wall Street Journal). **2** the quality of exciting the appetite or of being odd or pleasantly sharp to the taste.

**pi|quant** (pē′kənt), *adj.* **1** stimulating to the mind or interest: *a piquant bit of news.* **2** interestingly attractive: *a piquant smile.* **3** pleasantly sharp; stimulating to the taste; appetizing: *a piquant sauce, piquant pickles.* **4** *Archaic.* unpleasantly sharp or biting; stinging. [< Old French *piquant,* present participle of *piquer* to prick, sting; see etym. under **pique**] —**pi′quant|ly,** *adv.* —**pi′quant|ness,** *n.*

**pi|quante** (pē känt′), *adj.* = piquant. [< French *piquante,* feminine of *piquant* piquant]

**pique** (pēk), *n., v.,* **piqued, pi|quing.** —*n.* **1** a feeling of anger at being slighted; wounded pride: *In a pique, she left the party. It should comfort no one that a group of men are powerful enough to legislate by pique* (Wall Street Journal). **SYN:** umbrage. **2** *Archaic.* a fit of ill feeling between persons; personal quarrel: *Her sudden freak ... must have been caused by some little pique or misunderstanding between them* (George Eliot). [< Middle French *pique* < Old French *piquer* to prick; see the verb]
—*v.t.* **1** to cause a feeling of anger in; wound the pride of: *It piqued her that we had a secret she did not share.* **2** to arouse; stir up: *The boy's curiosity was piqued by the locked trunk.* **3** *Aeronautics, Obsolete.* to dive at in an attack.
**pique oneself on** (or **upon**), to feel proud about; take pride in: *Men who are thought to pique themselves upon their wit* (Alexander Pope).
[< French, Old French *piquer* to prick, sting < *pic* a pick[2], perhaps < Germanic (compare Old English *pīc*)]

**pi|qué** (pi kā′), *n.* a fabric of cotton, rayon, or silk, woven with narrow ribs or raised stripes. [< French *piqué* (literally) quilted, past participle of *piquer* to backstitch < Old French, to prick; see etym. under **pique,** verb]

**pi|quet** (pi ket′), *n.* a complicated card game for two, played with a deck of 32 cards, all below the seven being discarded. Also, **picquet.** [< French *piquet,* earlier *picquet,* perhaps < *pic* a score in the game, or < *piquer* pique, verb]

**pi|ra|cy** (pī′rə sē), *n., pl.* **-cies. 1** robbery on the sea. **2** *Figurative.* **a** the act of publishing or using a book, play, invention, musical composition, or the like, without permission. **b** the appropriation or use of anything that belongs to another or that has been assigned to the use of another: *drug piracy, piracy of the airwaves.* [< Medieval Latin *piratia,* earlier *pirata* < unrecorded Medieval Greek *peirateia* < Greek *peirātēs* pirate]

**pi|ra|gua** (pə rä′gwə, -rag′wə), *n.* = pirogue. [< Spanish *piragua* < a Carib (South America) word meaning a large dug-out canoe. See etym. of doublet **pirogue.**]

**Pronunciation Key:** hat, āge, cãre, fär; let, ēqual, tėrm; it, īce; hot, ōpen, ôrder; oil, out; cup, pu̇t, rüle; child; long; thin; ᴛʜen; zh, measure;
ə represents **a** in about, **e** in taken, **i** in pencil, **o** in lemon, **u** in circus.

**Pi|ran|del|li|an** (pir′ən del′ē ən), *adj.* of, having to do with, or in the style of Luigi Pirandello (1867-1936), Italian playwright, poet, and novelist.

***pi|ra|nha** (pi rän′yə), *n., pl.* **-nhas** or (*collectively*) **-nha.** a small South American fish that attacks man and other large mammals; caribe. [< Portuguese *piranha* < Tupi (Brazil) *pira nya,* variant of *pira'ya* (literally) scissors]

***piranha**

**pi|ra|ru|cu** (pə rä′rə kü), *n.* a very large South American fish; arapaima. [< Tupi *pirarucu*]

**pi|rate** (pī′rit), *n., v.,* **-rat|ed, -rat|ing,** *adj.* —*n.* **1** a person who attacks and robs ships; robber on the seas; buccaneer; freebooter: *Blackbeard became one of the most feared pirates operating in the West Indies* (Willard H. Bonner). **2** a ship used by pirates: *Squadrons of pirates hung yet about the smaller islands* (James A. Froude). **3** anyone who roves about in quest of plunder; marauder: *Pirates of the desert ...* (Washington Irving). **4** *Figurative.* a person, company, or organization that appropriates or uses something to which another has the exclusive rights: *A law was passed to squash the pirates, whose offshore transmissions were unauthorized* (T. J. Hickey).
—*v.i.* to be a pirate or commit an act of piracy.
—*v.t.* **1** to commit piracy upon; plunder as a pirate. **2** to rob; plunder. **3** *Figurative.* **a** to publish or use without the author's permission: *to pirate a book.* **b** to appropriate or use (something, the exclusive rights to which have been assigned to another): *to pirate a wave-length. Rather than investing millions of dollars in research, development and testing, they ... pirate drugs from the West* (Science News Letter).
—*adj.* that engage in piracy: *a pirate radio station. Pirate syndicates are already forming to try to exploit the game on the West Coast* (Alistair Cooke).
[< Latin *pīrata* < Greek *peirātēs* < *peirân* to attack; (originally) to try, make a hostile attempt on] —**pi′rate|like′,** *adj.*

**pirate perch,** a small, voracious fish of a dark-olive to pinkish color profusely dotted with black, found in sluggish waters of the eastern United States and the Mississippi Basin.

**pirate spider,** a kind of spider that does not spin webs but creeps into the webs of other spiders and kills them.

**pi|rat|ic** (pī rat′ik), *adj.* = piratical.

**pi|rat|i|cal** (pī rat′ə kəl), *adj.* **1** of pirates; like pirates. **2** like piracy. —**pi|rat′i|cal|ly,** *adv.*

**Pi|rith|o|us** (pī rith′ō əs), *n. Greek Legend.* a king of the Lapithae, who accompanied Theseus on his journey to Hades in order to abduct Persephone, but was imprisoned forever by Pluto.

**pirn** (pėrn), *n. Scottish.* **1** a weaver's bobbin, spool, or reel. **2** a fishing reel. [Middle English *pyrne;* origin uncertain]

**pi|ro|gen** (pi rō′gən), *n.pl.* = piroshki. [< Yiddish *pirogen,* plural of *pirog* stuffed pastry < Russian; see etym. under **piroshki**]

**pi|ro|gi** (pi rō′gē), *n.pl.* = piroshki. [< Russian *pirogi,* plural of *pirog;* see etym. under **piroshki**]

**pi|rogue** (pə rōg′), *n.* **1** a canoe hollowed from the trunk of a tree; dugout. **2** any relatively heavy canoe or small boat that somewhat resembles this, made in various parts of the world. **3** a two-masted, flat-bottomed sailing barge, used especially in the Caribbean and in the Atlantic coastal waters southward to Brazil. [< French *pirogue* < Spanish *piragua.* See etym. of doublet **piragua.**]

**pir|o|plasm** (pir′ə plaz′əm), *n., pl.* **-plasms, -plasma|ta** (-plaz′mə tə). the parasitic protozoan that infects the red blood cells of animals and causes piroplasmosis. [< *Piroplasma,* the genus name; see etym. under **piroplasmosis**]

**pir|o|plas|mo|sis** (pir′ə plaz mō′sis), *n.* any one of various infectious diseases of cattle, sheep, horses, and other livestock, caused by a protozoan parasite and transmitted by ticks. [< *Piroplasma,* the genus name of the protozoan (< Latin *pirum* pear + New Latin *plasma* plasma) + *-osis*]

**pi|rosh|ki** (pi rôsh′kē, -rosh′-), *n.pl.* small turnovers stuffed with meat, fish, chicken, or egg and vegetables. [< Russian *pirozhki,* plural of *pirozhok* (diminutive) < *pirog* stuffed pastry]

**pir|ou|ette** (pir′ù et′), *n., v.,* **-et|ted, -et|ting.** —*n.* the act of spinning around on one foot or on the toes in dancing: *A rotation which would put to shame the most finished pirouettes of the opera-dancer* (Robert Patterson).
—*v.i.* to spin around on the toe; move with a whirling motion: (*Figurative.*) *I can see myself chasing about the barn ... while the Guernsey gaily pirouettes from manger to door and back again* (Harper's).
[< Middle French *pirouette* (originally) a spinning top, whirligig < Italian *piruolo* whirligig + French *-ouette,* a diminutive suffix] —**pir′ou|et′ter,** *n.*

**pis al|ler** (pē zà lā′), *French.* **1** the least of possible evils; last resource; makeshift. **2** (literally) to go worse.

**Pi|san** (pē′zən), *adj., n.* —*adj.* of or having to do with Pisa, Italy: *Pisan architecture.*
—*n.* a native or inhabitant of Pisa.

**pis|ca|ry** (pis′kər ē), *n., pl.* **-ries. 1** *Law.* the right or privilege to fish in a body of water owned by another. **2** a place for catching fish; fishery. [< Late Latin *piscaria* < Latin, a fish market]

**pis|ca|tol|o|gy** (pis′kə tol′ə jē), *n.* **1** the science of fishing, including the methods of fishermen and the nature and habits of fish, as the object of systematic study. **2** *Obsolete.* ichthyology. [< Latin *piscātus* a fishing + English *-logy*]

**pis|ca|tor** (pis kā′tər), *n.* a fisherman; angler. [< Latin *piscātor* < *piscis* fish]

**pis|ca|to|ri|al** (pis′kə tôr′ē əl, -tōr′-), *adj.* **1** of or having to do with fishermen or fishing. **2** characteristic of fishermen or fishing. **3** employed in or addicted to fishing. [< Latin *piscātōrius* (< *piscātor, -ōris* fisherman < *piscis* fish) + English *-al*[1]] —**pis′ca|to′ri|al|ly,** *adv.*

**pis|ca|to|ry** (pis′kə tôr′ē, -tōr′-), *adj.* = piscatorial.

**Pis|ce|an** (pis′ē ən, pī′sē-), *n., adj.* —*n.* a person born under the sign of Pisces, February 19–March 20: *"strong-willed ambitious" Pisceans* (Time). —*adj.* of or having to do with Pisceans.

**Pis|ces** (pis′ēz, pī′sēz), *n.pl., genitive* (def. 1) **Pis|ci|um. 1** a northern constellation between Aquarius and Aries, seen by ancient astronomers as having the rough outline of fishes; the Fishes: *In modern times, the sun is seen against the background of Pisces, the Fishes, when it crosses the equator about March 21* (Bernhard, Bennett, and Rice). **2** the twelfth sign of the zodiac, which the sun enters about February 19; the Fishes. **3** = Piscean. **4** Also, **pisces.** a superclass of aquatic vertebrate animals comprising all the fishes. Pisces have gills and fins, two pairs of which are used for movement. [< Latin *Piscēs,* plural of *piscis* a fish]

**pis|ci|cide** (pis′ə sīd), *n.* the extermination of fish, especially all fish in a given area. [< Latin *piscis* fish + English *-cide*[2]]

**pis|ci|cul|tur|al** (pis′i kul′chər əl), *adj.* of or having to do with pisciculture.

**pis|ci|cul|ture** (pis′i kul′chər), *n.* the breeding, rearing, conservation, and study of fish by means that supplement or replace those normally available in nature. [< Latin *piscis* fish + *culture*]

**pis|ci|cul|tur|ist** (pis′i kul′chər ist), *n.* a person engaged or interested in pisciculture.

**pis|ci|form** (pis′ə fôrm), *adj.* fish-shaped. [< Latin *piscis* fish + English *-form*]

**pis|ci|na** (pi sī′nə, -sē′-), *n., pl.* **-nae** (-nē). a basin with a drain to carry away the water, used in churches in ritual ablutions, now usually placed in the sacristy. [< Medieval Latin *piscina* basin in a church < Latin *piscīna* fish pond < *piscis* a fish]

**pis|cine** (pis′īn, -in), *adj.* **1** of or having to do with a fish or fishes. **2** characteristic of a fish or fishes. [< Latin *piscis* a fish + English *-ine*[1]]

**Pis|ci|um** (pis′ē əm), *n.* genitive of **Pisces.**

**pis|civ|o|rous** (pi siv′ər əs), *adj.* feeding solely or chiefly on fish; fish-eating. [< Latin *piscis* fish + *vorāre* devour]

**pis|co** (pis′kō, pēs′-), *n.* a Peruvian brandy made from the dregs left in a wine press. [< *Pisco,* a city in Peru]

**pi|sé** (pē zā′), *n.* stiff earth or clay, often mixed with gravel or grass, used to form walls or floors by ramming until it becomes hard. [< French *pisé,* past participle of *piser* to beat, pound, ultimately < Latin *pīsāre, pinsāre*]

**pish** (pish, psh), *interj., n., v.* —*interj., n.* a sound made to express mild contempt or impatience.
—*v.i.* to make such a sound: *The Captain kept Pishing and Tushing and presently ... swearing* (H. G. Wells). —*v.t.* to say "pish" to. [imitative]

**pi|si|form** (pī′sə fôrm), *adj., n.* —*adj.* **1** of small globular form; pea-shaped. **2** designating or having to do with the pisiform bone.
—*n.* = pisiform bone.
[< New Latin *pisiformis* < Latin *pisum* pea (probably < Greek *písos*) + *forma* shape, form]

**pisiform bone,** a pea-shaped bone of the human wrist (carpus) in the proximal row of carpal bones.

**pis|mire** (pis′mīr′), *n. Archaic.* an ant: *The spider's skill,—The pismire's care to garner up his wheat* (Thomas Hood). [Middle English *pissemire* < *pisse* urine (because of the acrid smell of an anthill) + *mire* ant < Germanic (compare Norwegian *myre,* Middle Dutch *miere*)]

**pi|so|lite** (pī′sə līt), *n.* a variety of limestone consisting of rounded grains about the size of small peas. [adaptation of New Latin *pisolithus* < Greek *písos* pea + *líthos* -lite]

**pi|so|lit|ic** (pī′sə lit′ik), *adj.* **1** having to do with pisolite. **2** characteristic of pisolite. **3** having the structure of pisolite.

**piss** (pis), *v., n. Slang* (usually considered vulgar).
—*v.i.* to urinate.
—*v.t.* to discharge as or with the urine.
—*n.* urine.
[Middle English *pissen* < Old French *pissier*]

**pis|soir** (pē swär′), *n.* a public urinal, especially one situated on the street. [< French *pissoir* < *pisser* urinate]

***pis|ta|chi|o** (pis tä′shē ō, -tash′ē-), *n., pl.* **-chi|os,** *adj.* —*n.* **1** a nut with a greenish kernel having a flavor that suggests almond; green almond. **2** the kernel, used for flavoring. **3** the flavor. **4** the small tree that it grows on. It belongs to the cashew family and is a native of western Asia, and is also much grown in southern Europe. **5** a light green with a tinge of yellow.
—*adj.* light-green.
[< Old French *pistache* the tree, and Italian *pistacchio* the nut, both learned borrowings from Latin *pistācium* < Greek *pistákion* < *pistákē* the pistachio tree]

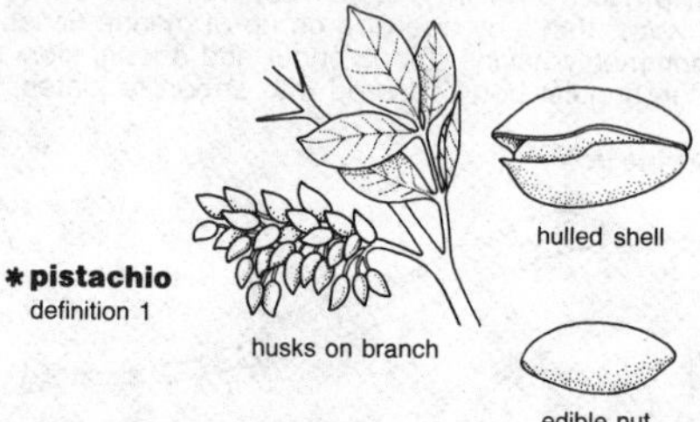

***pistachio**
definition 1

**pis|ta|reen** (pis tə rēn′), *n., adj.* —*n.* the former Spanish peseta, nominally worth two reals, used especially in the Spanish colonies in America.
—*adj.* petty; paltry.
[American English, apparently < a diminutive form of Spanish *peseta* peseta]

**piste** (pēst), *n.* **1** a skiing track or trail. **2** the beaten track of a horse or other animal. [< French *piste* < Latin *pista* (*via*) beaten track < *pīnsere* to pound[2]]

**pis|til** (pis′təl), *n.* **1** the part of a flower that produces seeds. It consists, when complete, of an ovary, a style, and a stigma. *The pistils of the columbine and pea are made up of single carpels* (Heber W. Youngken). See picture under **flower. 2** such organs taken collectively, when there are more than one; gynoecium. [< French *pistile* < New Latin *pistillum* pistil < Latin *pistillum* pestle. See etym. of doublet **pestle.**]

**pis|til|late** (pis′tə lāt, -lit), *adj.* **1** having a pistil or pistils. **2** having a pistil or pistils and no stamens: *If one or more pistils are present and stamens wanting, the flower is called pistillate or female* (Heber W. Youngken). [< *pistil* + *-ate*[1]]

**pis|til|lo|dy** (pis′tə lō′dē), *n.* the metamorphosis of other organs of a flower, as the perianth, sepals, or stamens, into pistils or carpels. [< New Latin *pistillodium* < *pistillum* pistil]

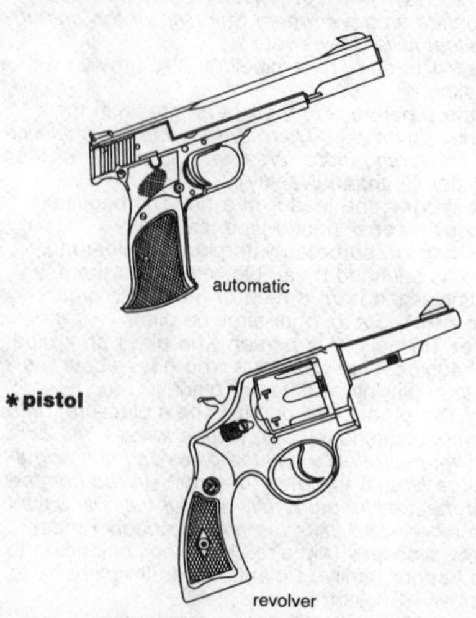

***pistol**

***pis|tol** (pis′təl), *n., v.,* **-toled, -tol|ing** or (*especially British*) **-tolled, -tol|ling.** —*n.* a small, short gun held and fired with one hand; handgun. The two chief classes of pistols in modern use are revolvers and automatics.

—*v.t.* to kill or wound by shooting with a pistol: *This varlet . . . threatened to pistol me* (John Evelyn).

[< obsolete French *pistole* < German *Pistole* < Czech *píšťala* firearm; (originally) pipe]

**pis|tole** (pis tōl′), *n.* **1** a former Spanish gold coin, worth $4. **2** any one of various former European gold coins, worth about the same amount. [< French *pistole* coin; (originally) pistol]

**pis|to|leer** or **pis|to|lier** (pis tə lir′), *n. Archaic.* **1** a person who uses or is skilled in the use of a pistol. **2** a soldier armed with a pistol. [< *pistol* + *-eer,* or < obsolete French *pistolier* < *pistole* pistol]

**pis|to|le|ro** (pis′tə lãr′ō), *n., pl.* **-ros.** a Latin-American gunman: *He ran away to Mexico and grew up a pistolero in the service of a provincial dictator* (Time). [American English < Spanish *pistolero* gunman < *pistola* pistol]

**pistol grip,** a grip or handle resembling the butt of a pistol, on the underside of the stock of a rifle or gun, to afford a better hold for the hand.

**pis|tol-whip** (pis′təl hwip′), *v.t.,* **-whipped, -whipping.** to beat (a person) with a pistol, usually with the barrel of the pistol.

***pis|ton** (pis′tən), *n.* **1** a disk or short cylinder of wood or metal, fitting closely inside a tube or hollow cylinder in which it is moved back and forth by some force, such as the pressure of steam. A piston receives or transmits motion by means of a rod that is attached to it. Pistons are used in pumps, engines, and compressors. **2** a sliding valve in a brass-wind instrument that moves in a cylinder by finger pressure, opening the air passage into additional tubings (crooks) which extend the effective length of the air passage and lower the pitch (a half step, whole step, or one and a half steps lower). [< earlier French *piston* < Italian *pistone* < *pistare* to pound[2] < Late Latin *pistāre* (frequentative) < *pīnsere* to pound[2]] —**pis′ton|like′,** *adj., adv.*

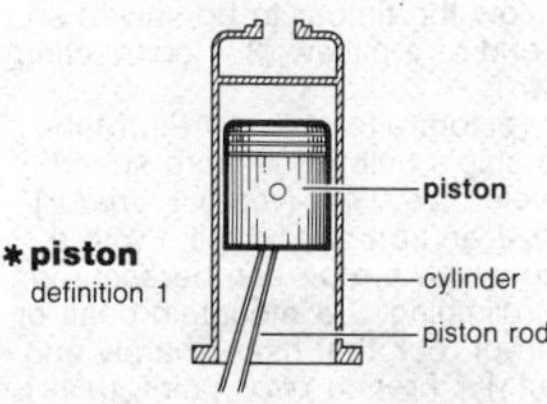


***piston** definition 1

**pis|ton|head** (pis′tən hed′), *n.* the movable disk or cylinder to which the piston rod is attached; piston.

**piston pin,** a shaft connecting the piston to the connecting rod in automobile engines.

**piston ring,** a metal packing ring, usually split so it can expand, fitted in a groove around a piston to insure a tight fit against the cylinder wall.

**piston rod,** a rod by which a piston imparts motion, or by which motion is imparted to it: **a** the rod connecting the piston to the crosshead and connecting rod of a double-acting engine. **b** = connecting rod.

**pit[1]** (pit), *n., v.,* **pit|ted, pit|ting.** —*n.* **1** a natural hole in the ground: *Water collected in the pit left when the old tree was uprooted.* **2a** an open hole or excavation made in digging for some mineral deposit, such as coal; shaft: *The pit of this mine is about 1000 feet deep.* **b** the mine as a whole: *They were playing havoc with legitimate union demands, and acting in a manner prejudicial to others at the pit and contrary to the spirit of trade unionism* (London Times). **3** a deep place; gulf; abyss. **4** a hollow on the surface of anything; hole. **5** a natural hollow or depression in the body: *to be hit in the pit of the stomach.* **6** a small depressed scar, such as one left on the skin after smallpox; pockmark. **7** a covered hole used as a trap for wild animals; pitfall. SYN: snare. **8** *Figurative.* an unsuspected danger or trap. **9** a place where dogs or cocks are made to fight. **10** *British.* **a** (before about 1850) the parquet or orchestra section of a theater. **b** (after about 1850) the rear part of the main floor of a theater, where the seats are cheaper. **c** the people who sit there. **11** the area in front of the stage in a theater where the musicians sit. **12** *U.S.* that portion of the floor of an exchange, especially a commodity exchange, devoted to trade in a particular item: *the wheat pit. An early sinking spell was overcome in most pits by short covering and replacement demand* (Wall Street Journal). **13** a large grave for many bodies. **14a** the portion of a garage used for greasing cars. **b** an area at the side of an automobile race track for repairing or refueling cars. **15** the enclosure at the end of a bowling alley where the pins fall. **16** an area at a sports track filled with sawdust, sand, or a canvas-covered net to soften the impact of landing after a pole vault or other jump. **17** the part of a casino containing the gambling tables.

—*v.t.* **1** to mark with small depressed scars or pits: *a little swarthy young man . . . much pitted with the smallpox* (George du Maurier). **2** to set (gamecocks, terriers, or other animals) to fight for sport. **3** *Figurative.* to set to fight or compete; match: *The little man pitted his brains against the big man's strength. She had pitted herself against Fate* (John Galsworthy). *The game will pit civilian all-stars against military all-stars of the Midnight Sun League* (New York Times). **4** to put or cast into a pit. —*v.i.* **1** to become marked with pits or small depressions. **2** *Medicine.* (of skin or tissue) to retain for a time the mark of pressure made by a finger, or instrument.

**the pit,** hell, or some part of it.

**the pits, a** a place for repair, refueling, or inspection of motor vehicles beside the track of an automobile racing course: *The second Vanwall . . . stopped at the pits on the seventh lap for carburetor adjustment* (London Times). **b** *U.S. Slang.* something that is very bad: *This state was good enough for them for about 55 years. Suddenly, it's the pits'* (New York Post).

[Old English *pytt,* ultimately < Latin *puteus* well[2]]

**pit[2]** (pit), *n., v.,* **pit|ted, pit|ting.** —*n.* the stone of a cherry, peach, plum, date, or similar fruit.

—*v.t.* to remove the pit from (fruit).

[American English < Dutch *pit* kernel, marrow. See related etym. at **pith.**] —**pit′ter,** *n.*

**pi|ta[1]** (pē′tə), *n.* **1** a tough fiber obtained from the leaves of the century plant and certain other agaves, used especially for cordage. **2** any one of these plants. **3** a similar fiber obtained from other plants, such as varieties of yucca. **4** any one of these plants. [< Spanish *pita* < Quechua (Peru), fine thread made of bast[1]]

**pi|ta[2]** (pē′tä, pē tä′), *n.* a flat, round barley or flour bread eaten in the Middle East. [< Hebrew *pīta,* Arabic *bīta*]

**pit|a|pat** or **pit-a-pat** (pit′ə pat′), *adv., n., v.,* **-pat|ted, -pat|ting.** —*adv.* with a quick succession of beats or taps; flutteringly; patteringly.

—*n.* the movement or sound of something going pitapat; palpitation; pattering: *'Tis but the pit-a-pat of two young hearts* (John Dryden).

—*v.i.* to go pitapat; palpitate; patter. Also, **pitpat, pitter-patter, pittypat.** [reduplication of *pat*[1]]

**pit band,** *U.S.* an orchestra playing immediately in front of and below the stage of a theater.

**pit boss,** the supervisor of the gambling tables in a casino.

**pit bull, 1** a kind of bulldog formerly used in dog fighting; pit dog. **2** = bull terrier.

**pitch[1]** (pich), *v., n.* —*v.t.* **1** to throw or fling; hurl; toss: *to pitch a stone into a lake, to pitch the debris over a cliff. The men were pitching horseshoes.* SYN: cast, heave. **2** to pick up and fling (hay or straw) in a mass with a pitchfork onto a vehicle or into a barn. **3a** to throw (the ball) to the batter in a game of baseball: *to pitch curves and fast balls.* **b** to loft (a golf ball) so that it alights with little roll. **4** to set up as a temporary shelter or abode: *to pitch a tent, to pitch camp.* **5** to fix firmly: *In this half-circle I pitched two rows of strong stakes, driving them into the ground till they stood very firm like piles* (Daniel Defoe). **6** to put, set, or plant in a fixed or definite place or position: *Here is a place to build a breastwork; here ye can pitch a fort* (Rudyard Kipling). **7** to set at a certain value, point, degree, or level: *to pitch one's hopes too high.* **8** to determine the musical key of (a tune, instrument, or the voice): *He . . . pitched the tunes with his pitchpipe* (Harriet Beecher Stowe). **9** *U.S. Slang.* to sell or try to sell (a product or service), often by high-pressure means. **10** in card games: **a** to indicate one's choice of trump by an opening lead of (a card of the suit chosen). **b** to settle (the trump suit) thus. **11** *Archaic.* to put in order.

—*v.i.* **1** to throw; toss; hurl: *He nearly always pitches too far.* **2a** to throw the ball to the batter in a game of baseball. **b** to act as pitcher for a team. **c** to strike a golf ball with a lofted club so that it goes up in the air and alights with little roll: *Cary then pitched to within a yard of the flag, before tapping in a putt for a birdie* (New York Times). **3** to set up a tent or shelter; establish a camp; encamp. **4** to take up a position; settle; alight. **5** to fall or plunge forward; fall headlong: *The skier lost his balance and pitched into a snowdrift.* **6** to plunge with the bow rising and then falling: *The ship pitched about in the storm.* **7** to slope downward; incline; dip. **8** *U.S. Slang.* to sell or try to sell something, often by high-pressure means: *Before I got on radio and television . . . I pitched at state fairs and in hotels* (New York Times).

—*n.* **1** a throw; fling; hurl; toss: *It's more than one maybe will get a bloody head on him with the pitch of my stone* (John M. Synge). **2** that which is pitched. **3a** the act of pitching or throwing a ball. **b** the ball so delivered. **c** the manner of doing this: *He is starting a fast pitch.* **4** *Figurative.* a point or position on a scale; degree; stage; level: *The poor man has reached the lowest pitch of bad fortune.* **5** *Music.* **a** the degree of highness or lowness of a sound or tone. Notes in music with a low pitch have a slower rate of vibration than those with a high pitch. **b** a particular standard of pitch for voices and instruments, never internationally standardized, but now generally accepted as 440 vibrations per second for a′ (the first *a* above middle *c*): *East and West met in perfect harmony here today and agreed on a different pitch, not political but musical* (New York Times). **6** height: *the pitch of an arch.* **7** *Figurative.* the highest point or degree; acme; climax: *happy to the pitch of ecstasy* (H. G. Wells). **8** *Informal.* **a** a talk, argument, offer, or plan, used to persuade, as in selling, or to promote an idea, product, or undertaking: *to make a strong sales pitch. It will be packaged in an economy-size tube and, as a new pitch, he will also sell it in the form of candy* (Harper's). **b** a television or radio commercial: *Any blame for lengthy commercials belongs to the broadcasters and sponsors. The FCC has no jurisdiction over the length of pitches* (Newsweek). **9a** a place of pitching or encamping or taking up a position: *It was a pleasant little island of green they chose for their midday pitch* (H. G. Wells). **b** a spot in a street or market place where a peddler, street performer, or merchant of anything regularly stations himself; stand: *When he arrived at the market, the best pitches were gone* (Atlantic). **10** the quantity of hay or straw raised with a pitchfork at one time. **11** a steep place; declivity. **12** the amount of slope: *Some roads in the Rocky Mountains have a very steep pitch.* **13** the slope or steepness of a roof: *The roof had a sharp pitch.* **14** *Mining.* the inclination, as of a vein of ore or seam of coal, from the horizontal; dip or rise. **15** the distance between the centers of two successive teeth of a cogwheel, gearwheel, pinion, rack, or the like. **16** the distance between two successive lines or points, especially in screw threads, where it is measured parallel to the axis and indicates the distance the screw moves forward in one turn. **17** the distance an aircraft propeller would move forward in one revolution if turning in a semisolid. **18** the movement of the longitudinal axis of an aircraft up or down from the horizontal plane. **19** a plunge forward or headlong; lurch. **20** a downward plunging of the fore part of a ship in a rough sea. **21** *Cricket.* the ground between and around the wickets. **22** the act of pitching on or choosing a place to live in or camp: *Having made their pitch the Gypsies unhitched their ponies and began to cook dinner.* **23** a variety of seven-up, in which the trump is settled by the first card played. **24** the ring or circle into which the marbles are put at the start of a game of marbles.

**in there pitching,** *Slang.* putting forth one's best efforts; working hard, busily, or steadily: *I don't know which came first, the dishonest customer or the dishonest dealer, but they're both in there pitching* (Maclean's).

**make a pitch,** *Informal.* to make a persuasive request; make a bid: *Madison Avenue took a poke at— and made a pitch to— Wall Street* (New York Times).

**pitch in,** *Informal.* to work or begin to work hard: *All the neighbors pitched in to build the new barn. I took hold with Dan and pitched right in* (Rudyard Kipling).

**pitch into,** *Informal.* to attack: *If any man had told me, then . . . I should have pitched into him* (Dickens).

**pitch on** (or **upon**) , to fix or settle on; select; choose: *If one holy place was desecrated, the monks pitched upon another* (Cardinal Newman).

[Middle English *picchen,* perhaps Old English *pīcian* pick[1]]

**pitch[2]** (pich), *n., v.* —*n.* **1** a black, sticky substance made from tar or turpentine, used to fill the seams of wooden ships, to cover roofs, or to make pavements: *Though pitch is a solid at ordinary temperatures, it is classed by science as a liquid with a viscosity many billions of times greater than that of water* (Scientific American). **2** the resin or crude turpentine from pine and fir trees. **3** any one of several other resins.

—*v.t.* to cover, coat, or smear with pitch.

**Pronunciation Key:** hat, āge, cãre, fär; let, ēqual, tėrm; it, īce; hot, ōpen, ôrder; oil, out; cup, pu̇t, rüle; child; long; thin; ᴛʜen; zh, measure; ə represents **a** in about, **e** in taken, **i** in pencil, **o** in lemon, **u** in circus.

[Old English *pic* < Latin *pix, picis*] — **pitch′like′**, *adj.*

**pitch-and-putt** (pich′ən put′), *adj., n.* — ***adj.*** of or having to do with golf played on a small course, usually consisting of nine holes: *a pitch-and-putt player.*
— ***n.*** **1** the game of golf played on a pitch-and-putt course. **2** a pitch-and-putt course.

**pitch-and-run** (pich′ən run′), *n. Golf.* a chip shot that rolls a distance after being lofted in the air.

**pitch-and-toss** (pich′ən tôs′, -tos′), *n.* a game in which coins are thrown at a mark, and the player whose coin comes closest to the mark tosses all the coins played and keeps those which land heads up.

**pitch-black** (pich′blak′), *adj.* very black or dark; pitch-dark: *He groped along the pitch-black street* (Edith Wharton). [< *pitch*[2] + *black*]

**pitch|blende** (pich′blend′), *n.* a mineral consisting largely of an oxide of uranium, occurring in black, pitchlike masses. It is a source of uranium, radium, polonium, and actinium. [translation of German *Pechblende* < *Pech* pitch[2] + *Blende* blende]

**pitch circle**, the pitch line of a gearwheel.

**pitch-dark** (pich′därk′), *adj.* = pitch-black.

**-pitched**, *combining form.* **1** having a ___ pitch: *A high-pitched voice = a voice having a high pitch.*
**2** having a ___ pitch or slope: *A single-pitched roof = a roof having a single pitch.*

**pitched battle** (picht), a battle with troops properly arranged and tactics planned on both sides.

**pitch|er**[1] (pich′ər), *n.* **1** a container with a lip on one side and a handle on the other. Pitchers are used for holding and pouring out water, milk, and other liquids. *The water in the pitcher was frozen.* **SYN**: ewer, jug. **2** the amount that a pitcher holds: *to drink a pitcher of milk.* **3** a leaf, or a part of one, modified into the form of a pitcher; ascidium. [< Old French *pichier, picher,* alteration of *bichier* < Vulgar Latin *bicārium,* perhaps < Greek *bīkos* earthen jar. See etym. of doublet **beaker**.] — **pitch′er|like′**, *adj.*

**pitch|er**[2] (pich′ər), *n.* **1** the player on a baseball team who throws the ball for the batter to try and hit. **2** a person who pitches hay or straw. **3** a golf club with a metal head that slopes at a relatively flat angle, more than that of a mashie niblick, so as to give loft to the ball when it is hit. It is usually called a "number 7 iron." [< *pitch*[1] + *-er*[1]]

**pitch|er|ful** (pich′ər fu̇l), *n., pl.* **-fuls.** the quantity sufficient to fill a pitcher.

*** pitcher plant**, a plant with leaves somewhat like a pitcher. These leaves capture insects and digest them by means of a liquid secreted in the leaves.

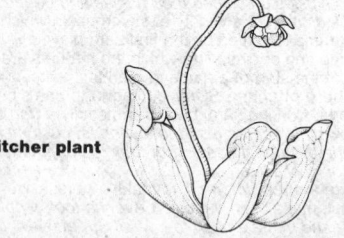

*** pitcher plant**

**pitch|fork** (pich′fôrk′), *n., v.* — ***n.*** a large fork with a long wooden handle, used in lifting and throwing hay or straw; hayfork. A pitchfork has two to four long, slightly curved steel prongs or tines.
— ***v.t.*** **1** to lift and throw with or as if with a pitchfork. **2** *Figurative.* to thrust (a person) forcibly or unsuitably into some position or office: *Here he was ... pitchforked into a coil of scandal* (Edith Wharton).

**pitch|ing niblick** (pich′ing), a golf club with a metal head that slopes at an angle flatter than that of a pitcher, but less than that of a niblick. It is usually called a "number 8 iron."

*** pitch line**, **1** an imaginary line passing through the teeth of a gearwheel, pinion, rack, or the like, so as to touch or coincide with the corresponding line in another gearwheel, pinion, rack, or the like, when the two are geared together. **2** (in marble games) the line from which the players lag. It is outside the playing circle, opposite the lag line.

**pitch|man** (pich′man′), *n., pl.* **-men.** *U.S. Informal.* **1** a person who sells small articles on the street or at fairs, carnivals, or the like. **2** a person who makes a sales pitch; one who sells or promotes a product, cause, idea, or undertaking, especially by high-pressure means; salesman: *a television pitchman. An adept pitchman, however, can get his customer half-hooked by telephone* (New York Times).

**pitch|out** (pich′out′), *n.* **1** (in baseball) a wide pitch thrown to prevent the batter from hitting the ball and to give the catcher a chance to catch a runner off base. **2** (in football) a lateral pass behind the line of scrimmage.

**pitch pine**, a pine tree which yields pitch or turpentine, especially a pine of eastern North America with reddish-brown bark, needles in groups of three, and persistent cones.

**pitch pipe**, a small musical pipe having one or more notes, used to give the pitch for singing or for tuning an instrument.

**pitch|stone** (pich′stōn′), *n.* obsidian or other vitreous rock that looks like hardened pitch.

**pitch|y** (pich′ē), *adj.,* **pitch|i|er, pitch|i|est. 1** full of pitch; bituminous or resinous. **2** coated, smeared, or sticky with pitch. **3** of the nature or consistency of pitch; sticky. **4** as black as pitch; pitch-black: *thick pitchy smoke* (Nicholas Wiseman). **5** *Figurative.* pitch-dark; intensely dark.

**pit dog**, = pit bull (def. 1).

**pit|e|ous** (pit′ē əs), *adj.* **1** to be pitied; moving the heart; deserving pity: *The starving children were a piteous sight.* **SYN**: pathetic, pitiable. See syn. under **pitiful**. **2** *Archaic.* full of pity; compassionate; merciful. **3** *Obsolete.* paltry; mean. [< Anglo-French *pitous,* variant of Old French *pitos* < Medieval Latin *pietosus* pitiful, dutiful < Latin *pietās* pity, piety < *pius* pious] — **pit′e|ous|ly**, *adv.* — **pit′e|ous|ness**, *n.*

**pit|fall** (pit′fôl′), *n.* **1** any trap or hidden danger: *The road to conquest of poliomyelitis, or infantile paralysis, has been long and full of pitfalls* (Science News Letter). **2** a hidden pit to catch animals or men in.

**pith** (pith), *n., v.* — ***n.*** **1a** the central, spongy tissue in the stems and branches of dicotyledonous plants; medulla: *The roots of most dicotyledonous plants lack a pith, the xylem extending to the center* (Harbaugh and Goodrich). **b** the internal parenchymatous tissue of certain other stems, such as palms and rushes: *Sago is made from the starchy pith of the palm trunk* (Arthur W. Galston). **c** a similar tissue occurring in other parts of plants, such as that lining the rind of the orange and certain other fruits. **2** the soft inner substance of a spinal column, bone, feather, or the like; marrow. **3** *Figurative.* the important or essential part; essence; substance: *the pith of a speech. It's his abominable pride, that's the pith of the matter* (Cardinal Newman). **SYN**: gist.
**4** strength; energy; vigor: *his look of native pith and genuine power* (Charlotte Brontë). **SYN**: force.
— ***v.t.*** **1** to remove or extract the pith from (plants). **2** to pierce or sever the spinal cord of (an animal) so as to kill it or render it insensible. [Old English *pitha*]

**pit|head** (pit′hed′), *n.* **1** the entrance to a mine. **2** the ground surrounding it.

**pith|e|can|throp|ic** (pith′ə kan throp′ik), *adj.* **1** = pithecanthropine. **2** = pithecanthropoid.

**pith|e|can|thro|pine** (pith′ə kan′thrə pīn), *adj., n.* — ***adj.*** of or having to do with the same group as Pithecanthropus: *a pithecanthropine skeleton.*
— ***n.*** a pithecanthropine animal: *The skeleton of the pithecanthropines is in every way hominid* (Ashley Montagu).

**pith|e|can|thro|poid** (pith′ə kan′thrə poid), *adj., n.* — ***adj.*** **1** resembling a Pithecanthropus. **2** related to a Pithecanthropus.
— ***n.*** a pithecanthropoid animal.

**Pith|e|can|thro|pus** (pith′ə kan thrō′pəs, -kan′thrə-), *n., pl.* **-pi** (-pī). one of a group of extinct ape men, approximating man in bodily form but with a much smaller brain capacity, whose existence about 500,000 years ago (in the Pleistocene) is assumed from remains first found in Java in 1891; Java man. The group has been viewed by some as a link between apes and men, and by others as a kind of man, and is considered to have been related to Peking man. [< New Latin *Pithecanthropus* < Greek *pithēkos* ape + *ánthrōpos* man]

**pi|the|coid** (pi thē′koid, pith′ə-), *adj.* **1** resembling the apes, especially the anthropoid apes; simian. **2** having to do with the apes. [< French *pithécoïde* < Greek *pithēkos* ape + *eîdos* form]

**pith helmet**, a helmet-shaped sun hat made originally of the dried pith of the East Indian sola or spongewood, but now made of various substances; sola topee.

**pi|thi|a|tism** (pi thī′ə tiz əm), *n. Medicine.* **1** a disorder caused by suggestion, such as forms of hysteria. **2** the cure of mental disorders by persuasion. [< Greek *peíthein* persuade + *iatós* curable + English *-ism*]

**pith|i|ly** (pith′ə lē), *adv.* in a pithy manner; tersely and forcibly; concisely.

**pith|i|ness** (pith′ē nis), *n.* the quality or character of being pithy.

**pith|less** (pith′lis), *adj.* without pith; wanting strength; weak. — **pith′less|ly**, *adv.*

**pith|os** (pith′os), *n.* a very large, wide-mouthed, earthenware jar of spheroidal form, used in ancient Greece for storing wine, oil, or grain. [< Greek *píthos*]

**pith|y** (pith′ē), *adj.,* **pith|i|er, pith|i|est. 1** full of substance, meaning, force, or vigor; crisply concise and to the point: *pithy phrases, a pithy speaker.* **SYN**: pointed. **2** of or like pith. **3** having much pith: *a pithy orange.*

**pit|i|a|ble** (pit′ē ə bəl), *adj.* **1** to be pitied; moving the heart; deserving pity: *The sick cat was a pitiable sight.* **SYN**: lamentable, deplorable. See syn. under **pitiful**. **2** deserving contempt; to be scorned; mean; contemptible; miserable: *His half-hearted attempts to help with the work were pitiable.* — **pit′i|a|ble|ness**, *n.* — **pit′i|a|bly**, *adv.*

**pit|i|er** (pit′ē ər), *n.* a person who pities.

**pit|i|ful** (pit′i fəl), *adj.* **1** to be pitied; moving the heart; deserving pity; piteous; lamentable: *a pitiful story, a pitiful sight.* **2** feeling pity; feeling sorrow for the trouble of others; tender: *The Lord is very pitiful, and of tender mercy* (James 5:11). **SYN**: compassionate, merciful. **3** deserving contempt; to be scorned; mean: *Driving away after hitting a dog is a pitiful act.* — **pit′i|ful|ly**, *adv.* — **pit′i|ful|ness**, *n.*
— *Syn.* **1 Pitiful, piteous, pitiable** mean arousing pity or to be pitied. **Pitiful** emphasizes the effect of pity aroused by someone or something felt to be touching or pathetic: *The deserted children were pitiful.* **Piteous** emphasizes the quality in the thing itself that makes it appeal for pity and move the heart: *Their sad faces were piteous.* **Pitiable** emphasizes arousing sorrow or regret, often mixed with contempt, for what deserves or needs to be pitied: *Their bodies and clothes were in a pitiable condition.*

**pit|i|less** (pit′ə lis), *adj.* without pity or mercy; merciless: *Ruffians, pitiless as proud* (William Cowper). *The pelting of this pitiless storm* (Shakespeare). **SYN**: ruthless. See syn. under **cruel**.
— **pit′i|less|ly**, *adv.* — **pit′i|less|ness**, *n.*

**pit|man** (pit′mən), *n., pl.* **-men** or (for def. 3) **-mans. 1** a man who works in a pit or mine, especially a coal mine. **2** a sawyer's helper who stands in a pit below the timber to be sawed and works the lower end of a pitsaw. **3** = connecting rod. [< *pit*[1] + *man*]

**pi|tom|e|ter log** (pi tom′ə tər, pē-), a Pitot tube projecting from a ship's hull to measure speed and distance traveled. [< *Pitot* (*tube*) + *-meter*]

**pi|ton** (pē′ton), *n.* **1** an iron bar or spike with a ring in one end to which a rope can be secured, used in mountain climbing. **2** a mountain peak or peaklike formation of rock that rises sharply and abruptly to a point. [< French *piton* point, peak]

**Pi|tot-stat|ic tube** (pē tō′stat′ik), a device combining a Pitot tube and a static tube, used to determine the speed of the air or other fluid by measuring the difference in pressure between moving and still fluid. The Pitot-static tube measures the ship or aircraft speed by variation in pressure.

**Pi|tot tube** (pē tō′), **1** a bent tube with an open end pointed against the flow of a gas or liquid, used for determining the velocity of fluids. **2** = Pitot-static tube. [< Henri *Pitot,* 1695-1771, a French physicist]

**pit|pat** (pit′pat′), *adv., n., v.,* **-pat|ted, -pat|ting.** = pitapat.

**pit pony**, *British.* a pony employed in coal mines.

**pit|prop** (pit′prop′), *n.* a beam or other heavy prop used to support the roof of a mine.

**Pit|res|sin** (pi tres′in), *n. Trademark.* vasopressin (def. 2).

**pits** (pits), *n.pl.* See under **pit**[1].

**pit|saw** (pit′sô′), *n.* a large saw with handles for two men, one working on the log and the other beneath it in a sawpit.

**pit|ta** (pit′ə), *n.* **1** any one of various plump, short-tailed, brightly colored perching birds, inhabiting forest floors of southeastern Asia, Australia, and Africa. **2** the ant thrush of South America. [< New Latin *Pitta* the typical genus < Telugu *pitta* anything small; a pet]

**pit|tance** (pit′əns), *n.* **1** a small allowance of money; very scanty wage or stipend: *a widow's pittance. She ... contrived to earn a pittance scarcely sufficient to support life* (Mary Shelley). **2** a small amount or share: *to retain at least a pittance of hope.* [Middle English *pitaunce* < Old French *pitance* piety, pity; later, portion of food allowed a monk < Vulgar Latin *pietantia* < Latin *pietās* pity, piety]

**pit|ter-pat|ter** (pit′ər pat′ər), *n., adv., v.* — ***n.*** a quick succession of light beats or taps; pitapat: *the pitter-patter of rain or of a child's steps.*
— ***adv.*** with a rapid succession of beats or taps.
— ***v.i.*** to go pitter-patter: *"Just go ahead as you normally would and let us pitter-patter around"* (New Yorker).
[Compare etym. under **pitapat**.]

**pit|ty|pat** (pit′ē pat′), *adv., n., v.i.,* **-pat|ted, -pat|ting.** = pitapat.

**pi|tu|i|tar|y** (pi tü′ə ter′ē, -tyü′-), *n., pl.* **-tar|ies,** *adj.* —*n.* **1** = pituitary gland. **2** any one of various extracts made from the pituitary gland and used in medical preparations.

—*adj.* **1** having to do with the pituitary gland. **2** designating a type of physique, obese and with large bone structure, thought to be caused by excessive secretion of the pituitary gland. **3** *Obsolete.* **a** of or having to do with mucus. **b** secreting mucus.

[< New Latin *pituitarius* < Latin *pītuītārius* relating to phlegm, mucus < *pītuīta* phlegm (because it was believed that the gland channeled mucus to the nose)]

**pituitary gland** or **body**, a small, oval endocrine gland situated at the base of the brain of most vertebrates, in a cavity of the sphenoid bone; hypophysis; master gland. It secretes hormones that promote growth, stimulate and regulate other glands, raise blood pressure, promote milk secretion, and regulate many other bodily functions. See diagram under **brain**.

**Pi|tu|i|trin** (pi tü′ə trin, -tyü′-), *n. Trademark.* a preparation or extract from the posterior lobe of the pituitary gland of cattle, used in treating diabetes insipidus shock and to aid in uterine contraction during childbirth.

**pit viper**, any one of a family of venomous snakes of America, the East Indies, Europe east of the lower Volga River, and Asia, having perforated fangs and a pit between the eye and nostril. Rattlesnakes, water moccasins, copperheads, fer-de-lances, and bushmasters are pit vipers.

**pit|y** (pit′ē), *n., pl.* **pit|ies,** *v.,* **pit|ied, pit|y|ing.** —*n.* **1** sorrow for another's suffering or distress; feeling for the sorrows of others; compassion; sympathy: *The policeman felt pity for the lost and crying child. Grief for the calamity of another is pity* (Thomas Hobbes). **2** a cause for pity or regret; thing to be sorry for: *It is a pity to be kept in the house in fine weather.*

—*v.t.* to feel pity for; be sorry for: *She pitied any child who was hurt. I pity those who are out in the cold tonight.*

—*v.i.* to feel pity; be compassionate.

**for pity's sake**, an exclamation of surprise or protest: *But for pity's sake, spare us that indignity!* (Time).

**have** (or **take**) **pity on**, to show pity for: *Have pity on the poor beggar.*

[< Old French *pite* < Latin *pīetās* piety, pity < *pīus* pious. See etym. of doublet **piety**.] —**pit′y|ing|ly,** *adv.*

—*Syn. n.* **1 Pity, compassion, sympathy** mean a feeling for the sorrows or sufferings of others. **Pity** means a feeling of sorrow for someone who is suffering or in sorrow or distress, and often felt to be weak or unfortunate: *The beggar's hungry look and ragged appearance aroused the stranger's pity.* **Compassion** adds the idea of tenderness and a strong desire to help or protect: *He felt compassion for the sobbing child.* **Sympathy** means a feeling with another in his sorrow and sharing and understanding it: *His friends expressed great sympathy for him when his mother died.*

**pit|y|ri|a|sis** (pit′ə rī′ə sis), *n.* **1** any one of various skin conditions characterized by the formation and eventual peeling off of small scales of skin. **2** a dry, scaly skin condition in domestic animals, occurring during the course of certain fungoid or filarial diseases. [< Greek *pitȳrīāsis* scurf, dandruff < *pítyron* bran + *-īāsis* -iasis]

**piu** (pyü), *adv. Music.* more (as part of a direction): *piu andante.* [< Italian *più*]

**Pi|ute** (pī′üt′), *n.* = Paiute.

**piv|ot** (piv′ət), *n., v., adj.* —*n.* **1** a short shaft, pin, or point on which something turns. The pin of a hinge or the end of an axle or spindle is a pivot. **2** a turn on a pivot. **3** *Figurative.* that on which something turns, hinges, or depends; central point: *His pitching was the pivot of our team's hopes. A permanent pivot in the center of one's inner life is also a stake beyond which one cannot range* (Edmund Wilson). **4a** *Basketball.* a way of moving while holding the ball in which a player may step in any direction with one foot, but he must keep the other foot in one spot on the floor. **b** the position of a pivotman.

—*v.t.* to mount on, attach by, or provide with a pivot or pivots: *The swinging door was pivoted on one side; the revolving door was pivoted in the center.*

—*v.i.* **1** to turn on or as if on a pivot: *to pivot on one's heel. There is a recess, and the board at the back pivots; a very simple hiding place* (Joseph Conrad). **2** to execute a dance figure suggesting pivoting. **3** *Basketball.* to use the pivot. **4** to change seats, as at a bridge table, when one player remains in his place, so that the partnerships change.

—*adj.* = pivotal.

[< Old French *pivot;* origin uncertain]

**piv|ot|a|ble** (piv′ə tə bəl), *adj.* that may be pivoted: *a pivotable shaft.*

**piv|ot|al** (piv′ə təl), *adj.* **1** of or having to do with a pivot. **2** *Figurative.* being that on which something turns, hinges, or depends; very important: *The Berlin problem is a pivotal issue between the United States and Soviet Russia.* SYN: central, cardinal, vital. —**piv′ot|al|ly,** *adv.*

**pivot joint**, a joint in which a bony pivot fits into a corresponding cavity or ring in another bone, permitting only rotating movement.

**piv|ot|man** (piv′ət man′), *n., pl.* **-men.** *Basketball.* a player who acts as an intermediary in receiving, passing, and shooting the ball.

**pix**[1] (piks), *n.* = pyx.

**pix**[2] (piks), *n.pl. Slang.* pictures. [probably short for *pictures*]

**pix|el** (pik′səl), *n.* one of the photographic elements of a televised image. [< *pix*[2] + *el*(ement)]

**pix|ie** (pik′sē), *n.* **1** = pixy. **2** a short hairstyle for women, popular in the 1950's.

**pix|i|lat|ed** (pik′sə lā′tid), *adj. U.S. Informal.* **1** slightly crazy: *The poor woman has been pixilated for years.* **2** foolish and amusing: *as pixilated as a cat filled with catnip.* [perhaps < *pixy,* perhaps patterned on *titillated*]

**pix|y** (pik′sē), *n., pl.* **pix|ies.** a fairy or elf. SYN: sprite. [origin uncertain]

**pix|y|ish** or **pix|ie|ish** (pik′sē ish), *adj.* like that of a pixy; mischievous: *a pixyish look.*

**pix|y-led** (pik′sē led′), *adj.* **1** led astray by pixies. **2** lost; bewildered.

**pi|zazz** (pə zaz′), *n. U.S. Slang.* **1** liveliness; pep: *Jazz and soul food, soul food and jazz, are thought to generate pizazz* (New Yorker). **2** flashy style or quality; ornateness: ... *the U.S. driver's growing fondness for pizazz* (Time). Also, **pizzazz, pazazz.** [origin unknown]

**pizz.,** *Music.* pizzicato.

**piz|za** (pēt′sə; *Italian* pēt′tsä), *n.,* or **pizza pie,** a spicy Italian dish made by baking a large flat cake of bread dough covered with cheese, tomato sauce, herbs, and often with anchovies, bits of sausage, or the like. [< Italian *pizza,* perhaps < *pesta* (thing) pounded, ultimately < Latin *pista,* feminine past participle of *pīnsere* to pound[2], beat]

**piz|zazz** (pə zaz′), *n. Slang.* = pizazz.

**piz|ze|ri|a** (pēt′sə rē′ə; *Italian* pēt′tsä rē′ä), *n.* a restaurant or bakery where pizzas are baked and sold. [< Italian *pizzeria* < *pizza;* see etym. under **pizza**]

**piz|zi|ca|to** (pit′sə kä′tō), *adj., n., pl.* **-ti** (-tē). *Music.* —*adj.* played on a violin, cello, viola, or bass viol, by plucking or pinching the string with the finger instead of using the bow.

—*n.* a tone or passage played in this way.

[< Italian *pizzicato* picked, pinched]

**P.J.,** **1** Presiding Judge. **2** Probate Judge.

**pjs** (pē′jāz′), *n.pl.,* or **p.j.'s,** *Slang.* pajamas.

**pk.,** **1** pack. **2** park. **3** peak. **4** peck.

**PK** (no periods), psychokinesis.

**pkg.,** package or packages.

**pks.,** **1** packs. **2** parks. **3** peaks. **4** pecks.

**pkt.,** packet.

**PKU** (no periods), phenylketonuria.

**pkwy.,** parkway.

**pl.,** **1** place. **2** plate or plates. **3** plural.

**Pl.,** Place.

**P.L.,** **1** Poet Laureate. **2** public law.

**PLA** (no periods), People's Liberation Army (the military forces of the People's Republic of China).

**P.L.A.,** Port of London Authority.

**pla|ca|bil|i|ty** (plā′kə bil′ə tē), *n.* the quality or character of being placable; readiness to be appeased or to forgive; mildness of disposition.

**pla|ca|ble** (plā′kə bəl), *adj.* that may be placated; easily quieted; forgiving or mild: *Methought I saw him placable and mild* (Milton). SYN: conciliatory. [< Latin *plācābilis* < *plācāre* placate] —**pla′ca|ble|ness,** *n.* —**pla′ca|bly,** *adv.*

**plac|ard** (*n.* plak′ärd; *v.* plə kärd′, plak′ärd), *n., v.* —*n.* a notice to be posted in a public place; poster. Placards are written or printed on one side of a single sheet. *There were also placards calling for men on nearly all the taxicabs* (H. G. Wells).

—*v.t.* **1** to put placards on or in: *The circus placarded the city with advertisements.* **2** to give public notice of with a placard or placards: *to placard a reward offered.* **3** to post or display as a placard: *to placard a bill or notice.*

[earlier, "sealed" document, plate of armor, an undergarment < Middle French *placard* < Old French *plaquier* to piece together, stick, plaster < Middle Dutch *placken.* Compare etym. under **plaque.**] —**pla|card′er,** *n.*

**pla|cate** (plā′kāt, plak′āt), *v.t.,* **-cat|ed, -cat|ing.** to soothe or satisfy the anger of; make peaceful; appease; pacify; conciliate: *to placate a person one has offended. A victory so complete ... failed to placate the indignant young actress* (Joseph Knight). SYN: propitiate. [< Latin *plācāre* (with English *-ate*[1]) be pleasing, soothe] —**pla′cat|er,** *n.* —**pla′cat|ing|ly,** *adv.*

**pla|ca|tion** (plā kā′shən), *n.* the act of placating; appeasing; pacifying. SYN: conciliation, propitiation.

**pla|ca|tive** (plā′kə tiv, plak′ə-), *adj.* = placatory.

**pla|ca|to|ry** (plā′kə tôr′ē, -tōr′-; plak′ə-), *adj.* tending or calculated to placate; conciliatory.

**place**[1] (plās), *n., v.,* **placed, plac|ing.** —*n.* **1** the part of space occupied by a person or thing; position in space or with reference to other bodies: *In the world I fill up a place, which may be better supplied when I have made it empty* (Shakespeare). **2** a particular portion of space; definite position in space; location: *We leave the well-loved place, where first we gazed upon the sky* (Tennyson). **3** a city, town, village, district, island, or the like: *What is the name of this place? What place do you come from?* **4** a building or spot used for some particular purpose: *A church is a place of worship. A store or office is a place of business.* **5** a house; house and grounds; dwelling: *His parents have a beautiful place in the country.* **6** a part or spot in a body or surface: *a sore place on one's foot. The dentist filled the decayed place in the tooth.* **7** a particular page or other point in a book or other writing: *to mark one's place. This is the place where the story gets most exciting.* **8** *Figurative.* a fitting or reasonable ground or occasion: *A funeral is not the place for humor. There is a time and place for everything.* **9** *Figurative.* right situation or usual position for a person or thing: *Each book is in its place on the shelf. The country is not a place for a person of my temper* (Richard Addison). **10** position or rank in any order of merit; standing: *a high place in society. We have not attempted to ascertain his place among historians* (William Gladstone). **11** social position; rank in society; station: *The servant filled his place well. In ancient times, a master and a slave had very different places in life.* **12a** the position of a competitor or team at the end of or during a race or contest: *last place. The team was still in seventh place on July 4.* **b** a ranking position, especially one of the first three, at the end of a race: *John outran his rival for a place.* **c** the second position at the end of a horse race. **13** position in time; part of time occupied by an event: *The performance went too slowly in several places.*

**14** space or a seat for a person, as in a theater, train, or coach: *We took our places at the table. Try to save me a place if you board the train before I do. Many of the boys ... will be found places at their nearest grammar schools* (Sunday Times). SYN: room. **15** a work, job, employment, post, or office: *He tried to get a place as a clerk in a store on Saturdays. I know my price, I am worth no worse a place* (Shakespeare). **16** official position; political power: *Nought's permanent among the human race, except the Whigs not getting into place* (Byron). **17** official function; duty; business: *It's not my place to find fault. It's not the place of a newspaper to print rumors.* **18** a step or point in any order of proceeding: *In the first place, the room is too small; in the second place, it is too dirty.* **19** the position of a figure in a number or series, in decimal or any other notation: *in the third decimal place.* **20** a short street or court (now usually as part of a name): *Waverley Place. Abbr:* Pl. **21** an open space or square in a city or town. **22** space in general; extension in three dimensions (especially as contrasted with *time*): *He passed the flaming bounds of Place and Time* (Thomas Gray). **23** *Astronomy.* the position of a heavenly body at any instant. **24** in falconry: **a** the pitch of a falcon or any other bird. **b** the greatest elevation which it attains in its flight: *a falcon, towering in her pride of place* (Shakespeare). **25** *Archaic.* space or room: *Place, nobles for the Falcon-Knight!* (Scott).

—*v.t.* **1** to put in a particular place; set in a specified position; station: *Guards had been placed at all the exits. The orphan was placed in a good home.* SYN: locate. See syn. under **put.** **2** to put in the proper order or position; arrange; dispose: *He had fewer troops than his enemy, but he placed them with more skill.* **3** to give the place, position, or condition of; identify: *I am sure I have met you before, but I cannot place you.* **4** to determine the date of; assign to an age: *Homer is usually placed about the 800's* B.C. **5** to appoint (a person) to a position or office; find a place or situation for: *He had resolved to place me happily in the world* (Samuel Johnson). SYN:

---

**Pronunciation Key:** hat, āge, cãre, fär; let, ēqual, tėrm; it, īce; hot, ōpen, ôrder; oil, out; cup, pu̇t, rüle; child; long; thin; ᴛʜen; zh, measure; ə represents **a** in about, **e** in taken, **i** in pencil, **o** in lemon, **u** in circus.

install. **6** to entrust, such as to an appropriate person or firm, for action, treatment, disposal, or the like: *Orders for next year's Christmas cards have already been placed.* **7** *Figurative.* to attribute or ascribe: *The people placed confidence in their leader.* **8** to decide or state the position of (a horse) at the end of a race, especially of the first three: *The favorite was not even placed.* **9** to produce (sounds of song or speech) with emphasis upon resonance assisted by the body organs involved; pitch. *—v.i.* **1** to finish among the leaders in a race or competition: *The favorite failed to place in the first heat and was eliminated.* **2** to finish second in a horse race.

**give** (or **make**) **place, a** to make room; step aside: *Make place! bear back there!* (Ben Jonson). **b** *Figurative.* to yield; give in: *His anger gave place to remorse.*

**go places,** *Informal.* to advance rapidly toward success; achieve success: *The young assistant manager is going places in his company.*

**in place, a** in the proper or usual place; in the original place: *books in place on shelves.* **b** *Figurative.* fitting, appropriate, or timely; seasonable: *If Mr. Manss were not a successful pastor, he would be very much in place as a journalist* (Chicago Advance).

**in (the) place of,** instead of: *to receive extra pay in place of a vacation. Use water in place of milk in this recipe.*

**know one's place,** to act according to one's position in life: *If you are hired as a typist, you must know your place and not act like an office manager.*

**out of place, a** not in the proper or usual place: *The second volume seems to be out of place; I cannot find it on the shelf.* **b** *Figurative.* inappropriate or ill-timed; unsuitable: *Talk about the depths of being ... is not always out of place, but it is mostly idle chatter* (J. M. Cameron).

**places,** *Mathematics.* the number of figures in a number or series, especially after the decimal point in a decimal: *to mark off three places.*

**put (a person) in his place,** to lower a person's dignity, as by a rebuke; humble or degrade: *The liberals had expected the Kennedy administration to put Franco sharply in his place* (Alastair Reid).

**take place, a** to happen; occur: *Mr. Wilson reminded the House that the exploratory talks had been taking place* (Manchester Guardian Weekly). **b** *Obsolete.* to take precedence: *Though Miss Crawford is in a manner at home at the Parsonage, you are not to be taking place of her* (Jane Austen).

[< Old French *place* < Vulgar Latin *plattia,* for Latin *platēa* courtyard; earlier, street < Greek *plateîa* (*hodós*) broad (way) < *platýs* broad. See etym. of doublets **plaza, piazza.**]

*—Syn. n.* **2 Place, position, location** mean a particular portion of space, or of the earth's surface. **Place** is the general term: *a quiet place, a strange place for storing books.* **Position** is place with respect to another place or places or within a framework or reference: *We are in a good position to see the parade.* **Location** may be used for either *place* or *position,* but it stresses a little more than either of these the uniqueness or isolation of a place in relation to anything or everything outside it: *a good location for a housing project. The Crocker Ridge location also should give fine views of the peaks of the northern Yosemite* (Sierra Club Bulletin).

**place**[2] (plȧs), *n. French.* a public square in a city or town; plaza.

**place|a|ble** (plā′sə bəl), *adj.* that can be placed.

**place aux dames** (plȧs ō dȧm′), *French.* (make) way for the ladies.

**pla|ce|bo** (plə sē′bō), *n., pl.* **-bos** or **-boes. 1** a pill, preparation, or treatment given to a person as medicine, but actually containing no active ingredients. Placebos are sometimes given for psychological effect, especially to satisfy or please a patient who actually needs no additional medicine. They are also used as controls in testing the effectiveness of new medicines. *The bottle, as the doctor had reason to know, contained a placebo—sugar pills* (Time). **2** *Figurative.* a thing said merely to flatter, please, or mollify: *So arbitrary a substance seems more a placebo to quiet the disturbed mind than a valid explanation of a physical phenomenon* (John R. Pierce). **3** the vespers of the office for the dead in the Roman Catholic Church, from the beginning of the opening antiphon with the word *placebo* (In the Bible, Psalms 114:9 of the Vulgate; Psalms 116:9 of the Authorized Version). [< Latin *placēbō* I shall please]

**placebo effect,** the beneficial effect of placebos on certain patients: *Some disorders, and some patients, are more susceptible to placebo effect than others—arthritics particularly* (Sunday Times).

**place card,** a small card with a person's name on it, marking his place at a table.

**place|hold|er** (plās′hōl′dər), *n. Mathematics.* a symbol that holds the place for numerals that are being considered.

**place in the sun,** a favorable position; as favorable a position as any occupied by others.

**place kick,** the kicking of a ball placed or held on the ground in football and soccer.

**place-kick** (plās′kik′), *v.i.* to make a place kick. *—v.t.* **1** to kick (a ball) as a place kick. **2** to score (points or a goal) by means of a place kick: *Tackle Bill Miller place-kicked four conversions* (New York Times). **—place′-kick′er,** *n.*

**place|less** (plās′lis), *adj.* **1** having no place or locality; not local. **2** having no employment or public office.

**place|man** (plās′mən), *n., pl.* **-men.** a person who holds or aspires to an appointment or office, especially public office, without regard to his fitness for it.

**place mat,** a mat of linen, plastic, paper, or wood put under each person's plate or place setting.

**place|ment** (plās′mənt), *n.* **1** the act or process of placing: *Representatives of the social agencies that really do the work of child placement answered* (New York Times). **2** the state of being placed; location; arrangement. **3** the act or process of finding work or a job for a person. **4a** the act of placing a football on the ground for an attempt to kick a goal by a place kick. **b** the position of the ball thus placed. **c** = place kick.

**place name,** a name of a place or locality; any geographical name.

**pla|cen|ta** (plə sen′tə), *n., pl.* **-tae** (-tē), **-tas. 1** the organ by which the fetus is attached to the inner wall of the uterus and nourished: *Until the moment of birth a developing baby is entirely dependent upon the placenta* (Scientific American). **2** the tissue of the ovary of flowering plants to which the ovules are attached, usually the enlarged or modified margins of the carpellary leaves. **3** a structure that bears the sporangia in ferns. [< New Latin *placenta* (*uterina*) (uterine) cake < Latin *placenta* flat cake < Greek *plakoûs, -oûntos* placenta; flat seed of the mallow, short for *plakóeis* flat < *pláx, plakós* flat surface]

**pla|cen|tal** (plə sen′təl), *adj., n.* *—adj.* **1** of or having to do with the placenta. **2** having a placenta.
*—n.* a placental mammal.

**plac|en|tar|y** (plas′ən ter′ē, plə sen′tər-), *adj., n., pl.* **-tar|ies.** *—adj.* **1** of or having to do with the placenta; placental. **2** made or done with reference to the placenta or to placentation: *a placentary classification.*
*—n.* a placental mammal.

**pla|cen|tate** (plə sen′tāt), *adj.* = placental.

**plac|en|ta|tion** (plas′ən tā′shən), *n.* **1** the formation and disposition of the placenta in the uterus. **2** the structure of the placenta. **3** *Botany.* the disposition or arrangement of the placenta or placentae in the ovary.

**pla|cen|ti|form** (plə sen′tə fôrm), *adj.* having the form of a placenta.

**plac|er**[1] (plas′ər), *n.* **1** a deposit of sand, gravel, or earth in the bed of a stream, containing particles of gold or other valuable minerals. **2** a place where gold or other minerals can be washed out of loose sand or gravel. [American English < Spanish *placer,* variant of *placel* sandbank < *plaza;* see etym. under **plaza**]

**plac|er**[2] (plā′sər), *n.* a person or thing that places, locates, or sets.

**placer mining,** the washing of loose sand or gravel for gold or other minerals. **—placer miner.**

**plac|es** (plā′siz), *n.pl.* See under **place**[1].

**place-seek|er** (plās′sē′kər), *n. British.* a person who seeks to gain public office; placeman.

**place setting,** the service of dishes or silverware, or table linen, set for one person at a table.

**pla|cet** (plā′sit), *n.* an expression of assent or sanction; permission. [< Latin *placet* it pleases]

**place value,** the value of a digit as determined by its place in a number. In 438.7, the place values of the digits are 4 x 100, 3 x 10, 8 x 1, and 7 x 1/10.

**plac|id** (plas′id), *adj.* pleasantly calm or peaceful; quiet: *a placid lake, a placid temper. The small restaurant had an intimate and placid atmosphere. I think I could ... live with animals, they are so placid and self-contained* (Walt Whitman). **SYN:** unruffled, tranquil, serene. See syn. under **peaceful.** [< Latin *placidus* < *placēre* to please] **—plac′id|ly,** *adv.* **—plac′id|ness,** *n.*

**pla|cid|i|ty** (plə sid′ə tē), *n.* calmness; peace; tranquility. **SYN:** serenity, peacefulness.

**plack** (plak), *n.* **1** a small coin of little value, formerly current in Scotland. **2** *Scottish.* a bit; scarcely anything: *His offer isn't worth a plack.* [origin uncertain]

**plack|et** (plak′it), *n.* **1** an opening or slit in a garment, especially at the top of a skirt, to make it easy to put on. **2** a pocket in a skirt. **3** *Archaic.* **a** an apron. **b** a petticoat. **c** a woman. [perhaps (originally) *placcat* a kind of undergarment or armor, apparently variant of *placard*]

**placket hole, 1** an opening to give access to a pocket in a skirt. **2** = placket.

**plac|o|derm** (plak′ə dėrm), *n.* any one of a class of extinct sharklike fishes having primitive jaws, and hard, bony plates covering the body. The placoderms were the marine counterparts of the armored dinosaurs. [< Greek *pláx, plakós* flat surface + *dérma* skin]

**plac|oid** (plak′oid), *adj., n.* *—adj.* **1** platelike, as the hard, spiny scales of a shark. **2** having platelike scales.
*—n.* any fish having placoid scales.
[< New Latin *Placoidei* the group name < Greek *pláx, plakós* flat surface + *eîdos* form]

**pla|cu|na** (pla kü′nə), *n.* any one of a genus of oysters with thin shells that are cut into small squares in the Philippines and fitted together to make a window. [< New Latin *Placuna* the genus name < Greek *pláx, plakós* flat surface]

**pla|fond** (plȧ fôɴ′), *n. Architecture.* a ceiling, either flat or vaulted, especially one of a decorative character. [< earlier French *plafond* ceiling < *plat* flat (see etym. under **plat**[1]) + *fond* bottom. Compare etym. under **fond**[2], **fund.**]

**pla|gal** (plā′gəl), *adj. Music.* **1** designating a cadence in which the chord of the subdominant immediately precedes that of the tonic. **2** (in Gregorian music) designating a mode that has its compass a fourth below that of the corresponding authentic mode. The keynote (final tone) is the same as in the authentic mode (the fourth tone of the plagal mode). [< Medieval Latin *plagalis* < *plaga* plagal mode, apparently alteration of *plagius* plagal < Medieval Greek *plagios* < Greek, oblique < *plágos* side]

**plage** (plȧzh), *n.* bright and intensely hot cloud in the sun's chromosphere, usually, but not always, accompanying and surrounding a sunspot. Plages are primarily composed of calcium and hydrogen and emit very short ultraviolet rays. [< French *plage* region, zone, learned borrowing from Latin *plaga*]

**pla|gia|rism** (plā′jə riz əm), *n.* **1** the act of plagiarizing: *If an author is once detected in borrowing, he will be suspected of plagiarism ever after* (William Hazlitt). **2** something plagiarized; an idea, expression, plot, or the like, taken from another and used as one's own. [< Latin *plagiārius* literary thief, kidnaper; earlier, plunderer (< *plaga* snare, net) + English *-ism*]

**pla|gia|rist** (plā′jər ist), *n.* a person who plagiarizes.

**pla|gia|ris|tic** (plā′jə ris′tik), *adj.* **1** like a plagiarist. **2** having to do with or like plagiarism. **—pla′gia|ris′ti|cal|ly,** *adv.*

**pla|gia|rize** (plā′jə rīz), *v.,* **-rized, -riz|ing.** *—v.t.* to take and use as one's own (the thoughts, writings, or inventions of another), especially, to take and use (a passage, plot, or the like) from the work of another writer: *I could not help plagiarizing Miss Hannah More's first line* (Harriet Beecher Stowe).
*—v.i.* to take ideas, passages, or the like, and represent them as one's own: *He even had doubts whether in 'The Silent Places,' he had been plagiarizing, more or less unconsciously, from Henry James's 'Great Good Place'* (H. G. Wells). **—pla′gia|riz′er,** *n.*

**pla|gia|ry** (plā′jər ē), *n., pl.* **-ries. 1** = plagiarism. **2** = plagiarist. [< Latin *plagiārius* literary thief; see etym. under **plagiarism**]

**pla|gi|o|clase** (plā′jē ə klās), *n.* a triclinic feldspar containing either sodium or calcium and having its two prominent cleavage directions oblique to one another. [< German *Plagioklas* < Greek *plágios* oblique + *klásis* cleavage]

**pla|gi|o|clas|tic** (plā′jē ə klas′tik), *adj. Mineralogy.* characterized by two different cleavage directions oblique to each other, as certain feldspars.

**pla|gi|o|trop|ic** (plā′jē ə trop′ik), *adj.* **1** of or having to do with plagiotropism. **2** exhibiting plagiotropism. **—pla′gi|o|trop′i|cal|ly,** *adv.*

**pla|gi|ot|ro|pism** (plā′jē ot′rə piz əm), *n.* the fact or process of turning by which the organs of certain plants take up an oblique position more or less divergent from the vertical, as the result of reacting differently to the influences of light, gravitation, and other external forces. [< Greek *plágios* oblique, slanting + English *tropism*]

**plague** (plāg), *n., v.,* **plagued, pla|guing.** *—n.* **1** a very dangerous disease that spreads rapidly

**Pronunciation Key:** hat, āge, cãre, fär; let, ēqual, tėrm; it, īce; hot, ōpen, ôrder; oil, out; cup, pu̇t, rüle; child; long; thin; ᴛʜen; zh, measure; ə represents **a** in about, **e** in taken, **i** in pencil, **o** in lemon, **u** in circus.

and often causes many deaths. Plague is caused by bacteria. It occurs in several forms, one of which is bubonic plague. The plague is common in Asia and has several times swept through Europe. *Plague, the dreaded "Black Death" of the Middle Ages, may exist in non-fatal chronic form, contrary to longstanding assumptions of medical science* (Science News Letter). **2** any epidemic disease; pestilence. **3** a punishment thought to be sent by God: *the ten plagues of Egypt.* **4** *Figurative.* a thing or person that torments, vexes, annoys, troubles, offends, or is disagreeable: *a plague of counterfeit money.* **5** *Informal, Figurative.* trouble.
—*v.t.* **1a** to cause to suffer from a plague: *The Lord plagued Pharaoh and his house with great plagues* (Genesis 12:17). **b** *Figurative.* to trouble or torment in any manner: *God save thee, ancient Mariner! From the fiends, that plague thee thus!* (Samuel Taylor Coleridge). **2** *Figurative.* to vex; annoy; bother: *The little boy plagued his father by begging over and over to go to the zoo.* **SYN:** trouble, worry, pester, harass. See syn. under **tease.**

**plague on** (or **take**), may a plague, or mischief of some kind, befall (a thing, person, etc.): *Plague take the fellow!*

[Middle English *plage* < Middle French *plague,* learned borrowing from Late Latin *plāga* pestilence, < Latin, blow[1], wound[1], probably related to *plangere* to strike] —**pla′guer,** *n.*

**plague spot,** **1** a spot on the body which is due to a plague or pestilence. **2** a locality where there is a plague. **3** *Figurative.* a seat of some grave or foul evil: *a plague spot of vice. The town was a plague spot of rebellion.*

**plague-strick|en** (plāg′strik′ən), *adj.* stricken with a plague or pestilence.

**pla|gui|ly** (plā′gə lē), *adv. Informal.* plaguy.

**pla|guy** or **pla|guey** (plā′gē), *adj., adv. Informal.* —*adj.* **1** troublesome; annoying. **2** excessive; very great.
—*adv.* vexatiously; exceedingly: *It was plaguy hard on a fellow ... to be gulled that way* (Harriet Beecher Stowe).

**plaice** (plās), *n., pl.* **plaice** or (*occasionally*) **plaices.** **1** a large European flatfish that is important for food in Great Britain and parts of Europe. It sometimes weighs more than ten pounds. **2** any one of various American flatfishes or flounders. [< Old French *plaïs* < Late Latin *platessa* flatfish < Greek *platýs* flat[1]]

**plaid** (plad), *adj., n.* —*adj.* having a pattern of crisscross stripes, usually of different widths, in various colors: *a plaid dress.* **SYN:** checkered.
—*n.* **1** any cloth with a pattern of crisscross stripes, usually of different widths, in various colors: *She bought a yard of beautiful red plaid to make a skirt.* **2** a pattern of this kind; tartan: *We looked at the chart to see if we could find the plaid of our ancestors.* **3** a long piece of twilled woolen cloth, usually having a pattern of stripes in many colors, worn over one shoulder by the Scottish Highlanders: *The Gael around him threw His graceful plaid of varied hue* (Scott).
[< Scottish Gaelic *plaide* blanket, mantle]

**plaid|ed** (plad′id), *adj.* **1** made of plaid. **2** having a plaid pattern. **3** wearing a plaid.

**plaid|o|yer** (pled′wə yā′), *n. Law.* the speech of an advocate; a pleading; plea: *Legally, the testimony of these witnesses was immaterial—Mr. Hauser did not mention one of them in his last plaidoyer* (Hannah Arendt). [< French, noun use of *plaidoyer* to plead < *plaid* plea; see etym. under **plea**]

***plain**[1] (plān), *adj., adv., n.* —*adj.* **1** without ornament, decoration, or bright color; simple: *a plain dress.* **SYN:** unembellished. **2** all of one color; without figured pattern or varied weave: *a plain blue dress.* **3** not rich or highly seasoned: *plain food, a plain diet.* **4** simple in manner; not distinguished, as by rank, culture, or position; common; ordinary: *a plain man of the people.* **5** not pretty; homely: *a plain girl.* **6** without obstructions; open: *in plain sight or view.* **7** easily seen or heard; clear; evident; obvious; manifest: *The meaning is plain. It was plain he was offended.* **SYN:** apparent. **8** not very hard; easy: *Tell me what you want in a few plain words.* **SYN:** intelligible, simple. **9** that is clearly what the name expresses; unmistakable; downright; absolute: *plain foolishness.* **SYN:** undisguised, sheer. **10** not intricate; uncomplicated: *plain sewing.* **11** straightforward; direct: *to give a plain answer to a question.* **12** frank; honest; sincere; outspoken; candid: *plain speech. I will sing a song if anybody will sing another; else, to be plain with you, I will sing none* (Izaak Walton). **SYN:** unaffected. **13** flat; level; smooth: *plain ground. The crooked shall be made straight, and the rough places plain* (Isaiah 40:4). **14** in cards: **a** not a court card or an ace. **b** not trumps.
—*adv.* in a plain manner; clearly: *Talk plain so I can understand you.*
—*n.* **1** a flat stretch of land; tract of level or nearly level land; prairie: *The settlers could see for miles over the plain ahead.* See picture below. **2** a broad, level expanse, such as a lunar sea: *Whether or not the maria were ever seas—now at least, they are and for millions of years have been what we call plains* (Bernhard, Bennet, and Rice).

**plains,** (especially in North America) a level, treeless, or almost treeless, tract of country; prairie: *the Great Plains. Cattle and horses wandered over the western plains.*

**the Plain,** (in French history) a moderate party in the Legislative Assembly and the National Convention of the French Revolution (so called from its occupying seats on the main floor).
[< Old French *plain* < Latin *plānus* flat[1], level. See etym. of doublets **piano**[2], **plan, plane**[1].]
—**plain′ly,** *adv.* —**plain′ness,** *n.*

**plain**[2] (plān), *v.i. Archaic and Dialect.* to complain. [< Old French *plaign-,* stem of *plaindre,* earlier *plaingre* < Latin *plangere* lament, (literally) beat the breast]

**plain chant,** = plain song.

**plain|clothes** (plān′klōz′, -klōᴛʜz′), *adj.* not in uniform when on duty.

**plain clothes,** the ordinary dress of civil life; nonofficial dress.

**plain|clothes|man** (plān′klōz′mən, -klōᴛʜz′-), *n., pl.* **-men.** a policeman or detective wearing ordinary clothes, not a uniform, when on duty.

**plain dealer,** a person who deals frankly and honestly with others.

**plain dealing,** frank, honest dealing with others.

**plain|er** (plā′nər), *n. Dialect.* a complainer.

**plain Jane,** a girl or woman who is ordinary, homely, or unsophisticated.

**plain-Jane** (plān′jān′), *adj. Informal.* homely; simple; ordinary: *From these plain-Jane foundations, the author builds a fascinating and terrifying tale* (New Yorker).

**plain-laid** (plān′lād′), *adj.* (of a rope) made by twisting three strands together from left to right or clockwise with the ends held away.

**Plain People,** any one of several religious groups, including the Amish and the Mennonites, who stress simplicity in clothing and in living.

**plains** (plānz), *n.pl.* See under **plain**[1].

**plain sail,** **1** the sails used in ordinary sailing, collectively, as distinguished from flying sails and special rigging. **2** any one of these sails.

**plain sailing,** **1** a simple or easy course of action; clear path or line of progress: *Albert had foreseen that his married life would not be all plain sailing* (Lytton Strachey). **2** sailing on a smooth, easy course, free of difficulty or obstruction.

**Plains Indian** (plānz), a member of any one of the tribes of North American Indians which formerly inhabited the Great Plains. They were of various linguistic stocks (Algonkian, Athapascan, Caddoan, Kiowan, Siouan, Uto-Aztecan), but shared a culture based on their nomadic following of the buffalo.

**plains|man** (plānz′mən), *n., pl.* **-men.** a man who lives on the plains; inhabitant or native of flat country.

**plain song,** or **plain|song** (plān′sông′, -song′),

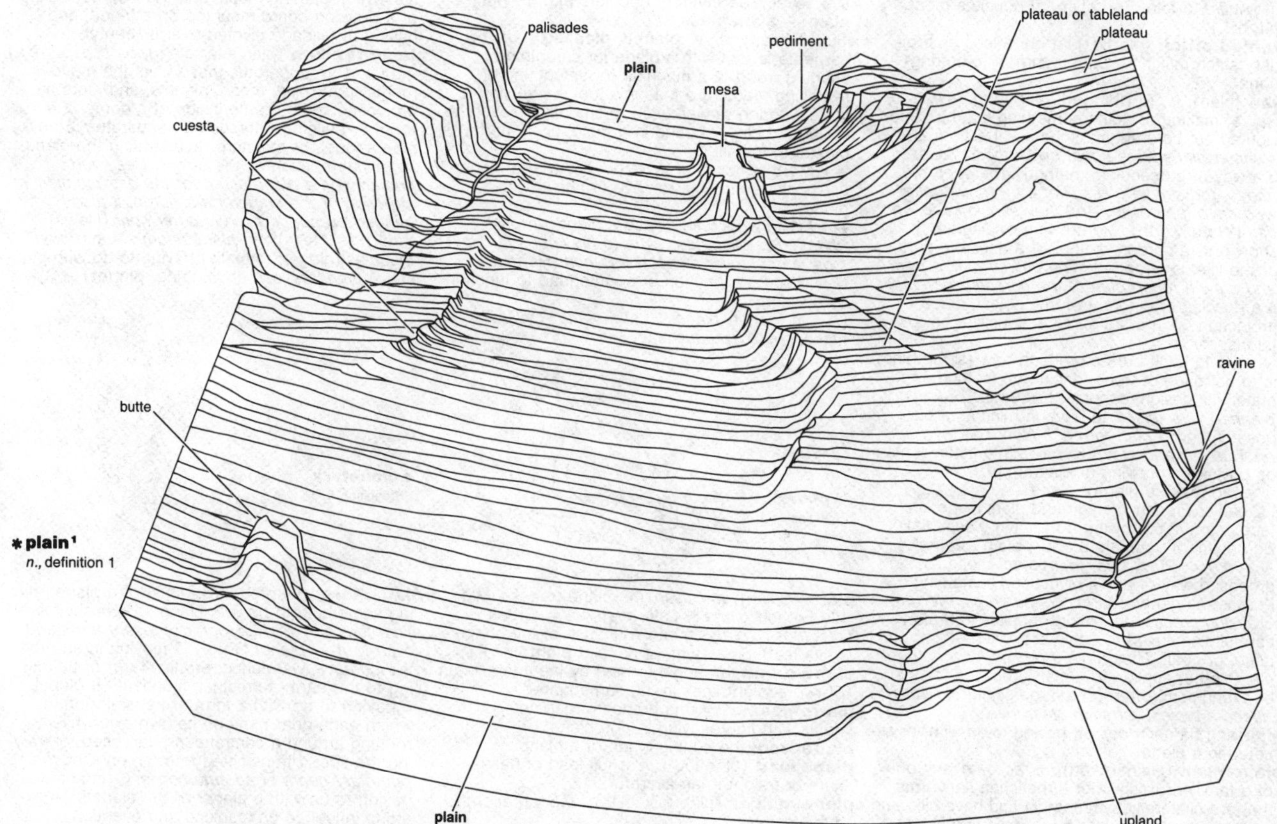


***plain**[1]
*n.,* definition 1

*n.* **1** vocal music used in the Christian church from the earliest times. Plain song is sung in unison. It is rhythmical, although the beats are not regular. **2** a melody taken as the theme for a contrapuntal treatment. **3** any simple melody or musical theme.

**plain-spo·ken** (plān′spō′kən), *adj.* plain or frank in speech: *a plain-spoken man, a plain-spoken rebuke.* SYN: blunt, outspoken, candid. —**plain′-spo′ken·ness**, *n.*

**plain·stones** (plān′stōnz′), *n.pl. Scottish.* flagstones.

**plaint** (plānt), *n.* **1** = complaint. **2** *Law.* an oral or written statement of the cause for an action. **3** *Archaic.* a lament. [< Old French *plaint* < Latin *plānctus, -ūs* lamentation < *plangere* to lament, beat the breast]

**plain·text** (plān′tekst′), *n.* **1** the text of any message that conveys an intelligible meaning in the language in which it is written, having no hidden meaning. **2** the intelligible text intended for, or derived from, a cryptogram: *Cryptography aims at making the message unintelligible to outsiders by various transformations of the plaintext* (Scientific American).

**plain·tiff** (plān′tif), *n.* a person who begins a lawsuit: *The plaintiff accused the defendant of fraud.* [< Anglo-French *plaintiff,* noun use of Old French *plaintif* complaining; see etym. under **plaintive**]

**plain·tive** (plān′tiv), *adj.* expressive of sorrow; mournful; sad: *a plaintive song, the plaintive cry of a bird.* SYN: melancholy, doleful, sorrowful. [< Old French *plaintif, plaintive* < *plaint* plaint] —**plain′tive·ly**, *adv.* —**plain′tive·ness**, *n.*

**plain tripe**, the walls of the first stomach or rumen of a ruminant animal, especially of a steer or cow, used as food.

**plain weave**, a simple weave of lengthwise threads set evenly with crosswise threads over one warp and under the next. Gingham, percale, shantung, and tweed are plain weave.

**plain-wo·ven** (plān′wō′vən), *adj.* woven with a plain weave, without twill, figure, or the like.

**plai·sance** (plā zäns′; *French* ple zäns′), *n.* a pleasure ground or place of amusements: *the Midway Plaisance at Chicago in 1893.* [< Old French *plaisance* pleasure. See etym. of doublet **pleasance**.]

**plais·ter** (plās′tər), *n., v.t. Obsolete.* plaster.

**plait** (*n., v. 1* plāt, plat; *n., v. 2* plāt, plēt), *n.* **1** a braid of hair, ribbon, and the like: *She wore her hair in a plait.* **2** = pleat.
—*v.t.* **1** to braid: *She plaits her hair.* **2** to pleat: [*He*] *wore his shirt plaited and puffed out* (Washington Irving).
[< Old French *pleit* fold[1], way of folding < Latin *plicitum,* variant of *plicātum,* neuter past participle of *plicāre* to fold. See etym. of doublets **pleat**, **plight**[1].]

**plait·ed stitch** (plā′tid, plat′id), a long embroidery stitch making a pattern similar to herringbone.

**plan** (plan), *n., v.,* **planned, plan·ning.** —*n.* **1** a way of making or doing something that has been worked out beforehand; scheme of action: *Our summer plans were upset by Mother's illness.* **2** a way of proceeding; method: *The good old rule ... the simple plan, That they should take, who have the power, And they should keep who can* (Wordsworth). **3** a drawing or diagram to show how a garden, a floor of a house, a park, or the like, is arranged: *The builder took a pencil and drew a rough plan of the garage on a plank.* **4** a drawing or diagram of any object, made by projection upon a flat surface, usually a horizontal plane.
—*v.t.* **1** to think out beforehand how (something) is to be made or done; decide on methods and materials; design, scheme, or devise: *Have you planned your trip?* **2** to have in mind as a purpose; intend: *I plan to reach New York by train on Tuesday and stay two days.* **3** to make a plan of; prepare a drawing or diagram of.
—*v.i.* to make a plan or plans.
[< earlier French *plan* ground plan; plane surface, learned borrowing from Latin *plānus* flat[1]. See etym. of doublets **piano**[2], **plain**[1], **plane**[1].]
—*Syn. n.* **1 Plan, design, project** mean a proposed way of doing or making something. **Plan** is the general term: *He has a plan for increasing production.* **Design** applies to a plan carefully contrived to achieve a given effect, purpose, or goal: *They have a design for a rich, full life.* **Project** applies to a plan proposed for trial or experiment, often on a large scale: *He introduced a project for slum clearance.*

**pla·nar** (plā′nər), *adj.* of, having to do with, or situated in a plane.

**pla·nar·i·an** (plə nãr′ē ən), *n., adj.* —*n.* any one of a family of freshwater turbellarian flatworms that are bilaterally symmetrical and have cilia and an intestine divided into three main branches: *A planarian can regenerate missing body parts. If the body is cut into two or three pieces, each piece can grow into a whole planarian* (J. A. McLeod). —*adj.* of or belonging to the planarians. [< New Latin *Planaria* the earlier genus name (< feminine of Late Latin *plānārius* level, as ground < Latin *plānus* flat[1], level) + English *-an*]

**pla·nar·i·ty** (plə nar′ə tē), *n.* the quality or state of being planar; flatness: *the planarity of the molecular structure.*

**pla·na·tion** (plā nā′shən), *n. Geology.* the process of erosion and deposition by which a stream produces a nearly level land surface. [< Latin *plānum* plane[1] + English *-ation*]

**planch** or **planche** (planch, plänch), *n.* **1** a slab or flat piece or metal, stone, or baked clay. **2** *Dialect.* **a** a plank; board. **b** a floor. [< Old French *planche* < Late Latin *planca* board, slab. See etym. of doublet **plank**.]

**plan·chet** (plan′chit), *n.* a flat piece of metal to be stamped to form a coin. [< *planch* + *-et;* see etym. under **planch**]

**plan·chette** (plan shet′), *n.* **1** a small board supported on two casters and a vertical pencil. The pencil is supposed to write words or phrases when a person rests his fingers lightly on the planchette. **2** the small board on legs that touches letters or words on an Ouija board. [earlier, small plank < French *planchette* (diminutive) < Old French *planche* plank; see etym. under **planch**]

**Planck's constant** (plangks), *Physics.* a universal constant having the value of the ratio of the energy of a quantum to its frequency, that is, energy equals Planck's constant times frequency. *Symbol:* h; *Value:* 6.624 $\times 10^{-27}$ erg-sec. [< Max *Planck,* 1858-1947, a German physicist, who first recognized it]

**plane**[1] (plān), *n., adj., v.,* **planed, plan·ing.** —*n.* **1** = airplane. **2** a level; grade: *Try to keep your work on a high plane.* **3** a flat or level surface: *The plane of the table was warped by dampness.* **4** a thin, flat, or curved supporting surface of an airplane. **5** a surface such that if any two points on it are joined by a straight line, the line will be contained wholly in the surface.
—*adj.* **1** flat; level; not convex or concave: *The plane lens was like a coin, without curvature.* **2** having a flat or level surface. **3** being wholly in a plane: *a plane figure.* **4** of or having to do with figures wholly in a plane. See also **plane geometry**.
—*v.i.* **1** to travel by airplane: *The President's son planed in from Washington* (Time). **2** to glide or soar, as an airplane does. **3** (of a boat or water skier) to rise slightly out of the water while moving at great speed.
[< Latin *plānum* level surface, and *plānus,* adjective, level. See etym. of doublets **piano**[2], **plain**[1], **plan**.] —**plane′ness**, *n.*

***plane**[2] (plān), *n., v.,* **planed, plan·ing.** —*n.* **1** a carpenter's tool with a blade for smoothing or shaping wood. **2** a machine for smoothing or removing metal. **3** a mason's tool resembling a large wooden trowel, used to smooth or level the surface of clay, of sand in a mold, or of mortar or plaster in a wall.
—*v.t.* **1** to smooth or level (wood) with a plane; use a plane on. **2** to remove or shave with a plane.
—*v.i.* **1** to work with or use a plane: *a rosy-cheeked Englishman ... up to his knees in shavings, and planing away at a bench* (Herman Melville). **2** to function or be intended to function as a plane.
[< Old French *plane* < Latin *plāna* < *plānāre* make level < *plānus* plain[1]]

blade

***plane**[2]
definition 1

**plane**[3] (plān), *n. British.* the plane tree. [< Middle French *plane* < Latin *platanus* < Greek *plátanos* < *platýs* broad (because of the shape of its leaf). See etym. of doublet **plantain**[1].]

**plane angle**, an angle formed by the intersection of two straight lines in the same plane.

**plane geometry**, the branch of geometry that deals with figures lying in one plane.

**plane iron**, the cutting blade of a plane.

**plane·load** (plān′lōd′), *n.* a full load of passengers or freight in an aircraft.

**plane·mak·er** (plān′mā′kər), *n. U.S.* an aircraft manufacturer.

**plane of symmetry**, a vertical plane that divides a symmetrical object, such as an aircraft, into symmetrical halves.

**plane-po·lar·ized** (plān′pō′lər īzd), *adj.* (of light) polarized so that all the vibrations of the waves take place in one plane.

**plane-post** (plān′pōst′), *v.t. British.* to send or convey (letters or other mail) by plane post.

**plane post**, *British.* a postal service conducted by airplane; air post.

**plan·er** (plā′nər), *n.* a person or thing that planes, especially a machine for planing wood or for finishing flat surfaces on metal.

**planer tree**, a small tree of the elm family, of the southeastern United States, producing a small, oval, nutlike fruit and having a hard, light-brown wood. [< New Latin *Planera* the genus name < Johann J. *Planer,* 1743-1789, a German botanist]

**plane sailing**, the navigation of a vessel in which courses are plotted and distances estimated as if the earth's surface were a plane.

**plane-shear** (plān′shir′), *n.* = plank-sheer.

**plane·side** (plān′sīd′), *n., adj.* —*n.* the area beside an airplane: *By the time I walk from planeside to a taxi, a cold wind sweeps across the airport* (Saturday Review).
—*adj.* at the planeside; beside an airplane: *a planeside interview.*

**plane spotter**, a person, usually a civilian volunteer, who watches for and reports the presence of enemy, or any unidentified, aircraft in an area of the sky.

**plan·et** (plan′it), *n.* **1** one of the heavenly bodies (except comets or meteors) that move around the sun in nearly circular paths. Mercury, Venus, Earth, Mars, Jupiter, Saturn, Uranus, Neptune, and Pluto are planets. Other planets are the asteroids or planetoids between Mars and Jupiter. *The planets vary in size from Jupiter, which has a diameter 11 times as large as the earth's, to Mercury, with a diameter less than half that of the earth* (Hyron Spinrad). **2** any similar body revolving around a star other than the sun: *Observe how system into system runs, What other planets circle other suns* (Alexander Pope). **3** (in astrology) a heavenly body supposed to influence people's lives and events. **4** *Figurative.* anything thought to exert such influence. **5** *Obsolete.* one of the seven heavenly bodies (the sun, the moon, Mercury, Venus, Mars, Jupiter, and Saturn) known since ancient times and distinguished by ancient peoples from the fixed stars in that they seem to move among the fixed stars, when viewed from Earth. [< Old French *planete,* learned borrowing from Late Latin *planētēs,* plural < Greek *planētēs* (*astéres*) wandering stars < *planâsthai* to wander] —**plan′et·like′**, *adj.*

**plane table**, an instrument used in the field for surveying, plotting maps, and the like, consisting of a drawing board mounted on a tripod, and having an alidade pivoted over its center.

**plan·e·tar·i·um** (plan′ə tãr′ē əm), *n., pl.* **-i·a** (-ē ə), **-i·ums.** **1** an apparatus that shows the movements of the sun, moon, planets, and stars by projecting lights on the inside of a dome. **2** a room or building with such an apparatus. **3** any plan, model, or structure representing the planetary system, such as the orrery: *Designed primarily as a planetarium for the astronomical instruction of the emperor's children, it also banged on gongs every quarter hour* (Newsweek). [< New Latin *planetarium* < Latin *planētārius* astrologer; (literally) having to do with planets < *planētēs;* see etym. under **planet**]

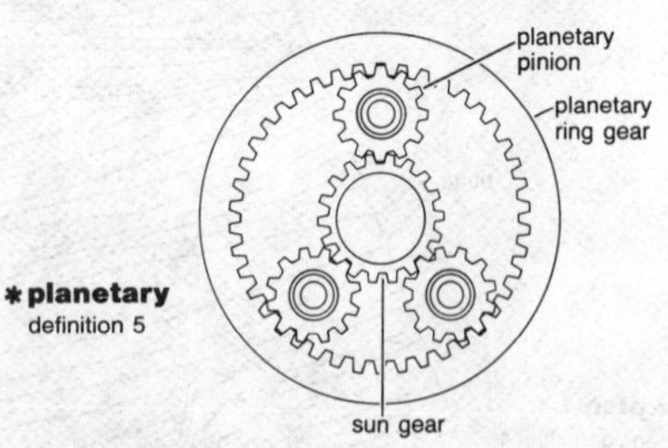


***planetary**
definition 5

***plan·e·tar·y** (plan′ə ter′ē), *adj.* **1** of a planet; having something to do with planets: *Planetary satellites turn only fast enough to present the same face to their planet* (Time). **2** moving in an orbit. **3** *Figurative.* wandering; erratic. **4a** of or belonging to the earth; terrestrial; mundane. **b** global. **5** having to do with a form of transmission in which each gear turns on its own axis while rotating around a central sun gear, used for varying the speed transmitted from an engine: *the planetary gears of an automobile.* **6** (in astrology) having to do with a planet or the planets as exerting influence on mankind and events.

**planetary nebula**, a nebula consisting of an envelope of gas many billions of miles in diameter surrounding a very hot star. The famous Ring Nebula in Lyra is a planetary nebula.

**planetary wave**, *Meteorology.* a strong current of air, 30,000 to 40,000 feet above the earth's surface, that circles the earth in the Northern Hemisphere, flowing generally from west to east.

**planetary wind**, = planetary wave.

**plan|e|tes|i|mal** (plan′ə tes′ə məl), *adj., n.* **—*adj.*** of or having to do with the planetesimal hypothesis.
**—*n.*** one of the minute bodies of the planetesimal hypothesis: *The mass of gas eventually cooled, congealing into small solid lumps, the planetesimals* (Atlantic).
[< *planet* + *-esimal,* as in *infinitesimal*]

**planetesimal hypothesis** or **theory**, the hypothesis that minute bodies in space move in planetary orbits and gradually unite to form the planets of a given planetary system.

**plan|et|oid** (plan′ə toid), *n.* a very small planet; asteroid: *Scientists like to think that these planetoids may be pieces of a big planet that once upon a time traveled around the sun between Mars and Jupiter* (Beauchamp, Mayfield, and West). [< *planet* + *-oid*]

**plan|et|oi|dal** (plan′ə toi′dəl), *adj.* of, having to do with, or like a planetoid.

**pla|net|o|khod** (plə net′ə ʜôt′), *n.* a vehicle like the Lunokhod designed by Soviet scientists for exploration of the planets. [< Russian *planetokhod* (literally) planet walker]

**plan|et|ol|o|gist** (plan′ə tol′ə jist), *n.* a person skilled in planetology.

**plan|et|ol|o|gy** (plan′ə tol′ə jē), *n.* the scientific study of the planets: *General planetology [is] a branch of astronomy that deals with the study and interpretation of the physical and chemical properties of planets* (New Scientist).

**plane tree**, any one of a group of tall, spreading trees, with broad, angular, palmately lobed leaves and bark that scales off in irregular patches; platan. One kind, a native of Iran and the Levant, is commonly planted as an ornamental tree in Europe. In the United States, plane trees are usually called buttonwood, sycamore, or buttonball.

**plan|et-strick|en** (plan′it strik′ən), *adj.* = planet-struck.

**plan|et-struck** (plan′it struk′), *adj.* **1** stricken by the supposed influence of a planet; blasted. **2** = panic-stricken.

**planet wheel**, any of the cogwheels, gears, or the like, in an epicyclic train, whose axes revolve around the common center, or central gear.

**plane wave**, the simplest kind of electromagnetic wave, moving through space in a straight line.

**plan|form** (plan′fôrm′), *n.* the form or shape of an object, as an airfoil, as seen from above: *A greater proportion of the planform might be filled with passengers* (New Scientist).

**plan|gen|cy** (plan′jən sē), *n.* the quality of being plangent.

**plan|gent** (plan′jənt), *adj.* **1** making the noise of waves breaking or beating on the shore: *the weltering of the plangent wave* (Sir Henry Taylor). **2** having a loud metallic or plaintive sound; resounding loudly: *St. Margaret's bells ... Hark! how those plangent comforters call and cry* (William Ernest Henley). [< Latin *plangēns, -entis,* present participle of *plangere* to beat the breast, lament] **—plan′gent|ly,** *adv.*

**plan|gor|ous** (plang′gər əs), *adj.* characterized by loud lamentation; wailing. [< Latin *plangor* (< *plangere* to lament) + English *-ous*]

**plan|hold|er** (plan′hōl′dər), *n.* a shareholder in a pension plan: *When the planholder reaches retirement, he draws a pension expressed in units—helping to offset subsequent rises in the cost of living* (Sunday Times).

**plan|i|fi|ca|tion** (plan′ə fə kā′shən), *n.* the act or process of planning: *economic planification.* [< French *planification* < *plan;* see etym. under **plan**]

**pla|nim|e|ter** (plə nim′ə tər), *n.* an instrument for measuring mechanically the area of plane figures by tracing their boundaries with a pointer. [< Latin *plānus* level + English *-meter*]

**plan|i|met|ric** (plan′ə met′rik), *adj.* having to do with planimetry or the measurement of plane surfaces.

**plan|i|met|ri|cal** (plan′ə met′rə kəl), *adj.* = planimetric.

**pla|nim|e|try** (plə nim′ə trē), *n.* the measurement of plane surfaces.

**pla|ni|ros|tral** (plā′nə ros′trəl), *adj.* having a broad, flat beak. [< Latin *plānus* flat + English *rostral*]

**plan|ish** (plan′ish), *v.t.* to flatten, smooth, or toughen (metal), especially by hammering lightly or rolling. [< obsolete French *planiss-,* stem of *planir* to smooth < *plan* plain¹, flat]

**plan|i|sphere** (plan′ə sfir), *n.* a projection or representation of the whole or a part of a sphere on a plane, especially a map of half or more of the celestial sphere with an adjustable device to show the part of the heavens visible at a given time. [< Medieval Latin *planisphaerium* < Latin *plānus* plain¹, flat + *sphaera* sphere < Greek *sphaîra*]

**pla|ni|spi|ral** (plā′nə spī′rəl), *adj.* = planospiral.

**plank** (plangk), *n., v.* **—*n.*** **1** a long, flat piece of sawed timber, thicker than a board, especially one more than two inches thick and four inches wide: *The deck of the sailing ship was made of thick planks.* **2** timber consisting of such pieces; planking. **3** a flat timber forming part of the outer side of a ship's hull. **4** *Figurative.* an article or feature of the platform of a political party or other organization: *State's rights ... a major plank in his election campaign* (New York Times). **5** *Figurative.* anything that supports or saves in time of need (with allusion to the use of a plank to save a shipwrecked man from drowning).
**—*v.t.*** **1** to cover or furnish with planks: *to plank a ship's deck.* **2** to cook and serve on a board, often with a decorative border of vegetables and potatoes: *planked steak or fish.* **3** *Informal.* to put or set with force: *He planked down the package. He finished the glass and planked it down firmly on the table* (Arnold Bennett). **4** *Informal.* to pay at once: *She planked down her money.*
**walk the plank, a** to be put to death by being forced to walk off a plank extending from a ship's side over the water. Pirates used to make their prisoners do this. *It would have been necessary for Howe and Nelson to make every French sailor whom they took walk the plank* (Macaulay). **b** *Figurative.* to be dismissed from one's job: *His work was unsatisfactory and it was not long before he walked the plank.*
[< Old North French, Old French *planche* < Late Latin *planca* board, marble slab. See etym. of doublet **planch.**]

**plank|ing** (plang′king), *n.* **1** the act or process of laying or covering with planks. **2** planks collectively. **3** the outer side of a ship's hull.

**plank-sheer** (plangk′shir′), *n.* one of the planks laid across the tops of the ribs or the frame of the hull of a ship at the line of the deck; gunwale.

**plank|ter** (plang′tər), *n.* any one of the organisms in a plankton: *The sediments are made up in part of the remains of the innumerable plankters that swarm in fertile seas* (Science News). [< Greek *planktēr* wanderer < *planktós* wandering; see etym. under **plankton**]

**plank|ton** (plangk′tən), *n.* the small animal and plant organisms that float or drift in water, especially at or near the surface. Plankton includes small crustaceans, algae, and protozoans, and serves as an important source of food for larger animals, such as fish. *Fine mesh nets are towed from a ship to bring up hundreds of kinds of microscopic sea life, lumped under the general name of plankton* (Science News Letter). [< German *Plankton* < Greek *planktón,* neuter of *planktós* wandering, drifting < *plázesthai* to wander]

**plank|ton|ic** (plangk ton′ik), *adj.* **1** of or having to do with plankton. **2** characteristic of plankton.

**plan|less** (plan′lis), *adj.* without a plan or design; haphazard; unsystematic. **SYN:** disorderly. **—plan′less|ly,** *adv.* **—plan′less|ness,** *n.*

**planned obsolescence**, the manufacture of products designed to deteriorate or become outdated after a shorter period of time than might normally be expected: *"planned obsolescence," the policy of redesigning each year to keep the buyers coming back* (Jerry M. Flint).

**planned parenthood**, regulation or limitation of the number of children in a family by means of birth control; family planning: *Planned parenthood in wedlock by the use of contraceptive devices cannot constitutionally be forbidden* (Arthur Krock).

**plan|ner** (plan′ər), *n.* a person who plans or makes a plan; deviser; arranger: *Secret intelligence reports on the Soviet Army have given U.S. planners an unexpected jolt* (Newsweek).

**plan|o|blast** (plan′ə blast), *n.* the free-swimming form of certain hydrozoans. [< Greek *plános* wandering + *blastós* germ, sprout]

***plano-concave**
***plano-convex**

plano-concave lens plano-convex lens

***pla|no-con|cave** (plā′nō kon′kāv, -kong′-), *adj.* flat on one side and concave on the other. [< Latin *plānus* flat + English *concave*]

***pla|no-con|vex** (plā′nō kon′veks), *adj.* flat on one side and convex on the other. [< Latin *plānus* flat + English *convex*]

**pla|no-cy|lin|dri|cal** (plā′nō sə lin′drə kəl), *adj.* flat on one side and cylindrical on the other. [< Latin *plānus* flat]

**pla|no|graph** (plā′nə graf, -gräf), *v., n.* **—*v.t.*** to print from a plane surface.
**—*n.*** a print or plate made by planography.

**plan|o|graph|ic** (plan′ə graf′ik), *adj.* **1** having to do with planography. **2** used in planography. **3** produced by planography: *Offset is a planographic technique.*

**plan|og|ra|phist** (pla nog′rə fist), *n.* a person who prints by means of planography.

**plan|og|ra|phy** (pla nog′rə fē), *n.* printing done from plane surfaces, as in lithography, collotype, and offset, in contrast to intaglio or relief work. [< Latin *plānus* level + English *-graphy*]

**pla|nom|e|ter** (plə nom′ə tər), *n.* a flat plate, usually of iron, used as a standard gauge for plane surfaces. [< Latin *plānus* flat + English *-meter*]

**pla|no|spi|ral** (plā′nō spī′rəl), *adj.* coiled in one plane: *The shell of the nautilus is planospiral.* [< Latin *plānus* flat + English *spiral*]

**plan position indicator**, a circular radarscope with a graduated scale and concentric rings that show the direction and distance of the object tracked, echoes from which appear on the screen as bright, arc-shaped blips. *Abbr:* PPI (no periods).

**plant** (plant, plänt), *n., v.* **—*n.*** **1** any living thing that is not an animal; a vegetable, in the widest sense. A plant is traditionally distinguished from an animal by the absence of locomotion and of special organs of sensation and digestion, and by its power of living wholly upon inorganic substances. Trees, shrubs, vines, grass, vegetables, seaweed, fungi, and algae are plants. *The oxygen in the air we breathe comes from plants* (Donald Mandell). **2** an herb or other living thing that has leaves, roots, and a soft stem, and is small in contrast with a tree or a shrub: *a tomato plant, a house plant.* **3** a shoot or slip recently sprouted from seed, or rooted as a cutting or layer. **4** a young growth ready to be set out in another place: *The farmer set out 100 cabbage plants.* **5** the buildings, machinery, and tools used in manufacturing some article, producing power, or carrying on some other industrial process: *an aircraft plant, a power plant.* **6** the workmen employed at a plant: *The whole plant is on strike.* **7** the complete apparatus used for a specific mechanical operation or process: *the heating plant on a ship.* **8** the complete equipment for any purpose: *a plant of a few hundred aeroplanes ... armed with machine guns, and the motor repair vans and so forth needed to go with the aeroplanes* (H. G. Wells). **9** the buildings, equipment, or any other material resources belonging to, or needed to maintain, an institution: *a college plant.* (*Figurative.*) *No one knows the total cost of bringing the U.S. educational plant up to the size required to handle expected enrollments* (Wall Street Journal). **10** *Slang.* a scheme or plot to swindle or defraud a person: *"It's a conspiracy," said Ben Allen. "A regular plant," added Mr. Bob Sawyer* (Dickens). **11** *Slang.* a person or thing so placed or a plan so devised as to trap, trick, lure, or deceive criminals or wrongdoers. **12** *Figurative.* a person, supposedly a member of the audience, who assists a performer on the stage: *a magician's plant.*
**—*v.t.*** **1** to put in the ground to grow, as seeds, young trees, shoots, or cuttings: *to plant potatoes.* **2** to lay out and prepare by putting seed or seedlings in the ground; furnish with plants: *to plant an orchard or a crop, to plant a field with trees. Growers are expected to plant 17,443,000 acres to cotton this year* (New York Times). **3** to set firmly; put; place: *Columbus planted the Spanish flag in the ground. The boy planted his feet far apart.* **4** to post; station: *to plant guards at an entrance.* **5** to establish (as a colony or city); settle. **6** to establish (a person) as a settler or colonist. **7** to colonize or settle (an area); stock, as with inhabitants or cattle. **8** to locate or situate: *a town planted at the mouth of a river.* **9** *Figurative.* to put in (ideas or feelings); introduce and establish firmly (a doctrine, religion, principle, or practice): *Parents try to plant ideas in their children. That noble thirst of fame and reputation which is planted in the hearts of all men* (Sir Richard Steele). **10** to introduce (a breed of animals) into a country. **11** to deposit (young fish, spawn, oysters), as in a river or tidal

**Pronunciation Key:** hat, āge, cãre, fär; let, ēqual, tėrm; it, īce; hot, ōpen, ôrder; oil, out; cup, pu̇t, rüle; child; long; thin; ᴛʜen; zh, measure; ə represents **a** in about, **e** in taken, **i** in pencil, **o** in lemon, **u** in circus.

water. 12 *Slang, Figurative.* to deliver (as a blow) with a definite aim. 13 *Slang, Figurative.* to hide (as something stolen). 14 *Slang, Figurative.* to place (a person or thing) as a plant, trap, or trick: *[He] denied that the story had been "planted" with him by a Government source* (New York Times). 15 *Slang.* to salt (a mine or claim). [partly Old English *plante* young plant, sprout, cutting (< Latin *planta* sprout), and partly < Old French *plante* plant < Medieval Latin *planta* plant < Latin] —**plant′like′**, *adj.*

**Plan|tag|e|net** (plan taj′ə nit), *n.* a member of the royal family that ruled England from 1154 to 1485. The English kings from Henry II through Richard III were Plantagenets. The houses of Lancaster and York were branches of this family.

**plan|ta|gi|na|ceous** (plan′tə jə nā′shəs), *adj.* belonging to the family of plants typified by the plantain. [< New Latin *Plantaginaceae* the family name (< Latin *plantāgo* plantain[2]) + English *-ous*]

**plan|tain**[1] (plan′tən), *n.* 1 a treelike, tropical, herbaceous plant closely related to the banana. 2 its fruit, longer and more starchy than the banana, and usually eaten cooked. It is one of the chief articles of food in tropical countries. [< Spanish *plátano,* learned borrowing from Latin *platanus* < Greek *plátanos* < *platýs* broad (because of the shape of its leaf). See etym. of doublet **plane**[3].]

**plan|tain**[2] (plan′tən), *n.* 1 a common weed with broad, flat leaves spread out close to the ground, and long, slender spikes carrying seeds and tiny greenish flowers. 2 any of several related herbs. [< Old French *plantain* < Vulgar Latin *plantanus* < Latin *plantāgo, -inis* < *planta* sole of the foot (because of its flat leaves)]

**plantain lily**, any lily of a group native to China and Japan, grown for its attractive ribbed foliage and tubular white or bluish flowers; funkia.

**plant-an|i|mal** (plant′an′ə məl), *n.* = zoophyte.

**plan|tar** (plan′tər), *adj.* of or having to do with the sole of the foot: *a plantar wart.* [< Latin *plantāris* < *planta* sole of the foot]

**plantar arch**, the main arch of the foot, extending from the heel to the ball of the foot.

**plan|ta|tion** (plan tā′shən), *n.* 1 a large farm or estate, especially in a tropical or semitropical climate, on which cotton, tobacco, sugar cane, coffee, rubber trees, or other crops are raised. The work on a plantation is done by laborers who live there. 2 a large group of trees or other plants that have been planted: *a rubber plantation. From its palm plantations comes much of the oil for Britons' soap and margarine* (Newsweek). 3 a colony; settlement: *the Virginia plantation.* 4 a local, minor civil division in Maine: *Local government is administered by the state's three classes of municipalities—towns, cities, and plantations* (Robert M. York). 5 the act of planting. [< Latin *plantātiō, -ōnis* a planting < *plantāre* to plant < *planta* a sprout]

**plant bug**, any one of various hemipterous insects that attack the flowers, leaves, and fruit of many plants.

**plant caterpillar**, a caterpillar, the larva of any one of several Australasian moths, within which a parasitic fungus is growing, killing the caterpillar and sending up a long shoot from the head.

**plant|er** (plan′tər, plän′-), *n.* 1 a person who owns or runs a plantation: *a cotton planter. One of the most considerable planters in the Brazils* (Daniel Defoe). 2 a machine for planting: *a corn planter.* 3 a person who plants. 4 an early settler; colonist. 5 a box, stand, or other holder, usually decorative, for house plants: *Hand-crafted, copper bound redwood planters in three smart shapes* (Wall Street Journal).

**planter's punch**, a sweet punch made with rum and flavored with lemon or lime juice.

**plant food**, any natural or chemical fertilizer.

**plant hopper**, = lantern fly.

**plant hormone**, any one of a group of substances that affect the growth of plants, including auxins, gibberellins, cytokinins, abscisic acid, and ethylene.

**plan|ti|grade** (plan′tə grād), *adj., n.* —*adj.* walking on the whole sole of the foot, as bears, raccoons, and men do. —*n.* a plantigrade animal. [< French *plantigrade* < Latin *planta* sole of the foot + *gradus, -ūs* step, related to *gradī* walk]

**plant|i|mal** (plan′tə məl), *n.* a living cell or organism formed by the fusion of animal and plant cells: *Three separate research groups have now successfully fused animal cells with plant cells to form the first ... "plantimals"* (Science News). [< *plant* + (an)*imal*]

**Plan|tin** (plôn taN′), *n.* a printing type of the old style, popular in Europe, based on the designs of the French printer Christophe Plantin, 1520-1589.

**plant kingdom**, all plants, as distinguished from animals and minerals; vegetable kingdom.

**plant|let** (plant′lit, plänt′-), *n.* 1 an undeveloped or rudimentary plant. 2 a small plant.

**plant louse**, an aphid or related insect which sucks juices from plants.

**plan|toc|ra|cy** (plan tok′rə sē), *n., pl.* **-cies.** 1 government by planters. 2 plantation owners as a class: *From sugar, rum, coffee, and slavery, a rich plantocracy grew* (Newsweek). [< *plant*(er) + *-ocracy,* as in *democracy*]

**plant pathologist**, an expert in plant pathology.

**plant pathology**, the study of plant diseases and their treatment.

**plant physiology**, the scientific study of the life processes or functions of plants.

**plants|man** (plants′mən), *n., pl.* **-men.** a nurseryman or florist.

**plan|u|la** (plan′yə lə), *n., pl.* **-lae** (-lē). the flat, ciliated, free-swimming larva of a coelenterate. [< New Latin *planula* (diminutive) < Latin *plānus* flat, level; see etym. under **plain**[1]]

**plan|u|lar** (plan′yə lər), *adj.* 1 of flattened form. 2 having to do with a planula or like a planula.

**plan|u|late** (plan′yə lit), *adj.* = planular.

**plap** (plap), *v.i.,* **plapped, plap|ping.** *n., adv. British.* plop. [imitative]

**plaque** (plak), *n.* 1 an ornamental tablet of metal, porcelain, plastic, or wood, intended to be hung up as a wall decoration or to be fixed to something, such as a piece of furniture: *Gregory Jackson ... presented to the Cardinal a plaque* (New York Times). 2 a platelike ornament or badge, especially one worn as the badge of an honorary order. 3 *Anatomy.* a small, flat discoidal formation, such as a blood platelet: *The accumulation of cholesterol in the blood vessels forms plaques which may eventually restrict the flow of blood* (New York Times). 4 a gelatinous deposit formed on the surface of teeth by food debris and bacteria: *Tartar begins as plaque, a film on your teeth that quickly hardens into this tough, cementlike substance* (Time). [< Middle French *plaque* < Middle Dutch *plak* flat board]

**pla|quette** (pla ket′), *n.* a small plaque.

**plash**[1] (plash), *v., n.* —*v.t., v.i.* to splash: *Far below him plashed the waters* (Longfellow). —*n.* 1 a splash: *the plash and murmur of the waves* (Hawthorne). 2 a shallow piece of standing water; puddle: *As he that leaves A shallow plash to plunge him in the deep* (Shakespeare). 3 *Scottish.* a heavy fall of rain. [probably imitative]

**plash**[2] (plash), *v.t.* 1 to bend and interweave (stems, branches, and twigs, sometimes partly cut) to form a hedge. 2 to make or repair (a hedge) in this way. [< Old French *plaissier,* and *plessier* < *plaisse,* and *plesse* hedge < Vulgar Latin *plectia,* variant of Latin *plecta* wickerwork, trellis < *plectere* to interweave] —**plash′er**, *n.*

**plash|y** (plash′ē), *adj.* 1 abounding in pools of water; marshy; wet: *Seek'st thou the plashy brink Of weedy lake?* (William Cullen Bryant). 2 plashing or splashing. 3 marked as if splashed with color: *a serpent's plashy neck* (Keats). [< *plash*[1] + *-y*[1]]

**plasm** (plaz′əm), *n.* = plasma.

**plas|ma** (plaz′mə), *n.* 1 the clear, almost colorless liquid part of blood or lymph, in which the corpuscles or blood cells float. It consists of water, salts, proteins, and other substances, and it makes up the largest part of the blood. Plasma can be kept indefinitely by freezing or drying and is often used in transfusions in place of whole blood. *In the capillaries some of the liquid part of the blood, the plasma, oozes through the walls into the spaces surrounding the cells* (Beauchamp, Mayfield, and West). 2 *Physiology.* the fluid contained in muscle tissue; muscle plasma. 3 the watery part of milk, as distinguished from the globules of fat. 4 *Biology.* protoplasm, especially the general body of protoplasm as distinct from the nucleus. 5 *Physics.* a highly ionized gas, consisting of almost equal numbers of free electrons and positive ions (atomic nuclei lacking their electron shells). 6 a faintly translucent, green variety of quartz, much used in ancient times for ornaments. [< New Latin *plasma* (in Late Latin, something molded, created) < Greek *plásma* < *plássein* to form, mold]

**plasma arc welding**, arc welding using the extremely high temperatures of a plasma jet to weld metal.

**plas|ma|blast** (plaz′mə blast), *n.* the parent or stem cell of a plasma cell. [< *plasma* + Greek *blastós* germ]

**plasma cell**, a mononuclear cell that produces antibodies in chronically inflamed connective tissue.

**plas|ma|cyte** (plaz′mə sīt), *n.* = plasma cell.

**plas|ma|gene** (plaz′mə jēn), *n.* a minute particle or element found in the cytoplasm of certain microorganisms, insects, and plants. It is regarded as being a hereditary factor corresponding in function to the genes found in the chromosome. [< *plasma* + *gene*]

**plasma jet**, a jet of highly ionized gas: *Plasma jets, the white-hot streams of gas used for such tasks as cutting and welding* (Science News Letter).

**plas|ma|lem|ma** (plaz′mə lem′ə), *n.* = plasma membrane.

**plasma membrane**, the thin membrane that forms the outer surface of the protoplasm of a cell; cell membrane.

**plas|ma|pause** (plaz′mə pôz′), *n.* the upper limits of the region above the atmosphere that contain layers of highly ionized gas: *The spacecraft will be far beyond the plasmapause, the outer boundary of the ionosphere, and beyond the magnetosphere for most of the time* (Science Journal).

**plas|ma|pher|e|sis** (plaz′mə fer′ə sis), *n.* the removal of blood from the body and the separation, by centrifugation, of the plasma from the cells, which are then washed in a saline solution and returned to the blood stream. This process is used to obtain plasma, as well as to treat certain pathological conditions. [< New Latin *plasmapheresis* < *plasma* + Greek *aphaíresis* a taking away; see etym. under **apheresis**]

**plasma physicist**, a person who studies plasma physics: *The plasma physicist must use such phenomena and tools as microwaves, X rays, ... particle counters, and spectrographs* (Richard F. Post).

**plasma physics**, a branch of physics dealing with highly ionized gas, especially as it appears in a wide range of cosmic phenomena and as it is used in controlled thermonuclear reactions: *Plasma physics owes much to astronomical studies of the motions of ionized and magnetized solar gases* (Scientific American).

**plas|ma|sphere** (plaz′mə sfir′), *n.* an envelope of highly ionized gas about a planet: *Since none of Jupiter's outer satellites seems to affect the planet's radiation, the plasmasphere evidently does not have a long tail extending to satellite orbits beyond Io* (New Scientist and Science Journal).

**plas|mat|ic** (plaz mat′ik), *adj.* of plasma; containing plasma; like plasma.

**plasma torch**, a device that produces plasma jets for vaporizing, melting, or reducing any substance, such as metal or waste products.

**plas|mic** (plaz′mik), *adj.* = plasmatic.

**plas|mid** (plaz′mid), *n.* = episome. [< (cyto)-*plasm* + *-id*[1]]

**plas|min** (plaz′min), *n.* an enzyme in the blood which can dissolve blood clots; fibrinolysin.

**plas|min|o|gen** (plaz min′ə jən), *n.* the inactive form of plasmin; profibrinolysin.

**Plas|mo|chin** (plaz′mə kin), *n. Trademark.* pamaquine.

**plas|mo|des|ma|ta** (plaz′mō dez′mə tə), *n.pl.* narrow strands of cytoplasm in plant cells that form connections between the plasma membranes of adjacent cells: *The existence of plasmodesmata in green plants is well known, and appears to be universal* (New Scientist). [< New Latin *plasmodesmata* < Greek *plásma* something molded + *désma* band]

**plas|mo|di|um** (plaz mō′dē əm), *n., pl.* **-di|a** (-dē ə). 1 a mass or sheet of naked protoplasm formed by the fusion, or by the aggregation, of a number of amebalike bodies, as in the slime molds. 2 any one of a group of parasitic protozoans, including the organisms which cause malaria. [< German *Plasmodium* < New Latin *plasmodium* < *plasma* plasma + *-odium,* a noun suffix]

**plas|mog|a|my** (plaz mog′ə mē), *n.* the fusion of cytoplasm in a living cell.

**plas|mo|gen** (plaz′mə jən), *n.* (used formerly in biology) formative protoplasm; the highest stage of protoplasm from which tissue and organs are formed. [< Greek *plásma* something molded + English *-gen*]

**plas|moid** (plaz′moid), *n.* a tightly packed, luminous pellet of plasma ions, formed when plasma moves across a magnetic field.

**plas|mol|y|sis** (plaz mol′ə sis), *n. Botany.* the contraction of protoplasm in a living cell, caused by the withdrawal of liquid when the cell is placed in a liquid of greater density than the cell sap: *Plasmolysis can be seen with the microscope if pieces of water plants are mounted in a 5 to 10 per cent solution of table salt* (Fred W. Emerson). [< Greek *plásma* something molded + *lýsis* a loosening]

**plas|mo|lyt|ic** (plaz′mə lit′ik), *adj.* 1 having to do with plasmolysis. 2 showing plasmolysis. 3 causing plasmolysis.

**plas|mo|lyze** (plaz′mə līz), *v.t., v.i.,* **-lyzed, -lyzing.** to contract by plasmolysis.

**Plas|mon** (plaz′mon), *n. Trademark.* an almost odorless and tasteless, flourlike food preparation obtained from milk, consisting essentially of the protein of milk. [coined from *plasma*]

**plas|mo|quine** (plaz′mə kwīn), *n.* = pamaquine.

**plas|mo|some** (plaz′mə sōm), *n. Biology.* a true nucleolus, as distinguished from a karyosome. [< Greek *plásma* something molded + *sôma* body]

**plas|ome** (plas′ōm), *n.* (formerly) one of the

smallest theoretical units of living substance; pangen; biophore; gemmule. [< German *Plasom,* earlier *Plasmatosom* < Greek *plásma* something created + *sôma* body]

**-plast,** *combining form.* a small body or structure, especially of living matter; particle or granule, as in *bioplast, blepharoplast, mesoplast, chloroplast.* [< Greek *plastós* formed, molded < *plássein* to form, mold]

**plas|ter** (plas′tər, pläs′-), *n., v.* —*n.* **1** a soft, sticky mixture, consisting mainly of lime, sand, and water, that hardens as it dries. Plaster is used especially for walls and ceilings. *Ordinary plaster is very similar to mortar save that it usually contains hair or other fibers to help hold it in place* (W. N. Jones). **SYN**: stucco. **2** = plaster of Paris. **3** a medical preparation, consisting of some substance spread on cloth that will stick to the body and protect cuts or relieve pain: *a mustard plaster.* **SYN**: poultice. **4** *Figurative.* a healing or soothing means or measure.
—*v.t.* **1** to cover (a wall or ceiling) with plaster. **2** to smear, bedaub, or fill in with plaster; apply plaster to. **3** to use plaster of Paris on or in making. **4** *Figurative.* to spread with anything thickly: *His shoes were plastered with mud. Smee plastered his sitters with adulation as methodically as he covered his canvas* (Thackeray). **5** *Figurative.* to make smooth and flat: *He plastered his hair down.* **SYN**: slick. **6** to apply a plaster to. **7** *Figurative.* to apply like a plaster: *to plaster posters on a wall.* **8** *U.S. Slang.* to punish, injure, or attack violently; wreak havoc, ruin, or destruction upon.
[noun (definition 1) < Old French *plastre,* learned borrowing from Medieval Latin *plastrum* a medical plaster, builder's plaster < Latin *emplastrum* < Greek *émplastron,* salve, plaster, ultimately < *en-* on + *plastós* molded < *plássein* to mold; noun (definition 3) Old English *plaster* < Medieval Latin *plastrum.* See etym. of doublet **piaster.**]
—**plas′ter|like′,** *adj.*

**plas|ter|board** (plas′tər bôrd′, -bōrd′; pläs′-), *n.* a thin board made of a layer of plaster between layers of pressed felt, covered with paper and used for walls and partitions.

**plaster cast,** **1** a mold, as of a piece of sculpture, made with plaster of Paris. **2** *Medicine.* a mold made from a bandage of gauze and plaster of Paris to hold a broken or dislocated bone in place.

**plas|tered** (plas′tərd, pläs′-), *adj. Slang.* drunk.

**plas|ter|er** (plas′tər ər, pläs′-), *n.* a person who plasters walls or anything else.

**plas|ter|ing** (plas′tər ing, pläs′-), *n.* a covering of plaster, especially on walls.

**plaster molding,** a casting process in which the metal is poured into a plaster mold.

**plaster of Paris,** a white, powdery substance which, when mixed with water, swells and hardens quickly. Plaster of Paris is made by calcining gypsum. It can be made into molds and casts by pouring, shaping, carving, and turning. *Plaster of Paris expands slightly when it sets—a requisite for any material that is to find use as a mold or a casting* (Monroe M. Offner).

**plaster saint,** lifeless embodiment of moral perfection: *Single men in barracks don't grow into plaster saints* (Rudyard Kipling).

**plas|ter|work** (plas′tər wėrk′, -pläs-′), *n.* work done with or in plaster, especially on walls and ceilings.

**plas|ter|y** (plas′tər ē, pläs′-), *adj.* like plaster; resembling plaster.

**plas|tic** (plas′tik), *n., adj.* —*n.* **1** any one of various substances that can be molded or shaped when softened, as by heat or pressure, and become hard when cooled. Glass and rubber are plastics. **2** a synthetic organic compound made from coal, water, limestone, or other similar basic raw materials, especially by polymerization. Plastics are molded, laminated, and extruded into various forms, such as sheets, fibers, and bottles. Nylon, vinyl, many cellulose products, Bakelite, polyethylene, and Lucite are plastics.
—*adj.* **1** made of plastic: *a plastic hose, a plastic bottle, a plastic dish.* **2** easily modeled or shaped: *Clay, wax, and plaster are plastic substances.* **3** molding or giving shape to material. **4** having to do with or involving molding or modeling; that expresses itself in three dimensions: *Sculpture is a plastic art.* **5** *Figurative.* easily influenced; impressionable; pliable: *the plastic mind of a child.* **6** *Figurative.* not natural or real; synthetic; artificial: *Now that so many of the young seem to wear their hearts on their sleeves, it is hard to tell which ones are real and which ones are plastic* (Harper's). **7** *Biology.* capable of forming, or being organized into, living tissue. **8** *Physics.* (of a substance) able to be deformed in any direction and to retain its deformed condition permanently without rupture. **9** *Archaic.* producing natural forms, especially living organisms; formative; procreative.
[< Latin *plasticus* < Greek *plastikós* able to be molded < *plastós* molded < *plássein* to form, mold] —**plas′ti|cal|ly,** *adv.*

**plas|ti|cate** (plas′tə kāt), *v.t.,* **-cat|ed, -cat|ing.** to grind or knead (rubber) to a pulp, especially by means of a plasticator.

**plas|ti|ca|tor** (plas′tə kā′tər), *n.* a machine for plasticating rubber.

**plastic bomb,** a puttylike mixture of two or more explosives, usually TNT and RDX, that can be molded into any shape.

**plastic deformation** or **flow,** *Physics.* the alteration of the shape of a solid by the application of a sufficient and sustained stress: *Plastic deformation of solids is brought about when planes of atoms in the component crystals slip along adjacent planes, in a few directions favored by the crystalline atomic arrangement* (Alan Holden).

**plastic foam,** a plastic having a soft, spongy texture, suitable for use in furniture cushions, mattresses, and upholstery: *Plastic foam is being used increasingly for insulating linings in clothing in addition to its cushioning application* (Wall Street Journal).

**Plas|ti|cine** (plas′tə sēn), *n. Trademark.* a composition that remains plastic for a long time, sometimes used by children and sculptors instead of modeling clay.

**plas|ti|cise** (plas′tə sīz), *v.t., v.i.,* **-cised, -cis|ing.** *Especially British.* plasticize. —**plas′ti|cis′er,** *n.*

**plas|ti|cism** (plas′tə siz əm), *n.* plastic quality; plasticity.

**plas|tic|i|ty** (plas tis′ə tē), *n.* **1** plastic quality: (*Figurative.*) *Yet it is this graphic weakness that gives his Hesiod etchings their strong plasticity and complicated charm* (New Yorker). **2** the capability of being molded, formed, or modeled. **3** *Physics.* the capability of being deformed permanently under externally applied forces without failure. **4** *Chemistry.* the property of particles of being displaced without removal from the sphere of attraction.

**plas|ti|ci|za|tion** (plas′tə sə zā′shən), *n.* **1** the act of plasticizing; a making or becoming plastic. **2** the state of being plasticized.

**plas|ti|cize** (plas′tə sīz), *v.,* **-cized, -ciz|ing.** —*v.t.* to make plastic.
—*v.i.* to become plastic.

**plas|ti|ciz|er** (plas′tə sī′zər), *n.* a chemical that causes a substance to become or remain soft, flexible, or viscous: *The new product has potentialities as both a good emulsifier and a paint plasticizer* (Wall Street Journal).

**plastic memory,** the tendency of certain plastics that have been molded into a distinct form to resume much the same form after they are melted and allowed to cool.

**plastic operation,** an operation involving plastic surgery.

**plastic surgeon,** a surgeon who specializes in plastic surgery.

**plastic surgery,** surgery that restores or improves the appearance or function of outer parts of the body, by replacing or repairing lost, damaged, or deformed parts.

**plas|tid** (plas′tid), *n. Biology.* **1** any one of various small differentiated masses of protoplasm in the cytoplasm of a plant cell, such as a chloroplast: *The cells of most plants contain protoplasmic bodies called plastids, which multiply by fission* (Harbaugh and Goodrich). **2** an individual mass or unit of protoplasm, such as a cell or one-celled organism. [< German *Plastiden,* plural < Greek *plástides,* feminine plural of *plástēs* one who molds < *plastós* molded]

**plas|tique** (plas tēk′), *n.* **1** controlled movement and statuelike posing in ballet. **2** = plastic bomb. [< French *plastique* plastic]

**plas|ti|queur** (plas′ti kœr′), *n.* a person who throws plastic bombs: *Plastiqueurs have blown up two flats in the next street* (Punch). [< French *plastiqueur* < *plastique*]

**plas|ti|sol** (plas′tə sol, -sōl), *n.* a plasticized liquid dispersion of resin particles, used for coating steel, for padding, and in the manufacture of toys. [< *plasti*(c) + *sol*[4] solution]

**plas|tom|e|ter** (plas tom′ə tər), *n.* a device used to measure the plasticity of materials.

**plas|tral** (plas′trəl), *adj. Zoology.* of, having to do with, or like a plastron.

**plas|tron** (plas′trən), *n.* **1** a breastplate, especially of steel, worn under a coat of mail. **2** a leather guard worn over the chest by a fencer. **3** an ornamental, detachable front of a woman's bodice: *One in navy wool rivets eyes on a chest-high square plastron, which unbuttons to show beneath still another plastron of white piqué* (Sunday Times). **4** the starched front of a man's shirt. **5** the ventral part of the shell of a turtle or tortoise; breastplate. [< Middle French *plastron* breastplate, shirt front adaptation of Italian *piastrone* (augmentative) < *piastra* plate of metal, piastre < Medieval Latin *plastrum* plaster]

**plas|trum** (plas′trəm), *n.* = plastron.

**-plasty,** *combining form.* molding; formation; plastic surgery, as in *mammoplasty, neoplasty, osteoplasty.* [< Greek *-plastia* + *plástēs* one who molds < *plastós* molded < *plássein* to mold]

**plat**[1] (plat), *n., v.,* **plat|ted, plat|ting.** —*n.* **1** a map, chart, or plan, especially of a town or other group of buildings proposed to be built. **2** a small piece of ground; plot: *smooth plats of fruitful ground* (Tennyson).
—*v.t.* to map out in detail; chart; plan.
[apparently variant of *plot;* influenced by obsolete *plat* flat surface < Old French *plat* < Vulgar Latin *plattus* < Greek *platýs* broad, flat]

**plat**[2] (plat), *n., v.,* **plat|ted, plat|ting.** *Especially Dialect.* —*n.* a braid; plait.
—*v.t.* to braid; plait: *And they clothed him with purple, and platted a crown of thorns, and put it about his head* (Mark 15:17).
[variant of *plait*]

**plat**[3] (plȧ), *n. French.* **1** a plate or dish. **2** a dish of food, as served at the table.

**plat.,** platoon.

**plat|an** or **plat|ane** (plat′ən), *n.* a plane tree: *Three tall platanes … very poor as to foliage* (Joseph Conrad). [< Latin *platanus* plane tree]

**plat|a|na|ceous** (plat′ə nā′shəs), *adj.* belonging to or having to do with the family of plants typified by the plane tree. [< New Latin *Platanaceae* the family name (< Latin *platanus* plane tree) + English *-ous*]

**pla|ta|no** (plä′tä nō, -tə-), *n., pl.* **-nos.** in Latin America: **1** the fruit of the tropical plantain. **2** a banana. [< Spanish *plátano;* see etym. under **plantain**[1]]

**plat|band** (plat′band′), *n. Architecture.* **1** a flat, rectangular molding with a projection much less than the width. **2** a fillet between the flutings of a column. [< Middle French *platebande* < *plate* flat + *bande* band]

**plat du jour** (plȧ′ dʏ zhür′), *pl.* **plats du jour** (plȧ′ dʏ zhür′). *French.* the specialty of the day in a restaurant.

**plate** (plāt), *n., v.,* **plat|ed, plat|ing.** —*n.* **1** a dish, usually round, that is almost flat. Our food is served on plates: *a china dinner plate, a pie plate.* **2** the contents of such a dish: *a plate of stew.* **3** = plateful. **4** something having the shape of a plate: *A plate is passed in church to receive the collection.* **5** a part of a meal, served on or in a separate dish; course. **6** the food served to one person at a meal: *We cooked enough for six plates of spaghetti.* **7a** dishes or utensils of silver or gold: *The family plate included a silver pitcher, candlesticks, and the usual knives, forks, and spoons.* **b** dishes and utensils covered with a thin layer of silver or gold; plated ware: *The knives are plate, not solid silver.* **8** a thin, flat sheet or piece of metal: *The warship was covered with steel plates.* **9** one of the pieces of steel welded together or riveted to form the hull of a ship: *to damage the bow plates in a collision.* **10** armor composed of thin pieces of iron or steel fastened together, or upon leather or heavy cloth; plate armor. **11** metal hammered, rolled, or cast in a sheet or sheets, as a material: *Plate has been running a close second to cold-rolled sheets as the tightest item on the steel list* (New York Times). **12** *Anatomy, Zoology.* a platelike part, organ, or structure, such as a lamina. Some reptiles and fishes have a covering of horny or bony plates. **13** a thin, flat piece, usually of metal or plastic, on which something is engraved. Plates are used for printing pictures. A metal copy of a page of type is a plate. **14** something printed from such a piece of metal or from a woodcut, especially a full-page illustration, sometimes printed on special paper: *a color plate.* **15** a thin sheet of glass, metal, or plastic, coated with chemicals that are sensitive to light. Plates are sometimes used in taking photographs. **16** = home plate (in baseball): *Another Braves' run crossed the plate in the seventh* (New York Times). **17** a piece of metal, plastic, or other firm material with false teeth set into it. **18** a thin cut of beef from the lower end of the ribs, used especially to make corned beef. **19** *Electronics.* the positive electrode in a vacuum tube. It is the electrode toward which the electrons flow, originally made in the form of a flat plate, but now usually cylindrical. **20** *Architecture.* a beam that supports the ends of rafters, usually running horizontally between corner posts. **21** = plate glass. **22** *Especially British.* **a** a gold or silver cup or other prize given to the winner of a race, especially a horse race. **b** a contest in which the prize is (or was originally) such an object. **23a** *British*

**Pronunciation Key:** hat, āge, cãre, fär; let, ēqual, tėrm; it, īce; hot, ōpen, ôrder; oil, out; cup, pu̇t, rüle; child; long; thin; ᴛʜen; zh, measure; ə represents a in about, e in taken, i in pencil, o in lemon, u in circus.

*Dialect.* a railroad rail. **b** Also, **plate rail**. an early type of rail with a raised flange along the outer edge. **24** one of the series of vast, platelike parts making up the crust of the earth according to the theory of plate tectonics: *Basically the idea is that both oceans and continents consist of rigid crustal plates—six major and several minor ones* (New Scientist). **25** *Historical.* precious metal; bullion. **26** *Obsolete.* silver coin. **27** *Slang.* a fashionably dressed person. *Abbr:* pl.
—*v.t.* **1** to cover with a thin layer of gold, silver, or other metal by mechanical, electrical, or chemical means: *to plate old silver again.* **2** to cover with metal plates for protection: *The Confederates plated the Merrimac, making the first American armored ship.* **3** to make a plate of (type) for printing. **4** to treat (paper) with polished metal plates or rollers to give it a glossy finish.
**on a plate**, *British.* without effort or exertion; on a platter: *If New Zealand has the EEC door slammed in her face ... car factories of Japan, to take one immediate example, would have a new market handed to them on a plate* (Manchester Guardian Weekly).
**plate out**, to cause the metal in a metallic solution to be deposited on the cathode in electrolysis.
[< Old French *plate,* feminine of *plat,* adjective, thin plate, leaf of metal < Vulgar Latin *plattus* flat < Greek *platýs*] —**plate′like′**, *adj.*

**plate armor**, plate; thin pieces of armor.

**pla|teau** (pla tō′), *n., pl.* **-teaus** or **-teaux** (-tōz′). **1** a plain in the mountains or at a height above the sea; large, high plain: *They found that chinchilla fur was ideal wear in the intense cold of the high mountain plateaux* (New Scientist). **SYN**: tableland. **2** a level, especially the level at which something is stabilized for a period, as would be shown on a graph by a horizontal line: *Some predicted a continued slow rise in economic activity, some a "plateau" for a while before a new rise* (Wall Street Journal). **3** *Psychology.* a temporary halt in the learning progress of an individual, depicted by a level stretch on the curve or chart showing the rate of learning. [< French *plateau* < Old French *platel* (diminutive) < *plat* flat; see etym. under **plate**]

**plate block**, *Philately.* a group of four or more connected stamps with the serial numbers of the plates from which the stamps were printed.

**plat|ed** (plā′tid), *adj.* **1** having one yarn on the face and another kind on the back: *plated fabric.* **2** overlaid with plates, as of metal, for protection or ornament. **3** overlaid with a coating or surface of a material more valuable than the body, especially with a thin film of gold or silver.

**plate|ful** (plāt′fu̇l), *n., pl.* **-fuls**. as much as a plate will hold.

**plate glass**, thick, very clear glass made in smooth, polished sheets and used for large windowpanes and mirrors: *Plate glass is made from higher grade ingredients than those used for ordinary window glass* (Monroe M. Offner).

**plate|hold|er** (plāt′hōl′dər), *n.* **1** *Photography.* a receptacle impervious to light, for holding a sensitized plate, used for exposing the plate within the camera by the removal of a slide, and for carrying the plate before and after using. **2** a bracket for holding plates and saucers.

**plate|lay|er** (plāt′lā′ər), *n. British.* a person who lays, keeps in order, and replaces the rails on a tramway or railway; tracklayer: *The first train ... set off at 7 A.M. packed with the line's toughest platelayers under the command of the company secretary* (Manchester Guardian).

**plate|let** (plāt′lit), *n.* **1** one of many small disks which float in the blood plasma and are involved in clotting. It is one of the three cellular elements of blood. *Platelets are colorless cells in the blood and are involved in blood clotting* (Science News Letter). **2** a small or minute plate. [< *plate* + *-let*]

**plat|en** (plat′ən), *n.* **1** a flat metal plate in a printing press, that presses the paper against the inked type so as to secure an impression. **2** a cylinder serving the same purpose. **3** the roller against which the paper rests in a typewriter. **4** a heated plate placed between wood fiber mats to consolidate them into hardboard. [< Old French *platine* < *plat* flat; see etym. under **plate**]

**plate paper**, **1** a heavy, spongy, unsized paper with a smooth, dull finish, used for taking impressions from engraved plates. **2** a similar heavy paper, such as that used for books. **3** a paper finished with a high gloss, as by supercalendering.

**plate proof**, *Printing.* a proof taken from an electrotype or stereotype plate.

**plat|er** (plā′tər), *n.* **1** a person or thing that plates. **2** an inferior race horse, especially one that changes owners frequently or may be presumed to be usable for sale; selling-plater. **3** *Obsolete.* a horse that runs mostly in plate races.

**plate race**, *Especially British.* a horse race with a plate as the prize.

**plate rail**, **1** a rail or narrow shelf attached to a wall to hold plates or other ornaments. **2** = plate (def. 23b).

**plat|er|esque** (plat′ə resk′), *adj.* in or resembling a style of architecture, especially of Spain, characterized by rich, excessively ornamented forms suggestive of silver work. [< Spanish *plateresco* < *platero* silversmith + *-esco-* esque]

**plate tectonics**, a theory that the earth's crust is divided into a series of vast, platelike parts that move or drift as distinct land masses; global tectonics: *Plate tectonics has been adequately tested in other parts of the world and has shown its ability to predict, amongst other things, the direction of the movement accompanying earthquakes* (Science Journal).

**plate tracery**, *Architecture.* tracery formed by cutting openings through stone, rather than by assembling pieces.

**plat|form** (plat′fôrm), *n., adj.* —*n.* **1** a raised level surface or structure formed with planks, boards, or the like: *The speakers stood above the crowd on a platform.* **2** the walk between or beside the tracks of a railroad station. **3** *U.S.* the floor beyond the inside doors at either end of a railroad passenger car; vestibule. **4** a piece of raised flooring, in a hall or in the open air, from which a speaker addresses his audience.
**5** *Figurative.* a plan of action or statement of the beliefs of a group: *The platform of the new political party demands lower taxes. But it is, in a sense, ratified by this far-ranging message which is intended to be a platform for the campaign* (Newsweek). **SYN**: policy, program. **6** *Figurative.* a draft or scheme of principles or doctrines, made by or on behalf of a religious party, church, or sect. **7** *Figurative.* **a** a place of public expression or discussion; forum: *The United Nations is meant to be ... a platform for the weakest nation* (New York Times). **b** a place of opportunity; springboard: *West Point was there to give a man a platform from which to pursue advanced studies* (Atlantic). **8a** a slightly raised level area on which a piece of artillery is mounted in a fortification. **b** a terrace; flat piece of ground: *Grove nods at grove, each alley has a brother, And half the platform just reflects the other* (Alexander Pope). **9a** a thick outer sole on a woman's, or some men's, shoes. **b** a shoe with such a sole; platform shoe. **10** *Aerospace.* a navigation system or radio-signal device to determine location. **11** *Obsolete.* a scheme; design.
—*adj.* of or having to do with a platform used by public speakers: *platform oratory.*
[< Middle French *plateforme,* earlier *platte fourme* (literally) flat form]

**platform car**, = flatcar.

**plat|form|er** (plat′fôr′mər), *n.* (in petroleum refining) a reformer in which the process of platforming is carried out. [< *plat*(inum) + (re)*former*]

**plat|form|ing** (plat′fôr′ming), *n.* the process in petroleum refining in which platinum is used as a catalyst in the presence of hydrogen to raise gasoline octane ratings. [< *plat*(inum) + (re)*forming*]

**platform scale**, a flat scale or a platform for weighing heavy bodies without lifting.

**platform shoe**, a woman's or man's cloglike shoe with a thick outer sole that usually extends solidly the length of the shoe, becoming thicker under the heel.

**platform spider**, a spider which spins a tangled web to catch flying insects and a flat web beneath to catch its falling prey.

**platform tennis**, a form of paddle tennis played on a wooden platform surrounded by walls of wire netting: *Platform tennis ... is unique in that it is played primarily in winter and always outdoors* (Time).

**platform ticket**, *British.* a ticket permitting a person other than a passenger to enter upon a railroad platform.

**plat|i|na** (plat′ə nə, plə tē′-), *n.* = platinum. [< earlier Spanish *platina* < *plata* silver (because it resembles silver)]

**plat|i|nate** (plat′ə nāt), *n. Chemistry.* a salt of platinic acid.

**plat|ing** (plā′ting), *n.* **1** a thin layer of silver, gold, or other metal. **2** a covering of metal plates. **3** the act of a person or thing that plates.

**pla|tin|ic** (plə tin′ik), *adj. Chemistry.* **1** of platinum. **2** containing platinum, especially with a valence of four.

**plat|i|nif|er|ous** (plat′ə nif′ər əs), *adj.* bearing or yielding platinum. [< *platin*(um) + *-ferous*]

**plat|in|i|rid|i|um** (plat′ən i rid′ē əm), *n.* a native alloy of platinum and iridium, occurring in whitish grains or cubes.

**plat|i|nize** (plat′ə nīz), *v.t.,* **-nized, -niz|ing.** to coat or treat with platinum.

**plat|i|no|cy|an|ic acid** (plat′ə nō sī an′ik), an acid of platinum and cyanide, formed by the decomposition of its salts in solution. *Formula:* $H_2Pt(CN)_4$

**plat|i|no|cy|a|nid** (plat′ə nō sī′ə nid), *n.* = platinocyanide.

**plat|i|no|cy|a|nide** (plat′ə nō sī′ə nīd), *n.* a salt of platinocyanic acid. [< *platinum* + *cyanide*]

**plat|i|noid** (plat′ə noid), *adj., n.* —*adj.* resembling platinum.
—*n.* **1** any one of a group of metals commonly found in association with platinum and resembling it in several properties, such as palladium, iridium, and osmium. **2** a platinumlike alloy consisting essentially of copper, nickel, zinc, and tungsten, used especially for electrical resistance coils.

**plat|i|no|type** (plat′ə nə tīp), *n.* **1** a process of photographic printing using a platinum salt and producing a print in platinum black. **2** a print made by this process.

**plat|i|nous** (plat′ə nəs), *adj. Chemistry.* **1** of platinum. **2** containing platinum, especially with a valence of two.

***plat|i|num** (plat′ə nəm), *n.* **1** a heavy metallic chemical element with a very high melting point. Platinum is a silver-white, precious metal which is resistant to acid and does not tarnish easily. It is ductile and malleable and is used as a catalyst, for chemical and industrial equipment, in dentistry, and for jewelry. *In the United States, platinum occurs in the gold-bearing deposits in California, Nevada, and Oregon* (Albert J. Phillips). **2** a light-gray color, less bright than silver and having a faint bluish tinge. [< New Latin *platinum,* alteration of *platina* platina]

***platinum**
definition 1

| symbol | atomic number | atomic weight | oxidation state |
|---|---|---|---|
| Pt | 78 | 195.09 | 2, 4 |

**platinum black**, a dull-black powder consisting of very finely divided metallic platinum. It is used as an oxidizing agent because it can condense large amounts of oxygen upon its surface.

**platinum blonde** or **blond**, **1** silvery blonde: *platinum blonde hair.* **2** a person, especially a woman, having silvery blonde hair.

**plat|i|tude** (plat′ə tüd, -tyüd), *n.* **1** a dull or commonplace remark, especially one spoken or written solemnly as if it were fresh and important: *"Better late than never" is a platitude.* **2** flatness; triteness; dullness; insipidity (as a quality of speech or writing): *even the platitude of her phraseology carries with it a curiously personal flavour* (Lytton Strachey). **SYN**: commonplaceness. [< French *platitude* < *plat* flat (saying); see etym. under **plate**]

**plat|i|tu|di|nar|i|an** (plat′ə tü′də nãr′ē ən, -tyü′-), *n.* a person given to platitudes.

**plat|i|tu|di|nize** (plat′ə tü′də nīz, -tyü′-), *v.i.,* **-nized, -niz|ing.** to utter platitudes.

**plat|i|tu|di|nous** (plat′ə tü′də nəs, -tyü′-), *adj.* **1** characterized by platitudes; using platitudes: *The fantastic Lorca imagery, mixture of the bizarre and the platitudinous, comes through particularly well in the translation* (Harper's). **2** being a platitude. —**plat′i|tu′di|nous|ly**, *adv.* —**plat′i|tu′di|nous|ness**, *n.*

**Pla|ton|ic** (plə ton′ik), *adj.* **1** of or having to do with Plato or his philosophy: *the Platonic philosophy.* **2** Also, **platonic. a** friendly but not like a lover; designating love or affection of a purely spiritual character, free from sensual desire: *without admission that their love could not remain platonic* (John Galsworthy). **b** feeling or professing such love. **3** *Figurative.* idealistic; not practical: *The League of Nations seemed a Platonic scheme to many people.* **SYN**: visionary, utopian. [< *Plato,* about 427-347 B.C., a Greek philosopher] —**pla|ton′i|cal|ly**, *adv.*

**Pla|ton|i|cal** (plə ton′ə kəl), *adj.* = Platonic.

**Platonic year**, = great year.

**Pla|to|nism** (plā′tə niz əm), *n.* **1** the philosophy or doctrines of Plato or his followers. **2** a Platonic doctrine or saying. **3** the doctrine or practice of Platonic love.

**Pla|to|nist** (plā′tə nist), *n.* a follower of Plato; adherent of Platonism.

**Pla|to|nis|tic** (plā′tə nis′tik), *adj.* **1** having to do with the Platonists or Platonism. **2** characteristic of the Platonists or Platonism.

**Pla|to|nize** (plā′tə nīz), *v.,* **-nized, -niz|ing.** —*v.t.* to make Platonic; give a Platonic character to; explain in accordance with Platonic principles.
—*v.i.* to follow the opinions or doctrines of Plato; reason like Plato: *The gentlemen and the maids Platonizing and singing madrigals had nothing else to do* (New Yorker).

**pla|toon** (plə tün′), *n., v.* —*n.* **1** a group of soldiers acting as a unit under a lieutenant. A platoon is made up of two or more squads. There are usually four platoons in a company. **2** a sub-

division of a police force. **3** *U.S. Sports.* a division of a team, especially in football, that specializes in either offensive or defensive play: *He has shifted Frank Gifford, his most versatile backfield man, from the defensive to the offensive platoon* (New York Times). **4** *Figurative.* a small group or company of people: *If you speak of the age, you mean your own platoon of people* (Emerson).
—*v.t., v.i. U.S. Sports.* to put or be put in a specialized play or position: *Later [Gil] Hodges decided to "platoon" him by playing him only against left-handed pitchers* (Time).
[< French *peloton* platoon, group of persons < Middle French, little ball (diminutive) < *pelote* ball; see etym. under **pellet**]

**platoon school**, an elementary school divided by classes into two groups that take turns attending classes in standard subjects and in special activities, such as music, drawing, cooking, and sewing.

**Platt|deutsch** (plät′doich′), *n.* the speech of North Germany, now often considered a nonstandard dialect; Low German. [< German *Plattdeutsch* < *platt* of the lowlands, (literally) flat (ultimately < Vulgar Latin *plattus;* see etym. under **plat**[1]) + *Deutsch* the German language]

**platte|land** (plät′land′), *n.* (in South Africa) a country district; rural area; hinterland: *The Africans reacted like lightning crackling across the platteland sky* (Time). [< Afrikaans *platteland* < Dutch < *platte* flat + *land* land]

**plat|ter**[1] (plat′ər), *n.* **1** a large, shallow dish for holding or serving food, especially meat and fish. A platter is usually longer than it is wide. SYN: trencher. **2** *Slang.* a phonograph record: *The long-play, 33⅓ r.p.m. platters, commonly known as albums* (Wall Street Journal). **3** *Slang.* home plate.
**on a (silver) platter**, without requiring any effort; very lightly or easily: *A former Army major ... charged that six years before, Mr. Hopkins had "handed" the Russians the A-bomb on a platter* (New York Times).
[< Anglo-French *plater* < Old French *plat* plate, dish, flat surface; see etym. under **plate**]

**plat|ter**[2] (plat′ər), *n.* a person who plats or plaits. [< *plat*[2] + *-er*[1]]

**platter pull**, a type of ski tow in which the skier is pulled up the slope by a disk attached to a towing cable. The skier straddles the extension so that the disk presses against him.

**plat|ting** (plat′ing), *n.* **1** the act or work of a person who plats. **2** straw, grass, or the like, platted into braid, or into some other form, as for hats. [< *plat*[2] + *-ing*[1]]

**plat|y**[1] (plā′tē), *adj.* consisting of or easily separating into plates, as mica; flaky.

**plat|y**[2] (plat′ē), *n., pl.* **plat|ys** or **plat|y.** a small, brilliantly colored, tropical freshwater fish that is a native of Mexico; moonfish. [< *Platy*(poecilus), the genus name]

**plat|y|fish** (plat′ə fish′), *n., pl.* **-fish|es** or (*collectively*) **-fish.** = platy[2].

**plat|y|hel|minth** (plat′ə hel′minth), *n.* any one of a phylum of worms having soft, usually flat, bilaterally symmetrical bodies, a distinct head, and no body cavity; flatworm. Tapeworms, turbellarians, and flukes belong to this phylum. [< *Platyhelminthes* the phylum name < Greek *platýs* flat + *hélmins, -inthos* worm, helminth]

**Plat|y|hel|min|thes** (plat′ə hel min′thēz), *n.pl.* the phylum of invertebrates comprising the platyhelminths.

***plat|y|pus** (plat′ə pəs), *n., pl.* **-pus|es, -pi** (-pī). an egg-laying mammal of Australia and Tasmania; duckbill: *The male platypus is as venomous as a poisonous snake* (Scientific American). [< Greek *platýpous* flat-footed < *platýs* flat + *poûs* foot]

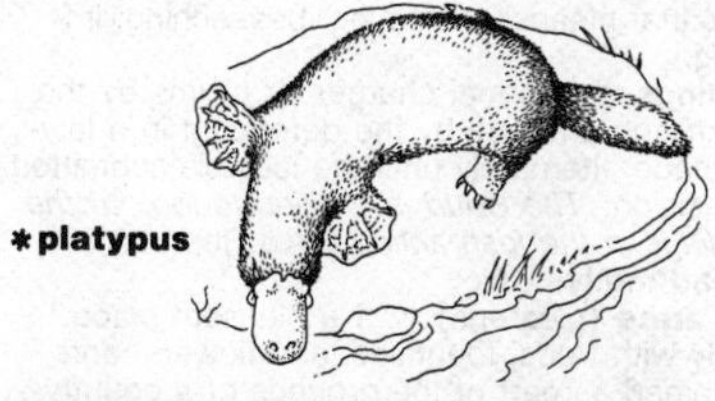
***platypus**

**plat|y|pus|ar|y** (plat′ə pə ser′ē), *n., pl.* **-ar|ies.** an artificial habitat designed for platypuses kept in captivity, including a water tank and burrowing bank.

**plat|y|rhyn|chous** (plat′ə ring′kəs), *adj.* having a broad, flat bill, as certain flycatchers. [< Greek *platýs* broad, flat + *rhýnchos* beak, bill + English *-ous*]

**plat|yr|rhine** (plat′ə rīn, -ər in), *adj., n.* —*adj.* having a broad, flat nose or a nasal index of from 51 to 58.
—*n.* a platyrrhine person, monkey, ape, or skull. [< New Latin *Platyrrhini* name of a division of apes < Greek *platýs* flat + *rhîs, rhīnós* nose]

**plat|yr|rhin|i|an** (plat′ə rin′ē ən), *adj.* = platyrrhine.

**plau|dit** (plô′dit), *n.* an enthusiastic expression of approval; acclaim. SYN: acclamation.
**plaudits**, a round of applause; clapping, or cheering, as an enthusiastic expression of approval or praise: *The actress bowed in response to the plaudits of the audience.*
[short for earlier *plaudite!* actor's request for applause < Latin, imperative of *plaudere* to applaud]

**plau|di|to|ry** (plô′də tôr′ē, -tōr′-), *adj.* applauding; laudatory.

**plau|si|bil|i|ty** (plô′zə bil′ə tē), *n.* the appearance of being true or reasonable; plausible quality: *The persuasiveness and plausibility of the book, however, are due to the author's ability* (Wall Street Journal).

**plau|si|ble** (plô′zə bəl), *adj.* **1** appearing true, reasonable, or fair: *For my own sake I've told a plausible lie at the club* (Joseph Conrad). **2** apparently worthy of confidence but often not really so: *a plausible liar.* [< Latin *plausibilis* deserving applause, pleasing < *plaudere* to applaud]
—**plau′si|ble|ness**, *n.*

**plau|si|bly** (plô′zə blē), *adv.* with an appearance of truth or trustworthiness; in a way that seems true or right; with fair show: *The story was plausibly told—whether it was true or not remains to be seen.*

**plau|sive** (plô′siv), *adj.* **1** having the quality of applauding; applausive. **2** *Obsolete.* plausible.

**plaus|tral** (plôs′trəl), *adj.* having to do with a wagon or cart. [< Latin *plaustrum* wagon, cart + English *-al*[1]]

**Plau|tine** (plô′tīn), *adj.* of or having to do with Plautus (254?-184 B.C.), Roman writer of comedies, or his works: *There is Plautine merriment at the Strand Theatre* (London Times).

**play** (plā), *n., v.* —*n.* **1** something done to amuse oneself; fun; sport; recreation: *The children are happy at play. Play consists of those activities which are not consciously performed for the sake of any reward beyond themselves* (Emory S. Bogardus). *All work and no play makes Jack a dull boy.* **2** an act or move in a game: *He made a good play at checkers.* **3** turn to play: *It is your play next.* **4** the carrying on or playing of a game: *Play was slow in the first half of the game.* **5** the manner or style of carrying on or playing a game: *Both sides showed brilliant play.* **6** a story written for or presented as a dramatic performance; drama: *"Peter Pan" is a charming play. A play, as we conceive of it ... is something which, by its nature, demands prose wherever prose will serve* (Atlantic). **7** a dramatic or theatrical performance, as on the stage. **8** *Figurative.* action or dealing of a specified kind (now used only in *fair play* and *foul play*). **9** *Figurative.* action; operation; working: *the lively play of fancy. He brought all his strength into play to move the rock. There was an engine in the room which was in full play.* **10** the act of lightly or briskly wielding or plying (used especially in combinations): *swordplay.* **11** a light, quick movement or change: *the play of sunlight on leaves, the play of light in a diamond.* **12** *Figurative.* freedom or opportunity for action; scope for activity: *to give free play to one's faculties. The boy gave his fancy full play in telling what he could do with a million dollars.* **13** free or unimpeded movement; the proper motion of a piece of mechanism, or a part of the living body: *the play of muscles.* **14** the space in or through which anything, especially a piece of mechanism, can or does move: *the play of a wheel on an axle.* **15** gambling: *to lose vast sums at play.* **16** *Obsolete.* a particular amusement; game: *The plays of children are nonsense but very educative nonsense* (Emerson). [Old English *plega* exercise]
—*v.t.* **1** to take part in (a game): *to play golf. Children play tag and ball.* **2** to perform, do, or execute: *He played a joke on his sister.* **3** to represent or imitate, especially for amusement: *to play spacemen, to play store.* **4** to take part in a game against: *Our team played the sixth-grade team. New York played Boston for the championship.* **5** to cause to play; use (a person) in a game; include in a team. **6** to act (a part) in a dramatic performance or in real life: *to play one's part well.* **7** *Figurative.* to act or behave as or like; perform the duties or characteristic actions of: *to play the host, to play the fool. Nor did the shift ... release a love of power for its own sake or an impulse to play the great man* (Edmund Wilson). **8** to act the part of: *to play Hamlet. The famous actress played Peter Pan.* **9** to perform or act (a drama, pageant, or incident) on or as if on the stage: *to play a tragedy.* **10** to give dramatic performances in: *to play the best theaters, to play the largest cities.* **11** to perform (music or a piece of music) on an instrument or instruments: *to play a symphony.* **12** to perform on (a musical instrument): *to play a piano.* **13** to cause to act or work; keep in continuous motion or exercise; operate: *to play a hose on a burning building.* **14** to cause to move or pass lightly: *The ship played its light along the coast.* **15** to stake or wager in a game: *to play five dollars.* **16** to gamble or bet on: *to play the horses.* **17** to put into action in a game: *Play your cards carefully and you will win the game.* **18** to allow (a hooked fish) to exhaust itself by pulling on the line: *M. A. Norden ... is shown playing a 137-lb. tarpon in a recent Alabama Deep Sea Fishing Rodeo* (Time).
—*v.i.* **1** to have fun; do something in sport; amuse or divert oneself: *The kitten plays with its tail. The children played in the yard.* SYN: frolic, revel. **2** to do something which is not to be taken seriously, but merely as done in sport. **3** to make believe; pretend in fun. **4** *Figurative.* to dally; trifle; toy: *to play with a new idea, to play with matches. He played with his watch-chain wearily* (Dickens). **5** to engage or take part in a game: *to play with skill.* **6** *Figurative.* to act, behave, or conduct oneself in some specified way: *to play fair, to play false, to play sick.* **7** to make music; perform on a musical instrument: *to play in an orchestra.* **8** to sound: *The music began to play.* **9** to act a part on or as if on a stage; perform: *to play in a tragedy.* **10** to move lightly or quickly, especially with alternating or irregular motion: *Leaves play in the wind. A breeze played on the water.* **11** to change or alternate rapidly, as colors do in iridescence: *the firelight playing on her red frock* (John Galsworthy). **12** to move or revolve freely, usually within a definite space, as a part of any mechanism: *The wheel plays in a track.* **13** to operate or act with continued or repeated action: *A fountain played in the garden.* **14** to gamble.
**bring** (or **call**) **into play**, to begin to exercise; bring into action; make active: *The intelligence and judgment of Mr. Ruskin ... are brought into play* (Matthew Arnold). *There is ... hardly a decision on such an issue that does not call into play an entire range of political and legal activities* (Saturday Review).
**in play, a** being used in the course of the game; in or during legitimate play: *Walton tried another big kick, but the ball fell in play, and was well returned by Strand-Jones* (Westminster Gazette). **b** as a joke: *He said it merely in play.*
**out of play**, not being used; not in or during legitimate play: *A runner cannot be tagged while the ball is out of play.*
**play back**, to replay (a phonograph or tape recording), especially just after it has been made: *We all laughed as we heard the tape recorder play back the conversation at dinner.*
**play ball.** See under **ball.**
**play by ear.** See under **ear.**
**play down, a** to make light of; de-emphasize; understate: *They want to play down politics, play up "good government" and "responsible leadership"* (Newsweek). **b** to lower one's standards to suit the demands of others; condescend: *Miss Holliday had won "a kind of immortality" with an art that never "played down"* (New York Times).
**play off, a** to play an additional game or match in order to decide (a draw or tie): *We're going to play off for the Wolcott cup* (Munsey's Magazine). **b** to pit (one person or thing against another), especially for one's own advantage: *to play off one party against another.*
**play on** (or **upon**), to take advantage of; make use of: *She played on her mother's good nature to get what she wanted.*
**play out, a** to perform to the end; bring to an end: *to play out a tragedy.* **b** *Figurative.* to exhaust; wear out: *The endless war was playing out both the men and the supplies.* **c** *Figurative.* to diminish; wear off: *When their initial lure had played out, the pioneers of the West found other attractions to induce them to stay on* (Ernest Gruening).
**play the field.** See under **field.**
**play the game.** See under **game.**
**play up,** *U.S.* to make the most of; exploit: *Happy customers and favorable reviews are quoted, successful promotions of the firm's books are played up* (Time).
**play up to,** *Slang.* to try to get into the favor of; flatter: *to play up to a celebrity.*
**play with, a** to touch or finger lightly, by way of amusement: *The Commissioner moved his legs, playing with a penknife* (Graham Greene).

**b** *Figurative.* to act carelessly; do foolish things; treat frivolously: *Don't play with matches. Montaigne ... could thus afford to play with life, and the abysses into which it leads us* (Cardinal Newman).
[Old English *plegian* to exercise, busy oneself with]
—*Syn. n.* **1 Play, sport, game** mean activity or exercise of mind or body engaged in for recreation or fun. **Play** is the general word: *Play is as necessary as work.* **Sport** applies to any form of athletics or an outdoor pastime, whether it requires much or little activity or is merely watched for pleasure: *Fencing, swimming, fishing, and horse racing are his favorite sports.* **Game** applies especially to an activity in the form of a contest, mental or physical, played by certain rules: *Tennis and chess are games.*

**pla|ya** (plä′yə), *n.* **1** *Southwestern U.S.* a plain of silt or mud, covered with water during the wet season. **2** *Geology.* the basin floor of an undrained desert which contains water at irregular periods. [American English < Spanish *playa* beach, strand < Late Latin *plagia* coast, side < Latin *plaga* place, region, something spread out]

**play|a|bil|i|ty** (plā′ə bil′ə tē), *n.* the quality of being playable: *He continued to study each of the eighteen holes, to see what could be done to improve its playability* (New Yorker).

**play|a|ble** (plā′ə bəl), *adj.* **1** that can be played. **2** fit to be played on.

**play-act** or **play|act** (plā′akt′), *v.i.* **1** to perform in a dramatic production. **2** *Figurative.* to make believe; pretend. —*v.t.* to act (a part); portray: (*Figurative.*) *just play-acting the bohemian* (Punch).

**play-act|ing** or **play|act|ing** (plā′ak′ting), *n.* **1** the acting of plays; dramatic performance. **2** *Figurative.* the action of making believe; pretending.

**play-ac|tion pass** (plā′ak′shən), *U.S. Football.* a play in which the quarterback passes the ball after faking a running play: *They ... caught Green Bay's own defenders napping with play-action passes that looked at first glance like handoffs into the line* (Time).

**play|ac|tor** (plā′ak′tər), *n.* an actor of plays; dramatic performer.

**play|back** (plā′bak′), *n.* the replaying of a sound recording, especially a tape recording, or of a videotape, especially just after it has been made.

**playback head**, a magnetic head for playing back tape recordings.

**play|bill** (plā′bil′), *n.* **1** a handbill or placard announcing a play. **2** a program of a play.

**play|book** (plā′bu̇k′), *n.* a book containing the diagrams of a football team's plays: *They spend most of their time ... studying the 'playbook' which sets out the dozens of moves they have to learn before the next match* (Sunday Times).

**play|boy** (plā′boi′), *n.* **1** *Informal.* a man, usually wealthy, whose chief interest is having a good time: *This takes me back to the Algonquin where over cocktails I met two playboys from Dallas, Texas* (Punch). **2** *Irish.* a man who seeks to play a role to his own advantage; clever or tricky pretender: *The Playboy of the Western World* (J. M. Synge).

**play-by-play** (plā′bī plā′), *adj. U.S.* denoting a running commentary, especially on a sports event.

**play|clothes** (plā′klōz′, -klōᴛʜz′), *n.pl.* comfortable clothes worn for play or recreation.

**play|day** (plā′dā′), *n.* a day given to pastime or diversion; holiday.

**play doctor**, *U.S.* a writer employed to revise a playscript prior to production.

**play|down** (plā′doun′), *n.* (in Canada) a play-off.

**played-out** (plād′out′), *adj.* suffering from overuse so as to be worn-out, worthless, or hackneyed: *played-out jokes.*

**play|er** (plā′ər), *n.* **1** a person who plays, or is qualified to play, in some game: *a baseball player, a card player, a tennis player.* **2** an actor in a theater: *All the world's a stage, And all the men and women merely players* (Shakespeare). **3** a musician. **4** a person who plays for stakes; gambler. **5** a thing or device that plays: *A phonograph is a record player.* **6** a mechanical device enabling a musical instrument, especially a piano, to be played automatically. **7** a person who plays rather than works; idler.

**player piano**, a piano played by machinery consisting of foot pedals that pump a pneumatic mechanism turning a paper roll with perforations which cause air pressure to move the piano keys.

**play|fel|low** (plā′fel′ō), *n.* = playmate.

**play field**, = playing field.

**play|ful** (plā′fəl), *adj.* **1** full of fun; fond of playing; frolicsome: *a playful puppy. The playful children just let loose from school* (Oliver Goldsmith). SYN: sportive. **2** not serious; joking: *a playful remark.* SYN: bantering, jesting, humorous, jocular. —**play′ful|ly**, *adv.* —**play′ful|ness**, *n.*

**play|girl** (plā′gėrl′), *n. Informal.* a woman or girl, usually wealthy, whose chief interest is having a good time.

**play|go|er** (plā′gō′ər), *n.* a person who goes often to the theater: *I'm in favor of introducing as many changes as possible to make the playgoer happy* (New York Times).

**play|go|ing** (plā′gō′ing), *adj., n.* —*adj.* going often to the theater.
—*n.* the practice or habit of going often to the theater: *His dapper discourses range from playgoing and Einstein's theory ... to the top hat* (Newsweek).

**play|ground** (plā′ground′), *n.* **1** a place for outdoor play, especially by children, often containing equipment for games and sports. **2** a recreation or resort area: *Over the past decade fashionable ... playgrounds such as Bermuda and Monte Carlo have been challenged* (London Times).

**play|group** (plā′grüp′), *n.* an informal nursery school, held usually in some neighborhood facility: *Mothers find difficulty in getting baby-sitters, but the playgroups in church premises and the adventure playgrounds are welcomed* (London Times).

**play|house** (plā′hous′), *n.* **1** a small house for a child to play in. **2** a small building separate from a main building, for the recreation of people of any age. **3** a toy house for a child; dollhouse. **4** a theater: *Successful periods in the playhouse do owe something to what is going on outside the playhouse* (Harper's).

**play|ing card** (plā′ing), a card used to play such games as poker, bridge, euchre, rummy, and pinochle, usually being one of a set of 52 cards arranged in four suits (spades, hearts, diamonds, and clubs) of 13 cards each.

**playing field**, **1** a field or piece of ground for games or a game: *It is being performed each night by floodlight on the playing fields beside the Avon* (London Times). **2** *U.S.* an area marked off as comprising that within which the play of a particular game may, according to the rules, take place; field of play.

**play|land** (plā′land′), *n.* = amusement park.

**play|let** (plā′lit), *n.* a short dramatic play: *The three playlets are almost identical in form and spirit* (New Yorker).

**play|mak|er** (plā′mā′kər), *n.* an offensive player, as in basketball, who sets up plays in which his teammates can score: *Cousy, having become the Celtics' acknowledged playmaker, began to direct their attack with a confidence that ... bordered on audacity* (New Yorker).

**play|mate** (plā′māt′), *n.* a person who plays regularly with another. SYN: playfellow.

**play-off** (plā′ôf′, -of′), *n.* **1** a game or series of games played after the regular season to decide a championship. **2** an extra game or round played off to settle a tie.

**play on** (or **upon**) **words**, = pun.

**play|pen** (plā′pen′), *n.* a small, folding pen for a baby or young child to play in. It is usually an enclosure with sides of wooden bars or netting.

**play|pit** (plā′pit′), *n. British.* a small pit, sometimes filled with sand, for children to play in: *The village shopping centres have good stores as well as sculpture and playpits for the children* (Manchester Guardian Weekly).

**play|room** (plā′rüm′, -ru̇m′), *n.* a room to play in, especially for children.

**play|script** (plā′skript′), *n.* the script of a play: *He's merely learning a part. There's the playscript in his hand* (New Yorker).

**play|some** (plā′səm), *adj.* = playful.

**play street**, a street temporarily or permanently closed to traffic to enable children to play outdoors safely.

**play suit**, **1** a matching outfit, usually consisting of shorts, a blouse and sometimes a skirt or jacket for women and girls. It is worn at the beach, on picnics, for tennis, or other leisure activity. *Here's the perfect play suit in luxurious white terry* (New Yorker). **2** playclothes for children.

**play therapy**, the therapeutic use of play, in the presence of a therapist, as a means of reducing a child's tensions and of promoting the child's emotional growth and health.

**play|thing** (plā′thing′), *n.* **1** a thing to play with; toy: *Some livelier plaything gives his youth delight* (Alexander Pope). **2** *Figurative.* something or someone treated as a thing to play with: *She is not a tragic heroine but merely a love-smitten plaything who quickly gets over her infatuation* (Winthrop Sargeant).

**play|time** (plā′tīm′), *n.* time for play or recreation.

**play|wear** (plā′wãr′), *n.* playclothes; leisurewear.

**play|wright** (plā′rīt′), *n.* a writer of plays; dramatist.

**play|writ|ing** (plā′rī′ting), *n.* the writing of plays; occupation of a playwright.

**pla|za** (plä′zə, plaz′ə), *n.* **1** a public square in a city or town. **2** *U.S.* **a** the wide area on a tollway where tollbooths are situated: *a toll plaza.* **b** an area with a restaurant, filling stations, and other services alongside an expressway: *a service plaza.* **3** *Especially Canadian.* a shopping center. [American English < Spanish *plaza*, learned borrowing from Latin *platēa* courtyard, broad street < Greek *plateîa* (*hodós*) broad (way). See etym. of doublets **piazza**, **place**[1].]

**pla|za de to|ros** (plä′thä dā tō′rōs, -sä), *Spanish.* a bull ring: *He was young, but he knew a lot about the injuries that occur in a plaza de toros* (Barnaby Conrad).

**plea** (plē), *n.* **1** a request, especially one made prayerfully or pleadingly; asking; appeal: *a plea for pity.* SYN: entreaty, prayer. **2** an argument or claim in defense; excuse: *The man's plea was that he did not see the stop sign.* **3a** the answer made by a defendant to a charge against him in a court of law. **b** an argument or allegation of fact made in support of one side in a lawsuit. **c** a plea which alleges some new fact on the basis of which the suit should be dismissed, delayed, or barred, but does not answer the charge; special plea. **4** *British, Law.* an action at law; lawsuit. [Middle English *plai, plaid* < Old French *plaid* lawsuit, decision plea < Late Latin *placitum* < Latin, (that) which pleases < *placēre* to please]

**plea bargaining**, an informal practice in which the prosecuting attorney in a criminal action agrees to allow a defendant to plead guilty to a lesser charge, in order to avoid a lengthy trial, assure a conviction, or gain the defendant's cooperation as a witness in a criminal action against another: *Plea bargaining in criminal cases was condemned ... by Lord Parker of Waddington, Lord Chief Justice* (London Times). *U.S. District Judge William J. Campbell ... believes "plea bargaining should be acknowledged, legitimatized, and encouraged"* (Jack Star).

**pleach** (plēch), *v.t.* to interweave (as growing branches or vines); intertwine or entwine: *Walking in a thick-pleached alley in mine orchard* (Shakespeare). [earlier form of *plash*[2], probably < dialectal Old French *plechier*, variant of *plessier*]

**plead** (plēd), *v.*, **plead|ed** or (*Informal*) **pled**, **plead|ing.** —*v.t.* **1** to offer reasons for or against; argue: *The boy pleaded his need for more time to finish the test.* **2** to offer as an excuse: *The woman who stole pleaded poverty.* **3a** to speak for or against in a court of law: *A good lawyer pleaded the case.* **b** to answer to a charge in a law court; make a plea of: *The defendant pleaded guilty to the theft.*
—*v.i.* **1** to ask earnestly; make an earnest appeal; beg; implore: *When the rent was due, the poor man pleaded for more time.* SYN: entreat, supplicate, beseech. **2a** to conduct a case in a court of law. **b** to make any allegation as part of an action at law, especially to present an answer or objection on the part of a defendant. **c** *Obsolete.* to go to law; litigate.
[Middle English *plaiden* < Old French *plaidier* < Vulgar Latin *placitāre* < Late Latin *placitum* plea < Latin *placēre* to please]

**plead|a|ble** (plē′də bəl), *adj.* that can be alleged, urged, or claimed in behalf of something: *a pleadable case.*

**plead|er** (plē′dər), *n.* **1** a person who pleads, especially in a court of law. **2** a person who entreats or intercedes.

**plead|ing** (plē′ding), *n., adj.* —*n.* **1** earnest entreaty; intercession; advocacy; supplication. **2a** the advocating of a case in a court of law. **b** the art or science of preparing or presenting pleas in legal cases. **c** a formal, usually written, allegation setting forth the cause of action or defense.
—*adj.* that pleads; entreating; beseeching; imploring.
**pleadings**, the formal charges or claims by the plaintiff and answers by the defendant in a lawsuit, made alternately until the issue is submitted for decision: *The Court is entitled to look at the pleadings in the Irish action* (Law Reports).
—**plead′ing|ly**, *adv.*

**pleas|ance** (plez′əns), *n.* **1** a pleasant place, usually with trees, fountains, and flowers, and maintained as part of the grounds of a country estate. **2** *Archaic.* delight; pleasure: *a feeling of solace and pleasance* (Scott). [< Old French *plaisance* pleasure < *plaisant* pleasant. See etym. of doublet **plaisance**.]

**pleas|ant** (plez′ənt), *adj.* **1** that pleases; giving pleasure; agreeable: *a pleasant outing in the country, a pleasant swim on a hot day.* **2** easy to get along with; friendly; agreeable: *a pleasant young man.* SYN: congenial, amiable. **3** fair; not stormy: *pleasant weather.* [< Old French *plaisant*, present participle of *plaisir* to please]

—**pleas′ant|ly,** *adv.* —**pleas′ant|ness,** *n.*

—*Syn.* **1 Pleasant, pleasing, agreeable** mean giving pleasure or satisfaction to the mind, feelings, or senses. **Pleasant** applies to the person or thing that gives pleasure: *We spent a pleasant evening.* **Pleasing** focuses attention on the person who receives pleasure: *It was pleasing to me because I wanted to see them.* **Agreeable** suggests being to a person's own taste or liking: *I think this cough medicine has an agreeable flavor.*

**pleas|ant|ry** (plez′ən trē), *n., pl.* **-ries. 1** a good-natured joke; jesting action or witty remark: *He ... made him the butt of his pleasantries* (Washington Irving). **SYN:** witticism, jest. **2** fun; joking. **SYN:** drollery, banter, raillery.

**please** (plēz), *v.,* **pleased, pleas|ing.** —*v.t.* **1** to be agreeable to; cause to be happy or glad: *Toys please children. Sunshine and flowers please most people.* **SYN:** gratify, delight, content, suit. **2** to be the will of (used impersonally): *May it please the court to show mercy.* —*v.i.* **1** to be agreeable; make someone happy or glad: *Such a fine meal cannot fail to please. For we that live to please must please to live* (Samuel Johnson). **2** to wish; like; think fit: *Do what you please.* **3** may it please you (now used merely as a polite addition to requests or commands): *Come here, please. Over the piano was printed a notice: Please do not shoot the pianist. He is doing his best* (Oscar Wilde).

**be pleased, a** to be moved to pleasure: *I was pleased with the quality of his work.* **b** to be disposed; like; choose: *The governor is pleased to doubt our having such letters as we mentioned* (Benjamin Franklin).

**if you please,** if you like or with your permission: *Pray sir, put your sword up if you please* (Shakespeare). *Will you take another cup? If you please* (Hugh Binning).

**please oneself, a** to gratify or satisfy oneself: *I purposed not so much to please myself, and a few, as to be beneficial* (Thomas Granger). **b** *Informal.* to do as one likes: *Since he didn't accept my advice, I told him to please himself.*

[Middle English *plesen* < Old French *plesir,* and *plaisir* < Latin *placēre*] —**pleas′er,** *n.*

▶ **Pleased** is followed by *with,* not *at: His boss was very pleased with his work.*

**pleas|ing** (plē′zing), *adj.* that gives pleasure or satisfaction; pleasant; agreeable: *a pleasing smile, a pleasing young man.* **SYN:** See syn. under **pleasant.** —**pleas′ing|ly,** *adv.* —**pleas′ing|ness,** *n.*

**pleas of the Crown, 1** (originally, in England) pleas or legal actions over which the Crown claimed exclusive jurisdiction. **2** (later, in England) all criminal actions or proceedings. **3** (in Scotland) the actions for robbery, rape, murder, and arson.

**pleas|ur|a|ble** (plezh′ər ə bəl, plā′zhər-), *adj.* pleasant; agreeable: *a pleasurable meeting between old friends.* **SYN:** gratifying. —**pleas′ur|a|ble|ness,** *n.*

**pleas|ur|a|bly** (plezh′ər ə blē, plā′zhər-), *adv.* in a pleasurable manner; with pleasure: *pleasurably entertained.*

**pleas|ure** (plezh′ər, plā′zhər), *n., v.,* **-ured, -ur|ing.** —*n.* **1** a feeling of being pleased; enjoyment; delight; joy: *The boy's pleasure in the gift was obvious. Pleasure, not gold, is now the quest* (New Yorker). **2** something that pleases; cause of joy or delight: *It would be a pleasure to see you again.* **3** anything that amuses; sport; play: *He takes his pleasure in riding and hunting.* **4** worldly or frivolous enjoyment; sensuous gratification. **5** one's will, desire, or choice: *What is your pleasure in this matter? Is it your pleasure to go now?*

—*v.t.* to give pleasure to; please; gratify. —*v.i.* **1** to take pleasure; delight. **2** *Informal.* to go out for pleasure.

**at one's pleasure,** as or when one pleases; at will; at discretion: *... whom the housekeeper ... huffed about at her pleasure* (Scott).

**during one's pleasure,** while one pleases: *... a Secretary ... who shall hold office during Her Majesty's pleasure* (Acts of Parliament).

**take pleasure,** to be pleased; delight: *I take pleasure in introducing the next speaker.*

[Middle English *plesir,* or *plesere* < Old French *plesir,* and *plaisir,* noun use of infinitive; see etym. under **please**; English spelling influenced by *measure*]

—*Syn. n.* **1 Pleasure, delight, joy** mean a feeling of satisfaction and happiness coming from having, experiencing, or expecting something good or to one's liking. **Pleasure** is the general word applying to this feeling, whether or not it is shown in any way: *The compliment gave her pleasure.* **Delight** means great pleasure, usually shown or expressed in a lively way: *He expressed his delight with a warm handshake.* **Joy** implies intense delight and happiness, often expressing itself in rejoicing: *The child clapped her hands with joy.*

**pleasure boat,** a boat designed or used for pleasure.

**pleas|ure-dome** (plezh′ər dōm′, plā′zhər-), *n.* a large and stately mansion, estate, hotel, or resort. [allusion to Samuel Taylor Coleridge's *Kubla Khan*]

**pleasure ground,** a piece of ground or land appropriated to pleasure or enjoyment.

**pleas|ure-house** (plezh′ər hous′, plā′zhər-), *n.* a house for purposes of pleasure or enjoyment.

**pleas|ure|less** (plezh′ər lis, plā′zhər-), *adj.* without pleasure; joyless.

**pleasure principle,** the instinct or drive to seek maximum pleasure or immediate gratification and minimum pain. According to Freudian psychology the pleasure principle originates in the libido and is the force that governs the id.

**pleat** (plēt), *n., v.* —*n.* a flat, usually narrow fold made in cloth by doubling it on itself, especially one of a series of folds by which the edge of a garment or drapery is symmetrically taken in. Pleats are arranged in many different fashions. *Twenty years ago it would have been possible to market all-wool fabrics with pleats of great durability, if only the pleater had been aware of research* (London Times).

—*v.t.* to fold or arrange in pleats: *a pleated skirt.* Also, **plait.**

[variant of *plait*] —**pleat′er,** *n.*

**pleat|less** (plēt′lis), *adj.* having no pleats: *The trends to ... two-button suits and pleatless trousers are expected to continue* (Wall Street Journal).

**pleb**[1] (pleb), *n. Slang.* a plebeian.

**pleb**[2] (pleb), *n. Slang.* a plebe.

**plebe** (plēb), *n. U.S.* a member of the lowest class at a military or naval academy, especially the United States Military Academy, the Naval Academy, or the Air Force Academy. [American English, perhaps short for *plebeian*]

**ple|be|ian** (pli bē′ən), *adj., n.* —*adj.* **1** belonging to or having to do with the common people: *the craftsmen and other plebeian inhabitants of the town* (Hawthorne). **2** belonging to or having to do with the lower class of citizens in ancient Rome. **3** *Figurative.* common; vulgar. **SYN:** coarse.

—*n.* **1** one of the common people. **SYN:** commoner. **2** one of the lower class of citizens in ancient Rome. **3** *Figurative.* a common, vulgar person: *To the brave, there is but one sort of plebeian, and that is the coward* (Edward G. Bulwer-Lytton). **SYN:** cad.

[< Latin *plēbēius* (< *plēbēs,* variant of *plēbs* the common people) + English *-an*] —**ple|be′ian|ly,** *adv.* —**ple|be′ian|ness,** *n.*

**ple|be|ian|ism** (pli bē′ə niz əm), *n.* plebeian character or ways.

**ple|bis|ci|tar|y** (plə bis′ə ter′ē, -tər-), *adj.* **1** relating to or of the nature of a plebiscite. **2** based on or favoring a plebiscite: *Swiss democracy is ... plebiscitary democracy* (Manchester Guardian).

**pleb|i|scite** (pleb′ə sīt, -sit), *n.* **1** a direct vote by the qualified voters of a country, state, or other political unit on some important question. **2** such a vote by the inhabitants of a territory to choose the country or ruler that will govern them: *The plebiscite in Kashmir desired by the U.N. has never taken place* (Wall Street Journal). [< French, Middle French *plébiscite,* learned borrowing from Latin *plēbiscītum* < *plēbēī,* genitive of *plēbs* the common people + *scītum* decree, ultimately < *scīre* to know]

**pleb|is|ci|tum** (pleb′ə sī′təm), *n., pl.* **-ta** (-tə). **1** a law enacted by the ancient Roman plebeians. **2** = plebiscite. [< Latin *plēbiscītum* plebiscite]

**plebs** (plebz), *n., pl.* **ple|bes** (plē′bēz). **1** the common people of ancient Rome. **2** the common people; the populace. **SYN:** hoi polloi. [< Latin *plēbs, plēbis*]

**plec|tog|nath** (plek′təg nath), *adj., n.* —*adj.* of or belonging to an order of teleost fishes having powerful jaws and teeth and (typically) bony or spiny scales, such as the triggerfish, puffer, and filefish. —*n.* a plectognath fish.

[< New Latin *Plectognathi* the order name < Greek *plektós* plaited, twisted (< *pléktein* to twist) + *gnáthos* jaw]

**plec|tog|na|thous** (plek tog′nə thəs), *adj.* = plectognath.

**plec|trum** (plek′trəm), *n., pl.* **-trums, -tra** (-trə). a small piece of ivory, horn, metal, or plastic, used for plucking the strings of a mandolin, lyre, zither, or other stringed instrument played without a bow; pick. [< Latin *plēctrum* < Greek *plēktron* (literally) thing to strike with < *plēssein* to strike]

**pled** (pled), *v. Informal.* pleaded; a past tense and past participle of **plead**: *The man pled for mercy.*

**pledge** (plej), *n., v.,* **pledged, pledg|ing.** —*n.* **1** a solemn promise: *a pledge to support a candidate. He made a pledge to give money to charity. The drunkard signed a pledge never to drink again.* **SYN:** covenant, vow. **2** something that secures or makes safe; security: *The knight left a jewel as pledge for the borrowed horse.* **SYN:** surety, guarantee. **3** the condition of being held as security: *to put bonds in pledge for a loan.* **4** *Law.* **a** the act of handing something over to another as security for the repayment of a debt or performance of a contract. **b** the contract by which such a delivery is formally made. **5** the drinking of a health or toast. **6** something given to show favor or love or as a promise of something to come; sign; token: *Bear her this jewel, pledge of my affection* (Shakespeare). **7** *U.S.* a person who has promised to join an organization but is serving a probationary period before membership: *Postcards sent out to undergraduates, pledges, and alumni of ... an academic fraternity* (Newsweek). **8** *Obsolete.* **a** a person who acts as surety for another. **b** a hostage.

—*v.t.* **1** to promise solemnly; undertake to give: *to pledge $100 to a charity. We pledge allegiance to the flag.* **2** to cause to promise solemnly; bind by a promise: *to pledge hearers to secrecy.* **3** to give as security: *to pledge one's honor, to pledge land for a loan.* **SYN:** pawn. **4** to drink in honor of (someone) and wish (him) well; drink a health to; toast: *The knights rose from the banquet table to pledge the king. Drink to me only with thine eyes, And I will pledge with mine* (Ben Jonson).

**take** (or **sign**) **the pledge,** to promise not to drink alcoholic liquor: *Once, the mere picture of a ragged urchin crouched outside a snowbound inn waiting for her father to emerge drunk with the comforts of beer ... was enough to make strong men sign the pledge* (Manchester Guardian Weekly).

[< Anglo-French, Old French *plege* < Medieval Latin *plegium, plevium* < *plevire* to incur risk for, go bail for; to warrant, apparently < a Germanic word. See related etym. at **plight**[2].] —**pledg′er,** *n.*

**pledg|ee** (ple jē′), *n.* **1** *Law.* a person with whom something is deposited as a pledge. **2** a person to whom a pledge is made.

**pledg|et** (plej′it), *n.* a small, absorbent compress of gauze, cotton, or the like, for use on a wound or sore: *He drew a pledget of linen ... through the wound* (John Henry). [origin uncertain]

**pledg|or** or **pledge|or** (ple jôr′), *n. Law.* a person who deposits something as a pledge.

**Ple|iad** (plē′ad, plī′-), *n.* any one of the Pleiades.

**ple|iad** (plē′ad, plī′-), *n.* a brilliant cluster or group of persons or things, especially of seven: *Donne, Chillingworth, Sir T. Browne, Jeremy Taylor, Milton, South, Barrow, form a pleiad ... such as no literature can match* (Thomas De Quincey). [< *Pleiad*]

**Ple|ia|des** (plē′ə dēz, plī′-), *n.pl.* **1** a group of several hundred stars in the constellation Taurus. The Pleiades are commonly spoken of as seven, though only six can normally be seen with the naked eye. **2** *Greek Mythology.* seven of the daughters of Atlas who were transformed by the gods into this group of stars.

**plein-air** (plān′ãr′), *adj.* of or having to do with certain impressionist schools and styles of painting that originated in France about 1870 and aimed at the representation of effects of atmosphere and light that cannot be observed in the studio; open-air. [< French *en plein air* in open air]

**plein-air|ism** (plān′ãr′iz əm), *n.* the principles or methods of the plein-air painters.

**plein-air|ist** (plān′ãr′ist), *n.* an artist of the plein-air school.

**Plei|o|cene** (plī′ə sēn), *n., adj.* = Pliocene.

**plei|o|tax|y** (plī′ə tak′sē), *n. Botany.* the condition of having more than the usual number of floral whorls. [< Greek *pleíōn* more + *táxis* arrangement]

**plei|o|trop|ic** (plī′ə trop′ik), *adj. Genetics.* controlling or effecting change in more than one character: *The mutation was pleiotropic* (Scientific American). [< Greek *pleíōn* more, comparative of *polýs* much, many + *trópos* a turning] —**plei′o|trop′i|cal|ly,** *adv.*

**plei|ot|ro|pism** (plī ot′rə piz′əm), *n.* = pleiotropy.

**plei|ot|ro|py** (plī ot′rə pē), *n. Genetics.* the condition of being pleiotropic.

**Pleis|to|cene** (plīs′tə sēn), *n., adj.* —*n.* **1** the geological epoch before the present period; ice age. It was characterized by vast glaciers and the presence of man in Europe. *Within the Quaternary most of the time is taken up by the Pleis-*

**Pronunciation Key:** hat, āge, cãre, fär; let, ēqual, tėrm; it, īce; hot, ōpen, ôrder; oil, out; cup, pu̇t, rüle; child; long; thin; ᴛʜen; zh, measure; ə represents a in about, e in taken, i in pencil, o in lemon, u in circus.

*tocene, estimated at 980,000 years, while the Holocene or Recent has lasted only 20,000 years* (Beals and Hoijer). **2** the deposits, such as of gravel, made in this epoch.
— ***adj.*** of this epoch or these deposits: *the great Pleistocene glaciers of Europe and North America.*
[< Greek *pleîstos* most, superlative of *polýs* much, many + *kainós* recent]

**plen.**, plenipotentiary.

**ple|na** (plē′nə), *n.* plenums; a plural of **plenum**.

**ple|na|ry** (plen′ər ē, plē′nər-), *adj., n., pl.* **-ries**.
— ***adj.*** **1** not lacking in any way; full; complete; absolute: *an ambassador with plenary power.* **SYN**: entire. **2** attended by all of its qualified members; fully constituted: *a plenary session of a committee.*
— ***n.*** a plenary session.
[< Late Latin *plēnārius* < Latin *plēnus* full] — **ple′na|ri|ly**, *adv.*

**plenary indulgence**, complete remission of temporal penalty for sin in the Roman Catholic Church.

**ple|ni|lune** (plē′nə lün, plen′ə-), *n. Poetic.* **1** a full moon. **2** the time of the full moon. [< Latin *plēnilūnium* < *plēnus* full + *lūna* moon]

**ple|nip|o|tence** (plə nip′ə təns), *n.* a fullness or completeness of power.

**ple|nip|o|tent** (plə nip′ə tənt), *adj., n. Rare.* — ***adj.*** invested with or possessing full power or authority; plenipotentiary.
— ***n.*** a plenipotent person; plenipotentiary.
[< Late Latin *plēnipotēns, -entis* < Latin *plēnus* full + *potēns* potent, empowered]

**plen|i|po|ten|ti|ar|y** (plen′ə pə ten′shē er′ē, -shər-), *n., pl.* **-ar|ies**, *adj.* — ***n.*** a diplomatic agent having full power or authority: *Each municipality was, as it were, a little sovereign, sending envoys to a congress to vote and to sign as plenipotentiaries* (John L. Motley).
— ***adj.*** having or giving full power and authority. The United States has either an ambassador or a minister plenipotentiary in most important countries.
[< Medieval Latin *plenipotentiarius* < Late Latin *plēnipotēns* plenipotent]

**plen|ish** (plen′ish), *v.t. Especially Scottish.* to fill up; furnish; supply; stock. [< Old French *pleniss-*, stem of *plenir* < Latin *plēnus* full]

**ple|nism** (plē′niz əm), *n.* the theory that all space is a plenum and that there is no such thing as a vacuum. — **ple′nist**, *n.*

**plen|i|tude** (plen′ə tüd, -tyüd), *n.* **1** fullness; completeness: *Her force of character, emerging at length in all its plenitude, imposed itself absolutely upon its environment* (Lytton Strachey). **2** plentifulness; abundance: *Its present deer population varies ... depending on the season and the plenitude of available forage* (Atlantic). **SYN**: copiousness. [< Latin *plēnitūdō, -inis* completeness, fullness < *plēnus* full]

**plen|i|tu|di|nous** (plen′ə tü′də nəs, -tyü′-), *adj.* stout; portly.

**plen|te|ous** (plen′tē əs), *adj.* **1** present or existing in full supply; plentiful; abundant; copious: *rich, plenteous tresses* (Charlotte Brontë). **2** bearing or yielding abundantly (of); prolific (in); fertile: *The seasons had been plenteous in corn* (George Eliot). — **plen′te|ous|ly**, *adv.* — **plen′te|ous|ness**, *n.*

**plen|ti|ful** (plen′ti fəl), *adj.* **1** more than enough; ample; abundant: *a plentiful supply of food. Ten gallons of gasoline is a plentiful supply for a seventy-mile trip. Apples are cheap now because they are plentiful.* **SYN**: copious, profuse. **2** furnished with or yielding abundance: *to set a plentiful table.* **SYN**: bountiful, generous. — **plen′ti|ful|ly**, *adv.* — **plen′ti|ful|ness**, *n.*

**plen|ti|tude** (plen′tə tüd, -tyüd), *n.* plentiful condition; plentifulness. [alteration of *plenitude*]

**plen|ty** (plen′tē), *n., pl.* **-ties**, *adj., adv.* — ***n.*** **1** a full supply; all that a person needs; large enough number or amount: *You have plenty of time to catch the train.* **SYN**: profusion, copiousness. **2** the quality or condition of being plentiful; abundance: *years of peace and plenty.*
— ***adj.*** enough; plentiful; abundant: *Six potatoes will be plenty.*
— ***adv. Informal.*** quite; fully: *plenty good enough.*
[Middle English *pleynte*, also *plenteth* < Old French *plente*, earlier *plentet* < Latin *plēnitās* fullness < *plēnus* full]

**ple|num** (plē′nəm), *n., pl.* **-nums** or **-na**, *adj.* — ***n.*** **1a** an enclosed quantity of air or other gas under greater pressure than the outside atmosphere. **b** such a condition of pressure. **2** a space that is filled, or conceived as being filled, with matter. **3** the whole of space regarded as being filled with matter. **4** a full assembly, such as a joint assembly of the upper and lower houses of a legislature. **5a** a condition of fullness. **b** a full place or thing.
— ***adj.*** of or having to do with a plenum.
[< Latin *plēnum* (*spatium*) full (space), (literally) neuter of *plēnus* full]

**ple|o|chro|ic** (plē′ə krō′ik), *adj.* showing different colors because of selective absorption of light when viewed in two or three different directions, as certain double-refracting crystals. [< Greek *pléōn* more, comparative of *polýs* much, many + *chróā* color + English *-ic*]

**ple|och|ro|ism** (plē ok′rō iz əm), *n.* the quality of being pleochroic.

**ple|o|mor|phic** (plē′ə môr′fik), *adj.* exhibiting different forms at different stages of the life cycle, as certain bacteria and fungi. [< Greek *pléōn* more, comparative of *polýs* much, many + *morphḗ* form + English *-ic*]

**ple|o|mor|phism** (plē′ə môr′fiz əm), *n. Biology.* **1** the existence of different forms or types, as in a species or genus. **2** the occurrence of more than one independent stage in the life cycle of a species.

**ple|o|nasm** (plē′ə naz əm), *n.* **1** the use of more words than are necessary to express an idea. "The two twins" is a pleonasm. **2** the unnecessary word, phrase, or expression. [< Late Latin *pleonasmos* < Greek *pleonasmós* < *pleonázein* to be redundant < *pléōn* more, comparative of *polýs* much]

**ple|o|nas|tic** (plē′ə nas′tik), *adj.* using more words than are needed; superfluous; redundant. — **ple′o|nas′ti|cal|ly**, *adv.*

**ple|o|nec|tic** (plē′ə nek′tik), *adj.* of or having to do with pleonexia.

**ple|o|nex|i|a** (plē′ə nek′sē ə), *n.* greed or grasping selfishness, especially as an indication of mental disorder. [< New Latin *pleonexia* < Greek *pleonexíā* < *pléōn* more, comparative of *polýs* much + *échein* to have]

**ple|o|pod** (plē′ə pod), *n.* = swimmeret. [< Greek *pleîn* to swim + *poûs, podós* foot]

**ple|rome** (plir′ōm), *n. Botany.* the innermost region of an apical meristem, composed of actively dividing cells: *Procambium or plerome originates the primary or first vascular bundles, the cambium, and sometimes the pith* (Heber W. Youngken). [< German *Plerom* < Greek *plḗrōma* a filling < *plēroûn* to fill < *plḗrēs* full]

**Ple|si|an|thro|pus** (plē′sē an′thrə pəs), *n.* an early manlike ape, considered to be one of the Australopithecines, whose bones have been found in South Africa. [< New Latin *Plesianthropus* the genus name < Greek *plēsíos* near + *ánthrōpos* man]

**ple|si|o|saur** (plē′sē ə sôr), *n.* any one of a group of large sea reptiles, now extinct, that had a long neck, small head, short tail, and four large flippers instead of legs. Plesiosaurs were common in the early Mesozoic era. [< New Latin *Plesiosaurus* the genus name < Greek *plēsíos* near + *saûros* lizard]

**ple|si|o|sau|rus** (plē′sē ə sôr′əs), *n., pl.* **-sau|ri** (-sôr′ī). = plesiosaur.

**ples|sor** or **ples|ser** (ples′ər), *n.* = plexor.

**pleth|o|ra** (pleth′ər ə), *n.* **1** excessive fullness; too much; superabundance: *a plethora of words, a plethora of food. This being the big Paris season, there is such a plethora of local and foreign attractions to look at and listen to that the real problem is to try and pick out the hundred best* (New Yorker). **SYN**: superfluity, oversupply, excess. **2** an abnormal condition caused by an excess of red corpuscles in the blood or an increase in the quantity of blood in the body: *Your character is like a person in a plethora, absolutely dying from too much health* (Richard Brinsley Sheridan). [< Late Latin *plēthōra* < Greek *plēthṓrā* fullness of humors < *plḗthein* be full < *plêthos* multitude, mass]

**ple|thor|ic** (ple thôr′ik, -thor′-; pleth′ər-), *adj.* **1** too full; inflated: *a plethoric style of writing, plethoric opulence.* **2** having too much blood or too many red corpuscles in the blood; afflicted with plethora: *a plethoric condition.* — **ple|thor′i|cal|ly**, *adv.*

**ple|thys|mo|graph** (plə thiz′mə graf, -gräf), *n.* a device for measuring and recording the variation in the size or volume of a part of the body, as altered by the flow of blood in it. [< Greek *plēthysmós* enlargement (< *plēthýs* fullness) + English *-graph*]

**ple|thys|mo|graph|ic** (plə thiz′mə graf′ik), *adj.* of or having to do with a plethysmograph.

**pleth|ys|mog|raph|y** (pleth′iz mog′rə fē), *n.* the use of a plethysmograph.

**pleu|ra**[1] (plůr′ə), *n., pl.* **pleu|rae** (plůr′ē). a thin membrane in the body of a mammal, covering each lung and folded back to make a lining for the thorax or chest cavity. [< New Latin *pleura* < Greek *pleurā́* the side, rib, or *pleurá* side, plural of *pleurón* rib]

**pleu|ra**[2] (plůr′ə), *n.* plural of **pleuron**.

**pleu|ral** (plůr′əl), *adj.* of the pleura: *pleural inflammation.*

**pleural cavity**, the space between the two layers of the pleura: *The space between the body wall and the lungs is designated the pleural cavity* (Harbaugh and Goodrich).

**pleu|rec|to|my** (plů rek′tə mē), *n., pl.* **-mies**. the surgical removal of part of the pleura.

**pleu|ri|sy** (plůr′ə sē), *n.* inflammation of the thin membrane covering the lungs and lining the thorax, often marked by fever, chest pains, and difficulty in breathing: *Pleurisy usually occurs as a complication of pneumonia, tuberculosis, and other infectious diseases* (M. D. Altschule). [< Old French *pleursie*, alteration of Late Latin *pleurisis* lung trouble, for Latin *pleurītis* pleurisy, pain in the side < Greek *pleurîtis* < *pleurā́* the side, rib; see etym. under **pleura**[1]]

**pleurisy root**, **1** the butterfly weed, whose root has been used as a popular remedy for pleurisy. **2** the root.

**pleu|rit|ic** (plů rit′ik), *adj.* **1** having pleurisy. **2** of pleurisy. **3** causing pleurisy.

**pleu|ri|tis** (plů rī′tis), *n.* = pleurisy.

**pleu|ro|dont** (plůr′ə dont), *adj., n.* — ***adj.*** **1** (of a tooth) not in a socket but issuing directly from and fixed to the upper or lower jawbone at the side or front. **2** having such teeth, as certain lizards.
— ***n.*** a pleurodont animal.
[< Greek *pleurón* side + *odoús, odóntos* tooth]

**pleu|ro|dyn|i|a** (plůr′ə din′ē ə, -dī′nē-), *n.* a virus infection causing painful inflammation of the muscles of the diaphragm and the chest and many symptoms similar to those of poliomyelitis; devil's grip; Bornholm disease. [< New Latin *pleurodynia* < Greek *pleurón* side + *odýnē* pain]

**pleu|ron** (plůr′on), *n., pl.* **pleu|ra**. a lateral part of the body of an arthropod, especially of a thoracic segment of an insect. [< New Latin *pleuron* < Greek *pleurón* rib, side]

**pleu|ro|per|i|to|ne|al** (plůr′ō per′ə tə nē′əl), *adj.* having to do with the pleura, or pleurae, and the peritoneum.

**pleu|ro|pneu|mo|nia** (plůr′ō nü mōn′yə, -mō′nē ə; -nyü-), *n.* **1** pneumonia complicated with pleurisy. **2** an infectious disease of cattle characterized by inflammation of both the pleura and the lungs, caused by a mycoplasma.

**pleu|ro|pneu|mo|nia-like organism** (plůr′ō nümōn′yə līk′, -mō′nē ə-; -nyü-), any one of the filterable microorganisms resembling both viruses and bacteria that cause such diseases as primary atypical pneumonia and pleuropneumonia of cattle; mycoplasma. *Abbr:* PPLO (no periods).

**plex|i|form** (plek′sə fôrm), *adj.* shaped like or resembling a plexus: *Its papilla is covered with a plexiform mesh of dilated vessels* (British Medical Journal). [< Latin *plexus* braid + English *-form*]

**Plex|i|glas** (plek′sə glas′, -gläs′), *n. Trademark.* plexiglass.

**plex|i|glass** (plek′sə glas′, -gläs′), *n.* a light, transparent thermoplastic, often used in place of glass. [< *pl*(astic) + (fl)*exi*(ble) + *glass*]

**plex|im|e|ter** (plek sim′ə tər), *n.* a small, thin plate, as of ivory, designed to be placed in contact with the body and struck with a plexor in diagnosis and examination by percussion. [< Greek *plêxis* stroke, percussion (< *plḗssein* to strike) + English *-meter*]

**plex|or** (plek′sər), *n.* a small hammer used for tapping the body in diagnosis and examination. Also, **plessor**, **plesser**. [< Greek *plêxis* a stroke (< *plḗssein* to strike) + English *-or*, as in *flexor*]

**plex|us** (plek′səs), *n., pl.* **-us|es** or **-us**. **1** a network of nerve fibers, blood vessels, or lymphatics. The solar plexus is a collection of nerves behind the stomach. **2** *Figurative.* a complex: *a plexus of mutual rights.* **SYN**: mass; web; network. [< New Latin *plexus* < Latin *plexus, -ūs* a braid < *plectere* to twine, braid]

**plf.**, plaintiff.

**pli|a|bil|i|ty** (plī′ə bil′ə tē), *n.* pliable condition or quality: (*Figurative.*) *Pliability in politics, if accompanied by honesty, is a virtue* (Henry Adams). **SYN**: flexibility.

**pli|a|ble** (plī′ə bəl), *adj.* **1** easily bent; flexible; supple: *Willow twigs are pliable.* **2** *Figurative.* easily influenced; yielding: *He is too pliable to be a good leader.* [< Middle French *pliable* < *plier* to bend; see etym. under **ply**[2]] — **pli′a|ble|ness**, *n.* — **pli′a|bly**, *adv.*

**pli|an|cy** (plī′ən sē), *n.* the fact of being easily bent; pliant condition or quality: (*Figurative.*) *To be overlooked for want of political pliancy, is a circumstance I need not blush to own* (Richard Watson). **SYN**: flexibility, pliability.

**pli|ant** (plī′ənt), *adj.* **1** bending easily; flexible; supple: *pliant leather.* **SYN**: pliable, limber. See syn. under **flexible**. **2** *Figurative.* easily influenced; yielding: *a pliant nature. It was his wish that Lord Granville, a young man whom he believed to be pliant to his influence, should be Palmerston's successor* (Lytton Strachey). **3** changing easily to fit different conditions; adaptable. [< Old French *pliant* bending, present participle of *plier;* see etym. under **ply**[2]]

—**pli′ant|ly**, *adv.* —**pli′ant|ness**, *n.*

**pli|ca** (plī′kə), *n., pl.* **-cae** (-sē). **1** a fold or folding of skin or membrane: *The mucous membrane lining of the intestinal wall has many plicae* (Carl C. Francis). **2** a matted, filthy condition of the hair caused by disease. [< Medieval Latin *plica* fold, pleat < Latin *plicāre* to fold, interweave]

**pli|cal** (plī′kəl), *adj.* having to do with or resembling a plica.

**pli|cate** (plī′kāt), *adj.* **1** folded like a fan; pleated. **2** folded along its ribs like a closed fan: *Thus birch leaves are plicate, folded several times lengthwise, like a fan* (New York Times). [< Latin *plicātus* folded, past participle of *plicāre* to fold] —**pli′cate|ly**, *adv.* —**pli′cate|ness**, *n.*

**pli|cat|ed** (plī′kā tid), *adj.* = plicate.

**pli|ca|tion** (plī kā′shən), *n.* **1a** the act or process of folding. **b** the fold. **2** plicate form or condition: *An artist of the Chinese school ... may accentuate folds of drapery by a kind of shadow beneath the plication* (W. Anderson).

*****pli|é** (plē ā′), *n. French.* **1** (in ballet) a movement or exercise with both knees bent but with the feet remaining on the floor and the back straight. **2** (literally) bent.

*****plié**
definition 1

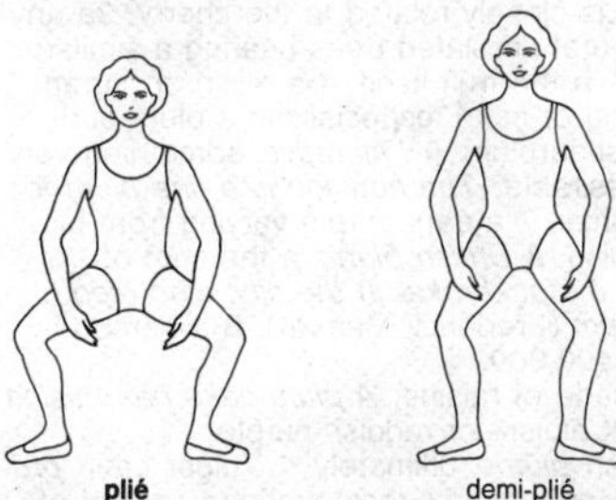


**plied** (plīd), *v.* the past tense and past participle of **ply**[1] and **ply**[2].

**pli|er** (plī′ər), *n.* **1** a person or thing that plies. **2** = pliers.

**pli|ers** (plī′ərz), *n., pl.* **-ers.** small pincers with long jaws for bending or cutting wire or holding small objects. [< *ply*[2], verb]

**plight**[1] (plīt), *n.* a condition or situation, now usually bad: *He was in a sad plight when he became ill and had no money. I think myself in better plight for a lender than you are* (Shakespeare). **SYN:** dilemma, scrape, fix. See syn. under **predicament.** [< Anglo-French *plit* (originally) manner of folding, for unrecorded *pleit;* confused with *plight*[2]. See etym. of doublet **plait.**]

**plight**[2] (plīt), *v., n.* —*v.t.* to promise solemnly; pledge: *to plight one's loyalty.* [Old English *plihtan* < *pliht,* noun]
—*n.* a solemn promise; pledge: *a mutual plight of faith* (George Meredith).
[Old English *pliht* (originally) danger; (later) the incurring of risk in warranting; pledge] —**plight′er,** *n.*

**plim|soles** (plim′səlz), *n.pl.* = plimsolls.

**Plim|soll mark** or **line** (plim′səl, -sol), one of a set of marks or lines on the hull of a ship that show how deep it may ride in the water, under varying conditions of water temperature and weather, after loading. A Plimsoll mark is required on British merchant ships and now appears on most other merchant ships. [< Samuel *Plimsoll,* 1824-1898, a member of Parliament who succeeded in having the law against overloading passed]

**plim|solls** (plim′səlz), *n.pl. British.* light canvas shoes with rubber soles; sneakers. [origin uncertain]

**plink** (plingk), *v., n.* —*v.t.* **1** to produce a tinkling sound. **2** to shoot or throw at a target, especially in a more or less casual way: *The neighborhood youngsters had gathered to plink tin cans off our yard fence* (Time).
—*v.i.* **1** to play on a musical instrument, etc., in a tinkling fashion: *So far he has done everything from Chinese-style plinking to jittering rock 'n' roll* (Newsweek). *The coin plinked on the glass counter.* **2** to shoot or throw something at a target.
—*n.* a tinkling sound: *the plinks of a piano.*
[imitative] —**plink′er,** *n.*

**plinth** (plinth), *n.* **1** the lower, square part of the base of a column. **2** a square base of a pedestal, as for a statue, bust, or vase. **3** the squared base of a piece of furniture. **4** a projecting part of a wall immediately above the ground, often consisting of a course (plinth course) or courses of bricks or stones. [< Latin *plinthus* < Greek *plínthos*]

**Pli|o|cene** (plī′ə sēn), *n., adj.* —*n.* **1** a geological epoch marked by the appearance of the first manlike apes, the rising of mountains in western America, and the migration of mammals between continents. The Pliocene is the last epoch of the Tertiary period of the Cenozoic era, after the Miocene. *We must of course have had direct ancestors during the Pliocene* (Alfred L. Kroeber). **2** the rocks formed in this epoch.
—*adj.* of this epoch or its rocks: *Pliocene beds.* Also, **Pleiocene.**
[< Greek *pleíōn* more, comparative of *polýs* much + *kainós* recent]

**Pli|o|film** (plī′ə film), *n. Trademark.* a clear, flexible plastic, a rubber hydrochloride, used to make raincoats and various kinds of moistureproof or protective bags and wrappings.

**Pli|o|hip|pus** (plī′ə hip′əs), *n.* any one of a group of extinct mammals of the horse family, living about 12,000,000 years ago. It is a direct ancestor of the modern horse and is the first horselike animal with a hoof having only one toe. [< *Plio*(cene) + Greek *hippos* horse]

**pli|o|saur** (plī′ə sôr), *n.* any one of a group of large Mesozoic sea reptiles related and similar to the plesiosaurs, but with a shorter neck, larger head, and stronger jaws and teeth. [< New Latin *Pliosaurus* the genus name < Greek *pleíōn* more + *saûros* lizard]

**plique-à-jour** (plēk′ä zhür′), *n.* a form of cloisonné enamel without a metal foundation. Plique-à-jours are the most translucent enamels because they have no background to stop the light. [< French *plique-à-jour,* probably alteration of *applique-à-jour* < *applique* application, apliquéd work + *à* in + *jour* opening]

**plis|ky** or **plis|kie** (plis′kē), *n., pl.* **-kies,** *adj. Scottish.* —*n.* a mischievous trick.
—*adj.* mischievous: *Auld Habkin o' the Pethfit, who was a plisky body* (John Service).
[origin unknown]

**plis|sé** or **plis|se** (plē sā′), *n.* a fabric like crepe, made of cotton, acetate, or rayon, which has the appearance of seersucker caused by a chemical shrinking with caustic soda. [< French *plissé,* (originally) past participle of *plisser* pleat < *pli;* see etym. under *ply*[2], noun]

**PLO** (no periods) or **P.L.O.,** Palestine Liberation Organization.

**plod** (plod), *v.,* **plod|ded, plod|ding,** *n.* —*v.i.* **1** to walk heavily or slowly; trudge: *The old man plods wearily along the road.* **SYN:** See syn. under **walk.** **2** *Figurative.* to proceed in a slow or dull way; work patiently with effort: *He plods away at his lessons until he learns them. The secret of good work—to plod on and still keep the passion fresh* (George Meredith).
—*v.t.* to walk heavily or slowly along or through: *The plowman homeward plods his weary way* (Thomas Gray).
—*n.* **1** the act or course of plodding. **2** a sound of heavy tread.
[perhaps imitative] —**plod′der,** *n.* —**plod′ding|ly,** *adv.*

**PL/1,** a general-purpose computer language that combines features of commercial- and scientific-oriented computer languages. [< *P*(rogramming) *L*(anguage) *1*]

**plonk**[1] (plongk), *v.t., v.i., n., adv.* = plunk.

**plonk**[2] (plongk), *n. Australian Slang.* cheap wine.

**plop** (plop), *n., v.,* **plopped, plop|ping,** *adv.* —*n.* **1** a sound like that of an object striking water without a splash: *The frog made a loud plop jumping into the water.* **2** the act or fact of falling with a plop.
—*v.i.* **1** to make a sound like that of an object striking water without a splash: *The noise of the frog as he plopped into the water, startled the ducks.* **2** to fall with such a sound.
—*v.t.* to cause (something) to plop, or fall with a plop.
—*adv.* with a plop: *The old ship went down all on a sudden with a lurch to starboard—plop* (Joseph Conrad).
[imitative]

**plosh** (plosh), *n.* = splash. [variant of *plash*[1]]

**plo|sion** (plō′zhən), *n. Phonetics.* explosion: *In plosive sounds the organs are separated with great rapidity and the plosion itself is thus heard as an instantaneous noise* (Simeon Potter). [< (ex)*plosion*]

**plo|sive** (plō′siv), *adj., n. Phonetics.* explosive: *We know that, of all the various vowels, plosives, fricatives and other sounds of speech, certain ones occur very often and others less so* (Colin Cherry). [< (ex)*plosive*]

**plot** (plot), *n., v.,* **plot|ted, plot|ting.** —*n.* **1** a secret plan, especially to do something wrong: *Two men formed a plot to rob the bank.* **SYN:** intrigue, conspiracy. **2** the plan or main story of a play, novel, poem, or other literary or theatrical piece: *Some people like plots filled with action and adventure.* **3** a small piece of ground: *a garden plot.* **4** a map or diagram: *He made a plot of the route of the hike.* **5** *Nautical.* the course or position, as of a ship or aircraft, drawn on a chart.
—*v.t.* **1** to plan secretly with others; plan: *to plot mischief or revenge.* **2** to divide (land) into plots: *The farm was plotted out into house lots.* **3** to make a map, diagram, or chart of: *The nurse plotted a chart to show the patient's temperature over several days.* **4** to mark the position of (something) on a map, diagram, or chart: *The nurse plotted the patient's temperature over several days.* **5** *Mathematics.* **a** to determine the location of (a point) by means of its coordinates; mark (a point) on graph paper. **b** to make (a curve) by connecting points marked out on a graph. **c** to represent (an equation or function) by means of a curve drawn through points on a graph.
—*v.i.* **1** to plan secretly with others to do something wrong; contrive a plot; conspire: *The rebels plotted against the government.* **2** to devise a literary plot.
[perhaps Old English *plot* patch of ground. Compare etym. under **plat**[1], **complot.**] —**plot′less,** *adj.* —**plot′less|ness,** *n.*
—*Syn. v.t.* **1**, *v.i.* **1. Plot, conspire, scheme** mean to plan secretly. **Plot** implies forming secretly, alone or together with others, a carefully designed plan, usually harmful or treacherous, against a person, group, or country: *Enemy agents plotted to blow up the plant.* **Conspire** implies combining with others to carry out an illegal act, especially treachery or treason: *They conspired to overthrow the government.* **Scheme** implies careful planning, often in a crafty or underhand way, to gain one's own ends: *He schemed to become president.*

**Plo|ti|nism** (plō tī′niz əm, plō′tə-), *n.* the philosophical system or teachings of Plotinus (205?-270?), the most noted exponent of Neoplatonism, who held that the material world is unreal and reality lies beyond life in the union of the soul with the mystical source of all truth, goodness, and beauty. —**Plo|ti′nist,** *n.*

**plot|line** (plot′līn′), *n.* the line or course along which the plot of a play, novel, or other literary or theatrical piece moves or develops: *a poorly constructed plotline.*

**plot|tage** (plot′ij), *n.* the area of a plot of land.

**plot|ter** (plot′ər), *n.* a person or thing that plots: *A suspected plotter was shot to death* (New York Times). *Another output device is the plotter, which can make plots from computer-generated data* (R. Clay Sprowls).

**plot|ting board** (plot′ing), a large board on which the positions of missiles, aircraft, ships, troops or civilian emergency services, parade routes, or any other people, equipment, or procedures, are plotted.

**plotting paper,** ruled paper on which curves, diagrams, or other functions can be plotted; graph paper.

**plot|ty** (plot′ē), *adj.,* **-ti|er, -ti|est.** *Informal.* characterized by an elaborate plot: *a plotty novel.*

**plough**[1] (plou), *n., v. Especially British.* plow.

**plough**[2] (plou), *v.t. British Slang.* to fail a student; flunk: *A Greek classmate of mine at Exeter was ploughed in preliminary Greek* (Joel Sayre). [special use of plough[1]]

**plough|back** (plou′bak′), *n. Especially British.* plowback.

**plough|boy** (plou′boi′), *n. Especially British.* plowboy.

**plough|land** (plou′land′), *n. Especially British.* plowland.

**plough|man** (plou′mən), *n., pl.* **-men.** *Especially British.* plowman.

**plough|share** (plou′shãr′), *n. Especially British.* plowshare.

**plov|er** (pluv′ər, plō′vər), *n., pl.* **-ers** or (*collectively*) **-er. 1** a small shore bird with a short bill, a tail like that of a pigeon, and long, pointed wings. The killdeer and the golden plover are two kinds. **2** any one of several related birds of the same family, such as the turnstones. **3** any one of various snipes and sandpipers. [< Anglo-French *plover,* Old French *plouvier* < Vulgar Latin *plovārius* (perhaps literally) rain bird < *plovēre* to rain, for Latin *pluere* < *pluvia* rain]

*****plow** (plou), *n., v.* —*n.* **1** a big, heavy, farm implement or piece of machinery for cutting the soil and turning it over: *The plow bottom lifts, turns, and breaks up the soil* (A. D. Longhouse). See picture on the following page. **2** a machine for removing snow; snowplow. **3** any one of various instruments, parts of machinery, or the like, resembling a plow in shape or action.
—*v.t.* **1** to turn up (the soil) with a plow; till: *to*

**Pronunciation Key:** hat, āge, cãre, fär; let, ēqual, tėrm; it, īce; hot, ōpen, ôrder; **oi**l, **ou**t; cup, pu̇t, rüle; **ch**ild; lo**ng**; **th**in; **ᴛʜ**en; **zh**, measure; ə represents **a** in about, **e** in taken, **i** in pencil, **o** in lemon, **u** in circus.

*plow a straight furrow.* **2** to remove with a plow or as if with a plow: *to plow snow, to plow up old roots.* **3** to furrow: *to plow a field,* (*Figurative.*) *wrinkles plowed in one's face by time.* **4** *Figurative.* **a** to cut the surface of (water): *The ship plowed the waves.* **b** to travel (a course) in this manner. —*v.i.* **1** to use a plow: *The farmer prefers to plow in the fall, so that he can begin seeding in the spring as soon as weather permits* (Colby and Foster). **2** to move as a plow does; advance slowly and with effort: *the ... horse-dealer whose caravans plowed through their fastnesses belly deep in snow* (Rudyard Kipling); (*Figurative.*) *to plow through a book.* **3** *Figurative.* to move through water by cutting the surface: *The ship plowed through the waves.* **4** to bear or admit of plowing: *The soil plows well.*

**plow back,** to reinvest (the profits of a business) in the same business: *Nearly 40 per cent of all the profits United States Steel has earned during this period has been plowed back into this program* (New York Times).

**plow into,** to invest in: *In the last ten years Imperial Oil has plowed a billion dollars into the Canadian economy* (Maclean's).

**plow out, a** to dig or thrust out (of the ground) with a plow: *to plow out roots or weeds.* **b** to remove; cast out; hollow out: *channels plowed out by a river.* (*Figurative.*) *God loves not to plow out the heart of our endeavours with ... sad tasks* (Milton).

**plow under, a** to bury in the soil by plowing (grass or legume) as a form of green manure: *This crop furnishes hay and perhaps some pasturage before it is plowed under* (Fred W. Emerson). **b** *U.S.* to reduce overproduction by plowing up (a crop): *to plow under acres of wheat.* **c** *Informal, Figurative.* to defeat or overwhelm; destroy; overcome: *The nation's educators are particularly worried about the possible "plowing under" of smaller colleges with lower standards* (Science News Letter).

**plow up, a** to break up (ground) by plowing: *The wild boar plows it* [*the earth*] *up like a furrow, and does irreparable damage in the cultivated lands* (Oliver Goldsmith). **b** to dig or thrust out (of the ground) by plowing: *to plow up crops.* **c** *Figurative.* to cut up; scratch deeply; bruise: *For he ... hath plowed up my heart* (William Barlow). Also, *especially British,* **plough.**

[Middle English *plow,* Old English *plōh*] —**plow′a·ble,** *adj.* —**plow′er,** *n.*

***plow**
definition 1

**Plow** (plou), *n.* **1** the Big Dipper; Charles's Wain. **2** the entire constellation Ursa Major. [< *plow*]

**plow|back** (plou′bak′), *n.* **1** a reinvestment of profits of a business in the same business. **2** the sum that has been reinvested.

**plow|boy** (plou′boi′), *n.* **1** a boy who guides a plow or the horses drawing it. **2** a country boy.

**plow|land** (plou′land′, -lənd), *n.* **1** an old English measure of land, usually 120 acres, considered as the area capable of being tilled with a team of eight oxen. **2** arable land.

**plow|man** (plou′mən), *n., pl.* **-men. 1** a man who guides a plow. **2** a farmworker.

**plow|share** (plou′shãr′), *n.* the blade of a plow, the part that cuts the soil; share.

**plow|tail** (plou′tāl′), *n.* the handle or handles of a plow.

**plow|wright** (plou′rīt′), *n.* a person who makes and repairs plows.

**ploy¹** (ploi), *n.* **1** *Informal.* a gambit or maneuver by which the advantage is or may be gained over another. **2** *British Informal.* an action or proceeding, especially one in which a person amuses himself: *Their "ploy" of that week happened to be rabbit-shooting with saloon-pistols* (Rudyard Kipling). [perhaps short for *employ,* noun, in obsolete meaning "use"]

**ploy²** (ploi), *v.i.* (of troops) to move from formation in a line to formation in a column: *There ... they acquire the art of ploying and deploying their troops* (Sir Charles Napier). [back formation < *deploy*] —**ploy′ment,** *n.*

**PLSS** (no periods), portable life-support system.

**plu.,** plural.

**pluck** (pluk), *v., n.* —*v.t.* **1** to pull off; pick: *to pluck a person out of bed. She plucked flowers in the garden.* **2** to pull at; pull; tug; jerk: *to pluck a person by the sleeve.* **SYN:** tweak. **3** to pull on (the strings of a musical instrument). **4** to pull off the feathers or hair from: *to pluck one's eyebrows. The farmer's wife was busy plucking chickens.* **5** *Slang, Figurative.* to rob; swindle; fleece. **6** *British Informal.* to reject (a candidate) in an examination.
—*v.i.* to pull sharply or forcibly; tug (at); jerk (at): *She plucked at the loose threads of her coat.*
—*n.* **1** the act of picking or pulling: *With a few plucks at the strings of his banjo everybody was singing along.* **2** *Figurative.* courage; boldness; spirit: *The cat showed pluck in fighting the dog. ... the pluck, daring, and admirable work of our aviators* (H. G. Wells). **SYN:** resolution, stamina. **3** the heart, liver, and lungs of an animal, used for food.

**pluck up, a** to get new courage; cheer up: *Even those passengers who were most distrustful of themselves plucked up amazingly* (Dickens). **b** to uproot; demolish: *I plucked up her social fiction* (Elizabeth Barrett Browning).

[Old English *pluccian, pluccian* to pull off, cull; later, to draw, snatch] —**pluck′a|ble,** *adj.* —**pluck′er,** *n.*

**pluck|y** (pluk′ē), *adj.,* **pluck|i|er, pluck|i|est.** having or showing courage: *a plucky dog.* **SYN:** brave, mettlesome, spirited. —**pluck′i|ly,** *adv.* —**pluck′i|ness,** *n.*

**plug** (plug), *n., v.,* **plugged, plug|ging.** —*n.* **1** a piece of wood or other substance, used to stop up a hole, to fill a gap, or to act as a wedge: *Put the plug in the drain before all the water runs out.* **SYN:** stopper, stopple. **2** a device to make an electrical connection. Some plugs screw into sockets; others have prongs. *When she put the plug in the socket, the light went on.* **3** a place where a hose can be attached; hydrant: *Water was pouring out of the plug onto the street.* **SYN:** cock. **4a** a cake of pressed tobacco. **b** a piece of this cut off for chewing. **5** = spark plug. **6** *Informal.* an advertisement or recommendation, especially one put in a radio or television program: *Mr. Harper reported the Democratic convention ... but ... has not mentioned it since last month and I want to put in a plug for it* (Bernard De Voto). **SYN:** endorsement. **7** *Informal.* a worn-out or inferior horse: *An old plug named Snowball kept getting in the way* (Time). **8** a fishing lure made of wood, metal, or plastic, and imitating the action or appearance of some natural food of a fish: *Some fishermen are taking fish on a jointed eel plug* (New York Times). **9** an iron wedge which is driven between two other wedges (feathers) to split rock. **10** a small clump of sod, especially sod sold to restore a lawn: *As the name implies, plugs are clumps of grass plants* (New York Times). **11** *Geology.* **a** a cylindrical mass of igneous rock formed in the crater of an extinct volcano. **b** a cylindrical mass of rock salt that has pushed its way upward through overlying rock and formed a dome, often containing quantities of oil and natural gas. **12** *U.S. Informal.* a shopworn or unsalable article. **13** *Slang.* a blow of the fist; punch. **14** *U.S. Slang.* a plug hat.
—*v.t.* **1** to stop up or fill with a plug: *He quickly plugged the drain to keep the bathwater from running out.* (*Figurative.*) *Opinion was sadly split as to how the air-defense gap could be plugged* (Newsweek). **SYN:** close. **2** to connect to an electric circuit by inserting a plug into an outlet: *Plug the radio into the tape recorder to tape the program. Five children were plugged into a tape recorder, listening to a story* (Atlantic). **3** *Informal.* to recommend or advertise, especially on a radio or television program: *to plug a new product.* **4** *Slang.* to put a bullet into; shoot. **5** *Slang.* to strike with the fist; punch. **6** to cut a small tapering piece from (a watermelon) in testing ripeness.
—*v.i.* **1** *Informal.* to work steadily; plod: *She plugged away at the typewriter.* **2** *Slang.* to hit; shoot.

**plug in, a** to make an electrical connection by inserting a plug into an outlet: *to plug in the television set.* [*He*] *brought a tape recorder into the Secretary's office, plugged it in, and asked a number of questions about Administration foreign policy* (Newsweek). **b** *U.S. Slang, Figurative.* to connect or relate (to anything said or happening): *She could tell I didn't plug in to what she was talking about* (W. J. J. Gordon).

**pull the plug,** to disconnect life-sustaining equipment, such as a respirator: *Establishing brain death as a judicial standard ... permits the physician to "pull the plug" without even committing an act of passive euthanasia. The patient will first be defined as dead; pulling the plug will merely be the harmless act of halting useless treatment on a cadaver* (Harper's).

[apparently < Dutch, Middle Dutch *plugge* a bung, stopper]

**plug|board** (plug′bôrd′, -bōrd′), *n.* **1** a switchboard in which the connections are made by inserting plugs. **2** a removable panel with many electric terminals into which connecting wire cords may be plugged to control a program or other process in a computer or punch-card machine; patchboard: *The instructions are programmed on the experimental equipment through a plugboard* (New Scientist).

**plug|ger** (plug′ər), *n.* **1** a person or thing that plugs. **2** a dentist's instrument, of various forms, for driving and packing a filling material into a hole, as in a decayed tooth.

**plug hat,** *U.S. Informal.* a man's high silk hat.

**plug-in** (plug′in′), *adj., n.* —*adj.* needing only to be plugged in to an electrical outlet to operate: *plug-in fryers and griddles.*
—*n.* a place where a piece of plug-in equipment can be connected.

**plug|o|la** (plə gō′lə), *n. U.S. Slang.* undercover payment for mentioning or displaying a product on another sponsor's radio or televison program. [< *plug* (def. 6) + (pay)*ola*]

**plug-ug|ly** (plug′ug′lē), *n., pl.* **-lies.** *Slang.* a ruffian; rowdy; tough: *In one Harrigan play, a plug-ugly enters, sneaking along menacingly and brandishing a club* (New Yorker).

**plum¹** (plum), *n., adj.* —*n.* **1** a round, juicy fruit with a smooth skin and a stone or pit. Plums are purple, blue, red, green, or yellow. **2** the tree that it grows on. The plum is a member of the rose family and is closely related to the cherry. **3a** any one of several unrelated trees bearing a similar edible fruit. **b** the fruit itself. **4** a raisin or currant in a pudding or cake, especially in a plum pudding. **5** = sugarplum. **6** *Figurative.* something very good or desirable: *The new job is a fine plum for him.* **SYN:** prize. **7** a dark purple varying from bluish to reddish. **8** *British Slang.* **a** the sum of £100,000: *a stockbroker in the city, who died worth a plum* (Frederick Marryat). **b** a person who has £100,000.
—*adj.* **1** made of raisins: *A plum cake has raisins in it.* **2** dark bluish- or reddish-purple.
[Old English *plūme,* ultimately < Vulgar Latin *prūna* < Latin *prūnum* < Greek *proûnon,* variant of *proûmnon.* See etym. of doublet **prune.**] —**plum′like′,** *adj.*

**plum²** (plum), *adj., adv.* = plumb.

**plum|age** (plü′mij), *n.* the feathers of a bird: *A parrot has bright plumage.* [< Old French *plumage* < *plume;* see etym. under **plume**]

**plum|aged** (plü′mijd), *adj.* furnished with or having plumage: *some common dull-plumaged little bird* (W. H. Hudson).

**plu|mate** (plü′māt, -mit), *adj. Zoology.* resembling a feather, as a hair or bristle that bears smaller hairs, or an insect's antenna covered with fine hairs. [< Latin *plūmātus,* past participle of *plūmāre* to provide with feathers < *plūma* feather]

**plumb** (plum), *n., adj., adv., v.* —*n.* a small weight on the end of a line used to measure the depth of water or to see if a wall is vertical; plummet; lead. See diagram under **plumb line.**
—*adj.* **1** vertical. **SYN:** perpendicular. **2** *Informal, Figurative.* complete; thorough: *plumb foolishness.* **SYN:** absolute.
—*adv.* **1** vertically. **2** *Informal.* completely; thoroughly: *That horse is plumb worn out.* Also, **plum.**
—*v.t.* **1** to test or adjust by a plumb line; test; sound: *Our line was not long enough to plumb the depths of the lake.* **2** *Figurative.* to get to the bottom of; fathom: *No one could plumb the deep mystery.* **3** to close with a lead seal. **4** *Informal.* to supply or repair the plumbing of. —*v.i.* **1** to be vertical; hang vertically. **2** *Informal.* to be employed as a plumber.

**out of** (or **off**) **plumb,** not vertical: *The column is seriously off plumb* (Pall Mall Gazette).

[Middle English *plum,* or *plumbe* < Old French *plom,* and *plomb* < Latin *plumbum* the element lead] —**plumb′a|ble,** *adj.* —**plumb′ness,** *n.*

**plum|bag|i|na|ceous** (plum baj′ə nā′shəs), *adj.* belonging to a family of dicotyledonous herbs and shrubs typified by the plumbago (leadwort). [< New Latin *Plumbaginaceae* the family name (< Latin *plumbāgō, -inis* plumbago) + English *-ous*]

**plum|bag|i|nous** (plum baj′ə nəs), *adj.* of the nature of or containing graphite (plumbago).

**plum|ba|go** (plum bā′gō), *n., pl.* **-gos. 1** = graphite. **2** any one of a group of herbaceous plants of warm regions, grown for their spikes of showy blue, white, or scarlet flowers; leadwort. [< Latin *plumbāgō, -inis* lead ore; leadwort < *plumbum* the element lead]

**plumb bob,** the weight at the end of a plumb line.

**plum|be|ous** (plum′bē əs), *adj.* made of or resembling lead; leaden. [< Latin *plumbeus* (with English *-ous*) leaden, dull < *plumbum* the element lead]

**plumb|er** (plum′ər), *n.* **1** a person whose work is putting in and repairing water pipes and fixtures such as toilets and sinks, in buildings: *When the water pipe froze, we sent for a plumber.* **2** *U.S. Informal.* a person assigned to stop leaks of secret information. [< Old French *plombier* < Latin (*artifex*) *plumbārius* (worker) in lead < *plumbum* the element lead]

**plumber's friend** or **helper**, a rubber suction cup at the end of a stick; plunger.

**plumb|er|y** (plum′ər ē), *n., pl.* **-er|ies.** **1** the shop or workplace of a plumber. **2** the work of a plumber; plumbing.

**plum|bic** (plum′bik), *adj.* **1** of or having to do with lead. **2** containing lead, especially with a valence of four. [< Latin *plumbum* the element lead]

**plum|bif|er|ous** (plum bif′ər əs), *adj.* containing or yielding lead. [< Latin *plumbum* the element lead + English *-ferous*]

**plumb|ing** (plum′ing), *n.* **1** the work or trade of a plumber. **2** the water pipes and fixtures in a building: *bathroom plumbing.* **3** the act of using a plumb line.

**plumb|ing|ware** (plum′ing wãr′), *n.* plumbing fixtures, as for a bathroom or kitchen.

**plum|bism** (plum′biz əm), *n.* = lead poisoning.

***plumb line**, **1** a line with a plumb at the end, used to find the depth of water or to see if a wall is vertical. **2** a line that is vertical, such as one formed by the surface of a wall.

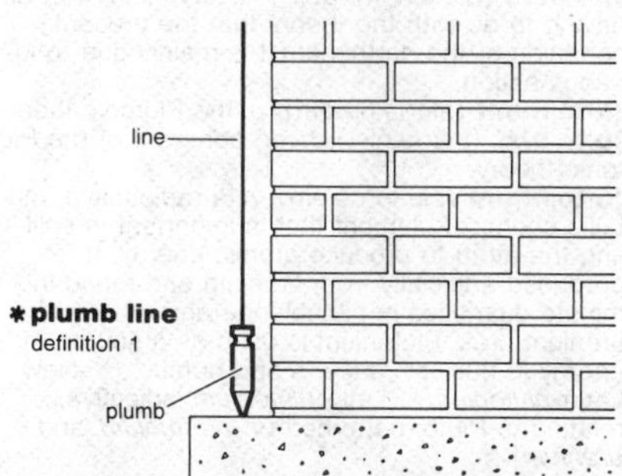

***plumb line** definition 1

**plum book**, *U.S. Informal.* an official publication listing available positions in the Federal government usually filled by presidential appointment: *The positions given Congressmen who have retired or been defeated in reelection campaigns are generally regarded as the best in the plum book* (New York Times). [< *plum*[1], def. 6]

**plum|bous** (plum′bəs), *adj.* **1** of lead. **2** containing lead, especially with a valence of two. [< Latin *plumbōsus* (with English *-ous*) < *plumbum*]

**plumb rule**, a narrow board fitted with a plumb line and bob, used by carpenters and masons for measuring angles from the vertical.

**plum|bum** (plum′bəm), *n. Chemistry* lead. *Symbol:* Pb [< Latin *plumbum*]

**plum cake**, a cake containing raisins, currants, and often other fruits.

**plum|cot** (plum′kot), *n.* a hybrid between the plum and the apricot. [< *plum*[1] + (apri)*cot*]

**plum curculio**, a brownish snout beetle with gray and black markings, that feeds on plum, peach, apricot, cherry, and apple trees. It lives east of the Rocky Mountains in the United States.

**plum duff**, a heavy pudding of flour, water, suet, and raisins or currants, boiled in a cloth or bag.

**plume** (plüm), *n., v.,* **plumed, plum|ing.** *—n.* **1** a feather, especially a large, long feather: *The rooster lost one of his plumes in the fight with the cat.* **2** a feather, bunch of feathers, or tuft of hair worn as an ornament on a hat or helmet: *Her photograph ... showed her stiff in her glories of plumes and satin* (Maurice H. Hewlett). **3** = plumage. **4** any feathered part or formation, such as of an insect, seed, or leaf. **5** something resembling a plume. **6** *Figurative.* an ornament or token of distinction or honor: *medals and other plumes of rank.* **7** the hollow cylinder of spray thrown up by an underwater atomic explosion. **8** the spray thrown up by a vessel at high speed.
*—v.t.* **1** to furnish with plumes: *The knight plumed his helmet with brilliant red feathers.* **2** to smooth or arrange the feathers of: *The eagle plumed its wing.* SYN: preen. *—v.i.* to form a plumelike cloud, as spray, vapor, or smoke does: *In the sub-zero weather, their exhausts pluming white in the gray streets* (Newsweek).
**plume oneself on**, to be proud of; show pride in oneself: *She plumed herself on skill in dancing.*
[< Old French *plume* < Latin *plūma* pinfeather, down] **—plume′less,** *adj.* **—plume′like′,** *adj.*

**plume|bird** (plüm′bėrd′), *n.* any one of a group of birds of New Guinea, notable for the luxuriance and brilliance of their plumage.

**plumed** (plümd), *adj.* **1** having plumes or plumelike parts. **2** adorned with or as with a plume or plumes: *plumed steeds.*

**plume|let** (plüm′lit), *n.* a small plume.

**plume poppy**, a showy plant of the poppy family, native to China and Japan, often cultivated in garden borders; tree celandine.

**plu|mi|corn** (plü′mə kôrn), *n.* one of a pair of hornlike or earlike tufts of feathers on the head of certain owls, such as the horned owls. [< Latin *plūma* feather + *cornū* horn]

**plum|met** (plum′it), *v., n.* **—v.i.** to plunge; drop: *to plummet into the sea.*
**—n.** **1** a weight fastened to a line; plumb. **2** *Figurative.* something that weighs down or depresses: *Ignorance itself is a plummet o'er me* (Shakespeare).
[< Old French *plommet* (diminutive) < *plom,* and *plomb* the element lead; see etym. under **plumb**]

**plum|my** (plum′ē), *adj.,* **-mi|er, -mi|est.** **1** full of or resembling plums: *a plummy crimson.* **2** *Informal, Figurative.* good; desirable: *Signing one's self over to wickedness for the sake of getting something plummy* (George Eliot). **3** *Informal, Figurative.* rich; full; mellow: *... a plummy, Lady Bountiful voice* (New Yorker). **—plum′mi|ly,** *adv.* **—plum′mi|ness,** *n.*

**plu|mose** (plü′mōs), *adj.* **1** having feathers or plumes; feathered. **2** like a plume; feathery. [< Latin *plūmōsus* < *plūma* pinfeather] **—plu′mose|ly,** *adv.*

**plu|mos|i|ty** (plü mos′ə tē), *n.* the state of being plumose.

**plump**[1] (plump), *adj., v.* **—adj.** rounded out; fat in an attractive way; chubby: *A healthy baby has plump cheeks.*
**—v.t., v.i.** to make or become plump: *Plump the pillows on your bed.*
[origin uncertain. Compare Middle Dutch *plomp,* Middle Low German *plump* blunt, thick, clumsy.] **—plump′ly,** *adv.* **—plump′ness,** *n.*

**plump**[2] (plump), *v., n., adv., adj.* **—v.i.** **1** to fall or drop heavily or suddenly: *All out of breath, she plumped down on a chair.* **2** *Informal.* to burst or plunge: *to plump into the water,* (*Figurative.*) *to plump out of a room.* **3** to vote at an election for one candidate alone: *I'll plump or I'll split for them as treat me the handsomest and are the most of what I call gentlemen* (George Eliot).
**—v.t.** **1a** to drop or let fall heavily or suddenly: *to plump down one's bags at the station.* **b** to pay at once and in one lot: *to plump down $10.* **2** *Informal, Figurative.* to utter abruptly; blurt: *If it ain't a liberty to plump it out ... what do you do for your living?* (Dickens).
**—n.** *Informal.* **1** a sudden plunge; heavy fall: *The frog made a huge plump and landed in the middle of the pond.* **2** the sound made by a plunge or fall: *We heard the plump of frogs as we approached the pond.*
**—adv.** **1** heavily or suddenly: *He ran plump into me.* **2** *Figurative.* directly or bluntly, as in speaking.
**—adj.** *Figurative.* direct; downright; blunt: *a plump denial.*
**plump for**, to give one's complete support to; champion vigorously; support wholeheartedly or unanimously: *to plump for lower taxes. The New Jersey delegation plumped for Jones.*
[imitative; probably < Middle Dutch *plompen,* or Middle Low German *plumpen* plunge abruptly into water, make a sound of hitting water. Perhaps related to **plump**[1].] **—plump′ly,** *adv.* **—plump′ness,** *n.*

**plump|en** (plum′pən), *v.t., v.i.* to make or become plump; swell out: *to plumpen geese* (v.t.). *The baby's cheeks plumpened* (v.i.).

**plump|er**[1] (plum′pər), *n.* **1** something that plumps or makes plump. **2** a small, light ball formerly sometimes carried in the mouth by women to fill out hollow cheeks. [< *plump*[1] + *-er*[1]]

**plump|er**[2] (plum′pər), *n.* **1** the act of plumping or falling heavily. **2a** a voter who plumps. **b** the vote of such a person. [< *plump*[2] + *-er*[5]]

**plump|ish** (plum′pish), *adj.* somewhat plump; roundish: *a plumpish figure.* **—plump′ish|ly,** *adv.*

**plum pudding**, a rich boiled or steamed pudding containing raisins, currants, and spices.

**plump|y** (plum′pē), *adj.* plump, as in body or form: *plumpy Bacchus* (Shakespeare).

**plu|mule** (plü′myül), *n.* **1** a small, soft feather. **2** the rudimentary terminal bud of the embryo of a seed, sometimes containing immature leaves. It is situated at the end of the hypocotyl, and is either within or enclosed by the cotyledon or cotyledons.[< Latin*plūmula*(diminutive)< *plūma* feather]

**plu|mu|lose** (plü′myə lōs), *adj.* having the form of a plumule.

**plum|y** (plü′mē), *adj.* **1** having plumes or feathers: *a flock of white plumy birds* (Charlotte Brontë). **2** adorned with a plume or plumes: *a plumy helmet.* **3** like a plume; feathery: *the plumy palms of Memphis* (Amelia B. Edwards).

**plun|der** (plun′dər), *v., n.* **—v.t.** **1** to rob by force; rob: *to plunder a bank. The pirates entered the harbor and began to plunder the town.* SYN: loot, sack. **2** to take (as goods or valuables) by illegal force or as an enemy: *The law of self-preservation had now obliged the fugitive Tartars to plunder provisions* (Thomas De Quincey).
**—v.i.** to commit a robbery or robberies, especially by force; loot.
**—n.** **1** things taken in plundering; booty; loot: *The pirates carried off the plunder in their ships.* **2** the act of robbing by force: *In olden times soldiers often gained great wealth by plunder of a conquered city.* **3** *U.S. Dialect.* **a** personal belongings or household goods. **b** luggage; baggage.
[probably ultimately < Middle Low German *plundern* < *plunder* household goods] **—plun′der|er,** *n.*
**—*Syn.*** *n.* **1 Plunder, booty, loot** mean things taken by force. **Plunder** applies to things carried off by invading soldiers during a war or by bandits and other robbers: *Much plunder from Europe reached Germany during World War II.* **Booty** applies particularly to things carried off and shared later by a band of robbers: *The bandits fought over their booty.* **Loot** applies particularly to things carried off from bodies and buildings in a city destroyed in war or the scene of a fire, wreck, or other disaster, but is used also of anything taken by robbery or other crime: *Much loot was sold after the great earthquake.*

**plun|der|a|ble** (plun′də rə bəl), *adj.* that can be plundered: *As plunderable matter increases, so will plunderage* (Jeremy Bentham).

**plun|der|age** (plun′dər ij), *n.* **1** the act of plundering; pillage; spoliation. **2** *Maritime Law.* **a** the embezzlement of goods on board a ship. **b** the goods embezzled.

**plun|der|ous** (plun′dər əs), *adj.* given to plundering: *plunderous troops.*

**plunge** (plunj), *v.,* **plunged, plung|ing,** *n.* **—v.t.** to throw or thrust with force into a liquid, place, or condition: *Plunge your hand into the water. The farmer plunged his pitchfork into the hay.* (*Figurative.*) *The quarrel between the two nations plunged the world into war.* SYN: immerse, submerge. See syn. under **dip.**
**—v.i.** **1** to throw oneself (into water, danger, a fight, or a condition): (*Figurative.*) *to plunge into debt, to plunge feverishly into study. He plunged into the river and saved the boy.* SYN: leap, dive. **2** to rush; dash: *to plunge into a burning building. The football player plunged ahead five yards for a touchdown.* **3** to pitch suddenly and violently: *The ship plunged about in the storm.* **4** *Informal.* to gamble or speculate recklessly or heavily.
**—n.** **1** the act of plunging: *The fullback made a 2-yard plunge for a first down.* **2** a jump or thrust; dash: *His plunge won the race.* **3** a dive into the water. **4** a place for diving.
**take the plunge**, to plunge into a new course of action, in spite of fear, reluctance, or risk: *Mr. Shonfield, brave man that he is, has taken the plunge and stated the fact in bald language* (New Yorker).
[< Old French *plungier* < Vulgar Latin *plumbicāre* to heave the sounding lead < Latin *plumbum* the element lead]

**plunge bath**, a bath which is large enough for the bather to be completely immersed in it.

**plunge pool**, the deep pool at the base of a waterfall which often cuts back under the falls, causing the overhanging rock face to collapse and moving the location of the falls further upstream.

**plung|er** (plun′jər), *n.* **1** a person, animal, or thing that plunges. **2a** a part of a machine, such as a piston in a pump, that works with a plunging motion; ram. **b** a rubber suction cup at the end of a long stick, used to free clogged pipes or drains by air pressure; plumber's friend. **3** a small pistonlike device in the valve of an automobile tire. **4** *Informal.* a reckless gambler or speculator.

**plung|ing fire** (plun′jing), gunfire, especially artillery fire, in which the projectiles descend on the target at an angle approaching the perpendicular, as by a battery firing from a higher elevation or in a high, looping trajectory.

**plunk** (plungk), *v., n., adv.* **—v.t.** **1** to pluck (a banjo, guitar, or other stringed musical instrument). SYN: pick. **2** to make a sound like the plucking of a stringed musical instrument: *It was cranked out by scores of organ-grinders and plunked out on a thousand parlor pianofortes* (New Yorker). **3** to throw, push, put, or drop heavily or suddenly.
**—v.i.** **1** to make a sudden sound like the plucking of a stringed musical instrument. **2** to fall or drop down abruptly; plump.
**—n.** *Informal.* **1** the act or sound of plunking:

---

**Pronunciation Key:** hat, āge, cãre, fär; let, ēqual, tėrm; it, īce; hot, ōpen, ôrder; **oi**l, **ou**t; cup, pu̇t, rüle; **ch**ild; lo**ng**; **th**in; **ᵺ**en; **zh**, measure; **ə** represents **a** in about, **e** in taken, **i** in pencil, **o** in lemon, **u** in circus.

*They played in such magnificent time that every high-stepping foot in all the line came down with the same jubilant plunk* (Booth Tarkington). **2** a direct, forcible blow. **3** *U.S. Slang.* a dollar: *I'll sell you the Candersen place for three thousand plunks* (Sinclair Lewis).
—*adv.* with a plunk.
**plunk down**, to hand over payment: *He plunked down four thousand dollars for the car.*
**plunk for**, *Informal.* to plump for: *He'll plunk for more public housing, federal aid for schools, hospitals, health measures* (Wall Street Journal).
[imitative]

**plu|per|fect** (plü'pėr'fikt), *n., adj.* —*n.* = past perfect.
—*adj.* **1** of, in, or having to do with the past perfect. **2** more than perfect; very excellent.
[short for Latin (*tempus praeteritum*) *plūs* (*quam*) *perfectum* (past tense) more (than) perfect]
—**plu'per'fect|ly**, *adv.*

**plu|per|fec|tion** (plü'pər fek'shən), *n.* the quality or state of being pluperfect.

**plupf.**, pluperfect.

**plur.**, **1** plural. **2** plurality.

**plu|ral** (plůr'əl), *adj., n.* —*adj.* **1** more than one: *plural citizenship.* **2** *Grammar.* **a** more than one in number: *"Boy" is singular; "boys" is plural.* **b** showing more than one in number: *the plural ending "-s," the plural form "fishes."* **3** having to do with or involving a plurality of persons or things; being one of such a plurality: *Better have none than plural faith* (Shakespeare).
—*n. Grammar.* **1** a form of a word to show it means more than one. *Books* is the plural of *book; men* is the plural of *man; are* is the plural of *is; we* is the plural of *I; these* is the plural of *this.* **2** a word or class of words used to show more than one. *Abbr:* pl.
[< Latin *plūrālis* < *plūs, plūris* more, comparative of *multus* much]

**plu|ral|ism** (plůr'ə liz əm), *n.* **1** the character, condition, or an instance of being plural. **2** *Sociology.* **a** a condition in which ethnic and other minority groups are able to maintain their identities in a society without conflicting with the dominant culture; the relative absence of assimilation in a society. **b** belief in or advocacy of such a condition. **3** the theory or belief, incorporated in or essential to various systems of philosophy, that reality has its essence or ultimate being in several or many principles or substances. **4** *Ecclesiastical.* the system or practice by which one person holds two or more offices, especially benefices, at the same time.

**plu|ral|ist** (plůr'ə list), *n., adj.* —*n.* **1** *Sociology, Philosophy.* an adherent or advocate of pluralism. **2** a person who holds two or more offices, especially ecclesiastical benefices, at the same time.
—*adj.* pluralistic.

**plu|ral|is|tic** (plůr'ə lis'tik), *adj.* of or having to do with pluralism; characterized by pluralism: *The United States has followed a pluralistic policy in permitting religious freedom for many different groups.* —**plu'ral|is'ti|cal|ly**, *adv.*

**plu|ral|i|ty** (plů ral'ə tē), *n., pl.* **-ties. 1a** the difference between the number of votes received by the winner of an election and the number received by the next highest candidate. **b** the number of votes received by the winner of an election which is less than a majority of the total vote. **2** the greater number; the majority. **3a** a large number; multitude. **b** the fact of being numerous; vastness; greatness: *The plurality of effort, which has been effective in finding the oil the nation needs, thus is also useful in developing methods to prevent its waste* (Atlantic). **4** the state or fact of being plural. **5** *Ecclesiastical.* **a** the simultaneous holding of two or more offices or benefices; pluralism. **b** any of the offices held under pluralism.

**plu|ral|ize** (plůr'ə līz), *v.t., v.i.,* **-ized, -iz|ing.** to make or become plural; express in the plural form. —**plu'ral|i|za'tion**, *n.*

**plu|ral|ly** (plůr'ə lē), *adv.* in the plural number; so as to express or imply more than one: *The "heavens" when used plurally ... remained expressive of the starry space beyond* (John Ruskin).

**plural marriage**, polygamy, especially with reference to the Mormons.

**plural wife**, any one of the wives of a polygamist, or in a plural marriage.

**pluri-**, *combining form.* having more than one ___; having many ___: *Pluriaxial = having more than one axis.* [< Latin *plūs, plūris* more]

**plu|ri|ax|i|al** (plůr'ē ak'sē əl), *adj.* **1** having more than one axis. **2** *Botany.* having flowers growing on secondary shoots.

**plu|ri|cel|lu|lar** (plůr'ə sel'yə lər), *adj.* having several cells; multicellular.

**plu|ri|dis|ci|pli|nar|y** (plůr'ə dis'ə plə ner'ē), *adj.* = multidisciplinary.

**plu|rip|o|tent** (plů rip'ə tənt) *adj.* capable of developing, growing, or producing in a number of ways: *pluripotent cells.*

**plu|ri|syl|la|ble** (plůr'ə sil'ə bəl), *n.* a word of more than one syllable.

***plus** (plus), *prep., adj., n.,* **plus|es** or **plus|ses**, *v.,* **plussed, plus|sing.** —*prep.* **1** added to; increased by: *3 plus 2 equals 5.* **2** and also: *The work of an engineer requires intelligence plus experience.*
—*adj.* **1a** and more; more than: *His mark was B plus.* **b** *Informal.* additional; extra: *a plus value.* **2** more than zero; positive: *a plus quantity.* **3** positively electrified; positive. **4** *Botany.* of or having to do with the strain of heterothallic fungi that acts as the male in reproduction.
—*n.* **1** the sign meaning that the quantity following it is to be added; plus sign. **2** *Figurative.* an added quantity; something extra; gain: *The pluses of his new job outweigh the disadvantages of having to move.* **SYN:** addition, increase. **3** *Figurative.* a positive quantity.
—*v.t. Informal.* **1** to add; gain: *He plussed two more points in the game.* **2** to add to; augment: *to plus a score.*
**be plus**, *Informal.* to have in addition: *Since his niece married he is plus a nephew.*
[< Medieval Latin *plus* < Latin *plūs* more, comparative of *multus* much]

***plus** *n., definition 1*

+ 39 + 13 = 52

***plus fours**, loose, baggy knickers that come down below the knee, worn especially by men for golf. [because they were originally four inches longer than ordinary knickers]

***plus fours**

**plush** (plush), *n., adj.* —*n.* a fabric, such as silk, cotton, wool, or rayon, like velvet but thicker and softer.
—*adj. Informal.* luxurious; expensive: *plush surroundings.*
[< French *pluche,* short for *peluche* (literally) hairy fabric < Vulgar Latin *pilūcea,* adjective < Latin *pilus* hair] —**plush'like'**, *adj.* —**plush'ly**, *adv.* —**plush'ness**, *n.*

**plush|y** (plush'ē), *adj.,* **plush|i|er, plush|i|est.** **1** of or like plush: *a plushy lawn.* **2** *Informal.* luxurious; plush: *plushy, elegant furniture.* —**plush'i|ness**, *n.*

**plus sign**, *Mathematics.* the sign indicating that the quantity following is to be added, or is a positive quantity.

**plus twos**, knickers like plus fours, but shorter and slimmer.

**Plu|tar|chan** (plü tär'kən), *adj.* **1** of or having to do with Plutarch, a Greek biographer of the century ending in A.D. 100. **2** of or like the group of famous Greeks and Romans whose lives were written by Plutarch.

**Plu|tar|chi|an** (plü tär'kē ən), *adj.* = Plutarchan.

***Plu|to** (plü'tō), *n.* **1** *Greek and Roman Mythology.* **a** the god of the region of the dead and husband of Persephone. He was also called Hades by the Greeks and Dis by the Romans. **b** a nymph who was the mother of Tantalus. **2** the eighth largest planet of the solar system and the farthest from the sun. It was discovered in 1930. See diagram under **solar system**.

***Pluto** definition 2

♇ symbol

**plu|toc|ra|cy** (plü tok'rə sē), *n., pl.* **-cies. 1** a government in which the rich rule. **2** a ruling class of wealthy people. [< Greek *plutokratiā* < *ploûtos* wealth (related to *polýs* much, many) + *krátos* power]

**plu|to|crat** (plü'tə krat), *n.* **1** a person who has power or influence because of his wealth. **2** a wealthy person. **SYN:** nabob, Croesus.

**plu|to|crat|ic** (plü'tə krat'ik), *adj.* **1** having power or influence because of wealth. **2** of or having to do with plutocrats or plutocracy. —**plu'to|crat'i|cal|ly**, *adv.*

**plu|tol|a|try** (plü tol'ə trē), *n.* the worship of wealth. [< Greek *ploûtos* wealth + *latreiā* worship]

**plu|tol|o|gy** (plü tol'ə jē), *n.* the science of wealth; political economy. [< Greek *ploûtos* wealth + English *-logy*]

**plu|ton** (plü'ton), *n.* a plutonic rock. [back formation < *plutonic*]

**Plu|to|ni|an** (plü tō'nē ən), *adj.* of or having to do with Pluto or the lower world: *He ... from the door of that Plutonian hall, invisible ascended his high throne* (Milton).

**plu|ton|ic** (plü ton'ik), *adj.* having to do with a class of igneous rocks that have solidified far below the earth's surface; abyssal. [< Latin *Plūtōn, -ōnis,* variant of *Plūtō* (< Greek *Ploútōn, -ōnos* god of the lower world, perhaps < *ploûtos* wealth) + English *-ic*]

**Plu|ton|ic** (plü ton'ik), *adj.* **1** = Plutonian. **2** of or having to do with the theory that the present condition of the earth's crust is mainly due to igneous action.

**Plu|to|nism** (plü'tə niz əm), *n.* the Plutonic theory.

**Plu|to|nist** (plü'tə nist), *n.* an adherent of the Plutonic theory.

***plu|to|ni|um** (plü tō'nē əm), *n.* a radioactive, metallic chemical element that is important in splitting the atom to produce atomic energy. It is produced artificially from uranium and found in minute quantities in pitchblende and other uranium ores. Plutonium is used as a source of energy in nuclear reactors and bombs. [< New Latin *plutonium* < Latin *plūtōnium,* adjective, relating to Pluto; patterned on *neptunium,* and *uranium*]

***plutonium**

| symbol | atomic number | mass number | oxidation state |
|---|---|---|---|
| Pu | 94 | 244 | 3, 4, 5, 6 |

**plu|to|nom|ic** (plü'tə nom'ik), *adj.* of or having to do with plutonomy.

**plu|ton|o|my** (plü ton'ə mē), *n.* the science of the production and distribution of wealth; political economy. [< Greek *ploûtos* wealth + *nómos* law]

**Plu|tus** (plü'təs), *n. Greek Mythology.* the god of riches and son of Demeter, blinded by Jupiter. [< Latin *Plūtus* < Greek *Ploûtos* (literally) wealth]

**plu|vi|al** (plü'vē əl), *adj., n.* —*adj.* **1** of or having to do with rain. **2** characterized by much rain; rainy. **3** caused by rain.
—*n.* a period of geological change in an area as a result of prolonged rainfall: *With the onset of the last pluvial, man was able to penetrate the deserts once more* (A. J. Arkell).
[< Latin *pluviālis* < *pluvia* rain]

**plu|vi|o|graph** (plü'vē ə graf, -gräf), *n.* a self-recording rain gauge. [< Latin *pluvia* rain + English *-graph*]

**plu|vi|om|e|ter** (plü'vē om'ə tər), *n.* an instrument for measuring the amount of rainfall; rain gauge. [< Latin *pluvia* rain + English *-meter*]

**plu|vi|o|met|ric** (plü'vē ə met'rik), *adj.* made by means of a pluviometer: *pluviometric observations.* —**plu'vi|o|met'ri|cal|ly**, *adv.*

**plu|vi|om|e|try** (plü'vē om'ə trē), *n.* the use of the pluviometer.

**Plu|vi|ôse** (plü'vē ōs; *French* ply vyōz'), *n.* the fifth month of the French Revolutionary calendar, extending from January 20 to February 18. [< French *Pluviôse* < Latin *pluviōsus* pluvious]

**plu|vi|ous** (plü'vē əs), *adj.* rainy; of rain. [< Latin *pluviōsus* (with English *-ous*) < *pluvia* rain]

**ply¹** (plī), *v.,* **plied, ply|ing.** —*v.t.* **1** to work with; use: *The dressmaker plies her needle.* **SYN:** employ. **2** to keep up work on; work at or on: *to ply one's trade. We plied the water with our oars.* **3** *Figurative.* to urge again and again: *She plied me with questions to make me tell her what was in the package.* **SYN:** importune. **4** to supply with in a pressing manner: *to ply a person with food or drink.* **5** to go back and forth regularly on: *Boats ply the river.*
—*v.i.* **1** to work busily or steadily: *Soon all the boats ... were dropped ... all the paddles plying* (Herman Melville). **2** to go back and forth regularly between certain places: *The bus plies from the station to the hotel.* **3** to travel; go; move: *Thither he plies* (Milton). **4** *Nautical.* to turn a sailing ship to windward. [Middle English *plyen,* probably short for *aplien* apply]

**ply²** (plī), *n., pl.* **plies**, *v.,* **plied, ply|ing.** —*n.* **1** a thickness or fold. **SYN:** layer. **2** a strand or twist of cord, yarn, or thread: *Three-ply rope is made of three twists.* **3** *Figurative.* an inclination of mind;

tendency of character. [< French *pli* a fold < Old French *plier* to fold; see the verb]
— ***v.t.*** *Dialect.* **1** to bend, fold, or shape. **2** *Obsolete.* to adapt.
— ***v.i.*** *Obsolete.* to bend or yield.
[< Old French *plier,* alteration of *pleiier,* and *ployer* < Latin *plicāre* to fold. Compare etym. under **pliant**.]

**ply|er** (plī′ər), *n.* = plier.

**ply|ers** (plī′ərz), *n., pl.* **-ers.** = pliers.

**Plymouth cloak,** *Archaic.* a staff; cudgel. [apparently because ruffians in Plymouth, England, wore no cloaks]

**Plymouth Rock,** any one of an American breed of medium-sized gray-and-black or white chickens kept for the production of both meat and eggs.

**ply|wood** (plī′wu̇d′), *n.* a building material made of several thin layers of wood glued together, usually with the grain of each layer at right angles to the next. Plywood is strong and relatively light. [< *ply*[2] + *wood*]

**p.m.,** **1a** after noon (Latin, *post meridiem*): *School ends at 3 p.m.* **b** the time from noon to midnight. **2** post-mortem.

**Pm** (no period), promethium (chemical element).

**P.M.,** an abbreviation for the following:
**1a** after noon (Latin, *post meridiem*). **b** the time from noon to midnight.
**2** Past Master.
**3** Paymaster.
**4** Police Magistrate.
**5** Postmaster.
**6** post-mortem.
**7** Prime Minister.
**8** Provost Marshal.

**PMA** (no periods), Production and Marketing Administration.

**P.M.G.** or **PMG** (no periods), **1** Paymaster General. **2** Postmaster General.

**PMH** (no periods), production per man-hour.

**pmk** (no period), postmark.

**pmkd** (no period), postmarked.

**PMLA** (no periods), Publications of the Modern Language Association of America.

**p.n.** or **P/N** (no periods), promissory note.

**PNdB** or **PNdb** (no periods), perceived noise decibel.

**pneum.,** **1** pneumatic. **2** pneumatics.

**pneu|ma** (nü′mə, nyü′-), *n.* spirit or soul. [< Greek *pneûma* spirit, breath, a wind < *pneîn* to blow, breathe]

**pneu|mat|ic** (nü mat′ik, nyü-), *adj., n.* — ***adj.*** **1** filled with air; containing air, especially air under pressure: *a pneumatic tire.* **2** worked by air, especially air under pressure: *a pneumatic drill.* **3** having to do with air and other gases. **4** containing or connected with air cavities, as the bones of birds or the swim bladder of fishes. **5** *Theology.* of or having to do with the spirit; spiritual.
— ***n.*** a pneumatic tire.
[< Latin *pneumaticus* < Greek *pneumatikós* of (the nature of) wind, spirit < *pneûma* a wind; see etym. under **pneuma**] — **pneu|mat′i|cal|ly,** *adv.*

**pneu|ma|tic|i|ty** (nü′mə tis′ə tē, nyü′-), *n.* the fact or condition of being pneumatic.

**pneu|mat|ics** (nü mat′iks, nyü-), *n.* the branch of physics that deals with the pressure, elasticity, weight, and other mechanical properties of air and other gases; pneumodynamics.

**pneumatic tube,** a tube through which notes, letters, or sales slips and cash are sent by means of air pressure.

**pneu|ma|to|cyst** (nü mat′ə sist, nyü-), *n.* an air sac, as in a hydrozoan. [< Greek *pneûma, -atos* breath, wind + English *cyst*]

**pneu|ma|tol|o|gy** (nü′mə tol′ə jē, nyü′-), *n.* **1** *Theology.* the doctrine of the Holy Spirit. **2** the doctrine of spirits or spiritual beings, in the 1600's considered a branch of metaphysics. **3** = pneumatics. **4** *Obsolete.* psychology. [< Greek *pneûma, -atos* spirit, breath + English *-logy*]

**pneu|ma|tol|y|sis** (nü′mə tol′ə sis, nyü′-), *n. Geology.* the process by which minerals and ores are formed by the action of vapors given off from igneous magmas. [< Greek *pneûma, -atos* breath, wind + *lýsis* a loosening]

**pneu|ma|to|lyt|ic** (nü′mə tō lit′ik, nyü′-), *adj. Geology.* of, having to do with, or formed by pneumatolysis.

**pneu|ma|tom|e|ter** (nü′mə tom′ə tər, nyü′-), *n.* an instrument for measuring the amount of air breathed in and out at each inspiration or expiration, or the force of inspiration or expiration. [< Greek *pneûma, -atos* breath + English *-meter*]

**pneu|ma|to|phore** (nü′mə tō fôr, -fōr; nyü′-; nü-mat′ə-, nyü-), *n.* **1** a structure supposed to serve as a channel for air, arising from the roots of various trees that grow in swampy places in the tropics. **2** a hollow structure containing gas in certain hydrozoans, serving as a float. [< Greek *pneûma, -atos* wind, breath + English *-phore*]

**pneu|mec|to|my** (nü mek′tə mē, nyü-), *n., pl.* **-mies.** the surgical removal of part of a lung. [< Greek *pneúmōn* lung + *ektomê* a cutting out]

**pneu|mo|ba|cil|lus** (nü′mō bə sil′əs, nyü′-), *n., pl.* **-cil|li** (-sil′ī). a bacillus commonly present in cases of pneumonia, pleurisy, and other diseases of the lungs, but considered almost certainly not the causative agent of the disease. [< New Latin *pneumobacillus* < Greek *pneúmōn* lung + Late Latin *bacillus* bacillus]

**pneu|mo|coc|cal** (nü′mə kok′əl, nyü′-), *adj.* having to do with or caused by a pneumococcus.

**pneu|mo|coc|cic** (nü′mə kok′sik, nyü′-), *adj.* = pneumococcal.

**pneu|mo|coc|cus** (nü′mə kok′əs, nyü′-), *n., pl.* **-coc|ci** (-kok′sī). the bacterium that causes lobar pneumonia. [< New Latin *pneumococcus* < Greek *pneúmōn* lung + New Latin *coccus* coccus]

**pneu|mo|co|ni|o|sis** (nü′mə kō′nē ō′sis, nyü′-), *n.* chronic inflammation of the lungs, produced by the inhalation of mineral dust; black lung. Also, **pneumonoconiosis.** [< New Latin *pneumoconiosis* < Greek *pneúmōn* lung + *kónis* dust + New Latin *-osis* -osis]

**pneu|mo|dy|nam|ics** (nü′mō dī nam′iks, nyü′-), *n.* = pneumatics.

**pneu|mo|gas|tric** (nü′mə gas′trik, nyü′-), *adj., n.* — ***adj.*** **1** of or having to do with the lungs and the stomach or abdomen. **2** of or having to do with a vagus nerve. — ***n.*** = vagus nerve. [< Greek *pneúmōn* lung + English *gastric*]

**pneumogastric nerve,** either of the vagus nerves.

**pneu|mo|graph** (nü′mə graf, -gräf; nyü′-), *n.* an instrument for automatically recording the movements of the human chest in respiration. [< Greek *pneúmōn* lung + English *-graph*]

**pneu|mog|ra|phy** (nü mog′rə fē, nyü-), *n.* **1** the recording of respiratory movement, especially by a pneumograph. **2** a method of X-raying tissues by introducing air into them.

**pneu|mo|nec|to|my** (nü′mə nek′tə mē, nyü′-), *n., pl.* **-mies.** the surgical removal of a lung. [< Greek *pneúmōn* lung + *ektomê* a cutting out]

**pneu|mo|nia** (nü mōn′yə, -mō′nē ə; nyü-), *n.* **1** a disease in which the lung or lungs are inflamed. Pneumonia is caused by a bacterium or virus. It is often an acute infection of the lung accompanied by high fever, pain, and a severe cough. Pneumonia in both lungs is called double pneumonia. **2** inflammation of the lung from irritants such as chemicals or foreign particles. [< New Latin *pneumonia* < Greek *pneumoniā* < *pneúmōn* lung < *pneûma* breath, spirit < *pneîn* to breathe, blow]

**pneu|mon|ic** (nü mon′ik, nyü-) *adj.* **1** having to do with, characterized by, or affected with pneumonia. **2** of, having to do with, or affecting the lungs; pulmonary.

**pneumonic plague,** a usually fatal, contagious disease, characterized by fever, chills, prostration, and infection of the lungs, usually transmitted by a flea that has bitten a rat infected with the plague bacillus.

**pneu|mo|ni|tis** (nü′mə nī′təs, nyü′-), *n.* any one of various acute inflammations of the lungs; pneumonia. [< Greek *pneúmōn* lung + English *-itis*]

**pneu|mo|no|co|ni|o|sis** (nü′mə nō kō′nē ō′sis, nyü′-), *n.* = pneumoconiosis.

**pneu|mo|stome** (nü′mə stōm, nyü′-), *n.* a small opening through which air passes to and from the mantle or respiratory cavity of gastropods. [< Greek *pneûma* wind + *stóma* mouth]

**pneu|mo|tho|rax** (nü′mō thôr′aks, -thōr′-; nyü′-), *n.* the presence of air or gas in the pleural cavity, as produced by the introduction of a needle into the cavity so as to collapse a lung in the treatment of pulmonary tuberculosis (artificial pneumothorax), or as produced by other than outside causes (spontaneous pneumothorax). [< Greek *pneûma* wind, spirit + English *thorax*]

**PNG** (no periods) or **P.N.G.,** persona non grata.

**p-n junction** (pē′en′), **1** a junction between a p-type region and an n-type region in a semiconducting crystal. **2** such a crystal, used as a rectifier or in transistors.

**pnxt.,** pinxit.

**PNYA** (no periods), Port of New York Authority.

**po.,** *Baseball.* putout or putouts.

**p.o.,** **1** post office. **2** *Baseball.* putout or putouts.

**Po** (no period), polonium (chemical element).

**P.O.,** an abbreviation for the following:
**1** Peninsular and Oriental (Steam Navigation Company).
**2** petty officer.
**3** pilot officer (in the Royal Air Force).
**4** postal order.
**5** post office.

**po|a|ceous** (pō ā′shəs), *adj.* of or belonging to the grass family of plants; gramineous. [< New Latin *Poa* the genus name (< Greek *póā* grass) + English *-aceous*]

**poach**[1] (pōch), *v.t.* **1** to trespass on (another's land), especially to hunt or fish: *The king's forests were poached by many hungry peasants.* **2** to take (game or fish) without any right: *The tramp poached a chicken from the farmer's henhouse.* **3** *Figurative: The rebel stevedores union ... was suspended from the congress for having poached members from the transport union* (New York Times). **4** to trample (soft ground) into muddy holes. **5a** to mix with water and reduce to a uniform consistency. **b** to mix thoroughly (paper pulp) with the bleach liquor.
— ***v.i.*** **1** to trespass on the lands or rights of another, especially to hunt or fish. SYN: encroach. **2** to take game or fish illegally or by unsportsmanlike means. **3** (of land) to become soft, miry, and full of holes by being trampled. **4** to sink into wet, heavy ground in walking.
[< Middle French *pocher* < Old French *pochier* poke out, gouge < Germanic (compare Low German *poken*). See related etym. at **poke**[1].]

**poach**[2] (pōch), *v.t.* **1** to cook (an egg) by breaking it into boiling water. **2** to cook (any of various foods, especially fish) by simmering for a short time in a liquid. [< Old French *pochier* (literally) to put in a bag (because the yolk is thought of as enclosed in the white of the egg) < *poche* cooking spoon < Late Latin *popia,* perhaps < a Gaulish word]

**poach|er**[1] (pō′chər), *n.* a person who poaches or trespasses, especially to hunt or fish illegally. [< *poach*[1] + *-er*[1]]

**poach|er**[2] (pō′chər), *n.* a vessel or pan for poaching, as eggs or fish. [< *poach*[2] + *-er*[1]]

**P.O.B.** or **POB** (no periods), Post Office Box.

**po|chard** (pō′chərd), *n., pl.* **-chards** or (*collectively*) **-chard.** **1** a European diving duck that has a reddish-brown head and neck. **2** any one of various related ducks, such as the redhead (American pochard) of North America. [origin uncertain]

**po|chette** (pô shet′), *n. French.* a small violin; kit.

**pock**[1] (pok), *n., v.* — ***n.*** a pimple, mark, or pit on the skin, caused by smallpox and certain other diseases. — ***v.t.*** **1** to pit, scar, or mark with or as if with pocks: *The tens of thousands of craters that pock the face of the moon* (Scientific American). **2** to scatter over (an area) like pocks. [Old English *pocc* a pustule. See related etym. at **poke**[2].]

**pock**[2] (pok), *n. Scottish.* a poke; bag.

**pock|et** (pok′it), *n., v., adj.* — ***n.*** **1** a small bag sewed into clothing for carrying money or small articles: *His money fell on the floor through a hole in his pocket.* **2** a hollow place; enclosed place: *a pocket of space in the milling crowd.* (*Figurative.*) *a pocket of silence, a pocket of air on a crowded train.* SYN: enclosure. **3** a small bag or pouch: *Lucy Locket lost her pocket* (nursery rhyme). SYN: reticule. **4** a bag at the corner or side of a pool or billiard table. **5a** a hole in the earth containing gold or other ore: *The miner struck a pocket of silver.* **b** a single lump of ore; small mass of ore. **c** a bin in which ore or rock may be stored. **d** a hole, as in a mine shaft or tunnel, containing poisonous or explosive gas. **6** any current or condition in the air that causes an aircraft to drop suddenly; air pocket. **7** a pouch in an animal body, especially the abdominal pouch of a marsupial or the cheek pouch of a squirrel, chipmunk, etc. **8** *Figurative.* an isolated group or collection of things: *The candidate met with pockets of resistance within his own political party. Pockets of unsold vehicles remain unobtrusively in fields and yards* (London Times). **9** a position in racing in which one is blocked or hemmed in by others. **10** a strip of cloth with open ends, sewed to a sail. A thin wooden spar is passed through it to stiffen the leech or side. **11** a space between certain pins at which a bowler aims: *... while a left-handed bowler tries to hit the pocket between the 1 and 2 pins* (Joe Wilman). **12** *U.S. Football.* a small, heavily protected area in the backfield for the passer: *[He] seldom runs a roll-out; he is a drop-back "pocket" passer* (Time).
— ***v.t.*** **1** to put in one's pocket: *He pocketed the letter* (Thomas Hardy). *He held out a pound to her and she pocketed it* (Graham Greene). **2** *Figurative.* to shut in; hem in; confine as in a pocket: *A voice pocketed deep in the throat, granular ... complaining* (Modern Writing No. 2). **3** *Figurative.* to hold back; suppress; hide: *Pocket your pride and say nothing.* SYN: stifle. **4** *Figurative.* to take and endure, without doing anything about it: *He pocketed the insult.* **5** *Figurative.* to

**Pronunciation Key:** hat, āge, cãre, fär; let, ēqual, tėrm; it, īce; hot, ōpen, ôrder; oil, out; cup, pu̇t, rüle; child; long; thin; ᴛʜen; zh, measure; ə represents **a** in about, **e** in taken, **i** in pencil, **o** in lemon, **u** in circus.

take secretly or dishonestly: *One partner pocketed all the profits.* SYN: steal. **6** to knock or drive into a pocket: *to pocket a billiard ball, to pocket a contestant in a race.* **7** *U.S.* to refrain from signing (a bill or other legislation) to keep it from becoming law.
—*adj.* **1** meant to be carried in a pocket: *a pocket handkerchief.* **2a** small enough to go in a pocket: *a pocket camera.* **b** small for its kind.
**in one's (hip) pocket**, under one's control or influence: *Even before he plunges into his program, ... [he] has his audience in his pocket* (Howard Taubman). *Britain, on the key issues, remained in America's pocket* (Drew Middleton).
**in pocket**, having or gaining money: *At the end of their peregrination, they are above a hundred crowns in pocket* (Tobias Smollett).
**line one's pocket** (or **pockets**), to make a large profit, especially in an unscrupulous manner: *Some people had gained control of a "handful of banks" to line their own pockets* (New York Times).
**out of pocket**, spending or losing money: *Besides the time he lost, he'll be out of pocket $25 for traveling expenses.*
[< Anglo-French *pokete* (diminutive) < Old North French *poke,* or *poque* poke[2]] —**pock′et|a|ble,** *adj.* —**pock′et|less,** *adj.* —**pock′et|like′,** *adj.*

**pocket battleship**, a swift, heavily armed cruiser, especially a German type used in World War II.

**pocket billiards**, = pool[2] (def. 1).

**pock|et|book** (pok′it bu̇k′), *n.* **1** a woman's purse: *She set her pocketbook down and took out her wallet.* SYN: handbag. **2** a small, flat or folded case for carrying money or papers in a pocket: *She had several large bills in her pocketbook.* SYN: wallet. **3** a person's supply of money; finances; funds: *a vacation easy on the pocketbook. This dress is too expensive for my pocketbook.* **4** Also, **pocket book.** a soft-covered or paperbound book of such size that it is easily carried in the pocket.

**pocket borough**, (formerly, in Great Britain) a borough whose parliamentary representation was controlled by a single person or family.

**pock|et|ful** (pok′it fu̇l), *n., pl.* **-fuls.** as much as a pocket will hold: ... *a whole pocketful of money* (Thackeray).

**pocket gopher**, any one of a group of burrowing rodents with large cheek pouches; gopher.

**pock|et-hand|ker|chief** (pok′it hang′kər chif), *n.* a handkerchief carried in the pocket.

**pock|et|knife** (pok′it nīf′), *n., pl.* **-knives.** a small knife with one or more blades that fold into the handle. See picture under **knife**.

**pocket money**, money for spending.

**pocket mouse**, any one of various small, mouselike American rodents with external cheek pouches, found in western North America, especially in desert areas or areas of sandy soil.

**pocket piece**, a coin, often one not current, carried habitually in the pocket, as for luck or for its associations.

**pocket rat**, any one of several rodents with cheek pouches, such as the pocket gopher and the kangaroo rat; pouched rat.

**pock|et-size** (pok′it sīz′), *adj.* **1** small enough to go in a pocket: *a pocket-size radio or camera.* **2** *Informal, Figurative: a pocket-size field. The pocket-size market of Switzerland, with a total population smaller than London* (London Times).

**pock|et-sized** (pok′it sīzd′), *adj.* = pocket-size.

**pocket veto**, **1** a method of vetoing a bill that can be used by the President of the United States on a bill presented to him within ten days of the end of a session of Congress. If the President does not sign the bill before Congress adjourns, it does not become a law. **2** a similar method used by the governor of a state.

**pock|et-ve|to** (pok′it vē′tō), *v.t.,* **-toed, -to|ing.** *U.S.* to veto (a bill) by means of the pocket veto.

**pock|mark** (pok′märk′), *n., v.* —*n.* a mark or pit on the skin; pock. —*v.t.* to disfigure or mark as if with pockmarks; pock: *Bomb craters ... pockmark surrounding rice paddies and hillsides* (New York Times). (*Figurative.*) *The field of inquiry is ... pockmarked with anomalies* (Manchester Guardian Weekly).

**pock|y** (pok′ē), *adj.,* **pock|i|er, pock|i|est.** **1** marked with pocks. **2** *Archaic.* of, having to do with, or like pocks or the pox.

**po|co** (pō′kō), *adv., adj. Music.* little; somewhat (used in directions to qualify other expressions). [< Italian *poco* < Latin *paucus* little, few]

**po|co a po|co** (pō′kō ä pō′kō), *Music.* little by little; gradually. [< Italian *poco a poco*]

**po|co|cu|ran|te** (pō′kō ku̇ ran′tē; *Italian* pō′kō kü-rän′tā), *adj., n.* —*adj.* caring little; careless; indifferent.
—*n.* a careless, indifferent person.
[< Italian *pococurante* < *poco* little (< Latin *paucus*) + *curante* caring, present participle of *curare* < Latin *cūrāre*]

**po|co|cu|ran|tism** (pō′kō ku̇ ran′tiz əm, -rän′-), *n.* the character, disposition, or habits of a pococurante.

**po|co|sin** (pə kō′sin), *n.* a tract of swampy land. [American English < Algonkian (language uncertain) *páquesen* or *poquosin* the land is in a watery state]

***pod**[1] (pod), *n., v.,* **pod|ded, pod|ding.** —*n.* **1** a shell or case in which plants such as beans and peas grow their seeds; legume or silique. A pod consists of two parts hinged together. **2** any dry, dehiscent pericarp, usually having several seeds, whether of one carpel or of several. **3** a streamlined cover over anything carried externally, especially on the wings or fuselage of an aircraft: *a gun pod or missile pod.* **4a** the case enclosing the eggs of a grasshopper. **b** any egg case or sac.
—*v.i.* **1** to bear or produce pods. **2** to fill out into a pod.
—*v.t.* to empty out of the pods; shell (peas).
[origin uncertain. Compare earlier *podder,* variant of *podware* food crops.] —**pod′like′,** *adj.*

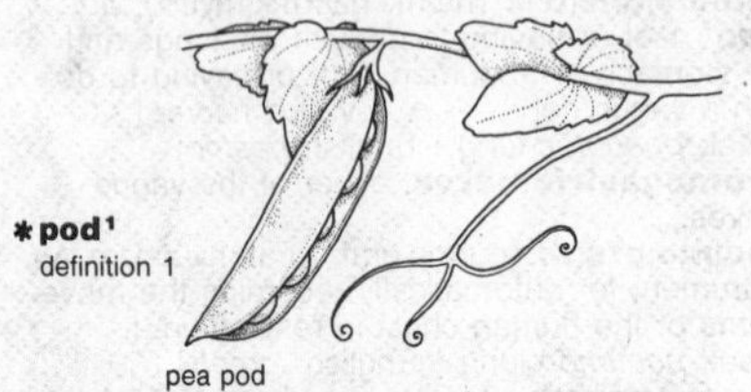

***pod**[1]
definition 1

**pod**[2] (pod), *n.* **1** a small herd, as of seals and whales. **2** a small flock of birds.

**pod**[3] (pod), *n.* **1** the straight groove in the body of certain augers and bits. **2** the socket in a brace in which the bit is inserted. [origin uncertain. Compare Old English *pād* a covering]

**p.o.d.**, pay on delivery.

**P.O.D.**, Post Office Department.

**po|dag|ra** (pə dag′rə), *n.* **1** gout in the foot. **2** gout generally. [< Latin *podagra* < Greek *podágrā* (literally) a foot trap < *poús, podós* foot + *ágrā* a catching, hunting]

**pod corn**, a variety of corn in which each grain or kernel is enclosed in an individual pod or husk, the whole ear being also in a husk. See picture under **corn**[1].

**Pod. D.**, Doctor of Podiatry.

**pod|dy** (pod′ē), *n. Australian.* a young calf, lamb, or other animal, taken from its mother and fed by hand.

**po|des|ta** (po des′tə; *Italian* pō′de stä′), *n.* in Italy: **1** a chief government official in medieval towns and republics. **2** a subordinate municipal judge in certain modern cities. **3** (under the Fascists) a city official or municipal judge. [< Italian *podestà* < Old Italian *podestate* < Latin *potestās, -ātis* power; public official, perhaps < *potest* he has power < *posse* to be able]

**po|de|ti|um** (pō dē′shē əm), *n., pl.* **-ti|a** (-shē ə). *Botany.* **1** a stalklike or shrubby outgrowth of the thallus of certain lichens, bearing the apothecium or fruiting body. **2** any stalklike elevation. [< New Latin *podetium* < Greek *poús, podós* foot]

**podg|y** (poj′ē), *adj.,* **podg|i|er, podg|i|est.** short and fat; pudgy: *I wish I had had a shake of that trembling, podgy hand* (Thackeray). SYN: dumpy. [variant of *pudgy*] —**podg′i|ly,** *adv.* —**podg′i|ness,** *n.*

**po|di|a|tric** (pə dī′ə trik), *adj.* of or having to do with podiatry.

**po|di|a|trist** (pə dī′ə trist), *n.* a person who treats disorders of the human foot; chiropodist.

**po|di|a|try** (pə dī′ə trē), *n.* the study and treatment of ailments of the human foot; chiropody. [< Greek *poús, podós* foot + *īātreíā* a healing]

**pod|ite** (pod′īt), *n.* a segment of the limb of a crustacean or other arthropod. [< Greek *poús, podós* foot + English *-ite*[1]]

**po|dit|ic** (pə dit′ik), *adj.* of or belonging to a podite.

**po|di|um** (pō′dē əm), *n., pl.* **-di|a** (-dē ə) or (especially for defs. 1 and 4) **-di|ums.** **1** a raised platform: *The speaker lectured from a podium. The conductor stepped up to the podium to lead the orchestra.* **2** a raised platform surrounding the arena in an ancient amphitheater. **3** a continuous projecting base or pedestal. **4** a continuous bench around a room. **5a** *Zoology.* an animal structure that serves as a foot. **b** *Botany.* a footstalk or other supporting part.
**take the podium**, to begin to address an audience or conduct an orchestra: *The conductor took the podium.*
[< Latin *podium* parapet, balcony < Greek *pódion* foot of a vase (diminutive) < *poús, podós* foot]

**pod|o|car|pus** (pod′ə kär′pəs), *n.* any one of a group of evergreen trees or shrubs of the Southern Hemisphere with a fleshy, drupelike fruit and a valuable wood, widely used in construction, cabinets, and carving. [< New Latin *Podocarpus* the genus name < Greek *poús, podós* foot + *karpós* fruit]

**pod|o|phyl|lin** (pod′ə fil′in), *n.* a yellow, bitter resin from the dried rhizome of the May apple, used as a cathartic. [< *podophyll*(um) + *-in*]

**pod|o|phyl|lum** (pod′ə fil′əm), *n.* the dried rhizome of the May apple. [< New Latin *Podophyllum* the genus name < Greek *poús, podós* foot + *phýllon* leaf]

**pod|sol** (pod′sol), *n.* = podzol.

**pod|sol|ic** (pod sol′ik), *adj.* = podzolic.

**Po|dunk** (pō′dungk), *n. U.S.* any small or insignificant town or village: *All such sufferers could well reflect upon the example set by the Mayo brothers, who converted Rochester, Minnesota, from a Podunk into a world center* (Harper's). [< Algonkian (Mohegan, or Massachusetts) *Potunk,* a place name, perhaps a corruption of *ptukohke,* a neck or corner of land]

**pod|zol** (pod′zol), *n.* a white or gray soil that is highly leached, found in certain cool, moist climates, especially northern Russia. Also, **podsol.** [< Russian *podzol* < *pod-* under + *zola* ashes]

**pod|zol|ic** (pod zol′ik), *adj.* of or having to do with podzol. Also, **podsolic.**

**pod|zo|li|za|tion** (pod′zə lə zā′shən), *n.* the process of development of a podzolic soil.

**P.O.E.** or **POE** (no periods), **1** port of embarkation. **2** port of entry.

**po|em** (pō′əm), *n.* **1** any composition in verse; arrangement of words in lines usually with a regularly repeated accent and often with rhyme. Poems are often highly imaginative or emotional, designed to express or convey deep feelings and thoughts. **2** a composition showing great beauty or nobility of language or thought: *a prose poem.* **3** something beautiful often likened to a poem: *a tone poem, a face that is a poem.* [< Old French *poeme,* learned borrowing from Latin *poēma* < Greek *póēma,* variant of *poíēma* < *poeîn,* variant of *poieîn* to make, compose]

**po|e|sy** (pō′ə sē, -zē), *n., pl.* **-sies.** **1** *Archaic.* **a** poetry. **b** a poem. **2** *Obsolete.* a motto or short inscription (often metrical, and usually in patterned or formal language). [< Old French *poësie,* learned borrowing from Latin *poēsis* < Greek *póēsis,* variant of *poíēsis* composition < *poieîn;* see etym. under **poem**.]

**po|et** (pō′it), *n.* **1** a person who writes poems. Longfellow and Scott were poets. SYN: bard. **2** a person who has great ability to feel and express beauty: *Herr Wieland is a poet with color* (New Yorker). [< Latin *poēta* < Greek *poētḗs,* variant of *poiētḗs* maker, author < *poieîn;* see etym. under **poem**.]

**poet.**, **1a** poetic. **b** poetical. **2** poetry.

**po|et|as|ter** (pō′it as′tər), *n.* a writer of rather poor poetry. SYN: rhymester. [< New Latin *poetaster* < Latin *poēta* poet + *-aster,* a diminutive suffix]

**po|et|as|ter|y** (pō′it as′tər ē, -trē), *n.* the work of a poetaster; poor poetry.

**po|et|ess** (pō′ə tis), *n.* a woman poet.

**po|et|ic** (pō et′ik), *adj., n.* —*adj.* **1** having to do with poems or poets: *the ranks of the poetic tribe* (William Cowper). **2** suitable for poems or poets: *"Alas," "o'er," "plenteous," and "blithe" are poetic words.* **3** showing beautiful or imaginative language, imagery, or thought: *She has such poetic fancies as calling the clouds sheep and the new moon a boat.* SYN: lyrical. **4** consisting of verse or poems: *a poetic translation.*
—*n.* = poetics. —**po|et′i|cal|ly,** *adv.* —**po|et′i|cal|ness,** *n.*

**po|et|i|cal** (pō et′ə kəl), *adj.* = poetic.

**po|et|i|cise** (pō et′ə sīz), *v.t., v.i.,* **-cised, -cis|ing.** *Especially British.* poeticize.

**po|et|i|cism** (pō et′ə siz əm), *n.* **1** overly poetic character or practice; overly poetic diction. **2** a banal or stereotyped expression in a poem.

**po|et|i|cize** (pō et′ə sīz), *v.,* **-cized, -ciz|ing.** —*v.t.* to make poetic; treat poetically; put into poetry: *The working class was ... idealized and poeticized by wayward genius* (Contemporary Review).
—*v.i.* to write or speak as a poet.

**poetic justice**, ideal justice with virtue being suitably rewarded and wickedness properly punished, as shown often in poetry, drama, and fiction.

**poetic license**, variation from regular usages and facts, such as is allowed in poetry.

**po|et|ics** (pō et′iks), *n.* **1** the part of literary criticism that deals with the nature and laws of poetry. **2** a formal or systematic study on poetry: *Aristotle's "Poetics."*

**po|et|i|cule** (pō et′ə kyül), *n.* a petty or insignificant poet; poetaster. [diminutive form < Latin *poēta* poet]

**po|et|ize** (pō′ə tīz), *v.,* **-ized, -iz|ing.** —*v.i.* to write poetry. —*v.t.* **1** to write poetry about. **2** to make poetic. —**po'et|iz'er**, *n.*

**poet laureate**, *pl.* **poets laureate**. **1** (in Great Britain) a poet appointed by the king or queen to write poems in celebration of court and national events. **2** the poet regarded as the best or most typical of his country or region. **3** any poet distinguished for excellence.

**po|et|ry** (pō'ə trē), *n.* **1** poems or verses as a form of literature; the writings of a poet or poets: *a collection of poetry.* **2** the art of writing poems: *Shakespeare and Milton were masters of English poetry.* **3** poetic quality; poetic spirit or feeling: *the poetry of nature. Poetry is the material out of which poems are made* (Atlantic). [< Old French *poetrie,* learned borrowing from Medieval Latin *poētria* < Latin *poēta* poet]

**poet's narcissus**, a narcissus with a short, trumpet-shaped tube that produces a single, wide-open white blossom on each stalk.

**po-faced** (pō'fāst'), *adj. British Informal.* poker-faced.

**pog|a|mog|gan** (pog'ə mog'ən), *n.* a war club of American Indians of the Great Lakes region and the Plains, having a slender handle and a heavy, knobbed head, used as a weapon and in ceremonies. [American English < Algonkian (Ojibwa) *pägämâgan* (literally) something used for striking]

**po|go|ni|a** (pə gō'nē ə, -gōn'yə), *n.* any North American orchid of a group that grows on the ground, such as the snakemouth. [< New Latin *Pogonia* the genus name < Greek *pōgon, pṓgōnos* beard]

**pog|o|nip** (pog'ə nip), *n. U.S.* a cold winter fog containing ice particles, that sometimes occurs in valleys in the Sierra Nevada Mountains. [American English < a Shoshonean word]

***po|go stick** (pō'gō), a toy consisting of a stick that contains a spring, and has footrests near the bottom and a handle at the top. A person can hop from place to place by jumping up and down on the footrests, while holding the handle. [< *Pogo,* a former trademark]

***pogo stick**

**po|grom** (pō grom', pō'grəm), *n.* an organized massacre, especially of Jews: *The only means of combating the pogroms is armed resistance* (London Daily News). [< Russian *pogrom* devastation]

**po|grom|ist** (pō grom'ist, pō'grə mist), *n.* an organizer of or a participant in a pogrom.

**po|gy** (pō'gē), *n., pl.* **-gies** or (*collectively*) **-gy**. **1** a perch of the western coast of the United States that bears live young. **2** = menhaden. [American English, apparently short for earlier *pauhagen, paughaden* the menhaden, perhaps < Algonkian (Abnaki) *pookagan* < a verb, meaning "one manures the land" (apparently the fish was used as fertilizer)]

**poh** (pō), *interj.* = pooh.

**poi** (poi), *n.* a Hawaiian food made of the root of the taro, baked, pounded, moistened, and fermented. [< Hawaiian *poi*]

**poign|ance** (poi'nəns, poin'yəns), *n.* = poignancy.

**poign|an|cy** (poi'nən sē, poin'yən-), *n.* the quality or condition of being poignant; piercing quality; sharpness: *poignancy of flavor,* (*Figurative.*) *poignancy of delight.*

**poign|ant** (poi'nənt, poin'yənt), *adj.* **1** very painful; piercing: *poignant suffering, a poignant reminder of one's failures.* **SYN**: severe. **2** *Figurative.* keen; intense: *a subject of poignant interest, a poignant delight.* **3** sharp to the taste or smell: *poignant sauces, poignant perfumes.* [< Old French *poignant,* present participle of *poindre* to prick < Latin *pungere*] —**poign'ant|ly**, *adv.*

**poi|ki|lo|therm** (poi'kə lə thėrm'), *n.* a cold-blooded animal.

**poi|ki|lo|ther|mal** (poi'kə lō thėr'məl), *adj.* having a body temperature that varies with that of the environment; cold-blooded: *poikilothermal animals.* [< Greek *poikílos* various, variegated + *thérmē* heat + English *-al*¹]

**poi|ki|lo|ther|mic** (poi'kə lō thėr'mik), *adj.* = poikilothermal.

**poi|ki|lo|ther|mous** (poi'kə lō thėr'məs), *adj.* = poikilothermal.

**poi|lu** (pwä'lü), *n.* a nickname for a French soldier. [< French *poilu* a French soldier in World War I; earlier, strong man; (literally) virile, hairy < Old French *pelu* < *peil, poil* hair < Latin *pilus*]

**poin|ci|an|a** (poin'sē an'ə), *n.* **1** any one of a genus of tropical trees or shrubs of the pea family, having showy scarlet, orange, or yellow flowers. **2** = royal poinciana. [< New Latin *Poinciana* the genus name < de *Poinci,* a governor of the Antilles in the 1600's, who wrote a natural history of the islands]

**poin|set|ti|a** (poin set'ē ə, -set'ə), *n.* a plant with large scarlet or white leaves that look like flower petals, and a small greenish-yellow flower. The poinsettia is a perennial tropical American plant that belongs to the spurge family, and is much used as Christmas decoration in the United States. [American English < New Latin *poinsettia* < Joel R. *Poinsett,* 1779-1851, discoverer of the plant]

**point** (point), *n., v.* —*n.* **1** a sharp end; something having a sharp end: *the point of a needle, a point of rock.* **2a** a tiny round mark; dot: *A period is a point. Use a point to set off decimals. Commas and points they set exactly right* (Alexander Pope). **b** a diacritical mark used in Semitic languages. **3** *Mathematics.* something that has position without length or width. Two lines meet or cross at a point. **4** a place; spot: *Stop at this point.* **5** any particular or definite position, condition, or time; degree; stage: *the freezing point, the boiling point, the point of death, a particular point in time. When it came to the point of shooting, he could not. The book is good—up to a point.* **6** *Figurative.* an item; small part; detail: *The speaker replied to the argument point by point.* **SYN**: particular. **7** *Figurative.* a special quality or feature: *Courage and endurance were his good points. Honesty is not her strong point.* **SYN**: trait, characteristic. **8** *Figurative.* a physical characteristic or feature of an animal, such as one used to judge excellence or purity of breed: *The good points in a cow aren't necessarily features of beauty* (Winston Churchill). **9** *Figurative.* **a** the main idea or purpose; important or essential thing: *to miss the point of a joke. I missed the point of your talk.* **SYN**: object. **b** any idea, argument, or point of view: *What's your point? You have a point there. The speaker made several points.* **10** *Figurative.* force; effectiveness: *He writes with point.* **11** *Figurative.* a particular aim, end, or purpose: *to carry one's point.* **12a** each of the 32 positions indicating direction marked at the circumference of the card of a compass. *North, south, east, and west are the four main, or cardinal, points on a compass.* **b** the interval between any two adjacent points of a compass; 11 degrees 15 minutes. **13** a piece of land with a sharp end sticking out into the water; cape: *The ship rounded the point and disappeared.* **14** a unit of scoring or measuring: *Our team won the game by ten points. The university credited him with five points for the semester's work. That stock has gone up a point. During the war meat was rationed by points per pound. Abbr:* pt. **15** *U.S.* a charge or fee discounted by a lender from a loan, usually one percent of the loan's face amount, by which the effective interest rate is substantially increased. **16** a unit for measuring printing type; about 1/72 inch. **17** *Informal, Figurative.* a hint; suggestion: *to get some points on farming.* **18** lace made with a needle; needlepoint. **19a** the tip of the angle formed by two rails of a frog in a railroad switch. **b** *British.* a railroad switch. **20a** the position of one of the players, such as in cricket or lacrosse. **b** the player in this position. **21** (in boxing) the tip of the chin. **22** (in hunting) the attitude, usually with muzzle pointing and one foreleg raised, assumed by a pointer or setter on finding game. **23** one of the 24 long pointed spaces of a backgammon board. **24a** one of two tungsten or platinum pieces, especially in the distributor of an automobile engine, for making or breaking the flow of current. **b** *Especially British.* an outlet; socket. **25** a short, musical strain, especially one sounded as a signal. **26** a small body of troops that patrols ahead of the advance guard or behind the rear guard to reconnoiter, as for obstacles or enemy forces. **27** a stroke with the bayonet. **28** *Phonetics.* the tip of the tongue. **29** *Archaic.* a tagged lace or cord used in the Middle Ages to lace or fasten various parts of the clothes: *Their points being broken—Down fell their hose* (Shakespeare). **30** *Obsolete.* **a** a conclusion; culmination. **b** condition; plight. **c** determination; resolution.
—*v.t.* **1** to sharpen: *Please point my pencil.* **2a** to mark with dots; punctuate. **b** to indicate decimals. **c** to mark points in (as the writing of Semitic languages or shorthand). **3** *Figurative.* to give force to (speech or action): *to point one's remarks. The preacher told a story to point his advice.* **4** to show (position or direction) with the finger; call attention to: *He pointed the way to the village over the hills.* **5** to turn (a finger, weapon, or the like) straight to or at; aim: *Don't point your gun at me. The fireman pointed his hose at the flames.* **SYN**: level. **6** to fill joints of (brickwork) with mortar or cement. **7** (of a dog) to show (game) by standing rigid looking toward it.
—*v.i.* **1** to indicate position or direction, or direct attention with, or as if with, the finger: *to point at a house.* **2** to tend; aim. **3** to have a specified direction: *The signboard points north. The ship pointed east.* **4** (of a dog) to show the presence of game by standing rigid and looking toward it. **5** (of an abscess) to come to a head.
**at the point of**, in the act of; very near to: *at the point of leaving.*
**beside the point**, having nothing to do with the subject; not appropriate; irrelevant: *He did what the others wanted; his own wishes were beside the point to them.*
**in point**, pertinent; apt: *a case in point.*
**in point of**, as regards: *States were too busy with their laws and too negligent in point of education* (Alexander Hamilton).
**make a point (of)**, to insist on; make a rule of: *He made a point of arriving on time. She made it a point to write home once a week.*
**on the point of**, just about (to do); on the verge of: *She was on the point of going out when a neighbor dropped in.*
**point off**, to mark off with points or dots: *To divide by 100 is done by only pointing off two figures for decimals* (Charles Hutton).
**point out**, to show or call attention to: *Please point out my mistakes.*
**points**, the extremities of an animal, such as the feet, ears, and tail: *That champion dog has many outstanding points.*
**point up**, to put emphasis on; call or give special attention to: *The report of the discussions points up the responsibility of teachers, school librarians, and all agencies ... to coordinate their efforts* (Saturday Review).
**stretch** (or **strain**) **a point**, **a** to exceed the reasonable limit; go further than one is entitled to go: *We've not quite so much proof as I could wish. It would be straining a point to arrest him, as it stands* (G. A. Lawrence). **b** to make a special exception; do more than one is bound to do: *I am not likely, I think, to ask anything very unreasonable, and if I did, they might have stretched a point* (Scott).
**to the point**, appropriate to the subject at hand; apt: *His speech was brief and to the point.*
[< Old French *point,* and *pointe* a prick, mark, sharp point; a small measure of space or time < Latin *pūnctum,* neuter, and *pūncta,* feminine, past participles of *pungere* to pierce]

**point after touchdown**, *U.S. Football.* a point scored for a successful conversion.

**point-blank** (*adj.* point'blangk'; *adv.* point'-blangk'), *adj., adv.* —*adj.* **1a** aimed straight at the mark, especially without the need to aim carefully because a target is so close: *a point-blank salvo.* **b** close enough for aim to be taken in this way: *He fired the gun from point-blank range.* **2** *Figurative.* plain and blunt; direct: *a point-blank question.*
—*adv.* **1** straight at the mark: *to fire point-blank.* **2** *Figurative.* plainly and bluntly; directly: *One boy gave excuses, but the other refused point-blank.*
[apparently < *point,* verb + *blank* the white mark in the center of a target]

**point count**, a system of bidding in bridge based upon point values given to the honor cards.

**point d'An|gle|terre** (pwaɴ' dän glə ter'), *French.* **1** a kind of delicate bobbin lace, originally Flemish. **2** (literally) lace of England.

**point d'ap|pui** (pwaɴ' dá pwē'), *French.* **1** a secure position serving as a base for operations, as in war or diplomacy. **2** (literally) point of support.

**point d'es|prit** (pwaɴ' des prē'), *French.* **1** a net fabric with dots woven into it singly or in groups. **2** (literally) lace of spirit.

**point-de|vice, point-de|vise** or **point-de-vyse** (point'di vīs'), *adj., adv. Archaic.* —*adj.* **1** perfect; precise. **2** scrupulously nice or neat.
—*adv.* completely; perfectly; exactly.
[Middle English *at poynt devys;* origin uncertain]

---

**Pronunciation Key:** hat, āge, cãre, fär; let, ēqual, tėrm; it, īce; hot, ōpen, ôrder; oil, out; cup, pu̇t, rüle; child; long; thin; ᴛʜen; zh, measure; ə represents **a** in about, **e** in taken, **i** in pencil, **o** in lemon, **u** in circus.

**point duty**, *British.* the duty of a policeman assigned to direct traffic at a point in a thoroughfare.

**pointe** (*French* pwaNt; *Anglicized* point), *n. Ballet.* **1** the toe, especially (as a dancing position) the tip of the toe. **2** the reinforced toe of the ballet slipper. [< French *pointe,* feminine of *point* point]

**point|ed** (poin′tid), *adj.* **1** having a point or points: *a pointed roof.* **SYN**: peaked. **2** *Figurative.* sharp; piercing: *a pointed wit.* **SYN**: keen. **3** *Figurative.* directed; aimed: *a pointed remark.* **SYN**: leveled. **4** *Figurative.* emphatic: *He showed her pointed attention.* **SYN**: marked. —**point′ed|ly**, *adv.* —**point′ed|ness**, *n.*

**pointed arch**, an arch that forms a point at the top, characteristic of the Gothic style of architecture.

**pointed fox**, the fur of red fox made to imitate that of silver fox, by dyeing it black and adding white or white-tipped hairs.

**pointed style**, the Gothic style of architecture, characterized by pointed arches.

***point|er** (poin′tər), *n.* **1** a person or thing that points: *Most little children are great pointers until they learn the names for things.* **2** a long, tapering stick used in pointing things out on a map or blackboard: *The teacher picked up the pointer and showed us Ireland on the map.* **3** the hand of a clock, compass, meter, or the like: *The pointer of the speedometer showed we were going 30 miles per hour.* **4** short-haired hunting dog with a smooth coat. A pointer is trained to show where game is by standing still with his head and body pointing toward it. See picture below. **5** any one of various other hunting dogs that point at game, such as the German short-haired pointer and the German wire-haired pointer. See picture below. **6** *Informal, Figurative.* a hint; suggestion: *She gave him some pointers on improving his tennis.* **SYN**: tip.

**Point|ers** (poin′tərz), *n.pl.* two stars in the Big Dipper. A line connecting them points approximately to the North Star in the Little Dipper.

**point|ful** (point′fəl), *adj.* full of point; meaningful; pertinent; apt: *... vivid and pointful in its portrayal of character* (Manchester Guardian Weekly). —**point′ful|ly**, *adv.* —**point′ful|ness**, *n.*

**poin|til|lism** (pwan′tə liz əm), *n.* a method of painting introduced by French impressionists, producing luminous effects by laying on the colors in points or dots of unmixed color that are blended by the eye. [< French *pointillisme* < *pointiller* to mark with little dots or points < *point* point]

**poin|til|list** (pwan′tə list), *n., adj.* —*n.* an artist who follows the style of pointillism.
—*adj.* of or characteristic of pointillism.

**poin|til|lis|tic** (pwan′tə lis′tik), *adj.* = pointillist.

**point lace**, lace made with a needle; needlepoint.

**point-laced** (point′lāst′), *adj.* trimmed with point lace.

**point|less** (point′lis), *adj.* **1** without a point: *a pointless sword, a pointless pencil.* **SYN**: blunt. **2** *Figurative.* without meaning or purpose: *a pointless story, a pointless question.* **SYN**: meaningless. —**point′less|ly**, *adv.* —**point′less|ness**, *n.*

**point man**, **1** *U.S. Military.* the man on the point of a patrol. **2** *Hockey.* an attacking defense player whose main job is to keep the puck in the attacking zone.

**point-of-aim** (point′əv ām′), *n.* a point just below the spot on the target which an archer wants to hit.

**point of fusion**, = melting point.

**point of honor**, a matter that affects a person's honor, principles, sense of duty, or the like.

**point of no return**, **1** the point in the flight of an aircraft at which it is safer to proceed than to turn back: *We also figure out the point of no return—the point beyond which we wouldn't have enough gas to turn around and get back* (New Yorker). **2** *Figurative.* a point reached in a course beyond which it is no longer possible to reverse or turn back to an earlier condition: *The majority of the children have passed the dreaded "point of no return," in this case medical phraseology for a victim of malnutrition who has become so dehydrated that death is only a matter of time* (New York Times).

**point of order**, a question raised as to whether proceedings are according to the rules.

**point-of-sale** (point′əv sāl′), *adj.* of or having to do with a computerized system of recording sales information when a sale is made: *The records are maintained inside the computer and are continuously updated by the point-of-sale information* (John R. Rice).

**point of tangency**, *Geometry.* the point where a straight line touches a circle: *The radius at the point of tangency makes a right angle with the tangent* (Rothwell Stephens).

**point of view**, **1** the position from which one looks at something: *a distant point of view.* **2** *Figurative.* an attitude of mind: *a stubborn point of view. Farmers and campers have different points of view toward rain.*

**points of the compass**, the 32 directions marked on a compass. North, south, east, and west are the four main, or cardinal, points of the compass.

**point source**, a source of light waves, radio waves, or other electromagnetic radiation which is so highly concentrated that it can be considered to come from a single point.

**point system**, **1** a system of promoting students by credits for individual subjects, rather than by the completion of a set program for each term. **2** a system of penalizing motorists for infractions of traffic rules and laws, each type of infraction carrying a certain number of penalty points. **3** a system of determining the winner of a game, race, or contest by adding up the number of points scored by each player or contestant. Point systems are often used in boxing and in motorcycle races. **4** *Printing.* a system of measuring type and leads, in which the pica body equals 12 points. **5** any of various systems of printing for the blind, as Braille, using raised dots in various combinations as symbols for letters.

**point-to-point** (point′tə point′), *n.* a cross-country or steeplechase horse race over a course marked by flags at the salient points.

**point|y** (poin′tē), *adj.,* **point|i|er**, **point|i|est**. having a point; coming to a point; pointed: *a small, merry-looking man with a pointy nose* (New Yorker).

**poise**[1] (poiz), *n., v.,* **poised**, **pois|ing**. —*n.* **1** mental balance, composure, or self-possession: *She has perfect poise and never seems embarrassed.* **SYN**: equanimity. **2** the way in which the body, head, or other part of the body are held; carriage: *the gladiatorlike poise of his small round head on his big neck and shoulders* (George du Maurier). **3** state of balance; equilibrium. **4** a pause between two periods of motion or change; suspense of movement: *At the poise of the flying year* (Richard Watson Gilder). **5** *Figurative.* the condition of being equally balanced between alternatives; state of indecision; suspense. **6** *Obsolete.* **a** the state of being heavy. **b** gravity; importance: *Occasions ... of some poise, Wherein we must have use of your advice* (Shakespeare). [< Old French *pois,* variant of *peis* < Vulgar Latin *pēsum,* for Latin *pēnsum* weight < *pendere* to weigh]
—*v.t.* **1** to balance: *Poise yourself on your toes.* **2** to hold or carry evenly or steadily: *The waiter poised the tray on his hand.* **3** *Figurative.* to consider; ponder: *A thousand resolutions ... weighed, poised and perpended* (Laurence Sterne). **4** *Obsolete.* to make stable, as by adding weight; ballast. **5** *Obsolete.* to weigh.
—*v.i.* **1** to be balanced or held in equilibrium. **2** to hang supported or suspended. **3** to hover, as a bird does in air: *A hummingbird can poise for several moments over a single flower.*
[< Anglo-French *poiser* < Old French *pois-,* stem of *peser* to weigh < Vulgar Latin *pēsare,* for Latin *pēnsāre* (intensive) < *pendere* to weigh]

**poise**[2] (poiz), *n.* a unit of measurement of viscosity in the centimeter-gram-second system. [< J. M. *Poiseuille,* 1797-1869, French physiologist]

**poised** (poizd), *adj.* **1** composed; self-possessed: *The young lady was beautiful and poised.* **2** ready; set: *The army was poised for battle.*

**poi|son** (poi′zən), *n., v., adj.* —*n.* **1** a drug or other substance very dangerous to life and health: Mustard gas, arsenic, and opium are poisons. **SYN**: venom. **2** *Figurative.* anything deadly or harmful: *Avoid the poison of hate.* **3** a substance that stops or weakens the action of a catalyst or enzyme.
—*v.t.* **1** to kill or harm by poison: *Farmers poison thousands of rats every year.* **2** to put poison in or on: *to poison food, to poison arrows.* **3** *Figurative.* to have a very harmful effect on: *Lies poison the mind. Whispering tongues can poison truth* (Samuel Taylor Coleridge). **4** to stop or weaken the action of (a catalyst or enzyme).
—*adj.* poisonous; toxic: *the poison waters of our polluted streams.*
[< Old French *poison,* earlier *puisun* < Latin *pōtiō, -ōnis.* See etym. of doublet **potion.**] —**poi′son|er**, *n.*

**poison claw**, either one of the first pair of legs of a centipede, having a claw that fills with poison from a gland in the head.

**poison dogwood** or **elder**, = poison sumac.

**poison gas**, a poisonous gas, such as mustard gas, used especially as a weapon in warfare.

**poison hemlock**, = hemlock (def. 1).

**poi|son|ing** (poi′zə ning), *n.* **1** the administering of a poison: *a case of murder by poisoning.* **2** the ingestion of a poison: *Death occurred by poisoning.*

***poison ivy**, **1** a shrub or climbing plant that looks like ivy, with white, berrylike fruit, glossy, green, compound leaves of three leaflets each, and a poisonous oil that causes a painful rash on most people if they touch the plant. Poison ivy is a North American plant, a variety of sumac, that belongs to the cashew family. **2** the rash caused by this plant.

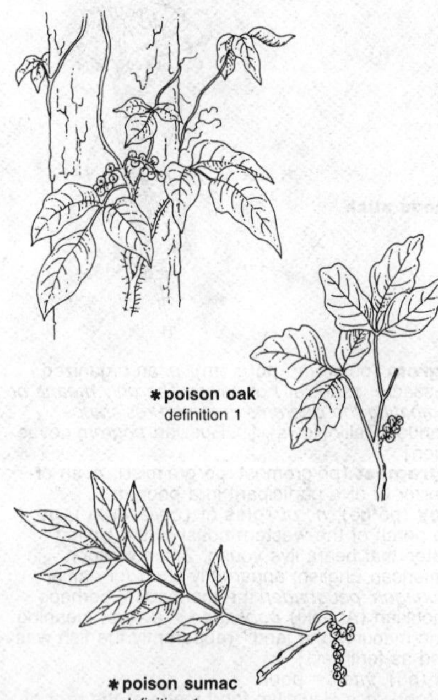

***poison ivy** definition 1

***poison oak** definition 1

***poison sumac** definition 1

***poison oak**, **1** a kind of poison ivy that grows as a shrub. It is found especially in the western United States. **2** = poison sumac. **3** the rash caused by either of these two plants.

**poi|son|ous** (poi′zə nəs), *adj.* **1** containing poison; very harmful to life and health; venomous: *The rattlesnake's bite is poisonous.* **2** *Figurative.* having a harmful effect: *a poisonous lie.* **SYN**: malevolent, malignant. —**poi′son|ous|ly**, *adv.* —**poi′son|ous|ness**, *n.*

**poi|son-pen** (poi′zən pen′), *adj.* designating vicious, slanderous, defamatory, and (usually) anonymous writings to or about a person: *the devastation wreaked upon a French village by a series of poison-pen letters* (New York Times).

***poison sumac**, **1** a shrub growing in swamps that has leaves composed of seven to thirteen leaflets that become brilliantly red in the autumn and white, berrylike fruit. It causes a very severe rash on most people if they touch it. Poison

***pointer** definitions 4, 5

pointer

German short-haired pointer

griffon

sumac is a tall North American shrub of the cashew family. 2 the rash caused by this plant.

**Pois|son distribution** (pwä sôɴ'), *Statistics.* a distribution differing from the normal curve that can be applied to distributions that are not continuous, as when the variable cannot have all values but is limited to particular values. The Poisson distribution is often used in bacteriological experiments when the variable is limited to the number of cells in an area. [< Denis *Poisson,* 1781-1840, a French mathematician]

**Poisson ratio,** *Physics.* a measure of the elasticity of a material, equal to the ratio of the lateral strain to the longitudinal strain when the material is subjected to tensile stress.

**poi|trel** (poi'trəl), *n.* a piece of armor for protecting the breast of a horse. Also, **peytral, peytrel.** [< Old French *poitral* < Latin *pectorāle* breastplate]

**po|kal** (pō käl'), *n.* an ornamental drinking cup or goblet, of silver, glass, or other material, especially one of German make. [< German *Pokal,* ultimately < Late Latin *baucalis* earthen wine cup < Greek *baúkalis*]

**poke¹** (pōk), *v.,* **poked, pok|ing,** *n.* —*v.t.* **1a** to push against with something pointed: *to poke the ashes of a fire. She poked me in the ribs with her elbow.* **SYN:** prod, nudge. **b** *Informal.* to hit with the fist; punch: *He poked me in the nose.* **2** to thrust; push: *The old gossip was always poking her nose into other people's business. He poked his head in the kitchen window.* **3** to make by poking: *He poked a hole in the paper.*
—*v.i.* **1** to make a thrust with the arm, fist, a stick, or the like: *to poke about in the ashes of a fire.* **2** *Figurative.* to search; grope; pry. **3** to go in a lazy way; loiter: *They ... dig out a canoe from a cotton-wood tree, and in this poke along shore silently* (Washington Irving). **SYN:** dawdle, potter. **4** to thrust itself or stick (out): *Pens and pencils poked out over the top of his coat pocket.*
—*n.* **1a** the act of poking; thrust; push: *When he gave the fire a poke it flared up.* **SYN:** nudge. **b** *Informal.* a blow with the fist; punch. **2** a slow, lazy person. **3** a device fastened on cattle, pigs, and other livestock to prevent them from breaking through fences.
[Middle English *poken.* Compare Middle Dutch, Middle Low German *pōken.* Perhaps related to **poach¹.**]

**poke²** (pōk), *n.* **1** *Dialect.* a bag; sack. **2** *Archaic.* a pocket: *not a penny in poke* (Robert Browning). **3** *Scottish.* the bag or wallet of a roving beggar. **4** *Slang.* a wallet; purse. [probably < Old North French *poke,* or *poque* < Germanic (compare Old English *pocca,* or *pohha* bag, pocket)]

**poke³** (pōk), *n.* **1** a bonnet or hat with a large brim in front. **2** the brim: *The close poke of her little black bonnet hid her face from him* (George Eliot). [(originally) brim of a bonnet; perhaps noun use of *poke¹*]

**poke⁴** (pōk), *n.* = pokeweed. [American English, short for Algonkian (Virginia) *puccoon* any plant used for dyeing]

**poke|ber|ry** (pōk'ber'ē, -bər-), *n., pl.* **-ries. 1** the deep-purple berry of the pokeweed. **2** = pokeweed. [American English < *poke⁴,* or *poke* (weed) + *berry*]

***poke bonnet,** a bonnet with a projecting brim.

***poke bonnet**

**poke check,** a quick poke with a hockey stick attempting to steal or push the puck from another player.

**pok|er¹** (pō'kər), *n.* **1** a person or thing that pokes. **2** a metal rod for stirring a fire: *He stirred the fire with a poker.* [< *pok*(e)¹ + *-er¹*]

**pok|er²** (pō'kər), *n.* a card game in which the players bet on the value of the cards that they hold in their hands, the winner taking the pool. [American English; origin uncertain. Compare Middle Low German, Middle Dutch *poken* to brag, also, to play]

**poker back,** an arthritic condition characterized by stiffening of the spine.

**poker face,** *Informal.* a face that does not show one's thoughts or feelings.

**po|ker-faced** (pō'kər fāst'), *adj.* having a poker face; expressionless: *The manager tried to look poker-faced but succeeded only in looking miserable* (New Yorker).

**poke|root** (pōk'rüt, -rut), *n.* = pokeweed.

**poker spine,** = poker back.

**pok|er|work** (pō'kər wėrk'), *n.* ornamental work executed by burning designs, as on wood or leather, with a hot instrument, originally a poker; pyrography.

**poke|sy** (pōk'sē), *adj.* slow-moving; easygoing. [variant of *pokey²*]

**poke|weed** (pōk'wēd'), *n.* any one of a group of tropical or subtropical plants, especially a tall, branching perennial herb of North America with greenish-white flowers, juicy, purple berries, and poisonous roots, sometimes called the inkberry; poke. The pokeweed is used in medicine, and its young shoots, somewhat like asparagus, are sometimes boiled and eaten. [American English < *poke⁴* + *weed*]

**pok|ey¹** (pō'kē), *n., pl.* **pok|eys.** *U.S. Slang.* a jail: *After all, if he'd said those things to the cop he'd have had a night in the pokey as well as the $25 fine* (Wall Street Journal). [origin uncertain]

**pok|y** or **pok|ey²** (pō'kē), *adj.,* **pok|i|er, pok|i|est. 1** moving or acting slowly; puttering; dull; slow: *I wouldn't have your pokey old husband* (Sinclair Lewis). *The firemen ... complained that the Russians had been too poky about reporting the fire* (New Yorker). **2** small; confined; cramped; mean: *Do you suppose I gave up my position at school in order to live in a poky little hole?* (Arnold Bennett). **3** shabby; dowdy. [< *pok*(e)¹ + *-y¹*] —**pok'i|ly,** *adv.* —**pok'i|ness,** *n.*

**pol** (pol), *n. Informal.* a politician: *Our committee offices used to be full of old pols and cigar smoke* (Maclean's).

**pol.,** 1 polar. 2 political. 3 politics.

**POL** (no periods), *Military.* petroleum, oil, and lubricants.

**Pol.,** 1 Poland. 2 Polish.

**Po|la|bi|an** (pō lā'bē ən), *adj., n.* —*adj.* of or having to do with a Slavic people who formerly lived in the basin of the Elbe River and on the Baltic coast of northern Germany and who became completely Germanized.
—*n.* **1** one of this people. **2** the Slavic language of this people, extinct since the 1700's.
[< Czech *Polabe* a Polabian (< *po* near, on + *Labe* the Elbe) + English *-ian*]

**po|lac|ca¹** (pō läk'kä), *n. Italian.* polonaise (sometimes used in musical directions).

**po|lac|ca²** (pə lak'ə), *n.* a merchant vessel with two or three masts, used on the Mediterranean. [< Italian *polacca*]

**Po|lack** (pō'läk *for 1;* pō'lak *for 2*), *n.* **1** *Slang.* a person of Polish descent (usually used in an unfriendly way). **2** *Obsolete.* **a** a native or inhabitant of Poland; Pole. **b** the king of Poland. [< Polish *Polak*]

**Po|la|col|or** (pō'lə kul'ər), *n. Trademark.* a special color film with its own developing and printing agents, from which a finished positive color print may be obtained in less than a minute after exposure. [< *Pola*(roid) + *color*]

**po|la|cre** (pə lä'kər), *n.* a two- or three-masted ship; polacca. [< French *polacre*]

**Po|land China hog** (pō'lənd), any one of an American breed of large black-and-white hogs.

**po|lar** (pō'lər), *adj.* **1** of or near the North or South Pole: *a polar wind. It is very cold in the polar regions.* **2** having to do with a pole or poles. **3** of the poles of a magnet, electric battery, or other charged source or matter. **4** *Figurative.* opposite in character, like the poles of a magnet: *Love and hatred are polar feelings or attitudes.* **SYN:** contrary. **5** *Geometry.* having to do with or reciprocal to a pole. **6** *Chemistry.* ionizing when dissolved or fused; ionic. **7** serving to guide; guiding. [< Medieval Latin *polaris* < Latin *polus* pole²]

**polar axis,** the axis in the mounting of an equatorial telescope that is parallel to the earth's axis.

***polar bear,** a large white bear of the arctic regions.

***polar bear**

**polar body** or **cell,** *Biology.* one of the tiny cells that arise by a very unequal meiotic division of the ovum at or near the time of fertilization.

**polar cap,** *Astronomy.* a white area at each pole of the planet Mars, resembling ice or snow, which increases and decreases with the changes of the planet's so-called seasons.

**polar circle,** either of two circles of the earth parallel to the equator, one of which is everywhere distant 23 degrees 30 minutes (23°30') from the North Pole and the other equally distant from the South Pole; Arctic or Antarctic Circle.

***polar coordinates,** *Mathematics.* coordinates defining a point in a plane, being the length of the straight line drawn to it from a fixed point and the angle which this line makes with a fixed initial line or axis.

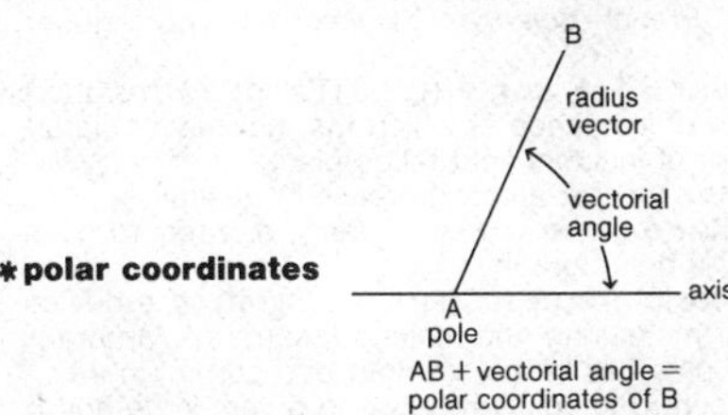


***polar coordinates**

**polar distance,** *Astronomy.* the complement of the declination of a heavenly body; codeclination.

**polar easterly,** a prevailing wind which blows from east to west between each of the poles and 60 degrees north or south latitude.

**polar front,** the boundary or boundary region between the cold polar winds and the warmer winds of tropical origin.

**polar hare,** = arctic hare.

**po|lar|im|e|ter** (pō'lə rim'ə tər), *n.* **1** an instrument used to measure the amount of polarized light received from a given source. **2** a form of polariscope for measuring the amount of rotation of the plane of polarization. [< *polari*(ze) + *-meter*]

**po|lar|i|met|ric** (pō'lər ə met'rik), *adj.* of or having to do with a polarimeter or polarimetry.

**po|lar|im|e|try** (pō'lə rim'ə trē), *n.* the use of a polarimeter; art or process of measuring or analyzing the polarization of light.

**Po|lar|is** (pō lãr'is), *n.* the North Star; polestar. [< Medieval Latin *Polaris* < Latin *polus;* see etym. under **pole²**]

**po|lar|i|scope** (pō lar'ə skōp), *n.* an instrument for showing the polarization of light, or for examining substances in polarized light.

**po|lar|i|scop|ic** (pə lar'ə skop'ik), *adj.* of or having to do with a polariscope.

**po|lar|ise** (pō'lə rīz), *v.t., v.i.,* **-ised, -is|ing.** *Especially British.* polarize. —**po'lar|is|er,** *n.*

**po|lar|i|ty** (pō lar'ə tē), *n., pl.* **-ties. 1** the possession of two opposed poles. A magnet or battery has polarity. **2** a positive or negative polar condition, as in electricity: *Reversing the polarity of an applied voltage, for instance, means interchanging the positive and negative conditions of the terminals to which it is applied* (Roy F. Allison). **3** *Figurative.* the possession of two opposite or contrasted principles or tendencies: *Many psychologists view polarity as an obvious factor in human behavior.*

**po|lar|iz|a|bil|i|ty** (pō'lə rī'zə bil'ə tē), *n.* the quality of being polarizable.

**po|lar|iz|a|ble** (pō'lə rī'zə bəl), *adj.* that can be polarized.

**po|lar|i|za|tion** (pō'lər ə zā'shən), *n.* **1** the act or process of polarizing or state of being polarized; production or acquistion of polarity. **2** the process by which gases produced during electrolysis are deposited on electrodes of a cell, giving rise to a reverse electromotive force. **3** *Optics.* **a** a state, or the production of a state, in which rays of light exhibit different properties in different directions, as when they are reflected from glass in a particular way, or when they are passed through a crystal of tourmaline that confines the light vibrations to a single plane. **b** the state in which all the vibrations of the waves take place in only one plane: *All light sources of practical importance emit radiation that exhibits little evidence of polarization. For this reason, the optical instruments based on the phenomena of polarization are provided with some element, such as a Nicol prism, for polarizing the natural light supplied by the source* (Hardy and Perrin). **4** *Figurative.* a splitting into opposing sides or extremes; division into opposite factions: *The polarization of the GOP into conservative and less-conservative*

---

*wings has become increasingly certain* (Wall Street Journal).

**po|lar|ize** (pō′lə rīz), *v.*, **-ized, -iz|ing.** —*v.t.* **1** to give polarity to; cause polarization in: *Some natural crystals, such as tourmaline, can polarize light. Tourmaline transmits the components that lie in one vibration-direction, and holds back others by absorbing them internally* (Richard T. Kriebel). **2** to give an arbitrary direction, or a special meaning or application, to: *to polarize a discussion.* **3** *Figurative.* to divide into opposing sides or extremes; split into opposite camps or factions: *People are tired of being polarized on emotional issues* (Time).
—*v.i.* to acquire polarity.
[< French *polariser* < *pôle* pole] —**po′lar|iz|er,** *n.*

**po|lar|iz|ing angle** (pō′lə rī′zing), *Optics.* the angle of incidence at which the maximum polarization of incident light takes place.

**polar lights,** aurora borealis or australis.

**po|lar|o|gram** (pō lar′ə gram), *n.* a record made by a polarograph.

**po|lar|o|graph** (pō lar′ə graf, -gräf), *n.* a device for measuring and making records (polarograms) of changes in the strength of a current in an electrolytic solution between a very large and a very small electrode as a result of changing the voltage difference between the electrodes, used in the qualitative and quantitative analysis of chemical mixtures. [< *polar*(ity) + *-graph*]

**po|lar|o|graph|ic** (pō lar′ə graf′ik), *adj.* of or having to do with a polarograph. —**po|lar′o|graph′i|cal|ly,** *adv.*

**po|lar|og|ra|phy** (pō′lə rog′rə fē), *n.* the analysis of chemicals with the polarograph.

**Po|la|roid** (pō′lə roid), *n.* **1** *Trademark.* a thin, transparent material that polarizes light, used especially in lamps, eyeglasses, and automobile glass, to reduce glare. **2** = Polaroid Land Camera.

**Polaroid Land Camera,** *Trademark.* a type of camera whose special film contains its own developing and printing agents so that a finished positive print is available about a minute after exposure. [< Edwin Herbert *Land,* born 1909, its American inventor]

**po|lar|on** (pō′lə ron), *n. Physics.* a conducting electron trapped by polarization charges in an ionic crystal lattice. [< *polar*(ization) + *-on*]

**polar orbit,** an orbit in which an earth satellite passes over or near the earth's poles instead of the equator.

**polar valence,** *Chemistry.* electrovalence.

**pol|der** (pōl′dər), *n.* a tract of low land reclaimed from the sea or other body of water and protected by dikes. [< Dutch *Polder*]

**pole¹** (pōl), *n., v.,* **poled, pol|ing.** —*n.* **1** a long, slender piece of wood, steel, or the like: *a telephone pole, a flagpole, a ski pole, a totem pole.* **2** the tapered wooden shaft of a vehicle; tongue. **3** a measure of length; rod; 5½ yards or 5.0292 meters. **4** a measure of area; square rod; 30¼ square yards or 25.289 square meters. **5a** a ship's mast: *We were scudding before a heavy gale, under bare poles* (Frederick Marryat). **b** any spar, especially a light spar. **6** the starting position nearest the inner rail or boundary fence of a race track: *to have the pole.*
—*v.t.* **1** to make (a boat) go with a pole: *Barges ... floated and sailed from upper rivers to New Orleans ... and were tediously ... poled back by hand* (Mark Twain). **2** to stir (molten metal or glass) with a pole of green wood, so as to reduce the oxygen in the mass by introducing carbon that reacts with the oxygen. **3** *Slang.* to hit (a long drive, especially a home run) in baseball.
—*v.i.* to pole a boat: *And poling upstream in white water, unassisted by a motor, is an art not easily acquired* (Atlantic).
[Old English *pāl,* ultimately < Latin *pālus* stake. See etym. of doublet **pale².**]

**pole²** (pōl), *n.* **1** either end of the earth's axis. The North Pole and South Pole are opposite each other. **2** either of two parts where opposite forces are strongest. A magnet or battery has both a positive pole and a negative pole. **3** *Geometry.* **a** either end of the axis of any sphere. **b** the origin or fixed point in a system of polar coordinates. **4** either celestial pole. **5** *Biology.* **a** each extremity of the main axis of an organism, nucleus, or cell, especially an egg cell. **b** each extremity of the spindle formed in a cell during mitosis. **c** the point on a nerve cell where a process originates. **6** each of two opposed or complementary principles.
**poles apart,** very different from one another; at opposite poles: *Mr. McKay and Mr. Lessing are poles apart in many of their views and judgments* (Wall Street Journal).
[< Latin *polus* end of an axis; the sky < Greek *pólos* axis, the sky < *pélein* come into being, be]

**Pole** (pōl), *n.* a person born or living in Poland, a country in central Europe between Germany and Russia. [< German *Pole,* singular of *Polen* the Poles < Middle High German *Polâne* < obsolete Polish *polanie* (literally) field dwellers < *pole* field]

**pole|ax** or **pole|axe** (pōl′aks′), *n., v.,* **-axed, -ax|ing.** —*n.* **1** an ax with a long handle and a hook or spike opposite the blade. **2** a kind of battle-ax with a short handle.
—*v.t.* to fell with or as if with a poleax.
[Middle English *pollax* < *polle* poll, head + *ax* ax; spelling influenced by *pole¹*]

**pole bean,** any one of various varieties of beans with long stems, grown by planting next to poles, wire, or fence, up which they may climb.

**pole|cat** (pōl′kat′), *n., pl.* **-cats** or (*collectively*) **-cat. 1** a small, dark-brown, European mammal which can emit a very disagreeable odor; fitch. It is a carnivorous animal related to the weasel. The domesticated ferret is closely related to it. **2** the North American skunk. **3** *U.S. Informal, Figurative.* a mean or contemptible person. [Middle English *polcat* < Old French *poule* fowl, hen (see etym. under **pullet**) + Middle English *cat* cat (perhaps because it preys on poultry)]

**pol. econ.,** political economy.

**pole horse,** a horse harnessed beside the pole of a vehicle; poler.

**po|leis** (pō′līs, -lās), *n.* plural of **polis.**

**pole|jump** (pōl′jump′), *v.i.* = pole-vault. —**pole′-jump′er,** *n.*

**pole jump,** = pole-vault.

**pole|man** (pōl′man′), *n., pl.* **-men.** a man using a pole, as in surveying, logging, or construction work.

**po|lem|ic** (pə lem′ik), *n., adj.* —*n.* **1** a disputing discussion; argument; controversy: *Writing polemics against a czar in a candlelit cellar could be dangerous* (Newsweek). **2** a person who takes part in a controversy or argument.
—*adj.* of controversy or disagreement; of dispute: *My father's little library consisted chiefly of books in polemic divinity* (Benjamin Franklin). **SYN:** controversial.
[< Greek *polemikós* belligerent < *pólemos* war] —**po|lem′i|cal|ly,** *adv.*

**po|lem|i|cal** (pə lem′ə kəl), *adj.* = polemic.

**po|lem|i|cist** (pə lem′ə sist), *n.* a writer of polemics: *The Church has had ... able ecclesiastics, effective polemicists and apologists* (Andrew M. Fairbairn).

**po|lem|i|cize** (pə lem′ə sīz), *v.i.,* **-cized, -ciz|ing.** to engage in polemics; carry on a controversy: *Skeptics have long theorized and polemicized about the phenomenon without producing a fully convincing natural explanation* (Time).

**po|lem|ics** (pə lem′iks), *n.* **1** the art or practice of disputation or controversy, especially in theology. **SYN:** argumentation. **2** *Theology.* the branch of theology that deals with the history or conduct of ecclesiastical controversy.

**pol|e|mist** (pol′ə mist), *n.* = polemicist.

**pol|e|mize** (pol′ə mīz), *v.i.,* **-mized, -miz|ing.** = polemicize.

**po|le|mo|log|i|cal** (pə lem′ə loj′ə kəl), *adj.* of or having to do with polemology.

**po|le|mol|o|gy** (pō lə mol′ə jē), *n.* the study of conflicts, especially of war among nations. [< French *polémologie* < Greek *pólemos* war + French *-logie* -logy]

**pol|e|mo|ni|a|ceous** (pol′ə mō′nē ā′shəs), *adj.* belonging to a family of dicotyledonous herbs including many ornamental flowers, such as the phlox and Jacob's-ladder. [< New Latin *Polemoniaceae* the family name (< Greek *polemônion* Greek valerian < *pólemos* war) + English *-ous*]

**po|len|ta** (pō len′tə), *n.* a thick porridge made of corn meal, commonly eaten in Italy. [< Italian *polenta* < Latin, peeled barley]

**pole of cold,** the place in either polar region where the lowest winter temperature occurs, such as Verkhoyansk in northern central Asia.

**pole of inaccessibility,** the point on the Antarctic continent which is the geographic center, being the point farthest from the coast in every direction.

**pole|piece** (pōl′pēs′), *n.* a piece of iron forming the end of an electromagnet, through which the lines of magnetic force are concentrated and directed.

**pole plate,** a horizontal timber (plate) laid across the tie beams and supporting the ends of rafters in a roof.

**pole position, 1** (in racing) the position of a contestant who is on the inside of the track, which gives him an advantage, since his opponents must cover a larger circumference in attempting to pass him. **2** *Figurative.* an advantageous position: *The German company retained a pole position in hormone research which led to the Pill* (Sunday Times).

**pol|er** (pō′lər), *n.* **1** a person who poles a boat. **2** an animal harnessed beside the pole of a vehicle; pole horse.

**pole|star** (pōl′stär′), *n.* **1** the North Star, a star that is almost directly above the North Pole, and was formerly much used as a guide by sailors. **SYN:** Polaris. **2** a guiding principle; guide. **3** (*Figurative.*) the center of attraction, interest, or attention.

**pole strap,** = martingale.

**pole trap,** a circular steel trap set on the top of a post.

***pole vault,** a vault over a high, horizontal bar between uprights, by using a long pole.

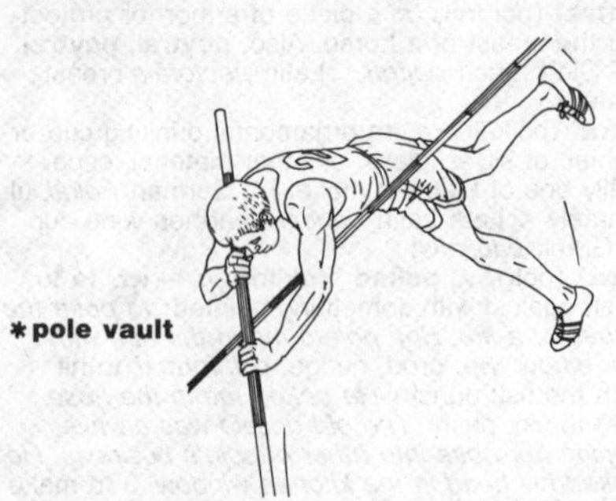

***pole vault**

**pole-vault** (pōl′vôlt′), *v.i.* to jump or leap over a high horizontal bar by using a long pole. —**pole′-vault′er,** *n.*

**pole-vault|ing** (pōl′vôl′ting), *n.* the act or practice of vaulting with the aid of a pole.

**pole|ward** (pōl′wərd), *adj., adv.* toward the North or the South Pole: *The air about the equator rises, and flows poleward in both directions* (J. W. Powell).

**pole|wards** (pōl′wərdz), *adv.* = poleward.

**po|ley** (pō′lē), *adj. Australian.* hornless; polled: *a poley cow.*

**po|lice** (pə lēs′), *n., v.,* **-liced, -lic|ing.** —*n.* **1** persons whose duty is keeping order and arresting people who break the law: *It is the function of the police to be on the watch for antisocial conduct and to apprehend the offender as soon as possible* (Emory S. Bogardus). **SYN:** constabulary, gendarmery. **2** the department of a government that keeps order and arrests persons who break the law. **3** regulation and control of a community, especially with reference to matters of public order, safety, health, and morals; public order. **4a** the act of cleaning and keeping in order an area, such as a military camp. **b** the soldiers detailed to do this.
—*v.t.* **1** to keep order in: *to police the streets, to police the seas.* **2** *Figurative.* to control, regulate, or administer (a law, operation, program, industry, or association) to discover or prevent the breaking of a law, rule, or agreement: *... authority to police prescription-drug advertising* (Wall Street Journal). **3** to keep clean and in order: *to police an army camp, to police a hospital kitchen.* **4** *Obsolete.* to regulate (a state or country).
[< Middle French *police,* learned borrowing from Medieval Latin *politia* the state, settled order of government < Late Latin *polītīa.* See etym. of doublets **policy¹, polity.**]

**police action,** a peacekeeping military action or campaign carried out against insurgent or aggressive forces in the interest of world peace: *The Korean war was not a war between sovereign nations, but a United Nations police action* (Bulletin of Atomic Scientists).

**police constable,** *British.* a policeman of the lowest rank; patrolman.

**police court,** a court for settling minor charges brought by the police. It has the power to hold people charged with serious offenses for trial in higher courts.

**police dog, 1** = German shepherd. **2** any dog trained to work with policemen or guards, or on their own, such as the Doberman pinscher or German shepherd.

**police force, 1** a body of policemen. **2** the police department of a city, town, state, or other area: *If you can identify the murderer ..., you probably belong on the police force yourself* (New Yorker). **3** a peacekeeping force: *The UN police force would stay in the Middle East indefinitely* (Harper's).

**police jury,** the central governing body of a parish (county) in Louisiana.

**police justice** or **magistrate,** a justice who presides at a police court.

**po|lice|man** (pə lēs′mən), *n., pl.* **-men.** a member of the police.

**police officer, 1** an officer in a police force. **2** = policeman.

**police power,** the power of the state to protect

the public welfare, safety, and order by controlling under law the actions of persons.

**police reporter**, a newspaper reporter who covers the police department.

**police state**, a state strictly policed by governmental authority, especially by a secret police, thus having only a minimum of social, economic, and political liberty.

**police station**, the headquarters of a police force for a particular precinct; station house.

**po|lice|wom|an** (pə lēs′wu̇m′ən), *n., pl.* **-women.** a woman who is a member of the police.

**pol|i|clin|ic** (pol′i klin′ik), *n.* a department of a hospital at which outpatients are treated. [< German *Poliklinik* < Greek *pólis* city + German *Klinik* bedside instruction (because the instruction was originally done in the patient's home instead of at the hospital). Compare etym. under **clinic.**]

**pol|i|cy**[1] (pol′ə sē), *n., pl.* **-cies. 1** a plan of action; way of management: *government policies. It is a poor policy to promise more than you can do. The tight-money policy was also reducing the pressure on prices* (Time). **2** practical wisdom; prudence: *In this ... he was actuated by policy rather than sentiment* (Edward A. Freeman). **3** political skill or shrewdness: *Never did base and rotten policy Colour her working* (Shakespeare). **4** *Obsolete.* the conduct of public affairs; government. [< Old French *policie,* learned borrowing from Late Latin *polītīa* state organization < Latin, citizenship < Greek *polīteiā* citizenship, polity < *polītēs* citizen < *pólis* city-state. See etym. of doublets **police, polity.**]

**pol|i|cy**[2] (pol′ə sē), *n., pl.* **-cies. 1** a written agreement about insurance; contract between insurer and insured: *My fire insurance policy states that I shall receive $35,000 if my house burns down.* **2** *U.S.* a method of gambling by betting that a certain number will be drawn in a lottery or will appear in a published statistic. [< Middle French *police* < Italian *polizza* written evidence of a transaction, ultimately < Latin *apodīxis* proof < Greek *apódeixis* proof, publication, declaration]

**pol|i|cy|hold|er** (pol′ə sē hōl′dər), *n.* a person who holds an insurance policy.

**pol|i|cy|mak|er** (pol′ə sē mā′kər), *n.* a person who is qualified or authorized to devise policies; high official.

**pol|i|cy|mak|ing** (pol′ə sē mā′king), *n., adj.* **—*n.*** the act or process of devising policy on a high level, especially by a government or administration of a country. **—*adj.*** having to do with or charged with policymaking.

**policy racket**, = numbers game. [American English, probably < (*wagering*) *policy*]

**policy shop**, *U.S.* a place where bets are made in policy gambling.

**pol|i|me|tri|cian** (pol′i mə trish′ən), *n.* a political scientist who specializes in mathematical and statistical methods of study and research.

**po|li|o** (pō′lē ō), *n.* an acute, infectious virus disease that destroys nervous tissue in the spinal cord, causing fever and paralysis of various muscles; infantile paralysis. [short for *poliomyelitis*]

**po|li|o|my|e|li|tis** (pō′lē ō mī′ə lī′tis, pol′ē-), *n.* **1** = polio. **2** any inflammation of the gray matter of the spinal cord. [< New Latin *poliomyelitis* < Greek *poliós* gray + *myelós* marrow + English *-itis*]

**polio vaccine**, a vaccine given to prevent polio, prepared from a killed poliovirus that has been grown in monkeys, such as the Salk vaccine, or from a weakened live virus, such as the Sabin vaccine.

**po|li|o|vi|rus** (pō′lē ō vī′rəs), *n.* any one of several types of viruses containing ribonucleic acid that cause polio: *Polioviruses are primarily parasites of the human gut* (New Scientist).

**po|lis** (pō′ləs), *n., pl.* **-leis.** a city-state in ancient Greece. [< Greek *pólis*]

**Po|li|sa|rio** (pō′li sär′yō), *n.* a guerrilla force fighting against the governments of Morocco and Mauritania for control of Western Sahara (the former Spanish Sahara): *Algeria ... declared its firm support for Polisario* (Philippe Decraene). [< *Po*(pular Front for the) *Li*(beration of) *Sa*(guia el Hamra and) *Rio* (de Oro), the two zones of Western Sahara]

**pol|ish** (pol′ish), *v., n.* **—*v.t.* 1** to make smooth and shiny: *to polish shoes.* SYN: burnish, brighten. **2** to remove by smoothing. **3** *Figurative.* to put into a better condition; improve: *to polish one's French, to polish a manuscript.* **4** *Figurative.* to make elegant; refine: *to polish manners.*
**—*v.i.* 1** to become smooth and shiny; take on a polish. **2** to become improved or more refined.
**—*n.* 1** a substance used to give smoothness or shine: *silver polish.* **2** a polished condition; smoothness or shine: *The polish of the furniture reflected our faces like a mirror.* **3** the act or process of polishing. **4** the condition of being polished. **5** *Figurative.* culture; elegance; refinement: *Travel with polite people gave polish to her manners.* **6** the outer hulls of rice, as removed by the milling process, used as a livestock feed.
**polish off,** *Informal.* **a** to get done with or rid of; finish: *We nearly polished off the Licensing Bill in the Commons* (Punch). **b** to defeat: *Northampton Town failed to polish off their rivals* (London Times). **c** to eat up or drink up: *An hour and a half before he was to walk on stage, he unconcernedly primed himself by heartily polishing off a steak and playing pingpong* (Time).
**polish up,** to get into a better condition; improve: *... to dot his i's and cross his t's and polish up his manuscript* (Manchester Examiner).
[Middle English *polisen* < Old French *poliss-,* stem of *polir* < Latin *polīre*] **—pol′ish|er,** *n.*
**—*Syn. n.* 2 Polish, luster, sheen** mean the shine of a surface. **Polish** suggests the shine given a surface by rubbing: *Rain spoiled the car's bright polish.* **Luster** suggests the shine of reflecting light, often of shifting colors: *Furniture that has been waxed has a luster.* **Sheen** suggests a more steady gleam or brilliance: *Highly polished metal has a sheen.*

**Pol|ish** (pō′lish), *adj., n.* **—*adj.*** of or having to do with Poland, a country in central Europe between Germany and Russia, its people, or language.
**—*n.* 1** the West Slavic language of Poland. **2** any one of a breed of light, European chickens, with a drooping crest of feathers on its head and, in some varieties, a beard.

**pol|ished** (pol′isht), *adj.* **1** that has been polished; glossy and smooth. **2** having naturally a smooth, glossy surface. **3** *Figurative.* refined; cultured; elegant: *I consider it as one of the first refinements of polished societies* (Jane Austen).

**polit., 1** political. **2** politics.

**Po|lit|bu|ro** (pə lit′byu̇r′ō), *n.* **1** the Communist Party executive committee which examines and controls policy and matters of state in the Soviet Union. It was known as the Presidium from 1952 until 1966. **2** a similar executive committee in any one of various countries, such as Hungary or Bulgaria. **3** any political group which controls state policy in the manner of a Communist Politburo. [< Russian *Politbjuro* Political Bureau]

**po|lite** (pə līt′), *adj.* **1** having or showing good manners; characterized by courtesy and consideration; behaving properly: *a polite reply. The polite boy gave the lady his seat on the bus.* **2** refined; characterized by civilized taste; elegant: *She wished to learn all the customs of polite society.* SYN: polished, cultured. [< Latin *polītus* refined; (literally) polished, past participle of *polīre* to polish] **—po|lite′ly,** *adv.* **—po|lite′ness,** *n.*
**—*Syn.* 1 Polite, civil, courteous** mean having the manners necessary in social relations. **Polite** means having and showing good manners at all times, and emphasizes following the rules for proper behavior: *That polite boy opened the door for me.* **Civil** means being just polite enough not to be rude: *Anyone should be able to give a civil answer.* **Courteous** adds to *polite* the idea of showing thoughtful attention to the feelings and wishes of others: *I go to that store because the clerks are courteous.*

**pol|i|tesse** (pol′i tes′; *French* pô lē tes′), *n.* formal manners; courtesy; politeness: *Diplomatic politesse has been thrown aside; that happens during war* (New York Times). [< French *politesse* < Italian *politezza* courtliness, cleanliness < *polito* polite < Latin *polītus*]

**pol|i|tic** (pol′ə tik), *adj., n.* **—*adj.* 1** wise in looking out for one's own interests; prudent: *The politic man tried not to offend people.* SYN: shrewd, astute. **2** showing wisdom or shrewdness: *a politic answer.* **3** scheming; crafty. **4** = political: *The state is a body politic.*
**—*n.*** a relationship in which one person or group governs or exerts power upon another: *It may just be that the phenomenon of sexual encounter depends on a sexual politic* (Time).
[< Latin *polīticus* < Greek *polītikós* an official; having to do with citizens < *polītēs* citizen < *pólis* city] **—pol′i|tic|ly,** *adv.*

**po|lit|i|cal** (pə lit′ə kəl), *adj.* **1** of or concerned with politics: *political parties, political wisdom. We have the right to vote on a political question. The whirlpool of political vicissitude which makes the tenure of office generally so fragile* (Hawthorne). **2** having to do with citizens or government: *Treason is a political offense.* SYN: civil, civic. **3** of politicians or their methods: *a political slogan, a political meeting.* **4** of or having to do with governing or a government; governmental: *political districts.* **5** having an organized system of government: *Modern man is a political species.* **—po|lit′i|cal|ly,** *adv.*

**political animal**, a person who is gifted in politics; one knowledgeable as a politician.

**political asylum**, the granting of protection and the right of residence and freedom of movement to a national of another country who has fled his own country: [*He*] *identified himself as an Estonian, begged political asylum* (Time).

**political economist**, a person skilled in political economy.

**political economy**, = economics.

**political geography**, the branch of geography that deals with the political divisions or states of the earth, their boundaries, possessions, and centers of population.

**po|lit|i|cal|ize** (pə lit′ə kə līz), *v.t., v.i.* **-ized, -izing.** = politicize.

**political science**, the science of the principles and conduct of government.

**political scientist**, a person skilled in political science.

**po|lit|i|cas|ter** (pə lit′ə kas′tər), *n.* a petty politician. [< *politic*(ian) + Latin *-aster,* a diminutive suffix]

**pol|i|ti|cian** (pol′ə tish′ən), *n.* **1** a person who gives much time to political affairs; a person who is experienced in politics: *Politicians are busy near election time.* **2** a person active in politics chiefly for his own profit or that of his party. **3** a person holding political office: *The shallow politicians who now labour at the helm of administration* (Tobias Smollett). **4** an expert in the theory or science of government and the art of governing; person skilled in statecraft.
**—*Syn.* 1 Politician, statesman** mean someone active or skilled in political or governmental affairs. **Politician** especially suggests ability to deal with people and accomplish things for the good of the people and the country, but in America often is used slightingly or contemptuously to suggest a man without principles scheming for his own or his party's good: *All officeholders are politicians.* **Statesman,** always in a good sense, emphasizes sound judgment, farsightedness, and skill in dealing with and managing national and international affairs: *Winston Churchill was a statesman.*

**po|lit|i|cize** (pə lit′ə sīz), *v.,* **-cized, -cizing.**
**—*v.t.*** to give a political character to: *Like America, Great Britain is a modern, large-scale society with a politicized population* (Bulletin of Atomic Scientists).
**—*v.i.*** to participate in or discuss politics: *We talk and squabble and politicize about education as a vote-catching agency* (Pall Mall Gazette). **—po|lit′i|ci|za′tion,** *n.*

**pol|i|tick** (pol′ə tik), *v.i.* to practice politics; engage in political activity: *The President put in a busy day of politicking* (Wall Street Journal).
**—pol′i|tick|er,** *n.*

**po|lit|i|co** (pə lit′ə kō), *n., pl.* **-cos.** = politician. [< Italian *politico,* or Spanish *político* (literally) politic < Latin *polīticus*]

**politico-,** *combining form.* political (and), as in *politico-military.*

**po|lit|i|co-mil|i|tar|y** (pə lit′ə kō mil′ə ter′ē), *adj.* having to do with politics and military activity: *In his new post ...* [*he*] *is expected to fill ... the role of White House politico-military adviser* (Atlantic).

**pol|i|tics** (pol′ə tiks), *n.* **1** the management of political affairs: *Theodore Roosevelt was engaged in politics for many years.* **2** political principles or opinions: *His politics were against rule by one man. A man's politics are his own affair.* **3** political methods or maneuvers: *the politics of the last election.* **4a** the science and art of government, concerned with the form, organization, and administration of a state or states and the relationship between states. **b** = political science.
**play politics,** to use a political issue or issues for some gain or advantage without regard to what is just or right: *All this provides ammunition for those in both parties who want to play politics with the issue* (New York Times).
► **Politics** is used as either singular or plural: *Politics is a good topic for discussion. His politics were a matter of great concern to his friends.*

**pol|i|ty** (pol′ə tē), *n., pl.* **-ties. 1** = government. **2** a particular form or system of government: *that the true historical polity of the Netherlands was a representative, constitutional government* (John L. Motley). **3** a community with a government; state: *The Jewish polity was utterly destroyed, and the nation dispersed over the face of the earth* (Joseph Butler). **4** the condition of having a government or civil organization: *races without polity.* [< Middle French *politie,* learned borrowing from Late Latin *polītīa* government < Latin, citizenship < Greek *polīteiā* < *polītēs* citizen; of one's city < *pólis* city. See etym. of doublets **police, policy**[1].]

**pol|ka** (pōl′kə, pō′kə), *n., v.,* **-kaed, -ka|ing. —*n.***

---

**Pronunciation Key:** hat, āge, cãre, fär; let, ēqual, tėrm; it, īce; hot, ōpen, ôrder; **oi**l, **ou**t; cup, pu̇t, rüle; **ch**ild; lo**ng**; **th**in; **ᵺ**en; **zh**, measure; **ə** represents **a** in about, **e** in taken, **i** in pencil, **o** in lemon, **u** in circus.

1 a kind of lively dance. It is performed usually by couples, in duple time, and consists of a pattern of three steps and a skip or hop. It originated in Bohemia. 2 music for it.
— *v.i.* to dance a polka.
[< French *polka*, German *Polka*, apparently < Czech *polka* (a name given in Prague in 1831 in tribute to the Poles who revolted unsuccessfully against Russia in 1830)]

**pol|ka dot** (pō′kə), **1** a dot or round spot repeated to form a pattern on cloth. **2** a pattern or fabric with such dots. [< *polka* (because of the popularity of the dance in the 1800's)] — **pol′ka-dot′**, *adj.*

**pol|ka-dot|ted** (pō′kə dot′id), *adj.* covered with polka dots.

**polka mazurka**, **1** a modification of a mazurka to the movement of a polka, with music in triple time. **2** a piece of music for this dance or in its rhythm.

**poll**[1] (pōl), *n., v., adj.* — *n.* **1** a survey of public opinion concerning a particular subject: *In 1968, the polls declared the election too close to call* (Cantril and Hart). **2** a collection of votes; voting: *to exclude women from the poll. The class had a poll to decide where it would have its picnic.* **3** the number of votes cast: *If it rains on election day, there is usually a light poll.* **4** the result of these votes: *He was returned at the head of the poll* (James A. Froude). **5a** a list of persons, especially a list of voters. **b** a person or individual in a number or list. **6** = poll tax. **7** the head, especially the part of it on which the hair grows: *He scratched his grizzled poll.* **8** the blunt end of a pick, hammer, or other tool, used to pound or crush.
— *v.t.* **1** to question or canvass in a poll of public opinion: *For production materials, four out of five purchasing agents polled are buying in the 60-day and under range* (Wall Street Journal). **2** to receive at an election: *The mayor polled a record vote.* **3** to cast (a vote); vote: *A large vote was polled for president. Sir Anthony Eden ... said: "We must poll every vote"* (London Times). **4** to take the votes of: *to poll a village on the matter of building a new school.* **5** to enter in a list or roll, as for the purpose of levying a poll tax. **6** to cut off or cut short the hair, wool, horns, or branches of: *Avenues of peculiarly polled plane trees* (New Yorker).
— *v.i.* to vote at a poll; give one's vote.
— *adj.* *Especially British.* polled; hornless: *So far three of the bulls bred have proved pure* (*homozygous*) *for the poll character, and produce brown and white poll calves* (London Times).
**polls**, the place where votes are cast and counted: *The polls will be open all day. 26 million Frenchmen were to go to the polls and with their ballots reveal what the politicians called "tomorrow's secret"* (Time).
[origin uncertain. Compare Middle Dutch *polle* top of the head, Middle Low German *pol* head]
— **poll′er**, *n.*

**poll**[2] (pol), *n.* **the poll**, *British Slang.* those students at Cambridge University who obtain a pass degree or degree without honors. [apparently < Greek *hoi polloi* plural, the many]

**Poll** (pol), *n.* a common name for a parrot. [< *Poll*, variant of *Moll*, a woman's name]

**pol|lack** (pol′ək), *n., pl.* **-lacks** or (*collectively*) **-lack.** any one of several saltwater food fishes related to the haddock and the cod. Pollacks are caught along the east coast of North America in seine nets. They are also caught along the Atlantic coast of Europe. [origin uncertain. Compare Gaelic *pollag* the freshwater herring]

**pol|lard** (pol′ərd), *n., v.* — *n.* **1** a tree that has had its branches cut back nearly to the trunk, so as to produce a thick, close growth of young branches. **2** an animal, such as a stag, ox, sheep, or goat without horns.
— *v.t.* to make a pollard of, as a tree; poll.
[< *poll*[1] to cut off + *-ard*, an obsolete suffix]

**polled** (pōld), *adj.* **1** = hornless. **2** shorn; shaven. **3** = bald.

**poll|ee** (pō lē′), *n.* a person who is questioned in a public-opinion poll.

**pol|len** (pol′ən), *n.* a fine, yellowish powder formed in the anthers of flowers. Grains of pollen carried to the pistils of flowers fertilize them. *Scientists have estimated that the male flowers of a corn plant produce more than 50 million grains of pollen* (William C. Beaver). [< New Latin *pollen* < Latin, mill dust, fine flour]

**pollen basket**, a smooth area on the outside of each of the back legs of a worker bee that is surrounded by stiff hairs and is used to carry pollen.

**pollen count**, the number of grains of pollen to be found at a specified time and place in a cubic yard of air: *Hay fever sufferers will profit more from a forecast of wind speed and direction than from local pollen counts* (Science News Letter).

**pol|le|no|sis** (pol′ə nō′sis), *n.* = pollinosis.

**pollen sac**, the baglike structure in the anther of a flower in which the pollen is produced.

**pollen tube**, a tube that grows from a pollen grain on the stigma of a flower down through the style into the ovary. Male reproductive cells move through the pollen tube to the ovary and fertilize the egg cell.

*__pol|ler|a__ (pə yär′ə), *n.* a colorful, embroidered costume for women which is traditional at Latin-American fiestas, having a full skirt and a flaring blouse worn off the shoulder. [< American Spanish *pollera* (literally) hooped petticoat < Spanish *pollera* chicken coop < *pollo* chicken < Latin *pullus*; see etym. under **poultry**]

***pollera**

**poll evil** (pōl), an inflamed or ulcerous sore in horses between the ligament of the neck and the first bone of the neck, caused by bruising followed by infection.

**pol|lex** (pol′eks), *n., pl.* **pol|li|ces** (pol′ə sēz). the innermost digit of the forelimb; the thumb or a part corresponding to it. [< Latin *pollex, -icis* the thumb; big toe]

**pol|li|cal** (pol′ə kəl), *adj.* of or having to do with the pollex: *the pollical muscles.*

**pol|li|ce ver|so** (pol′ə sē vėr′sō), *Latin.* with thumb turned downward or reversed (a sign used by the ancient Romans to indicate death for a gladiator who had been defeated).

**pol|li|nate** (pol′ə nāt), *v.t.,* **-nat|ed, -nat|ing.** to carry pollen from stamens to stigmas of; shed pollen on: *Many flowers are pollinated by bees.* [< New Latin *pollen, -inis* pollen + English *-ate*[1]]

*__pol|li|na|tion__ (pol′ə nā′shən), *n.* the act or process of carrying pollen from the anthers to the stigmas of flowers for fertilization, as by insects or the wind: *A considerable time, occasionally even months, often elapses between pollination and fertilization; but commonly only a few days or hours* (Bennett and Dyer). See diagram below.

**pol|li|na|tor** (pol′ə nā′tər), *n.* any insect or other agent that pollinates plants.

**poll|ing** (pō′ling), *adj.* **1** of, for, or having to do with the registering or casting of votes: *polling day, a polling place.* **2** that polls.

**pol|lin|ic** (po lin′ik), *adj.* of or having to do with pollen.

**pol|li|nif|er|ous** (pol′ə nif′ər əs), *adj.* **1** producing or bearing pollen. **2** carrying or adapted for carrying pollen, as certain organs of bees. [< New Latin *pollen, -inis* pollen + English *-ferous*]

**pol|lin|i|um** (pə lin′ē əm), *n., pl.* **-i|a** (-ē ə). an agglutinated or coherent mass or body of pollen grains, characteristic of plants of the milkweed and orchid families. [< New Latin *pollinium* < *pollen, -inis* pollen + *-ium*, a diminutive suffix]

**pol|li|nize** (pol′ə nīz), *v.t.,* **-nized, -niz|ing.** = pollinate.

**pol|li|no|sis** (pol′ə nō′sis), *n.* = hay fever. Also, **pollenosis.** [< New Latin *pollinosis* < *pollen, -inis* pollen + *-osis* -osis]

**pol|li|wog** (pol′ē wog), *n.* **1** = tadpole. **2** a person who has not crossed the equator on shipboard. [apparent alteration of Middle English *polwygle* < *polle* poll, head + *wiglen* to wiggle. Compare etym. under **tadpole.**]

**pol|lock** (pol′ək), *n., pl.* **-locks** or (*collectively*) **-lock.** = pollack.

**poll parrot** (pol), = parrot.

**polls** (pōlz), *n.pl.* See under **poll**[1].

**poll|ster** (pōl′stər), *n.* **1** a person who takes a public-opinion poll. **2** a person who takes, or evaluates the results of, public-opinion polls, as a trade or profession: *The pollsters assume that what is true of a sample of a few hundred is true of everybody* (Harper's).

**poll|tak|er** (pōl′tā′kər), *n.* = pollster.

**poll tax** (pōl), a tax levied on every adult citizen; head tax. It was declared unconstitutional in the United States as a prerequisite to voting in national elections in 1964, and in state and local elections in 1966.

**poll-tax|er** (pōl′tak′sər), *n. U.S. Informal.* person supporting the levy of a poll tax.

**pol|lu|tant** (pə lü′tənt), *n.* a polluting agent or medium: *Two other auto exhaust pollutants ... play a much larger role in the formation of smog* (Atlantic).

**pol|lute** (pə lüt′), *v.t.,* **-lut|ed, -lut|ing.** **1** to make physically impure, foul, or dirty; contaminate: *The water at the bathing beach was polluted by refuse from the factory. Nature, as well as man, pollutes the air in myriad ways* (Scientific American). **2** to make ceremonially or morally impure; defile; sully. [< Latin *pollūtus*, past participle of *polluere* to soil, defile] — **pol|lut′er**, *n.*

**pol|lut|ed** (pə lü′tid), *adj.* **1a** contaminated, as by smoke particles, fuel exhaust, and gases: *polluted air.* **b** contaminated by waste matter: *polluted water.* **2** impure; unclean: *Leave them to their polluted ways* (Milton). **3** *Slang.* drunk. — **pol-lut′ed|ness**, *n.*

**pol|lu|tion** (pə lü′shən), *n.* **1** the act or process of polluting; defiling; uncleanness: *One of the principal difficulties of freeing the river from pollution was that certain persons had prescriptive rights to pass their sewage into the Thames* (London Daily News). **2** = air pollution.

**pol|lu|tive** (pə lü′tiv), *adj.* causing pollution.

**Pol|lux** (pol′əks), *n.* **1** *Greek and Roman Mythology.* one of the twin sons of Zeus and Leda. Pollux was immortal; his brother, Castor, was mortal. **2** the brighter of the two brightest stars in the constellation Gemini.

**Pol|ly** (pol′ē), *n.* a common name for a parrot.

**Pol|ly|an|na** (pol′ē an′ə), *n.* a person, especially a girl or woman, who is untiringly cheerful and optimistic, usually to excess or to the point of foolishness, in the face of difficulty, trouble, or disaster: *Now it would take a veritable Pollyanna to believe that it makes no difference to the governing of a country whether a President is sick or well* (Wall Street Journal). [< *Pollyanna*, the heroine of several novels by Eleanor Porter, 1868-1920, an American writer]

**Pol|ly|an|na|ish** (pol′ē an′ə ish), *adj.* characteristic of a Pollyanna; untiringly cheerful and optimistic.

**pol|ly|wog** (pol′ē wog), *n.* = polliwog.

***polo**
definition 1

*__po|lo__ (pō′lō), *n.* **1** a game like hockey, played on horseback with long-handled mallets and a wooden ball. **2** = water polo. [Anglo-Indian < a native word of Northern India]

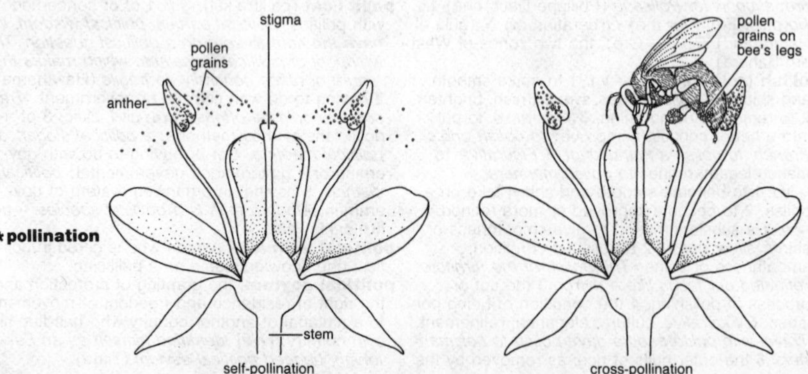

***pollination**

**polo coat**, a tailored, double-breasted topcoat of camel's hair or a similar, usually soft fabric.

**po|lo|ist** (pō′lō ist), *n.* a person who plays polo.

**pol|o|naise** (pol′ə nāz′, pō′lə-), *n.* **1** a slow, stately dance of Polish origin, in three-quarter time. It consists chiefly of a march or promenade of couples. **2** music for it. **3** a one-piece woman's overdress with a waist and an open skirt, popular especially in the 1700's and 1800's. [< French *polonaise,* feminine adjective, (literally) Polish]

***po|lo|ni|um** (pə lō′nē əm), *n.* a radioactive, metallic chemical element found in pitchblende or produced artificially from bismuth; radium F. It decays into an isotope of lead by the emission of alpha rays. [< New Latin *polonium* < medieval Latin *Polonia* Poland (because Poland was the homeland of Marie Curie)]

***polonium**

| symbol | atomic number | mass number | oxidation state |
|---|---|---|---|
| Po | 84 | 209 | 2, 4 |

**Po|lo|ni|us** (pə lō′nē əs), *n.* a pompous old man, the father of Ophelia in Shakespeare's *Hamlet.*

**Po|lo|nize** (pō′lə nīz), *v.t.,* **-nized, -niz|ing.** to make Polish as in customs or language. [< *Polonia,* Latinized form of *Poland* + English *-ize*] **—Po′lo|ni|za′tion,** *n.*

**po|lo|ny** (pə lō′nē), *n., pl.* **-nies.** *Especially British.* a sausage made of partly cooked pork: *I've chickens and conies, and pretty polonies, And excellent peppermint drops* (W. S. Gilbert). [origin uncertain]

**polo shirt**, a close-fitting shirt of knitted cotton, jersey, or synthetic fiber, with short sleeves, with or without a collar, pulled on over the head, worn by men and women for sports.

**pol|ter|geist** (pōl′tər gīst), *n.* a spirit or ghost that is supposed to make its presence known by tappings, the slamming of doors, or other sounds or happenings that cannot be explained. [< German *Poltergeist* < *poltern* make a noise + *Geist* spirit, ghost]

**pol|troon** (pol trün′), *n., adj.* **—*n.*** a wretched coward: *What a miserable little poltroon had fear ... made of me* (Charlotte Brontë). **—*adj.*** base; cowardly; contemptible. [< Middle French *poltrôn* < Italian *poltrone* (originally) colt, coward (because of a colt's habit of taking fright and running), or perhaps < *poltro* lazy]

**pol|troon|er|y** (pol trü′nər ē), *n.* the behavior of a poltroon; cowardice.

**pol|troon|ish** (pol trü′nish), *adj.* like a poltroon; cowardly. **—pol|troon′ish|ly,** *adv.*

**Pol|warth** (pōl′wərth), *n.* any one of a breed of sheep found in Australia, a cross between the Merino and the Lincoln.

**pol|y** (pol′ē), *n., pl.* **pol|ys.** *Informal.* **1** a polymer. **2** a polytechnic school.

**poly-**, *combining form.* **1** more than one; many; multi-, as in *polysyllable, polysyllabic, polynomial.* **2** polymeric, as in *polyester, polystyrene.* [< Greek *polýs* much, many]

**pol|y|ac|id** (pol′ē as′id), *adj. Chemistry.* equivalent in combining capacity to an acid radical of valence greater than unity as a base.

**pol|y|ac|ryl|am|ide** (pol′ē ak′rə lam′īd, -id; -ə kril′ə mīd, -mid), *n.* a polymer of acrylamide, used especially as a thickening agent: *Another method used for binding enzymes is to trap them in a gel—most commonly a polyacrylamide gel* (New Scientist).

**pol|y|a|cryl|ic acid** (pol′ē ə kril′ik), a polymer of acrylic acid, used in manufacturing nylon.

**pol|y|ac|ry|lo|ni|trile** (pol′ē ak′rə lō nī′trəl, -trīl, -trēl; -ə kril′ō nī′-), *n.* a polymer of acrylonitrile used in manufacturing synthetic fibers, such as Orlon.

**pol|y|a|del|phous** (pol′ē ə del′fəs), *adj. Botany.* having the stamens united in three or more bundles or groups. [< *poly-* + Greek *adelphós* (with English *-ous*) brother]

**pol|y|aes|the|sia** (pol′ē əs thē′zhə), *n. Medicine.* a morbid condition of the sense of touch, as in locomotor ataxia, in which a single stimulus, as the prick of a pin, is felt at two or more places.

**pol|y|al|pha|bet|ic** (pol′ē al′fə bet′ik), *adj. Cryptography.* having to do with or using several cipher alphabets for a single message: *a polyalphabetic cryptogram.* **—pol′y|al′pha|bet′i|cal|ly,** *adv.*

**pol|y|am|id** (pol′ē am′id), *n.* = polyamide.

**pol|y|am|ide** (pol′ē am′īd, -id), *n.* a chemical compound containing two or more amide (-$NH_2$) radicals, especially a polymeric amide.

**pol|y|a|mine** (pol′ē ə mēn′, -am′in), *n.* a chemical compound containing more than one amino group.

**pol|y|an|dric** (pol′ē an′drik), *adj.* of or having to do with polyandry.

**pol|y|an|drous** (pol′ē an′drəs), *adj.* **1** having more than one husband at the same time: *Polyandrous families, for instance, need not be restricted to one wife but may have two or more; in other words, they may practice polyandry and polygamy at once* (New Yorker). **2** *Botany.* having numerous stamens, of an indefinite number.

**pol|y|an|dry** (pol′ē an′drē, pol′ē an′-), *n.* **1** the practice or condition of having more than one husband at the same time. **2** *Botany.* the condition of being polyandrous. [< Greek *polyandría* < *polyándros* having many men or mates < *polýs* many + *anḗr, andrós* man, husband]

**pol|y|an|gu|lar** (pol′ē ang′gyə lər), *adj.* having many angles; polygonal.

**pol|y|an|tha rose** (pol′ē an′thə), one of a group of hybrid roses bearing large clumps of flowers on low, bushy plants, obtained by crossing several species of the rose. [< Greek *polýanthos;* see etym. under **polyanthus**]

**pol|y|an|thus** (pol′ē an′thəs), *n.* **1** a kind of narcissus bearing clusters of small yellow or white flowers. **2** a hybrid primrose bearing a single umbrel of many flowers. **3** = oxlip. [< New Latin *polyanthus* < Greek *polýanthos,* variant of *polyanthḗs* blooming prolifically < *polýs* many + *ánthos* flower]

**pol|y|ar|chy** (pol′ē är′kē), *n., pl.* **-chies.** government of a state or city by many. [< Greek *polyarchía* < *polýs* many + *archós* ruler]

**pol|y|ar|te|ri|tis** (pol′ē är′tə rī′təs), *n.* a disease characterized by inflammation and lesions of the external walls of the smaller arteries and by the formation of nodules within the arteries, resulting in a weakening and damaging of the surrounding tissues and organs.

**pol|y|ar|thrit|ic** (pol′ē är thrit′ik), *adj.* having to do with or suffering from polyarthritis.

**pol|y|ar|thri|tis** (pol′ē är thrī′tis), *n.* an inflammation of several or many joints.

**pol|y|ar|tic|u|lar** (pol′ē är tik′yə lər), *adj.* **1** having many joints. **2** affecting many joints.

**pol|y|a|tom|ic** (pol′ē ə tom′ik), *adj.* containing more than two atoms, especially having many replaceable hydrogen atoms.

**pol|y|ba|sic** (pol′ē bā′sik), *adj.* having two or more hydrogen atoms that can be replaced by basic atoms or radicals: *a polybasic acid.*

**po|lyb|a|site** (pə lib′ə sīt), *n.* a blackish mineral with a metallic luster, consisting essentially of silver, sulfur, and antimony. It is a valuable silver ore. [< German *Polybasit* < *poly-* poly- + *Base* (< Latin *basis*) base + *-it* -ite[1]]

**pol|y|bro|mi|nat|ed biphenyl** (pol′ē brō′mə nā′tid), any one of a group of poisonous and persistent chemicals related to the polychlorinated biphenyls, used as a fire retardant and additive to plastics, and regarded as a dangerous contaminant. *Abbr:* PBB (no periods).

**pol|y|but|a|di|ene** (pol′ē byü′tə dī′ēn, -dī ēn′), *n.* an improved type of synthetic rubber produced from butadiene and occurring in several polymeric forms.

**pol|y|car|bo|nate** (pol′ē kär′bə nāt), *n.* any plastic resin of a group, derived from phosgene and a phenol, resistant to impact and heat softening.

**pol|y|car|pel|lar|y** (pol′ē kär′pə ler′ē), *adj. Botany.* having or consisting of many carpels.

**pol|y|car|pic** (pol′ē kär′pik), *adj.* = polycarpous.

**pol|y|car|pous** (pol′ē kär′pəs), *adj. Botany.* consisting of many or several carpels. [< Greek *polýkarpos* fruitful < *polýs* much + *karpós* fruit]

**pol|y|cen|tric** (pol′ē sen′trik), *adj.* **1** having several centers or central parts: *polycentric chromosomes.* **2** of or characterized by polycentrism: *"Polycentric" Communism ... means adjusting party methods in each country to national traditions and requirements* (New York Times).

**pol|y|cen|trism** (pol′ē sen′triz əm), *n.* a principle of Communism that permits moderately independent leadership and variations in political dogma among Communist parties of the world.

**pol|y|cen|trist** (pol′ē sen′trist), *n., adj.* **—*n.*** one who advocates or practices polycentrism. **—*adj.*** of or characterized by polycentrism; polycentric: *Rumania would not take sides in the dispute, but preferred the "polycentrist" approach* (Time).

**pol|y|chaete** (pol′ē kēt), *n., adj.* **—*n.*** any annelid worm of a class including most of the common marine worms, having a series of unsegmented appendages or parapodia covered with many bristles or setae. **—*adj.*** of or belonging to the polychaetes. [< New Latin *Polychaeta* the class name < Greek *polychaítēs* having much hair < *polýs* much + *chaítē* mane, bristle]

**pol|y|chae|tous** (pol′ē kē′təs), *adj.* = polychaete.

**pol|y|cha|si|al** (pol′ē kā′zē əl), *adj.* of or having to do with a polychasium.

**pol|y|cha|si|um** (pol′ē kā′zē əm), *n., pl.* **-si|a** (-zē ə). *Botany.* a form of cymose inflorescence in which each axis produces more than two lateral axes. [< New Latin *polychasium* < Greek *polýs* much + *chásis* division < *cháskein* to yawn, gape. Compare etym. under **chasm.**]

**pol|y|chlo|rin|at|ed biphenyl** (pol′ē klôr′ə nā′tid, -klōr′-), any one of a group of poisonous chemicals used in industry as electrical insulators and in plastics manufacture, found in wildlife at levels approaching the concentration of DDT and similar insecticides. *Abbr:* PCB (no periods).

**pol|y|chlo|ro|bi|phen|yl** (pol′ē klôr′ō bī fen′əl, -fē′nəl; -klōr′-), *n.* = polychlorinated biphenyl.

**pol|y|chot|o|mous** (pol′ē kot′ə məs), *adj.* divided or dividing into many parts. [< *poly-* + (di)*chotomous*]

**pol|y|chot|o|my** (pol′ē kot′ə mē), *n., pl.* **-mies.** division into many parts. [< *poly-* + (di)*chotomy*]

**pol|y|chro|mat|ic** (pol′ē krō mat′ik), *adj.* = polychrome.

**pol|y|chrome** (pol′ē krōm), *adj., n., v.,* **-chromed, -chrom|ing.** **—*adj.*** having many or various colors; decorated or executed in many colors. **—*n.*** **1** a work of art in several colors, such as a colored statue. **2** a combination of many colors. **—*v.t.*** to decorate in several colors; paint by using polychromy: *to polychrome statuary.* [< French *polychrome* < Greek *polýchrōmos* < *polýs* many + *chrôma, -atos* color]

**pol|y|chrom|ic** (pol′ē krō′mik), *adj.* = polychrome.

**pol|y|chro|my** (pol′ē krō′mē), *n.* **1** polychrome coloring. **2** the art of painting or decorating in several colors, especially as anciently used in pottery and architecture.

**Pol|y|cle|tan** (pol′i klē′tən), *adj.* = Polyclitan.

**pol|y|clin|ic** (pol′ē klin′ik), *n.* a clinic or hospital dealing with many different diseases.

**Pol|y|cli|tan** (pol′i klī′tən), *adj.* **1** of or having to do with Polyclitus, or Polycletus, of Argos, a celebrated Greek sculptor of the 400's B.C., whose statue of the Doryphorus (spear bearer) long served as a standard of the perfect human proportions. **2** having to do with or observing the principles of art laid down by Polyclitus.

**pol|y|con|ic** (pol′ē kon′ik), *adj.* having to do with or based upon many cones.

**polyconic projection**, a system of map projection in which each parallel of latitude is represented as if projected on a cone touching the earth's surface along that parallel.

**pol|y|cot|y|le|don** (pol′ē kot′ə lē′dən), *n.* a plant of which the seed contains more than two cotyledons.

**pol|y|cot|y|le|don|ous** (pol′ē kot′ə lē′də nəs, -led′ə-), *adj.* having more than two cotyledons in the seed, as many gymnosperms.

**pol|y|crys|tal|line** (pol′ē kris′tə lin, -līn), *adj.* **1** composed of many crystals: *Most solids are polycrystalline* (Scientific American). **2** composed of crystals with different space lattices: *a polycrystalline metal.*

**pol|y|cy|clic** (pol′ē sī′klik, -sik′lik), *adj.* **1** having many rounds, turns, or whorls, as a shell. **2** *Electricity.* having many cycles or circuits. **3** *Chemistry.* having more than one ring in a molecule.

**pol|y|cyst|ic** (pol′ē sis′tik), *adj.* having or consisting of several cysts: *a polycystic tumor.*

**pol|y|cy|the|mi|a** or **pol|y|cy|thae|mi|a** (pol′ē-sī thē′mē ə), *n.* a disease caused by overactivity of the bone marrow, producing an excessive number of red blood corpuscles and a hemoglobin count that is too high. [< *poly-* + *cyt-* + *-emia*]

**pol|y|cy|the|mic** or **pol|y|cy|thae|mic** (pol′ē sī-thē′mic), *adj.* of, having to do with, or caused by polycythemia.

**pol|y|dac|tyl** or **pol|y|dac|tyle** (pol′ē dak′təl), *adj., n.* **—*adj.*** having many or several fingers or toes, especially more than the normal number. **—*n.*** a polydactyl animal. [< French *polydactyle* < Greek *polydáktylos* < *polýs* many + *dáktylos* finger, toe]

**pol|y|dac|tyl|ism** (pol′ē dak′tə liz əm), *n.* the condition or state of being polydactyl.

**pol|y|dac|tyl|ous** (pol′ē dak′tə ləs), *adj.* = polydactyl.

**pol|y|dac|tyl|y** (pol′ē dak′tə lē), *n.* = polydactylism.

**pol|y|de|mon|ism** or **pol|y|dae|mon|ism** (pol′ē-dē′mə niz əm), *n.* the belief in many supernatural powers or evil spirits.

**pol|y|de|mon|is|tic** or **pol|y|dae|mon|is|tic** (pol′ē dē′mə nis′tik), *adj.* having to do with or characterized by polydemonism.

**pol|y|dip|si|a** (pol′ē dip′sē ə), *n.* abnormally excessive thirst. [< New Latin *polydipsia* < Greek *polýs* much + *dípsa* thirst]

**pol|y|di|rec|tion|al** (pol′ē də rek′shə nəl, -dī-), *adj.* = multidirectional.

**pol|y|dis|perse** (pol′ē dis pėrs′), *adj. Chemistry.*

**Pronunciation Key:** hat, āge, cãre, fär; let, ēqual, tėrm; it, īce; hot, ōpen, ôrder; oil, out; cup, pu̇t, rüle; child; long; thin; ᴛʜen; zh, measure; ə represents **a** in about, **e** in taken, **i** in pencil, **o** in lemon, **u** in circus.

having to do with or made up of heterogeneous particles, as in a colloidal system.

**Pol|y|do|rus** (pol′i dôr′əs, -dōr′-), *n. Greek Legend.* the youngest son of Priam, killed by Achilles.

**pol|y|e|lec|tro|lyte** (pol′ē i lek′trə līt), *n.* an electrolyte of high molecular weight that dissociates unevenly in solution, leaving positive or negative ions joined to the polymer structure. Polyelectrolytes are used as soil conditioners and flocculating agents.

**pol|y|em|bry|o|ny** (pol′ē em′brē ō′nē, -brē ə-), *n. Botany.* the formation or presence of more than one embryo in a seed. [< *poly-* + Greek *émbryon* embryo + English *-y*[3]]

**pol|y|ene** (pol′ē ēn), *n.* any chemical compound of a group characterized by a number of coupled double bonds.

**pol|y|es|ter** (pol′ē es′tər), *n.* any one of a large group of synthetic polymeric resins made by changing various acids into esters with alcohols, glycerol, or glycols. Polyesters are used in the manufacture of paints, synthetic fibers, films, and reinforced plastics for construction.

**polyester fiber**, a synthetic, wrinkle- and abrasion-resistant fiber made by the condensation of terephthalic acid and glycol, used alone or in combination with other fibers in shirts, suits, and fabric for other articles.

**pol|y|e|ther foam** (pol′ē ē′thər), a polyurethane made from a polymer chain composed of repeating units of ether and oxygen.

**pol|y|eth|nic** (pol′ē eth′nik), *adj.* belonging to or containing many nations or races.

**pol|y|eth|y|lene** (pol′ē eth′ə lēn), *n.* any one of various very durable thermoplastics produced by the polymerization of ethylene, used especially for containers, insulation, and tubing. *Formula:* $(C_2H_4)_n$

**polyethylene glycol**, any one of various colorless and odorless polymers of ethylene glycol, ranging from viscous liquids, with molecular weights of about 200, to waxy solids, with molecular weights of about 6000. Polyethylene glycols are used as lubricants, solvents, intermediates, and bases for cosmetics. *Formula:* $HOCH_2(CH_2OCH_2)_nCH_2OH$

**pol|y|foil** (pol′ē foil′), *adj., n. Architecture.* **—*adj.*** consisting of or decorated with more than five foils; multifoil: *a polyfoil window, a polyfoil arch.* **—*n.*** a polyfoil opening or ornament; multifoil.

**po|lyg|a|la** (pə lig′ə lə), *n.* any one of a large group of herbs and shrubs, commonly known as milkworts, such as the fringed polygala of North America. [< New Latin *Polygala* the typical genus < Latin *polygala* the milkwort < Greek *polýgalon* < *polýs* much + *gála* milk]

**pol|y|ga|la|ceous** (pol′ē gə lā′shəs, pə lig′ə-), *adj.* belonging to the milkwort family of plants typified by the milkwort or polygala.

**po|lyg|a|mist** (pə lig′ə mist), *n.* a person who practices or favors polygamy.

**po|lyg|a|mous** (pə lig′ə məs), *adj.* **1a** having more than one wife at the same time. **b** (less commonly) having more than one husband at the same time. **2** *Botany.* bearing both unisexual and hermaphrodite flowers on the same plant or on different plants of the same species. **3** *Zoology.* **a** having several mates at the same time: *The war is, perhaps, severest between the males of polygamous animals* (Charles Darwin). **b** characterized by polygamy: *a polygamous species.* **—po|lyg′a|mous|ly**, *adv.*

**po|lyg|a|my** (pə lig′ə mē), *n.* **1a** the practice or condition of having more than one wife at the same time. The Moslem religion permits men to practice polygamy. **b** (less commonly) the practice or condition of having more than one husband at the same time. **2** *Zoology.* the practice of having several mates at the same time, usually one male with several females. [< Greek *polygamiā* < *polýgamos* often married < *polýs* many + *gámos* marriage]

**pol|y|gene** (pol′ē jēn′), *n.* any one of a group of genes whose individually small but cumulatively powerful operation controls a complex hereditary character, such as height. [< *poly-* + *gene*]

**pol|y|gen|e|sis** (pol′ē jen′ə sis), *n. Biology.* the theory of the origination of a race or species from several independent ancestors or germ cells.

**pol|y|ge|net|ic** (pol′ē jə net′ik), *adj.* **1** *Biology.* of or having to do with polygenesis. **2** having more than one origin; formed in several different ways or at several different times.

**pol|y|gen|ic** (pol′ē jen′ik), *adj.* **1** of or having to do with polygeny. **2** of or having to do with polygenes.

**polygenic inheritance**, the presence of complex hereditary characters that have developed from a relatively large number of genes operating collectively.

**po|lyg|e|ny** (pə lij′ə nē), *n.* the theoretical origination of mankind or a human race from several separate and independent pairs of ancestors.

**pol|y|glass** or **pol|y|glas tire** (pol′ē glas′, -gläs′), an automobile tire with a polyester-fiber cord and a fiberglass belt molded around the outside, designed for better traction and longer tread wear. [< *poly*(ester) + (fiber)*glass* or (Fiber)*glas*]

**pol|y|glot** (pol′ē glot), *adj., n.* **—*adj.*** **1** speaking or writing several languages: *The new school had a large and polyglot student body* (Atlantic). **2** written in several languages: *a polyglot Bible.* **—*n.*** **1** a person who speaks or writes several languages. **2** a book written in several languages. **3** a mixture or confusion of several languages. [< Greek *polýglōttos* < *polýs* many + *glôtta* tongue, variant of *glôssa*]

**pol|y|glot|tal** (pol′ē glot′əl), *adj.* speaking several languages.

**pol|y|glot|ter|y** (pol′ē glot′ər ē), *n.* knowledge of many languages; the skill of a polyglot.

**pol|y|glot|tic** (pol′ē glot′ik), *adj.* = polyglottal.

***pol|y|gon** (pol′ē gon), *n.* a closed plane figure having three or more angles and straight sides. [< Latin *polygōnum* < Greek *polýgōnon* (originally) neuter of *polýgōnos* polygonal < *polýs* many + *gōniā* angle]

***polygon**

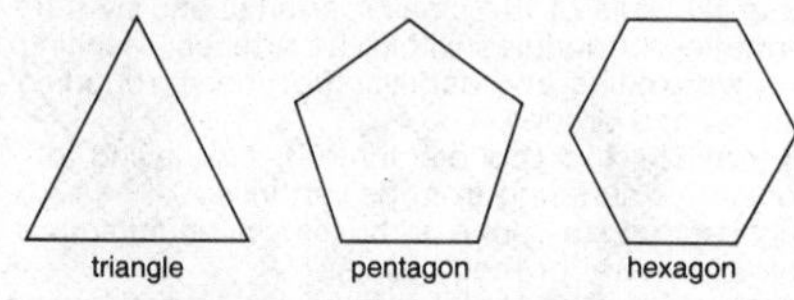


**pol|y|go|na|ceous** (pol′ē gə nā′shəs), *adj.* belonging to the buckwheat family of plants, including the knotgrass, jointweed, and dock. [< New Latin *Polygonaceae* the family name (< Latin *polygonon* polygonum) + English *-ous*]

**po|lyg|o|nal** (pə lig′ə nəl), *adj.* having more than three angles and three sides. **—po|lyg′o|nal|ly**, *adv.*

**po|ly|go|no|met|ric** (pə lig′ə nə met′rik), *adj.* of or having to do with polygonometry.

**pol|y|go|nom|e|try** (pol′ē gə nom′ə trē), *n.* a branch of mathematics dealing with the measurement and properties of polygons.

**po|lyg|o|num** (pə lig′ə nəm), *n.* any plant of a large and widely distributed group of the buckwheat family, consisting mainly of herbs, characterized by a stem with swollen joints sheathed by the stipules, such as the knotgrass, bistort, and smartweed. [< New Latin *Polygonum* the genus name < Latin *polygonon* knotgrass < Greek *polýgonon* < *polýs* many + *góny* knee, joint (because it has many joints)]

**po|lyg|o|ny** (pə lig′ə nē), *n.* = polygonum.

**pol|y|graph** (pol′ē graf, -gräf), *n.* **1** = lie detector. **2** *Medicine.* an instrument for recording several pulsations, as of an artery, a vein, and the heart, all at once. **3** an apparatus resembling a pantograph, used for making two or more identical drawings or writings simultaneously. **4** a prolific or versatile author. [probably < *poly-* + *-graph.* Compare French *polygraphe* instrument that makes simultaneous drawings, Greek *polygráphos* one that writes much.]

**pol|y|graph|ic** (pol′ē graf′ik), *adj.* **1** having to do with multiplication of copies of a drawing or writing: *a polygraphic instrument.* **2** done with a polygraph.

**pol|y|graph|i|cal** (pol′ē graf′ə kəl), *adj.* = polygraphic.

**po|lyg|y|nist** (pə lij′ə nist), *n.* a person who practices or favors polygyny.

**po|lyg|y|nous** (pə lij′ə nəs), *adj.* **1** having more than one wife at the same time. **2** of, having to do with, or involving polygyny. **3** *Botany.* having many pistils or styles.

**po|lyg|y|ny** (pə lij′ə nē), *n.* **1** the practice or condition of having more than one wife at the same time. The Moslem religion permits polygyny. **2** the practice of a male animal of having several mates. **3** *Botany.* the state of having many pistils or styles. [< *poly-* + Greek *gynḗ* woman, wife; patterned on *polygamy, polyandry*]

**pol|y|hal|ite** (pol′ē hal′īt), *n.* a mineral consisting essentially of a hydrous sulphate of calcium, magnesium, and potassium, occurring usually in fibrous masses, and of a brick-red color caused by the presence of iron. [< German *Polyhalit* < *poly-* poly- + Greek *háls* salt + German *-it* -ite[1]]

**pol|y|he|dral** (pol′ē hē′drəl), *adj.* **1** of or having to do with a polyhedron. **2** having many faces. **3** having to do with or causing polyhedrosis: *a polyhedral virus.*

***pol|y|he|dron** (pol′ē hē′drən), *n., pl.* **-drons, -dra** (-drə). a solid figure having four or more faces. [< New Latin *polyhedron* < Greek *polýedron,* neuter of *polýedros* < *polýs* many + *hédra* side, base]

***polyhedron**

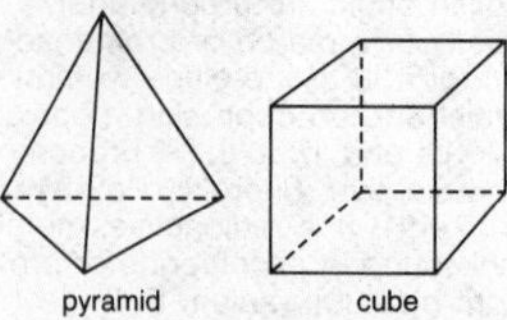


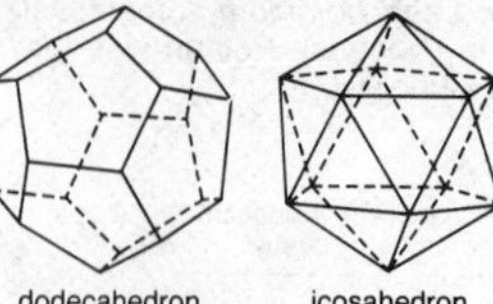


**pol|y|he|dro|sis** (pol′ē hē drō′sis), *n.* any one of several diseases of insect larvae, such as the corn earworm, caused by a type of virus that forms polyhedral protein granules inside the nuclei of the larval cells. [< *polyhedron* + *-osis*]

**pol|y|his|tor** (pol′ē his′tər), *n.* a person of great or varied learning; polymath. [< Greek *polyī́stōr* < *polýs* much + *hístōr* one who learns by inquiry or study. Compare etym. under **history.**]

**pol|y|his|to|ri|an** (pol′ē his tôr′ē ən, -tōr′-), *n.* = polyhistor.

**pol|y|his|tor|ic** (pol′ē his tôr′ik, -tor′-), *adj.* of or exhibiting polyhistory or wide and varied knowledge.

**pol|y|his|to|ry** (pol′ē his′tər ē, -his′trē), *n.* great or varied learning.

**pol|y|hy|dric** (pol′ē hī′drik), *adj.* = polyhydroxy.

**pol|y|hy|drox|y** (pol′ē hī drok′sē), *adj. Chemistry.* having several hydroxyl (-OH) radicals. [< *poly-* + *hydrox*(yl) + *-y*[3]]

**Pol|y|hym|ni|a** (pol′ē him′nē ə), *n. Greek Mythology.* the Muse of religious poetry. [< Latin *Polyhymnia* < Greek *Polýmnia,* short for *Polyýmnia* < *polýs* many + *hýmnos* song]

**pol|y I:C** (pol′ē ī′sē′), a synthetic chemical compound that stimulates the body to produce interferon by its resemblance to the RNA core of infectious viruses: *Poly I:C was ... highly effective against eye infections caused by herpes virus* (New Scientist). [< *polyi*(nosinic:poly)-*c*(ytidylic acid)]

**pol|y|im|ide** (pol′ē im′īd), *n.* any one of a class of tough, heat-resistant polymeric resins used as ablators, adhesives, semiconductors, and insulators.

**pol|y|i|so|bu|ty|lene** (pol′ē ī′sə byü′tə lēn), *n.* any one of a group of polymers derived from petroleum hydrocarbons catalyzed at low temperatures, ranging from oils to solids much like rubber.

**pol|y|i|so|cy|an|ate** (pol′ē ī′sə sī′ə nit, -nāt), *n.* = polyurethane.

**pol|y|i|so|prene** (pol′ē ī′sə prēn), *n.* one of the chief constituents of natural rubber. Polyisoprene can also be made synthetically from isoprene and used as a substitute for natural rubber.

**pol|y|lin|gual** (pol′ē ling′gwəl), *adj.* **1** speaking, reading, or writing many languages. **2** written in many languages.

**pol|y|lin|guist** (pol′ē ling′gwist), *n.* a person learned in many languages.

**pol|y|lith** (pol′i lith), *n.* a structure, such as a monument or column, built up of many or several stones. [< *poly-* + Greek *líthos* stone]

**pol|y|lith|ic** (pol′ē lith′ik), *adj.* consisting of many stones; built up of several blocks, as a shaft or column.

**pol|y|math** (pol′ē math), *n., adj.* **—*n.*** a man of much or varied learning; polyhistor: *Even a lifetime of sixty-seven years is hardly sufficient to become a serious polymath* (Atlantic). **—*adj.*** having great or varied learning. [< Greek *polymathḗs* having learned much < *polýs* much + *manthánein* learn]

**pol|y|math|ic** (pol′ē math′ik), *adj.* having to do with or characterized by polymathy.

**po|lym|a|thy** (pə lim′ə thē), *n.* great learning.

**pol|y|mer** (pol′i mər), *n.* a chemical compound in which each molecule is made up of two or more simpler molecules strung together. Nylon and cellulose are polymers. *Like cellulose, lignin is a polymer, that is, a giant molecule built up from identical or similar smaller molecular units* (Scientific American). [back formation < *polymeric*]

**pol|y|mer|ase** (pol′i mə rās), *n.* an enzyme that polymerizes nucleotides to form nucleic acid. [< *polymer* + *-ase*]

**pol|y|mer|ic** (pol′ē mer′ik), *adj.* having the same elements combined in the same proportions by weight, but differing in molecular weight and in chemical and physical properties. Acetylene, $C_2H_2$, and benzene, $C_6H_6$, are polymeric compounds. [< German *polymerisch* < Greek *polymerēs* (< *polýs* many + *méros* part, section) + German *-isch* -ic]

**pol|y|mer|ise** (pol′i mə rīz, pə lim′ə-), *v.t., v.i.,* **-ised, -is|ing.** *Especially British.* polymerize.

**po|lym|er|ism** (pə lim′ə riz əm, pol′i mə-), *n.* **1** *Chemistry.* the condition of being polymeric. **2** *Botany.* the condition of being polymerous.

**pol|y|mer|i|za|tion** (pol′i mər ə zā′shən, pə lim′ər ə-), *n. Chemistry.* **1** a reaction in which two or more molecules unite, forming a more complex molecule with a higher molecular weight and different chemical and physical properties (the new molecule retaining the same elements in the same proportion as the parent substance), as $CH_3CHO = (CH_3CHO)_3$, by which is indicated the formation of paraldehyde from acetaldehyde: *Polymerization is the opposite of cracking* (William B. Harper). *Polymerization is ... important in the production of synthetic rubber, plastics, paints, and artificial fibers* (James S. Fritz). **2** the conversion of one compound into another by such a process: *the polymerization of acetylene to benzene.*

**pol|y|mer|ize** (pol′i mə rīz, pə lim′ə-), *v.t., v.i.,* **-ized, -iz|ing.** to make or become polymeric; form a polymer; undergo or cause to undergo polymerization.

**po|lym|er|ous** (pə lim′ər əs), *adj.* **1** *Biology.* composed of many parts, members, or segments. **2** *Botany.* having many members in each whorl: *a polymerous flower.* [< *poly-* + Greek *méros* (with English *-ous*) part, section]

**pol|y|mix|in** (pol′ē mik′sin), *n.* = polymyxin.

**Po|lym|ni|a** (pō lim′nē ə), *n.* = Polyhymnia.

**pol|y|morph** (pol′ē môrf), *n.* **1** a polymorphous organism. **2a** a substance that crystallizes in two or more different forms. **b** one of these forms.

**pol|y|mor|phic** (pol′ē môr′fik), *adj.* = polymorphous.

**pol|y|mor|phism** (pol′ē môr′fiz əm), *n.* polymorphous state or condition.

**pol|y|mor|pho|nu|cle|ar** (pol′ē môr′fō nü′klē ər, -nyü′-), *adj.* having nuclei of various shapes, especially nuclei that have lobes: *polymorphonuclear leucocytes.*

**pol|y|mor|phous** (pol′ē môr′fəs), *adj.* **1** having, assuming, or passing through many or various forms or stages, as the honeybee does. **2** crystallizing in two or more forms, especially in forms belonging to different systems. [< Greek *polýmorphos* (with English *-ous*) < *polýs* many + *morphḗ* form] —**pol′y|mor′phous|ly,** *adv.* —**pol′y|mor′phous|ness,** *n.*

**pol|y|myx|in** (pol′ē mik′sin), *n.* any antibiotic substance of a group produced by certain bacilli, used against infections caused by Gram-negative bacteria. [< New Latin *polymyxa* a species of bacteria (< *poly-* + Greek *mýxa* mucus) + English *-in*]

**Pol|y|ne|sian** (pol′ə nē′zhən, -shən), *n., adj.* —*n.* **1** a member of any one of the brown peoples that live in Polynesia, a group of islands in the Pacific, east of Australia and the Phillippines. **2** the Austronesian languages of Polynesia, including Maori and Hawaiian.
—*adj.* of or having to do with Polynesia, its people, or their languages.

**pol|y|neu|ri|tis** (pol′ē nu̇ rī′tis, -nyu̇-), *n.* = multiple neuritis.

**po|lyn|ia** (pə lin′yə, pol′ən yä′), *n.* a space of open water in the midst of ice, especially in the arctic seas. [< Russian *polyn'ja*]

**Pol|y|ni|ces** (pol′ə nī′sēz), *n. Greek Legend.* a son of Oedipus, slain by his brother Eteocles in the expedition of the Seven against Thebes, and buried by his sister Antigone at the cost of her own life.

**pol|y|no|mi|al** (pol′ē nō′mē əl), *n., adj.* —*n.* **1** an algebraic expression consisting of two or more rational and integral terms. *Examples:* ab, $x^2y$, and 3npq are monomials; ab + $x^2y$ and pq − $p^2$ + q are polynomials. **2** *Biology.* a name of a variety, species, or the like, consisting of two or more terms.
—*adj.* consisting of two or more terms: *"Homo sapiens" is a polynomial expression.*
[< *poly-* + *-nomial,* as in *binomial*]

**pol|y|no|sic** (pol′ē nō′sik), *adj., n.* —*adj.* having to do with or designating a modified viscose fiber developed in Great Britain: *polynosic rayon staple.*
—*n.* a polynosic textile, plastic, or fiber.
[< *poly*(vi)*n*(yl) + (visc)*os*(e) + *ic*]

**pol|y|nu|cle|ar** (pol′ē nü′klē ər, -nyü′-), *adj.* having several nuclei.

**pol|y|nu|cle|o|tide** (pol′ē nü′klē ə tīd, -nyü′-), *n.* a substance composed of a number of nucleotides, such as nucleic acid.

**po|lyn|ya** (pə lin′yə, pol′ən yä′), *n.* = polynia.

**pol|y|ol** (pol′ē ōl, -ol), *n.* any one of various alcohols, such as sorbitol, that contain many hydroxyl radicals, used especially as surfactants and in plastics. [< *poly-* + (alcoh)*ol*]

**pol|y|o|le|fin** (pol′ē ō′lə fin), *n.* any olefin of a large group, including polyethylene and polystyrene, produced by polymerization with catalysts at low pressure.

**pol|y|o|ma** (pol′ē ō′mə), *n.,* or **polyoma virus,** a virus containing DNA, associated with various tumors formed in rodents: *A number of viral agents of cancer in lower animals, such as the polyoma virus in mice, Rous sarcoma virus in chickens, and certain leukemia viruses in mice and hamsters, provide models for study of related human diseases* (James G. Shaffer). [< *poly-* + *-oma*]

**pol|y|om|i|no** (pol′ē om′ə nō), *n., pl.* **-noes** or **-nos.** a many-sided piece so shaped that it can cover a number of squares on a game board and join other similar pieces. [< *poly-* + (d)*omino*]

**pol|y|ox|y|meth|y|lene** (pol′ē ok′sə meth′ə lēn), *n.* a polymerized form of formaldehyde. It is a thermoplastic resin.

**pol|yp** (pol′ip), *n.* **1** a rather simple form of water animal, consisting largely of a stomach and a mouth with fingerlike tentacles around the edge to gather in food. Polyps are coelenterates and often grow in colonies with their bases connected. Hydras, sea anemones, and corals are polyps. Some polyps produce a swimming stage called a medusa. **2** a tumor or similar mass of enlarged tissue arising from a mucous or serous surface, such as one in the nose or stomach. [< French *polype,* learned borrowing from Latin *polypus* < Greek *polýpous* < *polýs* many + *poús, podós* foot]

**pol|y|par|y** (pol′ē per′ē), *n., pl.* **-par|ies.** the common stem, stock, or supporting structure of a colony of polyps, such as corals. [< New Latin *polyparium* < Latin *polypus* + *-ārium* -ary]

**pol|y|pep|tid** (pol′ē pep′tid), *n.* = polypeptide.

**pol|y|pep|tide** (pol′ē pep′tīd, -tid), *n.* a peptide containing many molecules of amino acids.

**pol|y|pet|al|ous** (pol′ē pet′ə ləs), *adj.* **1** having the petals distinct or separate; choripetalous. **2** having many petals.

**pol|y|phage** (pol′i fāj), *n.* a person that eats much or to excess.

**pol|y|pha|gi|a** (pol′ē fā′jē ə), *n.* **1** *Medicine.* **a** excessive eating. **b** excessive appetite; bulimia. **2** *Zoology.* the habit of feeding on many different kinds of food. [< New Latin *polyphagia* < Greek *polyphagiā* < *polyphágos* voracious < *polýs* much + *phágeîn* to eat]

**po|lyph|a|gous** (pə lif′ə gəs), *adj.* eating many different kinds of food.

**po|lyph|a|gy** (pə lif′ə jē), *n. Medicine, Zoology.* polyphagia.

**pol|y|phar|ma|cy** (pol′ē fär′mə sē), *n.* the use of many different drugs or medicines, usually indiscriminately, in the treatment of a disease.

**pol|y|phase** (pol′ē fāz), *adj.* **1** having different phases: *In a polyphase alloy, the proportion of the various metals varies from one phase to another.* **2** of or having to do with a system combining two or more alternating electric currents of identical frequency but differing from one another in phase.

**Pol|y|phe|mus** (pol′ē fē′məs), *n. Greek Legend.* the Cyclops who captured Odysseus and his companions and ate two of them every day. Odysseus blinded him and escaped with his remaining men.

**Polyphemus moth,** a large, tan American silkworm moth, that has an eyespot on each hind wing.

**pol|y|phen|yl|ene oxide** (pol′ē fen′ə lēn, -fē′nə-), a thermoplastic substance that is highly resistant to acids, bases, and detergents, derived by oxidative polymerization of xylenol and used for making nose cones, dielectric components, and laboratory and industrial equipment. *Abbr:* PPO (no periods).

**pol|y|phone** (pol′ē fōn), *n. Phonetics.* a polyphonic symbol.

**pol|y|phon|ic** (pol′ē fon′ik), *adj.* **1** *Music.* having two or more voices or parts, each with an independent melody but all harmonizing; contrapuntal. **2** that can produce more than one tone at a time, as a piano or harp can. **3** producing many sounds; many-voiced. **4** *Phonetics.* representing more than one sound. English *oo* in *food, good* is polyphonic. —**pol′y|phon′i|cal|ly,** *adv.*

**polyphonic prose,** writing printed like prose but incorporating a definite rhythmic pattern or rhyme, so as to give the effect of verse when read, especially when read aloud.

**po|lyph|o|nist** (pə lif′ə nist), *n.* a polyphonic composer or theorist; contrapuntist.

**po|lyph|o|nous** (pə lif′ə nəs), *adj.* = polyphonic. —**po|lyph′o|nous|ly,** *adv.*

**po|lyph|o|ny** (pə lif′ə nē), *n.* **1** *Music.* polyphonic composition; counterpoint. **2** a multiplicity of sounds. **3** *Phonetics.* the representation of more than one sound by the same letter or symbol. [< Greek *polyphōniā* < *polýphōnos* having many sounds or voices < *polýs* many + *phōnḗ* sound]

**pol|y|phy|let|ic** (pol′ē fī let′ik), *adj.* developed from more than one ancestral type, as a group of animals. [< German *polyphyletisch* < Greek *polýs* many + *phȳlḗ, -etos* clan, tribe + German *-isch* -ic] —**pol′y|phy|let′i|cal|ly,** *adv.*

**pol|y|phyl|lous** (pol′ē fil′əs), *adj. Botany.* **1** having distinct or separate leaves. **2** having or consisting of many leaves. [< Greek *polýphyllos* (with English *-ous*) having many leaves < *polýs* many + *phýllon* leaf]

**po|lyp|i|dom** (pə lip′ə dəm), *n.* = polypary.

**pol|y|pite** (pol′i pīt), *n.* an individual zooid of a compound polyp.

**pol|y|ploid** (pol′ē ploid), *adj., n.* —*adj.* having three or more sets of chromosomes.
—*n.* a polyploid organism or cell.
[< *poly-* + *-ploid,* as in *haploid*]

**pol|y|ploi|dic** (pol′ē ploi′dik), *adj.* = polyploid.

**pol|y|ploi|dy** (pol′ē ploi′dē), *n.* **1** the natural condition of being polyploid. **2** a polyploid condition brought about by use of chemicals, hormones, or other special means, in order to develop new species of plants.

**pol|yp|ne|a** or **pol|yp|noe|a** (pol′ip nē′ə, pə lip′nē-), *n. Medicine.* very rapid breathing; panting. [< New Latin *polypnea, polypnoea* < *poly-* + Greek *pneîn* breathe]

**pol|y|po|di|a|ceous** (pol′ē pō′dē ā′shəs), *adj.* belonging to the chief family of ferns, including the polypody, spleenwort, walking fern, maidenhair, brake, and certain tree ferns. [< New Latin *Polypodiaceae* the family name (< Latin *polypodium* polypody) + English *-ous*]

**pol|y|po|dy** (pol′ē pō′dē), *n., pl.* **-dies.** any fern of a group, especially a widely distributed species that grows on moist rocks, old walls, and trees, and has naked, round spore cases, deeply pinnate fronds, and creeping stems. [< Latin *polypodium* < Greek *polypódion* a kind of fern; (literally, diminutive) < *polýpous, -podos* many-footed < *polýs* many + *poús, podós* foot (because its rootstock has many branches)]

**pol|y|poid** (pol′ē poid), *adj.* resembling a polyp (animal).

**pol|y|po|sis** (pol′ē pō′sis), *n.* the forming of many tumors or polyps on a part of the body.

**pol|y|pous** (pol′ə pəs), *adj.* of, having to do with, or like a polyp.

**pol|y|prag|mat|ic** (pol′ē prag mat′ik), *adj.* busy about many affairs; officious; meddlesome.

**pol|y|pro|pyl|ene** (pol′ē prō′pə lēn), *n.* a lightweight thermoplastic resin, similar in appearance to polyethylene but harder and having a higher melting point, used for films, insulating material, piping, baby bottles, and other molded plastics. It is a polymerized form of propylene gas. *Formula:* $(C_3H_6)_n$

**pol|yp|tych** (pol′ip tik), *n.* a combination of more than three panels or frames folded or hinged together, bearing pictures, carvings, or the like, as a picture or an altarpiece. [< Late Latin *polyptycha,* neuter plural, account books, ledgers < Greek *polýptychos* manifold < *polýs* many + *ptychḗ* a fold]

**pol|y|pus** (pol′ə pəs), *n., pl.* **-pi** (-pī). = polyp. [< Latin *polypus* polyp]

**pol|y|rhythm** (pol′ē riᴛʜ′əm), *n.* a complex of different rhythms used simultaneously in a musical piece or rendition.

**pol|y|rhyth|mic** (pol′ē riᴛʜ′mik), *adj.* having or using different rhythms simultaneously.

**pol|y|ri|bo|nu|cle|o|tide** (pol′ē rī′bō nü′klē ə tīd, -nyü′-; -tid), *n.* a polynucleotide synthesized by the action of RNA polymerase.

**pol|y|ri|bo|so|mal** (pol′ē rī′bə sō′məl), *adj.* of or having to do with polyribosomes.

**pol|y|ri|bo|some** (pol′ē rī′bə sōm), *n.* a cluster of ribosomes that are linked by messenger RNA and function as a unit in synthesizing proteins: *The ribosomes on the surface of the endoplasmic reticulum are arranged as polyribosomes with a spiral configuration* (J. Cronshaw).

**pol|y|sac|cha|rid** (pol′ē sak′ər id), *n.* = polysaccharide.

**pol|y|sac|cha|ride** (pol′ē sak′ə rīd, -ər id), *n.* any carbohydrate of a class, such as starch, dextrin, and insulin, that can be decomposed into two or more simple sugars by hydrolysis.

**pol|y|se|mic** (pol′ē sē′mik), *adj.* of or having to do with polysemy.

**pol|y|se|mous** (pol′ē sē′məs), *adj.* = polysemic.

**pol|y|se|my** (pol′ē sē′mē), *n. Linguistics.* the property of having many meanings; semantic diversity: *Words like "foot" and "head" show*

---

**Pronunciation Key:** hat, **ā**ge, c**ã**re, f**ä**r; let, **ē**qual, t**ė**rm; it, **ī**ce; hot, **ō**pen, **ô**rder; **oi**l, **ou**t; cup, p**u̇**t, r**ü**le; **ch**ild; lo**ng**; **th**in; **ᴛʜ**en; **zh**, measure; **ə** represents **a** in about, **e** in taken, **i** in pencil, **o** in lemon, **u** in circus.

*polysemy to a high degree.* [< Greek *polýsēmos* having many meanings < *polýs* many + *sêma* sign]

**pol|y|sep|a|lous** (pol′ē sep′ə ləs), *adj. Botany.* **1** having the sepals distinct or separate; chorisepalous. **2** having numerous sepals.

**pol|y|some** (pol′ē sōm), *n.* = polyribosome.

**pol|y|so|mic** (pol′ē sō′mik), *adj., n.* —*adj.* **1** having more than the normal number or sets of chromosomes. **2** = polyploid.
—*n.* a polysomic organism or cell.

**pol|y|sper|mous** (pol′ē spėr′məs), *adj. Botany.* containing or producing many seeds.

**pol|y|sty|rene** (pol′ē stī′rēn, -stir′ən), *n.* a colorless, transparent plastic used for insulation and in making toys, household appliances, luggage, reeds for musical instruments, synthetic rubber, dishes, tile, and implements. It is a polymerized form of styrene. *Formula:* $(C_8H_8)_n$

**pol|y|sul|fide** or **pol|y|sul|phide** (pol′ē sul′fīd, -fid), *n.* a chemical compound containing more than one atom of sulfur combined with another atom or radical.

**pol|y|sul|fone** (pol′ē sul′fōn), *n.* a hard, rigid, corrosion-resistant synthetic polymer used in the manufacture of mechanical and electrical equipment.

**pol|y|syl|lab|ic** (pol′ē sə lab′ik), *adj.* **1** of more than three syllables: *a polysyllabic word.* **2** having words of more than three syllables: *a polysyllabic language.* —**pol′y|syl|lab′i|cal|ly**, *adv.*

**pol|y|syl|lab|i|cal** (pol′ē sə lab′ə kəl), *adj.* = polysyllabic.

**pol|y|syl|la|ble** (pol′ē sil′ə bəl), *n.* a word of more than three syllables. *Politician* and *possibility* are polysyllables. [adaptation of Medieval Latin *polysyllaba* (*vox*) many-syllabled (word), feminine of *polysyllabus* < Greek *polysýllabos* < *polýs* many + *syllabê* syllable]

**pol|y|syn|apse** (pol′ē si naps′, -sin′aps), *n.* a synapse involving two or more adjacent nerve cells.

**pol|y|syn|ap|tic** (pol′ē si nap′tik), *adj.* of or having to do with a polysynapse: *a polysynaptic response, polysynaptic sites in the brain.*

**pol|y|syn|de|ton** (pol′ē sin′də ton), *n. Rhetoric.* the use of several conjunctions in close succession. *Example: And* the rain descended, *and* the floods came, *and* the winds blew, *and* beat upon that house; *and* it fell: *and* great was the fall of it (Matthew 7:27). [< New Latin *polysyndeton* < *poly-* poly- + *syndeton* < Greek *sýndetos* connected < *syndeîn* bind together < *syn-* together + *deîn* to bind. Compare etym. under **a syndeton, syndetic.**]

**pol|y|syn|the|sis** (pol′ē sin′thə sis), *n., pl.* **-ses** (-sēz). **1** the synthesis of many elements. **2** the combination of several words of a sentence into one word, such as in the languages of the North American Indians. In the North American Indian language, Oneida, *g-nagla′-sl-i-zak-s,* means "I search for a village."

**pol|y|syn|thet|ic** (pol′ē sin thet′ik), *adj.* characterized by polysynthesis.

**pol|y|tech|nic** (pol′ē tek′nik), *adj., n.* —*adj.* having to do with or dealing with many crafts or sciences: *a polytechnic school.*
—*n.* a technical school.
[< French *polytechnique* < Greek *polýtechnos* skilled in many arts < *polýs* many + *téchnē* art, skill]

**pol|y|tech|ni|cal** (pol′ē tek′nə kəl), *adj.* = polytechnic.

**pol|y|tene** (pol′ē tēn), *adj.* having a structure made up of many strands like a rope: *Polytene chromosomes develop ... by means of a process in which the chromosomes repeatedly replicate but do not separate* (Scientific American). [< *poly-* + Latin *taenia* band]

**pol|y|tet|ra|flu|or|o|eth|y|lene** (pol′ē tet′rə flü′ər-ə eth′ə lēn), *n.* a slippery, acid-resistant plastic resin that is easily shaped and can be cut with a knife, even at extreme temperatures, used for replacing surfaces of diseased joints, coating frying pans and other utensils, and as a dry lubricant, substituting for oil in some machinery; Teflon. It is a polymerized form of tetrafluoroethylene. *Formula:* $(C_2F_4)_n$ *Abbr:* PTFE (no periods).

**pol|y|the|ism** (pol′ē thē′iz əm), *n.* the belief in or worship of more than one god: *A number of advanced groups like the Egyptians, Greeks, and Romans had polytheism, a hierarchy of gods* (Ogburn and Nimkoff).
[< French *polythéisme* < Greek *polýtheos* of many gods (< *polýs* many + *theós* god) + French *-isme* -ism]

**pol|y|the|ist** (pol′ē thē′ist), *n., adj.* —*n.* a person who believes in or worships more than one god.
—*adj.* = polytheistic.

**pol|y|the|is|tic** (pol′ē thē is′tik), *adj.* having to do with or characterized by belief in or worship of more than one god. —**pol′y|the|is′ti|cal|ly**, *adv.*

**pol|y|the|is|ti|cal** (pol′ē thē is′tə kəl), *adj.* = polytheistic.

**pol|y|thene** (pol′ē thēn), *n.* = polyethylene.

**pol|y|to|nal** (pol′ē tō′nəl), *adj. Music.* having or using different harmonic keys simultaneously.
—**pol′y|to′nal|ly**, *adv.*

**pol|y|to|nal|i|ty** (pol′ē tō nal′ə tē), *n. Music.* **1** the use of different harmonic keys simultaneously. **2** the sounds produced by using different harmonic keys simultaneously.

**pol|y|tone** (pol′ē tōn′), *n.* variance of tone, especially in ordinary speech.

**pol|y|troph|ic** (pol′ē trof′ik), *adj.* subsisting on a variety of organic substances, as pathogenic bacteria. [< Greek *polýtrophos* highly nourished (< *polýs* much + *tréphein* nourish) + English *-ic*]

**pol|y|type** (pol′ē tīp′), *n.* **1** a cast produced by pressing a woodcut or other plate into semifluid metal. **2** a copy of an engraving or of printed matter made from a cast thus produced.

**pol|y|typ|ic** (pol′ē tip′ik), *adj.* having or involving many or several different types.

**pol|y|typ|i|cal** (pol′ē tip′ə kəl), *adj.* = polytypic.

**pol|y|un|sat|u|rate** (pol′ē un sach′ər it, -ə rāt), *n.* a polyunsaturated oil or fat, such as certain vegetable oils or fish oil, often used in low-cholesterol diets: *Richest of all in polyunsaturates are vegetable oils from corn, cottonseed, safflower, soybeans, and (if not artificially hydrogenated) peanuts and some olives* (Time).

**pol|y|un|sat|u|rat|ed** (pol′ē un sach′ə rā′tid), *adj.* having many double or triple bonds and free valences: *a polyunsaturated vegetable oil.*

**pol|y|u|re|than** (pol′ē yůr′ə than), *n.* = polyurethane.

**pol|y|u|re|thane** (pol′ē yůr′ə thān), *n.* a strong plastic resin that resists fire, the effects of weather, and the corrosive action of acids and oxygen, made in the form of rigid or flexible foams or solids. The wide variations of density and form make polyurethane's uses varied, and it is now used as a substitute for foam rubber in the form of a flexible foam, as a binder, filler, and strengthener for fractured bones in the form of a rigid solid, and as insulation in building construction or as a stiffener for sheet-metal structures in the form of a rigid foam. *Abbr:* PU (no periods).

**pol|y|u|ri|a** (pol′ē yůr′ē ə), *n. Medicine.* an excessive excretion of urine, as in diabetes and certain nervous diseases.

**pol|y|u|ric** (pol′ē yůr′ik), *adj.* of or having to do with polyuria.

**pol|y|u|ro|nide** (pol′ē yůr′ə nīd), *n.* a natural gum or resin found in humus or decaying vegetation which improves soil condition by binding the particles together.

**pol|y|va|lence** (pol′ē vā′ləns, pə liv′ə-), *n. Chemistry.* multivalence.

**pol|y|va|lent** (pol′ē vā′lənt, pə liv′ə-), *adj.* **1** *Chemistry.* multivalent. **2** containing the proper antibodies or antigens to resist more than one species or strain of disease organisms: *a polyvalent serum.*

**pol|y|ver|si|ty** (pol′ē vėr′sə tē), *n., pl.* **-ties.** = multiversity.

**pol|y|vi|nyl** (pol′ē vī′nəl), *adj.* of or having to do with any one of a group of chemical compounds formed by the polymerization of one or more compounds that have the vinyl ($CH_2$:CH-) group. Many polyvinyl compounds are important as thermoplastic resins.

**polyvinyl acetate**, a transparent thermoplastic resin formed by the polymerization of vinyl acetate, used in making adhesives, paints, lacquers, and plastics.

**polyvinyl alcohol**, a resin made from polyvinyl acetate, used especially as an adhesive, for coating materials and in molding.

**polyvinyl chloride**, a themoplastic synthetic resin formed by the polymerization of vinyl chloride, used especially in fabrics, pipes, and floor coverings, for its hardness and resistance to chemicals. *Abbr:* PVC (no periods).

**pol|y|vi|nyl|i|dene chloride** (pol′ē vī nil′ə dēn), a thermoplastic synthetic resin formed by the polymerization of vinylidene chloride, used for moldings and filaments.

**polyvinylidene resin**, = vinylidene resin.

**polyvinyl pyr|ro|li|done** (pi rō′lə dōn), a substance made from formaldehyde and acetylene, used chiefly with iodine and other antiseptics as an effective agent against bacteria, fungus, and virus, as a substitute for blood plasma in a time of shortage, and also in cosmetics and detergents. *Formula:* $(C_6H_9NO)_n$

**polyvinyl resin**, = vinyl resin.

**pol|y|wa|ter** (pol′ē wôt′ər, -wot′-), *n.* a supposedly new type of water that is denser than ordinary water and does not freeze, thought to have been discovered by a Soviet scientist in the 1960's but shown to be only ordinary water containing ionic impurities that cause it to have unusual properties; anomalous water; orthowater. [< *poly*(mer) + *water*]

**Po|lyx|e|na** (pə lik′sə nə), *n. Greek Legend.* a daughter of Priam and Hecuba, and the bride of Achilles. At her wedding Achilles was slain by Paris, and Polyxena was later sacrificed by the Greeks on his funeral pyre.

**pol|y|zo|an** (pol′ē zō′ən), *n., adj.* = bryozoan. [< New Latin *Polyzoa* (< Greek *polýs* many + *zôion* animal) + English *-an*]

**pol|y|zo|ar|i|al** (pol′ē zō är′ē əl), *adj.* of or having to do with a polyzoarium.

**pol|y|zo|ar|i|um** (pol′ē zō är′ē əm), *n., pl.* **-i|a** (-ē ə). a colony of bryozoans or its supporting skeleton. [< New Latin *polyzoarium* < *Polyzoa* polyzoan + *-arium* -ary]

**pol|y|zo|ic** (pol′ē zō′ik), *adj. Zoology.* **1** of or like the bryozoans. **2** composed of a number of individual zooids existing in the form of a colony. **3** of or having to do with a spore that produces many sporozoites.

**pol|y|zon|al** (pol′ē zō′nəl), *adj.* having several or many zones (applied especially to a type of lens composed of a number of annular segments).

**pol|y|zo|on** (pol′ē zō′on), *n., pl.* **-zo|a** (-zō′ə). = bryozoan. [< New Latin *polyzoōn* < Greek *polýs* many + *zôion* animal]

**pom** or **Pom** (pom), *n. Australian Slang.* a British immigrant; Briton. [back formation < *pommy*]

**pom|ace** (pum′is), *n.* **1** apple pulp or similar fruit pulp before or after the juice has been pressed out. **2** what is left after oil has been pressed out of something, such as the substance of certain fish. [< Medieval Latin *pomacium* cider < Latin *pōmum* apple]

**pomace fly**, any one of a group of several flies whose larvae live in decaying fruit; fruit fly.

**po|ma|ceous** (pə mā′shəs), *adj.* **1** belonging to a group of plants of the rose family bearing pomes or pomelike fruits, such as the apple and hawthorn; malaceous. **2** of or having to do with apples. **3** of the nature of a pome or apple. [< New Latin *pomaceus* (with English *-ous*) < Latin *pōmum* fruit; apple]

**po|made** (pə mād′, -mäd′), *n., v.,* **-mad|ed, -mad|ing.** —*n.* a perfumed ointment for the scalp and hair.
—*v.t.* to dress (the scalp and hair) with pomade.
[< Middle French *pommade* < Italian *pomata* < *pomo* apple < Latin *pōmum;* see etym. under **pome** (because it originally contained apple pulp)]

**Po|mak** (pō mäk′), *n.* any one of a group of Bulgarian Moslems living near the border with Greece.

**po|man|der** (pə man′dər, pō′man-), *n.* **1** a ball of mixed aromatic substances formerly carried for perfume or as a guard against infection. **2** the case in which this was carried, usually a hollow ball of gold or silver in the shape of an apple or orange. [alteration of Old French *pome d'ambre* < *pome* apple (see etym. under **pome**) + *d'ambre* of amber]

**po|ma|rine jaeger** (pō′mə rīn), a hawklike sea bird, a variety of jaeger with broad, blunt, elongated central tail feathers.

**po|ma|to** (pə mā′tō), *n., pl.* **-toes.** a small tomatolike fruit grown on a potato vine. It was developed by Luther Burbank by selection from the fruits of the potato. [blend of *potato* and *tomato*]

**po|ma|tum** (pō mā′təm, -mä′-), *n., v.t.* = pomade. [< New Latin *pomatum* < Italian *pomata* pomade]

**pome** (pōm), *n.* a fruit consisting of firm, juicy flesh surrounding a core that contains several seeds. Apples, pears, and quinces are pomes. See picture under **fruit.** [earlier, ball, apple < Old French *pome* < Vulgar Latin *pōma* < Latin *pōmum* fruit; apple] —**pome′like′**, *adj.*

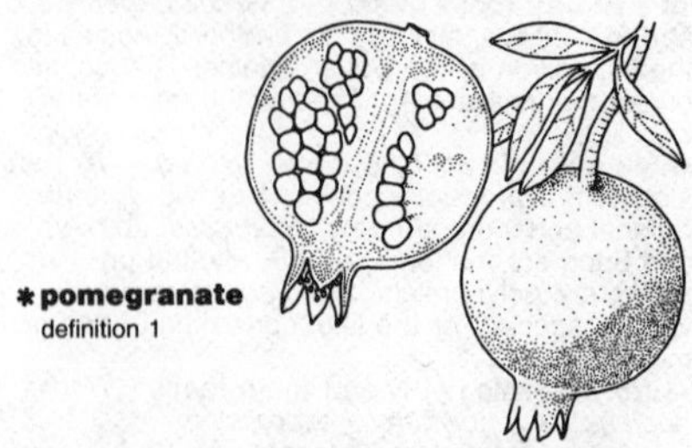

***pomegranate**
definition 1

***pome|gran|ate** (pom′gran′it, pum′-; pom gran′-), *n.* **1** a reddish-yellow fruit with a thick skin and with many seeds enveloped in a juicy red pulp. The pulp has a pleasant, slightly sour taste. The pomegranate is a large, roundish, many-celled berry. **2** the tree it grows on. It is a tropical Asian and African tree, widely cultivated in subtropical regions. **3** *Australian Slang.* a British immigrant; pommy. [alteration of Old French *pome grenate* < *pome* (see etym. under **pome**) + *grenate* having grains, ultimately < Latin *grānāta,* feminine < *grānum* grain. Compare etym. under **grenade.**]

**pom|e|lo** (pom′ə lō), *n., pl.* **-los.** **1** = grapefruit.

2 = shaddock. Also, **pummelo.** [origin uncertain]

**Pom|er|a|ni|an** (pom′ə rā′nē ən), *adj., n.* — ***adj.*** of or having to do with Pomerania, on the south coast of the Baltic Sea, or its people.
— ***n.*** **1** a native or inhabitant of Pomerania. **2** any one of a breed of small dogs, weighing from 3 to 7 pounds, with a sharp nose, pointed ears, and long, thick, silky hair. It is related to the chow and the spitz.

**pom|fret** (pom′frit, pum′-), *n.* **1** a fish of the Indian and Pacific oceans, used as food. **2** a kind of sea bream found near Bermuda. [apparently earlier *pamplee* < French *pample*]

**po|mi|cul|ture** (pō′mə kul′chər), *n.* the cultivation or growing of fruit. [< Latin *pōmum* fruit, apple + *cultūra* culture]

**po|mi|cul|tur|ist** (pō′mə kul′chər ist), *n.* a person who cultivates or raises fruit.

**po|mif|er|ous** (pō mif′ər əs), *adj.* bearing pomes or pomelike fruits. [< Latin *pōmifer* < *pōmum* fruit + *ferre* to bear + English *-ous*]

**pom|mé** or **pom|mée** (pô mā′), *adj. Heraldry.* having arms that terminate in knobs, globes, or balls: *a cross pommé.* See diagram under **cross.** [< French *pommé,* past participle of *pommer* to end in a round head < *pomme* apple]

**pom|mel** (pum′əl, pom′-), *n., v.,* **-meled, -mel|ing** or (*especially British*) **-melled, -mel|ling.** — ***n.*** **1** the part of a saddle that sticks up at the front. See picture under **saddle. 2** a rounded knob on the end of the hilt of a sword, dagger, or the like. Also, **pummel.** — ***v.t.*** to pummel; beat with the fists; strike or beat.
[< Old French *pomel* a rounded knob < *pom* hilt of a sword, (originally) variant of *pome;* see etym. under **pome**] — **pom′mel|er,** *n.*

**pom|my** (pom′ē), *n., pl.* **-mies.** *Australian Slang.* a British immigrant who has recently come to Australia; pomegranate.

**Po|mo** (pō′mō), *n., pl.* **-mo** or **-mos. 1** a member of a North American Indian tribe that once occupied the Russian River valley of northwestern California. The Pomo are noted for their excellent basketry. **2** the Hokan language of this tribe.

**po|mo|log|i|cal** (pō′mə loj′ə kəl), *adj.* of or having to do with pomology. — **po′mo|log′i|cal|ly,** *adv.*

**po|mol|o|gist** (pō mol′ə jist), *n.* an expert in pomology.

**po|mol|o|gy** (pō mol′ə jē), *n.* the branch of science that deals with fruits and fruit growing. [< New Latin *pomologia* < Latin *pōmum* fruit; apple + *-logia* -logy]

**Po|mo|na** (pə mō′nə), *n. Roman Mythology.* the goddess of fruits and fruit trees, wooed and wedded by Vertumnus, the god of the seasons. [< Latin *Pōmōna* < *pōmum* fruit; apple]

**Pomona glass,** a kind of glassware made in the United States in the late 1880's, consisting of clear glass etched and tinted after being blown into a mold.

**pomp** (pomp), *n., v.* — ***n.*** **1** a stately display; splendor; magnificence: *The king was crowned with great pomp.* **SYN:** flourish, grandeur. **2** a showy display; boastful show: *the pomps and vanities of the world.* **3** *Archaic.* a triumphal or ceremonial procession or pageant: *The heavens … rung … While the bright pomp ascended jubilant* (Milton).
— ***v.t.*** to dress with pomp.
[< Old French *pompe* < Latin *pompa* < Greek *pompē* procession, parade; (literally) a sending, ultimately < *pémpein* to send]

**Pom|pa|dour** (pom′pə dôr, -dōr, -dúr), *adj.* having to do with or named after the Marquise de Pompadour, the mistress of Louis XV of France: *Pompadour ribbons.*

***pom|pa|dour** (pom′pə dôr, -dōr, -dúr), *n.* **1** an arrangement of a woman's hair, in which it is puffed high over the forehead. **2** an arrangement of a man's or woman's hair in which it is brushed straight up and back from the forehead. **3** the hair so arranged. **4** a shade of crimson or pink. **5** a fabric with small floral designs of bright colors, especially crimson. [< *Pompadour*]

***pompadour**
definitions 1, 2

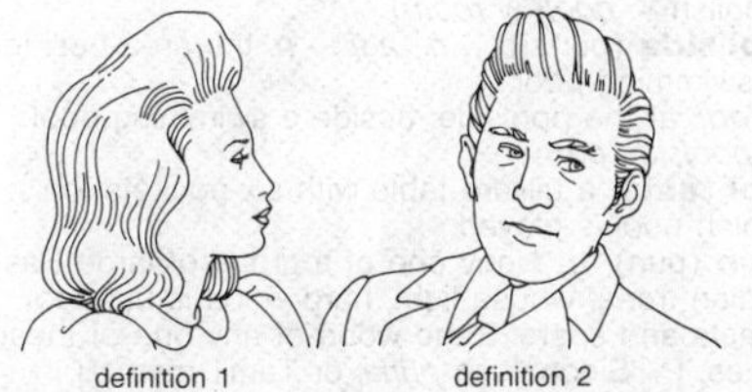

definition 1 definition 2

**pom|pa|no** (pom′pə nō), *n., pl.* **-nos** or (*collectively*) **-no. 1** any one of a group of food fishes of the West Indies and the coasts of southern North America. **2** a similar fish of the California coast. [American English < American Spanish *pámpano* any of various fish < Spanish, a vine tendril, or scion]

**Pom|pei|an** (pom pā′ən, -pē′-), *adj., n.* — ***adj.*** of or having to do with Pompeii, an ancient city of southeastern Italy, or its people. Pompeii was buried by an eruption of Mount Vesuvius in A.D. 79.
— ***n.*** a native or inhabitant of Pompeii.

**pom|pier** (pôɴ pyā′), *n., adj. French.* — ***n.*** **1** a fireman. **2** a thoroughly conventional and uninspired artist.
— ***adj.*** thoroughly conventional; unimaginative; hackneyed: *a pompier artist, pompier band music.*

**pom|pi|on** (pum′pē ən), *n. Dialect.* a pumpkin.

**pom-pom** (pom′pom′), *n.* **1** an automatic antiaircraft gun used especially on shipboard during World War II. It usually consisted of four gun barrels mounted as a unit, each with its own magazine of explosive shells. **2** any one of various other automatic weapons, such as the Maxim one-pounder used in the Boer War on the Hotchkiss heavy machine gun used in World War I. [imitative of the sound of its firing]

**pom|pon** (pom′pon), *n.* **1** an ornamental tuft or ball of yarn, feathers, silk, or the like, worn on a hat or dress, on shoes, or on a costume: *The clown had large green pompons down his front in place of buttons.* **2** a ball of wool, worn on the front or top of a certain kind of soldier's or sailor's hat. **3** a kind of chrysanthemum or dahlia with very small, rounded flowers; fairy dahlia. [< French *pompon,* perhaps < Old French *pompe* pomp]

**pom|poned** (pom′pond), *adj.* having a pompon or pompons: *a pomponed cap.*

**pom|pos|i|ty** (pom pos′ə tē), *n., pl.* **-ties. 1** pompous quality. **2** a pompous show of self-importance. [< Late Latin *pompōsitās* ostentation < *pompōsus* pompous]

**pom|pous** (pom′pəs), *adj.* **1** trying to seem magnificent or very important; fond of display; acting too proudly; self-important: *The leader of the band bowed in a pompous manner.* **SYN:** pretentious, grandiose, vain-glorious. **2** overly flowery or high-flown; inflated: *pompous language.* **SYN:** ostentatious, lofty. **3** characterized by pomp; splendid; magnificent; stately: *It was a glorious spectacle … to behold this pompous pageant issuing forth … the pennons and devices … fluttering above a sea of crests and plumes* (Washington Irving).
[< Late Latin *pompōsus* (with English *-ous*) < Latin *pompa* pomp] — **pom′pous|ly,** *adv.* — **pom′pous|ness,** *n.*

**ponce** (pons), *n., v.,* **ponced, ponc|ing.** *British Slang.* — ***n.*** a pimp; procurer.
— ***v.i.*** **1** to be or act as a pimp. **2** to go about in a flashy, showy way: *I was invited to Cannes, but what do I want to go poncing about Cannes for?* (Sunday Times).
[perhaps < *pounce*[1], verb]

**pon|ceau** (pon sō′), *n.* **1** the bright red color of the corn poppy; coquelicot. **2** any one of several red coal-tar dyes. [< French *ponceau* < Old French *pouncel* poppy]

**ponce|let** (pons′lit), *n. Physics.* a unit of power equivalent to 100 kilogram-meters per second. [< Jean-Victor *Poncelet,* 1788-1867, a French mathematician and engineer]

**pon|cho** (pon′chō), *n., pl.* **-chos.** a large piece of cloth, often waterproof, with a slit in the middle for the head to go through. Ponchos are worn in South America as cloaks. Waterproof ponchos are used in the armed forces and by hikers and campers. [< American Spanish *poncho* < Araucanian (Chile) *pontho* woolen fabric]

**pond** (pond), *n.* a body of still water, smaller than a lake: *a duck pond, a mill pond. In New Hampshire and beyond They like to call a lake a pond* (New Yorker). [probably (originally) variant of *pound*[3]]

**pond|age** (pon′dij), *n.* the capacity of a pond.

**pond|ed** (pon′did), *adj.* confined in a pond; dammed up: *The storm water remained ponded for weeks* (Harper's).

**pon|der** (pon′dər), *v.i.* to consider carefully; think over: *pondering on his unhappy lot* (Dickens).
— ***v.t.*** to weigh (as a matter or words); meditate upon: *to ponder a problem.* [< Old French *ponderer* to weigh, balance < Latin *ponderāre* to weigh < *pondus, -eris* weight, related to *pendēre* to hang] — **pon′der|er,** *n.* — **pon′der|ing|ly,** *adv.*

**pon|der|a|bil|i|ty** (pon′dər ə bil′ə tē), *n.* the property of being ponderable.

**pon|der|a|ble** (pon′dər ə bəl), *adj.* that can be weighed or considered; appreciable: *Not all the advantages of a good education are ponderable.*

**pon|de|ro|sa pine** (pon′də rō′sə), a pine tree of western North America that grows to great size, valuable as a lumber source; western yellow pine. [< New Latin *ponderosa* the species name < Latin *ponderōsus* ponderous]

**pon|der|os|i|ty** (pon′də ros′ə tē), *n.* a ponderous character or quality.

**pon|der|ous** (pon′dər əs), *adj.* **1** very heavy: *a ponderous mass of iron.* **SYN:** weighty, massive. **2** heavy and clumsy: *A hippopotamus is ponderous.* **SYN:** unwieldy, cumbersome. **3** *Figurative.* dull; tiresome: *The speaker talked in a ponderous way.* [< Latin *ponderōsus* (with English *-ous*) < *pondus, -eris* weight; see etym. under **ponder**] — **pon′der|ous|ly,** *adv.* — **pon′der|ous|ness,** *n.*

**pond fish,** any one of various fishes found in ponds, especially any of numerous small American freshwater sunfishes.

**pond lily,** = water lily.

**Pon|do** (pon′dō), *n., pl.* **-dos** or **-do. 1** a member of a people living in the Cape of Good Hope province in the Republic of South Africa. **2** the Bantu language of this people. Also, **Mpondo.**

**pond scum, 1** any free-floating, freshwater alga that forms a green scum on stagnant water, such as a spirogyra or related alga. **2** the green film formed by these algae.

**pond snail,** a common freshwater snail with a thin shell, commonly used in aquariums.

**pond|weed** (pond′wēd′), *n.* any one of a large genus of water plants that grow in quiet water, usually having oval leaves on the surface of the water and grasslike leaves under water.

**pone**[1] (pōn), *n. U.S.* **1** bread made of corn meal, popular in the southern United States. **2** a loaf or cake of this bread. [American English, earlier *ponap,* and *appone* < Algonkian (Powhatan) *äpan* something baked < *äpen* she bakes]

**pone**[2] (pōn), *n.* the player at the dealer's right in certain card games. [< Latin *pōnere* place]

**po|nent** (pō′nənt), *n., adj.* — ***n.*** *Obsolete.* the west.
— ***adj.*** *Archaic.* western; west: *Forth rush the Levant and the Ponent winds* (Milton).
[< Italian *ponente* < Medieval Latin *ponens, -entis* the west; (literally) setting sun < Latin *pōnere* to put, set down]

**po|ne|rine** (pō′nə rīn, -rin), *adj., n.* — ***adj.*** of or belonging to a subfamily comprising the most primitive ants, found especially in Australia and including the bulldog ant. Ponerine ants are wasplike in appearance and predatory.
— ***n.*** a ponerine ant.
[< New Latin *Ponerinae* the subfamily name < Greek *ponērós* wicked]

**pon|gee** (pon jē′), *n.* **1** a kind of soft silk, usually left in natural brownish-yellow color. The thread for it is obtained from the cocoon of a silkworm native to China. **2** a similar cloth of cotton or rayon, or of dyed silk. [< Chinese (Mandarin) *penchi* one's own machine; loom]

**pon|gid** (pon′jid), *adj.* of or having to do with the anthropoid apes most closely related to man, such as the chimpanzee. [< New Latin *Pongidae* the ape family < *Pongo* the typical genus < a native name in Africa]

**pon|gyi** (pon′jē, pun′-), *n.* a Buddhist priest or monk in Burma. Also, **phongyi.** [< Burmese *hpōngyī* < *hpōn* glory + *kyī* great]

**pon|iard** (pon′yərd), *n., v.* — ***n.*** a short, slender dagger: *She speaks poniards and every word stabs* (Shakespeare).
— ***v.t.*** to kill or wound by stabbing with a poniard: *We could have poniarded these geese by touch, but we could not pistol them* (Atlantic).
[< Middle French *poignard* < Old French *poing* fist < Latin *pūgnus,* related to *pugil* pugilist]

**pons** (ponz), *n., pl.* **pon|tes** (pon′tēz). *Anatomy.* **1** a part that connects two parts, as if bridging the space between them. **2** pons Varolii. [< Latin *pōns* bridge]

**pons as|i|no|rum** (as′ə nôr′əm, -nōr′-), **1** asses' bridge; a reference to the fifth proposition in the first book of Euclid which was difficult to "get over" for beginners. **2** any problem that is difficult for beginners. [< New Latin *pons asinorum* < Latin *pōns* bridge, *asinōrum,* genitive plural of *asinus* ass]

**pons Va|ro|li|i** (və rō′lē ī), a band of nerve fibers in the brain, just above the medulla oblongata, consisting of transverse fibers connecting the two lobes of the cerebellum, and longitudinal fibers connecting the medulla with the cerebrum. See diagram under **brain.** [< New Latin *pons Varolii* Varoli's bridge < Costanzo *Varoli,* about 1543-1575, an Italian anatomist]

**pon|tal** (pon′təl), *adj.* of or having to do with a bridge or bridges. [< Latin *pōns, pontis* bridge + English *-al*[1]]

**Pon|tic** (pon′tik), *adj.* of or having to do with Pontus or the Black Sea, or with Pontus, an ancient country south of it. [< Latin *Ponticus* < Greek *Pontikós* < *póntos* sea, especially, the Black Sea]

**Pronunciation Key:** hat, āge, cãre, fär; let, ēqual, tėrm; it, īce; hot, ōpen, ôrder; oil, out; cup, pu̇t, rüle; child; long; thin; ᴛʜen; zh, measure; ə represents **a** in about, **e** in taken, **i** in pencil, **o** in lemon, **u** in circus.

**pon|ti|cel|lo** (pon′tə chel′ō), *n., pl.* **-los.** the bridge of a stringed musical instrument. [< Italian *ponticello* (diminutive) < *ponte* bridge < Latin *pōns, pontis*]

**pon|ti|fex** (pon′tə feks), *n., pl.* **-tif|i|ces. 1** a member of the principal college of priests in ancient Rome, not assigned to the service of any particular god. The chief pontifex (pontifex maximus) was the highest religious authority of the state. **2** the Pope; pontiff. [< Latin *pontifex, -ficis* a high priest of Rome, perhaps < *pōns, pontis* bridge + *facere* make. See etym. of doublet **pontiff.**]

**pon|tiff** (pon′tif), *n.* **1** = pope. **2** a bishop. **3** a chief priest or high priest. **4** a member of the principal college of priests in ancient Rome; pontifex. [< Middle French *pontife,* learned borrowing from Latin *pontifex.* See etym. of doublet **pontifex.**]

**pon|tif|i|cal** (pon tif′ə kəl), *adj., n.* —*adj.* **1** of or having to do with the Pope; papal. **2** of or having to do with a bishop; episcopal. **3a** characteristic of a pontiff; stately; dignified; pompous. **b** = dogmatic.
—*n.* a book containing the forms for sacraments and other rites and ceremonies to be performed by bishops.
**pontificals,** the vestments and marks of dignity used by cardinals and bishops at certain ecclesiastical functions or ceremonies: *For a bishop to ride on hunting in his pontificals ... is against public honesty* (Jeremy Taylor).
—**pon|tif′i|cal|ly,** *adv.*

**pon|tif|i|cate** (*n.* pon tif′ə kit, -kāt; *v.* pon tif′ə-kāt), *n., v.,* **-cat|ed, -cat|ing.** —*n.* the office or term of office of a pontiff.
—*v.i.* **1** to behave or speak pompously. **2** to officiate as a pontiff, especially as a bishop.
[< Latin *pontificātus, -ūs* office of a pontifex (< *pontifex, -ficis*) + English *-ate*[3]]

**pon|tif|i|ca|tion** (pon tif′ə kā′shən), *n.* **1** the act of pontificating: [*A*] *study of a question that has recently been a subject for much pontification but very little analysis* (Economist). **2** something said or written in a pompous manner: *After these pontifications it is truly startling to turn to twelve pages of epilogue* (Economist).

**pon|tif|i|ces** (pon tif′ə sēz), *n.* plural of **pontifex.**

**pon|til** (pon′təl), *n.* = punty.

**pon|tine** (pon′tīn, -tin), *adj.* of or having to do with the pons.

**Pont l'É|vêque** or **pont l'é|vêque** (pôɴ′ lā-vek′), a soft Cheddar cheese made of cream thickened by heat. [< *Pont l'Évêque,* a region in France where this cheese was first made]

**pont|lev|is** (pont lev′is), *n.* = drawbridge. [< French *pont-levis* < *pont* bridge (see etym. under **pontoon**[1]) + *levis* movable (up and down), ultimately < Latin *levāre* raise]

**Pon|to|caine** (pon′tə kān), *n. Trademark.* tetracaine hydrochloride.

**pon|ton** (pon′tən), *n. U.S. Army.* pontoon[1] (def. 1). [< French *ponton*]

**ponton bridge** = pontoon bridge.

**pon|to|nier** (pon′tə nir′), *n.* a soldier or officer in charge of bridge equipment or the building of pontoon bridges. [< French *pontonnier* < *ponton;* see etym. under **pontoon**[1]]

**pon|toon**[1] (pon tün′), *n.* **1** a low, flat-bottomed boat, or some other floating structure, used as one of the supports of a temporary bridge. **2** either of the two boat-shaped parts of an airplane, for landing on or taking off from water; float. Pontoons are watertight and are filled with air. **3** a caisson, especially a caisson used in salvage work at sea, as in raising a sunken ship or removing wreckage. [< French, Middle French *ponton* < Latin *pontō, -ōnis* < *pōns, pontis* bridge]

**pon|toon**[2] (pon tün′), *n. British.* a card game; twenty-one. [origin uncertain]

**∗pontoon bridge**

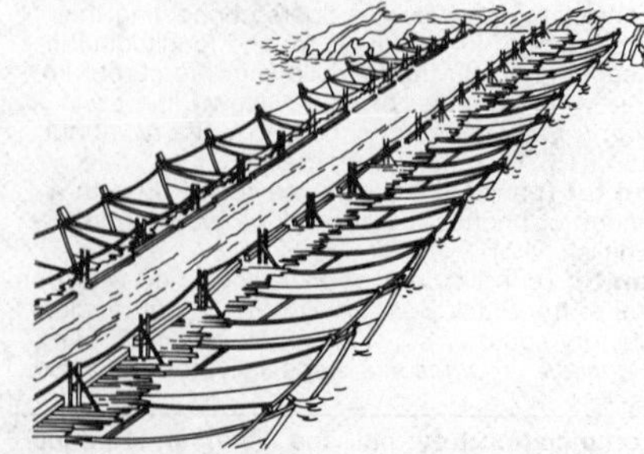

**∗pontoon bridge,** a temporary bridge supported by low, flat-bottomed boats or other floating structures.

**pontoon train,** *Military.* a train of vehicles carrying pontoons and other bridge equipment.

**po|ny** (pō′nē), *n., pl.* **-nies,** *v.,* **-nied, -ny|ing.** —*n.* **1** a kind of small horse, such as the Shetland pony. Ponies are usually less than five feet tall at the shoulder. **2** any small horse. **3** *Informal.* **a** a translation of a book, which a pupil uses instead of translating the book himself; trot. **b** any notes or help used by a student instead of doing his schoolwork; crib. **4** *Informal.* **a** a small glass, usually holding less than two ounces, for alcoholic liquor. **b** the amount such a glass will hold: *to drink a pony of brandy.* **5** something small of its kind. **6** *British Slang.* the sum of 25 pounds sterling.
—*v.t., v.i. U.S. Slang.* to translate with the aid of a pony.
**pony up,** *U.S. Slang.* **a** to pay (money), especially in settling an account: *I wish you'd pony up your end of the legal fee to Swineforth* (New Yorker). **b** to come up with; produce: *The man of doubtful social habits and temperamental vagaries cannot pony up the required quota of references* (Harper's).
[< French *poulenet* a little foal (diminutive) < *poulain* foal, ultimately < Latin *pullus* young animal]

**pony edition,** an edition of a newspaper or magazine that is smaller than the main edition, often through omission of advertising or local news items, designed especially for shipment by air to overseas subscribers.

**pony engine,** a small locomotive for switching railroad cars.

**pony express,** a system of carrying letters and very small packages in the western United States in 1860 and 1861 by relays of men riding fast ponies or horses.

**Pony League,** a group of baseball clubs for children thirteen and fourteen years old: *In Little League, players perform on a half-sized diamond ... Pony Leagues use a diamond three-quarters the regulation size* (Wall Street Journal).

**po|ny|skin** (pō′nē skin′), *n.* **1** the skin of a pony with the hair left on. **2** a fabric made like this in markings and texture.

**∗po|ny|tail** (pō′nē tāl′), *n.* an arrangement of a woman's or girl's hair in which it is pulled back and bound, with the ends falling free from where the hair is gathered, close to the crown of the head.

**∗ponytail**

**po|ny|tailed** (pō′nē tāld′), *adj.* wearing a ponytail.

**po|ny|trek|king** (pō′nē trek′ing), *n. Especially British.* travel by pony.

**pony truck,** a two- or four-wheeled leading or trailing truck, on some locomotives.

**pooch** (püch), *n. Slang.* a dog. [American English; origin unknown]

**pood** (püd), *n.* a Russian weight, equal to 36.113 pounds. [< Russian *pud* < Scandinavian (compare Norwegian, Old Icelandic *pund*), ultimately < Latin *pondus* weight]

**poo|dle** (pü′dəl), *n.* a dog with thick, curly hair often clipped and shaved in an elaborate manner. Poodles are black, brown, gray, or white. They were originally bred for use as gundogs but now are virtually always kept as pets. There are standard, miniature, and toy varieties. [< German *Pudel,* short for *Pudelhund* < dialectal German *pudeln* to splash water] —**poo′dle|like′,** *adj.*

**poodle cloth,** a woolly cloth with a nubby texture caused by the large knots in the weaving.

**poodle cut,** an arrangement of a woman's hair in short, small, close ringlets resembling a poodle's fur.

**poof**[1] (püf), *n., interj.* —*n.* a sound imitating a short sharp puff of the breath as in blowing out a candle.
—*interj.* an expression of contemptuous rejection. Also, **pouf.**
[imitative]

**poof**[2] (püf), *n., pl.* **poofs** or **pooves.** *British Slang.* a male homosexual. [ultimately < French *pouffe* puff]

**pooh** (pü), *interj., n., v.* —*interj., n.* an exclamation of contempt: *Pooh! You don't dare jump. "Pooh! pooh" cries the squire; "all stuff and nonsense"* (Henry Fielding).
—*v.t., v.i.* to pooh-pooh.

**Pooh-Bah** or **pooh-bah** (pü′bä′), *n.* **1** a person holding many offices or positions, especially many small offices without much authority. **2** a very pompous person. [< *Pooh-Bah,* a character in *The Mikado,* by Gilbert and Sullivan, who fills many insignificant offices]

**pooh-pooh** (pü′pü′), *v., interj.* —*v.t.* to express contempt for; make light of: *An authority on nutrition pooh-poohed the idea that we are better off with less fat in hot weather* (New York Times).
—*v.i.* to pooh-pooh someone or something.
—*interj.* an exclamation of contempt.

**poo|ka** (pü′kə), *n.* (in Irish legend) an evil spirit, sometimes in the form of an animal, such as a horse or rabbit: *Ireland's Celtic saints built Christian shrines of turf and mud to fend off pixies, pookas, hobgoblins and leprechauns* (Time). [Old English *pūca*]

**pool**[1] (pül), *n.* **1** a tank of water to swim or bathe in: *a swimming pool.* **2** a small body of still water; small pond: *There were several deep pools in the old stone quarry where the boys went swimming.* **3** a still, deep place in a stream. **4** a puddle: *After the heavy rains the fields were filled with pools of water.* (*Figurative.*) *On the floor I saw ... A little pool of sunlight* (G. Macdonald). **5** a section of an oil field in which petroleum is accumulated in the pores of sedimentary rock; oil pool. **6** *Medicine.* a collection of an abnormal quantity of blood in some part of the circulatory system of the body. [Old English *pōl*]

**∗pool**[2] (pül), *n., v.* —*n.* **1** a game, a form of billiards, played on a special table with six pockets. The players try to drive numbered and colored balls into the pockets with long sticks called cues. They usually use 15 object balls and a cue ball. **2a** things or money put together by different persons for common advantage: *The hikers put all their food and money in a pool.* **b** a group of people, usually having the same skills, who are drawn upon as needed: *the labor pool, a secretarial pool.* **c** a group, as of people, having the same need, or a group of public utilities having the same service: *an electric pool, a car pool to get to work.* **3** an arrangement between several companies or groups to prevent competition by controlling prices. **4** the persons who form a pool. **5a** a fund raised by a group of persons for purposes of speculation in the stock market, commodities, or the like. **b** the members of such a group. **6a** the total of the stakes played for or raced for in some games; pot. The pool may be won or may supply the winnings. **b** the total staked by a group of players, who will share proportionately in the event of winning. **c** the participants in such a game or race, or the members of such a group. **7** *Fencing.* a contest in which each member of one team fights each member of the other.
—*v.t.* to put (things or money) together for common advantage: *The three boys pooled their savings to buy a boat. They work as a team, pooling their knowledge and their talents* (New Yorker).
—*v.i.* to enter into or form a pool.
[< French *poule* booty, hen, perhaps < Old French *poule* hen, young fowl < Late Latin *pulla* chick < Latin *pullus;* meaning influenced by *pool*[1]]

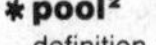

**∗pool**[2]
definition 1

**pool hall,** = poolroom.

**pool|room** (pül′rüm′, -ru̇m′), *n.* **1** a room or place in which the game of pool is played. **2** a place where people bet on races or games. [American English < *pool*[2] + *room*]

**pool|side** (pül′sīd′), *n., adj.* —*n.* the area beside a swimming pool.
—*adj.* at the poolside; beside a swimming pool: *a poolside party.*

**pool table,** a billiard table with six pockets, on which pool is played.

**poon** (pün), *n.* **1** any one of a group of large East Indian trees, whose light, hard wood is used for masts and spars. **2** the wood of any one of these trees. [< Singhalese *pūna,* or Tamil *punnai*]

**poop**[1] (püp), *n., v.* —*n.* **1** a deck at the stern above the ordinary deck, often forming the roof of a cabin. **2** the stern of a ship.
—*v.t.* **1** (of a wave) to break over the stern of (a ship): *The frigate was pooped by a tremendous*

*sea* (Frederick Marryat). **2** (of a ship) to receive (a wave) over the stern.
[< Old French *poupe,* earlier *pope* < Italian *poppa* < Latin *puppis, -is* stern]

**poop²** (püp), *v.t., v.i. Slang.* to make or become exhausted: *A set of tennis in the hot sun really poops me.*
**poop out,** to become exhausted, lose vigor: *This ivy was green at a time when other ivies had pooped out* (New Yorker).
[origin unknown]

**poop³** (püp), *n. U.S. Slang.* information; gossip: *The current astronomical poop is that canals are ... optical illusions* (New Yorker). [origin unknown]

**poop⁴** (püp), *n.* = nincompoop.

**poop deck,** = poop¹ (def. 1).

**pooped** (püpt), *adj. Slang.* tired; exhausted: *I'm too pooped to think any more* (New Yorker).

**-pooped,** *combining form.* having a ___ poop: *High-pooped* = *having a high poop.*

**poor** (pu̇r), *adj., n.* —*adj.* **1** having few things or nothing; lacking money or property; needy: *The children were so poor that they had no shoes. The poor man had nothing, save one little ewe lamb* (II Samuel 12:3). **2** not good in quality; lacking something needed: *poor soil, poor milk, a poor story.* **3** small in amount; scanty: *a poor crop. Upon this discovery the treasure-seekers, already reduced to a poor half dozen ... fled outright* (Robert Louis Stevenson). SYN: insufficient, inadequate. **4** lacking ability; inefficient: *a poor cook, a poor head for figures.* **5** not satisfactory; frail: *poor health.* **6** needing pity; unfortunate: *This poor child is hurt. The voter who seems likely to be commiserated with most ... is the poor taxpayer* (Newsweek). **7** not favorable: *a poor chance for recovery.* **8** shabby; worn-out: *a poor, threadbare coat.*
—*n.* **the poor,** persons who have very little or nothing: *The destruction of the poor is their poverty* (Proverbs 10:15).
[Middle English *pore,* short for *pouere* < Old French *povre* < Latin *pauper, -eris,* related to *paucus* few. See etym. of doublet **pauper.**]
—**poor′ness,** *n.*
—*Syn. adj.* **1 Poor, penniless, impoverished** mean with little or no money or property. **Poor** has a rather wide range of meaning, from being needy and dependent on charity for the necessities of life, to having no money to buy comforts or luxuries: *She is a poor widow.* **Penniless** means without any money at all, but sometimes only temporarily: *She found herself penniless in a strange city.* **Impoverished** means reduced to poverty from comfortable circumstances, even wealth: *Many people became impoverished during the depression of the 1930's.*

**poor box,** a box for receiving contributions of money for the relief of the poor, usually set at the entrance of a church.

**poor boy,** *U.S. Slang.* a hero sandwich.

**poor boy sweater,** a kind of close-fitting, knitted pullover.

**Poor Clare** (klãr), a member of an order of Franciscan nuns founded by St. Clare at Assisi in 1212. Poor Clares live under varying rules of poverty, at one time being absolutely dependent upon alms.

**poor farm,** *U.S.* a farm maintained at public expense by a government, especially a county government, as a place in which very poor people may live and work.

**poor|house** (pu̇r′hous′), *n.* formerly, a house in which paupers lived at public expense; almshouse; workhouse.

**poor|ish** (pu̇r′ish), *adj.* somewhat poor; of rather poor quality.

**poor law,** a law providing for the relief or support of the poor.

**poor|ly** (pu̇r′lē), *adv., adj.* —*adv.* in a poor manner; not enough; badly; meanly: *A desert is poorly supplied with water. Tom did poorly in the test.*
—*adj. Informal.* in bad health.

**poor man's,** that is a smaller, cheaper, easier, lighter, or otherwise lesser version of something or someone: ... *Spengler, the poor man's Nietzsche* (New Statesman). *Blue Scout Junior* [*is*] *called the "poor man's rocket" because of its low cost* (New York Times).

**poor man's weatherglass,** = scarlet pimpernel.

**poor mouth,** *Dialect or Informal.* **1** a claim or complaint of poverty, especially when exaggerated: *We read the news article ... accusing us of making a poor mouth about Princess Margaret's bills* (New York Times). **2** a person who makes such a claim or complaint: *Roblin* [*was*] *castigating his opponents as "poor mouths" ... who had no faith in Manitoba's future* (Canadian Saturday Night).

**poor-mouth** (pu̇r′mouᴛʜ′), *v.i., v.t. Informal.* to complain of one's economic or other circumstances; speak belittlingly or apologetically of oneself or one's position: *Players from 28 nations ... whizzed in on a chartered plane ... poor-mouthing in many tongues that they were used to clay courts and expected to play miserably on the grass* (Time). *"I sell a few hides to pay the taxes," he poor-mouthed* (Atlantic).

**poor relation,** **1** a relative in humble circumstances: *A Poor Relation ... is a preposterous shadow, lengthening in the noontide of your prosperity* (Charles Lamb). **2** a person or thing of inferior circumstances, secondary importance, or otherwise the lesser in comparison to: *Until a short time ago sculpture in Canada was a poor relation,* [*for*] *sculptors found little sponsorship and a small market* (Atlantic).

**poor-spir|it|ed** (pu̇r′spir′ə tid), *adj.* having or showing a poor, cowardly, or abject spirit.

**poor|tith** (pôr′tith, pōr′-), *n. Scottish.* condition of being poor; poverty. [< Old French *povretet* < Latin *paupertās;* see etym. under **poverty**]

**poor white,** a white person (especially in the southern United States) having little or no money and low social position (often used in an unfriendly way).

**poor|will** (pu̇r′wil), *n.* a bird of western North America that feeds on insects and closely resembles the whippoorwill. It is definitely proved that the poorwill hibernates. [imitative of its note]

**pooves** (püvz), *n.* poofs; a plural of **poof².**

**poov|ey** or **poov|y** (pü′vē), *adj.,* **poov|i|er, poov|i|est.** *British Slang.* of or like pooves; homosexual.

**pop¹** (pop), *v.,* **popped, pop|ping,** *n., adv.* —*v.i.* **1** to make a short, quick, explosive sound: *The firecrackers popped in bunches.* **2** to burst open with a pop: *The chestnuts were popping in the fire.* **3** to move, go, or come suddenly or unexpectedly: *Our neighbor popped in for a short call.* **4** *Informal.* to shoot; fire a gun or pistol. **5** to bulge; protrude: *The surprise made her eyes pop.* **6** *Informal.* to give birth: *Our mammals are popping all the time. Our Bengal tigers had four cubs last year; most of the deer present us with young* (New Yorker). **7** to hit a short, high ball over the infield in baseball. **8** *Slang.* to swallow (a drug in pill form), especially habitually: *Executives ... are popping pills these days to tranquilize their nerves* (New York Times). **9** *British.* to fasten with poppers: *The invaders don midi leather skirts popped up the side with three-quarters of the poppers undone* (London Times).
—*v.t.* **1** to thrust or put suddenly: *She popped her head through the window.* **2** to put (a question) suddenly. **3** to cause to make a sudden explosion; cause to burst open with a pop: *He popped the balloon.* **4** *U.S.* to heat or roast (popcorn) until it bursts with a pop.
—*n.* **1** a short, quick, explosive sound: *We heard the pop of a cork.* **2** a shot from a gun or pistol. **3** a bubbling soft drink: *strawberry pop.* **4** a fly ball in baseball that can easily be caught; pop fly.
—*adv.* with a pop; suddenly.
**pop off,** *Slang.* **a** to fall asleep: *All I need to do is lie down, and I can pop right off.* **b** to die: *I am afraid I shall pop off just when my mind is able to run alone* (Keats). **c** to state loudly as a complaint: *Many of his older colleagues, observing him sourly and listening to him pop off ... thought he was at least partly insane* (New Yorker).
**pop out** (or **up**), to hit a fly ball which is caught by a baseball fielder: *to pop out to left field.*
[imitative]

**pop²** (pop), *adj., n.* —*adj.* **1** *Informal.* popular: *pop songs.* **2** Also, **Pop.** having to do with pop art: *pop paintings.* **3** of or having to do with the popular arts and fashions, especially those reflecting the values and mores of the younger generation: *pop culture. I just don't believe that many young persons in this swinging pop society are left ignorant of the facts of life because of inertia or reticence on the part of our official guardians* (New Scientist).
—*n.* **1** a popular song or tune. **2** Also, **Pop.** = pop art.
[(originally) abbreviation of *popular*]

**pop³** (pop), *n. Informal.* papa; father. [variant of *papa*]

**pop., 1a** popular. **b** popularly. **2** population.

**pop art** or **Pop art,** an art form that uses everyday objects, especially popular mass-produced articles such as comic strips, soup cans, and posters, as its subject matter and sometimes also as the artistic material or medium itself: *Pop art is thought to be the art of everyday things and banal images—bathroom fixtures, Dick Tracy—but its essential character consists in redoing works of art. Its scope extends from Warhol's rows of Coca-Cola bottles to supplying the "Mona Lisa" with a mustache* (New Yorker).

**pop artist,** an artist who produces works of pop art.

**pop|corn** (pop′kôrn′), *n.* **1** a kind of Indian corn, the kernels of which burst open and puff-out when heated. See picture under **corn¹. 2** the white, puffed-out kernels. [American English < *pop¹* + *corn¹*]

**pope** or **Pope** (pōp), *n.* **1** Usually, **the Pope.** the supreme head of the Roman Catholic Church: *the last three popes.* The Pope is the bishop of Rome. **2** (in early times) a bishop of the Christian Church. **3** in the Eastern Orthodox Churches: **a** the bishop or patriarch of Alexandria. **b** a parish priest; papa. **4** *Figurative.* a person who assumes, or is considered to have, a position or authority like that of a pope: *Art Nouveau architecture exists, and the pope of it was, of course, Gaudi* (Listener). [Old English *pāpa* < Late Latin *pāpa,* and *pappa* pope < Latin *pāpa* bishop, tutor, in these senses < Greek *páppa,* or *páppas* patriarch, bishop; (originally) father]

**pope|dom** (pōp′dəm), *n.* **1** the office or dignity of a pope. **2** the tenure of office of a pope. **3** the papal government; papacy. **4** a system resembling the papacy.

**Pope Joan,** a card game resembling stops.

**pop|er|y** (pō′pər ē), *n.* the doctrines, customs, and ceremonies of the Roman Catholic Church (used in an unfriendly way).

**pope's nose,** *Slang.* the projecting, terminal portion of a bird's body from which the tail feathers spring.

**pop|eye** (pop′ī′), *n.* a bulging, prominent eye.

**pop|eyed** (pop′īd′), *adj.* having bulging, prominent eyes: *a popeyed, squatting frog.*

**pop fly,** *Baseball.* a short, high fly ball which can be caught quite easily; pop-up.

**pop|gun** (pop′gun′), *n.* a toy gun that shoots a pellet by compressed air, causing a popping sound.

**pop|in|jay** (pop′in jā), *n.* **1** a vain, overly talkative person; conceited, silly person: *as pert and as proud as any popinjay* (Scott). **2** the figure of a parrot, formerly used as a mark to shoot at. **3** *Obsolete.* a parrot. **4** *British.* the green woodpecker. [< Old French *papingay, papegay* < Spanish *papagayo* < Arabic *babaghā'* < Persian *babghā*]

**pop|ish** (pō′pish), *adj.* of or having to do with the Roman Catholic Church (used in an unfriendly way). —**pop′ish|ly,** *adv.* —**pop′ish|ness,** *n.*

**pop|lar** (pop′lər), *n.* **1a** a tree that grows very rapidly and produces light, soft wood. The Lombardy poplar, the cottonwood, and the aspen are three kinds of poplar. Poplars belong to the willow family and are native to temperate regions. **b** its wood. **2a** a tree resembling these in some way, especially the tulip tree. **b** the wood of any one of these trees. [< Old French *poplier,* extended < *pouple* poplar < Latin *pōpulus*]

**pop|lin** (pop′lin), *n.* a ribbed fabric, made of silk and wool, cotton and wool, rayon, or cotton, and used for making dresses, pants, suits, coats and other clothing, curtains, and tents. [< French *popeline,* or *papeline* < Italian *papalina,* feminine (literally) papal, perhaps < the papal capital of Avignon]

**pop|lit|e|al** (pop lit′ē əl, pop′lə tē′-), *adj. Anatomy.* of, having to do with, or in the region of the ham (the hollow part of the leg back of the knee). [< New Latin *popliteus* (*musculus*) (muscle) of the ham (< Latin *poples, -itis* ham, back of the knee) + English *-al¹*]

**pop|off** (pop′ôf′, -of′), *n. U.S. Informal.* a person who expresses complaints or opinions in a noisy, pretentious, or irresponsible way: [*He*] *has seemed irritable, withdrawn ... a reckless popoff in his informal pronouncements* (Time).

**pop|out** (pop′out′), *n. Surfing.* a poorly made surfboard: *"A lot of gremmies come out just to impress girls, and all they do is sit on their popouts"* (New Yorker).

**pop|o|ver** (pop′ō′vər) *n.* a very light and hollow muffin made from a batter similar to that used for Yorkshire pudding. [American English < *pop¹* + *over*]

**pop|pa** (pop′ə), *n. U.S. Informal.* **1** father. **2** any elderly man.

**pop|per** (pop′ər), *n.* **1** a person or thing that pops. **2** *U.S.* a wire basket or metal pan used for popping popcorn. **3** *British.* a snap fastener; press-stud.

**pop|pet** (pop′it), *n.* **1** a valve that controls flow, such as of water or gas, by moving straight up and down instead of being hinged. **2a** one of the small pieces of wood on the gunwale of a boat forming the rowlocks. **b** a timber placed beneath a ship's hull to support the ship in launching: *The workers then build strong supports called pop-*

---

**Pronunciation Key:** hat, āge, cãre, fär; let, ēqual, tėrm; it, īce; hot, ōpen, ôrder; **oil, out;** cup, pu̇t, rüle; **ch**ild; lo**ng**; **th**in; ᴛʜen; **zh,** measure; ə represents **a** in about, **e** in taken, **i** in pencil, **o** in lemon, **u** in circus.

*pets on the launching timbers at the bow and the stern* (Robert S. Burns). **3** a bead that can be attached to other beads by a snap coupling to form a chain. Poppets are used especially to make necklaces, bracelets, etc., adjustable in length. **4** *Especially British.* a small or dainty person, especially a pretty child or girl; pet: *"Little poppet!" she murmured to herself, maternally reflecting upon Florence's tender youth* (Arnold Bennett). **5** *Obsolete.* **a** a doll. **b** a puppet. [Middle English variant of *puppet*]

**pop|pet|head** (pop′it hed′), *n.* the tailstock or the headstock of a lathe.

**pop|pied** (pop′ēd), *adj.* **1** covered or adorned with poppies. **2** affected by or as by opium; listless.

**pop|ping crease** (pop′ing), *Cricket.* a line parallel to the wicket, marking the batsman's position.

**pop|ple**[1] (pop′əl), *v.,* **-pled, -pling,** *n.* —*v.i.* to move in a tumbling, irregular manner, as boiling water.
—*n.* a rolling or tossing of water in choppy tumultuous waves.
[probably imitative. Compare Middle Dutch *popelen* to murmur, babble.]

**pop|ple**[2] (pop′əl), *n. Dialect.* a poplar.

**pop|py** (pop′ē), *n., pl.* **-pies.** **1** a kind of plant with delicate, showy, red, yellow, or white flowers and roundish capsules containing many small seeds. The juice from the capsule of one variety is used to make opium. **2** any one of various related plants, such as the California poppy. **3** the flower of any one of these plants. **4** a bright red; poppy red. **5** *U.S.* an artificial flower resembling a poppy sold in an annual drive by the American Legion and several other veterans' groups as a means of raising funds for their charitable activities. [Old English *popig,* earlier *popæg,* perhaps ultimately < Latin *papāver*]

**pop|py|cock** (pop′ē kok′), *n., interj. Informal.* nonsense; bosh: *All this profit-sharing and welfare work and insurance ... is simply poppycock* (Sinclair Lewis). [American English, perhaps < Dutch *poppekak* (literally) soft dung]

**Poppy Day,** *U.S.* a day when artificial poppies are sold to help disabled veterans, usually any day of the week which ends on the Saturday before Memorial Day, or Memorial Day proper.

**poppy family,** a group of dicotyledonous herbs, widely distributed in north temperate regions, having a milky juice and flowers of various colors. The family includes the poppy, bloodroot, celandine, and California poppy.

**pop|py|head** (pop′ē hed′), *n. Architecture.* an ornamental finial, often richly carved, as at the top of the upright end of a bench or pew.

**poppy red,** = poppy (def. 4).

**poppy seed,** the seed of the poppy, used in baking to flavor rolls, bread, and cookies, especially by scattering over the top, and as a filling in cakes and pastries.

**pops** (pops), *adj. Slang.* having to do with or performing musical pieces of general or popular appeal: *a pops concert.* [< plural of *pop*[2]]

**Pop|si|cle** (pop′sə kəl), *n. Trademark.* molded ice cream or fruit-flavored ice on a stick.

**pop|skull** (pop′skul), *n. U.S. Slang.* bootleg whiskey or other liquor.

**pop|ster** (pop′stər), *n. U.S. Slang.* a pop artist.

**pop|sy** (pop′sē), *n., pl.* **-sies.** *Slang.* an affectionate name for a girl; a pretty girl. [< dialectal *pop* (< *poppet*) + *-sy,* as in *fubsy*]

**pop-top** (pop′top′), *adj., n.* —*adj.* provided with a tab or other device for opening without a can opener or bottle opener: *a pop-top beer can.*
—*n.* a pop-top container.

**pop|u|lace** (pop′yə lis), *n.* the common people; the masses: *The populace, who hated Pompey, threw flowers upon the tribune as he passed* (James A. Froude). [< French *populace* < Italian *popolaccio* < *popolo* people < Latin *populus*]

**pop|u|lar** (pop′yə lər), *adj., n.* —*adj.* **1** liked by most people: *a popular song.* **2** liked by acquaintances or associates: *Her good nature makes her the most popular girl in school.* **3** of the people; by the people; representing the people: *a popular election. The United States has a popular government.* **SYN:** See syn. under **general. 4** widespread among many people; common: *It is a popular belief that black cats bring bad luck.* **SYN:** prevalent, prevailing, current. **5** suited to the people: *popular prices, books on popular science.*
—*n. British.* a newspaper or magazine designed to appeal to the general public: *There were perplexing shifts in public taste which seemed to benefit the "quality" papers at the expense of the "populars"* (Manchester Guardian Weekly).
[< Latin *populāris* < *populus* people]

**popular front** or **Popular Front,** a coalition of communist, socialist, and moderate political parties against fascism, especially in France.

**pop|u|lar|ise** (pop′yə lə rīz), *v.t.,* **-ised, -is|ing.** *Especially British.* popularize.

**pop|u|lar|ist** (pop′yə lə rist), *adj.* seeking popular interest or participation; appealing to or involving the general public: *a popularist administration.*

**pop|u|lar|i|ty** (pop′yə lar′ə tē), *n.* the fact or condition of being liked by most of the people: *Few Presidents in history ever have achieved anywhere near the popularity of Mr. Eisenhower* (Newsweek).

**pop|u|lar|i|za|tion** (pop′yə lər ə zā′shən), *n.* **1** the act of popularizing: *The Bulletin, therefore, thinks it proper to devote its pages once again to a task of scientific popularization* (Bulletin of Atomic Scientists). **2** the state of being popularized.

**pop|u|lar|ize** (pop′yə lə rīz), *v.t.,* **-ized, -iz|ing.** to make popular, especially by writing about (a subject) in a way that is understandable to most people. —**pop′u|lar|iz′er,** *n.*

**Popular Latin,** the popular or commonly used form of Latin which was the main source of French, Spanish, Italian, Portuguese, and Romanian; Vulgar Latin.

**pop|u|lar|ly** (pop′yə lər lē), *adv.* **1** in a popular manner: *The book is popularly written ... and contains only a modest amount of technical information* (Bulletin of Atomic Scientists). **2** by the people; in general: [*He was*] *seeking to be the first popularly elected Democratic Senator in the history of this usually rock-ribbed Republican state* (Wall Street Journal).

**popular sovereignty, 1** the political principle that sovereignty rests in the people, who rule themselves through their representatives. The French Revolution and the American Revolution were based on the idea of popular sovereignty. **2** *U.S.* a doctrine advocated before the Civil War that the settlers of new territories had the right to decide in their own legislatures whether or not they wanted slavery; squatter sovereignty.

**popular vote,** the vote of the entire electorate, thought of as including all the people, as opposed to the electoral vote.

**pop|u|late** (pop′yə lāt), *v.t.,* **-lat|ed, -lat|ing. 1** to live in; inhabit: *This city is densely populated. The novels were populated with people who ... were fated ... to be baulked of the success they deserved* (London Times). **2** to furnish with inhabitants: *Europe populated much of America.* **SYN:** people. [< Medieval Latin *populare* (with English *-ate*[1]) < Latin *populus* people]

**pop|u|la|tion** (pop′yə lā′shən), *n.* **1** the people of a city, country, or district: *The impending overpopulation of the earth can be prevented only by a policy of stabilizing the population of every country* (F. S. Bodenheimer). *Population ... increases in a geometrical ratio, subsistence in an arithmetical ratio* (Thomas R. Malthus). **2** the number of people: *a population of 1,000,000, an increasing population.* **3** a part of the inhabitants distinguished in any way from the rest: *the urban population.* **4** the act or process of furnishing with inhabitants. **5** *Statistics.* the entire group of items or individuals from which the samples under consideration are presumed to come. **6** *Biology.* **a** the aggregate of organisms that inhabit a particular locality or region. **b** a (specified) portion of this aggregate: *the deer population of North America.* **7** Also, **Population.** *Astronomy.* one of two numbered groups (Population I and II) into which the stars of the various galaxies have been divided for classification, as on the basis of color or position: *The type I population ... is represented by our region of the galaxy and was accordingly the first to be recognized* (Robert H. Baker).

**pop|u|la|tion|al** (pop′yə lā′shə nəl), *adj.* of or having to do with population: *Speech tends to be one of the most persistent populational characters* (A. L. Kroeber).

**population explosion,** a rapid increase in population caused by a rise in the birth rate, usually accompanied by a decline in the death rate, because of advances, such as in medicine and agricultural output: *There was growing understanding of the danger of the population explosion that threatens the world* (Science News Letter).

**population inversion,** *Physics.* a state in which enough gas molecules are brought down to a lower energy level to prevent the loss of energy all at once.

**population parameter,** *Statistics.* a quantity that is constant for a particular distribution of a population but varies for other distributions.

**pop|u|la|tor** (pop′yə lā′tər), *n.* a person or thing that populates or peoples.

**pop|u|lism** (pop′yə liz əm), *n.* belief in or devotion to the needs, rights, and aspirations of the common people: *He imbibed ... their populism, their bias against the bigwigs and entrenched power* (Saturday Night).

**Pop|u|lism** (pop′yə liz əm), *n. U.S.* the principles and policies of the Populists.

**pop|u|list** (pop′yə list), *adj., n.* —*adj.* characterized by or based upon populism: *populist liberalism.*
—*n.* a supporter or advocate of populism.
[< *Populist*]

**Pop|u|list** (pop′yə list), *n., adj. U.S.* —*n.* a member or supporter of the People's Party, a political party formed in the United States in 1891. The Populists advocated government control of the railroads, limitation of private ownership of land, an increase in currency, and an income tax.
—*adj.* = Populistic.
[American English < Latin *populus* people + English *-ist*]

**Pop|u|lis|tic** (pop′yə lis′tik), *adj.* of or having to do with Populism or Populists.

**Populist Party,** = People's Party.

**pop|u|lous** (pop′yə ləs), *adj.* **1** full of people; having many people per square mile: *the most populous state of the United States.* **2** *Figurative.* plentiful; abundant: *Mormon crickets, on the other hand, will be less populous this year* (Science News Letter). [< Latin *populōsus* < *populus* people] —**pop′u|lous|ly,** *adv.* —**pop′u|lous|ness,** *n.*

**pop-up** (pop′up′), *n., adj.* —*n.* **1** *Baseball.* a pop fly: *A full swing might produce a useless strike-out or pop-up* (New Yorker). **2** a part of a book, greeting card, or child's game, that springs up when a cover or thing it is attached to is opened.
—*adj.* of or having to do with something that pops up: *a pop-up book, a pop-up toaster.*

**p.o.r.,** pay on return.

**por|bea|gle** (pôr′bē′gəl), *n.* a voracious shark of northern waters, that attains a length of from 10 to 12 feet. [< a dialectal Cornish word]

**por|ce|lain** (pôr′sə lin, pōr′-; pôrs′lən, pōrs′-), *n.* **1** a very fine earthenware, usually having a translucent white body and a transparent glaze; china: *Teacups are often made of porcelain.* (*Figurative.*) *The precious porcelain of human clay* (Byron). **2** a dish or other object made of this material. [< French *pourcelaine* < Italian *porcellana* a cowrie shell; chinaware < *porcella* young sow < Latin *porcus* hog (because the shell is shaped like a pig's back)]

**porcelain clay,** = kaolin.

**por|ce|lained** (pôr′sə lind, pōr′-; pôrs′lənd, pōrs′-), *adj.* covered or lined with porcelain.

**porcelain enamel,** = enamel (def. 1).

**por|ce|lain|ize** (pôr′sə lə nīz, pōr′-; pôrs′lə-, pōrs′-), *v.t.,* **-ized, -iz|ing.** to coat (a surface) with something hard like porcelain.

**por|ce|la|ne|ous** or **por|cel|la|ne|ous** (pôr′sə-lā′nē əs, pōr′-), *adj.* resembling porcelain.

**por|cel|la|nite** (pôr′sə lə nīt, pōr′-; pôr sel′ə nīt, pōr-), *n.* a clay hardened by natural baking, somewhat resembling porcelain or jasper.

**porch** (pôrch, pōrch), *n.* **1** a covered entrance to a building. **2** *U.S.* **a** a veranda. **b** a room open to the outside air, often having no walls, or walls of screen or glass: *a sleeping or dining porch.* **3** = portico. [< Old French *porche* < Latin *porticus, -ūs.* See etym. of doublet **portico.**]

**Porch** (pôrch, pōrch), *n.* **the, 1** the Stoic school of philosophy. **2** = Stoa. [translation of Greek *stoâ* porch (because of the public covered walk in ancient Athens where the philosopher Zeno taught)]

**porch climber,** *Informal.* a thief who gains entrance to a house by climbing a porch or veranda.

**por|cine** (pôr′sīn, -sin), *adj.* **1** of pigs or hogs. **2** like or characteristic of pigs or hogs; swinish: *The porcine head of the churchwarden was not on his shoulders by accident* (George MacDonald). [< Latin *porcīnus* < *porcus* hog]

***porcupine**

***por|cu|pine** (pôr′kyə pīn), *n., pl.* **-pines** or (*collectively*) **-pine.** an animal covered with quills or spines growing in its coarse hair. The porcupine is a rodent and there are several kinds, such as the North American porcupine with short quills or the European porcupine with long quills. [< Old French *porc-espin* < Latin *porcus* hog, pig + *spīna* thorn, spine]

**porcupine anteater,** = echidna.

**porcupine fish,** = sea porcupine.

**porcupine grass**, = spinifex.

**pore**[1] (pôr, pōr), *v.i.*, **pored, por|ing.** **1** to gaze earnestly or steadily: *She pored over the picture book in silence enjoying the colors.* **2** to study long and steadily: *He would rather pore over a book than play.* **3** to meditate or ponder intently: *He pored over the problem until he solved it.* [Middle English *pouren;* origin uncertain] —**porʹer,** *n.*

**pore**[2] (pôr, pōr), *n.* **1** a very small opening. Sweat comes through the pores in the human skin, and pores in leaves allow for the passage of water and carbon dioxide. The surfaces of pottery and lumber have pores. *Like human skin, soil has holes that are called pores* (Science News Letter). See diagram under **skin.** **2** *Astronomy.* one of many dark spots on the surface of the sun. [< Old French *pore,* learned borrowing from Latin *porus* < Greek *póros* (literally) passage < *perân* to penetrate, pass]

**por|gy** (pôrʹgē), *n., pl.* **-gies** or (*collectively*) **-gy.** any of various saltwater food fishes of Mediterranean and Atlantic waters. The scup and the sea bream or red porgy are two kinds. [American English; origin uncertain]

**Po|rif|er|a** (pə rifʹər ə), *n.pl.* the phylum comprising the poriferans.

**po|rif|er|an** (pô rifʹər ən, pō-), *n., adj.* —*n.* any one of a phylum of water animals with highly porous bodies, through which water passes continuously, that live attached to the sea-bottom; sponge.
—*adj.* of or having to do with the sponges.
[< New Latin *Porifera* the phylum (< Late Latin *porus* hole, passage (see etym. under **pore**[2]) + Latin *ferre* to bear) + English *-an*]

**po|rif|er|ous** (pô rifʹər əs, pō-), *adj.* **1** having pores. **2** of or having to do with the sponges; poriferan.

**po|rism** (pôrʹiz əm, pōrʹ-), *n. Geometry.* any one of various differently defined propositions of the ancient Greek mathematicians, especially as an extra proposition or corollary inserted by Euclid's commentators, or as a proposition affirming the possibility of finding such conditions as will make a certain problem indeterminate, or capable of innumerable solutions. [< Late Latin *porisma* < Greek *pórisma* a deduction, a corollary < *porízein* to deduce, carry < *póros* way, path, ford]

***pork** (pôrk, pōrk), *n.* **1** the meat of a pig or hog, used for food: *salt pork, a roast of pork.* **2** *U.S. Slang.* money from Federal or state appropriations, taxes, licenses, or other fees, spent to confer local benefits for political reasons. [< Old French *porc* < Latin *porcus* hog, pig]

***pork**
definition 1

bacon

loin chops

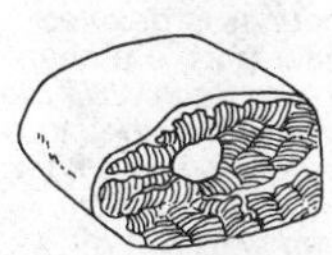
shoulder arm roast

rib chops

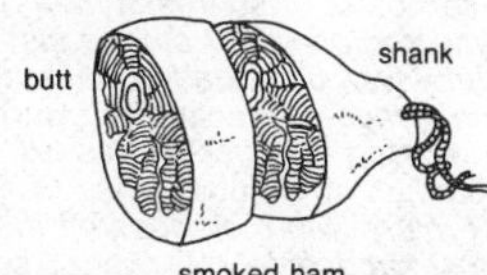

smoked ham

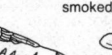

spareribs

tenderloin

**pork barrel**, *U.S. Slang.* a Federal or state appropriation for a project that will benefit or appeal to a particular body of constituents, although it may not fulfill a need: *Democrats are counting, too, on the traditional election-year pork barrel to help a troubled candidate here and there* (Wall Street Journal). —**porkʹ-barʹrel,** *adj.*

**pork-bar|rel|ing** (pôrkʹbarʹə ling, pōrkʹ-), *n., adj. U.S. Slang.* —*n.* the use of Federal or state appropriations for private or political advantage.
—*adj.* given to or engaged in pork-barreling: *pork-barreling politicians.*

**pork|er** (pôrʹkər, pōrʹ-), *n.* a pig, especially one fattened to eat: *Beechmast is very good feeding for swine to make them porkers, and for bacon* (Captain John Smith).

**pork|fish** (pôrkʹfishʹ, pōrkʹ-), *n., pl.* **-fish|es** or (*collectively*) **-fish.** a fish of the Atlantic coast from Florida to Brazil, resembling a sea bream; grunt.

**pork|ling** (pôrkʹling, pōrkʹ-), *n.* a young pig.

**pork|pie** (pôrkʹpīʹ, pōrkʹ-), *n.,* or **pork pie, 1** a hat with a low, round crown, flat on top, and resembling the meat pie in shape. **2** *British.* a deep, circular pie of pastry enclosing minced pork.

**porkpie** or **pork-pie hat,** = porkpie (def. 1).

**pork|y** (pôrʹkē, pōrʹ-), *adj.,* **pork|i|er, pork|i|est.** **1** of or like pork: *a porky taste.* **2** fat: *a porky face.*

**porn** (pôrn), *n., adj. Slang.* —*n.* **1** pornography: *Printed matter is still the most common form of porn* (Time). **2** = porno (defs. 2 and 3).
—*adj.* pornographic: *porn films.*

**por|no** (pôrʹnō), *n., pl.* **-nos,** *adj. Slang.* —*n.* **1** = pornography. **2** a pornographic motion picture. **3** a writer of pornography.
—*adj.* = pornographic.

**por|nog|ra|pher** (pôr nogʹrə fər), *n.* a person who writes, sells, or distributes pornography.

**por|no|graph|ic** (pôrʹnə grafʹik), *adj.* of or having to do with pornography; obscene. —**porʹno-graphʹi|cal|ly,** *adv.*

**por|nog|ra|phy** (pôr nogʹrə fē), *n.* **1** writings or pictures dealing with sexual matters in a manner intended to incite lust, and therefore considered obscene: *Local penalties against possession and distribution of pornography are small and not enforced effectively* (Newsweek). **2** a description or portrayal of any activity regarded as obscene: *In recent years the movies and television have developed a pornography of violence far more demoralizing than the pornography of sex* (Arthur Schlesinger, Jr.). [ultimately < Greek *pórnē* harlot + English *-graphy*]

**po|ro|mer|ic** (pôʹrə merʹik, pōʹ-), *adj., n.* —*adj.* (of a plastic) having a very high degree of porosity; consisting of millions of microscopic pores: *poromeric shoe material.*
—*n.* a poromeric plastic material: *The poromerics—because they "breathe" and thus simulate the properties of leather—are still the only suitable alternative to natural leather in men's footwear* (New Scientist and Science Journal).
[< *poro*(us) + (poly)*meric*]

**po|ros|i|ty** (pô rosʹə tē, pō-), *n., pl.* **-ties.** **1** a porous quality or condition. **2** a porous part or structure. **3** the ratio of the number of pores of a substance to the volume of its mass.

**po|rous** (pôrʹəs, pōrʹ-), *adj.* full of pores or tiny holes; permeable, as by water, air, or light: *the soil retains or even improves its desirable porous structure* (K. S. Spiegler). *Cloth, blotting paper, and ordinary earthenware are porous.* —**poʹrous|ly,** *adv.* —**poʹrous|ness,** *n.*

**por|phyr|i|a** (pôr firʹē ə), *n.* a metabolic disorder marked by the presence of excess porphyrins, especially in the body tissue, blood, and urine. [< New Latin *porphyria* < *porphyrin*]

**por|phyr|ic** (pôr firʹik), *adj., n.* —*adj.* affected with porphyria.
—*n.* a person affected with porphyria.

**por|phy|rin** (pôrʹfər in), *n. Biochemistry.* any one of a group of derivatives of pyrrole, especially an iron-free decomposition product of hematin or a magnesium-free decomposition product of chlorophyll. Porphyrins occur as basic substances especially in body tissue, blood, and urine. [< Greek *porphýrā* purple + English *-in*]

**por|phy|rite** (pôrʹfə rīt), *n.* a kind of porphyry containing triclinic feldspar and no quartz. [< Latin *porphyrītēs* < Greek *porphyrítēs* like purple < *porphýros* purple]

**por|phy|rit|ic** (pôrʹfə ritʹik), *adj.* **1** of, having to do with, containing, or resembling porphyry. **2** of the nature or structure characteristic of porphyry; containing distinct crystals embedded in a compact groundmass. —**porʹphy|ritʹi|cal|ly,** *adv.*

**por|phy|roid** (pôrʹfə roid), *n.* a rock resembling porphyry or of porphyritic structure, especially a sedimentary or igneous rock that has been altered by some metamorphic agency and has taken on a more or less perfectly developed porphyritic structure.

**por|phy|rop|sin** (pôrʹfə ropʹsin), *n.* a purple carotenoid pigment found in the rods of the retinas of freshwater fishes and certain frogs, analogous to rhodopsin. [< Greek *porphýrā* purple + *ópsis* sight + English *-in*]

**por|phy|ry** (pôrʹfər ē), *n., pl.* **-ries.** **1** a hard red or purplish rock of ancient Egypt containing crystals of feldspar. **2** any igneous rock in which coarse crystals are scattered through a mass of finer-grained minerals. [< Old French *porphyre, porfire* < Italian *porfiro,* ultimately < Greek *porphýros* purple]

**por|poise** (pôrʹpəs), *n., pl.* **-pois|es** or (*collectively*) **-poise,** *v.,* **-poised, -pois|ing.** —*n.* **1** a sea animal with a blunt, rounded snout, that looks like a small whale. Porpoises are mammals, related to the whale, and live in groups in the northern Atlantic and Pacific oceans. Porpoises eat fish. They are blackish in color with a somewhat paler belly. *The porpoise is a superior animal with a sense of humor, curiosity, and imagination more highly developed than that of a dog* (Atlantic). **2** any one of several other small sea mammals, especially the common dolphin or the bottle-nosed dolphin.
—*v.i.* to move, travel, or dive in the manner of a porpoise; make a series of bumps or plunges: *The Coroner asked ... if it was usual for a machine ... to porpoise when taking off on a perfectly smooth sea* (London Times).
[< Old French *porpeis,* also *porpois,* ultimately < Latin *porcus* hog + *piscis* fish]

**por|ra|ceous** (pə rāʹshəs), *adj.* = leek-green. [< Latin *porrāceus* (with English *-ous*) < *porrum* leek]

**por|rect** (pə rektʹ, pô-), *adj., v.* —*adj. Zoology.* stretched out; extended, especially forward: *porrect mandibles.*
—*v.t.* **1** *Zoology.* to stretch out; extend (a part of the body). **2** *Law.* to put forward; tender (as a document) for examination or correction.
[< Latin *porrectus,* past participle of *porrigere* to stretch forth < *por-* forth + *regere* to stretch, direct]

**por|ridge** (pôrʹij, porʹ-), *n.* a food made of oatmeal or other cereal boiled in water or milk until it thickens: *oatmeal porridge.*
**do (one's) porridge,** *British Slang.* to serve time in prison: *"Some right villains now doing porridge ... could turn out for our lot"* (London Times).
[apparently variant of *pottage*]

**por|ridg|y** (pôrʹij ē, pōrʹ-), *adj.* resembling porridge.

**por|rin|ger** (pôrʹən jər, porʹ-), *n.* **1** a small dish from which soup, porridge, bread and milk, or other runny food can be eaten. It is deeper than a plate or saucer. **2** a small bowl, especially one intended to be used by a child. [Middle English *pottinger,* alteration of earlier *potager* < Old French < *potage* pottage, porridge]

**port**[1] (pôrt, pōrt), *n.* **1** a place where ships and boats can be sheltered from storms; harbor: *The ship sailed into port behind the reef where huge waves were smashing.* **SYN:** See syn. under **harbor.** **2** a place where ships and boats can load and unload; city or town by a harbor: *New York and San Francisco are important ports.* **SYN:** See syn. under **harbor.** **3** = port of entry. **4** *Figurative.* a place, position, or condition in which one takes or may take refuge; haven. [Old English *port* < Latin *portus*]

**port**[2] (pôrt, pōrt), *n.* **1** an opening in the side of a ship to let in light and air or for loading and unloading; porthole: *a cargo port.* **2** a cover for such an opening. **3** an opening in the side of a ship, or in a wall, through which to shoot. **4** an opening in a pipe or cylinder for steam, air, or water to pass through: *The ship pumped water out of its hold from a port near the waterline.* **5** a gate, especially that of a city. [Old French *porte* < Latin *porta* gate]

**port**[3] (pôrt, pōrt), *n., adj., adv., v.* —*n.* the left side of a ship or aircraft when on board facing the bow or front.
—*adj.* **1** on the left side of a ship or aircraft: *the port side of the main deck* (Joseph Conrad). **2** on the left: *Southpaws customarily are reserved for rivals whose principal thumpers swing from the port side* (New York Times). —*adv.* to or toward the left side of a ship or boat.
—*v.t., v.i.* to turn or shift to the left side: *Port the helm.*
[origin uncertain; perhaps < *port*[1]]

**port**[4] (pôrt, pōrt), *n., v.* —*n.* **1** the way of holding one's head and body; bearing: *regal port. She dressed well, and had a presence and port calculated to set off handsome attire* (Charlotte Brontë). **SYN:** carriage, mien. **2** the position of a weapon when ported.
—*v.t.* to bring, hold, or carry (a rifle or sword) across and close to the body with the barrel or blade near the left shoulder.
[< Old French *port* < *porter* to carry < Latin *portāre*]

**port**[5] (pôrt, pōrt), *n.* a strong, sweet wine, that is dark red or tawny, or occasionally white, originally from Portugal. [short for *Oporto* (in Portuguese *O Porto* the Port), a city in Portugal, from which it is shipped]

**port**[6] (pôrt, pōrt), *n. Australian.* a traveling bag; portmanteau.

**Pronunciation Key:** hat, āge, cãre, fär; let, ēqual, tėrm; it, īce; hot, ōpen, ôrder; oil, out; cup, pu̇t, rüle; child; long; thin; ᴛʜen; zh, measure; ə represents **a** in about, **e** in taken, **i** in pencil, **o** in lemon, **u** in circus.

**Port.**, 1 Portugal. 2 Portuguese.
**port|a|bil|i|ty** (pôr′tə bil′ə tē, pōr′-), *n.* 1 the state of being portable; portableness. 2 the condition permitting a worker to transfer his contributions to a pension fund and rights to a pension from the pension fund of one employer to another, or to continue his rights in the same fund in spite of a change in jobs for the same employer.
**port|a|ble** (pôr′tə bəl, pōr′-), *adj., n.* —*adj.* 1 capable of being carried or moved; easily carried: *A portable typewriter can be moved from place to place.* 2 having to do with or designating a pension plan under which a worker's contributions and privileges are carried over from one job or employer to another: *a portable pension plan or legislation.* 3 *Obsolete.* that can be borne or tolerated; bearable: *How light and portable my pain seems now!* (Shakespeare).
—*n.* something designed to be carried or readily moved, such as a typewriter or radio: *My sister's TV is a portable.*
[< Late Latin *portābilis* < Latin *portāre* to carry] —**port′a|ble|ness**, *n.*
**por|ta|ca|val** (pôr′tə kā′vəl, pōr′-), *adj. Anatomy.* having to do with the portal vein and the vena cava.
**por|tage** (pôr′tij, pōr′-; *for n. 1, 2 and v. also* pôr tazh′, pōr-), *n., v.,* **-taged, -tag|ing.** —*n.* 1 the action or work of carrying boats, provisions, or goods overland from one river or lake to another or around a falls, rapids, or shallow water: *The portage of canoes from one lake to the other took two days of tugging and carrying.* 2 the place over which this is done: *As we were carrying the canoe upon a rocky portage, she fell, and was entirely bilged* (Robert Louis Stevenson). 3 the action or work of carrying anything. 4 the cost of carrying; freight charges; porterage. 5 (formerly) **a** the part of a ship's cargo that was set aside as all or part of a seaman's wages. **b** the space set aside for such cargo. **c** the tonnage of a vessel.
—*v.t., v.i.* 1 to carry (boats, provisions, or goods) overland between navigable waters. 2 to make a portage over (a place) or around (rapids, a cataract, or shallow water).
[< Old French *portage* < *porter* to carry]
**por|tal**[1] (pôr′təl, pōr′-), *n.* a door, gate, or entrance, usually an imposing one, such as one in a cathedral. [< Medieval Latin *portale,* noun use of neuter adjective *portalis* portal < Latin *porta* gate]
**por|tal**[2] (pôr′təl, pōr′-), *adj., n.* —*adj.* 1 of or having to do with the transverse fissure of the liver, through which the blood vessels enter. 2 of or having to do with the portal vein.
—*n.* = portal vein.
[< Medieval Latin *portale,* neuter adjective < Latin *porta* gate]
**portal circulation**, the part of the systemic circulation that carries blood from the stomach, pancreas, small intestine, and spleen to the liver.
**por|tal-to-por|tal pay** (pôr′təl tə pôr′təl, pōr′təl- tə pōr′təl), wages paid to an employee for the time he spends going to, and coming from, his actual place of work after having arrived on the grounds of the employer.
**portal vein**, the large vein which carries blood from the small intestine, stomach, pancreas, and spleen to the liver.
**por|ta|men|to** (pôr′tə men′tō, pōr′-; *Italian* pôr′tä men′tō), *n., pl.* **-ti** (-tē). *Music.* a gliding continuously without break from one pitch or tone to another, as in singing or in playing a stringed instrument.
[< Italian *portamento* (literally) a carrying < *portare* to carry < Latin *portāre*]
**por|tance** (pôr′təns, pōr′-), *n. Archaic.* 1 carriage; bearing. 2 conduct; behavior. [< Middle French *portance* action of carrying, favor < Old French *porter;* see etym. under **port**[4]]
**port arms**, 1 the command to bring or hold a rifle or other weapon in front of and diagonally across the body with the barrel up, while standing at attention. 2 the position in which a weapon is thus held.
**por|ta|tive** (pôr′tə tiv, pōr′-), *adj.* 1 easily carried; portable. 2 of, or having the power or function of, carrying. [< Old French *portatif, portative* < *porter* to carry; see etym. under **port**[4]]
**port authority**, a commission appointed to manage a port.
**port|cray|on** (pôrt′krā′ən, pōrt′-), *n.* a holder or handle for a drawing crayon. [< French *portecrayon* (literally) carry crayon]
*****port|cul|lis** (pôrt kul′is, pōrt-), *n.* a strong gate or grating of iron that can be raised or lowered, used to close or open the gateway of an ancient castle or fortress: *Up drawbridge, grooms—what, Warder, ho! Let the portcullis fall!* (Scott). [< Old French *porte coleïce* sliding gate, ultimately < Latin *porta* gate, *cōlāre* to filter through < *cōlum* colander]

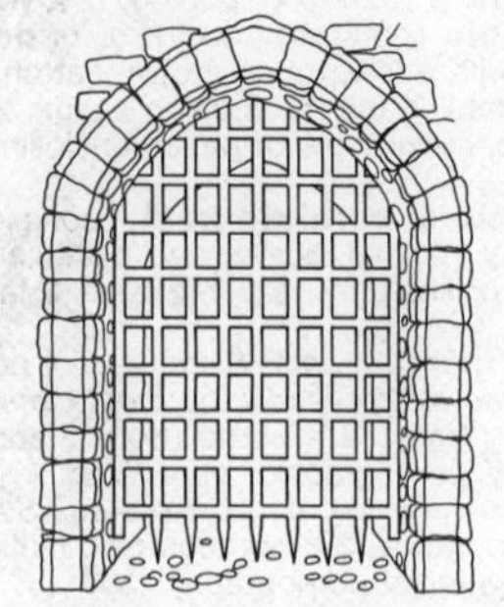
***portcullis**

**port de bras** (pôr də brä′), *pl.* **ports de bras** (pôr də brä′). *French.* 1 the technique of moving the arms in ballet. 2 an exercise or figure through which this technique is developed or displayed.
**Port du Sa|lut** (pôr′ dʏ sȧ lʏ′), a cheese with a hard rind and a soft interior that tastes much like Swiss cheese. Also, **Port Salut.** [< *Port du Salut,* a Trappist monastery in Bayonne, France]
**Porte** (pôrt, pōrt), *n.* the Turkish government before 1923. [< Middle French *porte,* short for *la Sublime Porte* (literally) High Gate, translation of the Turkish official title, with reference to the palace gate at which justice was administered]
*****porte-co|chere** or **porte-co|chère** (pôrt′kō shãr′, pōrt′-), *n.* 1 a porch at the door of a building under which carriages and automobiles stop so that persons getting in or out are sheltered: *They alighted under a porte-cochère with a glass roof* (Winston Churchill). 2 *Archaic.* an entrance for carriages, leading into a courtyard. [< French *porte-cochère* coach gate]

***porte-cochere**
definition 1

**porte-mon|naie** (pôrt′mun′ē, pōrt′-; *French* pôrt′ mô ne′), *n.* a purse; pocketbook. [< French *porte-monnaie* (literally) carry money < *porter* carry + *monnaie* money]
**por|tend** (pôr tend′, pōr-), *v.t.* 1 to indicate beforehand; give warning of; be a portent of: *Black clouds portend a storm.* SYN: foreshadow, betoken, forebode. 2 *Obsolete.* to mean. [< Latin *portendere* < *por-* before + *tendere* to extend]
**por|te|ño** (pôr tān′yō), *n.* a native or resident of Buenos Aires, Argentina. [< American Spanish *porteño* (literally) a port dweller]
**por|tent** (pôr′tent, pōr′-), *n.* 1 a warning, usually of coming evil; sign; omen: *The black clouds were a portent of bad weather.* SYN: token, presage. 2 the fact or quality of portending; ominous significance: *an occurrence of dire portent.* 3 a prodigy; wonder; marvel: *There have been great captains ... But Frederic was not one of those brilliant portents* (Macaulay). [< Latin *portentum,* (originally) neuter past participle of *portendere* to portend]
**por|ten|tous** (pôr ten′təs, pōr-), *adj.* 1 indicating evil to come; ominous; threatening: *direful omens and portentous sights and sounds in the air* (Washington Irving). SYN: foreboding, warning. 2 amazing; extraordinary: *The cause of that celestial anger—the gay, portentous Palmerston* (Lytton Strachey). SYN: wonderful, marvelous. —**por|ten′tous|ly**, *adv.* —**por|ten′tous|ness**, *n.*
**por|ter**[1] (pôr′tər, pōr′-), *n., v.* —*n.* 1 a man employed to carry loads or baggage, especially at a hotel, railroad station, or airport: *Give your bags to the porter.* 2 *U.S.* an attendant in a parlor car or sleeping car of a railway train.
—*v.t.* to carry as a porter: *Enough drink had been portered on the big trays to inflame an army* (New Yorker).
[< Old French *porteour* < Late Latin *portātor* < Latin *portāre* to carry]
**por|ter**[2] (pôr′tər, pōr′-), *n.* 1 a person who guards a door or entrance; doorman: *The porter let them in.* 2 = janitor. [< Anglo-French *porter,* Old French *portier* < Late Latin *portārius* < Latin *porta* gate]
**por|ter**[3] (pôr′tər, pōr′-), *n.* 1 a heavy, dark-brown beer. 2 *Obsolete.* a mixture of light beer, or ale, and stout, resembling this in flavor and color. [short for *porter's ale,* apparently < *porter*[2] (the original consumers)]
**por|ter|age** (pôr′tər ij, pōr′-), *n.* 1 the act or work of a porter. 2 the charge for this.
**por|ter|ess** (pôr′tər is, pōr′-), *n.* = portress.
**por|ter|house** (pôr′tər hous′, pōr′-), *n.* 1 a choice beefsteak cut from the thick end of the short loin and containing the tenderloin. See picture under **beef.** 2 *Archaic.* **a** an establishment at which porter and other malt liquors are sold. **b** a chophouse. [(def. 1) because this cut was allegedly popularized about 1814 by the keeper of a New York porterhouse]
**porterhouse steak**, = porterhouse (def.1).
**port|fo|li|o** (pôrt fō′lē ō, pōrt-), *n., pl.* **-li|os.** 1 a portable case, as for loose papers or drawings; briefcase: *adding to the many notes and tentative essays which had already accumulated in his portfolios* (Samuel Butler). 2 *Figurative.* the position and duties of a cabinet member, diplomat, or minister of state: *The Foreign Minister resigned his portfolio.* 3 *Figurative.* holdings in the form of stocks, bonds, or other securities: *There has been increased buying ... by the managers of larger investment portfolios* (Wall Street Journal). [alteration of earlier *porto folio* < Italian *portafoglia* < *portare* to carry (< Latin *portāre*) + *foglio* sheet, leaf < Latin *folium*]
**port|hole** (pôrt′hōl′, pōrt′-), *n.* 1 an opening in the side of a ship to let in light and air. 2 an opening in a fort, pillbox, side of a tank, ship, or wall, through which to shoot. 3 a port or opening for passage, as of steam or air.
**Por|tia** (pôr′shə, pōr′-), *n.* 1 heroine of Shakespeare's *Merchant of Venice,* who disguises herself and acts as a lawyer. 2 a woman lawyer.
*****por|ti|co** (pôr′tə kō, pōr′-), *n., pl.* **-coes** or **-cos.** a roof supported by columns, forming a porch or a covered walk. [< Italian *portico* < Latin *porticus, -ūs* < *porta* gate. See etym. of doublet **porch.**]

***portico**

**por|ti|coed** (pôr′tə kōd, pōr′-), *adj.* having a portico or porticoes.
**por|tiere** or **por|tière** (pôr tyãr′, pōr-), *n.* a curtain hung across a doorway. [< Middle French *portière* < Old French *porte* door, port[2]]
**por|tion** (pôr′shən, pōr′-), *n., v.* —*n.* 1 a part or share: *A portion of each school day is devoted to arithmetic.* SYN: See syn. under **part.** 2 a quantity of food served for one person: *Each child ate his portion.* 3 the part of an estate that goes to an heir; property inherited. 4 = dowry. 5 one's lot; fate: *This is the portion of a wicked man from God, and the heritage appointed unto him by God* (Job 20:29). SYN: destiny.
—*v.t.* 1 to divide into parts or shares: *When he died his money was portioned out among his children. The country was portioned out among the captains of the invaders* (Macaulay). SYN: apportion. 2 to give (a thing to a person) as a share; give a portion, as of an inheritance or dowry, to: *When I marry with their consent they will portion me most handsomely* (Dickens). SYN: apportion. 3 to provide with a lot or fate.
[< Old French *porcioun, portion,* learned borrowing from Latin *portiō, -ōnis,* related to *pars, partis* part] —**por′tion|er**, *n.*
**por|tion|less** (pôr′shən lis, pōr′-), *adj.* 1 having no portion or share. 2 having no dowry: *a portionless maid.*
**port|land cement** (pôrt′lənd, pōrt′-), cement of burned limestone and clay ground to a fine powder, used in making mortar and concrete. [< the Isle of *Portland,* a peninsula in Dorset, England]
**Portland stone**, a white limestone used in building, quarried in the Isle of Portland, a peninsula in Dorset, England.
**port|li|ness** (pôrt′lē nis, pōrt′-), *n.* portly condition.
**port|ly** (pôrt′lē, pōrt′-), *adj.,* **-li|er, -li|est,** *n., pl.* **-lies.** —*adj.* 1 having a large body; stout; corpulent: *a portly, rubicund man of middle age* (Winston Churchill). SYN: See syn. under **fat.** 2 stately; dignified.
—*n.* 1 a stout man: *Portlies have always had a propensity for double-breasted suits* (Newsweek).

**2** a suit made for a stout man: *Only a few stores carry portlies.*
[< *port*[4]]

**port|man|teau** (pôrt man′tō, pōrt-), *n., pl.* **-teaus** or **-teaux** (-tōz), *adj.* —*n.* a stiff, oblong traveling bag with two compartments opening like a book.
—*adj.* combining two or more different things of the same kind: *a portmanteau revue.*
[< Middle French *portmanteau* < *porter* to carry (see etym. under **port**[4]) + *manteau* mantle]

**portmanteau word**, a word made by combining parts of two words; blend.

**port of call**, a port where ships usually stop to discharge and receive cargo and passengers and take on supplies: *Manila is a port of call for practically all ships plying between India and Eastern Asia* (Colby and Foster).

**port of entry**, a city with a custom house, through which persons or merchandise may enter legally into a country; port.

**por|to|la|no** (pôr′tə lä′nō, pōr′-), *n., pl.* **-nos, -ni** (-nē). **1** a book of sailing directions accompanying a chart, used in the Middle Ages. It was usually drawn on sheepskin and showed the outline of coasts and harbors. **2** any chart or map.
[< Italian *portolano* harbor master, ship pilot]

**Port Or|ford cedar** (ôr′fərd), **1** a tall tree of the cypress family, native to Oregon and northern California; Lawson cypress. **2** the beautiful spotty-grained wood of this tree.

**Por|to Ri|can** (pôr′tə rē′kən, pōr′-), = Puerto Rican.

**por|trait** (pôr′trit, -trāt; pōr′-), *n.* **1** a picture of a person, especially of the face, as in a painting, drawing, or photograph: *Each face that hung in the hall was a portrait of a President.* **2** *Figurative.* a picture in words; description: *That character ... is almost the only exact portrait in the whole book* (Charles Kingsley). **3** a drawing, painting, sketch, or photograph, of any object: *The most ancient extant portrait anyways purporting to be the whale's* (Herman Melville). [< Old French *portrait,* (originally) past participle of Old French *portraire* to portray]

**por|trait|ist** (pôr′trā tist, pōr′-), *n.* a person who paints portraits.

**por|trai|ture** (pôr′trə chůr, -chər; pōr′-), *n.* **1** the act of portraying: *the portraitures of insignificant people by ordinary painters* (Sir Richard Steele). **2** a portrait or portraits. **3** *Figurative.* a picture in words. [< Old French *portraiture* < *portrait* portrait]

**por|tray** (pôr trā′, pōr-), *v.t.* **1** to make a likeness of in a drawing or painting; make a picture of: *to portray a historical scene.* **2** *Figurative.* to picture in words; describe: *The book "Black Beauty" portrays the life of a horse.* SYN: depict. **3** *Figurative.* to represent in a play or motion picture; impersonate; act. [< Old French *pourtraire* < Latin *prōtrahere* reveal, prolong (in Medieval Latin, to draw, paint) < *prō-* forth + *trahere* draw] —**por|tray′er**, *n.*

**por|tray|a|ble** (pôr trā′ə bəl, pōr-), *adj.* that can be portrayed.

**por|tray|al** (pôr trā′əl, pōr-), *n.* **1** a portraying by drawing or in words. **2** a picture or description. **3** the acting of a rôle in a play.

**por|tress** (pôr′tris, pōr′-), *n.* a female porter; woman who acts as a porter.

**Port Sa|lut** (pôr′ sȧ ly′; pôrt′ sə lüt′; pōrt′), = Port du Salut.

**port|side**[1] (pôrt′sīd′, pōrt′-), *n., adj., adv.* —*n.* the left side of a ship when facing the bow; port: *[The] motor whaleboat approached the trawler's starboard quarter, was waved to the portside where a ladder was lowered* (Time).
—*adj.* on the left side; port: *The manager took out his next batter, replaced him with a portside swinger as a pinch hitter.*
—*adv.* to or toward the left side: *The S.S. Champlain slid through morning mist, and, portside, Staten Island dimly floated past* (Atlantic).

**port|side**[2] (pôrt′sīd′, pōrt′-), *n., adj.* —*n.* the waterfront of a port.
—*adj.* waterfront: *portside docks.*

**port|sid|er** (pôrt′sī′dər, pōrt′-), *n. Slang.* a left-handed person, especially a baseball pitcher.

**Por|tu|guese** (pôr′chə gēz′, -gēs′; pōr′-), *n., pl.* **-guese**, *adj.* —*n.* **1** a person born or living in Portugal. **2** the Romance language of Portugal. Portuguese is also the chief language of Brazil.
—*adj.* of or having to do with Portugal, its people, or their language.

**Portuguese cabbage**, a plant related to the cabbage, having thick, broad, edible leaves like those of the cabbage, originally cultivated by the Portuguese of Bermuda.

**Portuguese man-of-war**, *pl.* **Portuguese men-of-war.** a large marine hydrozoan, having a large air sac that acts as a float, and many long thin tentacles. It is noted for brilliant coloring and great power of stinging.

**por|tu|lac|a** (pôr′chə lak′ə, pōr′-), *n.* **1** a low-growing plant with thick, fleshy leaves. It is an herb of the purslane family. **2** its dainty white, yellow, red, or purple flower. [< Latin *portulāca*]

**por|tu|la|ca|ceous** (pôr′chə lə kā′shəs, pōr′-), *adj.* belonging to the purslane family of plants.

**port|wide** (pôrt′wīd′, pōrt′-), *adj.* of or having to do with an entire port: *The threat of a portwide strike by longshoremen receded yesterday* (New York Times).

**port-wine mark** (pôrt′wīn′, pōrt′-), a deep-purple or dark-red birthmark composed of capillaries, usually on the face.

**pos.**, **1** positive. **2** possessive.

**po|sa|da** (pō sä′də; *Spanish* pō sä′ᴛʜä), *n.* **1** an inn. **2** a religious ceremony held in many Mexican homes on the nine nights before Christmas. [< Spanish *posada* < *posar* to lodge < Latin *pausāre;* see etym. under **pose**[1]]

**pose**[1] (pōz), *n., v.,* **posed, pos|ing.** —*n.* **1** a position of the body; way of holding the body: *a natural pose, a pose taken in exercising. She too got up ... Her pose had a kind of defiance in it* (Mrs. Humphry Ward). **2** *Figurative.* an attitude assumed for effect; pretense; affectation: *She takes the pose of being an invalid when really she is well and strong. Her interest in others is real, not just a pose.*
—*v.i.* **1** to hold a position: *He posed an hour for his portrait.* **2** *Figurative.* to take a false position or attitude for effect; make a false pretense: *He posed as a rich man though he owed more than he owned.*
—*v.t.* **1** to put in a certain position; put: *The photographer posed the family before taking the picture.* **2** to put forward for discussion; state: *to pose a question.*
[< Old French *poser* < Late Latin *pausāre* to pause < Latin *pausa* a pause; in Romance languages, influenced by *pos-,* the perfect stem of Latin *pōnere* to place (from the meaning "cause to pause, set down"); this influence spread to many English compounds, such as *compose, dispose, oppose*]

**pose**[2] (pōz), *v.t.,* **posed, pos|ing. 1** to puzzle completely; perplex; nonplus: *Kolory himself would be effectually posed were he called upon to draw up the articles of his faith* (Herman Melville). **2** *Obsolete.* to examine by questioning; interrogate. [variant of *oppose,* or perhaps of *appose*]

**Po|sei|don** (pə sī′dən), *n. Greek Mythology.* the god of the sea and of horses, son of Cronus and Rhea. The Romans called him Neptune. His weapon and attribute is the trident.

**pos|er**[1] (pō′zər), *n.* a person who poses, especially a poseur. [< *pos*(e)[1] + *-er*[1]]

**pos|er**[2] (pō′zər), *n.* **1** a very puzzling problem or question. **2** *Archaic.* a person who examines by questions. [< *pos*(e)[2] + *-er*[1]]

**po|seur** (pō zœr′), *n.* an affected person; one who poses to impress others: *I was ... a little of a prig and poseur in those days* (H. G. Wells). [< French *poseur* < *poser* pose[1]]

**po|seuse** (pō zœz′), *n.* a woman poseur.

**posh** (posh), *adj. Informal.* elegant or fine in appearance; stylish; luxurious: *posh restaurants.* [origin unknown]

**po|sied** (pō′zēd), *adj.* **1** furnished with posies or nosegays. **2** *Archaic.* inscribed with a posy or motto: *Many a ring of posied gold* (Shakespeare).

**pos|i|grade** (poz′ə grād), *adj. Aerospace.* **1** having positive acceleration; going or thrusting forward: *posigrade motion, posigrade rockets.* **2** of or from a posigrade rocket: *a posigrade maneuver.* [< *posi*(tive) + (retro) *grade*]

**pos|it** (poz′it), *v.t.* **1** to lay down or assume as a fact or principle; affirm the existence of; postulate. **2** to place, put, or set. [< Latin, *positus,* past participle of *pōnere* to set, place]

**po|si|tion** (pə zish′ən), *n., v.* —*n.* **1** the place where a thing or person is; place with respect to another place: *The flowers grew in a sheltered position behind the house.* SYN: situation, site, location. See syn. under **place**[1]. **2** a way of being placed: *Put the baby in a comfortable position.* **3** the proper place: *Each soldier got into position to defend the fort.* **4** a condition with reference to place or circumstances: *He maneuvered for position before shooting the basketball.* (*Figurative.*) *Your careless remark put me in an awkward position.* **5** *Figurative.* a job: *He lost his position because he was not honest.* **6** *Figurative.* standing, especially high standing; rank: *He was raised to the position of captain in the navy.* SYN: status. **7** *Figurative.* a way of thinking; set of opinions: *What is your position on this question?* **8** *Greek and Latin Prosody.* the situation of a short vowel before two or more consonants or their equivalent, making the syllable metrically long.
—*v.t.* **1** to place in a certain position; place: *The photographer positioned us so that the tall students stood behind the shorter ones. By adjusting the controls, the nails are fed out of slotted storage banks and positioned as desired* (Wall Street Journal). **2** to determine the position of; locate. **3** to market or advertise (a product) by appealing to a particular type of consumer or specific segment of the public: *The main difficulty manufacturers have in positioning a new product is [that] they want everybody to love their product* (Jack Springer).
[< Latin *positiō, -ōnis* < *pōnere* to set]
—*Syn. n.* **5 Position, situation, job** mean employment. **Position** is somewhat formal and usually suggests white-collar work: *She has a position in a bank.* **Situation** is chiefly used in employment advertising: *situations available.* **Job** is the informal word for employment of any kind, but emphasizes the idea of work to do: *He has a job on a ranch this summer. I don't envy the President his job.*

**po|si|tion|al** (pə zish′ə nəl), *adj.* of, having to do with, or depending on position.

**po|si|tion|er** (pə zish′ə nər), *n.* a person or thing that puts another in a certain position.

**position paper**, a formal statement defining the position of a person or group on a particular issue: *Great stress was laid on agreed position papers ... by the staff of the National Security Council* (Harper's).

**pos|i|tive** (poz′ə tiv), *adj., n.* —*adj.* **1** permitting no question; without doubt: *positive proof. We have positive knowledge that the earth moves around the sun.* SYN: unquestionable, unmistakable, indisputable. **2** sure; confident: *Are you positive you can go? Nor is Socrates positive of anything but the duty of enquiry* (Benjamin Jowett). **3** too sure; too confident: *A positive manner annoys some people. He was a very positive man—the embodiment of authority* (Harper's). SYN: dogmatic. **4a** definite; emphatic: *"No. I will not," was his positive refusal.* SYN: imperative, express. **b** *Informal.* downright; out-and-out: *Most of the luxuries ... are positive hindrances to the elevation of mankind* (Thoreau). **5** that can be thought of as real and present: *Light is a positive thing; darkness is only the absence of light.* **6** showing that a particular disease, condition, germ, or agent is present. **7** that surely does something or adds something; practical: *Don't just make negative criticisms; give us some positive help. The children's constant thought of one another constitutes a positive value* (Saturday Review). **8** tending in the direction thought of as that of increase or progress: *Motion in the direction that the hands of the clock move is positive.* **9** greater than zero; plus: *Five above zero is a positive quantity.* **10a** of the kind of electricity produced on glass when it is rubbed with silk; lacking electrons. **b** characterized by the presence or production of such electricity. **11** having a tendency to lose electrons, and thus to become charged with positive electricity: *Hydrogen and the metals have a positive valence.* **12** *Photography.* having the lines and shadows in the same position as in the original: *the positive image on a print.* **13** of the simple form of an adjective or adverb. **14** *Biology.* moving or turning toward light, the earth, or any other stimulus: *If a plant organ reacts by turning toward the source of a stimulus, it exhibits a positive tropism* (Fred W. Emerson). **15** arbitrarily laid down or imposed; determined by enactment or convention: *positive law.* **16** *Philosophy.* concerned with or based on matters of experience; not speculative or theoretical; empirical. **17** having no relation to or comparison with other things; absolute; unconditional. **18** in machinery: **a** dependable because determined by a firm structure or by exactly controlled forces or movements: *a positive stroke.* **b** functioning for the special purpose required: *positive lubrication.* **19** *U.S.* of or having to do with commodities which cannot be shipped to other countries without an individual export license: *The Commerce Department added several scientific items to its positive list and eased restrictions on others* (Wall Street Journal).
—*n.* **1** a positive degree or quantity. **2** the positive element in an electric battery. **3** *Photography.* a print made from a photographic film or plate. **4** the simple form of an adjective or adverb as distinct from the comparative and superlative. *Fast* is the positive; *faster* is the comparative; *fastest* is the superlative.
[< Latin *positīvus,* ultimately < *pōnere* to set]
—**pos′i|tive|ness**, *n.*

**positive acceleration**, an increase in velocity.

**positive angle**, *Mathematics.* an angle formed by a line rotating in a counterclockwise direction.

**Pronunciation Key:** hat, āge, cãre, fär; let, ēqual, tėrm; it, īce; hot, ōpen, ôrder; **oi**l, **ou**t; cup, pu̇t, rüle; **ch**ild; lo**ng**; **th**in; ᴛʜen; **zh**, measure; ə represents **a** in about, **e** in taken, **i** in pencil, **o** in lemon, **u** in circus.

**positive electricity**, electricity in which the proton is the elementary unit.

**positive eugenics**, eugenics which attempts to increase the genetic transmission of favorable traits by encouraging persons who are above average mentally and physically to have more children.

**positive feedback**, feedback in which the output of a process is returned to its input in such a way that the effect of the process is augmented: *Positive feedback, where the result of an action is used to effect an increase in that action, explains the explosive buildup characterizing the growth of a population* (Frank S. Beckman).

**positive lens**, a convex lens that converges light rays.

**pos|i|tive|ly** (poz′ə tiv lē, poz′ə tiv′lē), *adv.* **1** in a positive way: *He knew positively that he liked camping out.* **2** to an extreme degree; absolutely: *The player was positively furious when the umpire called him out.*

**positive number**, a number that is more than or above zero, indicated by the plus sign. For every positive number, such as +9, there is a negative number of the same arithmetical size (−9). *We must say that the product of two negative numbers is a positive number* (John R. Pierce).

**pos|i|tiv|ism** (poz′ə tə viz′əm), *n.* **1** a philosophical system founded by Auguste Comte, a French philosopher and sociologist, that deals only with positive facts and phenomena, rejecting abstract speculation. **2** a positive condition or quality; definiteness; assurance; dogmatism. [< French *positivisme* (coined by Comte) < *positif* positive + *-isme* -ism]

**pos|i|tiv|ist** (poz′ə tə vist), *n.* a person who maintains the doctrines of positivism.

**pos|i|tiv|is|tic** (poz′ə tə vis′tik), *adj.* of or having to do with the positivists or positivism.

**pos|i|tiv|i|ty** (poz′ə tiv′ə tē), *n.* the state or character of being positive.

**pos|i|tron** (poz′ə tron), *n.* an elementary particle having the same magnitude of mass and charge as an electron, but exhibiting a positive charge, present in cosmic rays and also emitted in beta decay; antiparticle of an electron; positive electron.

**pos|i|tro|ni|um** (poz′ə trō′nē əm), *n. Physics.* an electrically neutral atom consisting of an electron and a positron which destroy each other in less than a millionth of a second: *The source is positronium, a short-lived stuff made of the simplest atom yet discovered* (Science News Letter).

**pos|net** (pos′net), *n. Archaic.* a metal pot or vessel for use in cooking. [< Old French *poçonnet* (diminutive) < *poçon* pot, vessel]

**po|sol|o|gy** (pə sol′ə jē), *n.* the branch of medical science that is concerned with the doses in which medicines should be administered. [< Greek *pósos* how much + English *-logy*]

**poss.**, **1** possession. **2** possessive. **3a** possible. **b** possibly.

**pos|se** (pos′ē), *n.* **1** a group of men summoned by a sheriff to help him: *The posse chased the bandits across the prairie.* **2** = posse comitatus (def. 1). **3** a band, company, or assemblage: *a posse of spectators. A posse of children came down for the summer holidays* (Leonard Merrick). [< Medieval Latin *posse* body of men, power < Latin *posse* to be able]

**pos|se com|i|ta|tus** (pos′ē kom′ə tā′təs), **1** the entire body of male citizens, as the body from which a sheriff is authorized to call for aid in keeping the peace and carrying out certain of his other duties as an officer of the law: *It was his auxiliary duty to muster a posse comitatus or call upon the law-abiding members of the county to set up a "hue and cry" and join the chase* (New Yorker). **2** a group of men summoned by a sheriff to help him; posse. [< Medieval Latin (England) *posse comitatus* force of the county]

**pos|sess** (pə zes′), *v.t.* **1** to own; have as belonging to one: *Washington possessed great force and wisdom.* **2a** to hold as property; hold; occupy: *The first settlers in America possessed great tracts of land that they were to give to other settlers to possess.* **b** to hold as a tenant. **3** to influence strongly; control: *She was possessed by a desire to be rich. ... a naturally taciturn man possessed by an idea* (Joseph Conrad). **4** to control by an evil spirit: *He fought like one possessed. Frank Carney's drama about a young Irish girl who is supernaturally possessed is exciting* (New Yorker). **5** to maintain; keep: *Possess your soul in patience.* **6** *Archaic.* to take; win. **7** *Obsolete.* to put in possession of; give to. [probably back formation < *possession*]

**pos|sessed** (pə zest′), *adj.* **1** dominated by or as by an evil spirit or influence; demoniac; lunatic; mad; crazy: *He upset the table ... and rushed through the coffee-room like one possessed* (Charles J. Lever). **2** having or owning as property or a quality: *a man possessed of more wealth than brains.* **3** remaining calm or steady; composed; self-possessed. —**pos|sessed′ly**, *adv.* —**pos|sessed′ness**, *n.*

**pos|ses|sion** (pə zesh′ən), *n.* **1** a possessing; holding: *Our soldiers fought hard for the possession of the hilltop.* SYN: tenure. **2a** ownership: *At his father's death he came into possession of a million dollars.* **b** the holding or control of a thing as a tenant. **3** a thing possessed; property: *Please move your possessions from my room.* SYN: belonging. **4** a territory under the rule of a country: *Guam is a possession of the United States.* **5** domination as by a particular feeling, idea, or evil spirit: *Under states of possession, devotees experience a change in their customary behavior, even the timbre and pitch of their voice may alter* (Melville J. Herskovits). **6** self-control; composure. [< Latin *possessiō, -ōnis* < *possidēre* to possess]

**pos|ses|sive** (pə zes′iv), *adj., n.* —*adj.* **1** of possession. **2** showing possession. *My, your, his,* and *our* are possessive forms because they indicate who possesses or owns. **3** desirous of ownership: *a possessive nature.* **4** asserting or claiming ownership: *a possessive manner.*
—*n.* **1a** the possessive form of a word or the possessive case. **b** a word showing possession. In "the boy's books," *boy's* is a possessive. **2a** a group of words having the meaning or function of the possessive case. *Example:* of the boy, of the boy's. **b** a possessive pronoun or adjective.
—**pos|ses′sive|ly**, *adv.* —**pos|ses′sive|ness**, *n.*

**possessive adjective**, an adjective that shows possession, formed from a personal pronoun. *My, your, his,* etc., are possessive adjectives.

**possessive case**, *Grammar.* the case that expresses possession, origin, or various other relationships; genitive case. It is regularly formed in singular nouns by the addition of *'s*, as in *the boy's book, James's money, Socrates's wife* (the *s* being sometimes omitted, as in *for conscience' sake, Socrates' wife, Moses' mandates,* either by a natural contraction of two sibilant sounds into one or in order to avoid an unpleasant sequence of sibilants), and in plural nouns ending in *s* by the addition of the apostrophe alone, as in *the boys' books,* and in other plural nouns by the addition of *'s*, as in *men's wear.*

**possessive pronoun**, a pronoun that shows possession. There are two kinds, the substantive form (as *mine* or *yours*), and the attributive form (as *my* or *your*). The latter is also called a possessive adjective.

**pos|ses|sor** (pə zes′ər), *n.* a person who possesses; owner; holder.

**pos|ses|sor|ship** (pə zes′ər ship), *n.* the condition of a possessor.

**pos|ses|so|ry** (pə zes′ər ē), *adj.* **1** having to do with a possessor or possession. **2** arising from possession: *a possessory interest.* **3** having possession.

**pos|set** (pos′it), *n., v.,* **-set|ed, -set|ing** or (*sometimes*) **-set|ted, -set|ting.** —*n.* a hot drink made of milk curdled, as by ale or wine, and sweetened and spiced. It was formerly widely used as a remedy for colds.
—*v.t.* **1** to give or administer a posset to: *As she laid him in bed and possetted him, how frail and fragile he looked* (Arnold Bennett). **2** *Obsolete.* to curdle like a posset.
[Middle English *possot*]

**posset cup**, a cup, often with two or more handles, used in drinking posset.

**pos|si|bil|i|ty** (pos′ə bil′ə tē), *n., pl.* **-ties.** **1** the condition of being possible: *There is a possibility that the train may be late.* **2** a possible thing, circumstance, person, or event: *There are many possibilities. A whole week of rain is a possibility. Her clearer intellect saw possibilities which did not occur to him* (Anthony Trollope).

**pos|si|ble** (pos′ə bəl), *adj., n.* —*adj.* **1** that can be; that can be done; that can happen: *Come if possible.* **2** that can be true or a fact: *It is possible that she went.* **3** that can be done, chosen, etc., properly: *the only possible action, the only possible candidate.*
—*n.* a possible candidate or winner: *The President and party leaders considered two dozen possibles* (Time).
[< Latin *possibilis* < *posse* be able]
—*Syn. adj.* **1 Possible, practicable, feasible** mean capable of happening or being done. **Possible** means that with suitable conditions and methods something may exist, happen, or be done: *It is possible to cure tuberculosis.* **Practicable** means that under present circumstances or by available means something (a plan, method, invention) can easily or effectively be carried out, done, or used: *The X ray is a practicable way of discovering unsuspected diseases.* **Feasible** suggests that which is likely to work satisfactorily: *No method of preventing cancer is yet feasible.*

**pos|si|bly** (pos′ə blē), *adv.* **1** by any possibility; no matter what happens: *I cannot possibly go.* **2** perhaps: *Possibly you are right.*

**pos|sie** (pos′ē), *n. Australian Slang.* position. Also, **possy.**

**pos|sum** (pos′əm), *n.* **1** = opossum. **2** (in Australia) any one of various phalangers.
**play possum**, to put on a false appearance; pretend ignorance or illness.
[American English, short for *opossum* (which pretends to be dead when attacked)]

**Pos|sum** (pos′əm), *n. British.* a nickname for an electronic device or equipment by means of which a paralyzed person may telephone, type, or operate certain types of machines. [< Latin *possum* I am able, used because of its resemblance to the initials of the technical name of this device, *P*(atient) *O*(perated) *S*(elector) *M*(echanisms)]

**pos|sum|haw** (pos′əm hô′), *n.* **1** a shrub or small tree, a variety of holly, having small, red or orange fruit and growing in the southeastern United States; bearberry. **2** a shrub of the honeysuckle family found in wet areas of the southeastern United States; withe rod.

**pos|sy** (pos′ē), *n., pl.* **-sies.** = possie.

**post**[1] (pōst), *n., v.* —*n.* **1** a piece of timber, metal, or other solid substance firmly set up, usually as a support: *the posts of a door, gate, or bed; a hitching post.* **2a** a post or line where a race starts or ends: *She kept switching her tail while she was being saddled and all during the parade to the post* (New Yorker). **b** = goal post.
—*v.t.* **1** to fasten (a notice) up in a place where it can easily be seen: *The list of winners will be posted soon.* **2** to make known by or as if by a posted notice; make public: *to post a reward. The store posted prices clearly on its shelves.* **3** to put (a name) in a list that is published or posted up: *to post three ships as missing. Her plane is posted on time.* **4** to cover (a wall or fence) with notices or bills. **5** to put up notices warning people to keep out of: *That farmer posts his land against fishing, hunting, camping, and trespassing.*
**pip at** (or **on**) **the post**, *British Informal.* to beat to a goal; defeat at the last minute: *Oxford University having been just pipped on the post by the Australians, are at home to Gloucester* (London Times).
[Old English *post* < Latin *postis, -is* post, (apparently, originally) projecting, perhaps < *por-* forth (for *per-*) + *stāre* to stand]

**post**[2] (pōst), *n., v.* —*n.* **1** the place where a soldier, policeman, fireman, or other guardian is stationed; place where one is supposed to be when one is on duty: *When the fire alarm sounds, each man rushes to his post. Men like soldiers may not quit the post Allotted by the Gods* (Tennyson). **2** a place where soldiers are stationed, especially a military station or fort, or where a policeman is stationed, often for some special duty: *One southern post commander called out his troops and seized a Tunisian road block* (Wall Street Journal). **3** the soldiers occupying a military station, or a policeman occupying a station, often as some special duty. **4** *U.S.* a local branch of a veterans' organization, such as the American Legion or the Veterans of Foreign Wars. **5** a job or position: *the post of secretary, a diplomatic post.* **6** a trading station, especially in an uncivilized or unsettled country; trading post: *Fort Laramie is one of the posts established by the American fur company ... Here ... the arm of the United States has little force* (Francis Parkman). **7** a place on the floor of a stock exchange for trading in certain securities. **8** either or two bugle calls (first post and last post) calling soldiers in the British Army to their quarters for the night.
—*v.t.* **1** to station at a post; place (troops, policemen, or other guardians) at a particular point: *The captain posted guards at the door. Kim felt sure that the boy had been posted to guide him* (Rudyard Kipling). **2** to make a deposit of: *to post bail.* **3** to appoint to a post of command in the armed forces.
**take post**, **a** (formerly in the British Navy) to be commissioned as captain of a ship of not less than 20 guns: *Sir William Sanderson [and others] take post by a general order* (John Chamberlayne). **b** *Military.* to occupy a position: *A body of two thousand men ... were directed to take post at the bridge of Alcantara* (William F. P. Napier).
[< Middle French *poste* < Italian *posto* < Latin *positus,* past participle of *pōnere* to station, place, put]

**post**[3] (pōst), *n., v., adv.* —*n.* **1** a system for carrying letters, papers, or packages; the mail: *I shall send the packages by post.* **2** a single delivery of mail: *This morning's post has come.* **3** *Archaic.* a postman. **4** *Archaic.* a person, vehicle, or ship that carries mail. **5** = post office (def. 1). **6** = letter box. **7a** one of a series of fixed stations along a route for furnishing relays of men and horses for carrying the mail and supplying service to travelers by post horse or post chaise: *The town began as a pony express post and later grew into an important mining center.* **b** the distance between one post or station and the next; stage. **8** a size of paper, about 16 × 20 inches. **9** a newspaper or magazine: *the Saturday Evening Post.* **10** *Obsolete.* a courier; postrider.

**—*v.t.*** **1** to send by post; mail: *to post a letter.* **2** *Informal.* to supply with up-to-date information; inform: *to be well posted on current events. Baseball fans always post themselves as to the standing of the teams.* **3** *Bookkeeping.* **a** to transfer (an entry) from journal to ledger. **b** to enter (an item) in due place and form. **c** to make all requisite entries in (a ledger or other book of account). **—*v.i.*** **1** to travel with post horses or by post chaise: *His father and mother were with him, having posted from home in their carriage* (Samuel Butler). **2** to travel with haste; hurry: *He posted upstairs, taking three steps at once* (Scott). **SYN**: hasten. **3** to rise and fall in the saddle in rhythm with the horse's trot.

**—*adv.*** by post; speedily.

[< Middle French *poste* (originally) relay of horses for couriers < Italian *posta* < Latin, variant of *posita,* feminine past participle of *pōnere* to place]

**post-**, *prefix.* **1** after in time; later: *Postwar = after a war.*

**2** after in space; behind: *Postnasal = behind the nasal cavity.*

**3** after and more or less caused by, as in *postoperative, posttraumatic.*

[< Latin *post-* < *post* after, behind]

**post|age** (pōs′tij), *n.* **1** the amount paid on anything sent by mail: *The postage for airmail is greater than that for regular mail.* **2** the stamp or stamps used to send a letter or package.

**postage meter**, a machine that stamps postage on a letter or package and postmarks it.

**postage stamp**, an official stamp placed on mail to show that postage has been paid.

**post|al** (pōs′təl), *adj., n.* **—*adj.*** having to do with mail and post offices: *postal regulations, a postal clerk.*

**—*n.*** *U.S.* a post card. **—post′al|ly,** *adv.*

**postal card**, **1** a card with a printed postage stamp, issued by the government and used to send a message through the mail. **2** a similar card without a printed postage stamp; post card.

**postal code**, *Canadian.* a combination of six letters and numbers used to identify a mail-delivery zone in Canada. It corresponds to the U.S. Zip Code and the British postcode.

**postal note**, a type of money order formerly issued by U.S. post offices for amounts up to $10.

**postal order**, *British.* a type of money order issued by a post office for one of a number of fixed sums.

**postal service** or **postal system**, the department or agency of a government, in charge of mail: *Benjamin Franklin organized Canada's postal service in 1763.*

**Postal Service**, an independent agency of the United States government, that handles mail, sells postage stamps, and assists in the handling of passports and registration of aliens. It replaced the U.S. Post Office Department in 1971.

**post|au|dit** (pōst ô′dit), *n.* an audit conducted after a transaction has been settled or completed.

**post|ax|i|al** (pōst ak′sē əl), *adj.* **1** behind the axis. **2** of, having to do with, or on the posterior side of the limb of a vertebrate. **—post|ax′i|al|ly,** *adv.*

**post|bag** (pōst′bag′), *n. British.* **1** a mailbag. **2** mail.

**post beetle**, any one of various beetles whose larvae bore into posts and other timber.

**post-bel|lum** (pōst′bel′əm), *adj.* **1** after the war. **2** *Especially U.S.* after the American Civil War: *The cowboy migrations westward were a post-bellum phenomenon* (Horace Gregory). [American English < Latin *post bellum* after the war]

**post|box** (pōst′boks′), *n.* = mailbox.

**post|boy** (pōst′boi′), *n.* **1** a man who rides one of the horses drawing a carriage; postilion. **2** a boy or man who carries mail.

**post|ca|non|i|cal** (pōst′kə non′ə kəl), *adj.* of later date than the canon; written later than the canon of Scripture.

**post card**, or **post|card** (pōst′kärd′), *n.* **1** a card without postage printed on it, usually with a picture on one side, used to send a message through the mail. It is made by a private company. **2** a similar card with a printed postage stamp, issued by the government; postal card.

**post chaise**, a hired four-wheeled carriage that was used for traveling and to carry mail in the 1700's and early 1800's before there were railroads. It usually had seats for two to four people.

**post|clas|sic** (pōst klas′ik), *adj.* = postclassical.

**post|clas|si|cal** (pōst klas′ə kəl), *adj.* existing or occurring after the classic or classical period, especially of Greek and Latin literature or art.

**post|coach** (pōst′kōch′), *n.* a stagecoach used for carrying mail.

**post|code** (pōst′kōd′), *n. British.* a combination of letters and numbers identifying a postal area in Great Britain, used for accelerating mail deliveries. The corresponding system in the United States is the Zip Code.

**post|co|lo|ni|al** (pōst′kə lō′nē əl), *adj.* after a state of colonialism: *postcolonial Africa, a post-colonial regime.*

**post-com|mun|ion** (pōst′kə myün′yən), *n., adj.* **—*n.*** the prayer or prayers said at the end of the Communion service.

**—*adj.*** following the Communion service: *a post-communion address or hymn.*

**post|con|cil|i|ar** (pōst′kən sil′ē ər), *adj.* existing or occurring after the Vatican ecumenical council of 1962-1965.

**post|con|so|nan|tal** (pōst′kon sə nan′təl), *adj.* following immediately after a consonant.

**post-cost** (pōst′kôst′, -kost′), *v.t., v.i.,* **-cost, -cost|ing.** *British.* to review prices and costs in (government contracts) retrospectively.

**post|date** (pōst′dāt′), *v.t.,* **-dat|ed, -dat|ing.** **1** to give a later date than the true date to (a letter, check, document, or publication): *Many of the Berlin newspapers which are published in the evening are postdated by a day* (Charles Lowe). **2** to follow in time.

**post|deb** (pōst deb′), *n. Informal.* a post-debutante.

**post|deb|u|tante** (pōst deb′yə tänt, -tant; pōst′-deb yə tänt′), *n.* a girl who is past her first formal appearance, in society.

**post-di|lu|vi|an** (pōst′də lü′vē ən, -dī-), *adj., n.* **—*adj.*** existing or occurring after the Flood.

**—*n.*** a person who has lived since the Flood.

**post|doc|tor|al** (pōst dok′tər əl), *adj., n.* **—*adj.*** having to do with advanced academic work after the doctorate: *postdoctoral fellowships, postdoctoral research.*

**—*n.*** = postdoctorate.

**post|doc|tor|ate** (pōst dok′tər it), *adj., n.* **—*adj*** = postdoctoral: *Specialization requires two to five years in formal postdoctorate training* (T. B. Eveleth).

**—*n.*** a person who does postdoctoral work: *About half of our scientists are graduate students and young postdoctorates* (Max Perutz).

**post|ed price** (pōs′tid), the price a seller declares for something, such as that set on a barrel of crude oil by an oil-producing country: *Nigeria and Venezuela ... raised posted prices (a theoretical base figure for taxes that influences the actual selling price) to more than $14 per bbl.* (Time).

**post|em|bry|on|ic** (post em′brē on′ik), *adj.* following the embryonic stage of life or growth.

**post|er**[1] (pōs′tər), *n., adj.* **—*n.*** **1** a large printed sheet or notice put up in some public place. Posters usually contain attractive pictures or designs to catch people's attention. **2** a person who posts notices.

**—*adj.*** *Informal.* having posts: *a four-poster bed.* **—post′er|like′,** *adj.*

**post|er**[2] (pōs′tər), *n.* **1** = post horse. **2** *Obsolete.* a person who travels swiftly.

**poste res|tante** (pōst′ res tänt′), **1** a direction written on mail which is to remain at the post office till called for. **2** a post-office department in charge of such mail. [< French *poste restante* < *poste* post[3], *restante* remaining < Old French *rester* to rest]

**pos|te|ri|or** (pos tir′ē ər), *adj., n.* **—*adj.*** **1** situated behind; back; rear; hind: *The tail of an animal is on the posterior part of the body.* **2** later; coming after. **SYN**: subsequent, succeeding, following. **3** *Botany.* situated on the side nearest the axis; superior.

**—*n.*** Often, **posteriors**, the buttocks: *He drops upon his knees or posteriors* (Edward Ward).

[< Latin *posterior,* comparative of *posterus* subsequent < *post* after] **—pos|te′ri|or|ly,** *adv.*

**pos|te|ri|or|i|ty** (pos tir′ē ôr′ə tē, -or′-), *n., pl.* **-ties.** **1** the state or quality of being posterior. **2** a posterior position or date.

**post|er|ish** (pōs′tər ish), *adj.* characteristic of or resembling a poster: *posterish paintings.*

**pos|ter|i|ty** (pos ter′ə tē), *n.* **1** generations of the future: *If we burn up all the coal and oil in the world, what will posterity do? Posterity would remember him as the author of many fine poems* (Atlantic). **2** anyone's children, and their children, and their children, and so on and on; all of a person's descendants: *that the inheritance of the king should to to his posterity alone* (Ecclesiasticus 45:25). **SYN**: progeny. [< Latin *posteritās* < *posterus;* see etym. under **posterior**]

**pos|tern** (pōs′tərn, pos′-), *n., adj.* **—*n.*** **1** a back door or gate: *We came through the postern at the rear of the great castle wall.* **2** any small door or gate or private entrance: *We slipped out of the side postern into a night of darkness* (Robert Louis Stevenson).

**—*adj.*** **1** rear; lesser: *The castle had a postern door.* **2** of or like a postern.

[< Old French *posterne,* ultimately < Latin *posterus* behind; see etym. under **posterior**]

**Post Exchange** or **post exchange**, a general store at a military post that sells merchandise and services to military personnel and their dependents. *Abbr:* PX (no periods).

**post|ex|il|i|an** (pōst′eg zil′ē ən, -ek sil′-), *adj.* following the Babylonian exile or captivity of the Jews in the early 500's B.C.

**post|ex|il|ic** (pōst′eg zil′ik, -ek sil′-), *adj.* = postexilian.

**post|face** (pōst′fis), *n.* an explanatory note following the body of a text; afterword. [< *post-* + *-face,* as in *preface*]

**post|fig|ur|a|tive** (pōst fig′yər ə tiv), *adj. Anthropology.* of or designating a form of society in which the values of the adult or older generation predominate.

**post|fix** (*v.* pōst fiks′; *n.* pōst′fiks), *v., n.* **—*v.t.*** to affix at the end of something; append; suffix.

**—*n.*** a word, syllable, or letter added to the end of a word; suffix. [< *post-* + *fix,* verb; patterned on *prefix*]

**post|form|a|ble** (post′fôr′mə bəl), *adj.* that can undergo postforming: *postformable aluminum-polyethylene laminate.*

**post|form|ing** (pōst′fôr′ming), *n., adj.* **—*n.*** the process of bending or shaping a partially hardened thermosetting laminate.

**—*adj.*** used for bending or shaping in this process: *postforming treatment, a postforming table.*

**post|free** (post′frē′), *adj.* **1** free from postage charge. **2** *Especially British.* with the postage prepaid; postpaid.

**post|fron|tal** (pōst frun′təl), *adj.* **1** behind the forehead. **2** toward the rear of the frontal lobe of the cerebrum.

**post|gan|gli|on|ic** (pōst′gang lē on′ik), *adj.* lying within or behind a ganglion. A postganglionic neuron of the autonomic nervous system has its cell body in a ganglion, with its axon extending to an organ.

**post|gla|cial** (pōst glā′shəl), *adj.* coming after the glacial period or ice age; Recent.

**post|grad** (pōst grad′), *n., adj. Informal.* postgraduate.

**post|grad|u|ate** (pōst graj′ù it), *n., adj.* **—*n.*** a student who continues studying in college or at school after graduation; graduate student.

**—*adj.*** **1** taking a course of study after graduation. **2** of or for postgraduates: *postgraduate medical study.*

**posth.**, posthumous.

**post|haste** (pōst′hāst′), *adv., adj., n.* **—*adv.*** very speedily; in great haste: *This ... brought Mr. Beaulieu Plummer posthaste from the estate office up to the house* (H. G. Wells).

**—*adj.*** *Archaic.* done in great haste; very speedy: *The Duke ... requires your haste, post-haste appearance, even on the instant* (Shakespeare).

**—*n.*** *Archaic.* haste or speed like that of a messenger; great speed: *Norfolk and myself, In haste, post-haste, are come to join with you* (Shakespeare).

[apparently < *post*[3] courier + *haste,* noun; perhaps influenced by former letter directions, *haste post! haste*]

**post hoc** (pōst′ hok′), *Latin.* after this; subsequent: *Though all this has been post hoc to the formation of CND, it is of course by no means certain that it has been in any way propter hoc* (Punch).

**post hoc, er|go prop|ter hoc** (pōst′ hok ėr′gō prop′tər hok), *Latin.* after this, therefore as a result of this (a phrase used to denote a common logical fallacy that what comes before an event must also be its cause): *But no cancer-causing agent was known in tobacco smoke, so medical researchers were careful not to fall into the arguing post hoc, ergo propter hoc* (Time).

**post|hole** (pōst′hōl′), *n.* a hole dug in the ground to receive the end of a post.

**post|horn** (pōst′hôrn′), *n.* a small horn similar to a bugle, formerly used by a postrider or the guard of a mail coach to announce arrival. [< *post*[3] + *horn*]

**post horse**, a horse used by persons riding post or hired by travelers.

**post|house** (pōst′hous′), *n.* (formerly) a house where relays of post horses were kept for the convenience of travelers.

**Pronunciation Key:** hat, āge, cãre, fär; let, ēqual, tėrm; it, īce; hot, ōpen, ôrder; **oi**l, **ou**t; cup, pu̇t, rüle; **ch**ild; lo**ng**; **th**in; **ᴛʜ**en; **zh**, measure; **ə** represents **a** in about, **e** in taken, **i** in pencil, **o** in lemon, **u** in circus.

**post|hu|mous** (pos′chu̇ məs), *adj.* **1** happening after death: *posthumous fame.* **2** published after the death of the author: *a posthumous book.* **3** born after the death of the father: *a posthumous child.* [< Late Latin *posthumus,* (with English *-ous*) variant of Latin *postumus* last born; (originally) superlative of *post* after; the *h* appeared because it was erroneously taken as < *post* after + *humus* earth; the grave] —**post′hu|mous|ly,** *adv.* —**post′hu|mous|ness,** *n.*

**post|hyp|not|ic** (pōst′hip not′ik), *adj.* **1** after hypnosis: *a posthypnotic trance.* **2** intended to be carried out after the subject has emerged from hypnosis: *Scientists used posthypnotic suggestion to induce people to ... dream about certain subjects* (Morris Fishbein). —**post′hyp|not′i|cal|ly,** *adv.*

**pos|tiche** (pôs tēsh′), *adj., n.* —*adj.* **1** added inappropriately, as ornament. **2** false; counterfeit. —*n.* **1** an imitation or substitute: *Fastidiousness, at any rate, is very good postiche for modesty* (Ouida). **2** = pretense. **3** a false hairpiece. [< French *postiche* < Italian *apposticcio* < Late Latin *appositīcius* additional < Latin *appōnere* to add to. Compare etym. under **apposite.**]

**pos|ti|cous** (pos tī′kəs), *adj. Botany.* **1** posterior; turning outward. **2** placed on the outer side of a stamen. [< Latin *postīcus* (with English *-ous*) posterior < *post* behind]

**post|ie** (pōs′tē), *n. British Informal.* postman.

**pos|til|ion** or **pos|til|lion** (pōs til′yən, pos-), *n.* a person who guides a team of horses drawing a carriage or post chaise by riding the left-hand horse when one pair is used, or the left-hand horse of the leading pair when two or more pairs are used. [< French *postillon* < Italian *postiglione* < *posta* post, mail]

**post|im|pres|sion|ism** (pōst′im presh′ə niz əm), *n.* a style of painting developed by a group of French artists at the end of the 1800's, which departed from impressionism by its freer use of color, form, design, and expression. Cubism is a later development of postimpressionism.

**post|im|pres|sion|ist** (pōst′im presh′ə nist), *n., adj.* —*n.* an artist who practices postimpressionism. —*adj.* = postimpressionistic.

**post|im|pres|sion|is|tic** (pōst′im presh′ə nis′tik), *adj.* of or having to do with postimpressionism.

**post|in|dus|tri|al** (pōst′in dus′trē əl), *adj.* existing or occurring after industrialization: *Australia has already entered the "postindustrial age"—about half the work force is now white-collar workers* (Donald Horne).

**post|ing**[1] (pōs′ting), *n.* an assignment to a post, station, or position: *the posting of a soldier or policeman.* [< *post*[2] + *-ing*[1]]

**post|ing**[2] (pōs′ting), *n. Bookkeeping.* **1** the transferring of an entry from journal to ledger. **2** the entry of an item in due place and form. **3** the bringing of account books up to date. [< *post*[3] + *-ing*[1]]

**post-Kant|i|an** (pōst kan′tē ən), *adj., n.* = neo-Kantian.

**post-Keynes|i|an** (pōst kān′zē ən), *adj., n.* = neo-Keynesian.

**post|lap|sar|i|an** (pōst′lap sãr′ē ən), *adj.* **1** of the time or condition after a fall, especially the fall of man: *man's ability to establish a new secular humanism in a world not only postlapsarian, but also ... collectivist* (Saturday Review). **2** = sublapsarian. [< *post-* + Latin *lapsus* fall + English *-arian,* as in *prelapsarian*]

**post|lim|i|nar|y** (pōst lim′ə ner′ē), *adj.* of or having to do with the right of postliminy.

**post|lim|i|ny** (pōst lim′ə nē), *n.* (in international law) the right by which persons or things taken in war are restored to their former status when coming again under the control of the nation to which they belonged. [< Latin *postlīminium* a return behind one's own threshold < *post* behind + *līmen, -inis* threshold]

**post|lude** (pōst′lüd), *n.* **1** a concluding musical piece or movement. **2** music, especially an organ solo or voluntary, played at the end of a church service. **3** *Figurative.* any concluding part: *He looked upon the United Nations as, in its own way, a postlude to the League of Nations* (New York Times). [< *post-* + *-lude,* as in *prelude*]

**post|lu|di|al** (pōst lü′dē əl), *adj.* of or like a postlude; concluding: *postludial music.*

**post|man** (pōst′mən), *n., pl.* **-men.** **1** = mailman. **2** *Obsolete.* a postrider.

**postman's knock,** *British.* post office (def. 3).

**post|mark** (pōst′märk′), *n., v.* —*n.* an official mark stamped on mail to cancel the postage stamp and record the place and date of mailing. —*v.t.* to stamp with a postmark: *to postmark a letter.*

**post|mas|ter** (pōst′mas′tər, -mäs′-), *n.* **1** a person in charge of a post office. **2** *Obsolete.* the master of a station for supplying post horses to travelers.

**postmaster general,** *pl.* **postmasters general.** **1** the person at the head of the postal system of a country. **2 Postmaster General,** the chief executive officer of the U.S. Postal Service. He was formerly a member of the President's cabinet.

**post|mas|ter|ship** (pōst′mas′tər ship, -mäs′-), *n.* the office or term of office of a postmaster.

**post|men|o|paus|al** (post′men ə pô′zəl), *adj.* being or occurring after the menopause.

**post|men|stru|al** (pōst men′strú əl), *adj.* being or occurring after menstruation.

**post|me|rid|i|an** (pōst′mə rid′ē ən), *adj.* occurring after noon; of or having to do with the afternoon: *the postmeridian sun.* [< Latin *postmerīdiānus* < *post merīdiem* post meridiem]

**post me|rid|i|em** (mə rid′ē əm), after noon. *Abbr:* p.m., P.M. [< Latin *post merīdiem* after midday; *merīdiem,* accusative of *merīdiēs* < *medius* middle + *diēs* day. Compare etym. under **meridian.**]

**post|mil|le|nar|i|an** (pōst′mil ə nãr′ē ən), *n.* = postmillennialist.

**post|mil|le|nar|i|an|ism** (pōst′mil ə nãr′ē ə niz′əm), *n.* = postmillennialism.

**post|mil|len|ni|al** (pōst′mə len′ē əl), *adj.* of or having to do with the period following the millennium.

**post|mil|len|ni|al|ism** (pōst′mə len′ē ə liz′əm), *n.* the doctrine or belief that the second coming of Christ will follow the millennium.

**post|mil|len|ni|al|ist** (pōst′mə len′ē ə list), *n.* a believer in postmillennialism.

**post|mis|tress** (pōst′mis′tris), *n.* a woman in charge of a post office.

**post-mod|ern** (pōst mod′ərn), *adj.* that develops after a period or movement called *modern.* In the arts the post-modern period is sometimes characterized by an appearance of spontaneous creation or by a markedly identifiable inclusion of elements from past developments of style and technique, *post-modern dance. By now, a large number of architects and critics have conceded that the glass, steel and concrete vocabulary of modern architecture has lost its potency and ... a new, "post-modern" style is evolving* (Paul Goldberger).

**post-mod|ern|ism** (pōst mod′ər niz əm), *n.* a movement, especially in art and design, that embraces post-modern practices of style and technique.

**post-mod|ern|ist** (pōst mod′ər nist), *n., adj.* —*n.* a person who practices or adheres to post-modern style. —*adj.* of or having to do with post-modernists or post-modernism.

**post-mor|tem** or **post|mor|tem** (pōst môr′təm), *adj., n., v.* —*adj.* **1** after death: *A post-mortem examination showed that the man had been poisoned.* **2** of or used in an autopsy or autopsies. **3** *Figurative.* following, and concerned with, some event, often one that is difficult or unpleasant: *a post-mortem debate or discussion.*
—*n.* **1** an examination after death; autopsy: *He carried out a post-mortem on the body ... the first he had carried out on a death caused by a blow* (London Times). **2** *Figurative.* a discussion following, and concerned with, some event, often one that is difficult or unpleasant, such as the loss of an election or the failure of a new play: *a post-mortem in the local coffee shop.*
—*v.t., v.i.* to make or perform an autopsy.
[< Latin *post* after, *mortem,* accusative of *mors, mortis* death]

**post|na|sal** (pōst nā′zəl), *adj.* behind the nose or nasal cavity.

**postnasal drip,** a condition occurring especially in catarrh and sinusitis, in which mucus from the back of the nose drips down the back of the throat, sometimes infecting the bronchial tubes and causing bronchitis.

**post|na|tal** (pōst nā′təl), *adj.* **1** after childbirth: *postnatal care.* **2** occurring after birth: *postnatal diseases of children.* —**post|na′tal|ly,** *adv.*

**post|ne|o|na|tal** (pōst′nē ō nā′təl), *adj.* after being newborn; of the first year of infancy.

**post|nup|tial** (pōst nup′shəl), *adj.* after marriage: *a postnuptial gift to a wife.* —**post|nup′tial|ly,** *adv.*

**post-o|bit** (pōst ō′bit, -ob′it), *n., adj.* —*n.* a written agreement signed by a borrower promising to pay a certain sum of money to the lender on the death of a person whose heir the borrower expects to be.
—*adj.* effective after a person's death.
[short for Late Latin *post obitum* after death < Latin *post* after, *obitum,* accusative of *obitus, -ūs* destruction, death; (literally) an approach to anything < *ob-* to + *-īre* to go]

**post ob|i|tum** (pōst ob′ə təm), *Latin.* after death.

**post office, 1** a place where mail is handled and postage stamps are sold. **2** Often, **Post Office.** the former United States government department in charge of mail, replaced by the Postal Service in 1971: *The Post Office has mechanized the handling of paper work* (Newsweek). **3** a children's game in which players are called to another room (the post office) to be kissed (to get mail). Each player calls for the next.

**post-of|fice box** (pōst′ôf′is, -of′-), Also, **Post Office Box.** a rented box or pigeonhole at a post office, in which all the letters and papers for a private person, firm, or organization are put and kept till called for. *Abbr:* P.O.B.

**post|op|er|a|tive** (pōst op′ə rā′tiv, -ər ə-), *adj.* occurring after a surgical operation: *postoperative care.* —**post|op′er|a′tive|ly,** *adv.*

**post|or|bit|al** (pōst ôr′bə təl), *adj.* situated behind the socket or orbit of the eye.

**post|paid** (pōst′pād′), *adj.* with the postage paid for.

**post-paint|er|ly** (pōst′pān′tər lē), *adj.* of or characterized by a style of painting using traditional painterly qualities of color, form, and texture in producing nonobjective works, such as hard-edges.

**post|par|tum** (pōst pär′təm), *adj.* taking place after the birth of a child: *postpartum hemorrhage.* [< Latin *post* after + *partum,* accusative of *partus, -ūs* a giving birth < *parere* to bring forth]

**post|pone** (pōst pōn′), *v.,* **-poned, -pon|ing.** —*v.t.* **1** to put off till later; put off to a later time; delay: *The ball game was postponed because of rain. He postponed his departure until after supper* (H. G. Wells). SYN: defer. See syn. under **delay.** **2** to place after in order of importance or estimation; subordinate: *to postpone private gain to the public welfare.* —*v.i.* **1** = delay. SYN: defer. See syn. under **delay.** **2** *Medicine.* to be later in coming on or recurring, as an attack of malaria. [< Latin *postpōnere* < *post-* after + *pōnere* to put, place] —**post|pon′a|ble,** *adj.* —**post|pon′er,** *n.*

**post|pone|ment** (pōst pōn′mənt), *n.* the act or fact of putting off till later; putting off to a later time; delay: *The postponement of the ball game disappointed many people.* SYN: deferment.

**post|po|si|tion** (pōst′pə zish′ən), *n.* **1** the act of placing after. **2** the state of being placed after. **3** *Grammar.* a word or particle placed after or at the end of a word, as a modifier or to show syntactical relationship. *Example:* In *postmaster general* the adjective *general* is a postposition. [< Late Latin *postpositiō, -ōnis* < Latin *postpōnere* postpone]

**post|po|si|tion|al** (pōst′pə zish′ə nəl), *adj.* of or having to do with a postposition.

**post|pos|i|tive** (pōst poz′ə tiv), *adj., n. Grammar.* —*adj.* placed after or at the end of a word; enclitic. —*n.* a postpositive word or particle. —**post|pos′i|tive|ly,** *adv.*

**post|pran|di|al** (pōst pran′dē əl), *adj.* after-dinner: *postprandial speeches, a postprandial nap.* [< *post-* + *prandial*] —**post|pran′di|al|ly,** *adv.*

**post|rid|er** (pōst′rī′dər), *n.* a person who carries mail or dispatches on horseback.

**post road, 1** a road or route over which mail is carried. **2** a road with stations which furnish horses.

**post|ro|man|tic** (pōst′rō man′tik), *adj.* = neoromantic.

**post|script** (pōst′skript), *n.* **1** an addition to a letter, written after the writer's name has been signed: *Sir Gervaise, like a woman, had written his mind in his postscript* (James Fenimore Cooper). *Abbr:* P.S. **2** *Figurative.* a supplementary part added to any composition or literary work: *Lazarsfeld ... touches the nerve of the matter in his postscript to the study* (Saturday Review). SYN: addendum, appendix. [short for earlier *postscriptum* < Medieval Latin, (originally) neuter past participle of *postscribere* < Latin *post-* after + *scrībere* to write]

**post|syn|ap|tic** (pōst′si nap′tik), *adj.* occurring after a synapse. —**post′syn|ap′ti|cal|ly,** *adv.*

**post-synch** (pōst singk′), *v.* = post-synchronize.

**post-syn|chro|nize** (pōst sing′krə nīz), *v.t.,* **-nized, -niz|ing.** to synchronize (speech and other sounds) with motion-picture action after a scene or film has been photographed: *The whole film has post-synchronized dialogue, recorded in the peace and concentration of a studio* (Sunday Times). —**post-syn′chro|ni|za′tion,** *n.*

**post ten|e|bras lux** (pōst ten′ə bras luks), *Latin.* after darkness light.

**post|ten|sion** (pōst ten′shən), *v.t.* to subject (concrete) to internal stress after it has hardened.

**post time,** the time set for the start of a horse race.

**post|trau|mat|ic** (pōst′trô mat′ik), *adj.* occurring after a wound: *a posttraumatic disorder.*

**pos|tu|lan|cy** (pos′chə lən sē), *n., pl.* **-cies.** **1** the condition of being a postulant. **2** the period during which this condition lasts.

**pos|tu|lant** (pos′chə lənt), *n.* **1** a candidate, especially for admission to a religious order: *Each year some 75 young women between the ages of 16 and 30 are accepted as postulants* (Time). **2** a person who asks or applies for something; petitioner. [< Latin *postulāns, -antis,* present participle of *postulāre* to demand]

**pos|tu|late** (*n.* pos′chə lit; *v.* pos′chə lāt), *n., v.,* **-lat|ed, -lat|ing.** —*n.* something taken for granted or assumed as a basis for reasoning; fundamental principle; necessary condition: *One postulate*

*in geometry is that a straight line is the shortest distance between any two points. The underlying postulate ... was that knowledge is good and that those who advance knowledge need no further justification for their existence* (Bertrand Russell). **SYN**: hypothesis.
— ***v.t.*** **1** to assume without proof as a basis of reasoning; take for granted; require as a fundamental principle or necessary condition: *Geometry postulates certain things as a basis for its reasoning.* **2** to require; demand; claim.
[< New Latin *postulatum* < Latin *postulāre* to demand] — **pos'tu|la'tion**, *n.*

**pos|tu|la|tion|al** (pos'chə lā'shə nəl), *adj.* of or having to do with postulating.

**pos|tu|la|tor** (pos'chə lā'tər), *n.* **1** a person who postulates. **2** *Roman Catholic Church.* an official appointed to plead for the beatification or canonization of a person.

**pos|tur|al** (pos'chər əl), *adj.* of or having to do with posture: *exercises to correct a postural defect.*

**pos|ture** (pos'chər), *n., v.,* **-tured, -tur|ing.** — ***n.*** **1** the position of the body; way of holding the body: *Good posture is important to health.* **SYN**: carriage, bearing, stance. **2** *Figurative.* a condition; situation; state: *In the present posture of public affairs it is difficult to predict what will happen.* **SYN**: phase. **3** *Figurative.* a mental or spiritual attitude: *A firm policy is likely to be lacking until the President determines what should be the total American posture toward Russia* (Atlantic). **SYN**: outlook. **4** a pose, as of an artist's model; the attitude of a figure in a painting, etc. **5** *Figurative.* an affected or unnatural attitude; contortion of the body: *He would ... dance about him, and make a thousand antic postures and gestures* (Daniel Defoe).
— ***v.i.*** **1** to take a certain posture: *The dancer postured before the mirror, bending and twisting her body.* **2** *Figurative.* to pose for effect.
— ***v.t.*** to put in a certain posture: *Alice had been playing with the mirror's reflections—posturing her arms ... clasping her hands behind her neck* (Booth Tarkington).
[< French *posture* < Italian *postura* < Latin *positūra* < *pōnere* to place] — **pos'tur|er**, *n.*

**pos|tur|ize** (pos'chə rīz), *v.i., v.t.,* **-ized, -iz|ing.** to pose; posture.

**post|ver|te|bral** (pōst'vėr'tə brəl), *adj.* behind the vertebrae. Postvertebral muscles hold the body erect and allow the back to be extended.

**post|vo|cal|ic** (pōst'vō kal'ik), *adj.* following immediately after a vowel.

**post|war** (pōst'wôr'), *adj., adv.* after a war: *postwar economy.*

**post|ward** (pōst'wərd), *adv.* toward the post, as in a race or game: *Vitriolic goes postward tomorrow with ... opposition from five other colts* (New York Times).

**post|wards** (pōst'wərdz), *adv.* = postward.

**po|sy** (pō'zē), *n., pl.* **-sies. 1** a flower. **2** a bunch of flowers; bouquet. **SYN**: nosegay. **3** a motto or line of poetry engraved within a ring. [variant of *poesy*]

**pot**[1] (pot), *n., v.,* **pot|ted, pot|ting.** — ***n.*** **1** a kind of vessel or dish. There are many different kinds and shapes of pots. They are made of iron, tin, earthenware, and other substances. A pot may hold food or drink or contain earth for flowers to grow in. **2a** the amount a pot can hold; potful: *He ate a small pot of beans.* **b** a pot and what is in it. **3** alcoholic liquor: *He carries her into a public-house to give her a pot and a cake* (Daniel Defoe). **4** a basket used to catch fish or lobsters. **5** *Informal.* a large sum of money: *If a man brings in a big new client, his share of the pot can be upped in a single partnership meeting* (Harper's). **6** *Informal.* all the money bet at one time. **7a** = chamber pot. **b** = chimney pot. **8** = potshot. **9** *Slang.* a potbelly. **10** *British Slang.* a person of importance: *one of the principal men out there—a big pot* (Joseph Conrad). **11** *U.S. Slang.* marijuana.
— ***v.t.*** **1** to put into a pot: *to pot young tomato plants.* **2** to cook and preserve in a pot or can. **3** to cook (meat) thoroughly by simmering or braising in a pot. **4** to take a potshot at; shoot: *We had got to within sixty yards' range ... and were just about to sit down comfortably to "pot" them* [*two lions*]*, when they suddenly surprised us by ... bolting off* (J. H. Patterson). **5** *Informal, Figurative.* to seize; win; secure.
— ***v.i.*** **1** to take a potshot; shoot: *These "townies" pot at game birds and animals* (Manchester Guardian Weekly). **2** *Obsolete.* to drink liquor: *I learned it in England, where indeed they are most potent in potting* (Shakespeare).
**go to pot,** to go to ruin: *After losing his job he took to drinking and went to pot.*
**in one's pots,** drunk: *In their pots* [*they*] *will promise anything* (Fynes Moryson).
**keep the pot boiling,** *Informal.* **a** to make a living: *He doesn't earn much money—just enough to keep the pot boiling.* **b** *Figurative.* to keep things going in a lively way: *His lieutenants keep the rebellion pot boiling in ... Ireland* (London Times).
[Old English *pott*] — **pot'like'**, *adj.*

**pot**[2] (pot), *n. Scottish.* a deep hole in the ground; pit. [Middle English *pot;* perhaps special use of *pot*[1]]

**pot.**, potential.

**po|ta|bil|i|ty** (pō'tə bil'ə tē), *n.* potable quality: *the potability of sea water.*

**po|ta|ble** (pō'tə bəl), *adj., n.* — ***adj.*** fit for drinking; drinkable: *In dozens of places where the water was not potable, they set up purifying systems* (Newsweek).
— ***n.*** Usually, **potables, a** anything drinkable: *He bought eatables and potables.* **b** alcoholic liquor.
[< Late Latin *pōtābilis* < Latin *pōtāre* to drink] — **po'ta|ble|ness**, *n.*

**po|tage** (pô tȧzh'), *n. French.* soup.

**po|tam|ic** (pə tam'ik), *adj.* having to do with rivers. [< Greek *potamós* river + English *-ic*]

**pot|a|mol|o|gy** (pot'ə mol'ə jē), *n.* the scientific study of rivers. [< Greek *potamós* river + English *-logy*]

**pot|ash** (pot'ash'), *n.* **1** any one of several substances made from various minerals, wood ashes, blast furnace dust, or the like, and used in making soap, fertilizers, and glass. It is mainly impure potassium carbonate. When purified, it is known as pearlash. **2** potassium or any compound containing potassium. **3** = potassium hydroxide. [< earlier *pot-ashes,* translation of Dutch *potasschen* (literally) pot ashes]

**potash alum,** = alum.

**potash bulbs,** a combination of glass bulbs for holding a solution of potassium hydroxide, used in chemical analysis of organic substances.

**potash feldspar,** = orthoclase.

**po|tass** (pō tas'), *n.* **1** = potash. **2** = potassium.

**po|tas|sa** (pō tas'ə), *n.* potass; potash.

**po|tas|sic** (pə tas'ik), *adj.* **1** of or having to do with potassium. **2** containing potassium.

***po|tas|si|um** (pə tas'ē əm), *n.* a soft, silverwhite, metallic chemical element that occurs in nature only in compounds, such as saltpeter. Potassium is one of the most abundant elements in the earth's crust, and is essential for the growth of plants. It is an alkali metal and oxidizes rapidly when exposed to the air. Its compounds are used in making soap and fertilizers. Potassium is the lightest metal known except lithium. [earlier *potass* (< French *potasse* < New Latin *potassa*) + *-ium,* as in *sodium*]

***potassium**

| symbol | atomic number | atomic weight | oxidation state |
|---|---|---|---|
| K | 19 | 39.102 | 1 |

**po|tas|si|um-ar|gon dating** (pə tas'ē əm är'gon), a method of dating organic, geological, or archaeological specimens by measuring in the rock in which a specimen is found the amount of argon accumulated through the decay of radioactive potassium: *By means of potassium-argon dating, the age of the African man, Zinjanthropus, has been determined to be 1,750,000 years in the past* (Science News Letter).

**potassium bicarbonate,** a colorless, odorless substance with a slightly salty taste, obtained by passing carbon dioxide into a solution of potassium carbonate in water, and used in baking in place of baking powder or yeast, in medicine, and as a fire-extinguishing agent. *Formula:* $KHCO_3$

**potassium bisulfate,** a colorless salt, used in fusing metals and converting tartrates into potassium bitartrate. *Formula:* $KHSO_4$

**potassium bitartrate,** = cream of tartar.

**potassium bromide,** a white, crystalline substance with a pungent, salty taste, used in medicine as a sedative and in photography. *Formula:* KBr

**potassium carbonate,** a white, alkaline salt obtained from wood ashes, etc., used in making glass, soft soaps, and fertilizers; potash. *Formula:* $K_2CO_3$

**potassium chlorate,** a colorless, poisonous, crystalline substance used as an oxidizing agent in explosives and matches. *Formula:* $KClO_3$

**potassium chloride,** a colorless or white, crystalline compound obtained chiefly from carnallite, used in fertilizers and explosives. *Formula:* KCl

**potassium citrate,** a white, crystalline substance used in medicine as a diuretic, expectorant, and antacid. In certain heart operations, potassium citrate is introduced into the coronary blood vessels to arrest heartbeat. *Formula:* $K_3C_6H_5O_7 \cdot H_2O$

**potassium cyanate,** a white crystal or powder used in the manufacture of drugs, in organic synthesis, and to kill weeds and crab grass. *Formula:* KCNO

**potassium cyanide,** a very poisonous, white, crystalline compound used for removing gold from ore, in electroplating, as an insecticide, and in photography. *Formula:* KCN

**potassium dichromate,** a poisonous, yellowish-red, crystalline salt used in dyeing, in photography, and as an oxidizing agent. *Formula:* $K_2Cr_2O_7$

**potassium fluoride,** a white, crystalline, poisonous powder, used as a preservative and a disinfectant, in insecticides, and in etching glass. *Formula:* KF

**potassium hydroxide,** a white, solid substance which releases great heat when it dissolves in water; caustic potash. It is a very strong alkali used in bleaching, in making soft soap, as a reagent, and in medicine. *Formula:* KOH

**potassium iodide,** a colorless or white, crystalline compound, used in manufacturing photographic emulsions, as an additive in iodized table salt, and in medicine as an expectorant. *Formula:* KI

**potassium nitrate,** a white or colorless crystalline compound with a salty taste, produced from sodium nitrate and another potassium compound; niter; saltpeter. It is used as an oxidizing agent, in gunpowder, explosives, and fertilizers, in preserving meat, and in medicine. *Formula:* $KNO_3$

**potassium permanganate,** a dark purple crystalline compound used as an oxidizing agent and disinfectant. *Formula:* $KMnO_4$

**potassium sodium tartrate,** = Rochelle salt.

**potassium sulfate,** a colorless or white, crystalline salt used as a reagent, in fertilizers, in medicine as a cathartic, and in making glass. *Formula:* $K_2SO_4$

**po|ta|tion** (pō tā'shən), *n.* **1** the act of drinking. **2** a drink, especially of alcoholic liquor. [< Old French *potacion,* or *potation,* learned borrowing from Latin *pōtātiō, -ōnis* < *pōtāre* to drink]

**po|ta|to** (pə tā'tō), *n., pl.* **-toes. 1** a plant with a starchy tuber used as a vegetable. It originated in South America and belongs to the nightshade family. Potatoes have trumpet-shaped flowers that are white, bluish, or purplish. **2** this vegetable, which is round or oval, hard, and has a very thin skin; white potato; Irish potato. The potato is one of the most widely used vegetables in Europe and America. **3** = sweet potato. [< Spanish *patata* < Carib (perhaps Taino) *batata* sweet potato]

**potato beetle,** a black-and-yellow striped beetle that devours the leaves of potato plants; Colorado potato beetle.

**potato blight,** a destructive disease of the potato in which the leaves and stem develop yellow, brown, and black spots, caused by a parasitic fungus; late blight.

**potato bug,** = potato beetle.

**po|ta|to-bug bird** (pə tā'tō bug'), = rose-breasted grosbeak.

**potato chip,** a thin slice of raw potato fried in deep fat and salted.

**potato crisp,** *British.* a potato chip.

**potato psyllid,** an insect related to the aphids that attacks potato plants, transmitting a viral disease which causes extensive damage to the leaves.

**potato race,** a race in which each runner picks up and carries to a receptacle, one at a time, potatoes placed at intervals along the course. The potato is often carried with a spoon or knife.

**po|ta|to|ry** (pō'tə tôr'ē, -tōr'-), *adj.* of, having to do with, or given to drinking. [< Late Latin *pōtātōrius* < Latin *pōtāre* to drink]

**potato vine, 1** the potato plant, especially the part above ground. **2** a North American vine of the morning-glory family, having large, white and purplish, funnel-shaped flowers and a large root; man-of-the-earth.

**potato worm,** the larva of a sphinx or hawk moth which attacks potatoes, tomatoes, tobacco, and related plants.

**pot-au-feu** (pô'tō fœ'), *n. French.* **1** beef and vegetables cooked together as a stew. **2** (literally) pot on the fire.

**Pot|a|wat|o|mi** (pot'ə wot'ə mē), *n., pl.* **-mi** or **-mis. 1** a member of a tribe of North American Indians inhabiting the area of Lakes Michigan and Superior. **2** the Algonkian language of this tribe.

**pot barley,** barley which has been ground enough to remove the husks.

**pot|bel|lied** (pot'bel'ēd), *adj.* having a potbelly: *a potbellied bug.*

---

**Pronunciation Key:** hat, āge, cãre, fär; let, ēqual, tėrm; it, īce; hot, ōpen, ôrder; oil, out; cup, pu̇t, rüle; child; long; thin; ᴛʜen; zh, measure;
ə represents **a** in about, **e** in taken, **i** in pencil, **o** in lemon, **u** in circus.

**pot|bel|ly** (pot′bel′ē), *n., pl.* **-lies. 1** a distended or protuberant belly. SYN: paunch. **2** a person who has such a belly. **3** = potbelly stove.

***potbelly** or **potbellied stove**, a round, squat, bulging wood- or coal-burning stove used for heating.

***potbelly stove**

**pot|boil** (pot′boil′), *v.t., v.i. Informal.* to write or otherwise produce (potboilers): *For ten years, hopeful author [Marjorie] Rawlings worked on newspapers, potboiled syndicated verse, wrote (but seldom sold) short stories* (Time).

**pot|boil|er** (pot′boi′lər), *n. Informal.* an inferior work of literature or art produced merely to make a living. [the "boiling pot" is symbolic of the necessities of life]

**pot|bound** (pot′bound′), *adj.* having roots that have grown practically to fill the pot, so the plant cannot grow more without repotting: *a potbound house plant.*

**pot|boy** (pot′boi′), *n.* a man or boy who works in a tavern, serving customers, washing glasses, and doing other chores, especially in the kitchen.

**pot cheese**, *U.S.* cottage cheese, usually in large curds.

**po|teen** (pō tēn′), *n.* (in Ireland) illicitly distilled whiskey. Also, **potheen.** [< Irish *poitīn* (diminutive) < *pota* pot]

**Po|tem|kin Village** (pō tem′kin), a false facade intended to cover up a bad situation or activity: *The Party's myth of a bright future might seem to Russian poets like the biggest Potemkin Village of them all* (New Yorker). [< Prince Grigori *Potemkin,* 1739-1791, a Russian statesman and governor of the Crimea, who is said to have fooled Catherine the Great during her tour of the Crimea in 1787 by building sham villages to hide the area's actual poverty]

**po|tence** (pō′təns), *n.* = potency.

**po|ten|cy** (pō′tən sē), *n., pl.* **-cies. 1** power; strength; being potent: *the potency of an argument, the potency of a drug.* SYN: force, efficacy. **2** power to develop: *Books ... do contain a potency of life in them to be as active as that soul was whose progeny they are* (Milton). SYN: potentiality. [< Latin *potentia* < *potēns, -entis;* see etym. under **potent**]

**po|tent** (pō′tənt), *adj.* **1** having great power; powerful; strong: *a potent ruler, a potent remedy for a disease, potent reasons.* SYN: mighty. **2** exercising great moral influence: *if bravery be the most potent charm to win the favor of the fair* (Francis Parkman). *His good deeds had a potent effect on his comrades.* **3** capable of having sexual intercourse. **4** *Heraldry.* (of a cross) having arms that end in a form like the head of a crutch. See diagram under **cross.** [< Latin *potēns, -entis,* present participle of unrecorded Old Latin *potēre* be powerful, able < *potis* powerful] — **po′tent|ly,** *adv.* — **po′tent|ness,** *n.*

**po|ten|tate** (pō′tən tāt), *n.* **1** a person having great power: *In the base camps of the Big Four, a panoply of potentates and elected chieftains made ready for the fateful journey* (Time). SYN: autocrat. **2** a ruler. Kings, queens, and emperors are potentates. SYN: monarch, sovereign. **3** a powerful city, state, or the like. [< Late Latin *potentātus, -ūs* potentate < Latin, power, dominion < *potēns;* see etym. under **potent**]

**po|ten|tial** (pə ten′shəl), *adj., n.* — *adj.* **1** possible as opposed to actual; capable of coming into being or action: *There is a potential danger of being bitten when one plays with a strange dog. The potential efficiency of modern chemical weapons is generally comparable to that of atomic weapons* (Bulletin of Atomic Scientists). **2** *Grammar.* expressing possibility, as by the use of *may, might, can,* and *could: the potential subjunctive or potential mood of a verb.* **3** *Physics.* existing in a positional form, not as motion. **4** having to do with voltage.
— *n.* **1** something potential; possibility: *Many markets of massive potential await American wares abroad* (Wall Street Journal). SYN: See syn. under **latent. 2** *Grammar.* **a** the potential subjunctive or potential mood. **b** a verb form or verbal phrase used thus. **3** the amount of electrification of a point with reference to some standard; electromotive force expressed in volts. A current of high potential is used in transmitting electric power over long distances. *When the ends of a wire are connected to two points ... such as the terminals of a cell or generator, there will be a current in the wire but the potential of each point of the wire remains constant in time* (Sears and Zemansky). **4** *Physics.* a function or quantity that expresses force, such as electromotive force.
[< Late Latin *potentiālis* < Latin *potentia* potency < *potēns* potent] — **po|ten′tial|ly,** *adv.*

**potential difference**, the difference in the electrical states of two points which causes the flow of current between them. Potential difference is measured by the work required to transfer a unit charge of electricity from one point to the other.

**potential energy**, energy that is due to position or structure not to motion. A tightly coiled spring or a raised weight has potential energy. *The potential energy stored up in a pair of attracting bodies is equal to the work that would be necessary to pull them infinitely apart* (Scientific American).

**po|ten|ti|al|i|ty** (pə ten′shē al′ə tē), *n., pl.* **-ties. 1** potential condition or quality; possibility as opposed to actuality; possible power or capacity: *We feel that the potentialities of the human brain are inexhaustible* (Scientific American). **2** something potential; possibility.

**po|ten|ti|ate** (pə ten′shē āt), *v.t.,* **-at|ed, -at|ing.** to give power or potency to; make more active; strengthen: *Certain narcotics potentiate the effects of alcohol in the body.* SYN: increase, intensify. — **po|ten′ti|a′tion,** *n.* — **po|ten′ti|a′tor,** *n.*

**po|ten|til|la** (pō′tən til′ə), *n.* any one of a large group of low plants of the rose family that have mainly pinnate or palmate compound leaves, and are widely found in temperate regions; cinquefoil. [< New Latin *Potentilla* the genus name < Medieval Latin *potentilla* garden valerian < Latin *potēns, -entis* potent + *-illa,* a diminutive suffix]

**po|ten|ti|om|e|ter** (pə ten′shē om′ə tər), *n.* **1** an instrument for measuring electromotive force. **2** an instrument for changing or controlling electromotive force.

**po|ten|ti|o|met|ric** (pə ten′shē ə met′rik), *adj.* of or by means of a potentiometer.

**po|ten|ti|om|e|try** (pə ten′shē om′ə trē), *n.* the measurement of electromotive force by means of a potentiometer.

**pot|ful** (pot′fu̇l), *n., pl.* **-fuls.** as much as a pot can hold.

**pot furnace**, a furnace in which there are pots for melting small amounts of glass.

**pot|hang|er** (pot′hang′ər), *n.* a rack, bar, or the like, for hanging a pothook or a pot at different heights over an open fire.

**pot|head** (pot′hed′), *n. Slang.* a person who smokes marijuana: *He fears that some potheads will be led on to more dangerous experimentation with the hard drug, heroin* (Saturday Night).

**poth|e|car|y** (poth′ə kãr′ē), *n., pl.* **-car|ies.** *Archaic.* apothecary.

**po|theen** (pō thēn′), *n.* = poteen.

**poth|er** (poтн′ər), *n., v.* — *n.* **1** confusion; disturbance; fuss: *The children are making a great pother about the picnic.* SYN: commotion, flurry. **2** a choking cloud of dust or smoke. **3** mental disturbance.
— *v.t.* to bother; worry. SYN: harass.
— *v.i.* = fuss.
[earlier *puther;* origin uncertain; pronunciation influenced by *bother*]

**pot|herb** (pot′ėrb′, -hėrb′), *n.* **1** any plant whose leaves and stems are boiled for use as a vegetable, such as spinach. **2** a plant used as seasoning in cooking, such as sage or parsley.

**pot|hold|er** (pot′hōl′dər), *n.* a thick pad of cloth or other material for handling hot pots and other utensils.

**pot|hole** (pot′hōl′), *n., v.,* **-holed, -hol|ing.** — *n.* **1** a depression or hollow part forming a defect in the surface of a street or road: *They need frequent wheel alignment because they drive up on curbs and don't bother to steer around potholes* (Maclean's). **2** a deep, round hole, especially one made in the rocky bed of a river by stones and gravel being spun around in the current. **3** a cave entered from the surface.
— *v.i.* to explore caves as a sport or hobby: *Four potholers were ... potholing on the Pennines at Casterton* (London Times).

**pot|holed** (pot′hōld′), *adj.* having many potholes: *potholed streets.*

**pot|hol|er** (pot′hō′lər), *n.* a person who explores caves as a sport or hobby; spelunker.

**pot|hook** (pot′hu̇k′), *n.* **1** a hook for hanging a pot or kettle over an open fire. **2** a rod with a hook for lifting hot pots, or the like. **3** an S-shaped stroke in writing, especially one made by children in learning to write.

**pot|house** (pot′hous′), *n.* a tavern or alehouse.

**pot|hunt|er** (pot′hun′tər), *n.* **1** a person who shoots anything he comes upon regardless of the rules of sport: *flocks [of birds] that have escaped the murderous gun of the pothunter* (George W. Cable). **2** a person who takes part in contests merely to win prizes. **3** a person who hunts for food or for profit. **4** a person who digs up or hunts for archaeological objects as a hobby; amateur archaeologist.

**pot|hunt|ing** (pot′hun′ting), *n., adj.* hunting as a pothunter.

**po|tiche** (pō tēsh′), *n., pl.* **-tiches** (-tēsh′). a vase or jar of Chinese or Japanese style with a rounded or polygonal body narrowing at the top. [< French *potiche* an Oriental porcelain vase < *pot* pot, vessel < Vulgar Latin *pottus*]

**po|ti|cho|ma|ni|a** (pō′tə shō mā′nē ə), *n.* the art or process of imitating Japanese or other painted porcelain by coating the inner surface of glass vessels with designs painted on paper or linen. [< French *potichomanie* < *potiche* (see etym. under **potiche**) + *manie* mania]

**po|tion** (pō′shən), *n.* **1** a drink, especially one used as a medicine or poison, or in magic: *a pitchlike potion of gin and molasses ... a sovereign cure for all colds and catarrhs* (Herman Melville). *You promised me that your charms and potions would secure me her acceptance* (Nicholas P. S. Wiseman). **2** a kind of drink or beverage: *As to the intoxicating potion sold for wine, it is a vile, unpalatable, and pernicious sophistication* (Tobias Smollett). [< Old French *pocion,* or *potion* < Latin *pōtiō, -ōnis.* See etym. of doublet **poison.**]

**Pot|i|phar** (pot′ə fər), *n.* an officer of Pharaoh, who owned Joseph as a slave. Potiphar's wife tried to seduce Joseph (in the Bible, Genesis 39:1-20).

**pot|latch** (pot′lach′), *n., v.* — *n.* **1** a gift or present among certain American Indians of the northern Pacific coast. **2** Also, **Potlatch.** a ceremonial festival among these Indians at which gifts are bestowed on the guests. **3** *U.S. Informal.* a feast at which presents are given and received: *That night there was a grand wedding and a potlatch* (Jack London).
— *v.i.* to give or hold a potlatch: *Accession to political position requires potlatching; no one may inherit rank, found a household, or otherwise acquire rank without giving an elaborate potlatch* (Beals and Hoijer).
[American English < Chinook jargon *potlatch* < Wakashan (Nootka) *patshatl* giving, or a gift]

**pot|lead** (pot′led′), *n., v.* — *n.* a form of graphite or black lead, used to coat the bottom of a racing boat to reduce the friction of the water.
— *v.t.* to treat (a boat) with potlead.

**pot|lick|er** or **pot|lik|ker** (pot′lik′ər), *n.* = pot liquor.

**pot|line** (pot′līn′), *n.* a series of electrolytic cells in which aluminum is produced from alumina dissolved in a cryolite solution.

**pot liquor**, the liquid in which meat or vegetables have been cooked, used as broth, for gravy, or stock for soup.

**pot|luck** (pot′luk′), *n.* **1** whatever food happens to be ready or on hand for a meal: *Come in the house and take potluck with me. Lapham's idea of hospitality was still to bring a heavy-buying customer home to potluck* (William D. Howells). **2** *Figurative.* whatever happens or is available by chance: *If there won't be lamps at the auction I'll take potluck.*

**pot|man** (pot′mən), *n., pl.* **-men.** *British.* a man who works as a potboy.

**pot marigold**, a calendula whose flower heads are sometimes used for seasoning.

**pot of gold**, a rich source of profits: *A down-at-the-heels dowager of industrial high society has discovered a pot of gold in the corporate attic* (Wall Street Journal).

**po|too** (pō tü′), *n.* a large goatsucker of the West Indies and Central America. [imitative of its cry]

**po|to|roo** (pō′tə rü′), *n., pl.* **-roos** or (*collectively*) **-roo.** = kangaroo rat. [< an Australian native word]

**pot|pie** (pot′pī′), *n.* **1** a baked meat pie. **2** a stew, as of chicken or veal, with dumplings.

**pot|pour|ri** (pō′pu̇ rē′, pot pu̇r′ē), *n., pl.* **-ris. 1** a musical or literary medley or mixture: *The orchestra played a potpourri of Italian, French, and Austrian folksongs.* **2** a fragrant mixture of dried flower petals and spices. [earlier, a mixed stew < French *pot pourri,* translation of Spanish *olla podrida* rotten pot. Compare etym. under **olla-podrida.**]

**pot roast**, a cut of beef browned in a pot and cooked slowly with only a little water.

**pot|sherd** (pot′shėrd′), *n.* a broken piece of earthenware. [< *pot*[1] + *sherd*]

**pot|shoot** (pot′shüt′), *v.t., v.i.,* **-shot, -shoot|ing.** to shoot or attack with potshots: *I'm off potshooting eiders ... on the banks of the Northwest River* (Dave Godfrey). (*Figurative.*) *Even such ordinarily responsible papers as ... the weekly Ob-*

*server have joined the raucous "popular" press in potshooting at an old friend* (Time). —**pot′shoot′er**, *n.*

**pot|shot** (pot′shot′), *n., v.,* **-shot|ted, -shot|ting.** —*n.* **1** a shot fired at game to get food, with little regard to skill or the rules of sport. **2** a quick shot at or attack against something from close range or from ambush and without careful aim: *Chinese Reds and their Nationalist enemies are taking potshots at each other between China's mainland and Quemoy* (Wall Street Journal). **3** a random or careless shot: *Ammunition, once scarce, is now plentiful enough to be wasted on potshots at coconuts* (Time). **4** Often, **potshots.** *Figurative.* random or scattered criticism: *Potshots are aimed at a few cherished military institutions, from security checks to the medical corps* (Saturday Review). *He is not afraid to take potshots at some of the widely-held theories of his associates* (New York Times).
—*v.t., v.i.* to take potshots (at); potshoot. —**pot′shot′ter**, *n.*

**pot still**, a still in which heat is applied directly to a pot which contains the mash: *Irish whiskey is made in a pot still, which is simply a pot surrounded by Irish anthracite coal from Kilkenny* (Brendan Behan).

**pot|stone** (pot′stōn′), *n.* a kind of soapstone formerly used to make household utensils.

**pot|sy** (pot′sē), *n., pl.* **-sies. 1** = hopscotch. **2** the pebble used in hopscotch. [origin unknown]

**pot|tage** (pot′ij), *n.* a thick soup of vegetables or of vegetables and meat. [Middle English *potage* < Old French < *pot* pot (< Vulgar Latin *pottus*) + *-age* -age]

**pot|ted** (pot′id), *adj.* **1** put into a pot: *a potted plant.* **2** cooked and preserved in pots or cans: *potted beef.* **3** *Slang, Figurative.* drunk; intoxicated. **4** *British Slang.* **a** shortened; condensed: *a potted biography.* **b** recorded; canned: *potted music.*

**pot|ter**[1] (pot′ər), *n.* a person who makes pots, dishes, or vases out of clay. [Old English *pottere* < *pott* pot + *-ere* -er[1]]

**pot|ter**[2] (pot′ər), *v.i., v.t.* to keep busy in a rather useless way; putter: *She potters about the house all day, but gets little done.* [(apparently frequentative) < obsolete *pote,* Old English *potian* to push, poke. See related etym. at **put**[1], **putter**[1].]
—**pot′ter|er**, *n.* —**pot′ter|ing|ly**, *adv.*

**potter's clay**, clay that is free or nearly free from iron, suitable for making pottery.

**potter's field**, **1** a piece of ground set aside for the burial of people who die without friends or money. **2** a field bought for the 30 pieces of silver which Judas received for betraying Jesus, used as a burial place for strangers (in the Bible, Matthew 27:7-8).

**potter's ore**, coarsely grained galena, used to glaze pottery.

***potter's wheel**, a rotating horizontal disk upon which clay is molded into pottery.

***potter's wheel**

**potter wasp**, any one of various solitary wasps that make vaselike mounds of mud and sand for their young.

**pot|ter|y** (pot′ər ē), *n., pl.* **-ter|ies. 1** pots, dishes, or vases made from clay and hardened by heat. The finest type of pottery is called porcelain. All other pottery is called earthenware or stoneware. **2** the art or business of making them; ceramics: *She has taken up pottery as a hobby.* **3** a place where such pots, dishes, or vases are made: *Large potteries in Ohio and West Virginia make most of the stoneware produced today* (Eugene F. Bunker, Jr.). [< Old French *poterie* < *potier* potter < *pot* pot < Vulgar Latin *pottus*]

**pot|tle** (pot′əl), *n.* **1** a former liquid measure equal to two quarts. **2** a pot or tankard holding two quarts. **3** the liquid in it. **4** alcoholic liquor. **5** a small wicker basket: *a pottle of fine strawberries* (Tobias Smollett). [< Old French *potel* (diminutive) < *pot* pot < Vulgar Latin *pottus*]

**pot|to** (pot′ō), *n., pl.* **-tos. 1** a small, sluggish, African mammal resembling a lemur. It spends most of its time in trees, and is unique in having the spines of its vertebrae exposed. **2** = kinkajou. [< a West African word]

**Pott's disease** (pots), tuberculosis of the spinal column, often resulting in a marked curvature of the spine caused by the destruction of affected vertebrae. [< Percival *Pott,* 1713-1788, a British surgeon, who described the condition resulting from this disease]

**pot|ty**[1] (pot′ē), *adj.,* **-ti|er, -ti|est.** *British Informal.* **1** foolish; crazy: *The pottier their ideas the better I like them* (Listener). **2** petty; insignificant. [origin uncertain]

**pot|ty**[2] (pot′ē), *n., pl.* **-ties.** *Informal.* **1** a small chamber pot. **2** = potty-chair. [< *pot*[1] + *-y*[2]]

**pot|ty-chair** (pot′ē chãr′), *n.* a child's chair with an open seat fitting over a chamber pot, used for toilet training.

**pot-val|iant** (pot′val′yənt), *adj.* brave through drink: *a man who has drunk himself pot-valiant* (Tobias Smollett).

**pot-wal|lop|er** (pot′wol′ə pər), *n.* (formerly in some British boroughs) a man who qualified as a voter by having a separate fireplace over which his own pots boiled. [alteration of earlier *pot-waller* < *pot*[1] + *waller* < *wall* to boil, Old English *weallan;* influenced by dialectal *wallop* boil hard]

**pouch** (pouch), *n., v.* —*n.* **1** a bag; sack: *a mailman's pouch, a pouch of tobacco.* **2** a small bag to hold money: *a poor devil without penny in pouch* (Washington Irving). **3** a bag for carrying documents: *a diplomat's pouch.* **4** a fold of skin that is like a bag: *A kangaroo carries its young in a pouch. Chipmunks carry food in their cheek pouches. The old man had pouches under the eyes.* **5a** a baglike cavity or cyst in a plant; silicle. **b** any pocketlike space in the body: *the pharyngeal pouch, ileocecal pouch.* **6** *Especially Scottish.* a pocket in a garment.
—*v.t.* **1** to put into a pouch or pocket; pocket. **2** (of a fish or bird) to swallow. **3** to submit to without protest: *I will pouch up no such affront* (Scott). **4** *Informal.* to provide with money; give a present of money to: *Coningsby ... had been pouched in a manner worthy of a Marquess* (Benjamin Disraeli).
—*v.i.* to form a pouch or pouchlike cavity.
[< Old North French *pouche,* Old French *poche* < a Germanic word. See related etym. at **poke**[2].]
—**pouch′like′**, *adj.*

**pouched** (poucht), *adj.* having a pouch, as pelicans, gophers, and kangaroos do.

**pouched bear**, = koala.

**pouched rat**, **1** = gopher (def. 1). **2** = kangaroo rat. **3** any one of various pouched rodents of Africa.

**pouch|y** (pou′chē), *adj.,* **pouch|i|er, pouch|i|est.** having pouches; like a pouch; baggy.

**pou|dreuse** (pü drœz′), *n.* a small dressing table or vanity: *A Louis XV kingwood poudreuse [went] for £300* (London Times). [< French *poudreuse* < *poudre* powder]

***pouf** (püf), *n., interj.* —*n.* **1** a kind of women's headdress fashionable at the end of the 1700's. It has reappeared in a modified form called bouffant. **2** a high roll or pad of hair worn by women. **3** any part of a dress gathered up in a bunch: *There are folds around it to the hips; below, in back, great butterfly-wing poufs spread outward* (New Yorker). **4** a very soft, stuffed, backless ottoman or couch. **5** = poof[1].
—*interj.* = poof[1].
[< French *pouf* < Middle French; (originally) imitative of a sound; later extended to objects that appeared inflated, or puffed out. Compare etym. under **puff.**]

***pouf**
definition 1

**pouff** or **pouffe** (püf), *n. Especially British.* pouf.

**Pou|jad|ism** (pü zhä′diz əm), *n.* the movement, principles, and practices of the Poujadists.

**Pou|jad|ist** (pü zhä′dist), *n., adj.* —*n.* a member of a right-wing French political movement or party composed chiefly of small businessmen and favoring drastic reduction in taxation.
—*adj.* of the Poujadists or Poujadism.
[< French *Poujadiste* < Pierre *Poujade,* a store owner in central France, who started the movement in 1953 + French *-iste* -ist]

**pou|laine** (pü lān′), *n.* **1** a long, tapering point into which the toe of a shoe or slipper was prolonged, in a fashion of the 1300's and 1400's. **2** a shoe or the like with such a point; crackowe. [< Old French *poulaine, Poulaine* Poland (because this kind of shoe was worn there)]

**pou|lard** or **pou|larde** (pü lärd′), *n.* a young fattened hen, especially one spayed to improve the flesh for use as food. [< Middle French *poularde* < *poule* hen + *-arde,* a noun suffix; see etym. under **poultry**]

**poulard wheat**, a tall, stout-stemmed variety of wheat which produces coarse grain and straw.

**poult** (pōlt), *n.* a young turkey, pheasant, or other domestic fowl. [Middle English *poult,* short for *poullet* pullet < Old French *poulet;* see etym. under **poultry**]

**poult-de-soie** (pü′də swä′), *n. French.* a soft, rich, corded silk fabric of the grosgrain type.

**poul|ter|er** (pōl′tər ər), *n.* a dealer in poultry. [< obsolete *poulter* dealer in poultry < Old French *pouletier* < *poulet* pullet; see etym. under **poultry**]

**poul|tice** (pōl′tis), *n., v.,* **-ticed, -tic|ing.** —*n.* a soft, moist mass, especially of mustard, herbs, or flaxseed, applied hot to the body as a medicine.
—*v.t.* **1** to put a poultice on. **2** *Figurative.* to soothe; salve: *I am not willing to spend ... hours listening to someone denounce me in an effort to poultice his private wounds* (Harper's).
[alteration of earlier *pultes* < Latin *pultēs,* plural of *puls, pultis* mush < Greek *póltos* porridge. Compare etym. under **pulse**[2].]

***poul|try** (pōl′trē), *n.* birds raised for their meat or eggs, such as chickens, turkeys, geese, or ducks: *These aging birds provide much of the meat for firms that can poultry and turn out frozen chicken pies* (Wall Street Journal). [< Old French *pouleterie* < *poulet* pullet (diminutive) < *poule* hen < Vulgar Latin *pulla* < Latin *pullus* young fowl; young of animals in general]

***poultry**

**poul|try|man** (pōl′trē mən), *n., pl.* **-men. 1** a man who raises poultry commercially. **2** a man who sells poultry, eggs, and, sometimes, butter and cheese.

**pounce**[1] (pouns), *v.,* **pounced, pounc|ing,** *n.*
—*v.i.* **1** to jump suddenly and seize something: *The cat pounced upon the mouse.* (*Figurative.*) *His mother would pounce ... on his remarks as a barn-owl pounces upon a mouse* (Samuel Butler). **2** to dash suddenly; come suddenly: *to pounce onto the stage.*
—*v.t.* to swoop down upon and seize suddenly: *As if an eagle ... Stoop'd from his highest pitch to pounce a wren* (William Cowper). [< noun]
—*n.* **1** a sudden swoop or pouncing. **2** the claw or talon of a bird of prey.
[apparently contraction of Middle English *ponchoun* an instrument for punching < Old French *poinchon;* see etym. under **puncheon**[2]. See related etym. at **punch**[1].]

**pounce**[2] (pouns), *n., v.,* **pounced, pounc|ing.**
—*n.* **1** a fine powder formerly used to prevent ink from spreading in writing, or to prepare parchment for writing. **2** a fine powder used for transferring a design through a stencil.
—*v.t.* **1** to sprinkle, smooth, or prepare with pounce. **2** to trace (a design) with pounce rubbed through perforations.
[< French, Old French *ponce* < Late Latin *pōmex,* for Latin *pūmex, -icis.* See etym. of doublet **pumice.**] —**pounc′er**, *n.*

**pounce box**, a box with a perforated lid for sprinkling or transferring pounce.

**poun|cet box** (poun′sit), *Archaic.* a small box, with a perforated lid, for holding perfumes. [per-

**Pronunciation Key:** hat, āge, cãre, fär; let, ēqual, tėrm; it, īce; hot, ōpen, ôrder; oil, out; cup, pu̇t, rüle; child; long; thin; ᴛʜen; zh, measure; ə represents a in about, e in taken, i in pencil, o in lemon, u in circus.

haps for *pounced box* (that is, perforated)]

***pound**¹ (pound), *n., pl.* **pounds** or (*collectively*) **pound.** **1** a measure of weight. 1 pound avoirdupois = 16 ounces or 453.6 grams. 1 pound troy = 12 ounces or 373.24 grams. *A jet plane traveling 1,500 mph hits the rain drops with a force of 70,000 pounds per square inch* (Newsweek) *Abbr:* lb. **2a** a unit of money of Great Britain, formerly equal to 240 pence or 20 shillings, and since 1971 equal to 100 pence; pound sterling. **b** a unit of money of certain countries in the Commonwealth of Nations. **3** a unit of money of certain Middle Eastern countries, such as Egypt, Israel, Lebanon, Syria, and Turkey, having various values. **4** a former Scottish money of account. **5** (in the New Testament) a mina (a Semitic unit of money). [Old English *pund* < Latin *pondō*, adverb, (originally) for *lībra pondō* a pound by weight, ultimately < *pondus, -eris* weight, related to *pendēre* hang, and to *pendere* to weigh]

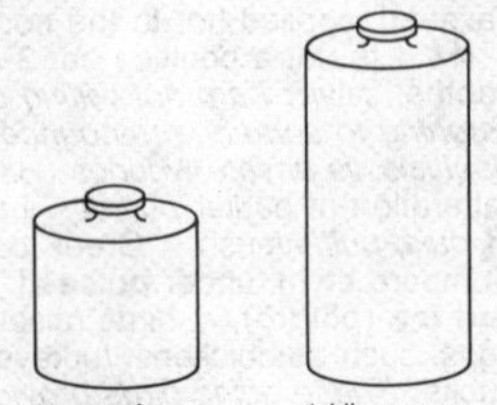

***pound¹** definitions 1, 2a | 1 pound= 16 ounces or 0.4536 kilogram | 1 kilogram= 1,000 grams or 2.2046 pounds

£ symbol definition 2a

**pound²** (pound), *v., n.* —*v.t.* **1** to hit hard again and again; hit heavily: *He pounded the door with his fist. The Germans suddenly got the range ... and began to pound us with high explosive* (H. G. Wells). **SYN:** thump. See syn. under **beat. 2** to crush to powder or pulp by beating: *to pound drugs with a pestle in a mortar.* **SYN:** pulverize, triturate. **3** to produce (sound) by pounding or as if by pounding: *to pound out a tune on a piano.* **4** to make solid or firm by beating.
—*v.i.* **1** to beat hard; throb: *After running fast you can feel your heart pound.* **2** to move with a pounding sound: *She pounded down the hill to catch the bus.* **3** to produce sound by pounding or as if by pounding: *We could hear drums pounding in the distance.* **4** (of a ship) to force its way through heavy waves.
—*n.* **1** the act of pounding. **2** a heavy beat or forcible blow; thump. **3** the sound of a beat or blow; thud.
[Old English *pūnian;* the *-d* is a later addition. Compare etym. under **sound¹.**]

**pound³** (pound), *n., v.* —*n.* **1** an enclosed place in which to keep stray animals: *a dog pound.* **2** an enclosure for keeping, confining, or trapping animals. **3** *Figurative.* a place of confinement, such as a prison, or an area of water enclosed by nets to catch fish or lobsters: *In his opinion, the nine-mile pound could be adequately provided with water* (London Times).
—*v.t.* **1** to shut up in a pound. **2** *Figurative.* impound or imprison.
[Old English *pund,* in *pund-fald* pinfold. Compare *pyndan* to enclose.]

**pound|age¹** (poun′dij), *n.* **1** a tax, commission, or rate, of so much per pound of British money or per pound of weight. **2** the weight, as of a person or product, in pounds: *Extra poundage often goes hand in hand with a beautiful glowing complexion* (New York Times). [< *pound¹* + *-age*]

**pound|age²** (poun′dij), *n.* **1** the act of putting in a pound. **2** the fee for release from a pound.

**pound|al** (poun′dəl), *n.* the unit of force equal to the force necessary to give a mass of one pound an acceleration of one foot per second per second. 1 poundal = 13,825 dynes.

**pound cake, 1** a cake, usually made with a pound of sugar and a pound of butter for each pound of flour, and plenty of eggs. **2** a rich, sweet cake somewhat like this.

**pound|er¹** (poun′dər), *n.* a person or thing that pounds, pulverizes, or beats. [Old English *punere.* See etym. under **pound².**]

**pound|er²** (poun′dər), *n.* **1** a person or thing weighing a specified number of pounds: *The baby was a nine-pounder. The bass was a fine seven-pounder.* **2** a gun firing a shell that weighs a specified number of pounds: *fine cannon, eighteen-pounders, with their carriages* (Benjamin Franklin). **3** a bank note, jewel, or other valuable article, worth a specified number of pounds sterling: *I pocketed the little donation—it was a ten-pounder* (Frederick Marryat).

**pound-fool|ish** (pound′fü′lish), *adj.* foolish or careless in regard to large sums of money: *a badly organized, penny-wise, pound-foolish effort* (Newsweek).

**pound force,** = poundal. *Abbr:* lbf (no periods).

**pound net,** fishnets arranged to form an enclosed space with a narrow opening.

**pound sterling,** the unit of money of Great Britain; pound. Since February 1971, 1 pound sterling = 100 pence, or before 1971, 1 pound sterling = 240 pence or 20 shillings.

**pounds|worth** (poundz′wėrth′), *n. British.* as much as can be bought for a pound.

**pour** (pôr, pōr), *v., n.* —*v.t.* **1** to cause to flow in a steady stream: *to pour milk from a bottle, to pour coal on a fire, to pour shells into the enemy trenches, to pour money into undeveloped areas.* **2** *Figurative.* to make known freely or without reserve: *The melancholy poet poured forth his sorrow in a song. I could pour out to her all my little worries* (Samuel Butler).
—*v.i.* **1** to flow in a steady stream: *The rain poured down. The cold blasts poured down from the mountains* (James Fenimore Cooper). (*Figurative.*) *The crowd poured out of the church.* **2** to rain heavily: *It's pouring.*
—*n.* **1** the act of pouring. **SYN:** outpouring, effluence. **2** a heavy rain; downpour. **3** the amount of molten metal poured at a time. **4** *Scottish.* a great quantity.
**pour it on,** *U.S. Informal.* **a** to do or express something with great vigor and enthusiasm, especially in advancing one's interest, using persuasion, or the like: *The salesman poured it on so well that the customers believed they really wanted to buy. On his first night in Manhattan he went before the United Nations General Assembly and poured it on—5,500 words* (Time). **b** to keep increasing one's score or advantage in a game, even when victory is no longer at issue: *Our team was leading 60-0, but the crowd kept yelling, "Pour it on!"*
[Middle English *pouren;* origin uncertain] —**pour′a|ble,** *adj.* —**pour′er,** *n.* —**pour′ing|ly,** *adv.*

**pour ac|quit** (pür à kē′), *French.* **1** received payment. **2** (literally) for receipt.

**pour|boire** (pür bwȧr′), *n. French.* **1** a small present of money; tip; gratuity. **2** (literally) (money) for drinking.

**pour le mé|rite** (pür lə mā rēt′), *French.* for merit.

**pour le sport** (pür lə spôr′), *French.* for sport: *... all beautifully dressed pour le sport* (Harper's).

**pour|par|ler** (pür pȧr lā′), *n.* an informal conference; preliminary discussion: *... the end of the opening pourparlers between the French and Algerian diplomats* (New Yorker). [< French *pourparler,* noun use of infinitive, to discuss, plot < *pour-* before + *parler* to talk; see etym. under **parley**]

**pour|point** (pür′point′), *n.* a stuffed and quilted doublet worn by men in the 1300's and 1400's. [< Old French *pourpoint,* quilt]

**pour point** (pôr, pōr), *Chemistry.* the lowest temperature at which engine oil or some other substance will flow under test conditions.

**pousse-ca|fé** (püs′kȧ fā′), *n., pl.* **-fés** (-fā′). **1** a small glass of liqueur served with or after coffee. **2** *U.S.* a small glass of various liqueurs arranged in layers. [< French *pousse-café* (literally) push coffee]

**pousse-pousse** (püs′püs′), *n. French.* a jinrikisha.

**pous|sette** (pü set′), *n., v.,* **-set|ted, -set|ting.** —*n.* a dancing round and round with hands joined, as of a couple in a country-dance.
—*v.i.* to dance in this way: *The turf-cutter seized old Olly Dowden, and ... poussetted with her* (Thomas Hardy).
[< French *poussette* (literally) little push < Middle French *pousse* a push < Old French *pousser* to push < Latin *pulsāre*]

**pou sto** (pü stō′, pou), a place to stand on; basis of operations: *She ... Who learns the one pou sto whence after-hands May move the world* (Tennyson). [< Greek *poû stô* (a place) where I may stand; from the saying (about the lever principle) attributed to Archimedes, "Give me a place where I may stand and I will move the world"]

**pout¹** (pout), *v., n.* —*v.i.* **1** to thrust or push out the lips, as a displeased or sulky child does: *Her whole face looked silly as she stood there pouting.* **2** to show displeasure. **3** to swell out; protrude.
—*v.t.* **1** to push out or protrude, especially the lips. **2** to say with a pout: *"That's the reason," pouted Louisa* (Dickens).
—*n.* **1** the act of pushing out of the lips when one is displeased or sulky: *A pout makes a person look very silly.* **2** a fit of sullenness: *There ensued a puerile tussle that put me in a precious pout, that I should be kept waiting by such things* (George W. Cable).
**in the pouts,** in a pouting mood; sulky: *Panurge somewhat vexed Friar John, and put him in the pouts* (Peter A. Motteux).
[Middle English *pouten,* probably imitative of pursing the lips. Compare etym. under **pooh.**]

**pout²** (pout), *n., pl.* **pouts** or (*collectively*) **pout. 1** any one of various freshwater catfishes, such as the hornpout. **2** = eelpout. [Old English *-pūte,* in *ǣlepūte* eelpout]

**pout|er** (pou′tər), *n.* **1** a person who pouts. **2** one of a breed of domestic pigeons that puff out their crops.

**pout|y** (pou′tē), *adj.,* **pout|i|er, pout|i|est.** *Informal.* inclined to pout; sulky.

**pov|e|ra** (pov′er ə), *adj.* of or having to do with a form of art that regards the artistic idea or process as more important than the finished product. [< Italian (arte) *povera* impoverished (art)]

**pov|er|ty** (pov′ər tē), *n.* **1** the condition of being poor: *Being out of work usually causes poverty.* **2** lack of what is needed; poor quality: *The poverty of the soil makes the crops small.* **SYN:** deficiency. **3** *Figurative.* a small amount; fewness: *A dull person's talk shows poverty of ideas.* [< Old French *pouerte* < Latin *paupertās* < *pauper* poor]
—*Syn.* **1 Poverty, want, destitution** mean the condition of being poor. **Poverty** emphasizes, more strongly than *poorness* does, owning nothing at all or having not enough for all the necessities of life: *Their tattered clothing and broken furniture indicated their poverty.* **Want** emphasizes extreme need, having too little to live on: *Welfare agencies help those in want.* **Destitution** emphasizes complete lack even of food and shelter, and often suggests having been deprived of possessions once had: *The Red Cross relieved the destitution following the floods.*

**poverty line,** a minimum income, the standard of adequate subsistence, below which a person or family is classified as living in poverty.

**pov|er|ty-strick|en** (pov′ər tē strik′ən), *adj.* extremely poor: *The poverty-stricken exiles contributed far more, in proportion ... than the wealthy merchants* (John L. Motley). **SYN:** indigent, destitute, penniless.

**pow¹** (pou), *n., interj.* a sudden explosive sound; bang: *I heard a "pow" over my head* (Jim Bentley). *Pow! ... flashbulbs popped* (Time). [imitative]

**pow²** (pō, pou), *n. Scottish.* poll; a head.

**POW** (no periods) or **P.O.W.,** prisoner of war.

**pow|der** (pou′dər), *n., v.* —*n.* **1** a solid reduced to dust by pounding, crushing, or grinding. **2** some special kind of powder: *face powder, talcum powder. The doctor gave her powders to take as a medicine.* **3** gunpowder or any similar explosive: *Soldiers used to carry their powder in a powder horn.*
—*v.t.* **1** to make into powder; pulverize. **2** to sprinkle or cover with powder. **3** to put powder on: *to powder one's nose.* **4** to sprinkle: *The ground was lightly powdered with snow.*
—*v.i.* **1** to become powder: *The soil powdered in the heat.* **2** to use powder as a cosmetic: *She saw herself going down the years, powdering a little more, painting a little more* (John Galsworthy). **3** *British Informal.* to rush; hurry.
**take a powder,** *U.S. Slang.* to go or run away; disappear; vanish: *When the police arrived, the burglars took a powder over the back fence.*
[Middle English *poudre* < Old French, earlier *poldre* < Latin *pulvis,* and *pulver* dust] —**pow′der|er,** *n.* —**pow′der|less,** *adj.*

**powder blue,** a light blue. —**pow′der-blue′,** *adj.*

**powder chest,** a chest for holding gunpowder.

**powder down,** downy feathers that grow indefinitely and continually crumble at their ends into a kind of powder. They are found especially in the herons.

**pow|dered milk** (pou′dərd), = dried milk.

**powdered sugar,** a sugar produced by grinding granulated sugar: *Confectioners' sugar is very fine powdered sugar.*

**powder flask,** a flask or case of horn, metal, or leather for carrying gunpowder.

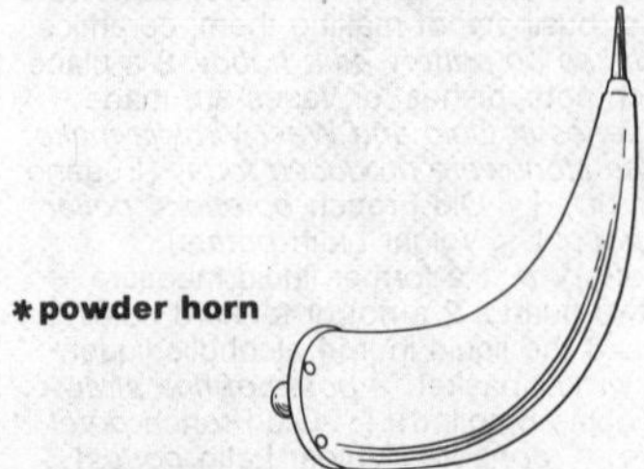

***powder horn**

***powder horn,** a flask made of the horn of an animal, used to carry gunpowder.

**powder keg**, 1 a small barrel for storing gunpowder: *When their powder kegs were empty, they surrendered* (Atlantic). 2 *Figurative.* something that threatens to explode suddenly or without warning: *It is part of the whole development which makes the Middle East the powder keg that it is today* (Atlantic).

**powder magazine**, a place where gunpowder is stored.

**powder metallurgy**, the technique or process of making metallic articles by shaping and coalescing powdered metals and alloys under heat and pressure.

**powder mill**, a mill for making gunpowder.

**powder monkey**, 1 a boy formerly employed on warships or in a fort, to carry powder to the guns. 2 a person skilled in the use of dynamite and other explosives, especially as used in construction work.

**powder puff**, a soft puff or pad for applying powder to the skin.

**pow|der-puff** (pou′dər puf′), *adj. Informal.* soft; weak; feeble: *Some critics sneered that he* [*a boxer*] *was a powder-puff puncher* (Time).

**powder room**, a lavatory, especially one for women, with a dressing table.

**pow|der|y** (pou′dər ē), *adj.* 1 of powder: *the powdery dust of flour.* 2 like powder; in the form of powder; dusty: *The snow was too dry and powdery to make good snowballs.* SYN: mealy. 3 easily made into powder. 4 sprinkled or covered with powder: *a powdery wig.*

**powdery mildew**, 1 any one of various fungi that attack many plants such as the pea, peach, rose, apple, grape, and cereal grains. It produces a light, powdery coat of conidia on the leaves. 2 the diseased condition produced by these fungi.

**Pow|ell|ism** (pou′ə liz əm), *n.* a movement in British politics led by (John) Enoch Powell (born 1913), Conservative Member of Parliament, advocating laissez-faire economics and exclusion of black immigrants from Great Britain: *Powellism is a combination of racism, archconservative economics, and a touch of prickly isolationism* (Time).

**Pow|ell|ist** (pou′ə list), *adj.* = Powellite.

**Pow|ell|ite** (pou′ə līt), *n., adj.* — *n.* a follower or supporter of Enoch Powell; adherent of Powellism.
— *adj.* of or having to do with Powellites or Powellism.

***pow|er** (pou′ər), *n., adj., v.* — *n.* 1 strength or force; might: *great physical power, the power of Samson. Penicillin is a medicine of great power. In a world of power, diplomacy cannot afford sentimentality* (Newsweek). 2 the ability to do or act: *I will give you all the help in my power.* 3 a particular ability: *He has great powers of concentration.* SYN: faculty. 4 authority; right; control; influence: *Congress has the power to declare war.* SYN: command, sway, dominion. 5 a person or thing that has authority or influence, such as an important nation: *Five powers held a peace conference. Dr. Adenauer declared that the establishment of the unity of Germany constitutes an obligation arising for the four Powers* (London Times). 6 energy or force that can do work: *Running water can be used to operate a turbine and produce electric power. Man is feeling his way gingerly toward harnessing thermonuclear power* (Scientific American). 7 the product of a number multiplied by itself one or more times: *16 is the 4th power of 2.* 8 *Physics.* the capacity of an instrument to magnify. An object seen through a microscope with a power of ten looks ten times its actual size. *Magnifying power of a given objective varies with the ocular* (*eyepiece*) *used* (Bernhard, Bennett, and Rice). 9 = simple machine. 10 *Physics.* the capacity for exerting mechanical force, as measured by the rate at which it is exerted or at which the work is done. Power is expressed in foot-pounds per minute, ergs per second, horsepower, watts, and other units. *The power is equal to the product of the current and the potential difference* (Sears and Zemansky). 11 a seizure of uncontrollable religious enthusiasm. 12 *Archaic.* a military or naval force: *Brutus and Cassius are levying powers* (Shakespeare). 13 *Dialect.* a large number or amount: *I've heard a power of queer things of yourself* (J. M. Synge).
— *adj.* 1 of electric power: *a power failure, a power cable, power lines.* 2 worked or driven by motive power; motor-driven: *a power lawn mower, a power saw.* 3 of or having to do with the use or exertion of power over others: *a power struggle, a power elite.*
— *v.t.* to provide (something) with power or energy: *a boat powered by an outboard motor. Spun by hot gases from the combustion chamber, the turbine or "windmill" powers the turbocar* (Maclean's).
— *v.i.* to move by means of power or force: *The young player powered into the finals.*

**in power**, having control or authority: *He* [*Pitt*] *had often declared that, while he was in power, England should never make a peace of Utrecht* (Macaulay).

**power down**, to reduce the power consumption of (a spacecraft): *"I would like to make sure that the LM* [*lunar module*] *is okay before we power down the CSM* [*command and service modules*]*"* (Glynn Lunney).

**powers, a** deity; divinity: *Then adore the woodland pow'rs with pray'r* (John Dryden). **b** the sixth of the nine orders of angels in medieval theology: *... the powers and thrones above* (John Keble).

**power up**, to increase the power consumption of (a spacecraft): *Because of the cold which had restricted the astronauts' sleep to only two or three hours and caused them considerable discomfort, the lunar module was powered up three hours earlier than planned—nine hours before entry into the earth's atmosphere* (London Times).

**the powers that be**, those who have control or authority: *Participation in the Hungarian rising was a criminal act from the point of view of the powers that be in Hungary* (Economist).

**to the nth power**. See under **nth**.

[Middle English *pouer* < Anglo-French *poër, pouair,* variants of Old French *poeir,* noun use of infinitive < Vulgar Latin *potere,* for Latin *posse* to be able]

— *Syn. n.* 1 **Power, strength, force** mean ability to do something or capacity for something. **Power** is the general word applying to any physical, mental, or moral ability or capacity, whether used or not: *Every normal, healthy person has power to think.* **Strength** means a natural or innate power within the person or thing to do, bear, or resist much: *She had the strength of character to endure the death of her only child.* **Force** means active use of power or strength to get something done or overcome opposition: *The force of his argument convinced me. We had to use force to get into the house.*

power product
$2^6 = 64$
base

***power**
*n.,* definition 7 2 to the 6th power is 64
or 2 x 2 x 2 x 2 x 2 x 2 = 64

**power amplifier**, an amplifier which has a relatively high output of current, as in a radio.

**power base**, *U.S.* a foundation of political support, especially for a campaign or a policy: *These progressives are young and ambitious, confident of their ability to build an effective power base in Georgia without the rural white supremacists* (New York Times).

**pow|er|boat** (pou′ər bōt′), *n.* a boat propelled by an engine on board; motorboat.

**pow|er|boat|ing** (pou′ər bō′ting), *n.* = motorboating.

***power brake**, a brake in a motor vehicle that uses the vacuum produced by the engine to force hydraulic fluid or compressed air to the brake shoes of the wheel, requiring very little pressure on the brake pedal to stop the vehicle.

***power brake**

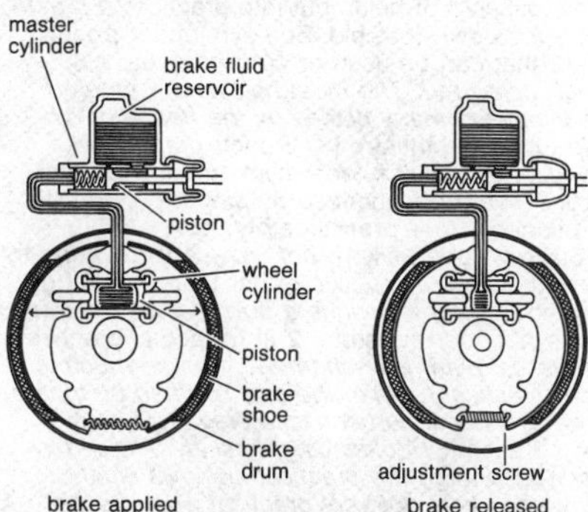


**power broker**, *U.S.* a person who manipulates power by influencing people in positions of power.

**power dive**, a dive made by an airplane at or nearly at peak power, especially as a maneuver in bombing or aerial fighting.

**pow|er-dive** (pou′ər dīv′), *v.,* **-dived** or (*U.S. Informal and British Dialect*) **-dove, -dived, -diving.** — *v.i.* to make a power dive.
— *v.t.* to cause (an airplane) to make a power dive.

**power drill**, a drill worked by a motor, not by hand.

**pow|ered** (pou′ərd), *adj.* 1 having power: *a powered lawn mower.* 2 using power of a specific kind or degree: *a high-powered racing car, a gasoline-powered engine.*

**power egg**, *Slang.* the gondola of an airship.

**pow|er|ful** (pou′ər fəl), *adj., adv.* — *adj.* 1 having great power or force; mighty; strong: *a powerful nation, a powerful medicine, a powerful opponent, a powerful argument.* SYN: potent. See syn. under **mighty**. 2 *Dialect.* great in quantity or number: *a powerful deal o' trouble* (Harriet Beecher Stowe).
— *adv. Dialect or Informal.* very; exceedingly; greatly: *powerful weary, a powerful cold day, powerful wet weather.* — **pow′er|ful|ly**, *adv.* — **pow′er|ful|ness**, *n.*

**pow|er|house** (pou′ər hous′), *n.* 1 a building containing boilers, engines, or generators for producing electric power. 2 *Informal, Figurative.* a powerful, energetic, or highly effective person or group: *A powerhouse of physical energy, he bounces and bounds with swift, long strides* (Time).

**pow|er|less** (pou′ər lis), *adj.* without power; lacking ability to produce an effect; helpless: *a powerless hand* (Shakespeare). *The mouse was powerless in the cat's claws. I now felt powerless to escape* (W. H. Hudson). SYN: weak, impotent. — **pow′er|less|ly**, *adv.* — **pow′er|less-ness**, *n.*

**power line**, a heavy wire for carrying electricity: *Every light in the district ... blinked out—somebody had hit the power line* (Time).

**power loading**, the gross weight of a propeller-driven aircraft divided by the horsepower of its engines.

**power loom**, a loom worked by steam, electricity, water power, or other force, not by hand.

**power of appointment**, authority given to one person over the property of another.

**power of attorney**, a written statement giving one person legal power to act for another: *The banker signed the agreement for his customer under power of attorney.*

**power pack**, an assemblage of electrical units used to change the voltage of a power line or battery to the voltage needed for various electronic circuits: *It requires no cumbersome power pack because it operates at very low voltage* (Science News Letter).

**power plant**, 1 a building with machinery for generating power. 2 a motor or engine: *The power plant of the automobile was a small four-cylinder engine.*

**power play**, 1 *Sports.* a play in which members of the offensive team converge at a given point to exert mass force or pressure on the defense: *a five-man power play in ice hockey.* 2 *Figurative.* any action, move, or play in which strong force or pressure is used to attain a goal: *Russia's squeeze on West Berlin now had become a subtle power play* (Newsweek).

**power point**, *British.* an electrical outlet; a wall socket.

**power politics**, 1 diplomacy in international affairs which uses the threat of superior military power: *The language of military power is the only language which disciples of power politics understand* (Patrick Anderson). 2 the use of power or coercion for political purposes: *In short, the only politics is power politics, and the only hope of dealing with the political power of the minorities is in the active, organized power of the majority* (James Reston).

**power press**, a printing press worked by a motor or engine, not by hand.

**power reactor**, any one of several types of nuclear reactors used to produce power for generating heat or electricity, or operating a ship or plane.

**pow|ers** (pou′ərz), *n.pl.* See under **power**.

**power saw**, a saw worked by a motor, not by hand.

**power series**, *Mathematics.* a series in which some quantity is raised to successively higher powers. The simplest power series is $1 + x + x^2 + x^3 + x^4 + x^5$ and so on.

**Pronunciation Key:** hat, āge, cãre, fär; let, ēqual, tėrm; it, īce; hot, ōpen, ôrder; oil, out; cup, pu̇t, rüle; child; long; thin; ᴛʜen; zh, measure; ə represents **a** in about, **e** in taken, **i** in pencil, **o** in lemon, **u** in circus.

***power shovel**, a machine for digging, operated by a diesel or gasoline engine, or formerly by steam power: *Siberia's great shallow coal seams can be mined with power shovels* (Newsweek).

***power shovel**

**power station**, = powerhouse (def. 1).
***power steering**, a steering mechanism in a motor vehicle that uses mechanical or hydraulic aid enabling the wheels to be turned easily.

***power steering**

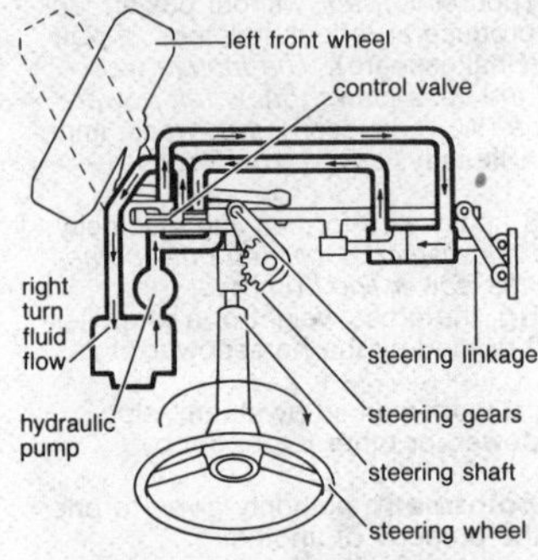


**power structure**, the established persons, groups, or institutions that hold power, as in a country, city, or organization: *an advocate of inner-city forces rebelling against the power structure and establishment of the city* (New York Times).
**power take-off**, a mechanism on a tractor or truck that provides power for other machines, often ones that are either mounted on or pulled by it. The coupling device between the power take-off and the equipment can be a pulley and belt or a drive shaft. *Abbr:* PTO (no periods).
**power train**, the parts of a motor vehicle which transmit power from the engine to the wheels, including the transmission, drive shaft, clutch, differential, and axles: *The power train ... is covered by a warranty for five years or 50,000 miles* (London Times).
**Pow|ha|tan** (pou′ə tan′, pou hat′ən), *n., pl.* **-tan** or **-tans**. **1** a member of an Indian tribe of eastern North America that once controlled a confederacy which included thirty different tribes. **2** the Algonkian language of this tribe.
**pow|wow** (pou′wou′), *n., v.* —*n.* **1** a ceremony of North American Indians, usually accompanied by magic, feasting, and dancing, performed for the cure of disease, success in hunting, victory in war, or other purposes. **2** a council or conference of or with North American Indians. **3** *Informal.* any conference or meeting: *I'll be back early, for a last powwow on the terrace* (Edith Wharton). **4** an American Indian priest or medicine man.
—*v.i.* **1** to hold an Indian powwow. **2** *Informal.* to confer: *We would go to the cave and powwow over what we had done* (Mark Twain).
[American English < Algonkian (probably Narragansett) *powwow* shaman, medicine man < a verb meaning "use divination"]
**pox** (poks), *n., v.* —*n.* **1** any disease that covers the body or parts of the body with sores, such as chicken pox or smallpox. **2** = syphilis.
—*v.t.* **1** to infect with pox: *Maggie May—who poxed up many a whaler* (Listener). **2** to curse with the pox or some other evil: *The dean friendly! The dean be pox't* (Jonathan Swift).
**pox on**, a plague on; may a pox or some other evil befall (a thing or person): *A pox on him, he's a cat still* (Shakespeare).
[spelling alteration of *pocks,* plural of *pock*]
**pox|vi|rus** (poks′vī′rəs), *n.* any one of a group of large, complex viruses containing DNA, including those causing smallpox, cowpox, and mouse pox.
**poz|zo|la|na** (pot′sō lä′nə), *n.* = pozzuolana.
**poz|zo|la|nic** (pot′sō lä′nik), *adj.* = pozzuolanic.
**poz|zuo|la|na** (pot′swō lä′nə), *n.* a volcanic rock or ash used in making hydraulic cement and containing silica, alumina, and lime: *The aqueducts of ancient times were generally built of stone, brick, or pozzuolana* (Hope Holway). [< Italian *pozzuolana,* noun use of feminine adjective < *Pozzuoli,* Italy, where it was first found]
**poz|zuo|la|nic** (pot′swō lä′nik), *adj.* consisting of or resembling pozzuolana.
**pp** (no period), pianissimo.
**pp.**, an abbreviation for the following:
**1** pages.
**2** past participle.
**3** pianissimo.
**4** privately printed.
**p.p.**, an abbreviation for the following:
**1** parcel post.
**2** parish priest.
**3** past participle.
**4** postpaid.
**P.P.**, an abbreviation for the following:
**1** Parcel Post.
**2** Parish Priest.
**3** past participle.
**4** postpaid.
**p.p.b.** or **ppb** (no periods), parts per billion.
**PPB** (no periods), Planning-Programming-Budgeting (a system of planning in which possible benefits are measured in relation to final costs).
**ppd.**, **1** postpaid. **2** prepaid.
**PPD** (no periods), purified protein derivative.
**PPE** (no periods) or **P.P.E.**, philosophy, politics, and economics: *an Oxford PPE graduate.*
**PP factor**, pellagra-preventive factor; nicotinic acid.
**pph.**, pamphlet.
**p.p.i.**, policy proof of interest.
**PPI** (no periods), plan position indicator: *The PPI screen shows a flat map of the circular region above the radar* (Scientific American).
**PPLO** (no periods), pleuropneumonia-like organism.
**p.p.m.** or **ppm** (no periods), parts per million.
**PPO** (no periods), polyphenylene oxide.
**ppr.** or **p.pr.**, present participle.
**P.P.S.** or **p.p.s.**, **1** a second postscript (Latin, *post postscriptum*). **2** *British.* Parliamentary Private Secretary.
**p.p.t.** or **ppt** (no periods), parts per thousand.
**PPWP** (no periods), Planned Parenthood-World Population.
**p.q.**, previous question.
**P.Q.**, **1** parliamentary question. **2** previous question. **3** Province of Quebec.
**pr.**, an abbreviation for the following:
**1** pair or pairs.
**2** paper.
**3** power.
**4** preferred (stock).
**5** present.
**6** price.
**7** priest.
**8** printing.
**9** pronoun.
**Pr** (no period), praseodymium (chemical element).
**Pr.**, **1** preferred (stock). **2** Provençal.
**PR** (no periods), **1** proportional representation. **2** public relations: *To hire a PR firm to manage an entire major campaign would involve an unthinkable degree of abdication for a self-respecting political leader* (Harper's). **3** Puerto Rico (with postal Zip Code).
**P.R.**, **1** proportional representation. **2** Puerto Rico.
**PRA** (no periods), Public Roads Administration.
**prac|ti|ca|bil|i|ty** (prak′tə kə bil′ə tē), *n., pl.* **-ties**. the quality of being practicable.
**prac|ti|ca|ble** (prak′tə kə bəl), *adj.* **1** that can be done; capable of being put into practice: *a practicable idea.* **SYN**: feasible. See syn. under **possible**. **2** that can be used or crossed over: *a practicable road. The moat had been rendered practicable in many places by the heaps of rubbish* (John L. Motley). [< French *praticable* < *pratiquer* to practice (see etym. under **practical**); English spelling influenced by *practic*] —**prac′ti|ca|ble|ness**, *n.* —**prac′ti|ca|bly**, *adv.*
**prac|ti|cal** (prak′tə kəl), *adj., n.* —*adj.* **1** having to do with action or practice rather than thought or theory: *Earning a living is a practical matter.* **SYN**: See syn. under **sensible**. **2** fit for actual practice: *a practical plan. My scheme ... was so much more practical ... than the one hatched by those three simple-minded conspirators* (W. H. Hudson). **3** useful: *Bookbinding, basketwork, and interior decoration are practical arts. His legal knowledge was not very practical when he became a chemist.* **4** having good sense; using common sense: *A practical person does not spend his time and money foolishly.* **5** inclined toward or fitted for action rather than thought or imagination; matter-of-fact; prosaic: *a practical mind. A common-place, practical reply ... was, I was sure, the best* (Charlotte Brontë). **6** engaged in actual practice or work: *A practical farmer runs a farm.* **7** being such in effect; virtual: *So many of our soldiers were captured that our victory was a practical defeat.*
—*n.* **1** an examination of practical knowledge in some subject: *She had arrived in Edinburgh still "stiff as a board" after some exhausting practicals as a physical education student* (London Times). **2** a pragmatic or practical person: *Visionaries disagreed with practicals and writers of sensibility with social historians* (Saul Bellow).
[extension of *practic* < Old French *practique,* learned borrowing from Late Latin *practicus* < Greek *prāktikós* < *prāktós* < *prāttein,* variant of *prâssein* do, act] —**prac′ti|cal|ness**, *n.*
**prac|ti|cal|i|ty** (prak′tə kal′ə tē), *n., pl.* **-ties**. **1** the quality of being practical; practical usefulness; practical habit of mind: *Company officials believe they can prove the practicality of an increased number of machines* (Wall Street Journal). **2** a practical matter.
**prac|ti|cal|ize** (prak′tə kə līz), *v.t.,* **-ized**, **-iz|ing**. to make practical or workable: *Some [color measurements] may serve better, if modified or practicalized* (Matthew Luckiesh).
**practical joke**, a trick played on someone to have a laugh at him: *brutal practical jokes.*
**practical joker**, a person who plays practical jokes.
**prac|ti|cal|ly** (prak′tə klē), *adv.* **1** really; so far as the results will be; in effect: *He is only a clerk, but he is in the store so much of the time that he practically runs the business.* **SYN**: virtually. **2** *Informal.* almost; nearly: *Our house is around the corner, so we are practically home.* **3** in a practical way; in a useful way: *You must stop wishing and start thinking practically.* **4** by actual practice: *I learned the game practically, not just by watching others play.*
**practical nurse**, a person whose occupation is to care for the sick, but who does not have the hospital training or diploma of a registered nurse.
**prac|ti|cant** (prak′tə kənt), *n.* = practitioner.
**prac|tice** (prak′tis), *n., v.,* **-ticed**, **-tic|ing**. —*n.* **1** an action done many times over for skill: *Practice makes perfect. Practice is as essential to the great writer as it is to the great violinist* (Atlantic). **SYN**: drill, exercise. **2** skill gained by experience or exercise: *He was out of practice at batting.* **3** the action or process of doing or being something: *Your plan is good in theory, but not in actual practice.* **4** the usual way; custom: *It is the practice at the factory to blow the whistles at noon.* **SYN**: habit. See syn. under **custom**. **5** the working at or following of a profession or occupation: *He is engaged in the practice of law.* **6** the business of a lawyer or doctor: *The old doctor sold his practice to the younger doctor.* **7** *Law.* the established method of conducting legal proceedings. **8a** *Archaic.* a scheme; plot. **b** plotting; trickery.
[< verb]
—*v.t.* **1** to do (some act) again and again to learn to do it well: *to practice playing the piano. He practiced pitching the ball.* **SYN**: See syn. under **exercise**. **2** to make a custom of; do usually: *Practice what you preach.* **3** to follow, observe, or use day after day: *People who are fat must learn to practice moderation in what they eat. We practised republican principles long before a republic was thought of* (Joseph Conrad). **4** to work at or follow as a profession, art, or occupation: *to practice medicine.* **5** to give training to; drill. **SYN**: train. **6** to take advantage of. **7** to carry out; do: *lest some treachery should be suddenly practised by the enemies* (II Maccabees 14:22). **8** *Obsolete.* to plot: *I doubt My uncle practises more harm to me* (Shakespeare).
—*v.i.* **1** to do something again and again to learn to do it well: *to practice with the rifle. She practices on the piano every day.* **2** to do something as a habit or practice: *to practice as well as preach.* **3** to practice a profession: *That young man is just beginning to practice as a lawyer.* **4** *Archaic.* to scheme; plot.
**practices**, actions; acts (usually in a bad sense): *the practices of criminals.*
[< Old French *practiser,* earlier *practiquer* < Medieval Latin *practicare* < Late Latin *prācticus* practical] —**prac′tic|er**, *n.*
► **practice, practise**. The noun is always spelled *practice* in American usage; the verb is either *practice* or *practise.* Noun: *Practice makes perfect.* Verb: *We must practice* (or *practise*) *what we preach.*
**prac|ticed** or **prac|tised** (prak′tist), *adj.* **1** skilled; expert; experienced; proficient: *Years of study have made him a practiced musician.* **SYN**: versed, accomplished. **2** acquired or perfected through practice: *practiced charm.*
**prac|tic|es** (prak′tə siz), *n.pl.* See under **practice**.
**prac|tice-teach** (prak′tis tēch′), *v.i.,* **-taught**, **-teach|ing**. to teach at a school for a certain period as part of one's college or university train-

ing in order to qualify for a teacher's certificate or diploma.

**practice teacher**, a person who practice-teaches; student teacher.

**prac|ti|cum** (prak′tə kəm), *n., pl.* **-cums, -ca** (-kə). a course in colleges and schools in practical work or in independent research, or an exercise of a practical nature, as in laboratory or field work. [< German *Praktikum* < New Latin (*collegium*) *practicum* practical (course) < Medieval Latin *practicare* to practice]

**prac|tise** (prak′tis), *n., v.t., v.i.,* **-tised, -tis|ing.** = practice. —**prac′tis|er,** *n.*

**prac|ti|tion|er** (prak tish′ə nər, -tish′nər), *n.* **1** a person engaged in the practice of a profession: *He was a medical practitioner for ten years; later he taught medicine. Science enriches ... the lives of its practitioners* (Polykarp Kusch). **2** a person who makes a practice of anything: *To these simple practitioners of the open-air life the settled populations seemed corrupt, crowded, vicious* (H. G. Wells). **3** a person authorized as a Christian Science healer. [earlier *practician* (< Old French *practicien* < *practique* (see etym. under **practical**) + *-er*[1]]

**prad** (prad), *n. Especially British Slang.* a horse. [by metathesis < Dutch *paard* < Late Latin *paraverēdus* a horse for outlying districts; see etym. under **palfrey**]

**pra|do** (prä′dō), *n., pl.* **-dos.** a fashionable boulevard or promenade, especially in a Spanish-speaking country. [< Spanish *prado* (originally) field, pasture < Latin *prātum* meadow]

**praec|i|pe** (pres′ə pē), *n. Law.* a writ requiring something to be done, or demanding a reason for its nonperformance. Also, **precipe.** [< Latin *praecipe,* imperative of *praecipere* to order, advise; see etym. under **precept**]

**prae|co|cial** (pri kō′shəl), *adj.* = precocial.

**prae|di|al** (prē′dē əl), *adj.* = predial.

**prae|fect** (prē′fekt), *n.* = prefect.

**prae|lect** (pri lekt′), *v.i.* = prelect.

**prae|mu|ni|re** (prē′myů nī′rē), *n.* in English law: **1** a writ of summons on the charge of resorting to a foreign court or authority, such as that of the pope, and so disregarding the supremacy of the sovereign. **2** this offense. **3** the penalty, as of forfeiture, imprisonment, or outlawry, incurred for it. [short for *praemunire facias* (words occurring in the writ), (literally) that thou do warn; *praemunire* warn < Medieval Latin confusion of Latin *praemunīre* to fortify, and *praemonēre* to warn]

**prae|no|men** (prē nō′mən), *n.pl.* **-no|mens, -nom|i|na** (-nom′ə nə). the first or personal name of a Roman citizen, such as *Marcus* in *Marcus Tullius Cicero.* Also, **prenomen.** [< Latin *praenōmen* forename < *prae-* before + *nōmen* name]

**prae|nom|i|nal** (prē nom′ə nəl), *adj.* of or having to do with a praenomen.

**prae|pos|i|tor** (prē poz′ə tər), *n.* = prepositor.

**prae|pos|tor** (prē pos′tər), *n.* = prepositor.

**prae|sid|i|um** (pri sid′ē əm), *n.* = presidium.

**prae|tex|ta** (prē teks′tə), *n., pl.* **-tae** (-tē). a white toga with a purple border worn by boys in ancient Rome until they were entitled to wear the toga of manhood and by girls until they were married: *the usual youth's garment, the short praetexta, reaching below the knee* (Nicholas P. S. Wiseman). [< Latin *praetexta,* short for *toga praetexta* toga fringed in front]

**prae|tor** (prē′tər, -tôr), *n.* **1** a magistrate or judge in ancient Rome. A praetor ranked next below a consul. **2** a consul as leader of the ancient Roman army. [< Latin *praetor, -ōris* < unrecorded *prae-itor* one who goes before < *prae-* before + stem of *īre* to go]

**prae|to|ri|al** (prē tôr′ē əl, -tōr′-), *adj.* of or having to do with a Roman praetor.

**prae|to|ri|an** (prē tôr′ē ən, -tōr′-), *adj., n.* —*adj.* **1** of or having to do with a praetor. **2** Often, **Praetorian.** having to do with the bodyguard of a Roman commander or emperor.
—*n.* **1** Often, **Praetorian.** a soldier of the bodyguard of a Roman commander or emperor. **2** a man having the rank of a praetor. Also, **pretorian.**

**Praetorian Guard**, the bodyguard of a Roman emperor.

**prae|to|ri|an|ism** (prē tôr′ē ə niz əm, -tōr′-), *n.* **1** any system like that of the Roman praetorian organization. **2** *Figurative.* military despotism, especially when corrupt: *The actions of the Peruvian military ... giving rise to fears that praetorianism would spread through others of the politically "soft" republic* (K. H. Silvert).

**prae|to|ri|um** (prē tôr′ē əm, -tōr′-), *n., pl.* **-to|ri|a** (-tôr′ē ə, -tōr′-). **1** the commander's headquarters in an ancient Roman camp. **2** the official residence of the governor of an ancient Roman province. Also, **pretorium.** [< Latin *praetorium* < *praetor* praetor]

**prae|tor|ship** (prē′tər ship), *n.* the office, dignity, or term of office of a praetor.

**prag|mat|ic** (prag mat′ik), *adj., n.* —*adj.* **1** concerned with practical results or values; viewing things in a matter-of-fact way. **2** of or having to do with pragmatism: *a pragmatic philosophy.* **3** having to do with the affairs of a state or community. **4** busy; active. **5** meddlesome; interfering. **SYN:** officious. **6** conceited; opinionated. **7** matter-of-fact: *Their pragmatic ... approach increasingly fits the apolitical mood of the workers* (Economist). **8** treating the facts of history systematically, with special reference to their causes and effects.
—*n.* **1** = pragmatic sanction. **2** = busybody. **3** a conceited person.
[< Latin *prāgmaticus* < Greek *prāgmatikós* efficient, one skilled in business or civil affairs < *prâgma, -atos* civil business; deed, act < *prâssein* to do, act. Compare etym. under **practical.**]
—**prag|mat′i|cal|ly,** *adv.* —**prag|mat′i|cal|ness,** *n.*

**prag|mat|i|cal** (prag mat′ə kəl), *adj.* = pragmatic.

**prag|mat|i|cism** (prag mat′ə siz əm), *n.* the system of pragmatism founded by the American philosopher Charles S. Peirce (1839-1914), as distinguished from that of William James.

**prag|mat|ics** (prag mat′iks), *n.* a division of semiotics which studies the relations between signs and their users.

**pragmatic sanction**, any one of various imperial decrees issued as fundamental law by former European emperors or monarchs.

**prag|ma|tism** (prag′mə tiz əm), *n.* **1** the philosophy that tests the value and truth of ideas by their practical consequences. Pragmatism originated in America in the 1800's. *The American philosophers who gave form to the doctrines of pragmatism—William James, Charles Peirce, and John Dewey ... claimed that an idea could be said to "work" only when actions based upon it resulted in the predicted results* (Goodwin Watson). **2** pragmatic quality or condition; concern with practical results or values. **3** officiousness. **4** dogmatism. **5** a matter-of-fact way of viewing things.

**prag|ma|tist** (prag′mə tist), *n., adj.* —*n.* **1** a person who believes in pragmatism: *If the individual was to be justified by the pragmatist's idea that "a thing is true if it works," it could only be done in terms of the outer ... world, where things can be seen, tested, and measured* (Wall Street Journal). **2** a busybody.
—*adj.* = pragmatistic.

**prag|ma|tis|tic** (prag′mə tis′tik), *adj.* of or having to do with pragmatism or pragmatists.

**prag|ma|tize** (prag′mə tīz), *v.t.,* **-tized, -tiz|ing.** to represent as real or material. —**prag′ma|tiz′er,** *n.*

**pra|hu** (prä′hü, -ü), *n.* = proa.

**Prai|rial** (pre ryȧl′), *n.* the ninth month of the French Revolutionary calendar, extending from May 20 to June 18. [< French *Prairial* < *prairie* meadow, prairie]

**prai|rie** (prãr′ē), *n.* **1** a large area of level or rolling land with grass but few or no trees, especially such an area making up much of central North America: *We saw the green, oceanlike expanse of prairie, stretching swell over swell to the horizon* (Francis Parkman). **2** *U.S. Dialect.* a small open space in a forest. [American English < French *prairie* < Old French *praerie* < Vulgar Latin *prātaria* < Latin *prātum* meadow]

**Prai|rie** (prãr′ē), *adj., n.* —*adj.* of or having to do with the Prairie Provinces (Manitoba, Saskatchewan, and Alberta) of western Canada.
—*n.* a Prairie Province: *The rural-urban split in Canada is greater than ever; and the Prairies are as solidly conservative as in 1962* (John Meisel).

**prairie chicken**, **1** any one of several varieties of brown, black, and white grouse that live on the prairies of North America, especially the greater prairie chicken and the lesser prairie chicken. The prairie chicken is noted for its elaborate courtship. **2** = sharp-tailed grouse.

**prairie clover**, any one of various herbs of the pea family with small, pink, purple, or white flowers in dense heads or spikes.

**prairie crocus**, the American species of pasqueflower, with fuzzy leaves and lavender to deep purple flowers, growing throughout the Midwestern plains of North America.

**prai|ried** (prãr′ēd), *adj.* having many prairies; bordered by prairies.

**prairie dog**, a burrowing animal like a woodchuck but smaller, found on the Great Plains and in the Rocky Mountain region. There are several kinds, making up a genus of rodents. Prairie dogs sometimes live in large colonies and have a shrill bark like that of a small dog. *Prairie dogs live in a "dog society" highly organized with respect to economic needs, social behavior and population control* (Science News Letter).

**prairie falcon**, a brownish falcon about the size of the duck hawk, found in the prairies and open areas of western North America.

**prairie oyster**, a raw egg, peppered and salted, and drunk in vinegar or brandy.

**prairie pigeon**, = Franklin's gull.

**prairie rattlesnake**, a rather small variety of rattlesnake of western North America, having a maximum length of about five feet.

**prairie schooner**, a large covered wagon used in crossing the plains of North America before the railroads were built. See picture under **covered wagon.**

**prairie squirrel**, any one of various burrowing rodents of western North America; gopher.

**Prairie State**, a nickname for Illinois.

**prairie warbler**, a warbler of the eastern United States having yellow underparts with black stripes on the sides and face.

**prairie wolf**, = coyote.

**praise** (prāz), *n., v.,* **praised, prais|ing.** —*n.* **1** the act or fact of saying that a thing or person is good; words that tell the worth or value of a thing or person: *Everyone heaped praise upon the winning team.* **SYN:** commendation, acclaim. **2** words or song worshiping God. **3** *Archaic.* a ground for praise or merit: *A restless crowd ... Whose highest praise is that they live in vain* (William Cowper). [< verb]
—*v.t.* **1** to speak well of: *The coach praised the team for its fine playing. She was enthusiastically praising the beauties of Gothic architecture* (F. Marion Crawford). **2** to worship in words or song: *to praise God.* —*v.i.* to give praise.
**damn with faint praise**, to praise with so little enthusiasm as to condemn: *Damn with faint praise, assent with civil leer* (Alexander Pope).
**sing the praises of**, to praise with enthusiasm: *Whitman's poems sing the praises of the United States and of democracy* (Gay W. Allen).
[< Old French *preisier* < Late Latin *pretiāre* to value, prize < Latin *pretium* a prize, price. See etym. of doublet **prize**[3].] —**prais′er,** *n.*
—*Syn. v.t.* **1 Praise, approve, commend** mean to think or speak well of. **Praise** means to express heartily a high opinion or admiration of someone or something: *The principal praised the students who had won scholarships.* **Approve** means to have or express a favorable opinion of: *Everyone approved her idea.* **Commend** suggests a formal expression of favorable opinion: *The mayor commended the boys for their quick thinking at the disaster.*

**praise|ful** (prāz′fəl), *adj.* **1** giving praise: *praiseful words.* **2** *Obsolete.* praiseworthy.

**praise|wor|thy** (prāz′wėr′ᴛʜē), *adj.* **-thi|er, -thi|est.** worthy of praise; deserving approval; commendable; laudable: *He does not ask what is allowable, but what is commendable and praiseworthy* (William Law). **SYN:** meritorious.
—**praise′wor′thi|ly,** *adv.* —**praise′wor′thi|ness,** *n.*

**Pra|krit** (prä′krit), *n.* any one of the Indo-European vernacular languages or dialects of northern and central India, especially those of the ancient and medieval periods. [< Sanskrit *prākṛta* natural, common, vulgar. Compare etym. under **Sanskrit.**]

**pra|line** (prä′lēn), *n.* a small cake of brown candy made of brown sugar or maple syrup and nuts, usually pecans or almonds. [American English < French *praline* < Marshal Duplessis-*Praslin,* 1598-1675, whose cook invented it]

**prall|tril|ler** (präl′tril′ər), *n. Music.* a melodic embellishment consisting of the rapid alternation of a principal tone with one usually a step above it; an inverted mordent. See picture under **mordent.** [< German *Pralltriller* < *Prall* recoil + *Triller* a trill]

**pram**[1] (pram), *n. British Informal.* a perambulator; baby carriage.

pram with sail

***pram**[2] (pram), *n.* a small rowboat with a flat bottom and a rectangular bow. [< Dutch *praam,* ultimately < a Slavic word]

**Pronunciation Key:** hat, āge, cãre, fär; let, ēqual, tėrm; it, īce; hot, ōpen, ôrder; oil, out; cup, pu̇t, rüle; child; long; thin; ᴛʜen; zh, measure; ə represents **a** in about, **e** in taken, **i** in pencil, **o** in lemon, **u** in circus.

**pram park**, *British.* an area reserved for parking baby carriages.

**prance** (prans, präns), *v.*, **pranced**, **pranc|ing**, *n.* —*v.i.* **1** to spring about as if dancing; move with high steps or with leaps from the hind to the front legs: *Horses prance when they feel lively.* **2** to ride on a horse doing this: *The insulting tyrant, prancing o'er the field ... His horse's hoofs wet with patrician blood* (Joseph Addison). **3** to move gaily or proudly; swagger: *The children pranced about in their new Halloween costumes.* **4** to caper; dance.
—*v.t.* to cause to prance.
—*n.* the act of prancing.
[Middle English *prancen,* and *prauncen;* origin uncertain] —**pranc′er**, *n.* —**pranc′ing|ly**, *adv.*

**pranc|y** (pran′sē, prän′-), *adj.*, **pranc|i|er**, **pranc|i|est**. that prances; characterized by prancing.

**pran|di|al** (pran′dē əl), *adj.* of or having to do with a meal, especially dinner. [< Latin *prandium* luncheon; meal + English *-al*[1]]

**Prandt|l number** (prän′təl), *Physics.* the specific heat of a fluid at constant pressure multiplied by its viscosity, and the product divided by its viscosity, and the product divided by its thermal conductivity.
[< Ludwig *Prandtl,* 1875-1953, a German physicist]

**prang** (prang), *n., v. Slang.* —*n.* a crash of or in an aircraft.
—*v.t., v.i.* **1** to crash (an aircraft): *Suppose I start cornering a little too fast ... and I prang the crate?* (New Yorker). **2** to destroy (a target or enemy aircraft).
[imitative]

**prank**[1] (prangk), *n., v.* —*n.* a piece of mischief; playful trick: *On April Fools' Day people often play pranks on each other. They ... played all manner of mischievous pranks* (Herman Melville). SYN: antic.
—*v.i.* to indulge in a prank or pranks.
[origin uncertain]

**prank**[2] (prangk), *v.t.* to dress in a showy way; adorn: *when violets pranked the turf with blue* (Oliver Wendell Holmes).
—*v.i.* to make a show or display; show off: *White houses prank where once were huts* (Matthew Arnold). [origin uncertain. Compare Middle Low German *prank* showiness, Dutch *pronken* to show off, strut.]

**prank|ish** (prang′kish), *adj.* **1** full of pranks; fond of pranks: *a prankish pupil.* **2** like a prank: *a prankish idea.* —**prank′ish|ly**, *adv.* —**prank′ishness**, *n.*

**prank|some** (prangk′səm), *adj.* = prankish.

**prank|ster** (prangk′stər), *n.* a person who plays practical jokes or other pranks.

**prank|y** (prang′kē), *adj.*, **prank|i|er**, **prank|i|est**. fond of pranks; prankish.

**prao** (prou), *n.* = proa.

**prase** (prāz), *n.* an indistinctly crystalline variety of green quartz. [< French *prase,* learned borrowing from Latin *prasius* < Greek *prásios* (*líthos*) leek-green (stone) < *práson* leek]

***pra|se|o|dym|i|um** (prā′zē ō dim′ē əm, -sē), *n.* a yellowish-white, rare-earth metallic chemical element which occurs with neodymium. Its green salts are used to tint ceramics. [< New Latin *praseodymium* < Greek *prásios* leek-green (see etym. under **prase**) + New Latin *didymium* < Greek *dídymos* twin < *dýo* double, twofold, two]

***praseodymium**

| symbol | atomic number | atomic weight | oxidation state |
|---|---|---|---|
| Pr | 59 | 140.907 | 3 |

**prat** (prat), *n. Slang.* the buttocks. [origin unknown]

**prate** (prāt), *v.*, **prat|ed**, **prat|ing**, *n.* —*v.i.* to talk a great deal in a foolish way: *to prate without ceasing.* —*v.t.* to say in an empty or foolish way.
—*n.* a prating; empty or foolish talk: *Hold your prate* (Samuel Lover). SYN: chatter, prattle.
[Middle English *praten;* origin uncertain. Compare Middle Dutch *praeten,* Middle Low German *praten.*] —**prat′er**, *n.* —**prat′ing|ly**, *adv.*

**prat|fall** (prat′fôl′), *n. U.S. Slang.* **1** a fall on the backside taken as part of a comic, roughhouse, or slapstick routine: *There is not a person alive who can suppress a guffaw at a perfectly timed pratfall* (Time). **2** any laughable mischance.

**prat|in|cole** (prat′ing kōl, prā′tin-), *n.* any one of a group of swallowlike shore birds of the Eastern Hemisphere, related to the plovers. [< New Latin *pratincola* the species name < Latin *prātum* meadow + *incola* inhabitant, resident < *incolere* < *in-* in + *colere* to dwell; also, cultivate]

**pra|tique** (pra tēk′, prat′ik), *n.* permission or license granted to a ship to carry on commerce with a port after passing quarantine or showing a clean bill of health. [< Old French *pratique,* earlier *practique* usage, practice]

**prat|tle** (prat′əl), *v.*, **-tled**, **-tling**. *n.* —*v.i.* **1** to talk as a child does; tell freely and carelessly: *The two neighbors prattled on and on about their private lives.* **2** to talk or tell in a foolish way; chatter: *to prattle in the most babyish way.* **3** *Figurative.* to sound like baby talk; babble: *the prattling of a brook or of leaves.*
—*v.t.* **1** to say in a childish way. **2** to say by chattering or babbling: *prattling scandal as he goes* (William Cowper).
—*n.* **1** childish or foolish talk: *The child had plenty of prattle in him* (Samuel Butler). **2** baby talk. **3** *Figurative.* sounds like baby talk; babble: *the prattle of a brook.*
[(frequentative) < *prate.* Compare Middle Low German *pratelen.*] —**prat′tler**, *n.* —**prat′tling|ly**, *adv.*

**pra|u** (prä′ü, prou), *n.* = proa.

**prav|i|ty** (prav′ə tē), *n., pl.* **-ties**. bad or corrupt state; depravity. [< Latin *prāvitās* < *prāvus* crooked, perverse]

***prawn** (prôn), *n., v.* —*n.* any one of several shellfish used for food. Prawns are much like shrimp but larger. They are related to shrimp.
—*v.i.* to fish for or catch prawns.
[Middle English *prayne,* and *prane;* origin uncertain] —**prawn′er**, *n.*

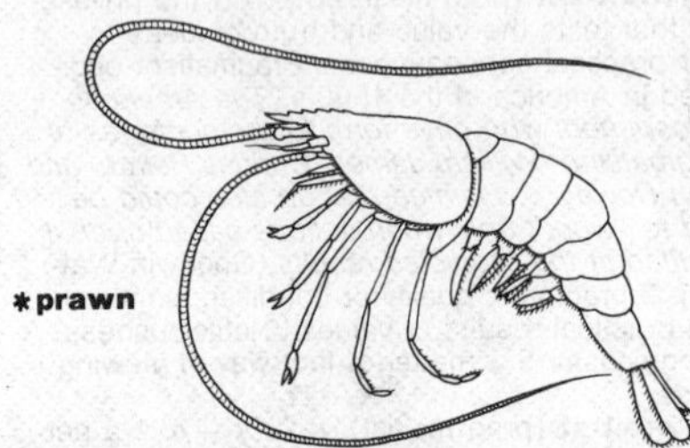

***prawn**

**prax|i|ol|o|gy** or **prax|e|ol|o|gy** (prak′sē ol′ə jē), *n.* the study of practice and custom in human relations. [< *praxis* + *-logy*]

**prax|is** (prak′sis), *n.* **1** practice, especially as contrasted with theory. **2** custom; use. **3** an example or group of examples for practice. [< Medieval Latin *praxis* < Greek *prâxis* a doing, acting < *prâssein* to do, act. Compare etym. under **practical**.]

**Prax|it|e|le|an** (prak sit′ə lē′ən), *adj.* having to do with or characteristic of Praxiteles, a Greek sculptor who lived about 350 B.C., or of his sculpture.

**pray** (prā), *v.i.* **1** to speak to God in worship; enter into spiritual communion with God; offer worship: *The entire congregation bowed their heads to pray.* **2** to ask from God or from any other object of worship: *to pray for help, to pray for one's family.* —*v.t.* **1** to ask earnestly: *There is nothing that we can do now but pray God to help.* SYN: entreat, implore, beseech, beg. **2** to ask earnestly for: *to pray someone's forgiveness. I know not how to pray your patience* (Shakespeare). SYN: crave. **3** to bring or get by praying: *to pray souls out of purgatory.* **4** please: *Pray come with me.* **5** to offer (a prayer). [< Old French *preier,* and *prier* < Late Latin *precāre* to pray for < Latin *precārī* < *prex, precis* prayer]

**prayer**[1] (prãr), *n.* **1** the act of praying: *Prayer as communion with the deity is not characteristic of Japanese Buddhism* (Atlantic). **2** the thing prayed for: *Their prayer was for peace. Our prayers were granted.* **3** a form of words to be used in praying: *The Lord's Prayer begins, "Our Father, which art in heaven." The farmers offered prayers for rain.* **4** a form of worship; religious service consisting mainly of prayers: *Prayer is one of the principal categories of worship* (Melville J. Herskovits). **5** an earnest request: *The flood victims broadcast a prayer for aid.* **6** the part of a pleading in a court proceeding or in a petition to a public body that states the action or relief desired. **7** *U.S. Slang.* a chance: *The other candidate didn't have a prayer* (New Yorker). [Middle English *praiere* < Old French *preiere* < Vulgar Latin *precāria* < Latin *precārius* (literally) things obtained by entreaty < *precārī* to pray, entreat] —**prayer′less**, *adj.*

**pray|er**[2] (prā′ər), *n.* a person who prays. [< *pray* + *er*[1]]

**prayer beads** (prãr), = rosary.

**prayer book** (prãr), a book of prayers: *A well-known prayer book is the Book of Common Prayer used by the Church of England* (Bernard Ramm).

**prayer|ful** (prãr′fəl), *adj.* having the habit of praying often; devout: *the prayerful life of monks. A prayerful silence filled the church.* SYN: pious, reverent. —**prayer′ful|ly**, *adv.* —**prayer′ful|ness**, *n.*

**prayer meeting** (prãr), a meeting for prayer and religious exercises, usually one at which several participants offer prayer.

**prayer rug** (prãr), a rug to kneel on during prayer, used especially by Moslems: *He rises every morning at 4 to read the Koran, prays five times a day in the mosque or on a prayer rug* (Time).

**prayer shawl** (prãr), = tallith.

**prayer stick** (prãr), a decorated stick used by some American Indians in religious ceremonies.

***prayer wheel** (prãr), a cylinder inscribed with or containing prayers, used by the Buddhists of Tibet. When it is rotated each turn counts as an uttered prayer.

***prayer wheel**

handheld

mounted

**pray-in** (prā′in′), *n.* a gathering of people to listen to sermons, improvise prayers, and sing religious songs, as a protest demonstration: *More than 3,000 Roman Catholics went to Westminster Cathedral for a "pray-in" called by an ad hoc group of laity, opposed to the Pope's ruling* (Sunday Times).

**pray|ing mantis** (prā′ing), = mantis.

**PRC** (no periods) or **P.R.C.**, People's Republic of China.

**pre-**, *prefix.* **1** before: *Prewar = before the war. Pre-Cambrian = before the Cambrian.*
**2** beforehand: *Preview = view beforehand.*
**3** before, as in position or space; in front of: *Premolar = in front of the molars.*
[< Latin *prae-* < *prae* before]
▶When **pre-** is joined to a root with initial *e,* the latter has usually been spelled with *ë* or preceded by the hyphen: *preëmpt, pre-empt;* most writers and editors now omit these marks: *preempt, preexistence.* The hyphen is also used before roots with an initial capital letter: *pre-Christian.* Otherwise prefix and root are joined directly without any mark: *preoccupy, prescription.*

**Words not separately defined in this dictionary appear in the following listing:**

**pre ab′do|men**
**pre′ac|cept′**
**pre′ac|cept′ance**
**pre|ac′cess**
**pre′ac|ces′si|ble**
**pre′ac|cord′**
**pre′ac|count′**
**pre′ac|cu′mu|late**
**pre′ac|cu′mu|la′tion**
**pre′ac|cu|sa′tion**
**pre′ac|cuse′**
**pre′ac|knowl′edge**
**pre′ac|knowl′edg|ment**
**pre′ac|quaint′**
**pre′ac|quaint′ance**
**pre′ac|quire′**
**pre′ac|quired′**
**pre′ac|quit′**
**pre′ac|quit′tal**
**pre|act′**
**pre|ac′tion**
**pre′a|dapt′**
**pre′a|dapt′a|ble**
**pre′ad|ap|ta′tion**
**pre′ad|just′**
**pre′ad|just′a|ble**
**pre′ad|just′ment**
**pre′ad|min′is|tra′tion**
**pre′ad|min′is|tra′tive**
**pre′ad|min′is|tra′tor**
**pre′ad|mis′sion**
**pre′ad|mit′**
**pre′ad|mon′ish**
**pre′ad|mo|ni′tion**
**pre′ad|o|les′cent**
**pre′a|dopt′**
**pre′a|dop′tion**
**pre′a|dult′**
**pre′a|dult′hood**
**pre′ad|vert′en|cy**
**pre′ad|vert′ent**
**pre|ad′ver|tise**
**pre′ad|ver|tise′ment**
**pre|ad′ver|tis′er**
**pre′ad|vice′**
**pre′ad|vis′a|ble**
**pre′ad|vise′**
**pre′ad|vis′er**
**pre′ad|vi′so|ry**
**pre′af|fect′**
**pre′af|fec′tion**
**pre′af|fil′i|a′tion**
**pre′af|fir|ma′tion**
**pre′af|ter|noon′**
**pre′ag|gres′sion**
**pre′ag|gres′sive**
**pre′a|gree′ment**
**pre′ag|ri|cul′tur|al**
**pre′a|larm′**
**pre′al|co|hol′ic**
**pre′al|le|ga′tion**
**pre′al|lege′**
**pre′al|li′ance**
**pre′al|lied′**
**pre′al|lot′**
**pre′al|lot′ment**

pre′al|low′
pre′al|ly′
pre|al′pha|bet
pre|al′tar
pre′al|ter|a′tion
pre′a|mal′ga|ma′tion
pre|am′bu|lar
pre|a′nal
pre′a|nal′y|sis
pre′an|es|thet′ic
pre′an|nex′
pre′an|nounce′
pre′an|nounce′ment
pre′an|te|pe′nult
pre′an|tiq′ui|ty
pre′a|or′tic
pre′ap|pear′ance
pre′ap|per|cep′tion
pre′ap|point′
pre′ap|point′ment
pre′ap|pre|hen′sion
pre′ap|prise′
pre′ap|prov′al
pre′ap|prove′
pre|ap′ti|tude
pre′ar|raign′
pre′ar|raign′ment
pre′ar|range′ment
pre′ar|rest′
pre′-Ar|thu′ri|an
pre′ar|tis′tic
pre-Ar′y|an
pre′as|cer|tain′
pre′as|cer|tain′ment
pre′as|sem′ble
pre′as|sign′
pre′as|sume′
pre′as|sur′ance
pre′as|sure′
pre′-As|syr′i|an
pre′at|tach′ment
pre′at|tune′
pre-Au′gus|tine
pre′a|vow′al
pre|ax′i|ad
pre′-Bab|y|lo′ni|an
pre|bach′e|lor
pre|bac′il|lar′y
pre′-Ba|co′ni|an
pre′bap|tis′mal
pre|bap′tize
pre|bar′gain
pre|bas′al
pre|bas′i|lar
pre′ben|e|dic′tion
pre′be|troth′al
pre′block|ade′
pre|bod′ing
pre|boil′
pre|boy′hood
pre|break′fast
pre|breathe′
pre-Brit′ish
pre|broad′cast′
pre′bro|mid′ic
pre|bron′chi|al
pre|buc′cal
pre-Bud′dhist
pre|budg′et
pre|budg′et|ar′y
pre-Byz′an|tine
pre|cal′cu|la|ble
pre|cal′cu|late
pre′cal|cu|la′tion
pre′cam|paign′
pre|can′di|da|cy
pre|can′vass
pre|cap′il|lar′y
pre|cap′i|tal|ist
pre′cap|i|tal|is′tic
pre|cap′ture
pre′-Car|bon|if′er|ous
pre|car′di|ac
pre|car′ni|val
pre′-Car|o|lin′gi|an
pre-Cath′o|lic
pre|cau′dal
pre-Celt′ic
pre|cen′sure
pre|cen′sus
pre′-Cen|ten′ni|al
pre|cen′tral
pre|cer′e|bral
pre′cer|ti|fi|ca′tion
pre|cer′ti|fy
pre|charge′
pre′-Chau|ce′ri|an
pre|check′
pre-Chel′le|an
pre|child′hood
pre′-Chi|nese′
pre|choose′
pre|cho′roid
pre′-Chris|ti|an′ic
pre-Christ′mas
pre′cir|cu|la′tion
pre′ci|ta′tion
pre|cit′ed
pre′civ|i|li|za′tion
pre|claim′
pre|claim′ant
pre|clas′sic
pre|clas′si|cal
pre′clas|si|fi|ca′tion
pre|clas′si|fied
pre|clas′si|fy
pre′cog|i|ta′tion
pre|cog′ni|za|ble
pre|cog′ni|zant
pre|coil′
pre|co′i|tal
pre′col|laps′i|ble
pre′col|lect′
pre′col|lect′a|ble
pre′col|lec′tion
pre|col′lege
pre′col|le′gi|ate
pre′com|bus′tion
pre′com|mend′
pre|com′ment
pre′com|mer′cial
pre′com|mit′
pre′com|mun′ion
pre′com|pli′ance
pre|com′pli|cate
pre′com|pose′
pre′com|pre|hen′sion
pre′com|pre|hen′sive
pre′com|press′
pre′com|pute′
pre′con|ceal′
pre′con|cede′
pre′con|ceiv′a|ble
pre|con′cen|trat′ed
pre′con|cen|tra′tion
pre′con|cep′tion|al
pre′con|ces′sion
pre′con|clude′
pre′con|clu′sion
pre′con|cur′
pre′con|cur′rence
pre′con|cur′rent
pre′con|demn′
pre′con|dem|na′tion
pre′con|den|sa′tion
pre′con|dense′
pre′con|duct′
pre′con|duc′tor
pre′con|fer′
pre|con′fer|ence
pre′con|fess′
pre′con|fes′sion
pre′con|fide′
pre′con|fig′ure
pre′con|fine′
pre′con|fine′ment
pre′con|firm′
pre′con|fir|ma′tion
pre′con|form′
pre′con|form′i|ty
pre′con|ges′tion
pre-Con′gress
pre′con|gres′sion|al
pre′con|jec′ture
pre′con|nu′bi|al
pre|con′se|crate
pre′con|se|cra′tion
pre′con|sent′
pre′con|sid′er
pre′con|sid′er|a′tion
pre′con|sol′i|date
pre′con|sol′i|dat′ed
pre′con|sol′i|da′tion
pre′con|stit′u|ent
pre|con′sti|tute
pre′con|struct′
pre′con|struc′tion
pre′con|sul|ta′tion
pre′con|sume′
pre′con|tained′
pre|con′tem|plate
pre′con|tem|pla′tion
pre′con|ti|nen′tal
pre′con|tract′
pre′con|trac′tive
pre′con|trac′tu|al
pre′con|triv′ance
pre′con|trive′
pre′con|ven′tion
pre′con|ver′sion
pre′con|vert′
pre′con|vey′
pre′con|vey′ance
pre′con|vict′
pre′con|vic′tion
pre|cook′
pre|cook′er
pre′-Co|per′ni|can
pre|cop′y
pre′cor|o|na′tion
pre′cor|rec′tion
pre′cor|res|pond′ent
pre|cor′ri|dor
pre′cor|rupt′
pre′cor|rup′tion
pre|cos′mic
pre|cos′mi|cal
pre|cos′tal
pre|coun′sel
pre|coun′sel|lor
pre′cre|ate′
pre′cre|a′tion
pre′cre|a′tive
pre|crit′i|cism
pre|cru′cial
pre′-Cru|sade′
pre|crys′tal|line
pre|cul′ti|vate
pre′cul|ti|va′tion
pre|cul′tur|al
pre|cul′ture
pre|cure′
pre′cur|ric′u|lar
pre′cur|ric′u|lum
pre|cut′
pre|cyst′ic
pre|damn′
pre′dam|na′tion
pre′-Dar|win′i|an
pre|day′light′
pre|day′time′
pre′de|cide′
pre′de|ci′sion
pre′de|ci′sive
pre′dec|la|ra′tion
pre′de|clare′
pre′dec|li|na′tion
pre′de|cline′
pre|ded′i|cate
pre′ded|i|ca′tion
pre′de|fine′
pre′def|i|ni′tion
pre|del′e|gate
pre′del|e|ga′tion
pre′de|lib′er|a′tion
pre′de|lin′quen|cy
pre′de|lin′quent
pre|dem′on|strate
pre′dem|on|stra′tion
pre|den′tal
pre′de|part|men′tal
pre′de|pres′sion
pre′de|scribe′
pre′de|scrip′tion
pre′de|sert′
pre′de|sert′er
pre′de|ser′tion
pre′de|sign′
pre′de|tain′
pre′de|tain′er
pre′de|ten′tion
pre′de|ter′mi|nate
pre′de|vel′op
pre′de|vel′op|ment
pre′de|vise′
pre′di|ag|no′sis
pre′di|ag|nos′tic
pre′di|as|tol′ic
pre′-Dick|en′si|an
pre|di′e|tar′y
pre|dig′i|tal
pre|din′ner
pre′dip|lo|mat′ic
pre′di|rect′
pre′di|rec′tion
pre′di|rec′tor
pre′dis|a|gree′ment
pre|dis′ci|pline
pre′dis|clo′sure
pre|dis′count
pre′dis|cour′age
pre′dis|cour′age|ment
pre|dis′course
pre′dis|cov′er
pre′dis|cov′er|er
pre′dis|cov′er|y
pre′dis|cus′sion
pre′dis|perse′
pre′dis|per′sion
pre′dis|pos′a|ble
pre′dis|pos′al
pre′dis|rupt′
pre′dis|rup′tion
pre′dis|so|lu′tion
pre′dis|solve′
pre′dis|suade′
pre′dis|tin′guish
pre|doc′tor|al
pre|doc′tor|ate
pre′doc|u|men′ta|ry
pre′do|mes′tic
pre|doom′
pre-Dor′ic
pre|dor′sal
pre|draft′
Pre′-Dra|vid′i|an
pre|draw′
pre|drill′
pre|dry′
pre|dusk′
pre-Dutch′
pre-East′er
pre′e|co|nom′ic
pre′e|co|nom′i|cal
pre|ed′it
pre′e|di′tion
pre′ed|i|to′ri|al
pre|ed′u|cate
pre′ed|u|ca′tion
pre′ed|u|ca′tion|al
pre′e|lec′tric
pre′e|lec′tri|cal
pre′el|e|men′tal
pre′el|e|men′ta|ry
pre′-E|liz′a|be′than
pre′e|man′ci|pa′tion
pre′em|bar′rass
pre′em|bar′rass|ment
pre′em|bod′i|ment
pre′em|bod′y
pre′e|mer′gen|cy
pre′e|mo′tion
pre′e|mo′tion|al
pre-Em′pire
pre′em|ploy′
pre′em|ploy′ment
pre′en|a′ble
pre′en|act′
pre′en|ac′tion
pre′en|close′
pre′en|clo′sure
pre′en|coun′ter
pre′en|deav′or
pre′en|dorse′
pre′en|dorse′ment
pre′en|force′
pre′en|force′ment
pre′en|gage′
pre′en|gage′ment
pre′en|gi|neered′
pre′en|gi|neer′ing
pre′en|large′
pre′en|large′ment
pre′en|light′en
pre′en|light′en|ing
pre′en|light′en|ment
pre′en|list′
pre′en|list′ment
pre′en|roll′
pre′en|roll′ment
pre|en′ter
pre′en|ter|tain′
pre′en|ter|tain′er
pre′en|ter|tain′ment
pre|en′trance
pre|en′try
pre′e|nu′mer|ate
pre′e|nu′mer|a′tion
pre′en|vel′op
pre′en|vel′op|ment
pre′en|vi′ron|men′tal
pre′ep|i|dem′ic
pre|ep′och|al
pre′e|quip′
pre′e|quip′ment
pre′e|rect′
pre′e|rec′tion
pre′e|rupt′
pre′e|rup′tion
pre′e|rup′tive
pre′es|sen′tial
pre′es|tab′lish
pre′es|tab′lish|ment
pre|es′ti|mate
pre′es|ti|ma′tion
pre′e|vap′o|rate
pre′e|vap′o|ra′tion
pre′ev|o|lu′tion|al
pre′ev|o|lu′tion|ar′y
pre′ex|act′
pre′ex|ac′tion
pre′ex|am′i|na′tion
pre′ex|am′ine
pre′ex|am′in|er
pre′ex|change′
pre′ex|clude′
pre′ex|clu′sion
pre′ex|clu′sive
pre′ex|cuse′
pre|ex′e|cute
pre′ex|e|cu′tion
pre′ex|empt′
pre′ex|emp′tion
pre′ex|haust′
pre′ex|haus′tion
pre′ex|hib′it
pre′ex|hi|bi′tion
pre′ex|hib′i|tor
pre′ex|pe|di′tion
pre′ex|pe|di′tion|ar′y
pre′ex|per′i|men′tal
pre′ex|pose′
pre′ex|po|si′tion
pre′ex|tin′guish
pre′ex|tin′guish|ment
pre|fab′u|lous
pre|fash′ion
pre|fed′er|al
pre|fes′ti|val
pre|feu′dal
pre|feu′dal|ism
pre|film′
pre|flow′er|ing
pre|fo′cus
pre′foun|da′tion
pre′fra|ter′nal
pre′fra|ter′nal|ly
pre|freeze′
pre-French′
pre|fresh′man
pre-Freud′i|an
pre|fur′lough
pre|fur′nish
pre|gain′
pre′-Gal|i|le′an
pre|gal′va|nize
pre′game
pre|gath′er
pre|gath′er|ing
pre′ge|o|log′i|cal
pre-Geor′gian
pre-Ger′man
pre′-Ger|man′ic
pre|girl′hood
pre|gla′cial
pre-Goth′ic
pre′grad|u|a′tion
pre′grat|i|fi|ca′tion
pre|grat′i|fy
pre-Greek′
pre′guar|an|tee′
pre|hard′en
pre|har′vest
pre|haunt′
pre|hear′ing
pre|heat′ed
pre-He′brew
pre′-Hel|len′ic
pre′-His|pan′ic
pre|hol′i|day
pre′-Ho|mer′ic
pre|hu′man
pre|im′age
pre′i|mag′i|nar′y
pre′i|mag′i|na′tion
pre′i|mag′ine
pre′im|bibe′
pre′im|bue′
pre|im′i|tate
pre′im|i|ta′tion
pre|im′i|ta′tive
pre′im|pe′ri|al
pre′im|press′
pre′im|pres′sion
pre′im|pres′sive
pre′in|au′gu|ral
pre′in|au′gu|rate
pre-In′ca
pre′in|car|na′tion
pre′in|cen′tive
pre′in|cli|na′tion
pre′in|cline′
pre′in|cor′po|rate
pre′in|cor′po|ra′tion
pre′in|de|pend′ence
pre′in|de|pend′ent
pre-In′di|an
pre|in′di|cate
pre′in|di|ca′tion
pre′in|dis|pose′
pre′in|dis′po|si′tion
pre′in|duc′tion
pre′in|duc′tive
pre′in|flec′tion|al
pre′in|flict′
pre′in|flic′tion
pre′in|form′
pre′in|for|ma′tion
pre′in|hab′it
pre′in|hab′it|ant
pre′in|hab′i|ta′tion
pre′in|here′
pre′in|her′it
pre′in|her′it|ance
pre′in|i′tial
pre′in|i′ti|ate
pre′in|i′ti|a′tion
pre′in|qui|si′tion
pre′in|scribe′
pre′in|scrip′tion
pre′in|sert′
pre′in|ser′tion
pre′in|spect′
pre′in|spec′tion
pre′in|stall′
pre′in|stal|la′tion
pre′in|still′
pre′in|stil|la′tion
pre′in|struct′
pre|in′su|late
pre′in|su|la′tion
pre′in|sur′ance
pre′in|sure′
pre′in|tend′
pre′in|ten′tion
pre|in′ter|change′
pre|in′ter|est
pre′in|ter′pret
pre′in|ter′pre|ta′tion
pre|in′ter|view
pre|in′ti|mate
pre′in|ti|ma′tion
pre|in′ven|to′ry
pre′in|vest′ment
pre′in|volve′
pre′in|volve′ment
pre|i′on|i|za′tion
pre|i′on|ize
pre-I′rish
pre-Is′lam
pre′-Is|lam′ic
pre-Is′lam|ite
pre′i|som′er|ize
pre|is′sue
pre-Jew′ish
pre′-John|so′ni|an
pre|jun′ior
pre′jus|ti|fi|ca′tion
pre|jus′ti|fy
pre-Keynes′i|an
pre|kin′der|gar′ten
pre|kin′dle
pre|know′
pre|knowl′edge
pre′-Ko|ran′ic
pre|la′bel
pre|lac′te|al
pre|lam′i|nate
pre-Lat′in
pre|launch′
pre|law′
pre|law′ful
pre|le′gal
pre|leg′is|la′tive
pre|li′cense
pre|lim′it
pre′lin|guis′tic
pre′-Lin|nae′an
pre|lit′er|ar′y
pre|lit′er|a|ture
pre|load′
pre|loan′
pre|lo′cate
pre|log′i|cal
pre|lu′bri|cate
pre|lum′bar
pre-Lu′ther|an
pre′ma|chine′
pre|mad′ness
pre|make′
pre|mak′er
pre′-Ma|lay′an
pre′ma|lig′nant
pre′man|dib′u|lar
pre′ma|ni′a|cal
pre′man|u|fac′ture
pre|mar′i|tal
pre|mar′riage
pre|mar′ry
pre-Marx′i|an
pre|match′
pre′ma|te′ri|al
pre′mat|ri|mo′ni|al
pre|meas′ure
pre|meas′ure|ment
pre|med′i|cate

**Pronunciation Key:** hat, āge, cãre, fär; let, ēqual, tėrm; it, īce; hot, ōpen, ôrder; **oi**l, **ou**t; cup, pu̇t, rüle; **ch**ild; lo**ng**; **th**in; ᴛʜen; **zh**, measure; ə represents **a** in about, **e** in taken, **i** in pencil, **o** in lemon, **u** in circus.

**pre′med|i|ca′tion**
**pre′me|di|e′val**
**pre′mem|o|ran′dum**
**pre′me|mo′ri|al**
**pre′men|o|pau′sal**
**pre|merg′er**
**pre′-Mes|si|an′ic**
**pre-Meth′od|ist**
**pre|mid′night**
**pre|mid′sum′mer**
**pre|min′is|ter**
**pre|mix′ture**
**pre|mod′el**
**pre|mod′ern**
**pre′-Mo|ham′me|dan**
**pre|mold′**
**pre′mo|nar′chi|cal**
**pre|mon′e|tar′y**
**pre′-Mon|go′li|an**
**pre′mon|u|men′tal**
**pre|mor′al**
**pre′mo|ral′i|ty**
**pre|mor′al|ly**
**pre|morn′ing**
**pre|mor′tal**
**pre′mo|sa′ic**
**pre′-Mo|sa′ic**
**pre-Mos′lem**
**pre|mourn′**
**pre|move′**
**pre′mu|nic′i|pal**
**pre|mu′si|cal**
**pre|mus′ter**
**pre′-My|ce|nae′an**
**pre|myth′i|cal**
**pre′-Na|po′le|on′ic**
**pre|na′tion|al**
**pre|na′tive**
**pre|nat′u|ral**
**pre|na′val**
**pre|neb′u|lar**
**pre′ne|go′ti|ate**
**pre′ne|go′ti|a′tion**
**pre′ne|o|lith′ic**
**pre′ne|phrit′ic**
**pre′-New|to′ni|an**
**pre-Nor′man**
**pre-Norse′**
**pre|num′ber**
**pre|num′ber|ing**
**pre|nup′tial**
**pre|nurs′er|y**
**pre′ob|jec′tion**
**pre′ob|li|ga′tion**
**pre′ob|serv′ance**
**pre′ob|ser|va′tion**
**pre′ob|ser|va′tion|al**
**pre′ob|serve′**
**pre′ob|tain′**
**pre′ob|tain′a|ble**
**pre′oc|cip′i|tal**
**pre′oc|clu′sion**
**pre|oc′cu|pant**
**pre|of′fer**
**pre|o′pen**
**pre|o′pen|ing**
**pre|op′er|at′ing**
**pre|op′er|a′tion|al**
**pre|op′tic**
**pre|or′bit|al**
**pre′or|dained′**
**pre′or|dain′ment**
**pre|or′der**
**pre′or|gan′ic**
**pre′o|rig′i|nal**
**pre′o|rig′i|nal|ly**
**pre|o′vu|la|to′ry**
**pre′-Pa|le|o|zo′ic**
**pre′par|lia|men′ta|ry**
**pre′par|oc|cip′i|tal**
**pre|par′ti|san**
**pre′par|ti′tion**
**pre|part′ner|ship**
**pre|pat′ent**
**pre-Paul′ine**
**pre|pen′e|trate**
**pre′pen|e|tra′tion**
**pre|peo′ple**
**pre′per|cep′tion**
**pre′per|i|to|ne′al**
**pre-Per′mi|an**
**pre-Pe′trine**
**pre′pig|men′tal**
**pre|pi′ous**
**pre′pi|tu′i|tar′y**
**pre|place′**
**pre′pla|cen′tal**
**pre|planned′**
**pre|plant′**
**pre|plot′**
**pre|pol′ish**
**pre-Pol′ish**
**pre|pol′i|tic**
**pre′po|lit′i|cal**
**pre′por|tray′**
**pre′por|tray′al**
**pre′po|ten′tial**
**pre′prep|a|ra′tion**
**pre|price′**
**pre|pri′ma′ry**
**pre|prim′er**
**pre′pro|duc′tion**
**pre′pro|fess′**
**pre′pro|hi|bi′tion**
**pre′pro|nounce′**
**pre′pro|nounce′ment**
**pre′pro|phet′ic**
**pre|prove′**
**pre′pro|vide′**
**pre′psy|chol′o|gy**
**pre|pu′ber|tal**
**pre′pub|li|ca′tion**
**pre′pub|lic′i|ty**
**pre|pub′li|cize**
**pre|pub′lish**
**pre|punch′**
**pre′qual|i|fi|ca′tion**
**pre|qual′i|fy**
**pre|quar′an|tine**
**pre|ques′tion**
**pre|race′**
**pre|rail′road′**
**pre|rail′way′**
**pre-Raph′a|el**
**pre|ra′tion|al**
**pre|read′i|ness**
**pre′re|ceipt′**
**pre′re|ceive′**
**pre′re|ceiv′er**
**pre′re|ces′sion**
**pre|rec|og|ni′tion**
**pre′rec|om|mend′**
**pre|rec′on|cile**
**pre|rec′on|cile′ment**
**pre′-Re|con|struc′tion**
**pre|rec′tal**
**pre′re|deem′**
**pre′re|demp′tion**
**pre|ref′er|ence**
**pre′re|fine′ment**
**pre′re|form′**
**pre|ref|or|ma′tion**
**pre′-Ref|or|ma′tion**
**pre′re|form′a|to′ry**
**pre|reg′is|ter**
**pre′reg|is|tra′tion**
**pre′reg|u|la′tion**
**pre′re|lease′**
**pre′re|li′gious**
**pre′re|mit′tance**
**pre′re|morse′**
**pre-Ren′ais|sance**
**pre|re′nal**
**pre′rep|re|sent′**
**pre′rep|re|sen|ta′tion**
**pre′re|quire′**
**pre′re|quire′ment**
**pre′re|sem′blance**
**pre′re|sem′ble**
**pre′re|solve′**
**pre′res|pi|ra′tion**
**pre′re|spire′**
**pre′-Res|to|ra′tion**
**pre′re|stric′tion**
**pre′re|veal′**
**pre′rev|e|la′tion**
**pre′re|view′**
**pre′re|vi′sion**
**pre′re|viv′al**
**pre′-Rev|o|lu′tion**
**pre′rev|o|lu′tion|ar′y**
**pre-Ro′man**
**pre′ro|man′tic**
**pre′ro|man′ti|cism**
**pre|roy′al**
**pre|sa′cral**
**pre′sal|va′tion**
**pre|sanc′ti|fy**
**pre|san′i|tar′y**
**pre′sar|to′ri|al**
**pre|sav′age**
**pre|sav′age|ry**
**pre-Sax′on**
**pre′scho|las′tic**
**pre′sci|en|tif′ic**
**pre|score′**
**pre|scout′**
**pre|screen′**
**pre|seal′**
**pre|search′**
**pre|sea′son**
**pre|sea′son|al**
**pre|sec′u|lar**
**pre′se|cure′**
**pre′se|lect′**
**pre′se|lec′tion**
**pre|sell′**
**pre|sem′i|nar′y**
**pre′-Se|mit′ic**
**pre|se′nile**
**pre|sen′si|tize**
**pre|sen′tence**
**pre|serv′ice**
**pre|ses′sion**
**pre|set′tle**
**pre|set′tle|ment**
**pre|shad′ow**
**pre-Shake′speare**
**pre′-Shake|spear′i|an**
**pre|shape′**
**pre|sharp′en**
**pre|ship′**
**pre|ship′ment**
**pre|show′**
**pre|shrink′**
**pre|sift′**
**pre|sig′nal**
**pre′-Si|lu′ri|an**
**pre|slav′er|y**
**pre|so′cial**
**pre′-So|crat′ic**
**pre|so′lar**
**pre|soph′o|more**
**pre|space′**
**pre-Span′ish**
**pre|spi′nal**
**pre|sput′nik**
**pre|stamp′**
**pre′stand|ard|i|za′tion**
**pre|stand′ard|ize**
**pre|steam′**
**pre|ster′i|lize**
**pre|stim′u|lus**
**pre|stock′**
**pre|strength′en**
**pre|stretch′**
**pre′strike′**
**pre|stud′y**
**pre′sub|sist′ence**
**pre′sub|sist′ent**
**pre′suc|cess′**
**pre′suc|cess′ful**
**pre′sup|ple|men′ta|ry**
**pre|sur′ger|y**
**pre|sur′gi|cal**
**pre′sus|pect′**
**pre|symp′tom**
**pre-Syr′i|an**
**pre′sys|tol′ic**
**pre|taste′**
**pre|tast′er**
**pre′tax|a′tion**
**pre|tel′e|graph**
**pre′tel|e|graph′ic**
**pre|tel′e|phone**
**pre′tel|e|phon′ic**
**pre|tem′po|ral**
**pre|ter′mi|nal**
**pre′ter|res′tri|al**
**pre-Ter′ti|ar′y**
**pre′-Thanks|giv′ing**
**pre′tho|rac′ic**
**pre|tib′i|al**
**pre|tinc′ture**
**pre|tour′na|ment**
**pre|tra′che|al**
**pre′tra|di′tion|al**
**pre|train′**
**pre|trea′ty**
**pre|trib′al**
**pre′tu|ber′cu|lous**
**pre-Tu′dor**
**pre′un|der|stand′**
**pre|un′ion**
**pre′u|nite′**
**pre|vac′ci|nate**
**pre′vac|ci|na′tion**
**pre′val|u|a′tion**
**pre|val′ue**
**pre|ver′bal**
**pre|ver′nal**
**pre|ver′te|bral**
**pre|ves′i|cle**
**pre′-Vic|to′ri|an**
**pre′-Vir|gil′i|an**
**pre|vis′it**
**pre|vis′i|tor**
**pre|vo′cal**
**pre|vo′cal|ly**
**pre′vo|li′tion|al**
**pre-Vol′stead**
**pre|vote′**
**pre|warn′**
**pre|weigh′**
**pre|wire′**
**pre|wrap′**

**preach** (prēch), *v., n.* —*v.i.* **1** to speak publicly on a religious subject: *Our minister preaches on Sunday morning. Who is going to preach at the Christmas Service?* **2** to give earnest advice. **3** to give advice earnestly, usually in a meddling or tiresome way: *My great-aunt is forever preaching about good table manners.*
—*v.t.* **1** to deliver (a sermon): *Dr. Clark preached a very eloquent sermon.* **2** to make known by preaching; proclaim: *to preach the Gospel.* **3** to recommend strongly; urge: *The coach was always preaching exercise and fresh air. Practice what you preach.* **SYN:** advocate.
—*n. Informal.* a sermon; religious discourse.
[< Old French *preche,* French *prêche* a preaching; from the verb]
**preach down, a** to condemn by preaching; speak against: *to preach down war and violence.* **b** to suppress or silence by preaching: *to preach down criticism.*
**preach up,** to commend by preaching; speak in favor of: *Philosophy and Christianity both preach up forgiveness of injuries* (Henry Fielding).
[< Old French *prechier,* short for *preëchier* < *predichier,* learned borrowing from Latin *praedicāre* declare publicly (in Late Latin, to preach). See etym. of doublet **predicate.**]

**preach|er** (prē′chər), *n.* a person who preaches; clergyman; minister; pastor: *I think they come under the heading of what the old preacher called vanity* (New Yorker).
**the Preacher,** a title given to the author or narrator of the book of Ecclesiastes; the Ecclesiast: *These are the words of the Preacher, the son of David, King of Jerusalem* (Miles Coverdale).

**preacher bird,** = red-eyed vireo.

**preach|er|ship** (prē′chər ship), *n.* the office of a preacher.

**preach|i|fy** (prē′chə fī), *v.i.,* **-fied, -fy|ing.** *Informal.* to preach or moralize too much, or in a tedious or pompous way.

**preach|ing** (prē′ching), *n.* **1a** what is preached; sermon. **b** a public religious service with a sermon. **2** the act or practice of a person who preaches: *France combines an imperishable structure with the perpetual preaching of insurrection* (Newsweek). —**preach′ing|ly,** *adv.*

**preaching cross,** a cross formerly erected to mark a place for open-air preaching, as by monks.

**preach|ment** (prēch′mənt), *n.* **1** the act or practice of preaching. **2** a long, tiresome sermon or speech: *Most parents tend to rely on preachments to impart their values to their children* (Sidonie M. Gruenberg).

**preach|y** (prē′chē), *adj.,* **preach|i|er, preach|i|est.** *Informal.* **1** inclined to preach: *Of the 1,400-odd books ... many, of course, are teachy, preachy pills of moralism* (Newsweek). **SYN:** didactic. **2** suggestive of preaching. —**preach′i|ly,** *adv.* —**preach′i|ness,** *n.*

**pre|a|dam|ic** (prē′ə dam′ik), *adj.* before Adam.

**pre|ad|a|mite** (prē ad′ə mīt), *n., adj.* —*n.* **1** a person believed to have lived before Adam. **2** a person who holds that there were men in existence before Adam.
—*adj.* **1** that existed before Adam: *detached broken fossils of preadamite whales* (Herman Melville). **2** having to do with the preadamites.
[< New Latin *Praeadamitae,* plural < Latin *prae-* before + *Adam* Adam + *-itae* -ite[1]]

**pre|ad|o|les|cence** (prē′ad ə les′əns), *n.* **1** the period of life between childhood and adolescence: *Almost all little girls, caught in the special exaltations of preadolescence, ... long to be some kind of heroine* (Maclean's). **2** = prepuberty.

**pre|al|bu|mi|nu|ric** (prē al byü′mə nůr′ik, -nyůr′-), *adj.* preceding the occurrence of albuminuria: *the prealbuminuric stage of Bright's disease.*

**pre|am|ble** (prē′am′bəl), *n.* **1** a preliminary statement; introduction to a speech or a writing. The reasons for a law and its general purpose are often stated in a preamble. *This is a long preamble of a tale* (Chaucer). **2** a preliminary or introductory fact or circumstance, especially one showing what is to follow: *This was the preamble of the great troubles that ... followed* (Robert Blair). [< Old French *preambule,* learned borrowing from Medieval Latin *praeambulum,* noun use of adjective, preliminary (in Late Latin, walking before) < Late Latin *praeambulāre* < Latin *prae-* before + *ambulāre* to walk]

**pre|amp** (prē amp′), *n.* = preamplifier.

**pre|am|pli|fi|er** (prē am′plə fī′ər), *n.* a unit that gives preliminary amplification to very weak impulses, bringing them to a level suitable for further amplification.

**pre|ar|range** (prē′ə rānj′), *v.t.,* **-ranged, -ranging.** to arrange beforehand.

**pre|a|tom|ic** (prē′ə tom′ik), *adj.* before August 6, 1945, the first military use of the atom bomb, at Hiroshima: *Preatomic age radioactivity was caused by naturally occurring radioisotopes and cosmic radiation* (Science News Letter).

**pre|au|dit** (prē ô′dit), *n.* an audit conducted before a transaction has been settled or completed.

**pre|ax|i|al** (prē ak′sē əl), *adj.* **1** in front of the body. **2** of or having to do with the inner side of the arm or of the leg. —**pre′ax′i|al|ly,** *adv.*

**preb|end** (preb′ənd), *n. British.* **1** the salary given to a clergyman connected with a cathedral or a collegiate church. **2** the particular property or church tax from which the money comes for this salary. **3** = prebendary. [< Old French *prebende,* learned borrowing from Late Latin *praebenda* allowance < Latin, (literally) things to be furnished < *praebēre* to furnish, offer, short for *praehibēre* < *prae-* before + *habēre* to hold. See etym. of doublet **provender.**]

**pre|ben|dal** (pri ben′dəl), *adj.* having to do with a prebend or a prebendary.

**preb|en|dar|y** (preb′ən der′ē), *n., pl.* **-dar|ies.** *British.* a clergyman who has a prebend.

**pre|bi|o|log|i|cal** (prē bī′ə loj′ə kəl), *adj.* = prebiotic.

**pre|bi|ot|ic** (prē′bī ot′ik), *adj.* before the appearance of living things: *... assumes that the earth's atmosphere in prebiotic times contained methane, nitrogen, and water* (Leonard Nelson).

**prebiotic soup,** = primordial soup.

**prec.,** preceding.

**pre|cal|cic** (prē kal′sik), *adj.* (of certain minerals) mostly calcic.

**Pre-Cam|bri|an** or **Pre|cam|bri|an** (prē kam′brē ən), *n., adj.* —*n.* **1** the earliest geological era, including all the time before the Cambrian; the Azoic, Archeozoic, and Proterozoic eras together: *The Pre-Cambrian includes all the history of the earth from its supposed origin until the invasion of the Cambrian seas over the eroded continents. This span of time involved is at least a billion and a half years* (Robert M. Garrels). **2** the rocks formed in this era.
—*adj.* of this era or its rocks.

**pre|can|cel** (prē kan′səl), *v.,* **-celed, -cel|ing** or (*especially British*) **-celled, -cel|ling,** *n.* —*v.t.* to put a mark of cancellation on (a postage stamp) before sale for use on bulk mail or parcel post.
—*n.* a precanceled postage stamp.

**pre|can|cel|la|tion** (prē′kan sə lā′shən), *n.* the act of precanceling or state of being precanceled.

**pre|can|cer|ous** (prē kan′sər əs), *adj.* of or having to do with a condition of the tissues which, while not now cancerous, may develop into cancer, as certain skin growths: *Examination of the lungs of cigarette smokers under the microscope reveals precancerous changes* (Atlantic).

**pre|car|i|ous** (pri kãr′ē əs), *adj.* **1** not safe or secure; uncertain; dangerous; risky: *Soldiers on the battlefield lead a precarious life. His poor hold on the branch was precarious. His power was more precarious than ... he was willing to admit* (Scott). **SYN**: perilous, hazardous. **2** dependent on chance or circumstance. **3** poorly founded; doubtful; assumed: *a precarious opinion or conclusion.* [< Latin *precārius* (with English *-ous*) obtainable by entreaty; dependent on another's will, uncertain < *prex, precis* prayer] —**pre|car′i|ous|ly**, *adv.* —**pre|car′i|ous|ness**, *n.*

**pre|cast** (prē kast′, -käst′), *v.t.*, **-cast, -cast|ing.** to cast (a building material) into blocks before using it for building.

**prec|a|tive** (prek′ə tiv), *adj.* expressing entreaty or desire; supplicatory. [< Late Latin *precātīvus* < Latin *precārī* entreat]

**prec|a|to|ry** (prek′ə tôr′ē, -tōr′-), *adj.* of, like, or expressing entreaty or supplication. [< Late Latin *precātōrius* < Latin *precātor, -ōris* entreater < *precārī* to entreat, pray]

**pre|cau|tion** (pri kô′shən), *n.* **1** care taken beforehand; thing done beforehand to ward off evil or secure good results: *Locking doors is a precaution against thieves.* **SYN**: safeguard. **2** a taking care beforehand; prudent foresight: *Proper precaution is prudent.* **SYN**: forethought. [< Late Latin *praecautiō, -ōnis* < Latin *praecavēre* guard against beforehand < *prae-* before + *cavēre* be on one's guard]

**pre|cau|tion|al** (pri kô′shə nəl), *adj.* = precautionary.

**pre|cau|tion|ar|y** (pri kô′shə ner′ē), *adj.* of or using precaution: *He wore warm clothes as a precautionary measure against catching a cold. ... throwing a precautionary glance around, as if to assure himself that we were not alone* (Charles Lever).

**pre|cau|tious** (pri kô′shəs), *adj.* using or showing precaution: *This precautious way of reasoning and acting has proved ... an uninterrupted source of felicity* (Sir Richard Steele). —**pre|cau′tious|ly**, *adv.*

**pre|cede** (prē sēd′), *v.*, **-ced|ed, -ced|ing.** —*v.t.* **1** to go or come before in order, place, or time: *A precedes B in the alphabet. A band preceded the soldiers in the parade. She preceded me into the room. Mr. Eisenhower preceded Mr. Kennedy as President.* **2** to be higher than in rank or importance: *A major precedes a captain. A knight precedes a pawn in the game of chess.* **3** to introduce by something preliminary; preface. —*v.i.* to go or come before in rank, order, place, or time. [< Latin *praecēdere* < *prae-* before + *cēdere* to go. Compare etym. under **precession**.]

**prec|e|dence** (pres′ə dəns, pri sē′-), *n.* **1** the act or fact of preceding; going or coming before in time or order. **SYN**: antecedence. **2** higher position or rank; greater importance: *This work takes precedence over all other work.* **SYN**: priority. **3** the right to precede others in ceremonies or social affairs; social superiority: *A Senator takes precedence over a Representative.*

**prec|e|den|cy** (pres′ə dən sē, pri sē′-), *n.*, *pl.* **-cies.** = precedence.

**prec|e|dent** (*n.* pres′ə dənt; *adj.* pri sē′dənt, pres′ə-), *n., adj.* —*n.* **1** an action that may serve as an example or reason for a later action: *Last year's school picnic set a precedent for having one this year. There was no precedent for Roosevelt's election to a third term as President.* **2** *Law.* a judicial decision, case, or proceeding that serves as a guide or pattern in future similar or analogous situations: *A decision of a court often serves as a precedent in another court. Precedent to a court is what past performances are to sports and the theater* (Wall Street Journal). [< adjective]
—*adj.* = preceding. [< Latin *praecēdēns, -entis,* present participle of *praecēdere* precede] —**pre|ced′ent|ly**, *adv.*

**prec|e|den|tial** (pres′ə den′shəl), *adj.* **1** of, being, or like a precedent: *If he is appointed, any applicant ... can claim ... appointment on the strength of this precedential case* (New York Independent). **2** having precedence; preceding: *It becomes necessary to distinguish the several precedential or introductory facts ... from the ultimate principal fact* (Jeremy Bentham). **3** having to do with social precedence: *Charles the Fifth settled a precedential hubbub between two dames of high degree* (Fraser's Magazine).

**pre|ced|ing** (prē sē′ding), *adj.* going before; coming before; previous: *Turn back and look on the preceding page for the answer. The preceding winter weeks had been dull and gloomy so that today's spring sunshine was a welcome change.* **SYN**: See syn. under **previous**.

**pre|cen|sor** (prē sen′sər), *v.t.* to censor before publication, exhibition, or release: *to precensor a motion picture. Most Russian authors ... precensor their works before submitting them to the state-owned publishing houses* (Time).

**pre|cen|sor|ship** (prē sen′sər ship), *n.* the act, process, or practice of precensoring a publication, motion picture, television program, or news release.

**pre|cent** (pri sent′), *v.t., v.i.* to act as precentor. [perhaps back formation < *precentor*]

**pre|cen|tor** (pri sen′tər), *n.* a person who leads and directs the singing of a church choir or congregation: *Observe a bevy of them ... joining in tiny chorus to the directing melody of an elder precentor* (Cowden Clarke). [< Latin *praecentor, -ōris* < *praecinere* sing before < *prae-* before + *canere* sing]

**pre|cen|to|ri|al** (prē′sen tôr′ē əl, -tōr′-), *adj.* of or having to do with a precentor.

**pre|cen|tor|ship** (pri sen′tər ship), *n.* the office, position, or function of a precentor.

**pre|cept** (prē′sept), *n.* **1** a rule of action or behavior; maxim: *"If at first you don't succeed, try, try again" is a familiar precept. His high-school science course covered many of the basic precepts of modern physics.* **SYN**: teaching, adage, axiom, direction. **2** *Law.* a writ; warrant; a written order issued pursuant to law. [< Anglo-French *precep,* and *precept,* learned borrowing from Latin *praeceptum* (originally) neuter past participle of *praecipere* to order, advise, anticipate < *prae-* before + *capere* to take]

**pre|cep|tive** (pri sep′tiv), *adj.* of the nature of or expressing a precept; instructive. —**pre|cep′tive|ly**, *adv.*

**pre|cep|tor** (pri sep′tər), *n.* **1** an instructor; teacher; tutor. **SYN**: schoolmaster. **2** the head of a preceptory. [< Latin *praeceptor, -ōris* < *praecipere;* see etym. under **precept**]

**pre|cep|to|ral** (pri sep′tər əl), *adj.* = preceptorial.

**pre|cep|tor|ate** (pri sep′tər it), *n.* the office of a preceptor.

**pre|cep|to|ri|al** (prē′sep tôr′ē əl, -tōr′-), *adj.* **1** of a preceptor; like that of a preceptor: *Wilson immediately proposed the preceptorial system to supplement the stultifying lectures of the day* (Newsweek). **2** using preceptors.

**pre|cep|tor|ship** (pri sep′tər ship), *n.* the office or position of a preceptor.

**pre|cep|to|ry** (pri sep′tər ē), *n., pl.* **-ries,** *adj.* —*n.* **1** a subordinate house or community of the Knights Templars. **2** the estate or manor of such a community.
—*adj.* = preceptive.
[< Medieval Latin *praeceptoria* (literally) having to do with a preceptor, or instructor]

**pre|cep|tress** (pri sep′tris), *n.* a woman preceptor.

**pre|ce|ram|ic** (prē′sə ram′ik), *adj.* of or having to do with a period or culture that existed before the making of pottery: *Associated human artifacts indicated occupation by preceramic Basket Makers estimated to date between 1500 and 2500 years ago* (Science).

**pre|cess** (prē ses′), *v.i.* to undergo precession: *When a steady twist is applied to a top ... the top wobbles or precesses slowly at right angles to the direction of the disturbing forces* (J. Little).

**pre|ces|sion** (prē sesh′ən), *n.* **1** the act or fact of going first; precedence. **2** the rotation of a spinning rigid body that has been tipped from its vertical axis by an external force acting on it. This phenomenon is illustrated by the wobble of a top and the gyration of the earth's axis. *The cross has shifted southward in the sky due to the earth's precession* (I. M. Levitt). **3** = precession of the equinoxes. [< Late Latin *praecessiō, -ōnis* < Latin *praecēdere* precede]

**pre|ces|sion|al** (prē sesh′ə nəl), *adj.* of or caused by precession, especially the precession of the equinoxes.

**precession of the equinoxes, 1** the earlier occurrence of the equinoxes in each successive sidereal year. **2** this motion of the equinoctial points. **3** this change in the direction of the earth's axis.

**pre|chor|dal** (prē′kôr′dəl), *adj.* situated in front of the notochord, especially of the embryos of higher vertebrates.

**pre-Chris|tian** (prē kris′chən), *adj.* **1** of or having to do with the times before the birth of Christ; before Christ. **2** before the introduction of Christianity: *The Yule log and the holly wreath are only two of the many Christmas symbols that originated in pre-Christian times.*

**pré|cieuse** (prā syœz′), *n., adj. French* —*n.* **1** a woman who affects too much refinement, as of taste or language. **2** (literally) precious.
—*adj.* overrefined; precious: *Her conversation is natural and reasonable, not précieuse and affected* (Horace Walpole).

**pré|cieux** (prā syœ′), *n., adj. French.* —*n.* **1** a man who affects too much refinement, as of taste or language. **2** (literally) precious.
—*adj.* overrefined; precious.

**pre|cinct** (prē′singkt), *n.* **1** a part or district, especially of a city: *a police precinct. There are over 300 election precincts in that city.* **2** Often, **precincts. a** the space within a boundary: *Do not leave the school precincts during school hours. The slightest invasion of the precincts which had been assigned to another tribe produced desperate skirmishes* (Scott). **b** the region immediately surrounding a place; environs: *a factory and its precincts.* **3** the ground immediately surrounding a church, temple, or the like: *They reached the precinct of the God. And on the hallowed turf their feet now trod* (William Morris). **precincts,** a boundary; limit: *The parade will be held within the precincts of the town. The whole population of the valley seemed to be gathered within the precincts of the grove* (Herman Melville).
[< Medieval Latin *praecinctum,* (originally) neuter past participle of Latin *praecingere* enclose < *prae-* before + *cingere* to gird, surround]

**pre|ci|os|i|ty** (presh′ē os′ə tē), *n., pl.* **-ties. 1** too much refinement; affectation, especially in the use of language. *Her work was sick, he told her—cramped with preciosity and mannerisms* (New Yorker). **SYN**: fastidiousness. **2** the persons showing such refinement: *All London had indeed been present ... The entire preciosity of the metropolis* (Arnold Bennett).
**preciosities,** precious things; articles of value: *five invaluable trunks, full of preciosities* (Arnold Bennett).
[< Old French *preciosite* < *precieux,* earlier *precios* precious]

**pre|cious** (presh′əs), *adj., adv.* —*adj.* **1** having great value; worth much; valuable; of great importance. Gold, silver, and platinum are often called the precious metals. *They were folk to whom sleep was precious* (John Galsworthy). **SYN**: See syn. under **valuable**. **2** much loved; dear: *a precious child.* **3** too nice; overrefined: *precious language. His poetry is flowery, effeminate, almost precious in tone.* **4** *Informal.* very great: *He's put things in a precious mess!* **5** of great moral or spiritual worth: *the precious blood of Christ* (I Peter 1:19). **6** choice; fine: *Did you ever see such a precious set of villians?* (Frederick Marryat). **7** gross; arrant: *Here, Mr. Speaker, is a precious mockery* (Edmund Burke).
—*adv. Informal.* very; extremely: *precious little money. I'll take precious good care never to sing in a theatre again* (George Du Maurier).
[< Old French *precios* (with English *-ous*), learned borrowing from Latin *pretiōsus* < *pretium* value, price] —**pre′cious|ly**, —**pre′cious|ness**, *n.*

**precious coral,** a species of coral with a hard internal skeleton of a red, rose, or pink color, used for jewelry and ornaments; red coral. Precious coral grows in bushlike formations in the Mediterranean Sea and the Sea of Japan.

**precious garnet,** a variety of garnet sometimes used as a gem; pyrope.

**precious stone,** a jewel; gem: *Diamonds, rubies, and sapphires are precious stones.*

**prec|i|pe** (pres′ə pē), *n.* = praecipe.

**prec|i|pice** (pres′ə pis), *n.* **1** a very steep cliff or slope; cliff, crag, or steep mountainside: *A few steps more, and I was standing on the very edge of a bank, a precipice not less than fifty feet deep* (W. H. Hudson). **SYN**: escarpment. **2** *Figurative.* a situation of great peril; critical position: *By giving the nation the feeling of hanging on a precipice, they succeeded in mobilizing public opinion behind them* (Newsweek). [< French *précipice,* learned borrowing from Latin *praecipitium* < *praeceps, -cipitis* steep; (literally) headlong < *prae-* forth, ahead + *caput, capitis* head]

**pre|cip|i|ta|bil|i|ty** (pri sip′ə tə bil′ə tē), *n.* the quality of being precipitable.

**pre|cip|i|ta|ble** (pri sip′ə tə bəl), *adj.* that can be precipitated, as from solution: *The amount of precipitable water contained in the world's atmosphere is only equivalent to 1 in. of rainfall* (J. D. Ovington).

**pre|cip|i|tance** (pri sip′ə təns), *n.* headlong haste; rashness: *The youth expects to force his way by genius, vigour, and precipitance* (Samuel Johnson).

**pre|cip|i|tan|cy** (pri sip′ə tən sē), *n., pl.* **-cies.** = precipitance.

**pre|cip|i|tant** (pri sip′ə tənt), *adj., n.* —*adj.* **1** very sudden or abrupt. **2** acting in a hasty or rash manner. **3** falling or rushing headlong; directed

**Pronunciation Key:** hat, āge, cãre, fär; let, ēqual, tėrm; it, īce; hot, ōpen, ôrder; oil, out; cup, pu̇t, rüle; child; long; thin; ᴛʜen; zh, measure; ə represents **a** in about, **e** in taken, **i** in pencil, **o** in lemon, **u** in circus.

straight downward: *Our men put the enemy to precipitant flight.* **4** falling to the bottom as a precipitate.

—***n.*** a substance that causes another substance in solution in a liquid to be separated out of solution as a solid.

[< Latin *praecipitāns, -antis,* present participle of *praecipitāre;* see etym. under **precipitate**] —**pre·cip′i|tant|ly,** *adv.*

**pre|cip|i|tate** (*v.* pri sip′ə tāt; *adj., n.* pri sip′ə tāt, -tit), *v.,* **-tat|ed, -tat|ing,** *adj., n.* —***v.t.*** **1** to hasten the beginning of; bring about suddenly: *to precipitate a war, to precipitate an argument; ... the depression of the forties which had precipitated the events of '48* (Edmund Wilson). **2** to throw down, hurl, or plunge in a violent or sudden manner: *to precipitate a rock down a cliff,* (*Figurative.*) *to precipitate oneself into a struggle.* **3** to separate (a substance) out from a solution as a solid: *The plate was prepared by the all but impossible process of precipitating silver chloride from solution* (A. W. Haslett). **4** to condense (water vapor) from the air in the form of rain, dew, or snow. —***v.i.*** **1** to be deposited from solution as a solid. **2** to be condensed as rain, dew, or snow. **3** *Figurative.* to rush headlong. **4** *Obsolete.* to fall headlong. [< Latin *praecipitāre* (with English *-ate*[1]) < *praeceps, -cipitis* headlong; see etym. under **precipice**]

—***adj.*** **1** very hurried; sudden: *A cool breeze caused a precipitate drop in the temperature.* **2** *Figurative.* with great haste and force; plunging or rushing; headlong: *the precipitate course of a river through a steep gorge.* **3** hasty; rash: *precipitate action.*

—***n.*** **1** a substance, usually crystalline, separated out from a solution as a solid. **2** moisture condensed from vapor by cooling and deposited in drops as rain, dew, or the like.

[< New Latin *praecipitatum,* neuter noun, < Latin *praecipitāre;* see the verb] —**pre|cip′i|tate′ly,** *adv.* —**pre|cip′i|tate′ness,** *n.* —**pre|cip′i|ta′tor,** *n.*

**precipitate copper,** copper obtained by leaching, from 60 to 90 per cent pure.

**pre|cip|i|ta|tion** (pri sip′ə tā′shən), *n.* **1** the act or condition of precipitating; throwing down or falling headlong: *the tragic precipitation of the climbers over the side of the mountain.* **2** the action of hastening or hurrying. **3** *Figurative.* the act or fact of bringing on suddenly: *the precipitation of a quarrel, the precipitation of war without warning.* **4** *Figurative.* unwise or rash rapidity; sudden haste. **5a** the process of separating a substance from a solution as a solid. **b** the substance separated out from a solution as a solid; precipitate. **6a** the act or fact of depositing moisture in the form of rain, snow, sleet, ice, or hail: *In steppe lands and arid regions, evaporation is greater than precipitation* (R. N. Elston). **b** something that is precipitated, such as rain, dew, or snow. **c** the amount that is precipitated. **7** = materialization (in spiritualism).

**pre|cip|i|ta|tive** (pri sip′ə tā′tiv), *adj.* having to do with precipitation; tending to precipitate.

**pre|cip|i|tin** (pri sip′ə tin), *n.* an antibody formed in blood serum as a result of inoculating with a foreign protein; coagulin. When the antibody is brought into contact with its soluble antigen, a precipitate forms.

**pre|cip|i|tous** (pri sip′ə təs), *adj.* **1** like a precipice; very steep: *precipitous cliffs. Access was gained by precipitous stone steps carved into the walls of rock* (Newsweek). **SYN:** See syn. under **steep.** **2** *Figurative.* hasty; rash. **3** rushing headlong; very rapid: *The sweep Of some precipitous rivulet to the wave* (Tennyson). [< Latin *praeceps, -cipitis* (see etym. under **precipice**) + English *-ous*] —**pre|cip′i|tous|ly,** *adv.* —**pre|cip′i|tous|ness,** *n.*

**pré|cis** (prā′sē, prā sē′), *n., pl.* **-cis.** a concise or abridged statement; abstract; summary: *Morton trotted up to the Capitol with the President's précis of the proposal to brief the Senate's leaders* (Time). **SYN:** compendium. [< French, Middle French *précis,* noun use of adjective, condensed, precise < Latin *praecīsus.* See etym. under **precise.**]

**pre|cise** (pri sīs′), *adj.* **1** exact; accurate; definite: *a precise instrument. The directions he gave us were so precise that we found our way easily. The precise sum was 34 cents. The essential criterion must always be that the information sought is reducible to a precise formula* (Anthony H. Richmond). **SYN:** correct. **2** careful; scrupulous; fastidious: *precise handwriting. She was precise in her manners.* **3** strict; particular: *We had precise orders to come home by nine o'clock.* [< Middle French *précis, précise,* learned borrowings from Latin *praecīsus* abridged, cut off < *praecīdere* to cut short < *prae-* in front + *caedere* to cut] —**pre|cise′ly,** *adv.* —**pre|cise′ness,** *n.*

**pre|ci|sian** (pri sizh′ən), *n.* **1** a person who is rigidly precise in the observance of rules or forms: *A profane person calls a man of piety a precisian* (Isaac Watts). **2** a person who is precise in religious observance, such as an English Puritan of the 1500's and 1600's. [< *precis*(e) + *-ian*]

**pre|ci|sian|ism** (pri sizh′ə niz əm), *n.* **1** the quality or state of being a precisian. **2** the doctrine or conduct of precisians.

**pre|ci|sion** (pri sizh′ən), *n., adj.* —***n.*** **1** the fact or condition of being precise; accuracy; being exact; definiteness: *to speak with precision, the precision of a machine. A weapon of precision is one that can be delivered precisely where it is wanted* (Bulletin of Atomic Scientists). **SYN:** correctness, preciseness, exactness. **2** careful exactness: *to dress with precision.*

—***adj.*** having to do with or characterized by precision: *precision instruments. The rendezvous was an extraordinary demonstration of precision control* (New York Times).

**precision bombing,** the dropping of bombs from an aircraft on a specific building, group of buildings, or other narrowly defined target, usually with the aid of a special bombsight or from a relatively low altitude.

**pre|ci|sion|ism** (pri sizh′ə niz əm), *n.* **1** the practice of precision; insistence on precision. **2** = purism (def. 3).

**pre|ci|sion|ist** (pri sizh′ə nist), *n., adj.* —***n.*** a person who insists on or affects precision, especially in expression or language; purist.

—***adj.*** of precisionism or the precisionists.

**pre|clear** (prē clir′), *v.t.* to clear in advance; certify as safe beforehand: *legislation giving FDA broad authority to preclear all types of medical devices* (Science News).

**pre|clin|i|cal** (prē klin′ə kəl), *adj.* **1** coming or occurring before clinical use: *a preclinical test of a new drug.* **2** preceding or preparing for clinical studies or aspects of medicine: *preclinical students.*

**pre|clude** (pri klüd′), *v.t.,* **-clud|ed, -clud|ing.** to shut out; make impossible; prevent: *The heavy thunderstorm precluded our going to the beach. Constant vigilance precludes surprise.* **SYN:** exclude, hinder. [< Latin *praeclūdere* < *prae-* before, ahead + *claudere* to shut]

**pre|clu|sion** (pri klü′zhən), *n.* the act or fact of precluding or condition of being precluded: *The preclusion of disturbance and indecorum in Christian assemblies* (Samuel Taylor Coleridge). [< Latin *praeclūsiō, -ōnis* < *praeclūdere* preclude]

**pre|clu|sive** (pri klü′siv), *adj.* tending or serving to preclude. [< Latin *praeclūsus,* past participle of *praeclūdere* + English *-ive*] —**pre|clu′sive|ly,** *adv.*

**pre|co|cial** (pri kō′shəl), *adj.* of or having to do with birds, such as grouse, whose chicks are downy when hatched and able to run about: *The common song birds are all altricial, while domestic fowls, partridges, most wading birds, and the various ducks are precocial* (A. Franklin Shul). Also, **praecocial.** [< Latin *praecox, -cocis* precocious + English *-al*[1]]

**pre|co|cious** (pri kō′shəs), *adj.* **1** developed earlier than usual in knowledge, skill, or the like: *This very precocious child could read well at the age of four.* **2** developed too early; occurring before the natural time: *a precocious taste for beer.* [*The*] *furniture, too, shows precocious dilapidation* (New Statesman). **3** of, having to do with, or indicating premature development: *Her imperfect articulation was the least precocious thing she had about her* (Charlotte Brontë). **4** flowering or fruiting early, as before the appearance of leaves. [< Latin *praecox, -cocis* (with English *-ous*) maturing early < *praecoquere* to ripen fully < *prae-* before its time + *coquere* to ripen; (literally) to cook] —**pre|co′cious|ly,** *adv.* —**pre|co′cious|ness,** *n.*

**pre|coc|i|ty** (pri kos′ə tē), *n.* precocious development; early maturity: *Macaulay's precocity was extraordinary, for when he was only four years old, he began to write a history of the world.*

**pre|cog|ni|tion** (prē′kog nish′ən), *n.* **1** previous cognition or knowledge; foreknowledge: *He further claims the laboratory proof of precognition* (*as in preguessing the order of a pack of cards which is to be mechanically shuffled*) (Newsweek). **2** in Scots law: **a** a preliminary examination, as of witnesses. **b** the evidence taken at it.

**pre|cog|ni|tive** (prē kog′nə tiv), *adj.* of the nature of or giving foreknowledge: *a precognitive dream.*

**pre|co|lo|ni|al** (prē′kə lō′nē əl), *adj.* before a state of colonialism: *precolonial Africa.*

**pre-Co|lum|bi|an** (prē′kə lum′bē ən), *adj.* of or belonging to the period before the arrival of Columbus in America; representative of American culture during or before the 1400's: *pre-Columbian Mexican sculpture.* [*There*] *is a selection of pre-Columbian figurines, mainly from terra cotta and dating from around 1000* B.C. *to 900* A.D. (New Yorker).

**pre|con|ceive** (prē′kən sēv′), *v.t.,* **-ceived, -ceiv|ing.** to form an idea or opinion of beforehand: *The beauty of the scenery surpassed all our preconceived notions. The Coliseum was very much what I had preconceived it* (Nathaniel Hawthorne).

**pre|con|cep|tion** (pri′kən sep′shən), *n.* **1** an idea or opinion formed beforehand: *the incapacity of actual objects for satisfying our preconceptions of them* (Charles Lamb). **SYN:** prejudgment. **2** the act of preconceiving.

**pre|con|cert** (*v.* prē′kən sėrt′; *n.* prē kon′sərt), *v., n.* —***v.t.*** to arrange beforehand: *At a preconcerted signal the policemen rushed into the thieves' hideout.*

—***n.*** a previous arrangement; preconcerted agreement or action: *We arose, as if by preconcert, to make examination of our treasure* (Edgar Allan Poe).

**pre|con|cil|i|ar** (prē′kən sil′ē ər), *adj.* existing or occurring prior to the Vatican ecumenical council of 1962-1965: *Everyone tends to exaggerate the mutual isolation of preconciliar days and to forget what two world wars accomplished in bringing Christians together* (Cardinal John Heenan).

**pre|con|di|tion** (prē′kən dish′ən), *n., v.* —***n.*** a condition required to be fulfilled beforehand; prerequisite: *Nonconformity is the basic precondition of art, as it is the precondition of good thinking* (Ben Shahn).

—***v.t.*** to condition beforehand: *For a weekend trip, the pilot will be preconditioned by eating a low residue diet* (Time).

**pre|co|nize** (prē′kə nīz), *v.t.,* **-nized, -niz|ing.** **1a** to proclaim; announce publicly. **b** to commend publicly. **2** (of the pope) to confirm publicly and officially the appointment of (a bishop, cardinal, or other high ecclesiastic). [< Medieval Latin *praeconizare* < Latin *praecō, -ōnis* public crier, herald]

**pre|con|quest** (prē kon′kwest, -kong′-), *adj.* existing or occurring before the conquest of a nation.

**Pre-Con|quest** (prē kon′kwest, -kong′-), *adj.* of or belonging to the period before the Conquest; of the times before the conquest of England by William the Conqueror: *Pre-Conquest churches, the Pre-Conquest English.*

**pre|con|scious** (prē kon′shəs), *adj., n.* —***adj.*** **1** not in the conscious mind but readily recalled; foreconscious: *preconscious memories. Now it was time to discover whether humans could make use of preconscious information* (Wall Street Journal). **2** before or preceding consciousness.

—***n.*** the part of the mind between the conscious and the subconscious; foreconscious: *Being repressed ... means being unable to pass out of the unconscious system because of the doorkeeper's refusal of admittance into the preconscious* (Sigmund Freud). —**pre|con′scious|ly,** *adv.*

**pre|con|scious|ness** (prē kon′shəs nis), *n.* = preconscious.

**pre|con|so|nan|tal** (prē′kon sə nan′təl), *adj.* immediately preceding a consonant.

**pre|cool** (prē kül′), *v.t.* to cool ahead of time; cool (as produce or meat) by artificial means before shipping: *It* [*Tasmania*] *will need greater facilities for storing and precooling its export apples* (Gordon Greenwood). —**pre|cool′er,** *n.*

**pre|curse** (pri kėrs′), *v.t.,* **-cursed, -curs|ing.** to run or go before; forerun, precede, and indicate the approach of. [< Latin *praecursus,* past participle of *praecurrere;* see etym. under **precursor**]

**pre|cur|sive** (pri kėr′siv), *adj.* = precursory.

**pre|cur|sor** (pri kėr′sər), *n.* **1** a forerunner: *A severe cold may be the precursor of pneumonia.* **SYN:** herald, harbinger. **2** an early stage or substance which precedes or gives rise to a more important or definitive stage or substance: *Proinsulin was identified ... as a substance within the pancreas that is a precursor of insulin* (Science News). **SYN:** predecessor. [< Latin *praecursor, -ōris* < *praecurrere* < *prae-* before, ahead + *currere* to run]

**pre|cur|so|ry** (pri kėr′sər ē), *adj.* indicative of something to follow; introductory. **SYN:** prefatory, preliminary.

**pred.,** **1** predicate. **2a** predicative. **b** predicatively.

**pre|da|cious** or **pre|da|ceous** (pri dā′shəs), *adj.* living by prey; predatory: *Gaudy, fast on the wing and deadly to its prey, the dragonfly ... is highly predacious* (Science News Letter). [< Latin *praedārī* to rob (< *praeda* prey) + English *-aceous*] —**pre|da′cious|ness, pre|da′ceous|ness,** *n.*

**pre|dac|i|ty** (pri das′ə tē), *n.* the fact or quality of being predacious.

**pre|date** (prē dāt′), *v.t.,* **-dat|ed, -dat|ing.** **1** to date before the actual time: *to predate a check.* **2** to precede in date; antedate: *The younger ones had troubles of their own, predating the controversy* (Joseph Hitrec).

**pre|da|tion** (prē dā′shən), *n.* **1** the act or habit of preying on another animal or animals; predatory behavior: *Any food chain, after the first plant-eating animal, is a succession of predations* (Tracy I. Storer). **2** *Obsolete.* the act of plundering or pillaging; depredation. [< Latin *praedātiō, -ōnis* < *praedārī;* see etym. under **predator**]

**predation pressure**, the impact of predatory animals on a given environment, constituting a continuing factor in the ecological balance between predator and prey.

**pred|a|tism** (pred′ə tiz əm), *n.* the state of being predatory.

**pred|a|tor** (pred′ə tər), *n.* an animal or person that preys upon another or others: *Predators must be nocturnal if their prey comes out only at night* (Cloudsley and Thompson). [< Latin *praedātor, -ōris* < *praedārī* to plunder < *praeda* prey, booty] —**pred′a|to′ri|ly**, *adv.* —**pred′a|to′ri|ness**, *n.*

**pred|a|to|ry** (pred′ə tôr′ē, -tōr′-), *adj.* **1a** living by preying upon other animals. Lions and tigers are predatory animals; hawks and owls are predatory birds. *Field trials were then set up in semi-arid bush country ... under completely natural conditions, which included the presence of foxes and other predatory animals* (Fenner and Day). **b** feeding upon and destructive, as to crops, trees, or buildings: *predatory insects.* **2** inclined to plundering or robbery: *predatory border warfare. Predatory pirates infested the seas.* **SYN:** marauding, thieving, rapacious. **3** *Figurative.* intentionally destructive: *Predatory price-cutting is sometimes used to destroy competing firms.* [< Latin *praedātōrius* < *praedātor* predator]

**pre|dawn** (prē dôn′, prē′dôn), *n., adj.* —*n.* the part of the day just before the dawn: *The predawn's copper haze ...* (Robert Irwin).
—*adj.* of the time preceding the dawn: *The ring of the telephone shattered the predawn stillness* (New York Times).

**pre|de|cease** (prē′di sēs′), *v.t.*, **-ceased**, **-ceas|ing.** to die before: *His friend and colleague Gilbert Hare ... predeceased him by only a few months* (London Times).

**pred|e|ces|sor** (pred′ə ses′ər), *n.* **1** a person holding a position or office before another: *John Adams was Jefferson's predecessor as President.* **2** a thing that came before another. **3** *Archaic.* an ancestor; forefather. [< Late Latin *praedēcessor* < Latin *prae-* before + *dēcessor, -ōris* retiring official (of a province) < *dēcēdere* go away]

***pre|del|la** (pri del′ə), *n.* **1** the platform on which an altar is placed: *The step or base (predella) on which the altar stands often is considered a part of the altar* (James Chillman). **2** a raised shelf at the back of an altar. **3** a painting or sculpture on the front of this, often forming an appendage to an altarpiece. **4** any painting forming a similar appendage to another painting. [< Italian *predella* stool, probably < Old High German *pret* board + Italian *-ella,* a diminutive suffix]

***predella**
definitions 2, 3

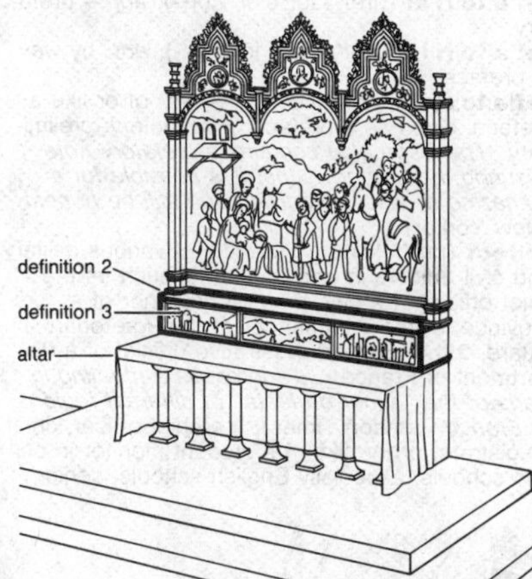


**pre|des|ig|nate** (prē dez′ig nāt), *v.t.*, **-nat|ed**, **-nat|ing.** **1** to designate beforehand; specify in advance. **2** *Logic.* to designate the range of (the predicate) by annexing to the subject a quantitative particle such as "one," "alone," or "nothing but." —**pre′des|ig|na′tion**, *n.*

**pre|des|ti|nar|i|an** (prē des′tə nãr′ē ən), *adj., n.* —*adj.* of, having to do with, or believing in predestination. —*n.* a person who believes in or upholds the doctrine of predestination.

**pre|des|ti|nar|i|an|ism** (prē des′tə nãr′ē ə niz′əm), *n.* the system or doctrines of the predestinarians.

**pre|des|ti|nate** (*v.* prē des′tə nāt; *adj.* prē des′tə nit, -nāt), *v.*, **-nat|ed**, **-nat|ing**, *adj.* —*v.t.* **1** to decree or ordain beforehand. **2** *Theology.* to foreordain by divine purpose. —*adj. Archaic.* predestined. [< Latin *praedēstināre* (with English *-ate*[1]) appoint beforehand < *prae-* before + *dēstināre* establish, make fast, apparently ultimately < *dē-* (intensive) + *stāre* to stand]

**pre|des|ti|na|tion** (prē′des tə nā′shən), *n.* **1** the act or fact of ordaining beforehand; destiny; fate: *a kind of moral predestination, or overruling principle which cannot be resisted* (Samuel Johnson). **2** the action of God in deciding beforehand what shall happen. **3** the doctrine that by God's decree certain souls will be saved and others lost: *... one of the most disastrous of human ideas, the doctrine of predestination!* (New Yorker).

**pre|des|ti|na|tor** (prē des′tə nā′tər), *n.* **1** a person who predestinates or foreordains. **2** a person who believes in predestination; predestinarian.

**pre|des|tine** (prē des′tən), *v.t.*, **-tined**, **-tin|ing.** to determine or settle beforehand; foreordain. [< Old French *predestiner,* learned borrowing from Latin *praedēstināre* to predestinate]

**pre|de|ter|mi|na|tion** (prē′di tėr′mə nā′shən), *n.* the act or process of predetermining or state of being predetermined.

**pre|de|ter|mi|na|tive** (prē′di tėr′mə nā′tiv), *adj.* having the quality of predetermining.

**pre|de|ter|mine** (prē′di tėr′mən), *v.t.*, **-mined**, **-min|ing.** **1** to determine or decide beforehand: *We met at a predetermined time.* **2** to direct or impel beforehand (to something): *Two world wars predetermined the henceforth inevitable symbiosis of scientific activity and political decision* (Bulletin of Atomic Scientists).

**pre|di|a|be|tes** (prē dī′ə bē′tis, -tēz), *n.* the period or condition in prediabetic persons that precedes the onset of overt diabetes.

**pre|di|a|bet|ic** (prē dī′ə bet′ik, -bē′tik), *adj., n.* —*adj.* exhibiting metabolic changes that indicate a predisposition to diabetes: *In addition, a blood sugar test showed that the twins were "prediabetic"* (Science News Letter).
—*n.* a prediabetic person: *The reason for the poor performance of the cells taken from prediabetics is not yet known but it may be due to more rapid aging of the diabetic cells* (Barbara Ford).

**pre|di|al** (prē′dē əl), *adj.* **1** consisting of land. **2** having to do with, arising from, or attached to land: *predial tithes, predial serfs.* Also, **praedial.** [< Medieval Latin *praedialis* < Latin *praedium* farm, estate]

**pred|i|ca|bil|i|ty** (pred′ə kə bil′ə tē), *n.* the quality of being predicable.

**pred|i|ca|ble** (pred′ə kə bəl), *adj., n.* —*adj.* that can be predicated or affirmed; assertable.
—*n.* **1** a thing that can be predicated; attribute. **2** *Logic.* any one of the various kinds of predicate that can be used of a subject. According to Aristotle they were genus, definition, difference, property, and accident, but subsequently definition was omitted and species added. —**pred′i|ca|bly**, *adv.*

**pre|dic|a|ment** (pri dik′ə mənt), *n.* **1** an unpleasant, difficult, or dangerous situation: *She was in a predicament when she missed the last train home.* **2** any condition, state, or situation. **3** that which can be predicated; attribute. **4** *Logic.* one of the categories or classes of predication. [< Late Latin *praedicāmentum* quality, category; (literally) something predicated < Latin *praedicāre;* see etym. under **predicate**]
—*Syn.* **1 Predicament, plight, dilemma** mean a bad situation. **Predicament** implies that it is perplexing or difficult to get out of it: *The people inside the burning house were in a dangerous predicament.* **Plight** implies that it is unfortunate or even hopeless: *We are distressed by the plight of refugees caught in the midst of war.* **Dilemma** implies that it involves a choice between two things, both disagreeable: *She is faced with the dilemma of telling a lie or betraying her friend.*

**pre|dic|a|men|tal** (pri dik′ə men′təl), *adj.* of or having to do with predicaments.

**pred|i|cant** (pred′ə kənt), *adj., n.* —*adj.* given to or characterized by preaching.
—*n.* a preacher, especially a member of a predicant religious order.
[< Late Latin *praedicāns, -antis,* present participle of Latin *praedicāre;* see etym. under **predicate**]

**pred|i|cate** (*n., adj.* pred′ə kit; *v.* pred′ə kāt), *n., adj., v.*, **-cat|ed**, **-cat|ing.** —*n.* **1** *Grammar.* the word or words in a sentence that tell what is said about the subject. In "Men work," "The men dug wells," "The men are soldiers," *work, dug wells,* and *are soldiers* are all predicates. **2** *Logic.* that which is said of the subject in a proposition; the second term in a proposition. *Examples:* No feathered animals are *elephants.* All birds are *feathered animals.* No birds are *elephants.* In the three propositions of this syllogism, *elephants, feathered animals,* and *elephants* are predicates. [< Late Latin *praedicātum* (originally) neuter past participle of Latin *praedicāre;* see the verb]
—*adj.* **1** *Grammar.* belonging to the predicate. In "Horses are strong," *strong* is a predicate adjective. In "The men are soldiers" *soldiers* is a predicate noun. *When the predicate tells more than one thing about the subject, it is called a compound predicate* (Harold B. Allen). **2** predicated.
—*v.t.* **1** to found or base (as a statement or action) on something. **2** to declare, assert, or affirm to be real or true: *Most religions predicate life after death.* **3** to connote; imply. **4** to declare to be an attribute or quality (of some person or thing): *We predicate goodness and mercy of God.* **5** *Logic.* **a** to state or assert (something) about the subject of a proposition. **b** to make (a term) the predicate in a proposition. **6** *Informal.* to predict. —*v.i.* to make a statement; assert; affirm: *Your mentality, too, is bully, as we all predicate* (Max Beerbohm).
[< Latin *praedicāre* (with English *-ate*[1]) declare publicly < *prae-* before + *dicāre* consecrate, dedicate. See etym. of doublet **preach.**]
▶ **predicate.** The predicate of a clause or sentence, in grammar, is the verb with its modifiers, object, and complement. It may be a simple verb of complete meaning (The big bell *tolled*), a verb and its modifier (The sun *sank quickly*), a transitive verb and its object (He finally *landed the big fish*), a linking verb and a complement, either a predicate adjective (The man *was sick*) or a predicate noun (The man *was a thief*).

**predicate calculus**, = functional calculus.

**predicate nominative**, a noun or pronoun complement that follows a linking verb.

**pred|i|ca|tion** (pred′ə kā′shən), *n.* **1** the act or fact of predicating; affirming; assertion. **2** *Grammar.* the use of predicates: *It may confidently be assumed that predication is common to all Indo-European languages* (Simeon Potter). **3** something predicated. **4** *Logic.* the assertion of something about or of a subject.

**pred|i|ca|tive** (pred′ə kā′tiv), *adj.* **1** predicating; expressing predication. **2** acting as a predicate. —**pred′i|ca′tive|ly**, *adv.*

**pred|i|ca|to|ry** (pred′ə kə tôr′ē, -tōr′-), *adj.* **1** of or having to do with a preacher; preaching. **2** characterized by being proclaimed or preached.

**pre|dict** (pri dikt′), *v.t.* to announce or tell beforehand; forecast; prophesy: *The weather service predicts rain for tomorrow.* **SYN:** foretell, presage. —*v.i.* to utter prediction; prophesy.
[< Latin *praedictus* < *praedīcere* < *prae-* before + *dīcere* to say] —**pre|dict′a|bly**, *adv.*

**pre|dict|a|bil|i|ty** (pri dik′tə bil′ə tē), *n.* the quality of being predictable.

**pre|dict|a|ble** (pri dik′tə bəl), *adj.* that can be predicted: *Every generation demonstrates some events to be regular and predictable, which the preceding generation had declared to be irregular and unpredictable* (Henry T. Buckle).

**pre|dic|tion** (pri dik′shən), *n.* **1** a thing predicted; prophecy: *The official predictions about the weather often come true. Many authorities ... insist economists should never make precise predictions* (Newsweek). **SYN:** augury, prognostication. **2** the act of predicting.

**pre|dic|tive** (pri dik′tiv), *adj.* foretelling; prophetic: *There is probably more interest in their methodological approach than in the predictive powers of their theories* (F. H. George). —**pre|dic′tive|ly**, *adv.*

**pre|dic|tor** (pri dik′tər), *n.* **1** a person or thing that predicts or foretells. **2** an instrument that calculates fire data on moving targets, especially aircraft.

**pre|di|gest** (prē′di jest′, -dī-), *v.t.* **1** to treat (food) by an artificial process similar to digestion, in order to make it more easily digestible. **2** to digest beforehand: *Foods are pre-mixed, pre-breaded, pre-fried—everything but predigested* (Harper's). (*Figurative.*) *Everything is predigested for us* (Time).

**pre|di|ges|tion** (prē′di jes′chən, -dī-), *n.* the digestion (of food) by artificial means before introduction into the stomach.

**pre|di|kant** (prā′di känt′), *n.* a clergyman of the Dutch Reformed Church in South Africa. [< Afrikaans *predikant* < Dutch < Late Latin *praedicāns;* see etym. under **predicant**]

**pre|di|lec|tion** (prē′də lek′shən, pred′ə-), *n.* a lik-

**Pronunciation Key:** hat, āge, cãre, fär; let, ēqual, tėrm; it, īce; hot, ōpen, ôrder; oil, out; cup, pu̇t, rüle; child; long; thin; ᴛʜen; zh, measure; ə represents **a** in about, **e** in taken, **i** in pencil, **o** in lemon, **u** in circus.

ing; preference: *In spite of her predilection for my powerful rival, she liked to flirt with me* (Washington Irving). **SYN**: partiality, predisposition. [< Middle French *prédilection* < Medieval Latin *praedilectus* well beloved, (literally) past participle of *praediligere* prefer before others < Latin *prae-* before + *dīligere* choose. Compare etym. under **diligent**.]

**pre|dis|pose** (prē′dis pōz′), *v.t.*, **-posed, -pos|ing. 1** to give an inclination or tendency to; make liable or susceptible: *A cold predisposes a person to other diseases.* **2** to put into a favorable or suitable frame of mind or emotional condition: *He is predisposed to be generous to his friends.* **3** to dispose of, give away, or bequeath before the usual or specified time.

**pre|dis|po|si|tion** (prē′dis pə zish′ən), *n.* a being predisposed; previous inclination or tendency; liability or susceptibility: *a predisposition to look on the dark side of things, a predisposition to colds.*

**pred|nis|o|lone** (pred nis′ə lōn), *n.* a powerful steroid hormone, used in treating arthritis, inflammatory diseases, asthma, and certain allergies; metacortandralone. It does not upset the water balance of the body and has fewer unpleasant side effects than cortisone. *Formula:* $C_{21}H_{28}O_5$ [< *pre*(gnane) + *d*(ie)*n*(e) + (cort)*isone* ( + connective *-ol*[1])]

**pred|ni|sone** (pred′nə sōn), *n.* a drug very similar to prednisolone, usually administered orally; metacortandracin. *Formula:* $C_{21}H_{26}O_5$

**pre|dom|i|nance** (pri dom′ə nəns), *n.* **1** the state or quality of being predominant; prevalence: *the predominance of weeds in the deserted garden.* **2** *Astrology.* superior influence; ascendancy.

**pre|dom|i|nan|cy** (pri dom′ə nən sē), *n.* = predominance.

**pre|dom|i|nant** (pri dom′ə nənt), *adj.* **1** having more power, authority, or influence than others; superior: *The United States became the predominant nation in the Western Hemisphere.* **SYN**: controlling, ruling. See syn. under **dominant**. **2** most extensive; noticeable; prevailing: *Green was the predominant color in the forest.* —**pre|dom′i|nant|ly**, *adv.*

**pre|dom|i|nate** (*v.* pri dom′ə nāt; *adj.* pri dom′ə nit), *v.*, **-nat|ed, -nat|ing**, *adj.* —*v.i.* to be greater in power, strength, influence, or numbers: *Sunny days predominate over rainy days in desert regions. In this character of the Americans, a love of freedom is the predominating feature* (Edmund Burke). *Life is made up of sobs, sniffles, and smiles, with sniffles predominating* (O. Henry). *Knowledge will always predominate over ignorance, as man governs the other animals* (Samuel Johnson).
—*v.t.* to dominate; control: *Let your close fire predominate his smoke* (Shakespeare).
—*adj.* = predominant. —**pre|dom′i|nat′ing|ly**, *adv.*

**pre|dom|i|na|tion** (pri dom′ə nā′shən), *n.* the fact or condition of predominating; superior power or influence; prevalence: *You would not trust to the predomination of right, which, you believe, is in your opinions* (Samuel Johnson).

**pre|dom|i|na|tor** (pri dom′ə nā′tər), *n.* a person or thing that predominates.

**pre|dy|nas|tic** (prē′dī nas′tik), *adj.* existing before the recognized dynasties, especially of Egypt before 3100 B.C.

**pree** (prē), *v.*, **preed, pree|ing**, *n. Scottish.* —*v.t.* to make proof or trial of, especially by tasting.
—*n.* a trial; taste.
**pree the mouth of**, to kiss: *He had no thought o' preeing lasses' mouths now* (James M. Barrie).
[short for obsolete *preve, prieve,* variants of *prove*]

**pre-ech|o** (prē ek′ō), *n., pl.* **-ech|oes**, *v.*, **-ech|oed, -ech|o|ing**. —*n.* **1** an echo heard on a phonograph record before hearing the sound that causes it, due to a defect in the record: *A new and exciting Leinsdorf is marred by pre-echo* (Atlantic). **2** a foreshadowing.
—*v.t.* to show or hint at beforehand; prefigure; foreshadow: *Fittingly, the disturbance pre-echoed a scene in the play* (Time). *One after another his familiar devices are pre-echoed—the cello obbligato, the divided cellos, the flutter of the woodwind* (London Times).

**pre|e|lect** or **pre-e|lect** (prē′i lekt′), *v.t.* to elect or choose beforehand.

**pre|e|lec|tion** or **pre-e|lec|tion** (prē′i lek′shən), *n., adj.* —*n.* an anticipatory election; previous choice.
—*adj.* before an election: *a preelection campaign.*

**pre|e|mer|gence** or **pre-e|mer|gence** (prē′i mėr′jəns), *adj.* before emerging or appearing: *A preemergence herbicide kills weeds before the plants push up through the soil.*

**pre|e|mer|gent** or **pre-e|mer|gent** (prē′i mėr′jənt), *adj.* = preemergence.

**pree|mie** (prē′mē), *n. Informal.* a premature baby: *To examine the eyes of these very small "preemies," the doctors must use special techniques* (Newsweek). Also, **premie**.

**pre|em|i|nence** or **pre-em|i|nence** (prē em′ə nəns), *n.* a being outstanding or preeminent; superiority; excellence: *the preeminence of Edison among the inventors of his day.*

**pre|em|i|nent** or **pre-em|i|nent** (prē em′ə nənt), *adj.* standing out above all others; superior to others. [< Latin *praeēminēns, -entis,* present participle of *praeēminēre* excel; rise above < *prae-* before + *ēminēre* stand out] —**pre|em′i|nent|ly, pre-em′i|nent|ly**, *adv.*

**pre|empt** or **pre-empt** (*v.* prē empt′; *n.* prē′empt), *v., n.* —*v.t.* **1** to secure before someone else can; acquire or take possession of beforehand: *The cat had preempted the comfortable chair. When Istanbul's mayor raised a feeble protest, the Premier, it was said, suggested he take a long vacation and promptly pre-empted his office* (Time). **2** to take over; displace: *Our policy permits candidates to preempt regular programs* (Robert E. Kintner). *Lots of Americans don't like ... when a special news show preempts the time of a popular evening program* (Harper's). **3** *U.S. and Canada.* to settle on (land) with the right to buy it before others: *He preempted the land by occupying it.* **4** *Cards.* to shut out (other bids) by making an opening bid at a high level.
—*v.i.* **1** to preempt, as a thing or place. **2** *Cards.* to bid at a high level to prevent one's opponents from bidding or exchanging informational bids, or to keep one's partner from changing the declaration, especially at whist or bridge.
—*n. Cards.* the act or practice of preempting: *It is amazing how often pre-empts induce the most cautious bidders to make risky bids* (Manchester Guardian Weekly).
[American English, back formation < *preemption*] —**pre|empt′er, pre-empt′er**, *n.*

**pre|emp|tion** or **pre-emp|tion** (prē emp′shən), *n.* **1** *U.S. and Canada.* the act or right of purchasing before others or in preference to others: *It is neither right nor legal that Mr. Hardy's preemption should gobble up over 250 acres of hay lands* (Regina Journal). **2** the act of seizing or taking possession beforehand; appropriation before others: ... *Federal preemption of the avocado problem* (New York Times). **3** the act or fact of displacing; replacement: *Sale of network time to candidates involves pre-emption of better paying advertisers* (Frank Stanton). [< *pre-* + Latin *ēmptiō, -ōnis* buying < *emere* to buy]

**pre|emp|tive** or **pre-emp|tive** (prē emp′tiv), *adj.* **1** of or having to do with preemption: *preemptive purchase of land.* **2** initiated before other launched beforehand: *a preemptive war. The preemptive strike ... would be a last-minute desperate attempt to destroy as much as possible of an enemy's forces because we were convinced that he was about to attack us* (Bulletin of Atomic Scientists). **3** *Finance.* allowing stockholders to have first choice of purchasing newly issued stock of a company: *They also defeated shareholder proposals for ... pre-emptive rights on new financing* (Wall Street Journal). **4** *Cards.* of or for preempting: *a preemptive bid.*
—**pre|emp′tive|ly, pre-emp′tive|ly**, *adv.*

**pre|emp|tor** or **pre-emp|tor** (prē emp′tər), *n.* a person who preempts, especially one who takes up land with the privilege of preemption.

**pre|emp|to|ry** or **pre-emp|to|ry** (prē emp′tər ē), *adj.* preemptive.

**preen**[1] (prēn), *v.t., v.i.* **1** to smooth or arrange (the feathers) with the beak, as a bird does: *Past the Ryemeadow's lonely woodland nook Where many a stubble gray goose preens her wing* (John Masefield). **2** to dress (oneself) carefully; primp. **3** to pride or please (oneself): *Prince, we may preen ourselves on gain, but is there not some tinge of loss?* (New Yorker). [perhaps variant of *prune*[3] to preen, dress carefully; influenced by dialectal *preen* to pin up, sew up < *preen*[2]. Compare etym. under **prune**[3].] —**preen′er**, *n.*

**preen**[2] (prēn), *n. Scottish.* a pin; brooch. [Old English *prēon* a pin, brooch]

**preen gland**, the uropygial gland: *Most birds have a pair of preen glands over the tail ... that secretes a preening ointment* (Scientific American).

**pre-Eng|lish** (prē ing′lish), *n., adj.* —*n.* the ancient continental West Germanic dialect which later became English.
—*adj.* **1** having to do with this dialect. **2** of or having to do with Britain or its peoples or languages before the Anglo-Saxon conquest.

**pre|ex|il|i|an** or **pre-ex|il|i|an** (prē′eg zil′ē ən, -ek sil′-), *adj.* **1** before the Babylonian Captivity or Exile of the Jews; before 586 B.C. **2** before exile.

**pre|ex|il|ic** or **pre-ex|il|ic** (prē′eg zil′ik), *adj.* preexilian.

**pre|ex|ist** or **pre-ex|ist** (prē′ig zist′), *v.i.* to exist beforehand, or before something else. —*v.t.* to exist before (something).

**pre|ex|ist|ence** or **pre-ex|ist|ence** (prē′ig zis′təns), *n.* previous existence, especially of the soul before its union with the body.

**pre|ex|ist|ent** or **pre-ex|ist|ent** (prē′ig zis′tənt), *adj.* existing previously.

**pref.**, an abbreviation for the following:
**1** preface.
**2** preference.
**3** preferred.
**4a** prefix. **b** prefixed.

***pre|fab** (prē′fab′), *n., v.*, **-fabbed, -fab|bing**, *adj. Informal.* —*n.* something prefabricated, especially a house: *Its scattering of prefabs and trailers and barracks, indeed gave the appearance of being at the edge of the civilized world* (New Yorker). See picture below.
—*v.t.* = prefabricate.
—*adj.* = prefabricated.
[American English, short for *prefabricate*]

**pre|fab|ri|cate** (prē fab′rə kāt), *v.t.*, **-cat|ed, -cat|ing. 1** to make all standardized parts of (as a house). The erection of a prefabricated house requires merely the assembling of the various sections. **2** to prepare in advance: [*The*] *Secretary ... says he has brought no prefabricated American plan to the London conference on German rearmament* (Wall Street Journal). —**pre′fab|ri|ca′tion**, *n.* —**pre|fab′ri|ca′tor**, *n.*

**pref|ace** (pref′is), *n., v.*, **-aced, -ac|ing**. —*n.* **1** an introduction to a book, writing, or speech: *Does your history book have a preface written by the author?* **SYN**: See syn. under **introduction**. **2** *Figurative.* something preliminary or introductory: *He ... seemed to look upon a certain mass of disappointment as the natural preface to all realizations* (Thomas Hardy). **3** Also, **Preface**. the introduction to the Canon of the Mass, ending with the Sanctus.
—*v.t.* **1** to introduce by written or spoken remarks; give a preface to. **2** to be a preface to; begin: *A depressing and difficult passage has prefaced every new page I have turned in life* (Charlotte Brontë).
[< Old French *preface,* ultimately < Latin *praefātiō* < *praefārī* to preface, foretell < *prae-* before + *fārī* speak]

**pref|a|to|ri|al** (pref′ə tôr′ē əl, -tōr′-), *adj.* = prefatory.

**pref|a|to|ri|ly** (pref′ə tôr′ə lē, -tōr′-), *adv.* by way of preface.

**pref|a|to|ry** (pref′ə tôr′ē, -tōr′-), *adj.* of or like a preface; given as a preface; introductory; preliminary: *The issue also contains a prefatory note assuring the reader ... that it is possible for a magazine to take advertising and still be honest* (New Yorker).

**pre|fect** (prē′fekt), *n.* **1** the title of various military and civil officers in ancient Rome, such as the chief official of a city, the civil governor of a province, or the commander of the Praetorian Guard. **2** the chief administrative official of a department of France: ... *addressed a meeting in Paris of the "super prefects" of different regions of France* (London Times). **3** a chief officer, chief magistrate, or the like. **4** a student monitor in certain schools, especially English schools; senior

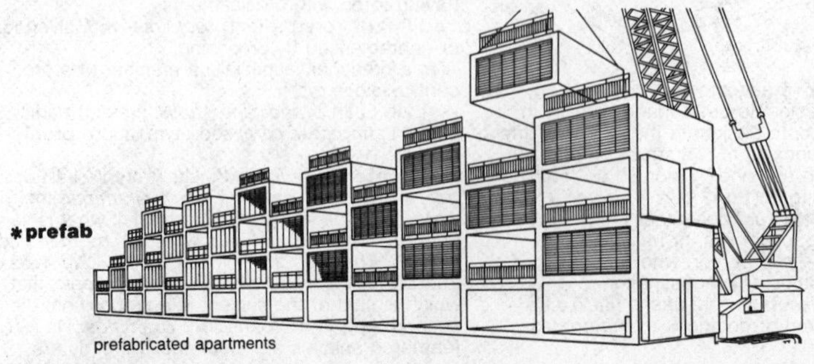

***prefab**

prefabricated apartments

student who has some authority over other students; prepositor: *Her face ... regarded him as she must have learned, ten years ago, when she was a school prefect, to regard one of the girls* (Harper's). **5** a dean in Jesuit schools or colleges. Also, **praefect.** [< Old French *prefect,* learned borrowing from Latin *praefectus* public overseer, (originally) one put in charge; (literally) past participle of *praeficere* < *prae-* in front, before + *facere* to make]

**pre|fec|to|ri|al** (prē′fek tôr′ē əl, -tōr′-), *adj.* having to do with a prefect or a prefecture.

**pre|fec|tur|al** (pri fek′chər əl), *adj.* of or belonging to a prefecture.

**pre|fec|ture** (prē′fek chər), *n.* the office, jurisdiction, territory, or official residence of a prefect: *The country [Morocco] is divided into 19 provinces and 5 urban prefectures* (James S. Coleman). [< Latin *praefectūra* < *praefectus* prefect]

**pre|fer** (pri fėr′), *v.,* **-ferred, -fer|ring.** — ***v.t.*** **1** to like better; choose rather: *She prefers reading to sewing. He prefers golf as a sport, but I prefer to swim rather than golf. My students preferred fiction over history. We would prefer that they draw their own conclusions.* **2** to put forward; present: *to prefer a claim to property. The policeman preferred charges of speeding against the driver.* **3** to advance; promote: *The captain was preferred to the rank of major.* **4** *Law.* to give preference to, as a creditor.
— ***v.i.*** to have or express a preference: *I will come later, if you prefer.*
[< Old French *preferer,* learned borrowing from Latin *praeferre* < *prae-* before + *ferre* to carry]
— **pre|fer′rer,** *n.*

**pref|er|a|bil|i|ty** (pref′ər ə bil′ə tē, pref′rə-), *n.* the state or quality of being preferable.

**pref|er|a|ble** (pref′ər ə bəl, pref′rə-), *adj.* to be preferred; more desirable. — **pref′er|a|ble|ness,** *n.*

**pref|er|a|bly** (pref′ər ə blē, pref′rə-), *adv.* by choice: *He wants a secretary, preferably one who is a college graduate.*

**pref|er|ence** (pref′ər əns, pref′rəns), *n.* **1** the act or attitude of liking better: *My preference is for beef rather than lamb.* **SYN:** selection, election. See syn. under **choice. 2** a thing preferred; first choice: *My preference in reading is a mystery story.* **3** the action of favoring, or fact of being favored, one above another: *A teacher should not show preference for any one of her pupils.* **4** the act or fact of favoring one country or group of countries in international trade by admitting their products at a lower import duty than that levied on others. **5** *Law.* priority of payment given to a certain debt or class of debts. **6** a type of card game for three players, using a deck of 32 cards. [< Middle French *preference,* learned borrowing from Medieval Latin *praeferentia* < Latin *praeferēns, -entis,* present participle of *praeferre* prefer]

**preference share** or **stock,** *British.* preferred stock.

**pref|er|en|tial** (pref′ə ren′shəl), *adj.* **1** of, giving, or receiving preference: *preferential treatment. Workers who lose their jobs to an automatic device should be given preferential hiring status* (Wall Street Journal). **2** having import duties favoring particular countries: *a preferential tariff.* **3** indicating or permitting indication of the order of one's preference: *a preferential vote, preferential voting. Both ... were unopposed in the preferential portion of the primary—a sort of popularity poll* (Wall Street Journal). **4** giving preference to union members in hiring, training, and promotion: *a preferential shop.* — **pref′er|en′tial|ly,** *adv.*

**pref|er|en|tial|ism** (pref′ə ren′shə liz əm), *n.* the system of giving preference in the fixing of a tariff: *The old-fashioned protectionism, which is now popping up again under the guise of Colonial preferentialism* (Liberty Review).

**pref|er|en|tial|ist** (pref′ə ren′shə list), *n.* a supporter of preference in tariff relations.

**preferential shop,** a shop giving preference to union members in hiring, training, and promotion.

**preferential voting,** a system of voting in which the voter indicates the order of his choice of candidates for an office, so that if no candidate has a majority of first choices, the election may be determined by totaling the first-choice, second-choice, etc., votes cast for each contestant.

**pre|fer|ment** (pri fėr′mənt), *n.* **1** advancement; promotion: *to seek preferment in one's job. That captain hopes for preferment in the army.* **2** a position or office giving social or financial advancement, especially one in the church: *their hunger for lands and office and preferment* (James A. Froude). **3** the act of preferring.

**pre|ferred stock** (pri fėrd′), stock on which dividends must be paid at a predetermined rate before any can be paid on the common stock.

**pre|fig|ur|a|tion** (prē′fig yə rā′shən), *n.* **1** the act of prefiguring; representation beforehand by a figure or type. **2** that in which something is prefigured; prototype.

**pre|fig|ur|a|tive** (prē fig′yər ə tiv), *adj.* **1** showing by previous figures, types, or similarity. **2** *Anthropology.* of or designating a form of society in which the values of the younger generation predominate. — **pre|fig′ur|a|tive|ly,** *adv.* — **pre|fig′ur|a|tive|ness,** *n.*

**pre|fig|ure** (prē fig′yər), *v.t.,* **-ured, -ur|ing. 1** to represent beforehand by a figure or type: *In one painting of Christ, His shadow is that of a cross, prefiguring the Crucifixion.* **2** to imagine or picture to oneself beforehand: *My first sensations ... were far from being so flattering as I had prefigured them* (Laurence Sterne). [< Latin *praefigūrāre* < *prae-* before + *figūrāre* to form, shape < *figūra* a form]

**pre|fig|ure|ment** (prē fig′yər mənt), *n.* the act of prefiguring.

**pre|fin|ish** (prē fin′ish), *v.t.* to finish (as a panel, window, or wall section) prior to installation in a building: *The window is to be prefinished and pre-glazed* (Harper's).

***pre|fix** (*n.* prē′fiks; *v.* prē fiks′), *n., v.* — ***n.*** **1** a syllable, syllables, or word put at the beginning of a word to change its meaning or to make another word. *Pre-* in *pre*paid, *under-* in *under*line, *dis-* in *dis*appear, *un-* in *un*like, and *re-* in *re*open are prefixes. *Prefixes are affixes which precede the root with which they are most closely associated* (H. A. Gleason). **2** a title put before a person's name, such as Mr., Dr., Sir, Rev., or Hon. **3** *Logic, Mathematics.* a symbol, number, or statement, that is put before a formula or proposition. [< New Latin *praefixum,* noun use of neuter of Latin *praefīxus* < *praefīgere* < *prae-* in front + *fīgere* to fix in, establish]
— ***v.t.*** **1** to fix beforehand. **2** *Obsolete.* to fix in one's mind beforehand.
**prefix to, a** to put (something) before: *We prefix "Mr." to a man's name.* **b** to add as a prefix: *to prefix a syllable to a word.*
[perhaps < Middle French *prefixer* < *pre-* before + *fixer* to fix, place; or < Middle French *prefix,* learned borrowing from Latin *praefīxus;* see noun]

***prefix** definition 1

con - figur - ation
prefix root suffix

**pre|fix|al** (prē′fik səl, prē fik′-), *adj.* **1** of the nature of a prefix. **2** characterized by prefixes. — **pre′fix|al|ly,** *adv.*

**pre|fix|a|tion** (prē′fik sā′shən), *n.* the use or forming of prefixes.

**pre|fix|ion** (prē fik′shən), *n.* the act of prefixing.

**pre|flight** (prē′flīt′), *adj.* preceding or occurring before flight, as of an aircraft, missile, or satellite: *a preflight inspection of a plane, preflight training.*

**pre|form** (prē fôrm′), *v.t.* to form or shape beforehand.

**pre|for|ma|tion** (prē′fôr mā′shən), *n.* **1** the act or process of shaping beforehand. **2** an old theory of generation according to which the individual exists complete in the germ cell, further development being merely in size.

**pre|for|ma|tion|ist** (prē′fôr mā′shə nist), *n.* a person who accepts the theory of preformation.

**pre|for|ma|tive** (prē fôr′mə tiv), *adj.* determining form beforehand; preforming.

**pre|fron|tal** (prē frun′təl), *adj., n.* — ***adj.*** of or having to do with the anterior portion of the frontal part of the brain.
— ***n.*** a bone in the anterior part of the skull of certain vertebrates, especially in amphibians and reptiles.

**prefrontal leucotomy,** = prefrontal lobotomy.

**prefrontal lobotomy,** a brain operation in which the nerves between the hypothalamic region and the cerebral cortex are cut to relieve the symptoms of mental illness.

**pre|gan|gli|on|ic** (prē′gang glē on′ik), *adj.* lying in front of or preceding a ganglion: *preganglionic neurons.*

**preg|gers** (preg′ərz), *adj. British Slang.* pregnant.

**preg|na|bil|i|ty** (preg′nə bil′ə tē), *n.* capability of being attacked; vulnerability.

**preg|na|ble** (preg′nə bəl), *adj.* open to attack; assailable; vulnerable. [< Old French *prenable,* and *pregnable* < stem of *prendre* < Latin *prendere,* short for *prehendere* to seize, take]

**preg|nan|cy** (preg′nən sē), *n., pl.* **-cies. 1** pregnant quality or condition: *to go through the last months of pregnancy,* (*Figurative.*) *a remark of obvious pregnancy.* **2** the period of being pregnant.

**pregnancy disease,** a disease of ewes caused by carbohydrate deficiency and occurring in the last month of pregnancy, most often in older ewes carrying twins or triplets; twin lamb disease.

**preg|nane** (preg′nān), *n.* a steroid hydrocarbon, the parent substance of the adrenocorticotropic hormones, a form of which is found in urine during pregnancy. *Formula:* $C_{21}H_{36}$ [< *pregn*(ancy) + *-ane*]

**preg|nant¹** (preg′nənt), *adj.* **1** soon to have a baby; having an embryo or embryos developing in the uterus; being with child or young. **2** filled; loaded: *The silence was pregnant with tragedy* (Harper's). **3** *Figurative.* fertile; rich; abounding: *a mind pregnant with ideas.* **4** *Figurative.* filled with meaning; significant: *Most proverbs are pregnant sayings. Historians will one day record our country's successes and failures in world affairs during these pregnant middle years of the twentieth century* (Atlantic). **5** *Obsolete.* disposed; ready: *The pregnant instrument of wrath Prest for this blow* (Shakespeare). [< Latin *praegnāns, -antis,* variant of *praegnās, -ātis* < *prae-* before + unrecorded *gna-* to bear young] — **preg′nant|ly,** *adv.*

**preg|nant²** (preg′nənt), *adj. Archaic.* (of an argument, evidence, reason, or the like) urgent; weighty; compelling: *One of the constables, besides the pregnant proof already produced, offers to make oath* (Scott). **SYN:** cogent. [< Old French *pregnant,* and *preignant* violent, pressing; (literally) present participle of *preindre* < Latin *premere* to press]

**pregnant mare's serum,** a serum containing a hormone taken from pregnant mares and injected into ewes or cows to control ovulation.

**preg|nen|o|lone** (preg nen′ə lōn), *n.* a drug obtained from stigmasterol and other steroids, used in the treatment of extreme fatigue, arthritis, and certain diseases. *Formula:* $C_{21}H_{32}O_2$ [< *pregn-*(ane) + *-ene* + *-ol¹* + *-one*]

**pre|hal|lux** (prē hal′əks), *n.* a rudimentary structure found on the inner side of the tarsus of some mammals, reptiles, and amphibians, supposed to represent an additional digit. [< *pre-* + *hallux*]

**pre|heat** (prē hēt′), *v.t.* to heat before using: *to preheat a pot before making tea.*

**pre|heat|er** (prē hē′tər), *n.* a furnace, hot chamber, or the like, in which something is placed, or through which something is passed, in order to be preheated.

***pre|hen|sile** (prē hen′səl), *adj.* adapted for seizing, grasping, or holding on. Many monkeys have prehensile tails. [< French *préhensile* < Latin *prehēnsus* < *prehendere* to grasp]

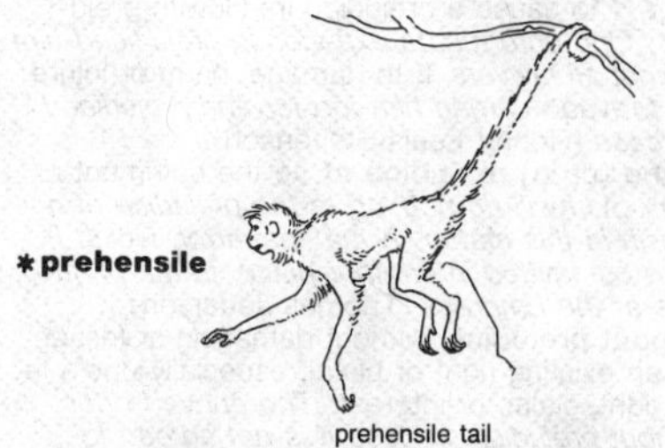

***prehensile**

prehensile tail

**pre|hen|sil|i|ty** (prē′hen sil′ə tē), *n.* the character of being prehensile.

**pre|hen|sion** (prē hen′shən), *n.* **1** the act of taking hold physically; grasping; seizing. **2** *Figurative.* grasping with the mind; mental apprehension. [< Latin *prehēnsiō, -ōnis* < *prehendere* to grasp]

**pre|hen|sive** (prē hen′siv), *adj.* **1** seizing or laying hold of. **2** *Figurative.* apprehending: *a prehensive mind.*

**pre|hen|so|ry** (prē hen′sər ē), *adj.* = prehensive.

**pre|his|to|ri|an** (prē′his tôr′ē ən, -tōr′-), *n.* a person who studies the remains, customs, and conditions of prehistoric times.

**pre|his|tor|ic** (prē′his tôr′ik, -tor′-), *adj.* of or belonging to times before histories were written: *Some prehistoric people lived in caves. Prehistoric men and animals are known from skeletal materials found in the crust of the earth* (Beals and Hoijer). — **pre′his|tor′i|cal|ly,** *adv.*

**pre|his|tor|i|cal** (prē′his tôr′ə kəl, -tor′-), *adj.* = prehistoric.

**pre|his|to|ry** or **pre-his|to|ry** (prē his′tər ē, -trē), *n.* history before recorded history; prehistoric matters or times: *A team of archeologists ... has discovered in that unexplored waste traces of a lost people of pre-history* (Harper's).

**prehn|ite** (prā′nīt, pren′īt), *n.* a mineral consisting of a hydrous silicate of aluminum and calcium, occurring in crystalline aggregates, and usually of a pale-green color. *Formula:* $Ca_2Al_2Si_3O_{10}(OH)_2$ [< German *Prehnit* < Colonel van *Prehn,* a Dutch governor of Cape Colony, who brought it to Europe in the late 1700's]

**pre·hom·i·nid** (prē hom′ə nid), *adj., n.* —***adj.*** of or having to do with a group of extinct, manlike primates regarded as immediate ancestors of the hominids.
—***n.*** a prehominid animal: *Walking upright was initiated by prehominids* (New Yorker).

**pre·hor·mone** (prē hôr′mōn), *n.* a rudimentary or incipient hormone.

**pre·ig·ni·tion** (prē′ig nish′ən), *n.* the ignition of the explosive mixture in an internal-combustion engine before the piston is in a position to begin its working stroke, especially before the inlet valve has closed or before full compression of the mixture is reached in the cylinder; autoignition.

**pre·in·dus·tri·al** (prē′in dus′trē əl), *adj.* existing or occurring before industrialization: *It would take ... 500 years for Lake Michigan to return to its preindustrial purity* (Atlantic).

**pre·judge** (prē juj′), *v.,* **-judged, -judg·ing.** —***v.t.*** to pass judgment on (a person, opinion, action, or condition) beforehand, especially without knowing all the facts: *The jury was reminded to keep an open mind during the trial and not to prejudge the case.*
—***v.i.*** to judge beforehand; judge without knowing all the facts.
[< French *préjuger,* alteration (influenced by earlier *juger*) of Latin *praejūdicāre* to prejudge, prejudice < *prae-* before + *jūdicāre* to judicate < *jūdex, -icis* a judge] —**pre·judg′er,** *n.*

**pre·judge·ment** (prē juj′mənt), *n. Especially British.* prejudgment.

**pre·judg·ment** (prē juj′mənt), *n.* the act of prejudging; judgment before full knowledge or examination of the case; decision or condemnation in advance: *I listen that I may know, without prejudgment* (George Eliot).

**prej·u·dice** (prej′ə dis), *n., v.,* **-diced, -dic·ing.**
—***n.*** **1** an opinion formed without taking time and care to judge fairly: *a prejudice toward doctors. Many people have a prejudice against foreigners. I am ... a bundle of prejudices—made up of likings and dislikings* (Charles Lamb). **2** harm or injury as the consequence of some action or judgment: *The attorney argued that the decision involved prejudice to his client.*
—***v.t.*** **1** to cause a prejudice in; fill with prejudice: *One unfortunate experience prejudiced him against all lawyers.* **2** to damage; harm or injure: *His bravado carried him too far and prejudiced his case* (Robert Louis Stevenson).
**to the** (or **in**) **prejudice of,** to the detriment or injury of: *I will do nothing to the prejudice of my cousin in this matter. A material error, which I have committed in another place, to the prejudice of the Empress* (Thomas Jefferson).
**without prejudice,** without damaging or lessening an existing right or claim, especially one's legal right, claim, or interest: *The above I offer without prejudice, in case it is not agreed to* (Manning and Granger).
[< Old French *prejudice,* learned borrowing from Latin *praejūdicium* < *prae-* before + *jūdicium* judgment < *jūdex, -icis* a judge]
—***Syn.*** *n.* **1 Prejudice, bias** mean an opinion, attitude, or tendency formed unfairly or unjustly. **Prejudice** applies to an opinion or judgment, usually unfavorable, formed beforehand with no basis except personal feelings: *She has a prejudice against modern furniture.* **Bias** applies to a strong leaning or propensity against or in favor of someone or something because of personal liking or a fixed idea: *He often does foolish things because of his bias in favor of the underdog.*

**prej·u·di·cial** (prej′ə dish′əl), *adj.* causing prejudice or disadvantage; hurtful: *They were playing havoc with legitimate union demands, and acting in a manner prejudicial to others at the pit and contrary to the spirit of trade unionism* (London Times). **SYN:** detrimental, damaging. —**prej′u·di′cial·ly,** *adv.*

**prel·a·cy** (prel′ə sē), *n., pl.* **-cies. 1** the position or rank of a prelate. **2** prelates as a group. **3** church government by prelates.

**pre·lap·sar·i·an** (prē′lap sãr′ē ən), *adj.* of the time or condition before a fall, especially the fall of man: *The monks and hermits were trying ... to re-create the life of prelapsarian Adam* (Manchester Guardian). [< *pre-* + Latin *lapsus* fall + English *-arian,* as in *infralapsarian*]

**prel·ate** (prel′it), *n.* a clergyman of high rank, such as a bishop. [< Medieval Latin *praelatus* prelate (in Late Latin, noble) < Latin, (literally) one that is preferred, past participle of *praeferre* prefer]

**prel·ate·ship** (prel′it ship), *n.* the office or rank of a prelate.

**pre·lat·ic** (pri lat′ik), *adj.* of or having to do with a prelate or prelates.

**prel·at·ism** (prel′ə tiz əm), *n.* = prelacy.

**prel·a·ture** (prel′ə chər), *n.* = prelacy. [< Medieval Latin *praelatura* < *praelatus* prelate]

**pre·lect** (pri lekt′), *v.i.* to discourse publicly; deliver a lecture. Also, **praelect.** [< Latin *praelēctus,* past participle of *praelegere* read to others, lecture upon < *prae-* before + *legere* read]
—**pre·lec′tion,** *n.* —**pre·lec′tor,** *n.*

**pre·li·ba·tion** (prē′lī bā′shən), *n.* a tasting beforehand; foretaste. [< Latin *praelībātiō, -ōnis* anticipation, a taste < *praelībāre* < *prae-* before + *lībāre* to taste]

**pre·lim** (pri lim′), *n., adj. Informal.* —***n.*** a preliminary examination. Prelims are given to some candidates for the doctorate before writing the dissertation. *He was miserably lonely, failed his "prelims" and had to leave at the end of his first year* (Sunday Times).
—***adj.*** = preliminary.

**prelim.,** preliminary.

**pre·lim·i·nar·y** (pri lim′ə ner′ē), *adj., n., pl.* **-nar·ies.** —***adj.*** coming before the main business; leading to something more important: *After the preliminary exercises of prayer and song, the speaker of the day gave an address.* **SYN:** prefatory, introductory.
—***n.*** **1** a preliminary step; something preparatory: *A physical examination is a preliminary to joining the army. The ambassadors dispensed with formal preliminaries and opened their discussions immediately.* **2** a preliminary examination. **3** an athletic contest or match preceding the main event, especially in boxing or wrestling.
[< New Latin *praeliminaris* < Latin *prae-* before + *līmen, -inis* threshold] —**pre·lim′i·nar′i·ly,** *adv.*

**pre·lit·er·ate** (prē lit′ər it), *adj.* being at a stage before the use of writing: *a preliterate society or culture.*

**prel·ude** (prel′yüd, -üd; prē′lüd, prā′-), *n., v.,* **-ud·ed, -ud·ing.** —***n.*** **1** anything serving as an introduction; preliminary performance: *The German invasion of Poland was a prelude to World War II. The treaty is regarded as a prelude to such a conference* (New York Times). **2a** a piece of music, or part of it, that introduces another piece or part: *But remember that the preludes and fugues were first of all reverie pieces used in the church service* (Atlantic). **b** an independent instrumental movement or piece of an imaginative, improvised nature, usually short and following no special form. **c** a composition played at the beginning of a church service, especially an organ solo: *We heard the organist play a prelude to the church service.*
—***v.t.*** **1** to be a prelude or introduction to: *When the gray of morn preludes the splendour of the day* (John Dryden). **2** to introduce with a prelude: *He preluded his address with a sonorous blast of the nose* (Washington Irving). **3** *Music.* to play as a prelude.
—***v.i.*** **1** to give a prelude or introductory performance. **2** *Music.* to play a prelude.
[< Middle French *prélude,* learned borrowing from Medieval Latin *praeludium* < Latin *praelūdere* to preface < *prae-* before + *lūdere* to play]

**pre·lud·er** (pri lü′dər, prel′yə-), *n.* **1** a person who preludes. **2** a person who plays a musical prelude.

**pre·lu·di·al** (pri lü′dē əl), *adj.* of or like a prelude; introductory: *preludial music, a preludial dinner.*

**pre·lu·sion** (pri lü′zhən), *n.* a prelude or introduction. [< Latin *praelūsiō, -ōnis* a prefacing < *praelūdere* to perform before; see etym. under **prelude**]

**pre·lu·sive** (pri lü′siv), *adj.* serving as a prelude; preliminary; introductory. —**pre·lu′sive·ly,** *adv.*

**pre·lu·so·ri·ly** (pri lü′sər ə lē), *adv.* by way of introduction or prelude.

**pre·lu·so·ry** (pri lü′sər ē), *adj.* = prelusive.

**prem.,** premium.

**pre·man** (prē′man′), *n., pl.* **-men.** a prehistoric man: *arboreal premen.*

**pre·ma·ture** (prē′mə chůr′, -tůr′, -tyůr′), *adj.* **1** before the proper time; too soon. A premature baby is one born more than two weeks early or weighing less than 5½ pounds. *His arrival an hour before the party began was premature. He was already decrepit with premature old age* (John L. Motley). **2** hasty; rash, as in action: *I had been a little too premature in coming to this conclusion* (Herman Melville). [< Latin *praemātūrus* < *prae-* beforehand, early + *mātūrus* ripe]
—**pre′ma·ture′ly,** *adv.* —**pre′ma·ture′ness,** *n.*

**pre·ma·tu·ri·ty** (prē′mə chůr′ə tē, -tůr′-, -tyůr′-), *n.* the quality or state of babies being premature: *For most of the deaths of babies under one month, prematurity is the chief cause* (Newsweek).

**pre·max·il·la** (prē′mak sil′ə), *n., pl.* **-max·il·lae** (-mak sil′ē). one of a pair of bones of the upper jaw of vertebrates, situated in front of and between the maxillary bones. [< New Latin *praemaxilla* < Latin *prae-* before, forward + *maxilla* maxilla]

**pre·max·il·lar·y** (prē mak′sə ler′ē), *adj., n., pl.* **-lar·ies.** —***adj.*** **1** in front of the maxillary bones. **2** of or having to do with premaxillae.
—***n.*** = premaxilla.

**pre·med** (prē′med, prē med′), *n., adj. Informal.*
—***n.*** a premedical student.
—***adj.*** premedical.

**pre·med·ic** (prē med′ik), *n.* = premed.

**pre·med·i·cal** (prē med′ə kəl), *adj.* preparing for the study of medicine: *a premedical student, a premedical course.*

**pre·med·i·tate** (prē med′ə tāt), *v.t., v.i.,* **-tat·ed, -tat·ing.** to consider or plan beforehand: *The murder was premeditated. The general premeditated his plan before giving the order to attack.* [< Latin *praemeditārī* (with English *-ate*[1]) < *prae-* before + *meditārī* to meditate]

**pre·med·i·tat·ed·ly** (prē med′ə tā′tid lē), *adv.* with premeditation; deliberately.

**pre·med·i·ta·tion** (prē′med ə tā′shən), *n.* previous deliberation or planning.

**pre·med·i·ta·tive** (prē med′ə tā′tiv), *adj.* characterized by premeditation. —**pre·med′i·ta′tive·ly,** *adv.*

**pre·med·i·ta·tor** (prē med′ə tā′tər), *n.* a person who premeditates.

**pre·men·stru·al** (prē men′strü əl), *adj.* being or occurring before menstruation: *premenstrual women.* —**pre·men′stru·al·ly,** *adj.*

**pre·mie** (prē′mē), *n.* = preemie.

**pre·mier** (*n.* pri mir′, prē′mē ər; *adj.* prē′mē ər, prem′yər), *n., adj.* —***n.*** a prime minister; chief officer: *It has been my aim to get the premiers of the four provinces working closer together than ever before* (Maclean's). [short for *premier minister* (literally) first minister]
—***adj.*** **1** first in rank or importance; chief: *a premier product. The show directors, faced with rising costs ... to stage Scotland's premier agricultural event, were disappointed* (London Times). **2** first in time; earliest: *the premier occurrence of a contagious disease.*
[< Old French *premier* first < Latin *prīmārius* < *prīmus* first. See etym. of doublet **primary.**]

**pre·mier dan·seur** (prə myā′ dän sœr′), *French.* the leading male dancer in a ballet or ballet company.

**pre·miere** or **pre·mière** (pri mir′, prə myãr′), *n., adj., v.,* **-miered, -mier·ing** or **-mièred, -mièr·ing.**
—***n.*** **1** a first public performance: *the premiere of a new play.* **2** the leading woman (in a play or the like).
—***adj.*** = premier; first.
—***v.t.*** to give the first public performance or showing of (as a play or motion picture): *The romantic opera "Louise" was premièred in 1900* (Time).
—***v.i.*** to have the first public performance or showing: *The new movie is premiering this month.* **2** to perform publicly for the first time, especially as a star: *She premiered in London.* **3** to appear for the first time: *The magazine is scheduled to premiere next fall.*
[< French *première,* (originally) feminine of *premier* first; see etym. under **premier**]

**pre·mière dan·seuse** (prə myer′ dän sœz′), *French.* the leading woman dancer in a ballet or ballet company.

**pre·mier·ship** (pri mir′ship, prē′mē ər-), *n.* **1** the office or rank of a prime minister: *Andre Tardieu, perhaps the most brilliant politician of the years between the two world wars, abandoned politics after two premierships* (Wall Street Journal). **2** the state of being first or foremost.

**pre·mil·le·nar·i·an** (prē′mil ə nãr′ē ən), *n., adj.*
—***n.*** a supporter of premillennialism.
—***adj.*** = premillennial.

**pre·mil·le·nar·i·an·ism** (prē′mil ə nãr′ē ə niz′əm), *n.* = premillennialism.

**pre·mil·len·ni·al** (prē′mə len′ē əl), *adj. Theology.* preceding the millenium; having to do with the world as it now is.

**pre·mil·len·ni·al·ism** (prē′mə len′ē ə liz′əm), *n.* the belief that Christ will come again before the millennium and reign a thousand years upon a righteous, happy earth.

**pre·mil·len·ni·al·ist** (prē′mə len′ē ə list), *n.* = premillenarian.

**prem·ise** (*n.* prem′is; *v.* pri mīz′), *n., v.,* **-ised, -is·ing.** —***n.*** **1** *Logic.* a statement assumed to be true and used to draw a conclusion. *Example:* Major premise: Children should go to school. Minor premise: He is a child. Conclusion: He should go to school. **2** any assumption or presupposition; postulate: *Every premise on which our democracy is based depends on a prompt and fair system of justice* (Robert P. Patterson, Jr.).
—***v.t.*** **1** to set forth as an introduction or explanation; mention beforehand: *Having premised these circumstances, I will now let the nervous gentleman proceed with his stories* (Washington Irving). **2** to have as a premise; base or imply beforehand; presuppose; postulate: *The original American dream ... was premised not specifically*

*on materialism but on a broad humanism* (Charles A. Reich).
— ***v.i.*** to make a premise.

**premises, a** a house or building with its grounds: *Each had entered the Brink's premises several times at night to study the layout* (Newsweek). **b** a piece or tract of land. **c** *Law.* things mentioned previously, such as the names of the parties concerned, a description of the property, the price, grounds for complaint, etc.: *The court having considered the premises are of the opinion ...* (Bloomfield's American Law Reports). **d** *Law.* the property forming the subject of a document: *Alice Higgins devised the premises, being a term for 999 years, to trustees, in trust to herself for life, remainder to H. Higgins, her son, and Mary, his wife* (William Cruise).
[< Old French *premisse,* learned borrowing from Latin *praemissa* (*propositiō*) (the proposition) put before; (originally) feminine past participle of *praemittere* < Latin *prae-* before + *mittere* to send]

**prem|iss** (prem′is), *n. Logic.* premise.

**pre|mi|um** (prē′mē əm), *n., pl.* **-ums,** *adj.* — ***n.*** **1** a reward, especially given as an incentive to buy; prize: *Some magazines give premiums for obtaining new subscriptions.* **2** something more than the ordinary price or wages: *Mr. Brown has to pay 6 per cent interest on his loan, and also a premium of two hundred dollars.* **3** the amount of money paid for insurance: *He pays premiums on his life insurance four times a year.* **4** the excess value of one form of money over another of the same nominal value, as of gold or silver coins over paper currency. **5** *Figurative.* an unusual or unfair value: *Most parents put a high premium on neatness and punctuality. Giving money to beggars may put a premium on idleness.* **6** a fee paid for instruction in some occupation.
— ***adj.*** of a higher grade or quality: *premium gasoline. A new low profile nylon cord premium tire ... will give up to 40 per cent more mileage* (Wall Street Journal).
**at a premium, a** at more than the usual value or price: *... entitled to extra seats for every football game, which could be sold to lesser fry at a handsome premium* (New Yorker). **b** *Figurative.* in high esteem; very valuable; much wanted: *John Lyon put their charms at a premium* (Harrovian).
[< Latin *praemium* reward, booty < *prae-* before + *emere* to buy]

**premium pay,** wages at more than the basic rate for overtime work or for work on holidays or weekends: *The union retains six paid holidays, with provision for premium pay if a worker was required to work on those days* (New York Times).

**pre|mix** (prē′miks′), *n., adj., v.* — ***n.*** any product mixed beforehand: *Bottlers like the premix because it gives them complete quality control over the product* (Wall Street Journal).
— ***adj.*** of a premix.
— ***v.t.*** to prepare by mixing beforehand.

**pre|mo|lar** (prē mō′lər), *n., adj.* — ***n.*** **1** one of the permanent teeth between the canine teeth and the molars; bicuspid: *In mammals, the teeth are specialized to accomplish specific functions. Premolars and molars* [*are*] *for grinding* (A. M. Winchester). **2** one of the molars of the milk teeth, preceding the permanent molars.
— ***adj.*** of the premolars.

**pre|mon|ish** (prē mon′ish), *v.t.* to advise; caution; forewarn. — ***v.i.*** to give warning beforehand. [< *pre-* + (ad)*monish*]

**pre|mo|ni|tion** (prē′mə nish′ən, prem′ə-), *n.* a notification or warning of what is to come; forewarning: *a vague premonition of disaster.* [< Middle French *premonicion,* learned borrowing from Latin *praemonitiō, -ōnis* < *praemonēre* < *prae-* before + *monēre* to warn]

**pre|mon|i|to|ri|ly** (pri mon′ə tôr′ə lē, -tōr′-), *adv.* by way of premonition.

**pre|mon|i|to|ry** (pri mon′ə tôr′ē, -tōr′-), *adj.* giving warning beforehand: *It is established practice in this country to get anyone showing premonitory symptoms of major drama away from the theatre* (Observer).

**Pre|mon|strant** (prē mon′strənt), *adj., n.* = Premonstratensian.

**Pre|mon|stra|ten|sian** (prē mon′strə ten′shən), *adj., n.* — ***adj.*** of or having to do with a Roman Catholic religious order founded by Saint Norbert at Prémontré, near Laon, France, in 1120.
— ***n.*** a member of the Premonstratensian order; white canon.
[< Medieval Latin *Premonstratensis* (< *Prémontré,* a city in France) + English *-ian*]

**pre|morse** (pri môrs′), *n. Botany.* having the end abruptly truncate, as if bitten or broken off, as certain roots. [< Latin *praemorsus,* past participle of *praemordēre* to bite in front < *prae-* before + *mordēre* to bite]

**pre|mun|dane** (prē mun′dān), *adj.* existing or occurring before the creation of the world; antemundane.

**pre|na|tal** (prē nā′təl), *adj.* **1** before childbirth: *A woman soon to have a baby requires prenatal care.* **2** occurring before birth: *prenatal damage to the skull.* — **pre|na′tal|ly,** *adv.*

**pre|no|men** (prē nō′mən), *n., pl.* **-no|mens** or **-nom|i|na** (-nom′ə nə). = praenomen.

**pre|nom|i|nate** (pri nom′ə nāt), *adj., v.,* **-nat|ed, -nat|ing.** *Obsolete.* — ***adj.*** named before; named above.
— ***v.t.*** to name beforehand; mention or specify in advance.
[< Latin *praenōminātus* < *praenōmināre* to name in the first place]

**pre|no|tion** (prē nō′shən), *n.* a previous notion; preconceived idea; preconception. [< Latin *praenōtiō, -ōnis* preconception < *prae-* before + *nōtiō, -ōnis* concept, definition < *nōscere* become acquainted]

**pren|tice** (pren′tis), *n., adj. Archaic.* — ***n.*** = apprentice.
— ***adj.*** of or like an apprentice; inexperienced; unskilled: *one's prentice years, formed by a prentice hand.*

**pre|nu|cle|ar** (prē nü′klē ər, -nyü′-), *adj.* **1** before the age of nuclear weapons: *In earlier, prenuclear times, American Presidents responded to such depredations with fleets, Marines, and righteous cannon fire—as when Thomas Jefferson dispatched U.S. frigates under Stephen Decatur to clean out the Barbary pirates who menaced American trade in the Mediterranean* (Time). **2** lacking a visible nucleus: *These other organisms have cells with nuclei and specialized organelles or specialized intracellular structures; they are called eukaryotic* (*truly nucleated*), *whereas bacteria and blue-green algae are prokaryotic* (*prenuclear*) (Scientific American).

**pre|oc|cu|pan|cy** (prē ok′yə pən sē), *n., pl.* **-cies.** the fact of occupying previously; earlier occupancy.

**pre|oc|cu|pa|tion** (prē ok′yə pā′shən), *n.* **1** the act of preoccupying. **2** the condition of being preoccupied; absorption.

**pre|oc|cu|pied** (prē ok′yə pīd), *adj.* **1** absorbed in thought; engrossed; abstracted: *That preoccupied reader didn't hear the telephone ring.* **2** occupied previously. **3** *Biology.* (of a generic or specific name) already used for something else and therefore unavailable as a name for another group.

**pre|oc|cu|py** (prē ok′yə pī), *v.t.,* **-pied, -py|ing.** **1** to take up all the attention of; absorb: *The question of getting to New York preoccupied her mind.* **2** to occupy beforehand; take possession of before others: *Our favorite seats had been preoccupied.* **3** *Obsolete.* to prepossess; bias.

**pre|op|e|ra|tive** (prē op′ər ə tiv, -ə rā′tiv), *adj.* occurring before a surgical operation: *preoperative treatment.* — **pre|op′e|ra|tive|ly,** *adv.*

**pre|o|ral** (prē ôr′əl, -ōr′-), *adj. Zoology.* situated in front of the mouth. — **pre|o′ral|ly,** *adv.*

**pre|or|dain** (prē′ôr dān′), *v.t.* to decide or settle beforehand; foreordain.

**pre|or|di|na|tion** (prē′ôr də nā′shən), *n.* the act of preordaining or condition of being preordained.

**prep** (prep), *adj., v.,* **prepped, prep|ping,** *n.* — ***adj.*** *Informal.* preparatory: *a good prep course in business English.*
— ***v.i.*** **1** *U.S. Informal.* to attend preparatory school: *they went to high schools instead of prepping* (Harper's). **2** *Informal.* to study; prepare: *She prepped for the real thing in a succession of out-of-town productions, from Munich, Germany to Pocatello, Idaho* (Time). — ***v.t.*** *U.S. Informal.* to prepare: *prepping a part in the school play.*
— ***n.*** **1** Often, **Prep.** a preparatory school: *He goes to Poly Prep.* **2** *Informal.* preparation of lessons; homework: *It is necessary to devote the long winter evenings to long weary hours of prep* (Punch).

**prep., 1** preparation. **2** preparatory. **3** preposition.

**pre|pack** (prē pak′), *v.t.* = prepackage.

**pre|pack|age** (prē pak′ij), *v.t.,* **-aged, -ag|ing.** to package (foods and other articles) in certain weights, sizes, or grades, usually with the price attached, before putting up for sale: *Most meat now sold in such self-service departments is prepackaged in the store rather than by packers* (Wall Street Journal).

**pre|paid** (prē pād′), *v.* the past tense and past participle of **prepay**: *Send this shipment prepaid.*

**prep|a|ra|tion** (prep′ə rā′shən), *n.* **1** the act of preparing; making ready: *He sharpened his knife in preparation for carving the meat.* **2** the state of being prepared. **3** a thing done to get ready: *He made thorough preparations for his trip by carefully planning which way to go.* **4** a medicine, food, or mixture of any kind made by a special process: *The preparation for his cough included camphor.* **5** an animal body or part of one prepared for dissection, or preserved for examination. **6** *Music.* **a** the leading up to a discord by sounding the dissonant tone in it as a consonant tone in the preceding chord. **b** the consonance which becomes dissonance (usually the suspension) in the next chord. [< Old French *preparacion,* learned borrowing from Latin *praeparātiō, -ōnis* < *praeparāre;* see etym. under **prepare**]

**pre|par|a|tive** (pri par′ə tiv), *adj., n.* — ***adj.*** = preparatory.
— ***n.*** something that prepares, or helps to prepare; preliminary; preparation: *if discontent and misery are preparatives for liberty* (Charles Kingsley). — **pre|par′a|tive|ly,** *adv.*

**pre|par|a|tor** (pri par′ə tər), *n.* a person who prepares food or medicine by a special process or prepares animals for dissection.

**pre|par|a|to|ry** (pri par′ə tôr′ē, -tōr′-), *adj.* **1** of or for preparation; preparing; making ready. Preparatory courses fit pupils for college. **2** as an introduction; preliminary: *preparatory remarks.*
— **pre|par′a|to′ri|ly,** *adv.*

**preparatory school, 1** *U.S.* a private school, usually from grades 9 through 12, that prepares boys or girls for college. **2** *British.* a private school that prepares boys of 6 to 14 for the public schools.

**pre|pare** (pri pãr′), *v.,* **-pared, -par|ing.** — ***v.t.*** **1** to make ready; put in condition for something: *to prepare a room for a guest, to prepare a boy for college. He prepares his lessons while his mother prepares supper.* **2** to make by a special process: *to prepare the medicine prescribed, to prepare steel from iron.* **SYN:** devise, contrive. **3** *Music.* to lead up to (a discord) by sounding the dissonant tone as a consonant tone in the preceding chord. **4** *Archaic.* to provide; furnish.
— ***v.i.*** to get ready; put oneself, or things, in readiness: *to prepare for a test. The thunderbolt Hangs silent; but prepare. I speak, it falls* (Tennyson).
[< Latin *praeparāre* < *prae-* before + *parāre* make ready] — **pre|par′er,** *n.*

**pre|par|ed|ly** (pri pãr′id lē), *adv.* with suitable preparation.

**pre|par|ed|ness** (pri pãr′id nis, -pãrd′nis), *n.* **1** the state of being prepared; readiness. **2** the state of having adequate military forces and defenses to meet threats or outbreaks of war.

**prepared piano, 1** a piano that has had its timbre altered to produce unconventional sounds by attaching various objects to the strings. **2** the method of playing such a piano.

**pre|pa|tel|lar** (prē′pə tel′ər), *adj.* situated in front of the patella: *the prepatellar bursa.*

**pre|pay** (prē pā′), *v.t.,* **-paid, -pay|ing.** **1** to pay in advance: *We prepay the post office by putting a stamp on a letter before sending it.* **2** to pay for in advance: *He prepaid the shipping charges to make sure the package would arrive on time.*
— **pre|pay′a|ble,** *adj.* — **pre|pay′ment,** *n.*

**pre|pense** (pri pens′), *adj.* planned beforehand; premeditated; deliberate. [alteration of Middle English *purpense* < Old French *purpenser* < *pour-* forward + *penser* to think; see etym. under **pensive**] — **pre|pense′ly,** *adv.*

**pre|plan** (prē plan′), *v.t., v.i.,* **-planned, -plan|ning.** to plan beforehand; plan ahead: *The academic curriculum must be preplanned at different levels of difficulty* (Atlantic). *There has also been "preplanning for air delivery" of the equipment* (New York Times).

**pre|pol|lex** (prē pol′eks), *n., pl.* **-pol|li|ces** (-pol′ə sēz). a rudimentary structure found in some animals on the radial edge of the hand or forefoot, supposed to represent an additional digit. [< *pre-* + *pollex*]

**pre|pon|der|ance** (prē pon′dər əns), *n.* **1** a greater number; greater weight; greater power or influence: *In July the hot days have the preponderance.* **2** *Figurative.* the fact or condition of being the chief or most important element: *the preponderance of oaks in these woods.*

**pre|pon|der|an|cy** (prē pon′dər ən sē), *n., pl.* **-cies.** = preponderance.

**pre|pon|der|ant** (prē pon′dər ənt), *adj.* **1** weighing more; being stronger or more numerous; having more power or influences. **2** *Figurative.* chief; most important; predominant: *Greed is a miser's preponderant characteristic. Faithfulness is one of the preponderant characteristics of dogs.* [< Latin *praeponderāns, -antis,* present participle of *praeponderāre* preponderate] — **pre|pon′der|ant|ly,** *adv.*

**pre|pon|der|ate** (prē pon′də rāt), *v.,* **-at|ed, -at|ing.** — ***v.i.*** **1** to be greater than something else in weight, power, force, influence, number, or

---

**Pronunciation Key:** hat, āge, cãre, fär; let, ēqual, tėrm; it, īce; hot, ōpen, ôrder; oil, out; cup, pu̇t, rüle; child; long; thin; ᴛʜen; zh, measure; ə represents **a** in about, **e** in taken, **i** in pencil, **o** in lemon, **u** in circus.

amount: *The good in this state of existence preponderates over the bad* (Dickens). **2** *Figurative.* to be chief; be most important; predominate: *Oaks and maples preponderate in our woods.*
— ***v.t.*** to be greater than; outweigh.
[< Latin *praeponderāre* (with English *-ate*[1]) outweigh < *prae-* before + *ponderāre* to weigh < *pondus, -eris* weight] — **pre|pon′der|at′ing|ly,** *adv.* — **pre|pon′der|a′tion,** *n.*

**pre|pon|der|ous** (prē pon′dər əs), *adj.* = preponderant. — **pre|pon′der|ous|ly,** *adv.*

**prep|o|si|tion** (prep′ə zish′ən), *n.* a word that shows certain relations between other words. *With, for, by,* and *in* are prepositions in the sentence "A man *with* rugs *for* sale walked *by* our house *in* the morning." [< Latin *praepositiō, -ōnis* < *praepōnere* < *prae-* before + *pōnere* put]
▶ **preposition at end of sentence.** Though formerly sometimes censured in textbooks, the use of a preposition at the end of a sentence is not always objectionable or easily avoidable (*What did you do it for?*). The effort to avoid it (*Tell me what you object to*) sometimes produces a clumsy (*Tell me to what you object*) or fussy effect (*Tell me what it is to which you object*).

**prep|o|si|tion|al** (prep′ə zish′ə nəl), *adj.* **1** having to do with a preposition. **2** having the nature or function of a preposition. **3** made up of a preposition and its object: *a prepositional phrase.*
— **prep′o|si′tion|al|ly,** *adv.*

**pre|pos|i|tive** (prē poz′ə tiv), *adj., n. Grammar.*
— ***adj.*** put before; prefixed.
— ***n.*** prepositive word or particle. — **pre|pos′i|tive|ly,** *adv.*

**pre|pos|i|tor** (prē poz′ə tər), *n.* any one of the senior boys at some English public schools who discipline the younger students, especially out of the classroom; monitor. Also, **praepositor, praepostor, prepostor.** [< Latin *praepositus* chief, head; (literally) one placed in authority, (originally) past participle of *praepōnere* (see etym. under **preposition**) + English *-or*]

**pre|pos|i|to|ri|al** (prē poz′ə tôr′ē əl, -tōr′-), *adj.* of or having to do with prepositors.

**pre|pos|sess** (prē′pə zes′), *v.t.* **1** to fill with a favorable feeling or opinion, especially beforehand or at the outset: *We were prepossessed by the boy's modest behavior.* **2** to fill with a feeling or opinion: *The teacher ... did not prepossess me in favour of his pursuits* (Mary Shelley). **3** to take or get possession of beforehand.

**pre|pos|sess|ing** (prē′pə zes′ing), *adj.* making a favorable first impression; attractive; pleasing: *a most prepossessing young man. Clean clothes and good manners are prepossessing.* — **pre′pos|sess′ing|ly,** *adv.* — **pre′pos|sess′ing|ness,** *n.*

**pre|pos|ses|sion** (prē′pə zesh′ən), *n.* **1** a favorable feeling or opinion formed beforehand; prejudice; bias: *A well-written letter applying for a position will create a prepossession toward the writer.* **2** prior possession or occupancy.

**pre|pos|ter|ous** (pri pos′tər əs, -trəs), *adj.* against nature, reason, or common sense; absurd; senseless; foolish: *It would be preposterous to shovel snow with a teaspoon. That the moon is made of green cheese is a preposterous notion.* SYN: nonsensical. See syn. under **ridiculous.** [< Latin *praeposterus* (with English *-ous*) absurd; (originally) in reverse order < *prae-* before + *posterus* coming after < *post* after] — **pre|pos′ter|ous|ly,** *adv.* — **pre|pos′ter|ous|ness,** *n.*

**pre|pos|tor** (prē pos′tər), *n.* = prepositor.

**pre|po|tence** (prē pō′təns), *n.* = prepotency.

**pre|po|ten|cy** (prē pō′tən sē), *n., pl.* **-cies. 1** superior power or influence; predominance: *The "prepotency" of pain [is seen in] ... its ability to suffuse the entire field of consciousness with distress and to crowd out all other thoughts* (Martin E. Spencer). **2** *Genetics.* the marked power of one parent, variety, or strain, to transmit a special character or characters to the progeny.

**pre|po|tent** (prē pō′tənt), *adj.* **1** having greater power or influence than others; predominant: *An ambiguous, prepotent figure had come to disturb the ... jealously guarded balance of the English constitution* (Lytton Strachey). **2** *Genetics.* **a** of prepotency. **b** exhibiting prepotency. [< Latin *praepotens, -entis,* present participle of *praeposse* be superior, very powerful < *prae-* before + *posse* be able] — **pre|po′tent|ly,** *adv.*

**prep|pie** or **prep|py** (prep′ē), *n., pl.* **-pies.** *U.S. Slang.* a student or graduate of a preparatory school: *No longer believe that Harvard students are all rich preppies tracing their Harvard histories back almost as far as the Saltonstalls ...* (Harper's). [< *prep* + *-ie*]

**pre|pran|di|al** (prē pran′dē əl), *adj.* preceding a dinner, banquet, or the like: *preprandial conversation. Fortifying himself with a preprandial dry martini* (Saturday Review). [< *pre-* + *prandial*]

**pre|preg** (prē′preg), *n.* a plastic or other synthetic material impregnated with the full complement of resin before it is molded. [< *pre-*(im)*preg*(nated)]

**pre|pri|ma|ry school** (prē prī′mer′ē, -mər-), a school for very young children; a combination of nursery school and kindergarten.

**pre|print** (prē′print′), *n., v.* — ***n.*** a printing in advance, especially a portion of a work issued before publication of the whole.
— ***v.t.*** to print in advance of publication: *The ads are preprinted by gravure in a continuous roll* (Sunday Times).

**pre|proc|ess** (prē pros′es; *especially British* -prō′ses), *v.t.* to process beforehand: *to preprocess ore or timber.*

**pre|proc|es|sor** (prē pros′es ər; *especially British* -prō′səs-), *n.* a device for preprocessing data: *... preprocessors to check, edit, and compile programmes* (Kenneth Owen).

**pre|pro|fes|sion|al** (prē′prə fesh′ə nəl, -fesh′nəl), *adj.* of or in preparation for a profession: *The program will ... be tailored to provide preprofessional training* (Saturday Review).

**pre|pro|gram** (prē prō′gram, -grəm), *v.t.,* **-grammed, -gram|ming** or **-gramed, -gram|ing.** to program beforehand, especially for automatic control: *How does one reconcile the known malleability of behavior with a preprogrammed and rigidly "wired" nervous system?* (Scientific American).

**prep school,** *Informal.* a preparatory school.

**pre|psy|chot|ic** (prē′sī kot′ik), *adj.* showing indications of psychosis; occurring before or leading to psychosis: *prepsychotic subjects.*

**pre|pu|ber|ty** (prē pyü′bər tē), *n.* the period of life just prior to puberty: *Estrogen ..., given over a prolonged period in prepuberty, has been used clinically to cut down the ultimate height of tall girls* (Nathan Dreskin).

**pre|pu|bes|cent** (prē′pyü bes′ənt), *adj.* having to do with prepuberty; immature: (*Figurative.*) *It relies for its climax on an offstage sound effect of prepubescent ... humor* (Time).

**pre|puce** (prē′pyüs), *n.* **1** the fold of skin covering the end of the penis; foreskin. **2** a similar fold of skin covering the end of the clitoris. [< Middle French, Old French *prepuce,* learned borrowing from Latin *praepūtium*]

**pre|pu|pa** (prē pyü′pə), *n., pl.* **-pae** (-pē), **-pas. 1** the inactive stage before pupation in the development of many insects. **2** the form of an insect in this stage: *We inject hemolymph from these prepupae into young larvae* (Scientific American).

**pre|pu|pal** (prē pyü′pəl), *adj.* of, having to do with, or in the form of a prepupa.

**pre|pu|tial** (prē pyü′shəl), *adj.* of or having to do with the prepuce.

**Pre-Raph|a|el|ite** (prē raf′ē ə līt, -rā′fē-), *n., adj.*
— ***n.*** **1** any Italian painter preceding Raphael. **2** one of a group of English artists and poets formed in 1848, including John Everett Millais and Dante Gabriel Rossetti, who aimed to work in the spirit that prevailed before the time of Raphael: *In any review of Pre-Raphaelite poetry and painting it will be clearly seen that it is one of the unique movements in European art in that it was both distinctly literary and distinctly graphic at the same time* (James D. Merritt). **3** any modern artist or writer having similar aims or methods.
— ***adj.*** **1** existing before Raphael. **2** of or belonging to the Pre-Raphaelites: *Of the many forces which exerted an influence upon the young Picasso, ... one was the PreRaphaelite movement* (Listener). **3** characteristic of or resembling the Pre-Raphaelites or their principles and style.

**Pre-Raph|a|el|it|ism** (prē raf′ē ə lī′tiz əm, -rā′fē-), *n.* **1** the style of painting in vogue from the time of Giotto to that of Raphael. **2** the revival of this style by the Pre-Raphaelites.

**pre|re|cord** (prē′ri kôrd′), *v.t.* to record in advance for later use: *to prerecord a television program on videotape.*

**pre|req|ui|site** (prē rek′wə zit), *n., adj.* — ***n.*** something required beforehand: *The completion of a high-school course is the usual prerequisite to college work.*
— ***adj.*** required beforehand.

**pre|rog|a|tive** (pri rog′ə tiv), *n., adj.* — ***n.*** **1** a right or privilege that nobody else has: *The government has the prerogative of coining money.* SYN: See syn. under **privilege. 2** a special superiority of right or privilege, such as may derive from an official position or office; precedence.
— ***adj.*** **1** having or exercising a prerogative. **2** *Law.* of or having to do with a prerogative court.
**the Royal Prerogative,** the original nonstatutory powers of the British sovereign recognized by common law, now constitutionally exercised by, or on the advice of, ministers responsible to Parliament: *In his opinion, the very lowest claim of the Royal Prerogative should include "a right on the part of the King to be the permanent President of his Ministerial Council"* (Lytton Strachey).
[< Latin *praerogātīva* privilege, favoring token; (originally) feminine adjective, allotted to vote first < *praerogāre* ask for a vote first < *prae-* before + *rogāre* ask]

**prerogative court, 1** (in Great Britain) a former ecclesiastical court for the trial of certain testamentary cases. **2** (in the state of New Jersey) the probate court.

**pres., 1** present. **2** presidency. **3** president.

**Pres., 1** Presbyterian. **2** President.

***pre|sa** (prā′sä), *n., pl.* **-se** (-sā). a notation in music used in a canon to show where the successive voice parts are to take up the theme. [< Italian *presa* a taking]

***presa**

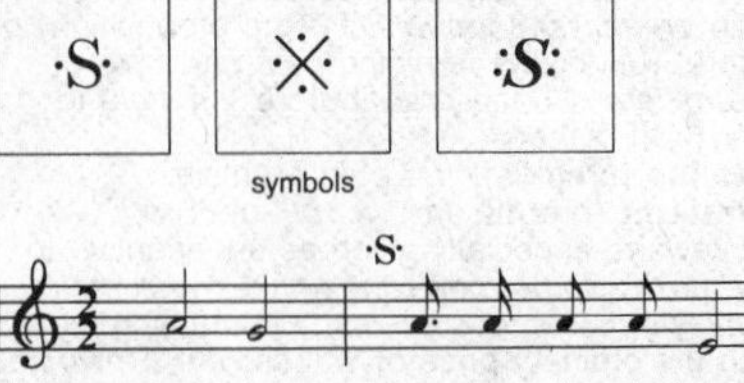


**pres|age** (*n.* pres′ij; *v.* pri sāj′), *n., v.,* **pre|saged, pre|sag|ing.** — ***n.*** **1** a sign felt as a warning; omen. **2** a feeling that something is about to happen; presentiment; foreboding: *She could not sleep at night and was haunted by a presage of disaster* (Samuel Butler). **3** a prediction; prognostication.
— ***v.t.*** **1** to give warning of; predict: *The farmer told us that a circle around the moon presages a storm.* **2** to have or give a prophetic impression of.
— ***v.i.*** to form or utter a presage or prediction.
[< Latin *praesāgium* < *praesāgīre* to forebode < *praesāgus* foreboding, adjective < *prae-* before + *sāgus* prophetic] — **pre|sag′er,** *n.* — **pre-sag′ing|ly,** *adv.*

**pre|sage|ful** (pri sāj′fəl), *adj.* **1** full of presage; foreboding. **2** = ominous.

**Presb.,** Presbyterian.

**pres|by|cu|sis** (prez′bə kyü′sis), *n.* hearing impairment due to aging. [< Greek *présbys* old man + *ákousis* hearing]

**pres|by|ope** (prez′bē ōp), *n.* a person having presbyopia.

**pres|by|o|pi|a** (prez′bē ō′pē ə), *n.* a condition of the eye occurring in middle and old age, in which only distant objects may be seen distinctly, unless glasses with corrective lenses are worn; normal loss of accommodation in the eyesight as the lens of the eye becomes less elastic and loses some of its ability to focus on objects close to the eyes. [< New Latin *presbyopia* < Greek *présbys* old man + New Latin *-opia* < Greek *ôps* eye]

**pres|by|op|ic** (prez′bē op′ik), *adj.* **1** having to do with presbyopia. **2** affected with presbyopia.

**pres|by|ter** (prez′bə tər, pres′-), *n.* **1** an elder in the early Christian Church. **2** a minister or a lay elder in the Presbyterian Church. **3** a minister or a priest in the Episcopal Church. [< Latin *presbyter* an elder < Greek *presbýteros,* (originally) comparative of *présbys* old (man). See etym. of doublet **priest.**]

**pres|byt|er|al** (prez bit′ər əl, pres-), *adj.* = presbyterial.

**pres|byt|er|ate** (prez bit′ə rāt, pres-), *n.* **1** the office of presbyter. **2** a body of presbyters; presbytery.

**pres|by|te|ri|al** (prez′bə tir′ē əl, pres′-), *adj.* **1** of or having to do with presbyters or a presbytery. **2** = presbyterian.

**Pres|by|te|ri|an** (prez′bə tir′ē ən, pres′-), *adj., n.*
— ***adj.*** of or belonging to a Protestant denomination or church governed by elected presbyters or elders, all of equal rank, and having beliefs based on Calvinism: *The Presbyterian Church in the U.S.* (*Southern*) *has taken a revamped stand on the question of marriage of divorced persons* (Newsweek).
— ***n.*** **1** a member of a Presbyterian church. **2** a supporter of Presbyterianism.
[< Latin *presbyterium* presbytery + English *-an*]

**pres|by|te|ri|an** (prez′bə tir′ē ən, pres′-), *adj.* having to do with or based on the principle of ecclesiastical government by presbyters or presbyteries.

**Pres|by|te|ri|an|ism** (prez′bə tir′ē ə niz′əm, pres′-), *n.* **1** the system of church government by elders all (including ministers) of equal rank. **2** the beliefs and organizational system of Presbyterian churches.

**pres|by|ter|y** (prez′bə ter′ē, pres′-), *n., pl.* **-ter|ies. 1** a meeting or court of all the ministers and certain of the elders within a district of a Presbyterian church. **2** the district under the jurisdiction of such a meeting or court. **3** the part of a church set aside for the clergy. **4** a priest's house in the Roman Catholic Church; rectory. **5** a body of presbyters or elders. [< Latin *presbyterium* < Greek *presbytérion* council of elders; also, its meeting place < *presbýteros* presbyter]

**pre|school** (prē′skül′), *adj., n.* —*adj.* before the age of going to regular school, usually from infancy to the age of five or six: *preschool training, preschool children.*
—*n.* a school for the observation or training of young children, usually under five years of age, sometimes divided in groups according to age.

**pre|school|er** (prē′skü′lər), *n. Informal.* a young child in or eligible for preschool: *It is not easy to fit the restless, busy, curious preschooler into a smooth-running household* (Sidonie M. Gruenberg).

**pre|sci|ence** (prē′shē əns, presh′ē-), *n.* knowledge of things before they exist or happen; foreknowledge; foresight: *a man of considerable prescience. People used to believe that animals have an instinctive prescience of the approach of danger. The day Archduke Franz Ferdinand was assassinated at Sarajevo, Mussolini, with quite a bit of prescience, remarked ... that it looked like the start of a major European war* (New Yorker). [< Old French *prescience,* learned borrowing from Latin *praescientia* < Latin *praesciēns, -entis,* present participle of *praescīre* to foreknow < *prae-* before + *scīre* to know]

**pre|sci|ent** (prē′shē ənt, presh′ē-), *adj.* knowing beforehand; foreseeing: *the sharks ... following them in the same prescient way that vultures hover over the banners of marching regiments* (Herman Melville). —**pre′sci|ent|ly,** *adv.*

**pre|scind** (pri sind′), *v.t.* to cut off, detach, or separate from. [< Latin *praescindere* < *prae-* in front + *scindere* to cut]

**pre|scribe** (pri skrīb′), *v.,* **-scribed, -scrib|ing.** —*v.t.* **1** to lay down as a rule to be followed; order; direct: *Good citizens do what the laws prescribe.* **SYN:** command, assign, set, appoint, ordain, enjoin. **2** to order as medicine or treatment: *The doctor prescribed a complete rest for her.* **3** *Law.* to make invalid or outlawed because of the passage of time.
—*v.i.* **1** to lay down a rule or rules; dictate; direct: *to do as the law prescribes.* **SYN:** command, assign, set, appoint, ordain, enjoin. **2** to give medical advice; issue a prescription. **3** *Law.* to claim a right or title to something by virtue of long use and enjoyment of it. **4** (in Scots law) to become invalid because of the passage of time. [< Latin *praescrībere* < *prae-* before + *scrībere* to write] —**pre|scrib′er,** *n.*

**pre|script** (*n.* prē′skript; *adj.* pri skript′, prē′skript), *n., adj.* —*n.* that which is prescribed; rule; order; direction.
—*adj.* prescribed; ordained; appointed. [< Latin *praescriptum,* neuter past participle of *praescrībere* prescribe]

**pre|scrip|ti|ble** (pri skrip′tə bəl), *adj.* **1** liable to prescription. **2** derived from or founded on prescription.

**pre|scrip|tion** (pri skrip′shən), *n.* **1** the act of prescribing. **2** something prescribed; order; direction: (*Figurative.*) *He was carrying no "prescription" for peace in the Far East in his mission to Peiping* (New York Times). **3** a written direction or order given by a doctor or dentist for preparing and using a medicine: *a prescription for a cough. Their task ... is to make a quick diagnosis—take a case history, make a physical examination, write a prescription* (Time). **4** the medicine. **5** *Law.* **a** possession or use of a thing long enough to give a right or title to it: *to claim a right by prescription, to acquire a thing by prescription.* **b** the right or title so established. **c** the process of so establishing a right or title. **d** a limitation of the time within which a claim may be made or an action brought; negative prescription.

**pre|scrip|tive** (pri skrip′tiv), *adj.* **1** prescribing: *a prescriptive system of grammar. In his [Johnson's] concept of a descriptive rather than prescriptive dictionary he discovered what the twentieth century takes for granted* (Saturday Review). **2** depending on legal prescription: *a prescriptive title.* **3** established by long use or custom: *the prescriptive respectability of a family with a mural monument and venerable tankards* (George Eliot). —**pre|scrip′tive|ly,** *adv.* —**prescrip′tive|ness,** *n.*

**pres|ence** (prez′əns), *n.* **1** the fact or condition of being present in a place: *I just learned of his presence in the city. "Liberal" intellectuals and "conservative" politicians both shared the unthinking assumption ... that the American "presence" abroad is by definition always good* (Manchester Guardian Weekly). **2** the place where a person is: *The messenger was admitted to my grandfather's presence.* **3** formal attendance upon a person of very high rank: *The knight retired from the royal presence.* **4** appearance; bearing: *The king was a man of noble presence.* **5** something present, especially a ghost, spirit, or the like: *She really felt drawn to worship him, as if he were the shrine ... of that Presence to which he bore such solemn witness* (Cardinal Newman). **6** the feeling or illusion of being in the place in which sound originated rather than listening to a recording of it: *They have the benefit of the latest techniques ... mostly in the intangible matter of "projection," or "presence"* (Musical America). **7** a living person, especially one of very high rank: *Slowly passed that august Presence Down the thronged and shouting street* (John Greenleaf Whittier). **8** *Obsolete.* an assembly, especially of people of high rank; company: *Here is like to be a good presence of Worthies* (Shakespeare). **9** *Obsolete.* a presence chamber.
**in the presence of,** in the sight or company of: *in the presence of danger. He signed his name in the presence of two witnesses.*
**saving your presence,** with an apology for doing or saying this in your presence: *Some of the members of your organization are unscrupulous schemers, saving your presence.*
[< Old French *presence* < Latin *praesentia* < *praesēns* present, beside. See etym. under **present**¹.]

**presence chamber,** the room in which a king or some very important person receives guests.

**presence of mind,** the ability to think calmly and quickly when taken by surprise.

**presence room,** a presence chamber.

**pres|ent**¹ (prez′ənt), *adj., n.* —*adj.* **1** being in the place or thing in question; at hand, not absent: *Every member of the class was present. Oxygen is present in the air.* **2** at this time; being or occurring now; current: *present prices, the present ruler. Let this great truth be present night and day* (Alexander Pope). **SYN:** See syn. under **current.** **3** *Grammar.* of or expressing the present tense: *The present forms of "ate" and "smiled" are "eat" and "smile." Abbr:* pr. **4** *Obsolete.* **a** attentive. **b** having presence of mind; self-possessed. **c** prompt to act; ready: *God is our refuge and strength, a very present help in trouble* (Psalms 46:1). **5** *Obsolete.* immediate.
—*n.* **1** *Grammar.* **a** the present tense. **b** a verb form or verbal phrase in that tense. **2** *Obsolete.* the thing or person that is present; affair in hand; present occasion.
**at present,** at the present time; now: *At present people need courage.*
**by these presents,** by these words; by this document: *know all men by these presents.*
**the present,** the time being; this time; now: *That will be enough for the present. The present is only a second away from the past.*
[< Latin *praesēns, -entis* present, (originally) present participle of *praeësse* to be before a thing, to rule over < *prae-* before + *esse* to be]

**pre|sent**² (*v.* pri zent′; *n.* prez′ənt), *v., n.* —*v.t.* **1** to give: *to present a book as a prize to the winner. They presented flowers to their teacher.* **SYN:** See syn. under **give.** **2** to offer; offer formally: *The servant presented the tray of sandwiches to each guest.* **3** to bring before the mind; offer for consideration: *He presented reasons for his action. She presented her ideas to the committee. Augustin Thierry ... had presented the Norman Conquest in terms of a class struggle between the conquerors and the Saxons* (Edmund Wilson). **4** to offer to view or notice: *The new library presents a fine appearance.* **5** to bring before the public; give a public performance of: *Our school presented a play.* **6** to set forth in words: *The speaker presented arguments for his side.* **7** to hand in; send in: *The grocer presented his bill.* **8** to introduce (one person to another); make acquainted; bring (a person) before somebody; introduce formally: *She was presented at court. Miss Smith, may I present Mr. Brown?* **SYN:** See syn. under **introduce.** **9** to direct; point; turn: *The soldier presented his face to the enemy. The handsome actor presented his profile to the camera.* **10** to aim or salute with (a weapon). **11** to recommend (a clergyman) for a benefice. **12** *Law.* **a** to bring a formal charge against (a person, etc.). **b** to bring (an offense or any violation) to the notice of a court, magistrate, or person in authority. **13** *Archaic.* to represent (a character) on the stage.
—*v.i.* **1** to point, face, or project in a particular direction. **2** to aim or level a weapon. **3** to present a clergyman for a benefice. [< Old French *presenter* < Latin *praesentāre* < *praesēns* present¹, beside]
—*n.* something given; gift: *I can make no marriage present; Little can I give my wife* (Tennyson). **SYN:** See syn. under **gift.**
**present with,** to give to; furnish with (something as a gift): *Our class presented the school with a picture.*
[< Old French *present,* in *en present* (to offer) in the presence of] —**pre|sent′er,** *n.*

**pre|sent|a|bil|i|ty** (pri zen′tə bil′ə tē), *n.* presentable condition or quality.

**pre|sent|a|ble** (pri zen′tə bəl), *adj.* **1** fit to be seen: *to make a house presentable for company.* **2** suitable in appearance, dress, or manners for being introduced into society or company: *a very presentable young man.* **3** suitable to be offered or given. —**pre|sent′a|ble|ness,** *n.* —**pre|sent′a-bly,** *adv.*

***pre|sent arms** (pri zent′), **1** to bring a rifle, etc., to a vertical position in front of the body. **2** this position. **3** a command to assume this position.

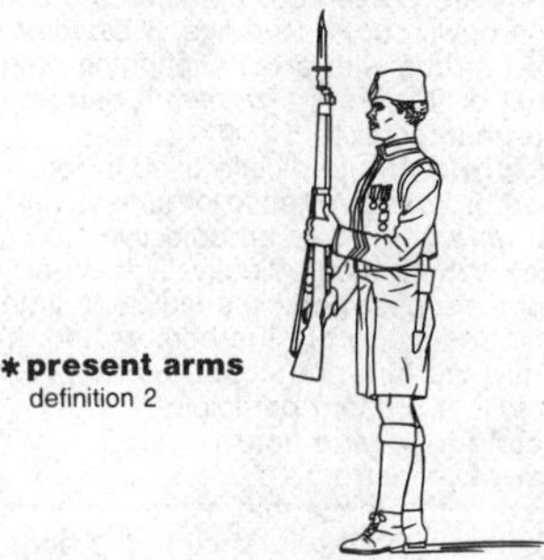

***present arms**
definition 2

**pres|en|ta|tion** (prez′ən tā′shən, prē′zən-), *n.* **1** the act of giving; delivering: *the presentation of a gift.* **2** the gift that is presented: *The presentation to the ambassador was a beautiful sword.* **3** the act of bringing forward; offering to be considered: *the presentation of a plan. The subject matter of all science is essentially the same: systematic observation and systematic presentation of the observations in communicable form* (F. H. George). **4** an offering to be seen; exhibition; showing: *the presentation of a play or a motion picture.* **5** a formal introduction: *the presentation of a lady to the queen.* **6** the act or right of presenting a clergyman to the bishop as a candidate for a benefice. **7** the presenting of a bill, draft, note, or other commercial obligation, as for payment or acceptance. **8** the position taken by the fetus during labor: *shoulder presentation.* **9** *Psychology.* an idea; cognition.

**pres|en|ta|tion|al** (prez′ən tā′shə nəl, prē′zən-), *adj.* **1** of or having to do with presentation. **2** (of words) presentive; notional.

**pres|en|ta|tion|ism** (prez′ən tā′shə niz əm, prē′zən-), *n.* the theory that perception by the senses gives knowledge of reality. —**pres′en|ta′tion|ist,** *n., adj.*

**pre|sen|ta|tive** (pri zen′tə tiv), *adj.* **1** knowable by perception. **2** being capable of or having to do with ecclesiastical presentation.

**pres|ent-day** (prez′ənt dā′), *adj.* of the present time; current: *All five of these men, Darwin perhaps excepted, ... would be regarded as misfits in present-day society* (New York Times).

**pres|en|tee** (prez′ən tē′), *n.* **1** a person to whom something is presented. **2** a person who is presented. **3** a clergyman presented for institution to a benefice.

**pre|sen|tient** (pri sen′shənt), *adj.* feeling beforehand; having a presentiment.

**pre|sen|ti|ment** (pri zen′tə mənt), *n.* a feeling or impression that something, especially something evil, is about to happen; vague sense of approaching misfortune; foreboding: *a presentiment of death.* [< Middle French *presentiment* < *pre-* before + *sentiment* impression, sentiment]

**pre|sen|ti|men|tal** (pri zen′tə men′təl), *adj.* relating to a presentiment.

**pre|sen|tive** (pri zen′tiv), *adj., n.* —*adj.* (of words) presenting an object or conception directly to the mind.
—*n.* a presentive word. —**pre|sen′tive|ly,** *adv.* —**pre|sen′tive|ness,** *n.*

**pres|ent|ly** (prez′ənt lē), *adv.* **1** before long; soon: *The clock will strike presently. Love was the wish to understand, and presently with constant failure the wish died* (Graham Greene). **SYN:** shortly. See syn. under **immediately.** **2** at the present time; at this time; now: *Most nine-year-old children are presently in fourth grade. I am presently working as a clerk. The vessel is presently in the Government's mothball fleet* (Wall Street Journal). **SYN:** currently. **3** *Archaic.* at once.

---

**Pronunciation Key:** hat, āge, cãre, fär; let, ēqual, tėrm; it, īce; hot, ōpen, ôrder; oil, out; cup, pu̇t, rüle; child; long; thin; ᴛʜen; zh, measure; ə represents **a** in about, **e** in taken, **i** in pencil, **o** in lemon, **u** in circus.

**pre|sent|ment** (pri zent′mənt), *n.* **1** the action of bringing forward; offering to be considered. **2** a showing; offering to be seen. **3** something brought forward or shown. **4** a representation on the stage or by a portrait. **5** a statement by a grand jury of an offense from their own knowledge: *In its presentment, regarded as one of the most bitter ever handed up in the county, the grand jury asserted that the men had misled the taxpayers* (New York Times). **6** the act of presenting a bill, note, or other commercial obligation, as for payment or acceptance. **7** a bringing to mind; suggestion. [< Old French *presentement* < *presenter* to present, bestow]

**pres|en|toir** (prez′ən twär′), *n.* **1** a tray or salver on which things are presented. **2** a kind of stand or holder for a bowl, cup, or the like. **3** *Obsolete.* a shallow bowl or cup with a tall supporting stem, for holding fruit or flowers. [< *present*², verb + French *-oir,* a noun suffix]

**present participle**, the participle used in forming the English progressive tense or aspect (is *running,* was *running*) and as an adjective (the *running* horse). When used adjectivally, neither the present nor the past participle indicates time, which must be deduced from the context. In "Singing merrily, we turn our steps toward home," *singing* is a present participle.
► See **participle** for usage note.

**present perfect**, = perfect.

**present tense**, **1** the tense that expresses time that is now, either without reference to the duration of the action ("He *runs,*" sometimes called *simple present*) or as being in progress, recurring, or habitual ("He *is running,*" called *present progressive*). **2** a verb form in the present tense.

**present value** or **worth**, (of a sum payable at a given future date) an amount which, plus the interest upon it for the time from the actual date to the given future date, will equal the sum then due: *The present value of $1,060 due one year from date, interest being allowed at 6 per cent, is $1,000.*

**pre|se|pio** (prā ze′pyō), *n., pl.* **-pios.** a representation of the Nativity; crèche. [< Italian *presepio* (literally) stable, manger < Latin *praesaepium*]

**pre|serv|a|ble** (pri zėr′və bəl), *adj.* that can be preserved.

**pres|er|va|tion** (prez′ər vā′shən), *n.* **1** the act or process of preserving; keeping safe: *Doctors work for the preservation of our health.* **2** the fact or condition of being preserved; being kept safe: *Egyptian mummies have been in a state of preservation for thousands of years. They* [*the villas*] *contain frescoes ... worthy of preservation* (Newsweek).

**pres|er|va|tion|ist** (prez′ər vā′shə nist), *n.* a person who believes in and advocates preservation of traditional things: *Then there are the total preservationists who would permanently maintain these significant examples even if they impede a sound new development* (New Yorker).

**pre|serv|a|tive** (pri zėr′və tiv), *n., adj.* —*n.* any substance that will prevent decay or injury. Paint is a preservative for wood surfaces. Salt is a preservative for meat.
—*adj.* that preserves.

**pres|er|va|tor** (prez′ər vā′tər), *n. U.S.* a person in charge of preserving a historic site or other landmark restoring it to its original form: *A Columbia University professor of architectural history will be named the first Preservator of Central Park* (New York Times).

**pre|serv|a|to|ry** (pri zėr′və tôr′ē, -tōr′-), *adj., n., pl.* **-ries.** —*adj.* = preservative.
—*n.* **1** = preservative. **2** an apparatus for preserving substances for food. **3** a place where the preserving of food products is carried on.

**pre|serve** (pri zėrv′), *v.,* **-served, -serv|ing,** *n.* —*v.t.* **1** to keep from harm or change; keep safe; protect: *those who wish to preserve the present order of society* (Charles Kingsley). **SYN:** save, shield, guard. **2** to keep up; maintain: *Mr. Travers preserved an immobility which struck D'Alcacer as obviously affected* (Joseph Conrad). **3** to keep from spoiling: *Ice helps to preserve food.* **4** to prepare (food) to keep it from spoiling. Boiling with sugar, salting, smoking, and pickling are different ways of preserving food. **5** to protect (game or fish) for personal use. **6** *Archaic.* to keep alive.
—*v.i.* **1** to make preserves, especially of fruit. **2** to raise and protect game for special use.
—*n.* a place where wild animals, fish, or trees and plants are protected: *People are not allowed to hunt on the preserve.*
**preserves**, fruit or the like cooked with sugar and sealed from the air: *She made plum preserves.*
[< Old French *preserver* < Late Latin *praeservāre* to preserve, observe a custom < Latin *prae* before + *servāre* keep]

**pre|serv|er** (pri zėr′vər), *n.* a person or thing that saves and protects from danger. Life preservers help to save people from drowning.

**pre|set** (prē set′), *v.t.,* **-set, -set|ting.** to set in advance: *If it is known in advance which elements are to be watched for, the instrument can be preset so that only relevant wavelengths are scanned* (A. Haslett).

**pre|set|ta|ble** (prē set′ə bəl), *adj.* that can be preset: ... *FM equipment with five presettable station selectors—push the appropriate button and hear one of the five stations of your choice* (Saturday Review).

**pre|side** (pri zīd′), *v.i.,* **-sid|ed, -sid|ing.** **1** to hold the place of authority; have charge of a meeting: *Our principal will preside at our election of school officers.* **2** to have authority; have control: *The manager presides over the business of this store.* **3** to serve as hostess; receive and entertain guests: *Zachary Taylor's wife refused to attend social affairs. Her daughter, Betty Bliss, presided for her* (Helen E. Marshall). [< Middle French *présider,* learned borrowing from *praesidēre* preside over, guard < *prae-* before, ahead + *sedēre* to sit] —**pre|sid′er**, *n.*

**pres|i|dence** (prez′ə dəns, prez′dəns), *n.* **1** the act or function of presiding. **2** the office of president.

**pres|i|den|cy** (prez′ə dən sē, prez′dən-), *n., pl.* **-cies.** **1** the office of president: *She was elected to the presidency of the Junior Club.* **2** the time during which a president is in office. **3** a local administrative board in the Mormon Church. **4** Often, **Presidency.** one of three former administrative divisions (Madras, Bombay, and, originally, Bengal) of British India.

**Pres|i|den|cy** (prez′ə dən sē, prez′dən-), *n., pl.* **-cies.** **1** the office of President of the United States: *to seek the Presidency. As Mr. Eisenhower completed his third year in the Presidency, his intimates ticked off the changes that had taken place in the man* (Newsweek). **2** the time of office of a President: *The United States entered World War II in the Presidency of Franklin D. Roosevelt.*

**pres|i|dent** (prez′ə dənt, prez′dənt), *n.* **1** the chief officer of a company, corporation, college, society, or club: *a bank president, the president of Columbia University.* **2** the highest executive officer of a republic: *the president of Argentina.* **3** the chief of state in a republic with a parliamentary government which is headed by a prime minister: *The duties of the president of Israel are largely ceremonial.* **4** the presiding officer of a city council or other governmental body: *New York City has five borough presidents.* **5** a person who presides at a meeting or assembly; chairman: *The vice-president of the United States is president of the Senate.* **6** the chief officer of the Mormon hierarchy. **7** the mayor of a town or city in Mexico. [< Latin *praesidēns, -entis* (literally) one presiding, present participle of *praesidēre* to preside]

**Pres|i|dent** (prez′ə dənt, prez′dənt), *n.* **1** the highest executive officer and chief of state of the United States: *They wanted a President who would stand above petty partisanship, who would be a President of all the people* (Newsweek). **2** the highest executive officer of any republic, especially in South America, Italy, and France.

**pres|i|dent-e|lect** (prez′ə dənt i lekt′, prez′dənt-), *n.* a president who has been elected but not yet inaugurated. [American English < *president* + *elect*]

**pres|i|den|tial** (prez′ə den′shəl), *adj.* of or having to do with a president or presidency: *a presidential election, a presidential candidate. The steel price rises ... brought presidential wrath on the industry* (New York Times). —**pres′i|den′tial|ly**, *adv.*

**presidential government**, a system of government in which the president has strong powers to function as head of the government, independent of the legislature. Both Mexico and the United States have presidential government.

**Presidential Medal of Freedom**, a decoration given by the United States to a civilian, or to a member of the armed forces of a friendly nation.

**presidential primary**, a direct primary that allows voters to express their preference for presidential candidates by voting for the presidential nominees or for delegates to party conventions pledged to particular nominees.

**president pro tem** or **president pro tempore**, a United States senator who is elected by members of the Senate to act as temporary president in the absence of the Vice-President, who is the permanent president of the Senate. The president pro tem is a member of the majority party and he is fourth in the line of succession to the Presidency, after the Speaker of the House and the Vice-President.

**pres|i|dent|ship** (prez′ə dənt ship, prez′dənt-), *n.* **1** the office or function of a president; presidency. **2** the term of office of a president.

**pre|sid|i|al** (pri sid′ē əl), *adj.* **1** of or having to do with a garrison. **2** of or having to do with a presidio.

**pre|sid|i|ar|y** (pri sid′ē er′ē), *adj.* = presidial.

**pre|sid|ing elder** (pri zī′ding), a former title of a district superintendent in the Methodist Church, a clergyman who supervises a number of churches and makes recommendations to the bishop.

**pre|sid|i|o** (pri sid′ē ō), *n., pl.* **-i|os.** **1** a garrisoned fort or military post in Spanish America or, during the period of Spanish or Mexican control, in the southwestern United States and California: *An expedition led by Captain Gaspar de Portolá ... established presidios, or military forts, at the site of San Diego* (George Shaftel). **2** a Spanish penal settlement in a colony or other Spanish possession. [American English < Spanish *presidio* < Latin *praesidium* presidium]

**pre|sid|i|um** (pri sid′ē əm), *n., pl.* **-i|a** (-ē ə), **-i|ums.** **1** a group of people elected by a body to serve as its executive or administrative committee: ... *a member of the presidium of the Union of Orthodox Rabbis of the United States and Canada* (New York Times). **2** Also, **Presidium.** an executive committee, usually permanent, in the government of various Communist countries, which acts for the legislature or makes the laws that the legislature ratifies: *the Presidium of Albania, the Romanian and Czech presidia.* [< Latin *praesidium* a presiding over < *praesidēre* to preside]

**Pre|sid|i|um** (pri sid′ē əm), *n., pl.* **-i|a** (-ē ə), **-i|ums.** **1** a permanent executive committee of the Supreme Soviet that acts for this legislature between its two yearly sessions. Its chairman is the head of state of the Soviet Union. **2** the chief executive and policy-making body of the Soviet Communist Party from 1952 to 1966, thereafter officially known as the Politburo. **3** = presidium (def. 2). [< Russian *Prezidium* < Latin *praesidium* presidium]

**pre|sig|ni|fy** (prē sig′nə fī), *v.t.,* **-fied, -fy|ing.** to signify beforehand; foreshow. [< Latin *praesīgnificāre* < *prae-* before + *sīgnificāre* signify]

**pre|soak** or **pre-soak** (*n.* prē′sōk′; *v.* prē sōk′), *n., v.* —*n.* a stain-removing substance put into water to soak laundry before washing: *The difference between a pre-soak and a detergent is mainly a difference in the concentration of active ingredients. However, both products contain essentially the same ingredients—enzymes, phosphates, and surfactant, a cleaning agent* (Time).
—*v.t., v.i.* to soak beforehand: *After pre-soaking in a processing solution, the ... film is placed in face contact with the exposed negative* (George T. Eaton).

**pre|sort** or **pre-sort** (prē sôrt′), *v.t.* to sort (mail) before delivery to the post office. *mandatory presorting of business mail* (New York Times).

**press**¹ (pres), *v., n.* —*v.t.* **1** to use force or weight steadily against; push with steady force; force: *Press the button to ring the bell.* **2** to squeeze; squeeze out: *to press apples for cider. Press all the juice from the oranges.* **3** to make smooth; flatten: *Press clothes with an iron. ... real butterflies and vari-colored leaves, pressed between layers of vinyl plastic* (New Yorker). **4** to clasp; hug: *Mother pressed the baby to her. He pressed my hand in greeting.* **5** to move by pushing steadily (up, down, or against). **6** to give a desired shape, texture, or condition to by pressure: *to press cotton into bales, to press phonograph records, to press steel.* **7** *Figurative.* to urge onward; cause to hurry. **8** *Figurative.* to keep asking (somebody) earnestly; entreat: *Because it was so stormy, we pressed our guest to stay all night.* **9** *Figurative.* to lay stress upon; insist on: *The need for this legislation has been pressed in the Senate.* **10** to constrain; compel; force. **11** *Figurative.* to urge for acceptance: *to press the need for vigilance.* **12** *Figurative.* to weigh heavily upon (the mind or conscience of a person). **13** (in weight lifting) to lift (a bar) in the press. **14** *Archaic.* to crowd upon; throng.
—*v.i.* **1** to use force steadily. **2** to push ahead with eagerness or haste; keep on pushing one's way: *I pressed on in spite of the wind.* **3** to crowd; throng: *The crowd pressed about the famous actor. A great roar of a cheer went up from a crowd that was pressing all around* (Edmund Wilson). **4** to iron clothes. **5** *Figurative.* to ask insistently; refer to something often and with emphasis: *Don't press for an answer yet. We now agree on two of the three major principles for which we have pressed* (Wall Street Journal). **6** *Figurative.* to harass; oppress; trouble: *The reflection that he had wasted his time ... pressed upon his mind* (Maria Edgeworth). **7** *Figurative.* to be urgent; demand prompt attention: *We must be up and away at once; the hour presses.*
—*n.* **1** the act or fact of pressing; pressure; push; force: *Give the button a slight press and the light will go on.* (*Figurative.*) *the press of ambition.*

(*Figurative.*) *The press of many duties keeps the President very busy.* **2** a pressed condition: *These trousers will hold a press.* **3** any one of various instruments or machines for exerting pressure: *a tie press, a cider press, a steel press.* **4** a machine for printing; printing press. **5** an establishment for printing books, a newspaper, or the like. **6** the process or art of printing. **7** the business of printing newspapers and magazines: *Many editors, writers, and printers work for the press.* **8** newspapers and magazines and those who write for them: *to release a story to the press, the freedom of the press. Our school picnic was reported in the press.* **9** notice given in newspapers or magazines: *The Senator's remarks got a good press.* **10** a crowd; throng: *The little boy was lost in the press.* **11** the act of pressing forward or together; crowding: (*Figurative.*) *the press of memories into his mind.* **12** *Figurative.* urgency; hurry: *There is no press about answering my note.* **13** a cupboard or closet, as for clothes or books. **14** (in weight lifting) the lifting of a bar off the floor to the chest, holding it there a few seconds, and then putting it up over the head. **15** *Basketball.* a play in which defensive players guard offensive players closely.

**go to press**, to begin to be printed: *The newspaper goes to press at midnight.*

[< Old French *presser* < Latin *pressāre* (frequentative) < *premere* to press]

**press²** (pres), *v., n.* —*v.t.* **1a** to force into service, often for which a person is not trained, or a thing is not designed: *Several mothers were pressed into service as kindergarten teachers.* **b** to force into naval or military service; impress. Naval officers used to visit towns and merchant ships to press men for the fleet. **2** to seize and use, as land or a building.

—*n.* **1** an impressment into service, usually naval or military. **2** an order for such impressment.

[< obsolete *prest* to engage by loan, to pay in advance. Compare etym. under **prest¹**.]

**press.**, pressure.

**press agent**, an agent employed to secure favorable publicity, as for a person or organization; publicist: *There are no press agents any more. They are all public relations counselors* (New York Times).

**press-a|gent** (pres′ā′jənt), *v.t. Informal.* to give publicity to or advertise, as a press agent does, or through a press agent: [*He*] *has not press-agented himself as an expert on schooling* (Tuscaloosa News).

**press-a|gen|try** (pres′ā′jən trē), *n. Informal.* the profession or activities of a press agent: *Many companies also fail to realize the difference between press-agentry and public relations* (Time).

**press association**, an agency subscribed to by newspapers, that gathers and distributes news (other than local) to them.

**press baron**, a powerful newspaper publisher.

**press|board** (pres′bôrd′, -bōrd′), *n.* a smooth pasteboard or heavy paper used in a press, as for finishing cloth.

**press box**, *U.S.* an enclosed space in a sports arena, usually high above the playing field, set aside for reporters: *Women are barred from the press box in all major-league baseball parks, and from many a football press box as well* (Newsweek).

**press bureau**, an office or department that does the work of a press agent.

**press|but|ton** (pres′but′ən), *n. Especially British.* push button: *The pressbutton marks a code on the underside of the tray* (New Scientist).

**press|cake** (pres′kāk′), *n.* a cake of compressed material: *Low cost protein foods have been developed from such indigenous resources as oilseed meals and presscakes* (Rose and Sherman).

**press camera**, a camera equipped for widely varying conditions of light and speed, made especially for newspaper and magazine photography. A press camera usually has a focal-plane shutter, a fitting for easily interchangeable lenses with shutters, and a synchronized range finder and flashbulb attachment.

**press clipping**, a piece, usually a paragraph, article, or notice, cut out from a newspaper: *A selection of press clippings ... shows that 46 were hostile* (Harper's).

**press conference**, = news conference: *The President gave the press conference a strong speech in defense of the foreign aid in general* (Wall Street Journal).

**press corps**, a group of newsmen from various publications and news agencies who regularly report news from a particular place.

**press correspondent**, a newspaper correspondent.

**pressed glass** (prest), glass made by pressing molten glass in a mold with a plunger.

**press|er** (pres′ər), *n.* a person or thing that presses: *Pressers iron the wrinkles out of the completed garments and press the inside edges of seams flat* (Betsy Talbot Blackwell).

**presser foot**, the part of a sewing machine that holds the cloth firmly in position; foot.

**press-forge** (pres′fôrj′), *v.t.,* **-forged, -forg|ing.** to forge by means of a forging press: *Automobile crankshafts could be press-forged at 150 per hour, compared with one-third that number for drop-forging* (Burnham Finney).

**press gallery**, a gallery for reporters: *I closely watched Senator Symington for years from the press gallery as a Senate correspondent* (Harper's).

**press gang**, a group of men formerly employed to impress other men for service, especially in the British navy or army in the 1700's: *A press gang, that was in need of men for a man-of-war, came aboard and pressed poor Charles* (John Galt).

**press-gang** (pres′gang′), *v.t. Especially British.* **1** to force into naval or military service; press: *The greater the efforts to press-gang conscripts, the more recruits the Vietcong get* (Manchester Guardian Weekly). **2** to force, impress, or lure into any activity: *East Germans are press-ganged to the polls* (Manchester Guardian Weekly).

**press|ing** (pres′ing), *adj., n.* —*adj.* requiring immediate action or attention; urgent: *A man with a broken leg is in pressing need of a doctor's help. He left town quickly on some pressing business. The danger now became too pressing to admit of longer delay* (James Fenimore Cooper).

—*n.* **1** a phonograph record: *The stereo pressings have the prefix SXL* (London Times). **2** all the phonograph records pressed at one time: ... *RCA Victor recording of the Tchaikovsky concerts* (*first pressing: 150,000 copies*) (Time).

—**press′ing|ly**, *adv.* —**press′ing|ness**, *n.*

**press lord**, = press baron.

**press|man** (pres′mən), *n., pl.* **-men.** **1** a man who operates or has charge of a printing press. **2** a reporter; newspaperman: *When I learned at the press conference that stories of this kind were on the censored list I at once revoked the order and told the pressmen to write as they pleased* (Dwight D. Eisenhower).

**press|mark** (pres′märk′), *n.* a mark put on a book or other volume to indicate its location in a library.

**press money**, money paid to a soldier or sailor on enlistment.

**press of sail** or **canvas**, all the sail the wind allows: *The British fleet was just out of sight with the exception of one or two stragglers, under a press of canvas* (Joseph Conrad).

**pres|sor** (pres′ər), *adj. Physiology.* increasing blood pressure; stimulating. A pressor nerve is one whose stimulation causes an increase of blood pressure.

**press release**, a news story, item, or piece of publicity issued by or on behalf of the individual or group involved to a newspaper or newspapers for publication.

**press|room** (pres′rüm′, -rům′), *n.* a room containing printing presses.

**press|run** (pres′run′), *n.* **1** the run of a printing press for a specific number of copies: *As TIME's pressrun begins in Chicago* ... (Time). **2** the number of copies run off: *El Diario ... doubled its regular 75,000 copy pressrun* (Newsweek).

**press secretary**, a secretary who handles the public relations and arranges press conferences of a politician, organization, or institution: *At 47, he is the most influential Presidential press secretary in U.S. history* (Newsweek).

**press-show** (pres′shō′), *v.t.,* **-showed, -shown** or **-showed, -show|ing.** to show to the press before public presentation; preview: *So far I have press-shown 18 films, to the first four of which only one critic turned up* (Derek Hill).

**press-stud** (pres′stud′), *n. British.* a snap fastener.

**press-up** (pres′up′), *n. Especially British.* pushup.

**pres|sur|al** (presh′ər əl), *adj.* of the nature of mechanical pressure.

**pres|sure** (presh′ər), *n., v.,* **-sured, -sur|ing.** —*n.* **1** the continued action of a weight or force: *The small box was flattened by the pressure of the heavy book on it. The pressure of the wind filled the sails of the boat.* **2** the force per unit of area: *There is a pressure of 20 pounds to the square inch on this tire. At sea level, air exerts a pressure in all directions of about 14.7 pounds per square inch* (Thomas A. Blair). **3** *Figurative.* a state of trouble or strain: *the pressure of poverty, working under pressure.* **4** *Figurative.* a compelling influence or force: *He changed his mind under pressure from others. Pressure was brought to bear on him to do better work. Society was constantly changing under the pressure of economic necessities* (Edmund Wilson). **5** *Figurative.* the need for prompt or decisive action; urgency: *the pressure of business affairs.* **6** = atmospheric pressure. **7** = electromotive force. **8** *Obsolete.* an impression; image; stamp.

—*v.t., v.i.* to force or urge by exerting pressure; press (for): *The salesman tried to pressure my father into buying the car. Legislators cannot be pressured into voting for something that is unconstitutional* (New York Times).

[< Old French *pressure,* learned borrowing from Latin *pressūra* < *premere* to press]

**pressure cabin**, an airplane cabin that can be pressurized.

**pres|sure-cook** (presh′ər kůk′), *v.t., v.i.* to cook in a pressure cooker: *These exotic ingredients were pressure-cooked on location* (Time).

**pressure cooker**, an airtight container for cooking with steam under pressure.

**pres|sure-fed** (presh′ər fed′), *adj.* supplied by the force of pressure, such as that of a pump: *a pressure-fed fuel system.*

**pressure feed**, the act or process of supplying by pressure.

**pressure flak|ing** (flā′king), a flaking of flint tools by applying pressure with a hard point.

***pressure gauge**, **1** a device for measuring pressure, such as an attachment for indicating the pressure of steam in a boiler: *Pressure gauges will tell what portions of the foundations bear the most weight* (Science News Letter). **2** a device used in gunnery to measure the pressure in the bore or chamber of a gun when the charge explodes.

***pressure gauge**
definition 1

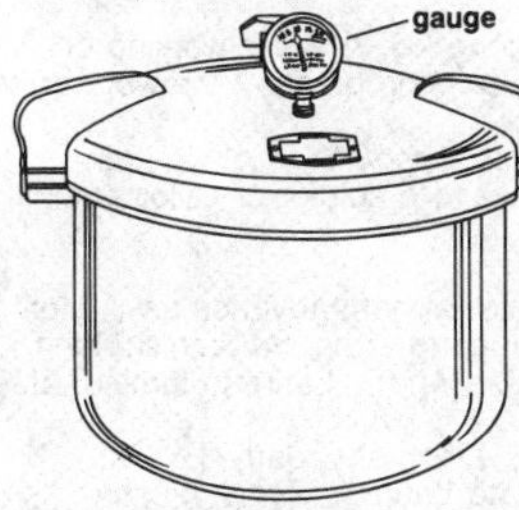

gauge

pressure cooker

**pressure gradient**, the rate at which atmospheric pressure decreases by units of horizontal distance along the line in which the pressure decreases most rapidly.

**pressure group**, any business, professional, or labor group which attempts to further its own interests by exerting pressure on legislative bodies or administrative departments or agencies: *The guild helps its members in many other ways, by bargaining energetically with local councils and by forming a pressure group for showmen's interests in Parliament* (Economist).

**pressure head**, *Physics.* the pressure of a liquid, such as at a given point in a pipe, expressed in terms of the height of a column of the liquid that would exert an equivalent pressure.

**pressure hull**, the hull, or part of the hull, of a submarine designed to withstand the pressure of the sea when submerged.

**pressure ice**, ice forced together by tides of arctic waters, forming a kind of ridge.

**pressure jump**, a sudden, slight increase in barometric pressure, occurring along an atmospheric front and preceding a tornado or other storm.

**pressure mine**, an underwater mine that is exploded by a change in water pressure caused by a passing ship.

**pressure plate**, the plate in a friction clutch that presses against the flywheel to transmit power to the transmission.

**pressure point**, **1** a point on the body where pressure applied to a blood vessel can check bleeding. **2** a point in the skin where the terminal organs of nerves are located, making it extremely sensitive to pressure. **3** the point at which the brakes of a vehicle take hold when the brake pedal is pushed down.

**pressure ridge**, a ridge of ice in arctic waters caused by lateral pressure.

**pres|sure-sen|si|tive** (presh′ər sen′sə tiv), *adj.* sealing when pressure is applied: *Pressure-sensitive adhesive tape used to cover underground pipelines* (Wall Street Journal).

**pressure suit**, a garment that provides pressure

upon the body so that respiration and circulation can continue normally, or nearly so, under low-pressure conditions such as occur at high altitudes: *... struggled into a silver-tinted pressure suit that had been tailored to a skintight fit* (Time).

**pressure tank**, a tank which holds air, fuel, or other fluid, under greater pressure than is normal in open atmospheric conditions: *Present launching sites of liquid-propelled missiles require ... heavily shielded bunkers of caves, containing corrosion-resistant pressure tanks for the dangerous liquids* (Scientific American).

**pres|sur|ize** (presh′ə rīz), *v.t.*, **-ized, -iz|ing. 1** to keep the atmospheric pressure inside (the cabin of an aircraft or spacecraft) at a normal level in spite of the altitude: *The pilot will have to be provided with air, presumably by pressurizing his cabin* (Time). **2** to place under high pressure: *If in some way hydrogen can be heated and pressurized, and it alone be the rocket propellant, we would realize a large gain in the velocity of the propellant* (Scientific American). *The reactor coolant system does not have to be pressurized* (New York Times). — **pres′sur|i|za′tion**, *n.*

**pres|sur|ized water reactor** (presh′ə rīzd), an atomic reactor using a slightly enriched natural uranium as fuel, in which water under high pressure carries the heat from the reactor to make steam for turbines that produce electric power.

**pres|sur|iz|er** (presh′ə rī′zər), *n.* a device that regulates air pressure in an enclosure: *The cab includes features such as a ... pressurizer that keeps the cab free of dust, dirt, and pollen* (London Times).

**press|work** (pres′wėrk′), *n.* **1** the working or management of a printing press. **2** the work done by a printing press.

**prest**[1] (prest), *n., v. Obsolete.* —*n.* **1** a loan. **2** advance payment to a soldier or sailor at enlistment.
—*v.t.* to enlist.
[< Old French *prest* a loan, advance pay; (literally) action of preparing < *prester* furnish, lend < Late Latin *praestāre* lend < Latin, to furnish, offer, vouch for]

**prest**[2] (prest), *adj. Obsolete.* ready. [< Old French *prest* < Late Latin *praestus* < Latin *praestō* (*esse*) (to be) at hand]

**pres|ta|tion** (pres tā′shən), *n.* a payment, as of money or service, made or exacted as a feudal or customary duty.

**pres|ter** (pres′tər), *n. Obsolete.* a priest. [< Old French *prestre* priest; see etym. under **priest**]

**Prester John**, a legendary Christian priest and king of the Middle Ages, said to have ruled a kingdom somewhere in Asia or Africa.

**pres|ti|dig|i|ta|tion** (pres′tə dij′ə tā′shən), *n.* = sleight of hand. [< French *prestidigitation* < *prestidigitateur* prestidigitator]

**pres|ti|dig|i|ta|tion|al** (pres′tə dij′ə tā′shə nəl), *adj.* of or having to do with prestidigitation.

**pres|ti|dig|i|ta|tor** (pres′tə dij′ə tā′tər), *n.* a person skilled in sleight of hand; conjurer: [*They are*] *watching a prestidigitator, and waiting to see what cute little animal will pop out of his hat next* (Howard Taubman). [< French *prestidigitateur*, apparently coined < *preste* nimble (< Italian *presto* presto) + Latin *digitus* finger + French *-ateur*, an agent suffix < Latin *-ator*]

**pres|tige** (pres tēzh′, pres′tij), *n., adj.* —*n.* reputation, influence, or distinction based on what is known of one's abilities, achievements, opportunities, or associations: *His prestige rose when the boys learned that his father was a ship's captain. After Napoleon's first battles, prestige did half his work for him* (George Meredith). *Thus it happened that while by the end of the reign the power of the sovereign had appreciably diminished, the prestige of the sovereign had enormously grown.* (Lytton Strachey).
—*adj.* prestigious: *Founding a prestige college is almost like trying for artificially aged wine* (New York Times).
[< Middle French *prestige* illusion, magic spell, (in plural) juggler's tricks, learned borrowing from Latin *praestīgiae*, plural]

**pres|tig|i|a|tion** (pres tij′ē ā′shən), *n.* = prestidigitation. [< Latin *praestigiāre* to deceive with juggling tricks]

**pres|tig|i|a|tor** (pres tij′ē ā′tər), *n.* = prestidigitator.

**pres|ti|gious** (pres tij′əs), *adj.* **1** having prestige: *The holder of the most prestigious job in journalism today is ... the TV critic* (Newsweek). **2** *Obsolete.* practicing or involving magic or jugglery; deceptive. — **pres|ti′gious|ly**, *adv.* — **pres|ti′gious|ness**, *n.*

**pres|tis|si|mo** (pres tis′ə mō), *adv., adj., n., pl.* **-mos.** *Music.* —*adv., adj.* very quick (used as a direction).
—*n.* a very quick part.
[< Italian *prestissimo*, superlative of *presto* presto]

**pres|to** (pres′tō), *adv., adj., n., pl.* **-tos**, *interj.*
—*adv.* very quickly (used especially as a musical direction).
—*adj.* **1** *Music.* very quick. **2** quick; sudden: *with the presto agility of a magician.*
—*n.* a very quick part in a piece of music.
—*interj.* right away; at once (an exclamation used to express quick or sudden action): *Then—presto!—the job was done. Drive several miles down the turnpike, around a cloverleaf, under an overpass, over an underpass, across a throughway, through a crossway, and presto! there we are* (Atlantic).
[< Italian *presto* < Latin *praestus* ready < Latin *praestō*, adverb, ready]

**presto chan|go** (chān′jō), *Slang.* change immediately or suddenly, as if by magic (used as an interjection): *Presto chango, it is now a low table* (New York Times).

**pre|stress** (prē stres′), *v.t.* to subject (a material) to heavy internal stress in making or casting to help withstand subsequent external loads or stresses. Bricks, concrete, and structural steel are prestressed by embedding steel wires or rods that are under tension. *It was found that prestressing doubled the ability of one aluminum alloy, used in the aircraft industry, to carry an external load* (Science News Letter). *Consulting engineers said that prestressed concrete might lead to the solution of these pavement problems* (New York Times).

**pre|sum|a|ble** (pri zü′mə bəl), *adj.* that can be presumed or taken for granted; probable; likely: *Unless they lose their way, noon is the presumable time of their arrival.*

**pre|sum|a|bly** (pri zü′mə blē), *adv.* as may be reasonably supposed; probably.

**pre|sume** (pri züm′), *v.,* **-sumed, -sum|ing.** —*v.t.* **1** to take for granted without proving; suppose: *You will play out of doors, I presume, if there is sunshine. The law presumes innocence until guilt is proved.* **2** to take upon oneself; venture; dare: *May I presume to tell you you are wrong? The plan which I shall presume to suggest* (Edmund Burke).
—*v.i.* **1** to take something for granted; assume. **2** to take an unfair advantage (on, upon): *Don't presume on his good nature by borrowing from him every week.* **3** to act with improper boldness; take liberties: *It would be presuming to camp in a person's yard without permission.*
[< Latin *praesūmere* anticipate, be arrogant (in Late Latin, take for granted) < *prae-* before + *sūmere* take] — **pre|sum′er**, *n.* — **pre|sum′ing|ly**, *adv.*

**pre|sum|ed|ly** (pri zü′mid lē), *adv.* as is or may be supposed; presumably.

**pre|sump|tion** (pri zump′shən), *n.* **1** unpleasant boldness: *It is presumption to go to a party when one has not been invited.* **SYN**: forwardness, effrontery. **2a** a thing taken for granted; assumption; supposition: *As his mouth was sticky, the presumption was that he had eaten the cake. The innocence of the accused is a necessary presumption under American law.* **b** *Law.* an inference that something not known to be true is a fact, based on the proved existence of some other fact. **3** a cause or reason for presuming; probability: *The more he disliked a thing the greater the presumption that it was right* (Samuel Butler). **4** the act of presuming: *This is a matter that concerns myself only, and it is presumption on his part to interfere in it* (W. H. Hudson). [< Latin *praesumptiō, -ōnis* < *praesūmere* presume]

**pre|sump|tive** (pri zump′tiv), *adj.* **1** based on likelihood; presumed: *a presumptive title to an estate.* **2** giving ground for presumption or belief: *The man's running away was regarded as presumptive evidence of his guilt.* — **pre|sump′tive|ly**, *adv.*

**presumptive heir**, = heir presumptive.

**pre|sump|tu|ous** (pri zump′chü əs), *adj.* **1** acting without permission or right; too bold; forward; daring too much: *But it is presumptuous and untrue to insist that God must back us up whatever we do* (Atlantic). **SYN**: overbold, impudent, arrogant, presuming, impertinent. **2** *Obsolete.* presumptive. [< Late Latin *praesumptuōsus* < Latin *praesumptiō, -ōnis* audacity, presumption; patterned on *sumptuōsus* expensive < *sumptus, -ūs* expense] — **pre|sump′tu|ous|ly**, *adv.* — **pre|sump′tu|ous|ness**, *n.*

**pre|sup|pose** (prē′sə pōz′), *v.t.*, **-posed, -pos|ing. 1** to take for granted in advance; assume beforehand: *Let's presuppose that we are going and make some plans.* **2** to require as a condition; imply: *A fight presupposes fighters.*

**pre|sup|po|si|tion** (prē′sup ə zish′ən), *n.* **1** the action of presupposing: *Acting on the presupposition that a flu epidemic will break out this winter, the Department of Health is issuing a vaccine.* **2** the thing presupposed: *The detective acted upon the presupposition that the thief knew the value of the jewels. Professor Sidarov outlined the fundamental presupposition of all Soviet historical works* (London Times).

**pre|sur|mise** (prē′sėr mīz′), *v.,* **-mised, -mis|ing,** *n.* —*v.t.* to surmise beforehand.
—*n.* a surmise previously formed.

**pre|syn|ap|tic** (prē′si nap′tik), *adj.* occurring before a synapse. — **pre′syn|ap′ti|cal|ly**, *adv.*

**pret.**, preterit.

**prêt-à-por|ter** (pre tà pôr tā′), *adj., n. French.* ready-to-wear: *prêt-à-porter fashions. The* [*Paris*] *designers these days trend more to mass-market ready-to-wears, known as prêt-à-porter* (Time).

**pre|tax** (prē′taks′), *adj.* = before-tax.

**pre-teen** or **pre|teen** (prē tēn′), *n., adj. Especially U.S.* —*n.* a person close to his teens; a boy or girl approaching adolescence: *The suits are for toddlers and preteens* (New York Times).
—*adj.* close to the teens; approaching adolescence: *Darlene* [*is*] *mother of two pre-teen children* (A. C. Wehrwein).

**pre|tence** (pri tens′, prē′tens), *n.* = pretense.

**pre|tend** (pri tend′), *v., adj.* —*v.t.* **1** to claim falsely: *She pretended to like the meal so she wouldn't offend the hostess.* **2** to claim falsely to have: *to pretend illness.* **3** to claim: *I don't pretend to be a musician. Speak in honest language and say the minority will be in danger from the majority. And is there an assembly on earth where this danger may not be equally pretended?* (Thomas Jefferson). **4** to make believe: *Let's pretend that we are soldiers.* **5** to venture; attempt; presume: *I cannot pretend to judge between them.* **6** *Obsolete.* to extend or hold (something) in front of or over, as for concealment or defense.
—*v.i.* **1** to make believe: *Kittens are not fighting when they cuff each other; they're only pretending.* **2** to lay claim: *James Stuart pretended to the English throne.* **3** to make pretensions (to): *a square white house pretending neither to beauty nor state* (Mrs. Humphry Ward). **4** to aspire (to), as a candidate or suitor: *A ... fellow ... might pretend surely to his kinswoman's hand* (Thackeray).
—*adj.* pretended; feigned: *It is a pretend meal this evening, with nothing whatever on the table* (James M. Barrie).
[< Latin *praetendere* < *prae-* before + *tendere* to stretch]
—*Syn. v.t.* **1,2 Pretend, affect, assume** mean to give a false impression by word, manner, or deed. **Pretend** implies a conscious intent to deceive: *She pretends ignorance of the whole affair.* **Affect** suggests using a false manner, more for effect than to deceive: *When she applied for a job, she affected simplicity.* **Assume** suggests putting on an appearance which, though not really genuine, is not wholly false: *She assumed a cheerful manner despite the upsetting news.*

**pre|tend|ed** (pri ten′did), *adj.* **1** claimed falsely; asserted falsely. **2** fictitious; counterfeit; feigned.
— **pre|tend′ed|ly**, *adv.*

**pre|tend|er** (pri ten′dər), *n.* **1** a person who pretends. **2** a person who lays claim, especially falsely, to a title or throne.

**pre|tense** (pri tens′, prē′tens), *n.* **1** make-believe; pretending: *My anger was all pretense.* **2** a false appearance: *Under pretense of picking up the handkerchief, she took the money. In this great barrage against the pretensions and pretenses of his contemporaries, Lewis ... by no means exhausted his creative energies* (New Yorker). **3** a false claim: *The girls made a pretense of knowing the boys' secret.* **4** a claim: *He makes no pretense to special knowledge.* **5** a showing off; display: *Her manner is modest and free from pretense.* **SYN**: ostentation. **6** anything done to show off. **7** *Obsolete.* an expressed aim or intention. Also, **pretence.** [< Anglo-French *pretensse*, ultimately < Latin *praetendere* pretend]

**pre|ten|sion**[1] (pri ten′shən), *n.* **1** a claim: *The young prince has pretensions to the throne. He makes no pretensions to special wisdom.* **2** the action of putting forward a claim; laying claim to; demand. **3** a doing things for show or to make a fine appearance; showy display: *The other girls were annoyed by her pretensions.* **4** an intention; design; aim.

**pre|ten|sion**[2] (prē ten′shən), *v.t.* = prestress.

**pre|ten|tious** (pri ten′shəs), *adj.* **1** making claims to excellence or importance: *a pretentious person, a pretentious book, a pretentious speech.* **2** doing things for show or to make a fine appearance; showy; ostentatious: *a pretentious style of entertaining guests.* [< French *prétentieux* (with English *-ous*), ultimately < Latin *praetendere* pretend] — **pre|ten′tious|ly**, *adv.* — **pre|ten′tious|ness**, *n.*

**pre|ter|hu|man** (prē′tər hyü′mən), *adj.* beyond what is human. [< Latin *praeter* beyond + English *human*]

**pret|er|it** or **pret|er|ite** (pret′ər it), *n., adj.* —*n. Grammar.* a tense (preterit tense) or verb form that expresses occurrence in the past; past tense. *Examples: Obeyed* is the preterit of *obey; spoke,* of *speak;* and *saw,* of *see.* See also **past tense.**
—*adj.* **1** *Grammar.* expressing past time. **2** *Obsolete.* bygone; past.
[< Latin *praeteritus* < *praeter-* beyond + *īre* go]
**preterit** or **preterite present,** *Grammar.* **1** preterit form with present meaning (applied specifically to certain Germanic or Old English verbs). **2** a preterit present verb or verb form.
**pret|er|i|tion** (pret′ə rish′ən), *n.* **1a** omission; neglect. **b** an instance of this. **2** the passing over by a testator of someone who would normally be an heir, such as a son. **3** the passing over by God of those not elected to salvation. [< Late Latin *praeteritiō, -ōnis* < Latin *praeteritus;* see etym. under **preterit**]
**pre|ter|i|tive** (pri ter′ə tiv), *adj. Grammar.* **1** expressing past time. **2** limited to past tenses: *preteritive verbs.*
**pre|ter|le|gal** (prē′tər lē′gəl), *adj.* beyond what is legal; not according to law. [< Latin *praeter* beyond + English *legal*]
**pre|ter|mis|sion** (prē′tər mish′ən), *n.* an omission; neglect.
**pre|ter|mit** (prē′tər mit′), *v.t.,* **-mit|ted, -mit|ting.** **1** to leave out or leave undone; omit. **2** to let pass without notice; overlook intentionally. **3** to leave off for a time; interrupt or suspend. [< Latin *praetermittere* < *praeter-* past, beyond + *mittere* let go, send]
**pre|ter|nat|u|ral** (prē′tər nach′ər əl, -nach′rəl), *adj.* **1** out of the ordinary course of nature; abnormal; exceptional; unusual: *preternatural keenness of sight* (W. H. Hudson). **2** due to something above or beyond nature; supernatural: *Eglinton Wood—a place well noted from ancient times for preternatural appearances* (John Galt). [< Medieval Latin *praeternaturalis* < Latin *praeter nātūram* (*praeterque fātum*) beyond nature (and beyond fate) < *praeter-* beyond + *nātūra* nature] —**pre′ter|nat′u|ral|ly,** *adv.* —**pre′ter|nat′u|ral|ness,** *n.*
**pre|ter|nat|u|ral|ism** (prē′tər nach′ər ə liz′əm, -nach′rə liz′-), *n.* **1** preternatural character or condition. **2** the recognition of the preternatural.
**pre|ter|nor|mal** (prē′tər nôr′məl), *adj.* beyond what is normal. [< Latin *praeter* beyond + English *normal*]
**pre|test** (*v.* prē test′; *n.* prē′test′), *v., n.* —*v.t.* **1** to test (a product, method, or object) in advance of regular use or application: *Aircraft builders and designers ... pretest structural parts and whole aircraft in simulated flights* (J. J. Jaklitsch). **2** to subject (students) to a preliminary test.
—*n.* the act or process of pretesting; preliminary test.
**pre|text** (prē′tekst), *n.* a false reason concealing the real reason; misleading excuse; pretense: *He used his sore finger as a pretext for not going to school. She did not go, on the pretext of being too tired.* [< Latin *praetextus* < *praetexere* to disguise, cover < *prae-* in front + *texere* to weave]
**pre|time** (prē tīm′), *v.t.,* **-timed, -tim|ing.** to preset for a particular time or times: *Traffic signals were pretimed, rather than responsive to the presence of vehicles* (New Scientist). *To use seconds in pretiming a complicated business involving thousands of participants ... was bold indeed* (New Yorker).
**pre|ti|um la|bo|rum non vi|le** (prē′shē əm lə bôr′əm non vī′lē, -bōr′-), *Latin.* no mean reward for labor (the motto of the Order of the Golden Fleece).
**pre|tor** (prē′tər), *n.* = praetor.
**pre|to|ri|al** (prē tôr′ē əl, -tōr′-), *adj.* = praetorial.
**pre|to|ri|an** (prē tôr′ē ən, -tōr′-), *adj., n.* = praetorian.
**pre|to|ri|um** (prē tôr′ē əm, -tōr′-), *n., pl.* **-to|ri|a** (-tôr′ē ə, -tōr′-). = praetorium.
**pre|tor|ship** (prē′tər ship), *n.* = praetorship.
**pre|treat** (prē trēt′), *v.t.* to treat beforehand: *... techniques for pretreating sewage and industrial waste so that it need not pollute the nation's waters* (Time).
**pre|treat|ment** (prē trēt′mənt), *n.* a treatment beforehand: *Phosphate fertilizers could be produced by pretreatment of seawater with phosphoric acid* (Atlantic).
**pre|tri|al** (prē′trī′əl), *n., adj.* —*n.* a meeting held by a judge or other arbitrator before a trial to clarify the issues so as to save time and costs at the trial: *There is nothing wrong with pressure to settle the case at pretrial rather than years later* (New York Times).
—*adj.* **1** having to do with such a meeting. **2** occurring or existing before a trial: *Pretrial publicity had prejudiced the jury.*
**pret|ti|fi|ca|tion** (prit′ə fə kā′shən), *n.* the fact or process of prettifying: *Fortunately, for all their painstaking prettification of their product, English apple-growers have not prettified the taste out of the fruit* (Sylvia Haymon).
**pret|ti|fi|er** (prit′ə fī′ər), *n.* a person or thing that prettifies: *... the work of the spoiler and prettifier in Cornwall* (W. T. Oliver).
**pret|ti|fy** (prit′ə fī), *v.t.,* **-fied, -fy|ing.** to make artificially pretty: *Until the last few decades, "restorers" hid more pictures, under new and falsely prettifying layers of paint and varnish, than they cleaned* (Time).
**pret|ti|ly** (prit′ə lē), *adv.* in a pretty manner; pleasingly; gracefully; nicely.
**pret|ti|ness** (prit′ē nis), *n.* **1** the condition or quality of being pretty; pleasing appearance: *Prettiness may be considered a superficial or surface quality* (Matthew Luckiesh). **2** a pretty thing or person, generally suggesting triteness: *Surburban villas, Belgrave terraces, and other such prettinesses* (Hawthorne).
**pret|ty** (prit′ē), *adj.,* **-ti|er, -ti|est,** *n., pl.* **-ties,** *adv., v.,* **-tied, -ty|ing.** —*adj.* **1** pleasing: *a pretty face, a pretty dress, a pretty tune, pretty manners.* Pretty is used to describe people and things that are good-looking in a feminine or childish way, dainty, sweet, or charming, but not stately, grand, elegant, or very important. **2** not at all pleasing: *This is a pretty mess, indeed.* **3** *Informal.* considerable in amount or extent: *He paid a pretty sum.* **4** fair; fine; nice: *a pretty day.* **5** too dainty or delicate; foppish: *He talks well, but can the pretty little man fight?* **6** *Archaic.* brave; bold; fine: *Robin Hood was a pretty fellow.*
—*n.* **1** a pretty person or thing. **2** *Archaic.* a brave, bold man or boy: *Back to back, my pretties* (Oliver Goldsmith).
—*adv.* fairly; rather; quite: *It is pretty late. It is pretty difficult to legislate against frenzy or against fools* (Time).
—*v.t.* to make pretty: *... prettied by formal bouquets of red and white carnations* (Maclean's).
**pretty much** (or **nearly** or **well**), almost; nearly: *pretty much a thing of the past.*
**pretty up,** to prettify: *The administrative budget pretties up the picture of Government cost and power* (Wall Street Journal).
**sitting pretty,** in an advantageous position; well off: *His uncle died and left him enough to be sitting pretty.*
[Old English *prættig* cunning, skillful, artful < *prætt* trick, wile, craft]
**pret|ty|ish** (prit′ē ish), *adj. Informal.* rather pretty.
**pretty penny,** *Informal.* a large sum of money: *Highways, already costing states a pretty penny, are going to eat into state treasuries at a faster pace* (Wall Street Journal).
**pret|ty-pret|ty** (prit′ē prit′ē), *adj., n., pl.* **-ties.**
—*adj.* pretty in an overdone or mawkish way: *pretty-pretty pictures or verse. [The] make-up was softly feminine without being pretty-pretty* (London Times).
—*n.* knickknack.
**pretty-pretties,** pretty things; ornaments: *This room contains a small fortune in pretty-pretties* (Bow Bells Weekly).
**pre|typ|i|fy** (prē tip′ə fī), *v.t.,* **-fied, -fy|ing.** to typify beforehand; prefigure; foreshadow.
**pret|zel** (pret′səl), *n.* a hard biscuit, usually in the form of a knot or stick, glazed and salted on the outside: *The order of the evening is beer, pretzels, and pristine jazz* (New Yorker). [American English < German *Brezel, Bretzel* < Old High German *brezitella* < a diminutive form of unrecorded Medieval Latin *brachitum* a kind of biscuit baked in the shape of folded arms < Latin *brachium* arm < Greek *brachī́ōn* upper arm]
**pre|vail** (pri vāl′), *v.i.* **1** to exist in many places; be in general use: *Making resolutions on New Year's Day is a custom that still prevails. The custom still prevails of hanging up stockings the night before Christmas.* **2** to be the most usual or strongest: *Sadness prevailed in our minds.* **3** to be the stronger; win the victory; succeed: *The knights prevailed against their foe. Reason prevailed over emotion. I decline to accept the end of man ... I believe that man will not merely endure: he will prevail* (William Faulkner). **4** to be effective: *But why Prevail'd not thy pure prayers?* (Tennyson).
**prevail on** (or **upon** or **with**), to persuade: *Can't I prevail upon you to stay for dinner? The governor prevailed with me to take charge of our Northwestern frontier* (Benjamin Franklin).
[< Latin *praevalēre* < *prae-* before + *valēre* have power]
**pre|vail|ing** (pri vā′ling), *adj.* **1** in general use; common: *a prevailing style. The prevailing summer winds here are from the west.* **SYN:** See syn. under **current.** **2** that prevails; having superior force or influence; victorious: *Yellow is the prevailing color in her room.* —**pre|vail′ing|ly,** *adv.* —**pre|vail′ing|ness,** *n.*
**prevailing westerlies,** the usual westerly winds that blow between 30 degrees and 60 degrees latitude, both north and south of the equator.
**prev|a|lence** (prev′ə ləns), *n.* widespread occurrence; general use: *the prevalence of complaints about the weather, the prevalence of automobiles.*
**prev|a|lent** (prev′ə lent), *adj.* **1** widespread; in general use; common: *Colds are prevalent in the winter.* **SYN:** usual, ordinary, prevailing. **2** predominant; victorious. [< Latin *praevalēns, -entis,* present participle of *prevalēre* prevail] —**prev′a|lent|ly,** *adv.*
**pre|var|i|cate** (prē var′ə kāt), *v.i.,* **-cat|ed, -cat|ing.** **1** to turn aside from the truth in speech or action; lie. **2** to speak evasively; equivocate. [< Latin *praevāricārī* make a sham accusation, deviate; (literally) walk crookedly < *prae-* before + *vāricāre* to straddle < *vāricus* straddling < *vārus* knockkneed, crooked]
**pre|var|i|ca|tion** (prē var′ə kā′shən), *n.* the act of prevaricating; turning aside from the truth; lie.
**pre|var|i|ca|tor** (prē var′ə kā′tər), *n.* a person who turns aside from the truth in speech or action.
**pre|ve|nance** (prē′və nəns), *n.* anticipation, especially of the wants of others. [< French *prévenance*]
**pre|ven|ience** (prē vēn′yəns), *n.* **1** = antecedence. **2** = anticipation.
**pre|ven|ient** (prē vēn′yənt), *adj.* **1** coming before. **2** = anticipatory. **3** tending to prevent. [< Latin *praeveniēns, -entis,* present participle of *praevenīre* to anticipate, come before; see etym. under **prevent**] —**pre|ven′ient|ly,** *adv.*
**prevenient grace,** *Theology.* divine grace turning the heart toward God.
**pre|vent** (pri vent′), *v.t.* **1** to stop or keep (from): *Illness prevented him from doing his work.* **2** to keep from happening: *Rain prevented the game.* **3** *Archaic.* to come before; go before; do before.
—*v.i.* to hinder: *I will meet you at six if nothing prevents.* [< Latin *praeventus,* past participle of *praevenīre* < *prae-* before + *venīre* to come]
—**pre|vent′er,** *n.*
—*Syn. v.t.* 1,2, *v.i.* **Prevent, hinder, impede** mean to get in the way of action or progress. **Prevent** means to keep a person or thing from doing something or making progress, acting or setting up an obstacle to stop him or it: *Business prevented my going.* **Hinder** means to hold back, so that making, starting, going ahead, or finishing is late, difficult, or impossible: *The wrong food hinders growth.* **Impede** means to slow up movement and progress by putting something binding or fouling on or in the way: *Muddy roads impeded our journey.*
**pre|vent|a|ble** (pri ven′tə bəl), *adj.* that can be prevented: *preventable infectious diseases.*
**pre|vent|a|tive** (pri ven′tə tiv), *adj., n.* = preventive.
**pre|vent|i|ble** (pri ven′tə bəl), *adj.* = preventable.
**pre|ven|tion** (pri ven′shən), *n.* **1** the action of preventing; hindering: *the prevention of fire.* **2** something that prevents: *The precautions were a prevention against fire.*
**pre|ven|tive** (pri ven′tiv), *adj., n.* —*adj.* that prevents or hinders: *preventive measures against disease.*
—*n.* something that prevents: *Vaccination is a preventive against polio.* —**pre|ven′tive|ly,** *adv.* —**pre|ven′tive|ness,** *n.*
**preventive detention,** **1** *U.S. Law.* the imprisonment of a criminal suspect without bail to prevent his committing any possible criminal acts before his trial is held: *Even if the courts uphold preventive detention ... the net result would be to put more prisoners into a prisons system that is already overcrowded, understaffed, underfinanced, and a breeding-ground for professional criminals* (New York Times). **2** *British Law.* the imprisonment of persistent offenders, usually for a period of from 5 to 10 years, to prevent them from committing more offenses.
**preventive medicine,** the branch of medicine concerned with the prevention of disease.
**preventive war,** an aggressive war waged against another nation, supposedly started in anticipation of attack by that nation: *The Turks have no nervous apprehension of an attack from Syria which might provoke them into a preventive war* (Wall Street Journal).
**pre|ven|to|ri|um** (prē′ven tôr′ē əm, -tōr′-), *n., pl.* **-to|ri|ums, -to|ri|a** (-tôr′ē ə, -tōr′-). an institution for preventing the spread of a disease, especially tuberculosis, as by the treatment of persons in an incipient stage of the disease or in danger of the disease: *"Preventoria" flourished [as] summer camps where youngsters exposed to TB*

**Pronunciation Key:** hat, āge, cãre, fär; let, ēqual, tėrm; it, īce; hot, ōpen, ôrder; oil, out; cup, pu̇t, rüle; child; long; thin; ᴛʜen; zh, measure; ə represents **a** in about, **e** in taken, **i** in pencil, **o** in lemon, **u** in circus.

*were fed milk, eggs, and other nourishing foods and given plenty of fresh air and sunlight* (Jonathan Spivak). [< *prevent* + *-orium* as in *sanatorium*]

**pre|view** (prē′vyü′), *n., v.* —*n.* **1** a previous view, inspection, or survey: *a preview of things to come.* **2** an advance showing of a performance or scenes from a motion picture, play, or television program, or a display of a new product: *The previews ... turned out to be, for the most part, regular concerts with explanatory remarks by Mr. Bernstein* (Francis D. Perkins).
—*v.t.* to view or display beforehand.

**pre|vi|ous** (prē′vē əs), *adj.* **1** coming or going before; that came before; earlier: *She did better in the previous lesson.* **2** *Informal.* quick; hasty; premature. *Don't be too previous about refusing.*
**previous to,** before; preceding: *Previous to her departure she gave a party.*
[< Latin *praevius* (with English *-ous*) leading the way < *prae-* before + *via* road] —**pre′vi|ous|ness,** *n.*
—*Syn.* **1 Previous, preceding, prior** mean coming before something. **Previous** means earlier: *I cannot go, for I have a previous engagement* (one made before). **Preceding** means coming immediately before: *Check the preceding statement.* **Prior** adds to *previous* the idea of coming first in order of importance: *I have a prior engagement* (one that has first call).

**Previous Examination,** *British.* the first examination for the degree of B.A. at Cambridge University.

**pre|vi|ous|ly** (prē′vē əs lē), *adv.* at a previous time; before: *I spoke to him previously.*

**previous question,** a motion to vote immediately on the main question without further debate. *Abbr:* p.q.

**pre|vise** (pri vīz′), *v.t.,* **-vised, -vis|ing. 1** to foresee; forecast. **2** = forewarn. [< Latin *praevīsus,* past participle of *praevidēre* < *prae-* before + *vidēre* to see]

**pre|vi|sion** (pri vizh′ən), *n.* **1** foresight; foreknowledge: *She knew by prevision what most women learn only by experience* (Thomas Hardy). **2** a prophetic vision or perception: *Some prevision warned the explorer of danger.* [< *pre-* + *vision*]

**pre|vi|sion|al** (pri vizh′ə nəl), *adj.* of or having to do with prevision; foreseeing; forecasting. —**pre-vi′sion|al|ly,** *adv.*

**pre|vo|cal|ic** (prē′vō kal′ik), *adj.* immediately preceding a vowel.

**pre|vo|ca|tion|al** (prē′vō kā′shə nəl), *adj.* of or having to do with training taken before entering a vocational school.

**pre|voy|ance** (pri voi′əns), *n.* foresight; forethought. [< French *prévoyance* < *prévoir* < Latin *praevidēre* to foresee; see etym. under **previse**]

**pre|vue** (prē′vyü′), *n. U.S.* preview (def. 2).

**pre|war** (prē′wôr′), *adj., adv.* before a war: *... so security-conscious a regime as the one that ruled prewar and wartime Japan* (New Yorker).

**prex** (preks), *n. U.S. Slang.* prexy.

**prex|y** (prek′sē), *n., pl.* **prex|ies.** *U.S. Slang.* a president, especially of a college or university: *The gentleman ... is still prexy of one of the land's snootiest colleges* (Saturday Review).

**prey** (prā), *n., v.* —*n.* **1** any animal or animals hunted or seized for food by another animal: *Mice and birds are the prey of cats. The relative number of predatory fish ... increased significantly compared with their prey* (F. S. Bodenheimer). **2** the habit of hunting and killing other animals for food: *Hawks are birds of prey.* **3** *Figurative.* a person or thing injured; victim: *to be a prey to fear, be a prey to disease. Meanwhile, Victoria, in growing agitation, was a prey to temper and to nerves* (Lytton Strachey). **4** *Archaic.* booty; spoil; plunder.
—*v.i.* **prey on** (or **upon**), **a** to hunt or kill for food: *Cats prey upon mice.* **b** *Figurative.* to do harm; be a strain upon; injure; irritate: *Worry about her debts preys on her mind.* **c** to rob; plunder: *A succession of ferocious invaders descended through the western passes, to prey on the defenceless wealth of Hindostan* (Macaulay).
[< Old French *preie* < Vulgar Latin *prēda,* for Latin *praeda*] —**prey′er,** *n.*

**pri|a|can|thid** (prī′ə kan′thid), *n., adj.* —*n.* any one of various small, carnivorous, acanthopterygian fish of tropical seas, occasionally found off the coast of the United States.
—*adj.* belonging or having to do with these fish.
[< New Latin *Priacanthidae* the family name < Greek *priōn* saw, tool + *ákantha* thorn]

**Pri|am** (prī′əm), *n. Greek Legend.* the king of Troy at the time of the Trojan War. He was the father of many children, including Hector, Paris, and Cassandra.

**Pri|a|pe|an** (prī′ə pē′ən), *adj.* = Priapic.

**Pri|ap|ic** or **pri|ap|ic** (prī ap′ik, -ā′pik), *adj.* **1** of or having to do with Priapus and his worship. **2** = phallic. —**Pri|ap′i|cal|ly, pri|ap′i|cal|ly,** *adv.*

**pri|a|pism** (prī′ə piz əm), *n.* licentiousness; intentional indecency.

**Pri|a|pus** (prī ā′pəs), *n. Greek and Roman Mythology.* the Greek and Roman god of procreation. He protected gardens, vineyards, and flocks.

**pri|a|pus** (prī ā′pəs), *n.* = phallus.

**price** (prīs), *n., v.,* **priced, pric|ing.** —*n.* **1** the amount for which a thing is sold or can be bought; cost to the buyer: *The price of this hat is $10.* **2** a reward offered for the capture of a person alive or dead: *Every member of the gang has a price on his head.* **3** *Figurative.* what must be given, done, or undergone to obtain a thing; amount paid for any result: *to secure wealth at the price of health. We paid a heavy price for the victory, for we lost ten thousand soldiers.* **4** value; worth: *a diamond of great price.* **5** money or other consideration for which a person's support or consent may be obtained.
—*v.t.* **1** to put a price on; set the price of: *The hat was priced at $10.* **2** *Informal.* to ask the price of; find out the price of: *Mother is pricing rugs.*
**at any price,** at any cost, no matter how great: *We wanted to win at any price.*
**beyond** (or **without**) **price,** so valuable that it cannot be bought or be given a value in money: *a painting beyond price. A robe of samite without price ... clung about her lissome limbs* (Tennyson).
[Middle English *pris* (originally) honor, praise, reward < Old French < Latin *pretium.* Compare etym. under **prize**[1], **praise.**] —**pric′er,** *n.*
—*Syn. n.* **1 Price, charge, cost** mean the amount asked or paid for something. **Price** is used mainly of goods and supplies, especially of what the seller asks for them: *The price of meat is high now.* **Charge** is used mainly of services rather than goods: *There is no charge for delivery.* **Cost** is used of either goods or services, and applies to whatever is spent, whether money, effort, etc.: *The cost of the house was high.*

**price commission,** *U.S.* a governmental commission in charge of regulating price and rent increases, especially to curb inflation.

**price control,** the fixing of prices, usually by a government agency, especially by establishing maximum or minimum prices for commodities and rents: *Rationing and price controls locked up the excess purchasing power in savings and staved off the worst of the inflation until the end of the war* (Bulletin of Atomic Scientists).

**price cutter,** a person or group that practices price cutting.

**price cutting,** a sharp reduction of prices, especially when undertaken at a loss in order to eliminate competitors: *As to stabilizing the industry, minimum prices did tend to diminish price cutting* (New York Times). —**price′-cut′ting,** *adj.*

**price-earn|ings ratio** (prīs′ėr′ningz), the ratio between the market price of a stock and its dollar earnings per share. A price of $64 with earnings of $8 per share has a ratio of 8 to 1. *The price-earnings ratios of many blue-chip ... which had swollen far out of proportion* (Newsweek).

**price fixer,** a manufacturer that engages in price fixing.

**price fixing, 1** the control of prices by a governmental agency. **2** an illegal agreement among several manufacturers to set a noncompetitive price on a product which they all make: *It was the first large-scale criminal price fixing case against the industry in more than 20 years* (Time). **3** the practice of setting and maintaining a retail price for one's products. —**price′-fix′ing,** *adj.*

**price index,** = consumer price index: *The price index is designed to show the month-to-month change in prices of goods and services bought by urban wage earners and clerical worker families* (Wall Street Journal).

**price|less** (prīs′lis), *adj.* **1** beyond price; extremely valuable: *Many museums have collections of priceless paintings by famous artists.* **2** *Informal.* very amusing or absurd; delightful: *Send me some of your priceless little sketches for my rummage sale on the 26th* (Punch).
—**price′less|ness,** *n.*

**price level, 1** the general level of prices, as may be shown by a consumer price index: *But until the public shows strong and definite hostility toward inflationary wage settlements, we must expect rising labor costs to push the price level slowly upward* (Sumner H. Slichter). **2** the average price of any product during a certain period: *The whole TV price level slid downhill with [the] introduction of portable sets priced substantially below table or console models* (Time).

**price prop,** = price support.

**price ring,** *Especially British.* a number of manufacturers who act together to set a noncompetitive price on a product which they all make.

**price support,** artificial support, generally provided by a government, to keep prices of products or commodities or foreign exchange rates from falling below certain stipulated levels. It may take the form of direct subsidy to the producer, or of government purchase at the level of support when the price in the open market falls below that level, or of loans to permit producers to hold back their production in storage pending a rise in price in the open market or an increase in protective tariffs.

**price-sup|port|ed** (prīs′sə pôr′tid, -pōr′-), *adj.* that is given price support: *price-supported agricultural commodities.*

**price tag, 1** a tag or ticket marked with the price of the article to which it is attached. **2** *Informal, Figurative.* an estimated worth or cost; value: *To answer these questions means putting a price tag on events which are obviously incalculable* (Newsweek).

**price war,** a period of intense competition between merchants, especially retail merchants, in which prices are progressively slashed until they may drop below cost.

**price|wise** (prīs′wīz), *adv.* with respect to price or prices: *Shipping men say that Swedish pulp isn't able to compete pricewise with the Canadian product* (Wall Street Journal).

**pric|ey** (prī′sē), *adj.,* **pric|i|er, pric|i|est.** *British Informal.* expensive: *When we travel ... we avoid the pricey hotels* (Sunday Times). Also, **pricy.**

**prick** (prik), *n., v.* —*n.* **1** a sharp point. **2** a little hole or mark made by a sharp point; puncture. **3** a pricking. **4** a pain like that made with a sharp point. **5** that which pricks or pierces, such as a goad for oxen. **6** *Figurative.* stinging compunction; remorse: *the prick of conscience.*
—*v.t.* **1** to make a little hole in with a sharp point: *The thorn pricked my thumb.* **SYN:** puncture. **2** to mark with a sharp point: *I pricked the map with a pin to show our route.* **3** to cause sharp pain to: *The cat pricked me with its claws.* (*Figurative.*) *My conscience pricked me.* **4** to raise or erect: *The dog pricked his ears at the sound of footsteps.* **5** *Archaic.* to spur; urge on: *My duty pricks me on to utter that Which else no worldly good should draw from me* (Shakespeare). **6** to transplant (seedlings). **7** to shoe (a horse) improperly, by driving a nail into the quick.
—*v.i.* **1** to pierce a little hole in something. **2** to cause or feel a sharp pain: *Thorns prick.* **SYN:** sting. **3** *Archaic.* to ride fast.
**kick against the pricks,** to make useless resistance that only hurts oneself: *He found it hard to kick against the pricks, yet, for that reason, kicked every day the harder* (London Times).
**prick up, a** to point upward; stand erect: *The spires of churches are to be seen pricking up through the greenery* (Blackwood's Magazine). **b** *Nautical.* to chart with dividers: *The captain ordered the ship's course to be pricked up.*
**prick (up) the ears.** See under **ear.**
[Old English *prica* a point, puncture, particle]
—**prick′ing|ly,** *adv.*

**prick-eared** (prik′ird′), *adj.* **1** having erect ears (used especially of dogs). **2** having the hair cut short so that the ears are prominent (used originally in England in the 1640's of the Roundheads by the Cavaliers).

**prick|er** (prik′ər), *n.* **1** a person or thing that pricks. **2** any sharp-pointed instrument. **3** *Archaic.* a horseman.

**prick|et**[1] (prik′it), *n.* **1** a sharp metal point on which to stick a candle. **2** a candlestick with such a point or points. [Middle English *pryket,* perhaps < *pryk* prick + *-et* -et]

**prick|et**[2] (prik′it), *n.* a buck in his second year, with straight, still unbranched horns. [perhaps < *pricket*[1]. Perhaps related to **brocket.**]

**prick|le** (prik′əl), *n., v.,* **-led, -ling.** —*n.* **1a** a small, sharp point; thorn; spine: *One of the prickles on the rosebush caught in my thumb.* **b** *Botany.* a sharp point growing from the bark of a plant like a thorn but able to be peeled off. **2** a prickly or smarting sensation: (*Figurative.*) *I feel the old, familiar prickle of excitement* (Punch).
—*v.i.* to feel a prickly or smarting sensation: *Her skin prickled when she saw the big snake.*
—*v.t.* **1** to cause such a sensation in: *I ... Felt a horror over me creep, Prickle my skin and catch my breath* (Tennyson). **2** *Figurative.* to goad; prod.
[Old English *pricel,* variant of *pricels* thing to prick with < *prician* to prick; later fused with *prickle* (diminutive) < *prick,* noun]

**prick|ly** (prik′lē), *adj.,* **-li|er, -li|est. 1** having many sharp points or thorns: *a prickly rosebush, the prickly porcupine.* **2** sharp and stinging; smarting; itching: *Heat sometimes causes a prickly rash on the skin.* **3** *Figurative.* hard to deal with: *a prickly question.* —**prick′li|ness,** *n.*

**prickly ash,** a shrub or small tree of the rue family, with strong prickles and leaves like those of the ash. Its bark is used in medicine.

**prickly heat**, a red, itching rash on the skin, caused by inflammation of the sweat glands; miliaria: *Known as prickly heat, this rash seems to bother babies less than it does mothers* (Sidonie M. Gruenberg).

**prickly pear**, **1** the round or pear-shaped fruit of a certain kind of cactus. The kinds that are good to eat are called tunas and are raised as food for people and livestock. **2** any cactus that it grows on; nopal; Indian fig. There are several species of prickly pear, making up a genus of cactuses. They are spiny or hairy, with showy green, yellow, or red flowers, and may grow from several inches to over 20 feet high. See picture under **cactus family**.

**prickly poppy**, any of a group of plants of the poppy family, of the southwestern United States, Mexico, and South America, with prickly foliage and orange, yellow, or white flowers, as the Mexican poppy.

**prick|spur** (prik′spėr′), *n.* an early form of horseman's spur with a single pricking point.

**pric|y** (prī′sē), *adj.*, **pric|i|er, pric|i|est.** *British Informal.* expensive; pricey.

**pride** (prīd), *n., v.,* **prid|ed, prid|ing.** —*n.* **1** a high opinion of one's own worth or possessions: *Pride in our city should make us help to keep it clean. He left Temple's protection only to learn that pride is a luxury to the poor* (Time). **2** pleasure or satisfaction in something concerned with oneself: *to take pride in a hard job well done.* **3** something that a person is proud of: *Her youngest child is her great pride. Glasgow is the pride of Scotland* (Tobias Smollett). **4** too high an opinion of oneself; conceit: *Pride goes before a fall.* **SYN**: vanity, arrogance. **5** an acting as if better than others; scorn of others; haughtiness. **6** the best part; most flourishing period; prime: *in the pride of manhood. The bees humming round the gay roses Proclaim it the pride of the year* (Robert Burns). **7** a group of lions living together: *Each pride has from one to three adult males, several lionesses, and cubs* (George B. Schaller). **8** *Archaic.* splendor; pomp: *... all Quality, Pride, Pomp, and Circumstance of glorious war* (Shakespeare). **9** *Archaic.* high spirit; mettle. **10** *Obsolete.* sexual desire in a female animal; heat.
—*v.t.* **pride oneself on,** to be proud of: *We pride ourselves on our clean streets. I pride myself on my memory.*
[Old English *prȳde* < *prūd* proud]
—*Syn. n.* **1 Pride, conceit** mean a high opinion of oneself. **Pride** implies pleased satisfaction with what one is, has, or has done, and suggests either proper self-respect and personal dignity because of real worth or excessive self-love and arrogance because of imagined superiority: *A man without pride deserves contempt.* **Conceit** implies much too high an opinion of one's own abilities and accomplishments, and often suggests an unpleasantly assertive manner: *Conceit makes the criminal think he is too clever to be caught.*

**pride|ful** (prīd′fəl), *adj.* proud: *"Depart," he cried, "perverse and prideful nymph"* (William Richardson). —**pride′ful|ly,** *adv.* —**pride′ful|ness,** *n.*

**pride|less** (prīd′lis), *adj.* without pride.

**pride of China** or **India,** = chinaberry (def. 1).

**pride of place,** *Especially British.* the highest position; the honor, pride, or distinction of first place.

**pried** (prīd), *v.* the past tense and past participle of **pry**[1] and **pry**[2].

*** prie-dieu** (prē dyœ′), *n.* a small desk for a prayer book or the like, with a piece on which to kneel. [< French *prie-dieu* (literally) pray God; *prie,* imperative of *prier* pray; *Dieu* God < Latin *deus*]

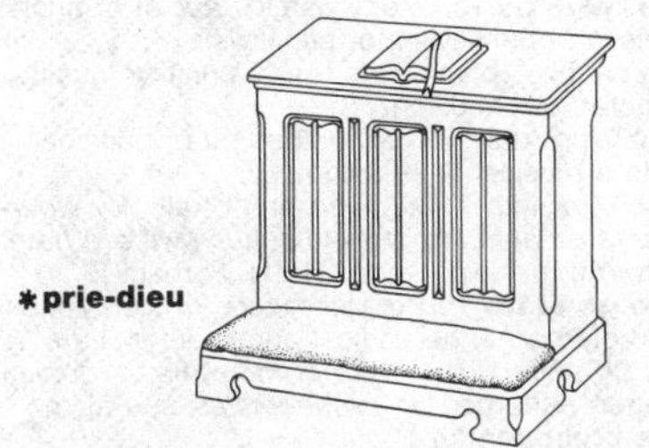
***prie-dieu**

**pri|er** (prī′ər), *n.* a person who pries; inquisitive person. [< *pry*[1], verb + *-er*[1]]

**priest** (prēst), *n.* **1** a clergyman or minister of a Christian church. **2** a clergyman authorized to administer the sacraments and pronounce absolution. **3** a special servant of a god, who performs certain public religious acts: *a priest of Apollo.* **4** *Figurative.* a person who has a position of leadership in some field: *a high priest of science.* [Old English *prēost,* ultimately < Latin *presbyter.* See etym. of doublets **presbyter, prester.**]

**priest|craft** (prēst′kraft′, -kräft′), *n.* the skills and knowledge of priests, especially when applied to worldly ends: *It is better that men should be governed by priestcraft than by brute violence* (Macaulay).

**priest|ess** (prēs′tis), *n.* a woman who serves at an altar or in sacred rites: *a priestess of Diana, a priestess of beauty.*

**priest|fish** (prēst′fish′), *n., pl.* **-fish|es** or (*collectively*) **-fish.** a rockfish of a slaty-black color, abundant along the Pacific coast of the United States.

**priest|hood** (prēst′hu̇d), *n.* **1** the position or rank of priest: *He was admitted to the priesthood.* **2** priests as a group: *the priesthood of Spain.* [Old English *prēosthād* < *prēost* priest + *-hād* hood]

**priest-king** (prēst′king′), *n.* a temporal ruler regarded as the direct representative of a god.

**priest|like** (prēst′līk′), *adj.* = priestly.

**priest|ly** (prēst′lē), *adj.,* **-li|er, -li|est. 1** of or having to do with a priest: *the priestly office.* **SYN**: sacerdotal. **2** like a priest; suitable for a priest: *priestly sobriety.* —**priest′li|ness,** *n.*

**priest-rid|den** (prēst′rid′ən), *adj.* dominated by priests (used in an unfriendly way).

**priest's crown,** = dandelion (so called because of the bald appearance after the pappus has blown off).

**prig**[1] (prig), *n.* a person who is too particular about speech and manners, and prides himself on being better than others: *A prig is a fellow who is always making you a present of his opinions* (George Eliot). [origin uncertain]

**prig**[2] (prig), *v.,* **prigged, prig|ging,** *n. Especially British.* —*v.i.* **1** to quarrel or haggle about a price, terms, or the like. **2** to beg; importune.
—*v.t.* to pilfer or steal: *I think we'd find that Mr. Beeton has been prigging little things out of the rooms here and there* (Rudyard Kipling).
—*n.* a petty thief.
[origin uncertain]

**prig|ger|y** (prig′ər ē), *n., pl.* **-ger|ies.** the conduct or character of a prig.

**prig|gish** (prig′ish), *adj.* too particular about doing right in things that show outwardly; priding oneself on being better than others. —**prig′gish|ly,** *adv.* —**prig′gish|ness,** *n.*

**prig|gism** (prig′iz əm), *n.* priggishness.

**prill** (pril), *n., v.* —*n.* a small ball or pellet roughly the size of small shot.
—*v.t.* to form (balls or pellets), as of metal or chemicals.
[origin uncertain]

**prim** (prim), *adj.,* **prim|mer, prim|mest,** *v.,* **primmed, prim|ming.** —*adj.* precise, neat, proper, or formal in a stiff way: *friends ... staid and prim, of evangelical tendencies* (Samuel Butler).
—*v.t.* **1** to form (the face or mouth) into an expression of stiff demureness. **2** to make (a person, thing, or place) prim. —*v.i.* to draw up the mouth in an affectedly nice way: *They mince and prim and pout, and are sigh-away* (George Meredith). —**prim′ly,** *adv.* —**prim′ness,** *n.*

**prim.,** **1** primary. **2** primate. **3** primitive.

**pri|ma bal|le|ri|na** (prē′mə bal′ə rē′nə), *pl.* **pri|ma bal|le|ri|nas.** the principal woman dancer in a ballet company. [< Italian *prima ballerina*]

**pri|ma|cy** (prī′mə sē), *n., pl.* **-cies. 1** the fact or condition of being first, as in order, rank, or importance. **SYN**: preeminence. **2** the position or rank of a bishop of the highest rank. **3** the supreme power of the pope in the Roman Catholic Church. [< Old French *primacie,* learned borrowing from Medieval Latin (England) *primatia,* for Latin *prīmātus, -ūs* < *prīmās, -ātis* of first rank; see etym. under **primate**]

**pri|ma don|na** (prē′mə don′ə, prim′ə), *pl.* **pri|ma don|nas. 1** the principal woman singer in an opera, operatic company, or concert group. **SYN**: diva. **2** *Figurative.* a temperamental person: *[His] genius was for making men work as a team. He had to handle the prima donnas of a dozen different nations* (Newsweek). [< Italian *prima donna* first lady < Latin *prīma domina.* Compare etym. under **prime**[1], noun, **donna.**]

**pri|ma fa|ci|e** (prī′mə fā′shē ē, fā′shē), at first view; before investigation. [< Latin *prīmā faciē,* ablative of *prīma faciēs* first appearance. Compare etym. under **prime**[1], noun, **face.**] —**pri′ma-fa′ci|e,** *adj.*

**prima-facie case,** *Law.* a case supported by prima-facie evidence.

**prima-facie evidence,** *Law.* evidence sufficient to establish a fact, or raise a presumption of fact, unless rebutted.

**pri|mage** (prī′mij), *n.* a small allowance formerly paid by a shipper to the master and crew of a vessel for the loading and care of goods.

**pri|ma in|ter pa|res** (prī′mə in′tər pãr′ēz), *Latin.* first among her peers.

**pri|mal** (prī′məl), *adj.* **1** of early times; first; primeval: *It hath the primal eldest curse upon it, A brother's murder* (Shakespeare). **SYN**: original. **2** chief; fundamental. [< Medieval Latin *primalis* < Latin *prīmus* first] —**pri′mal|ly,** *adv.*

**primal therapy** or **primal scream therapy,** a form of group psychotherapy which encourages members to reenact experiences of early childhood to release their repressed anger or pain: *The main technique that primal therapy uses is to persuade the patient to become a baby* (New Scientist).

**pri|ma|quine** (prī′mə kwin), *n.* a synthetic drug used to cure some forms of malaria. *Formula:* $C_{15}H_{21}N_3O$ [< *prima*(ry) + *quin*(olin)*e*]

**pri|ma|ri|ly** (prī′mer′ə lē, -mər-; prī mãr′-), *adv.* **1** above all; chiefly; principally: *Ulysses S. Grant was primarily a general.* **SYN**: preeminently. **2** at first; originally.

**pri|ma|ri|ness** (prī′mer′ē nis, -mər-), *n.* the state of being primary.

**pri|ma|ry** (prī′mer′ē, -mər-), *adj., n., pl.* **-ries.**
—*adj.* **1** first, as in order, time, or place: *a primary layer of tissue, the primary causes of unemployment.* **SYN**: See syn. under **elementary. 2** first in importance; chief: *a primary task. Education is the primary purpose of a school. A balanced diet is primary to good health.* **SYN**: principal, prime. **3** from which others have come; original; fundamental: *The historian searched for primary sources of information about the past.* **4** *Electricity.* denoting or having to do with the inducing circuit, coil, or current in an induction coil or the like. **5** *Chemistry.* **a** characterized by the replacement of a single atom or group. **b** formed by replacing a single atom or group. **6** *Geology.* **a** formed or developed directly from magma: *a primary rock or ore.* **b** *Obsolete.* Archeozoic. **7** *Grammar.* **a** (of word structure) consisting of a single free morpheme (*boy*) or of two or more bound morphemes (*receive*). **b** (of suffixes) added directly to an unanalyzable root. **c** (of tenses in certain older Indo-European languages) expressing present or future time. **8** utilizing the crude products of nature as raw materials: *Some industries also are classed as primary because they use only the crude products of the soil, forest, or mine as their raw materials* (Finch and Trewartha). **9** *Metallurgy.* derived from ore rather than from a combination of ore and scrap or from scrap alone.
—*n.* **1** anything that is first in order, rank, or importance. **2** an election in which members of a political party choose candidates for office; primary election. Primaries are held before the regular election. **3** = primary color. **4** a primary coil or circuit. **5** a heavenly body around which another revolves. **6** = primary feather. **7** a cosmic-ray particle traveling at high velocity that is commonly stopped on entering the earth's atmosphere by collision with an atom of other matter, the collision resulting in the formation of a number of secondary particles.
[< Latin *prīmārius* of the first rank, chief < *prīmus* first. See etym. of doublet **premier.**]

**primary accent, 1** the strongest accent in the pronunciation of a word, as on the first syllable of *sec′re tar′y.* **2** a mark (**′**) used to show this.

**primary atypical pneumonia,** a form of pneumonia, rarely fatal, that is caused by the Eaton agent and associated viruses.

**primary cell,** an electric cell that cannot be recharged electrically. The cells used in flashlights and portable radios are primary cells.

**primary coil,** a coil connected to the source of current through which voltages are induced in the secondary coil, as in a transformer.

**primary color,** a color of a group of colors which, mixed together, will produce all other colors. Red, yellow, and blue are the primary colors in pigments. In light they are red, green, and blue. In psychology, yellow, blue, green, and red are primary colors. *Color television ... is based on three primary colors—red, green, and blue—which can be mixed together so as to produce any visible color* (Kenneth Harwood).

**primary consumer,** *Ecology.* an animal in a food chain, such as a rabbit or deer, that eats grass and other green plants.

**primary crusher,** a machine in which rock is broken down into large pieces before being ground down further.

**primary election,** an election to choose candidates for office from a certain political party: *The letter recommended that Mr. Eisenhower enter* *his name in all Presidential primary elections* (Newsweek).

**primary feather**, one of the large flight feathers growing on the distal section of a bird's wing.

**primary grades**, *U.S.* the first three or four grades of elementary school.

**primary group**, *Sociology.* a group whose members have direct, intimate contact with each other: *By primary groups I mean those characterized by intimate face-to-face association and cooperation* (Ogburn and Nimkoff).

**primary intention**, = first intention.

**primary producer**, *Ecology.* a green plant in a food chain, such as a grass or a tree, that gets energy from the sun and nutrients from the soil, and provides food for primary consumers.

**primary root**, *Botany.* the single root which develops from the embryo itself.

**primary school**, the first three or four grades of the elementary school.

**primary stress**, = primary accent.

**primary structure**, a minimal sculpture.

**primary structurist**, a minimal sculptor.

**primary syphilis**, the first stage of syphilis, indicated by a painless chancre, usually on the genitals.

**primary teeth**, baby teeth or milk teeth.

**primary wave**, an earthquake wave traveling through solids faster than the secondary wave, and causing rocks to vibrate parallel with the wave.

**pri|mate** (prī′mit, -māt), *n.* **1** an archbishop or bishop ranking above all other bishops in a country or church province. SYN: metropolitan. **2** any of the highest order of mammals, including human beings, apes, monkeys, and lemurs. **3** a person who is first in rank or importance; chief; leader. [(definition 1) < Latin *prīmās, -ātis* of first rank (in Medieval Latin, a superior bishop or archbishop) < *prīmus* first; probably influenced by Old French *primat;* (definition 2) < New Latin *Primates,* the order name; (literally) plural of Latin *prīmās* first]

**pri|mate|ship** (prī′mit ship, -māt-), *n.* the position or rank of a church primate.

**pri|ma|tial** (prī mā′shəl), *adj.* of or characteristic of a primate or primateship: *primatial duties.*

**pri|ma|to|log|i|cal** (prī′mə tə loj′ə kəl), *adj.* of or having to do with primatology.

**pri|ma|tol|o|gist** (prī′mə tol′ə jist), *n.* a person skilled in primatology.

**pri|ma|tol|o|gy** (prī′mə tol′ə jē), *n.* the study of the origin, structure, development, and behavior of primates.

**pri|ma|ver|a** (prē′mə vär′ə), *n.* **1** a tall tree of Mexico and Central America whose bright yellow flowers appear in the early spring. **2** its wood, used in cabinetmaking. [< Spanish *primavera* springtime]

**pri|ma|ver|al** (prē′mə vir′əl), *adj.* of or having to do with the early springtime. [< Spanish *primavera* springtime + English *-al*[1]]

***prime**[1] (prīm), *adj., n.* —*adj.* **1** first in rank or importance; chief: *His prime object was to get enough to eat. The community's prime need is a new school.* SYN: principal. **2** *Figurative.* first in time or order; primary; fundamental; original: *the prime causes of war.* SYN: primordial. **3** first in quality; first-rate; excellent: *prime interest rates, a prime cut of meat.* **4** having no common integral divisor but 1 and the number itself: *7, 11, and 13 are prime numbers.* **5** having no common integral divisor but 1: *2 is prime to 9.* **6** ranking high or highest in some scale or rating system: *prime borrowers, prime time on television.* **7** (of beef and veal) being the best grade of meat; having red flesh that is firm, flavorful, and somewhat fatty: *Roughly 88 per cent of the cattle packers ... are slaughtering grades prime and choice* (Wall Street Journal). [partly < Latin *prīmus* first, partly < Old French *prime,* learned borrowing from Latin]

—*n.* **1** the best time; best condition: *A man of forty is in the prime of life.* **2** the best part. **3** *Figurative.* the first part; beginning: *We see how quickly sundry arts mechanical were found out, in the very prime of the world* (Richard Hooker). **4** springtime: *And brought him presents, flowers, if it were prime, Or mellow fruit if it were harvest time* (Edmund Spenser). **5** early manhood or womanhood; youth: *They were now in the happy prime of youth* (Hawthorne). **6** Also, **Prime.** the second of the seven canonical hours, or the service for it, originally fixed for the first hour of the day (beginning at 6 A.M.). **7** = prime number. **8a** one of the equal parts into which a unit is divided, especially one of the sixty minutes in a degree. **b** the mark indicating such a part, also used to distinguish one letter, quantity, etc., from another. B′ is read "B prime." **9** *Music.* **a** the same tone or note in another octave. **b** the octave or octaves between two such tones or notes. **c** the tonic or keynote. **10** the first defensive position in fencing.

[Old English *prīm* (noun definition 6); later, the first period (of the day) < Late Latin *prīma* the first service < Latin *prīma* (*hōra*) first hour (of the Roman day)] —**prime′ness,** *n.*

***prime**[1] definition 8b: A′ is to A as B′ is to B

**prime**[2] (prīm), *v.,* **primed, prim|ing,** *n.* —*v.t.* **1** to prepare by putting something in or on, such as gasoline into a carburetor or cylinder, to facilitate starting the engine. **2** to supply (a gun) with powder, especially to set off the main charge: *Our two combatants had taken the ground, and were priming their pistols* (Tobias Smollett). **3** to cover (a surface) with a first coat of paint, oil, or sizing, so that the finishing coat of paint will not soak in. **4** *Figurative.* to equip (a person) with information, words, arguments, or the like: *to prime a person with a speech.* **5** to pour water into (a pump) to start action.

—*v.i.* **1** to prime a firearm, charge, pump, or the like. **2** (of a boiler or steam engine) to let water pass to the cylinder in the form of spray along with the steam.

—*n.* something that primes; priming.

[origin uncertain. Perhaps related to *prime*[1] as a "first operation" or to *primage* as a "loading."]

**prime conductor**, a conductor that collects and retains positive electricity.

**prime cost**, the cost of the labor and material in production.

**prime factor**, *Mathematics.* a factor that has no other integral factors except itself and 1; factor that is itself a prime number.

**prime|ly** (prīm′lē), *adv. Informal.* exceedingly well; excellently: *primely cooked venison.*

**prime meridian**, the meridian from which the longitude east and west is measured. It passes through Greenwich, England, and its longitude is 0 degrees.

**prime minister**, the chief minister in certain governments. He is the head of the cabinet and the chief of state. SYN: premier.

**prime-min|is|te|ri|al** (prīm′min′ə stir′ē əl), *adj.* of or having to do with a prime minister: *prime-ministerial duties.*

**prime ministership**, the office of a prime minister; prime ministry.

**prime ministry**, the office or position of prime minister.

**prime mover**, **1** the first agent that puts a machine in motion, such as wind or electricity. **2** a machine, such as a water wheel or steam engine, that receives and modifies energy supplied by some natural source: *[The] Windmill is a machine that is a member of the class known as prime movers. It uses the energy of the wind to produce power* (A. D. Longhouse). **3** *Figurative.* a person or thing that starts or does the most for any enterprise. **4** *Philosophy.* that from which all movement derives, but which itself neither moves nor intervenes in the later action.

***prime number**, a whole number that cannot be divided without a remainder by any whole number except itself and 1; prime. 2, 3, 5, 7, 11, and 13 are prime numbers; 4, 6, and 9 are composite numbers.

***prime number**

| | | | | |
|---|---|---|---|---|
| 2 | 13 | 31 | 53 | 73 |
| 3 | 17 | 37 | 59 | 79 |
| 5 | 19 | 41 | 61 | 83 |
| 7 | 23 | 43 | 67 | 89 |
| 11 | 29 | 47 | 71 | 97 |

prime numbers

**prim|er**[1] (prim′ər; *British for 1, 2, 4* prī′mər), *n.* **1** a first book in reading. **2** a first book; beginner's book: *a primer in arithmetic.* **3** either of two sizes of printing type, great primer, 18-point type, or long primer, 10-point type. **4** *Archaic.* a prayer book used to teach children to read. [< Medieval Latin *primarius* (originally) a simplified collection of prayers and services < Latin *prīmārius* adjective, first in rank; see etym. under **primary**]

**prim|er**[2] (prī′mər), *n.* **1** a person or thing that primes. **2** a cap or cylinder containing a little gunpowder, used for firing a charge. **3** a first coat of paint, oil, or sizing: *a plaster or wood primer.* [apparently < *prim*(e)[2] + *-er*[1]]

**prime rate**, the lowest rate of interest charged by banks to large commercial customers with very high credit ratings: *Rates for all other customers are scaled upward from the prime rate* (Wall Street Journal).

**pri|me|ro** (pri mär′ō), *n.* a card game popular in England in the 1500's and 1600's. [apparently alteration of Spanish *primera,* (literally) feminine of *primero* first]

**prime time**, the peak hours of television viewing (in the United States, approximately 6 to 11 p.m.): *The network was ... gambling on soap opera in prime time* (Time). —**prime′-time′,** *adj.*

**pri|meur** (prē mœr′), *n. French.* a fruit or vegetable before its ordinary season.

**pri|me|val** (prī mē′vəl), *adj.* **1** of or having something to do with the first age or ages, especially of the world: *In its primeval state the earth was without any forms of life. A semi-mystical attitude is that not only space but also time itself began with the primeval atom* (Time). **2** ancient: *primeval forests untouched by the ax.* SYN: prehistoric. [< Latin *prīmaevus* early in life (< *prīmus* first + *aevum* age) + English *-al*[1]] —**pri|me′val|ly,** *adv.*

**pri|mi|done** (prī′mi don), *n.* = Mysoline. [< *p*(y)*rimid*(ine) + *-one*]

**pri|mine** (prī′min), *n. Botany.* the outer integument of an ovule. [< French *primine* (originally) the outer coat < Latin *prīmus* first + French *-ine* -ine[1]]

**prim|ing** (prī′ming), *n.* **1** powder or other material used to set fire to an explosive. **2** a first coat of paint, oil, or sizing.

**pri|mip|a|ra** (prī mip′ər ə), *n., pl.* **-a|ras, -a|rae** (-ə rē). **1** a woman who has borne only one child. **2** a woman who is having her first baby. [< Latin *prīmipara* < *prīmus* first + *-para,* feminine of *-parus* < *parere* to bear young]

**pri|mi|par|i|ty** (prī′mə par′ə tē), *n.* primiparous condition.

**pri|mip|a|rous** (prī mip′ər əs), *adj.* bearing a child, or young, for the first time.

**prim|i|tive** (prim′ə tiv), *adj., n.* —*adj.* **1** of early times; of long ago: *Primitive people often lived in caves.* SYN: prehistoric. **2** first of the kind: *primitive Christians.* **3** very simple; such as people had early in human history: *A primitive way of making a fire is by rubbing two sticks together. A trip to Africa opened their eyes to primitive art* (Time). **4** original; primary: *a primitive word.* **5** *Biology.* **a** primordial. **b** representing or related to an ancient group or species.

—*n.* **1** an artist belonging to an early period, especially before the Renaissance. **2a** an artist who does not use the techniques of perspective, shading, or the like in painting. **b** any artist who lacks artistic training or sophistication: *The Civil War photographers ... were often called primitives, meaning that they were innocent of a sense of themselves as fine artists* (John Szarkowski). **c** a work produced by such an artist: *The shows include an exhibition of modern French and Dutch primitives* (New Yorker). **3** a person living in a primitive society or in primitive times. **4** an algebraic or geometrical expression from which another is derived. **5** a word from which another is derived.

[< Latin *prīmitīvus* < *prīmitiae* first things, first fruits < *prīmus* first] —**prim′i|tive|ly,** *adv.* —**prim′i|tive|ness,** *n.*

**primitive area**, *U.S.* an area of forestland set aside to preserve the natural landscape under the supervision of the Forest Service.

**Primitive Methodist**, a member of a Methodist sect formed in the early 1800's in England.

**prim|i|tiv|ism** (prim′ə tə viz′əm), *n.* preference for the primitive, especially in art or religion: *Primitivism, for example, as illustrated by Picasso's concern with Negro art* (Atlantic).

**prim|i|tiv|ist** (prim′ə tə vist), *n., adj.* —*n.* a person who has a preference for the primitive, especially in art or religion.

—*adj.* **1** of or having to do with primitive art or artists: *Jacob Epstein's primitivist work was not his best; he was really a portrait sculptor* (New Yorker). **2** = primitivistic.

**prim|i|tiv|is|tic** (prim′ə tə vis′tik), *adj.* of or characteristic of primitivism or primitivists.

**prim|i|tiv|i|ty** (prim′ə tiv′ə tē), *n.* primitive quality, character, or condition.

**pri|mo**[1] (prē′mō), *n. Italian.* the first or principal part in a musical duet or trio.

**pri|mo**[2] (prē′mō), *adv. Latin.* first of all: *My eiderdown fascinates me, primo because we are having cold winter weather ...* (P. N. Furbank).

**pri|mo|gen|i|tor** (prī′mə jen′ə tər), *n.* **1** an ancestor; forefather. **2** the earliest ancestor. [< Late Latin *prīmōgenitor* < Latin *prīmō* at first + *genitor* begetter; patterned on *prīmōgenitus;* see etym. under **primogeniture**]

**pri|mo|gen|i|ture** (prī′mə jen′ə chůr, -chər), *n.* **1** the condition or fact of being the first-born among the children of the same parents. **2** the right or rule by which the eldest son inherits his father's land and buildings; inheritance by the first-born. [< Medieval Latin *primogenitura* < Latin *prīmōgenitus* first-born < *prīmō* at first (< *prīmus* first) + *gignere* to beget, produce]

**pri|mor|di|al** (prī môr′dē əl), *adj.* **1** existing at the very beginning; primitive: *primordial rock. Primordial man could have had little or no tradition before the development of speech* (H. G. Wells). **2** original; elementary: *primordial laws.* [< Latin *prīmōrdiālis* < *prīmōrdium* the beginning; see etym. under **primordium**] —**pri|mor′di|al|ly**, *adv.*

**primordial broth**, = primordial soup: *Threadlike filament of organic matter resembling decomposed plant tissue is another kind of fossil that ... might conceivably be polymerized abiotic molecules from the "primordial broth"* (Scientific American).

**primordial meristem**, *Botany.* the actively dividing cells lying behind the root cap.

**primordial soup**, the mixture of chemicals which gave rise to life on earth; prebiotic soup; protobiotic soup: *Polymers of amino acids forming primitive proteins are formed much more readily in those dramatic laboratory reconstructions of the primordial "soup" than are crude nucleic acids constructed from nucleotides* (New Scientist).

**pri|mor|di|um** (prī môr′dē əm), *n., pl.* **-di|a** (-dē ə). **1** the very beginning; earliest stage. **2** *Embryology.* the first cells in the earliest stages of the development of an organ or structure. [< Latin *prīmōrdium,* (literally) neuter of *prīmōrdius* original < *prīmus* first + *ōrdīrī* to begin]

**pri|most** (prē′most), *n.* an unripened Norwegian soft cheese made from whey. [< Norwegian *primost* < *prim* a cheese spread + *ost* cheese]

**primp** (primp), *v.t.* to dress (oneself) for show; prink: *to primp oneself for a party, to primp up the hair.* —*v.i.* to dress carefully. [apparently variation of *prim,* verb]

**prim|rose** (prim′rōz), *n., adj.* —*n.* **1** any one of a large group of plants with flowers of various colors, growing chiefly in the north temperate regions of Europe and Asia. The primrose is a perennial belonging to the primrose family. There are many kinds, making up a genus of plants. The common primrose of Europe is pale yellow. **2** = evening primrose. **3** the flower of any of these plants. **4** a pale yellow.
—*adj.* **1** pale-yellow. **2** *Figurative.* of or like a primrose; gay; pleasant. SYN: flowery.
[< Old French *primerose,* adaptation of Medieval Latin *prima rosa* primula; (literally) first rose]

***primrose family**, a group of dicotyledonous herbs found chiefly in northern temperate regions, grown for their showy flowers. The family includes the primrose, cyclamen, shooting star, brookweed, and pimpernel.

***primrose family**

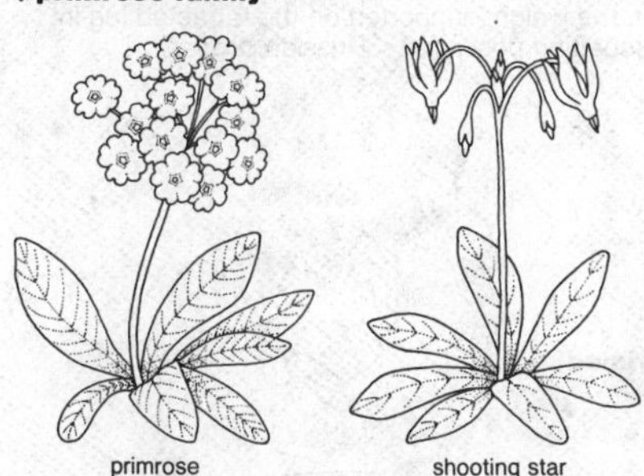


**primrose path**, **1** a pleasant or easy way. **2** a path of pleasure: *He also can try to wheedle his way out of the arms of the anxious lady who has led him down the primrose path* (New York Times).

**primrose yellow**, pale yellow.

**prim|u|la** (prim′yə lə), *n.* = primrose (def. 1). [< Medieval Latin *primula veris* cowslip; later, daisy; (literally) firstling of spring]

**prim|u|la|ceous** (prim′yə lā′shəs), *adj.* belonging to the primrose family. [< New Latin *Primulaceae* the family name]

**pri|mum mo|bi|le** (prī′məm mob′ə lē), **1** = prime mover: *Man may be unique ... in a way that has nothing to do with our being the wound-up and running-down toy of some ancient god or primum mobile* (New Yorker). **2** (in medieval astronomy) the sphere of the fixed stars. [< Medieval Latin *primum mobile* (literally) first moving thing]

**pri|mus** (prī′məs), *n., pl.* **-mus|es.** the senior bishop of the Scottish Episcopal Church. He is chosen by the other bishops, presides at all their meetings, and has ceremonial privileges, but no metropolitan authority. [< Latin *prīmus* first]

**Pri|mus** (prī′məs), *n. Trademark.* a portable stove which burns vaporized oil.

**pri|mus in|ter pa|res** (prī′məs in′tər pãr′ēz), *Latin.* first among equals: *The idea of the Soviet Communist Party as primus inter pares was not abandoned for ten years* (Atlantic).

**prim|y** (prī′mē), *adj.* at the prime or best stage: *a violet in the youth of primy nature* (Shakespeare). [< *prim*(e)[1] + *-y*[1]]

**prin.**, **1a** principal. **b** principally. **2** principle.

**prince** (prins), *n.* **1a** a male member of a royal family. **b** a son of a king or queen; son of a king's or queen's son. **2** a sovereign. **3** the ruler of a small state subordinate to a king or emperor. **4** the English equivalent of certain titles of nobility of varying importance or rank in other countries. **5** *Figurative.* a man of highest rank; the greatest or best of a group; chief: *a merchant prince, a prince of artists. That prince of pioneers* [*Daniel Boone*] (Francis Parkman). [< Old French *prince* < Latin *prīnceps, -cipis* chief < *prīmus* first + *-cip,* stem related to *capere* to take]

***Prince Al|bert** (al′bərt), a long, double-breasted coat, worn by men. [American English, probably < *Prince Albert* of England, husband of Queen Victoria]

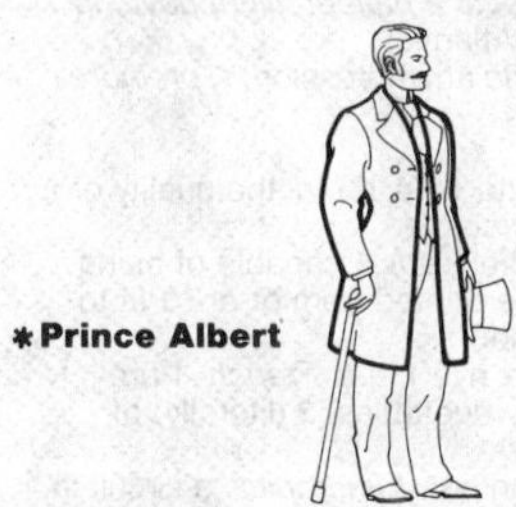

***Prince Albert**

**prince-bish|op** (prins′bish′əp), *n.* a bishop who is also a prince, especially formerly a German bishop who had the temporal authority and possessions of a bishopric. [translation of German *Fürstbischof*]

**Prince Charles spaniel** (chärlz), a black, tan, and white variety of the English toy spaniel.

**Prince Charming**, **1** the fairy-tale prince who marries Cinderella. **2** *Figurative.* an ideal type of man; a perfect lover: *... a dance palace where young Cinderellas could meet their Prince Charmings* (New York Times).

**prince consort**, a prince who is the husband of a queen or empress ruling in her own right; one who is a prince in his own right or (occasionally) one granted princely status by the marriage.

**prince|dom** (prins′dəm), *n.* **1** the lands ruled by a prince. **2** the title, rank, position, or dignity of a prince.
**princedoms**, principalities, an order of angels: *The angelic hosts, the archangelic pomps, thrones, dominations, princedoms, rank on rank* (Elizabeth Barrett Browning).

**prince|kin** (prins′kin), *n.* = princeling.

**prince|let** (prins′lit), *n.* = princeling.

**prince|li|ness** (prins′lē nis), *n.* princely quality or condition.

**prince|ling** (prins′ling), *n.* a young, little, or petty prince.

**prince|ly** (prins′lē), *adj.,* **-li|er, -li|est,** *adv.* —*adj.* **1** of a prince or his rank; royal: *princely power, the princely families of Europe.* **2** like a prince; noble; stately: *a princely manner.* SYN: courtly. **3** *Figurative.* fit for a prince: *Some presidents of businesses earn princely salaries.* SYN: magnificent, sumptuous.
—*adv.* in the manner of a prince; royally.

**Prince of Darkness**, the Devil; Satan.

**Prince of Peace**, Jesus Christ.

**Prince of Wales**, the title conferred on the eldest son, or heir apparent, of the British sovereign.

**prin|ceps** (prin′seps), *n., pl.* **-ci|pes** (-sə pēz). **1** among the ancient Romans: **a** a title for a civil or military official. **b** the title under which Augustus Caesar and his successors ruled the Roman Empire. **2** a chief or lord among the ancient Teutons, generally corresponding to the Anglo-Saxon alderman. [< Latin *prīnceps, -cipis* chief; see etym. under **prince**]

**prince regent**, a prince who acts as the regent of a country.

**prince royal**, the oldest son of a king or queen.

**Prince Ru|pert's metal** (rü′pėrts), = Prince's metal. [< *Prince Rupert,* 1619-1682, British soldier and inventor, grandson of James I of England]

**prince's-feath|er** (prin′siz feᴛʜ′ər), *n.* a tall, handsome annual garden plant of the amaranth family with thick, feathery red spikes.

**prince|ship** (prins′ship), *n.* **1** the position, rank, or dignity of a prince. **2** the rule of a prince.

**Prince's metal**, an alloy of about three parts of copper and one of zinc, resembling gold in color and once used in cheap jewelry. [< *Prince* Rupert; see etym. under **Prince Rupert's metal**]

**prin|cess** (prin′ses, -sis), *n., adj.* —*n.* **1** a daughter of a king or queen; daughter of a king's or queen's son. **2** the wife or widow of a prince. **3** a woman having the rank of a prince.
—*adj.* = princesse.
[< Old French *princesse,* feminine of *prince* prince]

**prin|cesse** (prin ses′; prin′ses, -sis), *adj., adv.* one-piece and close-fitting with a flaring skirt and vertical seams: *a princesse coat. Her dress was white linen, cut princesse over the hips, long and full-skirted* (New Yorker). [< French *princesse*]

**prin|cess|ly** (prin′ses lē, -sis-), *adj.* of, like, or befitting a princess: *She is handsome ... and her manners are princessly* (Byron).

**princess marble**, = sodalite.

**Princess Royal**, the title conferred on the oldest daughter of the British sovereign.

**princess tree**, a Chinese tree of medium height, with downy leaves and fragrant violet flowers, which has become naturalized in the eastern coastal United States.

**prin|ci|pal** (prin′sə pəl), *adj., n.* —*adj.* most important; chief; main: *Chicago is the principal city of Illinois.* SYN: cardinal, foremost, prime, leading, prominent.
—*n.* **1** the chief person; one who gives orders: *She is one of the principals of the Royal Ballet* (Maclean's). **2a** the head, or one of the heads, of an elementary or secondary school: *The principal told the teachers to dismiss school during the heavy snowstorm.* **b** the head of a college, especially in Great Britain. **3** a sum of money on which interest is paid. **4** money or property from which income or interest is received. **5** a person who hires or authorizes another person to act for him: *Mr. Smith does the business of renting the houses for Mr. Jones, his principal.* **6** a person directly responsible for a crime. **7** a person responsible for the payment of a debt that another person has endorsed. **8** *Music.* an organ stop whose tones are of the same quality as the open diapason but an octave higher. **9** anything of chief importance, such as a main truss or rafter in a building: *Our lodgings ... Shook as the earth did quake; the very principals did seem to rend, And all to topple* (Shakespeare). **10** each of the combatants in a duel.
[< Old French *principal,* learned borrowing from Latin *prīncipālis* first; later, princely (in Late Latin, noun, overseer) < *prīnceps* chief; see etym. under **prince**]
► **Principal, principle** are often confused in spelling even though they have entirely different meanings. *Principal* as an adjective means chief (*a principal ally*) and as a noun, chief person or head (*the school principal*). *Principle* is used only as a noun, meaning a basic truth or belief (*the principles of democracy*), or a rule of conduct (*Good character depends upon high principles*).

**principal boy**, *British.* a female player who takes the leading male part in a pantomime.

**prin|ci|pal|i|ty** (prin′sə pal′ə tē), *n., pl.* **-ties. 1** a small state or country ruled by a prince: *In that province* [*Normandy*] *they found a mighty state, which gradually extended its influence over the neighbouring principalities of Brittany and Maine* (Macaulay). **2** the country from which a prince gets his title. **3** supreme power: *Josephus ... calls the Commonwealth of the Hebrews a Theocracy, because the principality was in God only* (Milton). **4** chief place or rank: *Christ hath the primacy of order and the principality of influence* (Thomas Manton).
**principalities**, the order of angels next above the powers: *For we wrestle not against flesh and blood, but against principalities* (Ephesians 6:12).

**prin|ci|pal|ly** (prin′sə pə lē, -sə plē), *adv.* for the most part; above all; chiefly: *What I principally insist on, is due execution* (Jonathan Swift). SYN: mainly. See syn. under **especially**.

**principal parts**, the main parts of the verb or a set of verb forms from which all the other forms of the verb can be derived. In Modern English the principal parts are the infinitive, past tense or preterit, and past participle. *Examples:* go, went, gone; do, did, done; drive, drove, driven; push, pushed, pushed.

**prin|ci|pal|ship** (prin′sə pəl ship), *n.* the position or office of a principal.

**prin|ci|pate** (prin′sə pāt), *n.* **1** a chief place or authority: *Under two metaphors the principate of the whole church was promised* (Isaac Barrow). **2** = principality. **3** the period of the ancient Roman Empire when Augustus and his successors ruled as republican heads of the Senate. [< Latin *prīncipātus, -ūs* the first place (in an army or state) < *prīnceps, -cipis* chief + *-ātus* -ate[3]; see etym. under **prince**]

**Pronunciation Key:** hat, āge, cãre, fär; let, ēqual, tėrm; it, īce; hot, ōpen, ôrder; oil, out; cup, pu̇t, rüle; child; long; thin; ᴛʜen; zh, measure; ə represents **a** in about, **e** in taken, **i** in pencil, **o** in lemon, **u** in circus.

**prin|ci|pe** (*Italian* prēn′chē pā; *Spanish* prēn′thē-pā, -sē-; *Portuguese* prēɴ′si pə), *n., pl. Italian* **-pi** (-pē); *Spanish* **-pes** (-pās); *Portuguese* **-pes** (-pəs). *Italian, Spanish, Portuguese.* a prince.

**prin|ci|pes|sa** (prēn′chē pās′sä), *n., pl.* **-se** (-sā). *Italian.* a princess.

**prin|cip|i|a** (prin sip′ē ə), *n.* plural of **principium**.

**prin|cip|i|um** (prin sip′ē əm), *n., pl.* **-i|a**. a principle, especially a first principle or element. [< Latin *prīncipium* beginning, origin < *prīnceps, -cipis* first, chief; see etym. under **prince**]

**prin|ci|ple** (prin′sə pəl), *n., v.,* **-pled, -pling**. —*n.* **1** a truth that is a foundation for other truths; fundamental, primary, or general truth: *the principles of democratic government.* **2** a fundamental belief: *religious principles.* SYN: tenet. **3** a rule of action or conduct: *I make it a principle to save some money each week.* SYN: precept. **4** uprightness; honor: *Washington was a man of principle. Not only was it right as a matter of principle to bring the question ... out into the open, they said; it also was good politics* (Newsweek). SYN: integrity. **5** a rule of science explaining how something works: *the principle of the lever, the principle by which a machine acts. A jet engine is based on a principle known since ancient times.* **6** the method of operation, as of a machine. **7** a first cause or force; source; origin: *Thales said that the first principle of all things was water* (John Stuart Blackie). **8** one of the elements that compose a substance, especially one that gives some special quality or effect: *the bitter principle in a drug.* SYN: constituent, ingredient, component. **9** an original tendency or faculty; natural or innate disposition. **10 Principle**. God (in the belief of Christian Scientists).

—*v.t. Obsolete.* to teach the basic facts of a subject; impress; indoctrinate.

**in principle**, as regards the general truth or rule: *to approve something in principle.*

**on principle, a** according to a certain principle: *There was a time when I could not read Pope, but disliked him on principle* (James Russell Lowell). **b** for reasons of right conduct: *Outward acts, done on principle, create inward habits* (Cardinal Newman).

[< Old French *principe,* learned borrowing from Latin *prīncipium* principium; pattern of *participle*]

►See **principal** for usage note.

**prin|ci|pled** (prin′sə pəld), *adj.* having principles; that is so or such on principle: *She was firm and very principled.*

**-principled**, *combining form.* having a ____ principle or principles: *High-principled = having high principles.*

**principle of relativity**, = relativity (def. 4).

**prin|cock** (prin′kok), *n. Obsolete.* a pert or conceited young fellow. [origin uncertain]

**prin|cox** (prin′koks), *n. Obsolete.* princock.

**prink** (pringk), *v.t.* to dress for show; decorate: *A sixteen-storey tower packed with families and nattily prinked out in rectangles of daffodil and grey* (Punch). —*v.i.* to fuss about appearance. [origin uncertain. Perhaps related to **prank**[2]. Compare German *prangen.*] —**prink′er**, *n.*

**print** (print), *v., n.,* —*v.t.* **1** to use something, such as type, blocks, or plates, and ink or dye to stamp (words, pictures, or designs) on paper, cloth, or the like: *The company printed its name and address on all of its bills.* **2** to use type or plates and ink to stamp letters, words, or designs on (paper, cloth, or the like): *Who prints this newspaper? Some presses print rolls rather than sheets of paper.* **3** to cause to be printed; publish: *to print books. Most newspapers are printed daily.* **4** to write (something) in words or letters that are not connected by lines and look like printing type instead of writing with flowing strokes and the letters joined: *Print your name clearly.* **5** to mark (cloth or paper) with designs or patterns: *This machine prints wallpaper.* **6a** to make (marks) by pressure; stamp. **b** to make marks on; produce marks or figures on by pressure; impress: *Little footsteps lightly print the ground* (Thomas Gray). **7** *Figurative.* to fix (in the heart, mind, or memory); impress: *The scene is printed in my memory.* **8** to produce a photograph by light through (a negative).

—*v.i.* **1** to produce, as books or newspapers by a printing press. **2** to make letters or words the way they look in print instead of in writing. **3** to take an impression from type or plates. **4** (of type, a block, or plate) to give an impression on paper, cloth, or the like. **5** to be a printer; use a press in printing.

—*n.* **1** words in ink stamped by type: *This book has clear print.* **2** printed condition: *to put an article into print.* **3** a printed publication; newspaper or magazine: *the story they had read ... in the public prints* (Booth Tarkington). **4** an edition or impression of a book, newspaper, or magazine, made at one time. **5a** cloth with a pattern printed on it: *She has two dresses made of print.* **b** a dress made of such cloth: *She wore a cotton print.* **6** the pattern or design so printed. **7** a printed picture or design: *prints of race horses.* **8** a mark made by pressing or stamping: *the print of a foot in the ground.* **9** something that prints; stamp; die. **10** something that has been marked or shaped by pressing or stamping. **11** a photograph produced from a negative.

**in print, a** in printed form: *'Tis pleasant, sure, to see one's name in print* (Byron). **b** still available for purchase from the publisher: *Author and Title Entries of Books in Print and for Sale* (The American Catalogue).

**out of print**, no longer sold by the publisher: *Many books that are out of print are reissued in paperback form.*

**print out**, to produce (information or output) in printed or readable form: *The computer quickly prints out which defects a patient might have, in order of probability* (Atlantic).

[< Old French *priente* an impression < *preindre* to press]

**print.**, printing.

**print|a|bil|i|ty** (prin′tə bil′ə tē), *n.* the quality or condition of being printable.

**print|a|ble** (prin′tə bəl), *adj.* **1** capable of being printed. **2** that can be printed from or on. **3** fit to be printed or published.

**prin|ta|nier** (praɴ tȧ nyā′), *adj. French.* **1** prepared with chopped vegetables. **2** (literally) of spring.

**print|ed circuit** (prin′tid), *Electronics.* a circuit in which components or connections are printed, painted, or sprayed, on an insulating surface with a conducting material such as silver oxide.

**print|er** (prin′tər), *n.* **1** a person whose business or work is printing or setting type. **2** an instrument or appliance used for printing. **3** a computer printout mechanism.

**printer's devil**, a young helper or errand boy in a printing shop.

**printer's mark** or **device** = colophon (def. 1).

**printer's ream**, = perfect ream.

**print|er|y** (prin′tər ē), *n., pl.* **-er|ies**. **1** a shop with printing presses. **2** = printworks.

**print|ing** (prin′ting), *n.* **1** the act or process of producing written matter or pictures, such as books, newspapers, or magazines, by stamping in ink or dye from movable type, plates, or blocks: *The printing of the city's newspapers is not considered a part of the printing industry proper, since the big newspapers set their own type and have their own presses* (New York Times). **2** printed words or pictures: *The printing in that book is not very clear.* **3** all the copies printed at one time: *The first printing was swallowed up before publication* (New Yorker). **4** letters made like those in print.

**printing ink**, ink used in typographic printing.

**printing out**, *Photography.* the act or process of printing an image on a kind of sensitized paper so that it is visible and complete in detail, and need not be brought out by developing; printout.

**printing press**, a machine for printing from types, plates, or blocks.

**print|less** (print′lis), *adj.* making, leaving, or showing no print or trace.

**print|mak|er** (print′mā′kər), *n.* a person who makes a picture or design printed from a block or plate.

**print|mak|ing** (print′mā′king), *n.* the art or process of printing pictures or designs from a block or plate.

**print|out** (print′out′), *n.* **1a** the printed output of a computer or a printing press: *The computer's results can be presented in any of several different forms. One form of printout consists of all the numbers describing the flow in each frame* (Scientific American). **b** the act of producing such an output. **2** = printing out.

**print paper**, paper of a kind or class used for printing on.

**print shop**, **1** a shop where printing is done. **2** a shop where printed pictures are sold.

**print|works** (print′wėrks′), *n.* an establishment for printing textiles, such as calico.

**pri|on** (prī′on), *n.* any one of four similar petrels of the Southern Hemisphere whose bills are edged with projections resembling the teeth of a saw. [< Greek *priōn* a saw]

**pri|or**[1] (prī′ər), *adj.* coming before; earlier: *prior generations of man. I can't go with you because I have a prior engagement.* SYN: See syn. under **previous**.

**prior to**, coming before in time, order, or importance; earlier than; before: *An agreement was reached prior to the outbreak of the war. The thought is always prior to the fact* (Emerson).

[< Latin *prior, -ōris* former, earlier, superior]

**pri|or**[2] (prī′ər), *n.* **1** the head of a priory or monastery for men. Priors usually rank below abbots. **2** the superior of a house of canons regular or of friars. **3** a chief magistrate, such as in the medieval republic of Florence. [Old English *prior* < Medieval Latin, noun use of Latin *prior, -ōris* prior, superior]

**prior art**, earlier patents or inventions that bar a proposed invention from becoming patentable.

**pri|or|ate** (prī′ər it), *n.* **1** the office, rank, or time of service of a prior. **2** = priory.

**pri|or|ess** (prī′ər is), *n.* a woman at the head of a convent or priory for women. Prioresses usually rank below abbesses.

**pri|or|i|tize** (prī ôr′ə tīz, -or′-), *v.t.,* **-tized, -tiz|ing**. to arrange in order of importance: *The persons attending the Quarterly Parish meeting Wednesday night all prioritized these goals* (Elizabeth Kent). [< *priority* + *-ize*]

**pri|or|i|ty** (prī ôr′ə tē, -or′-), *n., pl.* **-ties**. **1** the state or fact of being earlier in time: *The priority of the visit of the Norsemen to America to that of Columbus has been established.* **2** the act of fact or coming before in order or importance: *Fire engines and ambulances have priority over other traffic.* SYN: precedence. **3** a government rating giving preference to persons or things in order of their importance to national defense or other essential affairs of state: *A system of priorities for spending on weapons and equipment in the next decade has been sketched by the defence department* (Vancouver Sun). **4** a preferential position allotted to any project, research, development, or the like, which gives it first claim to the necessary resources.

**priority mail**, *U.S.* a class of mail consisting of first-class matter weighing over 12 ounces and airmail weighing over 8 ounces.

**prior restraint**, *U.S.* a court injunction prohibiting a newspaper or magazine in advance from publishing an article whose contents may in the opinion of the court endanger due process, national security, or the like: *Lawyers for the newspapers told the judge this morning that they regarded "prior restraint" ... as clearly unconstitutional* (Martin Waldron).

**pri|or|ship** (prī′ər ship), *n.* the office, rank, or time of service of a prior.

**pri|o|ry** (prī′ər ē), *n., pl.* **-ries**. **1** a religious house governed by a prior or prioress. A priory is often, but not necessarily, dependent on an abbey. **2** = priorate. [Middle English *priorie* < Anglo-French, apparently learned borrowing from Medieval Latin *prioria* < *prior* prior]

**prise** (prīz), *v.t.,* **prised, pris|ing**, *n. Especially British.* prize[4].

***pris|iad|ka** (pris yäd′kə), *n.* a step of Slavic folk dancing, in which the legs are alternately kicked out, the weight supported on the retracted leg in a squatting position. [< Russian *prisyadka*]

***prisiadka**

***prism** (priz′əm), *n.* **1** a solid whose bases or ends have the same size and shape and are parallel to one another, and each of whose sides has two pairs of parallel edges. A six-sided pencil before it is sharpened has the shape of one kind of prism. **2** a transparent solid, often of glass, having the shape of a prism, usually with three-sided ends. A prism separates white light passing through it into the colors of the rainbow. **3** a crystal form consisting of three or more planes parallel to the vertical axis of the crystal. [< Late Latin *prisma* < Greek *prîsma, -atos* (originally) a thing sawed off < *prīzein* to saw, earlier *prīein*]

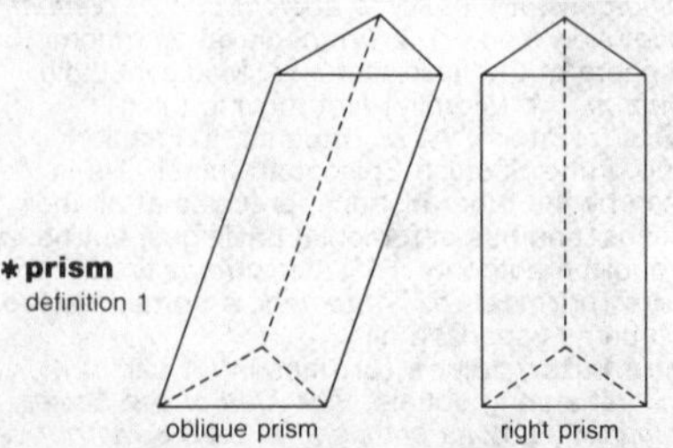


***prism**
definition 1

**pris|mat|ic** (priz mat′ik), *adj.* **1** of or like a prism: *These hoods were fitted with prismatic lenses having their broad bases outward* (Scientific

American). **2** formed by a transparent prism. **3** varied in color; brilliant. **SYN**: polychrome. [< Greek *prîsma, -atos* prism + English *-ic*] —**pris-mat′i|cal|ly**, *adv.*

**pris|mat|i|cal** (priz mat′ə kəl), *adj.* = prismatic.

**prismatic colors**, the seven colors formed when white light is passed through a prism; red, orange, yellow, green, blue, indigo, and violet. These are the colors of the spectrum.

**prismatic layer**, the middle layer of the shell of most mollusks.

**pris|ma|toid** (priz′mə toid), *n.* a polyhedron whose vertices lie in two parallel lines.

**prism binoculars**, binoculars in which two pairs of triangular prisms are introduced to shorten the length of the apparatus and form an erect image.

**pris|moid** (priz′moid), *n.* a solid like a prism except that one end is smaller than the other. [< *prism* + *-oid*]

**pris|moi|dal** (priz moi′dəl), *adj.* of or having to do with the form of a prismoid.

**pris|my** (priz′mē), *adj.* = prismatic.

**pris|on** (priz′ən), *n., v.* —*n.* **1** a public building in which criminals are confined; jail or penitentiary: *Burglars are put in prison.* **2** any place where a person or animal is shut up against his will: *The small apartment was a prison to the big dog from the farm.* **3** captivity or confinement; imprisonment.
—*v.t.* = imprison.
[Middle English *prisun,* alteration of Old French *preson* (originally) act of detaining < Latin *prehēnsiō, -ōnis* a seizing, arrest < *prehendere* seize] —**pris′on|like′**, *adj.*

**prison camp**, a camp used for the confinement of prisoners, especially prisoners of war or political prisoners.

**pris|on|er** (priz′ə nər, priz′nər), *n.* **1** a person who is under arrest or held in a jail or prison. **2** a person who is kept shut up against his will or who is not free to move: (*Figurative.*) *An untimely ague stay'd me a prisoner in my chamber* (Shakespeare). **3** a person taken by the enemy in war; prisoner of war: *The enemy prisoners were interned in prison camps.*

**prisoner of conscience**, a political prisoner: *A great many prisoners of conscience, it claims, are sent with or without trial "to the so-called special psychiatric hospitals, where they are given forcible treatment for their supposed mental ailments"* (London Times).

**prisoner of war**, a person taken by the enemy in war, especially a member of the armed forces who is captured by the enemy. *Abbr:* POW (no periods).

**prisoners' base**, an old game for children, a form of tag.

**prison house**, **1** a house or place of imprisonment; prison. **2** imprisonment; confinement: (*Figurative.*) *to escape from the prison house of London streets and factories* (London Daily Chronicle).

**pris|sy** (pris′ē), *adj.,* **-si|er, -si|est.** *U.S. Informal.* **1** too precise and fussy: *For nearly three hours—poised, precise, prissy—[he] detailed his secret career as a Communist and a spy* (Time). **2** too easily shocked; overnice: *a prissy mama's boy.* [American English, perhaps humorous alteration of *precise,* or *precious*] —**pris′si|ly**, *adv.* —**pris′si|ness**, *n.*

**pris|tane** (pris′tān), *n.* a complex hydrocarbon that is a product of the breakdown of chlorophyll and is found together with phytane in oil-bearing rocks: *Certain hydrocarbons, such as the branched-chain compounds phytane and pristane, can if found be taken to be definite evidence of life* (New Scientist). *Formula:* $C_{19}H_{40}$ [< Latin *pristis* shark, whale (because the substance was originally found in the fats of large sea animals) + *-ane*]

**pris|tine** (pris′tēn, -tin, -tīn), *adj.* as it was in its earliest time or state; original; primitive: *The colors of the paintings inside the pyramid had kept their pristine freshness in spite of their age. Much of Congress' effort in the security field since 1946 has been spent in the endeavor to retain the pristine secrecy of atomic energy information* (Bulletin of Atomic Scientists). **SYN**: primeval, primordial. [< Latin *pristinus* < *prīs-*, stem related to *prīmus* first] —**pris′tine|ly**, *adv.*

**prith|ee** (priᴛʜ′ē), *interj. Archaic.* I pray thee; I ask you: *Prithee, come hither. Prithee, who art thou?* [earlier *preythe* (literally) reduction of (*I*) *pray thee*]

**prit|tle-prat|tle** (prit′əl prat′əl), *n.* empty, trifling talk; chatter. [varied reduplication of *prattle*]

**priv.**, privative.

**pri|va|cy** (prī′və sē; *British also* priv′ə sē), *n., pl.* **-cies. 1** the condition of being private; being away from others; seclusion: *in the privacy of one's home.* **SYN**: solitude. **2** the absence of publicity; secrecy: *He told me his reasons in strict privacy.* **SYN**: concealment. **3** a private matter: *So few of the new generation seemed aware that there were any privacies left to respect* (Edith Wharton).

**privacies**, private places; places of retreat: *Beautiful glooms ... Wildwood privacies* (Sidney Lanier).

**pri|vat|do|cent** (prē vät′dō tsent′), *n., pl.* **-do|cen|ten** (-dō tsen′tən). (in German universities) a teacher or lecturer recognized by the university, but paid by students' fees. [< German *Privatdocent* < *privat* private (because he was not on the state payroll) + *Docent,* or *Dozent* teacher < Latin *docēns, -entis,* present participle of *docēre* to teach]

**pri|vat|do|zent** (prē vät′dō tsent′), *n., pl.* **-do|zen|ten** (-dō tsen′tən). = privatdocent.

**pri|vate** (prī′vit), *adj., n.* —*adj.* **1** not for the public; for just a few special people or for one: *a private road, a private house, a private secretary.* **2** not public; personal; individual: *the private life of a famous person, my private opinion, private property. A diary is a private journal.* **3** secret; confidential: *News reached her through private channels. He put the purse in a private pocket.* **4** secluded: *some private corner.* **SYN**: isolated. **5** alone: *He wishes to be private.* **SYN**: solitary. **6** having no public office: *a private citizen.* **7** operating or working independently: *a private educational institution, a private investigator.*
—*n.* **1** a common soldier, not an officer; a soldier or marine of the lowest rank: *His brother was promoted from private to corporal last week. Abbr:* Pvt. **2** *Obsolete.* a private citizen. **3** *Obsolete.* a private or personal matter.
**in private**, **a** not publicly: *They do desire some speech with you in private* (Ben Jonson). **b** secretly: *The rebels met in private to plot against the government. Confess they do, but not greatly in private* (George Sandys).
**privates**, the external sex organs; genitals.
[< Latin *prīvātus* apart from the public life, private, past participle of *prīvāre* deprive, free, release from < *prīvus* one's own, single, individual. See etym. of doublet **privy**.] —**pri′vate|ly**, *adv.* —**pri′vate|ness**, *n.*

**private bank**, a bank conducted by an individual or group of individuals on an unincorporated basis.

**private bill**, (in the House of Representatives and the House of Commons) a bill or act affecting the interests of a particular individual, place, or corporation only.

**private detective**, a detective who is employed by private citizens for certain specified lawful purposes; detective not on the public payroll.

**private enterprise**, **1** the business of a person, company, or store, of making and selling things, as contrasted with government control; free enterprise: *And there are those of us who feel the Government has already eaten too much of the pie of private enterprise—to the point of indigestion* (Wall Street Journal). **2** an economic system based on such individual enterprise.

**pri|va|teer** (prī′və tir′), *n., v.* —*n.* **1** an armed ship owned by private persons and holding a government commission to attack and capture enemy ships: *There were perhaps 3,700 scattered privateers serving as the great bulk of the American Navy* (Newsweek). **2** the commander of a privateer or one of its crew.
—*v.i.* to cruise as a privateer.
[< *privat*(e) + *-eer*]

**pri|va|teers|man** (prī′və tirz′mən), *n., pl.* **-men.** an officer or sailor of a privateer.

**private eye**, *Slang.* a private detective.

**private first class**, a soldier or marine ranking next below a corporal and next above a private. He wears an insigne of one chevron. *Abbr:* Pfc.

**pri|vate-la|bel** (prī′vit lā′bəl), *adj.* bearing the brand or label of the company offering it for retail sale rather than the brand of the manufacturer or processor: *private-label merchandise.*

**private law**, that branch of the law which deals with the rights and duties of persons in their relations with one another as private individuals.

**private member**, *British.* a member of the House of Commons who is not a member of the Ministry or an active leader of the opposition party; back-bencher.

**private parts**, the genitals; privates.

**pri|vates** (prī′vits), *n.pl.* See under **private**.

**private school**, **1** *U.S.* an educational institution, such as a preparatory school or parochial school, owned and operated by other than a government authority. **2** *British.* a school owned and operated by a person or persons for private profit.
▶ **Private school, public school** mean very different things in the United States and Great Britain. In Great Britain, a "public school" is one of the schools such as Eton, Harrow, and Winchester, that operates under a royal charter as a private foundation; such schools would be called "private schools" in the United States. The British equivalent of the American "public school" is the "council school" or any one of various other institutions owned and operated by a public authority and supported by public funds.

**private sector**, the segment of business and industry engaged in private enterprise: *While city commissioners' salaries of $25,000 to $35,000 are not lightly regarded, they are not readily competitive with those of the private sector* (New York Times).

**pri|vate-wire system** (prī′vit wīr′), a telephone or teletype system privately operated.

**pri|va|tion** (prī vā′shən), *n.* **1** a lack of the comforts or of the necessities of life: *Many children were hungry and homeless because of privation during the war. The Parisians had had five months of siege, were reduced to the direst privation, and saw France ... now bound over to the Germans by the Republic* (Edmund Wilson). **SYN**: need, destitution. **2** loss; absence; being deprived: *Privation of the company of all other human beings is a serious hardship.* **3** *Logic.* the loss or absence of a quality; negative quality. [< Latin *prīvātiō, -ōnis* < *prīvāre* to deprive; see etym. under **private**]

**pri|vat|ism** (prī′və tiz əm), *n. U.S.* avoidance of involvement in matters outside of one's own private life; retreat into privacy.

**pri|va|tis|tic** (prī′və tis′tik), *adj.* **1** given to or fond of privacy; seclusive: *At Harvard he is known for his privatistic ways* (Atlantic). **2** favoring or based upon the use of private enterprise, as distinguished from collectivism: *a privatistic economy.*

**priv|a|tive** (priv′ə tiv), *adj., n.* —*adj.* **1** *Grammar and Logic.* expressing deprivation or denial of something. *Un-* is a privative prefix; *unwise* means *not wise. Never* is a privative word. **2** *Obsolete.* having the quality of depriving.
—*n. Grammar.* a privative word, prefix, or suffix.
[< Latin *prīvātīvus* < *prīvāre* to deprive; see etym. under **private**] —**priv′a|tive|ly**, *adv.*

**pri|va|tize** (prī′və tīz), *v.t.,* **-tized, -tiz|ing.** to make private: *to privatize grief. I do not believe in nationalizing losses and privatizing gains* (London Times). —**pri′va|ti|za′tion**, *n.*

**priv|et** (priv′it), *n.* **1** a shrub much used for hedges. Privet belongs to the olive family and is native to Japan and the Mediterranean region. There are several kinds, some of which are evergreen. Privet has smooth, dark-green leaves and clusters of small, white flowers, succeeded by small, shining black berries. **2** any one of several other related plants, also planted for hedges. **3** a related shrub, of swamps of the southern United States. [origin unknown]

**priv|i|lege** (priv′ə lij, priv′lij), *n., v.,* **-leged, -leg|ing.** —*n.* **1** a special right, advantage, or favor: *He has given us the privilege of using his television set. Immunity from most laws is the privilege of an ambassador to another country.* **2** a contract containing an option to buy, sell, or both buy and sell.
—*v.t.* to give a privilege to: *The Constitution privileges Senators from slander when speaking in the Senate.*
[< Old French *privilege,* learned borrowing from Latin *prīvilēgum* law applying to one individual < *prīvus* individual, single + *lex, lēgis* law]
—*Syn. n.* **1 Privilege, prerogative** mean a special right. **Privilege** means a benefit or advantage granted for any reason: *Alumni have the privilege of buying football tickets at special rates.* **Prerogative** refers to a right, often an official right, belonging to a person, class, or the like by reason of status of some kind: *The right to coin money is a prerogative of the state. Changing her mind is often jokingly called a woman's prerogative.*

**priv|i|leged** (priv′ə lijd, priv′lijd), *adj.* **1** having some privilege or privileges: *The nobility in Europe was a privileged class.* **2** not subject to court action, as for slander: *Words spoken by a Senator on the Senate floor are privileged.*

**privileged communication**, *Law.* a communication which a witness cannot legally be compelled to disclose.

**priv|i|ly** (priv′ə lē), *adv.* in a private manner; secretly: *He took him aside, and told him the news privily and briefly* (Edward A. Freeman). **SYN**: confidentially.

**priv|i|ty** (priv′ə tē), *n., pl.* **-ties. 1** private knowledge: *There had been five ... attempts to assassinate the Prince, all of them with the privity of the Spanish government* (John L. Motley). **2** = complicity. **3** a legally recognized relation between two people, such as that of owner and

**Pronunciation Key:** hat, **ā**ge, c**ã**re, f**ä**r; let, **ē**qual, t**ė**rm; it, **ī**ce; h**o**t, **ō**pen, **ô**rder; **oi**l, **ou**t; cup, p**u̇**t, r**ü**le; **ch**ild; lo**ng**; **th**in; **ᴛʜ**en; **zh**, measure; **ə** represents **a** in about, **e** in taken, **i** in pencil, **o** in lemon, **u** in circus.

tenant or employer and servant. [< Old French *privite,* and *privete* < *prive* privy]

**priv|y** (priv′ē), *adj., n., pl.* **priv|ies.** —*adj.* **1** private: *What I may do ... must remain privy* (Punch). **2** *Archaic.* secret; hidden.
—*n.* **1** a small outhouse used as a toilet: *He introduced soakage pits and compost heaps, improved wells, and privies* (Atlantic). **2** a person who has a legal interest or part in any action or is directly affected by it.
**privy to,** having secret or private knowledge of: *The Vice President was privy to the plans of the President.*
[< Old French *prive* < Latin *prīvātus* private; as noun, a private friend or place. See etym. of doublet **private.**]

**privy chamber, 1** a private apartment in a royal residence, as in Great Britain. **2** *Archaic.* a room reserved for the private or exclusive use of some particular person or persons.

**privy council,** a group of personal advisers to a ruler or other person of high rank or authority.

**Privy Council, 1** (in Great Britain) the body of persons acting as personal advisers to the sovereign in matters of state, the welfare of the Crown, or the security of the realm. Most of its duties are now performed by the cabinet or committees of Parliament. **2** a similar body of advisers, as in certain Commonwealth nations or colonies and in Japan until it was abolished in 1947. [< *privy council*]

**privy councillor,** *Especially British.* privy councilor.

**privy councilor,** a member of a privy council.

**privy purse,** an allowance for the private expenses of the British sovereign.

**privy seal,** (formerly, in Great Britain) the seal affixed to grants and bills that were afterwards to receive the great seal, and to documents that do not require the great seal.

**prix** (prē), *n. French.* prize; price.

**prix fixe** (prē′ fēks′), *French.* **1** a meal served at a fixed price; table d'hôte: *For the three-thousand-franc prix fixe, the lobster was succulent, the champagne dry ... the gossip unbridled* (New Yorker). **2** the price of such a meal. **3** (literally) fixed price.

**prize[1]** (prīz), *n., adj.* —*n.* **1** a reward won after trying against other people: *Prizes will be given for the three best stories.* **SYN:** award, premium. **2** *Figurative.* any reward worth working for: *The beautiful Miss Mannering, of high family, with an Indian fortune, was a prize worth looking after* (Scott). **3** *Archaic.* an advantage; privilege: *It is war's prize to take all vantages* (Shakespeare).
—*adj.* **1** given as a prize: *a prize ribbon, a prize medal.* **2** that has won a prize: *a prize student.* **3** *Figurative.* worthy of a prize: *prize vegetables, a prize blunder.*
[alteration of Middle English *pris;* see etym. under **price[1]**]

**prize[2]** (prīz), *n., v.,* **prized, priz|ing.** —*n.* a thing or person that is taken or captured in war, especially an enemy's ship and its cargo taken at sea.
—*v.t.* to capture as a prize.
[Middle English *prise* < Old French, seizure, alteration of Vulgar Latin *prēsa,* ultimately < Latin *prehendere* to seize]

**prize[3]** (prīz), *v.t.,* **prized, priz|ing. 1** to value highly; think much of: *Mother prizes her best china.* **SYN:** esteem. **2** to estimate the value of; appraise. **SYN:** rate.
[Middle English *prisen* < Old French *prisier,* variant of *preisier* < Late Latin *pretiāre* < Latin *pretium* prize, reward, price. See etym. of doublet **praise.**]

**prize[4]** (prīz), *v.,* **prized, priz|ing,** *n.* —*v.t.* to raise or move by force; pry.
—*n.* **1** the act of prizing; leverage. **2** *Dialect.* an instrument used for prizing; lever. Also, *especially British,* **prise.**
[Middle English *prize* a lever < Old French *prise* a taking hold, grasp; see etym. under **prize[2]**]

**prize court,** a court that makes decisions concerning ships and other property captured at sea during a war.

**prize|fight** (prīz′fīt′), *n.* a boxing match between professional fighters that people pay money to see.

**prize|fight|er** (prīz′fī′tər), *n.* a man who boxes for money.

**prize|fight|ing** (prīz′fī′ting), *n.* boxing for money.

**prize|giv|ing** (prīz′giv′ing), *n. British.* a ceremony at which prizes are awarded: *a school prizegiving* (London Times).

**prize|man** (prīz′mən), *n., pl.* **-men.** *Especially British.* the winner of a prize, especially in a college or school: *a prizeman in classics.*

**prize money,** money obtained by the sale of ships and other property captured at sea in the course of a war.

**priz|er** (prī′zər), *n. Archaic.* a person who competes for a prize.

**prize ring, 1** a square space enclosed by ropes, used for prizefights. **2** = prizefighting.

**prize|win|ner** (prīz′win′ər), *n.* a person or thing that wins a prize: *A biochemist and Nobel prizewinner* (London Times).

**prize|win|ning** (prīz′win′ing), *adj.* that has won a prize: *a prizewinning novel.*

**prize|wor|thy** (prīz′wėr′ᴛʜē), *adj.* deserving of a prize: *a prizeworthy invention.*

**PRN** (no periods) or **P.R.N.,** pro re nata; as the occasion requires (used in prescriptions).

**pro[1]** (prō), *adv., adj., n., pl.* **pros.** —*adv., adj.* in favor of; for: *to argue a question pro and con* (adv.). *Being pro one usually meant being anti the other* (New Yorker) (adj.).
—*n.* **1** a reason in favor of. The pros and cons of a question are the arguments for and against it. **2a** a person who votes in favor of something. **b** an affirmative vote.
[abstracted from *pro and con,* or independent use of *pro-*[1]]

**pro[2]** (prō), *n., pl.* **pros,** *adj. Informal.* professional: *Television also has its circus of seasoned pros whom one sees week after week* (Listener). *Early in his pro career Moore had difficulty getting fights in this country* (New York Times).

**pro[3]** (prō), *prep. Latin.* before; for; forth.

**pro-[1],** *prefix.* **1** forward, as in *proceed, project.* **2** forth; out, as in *prolong, proclaim, prolapse.* **3** on the side of; in favor of; in behalf of, as in *pro-British, proclerical.* **4** in place of; acting as, as in *pronoun, proconsul.*
[< Latin *prō-,* prefix, and *prō,* preposition, or adverb]

**pro-[2],** *prefix.* **1** before; preceding; prior to, as in *prologue, proinsulin, proseminar.* **2** in front of; anterior, as in *prothorax, proscenium.*
[< Greek *pro-* < *pró,* preposition, before, forward]

**PRO** (no periods) or **P.R.O.,** Public Relations Officer: *Those who get in his way ... end up as small-time P.R.O.s at remote Engineer Corps posts* (New Yorker). *Churches throughout Surrey were "gratifyingly packed," according to the Archbishop of Canterbury's PRO* (Punch).
► Originally **PRO** or **P.R.O.** was used in the armed forces for an officer in charge of public relations. Since World War II the use of the abbreviation has become extended, especially in Great Britain, to any person in the field of public relations. In the United States the variant *PR man* is frequently used.

**P.R.O.,** Public Record Office (of Great Britain).

**pro|a** (prō′ə), *n.* a swift Malay sailing boat built with one side flat and balanced by an outrigger. Also, **prau.** [earlier *parao* < Malay *parahu;* spelling influenced by English *prow* and Portuguese *proa* prow]

**pro|ac|tive** (prō ak′tiv), *adj. Psychology.* characterized by the dominance of first-learned material over material learned subsequently: *The word-recall experiments also reveal that, 24 hours after having learned List I and List II, a subject's recall of List II words diminishes but his recall of List I words does not. This phenomenon, which demonstrates that interference by List I can affect recall of List II is termed "proactive inhibition"* (Scientific American). [< *pro-*[1] + *active,* as in *retroactive*]

**pro-am** (prō′am′), *adj., n.* —*adj.* including both professional and amateur players; professional and amateur: *a pro-am match, a pro-am event.*
—*n.* a pro-am game, match, or tournament: *Pro-ams are increasingly part of the golfing scene* (London Times).

**prob., 1a** probable. **b** probably. **2** probate. **3** problem.

**prob|a|bil|ism** (prob′ə bə liz′əm), *n.* **1** the philosophical doctrine that certainty is impossible and that probability suffices to govern faith and practice. **2** (in the Roman Catholic Church) the doctrine that where authorities differ as to the lawfulness of an action, either opinion may be followed.

**prob|a|bil|ist** (prob′ə bə list), *n.* a person who holds the doctrine of probabilism.

**prob|a|bil|is|tic** (prob′ə bə lis′tik), *adj.* **1** having to do with or based on probability: *Clausius, Maxwell, and Boltzmann showed how to derive the laws of gases from probabilistic assumptions about the behavior of individual molecules* (Scientific American). **2** of probabilists or probabilism in theology. —**prob′a|bil|is′ti|cal|ly,** *adv.*

**prob|a|bil|i|ty** (prob′ə bil′ə tē), *n., pl.* **-ties. 1** the quality or fact of being likely or probable; good chance: *There is a probability of rain.* **2** something likely to happen: *A storm is one of the probabilities for tomorrow.* **3** the likelihood that an event will occur, estimated as the ratio $\frac{p}{p+q}$, where p is the probable number of occurrences and q is the probable number of nonoccurrences: *But this process proved to be one that was regulated by chance and the laws or probability rather than by the causal or determinative principles* (Atlantic). **4** the science or study of probability theory: *Work in the honors section leads ... to a fifth year of study that includes probability and statistics* (Atlantic).
**in all probability,** probably: *In all probability I will go with you. ... these cliffs corresponding in all probability to ancient lines of fault* (Samuel Haughton).

**probability curve,** *Statistics.* a bell-shaped curve; normal curve.

**probability theory,** a branch of mathematics dealing with chance or random phenomena, and forming the theoretical basis of statistics: *Probability theory, as a mathematical discipline, is concerned with the problem of calculating the probabilities of complex events consisting of collections of "elementary" events whose probabilities are known or postulated* (Scientific American).

**prob|a|ble** (prob′ə bəl), *adj.* **1** likely to happen: *Cooler weather is probable after this shower.* **2** likely to be true: *Something he ate is the probable cause of his pain.* **3** affording ground for belief: *probable evidence.* [< Latin *probābilis* < *probāre* to try, test; see etym. under **prove**]

**probable cause,** *Law.* good reason for assuming that a charge has sufficient evidence.

**probable error,** *Statistics.* the amount by which the arithmetical mean of a sample is expected to vary because of chance alone: *The probable error means that in sampling data some error is bound to occur* (Emory S. Bogardus).

**prob|a|bly** (prob′ə blē), *adv.* more likely than not: *He will probably refuse the offer.* **SYN:** presumably.

**pro|bang** (prō′bang), *n. Medicine.* a slender, elastic rod tipped with a sponge, ball, or the like, used to remove foreign bodies, as from the esophagus. [earlier *provang;* influenced by *probe*]

**pro|bate** (prō′bāt), *n., adj., v.,* **-bat|ed, -bat|ing.** *Law.* —*n.* **1** the official proving of the will of a person who has died as genuine. **2** a true copy of a will with a certificate that it has been proved genuine.
—*adj.* of or concerned with the probating of wills or a probate court: *a probate judge.*
—*v.t.* to prove by legal process the genuineness of (a will).
[< Latin *probātum,* neuter past participle of *probāre* prove, test, consider good]

**probate court,** a court concerned with the probate of wills and the settlement of the estates of dead persons.

**pro|ba|tion** (prō bā′shən), *n.* **1** a trial or testing of conduct, character, or qualifications: *the general doctrine of religion, that our present life is a state of probation for a future one* (Joseph Butler). *After a period of probation a novice becomes a nun.* **2** any act or process of testing. **3a** the system of letting young offenders against the law, or first offenders, go free without receiving the punishment which they are sentenced to, unless there is a further offense: *The person on probation makes monthly reports, pays the fine ..., and makes restitution ... to the person or persons injured by him* (Emory S. Bogardus). **b** the status of an offender freed in this way. **4** a status or period of trial for students who have failing marks, have broken rules, etc.: *He was admitted to the sixth grade on probation.* **5** proof; demonstration. [< Latin *probātiō, -ōnis* a proving < *probāre* prove, test, consider good]

**pro|ba|tion|al** (prō bā′shə nəl), *adj.* = probationary.

**pro|ba|tion|ar|y** (prō bā′shə ner′ē), *adj.* **1** of or having to do with probation: *Pythagoras ... required from those he instructed in philosophy a probationary silence of five years* (Samuel Johnson). **2** on probation: *The College elected him probationary Fellow* (W. J. Courthope).

**pro|ba|tion|er** (prō bā′shə nər), *n.* a person who is on probation. **SYN:** novice, novitiate.

**pro|ba|tion|er|ship** (prō bā′shə nər ship), *n.* the condition or period of a probationer.

**probation officer,** an officer appointed to supervise offenders who have been placed on probation.

**pro|ba|tive** (prō′bə tiv, prob′ə-), *adj.* **1** giving proof or evidence: *... the probative fact* (Jeremy Bentham). **SYN:** demonstrative. **2** for a trial or test: *Some are only probative, and designed to ... stir up those virtues which before lay dormant in the soul* (Robert South).

**pro|ba|to|ry** (prō′bə tôr′ē, -tōr′-), *adj.* = probative.

**probe** (prōb), *v.,* **probed, prob|ing,** *n.* —*v.t.* **1** to search into; examine thoroughly; investigate: *to probe a person's thoughts or feelings to find out why he acted as he did. Man in his unquenchable thirst for oil has probed ever deeper into the desert wastes of the Middle East* (Newsweek).

**SYN**: scrutinize. **2** to examine with a probe. **3** *Military.* to test the strength or defenses of (the enemy), as by a raid: *An enemy unit of undetermined strength briefly probed a central sector position* (New York Times).

— ***v.i.*** to search; penetrate: *to probe into the causes of crime. We searched our minds in long discussions late each night and didn't spare each other as we probed for answers* (Norman Cousins). [< noun]

— ***n.*** **1** a thorough examination; investigation: *a probe into juvenile delinquency.* **2** an investigation, usually by a lawmaking body or a committee of its members in an effort to discover evidences of law violation: *An energetic, youthful trustbuster will guide the Senate probe* (Wall Street Journal). **3** a slender instrument for exploring something. A doctor or dentist uses a probe to explore the depth or direction of a wound or a cavity in the body. A Geiger counter uses a probe to detect the amount of radiation in radioactive matter, such as rocks. **4** a rocket, satellite or other unmanned spacecraft carrying scientific instruments, to record or report back information about space, other planets, or other objects in outer space: *a lunar probe. Probes ... pass in the vicinity of either Venus or Mars ... now well within the reach of rocket technology* (Harper's). **5** the launching of such a spacecraft. **6** *Military.* a testing of the strength or defenses of the enemy: *Light enemy probes and scattered patrol contacts have been reported* (New York Times). **7** a projecting pipelike device on an airplane which receives the fuel from a tanker plane when refueling in flight.

[< Late Latin *proba* a proof < Latin *probāre* prove. See etym. of doublet **proof.**] — **prob′er,** *n.* — **prob′ing\|ly,** *adv.*

***probe-and-drogue** (prōb′ən drōg′), *n.* a method of refueling planes in flight. The plane to be refueled inserts a pipelike probe into the funnel-shaped drogue that hangs on the end of a long flexible hose from a tanker plane.

***probe-and-drogue**

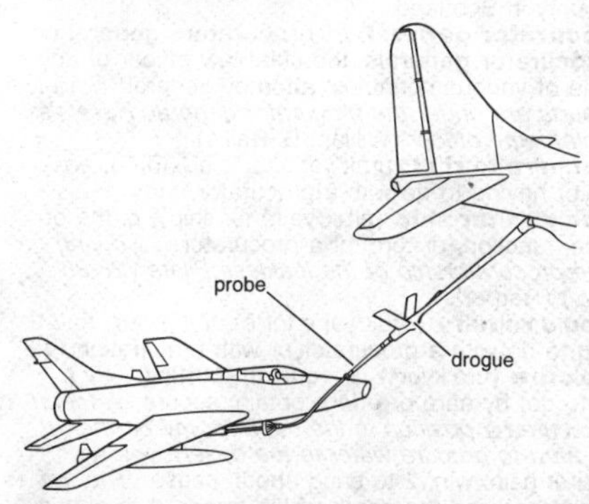


**pro\|ben\|e\|cid** (prō ben′ə sid), *n.* a drug stimulating the excretion of uric acid, used in treating gouty arthritis and other conditions. *Formula:* $C_{13}H_{19}NO_4S$ [< *pro*(pyl) + *ben*(zoic) (a)*cid*]

**pro\|bi\|ty** (prō′bə tē, prob′ə-), *n.* high principle; uprightness; honesty: *a man of unquestioned probity.* **SYN**: integrity, rectitude. [< Latin *probitās* < *probus* righteous, proper, worthy]

**prob\|lem** (prob′ləm), *n., adj.* — ***n.*** **1** a question, especially a difficult question: *How to do away with poverty is a problem that concerns the government. In biology there is still the problem of the basic chemistry of life* (Atlantic). **2** a matter of doubt or difficulty: *The president of a large company has to deal with many problems. This important constitutional problem [must not] remain clouded in doubt* (Newsweek). **3** something to be worked out: *a problem in arithmetic.*

— ***adj.*** **1** that causes difficulty: *a problem child.* **2** having a plot based on a problem, especially a problem of social conduct, relationship, or responsibility: *a problem novel.*

[< Latin *problēma* < Greek *próblēma, -atos* < *probállein* propose, put forth < *pro-* forward + *bállein* to throw]

**prob\|lem\|at\|ic** (prob′lə mat′ik), *adj.* having the nature of a problem; doubtful; uncertain; questionable: *What the weather will be is often problematic.* **SYN**: dubious, disputable. [< Late Latin *problematicus* < Greek *problēmatikós* < *próblēma, -atos* problem] — **prob′lem\|at′i\|cal\|ly,** *adv.*

**prob\|lem\|at\|i\|cal** (prob′lə mat′ə kəl), *adj.* = problematic.

**prob\|lem\|at\|ics** (prob′lə mat′iks), *n.pl.* problematic matters.

**prob\|lem\|ist** (prob′lə mist), *n.* a person who makes up or solves problems, as in chess or mathematics.

**pro bo\|no pu\|bli\|co** (prō bō′nō pub′lə kō), *Latin.* for the public welfare.

**pro\|bos\|cid\|e\|an** or **pro\|bos\|cid\|i\|an** (prō′bə sid′ē ən), *adj., n.* — ***adj.*** **1** belonging to or having to do with the order consisting of the elephants, and similar animals now extinct. **2a** having a proboscis. **b** having to do with or like a proboscis.

— ***n.*** an elephant, mammoth, or the like.

[< New Latin *Proboscidea* the order name (< Latin *proboscis, -idis* proboscis) + English *-an*]

**pro\|bos\|cis** (prō bos′is), *n., pl.* **-bos\|cis\|es, -bos\|ci\|des** (-bos′ə dēz). **1** an elephant's trunk. **2** a long, flexible snout, such as that of the tapir or certain monkeys. **3** the tubelike mouthparts of some insects developed to great length for piercing or sucking: *the proboscis of a fly or a mosquito.* **4** any similar organ, such as: **a** an organ of many worms, such as annelids and nemerteans, usually eversible and opening above the mouth. **b** the tongue of certain gastropods. **5** *Humorous.* a person's nose. [< Latin *proboscis, -idis* < Greek *proboskís, -ídos* (literally) a means for taking in food < *pró* forth + *bóskein* to feed, nourish]

**proboscis monkey,** a large, long-tailed monkey of Borneo, having a long nose.

**proc.,** **1** proceedings. **2** process.

**pro\|ca\|cious** (prō kā′shəs), *adj.* bold; forward; pert: *... a vain, proud, procacious, tempting mind* (Richard Baxter). [< Latin *procāx, -cācis* (with English *-ous*) < *procāre* ask]

**pro\|cac\|i\|ty** (prō kas′ə tē), *n.* impudence; petulance.

**pro\|caine** (prō kān′, prō′kān), *n.* a drug used as a local anesthetic, similar to, but much less toxic than, cocaine; novocaine. *Formula:* $C_{13}H_{20}N_2O_2 \cdot HCl$ [< *pro-*[1] + (co)*caine*]

**procaine amide,** a compound related to procaine used in the treatment of arrhythmia. *Formula:* $C_{13}H_{21}ON_3$

**pro\|cam\|bi\|al** (prō kam′bē əl), *adj.* of the procambium.

**pro\|cam\|bi\|um** (prō kam′bē əm), *n. Botany.* any undifferentiated tissue from which the vascular bundles are developed. [< New Latin *procambium* < *pro-* pro-[1] + *cambium* cambium]

**pro\|carp** (prō′kärp), *n.* the female sex organ of certain algae and fungi. [< New Latin *procarpium* < Greek *pró* pro-[2] + *karpós* fruit]

**pro\|car\|y\|ote** (prō kar′ē ōt), *n.* a cell or organism without a visible nucleus or nuclei: *Procaryotes were found in the Beck Spring Dolomite in association with the primitive eucaryotes* (Scientific American). Also, **prokaryote.** [< *pro-*[2] + Greek *káryon* nut, kernel]

**pro\|car\|y\|ot\|ic** (prō kar′ē ot′ik), *adj.* not having a visible nucleus or nuclei: *Procaryotic cells, which lack a nucleus and divide by simple fission, were a more primitive form of life than the eucaryotes and persist today in the bacteria and blue-green algae* (Scientific American). Also, **prokaryotic.**

**pro\|ca\|the\|dral** (prō′kə thē′drəl), *n.* a church used temporarily as a cathedral.

**pro\|ce\|den\|do** (prō′sə den′dō), *n., pl.* **-dos.** *Law.* a writ of a superior court commanding a subordinate court to proceed to judgment. [< Latin *prōcēdendo* (*ad jūdicium*) (literally) proceeding (to judgment)]

**pro\|ce\|dur\|al** (prə sē′jər əl), *adj.* of or having to do with procedure: *The recommendations the Commission made ... were purely procedural ones* (New Yorker). — **pro\|ce′dur\|al\|ly,** *adv.*

**pro\|ce\|dure** (prə sē′jər), *n.* **1** a way of proceeding; method of doing things: *What is your procedure in making bread?* **2** the customary manners or ways of conducting some business: *parliamentary procedure, legal procedure.* **3** *Obsolete.* the going on of an action; progress; course. [< Middle French *procédure* < Old French *proceder* to proceed, learned borrowing from Latin *prōcēdere*]

**pro\|ceed** (*v.* prə sēd′, prō-; *n.* prō′sēd), *v., n.* — ***v.i.*** **1** to go on after having stopped; move forward: *Please proceed with your story. The train proceeded at the same speed as before.* **SYN**: continue, progress. See syn. under **advance.** **2** to be carried on; take place: *The trial may proceed.* **3** to carry on any activity: *He proceeded to light his pipe.* **4** *Figurative.* to come forth; issue; go out: *Heat proceeds from fire.* **SYN**: emanate. **5** to advance to a higher status: *to proceed to master of arts.* **6** to begin and carry on an action at law: *Though rebellion is declared, it is not proceeded against as such* (Edmund Burke).

— ***n.*** **proceeds, 1** money obtained from a sale or some other activity or transaction: *The proceeds from the school play will be used to buy a new curtain for the stage.* **2** the amount remaining after a discount or charges have been deducted from the face value of a promissory note, an insurance policy, or the like.

[< Latin *prōcēdere* < *prō-* forward + *cēdere* to move] — **pro\|ceed′er,** *n.*

**pro\|ceed\|ing** (prə sē′ding), *n.* what is done; action; conduct; performance: *He wrote a memorandum, pointing out the unconstitutional nature of Lord Melbourne's proceedings* (Lytton Strachey). **SYN**: dealing, doing. *Abbr:* proc.

**proceedings, a** the action in a case in a law court: *Having already as much law proceedings on his hands as he could manage ...* (James H. Monk). **b** a record of what was done at the meetings of a society or club; minutes: *Proceedings of the Philological Society* (a title).

**pro\|ceeds** (prō′sēdz), *n.pl.* See under **proceed.**

**proc\|el\|lar\|i\|an** (pros′ə lãr′ē ən), *adj.* of or having to do with a group of sea birds that includes the petrels and related birds. [< New Latin *Procellaria* the genus name (< Latin *procella* storm) + English *-an*]

**pro\|ce\|phal\|ic** (prō′sə fal′ik), *adj.* having to do with or forming the forepart of the head: *procephalic processes, the procephalic lobe.* [< *pro-*[2] + *cephalic*]

**proc\|ess**[1] (pros′es; *especially British* prō′ses), *n., v., adj.* — ***n.*** **1** a set of actions or changes in a special order: *the process of reading, a process of decay. By what process or processes is cloth made from wool?* **SYN**: operation. **2** a course of action; procedure: *the democratic process.* **3** a part that grows out or sticks out: *the process of a bone.* **4** a written command or summons to appear in a law court. **5** the proceedings in a legal case or action. **6** forward movement; progress; course: *Saturnian Juno now, with double care, Attends the fatal process of the war* (Dryden).

— ***v.t.*** **1** to treat, prepare, or handle by some special method: *to process fruit and vegetables for market. This cloth has been processed to make it waterproof. Computing machines process information very quickly. [Fort] Dix ... processes men for overseas duty and on their return to this country* (New York Times). **2** to start legal action against, especially by serving a process on.

— ***adj.*** **1** treated or prepared by some special method: *process foods.* **2** used in some process: *process heat.* **3** involving special optical effects: *a process camera, a process shot.*

**in process, a** in the course or condition: *In process of time the house will be finished.* **b** in the course or condition of being done: *The author has just finished one book and has another in process.*

[< Old French *proces* a journey, going < Latin *prōcessus, -ūs* progress < *prōcēdere* to proceed] — **proc′ess\|a\|ble,** *adj.*

▶ The plural of **process** is regular and pronounced (pros′ə siz). The pronunciation (pros′ə sēz), apparently on the analogy of *indices* and *analyses,* is now also widely used.

**pro\|cess**[2] (prə ses′), *v.i. British.* to go, walk, or march in procession: *The pilgrims process energetically around the courtyard with their candles ... led by jolly bearded monks* (Manchester Guardian Weekly). [back formation < *procession*]

**process art,** = conceptual art.

**process cheese,** a cheese mixture prepared by melting various hard cheeses, especially cheddars, emulsifying them, and mixing them with whey, water, tartrate and phosphate salts, or other ingredients.

**proc\|ess\|ing tax** (pros′es ing), *U.S.* a Federal tax placed on processes involved in handling certain commodities, especially agricultural commodities.

**pro\|ces\|sion** (prə sesh′ən), *n., v.* — ***n.*** **1** something that moves forward; persons marching or riding: *a procession of ants. A funeral procession filled the street.* **SYN**: cortege. **2** an orderly moving forward: *We formed lines to march in procession onto the platform.*

— ***v.i.*** to move in procession.

[< Late Latin *prōcessiō, -ōnis* a ceremonial marching (in Latin, a marching onwards) < Latin *prōcēdere* to proceed]

**pro\|ces\|sion\|al** (prə sesh′ə nəl), *adj., n.* — ***adj.*** **1** of a procession: *Crowds ... lining the processional route* (Punch). **2** used or sung in a procession: *a processional hymn; ... the great processional elephant* (B. M. Croker).

— ***n.*** **1** processional music: *The choir and clergy marched into the church singing the processional.* **2** a book containing hymns, litanies, etc., for use in religious processions. — **pro\|ces′sion\|al\|ly,** *adv.*

**pro\|ces\|sion\|ar\|y** (prə sesh′ə ner′ē), *adj.* **1** consisting of a formal or solemn procession. **2** forming and moving in a procession: *processionary caterpillars.*

---

**Pronunciation Key:** hat, āge, cãre, fär; let, ēqual, tėrm; it, īce; hot, ōpen, ôrder; oil, out; cup, pu̇t, rüle; **child**; long; **thin**; **ᴛʜen**; **zh**, measure; ə represents **a** in about, **e** in taken, **i** in pencil, **o** in lemon, **u** in circus.

**proc|es|sor** (pros′es ər; *Especially British* prō′ses-), *n.* **1** a person who processes something, such as a worker who prepares food or food products especially for commercial canning or freezing. **2a** the unit that controls the processing operations in a computer: *Mercury units have become more costly than processors, because of the large amount required* (Science Journal). **b** the part of a computer that includes the processor, arithmetic unit, and magnetic-core memory: *In the past Digital's customers have usually bought a processor and written their own software for it* (New Scientist). **c** any device for handling or processing information, such as a data processor. **3** an artist who creates works of process art.

**process patent**, a patent on the method of producing a product.

**process printing**, a method of printing pictures in color, by which almost any shade can be reproduced from a combination of half-tone plates in red, yellow, blue, and, usually, black.

**process server**, a person who serves summonses, subpoenas, or other legal orders.

**pro|cès-ver|bal** (prō sā′ver bäl′; *French* prô se′ver bȧl′), *n., pl.* **-baux** (-bō′). a report of proceedings, as of an assembly; minutes: ... *when French and American experts would also meet to draw up the procès-verbal of the talks* (London Times).
[< French *procès- verbal* < *procès* process, report of proceedings + *verbal* verbal]

**pro|chan|cel|lor** (prō chan′sə lər), *n.* a deputy or assistant of the vice-chancellor in certain British universities.

**pro|chlor|per|a|zine** (prō′klôr per′ə zēn), *n.* a synthetic drug used as a tranquilizer and to stop vomiting. *Formula:* $C_{20}H_{24}ClN_3S$ [< *pro*(pyl) + *chlor-* + (pi)*perazine*]

**pro|cho|os** (prō′kō os), *n., pl.* **-cho|oi** (-kō oi). a pitcherlike vessel, resembling the oinochoe but usually more slender, used in ancient Greece for pouring out wine and for pouring water on the hands before a meal. [< Greek *próchoos* < *procheîn* pour forth < *pro-* before + *cheîn* to pour]

**pro|chro|nism** (prō′krə niz əm), *n.* the assigning of an event to a period earlier than its actual date: *It is a prochronism to talk of the May fly, for ... the first ten days of June usually constitute the May-fly season* (J. A. Gibbs). [< *pro-*[2] + Greek *chrónos* time + English *-ism*]

**pro|claim** (prə klām′, prō-), *v.t.* **1** to make known publicly and officially; declare publicly: *War was proclaimed. The people proclaimed him king.* (*Figurative.*) *His actions proclaim his love.* **SYN**: publish. See syn. under **announce. 2a** to declare (a person) to be an outlaw; denounce: *I heard myself proclaim'd; And by the happy hollow of a tree escaped the hunt* (Shakespeare). **b** to subject (a place) to legal restrictions. [< Latin *prōclāmāre* < *prō-* forth + *clāmāre* to shout; spelling influenced by *claim,* verb] — **pro|claim′er**, *n.*

**proc|la|ma|tion** (prok′lə mā′shən), *n.* an official announcement; public declaration: *Every year the President issues a Thanksgiving Day proclamation. The revolution broke out in France in February, 1848 ... with the immediate fall of Louis-Philippe and the proclamation of the French Republic* (Edmund Wilson).
— ***Syn.*** **Proclamation, edict** mean a notice or order issued by authority. **Proclamation** means an official public announcement by an executive or administrative officer, such as a president, governor, or mayor: *Lincoln issued a proclamation declaring the emancipation of slaves.* **Edict** means a public order or decree proclaimed by the highest authority, usually a ruler or court with supreme or absolute authority: *The dictator issued an edict ordering seizure of the mines.*

**pro|clam|a|to|ry** (prō klam′ə tôr′ē, -tōr′-), *adj.* in the manner of making a proclamation: *proclamatory style.*

**pro|clit|ic** (prō klit′ik), *adj., n.* — ***adj.*** (of a word) so closely connected with a following word as to have no independent accent.
— ***n.*** a proclitic word. In the following example *to* is a proclitic word: *to see and to do.*
[< New Latin *procliticus* < Greek *proklī́nein* bend forward; patterned on Greek *enklitikós* enclitic] — **pro|clit′i|cal|ly**, *adv.*

**pro|cliv|i|ty** (prō kliv′ə tē), *n., pl.* **-ties**. tendency; inclination; predisposition; leaning; propensity: *The old woman had a proclivity for finding fault. There are many spots in Florida that attract people with a proclivity for uncrowded but urbane resort life* (New Yorker). **SYN**: bias, bent. [< Latin *prōclīvitās* < *prōclīvis* prone to; (literally) sloping, inclining < *prō-* forward + *clīvus* a slope, related to *clīnāre* to bend. Compare etym. under **acclivity.**]

**Proc|ne** (prok′nē), *n. Greek Mythology.* Philomela's sister, who was turned into a swallow.

**pro-Com|mu|nist** (prō kom′yə nist), *adj., n.* — ***adj.*** favoring, aligned with, or committed to the Communists or Communism.
— ***n.*** a member of a pro-Communist armed forces or political group: *Malaya proposes to prevent pro-Communists among the Singapore Chinese from penetrating the Borneo territories* (New York Times).

**pro|con|sul** (prō kon′səl), *n.* **1** a governor or military commander of an ancient Roman province, with duties and powers like a consul's. **2** the governor of a colony or other dependent territory, especially during British or French colonial expansion. [< Latin *prōcōnsul,* probably < *prō cōnsule* in place of a consul]

**Pro|con|sul** (prō kon′səl), *n.* a manlike ape of the Miocene epoch, which lived in Africa approximately 25,000,000 years ago and is considered by some anthropologists to be an ancestor of man.

**pro|con|su|lar** (prō kon′sə lər), *adj.* of, having to do with, or governed by a proconsul: *proconsular rule.*

**pro|con|su|late** (prō kon′sə lit), *n.* the position or term of a proconsul.

**pro|con|sul|ship** (prō kon′səl ship), *n.* = proconsulate.

**pro|cras|ti|nate** (prō kras′tə nāt), *v.i., v.t.,* **-nat|ed, -nat|ing.** to put things off until later; delay, especially repeatedly: *to procrastinate until an opportunity is lost.* **SYN**: defer, postpone. [< Latin *prōcrāstināre* (with English *-ate*[1]) < *prō-* forward + *crāstinus* belonging to tomorrow < *crās* tomorrow] — **pro|cras′ti|na′tor**, *n.*

**pro|cras|ti|na|tion** (prō kras′tə nā′shən), *n.* the act or habit of putting things off till later; delay: *Procrastination is the thief of time* (Edward Young). **SYN**: dilatoriness, postponement.

**pro|cras|ti|na|tive** (prō kras′tə nā′tiv), *adj.* procrastinating; dilatory.

**pro|cras|ti|na|to|ry** (prō kras′tə nə tôr′ē, -tōr′-), *adj.* = procrastinative.

**pro|cre|ant** (prō′krē ənt), *adj.* generating; having to do with procreation: *procreant cause. Always the procreant urge of the world* (Walt Whitman). [< Latin *prōcreāns, -antis,* present participle of *prōcreāre* to procreate]

**pro|cre|ate** (prō′krē āt), *v.,* **-at|ed, -at|ing.** — ***v.t.*** **1** to become father to; beget. **2** to bring into being; produce: *Only two on an average survive to procreate their kind* (Charles Darwin).
— ***v.i.*** to produce offspring; reproduce.
[< Latin *prōcreāre* (with English *-ate*[1]) < *prō-* forth + *creāre* to create, bring forth, beget]

**pro|cre|a|tion** (prō′krē ā′shən), *n.* **1** the act or process of producing offspring; reproduction; begetting; becoming a father. **2** *Figurative.* production.

**pro|cre|a|tive** (prō′krē ā′tiv), *adj.* **1** producing offspring; begetting; bringing into being. **2** of or having to do with procreation: *the procreative faculty.* — **pro′cre|a′tive|ness**, *n.*

**pro|cre|a|tor** (prō′krē ā′tər), *n.* a person who begets; parent.

**Pro|crus|te|an** (prō krus′tē ən), *adj.* **1** of or having to do with Procrustes or his bed. **2** tending to produce conformity by violent or arbitrary means: *The Federal statutes of constitutionality now applicable to the states* [*are*] *not so strict as to be "Procrustean"* (New York Times).

**Pro|crus|tes** (prō krus′tēz), *n. Greek Legend.* a robber who stretched his victims or cut short their legs to make them fit the length of his bed.

**Procrustes' bed**, anything with which people or things are forced to conform, especially by violent and arbitrary means: *It is becoming increasingly necessary to find some way of breaking out of the Procrustes' bed that the British press has got itself clamped into ... as a result of its excessive dependence on advertising subsidies* (Francis Williams).

**proc|to|de|um** or **proc|to|dae|um** (prok′tə dē′əm), *n.* an invagination of ectodermal tissue in the embryo which forms part of the anal passage. [< Greek *prōktós* anus + *odaîos* (thing) that is on the way + New Latin *-um,* a noun suffix]

**proc|to|log|ic** (prok′tə loj′ik), *adj.* of or having to do with proctology.

**proc|to|log|i|cal** (prok′tə loj′ə kəl), *adj.* = proctologic.

**proc|tol|o|gist** (prok tol′ə jist), *n.* a person skilled in proctology.

**proc|tol|o|gy** (prok tol′ə jē), *n.* the branch of medicine dealing with the rectum and anus. [< Greek *prōktós* anus + English *-logy*]

**proc|tor** (prok′tər), *n., v.* — ***n.*** **1a** an official in a college, university, or school who keeps order. **b** a person who supervises students during an examination. **2** a person employed to manage another's case in a law court. **SYN**: attorney, counselor.
— ***v.t.*** to serve as a proctor at (an examination).
[reduction of *procurator*]

**proc|to|ri|al** (prok tôr′ē əl, -tōr′-), *adj.* of or having to do with a proctor. — **proc|to′ri|al|ly**, *adv.*

**proc|tor|ship** (prok′tər ship), *n.* the position of a proctor.

**proc|to|scope** (prok′tə skōp), *n.* an instrument for inspecting the rectum. [< Greek *prōktós* anus + English *-scope*]

**proc|tos|co|py** (prok tos′kə pē), *n., pl.* **-pies**. an examination of the rectum, especially with a proctoscope.

**pro|cum|bent** (prō kum′bənt), *adj.* **1** lying face down; prone; prostrate. **2** lying or trailing along the ground but not sending down roots: *a procumbent plant or stem.* **SYN**: trailing. [< Latin *prōcumbēns, -entis,* present participle of *prōcumbere* lean or fall forward < *prō-* forward + *cubāre* to lie, recline]

**pro|cur|a|ble** (prə kyůr′ə bəl), *adj.* that can be procured; obtainable.

**proc|u|ra|cy** (prok′yər ə sē), *n., pl.* **-cies**. the office or service of a procurator.

**pro|cu|ra|dor** (prō′kü rə dôr′, -dōr′), *n., pl.* **-do|res** (-dôr′ās, -dōr′). a member of the national legislature of Spain. [< Spanish *procurador* (literally) attorney, proctor]

**pro|cur|ance** (prə kyůr′əns), *n.* the act of procuring.

**proc|u|ra|tion** (prok′yə rā′shən), *n.* **1** the act of procuring. **2** management for another; agency. **3a** the appointment of an agent. **b** the authority given; power of attorney.

**proc|u|ra|tor** (prok′yə rā′tər), *n.* **1** a person employed to manage the affairs of another; person authorized to act for another; agent. **2** a financial agent or administrator of an ancient Roman province: *A few minor provinces were rather more directly controlled by the emperor and administered by his agents* (*procurators*). *Judea, in the time of Our Lord, with its procurator, Pontius Pilate, is the best known of these* (Harold Mattingly). **3** an attorney for the government in the Soviet Union; district attorney; prosecutor. [< Latin *prōcūrātor, -ōris* < *prōcūrāre;* see etym. under **procure**]

**procurator fiscal**, the public prosecutor of a county in Scotland.

**procurator general**, *pl.* **procurators general** or **procurator generals**. the chief law officer of any one of various countries; attorney general: *Soviet courts are under the procurator general, Russia's chief legal officer* (William B. Ballis).

**proc|u|ra|to|ri|al** (prok′yər ə tôr′ē əl, -tōr′-), *adj.* of or having to do with a procurator.

**proc|u|ra|tor|ship** (prok′yə rā′tər ship), *n.* the office, function, or term of a procurator: ... *during the procuratorship of the luckless Pilate* (*26-36* A.D.) (Harper's).

**proc|u|ra|to|ry** (prok′yər ə tôr′ē, -tōr′-), *adj.* having to do with a procurator or with procuration.

**pro|cure** (prə kyůr′), *v.,* **-cured, -cur|ing.** — ***v.t.*** **1** to get by care or effort; obtain; secure: *A friend procured a position in the bank for my brother. It is hard to procure water in the desert.* **SYN**: acquire, gain, win. **2** to bring about; cause: *The traitors procured the death of the prince.* **3** to obtain (women) for the gratification of lust.
— ***v.i.*** to act as a procurer or procuress: *How doth my dear morsel, thy mistress? Procures she still?* (Shakespeare).
[< Latin *prōcūrāre* manage, take care of < *prō-* on behalf of + *cūrāre* take care about < *cūra* care] — **pro|cure′ment**, *n.*

**pro|cur|er** (prə kyůr′ər), *n.* **1** a person who procures. **2** a pander; pimp.

**pro|cur|ess** (prə kyůr′is), *n.* a woman procurer; bawd.

**Pro|cy|on** (prō′sē on), *n.* a star of the first magnitude in the constellation Canis Minor. [< Latin *Procyōn* < Greek *Prokýōn* < *pró* before + *kýōn* dog (because it rises before the Dog Star, Sirius)]

**prod** (prod), *v.,* **prod|ded, prod|ding,** *n.* — ***v.t.*** **1** to poke or jab with something pointed: *to prod an animal with a stick.* **2** *Figurative.* to stir up; urge on; goad: *to prod a lazy boy to action by threats. The lateness of the hour prodded me to finish quickly. I have vitality enough to kick when prodded* (Thomas Huxley). **SYN**: incite. **3** to make by poking: *The lady has prodded little spirting holes in the damp sand ... with her parasol* (Dickens).
— ***n.*** **1** a poke; thrust: *That prod in the ribs hurt.* **2** a stick with a sharp point; goad: *a cattle prod.* **3** *Figurative.* words, actions, or feelings that prod: *Weekends I call my salesmen on the phone and give them a prod* (New Yorker).
[origin uncertain]

**Prod** (prod), *n.* (in Ireland) a Protestant (used in an unfriendly way).

**prod.**, produced.

**prod|der** (prod′ər), *n.* a person or thing that prods.

**prod|i|gal** (prod′ə gəl), *adj., n.* — ***adj.*** **1** spending too much; wasting money or other resources;

wasteful: *a prodigal son, to be prodigal of affection. America has been prodigal of its forests.* SYN: extravagant. **2** abundant; lavish; giving or yielding lavishly or profusely: *God's prodigal mercies. Of these things I shall be very prodigal in my discourse* (Henry Neville).
—*n.* a person who is wasteful or extravagant; spendthrift: *The father welcomed the prodigal.*
[< Latin *prōdigus* (see etym. under **prodigality**) + English *-al*¹] —**prod′i|gal|ly**, *adv.*

**prod|i|gal|i|ty** (prod′ə gal′ə tē), *n., pl.* **-ties.** **1** wasteful or reckless extravagance: *It is often surprising how men begin to curb their prodigality when convinced they must pay for it* (Wall Street Journal). **2** rich abundance; profuseness: *the prodigality of jungle growth.* SYN: profusion. [< Late Latin *prōdigālitās* < Latin *prōdigus* wasteful < *prōdigere* to squander, (literally) drive forth < *prōd-*, variant of *prō-* forth + *agere* to drive]

**pro|dig|i|o|sin** (prō dij′ē ō′sin), *n.* an antibiotic used against coccidioidomycosis. *Formula:* $C_{20}H_{25}N_3O$ [< New Latin (*Chromobacterium*) *prodigiosum,* the name of the bacteria which produce it + English *-in*]

**pro|di|gious** (prə dij′əs), *adj.* **1** very great; huge; vast: *The ocean contains a prodigious amount of water.* SYN: immense. **2** wonderful; marvelous; amazing: *a prodigious feat.* SYN: astonishing. **3** out of the ordinary; abnormal; monstrous: *Nature breeds, Perverse, all monstrous, all prodigious things* (Milton). **4** *Obsolete.* being a portent. [< Latin *prōdigiōsus* < *prōdigium* prodigy, omen] —**pro|di′gious|ly**, *adv.* —**pro|di′gious|ness**, *n.*

**prod|i|gy** (prod′ə jē), *n., pl.* **-gies.** **1** a marvel; wonder; surprise. A child prodigy is a child remarkably brilliant in some respect. **2** a marvelous example: *The warriors performed prodigies of valor. Samson performed prodigies of strength.* **3** a wonderful sign or omen: *An eclipse of the sun seemed a prodigy to early man. The old men paid careful attention to omens and prodigies, and especially to their dreams* (Francis Parkman). **4** something out of the ordinary; abnormality. [< Latin *prōdigium* omen < *prōd-*, variant of *prō-* forth + *-igium,* related to *aiō* I speak]

**pro|do|mos** (prō dō′mos), *n., pl.* **-moi** (-moi). a roofed, open space with pillars on one side. [< Greek *pró* before + *dómos* house]

**prod|ro|mal** (prod′rə məl), *adj.* (of disease symptoms) preliminary; premonitory.

**pro|drome** (prō′drōm), *n.* a symptom giving warning of illness. [< Middle French *prodrome,* learned borrowing from New Latin *prodromus* < Greek *pródromos* (one) going before < *pro-* forward + *drómos* a running, related to *drameîn* to run]

**pro|drom|ic** (prə drom′ik), *adj.* = prodromal.

**pro|duce** (*v.* prə düs′, -dyüs′; *n.* prod′üs, -yüs; prō′düs, -dyüs), *v.,* **-duced, -duc|ing,** *n.* —*v.t.* **1** to bring into existence by labor or effort; create: *to produce a work of art.* SYN: make. **2** to make from raw or other material; manufacture: *to produce steel. This factory produces stoves.* **3** to yield, furnish, or supply: *to produce hydroelectric power. His business produced a large profit.* **4** to cause to grow; raise: *to produce vegetables.* **5** to bring forth; bear: *to produce young. Hens produce eggs.* **6** to bring about; cause: *His hard work produced success.* SYN: effect. **7** to bring forward; show: *Produce your proof.* **8** to bring (a play or other performance) before the public: *Our class produced a play.* **9** to extend (a line or plane); continue. **10** *Obsolete.* to prolong; lengthen.
—*v.i.* to bring forth or yield offspring, crops, products, dividends, interest, etc.
—*n.* **1** what is produced; yield: *Vegetables are a garden's produce.* **2** offspring; progeny.
[< Latin *prōdūcere* < *prō-* forth + *dūcere* to bring, lead]

**pro|duce|a|ble** (prə dü′sə bəl, -dyü′-), *adj.* = producible.

**pro|duc|er** (prə dü′sər, -dyü′-), *n.* **1** a person or thing that produces, especially a person who grows or makes things that are to be used by others. **2a** a person in charge of the production of a play, a motion picture, or a television or radio show. **b** *British.* a director of a motion picture, play, etc. **3** a furnace for manufacturing producer gas. **4** a producing oil well: *During the past three months the Company participated in completing 8 producers and 7 dry holes* (Wall Street Journal).

**producer gas,** a gas that is a mixture of carbon monoxide, hydrogen, and oxygen, produced by the incomplete combustion of coke or coal, or by passing air and steam over burning coke or coal; air gas. It is used mainly as an industrial fuel.

**producer goods,** articles used in the production of other articles, such as machinery, tools, timber, and ore.

**pro|duc|i|bil|i|ty** (prə dü′sə bil′ə tē, -dyü′-), *n.* the quality of being producible.

**pro|duc|i|ble** (prə dü′sə bəl, -dyü′-), *adj.* that can be produced: ... *wealth being no more producible without painful toil than any other crop* (Spectator).

**prod|uct** (prod′əkt, -ukt), *n.* **1** that which is produced; result of work or of growth: *factory products, farm products. The products of respiration help indirectly to make certain soil minerals available to plants* (Fred W. Emerson). **2** a number or quantity resulting from multiplying two or more numbers or quantities together: *40 is the product of 8 and 5.* **3** *Chemistry.* a substance obtained from one or more other substances as a result of chemical reaction. [< Latin *prōductum,* noun use of neuter past participle of *prōdūcere* to produce]

**pro|duc|tion** (prə duk′shən), *n.* **1a** the act of producing; manufacture; creation: *His business is the production of automobiles. A farmer's business is the production of food. Chile ... ranks as a leader in total copper production* (Preston E. James). **b** *Slang.* the act of exaggerating something out of proportion to its importance: *to make a production out of taking snapshots.* **2** something that is produced; product: *the yearly production of a farm. That worthless gadget is the production of an ignorant inventor.* **3** the amount produced: *a decline in production.* **4** an artistic work: *a literary production.* **5** a presentation, as of a play or other artistic performance: *a lavish Broadway production.*

**pro|duc|tion|al** (prə duk′shə nəl), *adj.* of or having to do with production.

**production car,** *Especially British.* a stock car (defs. 1, 2).

**production control,** control of materials, time, allocation, and other factors in the manufacture of a product.

**pro|duc|tion|ize** (prə duk′shə nīz), *v.t.,* **-ized, -iz|ing.** to put into production: *A parallel programme inside the factory was devoted to productionizing the equipment* (Science Journal).

**production line,** a line in a factory along which a product is assembled part by part in a certain order and at a certain speed by workers, each of whom is responsible for a single operation. The production line is the basis of mass production and the standardization of products.

**production model,** a standard product; product as it comes from regular production.

**production well,** a well drilled in a proven area to extract oil or gas.

**pro|duc|tive** (prə duk′tiv), *adj.* **1** producing much; fertile: *a productive farm, a productive writer.* SYN: See syn. under **fertile.** **2** producing food or other articles of commerce: *Farming is productive labor.* **3** bringing forth; producing: *That field is productive only of weeds. Hasty words are productive of quarrels.* **4** used in forming new words: *-able is a productive suffix.* —**pro|duc′tive|ly**, *adv.* —**pro|duc′tive|ness**, *n.*

**pro|duc|tiv|i|ty** (prō′duk tiv′ə tē), *n.* the power to produce; productiveness: *There is only one effective way to control long-range inflationary pressures, and that is increased productivity* (Harper's).

**product liability,** responsibility of the manufacturer for any hazardous quality of his product: *insurance companies and others are intensely studying a new directive on product liability ... [which] would impose on manufacturers a large degree of responsibility for the safety of their products* (New York Times).

**pro|em** (prō′em), *n.* an introduction; preface; preamble: *Thus much may serve by way of proem, Proceed we therefore to our poem* (Jonathan Swift). SYN: foreword, exordium. [Middle English *proheme* < Old French, learned borrowing from Latin *proemium* < Greek *prooímion* < *pro-* before + *oímos* melodic line of a song; (literally) course, way, road]

**pro|e|mi|al** (prō ē′mē əl), *adj.* introductory; prefatory; preliminary.

**pro|en|zyme** (prō en′zīm), *n.* a protein formed in the cells of an organism, the inactive forerunner of an enzyme, which is converted into an active enzyme by a further reaction; zymogen.

**pro|es|trum** (prō es′trəm, -ēs′-), *n. Zoology.* the period just before estrus in the estrous cycle.

**pro|ette** (prō et′), *n.* a female professional in sports, especially golf. [< *pro*² + *-ette*]

**pro-Eu|ro|pe|an** (prō yůr′ə pē′ən), *adj., n.* —*adj.* **1** supporting or advocating the social, cultural, or economic unification of western European countries. **2** favoring membership in or cooperation with the European Common Market.
—*n.* a person who is pro-European.

**prof** (prof), *n. Informal.* professor.

**Prof.** or **prof.,** professor.

**prof|a|na|tion** (prof′ə nā′shən), *n.* the act of showing contempt or disregard toward something holy; treatment of something sacred as it should not be treated: *Reverence forbids quotation, for the profanation of divine names and ideas becomes revolting and unbearable* (Atlantic). SYN: desecration, defilement.

**pro|fan|a|to|ry** (prə fan′ə tôr′ē, -tōr′-), *adj.* profaning.

**pro|fane** (prə fān′), *adj., v.,* **-faned, -fan|ing.** —*adj.* **1** with contempt or disregard for God or holy things: *a profane man using profane language.* SYN: irreverent, blasphemous. **2** not sacred; worldly: *profane literature.* SYN: secular. **3** ritually unclean or polluted. **4** not initiated into religious rites or mysteries. **5** common; vulgar: *the profane rites of savages.*
—*v.t.* **1** to treat (holy things) with contempt or disregard: *Soldiers profaned the church when they stabled their horses in it.* SYN: desecrate, violate. **2** to put to wrong or unworthy use: *I feel me much to blame, So idly to profane the precious time* (Shakespeare).
[< Old French *prophane,* learned borrowing from Latin *profānus* (literally) not consecrated *prō-* outside of + *fānum* shrine] —**pro|fane′ly**, *adv.* —**pro|fane′ness**, *n.* —**pro|fan′er**, *n.*

**pro|fan|i|ty** (prə fan′ə tē), *n., pl.* **-ties.** **1** the use of profane language; swearing: *Profanity is seldom pleasant to listen to.* **2** the fact or quality of being profane; lack of reverence: *religious profanity.* **3** profane conduct or language.

**pro|fert** (prō′fərt), *n. Law.* an exhibition of a record or paper in open court, or a formal allegation that it is so exhibited. [< Latin *prōfert* (*in cūriā*) he produces (in court), third person present of *prōferre* bring forward < *prō-* forth + *ferre* to bear]

**pro|fess** (prə fes′), *v.t.* **1** to claim to have; lay claim to; claim: *to profess innocence. He professed the greatest respect for the law. I don't profess to be an expert in chemistry.* SYN: assume, pretend. **2** to declare one's belief in: *Christians profess Christ and the Christian religion.* **3** to declare openly: *He professed his loyalty to the United States. We profess Ourselves to be the slaves of chance* (Shakespeare). SYN: own, aver, acknowledge. **4** to have as one's profession or business: *to profess law.* **5** to receive or admit into a religious order. —*v.i.* to make a profession or professions. [back formation < (to be) *professed*]

**pro|fessed** (prə fest′), *adj.* **1** avowed or acknowledged; openly declared: *a professed liar.* **2** alleged; pretended: *How hast thou the heart, Being ... my friend profess'd, To mangle me with that word "banished"?* (Shakespeare). **3** having taken the vows of, or been received into, a religious order: *a professed nun.* [Middle English *professed,* earlier *profess* < Old French *profes,* or *professe,* ultimately < Latin *prōfitērī* < *prō-* forth + *fatērī* confess] —**pro|fess′ed|ly**, *adv.*

**pro|fes|sion** (prə fesh′ən), *n.* **1** an occupation requiring special education, such as law, medicine, teaching, or the ministry. **2** any calling or occupation by which a person habitually earns his living: *a librarian by profession, the acting profession.* **3** the people engaged in such an occupation: *The medical profession favors this law.* **4** the act of professing; open declaration: *I don't believe her profession of friendship for us.* **5** a declaration of belief in a religion. **6** the religion or faith professed. **7** taking the vows and entering a religious order.

**pro|fes|sion|al** (prə fesh′ə nəl, -fesh′nəl), *adj., n.* —*adj.* **1** of or having to do with a profession; appropriate to a profession: *Dr. Smith has a professional seriousness very unlike his ordinary joking manner.* **2** engaged in a profession: *A lawyer or a doctor is a professional person.* **3** following an occupation as one's profession or career: *a professional soldier, a professional writer.* **4** making a business or trade of something that others do for pleasure: *a professional musician, a professional ballplayer.* **5** undertaken or engaged in by professionals rather than amateurs: *a professional ball game.* **6** making a profession of something not properly regarded as a profession: *a professional busybody.*
—*n.* **1** a person who makes a business or trade of something that others do for pleasure, such as singing or dancing: *Only one member of the band is a professional; the others are amateurs. The musician is a professional who tours the country.* **2** a person engaged in a profession; professional man or woman: *The medical conference was attended by both laymen and professionals.*

**pro|fes|sion|al|ism** (prə fesh′ə nə liz′əm, -fesh′nə liz-), *n.* **1** professional character, spirit, or methods: *The production is marked by an assured professionalism* (Wall Street Journal). **2** the

**Pronunciation Key:** hat, āge, cãre, fär; let, ēqual, tėrm; it, īce; hot, ōpen, ôrder; **oi**l, **ou**t; cup, půt, rüle; **ch**ild; lo**ng**; **th**in; **ŦH**en; **zh**, measure; ə represents **a** in about, **e** in taken, **i** in pencil, **o** in lemon, **u** in circus.

standing, practice, or methods of a professional, as distinguished from those of an amateur.

**pro|fes|sion|al|ize** (prə fesh′ə nə līz, -fesh′nə-), *v.t., v.i.*, **-ized, -iz|ing.** to make or become professional. — **pro|fes′sion|al|i|za′tion,** *n.*

**pro|fes|sion|al|ly** (prə fesh′ə nə lē, -fesh′nə-), *adv.* **1** in a professional manner. **2** in professional matters; because of one's profession: *Do you wish to consult me professionally?* (Mary E. Braddon).

**pro|fes|sor** (prə fes′ər), *n.* **1** a teacher of the highest rank in a college or university: *The English professor is popular among the students. Abbr:* Prof. **2** *Informal.* **a** a teacher. **b** a person who claims special knowledge of or proficiency in any field: *The old professor tried to sell his snake oil at the fair but the crowd only laughed at his claims.* **3** a person who professes: *professors of various creeds. There is no error ... which has not had its professors* (John Locke). **4** a person who declares his belief in a religion. **5** *U.S. Slang.* a piano player in a cheap saloon, theater, or brothel. [< Latin *prōfessor, -ōris* < *prōfitērī* to profess, declare publicly; see etym. under **professed**]

**pro|fes|sor|ate** (prə fes′ər it), *n.* **1** the office or term of service of a professor. **2** a group of professors. [< *professor* + *-ate*[3]]

**pro|fes|so|ri|al** (prō′fe sôr′ē əl, -sōr′-; prof′ə-), *adj.* of, having to do with, or characteristic of a professor: *[His] speeches are grave and professorial, not rabble-rousing* (Harper's). — **pro′fes|so′ri|al|ly,** *adv.*

**pro|fes|so|ri|ate** or **pro|fes|so|ri|at** (prō′fe sôr′ē it, -sōr′-; prof′ə-), *n.* **1** a group of professors. **2** a professorship.

**pro|fes|sor|ship** (prə fes′ər ship), *n.* the position or rank of a professor: *Most of the great American historians of the nineteenth century held no professorships* (Atlantic).

**prof|fer** (prof′ər), *v., n.* — *v.t.* to offer for acceptance; present; tender: *We proffered regrets at having to leave so early.* **SYN**: See syn. under **offer.**
— *n.* an offer made: *Her proffer of advice was accepted. Hoping that the enemy ... would make a proffer of peace* (Edmund Burke).
[Middle English *proffren* < Anglo-French *proffrir* < earlier Old French *poroffrir* < *pour-* forth (< Latin *prō-* pro-[1]) + *offrir* offer < Latin *offerre*]

**pro|fi|bri|no|ly|sin** (prō fī′brə nō lī′sin, -nol′ə-), *n.* a proenzyme in the blood from which fibrinolysin is formed by certain blood activators.

**pro|fi|cien|cy** (prə fish′ən sē), *n., pl.* **-cies.** the state or quality of being proficient; knowledge; skill; advanced state of expertness: *Don Geronimo had been educated in England ... which ... accounted for his proficiency in the English language* (George H. Borrow).

**pro|fi|cient** (prə fish′ənt), *adj., n.* — *adj.* advanced in any art, science, or subject; skilled; expert: *She was very proficient in music.* **SYN**: versed, qualified, adept, competent. See syn. under **expert.**
— *n.* an expert: *He was a proficient in golf.*
[< Latin *prōficiēns, -entis* accomplish, make progress, be useful; (literally) present participle of *prōficere* < *prō-* forward + *facere* to make]
— **pro|fi′cient|ly,** *adv.*

**pro|file** (prō′fīl), *n., v.,* **-filed, -fil|ing.** — *n.* **1** a side view, especially of the human face: *In profile his long nose stuck out quite far.* **2** an outline: *The engineer gave a detailed profile of the project.* **SYN**: See syn. under **outline. 3** a drawing of a transverse vertical section of a building, bridge, or other structure. **4** a concise description of a person's abilities, personality, or career: *In a lengthy profile a few years ago, the Harvard Law Record called him "A scholar on the Bench"* (New York Times). **5** *Psychology.* a diagram showing a person's abilities or traits. **6** a diagram of collected data or measurements, as of a natural phenomenon or other scientific data: *If we took gravity readings all over the earth and corrected them to sea level, we would have a gravity profile of the geoid* (Scientific American). **7** sharpness of outline or delineation; clarity of definition: *As a whole, his work lacks a little in profile, due largely to a certain neutralness in its melodic substance* (Harold C. Schonberg).
— *v.t.* **1** to draw a profile of. **2** to write a profile of: *Who will The Observer profile next Sunday?* (New Scientist).
[< earlier Italian *profilo* < *profilare* to draw in outline < Latin *prō-* forth + *fīlum* thread]

**profile drag,** *Aeronautics.* the part of the drag of an airfoil resulting from its shape and the skin friction.

**pro|fil|er** (prō′fī lər), *n.* **1** a writer of journalistic or literary profiles: *Lillian Ross, crack profiler for The New Yorker magazine, [was] in Switzerland working up a series on Charlie Chaplin* (Newsweek). **2** a device for producing profiles of natural phenomena: *a seismic profiler. On the rig was a temperature profiler designed to obtain a continuous record of water temperature from the surface to the bottom as well as a detailed profile of the temperature gradients within the uppermost layer of sediment* (Saturday Review).

**prof|it** (prof′it), *n., v.* — *n.* **1** Often, **profits.** the gain from a business; what is left when the cost of goods and of carrying on the business is subtracted from the amount of money taken in: *The profits in this business are not large.* **SYN**: revenue, returns, proceeds. **2** the gain from any transaction: *to make a profit from the sale of stock.* **3** advantage; benefit; any gain resulting in mental or spiritual betterment: *What profit is there in worrying?* **SYN**: See syn. under **advantage.**
— *v.i.* **1** to make a gain from a business; make a profit: *to profit handsomely from a good business deal.* **2** to get advantage; gain; benefit: *A wise person profits by his mistakes.* **3** *Obsolete.* to make progress; advance.
— *v.t.* to be an advantage or benefit to: *For what shall it profit a man, if he shall gain the whole world, and lose his own soul?* (Mark 8:36).
[< Old French *profit* < Latin *prōfectus, -ūs* an advance < *prōficere;* see etym. under **proficient**]
— **prof′it|er,** *n.*

**prof|it|a|bil|i|ty** (prof′ə tə bil′ə tē), *n.* the quality or state of being profitable: *Profitability and the growth of the firm are the criteria of success in a business* (Scientific American).

**prof|it|a|ble** (prof′ə tə bəl), *adj.* **1** yielding a financial profit; lucrative; gainful: *The sale held by the Girl Scouts was very profitable.* **2** giving a gain or benefit; useful: *We spent a profitable afternoon in the library.* **SYN**: beneficial, fruitful. — **prof′it|a|ble|ness,** *n.*

**prof|it|a|bly** (prof′ə tə blē), *adv.* with profit: *I think it may be profitably taught in the Universities* (Thomas Hobbes).

**profit and loss,** an accounting record to show net profit or loss. — **prof′it-and-loss′,** *adj.*

**prof|it|eer** (prof′ə tir′), *n., v.* — *n.* a person who makes an unfair profit by charging excessive prices for scarce goods: *Profiteers made much money in World War I.*
— *v.i.* to seek or make such unfair profits.
[< *profit* + *-eer*]

**pro|fit|e|role** (prə fit′ə rōl′), *n.* a small, light puff of pastry or an hors d'oeuvre, with such filling as ice cream, whipped cream, fruit, or creamed meat or fish. [< Middle French *profiterole* < Old French *profit* (see etym. under **profit**) + *-erole,* a diminutive suffix]

**prof|it|less** (prof′it lis), *adj.* without profit, gain, or advantage; unprofitable: *... hours of utterly profitless talk* (Manchester Examiner). — **prof′it|less|ly,** *adv.*

**prof|it-mak|ing** (prof′it mā′king), *adj.* that makes a profit: *the only profit-making political organization in the world* (Harper's).

**profit margin,** the amount by which selling price exceeds costs: *Business has tended to become more competitive and profit margins have been reduced* (London Times).

**profit motive,** the expectation or goal of making profit as an incentive for investing in or starting a business: *The students ... refer to the profit motive as the "reward structure"* (Harper's).

**profit sharing,** the sharing of profits between employer and employees. — **prof′it-shar′ing,** *adj.*

**profit squeeze,** a narrow or narrowing profit margin: *Retail concerns are confronted with a "profit squeeze from rising expenses"* (Wall Street Journal).

**profit taking,** the selling of stocks, commodities, or real estate to take a profit: *Frequently in the new year there is profit taking by those who, for tax reasons, have not wanted to sell stocks in the year just passed* (Wall Street Journal).

**prof|li|ga|cy** (prof′lə gə sē), *n.* **1** great wickedness; vice. **2** reckless extravagance.

**prof|li|gate** (prof′lə git), *adj., n.* — *adj.* **1** very wicked; shamelessly bad: *a profligate wretch without any sense of principle, morality, or religion* (Tobias Smollett). **2** recklessly extravagant.
— *n.* a person who is very wicked or extravagant.
[< Latin *prōflīgātus* (literally) ruined, past participle of *prōflīgāre* < *prō-* down, forth + *flīgere* to strike, dash] — **prof′li|gate|ly,** *adv.* — **prof′li|gate|ness,** *n.*

**prof|lu|ent** (prof′lu̇ ənt), *adj.* flowing forth or along: *the profluent stream* (Milton). [< Latin *prōfluēns, -entis,* present participle of *prōfluere* flow forth or onward < *prō-* forth + *fluere* to flow]

**pro for|ma** (prō fôr′mə), *Latin.* for the sake of form; as a matter of form: *Later, after a pro forma floor debate, they dropped the signboard ban* (Time).

**pro|found** (prə found′), *adj., n.* — *adj.* **1** very deep: *a profound sigh, a profound sleep.* **2** felt strongly; very great: *profound despair; profound sympathy.* **3** going far deeper than what is easily understood; having or showing great knowledge or understanding: *a profound book, a profound thinker, a profound thought. Could this conflict of attachments be resolved by a profounder understanding of the principle of loyalty?* (Atlantic). **SYN**: abstruse, recondite. **4** carried far down; going far down; low: *a profound bow.*
— *n.* **1** the deep; the sea; the ocean. **2** an immeasurable abyss, as of space or time.
[Middle English *profound* < Old French *parfond,* and *profond,* learned borrowing from Latin *profundus* < *prō-* forth + *fundus* bottom] — **pro|found′ly,** *adv.* — **pro|found′ness,** *n.*

**pro|fun|di|ty** (prə fun′də tē), *n., pl.* **-ties. 1** the quality of being profound; great depth. **2** a very deep thing or place; an abyss: *through the vast profundity obscure* (Milton).
**profundities,** profound or deep matters: *I am ... not able to dive into these profundities ... not able to understand, much less to discuss* (Robert Burton).
[< Latin *profunditās* < *profundus* profound]

**pro|fuse** (prə fyüs′), *adj.* **1** very abundant: *profuse thanks.* **2** spending or giving freely; lavish; extravagant: *a profuse spender.* [< Latin *profūsus* poured forth, past participle of *profundere* < *prō-* forth + *fundere* to pour] — **pro|fuse′ly,** *adv.* — **pro|fuse′ness,** *n.*
— *Syn.* **1, 2 Profuse, lavish** mean occurring, spending, or giving freely. **Profuse** suggests great generosity, often excessive or insincere: *They were profuse in their praise.* **Lavish** suggests unstinting generosity but not necessarily extravagance: *It was a lavish display of gifts.*

**pro|fu|sion** (prə fyü′zhən), *n.* **1** great abundance: *a certain fruit which grew in profusion there* (Joseph Conrad). **2** extravagance; lavishness.

**pro|fu|sive** (prə fyü′siv), *adj.* profuse; lavish; prodigal: *a profusive variety of spring flowers* (Harper's). — **pro|fu′sive|ly,** *adv.* — **pro|fu′sive|ness,** *n.*

**prog**[1] (prog), *n. British Informal.* a progressive.

**prog**[2] (prog), *v.,* **progged, prog|ging,** *n. Dialect.*
— *v.i.* **1** to search or prowl about, especially for food. **2** to beg.
— *n.* food, especially for a journey.
[origin uncertain]

**prog.,** progressive.

**pro|gen|i|tive** (prō jen′ə tiv), *adj.* producing offspring; reproductive.

**pro|gen|i|tor** (prō jen′ə tər), *n.* an ancestor in the direct line; forefather. [< Latin *prōgenitor, -ōris* < *prōgignere* < *prō-* forth + *gignere* to produce]

**pro|gen|i|to|ri|al** (prō jen′ə tôr′ē əl, -tōr′-), *adj.* having to do with or being a progenitor.

**pro|gen|i|tor|ship** (prō jen′ə tər ship), *n.* the position or fact of being a progenitor: (*Figurative.*) *Cicero would [disown] the intellectual progenitorship of a cicerone* (Blackwood's Magazine).

**pro|gen|i|tress** (prō jen′ə tris), *n.* a woman progenitor.

**pro|gen|i|ture** (prō jen′ə chər), *n.* **1** the act of begetting; birth. **2** offspring; progeny.

**prog|e|ny** (proj′ə nē), *n., pl.* **-nies. 1** children or offspring; descendants: *Kittens are a cat's progeny.* **2** *Figurative.* something that is produced by or originates from something: *Around this fort a progeny of little Dutch-built houses ... soon sprang up* (Washington Irving). [< Old French *progenie,* learned borrowing from Latin *prōgeniēs* < *prōgignere* to beget; see etym. under **progenitor**]

**pro|ge|ri|a** (prō jir′ē ə), *n.* **1** the condition of being prematurely old. **2** a children's disease characterized by premature aging and a high susceptibility to diseases of old people. A child having progeria develops a wrinkled skin and loses his hair. [< New Latin *progeria* < Greek *progêros* prematurely old < *pró* before + *gêras* old age]

**pro|ges|ta|gen** (prō jes′tə jən), *n.* any one of various synthetic hormones similar to progesterone in action.

**pro|ges|ta|tion|al** (prō′jes tā′shə nəl), *adj.* of or characteristic of the part of the menstrual cycle immediately before menstruation.

**pro|ges|ter|one** (prō jes′tə rōn), *n.* a hormone secreted by the corpus luteum and placenta that makes the lining of the uterus ready to receive a fertilized ovum. It is used medically to treat such disorders as those of the uterus or arthritis. *Formula:* $C_{21}H_{30}O_2$ [< *proge*(stin) + *ster*(ol) + *-one*]

**pro|ges|tin** (prō jes′tin), *n.* any substance that makes the lining of the uterus readier to receive a fertilized ovum, such as progesterone. [< *pro-*[1] + Latin *gestāre* to bear + English *-in*]

**pro|ges|to|gen** (prō jes′tə jən), *n.* = progestagen.

**pro|glot|tic** (prō glot′ik), *adj.* of or having to do with the proglottis.

**pro|glot|tid** (prō glot′id), *n.* = proglottis.

**pro|glot|tis** (prō glot′is), *n., pl.* **-glot|ti|des** (-glot′ə dēz). one of the segments or joints of a tapeworm, containing both male and female sexual organs. [< New Latin *proglottis, -idis* < Greek *pro-* before + *glôtta* tongue (because of its shape)]

**prog|nath|ic** (prog nath′ik), *adj.* = prognathous.

**prog|na|thism** (prog′nə thiz əm), *n.* a prognathous condition.

**prog|na|thous** (prog′nə thəs, prog nā′-), *adj.* **1** having the jaws protruding beyond the upper part of the face: *a prognathous skull.* **2** protruding: *prognathous jaws.* [< *pro-*² forward + Greek *gnáthos* jaw + English *-ous*]

**prog|na|thy** (prog′nə thē), *n.* = prognathism.

**prog|no|sis** (prog nō′sis), *n., pl.* **-ses** (-sēz). **1** a forecast of the probable course of a disease. **2** an estimate of what will probably happen: *The prognosis, on this practical level, does not appear favorable* (New Yorker). [< Late Latin *prognōsis* < Greek *prógnōsis* < *progignṓskein* know beforehand < *pro-* before + *gignṓskein* to recognize]

**prog|nos|tic** (prog nos′tik), *adj., n.* —*adj.* indicating something in the future. —*n.* **1** an indication; sign. **2** a forecast; prediction: *Philosophers ... awaited in anxious impatience the fulfilment of their prognostics* (Washington Irving). [< Latin *prognōsticum* < Greek *prognōstikón* omen < *prognṓstikein,* related to *progignṓskein;* see etym. under **prognosis**]

**prog|nos|ti|cate** (prog nos′tə kāt), *v.t.,* **-cat|ed, -cat|ing.** **1** to predict from facts; forecast: *He did prognosticate ... that on the eighteenth of April a storm should burst over this land* (Jane Porter). **2** to indicate beforehand.

**prog|nos|ti|ca|tion** (prog nos′tə kā′shən), *n.* **1** a forecast; prediction: *The Doctor's prognostication in reference to the weather was speedily verified* (Dickens). **2** the act of foretelling.

**prog|nos|ti|ca|tive** (prog nos′tə kā′tiv), *adj.* having the character of a prognostic; predictive: *The comet ... was thought prognostications of the fall of Islamism* (John C. Hobhouse).

**prog|nos|ti|ca|tor** (prog nos′tə kā′tər), *n.* a person or thing that prognosticates.

**pro|gram** (prō′gram, -grəm), *n., v.,* **-grammed, -gram|ming** or **-gramed, -gram|ing.** —*n.* **1** a list of items or events set down in order with a list of the performers. There are concert programs, theater programs, and programs of meetings. **2** the items making up an entertainment: *The entire program was delightful.* **3** a plan of what is to be done: *a school program, a business program, a government program. On top of a big military program they have piled a large capital investment program* (Newsweek). **4** a set of instructions outlining the steps to be performed in a specific operation by an electronic computer or other automatic machine. **5** (in programmed instruction) a series of statements and questions to each of which a student is required to respond before he can go on to the next and usually more difficult level. **6** *Obsolete.* a public notice. **7** *Obsolete.* a prospectus; syllabus.
—*v.t.* **1** to arrange or enter in a program: *She had no discernible talent ... for the Chopin works she programed* (New York Times). **2** to draw up a program or plan for: *Today's farmer has numerous choices in programming his year's activities* (Wall Street Journal). **3** to prepare a set of instructions for (a computer or other automatic machine): *General-purpose computers now on the market can be programmed to do translation* (Scientific American). **4** to arrange (information) in a series of statements and questions in a sequence suitable for programmed instruction. **5** to cause to follow any planned sequence of steps or operations; to direct, control, or channel in accordance with a plan, schedule, or code: *Insects possess a biological clock that programs ... the insect's growth, reproduction, and dormant periods* (James A. Pearre). *The project hoped to show that "the legitimate hostilities and aggressions of black youth" could be programed to benefit the slum community* (Donald Janson). **6** to arrange programmed instruction for (a teaching machine, textbook, or computer).
—*v.i.* **1** to construct a sequence of steps or operations, as for a computer: *The ability to write a computer program will become as widespread as the ability to drive a car. Not knowing how to program will be like living in a house full of servants and not speaking their language* (Scientific American). **2** to follow a prearranged plan, schedule, scheme, or code: *It is broadly hinted by the casework staff* [*in the penitentiary*] *that if the inmate "programs," the U.S. Board of Parole will look more favorably at his case* (Atlantic). [< Late Latin *programma* < Greek *prógramma, -atos* proclamation < *prográphein* write publicly < *pro-* forth + *gráphein* to write]

**program director**, a person in charge of programming for a radio or television station.

**pro|gram|ma|bil|i|ty** (prō′gram ə bil′ə tē), *n.* the quality or condition of being programmable.

**pro|gram|ma|ble** (prō′gram ə bəl, -grə mə-), *adj.* capable of being programmed.

**pro|gram|mat|ic** (prō′grə mat′ik), *n.* **1** having to do with or of the nature of a program: *One wishes freedom for the individual investigator, yet programmatic research is the essence of applied research* (James B. Conant). **2** of the nature of program music. —**pro′gram|mat′i|cal|ly,** *adv.*

**pro|gramme** (prō′gram, -grəm), *n., v.,* **-grammed, -gram|ming.** *Especially British.* program.

**programmed instruction**, a progressive sequence of written material presented in small units which a student must learn before being allowed to read the next unit. Programmed instruction is used especially in teaching machines or programmed textbooks.

**programmed learning**, = programmed instruction.

**pro|gram|mer** or **pro|gram|er** (prō′gram ər, -grə mər), *n.* **1** a person who writes and codes the instructions which control the work of a computer or other automatic machine: *The need for programmers, persons who can convert problems into machine language, will continue to grow* (Science News Letter). **2** a person who prepares any program: *an educational programmer.*

**pro|gram|met|ry** (prō′gram ə trē), *n.* the measurement of the efficiency of a computer program or programmer: *In the area known as programmetry ... a sampling method is used which enables the machine time consumed to be metered for variable units of program size* (Science Journal).

**pro|gram|ming** or **pro|gram|ing** (prō′gram ing, -grə ming), *n.* **1** the planning and arranging of a program or programs, especially for radio and television. **2** the technique or process of preparing instructions for a computer or other automatic machine.

**programming language**, = computer language.

**program music**, music intended to convey impressions of images, scenes, or events.

**prog|ress** (*n.* prog′res; *especially British* prō′gres; *v.* prə gres′), *n., v.* —*n.* **1** an advance; growth; development; improvement: *the progress of science, the progress of a disease. He is showing rapid progress in his studies.* **2** the act or fact of moving forward; going ahead: *to make rapid progress on a journey, the progress of the earth around the sun.* **3** a journey or official tour, especially by a ruler or a judge: *How Summer's royal progress shall be wrought* (John Masefield). **4** *Sociology.* the development of mankind, a group, or an individual toward an objective recognized as desirable. **5** *Biology.* increasing specialization and adaptation, as to environment or ultimate function, during development or evolution.
—*v.i.* **1** to get better; advance; develop: *We progress in learning step by step. Our country ... is fast progressing in its political importance and social happiness* (George Washington). SYN: improve, grow. **2** to move forward; go ahead: *The building of the new school progressed quickly during the summer. The nation's economy has progressed some time without a recession.*
—*v.t.* to cause to move onward or advance; push forward: *Pending litigation will be progressed* (New York Times).
**in progress**, being carried out or on; taking place: *work in progress.*
[< Latin *prōgressus, -ūs* < *prōgredī* go forward < *prō-* forward + *gradī* to walk]

***pro|gres|sion** (prə gresh′ən), *n.* **1** the act or process of moving forward; going ahead: *Creeping is a slow method of progression.* **2** *Mathematics.* a series of numbers in which there is always the same relation between each quantity and the one succeeding it. 2, 4, 6, 8, 10 are in arithmetical progression. 2, 4, 8, 16, 32 are in geometric progression. **3** the apparent or actual motion of a planet from west to east. **4** *Music.* **a** the act of passing from one tone to another in melody, or from one chord to another in harmony. **b** = sequence.

1, 2, 3, 4, 5, 6
arithmetical progression

***progression**
definition 2

2, 4, 8, 16, 32
geometric progression

**pro|gres|sion|al** (prə gresh′ə nəl), *adj.* having to do with progression, advance, or improvement: *... the progressional force of civilization* (American Anthropologist).

**pro|gres|sion|ism** (prə gresh′ə niz əm), *n.* belief in or devotion to progress.

**pro|gres|sion|ist** (prə gresh′ə nist), *n.* a person who favors or believes in progress, as in politics or evolution.

**prog|ress|ist** (prog′res ist, prō′gres-), *n.* a person who favors progress; progressive.

**pro|gres|sive** (prə gres′iv), *adj., n.* —*adj.* **1** making progress; advancing to something better; improving: *a progressive nation.* **2** favoring progress; wanting improvement or reform in government, religion, or business: *He is blamed ... for helping to keep the Administration on a progressive course* (Time). **3** moving forward; going ahead; developing: *a progressive disease.* **4** going from one to the next; involving shifts of players or guests from one table to another: *progressive bridge.* **5** of, following, or based on the theories and practices of progressive education: *a progressive school; ... a progressive curriculum which includes regular courses* (Newsweek). **6** *Grammar.* showing the action as going on. *Is reading, was reading,* and *has been reading* are progressive forms of *read.* **7** *Phonetics.* (of assimilation) in which a preceding sound influences one that follows. **8** increasing in proportion to the increase of something else: *A progressive income tax is one whose rate goes up as a person's earnings increase.*
—*n.* **1** a person who favors improvement and reform in government, religion, or business: *Our doctor is a progressive in his beliefs.* **2** = progressivist. —**pro|gres′sive|ly,** *adv.* —**pro|gres′sive|ness,** *n.*

**Pro|gres|sive** (prə gres′iv), *adj., n.* —*adj.* of a Progressive Party.
—*n.* a member of a Progressive Party.

**Progressive Conservative**, **1** a member of the Progressive Conservative Party. **2** of or having to do with the Progressive Conservative Party.

**Progressive Conservative Party**, the former Conservative Party of Canada.

**progressive education**, a system of education based on the principles of John Dewey and his followers, characterized by emphasis on fitting a course of study to the abilities and interests of the pupils rather than fitting the pupils to a given curriculum.

**progressive jazz**, a jazz style closely resembling bebop, but technically more elaborate and experimental.

**Progressive Party**, **1** a political party formed in 1912 under the leadership of Theodore Roosevelt, advocating direct primaries, the initiative, the referendum, the recall, and woman suffrage. It was also called the Bull Moose Party. **2** a similar political party organized in 1924 and led by Senator Robert M. La Follette. **3** a political party formed in 1948 and led by Henry A. Wallace.

**pro|gres|siv|ism** (prə gres′ə viz əm), *n.* the principles and practices of progressives.

**Pro|gres|siv|ism** (prə gres′ə viz əm), *n. U.S.* the doctrines of a Progressive Party.

**pro|gres|siv|ist** (prə gres′ə vist), *n., adj.* —*n.* **1** a person who believes in progressive education. **2** = progressive.
—*adj.* = progressivistic.

**pro|gres|siv|is|tic** (prə gres′ə vis′tik), *adj.* of progressivists; characterized by progressivism.

**prog|res|siv|i|ty** (prog′rə siv′ə tē, prō′grə-), *n.* progressive quality; progressiveness.

**pro|gym|no|sperm** (prō jim′nə spėrm), *n.* any of the fossil plants believed to be progenitors of the gymnosperms.

**pro|hib|it** (prō hib′it), *v.t.* **1** to forbid by law or authority: *to prohibit the sale of alcoholic beverages. Picking flowers in this park is prohibited.* SYN: See syn. under **forbid**. **2** to prevent; hinder: *Rainy weather and fog prohibited flying. Good manners prohibit me from so rude an answer.* SYN: preclude, debar. [< Latin *prohibitus,* past participle of *prohibēre* < *prō-* away, forth + *habēre* to keep]
► **Prohibited** is followed by *from,* not *against: We are prohibited from smoking on school grounds.* The noun *prohibition* is followed by *against: The prohibition against smoking on school grounds is strictly enforced.*

**pro|hi|bi|tion** (prō′ə bish′ən), *n.* **1** the act of prohibiting or forbidding: *The prohibition against swimming in the city's reservoirs is sensible.* **2** a law or laws that prohibits. **3** a law or laws against making or selling alcoholic liquors. National prohibition existed in the United States between 1920 and 1933. **4** the period when national prohibition was in force in the United States.
► See **prohibit** for usage note.

**pro|hi|bi|tion|ism** (prō′ə bish′ə niz əm), *n.* the principles and practices of prohibitionists: *The bad saloon did more harm to the liquor trade than prohibitionism* (North American Review).

**pro|hi|bi|tion|ist** (prō′ə bish′ə nist), *n.* a person who favors laws against the manufacture and

**Pronunciation Key:** hat, āge, cãre, fär; let, ēqual, tėrm; it, īce; hot, ōpen, ôrder; oil, out; cup, pu̇t, rüle; child; long; thin; ᴛʜen; zh, measure; ə represents **a** in about, **e** in taken, **i** in pencil, **o** in lemon, **u** in circus.

sale of alcoholic liquors.

**Pro|hi|bi|tion|ist** (prō′ə bish′ə nist), *n.* a member of the Prohibition Party.

**Prohibition Party**, a political party, organized in 1869, advocating the prohibition by law of the manufacture and sale of alcoholic liquor.

**pro|hib|i|tive** (prō hib′ə tiv), *adj.* enough to prohibit or prevent something; prohibiting; preventing: *Gold would make excellent roofs, if the price were not prohibitive.* —**pro|hib′i|tive|ly**, *adv.* —**pro|hib′i|tive|ness**, *n.*

**pro|hib|i|tor** (prō hib′ə tər), *n.* a person who prohibits.

**pro|hib|i|to|ry** (prō hib′ə tôr′ē, -tōr′-), *adj.* = prohibitive.

**pro|hor|mone** (prō hôr′mōn), *n.* the inactive forerunner of a hormone; substance from which a hormone is built: *In the body, the molecule is first synthesized in the parathyroid gland as a prohormone, a long chain of 106 amino acids that are chemically linked together* (Earl A. Evans).

**pro|in|su|lin** (prō in′sə lin), *n.* a single-chain protein that is a precursor of insulin in the pancreas and converted by an enzyme into insulin. [< *pro-*[2] + *insulin*]

**proj|ect** (*n.* proj′ekt; *v.* prə jekt′), *n., v.* —*n.* **1** a plan; scheme: *Flying in a heavy machine was once thought an impossible project.* **SYN**: See syn. under **plan**. **2** an undertaking; enterprise: *to grant funds for a research project.* **3** a special assignment planned and carried out by a student, a group of students, or an entire class. **4** *U.S.* a group of apartment buildings built and run as a unit; a housing project: *Lucretia ... lives in the same project, one flight up* (New Yorker). [< Latin *prōjectum* < *prōjicere;* see the verb]
—*v.t.* **1a** to plan; scheme: *The government projected a tax decrease. I projected and drew up a plan for the union* (Benjamin Franklin). **SYN**: devise, contrive. **b** to make a forecast for (something) on the basis of past performance: *to project a population increase of 20 per cent in ten years.* **SYN**: foresee, forecast. **2** to throw or cast forward: *to project a missile into space. A cannon projects shells.* **3** to cause to fall on a surface or into space: *Motion pictures are projected on the screen. The tree projects a shadow on the grass.* **4** to cause to stick out or protrude: *to project a pier out into the lake.* **5** to draw lines through (a point, line or figure) and reproduce it on a line, plane, or surface. **6** *Psychology.* to treat as objective and external (what is essentially subjective).
—*v.i.* **1** to stick out: *The rocky point projects far into the water.* **SYN**: protrude. **2** *U.S. Dialect.* to make plans, especially in an ineffective way.
[< Latin *prōjectus,* past participle of *prōjicere* stretch out, expel < *prō-* forward + *jacere* to throw] —**proj|ect′a|ble**, *adj.*

**pro|jec|tile** (prə jek′təl), *n., adj.* —*n.* an object that can be thrown, hurled, or shot, such as a stone, spear, or bullet: *In this chapter we shall discuss the motion of a projectile, such as a baseball or golf ball, a bomb released from a plane, a rifle bullet, or the shell of a gun* (Sears and Zemansky).
—*adj.* **1** that can be thrown, hurled, or shot: *Bullets and arrows are projectile weapons.* **2** forcing forward; impelling: *a projectile force.* **3** that can be thrust forward: *the projectile jaws of a fish.*
[< New Latin *projectilis* < Latin *prōjicere;* see etym. under **project**]

**pro|jec|tion** (prə jek′shən), *n.* **1** a part that projects or sticks out: *rocky projections on the face of a cliff.* **2** the act or fact of sticking out: *The projection of that pole out into the hall may cause someone to trip and fall.* **3** the act or fact of throwing or casting forward: *the projection of a shell from a cannon, the projection of motion pictures on a screen.* **4** the representation, upon a flat surface, of all or part of the surface of the earth or the celestial sphere. **5** *Geometry.* the act or fact of projecting a figure, upon a line, plane, or surface. **6** *Figurative.* the act or fact of forming projects or plans: *The mayor's projections for rebuilding the slum areas of the city have found wide acceptance.* **7** *Figurative.* an estimate of what will happen; forecast made especially on the basis of past performance: *None of this means that the latest projections are wrong or that a recession is about to start* (Wall Street Journal). *If the present projections are realized, there will be twice as many people in Latin America as in North America by the year 2000* (Atlantic). **8** *Psychology, Psychiatry.* the treating of what is essentially subjective as objective and external; attributing one's own ideas or feelings to another person or group. **9** *Alchemy.* the casting of the powder of the philosophers' stone upon metal in fusion in order to transmute it into gold or silver.

**pro|jec|tion|al** (prə jek′shə nəl), *adj.* of or having to do with projection.

**projection booth**, = projection room.

**pro|jec|tion|ist** (prə jek′shə nist), *n.* **1** the operator of a motion-picture projector. **2** a television cameraman. **3** a person who draws a representation, such as a Mercator projection, of a curved surface upon a plane.

**projection print**, a photographic enlargement made by projecting an image onto a sensitized surface: *The two common types of photographs are contact prints and projection prints.*

**projection room**, a room for the projection of motion pictures: *The light in the projection room went on ... and there was a pause while the operator loaded a new reel* (New Yorker).

**pro|jec|tive** (prə jek′tiv), *adj.* **1** of or having to do with projection; produced by projection. **2** projecting. —**pro|jec′tive|ly**, *adv.*

**projective geometry**, the branch of geometry that deals with those properties of geometric figures that are unchanged after projection.

**projective technique**, *Psychology.* a method of evaluating personality factors, as by having the individual explain pictures and ink dots and supply dialogue.

**pro|jec|tiv|i|ty** (prō′jek tiv′ə tē), *n.* the character of being projective, as two plane figures.

**pro|jec|tor** (prə jek′tər), *n.* **1** an apparatus for projecting an image on a screen: *a motion-picture projector, a slide projector.* **2** a person who forms projects; schemer.

**pro|jet** (prô zhe′), *n. French.* **1** a plan; project. **2** a draft of a proposed treaty.

**pro|kar|y|ote** (prō kar′ē ōt), *n.* = procaryote.

**pro|kar|y|ot|ic** (prō kar′ē ot′ik), *adj.* = procaryotic.

**prol.**, prologue.

**pro|lac|tin** (prō lak′tin), *n.* a hormone from the anterior part of the pituitary gland that induces the mammary glands to give milk and affects the activity of the corpus luteum. [< *pro-*[1] + Latin *lac, lactis* milk + English *-in*]

**pro|lam|in** (prō lam′in, prō′lə min), *n.* any one of a group of simple proteins that are soluble in dilute alcohol but insoluble in water and absolute alcohol, such as gliadin. The prolamins are present in cereals. [< *pr*(otein) + *-al*[1] + *amin*(e)]

**pro|lam|ine** (prō lam′in, -ēn; prō′lə min, -mēn), *n.* = prolamin.

**pro|lan** (prō′lan), *n.* either of two hormones secreted by the pituitary gland that influence the activity of the gonads. They are present in urine during pregnancy. [< German *Prolan* < Latin *prōlēs* offspring]

**pro|lapse** (prō laps′), *n., v.,* **-lapsed, -laps|ing.** —*n.* the slipping out of an organ of the body from its normal position: *a prolapse of the uterus.*
—*v.i.* (of an organ) to fall; slip out of place.
[< Late Latin *prōlapsus, -ūs* < Latin *prolābī* slip forward or down < *prō-* forth + *lābī* to slip, slide]

**pro|lap|sus** (prō lap′səs), *n., pl.* **-sus.** = prolapse.

**pro|late** (prō′lāt), *adj.* **1** elongated in the direction of the polar diameter: *A football is a prolate spheroid. A prolate spheroid is generated by the revolution of an ellipse about its longer axis.* **2** extended or extending in width. [< Latin *prōlātus,* past participle of *prōferre* extend, bring forward < *prō-* forth + *ferre* bring, bear]

**prole** (prōl), *n. Slang.* a proletarian.

**pro|leg** (prō′leg′), *n.* an abdominal leg of a caterpillar or other larva.

**pro|le|gom|e|nar|y** (prō′lə gom′ə ner′ē), *adj.* = prolegomenous.

**pro|le|gom|e|non** (prō′lə gom′ə non), *n., pl.* **-na** (-nə). **1** preliminary material in a book, treatise, or the like; preface; introduction: *This book ... is consciously designed to serve as the prolegomenon to, and an explanation of, political history* (John Kenyon). **2** a preliminary statement or remark: *He, after some ambiguous prolegomena, roundly proposed I should go shares with him* (Robert Louis Stevenson). [< Greek *prolegómenon* anything said beforehand < *prolégein* say beforehand < *pró-* before + *légein* to say]

**pro|le|gom|e|nous** (prō′lə gom′ə nəs), *adj.* of or having to do with prolegomena: *It may not be amiss in the prolegomenous or introductory chapter, to say something of that species of writing* (Henry Fielding).

**pro|lep|sis** (prō lep′sis), *n., pl.* **-ses** (-sēz). **1** = anticipation. **2** anticipation of objections in order to answer them in advance. **3** an epithet in anticipation of its becoming applicable. *Example:* "The murdered king falls by a traitor's hand." **4** = anachronism. [< Latin *prolepsis* < Greek *prólēpsis* (rhetorical) anticipation; preconception < *prolambánein* anticipate < *pró-* before + *lambánein* show forth, seize; grasp with the senses or mind]

**pro|lep|tic** (prō lep′tik), *adj.* **1** = anticipative: *A proleptic instinct made him look forward* (Eden Philpotts). **2** involving prolepsis. —**pro|lep′ti|cal|ly**, *adv.*

**pro|le|tar|i|an** (prō′lə tãr′ē ən), *adj., n.* —*adj.* **1** of or belonging to the proletariat: *... irreverent proletarian humor* (Newsweek). **2** of or belonging to the proletary of ancient Rome. **3** *Obsolete.* low; vulgar.
—*n.* a person belonging to the proletariat: *The proletarians had not come from their factories at this hour* (Booth Tarkington).
[< Latin *prōlētārius* furnishing the state only with children (< *prōlēs* offspring < *prō-* forth + *alere* nourish, sustain) + English *-an*] —**pro′le|tar′i|an|ly**, *adv.*

**pro|le|tar|i|an|ism** (prō′lə tãr′ē ə niz′əm), *n.* the condition of being proletarian: *They had overturned feudalism, and now they had created proletarianism* (John Rae).

**pro|le|tar|i|an|i|za|tion** (prō′lə tãr′ē ə nə zā′shən), *n.* the act or process of proletarianizing: *the "petty bourgeoisie" struggling against proletarianization* (Manchester Guardian Weekly).

**pro|le|tar|i|an|ize** (prō′lə tãr′ē ə nīz), *v.t.,* **-ized, -iz|ing.** to make a proletarian of; cause to become proletarian: *In addition, there is the dual educational objective of intellectualizing the proletariat and proletarianizing the intellectuals* (Saturday Review).

**pro|le|tar|i|at** (prō′lə tãr′ē ət), *n.* **1** the lowest class in economic and social status. The proletariat includes unskilled laborers, casual laborers, and tramps. *The West has faced the task of absorbing its proletariat ... and of giving it the feeling of fully belonging* (Saturday Review). **2** the laboring class in Europe, especially as contrasted by the socialists formerly with slaves and serfs, and now with the middle class: *the dictatorship of the proletariat* (Karl Marx). **3** the proletaries in ancient Rome. [< French *prolétariat* < Latin *prōlētārius* proletarian + French *-at* -ate[3]]

**pro|le|tar|i|ate** (prō′lə tãr′ē it), *n.* = proletariat.

**pro|le|tar|y** (prō′lə ter′ē), *n., pl.* **-tar|ies.** *adj.* —*n.* a person of the poorest class in ancient Rome, regarded as contributing nothing but children to the state.
—*adj.* belonging to the lowest or poorest class.
[< Latin *prōlētārius;* see etym. under **proletarian**]

**pro-life** (prō′līf′), *adj.* = right-to-life. —**pro′-lif′er**, *n.*

**pro|lif|er|ate** (prō lif′ə rāt), *v.i., v.t.,* **-at|ed, -at|ing.** **1** to grow or produce by multiplication of parts, as in budding or cell division. **2** to multiply; spread; propagate: *These conferences proliferate like measles spots* (Harper's). [back formation < *proliferation*]

**pro|lif|er|a|tion** (prō lif′ə rā′shən), *n.* **1** reproduction, as by budding or cell division. **2** a spreading; propagation: *The draft of the test ban treaty contained an expression of desire to prevent the proliferation of nuclear weapons* (Seymour Topping). [< French *prolifération* < *prolifère* < Medieval Latin *prolifer;* see etym. under **proliferous**]

**pro|lif|er|a|tive** (prō lif′ə rā′tiv), *adj.* characterized by or tending to proliferation: *proliferative cancer cells.*

**pro|lif|er|ous** (prō lif′ər əs), *adj.* **1** producing new individuals, as by budding or cell division. **2** producing an addition from a part that is normally ultimate, such as a shoot or a new flower from the midst of a flower. [< Medieval Latin *prolifer* < Latin *prōlēs* offspring (see etym. under **proletarian**) + *-fer* bearing + English *-ous*] —**pro|lif′er|ous|ly**, *adv.*

**pro|lif|ic** (prə lif′ik), *adj.* **1** producing many offspring: *Rabbits are prolific animals.* **2** producing much: *a prolific tree, a prolific garden, a prolific writer,* (*Figurative.*) *a prolific imagination.* **SYN**: fertile. **3** characterized by abundant production: *a garden prolific of weeds.* **4** conducive to growth or fruitfulness: *a prolific climate.* [< Medieval Latin *prolificus* < Latin *prōlēs* offspring (see etym. under **proletarian**) + *facere* to make] —**pro|lif′ic|ly**, *adv.* —**pro|lif′ic|ness**, *n.*

**pro|lif|i|ca|cy** (prə lif′ə kə sē), *n.* the quality or state of being prolific: *The only feature which keeps oysters from extinction is their prolificacy* (Hegner and Stiles).

**pro|lif|i|cal|ly** (prə lif′ə klē), *adv.* in a prolific manner.

**pro|li|fic|i|ty** (prō lə fis′ə tē), *n.* = prolificacy.

**pro|line** (prō′lēn, -lin), *n.* an amino acid, a product of the decomposition of certain proteins. *Formula:* $C_5H_9NO_2$ [< German *Prolin*]

**pro|lix** (prō liks′, prō′liks), *adj.* using too many words; too long; tedious: *Conscious dullness has little right to be prolix* (Samuel Johnson). **SYN**: wordy, verbose. [< Latin *prōlixus* (literally) poured out < *prō-* forth + *lix-,* a root related to *liquēre* to flow, be liquid] —**pro|lix′ly**, *adv.* —**pro|lix′ness**, *n.*

**pro|lix|i|ty** (prō lik′sə tē), *n., pl.* **-ties.** too great length; tedious length of speech or writing: *the insufferable prolixity of the most prolix of hosts* (Charles J. Lever).

**pro|loc|u|tor** (prō lok′yə tər), *n.* **1** = chairman. **2** = spokesman. [< Latin *prolocūtor* pleader, advocate < *prōloquī* speak out < *prō-* forth + *loquī* to speak]

**Pro|loc|u|tor** (prō lok′yə tər), *n.* the Lord Chancellor, as chairman of the House of Lords.

**pro|loc|u|tor|ship** (prō lok′yə tər ship), *n.* the office or position of a prolocutor.

**pro|logue** or **pro|log** (prō′lôg, -log), *n.* **1** an introduction to a novel, poem, film, or other literary or dramatic work. **2** a speech or poem addressed to the audience by one of the actors at the beginning of a play. **3** *Figurative.* any introductory act or event: *The conference ... had a prologue and epilogue of arrivals and departures* (New Yorker). **4** the actor who speaks the prologue to a play. [< Latin *prōlogus* < Greek *prólogos* < *pro-* before + *lógos* speech]

**pro|logu|ize** or **pro|log|ize** (prō′lô gīz, -lo-), *v.i.*, **-ized, -iz|ing. 1** to compose a prologue. **2** to deliver a prologue: *There may prologuize the spirit of Philip* (Milton). —**pro′logu|iz′er, pro′log|iz′er,** *n.*

**pro|long** (prə lông′, -long′), *v.t.* **1** to make longer; extend; stretch: *Good care may prolong a sick person's life. The author cleverly prolonged the suspense in his mystery novel. It was useless to prolong the discussion* (Edith Wharton). **SYN:** protract. See syn. under **lengthen. 2** *Obsolete.* to put off in time; postpone: *This wedding-day Perhaps is but prolong'd: have patience* (Shakespeare). [< Late Latin *prōlongāre* < *prō-* forth + *longus* long. Compare etym. under **purloin.**] —**pro|long′a|ble,** *adj.* —**pro|long′er,** *n.* —**pro-long′ment,** *n.*

**pro|lon|gate** (prə lông′gāt, -long′-), *v.t.*, **-gat|ed, -gat|ing.** = prolong.

**pro|lon|ga|tion** (prō′lông gā′shən, -long-), *n.* **1** the action of lengthening in time or space; extension: *the prolongation of one's school days by a year of graduate study. ... the sofas resembling a prolongation of uneasy chairs* (George Eliot). **2** an added part: *The mountains to the right formed a prolongation of the range.*

**pro|longe** (prō lonj′; *French* prô lôNzh′), *n.* a strong rope with a hook at one end and a toggle at the other, formerly used in moving unlimbered guns. [< French *prolonge* < *prolonger* to prolong]

**pro|longed** (prə lôngd′, -longd′), *adj.* **1** lengthened; extended: *the last guest who had made a prolonged stay in his hotel* (Joseph Conrad). **2** beyond the ordinary, especially in length: *The dog uttered prolonged howls whenever the family left the house. ... a lean, lank, dark, young man with ... irregular, rather prolonged features* (H. G. Wells).

**pro|lo|ther|a|py** (prō′lō ther′ə pē), *n.* an orthopedic treatment for healing and hardening torn spinal ligaments by the injection of a substance that causes scar tissue to proliferate. [< *prol(iferative) therapy*]

**pro|lu|sion** (prō lü′zhən), *n.* **1** a preliminary: *But why such long prolusion and display, Such turning and adjustment of the harp?* (Robert Browning). **2** an introductory exercise, performance, essay, or the like: *All this tiresome prolusion is only to enable you to understand* (W. H. Hudson). [< Latin *prōlūsiō, -ōnis* < *prōlūdere* to play or practice beforehand < *prō-* before + *lūdere* to play]

**pro|lu|so|ry** (prō lü′sər ē), *adj.* serving for prolusion; introductory.

**prom**[1] (prom), *n. Informal.* a dance or ball given by a college or high-school class. [American English; short for *promenade*]

**prom**[2] or **Prom** (prom), *n. British Informal.* a promenade concert.

**prom.,** **1** promontory. **2** promoted.

**pro|ma|zine** (prō′mə zēn, -zin), *n.* a tranquilizing drug used to relieve anxiety and tension in mental illness, alcoholism, and drug addiction. *Formula:* $C_{17}H_{20}N_2S$ [< *pro*(pyl) + *m*(ethyl) + *azine*]

**pro me|mo|ri|a** (prō mə môr′ē ə, -mōr′-), *Latin.* for remembrance; for a memorial.

**prom|e|nade** (prom′ə nād′, -näd′), *n., v.,* **-nad|ed, -nad|ing.** —*n.* **1** a walk for pleasure or for show: *a promenade in the park. The Easter promenade is well known as a fashion show.* **2** a public place for such a walk: *The boardwalk at Atlantic City is a famous promenade along the beach.* **3** a dance or ball; prom. **4** a march of all the guests at the opening of a formal dance. **5** a ride, drive, or excursion in a boat: *What do you think of a little promenade at sea?* (Joseph Conrad). **6** a square-dancing figure in which a couple or, usually, all the couples of a set march once around the square, circle, or the hall.
—*v.i.* to walk about or up and down for exercise, for pleasure, or for show: *He promenaded back and forth on the ship's deck.*
—*v.t.* **1** to walk through; walk about. **2** to take on a promenade.
[< earlier French *promenade* < *promener* take for a walk, for Old French *pourmener* < Latin *prōmināre* drive (a beast) on < *prō-* forward + *mināre* drive with shouts < *minae* threats] —**prom′e|nad′er,** *n.*

**promenade concert,** *British.* a concert at which the audience stands instead of being seated.

**promenade deck,** a space, usually enclosed, on an upper deck of a ship where passengers can walk about without being exposed to the weather.

**pro|meth|a|zine** (prō meth′ə zēn), *n.* = Phenergan. [< *pro*(pyl) + *meth*(yl) + (thi)*azine*]

**Pro|me|the|an** (prə mē′thē ən), *adj.* of, having to do with, or suggestive of Prometheus, especially in his skill or art; daringly original: *Andrews is drawn to whatever in architecture is boldly marked with personality, whatever is Promethean and existential* (Harper's).

**Pro|me|the|us** (prə mē′thē əs, -thüs), *n. Greek Mythology.* one of the Titans. He stole fire from heaven and taught men its use, for which Zeus punished him by chaining him to a rock.

***pro|me|thi|um** (prə mē′thē əm), *n.* a radioactive metallic chemical element which is the product of the fission of uranium, thorium, and plutonium; (formerly) illinium: *The only rare earth not found in nature is promethium* (Science News Letter). [< *Prometheus* + New Latin *-ium,* a suffix meaning "element"]

***promethium**

| symbol | atomic number | mass number | oxidation state |
|---|---|---|---|
| Pm | 61 | 145 | 3 |

**Pro|min** (prō′min), *n. Trademark.* a drug derived from sulfone, used in the treatment of leprosy and tuberculosis. *Formula:* $C_{24}H_{34}N_2Na_2O_{18}S_3$

**prom|i|nence** (prom′ə nəns), *n.* **1** the quality or fact of being prominent, distinguished, or conspicuous: *the prominence of Washington as a leader, the prominence of football as a sport, the prominence of athletics in some schools.* **2** something that juts out or projects, especially upward; projection. A hill is a prominence. **3** a cloud of gas which erupts from the sun and is seen as either a projection from, or a dark spot on, the surface of the sun: *Spectacular upsurgings of gases in the chromosphere, known as prominences, are sometimes seen: these may shoot out to distances of the order of a few hundred thousand miles* (A. J. Higgs).

**prom|i|nent** (prom′ə nənt), *adj., n.* —*adj.* **1** well-known or important; distinguished: *a prominent citizen.* **SYN:** leading. See syn. under **eminent. 2** easy to see; that catches the eye: *A single tree in a field is prominent.* **3** standing out; projecting: *Some insects have prominent eyes.*
—*n.* = puss moth.
[< Latin *prōminēns, -entis,* present participle of *prōminēre* to jut or stand out < *prō-* forward + *minēre* to jut < *minae, -ārum* projecting points (of mountains); threats] —**prom′i|nent|ly,** *adv.*
—*Syn.* **2 Prominent, conspicuous** mean attracting attention and easily seen. **Prominent** describes something that stands out from its surroundings or background in a very noticeable manner: *He hung her picture in a prominent position in the living room.* **Conspicuous** describes something so plainly visible that it is impossible not to see it: *The uniformed soldier looked conspicuous among the group of civilians.*

**prom|is|cu|i|ty** (prom′is kyü′ə tē, prō′mis-), *n., pl.* **-ties.** the fact or condition of being promiscuous.

**pro|mis|cu|ous** (prə mis′kyü əs), *adj.* **1** mixed and in disorder: *a promiscuous heap of clothing on a closet floor.* **SYN:** miscellaneous. **2** making no distinctions; not discriminating: *promiscuous friendships.* **3** not confining one's sexual relationships to one person. **4** *Informal.* casual. [< Latin *prōmiscuus* (with English *-ous*) mixed < *prō miscuō* as common < *miscēre* to mix] —**pro-mis′cu|ous|ly,** *adv.* —**pro|mis′cu|ous|ness,** *n.*

**prom|ise** (prom′is), *n., v.,* **-ised, -is|ing.** —*n.* **1** words said or written, binding a person to do or not to do something: *to give a promise to help. A man of honor always keeps his promise.* **SYN:** vow, pledge, covenant. **2** *Figurative.* **a** an indication of what may be expected: *The clouds give promise of rain. In each dewdrop of the morning lies the promise of a day* (Thoreau). **b** an indication of future excellence; something that gives hope of success: *a pupil of promise in music, a young scholar who shows promise.*
—*v.i.* **1** to give one's word; make a promise: *He promised to stay till we came.* **2** *Figurative.* to give promise; give ground for expectation: *He thought that voyage promised very fair, and that there was a great prospect of advantage* (Daniel Defoe).
—*v.t.* **1** to make a promise of (something) to (a person): *to promise help to a friend.* **2** to obligate oneself by a promise to: *to promise a friend to help.* **3** *Figurative.* to give indication of; give hope of; give ground for expectation of: *a young man who promises much. The rainbow promises fair weather.* **4** to assure: *Good manners are never out of place, I promise you.*
[< Latin *prōmissum* < *prōmittere* send forth, foretell; promise < *prō-* before + *mittere* to put, send] —**prom′is|er,** *n.*

**Prom|ised Land** (prom′ist), **1** the country promised by God to Abraham and his descendants; Canaan (in the Bible, Genesis 15:18; 17:1-8). **2** = heaven (def. 1a).

**promised land,** a place or condition of expected happiness: *America has been a promised land for many immigrants.*

**prom|is|ee** (prom′ə sē′), *n.* a person to whom a promise is made.

**prom|is|ing** (prom′ə sing), *adj.* likely to turn out well; hopeful: *a promising beginning, a promising young writer.* —**prom′is|ing|ly,** *adv.*

**prom|i|sor** (prom′ə sôr, prom′ə sôr′), *n.* a person who makes a promise.

**prom|is|so|ry** (prom′ə sôr′ē, -sōr′-), *adj.* containing or implying a promise: *promissory oaths.*

**promissory note,** a written promise to pay a stated sum of money to a certain person at a certain time.

**Pro|mi|zole** (prō′mə zōl), *n. Trademark.* a drug used in the treatment of leprosy and, combined with streptomycin, in the treatment of tubercular diseases. *Formula:* $C_9H_9N_3O_2S_2$

**pro|mo** (prō′mō), *n., pl.* **-mos.** *U.S. Informal.* **1** a television announcement of a forthcoming program on the same network. **2** the promotion of a product in a radio or television program: *There were other tie-in "promos," involving among others, a rifle firm, a hat company, a food packer, and even the U.S. Air Force Academy* (Saturday Review). [short for *promotion*]

**prom|on|to|ry** (prom′ən tôr′ē, -tōr′-), *n., pl.* **-ries. 1** a high point of land extending from the coast into the water; headland: *that bold green promontory, known to seamen as Java Head* (Herman Melville). See picture under **peninsula. 2** *Anatomy.* a part that bulges out. [< Medieval Latin *promontorium,* variation (influenced by Latin *mōns* mount) of Latin *prōmunturium*]

**pro|mot|a|bil|i|ty** (prə mō′tə bil′ə tē), *n.* promotable state: *the promotability of a product.*

**pro|mot|a|ble** (prə mō′tə bəl), *adj.* that can be promoted; qualified for or deserving promotion.

**pro|mote** (prə mōt′), *v.t.,* **-mot|ed, -mot|ing. 1** to raise in rank, condition, or importance: *Pupils who pass the test will be promoted to the next higher grade.* **SYN:** advance, elevate, exalt. **2** to help to grow or develop; help to success: *An understanding and appreciation of the culture of other countries may promote peace.* **3** to help to organize; start: *Several bankers promoted the new company.* **4** to further the sale or acceptance of (a product or service) by advertising and publicity: *Color TV has been more aggressively promoted as more manufacturers have joined the competition* (Wall Street Journal). **5** *U.S. Slang.* to get by cheating or trickery: *to promote a television set.* **6** *Chess.* to exchange (a pawn reaching the last rank) for a queen, rook, bishop, or knight of the same color. **7** *Chemistry.* to make (a catalyst) more active: *The catalyst is preferably promoted ... by the addition of small amounts of aluminum oxide and potassium oxide* (Anthony Standen). [< Latin *prōmōtus,* past participle of *prōmovēre* < *prō-* forward + *movēre* to move]
—*Syn.* **2 Promote, further** mean to help something move toward a desired end. **Promote** applies to any phase or stage of development, including the initial one: *These scholarships will promote better understanding of Latin America.* **Further** applies especially to any stage beyond the initial one: *Getting a scholarship will further her education.*

**pro|mot|ee** (prə mō′tē, -mō′tē′), *n.* a person who is promoted.

**pro|mot|er** (prə mō′tər), *n.* **1** a person or thing that promotes, encourages, or furthers something: *Good humor is a promoter of friendship.* **2** a person who organizes new companies or other projects or enterprises and secures capital for them: *a railroad promoter. A boxing promoter stages and finances prize fights.* **3** *Chemistry.* a substance that promotes a catalyst. **4** *Genetics.* a functional element in the Jacob-Monod model of the operon: *A gene consists of 3 elements, together called an operon. The elements are a "promoter" that produces the repressor; an "operator" that starts the gene operating but is nor-*

**Pronunciation Key:** hat, āge, cãre, fär; let, ēqual, tėrm; it, īce; hot, ōpen, ôrder; oil, out; cup, pu̇t, rüle; child; long; thin; ᴛʜen; zh, measure; ə represents **a** in about, **e** in taken, **i** in pencil, **o** in lemon, **u** in circus.

*mally dampened by the repressor; and a "structural" portion, which is placed into action by the operator and does the main work of the gene* (Robert Reinhold).

**Promoter of the Faith**, = devil's advocate.

**pro|mo|tion** (prə mō′shən), *n.* **1** an advance in rank or importance: *The clerk was given a promotion and an increase in salary.* **2** the act of helping to grow or develop; helping along to success: *The local doctors were busy in the promotion of a health campaign.* **3** the action of helping to organize; starting: *It took much time and money for the promotion of the new company.* **4** the act of furthering the sale or acceptance of a product or service by advertising and publicity: *Public relations firms and advertising agencies both engage in promotion.*

**pro|mo|tion|al** (prə mō′shə nəl), *adj.* having to do with or used in the promotion of a person, product, or enterprise: *The publishing firm mailed out a million promotional pamphlets in the course of a year.*

**pro|mo|tive** (prə mō′tiv), *adj.* tending to promote: *promotive of business interests.* — **pro|mo′tive|ness**, *n.*

**Pro|mo|tor Fi|de|i** (prō mō′tər fī′dē ī), *pl.* **Pro|mo|to|res Fidei** (prō′mō tō′rēz). Promoter of the Faith. [< New Latin *Promotor Fidei*]

**prompt** (prompt), *adj., v., n.* — *adj.* **1** ready and willing; on time; quick: *Be prompt to obey. But he learns to tell time much earlier than he learns to be prompt* (Sidonie M. Gruenberg). **SYN**: punctual. See syn. under **ready**. **2** done at once; made without delay: *I expect a prompt answer.* **SYN**: immediate, swift. **3** *Especially British.* of a prompter; used in prompting: *a prompt box, the prompt side of the stage.*
— *v.t.* **1** to cause (someone) to do something: *His curiosity prompted him to ask questions.* **SYN**: incite, impel, induce. **2** to give rise to; suggest; inspire: *A kind thought prompted the gift.* **3** to remind (a learner, speaker, or actor) of the words or actions needed: *Please prompt me if I forget my lines.*
— *v.i.* to act as prompter.
— *n.* **1** an act of prompting. **2** something that prompts. **3** *Commerce.* **a** a limit of time allowed for payment of goods purchased. **b** the contract determining this limit of time.
[< Latin *promptus* ready, at hand; (originally) past participle of *prōmere* bring to light < *prō-* forward + *emere* buy, (originally) take. See etym. of doublet **pronto**.] — **prompt′ly**, *adv.* — **prompt′ness**, *n.*

**prompt|book** (prompt′bu̇k′), *n.* a copy of a play prepared for the prompter's use, containing the text as it is to be spoken and directions for the performance.

**prompt|er** (promp′tər), *n.* **1** a person who tells actors or speakers what to say when they forget. **2** a device for prompting a speaker, such as a TelePrompTer: *The President read his message from an electrically-operated prompter* (New York Times).

**promp|ti|tude** (promp′tə tüd, -tyüd), *n.* readiness in acting or deciding; promptness: *Our borrowers generally have met the repayment installments on their loans with a commendable promptitude* (London Times).

**prompt neutron**, a neutron emitted in nuclear fission with almost zero delay, as distinguished from a delayed neutron.

**prompt note**, a note reminding a person of the date a loan is due.

**prompt side**, *Theater.* the left side of the stage as one faces the audience.

**pro|mul|gate** (prō mul′gāt; *especially British* prom′əl gāt), *v.t.*, **-gat|ed, -gat|ing.** **1** to announce officially; proclaim formally: *The king promulgated a decree. The constitution probably will soon be promulgated and elections are promised within a year* (Newsweek). **2** to spread far and wide: *Schools try to promulgate knowledge and good habits.* [< Latin *prōmulgāre*] — **pro|mul′ga|tor**, *n.*

**pro|mul|ga|tion** (prō′mul gā′shən; *especially British* prom′əl gā′shən), *n.* **1** the act or process of promulgating: *the very promulgation of the gospel* (Richard Hooker). **2** the state of being promulgated. **3** the official publication of a new law or decree.

**pro|my|ce|li|al** (prō′mī sē′lē əl), *adj.* of or having to do with the promycelium.

**pro|my|ce|li|um** (prō′mī sē′lē əm), *n., pl.* **-li|a** (-lē ə). *Botany.* the filamentous product of the germination of a spore. [< *pro-*[2] + *mycelium*]

**prom|y|shlen|nik** (prom′ə shlen′ik), *n., pl.* **-shlen|ni|ki** (-shlen′ə kē). a Russian frontiersman of Siberia, the Aleutian Islands, or Alaska. [< Russian *promyshlennik*]

**pron.**, **1a** pronominal. **b** pronoun. **2a** pronounced. **b** pronunciation.

**pro|na|os** (prō nā′os), *n., pl.* **-na|oi** (-nā′oi). the porch or vestibule in front of the cella of a temple: *The chapel has an atrium, or pronaos, supported by slender Corinthian columns* (New Yorker). [< Latin *pronāos* < Greek *prónāos* < *pró* before + *nāós* temple]

**pro|na|tal|ist** (prō nā′tə list), *adj.* favoring a high rate of birth: ... *a reluctance to develop pronatalist policies* (London Times).

**pro|nate** (prō′nāt), *v.*, **-nat|ed, -nat|ing.** — *v.t.* **1** to hold (the hand or forelimb) with the palm down. **2** *Golf.* to rotate (the wrist) so that the right hand rolls over the left. **3** to make prone.
— *v.i.* **1** to be pronated. **2** *Golf.* to pronate the wrist.
[< Late Latin *prōnāre* (with English *-ate*[1]) throw (oneself) face down, bow to the ground < *prōnus* prone]

**pro|na|tion** (prō nā′shən), *n.* **1a** the act of rotating the hand or forelimb so that the palm turns down. **b** a similar movement, as of the foot, hindlimb, or shoulder. **c** *Golf.* the act of pronating the wrist. **2** the position taken in pronating. **3** a making prone.

**pro|na|tor** (prō nā′tər), *n.* a muscle that effects or assists in pronation.

**prone** (prōn), *adj.* **1** inclined; liable: *We are prone to think evil of people we don't like.* **SYN**: disposed, apt. **2** lying face down: *to be prone on a bed.* **3** lying flat: *to fall prone on the ground.* **SYN**: recumbent, prostrate. **4** having a downward slope or direction: *The sun ... was hasting now with prone career To the ocean isles* (Milton). **5** abject; base. [< Latin *prōnus* bent forward; inclined to < *prō-* forward] — **prone′ly**, *adv.* — **prone′ness**, *n.*

**pro|neph|ric** (prō nef′rik), *adj.* of or having to do with the pronephros: *the pronephric duct.*

**pro|neph|ros** (prō nef′ros), *n., pl.* **-roi** (-roi). *Embryology.* the most anterior part of the renal organ of vertebrate embryos. [< New Latin *pronephros* < Greek *pró* pro-[2] + *nephrós* kidney]

**prong** (prông, prong), *n., v.* — *n.* **1** one of the pointed ends of a fork or antler: *The prongs of his fork held the meat while he cut it with a knife.* **2** a branch or fork of a small stream: *Carpenter's Creek, a branch of Jackson's, which is the principal prong of the James River* (George Washington). **3** *Figurative.* any branch, fork, division, or section: *200 guerrillas ... struck in three prongs* (New York Times).
— *v.t.* **1** to pierce or stab with a prong. **2** to supply with prongs. **3** to turn up the soil with a fork; fork.
[origin uncertain]

**pronged** (prôngd, prongd), *adj.* having prongs, sections, aspects, branches, or divisions: *a three-pronged thrust consisting of sabotage, infiltration, and ultimate invasion* (New York Times).

**prong|horn** (prông′hôrn′, prong′-), *n., pl.* **-horns** or (*collectively*) **-horn.** a ruminant mammal like an antelope, living on the plains of western North America. Both sexes have bony horns with one short branch or prong jutting forward and with a black covering which is shed annually. [American English; short for earlier *pronghorn*(ed antelope)]

**pronghorn antelope**, = pronghorn.

**pro|nom|i|nal** (prō nom′ə nəl), *adj., n.* — *adj.* of or having to do with pronouns; having the nature of a pronoun. *This, that, any, some,* and so forth, are pronominal adjectives.
— *n.* a pronominal word.
[< Late Latin *prōnōminālis* < Latin *prōnōmen, -inis* pronoun] — **pro|nom′i|nal|ly**, *adv.*

**pro|noun** (prō′noun), *n.* **1** a word used to indicate without naming; word used instead of a noun. In "John did not like to go because he was sick," *he* is a pronoun used in the second part of the sentence to avoid repeating *John.* **2** the part of speech or form class to which such words belong. *Examples: I, we, you, he, it,* and *they* are personal pronouns; *my, mine, your, yours, his, our, ours, their,* and *theirs* are possessive pronouns; *who, whose, which,* and *whatever* are interrogative pronouns; *who, that, which,* and *what* are also relative pronouns; *this* and *that* are demonstrative pronouns or pronominal adjectives; *each, every, either,* and *neither* are distributive pronouns or pronominal adjectives; *any, some, one, other, another,* and *none* are indefinite personal or possessive pronouns or indefinite pronominal adjectives. *Abbr:* pron. [< *pro-*[1] in place of + *noun,* as translation of Latin *prōnōmen* < *prō-* in place of + *nōmen* name]

**pro|nounce** (prə nouns′), *v.*, **-nounced, -nounc|ing.** — *v.t.* **1** to make the sounds of; speak: *Pronounce your words clearly. In the word "dumb" you don't pronounce the "b."* **2** to declare (a person or thing) to be: *The doctor pronounced her cured.* **3** to declare solemnly or positively: *The judge pronounced sentence on the criminal. "Raise your right hands with me, ... and silently pronounce a vow of secrecy"* (James T. Farrell).
— *v.i.* **1** to pronounce words: *In speaking, they pronounce through the nose and throat* (Jonathan Swift). **2** to give an opinion or decision: *Only an expert should pronounce on this case.*
[< Old French *pronuncier,* learned borrowing from Latin *prōnūntiāre* < *prō-* forth + *nūntiāre* announce < *nūntius* messenger; information, report] — **pro|nounce′a|ble**, *adj.* — **pro|nounc′er**, *n.*

**pro|nounced** (prə nounst′), *adj.* strongly marked; emphatic; decided: *She held pronounced opinions on gambling. She has very pronounced likes and dislikes. The injured boy walks with a pronounced limp.* — **pro|nounc′ed|ly**, *adv.*

**pro|nounce|ment** (prə nouns′mənt), *n.* **1** a formal or authoritative statement; declaration: *The judge gave his pronouncement at the end of the trial.* **2** an opinion or decision.

**pro|nounc|ing** (prə noun′sing), *adj.* showing pronunciation; helping in pronunciation: *a pronouncing alphabet, a pronouncing dictionary of British English.*

**pron|to** (pron′tō), *adv. U.S. Informal.* promptly; quickly; right away: *Immigration authorities had him arrested and deported pronto* (Liberty). [American English < Spanish *pronto* < Latin *promptus.* See etym. of doublet **prompt**.]

**Pron|to|sil** (pron′tə səl), *n. Trademark.* a dye product formerly used in the treatment of streptococcal infections. It was found in 1932 to contain sulfanilamide, the first of the sulfa drugs to be widely used. *Formula:* $C_{12}H_{13}N_5O_2S{\cdot}HCl$

**pro|nu|cle|ar** (prō nü′klē ər, -nyü′-), *adj. Biology.* of or having to do with the pronucleus.

**pro|nu|cle|ate** (prō nü′klē it, -nyü′-), *adj.* = pronuclear.

**pro|nu|cle|us** (prō nü′klē əs, -nyü′-), *n., pl.* **-cle|i** (-klē ī). *Biology.* the nucleus of a sperm or of an ovum, just before these unite in fertilization to form the nucleus (synkaryon) of the zygote. [< New Latin *pronucleus* < Greek *pró* pro-[2], earlier + New Latin *nucleus* nucleus]

**pro|nun|ci|a|men|to** (prə nun′sē ə men′tō, -shē-), *n., pl.* **-tos.** a formal announcement; proclamation; manifesto. [American English < Spanish *pronunciamento* < *pronunciar* to pronounce < Latin *prōnūntiāre*]

**pro|nun|ci|a|tion** (prə nun′sē ā′shən), *n.* **1** a way of pronouncing: *a foreign pronunciation. This book gives the pronunciation of each main word. The British pronunciation of "been" is* (bēn). **2** the act of making the sounds of words; speaking; pronouncing; saying a word or words aloud: *Speech is pronunciation. Radio announcers practice pronunciation. Repeated pronunciation of a new word helps to remember it.* [< Latin *prōnūntiātiō, -ōnis* < *prōnūntiāre* to pronounce]

**pro|nun|ci|a|tion|al** (prə nun′sē ā′shə nəl), *adj.* of or having to do with pronunciation.

**proof** (prüf), *n., adj., v.* — *n.* **1** a way or means of showing beyond doubt the truth of something: *Is what you say a guess, or have you proof?* **SYN**: See syn. under **evidence**. **2** the establishment of the truth of anything; demonstration: *In proof of this theory, I shall make certain studies.* **SYN**: confirmation, corroboration. **3** an act of testing; trial: *That box looks big enough; but let us put it to the proof.* **SYN**: experiment. **4** the condition of having been tested and approved. **5** a trial impression from type. A book is first printed in proof so that errors can be corrected and additions made. *Did the author correct the page proofs?* **6** a trial print of an etching, photographic negative, or the like. **7** a proof coin: *The artist and coin designer T. H. Paget had offered a number of trial strikings and artist's proofs of pieces of his design* (London Times). **8** the strength of an alcoholic liquor with reference to the standard in which 100 proof spirit contains about 50% alcohol and about 50% water. Brandy of 90 proof is about 45% alcohol.
— *adj.* **1** of tested value against something: *proof against being taken by surprise.* **2** used to test or prove; serving for a trial. **3** of standard strength of alcohol.
— *v.t.* **1** to render proof against something; make resistant to something. **2a** = proofread. **b** to make a proof of.
[< Old French *prouve,* alteration (influenced by *prouver* to prove) of earlier *prueve* < Late Latin *proba* < Latin *probāre* prove. See etym. of doublet **probe**.] — **proof′er**, *n.*

**-proof**, *suffix.* protected against ___; safe from ___: *Fireproof = safe from fire. Waterproof = protected against water.*

**proof coin**, **1** a coin struck as a test of a new die. **2** one of a limited number of early impressions, especially struck by a mint for dealers and collectors.

**proof gallon**, a gallon of proof spirit.

**proof|ing** (prü′fing), *n.* the treating of something to make it resistant: *"Pigeon proofing" of buildings ... involves the use of screens and spikes* (Wall Street Journal).

**proof|less** (prüf′lis), *adj.* without proof.

**proof|like** (prüf′līk′), *adj.* like a proof coin in quality or appearance: *a prooflike specimen, prooflike silver dollars.*

**proof-lis|ten|er** (prüf′lis′ə nər), *n.* a person who listens to talking books to correct errors in pronunciation, context, or the like: *She is a proof-listener for the American Foundation for the Blind* (New York Times). [patterned after *proof-reader*]

**proof of loss**, a written statement from an insured person claiming payment of loss under an insurance policy: *Nor did he remember that in order to collect fully on a fire insurance policy, proof of loss must be supplied within sixty days* (New Yorker).

**proof positive**, incontrovertible proof: *He had won ascendancy again, and it was all a tribute to his dreams, proof positive of his skill in making his myths come true* (Listener).

**proof|read** (prüf′rēd′), *v.t., v.i.,* **-read** (-red′), **-read|ing.** to read (printers' proofs or typed copy) and mark errors to be corrected. [American English; probably back formation < *proofreading,* or *proofreader*] —**proof′read′er,** *n.*

**proof|read|ing** (prüf′rē′ding), *n.* the act of reading printers' proofs and marking errors to be corrected.

**proof set**, a set of proof coins for dealers and collectors: *The coins in a proof set are of a higher relief and polish than ordinary coins, making them more attractive to collectors* (Edward C. Rochette).

**proof sheet**, a printers' proof.

**proof spirit**, **1** *U.S.* an alcoholic liquor, or mixture of alcohol and water, with a specific gravity of .93353 and with half of its volume consisting of alcohol of a specific gravity of .7939 at 60 degrees Fahrenheit. **2** (in Great Britain) a similar alcoholic liquor with a specific gravity of .91984.

**proof-test** (prüf′test′), *v.t.* to subject (a product or material) to a conclusive test of its capacities or condition: *to proof-test a missile or a nuclear reactor. Both the concrete and the steel can be proof-tested before operation of the machine begins* (New Scientist).

**proof text**, a passage of Scripture brought forward to prove a special doctrine or belief.

**prop**[1] (prop), *v.,* **propped, prop|ping,** *n.* —*v.t.* **1** to hold up by placing a support under or against: *Prop the broken chair with a stick. He was propped up in bed with pillows.* **2** *Figurative.* to support; sustain: *to prop a failing cause. Justice should not be propped up by injustice* (Edward Miall). —*v.i. Australian.* (of a horse) to stop suddenly. [< noun]
—*n.* a thing or person used to support another: *The boys used two sticks as props for the sagging tent.* (*Figurative.*) *Advertising is an indispensable prop to the women's clothing business.*
**SYN:** support, brace, stay.
[origin uncertain. Compare Middle Dutch *proppe.*]

**prop**[2] (prop), *n.* **1** an object, such as a weapon or chair, used in a play or motion picture, not including costumes, scenery, and equipment that is part of the stage, or cameras and lighting; property: *a stage prop, the props used in a television commercial.* **2** *Informal.* a property man. [short for *property*]

**prop**[3] (prop), *n. Informal.* an airplane propeller. [short for *propeller*]

**prop.**, **1** properly. **2** property. **3** proposition. **4** proprietor.

**pro|pae|deu|tic** (prō′pi dü′tik, -dyü′-), *adj., n.* —*adj.* of, having to do with, or of the nature of preliminary instruction; introductory to some art or science.
—*n.* a propaedeutic subject or study.
[< Greek *propaideúein* teach beforehand (< *pró* before + *paideúein* teach, bring up) + inserted English *-t* + *-ic*]

**prop|a|ga|bil|i|ty** (prop′ə gə bil′ə tē), *n.* propagable quality.

**prop|a|ga|ble** (prop′ə gə bəl), *adj.* that can be propagated: ... *the olive not being successfully propagable by seed* (Thomas Browne).

**prop|a|gan|da** (prop′ə gan′də), *n.* **1** systematic efforts to spread opinions or beliefs; any plan or method for spreading opinions or beliefs: *The insurance companies engaged in health propaganda. Clever propaganda misled the enemy into believing that it could not win the war.* **2** the opinions or beliefs thus spread: *Our doctor said the health propaganda was true. The enemy spread false propaganda about us. None the less, national propaganda in its historical forms has been resisted* (London Times). [< New Latin (*congregatio de*) *propaganda* (*fide*) (congregation for) propagating (the faith); *propaganda,* ablative feminine gerundive of Latin *prōpāgāre* to propagate]

**prop|a|gan|dism** (prop′ə gan′diz əm), *n.* the use of propaganda.

**prop|a|gan|dist** (prop′ə gan′dist), *n., adj.* —*n.* a person who gives time or effort to the spreading of some opinion, belief, or principle: *The monks ... were the chief propagandists of Christianity in Palestine* (Alexander W. Kinglake).
—*adj.* of propaganda or propagandists.

**prop|a|gan|dis|tic** (prop′ə gan dis′tik), *adj.* of or having to do with propagandists or the use of propaganda: *There are obvious propagandistic advantages in popularizing English art abroad* (New Yorker). —**prop′a|gan|dis′ti|cal|ly,** *adv.*

**prop|a|gan|dize** (prop′ə gan′dīz), *v.,* **-dized, -diz|ing.** —*v.t.* **1** to propagate or spread (doctrines, opinions, or beliefs) by propaganda. **2** to subject to propaganda: *to propagandize voters. Officially, of course, she is doing her job of propagandizing the workers* (Harper's).
—*v.i.* to carry on propaganda: *The Ministry of Health, in propagandizing, is not so far forward as the Ministry of Agriculture* (J. W. R. Scott).
—**prop′a|gan′diz|er,** *n.*

**prop|a|gate** (prop′ə gāt), *v.,* **-gat|ed, -gat|ing.**
—*v.i.* to produce offspring; reproduce: *Pigeons propagate at a fast rate.* —*v.t.* **1** to increase in number or intensity: *Trees propagate themselves by seeds.* **SYN:** multiply. **2** to cause to increase in number by the production of young: *Cows and sheep are propagated on farms.* **3** to spread (news or knowledge): *Don't propagate unkind reports.* **SYN:** extend, diffuse. **4** to pass on; send further: *Sound is propagated by vibrations.*
[< Latin *prōpāgāre* (with English *-ate*[1]) to multiply plants by slips or layers < *prō-* forth + *pag-,* root of *pangere* make fast, pin down]

**prop|a|ga|tion** (prop′ə gā′shən), *n.* **1** the act or process of breeding plants or animals: *The propagation of poppies is by seed and of roses by cuttings.* **2** the act or process of making more widely known; getting more widely believed; spreading: *the propagation of the principles of science.* **3** the act or fact of passing on; sending further; spreading or extending: *the propagation of the shock of an earthquake, the propagation of a family trait from father to son.* **4** the travel of electromagnetic or sound waves through a medium such as air or water.

**prop|a|ga|tion|al** (prop′ə gā′shə nəl), *adj.* of or having to do with propagation.

**prop|a|ga|tive** (prop′ə gā′tiv), *adj.* serving or tending to propagate.

**prop|a|ga|tor** (prop′ə gā′tər), *n.* a person or thing that propagates: *A zealous propagator of Christianity* (Edward A. Freeman).

**prop|a|gule** (prop′ə gyül), *n. Botany.* a bud or other offshoot able to develop into a new plant. [< New Latin *propagulum* < Latin *propāgo* shoot, slip]

**pro|pane** (prō′pān), *n.* a heavy, colorless, flammable gas, a hydrocarbon of the methane series. Propane occurs in crude petroleum and in natural gas and is used as a fuel, refrigerant, or solvent. *Formula:* $C_3H_8$ [< *prop*(ionic acid) + *-ane*]

**pro|pa|nol** (prō′pə nōl, -nol), *n.* = propyl alcohol. [< *propan*(e) + *-ol*[1]]

**pro|par|ox|y|tone** (prō′par ok′sə tōn), *adj., n., v.,* **-toned, -ton|ing.** *Greek Grammar.* —*adj.* having an acute accent on the antepenult.
—*n.* a proparoxytone word.
—*v.t.* to accent on the antepenult.
[< Greek *proparoxýtonos* < *pro-* before + *paroxýtonos* paroxytone]

**pro|par|ox|y|ton|ic** (prō′par ok′sə ton′ik), *adj.* = proparoxytone.

**pro pa|tri|a** (prō pā′trē ə, pat′rē ə), *Latin.* for one's country or native land.

**pro|pel** (prə pel′), *v.t.,* **-pelled, -pel|ling.** **1** to drive or push forward; force ahead: *to propel a boat by oars.* **2** *Figurative.* to impel or urge onward: *a person propelled by ambition.* [< Latin *prōpellere* < *prō-* forward + *pellere* to push]
—**pro|pel′la|ble,** *adj.*

**pro|pel|lant** (prə pel′ənt), *n.* something that propels, especially an explosive that propels a projectile, or a fuel and an oxidizer that propels a rocket: *In a rocket, the propellant is some material carried along in tanks* (Christian Science Monitor). [alteration of earlier *propellent*]

**pro|pel|lent** (prə pel′ənt), *adj., n.* —*adj.* propelling; driving forward: *The mayor was the propellent force for new street lights.*
—*n.* a thing or person that propels; propellant.
[< Latin *prōpellēns, -entis,* present participle of *prōpellere* propel]

***pro|pel|ler** (prə pel′ər), *n.* **1** a revolving hub with blades, for propelling boats and aircraft: *However, a propeller is still far more effective than a jet at low flying speed* (J. M. Stephenson). **2** a person or thing that propels.

**pro|pend** (prō pend′), *v.i. Archaic.* to incline; tend. [< Latin *prōpendēre* incline to; see etym. under **propensity**]

**pro|pense** (prō pens′), *adj. Archaic.* inclined; disposed.

**pro|pen|sion** (prō pen′shən), *n. Archaic.* inclination; tendency.

**pro|pen|si|ty** (prə pen′sə tē), *n., pl.* **-ties.** a natural inclination or bent; inclination; leaning: *the natural propensity to find fault* (James Fenimore Cooper). *Most boys have a propensity for playing with machinery.* [< Latin *prōpēnsus,* past participle of *prōpendēre* incline to; weigh over (< *prō-* forward + *pendēre* hang) + English *-ity*]

**pro|pe|nyl** (prō′pə nəl), *n.* any one of certain hydrocarbon radicals of the formula $C_3H_5$

**prop|er** (prop′ər), *adj., adv., n.* —*adj.* **1** right for the occasion; fitting; correct: *soil in proper condition for planting, to use a word in its proper sense. Night is the proper time to sleep, and bed the proper place.* **SYN:** suitable, becoming, appropriate. **2** in the strict sense of the word; strictly so called: *England proper does not include Wales. Puerto Rico is not part of the United States proper. Footnotes are clearly set off from the text proper.* **3** decent; respectable: *proper conduct.* **SYN:** seemly, decorous. **4** *Grammar.* belonging to one or a few; not common to all; designating a particular person, place, or thing. *France* is a proper noun, *French* is a proper adjective. **5** designating a liturgical service, psalm, or lesson, appointed for a particular day or season. **6** *Informal.* complete; thorough; fine; excellent: *a proper jest, and never heard before* (Shakespeare). **7** *Archaic.* good-looking; handsome: *By St. Anne! but he is a proper youth* (Scott). **8** belonging exclusively or distinctively: *qualities proper to a substance.* **9** *Heraldry.* represented in its natural colors: *an eagle proper.* **10** *Archaic.* belonging to oneself; own: *to shroud me from my proper scorn* (Tennyson).
—*adv. Informal.* properly; completely; thoroughly: *Had 'em that time—had 'em proper!* (Sir Arthur Conan Doyle).
—*n. Ecclesiastical.* Also, **Proper. 1** the parts of the Mass which vary according to the day or festival. **2** the service or prayers appointed for a particular day or season. **3** the section of a missal or breviary containing these parts.
[< Old French *propre,* learned borrowing from Latin *proprius* one's own]

**proper adjective**, an adjective derived from a proper noun, such as *Italian* in *the Italian language.*
▶ **Proper adjectives.** Proper nouns used as adjectives and adjectives directly derived from proper names are regularly capitalized. When their reference to a particular person, place, or thing has been weakened or lost, they become simple adjectives and are usually not capitalized: *the French language, Roman ruins* (but *roman type*).

**prop|er|din** (prop′ər din), *n.* a protein substance present in blood plasma, held to be capable of inactivating or killing various bacteria and viruses and of reducing the effects of radiation. [< *pro*[1] + Latin *perdere* to destroy + English *-in*]

**proper fraction**, a fraction in which the numerator is smaller than the denominator; fraction less than 1. 2/3, 1/8, 3/4, and 199/200 are proper fractions.

**prop|er|ly** (prop′ər lē), *adv.* **1** in a proper, correct, or fitting manner: *to eat properly, to be dressed properly for cold weather.* **2** rightly; justly: *An honest man is properly indignant at the offer of a bribe.* **3** strictly: *Properly speaking, a whale is not a fish.* **4** *Informal.* thoroughly; completely; excellently.

**proper motion**, *Astronomy.* the apparent angular motion of a star across the sky after allowing for precession, nutation, and aberration, due to real motions of the star itself.

***propeller**
definition 1

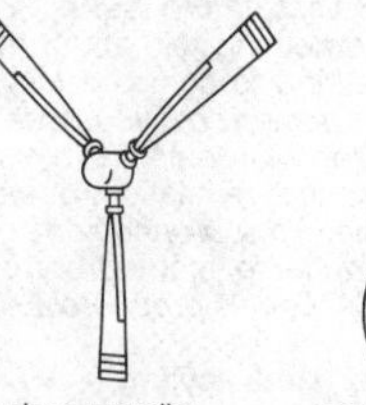

airplane propeller | screw propeller of a ship

**proper name**, = proper noun.

**proper noun**, a classification of nouns naming a particular person, place, or thing, written with an initial capital letter. *John, Chicago, Monday,* and *World War* are proper nouns; *boy, city,* and *day* are common nouns.

**Pronunciation Key:** hat, āge, cãre, fär; let, ēqual, tėrm; it, īce; hot, ōpen, ôrder; **oi**l, **ou**t; cup, pu̇t, rüle; **ch**ild; lo**ng**; **th**in; **ᴛʜ**en; **zh**, measure;
**ə** represents **a** in about, **e** in taken, **i** in pencil, **o** in lemon, **u** in circus.

**prop|er|tied** (prop′ər tēd), *adj.* owning property: *the propertied classes.*

**prop|er|ty** (prop′ər tē), *n., pl.* **-ties. 1** a thing or things owned; possession or possessions: *This house is that man's property. When the main forms of property are intangible the difficulty of defining rights and duties is much greater* (Atlantic). *He has developed a publication that is one of the "hottest properties" in publishing* (Harper's). **2** ownership; the right of ownership. **3** a piece of land or real estate: *a property on Main Street. He owns some property out West.* **4** any object, such as a piece of furniture or a walking stick (but not scenery, clothing, nor stage, camera, or lighting equipment), that is used in staging a play, a motion-picture scene, a television show, or the like: *The sofa was the first property to be put on the set. I will draw a bill of properties such as our play needs* (Shakespeare). **5** a story on which a motion picture is based: *Most properties come from such sources as novels, plays, and musical comedies* (Arthur Knight). **6** *Informal.* an actor, athlete, or employee, under contract: *Overnight the lanky Canadian turned into one of the most valuable "properties" in the music business* (Maclean's). **7** a quality or power belonging specially to something: *Soap has the property of removing dirt. All bodies when placed in a suitably large magnetic field develop magnetic properties* (W. D. Corner). **SYN**: See syn. under **quality. 8** *Logic.* a quality that is common to all the members of a class, but does not necessarily distinguish that class from other classes. [Middle English *proprete* < Old French *propriete* < Latin *proprietās* < *proprius* one's own, proper. See etym. of doublet **propriety.**] —**prop′er|ty|less,** *adj.*

—*Syn.* **1 Property, goods, effects** mean what someone owns. **Property** means whatever someone legally owns, including land, buildings, animals, money, stocks, documents, objects, and rights: *Property is taxable.* **Goods** means movable personal property, as distinguished from land and buildings, but applies chiefly to things of use in the house or on the land, such as furniture, furnishings, implements, never to money or papers: *Professional movers packed our goods.* **Effects** means personal possessions, including goods, clothing, jewelry, personal belongings, and papers, often of one who has died: *We gathered together his few effects to send them to his family. I packed our other effects.*

**property man,** a man employed in a theater to look after the stage properties; prop man.

**property tax,** a tax levied on real estate and personal property, the rate usually being based on a percentage of the property's total value as determined by the government: *In the United States and Canada, only provincial, state, and local governments levy property taxes* (Charles J. Gaa).

**pro|phage** (prō′fāj), *n.* a fusion of the genetic material of a virus with that of a host bacterium, capable under certain circumstances of becoming a group of viral particles; provirus. [< *pro-*² + Greek *phageîn* eat]

**pro|phase** (prō′fāz′), *n. Biology.* **1** the first stage in mitosis, that includes the formation of the spindle and the lengthwise splitting of the chromosomes. See diagram under **mitosis. 2** the first stage in meiosis, from the point at which the chromosomes appear (leptotene) to the point where the chromatids contract (diakinesis). [< *pro-*² + *phase*]

**proph|e|cy** (prof′ə sē), *n., pl.* **-cies. 1** the act of telling what will happen; foretelling future events: *Easing man's struggle against nature is the prophecy of science.* **2** something told about the future; indication of something to come: *A laughing face ... where scarce appeared The uncertain prophecy of beard* (John Greenleaf Whittier). **3** a divinely inspired utterance, revelation, or writing. **4** a book of prophecies: *the prophecy of Isaiah.* [< Old French *prophecie,* learned borrowing from Latin *prophētīa* < Greek *prophēteíā* < *prophḗtēs* prophet]

**proph|e|sy** (prof′ə sī), *v.,* **-sied, -sy|ing.** —*v.i.* **1** to tell what will happen: *The first explosion of the atomic bomb prophesied of change and a new age.* **2** to speak when or as if inspired by God: *Christians believe that Christ came to phophesy to mankind as the savior.* **3** *Obsolete.* to interpret or expound the Scriptures. —*v.t.* **1** to foretell; predict: *The sailor prophesied a severe storm.* **2** to utter in prophecy: *The prophets prophesy lies in my name* (Jeremiah 14:14). [(originally) spelling variant of Middle English *prophecy,* verb] —**proph′e|si′a|ble,** *adj.* —**proph′e|si′er,** *n.*

**proph|et** (prof′it), *n.* **1** a person who tells what will happen: *Don't be a bad-luck prophet.* **2** a person who preaches what he thinks has been revealed to him, especially any of the Biblical figures who taught and preached in the name of God, such as Isaiah and Jeremiah: *Every religion has its prophets.* **3** *Figurative.* a spokesman, as of some cause or doctrine: *Nothing could have been further from [Theodore] Roosevelt's intentions than to set up as the prophet of some great Reformation* (Baron Charnwood).

**the Prophet, a** Mohammed: *If but the Vine and Love-abjuring Band Are in the Prophet's Paradise to stand* (Edward FitzGerald). **b** Joseph Smith, the founder of the Mormon religion: *The Prophet, his brother Hyram, and other leading Mormons were seized* (John H. Blunt).

**the Prophets,** the books of the Old Testament written by prophets: *The Prophets are divided into the Major Prophets and Minor Prophets.*

[< Latin *prophēta,* or *prophētes* < Greek *prophḗtēs,* ultimately < *pro-* before + *phánai* to speak]

**proph|et|ess** (prof′ə tis), *n.* a woman prophet.

**proph|et|hood** (prof′it hu̇d), *n.* the character or office of a prophet.

**pro|phet|ic** (prə fet′ik), *adj.* **1** belonging to a prophet; such as a prophet has: *prophetic power.* **2** containing prophecy: *a prophetic saying.* **3** giving warning of what is to happen; foretelling: *Thunder is often prophetic of showers. It seem'd to those within the wall A cry prophetic of their fall* (Byron). —**pro|phet′i|cal|ly,** *adv.*

**pro|phet|i|cal** (prə fet′ə kəl), *adj.* = prophetic.

**proph|et|ism** (prof′ə tiz əm), *n.* the action or practice of a prophet or prophets, especially the system or principles of the Hebrew prophets: *Prophetism attained its apogee among the Semites of Palestine* (Thomas Huxley).

**pro|phy|lac|tic** (prō′fə lak′tik, prof′ə-), *adj., n.* —*adj.* **1** protecting from disease: *vaccination and other prophylactic measures. Hope of preventing tuberculosis by daily prophylactic doses of the drug isoniazid is now seen* (Science News Letter). **2** protective; preservative; precautionary. —*n.* **1** a medicine, treatment, or device that protects against disease: *He took vitamins as a prophylactic against colds.* **2** a precaution: *To keep the mind engrossed was the great prophylactic against fear* (John Buchan). **3** any contraceptive device, especially a condom.

[< Greek *prophylaktikós* < *prophylássein* take precautions against < *pro-* before + *phylássein,* dialectal variant of *phyláttein* to guard < *phýlax, -akos* a guard] —**pro′phy|lac′ti|cal|ly,** *adv.*

**pro|phy|lax|is** (prō′fə lak′sis, prof′ə-), *n.* **1** a protection from disease. **2** a treatment to prevent disease. [< New Latin *prophylaxis* < Greek *pro-* before + *phýlaxis* protection < *prophylássein*]

**pro|pine** (prō pēn′, -pīn′), *n., v.,* **-pined, -pin|ing.** *Scottish.* —*n.* a gift. [< Middle French *propine* < *propiner;* see the verb]

—*v.t.* **1** to offer (something) to one to drink. **2** to give; present. [< Middle French *propiner,* learned borrowing from Latin *propīnāre* supply with food or water; (originally) drink one's health < Greek *propieîn,* reduction of *propī́nein* drink a toast < *pró* forth + *pī́nein* to drink]

**pro|pin|qui|ty** (prō ping′kwə tē), *n.* **1** nearness in place, especially personal nearness. **2** nearness of blood; kinship. [< Latin *propinquitās* < *propinquus* near < *prope* near]

**pro|pi|ol|ic acid** (prō′pē ol′ik), a liquid organic acid with an odor resembling that of acetic acid. *Formula:* $C_3H_2O_2$ [< *propi*(onic) + *-ol*¹ + *-ic*]

**pro|pi|o|nate** (prō′pē ə nāt), *n.* a salt or ester of propionic acid.

**pro|pi|on|ic acid** (prō′pē on′ik, -ō′nik), a fatty acid with a pungent odor, found in perspiration and produced synthetically from ethyl alcohol and carbon monoxide. It is used in the form of its propionates to inhibit mold in bread and as an ingredient in perfumes. *Formula:* $C_3H_6O_2$ [< French *propionique* < *pro*(to)- first + Greek *pī́on* fat + French *-ique* -ic (because it is the first of the true carboxylic acids)]

**pro|pi|o|nyl** (prō′pē ə nəl), *n.* a univalent radical ($C_3H_5O$) contained especially in propionic acid. [< *propion*(ic) + *-yl*]

**pro|pi|ti|a|ble** (prə pish′ē ə bəl), *adj.* that may be propitiated.

**pro|pi|ti|ate** (prə pish′ē āt), *v.t.,* **-at|ed, -at|ing.** to prevent or reduce the anger of; win the favor of; appease or conciliate (one who is offended or likely to be): *Let fierce Achilles ... The god propitiate, and the pest assuage* (Alexander Pope). [< Latin *propitiāre* (with English *-ate*¹) < *propitius* propitious] —**pro|pi′ti|at′ing|ly,** *adv.*

**pro|pi|ti|a|tion** (prə pish′ē ā′shən), *n.* **1** the act of propitiating. **2** that which propitiates. **3** *Theology.* Christ, and His life and death, as the means by which reconciliation of God and mankind is attained.

**pro|pi|ti|a|tive** (prə pish′ē ā′tiv), *adj.* serving or tending to propitiate.

**pro|pi|ti|a|tor** (prə pish′ē ā′tər), *n.* a person who propitiates.

**pro|pi|ti|a|to|ry** (prə pish′ē ə tôr′ē, -tōr′-), *adj., n., pl.* **-ries.** —*adj.* intended to propitiate; making propitiation; conciliatory: *a propitiatory offering, a propitiatory prayer.* —*n.* = mercy seat.

**pro|pi|tious** (prə pish′əs), *adj.* **1** favorable: *propitious weather for our trip, a propitious reception. The seed of pessimism, once lodged within him, flourished in a propitious soil* (Lytton Strachey). **SYN**: auspicious, promising. **2** favorably inclined; gracious. [< Old French *propicius,* learned borrowing from Latin *propitius* (originally) falling forward < *prō-* forward + *petere* go toward] —**propi′tious|ly,** *adv.* —**pro|pi′tious|ness,** *n.*

**prop|jet** (prop′jet′), *n.* = turboprop.

**pro|plas|tid** (prō plas′tid), *n. Biology.* a protoplasmic body that is a precursor of a plastid. [< *pro-*² + *plastid*]

**prop man,** *Informal.* a man in charge of stage properties at a theater who furnishes them as needed; property man.

**prop|o|lis** (prop′ə lis), *n.* a reddish, resinous substance collected by bees from the buds of trees, used to stop up crevices in the hives and to strengthen the cells. [< Latin *propolis* < Greek *própolis* bee glue; (originally) suburb < *pró* before + *pólis* city (because it is used to line the outer part of the hive)]

**pro|pone** (prə pōn′), *v.t.,* **-poned, -pon|ing.** *Scottish.* to propose; propound. [< Latin *prōpōnere* < *prō-* before + *pōnere* to put, place]

**pro|po|nent** (prə pō′nənt), *n.* **1** a person who makes a proposal or proposition. **2** a person who supports something; advocate; favorer; supporter: *Proponents of the bill argued that Federal regulation of natural-gas production ... was discriminatory* (Newsweek). **3** *Law.* a person who submits a will for probate. [< Latin *prōpōnēns, -entis,* present participle of *prōpōnere;* see etym. under **propone**]

*__pro|por|tion__ (prə pôr′shən, -pōr′-), *n., v.* —*n.* **1** the relation of two things in size, number, amount, or degree: *Each girl's pay will be in proportion to the work she does. Mix water and orange juice in the proportions of three to one by taking three measures of water to every measure of orange juice.* **2** a proper relation between parts; balance; harmony: *His short legs were not in proportion to his long body. The commerce of your colonies is out of all proportion beyond the numbers of the people* (Edmund Burke). **3** a part; share: *A large proportion of Nevada is desert.* **4** *Mathematics.* **a** a statement of equality between two ratios. *Example:* 4 is to 2 as 10 is to 5. **b** a method of finding the fourth term of such a proportion when three are known.

—*v.t.* **1** to fit (one thing to another) so that they go together suitably: *The designs in that rug are well proportioned.* **2** to adjust in proper proportion or relation: *The punishment was proportioned to the crime.*

**proportions, a** size; extent: *He left an art collection of considerable proportions.* **b** dimensions: *He has the proportions of a dwarf.*

[< Latin *prōportiō, -ōnis* < unrecorded *prō portiōne* in relation to the part] —**pro|por′tion|er,** *n.*

**a : b = c : d**

**4 : 2 = 10 : 5**

direct proportion

*__proportion__ definition 4a

a : 1/b = c : 1/d

2 : 1/3 = 1/2 : 1/12

indirect proportion

**pro|por|tion|a|ble** (prə pôr′shə nə bəl, -pōr′-), *adj. Archaic.* being in due proportion; proportional: *For us to levy power Proportionable to the enemy Is all impossible* (Shakespeare).

**pro|por|tion|al** (prə pôr′shə nəl, -pōr′-), *adj., n.* —*adj.* **1** in the proper proportion; corresponding: *The increase in price is proportional to the improvement in the car. The pay will be proportional to the amount of time put in. The dwarf's long arms were not proportional to his height.* **2** *Mathematics.* having the same or a constant ratio: *The corresponding sides of mutually equiangular triangles are proportional.* —*n.* one of the terms of a proportion in mathematics.

**proportional counter,** a radiation counter similar to the Geiger counter, in which the amplitude of the pulse produced by the particle being counted is proportional to the amount of ionization it discharges. It is used in identifying various types of charged particles.

**pro|por|tion|al|ism** (prə pôr′shə nə liz′əm, -pōr′-), *n.* the theory or practice of proportional representation: *Proportionalism still rules in Austria and neither party wishes to be the first to disrupt it* (London Times).

**pro|por|tion|al|i|ty** (prə pôr′shə nal′ə tē, -pōr′-), *n.* the quality or condition of being in proportion.

**pro|por|tion|al|ly** (prə pôr′shə nə lē, -pōr′-), *adv.* in proportion: *The seats are then divided proportionally among the victorious group* (Time).

**proportional representation**, a system of electing members of a legislature so that each political party is represented in the legislature in proportion to its share of the total vote cast in an election.

**proportional tax**, a tax whose rate remains the same, whether it is applied to a small or a large sum. A tax levied on a fixed proportion of everyone's income, such as $5 for every $100 of income, is a proportional income tax.

**pro|por|tion|ate** (*adj.* prə pôr′shə nit, -pōr′-; *v.* prə pôr′shə nāt, -pōr′-), *adj., v.,* **-at|ed, -at|ing.** **—*adj.*** in the proper proportion; proportioned; proportional: *The money obtained by the fair was really not proportionate to the effort we put into it.*

**—*v.t.*** to make proportionate; proportion.
[< Latin *prōportiōnātus* < *prōportiō;* see etym. under **proportion**] **—pro|por′tion|ate|ness,** *n.*

**pro|por|tion|ate|ly** (prə pôr′shə nit lē, -pōr′-), *adv.* in proportion: *The money the boys earned was divided proportionately to the time each worked.*

**pro|por|tion|ment** (prə pôr′shən mənt, -pōr′-), *n.* **1** the act of proportioning. **2** the condition of being proportioned.

**pro|por|tions** (prə pôr′shənz, -pōr′-), *n.pl.* See under **proportion.**

**pro|pos|al** (prə pō′zəl), *n.* **1** what is proposed; plan, scheme, or suggestion: *a proposal to reduce taxes, constitutional proposals. The club will now hear this member's proposal.* **2** an offer of marriage. **3** the act of proposing: *Proposal is easier than performance.*

**—*Syn.* 1 Proposal, proposition** mean something put forward for consideration. **Proposal**, the more general term, applies to any suggestion, offer, or plan, however it may be stated: *The young people made a proposal to the City Council.* **Proposition** applies to a proposal stated in precise and specific terms: *The Council approved the idea, but not the proposition set forth.*

**pro|pose** (prə pōz′), *v.,* **-posed, -pos|ing. —*v.t.*** **1** to put forward for consideration, discussion, acceptance, or trial; suggest: *to propose a theory or explanation. She proposed that we take turns at the swing. Men must be taught as if you taught them not, And things unknown proposed as things forgot* (Alexander Pope). **SYN**: offer. **2** to present (the name of someone) for an office or membership: *I am proposing Jack for president.* **SYN**: nominate. **3** to present as a toast to be drunk. **4** to intend; plan: *She proposes to save half of all she earns.* **SYN**: design, purpose.

**—*v.i.*** **1** to make an offer of marriage. **2** to form a design or purpose: *Man proposes, God disposes.* [< Middle French, Old French *proposer* (< *pro-* forth + *poser;* see etym. under **pose**[1]) adaptation of Latin *prōpōnere;* see etym. under **propone**] **—pro|pos′er,** *n.*

**prop|o|si|tion** (prop′ə zish′ən), *n., v.* **—*n.*** **1** what is offered to be considered; proposal: *The tailor made a proposition to buy out his rival's business. To this rational proposition no objection could be raised* (James Fenimore Cooper). **SYN**: See syn. under **proposal. 2** a statement; assertion. *Example:* "All men are created equal." A proposition in logic is a statement to be proved either true or false. **3** a statement that is to be proved true, such as in a debate. *Example:* Resolved: that our school should have a store. **4** a problem to be solved: *a proposition in arithmetic, a proposition in geometry.* **5** *U.S. Informal.* a business enterprise; affair to be dealt with; undertaking: *a tough proposition, a paying proposition.* **6** *U.S. Informal.* a person or thing to be dealt with: *He's a cool proposition. The expense is a serious proposition that must be explored before purchase.*

**—*v.t.*** *Informal.* to propose a scheme, plan, or action to, often an improper one: *The social worker has so far put off propositioning him on taking a job as a dishwasher* (Maclean's).
[< Latin *prōpositiō, -ōnis* a setting forth < *prōpōnere;* see etym. under **propone**]

▶ **Proposition** as a synonym for *offer, plan, proposal* is largely confined to commercial jargon: *I have a proposition* (standard English *a plan*) *that may interest you.*

**prop|o|si|tion|al** (prop′ə zish′ə nəl), *adj.* **1** having to do with or constituting a proposition. **2** considered as a proposition. **—prop′o|si′tion|al|ly,** *adv.*

**propositional calculus**, the branch of symbolic logic that deals with connections such as *and, or, if* appearing in propositions; sentential calculus.

**propositional function**, **1** a combination of two or more propositions whose truth or falsity depends on the truth or falsity of the basic propositions and the way the function relates them. Propositional functions are used in truth tables. **2** an expression containing one or more variables that must be replaced with constants in order to have the expression become a declarative sentence; sentential function.

**pro|pos|i|tus** (prō poz′ə təs), *n. Law.* a person from whom descent or genealogical relationships are traced. [< Latin *prōpositus,* past participle of *prōpōnere;* see etym. under **propone**]

**pro|pound** (prə pound′), *v.t.* to put forward; propose: *to propound a theory, to propound a riddle, to propound a question.* [alteration of *propone*] **—pro|pound′er,** *n.*

**pro|pox|y|phene hydrochloride** (prə pok′sə fēn), a chemical compound used to relieve pain and as a sedative. It is a crystalline drug held to be as effective as codeine. *Formula:* $C_{22}H_{29}NO_2 \cdot HCl$ [< *prop*(ionic) + *oxy*(gen) + *phen*(yl)]

**prop|per** (prop′ər), *n.* a person or thing that props or supports.

**pro|prae|tor** or **pro|pre|tor** (prō prē′tər, -tôr), *n.* an officer who, after having served as praetor in ancient Rome, was sent to govern a province: *In 92 Sulla went as propraetor to Asia* (James A. Froude). [< Latin *prōpraetor* (literally) in place of the praetor < *prō* pro-[1] + *praetor* praetor]

**pro|pran|o|lol** (prō pran′ə lol), *n.* a drug which blocks nerve impulses in the heart, thereby reducing the heart's rate and force of contraction, used in the treatment of angina pectoris, arrhythmia, and other cardiac disorders. *Formula:* $C_{16}H_{21}NO_2$ [alteration of *propanol* + *-ol*[1]]

**pro|pri|e|tar|y** (prə prī′ə ter′ē), *adj., n., pl.* **-taries. —*adj.*** **1** belonging to a proprietor: *a proprietary right, a proprietary interest.* **2** holding property: *a proprietary class.* **3** owned by a private person or company; belonging to or controlled by a private person or company as property. A proprietary medicine is a patent medicine, that is, one which may be sold only by some one person or certain persons. *Proprietary drugs, such as aspirin, and cough remedies, can be sold without a prescription.* [< noun]

**—*n.*** **1** an owner; proprietor. **2** a group of owners: *The proprietary desired certain modifications in the existing policy* (Arnold Bennett). **3** the holding of property; ownership. **4** a proprietary medicine or drug. **5** the owner or group of owners of a grant from the king of England. William Penn was a proprietary.
[< Late Latin *proprietārius* < Latin *proprietās* ownership; see etym. under **propriety**]

**proprietary colony**, (in American history) a colony granted by the British government to some person or persons with full power of ownership, such as the power to appoint the governor and other high officials. Maryland, Delaware, and Pennsylvania were proprietary colonies.

**pro|pri|e|ties** (prə prī′ə tēz), *n.pl.* See under **propriety.**

**pro|pri|e|tor** (prə prī′ə tər), *n.* **1** a person who owns something as his possession or property; owner: *A number of boarding house proprietors are converting their rooms into flatlets* (London Times). **2** (in American history) the owner of a proprietary colony. [American English, probably alteration of *proprietary*]

**pro|pri|e|to|ri|al** (prə prī′ə tôr′ē əl, -tōr′-), *adj.* of or having to do with a proprietor: *proprietorial pride.*

**pro|pri|e|tor|ship** (prə prī′ə tər ship), *n.* = ownership.

**pro|pri|e|to|ry** (prə prī′ə tôr′ē, -tōr′-), *adj.* = proprietary.

**pro|pri|e|tress** (prə prī′ə tris), *n.* a woman owner or manager.

**pro|pri|e|ty** (prə prī′ə tē), *n., pl.* **-ties. 1** the quality or condition of being proper; fitness: *a remark of doubtful propriety.* **SYN**: aptness, suitability. **2** proper behavior: *She acts with propriety. Propriety demands that a boy rise from his seat when he is introduced to a lady.* **SYN**: etiquette, decorum, decency. **3** *Archaic.* proper or peculiar character: *Silence that dreadful bell; it frights the isle from her propriety* (Shakespeare). **4** *Obsolete.* property.

**proprieties**, the customs and rules of proper behavior: *The proprieties ... and even the graces, as far as they are simple, pure, and honest, would follow as an almost inevitable consequence* (Hannah More).
[< Old French *propriete,* learned borrowing from Latin *proprietās* appropriateness, peculiar nature < *proprius* one's own, proper. See etym. of doublet **property.**]

**pro|pri|o|cep|tion** (prō′prē ə sep′shən), *n.* a proprioceptive sense; the perception of internal bodily conditions, such as the state of muscular contraction.

**pro|pri|o|cep|tive** (prō′prē ə sep′tiv), *adj.* **1** receiving stimuli from within the body. **2** of or having to do with such stimuli. [coined < Latin *proprius* one's own + *-ceptus* taken (< *capere* to take) + English *-ive*]

**pro|pri|o|cep|tor** (prō′prē ə sep′tər), *n.* a sense organ that receives stimuli from within the body.

**pro|pri|o mo|tu** (prō′prē ō mō′tü, mō′tyü), *Latin.* of one's own accord.

**pro|proc|tor** (prō prok′tər), *n.* an assistant or deputy proctor in a British university.

**prop root**, a root that supports a plant by growing downward into the ground from above the soil, as in corn and the mangrove.

**prop|ter hoc** (prop′tər hok′), *Latin.* because of this: *Nevertheless, it is fair to admit that, perhaps not propter hoc, the situation has radically changed in Italy since the Luces arrived* (Harper's).

**prop|to|sis** (prop tō′sis), *n.* an abnormal protrusion, especially of the eyeball. [< Greek *próptōsis* a falling forward < *pro-* forward + *ptôsis* ptosis]

**pro|pug|nac|u|lum** (prō′pug nak′yə ləm), *n., pl.* **-la** (-lə). a bulwark; defense. [< Latin *prōpugnāculum* < *prōpugnāre* defend < *prō-* before + *pugnāre* to fight]

**pro|pul|sion** (prə pul′shən), *n.* **1** the act of driving forward or condition of being driven onward: *Propulsion before the wind in sailing ships was an ancient method of traveling.* **2** a propelling force or impulse: *Most large aircraft are powered by propulsion of jet engines.* [< Latin *prōpulsus,* past participle of *prōpellere* to propel + English *-ion*]

**pro|pul|sive** (prə pul′siv), *adj.* driving forward or onward; propelling.

**pro|pul|sor** (prə pul′sər), *n.* something intended to provide propulsion: *A propulsor for hydrofoil boats ... combines hot exhaust gases with cold water* (New York Times).

**pro|pul|so|ry** (prə pul′sər ē), *adj.* = propulsive.

**prop wash**, = slip stream.

**prop word**, a substantive which adds little or no meaning to that of the adjective modifying it. In the sentence *Which car will you take, the old or the new one,* "one" is a prop word.

**pro|pyl** (prō′pəl), *n.* the univalent radical, $C_3H_7$, of propane. [< *prop*(ionic) + *-yl*]

**prop|y|lae|um** (prop′ə lē′əm), *n., pl.* **-lae|a** (-lē′ə). a vestibule or entrance to a temple or other enclosure, especially when elaborate or of architectural importance. [< Latin *propylaeum* < Greek *propýlaion* entrance, gateway; (literally) neuter of *propýlaios,* adjective < *pró* before + *pýlē* gate]

**propyl alcohol**, a colorless liquid used as a solvent for waxes, oils, or resins; propanol. *Formula:* $C_3H_8O$

**pro|pyl|ene** (prō′pə lēn), *n.* a colorless, gaseous hydrocarbon homologous with ethylene, used in organic synthesis. *Formula:* $C_3H_6$ [< *propyl* + *-ene*]

**propylene glycol**, a colorless, viscous, liquid compound of propylene, used as an antifreeze, as a solvent, and in organic synthesis. *Formula:* $C_3H_8O_2$

**pro|pyl|ic** (prō pil′ik), *adj.* of, having to do with, or containing propyl.

**prop|y|lite** (prop′ə līt), *n.* a volcanic rock with triclinic feldspars greatly altered by hydrothermal action, occurring in regions of silver deposits. [American English < Greek *própylon,* variant of *propýlaion* gateway (see etym. under **propylaeum**) + English *-ite*[1] (because it was created at the start of the Tertiary period)]

**prop|y|lit|ic** (prop′ə lit′ik), *adj.* of or like propylite.

**prop|y|lon** (prop′ə lon), *n., pl.* **-lons, -la** (-lə). a monumental gateway standing before the actual entrance, or pylon, of a temple or avenue, in ancient Egypt. [< Greek *própylon,* variant of *propýlaion* gateway; see etym. under **propylaeum**]

**pro|pyl|thi|o|u|ra|cil** (prō′pəl thī′ō yůr′ə səl), *n.* a white, crystalline compound which inhibits thyroid activity, used to control hyperthyroidism. *Formula:* $C_7H_{10}N_2OS$

**pro ra|ta** (prō rā′tə, rä′tə), in proportion; according to the share, interest, etc., of each: *The preference issues will be offered pro rata to shareholders at 115* (London Daily Telegraph). [< Latin *prō ratā* (*parte*) according to (the portion) figured for each; *ratā,* ablative < *rērī* to count, figure]

**pro|rat|a|ble** (prō rā′tə bəl), *adj.* that can be prorated.

**pro|rate** (prō rāt′, prō′rāt′), *v.t., v.i.,* **-rat|ed, -rat|ing.** to distribute or assess proportionally: *We prorated the money according to the number of days each had worked. He is perfectly willing to prorate the special assessment* (Sinclair Lewis). [American English < *pro rata*]

**pro|ra|tion** (prō rā′shən), *n.* a prorating, especially a restriction, by law, of oil and gas production, limiting each producer to a set proportion of his total productive capacity. [< *prorat*(e) + *-ion*]

**prore** (prôr, prōr), *n. Poetic.* the prow of a ship: *The tall ship whose lofty prore Shall never stem the billows more* (Scott). [< Middle French *prore* < Latin *prōra*]

**pro re na|ta** (prō rē nā′tə), *Latin.* as the occasion requires; to meet the emergency. *Abbr:* PRN (no periods) or P.R.N.

**pro|ro|gate** (prō′rə gāt), *v.*, **-gat|ed, -gat|ing.** = prorogue. [< Latin *prōrogātus,* past participle of *prōrogāre* to defer; see etym. under **prorogue**]

**pro|ro|ga|tion** (prō′rə gā′shən), *n.* the discontinuance of the meetings of a lawmaking body without dissolving it. [< Latin *prōrogātiō, -ōnis* < *prōrogāre* to defer; see etym. under **prorogue**]

**pro|rogue** (prō rōg′), *v.t., v.i.,* **-rogued, -rogu|ing. 1** to discontinue the regular meetings of (a lawmaking body) for a time: *King Charles I prorogued the English Parliament. No opportunity was afforded ... of discussing the question before Parliament prorogued* (Westminster Gazette). **SYN:** adjourn. **2** *Obsolete.* to defer; postpone. [< Middle French *proroguer,* learned borrowing from Latin *prōrogāre* to defer, prolong < *prō-* forward + *rogāre* to ask for]

**pros.,** prosody.

**pro|sage** (prō′sij), *n.* a sausage which has pure vegetable protein instead of meat. [< *pro*(tein sau)*sage*]

**pro|sa|ic** (prō zā′ik), *adj.* **1** like prose; matter-of-fact; ordinary; not exciting: *a prosaic mind or style, to lead a prosaic life. No product is too prosaic or too mundane to profit greatly by attractive packaging* (Wall Street Journal). **SYN:** commonplace, humdrum, dull, tedious. **2** of, in, or having to do with prose. [< Late Latin *prōsaicus* < Latin *prōsa* prose] —**pro|sa′i|cal|ly,** *adv.* —**pro|sa′ic|ness,** *n.*

**pro|sa|i|cism** (prō zā′ə siz əm), *n.* = prosaism.

**pro|sa|ism** (prō′zā iz əm), *n.* **1** prosaic character. **2** a prosaic remark or expression.

**pro|sa|ist** (prō′zā ist, prō zā′ist), *n.* **1** a person who writes in prose; prose author. **2** a prosaic or unpoetic person.

**pro|sa|teur** (pro zȧ tœr′), *n. French.* a prose writer; prosaist.

**pro|sce|ni|um** (prō sē′nē əm), *n., pl.* **-ni|a** (-nē ə). **1** the part of the stage in front of the curtain. **2** the curtain and the framework that holds it. **3** the stage of an ancient theater. [< Latin *proscaenium* < Greek *proskēnion* < *pró-* in front of + *skēnē* stage, (originally) tent. Compare etym. under **scene.**]

**proscenium arch,** an arch or archway or equivalent opening in the wall between the stage and the auditorium of a theater.

**pro|sciut|to** (prō shü′tō), *n., pl.* **-ti** (-tē), **-tos.** dry-cured, spiced, and often smoked ham, sliced very thin and frequently served with melon or figs. [< Italian *prosciutto*]

**pro|scribe** (prō skrīb′), *v.t.,* **-scribed, -scrib|ing. 1** to prohibit as wrong or dangerous; talk against; condemn: *In earlier days, the church proscribed dancing and cardplaying. It is difficult to proscribe a party without infringing on the right of the individual to dissent* (Bulletin of Atomic Scientists). **SYN:** forbid, interdict. **2** to put outside of the protection of the law; outlaw. In ancient Rome, a proscribed person's property belonged to the state, and anyone might kill him. **3** to forbid to come into a certain place; banish. **SYN:** exile. [< Latin *prōscrībere* < *prō-* before (the public) + *scrībere* to write] —**pro|scrib′er,** *n.*

**pro|script** (prō′skript), *n.* a proscribed person: *As each proscript rose and stood From kneeling in the ashen dust* (Dante Gabriel Rossetti).

**pro|scrip|tion** (prō skrip′shən), *n.* the act of proscribing or condition of being proscribed; banishment; outlawry: *No one would raise a hand against the proscription of spinach from the national diet* (Atlantic). [< Latin *prōscriptiō, -ōnis* < *prōscrībere* proscribe]

**pro|scrip|tive** (prō skrip′tiv), *adj.* proscribing; tending to proscribe: *The Imperial ministers pursued with proscriptive laws, and ineffectual arms, the rebels whom they had made* (Edward Gibbon). —**pro|scrip′tive|ly,** *adv.*

**prose** (prōz), *n., adj., v.,* **prosed, pros|ing.** —*n.* **1** the ordinary form of spoken or written language; plain language not arranged in verses, especially the literary form, characterized by narration, description, and exposition, used in novels, plays, and articles: *The definition of good prose is—proper words in their proper places* (Samuel Taylor Coleridge). *Prose is a magnificent instrument of communication* (Atlantic). **2** *Figurative.* dull, ordinary talk.
—*adj.* **1** of prose; in prose. **2** *Figurative.* lacking imagination; matter-of-fact; commonplace.
—*v.i.* **1** to talk or write in a dull, commonplace way. **2** to compose or write prose.
—*v.t.* to write in prose; turn into prose.
[< Old French *prose,* learned borrowing from Latin *prōsa* (*ōrātiō*) straightforward (speech); (literally) feminine of *prōs* < *prōrsus,* for unrecorded *prōversus* straightway, direct < *prō-* forth, forward + *vertere* to turn]

**pro|sec|tor** (prō sek′tər), *n.* a person who dissects bodies as demonstrations for classes in anatomy. [< Latin *prōsector* anatomist < *prōsecāre* to cut up < *prō-* before + *secāre* to cut]

**pro|sec|to|ri|al** (prō′sek tôr′ē əl, -tōr′-), *adj.* of or having to do with a prosector.

**pros|e|cut|a|ble** (pros′ə kyü′tə bəl), *adj.* that can be prosecuted; liable to prosecution: *... the dearth of prosecutable crime* (New Yorker).

**pros|e|cute** (pros′ə kyüt), *v.,* **-cut|ed, -cut|ing.** —*v.t.* **1** to bring before a court of law: *Reckless drivers will be prosecuted.* **2** to carry out; follow up; pursue: *He started an inquiry into the causes of the fire, and prosecuted it for several weeks.* **3** to carry on (a business or occupation); practice: *Those polar fisheries could only be prosecuted in the short summer of that climate* (Herman Melville).
—*v.i.* **1** to bring a case before a law court. **2** to act as prosecuting attorney. [< Latin *prōsecūtus,* past participle of *prōsequī* to pursue < *prō-* forth + *sequī* follow. See related etym. at **pursue.**]

**pros|e|cut|ing attorney** (pros′ə kyü′ting), an attorney for the government; district attorney; public prosecutor.

**pros|e|cu|tion** (pros′ə kyü′shən), *n.* **1** the act or process of carrying on a lawsuit: *The prosecution will be stopped if the stolen money is returned.* **2** the side that starts action against another in a law court. The prosecution makes certain charges against the defense. **3** the act or process of carrying out; following up: *In the prosecution of his plan, he stored away a supply of food.*

**pros|e|cu|tor** (pros′ə kyü′tər), *n.* **1** the lawyer in charge of the government's side of a case against an accused person. **2** a person who starts legal proceedings against another person: *Who is the prosecutor in this case?* **3** a person who follows up or carries out any action, project, or business.

**pros|e|cu|to|ri|al** (pros′ə kyə tôr′ē əl, -tōr′-), *adj.* = prosecutory: *The book suffers from excessive prosecutorial zeal* (Saturday Review).

**pros|e|cu|to|ry** (pros′ə kyə tôr′ē, -tōr′-), *adj.* of or having to do with prosecution: *... fixed rules of law by which police, prosecutory, and judicial agencies ... must abide* (Atlantic).

**pros|e|lyte** (pros′ə līt), *n., v.,* **-lyt|ed, -lyt|ing.** —*n.* a person who has changed from one opinion, religious belief, or cause, to another: *These proselytes of the gate are as welcome as the true Hebrews* (Charles Lamb).
—*v.t.* **1** to convert from one opinion, religious belief, or cause, to another: *I have no wish to proselyte any reluctant mind* (Emerson). **2** to induce to join; enlist; solicit: *to proselyte high-school athletes for a college.*
—*v.i.* to make proselytes.
[< Latin *prosēlytus* < Greek *prosēlytos* one who has come over (to a faith); (literally) having arrived < *prós* toward + *ely-,* stem of *érchesthai* to come] —**pros′e|lyt′er,** *n.*

**pros|e|lyt|ism** (pros′ə lī tiz′əm, -lə-), *n.* **1** the act or fact of proselyting: *The spirit of proselytism attends this spirit of fanaticism* (Edmund Burke). **2** the condition of being a proselyte.

**pros|e|lyt|ist** (pros′ə lī′tist, -lə-), *n.* a person who proselytes; proselytizer: *The Mormon proselytists report unusual success in their missionary work* (New York Evangelist).

**pros|e|lyt|i|za|tion** (pros′ə lī′tə zā′shən), *n.* the act or work of proselytizing.

**pros|e|lyt|ize** (pros′ə lī tīz, -lə-), *v.,* **-ized, -iz|ing.** —*v.i.* to make converts; make proselytes.
—*v.t.* to make a proselyte of; convert: *One of these whom they endeavour to proselytize* (Edmund Burke). —**pros′e|lyt|iz′er,** *n.*

**pro|sem|i|nar** (prō sem′ə när), *n.* a preparatory seminar, especially for advanced college students. [< *pro-*[2] + *seminar*]

**pros|en|ce|phal|ic** (pros′en sə fal′ik), *adj.* of or having to do with the prosencephalon.

**pros|en|ceph|a|lon** (pros′en sef′ə lon), *n., pl.* **-la** (-lə). the anterior segment of the brain, consisting of the cerebral hemispheres, or their equivalent, and certain adjacent parts; forebrain; diencephalon and telencephalon. [< French *prosencéphalon* forebrain < Greek *prós* forward + *enképhalon* (literally) within the head < *en* in + *kephalē* head]

**pros|en|chy|ma** (pros eng′ki mə), *n.* a type of tissue characteristic of the woody and bast portions of plants, consisting of long, narrow cells with pointed ends that sometimes form ducts or vessels. [< Greek *prós* toward + English (par)*enchyma*]

**pros|en|chym|a|tous** (pros′eng kim′ə təs), *adj.* consisting of or having to do with prosenchyma.

**prose poem,** a work printed as prose but having elements of poetry in it, such as rhythms and poetic imagery; composition in polyphonic prose.

**prose poet,** a person who writes prose poems.

**prose poetry,** = polyphonic prose.

**pros|er** (prō′zər), *n.* **1** a person who talks or writes in a dull, commonplace way. **2** a writer of prose.

**Pro|ser|pi|na** (prō sėr′pə nə), *n. Roman Mythology.* the daughter of Jupiter and Ceres. She was carried off by Pluto and made queen of the lower world, but she was allowed to spend part of each year on the earth with her mother. At that time the earth blooms, but while Proserpina is in the lower world there is winter. The Greeks called her Persephone.

**Pro|ser|pi|ne** (pros′ər pīn, prō sėr′pə nē), *n.* = Proserpina.

**pros|i|ly** (prō′zə lē), *adv.* in a prosy manner; prosaically; tediously.

**pro|sim|i|an** (prō sim′ē ən), *n.* a primate belonging to the more primitive of the two divisions of primates, including all early fossil primates and modern lemurs, loris, tarsiers, and tree shrews. [< *pro-*[2] + *simian*]

**pros|i|ness** (prō′zē nis), *n.* prosy character or quality: *... settling down again to the prosiness of their everyday life* (G. Jackson).

**pro|sit** (prō′sit; *German* prō′zēt), *interj.* to your health!: *The man behind the counter poured us out a little something—and we murmured prosit!* (London Times). [< German *Prosit* < Latin *prōsit* (literally) may it be to your good (health), third person subjunctive of *prodesse* be good for]

**pro|slav|er|y** (prō slā′vər ē, -slāv′rē), *adj.* favoring slavery. [< *pro*[1] + *slavery*]

**pros|o|branch** (pros′ə brangk), *n., adj.* —*n.* any one of a group of marine gastropod mollusks having the gills in front of the heart.
—*adj.* of or belonging to this group.
[< New Latin *Prosobranchia* the order name < Greek *prósō* forward + *bránchia* gills]

**pro|so|di|ac** (prō sō′dē ak), *adj.* = prosodic.

**pros|o|di|a|cal** (pros′ə dī′ə kəl), *adj.* = prosodic.

**pro|sod|ic** (prō sod′ik), *adj.* of or having to do with prosody: *... prosodic features of the language—stress, transition, and pitch* (Harold Whitehall). —**pro|sod′i|cal|ly,** *adv.*

**pro|sod|i|cal** (prō sod′ə kəl), *adj.* = prosodic.

**pros|o|dist** (pros′ə dist), *n.* a person skilled in the technique of versification.

**pros|o|dize** (pros′ə dīz), *v.i.,* **-dized, -diz|ing.** to use prosody; versify: *His music sounds lyrical and accessible, and ... he is said to prosodize and melodize in manners appealing to concert singers* (Harper's).

**pros|o|dy** (pros′ə dē), *n.* **1** the science of poetic meters and versification. **2** any system or style of versification: *Latin prosody. Japanese prosody came to be based upon syllable-count because the language has no stress accent, as in English, or quantity, as in Latin* (Atlantic). [< Latin *prosōdia* < Greek *prosōidiā* accent, modulation and all the other features that characterize speech < *pros* in addition to + *ōidē* song, poem, ode]

**pro|so|ma** (prə sō′mə), *n. Zoology.* the anterior or cephalic segment of the body in certain animals, such as cephalopods, lamellibranchs, and cirripeds. [< New Latin *prosoma* < *pro-*[2] + Greek *sôma* body]

**pro|so|mal** (prə sō′məl), *adj.* of or belonging to the prosoma.

**pro|so|po|poe|ia** (prō sō′pə pē′ə), *n.* **1** = personification. **2** the representation of an imaginary or absent person as speaking or acting. [< Latin *prosōpopoeia* < Greek *prosōpopiīā* < *prósōpon* a person, face (< *prós* toward + *ōps, ōpós* face, countenance) + *poieîn* to make]

**pros|pect** (pros′pekt), *n., v.* —*n.* **1** a thing expected or looked forward to: *Seeing no prospect of success, we quit the attempt to climb the mountain.* **2** the act of looking forward; expectation: *The prospect of a vacation is pleasant.* **SYN:** anticipation. **3** outlook for the future: *Is there any prospect of rain?* **4** a person who may become a customer, candidate, or associate; prospective customer: *The salesman called on several prospects.* **5a** a view; scene: *The prospect from the mountain was grand.* **b** the direction in which a building, room, window, porch, or the like, faces; exposure; view: *the gate whose prospect is toward the east* (Ezekiel 42:15). **6** *Mining.* **a** an apparent indication of a metal, mineral deposit, etc. **b** a spot giving such indications. **c** a mine in an early stage.
—*v.i.* to explore a region for oil, gold, or other minerals; search or look: *to prospect for gold.*
—*v.t.* to search: *to prospect a region for silver.*
**in prospect,** looked forward to; expected: *Everything in prospect appears filled with good fortune.*
**prospects,** probabilities of success or profit: *good prospects in business, a young man's prospects in life. The prospects from our gardens are*

*good this year. With the death of Francis, the prospects of the Huguenots brightened* (Walter Besant).
[< Latin *prōspectus, -ūs* < *prōspicere* to look out, on; foresee < *prō-* forward + *specere* to look. See etym. of doublet **prospectus**.]

**pros|pec|tion** (prə spek′shən), *n.* **1** the action of looking forward; foresight. **2** the action of prospecting, as for gold: *Its object is to make an immediate, thorough archaeological prospection of the territory, for much certainly remains unknown* (Manchester Guardian).

**pro|spec|tive** (prə spek′tiv), *adj.* **1** that is looked forward to as likely or promised; probable; expected: *a prospective client. I won't have a prospective guest discussed* (Winston Churchill). **2** looking forward in time; future: *a prospective mother.*

**pro|spec|tive|ly** (prə spek′tiv lē), *adv.* in prospect or expectation; in the future.

**pros|pec|tor** (pros′pek tər, prə spek′-), *n.* a person who explores or examines a region, searching for gold, silver, oil, uranium, or other valuable ores, or estimating the value of some product of the region. [American English < *prospect,* verb + *-or*]

**pros|pects** (pros′pekts), *n.pl.* See under **prospect.**

**pro|spec|tus** (prə spek′təs), *n.* **1** a printed statement describing and advertising something, especially the description of a proposed enterprise, issued to potential investors: *the prospectus of a new company or issue of stock.* **2** *British.* a university or college catalog. [< Latin *prōspectus.* See etym. of doublet **prospect.**]

**pros|per** (pros′pər), *v.i.* to be successful; have good fortune; thrive; flourish: *His business prospered. Whatsoever he doeth shall prosper* (Psalms 1:3). *Well may you prosper!* (Shakespeare). — ***v.t.*** to make successful; cause to flourish: *Let every one of you lay by him in store, as God hath prospered him* (I Corinthians 16:2). [< Middle French *prosperer,* learned borrowing from Latin *prosperāre* < *prosperus* prosperous < *prō-* for, according to + *spēs* hope]

**pros|per|i|ty** (pros per′ə tē), *n., pl.* **-ties.** prosperous condition; good fortune; success: *Peace brings prosperity. ... the comforts and prosperities of his middle age* (H. G. Wells).

**Pros|per|o** (pros′pə rō), *n.* the exiled duke living on an enchanted island in Shakespeare's play *The Tempest,* who, by magic, restores his rank and wealth.

**pros|per|ous** (pros′pər əs), *adj.* **1** successful; thriving; doing well; fortunate: *a prosperous merchant.* **SYN:** flourishing, rich, wealthy. **2** favorable; helpful: *prosperous weather for growing wheat.* [< Latin *prosperus* (with English *-ous*); see etym. under **prosper**] — **pros′per|ous|ly,** *adv.* — **pros′per|ous|ness,** *n.*

**prost** (prōst), *interj.* = prosit.

**pros|ta|glan|din** (pros′tə glan′dən), *n.* any one of a group of hormonelike substances produced in the tissues of mammals by the action of enzymes on certain fatty acids, found in high concentrations in seminal fluid of the prostate gland, and thought to have a variety of important functions in reproduction, nerve-impulse transmission, muscle contraction, regulation of blood pressure, and metabolism. *Abbr:* PG (no periods). [coined by the Swedish physiologist Ulf S. von Euler < *prosta*(te) *gland* + *-in*]

**pros|tate** (pros′tāt), *n., adj.* — ***n.*** a large gland surrounding the male urethra just below the bladder, which secretes a substance used to transport sperm cells: *In later life, the prostate tends to become larger. It may press upon the urethral tube, interfering with the passage of urine. Surgeons may then have to remove either all, or part of, the gland* (R. F. Escamilla).
— ***adj.*** designating or having to do with this gland.
[< Medieval Latin *prostata* < Greek *prostátēs* one standing in front, ultimately < *pro-* before + *sténai* to stand]

**pros|ta|tec|to|my** (pros′tə tek′tə mē), *n., pl.* **-mies.** surgical removal of all or part of the prostate. [< *prostat*(e) + Greek *ektomḗ* a cutting out]

**pros|tat|ic** (pros tat′ik), *adj.* of or having to do with the prostate gland.

**pros|ta|tism** (pros′tə tiz əm), *n.* chronic obstruction to urination due to enlargement of the prostate.

**pros|ta|ti|tis** (pros′tə tī′tis), *n.* inflammation of the prostate gland.

**pros|ta|tot|o|my** (pros′tə tot′ə mē), *n., pl.* **-mies.** surgical incision into the prostate. [< *prostat*(e) + Greek *-tomiā* a cutting]

**pros|the|sis** (pros′thə sis), *n., pl.* **-the|ses** (-thə sēz). **1** the replacement of a missing tooth, leg, or other parts of the body, with an artificial one. **2** the part itself: *In the basement Dr. Michiels has established a modern dental laboratory, turning out expertly made prostheses and gold inlays* (Newsweek). **3** the art of making lifelike artificial parts for the human body. **4** the addition of a letter or syllable to a word, especially at the beginning, such as "be-" in "beknownst." [< Late Latin *prosthesis* (definition 4) < Greek *prósthesis* addition, ultimately < *prós* in addition to + *thésis* a placing or setting down < *tithénai* to put]

**pros|thet|ic** (pros thet′ik), *adj.* of or having to do with prosthesis: *prosthetic dentistry.* — **pros|thet′i|cal|ly,** *adv.*

**pros|thet|ics** (pros thet′iks), *n.* the branch of surgery or dentistry dealing with prosthetic devices.

**pros|the|tist** (pros′thə tist), *n.* **1** a specialist in prosthesis, as of limbs or other parts of the body. **2** = prosthodontist.

**pros|thi|on** (pros′thē on), *n.* the middle point of the anterior surface of the upper jaw. [< Greek *prósthion,* neuter of *prósthios* foremost, front]

**pros|tho|don|ti|a** (pros′thə don′shē ə, -don′shə), *n.* = prosthodontics. [< *prosth*(etic) + *-odontia,* as in *orthodontia*]

**pros|tho|don|tics** (pros′thə don′tiks), *n.* the branch of dentistry dealing with the making of crowns, bridges, or artificial teeth.

**pros|tho|don|tist** (pros′thə don′tist), *n.* a dentist who makes artificial teeth.

**Pro|stig|mine** (prō stig′min), *n. Trademark.* neostigmine.

**pros|ti|tute** (pros′tə tüt, -tyüt), *n., v.,* **-tut|ed, -tut|ing,** *adj.* — ***n.*** **1** a woman who has sexual relations with men for money. **SYN:** harlot, whore. **2** *Figurative.* a person who does base things for money.
— ***v.t.*** **1** to put to an unworthy or base use: *to prostitute artistic skills. The soup—alas! that I should so far prostitute the word* (Charles Lever). **SYN:** defile, debase. **2** to submit to immoral or unworthy behavior for money.
— ***adj.*** debased or debasing; corrupt: *I found how the world had been misled by prostitute writers* (Jonathan Swift).
[< Latin *prōstitūtus,* or *prōstitūta,* feminine, past participle of *prōstituere* to prostitute < *prō-* before (the public) + *statuere* cause to stand]

**pros|ti|tu|tion** (pros′tə tü′shən, -tyü′-), *n.* **1** the act or practice of a prostitute or prostitutes. **2** the use of one's body, honor, talents, or other gifts, in a base way.

**pros|ti|tu|tor** (pros′tə tü′tər, -tyü′-), *n.* a person or thing that prostitutes: (*Figurative.*) *prostitutors of the ballot* (New York Voice).

**pro|sto|mi|al** (prō stō′mē əl), *adj.* of, having to do with, or situated on the prostomium.

**pro|sto|mi|um** (prō stō′mē əm), *n.* the part of the body in front of the mouth of mollusks, worms, and certain other invertebrates. [< New Latin *prostomium* < Greek *prostómion* (literally) something in front of the mouth < *pró* before + *stóma* mouth]

**pros|trate** (pros′trāt), *v.,* **-trat|ed, -trat|ing,** *adj.* — ***v.t.*** **1** to lay down flat; cast down: *The captives prostrated themselves before the conqueror.* **2** *Figurative.* to make very weak or helpless; exhaust: *Sickness often prostrates people. In prostrating one enemy, he had mortified a hundred* (Scott).
— ***adj.*** **1** lying flat with face downward: *She was humbly prostrate in prayer.* **SYN:** prone. **2** lying flat: *He stumbled and lay prostrate on the floor.* **SYN:** prone. **3** *Figurative.* **a** helpless; overcome: *a prostrate enemy, to be prostrate with grief.* **b** submissive: *prostrate humility.* **4** *Botany.* lying along the ground: *a prostrate stem or plant.*
[< Latin *prōstrātus,* past participle of *prōsternere* < *prō-* forth + *sternere* to strew]

**pros|tra|tion** (pros trā′shən), *n.* **1** the act of prostrating; bowing down low or lying face down, as before a king, before idols, or before God. Prostration is an act of submission, respect, or worship. **2** *Figurative.* the condition of being very much worn out or used up in body or mind; exhaustion or dejection.

**pro|style** (prō′stīl), *adj., n.* — ***adj.*** having a portico in front, standing out from the walls of the building: *a prostyle Greek temple.*
— ***n.*** a prostyle portico or building.
[< Latin *prostȳlos* having pillars in front < unrecorded Greek *próstȳlos* < Greek *pro-* before + *stȳlos* pillar, column]

**pros|y** (prō′zē), *adj.,* **pros|i|er, pros|i|est.** like prose; commonplace; dull; tiresome: *an argument that was so prosy that many a head by and by began to nod* (Mark Twain).

**prot-,** *combining form.* the form of **proto-** before vowels, as in *protamine.*

**Prot.,** Protestant.

***protactinium**

| symbol | atomic number | mass number | oxidation state |
|---|---|---|---|
| Pa | 91 | 231 | 4,5 |

***pro|tac|tin|i|um** (prō′tak tin′ē əm), *n.* a very rare, heavy, radioactive metallic chemical element, which occurs in pitchblende and disintegrates to form actinium. Formerly, **protoactinium.** [< *prot-* + *actinium*]

**pro|tag|o|nist** (prō tag′ə nist), *n.* **1** the main character in a play, story, or novel. **2** a person who takes a leading part; active supporter; champion: *A new scene opened; and new protagonists—Mr. Gladstone and Mr. Disraeli—struggled together in the limelight* (Lytton Strachey). [< Greek *prōtagōnistḗs* < *prōtos* first + *agōnistḗs* actor < *agṓn* a contest, struggle < *ágein* to do]

**pro|ta|min** (prō′tə min), *n.* = protamine.

**pro|ta|mine** (prō′tə mēn, -min), *n.* any one of a group of basic proteins that are not coagulated by heat, are soluble in water, and form amino acids when hydrolyzed: *Nucleoproteins are formed by a salt-like union of a nucleic acid and a basic protein such as protamine or histone* (G. M. Wyburn). [< *prot-* + *amine*]

**pro|tan|dric** (prō tan′drik), *adj.* exhibiting proterandry; proterandrous: *The European oyster* [*is*] *protandric, the gonad of an individual first producing sperm and then eggs, in rhythmic alternation* (Tracy I. Storer).

**pro|tan|drous** (prō tan′drəs), *adj.* = proterandrous.

**pro|tan|dry** (prō tan′drē), *n.* = proterandry.

**pro|ta|nope** (prō′tə nōp), *n.* a person suffering from protanopia, having little or no perception of the red end of the spectrum: *A protanope confuses red and bluish green with gray, and, indeed, with each other* (Deane B. Judd).

**pro|ta|no|pi|a** (prō′tə nō′pē ə), *n.* a form of color blindness probably due to a lack of receptors sensitive to red light, which appears indistinguishable from dim green or yellow light, or may not be seen at all. [< New Latin *protanopia* < Greek *prôtos* first + *an-* not + *ṓps* eye]

**pro|ta|no|pic** (prō′tə nō′pik), *adj.* affected with protanopia: *One per cent of men is protanopic* (New Scientist).

**pro tan|to** (prō tan′tō), *Latin.* for so much; to that extent.

**prot|a|sis** (prot′ə sis), *n., pl.* **-ses** (-sēz). **1** *Grammar.* the clause expressing the condition in a conditional sentence. **2** the introduction of the characters and subject in the first part of a classical drama. [< Latin *protasis* < Greek *prótasis* < *proteínein* stretch ahead < *pro-* before + *teínein* to stretch]

**pro|te|a** (prō′tē ə), *n.* any one of a group of chiefly South African trees and shrubs with large cone-shaped heads of red or purple flowers that have no petals: *Note the proteas and silver trees that grew in profusion on what is now a built-up area* (Cape Times). [< New Latin *Protea* the genus name, alteration of *Proteus* (because there are many different forms of the plant)]

**Pro|te|an** (prō′tē ən, prō tē′-), *adj.* of or like Proteus, the Greek sea god who could take on many forms.

**pro|te|an¹** (prō′tē ən, prō tē′-), *adj.* readily assuming different forms or characters; exceedingly variable: *a protean artist or actor.* [< *Proteus* + *-an*]

**pro|te|an²** (prō′tē ən), *n.* any one of a group of insoluble compounds derived from protein by the action of water or enzymes. [< *prote*(in) + *-an*]

**pro|te|ase** (prō′tē ās), *n.* any one of various enzymes, such as pepsin, that break down proteins into simpler compounds. [< *prote*(olysis) + *-ase*]

**pro|tect** (prə tekt′), *v.t.* **1** to shield from harm or danger; shelter; defend; guard: *Protect yourself from danger. Protect the baby's eyes from the sun.* **SYN:** secure. See syn. under **guard.** **2** to guard (home industry) against foreign goods by taxing any which are brought into the country. **3** to provide money for the payment of (a draft, bond, or other obligation) when it falls due. [< Latin *prōtectus,* past participle of *prōtegere* < *prō-* in front + *tegere* to cover]

**pro|tect|ant** (prə tek′tənt), *n.* a substance that provides protection: *A new silicone metal protectant ... is the answer to many problems in corrosion* (Scientific American).

**pro|tect|ed cruiser** (prə tek′tid), a former type of light cruiser with armored decks but no armor on its sides.

**protected state,** a state or nation under the protectorate of a stronger power.

**pro|tect|ing** (prə tek′ting), *adj.* that protects: *To thy wings protecting shade My self I carry will* (Mary Herbert Pembroke).

**pro|tect|ing|ly** (prə tek′ting lē), *adv.* so as to protect.

**Pronunciation Key:** hat, āge, cãre, fär; let, ēqual, tėrm; it, īce; hot, ōpen, ôrder; oil, out; cup, pu̇t, rüle; child; long; thin; ᴛʜen; zh, measure; ə represents **a** in about, **e** in taken, **i** in pencil, **o** in lemon, **u** in circus.

**pro|tec|tion** (prə tek′shən), *n.* **1** the act of protecting, or condition of being kept from harm; defense: *We have policemen for our protection.* **SYN:** guard, security. **2** a thing or person that prevents damage: *An apron is a protection when doing dirty work.* **SYN:** shield, safeguard, bulwark. **3** the system of taxing foreign goods so that people are more likely to buy goods made in their own country; the opposite of free trade. **4** something that assures safe passage through a region; passport. **5** *Informal.* the payment of money to racketeers or gangsters as a form of tribute in order not to be molested. **6** *U.S.* a certificate of nationality issued to seamen who are citizens: *the out-ward-bound sailor in quest of a protection* (Hawthorne).

**pro|tec|tion|al** (prə tek′shə nəl), *adj.* having to do with, characterized by, or fostered by protection: *the protectional expansion of national commerce* (Henry Morley).

**pro|tec|tion|ism** (prə tek′shə niz əm), *n.* the economic system or theory of protection, in which high tariffs on imported goods give domestic producers encouragement and advantage: *The new upsurge of economic nationalism known in this country as protectionism ...* (New York Times).

**pro|tec|tion|ist** (prə tek′shə nist), *n., adj.* —*n.* **1** a person who favors protectionism: *The protectionists, who are usually protectionists for individual industries and areas, are vociferous as always* (Wall Street Journal). **2** a person who seeks to protect wildlife; a wildlife conservationist: *St. Cuthbert, the Northumbrian divine, ... has been given the credit of having been the first bird protectionist* (London Times).
—*adj.* of protectionism or protectionists: *protectionist tariffs, protectionist trade restrictions.*

**pro|tec|tive** (prə tek′tiv), *adj.* **1** being a defense; protecting: *the hard protective covering of a turtle. Marathon came up with protective packaging that made frozen food specialties practical* (Newsweek). **2** preventing injury to those around: *a protective device on a machine.* **3** guarding against foreign-made goods by putting a high tax or duty on them: *a protective tariff, protective legislation.* —**pro|tec′tive|ly**, *adv.* —**pro|tec′tiveness**, *n.*

**protective colloid**, a substance added to a colloidal suspension to keep the particles from coming together: *Gelatin and gum arabic are protective colloids in ice cream and India ink. Materials called protective colloids, or peptizing agents, are added to the mixture; and they apparently coat the suspended particles and so prevent their coalescing* (Offner).

**protective coloring** or **coloration**, a coloring some animals and plants have that makes them hard to distinguish from the things they live among, or makes them resemble something harmful or distasteful, and so protects them from their enemies.

**protective covenant**, an agreement among property owners in an area not to sell or rent property to members of certain specified ethnic or religious groups; a restrictive covenant.

**protective cover**, **1** the presence of fighter aircraft flying above friendly ships, troops, bombers, or installations, to repel enemy air attack on them: *Flying protective cover for these bombers, Sabre jets destroyed several enemy aircraft in air battles* (New York Times). **2** the aircraft giving this protection.

**protective custody**, imprisonment or arrest of a person supposedly for his protection: *13 other ministers taken into protective custody have been placed in a Jakarta military prison* (New York Times).

**protective mimicry**, a close resemblance of a defenseless animal to some different animal, which is less susceptible to attack from predators; Batesian mimicry. For example, the viceroy butterfly closely resembles the monarch, which is not eaten by birds because of its disagreeable taste.

**protective resemblance**, resemblance that some animals have to other animals or to some element in the environment that helps them hide from their enemies. The long body and broad, leaflike wings of the praying mantis is an example of protective resemblance.

**protective tariff**, a tariff chiefly to protect home industry against foreign competition, not to produce revenue: *Heavy revenue duties ... have the same effect as protective tariffs in obstructing free trade* (Time).

**pro|tec|tor** (prə tek′tər), *n.* **1a** a person who protects; defender. **SYN:** guardian. **b** a thing that protects: *The catcher in baseball wears a chest protector.* **2** the head of a kingdom when the king or queen cannot rule: *Oliver Cromwell was Lord Protector of England from 1653 to 1658.* **SYN:** regent.

**pro|tec|tor|al** (prə tek′tə rəl), *adj.* of or having to do with a protector.

**Pro|tec|tor|ate** (prə tek′tər it), *n.* the period (1653-1659) during which Oliver and Richard Cromwell were Lord Protectors of England. [< *protector* + *-ate*[3]]

**pro|tec|tor|ate** (prə tek′tər it), *n.* **1** a weak country under the protection and partial control of a strong country. Many parts of Africa were once European protectorates. **2** such protection and control. **3** the position or term of a protector. **4** government by a protector.

**pro|tec|tor|ship** (prə tek′tər ship), *n.* **1** the position or term of a protector. **2** the period during which a protector governs.

**pro|tec|to|ry** (prə tek′tər ē), *n., pl.* **-ries**. an institution for the care and training of homeless or delinquent children.

**pro|tec|tress** (prə tek′tris), *n.* a woman protector.

**pro|té|gé** (prō′tə zhā), *n.* **1** a person or group under the protection or kindly care of a friend or patron, especially of a person of superior position, influence, or skill: *The young pianist was a protégé of the celebrated composer.* **2** something under the care and protection of another: ... *with Formosa becoming a United Nations protégé and the people of Formosa, by plebiscite or otherwise, deciding their future* (London Times). [< French *protégé,* past participle of *protéger,* learned borrowing from Latin *prōtegere* protect]

**pro|té|gée** (prō′tə zhā), *n.* a woman protégé.

**pro|te|id** (prō′tē id), *n., adj.* —*n.* = protein.
—*adj.* containing much protein.

**pro|te|ide** (prō′tē īd, -id), *n., adj.* = protein.

**pro|tein** (prō′tēn, -tē in), *n., adj.* —*n.* **1** one of the substances containing nitrogen, carbon, hydrogen, and oxygen, that is a necessary part of the cells of animals and plants. Meat, milk, cheese, eggs, and beans contain protein. Proteins are built up of amino acids. They are complex organic compounds, essential to the functioning as well as the structure of all organic cells. **2** (formerly) the nitrogenous substances once thought to be the essential constituents of all animals and plants.
—*adj.* of or containing protein. [< German *Protein* < Greek *prōteîos* of the first quality (< *prôtos* first) + German *-in* -in] —**pro′tein|like′**, *adj.*

**pro|tein|a|ceous** (prō′tə nā′shəs, -tē ə-), *adj.* of or like protein: *A rather starchy seed like the wheat grain will imbibe relatively little water, while a proteinaceous one like the pea will absorb a great deal* (Science News Letter).

**pro|tein|ase** (prō′tə nās, -tē ə-), *n.* any of various proteases that change proteins to polypeptides.

**pro|tein|ic** (prō tēn′ik, -tē in′-), *adj.* = proteinaceous.

**pro|tein|oid** (prō′tə noid, -tē ə-), *n.* a proteinlike substance made by polymerization of a number of amino acids common to protein: *Proteinoids ... might represent the first evolutionary step along the road that led to the true proteins and eventually to life itself* (New Scientist).

**pro|tein|u|ri|a** (prō tə nůr′ē ə, -tē′ə-), *n.* the presence of protein in the urine.

**pro tem** (prō tem′), = pro tempore.

**pro tem.**, pro tempore.

**pro tem|po|re** (prō tem′pə rē), *Latin.* for the time being; temporarily: *president pro tempore, to appoint someone to an office pro tempore.* —**protem′po|re**, *adj.*

**pro|tend** (prō tend′), *v.t.* **1** to stretch forth; hold out before oneself. **2** to extend in one dimension, especially lengthwise: *His staff protending like a hunter's spear* (Wordsworth). **3** to extend in duration; prolong. [< Latin *prōtendere* < *prō-* before + *tendere* to stretch]

**pro|ten|sion** (prō ten′shən), *n.* = duration.

**pro|ten|sive** (prō ten′siv), *adj.* **1** extended in one dimension, especially lengthwise. **2** extended in time; prolonging.

**pro|te|ol|y|sis** (prō′tē ol′ə sis), *n.* the hydrolysis or breaking down of proteins into simpler compounds, as in digestion. [< *protein* + Greek *lýsis* a loosening]

**pro|te|o|lyt|ic** (prō′tē ə lit′ik), *adj.* **1** having to do with proteolysis. **2** bringing about proteolysis: *a proteolytic enzyme.*

**pro|te|ose** (prō′tē ōs), *n.* any one of a class of soluble compounds derived from proteins by the action of the gastric and pancreatic juices.

**pro|ter|an|drous** (prō′tə ran′drəs, prot′ə-), *adj.* exhibiting proterandry.

**pro|ter|an|dry** (prō′tə ran′drē, prot′ə-), *n.* **1** *Botany.* the maturation of the stamens and the discharge of the pollen before the pistils of the flower are mature. **2** *Zoology.* the maturation of the male organs or individuals of a hermaphroditic animal or a zooid colony before the female. [< Greek *próteros* prior (< *pró* before) + *anḗr, andrós* man, male + English *-y*[3]]

**prot|er|og|y|nous** (prot′ə roj′ə nəs), *adj.* exhibiting proterogyny.

**prot|er|og|y|ny** (prot′ə roj′ə nē), *n.* **1** *Botany.* the maturation of the pistils in a flower before the stamens have matured their pollen. **2** *Zoology.* the maturation of the female organs or individuals of a hermaphroditic animal or a zooid colony before the male. [< Greek *próteros* prior (< *pró* before) + *gynḗ* woman, female]

**Prot|er|o|zo|ic** (prot′ər ə zō′ik), *n., adj.* —*n.* **1** the geological era after the Archeozoic and before the Paleozoic, during which sponges, sea worms, and other forms of sea life appeared: *The Archeozoic probably began about 1,500 million years ago, and the Proterozoic 925 million years ago* (Beals and Hoijer). **2** the rocks formed in this era.
—*adj.* of this era or its rocks.
[< Greek *próteros* prior + *zōḗ* life + English *-ic*]

**pro|ter|vi|ty** (prə tėr′və tē), *n., pl.* **-ties**. **1** wantonness; petulance: ... *the peevishness and protervity of age* (Caleb D'Anvers). **2** an instance or show of this. [< Old French *protervite* < Latin *protervitās* < *protervus* violent, bold]

**Pro|tes|i|la|us** (prə tes′ə lā′əs), *n. Greek Legend.* the first Greek killed in the Trojan War.

**pro|test** (*n., adj.* prō′test; *v.* prə test′), *n., adj., v.* —*n.* **1** a statement that denies or objects strongly: *They yielded only after protest. A written protest, couched in the strongest terms, was dispatched ... for delivery* (London Times). **2** a solemn declaration: *The accused man was judged guilty in spite of his protest of innocence.* **3** a written statement by a notary public that a bill, note, check, or other commercial obligation has been presented to someone who has refused to pay it or accept it. **4** an attested declaration by the master of a ship in regard to some accident, injury, or loss during a voyage. **5** *Sports.* an objection to a player or a play as illegal.
—*adj.* characterized by protest; expressing protest or objection against some condition: *a protest meeting, a protest movement, a protest song. In the protest parade ... were businessmen, farmers, and housewives* (Wall Street Journal).
—*v.i.* **1** to make objections; object: *The children protested against having grown-ups in the game.* **2** to make a solemn declaration or affirmation: *The lady doth protest too much, methinks* (Shakespeare).
—*v.t.* **1** to object to: *He protested the umpire's decision.* **2** to declare solemnly; assert: *The accused man protested his innocence.* **3** to state that (a check, note, bill, or other commercial obligation) has not been paid. **4** to say in protest: *"Oh no, you didn't!" she protested, firmly* (Arnold Bennett). **5** *Obsolete.* to make known: *Do me right, or I will protest your cowardice* (Shakespeare). **6** *Obsolete.* to promise solemnly: *On Diana's altar to protest For aye austerity and single life* (Shakespeare). **7** *Obsolete.* to call to witness.
**under protest**, unwillingly; though objecting: *His insistent parents made him go to bed under protest.*
[< Middle French *protester* to protest; say publicly, learned borrowing from Latin *prōtestārī* < *prō-* forth, before + *testis* witness] —**pro|test′er**, *n.*

**Prot|es|tant** (prot′ə stənt), *n., adj.* —*n.* **1** a member of any one of certain Christian churches not governed by the Roman Catholic Church or the Eastern Church, such as those that split off from the Roman Catholic Church during the Reformation of the 1500's or developed thereafter. Lutherans, Baptists, Presbyterians, Methodists, Unitarians, Quakers, and many others are Protestants. **2** (in the 1600's) a Lutheran or an Anglican, as contrasted with a Calvinist, Presbyterian, Quaker, or other dissenter. **3** one of the German princes who protested the decision of the second diet of Speyer in 1529, which had denounced the Reformation.
—*adj.* of Protestants or their religion.
[< German or French *Protestant* one who protests < Latin *prōtestans, -antis,* present participle of *prōtestārī;* see etym. under **protest**]

**pro|tes|tant** (prə tes′tənt), *n., adj.* —*n.* a person who protests; protester: *One of the protestants, though his first reaction was milder than most, was Abraham Lincoln* (Atlantic).
—*adj.* protesting: *Alan Watt's [book] brings out well the gulf between the protestant lawlessness of the Dharma bums and the traditionalism of Zen Buddhism proper* (Manchester Guardian Weekly).
[noun use of French *protestant,* present participle of *protester;* see etym. under **protest**]

**Protestant Episcopal Church**, a church in the United States that has about the same principles and beliefs as the Church of England. It is a self-governing branch of the Anglican communion.

**Protestant ethic**, a set of values held to be the ideological basis of the capitalistic system, including the ideas of strict compliance with the law, the necessity and desirability of work and thrift, and encouragement of competition and the profit motive in everyday life: *The Protestant ethic and tradition of capitalism have made most middle-class Americans cherish their privacy and independence* (Lynne and Jack Waugh).

**Prot|es|tant|ism** (prot′ə stən tiz′əm), *n.* **1** the religion of Protestants. **2** their principles and beliefs. **3** Protestants or Protestant churches as a group.

**prot|es|tant|ism** (prot′ə stən tiz′əm), *n.* the condition of protesting; an attitude of protest. [< *Protestantism*]

**Prot|es|tant|ize** (prot′ə stən tīz), *v.t.,* **-ized, -iz|ing.** to make Protestant; change to Protestantism: *The introduction of a vernacular liturgy and congregational singing stirred many ... Catholics to feel that their church was being "Protestantized"* (Time).

**prot|es|ta|tion** (prot′ə stā′shən), *n.* **1** a solemn declaration; protesting: *to make a protestation of one's innocence. The Duke was ... vehement ... in his protestations of loyalty* (John L. Motley). **2** a protest; formal dissent or disapproval.

**pro|tes|ta|to|ry** (prə tes′tə tôr′ē, -tōr′-), *adj.* making protestation; expressing a protest.

**pro|test|ing** (prə tes′ting), *adj.* that protests; making a protest. —**pro|test′ing|ly,** *adv.*

**pro|tes|tor** (prə tes′tər), *n.* a person who makes a protest; protester.

**Pro|te|us** (prō′tē əs, -tyüs), *n.* **1** *Greek Mythology.* a sea god who could assume many different forms. **2** any person or thing capable of taking on various aspects or characters.

**pro|te|us** (prō′tē əs, -tyüs), *n.* **1** a blind salamander living in the subterranean waters of limestone caves in eastern Europe. It is related to the menobranch of North America. **2** any one of a group of microorganisms or bacteria, some of which are saprophytic and some pathogenic in man and fowl. [< New Latin *Proteus* the genus name < *Proteus*]

**pro|te|van|gel** (prō′ti van′jəl), *n.* = protevangelium.

**pro|te|van|gel|i|um** (prō′ti van jel′ē əm), *n.* the promise concerning the seed of the woman, regarded as the earliest announcement of the gospel. Genesis 3:15. [< New Latin *protevangelium* < Greek *prôtos* first + Latin *evangelium* evangel]

**pro|tha|la|mi|on** (prō′thə lā′mē on), *n., pl.* **-mi|a** (-mē ə). a song or poem to celebrate a marriage. [< Greek *pró* before + *thálamos* bridal chamber; probably patterned on *epithalamium*]

**pro|tha|la|mi|um** (prō′thə lā′mē əm), *n., pl.* **-mi|a** (-mē ə). = prothalamion.

**pro|thal|li|al** (prō thal′ē əl), *adj.* of a prothallium.

**pro|thal|line** (prō thal′īn, -in), *adj.* of, like, or belonging to a prothallium.

**pro|thal|li|um** (prō thal′ē əm), *n., pl.* **-thal|li|a** (-thal′ē ə). **1** the gametophyte of ferns, horsetails, club mosses, and other pteridophytes. **2** the analogous rudimentary gametophyte of seed-bearing plants. [< New Latin *prothallium* < Greek *pró* before + New Latin *thallus* thallus + *-ium,* a diminutive suffix]

**pro|thal|lus** (prō thal′əs), *n., pl.* **-thal|li** (-thal′ī). = prothallium.

**proth|e|sis** (proth′ə sis), *n.* **1a** the preparation of the Eucharistic elements in the Greek Church. **b** the table on which this is done. **c** the part of the sanctuary where this table stands. **2** prosthesis of a word or the human body. [< Greek *próthesis* a setting forth in public < *protithénai* < *pro-* before + *tithénai* to set, put]

**pro|thet|ic** (prō thet′ik), *adj.* having to do with or exhibiting prothesis. —**pro|thet′i|cal|ly,** *adv.*

**pro|thon|o|tar|i|al** (prō thon′ə tãr′ē əl), *adj.* of or belonging to a prothonotary.

**pro|thon|o|tar|y** (prō thon′ə ter′ē), *n., pl.* **-tar|ies.** **1** a chief clerk, secretary, or registrar, especially of a court of law. **2** the Roman Catholic official in charge of the registry of pontifical acts, canonizations, and the like. **3** the chief secretary of the patriarch of Constantinople in the Greek Church. **4** = prothonotary warbler. Also, **protonotary.** [< Medieval Latin *prothonotarius* < Medieval Greek *prōtonōtários* < *prôtos* first + Late Greek *nōtários* clerk, notary]

**pro|thon|o|tar|y|ship** (prō thon′ə ter′ē ship), *n.* the office of a prothonotary.

**prothonotary warbler,** a golden-yellow warbler of the central and eastern United States that has an olive back and bluish-gray wings and tail.

**pro|tho|rac|ic** (prō′thə ras′ik), *adj.* of or having to do with the prothorax: *the prothoracic cavity, a prothoracic gland.*

**pro|tho|rax** (prō thôr′aks, -thōr′-), *n., pl.* **-tho|rax|es, -tho|ra|ces** (-thôr′ə sēz, -thōr′-). the anterior division of an insect's thorax, bearing the first pair of legs. [< French *prothorax* < *pro-* pro-[1] + New Latin *thorax* thorax < Greek *thṓrāx* chest]

**pro|throm|base** (prō throm′bās), *n.* the proenzyme of thrombase.

**pro|throm|bin** (prō throm′bin), *n.* a substance in the blood plasma, essential to clotting, from which thrombin is derived; thrombogen. [< *pro-*[2] + *thrombin*]

**pro|tist** (prō′tist), *n., pl.* **pro|tists, pro|tis|ta** (pro-tis′tə). any one of the group of organisms that includes all one-celled animals and plants, such as the bacteria, protozoans, and yeasts: *Plantlike protists probably appeared several times through symbiotic unions between free-living, autotrophic prokaryote blue-green algae and various heterotrophic eukaryote protists* (Scientific American). [< German *Protista,* plural < Greek *prṓtistos* the very first, superlative of *prôtos* first (< *pró* before)]

**pro|tis|tan** (prō tis′tən), *adj., n.* —*adj.* of or having to do with protists.
—*n.* a single-celled organism; protist.

**pro|tis|tic** (prō tis′tik), *adj.* = protistan.

**pro|tis|tol|o|gy** (prō′tis tol′ə jē), *n.* the study of protists: *"The Protistan Kingdom: Protists and Viruses" [is] a nontechnical introduction to protistology: bacteria, ciliated cells, amebas, sporozoans, bacteriophages, and contagious germs* (Science News).

**pro|ti|um** (prō′tē əm, -shē-), *n.* the ordinary isotope of hydrogen, having a mass number of 1.0 *Symbol:* $H^1$ (no period). [< *prot*(on) + New Latin *-ium,* a noun suffix meaning "element" (because the nucleus contains one proton only)]

**proto-,** *combining form.* **1** first in time, as in *prototype.*
**2** first in importance; chief; primary, as in *protoplasm.*
Also, **prot-** before vowels.
[< Greek *prôto-* < *prôtos* first, superlative of *próteros* < *pró,* preposition, before; see etym. under **pro-**[2]]

**pro|to|ac|tin|i|um** (prō′tō ak tin′ē əm), *n.* the former name of protactinium.

**pro|to|an|throp|ic** (prō′tō an throp′ik), *adj.* of or belonging to the earliest period of the existence of man.

**pro|to|bi|ont** (prō′tō bī′ont), *n.* an elementary or primordial organism: *As a preliminary stage in the total process of organic evolution, chemical evolution of course reaches its climax when lifeless organic molecules are assembled by chance into a living organism. This first form of life is what the Russian biochemist A. I. Oparin calls a "protobiont"* (Scientific American).

**pro|to|bi|ot|ic soup** (prō′tō bī ot′ik), = primordial soup.

**pro|to|ca|non|i|cal** (prō′tō kə non′ə kəl), *adj.* of or forming a first or original canon.

**protocanonical books,** the books of the Bible whose canonicity has always been universally acknowledged in the church.

**pro|to|cat|e|chu|ic acid** (prō′tō kat′ə chü′ik, -shü′-), a crystalline compound derived from vanillin or produced synthetically, occurring naturally in various plants. *Formula:* $C_7H_6O_4$

**pro|toc|er|as** (prō tos′ər əs), *n.* an extinct ungulate mammal of North America, about the size of a sheep and distantly related to the chevrotains, with two or three pairs of horns on the head of the male. [< New Latin *Protoceras* the genus name < Greek *prôtos* first + *kéras* horn]

***pro|to|cer|a|tops** (prō′tō ser′ə tops), *n.* a species of hornless, plant-eating dinosaur, about six feet long, that lived during the late Cretaceous period in Asia and North America. [< New Latin *Protoceratops* < Greek *prôtos* first + *kéras, -atos* horn + *ôps* eye]

***protoceratops**

**pro|to|col** (prō′tə kol, -kôl), *n., v.,* **-colled, -col|ling.** —*n.* **1** the rules of etiquette of the diplomatic corps. **2** rules for any procedure. **3** a first draft or record from which a document, especially a treaty, is prepared. **4** a formal or official statement of a proceeding or transaction, such as a clinical report, or a report on a scientific experiment or on the preparation and testing of a drug. **5** *U.S.* the original record of a Spanish land grant made in parts of the Southwest and West.
—*v.i.* to draw up protocols.
—*v.t.* to embody in a protocol.
[< Old French *protocolle* minutes of a document, learned borrowing from Medieval Latin *protocollum* < Greek *prōtókollon* a first leaf (with date and contents) glued onto a papyrus roll < *prôtos* first + *kólla* glue]

**pro|to|col|ar** (prō′tə kol′ər), *adj.* = protocolary.

**pro|to|col|a|ry** (prō′tə kol′ər ē), *adj.* of or having to do with protocol or a protocol: *After these protocolary preliminaries, I got down to the main purpose of my visit* (New Yorker).

**pro|to|con|ti|nent** (prō′tō kon′tə nənt), *n.* = supercontinent.

**pro|to|derm** (prō′tə dėrm), *n.* = dermatogen.

**pro|to|dy|nas|tic** (prō′tō dī nas′tik), *adj.* of or having to do with the earliest royal dynasties of a country: *... fine stone vessels from protodynastic Egypt* (Joseph Alsop).

**pro|to|fas|cism** (prō′tō fash′iz əm), *n.* a movement or ideology characterized by fascist tendencies and ideas and usually associated with a political party of the far right.

**pro|to|fas|cist** (prō′tō fash′ist), *n., adj.* —*n.* **1** a member of a protofascist party. **2** a person who favors or supports protofascism.
—*adj.* of or having to do with protofascism or protofascists: *... the protofascist wing of the Syrian political spectrum* (Dwight J. Simpson).

**pro|to|gal|ax|y** (prō′tō gal′ək sē), *n., pl.* **-ax|ies.** **1** a hypothetical mass of contracting gas in space from which the galaxies may have formed as the result of a cosmic explosion of hydrogen. **2** a galaxy in the process of formation, before any stars have formed in it: *A protogalaxy consisting of an irregular cloud of gas and probably some dust, with a mass of a little less than a million times that of the sun, existed in intergalactic space somewhat more than 10 billion years ago* (Scientific American).

**Pro|to-Ger|man|ic** (prō′tə jėr man′ik), *adj., n.* —*adj.* of or having to do with the hypothetical language that was the ancestor of the Germanic languages.
—*n.* this language; primitive or original Germanic.

**pro|to|gine** (prō′tə jin, -jēn), *n.* a fine-grained variety of granite, occurring chiefly in the Alps. [< French *protogine,* ultimately < Greek *prôtos* first + *gígnesthai* be born]

**pro|tog|y|nous** (prō toj′ə nəs), *adj.* = proterogynous.

**pro|tog|y|ny** (prō toj′ə nē), *n.* = proterogyny.

**pro|to|his|tor|ic** (prō′tō his tôr′ik, -tor′-), *adj.* of or belonging to the beginnings of recorded history.

**pro|to|his|to|ry** (prō′tō his′tər ē, -trē), *n.* history at the dawn or beginnings of recorded history; protohistoric matters or times.

**pro|to|hu|man** (prō′tō hyü′mən), *adj.* resembling or preceding the earliest human; prehominid.

**pro|to|lan|guage** (prō′tō lang′gwij), *n.* a hypothetical, reconstructed language assumed to be the ancestor of one or more recorded or existing languages.

**pro|to|lith|ic** (prō′tə lith′ik), *adj.* of or having to do with the earliest Stone Age; eolithic. [< *proto-* + *lithic*[1]]

**pro|to|mar|tyr** (prō′tō mär′tər), *n.* **1** the first martyr in any cause: *The small city of St. Albans ... with its Roman theater, its place where a protomartyr was executed ...* (London Times). **2** Stephen, the first Christian martyr (in the Bible, Acts 7). [< Late Latin *prōtomartyr* < Greek *prōtómartys* < *prôtos* first + *mártys* martyr]

**pro|to|morph** (prō′tə môrf), *n.* a primitive form.

**pro|to|mor|phic** (prō′tə môr′fik), *adj.* = primitive. [< *proto-* + Greek *morphḗ* form + English *-ic*]

**pro|ton** (prō′ton), *n.* a tiny particle carrying one unit of positive electricity. All atoms are built up of electrons and protons. The number of protons in an atom is the atomic number of the element. A proton has a mass about 1,836 times that of an electron. [< Greek *prôton,* neuter of *prôtos* first]

**proton accelerator,** a device, such as a bevatron, for increasing the velocity of protons and other atomic particles, thereby increasing their energy.

**pro|ton|ate** (prō′tə nāt), *v.t.,* **-at|ed, -at|ing.** *Chemistry.* to provide with a proton; add a proton to: *A pesticide such as triazine is protonated when in contact with the clay* (J. J. Fripiat).

**pro|ton|a|tion** (prō′tə nā′shən), *n. Chemistry.* the addition of a proton: *The hydride complexes are usually obtained by reduction or protonation of suitable metal complexes. All the positively charged species listed in Table I were obtained by protonation, usually in very strong acid* (Science).

**proton beam,** a beam of high-energy protons as

**Pronunciation Key:** hat, āge, cãre, fär; let, ēqual, tėrm; it, īce; hot, ōpen, ôrder; oil, out; cup, pu̇t, rüle; child; long; thin; ᴛʜen; zh, measure; ə represents **a** in about, **e** in taken, **i** in pencil, **o** in lemon, **u** in circus.

developed by a proton accelerator.
**proton decay**, the radioactive transmutation of one chemical element into another by the emission of a proton from an unstable nucleus: *Proton decay ... is a process in which a nucleus emits a proton and decreases both atomic number and atomic weight by one* (Science News).
**pro|to|ne|ma** (prō′tə nē′mə), *n., pl.* **-ma|ta** (-mə tə). a filamentous structure in mosses from which the more visible, leafy portion grows. [< Greek *prôtos* first + *nêma, -atos* thread < *neîn* to spin]
**pro|to|ne|mal** (prō′tə nē′məl), *adj.* of or having to do with a protonema.
**pro|ton|ic** (prō ton′ik), *adj.* of or having to do with a proton or protons.
**pro|ton|o|tar|y** (prō ton′ə ter′ē), *n., pl.* **-tar|ies.** = prothonotary.
**pro|ton-pro|ton chain** (prō′ton prō′ton), a nuclear reaction believed to be the source of energy of the sun and other hydrogen-rich stars. It begins with the fusion of two protons to form a deuteron, the nucleus of a heavy hydrogen atom, which then changes in two stages into helium, releasing two protons to join the chain again. The reaction liberates tremendous energy.
**proton synchrotron**, = proton accelerator.
**pro|to|path|ic** (prō′tə path′ik), *adj. Biology, Psychology.* **1** having only primitive sense powers. **2** of or having to do with primitive receptors. [< *proto-* + Greek *páthos* a suffering, disease + English *-ic*]
**pro|to|phlo|em** (prō′tō flō′em), *n.* the first phloem tissue to develop, lying closest to the outer part of the stem; the primitive phloem of a vascular bundle. [< German *Protophloem* < Greek *prôtos* first + German *Phloem* phloem]
**pro|to|plan|et** (prō′tō plan′it), *n.* an earlier form of planet believed to have its origin in the condensation of solar gases and dust. The earth and other planets may have originated in this way.
**pro|to|plasm** (prō′tə plaz′əm), *n.* **1** living matter; the living substance of all plant and animal cells; the substance that is the physical basis of life. Protoplasm is a colorless matter somewhat like soft jelly or white of egg. It is a chemically active mixture of proteins, fats, and many other complex substances suspended in water. Metabolism, growth, and reproduction are manifested in protoplasm. **2** (formerly) cytoplasm. [< German *Protoplasma* < Greek *prôtos* first + *plásma* something molded < *plássein* to mold]
**pro|to|plas|mic** (prō′tə plaz′mik), *adj.* of or having to do with protoplasm: *Beneath the water was an intricate pattern of teeming protoplasmic life* (Time).
**pro|to|plast** (prō′tə plast), *n.* **1** the living unit of protoplasm within a plant cell, consisting of a nucleus, cytoplasm, and plasma membrane. **2a** the first formed; the original. **b** the hypothetical first man. [< Middle French *protoplaste,* learned borrowing from Latin *prōtoplastus* the first man < Greek *prōtóplastos* < *prôtos* first + *plastós* < *plássein* to form, mold]
**pro|to|plas|tic** (prō′tə plas′tik), *adj.* of or having to do with a protoplast.
**pro|top|o|dite** (prō top′ə dīt), *n.* the section or joint of an appendage which attaches to the body of a crustacean. [< *proto-* + Greek *poús, podós* foot + English *-ite*[1]]
**pro|to|pope** (prō′tə pōp), *n.* a priest of superior rank in the Greek Church; chief priest. [< *proto-* + *pope*]
**pro|to|por|phy|rin** (prō′tə pôr′fər in), *n.* a porphyrin or pigment occurring in cells and produced synthetically that is a basic part of hemoglobin in red blood and chlorophyll in green plants. *Formula:* $C_{34}H_{34}N_4O_4$
**pro|to|pro|te|ose** (prō′tō prō′tē ōs), *n.* any of various primary proteoses formed by the breakdown of proteins.
**pro|to|star** (prō′tō stär′), *n.* a star in the process of formation: *The photo also shows ... a typical dark globule—a dust cloud that is probably contracting to form a future protostar* (Science Journal).
**pro|to|stele** (prō′tə stēl, -stē′lē), *n. Botany.* the solid stele of most roots, and of the first-formed portion of some primitive stems.
**pro|to|ste|lic** (prō′tə stē′lik), *adj.* of or having to do with protostele.
**pro|to|troph** (prō′tə trof), *n.* an organism that gets its nourishment from inorganic substances; prototrophic organism.
**pro|to|troph|ic** (prō′tə trof′ik), *adj.* getting nourishment from inorganic substances: *Nitrobacteria are prototrophic organisms.* [< *proto-* + Greek *trophḗ* nourishment + English *-ic*]
**pro|to|typ|al** (prō′tə tī′pəl), *adj.* of, having to do with, or forming a prototype.
**pro|to|type** (prō′tə tīp), *n.* **1** the first or primary type of anything; original or model: *A modern ship has its prototype in the hollowed log used by primitive peoples. The prototype of the foreign agent is the spy* (Bulletin of Atomic Scientists). **2** *Biology.* a primitive form; archetype. [< Middle French *prototype* < New Latin *prototypon* < Greek *prōtótypon,* (originally) neuter of *prōtótypos* original, primitive < *prôtos* first + *týpos* type, model < *týptein* to strike]
**pro|to|typ|ic** (prō′tə tip′ik), *adj.* = prototypal.
**pro|to|typ|i|cal** (prō′tə tip′ə kəl), *adj.* = prototypal.
**pro|to|ver|a|trine** (prō′tō ver′ə trēn, -trin), *n.* an alkaloid drug obtained from the rhizomes of several false hellebores, used in treating hypertension.
**pro|to|vi|rus** (prō′tō vī′rəs), *n.* a primary type of virus that serves as a model for others of the same kind; prototype of a virus: *According to his hypothesis, normal cells manufacture RNA, which moves to neighboring cells in the form of a protovirus, or template, and stimulates the production of a new form of DNA* (Time).
**pro|tox|id** (prō tok′sid), *n.* = protoxide.
**pro|tox|ide** (prō tok′sīd, -sid), *n.* that member of a series of oxides which has the smallest proportion of oxygen. [< *prot-* + *oxide*]
**pro|to|xy|lem** (prō′tə zī′lem), *n.* the first xylem tissue to develop, lying closest to the pith; the primitive xylem of a vascular bundle. [< *proto-* + *xylem*]
**Pro|to|zo|a** (prō′tə zō′ə), *n.pl.* the phylum or subkingdom of invertebrates comprising the protozoans. [< New Latin *Protozoa* < Greek *prôtos* first + *zôa,* plural of *zôion* animal]
**pro|to|zo|al** (prō′tə zō′əl), *adj.* = protozoan.
**pro|to|zo|an** (prō tə zō′ən), *n., adj.* —*n.* any one of a group of microscopic animals that consist of a single cell. Protozoans, such as the ameba or the paramecium, are found in water or soil and reproduce by fission, budding, or dividing into spores. *The protozoans are the lowliest and simplest forms of animal life* (White and Renner).
—*adj.* belonging to or having to do with, or caused by, protozoans.
[< *protozo*(a) + *-an*]
**pro|to|zo|ic** (prō′tə zō′ik), *adj.* = protozoan.
**pro|to|zo|o|log|i|cal** (prō′tə zō′ə loj′ə kəl), *adj.* of or having to do with protozoology.
**pro|to|zo|ol|o|gist** (prō′tə zō ol′ə jist), *n.* a person skilled in protozoology.
**pro|to|zo|ol|o|gy** (prō′tə zō ol′ə jē), *n.* the branch of zoology or of pathology that deals with protozoans.
**pro|to|zo|on** (prō′tə zō′on), *n., pl.* **-zo|a** (-zō′ə). = protozoan.
**pro|tract** (prō trakt′), *v.t.* **1** to draw out; lengthen in time; prolong: *to protract a visit. He attempted ... to prevent, or at least to protract, his ruin* (Edward Gibbon). **2** to slide out; thrust out; extend. **3** to draw by means of a scale and protractor; plot: *to protract a piece of land in surveying.* [< Latin *prōtractus,* past participle of *prōtrahere* < *prō-* forward + *trahere* to drag]
**pro|tract|ed** (prō trak′tid), *adj.* lengthened. —**pro|tract′ed|ness**, *n.*
**pro|tract|ed|ly** (prō trak′tid lē), *adv.* in a protracted or drawn-out fashion: *His older brother, Ben ... dies somewhat protractedly of pneumonia in the second act* (New Yorker).
**pro|trac|tile** (prō trak′təl), *adj.* capable of being lengthened out, or of being thrust forth: *The turtle has a protractile head.*
**pro|trac|tion** (prō trak′shən), *n.* **1** the act of drawing out; extension. **2** a drawing that has exactly the same proportions as the thing it represents. **3** something that is protracted or plotted; plot.
**pro|trac|tive** (prō trak′tiv), *adj.* protracting; prolonging.
***pro|trac|tor** (prō trak′tər), *n.* **1** an instrument in the form of a semicircle for drawing or measuring angles. **2** a person or thing that protracts, such as a muscle that extends a part of the body.

***protractor**
definition 1

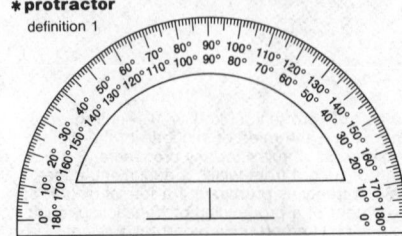

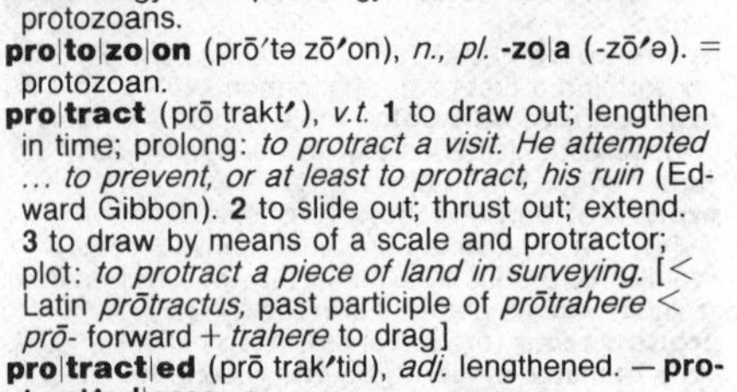

**pro|trud|a|ble** (prō trü′də bəl), *adj.* = protrusile.
**pro|trude** (prō trüd′), *v.,* **-trud|ed, -trud|ing.**
—*v.t.* to thrust forth; stick out: *The saucy child protruded her tongue.*
—*v.i.* to be thrust forth; project: *Her teeth protrude too far.*
[< Latin *prōtrūdere* < *prō-* forward + *trūdere* to thrust]
**pro|trud|ent** (prō trü′dənt), *adj.* protruding.
**pro|tru|si|ble** (prō trü′sə bəl), *adj.* = protrusile.
**pro|tru|sile** (prō trü′səl), *adj.* capable of being protruded: *An elephant's trunk is protrusile.*
**pro|tru|sion** (prō trü′zhən), *n.* **1** the action of protruding or condition of being protruded: *Starvation caused the protrusion of the poor cat's bones.* **2** something that sticks out; projection: *A protrusion of rock gave us shelter from the storm.* [< Latin *prōtrūsus,* past participle of *prōtrūdere* protrude + English *-ion*]
**pro|tru|sive** (prō trü′siv), *adj.* sticking out; projecting. —**pro|tru′sive|ly**, *adv.*
**pro|tu|ber|ance** (prō tü′bər əns, -tyü′-), *n.* **1** a part that sticks out; bulge; swelling: *From the protuberance in their father's coat pocket, the children guessed that he had brought them candy.* **2** a protuberant quality or condition.
**pro|tu|ber|an|cy** (prō tü′bər ən sē, -tyü′-), *n., pl.* **-cies.** = protuberance.
**pro|tu|ber|ant** (prō tü′bər ənt, -tyü′-), *adj.* bulging out; sticking out; prominent. [< Latin *prōtūberāns, -antis* bulging, present participle of *prōtūberāre* grow forth < *prō-* forward + *tūber, -eris* lump, tuber] —**pro|tu′ber|ant|ly**, *adv.*
**pro|tu|ber|ate** (prō tü′bə rāt, -tyü′-), *v.i.,* **-at|ed, -at|ing.** = bulge. [< Latin *prōtūberāre* (with English *-ate*[1]); see etym. under **protuberant**]
**pro|tu|ran** (prō tůr′ən), *n., adj.* —*n.* any one of a group of tiny primitive insects that live under bark and in damp places. Proturans are blind and wingless and are believed to represent a very early stage in the evolution of insects. *A new species of proturan, one of earth's most primitive insects, has been found in South America* (Science News Letter).
—*adj.* of or having to do with the proturans.
[< New Latin *Protura* the order or class name (< Greek *prôtos* first + *ourā́* tail) + English *-an*]
**pro|tyl** (prō′təl), *n.* = protyle.
**pro|tyle** (prō′tīl, -təl), *n.* the hypothetical, undifferentiated matter from which the chemical elements may have been derived. [< *prot-* + Greek *hýlē* matter]
**proud** (proud), *adj.* **1** thinking well of oneself: *The vile are only vain; the great are proud* (Byron). **2** feeling or showing great pleasure or satisfaction: *I am proud to call him my friend.* **3** having a becoming sense of what is due oneself, or one's position or character: *The hungry man was too proud to beg for food.* **4** thinking too well of oneself; haughty; arrogant: *a proud, insolent man. This proud fellow ... who scorns us all* (Tennyson). **5** very pleasing to one's feelings or one's pride; very honorable, creditable, or gratifying: *It was a proud moment for my cousin when he shook hands with the President.* **6** proceeding from pride; due to pride: *a proud smile, a father's proud look at his child.* **7** grand; magnificent; imposing; stately; majestic: *proud cities. The big ship was a proud sight.* **8** of exalted rank or station: *proud nobles.* **9** full of spirit or mettle: *a proud stallion.* **10** *Obsolete.* valiant; brave.
**do one proud**, *Informal.* to make proud; do very well; gratify highly: *They haven't done you very proud, have they?* (Graham Greene).
**proud of**, thinking well of; being well satisfied with; proud because of: *to be proud of oneself, to be proud of one's family.*
[Old English *prūd,* and *prūt,* probably < Old French *prod,* and *prud* valiant < Late Latin *prōde* profitable, of use, ultimately < Latin *prōdesse* be useful, profitable < *prō-* for + *esse* to be]
—**proud′ly**, *adv.* —**proud′ness**, *n.*
—*Syn.* **1 Proud, overbearing, supercilious** mean having or showing a high opinion of oneself. **Proud**, in a favorable sense, suggests dignity and self-esteem: *The grandee had a proud bearing.* **Overbearing**, always unfavorable, suggests being domineering or haughtily insulting in behavior and speech: *Promoted too quickly, the young man became overbearing.* **Supercilious**, also unfavorable, suggests being conceited, and revealing it in a coolly scornful attitude: *With a supercilious smile, he refused our invitation.*
**proud flesh**, the formation of granular tissue which occurs occasionally during normal healing of a wound or sore.
**proud|ful** (proud′fəl), *adv. Dialect.* full of pride; very proud.
**proud-heart|ed** (proud′här′tid), *adj.* having or showing pride; haughty: *And so, proud-hearted Warwick, I defy thee* (Shakespeare).
**Proust|i|an** (prüs′tē ən), *adj., n.* —*adj.* of, having to do with, or suggestive of the novelist Marcel Proust or his works: *The salutes, the flag being lowered at sunset, the bugler sounding recall—I found myself remembering every detail with an almost Proustian clarity* (New Yorker). *Best, perhaps, are the evocations of childhood, which reveal a Proustian sensibility* (Punch).
—*n.* a student or admirer of the works of Proust:

*I have heard Durrell fans celebrating the enchantments of Justine and Balthazar with the fervor one encounters among pious Proustians* (Atlantic).

**proust|ite** (prüs′tīt), *n.* a mineral consisting of a sulfide of arsenic and silver, occurring in crystals or masses of a red color; light ruby silver: *The ruby silver minerals, proustite and pyrargyrite, are of minor importance as sources of silver* (W. R. Jones). [< French *proustite* < Joseph-Louis *Proust,* 1754-1826, a French chemist, who discovered it + *-ite* -ite[1]]

**prov.**, an abbreviation for the following:
**1** provident.
**2** province.
**3** provincial.
**4** provincialism.
**5** provisional.
**6** provost.

**Prov.**, an abbreviation for the following:
**1** Provençal.
**2** Provence.
**3** Proverbs (book of the Old Testament).
**4** Province.
**5** Provost.

**prov|a|ble** (prü′və bəl), *adj.* that can be proved. Also, **proveable**. —**prov′a|ble|ness**, *n.* —**prov′a|bly**, *adv.*

**prov|and** (prov′ənd), *n. Archaic.* provender; provisions, especially food and fodder for an army. [apparently < Old French *provende;* see etym. under **provender**]

**prov|ant** (prov′ənt), *n. Archaic.* provand.

**prove** (prüv), *v.,* **proved**, **proved** or **prov|en**, **prov|ing**. —*v.t.* **1** to show as true and right; make certain; demonstrate the truth of by evidence or argument: *to prove that one is right, to prove a point.* **SYN**: corroborate, verify, confirm. **2** to give demonstration or proof of by action: *to prove one's skill. Ev'ry knight is proud to prove his worth* (John Dryden). **3** to establish the genuineness or validity of, especially of a will: *One [executor] alone is competent to prove a will and carry out its provisions* (Whitaker's Almanac). **4** to subject to some testing process; try out; test: *to prove a new tool.* **5** to test the correctness of (a mathematical calculation): *Prove these answers. Multiplication can be proved by division.* **6** to find out by experience; know because of having tested; have experience of; experience: *We have proved his good temper.* **7** *Law.* to obtain probate of (a will). **8** *Archaic.* to put to the test; try the qualities of: *The exception proves the rule. Prove all things; hold fast that which is good* (I Thessalonians 5:21). **9** *Printing.* to take a proof of (type, a plate, or engraving).
—*v.i.* **1** to be found to be; turn out: *This book proved interesting. He has proved capable as an administrator.* **2** *Obsolete.* to make a trial (of something).
**prove out**, to show or be shown, by means of a testing process, as ready and safe for use: *The ... irrigation project, a vast complex, can't prove out until a great deal more money is spent on it* (Wall Street Journal).
**prove up**, *U.S.* **a** to show that the requirements of the law for taking up (government land, mineral rights, or the like) have been fulfilled, so that a patent may be issued: *A number of promising discoveries had also been made and were now being proved up* (North Star). **b** to adduce the proof of right: *My wife proved up on her Cherokee blood* (J. H. Beadle).
[< Old French *prover* < Latin *probāre* < *probus* worthy]
► **proved**, **proven**. *Proved* is the usual verbal form, *proven* the usual adjectival form: *He had proved his ability. His proven ability could not be doubted.*

**prove|a|ble** (prü′və bəl), *adj.* = provable.

**pro|vec|tion** (prō vek′shən), *n. Linguistics.* the carrying of a terminal letter of a word to the beginning of the succeeding word, as in *a newt* for *an ewt.* [< Late Latin *prōvectiō, -ōnis* < Latin *prōvehere* < *prō-* forth + *vehere* carry]

**pro|ved|i|tor** (prō ved′ə tər), *n. Obsolete.* **1** a purveyor; steward. **2** an overseer. [< earlier Italian *proveditore* < *provedere* to provide < Latin *prōvidēre;* see etym. under **provide**]

**prov|en** (prü′vən), *v.* proved; a past participle of **prove**: *We do not wish guilty persons to get away. Neither do we wish innocent persons or persons not yet proven guilty to be subjected to unlawful and unconstitutional procedures* (New York Times).
► See **prove** for usage note.

**prov|e|nance** (prov′ə nəns), *n.* source; origin: *If a specimen fluoresces with a different color from that of a genuine specimen of the same provenance and period, the chances are that it is spurious* (George Savage). [< French *provenance* < Middle French *provenant,* present participle of *provenir* come forth, learned borrowing from Latin *prōvenīre*]

**Pro|ven|çal** (prō′vən säl′, prov′ən-), *n., adj.* —*n.* **1** a person born or living in Provence, a region in southeastern France bordering the Mediterranean. **2** the Romance language spoken in Provence; langue d'oc. In its medieval form, Old Provençal, it was widely known in Europe as one of the principal languages used by the troubadours.
—*adj.* of or having to do with Provence, its people, or their language.

**prov|en|der** (prov′ən dər), *n.* **1** dry food for animals, such as hay or corn. **2** *Informal.* food. [< Old French *provendre,* variant of *provende;* alteration of Vulgar Latin *prōbenda* < Latin *praebenda.* See etym. of doublet **prebend**.]

**pro|ve|ni|ence** (prō vē′nē əns, -vēn′yəns), *n.* source; origin. [probably alteration of *provenance*]

**prov|en|ly** (prü′vən lē), *adv.* = provably.

**pro|ven|tric|u|lus** (prō′ven trik′yə ləs), *n., pl.* **-li** (-lī). **1** the soft first (true or glandular) stomach of a bird, which secretes gastric juices. It lies between the crop and gizzard. **2** the digestive chamber between the crop and stomach (midgut) in insects. **3** a muscular crop in worms. [< New Latin *proventriculus* < Latin *prō-* before + *ventriculus* (originally) a pouch]

**prov|er** (prü′vər), *n.* **1** a person or thing that proves or tries. **2** a skilled workman employed to strike off proofs from engraved plates.

**prov|erb** (prov′ėrb), *n., v.* —*n.* **1** a short wise saying used for a long time by many people. "Haste makes waste" is a proverb. *Fast bind, fast find; A proverb never stale in thrifty mind* (Shakespeare). **SYN**: adage, maxim, saw. **2** *Figurative.* a well-known case: *He is a proverb for carelessness. This house ... will I cast out of my sight; and Israel shall be a proverb and a byword among all people* (I Kings 9:7).
—*v.t.* **1** to say in the form of a proverb; speak of proverbially. **2** *Figurative.* to make a byword of: *Am I not sung and proverbed for a fool in every street?* (Milton).
[Middle English *proverbe* < Old French, learned borrowing from Latin *prōverbium* < *prō-* forth + *verbum* word, (originally) a speaking, speech]
► See **epigram** for usage note.

**pro|ver|bi|al** (prə vėr′bē əl), *adj.* **1a** of a proverb. **b** expressed in a proverb: *proverbial wisdom.* **c** like a proverb: *proverbial brevity, a proverbial saying.* **2** that has become a proverb: *the proverbial stitch in time.* **3** *Figurative.* well-known: *the proverbial loyalty of dogs, the proverbial London fog.* **SYN**: unquestioned, familiar. —**pro|ver′bi|al|ly**, *adv.*

**pro|ver|bi|al|ist** (prə vėr′bē ə list), *n.* a person who originates, collects, or uses proverbs.

**Prov|erbs** (prov′ėrbz), *n.pl.* a book of the Old Testament made up of sayings of the wise men of Israel, including Solomon. *Abbr:* Prov.

**pro|vide** (prə vīd′), *v.,* **-vid|ed**, **-vid|ing**. —*v.t.* **1** to supply; furnish: *Sheep provide us with wool. The garden provides vegetables for the family.* **2** to arrange in advance; state as a condition beforehand: *Our club's rules provide that dues must be paid monthly.* **SYN**: stipulate. **3** to get ready; prepare beforehand: *Mother provides a good dinner. The wise ant her wintry store provides* (John Dryden).
—*v.i.* **1** to give what is needed or wanted; arrange to supply means of support: *to provide for one's family.* **2** to take care for the future: *to provide for old age, to provide against accident.*
[< Latin *prōvidēre* look after; (literally) foresee < *prō-* ahead + *vidēre* to see. See etym. of doublet **purvey**.]

**pro|vid|ed** (prə vī′did), *conj.* on the condition that; if: *She will go provided her friends can go also. I will tell you the real story, provided you won't quote me.* **SYN**: providing.

**prov|i|dence** (prov′ə dəns), *n.* **1** God's care and help: *Trusting in providence, the Pilgrims sailed for the unknown world.* **2** an instance of God's care and help: *There's a special providence in the fall of a sparrow* (Shakespeare). **3** care for the future; good management; being provident: *Greater providence on the parent's part would have kept the children from poverty.* **SYN**: foresight, prudence. **4** *Dialect.* the act of providing (for).
**make providence**, *Dialect.* to make provision: *Sudden death came to the fathers, and no providence made for the daughters* (John B. Berners).

**Prov|i|dence** (prov′ə dəns), *n.* = God: *Vigilant over all that he has made, Kind Providence attends with gracious aid* (William Cowper).

**prov|i|dent** (prov′ə dənt), *adj.* **1** having or showing foresight; careful in providing for the future: *Provident men save money for their families. He had been provident enough to take with him some of his best working tools* (Cardinal Newman). **SYN**: foreseeing, prudent. **2** economical; frugal: *We had tried to be reasonably provident in joint planning and management* (Atlantic). [< Latin *prōvidēns, -entis,* present participle of *prōvidēre;* see etym. under **provide**] —**prov′i|dent|ly**, *adv.*

**prov|i|den|tial** (prov′ə den′shəl), *adj.* **1** fortunate; happening by or as if by God's interventions: *Our delay seemed providential, for the train we planned to take was wrecked.* **SYN**: lucky, opportune. **2** of or proceeding from divine power or influence: *providential help, the providential nature of the universe.* —**prov′i|den′tial|ly**, *adv.*

**pro|vid|er** (prə vī′dər), *n.* a person or thing that provides.

**pro|vid|ing** (prə vī′ding), *conj.* on the condition that; if; provided: *I shall go providing it doesn't rain.*

**prov|ince** (prov′əns), *n.* **1** a big division of a country. Canada is divided into provinces instead of states. **2** *Figurative.* proper work or activity: *Astronomy is not within the province of Grade 4. The enforcement of law is not within the doctor's province.* **SYN**: sphere, domain. **3** *Figurative.* a division; department: *the province of science, the province of literature.* **SYN**: branch. **4** an ancient Roman territory outside Italy, ruled by a Roman governor. **5** any one of certain North American British colonies, some of which became states of the United States and the others of which became provinces of Canada. **6** a large church district governed by an archbishop.
**the provinces**, the part of a country outside the capital or the largest cities: *He was accustomed to city life and did not like living in the provinces.*
[< Old French *province,* learned borrowing from Latin *prōvincia*]

**pro|vin|cial** (prə vin′shəl), *adj., n.* —*adj.* **1** of a province: *a provincial government.* **2** belonging or peculiar to some particular province or provinces rather than to the whole country; local: *provincial English, provincial customs. This Tuscan speech was not a provincial dialect but ... it was essentially the speech of the educated society of one city, namely Florence* (Simeon Potter). **SYN**: regional, sectional. **3** having the manners, speech, dress, or point of view of people living in a province. **SYN**: rural. **4** *Figurative.* lacking refinement or polish; unsophisticated; countrified. **SYN**: rustic. **5** *Figurative.* lacking the broad-mindedness that is learned by experience with many people; narrow: *a provincial point of view. [Thoreau] was worse than provincial—he was parochial* (Henry James). **SYN**: intolerant.
—*n.* **1** a person born or living in a province. **2** a provincial person. **3** *Ecclesiastical.* **a** the head of a province. **b** a superior in some religious orders superintending his fraternity in a given district.
—**pro|vin′cial|ly**, *adv.*

**pro|vin|cial|i|sa|tion** (prə vin′shə lə zā′shən), *n. Especially British.* provincialization.

**pro|vin|cial|ise** (prə vin′shə līz), *v.t.,* **-ised**, **-is|ing**. *Especially British.* provincialize.

**pro|vin|cial|ism** (prə vin′shə liz əm), *n.* **1** provincial manners, habit of thought, or the like: *Neither "provincialism" nor "sectionalism" holds the South together but something deeper than these and essential to our system* (Harper's). **2** narrowmindedness. **3** a word, expression, or way of pronunciation peculiar to a district of a country. *Reckon* for *think* and *br'er* for *brother* are provincialisms. *Seldom has he sung an aria—never, perhaps, a complete role—without provincialisms; by which I mean an excessive or inappropriate use of aspirates, sobs, gulps, portamenti and the like* (New York Times). **SYN**: patois.

**pro|vin|cial|ist** (prə vin′shə list), *n.* **1** a supporter or advocate of the rights and claims of a province: *The "provincialists" are incapable of providing the Quebec wing of a Canadian party* (Canadian Forum). **2** a native or inhabitant of a province; provincial: *Such practical skill comes of itself in condensed masses of population, and it is this which gives the Londoner his advantage over the provincialist* (William Taylor).

**pro|vin|ci|al|i|ty** (prə vin′shē al′ə tē), *n., pl.* **-ties**. **1** provincial quality or character. **2** a provincial characteristic or trait.

**pro|vin|cial|ize** (prə vin′shə līz), *v.t.,* **-ized**, **-iz|ing**. **1** to make provincial; give a provincial character or name to. **2** to bring under the jurisdiction of a province: *Lesage wants to provincialize such federally administered plans as unemployment insurance and old-age pensions* (Maclean's). —**pro|vin′cial|i|za′tion**, *n.*

**prov|ing ground** (prü′ving), **1** a place, usually a large tract of land, for testing equipment, especially military weapons, vehicles, and other equipment: *The island is studded with the hallmark of* *the proving ground: towers* (Newsweek). **2** any place that affords the possibility of testing, as an idea, invention, or skill: *The whole southern portion of the southern hemisphere is an excellent proving ground for many large-scale meteorological theories* (E. F. Roots). (*Figurative.*) *Ellington himself, who [had] always used his orchestra as a proving ground for his compositions, [began] to write large, ambitious pieces again* (New Yorker).

**pro|vi|rus** (prō vī′rəs), *n.* a latent form of a virus, created by the fusion of the genetic material of a virus with that of the host bacterium: *The provirus may suddenly develop into virus and the bacterium give rise to a group of virus particles* (Scientific American).

**pro|vi|sion** (prə vizh′ən), *n., v.* **—*n.*** **1** a statement making a condition: *Our library has a provision that hands must be clean before books are taken out. A provision of the lease is that the rent must be paid promptly.* SYN: stipulation. **2** the act of providing; taking care for the future; preparation. **3** care taken for the future; arrangement made beforehand: *There is a provision for making the building larger if necessary.* **4** that which is made ready; supply; stock, especially of food; food: *Even the provision shops are closed, which seems to me the only reason why French housewives have refrigerators* (Punch). SYN: See syn. under **food**. **5** an appointment to an ecclesiastical office, especially by the pope to an office not yet vacant.
**—*v.t.*** to supply with provisions: *The cave was well provisioned; they had bread, oil, fruit, cheese, and wine.*
**make provision**, to take care for the future; make arrangements beforehand: *They made provision for their children's education.*
**provisions**, a supply of food and drinks: *They took plenty of provisions on their trip. The English for want of provisions were forced to break up siege* (Philemon Holland).
[< Latin *prōvīsiō, -ōnis* < *prōvidēre;* see etym. under **provide**]

**pro|vi|sion|al** (prə vizh′ə nəl), *adj., n.* **—*adj.*** for the time being; temporary: *a provisional agreement, a provisional governor.* SYN: provisory.
**—*n.*** **1** a postage stamp issued for use until the regular issue is available. **2** Often, **Provisional**. a member of the Provisional wing of the Irish Republican Army, consisting of militant extremists; Provo: *What is known is that the arms were destined for the breakaway I.R.A. group in the North— the so-called provisionals* (London Times).

**pro|vi|sion|al|ly** (prə vizh′ə nə lē), *adv.* **1** for the time being; temporarily. **2** = conditionally.

**pro|vi|sion|ar|y** (prə vizh′ə ner′ē), *adj.* **1** = provisional. **2** of or having to do with a provision.

**pro|vi|sion|er** (prə vizh′ə nər), *n.* a person who furnishes, or deals in provisions.

**pro|vi|sions** (prə vizh′ənz), *n.pl.* See under **provision**.

**pro|vi|so** (prə vī′zō), *n., pl.* **-sos** or **-soes**. a sentence or part of a sentence making a condition in a contract or other agreement; requirement; provision; condition: *He was admitted to the eighth grade with the proviso that he was to be put back if he failed any subject. They would accept a six-day conference, with the proviso . . . that its duration be fixed in advance* (New York Times). SYN: stipulation. [< Medieval Latin *proviso quod* it being provided that < Latin *prōvīsō,* ablative < *prōvidēre* provide]

**pro|vi|sor** (prə vī′zər), *n.* **1** *Ecclesiastical.* the holder of a papal provision. **2** *Obsolete.* **a** a purveyor. **b** a supervisor. [< Anglo-French *provisour,* Old French *proviseur* < Latin *prōvīsor* < *prōvidēre* provide]

**pro|vi|so|ri|ly** (prə vī′zər ə lē), *adv.* in a provisory way; provisionally; conditionally.

**pro|vi|so|ry** (prə vī′zər ē), *adj.* **1** containing a proviso; conditional. **2** = provisional.

**pro|vi|ta|min** (prō vī′tə min), *n.* a compound, such as carotene, that can be converted into a vitamin by chemical change within the body. [< *pro-*[2] before + *vitamin*]

**pro|vo** or **Pro|vo**[1] (prō′vō), *n., pl.* **-vos**. a Dutch or German political activist engaging in agitation, rioting, and disruptive activities. [ultimately short for French *provocateur*]

**Pro|vo**[2] (prō′vō), *n., pl.* **-vos**. Provisional: *Nevertheless, he believes, like any good Provo, that the fight must go on until . . . British soldiers have left the streets of Ulster* (Sunday Times).

**pro|vo|ca|teur** (prô vô kà tœr′), *n. French.* a person who provokes trouble or incites to violence or riot, especially one secretly hired or assigned to provoke such trouble; agent provocateur: *We shall combat ruthlessly provocateurs . . . and all those who disturb public order, threaten, or commit lynching* (Time).

**prov|o|ca|tion** (prov′ə kā′shən), *n.* **1** the act of provoking: *Ankara radio said yesterday that the Turkish authorities had arrested 2,124 persons "suspected of acts of provocation" in connexion with Tuesday's anti-Greek riots* (London Times). SYN: incitement. **2** something that stirs one up; cause of anger: *Their insulting remarks were a provocation, but he kept his temper.* SYN: affront. **3** *Obsolete.* a challenge. [< Latin *prōvocātiō, -ōnis* < *prōvocāre;* see etym. under **provoke**]

**pro|voc|a|tive** (prə vok′ə tiv), *adj., n.* **—*adj.*** **1** irritating; vexing: *Do not think I want to be provocative if I say it is inconceivable to establish normal relations between our States as long as this question is unsolved* (London Times). **2** tending or serving to call forth action, thought, laughter, anger, etc.: *a remark provocative of mirth. A Falstaff, almost as provocative of laughter as his prototype* (Hawthorne).
**—*n.*** something that rouses or irritates. **—pro|voc′a|tive|ly**, *adv.* **—pro|voc′a|tive|ness**, *n.*

**prov|o|ca|tor** (prov′ə kā′tər), *n.* a person who provokes trouble or incites to violence or riot, especially one secretly hired or assigned to provoke such trouble: *Is the uprising really the work of outside provocators?* (New York Times). *The bulletin, penned by still unknown provocators, . . . was full of crude fabrications* (London Times). [< French *(agent) provocateur*]

**pro|voc|a|to|ry** (prə vok′ə tôr′ē, -tōr′-), *adj.* = provocative.

**pro|voke** (prə vōk′), *v.t.,* **-voked, -vok|ing**. **1** to make angry; vex: *She provoked him by her teasing.* SYN: exasperate, nettle. See syn. under **irritate**. **2** to stir up; excite: *An insult provokes a person to anger.* SYN: rouse, kindle. **3** to bring about; start into action; call forth; cause: *The President's speech provoked much discussion.* **4** to induce (as a physical condition): *a drug which provokes a rise in temperature.* **5** *Obsolete.* to summon. [< Old French *provoker,* and *provoquer,* learned borrowings from Latin *prōvocāre* to appeal, challenge < *prō-* forth + *vocāre* to call] **—pro|vok′er**, *n.*

**pro|vok|ing** (prə vō′king), *adj.* that provokes; irritating: *a provoking mix-up. "It's very provoking," Humpty Dumpty said, "to be called an egg— very!"* (Lewis Carroll). **—pro|vok′ing|ly**, *adv.*

**pro|vo|lo|ne** (prō′vō lō′nā), *n.* a hard Italian cheese with a sharp, smoky flavor. [< Italian]

**prov|ost** (prov′əst; *especially Military* prō′vō), *n.* **1** a high-ranking administrator in some colleges and universities: *The title of the head of a college at Oxford depends on which college he is head of; at some colleges he is known as the Master, and at others as the Warden, the Provost . . .* (New Yorker). **2** the head or dean of the clergymen assigned to a cathedral. **3** the chief magistrate in a Scottish town. **4** = provost marshal. **5** *Obsolete.* a sheriff. [partly Old English *profost;* partly < Old French *provost,* both < Medieval Latin *propositus,* alteration of Latin *praepositus* a chief, prefect; (literally) placed in charge of; (originally) past participle of *praepōnere* < *prae-* at the head of, before + *pōnere* to place]

**provost court**, a military court set up within occupied enemy territory to try minor offenses committed by soldiers or civilians.

**provost guard**, a detail of soldiers under the provost marshal, especially a detail assigned for some special occasion or emergency.

**provost marshal**, **1** an officer in the army acting as head of police in a camp, fort, or district, and charged with the maintenance of order **2** an officer in the navy charged with the safekeeping of prisoners until their trial by court-martial.

**prov|ost|ship** (prov′əst ship), *n.* the position or authority of a provost.

**prow**[1] (prou), *n.* **1** the pointed front part of a ship or boat; bow: *The prow of the speeding motorboat cut through the water like a knife.* **2** something like it; projecting front of anything: *the prow of an aircraft.* **3** *Poetic.* a ship. [< Old French *proue* < dialectal Italian *prua* < Latin *prōra* < Greek *prôira*]

**prow**[2] (prou), *adj. Archaic.* valiant; brave; gallant. [< Old French *pru,* and *prou,* earlier *prud,* and *prod* valiant. See related etym. at **proud**.]

**prow|ess** (prou′is), *n.* **1** bravery; daring: *Two firemen showed great prowess by repeatedly rushing into the burning building to save many lives.* SYN: courage, valor. **2** brave or daring acts: *The President spoke of the prowess of the great soldier while awarding him the medal.* **3** unusual skill or ability: *The knights of old were famous for their prowess with the lance.* [< Old French *proece* < *prod* valiant, proud]

**prow|ess|ful** (prou′is fəl), *adj.* full of prowess; valorous; valiant.

**pro-West|ern** (prō wes′tərn), *adj.* on the side of the West; favoring the anti-Communist countries or their policies: *Most papers, basing their foreign coverage on dispatches from the West, have a pro-Western coloring* (Atlantic).

**prowl** (proul), *v., n.* **—*v.i.*** **1** to go about slowly and secretly, hunting for something to eat or steal: *Many wild animals prowl at night.* SYN: slink. **2** to wander: *He got up and prowled about his room.*
**—*v.t.*** to move over or through (a place or region) by prowling: *Lunt prowls the aisles in white tie and tails, picking up objects* (Newsweek).
**—*n.*** the act of prowling: *Some wild animal in its nightly prowl* (Jane Porter).
**on the prowl**, prowling about: *The patronage seekers are still on the prowl* (Harry S Truman).
[Middle English *prollen;* origin uncertain]
**—prowl′er**, *n.* **—prowl′ing|ly**, *adv.*

**prowl car**, a police car connected with headquarters by radio telephone; squad car.

**prox.**, proximo.

**prox|e|mic** (prok sē′mik), *adj.* of or having to do with the different degrees of proximity or congestion tolerated by various species of animals and various human cultures: *The proxemic patterns of Japanese culture permit what most North Americans would consider crowded conditions* (Leslie G. Freeman, Jr.). [< *prox(imity)* + *-emic,* as in *endemic, epidemic*]

**Prox|i|ma Centauri** (prok′sə mə), one of the three stars that constitute Alpha Centauri. It is closer to the earth than any other star except the sun, being 4.3 light-years away. [< New Latin *Proxima Centauri* (literally) nearest of *Centauri,* the star group *Alpha Centauri*]

**prox|i|mad** (prok′sə mad), *adv. Anatomy.* toward the point of origin, or proximal part. [< *proxim(al)* + Latin *ad* toward]

**prox|i|mal** (prok′sə məl), *adj.* **1** nearest. **2** *Anatomy* situated toward the point of origin or attachment, especially of a limb, bone, or other structure. [< Latin *proximus* nearest + English *-al*[1]] **—prox′i|mal|ly**, *adv.*

**prox|i|mate** (prok′sə mit), *adj.* **1** next; nearest: *The proximate cause offers the greater promise of rewarding investigation* (Observer). SYN: immediate, contiguous. **2** near the exact amount; approximate. [< Latin *proximātus,* past participle of *proximāre* come near < *proximus* nearest]
**—prox′i|mate|ness**, *n.*

**proximate analysis**, *Chemistry.* a form of analysis in which the constituent compounds of a complex mixture are determined.

**prox|i|mate|ly** (prok′sə mit lē), *adv.* next; very nearly; approximately.

**prox|i|me ac|ces|sit** (prok′sə mē ak ses′it), **1** a person who is second or next in line to the winner of an academic prize or honor: *Miles won the Dean's Prize in Biology, with Charlie Barefoot proxime accessit* (Richard Gordon). **2** a person who is second or next to another in importance: *He [R. A. Butler] was proxime accessit when Mr. Harold Macmillan . . . became Prime Minister* (London Times). [< Latin *proxime accessit* he has come very near]

**prox|im|i|ty** (prok sim′ə tē), *n.* nearness; closeness: *She and her cat enjoy their proximity to the fire. Marriages in proximity of blood are amongst us forbidden* (John Florio). SYN: propinquity, vicinity. [< Latin *proximitās* < *proximus* nearest]

**proximity fuse** or **fuze**, a tiny radio device set in the nose of a projectile that makes the shell explode when it comes within a certain distance of the target.

**proximity talks**, negotiations between belligerent countries or other disputing parties who occupy separate quarters in some confined area, such as a building, while a third party moves between them acting as a mediator: *He [Hafez al-Assad] again sank a U.S. proposal for Arab-Israeli "proximity" talks during the September UN General Assembly meeting* (F. Nicholas Willard).

**prox|i|mo** (prok′sə mō), *adv.* in or of the coming month: *on the 1st proximo.* [short for Latin *proximō mēnse* during next month; ablative singular of *proximus* near, *mēnsis* month]

**prox|y** (prok′sē), *n., pl.* **prox|ies**, *adj.* **—*n.*** **1** the action or agency of a deputy or substitute. In marriage by proxy, someone is substituted for the absent bride or bridegroom at the marriage service. **2** an agent; deputy; substitute, such as one appointed to vote for others at a stockholders' meeting: *Stockholders of national banks may vote by proxy, but bank clerks and tellers may not be proxies for the stockholders* (John A. Appleman). SYN: delegate, representative. **3** a writing authorizing a proxy to act or vote for a person: *A proxy is a sort of power of attorney.* **4** a vote so given: *The proxy with the most recent date is the one that's counted.*
**—*adj.*** **1** by means of a proxy or proxies: *proxy voting, a proxy marriage.* **2** of or having to do with stockholder's proxies; involving control of proxies: *a proxy fight between management and a group of stockholders.*
[Middle English *prockesye* < *procracie,* alteration of *procuracy* procuracy, the office of proctor]

**PRP** (no periods) or **P.R.P.**, People's Revolutionary Party (as of Mongolia or North Vietnam).

**prs.**, pairs.

**PRSA** (no periods) or **P.R.S.A.**, Public Relations Society of America.

**prude** (prüd), *n.* a person who is too proper or too modest in conduct, dress, or speech; a person who puts on extremely proper or modest airs. [< French *prude* < *prudefemme,* excellent woman < Old French *preudefemme,* and *prodfemme* < feminine of *prou* excellent, brave, earlier *prod* + *femme* woman. Compare etym. under **proud.**]

**pru|dence** (prü′dəns), *n.* **1** wise thought before acting; good judgment: *All the virtues range themselves on the side of prudence, on the art of securing a present well-being* (Emerson). **2** good management; economy.
—*Syn.* **1 Prudence, foresight** mean careful thought in acting and planning. **Prudence** emphasizes cautious good sense in giving thought to one's actions and their consequences: *Prudence dictates care in the use of natural resources.* **Foresight** emphasizes ability to see what is likely to happen and preparing for it accordingly: *He had the foresight to carry an umbrella.*

**pru|dent** (prü′dənt), *adj.* **1** planning carefully ahead of time; sensible; discreet: *A prudent man saves part of his wages.* SYN: judicious, wise, cautious. **2** characterized by good judgment or good management: *a prudent policy. I thought it prudent not to exacerbate the growing moodiness of his temper by any comment* (Edgar Allan Poe). SYN: judicious, wise, cautious. [< Latin *prūdēns, -entis,* short for *prōvidēns* provident] —**pru′dent|ly,** *adv.*

**pru|den|tial** (prü den′shəl), *adj.* **1** of, marked by, or showing prudence. **2** that may make decisions or give advice: *a prudential committee.* —**pru|den′tial|ly,** *adv.*

**prud|er|y** (prü′dər ē), *n., pl.* **-er|ies. 1** extreme modesty or propriety, especially when not genuine. **2** a prudish act or remark.

**prud'|homme** (prʏ dôm′), *n.* a member of a French tribunal appointed to arbitrate labor disputes. [< French *prud'homme* < Old French *prodhome* < *prod* brave, excellent + *ome, home* man]

**prud|ish** (prü′dish), *adj.* like a prude; excessively proper or modest; too modest about sex. SYN: priggish, prim. —**prud′ish|ly,** *adv.* —**prud′ish|ness,** *n.*

**pru|i|nose** (prü′ə nōs), *adj. Biology.* covered with a frostlike bloom or powdery secretion. [< Latin *pruīnōsus* frosty < *pruīna* hoarfrost]

**prune**[1] (prün), *n.* **1** a kind of sweet plum that is dried: *We had stewed prunes for breakfast.* **2** a plum suitable for drying. **3** *Slang.* a person thought to be unattractive, stupid, or unpleasant. **prunes and prism** (or **prisms**), a mincing or affectedly nice manner of speaking or behaving: *Papa, potatoes, poultry, prunes, and prism, are all very good words for the lips: especially prunes and prism* (Dickens).
[Middle English *prunne* < Old French *prune* a plum < Vulgar Latin *prūna.* See etym. of doublet **plum**[1].]

**prune**[2] (prün), *v.,* **pruned, prun|ing.** —*v.t.* **1** to cut superfluous or undesirable branches or twigs from (a bush, tree, or vine): *to prune fruit trees or grapevines.* **2** to cut off; cut out: *Prune all the dead branches.* (*Figurative.*) *The editor pruned the needless words from the writer's manuscript.* (*Figurative.*) *The financial proposals ... were severely pruned by the Commonwealth after consultation with the states* (Gordon Greenwood). **3** *Figurative.* to cut out useless or undesirable parts from: *The editor pruned the long text to a shorter and more readable length. The Senators pruned the President's budget.* SYN: trim.
—*v.i.* to cut off superfluous parts, especially twigs or branches: *Very often pruning brings about the introduction of fungus spores to the freshly cut or broken tissues* (Fred W. Emerson).
[Middle English *prouynen* < Old French *proignier,* and *proöignier* < Latin *pro-* for + *roöignier* clip, (originally) round off, ultimately < Latin *rotundus* round]

**prune**[3] (prün), *v.t., v.i.,* **pruned, prun|ing.** to dress carefully; preen. [Middle English *proynen,* and *pruynen;* origin uncertain. Apparently related to **preen**[1].]

**pru|nel|la** (prü nel′ə), *n.* **1** a strong, smooth fabric formerly used for the uppers of shoes. **2** a similar fabric, used for women's dresses. [probably < French, Old French *prunelle* sloe, wild plum (perhaps because of its color)]

**pru|nelle** (prü nel′), *n.* a small, yellow plum dried for the market, both skin and stone being removed. [earlier *prunella* < obsolete Italian, a small kind of plum, (diminutive) < *pruna* plum < Vulgar Latin *prūna;* spelling influenced by French *prunelle.* Compare etym. under **plum.**]

**prun|er** (prü′nər), *n.* a person or thing that prunes, or removes what is superfluous.

**prun|ing hook** (prü′ning), a long-handled tool with a hooked blade, used for pruning, as of fruit trees or brambles. [*pruning* < *prune*[2] + *-ing*[2]]

**pruning knife**, a knife, often with a curved blade, used for pruning.

**pruning shears**, strong, heavy shears used to prune vines, shrubs, or twigs.

**prunt** (prunt), *n.* **1** an ornamental stud or shaped piece of glass fixed on a glass vessel. **2** a tool with which such pieces are formed. [origin uncertain; perhaps dialectal variant of *print*]

**prunt|ed** (prun′tid), *adj.* ornamented with prunts.

**pru|ri|ence** (průr′ē əns), *n.* the quality or condition of being prurient; liking for or tendency towards lustfulness: *He had his inner and personal growths of vice, passion, even prurience* (Saul Bellow).

**pru|ri|en|cy** (průr′ē ən sē), *n., pl.* **-cies.** = prurience.

**pru|ri|ent** (průr′ē ənt), *adj., n.* —*adj.* **1** having lustful thoughts or wishes: *A survey disclosed that several books, with content and illustrations catering to prurient interests, are on sale in leading bookshops* (Atlanta Journal). SYN: lewd, lascivious. **2** being uneasy with desire, longing, or curiosity: *Prurient curiosity is presumably as old as the race and has a very rich American history* (Newsweek). **3** itching: *In filthy sloughs they roll a prurient skin* (Tennyson).
—*n.* a prurient person.
[< Latin *prūriēns, -entis,* present participle of *prūrīre* to itch; be wanton] —**pru′ri|ent|ly,** *adv.*

**pru|rig|i|nous** (prů rij′ə nəs), *adj.* **1** of, like, causing, or caused by prurigo. **2** uneasy. [< Latin *prūrīginōsus* < Latin *prūrīgō* prurigo]

**pru|ri|go** (prů rī′gō), *n.* a skin disease with violent itching and an eruption. [< Latin *prūrīgō* itching, lasciviousness < *prūrīre* to itch; perhaps influenced by *porrīgō* dandruff, scurvy]

**pru|rit|ic** (prů rit′ik), *adj.* of, having to do with, or like pruritus.

**pru|ri|tus** (prů rī′təs), *n.* itching, especially without visible eruption. [< Latin *prūrītus, -ūs* an itching < *prūrīre* to itch (for), be wanton]

**Prus.** or **Pruss., 1** Prussia. **2** Prussian.

**Prus|sian** (prush′ən), *adj., n.* —*adj.* of or having to do with Prussia, its people, or their language: *He leaned out of the window with a Prussian thrust, waving a bill and bellowing* (Atlantic).
—*n.* **1** a native or inhabitant of Prussia. **2** the dialect of German spoken in Prussia. **3** = Old Prussian.

**Prussian blue**, a deep-blue pigment, essentially a cyanogen compound of iron: *Prussian blue, another common pigment, can be identified by its stainlike character and tendency to bleach in the presence of alkalis* (Scientific American). *Formula:* $C_{18}Fe_7N_{18}$ [< *Prussia* (because it was discovered in 1704 in Berlin, the capital) + *-an*]

**Prus|sian|ism** (prush′ə niz əm), *n.* the spirit, system, policy, or methods of the Prussians, especially authoritarian methods associated with Bismarck (used in an unfriendly way): *Von Salomon's unreconstructed Prussianism and his violent hatred for the United States* (Harper's).

**Prus|sian|ize** (prush′ə nīz), *v.t.,* **-ized, -iz|ing.** to make Prussian or like Prussia in organization or character. —**Prus′sian|i|za′tion,** *n.*

**prus|si|ate** (prush′ē it, prus′-), *n.* **1** a salt of prussic acid; cyanide. **2** = ferricyanide. **3** = ferrocyanide. [< French *prussiate* < (*acide*) *prussique* prussic (acid) + *-ate* -ate[2]]

**prus|sic** (prus′ik), *adj.* = hydrocyanic.

**prussic acid**, = hydrocyanic acid. [< French *acide prussique* < *bleu de Prusse* Prussian blue]

**pru|ta** (prü′tä), *n., pl.* **pru|toth** (prü tôt′, -tōs′), **pru|ta,** or **pru|tas.** a former coin of Israel equal to 1/1000 of an Israeli pound: *The 50th anniversary stamp will have a face value of 120 pruta ... and the design shows a number of Tel Aviv public buildings* (Sunday Times). [< Hebrew *pərūṭāh*]

**pry**[1] (prī), *v.,* **pried, pry|ing,** *n., pl.* **pries.** —*v.i.* to look with curiosity; peep: *She likes to pry into the private affairs of others. They ask questions, dig and pry and dig again to find out what and why and where and who and how* (New Yorker).
—*n.* **1** an inquisitive person. SYN: busybody. **2** an inquisitive and rudely personal action, such as a glance or question.
[Middle English *prien;* origin uncertain]

**pry**[2] (prī), *v.,* **pried, pry|ing,** *n., pl.* **pries.** —*v.t.* **1** to raise, move, or separate by force, especially by force of leverage: *to pry the top off a bottle. Pry up that stone with a pickax. Run ... and fetch something to pry open the door* (Herman Melville). **2** *Figurative.* to get with much effort: *We finally pried the secret out of him.* [< noun]
—*n.* **1** a lever for prying. **2** the act of prying.
[< dialectal *prize* a lever, taken as a plural. See etym. under **prize**[4].]

**pry|er** (prī′ər), *n.* = prier.

**pry|ing** (prī′ing), *adj.* looking or searching too curiously; unpleasantly inquisitive. SYN: See syn. under **curious.** [< *pry*[1] + *-ing*[2]] —**pry′ing|ly** *adv.*

**pryt|a|neis** (prit′ə nēz, -nē əs), *n.pl.* the ten sections of the ancient Athenian council or senate, each section consisting of fifty members called prytanes. [< Greek *prytáneis,* plural of *prytaneiā* prytany]

**pryt|a|ne|um** (prit′ə nē′əm), *n., pl.* **-ne|a** (-nē′ə). a public hall in ancient Greek states or cities housing the official hearth of the community, especially that of Athens, in which the hospitality of the city was extended, as to honored citizens and ambassadors. [< Latin *prytanēum* < Greek *prytaneîon* < *prýtanis;* see etym. under **prytanis**]

**pryt|a|nis** (prit′ə nis), *n., pl.* **-nes** (-nēz). **1** a chief magistrate in certain ancient Greek states. **2** a member in ancient Athens of any one of the ten sections of the council or senate during the presidency of that section, each section presiding for a period of five weeks. [< Latin *prytanis* < Greek *prýtanis,* probably ultimately < *pró* before]

**pryt|a|ny** (prit′ə nē), *n., pl.* **-nies. 1** the office or dignity of a prytanis. **2** each of the ten sections of the ancient Athenian council or senate during the presidency of that section. **3** the period of five weeks during which each section presided.
[< Greek *prytaneiā* < *prýtanis* prytanis]

**pryth|ee** (priᴛʜ′i), *interj.* = prithee.

**Przhe|val|ski's** or **Prze|wal|ski's horse** (pər zhe väl′skiz), a wild horse native to the Altai Mountains of Mongolia. It is about four feet high and has a brushlike mane. [< Nikolai M. *Przhevalski* (or *Przewalski*), a Russian explorer of the 1800's]

**ps.**, pieces.

**p.s.**, postscript (Latin, *post scriptum*).

**Ps., 1** Psalm. **2** Psalms (a book of the Bible).

**PS** (no periods), proton synchrotron.

**P.S.**, an abbreviation for the following:
**1** passenger steamer.
**2** permanent secretary.
**3** postscript (Latin, *post scriptum*).
**4** private secretary.
**5** Privy Seal.
**6** *Theater.* prompt side.
**7** Public School.

**Psa., 1** Psalm. **2** Psalms (a book of the Bible).

**P.S.A.**, Photographic Society of America.

**PSAC** (no periods), President's Science Advisory Committee.

**psalm** (säm, sälm), *n., v.* —*n.* a sacred song or poem: *Hymns devout and holy psalms, Singing everlastingly* (Milton).
—*v.t.* to sing or celebrate in psalms: *The word is psalmed like a litany around the long table* (Manchester Guardian).
[Old English *sealm,* also *psealm* < Latin *psalmus* < Greek *psalmós* (originally) performance on a stringed instrument < *psállein* to pluck]

**Psalm** (säm, sälm), *n.* any one of the 150 sacred songs or hymns that together form a book of the Old Testament. [< *psalm*]

**psalm|book** (säm′bu̇k′, sälm′-), *n.* a book containing psalms, especially a collection of metrical translations of the Psalms prepared for public worship. SYN: Psalter.

**psalm|ist** (sä′mist, säl′-), *n.* the author of a psalm or psalms.

**Psalm|ist** (sä′mist, säl′-), *n.* **the,** King David, to whom many of the Psalms were traditionally ascribed.

**psal|mod|ic** (sal mod′ik), *adj.* **1** of or having to do with psalmody. **2** having the style or character of psalmody.

**psal|mo|dist** (sä′mə dist, säl′-, sal′-), *n.* a person who composes or sings psalms or hymns.

**psal|mo|dy** (sä′mə dē, säl′-, sal′-), *n., pl.* **-dies. 1** the act, practice, or art of singing psalms or hymns, especially in public worship: *All of them joined in the psalmody with strong marks of devotion* (Tobias Smollett). **2** psalms or hymns. **3** the arrangement of psalms for singing. [< Late Latin *psalmōdia* < Greek *psalmōidiā* < *psalmós* psalm + *ōidē* song, ode]

**Psalms** (sämz, sälmz), *n.* a book of the Old Testament consisting of 150 psalms; Psalter. Psalms is a part of the Hagiographa. *Abbr:* Ps.

**Psal|ter** (sôl′tər), *n.* **1** = Psalms. **2** a version of the Psalms for liturgical or devotional use. **3** a prayer book containing such a version: *Each pew contained several hymnbooks and psalters.* [Old English *saltere* < Late Latin *psaltērium* (in Latin, certain liturgical songs); (originally) a psaltery < Greek *psaltērion.* See etym. of doublet **psaltery.**]

---

**Pronunciation Key:** hat, āge, cãre, fär; let, ēqual, tėrm; it, īce; hot, ōpen, ôrder; **oi**l, **ou**t; cup, pu̇t, rüle; **ch**ild; lo**ng**; **th**in; ᴛʜen; **zh**, measure; **ə** represents **a** in about, **e** in taken, **i** in pencil, **o** in lemon, **u** in circus.

**psal|te|ri|an** (sôl tir′ē ən), *adj.* **1** having to do with the Psalter. **2** having the style of the Psalter.

**psal|te|ri|on** (sôl tir′ē on, sal-), *n.* = psaltery.

**psal|te|ri|um** (sôl tir′ē əm, sal-), *n., pl.* **-te|ri|a** (-tir′ē ə). the third stomach of a cow, deer, or other ruminant; omasum. [< Late Latin *psaltērium* a psalter book (because its folds are like leaves of a book)]

**psal|ter|y** (sôl′tər ē, -trē), *n., pl.* **-ter|ies**. an ancient musical instrument, played by plucking the strings. [Middle English *sautree* < Latin *psaltērium* < Greek *psaltērion* stringed instrument < *psállein* to pluck. Compare Old English *saltere* and Anglo-French *saltere, sautere.* See etym. of doublet **Psalter.**]

**Psal|ter|y** (sôl′tər ē, -trē), *n.* = Psalms. [< *psaltery*]

**psal|tress** (sôl′tris), *n. Rare.* a woman who plays on the psaltery.

**psam|mite** (sam′īt), *n.* = sandstone. [< French *psammite* < Greek *psámmos* sand + French *-ite* -ite[1]]

**psam|mit|ic** (sa mit′ik), *adj.* of, having to do with, or resembling psammite.

**PSAT** (no periods) or **P.S.A.T.**, Preliminary Scholastic Aptitude Test.

**PSC** (no periods) or **P.S.C.**, Public Service Commission.

***pschent** (psкent), *n.* the sovereign crown of all ancient Egypt, composed of the white crown or tall, pointed miter of southern Egypt combined with the red crown, square in front and rising to a point behind, of northern Egypt. [< Greek *pschént* < Egyptian *p-skhent* the double crown]

***pschent**

**psec** (no period), picosecond.

**pse|phite** (sē′fīt), *n.* any coarse fragmental rock. [< German *Psephit,* or French *pséphite* < Greek *psêphos* pebble + French *-ite* -ite[1]]

**pse|pho|log|i|cal** (sē′fə loj′ə kəl), *adj.* of or having to do with psephology.

**pse|phol|o|gist** (sē fol′ə jist), *n.* a person skilled or trained in psephology.

**pse|phol|o|gize** (sē fol′ə jīz), *v.i., v.t.,* **-gized, -giz|ing.** to investigate by psephological methods: *Scannon was ... busily psephologizing as one of the capital's most sought-after advisers on political trends* (Time). *The computer, for instance, is ... psephologizing eighteenth-century poll books* (London Times).

**pse|phol|o|gy** (sē fol′ə jē), *n.* the study of electoral systems and trends and of patterns of behavior in voting: [*He*] *will also be able, incidentally, to test the cube law of psephology, which says that if the ratio of the votes cast for two parties is A/B the ratio of parliamentary seats will be $A^3/B^3$* (New Scientist). [< Greek *psêphos* pebble used in voting + English *-logy*]

**pseud** (süd), *n. British Informal.* a false or insincere person; hypocrite; fraud: [*He*] *has an ear for this preposterous pseud who shelters behind hypocrisy* (Manchester Guardian Weekly). [< *pseudo-*]

**pseud-**, *combining form.* a form of **pseudo-** sometimes used before vowels, as in *pseudaxis.*

**pseud.**, pseudonym.

**pseu|dax|is** (sü dak′sis), *n. Botany.* a sympodium. [< *pseud-* + *axis*[1]]

**pseu|de|pig|ra|pha** or **Pseu|de|pig|ra|pha** (sü′də pig′rə fə), *n.pl.* spurious writings, especially certain writings professing to be Biblical in character, but not considered canonical, inspired, or worthy of a place in religious use. [< New Latin *pseudepigrapha,* ultimately < Greek *pseudepígraphos* falsely ascribed < *pseudês* false + *epigraphê* ascription; (originally) inscription. Compare etym. under **epigraph.**]

**pseu|de|pig|ra|phal** (sü′də pig′rə fəl), *adj.* = pseudepigraphic.

**pseu|dep|i|graph|ic** (sü′dep ə graf′ik), *adj.* of or having to do with the pseudepigrapha; spurious.

**pseu|dep|i|graph|i|cal** (sü′dep ə graf′ə kəl), *adj.* = pseudepigraphic.

**pseu|de|pig|ra|phous** (sü′də pig′rə fəs), *adj.* = pseudepigraphic.

**pseu|de|pig|ra|phy** (sü′də pig′rə fē), *n.* false ascription of authorship.

**pseu|do** (sü′dō), *adj., n., pl.* **-dos.** —*adj.* **1** false; sham; pretended: *a pseudo religion, pseudo anger.* **SYN:** spurious, counterfeit. **2** having only the appearance of: *Luxuries ... when long gratified, become a sort of pseudo necessaries* (Scott).
—*n. Informal.* a false or insincere person; fake; pretender; hypocrite: *The best parts of all of them put together wouldn't make one third-rate poet. They're all ... pseudos. Imitators of imitators* (New Yorker).
[< Greek *pseudês* false; see etym. under **pseudo-**]

**pseudo-**, *combining form.* **1** false; pseudo: *Pseudomorph = a false form. Pseudonym = a false name (used by an author). Pseudoscience = pretended science.*
**2** (in chemical terms) resembling; related to; isomeric with, as in *pseudonuclein.*
Also, **pseud-** before vowels.
[< Greek *pseudo-* < *pseûdos* falsehood, fallacy, or < *pseudês* false < *pseúdein* deceive]

**pseu|do|a|quat|ic** (sü′dō ə kwat′ik, -kwot′-), *adj.* not really aquatic, but growing in wet places.

**pseu|do|ar|cha|ic** (sü′dō är kā′ik), *adj.* not genuinely archaic.

**pseu|do|brook|ite** (sü′dō brůk′īt), *n.* an iron oxide of titanium that resembles brookite, found in some igneous rocks, such as andesite.

**pseu|do|carp** (sü′də kärp), *n.* a fruit that includes other parts in addition to the mature ovary and its contents, such as the apple, pineapple, or pear. [< *pseudo-* + Greek *karpós* fruit]

**pseu|do|car|pous** (sü′də kär′pəs), *adj.* of or having to do with a pseudocarp.

**pseu|do|cho|lin|es|ter|ase** (sü′dō kō′lə nes′tə rās, -kol′ə-), *n.* an enzyme present in the liver and blood plasma that is chemically similar to the enzyme cholinesterase in nerve tissue: *Pseudocholinesterase catalyzes hydrolysis of aspirin, succinylcholine, and other drugs* (Science News).

**pseu|do|clas|sic** (sü′də klas′ik), *adj., n.* —*adj.* pretending to be classic; falsely supposed to be classic.
—*n.* a pseudoclassic work of art or literature.

**pseu|do|clas|si|cal** (sü′dō klas′ə kəl), *adj.* = pseudoclassic.

**pseu|do|clas|si|cism** (sü′dō klas′ə siz əm) *n.* a false, spurious, or sham classicism.

**pseu|do|coel** (sü′də sēl), *n.* a body cavity in some primitive animals, similar to the coelom except that it is unlined: *In roundworms ... a cavity termed the pseudocoel, existing between the digestive tract and muscles, contains a body fluid which is set in circulation by the wriggling movements characteristic of such animals* (Harbaugh and Goodrich). [< *pseudo-* + Greek *koîlos* hollow]

**pseu|do|coe|lom** (sü′dō sē′ləm), *n.* = pseudocoel.

**pseu|do|cy|e|sis** (sü′dō sī ē′sis), *n.* illness in which the patient thinks herself pregnant and displays some of the appropriate symptoms; false pregnancy. [< *pseudo-* + Greek *kýēsis* conception]

**pseu|do|dox** (sü′də doks), *n.* an erroneous or false opinion. [< *pseudo-* + Greek *dóxa* opinion]

**pseu|do-e|vent** (sü′dō i vent′), *n.* a staged or contrived event; something arranged so that it may be publicized or reported in the news media: *The great enemy of healthy cultural and political life is ... the "pseudo-event"* (Manchester Guardian Weekly).

**pseu|do|glob|u|lin** (sü′dō glob′yə lin), *n.* any globulin that is soluble in pure water.

**pseu|do|he|mo|phil|i|a** (sü′dō hē′mə fil′ē ə, -hem′ə-), *n.* an abnormal condition of the blood platelets in which there is extensive bleeding from a cut or wound but faster clotting of the blood than in hemophilia; von Willebrand's disease.

**pseu|do|her|maph|ro|dite** (sü′dō hėr maf′rə dīt), *n., adj.* —*n.* a person affected by pseudohermaphroditism: *Pseudohermaphrodites ... can be helped by surgery to become normal men and women* (Time).
—*adj.* = pseudohermaphroditic.

**pseu|do|her|maph|ro|dit|ic** (sü′dō hėr maf′rə dit′ik), *adj.* affected by pseudohermaphroditism.

**pseu|do|her|maph|ro|dit|ism** (sü′dō hėr maf′rə dī tiz′əm), *n.* an appearance of hermaphroditism, as that due to a malformation of the external genitals: *pseudohermaphroditism, in which a boy or girl has the external sex characteristics of the opposite sex* (Newsweek).

**pseu|do|hex|ag|o|nal** (sü′dō hek sag′ə nəl), *adj.* falsely hexagonal; appearing to be hexagonal, though not really so: *The chromic acid in the ... stain distorts the spheroidal pollen grains to a pseudohexagonal shape* (Scientific American).

**pseu|do|hy|per|troph|ic** (sü′dō hī′pər trof′ik), *adj.* **1** producing or affected with pseudohypertrophy. **2** characterized by pseudohypertrophy: *such hereditary afflictions as pseudohypertrophic muscular dystrophy* (Harper's).

**pseu|do|hy|per|tro|phy** (sü′dō hī pėr′trə fē), *n., pl.* **-phies.** an enlargement of an organ by growth of fat or connective tissue as in hypertrophy, but with atrophy of the organ itself.

**pseu|do|in|tel|lec|tu|al** (sü′dō in′tə lek′chů əl), *adj., n.* —*adj.* pretending to be intellectual; falsely intellectual: *pseudointellectual snobbism.*
—*n.* a pseudointellectual person.

**pseu|do|lib|er|al** (sü′dō lib′ər əl, -lib′rəl), *adj., n.* —*adj.* not genuinely liberal; feigning liberalism; falsely liberal: *"The fashion in pseudoliberal circles dictates severe criticism of the FBI"* (Newsweek).
—*n.* a pseudoliberal person.

**pseu|do|log|i|cal** (sü′də loj′ə kəl), *adj.* having to do with or relating to pseudology. —**pseu′do|log′i|cal|ly,** *adv.*

**pseu|dol|o|gist** (sü dol′ə jist), *n.* a creator of falsehoods; systematic liar.

**pseu|dol|o|gy** (sü dol′ə jē), *n.* the act of lying, especially as an art or a subject of study. [< Greek *pseudologiā* < *pseudológos* speaking falsely < *pseudês* false + *lógos* speech]

**pseu|do|mon|ad** (sü′də mon′ad, -mō′nad), *n.* = pseudomonas.

**pseu|do|mon|as** (sü′də mon′as, -mō′nas), *n., pl.* **-a|des** (-ə dēz). any one of a group of motile, aerobic, Gram-negative bacteria, some of which are pathogenic: *Urinary tract infections caused by pseudomonas include everything from the serious kidney disease to cystitis* (Science News Letter). [< New Latin *Pseudomonas* the genus name < *pseudo-* + *monas* monad]

**pseu|do|morph** (sü′də môrf), *n.* **1** a false or deceptive form. **2** a mineral which has the form of another mineral. [< Medieval Greek *pseudómorphos* < Greek *pseudês* false + *morphê* form]

**pseu|do|mor|phic** (sü′də môr′fik), *adj.* **1** of or having to do with a pseudomorph. **2** like a pseudomorph.

**pseu|do|mor|phism** (sü′də môr′fiz əm), *n.* **1** the state of being a pseudomorph. **2** the process by which this is brought about.

**pseu|do|mor|phous** (sü′də môr′fəs), *adj.* having a false form, or a form proper to something else; characterized by pseudomorphism.

**pseu|do|nu|cle|in** (sü′də nü′klē in, -nyü′-), *n.* = paranuclein.

**pseu|do|nym** (sü′də nim), *n.* a name used by an author instead of his real name. Mark Twain is a pseudonym for Samuel Langhorne Clemens. *Moravia was then forbidden to write under his own name, and he adopted the pseudonym of Pseudo* (Atlantic). **SYN:** pen name, nom de plume. [< Greek *pseudṓnymon,* neuter of *pseudṓnymos* falsely named < *pseudês* false + dialectal *ónyma* name]

**pseu|do|nym|i|ty** (sü′də nim′ə tē), *n., pl.* **-ties.** the use of a pseudonym or false name; pseudonymous character.

**pseu|don|y|mous** (sü don′ə məs), *adj.* **1** bearing a false name: *a pseudonymous author.* **2** writing or written under an assumed or fictitious name. —**pseu|don′y|mous|ly,** *adv.* —**pseu|don′y|mous|ness,** *n.*

**pseu|do|pod** (sü′də pod), *n.* = pseudopodium.

**pseu|dop|o|dal** (sü dop′ə dəl), *adj.* = pseudopodial.

**pseu|do|po|di|al** (sü′də pō′dē əl), *adj.* **1** having to do with pseudopodia. **2** forming or formed by pseudopodia: *a pseudopodial process, pseudopodial movement.*

**pseu|do|po|di|um** (sü′də pō′dē əm), *n., pl.* **-di|a** (-dē ə). **1** a temporary protrusion of the protoplasm of a protozoan, serving as a means of locomotion and a way of surrounding and thereby absorbing food: *As the finger-like pseudopodium (the "false foot") of the amoeba advances, one sees the cytoplasm* (Scientific American). **2** the posterior extremity of a rotifer, serving chiefly as a swimming organ. [< New Latin *pseudopodium* < Greek *pseudês* false + *pódion* (diminutive) < *poús, podós* foot]

**pseu|do|preg|nan|cy** (sü′dō preg′nən sē), *n., pl.* **-cies. 1** a condition similar to pregnancy, found among dogs, rabbits, and other animals, after a sterile mating. **2** = pseudocyesis.

**pseu|do|preg|nant** (sü′dō preg′nənt), *adj.* affected with or characterized by pseudopregnancy: *Ova were transferred to the oviducts of three pseudopregnant females (that is, mice physiologically prepared for motherhood by mating with sterile males)* (New Scientist).

**pseu|do|ra|bies** (sü′dō rā′bēz), *n.* **1** a virus disease of cattle and swine which is transmitted by rats and is characterized by intense itching followed by inflammation of the tissues of the central nervous system; mad itch. **2** = lyssophobia.

**pseu|do-ran|dom** (sü′dō ran′dəm), *adj.* of or having to do with the use of computer-produced numbers in sequences which effectively imitate the actual randomness of a statistical sampling or distribution: *There are hundreds of ways in* *which computers can generate ... pseudo-random digits* (Scientific American). *Reduction in quantized brightness levels which must be transmitted ... to construct a TV picture can be achieved by pseudo-random coding* (Science Journal).

**pseu|do|sci|ence** (sü′dō sī′əns), *n.* false or pretended science: *Secrecy in science and the domination of ideological motives very often bring ... a flowering of pseudoscience and very costly research and construction projects* (Bulletin of Atomic Scientists).

**pseu|do|sci|en|tif|ic** (sü′dō sī′ən tif′ik), *adj.* of or having to do with pseudoscience; falsely scientific: *... a classical case of a man of genius who ventures into a branch of science for which he is ill prepared and dissipates his great energies on pseudoscientific nonsense* (Scientific American).

**pseu|do|sci|en|tist** (sü′dō sī′ən tist), *n.* a person who is engaged in pseudoscience or pseudoscientific pursuits.

**pseu|do|scope** (sü′də skōp), *n.* an optical instrument that makes concave parts appear convex, and convex parts concave: *It is possible to investigate some of the limits within which the mind will accept misinformation from the eyes by means of an instrument called the pseudoscope, a binocular-like device* (Scientific American).

**pseu|do|scop|ic** (sü′də skop′ik), *adj.* of or having to do with the pseudoscope or with pseudoscopy. **—pseu′do|scop′i|cal|ly,** *adv.*

**pseu|dos|co|py** (sü dos′kə pē), *n.* **1** the use of the pseudoscope. **2** the production of optical illusions similar to those caused by the pseudoscope.

**pseu|do|scor|pi|on** (sü′dō skôr′pē ən), *n.* an arachnid resembling the true scorpion but without tail or poison glands; book scorpion.

**pseu|do|so|phis|ti|ca|tion** (sü′dō sə fis′tə kā′shən), *n.* false or pretended worldliness, refinement, or urbanity; lack of true sophistication: *The script is full of pseudosophistication of the kind that high-school boys acquire on first looking into Krafft-Ebing* (New Yorker). *The pseudosophistication derived from association with generals, diplomats, and spooks most radically divorces a man from reality* (John Kenneth Galbraith).

**pseu|do|vi|ri|on** (sü′dō vī′rē on, -vir′ē-), *n.* a mature virus particle or virion whose nucleic-acid component has been partly absorbed from an animal cell.

**p.s.f.** or **psf** (no periods), pounds per square foot.

**pshaw** (shô), *interj., n., v.* **—*interj.*, *n.*** an exclamation expressing impatience, contempt, or dislike: *She writhed with impatience more than pain, and uttered "pshaws!" and "pishes!"* (Thomas Hood).
**—*v.t., v.i.*** to say "pshaw": *He fretted, pished, and pshawed* (Charlotte Brontë).
[< imitative]

***psi**[1] (sī, psē), *n.* the 23rd letter of the Greek alphabet, corresponding to the sound *s* or sometimes *ps* in English. [< Greek *psî*]

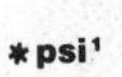
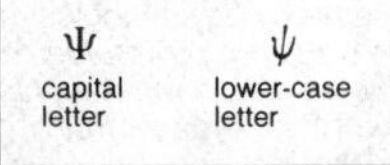


**psi**[2] (sī, psē), *n.* the group of psychological or nonphysical phenomena, including extrasensory perception, telepathy, and clairvoyance, that forms the subject matter of parapsychology: *Nonphysical though psi appears to be as judged by the familiar criteria of space and time, it is, nonetheless, a natural function of the normal personality* (Science). [< Greek *psî,* first letter of *psȳchê* breath, life, soul]

**p.s.i.** or **psi** (no periods), pounds per square inch: *It takes quite a sophisticated shelter to withstand 100 psi overpressure* (Harper's).

**p.s.i.a.** or **psia** (no periods), pounds per square inch absolute.

**p.s.i.g.** or **psig** (no periods), pounds per square inch gauge.

**psi|lan|thro|pism** (sī lan′thrə piz əm), *n.* the doctrine or belief that Jesus was a mere man. [< Greek *psīlós* bare, mere + *ánthrōpos* a man + English *-ism*]

**psi|lan|thro|pist** (sī lan′thrə pist), *n.* a person who believes that Jesus was a mere man.

**psi|lan|thro|py** (sī lan′thrə pē), *n.* = psilanthropism.

**psi|lo|cin** (sī′lə sən), *n.* a hallucinogenic substance that is related to and may be derived from psilocybin: *Included by name as "drugs having a potential for abuse because of their hallucinatory effect," were ... two other agents called psilocybin and psilocin* (New York Times). *Formula:* $C_{12}H_{16}N_2O$ [< *psiloc*(yb)*in*]

**psi|lo|cy|bin** or **psi|lo|cy|bine** (sī′lə sī′bin, -bēn), *n.* a hallucinogenic substance extracted from a Mexican mushroom and since synthesized, used experimentally to induce certain delusional and psychotic states. *Formula:* $C_{12}H_{17}N_2O_4P$ [ <*Psilocybe* (*mexicana*) the mushroom + English *-in, -ine*[2]]

**psi|lom|e|lane** (sī lom′ə lān), *n.* a common ore of manganese, a hydrated oxide, occurring in smooth, black, amorphous masses, or in botryoidal or stalactitic shapes. [< Greek *psīlós* bare, mere + *mélās, -anos* black]

**psi|lo|phyte** (sī′lə fīt), *n.* any one of a group of simple plants with upright branches that appeared in the early Paleozoic and were the first of the land plants. [< New Latin *Psilophyton* the genus name < Greek *psīlós* bare, mere + *phytón* plant]

**psi|lo|phyt|ic** (sī′lə fit′ik), *adj.* of or having to do with the psilophytes: *psilophytic flora of the Devonian period.*

**psi|lo|sis** (sī lō′sis), *n.* **1** the process of the hair falling out. **2** = sprue. [< New Latin *psilosis* < Late Latin *psīlōsis* stripping of flesh < Greek *psīlôsis* a stripping bare < *psīlós* bare]

**psi|on** (sī′on, psē′-), *n.* any one of a group of elementary particles related to and including the psi particle: *"Psions" ... are thought to possess charm as a hidden property* (New York Times). [< *psi* (particle) + *-on*]

**psi|on|ic** (sī on′ik, psē-), *adj.* of or resembling a psion or psions: *By now, something like nine members and cousins of the psionic family have been catalogued, and there may be more to come* (Science News).

**psi particle**, an electrically neutral elementary particle with a very large mass and long lifetime, produced by the collision of an electron and a positron; J particle: *A new fundamental particle, the psi particle, ... was thought possibly to consist of two new quarks* (John Newell).

**psit|ta|ceous** (si tā′shəs), *adj.* = psittacine.

**psit|ta|cine** (sit′ə sēn), *adj.* **1** of or having to do with a parrot or parrots: *Parrots and birds of the psittacine family, such as parakeets, may give psittacosis to their owners* (Science News Letter). **2** like a parrot. [< Greek *psittakós* parrot]

**psit|ta|cism** (sit′ə siz əm), *n.* a parrotlike use or repetition of words without awareness or understanding of their meaning. [< Greek *psittakós* parrot + English *-ism*]

**psit|ta|co|sis** (sit′ə kō′sis), *n.* a contagious virus disease occurring especially in parrots and related birds, communicable to people, in whom it is characterized by nausea, diarrhea, chills, and high fever; parrot fever. [< New Latin *psittacosis* < Greek *psittakós* parrot + New Latin *-osis* -osis]

**pso|ad|ic** (sō ad′ik), *adj.* of or having to do with the psoas muscles.

**pso|as** (sō′əs), *n.* either of two muscles of the loin. [< New Latin *psoas,* plural < Greek *psóa* loin muscle]

**pso|cid** (sō′sid), *n.* any one of a group of insects having an oval body, a large head, and chewing mouthparts, widely distributed in North America. Psocids are related to the book louse and feed on fungi and algae. [< New Latin *Psocidae* the family name, ultimately < Greek *psochôs* dust]

**pso|ra** (sôr′ə, sōr′-), *n.* **1** = scabies. **2** = psoriasis. [< Greek *psōrā* itch, mange < *psên* to rub]

**pso|ra|le|a** (sə rā′lē ə), *n.* any one of a group of herbs of the pea family, usually covered with glandular dots, such as the breadroot. [< New Latin *Psoralea* the genus name < Greek *psōraléos* scabby < *psōrā;* see etym. under **psora**]

**pso|ri|a|sis** (sə rī′ə sis), *n.* a chronic inflammatory skin disease characterized by dry, scaling patches and a reddened skin. [< New Latin *psoriasis* < Late Latin *psōriāsis* mange, scurvy < Greek *psōríāsis* a being itchy < *psōriân* have the itch < *psōrā;* see etym. under **psora**]

**pso|ri|at|ic** (sôr′ē at′ik, sōr′-), *adj.* **1** of the nature of psoriasis. **2** having psoriasis.

**P.SS.** or **p.ss.**, postscripts (Latin, *postscripta*).

**P.S.T., P.s.t.,** or **PST** (no periods), Pacific Standard Time.

**psych** (sīk), *n., v.* **—*n.*** *Informal.* psychology: *to major in psych, to take a psych course.*
**—*v.t.*** *Slang.* **1** to psychoanalyze or psychologize: *Bailey even used a hypnotist to help him pick and "psych" jurors, presumably by silent brain waves* (Time). **2** to use psychology on: *Westrum ... plans to "psych" the Mets with inspiration, optimism, and appeals to the spirit* (New York Times). **3** to trick, defeat, or overcome by the use of psychology: *It looked as if they had been "psyched" out of a vulnerable slam* (Scotsman). *Having discovered psychology, the cops induce "truth" by psyching the subject* (Time). **4** to stimulate; excite: *We were all psyched up, and as a result when we got there the shooting started, almost as a chain reaction* (Harper's).
**—*v.i.*** *Slang.* to break down psychologically: *"I boosted my bow hand, I think. I psyched out. I'll be damned if I know how"* (James Dickey).
[< *psych*(ology)]

**psych-**, *combining form.* a form of **psycho-** used in some cases before vowels.

**psych.**, **1** psychological. **2** psychology.

**psy|chal** (sī′kəl), *adj.* of or having to do with the soul; spiritual; psychic.

**psy|cha|nal|y|sis** (sī′kə nal′ə sis), *n.* = psychoanalysis.

**psy|chas|the|ni|a** (sī′kas thē′nē ə, -thə nī′-), *n.* mental exhaustion; mental weakness shown by fears, unreasonable ideas, etc. [probably < French *psychasthénie* < *psych-* psych- + *asthénie* weakness, asthenia < Greek *asthéneia*]

**psy|chas|then|ic** (sī′kas then′ik), *adj., n.* **—*adj.*** **1** of or having to do with psychasthenia. **2** having psychasthenia.
**—*n.*** a person suffering from psychasthenia.

**psy|che** (sī′kē), *n.* **1** the human soul or spirit. **2** the mind: *We need to know more about the interrelationship of the psyche and the soma, the mind and the body* (William C. Menninger). [< Latin *psȳchē* < Greek *psȳchê* breath; life < *psȳ́chein* breathe; blow]

**Psy|che** (sī′kē), *n. Greek and Roman Mythology.* the human soul or spirit pictured as a beautiful young girl, usually with butterfly wings. Psyche was loved by Cupid and was made immortal by Jupiter. [< Latin *Psȳchē* < Greek *Psȳchê* (literally) breath; life]

**psy|che|del|i|a** (sī′kə del′ē ə), *n.pl.* **1** the realm or world of psychedelic drugs and activities. **2** books, music, and artifacts that emphasize psychedelic activities. [< *psychedel*(ic) + *-ia,* as in *schizophrenia*]

**psy|che|del|ic** (sī′kə del′ik), *adj., n.* **—*adj.*** **1** revealing new areas of perception; expanding the consciousness: *Even a single dose of such psychedelic drugs as LSD may result in ... depression and suicidal or homicidal impulses* (New York Times). **2** of or having to do with psychedelic drugs or their use. **3** suggesting or resembling the effect of psychedelic drugs, as loud, bright, or kaleidoscopic: *psychedelic music.*
**—*n.*** **1** a drug or substance having an effect of seeming to expand consciousness and perception: *LSD and the other psychedelics including marijuana, present a serious social problem* (Maclean's). **2** a person who uses psychedelic drugs.
[< *psyche* + Greek *dêlos* visible + English *-ic*]
**—psy′che|del′i|cal|ly,** *adv.*

**Psyche knot**, an arrangement of hair in a twist which projects from the back of the head, such as classic Greek statues have.

**psy|chi|a|ter** (sī kī′ə tər, si-), *n. Obsolete.* a psychiatrist. [< Greek *psȳchê* soul, mind + *īātēr,* variant of *īātrós* physician]

**psy|chi|at|ric** (sī′kē at′rik), *adj.* of or having to do with the treatment of mental and emotional disorders: *Psychiatric case work is helping other persons to make adjustments* (Emory S. Bogardus). **—psy′chi|at′ri|cal|ly,** *adv.*

**psy|chi|at|ri|cal** (sī′kē at′rə kəl), *adj.* = psychiatric.

**psy|chi|a|trist** (sī kī′ə trist, si-), *n.* a doctor who treats mental and emotional disorders; expert in psychiatry: *The psychiatrist is concerned with minds that stray from the normal* (Science News Letter).

**psy|chi|a|try** (sī kī′ə trē, si-), *n.* the branch of medicine dealing with the treatment of mental and emotional disorders: *Psychiatry does not employ the technical methods of psychoanalysis* (Sigmund Freud). [probably < French *psychiatrie* < *psych-* psych- + Greek *īatreíā* cure < *īātrós* physician < *īâsthai* to heal]

**psy|chic** (sī′kik), *adj., n.* **—*adj.*** **1** of the soul or mind; mental: *illness due to psychic causes. Let us now consider the major categories under which psychic ... disorders are conveniently classified* (Sunday Times). **2** outside the known laws of physics; supernatural. A psychic force or influence is believed by spiritualists to explain second sight, telepathy, table moving and tappings. **SYN:** telepathic. **3** especially susceptible to psychic influences.
**—*n.*** **1** a person supposed to be specially sensitive or responsive to psychic force or spiritual influences; medium. **2** things that are psychic; the realm of parapsychology. **3** = psychic bid.
[< Greek *psȳchikós* < *psȳchê* soul, mind] **—psy′chi|cal|ly,** *adv.*

**psy|chi|cal** (sī′kə kəl), *adj.* = psychic.

**psychical** or **psychic research**, investigation and study of phenomena outside the field of normal psychology and ordinary laws of behavior, such as spiritualism and fortunetelling.

**Pronunciation Key:** hat, āge, cãre, fär; let, ēqual, tėrm; it, īce; hot, ōpen, ôrder; oil, out; cup, pu̇t, rüle; child; long; thin; ᴛʜen; zh, measure; ə represents **a** in about, **e** in taken, **i** in pencil, **o** in lemon, **u** in circus.

**psychic bid**, a bid in contract bridge made to mislead the opponents, on a hand lacking the values normally indicated by the bid.

**psychic energizer**, a drug that relieves or counteracts mental depression; antidepressant.

**psychic healer**, a person who practices psychic healing.

**psychic healing**, the alleviation or healing of disease or its symptoms by belief in the effects of the laying on of hands: *Of all the parapsychological arts, psychic healing is the one that has the greatest impact on the lives of the general public* (Peter Gwynne).

**psy|chics** (sī′kiks), *n.* **1** = psychology. **2** the study of psychic phenomena.

**psy|cho** (sī′kō), *n., pl.* **-chos**, *adj. Slang.* **—*n.*** a psychopath: *It turns upon getting rid of a bully by making out that he is a "psycho"* (Sunday Times). **—*adj.*** psychopathic: *psycho wards.*

**psycho-**, *combining form.* of the mind; mental ___: *Psychoanalysis = analysis of the mind. Psychotherapy = mental therapy. Psychology = science of the mind.* Also, **psych-** before some vowels. [< Greek *psycho-* < *psȳchḗ* soul, mind, life, breath]

**psy|cho|a|cous|tic** (sī′kō ə küs′tik, -kous′-), *adj.* of or having to do with psychoacoustics: *psychoacoustic responses to noise.* **—psy′cho|a|cous′ti|cal|ly**, adv.

**psy|cho|a|cous|ti|cal** (sī′kō ə küs′tə kəl, -kous′-), *adj.* = psychoacoustic.

**psy|cho|a|cous|tics** (sī′kō ə küs′tiks, -kous′-), *n.* the branch of acoustics that deals with the mental and auditory aspects of sound communication.

**psy|cho|ac|tive** (sī′kō ak′tiv), *adj.* acting on the mind; affecting or altering the mental state: *Marijuana is a psychoactive drug and can certainly cause problems if the basic personality structure of the user is weak* (New York Times).

**psy|cho|ac|tiv|i|ty** (sī′kō ak tiv′ə tē), *n.* psychoactive quality or condition: *The narcotic constituent of the mushroom is excreted with almost undiminished psychoactivity* (Richard E. Schultes).

**psy|cho|a|nal|y|sis** (sī′kō ə nal′ə sis), *n.* **1a** the examination of a person's mind to discover the unconscious desires, fears, anxieties, or motivating forces which produce certain mental and emotional disorders: *Psychoanalysis aims at and achieves nothing more than the discovery of the unconscious in mental life* (Sigmund Freud). **b** a method of psychotherapy based on such examination; analysis of mind or personality. **2** the body of theory originated and first developed by Freud.

**psy|cho|an|a|lyst** (sī′kō an′ə list), *n.* a person who practices psychoanalysis: *In the psychoanalyst's room the patient is first induced to talk about the subjects that he feels unable to discuss with anyone* (Listener).

**psy|cho|an|a|lyt|ic** (sī′kō an′ə lit′ik), *adj.* having to do with or of the nature of psychoanalysis. **—psy′cho|an′a|lyt′i|cal|ly**, *adv.*

**psy|cho|an|a|lyt|i|cal** (sī′kō an′ə lit′ə kəl), *adj.* = psychoanalytic.

**psy|cho|an|a|lyze** (sī′kō an′ə līz), *v.t.*, **-lyzed**, **-lyz|ing.** to examine by psychoanalysis. **—psy′cho|an′a|lyz′er**, *n.*

**psy|cho|bi|og|ra|pher** (sī′kō bī og′rə fər, -bi-), *n.* a person who writes psychobiographies: *Emily Dickinson continued to fascinate the psychobiographers* (Van Allen Bradley).

**psy|cho|bi|o|graph|i|cal** (sī′kō bī′ə graf′ə kəl), *adj.* of or having to do with psychobiography: *psychobiographical writings.*

**psy|cho|bi|og|ra|phy** (sī′kō bī og′rə fē, -bi-), *n., pl.* **-phies. 1** a biography that uses the methods and theories of psychoanalysis in recounting a person's life: *... the kind of psychobiography pioneered by Erik Erikson's "Young Man Luther"* (George Steiner). **2** the art or practice of writing such biographies: *There are various objections to psychobiography. First, few biographers have any formal training in psychoanalysis* (Bevis Hillier).

**psy|cho|bi|o|log|ic** (sī′kō bī′ə loj′ik), *adj.* = psychobiological.

**psy|cho|bi|o|log|i|cal** (sī′kō bī′ə loj′ə kəl), *adj.* of or having to do with psychobiology.

**psy|cho|bi|ol|o|gist** (sī′kō bī ol′ə jist), *n.* a person who studies the interrelationship of mental and biological functions.

**psy|cho|bi|ol|o|gy** (sī′kō bī ol′ə jē), *n.* the branch of biology which deals with the interrelationship of mental and biological functions as affecting personality.

**psy|cho|chem|i|cal** (sī′kō kem′ə kəl), *adj., n.* **—*adj.*** producing psychological changes or disorders; psychoactive: *a psychochemical agent or gas.* **—*n.*** a psychoactive chemical substance.

**psy|cho|del|ic** (sī′kō del′ik), *adj., n.* = psychedelic.

**psy|cho|dra|ma** (sī′kō drä′mə, -dram′ə), *n.* **1** the process of acting out a personal situation by a patient with the help of an audience or other actors, used in psychotherapy to reveal to the patient the social significance of his problems and aid in emotional adjustment: *Two patients volunteered to stage a psychodrama, one acting the submissive wife ... the other playing the domineering husband* (Time). **2** a psychological drama.

**psy|cho|dra|mat|ic** (sī′kō drə mat′ik), *adj.* of or having to do with psychodrama.

**psy|cho|dy|nam|ic** (sī′kō dī nam′ik), *adj.* of or having to do with mental powers or activities that relate to or derive from motivation or impulse: *I find them, in general, contradictory, puzzling, and confusing from a psychodynamic point of view* (New Yorker). **—psy′cho|dy|nam′i|cal|ly**, *adv.*

**psy|cho|dy|nam|ics** (sī′kō dī nam′iks), *n.* **1** the science, usually classified as a branch of psychology, that deals with psychodynamic phenomena. **2** psychodynamic factors or phenomena: *the psychodynamics of the intellectual reaction between people, books, and nature* (Edwin G. Boring).

**psy|cho|gal|van|ic** (sī′kō gal van′ik), *adj.* of or having to do with the electrical responses of the body to mental or emotional stimuli: *They are now using, ... scientific devices like the psychogalvanic skin response test to see how people like television programs* (Maclean's).

**psy|cho|gal|va|nom|e|ter** (sī′kō gal′və nom′ə tər), *n.* a galvanometer that records and measures decreases in the electrical resistance of the skin in response to emotional stimuli, such as those evoked by a series of selected questions or pictures.

**psy|cho|gen|e|sis** (sī′kō jen′ə sis), *n.* **1** the origin or development of the mind or soul. **2** animal evolution due to mental activity rather than to natural selection. [< *psycho-* + *genesis*]

**psy|cho|ge|net|ic** (sī′kō jə net′ik), *adj.* having to do with the formation of the mind by development. **—psy′cho|ge|net′i|cal|ly**, *adv.*

**psy|cho|gen|ic** (sī′kō jen′ik), *adj.* of mental origin: *psychogenic symptoms of a disorder.* **—psy′cho|gen′i|cal|ly**, *adv.*

**psy|cho|ger|i|at|ric** (sī′kō jer′ē at′rik), *adj.* of or having to do with psychogeriatrics: *Small psychogeriatric units attached to general hospitals ... avoid the stigma of a mental hospital* (London Times).

**psy|cho|ger|i|at|rics** (sī′kō jer′ē at′riks), *n.* the study of the psychological problems and mental illnesses of old age: *In the expanding field of psychogeriatrics these drugs will ... help to replace the present fear of death with the possibility of educating patients into the acceptance of their own forthcoming end* (New Scientist).

**psy|chog|no|sis** (sī kog′nə sis), *n.* the study of the mind or soul. [< *psycho-* + Greek *gnōsis* knowledge]

**psy|cho|gon|ic** (sī′kō gon′ik), *adj.* = psychogenetic.

**psy|chog|o|ny** (sī kog′ə nē), *n.* the origin and development of the soul or mind.

**psy|cho|gram** (sī′kə gram), *n.* **1** *Psychology.* a chart or record of a person's mental makeup. **2** a writing or message supposedly sent by a disembodied spirit or produced by a psychic agency: *The term "psychogram" ... rather mystically suggests a quasi-letter form which is the product of the subconscious mind* (London Times).

**psy|cho|graph** (sī′kə graf, -gräf), *n. Psychology.* a chart or biographical sketch indicating the various factors in a particular individual's personality.

**psy|cho|graph|ic** (sī′kō graf′ik), *adj.* of or having to do with psychography.

**psy|cho|graph|ics** (sī′kō graf′iks), *n.* the use of psychographs and psychography in market research: *Psychographics ... attempts to determine why people of similar educational and economic backgrounds develop different buying habits* (Time).

**psy|chog|ra|phy** (sī kog′rə fē), *n.* **1** the history or description of a person's mental processes: *You aim, then, at a sort of spiritual biography of your subject— what has recently been called a psychography* (London Daily Chronicle). **2** writing supposed to be due to a disembodied spirit. [< *psycho-* + *-graphy*]

**psy|cho|his|to|ri|an** (sī′kō his tôr′ē ən, -tōr′-), *n.* a person who writes about history from a psychological point of view.

**psy|cho|his|tor|i|cal** (sī′kō his tôr′ə kəl, -tor′-), *adj.* of or having to do with psychohistory or the psychological aspects of history: *psychohistorical insight.*

**psy|cho|his|to|ry** (sī′kō his′tər ē, -trē), *n., pl.* **-ries. 1** a historical account written from a psychological point of view. **2** the writing of such a history or histories: *Mazlish is at his worst fiddling around with "orality" and "anality" ... At his modest best, he offers this experiment in psychohistory as "a sketch" that "might inspire others to further effort"* (Newsweek).

**psy|cho|ki|ne|sis** (sī′kō ki nē′sis), *n.* the supposed ability of a person to exert influence upon the movement of inanimate objects, such as the rolling of dice or the turning of cards: *Psychokinesis (the "mind over matter" effect) is not yet a scientifically proven effect* (New Scientist).

**psy|cho|ki|net|ic** (sī′kō ki net′ik), *adj.* of or having to do with psychokinesis: *a study of telepathic and psychokinetic phenomena.*

**psychol.**, **1** psychological. **2** psychologist. **3** psychology.

**psy|cho|lin|guist** (sī′kō ling′gwist), *n.* a person who studies or is skilled in psycholinguistics.

**psy|cho|lin|guis|tic** (sī′kō ling gwis′tik), *adj.* of or having to do with psycholinguistics: *psycholinguistic phenomena.*

**psy|cho|lin|guis|tics** (sī′kō ling gwis′tiks), *n.* a branch of linguistics that deals with the mental states and processes in language and speech.

**psy|cho|log|ic** (sī′kə loj′ik), *adj.* = psychological.

**psy|cho|log|i|cal** (sī′kə loj′ə kəl), *adj.* **1** of the mind. Memories and dreams are psychological processes. *For three days the fathers faced a barrage of psychological tests, interviews, and group activities* (Newsweek). **2** of psychology or psychologists: *a psychological problem, a psychological explanation. It sought also to restore economic health, psychological self-confidence and military vigor* (New York Times). **3** like psychology.

**psy|cho|log|i|cal|ly** (sī′kə loj′ə klē), *adv.* **1** in a psychological manner. **2** in psychological respects: *It takes art to persuade us that psychologically we are all of us, in T.S. Eliot's phrase, eaten by the same worm* (Wall Street Journal).

**psychological moment**, **1** the very moment to get the desired effect in the mind. **2** the critical moment.

**psychological warfare**, the systematic efforts to affect morale, loyalty, or other motivating forces, especially of large national groups: *In West Germany the Russians were waging psychological warfare with a skill that was dangerous to underrate* (London Times).

**psy|chol|o|gism** (sī kol′ə jiz əm), *n.* **1** the use, especially the excessive use, of psychological methods or principles, as in history, philosophy, or literature: *In history Namier pretended to be advocating a ruthless materialism, while actually encouraging a crude kind of psychologism* (John Rex). **2** a term or idea used in or popularized by psychology: *... an odd assortment of flamboyant reach-me-down psychologisms* (H. R. F. Keating).

**psy|chol|o|gist** (sī kol′ə jist), *n.* an expert in psychology: *A psychologist ... is trained to understand the mind and its activities* (Marguerite Clark).

**psy|chol|o|gis|tic** (sī kol′ə jis′tik), *adj.* of or characterized by psychologism: *Fielding has been criticized again and again by a psychologistic age for his characters' total lack of interiority* (Kenneth Rexroth).

**psy|chol|o|gize** (sī kol′ə jīz), *v.i., v.t.*, **-gized**, **-giz|ing.** to investigate by psychological methods: *A man about town does not psychologize himself, he accepts his condition with touching simplicity* (John Galsworthy). **—psy|chol′o|giz′er**, *n.*

**psy|cho|logue** (sī′kə lôg, -log), *n.* = psychologist.

**psy|chol|o|gy** (sī kol′ə jē), *n., pl.* **-gies. 1** the science of the mind. Psychology tries to explain why people act, think, and feel as they do. *As psychology analyzes mental processes, so sociology analyzes social processes* (Emory S. Bogardus). **2** a textbook or handbook of psychology. **3** the mental states and processes of a person or persons; mental nature and behavior: *Mrs. Jones knew her husband's psychology. The long illness had a bad effect on the patient's psychology.* [< New Latin *psychologia* < Greek *psȳchḗ* soul, mind + New Latin *-logia* -logy]

**psy|cho|man|cy** (sī′kō man′sē), *n.* **1** occult communication between souls or with spirits. **2** *Obsolete.* necromancy. [< *psycho-* + Greek *manteiā* divination]

**psy|cho|man|tic** (sī′kō man′tik), *adj.* of or having to do with psychomancy.

**psy|chom|e|ter** (sī kom′ə tər), *n.* **1** an instrument used in psychometry. **2** a person supposed to possess the faculty of psychometry.

**psy|cho|met|ric** (sī′kō met′rik), *adj.* **1** having to do with psychometry. **2** of the nature of psychometry. **—psy′cho|met′ri|cal|ly**, *adv.*

**psy|cho|m et|ri|cal** (sī′kō met′rə kəl), *adj.* = psychometric.

**psy|cho|me|tri|cian** (sī′kō me trish′ən), *n.* = psychometrist.

**psy|cho|met|rics** (sī′kō met′riks), *n.* the measurement of mental facts and relations; psychometry.

**psy|chom|e|trist** (sī kom′ə trist), *n.* **1** a person skilled in psychometry. **2** a person supposed to possess the faculty of psychometry.

**psy|chom|e|trize** (sī kom′ə trīz), *v.t.*, **-trized, -triz|ing.** to practice the art of psychometry upon (an object).

**psy|chom|e|try** (sī kom′ə trē), *n.* **1** the measurement of mental facts and relations. **2** the alleged art or power of divining facts about an object or its owner through contact with it or proximity to it.

**psy|cho|mi|met|ic** (sī′kō mi met′ik, -mī-), *adj., n.* = psychotomimetic.

**psy|cho|mo|tor** (sī′kō mō′tər), *adj.* of or having to do with muscular activity directly related to or coming from mental processes: *In latent epilepsy, usually called … psychomotor epilepsy by doctors, the person goes into a trance* (New York Times).

**psy|cho|neu|ro|sis** (sī′kō nu̇ rō′sis, -nyu̇-), *n., pl.* **-ses** (-sēz). a mental disorder with physical symptoms but without apparent organic disease: *In both the actual neuroses and the psychoneuroses the symptoms proceed from the libido* (Sigmund Freud). [< New Latin *psychoneurosis* < *psycho-* psycho- + *neurosis* neurosis]

**psy|cho|neu|rot|ic** (sī′kō nu̇ rot′ik, -nyu̇-), *adj., n.* —*adj.* **1** of or having to do with psychoneurosis. **2** = neurotic.
—*n.* a person suffering from psychoneurosis.

**psy|cho|nom|ic** (sī′kə nom′ik), *adj.* of or having to do with psychonomics.

**psy|cho|nom|ics** (sī′kə nom′iks), *n.* the branch of psychology that deals with the laws of mental action, especially the relations of the individual mind to its environment. [< *psycho-* + Greek *nómos* law + English *-ics*]

**psy|cho|path** (sī′kə path), *n.* **1** a person who is mentally ill or unstable. **2** a person having a disorder of personality characterized by antisocial behavior, indifference to morality, and abnormal changes in mood and activity.

**psy|cho|path|ic** (sī′kə path′ik), *adj., n.* —*adj.* **1** of or having to do with mental disorders. **2** having a mental disorder. **3** of or characteristic of a psychopath. **4** likely to become insane.
—*n.* = psychopath. —**psy′cho|path′i|cal|ly,** *adv.*

**psy|cho|path|o|log|ic** (sī′kō path′ə loj′ik), *adj.* = psychopathological.

**psy|cho|path|o|log|i|cal** (sī′kō path′ə loj′ə kəl), *adj.* of or having to do with psychopathology: *psychopathological symptoms.* —**psy′cho|path′o|log′i|cal|ly,** *adv.*

**psy|cho|pa|thol|o|gist** (sī′kō pə thol′ə jist), *n.* an expert in psychopathology.

**psy|cho|pa|thol|o|gy** (sī′kō pə thol′ə jē), *n.* the science of mental disorders; abnormal psychology.

**psy|chop|a|thy** (sī kop′ə thē), *n.* **1** mental disease or disorder. **2** the treatment of disease by psychic means.

**psy|cho|phar|ma|ceu|ti|cal** (sī′kō fär′mə sü′tə kəl), *n.* a psychoactive drug.

**psy|cho|phar|ma|co|log|i|cal** (sī′kō fär′mə kə loj′ə kəl), *adj.* of or having to do with psychopharmacology.

**psy|cho|phar|ma|col|o|gist** (sī′kō fär′mə kol′ə jist), *n.* a person who studies psychopharmacology.

**psy|cho|phar|ma|col|o|gy** (sī′kō fär′mə kol′ə jē), *n.* a branch of pharmacology concerned with the effects of drugs on mental disturbances.

**psy|cho|phys|i|cal** (sī′kō fiz′ə kəl), *adj.* of or having to do with psychophysics: *The psychophysical methods … generally aim to connect stimulus and response, or stimulus and sensation* (F. H. George). —**psy′cho|phys′i|cal|ly,** *adv.*

**psy|cho|phys|i|cist** (sī′kō fiz′ə sist), *n.* a person who studies psychophysics.

**psy|cho|phys|ics** (sī′kō fiz′iks), *n.* the branch of psychology that deals with the physical relations of mental phenomena, especially the relations between physical stimuli and sensations.

**psy|cho|phys|i|o|log|ic** (sī′kō fiz′ē ə loj′ik), *adj.* = psychophysiological.

**psy|cho|phys|i|o|log|i|cal** (sī′kō fiz′ē ə loj′ə kəl), *adj.* of or having to do with psychophysiology.

**psy|cho|phys|i|ol|o|gist** (sī′kō fiz′ē ol′ə jist), *n.* a person who studies psychophysiology.

**psy|cho|phys|i|ol|o|gy** (sī′kō fiz′ē ol′ə jē), *n.* the branch of physiology which deals with mental phenomena.

**psy|cho|pomp** (sī′kō pomp), *n. Greek and Roman Mythology.* a conductor of souls to the place of the dead, especially Charon, Hermes, or Apollo. [< Greek *psȳchopompós* < *psȳchē* soul, spirit + *pompós* conductor < *pémpein* to send]

**psy|cho|pro|phy|lac|tic** (sī′kō prō′fə lak′tik, -prof′ə-), *adj.* of or having to do with psychoprophylaxis: *A fair slice of the population explosion has been born via the psychoprophylactic method* (Maclean's).

**psy|cho|pro|phy|lax|is** (sī′kō prō′fə lak′sis, -prof′ə-), *n.* a method of preparing women for natural childbirth by psychological conditioning: *A gynaecologist once pointed out … that a fundamental difference in approach to tasks—any tasks—may be one reason among many others why "psychoprophylaxis" works so well for some women in childbirth and so badly for others* (Manchester Guardian Weekly). [< *psycho-* + *prophylaxis*]

**psy|cho|sen|so|ry** (sī′kō sen′sər ē), *adj.* having to do with percepts or impulses that do not originate in the sense organs.

**psy|cho|sex|u|al** (sī′kō sek′shu̇ əl), *adj.* of or having to do with the psychological aspects of sex or both the mental and sexual processes: *psychosexual development, growth, or maturity.* —**psy′cho|sex′u|al|ly,** *adv.*

**psy|cho|sex|u|al|i|ty** (sī′kō sek′shu̇ al′ə tē), *n.* psychosexual character, quality, or condition.

**psy|cho|sis** (sī kō′sis), *n., pl.* **-ses** (-sēz). **1** any severe form of mental disturbance or disease which may also be associated with physical disease, and which produces deep and far-reaching disruption of normal behavior and social functioning: *Alcoholism may be a symptom of … psychosis, or may bring to notice an already existing psychosis* (Strecker, Ebaugh, and Ewalt). **2** = insanity. [< New Latin *psychosis* < Greek *psȳchē* soul, mind + New Latin *-osis* -osis]

**psy|cho|so|cial** (sī′kō sō′shəl), *adj.* of or having to do with the interrelationship of psychological and social processes, disciplines, and services: *a psychosocial study, psychosocial assistance, etc.* —**psy′cho|so′cial|ly,** *adv.*

**psy|cho|so|ci|o|log|i|cal** (sī′kō sō′sē ə loj′ə kəl, -shē-), *adj.* = psychosocial.

**psy|cho|so|ci|ol|o|gist** (sī′kō sō′sē ol′ə jist, -shē-), *n.* a person who studies the interrelationships of psychology and sociology.

**psy|cho|so|mat|ic** (sī′kō sō mat′ik), *adj., n.* —*adj.* of, having to do with, or caused by the interaction of mind and body, especially in the development of bodily disorders related to mental or emotional disturbances: *This is part of the growing belief of the psychosomatic (mind-body) experts that high blood pressure … [is] aided and abetted by upset emotions* (Marguerite Clark).
—*n.* a person having or showing a psychosomatic disorder.
[< *psycho-* + Greek *sōmatikós* somatic < *sôma* body] —**psy′cho|so|mat′i|cal|ly,** *adv.*

**psychosomatic medicine,** the use of the methods and principles of psychology in the treatment of physical ailments.

**psy|cho|so|mat|ics** (sī′kō sō mat′iks), *n.* = psychosomatic medicine.

**psy|cho|so|mat|ry** (sī′kō sō′mə trē), *n.* the interaction of the mind and body.

**psy|cho|sur|geon** (sī′kō sėr′jən), *n.* a doctor who performs psychosurgery.

**psy|cho|sur|ger|y** (sī′kō sėr′jər ē), *n.* brain surgery used in the treatment of certain psychoses.

**psy|cho|sur|gi|cal** (sī′kō sėr′jə kəl), *adj.* or or having to do with psychosurgery: *the psychosurgical procedure of prefrontal lobotomy.*

**psy|cho|tech|nol|o|gy** (sī′kō tek nol′ə jē), *n.* a branch of technology that deals with the application of psychology as a guide in handling practical problems.

**psy|cho|ther|a|peu|tic** (sī′kō ther′ə pyü′tik), *adj.* mentally healing. —**psy′cho|ther′a|peu′ti|cal|ly,** *adv.*

**psy|cho|ther|a|peu|tics** (sī′kō ther′ə pyü′tiks), *n.* the scientific basis of psychotherapy.

**psy|cho|ther|a|peu|tist** (sī′kō ther′ə pyü′tist), *n.* = psychotherapist.

**psy|cho|ther|a|pist** (sī′kō ther′ə pist), *n.* a person, such as a psychiatrist or psychoanalyst, who practices psychotherapy.

**psy|cho|ther|a|py** (sī′kō ther′ə pē), *n.* the treatment of mental or emotional disorders by psychological means, especially those involving intercommunication, as by psychoanalysis or hypnotism.

**psy|chot|ic** (sī kot′ik), *adj., n.* —*adj.* **1** having a psychosis; insane: *How absurd, I never heard of Communism, this is a witch hunt, my accuser is psychotic* (Eric Bentley). **2** of, having to do with, or caused by a psychosis.
—*n.* a psychotic person: *For the most part psychotics are aware of their disturbance—either because it itself makes them suffer or because others make them suffer for it* (Harper's). —**psy|chot′i|cal|ly,** *adv.*

**psy|chot|o|gen** (sī kot′ə jən), *n.* a drug that produces a psychotic state; psychotogenic drug: *A psychologist at Phipps Clinic foresees a future in which some hallucinogens, more precisely those described as psychotogens, will be used in ways that will benefit the functioning of the human brain* (John Hopkins Journal). [< *psychot*(ic) + connective *-o-* + *-gen*]

**psy|chot|o|ge|net|ic** (sī kot′ō jə net′ik), *adj.* = psychotogenic.

**psy|chot|o|gen|ic** (sī kot′ō jen′ik), *adj.* inducing or causing a psychotic state: *a psychotogenic drug. The effects of Vietnamese marijuana were sometimes surprisingly similar to those induced by hallucinogenic and psychotogenic agents such as L.S.D., mescaline and other so-called mind-expanders that have … proved harmful to the body and central nervous system of humans* (London Times).

**psy|chot|o|mi|met|ic** (sī kot′ō mi met′ik, -mī-), *adj., n.* —*adj.* producing a state resembling or symptomatic of psychosis: *They were conducting experiments with LSD and other psychotomimetic drugs* (Harper's).
—*n.* a psychotomimetic drug or substance: *LSD … was the first of the "modern" psychotomimetics* (Hannah Steinberg). Also, **psychomimetic.** —**psy|chot′o|mi|met′i|cal|ly,** *adv.*

**psy|cho|tox|ic** (sī′kō tok′sik), *adj.* harmful to the mind or personality; capable of producing mental disorder: *He asked for laws to control the production and sale of such drugs as barbiturates, amphetamines, and other psychotoxic drugs* (New York Times).

**psy|cho|tox|ic|i|ty** (sī′kō tok sis′ə tē), *n.* psychotoxic quality or condition.

**psy|cho|trop|ic** (sī′ko trop′ik), *adj., n.* —*adj.* affecting the mental processes: *a psychotropic drug.*
—*n.* a psychotropic drug or substance: *… possession of marijuana, hashish, or other psychotropics* (Science News).

**psy|cho|zo|ic** (sī′kō zō′ik), *adj.* of or belonging to the geological period of living creatures having minds or intelligence: *Our interest, … is in planets that may have intelligent life now, not in planets … whose "psychozoic era" has passed* (Scientific American).

**psychro-,** *combining form.* cold; coldness, as in *psychrometer, psychrotolerant.* [< Greek *psȳchrós* cold]

**psy|chrom|e|ter** (sī krom′ə tər), *n.* an instrument for measuring the relative humidity of the air, consisting of two thermometers, a dry-bulb and a wet-bulb thermometer. The difference between their temperature readings is a measure of the relative humidity.

**psy|chro|met|ric** (sī′krə met′rik), *adj.* of or having to do with a psychrometer.

**psy|chrom|e|try** (sī krom′ə trē), *n.* the branch of physics that deals with the measurement of the relative humidity in the air.

**psy|chro|phile** (sī′krə fīl), *n.* a psychrophilic microorganism.

**psy|chro|phil|ic** (sī′krə fil′ik), *adj.* requiring low temperatures for development: *psychrophilic bacteria. Psychrophilic microorganisms have been defined as organisms with the ability to grow well at 0°C* (J. L. Ingraham).

**psy|chro|tol|er|ant** (sī′krō tol′ər ənt), *adj.* able to endure cold: *Slime is caused by cold resistant, or psychrotolerant, bacteria which are not a health hazard but which produce an objectionable smell and change the colour of the meat* (Science Journal).

**psyl|la** (sil′ə), *n.* any one of a group of insects that suck the juices of plants and are serious pests of fruit trees, such as the pear psylla. [< New Latin *Psylla* the genus name < Greek *psylla* flea]

**psyl|lid** (sil′id), *adj.* of or belonging to the psyllas: *a psyllid bug.* [< New Latin *Psyllidae* the family name < *Psylla*]

**psyl|li|um** (sil′ē əm), *n.* a plantain whose fleaiike seeds are used as a laxative; fleawort. [< New Latin *psyllium* < Greek *psyllion* < *psylla* flea]

**psy|ops** (sī′ops′), *n.pl. Informal.* operations used in psychological warfare: *[He] also oversees the mission's psyops … such as the printing of propaganda leaflets* (New York Times). [< *psy*(chological) *op*(eration)*s*]

**psy|war** (sī′wôr′), *n. Informal.* psychological warfare.

**pt.,** an abbreviation for the following:
**1** part.
**2** past tense.
**3** pint or pints.
**4** point.
**5** port.
**6** preterit.

**p.t.,** **1** physical training. **2** pro tempore. **3** *British.* purchase tax.

**Pt** (no period), platinum (chemical element).

**P.t.,** Pacific time.

**P.T.,** **1** physical training. **2** *British.* purchase tax.

**pta.,** peseta.

**P.T.A.** or **PTA** (no periods), Parent-Teacher Association (an organization of the parents and teachers of a school, established to improve the environment of the community for children, especially by supporting the activities of the school).

---

**Pronunciation Key:** hat, āge, cãre, fär; let, ēqual, tėrm; it, īce; hot, ōpen, ôrder; oil, out; cup, pu̇t, rüle; child; long; thin; ᴛʜen; zh, measure; ə represents **a** in about, **e** in taken, **i** in pencil, **o** in lemon, **u** in circus.

**PTA deficiency**, a form of hemophilia caused by a deficiency in blood plasma of one of the factors necessary for blood clotting. [< *p*(lasma) *t*(hromboplastin) *a*(ntecedent) + *deficiency*]

**Ptah** (ptä, ptäH), *n.* (in ancient Egypt) the chief god of Memphis, father of men and gods and ruler of the world.

**ptar|mi|gan** (tär′mə gən), *n., pl.* **-gans** or (*collectively*) **-gan.** any one of several kinds of grouse that have feathered feet and are found in mountainous and cold regions. The plumage of most varieties is brownish in summer, white in winter. [< Scottish Gaelic *tàrmachan*]

***PT boat**, a small, fast motorboat which carries torpedoes, depth bombs, and light antiaircraft armament. [< *P*(atrol) *T*(orpedo) boat]

***PT boat**

**PTC** (no periods), phenylthiocarbamide.

**PTC deficiency**, = Christmas disease. [< *p*(lasma) *t*(hromboplastin *c*(omponent) + *deficiency*]

**Pte.**, Private (in the British Army): *And you with the Etruscan look not Pte. Maecenas by any chance?* (Listener).

**pter|an|o|don** (ter an′ə don), *n.* a large, toothless pterodactyl with a hornlike crest projecting from its head. [< New Latin *Pteranodon* the genus name < Greek *pterón* wing + *an-* without + *odoús, odóntos* tooth]

**pter|i|dine** (ter′ə dēn, -din), *n.* any one of various compounds derived from pigments in the wings of butterflies, characterized by a fused pyrazine and pyrimidine ring system. [< Greek *pterón* wing + English *-id* + *-ine*²]

**pter|i|do|log|i|cal** (ter′ə də loj′ə kəl), *adj.* having to do with pteridology.

**pter|i|dol|o|gist** (ter′ə dol′ə jist), *n.* an expert in the study of ferns.

**pter|i|dol|o|gy** (ter′ə dol′ə jē), *n.* the branch of botany that deals with ferns. [< Greek *pterís, -ídos* fern (< *pterón* feather) + English *-logy*]

**pter|i|do|phyte** (ter′ə də fīt), *n.* any one of a division of seedless and flowerless plants, having roots, stems, and leaves. Ferns, horsetails, and club mosses are pteridophytes. *The tissues of seed plants and pteridophytes are all derived from a fertilized egg (zygote) which has undergone repeated divisions* (Heber W. Youngken). [< Greek *pterís, -ídos* fern (< *pterón* feather) + English *-phyte*]

**pter|i|do|phyt|ic** (ter′ə də fit′ik), *adj.* of or having to do with pteridophytes.

**pter|i|doph|y|tous** (ter′ə dof′ə təs), *adj.* = pteridophytic.

**pter|i|do|sperm** (ter′ə də spėrm), *n.* any one of a group of fossil plants having the external aspect of ferns, but bearing true seeds; seed fern: *Fernlike pteridosperms are the earliest to start protecting their seeds* (New Scientist). [< Greek *pterís, -ídos* fern + English *sperm*]

**pter|in** (ter′in), *n.* a pigment or other compound containing a ring system such as that of pteridine. Folic acid and xanthopterin are pterins. [< Greek *pterón* wing + English *-in*]

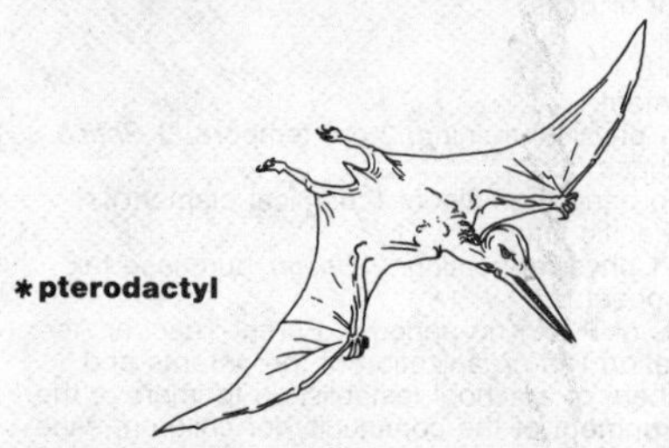
***pterodactyl**

***pter|o|dac|tyl** (ter′ə dak′təl), *n.* an extinct flying reptile that had wings somewhat like those of a bat. There were various kinds. The wings consisted of a strong, featherless membrane stretching from the elongated fourth digit of each foreleg to the body. Pterodactyls existed during the Jurassic and Cretaceous periods. [< Greek *pterón* wing + *dáktylos* finger, toe]

**pter|o|dac|tyl|oid** (ter′ə dak′tə loid), *adj.* having the form or characteristics of a pterodactyl.

**pter|o|dac|tyl|ous** (ter′ə dak′tə ləs), *adj.* of or like a pterodactyl.

**pte|ron** (ter′on), *n. Architecture.* a side row of columns in a classical temple. [< Greek *pterón* wing]

**pter|o|pod** (ter′ə pod), *adj., n.* —*adj.* of or belonging to a group of mollusks with lateral portions of the foot expanded into winglike lobes used in swimming.
—*n.* a pteropod mollusk.
[< New Latin *Pteropoda* a group or class name < Greek *pterópous, -podos* wingfooted < *pterón* wing, feather + *poús, podós* foot]

**pte|rop|o|dan** (tə rop′ə dən), *adj., n.* = pteropod.

**pte|rop|o|dous** (tə rop′ə dəs), *adj.* **1** = pteropod. **2** characteristic of a pteropod.

**pter|o|saur** (ter′ə sôr), *n.* an extinct flying reptile; pterodactyl: *On the land were the dinosaurs, in the sea the ichthyosaurs ... in the air the pterosaurs* (A. Franklin Shull). [< New Latin *Pterosauria* the order name < Greek *pterón* wing + *saûros* lizard]

**pter|o|sau|ri|an** (ter′ə sôr′ē ən), *adj., n.* —*adj.* **1** of or belonging to the same order as the pterodactyl. **2** like a pterodactyl.
—*n.* = pterodactyl.

**pte|ryg|i|um** (tə rij′ē əm), *n., pl.* **-i|ums, -i|a** (-ē ə). a triangular patch of thickened conjunctiva growing over the cornea that obscures vision. [< Greek *pterýgion* little wing, fin]

**pter|y|goid** (ter′ə goid), *adj., n.* —*adj.* **1** = winglike. **2** of or having to do with either of two processes of the spenoid bone.
—*n.* a pterygoid muscle, nerve, or other related part.
[< Greek *pterygoeidês* winglike < *ptéryx, -ygos* wing (< *pterón* wing, feather) + *eîdos* form, shape]

**pterygoid plate**, either of the two sections, the lateral section or the medial section, that make up a pterygoid process.

**pterygoid process**, **1** either of two processes descending, one on each side, from the point of juncture of the main body and the great wing of the sphenoid bone of the skull. Each process consists of a lateral and a medial section. **2** any one of the four pterygoid plates.

**pter|y|la** (ter′ə lə), *n., pl.* **-lae** (-lē). one of the definite tracts or areas on the skin of a bird, on which feathers grow. [< New Latin *pteryla* < Greek *pterón* feather + *hýlē* wood]

**pter|y|log|ra|phy** (ter′ə log′rə fē), *n., pl.* **-phies. 1** the description of pterylae. **2** a treatise on pterylosis. [< *pteryla* + *-graphy*]

**pter|y|lo|sis** (ter′ə lō′sis), *n.* the arrangement or disposition of the feathers of a bird in definite tracts, or pterylae. [< *pteryl*(a) + *-osis*]

**PTFE** (no periods), polytetrafluoroethylene.

**ptg.**, printing.

**PTH** (no periods), parathyroid hormone.

**ptis|an** (tiz′ən, ti zan′), *n.* a nourishing decoction often having a slight medicinal quality, originally one made from barley. [spelling alteration (influenced by Latin *ptisana*) of Middle English *tisane* < Old French *tisane,* learned borrowing from Late Latin *tisana,* variant of Latin *ptisana* crushed barley < Greek *ptisánē*]

**p.t.o.** or **P.T.O.**, *Especially British.* please turn over (a page).

**PTO** (no periods), power take-off: *The PTO drives the moving parts of mowing machines, hay balers, combines, potato diggers, and spray pumps* (A. D. Longhouse).

**Ptol|e|ma|ic** (tol′ə mā′ik), *adj.* **1** of or having to do with Ptolemy, an astronomer of the 100's A.D.: *The Ptolemaic constellations of the Horse, the Bird, and the Kneeler became respectively Pegasus, Cygnus, and Hercules* (Robert H. Baker). **2** of or having to do with the Ptolemies, who were rulers of Egypt from 323 B.C. to 30 B.C.

***Ptolemaic system**
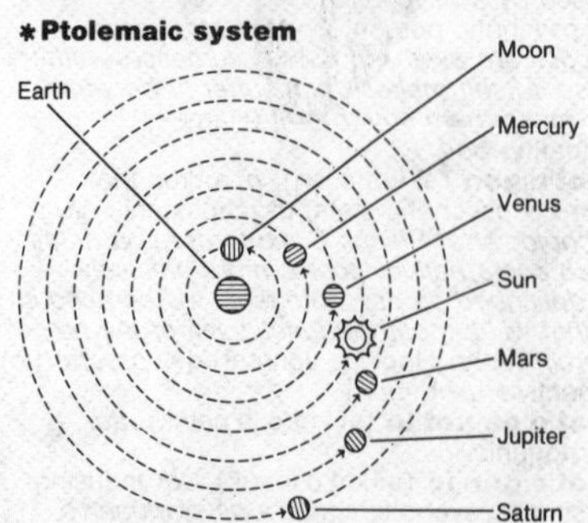


***Ptolemaic system**, the system of astronomy developed by the astronomer Ptolemy. It taught that the earth was the fixed center of the universe and that the sun, moon, and other heavenly bodies moved around the earth.

**Ptol|e|ma|ist** (tol′ə mā′ist), *n.* a supporter of the Ptolemaic system of astronomy.

**pto|maine** or **pto|main** (tō′mān, tō mān′), *n.* any one of several chemical compounds produced by bacteria in decaying matter. Improperly canned foods may contain ptomaines. Ptomaines are a group of basic, nitrogenous, organic compounds, some of which are poisonous. [< Italian *ptomaina* < Greek *ptôma* corpse, (literally) a fall; fallen thing < *pîptein* to fall]

**ptomaine poisoning**, **1** poisoning caused by ptomaines. **2** = food poisoning.

**pto|sis** (tō′sis), *n.* a slipping down of an organ, especially the drooping of the upper eyelid, caused by paralysis of the muscle that causes it to open. [< Greek *ptôsis* a falling < *pîptein* to fall]

**pto|tic** (tō′tik), *adj.* **1** having to do with or like ptosis. **2** affected with ptosis.

**pts.**, **1** parts. **2** pints. **3** points.

**PTV** (no periods), public television.

**Pty.**, **Pty** (no period), or **pty.**, proprietary.

**pty|a|lin** (tī′ə lin), *n.* an enzyme contained in the saliva of human beings and of certain other animals. It possesses the property of converting starch into dextrin and maltose, thus aiding digestion. [< Greek *ptýalon* saliva (< *ptýein* to spit) + English *-in*]

**pty|a|lism** (tī′ə liz əm), *n.* excessive secretion of saliva. [< Greek *ptýalon* saliva + English *-ism*]

**p-type** (pē′tīp′), *adj.* (of a semiconductor or its conductivity) positive type; having as the carrier of an electrical charge positive holes rather than negative electrons. [< *p*(ositive) *type*]

**Pu** (no period), plutonium (chemical element).

**PU** (no periods), polyurethane.

**pub** (pub), *n., v.,* **pubbed, pub|bing.** *Informal.*
—*n.* a saloon; tavern; public house: *I drove on and lunched very late at a remote pub overlooking the Blackmoor Vale* (Geoffrey Household).
—*v.i.* to visit or frequent pubs: *I was about to ask him to go pubbing with us when I noticed that he was carrying a book by T. S. Eliot* (H. Allen Smith).
[< *pub*(lic)]

**pub.**, an abbreviation for the following:
**1** public.
**2** publication.
**3** published.
**4** publisher.
**5** publishing.

**pub-crawl** (pub′krôl′), *v., n. Slang.* —*v.i.* to go from one pub or bar to another: *I'd rather pub-crawl than visit Whitehall* (Saturday Review).
—*n.* a round of several pubs made by one or more persons. —**pub′-crawl′er**, *n.*

**pu|ber|al** (pyü′bər əl), *adj.* of or at the age of puberty: *Two papers relate physique and puberal status to leadership and personality characteristics in junior high school boys* (Dale B. Harris). [< Late Latin *pūberālis* < Latin *pūber* a youth]

**pu|ber|tal** (pyü′bər təl), *adj.* = puberal.

**pu|ber|ty** (pyü′bər tē), *n.* the age or condition of becoming first able to produce offspring; the physical beginning of manhood and womanhood. Puberty comes at about 14 in boys and about 12 in girls. *The onset of puberty and adolescence is accompanied by numerous changes in both personality and behavior* (Beals and Hoijer). [< Latin *pūbertās* < *pūbēs, -eris* adult, full grown, manly]

**pu|ber|u|lent** (pyü ber′yə lənt), *adj. Botany.* covered with fine, short down; minutely pubescent. [< Latin *pūber* downy + *-ulent,* on the analogy of *pulverulent*]

**pu|ber|u|lous** (pyü ber′yə ləs), *adj.* = puberulent.

**pu|bes¹** (pyü′bēz), *n.* **1** the hair appearing on the lower abdomen at puberty. **2** the lower part of the hypogastrium. **3** *Botany.* pubescence. [< Latin *pūbēs*]

**pu|bes²** (pyü′bēz), *n.* plural of **pubis**.

**pu|bes|cence** (pyü bes′əns), *n.* **1** arrival at puberty. **2** a soft, downy growth on plants and some insects. **3** the fact of having such a growth.

**pu|bes|cent** (pyü bes′ənt), *adj., n.* —*adj.* **1** arriving or arrived at puberty. **2** covered with down or fine, short hair: *a pubescent stem or leaf.*
—*n.* an adolescent at the age of puberty.
[< Latin *pūbēscēns, -entis* reaching puberty, present participle of *pūbēscere* < *pūbēs, -eris* mature, adult]

**pu|bic** (pyü′bik), *adj.* **1** having to do with the pubis. **2** in the region of the pubis.

**pubic symphysis**, the place at the front of the pelvis where the pubis of one side is joined to the other.

**pu|bis** (pyü′bis), *n., pl.* **-bes.** the part of either hipbone that, with the corresponding part of the other, forms the front of the pelvis: *The pelvic structure is made up of three sets of paired bones, the ilium, the ischium and the pubis* (Scientific American). [< New Latin *os pūbis* bone of the groin < Latin *os* bone, *pūbis,* genitive of *pūbēs* the genital area]

**pub|keep|er** (pub′kē′pər), *n. Especially British.* a person who owns, manages, or keeps a public house.

**publ.,** 1 published. 2 publisher.

**pub|lic** (pub′lik), *adj., n.* — ***adj.*** **1** of or belonging to the people as a whole: *public affairs. The Restrictive Practices Court's ruling that the yarn spinners agreement is contrary to the public interest is a bitter pill for the cotton industry* (Manchester Guardian). **2** by the people: *public help for the poor.* **3** for the people as a whole: *public relief.* **4** open to all the people; serving all the people: *a public park, a public meeting, public libraries.* **5** of the affairs or service of the people: *a public official. Public employment does bring with it certain obligations beyond those required of citizens in private life* (Bulletin of Atomic Scientists). **6** known to many or all; not private: *The fact became public knowledge. He made public his intention to resign from the President's Cabinet.* **7** international: *public law.*
— ***n.*** **1** all the people; people in general: *to inform the public.* **2** a particular section of the people: *A popular actor has a large public. There is a separate public for every picture and every book* (John Ruskin). *At the other pole are the more stable groups called publics, characterized by deliberate discussion of issues confronting the group* (Ogburn and Nimkoff). **3** *British Informal.* a public house.
**go public,** to offer stocks or bonds for sale to the public for the first time: *To raise the money, family-owned Lykes went public in 1958, though the family still owns 64% of the stock* (Time).
**in public,** not in private or secretly; publicly; openly: *to stand up in public for what you believe.*
[< Latin *pūblicus,* earlier *poplicus* (influenced by *pūbēs* adult male population) < *populus* the people] — **pub′lic|ness,** *n.*

**public accountant, 1** an accountant who makes his services available to anyone for a fee or on a contract basis: *Auditing is one of the chief jobs of public accountants* (R. K. Mautz). **2** = certified public accountant.

**pub|lic-ad|dress system** (pub′lik ə dres′), an apparatus consisting of one or more microphones, amplifiers, and loudspeakers, by which speeches, announcements, music, or a motion-picture sound track may be made audible to a large audience, as on a public street or square, in an auditorium or a stadium for athletics, or in the various rooms of a building; P.A. system.

**pub|li|can** (pub′lə kən), *n.* **1** *British.* the keeper of a public house. **2a** a tax collector of ancient Rome. **b** any collector of tolls or tribute. [< Latin *pūblicānus* < *pūblicum* public revenue, (originally) neuter of *pūblicus* public]

**public assistance,** *U.S.* government payments under social security to needy persons, especially in the form of an annual income for the aged, the blind, and the disabled: *Persons receiving public assistance are generally allowed to earn small amounts of money without having their payments reduced* (Robert J. Myers).

**pub|li|ca|tion** (pub′lə kā′shən), *n.* **1** a book, newspaper, or magazine; anything that is published: *"Boy's Life" is a publication of the Boy Scouts. Abbr:* pub. **2** the printing and selling of books, newspapers, or magazines. **3** the first public sale of a book, magazine, or newspaper: *The first printing was swallowed up before publication* (New Yorker). **4a** the act of making known; public announcement: *There is prompt publication of any important news over the radio. The widespread publication of traffic laws helps prevent accidents.* **SYN:** promulgation, dissemination. **b** the fact or state of being made known. [< Latin *pūblicātiō, -ōnis* a publishing; (originally) a confiscation < *pūblicāre* to confiscate for public use < *pūblicus* public]

**public charge,** an indigent person who requires support or maintenance from public funds: *Since the wife ... had no way to support herself, it was her husband's job to see that she did not become a public charge* (Harper's).

**public defender,** an attorney designated by a court or other governmental agency, and paid from public funds, to defend persons involved in litigation or legal difficulties who do not have the means to hire their own attorney.

**public domain,** lands belonging to the state or the Federal government; public lands.
**in the public domain,** (of works, material, inventions, trade names, and the like) available for unrestricted use because unprotected by copyright, patent, or trademark: *Shakespeare's plays are in the public domain.*

**public enemy,** a person or thing, especially a criminal, that is a menace to the public.

**public funds,** *British.* the stock of the national debt, considered as a mode of investment.

**public health, 1** the health of the community taken as a whole. **2** measures taken to maintain and improve the general level of health, such as by preventive medicine, immunization, sanitation, and the organization of medical and hospital facilities.

**public house, 1** *British.* a place where alcoholic liquor is sold to be drunk; saloon or tavern. **2** an inn; hotel.

**public housing,** *U.S.* housing owned or operated by a municipality or other public body, usually through Federal aid, designed especially for families with low income: *A neighborhood that we remembered as an appalling slum ... is now abloom with public housing* (New Yorker).

**pub|lic-in|ter|est** (pub′lik in′tər ist, -trist), *adj.* of or having to do with class action suits and other legal means of protecting the interests of the public: *Meites chose public-interest law, he says, because "he couldn't bother with the conventional lawyer's willingness to take either side"* (Time).

**pub|li|cise** (pub′lə sīz), *v.t.,* **-cised, -cis|ing.** *Especially British.* publicize.

**pub|li|cist** (pub′lə sist), *n.* **1** a person skilled or trained in law or in public affairs. **2** a writer on law, politics, or public affairs. **3** a person who publicizes: *Dr. Tsuru is a leading publicist for the neutralist view of world affairs* (Atlantic). **4** = press agent.

**pub|lic|i|ty** (pub lis′ə tē), *n.* **1** public notice: *the publicity that actors desire.* **2** the measures used for getting, or the process of getting, public notice: *a campaign of publicity for a new automobile.* **SYN:** advertising, propaganda. **3** the articles, films, or devices, used in such measures or process: *to write publicity.* **4** the condition of being public; being seen by or known to many: *in the publicity of the streets.*

**pub|li|cize** (pub′lə sīz), *v.t.,* **-cized, -ciz|ing.** to give publicity to: *The means of picking the fights and publicizing them will be the classic device of Congressional inquiry* (New York Times). — **pub′li|ciz′a|ble,** *adj.*

**public lands,** all of the territory or land belonging to a national government, especially land that is open to sale, grant, or other method of disposal to anyone complying with the conditions prescribed by law.

**public law. 1** the branch of law that regulates the relationships between individuals and the government. One part of the public law defines and limits the powers of the government. Criminal law and international law are part of public law. **2** an act or statute that applies to the general public.

**pub|lic|ly** (pub′lə klē), *adv.* **1** in a public manner; openly: *Money for an election campaign must be recorded publicly.* **2** by the public: *The mayor was thought of publicly as the best man for the job.*

**public opinion,** the opinion of the people in a country or community on a matter of public interest or concern: *to make a survey of public opinion on the issue of gun-control laws. Public opinion can be wrong, misguided, mistaken* (Wall Street Journal).

**public policy,** the policy or general purpose of the law that protects the public from acts contrary to its welfare even when there is no positive statutory prohibition.

**public prosecutor,** = district attorney.

**public relations, 1** the activities of an organization, institution, or individual that are designed to win the favor of the general public and promote a better understanding of policies and purposes, especially by giving out information through the newspapers, magazines, radio, television, and motion pictures. **2** the attitude of the public toward a particular organization, institution, or individual: *to maintain good public relations.* **3** the business of such activities: *to take up public relations as a career. Abbr:* PR (no periods).

**Public Res.,** Public Resolution (used with a number).

**public school, 1** *U.S.* a free school maintained by taxes, especially an elementary or secondary school: *The chances of a private school graduate's making Who's Who are 6 to 1 over the public school man* (Newsweek). **2** *British.* an endowed private boarding school preparing students for university study or government service. — **pub′lic-school′,** *adj.*
► See **private school** for usage note.

**public servant, 1** a person who works for the government: *It is the function of every policeman to be an extremely valuable public servant* (Emory S. Bogardus). **2** *U.S.* a public-service corporation.

**public service, 1** government service: *His career, apart from public service sojourns in Washington, has been ... closely identified with Boston* (New York Times). **2** *U.S.* a service performed by a public utility. **3** something done for the general good: *The Citizens Union's annual award for public service will be presented tomorrow* (New York Times).

**pub|lic-serv|ice corporation** (pub′lik sėr′vis), a corporation formed or chartered to give service to the general public, as by furnishing gas or electricity, or bus or railroad transportation.

**public speaking,** the art or practice of making a speech before an audience: *Training in effective public speaking is an essential part of training for leadership in any field* (W. Hayes Yeager).

**pub|lic-spir|it|ed** (pub′lik spir′ə tid), *adj.* having or showing an unselfish desire for the public good: *A committee of 342 public-spirited men and women leaders ... has been organized* (New York Times). — **pub′lic-spir′it|ed|ly,** *adv.* — **pub′lic-spir′it|ed|ness,** *n.*

**public television,** *U.S.* noncommercial television broadcasting that features chiefly cultural and educational programs; educational television. *Abbr:* PTV (no periods).

**public utilities,** shares of stock or other securities issued by public-utility companies.

**public utility,** a company formed or chartered to render essential services to the public, such as a company furnishing gas, electricity, or water, or an airline, a railroad, or a bus line; utility. A public utility often has a monopoly on its particular service within an area or areas, and is subject to special governmental control or regulation.
— **pub′lic-u|til′i|ty,** *adj.*

**public works,** highways, dams, docks, canals, office buildings, and parks or other things built by the government at public expense for public use.

**pub|lish** (pub′lish), *v.t.* **1** to prepare and offer (a book, paper, map, a piece of music, or the like) for sale or distribution: [*He*] *is general editor for the volumes being published* (Time). **2** to bring out the books or works of: *Some American writers are published abroad before they achieve publication in this country.* **3** to make publicly or generally known: *Don't publish the faults of your friends. Publish it that she is dead* (Shakespeare). **SYN:** divulge, reveal, disclose. **4** to announce formally or officially. — ***v.i.*** **1** to come into circulation; be published: *The newspapers here publish every single day.* **2** to prepare a work for publication and distribution: *We have been publishing for many authors for many years.* [< Old French *publiss-,* stem of *publier,* learned borrowing from Latin *pūblicāre* < *pūblicus* (see etym. under **public**); spelling influenced by *astonish,* etc.] — **pub′lish|a|ble,** *adj.* — **pub′lish|ment,** *n.*

**pub|lish|er** (pub′li shər), *n.* **1** a person or company whose business is to produce and sell books, newspapers, or magazines: *Look at the bottom of the title page of this book for the publisher's name. Abbr:* pub. **2** a person who makes something public.

**pub|lish|ing** (pub′li shing), *n.* the business or activities of a publisher: *textbook publishing.*

**publishing house,** a company which publishes books or magazines; publisher: *Gide had long felt the need for ... a publishing house which would afford a hearing to young authors* (Atlantic).

**pu|bo|fem|o|ral** (pyü′bō fem′ər əl), *adj.* of, attached to, or common to the pubis and the femur: *pubofemoral fascia.*

**PUC** (no periods) or **P.U.C.,** Public Utilities Commission, a commission set up at various government levels to regulate public utilities.

**puc|coon** (pə kün′), *n.* **1** any one of various plants yielding a red dye, especially the bloodroot, and certain American plants of the borage family. **2** the pigment or dye obtained from any one of these plants. [American English < Algonkian (Powhatan) *pähkan,* a plant whose juice was used for dyeing < an Algonkian root meaning "blood." See related etym. at **poke**[4].]

**puce** (pyüs), *n., adj.* purplish brown. [< French *puce* (literally) a flea < Old French *pulce* < Latin *pūlex, -icis*]

**puck**[1] (puk), *n.* a malicious or mischievous spirit; elf or goblin. [Old English *pūca;* origin uncertain]

**puck**[2] (puk), *n.* a hard rubber disk used in the game of ice hockey. [probably < dialectal *puck* to strike or hit. See related etym. at **poke**[1].]

**Puck** (puk), *n.* a mischievous fairy in English folklore, who appears in Shakespeare's *A Midsummer Night's Dream.* [< *puck*[1]]

**puck|a** (puk′ə), *adj. Anglo-Indian.* **1** genuine; true; real. **2** reliable; good. **3** solid; substantial. **4** permanent. Also, **pukka.** [< Hindi *pakkā* substantial, solid; cooked, ripe]

**puck|er** (puk′ər), *v., n.* — ***v.t., v.i.*** to draw into wrinkles or irregular folds: *to pucker one's brow,*

---

**Pronunciation Key:** hat, āge, cãre, fär; let, ēqual, tėrm; it, īce; hot, ōpen, ôrder; oil, out; cup, pu̇t, rüle; child; long; thin; ᴛʜen; zh, measure; ə represents a in about, e in taken, i in pencil, o in lemon, u in circus.

*pucker cloth in sewing. The baby's lips puckered just before he began to cry. Trabert till that moment had looked tense and puckered up* (London Times). **SYN**: crease, purse.
— ***n.*** **1** an irregular fold; wrinkle: *This coat doesn't fit; there are puckers in the shoulders.* **2** *Informal, Figurative.* a dazed or perturbed condition: *She appeared to have stopped breathing; her flesh barely rippled. He recognized the symptoms; she was in a real pucker* (Atlantic). **3** *U.S. Slang.* the lips or mouth: *What's the good o' havin' music in your mind if you can't get it past your pucker?* (Louis Armstrong).
[apparently related to **poke**[2].]

**puck|er|y** (puk′ər ē), *adj.* tending to pucker; puckered; puckering.

**puck|ish** (puk′ish), *adj.* mischievous; impish: *a puckish twinkle of the eyes. He got a puckish delight out of teasing his sister.* — **puck′ish|ly**, *adv.* — **puck′ish|ness**, *n.*

**puc|ras** (puk′rəs), *n.* any one of various pheasants of the Himalaya region and parts of India and China, distinguished by the long crests and ear tufts of the males. Also, **pukras**. [< a native name]

**pud**[1] (pùd), *n.* = pood.

**pud**[2] (pud), *n. British Slang.* pudding.

**pud**[3] (pud), *n. Informal.* fist; hand. [origin unknown]

**pud|der** (pud′ər), *v.i.* **1** to go poking about; potter; dabble (in). **2** to poke or stir about, as with the hand or a stick.

**pud|ding** (pùd′ing), *n.* **1** a soft cooked food, usually sweet and often made with a milk base: *Rice pudding is nourishing.* **2** a dessert resembling a cake, flavored and sweetened and usually steamed or baked: *plum pudding.* **3** anything soft like a pudding. **4** *Scottish.* a kind of sausage. [origin uncertain. Compare French *boudin* stuffed sausage, Old English *puduc* wart, *puddewurst* black pudding.]

**pud|ding|head** (pùd′ing hed′, pùd′ən-), *n. Informal.* a stupid person.

**pud|ding|head|ed** (pùd′ing hed′id, pùd′ən-), *adj. Informal.* stupid.

**pudding stone**, a rock composed of pebbles held together by cementlike stone; conglomerate.

**pud|ding|y** (pùd′ing ē), *adj. Especially British.* having the appearance, shape, or consistency of a pudding.

**pud|dle** (pud′əl), *n., v.,* **-dled, -dling.** — ***n.*** **1** a small pool of water, especially dirty water: *a puddle of rain water.* **2** *Figurative: a puddle of ink.* **3** wet clay and sand stirred into a paste, used as a watertight lining for embankments, canals, etc. **4** the molten metal that flows before the flame of a welding torch and forms the weld when cooled: *Move the flame across the surface of the sheet metal, carrying the puddle along the surface* (Purvis and Toboldt).
— ***v.i.*** **1** to dabble or wade in puddles: *The children always puddle about in the garden after a rain.* **2** *Figurative.* to busy oneself in a disorderly way: *He puddled about at first one thing and another, never getting anything done.*
— ***v.t.*** **1** to make wet or muddy: *Tablecloths puddled with melted ice* (Thackeray). **2** to mix up (wet clay and sand) into a thick paste. **3** to use a mixture of wet clay and sand to stop water from running through: *Puddle up that hole in the wall.* **4** to stir (molten pig iron) along with an oxidizing agent to make wrought iron. **5** to prepare (soil) for planting while wet, as in a rice paddy. **6** to damage the texture of (soil, especially a heavy soil) by plowing, harrowing, or otherwise working before excess water has drained.
[Middle English *puddel*, apparently (diminutive) < Old English *pudd* ditch]

**pud|dle-jump** (pud′əl jump′), *v.t., v.i. Informal.* to fly a light airplane for short trips: *[He] has done some syndicated drawing and free-lance writing, puddle-jumped in his private plane* (Time).

**pud|dle-jump|er** (pud′əl jum′pər), *n.* **1** *Informal.* a lightweight airplane or helicopter: *We consider all types ... big and little transports or puddle-jumpers* (Newsweek). **2** *Slang.* an old or dilapidated automobile.

**pud|dler** (pud′lər), *n.* **1** a person or thing that puddles. **2** a person employed in the process of converting cast iron into wrought iron.

**pud|dling** (pud′ling), *n.* **1** the act or process of converting pig iron into wrought iron by stirring the molten metal along with an oxidizing agent. **2** the process of converting clay and sand into puddle. **3** the process of lining or filling something with puddle. **4** the clay and sand used in puddling; puddle.

**puddling furnace**, a furnace for converting pig iron into wrought iron.

**pud|dly** (pud′lē), *adj.* **1** full of puddles. **2** like a puddle.

**pud|dock** (pud′ək), *n. Dialect.* a paddock; toad.

**pu|den|cy** (pyü′dən sē), *n.* = modesty. [< Latin *pudentia* < *pudēns, -entis,* present participle of *pudēre* to make or be ashamed]

**pu|den|dal** (pyü den′dəl), *adj.* of or having to do with the pudenda.

**pu|den|dum** (pyü den′dəm), *n., pl.* **-da** (-də). the external genitals, especially of the female. [< Latin *pudendum* (literally) thing to be ashamed of, neuter gerundive of *pudēre* be ashamed]

**pudge** (puj), *n.* a pudgy person.

**pudg|y** (puj′ē), *adj.,* **pudg|i|er, pudg|i|est.** short and fat or thick: *a child's pudgy hand, a pudgy little man.* **SYN**: dumpy. Also, **podgy**. — **pudg′i|ly**, *adv.* — **pudg′i|ness**, *n.*

**pu|di|bund** (pyü′də bund), *adj.* shamefaced; modest; prudish. [< Latin *pudibundus* < *pudēre* be ashamed]

**pu|dic|i|ty** (pyü dis′ə tē), *n.* modesty; chastity. [< Middle French *pudicité*, ultimately < Latin *pudīcus* modest; chaste]

**pu|du** (pü′dü), *n.* the smallest deer known, about a foot high and weighing about 20 pounds; rabbit deer. Pudus live in the forests of western South America and have short, spikelike antlers and rough, brown or gray fur. [< American Spanish *pudu*]

**pueb|lo** (pweb′lō), *n., pl.* **-los.** an Indian village built of adobe and stone. The houses in a pueblo usually have roofs and are often several stories high. Pueblos were common in the southwestern United States, and some are still in use. [American English < Spanish *pueblo* a people, community < Latin *populus.* See etym. of doublet **people**.]

**Pueb|lo** (pweb′lō), *n., pl.* **-los,** *adj.* — ***n.*** a member of any one of a group of Indian tribes in the southwestern United States and northern Mexico living in pueblo villages. They are of several linguistic stocks. Pueblos were and are agricultural and known for such handicrafts as textiles and decorated earthenware.
— ***adj.*** of or having to do with the Pueblos or their culture: *Pueblo architecture.*
[< *pueblo*]

**Puel|che** (pwel′chē), *n., pl.* **-ches** or **-che.** a member of any one of various small groups of South American Indians formerly ranging the pampas of Argentina. Many of the gauchos of Argentina are descended from these groups.

**pu|er|ile** (pyü′ər əl; *especially British* pyü′ə rīl), *adj.* **1** foolish for a grown person to say or do; childish: *Such ravings, if invented by the pen of fiction, would seem puerile caricature* (John L. Motley). **SYN**: immature. **2** youthful; juvenile. [< Latin *puerīlis* < *puer* boy, child] — **pu′er|ile|ly**, *adv.* — **pu′er|ile|ness**, *n.*

**pu|er|il|ism** (pyü′ər ə liz′əm), *n.* childishness, especially that due to mental illness.

**pu|er|il|i|ty** (pyü′ə ril′ə tē), *n., pl.* **-ties. 1** childishness; foolishness. **2** a foolish act, idea, or statement.

**pu|er|pe|ra** (pyü ėr′pər ə), *n.* a woman in childbirth, or in the period immediately following parturition. [< Latin *puerpera* woman in childbirth < *puer* child, boy + *parere* to bear children]

**pu|er|per|al** (pyü ėr′pər əl), *adj.* of or having to do with childbirth: *puerperal pain.* [< New Latin *puerperalis* < Latin *puerpera;* see etym. under **puerpera**] — **pu|er′per|al|ly**, *adv.*

**puerperal fever**, = childbed fever.

**pu|er|pe|ri|um** (pyü′ər pir′ē əm), *n.* the state of a woman at and immediately following childbirth. [< Latin *puerperium* childbirth, childbed < *puerpera;* see etym. under **puerpera**]

**Puer|to Ri|can** (pwer′tə rē′kən), *adj., n.* — ***adj.*** of or having to do with Puerto Rico or its inhabitants. — ***n.*** a native or inhabitant of Puerto Rico.

**Puerto Rican cherry**, = acerola.

**puff** (puf), *v., n., adj.* — ***v.i.*** **1** to blow with short, quick blasts: *The bellows puffed on the fire.* **2** to breathe quick and hard: *She puffed as she climbed the stairs.* **3** to give out puffs; move with puffs: *The engine puffed out of the station.* **4** to move or come in puffs: *Smoke puffed out of the chimney.* **5** to smoke: *to puff away at a pipe.* **6** to become swollen or distended; swell: *A stung lip puffs up.*
— ***v.t.*** **1** to blow (air, vapor, or the like) in short, quick blasts; drive by puffing. **2** to put out with a puff of breath. **3** to smoke (a cigarette, pipe, or cigar): *The old man sat puffing his pipe contentedly.* **4a** to swell with air: *to puff out one's cheeks.* **b** *Figurative.* to swell with pride or conceit: *Victory had not puffed him up* (*Daniel Defoe*). **5** to arrange in soft, round masses; arrange softly and loosely: *to puff the hair.* **6** *Figurative.* to praise in exaggerated language: *They puffed him to the skies.*
— ***n.*** **1** a short, quick blast: *A puff of wind blew my hat off.* **2** a small quantity (of air, smoke, or other vapor) blown out in a short, quick blast: *a puff of smoke. The puffs depend on the presence of vapor in the atmosphere before the passage of the aircraft* (G. N. Lance). **3** a quick, hard breath. **4** the act or process of swelling: *With a huge puff the balloon was blown up and then suddenly burst.* **SYN**: distension. **5** a slightly swollen part; swelling. **6** a soft, round mass: *She wore her hair in three puffs.* **7** a small pad for putting powder on the skin: *She took the puff out of her compact and began to powder her nose.* **8** a light pastry filled with whipped cream, jam, or the like: *a cream puff.* **9** *Figurative.* extravagant praise: *Writing puffs for a fan magazine is a useful spur to the editorial imagination* (Newsweek). **SYN**: flattery. **10** a quilted bed coverlet filled with cotton, wool, down, or similar material. **11** a portion of material gathered and held down at the edges but left full in the middle, as in the sleeve of a dress. **12** *Dialect.* a puffball.
— ***adj.*** inflated with praise or commendation: *Does anybody claim that ... press junkets, and puff blurbs are confined to the securities business?* (Harper's).
[Middle English *puffen*, Old English *pyffan;* perhaps (originally) imitative. Compare Middle Dutch *puffen.*]

***puff adder**, **1** a large and very poisonous African snake that puffs loudly the air from its lungs when excited. **2** a harmless North American snake that puffs out its body; hognose snake: *Puff adders, if irritated, will roll over belly-side up, with tongue comically protuding and play dead* (Science News Letter).

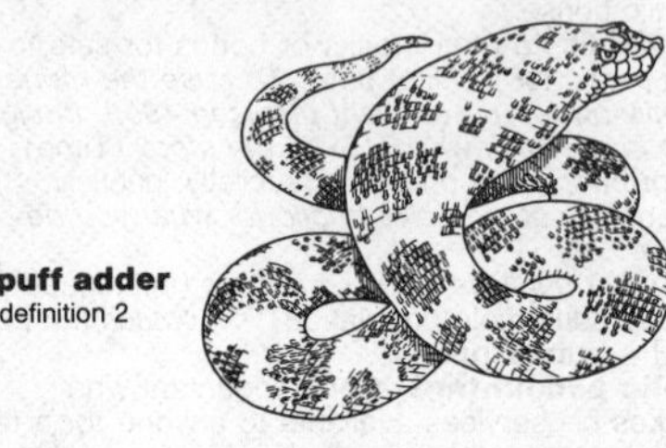

***puff adder**
definition 2

***puffball**

***puff|ball** (puf′bôl′), *n.* any one of various kinds of ball-shaped fungi that look somewhat like a mushroom and give off a dark cloud of tiny spores if suddenly broken when mature; devil's snuffbox. Immature puffballs are good to eat. *The young puffball is firm and white throughout but ... the tissues darken* (Fred W. Emerson).

**puff|bird** (puf′bėrd′), *n.* any one of a group of usually plain-colored, tropical American birds, so called from their habit of puffing out their feathers.

**puffed-up** (puft′up′), *adj.* **1** inflated with or as if with air. **2** swollen; distended: *Influenza left her with eyes too puffed-up to read.* **3** *Figurative.* overweening; conceited; pretentious.

**puff|er** (puf′ər), *n.* **1** a person or thing that puffs, such as a steam locomotive or steamboat: ... *there were literally hundreds of little fishing smacks and small puffers* (Lord Louis Mountbatten). **2** any one of various fishes capable of inflating the body by swallowing water or air, such as a blowfish, globefish, toadfish, or swellfish.

**puff|er|y** (puf′ər ē), *n., pl.* **-er|ies. 1** exaggerated praise: *publicity puffery.* **2** a puff in a dress or other garment.

**puff|i|ly** (puf′ə lē), *adv.* in a puffy manner.

**puf|fin** (puf′ən), *n.* a sea bird of arctic regions that has a thick body, a large head, a high narrow, furrowed bill of several colors, and vermilion feet; sea parrot. There are several kinds. [Middle English *poffin;* origin uncertain]

**puff|i|ness** (puf′ē nis), *n.* puffy condition or quality.

**puff|ing adder** (puf′ing), a small, harmless snake; hognose snake.

**puff paste**, a very light, flaky, rich dough for making pies, tarts, napoleons, and the like.

**puff|y** (puf′ē), *adj.,* **puff|i|er, puff|i|est. 1** puffed out; swollen: *Her eyes are puffy from crying.* **2** *Figurative.* puffed-up; vain: *His puffy airs were annoying to all around him.* **SYN**: conceited. **3** coming in puffs: *a puffy wind.* **4** fat; corpulent: *a very stout, puffy man* (Thackeray).

**pug**[1] (pug), *n.* **1** a small, heavy-bodied dog with a curly tail and a short, upturned nose on a wide, wrinkled face. Pugs are tan in color, with a short, smooth coat. **2** = pug nose. **3** = fox. [origin uncertain]

**pug**[2] (pug), *v.,* **pugged, pug|ging,** *n.* — ***v.t.*** **1** to mix (clay or loam) with water, as in brickmaking. **2** to stop or fill in with clay or the like. **3** to pack or cover with mortar to deaden sound.
— ***n.*** pugged clay.

[origin uncertain; perhaps imitative of the sound of the pounding of clay]

**pug³** (pug), *n. Slang.* a boxer. [short for *pugilist*]

**pug⁴** (pug), *n., v.,* **pugged, pug|ging.** *Anglo-Indian.* —*n.* the footprint (of an animal).
—*v.t.* to track (game) by footprints.
[< Hindi *pag* footprint]

**pug|dog** (pug′dôg′, -dog′), *n.* = pug¹ (def. 1).

**pug|ga|ree** or **pug|a|ree** (pug′ə rē), *n.* = puggree.

**pug|gree** (pug′rē), *n.* **1** a light turban worn in India. **2** a scarf wound around a hat or helmet and falling down behind, serving as protection against the sun. [< Hindustani *pagrī* turban]

**pug|gry** (pug′rē), *n., pl.* **-gries.** = puggree.

**pugh** (pü, pu̇), *interj.* an exclamation of contempt or disgust. [variant of *pooh*]

**pu|gil|ism** (pyü′jə liz əm), *n.* the art or sport of fighting with the fists; boxing. [< Latin *pugil, -ilis* boxer, related to *pūgnus* fist, and *pūgna* a fight]

**pu|gil|ist** (pyü′jə list), *n.* a person who fights with the fists; boxer.

**pu|gil|is|tic** (pyü′jə lis′tik), *adj.* of or having to do with boxing or boxers. —**pu′gil|is′ti|cal|ly,** *adv.*

**pug|mark** (pug′märk′), *n.* the footprint of an animal: *the pugmarks of a tiger.* [< *pug⁴* + *mark¹*]

**pug mill,** a mill which grinds and works clays and similar substances to make them plastic for use in brick or pottery, and in dressing ore.

**pug|na|cious** (pug nā′shəs), *adj.* having the habit of fighting; fond of fighting; quarrelsome: *a young cuckoo ... very fierce and pugnacious* (Gilbert White). **SYN:** combative. [< Latin *pugnāx, -ācis* (with English *-ous*) < *pugnāre* to fight] —**pug|na′cious|ly,** *adv.* —**pug|na′cious|ness,** *n.*

**pug|nac|i|ty** (pug nas′ə tē), *n.* a fondness for fighting; quarrelsomeness: *One must make some allowance for the critic's pugnacity and desire to shock* (Atlantic). **SYN:** belligerency.

**pug nose,** a short, turned-up nose.

**pug-nosed** (pug′nōzd′), *adj.* having a pug nose. **SYN:** snub-nosed.

**pug|ree** (pug′rē), *n.* = puggree.

**puir** (pʏr), *adj., n. Scottish.* poor.

**puis|ne** (pyü′nē), *adj., n.* —*adj. Law.* **1** inferior in rank; younger; junior: *The Lord Chief Justice can take direct responsibility rather than accept it on behalf of a puisne judge* (Manchester Guardian). **2** later: *a puisne mortgage.*
—*n.* **1** *Law.* a junior judge. **2** *Obsolete.* a junior. [early variant of *puny* < Old French *puisne*]

**pu|is|sance** (pyü′ə səns; pyü is′əns, pwis′-), *n.* power; might; strength; force: *to prove his puissance in battle brave* (Edmund Spenser).

**pu|is|sant** (pyü′ə sənt; pyü is′ənt, pwis′-), *adj.* having great power or strength; powerful; mighty; strong: *The star attraction was ... Rajpramukh of Rajasthan, descendant of the sun gods and a most puissant poloist* (Time). *I see in my mind a noble and puissant nation rousing herself like a strong man after sleep* (Milton). **SYN:** vigorous, forceful. [< Old French *puissant* being powerful < Vulgar Latin *possēns, -entis,* for Latin *potēns, -entis;* see etym. under **potent**] —**pu′is|sant|ly,** *adv.* —**pu′is|sant|ness,** *n.*

**pu|ja** (pü′jä), *n.* **1** any Hindu religious ceremony or rite. **2** rites performed in Hindu worship of idols. [< Sanskrit *pūjā*]

**puke** (pyük), *n., v.i., v.t.,* **puked, puk|ing.** *Informal.* vomit: *... the infant, Mewling and puking in the nurse's arms* (Shakespeare). [origin uncertain]
▶ **Puke** was accepted in standard English from the time of Shakespeare, until the middle of the 1800's, but is now generally avoided in polite speech or writing.

**Pukh|tan** (puʜ′tən), *n.* = Pathan.

**puk|ka** (puk′ə), *adj.* = pucka.

**pukka sahib,** *Anglo-Indian.* a good man; real gentleman: *His father was a pukka sahib in His Majesty's civil service* (Time).

**puk|ras** (puk′rəs), *n.* = pucras.

**pul** (pül), *n., pl.* **puls, pu|li** (pü′lē). a copper coin of Afghanistan, equal to 1/100 of an afghani. [< Persian *pūl*]

**pu|la** (pü′lä), *n., pl.* **-las.** a unit of money of Botswana, introduced in 1976: *The "pula"—a traditional ceremonial greeting meaning "rain" —will start at parity with the rand* (Manchester Guardian Weekly). [< Setswana *pula*]

**pul|chri|tude** (pul′krə tüd, -tyüd), *n.* physical beauty: *feminine pulchritude.* **SYN:** loveliness. [< Latin *pulchritūdō, -dinis* < *pulcher* beautiful]

**pul|chri|tu|di|nous** (pul′krə tü′də nəs, -tyü′-), *adj.* physically beautiful (often used as a humorous affectation).

**pule** (pyül), *v.i.,* **puled, pul|ing.** to cry in a thin voice, as a sick child does; whimper; whine. [perhaps imitative. Compare Old French *piauler.*]

**pul|er** (pyü′lər), *n.* a whiner; a sickly, complaining person.

**pu|li** (pü′lē), *n., pl.* **-lik** (-lēk), **-lis.** any medium-sized, long-haired sheep dog of a breed originally bred in Hungary and having a solid, usually gray or dull-black coat: *The Puli is frequently the Hungarian shepherd's only companion* (New Yorker). [< Hungarian *puli*]

**pul|ing** (pyü′ling), *adj.* whining; weakly querulous. —**pul′ing|ly,** *adv.*

**Pu|litz|er prize** (pyü′lit sər, pu̇l′it-), any one of various prizes given each year for distinguished work in American journalism, literature, drama, and music, established by Joseph Pulitzer and first awarded in 1917. Pulitzer prizes are awarded in such categories as the best play, novel, biography, history, book of poetry, editorial, news report, and cartoon. [< Joseph *Pulitzer,* 1847-1911, an American journalist]

**pulk** (pulk), *n.* a boatlike traveling sledge drawn by a single reindeer, used in Lapland. [< Finnish *pulkka*]

**pul|ka** (pul′kə), *n.* = pulk.

**pull** (pu̇l), *v., n.* —*v.t.* **1** to move (something) by grasping it and drawing it toward oneself: *Pull the door open.* **2** to move (something), usually with effort or force: *to pull a trigger, to pull a sled uphill.* **3** to take hold of and tug at (something): *to pull a rope. The boy pulled his sister's hair.* **4** to pick; pluck: *to pull flowers.* **5** to take hold of and draw out; extract: *to pull weeds. Father used the claw of his hammer to pull nails. I could hardly feel it when the dentist pulled my bad tooth.* **6** to tear, rend, or separate into parts by pulling; rip: *to pull a book into shreds. The baby pulled the top to pieces.* (*Figurative.*) *to pull an argument to pieces.* **7** to stretch too far; strain: *The football player pulled a muscle in his leg.* **8** *U.S.* to draw out (a gun or knife) in a threatening manner. **9a** to be provided or rowed with: *The boat pulls eight oars.* **b** to operate (an oar) in rowing or (a paddle) in canoeing. **c** to move (a boat) by rowing or (a canoe) by paddling. **10** *Informal.* to carry through; perform: *Don't pull any tricks on me.* **11** *Golf.* to hit (a ball) so that it curves to the left; hook: *He pulled his tee shot slightly and the ball seemed to be bound for a bunker* (News Chronicle). **12** *Baseball.* to hit (a ball) along or near the foul line on the same side of the plate as that on which the batter stands: *to pull the ball into right field.* **13** *Cricket.* to hit (a ball pitched on the wicket or on the off side) to the on side. **14** *Figurative.* to hold back, especially to keep from winning: *to pull a horse in a race, to pull punches in a fight.* **15** to take (an impression, proof, or copy) by printing: *Proofs of editorial and advertising matter are pulled on glossy enamel paper* (Time).
—*v.i.* **1** to tug: *He pulled at his tie nervously. The dog pulled at my sleeve to get my attention.* **2** to move, usually with effort or force: *I pulled ahead of the others in the race.* **3** to row or paddle: *Pull for the shore as fast as you can!* **4** to suck: *to pull on a cigar.* **5** to drink, especially heartily or thirstily.
—*n.* **1** the act of pulling; tug: *The boy gave a pull at the rope.* **2** an effort of pulling; difficult climb, journey, or other effort: *It was a hard pull to get up the hill.* **3** a handle, rope, ring, or other thing to pull by: *a bellpull, a curtain pull.* **4** a force that attracts: *magnetic pull.* **5** a drink. **6** a suck: *a long pull at a cigar.* **7** the act or fact of pulling the ball in golf, baseball, or cricket. **8** *Informal, Figurative.* influence; advantage: *to use political pull to get a job. They used their ... "pull" in Italian banking to favour German enterprises* (H. G. Wells). **9** an impression, proof, or copy taken by printing.

**pull apart, a** to separate into pieces by pulling: *The children pulled the flowers apart.* **b** *Figurative.* to be severely critical of: *to pull apart a term paper.*

**pull down, a** to demolish; destroy: *Desirous of pulling the house down and building a new one on its site* (Law Reports). **b** to lower: *He should pull down the blind* (Dickens). **c** to depress, as in health or spirits: *I did pull down myself, fasting* (Philip Sidney). **d** to earn (money or wages): *For all the money they demand and pull down, Brazilian dockers get precious little work done* (Time). **e** to depose or dethrone (a ruler); overthrow (a government) by force: *In such times a sovereign like Louis the Fifteenth ... would have been pulled down before his misgovernment had lasted for a month* (Macaulay). **f** to seize; overcome: *You weren't within half a field of the fair unknown when they pulled the fox down* (Hawley Smart).

**pull for,** *Informal.* **a** to give help to: *to pull for the underdog.* **b** to support enthusiastically: *The final, official word on the international grand prizes had gone out, ... and nothing could dampen the enthusiasm of those who had been pulling for Rauschenberg from the start* (Harper's).

**pull in, a** *Slang.* to arrest (a person): *to pull in every known gambler in town.* **b** to stop; check: *I must pull in, or my letter will never end* (Thomas Twining). **c** to arrive: *I pulled in this morning.*

**pull off, a** *Informal.* to do successfully; succeed in: *It is an exceptionally difficult trick, but they see no reason why with practice they should not pull it off* (Manchester Guardian). **b** to remove by or as if by stripping: *to pull off the bark of a sycamore branch. I could bash his head against the corner of the dock before the RCMP guard could pull me off* (Maclean's).

**pull oneself together,** to get control of one's mind or energies: *She pulled herself together and wrote a letter excusing her thoughtlessness.*

**pull out, a** to leave; move away: *The train pulled out of the station.* **b** *Figurative: He was pulling out of the Pike County project while there was still plenty of work* (Harper's).

**pull over,** to bring a vehicle to the side of the road or street and stop: *The policeman motioned the speeding driver to pull over. I considered that I had not time to pull over to my near side* (Morning Post).

**pull through,** to get through a difficult or dangerous situation, especially by recovering one's health: *They think she'll pull through—and the boy too* (Graham Greene).

**pull together,** to work in harmony; get on together: *Let ... danger appear ... then they all pulled together* (Frederick Marryat). *Where tenants for life and trustees did not pull together, sales could not in such cases be effected* (Law Times).

**pull up, a** to tear up; uproot: *The weeds themselves must be pulled up by the root* (Adam Dickson). **b** to bring or come to a halt; stop: *A car pulled up beside me.* **c** to check oneself in a course of action: *But it is a dangerous slope we are on, and unless we pull up now it may be hard to stop at the point we want* (Manchester Guardian). **d** *Figurative.* (1) to reprimand; rebuke: [*He*] *avowed his unalterable determination to "pull up" the cabman in the morning* (Dickens). (2) to jolt; startle: *The reader is pulled up more smartly when the general* [*MacArthur*] *records how he listened, then aged 70, to the cautious advice of a military conference on the Korean War* (London Times). **e** to move ahead, as in a race: *At forty yards Harding invariably led by a yard or more, but from this onward Cary pulled up, passing him at about sixty yards* (Outing).
[Old English *pullian*] —**pull′er,** *n.*
—*Syn. v.t.* **1, 2,** *v.i.* **1 Pull, tug, jerk** mean to draw toward oneself. **Pull** is the general word meaning to draw (or try to draw) toward or after oneself or in a specified or implied direction: *Pull the curtains across.* **Tug** means to pull hard or long, but does not always mean causing the thing or person to move: *The dog tugged at the tablecloth.* **Jerk** means to pull, push, or twist quickly and suddenly: *She jerked her hand away. He jerked his hat off.*

**pull|back** (pu̇l′bak′), *n.* **1** a withdrawal: *Washington hopes that the Kremlin may conceive it to be in its own interest to make further pullbacks* (Atlantic). **2** = retrenchment.

**pull date,** the date stamped on packaged food to show the limit of its shelf life. See also **open dating.**

**pull|down** (pu̇l′doun′), *adj.* that can be pulled down or lowered: *pulldown table legs.*

**pulled wool** (pu̇ld), wool removed from the pelts of slaughtered sheep.

**pul|let** (pu̇l′it), *n.* a young hen, usually less than a year old. [< Old French *poulet* young fowl, or *poulette* young hen (diminutives) < *poule* hen; see etym. under **poultry**]

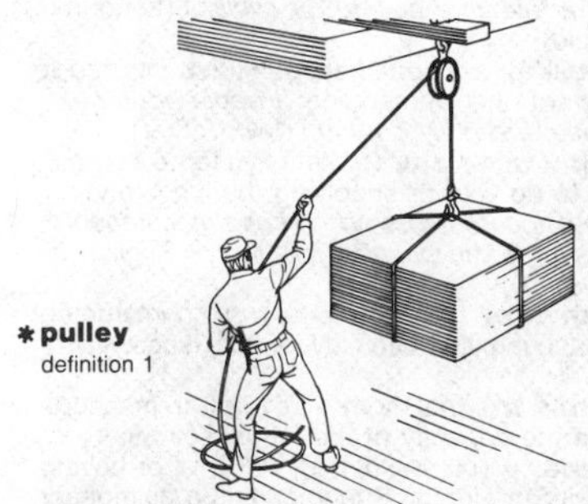

**✱pulley** definition 1

**✱pul|ley** (pu̇l′ē), *n., pl.* **-leys. 1** a wheel with a grooved rim in which a rope can run and so

**Pronunciation Key:** hat, āge, cãre, fär; let, ēqual, tėrm; it, īce; hot, ōpen, ôrder; oil, out; cup, pu̇t, rüle; child; long; thin; ᴛʜen; zh, measure; ə represents **a** in about, **e** in taken, **i** in pencil, **o** in lemon, **u** in circus.

change the direction of the pull. It is a simple machine and is used to lift weights. *Our flag is raised to the top of a pole by a rope and two pulleys.* **2** a set of such wheels, used to increase the power applied. **3** a wheel used to transfer power by driving a belt or being driven by a belt that moves some other part of the machine. [< Old French *poulie,* perhaps < Medieval Latin *poleia,* ultimately < Greek *polídion* (diminutive) < *pólos* axle, pole < *poleîn* to revolve]

**pull hitter**, a batter who consistently pulls the ball: *With a left-handed pull hitter coming to bat, the outfield was shifted to right.*

**pull-in** (pu̇l′in′), *n. British.* a place to obtain refreshments by the roadside; drive-in.

**Pull|man** (pu̇l′mən), *n.,* or **Pullman car**, **1** a railroad car with berths or small rooms for passengers to sleep in; sleeping car. **2** a railroad car with especially comfortable seats; parlor car. [American English < George M. *Pullman,* 1831-1897, an American inventor, who designed it]

**pullman slipper**, a soft slipper that can be folded compactly for traveling.

**pull-on** (pu̇l′on′, -ôn′), *adj., n.* —*adj.* that is pulled on to be worn, as a garment having no fastenings: *a pull-on blouse or sweater.*
—*n.* a pull-on garment: *Dotted black and white pull-ons match stretch nylon gloves* (New Yorker).

**pul|lo|rum disease** (pə lôr′əm, -lōr′-), a disease of chickens, turkeys, ducks, and some other birds, often fatal to the very young, caused by a toxin-forming bacterium. It affects the reproductive organs of hens with the consequence that chicks may have a well-developed infection when they are hatched. [< Latin *pullōrum,* genitive plural of *pullus* young fowl]

**pull|out** (pu̇l′out′), *n., adj.* —*n.* **1** a withdrawal, especially of troops: *The pullout may start this week; Gaza troops will exit by the overland motor route* (Wall Street Journal). **2** the action of an aircraft in recovering from a dive and returning to level flight: *Engineers and metallurgists worked for years to develop these planes that will withstand the centrifugal forces of high-speed turns and pullouts* (James Phinney Baxter III).
—*adj.* that pulls out: *a pullout shelf of a desk.*

**pull|o|ver** (pu̇l′ō′vər), *n., adj.* —*n.* a garment such as a sweater or shirt put on by pulling it over the head: *We hunted out an ancient pullover of her husband's* (Punch).
—*adj.* put on by pulling it over the head: *a pullover dress.*

**pull strap**, a small strap attached to the top of a shoe or boot to assist in pulling it on easily.

**pull-toy** (pu̇l′toi′), *n.* a toy that is intended to be pulled about on wheels by a child.

**pul|lu|late** (pul′yə lāt), *v.i.,* **-lat|ed, -lat|ing. 1** (of a seed) to sprout; germinate. **2** (of a plant or animal) to breed; multiply. **3** *Figurative.* **a** to be developed or produced abundantly. **b** to teem; swarm: *Patrons were assailed with ... mashed potatoes pullulating with marshmallow whip* (New Yorker). [< Latin *pullulāre* (with English *-ate*[1]) to sprout out and spread < *pullulus* a sprout or bud (diminutive) < *pullus* the young of any animal; sprout of a plant]

**pul|lu|la|tion** (pul′yə lā′shən), *n.* **1** sprouting; germination; generation; production. **2** offspring; progeny. **3** *Botany.* generation or reproduction by budding.

**pull-up** (pu̇l′up′), *n.* **1** (in calisthenics) the action of chinning oneself: *I've done push-ups and pull-ups and sit-ups until my muscles twitched like a thoroughbred's flanks* (Maclean's). **2** *British.* a pull-in: *a favourite pull-up for cyclists* (London Chronicle).

**pull|y** (pu̇l′ē), *adj.,* **pull|i|er, pull|i|est.** inclined to pull toward one; demanding: *People often get too close, too pully on you* (New Yorker).

**pul|mo|cu|ta|ne|ous** (pul′mō kyü tā′nē əs), *adj.* having to do with or supplying the lungs and skin: *pulmocutaneous arteries, pulmocutaneous vessels.* [< Latin *pulmō, -ōnis* lung + English *cutaneous*]

**pul|mom|e|ter** (pul mom′ə tər), *n.* an instrument for measuring the capacity of the lungs; spirometer.

**pul|mom|e|try** (pul mom′ə trē), *n.* the measurement of the capacity of the lungs; spirometry.

**pul|mo|nar|y** (pul′mə ner′ē), *adj.* **1** of or having to do with the lungs. Pneumonia is a pulmonary disease. **2** having lungs or similar organs. **3** occurring in the lungs. [< Latin *pulmōnārius* < *pulmō, -ōnis* lung. Related to Greek *pleúmōn,* or *pneúmōn* lung.]

**pulmonary anthrax**, = woolsorters' disease.

**pulmonary artery**, the artery which carries venous blood directly from the right ventricle of the heart to the lungs. See diagram under **heart**.

**pulmonary circulation**, the part of the human circulatory system that carries the blood from the heart to the lungs and back again.

**pulmonary tuberculosis**, tuberculosis of the lungs.

**pulmonary valve**, a set of three crescent-shaped flaps at the opening of the pulmonary artery; the semilunar valves: *When the ventricle contracts ... the pulmonary valve is opened and blood flows through* (Scientific American).

**pulmonary vein**, one of the four veins which carry oxygenated blood directly from the lungs to the left auricle of the heart. See diagram under **heart**.

**pul|mo|nate** (pul′mə nāt, -nit), *adj., n.* —*adj.* **1** having lungs or lunglike organs. **2** of or belonging to a group of gastropod mollusks that have lunglike sacs and include most land snails and slugs, and some aquatic snails.
—*n.* a pulmonate gastropod.
[< Latin *pulmō, -ōnis* lung + English *-ate*[1]]

**pul|mon|ic** (pul mon′ik), *adj.* **1** = pulmonary. **2** = pneumonic. [< French *pulmonique* < Latin *pulmō, -ōnis* lung + French *-ique* -ic]

**Pul|mo|tor** (pu̇l′mō′tər, pul′-), *n. Trademark.* a mechanical apparatus for producing artificial respiration which pumps air or oxygen in and out of the lungs, used in cases of drowning, asphyxiation, and heart attack; respirator.

**pulp** (pulp), *n., v.* —*n.* **1** the soft, fleshy part of any fruit or vegetable: *the pulp of an orange.* **2** the soft residue left when most of the liquid is pressed out of vegetables, fruit, etc. **3** the soft pith in the interior of the stem of a plant. **4** the soft inner part of a tooth, containing blood vessels and nerves: *Even teeth in which the pulps had been removed or destroyed were found to have some traces of radiophosphorus* (Shirley Hughes). **5** any soft, wet mass. Paper is made from wood or rags ground to pulp and mixed with water. **6** *Slang.* a magazine printed on cheap paper, and usually containing matter of a cheap, sensational nature: *Commercial writers who once filled the pulps and slicks with short stories have arrived here* (Maclean's). **7** *Mining.* **a** pulverized ore mixed with water. **b** dry pulverized ore.
—*v.t.* **1** to reduce to pulp: *Extracts from the various organs must then be removed and pulped and ... injected into the patient* (Punch). **2** to remove the pulp from.
—*v.i.* to become pulpy.
[< Latin *pulpa*]

**pul|pal** (pul′pəl), *adj.* of or having to do with pulp.

**pulp|board** (pulp′bôrd′, -bōrd′), *n.* a kind of millboard made directly from paper pulp instead of sheets of paper.

**pulp|er** (pul′pər), *n.* a machine for reducing fruit, wood, or other such substance, to pulp.

**pulp|i|fi|ca|tion** (pul′pə fə kā′shən), *n.* the act or process of converting into pulp.

**pulp|i|fi|er** (pul′pə fī′ər), *n.* = pulper.

**pulp|i|fy** (pul′pə fī), *v.t.,* **-fied, -fy|ing.** to reduce to pulp.

**pulp|i|ness** (pul′pē nis), *n.* the quality or state of being pulpy; softness; flabbiness.

***pul|pit** (pu̇l′pit), *n.* **1** a platform or raised structure in a church from which the minister preaches: *This eloquent and ornate carving on a church pulpit was done by Indian hands* (Newsweek). **2 a** preachers or preachings: *the influence of the pulpit. The pulpit is against horse racing on Sunday.* **b** the Christian ministry. **3** *Archaic.* any stage or rostrum used for public speeches or debates. **4** a safety rail, usually of iron, lashed to the end of the bowsprit of a whaling vessel to insure the safety of the harpooner. [< Late Latin *pulpitum* < Latin, scaffold, platform]

***pulpit**
definitions 1, 4

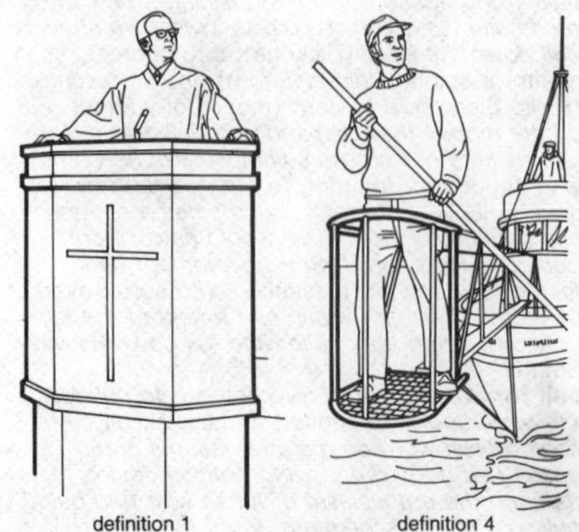

definition 1 definition 4

**pul|pit|eer** (pu̇l′pə tir′), *n.* a preacher by profession (used in an unfriendly way): *These words came from no Sunday pulpiteer, but from the assistant to the president* (Time). [< *pulpit* + *-eer*]

**pul|pit|er** (pu̇l′pə tər), *n.* = pulpiteer.

**pulp|less** (pulp′lis), *adj.* lacking pulp.

**pulp mill**, a mill to convert wood into pulp for making paper and other products.

**pul|pous** (pul′pəs), *adj.* = pulpy.

**pulp|wood** (pulp′wu̇d′), *n.* **1** wood reduced to pulp for making paper. **2** any soft wood, such as spruce, suitable for making paper.

**pulp|y** (pul′pē), *adj.,* **pulp|i|er, pulp|i|est.** of pulp; like pulp; fleshy; soft.

**pul|que** (pu̇l′kē; *Spanish* pül′kā), *n.* an alcoholic beverage made from the fermented juice of certain magueys. Pulque is much used in Mexico and Central America. [American English < Mexican Spanish *pulque,* apparently < a Nahuatl word]

**pul|sant** (pul′sənt), *adj.* pulsating; throbbing.

**pul|sar** (pul′sär), *n.* an astronomical source of powerful radio waves emitted in short, intense bursts or pulses at very precise intervals: *Pulsars have been found in all parts of the sky, but lie primarily in the Milky Way near the symmetry plane of the galaxy* (J. P. Ostriker). [< *pulse* + *-ar,* as in *quasar*]

**pul|sate** (pul′sāt), *v.i.,* **-sat|ed, -sat|ing. 1** to beat; throb; expand and contract rhythmically, as the heart or an artery does: *The patient's heart is pulsating rapidly.* (*Figurative.*) *What strains and strophes of unwritten verse pulsate through my soul* (Oliver Wendell Holmes). **2** to vibrate; quiver. [< Latin *pulsāre* (with English *-ate*[1]) (frequentative) < *pellere* to beat]

**pul|sa|tile** (pul′sə təl), *adj.* **1** pulsating; throbbing. **2** played by striking.

**pul|sa|til|la** (pul′sə til′ə), *n.* **1** any one of various perennial herbs of the crowfoot family with white or purplish flowers, certain kinds of which are used medicinally; pasqueflower. **2** an extract or preparation obtained from such a plant. [< New Latin *Pulsatilla* the genus name < Medieval Latin *pulsatilla* (diminutive) < Latin *pulsāta* driven about < *pulsāre* to pulsate (because the flower is easily driven about by the wind)]

**pul|sa|tion** (pul sā′shən), *n.* **1** the act of beating; throbbing; expanding and contracting: *This would suggest some slow pulsation taking place in the sun which gradually alters the strength of these solar streamers* (E. F. George). **2** a beat; throb. **3** the act of vibrating; quiver.

**pul|sa|tive** (pul′sə tiv), *adj.* pulsating. —**pul′sa-tive|ly**, *adv.*

**pul|sa|tor** (pul sā′tər), *n.* **1** a machine that pulsates, especially a kind of pump. **2** a device for separating diamonds from dirt. [< Latin *pulsātor, -ōris* a beater, knocker < *pulsāre* to pulsate]

**pul|sa|to|ry** (pul′sə tôr′ē, -tōr′-), *adj.* pulsating; throbbing.

**pulse**[1] (puls), *n., v.,* **pulsed, puls|ing.** —*n.* **1** the beating or a beat of the arteries caused by the changing flow of blood with each contraction of the heart. By feeling the pulse in the artery of the wrist, a person can count the number of times his heart beats each minute. *A wave of distention, the pulse, travels along the arteries* (Harbaugh and Goodrich). **2** any regular, measured beat: *the pulse in music, the pulse of an engine.* **3** *Figurative.* feeling; sentiment: *the pulse of the nation.* **4** *Electronics.* an electromagnetic wave, or a modulation of an electromagnetic wave, which lasts a short time: *In radar, for instance, the signals used are pulses, which rise and fall in amplitude over a short time* (John Pierce). [< Latin *pulsus, -ūs* < *pellere* to beat]
—*v.i.* **1** to beat; throb; vibrate: *My heart pulsed with excitement.* (*Figurative.*) *Theodore Dreiser could make a page pulse with life* (Newsweek). **2** *Electronics.* to emit or produce pulses.
**pulses**, each successive beat or throb of the arteries or heart: *This means that pulses, to be counted, must be analyzed by both detectors simultaneously* (Science).
[< Latin *pulsāre* (frequentative) < *pellere* to beat. See etym. of doublet **push**.] —**pulse′less**, *adj.* —**pulse′like′**, *adj.*

**pulse**[2] (puls), *n.* **1** the seeds of a group of plants, such as peas, beans, and lentils, used as food. **2** a plant that yields such seeds. [< Old French *pols,* and *pouls* < Latin *puls, pultis* porridge; see etym. under **poultice**]

**pulse|beat** (puls′bēt′), *n.* **1** a beat or pulsation of an artery: *The doctors noted irregular breathing movements and a possible heartbeat, although they could not detect a pulsebeat* (The Warren Report). **2** *Figurative.* a sign or suggestion of feeling or sentiment: *Instead of capturing the hypnotic quality of Marquand's even-tempered prose, the writer may find he has only reproduced Marquand's low emotional pulsebeat* (Time).

**pulse-code modulation** (puls′kōd′), a system of radio transmission in which successive electromagnetic waves of short duration are sampled periodically, quantized, and transmitted by code: *The result was the rapid development of pulse-*

*code modulation ... as a rival to amplitude modulation (AM) and frequency modulation (FM)* (Scientific American). *Abbr:* PCM (no periods).

**pulsed** (pulst), *adj.* that come in pulses; having pulsations: *The natural mode of communication with or between machines is by means of pulsed electrical signals* (John R. Pierce).

**pulse|jet** (puls′jet′), *n.*, or **pulsejet engine**, a type of jet engine into which the air necessary for the burning of the fuel is admitted by valves in spurts; resonant jet; aeroresonator: *This helicopter was powered with pulsejets, which is what the Nazi V-1 buzz bombs were* (Harper's).

**pulse-po|si|tion modulation** (puls′pə zish′ən), = pulse-time modulation.

**puls|er** (pul′sər), *n. Electronics.* an instrument that produces recurring high voltage pulses of short duration: *The voltage required ... is provided by an electronic pulser, which removes the voltage from the crystal in less than 10 nanoseconds* (New Scientist).

**puls|es** (pul′siz), *n.pl.* See under **pulse**[1].

**pulse-tak|er** (puls′tā′kər), *n. Informal.* a person who seeks to find out what views or sentiments are held and by what proportion of the people, or any particular segment of the people: *Farm pulse-takers now predict a similar outcome in votes late this year* (Wall Street Journal).

**pulse-tak|ing** (puls′tā′king), *n. Informal.* the process of conducting a survey to find out what views or sentiments are popular in respect to a subject.

**pulse-time modulation** (puls′tīm′), a system of radio transmission in which successive electromagnetic waves of short duration, timed to transmit the amplitude and pitch of the signal, are produced by modulation of the carrier. *Abbr:* PTM (no periods).

**pulse warmer**, a covering for the wrist to protect against cold; wristlet.

**pulse wave**, the wave of raised tension and arterial expansion which starts from the aorta with each ventricular systole and travels to the capillaries.

**pul|sim|e|ter** (pul sim′ə tər), *n.* an instrument for measuring and recording the strength or quickness of the pulse. [< Latin *pulsus* pulse, beat + English *-meter*]

**pul|sion** (pul′shən), *n.* the act of driving or pushing forward. [< Latin *pulsiō, -ōnis* < *pulsāre;* see etym. under **pulse**[1], verb]

**pul|som|e|ter** (pul som′ə tər), *n.* **1** a pump operated by steam but having no piston. **2** = pulsimeter. [< *pulse*[1] + *-meter*]

**pul|ta|ceous** (pul tā′shəs), *adj.* resembling pap; semifluid; pulpy. [< Latin *puls, pultis* pottage, mush + English *-aceous*]

**pu|lu** (pü′lü), *n.* a yellowish, silky, vegetable wool obtained from the base of the leafstalks of the Hawaiian tree ferns, formerly used for stuffing pillows and mattresses. [< Hawaiian *pulu* (literally) wet, soaked]

**pulv.**, powder (used in prescriptions). [< Latin *pulvis* dust]

**pul|ver|a|ble** (pul′vər ə bəl), *adj.* that can be reduced to dust or powder.

**pul|ver|ise** (pul′və rīz), *v.t., v.i.*, **-ised, -is|ing.** *Especially British.* pulverize.

**pul|ver|iz|a|ble** (pul′və rī′zə bəl), *adj.* = pulverable.

**pul|ver|ize** (pul′və rīz), *v.*, **-ized, -iz|ing.** —*v.t.* **1** to grind to powder or dust. **2** to break to pieces; demolish: *The hurricane pulverized the houses on the beach. (Figurative.) to pulverize a wall of prejudice, (Figurative.) to pulverize the hopes of the people.*
—*v.i.* to become dust: (*Figurative.*) *The stern old faiths have all pulverized* (Emerson).
[< Late Latin *pulverizāre* < Latin *pulvis, -eris* dust] —**pul′ver|i|za′tion**, *n.*

**pul|ver|iz|er** (pul′və rī′zər), *n.* **1** a person or thing that pulverizes. **2** a machine for breaking the soil, crushing stone, or grinding grain. **3** a bird that habitually rolls or wallows in the dust or takes sand baths.

**pul|ver|u|lence** (pul ver′yə ləns, -ver′ə-), *n.* dustiness; powder.

**pul|ver|u|lent** (pul ver′yə lənt, -ver′ə-), *adj.* **1** consisting of fine powder. **2** crumbling to dust: *pulverulent rock.* **3** covered with dust or powder. [< Latin *pulverulentus* full of dust < *pulvis, -eris* dust]

**pul|vil|lus** (pul vil′əs), *n., pl.* **-vil|li** (-vil′ī). a cushionlike pad or process on the foot of an insect, such as the fly, by which it can adhere to walls and ceilings. [< Latin *pulvillus* small pillow (diminutive) < *pulvīnus* cushion]

**pul|vi|nate** (pul′və nāt), *adj.* cushion-shaped; cushionlike. [< Latin *pulvīnātus* cushionlike < *pulvīnus* cushion, bulge]

**pul|vi|nat|ed** (pul′və nā′tid), *adj.* = pulvinate.

**pul|vi|nus** (pul vī′nəs), *n., pl.* **-ni** (-nī). any cushionlike swelling at the base of a leaf or leaflet at the point of junction with the axis. [< Latin *pulvīnus* cushion, bulge]

**pu|ma** (pyü′mə), *n., pl.* **-mas** or (*collectively*) **-ma.** **1** a large, tawny wildcat found in many parts of North and South America; cougar; mountain lion; panther. **2** its fur. [< Spanish *puma* < Quechua (Peru)]

**pum|ice** (pum′is), *n., v.*, **-iced, -ic|ing.** —*n.* a light, spongy natural glass thrown up from volcanoes, used for cleaning, smoothing, and polishing. Pumice can be used in both lump and powdered form. *Pumice, which comes from lava, has long been used for grinding and polishing, and for the building of roads* (Frank Press).
—*v.t.* to clean, smooth, or polish with pumice: *to pumice one's skin. The slab is then pumiced to reduce it to a level surface* (Ernest Spon).
[Middle English *pomice* < Old French *pomis,* learned borrowing from Late Latin *pōmex,* for Latin *pūmex, -icis.* See etym. of doublet **pounce**[2].]

**pu|mi|ceous** (pyü mish′əs), *adj.* consisting of or resembling pumice.

**pumice stone**, pumice in lump form.

**pum|mel** (pum′əl), *v.*, **-meled, -mel|ing** or (*especially British*) **-melled, -mel|ling,** *n.* —*v.t., v.i.* to strike or beat; beat with the fists; pommel.
—*n.* = pommel.
[variant of *pommel*]

**pum|me|lo** (pum′ə lō), *n., pl.* **-los.** = pomelo.

***pump**[1] (pump), *n., v.* —*n.* **1** a machine for forcing liquids, air, or gas into or out of things: *a water pump, an oil pump. The design of rocket pumps again demands careful choice of materials* (D. Hurden). **2** any medium or device used for raising atoms to an excited state. **3** the act of pumping. **4** *Informal.* the heart.
—*v.t.* **1** to move (liquids or gases) by a pump: *Pump water from the well into the pail.* **2** to remove water or other liquid or gas from by a pump: *to pump out a flooded cellar, to pump a well dry.* **3a** to provide (a laser) with the energy to raise atoms in its active medium, such as ruby or helium, to an excited state: *Many lasers ... are excited (or "pumped," as we say in the laboratory) by light. Others may be made to lase by radio waves, or by an electric current, or by chemical reactions* (National Geographic Magazine). **b** to raise (atoms) to an excited state by means of a light source or electron bombardment. **4** to move by a pump handle: (*Figurative.*) *He pumped my hand.* **5** *Figurative.* to draw, force, move up, pour forth, or eject, as if from a pump: *to pump air into one's lungs. Bill purchases by the Federal Reserve naturally have the opposite effect of pumping money into the banks* (Wall Street Journal). **6** *Figurative.* to shoot or fire in a stream: *to pump shells into the enemy lines.* **7** *Figurative.* to get information out of; try to get information out of: *Don't let them pump you.*
—*v.i.* **1** to work a pump. **2** *Figurative.* to work as a pump does: *to pump for words.* **3** *Figurative.* to move up and down like a pump handle.
**prime the pump, a** to stimulate business or the economy, especially by government spending: *The government can prime the pump by finding markets for equipment and by direct financial aid* (New Scientist). **b** to lead or encourage any activity or enterprise: *Meanwhile, he is priming the pump, with an eye on the political future which undoubtedly lies ahead of him* (Sunday Times).
**pump up,** to inflate (an automobile tire, a football, or other object that is filled with a fluid such as compressed air) by pumping air into it: *to pump up the tire on a bicycle.*
[Middle English *pompe,* perhaps < Germanic (compare earlier Dutch *pompe* a conduit)]

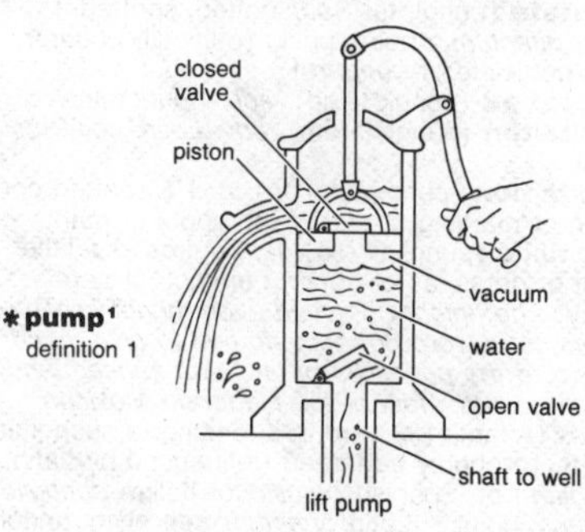


***pump**[1]
definition 1

***pump**[2]

***pump**[2] (pump), *n.* a low shoe with a thin sole and no fasteners: *black patent-leather dancing pumps.* [origin uncertain]

**pump|a|ble** (pum′pə bəl), *adj.* that can be pumped: *It is a major problem to maintain a low-viscosity, readily pumpable mud at a high specific gravity* (New Scientist).

**pump-ac|tion** (pump′ak′shən), *adj.* (of a shotgun or rifle) having a mechanism that ejects the used shell, reloads, and cocks the piece, by pushing a slide forward and back on the underside of the barrel.

**pump|age** (pum′pij), *n.* **1** the work done in pumping. **2** the quantity pumped: *Maximum pumpage rate of all stations totals 215,000,000 gallons daily* (Wall Street Journal).

**pumped storage** (pumpt), a system for generating electric power by using a man-made reservoir elevated over a body of water and pumping the water upwards by means of reversible turbines which then serve as generators as the water is released downwards.

**pump|er** (pum′pər), *n.* **1** a fire engine with pumps for pumping water through a hose. **2** a person or thing that pumps.

**pum|per|nick|el** (pum′pər nik′əl), *n.* a heavy, dark, slightly sour bread made from coarse, whole rye. [American English < German *Pumpernickel* (originally) bumpkin; perhaps (literally) lumbering Nicholas]

**pump gun**, a rifle or shotgun from which a used shell may be ejected and a fresh one placed in firing position from a magazine by pushing a slide on the underside of the barrel forward and back.

**pump house**, the place where a pump or pumps are installed and operate.

**pump|ing station** (pum′ping), an installation of pumps used to propel water, oil, or gas through a pipeline, irrigation canal, or electrical generator.

**pum|pi|on** (pum′pē ən), *n. Obsolete.* a pumpkin.

**pump|kin** (pump′kin, pung′-), *n.* **1** a large roundish, orange-yellow fruit of a vine, used for making pies, as a vegetable, as food for stock, and for jack-o'-lanterns. See picture under **gourd family.** **2** the coarse, trailing vine with broad, prickly leaves that it grows on. It belongs to the gourd family. **3** any one of certain large squashes that resemble the pumpkin in shape and color.
**some pumpkins** (or **punkins**), *U.S. Informal.* a person or thing of considerable consequence: *She is some punkins, that I wun't deny, For ain't she some related to you 'n' I?* (James Russell Lowell). *A man whose sneer can do all that is clearly some pumpkins* (New Yorker).
[alteration of earlier *pumpion* < earlier French *pompon,* for *pepon,* learned borrowing from Latin *pepō, -ōnis* melon, pumpkin < Greek *pépōn, -onos* (originally) cooked by the sun, ripe]

**pumpkin pine**, a variety of white pine noted for the fine grain of its wood: *... an antique dining table carved from pumpkin pine* (New York Times).

**pump|kin|seed** (pump′kin sēd′, pung′-), *n.* **1** the flattish, oval seed of a pumpkin. **2** a small freshwater sunfish of North America, mostly orange in color but with a bright red spot above the pectoral fin.

**pump-ox|y|gen|a|tor** (pump′ok′sə jə nā′tər), *n.* a mechanical device which oxygenates the blood and circulates it throughout the body, taking over the functions of the heart and lungs during major chest surgery; heart-lung machine.

**pump priming**, government expenditure, especially on public works, intended to stimulate business and thus to relieve depression and unemployment: *The Administration balked at the hysterical demands for unlimited pump priming and boondoggles* (Wall Street Journal). —**pump′-prim′ing**, *adj.*

**pump rod**, the piston rod of a pump.

**pump room**, **1** a room or building where a pump is worked. **2** a room or place at a spa or mineral spring where the water is dispensed, as for drinking.

**pump well**, **1** a well having a pump. **2** a compartment containing the pumps of a ship.

**pun**[1] (pun), *n., v.*, **punned, pun|ning.** —*n.* **1** the humorous use of a word where it can have different meanings, or of two or more words with the same or nearly the same sound but different meanings; play on words: *"We must all hang together, or we shall all hang separately" is a famous pun by Benjamin Franklin.* **2** a similar use of images, as in photography or art: *visual puns.*
—*v.i., v.t.* to make puns.
[origin uncertain. Compare Italian *puntiglio* fine point.]

---

**Pronunciation Key:** hat, āge, cãre, fär; let, ēqual, tėrm; it, īce; hot, ōpen, ôrder; oil, out; cup, pu̇t, rüle; child; long; thin; ᴛʜen; zh, measure; ə represents a in about, e in taken, i in pencil, o in lemon, u in circus.

**pun$^{2}$** (pun), *v.t.*, **punned**, **pun|ning**. *Especially British Dialect.* to pound; reduce to powder by beating; beat. [variant of *pound$^{2}$*]

**pu|na** (pü′nä), *n.* **1** a high, arid plateau, in the Peruvian Andes. **2** sickness due to high altitude. [< Spanish *puna* < Quechua (Peru)]

**punch$^{1}$** (punch), *v., n.* — ***v.t.*** **1** to hit with the fist: *They punched each other like boxers. You punch the ball too hard.* **SYN**: strike, poke, cuff. **2** *Informal.* to deliver with force or effectiveness: *... heroines and villains who punched home Verdi's galloping melodies with tremendous gusto* (New York Times). **3** to herd or drive (cattle): *Cowboys punch cows for a living.* — ***v.i.*** to give a punch or punches; hit; strike: *Boys punch; girls often slap.* **SYN**: strike, poke, cuff. [Middle English *punchen* goad (cattle); stab. Apparently related to **pounce$^{1}$**, **pounce$^{3}$**, **punch$^{2}$**, **puncheon$^{2}$**.]

— ***n.*** **1** a quick thrust or blow with the fist: *Patterson has a punch, exceptional poise for his age* (Newsweek). **2** *Informal.* vigorous force or effectiveness: *This story lacks punch. United States satellites, although smaller than the Russian sputniks, will pack as much scientific punch* (Science News Letter).

**beat to the punch**, *Informal.* to do anything sooner than (one's opponent): *There was no claim that Soviet scientists had beaten their American counterparts to the punch* (New York Times).

**pull (one's) punches**, *Informal.* to act or speak with fear, caution, or hesitation; be overly restrained: *The company is pulling its punches because of monopoly fears* (Wall Street Journal). [perhaps contraction of *puncheon$^{2}$*] — **punch′less**, *adj.*

**punch$^{2}$** (punch), *n., v.* — ***n.*** **1** a tool for making holes. **2** a tool or apparatus for piercing, perforating, or stamping materials, impressing a design, forcing nails beneath a surface, driving bolts out of holes, and the like.

— ***v.t.*** **1** to pierce, cut, stamp, force, or make with a punch: *to punch metal. The train conductor punched our tickets.* **SYN**: puncture, perforate. **2** to make (a hole) with a punch or any pointed instrument. **3** to cause to operate by pressing a key, lever, or other device: *to punch the time clock.*

— ***v.i.*** to register the time of one's arrival or departure by punching a time clock: *to punch in to work, to punch out at 5 P.M.*

[apparently contraction of *puncheon$^{2}$*. Apparently related to **punch$^{1}$**.]

**punch$^{3}$** (punch), *n.* a drink made of different liquids, often fruit juices, mixed together. [probably < Hindustani *pãnch* five < Sanskrit *pañca* (because of the number of ingredients in the drink)]

**Punch** (punch), *n.* a hook-nosed, humpbacked doll who quarrels violently with his wife Judy in the puppet show *Punch and Judy.*

**pleased as Punch**, very much pleased: *She was pleased as Punch with all her birthday presents.* [contraction of *Punchinello*]

**Punch-and-Ju|dy show** (punch′ ən jü′dē), a traditional English puppet show in which Punch quarrels violently with his wife Judy.

**punch|bag** (punch′bag′), *n.* **1** a stuffed or inflated bag punched for exercise or boxing practice; punching bag. **2** *Figurative.* a person or thing used to vent one's anger or annoyance.

**punch|ball** (punch′bôl′), *n.* a variation of baseball, usually played in city streets, in which a rubber ball is punched with the fist instead of being hit with a bat.

**punch|board** (punch′bôrd′, -bōrd′), *n.* a gambling device consisting of a board containing many holes in which are rolled slips of paper to be punched out by a player who pays for the privilege, a few of which reward him with a prize.

**punch bowl**, a large bowl for serving punch.

**punch card**, a card on which information is recorded by means of holes punched according to a code, for use in processing data by electronic computer: *Information ... is fed into the computer that turns out navigational data on punch cards* (Scientific American).

**punch-drunk** (punch′drungk′), *adj.* **1** (of a boxer) uncoordinated in movement or speech and disoriented as a result of brain concussion; afflicted with a condition resembling drunkenness to some extent: *I executed a nervous, almost dance-like step that characterized a punch-drunk boxer out of Hemingway* (New Yorker). **2** *Informal, Figurative.* dazed. — **punch′-drunk′en|ness**, *n.*

**punched card** (puncht), = punch card.

**punched tape**, paper tape punched for processing in various machines in the same fashion and for the same purposes as punch cards: *The punched tape may then be processed into the vital records and reports you need, either through your own electronic computer or at a computer service center* (Maclean's).

**pun|cheon$^{1}$** (pun′chən), *n.* **1** a large cask for liquor, varying in size from 70 to 120 gallons. **2** the amount that it holds, used as a unit of capacity. [< Old French *poinchon, poinçon,* and *ponson;* origin uncertain. The Old French forms are identical with those of *puncheon$^{2}$*, but there seems to be no connection between the words.]

**pun|cheon$^{2}$** (pun′chən), *n.* **1** a slab of timber or a piece of a split log, with a roughly smoothed face. **2** a short, upright piece of wood in the frame of a building. **3** *Obsolete.* an instrument for punching; punch. [< Old French *poinchon,* and *poinçon* < Vulgar Latin *pūnctiō, -ōnis* a punch, awl (in Latin, a pricking) < Latin *pungere* to pierce]

**punch|er** (pun′chər), *n.* **1** a person or thing that punches. **2** *Western U.S.* a cowpuncher: *Judge Henry gave me charge of him and some other punchers taking cattle* (Owen Wister). [American English < *punch$^{1}$* + *-er$^{1}$*]

**Pun|chi|nel|lo** (pun′chə nel′ō), *n.* **1** the principal character in a traditional Italian puppet show, the prototype of Punch. **2** = punchinello. [earlier *polichinello* < dialectal Italian *Pulcinella,* probably (originally) < diminutive form of *pulcino* chick < Latin *pullus* chick]

**pun|chi|nel|lo** (pun′chə nel′ō), *n., pl.* **-los** or **-loes**. **1** = clown. **2** any grotesque or absurd person or thing.

***punch|ing bag** (pun′ching), **1** a leather bag filled with air or stuffed, to be hung up and punched with the fists for exercise or boxing practice. **2** *Figurative.* a person or thing used to vent one's anger or annoyance.

***punching bag**

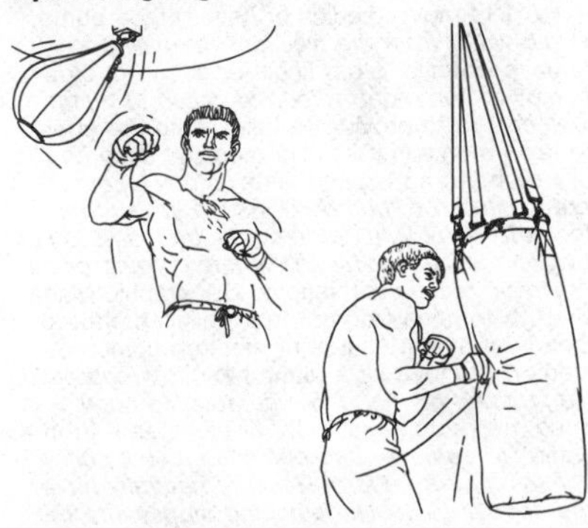

**punch line**, the line or sentence in a story, play, or drama which makes or enforces the point: *When you find five-year-old kids giving you the punch lines to classic jokes, it seems as though everybody's hep* (New Yorker).

**punch mark**, a mark punched on metal or a coin for identification or checking purposes.

**punch-out** (punch′out′), *n.* a section, as of paper or cardboard, having perforated edges, so that it may be easily pushed out; pushout: *Some coloring books have punch-outs of drawn figures, houses, and other objects.*

**punch press**, a press used to cut, indent, or shape metals.

**punch-up** (punch′up′), *n. British Informal.* a fight: *Enter the headmaster into a classroom punch-up* (London Times).

**punch|y** (pun′chē), *adj.*, **punch|i|er**, **punch|i|est**. *Informal.* **1** having lots of punch; forceful; terse; hard-hitting: *His ideas were ingenious, naïve, droll, and punchy* (New Yorker). **2** punch-drunk: *a punchy ex-fighter.*

**punc|tate** (pungk′tāt), *adj.* dotted; spotted. [< Latin *punctum* a point, prick; (originally) neuter past participle of *pungere*]

**punc|tat|ed** (pungk′tā tid), *adj.* = punctate.

**punc|ta|tim** (pungk tā′tim), *adv. Latin.* point for point.

**punc|ta|tion** (pungk tā′shən), *n.* **1** a spotted condition or marking. **2** one of the spots or marks.

**punc|til|i|o** (pungk til′ē ō), *n., pl.* **-i|os**. **1** a little point or detail, as of honor, conduct, or ceremony: *The knight observed every punctilio. The newcomers were not accustomed to give much regard to the punctilios of law, and consequently ran frequently afoul of the elaborate Mexican codes* (Atlantic). **2** care in attending to such little points. [probably patterned (influenced by Latin *punctum*) on Spanish *puntillo,* or Italian *puntiglio* < *punto* point < Latin *punctum;* see etym. under **punctate**]

**punc|til|i|ous** (pungk til′ē əs), *adj.* **1** very careful and exact: *A nurse should be punctilious in following the doctor's orders.* **SYN**: particular, meticulous. See syn. under **scrupulous**. **2** paying strict attention to details of conduct and ceremony: *From being reserved and punctilious, he is become easy and obliging* (Tobias Smollett). **SYN**: fastidious, ceremonious. — **punc|til′i|ous|ly**, *adv.* — **punc|til′i|ous|ness**, *n.*

**punc|tu|al** (pungk′chü əl), *adj.* **1** prompt; on time: *He is punctual to the minute.* **2** being a point; resembling a point. **3** *Mathematics.* of or having to do with a point: *punctual coordinates.* **4** *Archaic.* punctilious. [< Medieval Latin *punctualis* pertaining to a point < Latin *punctus, -ūs* point < *pungere* to pierce] — **punc′tu|al|ly**, *adv.* — **punc′tu|al|ness**, *n.*

**punc|tu|al|i|ty** (pungk′chü al′ə tē), *n.* the quality or condition of being on time; promptness: *Punctuality at meals was rigidly enforced at Gateshead Hall* (Charlotte Brontë).

**punc|tu|ate** (pungk′chü āt), *v.*, **-at|ed**, **-at|ing**.

— ***v.i.*** to use periods, commas, and other marks in writing or printing to help make the meaning clear.

— ***v.t.*** **1** to put punctuation marks in. **2** *Figurative.* to interrupt now and then: *His speech was punctuated with cheers. Three and a half years of continual internal strife punctuated at increasingly frequent intervals by the efforts of the party leaders to restore order* (London Times). **3** *Figurative.* to give point or emphasis to; emphasize: *He punctuated his remarks with gestures.* **SYN**: accentuate.

[< Medieval Latin *punctuare* (with English *-ate$^{1}$*) < Latin *punctus, -ūs* point < *pungere* to pierce]

**punc|tu|a|tion** (pungk′chü ā′shən), *n.* **1** the use of periods, commas, and other marks to help make the meaning of a sentence clear. Punctuation does for writing and printing what pauses and changes of voice do for speech. **2** = punctuation marks.

**punctuation marks**, marks used in writing or printing to help make the meaning clear. Periods, commas, question marks, semicolons, and colons are punctuation marks. *The punctuation marks, however, are not conceived of as representing features of speech* (Henry A. Gleason).

**punc|tu|a|tive** (pungk′chü ā′tiv), *adj.* serving to punctuate.

**punc|tu|a|tor** (pungk′chü ā′tər), *n.* a person who punctuates writing or printing.

**punc|tu|late** (pungk′chə lāt), *adj.* marked with small points, dots, or depressions. [< New Latin *punctulatus* < Latin *punctulum* (diminutive) < *punctum* point; see etym. under **punctate**]

**punc|tu|lat|ed** (pungk′chə lā′tid), *adj.* = punctulate.

**punc|tu|la|tion** (pungk′chə lā′shən), *n.* punctulate condition or marking.

**punc|tur|a|ble** (pungk′chər ə bəl), *adj.* that can be punctured.

**punc|ture** (pungk′chər), *n.,v.*, **-tured**, **-tur|ing**.

— ***n.*** **1** a hole made by something pointed: *a puncture in a tire.* **2** the act or process of puncturing: *Sewing is nothing more than puncture of a cloth by a needle drawing thread.* **3** *Zoology.* a minute, rounded pit or depression.

— ***v.t.*** **1** to make a hole in with something pointed: *If the nails fail, puncture their tires with a bullet* (George Bernard Shaw). **SYN**: pierce, prick, perforate. **2** *Figurative.* to reduce, spoil, or destroy as if by a puncture: *His ego was punctured by the criticism.* — ***v.i.*** to have or get a puncture.

[< Latin *punctūra* < *pungere* to prick, pierce]

**pun|dit** (pun′dit), *n.* **1** a very learned person; expert; authority: *Perhaps some clever pundit will be able to tell me what these words mean* (William H. Hudson). **2** a very learned Hindu. [< Hindi *paṇḍit* < Sanskrit *paṇḍita,* adjective, learned]

**pun|dit|i|cal** (pun dit′ə kəl), *adj.* of or having to do with a pundit or punditry: *A prodigious amount of punditical energy is used in trying to describe the difference between a Supreme Court liberal and a Supreme Court conservative* (Time).

**pun|dit|ry** (pun′də trē), *n.* **1** pundits collectively: *A resourceful thinker ... who is assuredly in the avant garde of socio-economic punditry* (Sunday Times). **2** the characteristics of a pundit; opinions or actions befitting a pundit: *When the President stuck by his policy of talking softly and backing the U.N., a new spate of punditry and radio-TV commentary bewailed his disappointing stand* (Time).

**pung** (pung), *n.* a sleigh with a boxlike body: *I have trouble in resisting the notion that I was somehow a son of pioneers, whose neighbors traveled in pungs* (Atlantic). [earlier *tom pung,* supposedly a variant of *toboggan*]

**pun|gen|cy** (pun′jən sē), *n.* pungent quality; sharpness (as of taste, smell, or feeling): *the pungency of pepper,* (*Figurative.*) *the pungency of wit.* (*Figurative.*) *In high-level conferences he expresses his views with pungency and vigor* (Harper's).

**pun|gent** (pun′jənt), *adj.* **1** sharply affecting the organs of taste and smell: *a pungent pickle, the pungent smell of burning leaves.* **SYN**: piquant, spicy. **2** *Figurative.* sharp; biting: *pungent criti-*

*cism.* SYN: caustic. 3 *Figurative.* stimulating to the mind; keen; lively: *a pungent wit.* SYN: poignant. 4 *Biology.* piercing; sharp-pointed. [< Latin *pungēns, -entis,* present participle of *pungere* to prick, pierce] — **pun′gent|ly**, *adv.* — **pun′gent-ness**, *n.*

**pung|ey** (pun′jē), *n., pl.* **-eys**. *U.S.* a kind of fast-sailing schooner used for oyster fishing and dredging in Chesapeake Bay. [origin unknown]

**pun|gi stick** or **stake** (pun′jē), a sharpened bamboo stick two or three feet high and often dipped in dung to infect the tip, stuck into the ground at an angle so as to puncture the foot of an enemy soldier. Also, **punji stick** or **stake**. [< Annamese *pungi*]

**pung|y** (pun′jē), *n., pl.* **pung|ies**. = pungey.

**Pu|nic** (pyü′nik), *adj., n.* — ***adj.*** **1** of or having to do with ancient Carthage or its inhabitants. **2** *Figurative.* treacherous; faithless.
— ***n.*** the Semitic language of ancient Carthage. [< Latin *Pūnicus* < *Poenus* a Carthaginian]

**Pu|ni|ca fi|des** (pyü′nə kə fī′dēz), *Latin.* Punic faith; perfidy or treachery.

**pu|ni|ly** (pyü′nə lē), *adv.* in a puny manner; weakly.

**pu|ni|ness** (pyü′nē nis), *n.* puny condition; weakness.

**pun|ish** (pun′ish), *v.t.* **1** to cause pain, loss, or discomfort to for some fault or offense: *Father sometimes punishes us when we do wrong. The government punishes criminals.* **2** to cause pain, loss, or discomfort for: *The law punishes crimes.* **3** *Informal.* to deal with severely, roughly, or greedily: *to punish a car by speeding. He punished my champagne* (Thackeray). — ***v.i.*** to subject to punishment. [< Old French *puniss-*, stem of *punir* < Latin *pūnīre*, related to *poena* a penalty < Greek *poinē* penalty, satisfaction] — **pun′-ish|er**, *n.*

**pun|ish|a|bil|i|ty** (pun′i shə bil′ə tē), *n.* the quality of being punishable; liability to punishment.

**pun|ish|a|ble** (pun′i shə bəl), *adj.* **1** liable to punishment: *a punishable criminal.* **2** deserving punishment: *One critic requested that the reading of American Wild West stories be made a punishable offense* (Newsweek). — **pun′ish|a|ble|ness**, *n.*

**pun|ish|a|bly** (pun′i shə blē), *adv.* in a punishable manner.

**pun|ish|ing** (pun′ish ing), *adj.* difficult; taxing: *His ninth trip which began last week—a punishing 28,000-mile, ten-day pilgrimage taking him as far as Australia and Samoa—was the longest thus far* (Time). — **pun′ish|ing|ly**, *adv.*

**pun|ish|ment** (pun′ish mənt), *n.* **1** the action of punishing or fact of being punished: *Courts administer the punishment of crime.* **2** pain, suffering, or loss for a fault or offense; penalty: *Her punishment for stealing was a year in prison.* **3** *Informal.* severe or rough treatment: *This engine can withstand a great deal of punishment.*

**pu|ni|tive** (pyü′nə tiv), *adj.* **1** concerned with punishment: *punitive laws. Julius Caesar's first invasion of Britain was a punitive military expedition.* **2** seeking to punish; inflicting punishment: *The judge imposed a punitive sentence on the prisoner. He had no comment on whether possible punitive action against the Teamsters will be discussed* (Wall Street Journal). [< Medieval Latin *punitivus* < Latin *pūnīre* to punish] — **pu′ni|tive-ly**, *adv.* — **pu′ni|tive|ness**, *n.*

**punitive damages**, *Law.* damages awarded by the court in addition to other damages when the wrongdoer has purposely harmed the other person; exemplary damages: *Punitive damages in libel cases—damages assessed as fines against the libeler but paid to the libeled person—are taxed as regular income* (Time).

**pu|ni|to|ry** (pyü′nə tôr′ē, -tōr′-), *adj.* = punitive.

**Pun|ja|bi** (pun jä′bē), *n., adj.* — ***n.*** **1** a native or inhabitant of the Punjab; Panjabi: *They were afraid the Punjabis would vote for somebody else* (Atlantic). **2** Panjabi; a language spoken in the Punjab.
— ***adj.*** of the Punjab, its people, or their language: *Eight little Pakistani girls did a Punjabi folk dance* (Time).
[< Hindi *pañjābī* < *Pañjāb* the Punjab < *pānj-*, and *pānch* five (< Sanskrit *pañca*) + *āb* waters]

**pun|ji stick** or **stake** (pun′jē), = pungi stick.

**punk** (pungk), *n., adj.* — ***n.*** **1** a spongy preparation that burns very slowly, usually of a light-brown color and made from fungus. A stick of punk is used to light fireworks: *To celebrate Fourth of July we all got an allotment of firecrackers, a stick of punk and half a dozen sparklers* (Guy Endore). **2** decayed wood used in a dry state for tinder; touchwood. **3** *Slang.* **a** a young hoodlum. **b** a young, inexperienced person: *The alderman is a young punk without enough brains to come in out of the rain* (Toronto Flash). **4** *Obsolete.* anything worthless. [American English < Algonkian (Delaware) *ponk;* see etym. under **punkie**]
— ***adj.*** *Slang.* **1** poor or bad in quality: *a punk day, a punk argument.* **2** not well; miserable: *to feel punk.*
[American English, perhaps < *punk,* noun, in sense of "rotten"]

**pun|kah** or **pun|ka** (pung′kə), *n.* (in India and Indonesia) a fan, especially a large swinging fan hung from the ceiling and kept in motion by a servant or by machinery: *The courtroom was sombre ... High up ... the punkahs were swaying short to and fro* (Joseph Conrad). [< Hindi *pankhā* < *pankh* feather < Sanskrit *pakṣa* wing]

**punk|ie** or **punk|y**[1] (pung′kē), *n., pl.* **punk|ies**. any one of various midges of the northern United States, which bite severely; biting midge; no-see-um. [American English < Dutch (of New York, New Jersey) *ponki* < Algonkian (Delaware) *ponk* (literally) living ashes (because of the painful bites of the insects)]

**pun|kin** (pung′kin), *n. U.S. Informal.* = pumpkin. **some punkins**. See under **pumpkin**.

**punk rock**, rock music performed in an aggressive, rowdy style: *Punk rock ... was not so much a return to 1950's hoodlumism as a clearing away of "progressive" fussiness* (John Rookwell). [< *punk,* def. 3a]

**punk|y**[2] (pung′kē), *adj.,* **punk|i|er**, **punk|i|est**. **1** containing, or of the nature of, punk or touchwood; spongy: *Sometimes a flame once kindled ... might lie dormant and unseen, smoldering slowly away within the punky wood of some rotting windfall* (Maclean's). (*Figurative.*) *The words of the Charter are soft and punky* (New Yorker). **2** (of fire) smoldering; burning slowly without flame.

**pun|ner** (pun′ər), *n.* a person who makes puns; punster.

**pun|net** (pun′it), *n.* a small, round, shallow chip basket, used chiefly for fruits and vegetables: *the big strawberries on top of the punnet* (Economist). [origin uncertain]

**pun|ni|ly** (pun′ə lē), *adv.* in a punny manner; punningly: *He plans to mix his printed material with occasional recordings called, punnily enough, "plattertudes"* (Time).

**pun|ning|ly** (pun′ing lē), *adv.* in a punning manner; by punning: ... *the punningly titled "Peace de Resistance" cookbook* (London Times).

**pun|ny** (pun′ē), *adj.,* **-ni|er**, **-ni|est**. having or consisting of a pun or puns: *a punny slogan. Episodes don't fit together very well in this ... often punny and occasionally hilarious mistresspiece* (Maclean's).

**pun|ster** (pun′stər), *n.* a person fond of making puns. [< *pun*[1] + *-ster*]

**punt**[1] (punt), *v., n.* — ***v.t.*** to kick (a football) before it touches the ground after dropping it from the hands. — ***v.i.*** to kick a football in this way.
— ***n.*** a kick given to a football released from the hands but not allowed to drop to the ground: *Tailback Jim Sears raced a punt back 69 yards* (New York Times).
[origin uncertain]

**punt**[2] (punt), *n., v.* — ***n.*** a shallow, flat-bottomed boat having square ends, usually moved by pushing with a pole against the bottom of a pond, river, or stream.
— ***v.t.*** **1** to propel (a boat) by pushing with a pole against the bottom of a pond, river, or stream. **2** to carry in a punt. — ***v.i.*** to use a punt; travel by punt.
[Old English *punt* < Latin *pontō, -ōnis* punt, a kind of ship; also, a floating bridge, pontoon < *pōns, pontis* bridge]

**punt**[3] (punt), *v., n.* — ***v.i.*** **1** to bet against the banker in a card game, such as faro. **2** = gamble. — ***n.*** **1** a player betting against the banker; punter. **2** a point in certain card games.
[< French *ponter* < Spanish *puntar,* ultimately < Latin *punctum* a point (originally) neuter past participle of *pungere* to pierce, prick]

**punt|er**[1] (pun′tər), *n.* a person who punts a boat: *To watch the punter in his pride, you have to catch him in an aquatic traffic jam* (London Times). [< *punt*[2] + *-er*[1]]

**punt|er**[2] (pun′tər), *n.* a person who punts a football. [< *punt*[1] + *-er*[1]]

**punt|er**[3] (pun′tər), *n.* a person who punts at faro or other games. [< *punt*[3] + *-er*[1]]

**pun|to** (pun′tō), *n., pl.* **-tos**. *Obsolete.* a thrust or pass in fencing. [< Italian *punto* point < Latin *punctum;* see etym. under **punt**[3]]

**pun|ty** (pun′tē), *n., pl.* **-ties**. an iron or steel rod used in glassmaking for handling the hot glass. [< French *pontil,* or Italian *pontello* (diminutive) < *punto* point < Latin *punctum;* see etym. under **punctate**]

**pu|ny** (pyü′nē), *adj.,* **-ni|er**, **-ni|est**. **1** of less than usual size and strength; small and weak: *My uncle was a thin, puny little man* (Washington Irving). SYN: undeveloped, stunted, feeble. **2** not important; petty: *this bloodstained rubbish of the ancient world, these puny kings and tawdry emperors* (H. G. Wells). *Over eighty per cent of the voting population went to the polls—a figure that makes American election intensities look puny* (New Yorker). SYN: trivial, insignificant. **3** *Obsolete.* inferior in rank; younger. [< Middle French *puîné* < Old French *puisne* born later < *puis* afterwards (ultimately < Latin *postea*) + *ne* born < Latin *nāscī* be born]

**pup** (pup), *n., v.,* **pupped**, **pup|ping**. — ***n.*** **1** a young dog; puppy: *The pup was lonesome when we first brought it home from the dog kennel.* **2** a young fox, wolf, seal, coyote, beaver, or other animal: *The pups played with the mother wolf.* **3** *Figurative.* a silly, conceited young man: *Baker loathed going to this red-haired young pup for supplies* (Atlantic).
— ***v.i.*** to bring forth pups.
[short for *puppy*]

**pu|pa** (pyü′pə), *n., pl.* **-pae** (-pē), **-pas**. **1** the stage in the life of an insect between the larval and the winged adult stage: *Finally, the larva seems to have eaten its fill and goes into a quiescent stage called the pupa* (A. M. Winchester). See diagram under **metamorphosis**. **2** an insect in this stage. Most pupae are unable to move about, and many are enclosed in a tough case or cocoon. *A somewhat different rhythm is seen in the moulting of insects, the hatching of their eggs and emergence of pupae* (Cloudsley and Thompson). [< New Latin *pupa* < Latin *pūpa* girl, doll]

**pu|pal** (pyü′pəl), *adj.* of, having to do with, or in the form of a pupa: *They were ready to emerge from their pupal shucks* (New Scientist).

**pu|par|i|um** (pyü pãr′ē əm), *n., pl.* **-i|a** (-ē ə). the hard pupal case formed, especially by certain dipterous insects, from the outermost larval skin. [< New Latin *puparium* < *pupa* pupa + *-arium* -ary]

**pu|pate** (pyü′pāt), *v.i.,* **-pat|ed**, **-pat|ing**. to become a pupa: *There is an increase in number after the majority of larvae have pupated* (F. S. Bodenheimer). [< *pup*(a) + *-ate*[1]]

**pu|pa|tion** (pyü pā′shən), *n.* **1** the act of pupating: *Materials secreted by a gland-like mass associated with the brain of these insects have a controlling influence upon the process of pupation* (Harbaugh and Goodrich). **2** the state of being a pupa; pupal condition. **3** the time during which an insect is a pupa.

**pup|fish** (pup′fish′), *n., pl.* **-fish|es** or (collectively) **-fish**. any one of various small fishes of the western United States related to the killifish, that can tolerate a wide range of temperatures and salinities.

**pu|pi|form** (pyü′pə fôrm), *adj.* having the form of a pupa. [< *pupa* + *-form*]

**pu|pil**[1] (pyü′pəl), *n.* **1** a person who is learning in school or being taught by someone: *The music teacher takes private pupils.* SYN: scholar, learner. See syn. under **student**. **2** *Law.* a boy or girl under the care of a guardian. [Middle English *pupille* a minor ward < Old French *pupille* < Latin *pūpillus,* and *pūpilla* ward (diminutives) < *pūpus* boy, and *pūpa* girl]

**pu|pil**[2] (pyü′pəl), *n.* the opening in the center of the iris of the eye which looks like a black spot. It is circular in human beings and most vertebrates. The pupil, which is the only place where light can enter the eye, expands and contracts, thus controlling the amount of light that strikes the retina. *The diameter of the pupil is changed automatically by the expansion or contraction of the iris* (Shortley and Williams). See diagram under **eye**. [< Latin *pūpilla* (originally) little doll, (diminutive) < *pūpa* girl, doll]

**pu|pil|age** or **pu|pil|lage** (pyü′pə lij), *n.* the state or condition of being a pupil, scholar, or ward: *One learnt what was and was not cricket during the period of pupilage* (London Times).

**pu|pil|ar|i|ty** or **pu|pil|lar|i|ty** (pyü′pə lar′ə tē), *n.* *Law.* the period between birth and puberty. [< Middle French *pupillarité,* ultimately < Latin *pūpillāris* having to do with an orphan or minor]

**pu|pil|lar|y**[1] (pyü′pə ler′ē), *adj.* belonging to a pupil, scholar, or ward. [perhaps < Middle French *pupillaire,* learned borrowing from Latin *pūpillāris* < *pūpillus* pupil]

**pu|pil|lar|y**[2] (pyü′pə ler′ē), *adj.* of or having to do with the pupil of the eye. [< New Latin *pupilla* pupil (of the eye) + English *-ary*]

**pu|pil|lom|e|ter** (pyü′pə lom′ə tər), *n.* an instrument for measuring the size of the pupil of the eye. [< New Latin *pupilla* pupil (of the eye)]

**pu|pip|a|rous** (pyü pip′ər əs), *adj.* bringing forth young that are already pupae: *Many ticks are pupiparous.* [< New Latin *pupa* pupa + Latin

---

**Pronunciation Key:** hat, āge, cãre, fär; let, ēqual, tėrm; it, īce; hot, ōpen, ôrder; oil, out; cup, pu̇t, rüle; child; long; thin; ᴛʜen; zh, measure; ə represents **a** in about, **e** in taken, **i** in pencil, **o** in lemon, **u** in circus.

*parere* to bear offspring + English *-ous*]

**pup|pet** (pup′it), *n., adj.* —*n.* **1a** a figure made to look like a person or animal, and moved by wires, strings, rods, or the hands: *Come ... let us shut up the box and the puppets, for our play is played out* (Thackeray). **b** *Figurative.* a person or group whose actions, while seemingly independent, are really manipulated or controlled by another: *She had ... acted but as a puppet in the hands of others* (Maria Edgeworth). *Chancellor Adenauer ... held that a neutralized Germany would inevitably become a Soviet puppet* (New York Times). **2** a small doll: ... *the motherly airs of my little daughters when they are playing with their puppets* (Joseph Addison).
—*adj.* **1** of a puppet or puppets: *a puppet theater.* **2** *Figurative.* manipulated or controlled by another: *a puppet ruler, a puppet government, a puppet regime.*
[earlier *poppet* < Old French *poupette* < a diminutive form of Vulgar Latin *puppa,* for Latin *pūpa* girl, doll] —**pup′pet|like′,** *adj.*

**pup|pet|eer** (pup′ə tir′), *n., v.* —*n.* a person who manipulates puppets: *An adroit puppeteer has put his marionettes through their paces* (Saturday Review).
—*v.t.* to manipulate (puppets).

**pup|pet|mas|ter** (pup′it mas′tər, -mäs′-), *n.* a person in charge of the performance in a puppet show.

**pup|pet|ry** (pup′ə trē), *n., pl.* **-ries. 1** the action of puppets. **2** *Figurative.* artificial action like that of a puppet. **3** the art or craft of making puppets, putting on puppet shows, and the like. **4** puppets collectively.

**puppet show,** a play performed with puppets on a small stage.

**Pup|pis** (pup′is), *n. Astronomy.* a constellation now considered as separate but formerly held to be a part of the larger constellation Argo. [< Latin *puppis* poop, stern]

**pup|py** (pup′ē), *n., pl.* **-pies. 1** Also, **puppy dog.** a young dog, usually less than a year old: *We've always had a dog, and this puppy is the smallest one yet.* **2** a young fox, wolf, seal, coyote, beaver, or other animal. **3** *Figurative.* a silly, conceited young man: *"You are an insolent puppy" Sir George stated* (Arnold Bennett). [probably < Old French *poupee* doll, toy < Vulgar Latin *puppa;* see etym. under **puppet**] —**pup′py|like′,** *adj.*

**puppy fat,** fatness occurring in children and adolescents: *Puppy fat was a myth, she said, ... an excuse used by parents and doctors for overweight teen-agers* (London Times).

**pup|py|hood** (pup′ē hu̇d), *n.* the state or period of being a puppy.

**pup|py|ish** (pup′ē ish), *adj.* of the nature or character of a puppy; proper to a puppy: *What began as an undergraduate romp, with all the puppyish vitality and touching bravura of adolescence, has declined into schoolboy humor* (Sunday Times).

**pup|py|ism** (pup′ē iz əm), *n.* the character or conduct of a puppy.

**puppy love,** the clumsy, short-lived romantic affection that exists between adolescent boys and girls; calf love: *A pretty little red-head to whom he plighted his puppy love when he was a schoolboy* (Time).

**pup tent,** a small, low tent, usually for one or two persons: *One burly lot of Yugoslav Communists pitched their U.S. Army pup tents beside the road* (Time).

**pur** (pėr), *n., v.i., v.t.,* **purred, pur|ring.** = purr.

**pur.,** purchasing.

**Pu|ra|na** or **pu|ra|na** (pu̇ rä′nə), *n.* (in Sanskrit literature) one of a class of sacred writings, of relatively late date, composed almost entirely in the epic couplet, and consisting of partly legendary and partly speculative histories of the universe, together with the genealogy and deeds of gods and heroes. There are eighteen principal Puranas. [< Sanskrit *purāṇá* belonging to former times < *purā* formerly]

**pur|blind** (pėr′blīnd′), *adj.* **1** nearly blind: *The deep joy we take in the company of people with whom we have just recently fallen in love is undisguisable, even to a purblind waiter* (New Yorker). **2** *Figurative.* slow to discern or understand: *O purblind race of miserable men* (Tennyson). **SYN:** dull, obtuse. **3** *Obsolete.* totally blind. [Middle English (originally) *pur blind* pure, in earlier sense "entirely," blind] —**pur′blind′ly,** *adv.* —**pur′blind′ness,** *n.*

**pur|chas|a|bil|i|ty** (pėr′chə sə bil′ə tē), *n.* the quality of being purchasable.

**pur|chas|a|ble** (pėr′chə sə bəl), *adj.* **1** that can be bought. **2** *Figurative.* venal; corrupt.

**pur|chase** (pėr′chəs), *v.,* **-chased, -chas|ing,** *n.* —*v.t.* **1** to get by paying a price; buy: *We purchased a new car.* **2** *Figurative.* to get in return for something: *to purchase safety at the cost of happiness.* **3** *Law.* to acquire other than by inheritance. **4** to hoist, haul, or draw by the aid of some mechanical device. **5** *Obsolete.* to go after and get possession of.
—*n.* **1** the act of buying: *the purchase of a new car.* **SYN:** See syn. under **buy. 2** the thing bought: *That hat was a good purchase. Next year's economic push will have to come from a combination of bigger business investment and rising government purchases* (Newsweek). **3** a firm hold to help move something or to keep from slipping: *Wind the rope twice around the tree to get a better purchase.* **4** a device for obtaining such a hold. **5** the annual income, such as rent, from land. **6** *Law.* an acquiring of property other than by inheritance. **7** *Obsolete.* booty. **8** *Obsolete.* acquisition; gain.
[< Anglo-French *purchacer* to pursue < *pur-* forth (< Latin *prō-* pro-[1]) + *chacer,* Old French *chacier* to chase, pursue]

**pur|chase|a|ble** (pėr′chə sə bəl), *adj.* = purchasable.

**purchase journal,** (in accounting) a book of original entry for recording purchases.

**pur|chas|er** (pėr′chə sər), *n.* = buyer.

**purchase tax,** *British.* a tax on retail sales of consumer goods, except food, fuel, and books, differing from the American sales tax in that the rate for each class of goods is based inversely on its estimated necessity in daily life: *It is suggested that the Government should sweep away all direct taxes, including turnover and purchase tax* (Sunday Times).

**pur|chas|ing agent** (pėr′chə sing), a buyer for a company who evaluates competitive bids on services or products needed, awards contracts, and orders new products.

**purchasing power, 1** the ability to buy things, as measured by the amount of money one earns or has available: *For the workers who did not share in the new round of raises, the higher prices would mean a decrease in real purchasing power* (Time). **2** the value of a unit of currency, as measured by the amount of things one can buy with it in a given period in comparison with some earlier period: *With a drop in purchasing power of the dollar, the depreciation allowances ... fall far short of the current cost of the needed replacement items* (Wall Street Journal).

**pur|dah** (pėr′də), *n.* in India: **1** a curtain serving to screen women from the sight of men or strangers: *The purdah hung, Crimson and blue ... Across a portal carved in sandalwood* (Edwin Arnold). *In Peshawar is the university and a college for women, where there are mixed debates with a purdah curtain dividing the sexes* (London Times). **2** the condition or system of being kept hidden from men or strangers: *He met and talked with everybody of any importance except for a few Moslem sultanas in purdah* (Harper's). [< Hindustani *pardah* < Persian, veil, curtain]

**pur|do|ni|an** or **pur|do|ni|on** (pėr dō′nē ən), *n. British.* purdonium.

**pur|do|ni|um** (pėr dō′nē əm), *n. British.* a coal scuttle for indoor use. [< *Purdon,* name of the designer of the box]

**pure** (pyu̇r), *adj.,* **pur|er, pur|est,** *n.* —*adj.* **1** not mixed with anything else; genuine; unadulterated: *pure gold. If a material contains only one element or only one compound, the chemist calls the material pure.* **SYN:** unalloyed. **2** perfectly clean; spotless: *pure hands.* **SYN:** immaculate. **3** without defects; perfect; correct: *to speak pure French. One would imagine that the words already in the English dictionary were all pure* (Guy Endore). **SYN:** faultless. **4** nothing else than; mere; sheer: *pure accident. They won by pure luck. His method of stating ideas ... contains a large element of pure incantation* (Edmund Wilson). **SYN:** utter. **5** with no evil; without sin; chaste: *a pure mind.* **SYN:** virtuous. **6** concerned with theory rather than practical use; not applied; abstract: *pure mathematics. If one insists that there are two kinds of science, pure and applied, then there are two kinds of scientific research, pure and applied* (Thomas M. Rivers). **7** keeping the same qualities or characteristics from generation to generation; of unmixed descent: *a pure Indian family. I saw that he was not a pure Indian, for ... he wore a beard and moustache* (William H. Hudson). **8** *Genetics.* homozygous, and therefore breeding true for at least one hereditary character: *Research mice ... which have been kept very close to "pure" through 275 generations by means of brother-sister mating* (Newsweek). **9** *Phonetics.* (of a vowel) constant in sound; not diphthongal. **10a** *Logic.* (of a proposition or syllogism) not modal. **b** *Philosophy.* independent of sense or experience: *pure knowledge, pure intuition.*
—*n.* that which is pure.
**pure and simple,** nothing else but; plainly and simply: *China ... declared that the Kremlin leaders were "accomplices of the U.S. imperialists, pure and simple"* (New York Times).
[< Old French *pur* < Latin *pūrus*] —**pure′ness,** *n.*

**pure|blood** (pyu̇r′blud′), *adj.* = pure-blooded.

**pure-blood|ed** (pyu̇r′blud′id), *adj.* **1** descended through a long line of unmixed ethnic or racial stock: *In Central America, Guatemala is 50 per cent pure-blooded Indian, the remainder Spanish or mestizo* (Newsweek). **2** = purebred.

**pure|bred** (pyu̇r′bred′), *adj., n.* —*adj.* of pure breed or stock; having ancestors known to have all belonged to one breed: *purebred Holstein cows. Many new seed varieties are the result of painstaking crossing of two purebred plants to produce a hybrid* (Wall Street Journal).
—*n.* a purebred animal.

**pure culture,** *Bacteriology.* a culture containing only a single species of organism.

**pure democracy, 1** a form of democracy in which the laws of a community are made directly by the people of the community instead of through representatives, as in ancient Athens from time to time and to an extent in the New England town meeting. **2** a community in which such a form of democracy is practiced.

**pu|rée** (pyu̇ rā′, pyu̇r′ā), *n., v.,* **-réed, -ré|ing.** —*n.* **1** food boiled to a pulp and put through a sieve or blender. **2** a thick dessert, entree, or soup made with this.
—*v.t.* to make into a purée.
[< French *purée,* (originally) past participle of Old French *purer* to strain; suppurate < Late Latin *purāre* < Latin *pūs, pūris* pus]

**pure-heart|ed** (pyu̇r′här′tid), *adj.* free from evil or guilt; guileless; sincere: *He has written about it, and revealed the pure-hearted ache for a better life that lies behind it* (Sunday Times).
—**pure′-heart′ed|ness,** *n.*

**Pure Land, 1** the paradise that awaits the believers in Amida, the Buddha of Amidism. **2** a sect that practices Amidism, such as Jodo and Shin. **3** the form of Mahayana Buddhism practiced by such a sect; Amidism.

**pure line,** *Genetics.* a strain of plants or animals that breeds true for one or more characters, obtained by continued inbreeding and selection or by self-fertilization: *the increased vigor of "hybrid" offspring as compared to the parental "pure lines"* (Bulletin of Atomic Scientists).

**pure|ly** (pyu̇r′lē), *adv.* **1** in a pure manner. **2** exclusively; entirely. **3** merely. **4** innocently; chastely.

**pur|fle** (pėr′fəl), *v.,* **-fled, -fling,** *n.* —*v.t.* to finish with an ornamental border: *a robe purfled with embroidery, a violin purfled with inlaid work.*
—*n.* an ornamental border.
[< Old French *pourfiler* < *pour-* (< Latin *prō-,* or *per-*) + *fil* thread < Latin *fīlum*]

**pur|fling** (pėr′fling), *n.* ornamental bordering. [< *purfl*(e) + *-ing*[1]]

**pur|ga|tion** (pėr gā′shən), *n.* the act or process of purging; cleansing: *a thorough purgation of the mind* (Henry Hallam).

**pur|ga|tive** (pėr′gə tiv), *n., adj.* —*n.* a medicine that causes emptying of the bowels. Castor oil is a purgative.
—*adj.* purging; cleansing: (*Figurative.*) *The coarse or macabre joke, on the part of the early Western writers, had often a purgative function* (New Yorker).
[< Late Latin *pūrgātīvus* < Latin *pūrgāre;* see etym. under **purge**] —**pur′ga|tive|ly,** *adv.* —**pur′ga|tive|ness,** *n.*

**pur|ga|to|ri|al** (pėr′gə tôr′ē əl, -tōr′-), *adj.* **1** of, like, or having to do with purgatory: *to enter into the purgatorial state of matrimony* (W. H. Hudson). **2** *Figurative.* of a spiritually cleansing or purifying quality: *It has been a period of complete satisfaction, and it came at the tail end of a long purgatorial experience* (Atlantic).

**pur|ga|to|ri|an** (pėr′gə tôr′ē ən, -tōr′-), *adj.* = purgatorial.

**pur|ga|to|ry** (pėr′gə tôr′ē, -tōr′-), *n., pl.* **-ries,** *adj.* —*n.* **1** (in Roman Catholic belief) a temporary condition or place in which the souls of those who have died penitent are purified from sin by punishment. **2** *Figurative.* any condition or place of temporary suffering or punishment: *I shuddered at the thought of spending another night in such a purgatory* (W. H. Hudson). *She wondered how long this purgatory was to last* (Thomas Hardy).
—*adj.* = purgative.
[< Medieval Latin *purgatorium,* (originally) neuter adjective, purging < Latin *pūrgāre;* see etym. under **purge**]

**purge** (pėrj), *v.,* **purged, purg|ing,** *n.* —*v.t.* **1** to wash away all that is not clean from; make clean: (*Figurative.*) *King Arthur tried to purge his land of sin.* **2** to clear of any undesired thing or person: (*Figurative.*) *He insisted that the Senate must be purged of its corrupt members* (James A. Froude). **3** to empty (the bowels). **4** *Figurative.* to clear of defilement or imputed guilt.

— *v.i.* **1** to become clean. **2** to undergo or cause emptying of the bowels. [< Old French *purgier* < Latin *pūrgāre*, earlier *pūrigāre* to cleanse, purify < *pūrus* pure + *agere* to drive, make]
— *n.* **1** the act of purging. **2** a medicine that purges; purgative. **3** *Figurative.* the elimination of undesired persons from a nation or party: *His career was helped somewhat by his ruthless execution of party purges in the satellites* (Newsweek). [(noun, def. 3) loan translation < Russian *chistka* cleaning, political purge < *chistit'* to clean, purge]

**purge|a|ble** (pėr′jə bəl), *adj.* that can be purged.

**purg|ee** (pėr jē′), *n.* a person who is purged, as from a country or political party: *The six purgees bellowed their protests from the convention podium* (Time).

**purg|er** (pėr′jər), *n.* **1** a person or thing that purges or cleanses. **2** = cathartic.

**purg|ing flax** (pėr′jing), an Old-World species of flax, a decoction of which is used as a cathartic and diuretic.

**pu|ri|fi|ca|tion** (pyůr′ə fə kā′shən), *n.* **1** the act or process of purifying: *We need laws to help with the purification of our water.* **2** the condition of being purified.

**Pu|ri|fi|ca|tion** (pyůr′ə fə kā′shən), *n.* a Christian festival, observed on February 2, commemorating the purifying of the Virgin Mary after the birth of Christ.

**pu|ri|fi|ca|tor** (pyůr′ə fə kā′tər), *n. Ecclesiastical.* a cloth used at Communion, especially for wiping the chalice.

**pu|ri|fi|ca|to|ry** (pyů rif′ə kə tôr′ē, -tōr′-), *adj.* serving to purify.

**pu|ri|fied protein derivative** (pyůr′ə fīd), a dried tuberculin, obtained from the filtrates of cultures of tubercle bacilli. *Abbr:* PPD (no periods).

**pu|ri|fi|er** (pyůr′ə fī′ər), *n.* **1** a person or thing that purifies or cleans: *Some 99,000 gallons of drinkable water were produced and distributed by the Army's new mobile purifier* (Science). **2** = purificator.

**pu|ri|form** (pyůr′ə fôrm), *adj.* having the form of pus; puslike. [< Latin *pūs, pūris* pus + English *-form*]

**pu|ri|fy** (pyůr′ə fī), *v.*, **-fied, -fy|ing.** — *v.t.* **1** to make pure: *Filters are used to purify water.* **2** to free from whatever is evil: *to purify the heart.* **3** to make ceremonially clean: *And the Jews' passover was nigh at hand: and many went out of the country up to Jerusalem before the passover, to purify themselves* (John 11:55). **4** to free of objectionable characteristics: *to purify a language.* **5** to clear or purge (of or from).
— *v.i.* to become pure. [< Old French *purifier* < Latin *pūrificāre* < *pūrus* pure + *facere* to make]

**Pu|rim** (pür′im, pyůr′-; *Hebrew* pü rēm′), *n.* a Jewish religious holiday, celebrated each year in February or March, commemorating Esther's saving of the Jews from being massacred by Haman (in the Bible, Esther 9:20-32). [< Hebrew *purim*, plural of *pur* lot, chance]

**pu|rin** (pyůr′in), *n.* = purine.

**pu|rine** (pyůr′ēn, -in), *n.* **1** a colorless, crystalline organic base containing nitrogen and related to uric acid. *Formula:* $C_5H_4N_4$ **2** any one of a group of compounds derived from it, such as caffeine, adenine, and guanine: *The purines and pterines contribute a major source of colour to the wings of butterflies* (B. Nickerson). [< German *Purin* < Latin *pūrus* pure + New Latin *ūricus* uric acid + German *-in* -ine²]

**Pu|rin|e|thol** (pyů rin′ə thol), *n. Trademark.* a drug used in the treatment of leukemia. *Formula:* $C_5H_4N_4S$

**pur|ism** (pyůr′iz əm), *n.* **1** strict or exaggerated observance of purity and correctness in language, art, style, and usage. **2** the insistence that others practice this. **3** the theory or methods of a group of French artists who, about 1918, revolted against cubism and stressed the portrayal of recognizable objects, using stylization and precise drawing to express the spirit of the machine age: *In 1918, with Amédée Ozenfant,* [*Le Corbusier*] *founded the painting movement called Purism* (New Yorker).

**pur|ist** (pyůr′ist), *n.* a person who is very careful or too careful about purity and correctness in language, art, style, and usage. A purist dislikes slang and all expressions that are not formally correct. *Even purists do not hesitate to say bedlam* (*Bethlehem*) (Scientific American). [< French *puriste* < Latin *pūrus* pure + French *-iste* -ist]

**pu|ris|tic** (pyů ris′tik), *adj.* very careful or too careful about purity and correctness in language, art, style, and usage: *Many linguists are as puristic as one could wish, turning quite pale in the presence of "the reason is because"* (Paul Roberts).

**Pu|ri|tan** (pyůr′ə tən), *n., adj.* — *n.* a person who wanted simpler forms of worship and stricter morals than others did in the Protestant Church during the 1500's and 1600's. Many Puritans settled in New England.
— *adj.* of the Puritans: *Singing the Hundredth Psalm, the grand old Puritan anthem* (Longfellow).
[< *purit*(y) + *-an*]

**pu|ri|tan** (pyůr′ə tən), *n., adj.* — *n.* a person who is very strict in morals and religion.
— *adj.* very strict in morals and religion.
[< *Puritan*]

**pu|ri|tan|ic** (pyůr′ə tan′ik), *adj.* = puritanical.

**Pu|ri|tan|i|cal** (pyůr′ə tan′ə kəl), *adj.* having to do with or like the Puritans.

**pu|ri|tan|i|cal** (pyůr′ə tan′ə kəl), *adj.* of or like a puritan; very strict or too strict in morals or religion. SYN: austere. [< *Puritanical*] — **pu′ri|tan′i|cal|ly**, *adv.* — **pu′ri|tan′i|cal|ness**, *n.*

**Pu|ri|tan|ism** (pyůr′ə tə niz′əm), *n.* the principles and practices of the Puritans.

**pu|ri|tan|ism** (pyůr′ə tə niz′əm), *n.* puritanical behavior or principles. [< *Puritanism*]

**pu|ri|tan|ize** (pyůr′ə tə nīz), *v.*, **-ized, -iz|ing.** — *v.i.* to practice puritanism. — *v.t.* to make puritan.

**pu|ri|ty** (pyůr′ə tē), *n.* **1** freedom from dirt or mixture; clearness; cleanness: *the purity of drinking water.* **2** freedom from evil; innocence: *No one doubts the purity of Joan of Arc's motives. Claude's agonizing longing for purity struggles against a sensuality that is wholly animal* (Saturday Review). **3** freedom from foreign or inappropriate elements; careful correctness: *purity of language, purity of style.* **4** saturation: *The purity of color is its amount of difference from gray of the same brightness. The purity of any spectrum color is of course 100%, and the purity of white is zero* (Sears and Zemansky). [< Old French *purete*, learned borrowing from Late Latin *pūritās* < Latin *pūrus* pure]

**Pur|kin|je cell** (pėr kin′jē), any one of the large branching cells, with cone-shaped bodies, that make up the intermediate layer of the cerebellar cortex: *Each Purkinje cell sends its message out of the cerebellum through a long threadlike axon* (Scientific American). [< Johannes E. *Purkinje*, 1787-1869, a Bohemian physiologist]

**Purkinje shift**, the adaptation of the eye to darkness by increasing sensitivity to light of shorter wavelength. [< Johannes E. *Purkinje*]

**purl¹** (pėrl), *v., n.* — *v.i.* **1** to flow with rippling motions and a murmuring sound: *A shallow brook purls.* **2** to pass with a sound like this: *The words ... purled out of Miss Foster's mouth like a bright spring out of moss* (Arnold Bennett).
— *n.* **1** a purling motion or sound. **2** the act of purling.
[perhaps < Scandinavian (compare Norwegian *purla* to ripple)]

*** purl²** (pėrl), *v., n.* — *v.t., v.i.* **1** to knit with inverted stitches by changing the yarn from one side of the needle to the other. **2** to border (material) with small loops. **3** *Archaic.* to embroider with gold or silver thread.
— *n.* **1** an inversion of stitches in knitting, producing a ribbed appearance. **2** a loop, or chain of small loops, along the edge of lace, braid, ribbon, or other material. **3** a thread of twisted gold or silver wire, used for bordering and embroidering. **4** *Obsolete.* the pleat or fold of a ruff or neckband.
[apparently variant of earlier *pirl* to twist; origin uncertain]

*** purl²**
definition 1

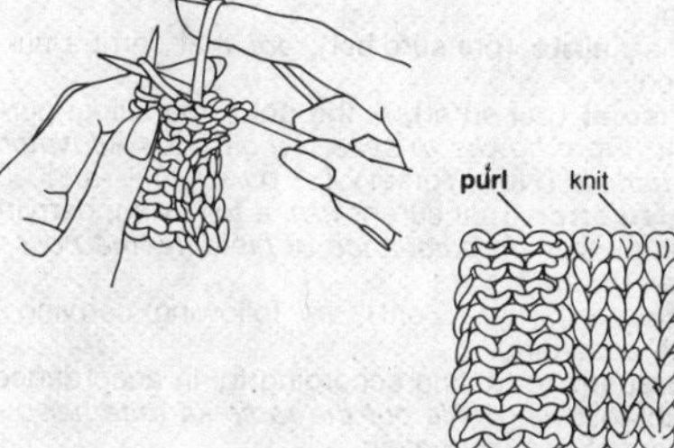


**purl³** (pėrl), *n.* **1** a medicated or spiced malt liquor. **2** a mixture of hot beer with gin and sometimes also sugar and ginger. [origin unknown]

**pur|li|cue** (pėr′lə kyü), *n.* the space enclosed by the extended forefinger and thumb: *Mr. Russet made a triangle of his purlicues and peered through it at his antagonist* (New Yorker). [origin uncertain]

**pur|lieu** (pėr′lü), *n.* **1** a piece of land on the border of a forest, especially one formerly included in the forest and still subject in part to the forest laws. **2** *Figurative.* one's haunt or resort; one's bounds. **3** any bordering, neighboring, or outlying region or district.
**purlieus, a** the parts around the border of any place: *A wolf ... was skulking about the purlieus of the camp* (Washington Irving). **b** nearby parts; vicinity; environs: (*Figurative.*) *to walk within the purlieus of the law.*
[alteration (influenced by French *lieu* place) of Anglo-French *puralee* (originally) a perambulation < *poraler* to go through < Old French *por-* forth, pro-¹ + *aler* to go]

**pur|lin** or **pur|line** (pėr′lən), *n.* a horizontal beam running the length of a roof and supporting the top rafters of the roof. [Middle English *purlyn;* origin uncertain]

**pur|loin** (pėr loin′), *v.t., v.i.* to steal: *A certain document of the last importance has been purloined from the royal apartments* (Edgar Allan Poe). [< Anglo-French *purloigner* to remove < *pur-* forth, pro-¹ + *loin* afar < Latin *longē*, adverb < *longus* long. See related etym. at **prolong**] — **pur|loin′er**, *n.*

**pu|ro|my|cin** (pyůr′ō mī′sin), *n.* an antibiotic drug produced from a soil actinomycete, used to treat certain protozoan diseases and to retard tumor growth. *Formula:* $C_{22}H_{29}N_7O_5$

**pur|ple** (pėr′pəl), *n., adj., v.,* **-pled, -pling.** — *n.* **1** a dark color made by mixing red and blue. **2** crimson. This was the ancient meaning of purple. **3** purple cloth or clothing, especially as worn by emperors, kings, and princes, to indicate high rank. **4** *Figurative.* imperial, royal, or high rank. A prince is born to the purple. **5** the rank or position of a cardinal. **6** any one of several gastropods having a gland that secretes a purplish fluid. One kind is common on both shores of the Atlantic.
— *adj.* **1** of the color of purple. **2** = crimson. **3** imperial; royal. **4** brilliant; gorgeous. **5** very ornate in style: *purple prose.*
— *v.t., v.i.* to make or become purple.
[Old English *purple*, variant of *purpure* < Latin *purpura* < Greek *porphýrā* a shell fish; the purple dye obtained from it]

**purple finch**, a sparrow-sized finch of eastern North America, the male of which has a rose-colored breast, head, and rump.

**pur|ple-fringed orchid** (pėr′pəl frinjd′), one of two North American orchids, with fringed, purplish flowers.

**purple gallinule**, a brilliantly colored gallinule, of the warmer regions of America, having bluish-purple head, neck, and underparts.

**purple grackle**, a large, purplish, iridescent blackbird found along the Atlantic coastal belt from southern New England and New York to Florida and Louisiana.

**pur|ple|heart** (pėr′pəl härt′), *n.* **1** a tree growing in tropical America whose wood is used for fine furniture and intricate inlaid work. **2** the wood itself, purple in color, and noted for its durability.

**purple heart**, *British Slang.* a narcotic drug sold in the form of a purple tablet; drinamyl: ... *the danger to teen-agers through the ease of getting purple hearts and pep pills* (Scotsman).

**Purple Heart**, a medal awarded to members of the armed forces of the United States for wounds received in action against an enemy or as a result of enemy action.

**purple heron**, a European heron resembling the common heron, but darker in coloration and in some places purplish: *The purple heron, with its angular wing and gorgeous body, kept us close company* (London Times).

**purple loosestrife**, a variety of loosestrife three feet or more in height with spikes of purple flowers, found in north temperate regions and Australia.

**purple martin**, a large, blue-black swallow of temperate North America, except the Pacific Coast region.

**purple medic**, = alfalfa.

**purple patch** or **passage**, a part or passage of a written work that is very ornate in style: *His narrative is robust, but it falls easily into the purple patches of a boys' magazine* (Punch).

**purple sandpiper**, a sandpiper with black or grayish head and back, found in arctic regions and, in the winter, south into the northern United States.

**purple vetch**, a weak-stemmed plant of the pea family with purple and white flowers, extensively grown in the Pacific Coast states for cattle feed and as ground cover.

**pur|plish** (pėr′plish), *adj.* somewhat purple.

**pur|ply** (pėr′plē), *adj.* = purplish.

**pur|port** (*v.* pər pôrt′, -pōrt′; pėr′pôrt, -pōrt; *n.* pėr′pôrt, -pōrt), *v., n.* — *v.t.* **1** to claim or profess:

**Pronunciation Key:** hat, āge, cãre, fär; let, ēqual, tėrm; it, īce; hot, ōpen, ôrder; oil, out; cup, půt, rüle; child; long; thin; ᴛʜen; zh, measure; ə represents **a** in about, **e** in taken, **i** in pencil, **o** in lemon, **u** in circus.

*The letter purported to be from the governor. The recommendations ... were purely procedural ones—or, at any rate, that is what they were intended to be and purported to be* (New Yorker). **2** to have as its main idea; mean: *a statement purporting certain facts.*
**—*n.*** the main idea; meaning: *The purport of her letter was that she could not come.* **SYN:** sense, gist, signification. See syn. under **meaning**.
[< Anglo-French *purporter* < *pur-* forth, pro-[1] + *porter* to carry < Latin *portāre*] **—pur|port′ed|ly,** *adv.*

**pur|port|less** (pėr′pôrt lis, -pōrt-), *adj.* without purport or meaning.

**pur|pose** (pėr′pəs), *n., v.,* **-posed, -pos|ing.** **—*n.*** **1** something one has in mind to get or do; plan; aim; intention: *His purpose was to discover how long these guests intended to stay* (Joseph Conrad). **SYN:** See syn. under **intention**. **2** the object or end for which a thing is made, done, or used: *The purpose of government he conceived to be the execution of justice* (James A. Froude).
**—*v.t., v.i.*** to plan; aim; intend: *my next experiment ... which I purpose to describe more at length* (Thoreau). *I purposed writing a little comment on each virtue* (Benjamin Franklin).
**on purpose,** with a purpose; not by accident; intentionally: *He tripped me on purpose. It was merely a mistake, but her Ladyship was convinced that it was done on purpose* (Maria Edgeworth).
**to good purpose,** with good results: *His letter may ... be made public to good purpose* (Freethinker).
**to little** (or **no**) **purpose,** with few or no results: *I used to insist on this ... but ... to no purpose* (Harriet Martineau).
**to the purpose,** to the point; relevant; pertinent: *His defending argument was well to the purpose.*
[< Old French *purpos* < *pourposer* to propose < *pour-* forth + *poser;* see etym. under **pose**[1]]

**pur|pose|ful** (pėr′pəs fəl), *adj.* having a purpose: *It has been my natural disposition to see this war as something purposeful* (H. G. Wells). **—pur′pose|ful|ly,** *adv.* **—pur′pose|ful|ness,** *n.*

**pur|pose|less** (pėr′pəs lis), *adj.* lacking a purpose. **—pur′pose|less|ly,** *adv.* **—pur′pose|less|ness,** *n.*

**pur|pose|ly** (pėr′pəs lē), *adv.* on purpose; intentionally: *Did you leave the door open purposely?*

**pur|pos|ive** (pėr′pə siv), *adj.* **1** acting with, having, or serving some purpose: *a purposive organ, a purposive structure.* **2** purposeful; resolute: *His mental processes were abnormally purposive* (Harper's). **3** of or having to do with purpose: *The purposive approach ... sees man as a composite body and mind whose controlling force is drive, motivation or purpose* (Scientific American). **—pur′pos|ive|ly,** *adv.* **—pur′pos|ive|ness,** *n.*

**pur|pres|ture** (pėr pres′chər), *n. Law.* an illegal enclosure of or encroachment upon property that belongs to the public or, formerly, to another person, such as the shutting up or obstruction of a highway or of navigable waters. [< Old French *purpresture* < *purprendre* usurp, occupy < *pur-* (< Latin *prō* before, for) + *prendre* < Latin *prehendere* seize, take]

**pur|pu|ra** (pėr′pyu̇r ə), *n.* any one of various diseases characterized by purple or livid spots on the skin or mucous membrane, caused by hemorrhages underneath the skin. [< Latin *purpura;* see etym. under **purple**]

**pur|pu|rate** (pėr′pyə rāt), *n. Chemical.* a salt of purpuric acid. [< *purpur*(ic acid) + *-ate*[2]]

**pur|pure** (pėr′pyu̇r), *n. Heraldry.* the purple color in coats of arms, in engraving represented by diagonal lines from the sinister chief to the dexter base. [Old English *purpure;* see etym. under **purple**]

**pur|pu|re|al** (pėr pyu̇r′ē əl), *adj. Poetic.* purple: *fields invested with purpureal gleams* (Wordsworth). [< Latin *purpureus* purple + English *-al*]

**pur|pu|ric** (pər pyu̇r′ik), *adj.* **1** having or producing a purple color. **2** of or like the disease purpura. **3** *Chemistry.* having to do with or derived from purpuric acid.

**purpuric acid,** a nitrogen-containing, organic acid, yielding salts which form purple or red solutions. *Formula:* $C_8H_5N_5O_6$

**pur|pu|rin** (pėr′pyər in), *n.* a red or orange, crystalline organic compound, originally obtained from madder, but now also prepared from alizarin, used in dyeing. *Formula:* $C_{14}H_8O_5$ [< Latin *purpura* purple dye + English *-in*]

**purr** (pėr), *n., v.* **—*n.*** a low, murmuring sound such as a cat makes when pleased.
**—*v.i., v.t.*** to make a low murmuring sound: *It* [*a young leopard*] *... purred like a cat when we stroked it with our hands* (Daniel Defoe). *... His engine purring almost inaudibly along the level road* (H. G. Wells). *The little girl purred content.* Also, **pur.** [imitative] **—purr′ing|ly,** *adv.*

**pur sang** (pyr sän′), *French.* **1** true-born; thoroughbred: *Why ... did a mathematician pur sang, as Boole certainly was, feel drawn to logic* (New Scientist). **2** (literally) pure blood.

**purse** (pėrs), *n., v.,* **pursed, purs|ing.** **—*n.*** **1** a small bag or container to hold small change, usually carried in a handbag or a pocket: *The little girl had her money for lunch in a purse she carried in her pocket.* **2** a woman's handbag: *The lady put her wallet in her purse.* **3** resources of money; funds; treasury: *He ... had no resources save the purse of his stepfather* (Arnold Bennett). **4** a sum of money: *A purse was made up for the orphans.* **5** any baglike receptacle, such as an animal's pouch, a seed capsule, or a covering for a golf club: *Then he fitted the golden head of his club with a chamois purse* (New Yorker).
**—*v.t.*** **1** to draw together; press into folds or wrinkles: *She pursed her lips and frowned.* **2** to put in a purse.
[Old English *purs* < Late Latin *bursa* < Greek *býrsa* hide, skin. See etym. of doublets **bourse, bursa, burse.**]

**purse crab,** = coconut crab.

**purse|ful** (pėrs′fu̇l), *n., pl.* **-fuls.** as much as a purse contains: ... *a purseful of profits* (Time).

**purse net,** = purse seine.

**purse-proud** (pėrs′proud′), *adj.* proud of being rich.

**purs|er** (pėr′sər), *n.* the officer who keeps the accounts of a ship or airplane, pays wages, attends to other matters of business, and is responsible for the welfare of passengers.

**pur|ser|ette** (pėr′sə ret′), *n.* a female purser on a ship or aircraft.

**purse seine,** a fishing net or seine which is pulled around a school of fish until the ends are brought together, the bottom then being drawn in under the fish to close as a bag.

**purse seiner,** a boat used in fishing with a purse seine.

**purse strings, 1** the strings pulled to close a purse. **2** *Figurative.* control of the money.
**control** (or **hold**) **the purse strings,** to control the expenditure of money: *Congress controls the purse strings* (New York Times). *The politicians hold the purse strings and therefore can enact the detailed regulations which the scientist must obey* (Science News Letter).
**loosen the purse strings,** to be generous in spending money: *Widespread loosening of the buying public's purse strings is bringing better business* (Wall Street Journal).
**tighten the purse strings,** to be sparing in spending money: *to tighten the purse strings after taking a cut in salary.*

**pur|si|ness** (pėr′sē nis), *n.* a pursy condition; shortness of breath.

**purs|lane** (pėrs′lān, -lən), *n.* **1** a common plant that has small, yellow flowers and small, thick leaves. It is a trailing herb, sometimes used for salads, for flavoring, or as a potherb. There are several kinds, comprising a genus of annual plants. *Purslane, a common garden weed, is flourishing this season despite the hot, dry weather* (New York Times). **2** any one of several plants like it that belong to the purslane family.
[< Old French *porcelaine,* alteration of Latin *porcilāca,* variant of *portulāca* portulaca < *portula* small door (diminutive) < *porta* gate (because of the open seed capsules which cover it)]

**purslane family,** a group of dicotyledonous herbs found chiefly in warm, arid regions. The family includes the purslane, claytonia, and bitterroot.

**pur|su|a|ble** (pər sü′ə bəl), *adj.* that can be pursued.

**pur|su|al** (pər sü′əl), *n.* the act of pursuing; pursuit: *From hawks to seas, To galaxies All Nature is pursual* (New Yorker). [< *pursu*(e) + *-al*[2]]

**pur|su|ance** (pər sü′əns), *n.* a following; carrying out; pursuit: *In pursuance of his duty, the policeman risked his life.*

**pur|su|ant** (pər sü′ənt), *adj.* following; carrying out; according.
**pursuant to,** acting according to; in accordance with; following: *We put the radio kit together pursuant to the instruction.*

**pur|su|ant|ly** (pər sü′ənt lē), *adv.* pursuant to.

**pur|sue** (pər sü′), *v.,* **-sued, -su|ing.** **—*v.t.*** **1** to follow to catch or kill; chase: *The policeman pursued the robbers. The dogs pursued the rabbit.* **SYN:** hunt, track. **2** to proceed along; follow in action; follow: *He pursued a wise course by taking no chances.* **3** to strive for; try to get; seek: *to pursue pleasure. Depart from evil, and do good; Seek peace, and pursue it* (Psalms 34:14). **4** to carry on; keep on with: *She pursued the study of music for four years. At Harvard he had the leisure to pursue his studies.* **5** *Figurative.* to follow closely and annoy or trouble; torment: *The boy pursued his father with questions.*
**—*v.i.*** to follow in pursuit: *The wicked flee when no man pursueth* (Proverbs 28:1).
[< Anglo-French *pursuer,* Old French *persuire,* or *poursuivre* < Latin *prōsequī;* see etym. under **prosecute**] **—pur|su′ing|ly,** *adv.*

**pur|su|er** (pər sü′ər), *n.* one who pursues; one who follows in haste with the purpose of overtaking.

**pur|suit** (pər süt′), *n.* **1** the act of pursuing: *the pursuit of game, the pursuit of pleasure, in the pursuit of science. The dog ran in pursuit of the cat. Man's aims are seen as pursuit of satisfaction* (*biological*) *and pursuit of security* (*cultural*) (Time). **2** an occupation; that which one engages in as a profession, business, or recreation: *Fishing is his favorite pursuit; reading is mine.* **3** a bicycle race: [*He*] *has been riding pursuit events for eight years, but at 30 feels the pursuit is becoming too much of a strain* (London Times). [< Anglo-French *purseute,* Old French *poursuite* < *persuire* to pursue]

**pursuit plane,** a fighter aircraft that has high speed and a high rate of climb, and can be maneuvered with ease.

**pur|sui|vant** (pėr′swə vənt), *n.* **1** an assistant to a herald; officer below a herald in rank. **2** *Figurative.* a follower; attendant: *sleep, the gracious pursuivant of toil* (Robert Bridges). **3** a herald or messenger: *these grey locks, the pursuivants of death* (Shakespeare). [< Old French *poursuivant,* (originally) present participle of *poursuivre* to pursue]

**pur|sy**[1] (pėr′sē), *adj.,* **-si|er, -si|est. 1** short-winded, especially because of fatness; puffy. **2** fat: *figures of little pursy cupids* (Washington Irving). [< Anglo-French *pursif,* variant of Old French *polsif* < *poulser* to pant < Latin *pulsāre* to beat; see etym. under **pulse**[1]]

**pur|sy**[2] (pėr′sē), *adj.,* **-si|er, -si|est. 1** having puckers; puckered. **2** rich; purse-proud: *The pursy man means by freedom the right to do as he pleases* (Emerson).

**pur|te|nance** (pėr′tə nəns), *n. Archaic.* the heart, liver, lungs, and windpipe of an animal. [perhaps < unrecorded Anglo-French *purtinaunce,* for Old French *pertinence* pertinence]

**pu|ru|lence** (pyu̇r′ə ləns, -yə-), *n.* the condition of forming, containing, or discharging pus; suppuration.

**pu|ru|len|cy** (pyu̇r′ə lən sē, -yə-), *n.* = purulence.

**pu|ru|lent** (pyu̇r′ə lənt, -yə-), *adj.* **1** forming, containing, or discharging pus; like pus: *a purulent sore, a purulent discharge from the nose during a cold.* **2** *Figurative.* corrupt; rotten; cheap: *It is an unintermitted eyesore of drive-ins, diners, souvenir stands, purulent amusement parks* (Harper's). [< Latin *pūrulentus* < *pūs, pūris* pus] **—pu′ru|lent|ly,** *adv.*

**pur|vey** (pər vā′), *v.t., v.i.* to supply (food or provisions); provide; furnish: *to purvey meat for an army, to purvey for a royal household.* [< Anglo-French *porveier,* or *purveier* < Latin *prōvidēre.* See etym. of doublet **provide.**]

**pur|vey|ance** (pər vā′əns), *n.* **1** the act of purveying. **2** provisions; supplies. **3** (formerly, in England) the right of the king or queen to supplies, use of horses, and personal service, especially when traveling.

**pur|vey|or** (pər vā′ər), *n.* **1** a person who supplies provisions: *a purveyor of fine foods and meats.* **2** a person who supplies anything: *a purveyor of gossip. He ... considered "fellows who wrote" as the mere paid purveyors of rich men's pleasures* (Edith Wharton). **3** (formerly, in England) an officer who provided or exacted food, horses, or personal service, in accordance with the right of purveyance.

**pur|view** (pėr′vyü), *n.* **1** the range, as of operation, activity, or concern; scope; extent: *matters within the purview of the government.* **2** the range of vision, thought, or understanding; outlook. **3** the main part of a statute, following the preamble. [< Anglo-French *purveu* (originally) past participle of *porveier* to purvey]

**pus** (pus), *n.* a thick, yellowish-white fluid found in infected sores in the body. It consists chiefly of white blood cells, bacteria, and serum. [< Latin *pūs, pūris*]

**Pu|sey|ism** (pyü′zē iz əm), *n.* the Oxford movement of the 1800's; Tractarianism. [< Edward B. *Pusey,* 1800-1882, one of the leaders of the Oxford movement]

**Pu|sey|ist** (pyü′zē ist), *n.* an adherent of Puseyism; Tractarianist.

**Pu|sey|ite** (pyü′zē īt), *n.* an adherent of Puseyism; Tractarianist.

**push** (pu̇sh), *v., n.* **—*v.t.*** **1** to move (something) away by pressing against it: *Push the door; don't pull it.* **2** to move up, down, back, forward, or in some other way, by pressing: *Push the dog outdoors.* **3** to thrust: *Trees push their roots down into the ground.* **4** to force (one's way): *We had to push our way through the crowd.* **5** *Figurative.* to make go forward; urge: *He pushed his plans strongly.* **6** to continue with; follow up: *to push a claim. Please push this job and get it done this*

week. **7** to extend: *Alexander pushed his conquests still farther east.* **8** *Figurative.* to urge the use, practice, or sale of: *to push used cars. They could also compel the chemists to "push" the sale of certain articles* (Cape Times). *Rival gangs pushed the drug [heroin] in the underworld generally* (Time). **9** *Figurative.* to press or bear hard upon: *to be pushed for cash.*
*—v.i.* to press hard: *We pushed with all our strength.* **2** to go forward by force: *to push through a crowd. I pushed into the next wigwam upon my hands and knees* (Byron). **3** to sit at an oar and row a boat with forward strokes: *to push down a stream.*
*—n.* **1** *Informal.* force; energy; power to succeed: *She has plenty of push. The seaway means push and purpose for the community* (Newsweek).
**2** an act of pushing: *Give the door a push.*
**3** *Figurative.* a hard effort; determined advance: *We made a push to finish the book on schedule.*
**4** (in Australia) a gang of larrikins.
**push around,** *Informal.* to treat roughly or with contempt; bully; harass: *The British people are tired of being pushed around* (Manchester Guardian).
**push off, a** to move from shore: *We pushed off in the boat.* **b** to depart; leave: *The corporation didn't want men who came to get rich quickly and then push off* (Manchester Guardian Weekly).
**push on,** to keep going; proceed: *We pushed on at a rapid pace. We pushed on for miles* (Punch).
[< Old French *pousser,* earlier *poulser* < Latin *pulsāre* to beat. See etym. of doublet **pulse**[1].]
*—Syn.* *v.t.* **1 Push, shove** mean to move someone or something by pressing against it. **Push** means pressing against the person or thing in order to move it ahead, aside, or in some other way, away from oneself or something else: *She pushed the drawer closed.* **Shove** means pushing roughly or with force and effort: *We shoved the piano across the room.*

***push|ball** (pu̇sh′bôl′), *n.* **1** a game played with a large, heavy ball, usually about six feet in diameter. Two sides of players try to push it toward opposite goals. **2** the ball used: (*Figurative.*) *Certain Congressmen may follow the Senate's lead in making this most serious matter a political pushball* (New York Times).

***pushball** definition 1

**push|bar** (pu̇sh′bär′), *n.* a bar which transmits a thrust or pushing force: *In no time the sled had more speed than we could keep up with ... without changing my grip on the pushbar I pivoted in behind him* (Canada Month).
**push bike,** *Especially British.* a bicycle operated by pedals rather than by a motor: *I was on a three-thousand-mile push bike ride through India with four Indian students* (Punch).
**push broom,** a long-handled, wide brush that is pushed like a mop to clean floors: *mechanized sweeper that does the work of 5 man-powered push brooms* (Wall Street Journal).
**push button,** a small button or knob pushed to turn an electric current on or off.
**push-but|ton** (pu̇sh′but′ən), *adj.* of or having to do with actions carried out by automatic or remote-controlled mechanisms: *push-button warfare, the push-button era.*
**push|cart** (pu̇sh′kärt′), *n.* a light cart pushed by hand: *The peddler's pushcart was filled with fruit.*
**push|chair** (pu̇sh′chãr′), *n. British.* a light baby carriage; stroller: *Tired, wonderful mothers bump pushchairs down ... staircases to get their babies into the light and air* (Manchester Guardian).
**push|er** (pu̇sh′ər), *n.* **1** a person or thing that pushes. **2** an airplane with propeller or propellers behind instead of in front: *In France the great early pioneers ... had tractor-type monoplanes, although Farman and Voisin also used pushers* (Atlantic). **3** *Informal.* an unlawful peddler of narcotics: *"Pushers" could be eliminated if the clinics made narcotics available legally under strict supervision* (New York Times).
**push|ful** (pu̇sh′fəl), *adj. Informal.* full of push; self-assertive; active and energetic in prosecuting one's affairs: *He was pushful and jittery under the most innocent circumstances* (Maclean's). **—push′ful|ly,** *adv.* **—push′ful|ness,** *n.*
**push|i|ly** (pu̇sh′ə lē), *adv.* in a pushy manner; aggressively.
**push|i|ness** (pu̇sh′ē nis), *n.* forwardness; self-assertiveness.
**push|ing** (pu̇sh′ing), *adj.* **1** that pushes. **2** *Figurative.* forward; aggressive; pushy: *the cocksureness of pushing vulgarity and self-conceit* (Samuel Butler). **3** *Figurative.* enterprising: *We ... are pleased with his pushing and persevering spirit* (Washington Irving). **—push′ing|ly,** *adv.* **—push′ing|ness,** *n.*
**push|out** (pu̇sh′out′), *n.* **1** a part or piece to be pushed out, such as a panel or an antenna. **2** = punch-out. **3** *U.S. Informal.* a student who drops out of school for failing in his studies; flunkee: *Much of the work of anti-dropout agencies boils down to ... random efforts at finding jobs for a handful of trainees whose numbers are dwarfed by new "pushouts" ... and other categories of school rejects* (Saturday Review).
**push|o|ver** or **push-o|ver** (pu̇sh′ō′vər), *n. Slang.* **1** something very easy to do: *It was a push-over, he added, with five days off a week* (Sunday Times). **2** a person very easy to beat in a contest: *He must have been the proverbial pushover* (Cape Times). **3** a person easily influenced or swayed or unable to resist a particular appeal: *I am not usually a pushover for newsreel shots or telecasts of races* (New Yorker). **4** the beginning of a dive in an airplane as the stick is pushed forward.
**push-over try,** *British. Rugby.* a try scored in the midst of or as the direct result of a scrummage: *Two scrums followed, and from the second the visitors achieved a push-over try* (Sunday Times).
**push|pin** (pu̇sh′pin′), *n.* **1** a thin tack with a glass head, that can be pushed into a wall, bulletin board, or the like, without leaving a noticeable mark. **2** a children's game played with pins. **3** child's play; triviality.
**push-pull** (pu̇sh′pu̇l′), *adj., n. Radio.* *—adj.* of or having such an arrangement of two circuit elements that the effect of one supplements the other: *a push-pull circuit or amplifier.*
*—n.* a push-pull arrangement.
**push|rod** (pu̇sh′rod′), *n.* a rod, as in an internal-combustion engine, that acts with a cam or cams to open and close the valves of the cylinders.
**Push|tu** (push′tü), *n.* = Pashto.
**Push|tun** (push tün′), *n.* = Pathan.
**push|up** or **push-up** (pu̇sh′up′), *n., adj.* *—n.* an exercise done by lying face down and raising the body with the arms while keeping the back, hips, and legs straight and the toes on the ground: *A few brisk pushups and you're in fine fettle for a chummy joust with Customs* (New Yorker).
*—adj.* that can be worn pushed up from the wrist: *pushup sleeves.*
**push|y** (pu̇sh′ē), *adj.,* **push|i|er, push|i|est.** forward; aggressive: *But what in the son was smirking and pushy was in the father shrewd and masterful* (New Yorker).
**pu|sil|la|nim|i|ty** (pyü′sə lə nim′ə tē), *n.* cowardliness; timidity.
**pu|sil|lan|i|mous** (pyü′sə lan′ə məs), *adj.* cowardly; fainthearted; mean-spirited; timid: *The pusillanimous man would not defend his own family ... an indignity which no prince, how inconsiderable or pusillanimous soever, could tamely endure* (Thomas W. Robertson). *One cannot contemplate this pusillanimous conduct of Montezuma without mingled feelings of pity and contempt* (William H. Prescott). syn: timorous, spiritless. [< Latin *pusillanimis* (with English *-ous*) < *pusillus* little + *animus* courage] **—pu′sil|lan′i|mous|ly,** *adv.* **—pu′sil|lan′i|mous|ness,** *n.*
**pus|ley** (pus′lē), *n.* = pussley.
**puss** (pu̇s), *n.* **1** = cat (def. 1). **2** = hare (def. 1). **3** a girl or woman: *The little puss seems already to have airs enough to make a husband ... miserable* (George Eliot). **4** *Slang.* the face; mouth: [*She*] *owns a deadpan puss and a willing set of lungs, all of which she puts to good use demolishing Tin Pan Alley tearjerkers* (New Yorker). [< Germanic (compare Dutch *poes,* Low German *puus, puus-katte*)]
**puss-in-the-cor|ner** (pu̇s′in ᴛʜə kôr′nər), *n.* a game for children, of whom one stands in the center and tries to capture one of the bases as the other players change places.
**puss|ley** (pus′lē), *n. U.S.* purslane: *Miss Alexander was up and helping weed pussley out of the garden* (New Yorker).
**puss|ly** (pus′lē), *n., pl.* **-lies.** = pussley.
**puss moth,** a large European moth, having the forewings of a whitish or light-gray color with darker markings and spots; prominent: *When searching poplars and willows, there is also a good chance of finding the buttonshaped eggs of the puss moth* (New Scientist).
**puss|y**[1] (pu̇s′ē), *n., pl.* **puss|ies. 1** = cat (def. 1). **2** a catkin, as of a willow. **3** = hare (def. 1). **4a** the game of tipcat. **b** the cat used in this game. [< *puss* + *-y*[2]]
**pus|sy**[2] (pus′ē), *adj.,* **-si|er, -si|est.** full of pus. [< *pus* + *-y*[1]]
**puss|y|cat** (pu̇s′ē kat′), *n.* a cat; pussy: *Whether I paint a skyscraper or a pussycat I want to make it more interesting* (Time).
**puss|y|foot** (pu̇s′ē fu̇t′), *v., n., pl.* **-foots.** *Informal.* *—v.i.* **1** to move softly and cautiously to avoid being seen. **2** to be cautious and timid about revealing one's opinions or committing oneself: *We have pussyfooted around on this boycott long enough and it has come time to be frank and honest* (Time).
*—n.* a person who pussyfoots.
***pussy willow, 1** a small North American willow with silky, grayish-white catkins. **2** any one of various similar willows.

***pussy willow** definition 1

**pus|tu|lant** (pus′chə lənt), *adj., n.* *—adj.* causing pustules.
*—n.* an irritant that causes pustules.
[< Latin *pustulāns, -antis,* present participle of *pustulāre;* see etym. under **pustulate**]
**pus|tu|lar** (pus′chə lər), *adj.* **1** of, like, or having to do with pustules. **2** characterized by pustules.
**pus|tu|late** (*v.* pus′chə lāt; *adj.* pus′chə lit), *v.,* **-lat|ed, -lat|ing,** *adj.* *—v.t., v.i.* to form pustules.
*—adj.* having pustules.
[< Latin *pustulāre* (with English *ate*[1]) < *pustula* pustule]
**pus|tu|la|tion** (pus′chə lā′shən), *n.* **1** the formation of pustules. **2** = pustule.
**pus|tule** (pus′chül), *n.* **1** a small bump on the skin filled with pus and inflamed at the base. **2** any swelling like a pimple or blister, such as the pustules of chicken pox. [< Latin *pustula*]
**pus|tu|lous** (pus′chə ləs), *adj.* = pustular.
**pusz|ta** (pu̇s′tä), *n.* the Hungarian steppe: *They saw the infinite horizons of the ... puszta* (New Yorker). [< Hungarian *puszta* (literally) barren, empty]
**put**[1] (pu̇t), *v.,* **put, put|ting,** *n.* *—v.t.* **1** to cause to be in some place or position; place; lay; set: *I put sugar in my tea. Put away your toys.* **2** to cause to be in some state, condition, position, or relation: *Put your room in order. He put himself under the care of a doctor. The murderer was put to death. We put the house on the market.* **3** to set (a person or animal) to do something, or upon some course of action: *to put someone to work.* **4** to express: *to put a French poem in English. Put the question in writing. The teacher puts things clearly.* **5** to set at a particular place, point, amount, distance, or other dimension or force, in a scale of estimation; appraise: *I put the distance at five miles.* **6** to propose or submit for answer, consideration, or deliberation: *We put several questions before the committee.* **7** to apply: *A doctor puts his skill to good use.* **8** to impose: *to put a tax on gasoline. C. suspected ... that he was putting a joke upon him* (Hawthorne). **9** to assign; attribute: *They put a wrong construction on my action.* **10** to throw or cast (an 8-pound, 12-pound, or 16-pound ball) from the hand placed close to the shoulder.
*—v.i.* **1** to take one's course; go; turn; proceed: *The ship put out to sea.* **2** *U.S. Informal.* to make off; be off: *to put for work.* **3** *Dialect.* (of a plant) to send forth shoots.
*—n.* **1** a throw or cast. **2** *Commerce.* the privilege of delivering a certain amount of stock or other securities, at a specified price within a certain period of time: *Puts, like calls, chiefly are bought by speculators* (Wall Street Journal).
**put about, a** to put (a ship) on the opposite tack: *The Stella was then put about, and the other broadside given* (Frederick Marryat). **b** to turn on to the other tack; change direction: *Down with the helm, and let us put about* (John Wilson). **c** to circulate: *Who has put this lie about?* (Mrs. Lynn Linton).
**put across,** *Informal.* **a** to carry out successfully: *The salesman put the deal across. And, gentlemen, we'll put it across! We'll do it by working!*

**Pronunciation Key:** hat, āge, cãre, fär; let, ēqual, tėrm; it, īce; hot, ōpen, ôrder; **oi**l, **ou**t; cup, pu̇t, rüle; **ch**ild; lo**ng**; **th**in; ᴛʜen; **zh**, measure; **ə** represents **a** in about, **e** in taken, **i** in pencil, **o** in lemon, **u** in circus.

(H. L. Foster). **b** to get accepted or understood; get across: *He could not put across his point of view to the audience.*

**put aside, a** to save for future use: *to put aside a dollar a week.* **b** to lay aside out of use: *A curious kind of egalitarian, humanitarian attitude has let us quickly put aside vice as a proposition, and go to misery* (Daniel P. Moynihan).

**put away, a** to save for future use: *The fruit should be ... carefully put away in bins* (Journal of the Royal Agricultural Society). **b** *Informal.* to consume as food or drink: *to put away a meal.* **c** *Informal.* to put in jail; imprison: *They never had enough on Duncan to make an actual arrest, but cops hear things ... and they were anxious to put him away* (John O'Hara). **d** *Informal.* to commit to a mental institution: *You knew their daughter had to be put away? It was a tragic thing ... she cut her wrists* (New Yorker). **e** *Informal.* to kill: *A reward, I should have greatly valued ... were he [a dog] not now in danger of being put away* (Anne Brontë).

**put by, a** to save for future use: *The old gentleman had put by a little money* (Dickens). **b** to turn aside; reject: *There is no putting by that crown; queens you must always be* (John Ruskin). **c** *Figurative.* to evade: *The chancellor ... smiling, put the question by* (Tennyson).

**put down, a** to put an end to; suppress; crush: *The rebellion was quickly put down. Sir Peter is such an enemy to scandal, I believe he would have it put down by parliament* (Richard Brinsley Sheridan). **b** to write down: *I have put you down in my will for a ring* (New Monthly Magazine). **c** to pay as a down payment: *to put down a deposit of $10 on a typewriter.* **d** *Informal, Figurative.* to lower in importance; slight or belittle; snub: *They sensed that even some of Mr. Johnson's normally solid supporters thought he should be put down a bit* (Atlantic). **e** *Informal.* to criticize: *"My friend here put me down pretty sharply—" Vivien interrupted. "Not sharply enough," she said* (Garson Kanin). **f** *Informal.* to kill: *If unwanted babies, why not "put down" our elderly parents, too?* (Manchester Guardian Weekly). **g** to land: *The plane put down at Shannon airport. We put down in Murmansk, but soon our stewardess jubilantly announced that our pilot had talked Vnukovo airport in Moscow into letting us come in* (Time).

**put forth, a** to send out; sprout; issue: *to put forth buds.* **b** to use fully; exert: *to put forth effort.* **c** to start, especially to sea: *to put forth on a voyage.* **d** to issue; publish: *to put forth an edict.* **e** to stretch forth or out: *He put forth his staff that he had in his hand* (Miles Coverdale).

**put forward,** to propose or submit for consideration or acceptance; propound; suggest: *His conclusions are hasty and the broad proposals which he puts forward contain no evidence that they could ever be successfully applied* (New Yorker).

**put in,** *Informal.* **a** to spend (time or other resources) as specified: *Put in a full day of work. I try and put in three miles before lunch* (Graham Greene). **b** to enter port: *The ship put in at Hong Kong.* **c** to enter a place for safety or supplies. **d** to enter; go in: *The ladies ... were busy at the bridge tables just off the center of the lobby on the afternoon I put in* (Saturday Review). **e** to sow; plant: *to put in crops.* **f** to get in (a word); interpose: *Baxter himself attempted to put in a word* (Macaulay). **g** to furnish in addition: *The Lords put in amendments which the Commons would not accept* (T. G. Tout).

**put in for,** to make a claim, plea, or offer for: *He put in for a loan at the bank.*

**put off, a** to lay aside; postpone: *to put off a meeting. Don't put off going to the dentist or your teeth will suffer from neglect. All things are now in readiness, and must not be put off* (John Dryden). **b** to go away; start out: *The Mayflower put off for America in 1620.* **c** to bid or cause to wait: *We refused to be put off any longer with such excuses.* **d** to hold back or stop from: *Don't let the formidable get-up ... put you off some extremely fine music-making* (Harper's). **e** *Figurative.* to get rid of; dispose of: *As to oxen, I put off two lots in the year* (Journal of the Royal Agricultural Society).

**put on, a** to present on a stage; produce (a play, lecture, or other entertainment): *The class put on a play. The Foundation for Integrative Education was putting on the last in a six-evening series of discussions* (New York Times). **b** to take on or add to oneself: *to put on weight,* (*Figurative.*) *to put on airs.* **c** to pretend: *to put on an air of innocence. Her surprise was all put on; she knew we were coming beforehand.* **d** to impose; inflict: *The fines were not fixed sums; the king could put on just what he liked* (M. J. Guest). **e** to apply or exert: *to put on speed, put on pressure.* **f** to set to work: *to put men on to clean up a job.* **g** to don; clothe with: *Mrs. Venn ... is going away to put on her things* (Thomas Hardy). **h** *Slang.* to play a trick on; tease playfully; poke fun at: *Are you putting me on?*

**put (one) over on,** to impose (something false or deceptive) on: *The discovery ... served to exacerbate the situation, confirming the eternal Cornish suspicion that Englishmen live only for the chance to put one over on them* (Punch).

**put out, a** to extinguish; make an end to; destroy: *to put out a candle, light, or fire.* **b** to set out on a voyage; go; turn; proceed: *The ship put out to sea. Dozens of Chinese would "cheerfully" put out in small boats to sell food to their enemies* (Punch). **c** to embarrass; disconcert; offend: *You must not be at all surprised or put out at feeling the difficulties you describe* (Cardinal Newman). **d** to provoke; annoy; irritate: *You must not be put out by the train delay. Sir Dene [was] ... thoroughly put out with the captain* (Mrs. Henry Wood). **e** to inconvenience: *Please don't put yourself out; I'll look for the book myself.* **f** to cause to be out in a game or sport: *to put out a batter at first base.* **g** to publish: *In its fourth communiqué put out in November of last year, the liaison office made an obvious effort ...* (New Yorker). **h** to eject: *He is ... put out by the constables* (Benjamin Jowett). **i** to destroy the sight of: *Will you put out mine eyes?* (Shakespeare). **j** to invest: *The syndicate in Toronto isn't interested in marijuana because the profits aren't high enough. Most of the people who put out are independent operators* (Maclean's).

**put over,** *Informal.* **a** to carry out successfully; put across: *You don't go into any business ... and put it over without running the risk of being shot* (Gertrude Atherton). **b** *Figurative.* to do or carry out by trickery: *to put over a fraud.* **c** to postpone; defer: *I wanted to put [the meeting] over until Sunday, so as not to interfere with my work* (New Yorker).

**put through, a** to cause to pass through any process: *We saw an ancient instructor putting his class of girls through what looked like early ballet exercises* (Maclean's). **b** *Figurative.* to carry out with success: *Taking prompt action ... to "put through" a certain nefarious design* (Longman's Magazine). **c** to send or pass between points, as a telegram, a telephone call, or a person: *to put a call through to London. Will you put me through to Chicago?*

**put to, a** to put in to shore; take shelter: *We ... were obliged to put to on account of the wind* (F. Baily). **b** to attach, as to a vehicle or train: *Bid him ... get the horses put to* (Laurence Sterne).

**put together, a** to form (a whole) by combining parts; construct; compose: *This toy can be taken apart and put together with ease.* **b** to combine mentally; take or consider collectively: *He knows more than the whole class put together.*

**put to it,** to force to a course; put in difficulty: *I was put to it to keep up with his pace.*

**put up, a** to raise; lift: *Shopkeepers had hastily put up their shutters* (Maxwell Gray). **b** to offer: *to put up a house for sale, to put up a prayer. Oughtn't the post ... to have been put up for public competition?* (Chambers's Journal). **c** to give or show: *to put up a brave front.* **d** to build: *to put up a monument.* **e** *Figurative.* to lay aside: *to put up one's work. I have put my complaint up again, for to my foes my bill I dare not show* (Chaucer). **f** to propose for election or adoption: *His name was put up for president of the club.* **g** to pack up or preserve (food): *to put up six jars of blackberries.* **h** to give or take lodging or food to: *The motel put him up for the night. He put up at the New Southern Hotel in Jackson* (New Yorker). **i** to pay; provide or deposit: *to put up the money for the show.* **j** to make up: *Prussia, together with the remaining states, puts up sixteen army corps* (Harper's Magazine). **k** to dress (hair): *to put up one's hair before a party.* **l** to cause (game) to rise from cover: *He noticed some teal and mallard in a stubble field and walking across, he put them up* (London Times). **m** to raise in amount: *Making preparations to put up the price still higher* (Saturday Review).

**put upon,** to impose upon; take advantage of; victimize: *However frustrated, distracted, and put upon the great press corps was, out of its agony came reading matter* (Newsweek).

**put up to, a** to inform of; make aware of: *He put me up to one or two things worth knowing* (Cornhill Magazine). **b** to get (a person) to do; stir up to; incite to: *Don't put her up to mischief.*

**put up with,** to bear with patience; endure; tolerate: *to put up with hot weather, put up with scorn.*

**stay put.** See under **stay**[1].

[< Old English *putian*]

—*Syn. v.t.* **1 Put, place, set** mean to cause someone or something to be in some place or position. **Put** emphasizes the action of moving something into or out of a place or position: *Put your hand in mine.* **Place** emphasizes the idea of a definite spot, more than action: *Place your hands behind your head.* **Set** emphasizes causing to be in a stated or certain position: *Set the box down over there.*

**put**[2] (put), *n. Dialect.* a stupid or silly fellow; bumpkin. [origin unknown]

**put**[3] (put), *v.t., v.i.,* **put|ted, put|ting,** *n.* = putt.

**put**[4] (put), *n.* a short, explosive sound, as that made by an outboard motor.

**pu|ta|men** (pyü tā′mən), *n., pl.* **-tam|i|na** (-tam′ə nə). **1** a hard or stony endocarp, such as the stone of a peach. **2** the outer zone of the extraventricular portion of the gray matter of the brain, thought by some to be the area of the brain reacting to sensations of pleasure. [< Latin *putāmen, -inis* < *putāre;* see etym. under **putative**]

**put-and-take** (pu̇t′ən tāk′), *n.* any gambling game played with a six-sided top or teetotum, in which all the players contribute to the pool from which winnings are taken: *It has been a game of put-and-take with all the accent on take* (New York Times).

**pu|ta|tive** (pyü′tə tiv), *adj.* supposed; reputed: *the putative author of a book.* [< Latin *putātīvus* < *putāre* to cleanse, trim, to prune trees; reckon, think] —**pu′ta|tive|ly,** *adv.*

**put-down** (pu̇t′doun′), *n. Informal.* **1** the act of slighting or belittling a person or thing: *The early church fathers would have examined Adam Ogilvy carefully for horns ... if they had heard his contemptuous put-down of patience, a paramount Christian virtue* (Time). **2** a comment, reply, or action intended to snub or belittle.

**put|log** (pu̇t′lôg, -log; put′-), *n.* one of the short horizontal members that support the flooring of a scaffold. [earlier *putlock,* perhaps < *put*[1]]

**put-off** (pu̇t′ôf, -of′), *n.* **1** the act of putting off or postponing; postponement. **2** the act or process of getting rid of by evasion or the like: *I would have asked farther, but Alan gave me the put-off* (Robert Louis Stevenson). **3** an evasion.

**put-on** (pu̇t′on′, -ôn′), *adj., n.* —*adj.* assumed; affected; pretended: ... *the put-on atheism of Left Bank beatniks* (Time).

—*n.* **1** a pretension or affectation. **2** *Slang.* a mischievous joke or trick played for fun; practical joke; hoax: *"Pop Art" is ... possibly a "put-on"* (New York Times).

**put-on artist,** *Slang.* a person skilled in the put-on: *Though he is usually forthright, he occasionally stirs suspicion that he is a bit of a put-on artist* (Time).

**put|out** (pu̇t′out′), *n.* the act of putting a player out in baseball or cricket: *Mantle made all three putouts in his lone inning at short* (New York Times).

**put-put** (put′put′), *n., v.,* **-put|ted, -put|ting.** —*n.* **1** the succession of sharp, explosive noises made by a small gasoline engine. **2** *Slang.* a boat or vehicle operated by such an engine.

—*v.i.* to go or travel by means of such an engine.

**pu|tre|fa|cient** (pyü′trə fā′shənt), *adj., n.* —*adj.* putrefying; putrefactive.

—*n.* an agent or substance that produces putrefaction.

**pu|tre|fac|tion** (pyü′trə fak′shən), *n.* the action or process of putrefying; decay; rotting.

**pu|tre|fac|tive** (pyü′trə fak′tiv), *adj.* **1** causing putrefaction. **2** characterized by or having to do with putrefaction. —**pu′tre|fac′tive|ness,** *n.*

**pu|tre|fi|a|ble** (pyü′trə fī′ə bəl), *adj.* likely to become putrefied.

**pu|tre|fi|er** (pyü′trə fī′ər), *n.* = putrefacient.

**pu|tre|fy** (pyü′trə fī), *v.i., v.t.,* **-fied, -fy|ing. 1** to break down by the action of bacteria and fungi, producing bad-smelling gases; rot; decay; decompose: *The meat putrefied because it was not refrigerated.* **2** to become or cause to be gangrenous. [< Middle French *putrefier,* learned borrowing from Latin *putrefierī,* and *putrefacere* < *puter* rotten (see etym. under **putrescent**) + *fierī* become, passive of *facere* make]

**pu|tresce** (pyü tres′), *v.i.,* **-tresced, -tresc|ing.** to begin to putrefy; become putrid.

**pu|tres|cence** (pyü tres′əns), *n.* **1** a putrescent condition. **2** putrescent matter.

**pu|tres|cent** (pyü tres′ənt), *adj.* **1** becoming putrid; rotting. **2** having to do with putrefaction. [< Latin *pūtrēscens, -entis,* present participle of *pūtrēscere* grow rotten < *pūtēre* to stink < *puter* rotten, related to *pūs, pūris* pus]

**pu|tres|ci|ble** (pyü tres′ə bəl), *adj., n.* —*adj.* likely to rot. —**n.** a substance that will rot.

**pu|tres|cine** (pyü tres′ēn, -in), *n.* a colorless, evil-smelling ptomaine, formed during the decay of animal tissue. *Formula:* $C_4H_{12}N_2$ [< Latin *pūtrēscere* (see etym. under **putrescent**) + English *-ine*[2]]

**pu|trid** (pyü′trid), *adj.* **1** decaying; rotten: *The* *meat became putrid in the hot sun.* **2** characteristic of putrefying matter; foul: *a putrid odor.* **3** *Figurative.* thoroughly corrupt or depraved; extremely bad. **4** gangrenous: *putrid flesh.* [< Latin *pūtridus* < *puter,* rotten; see etym. under **putrescent**] —**pu′trid|ly,** *adv.* —**pu′trid|ness,** *n.*

**pu|trid|i|ty** (pyü trid′ə tē), *n.* **1** putrid condition. **2** putrid matter.

**putsch** (pu̇ch), *n.* an uprising; insurrection: *The common political experience of Eastern Europe between wars was the putsch and persecution at home, jealousy and chauvinism abroad* (Newsweek). [< German *Putsch* (literally) push, thrust]

**putsch|ist** (pu̇ch′ist), *n.* a person who advocates or takes part in a putsch: *When he first began his guerrilla fight, ... Rodriguez himself laughed off Castro as a petty putschist* (Time).

**putt** (put), *v., n.* —*v.t., v.i.* to strike (a golf ball) gently and carefully in an effort to make it roll into or near the hole: *To putt well requires control.*

—*n.* **1** the stroke made in putting: *Bayliss had single putts on the first four greens coming back* (London Times). **2** the act of putting.

[variant of *put*[1]]

***put|tee** (put′ē, pu tē′), *n.* **1** a long, narrow strip of cloth wound around the leg from ankle to knee, formerly worn especially by sportsmen and soldiers: *He wore the ... short-sleeved tunic, boots and puttees of the Force Publique* (London Times). **2** a gaiter of cloth or leather reaching from ankle to knee, formerly worn especially by soldiers, riders, and many policemen and guards. Also, **puttie, putty.** [< Hindi *paṭṭī* a bandage, strip < Sanskrit *paṭī* cloth]

***puttee** definitions 1, 2

definition 1 definition 2

**put|ter**[1] (put′ər), *v.i.* to keep busy in a rather useless way: *She likes to spend the afternoon puttering in the garden.* Also, **potter.** [variant of *potter*[2]] —**put′ter|er,** *n.*

**putt|er**[2] (put′ər), *n.* **1** a golf player who putts. **2** a golf club used in putting. A putter has an upright face and a short, rigid shaft. [< *putt* + *-er*[1]]

**put|ter**[3] (pu̇t′ər), *n.* a person or thing that puts. [< *put*[1] + *-er*[1]]

***put|ti** (püt′ē), *n., pl. of* **put|to** (püt′ō). *Italian.* representations of cupidlike children used in art, especially during the Renaissance: *Two oil sketches of putti with swags of fruit ... were sold for £420* (London Times).

***putti**

**put|tie** (put′ē), *n.* = puttee.

**put|ti|er** (put′ē ər), *n.* a person who putties, such as a glazier. [< *putty*[1] + *-er*[1]]

**putt|ing green** (put′ing), **1** the smooth turf or sand around the hole into which a player putts a golf ball; that part of a golf course usually within 20 yards of the hole, except the hazards. **2** a similar area off the course, used to practice putting: *He put in another four and a half hours on the putting green.* [< *putt* + *-ing*[2]]

**put|ting-out system** (pu̇t′ing-out′), = cottage industry.

**put|tock** (put′ək), *n. Dialect.* any one of certain birds of prey, especially a kite or a buzzard. [Middle English *puttok*]

**putt-putt** (put′put′), *n., v.i.* = put-put.

**put|ty**[1] (put′ē), *n., pl.* **-ties,** *v.,* **-tied, -ty|ing.** —*n.* **1** a soft mixture of powdered chalk and linseed oil, used for fastening panes of glass in window frames and for filling cracks and holes in woodwork. Putty slowly hardens after it is applied. **2** a pipe-joint compound. **3** a very smooth mortar of lime and water mixed, used in plastering. **4** = putty powder. **5** = putty color.

—*v.t.* to stop up, fill up, or cover with putty: *He puttied up the holes in the woodwork before painting it.*

[< French *potée* (originally) potful < Old French *pot* pot, container < Vulgar Latin *pottus*]

**put|ty**[2] (put′ē), *n., pl.* **-ties.** = puttee.

**putty color,** a light gray. [< *putty*[1]]

**put|ty-col|ored** (put′ē kul′ərd), *adj.* light-gray.

**putty powder,** fine, abrasive powder, especially tin oxide, used to polish glass, stone, or metal.

**put|ty|root** (put′ē rüt′, -ru̇t′), *n.* a North American orchid, with racemes of brownish flowers; Adam-and-Eve. The corm it produces contains a glutinous matter that has been used as a cement.

**put-up** (pu̇t′up′), *adj. Informal.* planned beforehand, or deliberately, in a secret or crafty manner: *His election was a put-up job by the party bosses.*

**put-up|on** (pu̇t′ə pon′, -pôn′), *adj.* imposed upon; taken advantage of; victimized: *... a rich, overbearing builder and his put-upon, endlessly complaining family* (New Yorker).

**puy** (pwē), *n.* a small volcanic cone of a type common in Auvergne, central France. [< French *puy* hill < Old French, balcony, elevation. See etym. of doublet **pew.**]

**puz|zle** (puz′əl), *n., v.,* **-zled, -zling.** —*n.* **1** a hard problem: *How to get all my clothes into one suitcase was a puzzle.* **2** a problem or task to be done for fun: *A famous Chinese puzzle has seven pieces of wood to fit together.* **3** a puzzled condition: *The new student was in a puzzle about where to go.* **SYN:** bewilderment, quandary.

—*v.t.* to make unable to answer, solve, or understand something; fill with doubt or confusion; perplex: *How the dog got out of the house puzzled us.*

—*v.i.* **1** to be perplexed: *The dog stopped, puzzled over the disappearance of the scent of the fox by the river's edge.* **2** to exercise one's mind on something hard: *We tried to puzzle through something we didn't understand at all.*

**puzzle out,** to find out by thinking or trying hard: *to puzzle out the meaning of a sentence.*

**puzzle over,** to think hard about; try hard to do or work out: *He puzzled over his arithmetic for an hour.*

[origin uncertain] —**puz′zling|ly,** *adv.* —**puz′zling|ness,** *n.*

—*Syn. v.t.* **Puzzle, perplex, bewilder** mean to make a person uncertain what to think, say, or do. **Puzzle** suggests a problem having so many parts or sides and being so involved that it is hard to understand or solve: *The complicated instructions for building the radio puzzled him.* **Perplex** adds the idea of troubling with doubt about how to decide or act: *They were worried and perplexed by their son's behavior.* **Bewilder** emphasizes the idea of confusing and causing one to feel lost among all the various possibilities: *I was bewildered by the commotion of the city traffic.*

**puzzle box,** a box or pen from which an animal may learn to release itself, as by clawing a string or pressing a lever, used in experiments dealing with animal behavior or intelligence: *He [E. L. Thorndike] invented the puzzle box to investigate how such animals as cats and dogs solve problems* (B. F. Skinner).

**puz|zled|ly** (puz′əld lē), *adv.* in a puzzled manner.

**puz|zle|head** (puz′əl hed′), *n.* a person of confused ideas.

**puz|zle|head|ed** (puz′əl hed′id), *adj.* having or showing confused ideas.

**puzzle jug,** a jug with perforated sides from which one can drink without spilling only by closing a certain airhole with the finger: *He made ... the traditional instruments of rustic amusement, puzzle jugs which deluged the unwary with ale* (London Times).

**puz|zle|ment** (puz′əl mənt), *n.* **1** a puzzled condition: *He was just talking in a tone of sheer, hopeless ... puzzlement—bafflement* (A. S. M. Hutchinson). **2** something puzzling.

**puz|zle-mug** (puz′əl mug′), *n.* a drinking-vessel of pottery with perforated sides, several small spouts, and an inner tube through which the liquid contents may be drawn up to the mouth when a particular hole is closed with the finger.

**puz|zler** (puz′lər), *n.* **1** a person or thing that puzzles. **2** a person who occupies himself with puzzles.

**puz|zlist** (puz′ə list, puz′list), *n.* a writer or inventor of puzzles: *They [an arrangement of coins] are shown here in forms given by the English puzzlist Henry Ernest Dudeney to display bilateral symmetry for all of them* (Scientific American).

**PVA** (no periods), **1** polyvinyl acetate. **2** polyvinyl alcohol.

**PVC** (no periods), polyvinyl chloride: *The PVC coating protects it against ultraviolet radiation* (New Scientist).

**PVP** (no periods), polyvinyl pyrrolidone.

**Pvt.,** private: *Pvt. John E. Martin.*

**PW** (no periods) or **P.W.,** prisoner of war: *Captured airmen were separated from other P.W.s and taken to a place near Pyongyang* (Time).

**PWA** (no periods), Public Works Administration.

**P wave,** = primary wave.

**P.W.D.** or **PWD** (no periods), Public Works Department.

**pwe** (pwe), *n.* a Burmese celebration or entertainment in which groups of actors, singers, and dancers perform on outdoor stages: *A pwe ..., compounded of classical Burmese drama and dance and comic routines that are likely to dwell suggestively on either sex or politics* (New York Times). [< Burmese *pwe*]

**pwr** (no period), power.

**PWR** (no periods) or **P.W.R.,** pressurized water reactor.

**pwt.,** pennyweight.

**PX** (no periods) or **P.X.,** post exchange: *Her colleagues delighted in baked beans from the PX* (New Yorker).

**pxt.,** pinxit.

**py-,** *combining form.* the form of **pyo-** before vowels, as in *pyoid.*

**pya** (pyä), *n.* a unit of money of Burma, equal to 1/100 kyat. [< Burmese *pya*]

**py|ae|mi|a** (pī ē′mē ə), *n.* = pyemia.

**py|ae|mic** (pī ē′mik), *adj.* = pyemic.

**pyc|nid|i|um** (pik nid′ē əm), *n., pl.* **-i|a** (-ē ə). a spore fruit in some fungi. Typically it is a rounded or flask-shaped receptacle enclosing conidia borne on conidiophores. [< New Latin *pycnidium* < Greek *pyknós* thick, dense + New Latin *-idium,* a diminutive suffix]

**pyc|ni|o|spore** (pik′nē ə spôr, -spōr), *n. Botany.* a spermatium. [< Greek *pyknós* thick, dense + English *spore*]

**pyc|ni|um** (pik′nē əm), *n., pl.* **-ni|a** (-nē ə). *Botany.* **1** a spermogonium, especially of certain rust fungi. **2** a pycnidium. [< New Latin *pycnium* < Greek *pyknós* thick, dense + New Latin *-ium,* a noun suffix]

**pyc|nom|e|ter** (pik nom′ə tər), *n.* an instrument, consisting usually of a glass flask with a thermometer, for determining the relative density or specific gravity of liquids. [< Greek *pyknós* thick, dense]

**pyc|no|style** (pik′nə stīl), *adj., n. Architecture.* —*adj.* of or having to do with an arrangement of columns in which the intercolumniation measures one and a half diameters.

—*n.* a pycnostyle colonnade.

[< Latin *pycnostȳlos* < Greek *pyknóstȳlos* < *pyknós* thick, dense + *stȳlos* column]

**pye** (pī), *n.* a book of rules for finding the ecclesiastical service of the day; pie.

**pye-dog** (pī′dôg′, -dog′), *n.* an ownerless dog of low breed found in towns and villages of India and other parts of Asia. [< Hindi *pāhī* outsider + English *dog*]

**py|e|li|tis** (pī′ə lī′tis), *n.* inflammation of the pelvis of the kidney. [< New Latin *pyelitis* < Greek *pýelos* basin + New Latin *-itis* -itis]

**py|e|lo|gram** (pī′ə lə gram), *n.* an X-ray photograph of the kidney and ureter. [< Greek *pýelos* basin + English *-gram*]

**py|e|lo|graph** (pī′ə lə graf, -gräf), *n.* = pyelogram.

**py|e|lo|graph|ic** (pī′ə lə graf′ik), *adj.* of, having to do with, or obtained by pyelography.

**py|e|log|ra|phy** (pī′ə log′rə fē), *n.* the art of making X-ray pictures of the kidneys and ureters, after the injection of an opaque solution. [< Greek *pýelos* basin + English *-graphy*]

**py|e|lo|ne|phri|tis** (pī′ə lō nē frī′tis), *n.* an inflammation of the kidney and the pelvis: *Pyelonephritis as a cause of hypertension continues to be overlooked by many physicians* (Morris Fishbein). [< Greek *pýelos* basin + English *nephritis*]

**py|e|los|co|py** (pī′ə los′kə pē), *n.* fluoroscopic observation of the kidney, usually after injection of an opaque medium.

**py|e|mi|a** (pī ē′mē ə), *n.* a form of blood poisoning caused by bacteria that produce pus in the blood and characterized by the formation of multiple abscesses in different parts of the body. Also, **pyaemia.** [< New Latin *pyaemia,* perhaps < French *pyohémie* < Greek *pýon* pus + *haîma* blood]

**py|e|mic** (pī ē′mik), *adj.* **1** of or having to do with pyemia. **2** having pyemia. Also, **pyaemic.**

**py|garg** (pī′gärg), *n.* a kind of antelope, perhaps the addax (in the Bible, Deuteronomy 14:5). [< Latin *pȳgargus* < Greek *pȳ́gargos* < *pȳgê* rump + *argós* white]

**py|gid|i|al** (pī jid′ē əl), *adj.* of or having to do with the pygidium.

**Pronunciation Key:** hat, āge, cãre, fär; let, ēqual, tėrm; it, īce; hot, ōpen, ôrder; oil, out; cup, pu̇t, rüle; child; long; thin; ᴛʜen; zh, measure; ə represents **a** in about, **e** in taken, **i** in pencil, **o** in lemon, **u** in circus.

**py|gid|i|um** (pī jid′ē əm), *n., pl.* **-i|a** (-ē ə). the caudal part or terminal segment of the body in insects, crustaceans, and other invertebrates. [< New Latin *pygidium* < Greek *pȳgídion* (diminutive) < *pȳgḗ* rump]

**pyg|mae|an** or **pyg|me|an** (pig mē′ən), *adj.* very small, as in size, ability, or capacity; pygmy.

**Pyg|ma|li|on** (pig mā′lē ən, -māl′yən), *n. Greek Legend.* a sculptor and king of Cyprus, who fell in love with an ivory statue he had made. Aphrodite gave it life, and it became Galatea.

**pyg|moid** (pig′moid), *adj.* of the form of or resembling Pygmies: *The pygmoid Twa ... are rarely seen, being hunters and forest dwellers* (Atlantic).

**Pyg|my** (pig′mē), *n., pl.* **-mies,** *adj.* **—*n.*** **1** one of a group of dark-skinned people native to equatorial Africa who are less than five feet tall. **2** one of a race of very small humans mentioned in ancient history and legend as inhabiting parts of Ethiopia or India. **—*adj.*** of or having to do with the Pygmies. Also, **Pigmy.** [< Middle English *Pigmei* < Latin *pygmaei* < Greek *pygmaîoi* (originally) plural, adjective, dwarfish < *pygmḗ* cubit, fist < *pýx,* adverb, with the fist]

**pyg|my** (pig′mē), *n., pl.* **-mies,** *adj.* **—*n.*** **1** a very small person; dwarf: *... rumors of South American pygmies* (Science News Letter). **2** any very small animal or thing, especially when compared with something else or with a certain standard: *He proceeded to the 50,000-bird colony of Adélie Penguins (18-inch pygmies compared to the 40-inch Emperors)* (Newsweek).
**—*adj.*** **1** very small: *Pygmy marmosets live along the Amazon River in South America.* **2** *Figurative.* of very small capacity or power: *a pygmy mind.* Also, **pigmy.**

**pyg|my|ish** (pig′mē ish), *adj.* like a pygmy; dwarfish: *Compared with its giant kin ... the white [marlin] seems almost pygmyish* (Time).

**pyg|my|ism** (pig′mē iz əm), *n.* the condition or character of being a pygmy.

**pygmy nuthatch,** a small nuthatch inhabiting the coniferous forests of western North America.

**pygmy owl,** either of two small, grayish or reddish brown owls of western North America and South America, that often hunt during the day; gnome owl.

**py|ic** (pī′ik), *adj.* suppurating. [< *py-* + *-ic*]

**py|in** (pī′in), *n.* an albuminous substance found in pus.

**py|ja|mas** (pə jä′məz, -jam′əz), *n.pl.* pajamas.

**pyk|nic** (pik′nik), *adj., n. Anthropology.* **—*adj.*** characterized by rounded contours and a stocky form; plump and squat: *His pyknic Priestleyan features puckered in concentration* (Sunday Times).
**—*n.*** a person of this type: *When they go insane, pyknics are more likely to be manic-depressives* (Alfred L. Kroeber).
[< Greek *pyknós* thick, dense + English *-ic*]

**pyk|no|sis** (pik nō′sis), *n., pl.* **-ses** (-sēz). **1** a condition in which the nucleus of a cell stains more deeply than usual in microscopic study. This condition is thought to be a precursor of necrosis. **2** the thickening of a fluid or semisolid substance. [< Greek *pyknós* thick, dense + English *-osis*]

**pyk|not|ic** (pik not′ik), *adj.* having to do with or characterized by pyknosis: *pyknotic cells.*

**pyk|rete** (pī′krēt), *n.* a frozen slurry of water and wood pulp for use as building material in arctic regions. [< *Pyke,* the name of the inventor + (conc)*rete*]

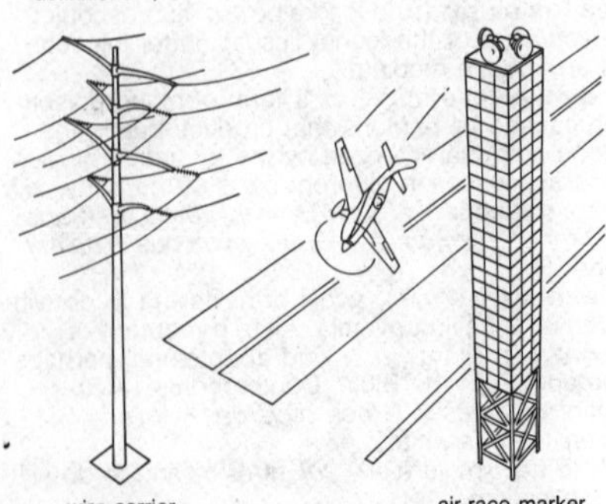

***pylon**
definitions 1, 2

***py|lon** (pī′lon), *n.* **1** a post or tower for guiding aviators, especially as a marker for the course to be flown in an air race. **2** a tall steel framework used to carry high-tension wires across country: *The caption ... implies that overhead lines in Borrowdale are to be erected on lattice towers—commonly referred to as "pylons"* (London Times). **3** one of a pair of high supporting structures of masonry marking an entrance at either side of a bridge. **4** a gateway, particularly of an Egyptian temple, usually consisting of two huge towers. **5** a horizontal structure attached to the underside of an airplane's wing, containing reserve fuel or weapons: *These devices, known as pylons, are part of the underbelly of F-84 Thunderjets* (Science News Letter). [< Greek *pylṓn* gateway < *pýlē* gate]

**py|lo|rec|to|my** (pī′lə rek′tə mē), *n., pl.* **-mies.** **1** the surgical removal of the pylorus. **2** the surgical removal of part of the stomach. [< *pylor*(us) + Greek *ektomḗ* a cutting out]

**py|lor|ic** (pī lôr′ik, -lor′-; pi-), *adj.* of or having to do with the pylorus: *pyloric glands, pyloric sphincter.*

**py|lor|o|spasm** (pī lôr′ə spaz əm, -lōr′-; pi-), *n.* a closing of the pylorus; spasm of the pylorus or of the part of the stomach close to the pylorus: *Heavy drinking may also produce in some people the condition called pylorospasm* (Scientific American).

**py|lo|rus** (pī lôr′əs, -lōr′-; pi-), *n., pl.* **-lo|ri** (-lôr′ī, -lōr′-). the opening that leads from the stomach into the intestine. [< Late Latin *pylōrus* < Greek *pylōrós* (originally) gatekeeper < *pýlē* gate + *oûros* watcher < *horân* to see]

**pyo-,** *combining form.* pus: *Pyogenesis = the formation of pus.* Also, **py-** before vowels. [< Greek *pýon* pus]

**py|o|der|ma** (pī′ə dėr′mə), *n.* any disease of the skin characterized by the formation of pus. [< *pyo-* + *derma*]

**py|o|der|mi|a** (pī′ə dėr′mē ə), *n.* = pyoderma.

**py|o|gen|e|sis** (pī′ə jen′ə sis), *n.* the formation of pus; suppuration. [< *pyo-* + *genesis*]

**py|o|gen|ic** (pī′ə jen′ik), *adj.* producing or generating pus; attended with or having to do with the formation of pus.

**py|og|e|nous** (pī oj′ə nəs), *adj.* = pyogenic.

**py|oid** (pī′oid), *adj.* of the nature of or resembling pus; purulent. [< *py-* + *-oid*]

**py|o|ne|phri|tis** (pī′ō ni frī′tis), *n.* suppurative inflammation of a kidney. [< *pyo-* + *nephritis*]

**py|o|per|i|car|di|um** (pī′ō per′ə kär′dē əm), *n.* the presence, or a collection, of pus in the pericardium.

**py|oph|thal|mi|a** (pī′of thal′mē ə), *n.* an inflammation of the eye that causes pus to form. [< *py-* + *ophthalmia*]

**py|o|pneu|mo|tho|rax** (pī′ō nü′mō thôr′aks, -nyü′-; -thōr′-), *n.* the presence of pus and air in the pleural cavities.

**py|or|rhe|a** or **py|or|rhoe|a** (pī′ə rē′ə), *n.* a disease of the gums in which pockets of pus form about the teeth, the gums shrink, and the teeth become loose: *The quantities of the two vitamins in body fluids of people with parodontal lesions, or pyorrhea, [are] lower than normal* (Science News Letter). [< New Latin *pyorrhoea* < Greek *pýon* pus + *rhoiā́* a flow < *rheîn* to flow]

**py|or|rhe|al** or **py|or|rhoe|al** (pī′ə rē′əl), *adj.* of or having to do with pyorrhea.

**py|o|sis** (pī ō′sis), *n.* the formation of pus; suppuration. [< New Latin *pyosis* < Greek *pýōsis* < *pýon* pus + New Latin *-osis* -osis]

**py|o|tho|rax** (pī′ō thôr′aks, -thōr′-), *n.* the collection of pus in the pleural cavities.

**py|o|u|re|ter** (pī′ō yu̇ rē′tər, -yür′ə-), *n.* the collection of pus in a ureter. [< *pyo-* + *ureter*]

**pyr-,** the form of **pyro-** that appears before *h,* and sometimes before vowels, as in *pyrene, pyrheliometer.*

**py|ra|can|tha** (pī′rə kan′thə, pir′ə-), *n.* any one of a group of thorny, evergreen shrubs; firethorn: *Pyracantha in the North has long since been denuded of its berries* (New York Times). [< Latin *pyracantha* < Greek *pyrákantha* < *pŷr* fire + *ákantha* thorn]

**pyr|a|lid** (pir′ə lid), *n., adj.* **—*n.*** any plain-colored moth of a large family with slender bodies, such as the meal moth.
**—*adj.*** belonging to or having to do with this family.
[< New Latin *Pyralidae* the family name < Latin *pyralis* a winged insect that supposedly lived in fire < Greek *pyralís* < *pŷr* fire]

**py|ral|i|dan** (pī ral′ə dən), *n., adj.* = pyralid.

**py|ral|i|did** (pī ral′ə did), *n., adj.* = pyralid.

**Py|ra|lin** (pī′rə lin), *n. Trademark.* a substance composed essentially of pyroxylin and camphor, variously colored to imitate ivory, amber, tortoise shell, and ebony, and used in the manufacture of many products, as combs and other toilet articles, knife handles, and trays.

***pyr|a|mid** (pir′ə mid), *n., v.* **—*n.*** **1** a solid having triangular sides meeting in a point. The base of a pyramid is a polygon. **2** anything having the form of a pyramid: *a pyramid of stones, a pyramid of cannonballs.* **3** a crystal each of whose faces intersects the vertical axis and one or two of the lateral axes. **3a** a very large structure built of stone or the like, with sloping sides meeting at a point and, usually, with a square base: *... the great pyramid of Cholula, the largest and most sacred temple in Mexico* (Joseph Gwilt). **b** Usually, **the Pyramids.** any one of the huge, massive stone pyramids, serving as royal tombs, built by the ancient Egyptians: *The largest of the Pyramids is the Great Pyramid at Giza, on the west bank of the Nile.* **4** *Anatomy.* a part or structure of more or less pyramidal form: **a** a mass of longitudinal nerve fibers on each side of the medulla oblongata. **b** one of the conical-shaped masses making up the medullary substance of the kidney. **5** *Figurative.* a pyramidal structure; an organization or hierarchy having the form of a pyramid: *a pyramid of power, a corporate pyramid. His references had come from the top of the unofficial power pyramid of American education* (New York Times). *The traditional pyramid, with a small upper class at the top, a somewhat larger middle class immediately below, and a much larger working class at the bottom ...* (New Scientist).
**—*v.i.*** **1** to form a pyramid: *The acrobats pyramided skillfully, one on top of the other.* **2** *Figurative.* to rise to the top or highest point: *Consumer lending had pyramided since the war* (Canada Month). **3** to be arranged in pyramidal form: *High scorers pyramid to the top, and highest scorer at the end of the final round is declared the winner* (New York Times). **4** *Finance.* to pyramid one's holdings in stocks. **—*v.t.*** **1** to put in the form of a pyramid. **2** *Figurative.* to raise or increase (as costs or wages) gradually: *They are pyramiding their costs in their pricing, just as steel is doing* (Wall Street Journal). **3** *Figurative.* to increase (as one's operations or holdings) in buying or selling stock on margin by using the profits to buy or sell more: *He pyramided his winnings and piled gold on gold ... and finally saw himself a millionaire three times over* (Percy Marks).
[< Latin *pȳramis, -idis* < Greek *pȳramís, -idos*]

***pyramid**
definition 1
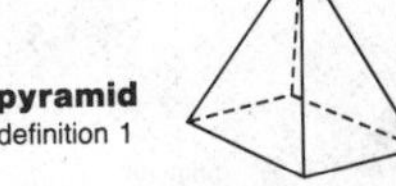
square base
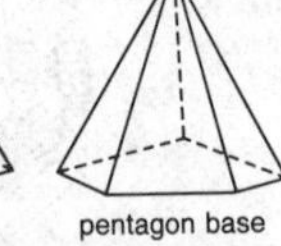
pentagon base

**py|ram|i|dal** (pə ram′ə dəl), *adj.* **1** shaped like a pyramid: *the pyramidal structures of ancient Egypt* (William H. Prescott). *The pyramidal cells in one hemisphere of the brain may activate the symmetrical region of the other hemisphere* (Scientific American). **2** *Figurative.* colossal; huge; extraordinarily great (a French use): *a pyramidal success.* **—py|ram′i|dal|ly,** *adv.*

**pyr|a|mid|ic** (pir′ə mid′ik), *adj.* pyramidal: *The enormous gate which rose O'er them in almost pyramidic pride* (Byron).

**pyr|a|mid|i|cal** (pir′ə mid′ə kəl), *adj.* = pyramidal. [< Greek *pȳramidikós* pyramidic (< *pȳramís, -idos* pyramid) + English *-al*[1]] **—pyr′a|mid′i|cal|ly,** *adv.* **—pyr′a|mid′i|cal|ness,** *n.*

**pyr|a|mid|i|on** (pir′ə mid′ē on), *n., pl.* **-i|ons, -i|a** (-ē ə). **1** a small pyramid forming the apex of an obelisk. **2** any small pyramid. [< New Latin *pyramidion*]

**Pyr|a|mus** (pir′ə məs), *n. Greek Legend.* a young Babylonian who loved Thisbe and killed himself because he thought that she had been devoured by a lion.

**py|ran** (pī′ran, pī ran′), *n.* one of two isomeric compounds, each having a ring of five carbon atoms and one oxygen atom. *Formula:* $C_5H_6O$ [< *pyr*(one) + *-an,* variant of *-ane*]

**py|rar|gy|rite** (pī rär′jə rīt), *n.* a dark-colored mineral consisting of a sulfide of silver and antimony, and showing, when transparent, a deep ruby-red color by transmitted light; dark ruby silver. *Formula:* $Ag_3SbS_3$ [probably < German *Pyrargyrit* < Greek *pŷr* fire + *árgyros* silver + German *-it* -ite[1] (probably because of its dark-red color)]

**py|ra|zin|a|mid** (pī′rə zin′ə mid), *n.* = pyrazinamide.

**py|ra|zin|a|mide** (pī′rə zin′ə mīd), *n.* a drug sometimes used in the treatment of tuberculosis, especially in conjunction with isoniazid or streptomycin, in persons who are resistant to or sensitive to other drugs. *Formula:* $C_5H_5N_3O$

**pyr|a|zine** (pir′ə zēn, -zin), *n. Chemistry.* **1** a feebly basic, crystalline organic compound, with an odor like heliotrope. *Formula:* $C_4H_4N_2$ **2** any one of various compounds derived from it: *The new TB medicine is a pyrazine chemical* (Science News Letter). [< *pyr-* + *azine*]

**pyre** (pīr), *n.* **1** a pile of wood for burning a dead body as a funeral rite: *Only within the past century have grieving widows been restrained from throwing themselves on their husbands' funeral* *pyres* (Newsweek). **2** any large pile or heap of burnable material. [< Latin *pyra* < Greek *pyrā́* < *pŷr* fire]

**py|rene¹** (pī′rēn), *n.* **1** a stone of a fruit, especially when there are several in one fruit. **2** = nutlet. [probably < New Latin *pyrena* < Greek *pȳrēn* stone of a fruit]

**py|rene²** (pī′rēn), *n.* a solid hydrocarbon, obtained from coal tar. *Formula:* $C_{16}H_{10}$

**Pyr|e|ne|an** (pir′ə nē′ən), *adj., n.* – ***adj.*** of or having to do with the Pyrenees, a mountain range between France and Spain: *Swarms of butterflies, dragonflies and other insects fly southwards over the Pyrenean passes* (Observer).
– ***n.*** **1** a native or inhabitant of the Pyrenees. **2** = Great Pyrenees.

**Pyr|e|nees** (pir′ə nēz), *n.* = Great Pyrenees.

**py|re|noid** (pī′rə noid, pī rē′-), *n.* a small protein structure resembling a nucleus, found in the chloroplast of certain algae, and associated with the formation and accumulation of starch. [< Greek *pȳrēn* stone of a fruit + English *-oid*]

**py|re|thrin** (pī rē′thrən, -reth′rən), *n.* one of the constituents or active principles of pyrethrum: *Insects cannot build resistance to pyrethrins because they are a natural insecticide* (Cape Times). [< *pyrethr*(um) + *-in*]

**py|re|thrum** (pī rē′thrəm, -reth′rəm), *n., pl.* **-thrums. 1** any one of various chrysanthemums, much cultivated for their showy while, lilac, or red flowers: *The rich "white highlands" whence comes most of Kenya's lucrative coffee, tea, sisal and pyrethrum* (Time). **2** an insecticide made of the powdered flower heads of any of certain of these: *With the appearance of the scientists on the field of battle, the old stand-bys of pyrethrum, oils and arsenic compounds were developed* (Science News Letter). [< Latin *pyrethrum* feverfew, pellitory < Greek *pȳrethron,* probably < *pŷr* fire]

**py|ret|ic** (pī ret′ik), *adj.* **1** of or having to do with fever. **2** producing fever: *Whenever the bodily temperature falls below normal, pyretic treatment is demanded* (H. C. Wood). **3** = feverish. [< New Latin *pyreticus* < Greek *pyretós* fever < *pŷr* fire]

**pyr|e|tol|o|gy** (pir′ə tol′ə jē, pī′rə-), *n.* the science of, or accumulated knowledge of, fevers. [perhaps < New Latin *pyretologia* < Greek *pyretós* fever (< *pŷr* fire) + New Latin *-logia* -logy]

**pyr|e|to|ther|a|py** (pir′ə tə ther′ə pē, pī′rə-), *n.* therapy in which fever is induced in the patient. [< Greek *pyretós* fever + English *therapy*]

**Py|rex** (pī′reks), *n. Trademark.* a kind of glassware that will not break when heated: *One of the newest glasses is borosilicate glass, widely advertised under the trade name "Pyrex"* (Monroe M. Offner).

**py|rex|i|a** (pī rek′sē ə), *n.* = fever. [< New Latin *pyrexia* < Greek *pyréssein* be feverish < *pyretós* fever; see etym. under **pyretic**]

**py|rex|i|al** (pī rek′sē əl), *adj.* of or having to do with a fever.

**py|rex|ic** (pī rek′sik), *adj.* = feverish.

**pyr|ge|om|e|ter** (pīr′jē om′ə tər, pir′-), *n.* an instrument for measuring the heat radiated outward into space from the earth's surface. [< *pyr-* + *geo-* + *-meter*]

**pyr|he|li|om|e|ter** (pīr hē′li om′ə tər, pir-), *n.* an instrument for measuring the intensity of the sun's heat.

**Pyr|i|ben|za|mine** (pir′ə ben′zə mēn, -min), *n. Trademark.* an antihistamine used especially in treating allergies. *Formula:* $C_{16}H_{21}N_3$

**py|rid|ic** (pī rid′ik), *adj.* of or related to pyridine.

**pyr|i|din** (pir′ə din), *n.* = pyridine.

**pyr|i|dine** (pir′ə dēn, -din), *n.* a liquid organic base with a pungent odor, occurring especially in coal tar, and serving as the parent substance of many compounds. It is used as a solvent and waterproofing agent, and in making various drugs and vitamins. *Formula:* $C_5H_5N$ [< *pyr*(role) + *-id* + *-ine²*]

**pyr|i|dox|al** (pir′ə dok′səl), *n.* an aldehyde or pyridoxine found in certain enzymes, such as carboxylase, and important in the synthesis of amino acids. *Formula:* $C_8H_9NO_3$

**pyr|i|dox|in** (pir′ə dok′sin), *n.* = pyridoxine.

**pyr|i|dox|ine** (pir′ə dok′sēn, -sin), *n.* vitamin $B_6$, essential to human nutrition, found especially in wheat germ, yeast, fish, and liver; adermin. *Formula:* $C_8H_{11}NO_3$ [< *pyrid*(ine) + *ox*(ygen) + *-ine²*]

**pyr|i|form** (pir′ə fôrm), *adj.* = pear-shaped. [< Medieval Latin *pyrum,* for Latin *pirum* pear + English *-form*]

**py|ri|meth|a|mine** (pī′rə meth′ə mēn, pir′ə-), *n.* a synthetic drug used in the treatment of malaria, often in combination with primaquine or chloroquine, and experimentally against some other diseases: *The antimalarial drug pyrimethamine ... is also quite effective against toxoplasmosis* (F. P. Mathews). *Formula:* $C_{12}H_{13}ClN_4$ [< *pyrim*(idine) + *eth*(yl) + (di)*amine*]

**py|rim|i|dine** (pī rim′ə dēn, pir′ə mə-; -din), *n.* **1** a liquid or crystalline organic base with a strong odor, whose molecular arrangement is a six-membered ring containing atoms of nitrogen. It is found in living matter and is a constituent of nucleic acid. *Formula:* $C_4H_4N_2$ **2** any one of a group of compounds derived from it, such as cytosine and thymine. [< German *Pyrimidin* < *Pyridin* pyridine]

**py|rite** (pī′rīt), *n., pl.* **-rites** (-rīts). a common yellow mineral with a metallic luster, a compound of iron and sulfur, which looks like and is often mistaken for gold; iron pyrites; fool's gold. It is used in making sulfuric acid. *Pyrite, in mistake for gold, was the first mineral shipped from America to England* (W. R. Jones). *Formula:* $FeS_2$ [< Latin *pyrītēs;* see etym. under **pyrites**]

**py|ri|tes** (pī rī′tēz, pi-; pī′rīts), *n.* **1** any one of various compounds of sulfur and a metal, such as tin pyrites, an ore of tin, or copper pyrites. **2** = pyrite. [< Latin *pyrītēs* < Greek *pyrītēs* (*líthos*) flint, (stone, or ore) of fire < *pŷr* fire]

**py|rit|ic** (pī rit′ik, pi-), *adj.* **1** having to do with pyrites. **2** consisting of or resembling pyrites.

**py|rit|i|cal** (pī rit′ə kal, pi-), *adj.* = pyritic.

**py|ro** (pī′rō), *n.* = pyrogallol.

**pyro-,** *combining form.* **1** of, having to do with, using, or caused by fire: *Pyromania = an obsession with fire. Pyrotechnics = the making of fireworks.*
**2** heat; high temperatures: *Pyrometer = an instrument that measures high temperatures.*
**3** formed by heat: *Pyroacid = an acid formed by heat.* Also, **pyr-** before *h* and some vowels. [< Greek *pyro-* < *pŷr, pyrós*]

**py|ro|ac|id** (pī′rō as′id, pir′ō-), *n.* any one of various acids obtained by subjecting other acids to heat. [< *pyr-* + *acid*]

**py|ro|cat|e|chin** (pī′rə kat′ə chin, -kin; pir′ə-), *n.* = pyrocatechol.

**py|ro|cat|e|chol** (pī′rə kat′ə kōl, -chōl, -kol; pir′ə-), *n.* a colorless, crystalline benzene derivative, occurring especially in certain plants and prepared from phenol by distillation of catechin. It is used in photography as a developer and medicinally as an antiseptic. *Formula:* $C_6H_6O_2$

**Py|ro|cer|am** (pī′rə ser′əm, -sə ram′; pir′ə-), *n. Trademark.* a light, crystalline ceramic material or product made from glass-ceramic and able to withstand sudden and extreme temperature and heat changes: *Pyroceram can be used to make items ranging from cooking pans to airplane skins* (Wall Street Journal).

**py|ro|chem|i|cal** (pī′rə kem′ə kəl, pir′ə-), *adj.* having to do with or producing chemical changes at high temperatures. – **py′ro|chem′i|cal|ly,** *adv.*

**py|ro|clas|tic** (pī′rə klas′tik, pir′ə-), *adj.* composed chiefly of fragments of volcanic origin: *pyroclastic flows, pyroclastic texture. Agglomerate and tuff are pyroclastic rocks.* [< *pyro-* + *clastic*]

**py|ro|con|duc|tiv|i|ty** (pī′rō kon′duk tiv′ə tē, pir′ō-), *n.* electrical conductivity induced by heat.

**py|ro|crys|tal|line** (pī′rə kris′tə lin, -līn; pir′ə-), *adj.* crystallized from a molten magma or highly heated solution.

**py|ro|e|lec|tric** (pī′rō i lek′trik, pir′ō-), *adj., n.* – ***adj.*** of, having to do with, or having pyroelectricity.
– ***n.*** a pyroelectric crystal.

**py|ro|e|lec|tric|i|ty** (pī′rō i lek′tris′ə tē, pir′ō-; -ē′-lek-), *n.* **1** the electrified state or electric polarity produced in certain crystals by a change in temperature. **2** the part of physics dealing with such phenomena.

**py|ro|gal|late** (pī′rə gal′āt, pir′ə-), *n.* an ether of pyrogallol. [< *pyro-* + *gall*(ic acid) + *-ate²*]

**py|ro|gal|lic** (pī′rə gal′ik, pir′ə-), *adj.* obtained from gallic acid by the action of heat.

**pyrogallic acid,** = pyrogallol.

**py|ro|gal|lol** (pī′rə gal′ōl, -ol; -gə lōl′; pir′ə-), *n.* a white, crystalline compound obtained by heating gallic acid with water, used as a photographic developer, in medicine, and as a reagent. Pyrogallol is a phenol but can be regarded as an acid. *Formula:* $C_6H_6O_3$ [< *pyro-* + *gall*(ic acid) + *-ol¹*]

**py|ro|gen** (pī′rə jən, pir′ə-), *n.* a substance that, when introduced into the blood, produces fever: *Pyrogens in pure form can, with advantage, replace the older materials and methods for producing a general stimulation of the defense mechanisms of the body* (London Times). [< *pyro-* + *-gen*]

**py|ro|gen|ic** (pī′rə jen′ik, pir′ə-), *adj.* **1** producing heat or fever. **2** produced by fire: *Volcanic rock is pyrogenic.*

**py|rog|e|nous** (pī roj′ə nəs, pi-), *adj.* = pyrogenic.

**py|rog|nos|tics** (pī′rəg nos′tiks, pir′əg-), *n.pl.* the characteristics of a mineral shown by the use of a blowpipe. [< *pyro-* fire + Greek *gnōstikós* having to do with knowledge]

**py|rog|ra|pher** (pī rog′rə fər, pi-), *n.* a person who is skilled in pyrography.

**py|ro|graph|ic** (pī′rə graf′ik, pir′ə-), *adj.* of, having to do with, or used in pyrography: *a pyrographic decoration.*

**Py|ro|graph|ite** (pī′rə graf′īt), *n. Trademark.* a strong graphite able to resist the effect of very high temperatures, used in missiles and other manufacture: *Pyrographite, a material it claims will solve the high-heat problems in the missile, nuclear reactor and industrial fields* (Wall Street Journal).

**py|rog|ra|phy** (pī rog′rə fē, pi-), *n., pl.* **-phies. 1** the art of burning designs as on wood, leather, or other surfaces. **2** objects decorated by pyrography. **3** a design or figure used in pyrography.

**py|ro|gra|vure** (pī′rō grə vyůr′, -grā′vyůr; pir′ō-), *n.* = pyrography.

**py|rol|a|ter** (pī rol′ə tər), *n.* a fire worshiper.

**py|rol|a|try** (pī rol′ə trē), *n.* the worship of fire: *Anything like pyrolatry or worship of fire, as a mere element, is foreign to the character of the Greeks* (Max Müller). [< *pyro-* + Greek *latreiā́* worship]

**py|ro|lig|ne|ous** (pī′rə lig′nē əs, pir′ə-), *adj.* produced by the distillation of wood. [< French *pyroligneux* (with English *-ous*) < Greek *pŷr, pyrós* fire + Latin *ligneus* of wood, ligneous]

**pyroligneous acid,** a crude acetic acid obtained by the destructive distillation of wood, and used in smoking meats; wood vinegar: *A portion of the distillate is converted to an acidic, watery fluid known as pyroligneous acid* (W. N. Jones).

**pyroligneous alcohol** or **spirit,** = methyl alcohol.

**py|ro|lig|nic** (pī′rə lig′nik, pir′ə-), *adj.* = pyroligneous.

**py|ro|log|i|cal** (pī′rə loj′ə kəl, pir′ə-), *adj.* having to do with or involving pyrology.

**py|rol|o|gist** (pī rol′ə jist, pi-), *n.* a person skilled in pyrology.

**py|rol|o|gy** (pī rol′ə jē, pi-), *n.* **1** the science of heat. **2** chemical or mineralogical analysis by the use of fire or the blowpipe. [< New Latin *pyrologia* < *pyro-* pyro- + *-logia* -logy]

**py|ro|lu|site** (pī′rə lü′sīt, pir′ə-; pī rol′yə-, pi-), *n.* native manganese dioxide, used as a source of manganese in glassmaking, and in making various chemicals, such as chlorine and oxygen. *Formula:* $MnO_2$ [< German *Pyrolusit* < Greek *pŷr, pyrós* fire + *loúein* to wash + German *-it* -ite¹]

**py|rol|y|sis** (pī rol′ə sis, pi-), *n.* chemical decomposition produced by exposure to high temperatures: *He established by pyrolysis that the strength of binding varies considerably in hydrocarbons* (New Scientist). [< *pyro-* + *lysis*]

**py|ro|lyt|ic** (pī′rə lit′ik, pir′ə-), *adj.* of, like, or by pyrolysis. – **py′ro|lyt′i|cal|ly,** *adv.*

**py|ro|lyze** (pī′rə līz, pir′ə-), *v.t.,* **-lyzed, -lyz|ing.** to decompose by pyrolysis: *The dried coal is then pyrolyzed ... at 850° F* (R. C. Phillips).
– **py′ro|lyz′er,** *n.*

**py|ro|mag|net|ic** (pī′rō mag net′ik, pir′ō-), *adj.* **1** having to do with magnetism as modified by heat. **2** of or depending upon the combined action of heat and magnetism.

**py|ro|man|cy** (pī′rə man′sē, pir′ə-), *n.* divination by fire, or by forms appearing in fire. [< Old French *pyromancie,* and *piromance,* learned borrowings from Medieval Latin *piromancia, pyromanteia* < Greek *pŷr, pyrós* fire + *manteiā́* divination]

**py|ro|ma|ni|a** (pī′rə mā′nē ə, pir′ə-), *n.* an uncontrollable desire to set things on fire; incendiarism.

**py|ro|ma|ni|ac** (pī′rə mā′nē ak, pir′ə-), *n.* a person with an uncontrollable desire to set things on fire.

**py|ro|ma|ni|a|cal** (pī′rō mə nī′ə kəl, pir′ō-), *adj.* **1** affected with or having a tendency toward pyromania. **2** caused by a pyromaniac: *a pyromaniacal fire.*

**Py|ro|men** (pī′rə mən), *n. Trademark.* a polysaccharide derived from certain bacteria, used to induce fever and treat allergies and skin diseases. It has been used on animals and a small number of humans to prevent the formation of scar tissue at the ends of a severed spine so as to permit nerve fibers to grow across and thus regain ability to function. *Pyromen helps virus-ravaged nerves to rebuild themselves so that they can again assert control over the muscles* (Time).

**py|ro|met|al|lur|gi|cal** (pī′rō met′ə lėr′jə kəl, pir′ō-), *adj.* of or having to do with pyrometallurgy: *The work is part of an experimental investigation of pyrometallurgical processing for nuclear fuel* (Scientific American).

**py|ro|met|al|lur|gy** (pī′rō met′ə lėr′jē, pir′ō-), *n.* the use of heat in refining ores, especially in order to hasten reactions and melt the metal.

**Pronunciation Key:** hat, āge, cãre, fär; let, ēqual, tėrm; it, īce; hot, ōpen, ôrder; **oi**l, **ou**t; cup, pu̇t, rüle; **ch**ild; lo**ng**; **th**in; ᴛʜen; **zh**, measure; **ə** represents **a** in about, **e** in taken, **i** in pencil, **o** in lemon, **u** in circus.

**py|rom|e|ter** (pī rom′ə tər, pi-), *n.* **1** an instrument for measuring very high temperatures: *An optical pyrometer ... tells the temperature of a substance, within five degrees, by its intensity of radiation* (New Yorker). **2** an instrument for measuring the expansion of solids by heat.

**py|ro|met|ric** (pī′rə met′rik, pir′ə-), *adj.* of or having to do with a pyrometer. —**py′ro|met′ri|cal|ly,** *adv.*

**py|ro|met|ri|cal** (pī′rə met′rə kəl, pir′ə-), *adj.* = pyrometric.

**pyrometric cone,** any one of a series of cones, each melting at different temperatures, used to measure the several degrees of heat in pottery kilns.

**py|rom|e|try** (pī rom′ə trē, pi-), *n.* **1** the measurement of very high temperatures. **2** the science of measuring very high temperatures.

**py|ro|mor|phite** (pī′rə môr′fīt, pir′ə-), *n.* a mineral consisting of chloride and phosphate of lead, occurring both in crystals and masses, green, yellow, brown, or whitish in color; green lead ore. [< German *Pyromorphit* < Greek *pŷr, pyrós* fire + *morphḗ* form + German *-it* -ite[1]]

**py|rone** (pī′rōn, pī rōn′), *n.* either of two isomeric compounds, one of which is the source of various natural yellow dyes. *Formula:* $C_5H_4O_2$ [< German *Pyron,* probably < Greek *pŷr* fire + German *-on* -one]

**py|rope** (pī′rōp), *n.* a deep-red variety of garnet, frequently used as a gem; precious garnet. [< Old French *pirope,* learned borrowing from Latin *pyrōpus* < Greek *pyrōpós* gold-colored bronze (literally) fire-eyed < *pŷr, pyrós* fire + *ṓps, ōpós* eye, face]

**py|ro|pho|bi|a** (pī′rə fō′bē ə, pir′ə-), *n.* a morbid dread of fire. [< *pyro-* + *-phobia*]

**py|ro|pho|bic** (pī′rə fō′bik, pir′ə-), *adj.* of, having to do with, or affected with pyrophobia.

**py|ro|phor|ic** (pī′rə fôr′ik, -for′-; pir′ə-), *adj.* **1** having the property of taking fire simply through exposure to air; that catches fire spontaneously, as certain compounds of phosphorus: *Many of the metals used in nuclear technology, notably uranium, plutonium, thorium and zirconium, are pyrophoric* (Scientific American). **2** (chiefly of an insect or marine organism) that is, or is like, a firefly; giving off light. [< New Latin *pyrophorus* (< Greek *pyrophóros* (literally) fire-bearing < *pŷr, pyrós* fire + *phórein* carry) + English *-ic*]

**py|ro|phor|ic|i|ty** (pī′rə fə ris′ə tē, pir′ə-), *n.* **1** spontaneous combustion upon exposure to air. **2** the tendency to react in this way; pyrophoric nature or quality.

**py|ro|phos|phate** (pī′rō fos′fāt, pir′ō-), *n.* a salt of pyrophosphoric acid.

**py|ro|phos|phor|ic acid** (pī′rō fos fôr′ik, -for′-; pir′ō-), a tetrabasic acid of phosphorus. *Formula:* $H_4P_2O_7$

**py|ro|pho|tom|e|ter** (pī′rō fō tom′ə tər, pir′ō-), *n.* a form of pyrometer, that measures temperatures by optical means.

**py|ro|phyl|lite** (pī′rə fil′īt, pir′ə-), *n.* a hydrous silicate of aluminum, usually of a whitish or greenish color. It is used as a filler and polisher, and in making slate pencils, lubricants, and cosmetics. *Pyrophyllite ... is for commercial purposes generally included in the statistics relating to talc* (W. R. Jones). *Formula:* $Al_2O_3 \cdot 4SiO_2 \cdot H_2O$ [< German *Pyrophyllite* < Greek *pŷr, pyrós* fire + *phýllon* leaf + German *-it* -ite[1] (because it leafs out under heat)]

**py|ro|sis** (pī rō′sis, pi-), *n.* = heartburn. [< New Latin *pyrosis* < Greek *pýrōsis* < *pŷr, pyrós* fire + New Latin *-osis* -osis]

**py|ro|stat** (pī′rə stat, pir′ə-), *n.* a thermostat for high temperature. Pyrostats are used to give warning of fire or to activate a sprinkler system. [< *pyro-* + (thermo)*stat*]

**py|ro|stilp|nite** (pī′rō stilp′nīt), *n.* a mineral, a sulfide of arsenic and silver, occurring in minute, bright-red, monoclinic crystals; fireblende. [< *pyro-* + Greek *stilpnós* shining + English *-ite*[1]]

**py|ro|sul|fate** (pī′rə sul′fāt, pir′ə-), *n.* a salt of pyrosulfuric acid.

**py|ro|sul|fu|ric acid** (pī′rō sul fyůr′ik, pir′ō-), a thick, fuming liquid acid, a powerful oxidizing and dehydrating agent; disulfuric acid. *Formula:* $H_2S_2O_7$

**py|ro|tech|nic** (pī′rə tek′nik, pir′ə-), *adj.* **1** of or having to do with fireworks: *a pyrotechnic display.* **2** *Figurative.* resembling fireworks; brilliant; sensational: *pyrotechnic eloquence, pyrotechnic dancing.* —**py′ro|tech′ni|cal|ly,** *adv.*

**py|ro|tech|ni|cal** (pī′rə tek′nə kəl, pir′ə-), *adj.* = pyrotechnic.

**py|ro|tech|ni|cian** (pī′rə tek nish′ən, pir′ə-), *n.* = pyrotechnist.

**py|ro|tech|nics** (pī′rə tek′niks, pir′ə-), *n.* **1** fireworks. Pyrotechnics used in military operations include signal rockets, flares, smoke bombs, and the like. **2** the act or process of making fireworks. **3** the use of fireworks. **4** a display of fireworks. **5** *Figurative.* a brilliant or sensational display, as of eloquence, anger, wit, or lightning: *The meanings of the prose are sacrificed to the mechanics of ... pyrotechnics* (Newsweek).

**py|ro|tech|nist** (pī′rə tek′nist, pir′ə-), *n.* a person skilled in pyrotechnics: *The whole skill of the pyrotechnists ... was employed to produce a display of fireworks which might vie with any that had been seen in the gardens of Versailles* (Macaulay).

**py|ro|tech|ny** (pī′rə tek′nē, pir′ə-), *n., pl.* **-nies.** pyrotechnics: [*They*] *make such a noise in the world ... with artificial volcanoes and puerile pyrotechny of all kinds* (Blackwood's Magazine). [< French *pyrotechnie* < Greek *pŷr, pyrós* fire + *téchnē* art, skill]

**py|ro|tox|in** (pī′rə tok′sin, pir′ə-), *n.* a toxin that causes fever.

**py|rox|ene** (pī′rok sēn), *n.* any one of a group of silicate minerals, usually calcium, magnesium, and iron silicate, but occurring in many varieties, often found in igneous rocks such as granites and lavas. [< French *pyroxène* < Greek *pŷr, pyrós* fire + *xénos* stranger (because it was not considered to be native to igneous rocks)]

**py|rox|en|ic** (pī′rok sen′ik), *adj.* of, having to do with, or containing a pyroxene or pyroxenes.

**py|rox|e|nite** (pī rok′sə nīt), *n.* any rock composed essentially, or in large part, of pyroxene of any kind.

**py|rox|man|gite** (pī′roks man′gīt), *n.* a yellowish-brown variety of pyroxene with a high manganese content. [< *pyrox*(ene) + *mang*(anese) + *-ite*[1]]

**py|rox|y|lin** or **py|rox|y|line** (pī rok′sə lin), *n.* any one of various substances made by nitrating certain forms of cellulose. Guncotton and the soluble cellulose nitrates used in making celluloid, and collodion, are pyroxylins. [< *pyro-* + Greek *xýlon* wood + English *-ine*[2]]

**Pyr|rha** (pir′ə), *n. Greek Mythology.* the wife of Deucalion. She and her husband were the only ones to survive a great flood sent by Zeus to destroy mankind.

**pyr|rhic**[1] (pir′ik), *n., adj.* —*n.* an ancient Greek dance: *A thrilling weapon dance, the pyrrhic, was performed by warriors* (Hanya Holm).
—***adj.*** of or having to do with a war dance.
[< Greek *pyrrhíchē* (*órchēsis*) perhaps (dance) of *Pýrrhichos,* supposedly the creator of the dance, or perhaps (as Aristotle says) < *pyrá* pyre (because it was first used at the funeral, that is, burning, of Patroclus)]

**pyr|rhic**[2] (pir′ik), *n., adj.* —*n.* a measure in poetry consisting of two short syllables or two unaccented syllables: *They intended to vary the ordinary rhythm by introducing an accentual pyrrhic* (English Metre). —***adj.*** consisting of or having to do with pyrrhics. [< Latin *pyrrhichius* < Greek *pyrrhíchios* (*poús*) pyrrhic (foot) < *pyrrhíchē;* see etym. under **pyrrhic**[1] (because the meter was used in that dance)]

**Pyr|rhic** (pir′ik), *adj.* of or having to do with Pyrrhus, a king of Epirus in Greece.

**Pyrrhic victory,** a victory won at too great a cost: *Out of the wreckage he salvaged a Pyrrhic victory, an amendment to get rid of the onerous provision for a two-thirds approval of tax bills* (Newsweek). [< *Pyrrhus,* king of Epirus in Greece, who defeated the Roman armies in 280 B.C., but lost so many men in doing so that he could not attack Rome itself + English *-ic*]

**Pyr|rho|nism** (pir′ə niz əm), *n.* skepticism; the philosophy of the Greek Pyrrho of Elis. Its central doctrine concerns the impossibility of attaining certainty of knowledge. *The Pyrrhonism of my opinions has at all times rendered me notorious* (Edgar Allan Poe).

**Pyr|rho|nist** (pir′ə nist), *n.* **1** an adherent of Pyrrhonism. **2** a person who doubts everything.

**Pyr|rho|nis|tic** (pir′ə nis′tik), *adj.* of or having to do with Pyrrhonists or Pyrrhonism: *These manners are brought together in a Pyrrhonistic unity which expresses perfectly the ambivalence of any East-West attitude* (Manchester Guardian Weekly).

**pyr|rho|tine** (pir′ə tēn, -tin), *n.* = pyrrhotite.

**pyr|rho|tite** (pir′ə tīt), *n.* a native iron sulfide having a bronze color and a metallic luster, occurring in crystals and masses. It often contains nickel and is usually slightly magnetic. *The dominant mineral being pyrrhotite, in which most of the pentlandite occurs as scattered grains* (W. R. Jones). [< Greek *pyrrhótēs* redness < *pyrrhós* fiery red < *pŷr* fire (because of its color) + English *-ite*[1]]

**pyr|rho|tit|ic** (pir′ə tit′ik), *adj.* of, having to do with, or containing pyrrhotite.

**pyr|rhu|lox|i|a** (pir′ə lok′sē ə), *n.* a gray finch with a reddish crest and tail, of the southwestern United States and Mexico, resembling and related to the cardinal. [< New Latin *Pyrrhuloxia* the genus name, perhaps < Greek *pyrrhós* fiery red]

**Pyr|rhus** (pir′əs), *n. Greek Legend.* a son of Achilles, who slew Priam and married Andromache. He was also called Neoptolemus.

**pyr|rol** (pir′ol, -ōl), *n.* = pyrrole.

**pyr|role** (pi rōl′, pī-; pir′ōl, pī′rōl), *n.* a colorless liquid, that smells like chloroform, obtained mostly from coal tar. It is the parent compound of chlorophyll, hemin, various proteins, and other important natural substances. *If in place of the hydrogens we attach to the nitrogen a ring made up of four carbon atoms, we get a compound called pyrrole* (Scientific American). *Formula:* $C_4H_5N$ [< German *Pyrrol* < Greek *pyrrhós* fiery red + German *-ol* -ole]

**pyr|ro|li|dine** (pi rō′lə dēn, -din; -rol′ə-), *n.* a colorless liquid, forming the base of proline and various alkaloids. *Formula:* $C_4H_9N$ [< *pyrrol*(e) + *-id* + *-ine*[2]]

**py|ru|vate** (pī rü′vāt, pi-), *n.* a salt or ester of pyruvic acid.

**py|ru|vic acid** (pī rü′vik, pi-), a colorless acid that smells like acetic acid, produced by the dry distillation of racemic acid or tartaric acid. It is an important intermediate product in carbohydrate and protein metabolism. *A severe thiamine deficiency state ... is characterized by the accumulation of pyruvic and lactic acids* (Time). *Formula:* $C_3H_4O_3$ [< *pyr-* + Latin *ūva* grape + English *-ic*]

**pyruvic aldehyde,** a substance, containing both an aldehyde and a ketone, used in organic synthesis and tanning. *Formula:* $C_3H_4O_2$

**pyruvic oxidase,** an enzyme which changes pyruvic acid to acetic acid. It is a factor in converting carbon dioxide and water into sugars and starches.

**Py|thag|o|re|an** (pi thag′ə rē′ən), *adj., n.* —***adj.*** of or having to do with Pythagoras, a Greek philosopher, religious teacher, and mathematician, his teachings, or his followers.
—*n.* a follower of Pythagoras.

**Py|thag|o|re|an|ism** (pi thag′ə rē′ə niz əm), *n.* the doctrines of philosophy originated by Pythagoras, often especially with reference to the doctrine of transmigration of souls.

***Pythagorean Theorem** or **theorem,** the theorem that the square of the hypotenuse of a right triangle equals the sum of the squares of the other two sides: *Many Greek discoveries, such as the Pythagorean theorem ... were known long, long before to the Babylonians* (Science).

***Pythagorean Theorem**

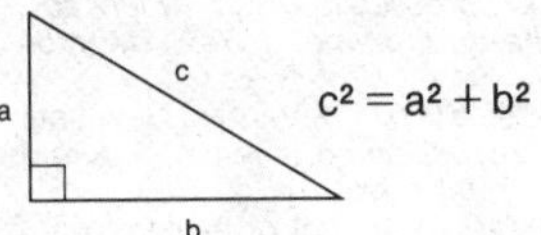


**Pyth|i|a** (pith′ē ə), *n.* the priestess of Apollo at Delphi, who delivered the divine responses to questions.

**Pyth|i|ad** (pith′ē ad), *n.* the period of four years intervening between two successive celebrations of the Pythian games.

**Pyth|i|an** (pith′ē ən), *adj.* **1** of or having to do with Apollo or the oracle at Delphi. **2** of or having to do with the Pythian games. [< Latin *Pȳthius* < Greek *Pýthios* of Delphi (earlier called Pytho), or the Delphic Apollo, + English *-an*]

**Pythian games,** one of the great national festivals of ancient Greece, held every four years at Delphi in honor of Apollo.

**Pyth|i|as** (pith′ē əs), *n. Roman Legend.* a man famous for his devoted friendship with Damon.

**Pyth|ic** (pith′ik), *adj.* = Pythian.

**py|tho|gen|ic** (pī′thə jen′ik, pith′ə-), *adj.* produced by putrefaction or filth (used especially of diseases, as typhoid fever). [< Greek *pȳ́thein* to rot + English *-gen* + *-ic*]

**Py|thon** (pī′thon, -thən), *n. Greek Mythology.* the huge serpent or monster that was hatched from the mud left after the deluge that only Deucalion and Pyrrha survived. It was slain by Apollo.

**py|thon** (pī′thon, -thən), *n.* **1** a large snake of Asia, Africa, and Australia, related to the boas, that kills its prey by crushing. Pythons usually live in trees near water. There are several kinds, making up a genus of reptiles. Some pythons are among the world's largest snakes. *The female python, on the other hand, coils around her eggs and incubates them with body heat* (New Yorker). **2** any large boa. **3** a spirit or demon that possesses some person. **4** a person so possessed. [< *Python*]

**py|tho|ness** (pī′thə nis), *n.* **1** the priestess of Apollo at Delphi, who gave out the answers of the oracle. **2** = prophetess. [earlier *pytoness* < Old French *phitonise,* learned borrowing from Late Latin *phȳthōnissa* < *Pȳthō, -ōnis* a familiar spirit, demon possessing a soothsayer < Greek *Pȳthō* region in which Delphi is]

**py|thon|ic** (pī thon′ik, pi-), *adj.* **1** having to do with the Python or with pythons. **2** snakelike. **3** = oracular.

**py|u|ri|a** (pī yůr′ē ə), *n.* the presence of pus in discharged urine. [< New Latin *pyuria*]

**pyx** (piks), *n.* **1** the vessel in which the consecrated Host is kept, or a small case used to carry it to the sick. **2** the box at the British mint in which specimen coins are kept to be tested for weight and purity.

**trial of the pyx**, the final official trial of the purity and weight of British coins. Also, **pix**.

[< Latin *pyxis, -idis* box < Greek *pyxís, -idos* < *pýxos* boxwood]

**Pyx|i|dis** (pik′sə dis), *n.* genitive of **Pyxis**.

**pyx|id|i|um** (pik sid′ē əm), *n., pl.* **-i|a** (-ē ə). a seed vessel that bursts open transversely into a top and bottom part, the top part acting as a lid. [< New Latin *pyxidium* < Greek *pyxídion* (diminutive) < *pyxís, -ídos* box; see etym. under **pyx**]

**pyx|ie** (pik′sē), *n.* **1** a very small, trailing evergreen shrub that has numerous small, white, star-shaped blossoms, found in pine barrens of the eastern United States. **2** *Botany.* a pyxidium. [American English, contraction of New Latin *Pyxidanthera* the genus name < Latin *pyxis* (see etym. under **pyx**) + *anthēra* anther (because its anthers open like a box lid)]

**pyx|is** (pik′sis), *n., pl.* **pyx|i|des** (pik′sə dēz). **1** a boxlike vase; casket. **2** *Botany.* pyxidium. [< Latin *pyxis, -idis* < Greek *pyxís, -ídos* a box; see etym. under **pyx**]

**Pyx|is** (pik′sis), *n., genitive* **Pyx|i|dis**. a small southern constellation, one of the four parts into which Argo was divided: *Near the Hydra's head lie Puppis and Pyxis, part of the old ship Argo* (Bernhard, Bennett, and Rice). [< New Latin *Pyxis nautica* the mariner's compass]

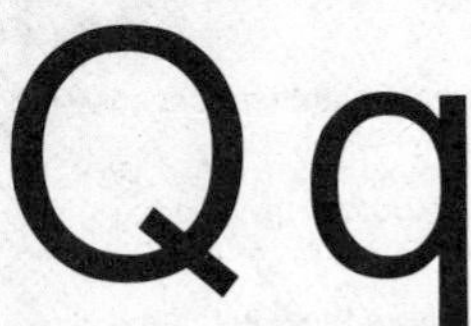

***Q¹** or **q** (kyü), *n., pl.* **Q's** or **Qs**, **q's** or **qs**. **1** the 17th letter of the English alphabet. *Q* is followed by *u* in most English words. **2** the sound represented by this letter. In modern English spelling, *q* is generally used in combination with *u* to stand for the sound represented by *kw*, as in *quiet* (kwī′ət), or represented by *k*, as in *antique* (an tēk′). **3** (used as a symbol for) the 17th, or more usually the 16th (of an actual or possible series, either *I* or *J* being omitted).

**Q²** (kyü), *n., pl.* **Q's**. anything shaped like the letter Q.

**q.**, an abbreviation for the following:
**1** farthing (Latin, *quadrans*).
**2** quart or quarts.
**3** quarter; one fourth of a hundredweight.
**4** quarterly.
**5** quarto.
**6** quasi.
**7** queen.
**8** query.
**9** question.
**10** quintal.
**11** quire.

**Q** (no period), a symbol or abbreviation for the following:
**1** quartermaster.
**2** *Chess.* queen.
**3** quetzal (a unit of money).
**4** a unit of heat energy equal to one quadrillion British thermal units ($10^{18}$ B.T.U.): *The U.S. Geological Survey estimates that the country contains 5,162 Q of oil, 3,317 Q of natural gas and 32,000 Q of coal* (Time).
**5** a unit used in electrical engineering to measure the amount of dissipation in an energy-storing system.

**Q.**, an abbreviation for the following:
**1** quarto.
**2** Quebec.
**3** Queen.
**4** Queensland.
**5** query.
**6** question.
**7** quire.

**qa.**, farthing (Latin, *quadrans*).

**qa|di** (kä′dē), *n., pl.* **-dis**. = cadi.

**Qa|dir|i|ya** (kä′di rē′yä), *n.* a Sufic order of ascetics founded in the 1100's and now centered in Baghdad. [< Arabic *Qadarīya* < Abd al-*Qadir* al Jilani, who founded the order]

**qa|id** (kä ēd′), *n.* = caid.

**Qa|jar** (kə jär′), *n., pl.* **-jars** or **-jar**. a member of the dynasty that ruled Iran from the late 1700's until the 1920's: *The Peacock Throne* [*was*] *built for Fath-Ali, a 19th-century Shah of the last Persian dynasty, the Qajars* (New York Times).

**qa|mis** (kə mēs′), *n. Arabic.* camise.

**qa|nat** (kä nät′), *n.* an underground tunnel dug in the hills to convey water to the plains below: *The desert counterpart of the Dutch dikes is the marvelous qanat* (Scientific American). *Qanats ... supply three-quarters of all the water used in Iran* (London Times). [< Arabic *qanāt* pipe, duct]

**Q. and A.**, question and answer: *Three busloads of foreign students got coffee, cocoa, cookies, and an hour of Q. and A.* (Newsweek).

**Qash|qai** (käsh′kī), *n., pl.* **-qai** or **-qais**. a member of a nomadic people of the mountains of Iran, speaking a Turkic language.

**qat** (kät), *n.* = kat.

**Qa|ta|ri** (kä′tä rē), *n., adj.* —*n.* a native or inhabitant of Qatar, a country in eastern Arabia: *Qatar is regarded by the neighbours as a protégé of Saudi Arabia, a point some Qataris indignantly deny* (Manchester Guardian Weekly).
—*adj.* of or having to do with Qatar or its people: *Foreign participation in Qatari commerce and industry is strictly controlled by legislation* (London Times).

**q.b.**, *Football.* quarterback.

**QB** (no periods), *Chess.* queen's bishop.

**Q.B.**, Queen's Bench.

**Q boat**, = Q ship.

**QC** (kyü′sē′), *adj.* quick-change: *QC jets can expand air cargo service to small cities* (K. E. Schaefte).

**Q.C.** or **QC** (no periods), Queen's Counsel.

**Q-clear|ance** (kyü′klir′əns), *n.*, or **Q clearance**, *U.S.* a high-level security clearance required by the Atomic Energy Commission before allowing access to secret information: *As an employee of an AEC contractor, he could not reveal restricted data to individuals not having a Q-clearance* (Bulletin of Atomic Scientists).

**q.d.**, **1** as if one should say (Latin, *quasi dicat*). **2** as if said (Latin, *quasi dictum*).

**Q.E.D.** or **QED¹** (no periods), which was to be proved (Latin, *quod erat demonstrandum*): *The layman ... may find it possible to believe that Euclid—or possibly Newton—wrote a concluding QED, to indicate the end of a complete collection of all mathematics* (New Scientist).

**QED²** (no periods), quantum electrodynamics.

**Q.E.F.**, which was to be done (Latin, *quod erat faciendum*).

**Q.E.I.**, which was to be found out (Latin, *quod erat inveniendum*).

**Q.F.**, quick-firing.

**Q-fac|tor** (kyü′fak′tər), *n. Electronics.* the ratio of the reactance of a capacitor or inductor to its resistance: *The Q-factor, for the frequency range studied, does not appear to vary with frequency and it has a value of approximately 1.7* (Science). [< *Q*(uality) *factor*]

**Q fever**, a rickettsial disease somewhat like influenza, usually lasting a short time, characterized by fever, headache, and chills: *In recent years many other odd infections have cropped up in the United States, among them rickettsial pox, Q fever* (Scientific American). [< short for *Queensland* fever (where the disease was first described), or for *query fever*, as the disease was first called]

**Qi|a|na** (kē ä′nə), *n. Trademark.* a washable and wrinkle-resistant synthetic fabric chemically related to nylon: *Qiana is said to have color, clarity, and luster equal to or better than most luxurious silks* (Frederick C. Price).

**q.i.d.**, (in prescriptions) four times a day (Latin, *quater in die*).

**qin|tar** (kin tär′), *n.* a unit of money in Albania, equal to 1/100 of a lek. [< Albanian *qintar*]

**qiv|i|ut** (kiv′ē ùt), *n.* the soft, silky underwool of the arctic musk ox, used as a textile fiber: *Teal feels that he has made progress toward his goal of showing that the oxen can support Northern man. His conviction hinges on the quality of their wool, called by the Eskimos "qiviut," a term that he translates as "golden fleece of the arctic"* (New Yorker). [< Eskimo]

**Qkt** (no periods), *Chess.* queen's knight.

**ql.**, quintal.

**q.l.** or **q.lib.**, as much as you please (Latin, *quantum libet*).

**Qld.**, Queensland.

**Q.M.** or **QM** (no periods), quartermaster.

**Q.M.C.** or **QMC** (no periods), Quartermaster Corps.

**Q.M.G.**, **QMG** (no periods), or **Q.M.Gen.**, quartermaster-general.

**Q.M.Sgt.**, quartermaster sergeant.

**qoph** (kōf), *n.* = koph.

**q. p.** or **q.pl.**, as much as you please (Latin, *quantum placet*).

**qq.**, questions.

**Qq** (no period), quartos.

**qq.v.**, which see (Latin, *quae vide;* used in referring to more than one item).

**qr.**, **1** farthing (Latin, *quadrans*). **2** quarter; one fourth of a hundredweight. **3** quire.

**QR** (no periods), *Chess.* queen's rook.

**qrs.**, **1** farthings (Latin, *quadrantes*). **2** quarters. **3** quires.

**q.s.**, **1** as much as suffices (Latin, *quantum sufficit*). **2** quarter section.

**Q scale**, a measure of how long vibrations in the surface of the earth take to die down: *On earth, such rubble would be a terrible conductor of tremors; on the geologist's "Q" scale ... it would rate about 10. By contrast the moon rubble scored at least 2,000* (Science News). [*Q*, for German *Querwellen* transverse waves]

**QSE** (no periods), *British.* qualified scientist and engineer.

**QSG** (no periods), quasi-stellar galaxy: *Many of what were believed to be faint blue stars, occurring by the thousands, are QSG's* (Roy K. Marshall).

**Q ship**, (in World War I) a merchant ship fitted with concealed guns and manned by a naval crew disguised as ordinary seamen, designed to decoy and destroy enemy submarines: *In 1916 as a young naval lieutenant, Campbell conceived* (*and executed*) *the idea of the top-secret Q ships—armed submarine hunters camouflaged as tramp steamers* (Newsweek).

**QSO** (no periods), quasi-stellar object.

**QSTOL** (kyü′stôl), *n.* quiet short take-off and landing (aircraft).

**Q-switch** (kyü′swich′), *n., v.* —*n.* any one of various devices for causing a crystal laser to produce a high-energy pulse of extremely short duration: *Q-switches are employed to obtain a very powerful pulsed output from a laser by allowing the laser to store up energy; when it reaches a maximum the blockage is quickly removed, and an intense pulse of laser radiation is emitted* (New Scientist).
—*v.t.* to cause (a crystal laser) to emit a high-energy pulse by means of a Q-switch: *Saturable absorbers have recently been used very successfully to Q-switch ruby and neodymium-doped lasers* (Michael Hercher).
[*Q*, abbreviation of *quantum*]

**Q-switched** (kyü′swicht′), *adj.* capable of emitting an extremely short, high-energy pulse by means of a Q-switch.

**Q-switch|ing** (kyü′swich′ing), *n.* the use of a Q-switch to obtain extremely short, high-energy laser pulses.

**qt.**, **1** quantity. **2** quart or quarts.

**q.t.**, (kyü′tē′), *n. Slang.* quiet.
**on the q.t.**, very quietly; secretly: *to do something on the q.t.*

**qto.**, quarto.

**qts.**, quarts.

**qu.**, an abbreviation for the following:
**1** quart.
**2a** quarter. **b** quarterly.
**3** queen.
**4** query.
**5** question.

**qua** (kwā, kwä), *adv.* as being; as; in the character or capacity of: *Qua father, he pitied the boy; qua judge, he condemned him. I find much to admire, qua sound, in these two discs* (Irving Kolodin). [< Latin *quā* by what way, how, where, adverb to *quī* who]

**Quaa|lude** (kwä′lüd), *n. Trademark.* a nonbarbiturate sedative, widely used as a narcotic and considered addictive: *Most popular among the downs are ... newer soporifics such as Quaaludes* (New York Times).

**qua|bird** (kwä′bėrd′), *n.* = black-crowned night heron. [< *qua* (imitative) + *bird*]

**quack¹** (kwak), *n., v.* —*n.* **1** the sound a duck makes: *the quack of ducks flying overhead.* **2** a sound resembling or imitating this.
—*v.i.* to make such a sound: *the sound of ducks quacking as they flew overhead.*
[probably imitative]

**quack²** (kwak), *n., adj., v.* —*n.* **1** a person who dishonestly pretends to be a doctor: *Running after quacks and mountebanks ... for medicines and remedies* (Daniel Defoe). **2** an ignorant pretender to knowledge or skill of any sort: *Don't pay a quack to tell your fortune. In painting ... Fortunato ... was a quack* (Edgar Allan Poe). SYN: charlatan.
—*adj.* **1** used by quacks: *quack medicine. The doctors of medicine ... offered me quack cures for imaginary diseases* (George Bernard Shaw). **2** not genuine: *a quack doctor.*
—*v.i.* **1** to be a quack. **2** to advertise or urge as a quack does.
—*v.t.* to treat by quack methods or medicines.
[short for *quacksalver*]

**quack³** (kwak), *n.* = quack grass.

**quack|er|y** (kwak′ə rē), *n., pl.* **-er|ies**. the practices or methods of a quack: *He warned against reaching into the medicine chest of economic quackery every time the slightest quiver runs through production and employment* (New York Times). SYN: charlatanry.

**quack grass**, a perennial, coarse, weedy grass

***Q¹**
definition 1

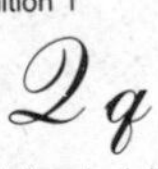

Script letters look like examples of fine penmanship. They appear in many formal uses, such as invitations to social functions.

Qq *Qq*

Handwritten letters, both manuscript or printed (left) and cursive (right), are easy for children to read and to write.

Qq *Qq*

Roman letters have *serifs* (finishing strokes) adapted from the way Roman stonecutters carved their letters. This is *Times Roman* type.

Qq *Qq*

Sans-serif letters are often called *gothic*. They have lines of even width and no serifs. This type face is called *Helvetica*.

Qq Qq

Between roman and gothic, some letters have thick and thin lines with slight flares that suggest serifs. This type face is *Optima*.

Q

Computer letters can be sensed by machines either from their shapes or from the magnetic ink with which they are printed.

which grows wild on sandy or gravelly soil; couch grass. [American English, perhaps variant of *quick grass*]

**quack|ish** (kwak′ish), *adj.* like a quack or charlatan; dealing in quackery: *Last week* [*his*] *purported cure for the ravages of age was exposed as merely the latest in an armlong list of quackish remedies* (Time).

**quack|sal|ver** (kwak′sal vər), *n.* **1** a quack doctor. **2** a quack; charlatan: *Brother Zeal-of-the-land is no vulgar impostor, no mere religious quacksalver* (Algernon Charles Swinburne). [< earlier Dutch *quacksalver* (literally) a hawker of salve < *quacken, kwakken* boast of, quack + *salf* salve]

**quack|y**[1] (kwak′ē), *adj.* having a flat, metallic quality, resembling the quack of a duck: *Our women's voices are, on the whole, ungentle ... they are pitched unpleasantly high and hardened by throat contractions into an habitual "quacky" or metallic quality* (F. Osgood).

**quack|y**[2] (kwak′ē), *adj.* suited to a quack; quackish; using the methods of quackery.

**quad**[1] (kwod), *n. Informal.* the quadrangle of a college.

**quad**[2] (kwod), *n. Informal.* a quadruplet.

**quad**[3] (kwod), *n., v.,* **quad|ded, quad|ding.** *Printing.* —*n.* a quadrat.
—*v.t.* to fill (a line) with quads in typesetting.

**quad**[4] (kwod), *n. British Slang.* quod; prison.

**quad**[5] (kwäd, kwod), *n. U.S. Informal.* Quaalude.

**quad.,** **1** quadrangle. **2** quadrant.

**quadr-**, *combining form.* the form of **quadri-** before vowels, as in *quadrant.*

**quad|ra** (kwod′rə), *n., pl.* **-rae** (-rē). **1** a square frame or border for enclosing a bas-relief. **2** any frame or border. [< Latin *quadra* square]

**quad|ra|ble** (kwod′rə bəl), *adj.* that can be squared. [< Latin *quadrāre* to square + English *-able*]

**quad|ra|disc** (kwod′rə disk′), *n.* a quadraphonic record.

**quad|ra|ge|nar|i|an** (kwod′rə jə nãr′ē ən), *adj., n.* —*adj.* **1** forty years old. **2** between forty and fifty.
—*n.* **1** a person who is forty years old. **2** a person between forty and fifty years old.
[< Latin *quadrāgēnārius* (literally) having forty (< *quadrāgēnī* forty each < *quadrāginta* forty, related to *quattuor* four)]

**Quad|ra|ges|i|ma** (kwod′rə jes′ə mə), *n.* **1** the first Sunday in Lent. **2** the forty days of Lent. [< Late Latin *Quadrāgēsima* (in Latin, fortieth) < *quadrāgēnī;* see etym. under **quadragenarian**]

**Quad|ra|ges|i|mal** (kwod′rə jes′ə məl), *adj.* **1** of or during Lent; suitable for Lent; Lenten. **2** Also, **quadragesimal.** lasting forty days, as the fast of Lent.

**Quadragesima Sunday**, the first Sunday in Lent.

**quad|ran|gle** (kwod′rang′gəl), *n.* **1** a four-sided space or court wholly or nearly surrounded by buildings: *the quadrangle of a palace, a college quadrangle.* **2** the buildings around a quadrangle: *There was a square court behind, round which the house, huts, and store formed a quadrangle* (Henry Kingsley). **3** a plane figure with four angles and four sides; quadrilateral. **4** the rectangular area represented by one of the United States Geological Survey topographic maps. The two common sizes are tracts about 13 miles wide by 17 miles north to south and 6½ miles wide by 8½ miles. [< Late Latin *quadrangulum,* neuter of Latin adjective *quadriangulus* < *quadri-* four + *angulus* angle]

**quad|ran|gled** (kwod′rang′gəld), *adj.* **1** = quadrangular. **2** containing a quadrangle.

**quad|ran|gu|lar** (kwod rang′gyə lər), *adj.* like a quadrangle; having four corners or angles: *a spacious, quadrangular house.*

**quad|ran|gu|lar|ly** (kwod rang′gyə lər lē), *adv.* in the form of a quadrangle.

***quad|rant** (kwod′rənt), *n.* **1a** a quarter of the circumference of a circle; arc of 90 degrees. **b** the area contained by such an arc and two radii drawn perpendicular to each other. **2** a thing or part shaped like a quarter circle. **3** an instrument with a scale of 90 degrees, used in astronomy, surveying, and navigation for measuring altitudes. **4** *Geometry.* one of the four parts into which a plane is divided by two straight lines crossing at right angles. The upper right-hand section is the first quadrant, and, in a counterclockwise direction, the others are the second, third, and fourth quadrants respectively. **5** *Embryology.* one of the four blastomeres in the four-cell stage of the ovum. [< Latin *quadrāns, -antis* a fourth, related to *quattuor* four]

**quad|ran|tal** (kwod ran′təl), *adj.* of or having to do with a quadrant; included in the fourth part of the surface of a circle.

**quadrantal deviation**, a compass error.

**Quad|ran|tid** (kwod ran′tid), *n.* one of a shower of meteors occurring early in January: *Shower meteors come from well-defined streams, of which the Perseids, the Leonids, and the Quadrantids are among the most celebrated* (New Scientist). [< New Latin *Quadrantis,* genitive of *Quadrans* (*Muralis*), a former constellation from which the showers seem to radiate]

**quadrant of safety**, the region toward which it is best for a person to run when he sees a tornado approaching.

**quad|ra|phon|ic** (kwod′rə fon′ik, -fō′nik), *adj.* of or having to do with high-fidelity sound transmission or reproduction over four different channels; four-channel: *Your car will, in addition to ordinary stereo, have equipment for the playing of quadraphonic cartridges* (London Times). Also, **quadriphonic, quadrophonic.** [< *quadra-* (alteration of *quadri-* four) + *phonic*] —**quad′ra|phon′i|cal|ly,** *adv.*

**quad|ra|phon|ics** (kwod′rə fon′iks, -fō′niks), *n.* = quadraphony.

**quad|raph|o|ny** (kwod raph′ə nē), *n.* quadraphonic sound reproduction.

**quad|ra|son|ic** (kwod′rə son′ik), *adj.* = quadraphonic. Also, **quadrisonic.**

**quad|ra|son|ics** (kwod′rə son′iks), *n.* = quadraphonics.

**quad|rat** (kwod′rət), *n.* **1** *Printing.* a piece of metal used for wide spaces in setting type; quad. **2** (in experimental agriculture) a square area of convenient size laid off for the purpose of accurate planting. **3** (in phytogeography) a similar square laid off for close study of the relative abundance of species or of other questions. [apparently variant of *quadrate,* noun]

**quad|rate** (*adj., n.* kwod′rit, -rāt; *v.* kwod′rāt), *adj., n., v.,* **-rat|ed, -rat|ing.** —*adj.* **1** square or rectangular. **2** of or designating the quadrate bone. **3** *Heraldry.* (of a cross) having arms which expand into a square at their junction. See picture under **cross. 4** *Astrology.* (of two heavenly bodies) 90 degrees distant from each other.
—*n.* **1** something square or rectangular; square; rectangle: *His person was a quadrate, his step massy and elephantine* (Charles Lamb). **2** = quadrate bone.
—*v.t., v.i.* **1** to square; agree. **2** to conform.
[< Latin *quadrātus* < *quadrus* square, related to *quattuor* four]

**quadrate bone**, one of the pair of bones in birds, fishes, amphibians, and reptiles that joins the lower jaw to the skull.

**quad|rat|ic** (kwod rat′ik), *adj., n.* —*adj.* **1** *Algebra.* of or having to do with an equation in which one or more of the terms is squared, but raised to no higher powers. **2** of or like a square; square.
—*n.* = quadratic equation.

**quad|rat|i|cal** (kwod rat′ə kəl), *adj.* = quadratic.

**quad|rat|i|cal|ly** (kwod rat′ə klē), *adv.* to the second degree.

**quadratic equation**, an equation involving a square or squares, but no higher powers, of the unknown quantity or quantities: *$x^2 + 3x + 2 = 12$ is a quadratic equation.*

**quad|rat|ics** (kwod rat′iks), *n.* the branch of algebra that deals with quadratic equations.

***quadrant**
definitions 1a,1b,3,4

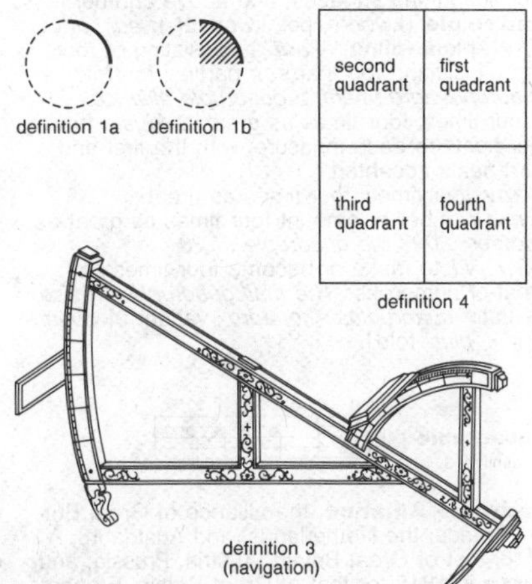


**quad|ra|trix** (kwod rā′triks), *n.* a curve used for finding a square equivalent in area to the figure bounded by a given curve, or for finding a straight line equal to a circle, arc, or the like. [< New Latin *quadratrix* < Latin *quadrāre* to square]

**quad|ra|ture** (kwod′rə chər), *n.* **1** the act of squaring. **2** the finding of a square equal in area to a given surface, especially one bounded by a curve. **3** *Astronomy.* **a** the position of a heavenly body that is 90 degrees away from another. See picture under **aspect. b** either of the two points in the orbit of a heavenly body halfway between the points of conjunction and opposition: *A half moon is visible at the quadratures of the moon.* [< Latin *quadrātūra* < *quadrātus* quadrate]

**quadrature of the circle**, the problem, insoluble by geometric methods alone, of squaring the circle, that is of finding a square whose area equals that of a given circle.

**quad|ren|ni|al** (kwod ren′ē əl), *adj., n.* —*adj.* **1** occurring every four years: *The United States has a quadrennial presidential election.* **2** of or for four years.
—*n.* **1** something that occurs every four years. **2** a fourth anniversary.
[< Latin *quadriennium* period of four years (see etym. under **quadrennium**) + English *-al*[1]]
—**quad|ren′ni|al|ly,** *adv.*

**quad|ren|ni|um** (kwod ren′ē əm), *n., pl.* **-ren|ni-ums, -ren|ni|a** (-ren′ē ə). a period of four years. [alteration of Latin *quadriennium* period of four years < *quadri-* four + *-enn-* < *annus* year]

**quadri-**, *combining form.* four; having four ___; four times: *Quadrilateral = having four sides* (*and four angles*). Also **quadr-** before vowels; **quadru-.** [< Latin *quadri-,* related to *quattuor* four]

**quad|ri|ad** (kwod′rē ad), *n.* a series of four; a group of four.

**quad|ric** (kwod′rik), *adj., n. Mathematics.* —*adj.* of the second degree (applied especially to functions or equations with more than two variables).
—*n.* an expression or surface of the second degree.

**quad|ri|cen|ten|ni|al** (kwod′rə sen ten′ē əl), *adj., n.* —*adj.* **1** of or having to do with 400 years or a 400th anniversary. **2** 400 years old.
—*n.* **1** a 400th anniversary. **2** its celebration.

**quad|ri|ceps** (kwod′rə seps), *n.* the large muscle of the front of the thigh, which extends the leg, and has four heads or origins. [< New Latin *quadriceps* < Latin *quadri-* four + *caput* head]

**quadriceps fem|o|ris** (fem′ə ris), = quadriceps. [< New Latin *quadriceps femoris* femoral quadriceps]

**quad|ri|cip|i|tal** (kwod′rə sip′ə təl), *adj.* having to do with the quadriceps.

**quad|ri|corn** (kwod′rə kôrn), *adj., n.* —*adj.* having four horns or hornlike parts: *quadricorn sheep.*
—*n.* a quadricorn animal.
[< New Latin *quadricornis* < Latin *quadri-* four + *cornū* horn]

**quad|ri|cor|nous** (kwod′rə kôr′nəs), *adj.* = quadricorn.

**quad|ri|cy|cle** (kwod′rə sī′kəl), *n.* a four-wheeled vehicle like a bicycle or tricycle. [< *quadri-* + *-cycle,* as in *bicycle*]

**quad|ri|en|ni|al** (kwod rē en′ē əl), *adj.* = quadrennial.

**quad|ri|en|ni|al|ly** (kwod rē en′ē ə lē), *adv.* = quadrennially.

**quad|ri|en|ni|um** (kwod rē en′ē əm), *n., pl.* **-en-ni|ums, -en|ni|a** (-en′ē ə). = quadrennium.

**quad|ri|far|i|ous** (kwod′rə fãr′ē əs), *adj.* **1** set or arranged in four rows or series. **2** having four parts; fourfold. [< Late Latin *quadrifarius* (with English *-ous*) fourfold < Latin *quadri-* four + *fārī* to speak]

**quad|ri|fid** (kwod′rə fid), *adj.* cleft or divided into four parts or lobes. [< Latin *quadrifīdus* < *quadri-* four + *fīd-,* a root of *findere* to split, divide]

**quad|ri|fo|li|ate** (kwod′rə fō′lē it), *adj.* having four leaves; having leaves in whorls of four. [< Latin *quadri-* four + *folium* leaf + English *-ate*[1]]

**quad|ri|fo|li|o|late** (kwod′ri fō′lē ə lāt, -fō lī′ə lit), *adj.* (of a compound leaf) having four leaflets.

**quad|ri|form** (kwod′rə fôrm), *adj.* having or combining four forms. [< Late Latin *quadriformis* < Latin *quadri-* four + *forma* form]

**quad|ri|fron|tal** (kwod′rə frun′təl), *adj.* having four fronts or faces.

**quad|ri|ga** (kwod rī′gə), *n., pl.* **-gae** (-jē). (in ancient Rome) a two-wheeled chariot pulled by four horses harnessed abreast. [< Latin *quadrīga* a team of four horses < *quadri-* four + *jugum* yoke, span]

***quad|ri|lat|er|al** (kwod′rə lat′ər əl), *adj., n.* —*adj.* having four sides and four angles.
—*n.* **1a** a plane figure having four sides and four angles. See the picture on the following page. **b** something having this form. **2** a figure formed by four straight lines which, if extended, intersect at six points; complete quadrilateral. **3** an area lying defended by four fortresses, one at each corner.

**Pronunciation Key:** hat, āge, cãre, fär; let, ēqual, tėrm; it, īce; hot, ōpen, ôrder; oil, out; cup, pu̇t, rüle; child; long; thin; ᴛʜen; zh, measure; ə represents **a** in about, **e** in taken, **i** in pencil, **o** in lemon, **u** in circus.

[< Latin *quadrilaterus* (< *quadri-* four + *latus, -eris* side) + English *-al*[1]]

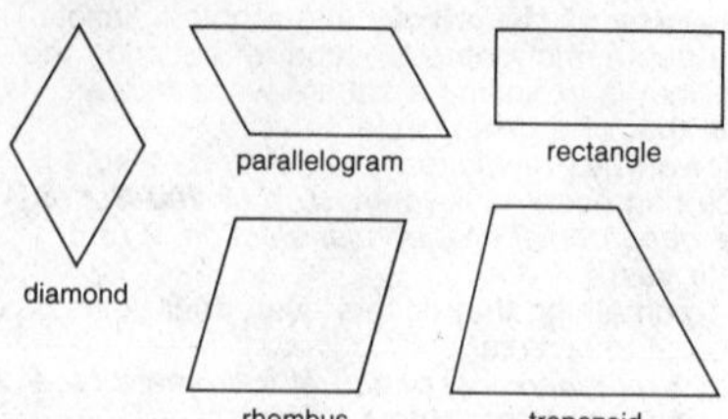


***quadrilateral**
definition 1a

**quad|ri|lin|gual** (kwod′rə ling′gwəl), *adj.* using or involving four languages: *A few blocks away ... petite Eartha Kitt took her listeners on a quadrilingual* (*English, French, Spanish, Turkish*) *tour* (Time). [< Latin *quadri-* four + *lingua* speech, tongue + English *-al*[1]]

**quad|ri|lit|er|al** (kwod′rə lit′ər əl), *adj., n.* —***adj.*** consisting of four letters or of four consonants.
—***n.*** a quadriliteral word or root.
[< Latin *quadri-* four + *lītera* letter + English *-al*[1]]

**quad|ril|lage** (kä drē läzh′), *n. French.* a system of defense in which an area is divided into small squares, and each square guarded by a small detachment of troops, sometimes used to protect the local population against guerrilla attacks.

**qua|drille**[1] (kwə dril′), *n.* **1** a square dance for four couples that usually has five parts or movements. **2** the music for such a dance. [< French *quadrille, cuadrille* < Spanish *cuadrilla* troop of horsemen < *cuadro* square (in battle) < Latin *quadrus* square]

**qua|drille**[2] (kwə dril′), *n.* a card game for four persons, popular in the 1700's: *Improving hourly in her Skill, To cheat and wrangle at Quadrille* (Jonathan Swift). [< French *quadrille, cuadrille,* alteration of Spanish *cuartillo* (diminutive) < *cuarto* fourth < Latin *quartus*]

**qua|drille**[3] (kwə dril′), *adj.* marked with squares; having a pattern composed of small squares: *a quadrille fabric.* [< French *quadrillé* < *quadrille* small square < Spanish *cuadrillo* < *cuadro* square < Latin *quadrus*]

**qua|drilled** (kwə drild′), *adj.* = quadrille[3].

**quad|ril|lion** (kwod ril′yən), *n., adj.* **1** (in the U.S., Canada, and France) 1 followed by 15 zeros. **2** (in Great Britain and Germany) 1 followed by 24 zeros. [alteration of French *quadrillon* < *quadri-* four + *million* million]

**quad|ril|lionth** (kwod ril′yənth), *n., adj.* —***n.*** **1** the last in a series of a quadrillion. **2** one of a quadrillion equal parts.
—***adj.*** last in a series of a quadrillion.

**quad|ri|nate** (kwod′rə nāt), *adj.* **1** = quadruple. **2** *Botany.* having four leaflets to a petiole; quadrifoliate. [< Latin *quadrīni* four each + English *-ate*[1]]

**quad|ri|no|dal** (kwod′rə nō′dəl), *adj.* having four nodes, as a vibrating string or organ pipe, or the oscillating surface of a seiche.

**quad|ri|no|mi|al** (kwod′rə nō′mē əl), *n., adj. Algebra.* —***n.*** an expression consisting of four terms, such as $a^2 \| ab + 4a \| b^2$.
—***adj.*** consisting of four terms. [< *quadri-* + *-nomial,* as in *binomial*]

**quad|ri|par|tite** (kwod′rə pär′tīt), *adj.* divided into or consisting of four parts. [< Latin *quadripartītus,* past participle of *quadripartīre* divide into four parts < *quadri-* four + *partīre* to divide < *pars, partis* part]

**quad|ri|par|ti|tion** (kwod′rə pär tish′ən), *n.* a dividing by four or into four parts. [< *quadri-* + *partition*]

**quad|ri|phon|ic** (kwod′rə fon′ik, -fō′nik), *adj.* = quadraphonic.

**quad|ri|ple|gi|a** (kwod′rə plē′jē ə), *n.* paralysis of both arms and both legs. [< New Latin *quadriplegia* < Latin *quadri-* four + Greek *plēgē* stroke]

**quad|ri|pleg|ic** (kwod′rə plej′ik, -plē′jik), *n.* a person afflicted with quadriplegia.

**quad|ri|reme** (kwod′rə rēm), *n.* an ancient ship with four rows of oars on each side, one above the other. [< Latin *quadrirēmis* < *quadri-* four + *rēmus* oar]

**quad|ri|sect** (kwod′rə sekt), *v.t.* to divide into four equal parts. [< *quadri-* + *-sect,* as in *bisect*]

**quad|ri|son|ic** (kwod′rə son′ik), *adj.* = quadraphonic.

**quad|ri|syl|lab|ic** (kwod′rə sə lab′ik), *adj.* **1** of or having to do with quadrisyllables. **2** consisting of four syllables.

**quad|ri|syl|la|ble** (kwod′rə sil′ə bəl), *n.* a word of four syllables. [< *quadri-* + *syllable*]

**quad|ri|va|lence** (kwod′rə vā′ləns, kwod riv′ə-), *n.* the quality of being quadrivalent.

**quad|ri|va|len|cy** (kwod′rə vā′lən sē, kwod-riv′ə-), *n.* = quadrivalence.

**quad|ri|va|lent** (kwod′rə vā′lənt, kwod riv′ə-), *adj., n. Chemistry.* —***adj.*** **1** having a valence of four; tetravalent. **2** having four different valences.
—***n.*** a quadrivalent atom or element. —**quad′ri-va′lent|ly,** *adv.*

**quad|riv|i|al** (kwod riv′ē əl), *adj., n.* —***adj.*** **1a** having four ways meeting in a point. **b** (of roads) leading in four directions. **2** belonging to the quadrivium. —***n.*** one of the four arts constituting the quadrivium. [< Medieval Latin *quadrivialis* < Latin *quadrivium* the meeting of four roads; see etym. under **quadrivium**]

**quad|riv|i|um** (kwod riv′ē əm), *n., pl.* **-i|ums, -i|a** (-ē ə). **1** (in ancient Rome and in the Middle Ages) arithmetic, geometry, astronomy, and music, the more advanced four of the seven liberal arts. **2** a place where four ways meet. [< Late Latin *quadrivium* < Latin, crossroads, meeting of four roads < *quadri-* four + *via* way]

**quad|ro** (kwad′rō), *n., pl.* **-ros.** a square section of a planned city or urban development, functioning as a residential unit with at least one apartment house and shopping center: *Within the one city he envisages quadros* (*single units of settlement*) *as in Brazilia, which will be of a small enough scale to engender community spirit* (New Scientist). [< Portuguese *quadro* a square]

**quad|ro|min|i|um** (kwod′rə min′ē əm), *n.* a building with four separately owned apartments: *In Chicago, Dayton and some West Coast areas, four-dwelling condominiums—or "quadrominiums" —have become the fastest selling form of housing* (Time). [< *quadr-* four + (cond)*ominium*]

**quad|roon** (kwod rün′), *n.* a person having one fourth Negro ancestry; child of a white person and a mulatto. [earlier *quarteron* < Spanish *cuarterón* < *cuarto* fourth < Latin *quartus*]

**quad|ro|phonic** (kwod′rə fon′ik, -fō′nik), *adj.* = quadraphonic.

**quadru-,** *combining form.* a variant of **quadri-,** as in *quadruped.*

**quad|ru|mane** (kwod′rů mān), *n.* a quadrumanous animal.

**quad|ru|ma|nous** (kwod rü′mə nəs), *adj.* **1** four-handed; using all four feet as hands, as monkeys do. **2** of or belonging to a former grouping of animals that included monkeys, apes, and lemurs. [< New Latin *quadrumanus* < Latin *quadru-,* variant of *quadri-* four + *manus* hand]

**quad|rum|vi|rate** (kwod rum′vər it), *n.* **1** a group of four men. **2** any association of four in office or authority. [< *quadr-* four + *-umvirate,* as in *triumvirate*]

**quad|ru|ped** (kwod′rů ped), *n., adj.* —***n.*** an animal that has four feet: *a hairy quadruped ... with a tail and pointed ears, probably arboreal in its habits* (Charles R. Darwin).
—***adj.*** having four feet.
[< Latin *quadrupēs, -pedis* < *quadru-,* variant of *quadri-* four + *pēs, pedis* foot]

**quad|ru|pe|dal** (kwod rü′pə dəl, kwod′rů ped′əl), *adj.* **1** of, having to do with, or like a quadruped; four-footed. **2** on hands and knees: *Seeing him just quadrupedal in the grass, the priest raised his eyebrows rather sadly* (Gilbert K. Chesterton).

**quad|ru|plane** (kwod′rů plān), *n.* an airplane with four supporting surfaces, one above another.

***quad|ru|ple** (kwod′rů pəl, kwod rü′-), *adj., adv., n., v.,* **-pled, -pling.** —***adj.*** **1** consisting of four parts; including four parts or parties; fourfold: *a quadruple agreement, a quadruple alliance.* **2** four times; four times as great. **3** *Music.* having four beats to each measure, with the first and third beats accented.
—***adv.*** four times; four times as great.
—***n.*** a number or amount four times as great as another: *80 is the quadruple of 20.*
—***v.t., v.i.*** to make or become four times as great or numerous: *The mail quadrupled in size.* [< Latin *quadruplus* < *quadru-,* variant of *quadri-* four + *-plus* -fold]

***quadruple**
definition 3

**Quadruple Alliance,** the alliance of Great Britain, France, the Netherlands, and Austria in 1718, that of Great Britain, Austria, Prussia, and Russia in 1815, or that of Great Britain, France, Spain, and Portugal in 1834.

**quadruple measure** or **time, 1** a musical measure of four beats with an accent on the first and third. **2** this rhythm.

**quad|ru|plet** (kwod′rů plit, kwod rü′-), *n.* **1** one of four children born at the same time of the same mother: *The quadruplets were three sisters and one brother.* **2** any group or combination of four: *The official form is in quadruplet and the writing on the last copy is not very dark.* **3** a group of four notes to be played in the time of three.

**quad|ru|plex** (kwod′rů pleks), *adj.* **1** = fourfold. **2** of or designating a system of telegraphy by which four messages, two in each direction, may be sent over one wire at the same time. [< Latin *quadruplex* fourfold < *quadru-,* variant of *quadri-* four + *-plex, -plicis,* related to *plaga* flat(ness), surroundings]

**quad|ru|pli|cate** (*adj., n.* kwod rü′plə kit; *v.* kwod-rü′plə kāt), *adj., v.,* **-cat|ed, -cat|ing,** *n.* —***adj.*** **1** fourfold; quadruple. **2** *Mathematics.* raised to the fourth power.
—***v.t.*** to make fourfold; quadruple.
—***n.*** one of four things, especially four copies of a document, exactly alike.
**in quadruplicate,** in four copies exactly alike: *The student filled out the form in quadruplicate for the registrar, bursar, dean, and academic adviser.*
[< Latin *quadruplicātus,* past participle of *quadruplicāre* < *quadruplex, -icis;* see etym. under **quadruplex**]

**quad|ru|pli|ca|tion** (kwod rü′plə kā′shən), *n.* **1** the act of making fourfold: *Of the current defense situation he says: "We have had quadruplication instead of unification"* (Newsweek). **2** something quadruplicated.

**quad|ru|plic|i|ty** (kwod′rů plis′ə tē), *n.* quadruple nature, character, or quality.

**quad|ru|ply** (kwod′rů plē), *adv.* in a fourfold manner or degree; to a fourfold extent or amount: *When the reconciliation did take place ... it was so doubly, trebly, quadruply sweet* (Atlantic).

**quad|ru|pole** (kwod′rə pōl′), *n.* a set or combination of two dipoles: *The current is made to flow along four rods, forming a quadrupole* (Science Journal). [< *quadru-* (variant of *quadri-*) + *pole*[2]]

**quae|re** (kwir′ē), *v. imperative, n.* —***v.*** query; ask (used to introduce or suggest a question): *Quaere, is this point fully proved? Quaere, whether the contrary is not more probable?*
—***n.*** a query or question: *I wondered a little at your quaere who Cheselden was?* (Jonathan Swift).
[< Latin *quaere* (literally) ask, imperative of *quaerere* to seek, ask for]

**quae|re ver|um** (kwir′ē vir′əm), *Latin.* seek the truth.

**quaes|tor** (kwes′tər, kwēs′-), *n.* **1** an official of ancient Rome in charge of the public funds; treasurer: *During the next 20 years, Caesar climbed nimbly up the ladder of state offices—quaestor, aedile, praetor, consul* (Time). **2** a public prosecutor in certain criminal cases in ancient Rome. Also, **questor.** [< Latin *quaestor,* variant of *quaesītor* an investigator < *quaerere* ask for]

**quaes|to|ri|al** (kwes tôr′ē əl, -tōr′-; kwēs-), *adj.* of or having to do with a quaestor or his position. Also, **questorial.**

**quaes|tor|ship** (kwes′tər ship, kwēs′-), *n.* the position or term of office of a quaestor. Also, **questorship.**

**quaff** (kwäf, kwaf, kwôf), *v., n.* —***v.i., v.t.*** to drink in large swallows; drink deeply and freely: *Last night among his fellow roughs he jested, quaffed and swore* (Francis H. C. Doyle). (*Figurative.*) *Felicity ... is quaffed out of a golden cup in every latitude* (Joseph Conrad).
—***n.*** **1** the act of quaffing. **2** something quaffed; deep drink.
[earlier *quaft;* origin uncertain]

**quaff|er** (kwäf′ər, kwaf′-, kwôf′-), *n.* a person who quaffs or drinks deeply.

**quag**[1] (kwag, kwog), *n.* a quagmire; bog: *Let me get off the bridge ... that firm bit by the quag will do* (John Masefield).

**quag**[2] (kwag, kwog), *v.i.,* **quagged, quag|ging.** *British Dialect.* to shake: (*Figurative.*) *Many a poor head will ache, and many a poor belly quag, if it is so bad as they tell me* (Richard Blackmore). [perhaps imitative. Compare etym. under **quake.**]

**quag|ga** (kwag′ə), *n.* a zebra of southern Africa closely related to the dauw but having distinct stripes on its head, neck, and shoulder only. It became extinct in the 1870's. *The poor quagga ... is a timid animal with a gait and figure much resembling those of an ass* (T. Pringle). [apparently < a Hottentot name]

**quag|ger|y** (kwag′ər ē, kwog′-), *n., pl.* **-ries.** a bog or marsh.

**quag|gy** (kwag′ē, kwog′-), *adj.,* **-gi|er, -gi|est.** **1** soft and muddy; boggy; miry; swampy: *Some dismal rood of quaggy land about the river's edge* (William Morris). SYN: marshy. **2** *Figurative.* soft and flabby: *quaggy flesh.*

**quag|mire** (kwag′mīr′, kwog′-), *n.* **1** soft, muddy ground; boggy or miry place; quag: *Many streets are unpaved and unlighted; in heavy rain they turn to quagmires* (Time). **2** *Figurative.* a difficult situation: *I have followed Cupid's Jack-a-lantern, and find myself in a quagmire at last* (Richard Brinsley Sheridan).

**qua|hog** or **qua|haug** (kwô′hog, -hôg; kwə hog′,

-hôg′), *n.* an almost circular, edible American clam; hard clam. Its shell was one of the main sources of wampum. *We were able to make a more detailed study of how amino acids are preserved in the edible clam, or quahog, of the Atlantic coast* (Scientific American). [American English < Algonkian (probably Pequot) *p'quaghhaug* hard clam]

**quai** (kā), *n., pl.* **quais** (kā). *French.* a quay.

**quaich** or **quaigh** (kwāʜ), *n. Scottish.* a shallow drinking cup with two handles. [< Scottish Gaelic *cuach* cup]

**Quai d'Or|say** (kā′ dôr sā′), **1** the French foreign office. **2** the French government. **3** a street in Paris along the left bank of the Seine River.

**quail**[1] (kwāl), *n., pl.* **quails** or (*collectively*) **quail.** **1** any one of various plump game birds belonging to the same family as chickens and pheasants, especially the bobwhite and the Gambel's quail: *If you were to ask whether the bobwhite is a quail or a partridge, the answer would depend on the part of the country you were in. In the East, the name quail is used interchangeably with bobwhite: bobwhite is quail and quail is bobwhite. In the South bobwhite is called partridge* (Science News Letter). **2** *U.S. Slang.* a good-looking young woman. **3** *Archaic.* a courtesan: *Here's Agamemnon—an honest fellow enough, and one that loves quails* (Shakespeare). [< Old French *quaille* < Germanic (compare Old High German *quatala,* and *wahtala*)]

**quail**[2] (kwāl), *v.i.* **1** to be afraid; lose courage; shrink back in fear: *The slave quailed at his master's look. They ... felt their hearts quailing under their multiplied hardships* (Washington Irving). *She made Barnes quail before her by the shafts of contempt which she flashed at him* (Thackeray). **SYN**: quake, cower, flinch. **2** to bend or shake as if in fear: *trees that quail before a blast of wind.* [apparently < Old French *coaillier* to coagulate < Latin *coāgulāre*]

**quaint** (kwānt), *adj.* **1a** strange or odd in an interesting, pleasing, or amusing way: *Old photographs seem quaint to us today.* **b** old-fashioned but picturesque or attractive: *a quaint old house.* **2** *Obsolete.* wise; skilled; clever: *to show how quaint an orator you are* (Shakespeare). **3** *Obsolete.* skillfully made; pretty; elegant; fine: *I never saw a better-fashion'd gown, More quaint, more pleasing* (Shakespeare). **4** *Obsolete.* strange; odd; singular: *In his wizard habit strange, Came forth,—a quaint and fearful sight* (Scott). [< Old French *cointe,* and *queinte* pretty, clever, knowing < Latin *cognitus* known, past participle of *cognōscere* to know] —**quaint′ly,** *adv.* —**quaint′ness,** *n.*

**quake** (kwāk), *v.,* **quaked, quak|ing,** *n.* —*v.i.* **1** to shake or tremble: *She quaked with fear. Quake in the present winter's state and wish That warmer days would come* (Shakespeare). **SYN**: See syn. under **shiver**[1]. **2** to move convulsively; rock violently: *The earth quaked. The mountains quake at him, and the hills melt, and the earth is burned at his presence* (Nahum 1:5).
—*n.* **1** a shaking or trembling. **2** an earthquake. [Old English *cwacian*]

**quake grass,** = quaking grass.

**quak|er** (kwā′kər), *n., adj.* —*n.* **1** a person or thing that quakes. **2** any one of various plain-colored birds and moths.
—*adj.* of or having to do with a quaker or Quaker.

**quakers,** *British Dialect.* quaking grass: *It's this green all along this valley, ... the quakers on the slopes, and the pines up there on the crests* (Berton Roueché).

**Quak|er** (kwā′kər), *n.* a member of a Christian church called the Society of Friends that believes in simple manners and clothes and simple religious services; Friend. Quakers are opposed to war and to taking oaths. The Quakers were founded by George Fox in the mid-1600's. *What a balm and a solace it is ... to ... seat yourself for a quiet half hour ... among the gentle Quakers* (Charles Lamb). [< *quake,* verb; reputedly from the fact that George Fox, the founder, told his followers to "tremble at the word of the Lord"; earlier used also of a foreign sect]

**Quaker City,** *U.S.* Philadelphia.

**Quak|er|ess** (kwā′kər is), *n.* a Quaker woman or girl.

**quaker grass,** = quaking grass.

**Quaker gun,** a dummy gun, as in a ship or fort. [from the opposition of Quakers to all warfare]

**Quak|er|ish** (kwā′kər ish), *adj.* like the Quakers; suitable for Quakers: *Don't address me as if I were a beauty; I am your plain Quakerish governess* (Charlotte Brontë).

**Quak|er|ism** (kwā′kə riz əm), *n.* the principles and customs of the Quakers: *He has once or twice referred to Quakerism as the wellspring of his beliefs* (Harper's).

**quak|er-la|dy** (kwā′kər lā′dē), *n., pl.* **-dies.** a small, delicate plant with bluish flowers; innocence or bluet.

**Quak|er|ly** (kwā′kər lē), *adj., adv.* —*adj.* like or suitable for a Quaker.
—*adv.* after the fashion of the Quakers.

**Quaker meeting, 1** a religious service of Quakers, during which there may be long periods of silence. **2** *Informal.* a silent group.

**quak|ers** (kwā′kərz), *n.pl.* See under **quaker.**

**Quaker State,** a nickname for Pennsylvania.

**quak|i|ly** (kwā′kə lē), *adv.* = quakingly.

**quak|i|ness** (kwā′kē nis), *n.* the condition of being quaky or shaking: *the quakiness of a bog.*

**quak|ing** (kwā′king), *adj.* that quakes; shaking; trembling. —**quak′ing|ly,** *adv.*

**quaking aspen,** an American poplar tree with flat, delicate stems and leaves that tremble in the slightest breeze.

**quaking grass,** any one of various grasses having spikelets on the slender branches of the panicle that move at the slightest breeze.

**quak|y** (kwā′kē), *adj.,* **quak|i|er, quak|i|est.** inclined to quake; quaking; trembling.

**qua|le** (kwä′lē), *n., pl.* **qua|li|a** (kwä′lē ə). *Philosophy.* a quality thought of apart from any object or real thing; an abstraction. *Sweetness* is a quale when it is considered separately from any particular thing, such as an apple. [< Latin *quāle,* neuter singular of *quālis* of what sort]

**qual|i|fi|a|ble** (kwol′ə fī′ə bəl), *adj.* that can be qualified or modified.

**qual|i|fi|ca|tion** (kwol′ə fə kā′shən), *n.* **1** that which makes a person fit for a job, task, office, or function: *To know the trail is one qualification for a guide.* **2** a necessary condition which must be fulfilled or complied with before a certain right can be acquired or exercised or an office held: *the qualifications for voting.* **3** that which limits, changes, or makes less free and full: *His pleasure had one qualification; his friends could not enjoy it, too.* **4** a modification; limitation; restriction: *The statement was made without any qualification.* **5** the process of qualifying. **6** the state of being qualified.

**qual|i|fi|ca|tive** (kwol′ə fə kā′tiv), *adj., n.* —*adj.* serving to qualify or modify.
—*n.* something serving to qualify, such as a qualifying term or expression: *These pedagogical reflections were interrupted by a fellow farther along the bar, who was using qualificatives that the bartender on duty ... couldn't go along with* (New Yorker).

**qual|i|fi|ca|tor** (kwol′ə fə kā′tər), *n.* an officer in the Roman Catholic Church whose business it is to examine causes and prepare them for trial.

**qual|i|fied** (kwol′ə fīd), *adj.* **1** having the desirable or required qualifications; fitted; competent: *a vessel qualified for use at sea, a qualified voter. To be qualified, an airplane pilot must have good eyesight and hold a license to fly.* **SYN**: adapted. **2** limited, modified, or restricted in some way: *qualified acceptance. His qualified answer was, "I will go, but only if you will come with me."* **3** *British Slang.* a euphemism for various oaths: *He was ... told not to make a qualified fool of himself* (Rudyard Kipling). —**qual′i|fied′ly,** *adv.* —**qual′i|fied′ness,** *n.*

**qualified endorsement,** (in business) an endorsement with the words "without recourse" added.

**qual|i|fi|er** (kwol′ə fī′ər), *n.* **1** a person, animal, or thing that qualifies: *Other qualifiers with their four-lap average speeds* (New York Times). **2** a word that limits or modifies the meaning of another word. Adjectives and adverbs are qualifiers. **SYN**: modifier.

**qual|i|fy** (kwol′ə fī), *v.,* **-fied, -fy|ing.** —*v.t.* **1** to make fit or competent: *Can you qualify yourself for the job?* **SYN**: prepare, equip. **2** to furnish with legal power; make legally capable: *No one but a landholder was qualified to be elected into that body* (George Bancroft). **3** to make less strong; change somewhat; limit; modify: *Qualify your statement that dogs are loyal by adding "usually."* **SYN**: moderate, temper, adapt. **4** to characterize by attributing some quality to; give a descriptive name to: *The "Devil's drawing-room," As some have qualified that wondrous place* (Byron).
**5** *Grammar.* to limit or modify the meaning of: *Adverbs qualify verbs.* **6** to modify the strength or flavor of (a liquid): *Tea which he drank ... qualified with brandy* (Tobias Smollett).
—*v.i.* **1** to become fit; show oneself fit: *Can you qualify for the Boy Scouts?* **2** to become legally capable: *to qualify as a voter.* **3** to gain the right to compete in a race, contest, or tournament.
[< Medieval Latin *qualificare* < Latin *quālis* of what sort + *facere* to make] —**qual′i|fy′ing|ly,** *adv.*

**qual|i|ta|tive** (kwol′ə tā′tiv), *adj.* concerned with quality or qualities: *The qualitative facts about food have to do with its vitamin content and its nutritional value. How the strength of the winds is related to the intensity of the differential heating is still a mystery. The qualitative working of the atmospheric heat is understood, but not its quantitative operation* (Science News Letter). [< Late Latin *quālitātīvus* < Latin *quālitās, -ātis* quality]
—**qual′i|ta′tive|ly,** *adv.*

**qualitative analysis,** a testing of something to find out what chemical substances are in it: *It is, rather, a physicochemical treatment of the principles of chemical equilibrium as applied to aqueous solutions and a fundamental exposition of the theoretical principles of qualitative and quantitative analysis* (Science).

**qual|i|tied** (kwol′ə tēd), *adj.* having a quality or qualities; endowed.

**qual|i|ty** (kwol′ə tē), *n., pl.* **-ties,** *adj.* —*n.* **1** something special about an object that makes it what it is; essential attribute; characteristic: *One quality of iron is hardness; one quality of sugar is sweetness. She has many fine qualities. I chose my wife, as she did her wedding gown ... for ... such qualities as would wear well* (Oliver Goldsmith). **SYN**: trait, feature. **2** nature, kind, or character of something: *the refreshing quality of a drink. Much oratory and considerable action ... was centered on cleaning up the environment and bettering the "quality of life"* (Charles Boyle). *Trials often test a man's quality. You know the fiery quality of the duke* (Shakespeare). **3** grade of excellence: *food of poor quality. That is the finest quality of cloth.* **4** fineness; merit; excellence: *Look for quality rather than quantity. There is more difference in the quality of our pleasures than the amount* (Emerson). **5** high rank; good or high social position: *people of quality. The house ... is frequented by gentry of the best quality* (Henry Fielding). **6** *Dialect.* people of high rank: *It was "baker's bread"—what the quality eat; none of your low-down corn-pone* (Mark Twain).
**7** character; position; relation: *Dr. Smith was present, but in quality of friend, not physician.*
**8** an accomplishment; attainment: *A just deportment, manners grac'd with ease, Elegant phrase ... Are qualities that ...* (William Cooper).
**9** *Acoustics.* the character of sounds aside from pitch and volume or intensity; timbre: *The quality of a sound is determined by the number of overtones present and their respective intensities* (Sears and Zemansky). **10** *Logic.* the character of a proposition as affirmative or negative.
**11** *Phonetics.* the sound of a vowel as determined by the shape of the oral resonance chamber, especially by the position of the tongue and lips. **12** *Especially British.* a newspaper or magazine designed to appeal to a sophisticated or specialized group of readers: *The "qualities," for example, need to earn a greater percentage of their income from advertising than do the "populars"* (Manchester Guardian Weekly).
—*adj.* of good or high quality: *quality merchandise. The Superintendent declared: "Educational excellence for every child in this city means quality integrated education"* (Leonard Buder).
[< Old French *qualite,* learned borrowing from Latin *quālitās* (coined by Cicero) < *quālis* of what sort]
—*Syn. n.* **1 Quality, property** mean a distinguishing mark or characteristic of a thing. **Quality,** the more general term, applies to any distinctive or characteristic feature of an individual or class, and it may be applied to people as well as things: *Good nature and quick wit are among her outstanding qualities.* **Property** applies to a quality essential to the nature of a thing or always manifested by it: *Heaviness is a property of lead.*

**quality control,** the inspection of manufactured products from the raw materials that go into them to their finished form to insure that they meet the standards of quality set by the manufacturer.

**qualm** (kwäm, kwälm), *n.* **1** a sudden, disturbing feeling in the mind; uneasiness; misgiving or doubt: *I tried the test with some qualms. At the haunted house I felt a sudden qualm of apprehension and terror.* **2** a disturbance or scruple of conscience: *She felt some qualms about staying away from church. ... an ignorant ruffianly gaucho, who ... would ... fight, steal, and do other naughty things without a qualm* (W. H. Hudson). *She had no qualms, no foreboding, no doubious sensation of weakness* (Arnold Bennett). **SYN**: compunction. **3** a feeling of faintness or sickness, especially of nausea, that lasts for just a moment. **4** a sudden fit of anything: *Immediately after one of these fits of extravagance he will be taken with violent qualms of economy* (Washington Irving). [origin uncertain]

**qualm|ish** (kwä′mish, kwäl′-), *adj.* **1** inclined to have qualms: *Elizabeth was not desirous of peace. She was qualmish at the very suggestion* (John L. Motley). **2** having qualms. **3** apt to cause qualms. —**qualm′ish|ly**, *adv.* —**qualm′ish-ness**, *n.*

**qualm|less** (kwäm′lis, kwälm′-), *adj.* having or feeling no qualms: *Any qualms that she may have suffered in the beginning disappeared ... By the end of January she was qualmless* (Warwick Deeping).

**qualm|y** (kwä′mē, kwäl′-), *adj.* = qualmish.

**quam|ash** (kwom′ash, kwə mash′), *n.* = camass.

**quan|da|ry** (kwon′dər ē, -drē), *n., pl.* **-ries.** a state of perplexity or uncertainty; dilemma: *Having captured our men, we were in a quandary how to keep them* (Theodore Roosevelt). **SYN**: predicament, difficulty, puzzle. [origin unknown]

**quand même** (käɴ mem′), *French.* even though; notwithstanding; come what may.

**quan|dong** or **quan|dang** (kwon′dong′), *n.* **1** an Australian tree related to the sandalwood, that has an edible fruit and a nutlike seed with an edible kernel. **2** the fruit of this tree. **3** the seed or kernel. [< the native Australian name]

**quant** (kwant, kwont), *n., v. British.* —***n.*** Also, **quant pole.** a pole with a flat board or cap at one end to prevent it from sinking into the mud, used to propel a boat: *No quant pole ever enters the water at the point planned* (Punch).
—***v.t., v.i.*** to propel (a boat) with a quant. [perhaps < Latin *contus* boat pole < Greek *kontós* < *kenteîn* to goad]

**quan|ta** (kwon′tə), *n.* plural of **quantum**: *Quantum theory tells us that light comes in little packages of energy called quanta* (John R. Pierce).

**quan|tal** (kwon′təl), *adj.* having to do with quanta or the quantum theory.

**quan|ta|some** (kwän′tə sōm), *n.* one of the granules containing chlorophyll found inside the chloroplast of plant cells: *Through the electron microscope, small leaf particles, quantasomes, resemble the stipples on the rubber surface of a table-tennis paddle* (William C. Steere). [< *quanta* (plural of *quantum* smallest unit of energy) + *-some*$^3$ body; so called from its being regarded as the smallest unit of the cell]

**quan|tic** (kwon′tik), *n. Mathematics.* a homogeneous function of two or more variables. [< Latin *quantus* how much + English *-ic;* probably patterned on *cubic*]

**quan|ti|fi|a|bil|i|ty** (kwon′tə fī ə bil′ə tē), *n.* the quality or condition of being quantifiable.

**quan|ti|fi|a|ble** (kwon′tə fī′ə bəl), *adj.* that can be counted or measured.

**quan|ti|fi|ca|tion** (kwon′tə fə kā′shən), *n.* the action of quantifying: *The economist is inclined to overlook the fact that the basic data of economics are not sales-inventory ratios or the wholesale commodity index but human values and choices, hardly subject to quantification, or chart-reading* (Wall Street Journal).

**quan|ti|fi|ca|tion|al** (kwon′tə fə kā′shə nəl), *adj.* of or having to do with quantification: *Those arguments must be recast in a "suitably formalized language that provides for quantificational notation"* (Stephen Toulmin). —**quan′ti|fi|ca′tion|al|ly**, *adv.*

**quan|ti|fi|er** (kwon′tə fī′ər), *n.* **1** *Logic.* a symbol prefixed to a formula or proposition to express a quantity such as "every," "all," or "some." Quantifiers are studied in functional calculus. **2** *Linguistics.* a modifier that indicates quantity, such as *eight, ten, few, much, many.* **3** a person who is skilled in quantifying: [*They*] *agree that "both types of scientific personalities, the quantifiers and the pattern-recognizers—the 'counters' and the 'poets'—will continue to be needed"* (Time). **4** a person concerned with the quantification of data.

**quan|ti|fy** (kwon′tə fī), *v.t.,* **-fied, -fy|ing.** **1** to determine the quantity of; measure: *Anything that can be quantified ought to be quantified, everything that will submit to scientific measure ought to be measured* (Saturday Review). **2** to express or indicate the quantity of: *to quantify a syllable or verse.* **3** *Logic.* to make explicit the quantity or extent of: *We quantify the assertion "Men are sinners," by putting "all," "some," "most," "many," etc., before "men."* [< Medieval Latin *quantificare* < Latin *quantus* how much + *facere* to make]

**quan|tise** (kwon′tīz), *v.t.,* **-tised, -tis|ing.** *Especially British.* quantize. —**quan′tis|er**, *n.*

**quan|ti|tate** (kwon′tə tāt), *v.t.,* **-tat|ed, -tat|ing.** to determine the quantity of; measure: *Attempts ... are made to quantitate the output of those faculty members who have not gained tenure* (Bulletin of Atomic Scientists).

**quan|ti|ta|tive** (kwon′tə tā′tiv), *adj.* **1** concerned with quantity or quantities: *a quantitative change, quantitative superiority. Quantitative research during the first half of the present century on the numerical fluctuations of wild animal populations led to the flowering of the science of animal ecology and formed a solid foundation for a theory of animal populations* (Science News Letter). **2** that can be measured. **3** (of verse) having feet consisting of long and short, rather than stressed and unstressed, syllables: *Perhaps the best quantitative verses in our language ... are to be found in Mother Goose* (James Russell Lowell). **4** of or having to do with the quantity or duration of a speech sound. [< Medieval Latin *quantitativus* < Latin *quantitās, -ātis* quantity] —**quan′ti|ta′tive|ly**, *adv.* —**quan′ti|ta′tive|ness**, *n.*

**quantitative analysis**, the testing of something to find out not only what chemical substances are in it, but also just how much there is of each substance.

**quan|ti|ty** (kwon′tə tē), *n., pl.* **-ties.** **1** an amount: *Use equal quantities of nuts and raisins in the cake.* **SYN**: portion. **2** a large amount; indefinite but usually large number: *The baker buys flour in quantity. The professor owns quantities of books.* **3** the amount of something present: *to decrease the quantity of heat in a room.* **4** something that is measurable. **5** *Music.* the length of a note. **6** the length of a sound or syllable in speech or poetry: *But in quantity, or length, the "short a" in sand is actually longer than the "long a" in late* (American Pronunciation). **7** *Mathematics.* **a** something having magnitude, or size, extent, amount, etc. **b** a figure or symbol representing this. **8** *Logic.* **a** the character of a proposition as universal or particular. **b** how far a term or concept in a proposition is supposed to extend, as indicated by words like *all, some,* or *no.* [< Old French *quantite*, learned borrowing from Latin *quantitās* < *quantus* how much]

**quantity surveyor**, a surveyor who estimates or determines the quantities of work and materials needed for a job: *The plans of the buildings ... will be now submitted to the quantity surveyor, with a view to the quantities being taken out* (London Daily News).

**quantity theory**, *Economics.* the theory that the general level of prices depends directly on the amount of money in circulation and on the velocity of its circulation, varying inversely with the volume of trade.

**quan|ti|za|tion** (kwon′tə zā′shən), *n.* the fact or process of quantizing..

**quan|tize** (kwon′tīz), *v.t.,* **-tized, -tiz|ing.** **1** to apply quantum mechanics or the quantum theory to; measure (energy) in quanta: *He assumed that the processes are quantized not only in space but in time; that is, we have cycles during which all action takes place* (Scientific American). *Much of the behavior of atoms and electrons could be explained only on the assumption that the field in the atom is quantized* (Scientific American). **2** to restrict the magnitude of (an observable quantity) in all or some of its range to a set of distinct values, especially to multiples of a definite unit: ... *rotatory energy is limited to certain discrete values, or, as the physicist says, is "quantized"* (Scientific American).

**quan|tiz|er** (kwon′tī zər), *n.* a person or thing that quantizes.

**quan|tong** (kwon′tong′), *n.* = quandong.

**quan|tum** (kwon′təm), *n., pl.* **-ta.** **1** *Physics.* **a** the basic unit of radiant energy; the smallest amount of energy capable of existing independently. Light and heat are given off and absorbed in quanta. *One radiation quantum can modify the nucleus of a germ cell sufficiently to cause a mutation, an inheritable change of character; but only one in many million quanta will score that kind of bull's eye* (Atlantic). **b** this amount of energy regarded as a unit. **2** a sum; amount; quantity; share or portion: *Every member pressing forward to throw on his quantum of wisdom, the subject was quickly buried under a mountain of words* (Washington Irving). [< Latin *quantum*, neuter adjective, how(ever) much]

**quantum chemistry**, the quantum theory as applied to the study of chemical systems and processes.

**quantum electrodynamics**, the quantum theory as applied to electrodynamics: *Quantum electrodynamics ... is concerned with the interaction of the electron, the particle of electricity, with radiation* (Science News Letter).

**quantum electronics**, the quantum theory as applied to electronics.

**quantum jump**, **1** *Physics.* the change in the orbit of an electron in an atom accompanying the loss or gain of a quantum of energy: *The action of the solid-state maser also depends on quantum jumps, but they are jumps of electrons within individual atoms rather than energy transitions of whole molecules* (Scientific American). **2** *Figurative.* a sudden, spectacular advance; major breakthrough.

**quantum leap**, a great or major advance; quantum jump: *In 1980, cable television will have the ... structure for a quantum leap followed by an effectively wired nation a decade later* (New Yorker).

**quan|tum-me|chan|i|cal** (kwon′təm mə kan′ə-kəl), *adj.* of, having to do with, or characteristic of quantum mechanics. —**quan′tum-me|chan′i|cal-ly**, *adv.*

**quantum mechanics**, the quantum theory as applied to the physical measurement of atomic structures and related phenomena: *Quantum mechanics ... enables scientists to deal with small particles, such as the electron, that do not follow the laws of classical physics* (Harvey E. White). *Quantum mechanics assumes that both matter and radiation have particle and wave aspects* (Earle B. Brown).

**quan|tum me|ru|it** (kwon′təm mer′ů it), *Latin.* as much as one has merited or deserved.

**quan|tum mu|ta|tus ab il|lo** (kwon′təm myü tā′-təs ab il′ō), *Latin.* how greatly changed from what he was!

**quantum number**, one of a set of numbers assigned to an atomic system, specifying the number of quanta or units of energy in the system.

**quantum physics**, physics according to the quantum theory; modern or contemporary physics: *Quantum physics normally deals with natural phenomena on a submicroscopic scale* (Scientific American).

**quan|tum suf|fi|cit** (kwon′təm suf′ə sit), *Latin.* as much as is sufficient.

**quantum theory**, the theory that whenever radiant energy is transferred, the transfer occurs in pulsations rather than continuously, and that the amount transferred during each pulsation is a definite amount or quantum. It was introduced by Max Planck, a German physicist. *What the quantum theory explains is the distinctiveness and the individuality of the 90-odd elements of which the world is made. What a long way for a theory to have come, that started out as a theory of the recondite subject of black-body radiation* (Scientific American).

**quan|tum va|le|bat** (kwon′təm və lē′bat), *Latin.* as much as it was worth.

**quap** (kwop), *n.* a hypothetical nuclear particle consisting of an antiproton and a quark. [< *qu*(ark) + *a*(nti)*p*(roton)]

**Qua|paw** (kwä′pô), *n., pl.* **-paw** or **-paws.** a member of a Siouan Indian tribe of the Arkansas River Valley, first mentioned in an account of Hernando de Soto's expedition from 1539 to 1543.

**qua|qua|ver|sal** (kwā′kwə vėr′səl), *adj., n.* —***adj.*** turned, pointing, or dipping in all directions.
—***n.*** *Geology.* a domed structure with the strata dipping away in all directions from a center. [< Late Latin *quāquāversus* (< *quāquā* where + *versus* toward)]

**qua|qua|ver|sal|ly** (kwā′kwə vėr′sə lē), *adv.* in all directions from a central point or area.

**quar.**, **1** quarter. **2** quarterly.

**quar|an|tin|a|ble** (kwôr′ən tē′nə bəl, kwor′-), *adj.* **1** subject or liable to quarantine. **2** requiring or giving grounds for quarantine. **3** that quarantine can prevent from spreading: *A drug company official notes flu isn't a quarantinable disease* (Wall Street Journal).

**quar|an|tine** (kwôr′ən tēn, kwor′-), *v.,* **-tined, -tin-ing,** *n.* —***v.t.*** **1** to keep (a person, animal, plant, or ship) away from others for a time to prevent the spread of a contagious disease: *My brother was quarantined for three weeks when he had scarlet fever.* **2** *Figurative.* to isolate or exclude for any reason: *to quarantine a belligerent nation.* [< noun]
—***n.*** **1** the condition of being quarantined: *The house was in quarantine for three weeks when the child had scarlet fever.* **2** detention, isolation, and other measures taken to prevent the spread of a contagious disease. **3** a place where, or time for which, people, animals, plants, or ships are held until it is sure that they have no contagious diseases, insect pests, etc. **4** *Figurative.* isolation, exclusion, and similar measures taken against an undesirable person or group: *Nothing we know of at present justifies departure from the well-tried policy of vigilance and quarantine eschewing alarmism* (Jewish Chronicle).
[< Italian *quarantina* < *quaranta* forty < Latin *quadrāgintā*, related to *quattuor* four (from the 40 days of the original period of isolation)]

**quarantine flag**, = yellow flag.

**quare** (kwãr, kwär), *adj.* **1** *Dialect.* queer. **2** *Prison Slang.* condemned: ... *wait tensely for a reprieve to arrive for the quare fellow* (Time). [variant of *queer*]

**quark** (kwôrk), *n. Nuclear Physics.* one of a hypothetical set of three nuclear particles, each with an electric charge less than that of the electron, regarded as possible constituents of all atomic particles. The existence and properties of quarks were predicted by the eightfold way. [< the phrase "three *quarks*" in *Finnegans Wake,* a novel by James Joyce]

**quar·rel**[1] (kwôr′əl, kwor′-), *n., v.,* **-reled, -rel·ing** or (*especially British*) **-relled, -rel·ling.** —*n.* **1** an angry dispute or disagreement; fight with words; breaking off of friendly relations: *They have had a quarrel and don't speak to each other. Love quarrels are easily made up, but of money quarrels there is no end* (Maria Edgeworth). **2** a cause for a dispute or disagreement; reason for breaking off friendly relations: *A bully likes to pick quarrels. An honest man has no quarrel with the laws.* **3** one's cause or side in a dispute or contest: *The knight took up the poor man's quarrel and fought his oppressor.*
—*v.i.* **1** to fight with words; dispute or disagree angrily; break off friendly relations; stop being friends: *The two friends quarreled and now they don't speak to each other. The sisters quarrelled among themselves as all sisters will* (Winston Churchill). **SYN:** bicker, wrangle, squabble. **2** to find fault; complain: *It is useless to quarrel with fate because one does not have control over it.* **SYN:** cavil.
[< Old French *quarrel,* or *querele* < Latin *querella, querēla* complaint < *querī* complain]
—*Syn. n.* **1 Quarrel, feud** mean an angry disagreement or unfriendly relation between two people or groups. **Quarrel** applies to an angry dispute, soon over or ending in a fight or in severed relations: *The children had a quarrel over the division of the candy.* **Feud** applies to a long-lasting quarrel, usually marked by violence and revenge when between two groups, by bitterness and repeatedly unfriendly verbal attacks when between individuals: *The senator and the columnist carried on a feud.*

**quar·rel**[2] (kwôr′əl, kwor′-), *n.* **1** a bolt or arrow with a square head, used with a crossbow. **2** a small, square or diamond-shaped pane of glass, used in latticed windows. **3** a stonemason's chisel. **4** = quarry[3]. [< Old French *quarrel* < Medieval Latin *quadrellus* (diminutive) < Latin *quadrus* square]

**quar·rel·er** (kwôr′ə lər, kwor′-), *n.* a person who quarrels.

**quar·rel·ler** (kwôr′ə lər, kwor′-), *n. Especially British.* quarreler.

**quar·rel·some** (kwôr′əl səm, kwor′-), *adj.* too ready to quarrel; fond of fighting and disputing: *A quarrelsome child has few friends. On our idle days they were mutinous and quarrelsome, finding fault with their pork, the bread, etc., and in continual ill humor* (Benjamin Franklin). **SYN:** choleric, irascible, disputatious. —**quar′rel·some·ly,** *adv.* —**quar′rel·some·ness,** *n.*

**quar·ri·er** (kwôr′ē ər, kwor′-), *n.* a worker who quarries stone.

**quar·ry**[1] (kwôr′ē, kwor′-), *n., pl.* **-ries,** *v.,* **-ried, -ry·ing.** —*n.* **1** a place where stone is dug, cut, or blasted out for use in building: *an ancient quarry from which the stone has been cut out in smooth masses* (Amelia B. Edwards). **2** *Figurative.* a source of plentiful supply; mine: *Each sentence seems a quarry of rich meditations* (Sir George Mackenzie).
—*v.t.* **1** to obtain from a quarry: *We watched the workmen quarry out a huge block of marble.* **2** *Figurative.* to dig out by hard work: *This is the story of Sandburg's boyhood quarried with deftness and tact out of the rich profusion of "Always the Young Strangers"* (Saturday Review). **3** to make a quarry in.
—*v.i.* to dig in a quarry: (*Figurative.*) *He deliberately left buried* [*some stories*] *in the files of these magazines because he quarried from them later for his novels* (Norman Shrapnel).
[< Medieval Latin *quareia* < *quareria* < *quadraria* < Latin *quadrus* a square]

**quar·ry**[2] (kwôr′ē, kwor′-), *n., pl.* **-ries. 1** an animal chased in a hunt; game; prey: *a falcon swooping on its quarry* (Herbert Spencer). *The foxhunters chased their quarry for hours.* **2** *Figurative.* anything hunted or eagerly pursued: *Hunter and quarry under the same roof, all unbeknownst to one another* (New Yorker). [< Old French *cuiree* < *cuir* skin, hide < Latin *corium*]

**quar·ry**[3] (kwôr′ē, kwor′-), *n., pl.* **-ries,** *adj.* —*n.* **1** a small, square or diamond-shaped pane of glass, used in latticed windows; quarrel: *This window was filled with old painted glass in ... quarries* (Margaret O. W. Oliphant). **2** a tile or stone that is square or diamond-shaped: *What ground remains ... is flagged with large quarries of white marble* (Sir Richard Steele).
—*adj.* square or diamond-shaped: *quarry tile.*
[< *quarrel*[2]]

**quar·ry-faced** (kwôr′ē fāst′, kwor′-), *adj.* **1** (of building stone) rough-faced, as taken from the quarry. **2** built of such stone, as masonry.

**quar·ry·ing** (kwôr′ē ing, kwor′-), *n.* the work or business of taking large solid blocks or broken masses of limestone, marble, slate, or the like, from the earth and preparing them for building projects: *University College, Cardiff, Wales, instituted a degree course in quarrying* (L. R. Buckley).

**quar·ry·man** (kwôr′ē mən, kwor′-), *n., pl.* **-men.** a person who works in a quarry: *The fragmentation of the broken rock is a further factor which the miner and quarryman have to consider* (New Scientist).

**quarry sap,** = quarry water.

**quarry water,** the moisture contained in newly quarried stone.

*** quart**[1] (kwôrt), *n.* **1** a measure for liquids, equal to ¼ of a gallon; 32 fluid ounces or 0.9463 liter; in Britain and Canada, 40 fluid ounces or 1.1364 liters. *Abbr:* qt. **2** a measure for dry things, equal to ⅛ of a peck; 67.2 cubic inches or 1.1012 liters; in Britain and Canada, 69.35 cubic inches or 1.1364 liters. **3a** a container holding a quart. **b** the contents of such a container: *to drink a quart of milk, to eat a quart of berries.* **4** *Music.* the interval of a fourth. [< Old French *quarte* < Latin *quarta,* feminine adjective, fourth]

*** quart**[1]
definition 1

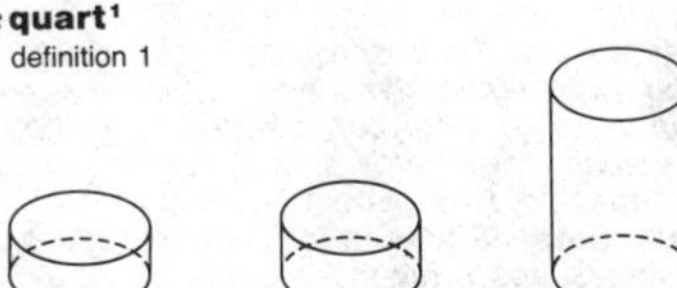


**quart**[2] (kärt), *n.* **1** a sequence of four cards in a suit: *Quart major means the sequence of the four highest cards of a suit.* **2** *Fencing.* the fourth in a series of eight parries; carte. [< Old French *quarte* (literally) fourth; see etym. under **quart**[1]]

**quart.,** **1** quarter. **2** quarterly.

**quar·tal** (kwôr′təl), *adj. Music.* of or having to do with a quart: *Quartal harmony is built in fourths, and clusters are built in seconds* (Grant Fletcher).

**quar·tan** (kwôr′tən), *adj., n.* —*adj.* recurring every fourth day, by inclusive counting.
—*n.* a fever or ague with two days between attacks.
[< Old French *quartaine* (*fievre*) < Latin (*febris*) *quartāna* quartan (fever), feminine adjective < *quartus* fourth]

**quartan malaria,** a mild, persistent form of malaria in which the attacks occur every 72 hours.

**quarte** (kärt), *n. Fencing.* the fourth in a series of eight parries; carte. [< French *quarte* < Old French; see etym. under **quart**[1]]

**quar·ter** (kwôr′tər), *n., v., adj.* —*n.* **1** one of four equal parts; half of a half; one fourth: *Each of the four boys had a quarter of an apple.* **2a** one fourth of a dollar; 25 cents: *These candies are one pound for a quarter.* **b** a copper and nickel coin of the United States, or a nickel coin of Canada, worth 25 cents. It was formerly made of silver. *Do you have change for a quarter?* **3a** one fourth of an hour; 15 minutes: *I've scarcely been ten minutes ... at least a quarter it can hardly be* (Byron). **b** the moment marking this period: *"The quarter's gone!" cried Mr. Tapley* (Dickens). **4a** one fourth of a year; 3 months: *Many savings banks pay interest every quarter.* **b** one fourth of a school year: *He had withdrawn Miss Mannering from the school at the end of the first quarter* (Scott). **c** one of four equal periods of play in certain games, such as football, basketball, soccer, or hockey. **5** one of the four periods of the moon, lasting about 7 days each. **SYN:** phase. **6a** one fourth of a yard; 9 inches. **b** one fourth of a mile; 440 yards: *He runs a fast quarter for a youngster.* **7a** one fourth of a hundredweight; 25 pounds in the United States or 28 pounds in Great Britain. **b** one fourth of a pound; 4 ounces avoirdupois or 3 ounces troy. **c** *British.* one fourth of a cartload of grain, about 8 bushels: *a quarter of oats.* **8** a region; place: *to visit a distant quarter. It was the opinion of Mark Lescarbot ... that the immediate descendants of Noah peopled this quarter of the globe* (Washington Irving). **SYN:** locality. **9** a section; district: *the French quarter. The quarter they lived in was near the railroad. ... the almost unmapped quarter inhabited by artists, musicians, and "people who wrote"* (Edith Wharton). **10** a certain part of a community, group, or the like: *information from a reliable quarter. The bankers' theory was not accepted in other quarters.* **11a** a point of the compass; direction: *We learned that each of the four principal points of the compass is called a quarter. From what quarter did the wind blow?* **b** one fourth of the distance between any two adjacent points of the 32 marked on a compass; 2 degrees 48 minutes 45 seconds. **12a** mercy shown a defeated enemy in sparing his life: *The pirates gave no quarter to their victims.* **b** *Figurative.* kindly or merciful treatment; indulgence: [*He*] *gave no quarter to his singers and extracted every ounce of power out of the orchestra* (London Times). **13a** one of the four parts into which an animal's carcass is divided in butchering: *a quarter of lamb.* **b** one of the four legs of an animal, with its adjoining parts: *The cattle were so small that a stout native could walk off with an entire quarter* (Herman Melville). **c** either side of a horse's hoof, between heel and toe. **14** the part of a ship's side near the stern: *All the stern and quarter of her was beaten to pieces with the sea* (Daniel Defoe). **15** *Heraldry.* **a** one of the four (or more) parts into which a shield is divided by lines at right angles. **b** an emblem occupying the upper right fourth of a shield. **16** the part of a boot or shoe above the heel and below the top of either side of the foot from the middle of the back to the vamp. **17** *Architecture.* an upright post in partitions, to which the laths are nailed. **18** *Music.* a quarter note: *That tone is held for two quarters.* **19** = quarterback. **20** *Archaic.* treatment; terms: *They will give thee fair quarter* (Scott).
—*v.t.* **1a** to divide into fourths: *Mother quartered the apple for the four boys.* **b** to divide into parts: *to quarter a chicken for frying.* **2a** to give a place to live in; station; lodge: *Coligny ... quartered all the women in the cathedral and other churches* (John L. Motley). **b** to impose (soldiers) on a household or community for food and lodging; billet: *Soldiers were quartered in all the houses of the town.* **3** to cut the body of (a person) into quarters as a sign of disgrace after hanging, a practice of former times. **4** to place or bear (heraldic bearings) in quarters of a shield: *The royal banner of England, quartering the lion, the leopard, and the harp* (Hawthorne). **5** to range over (ground) in every direction in search of game: *You could see the owls abroad ... before sunset, in quest of prey, quartering the ground like harriers* (W. H. Hudson). —*v.i.* **1** to live or stay in a place: *the village where he proposed to quarter for the night* (Scott). **2** *Nautical.* (of the wind) to blow on a ship's quarter: *She* [*a ship*] *came down upon us with the wind quartering* (Daniel Defoe). **3a** to range in every direction: *The dogs quartered, seeking game.* **b** to move in a slanting direction: *The swimmer quartered because of the strong current.* **4** to enter a new quarter: *The new moon's quartered in with foul weather* (Frederick Marryat).
—*adj.* **1** being one of four equal parts; being equal to only about one fourth of full measure: *a quarter inch, reduced to quarter rations.* **2** *Figurative.* less than half; far from complete; very imperfect (*used with a hyphen in combinations*): *a quarter-liberal, a quarter-baked theory. To take effective steps to discourage the purveying of such quarter-truths ... is described in your editorial columns as "censorship"* (London Times).

**at close quarters,** very close together; almost touching: *The cars had to pass at close quarters on the narrow mountain road. Living at close quarters, the father and mother quarreled constantly, and the boy had to witness these quarrels* (Edmund Wilson).

**cry (for) quarter,** to call for mercy: *Cry For quarter, or for victory* (Byron).

**quarters, a** a place to live or stay in: *The circus has its winter quarters in the South. The servants have quarters in a cottage.* **b** positions or stations assigned to members of a ship's company for battle, drill, or alerts: *Call the drummer ... and let him beat to quarters* (Frederick Marryat).
[< Old French *quartier* < Latin *quartārius* a fourth < *quartus* fourth]

**quar·ter·age** (kwôr′tər ij), *n.* **1** a quarterly payment, charge, or allowance: *A half-starved Clerk, eked out his lean quarterage, by these merry perquisites* (Benjamin Disraeli). **2a** the quartering of troops. **b** quarters for troops. [< Old French *quarterage* < *quartier* quarter + *-age* -age]

**quar·ter·back** (kwôr′tər bak′), *n., v.* —*n.* **1a** an offensive back who stands directly behind the center in football. The quarterback calls the plays on offense, and usually receives the ball directly from the center, handing it off to a running back or passing it to one of his receivers. **b** the position of quarterback. **2** *Figurative.* a person who directs any group or activity: *The third-base coach is the quarterback of the team; he calls the signals on a relay from the manager* (New York Times).

**Pronunciation Key:** hat, āge, cãre, fär; let, ēqual, tėrm; it, īce; hot, ōpen, ôrder; oil, out; cup, pu̇t, rüle; child; long; thin; ᴛʜen; zh, measure; ə represents **a** in about, **e** in taken, **i** in pencil, **o** in lemon, **u** in circus.

—*v.t.* to serve as quarterback of; direct the activities of: (*Figurative.*) *Fullback dad is the provider, mother quarterbacks the housekeeping* (Maclean's). (*Figurative.*) *A less wishful and probably sounder conjecture is that Ho has gone back to his old trick of standing behind the lines and quarterbacking Communist strategy for all Southeast Asia* (Time).

—*v.i.* to serve as a quarterback: (*Figurative.*) *So at the very least you would expect the Republican followers to show some interest, if no more than the Monday morning quarterbacking of indignation and disgust* (Wall Street Journal).

[American English, probably patterned on *halfback, fullback*]

**quarterback sneak**, *Football.* a play in which the quarterback does not hand off the ball, but keeps it and charges forward: *It was Lalla, on a quarterback sneak, who took the ball over from 1 foot out* (New York Times).

**quarter binding**, a style of bookbinding in which only the back is made of leather, as distinguished from half binding or three-quarter binding.

**quarter boat**, any boat hung on davits over a ship's quarter: *We ... lowered away the quarter boats, and went ashore* (Richard H. Dana).

**quar|ter-bound** (kwôr′tər bound′), *adj.* (of a book) bound in quarter binding.

**quarter crack**, a crack in the side wall of a horse's hoof resulting in lameness.

**quarter day**, a day beginning or ending a quarter of the year, especially for dating rents, salaries, or other arrangements. In England, the quarter days are March 25 (Lady Day), June 24 (Midsummer Day), September 29 (Michaelmas), and December 25 (Christmas).

**quar|ter|deck** (kwôr′tər dek′), *n., v.* —*n.* **1** the part of the upper deck between the mainmast and the stern of a sailing vessel, used especially by the officers of a ship. **2** a deck area on a modern naval vessel designated as the ceremonial post of the commanding officer: *Following as best they might, the newsmen could expect only rudeness or a quarterdeck tongue-lashing when they got close* (Time).

—*v.i.* to walk up and down as on a quarterdeck: (*Figurative.*) *He continued quarterdecking about the room for a few times in silence, and his annoyance subsided* (E. F. Benson).

**quar|ter|deck|er** (kwôr′tər dek′ər), *n. Informal.* a person, especially a ship's officer, who is looked upon more as a stickler for small points of etiquette than as a thorough master of his job.

**quarter eagle**, *U.S.* a former gold coin worth $2.50.

**quar|tered** (kwôr′tərd), *adj.* **1** divided into quarters: *yon cloudless, quartered moon* (Oliver Wendell Holmes). **2** furnished with rooms or lodging. **3** quartersawed. **4** having quarters as specified: *a short-quartered horse, low-quartered shoes.* **5** *Heraldry.* **a** (of a coat of arms) divided or arranged in quarters. **b** (of a cross) having a square piece missing in the center.

**quar|ter|fi|nal** (kwôr′tər fī′nəl), *n., adj.* —*n.* the round just before the semifinals in a tournament.

—*adj.* of or having to do with this round.

**quar|ter|fi|nal|ist** (kwôr′tər fī′nə list), *n.* a contestant or team in a quarterfinal.

**quarter grain**, the grain of wood shown when a log is quartered.

**quarter horse**, a strong horse originally bred for racing on quarter-mile tracks, now used by cowboys for sorting out cattle, in playing polo, and for riding: *The average racing quarter horse can dash over 20 seconds, often faster at this distance than some thoroughbreds* (Wall Street Journal).

**quar|ter-hour** (kwôr′tər our′), *n.* **1** fifteen minutes. **2** a point one fourth or three fourths of the way in an hour.

**quarter ill**, = blackleg (def. 3).

**quar|ter|ing** (kwôr′tər ing), *adj., n.* —*adj.* **1** (of a wind or sea) blowing on a ship's side near the stern: *Rolling and surging along, as we were now, through quartering seas, with an occasional shower of spray coming aboard as a whitecap slapped the guardrail* (Atlantic). **2** that quarters.

—*n.* **1** the act of dividing into fourths. **2** the act of assigning quarters, as for soldiers: *For an average of about $100 a month, a sum equal to the quartering allowance he gets from Uncle Sam, an Abilene airman will be able to rent a fully-furnished three-bedroom home complete with picture windows and carport* (Wall Street Journal). **3** *Heraldry.* **a** the division of a shield into quarters or parts. **b** one of such parts. **c** the coat of arms on it.

**quarterings**, the various coats of arms arranged on a shield: *a fat duchess, with fourteen quarterings* (Charles Lever).

**quarter light**, **1** a window in the side of a carriage, as distinguished from the windows in the doors. **2** *Especially British.* a small window in the side of an automobile which usually turns on a swivel, as distinguished from the ordinary windows.

**quar|ter|ly** (kwôr′tər lē), *adj., adv., n., pl.* **-lies.**

—*adj.* **1** happening or done four times a year: *to make quarterly payments on one's insurance.* **2** having to do with or covering a quarter of a year.

—*adv.* **1** once each quarter of a year: *to pay one's insurance premiums quarterly. Father pays his income tax quarterly.* **2** *Heraldry.* **a** in the quarters of a shield. **b** with division into quarters. **3** in or by quarters.

—*n.* a magazine published every three months. *Abbr:* quart.

**quar|ter|mas|ter** (kwôr′tər mas′tər, -mäs′-), *n.* **1** an officer in the army who has charge of providing quarters, clothing, rations, ammunition, fuel, and transportation, for troops. **2** a petty officer in the navy or merchant marine who has charge of the steering, the compasses, and the signals on a ship: *Deep water merchant mariners sailing into the Great Lakes via the St. Lawrence Seaway will find the fresh-water lingo quite different from ocean-going language ... Speed is reckoned in miles per hour not in knots, while the sailor steering the boat is a "wheelsman," not a "quartermaster"* (Wall Street Journal).

**Quartermaster Corps**, a former department of the United States Army that provided for the quarters, equipment, and other supplies, of troops. It was replaced by the Army Materiel Command in 1962.

**quar|ter|mas|ter-gen|er|al** (kwôr′tər mas′tər-jen′ər əl, -mäs′-; -jen′rəl), *n., pl.* **-als.** **1** *U.S. Military.* the staff officer in charge of the Quartermaster Corps. **2** *British Military.* a staff officer whose department is charged with all orders relating to the marching, embarking, billeting, and quartering, of troops. *Abbr:* Q.M.Gen.

**quar|ter-mi|ler** (kwôr′tər mī′lər), *n.* runner or racer who runs a quarter of a mile.

**quar|tern** (kwôr′tərn), *n.* **1** *British.* **a** a quarter; fourth part. **b** one fourth of a pint; gill. **c** one fourth of a peck or of a stone. **d** a quarter of a pound. **2** = quartern loaf. [Middle English *quartron* < Old French *quarteron* < *quart* fourth < Latin *quartus*]

**quartern loaf**, a large, round loaf of bread weighing about four pounds.

***quarter note**, a musical note played for one fourth as long a time as a whole note; crotchet.

***quarter note**
***quarter rest**

quarter notes

quarter rests

**quar|ter-phase** (kwôr′tər fāz′), *adj.* combining, producing, or carrying two alternating electric currents which differ in phase by one quarter of a cycle (90 degrees); diphase.

**quarter point**, one fourth of the angular distance between two adjacent points of the compass; 2 degrees 48 minutes 45 seconds.

**quarter racing**, a quarter-mile horse race along a straight path.

***quarter rest**, *Music.* a rest as long as a quarter note.

**quarter round**, a molding whose contour is exactly or approximately a quadrant; ovolo.

**quar|ters** (kwôr′tərz), *n.pl.* See under **quarter**.

**quar|ter|saw** (kwôr′tər sô′), *v.t.,* **-sawed, -sawed** or **-sawn, -saw|ing.** to saw (a log) lengthwise into quarters and then into boards. Logs are quartersawed so that the top and bottom surfaces of each board show a cross section of the annual rings of the wood.

**quarter section**, *U.S. and Canada.* a piece of land, usually square, containing 160 acres.

**quarter sessions**, **1** an English court, held quarterly, that has limited criminal jurisdiction and certain other powers. **2** any one of various other courts held quarterly, as in some states of the United States and in Scotland.

**quar|ter|staff** (kwôr′tər staf′, -stäf′), *n., pl.* **-staves.** **1** an old English weapon consisting of a stout pole 6 to 8 feet long, tipped with iron. **2** exercise or fighting with this weapon: *He was famous throughout the province for strength of arm and skill at quarterstaff* (Washington Irving).

**quar|ter|staves** (kwôr′tər stāvz′), *n.* plural of **quarterstaff**.

**quarter step**, a quarter tone in music.

**quarter tone**, half of a half-tone in music.

**quar|tet** or **quar|tette** (kwôr tet′), *n.* **1** a group of four singers or players performing together. **2** a piece of music for four voices or instruments. **3** any group of four; set of four. [< French *quartette* < Italian *quartetto* < *quarto* fourth < Latin *quartus*]

**quar|tic** (kwôr′tik), *adj., n. Mathematics.* —*adj.* of the fourth degree.

—*n.* an expression or surface of the fourth degree.

[< Latin *quartus* fourth + English *-ic*]

**quar|tier** (kàr tyā′), *n. French.* a section of a town or city; quarter.

**quar|tile** (kwôr′tīl, -təl), *n., adj.* —*n.* **1a** one of the points or marks dividing a frequency distribution into four parts, each having the same frequency. The upper quartile is the point reached or exceeded by 25 per cent of the cases plotted on the frequency scale. **b** any one of the four parts thus formed. **2** *Astrology.* the aspect of two heavenly bodies when their longitudes differ by 90 degrees.

—*adj.* of or having to do with quartiles; being a quartile.

[< Medieval Latin *quartilis* < Latin *quartus* fourth]

**quart major**, (in cards) a sequence of ace, king, queen, and jack of a suit.

**quar|to** (kwôr′tō), *n., pl.* **-tos**, *adj.* —*n.* **1** the page size (usually about 9 by 12 inches) of a book in which each leaf is one fourth of a whole sheet of paper. *Abbr:* 4°, Q. **2** a book having such pages.

—*adj.* of this size; having pages of this size.

[< Medieval Latin *in quarto* in the fourth (of a sheet)]

**quartz** (kwôrts), *n.* a very hard mineral composed of silica, found in many different types of rocks, such as sandstone and quartzite, and as an important constituent in granite, gneiss, and other rocks. Crystals of pure quartz are colorless and transparent. Colored varieties of quartz include flint, agate, and amethyst. Quartzes vary according to the size and purity of their crystals. Those with submicroscopic crystals are divided into fibrous varieties, or chalcedonies, and granular varieties. *Formula:* $SiO_2$ [< German *Quarz*]

—**quartz′like′**, *adj.*

**quartz clock**, an electric clock in which the frequency of current supplied to the clock motor is controlled by the vibrations of a quartz crystal: *The highly accurate standard quartz clocks at the Royal Greenwich Observatory and ... at the United States Naval Observatory, keep time to better than one part in ten thousand million* (New Scientist).

**quartz-di|o|rite** (kwôrts′dī′ə rīt), *n.* a variety of diorite having quartz as one of its main components.

**quartz glass**, a clear, vitreous solid, or glass, produced by fusion of a very pure form of quartz or rock crystal; fused quartz or silica; silica glass. Quartz glass is able to withstand large and rapid temperature changes and is specially transparent to the infrared, visible, and ultraviolet radiations. It is chiefly used in electronic and optical apparatus and equipment, such as vacuum tubes, insulating material, fluorescent and germicidal lamps.

**quartz|if|er|ous** (kwôrt sif′ər əs), *adj.* consisting of quartz; containing quartz.

**quartz-i|o|dine lamp** (kwôrts′ī′ə dīn, -din), an incandescent lamp made of quartz and containing iodine vapor and a tungsten filament, used especially in automobile headlights.

**quartz|ite** (kwôrt′sīt), *n.* a granular rock consisting mostly of quartz and formed by the metamorphism of sandstone: *Frank L. Hess reported uranium in quartzite of pre-Cambrian age very early in the century* (Bulletin of Atomic Scientists).

**quartz|it|ic** (kwôrt sit′ik), *adj.* of the nature of or consisting of quartzite.

**quartz lamp**, a mercury-vapor lamp that has a quartz vacuum tube, allowing ultraviolet rays to pass through: *The big advantage in using the quartz lamps to cook food is that their intense heat and rapid cooking cut down the moisture loss* (Wall Street Journal).

**quartz|ose** (kwôrt′sōs), *adj.* consisting mainly or wholly of quartz; quartzlike.

**quartz plate**, a quartz crystal cut so as to have electric polarity.

**qua|sar** (kwā′sär, kwä′-; -zär), *n.* a heavenly object which emits powerful blue light and radio waves; quasi-stellar object. A quasar is larger than a star and smaller than a galaxy. *The term quasar ... was originally applied only to the star-like counterparts of certain strong radio sources whose optical spectra exhibit red shifts much larger than those of galaxies. Before long, however, a class of quasi-stellar objects was discovered with large red shifts that have little or no emission at radio wavelengths. "Quasar" is now* *commonly applied to starlike objects with large red shifts regardless of their radio emissivity* (Scientific American).

**quash**[1] (kwosh), *v.t.* to put down completely; crush: *to quash a revolt. I wanted to scream, but the physical weariness had quashed down that nonsense* (Jane Carlyle). **SYN**: suppress, quell. [< Old French *quasser,* and *casser* < Latin *quassāre* shatter < *quatere* to shake]

**quash**[2] (kwosh), *v.t.* to make void; annul: *The judge quashed the charges against the defendant.* **SYN**: nullify, invalidate. [< Old French *quasser* < Late Latin *cassāre* < Latin *cassus* null; influenced in Old French by *quasser* quash[1]]

**qua|si** (kwā′sī, -zī; kwä′sē, -zē), *adj., adv.* **—*adj.*** seeming; not real; seemingly but not actually the same as; part; halfway: *quasi humor. The party was also said to have suggested that seven elected members should sit on the Executive Council as quasi Ministers* (London Times).
**—*adv.*** seemingly but not really; partly; almost: *a quasi-official statement.*
[< Latin *quasi* as if; as it were]

**quasi-**, *prefix.* quasi; partly: *Quasi-judicial = judicial to some degree.* [< *quasi*]

**qua|si|at|om** (kwā′sī at′əm, -zī-; kwä′sē-, -zē-), *n.* any one of various atomic structures formed by the combination of two or more subatomic particles: *Quasiatoms are generally unstable structures either because they are subject to matter-antimatter annihilation* (*positronium*) *or because one or more of their constituents is radioactively unstable* (*muonium*) (Science News).

**quasi contract**, a legal obligation similar to a contract.

**qua|si|fis|sion** (kwā′sī fish′ən, -zī-; kwä′sē-, -zē-), *n.* a type of nuclear fission in which a bombarded nucleus, instead of dividing into two new and nearly equal parts, reproduces the original projectile and target particles: *For heavy projectiles, say krypton, ... mostly quasifission occurs. It's called quasifission, but what seems incomplete about it is the fusion* (Dietrick E. Thomsen).

**qua|si-ju|di|cial** (kwā′sī jü dish′əl, -zī-; kwä′sē-, -zē-), *adj.* **1** having in some degree, or within a specified area, such authority as belongs to the judiciary: *Where so grave a matter as loyalty is involved, the defendant cannot constitutionally be condemned in a "quasi-judicial" procedure which denies him the right to confront his accusers* (New York Times). **2** judicial in nature but not under the authority or within the power of a judiciary: *quasi-judicial problems.* **—qua′si-ju|di′cial|ly,** *adv.*

**qua|si-leg|is|la|tive** (kwā′sī lej′is lā′tiv, -zī-; kwä′sē-, -zē-), *adj.* **1** having in some degree, or within a specified area, such authority as belongs to the legislature: *a quasi-legislative body.* **2** legislative in nature but not under the authority or within the power of the legislature: *... quasi-legislative questions brought by citizens seeking to vindicate the public good rather than with a concrete dispute* (Irving R. Kaufman).

**qua|si-mil|i|tar|y** (kwā′sī mil′ə ter ē, -zī-; kwä′sē-, -zē-), *adj.* partly military; semimilitary: *The history of the world shows that republics and democracies have generally lost their liberties by way of passing from civilian to quasi-military status* (Newsweek).

**quasi particle**, a unit particle or quantum, as of sound, light, or heat: *Soviet scientists had the honor of introducing the first quasi particles, the phonons* (*sound quanta in a crystal lattice*)*, and the concepts of two others: the exciton, a specially excited state of electrons in a crystal lattice; and the polaron, a conducting electron in an ionic lattice* (Mikhail D. Millionshchikov).

**qua|si-pub|lic** (kwā′sī pub′lik, -zī-; kwä′sē-, -zē-), *adj.* public in nature, function, or concern, but privately owned or controlled: *These institutions represent the unselfish cooperation of private, quasi-public, and foundations groups with public officials* (New York Times).

**qua|si-stel|lar** (kwā′sī stel′ər, -zī-; kwä′sē-, -zē-), *adj.* of, having to do with, or being various types of quasi-stellar objects: *a quasi-stellar radio source, a quasi-stellar blue galaxy.*

**quasi-stellar object**, any one of a group of celestial objects that are sources of powerful emissions of electromagnetic waves; quasar: *The extraordinary properties of quasi-stellar objects, or quasars, were not recognized until 1963, when Maarten Schmidt discovered the red shift of 3C 273. Much excitement was generated by the discovery of objects of stellar appearance which not only were strong radio sources but had large red shifts and which might therefore be the most distant observable objects in the universe* (Science). *Abbr:* QSO (no periods).

**quass** (kväs), *n.* = kvass.

**quas|sia** (kwosh′ə), *n.* **1** a bitter drug obtained from the wood of various tropical American trees, used as a tonic, a purge, and a substitute for hops. **2** the wood of any of these trees. **3** any one of these trees. [< New Latin *Quassia* the genus name of the trees < *Quassi,* a Surinam native of the 1700's, who first used the bark as a fever remedy]

**quassia family**, a group of dicotyledonous trees and shrubs of warm regions, having bitter bark and flowers in panicles or racemes. The family includes the quassia, mountain damson, and ailanthus.

**quas|sin** (kwos′in), *n.* the bitter principle of quassia, obtained as a white, crystalline substance. *Formula:* $C_{22}H_{30}O_6$ [< *quass*(ia) + *-in*]

**qua|ter|cen|te|nar|y** (kwā′tər sen′tə ner′ē), *adj., n., pl.* **-nar|ies.** **—*adj.*** of, comprising, or having to do with a period of 400 years.
**—*n.*** the 400th anniversary of some event, or its celebration.
[< Latin *quater* four times + English *centenary*]

**qua|ter|na|ry** (kwə tėr′nər ē), *n., pl.* **-ries,** *adj.*
**—*n.*** **1** a group of four. **2** the number four; 4.
**—*adj.*** **1** consisting of four things or parts. **2** arranged in fours.
[< Latin *quaternārius* < *quaternī* four each < *quater* four times, related to *quattuor* four]

**Qua|ter|na|ry** (kwə tėr′nər ē), *n., pl.* **-ries,** *adj.*
**—*n.*** **1** the present geological period, the later of the two periods making up the Cenozoic era, and including the Pleistocene and Recent epochs.
**2** the deposits made in this period.
**—*adj.*** of this period or these deposits.

**quaternary ammonium compound**, any derivative of ammonium in which the four hydrogen atoms have been replaced by organic radicals. Quaternary ammonium compounds are used as disinfectants and surface-active chemicals, and in various medicines.

**qua|ter|nate** (kwə tėr′nit), *adj.* **1** consisting of four; arranged in fours. **2** *Botany.* consisting of four leaflets.

**qua|ter|ni|on** (kwə tėr′nē ən), *n.* **1** a group or set of four: *four quaternions of soldiers* (Acts 12:4).
**2** *Mathematics.* the quotient of two vectors considered as depending on four geometrical elements and as expressible by an algebraic quadrinomial; hypercomplex number.
**quaternions,** the calculus of vectors in which a quaternion is employed: *... the value of quaternions for pursuing researches in physics* (Herbert Spencer).
[< Late Latin *quaterniō, -ōnis* < Latin *quaternī;* see etym. under **quaternary**]

**qua|ter|ni|ty** (kwə tėr′nə tē), *n., pl.* **-ties.** **1** a group or set of four persons or things: *A remarkable quaternity of great-grandmamma, grandmamma, mamma, and little daughter* (Saturday Review). **2** the state of being four. [< Late Latin *quaternitās* < *quaternī;* see etym. under **quaternary**]

**Qua|ter|ni|ty** (kwə tėr′nə tē), *n.* the union of four persons in one godhead.

**qua|ter|nize** (kwə tėr′nīz), *v.t.,* **-nized, -niz|ing.** to divide into four parts or components.

**qua|tor|zain** (kə tôr′zān, kat′ər-), *n.* **1** a poem of fourteen lines resembling a sonnet but not in strict sonnet form. **2** = sonnet. [< Middle French *quatorzaine* a set of 14 < *quatorze* quatorze]

**qua|torze** (kə tôrz′), *n.* 4 aces, kings, queens, or jacks, counting for 14 points in piquet. [< French *quatorze* fourteen < Latin *quattuordecim*]

**quat|rain** (kwot′rān), *n.* a stanza or poem of four lines, usually with alternate rhymes: *Who but Landor could have written the faultless and pathetic quatrain? I strove with none, for none was worth my strife; Nature I loved, and, next to Nature, Art; I warmed both hands before the fire of life; It sinks, and I am ready to depart* (Edmund C. Stedman). [< Middle French *quatrain* < Old French *quatre* four < Latin *quattuor*]

**qua|tre** (kä′tər; *French* kȧ′trə), *n.* a four in cards, dice, dominoes, or the like. [< Old French *quatre* four < Latin *quattuor*]

***quat|re|foil** (kat′ər foil′, -rə-), *n.* **1** a leaf or flower composed of four leaflets or petals. The four-leaf clover is a quatrefoil. **2** *Architecture.* an ornament having four lobes: *Another Longton Hall piece, a jug of lobed quatrefoil shape and baluster outline ... was sold to Messrs. Amor for £150* (London Times). [< Old French *quatre* four (see etym. under **quatre**) + *feuil* leaf < Latin *folium*]

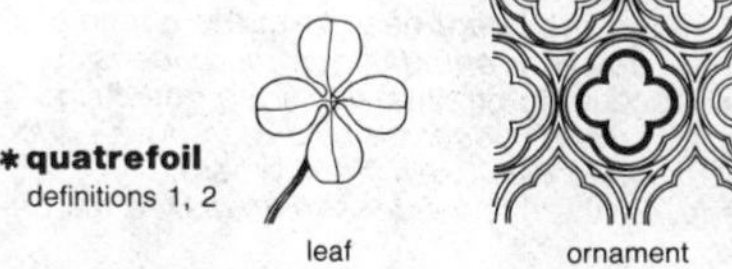

***quatrefoil** definitions 1, 2 — leaf — ornament

**quat|tro|cen|tist** (kwät′trō chen′tist), *n.* an Italian artist of the 1400's, of the style of art called quattrocento.

**quat|tro|cen|to** (kwät′trō chen′tō), *n., adj.* **—*n.*** the 1400's considered as an epoch of art or literature, especially in Italy. **—*adj.*** of this epoch, especially in art or architecture. [< Italian *quattrocento,* short for *mille quattrocento* one thousand and four hundred; *quattro* < Latin *quattuor* four]

**quat|tu|or|de|cil|lion** (kwät′yü ôr də sil′yən), *n.* **1** (in the U.S., Canada, and France) 1 followed by 45 zeros. **2** (in Great Britain and Germany) 1 followed by 84 zeros. [< Latin *quattuordecim* fourteen + English *-illion,* as in *million*]

**qua|ver** (kwā′vər), *v., n.* **—*v.i.*** **1** to shake; tremble: *The old man's voice quavered. Like rivers over reeds Which quaver in the current* (Philip J. Bailey). **2** to trill in singing or in playing on an instrument. **—*v.t.*** **1** to sing or say in trembling tones: *He quavered forth a quaint old ditty* (Washington Irving). **2** to sing with trills.
**—*n.*** **1** the act of shaking or trembling, especially the voice: *His voice ... had nothing of the tremulous quaver and cackle of an old man's utterance* (Hawthorne). **2** a trill in singing or in playing on an instrument. **3** *British.* an eighth note.
[frequentative form of earlier *quave* shake]
**—qua′ver|ing|ly,** *adv.*

**qua|ver|er** (kwā′vər ər), *n.* a person or thing that quavers.

**qua|ver|y** (kwā′vər ē), *adj.* that quavers; quavering; trembling.

***quay** (kē), *n., v.* **—*n.*** a solid landing place for ships, often built of stone: *to assign proper wharfs and quays in each port, for the exclusive landing and loading of merchandise* (William Blackstone). *Other stewards walked off and discussed on the quay whether they should return to the ship* (London Times). **SYN**: pier, wharf.
**—*v.t.*** to furnish with a quay or quays.
[< Old North French *cai, caie,* and *kay* < a Celtic word]

***quay**

**quay|age** (kē′ij), *n.* **1** a fee or charge for use of a quay: *docking quayage.* **2** quays collectively. **3** space on a quay or occupied by a quay. [< French *quayage* < Old French *cai* quay]

**quay|side** (kē′sīd′), *n.* the area immediately adjacent to a quay: *The great liner rises high above the quayside, a floating representative of the United States* (Manchester Guardian).

**Que.**, Quebec.

**quean** (kwēn), *n.* **1** a bold, impudent girl or woman; hussy: *Such is the sprinkling, which some careless quean Flirts on you from her mop* (Jonathan Swift). **2** = prostitute. **3** *Scottish.* a girl or young woman: *Queans, O' plump and strapping in their teens* (Robert Burns). [Old English *cwene*]

**quea|si|ly** (kwē′zə lē), *adv.* in a queasy manner; with squeamishness.

**quea|si|ness** (kwē′zē nis), *n.* **1** = nausea. **2** uneasiness or disgust. **3** = squeamishness.

**quea|sy** (kwē′zē), *adj.,* **-si|er, -si|est.** **1** inclined to nausea; easily upset: *a queasy stomach. Travelers who sit on the left side of a plane, particularly in the seats immediately aft of the wing, are more apt to be queasy, the doctors suggest* (Newsweek). **2** tending to unsettle the stomach. **3** *Figurative.* uneasy; uncomfortable: *But more and more observers are beginning to get queasy about the soaring consumer debt* (Wall Street Journal). **4** squeamish; fastidious. **SYN**: finical. **5** *Archaic.* uncertain; hazardous. [origin uncertain]

**Que|bec** (kwi bek′), *n. U.S.* a code name for the letter *q,* used in transmitting radio messages.

**Que|bec|er** or **Que|beck|er** (kwi bek′ər), *n.* a native or inhabitant of Quebec, a province and city in Canada: *Quebeckers resent the lack of adequate, senior representation in the federal cabinet* (Maclean's).

**Quebec heater**, (in Canada) a potbelly stove.

**Que|be|cois** (kā be kwä′), *n., pl.* **-cois.** *French.* a Quebecer.

---

**Pronunciation Key:** hat, āge, cãre, fär; let, ēqual, tėrm; it, īce; hot, ōpen, ôrder; oil, out; cup, pu̇t, rüle; child; long; thin; ᴛʜen; zh, measure; ə represents **a** in about, **e** in taken, **i** in pencil, **o** in lemon, **u** in circus.

**que|bra|cho** (kā brä′chō), *n., pl.* **-chos. 1** any one of several South American trees with very hard wood. The wood and sometimes the bark are used in tanning and dyeing. The bark of some kinds is used in medicine. The white quebracho belongs to the dogbane family. The red quebracho is of the cashew family. **2** the wood or bark of any of these trees: *Thinning agents presently in use are derived mostly from quebracho, an imported wood chemical product, or substitutes of it* (Wall Street Journal). [< Spanish *quebracho* (literally) break-ax < *quebrar* to break (< Latin *crepāre*) + *hacha* axe]

**Quech|ua** (kech′wä), *n.* **1** an Indian of the dominant tribal group in the Inca empire. **2** the language of the Quechuas. Certain dialects of Quechua are still spoken in parts of Peru, Ecuador, Bolivia, Argentina, and Chile. *An alphabet for writing Quechua, ancient language of the Incas still in common use, was devised and agreed upon by experts in the field* (Science News Letter).
[< Spanish *Quechua* < the native Quechua (Peru) name]

**Quech|uan** (kech′wən), *adj., n.* **—*adj.*** of or having to do with the Quechuas, their civilization, or their language.
**—*n.*** an Indian of the dominant tribal group in the Inca empire; Quechua.

**Quech|u|ma|ran** (kech′ü mä rän′), *n.* a linguistic stock that includes Quechua and Aymara. Also, **Kechumaran.** [< *Quechu*(a) + (Ay)*mara* + *-an*]

**queen** (kwēn), *n., v.* **—*n.* 1** the wife of a king: *The princess became a queen upon marrying the young king.* **2** a woman ruler: *England has a queen as head of her government.* **3** *Figurative.* **a** a woman who is very important: *the queen of society.* **b** a woman who is very stately or attractive: *a beauty queen, the queen of the May.* **4** a fully developed female in a colony of insects, such as bees or ants, that lays eggs. There is usually only one queen in a hive of bees. See pictures under **ant** and **bee**[1]. **5** a playing card with a picture of a queen. **6** the most powerful piece in the game of chess. It can move any number of squares in any straight or diagonal direction. **7** the chief, best, finest, or most: *the rose, queen of flowers.* **8** *Slang.* a male homosexual.
**—*v.i.* 1** Also, **queen it,** to act like a queen: *She's a fine girl … fit to queen it in any drawing-room* (George Meredith). **2** to reign as queen. **3** to become a queen in chess: *White's queen pawn had a clear path for queening* (Al Horowitz).
**—*v.t.*** to make a queen of: *to queen a pawn in chess.*
[Old English *cwēn*] **—queen′like′,** *adj.*

***Queen Anne** (an), **1** of or having to do with a style of English domestic architecture of the early 1700's, characterized by roomy and dignified buildings and by the use of red brick. **2** of or having to do with a style of furniture in England in the early 1700's, characterized by an emphasis on comfort and an increase in the use of upholstery. [< *Queen Anne* of Great Britain and Ireland, who reigned from 1702 to 1714]

***Queen Anne**
definition 2

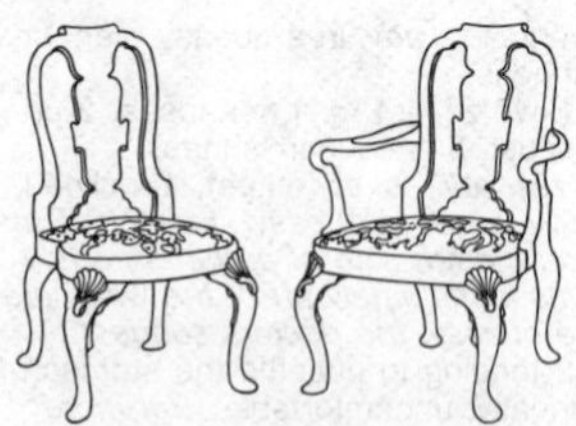

**Queen Anne cottage,** a kind of ornamental wooden cottage developed in England and the United States in the late 1800's.

**Queen Anne's lace,** a wild variety of the carrot, having lacy clusters of white flowers.

**queen bee,** the fully developed, fertile female in a colony of bees.

**queen butterfly,** a chocolate-brown and black butterfly of the southwestern United States and Mexico.

**queen consort,** the wife of a reigning king.

**queen|dom** (kwēn′dəm), *n.* **1** the realm of a queen. **2** the position or dignity of a queen.

**queen dowager,** the widow of a king.

**queen|fish** (kwēn′fish′), *n., pl.* **-fish|es** or (*collectively*) **-fish. 1** a small food fish with large scales, found on the coast of southern California. **2** = wahoo[3].

**queen|hood** (kwēn′hůd), *n.* the rank or dignity of a queen: *She* [*Queen Guinevere*] *… with all grace of womanhood and queenhood, answer'd him* (Tennyson).

**queen|ing** (kwē′ning), *n.* **1** any one of several varieties of apples. **2** (in chess) the promotion of a pawn which has reached the eighth rank to become a queen. [apparently < *queen* + *-ing*[1]]

**queen|less** (kwēn′lis), *adj.* without a queen: *Queenless worker bees will even desert young larvae to join in a group with a queen* (New Scientist).

**queen|let** (kwēn′lit), *n.* a petty queen.

**queen|li|ness** (kwēn′lē nis), *n.* the condition or quality of being queenly.

**queen|ly** (kwēn′lē), *adj.,* **-li|er, -li|est,** *adv.* **—*adj.* 1** of a queen; fit for a queen: *queenly rank or majesty.* **2** like a queen; like a queen's: *a queenly bearing or presence, queenly dignity. You are a queenly creature, not to be treated as any puny trollop of a handmaid* (George Meredith).
**—*adv.*** in a queenly manner; as a queen does: *Queenly responsive when the loyal hand Rose from the clay it work'd in as she past* (Tennyson).

**Queen Mab** (mab), a fairy queen in English folklore, who delivers dreams to men when she drives over their sleeping bodies in her chariot: *Even so dazzling a figure of romance as Maeve, the warrior queen of Connacht, survived only as the fragile Queen Mab of the English poets* (Scientific American).

**queen mother,** the widow of a king who is mother of a reigning king or queen.

**queen of the prairie,** a tall American perennial of the rose family with large clusters of pink flowers, growing in meadows and prairies.

**queen olive,** a large olive with a small pit.

**queen palm,** a palm native to Brazil, with feathery, curving leaves on long branches that reach nearly to the ground. Queen palms are often planted as specimen trees and along streets.

**queen|pin** (kwēn′pin′), *n. Slang.* the most important woman in a group: *In the working classes the oldest woman was the queenpin of the extended family, ruling over her daughters and their children* (Michael Young). [patterned after *kingpin*]

**queen post,** one of a pair of timbers extending vertically upward from the tie beam of a roof truss or the like, one on each side of its center. The queen post supports the rafter or rafters of the truss.

**queen regent, 1** a queen ruling in place of an absent or unfit king. **2** a queen ruling in her own right.

**queen regnant,** a queen ruling in her own right.

**queen|root** (kwēn′rüt′, -růt′), *n.* = queen's root.

**Queen's Bench** (kwēnz), *British.* a former court of record and the highest common-law court in England. *Abbr:* Q.B. Also (*when the ruler is a king*) **King's Bench.**

**Queensberry rules,** = Marquis of Queensberry rules: *The clash in Commons today will be fought under Queensberry rules* (Philip Rawstorne).

**Queen's Birthday,** a holiday observed in the Commonwealth on the actual or arbitrarily set birthday of the ruler. Also (*when the ruler is a king*) **King's Birthday.**

**Queen's Color** or **Colour,** the Union Jack as an emblem of, or carried with the colors of, a British regiment: *In brilliant sunshine on Saturday the Queen's Colour of the 2nd Battalion, Grenadier Guards, was trooped in the presence of the Queen in the Horse Guards Parade* (London Times). Also (*when the ruler is a king*) **King's Color** or **Colour.**

**queen's counsel,** *British.* a barrister or the body of barristers appointed counsel to the Crown. *Abbr:* Q.C. Also (*when the ruler is a king*) **king's counsel.**

**queen's English,** accepted English, especially correct British usage in speech and writing. Also (*when the ruler is a king*) **king's English.**

**queen's gambit,** a conventional series of moves, starting with the advance of the pawn in front of the queen, as the opening of a game of chess.

**queen|ship** (kwēn′ship), *n.* the dignity or office of a queen.

**queen|side** (kwēn′sīd′), *n., adj., adv. Chess.* **—*n.*** the side of the board nearest to the queen's starting position: *an attack on the queenside.*
**—*adj.*** occurring or situated on the queenside: *Black's strong queenside bind … proved enduring and victorious* (New York Times).
**—*adv.*** on the queenside: *White castled queenside.*

**queen-size** (kwēn′sīz′), *adj.* wider and longer than the standard size. A queen-size bed is 60 inches wide and 80 inches long.

**Queens|land|er** (kwēnz′lən dər), *n.* a native or inhabitant of Queensland, Australia: *… Baulch, a 23-year-old Queenslander, who is playing in his first British tournament* (David Gray).

**Queens|land hemp** (kwēnz′lənd), a tropical plant of the mallow family, a species of sida, that yields a useful fiber.

**Queensland nut,** = macadamia nut.

**queen's proctor,** (in British law) an officer representing the Crown who has the right to intervene in certain divorce and nullity cases. Also (*when the ruler is a king*) **king's proctor.**

**queen's root,** an herb of the spurge family of the southern United States, having a thick, woody root with alterative, emetic, and purgative properties.

**queen's shilling,** (in the British Army) a shilling formerly paid a recruit to make his enlistment binding. Also (*when the ruler was a king*) **king's shilling.**
**take the queen's shilling,** to enlist: *the dirtiest private that ever took the queen's shilling* (George Newby).

**Queen's speech,** a speech read by the queen at the opening of the British Parliament, prepared by the ministers of the government to explain domestic and foreign policy. Also (*when the ruler is a king*) **King's speech.**

**queen substance,** an acid found in the glandular secretion of queen bees that inhibits the normal development of the ovaries of worker bees: *The queen substance of the honey bee … will inhibit the normal development of the ovaries in other insects, including ants, flies and termites, and even in prawns* (New Scientist).

**queens|ware** (kwēnz′wãr′), *n.* cream-colored Wedgwood pottery: *His earthenware so impressed Queen Charlotte I that she made Wedgwood her court potter and ordered that pearly pottery be called queensware* (Time).

**queen truss,** the truss within queen posts.

**queer** (kwir), *adj., n., v.* **—*adj.* 1** not usual or normal; strange; odd; peculiar: *a queer way to repay a favor. That was a queer remark for her to make. The old three-cornered hat, And the breeches, and all that, Are so queer!* (Oliver Wendell Holmes). *I don't mind your queer opinions one little bit* (George Bernard Shaw). **SYN:** singular, curious, unusual. **2** *Informal.* probably bad; causing doubt or suspicion: *There is something very queer about her. His queer dealings caused him to lose a lot of business. All the world is queer but thee and me, and even thou art a little queer* (Robert Owen). **3** not well; faint; giddy: *The motion of the ship made her feel queer. They had given him brandy, rather a lot—that perhaps was the reason he felt so queer* (John Galsworthy). **4** *Slang.* **a** bad; counterfeit: *queer money.* **b** homosexual. **5** mentally unbalanced: *He … wondered if Zeena were also turning "queer"* (Edith Wharton).
**—*n.* 1** an odd or eccentric person. **2** *Slang.* a homosexual.
**—*v.t.*** *Slang.* to spoil; ruin: *to queer one's chances of success. I had a job as a sewer-pipe layer all fixed up … and that louse queered it thinking he could get it* (James T. Farrell).
[origin uncertain; perhaps < Low German *queer* across] **—queer′ly,** *adv.*

**queer|ish** (kwir′ish), *adj.* rather queer: *I still feel queerish* (New Yorker).

**queer|ness** (kwir′nis), *n.* **1** queer nature or behavior. **2** something strange or odd; peculiarity.

**Queer Street,** an imaginary street in which people in financial or other difficulties, or shady characters generally, are supposed to live: *Look out, fellow Christians, particularly you that lodge in Queer Street!* (Dickens). *The levy should not be applied so rigidly as to force companies into Queer Street if their costs rose faster than their incomes* (London Times).

**queest** (kwēst), *n.* the wood pigeon or ringdove: *The queest … has had to put up with a certain indifference on the part of naturalists because it is so common* (Robert Nye). [Middle English *quisht, quysht* cushat; see etym. under **cushat**]

**que|le|a** (kwē′lē ə), *n.* a red-billed weaverbird of Africa: *Sections of East Africa suffered greatly from the depredations of birds known as queleas* (E. I. Farrington). [< New Latin *quelea,* probably < an African word]

**quell** (kwel), *v., n.* **—*v.t.* 1** to put down; overcome; quash: *The police quelled the riot. The tumult … was not quelled until several had fallen on both sides* (Francis Parkman). **2** to put an end to; overcome; subdue: *to quell one's fears.* **SYN:** allay.
**—*n.* 1** the power or means to quell: *A sovereign quell is in his waving hands* (Keats). **2** *Obsolete.* a slaying; slaughter: *His spongy officers … shall bear the guilt of our great quell* (Shakespeare).
[Middle English *quellen* quell, Old English *cwellan* to kill]

**quell|er** (kwel′ər), *n.* a person or thing that quells or suppresses: *A dollop of the reeking riot queller* [*tear gas*] *spilled and gas masks were donned* (Time).

**que|ma|de|ro** (kā′mä dãr′ō), *n., pl.* **-dos.** a place of execution by fire: *And this is the quemadero, where criminals were burned to death* (Henry Roth). [< Spanish *quemadero* < *quemado,* past participle of *quemar* to burn]

**quench** (kwench), *v., n.* — ***v.t.*** **1** to put an end to; stop: *to quench a thirst.* **SYN**: allay, slake. **2** to drown out; put out: *Water quenched the fire. Not all its snow could quench our hearthfire's ruddy glow* (John Greenleaf Whittier). (*Figurative.*) *Hope seemed almost quenched in utter gloom* (W. H. Hudson). **SYN**: extinguish, stifle. **3** to cool suddenly by plunging into water or other liquid. Hot steel is quenched to harden it.
— ***v.i.*** to become quenched; be extinguished: *a thirst that will not quench.*
— ***n.*** **1** the act of quenching. **2** the state or fact of being quenched.
[Old English *-cwencan,* as in *ācwencan* quench, put out]

**quench|a|ble** (kwen′chə bəl), *adj.* that can be quenched.

**quench|er** (kwen′chər), *n.* a person or thing that quenches.

**quench-hard|en** (kwench′här′dən), *v.t.* to harden (an iron alloy) by heating it to a point above the temperature range where austenite forms and then cooling it.

**quench|less** (kwench′lis), *adj.* that cannot be quenched; inextinguishable: *quenchless thirst.*

**que|nelle** (kə nel′), *n.* a ball of seasoned, finely-chopped meat or fish cooked in water or stock. [< French *quenelle* < German *Knödel* dumpling < *knoten* to knot]

**Que|ran|dí** (kā′rän dē′), *n., pl.* **-dí** or **-dís.** a member of a South American Indian tribe of the Andean equatorial region.

**quer|cet|ic** (kwər set′ik, -sē′tik), *adj.* of or having to do with quercetin.

**quer|ce|tin** (kwėr′sə tin), *n.* a yellow, crystalline dye prepared from quercitrin. *Formula:* $C_{15}H_{10}O_7$ [< Latin *quercētum* an oak wood + English *-in*]

**quer|cine** (kwėr′sin, -sīn), *adj.* **1** of or having to do with the oak. **2** made of oak; oaken. [< Latin *quercīnus* < *quercus, -ūs* oak]

**quer|cit|rin** (kwėr′sit′rin), *n.* a yellow, crystalline powder extracted from the bark of the black oak. *Formula:* $C_{21}H_{20}O_{11}$

**quer|cit|ron** (kwėr′sit′rən), *n.* **1** = black oak (def. 1). **2** its inner bark, used in tanning, which yields a yellow dye. **3** the dye itself. [earlier *quereicitron* < Latin *quercus, -ūs* oak + English *citron* (probably because of the color)]

**quer|cus** (kwer′kəs), *n.* = oak. [< Latin *quercus, -ūs* oak]

**que|ri|da** (kā rē′də), *n. Southwestern U.S.* darling; sweetheart: *In every* [*court*] *in the Pecos some little señorita was proud to be known as his querida* (Walter N. Burns). [< Spanish *querida,* feminine past participle of *querer* to love, want < Latin *quaerere* seek]

**quer|i|mo|ni|ous** (kwir′i mō′nē əs), *adj.* complaining much.

**quer|i|mo|ny** (kwir′i mō′nē), *n., pl.* **-nies. 1** the act of complaining. **2** = complaint. [< Latin *querimōnia* < *querī* to complain]

**que|rist** (kwir′ist), *n.* a person who asks or inquires; questioner. [< Medieval Latin *quere* (< Latin *quaere* ask; see etym. under **quaere**) + English *-ist*]

**quern** (kwėrn), *n.* **1** a primitive hand mill for grinding grain, consisting commonly of two circular stones, the upper one being turned by hand: *a quern in its place, The grains it ground beside it—barley, wheat* (Atlantic). **2** a small hand mill used to grind pepper or other spices. [Old English *cweorn*]

**quer|u|lous** (kwer′ə ləs, -yə-), *adj.* **1** complaining; fretful; peevish; faultfinding: *a querulous remark. He is very querulous when he is sick.* **SYN**: petulant. **2** producing sounds as of complaining, or sounding as if uttered in complaint: *The brown-clad maidens ... Dance to the querulous pipe and shrill* (William Morris). *One querulous rook, unable to sleep, protested now and then* (Dickens). [< Late Latin *querulōsus* < Latin *querulus* < *querī* to complain] — **quer′u|lous|ly,** *adv.*

**quer|u|lous|ness** (kwer′ə ləs nis, -yə-), *n.* **1** the state of being querulous; disposition to complain. **2** the habit of murmuring.

**que|ry** (kwir′ē), *n., pl.* **-ries,** *v.,* **-ried, -ry|ing.** — ***n.*** **1** a question; inquiry. **SYN**: See syn. under **question. 2** a doubt. **3** the sign put after a question or used to express doubt about something written or printed; question mark.
— ***v.t.*** **1** to ask about; inquire into; ask. **2** to ask questions of. **3** to express doubt about. **4** to mark (a word, letter, or spacing) in a printer's proof with a question mark to indicate doubt of its correctness. — ***v.i.*** to ask questions: *prompt to query, answer, and debate* (Alexander Pope).
[< Medieval Latin *quere* < Latin *quaere* ask; see etym. under **quaere**]

**ques.**, question.

**que|so de bo|la** (kā′sō də bō′lä), a Mexican cheese similar to Edam or Dutch cheese. [< Spanish *queso de bola* (literally) ball cheese]

**quest** (kwest), *n., v.* — ***n.*** **1** a search or hunt: *She went to the library in quest of something to read.* **SYN**: pursuit. **2a** an expedition of knights: *There sat Arthur on the dais-throne, And those that had gone out upon the quest, Wasted and worn ... stood before the King* (Tennyson). **b** the knights in such an expedition. **c** the object sought for. **3a** = inquest. **b** a jury of inquest.
— ***v.t.*** to search or seek for; hunt.
— ***v.i.*** **1** to go about in search of something; search or seek: *This sense of man's balanced greatness and fallibility in the search for truth has made ours a profoundly questing civilization* (Adlai Stevenson). **2** of hunting dogs: **a** to search for game. **b** to bark when in sight of game; bay: *Who cry out for him yet as hounds that quest, And roar as on their quarry* (Algernon Charles Swinburne).
[< Old French *queste* < Vulgar Latin *quaesita* < Latin *quaerere* seek]

**quest|er** (kwes′tər), *n.* **1** a seeker or searcher. **2** a dog used to find game.

**ques|tion** (kwes′chən), *n., v.* — ***n.*** **1** a thing asked in order to find out; a sentence, in interrogative form, addressed to someone to get information; inquiry: *The teacher answered the children's questions about the story she had been reading to them.* **2** a matter of doubt or dispute; controversy: *A question arose about the ownership of the property.* **3a** a matter to be talked over, investigated, or considered: *the question of gun control. What is the question you have raised?* **b** a problem: *He could neither buy nor sell as well as his father. It was not a question of brains; it was a question of individuality* (Arnold Bennett). **4a** a matter to be debated or voted on: *The president asked if the club members were ready for the question. When the Clerk at the Table called the question I should of course have asked the indulgence of the House and begged that the question be put down a week later* (Sunday Times). **b** the taking of a vote on such a proposal. **5** the act of asking: *to examine by question and answer.* **6** a judicial examination or trial; interrogation.
— ***v.t.*** **1** to ask in order to find out; seek information from: *The teacher questioned the children about what happened in the story.* **2** to ask or inquire about: *We questioned the long delay. 'Tis safer to Avoid what's grown than question how 'tis born* (Shakespeare). **3** to doubt; dispute: *I question the truth of his story. No man can question whether wounds and sickness are not really painful* (Samuel Johnson). *The best English lawyers questioned ... the legality of a government by royal instructions* (George Bancroft). **SYN**: challenge.
— ***v.i.*** to ask a question or questions; inquire: *He that questioneth much shall learn much* (Francis Bacon).

**beg the question,** to take for granted the very thing being argued about: *Is this a work of history, or is it a beautifully packaged literary newsreel? Perhaps the "or" begs the question, for there is no reason why history cannot be vivid ... as well as reflective* (Telford Taylor).

**beside the question,** off the subject: *So many of the speaker's comments were beside the question the audience got bored.*

**beyond (all) question, a** without a doubt: *The statements in that book are true beyond question.* [*Alexander Pope's*] *The Dunciad ... is beyond all question full of coarse abuse* (Leslie Stephen). **b** inevitable; certain to happen: *Sometimes, when defeat is beyond question, nothing matters but the style of going down* (New Yorker).

**call in** (or **into**) **question,** to dispute; challenge: *He called my honor in question by suggesting that I cheated on the test. ... a person who was jealous lest his courage should be called in question* (Jonathan Swift).

**in question, a** under consideration or discussion: *His father ... had* (*besides this gentleman in question*) *Two other sons* (Shakespeare). **b** in dispute: *What is not in question is the difficulty of making good color plates* (John Shearman).

**out of the question,** not to be considered; impossible: *He began by agreeing ... that war now seemed out of the question* (New York Times).

**pop the question,** *Informal.* to propose marriage: *She agreed to marry him as soon as he popped the question.*

**without question,** without a doubt; not to be disputed: *He is without question the brightest student in the school. The architecture of the Old Quarter* [*of New Orleans*] *is a blend of Spanish and French ... and is without question the most fascinating bit of city housing in the United States* (David McReynolds).
[< Anglo-French *questiun,* Old French *question* legal inquest; torture, learned borrowing from Latin *quaestiō, -ōnis* a seeking < *quaerere* to seek] — **ques′tion|er,** *n.*
— ***Syn.*** *n.* **1 Question, query** mean something asked. **Question** applies to something which is asked to get definite information or to test knowledge and which therefore ordinarily calls for an answer: *I have some questions about today's lesson.* **Query** often applies to what has the form of a question but is really intended to express doubt or objection: *He put several queries concerning items in the budget.*
— *v.t.* **1 Question, ask, interrogate** mean to seek information from someone. **Ask** is the general word, and suggests nothing more: *I asked her why she did it.* **Question** often implies asking repeatedly or persistently: *I questioned the boy until he told all he knew about the subject.* **Interrogate** implies questioning formally and methodically: *The lawyer interrogated the witness.*

**ques|tion|a|ble** (kwes′chə nə bəl), *adj.* **1** open to question or dispute; doubtful; uncertain: *Whether your statement is true is questionable. The facts respecting him* [*Governor Van Twiller*] *were so scattered and vague, and divers of them so questionable in point of authenticity, that I have had to give up the search* (Washington Irving). **SYN**: debatable, disputable. **2** of doubtful propriety, honesty, morality, respectability, or the like: *questionable behavior, the questionable associates of a gambler.* **SYN**: dubious. **3** *Obsolete.* (of a person) open to questioning: *Thou comest in such a questionable shape That I will speak to thee* (Shakespeare).

**ques|tion|a|ble|ness** (kwes′chə nə bəl nis), *n.* doubtful character; suspicious state.

**ques|tion|a|bly** (kwes′chə nə blē), *adv.* in a questionable manner; doubtfully.

**ques|tion|ar|y** (kwes′chə ner′ē), *n., pl.* **-ar|ies,** *adj.* — ***n.*** = questionnaire.
— ***adj.*** questioning; interrogatory.

**ques|tion-beg|ging** (kwes′chən beg′ing), *n.* the act or fact of taking for granted the very thing argued about: *There is some question-begging here, but no matter ...* (Renata Adler).

**ques|tion|ing** (kwes′chə ning), *n., adj.* — ***n.*** the act of asking questions; inquiry; interrogation: *The committee members' questioning clearly suggested that few of them view favorably the Administration's tactics on the gold problem* (Wall Street Journal).
— ***adj.*** **1** that questions: *Like a ghost that is speechless, Till some questioning voice dissolves the spell of its silence* (Longfellow). **2** inquisitive: *Under ... the questioning eye of his father* (Charlotte Smith).

**ques|tion|ing|ly** (kwes′chə ning lē), *adv.* as one who questions; in a questioning manner.

**ques|tion|ist** (kwes′chə nist), *n.* a questioner; inquirer.

**ques|tion|less** (kwes′chən lis), *adj., adv.* — ***adj.*** **1** without question; beyond doubt. **2** unquestioning.
— ***adv.*** without question; beyond doubt: *a young man ... who can questionless write a good hand and keep books* (George Eliot).

* **question mark, 1** a mark put after a question in writing or printing; interrogation mark; query. **2** *Informal.* a difficult or debatable question; problem: *These are question marks that the next 48 hours will resolve one way or another* (London Times).

*** question mark**
definition 1

? Are you sure? When?

**ques|tion|mas|ter** (kwes′chən mas′tər, -mäs′-), *n. British.* a person who asks questions at a quiz show; quizmaster: *He was ... the first question-master on the first full quiz show broadcast by the B.B.C.* (London Times).

**ques|tion|naire** (kwes′chə nãr′), *n., v.,* **-naired, -nair|ing.** — ***n.*** a list of questions, usually a written or printed list. Questionnaires are mostly used to gather information or to obtain a sampling of opinion. *Upon Edmont alone Gilliéron relied for all his investigations, furnishing him with a questionnaire of some 1,920 words, including phrases, clauses and sentences* (Simeon Potter). *The unguided interview may be considered as*

*something between the free association technique of the psychiatrist and the use of a questionnaire* (Science News Letter).
— ***v.t.*** to submit a list of questions to: *What kind of man ... becomes an outstanding scientist? To answer his question, Bello interviewed or questionnaired 107 young ... scientists* (Time).
[< French *questionnaire*]

**question time**, **1** a period of about 45 minutes, usually four times a week, in which Ministers answer appropriate questions submitted in advance by Members of the British House of Commons. A Member submitting a question may also ask supplementary questions arising from the Minister's answer to the original question. **2** a similar period in a similar parliamentary body.

**ques|tor** (kwes′tər, kwēs′-), *n.* = quaestor.

**ques|to|ri|al** (kwes tôr′ē əl, -tōr′-; kwēs-), *adj.* = quaestorial.

**ques|tor|ship** (kwes′tər ship, kwēs′-), *n.* = quaestorship.

**quet|zal** (ket säl′), *n., pl.* **-zals, -za|les** (-sä′lās). **1** a Central American bird having brilliant golden-green and scarlet plumage. The adult male has long, flowing tail feathers. **2** the unit of money of Guatemala, equal to 100 centavos. Also, **quezal**. [< Mexican Spanish *quetzal,* earlier *quetzale* < Nahuatl *quetzalli* brilliant, resplendent (because of the bird's plumage)]

**Quet|zal|co|a|tl** (ket säl′kō ä′təl), *n.* a chief deity of the Aztecs and Toltecs in Mexico before the Spanish conquest, typically represented in sculpture as a plumed or feathered serpent: *And among the Aztecs of Yucatan the first Spanish explorers discovered a strong tradition of earlier European visitors. Was the blue-eyed god Quetzalcoatl perhaps a European?* (New York Times). [< Nahuatl *Quetzalcoatl* < *Quetzalli* (see etym. under **quetzal**) + *coatl* snake]

**queue** (kyü), *n., v.,* **queued, queu|ing** or **queue|ing.** — ***n.*** **1** a braid of hair hanging down from the back of the head: *His long, powdered locks hung in a well-tended queue down his back* (Harriet Beecher Stowe). **2** a number of persons, automobiles, or trucks arranged in a line waiting their turn: *There was a long queue at the theater. There are those who do not wish to make a lifetime career outside the United Kingdom but who would be prepared to go abroad for a short time provided they would not lose their place in the queue for a more permanent post in this country* (London Times). **3** a container for wine: *In Champagne it's called a queue and contains 216 liters* (Atlantic).
— ***v.i.*** to form or stand in a long line; take one's place in a queue: *Thirty-three vessels are queueing at the Mersey Bar 20 miles from port waiting to dock* (London Times). — ***v.t.*** to arrange (persons) in or as if in a queue or queues. Also, **cue**.
**queue up**, to line up: *Queuing up is a symbol of British fair play* (Time).
[< French *queue* < Old French *coue* < Latin *cōda,* variant of *cauda* tail]

**queue|ing theory** (kyü′ing), the mathematical study of the formation and behavior of queues or waiting lines, especially as applied to problems of traffic congestion and storage systems.

**queue-jump** (kyü′jump′), *v.i. British.* to go out of turn; go ahead of those who have been waiting: *To acknowledge that patients can queue-jump on any grounds other than medical is to open an enormous moral fester* (Linda Blandford).
— **queue′-jump′er**, *n.*

**queu|er** (kyü′ər), *n.* a person who stands in line: *The queuers were hoping for standing room. Reserved seats had been gone since July* (Time).

**quey** (kwā), *n. Scottish.* a heifer. [< Old Icelandic *kvīga,* apparently < *kū* cow]

**que|zal** (ke säl′), *n., pl.* **-zals, -za|les** (-sä′lās). = quetzal.

**quib|ble** (kwib′əl), *n., v.,* **-bled, -bling.** — ***n.*** **1** an unfair and petty evasion of the point or truth by using words with a double meaning: *a legal quibble. To a plain understanding his objections seem to be mere quibbles* (Macaulay). **SYN**: equivocation. **2** a play upon words; pun: *It was very natural ... that the common people, by a quibble ... should call the proposed "Moderation" the "Murderation"* (John L. Motley).
— ***v.i.*** to evade the point or the truth by twisting the meaning of words: *He was not averse to quibbling with* [the] *Department of Justice attorney over whether an associate in the rights congress was known as Marjorie Robinson or Margaret Robinson* (New York Times). *Oh, Miss Lucretia, who pride yourself on your plain speaking, that you should be caught quibbling!* (Winston Churchill).
[apparently, diminutive < obsolete *quib* quip < Latin *quibus,* dative and ablative plural of *quī* who, which (because it was much used in legal jargon)] — **quib′bling|ly**, *adv.*

**quib|bler** (kwib′lər), *n.* a person who evades plain truth by twisting the meaning of words.

**quib|ble|some** (kwib′əl səm), *adj.* tending to evade or confuse the real point or truth in petty ways: *Strauss can be evasive, quibblesome and not above beclouding a point with big handfuls of debater's dust* (Time).

**quiche** (kēsh), *n., pl.* **quiches** (kēsh). a custard pie baked in a rich crust and containing various ingredients: *scallop quiche, a quiche of lobster, quiches of onion, ham, or salmon.* [< French *quiche* < dialectal German (Alsace-Lorraine) *Küche* (diminutive) < German *Kuchen* cake]

**quiche lor|raine** (kēsh lô ren′), a quiche containing a mild cheese and crisply fried bits of bacon or minced ham. [< French *quiche Lorraine*]

**quick** (kwik), *adj., adv., n.* — ***adj.*** **1** fast and sudden; swift: *The cat made a quick jump. Many weeds have a quick growth. With a quick turn I avoided hitting the other car. Use an instant cake mix if you want a quick way to make a cake.* **2** begun and ended in a very short time: *a quick visit, a quick glance at the paper.* **3** coming soon; prompt; immediate: *a quick answer.* **4** (of movement) rapid; speedy: *a quick pace.* **5** not patient; hasty: *a quick temper.* **SYN**: impatient, irascible. **6** acting quickly; ready; lively; active: *a quick wit.* **SYN**: nimble, agile. **7** keen in perception: *Most dogs have a quick ear.* **8** understanding or learning fast: *a child who is quick in school.* **9** brisk: *a quick fire.* **10** sharp: *a quick curve.* **11** productive: *a quick vein of ore.* **12** readily convertible into cash. **13** having some quality or feature suggesting a living thing. **14** *Archaic.* living; alive.
— ***adv.*** quickly: *Run quick and fetch me some cream at the store.*
— ***n.*** **1** the tender, sensitive flesh under a fingernail or toenail: *The nervous child bit his nails to the quick.* **2** *Figurative.* the tender, sensitive part of one's feelings: *The boy's pride was cut to the quick by the words of blame.* **3** living persons: *the quick and the dead.* **4** *Especially British.* quickset.
[Old English *cwic* alive]
— ***Syn.*** *adj.* **1 Quick, fast, rapid** mean done, happening, moving, or acting with speed. **Quick** especially describes something done or made or happening with speed or without delay: *You made a quick trip.* **Fast** especially describes something moving or acting with speed: *I took a fast plane.* **Rapid** emphasizes the rate of speed or swiftness of the action or movement, or series of movements, performed: *I had to do some rapid planning.*

**quick-and-dir|ty** (kwik′ən dėr′tē), *n., pl.* **-ties.** *U.S. Slang.* a snack bar or lunch counter: *It was after one when he finished, and we stopped for lunch at a quick-and-dirty on East Ninety-sixth and talked shop, which he said was not unusual for him* (New Yorker).

**quick assets**, *Accounting.* cash or things that can be sold quickly, without appreciable loss.

**quick bread**, biscuits, corn bread, muffins, etc., prepared with a leavening agent that enables them to be baked as soon as the batter is mixed: *Of the 600 women questioned, 500 said that they used packaged cake mixes most often, then puddings, pastries and quick breads* (New York Times).

**quick-change** (kwik′chānj′), *adj.* **1** very quick in changing, as of one's mind, costume, or appearance: *She seems to be a very mousy character, and at the museum where she works nobody suspects that she is a mental quick-change artist* (New Yorker). **2** capable of being changed rapidly: *While engaged on the development of new types of quick-change cutting tools ...* (New Scientist).: *The first "quick-change" (QC) jets, passenger planes that can be converted for cargo in a matter of minutes, went into service in 1966* (Kenneth E. Schaefle).

**quick|en** (kwik′ən), *v.t.* **1** to cause to move more quickly; hasten: *Quicken your pace.* **SYN**: hurry, expedite, accelerate. **2** to stir up; make alive: *to quicken hot ashes into flames.* (*Figurative.*) *Reading adventure stories quickens my imagination. British shipbuilding needed to be streamlined, modernized, quickened up* (London Times). **SYN**: inspire, rouse, stimulate, animate. **3** to give or restore life to. — ***v.i.*** **1** to move more quickly; become faster: *His pulse quickened.* **2** to become more active or alive: (*Figurative.*) *Edwardian sportsmen were at their prime after the Press had quickened just enough to make them household names when they deserved it* (London Times). **3** to become living: *Summer flies ... that quicken even with blowing* (Shakespeare). **4** to grow bright or brighter: *The river, the mountain, the quickening east, swam before his eyes* (Bret Harte). **5a** (of a child in the womb) to show life by movements: *The baby's muscular activity as first felt by the mother is called quickening or "feeling life"* (Sidonie M. Gruenberg). **b** (of the mother) to enter that stage of pregnancy in which the movements of the child are felt.

**quick|en|er** (kwik′ə nər), *n.* **1** a person or thing that quickens. **2** something that reinvigorates.

**quick fire**, a rapid succession of shots.

**quick-fire** (kwik′fīr′), *adj.* = rapid-fire.

**quick-fir|ing** (kwik′fīr′ing), *adj.* = rapid-fire.

**quick-freeze** (kwik′frēz′), *v.t.,* **-froze, -fro|zen, -freez|ing.** to subject (food) to quick-freezing; cause to undergo rapid freezing before storage at freezing temperatures; sharp-freeze: *You can quick-freeze a month's supply of food, and keep it safely in your zero-zone freezer for up to one year* (Maclean's).

**quick-freez|ing** (kwik′frē′zing), *n.* a process in which food is subjected to rapid freezing before storage at freezing temperatures, in order to prevent the formation of ice crystals which damage the cells of some foods and cause them to leak their natural fluids during defrosting: *Quick-freezing might be considered to be any process that freezes food fast enough to prevent spoilage and that causes a minimum change in food cells* (John T. Nickerson).

**quick-fro|zen** (kwik′frō′zən), *adj., v.* — ***adj.*** (of food) prepared for storage by quick-freezing: *Mr. Birdseye gave the world its first packaged quick-frozen foods and laid the foundation for today's frozen food industry* (New York Herald Tribune).
— ***v.*** the past participle of **quick-freeze.**

**quick grass**, a western North American couch grass, ranging from Nebraska to British Columbia and south to Texas and Arizona. [< Middle English *quike,* variant of *quitch* (grass). Compare etym. under **quack grass.**]

**quick|hatch** (kwik′hach′), *n.* = wolverine. [alteration by folk etymology of Cree *kwekwuhakao*]

**quick|ie** (kwik′ē), *n., adj. Slang.* — ***n.*** **1** a motion picture, novel, or the like, produced cheaply and in haste: *But his book remains, somehow, for all its basic honesty, a sort of journalistic quickie in blackface* (New York Times). **2** a short drink of alcoholic liquor. **3** anything done very hastily: *Election year brought the usual flutter of campaign quickies* (Time).
— ***adj.*** **1** fast; quick; requiring little preparation: *a quickie training course for Directors, mostly on non-controversial matters* (Wall Street Journal). **2** giving little warning: *The turbulence that expressed itself in the early sit-down strikes and in hundreds of quickie shutdowns has yielded to a more cooperative relationship* (New York Times).

**quick|ish** (kwik′ish), *adj.* rather quick: *a quickish left-hander* (London Times).

**quick kick**, *Football.* a punt kicked on one of the first downs and not from the formation usual for kicking, intended to surprise the opponents and catch them out of position.

**quick-kick|er** (kwik′kik′ər), *n.* a football player skilled in kicking surprise punts over the other team's safety man: *His most famous pupil: North Carolina's All-American Charlie Justice, one of the game's finest quick-kickers* (Time).

**quick|lime** (kwik′līm′), *n.* a white, alkaline substance obtained by burning limestone and used especially for making mortar, glass, and insecticides; lime; calcium oxide.

**quick|ly** (kwik′lē), *adv.* rapidly; with haste; very soon: *Slum boys are tempted by dreams of "easy money" and quickly-won esteem* (Scientific American). *Leave the sickroom quickly and come into it quickly, not suddenly, nor with a rush* (Florence Nightingale). *Retaliation and vengeance quickly followed* (Leopold von Ranke).

**quick march**, a march in quick time.

**quick-mix** (kwik′miks′), *n.* food product offered for sale with most of the ingredients already mixed, usually requiring only the addition of a final ingredient and cooking: *Sales of quick-mix drinking chocolate in particular were so successful that they outstripped our supplies* (London Times).

**quick|ness** (kwik′nis), *n.* **1** = speed: *the quickness of motion.* **2** briskness; promptness: *the quickness of the imagination or wit.* **3** acuteness; keenness: *Would not quickness of sensation be an inconvenience to an animal that must lie still?* (John Locke). **4** sharpness; pungency.

**quick|sand** (kwik′sand′), *n.* **1** a very deep, soft, wet sand that will not hold up a person's weight. Quicksand may swallow up people and animals. **2** *Figurative: The roots of conflict, he believes, lie buried in the quicksands of human nature* (Newsweek). *It would have the great merit of eliciting information and perhaps revealing the location of any financial quicksands* (Wall Street Journal). *It is my duty ... to see that he is properly mated—not wrecked upon the quicksands of marriage* (George Meredith). **SYN**: treachery.

**quick|sand|y** (kwik′san′dē), *adj.,* **-sand|i|er, -sand|i|est.** of, like, or containing quicksand: *a quicksandy spot* (Vladimir Nabokov).

**quick|set** (kwik′set′), *n., adj. Especially British.* — ***n.*** **1** a plant or cutting, especially of hawthorn, set to grow in a hedge: *I am afraid I shall see*

*great neglects among my quicksets* (Jonathan Swift). **2** a hedge of such plants.
**–*adj.*** formed of such plants.

**quick-sight|ed** (kwik′sī′tid), *adj.* quick to see or discern: *a wonderfully active and quick-sighted person ... able to see what is going on all round* (W. H. Hudson). **–quick′-sight′ed|ness**, *n.*

**quick|sil|ver** (kwik′sil′vər), *n., v., adj.* **–*n.*** **1** = mercury (def. 1). **2** *Figurative.* something as shining, quick-moving, and elusive as mercury: *Emmett by contrast is a piece of quicksilver, brilliant but unpredictable* (London Times).
**–*v.t.*** to coat, treat, or mix with mercury.
**–*adj.*** bright and quick-moving; quicksilvery: *Dr. Pringle ... speaks swiftly, with quicksilver linking of thought and expression* (London Times).
[Old English *cwicseolfor,* translation of Latin *argentum vīvum* living silver; *vīvum,* neuter of *vīvus* living]

**quick|sil|ver|y** (kwik′sil′vər ē), *adj.* resembling quicksilver; bright and quick-moving: *The quicksilvery score, with its pastoral interludes and lavish descriptive effects, is a delight* (Time).

**quick|step** (kwik′step′), *n., v.,* **-stepped, -step|ping.** **–*n.*** **1** a step used in marching in quick time: *The Grand Army starts off to war with a rousing quickstep, soon changes its tune to fit a war for which ... hardly any of the soldiers were prepared* (Time). **2** music in a brisk march rhythm. **3** a lively dance step.
**–*v.i.*** **1** to march or progress at a lively pace: *But for all the explanations of the* [*ticker*] *tape-watchers there was one that underlay them all: The growing belief ... that the whole economy ... was once again quickstepping to new peaks* (Newsweek). **2** to dance the quickstep.

**quick study,** a person who memorizes rapidly: *Until a fortnight ago,* [*he*] *had never had Ravel's score in his hands, but he is what is known in the theatre as a quick study* (Time).

**quick-tem|pered** (kwik′tem′pərd), *adj.* easily angered. **SYN:** irascible, peppery.

**quick time,** a pace in marching of 120 thirty-inch steps per minute, the ordinary marching pace of the United States Army, Marine Corps, and other marching groups. In quick time, soldiers march four miles an hour.

**quick trick,** (in bridge) a card, such as an ace, or a combination of cards, such as a king and queen in the same suit, that may be counted upon to win a trick the first or second time a suit is played, unless trumped.

**quick-trig|gered** (kwik′trig′ərd), *adj.* **1** that shoots fast: *He had made his way, by jeep and on foot, into the wild, roadless fastness of Cuba's Sierra Maestra ... dodging quick-triggered army patrols* (Newsweek). **2** *Figurative.* quickly put in action or set in motion: *Igaya knows that only quick-triggered reflexes and a good memory stand between him and death* (Newsweek). *Actually the quick-triggered Seawolf got away before Mrs. Cole could strike her hard with the metal protected champagne bottle* (New York Times).

**quick-wit|ted** (kwik′wit′id), *adj.* having a ready wit; mentally alert; clever. **SYN:** keen, sharp.

**quick-wit|ted|ly** (kwik′wit′id lē), *adv.* cleverly; acutely.

**quick-wit|ted|ness** (kwik′wit′id nis), *n.* readiness of wit; cleverness.

**quid¹** (kwid), *n.* **1** a piece to be chewed. **2** a bite of chewing tobacco: *A large roll of tobacco was presented ... and every individual took a comfortable quid* (Tobias Smollett). [Old English *cwidu* cud]

**quid²** (kwid), *n., pl.* **quid** or **quids.** *British Slang.* one pound sterling; a sovereign: *I'll give you five quid for the lot.* [origin uncertain]

**quid|dit** (kwid′it), *n. Archaic.* quiddity. [short for *quiddity*]

**quid|di|ty** (kwid′ə tē), *n., pl.* **-ties.** **1** that which makes a thing what it is; essence: *The quiddity ... of poetry as distinguished from prose* (Thomas De Quincey). **2** a distinction of no importance; quibble: *How now, how now, mad wag! What, in thy quips and thy quiddities?* (Shakespeare). *His stylized manner and his quips and quiddities will grow stale* (Newsweek). [< Medieval Latin *quidditas* < Latin *quid* what, neuter of *quis* who]

**quid|dle** (kwid′əl), *v.,* **-dled, -dling,** *n. Dialect.*
**–*v.i.*** to trifle; fiddle; fuss: *I should like to know who's a going to stop a quiddle with young uns?* (Harriet Beecher Stowe).
**–*n.*** a person given to fussing: *The Englishman is ... a quiddle about his toast and his chop* (Emerson).
[origin uncertain. Perhaps related to **twiddle** or **fiddle.**]

**quid|nunc** (kwid′nungk′), *n.* an inquisitive person; gossip: *the crowd of village idlers, quidnuncs, tattlers and newsmongers* (Arnold Bennett). *At week's end the Russians themselves provided an unexpectedly fast answer for the quidnuncs* (Time). [< Latin *quid nunc* what now?; *quid,* neuter of *quis* who]

**quid pro quo** (kwid′ prō kwō′), *Latin.* **1** one thing in return for another; compensation: *A laughable quid pro quo ... occurred to him in a conversation* (Thackeray). *We must cease thinking of economic aid as a short-run political tool which calls for a military quid pro quo* (W. Averell Harriman). **2** (literally) something for something.

**quids** (kwidz), *n.pl. Especially British Slang.* money; cash: *"If only you boffins," (R.A.F. slang for a scientist) said Collins, "would give us a cheap way of locating an aircraft, then we'd be quids in"* (Time). [plural of *quid²*]

**¿quién sa|be?** (kyen sä′bā), *Spanish.* who knows?: *All climbed out carrying suitcases. "What are you going to do, rob the Treasury?" joshed a guard. "¿Quién sabe?" replied baby-faced José Alemán* (Time).

**qui|esce** (kwī es′), *v.i.,* **-esced, -esc|ing.** to become quiet or calm.

**qui|es|cence** (kwī es′əns), *n.* absence of activity; quiet state; stillness; motionlessness: *Movement, not quiescence, is the irrevocable lot of the inhabitants of a globe spinning at nineteen miles a second* (J. W. R. Scott). **SYN:** quietness, calmness, passivity.

**qui|es|cen|cy** (kwī es′ən sē), *n.* = quiescence.

**qui|es|cent** (kwī es′ənt), *adj.* quiet; inactive; still; motionless: *For a time he* [*a whale*] *lay quiescent* (Herman Melville). *And the debate, which had been relatively quiescent, became hotter than ever* (Newsweek). **SYN:** passive. [< Latin *quiēscēns, -entis,* present participle of *quiēscere* to rest < *quiēs* rest, quiet] **–qui|es′cent|ly,** *adv.*

**qui|et¹** (kwī′ət), *adj., v., adv.* **–*adj.*** **1** making no sound; with little or no noise; silent; hushed: *quiet footsteps, a quiet street. The holy time is quiet as a nun Breathless with adoration* (Wordsworth). **2** moving very little; still; calm: *a quiet lake, a quiet river.* **SYN:** See syn. under **still.** **3** saying little: *During dinner ... we were unusually quiet, even to gravity* (W. H. Hudson). **4** peaceful; gentle; not offending others: *a quiet girl, a quiet mind, quiet manners, a quiet night's sleep.* **SYN:** unobtrusive; inconspicuous. **5** not showy or bright: *Gray is a quiet color.* **6** at rest; not busy; not active: *a quiet evening at home, a quiet life in the country, a quiet trading on the stock exchange. The snow was piling up on the north side of the hogans and there was no smoke from the holes in the domeshaped roofs. All the chimneys were quiet* (Harper's). *All had been quiet since the news of the capitulation at Lerida* (James A. Froude).
**–*v.t.*** to make quiet: *The mother quieted her frightened child. In trying to quiet one set of malcontents, he had created another* (Macaulay).
**–*v.i.*** to become quiet: *The wind quieted down.*
**–*adv.*** in a quiet manner; quietly.
[< Latin *quiētus* resting, past participle of *quiēscere* to rest < *quiēs, -ētis* rest. See etym. of doublets **coy, quit,** adjective.] **–qui′et|ness,** *n.*

**qui|et²** (kwī′ət), *n.* **1** a state of rest; absence of motion or noise; stillness: *The first indications came in late June when orders began to improve after a long spell of quiet* (Wall Street Journal). **2** freedom from disturbance; peace: *Go to the library to read in quiet. His small force would be large enough to overawe them in times of quiet* (William H. Prescott). [< Latin *quiēs, -ētis* rest]

**qui|et|en** (kwī′ə tən), *Especially British.* **–*v.t.*** to make quiet: *At last ... to quieten them, I promised to ... write a short story* (Arnold Bennett).
**–*v.i.*** to become quiet: *Her heart had quietened down while she rested* (Joseph Conrad). *The situation will somehow quieten down one day, and the old order will be able to survive* (London Times).

**qui|et|er** (kwī′ə tər), *n.* a person or thing that quiets.

**qui|et|ish** (kwī′ə tish), *adj.* somewhat quiet: *After a quietish spell in the first fortnight of August, Elsey's horses have come back to form in no hesitant manner* (London Times).

**qui|et|ism** (kwī′ə tiz əm), *n.* **1** a form of religious mysticism requiring abandonment of the will, withdrawal from worldly interests, and passive meditation on God and divine things. **2** quietness of mind or life: *Dissent and deviation are treason, and quietism is sacrilege* (Atlantic). [< Italian *quietismo* < Latin *quiētus* quiet + Italian *-ismo* -ism]

**qui|et|ist** (kwī′ə tist), *n., adj.* **–*n.*** **1** a person who believes in or practices quietism. **2** a person who seeks quietness.
**–*adj.*** characterized by quietism; quietistic: *He accused Tolstoy of helping to bring about the failure of the 1905 Revolution because of his quietist influence on the peasantry* (Ernest J. Simmons).

**qui|et|is|tic** (kwī′ə tis′tik), *adj.* of or having to do with quietists or quietism: *Though the element of realism in this almost quietistic manifestation of the Baroque spirit is apparently derived from Caravaggio and the Spaniards, its essential characteristics are the peculiar result of the climate of independent thought in the France of Louis XIII* (London Times).

**qui|et|ly** (kwī′it lē), *adv.* **1** in a quiet manner; peacefully; calmly. **2** without motion. **3** without noise.

**qui|et-spo|ken** (kwī′ət spō′kən), *adj.* **1** speaking in a quiet, calm manner: *A reflective, quiet-spoken man,* [*he*] *is able to deal with it quite calmly* (Daniel Lang). **2** spoken quietly: *... a terse, quiet-spoken, but vigorous and very effective attack on M. Debrés' statements* (Manchester Guardian Weekly).

**qui|e|tude** (kwī′ə tüd, -tyüd), *n.* quietness; stillness; calmness: *That suave master of many roles ... whom the masters of Shangri-La have selected as the man to carry on their great tradition of quietude and culture* (Wall Street Journal). **SYN:** placidity, tranquillity. [< Late Latin *quiētūdō* < Latin *quiētus* quiet, adjective]

**qui|e|tus** (kwī ē′təs), *n.* **1** a final getting rid of anything; finishing stroke; anything that ends or settles: *The arrival of the militia gave the riot its quietus. At his press conference ... President Eisenhower rightly tried to put the quietus on the war talk of some in the Administration and Congress* (Wall Street Journal). **2** something that quiets: *The nurse ran to give its accustomed quietus to the little screaming infant* (Thackeray). **3** a discharge given on payment or settlement of accounts. [< Medieval Latin *quietus est* he is discharged < Latin *quiētus est* he is at rest; *quiētus* quiet, adjective]

**quiff** (kwif), *n.* **1** *British Slang.* a curl or lock of hair worn on the forehead: *Our eye was ...* [*on*] *that famous quiff of rebellious hair ritualistically uncovered three times as Lord Morrison took off his medieval hat and bowed to the Woolsack* (Manchester Guardian). **2** *Slang.* a cheap woman; prostitute. [perhaps < Italian *cuffia* coif]

**Quil|e|ute** (kwil′ə yüt), *n., pl.* **-ute** or **-utes.** **1** a member of a tribe of North American Indians living on the northwestern coast of the United States. **2** the language of this tribe, related to Quinault.

***quill** (kwil), *n., v.* **–*n.*** **1** a large, strong flight feather. **2** the hollow stem of a feather: *Each main shaft or quill sprouts forth some 600 dowls or barbs on either side to form the familiar vane of the feather* (Atlantic). **3** anything made from the hollow stem of a feather, such as a pen, a toothpick, or an instrument used for plucking the strings of a musical instrument. **4** a stiff, sharp hair or spine like the end of a feather. A porcupine or hedgehog has quills on its back. **5** a spool, bobbin, or spindle. **6** a piece of cinnamon or cinchona bark curled up in the form of a tube.
**–*v.t.*** to pleat (as fabric or garments) into small, cylindrical folds resembling quills.
**–*v.i.*** to wind thread or yarn on a quill: *The big textile machinery maker is boosting the loom winders as equipment which brings an "entirely new concept" to fabric production—integration of the quilling process with the loom* (Wall Street Journal).
[Middle English *quil* stiff hollow stalk, a reed; origin uncertain]

***quill**
definition 3

**quil|lai** (ki lī′), *n.* **1** a tree of Chile; soapbark. **2** its bark; soapbark. [< Spanish *quillái* < Araucanian (Chile) < *quillcan* to wash]

**quil|lai|a bark** (ki lī′ə, kwi lā′-), the bark of the quillai.

**quill|back** (kwil′bak′), *n., pl.* **-backs** or (collectively) **-back.** a large, carplike, freshwater fish of the central and eastern United States, having a very long second ray in its dorsal fin that suggests a quill.

**quill driver,** writer; clerk (used contemptuously).

**Pronunciation Key:** hat, āge, cãre, fär; let, ēqual, tėrm; it, īce; hot, ōpen, ôrder; oil, out; cup, pu̇t, rüle; child; long; thin; ᴛʜen; zh, measure; ə represents **a** in about, **e** in taken, **i** in pencil, **o** in lemon, **u** in circus.

**quill driving**, working with a pen; writing (used in a contemptuous way).
**quilled** (kwild), *adj.* **1** having quills: *a quilled mammal.* **2** having the form of a quill: *quilled bark.*
**quil|let** (kwil′it), *n.* a nicety; subtlety; quibble. [perhaps short for a variant of *quiddity*]
**quill feather**, one of the large feathers of the wing or tail of a bird.
**quill|ing** (kwil′ing), *n.* quilled strip of silk, lace, etc.; a fluted or pleated edging.
**quil|lon** (kē yôN′), *n. French.* either arm of a transverse piece forming a guard for the hand between the hilt and the blade of a sword: *The sword that went with the harness had a blade made in the Rhineland, a splendid gold and garnet pommel, two gold filigree mounts on the grip, gold quillons and two jeweled gold scabbard-bosses* (Scientific American).
**quill|work** (kwil′wėrk′), *n.* articles made with porcupine quills: *Indian quillwork.*
**quill|wort** (kwil′wėrt′), *n.* any one of a group of grasslike pteridophytic plants with quill-like leaves, growing especially in or near water.
**quilt** (kwilt), *n., v.* —*n.* **1** a cover for a bed, usually made of two pieces of cloth with a soft pad between, held in place by stitching. The top of a quilt often consists of bits and pieces of cloth sewed together in a design. **SYN**: comforter. **2** *Figurative.* anything resembling a quilt: *A quilt of gray clouds stretched across the chilly autumn sky.*
—*v.i.* to make quilts; do quilted work.
—*v.t.* **1** to stitch together with a soft lining: *to quilt a jacket. Whether dressed for palace or law court, Coke was always well turned out in handsome gown or doublet, quilted sleeves ...* (Atlantic). **2** to sew in lines or patterns: *The bedcover was quilted in a flower design.* **3** to sew up between pieces of material: *Secret papers were quilted in her belt.*
[< Old French *cuilte,* and *coultre* < Latin *culcita* cushion]
**quilt|er** (kwil′tər), *n.* **1** a person who quilts: *Seventeen-year-old Jane could tell the old time quilters the results of adding alum, chrome, tin, copper and iron to natural dyes such as great-great-grandmother used* (Science News Letter). **2** a sewing-machine attachment for quilting fabrics.
**quilt|ing** (kwil′ting), *n.* **1** quilted work. **2** material for making quilts. **3** a stout fabric woven so as to appear quilted. **4** the act or occupation of making a quilt or quilts. **5** = quilting bee.
**quilting bee**, *U.S.* a social gathering of women to make a quilt or quilts: *Quilting bees and threshings were community occasions* (Maclean's).
**quilting frame**, a frame to stretch and hold the fabrics and padding of a quilt in place while it is being sewed.
**quilt|work** (kwilt′wėrk′), *n.* articles made by quilting; quilted work.
**quin** (kwin), *n. Informal.* a quintuplet: *For a man, producing a book provides rather the same kind of fulfillment ... as childbirth does for a woman, but the author ... can go on having quins ... every other year for a lifetime* (James Morris).
**qui|na** (kē′nə, kwī′-), *n.* **1** = Peruvian bark. **2** = quinine. [< Spanish *quina* < Quechua (Peru) *kina* cinchona bark]
**quin|a|crine hydrochloride**, or **quin|a|crine** (kwin′ə krēn, -krin), *n.* a drug used in the treatment of malaria; Atabrine: *Atabrine is the trade name given this drug by the Germans and has been so commonly used that it is employed here. The official name in this country is quinacrine, in England mepacrine* (James Phinney Baxter III). [*quin*(ine) + *acr*(id)*ine*]
**qui|nal|dine** (kwi nal′din), *n. Chemistry.* a colorless, liquid compound occurring in coal tar and also obtained by synthetic methods, used in the preparation of certain dyes. *Formula:* $C_{10}H_9N$ [< *quin*(oline) + *ald*(ehyde) + (anil)*ine*]
**qui|na|ry** (kwī′nər ē), *adj., n., pl.* **-ries.** —*adj.* **1** having to do with the number five. **2** based on the number five. **3** consisting of five (things or parts).
—*n.* a group of five.
[< Latin *quīnārius* < *quīnī* five each < *quīnque* five]
**qui|nate** (kwī′nāt, -nit), *adj.* composed of five leaflets; quinquefoliolate: *a quinate leaf.* [< New Latin *quinatus* < Latin *quīnī* five each < *quīnque* five]
**Qui|nault** (kwə nult′), *n., pl.* **-nault** or **-naults.** **1** a member of a tribe of North American Indians living on the northwestern coast of the United States. **2** the Salishan language of this tribe.
**quin|az|o|lin** (kwi naz′ə lin), *n.* = quinazoline.
**quin|az|o|line** (kwi naz′ə lēn, -lin), *n.* **1** a colorless, crystalline substance generally considered as a quinoline derivative. *Formula:* $C_8H_6N_2$ **2** any one of various substances derived from this compound. [< *quin*(oline) + *azol*(e) + *-ine*[2]]
**quince** (kwins), *n.* **1** a hard, yellowish, acid, pear-shaped fruit, used for preserves and jelly. **2** the tree it grows on. It is a small Asian tree of the rose family. **3** any one of certain similar shrubs or trees grown for their blossoms, such as the Japanese quince. [(originally) plural of Middle English *quyne* < Old French *cooin* < Latin *cotōneum* (*mālum*), variant of *Cydōnium* < Greek *kydônion* (*málon*) (apple) of or from Cydonia, a town in Crete]
**quin|cen|te|nar|y** (kwin sen′tə ner′ē), *adj., n., pl.* **-nar|ies.** —*adj.* having to do with five hundred or a period of five hundred years; marking the completion of five hundred years.
—*n.* a five-hundredth anniversary, or its celebration.
**quin|cen|ten|ni|al** (kwin′sen ten′ē əl), *adj., n.* = quincentenary.
**quin|cun|cial** (kwin kun′shəl), *adj.* of, having to do with, or consisting of a quincunx.
**quin|cun|cial|ly** (kwin kun′shə lē), *adv.* in a quincuncial manner or order.
**quin|cunx** (kwin′kungks), *n., pl.* (*for defs. 1 and 2*) **-cunx|es.** **1** an arrangement of five things in a square or rectangle, one at each corner and one in the middle. **2** an overlapping arrangement of five petals or leaves, in which two are interior, two are exterior, and one is partly interior and partly exterior. **3** *Astrology.* an aspect of planets in which they are at a distance of five signs or 150 degrees from each other: *But the quincunx of heaven runs low, and 'tis time to close the five ports of knowledge* (Sir Thomas Browne). [< Latin *quīncūnx, -uncis* (literally) five-twelfths < *quīnque* five + *uncia* an ounce, a twelfth]
***quin|dec|a|gon** (kwin dek′ə gon), *n. Geometry.* a plane figure with 15 angles and 15 sides. [< Latin *quīndecim* fifteen < *quīnque* five + *decem* ten; patterned on English *decagon*]

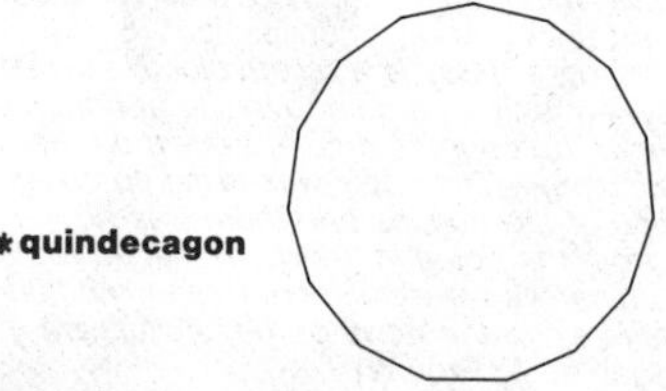


**quin|de|cem|vir** (kwin′di sem′vər), *n., pl.* **-vi|ri** (-və rī). in ancient Rome: **1** one of a body of fifteen men. **2** one of a body of fifteen priests who, at the close of the republic, had charge of the Sibylline Books. [< Latin *quīndecemvir* < *quīndecim* (see etym. under **quindecagon**) + *vir* man]
**quin|de|cen|ni|al** (kwin′di sen′ē əl), *adj., n.* —*adj.* of or having to do with fifteen years or a fifteenth anniversary.
—*n.* a fifteenth anniversary.
[< Latin *quīndecim* (see etym. under **quindecagon**); patterned on English *biennial*]
**quin|de|cil|lion** (kwin′də sil′yən), *n.* **1** (in the United States, Canada, and France) 1 followed by 48 zeros. **2** (in Great Britain and Germany) 1 followed by 90 zeros. [< Latin *quīndecim* fifteen + English *-illion,* as in *million*]
**quin|el|la** (kwi nel′ə), *n.* = quiniela: *The usual totalizator facilities operate on all races with quinellas on the first three and last races* (Cape Times).
**quin|gen|te|nar|y** (kwin jen′tə ner′ē), *adj., n., pl.* **-nar|ies.** = quincentenary. [< Latin *quīngentī* five hundred; patterned on *centenary*]
**quin|i|a** (kwin′ē ə), *n.* = quinine.
**quin|ic acid** (kwin′ik), a white, crystalline, organic acid, obtained from cinchona bark, coffee beans, etc. *Formula:* $C_7H_{12}O_6$
**quin|i|din** (kwin′ə din), *n.* = quinidine.
**quin|i|dine** (kwin′ə dēn, -din), *n. Chemistry.* an alkaloid isomeric with quinine, and associated with it in certain species of cinchona; conquinine: *Balm for some cases of disordered heart rhythm is quinidine. This chemical is a relative of the old anti-malaria drug, quinine* (Science News Letter). *Formula:* $C_{20}H_{24}N_2O_2$
[< *quin*(a) + *-id* + *-ine*[2]]
**quin|ie|la** or **quin|iel|la** (kwin yel′ə), *n.* a bet on a sporting event, especially horse racing, in which one picks the first two finishers but not necessarily in the order of finish: *... an old betting gimmick—the quiniela* (Audax Minor). *Exacta wagering calls for the bettor to pick the precise 1, 2 finish* (*unlike in quiniella gambling, in which 1, 2 or 2, 1 do not matter*) (New York Times). [< American Spanish *quiniela*]
**quin|in** (kwin′in), *n.* = quinine.
**qui|ni|na** (ki nē′nə), *n.* = quinine.
**qui|nine** (kwī′nīn; *especially British* kwi nēn′), *n.* **1** a bitter drug made from the bark of a cinchona tree, used especially in treating malaria and fevers and as a muscle relaxant. Quinine is a crystalline alkaloid. *Formula:* $C_{20}H_{24}N_2O_2 \cdot 3H_2O$ **2** any one of various salts of quinine used as medicine. [< *quin*(a) + *-ine*[2]]
**quinine water**, a carbonated drink containing a small amount of quinine and a little lemon and lime juice: *Sales of quinine water, a rising star on the fizz-water horizon, have moved up from about 100,000 cases in 1949 to about 1.2 million cases last year* (Wall Street Journal).
**quin|nat salmon**, or **quin|nat** (kwin′at), *n.* a large salmon of the Pacific coast; chinook salmon. [American English < Salishan *t'kwinnat*]
**qui|no|a** (kē′nō ä), *n.* **1** an annual plant of the amaranth family, found on the Pacific slopes of the Andes, cultivated in Chile and Peru as a grain. **2** an herb of the goosefoot family, also grown since early times by the natives of the Andean region, used to make bread, soup, and a beverage. **3** the seed of either of these plants. [American Spanish *quínoa*]
**quin|oid** (kwin′oid), *n., adj.* —*n.* a chemical compound having a structure like that of quinone.
—*adj.* like quinone in structure.
**qui|noi|din** (kwi noi′din), *n.* = quinoidine.
**qui|noi|dine** (kwi noi′dēn, -din), *n. Pharmacy.* a brownish-black, resinous substance consisting of amorphous alkaloids. It is obtained as a by-product in the manufacture of quinine, and used as a cheap substitute for it. [< *quin*(a) + *-oid* + *-ine*[2]]
**quin|ol** (kwin′ol, -ōl), *n.* = hydroquinone. [< *quin*(a) + *-ol*[2]]
**quin|o|lin** (kwin′ə lin), *n.* = quinoline.
**quin|o|line** (kwin′ə lēn, -lin), *n.* a nitrogenous organic base, a colorless, oily liquid with a pungent odor, occurring in coal tar and obtained from aniline. It is used as an antiseptic, as a solvent, and in the preparation of other compounds. *Formula:* $C_9H_7N$ [< *quinol* + *-ine*[2]]
**qui|none** (kwi nōn′, kwin′ōn), *n.* **1** a yellowish, crystalline compound with an irritating odor, obtained by the oxidation of aniline and regarded as a benzene with two hydrogen atoms replaced by two oxygen atoms. It is used in tanning and making dyes. *Quinone will, for example, oxidise another material and be itself reduced to hydroquinone* (New Scientist). *Woodward's synthesis starts with the simple coal-tar derivative quinone, proceeds directly and yields an abundance of reserpine* (Scientific American). *Formula:* $C_6H_4O_2$ **2** any one of a group of compounds, of which this is the type. [< *quin*(ic acid) + *-one*]
**qui|non|i|mine** (kwi non′ə mēn, -min), *n.* **1** a compound derived from quinone by the substitution of an -NH radical for one atom of oxygen. *Formula:* $C_6H_5NO$ **2** any compound similarly derived from quinone. [< *quinon*(e) + *imine*]
**quin|o|noid** (kwin′ə noid, kwi nō′-), *adj.* like quinone in structure. [< *quinon*(e) + *-oid*]
**quin|ox|a|lin** (kwi nok′sə lin), *n.* = quinoxaline.
**quin|ox|a|line** (kwi nok′sə lēn, -lin), *n.* a colorless, crystalline compound, used in organic synthesis. *Formula:* $C_8H_6N_2$ [< *quin*(oline) + (gly)*oxal*(in) + *-ine*[2]]
**quinqu-**, *combining form.* the form of **quinque-** before vowels, as in *quinquangular.*
**quin|qua|ge|nar|i|an** (kwin′kwə jə nãr′ē ən), *n., adj.* —*n.* a person 50 years old or between 50 and 60.
—*adj.* **1** 50 years old or between 50 and 60. **2** characteristic of one who is 50 years old.
[< Latin *quīnquāgēnārius* having fifty (< *quīnquāgēnī* fifty each < *quīnquāginta* fifty < *quīnque* five) + English *-an*]
**Quin|qua|ges|i|ma** (kwin′kwə jes′ə mə), *n.,* or **Quinquagesima Sunday**, the Sunday before the beginning of Lent; Shrove Sunday. [< Latin *quīnquāgēsima,* feminine adjective, fiftieth (in Late Latin, the period from Easter to Whitsunday)]
**quin|quan|gu|lar** (kwin kwang′gyə lər), *adj.* having five angles. [< Late Latin *quīnquangulus* (< Latin *quīnque* five + *angulus* angle) + English *-ar*]
**quinque-**, *combining form.* five; having five; five times ____: *Quinquefoliate = having five leaves. Quinquennium = a period of five years.* Also, **quinqu-** before vowels. [< Latin *quīnque-* < *quīnque*]
**quin|que|far|i|ous** (kwin′kwə fãr′ē əs), *adj.* fivefold; in five rows. [< *quinque-* + Latin *-farius* (with English *-ous*), an adjective suffix expressing quantity]
**quin|que|fid** (kwin′kwə fid), *adj.* split into five parts or lobes. [< *quinque-* + Latin *-fidus* cleft < *findere* to cleave, divide]
**quin|que|fo|li|ate** (kwin′kwə fō′lē it), *adj.* having five leaves or leaflets.
**quin|que|fo|li|o|late** (kwin′kwə fō′lē ə lāt, -fə lit), *adj.* having five leaflets; quinate.

**quin|que|loc|u|lar** (kwin′kwə lok′yə lər), *adj.* having five compartments.

**quin|quen|ni|ad** (kwin kwen′ē ad), *n.* a period of five years; quinquennium.

**quin|quen|ni|al** (kwin kwen′ē əl), *adj., n.* — *adj.* **1** occurring every five years: *A number of the permanent commissions of the congress, bodies whose work goes on in between the quinquennial meetings, read and debated separately* (London Times). **2** of or for five years.
— *n.* **1** something that occurs every five years. **2** something lasting five years.
[< Latin *quīnquennis* (< *quīnque* five + *annus* year) + English *-al*[1]] — **quin|quen′ni|al|ly**, *adv.*

**quin|quen|ni|um** (kwin kwen′ē əm), *n., pl.* **-quen|ni|a** (-kwen′ē ə). a period of five years. [< Latin *quīnquennium* < *quīnque* five + *annus* year]

**quin|que|par|tite** (kwin′kwə pär′tīt), *adj.* divided into or consisting of five parts. [< Latin *quīnquepartītus* < *quīnque* five + *partīrī* to divide < *pars, partis* past]

**quin|que|reme** (kwin′kwə rēm), *n.* a galley with five tiers of oars. [< Latin *quīnquerēmis* < *quīnque* five + *rēmus* oar. Compare etym. under **trireme**.]

**quin|que|va|lence** (kwin′kwə vā′ləns, kwing-kwev′ə-), *n.* **1** the condition of having a valence of five; pentavalence. **2** the condition of having five different valences.

**quin|que|va|len|cy** (kwin′kwə vā′lən sē, kwing-kwev′ə-), *n.* = quinquevalence.

**quin|que|va|lent** (kwin′kwə vā′lənt, kwing-kwev′ə-), *adj.* **1** having a valence of five; pentavalent. **2** having five different valences.

**quin|qui|va|lent** (kwin′kwə vā′lənt, kwing-kwiv′ə-), *adj.* = quinquevalent.

**quin|sy** (kwin′zē), *n.* tonsillitis with pus; very sore throat with an abscess in the tonsils; peritonsillar abscess. [Middle English *quinacy* < Medieval Latin *quinancia* < Greek *kynánchē* (originally) dog's collar < *kýōn, kynós* dog + *ánchein* to choke]

**quint**[1] (kwint), *n. Informal.* a quintuplet.

**quint**[2] (kwint, kint), *n.* **1** a set or sequence of five, such as in piquet. **2** *Music.* a fifth. [< French, Old French *quint,* or *quinte,* feminine < Latin *quīntus* and *quīnta* a fifth, related to *quīnque* five]

**quin|ta** (kin′tə), *n.* a country house or villa in Spain and Latin America: *... his presidential quinta in suburban Olivos* (Time). [< Spanish and Portuguese *quinta*]

***quin|tain** (kwin′tin), *n.* in the Middle Ages: **1** a post set up as a mark to be tilted at. **2** the exercise of tilting at a target. [< Old French *quintaine* < Medieval Latin *quintana,* apparently < Latin *quīntāna* market place of a Roman camp, (originally) placed between the stations of the fifth and sixth maniples < *quīntus* fifth (maniple)]

***quintain**
definition 1

**quin|tal** (kwin′təl), *n.* **1** a hundredweight. In the United States, a quintal equals 100 pounds; in Great Britain, 112 pounds. **2** a unit of mass in the metric system equal to 100 kilograms, or 220.46 pounds avoirdupois: *A million quintals of wheat ... and unspecified quantities of sugar and potatoes will be distributed* (New York Times). *Abbr:* ql. [< Medieval Latin *quintale* < Arabic *qinṭār* weight of a hundred pounds, probably ultimately < Latin *centēnārius* < *centum* hundred. Compare etym. under **kantar**.]

**quin|tan** (kwin′tən), *adj., n.* — *adj.* recurring every fifth day by inclusive count.
— *n.* a fever or ague with three days between attacks.
[< Latin *quīntāna* (*febris*) (literally) (fever) of the fifth (day, by Roman count) < *quīntus* fifth, related to *quīnque* five]

**quinte** (kaɴt), *n. Fencing.* the fifth in a series of eight parries. [< French *quinte,* feminine of *quint;* see etym. under **quint**[2]]

**quin|tes|sence** (kwin tes′əns), *n.* **1** the purest form of some quality; pure essence. **SYN:** pith. **2** the most perfect example of something: *Her costume was the quintessence of good taste and style.* **3** (in medieval philosophy) the ether of Aristotle, a fifth element (added to earth, water, fire, and air) permeating all things and forming the substance of the heavenly bodies. [< Middle French *quinte essence,* learned borrowing from Medieval Latin *quinta essentia* fifth essence, translation of Greek *pémptē ousíā* Aristotle's "fifth substance"]

**quin|tes|sen|tial** (kwin′tə sen′shəl), *adj.* having the nature of a quintessence; of the purest or most perfect kind: *Costain has created what amounts to a quintessential recapture of the English novel, from Smollett to Dickens* (Wall Street Journal). *They don't pay sufficient attention to the quintessential requirement: that it be easy for the reader to find what he is looking for* (Atlantic).

**quin|tes|sen|tial|ize** (kwin′tə sen′shə līz), *v.t.,* **-ized, -iz|ing.** to make quintessential; reduce or refine to a quintessence.

**quin|tes|sen|tial|ly** (kwin′tə sen′shə lē), *adv.* in a quintessential manner: *He is, quintessentially, the non-organization man ...* (Harper's).

**quin|tet** or **quin|tette** (kwin tet′), *n.* **1a** a group of five singers or players performing together. **b** a piece of music for five voices or instruments. **2** any group of five; set of five. **3** *Informal.* a men's basketball team. [probably < French *quintette* < Italian *quintetto* (diminutive) < *quinto* fifth < Latin *quīntus;* see etym. under **quintan**]

**quin|tic** (kwin′tik), *adj., n. Mathematics.* — *adj.* of the fifth degree: *a quintic equation.*
— *n.* a quantity, equation, or function, of the fifth degree. [< Latin *quīntus* fifth + English *-ic*]

**quin|tile** (kwin′təl, -tīl), *n., adj.* — *n.* **1a** one of the points or marks dividing a frequency distribution into five parts, each having the same frequency. **b** any one of the five parts thus formed. **2** *Astrology.* the aspect of two heavenly bodies when their longitudes differ by 72 degrees.
— *adj.* of or having to do with quintiles; being a quintile.
[probably < New Latin *quintus* fifth < Latin *quīntus;* patterned on English *quartile*]

**quin|til|lion** (kwin til′yən), *n., adj.* **1** (in the U.S., Canada, and France) 1 followed by 18 zeros. **2** (in Great Britain and Germany) 1 followed by 30 zeros. [< Latin *quīntus* fifth; patterned on English *million*]

**quin|til|lionth** (kwin til′yənth), *adj., n.* — *adj.* last in a series of a quintillion.
— *n.* **1** the last in a series of a quintillion. **2** one of a quintillion equal parts.

**quin|troon** (kwin trün′), *n.* a person having one sixteenth Negro ancestry. [alteration of Spanish *quinterón* < *quinto* fifth < Latin *quīntus* (because the person is fifth in descent from a Negro); after *quadroon*]

**quin|tu|ple** (kwin′tů pəl, -tyů-; kwin tü′-, -tyü′-), *adj., adv., n., v.,* **-pled, -pling.** — *adj.* **1** consisting of five parts; fivefold. **2** five times; five times as great.
— *adv.* five times; five times as great.
— *n.* a number or amount five times as great as another.
— *v.t., v.i.* to make or become five times as great or as numerous: *He had quintupled a fortune already considerable* (Henry James). *He has in seventeen years of pin-wheeling brilliance quintupled the magazine's circulation* (Newsweek).
[< French *quintuple* < Late Latin *quīntuplex* < Latin *quīntus* fifth + *-plex;* see etym. under **quaduplex**]

**quin|tu|plet** (kwin′tů plit, -tyů-; kwin tü′-, tyü′-), *n.* **1** one of five children born at the same time of the same mother: *The birth of quintuplets is so rare that it is reported on television and in the newspapers.* **2** any group or combination of five; set of five.

**quin|tu|pli|cate** (*adj., n.* kwin tü′plə kit, -tyü′-; *v.* kwin tü′plə kāt, -tyü′-), *adj., v.,* **-cat|ed, -cat|ing,** *n.* — *adj.* fivefold; quintuple.
— *v.t.* to make fivefold; quintuple.
— *n.* one of five things, especially five copies of a document, exactly alike.
**in quintuplicate,** in five copies exactly alike: *Such a person must fill out fifteen forms in quintuplicate ... showing just why he should be allowed a British bicycle* (New Yorker).

**quinze** (kwinz; *French* kaɴz), *n.* a card game somewhat similar to twenty-one, in which the object is to score fifteen, or as near as possible to that number, without exceeding it. [< French *quinze* < Latin *quīndecim;* see etym. under **quindecagon**]

**quip** (kwip), *n., v.,* **quipped, quip|ping.** — *n.* **1** a clever or witty saying: *I am generally known as a discouragingly slow man with a quip* (New Yorker). **SYN:** witticism. **2** a sharp, cutting remark: *If I sent him word again it was not well cut, he would send me word he cut it to please himself. This is called the Quip Modest* (Shakespeare). **SYN:** sarcasm. **3** = quibble. **4** something odd or strange. **5** = knickknack.
— *v.i.* to make quips.
— *v.t.* to sneer at.
[perhaps for earlier *quippy* < Latin *quippe* indeed! I dare say]

**quip|pish** (kwip′ish), *adj.* **1** clever; witty. **2** sarcastic; cutting: *The dialogue is more quippish than witty* (Time).

**quip|ster** (kwip′stər), *n.* a person who often makes quips.

***qui|pu** (kē′pü, kwip′ü), *n., pl.* **-pus.** a cord with knotted strings or threads of various colors, used by the ancient Peruvians to record events, keep accounts, and send messages. [earlier *quipo* < Spanish < Quechua (Peru) *quipu* knot]

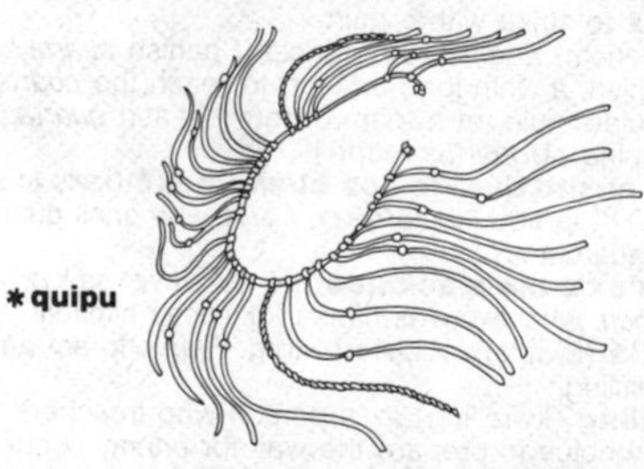

***quipu**

**quire**[1] (kwīr), *n., v.,* **quired, quir|ing.** — *n.* **1** 24 or 25 sheets of paper of the same size and quality. *Abbr:* qr. **2a** *Bookbinding.* a set of four sheets folded to make eight leaves. **b** to make eight leaves. **b** any similar set of sheets in proper order, but before binding.
— *v.t.* to arrange in quires; fold in quires.
**in quires,** in sheets and not bound: *I gave my book ... to the Heralds Office in quires* (Anthony Wood).
[< Old French *quaier,* earlier *quaer* < Late Latin *quaternus* < Latin *quaternī* four each, related to *quattuor* four. See etym. of doublets **cahier, casern**.]

**quire**[2] (kwīr), *n. Archaic.* choir.

**Quir|i|nal** (kwir′ə nəl), *n., adj.* — *n.* **1** one of the seven hills upon which Rome was built. **2** a palace built there, formerly the royal palace, now the official residence of the president of Italy: *Gronchi, unlike Einaudi,* [*refused*] *to live in the Quirinal, explaining "I don't want my children to develop crown-prince complexes"* (Newsweek). **3** the Italian government, as distinguished from the Vatican (representing the papacy).
— *adj.* **1** of or having to do with the Quirinal hill, the palace on it, or the Italian government. **2** of, relating to, or like Quirinus.
[< Latin *Quirīnālis* < *Quirīnus* Quirinus]

**Qui|ri|nus** (kwi rī′nəs), *n. Roman Mythology.* a god of war. Romulus was identified with him in early mythology. Later, Quirinus was viewed as the son of Mars.

**Qui|ri|tes** (kwi rī′tēz), *n.pl.* the citizens of ancient Rome considered in their civil capacity. [< Latin *Quirītēs,* plural of *Quirīs* (originally) citizens of the Sabine town of Cures]

**quirk** (kwėrk), *n., adj., v.* — *n.* **1** a peculiar way of acting: *The old man had many quirks. Every man had his own quirks and twists* (Harriet Beecher Stowe). **2** a clever or witty saying; quip: *Your rhymes ... your quirks and your conundrums* (William Godwin). **3** = quibble. **SYN:** shift, evasion. **4** the action of quibbling; equivocation. **5** a sudden twist or turn: *a quirk of fate, a mental quirk, a quirk in the road.* **6** a flourish in writing. **7** a sudden turn or flourish in a musical air: *light quirks of music, broken and uneven* (Alexander Pope). **8** *Architecture.* an acute angle or recess; a deep indentation.
— *adj.* having a quirk; quirked.
— *v.t.* to form with a quirk, especially in architecture. — *v.i.* to move with sudden twists or turns: *... to set an audience bounding and quirking* (George Meredith).

**quirked** (kwėrkt), *adj.* formed with a quirk or channel: *a quirked molding.*

**quirk|i|ly** (kwėr′kə lē), *adv.* in a quirky manner.

**quirk|i|ness** (kwėr′kē nis), *n.* the state or quality of being quirky: *Some jazz highbrows ... attribute Armstrong's fondness for Lombardo to the same inexplicable quirkiness that occasionally moves a thoroughbred race horse to pal around with a goat* (New Yorker).

**quirk|ish** (kwėr′kish), *adj.* having the character of a quirk; full of quirks, quibbles, or artful evasions.

**quirk|y** (kwėr′kē), *adj.,* **quirk|i|er, quirk|i|est.** full of quirks, twists, or shifts: *The writing has a quirky, personal quality that gives it an uncommon flavor* (New Yorker).

**quir|ley** (kwėr′lē), *n.* = quirly.

---

**Pronunciation Key:** hat, āge, cãre, fär; let, ēqual, tėrm; it, īce; hot, ōpen, ôrder; oil, out; cup, pu̇t, rüle; child; long; thin; ᴛʜen; zh, measure; ə represents **a** in about, **e** in taken, **i** in pencil, **o** in lemon, **u** in circus.

**quir|ly** (kwėr′lē), *n., pl.* **-lies.** *U.S. Slang.* a hand-rolled cigarette: *A cigarette is best called a quirly; it is seldom rolled or made, it is fashioned, shaped, spun, or built; it is not lit, fire is put to it* (Harper's).

**quirt** (kwėrt), *n., v.* —*n.* a riding whip with a short, stout handle and a lash of braided leather: *Our horses were lathered with sweat and it was use of quirt on rump rather than kindness in the voice that urged the horses on* (Maclean's).
—*v.t.* to strike with a quirt.
[American English < American Spanish *cuarta* < Spanish, a whip long enough to reach the *cuarta,* or guide mule, of a team of four < Latin *quarta,* feminine of *quartus* fourth]

**quis cus|to|di|et ip|sos cus|to|des?** (kwis kus-tō′dē et ip′sos kus tō′dēz), *Latin.* who shall guard the guardians?

**qui s'ex|cuse s'ac|cuse** (kē seks kyz′ sȧ kyz′), *French.* who excuses himself accuses himself.

**quis|le** (kwiz′əl), *v.i.,* **-led, -ling.** *Slang.* to act as a quisling.

**quis|ling** (kwiz′ling), *n.* a person who treacherously helps to prepare the way for enemy occupation of his own country; traitor. [< Norwegian *quisling* < Vidkun *Quisling,* 1887-1945, a Norwegian politician who was premier of the puppet government during the German occupation of Norway in World War II]

**quis se|pa|ra|bit?** (kwis sep′ə rā′bit), *Latin.* who shall separate (us)?

**quit**[1] (kwit), *v.,* **quit** or **quit|ted, quit|ting,** *n., adj.* —*v.t.* **1** to stop: *The men quit work at five.* SYN: cease, discontinue. **2** to go away from; leave: *He quit his room in anger. His big brother is quitting school this June.* **3** to give up; let go: *to quit a job, to quit school.* **4** to pay back; pay off (a debt): *A thousand marks ... To quit the penalty and to ransom him* (Shakespeare). SYN: repay. **5** to free; clear; rid: *to quit oneself of a nuisance.* **6** *Archaic.* to behave or conduct (oneself); acquit: *Quit yourselves like men, and fight* (I Samuel 4:9). —*v.i.* **1** to stop working: *It's almost five o'clock; time to quit.* **2** to leave: *If he doesn't pay his rent, he will receive notice to quit.* **3** *Informal.* to leave a position, job or assignment; resign: *If you don't like your job, quit.* [< Old French *quiter,* learned borrowing from Medieval Latin *quietare* to discharge debts < Latin *quiētus;* see etym. under **quiet**[1]]
—*n. U.S. Informal.* the act of leaving a position, job, or assignment; a quitting: *... to let normal quits, retirements, and deaths reduce work forces instead of layoffs* (Wall Street Journal).
—*adj.* free; clear; rid: *I gave him money to be quit of him.*
[< Old French *quite,* learned borrowing from Medieval Latin *quittus,* alteration of Latin *quiētus.* See etym. of doublets **quiet**[1], **coy.**]

**quit**[2] (kwit), *n.* any one of various small perching birds especially of the West Indies, such as the banana quit. [apparently imitative]

**quitch** (kwich), *n.,* or **quitch grass,** couch grass, a kind of spreading grass that is a common weed in gardens. [Old English *cwice,* related to *cwic* quick. Compare etym. under **quick grass.**]

**quit|claim** (kwit′klām′), *n., v.* —*n.* **1** the act of giving up a claim or right of action. **2** = quitclaim deed. [< Anglo-French *quiteclame* < *quiteclamer;* see the verb]
—*v.t.* to give up claim to (possession or right of action).
[< Anglo-French *quiteclamer* < *quite* free, quit, clear + *clamer* to claim]

**quitclaim deed,** a document in which a person gives up his claim, title, or interest in a piece of property to someone else but does not guarantee that the title is valid.

**quite** (kwīt), *adv.* **1** completely; wholly; entirely: *a hat quite out of fashion. I am quite alone. Are you quite satisfied?* SYN: totally. **2** actually; really; truly; positively: *quite the thing, quite a change in the weather.* **3** *Informal.* very; rather; somewhat; to a considerable extent or degree: *quite pretty. It is quite hot.* **4** absolutely; definitely (as an answer to a question or remark). [Middle English *quite,* (originally) variant of *quit*[1], adjective, clear, free]
▶ **quite.** The formal meaning of *quite* is "entirely, wholly." In informal English, it is generally used with the reduced meaning of "to a considerable extent or degree": Formal: *These charges are so serious you should be quite sure they are true before you proceed.* Informal: *He is quite worried. We hiked quite a distance.* A number of convenient phrases with *quite* are good informal usage: *quite a few* people, *quite a little* time, etc.

**qui trans|tu|lit sus|ti|net** (kwī trans′tyü lit sus′tə net, -tü-), *Latin.* he who transplanted (still) sustains (the motto of Connecticut, alluding to God's guidance of the first settlers and their descendants).

**quit|rent** (kwit′rent′), *n.* a fixed rent paid in money, instead of services rendered under a feudal system: *The courtly Laureate pays his quitrent ode, his peppercorn of praise* (William Cowper).

**quits** (kwits), *adj.* on even terms by having given or paid back something: *After he had repaid the dime he had borrowed from his brother, the boys were quits. Simply knock him off his horse, and then you will be quits* (William H. Hudson).
**be quits with,** to get even with; have revenge on: *A good chase and the old man felt he was quits with the boys who broke his window.*
**call it quits,** to break off an attempt to do something; stop for a time or permanently: *Since we could not manage to set up camp in the rain, we finally, called it quits and hiked home. Disarmament negotiators in London called it quits for now* (Wall Street Journal). *Mrs. Robinson retired at the age of 65. But she wasn't ready to call it quits* (New York Times).
**cry quits,** to admit that things are now even: *I should have fired at you, so we may cry quits on that score* (Frederick Marryat).
[< *quit*[1], adjective + *-s,* perhaps plural (because *quit* was taken as a noun)]

**quit|tance** (kwit′əns), *n.* **1** a release from debt or obligation. **2** the paper certifying this; receipt: *He then folded the quittance, and put it under his cap* (Scott). **3** the act of getting back at somebody; repayment; reprisal. SYN: retaliation, recompense, requital. [< Old French *quitance* < *quiter;* see etym. under **quit**[1], verb]

**quit|ter** (kwit′ər), *n. Informal.* **1** a person who shirks or gives up easily. SYN: shirker. **2** a person who gives up too easily; coward. [American English < *quit*[1], verb + *-er*[1]]

**quit|tor** (kwit′ər), *n.* an ulcer on a horse's foot. [earlier *quittor-bone,* apparently < Middle English *quiture* pus, a discharge from a sore < Old French *cuiture* (literally) cooking < Latin *coctūra* < *coquere* to cook]

**qui va là?** (kē vȧ lȧ′), *French.* who goes there?

**quiv|er**[1] (kwiv′ər), *v., n.* —*v.i.* to shake with a slight but rapid motion; shiver; tremble: *The dog quivered with excitement. Her lip quivered like that of a child about to cry* (Booth Tarkington). SYN: See syn. under **shake.**
—*v.t.* to cause to quiver: *Impotent as a bird with both wings broken, it still quivered its shattered pinions* (Charlotte Brontë).
—*n.* an act of quivering; tremble: *A quiver of his mouth showed that he was about to cry.*
[probably variant of *quaver;* perhaps influenced by *shiver*[1], *quiver*[3]]

***quiv|er**[2] (kwiv′ər), *n.* **1** a case to hold arrows: *a quiver of dogskin at his back, and a ... bow in his hand* (Francis Parkman). **2** the supply of arrows in such a case. [< Anglo-French *quiveir,* Old French *quivre,* probably < Germanic (compare Old High German *chohhāri*)]

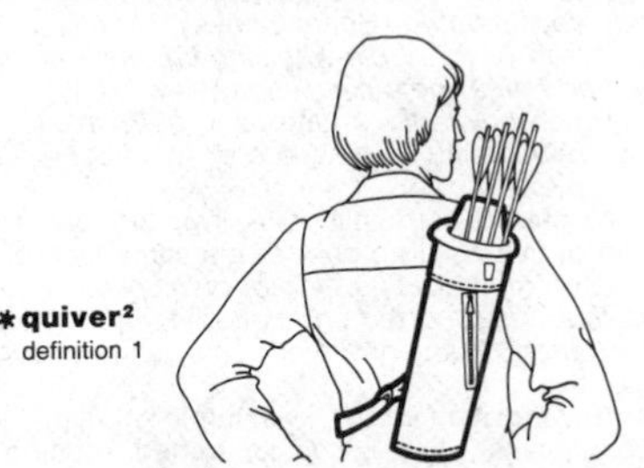
***quiver**[2]
definition 1

**quiv|er**[3] (kwiv′ər), *adj. Dialect.* nimble; quick. [Middle English *cwiver,* Old English *cwiferlīce* actively]

**quiv|ered** (kwiv′ərd), *adj.* **1** furnished with a quiver. **2** held in a quiver.

**quiv|er|ful** (kwiv′ər fu̇l), *n., pl.* **-fuls. 1** as much or as many as a quiver can hold. **2** *Figurative.* a sizable number or quantity: *Armed with a bad temper and a quiverful of sarcastic rejoinders ...* (Atlantic).

**quiv|er|y** (kwiv′ər ē), *adj.* shivery; tremulous: *She clung to him in the dances ... and afterwards hinted of a mood which made Clyde a little quivery and erratic* (Theodore Dreiser).

**qui vive?** (kē vēv′), who goes there?
**on the qui vive,** watchful; alert: *She looked quite stunning as she walked across the dining room to the table, not at all unlike a girl on the qui vive appropriate to a big college weekend* (J. D. Salinger). *Riled water is prized by fishermen, here as elsewhere, because their quarry is thought to be on the qui vive in it, looking for worms and other things that freshets wash their way* (New Yorker).
[< French *qui vive?* a sentinel's challenge (literally) (long) live who? expecting such a reply as *Vive le roi!* Long live the King!]

**Qui|xo|te** (kē hō′tē, kwik′sət), *n.* **Don,** a chivalrous, romantic, and very impractical knight who is the hero of a famous romance by Cervantes: *But he is no Quixote, for he recognizes a windmill when he sees one* (New York Times).

**quix|ot|ic** (kwik sot′ik), *adj.* **1** resembling Don Quixote; extravagantly chivalrous or romantic: *But, truly Irish to the last, they have declared with Quixotic bravado that they will never participate in the proceedings of a British Parliament which claims to exercise jurisdiction over any part of Ireland* (London Times). **2** visionary; not practical. SYN: utopian, impractical. —**quix|ot′i|cal|ly,** *adv.*

**quix|ot|i|cal** (kwik sot′ə kəl), *adj.* = quixotic.

**quix|ot|ism** (kwik′sə tiz əm), *n.* quixotic character or behavior.

**quix|ot|ry** (kwik′sə trē), *n.* = quixotism.

**quiz** (kwiz), *n., pl.* **quiz|zes,** *v.,* **quizzed, quiz|zing.** —*n.* **1** a short, informal test: *Each week the teacher gives us a quiz in geography.* **2** an act of quizzing or questioning: *My first lesson should be in the form of a quiz* (J. W. Brown). **3** a person who makes fun of others. **4** = practical joke. **5** an odd or eccentric person: *Young ladies have a remarkable way of letting you know that they think you a "quiz," without actually saying the words* (Charlotte Brontë).
—*v.t.* **1** to give a short, informal test to; test the knowledge of: *to quiz a class in history.* **2** to examine informally by questions; question; interrogate: *The lawyer quizzed the witness. In its annual pulse-taking, the NRDGA quizzed 312 stores, with a volume of $2.5 billion* (Newsweek). **3** to make fun of; mock: *Then let us walk about and quiz people* (Jane Austen). SYN: ridicule.

**quiz game,** a game, as on a quiz show, in which contestants compete in answering questions.

**quiz kid,** *U.S. Slang.* a child prodigy; whiz kid: *... being put on show to answer questions on baseball like some ... quiz kid* (Patrick Ryan).

**quiz|mas|ter** (kwiz′mas′tər, -mäs′), *n.* the master of ceremonies who conducts a quiz show and asks the questions: *What Moscow television's Sunday "Evening of Merry Questions" really needed, its quizmaster decided ..., was giveaway prizes, just like in America* (Newsweek).

**quiz program,** a quiz show: *So much of life is in question-and-answer form these days: the radio quiz programs, the loyalty investigations ...* (New Yorker).

**quiz show,** a radio or television show in which contestants are asked questions and win prizes if they answer correctly: *All three networks ... offer much the same fare: frivolous entertainment, consisting of Westerns, vaudeville, quiz shows, and an occasional detective story* (Harper's).

**quiz|zer** (kwiz′ər), *n.* a person who quizzes.

**quiz|zi|cal** (kwiz′ə kəl), *adj.* **1** that suggests making fun of others; teasing: *a quizzical smile. A little quizzical wrinkle of the brow that suggested a faintly amused attempt to follow my uncle's mental operations* (H. G. Wells). **2** questioning; baffled: *a quizzical expression on one's face.* **3** odd; queer; comical. —**quiz′zi|cal|ly,** *adv.*

**quiz|zi|cal|i|ty** (kwiz′ə kal′ə tē), *n.* a quizzical quality or expression: *There was a touch of quizzicality in one of her lifted eyebrows* (John Galsworthy).

**quiz|zing glass** (kwiz′ing), a single eyeglass; monocle: *There was a wee young man with a mop of black ringlets and a quizzing glass* (Max Beerbohm).

**Qum|ran Community** (ku̇m′rän), a monastic community about 100 years before Christ, located at Qumran, an area near the western shore of the Dead Sea, and described in the Dead Sea Scrolls; New Covenanters.

**quo'** (kwō), *v.t.* = quoth.

**quo|ad** (kwō′ad), *prep. Latin.* so far as; as to.

**quo|ad hoc** (kwō′ad hok′), *Latin.* as far as this; to this extent.

**quo a|ni|mo** (kwō an′ə mō), *Latin.* with what mind; with what intention.

**quod** (kwod), *n. British Slang.* prison: *a vagrant oft in quod* (Rudyard Kipling). Also, **quad.** [origin uncertain]

**quod|dy** (kwod′ē), *n., pl.* **-dies.** a double-ended sailboat formerly used for fishing along the Maine coast. [< (Passama)*quoddy* Bay, an inlet between Maine and New Brunswick]

**quod e|rat de|mon|stran|dum** (kwod er′at dem′ən stran′dəm), *Latin.* which was to be proved. *Abbr:* Q.E.D. or QED (no periods).

**quod e|rat fa|ci|en|dum** (kwod er′at fā′shē en′dəm), *Latin.* which was to be done. *Abbr:* Q.E.F.

**quod|li|bet** (kwod′li bet), *n.* **1** *Music.* **a** a fanciful harmonic combination of two or more melodies: *Singing several popular songs together creates a quodlibet* (Grant Fletcher). **b** = medley. **2** a scholastic argumentation upon a subject chosen at will, but almost always theological. [< Latin *quodlibet* < *quod* what + *libet* it pleases (one)]

**quod|li|bet|i|cal** (kwod′li bet′ə kəl), *adj.* of, having to do with, or like a quodlibet or quodlibets: *I* *must say that my question was disputatious as well as quodlibetical* (Harper's). —**quod'li|bet'i|cal|ly**, *adv.*

**quod vi|de** (kwod vī'dē), *Latin.* which see. *Abbr:* q.v.
▶ See **q.v.** for usage note.

**quoin** (koin, kwoin), *n., v.* —*n.* **1** an outside angle or corner of a wall or building. **2** a stone forming an outside angle of a wall; cornerstone. **3** a wedge-shaped block of wood, metal, or stone, used in building, especially one of the stones in the curve of an arch. **4** *Printing.* a short wedge used to lock up a form.
—*v.t.* **1** to provide or construct with quoins. **2** to secure or raise with quoins.
[variant of *coin.* Compare etym. under **coign.**]

***quoit** (kwoit), *n., v.* —*n.* a heavy, flattish, iron or rope ring thrown to encircle a peg stuck in the ground or to come as close to it as possible.
—*v.t.* to toss like a quoit.
**quoits,** a game, somewhat like horseshoes, played by tossing a heavy ring so that it will encircle a peg: *The game of quoits ... does not depend so much upon superior strength as upon superior skill* (Joseph Strutt).
[perhaps < Old French *coite* cushion; flat stone]

***quoit**

quoits

**quoit|er** (kwoi'tər), *n.* a person who plays at quoits; a quoit thrower.

**quo|mo|do** (kwō'mə dō, kwō mō'-), *n.* the manner, way, or means: *Mr. Northerton was desirous of departing that evening, and nothing remained for him but to contrive the quomodo* (Henry Fielding). [< Latin *quō modō* in what way?]

**quon|dam** (kwon'dəm), *adj.* that once was; former: *The quondam servant is now master. English law may come to be assessed by historians as the most valuable and lasting benefit conferred by this country on its quondam empire* (London Times). [< Latin *quondam* at one time, formerly]

***Quon|set hut** (kwon'sit), *Trademark.* a prefabricated building of corrugated metal, shaped like a half cylinder: *Steel Quonset huts are winning wide acceptance as an important "working tool" on the farm* (Time). [< *Quonset* Point, Naval Air Station, Rhode Island, where the hut was first built in 1941]

***Quonset hut**

**quo|rum** (kwôr'əm, kwōr'-), *n.* **1** the number of members of any society or assembly that must be present if the business done is to be legal or binding. More than one half the membership usually constitutes a quorum if no special rule exists. *Any ten male Jews over thirteen years of age can form ... the required quorum, and establish a congregation* (Maclean's). **2** *British.* **a** (originally) certain justices of the peace whose presence was necessary to make a session of court legal. **b** (later) all justices of the peace. **3** any select company or group. **4** (in the Mormon Church) any one of several groups or subdivisions of the Aaronic and Melchizedek orders of priesthood.
[< Latin *quōrum* of whom, genitive plural of *quī* (from the use of the word in commissions written in Latin)]

**quo|rum pars mag|na fu|i** (kwôr'əm pärz mag'nə fyü'ī, kwōr'əm), *Latin.* **1** in which I had a large share. **2** (literally) of which I was a great part.

**quot.,** quotation.

**quo|ta** (kwō'tə), *n., v.,* **-taed, -ta|ing.** —*n.* **1a** the share of a total due from or to a particular district, state, or person: *Each member of the club was given his quota of tickets to sell for the party. Each state in the United States was assigned its quota of soldiers during the first World War.* **b** a set number, amount, or portion: *I never exceed my quota of two cups of coffee a day. There had been, of course, the usual quota of shouting standees* (Saturday Review). SYN: allotment. **2** the number of immigrants of any specific nationality who are legally allowed to enter the United States in any year: *The quotas which the law allots to each country are based upon the balance of national origins in the U.S.* (New York Times).
—*v.t.* to assign or divide in shares; allot: *Every floor in every office building would have to have its quotaed shade of color* (New York Times).
[< Medieval Latin *quota* < Latin *quota* (*pars*) how large a part; *quota,* feminine of *quotus* how many, how much]

**quot|a|bil|i|ty** (kwō'tə bil'ə tē), *n.* fitness for being quoted.

**quot|a|ble** (kwō'tə bəl), *adj.* **1** that can be quoted: *And he gave them, as he often does, a quotable comment* (Harper's). **2** that can be quoted with propriety. **3** suitable for quoting: *His Senate prayers were pithy and quotable* (Newsweek).

**quot|a|ble|ness** (kwō'tə bəl nis), *n.* = quotability.

**quota system,** any system of quotas for regulating or restricting admission to an institution, profession, country, or groups; numerus clausus: *A quota system disregards qualifications, at best leads only to token jobs and is obviously discrimination in reverse* (New York Times). *The President ordered all government agencies to expunge any trace of a strict quota system for federal programs* (Robert L. Canfield).

**quo|ta|tion** (kwō tā'shən), *n.* **1** somebody's words repeated exactly by another person; passage quoted from a book or speech: *From what author does this quotation come? When the quotation is not only apt, but has in it a term of wit or satire, it is still the better qualified for a medal, as it has a double capacity of pleasing* (Joseph Addison). **2** the act of quoting; practice of citing: *Quotation is a habit of some preachers. Classical quotation is the parole of literary men all over the world* (Samuel Johnson). *Emerson ... believed in quotation, and borrowed from everybody ... not in any stealthy or shamefaced way, but proudly* (Oliver Wendell Holmes). **3a** the act or process of stating current price of a bond, stock, commodity, or other security. **b** the price stated: *What was today's market quotation on wheat?*

***quotation mark,** one of a pair of marks used to indicate the beginning and end of a quotation.
▶ A period coming at the end of a quotation is generally placed inside the final quotation marks, even when the period serves for the entire statement and not just the quoted material: *She spoke disparagingly of my "hero."*

***quotation mark**

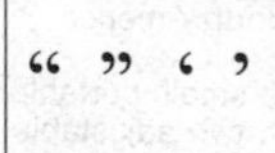

"She said 'I think not,' as I recall," I reported.

**quote** (kwōt), *v.,* **quot|ed, quot|ing,** *n.* —*v.t.* **1** to repeat the exact words of; give words or passages from: *to quote Shakespeare or one of his plays, to quote chapter and verse from the Bible.* **2** to bring forward as an example or authority: *The judge quoted various cases in support of his opinion.* **3** to give (a price): *The real-estate agent quoted a price on the house that was up for sale.* **4** to state the current price of (a bond, stock, commodity, or other security). **5** to enclose within quotation marks: *The dialogue in old books is not quoted.*
—*v.i.* to repeat exactly the words of another or a passage from a book: *The minister quoted from the Bible.*
—*n.* **1** = quotation: *American reporters abroad incessantly mine The Economist's pages for handy exportable quotes* (Newsweek). **2** = quotation mark.
[Middle English *coten* to mark in the margin < Medieval Latin *quotare* to number chapters < Latin *quotus* which or what number (in a sequence) < *quot* how many]
—*Syn. v.t.* **2 Quote, cite** mean to bring forward as authority or evidence. **Quote** means to use the words of another (either repeated exactly or given in a summary) and to identify the speaker: *The Commissioner was quoted as saying action will be taken.* **Cite** means to name as evidence or authority, but not to quote, a passage, author, or book, with exact title, page, and other such information: *To support his argument he cited Article 68, Chapter 10, of the Charter of the United Nations.*

**quot|er** (kwō'tər), *n.* a person who quotes or cites the words of an author or a speaker: *Next to the originator of a good sentence is the first quoter of it* (Emerson). *Mr. Roughead, a great reader and quoter of Dickens, is a little like another most kind-hearted man whose business lay with criminals, dear Mr. Wemmick in Great Expectations* (London Times).

**quoth** (kwōth), *v.t. Archaic.* said: *"Come hither," quoth the prince. Quoth the raven, "Nevermore"* (Edgar Allan Poe). [Middle English *quoth,* past tense of *quethen,* Old English *cwethan.* See related etym. at **bequeath.**]

**quoth|a** (kwō'thə), *interj. Archaic.* quoth he! indeed! (used ironically or contemptuously in repeating the words of another): *Here are ye clavering about the Duke of Argyle, and this man Martingale gaun to break on our hands, and lose us gude sixty pounds—I wonder what duke will pay that, quotha* (Scott). [< earlier *quoth'a* said he < *quoth* (see etym. under **quoth**) + *'a,* reduction of *he*]

**quo|tid|i|an** (kwō tid'ē ən), *adj., n.* —*adj.* reappearing daily; daily: *In quotidian matters this is not a smooth-running country—certainly not for the visitor who wants to make every day count; a travel agent, therefore, is worth his fee* (Atlantic).
—*n.* a fever or ague that occurs daily.
[< Latin *quotīdiānus,* variant of *cottīdiānus* < *cottīdiē* daily < *quotus* which or what number (in a sequence) + *diēs* day]

**quo|tient** (kwō'shənt), *n.* a number obtained by dividing one number by another: *If you divide 26 by 2, the quotient is 13.* [< Latin *quotiēns* how many times < *quot* how many]

**quo war|ran|to** (kwō wə ran'tō), *Law.* **1** a writ commanding a person to show by what authority he holds a public office or exercises a public privilege or franchise. It is a remedy for usurpation of office or of corporate franchises. **2** the legal proceedings taken against such a person. [< Medieval Latin *quo warranto* by what warrant < Latin *quō,* ablative of *quī* what + Medieval Latin *warrantō,* ablative of *warrantus.* Compare etym. under **warrant.**]

**Qu|r'an** (kü rän', -ran'), *n.* = Koran. [< Arabic *qur'ān*]

**Qu|raysh** (kü rīsh'), *n., pl.* **-raysh|es** or **-raysh.** a member of an Arabic tribe to which the prophet Mohammed belonged and from which the first series of caliphs came.

**qur|ush** (kür'üsh), *n., pl.* **-ush.** a unit of money in Saudi Arabia, equal to 1/20 of a riyal. [< Arabic *qurush*]

**q.v.,** which see (Latin *quod vide;* used in referring to a single item).
▶ The abbreviation **q.v.** is used in scholarly writing as a reference to another book, article, or the like, already mentioned, and indicates that further information will be found there. It has now been generally replaced in reference works by the English word *see.*

**qy.,** query.

***R¹** or **r** (är), *n., pl.* **R's** or **Rs, r's** or **rs. 1** the 18th letter of the English alphabet. There are two *r*'s in *carry.* **2** any sound represented by this letter.
**3** (used as a symbol for) the 18th, or more usually the 17th (of an actual or possible series, either *I* or *J* being omitted): *row R in a theater.*
**the three R's,** reading, (w)riting, and (a)rithmetic: *Middle-class schools, in which education is pushed beyond the three R's* (The Reader).

**R²** (är), *n., pl.* **R's**. anything shaped like the letter R.

**r** (no period), **1** *Statistics.* correlation coefficient.
**2** *Electricity.* resistance. **3** roentgen or roentgens.

**r.**, an abbreviation for the following:
**1** king (Latin, *rex*).
**2** queen (Latin, *regina*).
**3** rabbi.
**4** radium (dosage).
**5** radius.
**6a** railroad. **b** railway.
**7** rain.
**8** rare.
**9** *Commerce.* received.
**10** recipe.
**11** rector.
**12a** residence. **b** resides.
**13** retired.
**14** right.
**15** rises.
**16** river.
**17** road.
**18** rod or rods.
**19** roentgen.
**20** *Chess.* rook.
**21** royal.
**22** rubber.
**23** ruble or rubles.
**24** run or runs (in scoring baseball and cricket).
**25** rupee or rupees.

**R** (no period), an abbreviation or symbol for the following:
**1** *Physics, Chemistry.* gas constant.
**2** *Chemistry.* radical.
**3** radius.
**4** rand (unit of money).
**5** rare earth.
**6** ratio.
**7** Reaumur.
**8** *Electricity.* resistance.
**9** Restricted (a symbol used in the United States for motion pictures restricted to an adult audience): *The board wanted to rate the film ... R (anyone under 17 restricted unless accompanied by parent or guardian)* (Time).
**10** riyal.
**11** *Chess.* rook.

**R.**, an abbreviation for the following:
**1** King (Latin, *rex*).
**2** Queen (Latin, *regina*).
**3** rabbi.
**4a** railroad. **b** railway.
**5** range.
**6** Rankine.
**7** Reaumur.
**8** rector.
**9** redactor.
**10** Republican.
**11** respond or response (in church services).
**12** right (especially in stage directions).
**13** River.
**14** road.
**15** roentgen.
**16** Royal.
**17** ruble or rubles.
**18** rupee or rupees.

**Ra** (rä), *n.* the sun god and supreme deity of ancient Egypt, typically represented as a man with the head of a hawk, bearing the sun on his head. Also, **Re.** [< Egyptian *r'* the sun]

**Ra** (no period), radium (chemical element).

**RA** (no periods), Regular Army.

**R.A.**, an abbreviation for the following:
**1** rear admiral.
**2** Regular Army.
**3** *Astronomy.* right ascension.
**4a** Royal Academician (member of the Royal Academy). **b** Royal Academy (of Great Britain).
**5** Royal Artillery (of Great Britain).

**R.A.A.F.** or **RAAF** (no periods), Royal Australian Air Force.

**ra|bat** (rà bá', rə bat'), *n.* a breast cover, usually black, worn by certain clergymen, attached to a collar and hanging down over the breast, especially in the form of two flat or plaited bands. [< French *rabat* collar, turned-down collar < Old French *rabattre;* see etym. under **rebate**]

**ra|ba|to** (rə bā'tō, -bä'-), *n., pl.* **-toes.** = rebato.

***rab|bet** (rab'it), *n., v.,* **-bet|ed, -bet|ing.** —*n.*
**1** a cut, groove, or slot made on the edge or surface of a board or the like, to receive the end or edge of another piece of wood shaped to fit it.
**2** a joint so made.
—*v.t.* **1** to cut or form a rabbet in. **2** to join with a rabbet.
—*v.i.* to form a joint or bring pieces together with a rabbet. Also, **rebate.**
[< Old French *rabat* a beating down < *rabattre;* see etym. under **rebate**]

***rabbet**
definition 2

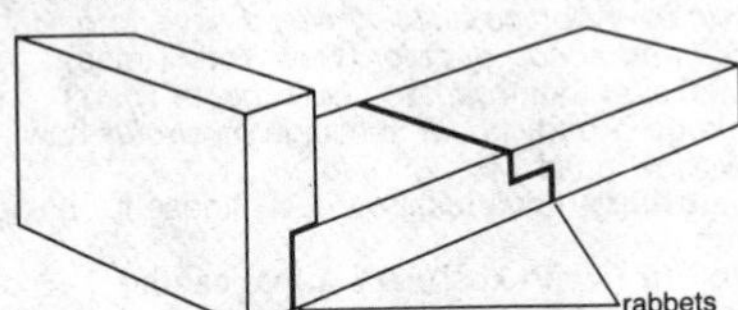


**rabbet joint,** a joint formed by a rabbet.

**rab|bi** (rab'ī), *n., pl.* **-bis** or **-bies. 1** a teacher of the Jewish religion; leader of a Jewish congregation; Jewish clergyman. **2** a Jewish title for a doctor or expounder of the law: *They said unto him, Rabbi,* (*which is to say, being interpreted, Master,*) (John 1:38). [Old English *rabbi* (originally) a term of address < Medieval Latin < Greek *rabbî* < Hebrew *rabbī* my master < *rabh* master]

**rab|bin** (rab'in), *n.* = rabbi. [< French *rabbin*]

**rab|bin|ate** (rab'ə nit, -nāt), *n.* **1** the office or position of a rabbi. **2** the period during which one is a rabbi. **3** rabbis as a group.

**rab|bin|ic** (rə bin'ik), *adj.* = rabbinical.

**Rab|bin|ic** (rə bin'ik), *n.* the Hebrew language or dialect as used by the rabbis in writings; the later Hebrew language.

**rab|bin|i|cal** (rə bin'ə kəl), *adj.* of or having to do with rabbis or their learning, teachings, or writings. — **rab|bin'i|cal|ly,** *adv.*

**rab|bin|ics** (rə bin'iks), *n.* rabbinical studies: *a professor of rabbinics.*

**rab|bin|ism** (rab'ə niz əm), *n.* **1** a rabbinical expression or phrase. **2** the teachings or traditions of the rabbis.

***rab|bit** (rab'it), *n., v.* —*n.* **1a** a burrowing animal about as big as a cat, with soft fur, a short, fluffy tail, long hind legs, and long ears. Rabbits can make long jumps and run very fast and they are sometimes raised for food or fur. They are rodentlike mammals that belong to the same order as the hare but produce young without fur, and include the gray European species and the American cottontails. **b** = hare. **2** the fur of a rabbit or hare. **3** = Welsh rabbit.
—*v.i.* to hunt or catch rabbits.
[Middle English *rabet*] — **rab'bit|er,** *n.*

**rabbit ball,** *Baseball Slang.* a very lively or bouncy baseball.

**rabbit brush** or **bush,** a desert plant of the aster family, common in western North America.

**rabbit deer,** = pudu.

**rabbit ear antenna,** *Informal.* a small, portable television receiving antenna, with two adjustable upright or diagonal rods resembling the ears of a rabbit.

**rabbit ears,** *U.S. Slang.* **1a** too much attention by an umpire, referee, or player to the reactions or attitudes of the spectators at a sporting event: *Rabbit ears in a boxing judge or referee ... affected more than one decision in the days before television* (New York Times). **b** the umpire, referee, or player at a sporting event characterized by this. **2** *Informal.* rabbit ear antenna.

**rabbit fever,** a disease of rodents and some other animals, communicable to people and transmitted chiefly by insects; tularemia.

**rab|bit|fish** (rab'it fish'), *n., pl.* **-fish|es** or (*collectively*) **-fish. 1** a chimaera or ratfish of the Atlantic Ocean. **2** an inedible, plant-eating fish of the Indian and Pacific oceans having a rabbitlike mouth and rounded nose.

**rabbit food,** *Slang.* green salads or raw vegetables.

**rab|bit|like** (rab'it līk'), *adj.* **1** like that of a rabbit: *rabbitlike ears.* **2** like a rabbit; timid or afraid.
**3** *Figurative.* prolific: *Mankind had been rabbitlike in the unplanned breeding of itself* (London Times).

**rabbit punch,** a sharp blow on the back of the neck, at or near the base of the skull. [because this is the typical method of stunning rabbits before butchering them]

**rab|bit|ry** (rab'ə trē), *n., pl.* **-ries. 1** a place where rabbits are kept. **2** a collection of rabbits.

**rabbit's foot, 1** the hind foot of a rabbit or hare, kept as a token of good luck. **2** a common species of clover.

**rab|bit|wood** (rab'it wůd'), *n.* a parasitic North American shrub related to the sandalwood, with oblong leaves, greenish-white flowers, and drupaceous fruit; buffalo nut.

**rab|bit|y** (rab'ə tē), *adj.,* **-bit|i|er, -bit|i|est.**
**1** somewhat like a rabbit or rabbits: *a rabbity look, rabbity creatures.* **2** of or full of rabbits: *a rabbity field.*

**rab|ble¹** (rab'əl), *n., v.,* **-bled, -bling,** *adj.* —*n.* a disorderly crowd; mob: *A rabble of angry citizens stormed the embassy.*
—*v.t.* to attack (a person or his property) as a rabble does; mob.
—*adj.* disorderly; rude; low.
**the rabble,** the lower classes of persons (used in an unfriendly way): *The proud nobles scorned the rabble. Theognis complains that the rabble rule the state with monstrous laws* (John Addington Symonds).
[Middle English *rabel.* Perhaps related to **rabble³.**]

***rabbit**
definitions 1a, b

cottontail
jack rabbit

**rab|ble²** (rab'əl), *n., v.,* **-bled, -bling.** —*n.* **1** an iron bar bent at one end, used for stirring, skimming, or gathering molten metal in puddling: *The slag is now drawn with a rabble into molds prepared for it* (Rossiter Raymond). **2** any similar instrument.
—*v.t.* to stir, skim, or gather with a rabble: *The molten metal is thoroughly stirred, or rabbled, to make it uniform* (Harper's).
[< French, Middle French *râble* < Old French *roable* < Latin *rutābulum* oven rake; fire shovel < *ruere* to fall; dig up]

**rab|ble³** (rab'əl), *v.t., v.i.,* **-bled, -bling.** *Dialect, Especially British.* to speak in a rapid, confused manner; gabble. [Middle English *rablen.* Compare Dutch *rabbelen.*]

**rab|ble|ment** (rab'əl mənt), *n.* **1** a mob; rabble.
**2** disorder; tumult.

***R¹**
definition 1

Script letters look like examples of fine penmanship. They appear in many formal uses, such as invitations to social functions.

Rr *Rr*

Handwritten letters, both manuscript or printed (left) and cursive (right), are easy for children to read and to write.

Rr *Rr*

Roman letters have *serifs* (finishing strokes) adapted from the way Roman stonecutters carved their letters. This is *Times Roman* type.

Rr *Rr*

Sans-serif letters are often called *gothic.* They have lines of even width and no serifs. This type face is called *Helvetica.*

Rr *Rr*

Between roman and gothic, some letters have thick and thin lines with slight flares that suggest serifs. This type face is *Optima.*

R

Computer letters can be sensed by machines either from their shapes or from the magnetic ink with which they are printed.

**rab|bler** (rab′lər), *n.* a person who works with or uses a rabble in puddling.

**rab|ble-rous|er** (rab′əl rou′zər), *n.* a person who tries to stir up groups of people with speeches tending to arouse them to acts of violence against some existing condition, usually to serve his own ends; agitator: *Hitler, although half-educated, was ... an eminently successful rabble-rouser* (Wall Street Journal).

**rab|ble-rous|ing** (rab′əl rou′zing), *adj., n.* —***adj.*** inciting or agitating as or like a rabble-rouser; demagogic: *a rabble-rousing speech or speaker.* —***n.*** the actions or methods of a rabble-rouser; demagoguery: *to engage in rabble-rousing, to stir up the public by rabble-rousing against the government.*

**rab|bo|ni** (ră bō′nī, -nē), *n.* master, a Jewish title of honor (applied especially to religious teachers and learned persons). John 20:16. [< Aramaic *rabbōni* my master]

**Rab|e|lai|si|an** (rab′ə lā′zē ən, -zhən), *adj.* **1** of or having to do with the French writer François Rabelais (1494?-1553). **2** suggesting Rabelais; characterized by broad, coarse humor: *Rabelaisian drinking parties* (Maclean's).

**Rab|e|lai|si|an|ism** (rab′ə lā′zē ə niz′əm, -zhə-niz-), *n.* broad, coarse humor.

**ra|bi** (rab′ē), *n.* the spring crop, sown in autumn in India: *Where indigo is grown in the kharif, barley is its usual accompaniment in the rabi* (Arthur H. Church). [< Arabic *rabī′* spring]

**Ra|bi I** (ră′bē), the third month of the Moslem year. It has 30 days. [< Arabic *Rabī′*]

**Rabi II**, the fourth month of the Moslem year. It has 29 days.

**ra|bic** (rā′bik), *adj.* **1** of or caused by rabies: *rabic symptoms.* **2** affected with rabies: *a rabic animal.*

**rab|id** (rab′id), *adj.* **1** unreasonably extreme; fanatical; violent: *The rebels are rabid idealists.* **SYN**: impassioned. **2** furious; raging: *He was rabid with anger.* **SYN**: frantic, raving. **3a** having rabies; mad: *a rabid dog.* **b** of rabies. [< Latin *rabidus* < *rabere* be mad < *rabiēs* madness] —**rab′id|ly**, *adv.* —**rab′id|ness**, *n.*

**ra|bid|i|ty** (rə bid′ə tē), *n.* = rabidness.

**ra|bies** (rā′bēz, -bē ēz), *n.* a virus disease that attacks the central nervous system of warm-blooded animals, causing mental disturbance, muscular spasms, and paralysis; hydrophobia. It is transmitted by the bite of a rabid animal, such as a mad dog or fox. *Rabies is almost sure death to both man and animals unless serum is given before symptoms of the disease appear* (Science News Letter). [< Latin *rabiēs*, related to *rabere* be mad. See etym. of doublet **rage**.]

**R.A.C.**, Royal Automobile Club (of Great Britain).

**ra|ca** (ră′kə, rā′-), *adj.* worthless (an ancient Jewish expression of contempt. In the Bible, Matthew 5:22) [< Late Latin *raca* foolish; empty < Greek *rakâ* < Aramaic *rēkā*]

**rac|coon** (ra kün′), *n.* **1** a small, grayish animal with a bushy, ringed tail. Raccoons are mammals that live in wooded areas of North America and South America near water and are active at night, living mostly in trees by day. **2** its fur. Also, **racoon.** [American English < Algonkian (Powhatan) *ärähkun* < *ärähkunĕm* he scratches with the hands (because of the animal's habit of leaving long scratches on the trees he climbs)]

**raccoon dog**, a small Asiatic wild dog, somewhat like a raccoon.

**race**¹ (rās), *n., v.,* **raced, rac|ing.** —***n.*** **1** any contest of speed, as in running, driving, riding, or sailing: *a horse race, a boat race. Often the races were run in foul weather, and often Dave ran barefoot* (Time). **2** Often, **races.** a series of horse races run at a set time over a regular course. **3** any contest that suggests a race: *a political race.* **SYN**: rivalry. **4** *Figurative.* onward movement; course: *the race of life.* **SYN**: progress. **5** a strong or fast current of water: *This evening the Talbot weighed and went back to the Cowes, because her anchor would not hold here, the tide set with so strong a race* (John Winthrop). **6** the channel of a stream: *The race, ... a canal 20 to 30 feet wide, ... carried ... through rocks and hills* (Jedidiah Morse). **7** a channel leading water to or from a place where its energy is utilized: *The water, brought through races by miles of fluming, spouted clear and strong over heaps of auriferous earth* (Rolf Boldrewood). **SYN**: sluice, conduit, canal. **8** a track, groove, or the like, for a sliding or rolling part of a machine, such as a channel for ball bearings: *... a split bushing was pressed in place between the main journal and the inner race of the ball bearings* (Purvis and Toboldt). **9** the current of air driven back by a propeller of an aircraft. **10** *Scottish.* the act of running; run: *The noble stag ... Held westward with unwearied race* (Scott). **11** (in Australia) a fenced path used to separate sheep from a fold. —***v.i.*** **1** to run to see who will win; engage in a contest of speed: *The boys raced to see who would get to the water fountain first.* **2** to run, move, or go swiftly: *Race to the doctor for help.* **SYN**: dash, rush. **3** (of a motor, wheel, propeller, or the like) to run faster than necessary when load or resistance is lessened or when the transmission is not engaged: *The motor engine raced before it was shut off* (Sinclair Lewis). —***v.t.*** **1** to try to beat in a contest of speed; run a race with: *I'll race you to the corner.* **2** to cause to run in a race: *The driver raced his car down the road at top speed.* **3** to cause to run, move, or go swiftly. **4** to make go faster than necessary; cause (a motor, wheel, propeller, or the like) to run too fast with reduced load or when the transmission is not engaged: *Don't race the motor while it's cold.*
[Middle English *ras* < Scandinavian (compare Old Icelandic *rās* strong current). Related to Old English *rǣs* a rush, running.]

**race**² (rās), *n.* **1** any one of the major divisions of mankind, each having distinctive physical characteristics and a common ancestry: *the white race, the yellow race. The whole concept of race, as it is traditionally defined, may be profoundly modified or even dropped altogether, once the genetic approach has been fully exploited* (Beals and Hoijer). **SYN**: See syn. under **people**. **2** a group of persons connected by common descent or origin: *the Nordic race. We were two daughters of one race* (Tennyson). *Troy's whole race thou wouldst confound* (Alexander Pope). **SYN**: See syn. under **people**. **3** human beings, as a group: *the human race, to which so many of my readers belong* (Gilbert K. Chesterton). *That ev'ry tribe ... Might feel themselves allied to all the race* (William Cowper). **4** a group of animals or plants having the same ancestry: *the canine race, the race of fishes.* **5** a group, class, or kind, especially of people: *the brave race of seamen.* **6a** the condition of belonging to a particular stock: *Race was considered important by the Nazis, who claimed that they were Aryans. Goodbye to the Anglo-Saxon race, Farewell to the Norman blood!* (A. L. Gordon). *... a planet unvexed by war, untroubled by hunger or fear, undivided by senseless distinctions of race, color, or theory* (Stephen Vincent Benét). **b** the qualities due to this. **7** stock of high quality: *The look of race, which had been hers since childhood* (Winston Churchill). **8** a lively or stimulating quality. **9** the characteristic taste of a particular type of wine. **10** *Zoology.* a variety characteristic of a given area: *The plains ... bred a generous race of horses* (Edward Gibbon). **11** *Botany.* any group whose characters continue from one generation to another: *A race, in this technical sense of the term, is a variety which is perpetuated with considerable certainty by sexual propagation* (Asa Gray). [< Middle French *race*, earlier *rasse* < Italian *razza;* origin uncertain]

**race**³ (rās), *n.* = rhizome: *a race or two of ginger* (Shakespeare). [< Old French *rais*, or *raiz* < Latin *rādīx, -īcis* root]

**race**⁴ (rās), *n.* a narrow white mark down the face of a horse or dog. [origin uncertain]

**race|a|bout** (rās′ə bout′), *n.* **1** a type of racing yacht with a short bowsprit and a rig like that of a sloop. **2** a type of automobile built or remodeled for racing: *a fully restored 1910 Simplex raceabout.*

**race-bait|er** (rās′bā′tər), *n.* a person given to race-baiting.

**race-bait|ing** (rās′bā′ting), *n.* the persecution of people of a different race or races: *As the Negroes begin to vote in ever larger numbers, race-baiting in Southern politics should decrease* (Atlantic).

**race card**, *British.* form sheet (def. 1).

**race course**, or **race|course** (rās′kôrs′, -kōrs′), *n.* ground laid out for racing; race track.

**race|go|er** (rās′gō′ər), *n.* a person who frequently goes to horse races, automobile races, or the like.

**race horse**, or **race|horse** (rās′hôrs′), *n.* a horse bred, trained, or kept for racing: *English race horses have come to surpass in fleetness and size the parent Arabs* (Charles Darwin).

**race knife**, a knife with a bent lip, as for marking or numbering. [< *race*, variant of *raze* + *knife*]

**ra|ce|mate** (rā sē′māt, -sem′āt; rə-), *n.* a salt or ester of racemic acid.

∗**ra|ceme** (rā sēm′, rə-), *n.* a simple flower cluster having its flowers on nearly equal stalks along a stem, the lower flowers blooming first. The lily of the valley, currant, and chokecherry have racemes. [< Latin *racēmus* cluster (of grapes or berries). See etym. of doublet **raisin.**]

**ra|cemed** (rā sēmd′, rə-), *adj.* arranged in racemes.

**race meeting**, *British.* a number of horse races held at the same time on one day or successive days.

**ra|ce|mic** (rā sē′mik, -sem′ik; rə-), *adj. Chemistry.* of or designating an optically inactive compound formed by the combination of dextrorotatory and levorotatory forms in equal molecular proportions. [< Latin *racēmus* cluster (of grapes or berries) + English *-ic*]

**racemic acid**, an optically inactive form of tartaric acid, occurring in the juice of grapes along with ordinary tartaric acid. *Formula:* $C_4H_6O_6$

**rac|e|mif|er|ous** (ras′ə mif′ər əs), *adj.* bearing racemes: *The vine its racemiferous branches spread* (Hans Busk).

**rac|e|mism** (ras′ə miz əm, rə sē′-), *n.* the joining of dextrorotatory and levorotatory molecules in an optically inactive substance.

**rac|e|mi|za|tion** (ras′ə mə zā′shən), *n. Chemistry.* the act or process of producing a racemic compound.

**rac|e|mize** (ras′ə mīz, rə sē′-), *v.t., v.i.,* **-mized, -miz|ing.** to make or become optically inactive through racemism.

**rac|e|mose** (ras′ə mōs), *adj.* **1** in the form of a raceme; characteristic of racemes. **2** arranged in racemes. [< Latin *racēmōsus* full of clusters < *racēmus* cluster (of grapes or berries); meaning influenced by English *raceme*]

**racemose gland**, a gland formed of a system of ducts which branch into sacs and resemble clusters of grapes, such as the pancreas.

**rac|er** (rā′sər), *n.* **1** a person, animal, boat, automobile, airplane, or bicycle that takes part in races. **2** any one of various harmless North American snakes that are able to move very rapidly, such as the blacksnake and the blue racer.

**race relations**, the way in which people of different racial groups live or work together or treat one another: *Race relations are a question of major significance, not only between white and coloured, but equally as important between Indians and Fijians* (Manchester Guardian).

**race riot**, a violent clash between people of different racial groups within the same community, especially between whites and Negroes: *In studies of race riots it has been found that they sometimes begin in the aggressiveness resulting from the frustrations of repressed minority groups* (Emory S. Bogardus).

**race runner**, or **race|run|ner** (rās′run′ər), *n.* a whip-tailed lizard of the southeastern United States, about 8 inches long, that can run very fast.

**race suicide**, the extinction of a people that tends to result when, by deliberate limitation of the number of children, the birth rate falls below the death rate.

**race track**, or **race|track** (rās′trak′), *n.* ground laid out for racing, usually round or oval; race course.

**race|track|er** (rās′trak′ər), *n.* = racegoer.

**race|way** (rās′wā′), *n.* **1** a passage or channel for water, especially for a mill. **2** a metal pipe enclosing electric wiring inside a building. **3** a track used for harness racing. **4** = race¹ (def. 8).

**Ra|chel** (rā′chəl), *n.* the favorite wife of Jacob, and the mother of Joseph and Benjamin (in the Bible, Genesis 29-35).

**rach|et** (rach′it), *n. Especially British.* ratchet.

**ra|chis** (rā′kis), *n., pl.* **ra|chis|es, rach|i|des** (rak′ə dēz, rā′kə-). **1** *Botany.* **a** a stem, such as those of grasses: *A spike is a cluster of flowers, sessile or nearly so, borne in the axils of bracts on an elongated rachis* (Heber W. Youngken). **b** a stalk, as of a pinnately compound leaf or frond. **2** the shaft of a feather. See picture under **feather**. **3** the spinal column. [< New Latin *rachis* < Greek *rháchis* backbone]

**ra|chit|ic** (rə kit′ik), *adj.* **1** having to do with rickets. **2** suffering from rickets.

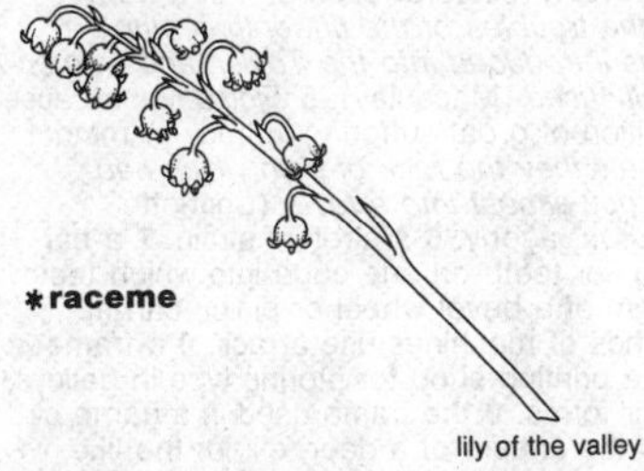

∗**raceme**

**rachitic rosary**, a row of nodules resembling a string of beads which often appears on the ribs of rachitic children at the junction of the ribs with their cartilages; rosary ribs.

---

**Pronunciation Key:** hat, āge, cãre, fär; let, ēqual, tėrm; it, īce; hot, ōpen, ôrder; oil, out; cup, pu̇t, rüle; child; long; thin; ᴛʜen; zh, measure; ə represents a in about, e in taken, i in pencil, o in lemon, u in circus.

**ra|chi|tis** (rə kī′tis), *n.* = rickets. [< New Latin *rachitis* < Greek *rhachîtis* a disease of the spine < *rháchis* spine + *-îtis* -itis]

**Rach|man|ism** (rak′mə niz əm, räk′-), *n. British.* unscrupulous practices by landlords, such as the extortion of high rents in rundown properties: *When we talk of Rachmanism, we are not talking so much of houses in bad condition, or overcrowded, as of those cases where landlords get rid of tenants by intimidation where they cannot do so by lawful means* (Lord Silkin). [< Peter *Rachman,* a speculator in London slum properties who died in 1962 + *-ism*]

**ra|cial** (rā′shəl), *adj.* **1** having to do with a race of persons, animals, or plants; characteristic of a race: *racial traits.* **SYN:** ethnic. **2** of or involving races: *racial dislikes, racial equality. The Commonwealth's outstanding characteristic is that it is a multi-racial association, and that its whole future depends on the absence of racial discrimination* (Manchester Guardian Weekly). **SYN:** ethnic. —**ra′cial|ly,** *adv.*

**ra|cial|ism** (rā′shə liz əm), *n.* unreasonable race prejudice: *The Prime Minister spoke on race relations, commenting that ... there had been less racialism in debate and more moderation* (London Times).

**ra|cial|ist** (rā′shə list), *n., adj.* —*n.* a person who supports racialism.
—*adj.* having to do with or characterized by racialism; racist: *Wilson ... would not tolerate any Rhodesia settlement based on the "racialist principle of the police state"* (Manchester Guardian Weekly).

**ra|cial|is|tic** (rā′shə lis′tik), *adj.* of or having to do with racialism or racialists.

**rac|i|ly** (rā′sə lē), *adv.* in a racy manner or style; piquantly; spicily.

**rac|i|ness** (rā′sē nis), *n.* the quality or condition of being racy; vigor; liveliness.

**rac|ing** (rā′sing), *n.* **1** the act of engaging in a race. **2** the business of arranging for or carrying on races, especially between horses.

**racing car,** any car used in automobile races, such as a stock car, a sports-racing car, a sprint car, or a dragster.

**racing form,** = form sheet.

**racing skate,** an ice skate with a long, straight blade and a lightweight shoe, built for speed.

**rac|ism** (rā′siz əm), *n.* **1** the belief that a particular race, especially one's own, is superior to other races: *... the biological racism which furnished a fraudulent scientific sanction for the atrocities committed in Hitler's Germany and elsewhere* (Science). **2** discrimination or prejudice against a race or races based on this belief: *Racism, which by definition involves a form of subjection of one race by another, is evil. "Apartheid" cannot succeed* (New York Times). **3** a political or social policy or system against a race or races based on this belief: *Racial determinism ... easily slips into the political field, where this approach is called racism* (Melville J. Herskovits).

**rac|ist** (rā′sist), *n., adj.* —*n.* a person who believes in, supports, or practices racism: *the bigotry of a racist.*
—*adj.* believing in, supporting, or practicing racism: *a racist attitude or speech.*

**rac|is|tic** (rā sis′tik), adj. = racist.

**rack**[1] (rak), *n., v.* —*n.* **1** a frame with bars, shelves, or pegs to hold, arrange, or keep things on: *a hatrack, a tool rack, a baggage rack.* **2** a framework set on a wagon for carrying hay or straw. **3** a frame of bars to hold hay and other food especially for cattle and horses. **4** an instrument once used for torturing people by stretching them between rollers at each end of a frame: *During the troubles of the fifteenth century, a rack was introduced into the Tower, and was occasionally used* (Macaulay). **5** *Figurative.* a cause or condition of great suffering in body or mind: *Little knew they the rack of pain which had driven Lucy almost into a fever* (Charlotte Brontë). **SYN:** agony. **6** a stretch; strain. **7** a bar with pegs or teeth on one edge into which teeth on the rim of a bevel wheel or pinion can fit. Many kinds of machines use a rack. **8** a framework in a printing shop for storing type in galleys, cases, or forms. **9** the frame used in a game of pool. **10** the antlers of a deer, elk, or the like, especially when large and spreading.
—*v.t.* **1** to hurt very much: *to be racked with grief. A toothache racked my jaw.* **SYN:** agonize. **2** to stretch; strain. **3** to torture on the rack. **4** to put (a thing) in or on a rack. **5a** to raise (rent) above a fair or normal amount: *He racked no rents to maintain the expenses of his establishment* (Quarterly Review). **b** to oppress (a person) with high rents or other demands for money: *Here are no hard landlords to rack us with high rents* (Captain John Smith).
**on** (or **upon**) **the rack,** in great pain or distress; suffering very much: *Let me choose, For as I am, I live upon the rack* (Shakespeare).
**rack up,** *U.S. Informal.* to accumulate: *More than a fourth of the nation's annual retail sales volume is racked up in November and December* (Wall Street Journal).
[Middle English *rakke;* origin uncertain] —**rack′er,** *n.*

**rack**[2] (rak), *n. Archaic.* wreck; destruction.
**go to rack and ruin,** to be destroyed: *Over the years, the vacant house went to rack and ruin first by vandals and then a fire.*
[variant of **wrack**[1]. Compare etym. under **rack**[4].]

**rack**[3] (rak), *n., v.* —*n.* **1** = single-foot. See picture under **gait. 2** = pace[1] (def. 4).
—*v.i.* to go at a rack: *No one ever saw him trotting or galloping; he only racks* (Frederick Marryat).
[origin uncertain] —**rack′er,** *n.*

**rack**[4] (rak), *n., v.* —*n.* flying, broken clouds driven by the wind: *Across the sky the driving rack of the rain cloud Grows for a moment then* (Longfellow).
—*v.i.* (of clouds or fog) to be driven before the wind.
[Middle English *rak,* perhaps < Scandinavian (compare Old Icelandic *rek* jetsam, wreckage). See related etym. at **wreck, wrack**[1].]

**rack**[5] (rak), *n.* the neck part of a forequarter of mutton, pork, or veal, especially when made into a roast for cooking: *a rack of lamb.* [origin uncertain]

**rack**[6] (rak), *v.t.* to draw off (wine or cider) from the lees. [< Middle French *raqué* pressed from marc of grapes. Compare Provençal *arracar* to rack, *raca* dregs.] —**rack′er,** *n.*

**rack**[7] (rak), *n.* **1** the track or trail made by an animal, especially that of a deer, as marked by gaps in hedges. **2** *Dialect.* a narrow path or track. [Middle English *rakke,* perhaps < Scandinavian (compare Old Icelandic *rāk* stripe)]

***rack car,** a railroad freight car with racks for carrying objects, such as automobiles or timber: *... three-tiered rack cars, which carry up to 18 autos* (Wall Street Journal).

***rack car**

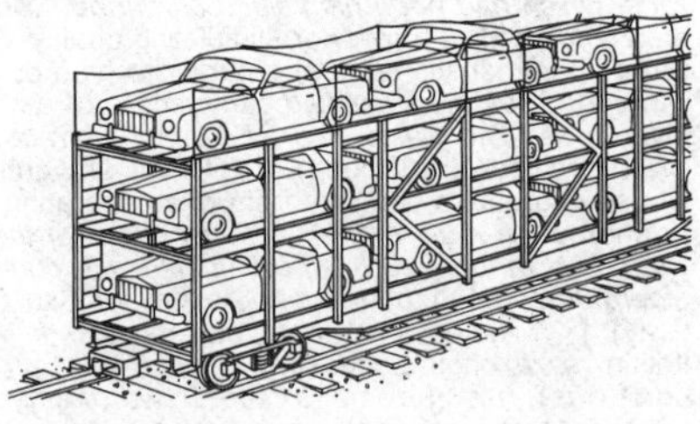

**rack|et**[1] (rak′it), *n., v.* —*n.* **1** a loud and confused noise or loud talk; din: *Don't make a racket when others are reading. Imagine the thunderous racket made by ... these carts ... returning empty* (W. H. Hudson). **SYN:** uproar, clamor, hubbub. **2** a time of gay parties and social excitement. **SYN:** revelry. **3** *Informal.* **a** a dishonest scheme for getting money from people, often by threatening to hurt them or what belongs to them: *The racket was to "sell" protection to store owners or beat them up and wreck their stores.* **b** any dishonest scheme: *Everyone wants the illegal drug racket broken and crime by addicts stopped* (Harper's). **4** *U.S. Slang.* an occupation. **5** strain or other adverse consequences.
—*v.i.* **1** to make a racket; move about in a noisy way: *I ... sometimes spent further hours a day racketing along underground in a thunderous, crowded, and filthy Bronx express* (Manchester Guardian). **2** to live a gay life; take part in social excitement: *He racketed round 'mong them nabobs* (Harriet Beecher Stowe).
**stand the racket,** to hold out against strain or wear and tear: *I like a quiet life ... Don't believe I could stand the racket* (Anthony Hope).
[probably < earlier British slang *racket* a type of fraud, scheme]

**rack|et**[2] (rak′it), *n.* **1a** an oval, wooden or metal frame with a network of strings and having a long handle. It is used for games like tennis or badminton. *The main object of modern lawn tennis is to meet the ball with a full racket* (Charles G. Heathcote). **b** a small wooden implement with a short handle, used to strike the ball in table tennis and paddle tennis; paddle. **2** a snowshoe that resembles a tennis racket. Also, **racquet.**
**rackets,** a game played in a walled court with a ball and rackets: *Rackets ... is, like any other athletic game, very much a thing of skill and practice* (William Hazlitt).
[< French *raquette,* perhaps < Spanish *raqueta* < Arabic *rāḥa* palm of the hand]
► **Rackets,** the game, is plural in form and singular in use: *Rackets is played in a walled court.*

**rack|et|eer** (rak′ə tir′), *n., v.* —*n.* a person who gets money from people through bribery, threats of violence, or other unlawful means: *They are convinced the crackdown is scaring off the racketeers* (Wall Street Journal).
—*v.i.* to extort money in this way.
[American English < *racket*[1] (definition 3) + *-eer*]

**rack|et|eer|ing** (rak′ə tir′ing), *n.* the business of a racketeer.

**rack|ets** (rak′its), *n.pl.* See under **racket**[2].

**racket store,** *Southwestern U.S.* a dime store.

**rack|et|tail** (rak′it tāl′), *n.* a hummingbird having two very long tail feathers with the ends shaped like rackets.

**rack|et|y** (rak′ə tē), *adj.,* **-et|i|er, -et|i|est.** **1** noisy: *rackety music.* **2** characterized by social excitement or dissipation. [< *racket*[1] + *-y*[1]]

**rack|ing|ly** (rak′ing lē), *adv.* in a racking or disturbing manner; torturingly.

**rack jobber,** a wholesale distributor who provides notions, housewares, and the like, and such services as price marking and display material to supermarkets, drugstores, and other retail outlets.

**rack|le** (rak′əl), *adj. Scottish.* hasty; rash; impetuous; headstrong. [origin uncertain. Perhaps related to **reck.**]

**rack rail,** a rail in a type of railway for very steep grades, having cogs or teeth with which the cogwheel of the locomotive engages; cograil.

**rack railway,** a railway using a rack rail; cog railway.

**rack-rent** (rak′rent′), *n., v.* —*n.* an unreasonably high rent, nearly equal to the value of the holding: *Agriculture cannot be expected to flourish where ... the husbandman begins on a rack-rent* (Tobias Smollett).
—*v.t.* to exact rack-rent from (a tenant) or for (land).
[< *rack*[1] to stretch + *rent*[1]]

**rack-rent|er** (rak′ren′tər), *n.* **1** a person subjected to rack-rent. **2** a person who exacts rack-rent.

**rack|work** (rak′wėrk′), *n.* **1** a mechanism in which a rack is used. **2** a rack and pinion, or the like.

**ra|clette** (rä klet′), *n.* **1** a Swiss fondue made by holding cheese to the fire and scraping off the part that melts onto crusty bread or boiled potatoes. **2** a local cheese used to make this dish. [< French *raclette* (literally) scraper < *racler* to scrape]

**ra|con** (rā′kon), *n. Especially U.S.* radar beacon. [< *ra*(dar) (bea)*con*]

**rac|on|teur** (rak′on tėr′), *n.* a person clever at telling stories, anecdotes, and the like: *There never was, in my opinion, a raconteur, from Charles Lamb or Theodore Hook down to Gilbert à Beckett or H. J. Byron, ... who spoke and told anecdotes at a dinner-table, ... that was not conscious that he was going to be funny* (Lester Wallack). [< French *raconteur* < Old French *raconter* relate, recount < *re-* again, re- + *aconter* recount]

**ra|con|teuse** (rak′on tœz′), *n. French.* a woman raconteur.

**ra|coon** (ra kün′), *n.* = raccoon.

**racoon dog,** = raccoon dog.

**rac|quet** (rak′it), *n.* = racket[2].
**racquets,** the game of rackets.

**rac|quet|ball** (rak′it bôl′), *n.* a game played on a walled court by two or four players using a stringed racket with a short handle and a ball that is slightly larger and softer than a handball.

**rac|y**[1] (rā′sē), *adj.,* **rac|i|er, rac|i|est. 1** vigorous; lively: *a racy discussion. In Whitman and Melville letters again became as racy as the jabber of a waterside saloon* (Lewis Mumford). **SYN:** spirited. **2** having an agreeably peculiar taste or flavor: *a racy apple.* **SYN:** piquant, spicy. **3** suggestive of indecency; somewhat improper; risqué: *a racy story, a racy dress.* **4** fresh; unspoiled; pure. [< *race*[2] (definition 9) + *-y*[1]]

**rac|y**[2] (rā′sē), *adj.* **rac|i|er, rac|i|est.** designed for, or as if for, racing; streamlined: *a racy sports car, a sloop with racy lines.* [< *race*[1] + *-y*[1]]

**rad** (rad), *n., pl.* **rad** or **rads.** a unit for measuring absorbed doses of radiation, equal to 100 ergs of energy per gram: *The quantity of total body radiation that is fatal in almost all cases is close to 800 rads* (Arnold L. Bachman). [< *rad*(iation)]

**rad.,** an abbreviation for the following:
1 radian.
2 radical (the mathematical sign).
3 radio.
4 radius.
5 radix (root).

**RADA** (no periods) or **R.A.D.A.,** Royal Academy of Dramatic Art.

**ra|dar** (rā′där), *n.* **1** an instrument for determining the distance, direction, and speed of unseen objects by the reflection of radio waves: *In fog,*

*rain, or snow, a ship's radar can spot other ships or icebergs in time to prevent collisions. ... Forecasters can look into a storm with radar and learn its size, shape, speed, direction of travel, and rate of development* (Robert C. Guthrie). **2** this and other instruments and techniques which have developed from it, as a field of electronics: *to study radar.* **3** a process by which the reflection of radio waves is measured: *The miracle underlying all radar is that men have learned ... to measure time in such infinitesimal amounts that radio echo ranges of objects miles away can be read with accuracy in yards* (James Phinney Baxter).
[American English < *ra*(dio) *d*(etecting) *a*(nd) *r*(anging)] – **ra′dar|like′**, *adj.*

**radar astronomy**, a branch of astronomy that studies planets and other heavenly bodies by analyzing the echoes or reflections of radar signals sent from the earth at specific targets.

**radar beacon**, a beacon that transmits radar waves to aid navigators to determine a plane's position.

**radar fence** or **screen**, a protective chain of radar posts so placed around an area that their field is continuous: *The defense of North America involves radar screens, military airplanes, and defense against submarines* (Bulletin of Atomic Scientists).

**ra|dar|man** (rā′där man′, -mən), *n., pl.* **-men.** a technician in a branch of the armed forces, who operates or services radar equipment.

**radar picket**, a ship or aircraft with radar, stationed near the outside boundary of some area to detect approaching aircraft.

**ra|dar|scope** (rā′där skōp), *n.* a screen or oscilloscope which displays the dots of light indicating the location of objects within the radar's range; scope.

**radar telescope**, a radio telescope used, in radar astronomy, as a radar receiver to study and measure the distance of objects in outer space.

**rad|dle¹** (rad′əl), *n., v.,* **-dled, -dling.** – ***n.*** **1** one of the many slender sticks fastened to or woven between upright stakes, as to form a fence. **2** such sticks. **3** a fence made of them.
– ***v.t.*** = interweave.
[< Anglo-French *reidele* a stick, Old French *reddalle*]

**rad|dle²** (rad′əl), *n., v.,* **-dled, -dling.** – ***n.*** red ocher; hematite.
– ***v.t.*** **1** to paint with red ocher. **2** to color heavily with rouge: *The second hussy ... being raddled with red paint* (George J. Whyte-Melville). Also, **reddle, ruddle.**
[variant of *ruddle*]

**rad|dled** (rad′əld), *adj.* coarsely streaked with red, as if painted with raddle: *raddled cheeks.* Also, **reddled, ruddled.**

**rad|dle|man** (rad′əl mən), *n., pl.* **-men.** a person who digs or sells red ocher. Also, **reddleman, ruddleman.**

**Ra|dha** (rä′dä), *n. Hindu Mythology.* a shepherdess who was the consort of Krishna: *Radha and Krishna are the archetypal lovers of Hindu India* (Manchester Guardian Weekly).

**ra|di|ac** (rā′dē ak), *n.* a device for detecting and measuring radioactivity. [< *r*(adio) *a*(ctivity) *d*(etection) *i*(dentification) *a*(nd) *c*(omputation)]

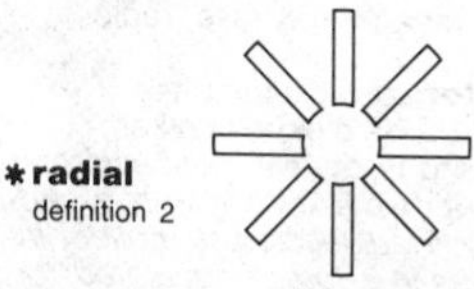
***radial** definition 2

radial pattern

***ra|di|al** (rā′dē əl), *adj., n.* – ***adj.*** **1** of or like radii or rays. **2** arranged like or in radii or rays: *At a little distance from the center the wind is probably nearly radial* (Science). **3** of the radius of a circle: *... the placing of a large fraction of the total mass at the radial distance assigned to the phosphorus atoms* (A. W. Haslett). **4** of or near the radius (a bone of the forearm): *a radial nerve; ... palpating the radial pulse at the wrist* (Time). **5** of or having to do with the arm of a starfish or other echinoderm.
– ***n.*** **1** = radial-ply tire. **2** *Biology.* a radial nerve, artery, or organ. **3** *Aeronautics.* any one of the lines of position radiating from a radio navigation facility, such as an omnirange or VOR. **4** = radial engine. – **ra′di|al|ly**, *adv.*

**radial engine**, an internal-combustion engine having radially arranged cylinders, formerly much used for aircraft.

**ra|di|al-ply tire** (rā′dē əl plī′), an automobile tire with parallel cords running at right angles to the center line of the tread.

***radial symmetry**, *Zoology.* a condition in which like parts are arranged about an axis, from which they radiate like the parts of a flower, as in many echinoderms.

**radial tire**, = radial-ply tire.

**radial velocity**, the velocity of a star along the line of sight of an observer, determined by measuring the positions of lines in the star's spectrum, usually with a spectroscope.

***radial symmetry**

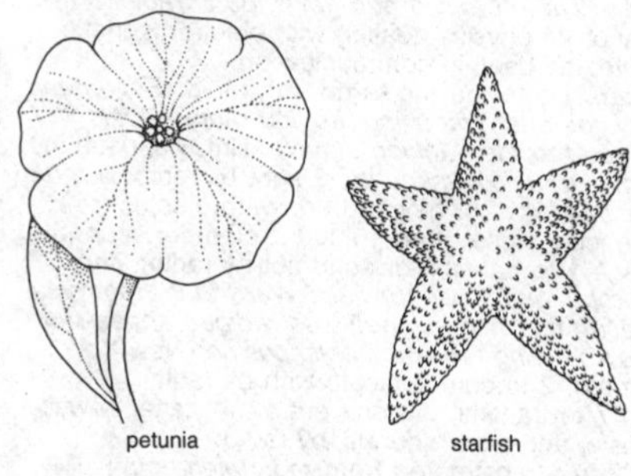


**ra|di|an** (rā′dē ən), *n.* the angle at the center of a circle, that subtends an arc of the circle equal in length to the radius; an angle of 57.2958+ degrees. *Abbr:* rad. [< *radi*(us) + *-an*]

**ra|di|ance** (rā′dē əns), *n.* **1** vivid brightness; brilliance: *the radiance of the sun,* (*Figurative.*) *the radiance of a smile.* **2** = radiation.

**ra|di|an|cy** (rā′dē ən sē), *n.* = radiance.

**ra|di|ant** (rā′dē ənt), *adj., n.* – ***adj.*** **1** shining; bright; beaming: *radiant sunshine,* (*Figurative.*) *a radiant smile.* **SYN:** See syn. under **bright. 2** sending out rays of light or heat: *The sun is a radiant body.* **3** bright with light: *The new house was radiant with light* (Arnold Bennett). **4** sent off in rays from some source; radiated: *We get radiant heat from the sun.* **5** strikingly fine or splendid, as looks or beauty, or the person: *He delighted in the radiant good looks of his betrothed* (Edith Wharton).
– ***n.*** **1** *Physics.* a point or object from which light or heat radiates. **2** the point in the heavens from which the meteors in a shower seem to have come: *The radiant of a meteoric shower is the vanishing point in the perspective of the parallel trails* (Robert H. Baker).
[< Latin *radiāns, -antis,* present participle of *radiāre* beam < *radius* beam, ray] – **ra′di|ant|ly**, *adv.*

**radiant energy**, waves of light, heat, or electricity (and, formerly, sound), that are sent out through space; energy in the form of waves, especially electromagnetic waves. X rays, radio waves, and visible light are forms of radiant energy. *Radiant energy lifted ocean water into the sky and then produced the rain that dropped to the earth to be collected and piped to your house* (Ralph E. Lapp).

**radiant flux**, *Physics.* the rate of emission of radiant energy, in watts or in ergs per second.

**radiant heat**, heat transmitted by electromagnetic radiation.

**radiant heating**, a system of heating in which a network of hot-water or steam pipes is enclosed within walls, floors, and ceiling, instead of using radiators; panel heating.

**ra|di|ate** (rā′dē āt), *v.,* **-at|ed, at|ing,** *adj., n.*
– ***v.t.*** **1** to give out rays of: *The sun radiates light and heat.* **2** to give out; send forth: (*Figurative.*) *Her face radiates joy.*
– ***v.i.*** **1** to give out rays; shine: *Many giant red stars are known to be radiating* (New Astronomy). **SYN:** glow. **2** to issue in rays: *Heat radiates from those hot steam pipes.* **3** to spread out from a center: *Roads radiate from the city in every direction.* **SYN:** diverge.
– ***adj.*** **1** having rays: *A daisy is a radiate flower.* **2** radiating from a center. **3** of an animal with a radial structure.
– ***n.*** invertebrate animal having a radial structure.
[< Latin *radiāre* (with English *-ate*¹); see etym. under **radiant**]

**ra|di|ate|ly** (rā′dē it lē), *adv.* = radially.

**ra|di|a|tion** (rā′dē ā′shən), *n.* **1** the act or process of giving out light, heat, electricity, or other radiant energy: *The sun, a lamp, or an electric heater all warm us by radiation.* **2** the energy radiated: *The steam pipes do not afford sufficient radiation for so large a room. The masses of the stars vary only from about a tenth of the solar mass to about 50 times that mass, while the total radiation emitted increases about 500,000 times* (W. H. Marshall). **3a** the action or process of giving forth radioactive rays by molecules and atoms of a radioactive substance, as a result of the disintegration of atomic nuclei: *In the high-temperature air of the shock wave ... ionization and radiation are taking place* (Atlantic). **b** the ray or rays sent out. Some radiations from atoms are alpha particles, beta particles, gamma rays, and neutrons. *The radiation from an atomic bomb is dangerous to life.* **4** divergence from a central point; radial arrangement or structure: *The beauty of a crest or bird's wing consists ... in the radiation of the plumes* (John Ruskin). **5** *Informal.* the radiators of a central heating system referred to collectively, or their capacity: *The plumbing contractor will figure out how much radiation you need.* – **ra′di|a′tion|less**, *adj.*

**ra|di|a|tion|al** (rā′dē ā′shə nəl), *adj.* of or having to do with radiation.

**radiation belt**, **1** either of two broad bands of radiation around the earth and centered on the earth's magnetic equator; Van Allen radiation belt. **2** any similar belt near either of these: *The satellite's radiation counters have revealed a radiation belt beneath the two Van Allen belts; the new belt consists of energetic protons* (Scientific American).

**radiation chemistry**, the branch of chemistry that studies the chemical influence of radiation on matter.

**radiation counter**, any device for detecting and counting radioactive rays in a given area, such as a Geiger counter.

**radiation fog**, a fog that forms when air near or along the ground at night loses warmth through outward radiation.

**radiation sickness**, a disease resulting from an overexposure to radiation from radioactive materials. It is usually characterized by nausea, diarrhea, and headache, and in severe cases by internal bleeding, changes in blood cells, loss of hair, and other symptoms.

**ra|di|a|tive** (rā′dē ā′tiv), *adj.* having to do with radiation; radiating.

**ra|di|a|tor** (rā′dē ā′tər), *n.* **1** a device for heating a room, consisting of pipes through which steam or hot water passes. **2** a device for cooling circulating water. The radiator of an automobile gives off heat very fast and so cools the water inside. **3** a person or thing that radiates: *Once their enormous distances are appreciated, it becomes clear that* [*stars*] *are radiators of vast power* (Bondi and Bondi). [< *radiat*(*e*) + *-or*]

**rad|i|cal** (rad′ə kəl), *adj., n.* – ***adj.*** **1** going to the root; fundamental; basic: *If she wants to grow thin, she must make radical changes in her diet. Radical departures from custom and tradition in dress were introduced in the 1960's.* **2** favoring extreme changes or reforms; extreme: *A global ideology ... has the power to capture radical revolutionary minds* (Newsweek). *I never dared be radical when young For fear it would make me conservative when old* (Robert Frost). **3** having to do with or forming the root of a number or quantity. **4** of or from the root or roots: *Since book is a simple word consisting of one morpheme, it may be said to contain one and only one root or radical element* (Simeon Potter). **SYN:** original, primary. **5** *Botany.* arising from the root or the base of the stem; basal. [< Late Latin *rādīcālis* < Latin *rādīx, -īcis* root]
– ***n.*** **1** a person who favors extreme changes or reforms, especially in politics; person with extreme opinions: *It was clear that he had awakened deep currents of resentment, and of hope, among young radicals in France* (Newsweek). *A radical is a man with both feet firmly planted in the air* (Franklin D. Roosevelt). **2** an atom or group of atoms acting as a unit in chemical reactions. Ammonium ($-NH_4$) is a radical in $NH_4OH$ and $NH_4Cl$, becoming part of those compounds without undergoing change, as if it were a single element instead of two or more. *Such radicals may be produced by the high-temperature decomposition of hydrocarbons such as methane,* $CH_4$*, which forms the methyl radical,* $CH_3$ (M. P. Barnett). **3** *Mathematics.* **a** an expression indicating the root of a quantity. *Examples:* $\sqrt{5}$, $\sqrt{x-3}$ **b** the mathematical sign put before an expression to show that some root of it is to be extracted; radical sign. **4** any one of a number of Chinese written characters common to many written words: *Chinese characters are classified in a dictionary under 214 radicals, or meaning indicators* (Shau Wing Chan). **5** *Linguistics, Grammar.* a word or a part of a word serving as a root on which other words are formed. *Love* is the radical of *lovely, loveliness,* and *loving.* **6** anything fundamental or basic.
[< adjective; (def. 1) < French *radical* < Middle French, adjective, learned borrowing from Late Latin *rādīcālis;* see the adjective]

**radical axis**, *Geometry.* the straight line joining

---

**Pronunciation Key:** hat, āge, cãre, fär; let, ēqual, tėrm; it, īce; hot, ōpen, ôrder; oil, out; cup, pu̇t, rüle; child; long; thin; ᴛʜen; zh, measure; ə represents **a** in about, **e** in taken, **i** in pencil, **o** in lemon, **u** in circus.

the points of intersection of two circles, or between two circles that do not intersect, from which tangents at any point to both circles will be of equal length.

**radical chic**, *U.S.* people of fashionable society who support or socialize with radicals.

**radical empiricism**, the philosophical theory proposed by William James that experience is the sole basis of and only norm for the perception of reality. —**radical empiricist**.

**radical expression**, *Mathematics.* an expression, especially an irrational number or quantity, involving a radical sign.

**rad|i|cal|ism** (rad′ə kə liz′əm), *n.* **1** the principles or practices of radicals; support or advocacy of extreme changes or reforms, especially in politics. **2** the state or condition of being radical.

**rad|i|cal|i|za|tion** (rad′ə kə lə zā′shən), *n.* **1** the process of making radical. **2** the process of becoming radical.

**rad|i|cal|ize** (rad′ə kə līz), *v.*, **-ized, -iz|ing.** —*v.t.* to make radical: *to radicalize a political system, to radicalize a student body.*
—*v.i.* to become radical: *When it* [*the Reform Bill*] *and the Catholic question were both carried ... Herbert Grimstone radicalized* (Lady Lytton).

**radical left**, = New Left.

**rad|i|cal|ly** (rad′ə klē), *adv.* **1** by root or origin; primitively; originally; naturally: *The language, which is called the Manx, is radically Erse, or Irish* (Jedidiah Morse). **2** in a radical manner; at the origin or root; fundamentally; essentially: *a radically defective system.*

**rad|i|cal|ness** (rad′ə kəl nis), *n.* the condition of being radical.

**radical right**, the reactionary or right-wing element in a country or political party that advocates radical or extremist policies: *One solution ... —to abolish the income tax—is proposed chiefly by some members of the radical right, who consider any income tax Socialistic or Communistic* (New Yorker).

**radical rightism**, the ideology of the radical right. —**radical rightist**.

***radical sign**, the mathematical sign put before a number or an expression to show that some root of it is to be found by calculation. $\sqrt{16} = $ the square root of 16 = 4. $\sqrt[3]{27} = $ the cube root of 27 = 3.

***radical sign**

$\sqrt{49}=7$

$\sqrt[3]{125}=5$

**rad|i|cand** (rad′ə kand′), *n.* the quantity placed under a radical sign. [< Latin *rādīcandus,* gerundive of *rādīcāre* take root]

**rad|i|cant** (rad′ə kənt), *adj. Botany.* producing roots from stems or leaves. [< Latin *rādīcans, -antis,* present participle of *rādīcāre;* see etym. under **radicate**]

**rad|i|cate** (rad′ə kāt), *v.*, **-cat|ed, -cat|ing,** *adj.* —*v.i.* to take root; produce roots: *Trees began ... to radicate where but lately a shrub wanted moisture* (Thomas Blount).
—*v.t.* to cause to take root; plant firmly: (*Figurative.*) *Radicate Thy Love within me, O my God, Let it be rooted deep* (Richard Welton).
—*adj. Biology.* rooted.
[< Latin *rādīcāre* (with English *-ate*[1]) < *rādīx, -īcis* root] —**rad′i|ca′tion**, *n.*

**rad|i|cel** (rad′ə səl), *n.* a little root; a rootlet or radicle. [< New Latin *radicella* (diminutive) < Latin *rādīcula* radicle]

**rad|i|ces** (rad′ə sēz, rā′də-), *n.* a plural of **radix**.

**ra|di|ci|da|tion** (rā′də sə dā′shən), *n.* the irradiation of food to destroy disease germs. [< *radi*(ation) + *-cide*[1] + *-ation*]

**rad|i|cle** (rad′ə kəl), *n.* **1** the part of a seed that develops into the main root. See picture under **embryo**. **2** a little root. **3** *Anatomy.* a rootlike part, such as one of the fibrils of a nerve fiber. **4** *Chemistry.* a radical. [< Latin *rādīcula* (diminutive) < *rādīx, -īcis* root]

**rad|ic-lib** (rad′ik lib′), *n. U.S. Informal.* a liberal with radical or leftist leanings; a radical liberal.

**ra|dic|u|lar** (ra dik′yə lər), *adj.* of or having to do with a radicle or radicles.

**ra|dic|u|lop|a|thy** (ra dik′yə lop′ə thē), *n.* a diseased condition of the roots of spinal nerves. [< Latin *rādīcula* radicle + English *-pathy*]

**ra|di|es|the|sia** (rā′dē es thē′zhə), *n.* sensitivity to invisible radiation from any source: *Radiesthesia may be involved in such psychic phenomena as reading print or identifying colors with the hands ... and dowsing* (Samuel Moffat). [< *radi*(ation) + *esthesia*]

**ra|di|i** (rā′dē ī), *n.* a plural of **radius**.

**ra|di|o** (rā′dē ō), *n., pl.* **-di|os,** *adj., v.,* **-di|oed, -di|o|ing.** —*n.* **1** the way of sending and receiving words, music, and other sounds by electric waves, without wires: *We can listen to music broadcast by radio.* **2** a device for receiving and making it possible to hear sounds so sent; receiver: *His radio cost $30.* **3** *Informal.* a message sent by radio. **4** the business of broadcasting by radio: *He left acting and got a job in radio.* **5** the branch of physics dealing with electromagnetic waves as used in communication.
—*adj.* **1** of or having to do with radio: *Seventeen minutes after launching, its first radio signals beeped to the tracking station* (Time). **2** used in radio: *a radio transmitter.* **3** sent by radio: *a radio program.* **4** of or having to do with electric frequencies higher than 15,000 cycles per second.
—*v.t.* **1** to transmit or send out by radio: *The ship radioed a call for help. Word that the proclamation had been signed was radioed ahead from the speeding Presidential limousine* (New York Times). **2** to communicate with by radio.
—*v.i.* to transmit or send out a message, news, music, and other sounds, by radio.
[< *radio-,* abstracted from *radiotelegraphy*]

**radio-**, *combining form.* **1** radio: *Radiobroadcast = a broadcast by radio.*
**2** radial; radially: *Radiosymmetrical = radially symmetrical.*
**3** radiant energy: *Radiometer = an instrument that measures radiant energy.*
**4** radioactive: *Radioisotope = a radioactive isotope.*
[< Latin *radius* (originally) ray, beam]

**ra|di|o|ac|ti|vate** (rā′dē ō ak′tə vāt), *v.t.,* **-vat|ed, -vat|ing.** to make radioactive.

**ra|di|o|ac|tive** (rā′dē ō ak′tiv), *adj.* **1** giving off radiant energy in the form of alpha, beta, or gamma rays by the breaking up of atoms. Radium, uranium, and thorium are radioactive metallic elements. *It takes some time for air currents to distribute radioactive dust across the world* (New Scientist). **2** of, having, or caused by radioactivity: *Further disposal studies showed that the 55-gallon oil drum containers, used to package radioactive wastes were very rugged* (Science News Letter). —**ra′di|o|ac′tive|ly**, *adv.*

**radioactive decay**, the spontaneous disintegration of a radioactive substance, at the characteristic rate of the particular radioisotope, and accompanied by the emission of nuclear radiation: *The spontaneous change taking place in an unstable atomic nucleus is known as radioactive decay* (The Effects of Atomic Weapons).

**radioactive series**, one of several series of isotopes of certain elements representing various stages of disintegration of a radioactive substance. Three of these series occur naturally (the actinium, thorium, and uranium series) and others, such as the neptunium series, are artificially produced.

**ra|di|o|ac|tiv|i|ty** (rā′dē ō ak tiv′ə tē), *n.* **1** the property (exhibited by certain elements) of giving off radiant energy in the form of alpha particles, beta particles, or gamma rays, as the result of spontaneous disintegration of the nuclei of atoms: *We'll have to learn to control radioactivity just as we learned to control fire* (Bulletin of Atomic Scientists). **2** the radiation given off: *How much liability insurance should a plant have against the not inconceivable possibility that it overheat and spew its radioactivity around the neighborhood?* (Newsweek).

**radio altimeter**, an altimeter which uses radio signals to measure height from the ground at low altitudes.

**radio astronomer**, an expert in radio astronomy.

**ra|di|o-as|tro|nom|i|cal** (rā′dē ō as′trə nom′ə kəl), *adj.* of or having to do with radio astronomy: *radio-astronomical observations.*

**radio astronomy**, the branch of astronomy dealing with the detection of objects in space by means of radio waves that these objects give off. Radio astronomy enables observers to study heavenly bodies beyond the range of ordinary telescopes.

**ra|di|o|au|to|graph** (rā′dē ō ô′tə graf, -gräf), *n.* a picture of an object produced on a sensitized surface, such as photographic film, by rays from some radioactive substance; autoradiograph: *Radioautographs showed that the new growing leaves drew on mature leaves for* [*phosphorus*] *until the old leaves were depleted and died* (Some Applications of Atomic Energy in Plant Science).

**ra|di|o|au|to|graph|ic** (rā′dē ō ô′tə graf′ik), *adj.* of a radioautograph or radioautography; autoradiographic.

**ra|di|o|au|tog|ra|phy** (rā′dē ō ô tog′rə fē), *n.* the process of producing radioautographs; autoradiography.

**radio beacon**, a radio station for sending special signals so that ships and airplanes can determine their position.

**radio beam**, a continuous signal by radio to show the proper course for an airplane, especially one giving the course to a certain airport.

**ra|di|o|bi|o|log|i|cal** (rā′dē ō bī′ə loj′ə kəl), *adj.* **1** of or having to do with radiobiology: *radiobiological phenomena or studies.* **2** caused by radiation: *Removal of oxygen before irradiation was found to protect cells against many kinds of radiobiological damage* (Science News Letter).

**ra|di|o|bi|ol|o|gist** (rā′dē ō bī ol′ə jist), *n.* an expert in radiobiology.

**ra|di|o|bi|ol|o|gy** (rā′dē ō bī ol′ə jē), *n.* the branch of biology dealing with the effects of radiation on animal bodies.

**ra|di|o|broad|cast** (rā′dē ō brôd′kast′, -käst′), *n., v.,* **-cast** or **-cast|ed, -cast|ing.** —*n.* **1** the action of broadcasting by radio. **2** such a broadcast.
—*v.t., v.i.* to broadcast by radio. —**ra′di|o|broad′cast′er**, *n.*

**radio car**, an automobile, such as a squad car, equipped with a two-way radio: *Several radio cars responded* (New York Times).

**ra|di|o|car|bon** (rā′dē ō kär′bən), *adj., n.* —*adj.* having to do with a method of determining the age of a substance, such as a fossil, by measuring its radioactive carbon content: *With the temperature cycles thus established, the next step was to date them by radiocarbon analysis* (Scientific American).
—*n.* a radioactive isotope of carbon, especially carbon 14.

**radiocarbon dating**, = carbon dating.

**ra|di|o|cast** (rā′dē ō kast′, -käst′), *v.,* **-cast** or **-cast|ed, -cast|ing,** *n.* —*v.t., v.i.* to broadcast by radio.
—*n.* a broadcast by radio; radiobroadcast: *In the rich voice with which he dominated the radiocast of the coronation, the archbishop was ranging through the state of Christianity around the world* (Time). —**ra′di|o|cast′er**, *n.*

**ra|di|o|ce|si|um** or **ra|di|o|cae|si|um** (rā′dē ō sē′zē əm), *n.* a radioisotope of cesium, used in radiotherapy.

**ra|di|o|chem|i|cal** (rā′dē ō kem′ə kəl), *adj., n.* —*adj.* of or having to do with radiochemistry.
—*n.* a chemical to which radioactive isotopes have been added: *It is offering a full range of radiochemicals with the addition of radioisotopes to its line of laboratory reagents* (New York Times).

**ra|di|o|chem|ist** (rā′dē ō kem′ist), *n.* an expert in radiochemistry.

**ra|di|o|chem|is|try** (rā′dē ō kem′ə strē), *n.* the branch of chemistry dealing with radioactive substances.

**ra|di|o|co|balt** (rā′dē ō kō′bôlt), *n.* a radioactive isotope of cobalt, used in radiology and radiotherapy: *A piece of radiocobalt, as big as a pea, can replace an X-ray set weighing several hundred pounds* (Atlantic).

**ra|di|o|com|pass** (rā′dē ō kum′pəs), *n.* a device for finding the direction from which radio messages are received, used to determine position, as of an aircraft or a ship at sea; radio direction finder.

**ra|di|o|con|duc|tor** (rā′dē ō kən duk′tər), *n.* a device that detects electric waves, such as a coherer in wireless telegraphy.

**ra|di|o|di|ag|no|sis** (rā′dē ō dī′əg nō′sis), *n.* medical diagnosis by means of X rays, radiographs, or the like.

**radio direction finder**, = radiocompass.

**ra|di|o|ec|o|log|i|cal** (rā′dē ō ek′ə loj′ə kəl, -ē′kə-), *adj.* of or having to do with radioecology.

**ra|di|o|e|col|o|gist** (rā′dē ō ē kol′ə jist), *n.* a specialist in radioecology: *Radioecologists collect insects and leaf samples in a forest inoculated with radioactive cesium 137* (Ralph E. Lapp).

**ra|di|o|e|col|o|gy** (rā′dē ō ē kol′ə jē), *n.* the study of radioactivity in the environment and its effect upon plants and animals, especially in a particular locality.

**ra|di|o|el|e|ment** (rā′dē ō el′ə mənt), *n.* a radioactive element, especially one produced artificially: *Weathering effects beyond two years will depend very critically upon the nature of the radioelements which then predominate in the fallout debris* (Bulletin of Atomic Scientists).

**radio emission**, the emission of radio waves by objects in space: *Giant antennae forming radio telescopes allow the observation of radio emissions of heavenly bodies* (Science News Letter).

**radio frequency**, **1** any electromagnetic wave frequency suitable for radio broadcasting, usually above 15,000 cycles per second: *Techniques using radio frequencies are therefore the method par excellence for studying low-energy transitions in atoms and molecules* (J. Little). *Abbr:* RF (no periods). **2** the frequency of the waves which transmit a particular radio broadcast. —**ra′di|o-fre′quen|cy**, *adj.*

**radio galaxy**, a galaxy that emits radio waves: *It*

*seemed likely ... that most radio sources in space ... were remote radio galaxies which emitted vast amounts of energy by unknown mechanisms* (London Times).

**ra|di|o|gen|ic** (rā′dē ō jen′ik), *adj.* **1** formed as a product of radioactivity: *radiogenic isotopes, radiogenic elements.* **2** suitable for radiobroadcasting. [< *radio-* + *-gen* + *-ic*]

**ra|di|o|ge|ol|o|gy** (rā′dē ō jē ol′ə jē), *n.* the branch of geology dealing with the relation of radioactivity to geology.

**ra|di|o|gold** (rā′dē ō gōld′), *n.* a radioisotope of gold, used in the treatment of cancer.

**ra|di|o|go|ni|om|e|ter** (rā′dē ō gō′nē om′ə tər), *n.* = radiocompass.

**ra|di|o|go|ni|o|met|ric** (rā′dē ō gō′nē ə met′rik), *adj.* **1** of or having to do with a radiogoniometer. **2** used in radiogoniometry.

**ra|di|o|go|ni|o|met|ri|cal** (rā′dē ō gō′nē ə met′rə kəl), *adj.* = radiogoniometric.

**ra|di|o|go|ni|om|e|try** (rā′dē ō gō′nē om′ə trē), *n.* the art of using a radiogoniometer.

**ra|di|o|gram**[1] (rā′dē ō gram), *n.* **1** a message transmitted by radio. **2** = radiograph.

**ra|di|o|gram**[2] (rā′dē ō gram), *n. British.* a radio-gramophone.

**ra|di|o|gram|o|phone** (rā′dē ō gram′ə fōn), *n. British.* a radio and phonograph combined in a single unit.

**ra|di|o|graph** (rā′dē ō graf, -gräf), *n., v.* —*n.* a picture produced by X rays or other rays on a photographic plate, commonly called an X-ray picture: *The radiograph was taken at the surgeon's request ... and two days later it was decided to operate* (Science News).
—*v.t.* to make a radiograph of: *At this plant the company manufactures projectors for radiographing metals* (Newsweek).

**ra|di|og|ra|pher** (rā′dē og′rə fər), *n.* a person skilled in radiography.

**ra|di|o|graph|ic** (rā′dē ō graf′ik), *adj.* of or having to do with radiographs or radiography: *a radiographic examination.*

**ra|di|o|graph|i|cal** (rā′dē ō graf′ə kəl), *adj.* = radiographic.

**ra|di|o|graph|i|cal|ly** (rā′dē ō graf′ə klē), *adv.* by radiography.

**ra|di|og|ra|phy** (rā′dē og′rə fē), *n.* the production of images on sensitized plates by means of X rays: *A field in which radium and its daughter product radon have been used for some time is industrial radiography* (Crammer and Peierls).

**ra|di|o|he|li|o|graph** (rā′dē ō hē′lē ə graf, -gräf), *n.* a device for studying and measuring radio noise emitted by the sun: *The radioheliograph has ... recorded an explosion on the sun which is one million times bigger than a 70 megaton H-bomb* (London Times).

**ra|di|o|im|mu|no|as|say** (rā′dē ō i myü′nō ə sā′, -as′ā), *n.* a method of assaying the amount or other characteristics of a substance by labeling it with a radioactive chemical and combining it with an antibody to induce an immunological reaction: *The availability of pure hormone has made possible the development of a very sensitive radioimmunoassay for the hormone* (D. Harold Copp).

**ra|di|o|im|mu|no|log|i|cal** (rā′dē ō i myü′nə loj′ə kəl), *adj.* involving the use of radioimmunoassay: *Estimation of the concentration of peptide hormones in plasma can be made by radioimmunological techniques* (John Watt McLaren).

**ra|di|o|i|o|dine** (rā′dē ō ī′ə dīn, -din, -dēn), *n.* a radioisotope of iodine, used in the treatment of thyroid disorders; iodine 131: *A given amount of radioiodine ingested appears to deliver considerably more radiation to infant thyroids than to those of adults* (Scientific American).

**ra|di|o|i|ron** (rā′dē ō ī′ərn), *n.* a radioisotope of iron, used in studying hemoglobin and red blood cells, and various kinds of anemia characterized by iron deficiency.

**ra|di|o|i|so|tope** (rā′dē ō ī′sə tōp), *n.* a radioactive isotope, especially one produced artificially: *A million medical patients are being diagnosed or treated with radioisotopes each year* (Bulletin of Atomic Scientists).

**ra|di|o|i|so|top|ic** (rā′dē ō ī′sə top′ik), *adj.* of or having to do with radioisotopes: *One satellite of each group had a radioisotopic nuclear generator* (New Scientist). —**ra′di|o|i′so|top′i|cal|ly**, *adv.*

**ra|di|o|la|beled** (rā′dē ō lā′bəld), *adj.* labeled with a radioactive isotope or other radioactive substance: *Dr. Wall ... will use radiolabeled THC [tetrahydrocannabinol] in studies of metabolism and biological distribution* (Science News).

***ra|di|o|lar|i|an** (rā′dē ō lãr′ē ən), *n., adj.* —*n.* any one of a large order of minute marine protozoans, often having a spherical body with numerous fine, radiating pseudopods and usually an outer spiny skeleton.
—*adj.* of or belonging to the radiolarians.
[< New Latin *Radiolaria* the order name < Late Latin *radiolus* (diminutive) < Latin *radius* ray]

**radio link**, the part of a communication system which transmits messages by radio waves rather than by cables or wires: *Changes in a capacitance vary the frequency of a signal transmitted by radio link to the shore* (New Scientist).

**ra|di|o|lo|ca|tion** (rā′dē ō lō kā′shən), *n. British.* the use of radar, sonar, and other electronic devices, to determine the position and course of an object.

**ra|di|o|lo|ca|tor** (rā′dē ō lō′kā tər, -lō kā′-), *n. British, Obsolete.* radar.

**ra|di|o|log|ic** (rā′dē ō loj′ik), *adj.* = radiological.

**ra|di|o|log|i|cal** (rā′dē ō loj′ə kəl), *adj.* **1** of or having to do with radiology. **2** of or having to do with the rays from radioactive substances: *A British physicist speculates on the composition and possible radiological effects of the superbomb tested in the Pacific last spring* (Bulletin of Atomic Scientists). —**ra′di|o|log′i|cal|ly**, *adv.*

**ra|di|ol|o|gist** (rā′dē ol′ə jist), *n.* an expert in radiology.

**ra|di|ol|o|gy** (rā′dē ol′ə jē), *n.* **1** the science dealing with X rays or the rays from radioactive substances, especially for medical diagnosis or treatment. **2** the art of using X rays to examine, photograph, or treat bones, organs, or certain manufactured products.

**ra|di|o|lu|cen|cy** (rā′dē ō lü′sən sē), *n.* the property of being radiolucent.

**ra|di|o|lu|cent** (rā′dē ō lü′sənt), *adj.* permitting X rays and other forms of radiation to pass through; partly or wholly radiotransparent.

**ra|di|ol|y|sis** (rā′dē ol′ə sis), *n.* the chemical decomposition of a substance resulting from the action of radiation: *Organic fluids in the radioactive environment of a reactor are subject to radiolysis* (Bulletin of Atomic Scientists). [< *radio-* + Greek *lýsis* a loosening]

**ra|di|o|lyt|ic** (rā′dē ō lit′ik), *adj.* having to do with or producing radiolysis.

**ra|di|o|man** (rā′dē ō man′), *n., pl.* **-men. 1** a member of the crew of a ship or aircraft in charge of sending and receiving radio messages. **2** a person who works in radiobroadcasting: *A group of radiomen [tried] to find out if anyone was still listening to radio in the nation's TV areas* (Time).

**ra|di|o|me|te|or|o|graph** (rā′dē ō mē′tē ər ə graf, -gräf; -mē′tē or′-), *n.* = radiosonde.

***ra|di|om|e|ter** (rā′dē om′ə tər), *n.* **1** an instrument used for indicating the transformation of radiant energy into mechanical force, consisting of an exhausted glass vessel containing vanes which revolve on an axis when exposed to light. **2** an instrument based on the same principle, but used for detecting and measuring small amounts of radiant energy.

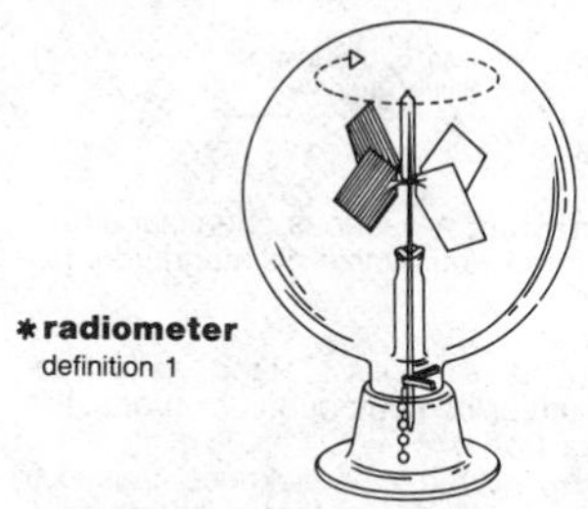
***radiometer**
definition 1

**ra|di|o|met|ric** (rā′dē ō met′rik), *adj.* having to do with the radiometer or with radiometry.

**ra|di|o|met|ri|cal|ly** (rā′dē ō met′rə klē), *adv.* by using radiometry.

**ra|di|om|e|try** (rā′dē om′ə trē), *n.* the measurement of radiant energy.

**ra|di|o|mi|crom|e|ter** (rā′dē ō mī krom′ə tər), *n.* a thermoelectric device for measuring minute changes in temperature. [< *radio-* + *micrometer*]

**ra|di|o|mi|met|ic** (rā′dē ō mi met′ik), *adj.* having an effect on living tissue almost identical with that of radiation: *a radiomimetic chemical, drug, or agent. The knowledge that substances can be "radiomimetic" is largely a product of World War II research in poison gases* (Scientific American).

**radio navigation**, navigation of an aircraft or ship with the aid of radio beacons, radiocompasses, loran, and other electronic navigational aids.

***radiolarian**

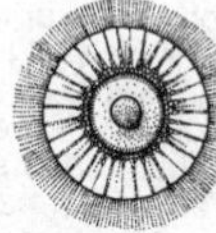

**ra|di|o|ne|cro|sis** (rā′dē ō nə krō′sis), *n., pl.* **-ses** (-sēz). necrosis brought about by irradiation.

**radio noise**, radio emission, especially from a radio star or pulsar, characterized by random or erratic changes of amplitude or frequency.

**ra|di|o|nu|clide** (rā′dē ō nü′klīd, -nyü′-), *n.* a nuclide that is radioactive: *The synthetic radioactive fallout is produced in a "hot" laboratory by processing the radionuclide, lanthanum 140* (Science News Letter).

**ra|di|o|paque** (rā′dē ō pāk′), *adj.* not transparent to X rays or other radioactive substances: *The velocity of blood flow—is easily determined by injecting a radiopaque substance into the bloodstream and measuring the rate of travel of its shadow on a film* (Scientific American).

**ra|di|o|phare** (rā′dē ō fãr), *n.* a radio station for determining the position of ships at sea. [< *radio-* + Greek *pháros* lighthouse]

**ra|di|o|phar|ma|ceu|ti|cal** (rā′dē ō fär′mə sü′tə kəl), *n.* a radioactive drug used especially for the treatment of tumors and for diagnostic purposes.

**ra|di|o|phone** (rā′dē ō fōn), *n.* = radiotelephone. [< *radio-* + *-phone*]

**ra|di|o|phon|ic** (rā′dē ō fon′ik), *adj.* having to do with the radiophone or radiophony. —**ra′di|o|phon′i|cal|ly**, *adv.*

**radio phonograph**, an appliance including both a radio receiver and a phonograph.

**ra|di|oph|o|ny** (rā′dē of′ə nē), *n.* the science or process of producing sound by the action of radiant energy.

**ra|di|o|phos|pho|rus** (rā′dē ō fos′fər əs), *n.* a radioisotope of phosphorus, used in the treatment of leukemia and other diseases of the blood.

**ra|di|o|pho|to** (rā′dē ō fō′tō), *n., pl.* **-tos. 1** = radiophotograph. **2** = radiophotography: *Still pictures taken a mere nine minutes before in London would be upon us in a moment having been miraculously transmitted by radiophoto across the broad stretches of the Atlantic* (New Yorker).

**ra|di|o|pho|to|graph** (rā′dē ō fō′tə graf, -gräf), *n.* a photograph transmitted by radio.

**ra|di|o|pho|to|graph|ic** (rā′dē ō fō′tə graf′ik), *adj.* of or by radiophotography.

**ra|di|o|pho|tog|ra|phy** (rā′dē ō fə tog′rə fē), *n.* the transmission of a photograph by radio.

**ra|di|o|phys|ics** (rā′dē ō fiz′iks), *n.* the branch of physics dealing with radioactive substances.

**radio pill**, a miniaturized radio transmitter enclosed in a plastic capsule that can be swallowed and used to transmit signals on gastrointestinal and other conditions as it passes through the body.

**ra|di|o|pro|tec|tion** (rā′dē ō prə tek′shən), *n.* protection against the effects of radiation.

**ra|di|o|pro|tec|tive** (rā′dē ō prə tek′tiv), *adj.* providing radioprotection: *Dopamine, an intermediate hormone formed by the adrenal glands in the synthesis of norepinephrine, is a good radioprotective agent* (J. Richard Thomson).

**ra|di|o|pro|tec|tor** (rā′dē ō prə tek′tər), *n.* a radioprotective drug or agent.

**radio range**, **1** the reach of a radio beam or beams emitted by a radio beacon. **2** the station emitting such beams; radio beacon.

**radio range beacon**, = radio beacon.

**ra|di|o|scope** (rā′dē ō skōp), *n.* **1** an instrument for studying and applying X rays. **2** a form of spinthariscope.

**ra|di|o|scop|ic** (rā′dē ō skop′ik), *adj.* of or having to do with the radioscope or radioscopy.

**ra|di|o|scop|i|cal** (rā′dē ō skop′ə kəl), *adj.* = radioscopic.

**ra|di|os|co|py** (rā′dē os′kə pē), *n.* the examination of opaque objects by means of X rays or other radioactive substances.

**ra|di|o|sen|si|tive** (rā′dē ō sen′sə tiv), *adj.* sensitive to X rays or other radioactivity: *a radiosensitive tumor. Another weed, Anisantha sterilis, was found remarkably radiosensitive since only 5,000 rad was lethal* (Science News Letter).

**ra|di|o|sen|si|tiv|i|ty** (rā′dē ō sen′sə tiv′ə tē), *n.* the sensitivity of tissues, organisms, or other objects, to X rays or other radioactivity: *The increased radiosensitivity of a child's body must be considered in contrast to that of the adult* (Bulletin of Atomic Scientists).

**ra|di|o|so|di|um** (rā′dē ō sō′dē əm), *n.* a radioisotope of sodium, used in studying blood circulation and water metabolism, and in the treatment of kidney and other diseases.

**ra|di|o|sonde** (rā′dē ō sond), *n.* an instrument carried into the stratosphere by means of a balloon, from which it descends by parachute, automatically reporting data on atmospheric temperature, pressure, and humidity to the ground by means of a small radio transmitter. [< *radio-* + French *sonde* depth sounding]

**radio source,** = radio star.

**radio spectrum,** the entire range of radio waves, from 3 centimeters to 30,000 meters.

**radio star,** a powerful mass of energy in space that emits radio waves instead of light waves. Radio stars are studied by radio astronomers: *There seem to be a great number of these radio stars: more than 200 are now known, and it is likely that vastly greater numbers will be found as radio telescopes are improved* (A. C. B. Lovell).

**radio station, 1** an installation consisting of radio-transmitting devices, broadcasting studios, and all other equipment necessary for radiobroadcasting. **2** an organization or department in the business of commercial broadcasting.

**ra|di|o|ster|il|i|za|tion** (rā′dē ō ster′ə lə zā′shən), *n.* sterilization of medical instruments, apparatus, and the like, by means of radioactive rays.

**ra|di|o|ster|il|ize** (rā′dē ō ster′ə līz), *v.t.,* **-ized, -iz|ing.** to sterilize by subjecting to radioactive rays: *In Europe and the U.S. several new plants for radiosterilizing medical supplies were built or ordered* (John H. Stump).

**ra|di|o|stron|ti|um** (rā′dē ō stron′shē əm, -tē-əm), *n.* a radioisotope of strontium that forms part of the fallout of a hydrogen bomb explosion; strontium 90: *Radiostrontium ... is the principal radioactive hazard to the farms and forests if atomic war comes* (Science News Letter).

**radio studio,** a room, usually with special acoustic properties, from which a radiobroadcast can be made.

**ra|di|o|sur|ger|y** (rā′dē ō sėr′jər ē), *n.* surgery involving the use of radioactive materials: *Radiosurgery on the brain without opening the skull was reported by Swedish and American neurosurgeons* (Science News Letter).

**ra|di|o|sym|met|ri|cal** (rā′dē ō si met′rə kəl), *adj.* radially symmetrical; actinomorphic.

**ra|di|o|tel|e|gram** (rā′dē ō tel′ə gram), *n.* a message transmitted by radiotelegraphy; radiogram.

**ra|di|o|tel|e|graph** (rā′dē ō tel′ə graf, -gräf), *n., v.* —*n.* **1** a telegraph transmitting by radio waves instead of by electric wires. **2** = radiotelegraphy. —*v.t., v.i.* to telegraph by radio.

**ra|di|o|tel|e|graph|ic** (rā′dē ō tel′ə graf′ik), *adj.* of or having to do with radiotelegraphy.

**ra|di|o|te|leg|ra|phy** (rā′dē ō tə leg′rə fē), *n.* system of telegraphing by radio; wireless telegraphy.

**ra|di|o|te|lem|e|ter** (rā′dē ō tə lem′ə tər), *n.* a device or apparatus for taking measurements by radiotelemetry.

**ra|di|o|tel|e|met|ric** (rā′dē ō tel′ə met′rik), *adj.* having to do with radiotelemetry.

**ra|di|o|te|lem|e|try** (rā′dē ō tə lem′ə trē), *n.* the automatic taking of measurements at distant or inaccessible points, as within a nuclear reactor, and the transmission of the data to a receiving point, specifically by means of radio: *Radiotelemetry, permitting study of heart function at any moment of exertion, had found the hidden defect in the 20-year-old runner after he had ... been checked by a cardiologist and been cleared for distance running* (San Francisco Chronicle).

**ra|di|o|tel|e|phone** (rā′dē ō tel′ə fōn), *n., v.,* **-phoned, -phon|ing.** —*n.* a radio transmitter using voice communication. —*v.t., v.i.* to telephone by radio: *[He] radiotelephoned to the White House a request to report to the nation on the crisis* (Time).

**ra|di|o|tel|e|phon|ic** (rā′dē ō tel′ə fon′ik), *adj.* of or having to do with a radiotelephone.

**ra|di|o|te|leph|o|ny** (rā′dē ō tə lef′ə nē), *n.* radio communication by means of voice signals.

**radio telescope,** a device used in radio astronomy for detecting and recording radio waves coming from stars and other objects in outer space. It consists of a radio receiver with an antenna fixed on a wide bowl-shaped reflector which collects and focuses the waves. *A great advantage of the radio telescope is that it can "see" much farther than optical instruments* (Scientific American).

**ra|di|o|ther|a|peu|tic** (rā′dē ō ther′ə pyü′tik), *adj.* of or having to do with the treatment of disease by means of X rays or radioactive agencies.

**ra|di|o|ther|a|peu|tics** (rā′dē ō ther′ə pyü′tiks), *n.* the branch of therapeutics that deals with the use of X rays or radioactive substances such as radium in the treatment of disease.

**ra|di|o|ther|a|pist** (rā′dē ō ther′ə pist), *n.* an expert in radiotherapy: *By dividing and spreading the dose radiotherapists can treat cancerous tissue with thousands of rads without excessive damage to the patient* (Scientific American).

**ra|di|o|ther|a|py** (rā′dē ō ther′ə pē), *n.* the treatment of disease by means of X rays or radioactive agencies: ... *kilocurie sources of radiocaesium for use in radiotherapy* (Bulletin of Atomic Scientists).

**ra|di|o|ther|my** (rā′dē ō thėr′mē), *n.* diathermy by a short-wave radio apparatus. [< *radio-* + Greek *thérmē* heat]

**ra|di|o|tho|ri|um** (rā′dē ō thôr′ē əm, -thōr′-), *n.* a radioactive isotope of thorium, having a mass number of 228. It is a disintegration product of mesothorium II. [< New Latin *radiothorium* < *radio-* radio- + *thorium* thorium]

**ra|di|o|tox|ic** (rā′dē ō tok′sik), *adj.* of or having to do with radiotoxins: *radiotoxic effects of irradiation.*

**ra|di|o|tox|in** (rā′dē ō tok′sən), *n.* a radioactive poison: *The radiotoxins in the [irradiated] extracts penetrate the cell nucleus and combine with certain proteins such as histones ... thus affecting the mechanism controlling the synthesis of nucleic acid* (Science Journal).

**ra|di|o|tox|o|log|ic** (rā′dē ō tok′sə loj′ik), *adj.* of or having to do with the study of radiotoxins.

**ra|di|o|trac|er** (rā′dē ō trā′sər), *n.* a radioisotopic tracer.

**ra|di|o|trans|par|ent** (rā′dē ō trans pãr′ənt), *adj.* transparent to X rays and other radioactive substances; not radiopaque: *The X rays would show exactly ... how deep the radiotransparent layers go* (Science News Letter).

**radio tube,** a vacuum tube used in a radio set.

**ra|di|o|ul|nar** (rā′dē ō ul′nər), *adj. Anatomy.* of the radius and the ulna (bones of the forearm). [< *radius* + *uln*(a) + *-ar*]

**ra|di|o|vi|sion** (rā′dē ō vizh′ən), *n.* television transmitted by radio waves.

**radio wave,** an electromagnetic wave within the radio frequencies: *Radio waves travel at the speed of light: 186,282 miles a second* (Arthur Hull Hayes).

**rad|ish** (rad′ish), *n.* **1** a small, crisp, root with a red, white, or blackish skin, used as a relish and in salads: *And under an old oak's domestic shade, Enjoy'd, spare feast! a radish and an egg* (William Cowper). **2** the plant. It belongs to the mustard family. See picture under **mustard family.** [< Middle French *radis* < Italian *radice* < Latin *rādīx, -īcis* root. See etym. of doublet **radix.**]

***ra|di|um** (rā′dē əm), *n.* a radioactive metallic chemical element found in very small amounts in uranium ores such as pitchblende. Radium is very unstable and gives off alpha particles and gamma rays as it breaks down in successive forms into radon, polonium, and, finally, lead. Radium is used in treating cancer and in making luminous paint. *Radium is never found free, but it is found combined in almost all rocks in extremely minute quantities* (Monroe M. Offner). [< New Latin *radium* < Latin *radius* ray, beam]

***radium**

| symbol | atomic number | mass number | oxidation state |
|---|---|---|---|
| Ra | 88 | 226 | 2 |

**radium emanation,** a gaseous chemical element, a product of radioactive disintegration; radon.

**radium F,** = polonium.

**ra|di|um|ize** (rā′dē ə mīz), *v.t.,* **-ized, -iz|ing.** to treat with radium or its compounds or products. —**ra′di|um|i|za′tion,** *n.*

**radium poisoning,** radiation sickness caused by the absorption of radium into the body and its deposition in bone-marrow tissue.

**ra|di|um|ther|a|py** (rā′dē əm ther′ə pē), *n.* the treatment of disease by means of radium.

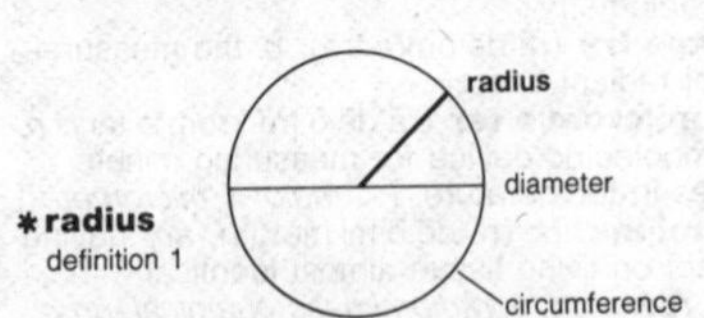


***radius**
definition 1

***ra|di|us** (rā′dē əs), *n., pl.* **-di|i** or **-di|us|es. 1** any line going straight from the center to the outside of a circle or sphere. Any spoke in a wheel is a radius. **2** a circular area measured by the length of its radius: *The explosion could be heard within a radius of ten miles.* **3a** the distance an airplane, ship, or other vehicle can travel and still have enough fuel to return: *a submarine with a cruising radius of 4,000 miles.* **b** *Figurative.* the field of operation or range of influence of anything: *the radius of Western culture.* **4a** that one of the two bones of the forearm, which is on the thumb side. **b** a corresponding bone in the forelimb of other vertebrates. **5** a line thought of as dividing an animal having radial symmetry into like parts. **6** the distance between the center and the axis of rotation in an eccentric; eccentricity. [< Latin *radius* ray, spoke of a wheel, radius bone. See etym. of doublet **ray**[1].]

**radius rod,** a rod flexibly connected, at one end to the chassis or underframe of an automobile, and at the other end to an axle.

**radius vector,** *pl.* **radii vectores** or **radius vectors. 1** *Mathematics.* a line segment, or its length, joining a fixed point and a variable point in a system of polar coordinates. See picture under **polar coordinates. 2** *Astronomy.* such a line, or distance, with the sun or other central body taken as a fixed point, and a planet, comet, or other body, as the variable point. [< New Latin *radius vector* < *radius* radius, *vector* vector]

**ra|dix** (rā′diks), *n., pl.* **rad|i|ces** or **ra|dix|es. 1** a root; radical; source or origin. **2** *Mathematics.* a number taken as the base of a system of numbers, logarithms, or the like: *The radix of the decimal system is ten.* **3** *Linguistics.* a root or etymon. **4** the root of a plant, especially a plant used in the preparation of a medicine. [< Latin *rādīx, -īcis* root. See etym. of doublet **radish.**]

**RAdm.** or **RADM.,** rear admiral.

**ra|dome** (rā′dōm), *n.* a domelike structure, usually a hemisphere of plastic, used to shelter a radar antenna that might otherwise suffer damage from the elements, as on an aircraft or in an arctic installation. [< *ra*(dar) + *dome*]

***ra|don** (rā′don), *n.* a heavy, inert, radioactive gas formed by the radioactive decay of radium. It is a rare chemical element. Radon is used in the treatment of cancer. *Radon, an alpha-emitting daughter of radium, is easily measured by its radioactivity* (Scientific American). Formerly, **niton.** [< *radium*]

***radon**

| symbol | atomic number | mass number |
|---|---|---|
| Rn | 86 | 222 |

**rad|u|la** (raj′ů lə), *n., pl.* **-lae** (-lē). a horny band in the mouth of a mollusk, set with tiny teeth: *[The limpet] gathers food into its mouth with a long tongue, or radula, which looks like a ribbon and is covered with rows of teeth* (William J. Clench). [< Latin *rādula* a scraper < *rādere* to scrape]

**rad|u|lar** (raj′ů lər), *adj.* of a radula; like a radula: *radular teeth.*

**R.A.F.** or **RAF** (no periods), Royal Air Force (of Great Britain).

**ra|fale** (rȧ fȧl′), *n. Military.* a sudden, brief, violent burst of artillery fire, repeated at intervals. [< French *rafale* (literally) squall]

**raff** (raf), *n.* **1** a quantity; heap. **2** the riffraff: *jostling with ... coal whippers, brazen women, ragged children, and the raff and refuse of the river* (Dickens). **3** *British Dialect.* rubbish. [apparently abstracted from Middle English *riffe and raff* one and all; see etym. under **riffraff**]

**raf|fi|a** (raf′ē ə), *n.* **1** the soft fiber from the leafstalks of a kind of palm tree growing on Madagascar, used in making baskets, and mats. **2a** Also, **raffia palm.** the tree from which this fiber is obtained. It is a palm tree with long, plumelike, pinnate leaves. **b** any other palm of this group. Also, **raphia.** [< Malagasy *rafia*]

**raf|fi|né** (rȧ fē nā′), *adj., n. French.* —***adj.*** refined; cultivated: *a raffiné aristocrat.* —*n.* a fashionable dandy or rake.

**raf|fi|nose** (raf′ə nōs), *n.* a colorless, crystalline sugar, present especially in sugar beets and cottonseed. It yields fructose, glucose, and galactose when hydrolyzed. *Formula:* $C_{18}H_{32}O_{16} \cdot 5H_2O$ [< French *raffiner* refine + English *-ose*[2]]

**raff|ish** (raf′ish), *adj.* **1** showy and cheap; tawdry. **2** rakish or disreputable; rowdy; dissipated. —**raff′ish|ly,** *adv.* —**raff′ish|ness,** *n.*

**raf|fle**[1] (raf′əl), *n., v.,* **-fled, -fling.** —*n.* a sale in which people each pay a small sum for a chance to win a prize: *She wore a cloth coat, preferring it to a mink stole she won in a raffle a year ago* (Newsweek). —*v.t.* to sell (an article) by a raffle. —*v.i.* to hold a raffle. [Middle English *rafle* a dice game < Old French *rafle* plundering, stripping, ultimately < Germanic (compare Dutch *rafelen* ravel, pluck)] —**raf′fler,** *n.*

**raf|fle**[2] (raf′əl), *n.* **1** = rubbish. **2** a tangle, especially of ropes, rags, and canvas. [< *raff* trash + *-le,* a diminutive suffix]

**raf|fle|sia** (ra flē′zhə), *n.* any one of a group of parasitic Malaysian plants without stems or leaves, and with a single large flower, sometimes 3 feet in diameter. [< New Latin *Rafflesia* the genus name < T. Stamford *Raffles,* 1781-1826, a British governor of Sumatra, who discovered the plant]

**raf|fle|si|a|ceous** (ra flē′zē ā′shəs), *adj.* of or belonging to the family of plants typified by the rafflesia.

**raft**[1] (raft, räft), *n., v.* —*n.* **1** logs or boards fastened together to make a floating platform: *Hav-*

*ing no boat, we had to cross the stream on a raft.* **2** any floating platform, such as used by swimmers or for life rafts.
—***v.t.*** **1** to send by raft; carry on a raft: *We crossed it* [*a river*] *... rafting over our horses and equipage* (Francis Parkman). **2** to make into a raft.
—***v.i.*** to use a raft; work on or guide a raft.
[Middle English *rafte* < Scandinavian (compare Old Icelandic *raptr* log, rafter)]

**raft**[2] (raft, räft), *n. Informal.* a large number; abundance: *a raft of troubles.* [variant of Middle English *raff* heap]

**raft|ed floe** (raf′tid), a floe in an ice field of the arctic regions that buckles and slides over another floe.

**raft|er**[1] (raf′tər, räf′-), *n.* a slanting beam of a roof: *He held the ridgepole up, and spiked again The rafters of the Home* (Edwin Markham). [Old English *ræfter*]

**raft|er**[2] (raf′tər, räf′-), *n.* a person who rafts timber.

**raft|ered** (raf′tərd, räf′-), *adj.* built with rafters; with rafters left exposed on a ceiling.

**rafts|man** (rafts′mən, räfts′-), *n., pl.* **-men.** a man who manages, or works on, a raft.

**rag**[1] (rag), *n., adj., v.,* **ragged, rag|ging.** —***n.*** **1** a torn or waste piece of cloth: *Use a clean rag to rub this mirror bright.* **2** a small piece of cloth: *We used part of an old shirt as a polishing rag.* **3** a small piece of anything of no value. **4** a shred, scrap, or fragmentary bit of anything. **5** a contemptuous or humorous term, such as for some article of clothing, a flag, a theater curtain, or a piece of paper money. **6** a beggarly, worthless, or wretched person. **7** a rough projection; jag. **8** the white, stringy core, as of an orange. **9** *Informal.* a piece of ragtime music.
—***adj.*** made from rags: *a rag rug, rag paper.*
—***v.t.*** to make ragged.
—***v.i.*** **1** to become ragged. **2** *U.S. Slang.* to dress in fine clothes.
**chew the rag,** *Slang.* to talk at length; chat: *The way as that Sam chewed the rag was just jammy* (Punch).
**rags, a** a tattered or worn-out clothes; tatters: *The base degree to which I now am fallen, These rags, this grinding ...* (Milton). **b** *Slang.* clothing: *I stood up and shook my rags off and jumped into the river* (Mark Twain). **c** extreme poverty: *We seem to have moved from rags to riches overnight* (New York Times).
[Middle English *ragge,* perhaps < Scandinavian (compare Old Icelandic *rögg* shaggy tuft), or perhaps unrecorded Old English *ragg,* implied in *raggig* raglike]

**rag**[2] (rag), *v.,* **ragged, rag|ging,** *n. Slang.* —***v.t.*** **1** to scold. **2** to play jokes on or make fun of; tease: *In a series of rough charades it rags with slapstick humour an oaf who tries to rise in society by a bourgeois marriage* (Punch). *I remember some kids were ragging me and they told me we were poor and I couldn't understand it* (Maclean's).
—***n.*** **1** the act of ragging. **2** *Especially British.* a boisterous public demonstration.
[origin uncertain]

**rag**[3] (rag), *n.* **1** a large roofing slate. **2** any one of various coarse rocks used in building: *Of shale and hornblende, rag and trap and tuff* (Tennyson). [Middle English *ragge;* origin unknown]

**ra|ga** (rä′gə), *n., pl.* **-gas.** a traditional Hindu melodic form, consisting of certain prescribed combinations of notes with regular ascending and descending patterns. [< Sanskrit *raga* (literally) color, mood]

**rag|a|muf|fin** (rag′ə muf′ən), *n.* **1** a ragged, disreputable fellow. **2** a ragged child. [probably < *rag*[1] + *muffin,* in an uncertain sense]

**rag|a|muf|fin|ly** (rag′ə muf′ən lē), *adj.* like a ragamuffin; ragged; slovenly.

**rag-and-bone man** (rag′ən bōn′), *Especially British.* a ragman.

**ra|ga-rock** (rä′gə rok′), *n.* a form of rock'n'roll using an Indian melodic form, such as the raga, and usually including a sitar or three-stringed Indian guitar among the instruments.

**ra|gaz|za** (rä gät′tsä), *n., pl.* **-ze** (-tsā). *Italian.* a girl or young woman.

**rag|bag** (rag′bag′), *n.* **1** a bag for storing rags, scraps of cloth, and the like. **2** *Figurative.* a motley collection: *The book is a ragbag of philosophical odds and ends.*

**rag bolt,** a bolt having the shank barbed so as to resist withdrawal. [< *rag*[1], in rare sense of "jagged projection" + *bolt*[1]]

**rag doll,** a limp doll made of rags or scraps of cloth: *Rag dolls are the most popular of all homemade dolls* (Nina R. Jordan).

**rage** (rāj), *n., v.,* **raged, rag|ing.** —***n.*** **1** violent anger; fury: *a voice quivering with rage. Mad with rage, he dashed into the flight.* **2** a fit of violent anger: *He flew into a rage when the other boy hit him.* **3** violence: *the rage of a savage tiger, the rage of a storm.* **4** great enthusiasm. **5** a violent feeling, appetite, or passion; frenzy: *Dinmont ... said little ... till the rage of thirst and hunger was appeased* (Scott). **6** *Obsolete.* madness; insanity: *The great rage, You see is kill'd in him* (Shakespeare).
—***v.i.*** **1** to be furious with anger. **2** to talk or move with furious anger: *Keep your temper; don't rage.* **3** to act violently; move, proceed, or continue with great violence: *The wind rages wildly. The fire raged. A heavy gulf thunderstorm was raging* (Joseph Conrad).
**the rage,** what everybody wants for a short time; the fashion; craze; fad: *Red ties were all the rage last year. Rocking chairs became the rage* (Carol L. Thompson).
[< Old French *rage* < Vulgar Latin *rabia* < Latin *rabiēs* madness. See etym. of doublet **rabies.**]
—***Syn.*** *n.* **1 Rage, fury** mean violent anger. **Rage** means anger so great and strong that a person or animal loses control over his feelings or good judgment and acts or speaks violently or coldly turns his mind to finding a way to get even: *In his rage at being publicly punished, he broke the teacher's favorite vase.* **Fury** means rage so wild and fierce that it destroys common sense and makes a person into an enraged wild animal, wanting to harm and destroy: *In its fury the mob went through the streets wrecking cars.*

**rage|ful** (rāj′fəl), *adj.* full of rage. —**rage′ful|ly,** *adv.*

**rag|ged** (rag′id), *adj.* **1** worn or torn into rags; tattered: *ragged clothing.* **SYN:** rent, frayed. **2** wearing torn or badly worn-out clothing: *a ragged urchin of the streets.* **3** not smooth and tidy; rough: *an old dog's ragged coat, a ragged garden.* **4** having loose shreds or bits: *a ragged wound.* **5** having rough or sharp points; uneven; jagged: *ragged rocks.* **6** harsh: *a ragged voice.* **7** faulty; imperfect; irregular: *ragged rhyme.*
—**rag′ged|ly,** *adv.* —**rag′ged|ness,** *n.*

**ragged edge,** the very edge; brink: *on the ragged edge of mental collapse.*

**ragged robin,** a perennial plant, a lychnis with ragged-looking, pink or white petals; cuckooflower.

**rag|ged|y** (rag′ə dē), *adj.,* **-ged|i|er, -ged|i|est.** ragged: *a raggedy coat. Oh, the Raggedy Man he works for Pa* (James Whitcomb Riley).

**rag|gee** or **rag|gi** (rag′ē), *n.* an East Indian cereal grass, grown in Asia for its grain. [< Hindustani *rāgī*]

**rag|get|y** (rag′ə tē), *adj.,* **-get|i|er, -get|i|est.** *Especially British.* raggedy.

**rag|gle** (rag′əl), *n.* a groove cut in stone, especially on a wall to receive the end or edge of a roof. [origin uncertain]

**rag|gle-tag|gle** (rag′əl tag′əl), *adj. Informal or Dialect.* slipshod; slovenly; raggedy: *Next came the pedlars, a genial, raggle-taggle, clownish company, all around the church* (Manchester Guardian). [< *ragtag*]

**rag|gy** (rag′ē), *adj.,* **-gi|er, -gi|est.** *Dialect.* ragged.

**rag|i** (rag′ē), *n.* = raggee.

**rag|ing** (rā′jing), *adj.* that rages; violent, as a tempest, or as disease or pain; furious: *a raging fever, raging anger.* —**rag′ing|ly,** *adv.*

***rag|lan** (rag′lən), *adj., n.* —***adj.*** having sleeves cut so as to continue up to the collar: *a raglan topcoat.*
—***n.*** a loose topcoat or overcoat with sleeves cut so as to continue up to the collar.
[< Baron *Raglan,* 1788-1855, British field marshal]

***raglan**
***raglan sleeve**

***raglan sleeve,** a sleeve cut so as to continue up to the collar.

**rag|like** (rag′līk′), *adj.* like a rag.

**rag|man** (rag′man′), *n., pl.* **-men.** a man who gathers, buys, or sells rags, old newspapers, and magazines.

**Rag|na|rok** (räg′nə rok′), *n. Norse Mythology.* the destruction of the world in the war between the gods and the forces of evil led by Loki; Twilight of the Gods.

**ra|gout** (ra gü′), *n., v.,* **-gouted** (-güd′), **-gout|ing** (-gü′ing), —***n.*** a highly seasoned stew of meat and vegetables.
—***v.t.*** to make into a ragout.
[< French *ragoût* < Middle French *ragoûter* restore the appetite < *re-* back, re- + *à* to (< Latin *ad*)+ *goût* < Latin *gustus, -ūs* taste]

**rag|pick|er** (rag′pik′ər), *n.* a person who picks up rags and other waste material from the streets, rubbish heaps, or trash baskets.

**rags** (ragz), *n.pl.* See under **rag**[1].

**rag|stone** (rag′stōn′), *n. British.* a roofing slate or building stone; a coarse sandstone. [< *rag*[3] + *stone*]

**rag|tag** (rag′tag′), *n., adj.* —***n.*** the riffraff; rabble.
—***adj.*** *U.S. Informal.* characteristic or consisting of riffraff: *His forces had been whittled down to a ragtag band* (Newsweek).

**ragtag and bobtail,** = ragtag.

**rag|time** (rag′tīm′), *n.* **1** a musical rhythm with regular beat in the base and accents falling at unusual places in the treble. **2** music with such a configuration of rhythm. It is generally considered a form of jazz. [American English; perhaps earlier *ragged time* (because of the rhythm)]

**rag trade,** *Slang.* the garment industry.

**rag trader,** *Slang.* a clothes merchant; retailer of clothing.

**rag|u|ly** (rag′yə lē), *adj. Heraldry.* (of a division on an escutcheon) having alternate projections and depressions like a battlement, but set obliquely. [origin uncertain] See picture at **heraldry.**

**rag|weed** (rag′wēd′), *n.* **1** any one of several coarse weeds whose pollen is one of the most common causes of hay fever. Ragweed belongs to the composite family. **2** *U.S. Dialect.* the marsh elder. **3** *British.* ragwort.

**rag|worm** (rag′wėrm′), *n.* any one of various nereid worms of the European coast, much used as bait.

**rag|wort** (rag′wėrt′), *n.* any one of various composite plants with irregularly lobed leaves and yellow flowers.

**rah** (rä), *interj., n.* = hurrah. [American English, short for *hurrah*]

**rah-rah** (rä′rä′), *interj., n., adj.* —***interj., n.*** = hurrah.
—***adj.*** *Informal.* characteristic of college cheering and youthful enthusiasm often associated with college life; collegiate: *rah-rah spectator sports.*

**raid** (rād), *n., v.* —***n.*** **1** an attack; sudden attack: *Each venture Is a new beginning, a raid on the inarticulate With shabby equipment always deteriorating* (T. S. Eliot). **2** a sudden attack, usually by a small force having no intention of holding the territory invaded: *an enemy air raid. The pirates planned a raid on the harbor.* **3** an entering and seizing what is inside: *a police raid. The hungry boys made a raid on the pantry.* **4** *Figurative.* a predatory, often unscrupulous incursion into the domain of another for the purpose of securing something: *a raid by one union on the membership of another, a raid by a college on the faculty of another.* **5** a deliberate attempt by speculators to force down prices on stock exchanges.
—***v.t.*** **1** to attack suddenly: *The enemy raided our camp.* **2** to force a way into; enter and seize what is in: *The police raided the house looking for stolen jewels.* **3** to make a raid upon: (*Figurative.*) [*The university*] *is out to raid faculties from coast to coast* (Time).
—***v.i.*** to engage in a raid.
[Northern English form of Old English *rād* a riding. Compare etym. under **road.**] —**raid′er,** *n.*

**rail**[1] (rāl), *n., v.* —***n.*** **1** a bar of wood or of metal: There are stair rails, fence rails, altar rails, and rails protecting monuments. Bars laid along the ground for a railroad track are called rails. **2** a fence enclosing a race track: *The jockey rode the horse near the rail.* **3** = railroad: *We travel by rail and by boat.* **4** the upper part of the bulwarks of a ship. **5** a horizontal board or piece in a framework or paneling: *a chair rail.*
—***v.t.*** **1** to furnish with rails. **2** to enclose with bars.
**off the rails,** *Especially British.* out of the proper or normal condition; out of control; haywire: *At that time it seemed to me the national government was going seriously off the rails* (Walter Gordon).
**rail in,** to enclose within a fence: *A space was railed in for the reception of the ... jurors* (Maria Edgeworth).
**rail off,** to separate by a fence: *They railed off a space for the horses. The footpaths were railed*

*off along the whole distance* (James A. Froude). [< Old French *reille* < Latin *rēgula* straight rod, related to *regere* to straighten. See etym. of doublet **rule**.]

**rail**[2] (rāl), *v.i.* to complain bitterly; use violent and reproachful language: *He railed at his hard luck. Poets, like disputants, when reasons fail, Have one sure refuge left, and that's to rail* (John Dryden). *Why rail at fate? The mischief is your own* (John G. Whittier). **SYN**: scold, revile, upbraid.
— *v.t.* to bring or force by railing. **SYN**: scold, revile, upbraid.
[< Middle French *railler* < Old Provençal *ralhar,* probably < Vulgar Latin *ragulāre,* for Late Latin *ragere* to bray, brawl. See etym. of doublet **rally**[2].] — **rail′er**, *n.*

**rail**[3] (rāl), *n., pl.* **rails** or (*collectively*) **rail**. a small, dull-colored wading bird with short wings, a plump body, long toes, and a harsh cry. It lives in marshes and swamps. There are numerous kinds. [< Old French *raale,* perhaps < *raler* to rattle; perhaps imitative]

**rail**[4] (rāl), *n. Archaic.* **1** a garment; cloak. **2** a kerchief. [Old English *hrægl*]

**rail|bird**[1] (rāl′bėrd′), *n. U.S. Slang.* a person fond of watching horse races and workouts from a position at the rail of the track.

**rail|bird**[2] (rāl′bėrd′), *n. U.S.* a rail, especially the Carolina rail or sora.

**rail|car** (rāl′kär′), *n.* a railroad car other than an engine, having its own power unit and used to transport passengers or freight.

**railcar train**, a passenger train pulled by a railcar: *Other ... railcar trains include the gas-turbine electric trains called turbo-trains* (Gus Welty).

**rail|head** (rāl′hed′), *n.* **1** the farthest point to which the rails of a railroad have been laid. **2** a place on a railroad where supplies for troops are unloaded. **3** the upper part of a steel rail with which the cars come in contact. **4** *Figurative.* a farthest point: *somewhere beyond the railheads Of reason, south or north, Lies a magnetic mountain Riveting sky to earth* (C. Day Lewis).

**rail|ing** (rā′ling), *n.* **1** a fence made of rails, rails and supports, or the like. **SYN**: balustrade. **2** material for rails. **3** rails: *A pile of railing lay by the barn.*

**rail joint**, = angle bar.

**rail|ler|y** (rā′lər ē), *n., pl.* **-ler|ies**. **1** good-humored ridicule; teasing; joking. **SYN**: badinage, persiflage. **2** a bantering remark. [< French *raillerie* < Middle French *railler;* see etym. under **rail**[2]]

**rail|man** (rāl′man′), *n., pl.* **-men**. **1** an owner or executive of a railroad company. **2** a person who works on a railroad; railroader.

**rail|road** (rāl′rōd′), *n., v.* — *n.* **1** a road or track with parallel steel rails on which the wheels of the cars go. Engines usually pull trains on railroads. **2a** the tracks, stations, trains, and other property of a system of transportation that uses rails, together with the people who manage them: *The Columbia was a turbulent river ... It had its era of steamboats, which gave way in time to the railroads* (Newsweek). **b** the people, such as a company or corporation, who manage a railroad. *Abbr:* R.R. **3** *Bowling.* a split, especially one that leaves the 7 and 10 pins standing. **4** (in court tennis) a hard overhead serve made near the wall at the left of the server as he faces the net: *Both men are left-handers and both consistently served a railroad* (London Times).
— *v.i.* to work on a railroad.
— *v.t. U.S.* **1** to send by railroad; carry on a railroad. **2** *Informal, Figurative.* to send along quickly or too quickly to be fair: *His enemies tried to railroad him to prison without a fair trial.*

**rail|road|er** (rāl′rō′dər), *n. U.S.* **1** a person who works on a railroad. **2** a person who owns or operates a railroad.

***railroad flat**, an apartment in which the rooms are lined up in a row like boxcars: *In some of the row houses, railroad flats run from front to back* (Harper's).

**rail|road|i|a|na** (rāl′rō dē ä′nə, -an′ə, -ā′nə), *n.pl.* a collection of books, documents, facts, and other paraphernalia, about railroads.

**rail|road|ing** (rāl′rō′ding), *n. U.S.* **1** the construction or operation of railroads. **2** *Informal, Figurative.* the act or process of hurrying (a thing or person) along: *The principal felt as if parents were railroading him into a decision.*

**rail|road|man** (rāl′rōd′man′, -mən), *n., pl.* **-men**. *Especially U.S.* a railroader.

**railroad worm**, = apple maggot.

**rail|split|ter** (rāl′split′ər), *n. U.S.* a person who splits logs into fence rails.
**the railsplitter** or **Railsplitter**, Abraham Lincoln: *The railsplitter had defeated the man full of words ... Truth gave the victory to Lincoln; a trick bestowed the Senatorship upon Douglas* (Margaret L. Coit).

**rail tongs**, tongs used by tracklayers for lifting rails.

**rail|way** (rāl′wā′), *n.* **1** *Especially British.* a railroad. *Abbr:* Ry. **2** any track made of rails: *a cog railway.* **3** a streetcar line.

**railway beetle**, a firefly of Paraguay, about three inches long, that emits flashes of red and green lights suggestive of railway signals.

**rail|wayed** (rāl′wād′), *adj.* having railways.

**rail|way|man** (rāl′wā′man′, -mən), *n., pl.* **-men**. *Especially British.* a railroader.

**railway stitch**, an embroidery stitch consisting of a loop of thread held in place by a small stitch.

**rail|work|er** (rāl′wėr′kər), *n.* a person who works for a railroad.

**rai|ment** (rā′mənt), *n.* clothing; garments. [Middle English *raiment,* short for *arraiment* < *array,* verb]

**rain** (rān), *n., v.* — *n.* **1** water falling in drops from the clouds. Rain is formed from moisture condensed from water vapor in the atmosphere. *The rain spattered the window.* **2** the fall of such drops; shower or rainstorm: *a hard rain.* **3** *Figurative.* a thick, fast fall of anything: *a rain of bullets, a rain of tears.*
— *v.i.* **1** to fall in drops of water: *It rained all day.* **2** *Figurative.* to fall like rain: *Sparks rained down from the burning roof.* **3** to pour down rain.
— *v.t.* **1** to send down (rain): *I will rain upon him ... an overflowing rain, and great hailstones* (Ezekiel 38:22). **2** *Figurative: The children rained flowers on the May queen.* **SYN**: shower.
**it never rains but it pours**, events of a kind, especially misfortunes, come all together: *As it never rains but it pours, news of another disaster was rife in the city in the evening* (Earl Dunmore).
**rain off**, *British.* to rain out: *An open-air meeting was rained off, but pickets patrolled the dock entrances* (London Times).
**rain out**, to cancel because of rain: *The second game of the scheduled double-header was rained out in the third inning with Cincinnati leading* (New York Times).
**the rains**, the rainy season; the seasonal rainfalls: *The heavy tropical rains are usually confined to definite periods* (Thomas Henry Huxley).
[Old English *regn*]

**rain|band** (rān′band′), *n.* a dark band in the solar spectrum, due to the water vapor in the atmosphere.

**rain|bar|rel** (rān′bar′əl), *n.* a barrel used to collect rain water for drinking or washing.

**rain|bird** (rān′bėrd′), *n.* any one of several kinds of birds, such as the green woodpecker or the Jamaican cuckoo, supposed to foretell rain by its cries or actions: *From a group of trees came the liquid call of the rainbird* (Cape Times).

***railroad flat**

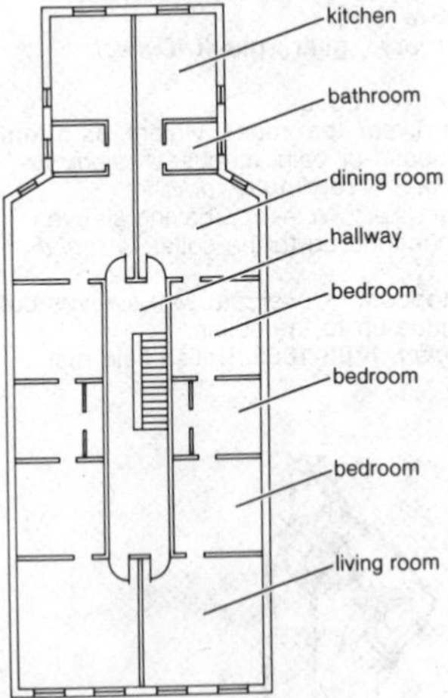


**rain|bow** (rān′bō′), *n., adj., v.* — *n.* **1** a bow or arch of seven colors seen sometimes in the sky, or in mist or spray when the sun shines on it from behind the observer; iris. A rainbow shows all the colors of the spectrum: violet, indigo, blue, green, yellow, orange, and red. *The rainbow, one of the most beautiful of natural phenomena, is a spectrum produced by the dispersion of sunlight by spherical raindrops* (John Charles Duncan). *There was a rainbow round about the throne* (Revelation 4:3). **2** anything similar, such as a lunar rainbow or moonbow. **3** = rainbow trout.
— *adj.* **1** having to do with a rainbow. **2** *Figurative.* having many colors like a rainbow: *the endless parrot-tribe with their rainbow hues* (William H. Prescott).
— *v.t.* to brighten or span with a rainbow: (*Figurative.*) *The great bridge rainbows the skyline* (Manchester Guardian Weekly).
— *v.i.* to take the form or color pattern of a rainbow: *The sails ... rainbowed with small signalling flags* (London Times).
[Old English *regnboga* < *regn* rain + *boga* bow, curve, arch]

**rainbow darter**, a brightly-colored darter, found in the tributaries of the Mississippi River and eastward.

**rainbow fish**, = guppy.

**rainbow horse**, = Appaloosa.

**rainbow lorikeet**, a lorikeet of many bright colors, found from the East Indies and Australia east to New Hebrides.

**rainbow runner**, a carangoid fish of the Indian and Pacific oceans, about four feet long, and having a very bright blue color on the back and a yellow stripe bordered with blue along the side of the body.

**rainbow snake**, a burrowing snake of the southeastern United States which has a red belly and red or yellow striped back; hoop snake.

**rainbow trout**, a large trout which is native to western North America and has been introduced in other areas, named for its bright pinkish coloring. A rainbow trout that has entered or returned from the sea is called a steelhead.

**rain|bow|y** (rān′bō′ē), *adj.* of or like a rainbow: *rainbowy colors.*

**rain|cape** (rān′kāp′), *n.* a waterproof cape for protection from rain.

**rain check**, **1** a ticket for future use, given to the spectators at a baseball game or other outdoor performance stopped by rain. **2** *Figurative: I can't accept your luncheon invitation today, but I'll gladly take a rain check on it.*

**rain cloud**, a cloud from which rain falls.

**rain|coat** (rān′kōt′), *n.* a waterproof coat worn for protection from rain.

**rain|coat|ed** (rān′kō′tid), *adj.* wearing a raincoat.

**rain crow**, a North American cuckoo, especially the black-billed cuckoo, so called from the belief that its frequent calls predict rain.

**rain dance**, a ritual dance, performed by many primitive peoples, to bring rain.

**rain|drop** (rān′drop′), *n.* a drop of rain: *Raindrops fall at a speed of about 500 to 1,000 feet a minute* (Science News Letter).

**rain|fall** (rāl′fôl′), *n.* **1** a shower of rain: *The existence of both crystals and droplets within one cloud will always greatly facilitate rainfall* (Eric Kraus). **2** the amount of water in the form of rain, sleet, or snow that falls within a given time and area: *The yearly rainfall in New York is much greater than that in Arizona.*

**rain forest**, a large, very dense forest in a region where rain is very heavy throughout the year. Rain forests are usually in tropical areas, but sometimes in northern areas, such as southeastern Alaska: *The ... dense, steamy rain forests of Australia and New Guinea, where the sun seldom penetrates* (Scientific American).

**rain|fowl** (rān′foul′), *n.* a bird supposed to foretell rain by its cries or actions, especially by being noisy or uneasy.

**rain gauge**, an instrument for measuring rainfall.

**rain|i|ly** (rā′nə lē), *adv.* in a rainy manner; with rain falling.

**rain|i|ness** (rā′nē nis), *n.* a rainy condition.

**rain|less** (rān′lis), *adj.* without rain: *a rainless region or season.* — **rain′less|ness**, *n.*

**rain|mak|er** (rān′mā′kər), *n.* a person who tries to produce rain, especially by supernatural or artificial means: *At least two states—Massachusetts and Maryland—are turning to professional rainmakers in an effort to get the farmers some moisture* (Wall Street Journal).

**rain|mak|ing** (rān′mā′king), *n., adj.* — *n.* the producing of rain by artificial or supernatural means. One method is to scatter crystals of silver iodide or dry ice into a cloud from an airplane. As the crystals heat up and expand they collect particles of moisture and build up a heavy moisture concentration within the cloud. When this becomes too heavy to hold, the cloud releases it as rain. *When scientific rainmaking was invented in the U.S. in the late 1940's, it seemed that at last man could do something about the weather* (Time).
— *adj.* producing or attempting to produce rain: *rainmaking ceremonies.*

**rain|out** (rān′out′), *n.* **1a** the postponement or cancellation of an outdoor event, such as a ball game or concert, because of rain: *In case of a rainout, the next two nights are available* (New York Times). **b** an event that is rained out. **2** precipitation of radioactive water droplets due to an underwater nuclear explosion or unfavorable atmospheric conditions.

**rain|proof** (rān′prüf′), *adj., v.* — *adj.* that will not let rain through; impervious to rain; waterproof.
— *v.t.* to make impervious to rain.

**rains** (rānz), *n.pl.* See under **rain**.

**rain|show|er** (rān′shou′ər), *n.* a shower of rain: *The Weather Bureau described it as "a good rainshower," but said only .02 inches had been measured* (New York Times).
**rain|spout** (rān′spout′), *n.* a spout draining the gutter of a roof; downspout.
**rain|squall** (rān′skwôl′), *n.* a sudden, violent wind accompanied by rain: *Recovery helicopters ... flapped blindly through rainsqualls and fog in a vain search for the spacecraft* (Time).
**rain|suit** (rān′süt′), *n.* a suit made to be worn in rain or rainy weather: *... poplin rainsuits with matching sou'westers* (Sunday Telegraph).
**rain|swept** (rān′swept′), *adj.* exposed to driving rain: *a rainswept courtyard.*
**rain|storm** (rān′stôrm′), *n.* a storm with much rain.
**rain tree**, = monkeypod.
**rain|wash** (rān′wosh′, -wôsh′), *n.* **1** the action of washing along or away by the force of rain: *Rainwash on hill slopes marks the initial stage in the movement of the surface waters that are gathered later into well-defined streams and rivers* (Gilluly, Waters, and Woodford). **2** displacement of soil, sand, or rocks, brought about by rainfall: *Shells were also found in pre-Roman rainwash at Northfleet* (London Times).
**rain water**, or **rain|wa|ter** (rān′wôt′ər, -wot′-), *n.* water that has fallen as rain.
**rain|wear** (rān′wãr′), *n.* clothes made to be worn in the rain, such as raincoats and rubbers; rainproof clothes.
**rain|y** (rā′nē), *adj.,* **rain|i|er, rain|i|est. 1** having rain; having much rain: *April is a rainy month. When the wind was easterly, the weather was gloomy, dark, and rainy* (John H. Moore). **2** bringing rain: *The sky is filled with dark, rainy clouds.* **3** wet with rain: *rainy streets.*
**rainy day**, a possible time of greater need in the future: *to save money for a rainy day.*
**rais|a|ble** (rā′zə bəl), *adj.* that can be raised.
**raise** (rāz), *v.,* **raised, rais|ing,** *n.* **—*v.t.* 1** to lift up; put up; move to a higher place: *Children in school raise their hands to answer a question. The soldiers raised a white flag.* **2** to set upright: *Raise the overturned lamp.* **3** to cause to rise: *The automobiles raised a cloud of dust.* **4** *Figurative.* to put or take into a higher position; make higher or nobler; elevate: *to raise a salesman to manager. The boy raised himself by hard study to be a great lawyer.* **SYN:** promote, advance, exalt. **5** to increase in amount, price, or pay: *to raise prices, to raise the rent.* **6** to increase in degree, intensity, or force: *to raise one's courage. I cannot hear you; please raise your voice.* **7** to make of higher pitch. **8** to bet or bid more than (another player or another bet or bid, as in poker or bridge or at an auction). **9** to bring together; get together; gather together; collect; manage to get: *to raise funds. The leader raised an army.* **SYN:** muster. **10** to make grow; help to grow; breed: *The farmer raises chickens and corn.* **11** to bring into being. **12** to cause to appear: *to raise the ghost of Napoleon.* **13** to bring about; cause: *A funny remark raises a laugh.* **14** to utter (as a cry); produce (a noise): *to raise a shout.* **15** to build; build up; set up; create; produce; start: *People raise monuments to soldiers who have died for their country.* **16** *Figurative.* to rouse; stir up: *to raise prejudice. The dog raised a rabbit from the underbrush and was chasing it.* **17** to bring up; rear: *Parents raise their children.* **18** to cause to become light and spongy in texture and to swell: *The action of yeast raises bread.* **19** to bring back to life: *to raise the dead.* **20a** to put an end to: *Our soldiers raised the siege of the fort by driving away the enemy.* **b** to break up and remove: *Captain Bonneville and his confederate Indians raised their camp* (Washington Irving). **21** to come in sight of: *After a long voyage the ship raised land.* **22** to call attention to; pose: *to raise a question.* **23** to falsify the value of (as a check or note) by making the sum larger.
**—*v.i.* 1** *U.S.* to rise to the top; attain a higher level or position: *The water having raised ... I could form no accurate judgment of the progress* (George Washington). **2** to increase one's bid or bet at an auction or in games.
**—*n.* 1** a raised place. **2** *U.S.* an increase in amount, price, or pay: *The janitor got a raise in his monthly wages.* **3** the amount of such an increase. **4** *Mining.* a passage or shaft driven upward to connect one level with a higher one.
[Middle English *reisen* < Scandinavian (compare Old Icelandic *reisa,* related to Old English *rǣran*). See related etym. at **rear**[2].]
**—*Syn.*** *v.t.* **1, 2 Raise, lift, elevate** mean to move something to a higher position. **Raise** means to bring something to a high or, especially, vertical position or to move it up from a lower to a higher level: *to raise a ladder or a window shade.* **Lift** means to take something, usually heavy, from the ground or other low level: *Please lift the table.* **Elevate**, a more formal term, means to bring something to a higher position or level: *The flag was elevated from half-mast to the top of the mast.*
► **raise, rear.** *Raise* is good informal usage in the sense of bring up: *He was born and raised in Oregon. Rear* is formal in this sense: *He was reared in the South. Bring up* in this sense is used in all levels: *He was brought up by his grandparents.*
**raised** (rāzd), *adj.* **1** made light with yeast, not with baking powder: *raised doughnuts.* **2** embossed: *the raised figure of a horse.*
**rais|er** (rā′zər), *n.* a person who grows or raises things: *a cattle raiser.*
**rai|sin** (rā′zən), *n.* **1** a sweet, dried grape. It is used especially in cooking and baking. **2** a dark-purple color with a bluish tinge. [< Old French *raizin* < Latin *racēmus* cluster (of grapes or berries). See etym. of doublet **raceme.**]
**rais|ing** (rā′zing), *n.* **1** the act of lifting up. **2** a raised place. **3** the process of bringing up the nap of cloth by carding with teasels. **4** the process of embossing or ornamenting sheet metal by hammering, spinning, or stamping.
**rai|son d'é|tat** (re zôɴ′ dā tá′), *French.* political reason; reason of state.
**rai|son d'ê|tre** (re zôɴ′ de′trə), *French.* reason for being; justification: *The raison d'être for a strategic weapon is to deter* (Bulletin of Atomic Scientists).
**rai|son|né** (re zô nā′), *adj. French.* systematic; logical.
**rai|son|neur** (re zô nœr′), *n.* a character, especially in a play or novel, who rationalizes, explains, or comments upon the actions of the other characters: *Ferdyshenko ... is brought on [in a stage production of Dostoevsky's "The Idiot"] as a guide and raisonneur, to nudge, chuckle and underline such points as have been elaborated before our eyes* (Manchester Guardian Weekly). [< French *raisonneur* reasoner, rationalizer]
**raj** (räj), *n.* (in India) rule; dominion: *the British raj.* [< Hindi *rāj*]
**Ra|jab** (rä jäb′), *n.* the seventh month of the Moslem year. It has 30 days. [< Arabic *Rajab*]
**ra|jah** or **ra|ja** (rä′jə), *n.* **1** a ruler or chief in India, Java, Borneo, and some other Eastern countries. **2** a title given to important Hindus in India. [< Hindi *rājā* < Sanskrit, nominative of *rājan* king]
**ra|jah|ship** or **ra|ja|ship** (rä′jə ship), *n.* **1** the office, rank, or authority of a rajah. **2** the territory ruled by a rajah.
**Ra|jas|tha|ni** (rä′jə stä′nē), *n., adj.* **—*n.* 1** the Indic language of Rajasthan, a state of northwestern India. **2** a native or inhabitant of Rajasthan.
**—*adj.*** of or having to do with Rajasthan or Rajasthanis: *Rajasthani dancing, Rajasthani customs.*
**Raj|put** or **Raj|poot** (räj′püt), *n.* a member of a Hindu military, landowning, and ruling caste. [< Hindi *rājpūt* < Sanskrit *rājaputra* king's son]
**Raj|ya Sab|ha** (räj′yə sub′hä), the upper house of the parliament of India: *The Union Parliament consists of the Council of States* (*Rajya Sabha*) *and a House of the People* (*Lok Sabha*) (Donovan Rowse).
**rake**[1] (rāk), *n., v.,* **raked, rak|ing. —*n.* 1a** a long-handled tool having a bar at one end with teeth in it. A rake is used for smoothing the soil or gathering together loose leaves, hay, or straw. **b** a machine used to gather mowed hay and place it in windrows. **2** any one of various tools or instruments similar to a rake. A croupier uses a rake to gather together money or chips at a gambling table.
**—*v.t.* 1** to move with a rake: *Rake the leaves off the grass.* **2** to make clear, clean, or smooth with a rake: *Rake the yard.* **3** to gather; gather together. **4** *Figurative.* to search carefully: *I raked the ads for a bicycle for sale.* **5** to fire guns along the length of (a ship or a line of soldiers). **6** to bring up (something) forgotten or unknown: *to rake up an old scandal.*
**—*v.i.* 1** to use a rake: *I like to rake.* **2** to search with a rake. **3** *Figurative.* to scrape or sweep: *The sea rakes against the shore.*
[Old English *raca*] **—rak′er,** *n.*
**rake**[2] (rāk), *n.* a person who shamelessly indulges in vice; immoral or dissolute person: *gambling half the day with the rakes and dandies of the fashionable club* (Edith Wharton). [short for *rakehell*]
**rake**[3] (rāk), *n., v.,* **raked, rak|ing. —*n.* 1** a slant; slope. A ship's smokestacks have a slight backward rake. **2** the inward slant between the leading and trailing edges on the wing tip of an airplane. **3** the angle between a cutting tool and the surface of the work.
**—*v.i., v.t.*** to slant or cause to slant.
[origin uncertain]
**rake**[4] (rāk), *v.i.,* **raked, rak|ing. 1** (of a hawk) to fly along after the game or to fly wide of it. **2** (of a dog) to hunt with the nose close to the ground. [probably Old English *racian*]
**ra|kee** (rä kē′, rak′ē), *n.* = raki.
**rake|hell** (rāk′hel′), *n., adj.* a dissolute or immoral person; rake; profligate: [*This*] *man of the world and Broadway rakehell, makes his true confession ...* (New York Times). [probably alteration of Middle English *rakel,* also *rackle* rough, hasty (perhaps influenced by *rake*[1] to search) + *hell*]
**rake|hell|y** (rāk′hel′ē), *adj.* profligate; dissolute; recklessly extravagant.
**rake-off** (rāk′ôf′, -of′), *n. U.S. Informal.* a share or portion, often an amount taken or received illicitly: *Her husband testified earlier that he was getting a rake-off on a dice game* (New York Times).
**rak|er|y** (rā′kər ē), *n., pl.* **-er|ies.** rakish conduct or practices; immorality: *He ... instructed his Lordship in all the rakery and intrigues of the lewd town* (Roger North).
**rake's progress**, a downhill course: *Compared with my rake's progress of the first three weeks, this week has been exasperatingly slow* (Observer). [< *The Rake's Progress,* a series of engravings by the English artist William Hogarth, 1697-1764, showing the progressive deterioration of a rake]
**ra|ki** (rä kē′, rak′ē), *n.* an alcoholic liquor distilled from grain, or from grapes, plums, or other fruit, flavored with anise, in southeastern Europe and the Near East. [< Turkish *raki* brandy, spirits]
**rak|ish**[1] (rā′kish), *adj.* **1** smart; jaunty; dashing: *a hat set at a rakish angle.* **2** suggesting dash and speed: *He owns a rakish boat.* [probably < *rake*[3] + *-ish*] **—rak′ish|ly,** *adv.* **—rak′ish|ness,** *n.*
**rak|ish**[2] (rā′kish), *adj.* like a rake; immoral; dissolute. **SYN:** licentious. [< *rake*[2] + *-ish*] **—rak′ish|ly,** *adv.* **—rak′ish|ness,** *n.*
**rale** or **râle** (räl), *n.* an abnormal crackling, whistling, or other sound accompanying the normal sounds of breathing, a symptom of certain pulmonary diseases. [< French *râle* (originally) death rattle < *râler* to rattle < Old French *raler.* Compare etym. under **rail**[3].]
**rall.,** *Music.* rallentando.
**ral|len|tan|do** (räl′len tän′dō), *adj., n., pl.* **-dos.** *Music.* **—*adj.*** becoming slower; slackening.
**—*n.*** a phrase or passage played or to be played in this manner.
[< Italian *rallentando* a slowing down, < *rallentare* to slow down < *lento* slow]
**ral|li|er** (ral′ē ər), *n.* a person who rallies.
**ral|li|form** (ral′ə fôrm), *adj.* (of birds) resembling the rails. [< New Latin *Rallus* the genus name + English *-form*]
**ral|line** (ral′īn, -in), *adj.* related to or resembling the rails. [< New Latin *Rallus* the genus name + English *-ine*[1]]
**ral|ly**[1] (ral′ē), *v.,* **-lied, -ly|ing,** *n., pl.* **-lies. —*v.t.* 1** to bring together; bring together again; get in order again: *The commander was able to rally the fleeing troops.* **2** to pull together; revive: *We rallied all our energy for one last effort.* **SYN:** summon.
**—*v.i.* 1** to come together again; reassemble: *There is Jackson standing like a stone wall. Rally behind the Virginians* (Barnard E. Bee). **2** to come together for a common purpose or action: *The girls at the camp rallied to get the meals when the cook was sick.* **3** to come to help a person, party, or cause: *He rallied to the side of his frightened sister.* **4** to recover health and strength: *The sick man may rally now.* **5** to recover more or less from a drop in prices. **6** to take part in a rally in tennis and similar games.
**—*n.* 1** the act of rallying; recovery. **SYN:** recuperation. **2** the act of coming together; meeting of many people: *a political rally.* **3a** the act of hitting the ball back and forth several times in tennis and similar games: *Kershaw was now increasing his own pace of stroke which led to many long rallies* (London Times). **b** an exchange or flurry of blows in a boxing match. **4** a rise following a drop in prices: *a sudden rally in the grain market.* **5** an automobile race: *The form of the rally has been altered since last year, in deference to the increasing restrictions placed on public-road motoring events by the authorities* (Sunday Times).
[< French *rallier* < *re-* again, re- + *allier* to ally]
**ral|ly**[2] (ral′ē), *v.,* **-lied, -ly|ing. —*v.t.*** to make fun of; tease: *The boys rallied him on his short haircut.*
**—*v.i.*** to indulge in teasing banter.
[< French, Middle French *railler.* See etym. of

**Pronunciation Key:** hat, āge, cãre, fär; let, ēqual, tėrm; it, īce; hot, ōpen, ôrder; oil, out; cup, pu̇t, rüle; child; long; thin; ᴛʜen; zh, measure; ə represents **a** in about, **e** in taken, **i** in pencil, **o** in lemon, **u** in circus.

doublet **rail**[2].] —**ral′ly|ing|ly**, *adv.*

**ral|ly|ing** (ral′ē ing), *n.* the sport of racing in automobiles: *There's no place one can take lessons in rallying, thus the ... old-timers in the sport keep getting better, and no new blood has a chance* (San Francisco Chronicle). [< *rally*[1] (def. 5) + *-ing*[1]]

**rallying cry**, a battle cry; war cry: *His voice was the rallying cry for thousands of workers-turned-saboteurs* (Harper's).

**rallying point**, a point or place at which to rally strength or resources: *She reached a rallying point in her fight against the disease.*

**ral|ly|ist** (ral′ē ist), *n.* a contestant in an automobile race.

**ram** (ram), *n., v.,* **rammed, ram|ming.** —*n.* **1** a male sheep. **2** a machine or part of a machine that strikes heavy blows, such as the plunger of a force pump, the weight of a pile driver, or the piston of a hydraulic press: *The central part of the ram of the press* (*the "mandrel"*) *pushes downwards and forces a hole right through the billet* (F. A. Fox). **3** a beak at the bow of a warship, used to break through the sides of enemy ships. **4** a ship with such a beak. **5** a pump in which the force of a descending column of water raises some of the water above its original level. **6** = battering ram. [Old English *ramm*]
—*v.t.* **1** to butt against; strike head-on; strike violently: *One ship rammed the other ship. I rammed my head against the door in the dark.* **2** to push hard; drive down or in by heavy blows: *to ram piles.* **3** to cram, stuff, or thrust: *He rammed all his clothes into the suitcase.* **4** to push (a charge) into a firearm or cannon, especially through the muzzle with a ramrod. **5** *Figurative.* to push or force: *to ram legislation through Congress. He tried to ram through drastic economic and social reforms* (Time).
—*v.i.* **1** to crash: *The skidding car rammed into a fence.* **2** to move very fast: *The motorcyclists rammed down the open highway.*
[Middle English *rammen* to tamp down earth, perhaps < *ram*, noun]

**Ram** (ram), *n.* Aries, a constellation and the first sign of the zodiac. [< *ram*]

**RAM** (no periods), random-access memory: *Appropriately programmed RAM's—up to 16 kbit [kilobit] per circuit—can store any program in the machine* (New Scientist).

**R.A.M.**, **1** Royal Academy of Music. **2** Royal Arch Mason.

**Ra|ma** (rä′mə), *n.* the sixth, seventh, and eighth incarnations of Vishnu. [< Sanskrit *Rāma*]

**Ra|ma|chan|dra** (rä′mə chun′drə), *n.* the eighth incarnation of Vishnu. [< Sanskrit *Rāmacandra*]

**Ram|a|dan** (ram′ə dän′), *n.* **1** the ninth month of the Moslem year. It has 30 days. **2** an annual Moslem religious observance held in this month, during which fasting is rigidly practiced daily from dawn until sunset. Because the Islamic calendar is based on lunar months Ramadan comes at different seasons. **3** the fasting itself. [< Arabic *Ramaḍān* (originally) the hot month < *ramiḍa* be burnt, scorched]

**ra|mal** (rā′məl), *adj.* **1** of or having to do with a branch or ramus: *A ramal leaf is one which is affixed directly to a branch* (Heber W. Youngken). **2** like a branch or ramus.

**Ra|man effect** (rä′mən), the scattering of incident light by the molecules of a transparent substance, in such a way that the wave lengths of the scattered light are lengthened or shortened. [< Sir Chandrasekhara V. *Raman*, 1888-1970, an Indian physicist, who discovered it]

**Ra|ma|pi|the|cus** (rä′mə pith′ə kəs), *n.* a manlike primate, similar to Kenyapithecus, originally discovered in the Siwalik Hills of northwestern India. [< *Rama* + Greek *píthēkos* ape]

**Ra|ma|ya|na** (rä mä′yə nə), *n.* the later of the two great ancient epics of Hinduism (the other is the *Mahabharata*) with Ramachandra as its hero, written in Sanskrit probably early in the Christian Era. [< Sanskrit *Rāmāyaṇa*]

**Ram|a|zan** (ram′ə zän′), *n.* = Ramadan.

**ram|ble** (ram′bəl), *v.,* **-bled, -bling,** *n.* —*v.i.* **1** to wander about: *We rambled here and there through the woods.* **SYN**: rove, range, meander. See syn. under **roam**. **2** to talk or write about first one thing and then another with no useful connections. **3** to spread irregularly in various directions: *Vines rambled over the wall.*
—*v.t.* to wander over: *I ramble the rough highland hills* (William Hone).
—*n.* a walk for pleasure, not to go to any special place.
[origin uncertain. Apparently related to Middle English *romblen* to roam.]

**ram|bler** (ram′blər), *n.* **1** a person or thing that rambles: *a rambler in the wood* (Thoreau). **2** any one of various climbing roses having clusters of small, red, yellow, or white flowers. The crimson rambler is a well-known kind. **3** *Informal.* a bungalow or ranch house.

**ram|bling** (ram′bling), *adj.* **1** that rambles; wandering about: *rambling roses.* **2** going from one subject to another without clear connections: *a rambling speech.* **3** extending in irregular ways in various directions; not planned in an orderly way: *a rambling old farmhouse.* **4** that is a ramble: *a rambling walk.* —**ram′bling|ly**, *adv.*

**Ram|bouil|let** (ram′bů lā; *French* räɴ bü ye′), *n.* any one of a breed of French sheep developed from the merino, raised for wool and meat. [< *Rambouillet*, a town in France, famous for its sheep and wool]

**ram|bunc|tious** (ram bungk′shəs), *adj. U.S. Informal.* **1** wild and uncontrollable; unruly: *Ever since she got out of college she's been too rambunctious to live with* (Sinclair Lewis). **2** noisy and violent; boisterous: *The gay rambunctious story revolves around a happy-go-lucky boy and two pretty girls on a spree* (Times of India). [American English, earlier *rambustious*, perhaps < *ram*, verb + *robustious*, or variant of *bumptious*] —**ram|bunc′tious|ly**, *adv.* —**ram|bunc′tious|ness**, *n.*

**ram|bu|tan** (ram bü′tən), *n.* **1** the bright-red, spiny, edible fruit of a Malayan tree of the soapberry family, having a pulp of a subacid flavor. **2** the tree itself. [< Malay *rambutan* < *rambut* hair (because of its appearance) + *-an*, a derivative suffix]

**ram|e|kin** or **ram|e|quin** (ram′ə kin), *n.* **1** a small, separately cooked portion of some food, especially one topped with cheese and breadcrumbs. **2** a small baking dish holding enough for one portion. [< French *ramequin*, perhaps < obsolete Dutch *rammeken* toasted bread, or < German *Rahm* cream]

**ra|men|tum** (rə men′təm), *n., pl.* **-ta** (-tə), *Botany.* a thin, membranous scale formed on the leaves or shoots of some ferns. [< Latin *rāmentum* piece scraped off < *rādere* to scrape]

**ra|met** (rā′met), *n. Horticulture.* one of the plants in a clone. [< Latin *rāmus* branch + English *-et*]

**ram|head** (ram′hed′), *n.* **1** part of the arm of a crane. **2** a block for guiding the halyards of a ship.

**ra|mi** (rā′mī), *n.* plural of **ramus**.

**ram|ie** (ram′ē), *n.* **1** a perennial Asian shrub of the same family as the nettle, that yields a strong, lustrous fiber; China grass. **2** this fiber, used to make fabrics, surgical dressings, and the like. Ramie's strength increases when it is wet, so it is suitable for ropes, canvas, nets, and life rafts. [< Malay *rami* plant]

**ram|i|fi|ca|tion** (ram′ə fə kā′shən), *n.* **1** a dividing or spreading out into branches or parts. **2** the manner or result of branching; offshoot; branch; part; subdivision.

**ram|i|form** (ram′ə fôrm), *adj.* **1** branchlike. **2** branched: *a ramiform plant.* [< Latin *rāmus* branch + English *-form*]

**ram|i|fy** (ram′ə fī), *v.,* **-fied, -fy|ing.** —*v.i.* to divide or spread out into parts resembling branches: *Quartz veins ramify through the rock in all directions* (F. Kingdon-Ward).
—*v.t.* to cause to branch out.
[< French, Old French *ramifier* < Medieval Latin *ramificari* < Latin *rāmus* branch + *facere* make]

**ram|jet** (ram′jet′), *n.* a type of jet engine in which the fuel is fed into air compressed by the speed of the airplane, guided missile, etc., in which it is contained. A ramjet must reach a speed of at least 300 miles an hour to operate efficiently. See diagram under **combustion chamber**. [< *ram*, verb + *jet* (engine)]

**ram|mer** (ram′ər), *n.* a person or thing that rams.

**ram|mish** (ram′ish), *adj.* **1** like a ram; rank in smell or taste. **2** = lustful.

**ra|mose** (rā′mōs, rə mōs′), *adj.* having many branches; branching. [< Latin *rāmōsus* < *rāmus* a branch] —**ra′mose|ly**, *adv.*

**ra|mous** (rā′məs), *adj.* **1** = ramose. **2** of or like a branch.

**ramp**[1] (ramp), *n.* a sloping way connecting two different levels, especially of a building or road; slope: *The passengers walked up the ramp to board the airplane.* [< Middle French *rampe* < Old French *ramper*; see etym. under **ramp**[2]]

**ramp**[2] (ramp), *v., n.* —*v.i.* **1** to rush wildly about; behave violently: *It is one thing to hear a lion in captivity ... quite another ... when he is ramping around ... one's fragile tent* (J. H. Patterson). **2** to jump or rush with fury. **3** *Heraldry.* to stand on the hind legs; raise the forepaws in the air (said especially of lions in coats of arms). **4** to take a threatening posture.
—*n.* an act of ramping.
[< Old French *ramper* to creep, climb < Germanic (compare Middle High German *rimpfen*, related to *rampf* cramp)]

**ramp**[3] (ramp), *n.* **1** a kind of wild onion of eastern North America, related to the ramson, and having a strongly-flavored edible root; wild leek: *Mountain folk traditionally gather ramps for festive occasions* [*in late April*] (New York Times). **2** = ramson. [< earlier *ramps*, variant of *rams*, Old English *hramsa*]

**ram|page** (*n.* ram′pāj; *v.* ram pāj′, ram′pāj), *n., v.,* **-paged, -pag|ing.** —*n.* a fit of rushing wildly about; spell of violent behavior; wild outbreak: *The mad elephant went on a rampage and killed its keeper.*
—*v.i.* to rush wildly about; behave violently; rage: *He could not lie still, but ... raged and rampaged up and down his ... bedroom* (George Du Maurier).

**ram|pa|geous** (ram pā′jəs), *adj.* violent; unruly; boisterous: *a rampageous free-for-all.* —**ram|pa′geous|ly**, *adv.* —**ram|pa′geous|ness**, *n.*

**ram|pag|ing** (ram pā′jing, ram′pā-), *adj.* violent; rampageous: *rampaging attacks.*

**ramp|an|cy** (ram′pən sē), *n.* the fact or condition of being rampant.

***ramp|ant** (ram′pənt), *adj.* **1** growing without any check: *The vines ran rampant over the fence.* **2** passing beyond restraint or usual limits; unchecked: *Anarchy was rampant after the dictator died.* **3** angry; excited; violent. **SYN**: furious, raging. **4** *Heraldry.* standing up on the hind legs. **5** (of animals) rearing. **6** *Architecture.* (of an arch or vault) having different levels of support for the two sides. [< Old French *rampant*, present participle of *ramper*; see etym. under **ramp**[2]] —**ramp′ant|ly**, *adv.*

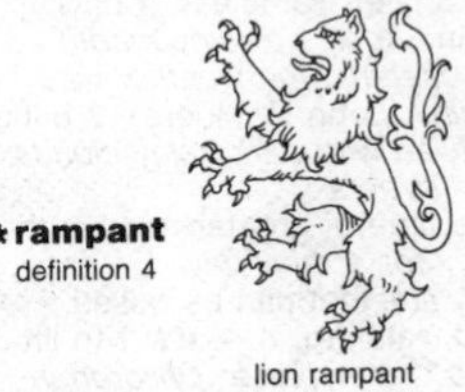

***rampant** definition 4

lion rampant

***ram|part** (ram′pärt), *n., v.* —*n.* **1** a wide bank of earth, often with a wall on top, built around a fort to help defend it: *O'er the ramparts we watched* (Francis Scott Key). **SYN**: embankment. **2** *Figurative: to strengthen the ramparts of freedom.* **SYN**: defense, protection, bastion, bulwark.
—*v.t.* to fortify or surround with, or as if with, a rampart: *Against our ramparted gates* (Shakespeare).
[< Middle French *rempart* < *remparer* to fortify < *re-* (< Latin *re-* back) + *emparer* fortify, ultimately < Latin *ante* before + *parāre* to prepare]

***rampart** definition 1

**ram|pike** (ram′pīk′), *n.* **1** a decaying or dead tree. **2** *Canadian.* the bleached or blackened trunk of a dead tree, especially one killed by fire. [origin uncertain]

**ram|pi|on** (ram′pē ən), *n.* **1** a European bellflower, whose white, tuberous roots are sometimes used for salad. **2** any one of a group of blue-flowered plants of the bellflower family, native to Europe and parts of Asia. [probably < a Romance form (ultimately diminutive) < Latin *rāpa* turnip]

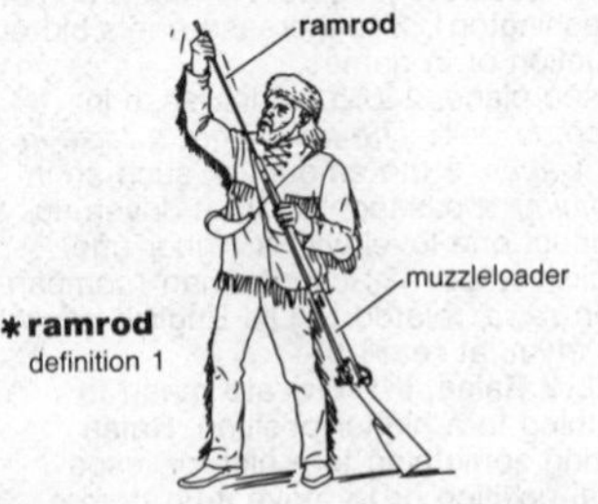


***ramrod** definition 1

***ram|rod** (ram′rod′), *n., adj., v.,* **-rod|ded, -rod|ding.** —*n.* **1** a rod for ramming down the charge

in a gun that is loaded from the muzzle. **2** a rod for cleaning the barrel of a gun. **3** *Figurative.* a stiff, unbending person.
—*adj.* stiff; rigid; unbending: *He ... walked ten times with ramrod dignity from the wings and bowed misty-eyed to the packed hall* (Time).
—*v.t. Informal.* to push forward vigorously; ram (through): *to ramrod a bill through Congress.*

**ram|shack|le** (ram′shak′əl), *adj.* **1** loose and shaky; likely to come apart: *The buildings on this farm are old and ramshackle.* **SYN:** rickety, dilapidated. **2** weak; feeble: *... the whole ramshackle structure of federal taxes* (Theodore H. White). **3** decadent: *He had also become an expert on the ramshackle politics of the Turkish empire* (Punch). [earlier *ramshackled,* variant of *ransackled* (ultimately frequentative) < *ransack*]

**ram's horn,** = shofar.

**ram's-horn snail** (ramz′hôrn′), a freshwater snail with a flat coiled shell, commonly found in aquariums.

**ram|son** (ram′zən, -sən), *n.* a kind of garlic with broad leaves.
**ramsons,** the bulbous root of this plant, used as a relish: *There were dishes of pickles, olives, and ramsons on the cocktail table.*
[Old English *hramsan* (originally) plural of *hramsa*]

**ram|stam** (ram′stam′), *adj., adv. Scottish.* —*adj.* impetuous; reckless.
—*adv.* in a rush; precipitately.
[perhaps < *ram* + dialectal *stam* to stamp]

**ram|til** (ram′təl), *n.* a composite African plant cultivated in India and parts of Africa for the oil produced from its seeds. [< Hindi *rāmtīl* < Sanskrit *Rāma* Rama + *tīla* sesame seed]

**ram|u|lose** (ram′yə lōs), *adj.* having many small branches. [< Latin *rāmulōsus* < *rāmulus* (diminutive) < *rāmus* branch]

**ram|u|lous** (ram′yə ləs), *adj.* = ramulose.

**ra|mus** (rā′məs), *n., pl.* **-mi** (-mī). a branch, as of a plant, a vein, or a bone. [< Latin *rāmus* branch]

**ran** (ran), *v.* the past tense of **run**: *The dog ran after the cat.*

**Ran** (rän), *n. Norse Mythology.* a sea goddess who caught drowning men in her net.

**rance** (rans), *n.* a red Belgian marble with blue and white veins. [probably < Middle French *rance*]

**ranch** (ranch), *n., v.* —*n.* **1** a very large farm and its buildings. Many ranches are for raising cattle, sheep, or horses. **2** any farm, especially one used to raise one kind of animal or crop: *a chicken ranch, a fruit ranch.* **3** the persons working or living on a ranch: *The entire ranch was at the party.* **4** = ranch house (def. 2).
—*v.i.* to work on a ranch or manage a ranch.
[American English < American Spanish *rancho* small farm, group of farm huts < Spanish, (originally) group of persons who eat together < Old High German *hring* circle, assembly]

**ranch|er** (ran′chər), *n.* a person who owns, manages, or works on a ranch.

**ran|che|ri|a** (ran′chə rē′ə), *n.* (in Spanish America and southwestern U.S.) a group of ranchos or rude huts for Indians or rancheros. [American English < Spanish *ranchería* < *rancho;* see etym. under **ranch**]

**ran|che|ro** (ran chăr′ō, rän-), *n., pl.* **-ros.** in Spanish America: **1** a rancher. **2** a herdsman on a ranch. [American English < American Spanish *ranchero* < *rancho;* see etym. under **ranch**]

**ranch house, 1** the main house on a ranch, in which the owner or manager and his family live. **2** a one-story dwelling, like most houses on a ranch, having a low roof.

**ranch|man** (ranch′man′), *n., pl.* **-men.** = rancher.

**ran|cho** (ran′chō, rän′-), *n., pl.* **-chos.** in Spanish America: **1** a ranch. **2** a rude hut or group of huts for herdsmen or laborers: *I put up for the night at the solitary mud rancho of an old herdsman* (W. H. Hudson). [American English < American Spanish *rancho;* see etym. under **ranch**]

**ran|cid** (ran′sid), *adj.* **1** stale; spoiled: *rancid butter.* **2** tasting or smelling like stale fat or butter: *a rancid odor.* **3** *Figurative.* nasty; disagreeable; odious: *He's a rancid fellow* (Robert Louis Stevenson). [< Latin *rancidus* < *rancēre* be rank] —**ran′cid|ly,** *adv.* —**ran′cid|ness,** *n.*

**ran|cid|i|ty** (ran sid′ə tē), *n.* rancid quality or condition.

**ran|cor** (rang′kər), *n.* bitter resentment or ill will; extreme hatred or spite: *This silly affair ... greatly increased his rancor against me* (Benjamin Franklin). **SYN:** malice, animosity. [< Old French *rancour,* and *rancor,* learned borrowings < Late Latin *rancor* rankness < Latin *rancēre* be rank]

**ran|cor|ous** (rang′kər əs), *adj.* spiteful; bitterly malicious: *a rancorous old man.* —**ran′cor|ous|ly,** *adv.* —**ran′cor|ous|ness,** *n.*

**ran|cour** (rang′kər), *n. Especially British.* rancor.

**rand**[1] (rand), *n.* **1** a strip of leather for leveling, set in a shoe at the heel before the lifts are attached. **2** *British Dialect.* **a** a border or margin, as of unplowed land around a field. **b** a strip of meat. [Old English *rand* border, margin]

**rand**[2] (rand), *n., pl.* **rand.** the unit of money of the Republic of South Africa equal to 100 cents. *Abbr:* R (no period). [< Afrikaans *rand* < Dutch, field border]

**ran|dan**[1] (ran′dan, ran dan′), *n. British Dialect.* disorderly behavior; a spree. [perhaps variant of Middle English *randun;* see etym. under **random**]

**ran|dan**[2] (ran′dan, ran dan′), *n.* **1** a style of rowing in which the middle one of three rowers in a boat uses a pair of sculls and the other two use one oar each. **2** a boat for such rowing. [origin uncertain]

**r & b, R & B,** or **R and B** (no periods), rhythm and blues: *R and B influenced the Beatles and other early groups* (Sunday Times).

**R & D** or **R and D,** (no periods), research and development: *"It would have been most unfortunate ... if, for example, in 1946 we had adopted a policy that all federally supported R & D should be carried out in Federal laboratories* (Science News).

**ran|dem** (ran′dəm), *adv., n.* —**adv.** with three horses harnessed tandem.
—*n.* a carriage or a team driven randem. [probably < *tandem;* form influenced by *random*]

**ran|dom** (ran′dəm), *adj., n.* —*adj.* by chance; with no plan, method, or purpose; casual: *to take a random guess, to make a random sampling of opinion. He was not listening and made a random answer to the teacher's question. Cancer is brought about through a random mutation or change in the character of body cells* (Observer).
—*n.* a random course or movement.
**at random,** by chance; with no plan or purpose: *The librarian took a book at random from the shelf. Laurence had chosen these illustrations ... quite at random* (William H. Mallock).
[Middle English *randun* impetuosity, speed < Old French *randon* rapid rush, disorder, perhaps < Germanic (compare Old High German *rant*)]
—**ran′dom|ly,** *adv.* —**ran′dom|ness,** *n.*
—*Syn. adj.* **Random, haphazard** mean made, done, happening, or coming by accident or chance. **Random** emphasizes the absence of any direction, purpose, or plan: *His random guess at the number of beans in the jar won the prize.* **Haphazard** emphasizes the effect or result of chance due to the absence of planning or direction: *Because of her haphazard way of buying clothes, she never looks well dressed.*

**random access,** access to the memory of a computer in which each successive source of information is chosen at random and independent of the location of previous sources: *Perhaps the most important attribute of random access to a memory is the ease with which it is possible to choose one or another command according to the process being executed, thus allowing branching into one or two or more possible programming sequences* (Scientific American). —**ran′dom-ac′cess,** *adj.*

**ran|dom|i|za|tion** (ran′də mə zā′shən), *n.* **1** the act or process of randomizing: *If the cards are dealt at random, any further randomization through the use of mixed strategies by the players is superfluous* (Scientific American). **2** the state of being randomized.

**ran|dom|ize** (ran′də mīz), *v.t., v.i.,* **-ized, -iz|ing.** to put, take, or perform at random, especially in order to control the variables, as of a scientific experiment or statistical procedure: *Shuffling randomizes a deck of ordered cards* (Scientific American). *If he tries to randomize in his head, unconscious biases creep in* (Martin Gardner). —**ran′dom|iz|er,** *n.*

**random sample,** *Statistics.* a sample so drawn from the total group that every item in the group has an equal chance of being chosen: *In economic and social studies it is difficult to apply the mechanical methods necessary to obtain a random sample* (Croxton and Cowden). *In theory, a random sample gives each case in the universe an equal chance of being included* (Albert E. Waugh).

**random sampling,** *Statistics.* the process of selecting a random sample: *Random sampling forms the basis of the work of the social scientists today* (Listener).

**random variable,** *Statistics.* a variate.

**random walk,** *Statistics.* any movement or process whose individual steps are determined at random or by chance: *The "random walk" model ... solved the mystery of Brownian motion, thus establishing the foundations of modern atomic theory* (Scientific American).

**r. & r.** or **r.-'n'-r.,** rock'n'roll.

**R and R** (no periods), *U.S. Military.* rest and recuperation or rest and recreation (a five-day vacation leave given to American servicemen, exclusive of the annual 30-day leave, during each one-year tour of duty.

**rand|y** (ran′dē), *adj.,* **rand|i|er, rand|i|est,** *n., pl.* **rand|ies.** —*adj.* **1** boisterous; coarse; disorderly: *Maire John herself was a randy old lady who would have delighted Apuleius in the days of silver Latin* (New Yorker). **2** lewd; lustful: *... randy and rakish in their sexual appetites* (G. S. Fraser).
—*n. Scottish.* **1** a rude beggar; rough tramp. **2** a virago.
[probably < dialectal *rand,* variant of *rant* + *-y*[1]]
—**ran′di|ly,** *adv.* —**ran′di|ness,** *n.*

**ra|nee** (rä′nē), *n.* **1** the wife of a rajah. **2** a ruling Hindu queen or princess. Also, **rani.** [< Hindi *rānī* < Sanskrit *rājñī*]

**rang** (rang), *v.* a past tense of **ring**[2]: *The telephone rang.*

**ran|ga|ti|ra** (ran′gə tir′ə), *n.* **1** a Maori chief. **2** a Maori master or mistress. [< Maori *rangatira*]

**range** (rānj), *n., v.,* **ranged, rang|ing,** *adj.* —*n.* **1** the distance between certain limits; extent: *a range of colors to choose from, range of prices from 5 cents to 25 dollars, the average daily range of temperature, vocal range, a limited range of ideas.* **2a** the distance a gun can shoot or a projectile, laser, radio, or other apparatus can operate: *to be within range of the enemy. The useful range of these hand-held radio's is about three miles.* **b** the distance from a gun, launching pad, radio transmitter, or other place or device, of an object aimed at or used: *to set the sights of a howitzer for a range of 1,000 yards. That camera lens is set for a range of three feet to infinity.* **3** the greatest distance an aircraft, rocket, or the like, can travel on a single load of fuel. **4** a place to practice shooting: *a missile range.* **5** land for grazing. **6** the act of wandering or moving about. **7** a row or line of mountains: *the Green Mountain range of the Appalachian system. Mount Rainier is in the Cascade Range.* **8** a row, line, or series: *The library has ranges of books in perfect order.* **9** a line of direction: *The two barns are in direct range with the house.* **10** a rank, class, or order: *The cohesion of the nation was greatest in the lowest ranges* (William Stubbs). **11** the district in which certain plants or animals live or naturally occur: *the reindeer, who is even less Arctic in his range than the musk ox* (Elisha K. Kane). **12** a stove for cooking: *Gas and electric ranges have replaced the coal and wood range.* **13** *Mathematics.* **a** the set of all the values a given function may take on. **b** = domain. **14** *Statistics.* the difference between the smallest and the greatest values which a variable bears in frequency distribution: *The range of this variation is unusually small.* **15a** *U.S.* a row of townships, each six miles square, between two meridians six miles apart. **b** *Canadian.* a subdivision of a township; concession: *A real ghost roams about township 14, range 15* (Neepawa, Manitoba, Star). **16** *Surveying.* a line extended so as to intersect a transit line. **17** the part of an animal hide near the tail. [probably < verb]
—*v.i.* **1** to extend between certain limits: *prices ranging from $5 to $10.* **2** to wander; rove; roam: *to range through the woods. Our talk ranged over all that had happened on our vacation.* **3** to run in a line; extend: *a boundary ranging from east to west.* **4** to be found; occur: *a plant ranging from Canada to Mexico.* **5** (of a gun, radio, laser, or other device) to have a particular range. **6** to find the distance or direction of something. **7** to take up or have a position in a line or other arrangement. **8** to search an area: *The eye ranged over an immense extent of wilderness* (Washington Irving).
—*v.t.* **1** to wander over: *Buffalo once ranged these plains.* **2** to put in a row or rows: *Range the books by size.* **3** to put in groups or classes; classify. **4** to put in a line on someone's side: *Loyal citizens ranged themselves with the king.* **5** to make straight or even: *to range lines of type.* **6a** to find the proper elevation for (a gun). **b** to give the proper elevation to (a gun). **7** to direct (a telescope) upon an object; train.
—*adj.* of or on land for grazing: *a range pony, range cattle.*
[< Old French *ranger* to array < *rang;* see etym. under **rank**[1]]
—*Syn. n.* **1 Range, scope, compass** mean the extent of what something can do or take in. **Range** emphasizes the extent (and variety) that can be covered or included by something in operation or action, such as the mind, the eye, a machine, or a force: *The car was out of my range of vision.* **Scope** emphasizes the limits beyond which the understanding, view, applica-

**Pronunciation Key:** hat, āge, cãre, fär; let, ēqual, tėrm; it, īce; hot, ōpen, ôrder; oil, out; cup, pu̇t, rüle; child; long; thin; ᴛʜen; zh, measure; ə represents **a** in about, **e** in taken, **i** in pencil, **o** in lemon, **u** in circus.

tion, or the like, cannot extend: *Some technical terms are outside the scope of this dictionary.* **Compass** also emphasizes limits, but implies more definite ones that are likely to be permanent: *Supernatural phenomena are beyond the compass of reason or science.*

**range finder**, an instrument for estimating the range or distance of an object: *This superb 35mm camera has lens-coupled range finder combined with view finder* (Time).

**range|find|ing** (rānj′fīn′ding), *n.* the act or process of estimating the range or distance of an object, as by a range finder: *There has been a great deal of speculation in the USA about the possibilities of using the laser for rangefinding, particularly in space* (New Scientist).

**range|land** (rānj′land′), *n.* land for grazing; range.

**rang|er** (rān′jər), *n.* **1** a person employed to guard a tract of forest: *Rangers also patrol roads in remote ranges towing a horse trailer so that they can take to horseback if necessary* (Newsweek). **2** Also, **Ranger**. one of a body of armed men employed in ranging over a region to police it: ... *the* [*Texas*] *Rangers, the oldest police force in the U.S. with statewide jurisdiction* (Newsweek). **3** Also, **Ranger**. a soldier in the United States Army trained for raids and surprise attacks; commando. **4** *Ranger,* a member of the Girl Guides from the ages of fourteen to eighteen. **5** a person or thing that ranges; rover. **6** *British.* the official title of the keeper of a royal park or forest.

**ranger alfalfa**, a hybrid variety of winter-hardy, wilt-resistant alfalfa with variegated flowers, grown in the northern United States.

**rang|er|ship** (rān′jər ship), *n.* the office of ranger or keeper of a forest or park.

**rang|i|ness** (rān′jē nis), *n.* the quality or condition of being rangy.

**rang|y** (rān′jē), *adj.,* **rang|i|er, rang|i|est. 1** fitted for ranging or moving about: *The ponies ... used for circle-riding in the morning have need to be strong and rangy* (Theodore Roosevelt). **2** slender and long-limbed: *a rangy horse.* **3** (in Australia) mountainous.

**ra|ni** (rä′nē), *n.* = ranee.

**rank**[1] (rangk), *n., v.* —*n.* **1** a row or line, usually of soldiers, placed side by side: *The Tuscan army ... Rank behind rank* (Macaulay). **2** position; grade; class: *He was promoted from the rank of captain to the rank of major. Los Angeles is a city of high rank. A zoo contains animals of all ranks. Coal is classified in ranks, according to the amount of heat it produces.* **SYN**: standing, status, station. **3** high position: *Dukes and generals are men of rank.* **SYN**: eminence, distinction. **4** orderly arrangement or array: *to break rank.* **5** one of the lines of squares extending left and right across a chess- or checkerboard. At the start of a game of chess, the pieces stand on first rank, and the pawns on the second rank.
—*v.t.* **1** to put in some special order in a list; classify: *Rank the states in the order of size.* **2** to be more important than; outrank: *A major ranks a captain.* **3** to arrange in a row or line: *The librarian ranked the jumbled books on the shelves.*
—*v.i.* **1** to have a certain place or position in relation to other persons or things: *He ranked low in the test. New York State ranks first in wealth.* **2** to form a rank or ranks; stand in rank: *The crowd ranked six deep along the parade route.* **3** *U.S.* to be the highest in rank or standing.
**pull rank**, *Especially U.S.* to use one's position to gain something: *The young lieutenant was bossy and always pulling rank.*
**ranks, a** an army; soldiers: *An advance party of 26 officers and 144 other ranks would sail from Sydney to Penang* (London Times). **b** = rank and file: *He regarded himself as a man in the ranks, the member of an awkward squad* (Graham Greene). **c** formation: *to open ranks, to close ranks.*
[< Old French *rang,* earlier *reng* < Germanic (compare Old High German *hring* circle, ring). Compare etym. under **ranch.**]

**rank**[2] (rangk), *adj.* **1** large and coarse: *rank grass.* **2** growing thickly and in a coarse way: *a rank growth of weeds.* **3** producing a dense but coarse growth: *a rank swamp.* **4** having a strong, bad smell or taste: *rank meat, rank tobacco. A rank cigar of the sort that they sell to students* (Rudyard Kipling). **SYN**: rancid. **5** *Figurative.* strongly marked; extreme: *rank ingratitude, rank nonsense.* **SYN**: flagrant, absolute. **6** coarse; indecent. **SYN**: obscene. **7** *Especially Law.* high or excessive in amount. [Middle English *ranke* luxuriant, vigorous, Old English *ranc* proud, overweening; full grown] —**rank′ly**, *adv.* —**rank′ness**, *n.*

**rank and file, 1a** common soldiers, not officers, especially those with the rank of corporal or below; ranks. **b** the people in a business, labor union, political party, or other institution or group, who are not a part of the management: *This sudden flurry of costly strikes points to a weakness in Britain's labor union structure which so often finds the leaders being flouted by the rank and file* (New York Times). **2** the common people.
—**rank′-and-file′**, *adj.*

**rank and filer**, a member of the rank and file: *Management and union rank and filers alike had hoped Congress would act swiftly* (Newsweek).

**rank|er** (rang′kər), *n.* **1** *Informal.* a person who ranks. **2** a soldier in the ranks: *Gentlemen-rankers out on the spree, Damned from hell to Eternity* (Rudyard Kipling). **3** an officer promoted from the ranks. [< *rank*[1] + *-er*[1]]

**Ran|kine** (rang′kən), *adj.* of, based on, or according to the Rankine scale: *528 degrees Rankine. Abbr:* R. [< William J. M. *Rankine,* 1820-1872, a Scottish scientist and engineer]

**Rankine cycle**, *Thermodynamics.* a kind of Carnot cycle, used as a standard of thermal efficiency. It comprises the introduction of water by pump, evaporation, adiabatic expansion, and condensation. [< William J. M. *Rankine*]

**Rankine scale**, a scale in which temperatures are measured as roughly 460 degrees plus the Fahrenheit value, absolute zero being minus 459.67 degrees Fahrenheit. See picture under **absolute scale**.

**rank|ing** (rang′king), *n., adj.* —*n.* a standing: *He has a poor ranking in his class. Stirling Moss, No. 2 driver in the world rankings ...* (Atlantic).
—*adj.* of highest standing; leading; foremost: *the ranking U.S. Senator.* [< *rank*[1] + *-ing*[1]]

**ran|kle** (rang′kəl), *v.,* **-kled, -kling.** —*v.i.* to be sore; cause soreness; continue to give pain: *The blister rankled as he walked.* (*Figurative.*) *The memory of the insult rankled in his mind.*
—*v.t.* to cause pain or soreness in or to.
[< Old French *rancler,* also *draoncler* < *draoncle* a festering sore, learned borrowing from Medieval Latin *dracunculus* sore, ulcer, apparently (diminutive) < Latin *dracō, -ōnis* serpent, dragon < Greek *drákōn, -ontos*]

**ranks** (rangks), *n.pl.* See under **rank**[1].

**RANN** (no periods), Research Applied to National Needs (a scientific research program established by the United States National Science Foundation in 1971).

**ran|sack** (ran′sak), *v.t.* **1** to search thoroughly through: *The thief ransacked the house for jewelry.* **SYN**: rummage. **2** to rob; plunder: *The invading army ransacked the city and carried off its treasures.* **SYN**: pillage. [< Scandinavian (compare Old Icelandic *rannsaka* search a house < *rann* house + *-saka* to search)] —**ran′sack|er**, *n.*

**ran|som** (ran′səm), *n., v.* —*n.* **1** the price paid or demanded before a captive is set free: *The robber chief held the travelers prisoners for ransom.* **2** a ransoming; redemption, as of a prisoner, slave, or captured goods, for a price. **3** a means of delivering or rescuing, as from sin or its consequences: *Even the Son of man came ... to give his life a ransom for many* (Mark 10:45).
—*v.t.* **1** to obtain the release of (a captive) by paying a price: *They ransomed the kidnaped child with a great sum of money. O come, O come, Emmanuel, And ransom captive Israel* (J. M. Neale). **2** to redeem or deliver, especially from sin or ignorance: *Poor sick people, richer in His eyes who ransomed us ... than I* (Tennyson). **3** to release upon payment. **4** to hold for ransom; demand a ransom for.
[Middle English *ranscun* < Old French *rançon,* earlier *raençon* < Latin *redemptiō, -ōnis.* See etym. of doublet **redemption.**] —**ran′som|er**, *n.*

**rant** (rant), *v., n.* —*v.i.* **1** to speak wildly, extravagantly, violently, or noisily. **SYN**: declaim, rave. **2** *Archaic.* **a** to carouse: *Wi' quaffing and laughing, They ranted and they sang* (Robert Burns). **b** to lead a dissolute life.
—*n.* **1a** extravagant, violent, or noisy speech: *Madly enough he preached ... with imperfect utterance, amid much frothy rant* (Thomas Carlyle). **b** ranting words: *He sometimes ... in his rants talked with Norman haughtiness of the Celtic barbarians* (Macaulay). **2** *Scottish.* a noisy spree.
**rant and rave**, to speak or scold wildly and violently: *Rant and rave as he might, the children blithely went on with their playing.*
[< earlier Dutch *ranten*] —**rant′er**, *n.* —**rant′ingly**, *adv.*

**rant|i|pole** (ran′tə pōl), *n., adj., v.,* **-poled, -poling.** —*n.* **1** a rude, romping boy or girl. **2** a boisterous, wild fellow. **3** = termagant.
—*adj.* boisterous; riotous; wild.
—*v.i.* to romp rudely; act in a boisterous, wild fashion.
[apparently < *ranty* + *poll*[1] head]

**rant|y** (ran′tē), *adj. British Dialect.* **1** raving or wild, as with passion, anger, or pain. **2** lively, boisterous, or riotous. [< *rant* + *-y*[1]]

**ran|u|la** (ran′yə lə), *n. Medicine.* a cystic tumor under the tongue, caused by the obstruction of the salivary ducts or glands. [< Latin *rānula* (diminutive) little frog; swelling on the tongue < *rāna* frog]

**ra|nun|cu|la|ceous** (rə nung′kyə lā′shəs), *adj.* belonging to the crowfoot family. [< New Latin *Ranunculaceae* the family name (< Latin *rānunculus* ranunculus) + English *-ous*]

***ra|nun|cu|lus** (rə nung′kyə ləs), *n., pl.* **-lus|es, -li** (-lī). any plant of a large and widely distributed genus of herbs, with divided leaves and five-petaled flowers, such as the buttercup. [< Latin *rānunculus* a medicinal plant; (originally) small frog < *rāna* frog (because of the shape)]

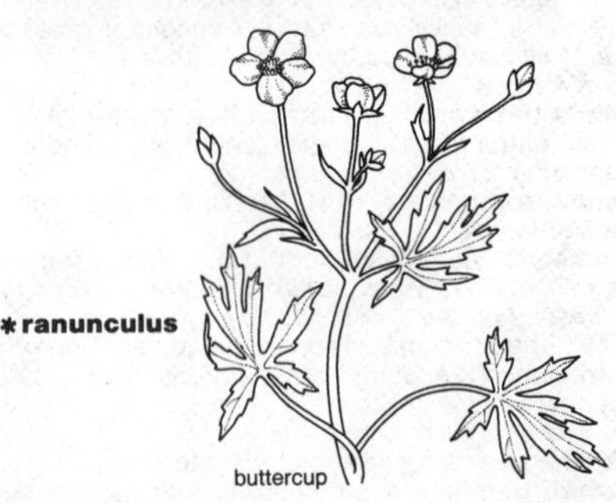

***ranunculus**

**ranz des vaches** (räns′ dā vàsh′, rän′), *French.* a Swiss herdsman's call to lead cattle to higher pastures.

**Ra|oult's law** (rä üls′), *Chemistry.* the statement or principle that the vapor pressure of a substance in solution is proportional to the molecular weight of the substance expressed in grams. [< François M. *Raoult,* 1830-1901, a French chemist]

**rap**[1] (rap), *n., v.,* **rapped, rap|ping.** —*n.* **1** a quick, light blow: *a rap on the head.* **2** a light, sharp knock: *Did I just hear a rap on the door?* **3** a sound, as of knocking, ascribed to spirits. **4** *Slang.* **a** blame; rebuke: *He got the rap for our mistake. He who has the bad taste to meddle with the caprices of believers ... gets the rap and the orders of dismissal* (Atlantic). **b** conviction; prison sentence: *He was either a big-shot bootlegger or a crook whom the government had had to prosecute for income-tax evasion because it could not hang a murder rap on him* (Harper's).
—*v.i.* to knock sharply; tap: *to rap on a door. The chairman rapped on the table for order.*
—*v.t.* **1** to strike sharply on: *She rapped him over the knuckles with her fan* (Tobias Smollett). **2** *U.S. Slang, Figurative.* to rebuke; criticize; condemn: *The chairman rapped the Cuban delegate for naming names* (Newsweek). **3** to answer (a spiritual medium) by raps. **4** *Obsolete.* to affect with joy: *What, dear sir, Thus raps you* (Shakespeare).
**beat the rap**, *U.S. Slang.* to escape conviction or prison sentence: *He almost beat the conspiracy rap when he was charged with forgery.*
**rap out**, to say sharply: *to rap out an answer. Adams then rapped out a hundred Greek verses* (Henry Fielding).
**take the rap**, *U.S. Slang.* to pay the penalty; take the blame: *History shows when the economy is down, the party in power takes the rap* (Wall Street Journal).
[probably imitative]

**rap**[2] (rap), *n.* **1** *Informal.* the least bit: *I don't care a rap.* **2a** a counterfeit coin, formerly used in Ireland for a halfpenny. **b** a coin of the smallest value, or the smallest amount of money: *Here is my hand to you with all my heart; but of money, not one rap* (Robert Louis Stevenson). [origin uncertain. Compare obsolete German *Rappen* a coin.]

**rap**[3] (rap), *v.t.,* **rapped** or **rapt, rap|ping.** *Archaic.* **1** to enrapture. **2** to carry off. **3** to seize; steal. [(definition 1) < *rapt,* adjective; (definition 2) perhaps related to dialectal German *rappen* to hasten]

**rap**[4] (rap), *v.,* **rapped, rap|ping,** *n. U.S. Slang.* —*v.i.* **1** to talk informally; converse: *I went with Officers Juan Morales and Pete DiBono to the juvenile guidance center where they rap once every week with the kids in jail* (Bill Moyers). **2** to get along; maintain rapport: *The candidate softly rakes "the voices of doubt and despair," claims to rap with the Silent Majority* (Time).
—*n.* informal talk; conversation: *"You may call it a rap, but here it's still called a powwow"* (New Yorker).
[< *rap*(port)]

**ra|pa|cious** (rə pā′shəs), *adj.* **1** seizing by force; plundering: *rapacious pirates.* **2** grasping; greedy: *a rapacious miser.* **SYN**: avaricious. **3** living by the capture of prey; predatory: *rapacious birds.* [<

Latin *rapāx, -ācis* (with English *-ous*) grasping < *rapere* to seize] — **ra|pa′cious|ly,** *adv.* — **ra|pa′cious|ness,** *n.*

**ra|pac|i|ty** (rə pas′ə tē), *n.* a rapacious spirit, action, or practice; greed: *the rapacity of the great claimants of lands who held seats in the council* (George Bancroft). SYN: voracity, cupidity, covetousness.

**rape**[1] (rāp), *n., v.,* **raped, rap|ing.** — *n.* **1** the act of seizing and carrying off by force. **2** the crime of having sexual intercourse especially with a woman or girl forcibly or without consent. **3** any violent seizure or hostile action against a weaker opponent: *Hitherto our attitude to this illegality has been unpleasantly reminiscent of Mr. Neville Chamberlain's comment on Hitler's rape of Czechoslovakia* (London Times). [< verb]
— *v.t., v.i.* **1** to seize and carry off by force. **2** to force (especially a woman or girl) to have sexual intercourse; commit rape on. **3** to rob or plunder: *I raped your richest roadstead, I plundered Singapore* (Rudyard Kipling).
[< Latin *rapere* to seize, lift]

**rape**[2] (rāp), *n.* a small European plant whose leaves are used as food for sheep and hogs. It belongs to the mustard family. The seeds of the rape yield an oil that is used as a lubricant. [< Latin *rāpa,* and *rāpum* turnip]

**rape**[3] (rāp), *n.* the refuse of grapes after the juice has been pressed out. [< French *râpe* < Old French, grater < Medieval Latin *raspa,* perhaps < Germanic (compare Old High German *raspōn* to grate)]

**rape**[4] (rāp), *n.* one of the six divisions of the county of Sussex, England, intermediate between a hundred and the shire. [Middle English *rape;* origin unknown]

**rape oil,** a brownish-yellow oil obtained from the rapeseed, used chiefly as a lubricant and in the manufacture of soap and rubber; colza oil. [< *rape*[2]]

**rape|seed** (rāp′sēd′), *n.* **1** the seed of rape. **2** the plant.

**rapeseed oil,** = rape oil.

**rap group,** *U.S. Slang.* a group that meets to discuss and work out problems together: *The New York chapter of the Vietnam Veterans ... instituted weekly "rap groups" where men meet and talk about their experiences and feelings* (New York Times). [< *rap*[4]]

**Raph|a|el** (raf′ē əl, rā′fē-), *n.* (in Hebrew and Christian tradition) one of the archangels; the healing angel. [ultimately < Greek *Rhaphaēl* < Hebrew *Rəfā'el* (literally) God healed]

**ra|phe** (rā′fē), *n.* **1** *Anatomy.* a seamlike union between two parts of an organ of the body. **2** *Botany.* **a** (in certain ovules) the vascular tissue connecting the hilum with the chalaza. **b** a median line or rib on a valve of a diatom. [< New Latin *raphe* < Greek *rhaphē* suture, seam; thing sewn < *rhaphis, -idos* needle < *rháptein* to stitch, sew. Compare etym. under **rhapsody.**]

**ra|phi|a** (rā′fē ə), *n.* = raffia.

**raph|i|des** (raf′ə dēz), *n., pl. of* **raphis.** minute needle-shaped crystals of calcium oxalate, that occur in the cells of many plants. [< New Latin *raphides* < Greek *rhaphis, -idos* a needle; see etym. under **raphe**]

**raph|is** (raf′is), *n.* one of the raphides.

**rap|id** (rap′id), *adj., n.* — *adj.* **1** moving, acting, or doing with speed; very quick; swift: *a rapid walk, a rapid worker.* SYN: fleet, speedy. See syn. under **quick. 2** going on or forward at a fast rate: *rapid growth, rapid development.* **3** fairly steep: *a rapid slope.* **4** arranged for brief exposures to light: *a rapid film.*
— *n.* **rapids,** a part of a river's course where the water rushes quickly, often over rocks near the surface: *The boat overturned in the rapids. Most hair-raising future project: A trip on the rapids of the Colorado River* (Newsweek).
[< Latin *rapidus* < *rapere* to hurry away; seize]
— **rap′id|ly,** *adv.* — **rap′id|ness,** *n.*

**rapid eye movement,** the frequent and rapid movements of the eyes which occur during the dreaming period or state known as paradoxical sleep; REM: *Dream experiments have only been possible since the discovery that rapid eye movements ... in a sleeping man indicate he is dreaming* (Science News).

**rap|id-fire** (rap′id fīr′), *adj.* **1** firing shots in quick succession. **2** *Figurative:* *rapid-fire remarks, rapid-fire commands, rapid-fire wit.*

**rap|id-fir|ing** (rap′id fīr′ing), *adj.* = rapid-fire.

**ra|pid|i|ty** (rə pid′ə tē), *n.* quickness; swiftness; speed.

**ra|pi|do** (rä′pē dō), *n., pl.* **-dos.** (in Italy, Spain, and Latin America) an express train. [< Italian *rapido,* Spanish *rápido* (literally) rapid]

**rap|ids** (rap′idz), *n.pl.* See under **rapid.**

**rapid transit,** a subway or elevated railroad, or other fast system of public transportation, in or near a city.

**ra|pi|er** (rā′pē ər), *n.* a long and light two-edged sword with a narrow, pointed blade, used for thrusting. See picture at **sword.** [< Middle French *rapière* < Old French *rapiere,* adjective < *râpe* a grater, rasp (because of its perforated guard)]

**ra|pi|er|like** (rā′pē ər līk′), *adj.* sharp; keen: *a rapierlike edge,* (*Figurative.*) *rapierlike wit.*

**rap|ine** (rap′in), *n.* a robbing by force and carrying off; plundering: *The soldiers in the enemy's land got their food by rapine.* [< Latin *rapīna* < *rapere* to seize, hurry off. See etym. of doublets **ravin, ravine.**]

**rap|ist** (rā′pist), *n.* a person who commits rape.

**rap|loch** (rap′lOH), *n., adj. Scottish.* — *n.* a coarse, undyed, homespun woolen.
— *adj.* coarse; rough; homely: *Tho' rough an' raploch be her measure, She's seldom lazy* (Robert Burns).

**rap|pa|ree** (rap′ə rē′), *n.* **1** an Irish freebooter, especially of the late 1600's. **2** = robber. [< Irish *rapaire* (originally) short pike; later, the wielder of the pike]

**rap|pee** (ra pē′), *n.* a strong snuff made from the darker and ranker kinds of tobacco leaves. [< French (*tabac*) *râpé* (literally) grated (tobacco) < Old French *râpe;* see etym. under **rape**[3]]

**rap|pel**[1] (ra pel′), *n.* the roll or beat of the drum to call soldiers to arms. [< French *rappel* < *rappeler* to recall; see etym. under **repeal**]

***rap|pel**[2] (ra pel′), *v.i.,* **-pelled, pel|ling.** to descend a cliff or rock face on a rope by means of short drops, the rope being secured above the climber and passed through a harness and karabiners or, traditionally, between the legs, across the chest, and over the shoulder, the other end hanging free. [< French *rappeler;* see etym. under **repeal**]

***rappel**[2]

**rap|pen** (rap′ən), *n., pl.* **-pen. 1** the Swiss centime. **2** a coin worth one rappen. [< German *Rappen* < Middle High German *rappe* a coin with the head of a bird on it < *rappe, rabe* raven]

**rap|per**[1] (rap′ər), *n.* **1** a person who raps, especially as a means of communication, in a séance. **2** a door knocker. [< *rap*[1] + *-er*[1]]

**rap|per**[2] (rap′ər), *n. U.S. Slang.* a person who raps; talker. [< *rap*[4] + *-er*[1]]

**Rapp|ite** (rap′īt), *n.* a member of the Harmonists. [< George *Rapp,* 1757-1847, the leader of the Harmonists + *-ite*[1]]

**rap|port** (ra pôrt′, -pōrt′; *French* rȧ pôr′), *n.* **1** relation; connection: *Some time might be necessary before sufficient rapport ... is built up between observer and observed* (Anthony H. Richmond). **2** agreement; harmony: *the rapport of close friends.* [< French *rapport* < *rapporter* bring back < *re-* again, re- + *apporter* < Latin *adportāre* bring < *ad-* to + *portāre* carry]

**rap|por|tage** (rȧ pôr tȧzh′), *n. French.* reportage.

**rap|por|teur** (rȧ pôr tœr′), *n. French.* **1** a reporter; recorder: *Mr. Goullart is a most delightful rapporteur and the reader remains spellbound* (Saturday Review). **2** a member of a legislative, military, or other official group, appointed to make or draw up a report: *Three rapporteurs were appointed to summarize the work of the conference and look into the possibility of a second meeting* (Bulletin of Atomic Scientists).

**rap|proche|ment** (rȧ prôsh mäN′), *n.* the establishment or renewal of friendly relations: *Such a rapprochement of the reformed and evangelical churches would carry one stage farther the cause of Christian unity* (London Times). [< French *rapprochement* < *rapprocher* bring near < *re-* re- + Old French *aprochier* to approach]

**rap|scal|lion** (rap skal′yən), *n.* a rascal; rogue; scamp: *A set of ferocious-looking rapscallions had boarded the steamer* (James Runciman). Also, **rascallion.** [earlier *rascallion* < *rascal*]

**rap session,** *U.S. Slang.* an informal discussion by a group of people, usually about a specific problem: *a church rap session at which a few hundred women came to talk about their abortions* (New Yorker). [< *rap*[4]]

**rap sheet,** *U.S. Slang.* a police record: *The "Rap Sheet" of most first-termers will show from one to three pages of brushes with the law, fines, county-jail time, and probation before these men got into a California prison, or for that matter, most American prisons* (Atlantic). [< *rap*[1]]

**rapt** (rapt), *adj., v.* — *adj.* **1** lost in delight: *rapt with joy.* SYN: enraptured, ecstatic. **2** so busy thinking of or enjoying one thing that one does not know what else is happening: *Rapt in his work, he did not hear the footsteps coming closer.* SYN: engrossed, spellbound, absorbed. **3** carried away in body or spirit from earth, life, or ordinary affairs: *Rapt into future times, the bard begun* (Alexander Pope). SYN: transported. **4** showing a rapt condition; caused by a rapt condition: *a rapt smile. The girls listened to the story with rapt attention.*
— *v.* a past tense and past participle of **rap**[3].
[< Latin *raptus,* past participle of *rapere* seize]
— **rapt′ly,** *adv.* — **rapt′ness,** *n.*

**rap|tor** (rap′tər, -tôr), *n.* any raptorial bird; bird of prey: *Some raptors never attack birds, others only occasionally* (W. H. Hudson). [< Latin *raptor;* see etym. under **raptorial**]

**rap|to|ri|al** (rap tôr′ē əl, -tōr′-), *adj.* **1** adapted for seizing prey; having a hooked beak and sharp claws suited for seizing prey. **2** belonging to or having to do with birds of prey, such as the eagles and hawks. [< Latin *raptor, -ōris* robber (< *rapere* seize) + English *-al*[1]]

**rap|ture** (rap′chər), *n., v.,* **-tured, -tur|ing.** — *n.* **1** a strong feeling that absorbs the mind; very great joy: *The mother gazed with rapture at her newborn baby.* **2** Often, **raptures.** an expression of great joy. **3** *Obsolete.* a carrying or transporting.
— *v.t.* = enrapture.
[< *rapt;* patterned on *capture*]
— *Syn. n.* **1 Rapture, ecstasy** are formal words meaning a feeling of being lifted high in mind and spirits. **Rapture** emphasizes being filled with and completely taken up in a feeling of delight or bliss: *In rapture the child listened to the talking doll.* **Ecstasy** implies being overwhelmed or carried away by strong emotion: *The intensity of religious ecstasy enables some people temporarily to forget their worldly cares.*

**rapture of the deep,** = nitrogen narcosis.

**rapture of the depths,** = nitrogen narcosis.

**rap|tur|ous** (rap′chər əs), *adj.* full of rapture; expressing or feeling rapture. SYN: ecstatic, blissful, transported. — **rap′tur|ous|ly,** *adv.* — **rap′tur|ous|ness,** *n.*

**rap|tus** (rap′təs), *n.* rapturous emotion; ecstatic feeling: *He respected the state of raptus in which all these poems were written* (Atlantic). [< Latin *raptus;* see etym. under **rapt**]

**ra|ra a|vis** (rãr′ə ā′vis), *pl.* **ra|rae a|ves** (rãr′ē ā′vēz). *Latin.* **1** a person or thing seldom met; rarity: *The once familiar village iceman is now rara avis* (Atlantic). **2** (literally) a rare bird.

**rare**[1] (rãr), *adj.,* **rar|er, rar|est. 1** seldom seen or found: *Peacocks and storks are rare birds in the United States. The three-o'clock in the morning courage which Bonaparte thought was the rarest* (Thoreau). **2** not happening often; unusual: *a rare event. Snow is rare in Florida.* SYN: infrequent, uncommon. **3** unusually good or great: *rare beauty. Edison had rare powers as an inventor.* **4** not dense; thin: *The higher you go above the earth, the rarer the air is.* [< Latin *rārus*] — **rare′ness,** *n.*
— *Syn.* **1 Rare, scarce** mean not often or easily found. **Rare** describes something uncommon or unusual at any time and often suggests excellence or value above the ordinary: *The Gutenberg Bible is a rare book.* **Scarce** describes something usually or formerly common or plentiful but not easily available at the present time: *Water is becoming scarce in some parts of the country.*

**rare**[2] (rãr), *adj.,* **rar|er, rar|est.** not cooked much: *a rare steak.* SYN: underdone. [variant of *rear*[3], Old English *hrēr* lightly cooked] — **rare′ness,** *n.*

**rare bird,** a rarity; rara avis: *Prokofiev's opera ... first saw production in Chicago and is a rare bird in England* (Manchester Guardian Weekly).

**rare|bit** (rãr′bit), *n.* = Welsh rabbit. [alteration of (Welsh) *rabbit*]

**rare earth, 1** an oxide of a rare-earth element: *Rare earths can be used in control rods for nuclear reactors, and also as a radiation shielding ingredient in concrete* (Science News Letter). **2** = rare-earth element.

**rare-earth** (rãr′ẽrth′), *adj.* of or having to do with rare earth.

**Pronunciation Key:** hat, āge, cãre, fär; let, ēqual, tėrm; it, īce; hot, ōpen, ôrder; **oi**l, **ou**t; cup, pu̇t, rüle; **ch**ild; lo**ng**; **th**in; **ᴛʜ**en; **zh**, measure; **ə** represents **a** in about, **e** in taken, **i** in pencil, **o** in lemon, **u** in circus.

**rare-earth element** or **metal**, any one of a series of metallic elements that have similar properties, ranging from lanthanum (atomic number 57) through lutetium (atomic number 71); lanthanide. Some series do not include lanthanum. *Relatively large proportions of the rare-earth elements are formed in fission and their separation was the subject of intense study as a part of the "Manhattan Project"* (K. S. Spiegler).

**rar|ee show** (rãr′ē), **1** a show carried about in a box; peep show. **2** any show or spectacle. [probably alteration of earlier *rare show*]

**rar|e|fac|tion** (rãr′ə fak′shən), *n.* **1** the action of rarefying. **2** the process of being rarefied. **3** *Physics.* **a** a decrease in density and pressure in a medium, such as air, due to the passing of a sound wave or other compression wave. **b** the region in which this occurs.

**rar|e|fac|tion|al** (rãr′ə fak′shə nəl), *adj.* = rarefactive.

**rar|e|fac|tive** (rãr′ə fak′tiv), *adj.* causing, attended with, or characterized by rarefaction. [< Latin *rārēfactum,* past participle of *rārēfacere* rarefy + English *-ive*]

**rar|e|fi|ca|tion** (rãr′ə fə kā′shən), *n.* = rarefaction.

**rar|e|fy** (rãr′ə fī), *v.,* **-fied, -fy|ing.** —*v.t.* **1** to make less dense: *The air on high mountains is rarefied.* **2** *Figurative.* to refine; purify: *Love is a gentle flame that rarefies ... her whole being* (William Hazlitt).
—*v.i.* **1** to become less dense. **2** *Figurative.* to make (an idea) subtle: *In some parts of the argument the abstraction is so rarefied as to become ... fallacious* (Benjamin Jowett). Also, **rarify.**
[< Latin *rārēfacere* < *rārē,* adverb, rare (< *rārus,* adjective) + *facere* make, -fy]

**rare gas,** = inert gas.

**rare|ly** (rãr′lē), *adv.* **1** not often or commonly; seldom; infrequently: *a sight rarely seen. A person who is usually on time is rarely late.* **2** unusually; unusually well: *a rarely carved panel.*
**rarely ever,** *Informal.* seldom: *I rarely ever go out for dinner.*

**rare|ripe** (rãr′rīp′), *adj., n.* —*adj.* coming early to maturity; ripening early in the year; early ripe: *rareripe fruit or grain.* —*n.* a fruit or vegetable that is ripe early, especially a variety of peach. [< *rare,* obsolete form of *rathe* + *ripe*]

**rar|i|fy** (rãr′ə fī), *v.t., v.i.,* **-fied, -fy|ing.** = rarefy.

**rar|ing** (rãr′ing), *adj. Informal.* very eager; full of desire: *raring to go. Members had come back to Westminster raring for a fight* (Punch). [< present participle of *rare,* dialectal variant of *rear*[2]]

**rar|i|ty** (rãr′ə tē), *n., pl.* **-ties. 1** something rare: *A person over one hundred years old is a rarity. He was that priceless rarity, an intuitive thinker who was able to assemble and grasp great generalities* (Atlantic). **SYN:** exception. **2** fewness; scarcity: *The rarity of diamonds makes them valuable.* **SYN:** paucity, infrequency. **3** rare or thin condition; lack of density; thinness: *The rarity of the air in the mountains is bad for people with weak hearts.* **SYN:** tenuity.

**ras** (ras), *n.* **1** a headland, promontory, or cape (used in many place names on the Arabian and African coasts). **2** a prince, governor, or chief in Ethiopia. [< Arabic *rās* head]

**ras|bo|ra** (raz bôr′ə, -bōr′-), *n., pl.* **-ras.** any one of a group of Asian minnows, especially a Malayan species having a black triangle on the posterior part of the body and often kept in aquariums. [< New Latin *Rasbora* the genus name < the native name in the East Indies]

**ras|cal** (ras′kəl), *n., adj.* —*n.* **1** a bad, dishonest person: *The thieving rascal stole my bicycle.* **2** a mischievous person, child, or animal; scamp: *Come here, you little rascal. He's a lucky young rascal. My sons are a pair of rascals at times.* **3** *Obsolete.* one of the rabble.
—*adj.* **1** low; mean; dishonest: *My days spent in rascal enterprises and rubbish selling* (H. G. Wells). **2** *Obsolete.* of low birth; baseborn; base.
[< Old French *rascaille* < *rasque* scurvy, filth < Vulgar Latin *rāsicāre* to scrape < Latin *rādere* to scrape, scratch]

**ras|cal|i|ty** (ras kal′ə tē), *n., pl.* **-ties. 1** rascally character or conduct: ... *a harlequin playing a clarinet and presumably representing the spirit of pure Gallic rascality* (New Yorker). **2** a rascally act or practice: *I don't want to be told about any of his rascalities* (Joseph Conrad). **3** rascals as a group.

**ras|cal|lion** (ras kal′yən), *n.* = rapscallion.

**ras|cal|ly** (ras′kə lē), *adj., adv.* —*adj.* of or like a rascal; mean or dishonest; bad: *To steal the poor boy's bicycle was a rascally trick. There was none of any quality, but poor and rascally people* (Samuel Pepys).
—*adv.* in a rascally manner.

**ras|casse** (ras kas′), *n.* a scorpionfish of the Mediterranean, used in preparing bouillabaisse. [< French *rascasse* < Provençal *rascasso*]

**rase** (rāz), *v.t.,* **rased, ras|ing.** = raze.

**rash**[1] (rash), *adj., adv.* —*adj.* **1** too hasty and careless; reckless; taking too much risk: *It is rash to cross the street without looking both ways.* **SYN:** impetuous. **2** characterized by undue haste: *a rash promise, a rash remark.* **3** *Obsolete.* quick and strong in action: *rash gunpowder* (Shakespeare).
—*adv. Obsolete.* in a rash manner; rashly: *Why do you speak so startlingly and rash?* (Shakespeare).
[Middle English *rasch* quick, probably < Middle Dutch, or Middle Low German, fast, quick, nimble] —**rash′ly,** *adv.* —**rash′ness,** *n.*
—*Syn. adj.* **1, 2 Rash, reckless** mean acting or speaking without due care or thought. **Rash** emphasizes being in too great a rush, speaking hastily or plunging into action without stopping to think: *Only a rash person would have rushed into the burning house to save some clothes.* **Reckless** emphasizes being without caution, acting carelessly without paying attention to possible consequences of what one does or says: *The dog was killed by a reckless driver.*

**rash**[2] (rash), *n.* **1** the act or fact of breaking out with many small red spots on the skin. Scarlet fever causes a rash. **2** *Informal, Figurative.* an outbreak: *a rash of investigations, a rash of letters. A few years ago the popular press broke out with a ... rash of editorials scolding American novelists for the way they were portraying their native country* (Harper's). [< Old French *rasche,* and *rasque* scurf, scurvy; see etym. under **rascal**]

**rash**[3] (rash), *n. Scottish.* rush (the plant).

**rash|er** (rash′ər), *n.* a thin slice of bacon or ham for frying or broiling. [origin uncertain; perhaps < obsolete *rash* to cut, slash]

**Ras|kol|nik** (räs kōl′nik), *n., pl.* **-niks, -ni|ki** (-nə kē). a dissenter from the Orthodox Church in Russia. [< Russian *Raskol′nik* < *raskolot′* split < *raskol* split < *raz-* apart + *kolot′* to split]

**ra|so|ri|al** (rə sôr′ē əl, -sōr′-), *adj.* of or having to do with birds that scratch the ground for food, such as the chicken. [< New Latin *Rasores,* the order name (< Latin *rādere* to scratch) + English *-ial*]

**ra|sor|ite** (rā′zər īt), *n.* = kernite. [< *Rasor,* a proper name + *-ite*[1]]

**rasp** (rasp, räsp), *v., n.* —*v.i.* **1** to make a harsh, grating sound: *The file rasped as he worked.* **2** *Figurative.* to produce a harsh effect; grate: *The sound rasped on his ears.*
—*v.t.* **1** to utter with a grating sound: *to rasp out a command.* **2** *Figurative.* to have a harsh, grating effect on; irritate: *Her feelings were rasped and exploded into anger.* **3** to scrape with a rough instrument.
—*n.* **1** a harsh, grating sound: *the rasp of katydids, the rasp in a person's voice.* **2** a coarse file with pointlike teeth. **3** the act of rasping, or rubbing with something like a rasp.
[< Old French *rasper,* related to *râpe;* see etym. under **rape**[3]]

**rasp|ber|ry** (raz′ber′ē, -bər-; räz′-), *n., pl.* **-ries,** *adj.* —*n.* **1** a small fruit that grows on bushes. It is hollow and shaped like a cone. Raspberries are usually red or black, but some kinds are white or yellow. Each berry is composed of many drupelets. **2** the bush that it grows on. The raspberry is a species of bramble and belongs to the rose family. **3** a reddish purple. **4** *Slang.* a sound of disapproval or derision made with the tongue and lips.
—*adj.* reddish-purple.
[earlier *raspis* raspberry (origin uncertain) + *berry*]

**raspberry sawfly,** a sawfly, whose pale-green larvae attack such plants as the raspberry and blackberry.

**rasped** (raspt, räspt), *adj.* **1** = raspy. **2** (of book edges) roughened to imitate a deckle edge, but left uncut.

**rasp|er** (ras′pər, räs′-), *n.* **1** a person or thing that rasps. **2** a machine for scraping sugar cane.

**rasp|ing** (ras′ping, räs′-), *adj.* = raspy. —**rasp′ing|ly,** *adv.*

**rasp|y** (ras′pē, räs′-), *adj.,* **rasp|i|er, rasp|i|est. 1** grating; harsh; rough. **2** *Figurative.* irritable: *a raspy disposition.*

**ras|se** (ras′ə, ras), *n.* a small civet cat, widely distributed from Malaya, China, and India to Madagascar, and often kept in captivity for the civet that it yields. [< Javanese *rase*]

**ras|sle** (ras′əl), *v.t., v.i.,* **-sled, -sling.** *Dialect.* wrestle.

**Ras Ta|far|i|an,** or **Ras|ta|far|i|an** (ras′tə fãr′ē ən), *n., adj.* —*n.* a member of a West Indian cult of black nationalists, especially in Jamaica, that worship the former Emperor of Ethiopia, Haile Selassie, as God.
—*adj.* of or having to do with this cult.
[< *Ras Tafari,* the title and surname of Emperor Haile Selassie + *-an*]

**ras|ter** (ras′tər), *n.* a pattern of close parallel lines in the cathode-ray tube on which the image is formed in a television set. [< German *Raster* screen, ultimately < Latin *rādere* to scratch]

**ra|sure** (rā′zhər), *n.* erasure; obliteration; effacement. [< Latin *rāsūra* < *rādere* to scrape, scratch]

∗**rat** (rat), *n., interj., v.,* **rat|ted, rat|ting.** —*n.* **1** a long-tailed rodent like a mouse but larger. Rats are gray, black, brown, or white. They are found in almost any place inhabited by man, are frequent spreaders of disease, and cause great damage. **2** any member of several groups of similar rodents of the New World, such as the wood rats, cotton rats, and kangaroo rats. **3** any one of various other mammals, such as the muskrat. **4** *Slang, Figurative.* a low, mean, disloyal person who abandons his party or associates, especially in time of trouble. **5** *Informal, Figurative.* a scab (workman). **6** *U.S.* a roll of hair or other material worn to puff out a woman's hair.
—*interj.* **rats,** *Slang.* an exclamation used to indicate scornful impatience or disbelief: *"We are alone at last," repeated Miss Vavasour ... "Oh rapture!" "Oh rats!" said the manager of the theater* (Leonard Merrick).
—*v.i.* **1** to hunt for rats; catch rats. **2** *Informal, Figurative.* to behave in a low, mean, disloyal way. **3** *Informal, Figurative.* to act as a rat or scab. **4** *U.S. Slang.* to turn informer against one's associates.
—*v.t. U.S.* **1** to provide with a roll of hair or other material worn to puff out the hair: *The ladies were beautifully ruffled and ratted.* **2** to puff out (hair): *When they made their hair bouffant they said that they ratted it* (New Yorker).
**rat around,** *Slang.* to run back and forth; scurry around: *"He doesn't like to be ratting around in hotel rooms"* (New Yorker).
**rat on,** *Slang.* to go back on; welsh: *to rat on an obligation or promise.*
**smell a rat,** to suspect a trick or scheme: *He'll be sure to smell a rat if I'm with you* (William Dean Howells).
[Old English *rætt,* apparently < Vulgar Latin *rattus*] —**rat′like′,** *adj.*

∗**rat**
definitions 1, 2, 3

**ra|ta** (rä′tə), *n.* **1** a large forest tree of New Zealand with dark red flowers and a hard, red wood. **2** a parasitic climbing vine of the same species. [< Maori *rata*]

**rat|a|bil|i|ty** (rā′tə bil′ə tē), *n.* the quality of being ratable. Also, **rateability.**

**rat|a|ble** (rā′tə bəl), *adj.* **1** that can be rated. **2** = proportional. **3** *British.* taxable. Also, **rateable.**

**rat|a|bly** (rā′tə blē), *adv.* in a ratable manner; proportionately. Also, **rateably.**

**rat|a|fee** (rat′ə fē′), *n.* = ratafia.

**rat|a|fi|a** (rat′ə fē′ə), *n.* **1** a cordial flavored with fruit kernels or almonds. **2** a sweet biscuit similarly flavored. [< French *ratafia* < Creole, also *tafia,* name for rum; origin uncertain]

**rat|al** (rā′təl), *n. British.* the amount on which rates or taxes are assessed.

**ra|tan** (ra tan′), *n.* = rattan.

**rat|a|plan** (rat′ə plan′), *n.* the sound of a drum; tattoo. [< French *rataplan;* imitative]

**rat-a-tat** (rat′ə tat′), *n.* a sound as of rapping; rat-tat: *the rat-a-tat of drumbeats.*

**rat-a-tat-tat** (rat′ə tat tat′), *n.* = rat-a-tat.

**rat|bag** (rat′bag′), *n. Australian Slang.* a queer person; crank; creep.

**rat|bite fever** or **disease** (rat′bīt′), a disease characterized by fever, ulceration, and a purplish rash, caused by the bite of a rat or other infected animal.

**rat·catch·er** (rat′kach′ər), *n.* a person or animal that catches rats; ratter.

**ratch** (rach), *n.* = ratchet. [perhaps < German *Rätsche,* or *Ratsche*]

**rat cheese,** = Cheddar: *It is also known, ... after one of its biggest fans,* [*as*] *rat cheese* (New York Times).

**ratch·et** (rach′it), *n., v.* —*n.* **1** a wheel or bar with teeth that come against a catch so that motion is permitted in one direction but not in the other. **2** the catch. **3** the entire device, wheel and catch or bar and catch.
—*v.t.* to operate or move by means of a ratchet: *One crew attached the chain, ... secured the cable, and ratcheted the lever with verve* (Punch).
—*v.i.* to move in the manner of a ratchet.
[< French *rochet* < Italian *rocchetto* bobbin, spindle, (diminutive) < *rocca* distaff < Germanic (compare Old High German *roccho* distaff)]

**ratchet bar,** a bar with pegs or teeth to hold against a ratchet wheel; rack.

**ratchet brace,** a carpenters' brace in which, by means of a ratchet, reciprocating motion of the handle is converted into rotary motion of the bit.

**ratchet drill,** a drill rotated by a ratchet wheel moved by a pawl and lever.

**ratchet jaw,** *U.S. Slang.* a chatterbox: *But even without the ratchet jaws, some CBers on crowded highways ... never get a chance to talk* (Robert K. Johnson).

**ratchet wheel,** a wheel with teeth and a catch that permits motion in only one direction. See picture under **pawl.**

**ratch·et·y** (rach′ə tē), *adj.* resembling the movement of a ratchet; jerky; clipping.

**rate[1]** (rāt), *n., v.,* **rat·ed, rat·ing.** —*n.* **1** a quantity, amount, or degree measured in proportion to something else: *The rate of interest is 6 cents on the dollar. The railroad rate is 4 cents a mile. Parcel post rates depend on weight.* **2** the degree of speed, progress, accumulation, or other measure: *The car was going at the rate of 40 miles an hour. The General posted along at a great rate* (Dickens). **3** a price: *the rates for a long-distance telephone call. We pay the regular rate.* **4** class; grade; rating: *first rate, second rate.* SYN: rank, order. **5** *British.* a tax on property for some local purpose. **6** *Obsolete.* a style of living: *Nor do I now make moan to be abridged From such a noble rate* (Shakespeare).
—*v.t.* **1** to put a value on: *We rated the house as worth $30,000.* **2** to consider; regard: *He was rated one of the richest men in town.* **3** to put in a certain class or grade: *I should be rated ship's boy* (Robert Louis Stevenson). **4** *Informal.* to be worthy of: *She rates the best seat in the house.* **5** to subject to a certain tax. **6** to fix at a certain rate. **7** to arrange for transporting (goods) at a certain rate. **8** to design for a certain speed. **9** to determine the speed of.
—*v.i.* to be ranked; be considered.
**at any rate,** in any case; under any circumstances; anyway: *Commercially the arrangement was not a success, at any rate for the firm* (Joseph Conrad).
**at that** (or **this**) **rate,** in that or this case; under such circumstances: *At this rate, overspeculation will be followed by declines, but there is a vast difference between a speculative reaction and a panic* (Boston Transcript).
[< Old French *rate* < Medieval Latin *rata* (*pars*) fixed (amount); *rata* < Latin *rērī* to reckon. Compare etym. under **prorate.**]

**rate[2]** (rāt), *v.t., v.i.,* **rat·ed, rat·ing.** to scold; berate: [*Elizabeth I*] *rated great nobles as if they were schoolboys* (John R. Green). [Middle English *răten;* origin uncertain. Compare Swedish *rata* to reject, find fault with.]

**ra·té** (rä tā′), *n. French.* a failure; bungler.

**rate·a·bil·i·ty** (rā′tə bil′ə tē), *n.* = ratability.

**rate·a·ble** (rā′tə bəl), *adj.* = ratable.

**rate·a·bly** (rā′tə blē), *adv.* = ratably.

**rate card,** a card listing rates for advertising.

**ra·tel** (rā′təl, rä′-), *n.* either of two badgerlike, carnivorous mammals, one found in South and East Africa and the other in southern Asia, having a gray back and black underside; honey badger. [< Afrikaans *ratel* < German *Ratel-Maus* (literally) rattle-mouse]

**rate meter,** a device in a radiation counter which indicates the rate at which ions are absorbed: *The whole soft-landing operation is a complex manoeuvre involving feedback from a ... radar rate meter* (New Scientist).

**rate-of-climb indicator** (rāt′əv klīm′), a flight instrument on a control panel that shows the rate of climb or descent of an airplane.

**rate of exchange,** the rate or price per unit at which the currency of one country may be exchanged for the currency of another.

**rate·pay·er** (rāt′pā′ər), *n. British.* a taxpayer.

**rate·pay·ing** (rāt′pā′ing), *adj. British.* paying a tax or taxes.

**rat·er[1]** (rā′tər), *n.* a person or thing that rates, estimates, measures, or otherwise evaluates: *His surveys had also uncovered a rather disquieting fact for TV raters who assumed everyone tuned in is watching* (Newsweek).

**rat·er[2]** (rā′tər), *n.* a person who scolds.

**rat·fink** (rat′fingk′), *n. Slang.* a mean or obnoxious person; fink.

**rat·fish** (rat′fish′), *n., pl.* **-fish·es** or (*collectively*) **-fish.** a cartilaginous fish with a long, thin tail and large crushing plates instead of teeth; chimaera: *Liver oil from ratfish is the richest source of butyl alcohol* (Science News Letter).

**rat flea,** any one of several species of fleas that infest rats and are carriers of diseases such as bubonic plague and typhus.

***rat·guard** (rat′gärd′), *n.* a sheet-metal disk attached to the moorings of a vessel to keep rats from boarding it.

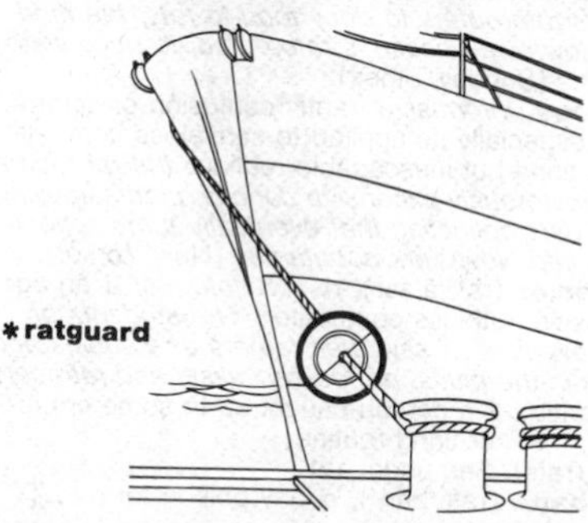

***ratguard**

**rath[1]** (rath, räth), *adj., adv. Archaic.* rathe.

**rath[2]** (räth), *n.* a fortified dwelling of an ancient Irish chief. [< Irish *rath*]

**rat·haus** (rät′hous), *n.* a German town hall. [< German *Rathaus* < *Rat* council, assembly + *Haus* house]

**rathe** (rāᴛʜ), *adj., adv. Archaic.* early; growing or blooming early: *the rathe primrose* (Milton); *men of rathe and riper years* (Tennyson). [Old English *hræth* quick]

**rath·er** (raᴛʜ′ər, räᴛʜ′-), *adv., interj.* —*adv.* **1** more willingly; more readily; by preference: *I would rather go today than tomorrow. She would rather play than rest.* **2** more properly; with better reason: *This is rather for your parents to decide than for you.* **3** more truly or correctly: *We sat up till one o'clock Monday night or, rather, Tuesday morning.* **4** to some extent; more than a little; somewhat: *After working so long he was rather tired.* **5** (with verbs) in some degree: *We rather felt that this was unwise.* **6** on the contrary: *The sick man is no better today; rather, he is worse. The lesson wasn't difficult to do; rather, it was easy.* **7** *Dialect.* earlier; sooner.
—*interj. British Informal.* yes, indeed! certainly! very much so!
**had rather,** would prefer to; would more willingly: *She had rather play than rest. I had rather err with Plato than be right with Horace* (Shelley).
[Old English *hrathor,* comparative of *hrathe* quickly]
► See **had** for usage note.

**rat·hole** (rat′hōl′), *n.* **1** a hole gnawed, as in woodwork, by a rat or rats. **2** *Figurative.* a disreputable place or condition: *Who routed you from a rathole ... to perch you in a palace?* (H. and J. Smith).
**down the rathole,** to nothing; down the drain: *His last pile of money—thirty-five thousand dollars—went down the rathole when he tried to save an old friend from bankruptcy* (New Yorker).

**raths·kel·ler** (räts′kel′ər, raths′-), *n.* a restaurant selling alcoholic drinks. It is usually below street level. [American English < German *Rathskeller* < *Rathaus* town hall (< *Rat* town council) + *Keller* cellar (because it was originally a wineshop in the town hall)]

**rat·i·cide** (rat′ə sīd), *n.* a poisonous substance for killing rats; rodenticide. [< *rat* + *-cide*[1]]

**rat·i·fi·ca·tion** (rat′ə fə kā′shən), *n.* confirmation; approval: *the ratification of a treaty by the Senate.*

**rat·i·fi·er** (rat′ə fī′ər), *n.* a person or thing that ratifies or sanctions.

**rat·i·fy** (rat′ə fī), *v.t.,* **-fied, -fy·ing.** to confirm; approve: *The two countries will ratify the agreement made by their representatives. The Senate ratified the treaty.* SYN: sanction, authorize. See syn. under **approve.** [< Old French *ratifier,* learned borrowing from Medieval Latin *ratificare* < Latin *rērī* to reckon + *facere* make]

**ra·tine** (ra tēn′), *n.* = ratiné.

**rat·i·né** (rat′ə nā′), *n.* any one of various fabrics, of wool or cotton, with a curled or tufted nap or a looped or rough surface: *Bouclé, ratiné, and éponge are all similar in character, made from a special three-ply yarn producing a curly surface and spongy cloth* (Bernice G. Chambers). [< French *ratiné,* past participle of *ratiner* < Old French *ratine,* earlier *rastin* cloth of frizzed wool; origin uncertain. See related etym. at **ratteen.**]

**rat·ing[1]** (rā′ting), *n.* **1** a class; grade. **2a** the position in a class or grade: *the rating of a seaman, the rating of a ship according to tonnage.* **b** an enlisted man, as in the Royal Navy or British merchant navy: *The Eagle ... will embark 400 relatives of officers and ratings for a day at sea* (Sunday Times). **3** *U.S.* a level of merit or popularity established by a survey: *a television program with a high rating. After a fortnight of low ratings and blows from the reviewers, an emergency meeting of network bigwigs was held to try to pep up the show* (Newsweek). **4** an amount fixed as a rate: *a rating of 80 per cent in English.* **5** = a credit rating. **6** *British.* the fixing of the amount of a tax. **7** the operating characteristics of a machine, such as voltage or horsepower.

**rat·ing[2]** (rā′ting), *n.* the act of scolding; reproving.

**ra·ti·o** (rā′shē ō, -shō), *n., pl.* **-ti·os. 1** the relation between two numbers or quantities expressed as a quotient; relative magnitude. "He has sheep and cows in the ratio of 10 to 3" means that he has ten sheep for every three cows, or 3 1/3 times as many sheep as cows. **2** a quotient expressing this relation. The ratio between two quantities is the number of times one contains the other. The ratio of 3 to 6 is written as 3:6, 3/6, or 1/2; the ratio of 6 to 3 is written as 6:3, 6/3, 6 ÷ 3, or 2. The ratios of 3 to 5 and 6 to 10 are the same. **3** proportional relation or rate, especially of gold to silver. [< Latin *ratiō, -ōnis* reckoning < *rērī* to reckon. See etym. of doublets **ration, reason.**]

**ra·ti·oc·i·nate** (rash′ē os′ə nāt), *v.i.,* **-nat·ed, -nat·ing.** to carry on a process of reasoning; reason: *Besides* (*I ratiocinated*) *I was not the first rogue male to fall for the charms of a young thing only five-sixths his age* (Punch). [< Latin *ratiōcinārī* (with English *-ate*[1]) < *ratiō, -ōnis;* see etym. under **ratio**] —**ra′ti·oc′i·na′tor,** *n.*

**ra·ti·oc·i·na·tion** (rash′ē os′ə nā′shən), *n.* **1** reasoning; process of reasoning: *On the way home, I tried to envision the rival patterns of ratiocination* (New Yorker). **2** a conclusion arrived at by reasoning: *subtle definitions, or intricate ratiocinations* (Samuel Johnson).

**ra·ti·oc·i·na·tive** (rash′ē os′ə nā′tiv), *adj.* of or characterized by close or careful reasoning: *Hoyle's book abounds in theories which make Sherlock Holmes's ratiocinative high jinks look as unexciting as an old calabash pipe* (Scientific American).

**ra·ti·oc·i·na·to·ry** (rash′ē os′ə nə tôr′ē, -tōr′-), *adj.* = ratiocinative.

**ra·tion** (rash′ən, rā′shən), *n., v.* —*n.* **1** a fixed allowance of food; daily allowance of food for a person or animal: *Rations of rice have been provided for those engaged on this work, and its distribution arranged by the village* (Science News). SYN: See syn. under **food. 2** a portion of anything dealt out: *rations of sugar, gasoline and oil rations.* SYN: share, allotment.
—*v.t.* **1** to allow only certain amounts to: *to ration citizens when supplies are scarce.* **2** to distribute in limited amounts: *to ration gasoline. Food is rationed to the public during times of shortage, such as crop failure.* **3** to supply with rations: *to ration an army.*
[< French, Middle French *ration,* learned borrowing from Latin *ratiō, -ōnis* (in Medieval Latin, share, proportion). See etym. of doublets **ratio, reason.**]

**ra·tion·al** (rash′ə nəl, rash′nəl), *adj., n.* —*adj.* **1** sensible; reasonable; reasoned out: *When people are very angry, they seldom act in a rational way.* SYN: sound, wise, judicious, sane. **2** able to think and reason clearly: *As children grow older, they become more rational. The patient appeared perfectly rational.* **3** of reason; based on reasoning: *There is a rational explanation for thunder and lightning.* **4** *Mathematics.* **a** of or having to do with a rational number. **b** involving no root that cannot be extracted. **5** *Prosody.* of or having to do with a syllable in Greek or Latin verse that has the metrical value needed to fit the pattern.
—*n.* **1** that which is rational or reasonable. **2** = rational number.
[< Latin *ratiōnālis* < *ratiō;* see etym. under **ratio**] —**ra′tion·al·ly,** *adv.* —**ra′tion·al·ness,** *n.*

**ra·tion·ale** (rash′ə nal′; -näl′ē, -nā′-), *n.* **1** the fundamental reason; the whys and wherefores:

*We must examine the rationale of the rule* (Edgar Allan Poe). **2** a statement of reasons; reasoned principles: *The rationale of this policy was spelled out in letters written by Stalin and published in "Bolshevik" on October 2, 1952* (W. Averell Harriman). [< Latin *ratiōnāle,* neuter of *ratiōnālis* rational < *ratiō;* see etym. under **ratio**]

**ra|tion|al|ise** (rash'ə nə līz, rash'nə-), *v.t., v.i.,* **-ised, -is|ing.** *Especially British.* rationalize.

**ra|tion|al|ism** (rash'ə nə liz'əm, rash'nə liz-), *n.* **1** the principle or habit of accepting reason as the supreme authority in matters of opinion, belief, or conduct. **2** the philosophical doctrine that reason is in itself a source of knowledge, independent of the senses. **3** *Theology.* the examination of dogma or the explanation of the supernatural by reason.

**ra|tion|al|ist** (rash'ə nə list, rash'nə-), *n., adj.* — *n.* **1** a person who accepts reason as the supreme authority in matters of opinion, belief, or conduct. **2** an adherent of the philosophical theory of rationalism. **3** a believer in the theological doctrine of rationalism.
— *adj.* = rationalistic.

**ra|tion|al|is|tic** (rash'ə nə lis'tik, rash'nə-), *adj.* of rationalism or rationalists: *Modern man has become so rationalistic in his attitude that his tendency is toward a nonrecognition and denial of the unconscious* (New Yorker). — **ra'tion|al|is'ti|cal|ly,** *adv.*

**ra|tion|al|is|ti|cal** (rash'ə nə lis'tə kəl, rash'nə-), *adj.* = rationalistic.

**ra|tion|al|i|ty** (rash'ə nal'ə tē), *n., pl.* **-ties. 1** the possession of reason; reasonableness: *The man is odd in some ways, but no one doubts his rationality.* **2** a rational or reasonable view, practice, reason, or doctrine.

**ra|tion|al|i|za|tion** (rash'ə nə lə zā'shən, rash'nə-), *n.* **1** the act of rationalizing: *Thus, what Taylor did for rationalization of physical work, the psychologists do for the mental and emotional aspect of the worker* (Erich Fromm). **2** the fact or state of being rationalized.

**ra|tion|al|ize** (rash'ə nə līz, rash'nə-), *v.,* **-ized, -iz|ing.** — *v.t.* **1** to make rational or conformable to reason: *When life has been duly rationalized by science, it will be seen that among a man's duties, care of the body is imperative* (Herbert Spencer). **2** to treat or explain in a rational manner. **3** to find (often unconsciously) an explanation or excuse for: *She rationalizes her gluttony by thinking, "I must eat enough to keep up my strength."* **4** to explain (myth, legend, or other belief) in terms of contemporary scientific knowledge. **5** to organize or run (a business, industry, operation, or institution) on economically sound or proven methods of administration and production: *He wanted the six hundred-odd societies to rationalize themselves and offer better terms* (Punch). **6** *Mathematics.* to clear from irrational quantities.
— *v.i.* to find excuses (often unconsciously) for one's desires. — **ra'tion|al|iz'er,** *n.*

**rational number,** any number that can be expressed as an integer or as a ratio between two integers, excluding zero as a denominator; real number. 2, 5, and -1/2 are rational numbers.

**ra|tion|ing** (rash'ə ning, rā'shə ning), *n.* the distribution of scarce foods, food, or other items in rations: *During World War II many countries imposed rationing to conserve materials needed for the war effort. Gasoline rationing is one method of allocating gas in fair shares during a gas shortage.*

**rat|ite** (rat'īt), *adj., n.* — *adj.* **1** having a flat breastbone with no keel: *Ostriches and emus are ratite birds.* **2** of or having to do with ratite birds.
— *n.* a ratite bird.
[< New Latin *Ratitae* the order name < Latin *ratis* raft, timber; spelling influenced by English *-ite*[1]]

**rat kangaroo,** any one of certain small kangaroos about the size of a rabbit, found in Australia and Tasmania.

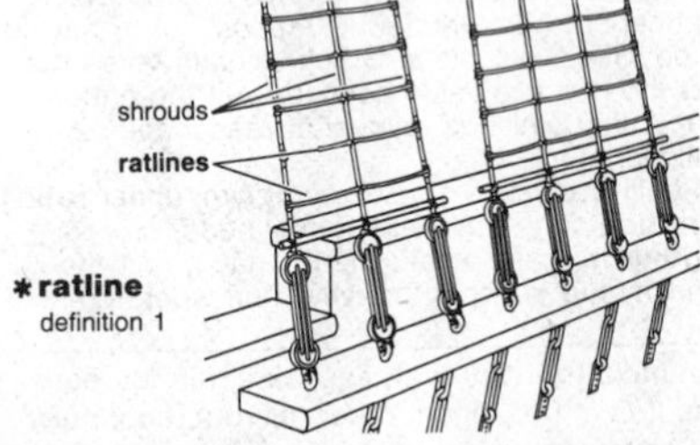

***ratline**
definition 1

***rat|line** or **rat|lin** (rat'lin), *n.* **1** one of the small ropes that cross the shrouds of a ship, used as steps for going aloft. **2** the small, tarred rope from which these are made. [Middle English *ratling,* and *radelyng;* origin uncertain; spelling influenced by English *line*[1]]

**ratline hitch,** = clove hitch.

**RATO** or **ra|to** (rā'tō), *n. Aeronautics.* a unit of one or more rockets, providing extra power to speed up an airplane during take-off. [< *r*(ocket) *a*(ssisted) *t*(ake)-*o*(ff)]

**ra|toon** (ra tün'), *n., v.* — *n.* a shoot springing up from the root of a plant after it has been cropped: *ratoons of sugar cane.*
— *v.i., v.t.* to send up or cause to send up new shoots after being cropped. Also, **rattoon.**
[< Spanish *retoño* < *retoñar* to sprout < *otoño* autumn < Latin *autumnus*]

**rat|proof** (rat'prüf'), *adj., v.* — *adj.* so made that rats cannot enter.
— *v.t.* to make ratproof: *The modern farmstead-ing is ratproofed, to deny food to rats; the modern town warehouse is ratproofed, to deny water to rats* (Sunday Times).

**rat race,** *Informal.* a frantic confusion or scramble, especially as applied to senseless competition; tiring but inescapable routine: *the rat race of preposterously expensive dances, clothes-buying, and date-collecting that eventually turns schoolgirls into New York debutantes* (New Yorker).

**rat|rac|er** (rat'rā'sər), *n. U.S. Informal.* **1** an aggressive, ruthless competitor: *The students of the twenties ... saw their fathers as Babbitts and stick-in-the-muds, not as capitalists and ratracers* (Atlantic). **2** a person caught up in some confusion, rush, or tiring routine.

**rats** (rats). See under **rat.**

**rats|bane** (rats'bān'), *n.* any poison for rats. [< *rats* + *bane*]

**rat snake,** any one of various snakes, such as the corn snake and the chicken snake of North America, that kill rats and other rodents and are sometimes domesticated for this purpose.

**rat|tail** (rat'tāl'), *adj., n.* — *adj.* having a tail or taillike part like that of a rat; long and slender: *Everything in the house, down to the last rattail hinge and hickory floor-peg, is historically accurate* (Atlantic).
— *n.* **1** something resembling a rat's tail. **2** a horse's tail with little or no hair. **3** a deep-sea fish with a long, tapering tail; grenadier.

**rattail cactus,** a cultivated cactus of Central America, with creeping, cylindrical stems and crimson flowers.

**rat-tailed** (rat'tāld'), *adj.* = rattail.

**rat-tail file,** a fine, round file used especially to enlarge holes in metal.

**rat|tan** (ra tan'), *n.* **1** Also, **rattan palm.** a kind of palm with very long, thin, jointed stems. It is a climbing plant of East India and Africa. **2** the stems of such palm trees, forming a tough, stringy material which are used especially for wickerwork and canes. **3** a cane, switch, or stick, especially a walking stick, made from a piece of such a stem. Also, **ratan.** [ultimately < Malay *rōtan*]

**rat-tat** (rat'tat'), *n.* a sound as of rapping: *Then came a sharp rat-tat at the door* (George Gissing). Also, **rat-a-tat, rat-a-tat-tat.**

**rat|teen** (ra tēn'), *n.* any one of various fabrics with tufted, looped, or rough surfaces. [< French *ratine;* origin uncertain. See related etym. at **ratiné.**]

**rat|ten** (rat'ən), *v.t.* **1** to damage or destroy (work, tools, machinery). **2** to frighten or coerce an employer or workman. — *v.i.* to practice rattening.
[perhaps related to **rat** (because of the rodent's frequent destructive habits)] — **rat'ten|er,** *n.*

**rat|ter** (rat'ər), *n.* **1** a person or animal that catches rats; ratcatcher: *Our terrier is a good ratter.* **2** *Slang.* a person who deserts, informs on, or betrays his associates.

**rat|tish** (rat'ish), *adj.* **1** of, having to do with, or resembling a rat. **2** infested with rats.

**rat|tle**[1] (rat'əl), *v.,* **-tled, -tling,** *n.* — *v.i.* **1** to make a number of short, sharp sounds: *The window rattled in the wind.* **2** to move with short, sharp sounds: *The old car rattled down the street.* **3** to talk quickly, on and on, in a lively but rather pointless manner: *They ... rattled on in a free, wild, racy talk* (William Dean Howells).
— *v.t.* **1** to cause to rattle: *She rattled the dishes. The door did not yield ... he rattled the handle violently* (Edith Wharton). **2** to say or do quickly: *He rattled off the dates without a moment's hesitation. He sat down to the piano, and rattled a lively piece of music* (Harriet Beecher Stowe). **3** *Informal.* to disturb; confuse; upset: *She was so rattled that she forgot her speech.* **4** *Informal.* to stir up; rouse. **5** to chase (game) vigorously.
— *n.* **1** a number of short, sharp sounds: *We used to hear the rattle of the milk bottles in the early morning.* **2** a toy or instrument that makes a noise when it is shaken: *The baby shakes his rattle.* **3** the series of horny pieces at the end of a rattlesnake's tail. **4** a sound in the throat caused by partial obstruction, occurring in some diseases of the lungs and also often just before death. **5** a racket; uproar. **6** any one of certain plants whose ripe seeds rattle in their cases. **7** trivial talk; chatter: *People took her rattle for wit* (George Meredith).
[Middle English *ratelen;* probably ultimately imitative. Compare Low German *ratelen.*]

**rat|tle**[2] (rat'əl), *v.t.,* **-tled, -tling.** to furnish with ratlines on: *to rattle the rigging down.* [back formation < *ratline,* taken as verbal noun *ratlin'*]

**rat|tle|box** (rat'əl boks'), *n.* **1** a boxlike toy for making a rattling sound; rattle. **2** any one of various plants of the pea family whose ripened seeds rattle in the inflated pod.

**rat|tle|brain** (rat'əl brān'), *n.* a giddy, thoughtless person.

**rat|tle|brained** (rat'əl brānd'), *adj.* like a rattlebrain; giddy; whimsical; foolish.

**rat|tle|head** (rat'əl hed'), *n.* = rattlebrain.

**rat|tle|head|ed** (rat'əl hed'id), *adj.* = rattlebrained.

**rat|tle|pate** (rat'əl pāt'), *n.* = rattlebrain.

**rat|tle|pat|ed** (rat'əl pā'tid), *adj.* like a rattlepate.

**rat|tler** (rat'lər), *n. Informal.* **1** = rattlesnake. **2** a machine or vehicle that rattles when used, especially because of age or hard use.

**rat|tle|root** (rat'əl rüt', -rút'), *n.* **1** any one of various plants whose roots have been considered a remedy for snake bite. **2** = senega. [< *rattle-*(snake) *root*]

***rat|tle|snake** (rat'əl snāk'), *n.* a poisonous American snake with a thick body and a broad, triangular head, that makes a rattling noise with the rattle at the end of its tail. Rattlesnakes are pit vipers and include the timber rattlesnake and the diamondback rattlesnake. *The rattlesnake is by far the most abundant and important of the poisonous snakes in the United States* (A. M. Winchester).
[American English < *rattle*[1] + *snake*]

***rattlesnake**
diamondback

**rattlesnake fern,** a fern characterized by clusters of sporangia that resemble the rattles of a rattlesnake.

**rattlesnake pilot,** *U.S.* a copperhead.

**rattlesnake plantain,** any one of various low terrestrial orchids with spotted leaves and whitish flowers, found in north temperate regions. See picture under **adder's-tongue.** [because of its spotted leaves]

**rattlesnake root, 1a** any one of various composite plants whose roots have been considered a remedy for snakebites. **b** the root of any of these plants. **2a** = senega. **b** its root. [because of its reputed value in cases of snakebite]

**rattlesnake weed, 1** a North American hawkweed, having leaves marked with purple veins. Its leaves and root are thought to be medicinal. **2** a weed of the parsley family, found in southern and western North America. **3** a marsh plant of the same family, found in the southeast United States. **4** = rattlesnake plantain. [because of its coloration, or its reputation as a remedy for snakebites]

**rat|tle|trap** (rat'əl trap'), *n., adj.* — *n.* **1** a rattling, rickety wagon or other vehicle: *Rattletraps have been a big cause of accidents on other turnpikes* (Wall Street Journal). **2** any shaky, rattling object. **3** *Slang.* a very talkative person; chatterbox.
— *adj.* rickety; rattling.
**rattletraps,** odds and ends: *Rattletraps for the mantelpiece, gimcracks for the table ...* (Mary C. Jackson).

**rat|tling** (rat'ling), *adj., adv.* — *adj.* **1** that rattles: *a rattling teakettle.* **2** fast and lively; brisk: *a rattling speech, a rattling pace.* **3** *Informal.* very fine; great; important: *He preached ... a sermon ... that gave him a rattling reputation* (Mark Twain).
— *adv. Informal.* remarkably; extremely; especially: *a rattling good time.* — **rat'tling|ly,** *adv.*

**rat|tly** (rat'lē), *adj.* that rattles; rattling.

**rat|ton** (rat'ən), *n. Dialect.* a rat. [< Old French *raton* < *rat* rat, probably < Vulgar Latin *rattus*]

**rat|toon** (ra tün'), *n., v.i., v.t.* = ratoon.

**rat|trap** (rat'trap'), *n., adj.* — *n.* **1** a trap for rats. **2** *Figurative.* a dilapidated building, as where rats are thought to abound: *These tenements were*

*rattraps and a disgrace* (Louise Meriwether). 3 *Figurative.* a hopeless situation: *A Peer ... finds himself in a rattrap from which politically there is no escape* (Contemporary Review).
— *adj.* of, having to do with, or like a rattrap.

**rat|ty** (rat′ē), *adj.*, **-ti|er, -ti|est.** 1 of rats; like rats: *ratty odors.* 2 full of rats: *Your German dungeons are mortal shivering ratty places* (George Meredith). 3 *Slang, Figurative.* **a** poor; shabby: *an old ratty deck of cards* (Mark Twain). **b** angry; irritable.

**rau|ci|ty** (rô′sə tē), *n.* hoarseness; harshness.

**rau|cous** (rô′kəs), *adj.* hoarse; harsh-sounding: *We heard the raucous caw of a crow in the field of corn.* SYN: husky. [< Latin *raucus* (with English *-ous*)] — **rau′cous|ly,** *adv.* — **rau′cous|ness,** *n.*

**raunch** (rônch, ränch), *n. U.S. Slang.* coarseness; vulgarity: *There are bars that are all elegance, and bars that are all raunch, and bars that breathe both elegance and raunch* (John Corry).

**raunch|y** (rôn′chē, rän′-), *adj.*, **raunch|i|er, raunch|i|est.** *U.S. Slang.* 1 carelessly untidy; sloppy; shabby: *... a bunch of raunchy, rebellious kids* (Harper's). 2 coarse; vulgar: *The material has ranged from the reasonable to the downright raunchy* (Time). [origin unknown] — **raunch′i|ly,** *adv.* — **raunch′i|ness,** *n.*

**rau|po** (rou′pō), *n.* a bulrush of New Zealand used for building native houses and thatching roofs. [< Maori *raupo*]

**rau|wol|fi|a** (rô wol′fē ə), *n.* 1 any one of a genus of tropical trees and shrubs of the dogbane family, especially a small, evergreen shrub of southern Asia: *Dr. Wilkins was the first Western physician to use the Indian snakeroot, rauwolfia, in the treatment of high blood pressure* (Science News Letter). 2 an alkaloid substance derived from the root of this shrub. It is the source of various drugs, such as reserpine, which are used for reducing high blood pressure and in the treatment of mental illness. [< New Latin *Rauwolfia* the genus name < Leonard *Rauwolf,* a German botanist of the 1500's]

**rav|age** (rav′ij), *v.*, **-aged, -ag|ing,** *n.* — *v.t.* to lay waste; damage greatly; destroy: *The forest fire ravaged many miles of country. Verdun, one of the oldest cities of France, has been a battleground ever since Attila the Hun ravaged it in A.D. 450* (Stefan T. Possony).
— *v.i.* to work destruction.
— *n.* violence; great damage; destruction; devastation: *War causes ravage.*
[< French *ravager* < Middle French *ravage* destruction, especially by rain and snowfall < *ravir;* see etym. under **ravish**] — **rav′ag|er,** *n.*

**rav|age|ment** (rav′ij mənt), *n.* destruction.

**rave[1]** (rāv), *v.*, **raved, rav|ing,** *n., adj.* — *v.i.* 1 to talk wildly. An excited, angry person raves; so does a madman. SYN: storm, rant. 2 to talk with very great or too much enthusiasm: *She raved about her food.* 3 to howl; roar; rage: *The wind raved about the lighthouse.*
— *v.t.* to express in a frenzied or wild manner.
— *n.* 1 the act of raving; frenzy or great excitement: *... after our little hour of strut and rave* (James Russell Lowell). 2 *Informal.* unrestrained praise: *Paris designer Pierre Cardin draws raves from fashion experts with his "going away look"* (Wall Street Journal). 3 *Slang.* an infatuation, especially such as occurs in adolescence. 4 a bright display: *Turn the classroom into an art studio, a rave of colour, a haven for these kids* (Manchester Guardian Weekly). 5 *British Slang.* a wild party; rave-up: *... all-night raves in airless cellars* (Punch).
— *adj. Informal.* unrestrainedly enthusiastic in praising: *The play got rave notices in the local press.*
[perhaps < Old French *raver,* variant of *rêver* to dream, wander, rave; origin uncertain]

**rave[2]** (rāv), *n.* one of the sidepieces in the body of a wagon, sleigh, or the like. [origin uncertain]

**rav|el** (rav′əl), *v.*, **-eled, -el|ing** or (*especially British*) **-elled, -el|ling,** *n.* — *v.i.* 1 to fray out; separate into threads: *The sweater has raveled at the elbow.* 2 to become tangled, involved, or confused: (*Figurative.*) *To hem the end of our history that it ravel not out* (Thomas Fuller).
— *v.t.* 1 to separate the threads of; fray: *Ravel a bit of the leftover cloth to mend the tear in your dress.* 2 *Figurative.* to make plain or clear; unravel: *Must I ravel out My weaved-up folly* (Shakespeare). SYN: disentangle. 3 to tangle; involve; confuse: (*Figurative.*) *The lawyer's arguments just ravel and complicate the contract.* SYN: enmesh.
— *n.* 1 an unraveled thread or fiber: *Since then the splits and ravels have shown up ... so that it is now doubtful whether the fabric can ever be repaired* (Harper's). 2 a tangle; complication; entanglement.
[probably < earlier Dutch *ravelen*] — **rav′el|er,** *especially British,* **rav′el|ler,** *n.*

**rave|lin** (rav′lin), *n.* a triangular outwork in a fortification, outside of the main ditch and having two embankments forming a projecting angle. [< Middle French *ravelin*]

**rav|el|ing** (rav′ə ling, rav′ling), *n.* something raveled out, such as a thread drawn from a woven or knitted fabric.

**rav|el|ment** (rav′əl mənt), *n.* 1 entanglement; confusion. 2 = raveling.

***ra|ven[1]** (rā′vən), *n., adj.* — *n.* a large, black bird like a crow but larger. Ravens inhabit Europe, Asia, and North America and have long been regarded as a portent of evil or death.
— *adj.* deep, glossy black: *She has raven hair.*
[Old English *hræfn*]

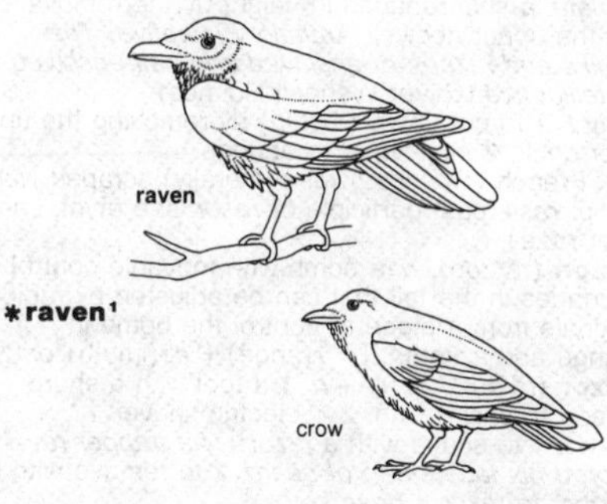


***raven[1]**

**rav|en[2]** (rav′ən), *v., n., adj.* — *v.t.* 1 to devour voraciously: *a roaring lion ravening the prey* (Ezekiel 22:25). 2 to prey on; plunder.
— *v.i.* to be ravenous: *The more they fed, they ravened still for more* (John Dryden).
— *n.* plunder; rapine; robbery.
— *adj.* ravin; ravenous.
[< Old French *raviner* (originally) fall impetuously or precipitously < *ravine* violent action; see etym. under **ravine**] — **rav′en|er,** *n.*

**Ra|ven** (rā′vən), *n.* the southern constellation Corvus. [< *raven*]

**rav|en|ing** (rav′ə ning), *adj.* greedy and hungry; ravenous: *a ravening wolf.* [< *raven*[2] + *-ing*[2]]

**rav|en|ous** (rav′ə nəs), *adj.* 1 very hungry: *Give the ravenous boy a snack.* SYN: famished. 2 greedy. SYN: gluttonous, voracious. 3 = rapacious. SYN: plundering. [< Old French *ravinos* (with English *-ous*) rapacious, violent < *ravine;* see etym. under **ravine**. See related etym. at **raven**[2].] — **rav′en|ous|ly,** *adv.* — **rav′en|ous|ness,** *n.*

**ra|ven|sa|ra nut** (rā′vən sā′rə), a kind of nutmeg obtained from a tree of Madagascar, used for making spice. [< the native name of the tree in Madagascar]

**rav|er** (rā′vər), *n.* a person who raves.

**rave-up** (rāv′up′), *n. British Slang.* a wild party: *all-night rave-ups.*

**ra|vi|gote** (rȧ vē gôt′), *n.* a sauce or dressing consisting of a mixture of spinach purée, tarragon, chervil, parsley, chives, and other herbs, used with vinegar as a seasoning. [< French *ravigote* < *ravigoter* revive]

**rav|in** (rav′ən), *n., v., adj.* — *n.* = rapine: *Blood and ravin and robbery are their characteristics* (George Rawlinson). — *v.t., v.i.* = raven[2]. — *adj.* = ravenous: *Better 'twere I met the ravin lion* (Shakespeare). [< Old French *ravine* robbery. See etym. of doublets **rapine, ravine.**]

**ra|vine** (rə vēn′), *n.* a long, deep, narrow valley eroded by running water: *The river had worn a ravine between the two hills.* See picture under **plain**[1]. [< French, Old French *ravine* violent rush, robbery < Latin *rapīna* < *rapere* to snatch. See etym. of doublets **rapine, ravin.**]

**ra|vined** (rə vēnd′), *adj.* filled or furrowed with ravines.

**ravine deer,** an East Indian antelope, the male of which has a second pair of small horns on the forehead in front of the principal pair. [because it frequents ravines]

**rav|ing** (rā′ving), *adj., n.* — *adj.* 1 that raves; delirious; frenzied; raging. 2 *Informal.* remarkable; extraordinary: *a raving beauty.*
— *n.* delirious, incoherent talk. — **rav′ing|ly,** *adv.*

**rav|i|o|li** (rav′ē ō′lē), *n. sing. or pl.* small, thin pieces of dough filled usually with chopped meat or cheese. Ravioli is cooked in boiling water and is usually served with a highly seasoned tomato sauce. [< Italian *ravioli,* or *raviuoli,* plural < *rapa* beet < Vulgar Latin *rāpa,* feminine singular < Latin, plural of *rāpum* beet, turnip]

**rav|ish** (rav′ish), *v.t.* 1 to fill with delight: *The prince was ravished by Cinderella's beauty.* SYN: enrapture, entrance, enchant, transport. 2 to carry off by force: *The wolf ravished the lamb from the flock.* 3 = rape. 4 to plunder; despoil: *the ease with which the Spaniards had ravished the city* (John L. Motley). [< Old French *raviss-,* stem of *ravir* < Vulgar Latin *rapīre,* for Latin *rapere* to seize. See related etym. at **rape**[1].]
— **rav′ish|er,** *n.* — **rav′ish|ment,** *n.*

**rav|ish|ing** (rav′i shing), *adj.* very delightful; enchanting: *jewels of ravishing beauty.* — **rav′ish|ing|ly,** *adv.*

**raw** (rô), *adj., n.* — *adj.* 1 not cooked: *raw meat, raw oysters. Many fruits are eaten raw.* 2 in the natural state; not manufactured, treated, or prepared: *raw cotton, raw hides. Raw milk has not been pasteurized. When raw umber is heated, it becomes burnt umber, which has a deep reddish color.* 3 not experienced; not trained: *a raw recruit.* SYN: ignorant, inexperienced. 4 with the skin off; sore: *a raw wound, a raw spot on a horse where the harness rubbed.* 5 damp and cold: *raw weather, a raw wind.* 6 *Figurative.* uncivilized; brutal: *the raw frontier.* 7 *Figurative.* having a crude quality; not refined in taste: *a raw piece of work, a raw story.* 8 *Informal.* harsh; unfair: *The firemen complained that they got a raw deal in the new contract with the city.*
— *n.* 1 the raw flesh. 2 a raw or sore spot on the body.
**in the raw, a** in an original, natural state: *life in the raw. Modern filtration and treatment methods can provide pure water from streams far less potable in the raw than the upper Hudson* (New York Times). **b** *Figurative.* naked; nude: *He swims in the raw when no one else is around.*
**on the raw,** *British.* in a sensitive spot; so as to be hurt, embarrassed, offended, or concerned: *Cancer ... is a subject which touches most people on the raw* (New Scientist).
[Old English *hrēaw*] — **raw′ly,** *adv.* — **raw′ness,** *n.*
— ***Syn.*** *adj.* 2 **Raw, crude** mean not processed or prepared for use. **Raw,** the more extensive term, applies to any natural product that has not yet been subjected to manufacture, treatment, or preparation for use: *Raw milk has not been pasteurized to make it safe to drink.* **Crude,** the more specific term, applies to a natural product that is in an impure state and needs refining, tempering, or treatment with chemicals and heat: *Crude rubber is treated with sulfur and heat to make it more elastic and durable.*

**raw-boned** or **raw|boned** (rô′bōnd′), *adj.* having little flesh on the bones; gaunt: *a camel's swaying, raw-boned gait* (New Yorker).

**raw|head** (rô′hed′), *n.* a goblin of ghastly appearance.

**raw|hide** (rô′hīd′), *n., v.*, **-hid|ed, -hid|ing.** — *n.* 1 the skin of cattle that has not been tanned. 2 a rope or whip made of this.
— *v.t.* to whip with a rawhide.

**ra|win** (rā′win), *n.* 1 the determination of wind speed and direction by the tracking of a balloon with radar or radiocompass. 2 wind tracked in this manner. [< *ra*(dar) + *win*(d)]

**ra|win|sonde** (rā′win sond), *n.* 1 the gathering of temperature, pressure, wind speed or other atmospheric information by means of a balloon-borne radiosonde tracked by radiocompass and sometimes radar. 2 a radiosonde used for this purpose. [< *rawin* + (radio)*sonde*]

**raw|ish** (rô′ish), *adj.* somewhat raw.

**raw material,** 1 a substance in its natural state; any product that comes from mines, farms, forests, or the like before it is prepared for use in factories, mills, and similar places. Coal, iron ore, petroleum, cotton, and animal hides are raw materials. *These imports are mainly raw materials that are duty-free, or have low tariff rates because the U.S. requires them* (Time). 2 *Figurative: Young men are the raw material of an army. You [the Press] deal with the raw material of opinion* (Woodrow Wilson).

**raw milk,** unpasteurized milk.

**raw packing,** the canning of fruits or vegetables by cold-packing them; cold pack.

**raw score,** the score in a psychological, educational, or other test as obtained originally, before making any adjustments.

**raw silk,** 1 silk reeled from the cocoons before being thrown or spun. 2 cloth woven from this silk.

**rax** (raks, räks), *Scottish.* — *v.i.* 1 to stretch. 2 to reach out. — *v.t.* 1 to stretch out. 2 to hand over. [Old English *raxan*]

**ray[1]** (rā), *n., v.* — *n.* 1 a line or beam of light: *rays of the sun.* SYN: See syn. under **beam**. **2a** a line or stream of heat, electricity, or other radiant energy: *X rays, the invisible rays of the spectrum.* **b** any stream of particles moving in the same line. 3 a thin line like a ray, coming out from a

**Pronunciation Key:** hat, āge, cãre, fär; let, ēqual, tėrm; it, īce; hot, ōpen, ôrder; **oi**l, **ou**t; cup, pu̇t, rüle; **ch**ild; lo**ng**; **th**in; ᴛʜen; **zh**, measure; ə represents **a** in about, **e** in taken, **i** in pencil, **o** in lemon, **u** in circus.

center: *Little rays shot out through the pane of glass where the stone hit it.* **4** a part like a ray, such as: **a** one of the arms or branches of a starfish. **b** the marginal portion of the flower head of certain composite plants, composed of ray flowers or petals. **c** one of these ray flowers. **d** a branch of an umbel. **e** one of the processes which support and extend the fin of a fish. **f** one of the vertical bands of tissue between the pith and the bark of a tree or other plant. **5** *Figurative.* a slight trace; faint gleam: *Not a ray of hope pierced our gloom.* **6** = half-line. **7** light; radiance: *lamps that shed at eve a cheerful ray* (Thomas Gray). **8** a line of sight. **9** a glance of the eye: *All eyes direct their rays On him* (Alexander Pope). **10** one of any system of lines, parts, or things radially arranged.
—*v.i.* **1** to extend in lines from the center. **2** to issue as rays. **3** to shine.
—*v.t.* **1** to send forth in rays; radiate. **2** to treat with rays, as with X rays. **3** to throw rays upon. [< Old French *rai* < Latin *radius.* See etym. of doublet **radius.**]

***ray²** (rā), *n.* any one of various fishes that have broad, flat bodies with very broad fins. Rays are related to the sharks. The electric ray has organs with which it shocks or kills its prey. Various rays include the sting rays, electric rays, devilfishes, and sawfishes. [< Old French *raie* < Latin *raia*]

***ray²**

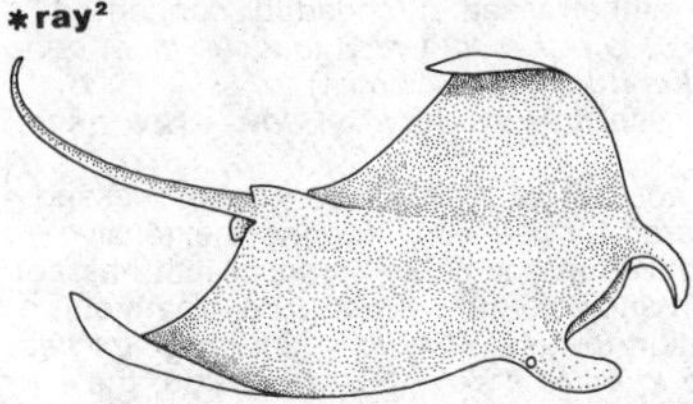

**ra|yah** or **ra|ya** (rä′yə), *n.* a Turkish subject who is not a Moslem. [< French *raïa* < Turkish *râya* < Arabic *ra'āyā* subjects, peasants < *ra'ā* he pastured]

**rayed** (rād), *adj.* having rays.

**ray-finned** (rā′find′), *adj.* having fins consisting of soft or spiny rays with a web of skin around them. Most fish living today are ray-finned.

**ray flower** or **floret**, one of the marginal flowers or florets of a daisy, aster, or other composite flower head, resembling a petal. See picture under **dimorphism.**

**ray fungus**, = actinomycete.

**ray gun**, **1** a gun or other instrument that is supposed to shoot radioactive rays. **2** anything resembling such a gun, as a scientific instrument producing a form of radiation.

**ray hair**, one of the slender filaments in the finfold of an embryo fish.

**ray|ing** (rā′ing), *n.* exposure to radioactivity.

**Ray|leigh wave** (rā′lē), a vertical, ripple-like wave on or just below the surface of the earth, caused by seismic disturbances: *Measurement of crustal thickness over the entire U.S. was made by noting dispersion in phase velocity of earthquake Rayleigh waves* (Science News Letter). [< J. W. S. *Rayleigh,* 1842-1919, a British physicist, who first described it in 1900]

**ray|less** (rā′lis), *adj.* **1** without rays. **2** sending out no rays. **3** *Figurative.* dark; gloomy: *rayless night.* —**ray′less|ness,** *n.*

**rayless goldenrod**, any one of various plants related to the goldenrod which contain the poisonous substance that causes trembles in cattle and sheep.

**Ray|naud's disease** (rā nōz′), a primary disorder of the vascular system, characterized by spasms and cyanosis of the extremities, especially in the fingers and toes, due to the obstruction of blood supply and local asphyxia. [< Maurice *Raynaud,* 1834-1881, a French physician]

**Raynaud's phenomenon**, a condition in which the hand or fingers turn white or blue, especially as a symptom of Raynaud's disease.

**ray|on** (rā′on), *n., adj.* —*n.* **1** a fiber or fabric made from cellulose treated with chemicals. Rayon is used instead of silk, wool, cotton, and similar fabrics and can be made to look like any one of these, especially silk. *Rayon ranks second only to cotton as the most widely used fiber* (Charles H. Rutledge). **2** cloth made of this fiber.
—*adj.* made of rayon: *a rayon sweater. If a rayon fiber is dyed and then the dye is leached out, the skin remains darker* (New Scientist).
[American English < *ray*¹ beam, light. Compare French *rayon* ray of light.]

**ray|on|nant** (rā′ə nənt), *adj.* **1** sending out rays. **2** having radiating lines, as some architectural or other decoration. [< French *rayonnant,* present participle of *rayonner* to send out rays < *rayon* ray of light, ultimately < Latin *radius*]

**ray|on|né** (rā′ə nā′), *adj. Heraldry.* (of a division on an escutcheon) having alternate pointed projections and depressions. [< French *rayonné,* past participle of *rayonner* to send out rays; see etym. under **rayonnant**]

**raze** (rāz), *v.t.,* **razed, raz|ing.** **1** to tear down; destroy completely; demolish: *The old firehouse was razed to the ground and a new one was built.* **SYN:** level. **2** *Obsolete.* to scrape off; erase. **3** *Obsolete.* to scrape. Also, **rase.** [< French, Old French *raser* to scrape, shave < Vulgar Latin *rāsāre* < Latin *rādere* to scrape, shave]

**ra|zee** (rā zē′), *n., v.,* **-zeed, -zee|ing.** —*n.* **1** *Obsolete.* a ship reduced in height by the removal of the upper deck. **2** *Archaic, Figurative: The hulks and razees of enslaved and half-enslaved intelligence* (Oliver Wendell Holmes).
—*v.t.* **1** to cut down (a ship) by removing the upper deck. **2** *Figurative.* to abridge.
[< French (*vaisseau*) *rasé* (literally) scraped warship; *rasé,* past participle of *raser;* see etym. under **raze**]

**ra|zon** (rā′zon), *n.* a bomb with movable control surfaces in the tail that can be adjusted by radio signals from a plane to control the bomb in range and azimuth. [< *r*(ange) + *az*(imuth) *on*(ly)]

**ra|zor** (rā′zər), *n., v.* —*n.* **1** a tool with a sharp blade to shave with. **2** = electric shaver.
—*v.t.* **1** to shave with a razor: *The trapper razored his face clean of beard.* **2** to remove with a razor: *to razor a beard.*
[< Old French *rasor,* and *rasour* < *raser* to scrape; see etym. under **raze**]

**ra|zor|a|ble** (rā′zər ə bəl), *adj.* fit to be shaved.

**ra|zor|back** (rā′zər bak′), *n.* **1** a kind of thin, half-wild hog with a ridged back. Razorbacks are common in the southern United States. **2** a finback (whale); rorqual. **3** a sharp ridge, as on a hill or mountain.
—*adj.* = razor-backed: ... *razorback hills covered with jungles* (Newsweek).

**ra|zor-backed** (rā′zər bakt′), *adj.* having a very sharp back or ridge: *a razor-backed animal.*

**ra|zor|bill** (rā′zər bil′), *n.* = razor-billed auk.

**ra|zor-billed auk** (rā′zər bild′), an auk of the North Atlantic resembling the great auk but smaller.

**razor clam** or **fish**, any one of various bivalve mollusks with a long, narrow shell.

**razor edge**, **1** a keen, razorlike edge. **2** *Figurative.* razor's edge.

**ra|zor-edged** (rā′zər ejd′), *adj.* **1** having a razor edge: *In recent works, he divides the painting into razor-edged triangles rimmed with black* (Time). **2** *Figurative.* keen; incisive; trenchant: *razor-edged wit.*

**razor haircut**, a haircut given with a razor instead of scissors.

**ra|zor's edge** (rā′zərz), **1** a keen edge. **2** *Figurative.* a precariously thin line or margin: *China is balanced on a razor's edge between victory and defeat* (Manchester Guardian Weekly). *He lived on a razor's edge between the two cultures, the world of art and the world of science* (Listener).

**ra|zor-sharp** (rā′zər shärp′), *adj.* sharp as a razor; very sharp: *Bellboys tiptoed by the razor-sharp scimitars of the fitfully dozing guards* (Newsweek). (*Figurative.*) *His poetic gift is delicate, razor-sharp, and very special* (Atlantic).

**razor shell**, **1** the shell of a razor clam. **2** = razor clam.

**ra|zor|strop** (rā′zər strop′), *n.* a strap of leather for sharpening a razor; strop.

**ra|zor-thin** (rā′zər thin′), *adj.* thin as a razor's edge; extremely thin or slight: *He sported a razor-thin red moustache* (Newsweek). (*Figurative.*) *His popular vote lead was razor-thin* (Wall Street Journal).

**razz** (raz), *v., n. Slang.* —*v.t.* **1** to laugh at; make fun of; tease. **2** to express disapproval of; boo: *The angry crowd razzed the umpire.*
—*v.i.* to tease.
—*n.* strong disapproval or criticism; derision: *The Red Swede got the grand razz handed to him* (Sinclair Lewis).
[American English, back formation < *raspberry*]

**raz|zi|a** (raz′ē ə), *n.* a plundering military raid. [< French *razzia* < Arabic *ghāzia,* variant of *ghazāh* war; foray < *ghasw* to make war]

**raz|zle** (raz′əl), *n.* = razzle-dazzle.

**raz|zle-daz|zle** (raz′əl daz′əl), *n., adj., v.,* **-zled, -zling.** —*n.* **1** *U.S. Slang.* dazzling glitter, excitement, or the like, such as to cause bewilderment: *The store sells anything from diapers to tombstones, and pulls customers in from six counties with a sales formula combining low prices and razzle-dazzle* (Wall Street Journal). **2** a revolving platform on which people are moved about in amusingly irregular ways. **3** an intricate movement by the players of a team in sports, especially football, intended to deceive or bewilder their opponents. **4** *Slang.* intoxication.
—*adj. U.S. Slang.* showy; bewildering: *He specializes in the razzle-dazzle finish, in which the hero gallops on to the scene when all seems darkest and the curtain falls* (New York Times).
—*v.t. U.S. Slang.* to bedazzle with glitter, excitement, or the like; confuse; bewilder: *She beat boys at mumblety-peg, whizzed past them in foot races and razzle-dazzled them in basketball* (Time).
[American English, varied reduplication of *dazzle*]

**raz|zle-daz|zler** (raz′əl daz′lər), *n. U.S. Slang.* **1** a person or thing that razzle-dazzles. **2** something that astonishes with its glaring incongruities.

**razz|ma|tazz** (raz′mə taz′), *n. U.S. Slang.* razzle-dazzle; fanfare: ... *a high-powered product, successfully designed for theatergoers with a taste of unabashed razzmatazz and schmaltz* (Christian Science Monitor).

**Rb** (no period), rubidium (chemical element).

**RBE** (no periods), relative biological effect (or efficiency).

**r.b.i., rbi** (no periods), or **RBI** (no periods), *Baseball.* run or runs batted in.

**R.C.** or **RC** (no periods), **1** Red Cross. **2** Reserve Corps. **3** Roman Catholic.

**RCA** (no periods), Royal Canadian Army.

**R.C.A.**, **1** Royal Canadian Academy of Arts. **2** Royal Canadian Army. **3** Royal College of Art.

**RCAF** (no periods) or **R.C.A.F.**, Royal Canadian Air Force.

**R.C.Ch.**, Roman Catholic Church.

**R.C.M.** or **RCM** (no periods), Royal College of Music.

**RCMP** (no periods) or **R.C.M.P.**, Royal Canadian Mounted Police.

**RCN** (no periods) or **R.C.N.**, Royal Canadian Navy.

**r-col|or** (är′kul′ər), *n. Phonetics.* an accompanying retroflex articulation of a vowel resulting in an *r*-like quality.

**r-col|ored** (är′kul′ərd), *adj. Phonetics.* pronounced with an r-color: *an r-colored vowel.*

**R.C.P.**, Royal College of Physicians (of England).

**RCS** (no periods) or **R.C.S.**, **1** reaction control system (of a rocket engine). **2** reentry control system.

**R.C.S.**, Royal College of Surgeons (of England).

**Rct** (no period), recruit.

**-rd**, a suffix added to the numeral 3 or any numeral ending with 3 (except 13) to indicate the ordinal number: *3rd Avenue, 93rd Street, the 23rd of April.*

**rd.**, **1** rix-dollar. **2** road. **3** rod or rods. **4** round.

**Rd** (no period), formerly, radium (chemical element). Now, **Ra** (no period).

**Rd.**, **1** rix-dollar. **2** Road.

**R/D** (no periods), *Banking.* refer to drawer.

**R.D.**, Rural Delivery.

**RDA** (no periods), recommended dietary allowance.

**RDB** (no periods), Research and Development Board.

**R.D.C.** or **RDC** (no periods), Rural District Council.

**RDF** (no periods), **1** radio direction finder. **2** radio direction finding.

**RDS** (no periods), respiratory distress syndrome.

**RDX** (no periods), a powerful and highly sensitive crystalline explosive used in combination with other explosive substances in bombs, depth charges, etc.; cyclonite: *RDX is far more violent than TNT, having at least 50% more power* (Science News Letter). *Formula:* $C_3H_6N_6O_6$ [perhaps < *R*(search and) *D*(evelopment E)*x*(plosive)]

**re¹** (rā), *n.* the second tone of the musical diatonic scale. [< Medieval Latin *re* < Latin *re*-(*sonāre*) to resound. See etym. under **gamut.**]

**re²** (rē), *prep.* with reference to; in the matter or case of; about; concerning: *re your letter of the 7th.* [< Latin (*in*) *rē* (in) the matter of]
▶ **Re** is used in the heading of certain legal documents and to some extent in business writing. In ordinary prose, the equivalent English prepositions are preferable.

**Re** (rā), *n.* = Ra. [< Egyptian *r'* the sun]

**re-**, *prefix.* **1** again; anew; once more: *Reopen* = *open again. Reappear* = *appear again.*
**2** back: *Repay* = *pay back.* Also, sometimes **red-** before vowels.
[< Latin *re-*, or < French, Old French *re-* < Latin]
▶ **re-**. Usually words formed of the prefix *re-* and another word are not hyphened: *rearrange, refine, remit.* However, words formed with the prefix *re-* meaning again are sometimes hyphened (1) when the word to which it is joined begins with *e: reecho* or *re-echo,* (2) when the form with hyphen can have a different meaning from the form without: *reform,* to make better—*re-form,* to shape again, (3) (rarely) for emphasis, as in "now *re-seated* in fair comfort," or in informal or humorous compounds: *re-remarried,* and (4) before roots with an initial capital letter: *re-Americanize.*

At one time words beginning with *e,* such as *echo* in *reecho* were written *reëcho* with the dieresis, but that device is now archaic in English according to most stylebooks and general use.

**The meaning of each of the following words is found by adding *again* or *anew* to the main part. The pronunciation of the main part is not changed.**

**re′a|bridge′**
**re′ab|solve′**
**re′ac|cel′er|ate**
**re′ac|cel′er|a′tion**
**re′ac|cept′**
**re′ac|cept′ance**
**re′ac|cli′mate**
**re′ac|cli′ma|tize**
**re′ac|com′plish**
**re′ac|com′plish|ment**
**re′ac|cost′**
**re′ac|count′**
**re′ac|cred′it**
**re′ac|cu′mu|late**
**re′ac|cu′mu|la′tion**
**re′ac|cu|sa′tion**
**re′ac|cus′tom**
**re′ac|knowl′edge**
**re′ac|knowl′edg|ment**
**re′ac|quaint′**
**re′ac|quaint′ance**
**re′ac|qui|si′tion**
**re′a|dapt′a|bil′i|ty**
**re′a|dapt′a|ble**
**re′ad|ap|ta′tion**
**re′a|dap′tive**
**re′ad|dict′**
**re′ad|here′**
**re′ad|he′sion**
**re′ad|ju′di|cate**
**re′ad|ju′di|ca′tion**
**re′ad|min′is|ter**
**re′ad|mi|ra′tion**
**re′ad|mire′**
**re′a|dop′tion**
**re′ad|vance′ment**
**re|ad′ver|tise**
**re′ad|ver|tise′ment**
**re′ad|vise′**
**re′aer|a′tion**
**re′af|fil′i|ate**
**re′af|fil′i|a′tion**
**re′af|fix′**
**re|ag′gre|gate**
**re|ag′i|tate**
**re′ag|i|ta′tion**
**re′a|line′**
**re′al|le|ga′tion**
**re′al|lege′**
**re′al|lot′**
**re′al|lot′ment**
**re′al|low′**
**re′al|low′ance**
**re|al′ter**
**re′al|ter|a′tion**
**re′a|mend′**
**re′a|mend′ment**
**re′-A|mer′i|can|ize**
**re|am′pli|fy**
**re′a|nal′y|sis**
**re|an′a|lyze**
**re|an′chor**
**re|an′no|tate**
**re′an|nounce′**
**re′an|nounce′ment**
**re′a|pol′o|gize**
**re′ap|plaud′**
**re|ap′pli|cant**
**re′ap|pli′er**
**re′ap|praise′ment**
**re′ap|prov′al**
**re′ap|prove′**
**re′a|rise′**
**re′a|rouse′**
**re′ar|raign′**
**re′ar|range′a|ble**
**re′ar|rang′er**
**re′ar|ray′**
**re′ar|rest′**
**re′ar|riv′al**
**re′ar|rive′**
**re′as|cend′ant**
**re′as|cend′en|cy**
**re′as|cend′ent**
**re|ask′**
**re′as|pire′**
**re′as|sail′**
**re′as|sault′**
**re′as|say′**
**re′as|sig|na′tion**
**re′at|tack′**
**re′at|tend′**
**re′at|tend′ance**
**re′at|tire′**
**re′at|tract′**
**re′at|trib′ute**
**re|au′dit**
**re′au|di′tion**
**re′au|then′ti|cate**
**re′au|then′ti|ca′tion**
**re′au|thor|i|za′tion**
**re|au′thor|ize**
**re′a|vail′**
**re′a|vail′a|ble**
**re′a|vow′**
**re′a|vow′al**
**re′a|wake′**
**re′a|wak′en|ment**
**re′a|ward′**
**re|bait′**
**re|bake′**
**re|bal′ance**
**re|bal′last**
**re|band′age**
**re|ban′ish**
**re|ban′ish|ment**
**re′bar|ba|ri|za′tion**
**re|bar′ba|rize**
**re|beau′ti|fy**
**re′be|gin′**
**re′be|gin′ning**
**re|bend′**
**re′be|stow′**
**re′be|stow′al**
**re|bite′**
**re|blast′**
**re|bless′**
**re|board′**
**re|bomb′**
**re|book′**
**re|bore′**
**re|bor′row**
**re|bot′tle**
**re|bounce′**
**re|bound′a|ble**
**re|brace′**
**re|branch′**
**re|break′**
**re|brew′**
**re|bring′**
**re|bub′ble**
**re|buck′le**
**re|bud′**
**re|budg′et**
**re|buf′fet**
**re|bunch′**
**re|bun′dle**
**re|bur′den**
**re|bur′i|al**
**re|burn′**
**re|bur′nish**
**re|but′ton**
**re|buy′**
**re|ca′ble**
**re|cal′ci|fi|ca′tion**
**re|cal′ci|fy**
**re|cal′cine**
**re|cal′cu|late**
**re′cal|cu|la′tion**
**re|cal′i|brate**
**re′cal|i|bra′tion**
**re|calk′**
**re′ca|nal′ize**
**re|can′vas**
**re|can′vass**
**re|cart′**
**re|carve′**
**re|cash′**
**re|cat′a|log**
**re|catch′**
**re|cat′e|gor|ize**
**re′ce|ment′**
**re|cen′ter**
**re|cen′tral|i|za′tion**
**re|cen′tral|ize**
**re|chain′**
**re|chart′**
**re|cheer′**
**re|chew′**
**re|cho′re|o|graph**
**re-Chris′tian|ize**
**re|civ′i|lize**
**re|clas′si|fi|ca′tion**
**re|clas′si|fy**
**re|clean′**
**re|cleanse′**
**re|clear′**
**re|climb′**
**re|clos′a|ble**
**re|close′**
**re′co|ag′u|late**
**re′co|ag′u|la′tion**
**re|coast′**
**re|coat′**
**re|cock′**
**re|code′**
**re′cod|i|fi|ca′tion**
**re|cod′i|fy**
**re|coin′er**
**re′col|late′**
**re′col|la′tion**
**re′com|mu′ni|cate**
**re′com|pare′**
**re′com|par′i|son**
**re′com|pel′**
**re|com′pen|sate**
**re′com|pi|la′tion**
**re′com|pile′**
**re′com|pile′ment**
**re′com|plain′**
**re′com|plete′**
**re′com|ple′tion**
**re|com′pli|cate**
**re′com|pli|ca′tion**
**re′com|pound′**
**re′con|ceal′**
**re′con|ceal′ment**
**re′con|cede′**
**re′con|ceive′**
**re′con|cep′tion**
**re′con|ces′sion**
**re′con|fer′**
**re′con|fess′**
**re′con|fine′**
**re′con|fine′ment**
**re′con|geal′**
**re′con|nec′tion**
**re|con′quer|or**
**re′con|sole′**
**re′con|strue′**
**re′con|sult′**
**re′con|sul|ta′tion**
**re|con′tact**
**re|con′tem|plate**
**re′con|tem|pla′tion**
**re′con|tin′u|ance**
**re′con|tin′ue**
**re′con|tract′**
**re′con|trac′tion**
**re′con|trast′**
**re′con|va|lesce′**
**re′con|va|les′cence**
**re′con|va|les′cent**
**re′con|verge′**
**re′con|vert′er**
**re′con|voke′**
**re|cook′**
**re|cool′**
**re|cop′y|right′**
**re|cork′**
**re′cor|rect′**
**re′cor|rec′tion**
**re|cost′**
**re′cos|tume′**
**re|cou′ple**
**re|cred′it**
**re|crew′**
**re|cru′ci|fy**
**re′cul|ti|va′tion**
**re|curl′**
**re|cush′ion**
**re|date′**
**re′de|bate′**
**re|deb′it**
**re′de|cay′**
**re′de|ci′sion**
**re′de|clare′**
**re′de|cline′**
**re|ded′i|ca|to′ry**
**re′de|feat′**
**re′de|fend′**
**re′de|fer′**
**re′de|fi′ance**
**re′de|fy′**
**re′de|lib′er|ate**
**re′de|lib′er|a′tion**
**re′de|liv′er|ance**
**re′de|liv′er|y**
**re′dem|on|stra′tion**
**re′de|scrip′tion**
**re′des|ig|na′tion**
**re′de|sire′**
**re′de|sir′ous**
**re′de|tect′**
**re′de|vote′**
**re|dic′tate**
**re′dic|ta′tion**
**re′dif|fer|en′ti|ate**
**re′dif|fer|en′ti|a′tion**
**re′dif|fuse′**
**re|dig′**
**re′di|ges′tion**
**re|dip′**
**re′dis|charge′**
**re|dis′ci|pline**
**re′dis|cuss′**
**re′dis|cus′sion**
**re′dis|patch′**
**re′dis|perse′**
**re′dis|play′**
**re′dis|po|si′tion**
**re′dis|pute′**
**re|dis′sol|u|ble**
**re′dis|so|lu′tion**
**re′dis|solv′a|ble**
**re′dis|tend′**
**re′dis|trib′ut|er**
**re′dis|trib′u|tive**
**re′dis|trib′u|tor**
**re′dis|trib′u|to′ry**
**re|dive′**
**re′di|vi′sion**
**re|dock′**
**re′do|mes′ti|cate**
**re|doom′**
**re|drain′**
**re|dream′**
**re|dredge′**
**re|drill′**
**re|dust′**
**re′e|di′tion**
**re′e|ject′**
**re′e|jec′tion**
**re′e|ject′ment**
**re′el|e|va′tion**
**re′em|bat′tle**
**re′em|bel′lish**
**re′em|brace′ment**
**re′em|i|gra′tion**
**re′e|mis′sion**
**re′em|pow′er**
**re′en|a′ble**
**re′en|a′ble|ment**
**re′e|nam′el**
**re′en|close′**
**re′en|clo′sure**
**re′en|dear′**
**re′en|dear′ment**
**re′en|dow′ment**
**re|en′er|gize**
**re′en|forc′er**
**re′en|fran′chise**
**re′en|fran′chise|ment**
**re′en|gen′der**
**re′en|join′**
**re′en|kin′dle**
**re′en|large′**
**re′en|large′ment**
**re′en|light′en**
**re′en|light′en|ment**
**re′en|list′er**
**re′en|liv′en**
**re′en|roll′**
**re′en|roll′ment**
**re′en|shrine′**
**re′en|sphere′**
**re′en|ter|tain′**
**re′en|ter|tain′ment**
**re′en|thrall′**
**re′en|tice′**
**re′en|ti′tle**
**re′en|tomb′**
**re′en|train′**
**re′en|trench′**
**re′e|nun′ci|ate**
**re′e|nun′ci|a′tion**
**re|e′qui|lib′rate**
**re′e|rec′tion**
**re|es′ca|la′tion**
**re′es|cape′**
**re′es|cort′**
**re′es|pous′al**
**re′es|pouse′**
**re′es|tab′lish|er**
**re′es|ti|ma′tion**
**re′e|vap′o|rate**
**re′ex|alt′**
**re|ex′ca|vate**
**re′ex|ca|va′tion**
**re′ex|ci|ta′tion**
**re′ex|cite′**
**re|ex′er|cise**
**re′ex|ert′**
**re′ex|hale′**
**re′ex|haust′**
**re′ex|hi|bi′tion**
**re′ex|ist′**
**re′ex|ist′ence**
**re′ex|ist′ent**
**re′ex|pect′**
**re′ex|pec|ta′tion**
**re′ex|per′i|ment**
**re′ex|pla|na′tion**
**re|ex′ploit**
**re′ex|pose′**
**re′ex|po′sure**
**re′ex|pound′**
**re′ex|press′**
**re′ex|pres′sion**
**re′ex|pul′sion**
**re′ex|tend′**
**re′ex|ten′sion**
**re′ex|tract′**
**re|fall′**
**re|fal′low**
**re|fan′**
**re′fer|ment′**
**re′fer|ti|li|za′tion**
**re|film′**
**re|fil′ter**
**re|find′**
**re|fin′ger**
**re|flame′**
**re|flash′**
**re|flesh′**
**re′float|a′tion**
**re|floor′**
**re|fo′li|ate**
**re|for′ward**
**re′foun|da′tion**
**re|frac′ture**
**re|fresh′en**
**re|fright′en**
**re|frus′trate**
**re|fry′**
**re|gar′nish**
**re|gar′ri|son**
**re|gas′i|fy**
**re|glo′ri|fied**
**re|gloss′**
**re|grasp′**
**re|grease′**
**re|grind′er**
**re|grip′**
**re|groove′**
**re|grow′**
**re′guar|an|tee′**
**re|guide′**
**re|hal′low**
**re|ham′mer**
**re|hard′en**
**re|har′ness**
**re|heap′**
**re|hoist′**
**re|hum′ble**
**re′hu|mil′i|ate**
**re|ice′**
**re′i|den′ti|fi|ca′tion**
**re′i|den′ti|fy**
**re′ig|ni′tion**
**re′il|lume′**
**re′il|lu′mi|nate**
**re′il|lu′mi|na′tion**
**re′il|lu′mine**
**re′i|mag′ine**
**re′im|bibe′**
**re′im|merse′**
**re′im|mer′sion**
**re|im′mi|gra′tion**
**re|im′mu|ni|za′tion**
**re|im′pact**
**re′im|part′**
**re′im|press′**
**re′in|car′cer|a′tion**
**re′in|duce′ment**
**re′in|duct′**
**re′in|duc′tion**
**re′in|dus′tri|al|i|za′tion**
**re′in|fer′**
**re′in|fest′**
**re′in|fes|ta′tion**
**re′in|fil′trate**
**re|in′fil|tra′tion**
**re′in|flict′**
**re|in′flu|ence**
**re′in|fu′sion**
**re′in|hab′i|ta′tion**
**re′in|her′it**
**re′i|ni′ti|ate**
**re′i|ni′ti|a′tion**
**re|in′jure**
**re|in′ju|ry**
**re|ink′**
**re′in|oc′u|late**
**re′in|oc′u|la′tion**
**re′in|quire′**
**re′in|quir′y**
**re′in|stal|la′tion**
**re′in|still′**
**re′in|sult′**
**re′in|ter′ro|ga′tion**
**re|in′ter|view**
**re′in|trude′**
**re′in|tru′sion**
**re′in|va′sion**
**re′in|ven′tion**
**re′in|ven′tor**
**re′in|vert′**
**re′in|voke′**
**re′in|volve′ment**
**re|i′so|late**
**re|lace′**
**re|lance′**
**re|land′**
**re|latch′**
**re|lead′**
**re|li′cense**
**re|lick′**
**re|lift′**
**re|lim′it**
**re′lim|i|ta′tion**
**re|liq′ue|fy**
**re|list′**
**re|lit′i|gate**
**re|lock′**
**re|lodge′**
**re|look′**
**re|loop′**
**re′mag|net|i|za′tion**
**re|mag′net|ize**
**re|mail′**
**re|man′tle**
**re′man|u|fac′ture**
**re|map′**
**re|march′**
**re′mas|ti|ca′tion**
**re|mate′**
**re′ma|te′ri|al|ize**
**re|meas′ure|ment**
**re|mem′o|rize**
**re|mend′**
**re′min|er|al|i|za′tion**
**re|min′er|al|ize**
**re|min′gle**
**re|mint′**
**re|mix′ture**
**re|mo′bi|lize**
**re|mort′gage**
**re|mus′ter**
**re′my|thol′o|gize**
**re|nor′mal|ize**
**re′no|ti|fi|ca′tion**
**re|no′ti|fy**
**re|num′ber**
**re′ob|ser|va′tion**
**re′ob|serve′**
**re′ob|tain′ment**
**re′oc|cur′**
**re′oc|cur′rence**
**re|of′fer**
**re′op|po|si′tion**
**re|or′ches|trate**
**re′or|ches|tra′tion**
**re|or′na|ment**
**re|out′fit**
**re′o|ver|flow′**
**re|own′**
**re′ox|i|da′tion**
**re|ox′i|dize**
**re|ox′y|gen|ate**
**re|pack′er**
**re|page′**
**re|pan′el**
**re|pa′per**
**re|par′a|graph**
**re|park′**
**re|patch′**
**re|pat′ent**
**re|pave′ment**
**re|pawn′**
**re|ped′dle**
**re|peg′**
**re|pen′**
**re|pe′nal|ize**
**re′per|form′**
**re′per|form′ance**
**re′pe|rus′al**
**re′pe|ruse′**
**re|phase′**
**re|pick′**
**re|pin′**
**re|pitch′**
**re|plane′**
**re|plate′**
**re|pleat′**
**re|plot′**

**Pronunciation Key:** hat, āge, cãre, fär; let, ēqual, tėrm; it, īce; hot, ōpen, ôrder; oil, out; cup, pu̇t, rüle; child; long; thin; ᴛʜen; zh, measure; ə represents **a** in about, **e** in taken, **i** in pencil, **o** in lemon, **u** in circus.

**re|plow′**
**re|plun′der**
**re|point′**
**re′pol|lute′**
**re|pol′y|mer|ize**
**re|pop′u|late**
**re|pow′der**
**re|pow′er**
**re′pre|cip′i|tate**
**re′pre|cip′i|ta′tion**
**re′pre|pare′**
**re-press′**
**re|pres′sure**
**re|pres′sur|ize**
**re|price′**
**re|prime′**
**re′pro|claim′**
**re′pro|cur′a|ble**
**re′pro|cure′**
**re′pro|nounce′**
**re′pro|por′tion**
**re′pro|pos′al**
**re′pro|pose′**
**re|pros′e|cute**
**re′pros|e|cu′tion**
**re-prove′**
**re|pub′lish**
**re|pump′**
**re|pun′ish**
**re|pun′ish|ment**
**re′pu|ri|fi|ca′tion**
**re|pu′ri|fy**
**re|pur′pose**
**re′pur|suit′**
**re′qual|i|fi|ca′tion**
**re|qual′i|fy**
**re|ques′tion**
**re|quick′en**
**re′quo|ta′tion**
**re|quote′**
**re|raise′**
**re|rate′**
**re|read′er**
**re′re|cord′**
**re|reel′**
**re′re|fine′**
**re′re|flect′**
**re′re|flec′tion**
**re′re|form′**
**re|reg′is|ter**
**re′reg|is|tra′tion**
**re′re|hearse′**
**re′re|it′er|ate**
**re′re|late′**
**re′re|lease′**
**re′re|mit′**
**re|rent′**
**re|rent′al**
**re′re|pair′**
**re′re|peat′**
**re′re|port′**
**re′rep|re|sent′**
**re′rep|re|sen|ta′tion**
**re′re|side′**
**re′re|solve′**
**re′re|veal′**
**re′rev|e|la′tion**
**re′re|vise′**
**re|rig′**
**re|ring′**
**re|riv′et**
**re-Ro′man|ize**
**re|rub′**
**re|sad′dle**
**re|salt′**
**re|scale′**
**re|scrub′**
**re|seal′**
**re′se|crete′**
**re′se|lect′**
**re|sen′tence**
**re|sew′**
**re|share′**
**re|shave′**
**re|sheathe′**
**re|shift′**
**re|shine′**
**re|shin′gle**
**re|show′**
**re|shut′**
**re|shut′tle**
**re|sight′**
**re|sil′ver**
**re|sing′**
**re|sink′**
**re|slash′**
**re|slay′**
**re|slide′**
**re|smelt′**
**re|smile′**
**re|smooth′**
**re|snub′**
**re|soak′**
**re|soil′**
**re′so|lid′i|fy**
**re-solve′**
**re|spar′kle**
**re|sphere′**
**re|spin′**
**re|splice′**
**re|split′**
**re|spot′**
**re|spring′**
**re|sprin′kle**
**re|sprout′**
**re|stack′**
**re|stain′**
**re|stamp′**
**re|steal′**
**re|steel′**
**re|stem′**
**re|stitch′**
**re|stress′**
**re|stuff′**
**re|sub′ju|gate**
**re′sub|li|ma′tion**
**re′sub|lime′**
**re′sub|merge′**
**re′sub|mis′sion**
**re′suc|ceed′**
**re|suf′fer**
**re′sug|gest′**
**re|suit′**
**re|sup′**
**re′sup|press′**
**re′sur|prise′**
**re′sur|ren′der**
**re′sus|pend′**
**re|swal′low**
**re|swell′**
**re|syn′the|size**
**re|tack′**
**re|tail′or**
**re|talk′**
**re|tar′get**
**re|taste′**
**re|taught′**
**re|tax′**
**re′tax|a′tion**
**re|teach′**
**re|tel′e|graph**
**re|tel′e|phone**
**re|tes′ti|fy**
**re|thatch′**
**re|thread′**
**re|throne′**
**re|tie′**
**re|tile′**
**re|till′**
**re|time′**
**re|tin′**
**re|tor′ture**
**re|toss′**
**re|track′**
**re′trans|plant′**
**re′trans|port′**
**re|trav′el**
**re′trav|erse′**
**re|trip′**
**re-turn′**
**re|twine′**
**re|twist′**
**re|un′du|late**
**re′un|fold′**
**re|urge′**
**re|ut′ter|ance**
**re|va′por|ize**
**re|ver′i|fy**
**re|ver′si|fy**
**re|vin′di|cate**
**re|vis′i|ta′tion**
**re|vis′u|al|ize**
**re|vow′**
**re|voy′age**
**re|warm′**
**re|wash′**
**re|wax′**
**re|weave′**
**re|weigh′**
**re|weight′**
**re|weld′**
**re|wet′**
**re|whirl′**
**re|whit′en**
**re|wid′en**
**re|yoke′**

**r.e.**, right end.
**Re** (no period), rhenium (chemical element).
**Re.**, rupee or rupees.
**RE** (no periods), religious education.
**R.E.**, an abbreviation for the following:
**1** Reformed Episcopal.
**2** Right Excellent.
**3** Royal Engineers of Great Britain.
**4** Royal Exchange of Great Britain.
**REA** (no periods) or **R.E.A.**, Rural Electrification Administration.
**re|ab|sorb** (rē′əb sôrb′, -zôrb′), *v.t.* to absorb again or anew. —**re′ab|sorp′tion**, *n.*
**re|ac|com|mo|date** (rē′ə kom′ə dāt), *v.t.*, **-dat|ed, -dat|ing.** to accommodate or adjust afresh or again: *The hotel refused to reaccommodate us in other rooms.*
**reach** (rēch), *v., n.* —***v.t.*** **1** to get to; arrive at; come to: *to reach the top of a hill, to reach the end of a book, to reach an agreement. Your letter reached me yesterday.* **SYN**: attain, gain. **2** to stretch out; hold out; extend: *to reach one's foot out. A tree reaches out its branches.* **3a** to extend to: *The radio reaches millions.* **b** to get in touch with (someone): *I could not reach you by telephone.* **4** to touch; get in touch with, as by anything extended or cast: *I cannot reach the top of the wall. The anchor reached bottom.* **5** to move to touch or seize (something); try to get: *to reach a package on a high shelf.* **6** *Figurative.* to get at; influence: *Some people are reached by flattery. The speaker reached the hearts of his hearers.* **7** to take and pass with the hand: *Please reach me the newspaper.* **8** *Figurative.* to amount to; be equal to: *The cost of the war reached billions.*
—***v.i.*** **1** to stretch: *to reach toward a book. A hand reached from the dark and seized him.* **2** to extend, as in space, time, or influence: *a dress reaching to the floor. The United States reaches from ocean to ocean.* (*Figurative.*) *The power of Rome reached to the ends of the known world.* **3** to get or come; function; carry: *farther than the eye can reach.* **4** to make a stretch in a certain direction; move as if to touch or seize something: *The man reached for his gun.* **5** to make a stretch of certain length with the hand, etc.: *I cannot reach to the top of the wall.* **6** *Figurative.* to amount (to): *amounts reaching to a considerable sum.* **7** to succeed in coming, as to a place, point, or person: *They could not reach back to the boat before it was dark* (Daniel Defoe). **8** to sail on a course with the wind forward of the beam.
—***n.*** **1** the act of stretching out; reaching: *By a long reach, the drowning man grasped the rope.* **2** the extent or distance of reaching: *out of one's reach. Food and water were left within reach of the sick dog.* **3** *Figurative.* range; power; capacity: *the reach of the mind. Philosophy is not beyond a child's reach; he can understand it.* **4** a continuous stretch or extent: *vast reaches of snow in the Antarctic, a reach of woodland.* **5** the course or distance sailed on one tack. **6** the part of a river, channel, or lake between bends. **7** the part of a canal between locks. **8** a pole from the rear axle of a wagon or carriage to the bar above the front axle.
[Old English *rǣcan*] —**reach′er**, *n.*
**reach|a|ble** (rē′chə bəl), *adj.* that can be reached; within reach: *a reachable goal.* **SYN**: accessible, attainable.
**reach|less** (rēch′lis), *adj.* beyond reach; unattainable; lofty: *the reachless height of an eagle nest.*
**reach-me-down** (rēch′mē doun′), *n., adj. British Informal.* hand-me-down.
**re|ac|quire** (rē′ə kwīr′), *v.t.*, **-quired, -quir|ing.** to acquire anew.
**re|act** (rē akt′), *v.i.* **1** to act back; have an effect on the one that is acting: *Unkindness often reacts on the unkind person and makes him unhappy.* **2a** to act in response: *Dogs react to kindness by showing affection.* **b** to respond in some manner; have an opinion of some proposal: *How did he react to the idea when you told him? Plants react to light.* **3** to act chemically. Acids react on metals. **4** to return, as to a previous state or level. —***v.t.*** to cause (a substance) to form a chemical reaction: *One way to make formaldehyde is to react methane with hydroxyl* (Science News). *Fertilizer manufacturers make superphosphate by reacting rock phosphate with sulphuric acid* (New Scientist).
**react against**, to act unfavorably toward or take an unfavorable attitude toward; act in opposition to (some force): *to react against oppression. Some individuals react against fads.*
[< *re-* back + *act*, verb. Compare Medieval Latin *reactus*, past participle of *reagere.*]
**re-act** (rē akt′), *v.t.* to act over again: *to re-act a scene from a play.* [< *re-* again + *act*]
**re|act|ance** (rē ak′təns), *n. Electricity.* that part, expressed in ohms, of the impedance of an alternating-current circuit which is due to inductance and capacitance, rather than resistance: *amplifiers ... for microwave amplification by variable reactance* (Wall Street Journal).
**re|act|ant** (rē ak′tənt), *n. Chemistry.* an element or compound that enters into a chemical reaction: *The influence of the concentrations of the reactants on the rates of chemical reactions was discovered very early in the development of chemical kinetics* (K. D. Wadsworth).
**re|ac|tion** (rē ak′shən), *n.* **1a** an action in response to some influence or force: *Our reaction to a joke is to laugh. The doctor observed carefully his patient's reactions to the tests.* **b** the response of the body to a test for immunization or the like: *A more general distinction depends on the extent of reaction shown by antiserum prepared against one strain of the virus* (A. W. Haslett). **c** the response of a nerve, muscle, or organ to a stimulus: *They were designed to elucidate the reaction of the human body to the various stresses* (E. F. Roots). **d** *Informal.* a response, such as to an idea or plan; attitude; feeling; opinion: *What was his reaction to the plan?* **2** an action in the opposite direction: *Fever is a common reaction from a chill.* **3a** a chemical action of two substances on each other which results in the formation of one or more additional substances. The reaction between nitrogen and hydrogen produces ammonia. *Putting an acid and a metal together causes a reaction.* **b** the change resulting from such chemical action: *... whether reaction occurs may depend on the timing of internal vibration of each of the molecules* (K. D. Wadsworth). **4** a process in which the nucleus of an atom becomes transformed, as in the disintegration of radioactive substances; nuclear reaction: *Reactions of the general type in which one of the two deuteron particles enters the hit nucleus and the other continues on its way* (A. W. Haslett). **5** a political tendency toward a previous, usually more conservative, state of affairs. **6** a drop in prices following a rise in prices, as on a stock market. **7** an equal and opposite force which a body exerts against a force that acts upon it: *... in no case is it of importance which of the equal and opposite forces is considered the action and which the reaction* (Shortley and Williams). —**re|ac′tion|less**, *adj.*
**re|ac|tion|al** (rē ak′shən əl), *adj.* of or having to do with reaction. —**re|ac′tion|al|ly**, *adv.*
**re|ac|tion|ar|y** (rē ak′shə ner′ē), *adj., n., pl.* **-ar|ies.** —***adj.*** having to do with or favoring a return to a previous, usually more conservative, state of affairs: *The economic recession brought about a reactionary attitude toward low tariffs.*
—***n.*** a person who favors a return to a previous, usually more conservative, state of affairs, especially in politics; extreme conservative.
**re|ac|tion|ar|y|ism** (rē ak′shə ner′ē iz′əm), *n.* = reactionism.
**reaction engine**, an engine which expels a stream of burned exhaust gases at high velocity, the reaction from which creates a forward accelerating force; thrustor; jet engine.
**re|ac|tion|ism** (rē ak′shə niz əm), *n.* reactionary principles and ideas; inclination toward a previous state of affairs, especially in politics; conservatism.
**re|ac|tion|ist** (rē ak′shə nist), *adj., n.* = reactionary.
**reaction key**, *Psychology.* an instrument to record movement of response in a reaction experiment.
**reaction time**, the interval of time between a stimulus or signal and the response to it.
**reaction turbine**, a water turbine whose wheels are turned by the weight or pressure of the water as well as by its speed of flow. Reaction turbines have movable vanes around the edge of the wheel to adjust the flow of water and direct it at the desired angle.
**re|ac|ti|vate** (rē ak′tə vāt), *v.t.*, **-vat|ed, -vat|ing.** to make active again; restore to active service: *The Army announced that the old 101st Airborne Division, famous for its stand at Bastogne in the second world war, will be reactivated at Fort Campbell, Kentucky* (Newsweek).
**re|ac|ti|va|tion** (rē′ak tə vā′shən), *n.* the act or process of reactivating or state of being reactivated: *The government has authorized this month the reactivation of thirteen more labor unions* (New York Times).
**re|ac|tive** (rē ak′tiv), *adj.* **1** tending to react: *Moreover, all the steps, apart from the first, require little or no energy of activation, because they are all reactions of highly reactive atoms with molecules* (K. D. Wadsworth). **2** having to do with or characterized by reaction, especially in politics, or reactance. —**re|ac′tive|ly**, *adv.* —**re|ac′tive|ness**, *n.*
**reactive circuit**, a circuit with impedance from inductance or capacity or to both.
**reactive coil**, a wire coil, often with an iron core, to produce reactance.
**reactive drop**, the fall of potential in a circuit from reactance.
**re|ac|tiv|i|ty** (rē′ak tiv′ə tē), *n.* the power or con-

dition of being reactive, as in a chemical combination: *The existence of such ... ions as intermediates in organic reactions is well established, and their reactivity can be readily measured by the rate at which they react with powerful acidic (negative) ions* (R. F. Homer).

**re|ac|tor** (rē ak′tər), *n.* **1** a device for splitting atoms to produce atomic energy without causing an explosion; pile; nuclear reactor; atomic reactor. Reactors are special assemblies for the production of a controlled chain reaction and consist of layers of fissionable material, such as uranium, spaced with moderators, such as graphite and heavy water, which slow down the speed and number of the neutrons intended for splitting the uranium nuclei. *The goal is to find economical ways of chemically treating water from the Columbia River so that it can be used to cool Hanford reactors operating at higher power than at present* (Science). **2** a person or animal that reacts positively to a medical test, such as for allergy. **3** a person or animal that reacts. **4** *Electricity.* a type of condenser characterized by slow resistance and high inductance.

**read**[1] (rēd), *v.,* **read** (red), **read|ing,** *n.* **—*v.t.*** **1** to get the meaning of (writing or printing): *We read books. The blind girl reads special raised print by touching it. I know enough German to read German.* **2** to find out from writing or print: *to read the news.* **3** to speak out loud (printed or written words); say aloud: *Please read this story to me.* **4** to show by letters, figures, or signs: *The thermometer reads 70 degrees. The ticket reads "From New York to Boston."* **SYN:** indicate, register. **5** to give as the word or words in a particular passage: *For "fail," a misprint, read "fall."* **6** to study (a subject): *He is reading law.* **7** *Figurative.* to get the meaning of; understand: *He could read distrust on my face. God reads men's hearts.* **SYN:** comprehend. **8** to receive and understand (a person's voice transmitting over radio): *"This is a pilot. I'm in the tower—if we can get you in we'll try to talk to you. Do you read me, 79-X ...?* (St. Louis Post-Dispatch). **9** *Figurative.* to give the meaning of; interpret: *A prophet reads the future.* **SYN:** explain, decipher. **10** *Figurative.* to introduce (something not expressed or directly indicated) by one's manner of understanding or interpreting: *She read a hostile intent in a friendly letter.* **SYN:** infer. **11** to bring or put by reading: *He reads himself to sleep.* **12** to give (a lecture or lesson) as a reprimand. **13a** to absorb information from (a punch card, magnetic tape, or other input device): *The ... Unit both punches and reads paper tape or unit cards that activate other equipment* (Wall Street Journal). **b** to absorb (information) this way: *If the computer is told to read the contents of address 105, it will read ... the column designated 105* (W. M. Chow and J. C. Sippl). **14** to decode (a genetic message): *Each transfer RNA is succeeded by another one, carrying its own amino acid, until the complete message in the messenger RNA has been "read"* (Scientific American).
**—*v.i.*** **1** to get the meaning of something written or printed: *to learn to read and write. The blind read with their fingers.* **2** to learn from writing or print: *We read of heroes of other days.* **3** to say aloud the words one sees or touches: *to read to a child before bedtime.* **4** to study by reading: *He ... was ... set to read with the best private tutors that could be found* (Samuel Butler). **5** to produce a certain impression when read; mean; be in effect when read: *This does not read like a child's composition.* **6** to convey a statement when read: *The telegram reads as follows.* **7** to be worded in a certain way: *This line reads differently in the first edition.* **8** *Figurative.* to admit of being read or interpreted: *a rule that reads two different ways.*
**—*n.*** *Informal.* **1** an act or spell of reading: *Woe betide those who settle down with this book to a steady read through 550 pages from beginning to end* (Economist). **2** a thing to read; matter for reading: *Serious critics dismiss her writing as nothing but "a jolly good read"* (Time). *The novel itself is ... a hard read* (Listener).
**read between the lines.** See under **line**[1].
**read in,** to feed information into a computer: *All data has to be read in to computers, and there is great interest in machines which can do their own reading* (New Scientist).
**read into,** to interpret in a certain way, often attributing more than intended: *He read into the statement a deep insult. He reads something of himself into the composition* (Arthur C. Ainger).
**read out, a** to transmit (data) by radio transmitter: *Three radio receiving stations, to read out telemetry data from the satellite, are being established in Brazil* (New York Times). **b** to transmit information from the storage of a computer: *This system will read out continuously in real-time to a new second generation of still relatively simple ... receivers* (Science Journal).
**read out of,** to expel from (a political party or other group): *[He] would be read out of the U.N. probably by the next General Assembly* (Newsweek).
**read up on,** to study by reading about: *to read up on the latest scientific advances.*
[Old English *rǣdan* to guess; read; counsel]

**read**[2] (red), *adj., v.* **—*adj.*** having knowledge gained by reading; informed: *a well-read man. He is widely read in history.*
**—*v.*** the past tense and past participle of **read**: *I read that book last year. She has read it too.*
[(originally) past participle of *read*[1]]

**read|a|bil|i|ty** (rē′də bil′ə tē), *n.* readable quality: *Some novels struck a balance between traditionalist readability and avant-garde obscurity* (Renato Barilli).

**read|a|ble** (rē′də bəl), *adj.* **1** easy or pleasant to read; interesting: *Treasure Island is a very readable story.* **2** capable of being read; legible.
**—read′a|ble|ness,** *n.* **—read′a|bly,** *adv.*

**re|a|dapt** (rē′ə dapt′), *v.t.* to adapt anew.

**re|ad|dress** (rē′ə dres′), *v.t.* **1** to put a new address on. **2** to speak to again. **3** to apply (oneself) anew.

**read|er** (rē′dər), *n.* **1** a person who reads: *a good reader, a light reader.* **2** a book for learning and practicing reading. **3** a person employed to read manuscripts and estimate their fitness for publication: *The ideal publisher's reader should have two perfections—perfect taste and perfect knowledge of what the various kinds of other people deem to be taste* (Arnold Bennett). **4** = proofreader. **5a** *Especially British.* an instructor in certain universities: *He came under Dr. Martin Johnson, the present Reader in Astrophysics at Birmingham* (New Scientist). **b** an assistant who grades and corrects examinations and reads papers for a professor. **6** a person who reads or recites to entertain an audience. **7** a person who reads aloud the lessons or other parts of the service in a church. **8** an electronic device that absorbs information from punch cards, magnetic tape, or other input devices: *The brain of the control is a punched-tape reader which simultaneously reads 140 channels, each of which provides information for a specific job* (Kenneth R. Burchard).

**read|er|ship** (rē′dər ship), *n.* **1** the reading audience, especially of a particular author, publication, or type of reading matter: *The distribution of readership has not been determined, but undoubtedly a large number of these readers are young* (Atlantic). **2** the office of reader, especially in a university.

**read|i|ly** (red′ə lē), *adv.* **1** quickly; promptly; without delay: *A bright boy answers readily when called on.* **2** easily; without difficulty: *Everything around me is within easy reach and readily accessible.* **3** willingly.

**read-in** (rēd′in′), *n.* **1** the feeding of information into a computer: *During read-in ... the source connected to any store can be changed by depressing the appropriate button* (New Scientist). **2** the reading of appropriate literary passages at a meeting as a protest against social ill.

**read|i|ness** (red′ē nis), *n.* **1** the condition of being ready; preparedness: *to be in readiness for any emergency. Everything is in readiness for the party.* **2** quickness; promptness: *His readiness in reacting prevented a dogfight.* **3** ease; facility: *readiness of thought.* **4** willingness: *Her cheerful readiness to help made her a valued worker.*

**read|ing** (rē′ding), *n., adj.* **—*n.*** **1** the act or process of getting the meaning of written or printed words: *The teaching of reading has not changed in a generation* (Time). **2** the study of books or other written material: *Reading has objective values, such as giving facts and arousing interests* (Emory S. Bogardus). *Reading maketh a full man* (Francis Bacon). **3** a speaking out loud of written or printed words; public recital: *Reading aloud requires stamina in the reader as well as the read to* (London Times). **4** the written or printed matter read or to be read: *It is in newspapers that we must look for main reading of this generation* (Thomas De Quincey). *Remembering his early love of poetry and fiction, she unlocked a bookcase, and took down several books that had been excellent reading in their day* (Hawthorne). **5** the amount shown by letters, figures, or signs on the scale of an instrument: *The reading of the thermometer was 96 degrees.* **6** the form of a given word or passage in a particular copy or edition of a book: *No two editions have the same reading for that passage.* **7** *Figurative.* interpretation: *Each actor gave the lines a different reading.* **8** the extent to which one has read; literary knowledge. **9** the formal recital of a bill, or part of it, before a legislature. In Congress, a bill is given three readings (usually by title only and as a formality) during its passage. The British Parliament also gives a bill three readings, the fullest one being the second reading.
**—*adj.*** **1** that reads: *the reading public.* **2** used in or for reading: *reading glasses.* **3** of or for reading: *good reading material.*

**reading accelerator,** a mechanical device adjusted for different speeds to limit the time for reading each line of a book, used to increase reading speed.

**reading chair,** a chair having high broad armrests and a reading desk attached to the back, so that a person could sit backwards on the chair and rest his elbows on the armrests while he reads. Reading chairs were first made in the 1700's.

**reading desk,** a desk to hold a book while a person reads, especially when standing; lectern.

**reading glass,** a magnifying glass usually used to read fine print or details of maps.

**reading room,** a special room for reading, such as that in a library or club.

**re|ad|journ** (rē′ə jėrn′), *v.t., v.i.* to adjourn again.
**—re′ad|journ′ment,** *n.*

**re|ad|just** (rē′ə just′), *v.t., v.i.* to adjust again; arrange again: *the day hospital ... for patients who ... need help in readjusting to the world at large* (Time). **—re′ad|just′er,** *n.* **—re′ad|just′ment,** *n.*

**re|ad|mis|sion** (rē′əd mish′ən), *n.* admission again or anew.

**re|ad|mit** (rē′əd mit′), *v.t.,* **-mit|ted, -mit|ting.** to admit again.

**re|ad|mit|tance** (rē′əd mit′əns), *n.* permission to enter again; readmission: *Humbly petitioning a readmittance into his college* (Thomas Warton).

**read-on|ly memory** (rēd′ōn′lē), a computer memory which stores permanent data: *Changing the program may require the physical replacement of a read-only memory* (Wallace B. Riley). *Abbr:* ROM (no periods).

**re|a|dopt** (rē′ə dopt′), *v.t.* to adopt again: *The boundary which had first passed was readopted by a large vote* (Bayard Taylor).

**re|a|dorn** (rē′ə dôrn′), *v.t.* to adorn anew.

**read|out** (rēd′out), *n.* **1** the display, usually in digits, of processed information by a computer: *This machine is a simple digital computer which allows the rating of up to 20 people ... After all members have made their choices the machine gives a digital readout of the mean rating for each member of the group* (New Scientist). **2** the transmission of quantitative data such as that taken by a telemeter. **3** a device used for facilitating such a display or transmission.

**re|ad|sorb** (rē′ad sôrb′, -zôrb′), *v.t.* to adsorb again or anew.

**read|y** (red′ē), *adj.,* **read|i|er, read|i|est,** *v.,* **read|ied, read|y|ing,** *n.* **—*adj.*** **1** prepared for action or use at once; prepared: *Dinner is ready. We were ready to start at nine. The soldiers are ready for battle. The cannons are pointed, and ready to roar* (Byron). **2** willing: *She is ready to forgive. The soldiers were ready to die for their country.* **SYN:** disposed. **3** quick; prompt: *a ready welcome.* **4** quick in thought or action; dexterous: *The speaker has a ready wit.* **5** likely; liable; apt: *She is too ready to find fault.* **SYN:** prone. **6** easy to get at; very easy to reach; immediately available: *ready money.*
**—*v.t.*** to make ready; prepare: *The explorers readied themselves for the winter expedition.*
**—*n.*** **1** the condition or position of being prepared for action: *The soldiers walked down the road with their guns at the ready.* **2** *Slang.* ready money; cash.
**make ready,** to prepare: *His companions made ready to fight* (William Longman).
**ready up,** to make ready; prepare for a special purpose: *It was the women's job to ready up the house for the party; the men went out to buy the food and drinks.*
[Middle English *redi* < Old English *rǣde* mounted (ready to ride) + *-ig* -y[1]. See related etym. at **ride.**]
**—*Syn.*** *adj.* **3, 4 Ready, prompt** mean quick to understand, observe, or act in response. **Ready,** chiefly describing a person, his mind, hands, or instrument, suggests being prepared to act or respond without delay: *With ready fingers the surgeon explored the wound.* **Prompt,** more often describing what is done, emphasizes being quick to act when the occasion demands or request is made: *He is prompt to help students.*

**read|y-made** (red′ē mād′), *adj., n.* **—*adj.*** **1** ready for immediate use; made for anybody who will buy; not made to order: *Department stores sell ready-made clothes.* **2** *Figurative.* having little or no individuality, as if made by mass production,

---

**Pronunciation Key:** hat, āge, cãre, fär; let, ēqual, tėrm; it, īce; hot, ōpen, ôrder; oil, out; cup, pu̇t, rüle; child; long; thin; ᴛʜen; zh, measure; ə represents **a** in about, **e** in taken, **i** in pencil, **o** in lemon, **u** in circus.

and kept in readiness for any use or occasion: *ready-made opinions. They were ... spies and agents ready-made for either party* (Robert Louis Stevenson).

—*n.* **1** a ready-made object: *Some maternity shops, in addition to selling ready-mades, will custom-design clothes* (Maclean's). **2** an ordinary object, such as a bicycle wheel or a metal rack, mounted and treated as if it were a work of art, especially in Dada: *Duchamp originally fathered the movement with "ready-mades," ordinary objects from our environment* (Atlantic).

**read|y-mix** (red′ē miks′), *adj., n.* —*adj.* that contains the proper inactive ingredients and is ready for use after mixing with water, milk, or other, usually liquid, substance: *ready-mix cement, ready-mix cake.*

—*n.* a preparation that is ready for use after mixing with a liquid solution: *The American consumer ... insists on better cuts of beef, fancier grades of vegetables,* [*and*] *ready-mixes* (Newsweek).

**ready reckoner,** *British.* a table, or collection of tables, showing at a glance the results of such arithmetical calculations as are most frequently required in ordinary business, housekeeping, or laboratory calculations.

**Ready Reserve,** *U.S.* reserve members of the armed forces who train at certain intervals in preparation for active duty in an emergency: *That service will consist of six months' training, at which time he will move into the Ready Reserve and have an obligation there for nine and one-half years* (New York Times).

**Ready Reservist,** a member of the Ready Reserve.

**ready room,** a room where members of an aircrew meet to receive a briefing or a call to fly.

**read|y-to-wear** (red′ē tə wãr′), *adj., n.* —*adj.* ready-made for wear: *Others prefer to make their own clothes because they feel that ready-to-wear garments have too little individuality* (Mary Ellen Roach).

—*n.* ready-made clothing: *He would like some day to design ready-to-wear to be manufactured in America* (New York Times).

**read|y|wit|ted** (red′ē wit′id), *adj.* mentally alert.

**re|af|firm** (rē′ə fėrm′), *v.t.* to affirm again or anew: *The electors have since ... reaffirmed and strengthened that decision* (Spectator). —**re′af|fir|ma′tion,** *n.* —**re′af|firm′er,** *n.*

**re|af|for|est** (rē′ə fôr′əst, -for′-), *v.t.* to cover again with forest; reforest. —**re′af|for′est|a′tion,** *n.*

**re|a|gent** (rē ā′jənt), *n.* a substance used to detect the presence of other substances by the chemical reactions it causes: *The addition to the blood of small amounts of reagents such as citrates, which can bind chemically and inactivate calcium ions ... prevents coagulation quite effectively* (K. S. Spiegler).

**re|a|gin** (rē′ə jin), *n.* **1** one of a group of antibodies that reacts with the allergens, as of hay fever or asthma. **2** a substance in serum and cerebrospinal fluid that behaves like an antibody in complement fixation and similar reactions. [< *reag*(ent) + *-in*]

**re|a|gin|ic** (rē′ə jin′ik), *adj.* having to do with or being a reagin: *reaginic activity, a reaginic antibody.* —**re′a|gin′i|cal|ly,** *adv.*

**re|al[1]** (rē′əl, rēl), *adj., adv., n.* —*adj.* **1** existing as a fact; not imagined or made up; actual; true: *real pleasure, a real experience, the real reason.* **2** genuine; not artificial: *the real thing, a real diamond, real money.* SYN: authentic. **3** *Law.* of or having to do with immovable property. Land and houses are called real property. **4** of or having to do with things. **5** *Mathematics.* either rational or irrational, not imaginary. **6** *Optics.* **a** of or having to do with an image formed by actual convergence of rays: *A real image can be caught on a screen, a virtual image cannot* (Shortley and Williams). **b** having to do with or designating a focus forming such an image. **7** *Economics.* measured by reference to useful goods rather than money: *In a period of rising prices, real incomes fall if money incomes remain steady.* **8** *Philosophy.* existing in or having to do with things, and not words or thought merely.

—*adv. Informal.* very; extremely: *real soon. It was real kind of you to come.*

—*n.* something real or having a real existence.

**for real,** *Slang.* **a** in reality; really: *Prove to your loved ones that you're a Christian, for real* (San Francisco Chronicle). **b** real; actual; possible. **c** genuine; authentic: *"Here's Love"—something about a Macy Santa Claus who thinks he's for real* (New Yorker).

[< Late Latin *reālis* < Latin *rēs, reī* matter, thing]

—*Syn. adj.* **1 Real, actual, true** all relate to fact. **Real** means that what is described is in fact what it seems, is thought, or is said to be, not pretended, imaginary, or made up: *Give your real name.* **Actual** means that what it describes has in reality happened or come into existence, and is not merely capable of happening or existing only in theory: *Name an actual instance of heroism.* **True** means in agreement with what is real or actual, not false: *Tell the true story.* **2** authentic.

**re|al[2]** (rē′əl; *Spanish* rä äl′), *n., pl.* **re|als,** *Spanish.* **re|a|les** (rä ä′läs). a former small silver coin of Spain and Spanish America, worth about 12½ cents. It was widely used in the American colonies at one time and was referred to as a *bit.* [< Spanish *real* < Latin *rēgālis* regal < *rēx, rēgis* king. See etym. of doublets **regal, royal.**]

**re|al[3]** (rä äl′), *n.* singular of **reis.**

**real estate,** land together with the buildings, fences, trees, water, and minerals that belong with it. —**real′-es|tate′,** *adj.*

**re|al|gar** (rē al′gər), *n.* a lustrous orange-red mineral, a sulfide of arsenic, used in fireworks. *Formula:* $As_2S_2$ [< Medieval Latin *realgar,* probably < Spanish *rejalgar* < Arabic *rahgh-al-ghār,* variant of *rahghu-lghār* (literally) powder of the cave; form apparently from a textual error for *rahghu-lfār* rat powder]

**re|al|i|a** (rē ā′lē ə), *n. pl.* actual objects, such as types of woods or fabrics, used as tools in teaching. [< Late Latin *reālia,* neuter plural of *reālis* real; see etym. under **real**[1]]

**re|a|lign** (rē′ə līn′), *v.t., v.i.* to align again or anew: *to realign wheels of a car. Just behind the film the carbon atoms realign themselves and form diamonds* (Scientific American). *Some political scientists have urged that the two major parties realign ... that all conservatives move into the Republican party and all liberals be driven into the Democratic party* (K. Colegrove and F. F. Blackly). —**re′a|lign′ment,** *n.*

**re|al|ise** (rē′ə līz), *v.t., v.i.,* **-ised, -is|ing.** *Especially British.* realize.

**re|al|ism** (rē′ə liz əm), *n.* **1** thought and action based on realities; practical tendency: *His realism caused him to dislike fanciful schemes. With the inexorable realism of her sex she easily dismissed ... theories, and accommodated herself to the fact* (Arnold Bennett). **2** Also, **Realism.** (in art and literature) the picturing of life as its actually is: *When we think of Realism we think of Ibsen ... because in his social plays he not only used the form but pressed it very close to its ultimate limits* (Arthur Miller). **3** the doctrine that material objects have a real existence independent of our consciousness of them. **4** the doctrine that general ideas have a real existence independent of the mind.

**re|al|ist** (rē′ə list), *n., adj.* —*n.* **1** a person interested in what is real and practical rather than what is imaginary or theoretical: *The multitude of protectionists do not dream. They are hard, if mistaken, realists* (Spectator). **2** a writer or artist who represents things as they are in real life. **3** a person who believes in realism.

—*adj.* realistic: *It can be seen as a dramatic and realist attempt to reveal ultimate degradation* (Punch).

**re|al|is|tic** (rē′ə lis′tik), *adj.* **1** like the real thing; lifelike. **2** representing life in literature or art as it actually is: *The realistic novel, which was created by Defoe under George I., was already foreshadowed in the admirable character sketches of Addison* (William E. H. Lecky). **3** seeing things as they really are; practical. **4** having to do with realists or realism. —**re′al|is′ti|cal|ly,** *adv.*

**re|al|i|ty** (rē al′ə tē), *n., pl.* **-ties. 1** actual existence; true state of affairs: *I doubted the reality of what he had seen; I thought he must have dreamed it. Ghosts have no place in reality.* SYN: actuality. **2** a real thing; actual fact: *Slaughter and destruction are terrible realities of war.* SYN: truth, verity.

**in reality,** really; actually; in fact; truly: *We thought he was serious, but in reality he was joking.*

**re|al|iz|a|ble** (rē′ə lī′zə bəl), *adj.* that can be realized: *a realizable goal, realizable capital.*

**re|al|i|za|tion** (rē′ə lə zā′shən), *n.* **1** the action of realizing or result of being realized: *The realization of her hope to be an actress made her happy.* SYN: consummation, fulfillment. **2** a clear understanding; full awareness; perception: *The explorers had a full realization of the dangers they would face.* SYN: comprehension. **3** the exchange of property for its money value. **4** the obtaining or acquiring (of money, a fortune, or property).

**re|al|ize** (rē′ə līz), *v.,* **-ized, -iz|ing.** —*v.t.* **1** to understand clearly; be fully aware of: *Does he fully realize the risks he's taking? She realizes how hard you worked.* SYN: comprehend, conceive. **2** to make real; bring into actual existence: *Her uncle's present made it possible for her to realize her dream of going to college.* SYN: achieve. **3** to cause to seem real. **4** to change (property) into money: *Before going to England to live, he realized all his American property.* **5** to obtain as a return or profit: *He realized $118 for his work.* **6** to bring as a return or profit: *The prices realized were disappointing to the sellers.*

—*v.i.* **1** to convert property into money: *He realized with great prudence while this mine was still at its full vogue* (Thackeray). **2** to make a profit. **3** to change an asset, right, or property into money or other real property. —**re′al|iz′er,** *n.*

**re|al|iz|ing** (rē′ə lī′zing), *adj.* that realizes; clear and vivid: *a realizing sense of danger.* —**re′al|iz′ing|ly,** *adv.*

**re|al-life** (rē′əl līf′), *adj.* true to life; existing in reality; real: *a real-life story. There seems to be a growing desire for toys that are ... closely related to real-life situations* (New Yorker).

**re|al|lo|cate** (rē al′ə kāt), *v.t.,* **-cat|ed, -cat|ing.** to allocate again or anew; assign or distribute again. —**re′al|lo|ca′tion,** *n.*

**re|al|ly** (rē′ə lē, rē′lē), *adv.* **1** actually; truly; in fact: *We should learn to accept things as they really are.* **2** indeed: *Oh, really?*

**re-al|ly** (rē′ə lī′), *v.,* **-lied, -ly|ing.** —*v.t.* **1** to form or arrange again; recompose: *The enemy did not pursue, which gave us time to stop and re-ally our men* (Sir Henry Slingsby). **2** to connect; unite.

—*v.i.* to come together again; rally: *They re-allied and assembled themselves together.*

**realm** (relm), *n.* **1** a kingdom: *the British realm.* **2** *Figurative.* a region or sphere in which something rules or prevails; range; extent: *The President's realm of influence is very wide. One realm we have never conquered—the pure present* (D. H. Lawrence). **3** *Figurative: the realm of biology, the realm of poetry.* SYN: province. **4** *Geography.* a prime division of the earth's surface, containing one or more regions; zoological region of the first order.

**abjure the realm,** (formerly, in England) to take an oath to leave the country and never return: *Even while abjurations were in force, such a criminal was not allowed to take sanctuary and abjure the realm* (William Blackstone).

[Middle English *realme* < Old French *realme,* alteration (influenced by *reial* royal) of *reiemme* < Gallo-Romance *regiminem,* accusative of Latin *regimen.* See etym. of doublets **regime, regimen.**]

**realm|less** (relm′lis), *adj.* without a realm.

**re|al|ness** (rē′əl nis, rēl′-), *n.* the state or condition of being or appearing real: *There is such a realness to his narration that one is willing to overlook his many deficiencies in the art of expression* (Science).

**real number,** any rational or irrational number.

**Re|al|po|li|tik** (rā äl′pō′li tēk′), *n. German.* political realism; practical politics: *Together with the Russian unideological Realpolitik, which means the Russians want us to keep what they have but are not out to conquer the world, there is another factor of accommodation, the spontaneous wishes of the Russian people* (Canadian Forum).

**real presence** or **Real Presence,** the doctrine that Christ's body and blood are actually present in the sacrament of the Eucharist.

**real property,** = real estate.

**Re|al|schu|le** (rā äl′shü′lə), *n., pl.* **-len** (-lən). a German secondary school that emphasizes science and modern languages. [< German *realschule* < *real* real, practical + *Schule* school]

**real tennis,** *British.* court tennis. [variant of *royal tennis*]

**real time,** equivalence in time or speed between the output of an electronic computer and a particular physical process which needs this output for its effective operation: *That thinking had to be done in what engineers call "real time"—quick decisions, made on the basis of information that becomes available almost instantaneously through the vast electronic communications network* (New York Times).

**re|al-time** (rē′əl tīm′), *adj.* operating in real time; producing data or solving problems simultaneously with a process which depends on the data or solutions for its continuation or completion: *The central theme is "real-time systems", which can be taken to mean systems that deal with problems as they appear ... the term "real-time" in this sense also covers, for example, a system that a scientist or engineer can turn to without leaving his desk* (New Scientist).

**Re|al|tor** or **re|al|tor** (rē′əl tər, -tôr), *n. U.S. Trademark.* a person engaged in the real-estate business who is a member of the National Association of Real Estate Boards. [American English, apparently < *realt*(y) + *-or*]

**re|al|ty[1]** (rē′əl tē), *n.* = real estate. [< *real*[1] (definition 3) + *-ty*]

**re|al|ty[2]** (rē′əl tē), *n. Obsolete.* sincerity; honesty. [< Old French *realte* < Medieval Latin *regalitas, -atis* < Latin *rēgālis;* see etym. under **regal**[1]]

**real wages,** wages measured in actual purchasing power.

**ream**[1] (rēm), *n.* **1** 480 or 500 sheets of paper of the same size and quality. **2** 516 sheets of printing paper; perfect ream. **3** *Figurative.* a very large quantity: *ream upon ream of nonsense.* [< Old French *raime,* or *rayme* < Spanish *resma* < Arabic *rizmah* bundle]

**ream**[2] (rēm), *v.t.* **1** to enlarge or shape (a hole). **2** to remove with a reamer. [Middle English *reamen;* origin uncertain]

**ream**[3] (rēm, rām), *n., v. Scottish.* —*n.* **1** cream. **2** a froth or scum.
—*v.i.* to froth or foam.
—*v.t.* to skim.
[Old English *rēam*]

**ream|er** (rē′mər), *n.* **1** a tool for enlarging or shaping a hole. **2** a utensil for squeezing the juice out of oranges, lemons, and the like.

**re|am|pu|ta|tion** (rē′am pyə tā′shən), *n.* amputation on a limb, a part of which has already been removed.

**re|an|i|mate** (rē an′ə māt), *v.t.,* **-mat|ed, -mat-ing.** to restore to life; give fresh spirit, vigor, or activity, to: *to reanimate discouraged troops,* (*Figurative.*) *to reanimate trade.*

**re|an|i|ma|tion** (rē′an ə mā′shən), *n.* **1** the act or operation of reanimating: *Whatever method of heating was used, artificial respiration was essential for reanimation* (New Scientist). **2** a reanimated state.

**re|an|nex** (rē′ə neks′), *v.t.* to annex again, as territory that has been disjoined: *Saint Quentin, which ... had been a Flemish town, was to be reannexed* (John L. Motley). —**re′an|nex|a′tion,** *n.*

**re|a|noint** (rē′ə noint′), *v.t.* to anoint again.

**reap** (rēp), *v.t.* **1** to cut (grain): *Giant machines reap the wheat grown in the midwestern United States.* **2** to gather (a crop): *It took many hands to reap a cotton crop before the invention of machinery.* **3** to cut grain or gather a crop from: *The farmer reaps his fields.* **4** *Figurative.* to get as a return or reward: *Kind acts often reap happy smiles.* **SYN:** earn. —*v.i.* **1** to reap a crop. **2** *Figurative.* to get a return. **SYN:** profit. [Old English *repan,* variant of *rīpan*]

**reap|a|ble** (rē′pə bəl), *adj.* that can be reaped.

**reap|er** (rē′pər), *n.* a person or machine that cuts grain or gathers a crop.

**reaper and binder,** a machine that cuts and gathers grain, and ties the stalks into bundles.

**reap|hook** (rēp′hu̇k′), *n.* a tool with a curved blade used especially for reaping grain.

**reap|ing machine** (rē′ping), = reaper.

**re|ap|par|el** (rē′ə par′əl), *v.t.,* **-eled, -el|ing** or (*especially British*) **-elled, -el|ling.** to clothe again.

**re|ap|pa|ri|tion** (rē′ap ə rish′ən), *n.* = reappearance.

**re|ap|pear** (rē′ə pir′), *v.i.* to come into sight again: *See! the dull stars roll round and reappear* (Alexander Pope).

**re|ap|pear|ance** (rē′ə pir′əns), *n.* the act or fact of reappearing.

**re|ap|pli|ca|tion** (rē′ap lə kā′shən), *n.* **1** the process of applying again. **2** the fact or condition of being reapplied.

**re|ap|ply** (rē′ə plī′), *v.t., v.i.,* **-plied, -ply|ing.** to apply again.

**re|ap|point** (rē′ə point′), *v.t.* to appoint again.

**re|ap|point|ment** (rē′ə point′mənt), *n.* a renewed appointment: *Reappointment in April for another four-year term of* [*the*] *U.S. Surgeon General* (Time).

**re|ap|por|tion** (rē′ə pôr′shən, -pōr′-), *v.t.* **1** to apportion again: *to reapportion property.* **2** *U.S.* to revise the apportionment of: *The 50 state legislatures have been reapportioned because the Court eventually came around to Justice Black's view that the Constitution required districts of equal population* (Anthony Lewis). —*v.i. U.S.* to undergo reapportionment: *Legislatures often refuse to reapportion because they wish to protect the seats of some members from underpopulated areas* (Robert G. Dixon, Jr.).

**re|ap|por|tion|ment** (rē′ə pôr′shən mənt, -pōr′-), *n.* **1** a new distribution or arrangement: *the reapportionment of the shares of an inheritance.* **2** *U.S.* a revising of the representation of an area within a deliberative body, especially by redrawing election districts: *Reapportionment is, strictly speaking, simply legislative redistricting, but in fact the process implies a reweighting of all the interests which contend for political influence* (Roger H. Davidson).

**re|ap|prais|al** (rē′ə prā′zəl), *n.* a new and fresh appraisal; reconsideration: *The situation calls for a reappraisal of all U.S. policies and contacts abroad, particularly in Latin America* (Wall Street Journal).

**re|ap|praise** (rē′ə prāz′), *v.t.,* **-praised, -prais-ing.** to reconsider; make a fresh valuation of: *Samuel Eliot Morison's "Strategy and Compromise" reappraises all the major strategic problems and decisions which faced the Allies during the war* (Newsweek).

**re|ap|proach** (rē′ə prōch′), *v.i., v.t.* to approach again.

**re|ap|pro|pri|ate** (rē′ə prō′prē āt), *v.t.,* **-at|ed, -at|ing.** to appropriate again.

**re|ap|pro|pri|a|tion** (rē′ə prō′prē ā′shən), *n.* a new or different appropriation.

**rear**[1] (rir), *n., adj.* —*n.* **1** the back part; back: *the rear of a car. The kitchen is in the rear of the house.* **2** the last part of an army, fleet, or other group engaged in a struggle, especially when farthest from the line of battle or other conflict: *Many helpers worked in the rear to help win the candidates election.* **3** the space or position behind, or at the back of, anything: *The soldiers ... fired upon them from the rear* (George Bancroft).
—*adj.* at the back; in the back: *Leave by the rear door of the bus. He returned to rear headquarters about fifteen miles behind the front lines.*
**at** (or **in**) **the rear of,** behind: *The houses were built in 1877; at the rear of them was a 9-inch sewer* (Law Times).
**bring up the rear,** to move onward as the rear part; come last in order: *Lauener was in front, ... while I brought up the rear* (John Tyndall).
[(originally) short for *arrear*]

**rear**[2] (rir), *v.t.* **1** to make grow; help to grow; bring up: *The mother was very careful in rearing her children.* **2** to breed (livestock). **3** to set up; build: *The men of old reared altars to the gods. The pioneers soon reared churches in their settlements.* **SYN:** erect. **4** to lift up; raise: *The snake reared its head.* (*Figurative.*) *The specter of revolt reared its head in Britain's American colonies long before the Revolution.* **SYN:** elevate. **5** *British Dialect.* to set upright: *Gently rear'd By the angel, on thy feet thou stood'st at last* (Milton). **6** to exalt. —*v.i.* to rise on the hind legs; rise: *The horse reared as the fire engine dashed past.*
**rear oneself,** to get up on one's feet; rise up: *The unruly beast presently reared himself* (Henry Fielding).
[Old English *rǣran* to raise, related to *rīsan* to rise] —**rear′er,** *n.*
► See **raise** for usage note.

**rear**[3] (rir), *adj. British Dialect.* rare; underdone. [Old English *hrēr*]

**Rear Adm.,** rear admiral.

**rear admiral,** a naval officer next in rank above a captain and next below a vice-admiral. *Abbr:* Rear Adm., RAdm.

**rear-driv|en** (rir′driv′ən), *adj.* driven by power transmitted to the rear wheels: *Most modern automobiles and trucks are rear-driven.*

**rear-end** (rir′end′), *adj.* at the rear end: *Reflecting sheeting outlining the rear of a motor vehicle, to lessen danger of rear-end collisions* (Science News Letter).

**rear-en|gine** (rir′en′jin), *adj.* having a rear-mounted engine: *a rear-engine sports car.*

**rear-en|gined** (rir′en′jind), *adj.* = rear-engine.

**rear|guard** (rir′gärd′), *adj.* designed or carried out to prevent, delay, or evade; diverting or delaying as a defensive measure: *rearguard tactics.* (*Figurative.*) *In seeking to keep races apart he is fighting a rearguard action against a world trend* (Manchester Guardian Weekly).

**rear guard,** the part of an army that protects the rear.

**re|ar|gue** (rē är′gyü), *v.t.,* **-gued, -gu|ing.** to argue over again.

**re|ar|gu|ment** (rē är′gyə mənt), *n.* the process of renewing an argument, as of a case in court; a new pleading upon the same matter: *The Court ... held the cases under advisement ... and then directed the reargument conducted last December* (Atlantic).

**rear|horse** (rir′hôrs′), *n.* = mantis. [< *rear*[2] to rise up + *horse* (because of the customary stance of the mantis)]

**rearing pond,** a pond in which the young are reared, usually at a fish hatchery.

**re|arm** (rē ärm′), *v.t., v.i.* **1** to arm again; arm oneself again. **2** to supply with new or better weapons. —**re|arm′er,** *n.*

**re|ar|ma|ment** (rē är′mə mənt), *n.* the act or process of rearming: *While the French generally are for the North Atlantic alliance they are not for German rearmament* (New York Times).

**rear|most** (rir′mōst), *adj.* farthest in the rear; last.

**rear-mount|ed** (rir′moun′tid), *adj.* **1** mounted in the rear, especially of a motor vehicle: *Enthusiasts ... rev up the rear-mounted 68-h.p. engine and zip along the Autobahn at speeds of up to 85 m.p.h.* (Time). **2** having a rear-mounted engine: *Jim Clark of Scotland rode a rear-mounted Lotus-Ford to a record-shattering victory* (New York Times).

**rear|mouse** (rir′mous′), *n., pl.* **-mice.** = reremouse.

**re|ar|range** (rē′ə rānj′), *v.t.,* **-ranged, -rang|ing.** **1** to arrange in a new or different way: *Mother rearranged the living room furniture to fit in more chairs for the party.* **2** to arrange again: *He had to rearrange his papers after the wind blew them on the floor.*

**re|ar|range|ment** (rē′ə rānj′mənt), *n.* a new or different arrangement.

**rear sight,** the sight closer to the eye of the user in a weapon that has a pair of sights.

**rear-view mirror** (rir′vyü′), a movable mirror inside an automobile or truck that gives the driver a view of what is behind him: *In the rear-view mirror he'd seen a car's headlights coming up behind him* (New Yorker).

**rear|ward** (rir′wərd), *adv., adj., n.* —*adv., adj.* toward or in the rear: *A rearward view discloses a fine grouping of the hills which have been passed* (Henry I. Jenkinson).
—*n.* the rear, especially of an army or fleet.
[< Anglo-French *rerewarde* < *rere* rear, back + *warde* ward, guard] —**rear′ward|ly,** *adv.*

**rear|wards** (rir′wərdz), *adv.* = rearward.

**re|as|cend** (rē′ə send′), *v.i., v.t.* to ascend again.

**re|as|cend|an|cy** (rē′ə sen′dən sē), *n.* a reascending; return to ascendancy.

**re|as|cen|sion** (rē′ə sen′shən), *n.* the act of reascending.

**re|as|cent** (rē′ə sent′), *n.* **1** the act of reascending. **2** a rise, such as of ground, following a descent.

**rea|son** (rē′zən), *n., v.* —*n.* **1** a cause or motive, as for an action or feeling; ground: *Tell me your reasons for not liking him. I have my own reasons for doing this.* **2** an explanation; justification: *Sickness is the reason for her absence. What is your reason for doing such poor work?* **3** the ability or power to think and draw conclusions; intelligence: *Of all the faculties of the human mind ... Reason stands at the summit* (Charles Darwin). **4** a reasonable or sensible view of a matter; right thinking; common sense: *to listen to reason.* **5** sanity: *That poor old man has lost his reason.* **6** *Obsolete.* justice; satisfaction: *to do one reason.*
—*v.i.* **1** to think things out; think logically; solve new problems: *An idiot cannot reason.* **2** to draw conclusions or inferences from facts or premises. **3** to consider; discuss; argue: *Reason with her and try to make her change her mind. They reasoned among themselves, saying, It is because we have taken no bread* (Matthew 16:7).
—*v.t.* **1** to persuade by reasoning: *Don't fancy that men reason themselves into convictions* (Charles Kingsley). **2** to argue, conclude, or infer: *to reason a point.* **3** to support with reasons. **4** to reason about or discuss (what, why, or how): *I will not reason what is meant hereby* (Shakespeare).
**bring to reason,** to cause to be reasonable: *The stubborn child was at last brought to reason.*
**by reason of,** on account of; because of: *I cannot go, by reason of a conflicting meeting.*
**in** (or **within**) **reason,** within reasonable and sensible limits: *If you want a cheque for yourself ... you can name any figure you like—in reason* (George Bernard Shaw). *I will do anything within reason to keep my promise to you.*
**reason away,** to get rid of by reasoning: *He is so blinded by his ideas that he finds no trouble in reasoning away their many contradictions and absurdities.*
**reason out,** to think through and come to a conclusion; think out: *By thus reasoning out the probable consequences of an action, motives ... may lose more or less of their force* (William B. Carpenter).
**stand to reason,** to be reasonable and sensible: *It stands to reason that he would resent your insults.*
**with** (**good**) **reason,** justly or properly; with justification: *If he continuously complains of a pain in his back, it is with reason. She decided not to borrow money, and with good reason.*
[< Old French *reson,* and *raisun* < Latin *ratiō, -ōnis.* See etym. of doublets **ratio, ration.**] —**rea′son|er,** *n.*
—*Syn. n.* **1 Reason, cause, motive** mean that which makes something happen. **Reason** applies to a ground or occasion that explains something that has happened, or one given as an explanation, which may or may not be the true cause or motive: *The reason he went to Arizona was the climate.* **Cause** applies to a person, thing, incident, or condition that directly brings about an action or happening: *The cause was his doctor's warning.* **Motive** applies to the feeling or desire that makes a person do what he does: *His mo-*

*tive was to regain his health.*

**rea|son|a|bil|i|ty** (rē′zə nə bil′ə tē, rēz′ nə-), *n.* reasonable quality or state.

**rea|son|a|ble** (rē′zə nə bəl, rēz′nə-), *adj.* **1** according to reason; sensible; not foolish: *When we are angry, we do not always act in a reasonable way. The jury had a reasonable doubt as to the defendant's guilt and therefore acquitted him.* **2** not asking too much; fair; just: *a reasonable offer.* **3** not high in price; inexpensive: *a reasonable dress.* **4** able to reason: *Man is a reasonable animal and can solve most of his problems.* —**rea′son|a|ble|ness,** *n.*

—*Syn.* **1 Reasonable, rational** mean according to reason. **Reasonable** suggests showing good judgment in everyday affairs because of the practical application of reason: *He took a reasonable view of the dispute and offered a solution that was fair, sensible, and practical.* **Rational** often suggests an unusual power to think logically and objectively, hence doing or saying what is sensible: *Her approach to the problem was rational.*

**rea|son|a|bly** (rē′zə nə blē, rēz′nə-), *adv.* in a reasonable manner; with reason.

**rea|soned** (rē′zənd), *adj.* based on reasoning or reasons; reasonable: *This editorial gave a very reasoned approach to the problem facing our nation* (Wall Street Journal).

**rea|son|ing** (rē′zə ning, rēz′ning), *n.* **1** the process of drawing conclusions from facts: *Philosophers have constantly failed to provide validity for principles of reasoning employed in science by reference to reason itself* (A. E. Bell). **2** reasons; arguments.

**rea|son|less** (rē′zən lis), *adj.* **1** lacking the power to reason: *reasonless creatures.* **2** lacking good judgment or sense. **3** without reason; unreasonable. —**rea′son|less|ly,** *adv.* —**rea′son|less|ness,** *n.*

**reason of state,** a political motive for some action or measure on the part of a ruler, government, or public officer, especially one not expedient to set forth publicly.

**re|as|sem|blage** (rē′ə sem′blij), *n.* second assemblage.

**re|as|sem|ble** (rē′ə sem′bəl), *v.t., v.i.,* **-bled, -bling.** to bring or come together again: *One by one, the 65 crystal chandeliers in the U.S. Capitol had been taken down, disassembled, washed prism by prism, reassembled and rehung* (Time).

**re|as|sem|bly** (rē′ə sem′blē), *n., pl.* **-blies.** a second assembly; reassemblage: *The reassembly of the atoms that compose the human body* (Samuel Johnson).

**re|as|sert** (rē′ə sėrt′), *v.t.* to assert again.

**re|as|ser|tion** (rē′ə sėr′shən), *n.* a repeated assertion of the same thing; the act of asserting again.

**re|as|sess** (rē′ə ses′), *v.t.* to assess again: *The rateable value of certain property having been reassessed at a much higher sum* (Law Times Report). —**re′as|sess′ment,** *n.*

**re|as|sign** (rē′ə sīn′), *v.t.* to assign again. —**re′as|sign′ment,** *n.*

**re|as|sim|i|late** (rē′ə sim′ə lāt), *v.t.,* **-lat|ed, -lat|ing.** to assimilate again. —**re′as|sim′i|la′tion,** *n.*

**re|as|so|ci|ate** (rē′ə sō′shē āt), *v.t., v.i.,* **-at|ed, -at|ing.** to come together again: *The Indian families ... separate in the winter season ... and reassociate in the spring and summer* (Alexander Henry). —**re′as|so′ci|a′tion,** *n.*

**re|as|sort** (rē′ə sôrt′), *v.t.* **1** to assort again. **2** to assort repeatedly. —**re′as|sort′ment,** *n.*

**re|as|sume** (rē′ə süm′), *v.t.,* **-sumed, -sum|ing.** to assume again or anew; resume: *He would, by letter, turn [his duties] over to the Vice-President until he recovered, at which time he could write another letter, reassuming his post* (Newsweek).

**re|as|sump|tion** (rē′ə sump′shən), *n.* a second assumption.

**re|as|sur|ance** (rē′ə shůr′əns), *n.* **1** new or fresh assurance. **2** the restoration of courage or confidence. **3** *British.* reinsurance: *The total of sums assured under new policies in the year was over £56,700,000, after deduction of reassurances* (London Times).

**re|as|sure** (rē′ə shůr′), *v.t.,* **-sured, -sur|ing. 1** to restore to confidence: *The captain's confidence during the storm reassured the passengers.* **2** to assure again or anew. **3** *Especially British.* to insure again.

**re|as|sur|ing** (rē′ə shůr′ing), *adj.* that reassures; comforting; encouraging: *reassuring words.* —**re′as|sur′ing|ly,** *adv.*

**reast|y** (rēs′tē), *adj.,* **reast|i|er, reast|i|est.** *Dialect.* rancid: *For six months the food ... was only some reasty bacon and Indian corn* (A. Welby). [< Old French *resté* left over, past participle of *rester* to remain; see etym. under **rest**²]

**re|a|ta** (rē ä′tə), *n.* = lariat: *Papa got on his horse and splashed out into the shallows, shaking a wide loop into his plaited Mexican horsehide reata* (New Yorker). [< Spanish *reata* rope]

**re|at|tach** (rē′ə tach′), *v.t.* to attach again. —**re′at|tach′ment,** *n.*

**re|at|tain** (rē′ə tān′), *v.t.* to attain again. —**re′at|tain′ment,** *n.*

**re|at|tempt** (rē′ə tempt′), *v., n.* —*v.t.* to attempt again.

—*n.* a new attempt.

**re|auc|tion** (rē ôk′shən), *v.t.* to auction again.

**Réaum.,** Réaumur thermometer.

**Re|au|mur** or **Ré|au|mur** (rā′ə myůr; *French* rā ō mYr′), *adj.* of or in accordance with the thermometric scale introduced about 1730 by René Antoine Ferchault de Réaumur, 1683-1757, a French physicist, in which the freezing point of water is 0 degrees and the boiling point 80 degrees. *Abbr:* R.

**reave**¹ (rēv), *v.t.,* **reaved** or **reft, reav|ing.** *Archaic.* **1** to deprive by force; strip; rob: *to reave the orphan of his patrimony* (Shakespeare). **2** to take by force; take away. [Old English *rēafian.* See related etym. at **bereave, rob, rover**².]

**reave**² (rēv), *v.t., v.i.,* **reaved** or **reft, reav|ing.** *Archaic.* to tear; split. [Middle English *reve;* apparently < *reave*¹; influenced by *rive*]

**reav|er** (rē′vər), *n.* a robber or plunderer; marauder; raider: *This paper is remarkable for the sagacity which tracks the footsteps of the literary reaver* (William Hamilton).

**re|a|wak|en** (rē′ə wā′kən), *v.t., v.i.* to awaken again or anew: *The consciousness of the truth ... reawakens* (Popular Science Monthly).

**reb** or **Reb**¹ (reb), *n. U.S. Historical.* a Confederate soldier in the American Civil War: *"Hello, Charley," he said, "Where you been?" ... "Out hearing the Rebs," he said* (Stephen Vincent Benét). [< *reb*(el)]

**Reb**² (reb), *n. Yiddish.* Mister or Rabbi (used as a title, especially before a given name): *Reb Mordecai.*

**re|bab** (rə bäb′), *n.* **1** an ancient stringed instrument with a pear-shaped or a long, narrow body, a vaulted back, and no neck. It was played originally with the fingers and later with a bow. **2** any one of various stringed instruments played with a bow, in use among the Moslems of northern Africa. [< Persian and Arabic *rabāb.* See related etym. at **rebec.**]

**re|bap|tism** (rē bap′tiz əm), *n.* a second baptism.

**re|bap|tize** (rē′bap tīz′), *v.t.,* **-tized, -tiz|ing. 1** to baptize a second time: *People called them Anabaptists, or "rebaptizers," because they rebaptized all who joined them* (Winfred E. Garrison). **2** to baptize by a new name; rename. —**re′bap|tiz′er,** *n.*

**re|bar|ba|tive** (ri bär′bə tiv), *adj.* **1** crabbed; cross: *a rebarbative old man.* **2** unattractive: *a rebarbative hat.* [< French *rébarbatif* < Old French < *rebarber* oppose, confront (literally, beard to beard) < *re-* + *barbe* beard < Latin *barba*]

**re|bat|a|ble** (ri bā′tə bəl), *adj.* that is or can be rebated: *rebatable taxes.*

**re|bate**¹ (rē′bāt, ri bāt′), *n., v.,* **-bat|ed, -bat|ing.** —*n.* a return of part of money paid; partial refund; discount: *An interesting feature of German price lists for the outside world is the appearance of rebates to shipbuilders—rebates for indirect exports, which recall the cartel* (London Times). [< Old French *rabat* < *rabatre* beat down; see the verb]

—*v.t.* **1** to return part of money paid: *to rebate one third of the price.* **2** to make dull; blunt: (*Figurative.*) *to rebate strong feelings.* [< Old French *rebatre* beat down < *re-* back + *abattre* beat down < *a-* to (< Latin *ad-*) + *batre* to beat < Latin *battuere*] —**re′bat|er,** *n.*

**re|bate**² (rē′bāt, rab′it), *n., v.t., v.i.,* **-bat|ed, -bat|ing.** = rabbet.

**re|ba|to** (rə bä′tō), *n., pl.* **-toes.** a stiff collar of lace worn by both men and women, especially in western Europe and England, from about 1590 to 1630. [alteration of French, Old French *rabat,* or < obsolete French *rabateau* < *rebatre;* see etym. under **rebate**¹, verb]

**Reb|be** or **reb|be** (reb′ə), *n. Yiddish.* **1** rabbi (used as a form of address). **2** a Hasidic rabbi or spiritual leader.

**re|bec** or **re|beck** (rē′bek), *n.* a three-stringed musical instrument, somewhat like a violin, used in the Middle Ages: *And the jocund rebecks sound* (Milton). [< Middle French *rebec,* alteration (influenced by Old French *bec* beak, because of the shape of the instrument) of Old French *rebebe,* or *rubebe,* probably < Old Provençal *rebec,* and *rebeb* < Arabic *rabāb* rebab]

**Re|bec|ca** or **Re|bek|ah** (ri bek′ə), *n.* the wife of Issac, and the mother of Esau and Jacob (in the Bible, Genesis 24-25).

**Rebekah lodge,** a woman's branch or chapter of the Independent Order of Odd Fellows.

**reb|el** (*n., adj.* reb′əl; *v.* ri bel′), *n., adj., v.,* **re|belled, re|bel|ling.** —*n.* **1** a person who resists or fights against authority instead of obeying: *The rebels armed themselves against the government.* **SYN:** insurgent. **2** Also, **Rebel.** *U.S. Historical.* a Confederate, especially a Confederate soldier: *The Rebels are reported to have ordered an entire fleet from French builders* (New Mexican Review). [< Old French *rebelle,* learned borrowing < Latin *rebellis* < *rebellāre;* see the verb]

—*adj.* **1** defying law or authority: *a rebel army.* **2** Also, **Rebel.** *U.S. Historical.* Confederate: *the Rebel flag.*

—*v.i.* **1** to resist or fight against law or authority: *The harassed soldiers decided to rebel.* **SYN:** revolt, mutiny. **2** *Figurative.* to feel a great dislike or opposition: *We rebelled at having to stay in on so fine a day.* [< Old French *rebeller* < Latin *rebellāre* < *re-* again + *bellāre* to wage war < *bellum* war. See etym. of doublet **revel.**] —**re|bel′ler,** *n.*

**reb|el|dom** (reb′əl dəm), *n.* **1** a region controlled by rebels. **2** rebels as a group. **3** = rebellion.

**re|bel|lion** (ri bel′yən), *n.* **1** a fight against one's government: *The American colonists were in rebellion against the British king.* **SYN:** insurrection, revolution, sedition. See syn. under **revolt. 2** resistance against any power or restriction: *The slaves rose in rebellion against their masters.* **3** the act or condition of rebelling; revolt. [< Latin *rebelliō, -ōnis* < *rebellis* rebel < *rebellāre;* see etym. under **rebel,** verb]

**re|bel|lious** (ri bel′yəs), *adj.* **1** defying authority; acting like a rebel; rebelling: *a rebellious army.* **SYN:** mutinous. **2** *Figurative.* hard to manage; hard to treat: *The rebellious boy would not obey the rules.* **SYN:** disobedient. —**re|bel′lious|ly,** *adv.* —**re|bel′lious|ness,** *n.*

**rebel yell,** a long, shrill yell given by Confederate soldiers while going into battle in the U.S. Civil War.

**re|bid** (*v.* rē bid′; *n.* rē′bid′), *v.,* **-bid, -bid|ding,** *n.* —*v.t.* to bid again: *Possibly he should have ... rebid one of his suits* (London Times).

—*n.* a subsequent bid made by a player: *The two no-trump was a demand for a rebid.*

**re|bill** (rē bil′), *v.t.* to bill again.

**re|bind** (rē bīnd′), *v.t.,* **-bound, -bind|ing.** to bind again or anew: *The book with the broken back needs rebinding.*

**re|birth** (rē′bėrth′, rē bėrth′), *n.* **1** a new birth; being born again. **2** the act or process of reviving; coming back into existence or into a former condition, as of strength or power: (*Figurative.*) *a rebirth of confidence,* (*Figurative.*) *a rebirth of national pride.*

**re|block** (rē blok′), *v.t.* **1** to provide with new block or a new block. **2** to remold: *to reblock a hat.*

**re|bloom** (rē blüm′), *v.i.* to bloom again.

**re|blos|som** (rē blos′əm), *v.i.* to blossom again.

**reb|o|ant** (reb′ō ənt), *adj.* resounding loudly: *The echoing dance Of reboant whirlwinds* (Tennyson). [< Latin *reboāns, -antis,* present participle of *reboāre* to resound, bellow back < *re-* again + *boāre* to bellow < Greek *boân*]

**re|boil** (rē boil′), *v.t.* to cause to boil again; subject again to boiling.

**re|boise|ment** (ri boiz′mənt), *n.* a conversion into woodland; reforestation. [< French *reboisement* < *reboiser* reforest < *re-* again (< Latin *re-*) + *boiser* to plant with trees < *bois* wood < Medieval Latin *boscus*]

**re|bop** (rē′bop′), *n. U.S. Slang.* bebop.

**re|born** (rē bôrn′), *adj.* born again.

**reb|o|so** (rā bō′sō), *n., pl.* **-sos.** = rebozo.

**re|bound**¹ (*v.* ri bound′; *n.* rē′bound′, ri bound′), *v., n.* —*v.i.* **1** to spring back: *I never think I have hit hard unless it rebounds* (Samuel Johnson). (*Figurative.*) *An evil example, that would rebound back on themselves* (Edmund Burke). **SYN:** recoil. **2** = resound. **3** to get back to a good condition; bounce back; recover: *Government securities rebounded yesterday after a week of steady declines* (Wall Street Journal). **4** *Archaic.* to leap; spring.

—*v.t.* **1** to cause to spring back. **2** to echo back.

—*n.* **1** the act or process of springing back; rebounding: *You hit the ball on the rebound in handball.* (*Figurative.*) *a rebound from a state of depression and shame* (John F. D. Maurice). **2** *Basketball.* a ball that bounds back off the backboard or the rim of the basket after a shot has been made.

**on the rebound,** in reaction to or as a result of the abrupt ending of a love affair: *to become engaged on the rebound. [He] had been interested in another girl altogether, and he had married this one on the rebound* (New Yorker).

[< Old French *rebondir* < *re-* back, re- + *bondir* to bound, spring, resound, perhaps < Gallo-Romance *bombītīre,* ultimately < Latin *bombus* a booming sound < Greek *bómbos*]

**re|bound**² (rē bound′), *v.* the past tense and past participle of **rebind**: *Send this book to be rebound.*

**re|bound|er** (rē′boun′dər), *n.* a basketball player skilled at catching and controlling a ball that rebounds from the backboard: *Brannum was the top rebounder of the contest with 13, one more than Gallatin* (New York Times).

**✱re|bo|zo** (rā bō′sō, -zō), *n., pl.* **-zos.** a shawl or long scarf worn by Spanish-American women over the head and shoulders. [American English < Spanish *rebozo* shawl; a muffling of oneself < *bozo* the area around the mouth]

**✱rebozo**

**re|breathe** (rē brēᴛʜ′), *v.t.,* **-breathed, -breath|ing.** to breathe again.

**re|breath|ing device** (rē brē′ᴛʜing), an underwater diving device that repurifies the diver's exhaled air to breathe again.

**re|broad|cast** (rē brôd′kast′, -käst′), *v.,* **-cast** or **-cast|ed, -cast|ing,** *n.* — ***v.t., v.i.*** **1** to broadcast again or anew: *His radio messages to the U.S.S.R. are now translated and rebroadcast* (Newsweek). **2** to relay by broadcast (messages, speeches, or music, received from a broadcasting station).
—***n.*** a program, message, or the like, rebroadcast: *Rebroadcasts of earlier Playhouse 90 productions on tape and film were to follow* (New Yorker).

**re|buff** (ri buf′), *n., v.* —***n.*** a blunt or sudden check to a person who makes advances, offers help, or makes a request; snub: *We tried to be friendly, but his rebuff made us think he wanted to be left alone.*
—***v.t.*** to give a rebuff to: *The playful dog was rebuffed by a kick.* **SYN:** check.
[< Middle French *rebuffe* < Italian *ribuffo,* and *rabuffo* < *rabuffare* disarrange, alteration of *baruffare* to scuffle < Germanic (compare Old High German *biroufan* to tussle, pluck out)]

**re|build** (*v.* rē bild′; *n.* rē′bild′), *v.,* **-built, -build|ing,** *n.* — ***v.t., v.i.*** to build again or anew: *They [children] are building new bone while adults are simply rebuilding some of their skeleton* (Newsweek). *When the Company proceeded to rebuild, they no longer did so in the massive and imposing style of the fourteenth century* (M. Pattison).
—***n.*** an act or instance of rebuilding: *A complete Bentley rebuild will cost at least £4,000* (Sunday Times). —**re|build′er,** *n.*

**re|built** (rē bilt′), *v.* the past tense and past participle of **rebuild:** *The damaged section of the school was entirely rebuilt.*

**re|buk|a|ble** (ri byü′kə bəl), *adj.* deserving of rebuke.

**re|buke** (ri byük′), *v.,* **-buked, -buk|ing,** *n.* —***v.t.*** **1** to express disapproval of; reprove: *The teacher rebuked the child for throwing paper on the floor.* **SYN:** reprimand, censure. See syn. under **reprove. 2** *Obsolete.* to repress; check: *Under him My genius is rebuk'd: as, it is said, Mark Antony's was by Caesar* (Shakespeare).
—***n.*** an expression of disapproval; scolding: *The child feared the teacher's rebuke.*
[< Anglo-French *rebuker,* Old French *rebuchier* < *re-* back + *buchier* to strike < *bûche,* and *busche* a log, wood < Vulgar Latin *būsca*] —**re|buk′er,** *n.* —**re|buk′ing|ly,** *adv.*

**re|buke|ful** (ri byük′fəl), *adj.* full of rebuke; of a rebuking character, as words.

**re|bunk|er** (rē bung′kər), *v.i., v.t.* to refill the bunkers with coal; coal again.

**re|bur|y** (rē ber′ē), *v.t.,* **-bur|ied, -bur|y|ing.** to bury again: *Reburied hastily at dead of night* (Thomas Carlyle).

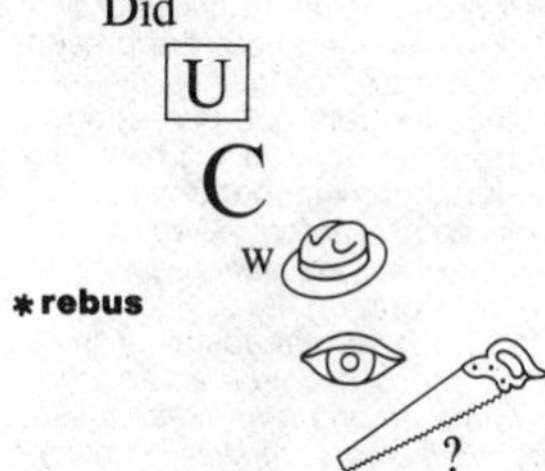


**✱rebus**

**✱re|bus** (rē′bəs), *n., pl.* **-bus|es.** a representation of a word or phrase by pictures, letters, numbers, or combinations of these to suggest the syllables or words. A picture of a cat on a log is a rebus for "catalog." A picture of an eye, followed by "CA" and a picture of a dog, may be a rebus for "I see a dog." [< Latin *rēbus* by means of objects, ablative plural of *rēs* thing, object]

**re|bus sic stan|ti|bus** (rē′bəs sik stan′tə bəs), *Latin.* things remaining the same: *There is a legal principle which holds that even the most solemnly recorded agreements are to be valid only for as long as they were intended to be valid—rebus sic stantibus, or while circumstances remain the same* (New Yorker).

**re|but** (ri but′), *v.t.,* **-but|ted, -but|ting. 1** to oppose by evidence on the other side or by argument; try to disprove: *to rebut the arguments of the other team in a debate.* **SYN:** refute, contradict, dispute. **2** *Obsolete.* to repel; repulse. [< Old French *reboter* < *re-* back + *boter* to butt, strike < Germanic (probably unrecorded Frankish *botan* to strike)]

**re|but|ta|ble** (ri but′ə bəl), *adj.* that can be rebutted; subject to rebuttal.

**re|but|tal** (ri but′əl), *n.* the act or process of rebutting: *The State Department issued a 2,700-word rebuttal, complete with texts of proposals and counterproposals* (Newsweek).

**re|but|ter[1]** (ri but′ər), *n.* **1** a person who rebuts. **2** an argument that rebuts. [< *rebut* + *-er*[1]]

**re|but|ter[2]** (ri but′ər), *n. Law.* an answer such as a defendant makes to a plaintiff's surrejoinder. [< Old French *reboter,* noun use of infinitive; see etym. under **rebut**]

**rec.,** an abbreviation for the following:
**1** receipt.
**2** recipe.
**3a** record. **b** recorded. **c** recorder.
**4** recreation.

**re|cal|ci|trance** (ri kal′sə trəns), *n.* a refusal to submit, conform, or comply.

**re|cal|ci|tran|cy** (ri kal′sə trən sē), *n.* = recalcitrance.

**re|cal|ci|trant** (ri kal′sə trənt), *adj., n.* —***adj.*** resisting authority or control; disobedient: *a recalcitrant child. The recalcitrant patient would not take his medicine.*
—***n.*** a recalcitrant person or animal.
[< Latin *recalcitrāns, -antis,* present participle of *recalcitrāre* kick back < *re-* back + *calx, calcis* heel]

**re|cal|ci|trate** (ri kal′sə trāt), *v.i.,* **-trat|ed, -trat|ing.** to show strong objections, opposition, or resistance.

**re|cal|ci|tra|tion** (ri kal′sə trā′shən), *n.* opposition; repugnance.

**re|ca|lesce** (rē′kə les′), *v.i.,* **-lesced, -lesc|ing.** to show recalescence.

**re|ca|les|cence** (rē′kə les′əns), *n.* the increased brilliancy and sudden emission of heat of a cooling metal, especially iron, at a certain temperature. [< Latin *recalēscēns, -entis,* present participle of *recalēscere* < *re-* again + *calēscere* grow warm. Compare etym. under **calescent.**]

**re|ca|les|cent** (rē′kə les′ənt), *adj.* that shows recalescence.

**re|call** (*v.t.* ri kôl′; *n.* ri kôl′, rē′kôl′), *v., n.* —***v.t.*** **1** to call back to mind; remember: *to recall a name. Mother can recall stories that she heard years ago.* **SYN:** recollect. See syn. under **remember. 2** to call back; order back: *The ambassador was recalled. The retired captain was recalled to duty.* **3** to bring back; restore; revive: *recalled to life.* **4** to take back; withdraw: *I shall recall my order for a new coat because I had one given to me.* **SYN:** revoke, retract.
—***n.*** **1** the act of recalling to mind: *A few people with remarkable memories are said to have "total recall."* **2** the act of calling back; ordering back: *The four major American carmakers recalled 8.7 million autos, and probably more than half the recalls involved safety* (New York Times). **3** a signal used in calling back men, ships, etc.
**4** *Figurative.* the act of taking back; undoing; revocation; annulment. **5** the procedure by which a public official can be removed from office by vote of the people before his term has expired.
—**re|call′er,** *n.*

**re|call|a|ble** (ri kô′lə bəl), *adj.* that can be recalled.

**re|call|ment** (ri kôl′mənt), *n.* **1** the act of calling back. **2** an invitation or summons to return.

**re|can|des|cence** (rē′kan des′əns), *n.* a growing brighter; renewed candescence.

**re|cant** (ri kant′), *v.t.* **1** to take back formally or publicly; withdraw or renounce (as a statement, opinion, or purpose): *The critics of the government publicly recanted their errors.* **2** to retract (as a promise or oath). **3** to give up (a purpose).
—***v.i.*** to renounce an opinion or allegiance: *Though he was tortured to make him change his religion, the prisoner would not recant. ... a bill ... which would make the threat of perjury more real and thus make it infinitely more dangerous to recant* (Saturday Review). [< Latin *recantāre* < *re-* back + *cantāre* (frequentative) < *canere* to sing] —**re|cant′er,** *n.*

**re|can|ta|tion** (rē′kan tā′shən), *n.* the act of recanting; public or formal renouncing: *The drama of the Inquisition lies in Galileo's abject recantation of his life's work* (Time).

**re|cap[1]** (*v.* rē′kap′, rē kap′; *n.* rē′kap′), *v.,* **-capped, -cap|ping,** *n.* — ***v.t.*** **1** to put a strip of rubber or similar material on the tread of (a worn surface of an automobile tire), by using heat and pressure to make a firm union. **2** to cap again or anew: *... front teeth newly recapped and visible behind a more or less constant smile* (Time).
—***n.*** a recapped tire: *Volume of retreading has been growing, with 32 million recaps sold last year* (Wall Street Journal).
[< *re-* again + *cap,* verb]

**re|cap[2]** (*v.* ri kap′; *n.* rē′kap), *v.,* **-capped, -cap|ping,** *n. Informal.* —***v.t., v.i.*** = recapitulate.
—***n.*** = recapitulation: *Here's a recap of Orange Bowlers' paths to Miami* (Birmingham News).
[short for *recapitulate*]

**re|cap|i|tal|ize** (rē kap′ə tə līz), *v.t., v.i.,* **-ized, -iz|ing.** to capitalize again; renew or alter the capitalization of. —**re|cap′i|tal|i|za′tion,** *n.*

**re|ca|pit|u|late** (rē′kə pich′ə lāt), *v.t., v.i.,* **-lat|ed, -lat|ing. 1** to repeat or recite the main points of; tell briefly; sum up: *The speaker concluded by recapitulating the ideas presented in his speech.* **2** *Biology.* to repeat or reenact successive steps in a process: *One evolutionary theory holds that the development of an organism recapitulates the life history of the race to which it belongs.* [< Latin *recapitulāre* (with English *-ate*[1]) < *re-* again + *capitulum* chapter, section (diminutive) < *caput, capitis* head]

**re|ca|pit|u|la|tion** (rē′kə pich′ə lā′shən), *n.* **1** a brief statement of the main points; summary: *One gets the notion that his book is in a sense an unconscious recapitulation of the process of growth* (New Yorker). **2** *Biology.* the repetition in the development of an embryo of stages in the evolution of the species. **3** *Music.* the section of a movement repeating the theme of the exposition, after the development.

**recapitulation theory** or **doctrine,** the theory that the development of an organism recapitulates the life history of the race to which it belongs.

**re|ca|pit|u|la|tive** (rē′kə pich′ə lā′tiv), *adj.* **1** having to do with or characterized by recapitulation; giving a summary of the chief parts or points. **2** of or having to do with the biological doctrine of recapitulation.

**re|ca|pit|u|la|tor** (rē′kə pich′ə lā′tər), *n.* a person or thing that recapitulates.

**re|ca|pit|u|la|to|ry** (rē′kə pich′ə lə tôr′ē, -tōr′-), *adj.* = recapitulative.

**re|cap|pa|ble** (rē kap′ə bəl), *adj.* that can be recapped: *a recappable tire.*

**re|cap|ture** (rē kap′chər), *v.,* **-tured, -tur|ing,** *n.*
—***v.t.*** **1** to capture again; have again. **2** *Figurative.* to recall: *The picture album recaptured the days of the horse and buggy.* **3** (of the government) to take (a company's excess profits).
—***n.*** **1** the act of taking or fact of being taken a second time: *"Mad Anthony" Wayne ... was the hero of the recapture of Stony Point, N.Y., a British post on the Hudson River, in 1779* (John R. Alden). **2** the thing that is taken. **3** *U.S.* the act of taking a company's excess profits, especially the profits of a public utility, by the government.

**re|car|bon** (rē′kär′bən), *v.t.* to supply (an arc lamp) with new carbons.

**re|car|ry** (rē kar′ē), *v.t.,* **-ried, -ry|ing. 1** to carry back, as in returning. **2** to carry again or in a reversed direction: *When the Turks besieged Malta or Rhodes ... pigeons were then relayed to carry and recarry letters* (Izaak Walton).

**re|cast** (*v.* rē kast′, -käst′; *n.* rē′kast′, -käst′), *v.,* **-cast, -cast|ing,** *n.* — ***v.t.*** **1** to cast again or anew: *to recast a bell.* **2** to make over; remodel: *to recast a sentence.*
—***n.*** **1** the act or process of recasting. **2** something formed by recasting.

**rec|ce** (rik′ē), *n. Informal.* reconnaissance: *An officer was told to make a 'recce' on a bank and return with plans to raid it* (London Times).

**recd.** or **rec'd.,** received.

**re|cede** (ri sēd′), *v.i.,* **-ced|ed, -ced|ing. 1** to go backward; move backward: *Houses and trees seem to recede as you ride past in a train.* **SYN:** retreat, retire. **2** to slope backward: *He has a chin that recedes.* **3** to withdraw: *to recede from an agreement.* **4** to go or fall back; decline in

---

**Pronunciation Key:** hat, āge, cãre, fär; let, ēqual, tėrm; it, īce; hot, ōpen, ôrder; oil, out; cup, pu̇t, rüle; child; long; thin; ᴛʜen; zh, measure; ə represents **a** in about, **e** in taken, **i** in pencil, **o** in lemon, **u** in circus.

character or value. [< Latin *recēdere* < *re-* back + *cēdere* to go]

**re-cede** (rē sēd′), *v.t.*, **-ced|ed, -ced|ing.** to cede again. [< *re-* back + *cede*]

**re|ced|ence** (ri sē′dəns), *n.* **1** the act or fact of receding. **2** = recession[1] (def. 4).

**re|ceipt** (ri sēt′), *n., v.* —*n.* **1** a written statement that money, a package, or a letter has been received: *Sign the receipt for this parcel.* **2** the act of receiving or fact of being received: *On receipt of the news he went home.* **3** *Dialect.* a recipe.
—*v.t.* **1** to write on (a bill or invoice) that something has been received or paid for: *Pay the bill and ask the grocer to receipt it.* **2** *U.S.* to acknowledge in writing the receipt of (money or goods). —*v.i. U.S.* to give a receipt.
**receipts,** money received; amount or quantity received: *Our expenses were less than our receipts.*
[alteration (influenced by Latin *recepta,* feminine past participle of *recipere*) of Middle English *receit* < Anglo-French *receite,* Old French *reçoite,* earlier *recete* < Latin *recipere;* see etym. under **receive**]
► **receipt, recipe.** Both words mean a formula, directions for preparing something to eat. Locally one or the other may be preferred by cooks, but they are interchangeable in meaning.

**re|ceipt|or** (ri sē′tər), *n.* **1** a person who receipts. **2** *U.S. Law.* a person to whom attached property is bailed.

**re|ceiv|a|ble** (ri sē′və bəl), *adj., n.* —*adj.* **1** fit for acceptance: *Gold is receivable all over the world.* **2** on which payment is to be received. Bills receivable is the opposite of bills payable. **3** which is to be received.
—*n.* **receivables,** assets in the form of obligations due, or soon due, from others: *The collection of receivables is so far behind that the hardware store may not be able to pay its own bills.*

**re|ceiv|al** (ri sē′vəl), *n.* the act of receiving.

**re|ceive** (ri sēv′), *v.,* **-ceived, -ceiv|ing.** —*v.t.* **1** to take (something offered or sent); take into one's hands or possession: *to receive gifts.* **2** to have (something) bestowed, conferred, or granted: *to receive a name, to receive a degree.* **3** to be given; get: *to receive payment. The boy at camp received a letter from his mother.* **4** to take in; support; bear; hold: *The boat received a heavy load. A bowl receives the water from the faucet.* **5** to take or let into the mind: *to receive new ideas, to receive news, to receive an education.* **6** to accept as true or valid: *a theory widely received.* **7** to experience; suffer; endure: *to receive a blow, to receive punishment.* **8** to let into one's house or society; accept: *The people of the neighborhood were glad to receive the new family.* **9** to meet (guests, visitors, or officials); greet upon arrival: *Crowds gathered to receive the queen.* **10** to admit to a place; give shelter to: *to receive strangers.* **11** to agree to listen to: *to receive confession.* **12** to admit to a state or condition: *to receive a person into the church.*
—*v.i.* **1** to be at home to friends and visitors: *She receives on Tuesdays.* **2** *Radio, Television.* to change electrical waves broadcast through the air into sound or picture signals: *Our television receives well since we had a new antenna put on.* **3** to take, accept, admit, or get something: *Freely ye have received, freely give* (Matthew 10:8). *Everyone shall receive according to his deserts* (Joseph Butler). **4** to take the sacrament of Holy Communion. **5** to return a served ball, as in tennis.
[< Old North French *receivre,* Old French *reçoivre* < Latin *recipere* < *re-* back + *capere* to take]
—*Syn. v.t.* **1 Receive, accept** mean to take what is given, offered, or delivered. **Receive** carries no suggestion of positive action or of activity of mind or will on the part of the receiver, and means nothing more than to take to oneself or take in what is given or given out: *He received a prize.* **Accept** always suggests being willing to take what is offered, or giving one's consent: *She received a gift from him, but did not accept it.*

**re|ceived** (ri sēvd′), *adj.* commonly accepted; commonplace: *They exchange with wary civility the well-worn coins of received ideas about the weather, politics, school, war, and Empire that they have spent a lifetime accumulating* (Brendan Gill).

**Received Pronunciation,** the pronunciation of English used by educated Englishmen everywhere.

**Received Standard,** the English spoken by educated Englishmen everywhere.

**re|ceiv|er** (ri sē′vər), *n.* **1** a person who receives: *The receiver of a gift should thank the giver.* **2** a thing that receives: *Public telephones have coin receivers for nickels, dimes, and quarters.* **3** the part of the telephone held to the ear; telephone receiver: *Even before I picked up the receiver, I knew that something was wrong* (New Yorker). **4** a device that changes electrical waves broadcast through the air into sound and picture signals: *a radio receiver, a television receiver.* **5** a person appointed by law to take charge of the property of others: *He will act as receiver for the firm that has failed in business.* **6** a player who catches a forward pass, kickoff, or punt in a football game. **7** a treasurer. **8** a person who knowingly receives stolen goods or harbors offenders. **9** *Chemistry.* **a** a vessel for receiving and condensing the product of distillation. **b** a vessel for receiving and containing gases.

**receiver general,** (in Massachusetts) an elected state official who collects assessments.

**re|ceiv|er|ship** (ri sē′vər ship), *n.* **1** the position of a receiver in charge of the property of others. **2** the condition of being in the control of a receiver.

**re|ceiv|ing blanket** (ri sē′ving), a small, light blanket used to wrap an infant in, especially after a bath: *Her husband has used more diapers and receiving blankets than she has in three years with two children* (New York Times).

**receiving end,**
**to be at** (or **on**) **the receiving end,** to be the recipient (of something, originally something unpleasant but now applied to anything): *Middle-aged obese housewives are the most common to be found at the receiving end, and about half of them are given the drugs because of primary diagnosis of depression* (Science Journal).

**receiving line,** a group of persons standing in line to receive the guests as they arrive, as at a formal reception or other social function.

**receiving set, 1** an apparatus for receiving sound, or sound and picture images, sent by radio waves; radio or television set. **2** an apparatus for receiving messages sent by telegraph or teletype.

**re|cel|e|brate** (rē sel′ə brāt), *v.t.,* **-brat|ed, -brat|ing.** to celebrate again.

**re|cel|e|bra|tion** (rē′sel ə brā′shən), *n.* **1** the act of celebrating a second time. **2** the state of being celebrated again.

**re|cen|cy** (rē′sən sē), *n.* the condition of being recent.

**re|cense** (ri sens′), *v.t.,* **-censed, -cens|ing.** to review; revise.

**re|cen|sion** (ri sen′shən), *n.* **1** the revision of a text, especially when critical. **2** a revised version of a text. [< Latin *recēnsiō, -ōnis* < *recēnsēre* survey, count over < *re-* again + *cēnsēre* count. See related etym. at **census.**]

**re|cen|sion|ist** (ri sen′shə nist), *n.* a person who reviews or revises, as an editor.

**re|cent** (rē′sənt), *adj.* **1** done or made not long ago: *recent events.* **2** not long past; modern: *a recent period in history.* **3** lately or newly come. [< Latin *recēns, -entis* new, fresh] —**re′cent|ly,** *adv.* —**re′cent|ness,** *n.*

**Re|cent** (rē′sənt), *n., adj.* —*n.* **1** the present geological epoch, after the Pleistocene epoch of the Cenozoic era; Holocene: ... *the Holocene or Recent has lasted only 20,000 years* (Beals and Hoijer). **2** the series of rocks formed during this epoch.
—*adj.* of or having to do with this epoch or its rocks.
[< *recent*]

**re|cept** (rē′sept), *n. Psychology.* an idea supposedly formed in animals' minds by the reception of similar percepts, such as successive percepts of the same object. [< Latin *receptum,* (originally) neuter past participle of *recipere;* see etym. under **receive**]

**re|cep|ta|cle** (ri sep′tə kəl), *n.* **1** any container or place used to put things in to keep them conveniently. Bags, baskets, and vaults are all receptacles. **2** the stalklike part of a flower that bears the sepals, petals, stamens, and pistils: *All these parts—calyx, corolla, stamens, and carpels—are attached to the receptacle, the somewhat specialized summit of the pedicel* (Fred W. Emerson). See picture under **flower. 3** a socket or outlet into which a plug can be inserted to make an electrical connection. [< Latin *receptāculum* (diminutive) < *recipere;* see etym. under **receive**]

**re|cep|ti|ble** (ri sep′tə bəl), *adj.* **1** that can be received; receivable. **2** that can receive.

**re|cep|tion** (ri sep′shən), *n.* **1** the act of receiving: *Her calm reception of the bad news surprised us.* **2** the fact of being received: *Her reception as a club member pleased her.* **3** the manner of receiving: *We were given a warm reception on returning home.* **4** a gathering to receive and welcome people; party; entertainment: *Our school gave a reception to welcome our new principal.* **5** *Radio, Television.* **a** the quality of the sound or picture reproduced in a receiving set: *Reception was poor because we were so far from the transmitter.* **b** the act or process of receiving radio waves. [< Latin *receptiō, -ōnis* < *recipere;* see etym. under **receive**]

**reception center,** a place at which people are received and taken care of in some way.

**re|cep|tion|ist** (ri sep′shə nist), *n.* a person employed to receive callers: *She is a receptionist in a doctor's office.*

**reception room,** a room for the reception of visitors.

**re|cep|tive** (ri sep′tiv), *adj.* able, quick, or ready to receive ideas, suggestions, impressions, or stimuli: *a receptive mind.* —**re|cep′tive|ly,** *adv.* —**re|cep′tive|ness,** *n.*

**re|cep|tiv|i|ty** (rē′sep tiv′ə tē), *n.* the ability or readiness to receive.

**re|cep|tor** (ri sep′tər), *n.* **1** a cell or group of cells sensitive to stimuli, such as a sense organ or the terminal portion of a sensory or afferent neuron: *The eye has two kinds of visual receptors, rods and cones* (Science News Letter). **2** a chemical radical in a cell, to which a virus or protein substance becomes attached. **3** = receiver. [< Latin *receptor* receiver]

**re|cess** (*n.* rē′ses *for 1,* ri ses′, rē′ses *for 2 and 3; v.* ri ses′), *n., v.* —*n.* **1** a time during which work stops: *Our school has an hour's recess at noon. There will be a short recess before the next meeting.* SYN: intermission. **2** a part in a wall, set back from the rest; alcove; niche: *This long bench will fit nicely in that recess.* **3** an inner place or part; quiet, secluded place: *the recesses of a cave,* (*Figurative.*) *the recesses of one's secret thoughts.*
—*v.i.* to take a recess: *The committee recessed for lunch.*
—*v.t.* **1** to put in a recess; set back: *to recess a window.* **2** to make a recess in: *to recess a wall.*
[< Latin *recessus, -ūs* a retreat < *recēdere;* see etym. under **recede**]

**re|ces|sion**[1] (ri sesh′ən), *n.* **1** the action or fact of going backward; moving backward. **2** the action or fact of sloping backward. **3** withdrawal, as of the minister and choir after the service in some churches. **4** a period of temporary business reduction, shorter and less extreme than a depression: *When the country entered the 1949 recession, many analysts again warned business to batten down the hatches* (Newsweek). [< Latin *recessiō, -ōnis* < *recēdere;* see etym. under **recede**]

**re|ces|sion**[2] (ri sesh′ən), *n.* the act of ceding back to a former owner. [< *re-* + *cession*]

**re|ces|sion|al** (ri sesh′ə nəl), *n., adj.* —*n.* a hymn or piece of music sung or played while the clergy and the choir retire from the church at the end of a service: *The attendant minister pronounced the benediction, the organ played the recessional* (Atlantic).
—*adj.* **1** of or having to do with a recessional: *a recessional hymn.* **2** of or having to do with recession.
[< *recession*[1] + *-al*[1]]

**recessional moraine,** a terminal moraine formed when a receding glacier halts temporarily. See picture under **glacier.**

**re|ces|sion|ar|y** (ri sesh′ə ner′ē), *adj.* of or having to do with a business recession: *He admits himself baffled by the combination of high inflationary symptoms in prices and interest rates with recessionary symptoms in output* (London Times).

**re|ces|sive** (ri ses′iv), *adj., n.* —*adj.* **1** likely to go back; receding. **2** *Biology.* of or having to do with a recessive character: *Blue eyes are recessive in a person, brown eyes dominant. In peas tallness is dominant, dwarfness recessive* (Heber W. Youngken). **3** (of accent) tending to move from one syllable of a word to a syllable nearer the beginning of the word: *recessive stress is a tendency in current English* (Simeon Potter).
—*n. Biology.* **1** a recessive character or gene: *In a heterozygote the genes are of two kinds, dominants and recessives* (Heber W. Youngken). **2** an individual possessing or transmitting a recessive character. —**re|ces′sive|ly,** *adv.* —**re|ces′sive|ness,** *n.*

**recessive character,** the one of any pair of contrasting characters that is latent or subordinate in an animal or plant when both are present in the germ plasm. *Example:* If a guinea pig inherits a gene for black fur from one parent and a gene for white fur from the other, it will have black fur, as black fur is dominant and white fur is recessive. *Recessive characters, even in the presence of dominant ones, are quite easily recognized* (G. Fulton Roberts).

**Rech|a|bite** (rek′ə bīt), *n.* a total abstainer from alcoholic drinks: *Yet snobs every bit as accomplished are to be found among both Rechabites and non-denominational water-drinkers* (Punch). [< Late Latin *Rechabīta,* plural, translation of Hebrew *Rēkābim* < *Rēkāb,* the father of the founder of a sect which refused to drink wine (in the Bible, Jeremiah 35:2-19); spelling influenced by English *-ite*[1])

**re|change** (rē chānj′), *v.*, **-changed, -chang|ing,** *n.* — ***v.t., v.i.*** to change again or anew.
— ***n.*** a second or further change.

**re|chan|nel** (rē chan′əl), *v.t.*, **-neled, -nel|ing** or (*especially British*) **-nelled, -nel|ling.** to channel in a new form or direction: *It is difficult to predict whether ... we can measurably rechannel the buying demands of the public* (Wall Street Journal).

**re|charge** (rē chärj′), *v.*, **-charged, -charg|ing,** *n.* — ***v.t., v.i.*** to charge again or anew; reload: *The storage battery is recharged by passing a current through the unit in the reverse direction of the discharge* (Wall Street Journal).
— ***n.*** a second or additional charge: *In recent years the artificial recharge of water-bearing strata has been carried out experimentally* (New Scientist).

**re|charge|a|ble** (rē chär′jə bəl), *adj.* chargeable again.

**re|char|ter** (rē chär′tər), *v.*, *n.* — ***v.t.*** to charter again or anew.
— ***n.*** **1** a chartering again. **2** a second or additional charter.

**re|chauf|fé** (rā′shō fā′), *n.*, *pl.* **-fés** (-fā′). **1** a warmed-up dish of food. **2** *Figurative.* a rehash, as of literary material. [< French *réchauffé* (literally) warmed over < *ré-* again + *échauffer* to warm up < *e-* out, ex-[1] + Old French *chaufer.* Compare etym. under **chafe.**]

**re|cheat** (ri chēt′), *n. Archaic, Hunting.* **1** the calling together of the hounds. **2** a call on the horn to gather the hounds at the beginning or end of a chase: *The chase was declared to be ended ... when the recheat should be blown* (Scott). [< Old French *racheter,* and *rachater* reassemble, rally]

**re|check** (*v.* rē chek′; *n.* rē′chek′), *v.*, *n.* — ***v.t., v.i.*** to check again.
— ***n.*** a checking again; double-check.

**re|cher|ché** (rə shãr′shā; *French* rə sher shā′), *adj.* **1** sought after; in great demand; rare: *The exhibition consists of a recherché choice of the finest productions of their archaic arts ever discovered* (New Yorker). **2** too studied; far-fetched. [< French *recherché* sought after < Old French *rechercher* seek after carefully < *re-* again + *chercher.* Compare etym. under **search.**]

**re|choose** (rē chüz′), *v.t.*, **-chose, -cho|sen.** to choose again: *The old-time ceremony of rechoosing a representative* (North Star).

**re|chris|ten** (rē kris′ən), *v.t.* to christen a second time; rename.

**re|cid|i|vate** (ri sid′ə vāt), *v.i.*, **-vat|ed, -vat|ing.** **1** to relapse into crime: *No sooner did he leave prison, than he recidivated into petty felonies.* **2** to fall back or relapse; return, as to a former state or way of acting: *Thus then to recidivate, and to go against her own act and promise ...* (Lancelot Andrewes). [< Medieval Latin *recidivatus,* past participle of *recidivare;* see etym. under **recidivist**]

**re|cid|i|va|tion** (ri sid′ə vā′shən), *n.* **1** a falling back, such as into a former state or way of acting; relapse. **2** the relapse of a criminal into crime.

**re|cid|i|vism** (ri sid′ə viz əm), *n.* a repeated or habitual relapse, especially into crime: *There is considerable recidivism among some juvenile offenders due to alcoholic liquor* (Clyde B. Vedder). [< *recidiv*(ist) + *-ism*]

**re|cid|i|vist** (ri sid′ə vist), *n.*, *adj.* — ***n.*** a person who relapses, especially a habitual criminal: *Major Lloyd-George ... described the recidivist, or persistent offender, as "the central problem of any penal system"* (London Times).
— ***adj.*** of recidivism: *Nobody can write off the condition of Quebec's jails and Quebec's appalling recidivist rate* (Maclean's).
[< French *récidiviste* < Middle French *recidiver* to relapse, learned borrowing from Medieval Latin *recidivare* < Latin *recidīvus;* see etym. under **recidivous**]

**re|cid|i|vis|tic** (ri sid′ə vis′tik), *adj.* = recidivous.

**rec|i|div|i|ty** (res′ə div′ə tē), *n.* a tendency to relapse, especially into crime.

**re|cid|i|vous** (ri sid′ə vəs), *adj.* liable to relapse, especially into crime. [< Latin *recidīvus* (with English *-ous*) < *recidere* fall back < *re-* back + *cadere* to fall]

**rec|i|pe** (res′ə pē), *n.* **1** a set of directions for preparing something to eat: *Give me your recipe for cookies.* **2** a set of directions for doing or preparing anything: *a recipe for gunpowder.* **3** *Figurative: a recipe for happiness. Hard work is his recipe for success.* **4** a medical prescription. **5** = receipt. [< Latin *recipe* take!, imperative of *recipere;* see etym. under **receive**]

**re|ci|pher** (rē sī′fər), *v.t.* to encipher an already coded message.

**re|cip|i|ence** (ri sip′ē əns), *n.* reception; a receptiveness.

**re|cip|i|en|cy** (ri sip′ē ən sē), *n.* = recipience.

**re|cip|i|ent** (ri sip′ē ənt), *n.*, *adj.* — ***n.*** a person or thing that receives something: *The recipients of the prizes had their names printed in the paper.*
— ***adj.*** willing to receive; receiving: *The price charged for surplus would have to be either nil or appreciably lower ... than the commercial price prevailing in the recipient country* (Wall Street Journal).
[< Latin *recipiēns, -entis,* present participle of *recipere;* see etym. under **receive**]

**re|cip|ro|cal** (ri sip′rə kəl), *adj.*, *n.* — ***adj.*** **1** in return: *Although I gave him many presents, I had no reciprocal gifts from him.* **2** existing on both sides; mutual: *reciprocal liking, reciprocal distrust. Kindness is generally reciprocal* (Samuel Johnson). **3** inversely proportional; inverse. **4** *Grammar.* expressing mutual action or relation. In "The two children like each other," *each other* is a reciprocal pronoun.
— ***n.*** **1** a number so related to another that when multiplied together they give one: *3 is the reciprocal of 1/3, and 1/3 is the reciprocal of 3.* **2** a thing that is reciprocal to something else; counterpart.
[< Latin *reciprocus* returning] — **re|cip′ro|cal|ly,** *adv.*

**re|cip|ro|cal|i|ty** (ri sip′rə kal′ə tē), *n.* the quality or state of being reciprocal.

**reciprocal ohm,** *Electricity.* the mho.

**reciprocal trade,** an arrangement between countries to reduce or do away with tariffs, duties, or import quotas, in trading with each other; a most-favored-nation trade agreement.

**reciprocal translocation,** *Genetics.* an interchange of parts between pairs of chromosomes.

**re|cip|ro|cate** (ri sip′rə kāt), *v.*, **-cat|ed, -cat|ing.** — ***v.t.*** **1** to give, do, feel, or show in return: *She likes me, and I reciprocate her liking.* **2** to cause to move with an alternating backward and forward motion.
— ***v.i.*** **1** to make return, as for something given; make interchange. **2** (of mechanical parts) to move with an alternate backward and forward motion. [< Latin *reciprocāre* (with English *-ate*[1]) < *reciprocus* returning, alternating]

**re|cip|ro|cat|ing engine** (ri sip′rə kā′ting), an engine in which the piston and piston rod move back and forth in a straight line, the reciprocating motion being changed to rotary motion.

**re|cip|ro|ca|tion** (ri sip′rə kā′shən), *n.* **1** the act of reciprocating; return: *the reciprocation of a favor received. With a sincere reciprocation of all your kindly feeling* (Dickens). **2** the state of being in a reciprocal or harmonious relation. **3** the backward and forward motion of mechanical parts.

**re|cip|ro|ca|tive** (ri sip′rə kā′tiv), *adj.* having to do with or characterized by reciprocation.

**re|cip|ro|ca|tor** (ri sip′rə kā′tər), *n.* a person or thing that reciprocates.

**re|cip|ro|ca|to|ry** (ri sip′rə kə tôr′ē, -tōr′-), *adj.* = reciprocative.

**rec|i|proc|i|tar|i|an** (res′ə pros ə tãr′ē ən), *adj.*, *n.* — ***adj.*** of or having to do with reciprocity especially of commercial privileges between two governments.
— ***n.*** a person who favors reciprocity, especially in trade agreements.

**rec|i|proc|i|ty** (res′ə pros′ə tē), *n.*, *pl.* **-ties.** **1** reciprocal state; mutual action: *We in the Central, at least, are not too proud to welcome a little reciprocity* (Wall Street Journal). **2** a mutual exchange, especially an exchange of special privileges in regard to trade between two countries, as by the mutual lowering of tariffs.

**re|cir|cle** (rē sėr′kəl), *v.t.*, *v.i.*, **-cled, -cling.** to circle again: *The airplane recircled the field.*

**re|cir|cu|late** (rē sėr′kyə lāt), *v.t.*, *v.i.*, **-lat|ed, -lat|ing.** to circulate anew: *As the amount of impurities picked up from the system is small, the water can be recirculated instead of running to waste* (New Scientist). — **re′cir|cu|la′tion,** *n.*

**re|ci|sion** (ri sizh′ən), *n.* a cutting back or away. [< Latin *recīsiō, -ōnis* < *recīdere* cut out < *re-* back + *caedere* to cut]

**ré|cit** (rā sē′), *n.* a short narrative: *He has given us a pleasant series of récits from the flow of his thinking and doing* (Saturday Review). [< French *récit* narrative < *réciter* to narrate < Latin *recitāre;* see etym. under **recite**]

**recit.,** *Music.* recitative[1].

**re|cit|al** (ri sī′təl), *n.* **1** the act of reciting; telling facts in detail: *Her recital of her experiences in the hospital bored her hearers.* **2** a story; account: *Which recital of the details is easier to understand?* **SYN:** narration. **3** a musical entertainment, usually given by a single performer: *All the music students in the class will give a recital Tuesday afternoon.* **4** a public performance given by a group of dancers (often dance pupils). **5** (formerly) a concert consisting of selections from one composer.

**re|cit|al|ist** (ri sī′tə list), *n.* a musician, singer, or actor who gives recitals: *Pianist de Groot was a two-handed recitalist of solid international reputation* (Time).

**re|ci|tan|do** (rā′chē tän′dō), *adj. Music.* reciting; half spoken or declaimed, after the manner of a recitative. [< Italian *recitando,* present participle of *recitare* recite]

**rec|i|ta|tion** (res′ə tā′shən), *n.* **1** the act of reciting; telling of facts in detail. **2** the act of reciting a prepared lesson by pupils before a teacher: *The teacher noted several mistakes in his recitation of the multiplication table of 9.* **3** the act of repeating something from memory before an audience: *The audience enjoyed the poet's moving recitation of several of his poems.* **4** a piece repeated from memory. [< Latin *recitātiō, -ōnis* < *recitāre;* see etym. under **recite**]

**rec|i|ta|tion|ist** (res′ə tā′shə nist), *n.* a person who recites poetry or prose before an audience.

**rec|i|ta|tive**[1] (res′ə tə tēv′), *n.*, *adj.* — ***n.*** **1** a passage, part, or piece of music which is sung with the rhythm and phrasing of ordinary speech. Operas often contain long recitatives. *Lerner's nimble recitatives and patter songs ... provide as agreeable a pattern as anyone could wish for* (Saturday Review). **2** this style of singing: *Operas often contain long passages of recitative. There's a lot of that recitative that is in the character of the songs and fits the opera perfectly* (Atlantic).
— ***adj.*** of or resembling recitative: *Kabuki actors must attain not only great control of the voice, for their parts are spoken in a "high" recitative style* (Atlantic).
[< Italian *recitativo* < Latin *recitāre;* see etym. under **recite**]

**rec|i|ta|tive**[2] (res′ə tā′tiv, ri sī′tə-), *adj.* **1** that recites. **2** having to do with a recital. [< *recit*(e) + *-ative;* perhaps influenced by *recitative*[1]]

**rec|i|ta|ti|vo** (res′ə tə tē′vō), *n.*, *pl.* **-vos,** *adj.*, = recitative[1]. [< Italian *recitativo*]

**re|cite** (ri sīt′), *v.*, **-cit|ed, -cit|ing.** — ***v.t.*** **1** to say over; repeat: *to recite a lesson. He can recite that poem from memory.* **SYN:** rehearse. **2** to give an account of in detail: *He recited the day's adventures. Will you recite the names of the pupils who have not been absent this term?* **SYN:** relate, narrate. **3** to repeat (as a poem or speech) to entertain an audience.
— ***v.i.*** **1** to repeat something; say part of a lesson: *The teacher called on me to recite.* **2** *Obsolete.* to relate, rehearse, or declare.
[< Latin *recitāre* < *re-* back, again + *citāre* call, summon (frequentative) < *ciēre* to rouse, call]
— **re|cit′er,** *n.*

**re|cit|ing note** or **tone** (ri sī′ting), a note in Gregorian music on which several syllables are recited in monotone.

**reck** (rek), *Archaic.* — ***v.i.*** **1** to care; heed: *The brave soldier recked little of danger.* **2** to be important or interesting; matter.
— ***v.t.*** **1** to have regard for: *May ye better reck the rede than ever did th' adviser!* (Robert Burns). **2** to matter to; concern: *Of night, or loneliness, it recks me not* (Milton).
[Old English *reccan*]

**reck|less** (rek′lis), *adj.* rash; heedless; careless: *Reckless driving causes many automobile accidents. Reckless of consequences, the boy played truant.* **SYN:** See syn. under **rash.** [Old English *recceléas,* related to *reccan* reck]
— **reck′less|ly,** *adv.* — **reck′less|ness,** *n.*

**reck|ling** (rek′ling), *n. British Dialect.* the smallest and weakest one in a litter of animals or a family of children: *There lay the reckling one, But one hour old!* (Tennyson). [origin unknown]

**reck|on** (rek′ən), *v.t.* **1** to find the number or value of; count up: *Reckon the cost before you decide to purchase the bicycle.* **SYN:** compute, calculate. **2** to consider; judge; account: *He is reckoned the best speller in the class.* **SYN:** regard, deem, esteem. **3** *Informal.* to think; suppose: *I reckon this always, that a man is never undone till he be hanged* (Shakespeare). — ***v.i.*** **1** to count; make a calculation. **SYN:** compute, calculate. **2** to depend; rely: *You can reckon on our help.* **3** to settle; settle accounts.
**reckon up,** to count up: *There were 786 small red roses ... at the first count and ... there will still be all those forget-me-nots to reckon up* (Punch).
**reckon with,** to take into consideration; deal with something or someone: *But in general what is in a politician's head is actual places and people, contingencies immediately to be reckoned with* (Edmund Wilson).

---

**Pronunciation Key:** hat, āge, cãre, fär; let, ēqual, tėrm; it, īce; hot, ōpen, ôrder; **oi**l, **ou**t; cup, pu̇t, rüle; **ch**ild; lo**ng**; **th**in; **ᴛʜ**en; **zh,** measure; **ə** represents **a** in about, **e** in taken, **i** in pencil, **o** in lemon, **u** in circus.

**reckon without one's host**. See under **host**[1].
[Middle English *recken*, Old English *gerecenian*]

**reck|on|a|ble** (rek′ə nə bəl), *adj.* capable of being reckoned: *They [statements] will be used to determine reckonable earnings quickly* (London Times).

**reck|on|er** (rek′ə nər), *n.* **1** a person who reckons. **2** a help in reckoning, such as a book of tables.

**reck|on|ing** (rek′ə ning, rek′ning), *n.* **1** a method of computing; count; calculation: *By my reckoning we are miles from home.* **2** the settling of an account: (*Figurative.*) *The day of the criminal's reckoning comes in court.* **3** a bill, especially at an inn or tavern: *The company having now pretty well satisfied their thirst, nothing remained but to pay the reckoning* (Henry Fielding). **4a** the calculation of the position of a ship. **b** the position calculated.

**re|claim** (ri klām′), *v.t.* **1** to bring back to a useful, good condition: *The farmer reclaimed the swamp by draining it. Society reclaims criminals by teaching them skills. Henrietta reclaimed him from a life of vice* (Macaulay). **SYN**: See syn. under **recover**. **2** to get from discarded things: *to reclaim rubber from old tires, to reclaim metal from old tin cans.* **3** to demand the return of: *The library reclaimed the book he borrowed a year ago.* **4** to make tame; subdue. — ***v.i.*** **1** to exclaim; protest. **2** *Obsolete.* to call out; cry loudly.
[< Old French *reclaimer*, and *reclamer* to protest; invoke, appeal, learned borrowings from Latin *reclāmāre* cry out loudly (against) < *re-* back + *clāmāre* cry out] — **re|claim′er**, *n.*

**re-claim** (rē klām′), *n.* a new or renewed claim.

**re|claim|a|ble** (ri klā′mə bəl), *adj.* that can be reclaimed.

**re|claim|ant** (ri klā′mənt), *n.* a person who reclaims.

**rec|la|ma|tion** (rek′lə mā′shən), *n.* **1** the act or process of reclaiming or state of being reclaimed; restoration to a useful, good condition: *the reclamation of deserts by irrigation.* **2** the act of protesting; protest: *My reclamation was not well received* (Richard A. Proctor). [< Latin *reclāmātiō, -ōnis* < *reclāmāre;* see etym. under **reclaim**]

**ré|clame** (rā klàm′), *n. French.* **1** advertisement; notoriety: *The vessel ... had achieved a certain dubious réclame shortly before* (New Yorker). **2** desire for publicity.

**re|clasp** (rē klasp′, -kläsp′), *v.t., v.i.* to clasp anew.

**re|clean|er** (rē klē′nər), *n.* the screening attachment of a bean thresher or pea huller that cleans beans or peas before they are put into bags.

**re|clin|a|ble** (ri klī′nə bəl), *adj.* capable of reclining or being reclined: *Both front seats are fully reclinable* (London Times).

**rec|li|nate** (rek′lə nāt), *adj. Botany.* bent or curved downward, as a leaf in a bud. [< Latin *reclīnātus*, past participle of *reclīnāre;* see etym. under **recline**]

**re|cline** (ri klīn′), *v.*, **-clined, -clin|ing.** — ***v.i.*** to lean back; lie down: *The tired girl reclined on the couch.* — ***v.t.*** to lay down.
[< Latin *reclīnāre* < *re-* back + *clīnāre* to lean] — **re|clin′er**, *n.*

**re|clothe** (rē klōᴛʜ′), *v.t.*, **-clothed, -cloth|ing.** to clothe again.

**rec|luse** (*n.* rek′lüs, ri klüs′; *adj.* ri klüs′), *n., adj.* — ***n.*** a person who lives shut up or withdrawn from the world: *a bachelor and something of a recluse in his private house, where he lived alone* (W. H. Hudson).
— ***adj.*** shut up or apart from the world: *a recluse life.*
[< Old French *reclus*, or *recluse*, feminine, past participle of *reclure* < Latin *reclūdere* to shut up, enclose < *re-* back + *claudere* to shut] — **re|cluse′ly**, *adv.* — **re|cluse′ness**, *n.*

**recluse spider**, = brown recluse.

**re|clu|sion** (ri klü′zhən), *n.* **1** the act of shutting up or condition of being shut up in seclusion. **2** solitary confinement. **3** the condition or life of a recluse: *She is one of the few nuns in the world with ecclesiastical permission to attempt the hermitlike life known as reclusion* (Time).

**re|clu|sive** (ri klü′siv), *adj.* characterized by seclusion; recluse. — **re|clu′sive|ly**, *adv.* — **re|clu′sive|ness**, *n.*

**re|coal** (rē kōl′), *v.t.* to supply again with coal: *to recoal a steamship.* — ***v.i.*** to take on a fresh supply of coal.

**rec|og|nise** (rek′əg nīz), *v.t., v.i.*, **-nised, -nis|ing.** *Especially British.* recognize.

**rec|og|ni|tion** (rek′əg nish′ən), *n.* **1** the act of recognizing; knowing again: *The prince bowed his head in recognition of the emperor's authority.* **2** the fact of being recognized: *By a good disguise he escaped recognition.* **3** acknowledgment or admission: *We insisted on complete recognition of our rights.* **SYN**: admission. **4** notice: *to seek recognition by the chair.* **5** favorable notice; attention; acceptance: *The actor soon won recognition from the public.* **SYN**: appreciation. **6** a formal acknowledgment conveying approval or sanction: *the recognition of a new country by the United Nations.* [< Latin *recognitiō, -ōnis* < *recognōscere;* see etym. under **recognize**]

**rec|og|ni|tion|al** (rek′əg nish′ən əl), *adj.* of or having to do with recognition.

**recognition color** or **mark**, a color on an animal supposed to be of use to others of its species as a means of recognition.

**re|cog|ni|tive** (ri kog′nə tiv), *adj.* having to do with recognition.

**re|cog|ni|to|ry** (ri kog′nə tôr′ē, -tōr′-), *adj.* = recognitive.

**rec|og|niz|a|bil|i|ty** (rek′əg nī′zə bil′ə tē), *n.* recognizable quality.

**rec|og|niz|a|ble** (rek′əg nī′zə bəl), *adj.* that can be recognized. **SYN**: identifiable. — **rec′og|niz′a|bly**, *adv.*

**re|cog|ni|zance** (ri kog′nə zəns, -kon′ə-), *n.* **1** *Law.* **a** a bond binding a person to do some particular act. **b** the sum of money to be forfeited if the act is not performed. **2** = recognition. **3** *Archaic.* a badge; token: *That recognizance and pledge of love which I first gave her* (Shakespeare). [alteration (influenced by Latin *recognōscere*) of Middle English *reconysaunce* < Old French *reconnaissance*, and *recognoissance* < *reconoistre;* see etym. under **recognize**. See etym. of doublet **reconnaissance**.]

**rec|og|nize** (rek′əg nīz), *v.*, **-nized, -niz|ing.** — ***v.t.*** **1** to know again; be aware of (someone or something) as already known: *to recognize an old friend. You have grown so much that I scarcely recognized you.* **2** to identify: *to recognize a person from a description.* **3** to acknowledge acquaintance with; greet: *to recognize a person on the street.* **4** to acknowledge; accept; admit: *to recognize a claim. A patriot recognizes his duty to defend his country. I recognize your right to ask that question.* **SYN**: concede, grant. **5** to take notice of: *Anyone who wishes to speak in a public meeting should stand up and wait till the chairman recognizes him.* **6** to show appreciation of: *Honesty and perseverance in students are quickly recognized by teachers.* **7** to acknowledge and agree to deal with: *For some years other nations did not recognize the new government.*
— ***v.i.*** *Law.* to bind a person by bond to do some particular act.
[alteration of Old French *reconuiss-*, stem of *reconoistre* < Latin *recognōscere* < *re-* again + *com-* (intensive) + *gnōscere* to learn. See etym. of doublet **reconnoiter**.]

**rec|og|nized** (rek′əg nīzd), *adj.* acknowledged, admitted, or approved: *a recognized method of procedure. Every newspaper and periodical of recognized standing ...* (Edward Bok).

**re|cog|ni|zee** (ri kog′nə zē′, -kon′ə-), *n. Law.* the person to whom a recognizance is made.

**rec|og|niz|er** (rek′əg nī′zər), *n.* a person who recognizes.

**re|cog|ni|zor** (ri kog′nə zôr′, -kon′ə-), *n. Law.* a person who enters into a recognizance.

**re|coil** (*v.* ri koil′; *n.* ri koil′, rē′koil), *v., n.* — ***v.i.*** **1** to draw back; shrink back: *Most people would recoil at seeing a snake in the path. The ... British had recoiled five and twenty miles* (H. G. Wells). **SYN**: flinch. **2** to spring back: *The gun recoiled after I fired.* **SYN**: kick. **3** to react: (*Figurative.*) *Revenge often recoils on the avenger.*
— ***n.*** **1** a drawing or springing back; recoiling: *This is the expulsion of a jet of gas or other substance in one direction causing a recoil or thrust in the opposite direction* (New York Times). **2** a state of having recoiled: *in recoil from danger.* **3** the distance or force with which a gun, spring, or other mechanism, springs back.
[< Old French *reculer* < *re-* back + *cule* rump < Latin *cūlus*] — **re|coil′er**, *n.*

**recoil cylinder**, a cylinder with a piston and piston rod that are forced through the length of the cylinder when a gun recoils.

**re|coil|less** (ri koil′lis), *adj.* having no appreciable recoil: *a recoilless rifle.*

**re|coil-op|er|at|ed** (rē′koil op′ə rā′tid), *adj.* (of an automatic or semiautomatic weapon) utilizing the force of recoil caused by gas pressure to unlock the bolt and activate the loading mechanism.

**recoil spring**, a spring to check a piece which recoils.

**recoil system**, a recoil-operated machine-gun mechanism.

**re|coin** (rē koin′), *v.t.* to coin again or anew.

**re|coin|age** (rē koi′nij), *n.* **1** coinage anew. **2** a new coinage.

**rec|ol|lect** (rek′ə lekt′), *v.t.* **1** to call back to mind; remember: *I know why I began the Memoir. It was an experiment to see how much I could really recollect if I once began to try* (William De Morgan). **SYN**: See syn. under **remember**. **2** to recall (oneself) to something temporarily forgotten. — ***v.i.*** to recall something; remember. [< Latin *recollectus*, past participle of *recolligere;* see etym. under **re-collect**]

**re-col|lect** (rē′kə lekt′), *v.t.* **1** to collect again. **2** to recover control of (oneself). [partly < Latin *recollectus*, past participle of *recolligere* < *re-* again + *colligere* (compare etym. under **collect**[1]), later partly < English *re-* + *collect*[1]]

**rec|ol|lect|ed** (rek′ə lek′tid), *adj.* remembered. [< *recollect* + *-ed*[2]] — **rec′ol|lect′ed|ness**, *n.*

**re-col|lect|ed** (rē′kə lek′tid), *adj.* composed; sure of oneself. [< *re-collect* + *-ed*[2]] — **re′-col|lect′ed|ness**, *n.*

**rec|ol|lec|tion** (rek′ə lek′shən), *n.* **1** the act or power of recalling to mind: *Recollection of the distant events is difficult.* **2** memory; remembrance: *This has been the hottest summer within my recollection.* **SYN**: See syn. under **memory**. **3** a thing remembered: *a vivid recollection of a dream.*

**rec|ol|lec|tive** (rek′ə lek′tiv), *adj.* having recollection; characterized by recollection. — **rec′ol|lec′tive|ly**, *adv.*

**re|col|o|nize** (rē kol′ə nīz), *v.t.*, **-nized, -niz|ing.** to colonize (a place) anew. — **re′col|o|ni|za′tion**, *n.*

**re|col|or** (rē kul′ər), *v.t.* to color or dye again. — ***v.i.*** to flush again: *The swarthy blush recolors in his cheeks* (Byron).

**re|comb** (rē kōm′), *v.t.* to comb again.

**re|com|bi|nant** (ri kom′bə nənt), *n., adj.* — ***n.*** **1** something that combines again. **2** *Biology.* an organism, cell, or other structure showing characteristics resulting from recombination: *The recombinants always inherit a larger fraction of their genetic characteristics from their mother than from their father* (Scientific American).
— ***adj.*** *Biology.* characterized by or showing recombination.

**recombinant DNA**, genetic material produced in the laboratory by combining DNA fragments from different types of cells or by transplanting them from one form of life, such as viruses, to other forms such as bacteria: *Work with recombinant DNA molecules or organisms containing them would be carried out in a hood that restricts movement of particles to or from the work area ... and all materials would be decontaminated or destroyed before leaving the laboratory* (James C. Copeland).

**re|com|bi|na|tion** (rē′kom bə nā′shən), *n.* **1** the act or process of recombining. **2** *Biology.* the formation of new combinations of genes in offspring, especially by the process of crossing over.

**re|com|bi|na|tive** (ri kom′bə nā′tiv), *adj. Biology.* of or having to do with recombination.

**re|com|bine** (rē′kəm bīn′), *v.t., v.i.*, **-bined, -bin|ing.** to combine again or anew.

**re|com|fort** (rē kum′fərt), *v.t. Archaic.* to comfort again; cheer; console.

**re|com|mence** (rē′kə mens′), *v.*, **-menced, -menc|ing.** — ***v.i.*** to begin again to be; begin anew. — ***v.t.*** to cause to begin again to be; begin again.
[< Old French *recommencer* < *re-* re- + *commencer.* Compare etym. under **commence**.]

**re|com|mence|ment** (rē′kə mens′mənt), *n.* the act or fact of beginning anew.

**rec|om|mend** (rek′ə mend′), *v., n.* — ***v.t.*** **1** to speak in favor of; suggest favorably: *The teacher recommended him for the job. Can you recommend a good adventure story? The waiter recommended fried chicken as the best dish on the menu.* **2** to advise; counsel: *The doctor recommended that she stay in bed.* **3** to make pleasing or attractive: *The location of the camp recommends it as a summer home.* **4** to hand over for safekeeping; commit; entrust: *He recommended his soul to God.*
— ***n.*** *Informal.* a recommendation.
[< Medieval Latin *recommendare* < Latin *re-* again + *commendāre.* Compare etym. under **commend**.]

**rec|om|mend|a|ble** (rek′ə men′də bəl), *adj.* worthy of being recommended.

**rec|om|men|da|tion** (rek′ə men dā′shən), *n.* **1** the act of recommending: *We stayed at that hotel on the cabdriver's recommendation.* **2** anything that recommends a person or thing: *We couldn't find much in the cooking that was a recommendation for eating at that restaurant again.* **3** words of advice or praise: *The recommendation in his letter got me the job.* **4** a person or thing recommended.

**rec|om|men|da|to|ry** (rek′ə men′də tôr′ē, -tōr′-), *adj.* serving to recommend; recommending: *I was to take with me letters recommendatory to a number of his friends* (Benjamin Franklin).

**rec|om|mend|er** (rek′ə men′dər), *n.* a person or thing that recommends.

**re|com|mis|sion** (rē′kə mish′ən), *v.t.* to commission anew: *The Royal Navy's oldest aircraft carrier, Victorious ... was recommissioned at Portsmouth yesterday* (London Times).

**re|com|mit** (rē′kə mit′), *v.t.,* **-mit|ted, -mit|ting.** **1** to commit again. **2** to refer again to a committee.

**re|com|mit|ment** (rē′kə mit′mənt), *n.* **1** the act or process of recommitting. **2** the state of being recommitted.

**re|com|mit|tal** (rē′kə mit′əl), *n.* = recommitment.

**rec|om|pense** (rek′əm pens), *v.,* **-pensed, -pens|ing,** *n.* — ***v.t.*** **1** to pay back; reward; pay (a person): *The travelers recompensed the man who so carefully directed them.* **SYN:** repay, compensate, remunerate, requite. **2a** to make a fair return for (an action, anything lost, damage done, or hurt received): *The insurance company recompensed him for the loss of his car. Liberally recompensing their services ... he took leave of his faithful followers* (William H. Prescott). **b** *Archaic.* to atone for: *... the future must recompense the past* (Robert Browning). **3** *Obsolete.* to give in return: *Recompense to no man evil for evil* (Romans 12:17).

— ***n.*** **1** a payment; reward: *He received $2,000 in recompense for the loss of his car.* **2** return; amends: *Some recompense To comfort those that mourn* (Robert Burns).

[< Late Latin *recompēnsāre* < Latin *re-* back + *compēnsāre.* Compare etym. under **compensate.**]

**re|com|pose** (rē′kəm pōz′), *v.t.,* **-posed, -pos|ing.** **1** to compose again: *Whatever is decomposed may be recomposed by the being who first composed it* (Joseph Priestley). **2** = rearrange. **3** to restore to composure: *Our spirits, when disordered, are not to be recomposed in a moment* (Henry Fielding).

**re|com|po|si|tion** (rē′kom pə zish′ən), *n.* **1** the act or process of recomposing: *I have taken great pains with the recomposition of this scene* (Charles Lamb). **2** the fact or state of being recomposed.

**re|com|press** (rē′kəm pres′), *v.t.* to compress again.

**re|com|pres|sion** (rē′kəm presh′ən), *n.* **1** the act of recompressing. **2** the state of being recompressed.

**re|com|pute** (rē′kəm pyüt′), *v.t.,* **-put|ed, -put|ing.** to compute again; recalculate. — **re′com|pu|ta′tion,** *n.*

**re|con**[1] (rē′kon), *n. Biology.* the smallest molecular unit of genetic material out of which the larger units, the muton and cistron, are built: *The ultimate unit of molecular structure, the "recon," was found equal to one base pair of nucleic acid. The muton was approximately ten base pairs long* (Science News Letter). [< *rec*(ombination) + *-on,* as in *muton*]

**re|con**[2] (ri kon′), *n., v. U.S. Informal.* — ***n.*** = reconnaissance.

— ***v.t., v.i.*** = reconnoiter.

**re|con|cen|trate** (rē kon′sən trāt), *v.t.,* **-trat|ed, -trat|ing.** **1** to concentrate again. **2** to bring (forces) together at some point: *to reconcentrate troops before an offensive.* — **re′con|cen|tra′tion,** *n.*

**re|con|cep|tu|al|i|za|tion** (rē′kən sep′chü ə lə zā′shən), *n.* **1** the process of conceptualizing again or anew: *The work involved a reconceptualization of an organization's problems and a redefining of assumptions and expectations* (Emory S. Bogardus). **2** a new conceptualization.

**rec|on|cil|a|bil|i|ty** (rek′ən sī′lə bil′ə tē), *n.* the fact or quality of being reconcilable.

**rec|on|cil|a|ble** (rek′ən sī′lə bəl), *adj.* that can be reconciled. — **rec′on|cil′a|ble|ness,** *n.*

**rec|on|cil|a|bly** (rek′ən sī′lə blē), *adv.* in a reconcilable manner.

**rec|on|cile** (rek′ən sīl), *v.t.,* **-ciled, -cil|ing.** **1a** to make friends again: *The children had quarreled but were soon reconciled. Being all now good friends, for common danger ... had effectually reconciled them* (Daniel Defoe). **b** to win over: *to reconcile a hostile person.* **2** to settle (a quarrel or difference): *The teacher had to reconcile disputes among her pupils.* **3** to make agree; bring into harmony: *It is impossible to reconcile his story with the facts. There is need for a procedure for reconciling power needs and environmental protection* (Joseph C. Swidler). **4** to make satisfied; make no longer opposed: *It is hard to reconcile oneself to being sick a long time. Custom reconciles us to everything* (Edmund Burke). **5** to purify by special ceremonies: *The places of old assembly ... were cleansed, or repaired, refitted and reconciled, and opened to ... public ... worship* (Nicholas P. S. Wiseman). [< Latin *reconciliāre* < *re-* back + *conciliāre.* Compare etym. under **conciliate.**] — **rec′on|cil′er,** *n.*

**rec|on|cile|ment** (rek′ən sīl′mənt), *n.* = reconciliation.

**rec|on|cil|i|a|tion** (rek′ən sil′ē ā′shən), *n.* **1** the act of reconciling; bringing together again in friendship: *the absence of any appearance of reconciliation between the theory and practice of life* (Emerson). **2** the fact of being reconciled; settlement or adjustment of disagreements or differences: *a reconciliation of opposite points of view.* **SYN:** agreement.

**rec|on|cil|i|a|to|ry** (rek′ən sil′ē ə tôr′ē, -tōr′-), *adj.* tending to reconcile.

**re|con|dense** (rē′kən dens′), *v.t., v.i.,* **-densed, -dens|ing.** to condense again: *Vapour, which rises in the air and is recondensed on mountain heights* (John Tyndall). — **re′con|den|sa′tion,** *n.*

**rec|on|dite** (rek′ən dīt, ri kon′-), *adj.* **1** hard to understand; profound: *The recondite principles of philosophy* (Henry Mackenzie). **SYN:** abstruse. **2** little known; obscure: *a recondite writer, recondite writings.* **3** hidden from view; concealed. [< Latin *reconditus,* past participle of *recondere* store away < *re-* back + *condere* to store < *com-* up + *dare* to put, lay] — **rec′on|dite′ly,** *adv.* — **rec′on|dite′ness,** *n.*

**re|con|di|tion** (rē′kən dish′ən), *v.t.* to restore to a good or satisfactory condition; put in good condition, as by repairing, making over, etc.: *to recondition an old house.* **SYN:** renovate. — **re′con|di′tion|er,** *n.*

**re|con|duct** (rē′kən dukt′), *v.t.* to conduct back or again: *Amidst this new creation want'st a guide To reconduct thy steps?* (John Dryden).

**re|con|fig|ure** (rē′kən fig′yər), *v.t.,* **-ured, -ur|ing.** to change the form or parts of (an aircraft, computer, or other apparatus or device): *The air traffic control and navigation complex which exists today is essentially a hodgepodge of war surplus systems which have been reconfigured using modern components* (Science News).

**re|con|firm** (rē′kən fėrm′), *v.t.* to confirm anew: *to reconfirm a reservation.*

**re|con|fir|ma|tion** (rē′kon fər mā′shən), *n.* **1** the act of reconfirming. **2** the state or condition of being reconfirmed: *a reconfirmation of the alliance.*

**re|con|nais|sance** (ri kon′ə səns), *n.* an examination or survey, especially for military purposes. [< French *reconnaissance* < Old French *recognoissance.* See etym. of doublet **recognizance.**]

**reconnaissance in force,** *Military.* an attack to discover the position and strength of an enemy.

**reconnaissance satellite,** an artificial satellite used to gather strategic information through photography, television, or other means of surveillance.

**re|con|nect** (rē′kə nekt′), *v.t.* to connect again: *The alliance ... would be a link reconnecting England with the Empire* (James A. Froude).

**re|con|nois|sance** (ri kon′ə səns), *n.* = reconnaissance.

**rec|on|noi|ter** (rek′ə noi′tər, rē′kə-), *v.t.* **1** to approach and examine or observe in order to learn something; make a survey of (the enemy, the enemy's strength or position, a region, or objective) in order to gain information for military purposes: *Our scouts will reconnoiter the enemy's position before we attack.* **2** to survey (a tract or region) for engineering or geological purposes.

— ***v.i.*** to approach a place and make a first survey of it: *It seemed wise to reconnoiter before entering the town.*

[< obsolete French *reconnoître* < Old French *reconoistre.* See etym. of doublet **recognize.**]

**rec|on|noi|ter|er** (rek′ə noi′tər ər, rē′kə-), *n.* a person who reconnoiters or makes a preliminary survey.

**rec|on|noi|tre** (rek′ə noi′tər, rē′kə-), *v.t., v.i.,* **-tred, -tring.** *Especially British.* reconnoiter.

**rec|on|noi|trer** (rek′ə noi′trər, rē′kə-), *n. Especially British.* reconnoiterer.

**re|con|quer** (rē kong′kər), *v.t.* to conquer again; recover by conquest.

**re|con|quest** (rē kon′kwest, -kong′-), *n.* the act of reconquering.

**re|con|se|crate** (rē kon′sə krāt), *v.t.,* **-crat|ed, -crat|ing.** to consecrate anew. — **re′con|se|cra′tion,** *n.*

**re|con|sid|er** (rē′kən sid′ər), *v.t.* to consider again: *The assembly voted to reconsider the bill. The judge reconsidered his decision.* — ***v.i.*** to take up a matter again.

**re|con|sid|er|a|tion** (rē′kən sid′ə rā′shən), *n.* **1** the act of reconsidering: *Her newest book is a reconsideration of some of the greatest Western writers* (Newsweek). **2** the state of being reconsidered.

**re|con|sign** (rē′kən sīn′), *v.t.* to consign again: *Officials said 4,000 tons will be sold in the open market and the remainder will be reconsigned to the original suppliers* (Wall Street Journal).

**re|con|sign|ment** (rē′kən sīn′mənt), *n.* **1** the act of consigning again. **2** a change of destination during transportation.

**re|con|sol|i|date** (rē′kən sol′ə dāt), *v.t.,* **-dat|ed, -dat|ing.** to consolidate anew: *A petrifying fluid, with which a broken stone will be reconsolidated like a broken limb* (Richard J. Sullivan). — **re′con|sol′i|da′tion,** *n.*

**re|con|stit|u|ent** (rē′kən stich′ü ənt), *adj., n.* — ***adj.*** **1** building up. **2** causing the formation of new tissues.

— ***n.*** a drug that reconstitutes what has been wasted by disease.

**re|con|sti|tute** (rē kon′stə tüt, -tyüt), *v.t.,* **-tut|ed, -tut|ing.** **1** to form again; bring back to its original form or consistency: *to reconstitute frozen orange juice by adding water.* **2** to pulverize (coarse or damaged leaves of tobacco), press the dust into sheets, and use them as material for cigars.

**re|con|sti|tut|ed** (rē kon′stə tü′tid, -tyü′-), *adj.* that has been formed again or brought back to its original consistency: *reconstituted milk, reconstituted lemon juice.*

**re|con|sti|tu|tion** (rē′kon stə tü′shən, -tyü′-), *n.* the act or process of reconstituting.

**re|con|struct** (rē′kən strukt′), *v.t.* to construct again; rebuild; make over; restore: *to reconstruct the facts of a story to understand how something happened.* **SYN:** renew, remodel. — ***v.i.*** to come together again in the original form: *The image hologram is sometimes confused with a "volume hologram," which will also reconstruct in white light* (New Scientist).

**re|con|struct|ed** (rē′kən struk′tid), *adj.* **1** made again. **2** artificially made from bits of real gems: *a reconstructed ruby.*

**re|con|struct|i|ble** (rē′kən struk′tə bəl), *adj.* that can be reconstructed: *Some of the statues were fragmentary but reconstructible* (William A. Ritchie).

**re|con|struc|tion** (rē′kən struk′shən), *n.* **1** the act of constructing again. **2** the state of being constructed again. **3** something reconstructed.

**Re|con|struc|tion** (rē′kən struk′shən), *n.* **1** the process by which the Southern states after the Civil War were reorganized and their relations with the national government were reestablished. **2** the period when this was done from 1865 to 1877.

**Re|con|struc|tion|ism** (rē′kən struk′shən iz əm), *n.* a movement in American Judaism which regards Judaism as a religious civilization and favors those institutions, customs, and religious laws, that are meaningful to Jews of all backgrounds and denominations.

**Re|con|struc|tion|ist** (rē′kən struk′shən ist), *adj., n.* — ***adj.*** of or having to do with Reconstructionism.

— ***n.*** a supporter of Reconstructionism.

**re|con|struc|tive** (rē′kən struk′tiv), *adj.* tending to reconstruct.

**reconstructive surgery,** a branch of surgery dealing with the repair of congenital or acquired defects or malformations of body tissues.

**re|con|struc|tor** (rē′kən struk′tər), *n.* a person who constructs or restores again.

**re|con|tam|i|nate** (rē′kən tam′ə nāt), *v.t.,* **-nat|ed, -nat|ing.** to contaminate again. — **re′con|tam′i|na′tion,** *n.*

**re|con|trol** (rē′kən trōl′), *v.,* **-trolled, -trol|ling,** *n.* — ***v.t.*** to put new controls upon; place again under price or rent control: *Four owners of the 29 establishments that had been recontrolled had filed plans with the Buildings Department to convert the building back to apartment house use* (New York Times).

— ***n.*** a recontrolling; renewal of controls.

**re|con|vene** (rē′kən vēn′), *v.i., v.t.,* **-vened, -ven|ing.** to convene again.

**re|con|ver|sion** (rē′kən vėr′zhən, -shən), *n.* **1** conversion back to a previous state or belief. **2** conversion again or anew.

**re|con|vert** (rē′kən vėrt′), *v.t., v.i.* **1** to convert back to a previous state or belief. **2** to convert again: *After the war, the factories that produced tanks were reconverted to produce tractors.*

**re|con|vey** (rē′kən vā′), *v.t.* **1** to convey again or back to a previous place or position. **2** *Law.* to make over again or restore to a former owner.

**re|con|vey|ance** (rē′kən vā′əns), *n.* conveyance again; conveyance back.

**re|con|vict** (rē′kən vikt′), *v.t.* to convict again. — **re′con|vic′tion,** *n.*

**re|cop|y** (rē kop′ē), *v.t.,* **-cop|ied, -cop|y|ing.** to copy again.

**re|cord** (*v.* ri kôrd′; *n., adj.* rek′ərd), *v., n., adj.* — ***v.t.*** **1** to set down in writing so as to keep for future use: *to record the proceedings at a meeting. Listen to the speaker and record what he says. A long inscription ... records how Amenhotep ... slew seven kings with his own hand* (Amelia B. Edwards). **2** to put in some permanent form; keep for remembrance: *We record history in books. The widespread destruction recorded*

---

**Pronunciation Key:** hat, āge, cãre, fär; let, ēqual, tėrm; it, īce; hot, ōpen, ôrder; oil, out; cup, pu̇t, rüle; child; long; thin; ᴛʜen; zh, measure; ə represents **a** in about, **e** in taken, **i** in pencil, **o** in lemon, **u** in circus.

*the effectiveness of the atomic bomb.* **3** to register, especially in permanent form: *A cardiograph records the movements of the heart.* **4** to put (music, words, or sounds) on a phonograph disk or on specially treated tape or wire: *Both will be recorded, and both brought their composers $1,200 each* (Newsweek).
— ***v.i.*** to make a phonograph disk or disks; put a song, speech, or other performance, on a record: *He recorded frequently and with apparent complete freedom* (New Yorker).
— ***n.*** **1** anything written and kept: *Her diary was a record of her childhood.* **2a** an official written account: *The secretary kept a record of what was done at the meeting. 43 out of 100 firms that lose their accounts receivable and other business records in a fire never reopen* (New Yorker).
**b** an official copy of a document: *The county clerk has a record of the deed to this house. The record of his case is in the court clerk's file.* **3** a disk or cylinder used on a phonograph. A record plays the sounds copied on its very small grooves. **4** the known facts about what a person, animal, or thing has done: *He has a fine record at school. That newspaper's record in promoting good causes has been unequaled. With a number of delays on its record, this train's schedule is not reliable.* **5** *U.S.* a criminal's recorded history of offenses, arrests, convictions, and other activity under legal supervision. **6** the best yet done; best or greatest amount, rate, or speed yet attained: *Who holds the record for the high jump?* **7** a recording or being recorded: *What happened is a matter of record.*
— ***adj.*** making or affording a record: *a record wheat crop.*
**break a** (or **the**) **record**, to make a better record: *He broke the record for the long jump.*
**go on record**, to state publicly for the record: *The candidate went on record as an opponent of nuclear tests.*
**off the record**, not to be recorded or quoted: *Politicians often say things off the record that it would be impolitic to say directly.*
**of record**, according to official record: *He says he and his wife and two adult children together own beneficially and of record 30,800 Libby shares* (Wall Street Journal).
**on record, a** recorded; set down; registered: *The date of her birth is on record in Dade County, Florida.* **b** to be recorded or quoted: *Big-state Democratic governors ... put themselves on record in favor of strong civil rights action* (Wall Street Journal).
[< Old French *recorder* < Latin *recordārī* remember, call to mind < *re-* back + *cor, cordis* heart, mind]

**re|cord|a|ble** (ri kôr′də bəl), *adj.* **1** that can be recorded: *... the smallest recordable activity is a few millionths of a volt* (Floyd and Silver). **2** worth recording.

**rec|or|da|tion** (rek′ər dā′shən), *n.* **1** the act of recording. **2** = record. **3** *Obsolete.* remembrance.
[< Latin *recordātiō, -ōnis* < *recordārī;* see etym. under **record**]

**re|cor|da|tive** (ri kôr′də tiv), *adj.* that records or keeps in memory; commemorative.

**re|cor|da|to|ry** (ri kôr′də tôr′ē, -tōr′-), *adj.* having to do with the keeping of records.

**record breaker**, a person, thing, or event that is faster, bigger, or in any way better than any other of the same class: *In his long term at New Haven, Kiphuth produced dozens of topflight swimmers, and many were record breakers* (Time).

**rec|ord-break|ing** (rek′ərd brā′king), *adj.* surpassing any recorded performance or production of its kind.

**record changer**, a turntable for a phonograph with a device that holds several records above the turntable, letting each record down automatically after the previous one has been played.

***re|cord|er** (ri kôr′dər), *n.* **1** a person whose business is to make and keep records: *The recorder in many of our local towns keeps the record of taxes paid and land ownership.* **SYN**: registrar. **2** a machine, or part of a machine, that records. A cashier's recorder adds up and prints the amount of sales made. *A microfilm recorder takes small pictures of documents.* **3** = tape recorder. **4** a title given to certain judges in some cities. **5** a wooden musical wind instrument with a mouthpiece shaped like a whistle, eight finger holes, and soft, mellow tones: *flutes and soft recorders* (Milton). *More recorders are being tootled nowadays than at any time since the development of the modern orchestra* (Newsweek). **6** a person who records sounds or sound effects for motion pictures or phonograph records: *There is no specialization among technical workers, except in the case of sound mixers and recorders* (New York Times).

***recorder**
definition 5

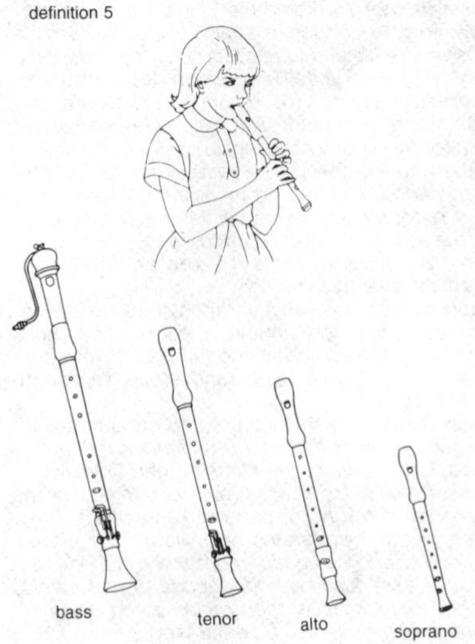


**re|cord|er|ship** (ri kôr′dər ship), *n.* the position or term of a recorder.

**rec|ord|hold|er** (rek′ərd hōl′dər), *n.* a person who holds the record for some achievement: *He defeated the world recordholder ... and won the 5000 meter race* (New York Times).

**re|cord|ing** (ri kôr′ding), *n.* **1** a record used on a phonograph: *Virtually all major-label recordings and most on small-company labels are now released in both stereo and mono (standard) form* (Harper's). **2** the original transcription of any sound or combination of sounds: *A recording of the Liverpool performance is to be broadcast on April 7* (Sunday Times). **3** = tape recording.

**recording head**, = magnetic head.

**re|cord|ist** (ri kôr′dist), *n.* a person who cuts phonograph records or makes tape recordings, especially as a hobby: *Like the photographer with his various darkroom techniques, the recordist has a number of methods at his disposal for the creation of compositions in sound* (Glen Southworth).

**record library**, a collection of phonograph records.

**rec|ord|mak|er** (rek′ərd mā′kər), *n.* a person or company that makes phonograph records: *Now the endless search for operatic treasure has driven the recordmakers back to Gluck* (Time).

**record player**, = phonograph.

**re|cor|o|na|tion** (rē′kôr ə nā′shən, -kor-), *n.* the act of recrowning or fact of being recrowned.

**re|count¹** (ri kount′), *v.t.* **1** to tell in detail; give an account of: *He recounted all the happenings of the day. They used to recount ... the exploits of their youth* (Gilbert White). **SYN**: describe. **2** to tell one by one; enumerate: *to recount the items in a list.* [< Anglo-French, Old French *reconter* < *re-* again + *conter* to relate. Compare etym. under **count¹**.]

**re-count** or **re|count²** (*v.* rē kount′; *n.* rē′kount′, rē kount′), *v., n.* — ***v.t.*** to count again: *The miser counted and re-counted his money.*
— ***n.*** a second count: *A re-count of the votes was made.*
[< *re-* + *count¹*]

**re|count|al** (ri koun′təl), *n.* = narration.

**re|coup** (ri küp′), *v., n.* — ***v.t.*** **1** to make up for: *He recouped his losses.* **2** to repay: *I will recoup you for any money you spend. It was necessary for parliament to intervene to compel the landlord to recoup the tenant for his outlay on the land* (W. S. Gregg). **SYN**: reimburse, recompense. **3** *Law.* to deduct: *The defendant may recoup damages before paying his lawyer's fee.*
— ***v.i.*** to make up for a loss.
— ***n.*** the act of recouping; deduction.
[< Old French *recouper* < *re-* back + *couper* to cut, divide with a stroke < *coup.* Compare etym. under **coup**.] — **re|coup′a|ble**, *adj.* — **re|coup′er**, *n.* — **re|coup′ment**, *n.*

**re|course** (rē′kôrs, -kōrs; ri kôrs′, -kōrs′), *n.* **1** the act of turning for help or protection; appealing: *Our recourse in illness is to a doctor.* **2** a person or thing appealed to or turned to for help or protection: *His only recourse in trouble was his family.* **3** the right to demand compensation from someone, especially the right which the holder of a bill of exchange has to come back upon the drawer and endorsers if the acceptor fails to meet it. **4** *Obsolete.* access; admission.
**have recourse to**, to appeal to; turn to for help: *If we do not know what a word means, we have recourse to a dictionary. If threats and persuasions proved ineffectual, he had often recourse to violence* (Edward Gibbon).
[< Old French *recours* < Latin *recursus, -ūs* a return, retreat < *recurrere;* see etym. under **recur**]

**re|cov|er** (ri kuv′ər), *v., n.* — ***v.t.*** **1** to get back (something lost, taken away, or stolen); regain: *to recover a lost ring, to recover one's temper or health.* **2** to make up for (something lost or damaged): *to recover lost time.* **3** to bring back to life, health, one's senses, or normal condition: *Our men ... took up three men; one of which was just drowning, and it was a good while before we could recover him* (Daniel Defoe). **4** to get back to the proper position or condition: *He started to fall but recovered himself.* **5** to obtain by judgment in a law court: *to recover damages.* **6** to regain in usable form; reclaim. Many useful substances are now recovered from materials that used to be thrown away. **7** to rescue; deliver. **8** to return (a bayonet, sword, or the like) to a certain position, as after use. **9** *Archaic.* to get to; reach.
— ***v.i.*** **1** to get well; get back to a normal condition: *She is recovering from a cold. The man recovered of the bite—The dog it was that died* (Oliver Goldsmith). **2** to obtain judgment in one's favor in a law court. **3** *Sports.* to make a recovery.
— ***n.*** *Sports.* a recovery, especially a getting back to the proper position in fencing or boxing.
[< Anglo-French *recoverer,* Old French *recovrer* < Latin *recuperāre.* See etym. of doublet **recuperate**.]
— *Syn.* *v.t.* **1 Recover, reclaim, retrieve** mean to get something back. **Recover** means to get something back again after losing it: *He recovered the stolen furs.* **Reclaim** means to get something back after temporarily giving it up: *At the end of the trip we reclaimed our luggage.* **Retrieve** means to get something back after letting it lapse or deteriorate: *It took him a long time to retrieve his reputation.*

**re-cov|er** (rē kuv′ər), *v.t.* **1** to put a new cover on: *We had our couch re-covered with new material.* **2** to put a cover back on.

**re|cov|er|a|bil|i|ty** (ri kuv′ər ə bil′ə tē), *n.* the state, property, or possibility of being recovered.

**re|cov|er|a|ble** (ri kuv′ər ə bəl), *adj.* **1** that can be regained. **2** that can be restored from sickness, faintness, or the like. **3** that can be brought back to a former condition. **4** that can be obtained from a debtor or possessor: *The debt is recoverable.*

**re|cov|er|er** (ri kuv′ər ər), *n.* **1** a person who recovers. **2** = recoveror.

**re|cov|er|or** (ri kuv′ər ər), *n. Law.* a person who obtains a judgment in his favor in a law court.

**re|cov|er|y** (ri kuv′ər ē, -kuv′rē), *n., pl.* **-er|ies**. **1** the act of recovering. **2** the process or fact of coming back to health or normal condition: *We heard of your recovery from fever.* **3** the fact or process of getting back something that was lost, taken away, stolen, or sent out: *The insurance company helped the police in the recovery of the stolen property. The recovery of Bagdad was impossible unless the British were driven back to the Sinai desert* (John Buchan). **4** the act or fact of getting back to a proper position or condition: *He tripped and almost fell, but made a quick recovery.* **5** the act of locating and repossessing a missile, nose cone, or package of scientific instruments, after a flight in space or balloon ascent in the upper atmosphere: *the recovery of a space capsule.* **6** the return to a position of guard after a lunge in fencing, an attack in boxing, etc. **7** the act or fact of obtaining some property or right by the judgment of a law court.

**recovery metallurgy**, = extractive metallurgy.

**recovery room**, a room used in a hospital to treat patients recovering immediately after an operation or childbirth: *The child spent the next critical hours in the recovery room* (Harper's).

**recpt.**, receipt.

**rec|re|ance** (rek′rē əns), *n.* = recreancy.

**rec|re|an|cy** (rek′rē ən sē), *n.* **1** = cowardice. **2** unfaithfulness; treason.

**rec|re|ant** (rek′rē ənt), *adj.* **1** lacking courage; cowardly: *a recreant knight who would run in the face of battle.* **SYN**: pusillanimous. **2** unfaithful, as to duty; false; disloyal; traitorous: *The recreant nobles forced King John to sign the Magna Charta.* **SYN**: faithless.
— ***n.*** **1** = coward. **2** = traitor. **SYN**: betrayer.
[< Old French *recreant* (one) confessing himself beaten, present participle of *recreire* to surrender allegiance, yield < Latin *re-* back + *crēdere* entrust (to), believe] — **rec′re|ant|ly**, *adv.*

**rec|re|ate** (rek′rē āt), *v.,* **-at|ed, -at|ing.** — ***v.t.*** to refresh, as with games, pastimes, or exercises.
— ***v.i.*** to take recreation.
[< Latin *recreāre* (with English *-ate¹*) to restore < *re-* again + *creāre* to create]

**re-cre|ate** (rē′krē āt′), *v.t.*, **-at|ed, -at|ing.** to create anew: *to re-create a scene.* [< *re-* + *create*]

**rec|re|a|tion** (rek′rē ā′shən), *n.* play or amusement. Walking, gardening, and reading are quiet forms of recreation. **SYN:** diversion, relaxation.

**re-cre|a|tion** (rē′krē ā′shən), *n.* **1** the act or process of creating anew: *His re-creation of the experiences of the Polonskys . . .* (Saturday Review). **2** a new creation.

**rec|re|a|tion|al** (rek′rē ā′shə nəl), *adj.* of or having to do with recreation: *the recreational facilities of the playground.*

**recreational therapist**, a person who treats disabled persons, guiding them in specific types of recreational activity to promote their rehabilitation.

**recreational vehicle**, a vehicle used for recreational activities, such as a camper, trailer, or dune buggy.

**rec|re|a|tion|ist** (rek′rē ā′shə nist), *n.* a person who is interested or engaged in recreational activities: *There is some fear by recreationists that the oil industry's proposals would spoil beaches* (New York Times).

**recreation room**, a room used for recreational purposes, such as games or dancing.

**rec|re|a|tive** (rek′rē ā′tiv), *adj.* refreshing; restoring.

**re-cre|a|tive** (rē′krē ā′tiv), *adj.* creating anew; re-creating.

**re|cre|a|tor** (rē′krē ā′tər), *n.* a person who creates anew: *Though [he] was thus a little disappointing as a recreator of monumental form, I found his virtues as a meticulous craftsman quite arresting* (New Yorker).

**rec|re|ment** (rek′rə mənt), *n.* **1** a substance which after having been separated from the blood is returned to it; a secretion from one part of the body that is absorbed by another, such as gastric juice. **2** the useless part of a substance; dross. [<French *récrément,* learned borrowing from Latin *recrēmentum* dross <*re-* back + *cernere* to separate, sift]

**rec|re|men|tal** (rek′rə men′təl), *adj.* of or having to do with recrement.

**rec|re|men|ti|tious** (rek′rə men tish′əs), *adj.* **1** consisting of recrement. **2** = useless.

**re|cres|cence** (ri kres′əns), *n.* regrowth, especially of lost parts of an organism.

**re|crim|i|nate** (ri krim′ə nāt), *v.i., v.t.*, **-nat|ed, -nat|ing.** to accuse (someone) in return: *He said she had lied, and she recriminated by saying he had lied too. To criminate and recriminate never yet was the road to reconciliation in difference among men* (Edmund Burke). **SYN:** countercharge. [< Medieval Latin *recriminare* (with English *-ate*[1]) < Latin *re-* again + *crīminārī* accuse < *crīmen, -inis* a charge]

**re|crim|i|na|tion** (ri krim′ə nā′shən), *n.* the act of accusing in return; counter accusation: *The quarreling children were full of recrimination.*

**re|crim|i|na|tive** (ri krim′ə nā′tiv, -nə-), *adj.* involving recrimination; recriminatory. **—re|crim′i-na′tive|ly,** *adv.*

**re|crim|i|na|to|ry** (ri krim′ə nə tôr′ē, -tōr′-), *adj.* of or involving recrimination: *a recriminatory remark.*

**rec room** (rek), *Informal.* recreation room: *We were playing ping-pong in the rec room* (Atlantic).

**re|cross** (rē krôs′, -kros′), *v.t., v.i.* **1** to cross again in returning: *to recross a border.* **2** to cross a second time or anew: *He crossed and recrossed his legs.*

**re|crown** (rē kroun′), *v.t.* to crown again.

**re|cru|desce** (rē′krü des′), *v.i.*, **-desced, -desc|ing.** to break out again; become active again. [< Latin *recrūdēscere* become raw, grow worse < *re-* again + *crūdēscere* become raw < *crūdus* raw]

**re|cru|des|cence** (rē′krü des′əns), *n.* a breaking out afresh; renewed activity: *the recrudescence of an influenza epidemic.* **SYN:** return, recurrence. [<Latin *recrūdēscēns, -entis,* present participle of *recrūdēscere;* see etym. under **recrudesce**]

**re|cru|des|cen|cy** (rē′krü des′ən sē), *n.* = recrudescence.

**re|cru|des|cent** (rē′krü des′ənt), *adj.* breaking out again.

**re|cruit** (ri krüt′), *n., v.* **—*n.*** **1a** a newly enlisted soldier, sailor, or other member of the armed forces: *To have a wholly Regular Army we should need about 100,000 regular recruits, of whom there is no sign* (London Times). **b** *Figurative: The Nature Club needs recruits. Mr. E. H. Machin ("that most enterprising and enlightened recruit to the ranks of theatrical managers")* (Arnold Bennett). **SYN:** novice, tyro. **2** *Archaic.* a fresh supply of something. [<obsolete French *recrute* <*recruter;* see the verb]

**—*v.t.*** **1a** to get (men and women) to join an army, navy, air force, or other branch of the armed forces. **b** to strengthen or supply (any branch of the armed forces) with new personnel. **c** *Figurative: to recruit new students, to recruit teachers for a school. The company is seeking to recruit young new executives.* **2** to increase or maintain the number of: *to recruit a colonial population with new settlers.* **3** to get a sufficient number or amount of; renew; replenish: *Before sailing, we recruited our provisions.* **4** to renew the health, strength, or spirits of; refresh: *The rest and the refreshment of the fruit . . . recruited him, and he moved on languidly* (Cardinal Newman).

**—*v.i.*** **1** to get new men and women for an army, navy, air force, or other branch of the armed forces: *The country's first act would be to recruit for the navy* (Edward Bok). **2** to renew health, strength, or spirits; recuperate: *After that Mr. Scott found it necessary to recruit for two months at Scarborough "with a course of quinine"* (Lytton Strachey). **3** *Archaic. to gain new supplies of anything lost or wasted.*

[<French *recruter* <*recrue* recruit; (literally) new growth <Old French *recroître* < *re-* again + *croître* to grow <Latin *crēscere.* Compare etym. under **crescent.**]

**re|cruit|a|ble** (ri krü′tə bəl), *adj.* that can be recruited: *The club is looking for recruitable members.*

**re|cruit|er** (ri krü′tər), *n.* a person who recruits, especially one who enlists men and women in an army, navy, or air force.

**re|cruit|ment** (ri krüt′mənt), *n.* **1** the act or business of recruiting: (*Figurative.*) *The recruitment and retention of individuals of outstanding ability became an element of national security* (Bulletin of Atomic Scientists). **2** the condition of being recruited.

**re|crys|tal|li|za|tion** (rē′kris tə lə zā′shən), *n.* repeated crystallization of the same substance: *Recrystallization has been found to take place mainly at temperatures near the freezing point ... as is broadly the case with most temperate glaciers* (E. F. Roots).

**re|crys|tal|lize** (rē kris′tə līz), *v.t., v.i.*, **-lized, -liz|ing.** to crystallize again.

**rec. sec.**, recording secretary.

**rect.**, an abbreviation for the following:
**1** receipt.
**2** rectangle.
**3** rectified.
**4** rector.
**5** rectory.

**rec|ta** (rek′tə), *n.* a plural of **rectum.**

**rec|tal** (rek′təl), *adj.* **1** of or having to do with the rectum. **2** near the rectum. **3** for use in the rectum: *a rectal thermometer.*

**rec|tal|ly** (rek′tə lē), *adv.* in or through the rectum.

***rec|tan|gle** (rek′tang′gəl), *n.* a four-sided figure with four right angles. [alteration of Medieval Latin *rectiangulum* <Late Latin, neuter of *rectiangulus* having a right angle <Latin *rēctus* right (<*regere* straighten, rule) + *angulus* angle, corner]

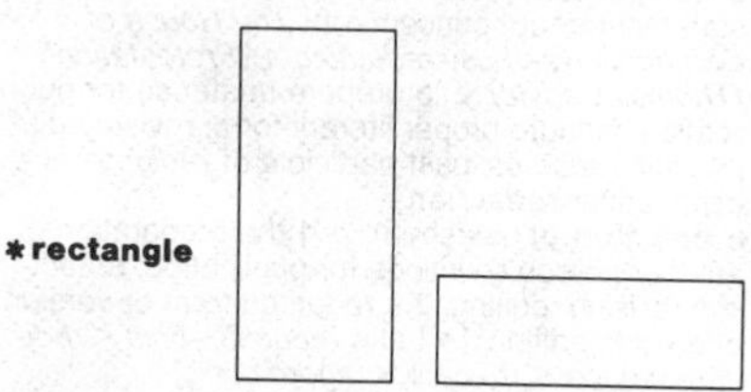

***rectangle**

**rec|tan|gled** (rek′tang′gəld), *adj.* **1** = right-angled. **2** *Heraldry.* formed with right angles or a right angle.

**rec|tan|gu|lar** (rek tang′gyə lər), *adj.* **1** shaped like a rectangle: *a small, rectangular house, almost square.* **2** having one or more right angles. **3** placed at right angles. **—rec|tan′gu|lar|ly,** *adv.* **—rec|tan′gu|lar|ness,** *n.*

**rectangular coordinates**, a system of Cartesian coordinates.

**rec|tan|gu|lar|i|ty** (rek′tang gyə lar′ə tē), *n.* rectangular quality or condition.

**rec|te et re|tro** (rek′tē et rē′trō), *Music, Latin.* **1** to be repeated backward. **2** (literally) right and backward.

**rec|ti** (rek′tī), *n.* plural of **rectus.**

**rec|ti|fi|a|ble** (rek′tə fī′ə bəl), *adj.* that can be rectified.

**rec|ti|fi|ca|tion** (rek′tə fə kā′shən), *n.* the act of rectifying.

**rec|ti|fi|ca|tive** (rek′tə fə kā′tiv), *adj.* rectifying; corrective.

**rec|ti|fi|ca|to|ry** (rek′tə fə kə tôr′ē, -tōr′-), *adj.* = rectificative.

**rec|ti|fi|er** (rek′tə fī′ər), *n.* **1** a person or thing that makes right, corrects, or adjusts. **2** a device for changing alternating current into direct current: *Biggest market for the rare metal is in rectifiers, devices used in radio* (Wall Street Journal).

**rec|ti|fy** (rek′tə fī), *v.t.*, **-fied, -fy|ing. 1** to make right; put right; adjust; remedy: *The storekeeper admitted his mistake and was willing to rectify it. It is ecology again which helps to analyze the situation and rectify it* (F. S. Bodenheimer). **SYN:** correct, amend. **2** to change (an alternating current) into a direct current. **3** to purify or refine: *to rectify a liquor by distilling it several times.* **4** *Geometry.* to determine the length of (a curve, arc, or the like). [< Medieval Latin *rectificare* <Latin *rēctus* right, correct (<*regere* straighten, rule) + *facere* to make]

**rec|ti|lin|e|al** (rek′tə lin′ē əl), *adj.* <rectilinear.

**rec|ti|lin|e|ar** (rek′tə lin′ē ər), *adj.* **1** in a straight line; moving in a straight line: *The simplest kind of displacement of a particle occurs in rectilinear motion, which is motion along a straight line* (Shortley and Williams). **2** forming a straight line. **3** bounded or formed by straight lines: . . . *flat and fertile fields, intensely green, and rectilinear roads edged with poplars, reminiscent of the large, geometric beauty of the Ile de France* (Harper's). **4** characterized by straight lines. [< Late Latin *rectilīneus* (<*rēctus* straight + *līnea* line) +English *-ar*] **—rec′ti|lin′e|ar|ly,** *adv.*

**rec|ti|tude** (rek′tə tüd, -tyüd), *n.* **1** upright conduct or character; honesty; righteousness: *The name of Brutus would be a guaranty to the people of rectitude of intention* (James A. Froude). **SYN:** integrity, virtue. **2** correctness: *rectitude of judgment.* **3** direction in a straight line; straightness. [<Late Latin *rēctitūdō* <Latin *rēctus* straight, correct]

**rec|ti|tu|di|nous** (rek′tə tü′də nəs, -tyü′-), *adj.* morally upright; virtuous: *He has spent 23 years in rectitudinous monogamy* (Time).

**rec|to** (rek′tō), *n., pl.* **-tos.** the right-hand page of an open book: *The title page is always on the right side or the recto, of the leaf; the left side is known as the verso* (Van Allen Bradley). [<Latin (*foliō*) *rēctō* facing (leaf of a book); *rēctō,* ablative of *rēctus* right (hand)]

**rec|to|cele** (rek′tə sēl), *n.* a rectal hernia extending into the vagina. [<*rectum* + Greek *kēlē* tumor, rupture]

**rec|tor** (rek′tər), *n.* **1** a clergyman in the Protestant Episcopal Church or the Church of England who has charge of a parish. **2** a priest in the Roman Catholic Church who has charge of a congregation or religious house. **3** the head of a school, college, or university: *After Jefferson's death in 1826, [Madison] became rector, or president, of the University of Virginia* (Ralph L. Ketcham). **4** the person in control; director. [< Latin *rēctor, -ōris* ruler <*regere* to rule; straighten]

**rec|tor|ate** (rek′tər it), *n.* the position, rank, or term of a rector. [<*rector* + *-ate*[3]]

**rec|to|ri|al** (rek tôr′ē əl, -tōr′-), *adj.* of a rector or a rectory: *rectorial tithes.*

**rec|tor|ship** (rek′tər ship), *n.* = rectorate.

**rec|to|ry** (rek′tər ē, -trē), *n., pl.* **-ries. 1** a rector's house; parsonage. **2** the church living with all its rights, tithes, and lands held by a rector.

**rec|tri|ces** (rek trī′sēz), *n.* plural of **rectrix.**

**rec|trix** (rek′triks), *n., pl.* **-tri|ces.** one of the strong feathers in the tail of a bird. The rectrices serve as a rudder in flight. [<Latin *rēctrīx, -īcis* <*regere* to straighten (because of their use in directing the flight)]

**rec|tum** (rek′təm), *n., pl.* **-ta** or **-tums.** the lowest part of the large intestine, extending from the last curve of the colon to the anus. See diagram under **digestion.** [<New Latin *rectum,* for Latin (*intestīnum*) *rēctum* straight (intestine); *rēctum,* (literally) neuter past participle of *regere* to straighten, rule]

**rec|tus** (rek′təs), *n., pl.* **-ti.** any one of several very straight muscles (as in the abdomen, thigh, and eye). [<New Latin (*musculus*) *rectus* straight (muscle); *rectus,* (literally) past participle of Latin *regere* to straighten, rule]

**re|cu|ler pour mieux sau|ter** (rə kʏ lā′pür myœ sō tā′), *French.* to draw back in order to leap better.

**re|cul|ti|vate** (rē kul′tə vāt), *v.t.*, **-vat|ed, -vat|ing.** to cultivate anew: *to recultivate land, to recultivate a friendship.*

**re|cum|ben|cy** (ri kum′bən sē), *n.* a recumbent position or condition.

**re|cum|bent** (ri kum′bənt), *adj.* **1** lying down; reclining; leaning. **2** *Figurative.* inactive; idle; listless. **3** *Biology.* leaning or resting on anything: *a recumbent plant.* [<Latin *recumbēns, -entis,* present participle of *recumbere* to recline <*re-*

**Pronunciation Key:** hat, āge, cãre, fär; let, ēqual, tėrm; it, īce; hot, ōpen, ôrder; oil, out; cup, pu̇t, rüle; child; long; thin; ᴛʜen; zh, measure; ə represents **a** in about, **e** in taken, **i** in pencil, **o** in lemon, **u** in circus.

back + *-cumbere* to lie down] **—re|cum′bent|ly,** adv.

**re|cu|per|ate** (ri kyü′pə rāt, -kü′-), *v.,* **-at|ed, -at|ing.** *—v.i.* to recover, as from sickness, exhaustion, or loss: *It took him a few days to recuperate after his tonsils were taken out.* *—v.t.* **1** to restore, as to health or strength. **2** to get back; recover; regain: *He recuperated gradually everything he had lost. Some of its heat will be recuperated to produce electric current* (New York Times).
[< Latin *recuperāre* (with English *-ate*[1]), apparently < *re-* back + *capere* to receive, take. See etym. of doublet **recover.**]

**re|cu|per|a|tion** (ri kyü′pə rā′shən, -kü′-), *n.* recovery, such as from sickness or loss.

**re|cu|per|a|tive** (ri kyü′pə rā′tiv, -kü′-), *adj.* **1** of recuperation: *the recuperative powers of youth.* **2** aiding recuperation: *a recuperative rest.* **—re-cu′per|a′tive|ness,** *n.*

**re|cu|per|a|tor** (ri kyü′pə rā′tər, -kü′-), *n.* **1** a person who recovers. **2** a device that utilizes normally waste heat from a furnace to heat incoming air.

**re|cu|per|a|to|ry** (ri kyü′pər ə tôr′ē, -kü′-; -tōr′-), adj. = recuperative.

**re|cur** (ri kėr′), *v.i.,* **-curred, -cur|ring. 1** to come up again; occur again; be repeated: *Leap year recurs every four years. My holiday visits ... seemed to them to recur too often, though I found them few enough* (Charles Lamb). **2** to return in thought or speech: *Old memories often recurred to him. The builder recurred to the matter of the cost of remodeling our house.* SYN: revert. **3** to have recourse; resort: *to recur to an expedient.* [< Latin *recurrere* < *re-* back + *currere* to run]

**re|cur|rence** (ri kėr′əns), *n.* an occurrence again; repetition; return: *More care in the future will prevent recurrence of the mistake.*

**re|cur|rent** (ri kėr′ənt), *adj.* **1** occurring again; repeated; recurring: *recurrent attacks of hay fever, a recurrent mistake.* **2** turned back so as to run in the opposite direction: *a recurrent nerve.* [< Latin *recurrēns, -entis,* present participle of *recurrere;* see etym. under **recur**] **—re|cur′rent|ly,** adv.

**re|cur|ring decimal** (ri kėr′ing), a circulating decimal.

**re|cur|sive** (ri kėr′siv), *adj.* **1** *Mathematics.* recurring; repeated: *recursive functions. The set 2, 4, 6, 8, ... is recursive because all its integers can be described as divisible by two* (Time). **2** capable of being returned to or used repeatedly: *One function Professor Miller considered was the ability to deal with "recursive" programmes, that is, to interrupt a course of action to undertake another— a "subroutine"— and then to interrupt this in turn with the same subroutine, and so on* (New Scientist).
[< Latin *recursus* (past participle of *recurrere* to recur) + English *-ive*] **—re|cur′sive|ly,** *adv.* **—re|cur′sive|ness,** *n.*

**re|cur|vate** (ri kėr′vit, -vāt), *adj.* recurved. [< Latin *recurvātus,* past participle of *recurvāre* < *re-* back + *curvus* curve]

**re|cur|va|ture** (ri kėr′və chùr), *n.* the fact or process of turning back upon a previous direction, usually from a westward path to an eastward one: *the recurvature of the path of a hurricane.*

**re|curve** (ri kėrv′), *v.t., v.i.,* **-curved, -curv|ing.** to curve back; bend back.

**rec|u|san|cy** (rek′yə zən sē, ri kyü′-), *n.* the act or fact of being recusant. SYN: recalcitrance.

**rec|u|sant** (rek′yə zənt, ri kyü′-), *adj., n.* *—adj.* **1** refusing to submit. **2** (formerly) refusing to attend the services of the Church of England or to acknowledge the ecclesiastical supremacy of the Crown.
*—n.* **1** a person who refuses to submit. **2** (formerly) a Roman Catholic who refused to attend the services of the Church of England.
[< Latin *recūsāns, -antis,* present participle of *recūsāre* refuse; see etym. under **recuse**]

**re|cuse** (ri kyüz′), *v.t.,* **-cused, -cus|ing. 1** = reject. **2** *Law.* to reject or challenge (a judge or juror) as disqualified to act. [< Old French *recuser,* learned borrowing from Latin *recūsāre* to refuse, object < *re-* back + *causāre* plead a cause < causa cause]

**re|cut** (rē kut′), *v.t.,* **-cut, -cut|ting.** to cut again.

**rec|vee** (rek′vē′), *n.* *U.S. Informal.* a vehicle used for recreational activities, such as a camper or trailer; recreational vehicle: *The travel trailer is the most popular of all the recvees* (Norman Strung).

**re|cy|cla|ble** (rē sī′klə bəl), *adj.* that can be recycled.

**re|cy|cle** (rē sī′kəl), *v.,* **-cled, -cling,** *n.* *—v.t.* to cause to undergo processes or treatment in order to be used again. Paper, aluminum, and glass are common products that are recycled. *There is nothing in untouched nature to compare with our extravagant use of energy and our failure to recycle essential materials* (Bulletin of Atomic Scientists).
*—v.i.* **1** to go through a cycle again; go through a new cycle: *Falcons often recycle (mate and lay more eggs in season) if the first batch is destroyed* (Nancy Hicks). **2** to put wastes, garbage, or the like, through a cycle of purification and conversion to useful products: *Officials agreed that recycling would have a chance to succeed only if separation of garbage were mandatory.*
*—n.* the act or process of recycling: *Because internal recycle builds up the chemicals, layer upon layer, the granules are spherical in shape* (Scotsman).

**red**[1] (red), *n., adj.,* **red|der, red|dest.** *—n.* **1** the color of blood or of a ruby. Red has the longest light wave in the color spectrum. **2** any shade of that color: *Red is obliged to include many of the browns, which are deep shades of red and hues closely akin to it* (Matthew Luckiesh). **3** a red pigment or dye. **4** red cloth or clothing: *to wear red.* **5** a red or reddish person, animal, or thing. **6** *Informal.* a person with extremely radical political ideas; Red: *He can hardly be called a pink, much less a red* (Time). **7** *U.S. Slang.* secobarbital.
*—adj.* **1** having the color of blood or of a ruby: *red paint, red velvet, red shoes.* **2** being like or suggesting the color of blood: *red hair.* **3** sore; inflamed: *red eyes.* **4** *Figurative.* blushing; flushed: *Tom's face was as red with delight, as his sister's had been with anger* (George Macdonald). **5** red-hot; glowing. **6** of or having to do with the north pole of a magnet. **7** = Red; radical; revolutionary.
**in the red,** *Informal.* in debt; losing money: *Promoter Frank J. Bruen declined to make any further estimates as to what the show would draw or whether there was a chance to save it from going heavily "in the red"* (Baltimore Sun).
**out of the red,** *Informal.* showing a profit: *About 966 copies more and the title will be out of the red* (Publishers' Weekly).
**see red,** *Informal.* to become very angry: *I saw red and before I knew it I had hit him.*
[Old English *rēad*]

**red**[2] (red), *v.t.,* **red, red|ding.** = redd[1].

**Red** (red), *adj., n.* *—adj.* **1** extremely radical; revolutionary. **2** having to do with the Soviet Union or any Communist country: *Red guns from the Chinese mainland lobbed 66 shells on the offshore Quemoy islands* (Wall Street Journal).
*—n.* **1** an extreme radical; revolutionary: *Communists, extreme socialists, and anarchists are often called Reds.* **2** a Communist, especially an inhabitant of the Soviet Union or any Communist country.
[< *red*[1] (the color of the flag of the International Communist Movement)]

**red-,** *prefix.* a form of **re-** in some cases before vowels, as in *redeem, redintegrate.*

**re|dact** (ri dakt′), *v.t.* **1** to draw up or frame (a statement or announcement): *The House of Commons was busy redacting a "Protestation" (Thomas Carlyle).* **2** to prepare (material) for publication; put into proper literary form; revise; edit. [< Latin *redactus,* past participle of *redigere;* see etym. under **redaction**]

**re|dac|tion** (ri dak′shən), *n.* **1** the preparation of another person's writings for publication; redacting; revising; editing. **2** a redacted form or version of a work; edition. [< Latin *redactiō, -ōnis* < *redigere* reduce < *re-* back + *agere* bring]

**re|dac|tor** (ri dak′tər), *n.* a person who redacts; editor.

**red adder,** = copperhead (snake).

**red admiral,** a butterfly having blue-black wings with white spots and red bands.

**red alder, 1** a commercially important hardwood tree of the Pacific Northwest. **2** its reddish-brown wood, used for furniture, cabinetwork, pulp, and woodenware.

**red alert, 1** an alert to warn that an attack by enemy aircraft is imminent, as when hostile aircraft appear in an air defense sector. **2** any state of readiness in the face of imminent danger: *Admissions to London hospitals [due to a flu epidemic] ... totalled slightly over 2,000, above the figure for a similar period during the last hospital "red alert"* (Manchester Guardian Weekly).

**red algae,** a class of characteristically red or purplish, mostly marine, algae, such as carrageen. The color depends on the combination of chlorophyll, red pigment, and in some, blue pigment. *Red algae supply agar-agar, an important substance used in bacteriology laboratories* (Lewis H. Tiffany).

**re|dan** (ri dan′), *n.* a fortification with two walls forming an angle that points outward. [< French *redan,* variant of *redent* a double notching < Latin *re-* again + *dēns, dentis* tooth]

**Red Angus,** any one of a breed of cattle developed from red calves born to black Aberdeen Angus cattle.

**red ant,** any one of various small, reddish ants, such as the Pharaoh's ant.

**red|ar|gue** (red är′gyü), *v.t.,* **-gued, -gu|ing.** *Scottish.* **1** to prove (a person) to be wrong by argument. **2** to prove (a statement or argument) to be false or incorrect. [< Latin *redarguere* disprove < *re-* back + *arguere* to argue]

**red|ar|gu|tion** (red′är gyü′shən), *n.* *Rare.* disproof of a statement or argument; refutation. [< Latin *redargūtiō, -ōnis* < *redarguere* redargue]

**red arsenic,** = realgar.

**red ash,** a variety of ash tree common in the eastern United States.

**red astrachan,** an early variety of apple having a yellowish skin spotted and streaked with red, and a crisp, juicy pulp of rich, acid flavor.

**red-backed mouse** (red′bakt′), = redback vole.

**red-backed sandpiper,** = dunlin.

**red-backed shrike,** a small European shrike, with a chestnut brown back and a gray crown.

***red-backed spider,** a poisonous spider related to the black widow, found in Australia, New Zealand, and the East Indies.

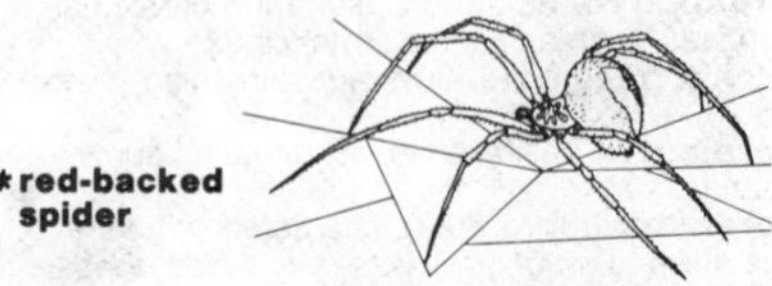

***red-backed spider**

**red|back vole** (red′bak′), any one of a group of voles with reddish fur on the back, found especially in northern regions.

**red-bait** (red′bāt′), *v.i., v.t.* to accuse or harass (a person or persons) with being Communist, usually without sufficient evidence: *In this buffeting from all sides, [he] is pictured as both "red-baiting" and "soft on Communism"* (Time).

**red-bait|er** (red′bā′tər), *n.* a person who is given to red-baiting.

**red|ball** (red′bôl′), *n.* *Railroading.* a fast freight train; hot-shot.

**red bat,** a North American migratory tree bat having reddish fur tipped with white.

**red bay,** an evergreen tree of the eastern and southern United States having dark blue fruit with red stalks and bluish-green leaves. It belongs to the laurel family.

**red beds,** *Geology.* a series of deep-red, sandy, sedimentary strata of the Permian or Triassic periods, often containing gypsum or salt deposits. It is a conspicuous formation in the Rocky Mountains.

**red beet,** the common beet.

**red-bel|lied terrapin** (red′bel′ēd), a large turtle with a reddish shell and abdomen, found along the Atlantic coast of the United States.

**red-bellied woodpecker,** a woodpecker of the eastern United States having black-and-white bars across the back of the head. The male red-bellied woodpecker also has red on the crown and the abdomen.

**red-billed tropic bird** (red′bild′), a white tropic bird with a bright orange-red bill. It is found throughout the warmer parts of the Atlantic and Pacific oceans.

**red birch,** = river birch.

**red|bird** (red′bėrd′), *n.* any one of several birds with red feathers, such as the cardinal, the scarlet tanager, the summer tanager, or the European bullfinch.

**red-blind** (red′blīnd′), *adj.* unable to distinguish the color red. **—red′-blind′ness,** *n.*

**red blood cell** or **corpuscle,** = red corpuscle.

**red-blood|ed** (red′blud′id), *adj.* full of life and spirit; virile; vigorous: *It is a fight which should fire the hearts of all red-blooded Americans and stir their wills to action* (Newsweek).

**red board,** *Railroading.* a signal to stop.

**red|bone** (red′bōn′), *n.* *U.S.* a hound with a red or reddish coat, used especially for hunting raccoons and boars.

**Red Branch,** (in Celtic legend) the group of heroes and warriors that included Cuchulainn. The feats of the Red Branch are described in the Ulster cycle.

**red brass,** an alloy of copper and zinc, with more copper than in the normal composition of brass; low brass; tombac.

**red|breast** (red′brest′), *n.* **1** = robin. **2** a small shore bird with a reddish breast in its spring plumage; knot.

**red-breast|ed bream** (red′bres′tid), a sunfish of the eastern United States with a reddish belly.

**red-breasted merganser,** a variety of merganser with a long crest and, in the male, white collar and reddish-brown breast, most common in marine waters of the Northern Hemisphere.

**red-breasted nuthatch,** a small nuthatch with reddish underparts, found in forested areas of northern North America.

**red-breasted sapsucker**, a sapsucker of the Pacific coast of North America. The adult of both sexes has the crown, throat, and breast entirely red.

**red|brick** (red′brik′), *adj., n. British.* —*adj.* of or having to do with a university other than Oxford or Cambridge: *Thus the prospects are not very bright for an ordinary man holding a B.Sc. gained at a redbrick university, however good he is* (New Scientist).
—*n.* Also, **Redbrick**. **1** a university other than Oxford or Cambridge. **2** a student or graduate of such a university: *Of the 175 University men, some 100, or 57 per cent, are Redbricks* (London Times).
[so called because of the buildings of red brick often characterizing the later universities, especially of the 1800's]

**red|bud** (red′bud′), *n.* any one of various North American trees or shrubs of the pea family, bearing many small, pink, budlike flowers early in the spring; Judas tree.

**red|bug** (red′bug′), *n.* **1** = chigger: *Chiggers, called redbugs down South, cause the most exquisite itching* (Science News Letter). **2** = cotton stainer.

**red cabbage**, a variety of cabbage with deep-purple leaves which become reddish when cooked.

**red|cap** (red′kap′), *n.* **1** a porter at a railroad station or bus station. He usually wears a red cap as part of his uniform. *No redcaps were in sight and Sam had two bags* (Harper's). **2** *British Slang.* a military policeman. He wears a hat with a red band as part of his uniform. **3** = European goldfinch.

**Red|cap** (red′kap′), *n.* any one of an English breed of chickens with a rose comb and black, brown, and deep-red plumage.

**red carpet**, a carpet laid down for royalty or other notable persons to walk on when being received formally or given preferential treatment.
**roll out the red carpet**, to receive or treat royally or preferentially by or as if by laying down a red carpet: *The hotel rolled out the red carpet for the President.*

**red-car|pet** (red′kär′pit), *adj.* royal or preferential; favored: *The visiting premier received red-carpet treatment.*

**red caviar**, salmon roe eaten as a delicacy.

**red cedar**, **1** any one of several varieties of North American juniper. **2** the wood, used especially in making pencils and for interior finishing. **3** = giant arbor vitae.

**red cell**, = red corpuscle.

**red cent**, *U.S. Informal.* a copper cent. It is no longer current.
**not worth a red cent**, worthless: *His advice about gardening wasn't worth a red cent.*

**Red Chamber**, the Senate of the Canadian Parliament.

**Red Chinese**, **1** the natives or inhabitants of Red China (the People's Republic of China, a Communist state). **2** of or having to do with Red China or its people: *the Red Chinese regime.*

**red clay**, *Geology.* a reddish-brown mud that covers the ocean bottoms at depths below 12,000 feet. It consists of very fine particles of volcanic ash, mica, quartz, pumice, and meteoritic material.

**red clover**, a species of clover that has rounded heads of reddish-purple flowers, cultivated as food especially for horses and cattle, and as a cover crop. It is the state flower of Vermont.

**red|coat** (red′kōt′), *n.* (in former times) a British soldier. During the American Revolution, a red coat was worn by most infantry and certain other regiments. *The redcoats are abroad ... these English must be looked to* (James Fenimore Cooper).

**red-cock|ad|ed woodpecker** (red′ko kā′did), a woodpecker of the southern United States having black-and-white bars across the back and white cheeks.

**red coral**, = precious coral.

**red corpuscle**, one of the tiny, red-colored cells in the blood, formed in bone marrow and containing hemoglobin, that carries oxygen from the lungs to the tissues of the body; red cell; red blood cell; erythrocyte. See diagram under **corpuscle**.

**Red Crescent**, the Moslem counterpart of the Red Cross.

**red cross**, a red Greek cross on a white ground, the emblem of the Red Cross.

**Red Cross**, **1** an international organization to care for the sick and wounded in war and to relieve suffering caused by floods, fire, diseases, and other calamities. In most countries, its badge is a red cross on a white background. In most Moslem countries the badge is a red crescent on a white background. **2** a national society that is a branch of this organization. **3** the cross of Saint George, England's national emblem.

**red crossbill**, a variety of crossbill of northern North America and the Appalachians, the male of which has dull-red plumage.

**red currant**, a European currant with red fruit, used in jams, jellies, and wine. It is less sharp in flavor than the black currant.

**redd**[1] (red), *v.t.*, **redd, redd|ing.** *Dialect.* to clear; clean; tidy. Also, **red.** [apparently Old English *rǣdan* arrange, put in order]

**redd**[2] (red), *n.* **1** the spawn of fish and frogs. **2** a nest made by a fish in which to spawn. [origin uncertain]

**red deer**, **1** a deer with reddish fur, about four feet high, native to the forests of Europe and Asia, and formerly very abundant in England. **2** the common deer of America in its summer coat.

**red|den** (red′ən), *v.t.* to make red. **SYN**: ruddy.
—*v.i.* **1** to become red. **2** *Figurative.* to blush.

**red|den|dum** (re den′dəm), *n., pl.* **-da** (-də). *Law.* a reservation in a deed giving the grantor a new share of a previous grant. [< Latin *reddendum*, neuter gerundive of *reddere;* see etym. under **render**]

**red|dish** (red′ish), *adj.* somewhat red. —**red′dish|ness**, *n.*

**reddish egret**, a grayish heron of the West Indies, Mexico, and the Gulf States with a cinnamon head and neck. There is also a pure white color phase.

**red|dle** (red′əl), *n., v.t.*, **-dled, -dling.** = raddle[2].

**red|dled** (red′əld), *adj.* = raddled.

**red|dle|man** (red′əl man), *n., pl.* **-men.** = raddleman.

**red dog**, **1** the lowest grade of flour produced in milling. **2** a mixture of slate, ash, and waste from a coal mine, used sometimes in surfacing temporary roads. **3** a card game in which each player bets on his ability to show a card from his hand of the same suit but higher than the one turned up from the remaining cards in the deck. **4** *Football Slang.* the defensive tactic of red-dogging; blitz.

**red-dog** (red′dôg′, -dog′), *v.t., v.i.* **-dogged, -dog|ging.** *Football Slang.* to pursue and harass (the passer); blitz.

**red drum** or **drumfish**, a large drumfish of the Atlantic Coast of North America.

**Red Duster**, = Red Ensign.

**red dwarf**, one of a group of faint stars of the main-sequence group having a cooler temperature and lower luminosity than the others.

**rede** (rēd), *v.*, **red|ed, red|ing,** *n. Archaic or Dialect.* —*v.t.* **1** to give counsel to; advise. **2** to interpret; explain. **3** to tell.
—*n.* **1** advice. **2** a story. **3** an interpretation. **4** a plan.
[Middle English *reden* Old English *rǣdan.* Compare etym. under **read**[1].]

**re|deal** (rē dēl′), *v.*, **-dealt, -deal|ing,** *n.* —*v.i., v.t.* to deal again.
—*n.* a dealing again; new deal.

**red-ear sunfish** (red′ir′), a small freshwater sunfish of the southeastern United States, having a reddish gill covering.

**re|de|ceive** (rē′di sēv′), *v.t.*, **-ceived, -ceiv|ing.** to deceive again.

**re|de|cide** (rē′di sīd′), *v.t.*, **-cid|ed, -cid|ing.** to decide again.

**re|dec|o|rate** (rē dek′ə rāt), *v.t., v.i.*, **-rat|ed, -rat|ing.** to decorate (as a room or building) again or anew, especially by painting or papering. —**re′dec|o|ra′tion**, *n.*

**re|ded|i|cate** (rē ded′ə kāt), *v.t.*, **-cat|ed, -cat|ing.** to dedicate anew: *Those who ... have rededicated themselves unto the Lord* (Charles Haddon Spurgeon).

**re|ded|i|ca|tion** (rē′ded ə kā′shən), *n.* the act of dedicating anew: *There was a rededication service at the church* (London Daily News).

**re|deem** (ri dēm′), *v.t.* **1** to buy back: *The property on which the money was lent was redeemed when the loan was paid back.* **SYN**: regain. **2** to pay off: *He redeemed the debt.* **3** to make up for; balance: *A very good feature will sometimes redeem several bad ones.* **4** to carry out; make good; fulfill: *We redeem a promise by doing what we said we would.* **5** to set free; rescue; save: *to be redeemed from sin. Like some merchant who, in storm, Throws the freight over to redeem the ship* (Robert Browning). **SYN**: liberate, deliver, release. **6** to reclaim (land): *a tract redeemed from the sea* (Thomas Hardy). [< Latin *redimere* < *re-* back + *emere* to buy]

**re|deem|a|bil|i|ty** (ri dē′mə bil′ə tē), *n.* redeemable quality or state.

**re|deem|a|ble** (ri dē′mə bəl), *adj.* **1** that can be redeemed. **2** that will be redeemed or paid: *These bonds are redeemable in five years.* —**re|deem′a|ble|ness**, *n.* —**re|deem′a|bly**, *adv.*

**re|deem|er** (ri dē′mər), *n.* a person who redeems.

**Re|deem|er** (ri dē′mər), *n.* Jesus Christ, the Saviour of the world.

**re|deem|ing** (ri dē′ming), *adj.* that redeems; saving: *a redeeming feature.*

**re|de|fect** (rē′di fekt′), *v.t.* to forsake again; defect afresh.

**re|de|fec|tion** (rē′di fek′shən), *n.* the act of defecting or deserting again. The desertion by a political refugee of the country in which he found asylum and his return to his original country is redefection. *The young Russians had no words to explain their redefection* (Time).

**re|de|fec|tor** (rē′di fek′tər), *n.* a person who commits a redefection.

**re|de|fine** (rē′di fīn′), *v.t.*, **-fined, -fin|ing.** to define again: *One of the ancient terms it might be well to revive and redefine* (William Minto).

**re|def|i|ni|tion** (rē′def ə nish′ən), *n.* the act or process of redefining: *The whole tenor of his labors was towards an assertion, purification, and redefinition of Transcendentalism* (David Masson).

**re|de|liv|er** (rē′di liv′ər), *v.t.* **1** to deliver back; return. **2** to deliver again.

**re|de|mand** (rē′di mand′, -mänd′), *v., n.* —*v.t.* **1** to demand back. **2** to demand again.
—*n.* a redemanding.

**re|dem|on|strate** (rē dem′ən strāt), *v.t.*, **-strat|ed, -strat|ing.** to demonstrate again.

**re|demp|tion** (ri demp′shən), *n.* **1** the act of redeeming or state of being redeemed; buying back; paying off: *Redemption of his mortgage took the farmer many years.* **2** = ransom: *The Austrians set the redemption of England's King Richard at many hundreds of English pounds.* **3** deliverance; rescue: *The floating board provided the sailor's redemption from drowning.* **4** deliverance from sin; salvation: *The minister worked hard to save drunks and gamblers whom the rest of us thought were beyond redemption.* [< Latin *redēmptiō, -ōnis* < *redimere;* see etym. under **redeem**. See etym. of doublet **ransom.**]

**re|demp|tion|al** (ri demp′shə nəl), *adj.* of or having to do with redemption.

**re|demp|tion|er** (ri demp′shə nər), *n.* one of the early emigrants to America, who gave the right to his services for a certain time in payment for his passage.

**Re|demp|tion|ist** (ri demp′shə nist), *n.* a member of the Roman Catholic Order of the Holy Trinity; Trinitarian.

**re|demp|tive** (ri demp′tiv), *adj.* serving to redeem.

**re|demp|tor** (ri demp′tər), *n.* = redeemer.

**Re|demp|tor|ist** (ri demp′tər ist), *n.* a member of the Congregation of the Most Holy Redeemer, a Roman Catholic order founded in Italy in 1732 and devoted to work among the poor. [< French *rédemptoriste* < Latin *redēmptor, -ōris* (< *redimere;* see etym. under **redeem**) + French *-iste* -ist]

**re|demp|to|ry** (ri demp′tər ē), *adj.* = redemptive.

**re|demp|tress** (ri demp′tris), *n.* a woman redeemer.

**re|demp|trix** (ri demp′triks), *n., pl.* **-demp|trix|es, -demp|tri|ces** (-demp′tri sēz). = redemptress.

**Red Ensign** or **red ensign**, **1** the form of the national flag of Great Britain used as an ensign by merchant ships, consisting of a red flag with the Union Jack in the upper corner close to the flagstaff. **2** (until 1965) the flag of Canada, consisting of a red flag containing the national arms of Canada, with the Union Jack in the upper corner close to the flagstaff. It has been replaced by a flag with a red maple leaf centered on a white background, and flanked by two broad, vertical, red bars.

**re|de|ny** (rē′di nī′), *v.t.*, **-nied, -ny|ing.** to deny again.

**re|de|ploy** (rē′di ploi′), *v.t.* **1** to change the position of (troops) from one theater of war to another: *At the same time, he will redeploy French forces for even more effective action against the rebel guerrillas* (Newsweek). **2** to move (anything or anyone) from one place or area to another: *to redeploy capital or funds towards the export trades. The Ministry of Labour, for example, is ... redeploying thousands of workers who have never been forced to contemplate a move before* (Manchester Guardian Weekly). —*v.i.* to undergo redeployment; be redeployed. —**re′de|ploy′ment**, *n.*

**re|de|pos|it** (rē′di poz′it), *v., n.* —*v.t.* to deposit again.
—*n.* a new deposit.

**re|dep|o|si|tion** (rē′dep ə zish′ən, -dē pə-), *n.* **1** the act of redepositing. **2** the state or condition

---

**Pronunciation Key:** hat, āge, cãre, fär; let, ēqual, tėrm; it, īce; hot, ōpen, ôrder; **oi**l, **ou**t; cup, pu̇t, rüle; **ch**ild; lo**ng**; **th**in; **ᴛʜ**en; **zh**, measure;
ə represents **a** in about, **e** in taken, **i** in pencil, **o** in lemon, **u** in circus.

of being redeposited: *Changes ... brought about by the deposition, removal, and redeposition of gravel, sand, and fine sediment* (Charles Lyell).

**re|de|scend** (rē′di send′), *v.i., v.t.* to descend again.

**re|de|scent** (rē′di sent′), *n.* a descending or falling again.

**re|de|scribe** (rē′di skrīb′), *v.t.*, **-scribed, -scrib|ing.** to describe a second time; describe again.

**re|de|sign** (rē′di zīn′), *v., n.* —*v.t.* to design again: *The t does not look well: I shall have to redesign it* (William Morris).
—*n.* **1** the act or process of redesigning: *There is still considerable scope for increasing the Caravelle's payload, but no prospect for improving its speed without a complete redesign of wing* (New Scientist). **2** a new design: *It's just a coincidence that large-scale redesigns ... are coming up at a time when the industry woefully needs some help* (Wall Street Journal).

**re|des|ig|nate** (rē dez′ig nāt), *v.t.*, **-nat|ed, -nat|ing.** to designate again.

**re|de|ter|mine** (rē′di tėr′mən), *v.t.*, **-mined, -min|ing.** to determine again: *To redetermine their boundaries after the subsidence of the flood* (John W. Draper). —**re′de|ter′mi|na′tion,** *n.*

**re|de|vel|op** (rē′di vel′əp), *v.t.* **1** to develop again. **2** *Photography.* to put into a second developer after bleaching to tone the image. **3** to improve (land or buildings), especially by rebuilding: *Eight downtown blocks now have been cleared and 7 million dollars are being spent to redevelop them for a parkway* (Newsweek). —*v.i.* to develop again.

**re|de|vel|op|er** (rē′di vel′ə pər), *n.* a person, thing, or company that redevelops land or buildings: *The federal government will then lend the locality the money it needs to acquire and clear blighted land for subsequent sale to private redevelopers* (Harper's).

**re|de|vel|op|ment** (rē′di vel′əp mənt), *n.* **1** the act or process of redeveloping. **2** the condition of being redeveloped.

**red|eye** (red′ī′), *n.* **1** any one of various fishes with reddish eyes, such as: **a** a cyprinoid fish with a red iris; rudd. **b** a blue-spotted freshwater sunfish of the eastern United States. **c** = rock bass. **2** = red-eyed vireo. **3** = copperhead. **4** *U.S. Slang.* strong, cheap whiskey.

**red-eyed** (red′īd′), *adj.* **1** having a red iris: *At his feet sat a white-coated, red-eyed dog* (Dickens). **2** having eyes surrounded by a red ring, as some birds: *The red-eyed flycatcher is an inhabitant of the whole of our forests* (James Audubon). **3** having the eyes reddened, as by tears, lack of sleep, or excessive fatigue: *Before it's all over, negotiators and labor reporters will be weary and red-eyed* (Newsweek).

**red-eyed towhee,** the common towhee of eastern North America.

**red-eyed vireo,** a large vireo of temperate North America with white underparts and a white stripe over the eye.

**redeye gravy,** *U.S.* gravy made from the grease of fried meat, especially ham: *She had been raised on corn dodgers and redeye gravy* (Time).

**red-faced** (red′fāst′), *adj.* **1** having a red face: *The stout, red-faced Dutch plantation owner ...* (Wall Street Journal). **2** flushed as with embarrassment or anger: *[He] retorted with a blistering lecture about the ethics of business and government, and sent them away red-faced with shock* (Newsweek). —**red′-faced′ly,** *adv.*

**red fescue,** a grass with small, reddish spikelets grown for pasture and used in lawns: *A good lawn mixture should also include red fescues* (Science News Letter).

**red|field|i|a** (red fēl′dē ə), *n.* a tall grass, with a loose, diversely spreading flower cluster, found in sandy parts of the western United States. [< New Latin *Redfieldia* the genus name < John H. *Redfield,* 1815-1895, an American botanist]

**Red|field's grass** (red′fēldz), = redfieldia.

**red|fin** (red′fin′), *n.* any one of various small, freshwater, cyprinoid fishes with reddish fins, as the shiner.

**red fir,** **1** any one of various firs of the western United States, especially a variety of Oregon, California, and Nevada growing to a height of over 200 feet. **2** their reddish wood. **3** = Douglas fir.

**red fire,** a chemical preparation that burns with a red light, used especially in fireworks and signals.

**red|fish** (red′fish′), *n., pl.* **-fish|es** or (*collectively*) **-fish. 1** = sockeye salmon. **2** = rosefish. **3** = red drum.

**red flag,** **1** a symbol of rebellion, revolution, etc. **2** a sign of danger. **3** *Figurative.* any thing that stirs up anger.

**red-foot|ed booby** (red′fu̇t′id), a gull-like sea bird about the size of a small goose, which lives on tropical islands.

**red fox,** **1** the common reddish fox of North America. **2** any one of various reddish foxes of Europe, Africa, and Asia. **3** the reddish fur of a fox.

**red fuming nitric acid,** a highly corrosive and unstable form of nitric acid used in combination with aniline in rocket fuels.

**red giant,** *Astronomy.* a star of great size and brightness which has a comparatively cool surface temperature.

**red grouper,** a grouper, often of a reddish color, found along the southern Atlantic coast as far as Brazil.

**red grouse,** a variety of grouse of Great Britain and Ireland that does not turn white in winter.

**Red Guard,** a member of a mass movement of young Chinese communists proclaiming rigid adherence to Maoist doctrines. The Red Guard were at the forefront of the Chinese cultural revolution of 1966-67.

**Red Guard|ism** (gär′diz əm), the movement of the Chinese Red Guards.

**red gum**[1], **1** any one of several Australian eucalyptus trees which yield a reddish gum, used as an astringent and for coughs. **2** = sweet gum. [< *red*[1] + *gum*[1]]

**red gum**[2], a reddish eruption of the skin affecting infants; strophulus. [alteration of earlier *red-gownd,* or *red-gowm,* apparently < *red*[1] + obsolete *gound* foul matter, Old English *gund* matter, pus; spelling influenced by *gum*[1]]

**red-haired** (red′hãrd′), *adj.* having red hair.

**red-hand** (red′hand′), *adj. Scottish.* red-handed.

**red-hand|ed** (red′han′did), *adv., adj.* **1** in the very act of committing a crime or mischief: *a man caught red-handed in robbery.* **2** having hands red with blood. —**red′-hand′ed|ly,** *adv.* —**red′-hand′ed|ness,** *n.*

**red hat,** **1** a cardinal's hat. **2** the position or rank of a cardinal. **3** a cardinal.

**Red|ha|ven** (red′hā′vən), *n.* a variety of freestone peach grown in the United States.

**red haw,** **1** = downy hawthorn. **2** any hawthorn.

**red|head** (red′hed′), *n.* **1** a person having red hair. **2** a kind of North American duck of the same genus as and resembling the canvasback but with a grayer body. The adult male has a reddish-brown head. **3** = redheaded woodpecker.

**red|head|ed** (red′hed′id), *adj.* **1** having red hair. **2** having a red head.

**redheaded woodpecker,** a black-and-white North American woodpecker with a bright-red head and neck.

**red heat,** **1** the condition of being red-hot. **2** the accompanying temperature.

**red herring,** **1** the common smoked herring. **2** something used to draw attention away from the real issue.

**red hind,** a kind of olive-colored grouper with red spots. It is an important food fish of the Caribbean.

**red|horse** (red′hôrs′), *n.* any one of various large suckers with red fins, found in lakes and rivers of North America.

**red-hot** (red′hot′), *adj., n. Informal.* —*adj.* **1** red with heat; very hot: *a red-hot iron.* **2** *Figurative.* **a** excited; violent: *a red-hot fanatic.* **b** enthusiastic; spirited: *a red-hot football team, a streak of red-hot pitching and batting.* **3** *Figurative.* fresh from the source: *red-hot rumors.*
—*n.* **1** Also, **red hot.** *U.S. Slang.* a frankfurter. **2** *U.S.* **a** a person who is enthusiastic or excited about something: *The lads like sports but aren't red hots* (San Francisco Chronicle). **b** a violent radical.

**red-hot poker,** **1** any African plant of a group of the lily family with tall, slender spikes of red and yellow flowers. **2** the flower of any of these plants.

**re|di|a** (rē′dē ə), *n., pl.* **-di|ae** (-dē ē). a larval stage in many trematodes, hatched from eggs formed in the sporocyst, and in turn developing into a cercaria: *Each redia has a small mouth, a muscular pharynx, and a simple intestine* (London Times). [< New Latin *redia* < Francesco *Redi,* an Italian naturalist of the 1600's]

**re|did** (rē did′), *v.* the past tense of **redo:** *We redid it as a collection of short stories* (Newsweek).

**re|dif|fu|sion** (rē′di fyü′zhən), *n.* **1** the act of rediffusing. **2** the state or condition of being rediffused.

**re|di|gest** (rē′də jest′, -dī-), *v.t.* to digest again: *Kant ate up all Hume and redigested him* (David Masson).

**red Indian,** a North American Indian: *I have always understood that the pipe originated among the red Indians of North America* (Sunday Times).
► See **American Indian** for usage note.

*** red|in|gote** (red′ing gōt), *n.* **1** an outer coat with long skirts overlapping in front, formerly worn by men. **2** a somewhat similar coat now worn by women, sometimes forming part of a dress: *Veneziani's redingote, to be worn over a dress or as a dress, is reproduced in black cotton faille* (New Yorker). [< French *redingote* < English *riding coat*]

*** redingote**
definitions 1, 2

definition 1

definition 2

**red ink,** **1** ink having a red color, used in bookkeeping for recording debit items and balances. **2** *U.S., Figurative.* financial loss; deficit: *Colleges battle red ink with a scattering of tuition fee hikes* (Wall Street Journal). —**red′-ink′,** *adj.*

**red|in|te|grate** (red in′tə grāt), *v.*, **-grat|ed, -grat|ing.** *Archaic.* —*v.t.* to make whole again; restore to a perfect state; renew; reestablish.
—*v.i.* to become whole again; be renewed.
[< Latin *redintegrāre* (with English *-ate*[1]) < *re-* again + *integrāre* make whole, renew < *integer* whole. Compare etym. under **integer.**]

**red|in|te|gra|tion** (red′in tə grā′shən), *n.* **1** restoration; renewal; reestablishment: *A redintegration of love began to take place between the Colonel and his relatives in Park Lane* (Thackeray). **2** *Psychology.* the tendency of elements once combined as parts of a single mental state to recall or suggest one another at a later time.

**red|in|te|gra|tive** (red in′tə grā′tiv), *adj.* of or having to do with redintegration.

**red|in|te|gra|tor** (red in′tə grā′tər), *n.* a person or thing that redintegrates.

**re|di|rect** (rē′də rekt′, -dī-), *v., adj., n.* —*v.t.* to direct again or anew.
—*adj. Law.* of or having to do with a second examination of a witness by the party calling him, after cross-examination.
—*n. Law.* such a second examination.

**re|di|rec|tion** (rē′də rek′shən, -dī-), *n.* the act or process of redirecting.

**re|dis|count** (rē dis′kount), *v., n.* —*v.t.* to discount again; discount (a bill of exchange) for another, who has already discounted it.
—*n.* **1** the act of rediscounting. **2** *Informal.* a commercial paper that has been rediscounted.

**re|dis|count|a|ble** (rē dis′koun tə bəl), *adj.* that can be rediscounted: *rediscountable bills of exchange.*

**rediscount rate,** the rate of discount charged by a Federal Reserve Bank on loans to commercial member banks.

**re|dis|cov|er** (rē′dis kuv′ər), *v.t.* to discover again or anew. —**re′dis|cov′er|er,** *n.*

**re|dis|cov|er|y** (rē′dis kuv′ər ē, -kuv′rē), *n., pl.* **-er|ies.** the act or process of discovering again.

**re|dis|lo|ca|tion** (rē′dis lō kā′shən), *n.* **1** repeated dislocation. **2** *Medicine.* dislocation recurring after reduction.

**re|dis|pose** (rē′dis pōz′), *v.t.*, **-posed, -pos|ing. 1** to dispose or adjust again. **2** = rearrange.

**re|dis|po|si|tion** (rē′dis pə zish′ən), *n.* **1** the act or process of disposing or adjusting again. **2** = rearrangement.

**re|dis|solve** (rē′di zolv′), *v.t., v.i.*, **-solved, -solv|ing.** to dissolve again.

**re|dis|till** (rē′dis til′), *v.t.* to distill again.

**re|dis|til|late** (rē′dis′tə lāt), *n.* something that is produced by a second or repeated distillation.

**re|dis|til|la|tion** (rē dis′tə lā′shən), *n.* the act or process of redistilling.

**re|dis|trib|ute** (rē′dis trib′yüt), *v.t.*, **-ut|ed, -ut|ing.** to distribute again or anew.

**re|dis|tri|bu|tion** (rē′dis trə byü′shən), *n.* a distribution made again or anew: *The first and most popular measure in an agrarian society usually calls for the expropriation and redistribution of land* (Preston E. James).

**re|dis|tri|bu|tion|al** (rē′dis trə byü′shə nəl), *adj.* of or having to do with redistribution.

**re|dis|trib|u|tive** (rē′dis trib′yə tiv), *adj.* = redistributional.

**re|dis|trict** (rē dis′trikt), —*v.t., v.i. U.S.* to divide into districts again, often for voting purposes: *to redistrict a state or county. A "radical redistricting" of school zones ... would provide in each school a percentage quota of Negroes and whites in direct ratio to the racial breakdown of the whole community* (Saturday Review). *New*

*York need not redistrict* (New York Times). [American English < *re-* again + *district,* verb]

**re|di|vide** (rē′də vīd′), *v.t., v.i.,* **-vid|ed, -vid|ing.** to divide again: *The Empire was redivided, and territorially reorganized* (Cornelius C. Felton).

**red|i|vi|vus** (red′ə vī′vəs), *adj.* alive again; restored; renewed. [< Latin *redivīvus* < *re-* again + *vīvus* living, alive]

**Red Jamaica,** a small, red-skinned variety of banana grown in the Caribbean region.

**red jasmine,** a tropical American shrub or tree of the same family as the dogbane, with large, fragrant red flowers; frangipani.

**red kangaroo,** a large, reddish kangaroo of Australia. It is one of the largest marsupials in existence, standing nearly seven feet tall.

**red lattice,** *Obsolete.* **1** a lattice painted red, formerly the sign of an alehouse. **2** = alehouse.

**red lead,** a red oxide of lead, used in paint, in making cement for pipes, and in making glass; minium. *A variety of red lead, "orange mineral," is used in making red paint, printing ink and dipping paint* (W. R. Jones). *Formula:* $Pb_3O_4$

**red lead ore,** = crocoite.

**red|leg** (red′leg'), *n.* an infectious disease of frogs, usually prevalent in the fall, characterized by hemorrhagic congestion of the legs and abdomen.

**red-leg|ged widow** (red′leg'id, -legd'), = red widow.

**red-let|ter** (red′let′ər), *adj.* **1** memorable; especially happy: *Graduation is a red-letter day in one's life.* **SYN:** notable. **2** marked by red letters.

**red light, 1** a red traffic signal which indicates that vehicles or pedestrians should stop. **2** any sign or signal of danger or warning. **3** a children's game of tag. One player turns his back and counts to ten while the others try to advance and tag him before he reaches ten and calls "red light."

**red-light** (red′līt′), *adj.* **1** having a red light or lights. **2** characterized by many brothels and disorderly places: *a red-light district.*

**red|line** (red′līn'), *v.,* **-lined, -lin|ing.** *U.S.* — ***v.t.*** **1** to cross out with, or as with, a red line; cancel: *to redline an item on a list.* **2** to exclude or discriminate against, especially by charging higher rates or refusing to grant mortgages or loans: *When banks redline a blighted area and shut off investment ...* (Harper's). **3a** to set a recommended limit on the speed of (an airplane). **b** to stop from flying; ground.— ***v.i.*** **1** to subject an area or community to economic discrimination: *Refusing to insure homes in a poor neighborhood is a form of redlining.* **2** to fly an airplane according to a recommended speed.

**red|ly** (red′lē), *adv.* with a red color or glow: *The blaze was redly reflected in the waters of the strait* (George Borrow).

**red man,** = American Indian.

**Red Man,** *U.S.* a member of the Improved Order of Red Men, a fraternal society.

**red mangrove,** a mangrove with a round top and thick oval leaves that grows along the coasts from Florida to northern South America. Its wood is used for wharf piles and fuel, and its bark for tanning hides and making dyes.

**red maple, 1** any one of several varieties of maple tree with reddish-brown wood and bright-red flowers that appear in the spring before the leaves, especially a large maple of eastern North America. **2** the wood of any one of these trees, used in cabinetwork.

**Red Mass,** a Mass celebrated in the Roman Catholic Church in honor of the Holy Ghost. The officiating priests wear red vestments.

**red meat,** a meat that is red when raw. Red meat includes beef, veal, pork, mutton, and lamb.

**red mite,** any one of several mites of a reddish color that are serious pests of citrus fruit.

**red mud, 1** = red clay. **2** residue of impurities, such as silicone oxide and iron oxide resulting from the processing of alumina.

**red mulberry,** a medium-sized mulberry of the eastern United States, having large, dark-green leaves and purplish fruit.

**red mullet,** any one of a group of reddish fishes valued as food.

**red|neck** (red′nek'), *n. U.S. Slang.* a poor, white, Southern farmer or sharecropper (often used in an unfriendly way).

**red-necked** (red′nekt′), *adj. U.S. Slang.* excitable; ill-tempered; angry.

**red-necked grebe,** = Holboell's grebe.

**red-necked wallaby,** a large, reddish and gray wallaby that lives largely in New South Wales.

**red|ness** (red′nis), *n.* the quality of being red; red color.

**red nightshade,** = pokeweed.

**red nose,** a disease of the upper respiratory tract of cattle; mucosal disease.

**Red No. 2,** an artificial coloring agent derived from coal tar, widely used in foods and cosmetics until banned in the United States as a possible carcinogen: *Belgium and Sweden have also restricted use of Red No. 2, but it is still used in many countries* (Vernon L. Sorenson).

**re|do** (*v.* rē dü′; *n.* rē′dü'), *v.,* **-did, -done, -do|ing,** *n.* — ***v.t.*** to do again; do over: *He ... ends by redoing the work of all of them* (Atlantic).
— ***n.*** **1** the act or process of redoing. **2** something redone; rehash: *... a redo of yesteryear's thumping theatrics* (R. E. Shepard).

**red oak, 1** any one of various North American oaks with hard, reddish-brown, coarse-grained wood. **2** the wood of any of these trees.

**red ocher,** an earthy, reddish hematite; raddle.

**red oil,** a dark, reddish-brown substance distilled from the leaves and tops of the female hemp plant and containing about 20% tetrahydrocannabinol, the intoxicating principle in marijuana.

**red|o|lence** (red′ə ləns), *n.* redolent condition or quality.

**red|o|len|cy** (red′ə lən sē), *n.* = redolence.

**red|o|lent** (red′ə lənt), *adj.* **1** having a pleasant smell; fragrant. **SYN:** aromatic. **2** smelling strongly; giving off an odor: *a house redolent of fresh paint.* **3** *Figurative.* suggesting thoughts or feelings: *"Ivanhoe" is a name redolent of romance. Oxford is redolent of age and authority* (Emerson). **SYN:** reminiscent. [< Latin *redolēns, -entis,* present participle of *redolēre* emit scent < *re-* back + *olēre* to smell] —**red′o|lent|ly,** *adv.*

**re|done** (rē dun′), *v.* the past participle of **redo.**

**red osier, 1** any one of various willows with reddish bark. **2** *U.S.* a dogwood having reddish branches and shoots resembling those of the osier.

**re|dou|ble** (rē dub′əl), *v.,* **-bled, -bling,** *n.* — ***v.t.*** **1** to double again: *After a long diet, he redoubled his weight in a month by eating cakes and pies.* **2** to increase greatly; double: *When he saw land ahead, the swimmer redoubled his speed.* **3** to repeat; echo. **4** (in games) to double (an opponent's double).
— ***v.i.*** **1** to double back: *The fox redoubled on his trail to escape the hunters.* **2** to be doubled; become twice as great: *The clamour redoubled when it was known that the convert ... had accepted the Deanery of Saint Paul's* (Macaulay). **3** to resound: *A stunning clang of massive bolts redoubling beneath the deep* (Shelley).
— ***n.*** the act of redoubling; a double of a double. [< Middle French *redoubler* < *re-* re- + *doubler* to double] —**re|dou′ble|ment,** *n.*

**re|doubt**[1] (ri dout′), *n.* **1** a small, usually temporary fort standing alone, especially on a ridge, as above or near a pass or river: *They will meet American power in the air and sea lanes between the mainland and the Nationalist redoubt* (New Yorker). **2** a fortified enclosure in front or on the flanks of a permanent fortification: (*Figurative.*) *Conservatism, entrenched in its immense redoubts* (Emerson). [< French *redoute* < earlier Italian *ridotta* < Vulgar Latin *reductus, -ūs* a retreat < Latin *redūcere;* see etym. under **reduce**; spelling influenced by *redoubt*[2]]

**re|doubt**[2] (ri dout′), *v.t., v.i.* = fear. [< Old French *redouter,* and *redoubter* < *re-* again + *doubter.* Compare etym. under **doubt.**]

**re|doubt|a|ble** (ri dou′tə bəl), *adj.* **1** that should be feared or dreaded: *a redoubtable warrior.* **SYN:** formidable. **2** commanding respect: *a redoubtable debater. ... that you marry this redoubtable couple together—Righteousness and Peace* (Oliver Cromwell). *Michael I. Pupin ... had become professor of electromechanics and a redoubtable inventor* (Harper's). [< Old French *redoutable* < *redouter* to dread < *re-* again + *douter.* Compare etym. under **doubt.**] —**re|doubt′a|ble|ness,** *n.* —**re|doubt′a|bly,** *adv.*

**re|doubt|ed** (ri dou′tid), *adj.* **1** dreaded; formidable. **2** respected; renowned.

**re|dound** (ri dound′), *v., n.* — ***v.i.*** **1** to come back as a result; contribute: *The noble deeds of women redound to the glory of womanhood.* **2** to come back; recoil: *Disgrace redounds upon a person who lies or cheats.* **3** to proceed; arise; issue: *the anxiety of spirit which redoundeth from knowledge* (Francis Bacon).
— ***n.*** the fact of redounding or resulting: *Not without redound Of use and glory to yourselves ye come* (Tennyson).
[< Old French *redonder,* learned borrowing from Latin *redundāre* overflow < *re-* back + *undāre* to surge, rise in waves < *unda* wave]

**red|out** (red′out'), *n.* a sudden rush of blood to the head producing a red blur before the eyes, experienced by pilots when flying loops, spins, and certain other maneuvers. [< *red*[1]; patterned on *blackout*]

**red|o|wa** (red′ə wə, -və), *n.* **1** a Bohemian dance popular in the 1800's. One form in triple time resembles the waltz or mazurka; another in duple time resembles the polka. **2** music for these dances. [< German *Redowa* < Czech *rejdovák* < *rejdovati* steer about, drive < *rejd* turn, circular dance]

**re|dox** (rē′doks), *n., adj.* — ***n.*** = oxidation-reduction.
— ***adj.*** of or having to do with oxidation-reduction. [< *red*(uction) + *ox*(idation)]

**red-pen|cil** (red′pen′səl), *v.t.,* **-ciled, -cil|ing** or (*especially British*) **-cilled, -cil|ling.** to correct or edit with or as if with a red lead pencil; blue-pencil: *I have been red-pencilling student papers for a good many years and I ought by now to have become resigned or cynical* (Wall Street Journal).

**red pepper, 1** any one of several varieties of pepper that have hollow, sweet or mild fruits which are red when ripe. They belong to the nightshade family. The sweet pepper and chili are two kinds. **2** the fruit of any of these plants, used as a seasoning. **3** = cayenne.

**red phalarope,** a phalarope with reddish underparts which breeds in arctic regions and winters at sea in southern waters.

**red phosphorus,** an allotropic form of phosphorus: *Red phosphorus is far less reactive than white phosphorus* (New Scientist).

**red pine, 1** a pine of the northern United States and Canada, often over 100 feet tall, with smooth, reddish, hard wood of low resin content: *Red pine, also called Norway Pine, is a large, straight tree much prized for its lumber* (Richard J. Preston). **2** the wood, much used for lumber in construction.

**red planet,** the planet Mars.

**red|poll** (red′pōl'), *n.* **1** any one of several varieties of small, brownish finches of arctic regions, the males of which have a pink or red cap on the head. During the winter they breed in the northern United States. **2** = Red Polled.

**red|polled** (red′pōld′), *adj.* having red on the top of the head.

**Red Polled** or **Poll,** any reddish, hornless, short-haired cattle of a breed raised in England.

**red porgy,** a porgy that is crimson with blue spots.

**Red Power,** a slogan used by American Indians: *As with Black Power the burgeoning Red Power movement has two components, one cultural, the other political* (Manchester Guardian Weekly).

**red quebracho,** a tree of the cashew family, growing in Argentina, whose wood and bright-red bark are used in tanning and dyeing.

**re|draft** (*v.* rē draft′, -dräft′; *n.* rē′draft', -dräft'), *v., n.*— ***v.t.*** to draft again or anew.
— ***n.*** **1** a second draft. **2** a draft on the drawers or endorsers of a protested bill of exchange for the amount of the bill plus costs and charges.

**red rag, 1** a source of extreme provocation or annoyance; something which excites violent anger (from the belief that a red rag will incite a bull): *The phrase "secret diplomacy" has long been a red rag to American public opinion* (Wall Street Journal). **2** a variety of rust in grain. **3** *Slang.* the tongue: *Stop that ... red rag of yours, will you* (William S. Gilbert).

**red rain,** rain colored by thick dust particles, found especially in areas where rain falls through clouds of volcanic dust.

**re|drape** (rē drāp′), *v.t.,* **-draped, -drap|ing.** to drape again.

**red raspberry,** the common European or American variety of raspberry.

**re|draw** (rē drô′), *v.t.,* **-drew, -drawn, -draw|ing.** to make a redraft of. —**re|draw′er,** *n.*

**re|dress** (*v.* ri dres′; *n.* rē′dres, ri dres′), *v., n.* — ***v.t.*** **1** to set right; repair; remedy: *King Arthur tried to redress wrongs in his kingdom.* **2** to adjust evenly again: *I called the New World into existence to redress the balance of the Old* (George Canning).
— ***n.*** **1** the act or process of setting right; relief; reparation: *Anyone who has been injured unfairly deserves redress. My griefs ... finding no redress, ferment and rage* (Milton). **SYN:** restitution. **2** the means of a remedy: *There was no redress against the lawless violence to which they were perpetually exposed* (John L. Motley).
[< Middle French *redresser* < *re-* again + Old French *dresser* to straighten, arrange. Compare etym. under **dress,** verb.] —**re|dress′er, re|dres′sor,** *n.*

**re-dress** (rē dres′), *v.t.* to dress again.

**re|dress|a|ble** (ri dres′ə bəl), *adj.* that can be redressed.

**re|dress|al** (ri dres′əl), *n.* the act or process of redressing or state of being redressed: *In spite of a redressal of the situation ... they lost five wickets for 116* (London Times).

**re|dress|ment** (ri dres′mənt), *n.* = redressal.

**Pronunciation Key:** hat, āge, cãre, fär; let, ēqual, tėrm; it, īce; hot, ōpen, ôrder; oil, out; cup, pu̇t, rüle; child; long; thin; ᴛʜen; zh, measure; ə represents **a** in about, **e** in taken, **i** in pencil, **o** in lemon, **u** in circus.

**re|drew** (rē drü′), *v.* the past tense of **redraw**.

**red rice**, a wild rice having all or part of the grain colored red, considered to be a weed in rice fields of the southern United States.

**re|drive** (rē drīv′), *v.t.,* **-drove** or (*Archaic*) **-drave, -driv|en, -driv|ing.** to drive back; drive again: *As to and fro the doubtful Galliot rides, Here driven by Winds, and there redriven by Tides* (John Dryden).

**red robin**, = herb Robert.

**red|root** (red′rüt′, -růt′), *n.* **1** a North American plant of the bloodwort family with sword-shaped leaves, woolly, yellow flowers, and a red root used in dyeing. **2** any one of various other plants with red roots, such as the bloodroot, the alkanet, and the giant pigweed.

**re|drop** (rē drop′), *v.i., v.t.,* **-dropped** or **-dropt, -drop|ping.** to drop again.

**red rose**, the emblem of the house of Lancaster.

**red rot**, a fungous disease which attacks sugar cane and sorghum, discoloring the pith and rotting the seeds and stalks.

**red rust**, a phase of certain rust fungi in which rapidly reproducing orange or brownish spores are formed.

**re|dry** (rē drī′), *v.t., v.i.,* **-dried, -dry|ing.** to dry again.

**red sage**, a tropical American plant of the verbena family, with yellow flowers that change to bright orange or red.

**red salmon**, = sockeye salmon.

**red sandalwood**, **1** an East Indian tree of the pea family, with dark-red wood. **2** its wood, used for construction and as the source of a red dye.

**red sanders** or **red sanderswood**, = red sandalwood.

**red scale**, a scale insect that attacks orange, grapefruit, and other citrus trees.

**red-shaft|ed flicker** (red′shaf′tid), a variety of flicker of western North America, with red feathers under the wings and tail.

**red|shank** (red′shangk′), *n.* an Old World bird related to the snipe, having red legs.

**red shift**, *Astronomy.* a shift of the light of stars, nebulae, and other luminous bodies toward the red end or longest wavelengths of the spectrum, indicating movement outward at increasing speed, and leading to the belief that the universe is constantly expanding at an ever greater rate of speed.

**red-shift** (red′shift′), *v.t.* to shift (the light, as of stars) toward the red end of the spectrum: *In the spectra of quasi-stellar objects, however, these ultraviolet lines* (*both emission and absorption*) *are red-shifted into the visible region of the spectrum* (Scientific American).

**red shirt**, a member of an organization who wore red shirts, especially a follower of Giuseppe Garibaldi in the struggle for Italian unity in the 1800's.

**red|shirt** (red′shėrt′), *n., v. U.S. Sports.* **—*n.*** a college student of marked athletic ability whose normal four-year course is deliberately extended by one year, usually the sophomore year, in order that he may develop further his athletic skills. **—*v.t.*** to keep out of varsity competition for a year as a redshirt.
[so called because of the red shirts often worn by such players during practice to distinguish them from members of the varsity]

**red-short** (red′shôrt′), *adj.* brittle when at a red heat: *Iron and steel with too much sulfur are red-short.* **—red′-short′ness,** *n.*

**red-shoul|dered hawk** (red′shōl′dərd), a common hawk of North America with broad wings and tail, that feeds on rodents and insects.

**Red Sindhi**, a red Brahma variety of cattle that originated in the province of Sind in Pakistan.

**red|skin** (red′skin′), *n., adj.* North American Indian: *We have had more difficulty with white desperadoes than with redskins* (Theodore Roosevelt). [American English < *red*[1] + *skin*]

**red snapper**, a reddish snapper of the Gulf of Mexico and the Caribbean region, much valued as a food fish.

**red snow**, **1** a growth of red algae in snow that makes the white surface seem lightly brushed with red. It is common in arctic and alpine regions. **2** snow containing such a growth.

**red sorrel**, = sheep sorrel.

**red spider**, a mite that damages fruit trees and evergreens by sucking the juice from leaves.

**red spruce**, an important commercial spruce that grows between Nova Scotia and North Carolina, and as far west as Tennessee. It has dark-red bark and its wood is used for pulp and lumber.

**red squad**, an intelligence unit of a police department: [*The*] *subcommittee chairman, characterized the files of such local intelligence units, generally known as "red squads," as unreliable* (John M. Crewdson).

**red squill**, a squill having a reddish bulb, used as a rat poison.

**red squirrel**, a common North American squirrel having reddish fur. See picture under **squirrel**.

**red|start** (red′stärt′), *n.* **1** a fly-catching warbler of America with orange-red or yellow markings on the tail and wings. **2** a small, common European songbird with a reddish tail. **3** = painted redstart.
[American English < *red*[1] + *start*[2] a tail]

**red stele**, a disease of strawberries caused by a fungus that attacks the roots, causing the plants either to become stunted or to die: *Red stele attacks the roots, turning the steles or central part of the plant roots red* (Science News Letter).

**red-stem fil|a|ree** (red′stem′ fil′ə rē), = alfilaria. [*filaree,* alteration of American Spanish *alfilerilla* alfilaria]

**red tab**, *British Slang.* a high-ranking military officer: *A carload of red tabs and brass hats arrives* ... (J. B. Priestley). [because of the red tabs on officers' collars]

**red|tail** (red′tāl′), *n.* = red-tailed hawk.

**red-tailed hawk** (red′tāld′), a common North American hawk with a reddish-brown tail.

**red-tailed tropic bird**, a tropic bird of the Indian and Pacific oceans, with a white body tinted with pink and a reddish tail.

**red tape**, **1** tape having a red color, formerly used for tying up official papers. **2** too much attention to details and forms; bureaucratic routine: *A House Banking subcommittee assailed what it called the red tape and delays in the program to eliminate slums* (Wall Street Journal). **—red′-tape′,** *adj.*

**red-tap|ism** (red′tā′piz əm), *n.* too much attention to details and form.

**red tetra**, = flame tetra.

**red-throat|ed diver** (red′thrō′tid), any small loon of a species distinguished by an elongated patch of dark bay color on the throat.

**red tide**, a reddish discoloration on the surface of seawater produced at times by the sudden clustering together of billions of one-celled organisms that are toxic to fish. Red tide appears in most waters of the tropics and semitropics around Africa, Asia, South America, and California, Texas, Florida and in the Gulf of Mexico. *Unusually sultry weather plus an abundant rainfall appears to be the reason for Florida's latest red tide* (Science News Letter).

**red|top** (red′top′), *n.* any one of several grasses grown for forage and pasture, especially a species having large, reddish, spreading flower clusters.

**re|duce** (ri düs′, -dyüs′), *v.,* **-duced, -duc|ing.** **—*v.t.*** **1** to make less; make smaller; decrease: *We have reduced expenses this year. She is trying to reduce her weight.* SYN: lessen, diminish. **2** to make lower, as in degree or intensity; weaken; dilute. **3** to bring down; lower: *Misfortune reduced that poor woman to begging.* SYN: humble, debase, degrade. **4** to bring to a different condition; change: *The teacher soon reduced the noisy class to order. I was reduced to tears by the cruel words.* **5** to change to another form without altering basic substance or value: *to reduce a statement to writing. The chalk was reduced to powder. If you reduce 3 ft., 6 in. to inches, you have 42 inches.* **6** to bring under control; conquer; subdue: *The army reduced the fort by a sudden attack.* **7** to restore to its proper place or normal condition; set: *A doctor can reduce a fracture or dislocation.* **8** *Chemistry.* **a** to combine with hydrogen. **b** to remove oxygen from. **c** to change (atoms or ions) to a lower valence by the gain of electrons. **9** *Mathematics.* to simplify (an expression, fraction, formula, or function). **10** = smelt: *to reduce the ores of silver or copper.* **11** *Biology.* to bring about meiosis in (a cell). **12** to thin (paint) with oil or turpentine. **13** to treat (a photographic negative) to make less dense. **14** *Astronomy.* to correct (observations) by making allowances.
**—*v.i.*** to become less; be made less; become less in weight: *His doctor advised him to reduce.*
[< Latin *redūcere* < *re-* back + *dūcere* bring, lead]

**re|duced** (ri düst′, -dyüst′), *adj.* **1** diminished in number, quantity, amount, or size: *I ... reproduced some of his plates on a reduced scale* (Clements R. Markham). **2** weakened; impaired: *The English leaders appear to have had no conception of the extremely reduced state of the French* (James Mill). **3** impoverished: ... *retired to the rural districts in reduced circumstances* (John Ruskin).

**reduced iron**, a fine, gray-black powder, obtained especially by the action of hydrogen on ferric oxide, used in medicine to increase the hemoglobin content of the blood.

**re|duc|er** (ri dü′sər, -dyü′-), *n.* **1** a person or thing that reduces. **2** a threaded cylindrical piece for connecting pipes of different sizes. **3** a solution for reducing the density of photographic negatives.

**re|duc|i|bil|i|ty** (ri dü′sə bil′ə tē, -dyü′-), *n.* the quality or state of being reducible.

**re|duc|i|ble** (ri dü′sə bəl, -dyü′-), *adj.* that can be reduced: *4/8 is reducible to ½.* **—re|duc′i|ble|ness,** *n.* **—re|duc′i|bly,** *adv.*

**re|duc|ing agent** (ri dü′sing, -dyü′-), any chemical substance that reduces or removes the oxygen in a compound.

**reducing furnace**, a furnace for reducing ores from oxides or separating metal from other substances by a nonoxidizing heat or flame.

**reducing gear**, a gear which slows down the speed it transmits.

**reducing sugar**, a saccharide, such as glucose or fructose, that causes the reduction of copper or silver salts in alkaline solutions.

**reducing valve**, a valve for automatically reducing the pressure, as of steam or air in a closed heating system or boiler.

**re|duc|tant** (ri duk′tənt), *n.* = reducing agent: *Chlorophyll is thus a very peculiar substance: it can act both as an oxidant and as a reductant* (Scientific American).

**re|duc|tase** (ri duk′tās, -tāz), *n.* any enzyme that promotes reduction of an organic compound. [< *reduct* (ion) + *-ase*]

**re|duc|ti|o ad ab|sur|dum** (ri duk′shē ō ad absėr′dəm), *Latin.* reduction to absurdity; method of proving something false by showing that conclusions to which it leads are absurd.

**re|duc|tion** (ri duk′shən), *n.* **1** the action or process of reducing or state of being reduced: *a reduction of 10 pounds in weight. Failure to obey orders caused the corporal's reduction to the rank of private.* **2** the amount by which a thing is reduced: *The reduction in cost was $5.* **3** the form of something produced by reducing; copy of something on a smaller scale. **4** *Biology.* meiosis. **5** *Chemistry.* **a** any reaction in which oxygen is removed from a compound. **b** a reaction in which an atom or group of atoms gains one or more electrons. The atom or group of atoms that lose electrons becomes oxidized. [< Latin *reductiō, -ōnis* < *redūcere;* see etym. under **reduce**]

**re|duc|tion|al** (ri duk′shə nəl), *adj.* of or having to do with reduction.

**reduction division**, = meiosis.

**reduction gear**, a gear that reduces the speed of rotation, as of a motor or turbine, to a lower speed in transmitting the driving force to a machine or device.

**re|duc|tion|ism** (ri duk′shə niz əm), *n.* the tendency to reduce differences, as in theories and ideas, to a single unifying principle, especially in science.

**re|duc|tion|ist** (ri duk′shə nist), *n., adj.* **—*n.*** a person who favors reduction or reductionism. **—*adj.*** favoring reduction or reductionism.

**re|duc|tion|is|tic** (ri duk′shə nis′tik), *adj.* = reductionist.

**re|duc|tive** (ri duk′tiv), *adj., n.* **—*adj.*** **1** tending to reduce; reducing. **2** of or having to do with minimal art; minimal: *To judge by art magazines and museum programs, nothing new has been done in the past few years but Happenings, optical displays, and so-called primary structures and reductive paintings* (Harold Rosenberg).
**—*n.*** a thing that reduces. **—re|duc′tive|ly,** *adv.*

**re|duc|tiv|ism** (ri duk′tə viz əm), *n.* = minimal art.

**re|duc|tiv|ist** (ri duk′tə vist), *n.* = minimalist.

**re|duc|tor** (ri duk′tər), *n.* a device reducing ferric sulfate to ferrous sulfate by zinc: *A reductor is used in the analysis of iron and steel.*

**re|dun|dance** (ri dun′dəns), *n.* = redundancy.

**re|dun|dan|cy** (ri dun′dən sē), *n., pl.* **-cies.** **1** more than is needed. **2** a redundant thing, part, or amount. **3** the use of too many words for the same idea; wordiness: *She is afflicted with a passion for redundancy* (Atlantic). **4** the part of a communication that can be omitted without loss of essential information. **5** *British.* an excess or surplus of workers, such as in a factory or industry, especially as a result of modernization or automation: *Workers at the ... factory, where about a thousand people are employed, became worried last month about redundancy and the introduction for some of them of a four-day week* (Manchester Guardian Weekly). **6** *Aerospace.* the ability to provide duplication or replacement of some function in case of a failure in equipment: *The Goldstone station was equipped with two completely separate systems to provide 100 percent redundancy in the reception and recording of the Ranger photographs* (Scientific American).

**re|dun|dant** (ri dun′dənt), *adj.* **1** extra; not needed: *In "We two both ate an apple each" the word "two" is redundant.* SYN: superfluous. **2** using too many words for the same idea; that says the same thing again; wordy: *redundant language. His style of writing is redundant.* **3** having some unneeded or unusual part, as a verb that has more than one form for a tense. **4** *British.* dismissed or facing dismissal from work because unneeded or superfluous: *redundant railwaymen.*

[< Latin *redundāns, -antis,* present participle of *redundāre;* see etym. under **redound**] —**re|dun′dant|ly,** *adv.*

**re|du|pli|cate** (*v.* ri dü′plə kāt, -dyü′-; *adj.* ri dü′plə kit, -dyü′-; -kāt), *v.,* **-cat|ed, -cat|ing,** *adj.*
—***v.t.*** **1** to double; repeat. **2a** to repeat (a letter or syllable) in forming a word. **b** to form by such repetition.
—***v.i.*** to become doubled.
—***adj.*** **1** doubled or repeated. **2** *Botany.* valvate, with the edges folded back so as to project outward.
[< Latin *reduplicāre* (with English *-ate*[1]) < *re-* again + *duplicāre.* Compare etym. under **duplicate.**]

**re|du|pli|ca|tion** (ri dü′plə kā′shən, -dyü′-), *n.* **1** the act of reduplicating or fact of being reduplicated; doubling; repetition. **2** something resulting from repeating; duplicate; copy: *To the prisoner each day seemed a reduplication of the preceding day.* **3a** repetition, as of a syllable or the initial part of a syllable: *Years might pass without my thinking of reduplication, but then suddenly a fresh double word, "tsetse fly" or "Berber", would come along* (Guy Endore). **b** a syllable so formed. **c** a word containing such a syllable: *Razzle-dazzle and bonbon are reduplications.*

**re|du|pli|ca|tive** (ri dü′plə kā′tiv, -dyü′-), *adj.* tending to reduplicate; having to do with or marked by reduplication. —**re|du′pli|ca′tive|ly,** *adv.*

**re|du|pli|ca|to|ry** (ri dü′plə kə tôr′ē, -tōr′-; -dyü′-), *adj.* reduplicative; repetitious.

**re|du|vi|id** (ri dü′vē id, -dyü′-), *adj., n.* —***adj.*** of or belonging to a family of bloodsucking insects that includes the assassin bugs.
—***n.*** an insect of this family.
[< New Latin *Reduviidae* the family name < Latin *reduvia* hangnail]

**re|dux** (rē′duks), *adj.* brought back or returned, as from a distance or from exile. [< Latin *redux* leading back < *redūcere;* see etym. under **reduce**]

**red|ward** (red′wərd), *adv.* toward the red end of the spectrum.

**red|ware**[1] (red′wãr′), *n.* a large brown seaweed found off northern Atlantic coasts. [< *red*[1] + (sea)*ware*]

**red|ware**[2] (red′wãr′), *n.* a coarse, unglazed pottery made of clay containing iron oxide. [< *red*[1] + *ware*[1]]

**red-wat** (red′wot′), *adj. Scottish.* soaked with blood.

**red|wa|ter** (red′wôt′ər, -wot′-), *n.,* or **red water, 1** a usually fatal, bacterial disease of cattle characterized by internal hemorrhages and red urine. **2** a malarial fever in cattle caused by a sporozoan parasite which is transmitted by ticks: *Blood parasites akin to the protozoa ... cause red water in cattle and malaria in man* (New Scientist).

**red widow,** a poisonous spider found in Florida that is closely related to the black widow; red-legged widow.

**red|wing** (red′wing′), *n.* **1** a blackbird of North America. The male has a scarlet patch on each wing. **2** a common European song thrush that has reddish color on the underside of the wings.

**red-winged blackbird** (red′wingd′), = redwing (def. 1).

**red wolf,** a grayish, reddish, or blackish wolf of areas of the southern United States, smaller than the gray or timber wolf.

**red|wood** (red′wu̇d′), *n.* **1a** an evergreen tree of the California and southern Oregon coasts; sequoia; big tree. It is among the world's largest trees, reaching a height of over 300 feet and an age of several thousand years. Redwoods are conifers belonging to the taxodium family. *The coast redwoods—Sequoia sempervirens—are not the oldest trees in California, although decidedly the tallest* (Newsweek). **b** its brownish-red wood. Redwood is a relatively light, straight-grained wood. **2a** any one of various trees, chiefly of tropical regions, with a reddish wood or from which a red dyestuff is obtained. **b** any red-colored wood.

**red|worm** (red′wėrm′), *n.* **1** a kind of reddish worm much used as bait; bloodworm. **2** a worm or grub that attacks grain.

**re|dye** (rē dī′), *v.t.,* **-dyed, -dye|ing.** to dye again.

**red-yel|low** (red′yel′ō), *n., adj.* —***n.*** a color between red and yellow. —***adj.*** of such hue.

**re|ech|o** or **re-ech|o** (rē ek′ō), *v.,* **-ech|oed, -ech|o|ing,** *n., pl.* **-ech|oes.** —***v.i., v.t.*** to echo back: *The thunder reechoed far behind. The house reechoes children's laughter.* **SYN:** resound, reverberate.
—***n.*** an echo of an echo.

***reed** (rēd), *n., adj., v.* —***n.*** **1** a kind of tall grass with a hollow, jointed stalk that grows in wet places. **2** such a stalk. **3** *Figurative.* anything or anyone like a reed, such as a person or thing that is frail, weak, or delicate: *Man is but a reed, the weakest in nature, but he is a thinking reed* (Blaise Pascal). *The United Nations is a fragile reed* (Wall Street Journal). **4** anything made from the stalk of a reed or anything like it, such as an arrow or a musical instrument played by blowing through it. **5a** a thin piece of wood, metal, or plastic in a musical instrument that produces sound when a current of air moves it. **b** = reed instrument. **6** a weaver's instrument for separating the threads of the warp and beating up the woof. **7** a small convex molding; reeding. **8** *British Dialect.* straw prepared for thatching. **9** (in the Bible) a Hebrew unit of length; six cubits.
—***adj.*** **1** producing tones by means of reeds: *a reed musician.* **2** = reedy.
—***v.t.*** **1** to thatch with reeds. **2** to decorate with reeding.
[Old English *hrēod*] —**reed′like′,** *adj.*

***reed**
definitions 1, 5a, b

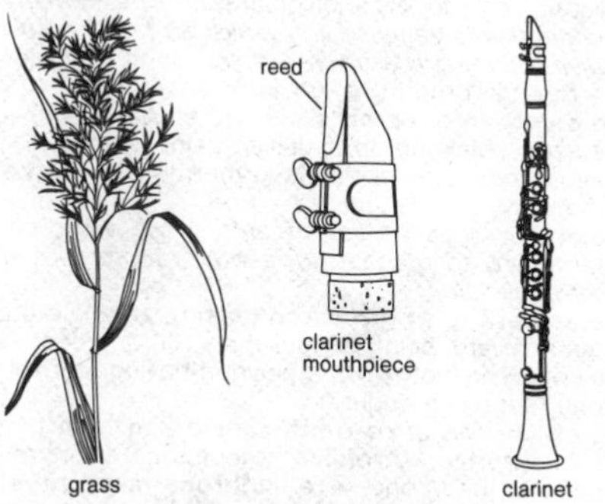

reed
clarinet mouthpiece
grass
clarinet

**reed|bird** (rēd′bėrd′), *n.* = bobolink.

**reed|buck** (rēd′buk′), *n., pl.* **-bucks** or (*collectively*) **-buck.** any one of several tan African antelopes that live in marshy regions. Only the males have horns. [translation of Afrikaans and Dutch *rietbok*]

**reed bunting,** a European bunting that lives in marshes.

**reed canary grass,** a common species of canary grass, grown in the Northern Hemisphere for use as fodder. A variegated form of it is the ribbon grass of gardens.

**re|ed|i|fy** or **re-ed|i|fy** (rē ed′ə fī), *v.t.,* **-fied, -fy|ing.** to rebuild; restore.

**reed|ing** (rē′ding), *n.* **1** a small convex molding. **2** these moldings on the surface of a column. **3** ornamentation consisting of such moldings.

**reed instrument,** a musical instrument that makes sound by means of a vibrating reed or reeds. Oboes, clarinets, and saxophones are reed instruments.

**re|ed|it** or **re-ed|it** (rē ed′it), *v.t.* to edit again.

**reed|ling** (rēd′ling), *n.* a small European bird that lives in reedy places; bearded tit. The male has a tuft of black feathers on each side of the head.

**reed mace,** *British.* the cattail plant.

**reed organ,** a musical instrument producing tones by means of small metal reeds and played by keys. Two common forms are the harmonium, in which the air is forced outward through the reeds, and the melodeon, in which the air is sucked inward.

**reed pipe,** an organ pipe with a reed.

**Reed-Stern|berg cell** (rēd′stėrn′bėrg), any one of the large phagocytic cells, usually with two nuclei, characteristic of Hodgkin's disease. [< D. *Reed,* 1874-1964, an American pathologist and C. *Sternberg,* 1872-1935, an Austrian pathologist]

**reed stop,** a set of reed pipes in an organ, controlled by one stop knob.

**re|ed|u|cate** or **re-ed|u|cate** (rē ej′u̇ kāt), *v.t.,* **-cat|ed, -cat|ing.** to educate again, especially to new ideas, methods, or habits, in order to reform or rehabilitate: *The author's ideal prison would be ... a walled city, where the prisoner would ... reeducate himself in preparation for the time he is released* (Saturday Review).

**re|ed|u|ca|tion** or **re-ed|u|ca|tion** (rē′ej u̇ kā′shən), *n.* **1** a reeducating. **2** a being reeducated.

**re|ed|u|ca|tion|al** or **re-ed|u|ca|tion|al** (rē′ej u̇ kā′shə nəl), *adj.* of, having to do with, or for reeducation.

**re|ed|u|ca|tive** or **re-ed|u|ca|tive** (rē ej′u̇ kā′tiv), *adj.* = reeducational.

**reed warbler,** a common European warbler found in wet, reedy places.

**reed wire,** a flattened wire used in musical instruments, as in the fastening of the mouthpieces of reeds.

**reed|y** (rē′dē), *adj.,* **reed|i|er, reed|i|est. 1** full of reeds: *a reedy pond, the broad, reedy fen* (Robert Louis Stevenson). **2** made of a reed or reeds. **3** like a reed or reeds: *reedy grass.* **4** sounding like a reed instrument: *a thin, reedy voice.* —**reed′i|ly,** *adv.* —**reed′i|ness,** *n.*

**reef**[1] (rēf), *n.* **1** a narrow ridge of rocks, sand, or coral at or near the surface of the water: *The ship was wrecked on a hidden reef.* **SYN:** shoal. **2** a vein or lode in mining. [probably < earlier Dutch *riffe,* or *rif.* Compare etym. under **riffle**[1].]

***reef**[2] (rēf), *n., v.* —***n.*** **1** a part of a sail that can be rolled or folded up to reduce the area exposed to the wind. **2** the size a sail is reduced to by reefing. **3a** the act of reefing. **b** a method of reefing.
—***v.t.*** **1** to reduce the area of (a sail) by rolling or folding up a part of it. **2** to reduce the length of (a topmast, bowsprit, spar, or yard) as by lowering.
[ultimately < Scandinavian (compare Old Icelandic *rif* rib, reef, ridge)]

***reef**[2]
definition 1

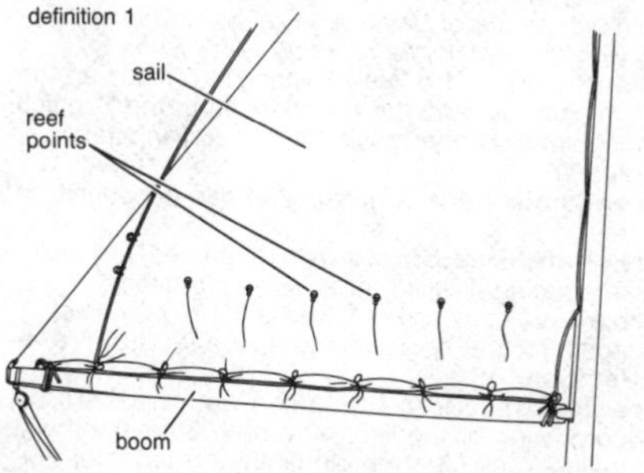

sail
reef points
boom

**reef band,** a band of canvas sewed across a sail to strengthen it for the strain of the reef points.

**reef|er**[1] (rē′fər), *n.* **1** a person who reefs. **2** a short coat of thick cloth, worn especially by sailors and fishermen. **3** *Informal.* a midshipman. **4** a long scarf or muffler.

**reef|er**[2] (rē′fər), *n. U.S. Slang.* a cigarette containing marijuana. [American English; origin uncertain, perhaps < *reef*[2] (because both the sail and cigarette are rolled)]

**reef|er**[3] (rē′fər), *n. U.S. Slang.* a refrigerator railroad car or truck trailer. [< *refrigerator*]

**reef|ing** (rē′fing), *n.* the process of taking out ore rock.

**reef knot,** = square knot.

**reef-knot** (rēf′not′), *v.t.,* **-knot|ted, -knot|ting.** to tie in a reef knot: *to reef-knot a line.*

**reef point,** one of the cords to reef a sail.

**reef|y** (rē′fē), *adj.,* **reef|i|er, reef|i|est. 1** marked by reefs or rocks: *the reefy entrance to a harbor.* **2** characterized by reefs: *a reefy coast.*

**reek** (rēk), *n., v.* —***n.*** **1** a strong, unpleasant smell; disagreeable fumes or odor; vapor: *We noticed the reek of cooking cabbage as we entered the hall. ... the pungent reek of camels* (Rudyard Kipling). **2** the condition of reeking: *in a reek of a sweat.* **3** *Dialect.* smoke. [Old English *rēc*]
—***v.i.*** **1a** to send out vapor or a strong, unpleasant smell: *a reeking pond of stagnant water, to reek with the smell of cooking. She reeked of cheap perfume.* **b** *Figurative: a manner reeking with arrogance, a government reeking with corruption.* **2** to be wet with sweat or blood: *their horses reeking with the speed at which they had ridden* (Scott).
—***v.t.*** **1** to dry or coat by smoking, as meat, or molds for steel. **2** to give out strongly or unmistakably: *His manner reeks arrogance.*
[Middle English *reken,* Old English *rēocan.* See related etym. at **reek,** noun.] —**reek′er,** *n.*

**reek|y** (rē′kē), *adj.,* **reek|i|er, reek|i|est.** reeking.

**reel**[1] (rēl), *n., v.* —***n.*** **1** a frame like a spool turning on an axis, for winding thread, yarn, a fish line, rope, wire, string, or anything that can be wound: *The fishing line was hopelessly snarled on the reel.* **2** a spool; roller: *The cat played with the empty reel rolling it along the floor.* **3** something wound on a reel: *two reels of motion-picture film.* **4** a length of motion-picture film on a reel.
—***v.t.*** **1** to wind on a reel. **2** to draw with a reel or by winding: *to reel in a fish.*
**off the reel,** *Informal.* quickly and easily: *[The story] seems to me to be so constituted as to require to be read off the reel* (Dickens). *He won five races off the reel* (St. James' Gazette).
**reel off,** to say, write, or make in a quick, easy way: *to reel off a list of names. He can reel off stories by the hour.*
[Old English *hrēol*]

**Pronunciation Key:** hat, āge, cãre, fär; let, ēqual, tėrm; it, īce; hot, ōpen, ôrder; oil, out; cup, pu̇t, rüle; child; long; thin; ᴛʜen; zh, measure; ə represents **a** in about, **e** in taken, **i** in pencil, **o** in lemon, **u** in circus.

**reel²** (rēl), *v., n.* — *v.i.* **1** to sway, swing, or rock under a blow or shock: *The boy reeled when the ball struck him. The ship shook and reeled in the storm.* **2** to sway in standing or walking: *The wounded man reeled and fell as he lurched toward the bear with a knife.* **3** to be in a whirl; be dizzy: *His head was reeling after the first dance.* **4** to go with swaying or staggering movements: *The dazed boy reeled down the street.* **5** to become unsteady; give way; sway; stagger; waver: *Our regiment reeled when the cavalry struck it.*
— *v.t.* to cause to reel or reel along.
— *n.* a reeling or staggering movement.
[Middle English *relen,* probably < *reel*¹, verb]
— *Syn.* *v.i.* **2 Reel, stagger** mean to stand or move unsteadily. **Reel** suggests dizziness and a lurching movement: *Sick and faint, he reeled when he tried to cross the room.* **Stagger** suggests moving with halting steps and without much sense of balance: *The boy staggered in with the heavy pile of wood in his arms.*

**reel³** (rēl), *n.* **1** a lively dance. Two kinds are the Virginia reel and the reel danced in the Scottish Highlands. **2** the music for a reel. [apparently < *reel*²]

**reel|a|ble** (rē′lə bəl), *adj.* that can be wound on a reel.

**reel-and-bead molding** (rēl′ən bēd′), a molding alternating disklike parts with long beads.

**re|e|lect** or **re-e|lect** (rē′i lekt′), *v.t.* to elect again for the same office. — **re′e|lec′tion, re′-e-lec′tion,** *n.*

**reel|er** (rē′lər), *n.* **1** a person who winds silk, cord, wire, or the like, on a reel. **2** a person who makes reels. **3** a motion picture in terms of the length of the film on a reel or reels. [< *reel*¹ + *-er*¹]

**re|el|e|vate** or **re-el|e|vate** (rē el′ə vāt), *v.t.,* **-vat|ed, -vat|ing.** to elevate again.

**re|el|i|gi|bil|i|ty** or **re-el|i|gi|bil|i|ty** (rē′el ə jə bil′ə tē), *n.* the condition of being reeligible.

**re|el|i|gi|ble** or **re-el|i|gi|ble** (rē el′ə jə bəl), *adj.* **1** qualified to be elected again to the same office. **2** once again eligible, as for parole or athletic competition: *a bill to make the tribunes legally reeligible* (James A. Froude).

**reel-to-reel** (rēl′tə rēl′), *adj.* consisting of or using two reels to wind up magnetic tape, film, or the like: *a reel-to-reel recorder unit, conventional reel-to-reel tape.*

**reel towel,** = roller towel.

**re|em|bark** or **re-em|bark** (rē′em bärk′), *v.t., v.i.* to embark again. — **re′em|bar|ka′tion, re′-em-bar|ka′tion,** *n.*

**re|em|bod|y** or **re-em|bod|y** (rē′em bod′ē), *v.t.,* **-bod|ied, -bod|y|ing.** to embody again.

**re|em|brace** or **re-em|brace** (rē′em brās′), *v.t., v.i.,* **-braced, -brac|ing.** to embrace again.

**re|em|broi|dered** or **re-em|broi|dered** (rē′em-broi′dərd), *adj.* overlaid with an embroidered design: *Another dance dress ... is of moonstone gray satin covered with reembroidered gray lace* (New Yorker).

**re|e|merge** or **re-e|merge** (rē′i mėrj′), *v.i.,* **-merged, -merg|ing.** to emerge again: *to reemerge from obscurity.*

**re|e|mer|gence** or **re-e|mer|gence** (rē′i mėr′jəns), *n.* the act of reemerging.

**re|e|mer|gent** or **re-e|mer|gent** (rē′i mėr′jənt), *adj.* reemerging.

**re|em|i|grate** or **re-em|i|grate** (rē em′ə grāt), *v.i.,* **-grat|ed, -grat|ing.** to emigrate again.

**re|e|mit** or **re-e|mit** (rē′i mit′), *v.t.,* **-mit|ted, -mit|ting.** **1** to emit again. **2** *Especially U.S.* to reissue (bills, banknotes, or the like).

**re|em|pha|sis** or **re-em|pha|sis** (rē em′fə sis), *n., pl.* **-ses** (-sēz). renewed emphasis: *Today there is a re-emphasis on healthy, hard-hitting selling* (Time).

**re|em|pha|size** or **re-em|pha|size** (rē em′fə-sīz), *v.t., v.i.,* **-sized, -siz|ing.** to emphasize again.

**re|em|ploy** or **re-em|ploy** (rē′em ploi′), *v.t.* to take back into employment. — **re′em|ploy′ment, re′-em|ploy′ment,** *n.*

**re|en|act** or **re-en|act** (rē′en akt′), *v.t.* to enact again, as a law or event.

**re|en|ac|tion** or **re-en|ac|tion** (rē′en ak′shən), *n.* the act of reenacting; reenactment.

**re|en|act|ment** or **re-en|act|ment** (rē′en akt′-mənt), *n.* the enactment a second time, as of a law or an event: *Dore Schary ... has agreed to produce on the Capitol Steps a re-enactment of Lincoln's second inauguration* (New York Times).

**re|en|coun|ter** or **re-en|coun|ter** (rē′en koun′-tər), *v., n.* — *v.t., v.i.* to meet again: *We do not reencounter the past* (Scientific American).
— *n.* a meeting again, as after separation or absence: *She had said it on that occasion of their first reencounter* (A. S. M. Hutchinson).

**re|en|cour|age** or **re-en|cour|age** (rē′en kėr′ij), *v.t.,* **-aged, -ag|ing.** to encourage again. — **re′en-cour′age|ment, re′-en|cour′age|ment,** *n.*

**re|en|dow** or **re-en|dow** (rē′en dou′), *v.t.* to endow again.

**re|en|force** or **re-en|force** (rē′en fôrs′, -fōrs′), *v.t.,* **-forced, -forc|ing.** = reinforce.

**re|en|force|ment** or **re-en|force|ment** (rē′en-fôrs′mənt, -fōrs′-), *n.* = reinforcement.

**re|en|gage** or **re-en|gage** (rē′en gāj′), *v.t., v.i.,* **-gaged, -gag|ing.** to engage again. — **re′en|gage′-ment, re′-en|gage′ment,** *n.*

**re|en|gine** or **re-en|gine** (rē en′jən), *v.t.,* **-gined, -gin|ing.** to provide with other engines: *to reengine a ship.*

**re|en|gi|neer** or **re-en|gi|neer** (rē′en jə nir′), *v.t.* to engineer again: *The intent is to reengineer an entire industry—operations, equipment, corporate structures and all* (Wall Street Journal).

**re|en|grave** or **re-en|grave** (rē′en grāv′), *v.t.,* **-graved, -grav|ing.** to engrave again.

**re|en|joy** or **re-en|joy** (rē′en joi′), *v.t.* to enjoy a second time. — **re′en|joy′ment, re′-en|joy′-ment,** *n.*

**re|en|list** or **re-en|list** (rē′en list′), *v.t., v.i.* to enlist again or for an additional term: *The Roman general was eager ... to reenlist so brave a soldier in the service of the empire* (John L. Motley). — **re′en|list′ment, re′-en|list′ment,** *n.*

**re|en|slave** or **re-en|slave** (rē′en slāv′), *v.t.,* **-slaved, -slav|ing.** to enslave again; cast again into bondage. — **re′en|slave′ment, re′-en|slave′-ment,** *n.*

**re|en|ter** or **re-en|ter** (rē en′tər), *v.i., v.t.* to enter again; go in again: *to reenter a room, to reenter public life.*

**re|en|ter|ing angle** (rē en′tər ing), an angle that turns inward, being greater than 180 degrees.

**reentering polygon,** a polygon having at least one reentering angle.

**re|en|throne** or **re-en|throne** (rē′en thrōn′), *v.t.,* **-throned, -thron|ing.** to enthrone again; restore to the throne. — **re′en|throne′ment, re′-en-throne′ment,** *n.*

**re|en|trance** or **re-en|trance** (rē en′trəns), *n.* **1** the act of entering a second time. **2** the act of coming back in after going out.

**re|en|trant** or **re-en|trant** (rē en′trənt), *adj., n.* — *adj.* that reenters.
— *n.* an angle, bend, or other configuration, that turns inward.

**re|en|try** or **re-en|try** (rē en′trē), *n., pl.* **-tries.** **1** the act of entering again or returning; new or fresh entry; second entry: *They will be barred from reentry into Singapore* (New York Times). **2** *Law.* the act or fact of taking possession again. **3** a playing card that will take a trick and thus let the player get the lead. **4** the return of a rocket or spacecraft into the earth's atmosphere after flight into outer space: *The "heat barrier" ... creates a reentry problem for rockets and satellites returning to earth* (Scientific American).

**re|e|quip** or **re-e|quip** (rē′i kwip′), *v.t.,* **-quipped, -quip|ping.** to equip again. — **re′e|quip′ment, re′-e|quip′ment,** *n.*

**re|e|rect** or **re-e|rect** (rē′i rekt′), *v.t.* to erect again.

**reest** (rēst), *v.i. Scottish.* (of horses) to balk. [probably variant of *rest*¹, verb. Compare Scottish *arreest* to arrest.]

**re|es|tab|lish** or **re-es|tab|lish** (rē′es tab′lish), *v.t.* to establish again; restore. SYN: reinstate. — **re′es|tab′lish|ment, re′-es|tab′lish|ment,** *n.*

**re|es|ti|mate** or **re-es|ti|mate** (*v.* rē′es′tə māt; *n.* rē′es′tə mit, -māt), *v.,* **-mat|ed, -mat|ing,** *n.* — *v.t., v.i.* to estimate again.
— *n.* the act or process of reestimating: *The Mayor promised that the reestimate of borrowing would not interfere with the ... budget* (New York Times).

**re|e|val|u|ate** or **re-e|val|u|ate** (rē′i val′yu̇ āt), *v.t., v.i.,* **-at|ed, -at|ing.** to evaluate again. — **re′e-val′u|a′tion, re′-e|val′u|a′tion,** *n.*

**reeve¹** (rēv), *n.* **1** the chief official of a town or district in England: *A lord "who has so many men that he cannot personally have all in his own keeping" was bound to set over each dependent township a reeve, not only to exact his lord's dues, but to enforce his justice within its bounds* (John R. Green). **2** a bailiff; steward; overseer. **3** a local official of a town or village in Canada: *There are several mayors, aldermen and reeves besides those I have already mentioned whose chances are fair* (Toronto Telegram). [Old English *gerēfa.* Compare etym. under **sheriff.**]

**reeve²** (rēv), *v.t.,* **reeved** or **rove, reev|ing.** **1** to pass (a rope) through a hole, ring, etc. **2** to fasten by placing through or around something. **3** to pass a rope through (a block, ring, etc.). [origin uncertain. Compare Dutch *reven* to reef a sail.]

**reeve³** (rēv), *n.* a female ruff (sandpiper). [perhaps related to **ruff**¹]

**reeve|ship** (rēv′ship), *n.* the position or term of office of a reeve.

**Reeves pheasant** (rēvz), a pheasant of northern China that has extremely long tail feathers which were once widely used to trim hats. [< John *Reeves,* 1774-1856, an English naturalist who lived in China]

**re|ex|am|i|na|tion** or **re-ex|am|i|na|tion** (rē′eg-zam′ə nā′shən), *n.* **1** a second or renewed examination: *Medical experts suggest that a reexamination of disabled veterans take place every year* (Harper's). **2** *Law.* the examination of a witness after cross-examination.

**re|ex|am|ine** or **re-ex|am|ine** (rē′eg zam′ən), *v.t.,* **-ined, -in|ing.** **1** to examine again. **2** *Law.* to examine (a witness) again after cross-examination.

**re|ex|change** or **re-ex|change** (rē′eks chānj′), *v.,* **-changed, -chang|ing,** *n.* — *v.t.* to exchange again or anew.
— *n.* **1** a second exchange. **2** *Commerce.* **a** the recovery of the amount plus expenses of inconvenience for a dishonored foreign bill of exchange. **b** the draft recovering the amount. **c** the expense of inconvenience.

**re|ex|hib|it** or **re-ex|hib|it** (rē′eg zib′it), *v., n.* — *v.t.* to exhibit again or anew.
— *n.* a second or renewed exhibit.

**re|ex|pand** or **re-ex|pand** (rē′ek spand′), *v.t., v.i.* to expand again after contraction.

**re|ex|pan|sion** or **re-ex|pan|sion** (rē′ek span′-shən), *n.* the act of reexpanding.

**re|ex|pel** or **re-ex|pel** (rē′ek spel′), *v.t.,* **-pelled, -pel|ling.** to expel again.

**re|ex|pe|ri|ence** or **re-ex|pe|ri|ence** (rē′ek-spir′ē əns), *n., v.,* **-enced, -enc|ing.** — *n.* a renewed or repeated experience.
— *v.t.* to experience again.

**re|ex|plain** or **re-ex|plain** (rē′ek splān′), *v.t., v.i.* to explain again or anew.

**re|ex|plore** or **re-ex|plore** (rē′ek splôr′, -splōr′), *v.t., v.i.,* **-plored, -plor|ing.** to explore again.

**re|ex|port** or **re-ex|port** (*v.* rē′ek spôrt′, -spōrt′; *n.* rē eks′pôrt, -pōrt), *v.t.* to export (imported goods). — *n.* **1** something that is reexported: *Reexports over the same period have been 14 per cent up on the year* (Manchester Guardian). **2** a reexporting or being reexported: *Foreign sugars have not been taken to Hawaii for reexport to the Pacific Coast* (American). — **re′ex|por|ta′tion, re′-ex|por|ta′tion,** *n.*

**ref** (ref), *n. Informal.* a referee.

**ref.,** an abbreviation for the following:
**1** referee.
**2** reference.
**3** referred.
**4** reformation.
**5** reformed.
**6** reformer.

**re|fab|ri|cate** (rē fab′rə kāt), *v.t.,* **-cat|ed, -cat-ing.** to fabricate afresh.

**re|face** (rē fās′), *v.t.,* **-faced, -fac|ing.** **1** to repair the face of (a building, wall, stone, or other surface). **2** to put a new facing in (a garment).

**re|fash|ion** (rē fash′ən), *v.t.* = reshape: *The nineteenth century historian, who refashions the past on the lines of his own mind* (Mrs. Humphry Ward).

**re|fas|ten** (rē fas′ən, -fäs′-), *v.t.* to fasten again: *It was so negligently refastened* (Scott).

**Ref. Ch.,** Reformed Church.

**re|fect** (ri fekt′), *v.t. Archaic.* to refresh with food or drink. [< Latin *refectus,* past participle of *reficere;* see etym. under **refectory**]

**re|fec|tion** (ri fek′shən), *n.* **1** refreshment by food or drink. **2** a meal; repast: *They sat on Meredith's big porch ... and ate a substantial refection* (Booth Tarkington). [< Latin *refectiō, -ōnis* < *reficere;* see etym. under **refectory**]

**re|fec|tion|er** (ri fek′shə nər), *n.* a person in a monastery, abbey, or the like, in charge of the refectory and of supplies of food.

**re|fec|to|ri|al** (rē′fek tôr′ē əl, -tōr′-), *adj.* **1** having to do with refection. **2** used for refection.

**re|fec|to|ry** (ri fek′tər ē), *n., pl.* **-ries.** a room for meals, especially in a monastery, convent, or school: *School was dismissed, and all were gone into the refectory to tea* (Charlotte Brontë). [< Late Latin *refectōrium* < Latin *reficere* to refresh < *re-* again + *facere* make]

***refectory table**

***refectory table,** a long, narrow, heavy table, especially one having simple lines and sturdy construction: *A beautiful oak refectory table ... used at meal times four hundred years ago by Italian monks* (Maclean's).

**re|fel** (ri fel′), *v.t.*, **-felled, -fel|ling.** *Obsolete.* **1** to refute. **2** to reject. **3** to repel. [< Latin *refellere* to disprove, refute < *re-* back + *fallere* deceive]

**re|fer** (ri fėr′), *v.*, **-ferred, -fer|ring.** —*v.i.* **1** to direct attention: *The minister often refers to the Bible.* **2** to relate; apply: *The rule refers only to special cases.* **3** to turn for information or help: *Writers often refer to a dictionary to find the meaning of words.*

—*v.t.* **1a** to send or direct for information, help, or action: *We referred him to the boss. Our librarian refers us to many good books. They referred me to another department.* **b** to direct the attention of: *The asterisk refers the reader to a footnote. These weird sisters ... referred me to the coming on of time, with "Hail, King that shalt be!"* (Shakespeare). **2** to hand over; submit: *Let's refer the dispute to the umpire. She treated me with a certain consideration, and often referred questions to me* (Francis M. Crawford). **3** to assign to or think of as caused by; assign: *Some people refer all their troubles to bad luck instead of to poor work.* **4** *Archaic.* to defer.

[< Latin *referre* < *re-* back + *ferre* take, bring]

—*Syn. v.i.* **1 Refer, allude** mean to speak of something in a way to turn attention to it. **Refer** means to make direct or specific mention: *In his speech he referred to newspaper accounts of the election campaign.* **Allude** means to mention indirectly: *She never referred to the incident, but often alluded to it by hinting.*

► **refer back.** Though *refer back* is not uncommon, it is redundant and regarded as nonstandard in some quarters, though logical parallels, such as *raise up* and *recede from*, do not seem to be as objectionable: *The relative pronoun refers (back) to its antecedent.*

**ref|er|a|ble** (ref′ər ə bəl), *adj.* that can be referred.

**ref|er|ee** (ref′ə rē′), *n.*, *v.*, **-eed, -ee|ing.** —*n.* **1** a judge of play in games and sports: *the referee in a football game.* **2** a person to whom something is referred for decision or settlement: *The Governor acted as referee in the dispute between the striking garbagemen and the city government.*

—*v.t., v.i.* to act as referee; act as referee in or of: *He had never refereed Saddler before, but he had heard about his propensity for bringing out the worst in other fighters' natures* (New Yorker).

**referee's position**, a starting position in amateur wrestling used after the first period of a match, in which one wrestler gets on hands and knees while the other stands at the opponent's side with an arm around the opponent's waist and a hand on the opponent's elbow. The referee determines which wrestler takes each position.

**ref|er|ence** (ref′ər əns, ref′rəns), *n., adj., v.*, **-enced, -enc|ing.** —*n.* **1** direction of the attention, as by a footnote: *This history book contains many references to larger histories.* **2** a statement or book referred to: *You will find that reference on page 16.* **3** something used for information or help: *A dictionary is a book of reference.* **4** a person who can give information about another person's character or ability: *He gave his bank as a reference for credit.* **5** a statement about someone's character or ability: *The boy had excellent references from men for whom he had worked.* **6** relation; respect; regard: *This test is to be taken by all pupils without reference to age or grade.* **7** the act of referring or fact of being referred.

—*adj.* used for information or help: *a reference section in the library.*

—*v.t.* **1** to provide with references or a point of reference: *... such control [is] not difficult when referenced to positions of fixed stars, or points on earth* (Bulletin of Atomic Scientists). **2** to assign as a reference: *This is a private communication and should be referenced as such* (Science).

**in** (or **with**) **reference to**, in relation to; with respect to; about; concerning: *The same notation ... was used to express the properties of the ellipse in reference to its axes* (Dionysius Lardner). *All existing lives must, with reference to their environment, be the best possible lives* (Henry Drummond).

**make reference to**, to mention: *Do not make any reference to his lameness.*

**reference beam**, the beam of laser light that is aimed at the photographic plate or film in holography.

**reference book**, **1** a book referred to for information on a special or general subject, often having the subject headings in alphabetical order. Dictionaries, encyclopedias, and almanacs are reference books. **2** a book held for consultation, but not available for loan from a library.

**reference group**, *Sociology.* a group of people whose standards and values are admired by an individual and have a greater influence on him than the standards and values of his own group or other groups.

**reference library**, a library consisting largely of reference books which are consulted only in the library.

**reference mark**, a number, letter, star, dagger, or other printing device, used to refer a reader from the text to a footnote, an appendix, or other reference.

**ref|er|end** (ref′ər ənd), *n.* a person or thing referred to; referent.

**ref|er|en|da|ry**[1] (ref′ə ren′dər ē), *n., pl.* **-ries.** **1** any one of various medieval court or state officials to whom petitions or other matters were referred. **2** = referee. [< Medieval Latin *referendarius* < Latin *referendus* one to whom a matter must be referred; (literally) gerundive of *referre;* see etym. under **refer**]

**ref|er|en|da|ry**[2] (ref′ə ren′dər ē), *adj.* of or like a referendum. [< *referend*(um) + *-ary*]

**ref|er|en|dum** (ref′ə ren′dəm), *n., pl.* **-dums, -da** (-də). **1** the principle or process of submitting a bill already passed by the lawmaking body to a direct vote of the citizens for approval or rejection. **2** a vote on such a bill. **3** the act or process of submitting any matter to a direct vote. [< Latin *referendum* that which must be referred; (literally) neuter gerundive of *referre;* see etym. under **refer**]

**ref|er|ent** (ref′ər ənt), *n., adj.* —*n.* **1** a person who is consulted. **2** a person, thing, or idea that a word stands for or refers to: *Individuals may differ widely in the referents they have for the same word* (Ogburn and Nimkoff).

—*adj.* containing a reference; referring.

[< Latin *referēns, -entis,* present participle of *referre;* see etym. under **refer**]

**ref|er|en|tial** (ref′ə ren′shəl), *adj.* of or making reference. —**ref′er|en′tial|ly,** *adv.*

**re|fer|ral** (ri fėr′əl), *n.* **1** the act of referring; directing or assigning of someone or something to a person, place, or position, for some purpose: *the referral of a patient by his family doctor to a specialist, the referral of an unemployed worker to a factory.* **2** a person who is referred.

**re|ferred pain** (ri fėrd′), pain that proceeds from a part or organ other than the part or organ actually affected or irritated: *Pain from the heart may be felt in the left arm. ... This referred pain may be accounted for by the fact that nerves from the involved structures enter the spinal cord at the same level* (Martin E. Spencer).

**re|fer|rer** (ri fėr′ər), *n.* a person who refers.

**re|fer|ri|ble** (ri fėr′ə bəl), *adj.* = referable.

**re|fer|ti|lize** (rē fėr′tə līz), *v.t.*, **-lized, -liz|ing.** to fertilize again.

**ref|fo** (ref′ō), *n., pl.* **-fos.** *Australian Slang.* a European refugee.

**re|fight** (rē fīt′), *v.t.*, **-fought, -fight|ing.** to fight again: *If we could each of us refight our battles, doubtless our tactics would be different* (Margaret Goodman).

**re|fig|ure** (rē fig′yər), *v.t., v.i.*, **-ured, -ur|ing.** to figure again.

**re|fill** (*v.* rē fil′; *n.* rē′fil′), *v., n.* —*v.t., v.i.* to fill again.

—*n.* **1** something to refill with: *Refills can be bought for some kinds of pens and pencils.* **2** the action of filling again, as of a medical prescription: *The doctor limited the antibiotic refills to two.*

**re|fill|a|ble** (rē fil′ə bəl), *adj.* that can be refilled.

**re|fi|nance** (rē fī′nans; rē′fī nans′, -fə-), *v.t.*, **-nanced, -nanc|ing.** to finance again or anew, as by arranging new terms, or borrowing to settle notes.

**re|fine** (ri fīn′), *v.*, **-fined, -fin|ing.** —*v.t.* **1** to make pure; free from impurities: *Sugar, oil, and metals are refined before being used. Over the past 100 years, the sugar industry has steadily improved its techniques for extracting ... and refining the crystallized grains* (Newsweek). **2** to make fine, polished, or cultivated: *Reading good books helped to refine her speech. Love refines the thoughts* (Milton). **3** to change or remove, as by polishing or purifying. **4** to make very fine, subtle, or exact.

—*v.i.* **1** to become pure; become free from impurities. **2** to become fine, polished, or cultivated. **3** to use nicety or subtlety of thought or language; make fine distinctions.

**refine on** (or **upon**), **a** to improve: *Our laws have considerably refined ... upon the invention* (William Blackstone). **b** to excel: *Chaucer has refined on Boccace, and has mended the stories which he has borrowed* (John Dryden).

[< *re-* + *fine*[1] make fine; probably patterned on Middle French *raffiner* < *re-* + Old French *affiner.* Compare etym. under **affine.**]

**re|fined** (ri fīnd′), *adj.* **1** freed from impurities; made pure: *refined sugar, refined gold. They claimed that the refined products of the crude oil were also theirs* (London Times). **2** freed or free from grossness, coarseness, crudeness, or vulgarity: *refined tastes, a refined voice.* **SYN:** polished, cultured. **3** having or showing nice feeling, taste, manners, or language; cultivated; well-bred: *refined manners.* **4** fine; subtle: *refined distinctions.* **5** minutely precise: *refined measurements.*

**re|fine|ment** (ri fīn′mənt), *n.* **1** fineness of feeling, taste, manners, or language: *Good manners and correct speech are marks of refinement.* **SYN:** culture, polish. **2** the act or result of refining: *Gasoline is produced by the refinement of petroleum.* **3** improvement; advance: *refinements in the design of a new engine.* **4** a fine point; subtle distinction. **5** an improved, higher, or extreme form of something: *Such refinements of cruelty as were practiced by Caligula* (Sir Winston Churchill).

**re|fin|er** (ri fī′nər), *n.* a person or thing that refines: *Oil refiners on the Gulf Coast trimmed bulk gasoline prices a quarter cent a gallon* (Wall Street Journal).

**re|fin|er|y** (ri fī′nər ē, -fīn′rē), *n., pl.* **-er|ies.** a building and machinery for purifying metal or sugar, distilling petroleum, or other such processes: *The Bureau of Mines has sold its shale-oil refinery at Rifle, Colo.* (Newsweek).

**re|fin|ish** (rē fin′ish), *v.t.* to put a new finish on (as wood or metal): *to refinish furniture.* —**re|fin′ish|er,** *n.*

**re|fire** (rē fīr′), *v.t.*, **-fired, -fir|ing.** to fire again: *to refire a furnace.*

**re|fit** (*v.* rē fit′; *n.* rē′fit, rē fit′), *v.*, **-fit|ted, -fit|ting,** *n.* —*v.t.* to fit, prepare, or equip for use again: *The old ship was refitted for the voyage.*

—*v.i.* to get fresh supplies: *His ship put into Portsmouth to refit* (Lytton Strachey).

—*n.* the act of refitting: *An explosion occurred ... in the diesel room of H.M.S. Daring under refit in Devonport dockyard* (London Times). —**re|fit′ment,** *n.*

**re|fix** (rē fiks′), *v.t.* to set up again; attach again in the same or another place. —**re′fix|a′tion,** *n.*

**refl.**, an abbreviation for the following:
**1** reflection.
**2a** reflective. **b** reflectively.
**3** reflex.
**4a** reflexive. **b** reflexively.

**re|flate** (ri flāt′), *v.t., v.i.*, **-flat|ed, -flat|ing.** = reinflate.

**re|fla|tion** (ri flā′shən), *n.* inflation stimulated to restore business conditions to their level before the recession: *You regard deflation as the danger and a little reflation as desirable?* (Punch). [< *re-* + (in)*flation*]

**re|fla|tion|ar|y** (ri flā′shə ner′ē), *adj.* of or inducing reflation: *reflationary measures.*

**re|flect** (ri flekt′), *v.t.* **1** to turn back or throw back (light, heat, sound, or the like): *The sidewalks reflect heat on a hot day.* **2a** to give back an image or likeness of: *A mirror reflects your face.* **b** *Figurative: The newspaper reflected the owner's opinions.* **3** to serve to cast or bring: *A brave act reflects credit on the person who does it.* —*v.i.* **1** to cast back light, heat, sound, etc.: *The sun's rays reflected on the ocean.* **2** to give back an image: *A mirror reflects.* **3** to think; think carefully: *Take time to reflect before doing important things.* **SYN:** meditate, ponder, deliberate. See syn. under **think.** **4** to cast blame, reproach, or discredit: *The child's bad behavior reflects on his home training.*

[< Latin *reflectere* < *re-* back + *flectere* to bend]

**re|flect|ance** (ri flek′təns), *n.* the amount of light reflected by a surface in proportion to the amount of light falling on the surface: *It is evident that reflectance is related in a general way to the lightness of the color perceived* (Deane B. Judd).

**re|flect|i|ble** (ri flek′tə bəl), *adj.* that can be reflected.

**re|flect|ing microscope** (ri flek′ting), a microscope that uses mirrors rather than lenses to magnify.

**reflecting telescope**, a telescope in which light from the object is gathered and focused by a concave mirror or speculum and the resulting image is magnified by the eyepiece. See picture under **telescope.**

**re|flec|tion** (ri flek′shən), *n.* **1** the act of reflecting or the condition of being reflected: *Radar uses the reflection of radio waves.* **2** something reflected: *An echo is a reflection of sound.* **3a** likeness; image: *You can see your reflection*

---

**Pronunciation Key:** hat, āge, cãre, fär; let, ēqual, tėrm; it, īce; hot, ōpen, ôrder; oil, out; cup, pu̇t, rüle; child; long; thin; ᴛʜen; zh, measure; ə represents **a** in about, **e** in taken, **i** in pencil, **o** in lemon, **u** in circus.

*in a mirror. See the reflection of the tree in this still water.* **b** *Figurative: The boy's mannerisms were a reflection of his father's.* **4** thinking, especially careful thinking: *On reflection, the plan seemed too dangerous.* **5** an idea or remark resulting from careful thinking; idea; remark: *He made very wise reflections and observations upon all I said* (Jonathan Swift). **6** a remark or action that casts blame or discredit. **7** blame; discredit. **8** *Anatomy.* **a** the bending of a part back upon itself. **b** the part bent back.

**re|flec|tion|al** (ri flek′shə nəl), *adj.* **1** of reflection. **2** caused by reflection.

**re|flec|tive** (ri flek′tiv), *adj.* **1** that reflects; reflecting: *the reflective surface of polished metal.* **2** thoughtful: *The judge had a reflective look.* **SYN:** contemplative, meditative. **3** reflected: *reflective light or glory.* — **re|flec′tive|ly,** *adv.* — **re|flec′tive-ness,** *n.*

**re|flec|tiv|i|ty** (rē′flek tiv′ə tē), *n.* the quality or state of being reflective.

**re|flec|tom|e|ter** (rē′flek tom′ə tər), *n.* an instrument for measuring the reflecting power of surfaces.

**re|flec|tom|e|try** (rē′flek tom′ə trē), *n.* the measurement of the reflecting power of surfaces, as with a reflectometer.

**re|flec|tor** (ri flek′tər), *n.* **1** any thing, surface, or device that reflects light, heat, sound, or the like, especially a piece of glass or metal for reflecting light in a particular direction. Reflectors are usually concave. *It is no coincidence that polished silver is the best light reflector known as well as being the best electrical conductor* (J. Crowther). **2** a telescope with a concave mirror which reflects and focuses light; reflecting telescope.

**re|flec|tor|ize** (ri flek′tə rīz), *v.t.,* **-ized, -iz|ing.** to treat with a substance that reflects light at night: *to reflectorize road signs, reflectorized cloth.*

**re|flec|to|scope** (ri flek′tə skōp), *n.* an electronic device for detecting flaws in metallic objects or parts by passing ultrasonic waves through them. The slightest flaw breaks the pattern of the waves.

**re|flet** (rə fle′), *n.* **1** the reflection of light or color. **2** luster; iridescence. [< French *reflet* reflection < Italian *riflesso,* learned borrowing from Latin *reflexus, -ūs* a bending back < *reflectere* reflect]

**re|flex** (*n., adj.* rē′fleks; *v.* ri fleks′), *n., adj., v.* — *n.* **1** an involuntary action in direct response to a stimulation of some nerve cells. Sneezing, vomiting, and shivering are reflexes. *Simple reflexes are considered to be independent of any learning process* (S. A. Barnett). **2** *Figurative.* something reflected; image; reflection: *A law should be a reflex of the will of the people.* **3** a copy. **4** a reflex receiving set.
— *adj.* **1** not voluntary; not controlled by the will; coming as a direct response to a stimulation of some sensory nerve cells. Yawning is a reflex action. *Sometimes he binds his limbs with rope so that reflex movements will not jar his hand* (Newsweek). **2** bent back; turned back: *reflex light.* **3** (of an angle) more than 180 degrees and less than 360 degrees. **4** coming as a reaction. **5** *Radio.* having amplifier tubes that function as both radio-frequency and audio-frequency amplifiers simultaneously.
— *v.t.* to bend back; turn back.
[< Latin *reflexus, -ūs* < *reflectere;* see etym. under **reflect**]

**reflex arc,** the nerve path in the body leading from stimulus to reflex action. The impulse travels inward to a nerve center and the response outward to the organ or part where the action takes place.

***reflex camera,** a camera in which the image received through the lens is reflected by a mirror onto a horizontal piece of ground glass, for viewing and focusing.

***reflex camera**

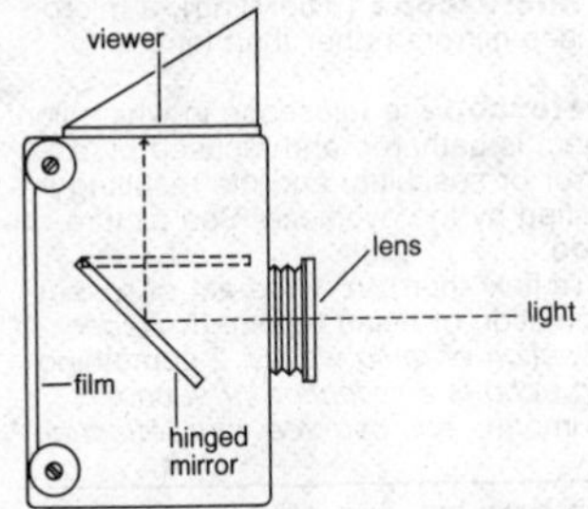

single-lens reflex camera

**re|flexed** (ri flekst′), *adj.* turned, bent, or folded back: ... *reflexed bracts that conceal the flowers* (Joseph Hooker).

**re|flex|i|ble** (ri flek′sə bəl), *adj.* that can be reflected.

**re|flex|i|bil|i|ty** (ri flek′sə bil′ə tē), *n.* ability to be reflected.

**re|flex|ion** (ri flek′shən), *n.* = reflection.

**re|flex|ion|al** (ri flek′shə nəl), *adj.* = reflectional.

**re|flex|ive** (ri flek′siv), *adj., n.* — *adj.* **1** *Grammar.* expressing an action that refers to the subject. **2** occurring in reaction. **3** *Obsolete.* reflective.
— *n. Grammar.* a reflexive verb or pronoun. In "The boy hurt himself," *hurt* and *himself* are reflexives. — **re|flex′ive|ly,** *adv.* — **re|flex′ive|ness,** *n.*

► **reflexive pronouns.** The pronouns such as *myself, yourself,* and *himself* are called *reflexive* when they refer to the subject and are used as direct objects, indirect objects, or objects of prepositions: *He shaves himself. She bought herself two hats.* When used as modifiers, they are called intensifying pronouns or adjectives: *He himself is going. He is going himself.*

**re|flex|iv|i|ty** (rē′flek siv′ə tē), *n.* the quality or condition of being reflexive.

**re|flex|ly** (rē′fleks lē), *adv.* in a reflex manner: *The cat continued to survive for many hours, an unconscious automaton, yet reacting reflexly to many stimuli* (New Scientist).

**re|flex|ness** (rē′fleks nis), *n.* the state or condition of being reflex.

**re|flex|o|log|i|cal** (ri flek′sə loj′ə kəl), *adj.* of or having to do with reflexology.

**re|flex|ol|o|gy** (rē′flek sol′ə jē), *n.* the study of behavior as a series of reflexes: *In reflexology and its offspring we have the beginnings ... of a rational account of behavior in terms of its bodily mechanisms, especially the central nervous system* (S. A. Barnett).

**re|float** (rē flōt′), *v.t.* to float, or set afloat, again: *to refloat a sunken vessel.*

**re|flo|res|cence** (rē′flô res′əns, -flō-), *n.* a blossoming again.

**re|flo|res|cent** (rē′flô res′ənt, -flō-), *adj.* coming into bloom again; reflowering.

**re|flour|ish** (rē flėr′ish), *v.i.* to revive, flourish, or bloom anew.

**re|flow** (*v.,* rē flō′; *n.* rē′flō), *v., n.* — *v.i.* **1** to flow back; ebb. **2** to flow again.
— *n.* the action or process of flowing back or flowing again: (*Figurative.*) *The reflow of funds ... into Britain has already begun* (New York Times).

**re|flow|er** (rē flou′ər), *v.i.* to flower again.
— *v.t.* to cause to flower or bloom again.

**ref|lu|ence** (ref′lu̇ əns), *n.* an ebb or backward movement.

**ref|lu|ent** (ref′lu̇ ənt), *adj.* flowing back; ebbing. [< Latin *refluēns, -entis,* present participle of *refluere* flow back < *re-* back + *fluere* to flow]

**re|flux** (*n.* rē′fluks; *v.* rē fluks′), *n., v.* — *n.* **1** the action or process of flowing back (as of water, air, or blood); reflow. **2** the act or process of refluxing.
— *v.t.* to boil (liquid) so that the vapor condenses and flows back to its source: *The formaldehyde solution was refluxed over the mineral kaolinite* (S. W. Fox and Angus Wood).

**re|flux|ion** (rē fluk′shən), *n.* reflux; reflow.

**re|foc|il|late** (ri fos′ə lāt), *v.t.,* **-lat|ed, -lat|ing.** to revive, refresh, reanimate, or comfort (as a person, the spirits, or senses): *About every three hours his man was to bring him a roll and a pot of ale to refocillate his wasted spirits* (John Aubrey). [< Late Latin *refocillātus,* past participle of *refocillāre* to warm into life again, revive < Latin *re-* back + *focillāre* to warm into life < *focus* hearth] — **re|foc′il|la′tion,** *n.*

**re|fo|cus** (rē fō′kəs), *v.t., v.i.,* **-cused, -cus|ing** or (*especially British*) **-cussed, -cus|sing.** to focus again: *to refocus one's sights, to refocus upon a goal.*

**re|fold** (rē fōld′), *v.t.* to fold again.

**re|for|est** (rē fôr′ist, -for′-), *v.t., v.i.* to replant with trees. — **re′for|est|a′tion,** *n.*

**re|forge** (rē fôrj′, -fōrj′), *v.t.,* **-forged, -forg|ing.** to forge or form again; to fabricate or fashion anew; make over. — **re|forg′er,** *n.*

**re|form** (ri fôrm′), *v., n., adj.* — *v.t.* **1** to make better: *Some prisons try to reform criminals instead of just punishing them.* **2** to improve by removing faults or abuses: *to reform a city administration.* **3** to crack and refine (petroleum or gas): *The use of a platinum-containing catalyst for the reforming of straight-run gasoline has undergone rapid acceptance by the petroleum industry* (Vladimir Haensel).
— *v.i.* to become better: *The boy promised to reform if given another chance.*
— *n.* an improvement, especially one made by removing faults or abuses; change intended to be an improvement: *The new government made many needed reforms. The most fundamental reform, then, is a reform in fundamental point of view* (Bulletin of Atomic Scientists).
— *adj.* of reform; favoring reform: *a reform movement within a party, a reform mayor.*
[< Latin *reformāre* < *re-* again + *formāre* to form < *forma* form]

**Re|form** (ri fôrm′), *adj.* of or having to do with the liberal branch of Judaism, as contrasted with the Orthodox and Conservative branches: *The Reform Branch ... members seek to interpret Jewish religious law in accordance with the needs of contemporary life* (New York Times). *The worship would be according to the relaxed rules of Reform Judaism* (Time). [< *reform*]

**re-form** (rē fôrm′), *v.t.* to form again. — *v.i.* **1** to take a new shape: *The effect ... is comparable to ... watching clouds form and re-form in the changing light of a hot afternoon* (Atlantic). **2** to form again.

**re|form|a|bil|i|ty** (ri fôr′mə bil′ə tē), *n.* the quality or condition of being reformable.

**re|form|a|ble** (ri fôr′mə bəl), *adj.* that can be reformed.

**ref|or|ma|tion** (ref′ər mā′shən), *n.* the act or process of reforming or condition of being reformed; change for the better; improvement.

**Ref|or|ma|tion** (ref′ər mā′shən), *n.* the great religious movement in Europe in the 1500's that aimed at reform within the Roman Catholic Church but led to the establishment of Protestant churches.

**re-for|ma|tion** (rē′fôr mā′shən), *n.* the act or process of formation over again.

**ref|or|ma|tion|al** (ref′ər mā′shə nəl), *adj.* of or having to do with reformation.

**Ref|or|ma|tion|al** (ref′ər mā′shə nəl), *adj.* of or having to do with the Reformation.

**re|for|ma|tive** (ri fôr′mə tiv), *adj.* that reforms; tending toward or inducing reform: *We are advised by the Prison Commissioners that periods of that kind are of very little value for reformative training* (Economist). — **re|for′ma|tive|ly,** *adv.* — **re|for′ma|tive|ness,** *n.*

**re-for|ma|tive** (rē fôr′mə tiv), *adj.* having the power of forming over again.

**re|form|a|to|ry** (ri fôr′mə tôr′ē, -tōr′-), *n., pl.* **-ries,** *adj.* — *n.* an institution for reforming young offenders against the laws; prison for young criminals; reform school: [*The prison farm*] *can be combined with any advantages in occupational training that reformatories may afford* (Emory S. Bogardus). — *adj.* serving to reform; intended to reform: *reformatory laws.*

**re|formed** (ri fôrmd′), *adj.* improved; amended.

**Re|formed** (ri fôrmd′), *adj.* of or having to do with the Protestant churches, especially the Calvinistic as distinguished from the Lutheran.

**reformed spelling,** any one of various systems designed to simplify the spelling of English words, especially by making the spelling consistent with pronunciation and omitting unpronounced letters. In various systems of reformed spelling words such as *knock, prologue, though,* and *photograph* have been spelled *nok, prolog, tho,* and *fotograf.*

**re|form|er** (ri fôr′mər), *n.* **1** a person who reforms, or tries to reform, some state of affairs, custom, or practice; supporter of reforms. **2** a device used especially to reform petroleum and natural gas.

**re|form|ism** (ri fôr′miz əm), *n.* social or political reform.

**re|form|ist** (ri fôr′mist), *n., adj.* — *n.* = reformer.
— *adj.* of reformists or reformism: *The move is part of the Government's stiffening resistance to the liberal and reformist influence of modern education and communications media* (New York Times).

**reform school,** = reformatory.

**re|for|mu|late** (rē fôr′myə lāt), *v.t.,* **-lat|ed, -lat|ing.** to formulate anew: *Luther's doctrine of justification by faith reformulated Gospel truth for the Reformation era* (Academy). — **re′for|mu|la′tion,** *n.*

**re|for|ti|fi|ca|tion** (rē′fôr tə fə kā′shən), *n.* **1** the action of fortifying again. **2** a new fortification.

**re|for|ti|fy** (rē fôr′tə fī), *v.t.,* **-fied, -fy|ing.** to fortify again: *I am repeating a judgment formed long ago, and often refortified* (John H. Skrine).

**re|fought** (rē fôt′), *v.* the past tense and past participle of **refight.**

**re|found**[1] (rē found′), *v.t.* to set up or found anew; reestablish: *Abingdon School, one of the oldest in the country, was founded or, as some aver, refounded in 1563* (London Times). [< *re-* + *found*[2]]

**re|found**[2] (rē found′), *v.t.* to cast or found anew; recast: *All our cannon ... needed to be refounded* (Thomas Carlyle). [< *re-* + *found*[3]]

**re|fract** (ri frakt′), *v.t.* to bend (a ray of light, sound waves, or a stream of electrons) from a straight course. Water refracts light. [< Latin *refractus,* past participle of *refringere* < *re-* back + *frangere* to break]

**re|frac|tile** (ri frak′təl), *adj.* exhibiting refraction; refractive.

**re|frac|til|i|ty** (rē′frak til′ə tē), *n.* the character of being refractile.

**re|fract|ing telescope** (ri frak′ting), a telescope in which light from the object is gathered and focused by a lens (the objective) and the resulting image is magnified by the eyepiece: *In combination, two double convex lenses can form a refracting telescope* (Robert H. Baker). See picture under **telescope**.

**re|frac|tion** (ri frak′shən), *n.* **1a** the process of turning or bending a ray of light when it passes at an angle from one medium into another of different density: *The refraction of light that gives a diamond its fire is based on certain mathematical laws* (New Yorker). **b** the process of turning or bending sound waves, a stream of electrons, etc., when passing from one medium to another of different density: *When a tracking radar is used for guidance of an ICBM or IRBM ... an error in apparent direction of the missile can be produced by refraction of the microwaves in clouds* (Kenneth F. Gantz). **2** the process of measuring refraction of the eye, a lens, or the like.

**re|frac|tion|al** (ri frak′shə nəl), *adj.* of or having to do with refraction.

**re|frac|tion|ate** (ri frak′shə nāt), *v.t.*, **-at|ed, -at|ing.** to fractionate again.

**refraction circle**, an instrument with a graduated circle for determining indexes of refraction.

**re|frac|tion|ist** (ri frak′shə nist), *n.* **1** a person skilled in determining the amount of refraction in a lens. **2** = optometrist.

**re|frac|tive** (ri frak′tiv), *adj.* **1** refracting; having power to refract. **2** having to do with or caused by refraction. **—re|frac′tive|ly,** *adv.* **—re|frac′tive|ness,** *n.*

**refractive index**, = index of refraction.

**re|frac|tiv|i|ty** (rē′frak tiv′ə tē), *n.* the quality or condition of being refractive.

**re|frac|tom|e|ter** (rē′frak tom′ə tər), *n.* **1** an instrument for measuring refraction: *Typical of automatic control of the quality of products is the recent commercial introduction of refractometers for monitoring processes involving liquids* (David M. Kiefer). **2** an instrument for determining the refractive condition of the eye.

**re|frac|to|met|ric** (ri frak′tə met′rik), *adj.* having to do with the measurement of refractive indexes.

**re|frac|tom|e|try** (rē′frak tom′ə trē), *n.* the use of refractometers.

**re|frac|tor** (ri frak′tər), *n.* **1** anything that refracts light rays, waves, sound, and other physical forces. **2** = refracting telescope.

**re|frac|to|ri|ly** (ri frak′tər ə lē), *adv.* stubbornly; obstinately.

**re|frac|to|ri|ness** (ri frak′tər ē nis), *n.* a refractory quality or condition.

**re|frac|to|ry** (ri frak′tər ē), *adj., n., pl.* **-ries.**
**—*adj.*** **1** hard to manage; stubborn; obstinate: *Mules are refractory.* **2** not yielding readily to treatment: *She had a refractory cough.* **3** hard to melt, reduce, or work: *Some ores are more refractory than others. The shock wave ... has a temperature ... several times the melting temperature of tungsten, the most refractory of metals* (Atlantic). **4a** (of a muscle, nerve, or other organ or organism) that responds less readily to stimulation after a response. **b** of the period in which this occurs.
**—*n.*** **1a** an ore, cement, ceramic material, or similar substance that is hard to melt, reduce, or work. **b** a brick made of refractory material, as used for lining furnaces. **2** *Obsolete.* a refractory person.

**re|frain¹** (ri frān′), *v.i.* to hold oneself back, especially from satisfying a momentary impulse; abstain: *Refrain from wrongdoing. I have hitherto refrained from appealing to you* (George Bernard Shaw). **—*v.t.*** **1** *Archaic.* to hold back; restrain: *I have refrained my feet from every evil way* (Psalms 119:101). **2** *Obsolete.* to keep from; abstain.
[< Old French *refrener,* learned borrowing from Latin *refrēnāre* < *re-* back + *frēnāre* to restrain, furnish with a bridle < *frēnum* a bridle]
**—re|frain′er,** *n.*
**—*Syn.*** *v.i.* **Refrain, abstain** mean to keep oneself from (doing) something. **Refrain** implies checking an impulse or urge to do it: *He politely refrained from saying what he thought of her hat.* **Abstain** implies holding back from it by force of will, deliberately doing without something one really wants but believes harmful or unnecessary: *He is abstaining from pie.*

**re|frain²** (ri frān′), *n.* **1a** a phrase or verse repeated regularly in a song or poem, especially at the end of each stanza; chorus. In "The Star-Spangled Banner" the refrain is "O'er the land of the free and the home of the brave." **b** *Figurative: One hears the same refrain across the country: "What difference would my vote make?"* (James Reston). *"We are not afraid, we are not afraid," the soldiers kept telling me, repeating a refrain as if they were trying to convince themselves* (Donald Kirk). **2** the music for the refrain of a song. [< Old French *refrain,* alteration of *refrait* (originally) past participle of *refraindre* break off, modulate < Vulgar Latin *refrangere* break off (in Late Latin, lessen), for Latin *refringere;* see etym. under **refract**]

**re|frame** (rē frām′), *v.t.*, **-framed, -fram|ing.** to frame anew.

**re|fran|gi|bil|i|ty** (ri fran′jə bil′ə tē), *n.* **1** the property of being refrangible. **2** the amount of refraction (as of light rays) that is possible.

**re|fran|gi|ble** (ri fran′jə bəl), *adj.* that can be refracted: *Rays of light are refrangible.* [< *re-* + Latin *frangere* to break + English *-ible*] **—re|fran′gi|ble|ness,** *n.*

**re|freeze** (rē frēz′), *v.t.*, **-froze, -fro|zen, -freez|ing.** to freeze a second time.

**re|fresh** (ri fresh′), *v.t.* **1** to make fresh again; renew: *His bath refreshed him. She refreshed herself with a cup of tea.* **SYN:** freshen, renovate, revive, enliven. **2** to restore to a certain condition by furnishing a fresh supply; replenish: *He refreshed his memory by a glance at the book. The trappers refreshed their winter food supplies by hunting.* **—*v.i.*** to become fresh again. [< Old French *refrescher* < *re-* again + *fresche* fresh < Germanic (compare Old High German *frisc,* Middle High German *fresch*)]

**re|fresh|er** (ri fresh′ər), *adj., n.* **—*adj.*** helping to renew knowledge or abilities, or to bring a person new needed knowledge: *to take a refresher course in typing.*
**—*n.*** **1** a person or thing that refreshes: *Lemonade on a hot day is a good refresher.* **2** a reminder. **3** *Especially British.* an extra fee paid to a lawyer in a prolonged case.

**re|fresh|ing** (ri fresh′ing), *adj.* **1** that refreshes: *a cool, refreshing drink, refreshing sleep.* **2** welcome as a pleasing change: *It was refreshing to have a steak after so many meals of hamburger.*
**—re|fresh′ing|ly,** *adv.* **—re|fresh′ing|ness,** *n.*

**re|fresh|ment** (ri fresh′mənt), *n.* **1** the act of refreshing or fact of being refreshed: *the refreshment of getting away from too much television.* **2** a thing that refreshes: *Iced tea is a good refreshment on a hot afternoon.*
**refreshments,** food or drink: *Cake and lemonade were the refreshments at our party.*

**re|frig|er|ant** (ri frij′ər ənt), *n., adj.* **—*n.*** **1** something that cools; refrigerating agent. Ice is a refrigerant. **2** a liquid or gas such as ammonia, used in mechanical refrigerators, freezers, and air conditioners to produce a low temperature. **3** a medicine for reducing fever: *Aspirin and quinine are refrigerants.*
**—*adj.*** **1** refrigerating; cooling. **2** reducing bodily heat or fever.

**re|frig|er|ate** (ri frij′ə rāt), *v.t.*, **-at|ed, -at|ing.** to make or keep (food, drinks, laboratory supplies, or scientific specimens) cold or cool: *Milk, meat, and ice cream must be refrigerated to prevent spoiling.* [< Latin *refrīgerāre* (with English *-ate*¹) < *re-* against + *frīgēre* to freeze, related to *frīgidus* cold, frigid]

**re|frig|er|a|tion** (ri frij′ə rā′shən), *n.* the act or process of cooling or keeping cold.

**re|frig|er|a|tive** (ri frij′ə rā′tiv), *adj., n.* **—*adj.*** that refrigerates.
**—*n.*** something that refrigerates.

**re|frig|er|a|tor** (ri frij′ə rā′tər), *n.* **1** a box, room, or other enclosed area for keeping foods and other items cool. An electric refrigerator cools without ice. **2** something that cools. [< obsolete French *refrigerateur,* ultimately < Latin *refrīgerāre;* see etym. under **refrigerate**]

**re|frig|er|a|to|ry** (ri frij′ər ə tôr′ē, -tōr′-), *adj., n., pl.* **-ries.** **—*adj.*** that refrigerates.
**—*n.*** a refrigerant or refrigerator.

**re|frin|gen|cy** (ri frin′jən sē), *n.* refringent or refractive power.

**re|frin|gent** (ri frin′jənt), *adj.* refracting; refractive: *a refringent prism.* [< Latin *refringēns, -entis,* present participle of *refringere;* see etym. under **refract**]

**Ref. Sp.,** reformed spelling.

**reft¹** (reft), *v. Archaic.* reaved; a past tense and a past participle of **reave**¹; deprived by force: *The barons reft King John of his power.*

**reft²** (reft), *v. Archaic.* reaved; a past tense and past participle of **reave**².

**re|fu|el** (rē fyü′əl), *v.*, **-eled, -el|ing** or (*especially British*) **-elled, -el|ling.** **—*v.t.*** to supply with fuel again.
**—*v.i.*** to take on a fresh supply of fuel: *A Boeing KC-97 tanker ... feeds a Boeing B-47 jet medium bomber by the "flying boom" method, one of two principal ways to refuel in midair* (New York Times).

**re|fu|el|a|ble** or (*especially British*) **re|fu|el|la|ble** (rē fyü′ə lə bəl), *adj.* that can be refueled: *a refuelable rocket booster.*

**re|fu|el|er** or (*especially British*) **re|fu|el|ler** (rē fyü′ə lər), *n.* a person or thing that refuels.

**ref|uge** (ref′yüj), *n., v.*, **-uged, -ug|ing.** **—*n.*** **1** shelter or protection from danger or trouble; safety; security: *The cat took refuge from the dogs in a tree.* **2** a place of safety or security. **3** a resort, shift, or expedient in any emergency: (*Figurative.*) *I consider proverbs as the refuge of weak minds* (Henry Kingsley).
**—*v.t.*** to give refuge to: *The political defector was refuged in an embassy.*
**—*v.i.*** to give refuge; take refuge: *Pirates refuged formerly in the Hebrides* (A. M. Johnson). *Topics range from statistical plant ecology ... to refuging* (Science News).
[< Old French *refuge,* learned borrowing from Latin *refugium* < *re-* back + *fugere* to flee + *-ium* place for]

**ref|u|gee** (ref′yə jē′, ref′yə jē), *n., v.*, **-geed, -gee|ing.** **—*n.*** a person who flees for refuge or safety, especially to a foreign country, in time of war, persecution, or disaster: *Many refugees came from Europe to America. The homeless refugees from the flooded town were helped by the Red Cross. ... the great drive of the Germans towards Antwerp ... which swept before it multitudes of Flemish refugees* (H. G. Wells).
**—*v.i.*** **1** to become a refugee. **2** to take refuge in another country.
[< French *réfugié* (literally) past participle of Middle French *réfugier,* learned borrowing from Latin *refugere* to flee; see etym. under **refuge**]

**re|ful|gence** (ri ful′jəns), *n.* a shining brightly; radiance; splendor. **SYN:** brightness.

**re|ful|gen|cy** (ri ful′jən sē), *n.* = refulgence.

**re|ful|gent** (ri ful′jənt), *adj.* shining brightly; radiant; splendid: *a refulgent sunrise.* [< Latin *refulgēns, -entis,* present participle of *refulgēre* < *re-* back + *fulgēre* to shine] **—re|ful′gent|ly,** *adv.*

**re|fund¹** (*v.* ri fund′; *n.* rē′fund), *v., n.* **—*v.t.*** **1** to pay back; repay; make restitution of (money received or taken): *If the shoes do not wear well, the shop will refund your money.* **2** *Obsolete.* to pour in or out again.
**—*v.i.*** to make repayment.
**—*n.*** **1** a return of money paid. **2** the money paid back.
[< Latin *refundere* < *re-* back + *fundere* pour]
**—re|fund′er,** *n.*

**re|fund²** (rē fund′), *v.t.* to change (as a debt or loan) into a new form: *These maturing obligations will either be redeemed ... or will be refunded into other obligations* (Andrew W. Mellon). [< *re-* + *fund*]

**re|fund|a|bil|i|ty** (ri fun′də bil′ə tē), *n.* the quality or condition of being refundable.

**re|fund|a|ble** (ri fun′də bəl), *adj.* capable of being refunded: *a refundable deposit. If you return the merchandise you bought in this store, the money you paid for it is refundable.*

**re|fund|ment** (ri fund′mənt), *n.* **1** the act or process of refunding; repayment. **2** a thing or amount refunded.

**re|fur|bish** (rē fėr′bish), *v.t.* to polish up again; do up anew; brighten; renovate: *to refurbish an old house.* **—re|fur′bish|ment,** *n.*

**re|fur|nish** (rē fėr′nish), *v.t.* to furnish over again.
**—re|fur′nish|ment,** *n.*

**re|fus|a|ble** (ri fyü′zə bəl), *adj.* that can be refused.

**re|fus|al** (ri fyü′zəl), *n.* **1** the act of refusing: *His refusal to play the game provoked the other boys.* **SYN:** denial, dissent. **2** the right to refuse or take a thing before it is offered to others: *He had a client who had first refusal on the painting* (Manchester Guardian Weekly).

**re|fuse¹** (ri fyüz′), *v.*, **-fused, -fus|ing.** **—*v.t.*** **1** to say no to; decline to accept; reject: *He refuses the offer. She refused him when he asked her to marry him.* **2** to deny (a request, demand, or invitation); decline to give or grant: *to refuse admittance.* **3** to say one will not do, give, or allow something; decline (to do something): *to refuse to discuss a question. He refuses to obey.* **4** to decline to jump over: *The black horse refused the fence.* **5** to hold or move (troops) back from the regular alignment, when about to meet the enemy. **6** *Obsolete.* to give up; abandon; renounce: *Deny thy father and refuse thy name* (Shakespeare).
**—*v.i.*** to say no; decline to accept or consent: *She is free to refuse.*
[< Old French *refuser* < Latin *refundere;* see etym. under **refund**¹] **—re|fus′er,** *n.*
**—*Syn.*** *v.t.* **1 Refuse, decline, reject** mean not to accept something offered. **Refuse** implies a direct and sometimes an ungracious denial: *He flatly refused to go with me after our quarrel.* **De-**

**Pronunciation Key:** hat, āge, cãre, fär; let, ēqual, tėrm; it, īce; hot, ōpen, ôrder; oil, out; cup, pu̇t, rüle; child; long; thin; ᴛʜen; zh, measure; ə represents **a** in about, **e** in taken, **i** in pencil, **o** in lemon, **u** in circus.

**cline** is more polite, implying reluctant rather than direct denial: *He declined my invitation because of a previous appointment.* **Reject** is more emphatic than *refuse*, implying a very positive denial: *He rejected my friendly advice upon further consideration.*

**ref|use²** (ref′yüs), *n., adj.*, —*n.* **1** useless stuff; waste; rubbish: *The garbagemen took away all refuse from the streets.* SYN: trash. **2** the scum, dregs, or outcast portions of something.
—*adj.* rejected as worthless or of little value; useless: *Every thing that was vile and refuse, that they destroyed utterly* (I Samuel 15:9).
[probably < Old French *refus* refusal; also, what is refused; (literally) past participle of *refuser;* see etym. under **refuse¹**]

**re|fus|nik** (ri fyüz′nik), *n.* a citizen of the Soviet Union who is refused permission by the authorities to leave the country: *Anatoly Scharansky, the celebrated 29-year-old refusnik was arrested ... at the Slepak apartment, where he had stayed for six months* (New York Post). [< *refuse¹* + *-nik*]

**ref|u|ta|bil|i|ty** (ref′yə tə bil′ə tē, ri fyü′-), *n.* the quality of being refutable.

**ref|u|ta|ble** (ref′yə tə bəl, ri fyü′-), *adj.* that can be refuted: *refutable illusions.*

**ref|u|ta|bly** (ref′yə tə blē, ri fyü′-), *adv.* in a refutable manner.

**ref|u|ta|tion** (ref′yə tā′shən), *n.* the disproof of a claim, opinion, or argument: *There is, however, more to life, and especially intellectual life, than the detection and refutation of error* (Bulletin of Atomic Scientists).

**re|fu|ta|tive** (ri fyü′tə tiv), *adj.* serving to refute.

**re|fu|ta|to|ry** (ri fyü′tə tôr′ē, -tōr′-), *adj.* = refutative.

**re|fute** (ri fyüt′), *v.t.*, **-fut|ed, -fut|ing.** **1** to show (a claim, opinion, or argument) to be false or incorrect; prove wrong; disprove: *How would you refute the statement that the cow jumped over the moon?* **2** to prove (a person) to be in error; confute. [< Latin *refūtāre* < *re-* back + *fūtāre* beat, drive] —**re|fut′er,** *n.*

**reg.,** an abbreviation for the following:
**1** regent.
**2** regiment.
**3** region.
**4** register.
**5** registered.
**6** registrar.
**7** registry.
**8a** regular. **b** regularly.
**9** regulation.
**10** regulator.

**Reg.,** **1** Queen (Latin *regina*). **2** Regent. **3** Regiment.

**re|gain** (*v.* ri gān′; *n.* rē′gān′), *v., n.* —*v.t.* **1** to get again; recover: *to regain health. I began by degrees to regain confidence* (Benjamin Jowett). **2** to get back to; reach again: *to regain the shore. You can regain the main road by turning left two miles ahead.*
—*n.* **1** the act or process of regaining; recovery: *Pakistan's strongest foreign policy has been ... regain of Kashmir* (Atlantic). **2** an amount regained or recovered.

**re|gain|a|ble** (ri gā′nə bəl), *adj.* that can be regained.

**re|gal¹** (rē′gəl), *adj.* **1** belonging to a king; royal: *The regal power descends from father to son.* SYN: See syn. under **royal.** **2** fit for a king; kinglike; stately; splendid; magnificent: *It was a regal banquet.* [< Latin *rēgālis* < *rēx, rēgis* king. See etym. of doublets **real², royal.**]

**re|gal²** (rē′gəl), *n.* a small, portable organ used in the 1500's and 1600's, having one, or sometimes two, sets of reed pipes played with keys by the right hand, while a small bellows was worked by the left hand. [< Middle French *régale,* perhaps < *régal* regal < Latin *rēgālis;* see etym. under **regal¹**]

**re|gale** (ri gāl′), *v.,* **-galed, -gal|ing,** *n.* —*v.t.* **1** to entertain very well; delight with something pleasing: *The old sailor regaled the boys with sea stories.* **2** to entertain or refresh with a choice meal.
—*v.i.* to feast: *The children regaled on raspberries and cream.*
—*n.* **1** a feast: *They indulged in a regale, relishing their buffalo beef* (Washington Irving). **2** choice food or drink. **3** regalement.
[< French *régaler* < Old French *regale,* noun < *gale* joy < *galer* make merry] —**re|gale′ment,** *n.* —**re|gal′er,** *n.*

**re|ga|li|a** (ri gā′lē ə, -gāl′yə), *n.pl.* **1** the emblems of royalty. Crowns and scepters are regalia. **2** the emblems or decorations of any society or order: *Tom joined the new order of Cadets of Temperance, being attracted by the showy character of their "regalia"* (Mark Twain). **3** clothes, especially fine clothes: *in party regalia.* **4** the rights and privileges of a king. [< Latin *rēgālia* royal things, neuter plural of *rēgālis;* see etym. under **regal¹**]

**re|gal|i|ty** (ri gal′ə tē), *n., pl.* **-ties.** **1** royalty; sovereignty; kingship. **2** a right or privilege having to do with a king. **3** a kingdom. **4** in Scotland: **a** a territory under the rule of a duke, baron, or other person appointed by the king. **b** such a grant by the king.

**re|gal|ly** (rē′gə lē), *adv.* = royally.

**regal moth,** a large, hairy moth with olive forewings and orange-red hind wings, both spotted with yellow. Its wingspread is about five inches.

**re|gal|va|nize** (rē gal′və nīz), *v.t.,* **-nized, -niz|ing.** to galvanize anew.

**Re|gan** (rē′gən), *n.* the wicked younger daughter in Shakespeare's play *King Lear.*

**re|gard** (ri gärd′), *v., n.* —*v.t.* **1** to think of; consider or look on: *He is regarded as the best doctor in town.* SYN: deem, hold. **2** to show thought or consideration for; care for; respect: *She always regards her parents' wishes. Regard the rights of others.* SYN: esteem. **3** to take notice of; pay attention to; heed: *None regarded her screams.* **4** to look at; look closely at; watch: *The cat regarded me anxiously when I picked up her kittens. He regarded me sternly.* **5** to concern; relate to.
—*v.i.* **1** to look closely. **2** to pay attention.
—*n.* **1** thoughtfulness of others and their feelings; care: *Have regard for the wishes of others.* SYN: See syn. under **respect.** **2** a look; steady look; gaze: *The man's regard seemed fixed upon some distant object. Claude turned and met the stranger's regard with a faint smile* (George W. Cable). **3** favor; good opinion; esteem: *Their boss has high regard for their ability. I once thought you had a kind of regard for her* (George Borrow). **4** a particular matter; point: *You are wrong in this regard.* **5** *Obsolete.* importance to others: *I am a bard of no regard Wi' gentlefolks, and a' that* (Robert Burns).
**as regards,** with respect to; concerning: *As regards money, I have enough. He was in a thoroughly sound condition as regards intellect* (Law Times).
**in** (or **with**) **regard to,** about; concerning; regarding; relating to: *The teacher wishes to speak to you with regard to being late. And in regard to remarkable persons in general, Michelet always shows them in relation to the social group which has molded them* (Edmund Wilson).
**regards,** good wishes; an expression of esteem: *I sent my regards.*
**without regard to,** not considering: *without regard to public opinion.*
[< Old French *regarder* < *re-* back + *garder,* earlier *guarder* guard; see etym. of doublet **reward.**]

**re|gard|a|ble** (ri gär′də bəl), *adj.* that can be or should be regarded.

**re|gard|ant** (ri gär′dənt), *adj. Heraldry.* looking backward: *a lion regardant.* [< Old French *regardant* (originally) present participle of *regarder* regard]

**re|gard|ful** (ri gärd′fəl), *adj.* **1** heedful or observant; mindful. **2** considerate; respectful. —**re|gard′ful|ly,** *adv.* —**re|gard′ful|ness,** *n.*

**re|gard|ing** (ri gär′ding), *prep.* with regard to; concerning; about: *a prophecy regarding the future of life on this planet. A letter regarding the boy's conduct was sent to his father.*

**re|gard|less** (ri gärd′lis), *adj., adv.* —*adj.* with no heed; careless: *A man who had been openly regardless of religious rites ...* (George Eliot).
—*adv.* in spite of all; anyway: *Time has proceeded regardless* (New Statesman). *The motive was perhaps shabby, but regardless, ... it was there to stay* (Sports Illustrated).
**regardless of,** in spite of; notwithstanding: *... a classic of the British theater mounted regardless of expense* (Show). *The President should run regardless of the state of his health* (Newsweek).
—**re|gard′less|ly,** *adv.* —**re|gard′less|ness,** *n.*

**re|gards** (ri gärdz′), *n.pl.* See under **regard.**

**re|gath|er** (rē gaᴛʜ′ər), *v.t., v.i.* to gather again or anew.

**re|gat|ta** (ri gat′ə), *n., pl.* **-tas.** **1** a series of boat races: *the annual regatta of the yacht club.* **2** a boat race. **3** a gondola race originally held in Venice. [< Italian *regata,* or dialectal (Venetian) Italian *regatta*]

**re|gauge** (rē gāj′), *v.t.,* **-gauged, -gaug|ing.** to gauge anew.

**regd.,** registered.

**re|gear** (rē gir′), *v.t.* to gear again: (*Figurative.*) *Specifically, it [a country] needs to regear and speed its missile program, and to reshape its alliances* (Time).

**re|ge|late** (rē′jə lāt, rR′jə lāt′), *v.i.,* **-lat|ed, -lat|ing.** to freeze together again.

**re|ge|la|tion** (rē′jə lā′shən), *n.* the action or fact of two pieces of ice having moist surfaces freezing together again at a temperature above the freezing point. [< *re-* again + Latin *gelātiō, -ōnis.* Compare etym. under **gelation.**]

***Ré|gence** (rē′jəns; *French* rā zhäɴs′), *adj.* of, having to do with, or characteristic of the French Regency, or the style of furniture of that period: *a Régence armchair.* [< French *Régence* < *régence* regency]

***Régence**

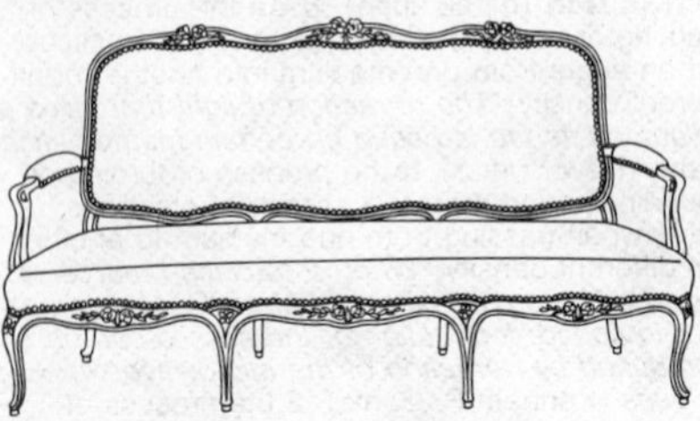

**re|gen|cy** (rē′jən sē), *n., pl.* **-cies.** **1** the position, office, or function of a regent or group of regents: *The Queen Mother held the regency till the young king became of age.* **2** a body of regents. **3** government consisting of regents. **4** the time during which there is a regency.

***Re|gen|cy** (rē′jən sē), *n., adj.* —*n.* **1** the period from 1811 to 1820 in English history, during which George, Prince of Wales, acted as regent. **2** the period from 1715 to 1723 in French history, during which Philippe, Duke of Orléans, acted as regent.
—*adj.* of or having to do with the English or French Regency or the style of furniture of these periods.

***Regency**

English Regency sofa

**re|gen|er|a|ble** (ri jen′ər ə bəl), *adj.* that can be regenerated.

**re|gen|er|a|cy** (ri jen′ər ə sē), *n.* regenerate state.

**re|gen|er|ate** (*v.* ri jen′ə rāt; *adj., n.* ri jen′ər it), *v.,* **-at|ed, -at|ing,** *adj., n.* —*v.t.* **1** to give a new and better spiritual life to: *Being converted regenerated the man. The doctrine of the Church is, that children are regenerated in holy baptism* (Charles Kingsley). **2** *Figurative.* to improve the moral condition of; put new life and spirit into; reform completely: *a band of Christian reformers, coming to purify and regenerate the land* (Washington Irving). **3** to grow again; form (new tissue, a new part, etc.) to replace what is lost: *If a young crab loses a claw, it can regenerate a new one.* **4** *Electronics.* to increase the amplification of, by transferring a portion of the power from the output circuit to the input circuit. **5** *Physics.* to cause (a substance) to return intermittently to its original state or condition. **6** to make use of (pressure, heat, energy, force, or some material) that would normally be unused: *They were testing a Boeing system for regenerating oxygen for space crews* (New Scientist).
—*v.i.* to reform; be regenerated: *Blood vessels regenerate very quickly* (Bernard Donovan).
—*adj.* **1** born again spiritually. **2** *Figurative.* made over in better form, especially as formed anew morally.
—*n. Biology.* a regenerated part, organ, or organism: *We would ... retrain both head and tail regenerates to see if either half showed any evidence of the prior conditioning* (New Scientist).
[< Latin *regenerāre* (with English *-ate¹*) make over < *re-* again + *generāre* to produce. Compare etym. under **generate.**] —**re|gen′er|ate|ly,** *adv.* —**re|gen′er|ate|ness,** *n.*

**re|gen|er|a|tion** (ri jen′ə rā′shən), *n.* **1** the action of regenerating or process or fact of being regenerated. **2** the rebirth of the spirit: *Spiritual regeneration begins naturally among the poor and humble* (James A. Froude). (*Figurative.*) *All great regenerations are the universal movement of the mass* (Edward G. E. Bulwer-Lytton). **3a** the formation of new animal tissue to repair the waste of the body or to replace worn-out tissue. **b** the reproduction of lost parts or organs. **4** *Electronics.* the amplification of the strength of a radio signal by transferring a portion of the power from the output circuit to the input circuit.

**re|gen|er|a|tive** (ri jen′ə rā′tiv, -ər ə-), *adj.* tending to regenerate; regenerating. —**re|gen′er|a′tive|ly,** *adv.*

**regenerative circuit,** a circuit formed in some incandescent lamps by the conversion of tungsten into a chemical before it evaporates and its subsequent redeposition on the filament as tungsten.

**re|gen|er|a|tor** (ri jen′ə rā′tər), *n.* **1** a person or thing that regenerates. **2** a device in a furnace, engine, or other mechanism, for heating incoming air.

**re|gent** (rē′jənt), *n., adj.* —*n.* **1** a person who rules when the regular ruler is absent, unfit, too young, or temporarily disqualified: *The Queen was the regent till the prince grew up.* **2** a member of a governing board. Many universities have boards of regents. *An individual alumnus, industrialist, regent or philanthropist can aid this effort by discussing the problem at the institutional level* (Newsweek). **3** *Obsolete.* a ruler; governor.
—*adj.* **1** acting as a regent. **2** *Obsolete.* ruling; governing.
[< Latin *regēns, -entis,* present participle of *regere* to rule, direct, straighten]

**re|gent|al** (rē′jən təl), *adj.* of or having to do with a regent or regents: *a regental board or committee.*

**regent bird,** an Australian bowerbird, the male of which has velvety, black-and-yellow feathers. [< the Prince *Regent* of England, afterward George IV, 1762–1830]

**re|gent|ship** (rē′jənt ship), *n.* the position of a regent; regency.

**re|ger|mi|nate** (rē jėr′mə nāt), *v.i.,* **-nat|ed, -nat|ing.** to germinate again: *This tree regerminates perpetually* (Thomas Taylor). —**re′ger|mi|na′tion,** *n.*

**re|ges** or **Re|ges** (rē′jēz), *n.* plural of **rex** or **Rex.**

**reg|gae** (reg′ā, rā′gā), *n.* a simple, lively, rhythmic form of rock'n'roll music of West Indian origin: *Reggae is characterized by a loping beat and sparing use of instrumental effects* (Ed Ward). [< a native name in the British West Indies]

**reg|i|cid|al** (rej′ə sī′dəl), *adj.* of or having to do with regicide or a regicide.

**reg|i|cide**[1] (rej′ə sīd), *n.* the crime of killing a king. [< Latin *rēx, rēgis* + English *-cide*[2]]

**reg|i|cide**[2] (rej′ə sīd), *n.* **1** a person who kills a king. **2** Often, **Regicide.** one of the judges who sentenced Charles I to death. [< Latin *rēx, rēgis* + English *-cide*[1]]

**ré|gie** (rā zhē′, rā′zhē), *n.* **1** an excise or revenue service or department, as in France. **2** a government monopoly, as of tobacco, used as a means of taxation. [< French *régie* < *régir* govern, learned borrowing from Latin *regere* to rule, straighten]

**re|gild** (rē gild′), *v.t.* to gild anew.

**re|gime** or **ré|gime** (ri zhēm′, rā-), *n.* **1** the system of government or rule; prevailing system: *Under the old regime women could not vote. The Russians may mean what they say when they describe their present régime as a transitory stage* (Bulletin of Atomic Scientists). **2** any prevailing political or social system. **3** the period or length of a regime. **4** *Informal.* a system of living; regimen: *The baby's regime includes two naps a day.* [< French *régime,* learned borrowing from Latin *regimen.* See etym. of doublet **regimen.**]

**reg|i|men** (rej′ə men, -mən), *n.* **1** a set of rules or habits of diet, exercise, or manner of living intended to improve health, reduce weight, cultivate the mind, or otherwise make something better or achieve some goal. **2** the act of governing; government; rule. **3** *Grammar.* the influence of one word in determining the case or mood of another; government. [< Latin *regimen, -inis* < *regere* to rule, straighten. See etym. of doublet **regime.**]

**reg|i|ment** (*n.* rej′ə mənt; *v.* rej′ə ment), *n., v.*
—*n.* **1** a unit of an army made up of several battalions or squadrons of soldiers organized into one large group, usually commanded by a colonel. It is smaller than a brigade. *Each division will comprise five battle groups (instead of the traditional three regiments)* (Newsweek). **2** *Figurative.* a large number: *He was living in that magnificent house all alone, with a whole regiment of servants* (Arnold Bennett). **3** *Archaic.* rule or authority.
—*v.t.* **1** to form into a regiment or organized group. **2** to assign to a regiment or group. **3** *Figurative.* to treat in a strict or uniform manner: *A totalitarian state regiments its citizens.* **4** to put in order or organize into some system.
[< Late Latin *regimentum* rule, direction < Latin *regere* to rule, straighten]

**reg|i|men|tal** (rej′ə men′təl), *adj., n.* —*adj.* of or having to do with a regiment: *He led the regimental band ashore at Normandy, on D Day* (Newsweek).
—*n.* **regimentals,** a military uniform: *Colonel Forster ... in his regimentals* (Jane Austen).
—**reg′i|men′tal|ly,** *adv.*

**reg|i|men|ta|tion** (rej′ə men tā′shən), *n.* **1** formation into organized or uniform groups. **2** the act or process of making uniform. **3** *Figurative.* subjection to control: *In time of war there may be regimentation of our work, play, food, and clothing. The whole plan would lead to complete regimentation of farming, with each farmer told exactly how many pounds or bushels of every crop he could sell* (Newsweek).

**re|gim|i|nal** (ri jim′ə nəl), *adj.* having to do with a regimen.

**re|gi|na** (ri jī′nə, -jē′-), *n.* = queen. [< Latin *rēgīna*]

**re|gi|nal** (ri jī′nəl), *adj.* = queenly. [< Medieval Latin *reginalis* < Latin *rēgīna* queen]

**re|gion** (rē′jən), *n.* **1** any large part of the earth's surface: *the region of the equator.* **2** a place, space, or area: *an unhealthful region, a mountainous region. No other region offers so much of everything industry needs ... as the Gulf South* (Newsweek). **3** a part of the body: *the region of the heart.* **4** *Figurative.* a field of thought or action; sphere; domain: *the region of art, the region of imagination.* **5** an administrative division: *He [Constantine] divided Constantinople into fourteen regions or quarters* (Edward Gibbon). **6** a division of the sea according to depth. **7** a division of the atmosphere according to height. **8** a division of the earth according to plant or animal life. [< Anglo-French *regiun,* Old French *region,* and *reion,* learned borrowings from Latin *regiō, -ōnis* direction (in space); country < *regere* to direct, rule, straighten]

**re|gion|al** (rē′jə nəl), *adj., n.* —*adj.* **1** of or in a particular region: *a regional storm.* **2** of a particular part of the body: *a regional disorder.*
—*n. U.S.* any one of a number of small stock exchanges located in various regions of the country and serving chiefly as a secondary market for shares traded on the larger exchanges: *Wall Street brokers say that a considerable amount of United States securities business is being diverted by Canadian brokers to the regionals* (New York Times). —**re′gion|al|ly,** *adv.*

**re|gion|al|ism** (rē′jə nə liz′əm), *n.* **1** strong or steadfast attachment to a certain region. **2** stress on regional customs or peculiarities in literature and art. *The regionalism of American writing falls into place beside that of Scotland or Ireland* (London Times). **3** an expression, dialect, custom, etc., peculiar to a region.

**re|gion|al|ist** (rē′jə nə list), *n., adj.* —*n.* a person who practices regionalism: *Their main platform, at first sight surprisingly, is a United Europe—"we are regionalists not nationalists nowadays," their spokesman insists* (Economist).
—*adj.* of or inclined to regionalism: *a regionalist writer or artist.*

**re|gion|al|is|tic** (rē′jə nə lis′tik), *adj.* of, having to do with, or characterized by regionalism.

**re|gion|al|i|ty** (rē′jə nal′ə tē), *n.* regional character.

**re|gion|al|ize** (rē′jə nə līz), *v.t.,* **-ized, -iz|ing.** to organize or divide by regions; decentralize: *to regionalize trade.* —**re′gion|al|i|za′tion,** *n.*

**regional metamorphism,** *Geology.* metamorphism involving very large bodies of rocks, caused by the heat and mountain-forming movements in the earth's crust.

**re|gird** (rē gėrd′), *v.t.,* **-girt** or **-gird|ed, -gird|ing.** to gird again.

**ré|gis|seur** (rā zhē sœr′), *n. French.* a stage manager or director of a theatrical production.

**reg|is|ter** (rej′ə stər), *v., n.* —*v.t.* **1** to write in a list or record: *Register the names of the new members. The government patent office registers all new trademarks.* **2** to have (a letter, package, or other mail) recorded in a post office, paying extra postage for special care in delivering: *He registered the letter containing the check.* **3** to indicate; record automatically: *The thermometer registers 90 degrees.* **4** to show (surprise, joy, anger, or other emotion) by the expression on one's face or by actions. **5** to cause (lines, columns, colors, or other presswork) to fit or correspond exactly in printing.
—*v.i.* **1** to write or have one's name written in a list or record: *to register at a hotel. A person must register before he can vote.* **2** to show surprise, joy, anger, or other emotion, by one's expression or actions. **3** (of lines, columns, colors, or other presswork) to fit or correspond exactly in printing.
—*n.* **1** a written or printed list or record: *A register of attendance is kept at our school.* **2** the book in which a list or record is kept: *a hotel register. Look up his record in the register.* **3** a thing that records. A cash register shows the amount of money taken in. **4a** the range of a voice or an instrument: *The last verse ... goes as low as my register will reach* (Rudyard Kipling). **b** a part of this range: *All voices are divided into "registers"—head, middle, and chest. The average person can recognize these registers when he yodels; yodelling is deliberately crossing the breaks between head and chest registers* (Winthrop Sargeant). **5a** an opening in a wall or floor with a device to regulate the amount of heated or cooled air that passes through: *Did you ever come into the house on a cold winter day and stand over the register of a hot-air heating system?* (Beauchamp, Mayfield, and West). **b** the plate for regulating the draft in a furnace. **6** registration or registry. **7** = registrar. **8** the set of pipes of an organ stop. **9** the exact fit or correspondence of lines, columns, colors, or other presswork, in printing. **10** the exact adjustment of the focus in a camera. **11** a customs document declaring the nationality of a ship. **12** a storage device in which the arithmetic unit of a computer stores data temporarily.
[< Medieval Latin *registrum,* alteration of Late Latin *regesta, -ōrum* list, (originally) things transcribed < Latin *regerere* to record < *re-* back + *gerere* carry, bear] —**reg′is|ter|er,** *n.*

**reg|is|tered** (rej′ə stərd), *adj.* **1** recorded: *a registered trademark. A registered bond is listed by name, number, etc., and interest is mailed to the owner.* **2** recognized by law; certified: *a registered accountant.* **3** sent by registered mail: *a registered letter.* **4** purebred; pedigreed: *a registered cow.*

**registered mail, 1** letters or parcels for which a special fee has been paid, the delivery of which is recorded by the post office. The person receiving registered mail must sign a postal receipt before the mail is given to him. **2** the postal service in charge of such mail.

**registered nurse,** a graduate nurse licensed by state authority to practice nursing. *Abbr:* R.N.

**registered player,** a tennis player of a category created by the International Lawn Tennis Federation, consisting of independent professionals who are eligible to play for prize money in open tournaments.

**register of wills,** a clerk of the probate court who records wills, reports from executors, and other matters dealing with estates or trusts.

**register ton,** a unit of measure of the internal capacity of a ship; 100 cubic feet or 2.83 cubic meters.

**reg|is|tra|bil|i|ty** (rej′ə strə bil′ə tē), *n.* the quality or condition of being able to register or be registered.

**reg|is|tra|ble** (rej′ə strə bəl), *adj.* that can be registered.

**reg|is|tral** (rej′ə strəl), *adj.* preserved in, copied from, and authenticated by a register.

**reg|is|trant** (rej′ə strənt), *n.* a person who registers: *the registrant of a patent.*

**reg|is|trar** (rej′ə strär, rej′ə strär′), *n.* an official who keeps a register; official recorder: *the registrar of a college. I married her before the registrar at Letchbury* (Samuel Butler). [variant of Middle English *registrer,* or earlier *registrary,* perhaps < *register,* verb, or < Medieval Latin *registrarius* < *registrum*]

**reg|is|trar|ship** (rej′ə strär ship, rej′ə strär′-), *n.* the office of registrar.

**reg|is|trate** (rej′ə strāt), *v.i.,* **-trat|ed, -trat|ing.** to use various organ stops while playing a piece of music. [apparently back formation < *registration*]

**reg|is|tra|tion** (rej′ə strā′shən), *n.* **1** the act of registering: *Registration of his new car took most of the afternoon to fill out the forms.* **2** an entry in a register: *The registration was smudged and difficult to read.* **3** the number of people registered: *Registration for this election is higher than for the last election.* **4** a legal document showing that some person or thing has been registered: *an automobile registration.* **5** the combination of organ stops for a piece of music. **6** the adjustment of lines, columns, colors, or other presswork, in printing; register.

**reg|is|tra|tion|al** (rej′ə strā′shə nəl), *adj.* of or having to do with registration: *registrational procedures.*

**registration area,** that section of a country in which births, deaths, and other vital statistics, officially registered by the local government serve as a basis for calculating the vital statistics of the country's population.

**registration statement,** *U.S.* a statement of information about a proposed issue of stock filed with the Securities and Exchange Commission before the issue is marketed.

---

**Pronunciation Key:** hat, āge, cãre, fär; let, ēqual, tėrm; it, īce; hot, ōpen, ôrder; oil, out; cup, pu̇t, rüle; child; long; thin; ᴛʜen; zh, measure; ə represents **a** in about, **e** in taken, **i** in pencil, **o** in lemon, **u** in circus.

**reg|is|try** (rej′ə strē), *n., pl.* **-tries. 1** the act of registering; registration. **2** (of a ship) the fact of being registered as the property of an individual or corporation of a particular country, under the flag of which it sails. **3** a place where a register is kept; office of registration. **4** a book in which a list or record is kept; register.

**re|gi|us** (rē′jē əs, -jəs), *adj.* = royal. [< Latin *rēgius* < *rēx, rēgis* king]

**regius professor**, a professor in a British university holding a position founded by a royal grant.

**ré|glage** (rā gläzh′), *n.* **1** regulation; adjustment. **2** *Military.* the regulation and spotting of artillery fire, especially by aircraft observation. [< French *réglage* < *régler* regulate < Late Latin *rēgulāre;* see etym. under **regulate**]

**re|glaze** (rē glāz′), *v.t.,* **-glazed, -glaz|ing.** to glaze again.

**reg|let** (reg′lit), *n.* **1** *Architecture.* a narrow, flat molding. **2** *Printing.* **a** a thin strip of wood used in place of leading to space lines of type. **b** the wood for making these strips. [earlier, column in a book < Middle French *réglet* (diminutive) < Old French *regle* < Latin *rēgula;* see etym. at **rule**]

**re|glo|ri|fy** (rē glôr′ə fī, -glōr′-), *v.t.,* **-fied, -fy|ing.** to glorify again.

**re|glow** (rē glō′), *v., n.* — *v.i.* to glow again. — *n.* the act of glowing again.

**re|glue** (rē glü′), *v.t.,* **-glued, -glu|ing.** to glue again.

**reg|ma** (reg′mə), *n., pl.* **-ma|ta** (-mə tə). a dry fruit of three or more carpels that separate from the axis at maturity, such as in various geraniums. [< New Latin *regma* < Greek *rhêgma, -atos* a break < *rhēgnýnai* to break]

**reg|nal** (reg′nəl), *adj.* of or having to do with a reigning sovereignty, or a reign: *the third regnal year of a king.* [< Medieval Latin *regnalis* < Latin *rēgnum* reign < *rēx, rēgis* king]

**reg|nan|cy** (reg′nən sē), *n., pl.* **-cies.** = reign.

**reg|nant** (reg′nənt), *adj.* **1** ruling; reigning: *Queen regnant. The members of virtually every royal house, regnant or deposed, in Europe are related to Europe's most prospering crown, Britain's* (Time). **2** *Figurative.* **a** exercising sway or influence; predominant. **b** prevalent; widespread: *The belief in witchcraft and diabolical contracts which was regnant in his day ...* (Matthew Arnold). [< Latin *rēgnāns, -antis,* present participle of *rēgnāre* to rule < *rēgnum* kingdom < *rēx, rēgis* king]

**reg|nat po|pu|lus** (reg′nat pop′yə ləs), *Latin.* the people rule (the motto of Arkansas).

**reg|num** (reg′nəm), *n. Latin* **1** dominion; rule. **2** a period of power or rule.

**reg|o|lith** (reg′ə lith), *n.* the layer of soil and loose rock fragments overlying solid rock; mantle rock. [< Greek *rhêgos* blanket (< *rhêgein* to dye) + *líthos* stone]

**re|gorge** (rē gôrj′), *v.,* **-gorged, -gorg|ing.** — *v.t.* **1** to disgorge; vomit. **2** to swallow again. — *v.i.* to flow back.

**Reg. Prof.,** Regius Professor.

**re|grade** (rē grād′), *v.t.,* **-grad|ed, -grad|ing.** to grade again.

**re|graft** (rē graft′, -gräft′), *v.t.* to graft again.

**re|grant** (*v.* rē grant′, -gränt′; *n.* rē′grant′, -gränt′), *v., n.* — *v.t.* to grant again. — *n.* the renewal of a grant.

**re|grass** (rē gras′, -gräs′), *v.t.* **1** to cause to produce grass again. **2** to bring back to the condition of good pastureland.

**re|grate** (ri grāt′), *v.t.,* **-grat|ed, -grat|ing. 1** to buy up (grain, provisions, or other commodities) to sell again at a profit in or near the same market. It was formerly forbidden by law. **2** to sell again (commodities so bought); retail. [< Old French *regrater;* origin uncertain]

**re|grat|er** or **re|gra|tor** (ri grā′tər), *n.* a person who regrates; retailer.

**re|greet** (rē grēt′), *v., n. Obsolete.* — *v.t.* **1** to greet again. **2** to greet in return. **3** to salute. — *n.* a greeting.

**re|gress** (*v.* ri gres′; *n.* rē′gres), *v.i.* **1** to go back; move in a backward direction: *They indicate a retreating area of sedimentation, as when a sea regresses from the land* (Raymond C. Moore). **2** to return to an earlier or less advanced state. — *v.t. Psychology.* to cause regression in (a person). — *n.* a going back; backward movement or course; return. [< Latin *regressus,* past participle of *regredī* < *re-* back + *gradī* to go, step]

**re|gres|sion** (ri gresh′ən), *n.* **1** the act of going back; backward movement. **2** *Psychology.* the reversion of a person to an earlier stage or way of thinking, feeling, or acting, as a way of trying to escape difficult problems by assuming the characteristics of childhood: *In regression the individual retreats from reality to a less demanding personal status—one which involves lowered aspiration and more readily accomplished satisfactions* (James C. Coleman). **3** *Biology.* the reversion of offspring to a less developed state or form or to an average type, such as a tendency of children of tall parents to be shorter than their parents. **4** *Statistics.* the tendency of one variable that is correlated with another to revert to the general type and not to equal the amount of deviation of the second variable.

**regression coefficient**, *Statistics.* the numerical value best expressing the regression of a variable.

**re|gres|sive** (ri gres′iv), *adj.* **1** showing regression; going back; backward: *I'm regressive, yes, but very tired, too* (Newsweek). **2** decreasing in proportion to the increase of something else: *A regressive tax is one whose rate becomes lower as the sum to which it is applied becomes larger.* **3** *Phonetics.* changing its sound by assimilation under the influence of the sound that follows. — **re|gres′sive|ly,** *adv.* — **re|gres′sive|ness,** *n.*

**re|gres|siv|i|ty** (rē′gre siv′ə tē), *n.* the quality of being regressive; retrograde tendency or policy.

**re|gres|sor** (ri gres′ər), *n.* a person or thing that regresses.

**re|gret** (ri gret′), *v.,* **-gret|ted, -gret|ting,** *n.* — *v.t.* to feel sorry for or about: *We regretted his absence from the party.* — *v.i.* to feel sorry; mourn: *Those are harsh words that he will regret later on. Those who had umbrellas were putting them up; those who had not were regretting and wondering how long it would last* (Elizabeth Gaskell). [< Old French *regretter* to regret, (originally) bewail (a death); origin uncertain; perhaps < Scandinavian (compare Old Icelandic *grāta* cry). Compare etym. under **greet**[2].]

— *n.* the feeling of being sorry; sorrow; sense of loss: *It was a matter of regret that I could not see my mother before leaving.* **regrets,** a polite reply declining an invitation: *She could not come but sent regrets.* [< Middle French *regret* < Old French *regretter;* see the verb]

— *Syn. n.* **Regret, remorse** mean a feeling of sorrow for a fault or wrongdoing. **Regret** suggests sorrow or dissatisfaction about something one has done or failed to do, sometimes something one could not help: *With regret he remembered his forgotton promise.* **Remorse** suggests the mental suffering of a gnawing or guilty conscience: *The boy was filled with remorse for the worry he had caused his mother.*

**re|gret|ful** (ri gret′fəl), *adj.* feeling or expressing regret; sorry; sorrowful. — **re|gret′ful|ly,** *adv.* — **re|gret′ful|ness,** *n.*

**re|gret|less** (ri gret′lis), *adj.* not feeling or showing regret.

**re|gret|ta|ble** (ri gret′ə bəl), *adj.* that should be or is regretted: *It is regrettable that many students cannot spell accurately.*

**re|gret|ta|bly** (ri gret′ə blē), *adv.* with regret; regretfully: *My mother and sisters, who have so long been regrettably prevented from making your acquaintance* (Henry James).

**re|gret|ter** (ri gret′ər), *n.* a person who regrets.

**re|grind** (rē grīnd′), *v.t.,* **-ground, -grind|ing.** to grind again.

**re|group** (rē grüp′), *v.t., v.i.* to group anew: *Children refine new ideas, regroup facts, and project their minds and their emotions outside of themselves* (Saturday Review). *As his army paused to regroup, the Premier broadcast "a solemn appeal to the rebels to lay down their arms"* (Time).

**re|group|ment** (rē grüp′mənt), *n.* a rearrangement in groups: *The talks yesterday reportedly concerned technical questions relating to regroupment of forces* (Wall Street Journal).

**re|growth** (rē grōth′), *n.* **1** the act or process of growing again. **2** new or second growth: *Amid the ruins ... he towered up, gigantic, glowering, indispensable, the sole agency by which time could be gained for healing and regrowth* (Wall Street Journal).

**regs** (regz), *n.pl. U.S. Informal.* regulations: *I know the new I.R.S.* [*Internal Revenue Service*] *regs by heart ... I even know the sections on farm income* (New Yorker).

**regt.,** regiment.

**Regt.,** **1** regent. **2** regiment.

**reg|u|la** (reg′yə lə), *n., pl.* **-lae** (-lē). *Architecture.* a band or fillet at the base of the Doric entablature, bearing droplike ornaments on the lower side. [< Latin *rēgula;* see etym. under **rule**]

**reg|u|la|ble** (reg′yə lə bəl), *adj.* = regulatable.

**reg|u|lar** (reg′yə lər), *adj., n.* — *adj.* **1** fixed by custom or rule; usual; normal: *Six o'clock was his regular hour of rising. Our regular sleeping place is in a bedroom.* **SYN:** typical, standard. **2** of the normal grade, quality, or value; not premium: *regular gasoline, regular grind coffee.* **3** following some rule or principle; according to rule: *A period is the regular ending for a sentence. S or es is the regular ending for a plural.* **4** coming, acting, or done again and again at the same time: *regular attendance at church. Sunday is a regular holiday.* **5** steady; habitual: *A regular customer trades often at the same store.* **SYN:** constant. See syn. under **steady. 6** even in size, spacing, or speed; well-balanced: *regular features, regular teeth, regular breathing.* **7** = symmetrical. **8** having all its angles equal and all its sides equal: *a regular polygon.* **9** having all the same parts alike in shape and size: *a regular flower.* **10** = isometric: *a regular crystal.* **11** orderly; methodical: *He leads a regular life.* **12** properly fitted or trained: *The regular cook in our cafeteria is sick.* **13** *Grammar.* having the usual endings; changing form in the usual way, especially to show tense, number, person, or mood. "Ask" is a regular verb. **14** *Informal.* **a** thorough; complete: *a regular bore.* **b** fine; agreeable; all-right: *He's a regular fellow.* **15** permanently organized: *If we had a wholly regular army we could meet our present commitments with at least 100,000 fewer men because of the saving in overheads, avoidance of waste in movements, and so forth* (London Times). **16** of or belonging to the permanent armed forces of a country: *The conscript or regular soldier ... could not conceive of anybody who was not sick belonging to an organised army* (Listener). **17** belonging to a religious order bound by certain rules: *The regular clergy live in religious communities.* **18** *U.S.* having to do with or conforming to the requirements of a political party or other organization: *the regular candidate, a regular ticket.* **19** *Sports.* first; varsity; best: *He was on the regular team for three seasons.*

— *n.* **1** a member of a regularly paid group of any kind: *The fire department was made up of regulars and volunteers.* **2** a member of the permanent armed forces of a country. **3** a person belonging to a religious order bound by certain rules. **4** *Sports.* a player who plays in all or most of a team's games: *Holmes, who replaced Jim Looney, injured regular, in the third quarter, took advantage of an erratic ... pass defense to score* (New York Times). **5** *U.S.* a party member who faithfully stands by his party. **6** a regular customer or contributor. **7** a size of garment for men of average height and weight: *Men's: shorts, regulars, longs in standard sizes* (New Yorker). **8** regular gasoline: *I bought a dollar's worth of regular from the lady in charge of the filling station* (Anthony Bailey).

[< Latin *rēgulāris* < *rēgula;* see etym. under **rule**]

**Regular Army**, the part of the Army of the United States that is made up of professionals and provides a permanent standing army.

**reg|u|lar|ise** (reg′yə lə rīz), *v.t.,* **-ised, -is|ing.** *Especially British.* regularize.

**reg|u|lar|i|ty** (reg′yə lar′ə tē), *n.* the fact or state of being regular; order; system; steadiness: *The seasons come and go with regularity.*

**reg|u|lar|i|za|tion** (reg′yə lər ə zā′shən), *n.* **1** the act or process of making regular: [*He*] *said that the Waterfront Commission had been facing up to the staggering problems of regularization of port conditions* (New York Times). **2** the state of being made regular.

**reg|u|lar|ize** (reg′yə lə rīz), *v.t.,* **-ized, -iz|ing.** to make regular: *Having regularized the procedure, we went on to the bars* (New Yorker). — **reg′u|lar|iz|er,** *n.*

**reg|u|lar|ly** (reg′yə lər lē), *adv.* **1** in a regular manner. **2** at regular times.

**regular year**, a year of 354 days in the Jewish calendar, as distinguished from an abundant year and a defective year.

**reg|u|lat|a|ble** (reg′yə lā′tə bəl), *adj.* that can be regulated.

**reg|u|late** (reg′yə lāt), *v.t.,* **-lat|ed, -lat|ing. 1** to control by rule, principle, or system: *Accidents happen in the best regulated kitchens. Private schools regulate the behavior of students.* **2** to put in condition to work properly: *My watch is losing time; I will have to regulate it.* **3** to keep at some standard: *This instrument regulates the temperature of the room.* **4** to put in good condition: *to regulate digestion.* **5** to systematize; regularize: *to regulate one's habits of work or leisure.* [< Late Latin *rēgulāre* < Latin *rēgula;* see etym. under **rule**]

**reg|u|la|tion** (reg′yə lā′shən), *n., adj.* — *n.* **1** control by rule, principle, or system: *The Bureau of Traffic controls the regulation of traffic on city streets.* **2** a rule; law: *traffic regulations. Government regulations controlled the prices of rooms* (Newsweek).

— *adj.* **1** required by a rule; standard: *a regulation tennis court. Soldiers wear a regulation uniform.* **2** usual; ordinary.

**reg|u|la|tion|ist** (reg′yə lā′shə nist), *n.* a person who favors regulations in a particular matter.

**reg|u|la|tive** (reg′yə lā′tiv), *adj.* regulating: *Patents are being used as ... regulative instruments in antitrust decrees* (Wall Street Journal).

**reg|u|la|tor** (reg′yə lā′tər), *n.* **1** a person or thing that regulates. **2** a device in a clock or watch to make it go faster or slower. **3** a very accurate clock used as a standard of time. **4** a valve to regulate passage, as of air, gas, steam, or water. **5** *Electricity.* a device to control the current, speed, voltage, or the like, as of a machine or transformer. **6** *U.S. History.* a member of any of various vigilance committees.

**reg|u|la|to|ry** (reg′yə lə tôr′ē, -tōr′-), *adj.* regulating: *The conferees will find out what regulatory moves are afoot in the various state legislatures* (Wall Street Journal).

**regulatory gene**, the part of an operon that regulates the structural genes; operator gene: *The first known class consists of structural genes, which determine the amino acid sequence and three-dimensional shape of proteins; the second is regulatory genes, which specify whether structural genes will function and therefore control the rate of enzyme synthesis* (Science News).

**reg|u|line** (reg′yə lin, -līn), *adj.* of or having to do with a regulus. [< *regul*(us) + *-ine*[1]]

**reg|u|lus** (reg′yə ləs), *n., pl.* **-lus|es, -li** (-lī). a product of the smelting of various ores, such as copper, lead, and silver, consisting of an impure metallic mass. [< Medieval Latin *regulus* (diminutive) < Latin *rēx, rēgis* king (because it combined readily with the king's metal, gold)]

**Reg|u|lus** (reg′yə ləs), *n.* a white star of the first magnitude in the constellation Leo. [< Latin *rēgulus* (diminutive) < *rēx, rēgis* king (because of its magnitude)]

**re|gur|gi|tate** (rē gėr′jə tāt), *v.,* **-tat|ed, -tat|ing.** —*v.i.* (of liquids, gases, undigested foods, sewage, or the like) to rush, surge, or flow back: *As the sewers clogged up, drains all through the apartment began to regurgitate.*
—*v.t.* to throw up; vomit: *Ants feed their young on regurgitated food. Many of the sea birds swallow fish and later regurgitate the partially digested fish to feed their young* (A. M. Winchester).
[< Medieval Latin *regurgitare* to overflow < Latin *re-* back + *gurges, -itis* whirlpool]

**re|gur|gi|ta|tion** (rē gėr′jə tā′shən), *n.* **1** the act of regurgitating. **2** the flow of blood back into the heart through a defective heart valve.

**re|gur|gi|ta|to|ry** (rē gėr′jə tə tôr′ē, -tōr′-), *adj.* regurgitating; throwing up.

**re|ha|bil|i|tant** (rē′hə bil′ə tənt), *n.* a person who has been rehabilitated: *Nearly 85 per cent of rehabilitants return to work* (Time).

**re|ha|bil|i|tate** (rē′hə bil′ə tāt), *v.,* **-tat|ed, -tat|ing.** —*v.t.* **1** to restore to a good condition; make over in a new form: *The old neighborhood is to be rehabilitated.* **2** to restore, as to a former standing, rank, rights, privileges, or reputation: *The man who had committed the theft completely rehabilitated himself and again became a trusted and respected citizen.* **3** to restore to a condition of good health, or to a level of useful activity, by means of medical treatment and therapy.
—*v.i.* to be or become rehabilitated; undergo rehabilitation: *New York and California now have such laws aimed at giving selected violators a chance to rehabilitate and to have a criminal conviction erased from their records* (New Scientist).
[< Medieval Latin *rehabilitare* (with English *-ate*[1]) < Latin *re-* again + *habilitāre* < *habilis* fit, suited < *habēre* to hold, have]

**re|ha|bil|i|ta|tion** (rē′hə bil′ə tā′shən), *n.* the act or process of rehabilitating something or someone: *the rehabilitation of an injured person. Vocational rehabilitation services could be available to ... newly disabled each year who could benefit from rehabilitation* (New York Times).

**re|ha|bil|i|ta|tive** (rē′hə bil′ə tā′tiv), *adj.* of or for rehabilitation: *... such rehabilitative techniques as prisons without bars* (Atlantic).

**re|ha|bil|i|ta|tor** (rē′hə bil′ə tā′tər), *n.* a person who rehabilitates others or believes in rehabilitation: *He should know that the rehabilitators have no stronger case than the get-tough school* (Sunday Times).

**re|ha|bit|u|ate** (rē′hə bich′ů āt), *v.t., v.i.,* **-at|ed, -at|ing.** to make or become habitual again: *The response ... rehabituated when repeated stimuli were reintroduced* (Scientific American).

**re|han|dle** (rē han′dəl), *v.t.,* **-dled, -dling.** to handle or have to do with again; remodel.

**re|hang** (rē hang′), *v.t.,* **-hung** or (*especially for execution or suicide*) **-hanged, -hang|ing.** to hang again: *He hung and rehung the pictures* (Thackeray).

**re|har|mo|nize** (rē här′mə nīz), *v.t.,* **-nized, -niz|ing.** **1** *Music.* to provide (a melody or theme) with a new harmony; rearrange harmonically. **2** to bring back into harmony or agreement.

**re|hash** (*v.* rē hash′; *n.* rē′hash), *v., n.* —*v.t.* to deal with again; work up (old material) in a new or different form: *The question had been rehashed again and again.*
—*n.* **1** the act of rehashing; putting something old into a new or different form. **2** something old put into a new or different form: *That composition is simply a rehash of an article in the encyclopedia.*

**re|hear** (rē hir′), *v.t.,* **-heard, -hear|ing.** to hear over again: *At the request of the New Jersey Bar Association the case was reheard last week* (New York Times).

**re|hear|ing** (rē hir′ing), *n.* **1** a second hearing; reconsideration. **2** *Law.* a second hearing or trial; a new trial in chancery, or a second argument of a motion or an appeal: *If by this decree either party thinks himself aggrieved, he may petition the chancellor for a rehearing* (Sir William Blackstone).

**re|hears|al** (ri hėr′səl), *n.* the act of rehearsing; performance beforehand for practice or drill: *More rehearsals might have helped the cast* (Newsweek).

**re|hearse** (ri hėrs′), *v.,* **-hearsed, -hears|ing.** —*v.t.* **1** to practice (a play, part, music, or reading) for a public performance: *We rehearsed our parts for the school play.* **2** to drill or train (as a person or group) by repetition. **3** to tell in detail; repeat: *The children rehearsed all the happenings of the day to their father in the evening.* **4** to tell one by one; enumerate: *An act of the English parliament rehearsed the dangers to be apprehended* (George Bancroft). **SYN:** relate, recount.
—*v.i.* to recite; rehearse a play, part, music, or reading: *You look as if you were rehearsing for a villain in a play* (Booth Tarkington).
[< Anglo-French *rehearser,* Old French *rehercier,* and *reherser* to rake over < *re-* again + *hercier* to rake, harrow < *herce,* or *herse* a harrow, rake < Latin *hirpex, -icis*] —**re|hears′er,** *n.*

**re|heat** (rē hēt′), *v., n.* —*v.t., v.i.* to heat over again: *Part of last night's dinner was reheated for lunch today.*
—*n.* = afterburner.

**re|heat|er** (rē hē′tər), *n.* something that reheats.

**re|heel** (rē hēl′), *v.t.* to supply a heel to, especially in knitting or mending.

**re|hire** (rē hīr′), *v.,* **-hired, -hir|ing,** *n.* —*v.t.* to hire again.
—*n.* a renewed hiring.

**Re|ho|bo|am** (rē′ə bō′əm), *n.* **1** a son of Solomon and the first king of Judah, who refused to lower taxes, thus causing the revolt and secession of the northern tribes of Israel: *Rehoboam ... was the son of Solomon and Naamah, a woman who belonged to the tribe of Ammon* (Hendrik van Loon) (in the Bible, I Kings 11:43, 12:1-24).
**2** Also, **rehoboam.** a bottle that holds 156 ounces.

**Re|ho|both** (rē′ə bōth), *n.* any one of a group of natives of southwestern Africa who are of mixed African and European ancestry.

**re|hos|pi|tal|i|za|tion** (rē hos′pə tə lə zā′shən), *n.* the act of rehospitalizing.

**re|hos|pi|tal|ize** (rē hos′pə tə līz), *v.t.,* **-ized, -iz|ing.** to hospitalize again.

**re|house** (rē houz′), *v.t.,* **-housed, -hous|ing.** to house again; provide with other houses: *There's enough quick-growing pulpwood in the Amazon Valley alone to let us rehouse the whole world every ten years* (New Yorker).

**re|hu|man|ize** (rē hyü′mə nīz), *v.t.,* **-ized, -iz|ing.** to humanize again; restore a human character or quality to: *Goods and gadgets will provide the basis for the civilized life as well as rehumanize the dehumanized* (John W. Aldridge). *It was to try to rehumanize Soviet theatre and let it treat people as something more than individuals who either do or don't do their duty by the Communist state* (London Times). —**re|hu′man|i|za′tion,** *n.*

**re|hu|mid|i|fy** (rē′hyü mid′ə fī), *v.t.,* **-fied, -fy|ing.** to make moist again; redampen.

**re|hy|drat|a|ble** (rē hī′drā tə bəl), *adj., n.* —*adj.* that can be rehydrated.
—*n.* a rehydratable food or other substance.

**re|hy|drate** (rē hī′drāt), *v.t.,* **-drat|ed, -drat|ing.** **1** to restore water or moisture to (something dehydrated): *to rehydrate vegetables, rehydrated chicken soup.* **2** *Chemistry.* to cause to become a hydrate again.

**re|hy|dra|tion** (rē′hī drā′shən), *n.* the act or process of rehydrating or condition of being rehydrated: *the rehydration of freeze-dried foods.*

**rei** (rā), *n.* a form sometimes used as the singular of **reis.**

**Reich** (rīH), *n.* Germany, as an empire or state; the German nation (a term applied to the Holy Roman Empire, 962-1806; the German Empire, 1871-1918; and Nazi Germany, 1933-1945). [< German *Reich* empire, realm < Middle High German *rīch* < Old High German *rīhhi,* ultimately < a Celtic word]

**Reichs|bank** (rīHs′bangk′; *German* rīHs′bängk′), *n.* the state bank of Germany. [< German *Reichsbank* < *Reich* Reich + *Bank* bank]

**Reichs|füh|rer** (rīHs′fy′rər), *n. German.* the leader of the Reich.

**reichs|mark** (rīHs′märk′), *n., pl.* **-marks** or **-mark.** the former unit of money of Germany, established in 1924. It was replaced by the Deutsche mark in West Germany in 1948. *Abbr:* Rm. [< German *Reichsmark* < *Reich* Reich + *Mark* mark, unit of currency]

**reichs|pfen|nig** (rīHs′pfen′ig), *n., pl.* **-pfen|nigs, -pfen|ni|ge** (-pfen′i gə). a small German coin that was worth about 1/100 of a reichsmark. [< German *Reichspfennig* < *Reich* Reich + *Pfennig.* Compare etym. under **pfennig.**]

**Reichs|rat** or **Reichs|rath** (rīHs′rät′), *n.* **1** (formerly) the parliament in the Austrian part of the Austro-Hungarian Empire. **2** the former national council of Germany under Hitler, now called the Bundesrat in West Germany. [< German *Reichsrat* < *Reich* Reich + *Rat* council]

**Reichs|tag** (rīHs′täk′), *n.* the former elective legislative assembly of Germany. The West German equivalent is now called the Bundestag. [< German *Reichstag* < *Reich* Reich + *tagen* to deliberate]

**Reichs|wehr** (rīHs′vār′), *n.* the limited military force that Germany was permitted to have instead of an army after the end of World War I. [< German *Reichswehr* < *Reich* Reich + *Wehr* defense]

**reif** (rēf), *n. Obsolete.* plunder. [Old English *rēaf.* See related etym. at **reave**[1].]

**re|i|fi|ca|tion** (rē′ə fə kā′shən), *n.* the regarding or treating of an idea as a thing; materialization.

**re|i|fy** (rē′ə fī), *v.t.,* **-fied, -fy|ing.** to make (an abstraction) material or concrete: *to reify an abstract concept.* [< Latin *rēs, reī* thing + English *-fy;* perhaps patterned on *deify*]

**reign** (rān), *n., v.* —*n.* **1** the period of power of a ruler: *The queen's reign lasted fifty years.* **2** the act of ruling; royal power; rule: *The reign of a wise ruler benefits his country.* **3** *Figurative.* existence everywhere; prevalence: *Our city must dedicate itself to a reign of law and order* (New York Times). **4** *Obsolete.* a kingdom; realm; domain: *Then stretch thy sight o'er all her rising reign* (Alexander Pope).
—*v.i.* **1** to be a ruler; rule: *A king reigns over his kingdom. The laws reigned, and not men* (George Bancroft). **2** *Figurative.* to exist everywhere; prevail: *On a still night silence reigns. Venice reigned as the major sea power of the Mediterranean during the Middle Ages* (Bernard Brodie).
[< Old French *reigne* reign, realm < Latin *rēgnum* < *rēx, rēgis* king]

**re|ig|nite** (rē′ig nīt′), *v.t.,* **-nit|ed, -nit|ing.** to ignite again: *Matters are straightened out by the gods, who reignite the flame with a bolt of lightning* (New Yorker).

**Reign of Terror**, a period of the French Revolution from about June, 1793, to July, 1794, during which many persons considered undesirable by the ruling group were ruthlessly executed.

**reign of terror**, a period or situation in which a community lives in fear of death or violence because of the extremist methods used by a political group to win or keep power: *Northern Rhodesia is in the grip of a "reign of terror" reminiscent of Nazi Germany* (New York Times).

**re|il|lu|sion** (rē′i lü′zhən), *v.t.* to restore one's faith or illusion: *They [the Conservatives] came to power because the electorate was disillusioned with the Labour Party rather than because they were reillusioned with the Conservatives* (London Times).

**re|im|burse** (rē′im bėrs′), *v.t.,* **-bursed, -burs|ing.** to pay back; refund. You reimburse a person for expenses made for you. [< *re-* + obsolete *imburse* put into a purse < Medieval Latin *imbursare* < *in-* into + *bursa* purse (in Late Latin, hide, skin); patterned on French, Middle French *rembourser* < *embourser*] —**re′im|burs′a|ble,** *adj.* —**re′im|burs′er,** *n.*

**re|im|burse|ment** (rē′im bėrs′mənt), *n.* a paying back; repayment (as for expenses or loss).

**re|im|plant** (rē′im plant′, -plänt′), *v.t.* to implant again. —**re′im|plan|ta′tion,** *n.*

**re|im|port** (*v.* rē′im pôrt′, -pōrt′; *n.* rē im′pôrt, -pōrt), *v., n.* —*v.t.* to import (something previously exported): *We used to grow cotton in America, export it to England, and then reimport it as finished cloth.*
—*n.* = reimportation. —**re′im|por|ta′tion,** *n.*

**re|im|pose** (rē′im pōz′), *v.t.,* **-posed, -pos|ing.** to impose again or anew: *Soviet overlordship could*

---

**Pronunciation Key:** hat, āge, cãre, fär; let, ēqual, tėrm; it, īce; hot, ōpen, ôrder; oil, out; cup, pu̇t, rüle; child; long; thin; ᴛʜen; zh, measure; ə represents **a** in about, **e** in taken, **i** in pencil, **o** in lemon, **u** in circus.

*be reimposed only by force* (Newsweek).

**re|im|po|si|tion** (rē′im pə zish′ən), *n.* **1** a reimposing. **2** a tax levied once more or in a new form: *Such reimpositions are always over and above the taille of the particular year in which they are laid on* (Adam Smith).

**re|im|preg|nate** (rē′im preg′nāt), *v.t.*, **-nat|ed, -nat|ing.** to impregnate again.

**re|im|pres|sion** (rē′im presh′ən), *n.* **1** a second impression. **2** the act or process of reprinting. **3** a reprint.

**re|im|print** (rē′im print′), *v.t.* to imprint anew; reprint.

**re|im|pris|on** (rē′im priz′ən), *v.t.* to imprison again. **—re′im|pris′on|ment,** *n.*

**rein** (rān), *n., v.* **—*n.*** **1** Usually, **reins.** a long, narrow strap or line fastened to a bridle or bit, by which to guide and control an animal. A driver or rider of a horse holds the reins in his hands. See picture under **harness. 2** *Figurative.* a means of control and direction: *Few kings now hold the reins of government.*

**—*v.t.*** **1** to check or pull with reins: *The coachman reins his smoking bays Beneath the elm-tree's shade* (Oliver Wendell Holmes). **2** *Figurative.* to guide and control: *He reined his horse well. Rein your tongue.* **3** to equip with reins. **—*v.i.*** **1** to bring, turn, draw, or pull something by means of reins. **2** to rein a horse.

**draw rein, a** to tighten the reins: *He drew rein to check the fleeing horse.* **b** *Figurative.* to slow down; stop: *The marchers drew rein in the square.*

**give rein to,** to let move or act freely, without control: *to give rein to one's feelings. The Romantic poets gave rein to their imaginations.*

**keep a tight rein on,** to check or restrain; control closely: *The past two governors may have submitted spendthrift budgets, but they weren't approved by the legislature, which has been keeping a tight rein on the purse* (Wall Street Journal).

**rein in** (or **up**), to cause to stop or go slower: *another rider, meeting him and reining in* (George W. Cable).

**take the reins,** to assume control: *Part of the Vice-President's job is to take the reins if the President falls ill.*

[< Old French *rene* < Vulgar Latin *retina* a bond, check < Latin *retinēre* to hold back; see etym. under **retain**]

**re|in|au|gu|rate** (rē′in ô′gyə rāt), *v.t.*, **-rat|ed, -rat|ing.** to inaugurate afresh.

**re|in|car|nate** (rē′in kär′nāt), *v.t.*, **-nat|ed, -nat|ing.** to give a new body to (a soul).

**re|in|car|na|tion** (rē′in kär nā′shən), *n.* **1** the rebirth of the soul in a new body. **2** a new incarnation or embodiment.

**re|in|car|na|tion|ist** (rē′in kär nā′shə nist), *n.* a person who believes in reincarnation.

**re|in|cite** (re′in sīt′), *v.t.*, **-cit|ed, -cit|ing.** to incite again; reanimate; reencourage: *The hurricane seemed to have been reincited instead of exhausted* (Charlotte Smith).

**re|in|cor|po|rate** (rē′in kôr′pə rāt), *v.t., v.i.*, **-rat|ed, -rat|ing.** to incorporate again.

**re|in|cor|po|ra|tion** (rē′in kôr′pə rā′shən), *n.* the action of reincorporating or condition of being reincorporated: *Potomac said it will seek stockholder approval of its reincorporation under the new District of Columbia Business Incorporation Act* (Wall Street Journal).

**re|in|crease** (rē′in krēs′), *v.t.*, **-creased, -creas|ing.** to increase again; augment; reinforce.

**re|in|cur** (rē′in kėr′), *v.t.*, **-curred, -cur|ring.** to incur a second time.

***reindeer**

***rein|deer** (rān′dir′), *n., pl.* **-deer** or **-deers.** a kind of large deer with branching antlers, living in northern regions of Europe, Asia, and North America. The North American variety was introduced into Alaska in the 1890's. It is used to pull sleighs and also for meat, milk, and hides. *Santa Claus' sleigh is drawn by reindeer. To the lowland Laplanders, the reindeer is horse, sheep, and cow, all in one* (Victor H. Cahalane). [< Scandinavian (compare Old Icelandic *hreindȳri* < *hreinn* reindeer + *dȳr* animal)]

**reindeer moss,** a gray, branched lichen, the chief winter food of reindeer: *Green woodland mosses and a yielding sponge of reindeer moss carpet the ground* (New Yorker).

**re|in|dict** (rē′in dīt′), *v.t.* to indict again: *The prosecution said it planned to reindict the remaining defendants on simpler charges* (Newsweek).

**re|in|doc|tri|nate** (rē′in dok′trə nāt), *v.t.*, **-nat|ed, -nat|ing.** to indoctrinate again. **—re′in|doc′tri|na′tion,** *n.*

**re|in|duce** (rē′in düs′, -dyüs′), *v.t.*, **-duced, -duc|ing. 1** to induce anew or again. **2** *Obsolete.* to bring back; reintroduce: *There was a design ... to reinduce Secular Priests into Monks' places* (Thomas Fuller).

**re|in|fect** (rē′in fekt′), *v.t.* to infect again.

**re in|fec|ta** (rē in fek′tə), *Latin.* the matter being unfinished.

**re|in|fec|tion** (rē′in fek′shən), *n.* infection a second time or subsequently.

**re|in|flame** (rē′in flām′), *v.t.*, **-flamed, -flam|ing.** to inflame anew; rekindle; warm again.

**re|in|flate** (rē′in flāt′), *v.t., v.i.*, **-flat|ed, -flat|ing.** to inflate again.

**re|in|fla|tion** (rē′in flā′shən), *n.* inflation again or anew.

**re|in|force** (rē′in fôrs′, -fōrs′), *v.*, **-forced, -forc|ing,** *n.* **—*v.t.*** **1** to strengthen with new force or materials: *to reinforce a garment with an extra thickness of cloth, to reinforce a wall or a bridge, to reinforce an army or a fleet.* **2a** to strengthen; make stronger or more effective: *to reinforce an argument, a plea, or an effect.* **b** to add to; increase; supplement: *to reinforce a stock or a supply.* **3** *Psychology.* **a** to encourage or strengthen (a response to a stimulus), usually by rewarding a correct response and withholding reward for an incorrect one: *If they happen to be particularly upset by their son's stomach pains ... and tend to play down the other effects, they will "reward" or reinforce the specific symptoms whenever they occur* (John E. Pfeiffer). **b** to reward (a person or animal) for responding to a stimulus: *We decided that this man who had been mute for 30 years had learned to be mute—or more technically had been reinforced (rewarded) by his environment for being mute* (Irene Kassorla).

**—*v.i.*** *Psychology.* to encourage or strengthen a response or stimulus: *With the red light on, push the manual feed switch to reward the bird every time it hits the switch. Continue to reinforce only as the bird pecks closer to the red light ... A pigeon can be trained in this way in as little as 15 minutes* (Scientific American).

**—*n.*** **1** something that reinforces or strengthens. **2** the thicker metal at the rear part of a cannon to strengthen the barrel where the charge is exploded. Also, **reenforce.**

[earlier *re-enforce* < *re-* + *enforce;* perhaps patterned on Middle French *renforcer*] **—re′in|forc′er,** *n.*

**re|in|forced concrete** (rē′in fôrst′, -fōrst′), concrete with metal embedded in it to make the structure stronger; ferroconcrete: *Reinforced concrete, or concrete in which steel rods are embedded, must be used for concrete structures like floors, arches, and tanks* (Monroe M. Offner).

**reinforced plastic,** plastic for construction strengthened with glass fibers and polyester resins, used in foundations, walls, roofs, boats, and tanks: *Limited quantities of complete sports-car bodies have been made of reinforced plastics and many automobile components are now made of this material* (F. H. Carmen).

**re|in|force|ment** (rē′in fôrs′mənt, -fōrs′-), *n.* **1** the act of reinforcing or state of being reinforced. **2** the act of strengthening or increasing in any way, especially as in learning or behavior processes. **3** something that reinforces.

**reinforcements,** extra soldiers, warships, planes, etc.: *Reinforcements were sent to the battlefield.* Also, **reenforcement.**

**reinforcement therapist,** a person who practices reinforcement therapy.

**reinforcement therapy,** psychiatric therapy designed to restore normal behavior by rewarding a patient whenever he responds normally to a stimulus, especially a stimulus in commonplace circumstance; operant conditioning. The rewards are supposed to reinforce normal responses until they become permanent.

**re|in|form** (rē′in fôrm′), *v.t.* to inform again or in a new way.

**re|in|fuse** (rē′in fyüz′), *v.t.*, **-fused, -fus|ing.** to infuse again or in a new way.

**re|in|gest** (rē′in jest′), *v.t.* to ingest again.

**re|in|hab|it** (rē′in hab′it), *v.t.* to inhabit again.

**re|in|ject** (rē′in jekt′), *v.t.* to inject again.

**rein|less** (rān′lis), *adj.* **1** without a rein or reins: *reinless steeds, a reinless rider.* **2** *Figurative.* unchecked; unrestrained: *reinless fury. The reinless play of the imagination ...* (John Ruskin).

**reins** (rānz), *n.pl. Archaic.* **1** the kidneys. **2** the lower part of the back. **3** the feelings: *The righteous God trieth the hearts and reins* (Psalms 7:9). [partly Old English *renys* < Latin *rēnēs,* plural of *rēn, rēnis* kidney, partly < Old French *reins,* or *rens* < Latin]

**re|in|scribe** (rē′in skrīb′), *v.t.*, **-scribed, -scrib|ing.** (in French law) to record or register a second time: *In Louisiana, originally a French colony, the old French law requires a mortgage to be periodically reinscribed in order to preserve its priority.*

**re|in|sert** (rē′in sėrt′), *v.t.* to insert again or in a new way: *All these deletions must be reinserted* (Atlantic).

**re|in|ser|tion** (rē′in sėr′shən), *n.* **1** the act of reinserting. **2** a second insertion.

**reins|man** (rānz′mən), *n., pl.* **-men.** a person who holds the reins; driver: *a skillful reinsman. The colts are members of the Del Miller stable, but the Pennsylvania reinsman will not drive either in the Delaware classic* (New York Times).

**re|in|spect** (rē′in spekt′), *v.t.* to inspect again: *We went to the Uffizi gallery, and reinspected the greater part of it* (Hawthorne).

**re|in|spec|tion** (rē′in spek′shən), *n.* the act of inspecting a second time.

**re|in|spire** (rē′in spīr′), *v.t.*, **-spired, -spir|ing.** to inspire again or in a new way.

**re|in|stall** (rē′in stôl′), *v.t.* to install over again.

**re|in|stall|ment** (rē′in stôl′mənt), *n.* **1** the act or process of reinstalling. **2** an additional installment.

**re|in|state** (rē′in stāt′), *v.t.*, **-stat|ed, -stat|ing.** to put back in a former position or condition; establish again: *to reinstate a member of the club. The broken glass hacked out and reinstated* (Samuel Butler).

**re|in|state|ment** (rē′in stāt′mənt), *n.* **1** the act or process of putting back in a former position or condition; establishing again: *The reinstatement and restoration of corruptible things is the noblest work of natural philosophy* (Francis Bacon). **2** *Psychoanalysis.* alleviation of anxiety by infantile ritualistic acts to please a supposed father or mother.

**re|in|sti|tute** (rē in′stə tüt, -tyüt), *v.t.*, **-tut|ed, -tut|ing.** to institute again.

**re|in|sti|tu|tion** (rē′in stə tü′shən, -tyü′-), *n.* the act of reinstituting or state of being reinstituted: *There will never again be any reinstitution of slavery* (Horace Bushnell).

**re|in|struct** (rē′in strukt′), *v.t.* to instruct again or in turn.

**re|in|struc|tion** (re′in struk′shən), *n.* the action of reinstructing: *A course of reinstruction in the dry rudiments of knowledge* (Pall Mall Gazette).

**re|in|sur|ance** (rē′in shůr′əns), *n.* **1** the act of reinsuring. **2** the amount covered by it.

**re|in|sure** (rē′in shůr′), *v.t.*, **-sured, -sur|ing.** to insure again; insure under a contract by which a first insurer relieves himself from the risk and transfers it to another insurer. **—re′in|sur′er,** *n.*

**re|in|te|grate** (rē in′tə grāt), *v.t.*, **-grat|ed, -grat|ing.** to integrate over again or in a new way.

**re|in|te|gra|tion** (rē′in tə grā′shən), *n.* a reintegrating; a making whole again.

**re|in|ter** (rē′in tėr′), *v.t.*, **-terred, -ter|ring.** to inter again.

**re|in|ter|ment** (rē′in tėr′mənt), *n.* **1** the act of reinterring. **2** the fact or state of being reinterred.

**re|in|ter|pret** (rē′in tėr′prit), *v.t.* to interpret anew: *It needs a scientific telescope, it needs to be reinterpreted and artificially brought near us* (John Martineau).

**re|in|ter|pre|ta|tion** (rē′in tėr′prə tā′shən), *n.* the act of reinterpreting.

**re|in|ter|ro|gate** (rē′in ter′ə gāt), *v.t.*, **-gat|ed, -gat|ing.** to interrogate again; question repeatedly: *For interrogated, say reinterrogated: for ... he must always have been interrogated in the first instance* (Jeremy Bentham).

**re|in|trench** (rē′in trench′), *v.t.* to intrench again or in a new way.

**re|in|tro|duce** (rē′in trə düs′, -dyüs′), *v.t.*, **-duced, -duc|ing.** to introduce again or in a new way: *to reintroduce a bill in Congress.*

**re|in|tro|duc|tion** (rē′in trə duk′shən), *n.* the act of reintroducing.

**re|in|vade** (rē′in vād′), *v.t.*, **-vad|ed, -vad|ing.** to invade again or in turn.

**re|in|vent** (rē′in vent′), *v.t.* to devise or create anew, independently, and without knowledge of a previous invention: *After Spenser ... had reinvented the art of writing well* (James Russell Lowell).

**re|in|vest** (rē′in vest′), *v.t., v.i.* **1** to invest again or in a new way. **2** to invest income obtained from a previous investment.

**re|in|ves|ti|gate** (rē′in ves′tə gāt), *v.t.*, **-gat|ed, -gat|ing.** to investigate again: *When I acquainted* *my friend with these facts he reinvestigated the specimen* (Jonathan Hutchinson).

**re|in|ves|ti|ga|tion** (rē′in ves′tə gā′shən), *n.* the act of reinvestigating.

**re|in|vest|ment** (rē′in vest′mənt), *n.* **1** the action of reinvesting. **2** a second investment.

**re|in|vig|or|ate** (rē′in vig′ə rāt), *v.t.*, **-at|ed, -at|ing.** to invigorate again; give fresh vigor to: *Spain ... was in some degree reinvigorated by the infusion of a foreign element into her government* (William E. H. Lecky).

**re|in|vig|or|a|tion** (rē′in vig′ə rā′shən), *n.* the act of reinforcement.

**re|in|vi|ta|tion** (rē′in və tā′shən), *n.* the act of inviting again; reinviting.

**re|in|vite** (rē′in vīt′), *v.t.*, **-vit|ed, -vit|ing.** to invite again.

**re|in|volve** (rē′in volv′), *v.t.*, **-volved, -volv|ing.** to involve anew.

**re|ir|ra|di|ate** (rē′i rā′dē āt), *v.t.*, **-at|ed, -at|ing.** to irradiate again.

**reis** (rās), *n., pl. of* **re|al.** a former Portuguese and Brazilian unit of money. Nine Portuguese reis or eighteen Brazilian reis were worth one United States cent. [< Portuguese *reis,* plural of *real* real³. Compare etym. under **real².**]

**re|is|su|ance** (rē ish′ü əns), *n.* the act of issuing again or state of being issued again.

**re|is|sue** (rē ish′ü, -yü), *v.*, **-sued, -su|ing,** *n.* —*v.t., v.i.* to issue again or in a new way: *The rifles are being reissued this week* (Newsweek). —*n.* a second or repeated issue: *the reissue of a best seller at a lower price. Its reissue is a lively event in a dull publishing season* (Time).

**REIT** (no periods), real estate investment trust: *... REITs, new kinds of companies that warned prospective investors in statements filed with the Security Exchange Commission that they were risky, speculative ventures* (Washington Post).

**rei|ter** (rī′tər), *n.* a German mounted soldier, especially in the wars of the 1500's and 1600's. [< German *Reiter* (literally) rider < *reiten* to ride]

**re|it|er|ate** (rē it′ə rāt), *v.t.*, **-at|ed, -at|ing.** to say or do several times; repeat again and again: *The girl did not move though the policeman reiterated his command that she go. The boy reiterated his assurances that he would be very careful with my bicycle.* **SYN:** See syn. under **repeat.** [< Latin *reiterāre* < *re-* again + *iterāre* to repeat < *iterum,* adverb, again]

**re|it|er|a|tion** (rē it′ə rā′shən), *n.* **1** a saying again; repetition. **2** something repeated.

**re|it|er|a|tive** (rē it′ə rā′tiv), *adj.* = repetitious. —**re|it′er|a′tive|ly,** *adv.*

**Rei|ter's syndrome** (rī′tərz), a disease characterized by inflammation of the joints, of the conjunctiva, and of the urethra: *Reiter's syndrome* [*is*] *a probable variant of rheumatoid arthritis* (George E. Ehrlich). [< Hans *Reiter,* born 1881, a German physician, who first described the disease]

**reiv|er** (rē′vər), *n. Scottish.* reaver; robber; raider. [ultimately < Old English *rēafian* to take by force. See related etym. at **bereave, rob.**]

**re|ja** (rā′hä), *n. Spanish.* a decorative screen or grating protecting a window or before an altar, chapel, or choir of a church.

**re|jas|er** (rē jā′sər), *n. U.S.* a person who engages in or practices rejasing.

**re|jas|ing** (rē jā′sing), *n. U.S.* the act or practice of putting rubbish or discarded items to useful purpose: *The biggest benefit of rejasing is that virtually indestructible objects never reach the garbage heap* (Time). [< *re*(using) *j*(unk) *a*(s) *s*(ometh)*ing* (else)]

**re|ject** (*v.* ri jekt′; *n.* rē′jekt), *v., n.* —*v.t.* **1** to refuse to take, use, believe, consider, or grant: *They rejected our help. He tried to join the army but was rejected because of poor health.* **SYN:** decline, rebuff, repulse. See syn. under **refuse. 2** to throw away as useless or unsatisfactory: *Reject all apples with soft spots.* **3** (of the body) to resist the introduction of (foreign tissue or other matter) by the mechanism of immunity: *Trouble is, the human body has a habit of trying to reject any tissue or organism that is foreign to its own chemistry* (Time). **4** to repulse or rebuff (a person or appeal). **5** to vomit. —*n.* a rejected person or thing: [*His*] *wardrobe must have been made up of Salvation Army rejects* (New Yorker). [< Latin *rejectus,* past participle of *rejicere* < *re-* back + *jacere* throw]

**re|ject|a|ble** (ri jek′tə bəl), *adj.* capable of being rejected; worthy or suitable to be rejected.

**re|jec|ta|men|ta** (ri jek′tə men′tə), *n.pl.* **1** things rejected as useless or worthless; refuse; waste. **2** = excrement. [< New Latin *rejectamenta* < Latin *rejectus;* see etym. under **reject**]

**re|ject|ant** (ri jek′tənt), *n.* an insect repellent derived from a substance in plants which insects reject: *To be of practical value ... a rejectant should be persistent and should be absorbed by the plant so that new plant growth would also be distasteful* (Science News).

**re|ject|ee** (ri jek′tē′, -jek′tē), *n.* = reject.

**re|ject|er** (ri jek′tər), *n.* a person or thing that rejects.

**re|jec|tion** (ri jek′shən), *n.* **1** the act of rejecting: *The inspector ordered the rejection of the faulty parts.* **2** the state of being rejected: *A child who feels unloved, unwanted, or unworthy of his parents' interest is said to be suffering from rejection* (Sidonie M. Gruenberg). **3** a thing rejected: *All rejections by the inspector were destroyed at once.* **4** *Biology.* immunological resistance of an organism to the grafting or implantation of foreign tissue: *It is well known that immunity problems, including rejection of transplants have been unsolved* (Science News Letter).

**re|jec|tion|ist** (ri jek′shə nist), *n.* any one of the Arab leaders or states that refuse to negotiate or work out a settlement with Israel: *The "rejectionists" ... have accused Syria of wanting to eliminate them so as to have a free hand to embark on what they call an Egyptian-type policy of accommodation with the United States and Israel* (Henry J. Tanner).

**rejection slip,** a note from a publisher rejecting the accompanying returned manuscript: *For the first time out of twenty tries I got a check instead of a rejection slip* (James Thurber).

**re|jec|tive** (ri jek′tiv), *adj.* that rejects; rejecting.

**rejective art,** = minimal art.

**re|jec|tiv|ist** (ri jek′tə vist), *n.* = minimalist.

**re|jec|tor** (ri jek′tər), *n.* = rejecter.

**re|jig** (*n.* rē′jig′; *v.* ri jig′), *n., v.*, **-jigged, -jig|ging.** *British Slang.* —*n.* an overhauling or streamlining. —*v.t.* to rejigger: *The Treasury rejigged an old wartime poster to read in effect "Spend to Defend the Right to be Free"* (Punch).

**re|jig|ger** (ri jig′ər), *v.t. Slang.* to change or rearrange, especially by clever handling or juggling; work over in a new form: *Sir Arthur ... had rejiggered his assistant's records* (Time).

**re|joice** (ri jois′), *v.*, **-joiced, -joic|ing.** —*v.i.* to be glad; be filled with joy: *Mother rejoiced at our success.* —*v.t.* **1** to make glad; fill with joy: *Good news rejoices the heart.* **SYN:** cheer, delight. **2** *Obsolete.* to be joyful at: *Ne'er mother Rejoiced deliverance more* (Shakespeare). [< Old French *rejoiss-,* stem of *rejoir* < *re-* again + *esjoïr* < *es-* (Latin *ex-*) out (of) + *joir* be glad < Vulgar Latin *gaudīre,* for Latin *gaudēre* be glad] —**re|joic′er,** *n.*

**re|joice|ful** (ri jois′fəl), *adj.* joyful; joyous.

**re|joic|ing** (ri joi′sing), *n.* **1** the feeling or expression of joy: *There were great festivities—illuminations, state concerts, immense crowds, and general rejoicings* (Lytton Strachey). **2** an occasion for joy. **3** *Obsolete.* a cause of joy: *Thy word was unto me the joy and rejoicing of mine heart* (Jeremiah 15:16). —**re|joic′ing|ly,** *adv.*

**re|join¹** (rē join′), *v.t.* **1** to join again; unite again: *The members of our family will be rejoined at Thanksgiving.* **2** to join the company of again: *The sailor will rejoin his comrades.* —*v.i.* to come together again; be reunited.

**re|join²** (ri join′), *v.t.* to answer; reply: *"Come with me!" "Not on your life," he rejoined.* —*v.i.* **1** to make answer to a reply or remark. **2** *Law.* to answer the plaintiff's reply to the defendant's plea. [< Old French *rejoindre* < *re-* back + *joindre.* Compare etym. under **join**]

**re|join|der** (ri join′dər), *n.* **1** an answer to a reply; response: *a debater's rejoinder.* **SYN:** retort. **2** *Law.* a defendant's answer to the plaintiff's reply to the defendant's plea. [< Middle French, Old French *rejoindre,* noun use of infinitive < *re-* back + *joindre.* Compare etym. under **join.**]

**re|judge** (rē juj′), *v.t.*, **-judged, -judg|ing.** to judge over again or in a new way.

**re|jug|gle** (rē jug′əl), *v.t.*, **-gled, -gling.** to juggle again.

**re|jus|ti|fi|ca|tion** (rē′jus tə fə kā′shən), *n.* the act of rejustifying.

**re|jus|ti|fy** (rē jus′tə fī), *v.t.*, **-fied, -fy|ing.** to justify again.

**re|ju|ve|nate** (ri jü′və nāt), *v.t.*, **-nat|ed, -nat|ing. 1** to make young or vigorous again; give youthful qualities to: *The long rest and new clothes have rejuvenated her.* **2** *Geology.* **a** to cause (a stream) to flow faster and erode land quicker by increasing the declivity of the land it flows over. **b** to begin a new cycle of erosion in (a region) by upheaval of the land surrounding a stream. [< *re-* + Latin *juvenis* young] —**re|ju′ve|nat′ing|ly,** *adv.*

**re|ju|ve|na|tion** (ri jü′və nā′shən), *n.* **1** the act or process of rejuvenating; restoration to youth, youthful appearance or vigor. **2** the condition of being rejuvenated.

**re|ju|ve|na|tor** (ri jü′və nā′tər), *n.* a person or thing that rejuvenates.

**re|ju|ve|nesce** (ri jü′və nes′), *v.t., v.i.*, **-nesced, -nesc|ing. 1** to make or become young again. **2** *Biology.* to undergo or produce rejuvenescence.

**re|ju|ve|nes|cence** (ri jü′və nes′əns), *n.* **1** the renewal of youth or youthful vigor. **2** *Biology.* **a** the process by which the contents of a cell break the cell wall and form a new cell with a new wall. **b** the renewal of vitality by the exchange of material between two distinct cells, as during conjugation. [< *re-* again + Latin *juvenēscēns, -entis,* present participle of *juvenēscere* grow young < *juvenis* young]

**re|ju|ve|nes|cent** (ri jü′və nes′ənt), *adj.* **1** becoming young again. **2** making young again.

**re|ju|ve|nize** (ri jü′və nīz), *v.t.*, **-nized, -niz|ing.** = rejuvenate.

**re|kin|dle** (rē kin′dəl), *v.t., v.i.*, **-dled, -dling.** to set on fire again; kindle anew. —**re|kin′dler,** *n.*

**re|kin|dle|ment** (rē kin′dəl mənt), *n.* **1** the act of rekindling. **2** the state of being rekindled.

**re|knit** (rē nit′), *v.t.*, **-knit|ted** or **-knit, -knit|ting.** to knit (up) again; refasten: (*Figurative.*) *The renewal of the parental reknits the fraternal tie* (W. R. Williams).

**rel.,** **1** relating. **2a** relative. **b** relatively. **3** religion.

**re|la|bel** (rē lā′bəl), *v.t.*, **-beled, -bel|ing.** to label again.

**re-laid** (rē lād′), *v.* the past tense and past participle of **re-lay:** *The pavement on our street has just been re-laid.*

**re|lapse** (ri laps′; *also for n.* rē′laps), *v.*, **-lapsed, -laps|ing,** *n.* —*v.i.* **1** to fall or slip back into a former state or way of acting: *After one cry of surprise she relapsed into silence.* **2** to fall back into wrongdoing; backslide. **3** to have a return of the symptoms of an illness following convalescence: *The next day the doctors were back; Tom had relapsed* (Mark Twain). —*n.* the state or process of falling or slipping back into a former state, or way of acting: *He seemed to be getting over his illness but had a relapse.* [< Latin *relāpsus,* past participle of *relābī* < *re-* back + *lābī* to slip] —**re|laps′er,** *n.*

**re|laps|ing fever** (ri lap′sing), any one of several infectious diseases characterized by recurrent episodes of chills, fever, and neuromuscular pain, and caused by spirochetes transmitted by lice or ticks.

**re|lat|a|ble** (ri lā′tə bəl), *adj.* **1** that may be related with something else: *Class sizes are not directly relatable to the quality and effectiveness of learning* (Manchester Guardian Weekly). **2** that may be told or narrated: *The story is too long to be relatable at one sitting.*

**re|late** (ri lāt′), *v.*, **-lat|ed, -lat|ing.** —*v.t.* **1** to give an account of; tell: *The traveler related his adventures.* **SYN:** recount, recite, narrate. **2** to connect in thought or meaning: *"Better" and "best" are related to "good."* —*v.i.* **1** to be connected in any way: *We are interested in what relates to ourselves. The critic eye ... examines bit by bit: How parts relate to parts, or they to whole* (Alexander Pope). **SYN:** pertain. **2** to have a friendly or close social relationship with another or others; be responsive or sympathetic: *Some teen-agers relate better to their friends than to their family. He flagellates himself equally for ... relating badly to his children and for not relating at all to the children of Pakistan* (Melvin Maddocks). **3** *Obsolete.* to give an account of something. [< Latin *relātus,* past participle of *referre;* see etym. under **refer**] —**re|lat′er,** *n.*

**re|lat|ed** (ri lā′tid), *adj.* **1** connected in any way: *Montesquieu had shown how human institutions were related to racial habit and climate* (Edmund Wilson). **2** belonging to the same family; connected by a common origin: *Cousins are related. French and Spanish are related languages.* **SYN:** allied, cognate, akin. **3** *Music.* relative. **4** narrated. —**re|lat′ed|ness,** *n.*

**re|la|tion** (ri lā′shən), *n.* **1** a connection in thought or meaning: *Your answer has no relation to the question.* **2** connection or dealings between persons, groups, or countries: *international relations. The relation of mother and child is the closest in the world. The relation between master and servant has changed greatly during the last century. Our firm has business relations with his firm.* **SYN:** alliance, relationship, affiliation. **3** a person who belongs to the same family as another, such as a father, brother, aunt, or relative. **4** reference; regard. **5a** the act of telling; account: *We were interested by the hunter's relation of his adventures.* **b** a narrative: *We must be content in our ignorance with a brief and summary relation* (Lytton Strachey). **6** *Mathematics.* a set of ordered pairs. **7** *Law.* **a** a reference to an earlier

---

**Pronunciation Key: h**a**t, ā**ge, c**ã**re, f**ä**r; l**e**t, **ē**qual, t**ė**rm; **i**t, **ī**ce; h**o**t, **ō**pen, **ô**rder; **oi**l, **ou**t; c**u**p, p**u̇**t, r**ü**le; **ch**ild; lo**ng**; **th**in; **ᴛʜ**en; **zh**, measure; **ə** represents **a** in about, **e** in taken, **i** in pencil, **o** in lemon, **u** in circus.

date. **b** the charge of the person who brings a lawsuit.

**in** (or **with**) **relation to**, in reference to; in regard to; about; concerning: *We must plan in relation to the future.*

[< Latin *relātiō, -ōnis* < *referre;* see etym. under **refer**]

**re|la|tion|al** (ri lā′shə nəl), *adj.* **1** having to do with relations. **2** that relates. **3** showing relation between elements in grammar. —**re|la′tion|al|ly,** *adv.*

**re|la|tion|ship** (ri lā′shən ship), *n.* **1** a connection: *What is the relationship of clouds to rain?* **2** the condition of belonging to the same family. **3** the state or condition that exists between people or groups that deal with one another: *a business relationship, a social relationship.*

**rel|a|tive** (rel′ə tiv), *n., adj.* —*n.* **1** a person who belongs to the same family as another, such as a father, brother, aunt, nephew, or cousin: *Moody put nearly all of his estate in a tax-exempt foundation, passing out only about $1.5 million to relatives and associates* (Newsweek). **2** a relative pronoun. *Who, what,* and *that* are relatives.

—*adj.* **1** related or compared to each other: *Before ordering our dinner, we considered the relative merits of chicken and roast beef.* **2** depending for meaning on a relation to something else: *East is a relative term; for example, Chicago is east of California but west of New York.* **3** *Grammar.* introducing a subordinate clause; referring to a person or thing mentioned. In "The man who wanted it is gone," *who* is a relative pronoun, and *who wanted it* is a relative clause. **4** *Music.* having a close harmonic relation; having the same signature: *a relative minor.*

**relative to, a** about; concerning: *The teacher asked me some questions relative to my plans for the summer. ... some inquiries relative to the character and usages of the remote Indian nations* (Francis Parkman). **b** in proportion to; in comparison with; for: *He is strong relative to his size. Price is relative to demand.*

[< Late Latin *relātīvus* < Latin *referre;* see etym. under **refer**] —**rel′a|tive|ness,** *n.*

▶ **relative clauses.** A relative clause is an adjective clause introduced by a relative pronoun (such as *that, which, who,* or *whose*), or a relative adverb (*where, when, why*), or by neither (an asyndetic clause): The ball *that had been lost* was found by the caddy. The man *whose ball was lost* was angry. Mike's plane, *which was lost in the storm,* landed safely in a field. This is the place *where they met.* The ring *he bought* was expensive (asyndetic).

▶ **relative pronouns.** There are two classes: (1) Those such as *that, which, of which, who, whose, what,* and *whom,* which introduce adjective clauses and refer to an antecedent in the main clause: A man *who* was there gave us the details. Our team, *which* scored first, had the advantage. We didn't take the same trail *that* they did. He did *what* he thought best. *Who* refers to persons; *which,* to animals or objects; *that,* to persons, animals, or objects; *what* to objects. (2) Those such as *whoever, whichever,* and *who,* which introduce noun clauses and have no definite antecedent: You may have *whichever* you like. I know *who* did it.

**relative frequency,** *Statistics.* the ratio of the number of actual occurrences to the possible occurrences. *Example:* If *E* occurs *x* times in *N* trials, then x/N is the relative frequency of *E.*

**relative humidity,** the ratio between the amount of water vapor in the air and the greatest amount the air could contain at the same temperature: *Relative humidity is most accurately measured by determining the dew point* (Shortley and Williams).

**rel|a|tive|ly** (rel′ə tiv lē), *adv.* **1** in relation to something else; comparatively: *One inch is a relatively small difference in a man's height.* **2** in relation or with reference (to): *the value of one thing relatively to other things.* **3** in proportion (to): *a subject little understood relatively to its importance. He is strong relatively to his size.*

**relative maximum,** *Mathematics.* a value of a variable greater than any values close to it.

**rel|a|tiv|ism** (rel′ə tə viz′əm), *n.* the philosophical doctrine of the relativity of knowledge, truth, or certainty.

**rel|a|tiv|ist** (rel′ə tə vist), *n., adj.* —*n.* **1** a person who believes in the theory of relativity: *The now dormant relativists may awaken to brave new concepts that will reorient us in the universe of matter and ideas* (Harlow Shapley). **2** a person who believes in relativism.

—*adj.* = relativistic: *In Dewey's relativist world consequences were the definite test of all thinking, and experience the only ultimate authority* (Newsweek).

**rel|a|tiv|is|tic** (rel′ə tə vis′tik), *adj.* **1** of or having to do with relativity: *Relativistic phenomena generally cause a lot of intellectual difficulties for the non-scientist* (Atlantic). **2** of or having to do with relativism or relativists. **3** *Physics.* having a speed so great relative to the speed of light that the values of mass and other properties are significantly altered: *Synchrotron radiation ... is produced when beams of relativistic electrons (electrons moving at speeds near that of light) are bent around the circular paths characteristic of many accelerators* (William E. Spicer).

**rel|a|tiv|is|ti|cal|ly** (rel′ə tə vis′tə klē), *adv.* **1** in a relativistic manner: *Most of the mass of the three quarks in a proton is relativistically converted into the tremendous energy that binds them together* (Time). **2** from a relativistic point of view: *Although the name of a particle, or its electric charge, is a relativistically invariant concept, its ... angular momentum is not* (David Park).

**rel|a|tiv|i|ty** (rel′ə tiv′ə tē), *n.* **1** the condition of being relative. **2** *Philosophy.* existence only in relation to the human mind. **3** *Physics.* the character of being relative rather than absolute, as ascribed to motion or velocity. **4a** a theory dealing with the physical laws which govern time, space, mass, motion, and gravitation, expressed in certain equations by Albert Einstein; special theory of relativity. According to it, the only velocity we can measure is velocity relative to some body, for if two systems are moving uniformly in relation to each other, it is impossible to determine anything about their motion except that it is relative, and the velocity of light is constant, independent of either the velocity of its source or an observer. Thus it can be mathematically derived that mass and energy are interchangeable, as expressed in the equation $E = mc^2$, where c = the velocity of light; that a moving object appears to be shortened in the direction of the motion to an observer at rest; that a clock in motion appears to run slower than a stationary clock to an observer at rest; and that the mass of an object increases with its velocity. *One of the fundamental postulates of relativity is that the velocity of light is the same in all circumstances, even when the source and the observer are in relative motion* (W. H. Marshall). **b** an extension of this theory, dealing with the equivalence of gravitational and inertial forces; general theory of relativity.

**relativity of knowledge, 1** *Philosophy.* the doctrine that all human knowledge is relative to the human mind. The mind can know only the effects which things produce upon it and not what the things themselves are. **2** *Psychology.* the theory that the consciousness of objects comes only from their relations to one another.

**rel|a|tiv|ize** (rel′ə tə vīz), *v.t.,* **-ized, -iz|ing.** to make relative: *Recognition of the reality of evil necessarily relativizes the good* (Carl G. Jung).

**re|la|tor** (ri lā′tər), *n.* **1** a person who relates or narrates. **2** *Law.* an individual who brings a charge that causes the state to initiate legal action. [< Latin *relātor* < *referre;* see etym. under **refer**]

**re|launch** (rē lônch′, -länch′), *v.t., v.i.* to launch again.

**re|laun|der** (rē lôn′dər, -län′-), *v.t., v.i.* to launder anew.

**re|lax** (ri laks′), *v.t.* **1** to make less stiff or firm; loosen: *Relax your muscles to rest them.* **2** to make less strict or severe; lessen in force: *Discipline was relaxed on the last day of school. Gloria ... slowly relaxes her threatening attitude* (George Bernard Shaw). **3** to relieve from work or effort; give recreation or amusement: *Relax your mind.* **4** to weaken; slacken; lessen in force or intensity: *to relax precautions against attack. Don't relax your efforts because the examinations are over.* —*v.i.* **1** to become less tense or firm; loosen up: *Relax when you dance. Her compressed lips relaxed as she became less angry.* **2** to become less strict or severe; grow milder: *Alick ... never relaxed into the frivolity of unnecessary speech* (George Eliot). **3** to be relieved from work or effort; take recreation or amusement; reduce strain and worry; be lazy and carefree: *Take a vacation and relax. They come for rest, for fun, for the pure luxury of relaxing in Nassau sunshine* (New Yorker). **4** to lessen in force or intensity; diminish: *The waves relaxed in their force until they did little more than play upon the side of the wreck* (Frederick Marryat).

[< Latin *relaxāre* < *re-* back + *laxāre* to undo < *laxus* loose. See etym. of doublet **release.**] —**re|lax′er,** *n.*

**re|lax|ant** (ri lak′sənt), *n., adj.* —*n.* a drug or other substance that produces relaxation: *Anesthesia proper begins with injections of thiopental and a muscle relaxant of the curare family* (Time).

—*adj.* of, causing, or characterized by relaxation: *relaxant medication.*

**re|lax|a|tion** (rē′lak sā′shən), *n.* **1** the act or process of loosening: *the relaxation of the muscles.* **2** the act or fact of lessening strictness, severity, or force: *the relaxation of discipline over the holidays.* **3** relief from work or effort; recreation; amusement: *Walking and reading were the only relaxations permitted on Sunday.* **4** the condition of being relaxed: *Mr. Lunt's always extraordinary relaxation on the stage has reached the point where practically everything he does gives the impression of being an immediate and happy improvisation* (New Yorker). **5** pardon; remission.

**relaxation time,** the time required, in many physical phenomena involving change or disturbance, for the elements of the process to recover equilibrium, or to effect some desired or expected result.

**re|lax|a|tive** (ri lak′sə tiv), *adj.* tending to relax; of the nature of relaxation.

**re|laxed** (ri lakst′), *adj.* **1** free from restraint or restrictions; not strict or precise: *Shakespeare ... is relaxed and careless in critical places* (William Hazlitt). **2** slackened, mitigated, or modified with respect to strictness: *When the law has become relaxed, public opinion takes its place* (James A. Froude).

**re|lax|ed|ly** (ri lak′sid lē), *adv.* in a relaxed manner.

**re|lax|in** (ri lak′sin), *n.* a hormone produced by the corpus luteum during pregnancy which relaxes the pelvic ligaments. It is used in medicine to control premature labor and ease normal labor. [< *relax* + *-in*]

**re|lax|or** (ri lak′sər), *n. U.S.* a substance that loosens or slackens closely curled hair: *The Afro ... severely scissored demand for straighteners and the other hair relaxors* (Time).

**re|lay** (rē′lā, ri lā′), *n., v.,* **-layed, -lay|ing.** —*n.* **1** a fresh supply: *New relays of men were sent to fight the fire. The distances at which we got relays of horses varied greatly* (Alexander W. Kinglake). **2a** = relay race. **b** one part of a relay race. **3** an electromagnetic device in which a weak current acts as a switch for a stronger current. A relay is used in transmitting telegraph or telephone messages over long distances. **4** a device that extends or reinforces the action or effect of an apparatus, such as a servomotor. **5** a group of persons taking turns in any work or activity; shift. **6** the act of passing on a ball, puck, or stick from one player to another.

—*v.t.* **1** to take and carry or send farther: *Messengers will relay your message. He relays to Marx the stories that are reaching him from friends in Germany* (Edmund Wilson). **2** to transmit by an electrical relay. **3** to provide or replace with a fresh supply.

—*v.i.* to relay signals, a message, a ball, puck, or stick in sports, or an impulse or force of energy.

[< Old French *relai* a reserve pack of hounds or other animals < *relaier* exchange tired animals for fresh < *re-* back + *laier* to leave, let] —**re-lay′er,** *n.*

**re-lay** (rē lā′), *v.t.,* **-laid, -lay|ing.** to lay again: *That floor must be re-laid. At the same time that more and more people were trying to drive, more and more highways were being torn up and re-laid* (Harper's). [< *re-* + *lay*[1]]

**relay race,** a race in which each member of a team runs, swims, or otherwise covers only a certain part of the distance.

**relay station,** an instrument or object that transmits or reflects electrical signals from one place to another: *The moon, long a symbol linked to lovers, may soon be used as a relay station for their intercontinental telephone calls* (Newsweek).

**relay switch,** a switch operating an electric relay.

**re|leap** (rē lēp′), *v.t., v.i.,* **-leaped** or **-leapt, -leap|ing.** to leap back or over again: *I resolved to pluck up courage and releap the dangerous abyss* (Edward G. Bulwer-Lytton).

**re|learn** (rē lėrn′), *v.t.,* **-learned** or **-learnt, -learn|ing.** to learn again: *We must relearn the lesson that St. Augustine is forever insisting upon* (Charles Gore).

**re|leas|a|bil|i|ty** (ri lē′sə bil′ə tē), *n.* releasable property or quality.

**re|leas|a|ble** (ri lē′sə bəl), *adj.* that can be released: *One pound of uranium carries more releasable energy than 1500 tons of coal.*

**re|lease** (ri lēs′), *v.,* **-leased, -leas|ing,** *n.*

—*v.t.* **1** to let go: *Release the catch and the box will open.* **2** to let loose; set free: *She released him from his promise.* **3** to relieve: *The nurse will be released from duty at seven o'clock. Release me from this life, From this intolerable agony!* (Robert Southey). See syn. under **dismiss. 4a** to give up (as a legal right or claim). **b** to make over to another (property or interest). **5** to permit to be published, shown, sold, or otherwise distributed: *to release a news dispatch, to release a motion picture.* **6** *Obsolete.* to pardon.

—*n.* **1** the act of letting go; setting free: *the release of strain from an engine. The end of the*

*war brought the release of the prisoners.* **2** freedom; relief: *This medicine will give you a release from pain.* **3** a part of a machine that sets other parts free to move: *Press the release and the turntable will begin to turn.* **4a** the legal surrender, such as of a right or estate, to another. **b** the document that does this. **5** permission for publication, exhibition, sale, or other form of distribution: *Now in the final stages of editing, the two-hour picture is scheduled for midsummer release* (Newsweek). **6a** an article, statement, or the like, distributed for publication: *a news release.* **b** a phonograph record, motion picture, or other mechanical recording similarly released: *One of the most satisfying of the recent releases [is] his "Blues in Orbit"* (Punch). **7** *Phonetics.* the act or fact of breaking the closure in the articulation of a stop, as *b, t,* and *k* sounds. **8** *Obsolete.* a pardon.
[< Old French *relaissier* < Latin *relaxāre.* See etym. of doublet **relax.**]
**—*Syn.*** *v.t.* **2 Release, free** mean to set loose from something that holds back or keeps confined. **Release** suggests relaxing the hold on the person or thing: *He released the brakes of the truck.* **Free** suggests removing or unfastening whatever is holding back: *He freed the bird from the cage.*

**re-lease** (rē lēs′), *v.t.,* **-leased, -leas|ing.** to lease again.

**re|leased time** (ri lēst′), *U.S.* time given up by public schools for religious education or other legally appointed instruction outside of school: *On Thursdays, the children at the elementary schools nearby are let out an hour early for released time* (New Yorker).

**re|leas|ee** (ri lē′sē), *n.* a person to whom a release is given: *The University of Illinois concluded a study of the ... careers of prisoners released from federal institutions, finding among other things that the most significant factor in the success of releasees was their ability to obtain a job* (Charles V. Bennett).

**re|lease|ment** (ri lēs′mənt), *n.* the act of releasing; release.

**re|leas|er** (ri lē′sər), *n.* **1** a person or thing that releases: *the releasers of the prisoner, a releaser of news.* **2** *Ethology.* a stimulus that releases a specific response in another animal: *The baby waxbill's special food-begging notes are what we call 'releasers'—the signals, in other words, that make the mother waxbill feed her young* (Konrad Z. Lorenz).

**re|leas|ing factor** (ri lē′sing), a substance that triggers the release of hormones from an endocrine gland: *There appears to be a chemically distinct releasing factor for each of the six anterior pituitary hormones* (New Scientist).

**rel|e|ga|ble** (rel′ə gə bəl), *adj.* that can be relegated.

**rel|e|gate** (rel′ə gāt), *v.t.,* **-gat|ed, -gat|ing. 1** to put away, usually to a lower position or condition: *to relegate a dress to the rag bag. We have not relegated religion (like something we were ashamed to show) to obscure municipalities or rustic villages* (Edmund Burke). **2** to send into exile; banish. **3** to hand over (as a matter or task). **4** to refer (a person), as for information. [< Latin *relēgāre* (with English *-ate*[1]) < *re-* back + *lēgāre* to dispatch < *lēgātus* having a commission or contract < *lēx, lēgis* law, contract]

**rel|e|ga|tion** (rel′ə gā′shən), *n.* the act of relegating or state of being relegated.

**re|lend** (rē lend′), *v.t.,* **-lent, -lend|ing.** to lend again.

**re|lent** (ri lent′), *v.i.* **1** to become less harsh or cruel; be more tender and merciful: *After hours of questioning the suspect, the police relented and allowed him to sleep a few hours. The captain at last relented, and told him that he might make himself at home* (Herman Melville). **2** *Obsolete.* to melt. **—*v.t. Obsolete.*** **1** to slacken. **2** to soften in feeling. **3** to make dissolve. [perhaps < Latin *re-* again + *lentus* slow, viscous]

**re|lent|less** (ri lent′lis), *adj.* without pity; not relenting; unyielding; harsh: *relentless determination. The storm raged with relentless fury.* **SYN:** ruthless, implacable. **—re|lent′less|ly,** *adv.* **—re|lent′less|ness,** *n.*

**re|let** (rē let′), *v.t.,* **-let, -let|ting.** to let anew, as a house.

**rel|e|vance** (rel′ə vəns), *n.* the quality or state of being relevant: *Today, however, reserve forces have lost much of their relevance, and the need is for men on the ground in peacetime* (London Times).

**rel|e|van|cy** (rel′ə vən sē), *n.* = relevance.

**rel|e|vant** (rel′ə vənt), *adj.* **1** bearing upon or connected with the matter in hand; to the point: *relevant questions. The witness' testimony is not relevant to the case.* **SYN:** applicable, appropriate. See syn. under **pertinent. 2** *Informal.* purposeful; meaningful: *Pushkin and Chekhov were attacked for their failure to be "relevant" and engagé (Atlantic). Museums should have a more involved or relevant public role* (New York Times). *The Walinsky campaign is energetic, relevant, and heavily financed* (Time). [< Latin *relevāns, -antis* relieving, present participle of *relevāre;* see etym. under **relieve**] **—rel′e|vant|ly,** *adv.*

**re|le|vé** (rə lə vā′), *n. French.* (in ballet) the raising of the body on the fully or partly pointed toe.

**re|li|a|bil|i|ty** (ri lī′ə bil′ə tē), *n.* the quality or state of being reliable; trustworthiness; dependability: *An employee has perfect reliability if he always does his work responsibly.*

**re|li|a|ble** (ri lī′ə bəl), *adj.* worthy of trust; that can be depended on: *reliable sources of news. Send him to the bank for money; he is a reliable boy.* **—re|li′a|ble|ness,** *n.*
**—*Syn.* Reliable, trustworthy** mean worthy of being depended on or trusted. **Reliable** implies that a person or thing can safely be trusted and counted on to do or be what is expected, wanted, or needed: *I have always found this to be a reliable brand of canned goods.* **Trustworthy** implies that a person is fully deserving of complete confidence, as in his truthfulness, honesty, and good judgment: *He is a trustworthy news commentator.*

**re|li|a|bly** (ri lī′ə blē), *adv.* in a reliable manner; to a reliable extent or degree.

**re|li|ance** (ri lī′əns), *n.* **1** trust or dependence: *A child has reliance on his mother.* **2** confidence: *His reliance on the products of that company was not justified by their claims of quality.* **3** a thing on which one depends.

**re|li|ant** (ri lī′ənt), *adj.* **1** trusting or depending; relying. **2** = confident. **3** relying on oneself; self-reliant. **—re|li′ant|ly,** *adv.*

**rel|ic** (rel′ik), *n.* **1** a thing, custom, or other remains, left from the past: *This ruined bridge is a relic of the Civil War. Another relic of colonialism in Macassar is the Grand Hotel* (New York Times). **2** something belonging to a holy person, kept as a sacred memorial. **3** an object having interest because of its age or its associations with the past; keepsake; souvenir.
**relics, a** remains; ruins: *It is only in this last period ... that we find the relics of the war chariot among the contents of the tomb* (Daniel Wilson). **b** *Archaic.* the remains of a person; corpse: *How long he lived after that year, I cannot tell, nor where his relics were lodg'd* (Anthony Wood).
[< Old French *relique* < Latin *reliquiae,* feminine plural, remains (in Late Latin, relics) < *re-* back + *linquere* leave]

**rel|ict** (rel′ikt), *n., adj.* **—*n.*** **1** = relic: *The Winchester bushel is the only existing relict of the old English system* (J. Q. Adams). **2** a plant or animal surviving from an earlier period. **3** *Geology.* a rock, feature, or structure which survives or persists after others have been replaced. **4** a man's widow.
**—*adj.*** remaining or surviving from an earlier period: *relict flora, relict rocks, relict permafrost.*
[< Late Latin *relicta* widow; (originally) feminine past participle of Latin *relinquere* leave < *re-* back + *linquere* leave]

**✱re|lief** (ri lēf′), *n., adj.* **—*n.*** **1** the fact or state of lessening or freeing from a pain, burden, or difficulty: *Relief from the pain came as the medicine began to work. To her great relief, the lost dog was found at once.* **2** something that lessens or frees from pain, burden, or difficulty; aid; help: *Relief was quickly sent to the sufferers from the great earthquake.* **3** help given to poor people: *Needy and handicapped people depend on government relief for their support.* **4** something that makes a pleasing change or lessens strain: *The clown's antics came as a welcome comic relief in the middle of the serious play.* **5** freedom from a post of duty, often by the coming of a substitute: *This nurse was on duty from seven in the morning until seven at night, with only two hours' relief.* **6** a change of persons on duty. **7** a person or persons who relieve others from duty: *The nurse's relief arrives at seven.* **8** the projection of figures or designs from a surface in sculpture or carving. **9** a figure or design standing out from the surface from which it is cut, shaped, or stamped: *Twenty-one paintings and reliefs make up the Nicholson collection* (New Yorker). **10** the appearance of standing out from a surface, given to a drawing or painting by the use of shadow, shading, color, or line. **11** differences in height between the summits and lowlands of a region; different heights of the earth's surface. **12** *Law.* **a** reparation; redress: *Habeas corpus relief was also granted in the case of a coerced confession* (R. L. Hirshberg). **b** (in feudal law) money which the heir of a deceased tenant paid to the lord on taking possession of the estate.
**—*adj.*** of or for the relief of poor people; having to do with people on relief: *the city relief rolls, relief checks, a relief center.*
**in relief, a** standing out from a surface: *Sculptors have carved figures in relief for thousands of years* (Florence Hope). ... *a church with its dark spire in strong relief against the clear, cold sky* (Washington Irving). **b** in a strong, clear manner; with distinctness: *His noble nature stood out in relief from the evil of his surroundings.*
**on relief,** receiving money to live on from public funds; on welfare: *His family has been on relief ever since he died.*
[< Old French *relief* < *relever;* see etym. under **relieve;** (def. 8) < Old French *relief* < Italian *rilievo;* see etym. under **relievo**]

**✱relief**
definition 8

bas-relief

high relief

**re|lief|er** (ri lē′fər), *n.* **1** *Baseball.* a relief pitcher: *Jim Konstanty, the reliefer responsible for the 1950 pennant, is now rated a starter* (Time). **2** *U.S. Informal.* a person who is on relief: ... *putting able-bodied reliefers to work for the city* (Wall Street Journal).

**relief map,** a map that shows the different heights of a surface by using shading, colors, or solid materials, such as clay, and in other ways.

**relief pitcher,** *Baseball.* a pitcher who enters a game to relieve another pitcher, usually a pitcher who specializes in this and seldom starts a game.

**relief printing,** letterpress; printing from type.

**relief valve,** a valve set to open at a given pressure of steam, air, or water; safety valve.

**re|li|er** (ri lī′ər), *n.* a person who relies.

**re|liev|a|ble** (ri lē′və bəl), *adj.* that can be relieved.

**re|lieve** (ri lēv′), *v.,* **-lieved, -liev|ing. —*v.t.*** **1** to make less; make easier; reduce the pain or trouble of: *Aspirin will usually relieve a headache.* **SYN:** alleviate, mitigate. **2** to set free: *Your coming relieves me of the bother of writing a long letter. This relieved Ernest of a good deal of trouble* (Samuel Butler). **3** to bring aid to; help: *Rescue workers were sent to relieve the trapped coal miners.* **4** to free (a person on duty) by taking his place: *to relieve a guard or sentry.* **5** to remove or release from a job or position: *[He] was relieved of his post ... by a revolutionary council* (Wallace Sokolsky). **6** to give variety or a pleasing change to: *The black dress was relieved by red trimming.* **7** to make stand out more clearly. **8** *Informal.* to deprive by theft; rob: *[She was] relieved in Las Vegas of a gold necklace and diamond ring valued at $5,300* (Time). **9** to empty the bladder or bowels of: *The little boy ... got off his bicycle to relieve himself* (New Yorker). **10** *Sports.* to substitute for (another player, such as a pitcher in a baseball game).
**—*v.i.*** **1** to stand out more clearly; appear in relief: *Relieving dark against their white walls were lines of troops* (Harper's). **2** *Sports.* to substitute for another player, especially as a relief pitcher.
[< Old French *relever* < Latin *relevāre* to lighten < *re-* back + *levāre* raise < *levis* light (weight)]

**re|liev|er** (ri lē′vər), *n.* **1** a person or thing that relieves. **2** *Baseball.* a relief pitcher: *Collins worked the reliever for a pass, filling the bases* (New York Times).

**re|lie|vo** (ri lē′vō), *n., pl.* **-vos.** relief, in painting, in sculpture, and other art forms. [alteration of Italian *rilievo* < *rilevare* to raise < Latin *relevāre;* see etym. under **relieve**]

**re|light** (rē līt′), *v.t., v.i.,* **-lighted** or **-lit, -light|ing.** to light again or anew: *The furnace relighted yesterday has a 250-ton capacity* (Wall Street Journal). [< *re-* + *light*[1]] **—re|light′er,** *n.*

**re|li|gieuse** (rə lē zhyœz′), *n., pl.* **-gieuses** (-zhyœz′). *French.* a nun.

**re|li|gieux** (rə lē zhyœ′), *n., pl.* **-gieux** (-zhyœ′). *French.* a man belonging to a religious order or community.

---

**Pronunciation Key:** hat, āge, cãre, fär; let, ēqual, tėrm; it, īce; hot, ōpen, ôrder; oil, out; cup, pu̇t, rüle; child; long; thin; ᴛʜen; zh, measure; ə represents **a** in about, **e** in taken, **i** in pencil, **o** in lemon, **u** in circus.

**religio-**, *combining form.* of religion; religious, as in *religio-ethical, religio-political.* [< Latin *religiō, -ōnis* religion]

**re|lig|i|o-eth|i|cal** (ri lij′ē ō eth′ə kəl), *adj.* having to do with or based upon both religion and ethics: *Islam arose as a movement of socioeconomic justice and reform backed by certain religio-ethical ideas about God, man, and the universe* (London Times).

**re|lig|i|o la|i|ci** (ri lij′ē ō lā′ə sī), *Latin.* the religion of the layman.

**re|lig|i|o lo|ci** (ri lij′ē ō lō′sī), *Latin.* the sacred character of a place.

**re|li|gion** (ri lij′ən), *n.* **1** belief in God or gods: *George Washington's religion was one of his chief supports during the hardships he suffered in the Revolution.* **2** worship of God or gods: *Christians and Jews believe in the same God but participate in religion on different days.* **3** a particular system of religious belief and worship: *the Christian religion, the Moslem religion.* **4** anything done or followed with reverence or devotion: *"In Turin football is a religion," observed the narrator* (Listener). *Park ... had not made a religion of camping out* (New Yorker).
**experience religion**, to become converted: *Some went so far as to doubt if she had ever experienced religion* (Oliver Wendell Holmes).
[< Latin *religiō, -ōnis* respect for what is sacred; religion; probably (originally) care for (worship and traditions) < *relegere* go through, or read again < *re-* again + *legere* to read; *religiō* was apparently strongly influenced, in popular thought, by the verb *religāre* to bind, in the sense "place an obligation on"]

**re|li|gion|ar|y** (ri lij′ə ner′ē), *adj.* having to do with religion: *religionary intolerance.*

**re|li|gion|ism** (ri lij′ə niz əm), *n.* **1** an excessive inclination toward religion. **2** an exaggerated zeal in religion.

**re|li|gion|ist** (ri lij′ə nist), *n.* **1** a person devoted to religion. **2** a religious zealot or bigot: *He plunged from the ark into the canal ... unsuccessfully pursued by a small band of whooping religionists* (New Yorker).

**re|li|gion|less** (ri lij′ən lis), *adj.* without religion; irreligious.

**re|lig|i|o-po|lit|i|cal** (ri lij′ē ō pə lit′ə kəl), *adj.* having to do with or based upon both religion and politics: *These are to draw into closer amity the two religio-political communities in the province* (London Times).

**re|li|gi|ose** (ri lij′ē ōs), *adj.* religious to excess; unduly occupied with religion.

**re|li|gi|os|i|ty** (ri lij′ē os′ə tē), *n.* **1** religious feeling or sentiment; piety. **2** affectation of religious feeling: *there is too much noisy religiosity on the public level in the U.S.* (Time). [< Latin *religiōsitās* < *religiōsus* religious < *religiō*; see etym. under **religion**]

**re|lig|i|o|so** (ri lij′ē ō′sō), *adj., adv. Music.* expressing religious sentiment; devotional: *What appeals to me as impressive and rewarding is Poulenc's willingness to follow his expressive urge where it leads him, whether the mode is ... secular, religioso, whatever* (Saturday Review). [< Italian *religioso* < Latin *religiōsus* religious]

**re|li|gious** (ri lij′əs), *adj., n., pl.* **-gious.** —*adj.* **1** of religion; connected with religion: *religious meetings, religious freedom, religious differences. Technically speaking a religious book is produced by a religious writer* (Harper's). **2** much interested in religion; devoted to the worship of God or gods: *She is very religious and goes to church every day.* SYN: pious, devout. **3** belonging to an order of monks, nuns, friars, or the like. **4** of or connected with such an order: *a shaven head, and a religious habit* (Joseph Addison). **5** strict; done with care; very careful: *Mother gave religious attention to the doctor's orders.* SYN: exact, scrupulous.
—*n.* **1** a monk, nun, friar, or the like; member of a religious order: *There are sixty religious teaching in this church school.* **2** such persons as a group: *One of Sister Benedicta's fellow religious at Echt soon received a brief message* (Time).
[perhaps < Anglo-French *religius,* Old French *religious,* learned borrowing from Latin *religiōsus* < *religiō*; see etym. under **religion**] —**re|li′gious|ly,** *adv.* —**re|li′gious|ness,** *n.*

**religious education**, instruction in the beliefs of a religion, as in Sunday school.

**re|line** (rē līn′), *v.t.,* **-lined, -lin|ing. 1** to mark with new lines; renew the lines of. **2** to put a new lining in: *Steel furnaces must be relined frequently* (Wall Street Journal). —**re|lin′er,** *n.*

**re|lin|quish** (ri ling′kwish), *v.t.* **1** to give up; let go; release: *The small dog relinquished his bone to the big dog.* **2** to abandon: *She has relinquished all hope of going to Europe this year.* **3** to renounce; resign: *to relinquish a throne.* **4** *Obsolete.* to withdraw from; leave: *Most of them relinquished Spain, as a country where they could no longer live in security* (Washington Irving).
[< Middle French, Old French *relinquiss-,* stem of *relinquir* < Latin *relinquere* < *re-* back + *linquere* leave] —**re|lin′quish|er,** *n.*

**re|lin|quish|ment** (ri ling′kwish mənt), *n.* the act or fact of giving up; abandonment; surrender: *The most important change is relinquishment of day-to-day Allied control over West Berlin legislation* (New York Times).

**rel|i|quar|y** (rel′ə kwer′ē), *n., pl.* **-quar|ies,** *adj.* —*n.* a small box or other receptacle for a relic or relics: *We stopt at St. Denis, [and] saw ... crucifixes, ... crowns, and reliquaries of inestimable value* (Thomas Gray).
—*adj.* of or having to do with a relic or relics: *... two most curious specimens of reliquary superstition* (George S. Faber). *There could be no doubt that here was an Italian 15th century reliquary bust* (Time).
[< French *réliquaire* < Old French *reliquaire* < *relique*; see etym. under **relic**]

**rel|ique** (rel′ik; *French* rə lēk′), *n. Archaic.* a relic. [< Middle French, Old French *relique;* see etym. under **relic**]

**re|liq|ui|ae** (ri lik′wē ē), *n.pl.* remains, as those of fossil animals or plants. [< Latin *reliquiae;* see etym. under **relic**]

**re|liq|ui|date** (rē lik′wə dāt), *v.t.,* **-dat|ed, -dat|ing.** to liquidate anew; adjust a second time.

**re|liq|ui|da|tion** (rē′lik wə dā′shən), *n.* a second or renewed liquidation; a renewed adjustment.

**rel|ish** (rel′ish), *n., v.* —*n.* **1** a pleasant taste; good flavor: *Hunger gives relish to simple food.* **2a** something to add flavor to food. Olives, pickles, and peppers are relishes. **b** chopped pickles, peppers, and other pickled fruit or vegetables, with slightly sweet seasoning. **3** a slight dash (of something). **4** liking; appetite; enjoyment: *The hungry boy ate with great relish.* (*Figurative.*) *The teacher has no relish for old jokes. The cheerfulness of the children added a relish to his existence* (Jane Austen). SYN: zest.
—*v.t.* **1a** to take pleasure or delight in; like the taste of; enjoy: *A cat relishes cream.* **b** *Figurative.* to care for or be pleased with; approve of or like: *We did not relish the prospect of staying after school. This doctrine ... was not much relished by a great part of the audience* (Robert Graves). **2** to give flavor to; make pleasing.
—*v.i.* to have a taste: *It will make everything relish of religion* (Jeremy Taylor).
[earlier *reles* < Old French, remainder < *relesser,* or *relaissier;* see etym. under **release**] —**rel′ish|er,** *n.* —**rel′ish|ing|ly,** *adv.*

**rel|ish|a|ble** (rel′i shə bəl), *adj.* that can be relished.

**re|lis|ten** (rē lis′ən), *v.i.* to listen again or anew: *The brook ... seems, as I relisten to it, Prattling the primrose fancies of the boy* (Tennyson).

**re|live** (rē liv′), *v.,* **-lived, -liv|ing.** —*v.t.* to live over or through again: *She relived the scene of their good-bye* (Lionel Merrick).
—*v.i.* to live again or anew.

**re|load** (rē lōd′), *v.t., v.i.* to load again.

**re|load|er** (rē lō′dər), *n.* a self-loading conveyor to collect and transport coal from a storage yard to railroad cars, vessels, or nearby storage places.

**re|loan** (rē lōn′), *v.t.* to loan again.

**re|lo|cat|a|bil|i|ty** (rē lō′kā tə bil′ə tē), *n.* the fact or condition of being relocatable: *The mobility and relocatability of the mobile home would appear ... particularly suitable for use in underdeveloped countries and in disaster areas* (London Times).

**re|lo|cat|a|ble** (rē lō′kā tə bəl, rē′lō kā′-), *adj.* that can be relocated or moved to a new location: *a relocatable building. Increasingly, cities are turning to the use of relocatable structures to offset the problems imposed by shifting city populations* (Saturday Review).

**re|lo|cate** (rē lō′kāt), *v.,* **-cat|ed, -cat|ing.** —*v.i.* to move to a new location; resettle: *The tenants of the burned building were forced to relocate. A hospital ... may relocate in the suburban area instead of rebuilding on a downtown site* (James A. Hamilton).
—*v.t.* to locate again or anew; put in a new location: *to relocate a family. Programs must be worked out to ease the impact of technological changes by retraining and relocating workers* (Wall Street Journal).

**re|lo|ca|tion** (rē′lō kā′shən), *n.* the action of relocating or state of being relocated.

**re|lo|ca|tor** (rē lō′kā tər), *n.* **1** one that relocates. **2** a device to find the range and direction of a target to aim shore batteries.

**rel. pron.**, relative pronoun.

**re|lu|cent** (ri lü′sənt), *adj.* **1** casting back light. **2** shining; bright. SYN: refulgent. [< Latin *relūcēns, -entis* < *relūcēre* to shine out, glow < *re-* back + *lūcere* to shine, related to *lūx, lūcis* light[1]]

**re|luct** (ri lukt′), *v.i.* **1** to offer resistance or opposition: *I ... reluct at the inevitable course of destiny* (Charles Lamb). **2** to be reluctant. [< Latin *reluctārī;* see etym. under **reluctant**]

**re|luc|tance** (ri luk′təns), *n.* **1** a reluctant feeling or action; unwillingness: *She took part in the game with reluctance. There is nothing we receive with so much reluctance as Advice* (Joseph Addison). SYN: disinclination. **2** slowness in action because of unwillingness: *Facts were never pleasing to him. He acquired them with reluctance and got rid of them with relief* (James M. Barrie). **3** *Physics.* the resistance offered to the passage of magnetic lines of force. It is equivalent to the ratio of the magnetomotive force to the magnetic flux.

**re|luc|tan|cy** (ri luk′tən sē), *n., pl.* **-cies.** = reluctance.

**re|luc|tant** (ri luk′tənt), *adj.* **1** showing unwillingness; unwilling: *The teacher led the reluctant boy to the principal. He put the flimsy paper down with a slow, reluctant movement* (H. G. Wells). **2** slow to act because unwilling: *I am reluctant to go out in very cold weather. He was very reluctant to give his money away.* **3** *Archaic.* resisting; opposing. [< Latin *reluctāns, -antis* struggling against, present participle of *reluctārī* < *re-* back + *luctārī* to struggle] —**re|luc′tant|ly,** *adv.*
—*Syn.* **1 Reluctant, loath** mean unwilling to do something. **Reluctant** implies mere lack of willingness, due to distaste for what is to be done, to irresolution, or simply to laziness: *She gave us her reluctant consent. He was reluctant to leave his cozy chair by the fire.* **Loath** implies strong unwillingness because one feels the thing to be done is extremely disagreeable or hateful: *His parents were loath to believe their son would steal.*

**re|luc|tate** (ri luk′tāt), *v.i.,* **-tat|ed, -tat|ing.** to offer resistance; show reluctance: *The child is commanded to do the thing that is right. He reluctates. He is punished* (Henry Ward Beecher).

**re|luc|ta|tion** (rē′luk tā′shən), *n.* resistance; reluctance.

**rel|uc|tiv|i|ty** (rel′ək tiv′ə tē), *n. Physics.* the ratio of the intensity of the magnetic field to the magnetic induction of a substance; the reciprocal of permeability.

**re|lume** (ri lüm′), *v.t.,* **-lumed, -lum|ing.** to relight or rekindle: (*Figurative.*) *I know not where is that Promethean heat That can thy light relume* (Shakespeare). [apparently < Latin *relūmināre* < *re-* again + *lūmināre* light up < *lūmen, -inis* light[1]]

**re|lu|mine** (ri lü′mən), *v.t.,* **-mined, -min|ing.** = relume.

**re|ly** (ri lī′), *v.i.,* **-lied, -ly|ing.** to depend; trust: *Rely on your own efforts. I relied upon your promise absolutely. The Assembly, which could not rely on the Armed Forces ... was too weak to defy Algiers* (Observer). [< Old French *relier* < Latin *religāre* bind fast < *re-* back + *ligāre* to bind]
—*Syn.* **Rely, depend** mean to have confidence in someone or something. **Rely** implies confidence that a person or thing will perform or be as one expects: *This is a product you can rely on.* **Depend** implies confidence that a person or thing will give the help or support expected or needed: *She depends on her friends to make her decisions.*

**rem** (rem), *n., pl.* **rem** or **rems.** a unit for measuring absorbed doses of radiation, equivalent to one roentgen of X rays or gamma rays. [< *r*(oentgen) *e*(quivalent) *m*(an)]

**REM** (rem), *n.* = rapid eye movement: *REMs occurred in varying stretches of five minutes to an hour, several times during a night's sleep* (Time).

**rem.**, remark or remarks.

**re|made** (rē mād′), *v.* the past tense and past participle of **remake.**

**re|main** (ri mān′), *v., n.* —*v.i.* **1** to continue in a place; stay: *We shall remain at the seashore till September.* SYN: See syn. under **stay. 2** to continue; keep on; last: *The town remains the same year after year.* **3** to be left: *A few apples remain on the trees. If you take 2 from 5, 3 remains.*
—*n.* **remains, a** what is left: *The remains of the meal were fed to the dog.* **b** a dead body: *Washington's remains are buried at Mount Vernon.* **c** a wreckage: *Remains of the DC-8F that crashed on Nov. 29 [were] reassembled in Montreal* (Canada Month). **d** a writer's works not yet published at the time of his death: *He left behind him many valuable remains, which Bion Proconnesius is said to have translated* (Jacob Bryant). **e** things left from the past, such as a building, a monument, or parts of an animal or plant: *the remains of an ancient civilization.*
[< Old French *remaindre* < Latin *remanēre* < *re-* back + *manēre* to stay]

**re|main|der** (ri mān′dər), *n., adj., v.* —*n.* **1** the part left over; the rest: *After studying an hour, she spent the remainder of the afternoon in play.* SYN: residue, remnant, balance, surplus. **2** in arithmetic: **a** the number left over after subtract-

ing one number from another: *If you take 2 from 9, the remainder is 7.* **b** the number left over after dividing one number by another: *If you divide 14 by 3, the quotient is 4 with a remainder of 2.* **3** one of the copies of a book left in the publisher's hands after the sale has practically ceased. **4** *Law.* a future estate so created as to take effect after another estate, such as a life interest, has come to an end.
—*adj.* remaining; left over: *Their memories are dimm'd and torn, Like the remainder tatters of a dream* (Thomas Hood).
—*v.t.* to sell as a remainder: *to remainder books.* **remainders**, stamps voided for postal use: *to collect remainders.*
[< Anglo-French *remainder,* Old French *remaindre,* noun use of infinitive; see etym. under **remain**]

**re|main|der|man** (ri mān′dər man′), *n., pl.* **-men.** *Law.* a person to whom a remainder is devised.

**re|mains** (ri mānz′), *n.pl.* See under **remain.**

**re|make** (*v.* rē māk′; *n.* rē′māk′), *v., n.,* **-made, -mak|ing,** *n.* —*v.t.* to make anew; make over: *They have united under God to remake the world* (Newsweek).
—*n.* a remade product, such as a new version of a motion picture or a recording: *This is a remake of Alfred Hitchcock's fondly remembered 1935 mystery ... based on the John Buchan novel* (Maclean's). —**re|mak′er,** *n.*

**re|man** (rē man′), *v.t.,* **-manned, -man|ning. 1** to furnish with a fresh supply of men: *to reman a fleet.* **2** to restore the manliness or courage of.

**re|man|ci|pa|tion** (rē′man sə pā′shən), *n.* (in Roman law) the act of retransferring.

**re|mand** (ri mand′, -mänd′), *v., n.* —*v.t.* **1** to send back. **2a** to send back (a prisoner or an accused person) into custody: *He is charged with treason and remanded for interrogation* (Time). **b** to send (a case) back to the court it came from for further action there. **3** to recall; revoke: *I will remand the order I despatched to my banker* (Charlotte Brontë).
—*n.* a remanding.
[< Late Latin *remandāre* < Latin *re-* back + *mandāre* to consign, order]

**remand home,** *British.* detention home: *Can detention in a remand home be regarded as educational?* (Manchester Guardian).

**re|mand|ment** (ri mand′mənt), *n.* the act of remanding.

**rem|a|nence** (rem′ə nəns), *n.* **1** the state or quality of being remanent. **2** *Physics.* the flux density remaining in a substance after the magnetizing force has ceased.

**rem|a|nent** (rem′ə nənt), *adj.* **1** remaining. **2** = additional. [< Latin *remanēns, -entis,* present participle of *remanēre;* see etym. under **remain**]

**re|ma|nié** (rə man yā′), *adj., n.* —*adj.* **1** (of fossils) derived from an older bed or layer. **2** recemented, such as a glacier formed by the falling of fragments of ice.
—*n.* **1** a characteristic portion of one formation occurring in another younger one. **2** a fossil found in a bed of more recent origin than that in which it was first buried.
[< French *remanié,* past participle of *remanier* to handle again, change < *re-* + *manier* to handle < *main* hand < Latin *manus*]

**re|mark** (ri märk′), *v., n.* —*v.t.* **1** to say in a few words; state; speak; comment: *He remarked that my hands would be better for a wash.* **2** to notice; observe: *Did you remark that queer cloud?* **SYN:** note. **3** *Obsolete.* to distinguish: *His manner remarks him; there he sits* (Milton).
—*v.i.* to make a remark; comment.
—*n.* **1** something said in a few words; short statement; comment: *The president made a few remarks.* **2** the act of noticing; observation. **3** = remarque.
[< French *remarquer* < *re-* again + Middle French *marquer,* variant of Old North French *merquier,* Old French *merchier* to mark, notice < Germanic (probably unrecorded Frankish *merkjan*)]

**re|mark|a|ble** (ri mär′kə bəl), *adj.* worthy of notice; unusual: *He has a remarkable memory. This story of Mongolian conquests is surely the most remarkable in all history* (H. G. Wells). **SYN:** notable, noteworthy, extraordinary, singular. —**re|mark′a|ble|ness,** *n.*

**re|mark|a|bly** (ri mär′kə blē), *adv.* notably; unusually: *The day of the blizzard was remarkably cold.*

**re|marque** (ri märk′), *n.* in the graphic arts: **1** a distinguishing mark indicating a particular stage of a plate, as a small sketch engraved on the margin of a plate, and usually removed after a fixed number of early proofs have been taken. **2** a proof, print, or plate having such a distinguishing mark. [< French *remarque* < *remarquer;* see etym. under **remark**]

**re|mar|riage** (rē mar′ij), *n.* any marriage after one's first one; second or subsequent marriage: *A special commission of the United Lutheran Church of America ... called for a relaxation of the church's strict laws on divorce, remarriage, and birth control* (Newsweek).

**re|mar|ry** (rē mar′ē), *v.t., v.i.,* **-mar|ried, -mar|ry|ing.** to marry again: *Widows might remarry if they liked* (Frederic W. Farrar). *His property was confiscated and his wife remarried to another* (George Grote).

**re|mas|ti|cate** (rē mas′tə kāt), *v.t.,* **-cat|ed, -cat|ing.** to chew again, as the cud; ruminate.

**re|match** (rē′mach′), *n.* a second or subsequent match, as between two opponents or teams.

**Rem|brandt|esque** (rem′bran tesk′), *adj.* in the manner or style of Rembrandt: *One goes through a vast Rembrandtesque shed opening upon a great sunny field* (H. G. Wells). [< *Rembrandt* van Rijn, 1606-1669, a Dutch painter + *-esque*]

**re|meas|ure** (rē mezh′ər, -mā′zhər), *v.t.,* **-ured, -ur|ing.** to measure again: *Measuring and remeasuring, with ... tremendous strides, the length of the terrace* (Scott).

**re|me|di|a|ble** (ri mē′dē ə bəl), *adj.* that can be remedied or cured. —**re|me′di|a|ble|ness,** *n.*

**re|me|di|a|bly** (ri mē′dē ə blē), *adv.* in a remediable manner or condition.

**re|me|di|al** (ri mē′dē əl), *adj.* **1** tending to relieve or cure; remedying; curing; helping; relieving. **2** intended to improve related study habits and skills: *Students who read poorly will have to take a course in remedial reading.* [< Late Latin *remediālis* < Latin *remedium;* see etym. under **remedy**] —**re|me′di|al|ly,** *adv.*

**re|me|di|a|tion** (ri mē′dē ā′shən), *n.* the act or process of remedying: *Only one instructor attempted to familiarize the student with the symptoms, causes and remediation of severe reading disabilities* (New Yorker).

**rem|e|di|less** (rem′ə dē lis), *adj.* without remedy; incurable; irreparable.

**rem|e|dy** (rem′ə dē), *n., pl.* **-dies,** *v.,* **-died, -dy|ing.** —*n.* **1** a means of removing or relieving diseases or any bad condition; cure: *Aspirin and a mustard plaster are two old cold remedies. (Figurative.) Religion, and not atheism, is the true remedy for superstition* (Edmund Burke). **SYN:** restorative, corrective. **2** a legal redress; legal means of enforcing a right or redressing a wrong. **3** (in coinage) an allowance at the mint for deviation from standard weight and fineness.
—*v.t.* to put right; make right; cure: *A thorough cleaning remedied the trouble.* **SYN:** See syn. under **cure.**
[probably < Anglo-French *remedie,* Old French *remede,* learned borrowing from Latin *remedium* < *re-* again + *medēri* to heal]

**re|melt** (rē melt′), *v.t., v.i.* to melt again.

**re|mem|ber** (ri mem′bər), *v.t.* **1** to call back to mind; recall: *I can't remember that man's name.* **2** to have (something) come into the mind again: *Then I remembered where I was. He suddenly remembered that he had left the windows open.* **3** to keep in mind; take care not to forget: *Remember me when I'm gone.* **4** to keep in mind as deserving a reward or gift; make a gift to; reward; tip: *Grandfather remembered us all in his will.* **5** to mention (a person) as sending friendly greetings; recall to the mind of another: *He asked to be remembered to you.* **6** *Archaic.* to remind.
—*v.i.* **1** to have memory: *Dogs remember.* **2** to recall something. **3** *Archaic.* to have recollection: *I remember Of such a time* (Shakespeare).
[< Old French *remembrer* < Latin *rememorārī* < *re-* again + *memor, -oris* mindful of] —**re|mem′ber|er,** *n.*
—*Syn. v.t.* **1, 2 Remember, recall, recollect** mean to think of something again by an act of memory. **Remember** applies whether the act requires conscious effort or not: *I remember many stray incidents from my childhood.* **Recall** (as well as *recollect*) applies particularly when the act requires conscious effort: *It took me a long time to recall one curious incident.* **Recollect** suggests that the thing remembered is somewhat hazy: *As I recollect, the incident occurred when I was about four.*

**re|mem|ber|a|ble** (ri mem′bər ə bəl), *adj.* that can be or is worthy of being remembered.

**re|mem|brance** (ri mem′brəns), *n.* **1** the power to remember or act of remembering; memory: *The old man's remembrance of the boyhood incident was dimmed by age.* **2** the condition of being remembered: *America holds its heroes in grateful remembrance.* **3** any thing or action that makes one remember a person; keepsake; souvenir: *His parents gave him a fine watch as a remembrance.*
**remembrances,** greetings: *Give my remembrances to your sister when you write to her.*

**Remembrance Day, 1** November 11, the anniversary of the end of World War I in 1918, set aside in Great Britain and Canada to honor the soldiers killed in World Wars I and II. **2** = Remembrance Sunday.

**re|mem|branc|er** (ri mem′brən sər), *n.* a person or thing that reminds one; reminder.

**Re|mem|branc|er** (ri mem′brən sər), *n. British.* **1** any of certain officials of the Court of the Exchequer. The King's (or Queen's) Remembrancer, who collects the sovereign's debts, is the only one still in existence and serves as an officer of the Supreme Court. **2** an officer of the corporation of the City of London.

**Remembrance Sunday,** the Sunday preceding or nearest to November 11, set aside in Great Britain to honor the soldiers killed in World Wars I and II.

**re|merge** (rē mėrj′), *v.i.,* **-merged, -merg|ing.** to merge again: *A remoter realm, out of which we emerged, and into which we again remerge* (Spectator).

**re|mex** (rē′meks), *n.* singular of **remiges.**

**rem|i|cle** (rem′ə kəl), *n.* **1** a small flight feather. **2** the outermost feather attached to the second phalanx of the middle finger of a bird's wing.

**rem|i|ges** (rem′ə jēz) *n., plural of* **re|mex** (rē′meks). the feathers of a bird's wing that enable it to fly; flight feathers. [< Latin *rēmiges,* plural of *rēmex, -igis* oarsman < *rēmus* oar, rudder]

**re|mig|i|al** (ri mij′ē əl), *adj.* of or having to do with the remiges. [< Latin *rēmex, -igis* oarsman (< *rēmus* oar, rudder) + English *-al*[1]]

**rem|i|grant** (rem′ə grənt), *n.* a person or animal that remigrates. Certain insects leave one plant and migrate to a different plant to breed, but a later generation returns to the original plant.

**re|mi|grate** (rē mī′grāt), *v.i.,* **-grat|ed, -grat|ing.** to migrate again or back.

**re|mi|gra|tion** (rē′mī grā′shən), *n.* the action of remigrating.

**re|mil|i|ta|ri|za|tion** (rē′mil ə tər ə zā′shən), *n.* **1** the act of remilitarizing: *The German Federal Republic entered upon the path of remilitarization and was included in the military grouping of the western powers* (London Times). **2** the state or condition of being remilitarized.

**re|mil|i|ta|rize** (rē mil′ə tə rīz), *v.t.,* **-rized, -riz|ing.** to militarize anew.

**re|mind** (ri mīnd′), *v.t.* to make (one) think (of something); cause to remember; bring to mind: *This picture reminds me of a story I heard. The time of year reminds me how the months have gone* (Dickens). —*v.i.* to bring something to mind. [< *re-* again + *mind*[1], verb]

**re|mind|er** (ri mīn′dər), *n.* something to help one remember: *She left a note as a reminder to call back.*

**re|mind|ful** (ri mīnd′fəl), *adj.* **1** reminiscent: *keepsakes remindful of one's friends.* **2** mindful: *to be remindful of one's duties.*

**rem|i|nisce** (rem′ə nis′), *v.i., v.t.,* **-nisced, -nisc|ing.** to talk or think about past experiences or events: *He reminisces of years gone by* (Commentary). *We have many biographies of this well-documented and heavily reminisced period* (Malcolm Bradbury). [back formation < *reminiscence*] —**rem′i|nis′cer,** *n.*

**rem|i|nis|cence** (rem′ə nis′əns), *n.* **1** the act or fact of remembering; recalling past persons or events or places where one has been. **2** Often, **reminiscences,** an account of something remembered; recollection: *reminiscences of college, reminiscences of an old man.* **3** a thing that makes one remember or think of something else. [< Latin *reminīscentia* < *reminīscēns, -entis,* present participle of *reminīscī* remember < *re-* again + *min-,* root of *meminī* to remember, related to *mēns* mind]

**rem|i|nis|cent** (rem′ə nis′ənt), *adj.* **1** recalling past persons or events, or places where one has been: *reminiscent talk.* **2** awakening memories of something else; suggestive: *a manner reminiscent of a statelier age.* —**rem′i|nis′cent|ly,** *adv.*

**rem|i|nis|cen|tial** (rem′ə nə sen′shəl), *adj.* of or having to do with reminiscence. —**rem′i|nis|cen′tial|ly,** *adv.*

**re|mise**[1] (ri mīz′), *v.t.,* **-mised, -mis|ing.** *Law.* to give up a claim to; surrender by deed: *to remise a right or property.* [< Middle French *remise* restoration, noun use of feminine past participle of Old French *remettre,* learned borrowing from Latin *remittere;* see etym. under **remit**]

**re|mise**[2] (ri mēz′), *n.* **1** a house for a carriage. **2** a carriage hired from a livery stable. [< French *remise* < Old French *remettre;* see etym. under **remise**[1]]

**re|miss** (ri mis′), *adj.* **1** careless or slack in doing

---

**Pronunciation Key:** hat, āge, cãre, fär; let, ēqual, tėrm; it, īce; hot, ōpen, ôrder; **oi**l, **ou**t; cup, pu̇t, rüle; **ch**ild; lo**ng**; **th**in; **ᴛʜ**en; **zh**, measure; **ə** represents **a** in about, **e** in taken, **i** in pencil, **o** in lemon, **u** in circus.

what one has to do; neglectful; negligent: *A policeman who lets a thief escape is remiss in his duty.* **SYN**: derelict, thoughtless. **2** characterized by carelessness, negligence, or inattention. **3** lacking force or energy. **SYN**: mild. [< Latin *remissus,* past participle of *remittere* < *re-* back + *mittere* let go, send] —**re|miss'ly,** *adv.* —**re-miss'ness,** *n.*

**re|mis|si|bil|i|ty** (ri mis'ə bil'ə tē), *n.* remissible quality or state.

**re|mis|si|ble** (ri mis'ə bəl), *adj.* that can be remitted.

**re|mis|sion** (ri mish'ən), *n.* **1** the action of letting off (as from debt or punishment): *The bankrupt sought remission of his debts.* **2** pardon; forgiveness: *Remission of sins is promised to those who repent.* **3** a decrease by lowering or lessening (as of pain, force, or labor): *The backbreaking work of harvesting continues without remission until the crops are in. The storm continued without remission.* **4** *Obsolete.* relaxation.

**re|mis|sive** (ri mis'iv), *adj.* **1** inclined to remission. **2** characterized by remission.

**re|mit** (ri mit'), *v.,* **-mit|ted, -mit|ting,** *n.* —*v.i.* **1** to send money to a person or place: *Enclosed is our bill: please remit.* **2** to become less. **SYN**: abate, slacken, diminish.
—*v.t.* **1** to send (money due). **2** to refrain from carrying out; refrain from exacting; cancel: *The governor remitted the prisoner's punishment.* **3** to pardon; forgive: *Christ gave His disciples power to remit sins.* **4** to make less; decrease: *After we had rowed the boat into calm water we remitted our efforts. In return the Government remits income tax on my subscriptions* (London Times). **SYN**: abate, slacken, diminish. **5** to send back (a case) to a lower court for further action. **6** *British.* to refer (a topic, problem, or other matter) for consideration or information. **7** to put back. **8** to postpone. **9** *Obsolete.* to send back, especially to prison.
—*n.* **1** the transfer of a case from one court or judge to another. **2** *British.* a matter submitted to someone for consideration or information; a subject of study or inquiry: *Given a remit about "environmental pollution in all its forms," Mr. Crossland finds himself concerned with land, sea, air, and water* (Manchester Guardian Weekly). **3** *Obsolete.* remission; pardon.
[< Latin *remittere* send back, let go < *re-* back + *mittere* let go, send]

**re|mit|ment** (ri mit'mənt), *n.* = remittance.

**re|mit|ta|ble** (ri mit'ə bəl), *adj.* that can be remitted: *Cash dividends could be paid in whatever currency might be remittable from Brazil* (Wall Street Journal).

**re|mit|tal** (ri mit'əl), *n.* = remission.

**re|mit|tance** (ri mit'əns), *n.* **1** the act of sending of money to someone at a distance. **2** the money that is sent: *Thus he was able to send his friend regular remittances; and in the August of 1851 a new source of income opened for Marx* (Edmund Wilson).

**remittance man,** an emigrant who is supported or assisted by remittances from home: *I was a combination Sorbonne student and remittance man* (New Yorker).

**re|mit|tence** (ri mit'əns), *n.* the act of remitting.

**re|mit|ten|cy** (ri mit'ən sē), *n.* the act of remitting.

**re|mit|tent** (ri mit'ənt), *adj.* lessening for a time; lessening at intervals: *a remittent type of fever.* —**re|mit'tent|ly,** *adv.*

**remittent fever,** a fever in which the symptoms lessen and then return, without ever disappearing entirely.

**re|mit|ter¹** (ri mit'ər), *n.* **1** *Law.* the principle or operation by which a person having two titles to an estate and receiving it by the later or more defective one is adjudged to hold it by the earlier and more valid one. **2** *Law.* the remitting of a case to another court for decision. **3** restoration, as to a former right or condition.

**re|mit|ter²** (ri mit'ər), *n.* a person or thing that remits.

**re|mit|tor** (ri mit'ər), *n. Law.* a person who makes a remittance.

**re|mix** (rē miks'), *v.t.,* **-mixed** or **-mixt, -mix|ing.** to mix again: *It may then be overhauled and remixed with more earth* (L. F. Allen).

**rem|nant** (rem'nənt), *n., adj.* —*n.* **1** a small part left: *Since the factory moved, this town has only a remnant of its former population. Though terribly offended, he retained some remnant of dignity.* **SYN**: rest, fragment. **2** a piece of cloth, ribbon, lace, or other material, left after the rest has been used or sold: *She bought a remnant of silk at a bargain.*
—*adj. Archaic.* remaining.
[< Old French *remenant,* present participle of *remenoir,* also *remanoir,* and *remaindre;* see etym. under **remain**]

**rem|nan|tal** (rem nan'təl), *adj.* of or having to do with a remnant.

**re|mod|el** (rē mod'əl), *v.t.,* **-eled, -el|ing** or (*especially British*) **-elled, -el|ling. 1** to model again. **2** to make over; change or alter: *The old barn was remodeled into a house.*

**re|mod|el|er** (rē mod'ə lər), *n.* a person who remodels: *In this historic neighborhood, remodelers were busy restoring to their original elegance dozens of 18th century row houses* (Time).

**re|mod|el|ler** (rē mod'ə lər), *n. Especially British.* remodeler.

**re|mod|el|ment** (ri mod'əl mənt), *n.* **1** the action of remodeling. **2** the condition of being remodeled.

**re|mod|i|fi|ca|tion** (rē'mod ə fə kā'shən), *n.* the act of modifying again; a repeated modification or change.

**re|mod|i|fy** (rē mod'ə fī), *v.t.,* **-fied, -fy|ing.** to modify again; shape anew; re-form: *Before America was remodified by the arts of Europe* (Thomas Hope).

**re|mo|lade** (rā'mə läd'), *n.* = remoulade.

**re|mold** (rē mōld'), *v.t.* to mold or shape over again or in a new way. —**re|mold'er,** *n.*

**re|mon|e|ti|za|tion** (rē mon'ə tə zā'shən, -mun'-), *n.* **1** the act of remonetizing. **2** the condition of being remonetized.

**re|mon|e|tize** (rē mon'ə tīz, -mun'-), *v.t.,* **-tized, -tiz|ing.** to restore to use as legal tender: *to remonetize silver.* [American English < *re-* again + *monetize;* probably patterned on *demonetize*]

**re|mon|strance** (ri mon'strəns), *n.* **1** the act of remonstrating; protest; complaint: *Almost every word ... is ... in the nature of remonstrance for some breach of decorum* (George Bernard Shaw). **2** *Historical.* a formal statement in protest to a ruler, government, or the like. **3** *Obsolete.* demonstration; manifestation: *remonstrance of my hidden power* (Shakespeare). [< Medieval Latin *remonstrantia* < *remonstrare;* see etym. under **remonstrate**]

**Re|mon|strant** (ri mon'strənt), *n.* a member of the Arminian party in the Dutch Reformed Church. [< Medieval Latin *remonstrans, -antis,* present participle of *remonstrare;* see etym. under **remonstrate**]

**re|mon|strant** (ri mon'strənt), *adj., n.* —*adj.* remonstrating; protesting.
—*n.* a person who remonstrates.
[< *Remonstrant*] —**re|mon'strant|ly,** *adv.*

**re|mon|strate** (ri mon'strāt), *v.,* **-strat|ed, -strat|ing.** —*v.i.* to object; protest; speak, reason, or plead in complaint or protest: *The teacher remonstrated with the boy about his low grades. The people of Connecticut ... remonstrated against the bill* (George Bancroft).
—*v.t.* **1** to reason or plead in protest. **2** *Obsolete.* to point out; show.
[< Medieval Latin *remonstrare* point out, show < Latin *re-* back + *mōnstrāre* point out < *mōnstrum* a sign. Compare etym. under **monster.**]

**re|mon|stra|tion** (rē'mon strā'shən, rem'ən-), *n.* the act of remonstrating: *He went many times over the case of his wife, the judgement of the doctor, his own repeated remonstration* (Harper's).

**re|mon|stra|tive** (ri mon'strə tiv), *adj.* remonstrating. —**re|mon'stra|tive|ly,** *adv.*

**re|mon|stra|tor** (ri mon'strā tər), *n.* = remonstrant.

**re|mon|tant** (ri mon'tənt), *adj., n.* —*adj.* blooming more than once in a season: *remontant roses.*
—*n.* a remontant rose.
[< French *remontant,* present participle of *remonter* < Old French; see etym. under **remount**]

**rem|on|toir** (rem'ən twär'), *n.* a device in a clock or watch that keeps action of a pendulum or balance uniform. [< French *remontoir* < *remonter;* see etym. under **remount**]

***remora**
definition 1

sucker

**remora attached to shark:**

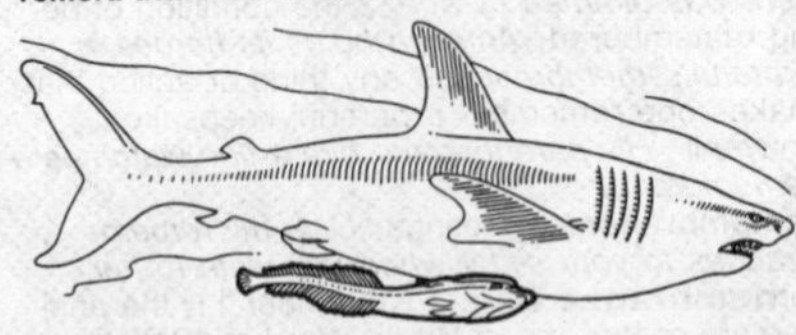

***rem|o|ra** (rem'ər ə), *n.* **1** any one of certain fishes, found especially in tropical waters, with a sucker on the top of the head by which it can attach itself especially to ships and other fishes for transportation: *This is the remora, hitchhiker of the oceans, known to seafaring men the world over as the "pilot fish" or "shark sucker"* (Science News Letter). **2** *Obsolete.* an obstacle; obstruction.
[< Latin *remora* delay, hindrance < *re-* back + *mora* a wait, pause (because it was believed that if it attached itself to a ship, the ship's course would be hindered)]

**re|morse** (ri môrs'), *n.* **1** a deep, painful regret for having done wrong: *Because the thief felt remorse for his crime, he confessed. The critic else proceeds without remorse, Seizes your fame* (Alexander Pope). **SYN**: compunction, contrition. See syn. under **regret. 2** *Obsolete.* sorrow; pity; compassion: *the tears of soft remorse* (Shakespeare). [< Old French *remors* < Latin *remordēre* to disturb < *re-* again + *mordēre* to bite]

**re|morse|ful** (ri môrs'fəl), *adj.* feeling or expressing remorse: *So groan'd Sir Lancelot in remorseful pain* (Tennyson). —**re|morse'ful|ly,** *adv.* —**re-morse'ful|ness,** *n.*

**re|morse|less** (ri môrs'lis), *adj.* **1** without remorse: *His hearty, remorseless laugh showed that the loss meant little to him.* **2** pitiless; cruel: *The remorseless master hit and kicked his dog.* —**re|morse'less|ly,** *adv.* —**re|morse'less|ness,** *n.*

**re|mote** (ri mōt'), *adj.,* **-mot|er, -mot|est,** *n.* —*adj.* **1** far away; far off: *a remote country. The North Pole is a remote part of the world.* **SYN**: See syn. under **distant. 2** out of the way; secluded: *Mail comes to this remote village only once a week.* **3** distant: *a remote relative, the remote past.* **4** *Figurative.* slight; faint: *I haven't the remotest idea what you mean.* **5** *Obsolete.* foreign or alien (to).
—*n.* a radio or television program originating outside of the studio: *We worked ... on a series of NBC Television remotes throughout the country* (Saturday Review).
[< Latin *remōtus,* past participle of *removēre;* see etym. under **remove**] —**re|mote'ness,** *n.*

**remote batch,** a large collection of input and output data passed back and forth between one or more locations and a remote central processor or main computer: *These machines [direct input computers] are therefore converging with small industrial real-time processors in their suitability for use as remote batch terminals and in other systems* (London Times).

**remote control,** the control from a distance of a machine, operation, action, etc., usually by electrical impulses or radio signals: *a calculator or television set operated by remote control. Some model airplanes can be flown by remote control. As air battle commanders watch the picture, they can direct interception by remote control* (Time).

**re|mote-con|trol** (ri mōt'kən trōl'), *adj.* by remote control: *remote-control steering or flying, remote-control television.*

**re|mote-con|trolled** (ri mōt'kən trōld'), *adj.* = remote-control.

**re|mote|ly** (ri mōt'lē), *adv.* in a remote manner; distantly: (*Figurative.*) *These points are not even remotely connected.*

**remote sensing,** observation or scanning, especially of natural features, from a great distance by means of radar, aerial infrared photography, seismography, and similar techniques: *Remote sensing involves the use of special cameras and other sophisticated instruments in orbiting earth satellites. These instruments see and record invisible as well as visible light waves given off by objects on earth. The result is a picture that is far more revealing than one obtained by regular photography* (George W. Irving, Jr.).

**remote sensor,** any instrument or apparatus used in remote sensing.

**re|mo|tion** (ri mō'shən), *n.* **1** = removal. **2** = remoteness. **3** *Obsolete.* departure.

**re|mou|lade** or **ré|mou|lade** (rā'mə läd'; *French* rā mü läd'), *n.* a sauce, usually containing hard-boiled egg yolks, eggs, capers, oil, and vinegar, but now often made with mayonnaise in place of the egg yolks and oil, used as a salad dressing and as a condiment to fish. Also, **remolade.** [< French *rémoulade,* earlier *ramolade;* origin unknown; form influenced by French *remoulade* farrier's unguent < Italian *remolata* < Late Latin *remolum*]

**re|mould** (rē mōld'), *v.t. Especially British.* remold.

**re|mount** (*v.* rē mount'; *n., adj.* rē'mount', rē-mount'), *v., n., adj.* —*v.t.* **1** to mount again: *to remount a picture. The fallen rider remounts his horse.* **2** to furnish with fresh horses.
—*v.i.* **1** to mount a horse or other animal again. **2** to move upward again.
—*n.* a fresh horse, or a supply of fresh horses, for use: *Some of the cavalry had received remounts* (Sir Arthur Conan Doyle).

—***adj.*** of or having to do with remounts.
[< Old French *remonter* < *re-* again + *monter.* Compare etym. under **mount**[1].]

**re|mov|a|bil|i|ty** (ri mü′və bil′ə tē), *n.* the quality or state of being removable.

**re|mov|a|ble** (ri mü′və bəl), *adj.* that can be removed. —**re|mov′a|ble|ness**, *n.*

**re|mov|a|bly** (ri mü′və blē), *adv.* so as to be removable.

**re|mov|al** (ri mü′vəl), *n.* **1** the act of removing; taking away: *After the removal of the soup, fish was served.* **2** change of place: *The store announces its removal to larger quarters.* **3** dismissal from an office or position: *Government officials who do not carry out their public trust are subject to removal.*

**re|move** (ri müv′), *v.*, **-moved, -mov|ing,** *n.* —***v.t.*** **1** to move from a place or position; take off; take away: *People remove their hats in a theater.* SYN: dislodge, shift, displace. **2** to get rid of; put an end to: *An experiment removed all our doubt about the fact that water is made up of two gases.* **3** to kill. **4** to dismiss from an office or position: *The mayor removed the chief of police for failing to do his duty.*
—***v.i.*** to go away; move away: *till Birnam wood remove to Dunsinane* (Shakespeare).
—***n.*** **1** the act of moving away: *It is an English proverb that three removes are as bad as a fire* (Cardinal Newman). **2** a step or degree of distance: *At every remove the mountain seemed smaller.* (*Figurative.*) *His cruelty was only one remove from crime. It's a far remove from Paradise Is Spanish port* (John Masefield). **3** *British.* one course of a meal.
[< Old French *remouvoir* < Latin *removēre* < *re-* back + *movēre* to move]

**re|moved** (ri müvd′), *adj.* **1** distant; remote: *a house far removed from the city.* **2** separated by one or more steps or degrees of relationship: *a cousin once removed.*

**re|mov|ed|ness** (ri mü′vid nis), *n.* the quality or state of being removed.

**re|mov|er** (ri mü′vər), *n.* a person or thing that removes: *a bottle of ink remover.*

**rem|pli** (räɴ plē′), *adj. Heraldry.* covered with a different tincture, except for a bordering space: *a rempli chief.* [< French *rempli,* past participle of *remplir* to fill up < *re-* again + *emplir* to fill < Latin *implēre.* Compare etym. under **implement.**]

**REM sleep,** = paradoxical sleep.

**re|mu|da** (*Spanish* rä mü′ᴛʜä; *Anglicized* ri myü′də), *n.* the saddle horses of a ranch, from which the cowboys choose their mounts for the day: *At night, it would make the wearer invisible, so he could steal horses from the best guarded remuda* (Harper's). [American English < American Spanish *remuda* spare horse < *re-* again + *mudar* to change < Latin *mūtāre*]

**re|mu|ner|ate** (ri myü′nə rāt), *v.t.*, **-at|ed, -at|ing.** to pay, as for work, services, or trouble; reward: *The boy who returned the lost jewels was remunerated. The harvest will remunerate the laborers for their toil.* SYN: recompense. See syn. under **pay.** [< Latin *remūnerāre* (with English *-ate*[1]) < *re-* back + *mūnerāre* to give < *mūnus, -eris* gift]

**re|mu|ner|a|tion** (ri myü′nə rā′shən), *n.* reward; pay; payment: *Remuneration to employes for the quarter was down $3 million* (Wall Street Journal).

**re|mu|ner|a|tive** (ri myü′nə rā′tiv, -nər ə-), *adj.* paying; profitable: *remunerative work.* —**re|mu′ner|a′tive|ly**, *adv.* —**re|mu′ner|a′tive|ness**, *n.*

**re|mu|ner|a|tor** (ri myü′nə rā′tər), *n.* a person who remunerates.

**re|mu|ner|a|to|ry** (ri myü′nə rə tôr′ē, -tōr′-), *adj.* profitable; remunerative.

**re|mur|mur** (rē mėr′mər), *Poetic.* —***v.i.*** to respond or resound with murmurs.
—***v.t.*** to repeat in murmurs: *The trembling trees ... Her fate remurmur to the silver flood* (Alexander Pope).

**Re|mus** (rē′məs), *n. Roman Mythology.* the twin brother of Romulus. As children they were nursed by a wolf; later Romulus founded Rome and slew Remus for leaping contemptuously over the wall of his new city.

**Ren|ais|sance** (ren′ə säns; ren′ə säns′, -zäns′; ri nā′səns), *n., adj.* —***n.*** **1** the great revival of art and learning in Europe during the 1300's, 1400's, and 1500's. **2** the period of time when this revival occurred. **3** the style especially of art and architecture of this period.
—***adj.*** of or having to do with the Renaissance: *Renaissance sculpture.*
[< French, Old French *renaissance* < *re-* again + *naissance* birth < Latin *nāscentia* birth, origin < *nāscī* be born. Compare etym. under **native.**]

**ren|ais|sance** (ren′ə säns; ren′ə säns′, -zäns′; ri nā′səns), *n.* **1** a new birth; revival: *a renaissance of interest in archaeology; ... a renaissance of free men* (Newsweek). **2** any revival, or period of marked improvement and new life, especially in art, literature, or music.

*****Renaissance architecture**, the style of architecture imitating the classical Roman. It originated in Italy in the first half of the 1400's, afterward spreading over Europe.

*****Renaissance architecture**

**Renaissance man,** a man who is knowledgeable in an unusually wide variety of the arts and sciences: *Plimpton is the Renaissance man; his abilities and interests run the full gamut. He is a tennis ace. He is a linguist, a poet, a wit, and a classical scholar* (New Yorker). *The two-volume manuscript finds of drawings and notes made by the epitome of the "Renaissance Man" will keep Leonardo da Vinci scholars enthralled and occupied for many years* (Fay Leviero).

**re|nais|sant** (ri nā′sənt), *adj.* reviving; renascent: *Rapidly rising output and renaissant business confidence and investment are normally a time at which profits rise* (London Times). [< French *renaissant*]

**Re|nais|sant** (ri nā′sənt), *adj.* of or having to do with the Renaissance.

**re|nal** (rē′nəl), *adj.* of the kidneys; having to do with or located near the kidneys: *a renal artery. The veins which carry blood to the kidneys constitute the renal portal system* (Hegner and Stiles). [< Latin *rēnālis* < *rēn, rēnis* kidney]

**renal corpuscle,** one of the filtering structures in the cortex of the kidney, composed of a glomerulus and Bowman's capsule; Malpighian body: *The renal corpuscles with the uriniferous tubules are the essential excretory units in the vertebrate animals generally* (A. Franklin Shull).

**renal gland** or **capsule,** = adrenal gland.

**re|name** (rē nām′), *v.t.*, **-named, -nam|ing.** to give a new name to; name again.

**Ren|ard** (ren′ərd), *n.* = Reynard.

**Re|nas|cence** (ri nas′əns, -nā′səns), *n.* = Renaissance.

**re|nas|cence** (ri nā′səns, -nas′əns), *n.* **1** a new birth; revival; renewal: *a renascence of religion. She wanted to lie ... and wait, as a patient animal waits, for her renascence* (New Yorker). **2** a being renascent: *a period of moral renascence* (H. G. Wells).

**re|nas|cent** (ri nā′sənt, -nas′ənt), *adj.* being born again; reviving; springing again into being or vigor. [< Latin *renāscēns, -entis,* present participle of *renāscī* < *re-* again + *nāscī* be born. Compare etym. under **native.**]

**re|na|tion|al|ise** (rē nash′ə nə līz, -nash′nə-), *v.t.*, **-ised, -is|ing.** *Especially British.* renationalize.

**re|na|tion|al|i|za|tion** (rē nash′ə nə lə zā′shən, -nash′nə-), *n.* the act or process of renationalizing or fact or condition of being renationalized: *With the return of the Conservative Government measures of renationalization ... are no longer risks to be discounted* (London Times).

**re|na|tion|al|ize** (rē nash′ə nə līz, -nash′nə-), *v.t.*, **-ized, -iz|ing.** to nationalize again; restore to government control: *Socialists have repeatedly threatened to renationalize steel as soon as possible if the conservatives denationalize it* (Newsweek).

**re|na|tur|a|tion** (rē nā′chə rā′shən), *n.* **1** the act or process of renaturing. **2** the fact or state of being renatured.

**re|na|ture** (rē nā′chər), *v.t.*, **-tured, -tur|ing.** to change back to a natural state after denaturing: *These double threads may be separated into single strands by experimental denaturation and can then be renatured into double strands once more* (Science Journal).

**re|nav|i|gate** (rē nav′ə gāt), *v.i., v.t.*, **-gat|ed, -gat|ing.** to navigate again.

**re|nav|i|ga|tion** (rē′nav ə gā′shən), *n.* the act of renavigating.

**ren|con|tre** (ren kon′tər; *French* räɴ kôɴ′trə), *n.* = rencounter.
[< French, Middle French *rencontre;* see etym. under **rencounter**]

**ren|coun|ter** (ren koun′tər), *n., v.* —***n.*** **1** a hostile meeting; conflict; battle; duel. **2** a chance meeting: *All my acquaintance with him was confined to an occasional rencounter in the hall* (Charlotte Brontë).
—***v.t.*** to come upon: *I had the good fortune to rencounter you at Durrisdeer* (Robert Louis Stevenson).
—***v.i.*** to meet in conflict.
[< Middle French, Old French *rencontre* < *rencontrer* to meet < *re-* again + *encontrer.* Compare etym. under **encounter.**]

**rend** (rend), *v.*, **rent, rend|ing.** —***v.t.*** **1** to pull apart violently; tear: *Wolves will rend a lamb in pieces.* **2** to split: *Lightning rent the tree.*
**3** *Figurative.* to disturb violently: *a mind rent by doubt. He was rent by a wish to keep the money he found and the knowledge that he ought to return it.* **4** to remove with force or violence: *I will surely rend the kingdom from thee* (I Kings 11:11). —***v.i.*** to rip.
[Old English *rendan*] —**rend′er**, *n.*

**ren|der** (ren′dər), *v., n.* —***v.t.*** **1** to cause to become; make: *An accident has rendered him helpless. Fright rendered me speechless.* **2** to give; do: *to render judgment. Can you render any aid? What service has he rendered to the school?* **3** to offer for consideration, approval, payment, or fulfillment; hand in; report: *to render a bill. The treasurer rendered an account of all the money spent.* **4** to give in return: *Render thanks for your blessings.* **5** to pay as due: *The conquered rendered tribute to the conqueror.* **6** to bring out the meaning of; represent: *The actor rendered the part of the villain well.* **7** to play or sing (music): *to render an old English ballad.* **8** to change from one language to another; translate: *Render that Latin proverb into English.* **9** to give up; surrender: *The knights rendered their swords to the victors.* **10** to melt (fat or other animal or vegetable matter); clarify or extract by melting. Fat from hogs is rendered for lard. **11** to cover (bricks, stone, or lath) with a first coat of plaster.
—***v.i.*** *Obsolete.* to make return or recompense.
—***n.*** **1** a first coat of plaster. **2** *Law.* a return; payment in money, kind, or service made by a tenant to his superior.
[< Old French *rendre* < Vulgar Latin *rendere,* alteration of Latin *reddere* give as due; to pay < *re-* back, again + *dare* give] —**ren′der|er**, *n.*

**ren|der|a|ble** (ren′dər ə bəl), *adj.* that can be rendered.

**ren|der|ing** (ren′də ring), *n.* **1a** the act of yielding, giving, offering, or paying: *Love itself is, in its highest state, the rendering of an exquisite praise to body and soul* (John Ruskin). **b** that which is rendered or given: *Alas! our renderings are nothing ...; we are like the barren field* (Philip Henry). **2** translation; interpretation: *Correct rendering is very often conspicuously absent from our authorized version of the Old Testament* (Matthew Arnold). **3a** reproduction; representation: *The painter has shown himself extremely skilful in his rendering of curious effects of light* (London Times). **b** performance: *The Opera Society had given an excellent rendering of "Patience" in the Founders' Hall* (Graham Greene).

**ren|dez|vous** (rän′də vü), *n., pl.* **-vous** (-vüz), *v.*, **-voused** (-vüd), **-vous|ing** (-vü′ing). —***n.*** **1** an appointment or engagement to meet at a fixed place or time; meeting by agreement: *Each tribe had usually some fixed place of rendezvous* (Scott). (*Figurative.*) *This country has a rendezvous with destiny* (Franklin D. Roosevelt). **2** a meeting place; gathering place: *The family had two favorite rendezvous, the living room and the lawn behind the house.* **3** a place agreed on for a meeting at a certain time, especially of troops or ships. **4** a meeting at a fixed place or time: *the rendezvous of a lunar module and the command ship.*
—***v.i.*** to meet at a rendezvous.
—***v.t.*** *U.S.* to bring together (as troops, ships, or space capsules) at a fixed place.
[< Middle French *rendezvous* < *rendez-vous* betake (literally, present) yourself < Old French *rendre* (see etym. under **render**), *vous* < Latin *vōs* you, plural]

**ren|di|tion** (ren dish′ən), *n.* **1** the act of rendering: *Not the newspaper articles which were a sensationalized rendition of his tour* (Saturday Review). **2** the rendering of a dramatic part or music, to bring out the meaning. **3** = translation. **4** the surrender of a place, person, position, or possession. [< Middle French *rendition* < Old French *rendre;* see etym. under **render**]

**rend|rock** (rend′rok′), *n.* an explosive mixture

**Pronunciation Key:** hat, āge, cãre, fär; let, ēqual, tėrm; it, īce; hot, ōpen, ôrder; oil, out; cup, pu̇t, rüle; child; long; thin; ᴛʜen; zh, measure; ə represents **a** in about, **e** in taken, **i** in pencil, **o** in lemon, **u** in circus.

used chiefly in blasting, containing nitroglycerin, kieselguhr, and wood pulp.

**ren|e|gade** (ren′ə gād), *n., adj., v.,* **-gad|ed, -gad|ing.** —*n.* a deserter, such as from a religious faith or a political party; traitor; one who abandons his principles or his people. **SYN:** apostate, recreant, backslider.
—*adj.* like a traitor; deserting; disloyal; apostate: *But he is not, like Joyce, a bitterly renegade Catholic* (The Reporter). **SYN:** traitorous.
—*v.i.* to turn renegade.
[< Spanish *renegado* renegado < Medieval Latin *renegare* to deny; see etym. under **renege**]

**ren|e|ga|do** (ren′ə gā′dō), *n., pl.* **-does,** *adj., v.i.,* **-doed, -doe|ing.** *Archaic.* renegade. [< Spanish *renegado* < Medieval Latin *renegare;* see etym. under **renege**]

**re|nege** (ri nig′, -nēg′), *v.,* **-neged, -neg|ing,** *n.*
—*v.i.* **1** to fail to play a card of the same suit as that first played, although one is able to do so; revoke. It is against the rules of cards to renege. **2** *Informal.* to back out; fail to follow up: *to renege on a promise or responsibility. Most of the 57 members who had backed an amendment to admit women reneged* (Newsweek).
—*v.t. Archaic.* to deny; renounce.
—*n.* a failure to follow suit in cardplaying when able to do so; revoke.
[< Medieval Latin *renegare* < Latin *re-* back + *negāre* deny] —**re|neg′er,** *n.*

**re|ne|go|ti|a|ble** (rē′ni gō′shē ə bəl, -shə bəl), *adj.* that can be renegotiated: *Average profits on the much larger renegotiable defense business have plummeted* (Wall Street Journal).

**re|ne|go|ti|ate** (rē′ni gō′shē āt), *v.t., v.i.,* **-at|ed, -at|ing.** to negotiate again or anew, especially a contract, to eliminate excessive profits.

**re|ne|go|ti|a|tion** (rē′ni gō′shē ā′shən), *n.* the act or process of renegotiating or condition of being renegotiated: *Far from encouraging is the threat of renegotiation of profits on Government contracts* (Wall Street Journal).

**re|nerve** (rē nėrv′), *v.t.,* **-nerved, -nerv|ing.** to restore vigor or courage to.

**re|new** (ri nü′, -nyü′), *v.t.* **1** to make new again; make like new; restore: *Rain renews the greenness of the field.* **2** to make spiritually new: *Grant that we ... may daily be renewed by thy holy spirit* (Book of Common Prayer). **3** to begin again; get again; say, do, or give again: *to renew an attack, one's youth, or one's vows. He renewed his efforts to open the window.* **4** to replace by new material or a new thing of the same sort; fill again: *She renewed the sleeves of her dress. The well renews itself no matter how much water is taken away.* **5** to give or get for a new period: *We renewed our lease for another year.*
—*v.i.* **1** to renew a lease, note, or other obligation or agreement. **2** to begin again. **3** to become new again. —**re|new′er,** *n.*
—*Syn. v.t.* **1 Renew, restore, renovate** mean to put back in a new or former condition. **Renew** means to put back in a condition like new something that has lost its freshness, force, or vigor: *She renewed the finish of the table.* **Restore** means to put back in its original, former, or normal condition something that has been damaged, worn out, or partly ruined: *That old Spanish mission has been restored.* **Renovate** means to put in good condition or make like new, as by cleaning, repairing, and redecorating: *The store was renovated.*

**re|new|a|bil|i|ty** (ri nü′ə bil′ə tē, -nyü′-), *n.* the quality or condition of being renewable: *The original complaint ... charged the company had misrepresented in advertising the renewability of its policies* (Wall Street Journal).

**re|new|a|ble** (ri nü′ə bəl, -nyü′-), *adj.* that can be renewed: *a renewable contract.*

**re|new|a|bly** (ri nü′ə blē, -nyü′-), *adv.* so as to be renewable.

**re|new|al** (ri nü′əl, -nyü′-), *n.* the act of renewing or fact of being renewed: *When hot weather comes there will be a renewal of interest in swimming and canoeing.*

**re|new|ed|ly** (ri nü′id lē, -nyü′-), *adv.* = anew.

**R. Eng.,** Royal Engineers.

***ren|i|form** (ren′ə fôrm, rē′nə-), *adj.* kidney-shaped: *a reniform leaf, a reniform shell.* [< Latin *rēn, rēnis* kidney + English *-form*]

**re|nin** (rē′nin), *n.* a protein enzyme in the kidney that raises blood pressure when injected into the bloodstream: *Page made important discoveries on the workings of renin, an enzyme secreted by the kidney when it is starved of blood* (Time). [< Latin *rēn, rēnis* kidney + English *-in*]

**ren|i|punc|ture** (ren′ə pungk′chər, rē′nə-), *n.* surgical puncture of the capsule of the kidney, for relief of pain. [< Latin *rēn, rēnis* kidney + English *puncture*]

**re|ni|ten|cy** (ri nī′tən sē, ren′ə-), *n.* resistance; recalcitrance.

**re|ni|tent** (ri nī′tənt, ren′ə-), *adj.* **1** resisting pressure; resistant. **2** = recalcitrant. [< French *rénitent,* learned borrowing from Latin *renītēns, -entis,* present participle of *renītī* to resist < *re-* back + *nītī* to struggle, fight]

**ren|net** (ren′it), *n.* **1** substance containing rennin, obtained from the stomach of a calf or other ruminant, used for curdling milk in making cheese and junket: *The milk proteins are clotted, either by the action of lactic acid produced by bacteria growing in the milk, or by the addition of rennet* (Science News). **2** a mass of curdled milk found in the fourth stomach of a calf or other ruminant. [Middle English *rennet* < *rennen* to run, Old English *rinnan,* or < Scandinavian (compare Old Icelandic *renna*)]

**rennet pepsin,** pepsin from the stomach of the calf.

**rennet stomach,** the abomasum of a ruminant.

**ren|nin** (ren′in), *n.* an enzyme in the gastric juice that coagulates or curdles milk. It occurs in young infants, in calves, and also in certain lower animals and plants.

**re|nog|ra|phy** (rə nog′rə fē), *n.* the study of the kidneys by means of radiography. [< Latin *rēn, rēnis* kidney + English *-graphy*]

**re|nom|i|nate** (rē nom′ə nāt), *v.t.,* **-nat|ed, -nat|ing.** to nominate again. —**re′nom|i|na′tion,** *n.*

**re|nounce** (ri nouns′), *v.,* **-nounced, -nounc|ing.**
—*v.t.* **1** to declare that one gives up; give up entirely; give up: *He renounces his claim to the money. The shipwrecked sailor renounced all hope of rescue.* **SYN:** forego, forsake, relinquish. **2** to cast off; refuse to recognize as one's own: *He renounced his wicked son.* **SYN:** repudiate, disown. **3** to give up, surrender, or resign by a greater or lesser sacrifice of one's own wishes or feelings: *The mind which renounces, once and for all, a futile hope, has its compensations in ever-growing calm* (George Gissing). **4** to play (a suit of cards) different from that led, having no card of the suit led.
—*v.i.* **1** to make formal surrender. **2** to play a card of a different suit from that led. [< Old French *renoncer,* learned borrowing from Latin *renūntiāre* < *re-* back + *nūntiāre* to announce < *nūntius* messenger] —**re|nounce′ment,** *n.* —**re|nounc′er,** *n.*

**ren|o|vate** (ren′ə vāt), *v.t.,* **-vat|ed, -vat|ing. 1** to make like new; make new again; make over; restore to good condition: *to renovate a garment. He had cleaned and renovated the dark little hole of a cabin* (Joseph Conrad). **SYN:** See syn. under **renew. 2** to restore to vigor; invigorate; refresh. **3** make over in a new or better form; regenerate: *We want men and women who shall renovate life and our social state* (Emerson). [< Latin *renovāre* (with English *-ate*[1]) < *re-* again + *novāre* make new < *novus* new] —**ren′o|va′tor,** *n.*

**ren|o|va|tion** (ren′ə vā′shən), *n.* the process of restoration to good condition; renewal.

**re|nown** (ri noun′), *n., v.* —*n.* **1** fame; being widely celebrated or held in high repute: *A doctor who finds a cure for a disease wins renown.* **SYN:** celebrity, distinction. **2** *Obsolete.* **a** a report; rumor. **b** reputation: *a young gentlewoman of a most chaste renown* (Shakespeare).
—*v.t.* to make famous: *The things of fame that do renown this city* (Shakespeare).
—*v.i.* to brag; swagger.
[< Anglo-French *renoun,* Old French *renon,* or *renom* < *renommer* make famous < *re-* again, re- + *nommer* to name < Latin *nōmināre* < *nōmen, -inis* name]

**re|nowned** (ri nound′), *adj.* famous; famed. **SYN:** See syn. under **famous.**

**rens|se|laer|ite** (ren′sə lə rīt, ren′sə lãr′īt), *n.* a variety of talc with a fine, compact texture that can be worked on a lathe. [American English < Stephen Van *Rensselaer,* 1764-1839, an American statesman]

***reniform**

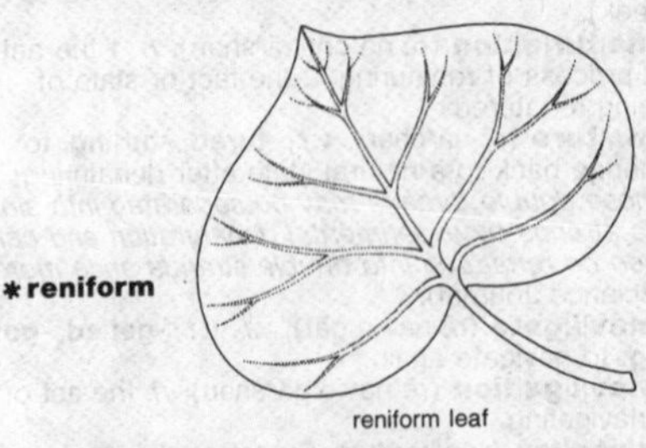

reniform leaf

**rent**[1] (rent), *n., v.* —*n.* **1** a regular payment for the use of property: *Rent for that six-room apartment is $500 a month.* **2** *Economics.* **a** what is paid for the use of natural resources. **b** = economic rent. **3** a house or other property for which rent is received. **4** *Obsolete.* a revenue; income: *What are thy rents? What are thy comings-in?* (Shakespeare).
—*v.t.* **1** to pay at regular times for the use of (property): *We rent a house from them.* **2** to receive regular pay for the use of (property): *The landlord rents several other houses.* —*v.i.* to be rented: *This farm rents for $1,500 a year.*
**for rent,** that can be had in return for rent paid: *That vacant apartment is for rent.*
[< Old French *rente* < Vulgar Latin *rendita* < *rendere;* see etym. under **render**]

**rent**[2] (rent), *n., adj., v.* —*n.* **1** a torn place; tear; split: *a rent in a shirt. See what a rent the envious Casca made* (Shakespeare). **SYN:** breach. **2** a break of relations; separation; schism; rupture. [< obsolete *rent* tear, variant of *rend*]
—*adj.* torn; split: *a rent shirt.*
—*v.* the past tense and past participle of **rend:** *The tree was rent by the wind.*
[past participle of *rend*]

**rent|a|bil|i|ty** (ren′tə bil′ə tē), *n.* the quality of being rentable.

**rent|a|ble** (ren′tə bəl), *adj.* that can be rented.

**rent-a-car** (rent′ə kär′), *n. U.S.* a car rented for a day, week, or other contracted time, for a fixed sum or according to mileage.

**rent|al** (ren′təl), *n., adj.* —*n.* **1** an amount received or paid as rent: *The yearly rental of her house is $4,000.* **2** a list of tenants and of rents received or due. **3** something rented, especially an apartment or house offered for rent: *There are not many rentals available in Fairfield County.*
—*adj.* having to do with or collecting rent: *a rental agent, rental value.*
[< Anglo-French or Medieval Latin (England) *rentale,* both < Old French *rente* < Vulgar Latin *rendita* < *rendere;* see etym. under **render**]

**rental library,** a circulating library that makes a charge for lending books.

**rent control,** the regulation of rent by a government.

**rente** (räɴt), *n. French.* income; revenue.

**ren|ten|mark** (ren′tən märk′), *n.* a temporary German mark used in 1923 and 1924, representing a mortgage of all German property: *All Reichsmarks were called in and rentenmarks issued in exchange—one trillion Reichsmarks for one rentenmark* (Wall Street Journal). [< German *Rentenmark* < *Rente* revenue (< French *rente*) + *Mark* mark, unit of currency]

**rent|er** (ren′tər), *n.* a person who pays rent for using another's property. **SYN:** lessee.

**rentes** (räɴt), *n.pl.* **1** the interest paid on French government bonds. **2** such bonds. [< French *rentes,* plural of *rente* rent, income, revenue < Old French *rente;* see etym. under **rent**[1]]

**ren|tier** (räɴ tyā′), *n. French.* a person who has a fixed income from investment, as in lands or stocks.

**rent party,** a party to which admission is charged for the purpose of paying the rent of the host.

**rent roll,** *Especially British.* a list of rents received or due.

**rent-seck** (rent′sek′), *n.* (formerly) a rent established with the agreement that if the tenant fell behind in payments the owner could not seize the tenant's goods.
[< Anglo-French *rente secque* (literally) dry rent; *rente* < Vulgar Latin *rendita* < *rendere* (see etym. under **render**), *secque* < Latin *siccus* dry, sec]

**rent strike,** *U.S.* a refusal by the tenants of a building to pay rent as a protest, especially against poor service: *The tenants of the apartments at West Madison and Albany were conducting a rent strike* (New Yorker).

**re|nu|mer|ate** (rē nü′mə rāt, -nyü′-), *v.t.,* **-at|ed, -at|ing.** to count or number again.

**re|nun|ci|ant** (ri nun′sē ənt), *n.* one who renounces, especially one who renounces the world.

**re|nun|ci|ate** (ri nun′sē āt), *v.t.,* **-at|ed, -at|ing.** = renounce.

**re|nun|ci|a|tion** (ri nun′sē ā′shən), *n.* the act of giving up a right, title, or possession; renouncing: *The bonzes preach only patience, humility and the renunciation of the world* (Edward Gibbon). **SYN:** rejection. [< Latin *renūntiātiō, -ōnis* < *renūntiāre;* see etym. under **renounce**]

**re|nun|ci|a|tive** (ri nun′sē ā′tiv), *adj.* that renounces.

**re|nun|ci|a|to|ry** (ri nun′sē ə tôr′ē, -tōr′-), *adj.* that renounces; renunciative.

**ren|ver|sé** (räN ver sā′), *n. Ballet.* a bending of the body from the waist during a turn. [< French *renversé,* past participle of *renverser* to turn back]

**re|oc|cu|pa|tion** (rē′ok yə pā′shən), *n.* the act of occupying again; renewed occupation.

**re|oc|cu|py** (rē ok′yə pī), *v.t.,* **-pied, -py|ing.** to occupy (a place or position) again: *After a lapse of years a new people with new fashions of pottery and implements reoccupied the site* (Scientific American).

**re|o|dor|ant** (rē ō′dər ənt), *n.* a preparation that replaces or masks an offensive odor.

**re|o|dor|ize** (rē ō′də rīz), *v.t.,* **-ized, -iz|ing.** to change an offensive odor in (a room) by replacing or masking it with a stronger perfumed or pleasant odor. —**re|o′dor|i|za′tion,** *n.*

**re|o|pen** (rē ō′pən), *v.t.* **1** to open again: *He reopened the window when it grew warmer.* **2** to discuss again or further: *to reopen a contract. The matter is settled and cannot be reopened.*
—***v.i.*** **1** to open again. **2** = resume: *School will reopen in September.* —**re|o′pen|er,** *n.*

**re|op|pose** (rē′ə pōz′), *v.t.,* **-posed, -pos|ing.** to oppose again.

**re|or|dain** (rē′ôr dān′), *v.t.* to ordain, appoint, or establish again.

**re|or|der** (rē ôr′dər), *v., n.* —***v.t., v.i.*** **1** to put in order again; rearrange. **2** to give a second or repeated order for goods; order again.
—***n.*** a second or repeated order for goods placed with the same company or person.

**re|or|di|na|tion** (rē′ôr də nā′shən), *n.* a second or repeated ordination.

**re|or|gan|ise** (rē ôr′gə nīz), *v.t., v.i.,* **-ised, -is|ing.** *Especially British.* reorganize.

**re|or|gan|i|za|tion** (rē′ôr gə nə zā′shən), *n.* **1** the act or process of reorganizing: *I have already commenced a reorganization of the cavalry* (Duke of Wellington). **2** the reconstruction or rehabilitation of a business that is in the hands of a receiver. **3** the condition of being reorganized.

**re|or|gan|i|za|tion|al** (rē′ôr gə nə zā′shə nəl), *adj.* of or having to do with reorganization: *reorganizational changes.*

**re|or|gan|ize** (rē ôr′gə nīz), *v.t., v.i.,* **-ized, -iz|ing.** **1** to organize anew; form again; arrange in a new way: *Classes will be reorganized after the first four weeks.* **SYN:** rearrange, readjust. **2** to form a new company to operate (a business in the hands of a receiver). —**re|or′gan|iz′er,** *n.*

**re|o|ri|ent** (rē ôr′ē ent, -ōr′-), *v.t., v.i.* to orient again or in a new way: *Those reoriented to the white man's ways and his eating habits, soon start picking up his citified diseases* (Maclean's). —**re|o′ri|en|ta′tion,** *n.*

**re|o|ri|en|tate** (rē ôr′ē en tāt, -ōr′-) *v.t., v.i.,* **-tat|ed, -tat|ing.** = reorient.

**re|o|vi|rus** (rē′ō vī′rəs), *n.* an echovirus associated with respiratory and intestinal infections and found also in certain animal and human tumors. [< *r*(espiratory) *e*(nteric) *o*(rphan) *virus*]

**rep¹** (rep), *n.* a ribbed fabric of wool, silk, rayon, or cotton. Woolen rep is used especially for upholstery. Also, **repp, reps.** [probably < French *reps;* origin uncertain]

**rep²** (rep), *n. Slang.* reputation: *We can't afford to have our reps ruined by being seen with you* (Sinclair Lewis).

**rep³** (rep), *n. Informal.* repertory (company or theater).

**rep⁴** (rep), *n. Informal.* representative.

**rep⁵** (rep), *n., pl.* **rep** or **reps.** a unit of radiation used especially to measure beta rays, equal to the amount of ionizing radiation that will transfer to living tissue 93 ergs of energy per gram. [< *r*(oentgen) *e*(quivalent) *p*(hysical)]

**rep.,** an abbreviation for the following:
**1** repeat.
**2a** report. **b** reported.
**3** reporter.
**4** representative.
**5** republic.

**Rep** (no period), *Slang.* Repertory Company or Theater.

**Rep.,** **1** Representative. **2** Republic. **3** Republican.

**re|pack** (rē pak′), *v.t., v.i.* to pack again: *to repack a suitcase.*

**re|pack|age** (rē pak′ij), *v.t.,* **-aged, -ag|ing.** to package again, especially in a more attractive container: *It plans to repackage the company's products with the aim of achieving greater eye-appeal and of preserving the product's freshness for a longer period* (Wall Street Journal). —**re-pack′ag|er,** *n.*

**re|paid** (ri pād′), *v.* the past tense and past participle of **repay:** *He repaid the money he had borrowed. All debts should be repaid.*

**re|paint** (*v.* rē pānt′; *n.* rē′pānt′), *v., n.* —***v.t., v.i.*** to paint again.
—***n.*** **1** the act or process of repainting: *The Coliseum would need new dressing rooms, ... technical equipment, and a repaint* (Sunday Times). **2** a part of a picture that has been repainted.

**re|pair¹** (ri pãr′), *v., n.* —***v.t.*** **1** to put in good condition again; mend: *He repairs shoes.* **SYN:** restore, renovate. See syn. under **mend.** **2** to make up for; remedy: *How can I repair the harm done? The loss of such a man could not easily be repaired* (Macaulay).
—***n.*** **1** the act or work of repairing: *He was hired to make an estimate and repair of all the broken windows.* **2** Often, **repairs.** an instance or piece of repairing: *Repairs on the school building are made during the summer.* **3** condition fit to be used: *The state keeps the roads in repair.* **4** condition for use with respect to repairing: *The house was in bad repair.*
[Middle English *reparen* < Latin *reparāre* < *re-* again + *parāre* prepare] —**re|pair′a|ble,** *adj.* —**re|pair′er,** *n.*

**re|pair²** (ri pãr′), *v., n.* —***v.i.*** **1** to go (to a place): *After dinner we repaired to the porch.* **2** *Obsolete.* to return.
—***n.*** **1** the act of repairing to a place. **2** a place repaired to; resort.
[< Old French *repairier* < Late Latin *repatriāre* return to one's own country. See etym. of doublet **repatriate.**]

**re|pair|man** (ri pãr′man′, -mən), *n., pl.* **-men.** a man whose work is repairing: *a television repairman.*

**re|pand** (ri pand′), *adj. Botany.* having the margin slightly uneven or wavy: *a repand leaf.* [< Latin *repandus* < *re-* back + *pandus* bent]

**rep|a|ra|ble** (rep′ər ə bəl, ri pãr′-), *adj.* that can be repaired or remedied. [< Latin *reparābilis* < *reparāre;* see etym. under **repair¹**] —**rep′a|ra|bly,** *adv.*

**rep|a|ra|tion** (rep′ə rā′shən), *n.* **1** compensation for wrong or injury done: *to make reparation.* **2** the act or fact of giving satisfaction or compensation for wrong or injury done. **3** the act of repairing or state of being repaired; restoration to good condition: *The building stood from century to century ... without need of reparation* (Samuel Johnson).
**reparations,** compensation for wrong or injury, especially payments made by a defeated country for the devastation of territory during war: *After World War I England and France demanded reparations from Germany.*
[< Old French *reparacion,* learned borrowing from Latin *reparātiō, -ōnis* < *reparāre;* see etym. under **repair¹**]

**re|par|a|tive** (ri par′ə tiv), *adj.* **1** tending to repair: *reparative power.* **2** having to do with or involving reparation.

**re|par|a|to|ry** (ri par′ə tôr′ē, -tōr′-), *adj.* = reparative.

**rep|ar|tee** (rep′ər tē′), *n.* **1** a witty reply or replies: *Droll allusions, good stories, and smart repartees ... fell thick as hail* (Charles J. Lever). **SYN:** sally, retort. **2** talk characterized by clever and witty replies: *accomplished in repartee.* **3** cleverness and wit in making replies: *framing comments ... that would be sure to sting and yet leave no opening for repartee* (H. G. Wells). [< French *repartie* < *repartir* to reply, set out again, ultimately < Latin *re-* back, again + *pars, partis* a part, portion, share]

**re|par|ti|mien|to** (rā pär′ti myen′tō), *n., pl.* **-tos** (-tōs). **1** a partition. **2** an allotment. **3** (in Spanish America) a territory granted by the early conquerors to their comrades and followers. It included the right to the labor of the native inhabitants. [< Spanish *repartimiento* < *repartir* < *re-* back (< Latin) + *partire* leave < Latin *partīrī* part]

**re|par|ti|tion** (rē′pär tish′ən, -pər-), *n., v.* —***n.*** **1** partition; distribution; allotment. **2** a redistribution.
—***v.t.*** to partition again or in a new way.

**re|pass** (rē pas′, -päs′), *v.t., v.i.* **1** to pass back: *to repass the gravy.* **2** to pass again: *to repass a car.*

**re|pas|sage** (rē pas′ij), *n.* **1** a passage back. **2** a passing again.

**re|past** (ri past′, -päst′), *n., v.* —***n.*** **1** a meal; attractive meal; food: *to serve a delicious repast. Breakfast at our house is a light repast.* **2** a taking of food; eating: *a brief repast.* **3** *Archaic.* mealtime.
—***v.i.*** to feed or feast (on, upon).
—***v.t.*** *Obsolete.* to feed.
[< Old French *repast* < Late Latin *repāscere* feed again < Latin *re-* again + *pāscere* to feed]

**re|pa|tri|ate** (rē pā′trē āt), *v.,* **-at|ed, -at|ing,** *n.* —***v.t.*** **1** to send back to one's own country: *After peace was declared, refugees and prisoners of war were repatriated.* **2** to restore to citizenship.
—***v.i.*** to go back to one's own country.
—***n.*** a repatriated person: *To provide the means of transportation necessary for the transfer of repatriates to the frontier of their countries* (New York Times).
[< Late Latin *repatriāre* (with English *-ate¹*) < Latin *re-* back + *patria* native land < *pater, patris* father. See etym. of doublet **repair².**] —**re|pa′tri-a′tion,** *n.*

**re|pave** (rē pāv′), *v.t.,* **-paved, -pav|ing.** to pave again or anew.

**re|pay** (ri pā′), *v.,* **-paid, -pay|ing.** —***v.t.*** **1** to pay back: *He repaid the money he had borrowed.* **SYN:** refund. **2** to give back; return: *to repay a blow, to repay a visit.* **3** to make return for: *No thanks can repay such kindness.* **4** to make return to: *The boy's success repaid the teacher for her efforts.*
—***v.i.*** to make repayment or return: *Vengeance is mine; I will repay, saith the Lord* (Romans 12:19).
[< Old French *repaier* < *re-* back, re- + *paier* to pay] —**re|pay′a|ble,** *adj.* —**re|pay′er,** *n.* —**re-pay′ment,** *n.*

**re|peal** (ri pēl′), *v., n.* —***v.t.*** **1** to take back; do away with; withdraw: *The law was repealed. The 18th amendment of the U.S. Constitution was repealed by the 21st.* **SYN:** revoke, rescind, annul, abrogate. **2** *Obsolete.* to call back.
—***n.*** the act of repealing; withdrawal; abolition: *He voted for the repeal of that law.* **SYN:** abrogation, revocation.
[< Anglo-French *repeler,* Old French *rapeler* < *re-* back + *apeler* to call, appeal < Latin *appelāre* accost, related to *appellere* < *ad-* to + *pellere* strike, hit] —**re|peal′a|ble,** *adj.*

**re|peal|er** (ri pē′lər), *n.* **1** a person or thing that repeals. **2** *U.S.* a bill, or a clause of a bill, to repeal some legislative measure.

***re|peat** (ri pēt′), *v., n., adj.* —***v.t.*** **1** to do or make again: *to repeat an error.* **2** to say again: *to repeat a word for emphasis. I do but repeat what has been said a thousand times* (Sir Richard Steele). **3** to say over; recite: *She can repeat many poems from memory.* **4** to say after another says: *Repeat the pledge to the flag after me.* **5** to tell to another or others: *I promised not to repeat the secret.*
—***v.i.*** **1** to do or say something again. **2** *U.S.* to vote more than once in an election. **3** (of food) to rise in the gullet, so as to be tasted again.
—***n.*** **1** the action of repeating. **2** a thing repeated: *"There's nothing on television tonight but repeats," Carl said to Louise* (Russell Baker). **3** *Music.* **a** a passage to be repeated. **b** a sign indicating this, usually a double line and a row of dots placed at the end of, or before or after, the passage. **4** *Commerce.* a reorder for goods.
—***adj.*** done again; repeated: *a repeat performance, repeat sales.*
**repeat itself,** to happen over again at a later time: *History repeats itself.*
**repeat oneself,** to say what one has already said: *A man must necessarily repeat himself who writes eighty-five stories ... in less than twenty years* (Leslie Stephen).
[< Old French *repeter,* learned borrowing from Latin *repetere* do or say again, attack again < *re-* again + *petere* aim at, seek] —**re|peat′a|ble,** *adj.* —**re|peat′a|bly,** *adv.*
—*Syn.* *v.t.* **1, 2,** *v.i.* **1 Repeat, reiterate** mean to do or say again. **Repeat,** the general word, means to say, do, make, or perform something over again, once or many times: *The orchestra will repeat the concert next week.* **Reiterate,** more formal, implies repeating again and again insistently and applies especially to something said: *We reiterated our requests for better bus service.*

***repeat**
*n.,* definition 3b

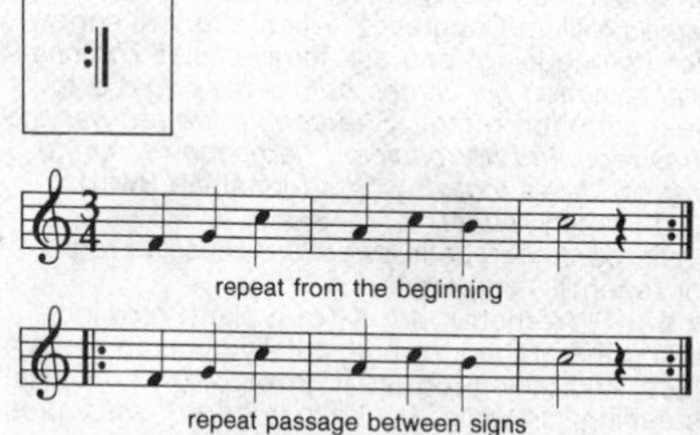

repeat from the beginning

repeat passage between signs

**re|peat|a|bil|i|ty** (ri pē′tə bil′ə tē), *n.* the fact or quality of being repeatable.

**re|peat|ed** (ri pē′tid), *adj.* said, done, or made more than once: *Her repeated efforts at last won success.*

**re|peat|ed|ly** (ri pē′tid lē), *adv.* again and again; more than once: *He pointed out repeatedly that there are four cuisines in France, not just one, each with rewards to the epicure* (Atlantic). **SYN:** frequently, often.

**re|peat|er** (ri pē′tər), *n.* **1** a type of gun that can be fired several times without reloading. A lever, bolt, or the like, must be moved after each shot. **2** a watch or clock that, if a spring is pressed, strikes the hour it struck last, plus the number of quarter hours, five-minute periods, or minutes

**Pronunciation Key:** hat, āge, cãre, fär; let, ēqual, tėrm; it, īce; hot, ōpen, ôrder; oil, out; cup, pu̇t, rüle; child; long; thin; ᴛʜen; zh, measure; ə represents **a** in about, **e** in taken, **i** in pencil, **o** in lemon, **u** in circus.

which have passed since then. **3** *U.S.* a person who votes more than once in an election. **4** *U.S.* a student who takes a course again or fails to pass on to the next grade. **5** *Informal.* a person who is repeatedly sent to prison or a reformatory; habitual criminal: *It sometimes has become the rule to place on probation adolescents who have become "repeaters"* (Emory S. Bogardus). **6a** a device that amplifies voice sounds in telephonic communication. Repeaters are built into underwater cables at certain intervals and relay the amplified sounds over long distances. **b** a similar device for amplifying and relaying radio, telegraph, and radar signals. **7** = repeating decimal. **8** = substitute (def. 4). **9** any person or thing that repeats.

**re|peat|ing decimal** (ri pē′ting), a decimal in which the same figure or series of figures is repeated infinitely. *Examples:* .3333+, .2323+.

**repeating rifle**, a rifle that fires several shots without reloading; repeater.

**re|pe|chage** (rep′ə shäzh; *French* rə pe shàzh′), *n. Sports.* a trial race in which runners-up in early heats receive a second chance to qualify for the final race. [< French *repêchage* (literally) fishing up again]

**re|pel** (ri pel′), *v.,* **-pelled, -pel|ling.** — ***v.t.*** **1** to force back; drive back; drive away: *They repelled the enemy. We can repel bad thoughts.* **2** to keep off or out; fail to mix with: *Oil and water repel each other. This tent repels moisture.* **3** to force apart or away by some inherent force: *The positive poles of two magnets repel each other.* **4** to be displeasing to; cause disgust in: *Spiders and worms repel me.* **5** to reject: *to repel a proposition, to repel a charge. Katy ... repelled this opinion with indignation* (James Fenimore Cooper).
— ***v.i.*** **1** to cause dislike; displease: *Evil odors invariably repel.* **2** to act with a force that drives or keeps away something.
[< Latin *repellere* < *re-* back + *pellere* to drive, strike] — **re|pel′ler**, *n.*

**re|pel|lan|cy** (ri pel′ən sē), *n. Especially British.* repellency.

**re|pel|lant** (ri pel′ənt), *adj., n. Especially British.* repellent. — **re|pel′lant|ly**, *adv.*

**re|pel|lence** (ri pel′əns), *n.* = repulsion.

**re|pel|len|cy** (ri pel′ən sē), *n.* = repulsion.

**re|pel|lent** (ri pel′ənt), *adj.* **1** disagreeable or distasteful; unattractive: *That disagreeable man has a cold, repellent manner. Cheating and lying are repellent to most people.* **SYN**: repugnant. **2** repelling; driving back.
— ***n.*** **1** anything that repels: *a water repellent. We sprayed insect repellent on our arms and legs before we went on the picnic. It is neither an attractant nor a repellent to unconditioned salmon* (Scientific American). **2** a medicine or application that reduces tumors, swellings, or eruptions.
— **re|pel′lent|ly**, *adv.*

**re|pent**[1] (ri pent′), *v.i.* **1** to feel sorry for having done wrong and seek forgiveness: *The sinner repented.* **2** to feel sorry; regret something done in the past: *Married in haste, we may repent at leisure* (William Congreve). — ***v.t.*** **1** to feel sorrow for (wrongdoing) and ask forgiveness: *The criminal repented his crimes before the priest.* **2** to feel sorry for; regret: *She bought the red hat and has repented her choice. I had soon reason to repent those foolish words* (Jonathan Swift). [< Old French *repentir* < *re-* again, re- + Vulgar Latin *pēnitire* < Latin *paenitēre* cause to regret or repent] — **re|pent′er**, *n.*

**re|pent**[2] (rē′pənt), *adj.* **1** (of a plant) growing along the ground, or horizontally beneath the surface, and taking root as it grows. **2** (of an animal) creeping; crawling. [< Latin *rēpēns, -entis,* present participle of *rēpere* to creep, crawl]

**re|pent|ance** (ri pen′təns), *n.* **1** sorrow for doing wrong: *Her repentance made everyone anxious to forgive her.* **SYN**: contrition. **2** sorrow; regret.

**re|pent|ant** (ri pen′tənt), *adj.* repenting; feeling regret; sorry for doing wrong: *a repentant criminal, repentant tears.* [< Old French *repentant,* present participle of *repentir* repent] — **re|pent′ant|ly**, *adv.*

**re|peo|ple** (rē pē′pəl), *v.t.,* **-pled, -pling. 1** to people anew. **2** to restock with animals.

**re|per|cus|sion** (rē′pər kush′ən), *n.* **1** an indirect influence or reaction from an event: *repercussions of war, repercussions of a scandal. The repercussions of this victory went round the country* (Time). **2** a sound flung back; echo: *Like the echo which is a repercussion of the original voice* (Cardinal Newman). **SYN**: reverberation. **3** the action of springing back; rebound; recoil: *the repercussion of a cannon.* **4** the action of driving back. **5** *Music.* **a** the repetition of a tone or chord. **b** the repetition of the theme in a fugue, especially the theme and answer in all voices. **6** *Medicine.* **a** a method of diagnosing pregnancy; ballottement. **b** the action of driving in or away, as of a tumor or eruption. [< Latin *repercussiō, -ōnis* < *repercutere* < *re-* back, again + *percutere* strike, beat. Compare etym. under **percussion.**]

**re|per|cus|sive** (rē′pər kus′iv), *adj.* **1** causing repercussion. **2** reverberated. — **re′per|cus′sive|ly**, *adv.*

**re|per|fo|rate** (ri pėr′fə rāt), *v.t.,* **-rat|ed, -rat|ing.** to perforate again.

**re|per|fo|ra|tor** (ri pėr′fə rā′tər), *n.* a machine that receives information on punched tape and duplicates it on a similar tape for retransmission.

**rep|er|toire** (rep′ər twär, -twôr), *n.* the list of plays, operas, parts, or pieces, that a company, an actor, a musician, or a singer is prepared to perform. [< French *répertoire,* learned borrowing from Late Latin *repertōrium.* See etym. of doublet **repertory.**]

**rep|er|to|ri|al** (rep′ər tôr′ē əl, -tōr′-), *adj.* of or having to do with a repertory.

**rep|er|to|ry** (rep′ər tôr′ē, -tōr′-), *n., pl.* **-ries. 1** = repertoire: *One of the best ... was the revival in the repertory of the Comédie-Française ... of Racine's Old Testament tragedy "Athalie"* (New Yorker). **2** any store or stock of things ready for use. **3** = storehouse. **SYN**: depository, depot. **4** = repertory company or theater. [< Late Latin *repertōrium* inventory < Latin *reperīre* to find, get < *re-* again + *parere* beget, produce. See etym. of doublet **repertoire.**]

**repertory company** or **theater**, a permanent organization of actors presenting a repertoire of plays, usually producing them alternately.

**rep|e|tend** (rep′ə tend, rep′ə tend′), *n.* **1** that part of a repeating decimal that is repeated indefinitely. **2** = refrain. [< Latin *repetendus,* gerundive of *repetere;* see etym. under **repeat**]

**ré|pé|ti|teur** (rā pā tē tœr′), *n. French.* a person who coaches singers.

**rep|e|ti|tion** (rep′ə tish′ən), *n.* **1** the act of repeating; doing or saying again: *Repetition helps learning. Any repetition of the offense will be punished. Nature is an endless combination and repetition of a very few laws* (Emerson). **2** a repeated occurrence; thing repeated: *The repetition soon became boring.* [< Latin *repetitiō, -ōnis* < *repetere;* see etym. under **repeat**]

**rep|e|ti|tious** (rep′ə tish′əs), *adj.* full of repetitions; repeating in a tiresome way. **SYN**: reiterative. — **rep′e|ti′tious|ly**, *adv.* — **rep′e|ti′tious|ness**, *n.*

**re|pet|i|tive** (ri pet′ə tiv), *adj.* of or characterized by repetition: *The text itself is loaded with clichés, grossly repetitive, and stylistically dull* (Scientific American). — **re|pet′i|tive|ly**, *adv.* — **re|pet′i|tive|ness**, *n.*

**re|pho|to|graph** (rē fō′tə graf, -gräf), *v.t.* to photograph again.

**re|phrase** (rē frāz′), *v.t.,* **-phrased, -phras|ing.** to phrase again; say or write in a new or different way: *to rephrase a question.*

**re|pine** (ri pīn′), *v.i.,* **-pined, -pin|ing.** to be discontented; fret; complain: *Through the long and weary day he repined at his unhappy lot* (Washington Irving). — **re|pin′er**, *n.*

**re|place** (ri plās′), *v.t.,* **-placed, -plac|ing. 1** to fill or take the place of: *He replaced his brother as captain. Most telephone operators have been replaced by dial telephones.* **2** to get another in place of: *I will replace the cup I broke.* **3** to put back; put in place again: *Please replace the books on the shelf.* — **re|place′a|ble**, *adj.* — **re|plac′er**, *n.*
— *Syn.* **1 Replace, supersede, supplant** mean to take the place of another. **Replace** means to fill as substitute or successor the place formerly held by another: *When one of the players on the team was hurt, another replaced him.* **Supersede**, a formal word used chiefly of things, suggests causing what is replaced to be put aside as out-of-date or no longer useful: *Buses have superseded streetcars.* **Supplant**, when used of a person, especially suggests forcing him out and taking over his place by scheming or treachery: *The dictator supplanted the president.*

**re|place|a|bil|i|ty** (ri plā′sə bil′ə tē), *n.* the fact or quality of being replaceable.

**re|place|ment** (ri plās′mənt), *n.* **1** the act of replacing: *The law required the replacement of wooden railroad cars by steel cars.* **2** the condition of being replaced. **3** something or someone that replaces, such as a man in military service who replaces another of similar training or skill. **SYN**: substitute. **4a** *Geology.* the process by which one mineral replaces another in a crystalline form. **b** the process by which an edge or angle of a crystal is worn off and replaced by one or more faces.

**replacement set**, *Mathematics.* domain.

**re|plan** (rē plan′), *v.t., v.i.,* **-planned, -plan|ning.** to plan again: *Our cities are being replanned for cars* (New Yorker).

**re|plant** (*v.* rē plant′, -plänt′; *n.* rē′plant′, -plänt′), *v., n.* — ***v.t.*** **1** to plant again: *to replant a garden. I'm going to have to replant all the bushes around the house* (Look). **2** to reinstate.
— ***v.i.*** to provide and set fresh plants: *After the killing frost, we had to replant.*
— ***n.*** something that is replanted.

**re|play** (*v.* rē plā′; *n.* rē′plā′), *v., n.* — ***v.t.*** to play (a match or game, or a phonograph record, magnetic tape, or motion-picture film) again.
— ***n.*** **1** a replayed match. **2** the action of replaying a phonograph record, magnetic tape, or the like: *Mariner IV was ordered to transmit the entire set a second time. We were anxious to see how closely a replay would duplicate the initial values* (Scientific American). **3** something replayed, especially a rerun of a videotaped portion of a game or match that is being televised: *We saw the touchdown again on the replay. "I saw a replay and it was a left," a reporter told Griffith* (New York Times). **4** *Figurative.* a repetition: *His comments sound like replays of earlier criticism.*

**re|plead** (rē plēd′), *v.i., v.t.,* **-plead|ed** or **-pled, -plead|ing.** to plead again.

**re|plead|er** (rē plē′dər), *n. Law.* **1** a second pleading. **2** the right of pleading again. [< *replead* + *-er*[5]]

**re|pled** (rē pled′), *v.* repleaded; a past tense and a past participle of **replead.**

**re|plen|ish** (ri plen′ish), *v.t.* to fill again; provide a new supply for: *to replenish one's wardrobe. Her supply of towels needs replenishing. You had better replenish the fire. One cannot take from a water supply at a greater rate than it is replenished* (R. N. Elston). **SYN**: refill, renew. — ***v.i.*** to fill again; become filled: *Her coffers began to replenish, her subjects were rich* (H. Stubbe). [< Old French *repleniss-,* stem of *replenir* < Latin *re-* again + *plēnus* full, related to *plēre* fill. Compare etym. under **replete.**] — **re|plen′ish|er**, *n.*
— **re|plen′ish|ment**, *n.*

**re|plete** (ri plēt′), *adj.* **1** abundantly supplied; filled: *The Disneyland tour was replete with unexpected thrills.* **SYN**: full, abounding. **2** sated (with food or drink); gorged: *The old men would sit at their tables, replete and sleepy* (H. G. Wells). [< Middle French *replète* < Latin *replētus,* past participle of *replēre* < *re-* again + *plēre* to fill, related to *plēnus* full] — **re|plete′ness**, *n.*

**re|ple|tion** (ri plē′shən), *n.* **1** the state of being replete; fullness. **2** excessive fullness. **3** *Medicine.* a disease caused by excess of red corpuscles in the blood or an increase in the quantity of blood in the body; plethora.

**re|plev|i|a|ble** (ri plev′ē ə bəl), *adj.* that can be replevied.

**re|plev|in** (ri plev′ən), *n., v.* — ***n.*** **1** the recovery of goods taken from a person upon his giving security that the case shall be tried in court and the goods returned if he is defeated. **2** the writ by which the goods are thus recovered.
— ***v.t.*** to recover (goods) by replevin.
[< Anglo-French *replevine* < *replever,* Old French *replevir;* see etym. under **replevy**]

**re|plev|y** (ri plev′ē), *v., n.,* **-plev|ied, -plev|y|ing,** *n., pl.* **-plev|ies.** — ***v.t., v.i.*** to recover by replevin.
— ***n.*** = replevin.
[< Old French *replevir* < *re-* again + *plevir* to pledge]

**rep|li|ca** (rep′lə kə), *n.* **1** a copy of a work of art, especially one made by the original artist: *The young artist made a replica of the famous painting.* **2** a copy; reproduction: *He is a replica of his father in looks and voice. There is a replica of the Mayflower in Plymouth, Massachusetts.* **SYN**: facsimile. [< Italian *replica* < *replicare* to reproduce < Latin *replicāre* unroll; see etym. under **reply**]

**rep|li|ca|ble** (rep′lə kə bəl), *adj.* that can be duplicated or reproduced: *It is meant to be a replicable project—one that can be copied in many different kinds of industries* (New York Times).

**rep|li|case** (rep′lə kās), *n.* an enzyme used in the replication of DNA and RNA; DNA polymerase or RNA polymerase: *In the research, new viral RNA was produced in the test tube with the help of an enzyme, called replicase, and strands of natural virus RNA* (New York Times).

**rep|li|cate** (*adj., n.* rep′lə kit; *v.* rep′lə kāt), *adj., n., v.,* **-cat|ed, -cat|ing.** — ***adj.*** **1** folded back on itself: *a replicate leaf.* **2** exactly reproduced; duplicated.
— ***n.*** any exact reproduction or duplicate.
— ***v.t.*** **1** to fold or bend back. **2** to copy exactly; reproduce; duplicate: *What then distinguishes virus DNA, which replicates itself at the expense of other pathways of cellular anabolism?* (Science). **3** to say in reply.
— ***v.i.*** **1** to fold or bend back. **2** to reproduce oneself or itself: *When the cell reproduces by the process of division known as mitosis, these homologous chromosomes replicate and separate, so that each of the two daughter cells has a full complement of 46 chromosomes* (Scientific American).

[< Latin *replicātus,* past participle of *replicāre* fold back; see etym. under **reply**]

**rep|li|ca|tion** (rep′lə kā′shən), *n.* **1** a fold. **2** the act or process of reproducing or duplicating: *Sometimes, because of a mistake in some step of the replication process, a daughter cell gets a gene carrying a garbled message* (Scientific American). **3** an exact copy; reproduction; duplication. **4** a reply; rejoinder. **5** reverberation; echo. **6** a plaintiff's reply to the defendant's plea.

**rep|li|ca|tive** (rep′lə kā′tive), *adj.* causing or taking part in replication.

**rep|li|ca|tor** (rep′lə kā′tər), *n.* a thing that replicates or causes replication.

**rep|li|con** (rep′lə kon), *n.* a theoretical unit of DNA replication. [< *replic*(ation) + *-on*]

**re|pli|er** (ri plī′ər), *n.* a person who replies.

**re|ply** (ri plī′), *v.,* **-plied, -ply|ing,** *n., pl.* **-plies.** — *v.i.* **1** to answer by words or action; answer; respond: *He replied with a shout. The enemy replied to the attack with heavy gunfire.* **2** *Law.* (of a plaintiff) to answer a defendant's plea.
— *v.t.* to give as an answer: *He replied that he had caught cold and could not come.*
— *n.* **1** the act of replying; response: *I wrote in reply to their inquiries.* **2** something replied; answer: *I didn't hear your reply to the question. What was the reply in your letter?*
[< Old French *replier* < Latin *replicāre* unroll, fold back < *re-* back + *-plicāre* to fold]

**re|po** (rē′pō), *n. U.S. Finance, Informal.* an agreement to buy back securities, especially government bonds, after a given period; repurchase agreement: *The Federal Reserve injected reserves into the banking system ..., first by negotiating weekend repurchase agreements and then by arranging six-day fixed-term "repo's"* (John H. Allen). [short for *repurchase*]

**re|po|lar|ize** (rē pō′lər īz), *v.t., v.i.,* **-ized, -iz|ing.** to polarize again.

**re|pol|ish** (rē pol′ish), *v.t.* to polish again.

**ré|pon|dez s'il vous plaît** (rā pôN dā′ sēl vü ple′), *French.* please reply (placed on formal invitations). *Abbr:* R.S.V.P.

**re|port** (ri pôrt′, -pōrt′), *n., v.* — *n.* **1** an account of something seen, heard, read, done, or considered: *The reports of my death are greatly exaggerated* (Mark Twain). **SYN:** narrative, description. **2** anything formally or officially expressed, generally in writing: *a school report, a committee report to the President, a court report of the judicial opinion.* **3** the sound of a shot or an explosion: *the report of a gun.* **4** common talk; rumor: *Report has it the neighbors left.* **SYN:** gossip, hearsay. **5** reputation: *a just man of good report.*
— *v.t.* **1** to make a report of; announce or state. **SYN:** narrate. **2** to give or bring an account of; state officially: *Our treasurer reports that all dues are paid up.* **3** to take down in writing; write an account of. **4** to repeat (what one has heard or seen); bring back an account of; describe; tell: *The radio reported the news and weather.* **5** to present (oneself): *We ... went on shore with the lieutenant to report ourselves to the admiral* (Frederick Marryat). **6** to announce as a wrongdoer; denounce: *to report a prowler to the police.*
— *v.i.* **1** to make a report; give an account of something: *The rules committee will report after lunch.* **2** to act as a reporter. **3** to relate; tell. **4** to present oneself; appear: *Report for work at eight.*
**report out,** to return (a bill) from committee to a lawmaking body with a formal report: *The Senate subcommittee ... has already reported out four civil-rights bills* (Newsweek).
[< Old French *report* < *reporter,* learned borrowing from Latin *reportāre* < *re-* back + *portāre* to carry] — **re|port′a|ble,** *adj.*

**re|port|age** (ri pôr′tij, -pōr′-), *n.* the act of reporting news or events, especially in the style of newspaper reporters.

**report card,** a report sent regularly by a school to parents or guardians, indicating the quality of a student's work.

**re|port|ed|ly** (ri pôr′tid lē, -pōr′-), *adv.* according to reports.

**re|port|er** (ri pôr′tər, -pōr′-), *n.* **1** a person who gathers news for a newspaper, magazine, or radio or television station: *In a very real sense, a newspaper can be only as good as its reporters* (New Yorker). **2** a person who takes down reports of law cases: *a court reporter.* **3** a person who reports: *The police were unable to find out who was the reporter of the fire.*

**rep|or|to|ri|al** (rep′ər tôr′ē əl, -tōr′-), *adj.* of or having to do with reporters: *a reportorial style of writing.* — **rep′or|to′ri|al|ly,** *adv.*

**re|pos|al** (ri pō′zəl), *n.* the act of reposing.

**re|pose**[1] (ri pōz′), *n., v.,* **-posed, -pos|ing.** — *n.* **1** rest or sleep: *Do not disturb her repose. They muttered prayers to themselves for the repose of the soul of their dead pal* (James T. Farrell). **2** quietness; ease: *She has repose of manner.* **SYN:** composure. **3** peace; calmness: *the repose of the country.* **SYN:** tranquillity. **4** a restful quality.
— *v.i.* **1** to lie at rest: *The cat reposed upon the cushion.* **2** to lie in a grave: *In quiet she reposes* (Matthew Arnold). **3** to rest from work or toil; take a rest: *Many people from the North repose in Florida during the winter season.* **4** to be supported. **5** to depend; rely (on): *The explorers reposed on the judgment of their Indian scout.*
— *v.t.* **1** to lay to rest: *Repose yourself in the hammock.* **2** to refresh by rest: *We stopped at a little public-house where we reposed ourselves* (Richard Graves).
[< Old French *repos* < *reposer* < Late Latin *repausāre* cause to rest < *re-* again + *pausāre* to pause. Compare etym. under **pose**[1].]

**re|pose**[2] (ri pōz′), *v.t.,* **-posed, -pos|ing.** to put; place: *We repose complete confidence in his honesty.* [< Latin *repositus,* past participle of *repōnere* < *re-* back + *pōnere* to place]

**re|pose|ful** (ri pōz′fəl), *adj.* calm; quiet: [*He*] *and his interior decorator ... have created a beautiful and reposeful interior* (Reporter). — **re|pose′ful|ly,** *adv.* — **re|pose′ful|ness,** *n.*

**re|pos|ing room** (ri pō′zing), a room in which the deceased is laid out at a funeral.

**re|pos|it** (ri poz′it), *v.t.* **1** = deposit. **2** to lay up; store. **3** to put back. [< Latin *repositus,* past participle of *repōnere;* see etym. under **repose**[2]]

**re|po|si|tion** (rē′pə zish′ən, rep′ə-), *v., n.* — *v.t.* **1** to restore (as a bone or organ of the body) to its normal position. **2** to place in a new position.
— *n.* **1** the act of depositing. **2** = replacement. **3** *Archaic.* restoration to office or possession.

**re|pos|i|to|ry** (ri poz′ə tôr′ē, -tōr′-), *n., pl.* **-ries,** *adj.* — *n.* **1** a place or container where things are stored or kept: *The box was the repository for old magazines. A library is a repository of information.* **2** a person to whom something is confided or entrusted: *Pepper alone had been the repository of my secret* (Thomas B. Aldrich).
— *adj. Medicine.* absorbed by degrees; acting slowly: *a repository drug.*
[< Latin *repositōrium* < *repōnere;* see etym. under **repose**[2]]

**re|pos|sess** (rē′pə zes′), *v.t.* **1** to possess again; get possession of again. **SYN:** recover. **2** to put in possession again. — **re′pos|ses′sion,** *n.*

**re|post** (ri pōst′), *n., v.i.* = riposte.

**re|pot** (rē pot′), *v.t.,* **-pot|ted, -pot|ting.** **1** to replace in pots. **2** to shift (plants) from one pot to another.

**re|pous|sé** (rə pü sā′), *adj., n.* — *adj.* **1** raised in relief by hammering on the reverse side. A repoussé design can be made on thin metal. **2** ornamented or made in this manner.
— *n.* repoussé work.
[< French *repoussé* < Middle French *repousser* < *re-* back + *pousser* to push]

**repp** (rep), *n.* = rep[1].

**repped** (rept), *adj.* transversely corded, like rep.

**repr.,** **1a** represented. **b** representing. **2a** reprint. **b** reprinted.

**rep|re|hend** (rep′ri hend′), *v.t.* to reprove or blame; rebuke. **SYN:** reproach, censure, reprimand, upbraid. [< Latin *reprehendere* (originally) pull back < *re-* back + *prehendere* to grasp]
▶ This word is often confused with *apprehend,* to take into custody, arrest.

**rep|re|hen|si|bil|i|ty** (rep′ri hen′sə bil′ə tē), *n.* the character of being reprehensible.

**rep|re|hen|si|ble** (rep′ri hen′sə bəl), *adj.* deserving reproof, blame, or rebuke: *Cheating is a reprehensible act.* **SYN:** blameworthy, culpable. — **rep′re|hen′si|bly,** *adv.*

**rep|re|hen|sion** (rep′ri hen′shən), *n.* reproof, rebuke, or blame. [< Latin *reprehēnsiō, -ōnis* < *reprehendere* reprehend]

**rep|re|hen|sive** (rep′ri hen′siv), *adj.* containing reprehension; reproving. — **rep′re|hen′sive|ly,** *adv.*

**rep|re|sent** (rep′ri zent′), *v.t.* **1** to stand for; be a sign or symbol of: *Letters represent sounds. The fifty stars in our flag represent the fifty states. A policeman represents the power of the law.* **2** to express by signs or symbols: *to represent ideas by words.* **3** to act in place of; speak and act for: *We chose a committee to represent us. The Colonies ... complain that they are taxed in a Parliament in which they are not represented* (Edmund Burke). **4** to act the part of: *Each child will represent an animal at the party.* **5** to show in a picture, statue, carving, or other form of art; give a likeness of; portray: *This painting by Leonardo da Vinci represents the Last Supper.* **6** to be a type of; be an example of: *A log represents a very simple type of boat.* **7** to be the equivalent of; correspond to. **8** to describe; set forth: *He represented the plan as safe, but it was not.* **9** to bring before the mind; make one think of: *His fears represented the undertaking as impossible.*
[< Latin *repraesentāre* < *re-* back + *praesēns, -entis* present[1]] — **rep′re|sent′a|ble,** *adj.* — **rep′re|sent′er,** *n.*

**re-pre|sent** (rē′pri zent′), *v.t.* to present over again or in a new way.

**rep|re|sen|ta|tion** (rep′ri zen tā′shən), *n.* **1** the act of representing: *the boy's representation of his class on the Student Council.* **2** the condition or fact of being represented: *"Taxation without representation is tyranny." The United States Congress is elected on the basis of proportional representation.* **3** representatives considered as a group. **SYN:** delegation. **4** a likeness, picture, or model: *Most representations of George Washington make him look very solemn.* **SYN:** image. **5** the performance of a play; presentation: *A representation of the story of Rip Van Winkle will be given in the school assembly today.* **SYN:** production. **6** the process or faculty of forming mental images or ideas. **7** an account; statement: *They deceived us by false representations.* **8** a protest; complaint: *to make representations to the police about a nuisance.* **SYN:** remonstrance. **9** *Law.* a statement of fact, implied or expressed, made by a party to a transaction and tending to facilitate conclusion of the transaction.

**rep|re|sen|ta|tion|al** (rep′ri zen tā′shə nəl), *adj.* **1** of or having to do with representation: *representational government.* **2** of or designating a form of art that emphasizes realistic and conventional representation of subjects and the use of traditional materials: *We have run through the satisfactions of representational art to the puzzling outlines of abstract art* (Atlantic). — **rep′re|sen|ta′tion|al|ly,** *adv.*

**rep|re|sen|ta|tion|al|ism** (rep′ri zen tā′shə nə liz′əm), *n.* **1** the theory or practice of representational art. **2** the philosophical doctrine that the perception of an object is only a representation of the real object in the external world. — **rep′re|sen|ta′tion|al|ist,** *n.*

**rep|re|sent|a|tive** (rep′ri zen′tə tiv), *n., adj.* — *n.* **1** a person appointed or elected to act or speak for others: *She is the club's representative at the convention. The Philippines also declined to send a representative, but are expected to send an observer* (New York Times). **SYN:** agent, deputy. **2** an example; type: *The tiger is a common representative of the cat family.*
— *adj.* **1** having its citizens represented by chosen persons: *a representative government.* **2** representing: *Images representative of animals were made by the children out of clay.* **3** enough like all those of its kind to stand for all the rest: *Balls, blocks, puzzles, and trains are representative toys. Oak, birch, and maple are representative American hardwoods.* **SYN:** typical. — **rep′re|sent′a|tive|ly,** *adv.* — **rep′re|sent′a|tive|ness,** *n.*

**Rep|re|sent|a|tive** (rep′ri zen′tə tiv), *n. U.S.* a member of the lower house of Congress (the House of Representatives) or of a corresponding body of any of certain state legislatures. *Abbr:* Rep.

**representative fraction,** a geographical scale expressed in the form of a fraction. *Example:* The representative fraction 1:62,500 or 1/62,500 shows that one unit of measurement on the map represents 62,500 of the same units on the earth's surface. *Abbr:* R.F.

**re|press** (ri pres′), *v.t.* **1** to prevent from acting; check: *She repressed an impulse to cough. To save his life he could not repress a chuckle* (Booth Tarkington). **SYN:** curb, restrain. **2** to keep down; put down; suppress: *The dictator repressed the revolt.* **3** *Psychoanalysis.* to make the object of repression; force (a painful or undesirable memory or impulse) from the conscious mind into the unconscious mind. [< Latin *repressus,* past participle of *reprimere* < *re-* back + *premere* to press] — **re|press′er,** *n.* — **re|press′i|ble,** *adj.*

**re|pres|sion** (ri presh′ən), *n.* **1** the act of repressing: *The repression of a laugh made him choke. Fourteen months of military repression ... plainly had failed* (Newsweek). **2** the condition of being repressed: *Repression by her strict parents only made her behave worse.* **SYN:** constraint. **3** *Psychoanalysis.* a defense mechanism by which unacceptable or painful impulses, emotions, or memories are put out of the conscious mind, their energy or effect remaining (according to Freudian theory) in the unconscious, where it influences personality and behavior.

**re|pres|sion|ist** (ri presh′ə nist), *n.* a person who advocates repression or repressive measures.

**re|pres|sive** (ri pres′iv), *adj.* tending to repress; having power to repress: *repressive laws.* **SYN:** inhibitory. — **re|pres′sive|ly,** *adv.* — **re|pres′sive|ness,** *n.*

**re|pres|sor** (ri pres′ər), *n.* **1** a person or thing

**Pronunciation Key:** hat, āge, cãre, fär; let, ēqual, tėrm; it, īce; hot, ōpen, ôrder; **oi**l, **ou**t; cup, pu̇t, rüle; **ch**ild; lo**ng**; **th**in; **ŦH**en; **zh**, measure; **ə** represents **a** in about, **e** in taken, **i** in pencil, **o** in lemon, **u** in circus.

that represses. **2** a substance that represses chemical or organic activity. **3** *Genetics.* a theoretical component of the operon whose function is to repress the action of the operator: *The repressor determines when the gene turns on and off by functioning as an intermediate between the gene and an appropriate signal* (Scientific American).

**re|priev|al** (ri prē′vəl), *n.* = reprieve.

**re|prieve** (ri prēv′), *v.,* **-prieved, -priev|ing,** *n.* — ***v.t.*** **1** to delay the punishment of (a person), especially the execution of (a person condemned to death): *At the last moment the governor reprieved the condemned prisoner for three weeks.* **2** to give relief from any evil or trouble. SYN: relieve.
— ***n.*** **1** a delay in carrying out a punishment, especially of the death penalty. **2** the order giving authority for such delay. **3** temporary relief from any evil or trouble.
[< obsolete *repry* to remand, detain < Old French *repris,* past participle of *reprendre* take back < Latin *reprehendere* (see etym. under **reprehend**); form perhaps influenced by Middle English *repreve* reprove]

**rep|ri|mand** (*n.* rep′rə mand, -mänd; *v.* rep′rə mand′, -mänd′), *n., v.* — ***n.*** a severe or formal reproof: *the sharp reprimands that were sure to follow every act of negligence* (John F. Kirk).
— ***v.t.*** to reprove severely or formally; censure: *The policeman reprimanded the driver for turning without a signal. Captain Wilson sent for the master, and reprimanded him for his oppression* (Frederick Marryat). SYN: reprehend. See syn. under **reprove.**
[< French *réprimande,* earlier *réprimende,* learned borrowing from Latin *reprimenda* a thing to be repressed, feminine gerundive of *reprimere* repress] — **rep′ri|mand′er,** *n.*

**re|print** (*v.* rē print′; *n.* rē′print′), *v., n.* — ***v.t.*** to print again; print a new impression of.
— ***n.*** **1a** the act or process of reprinting; new impression of a printed work without alteration: *the reprint of a book or article.* **b** anything reprinted, such as a book or article: *Reprints are less expensive than original editions. Reprints of articles from Engineering and Mining Journal pile high in his in-basket* (Saturday Review). **2** *Philately.* a stamp printed from the original plate after the issue has been discontinued. — **re|print′er,** *n.*

**re|pris|al** (ri prī′zəl), *n.* **1** injury done in return for injury, especially by one nation or group to another: *The policy of reprisals is the fruit of cold, unemotional ... reasoning* (Harper's). SYN: retaliation. **2** = compensation. [< Old French *reprisaille* < Italian *ripresaglia,* or < Medieval Latin *represalia,* ultimately < Latin *reprēnsus,* past participle of *reprēndere, reprehendere;* see etym. under **reprehend**]

**re|prise**[1] (rə prēz′), *n., v.,* **-prised, -pris|ing,** — ***n.*** **1** a renewal or resumption of an action; repetition: *Most of Van Fleet's testimony was a reprise of things he had said before* (Time). **2** *Music.* a repetition or return to the first theme or subject.
— ***v.t.*** to perform or present a reprise of; repeat: *Horror films used to reprise climactic sequences to clue us in on the previous material* (New Yorker). *There is joyful good fun ... in the title song, which is reprised near the end* (Saturday Review).
[< Old French *reprise,* feminine of *repris,* past participle of *reprendre* (literally) take back; see etym. under **reprieve**]

**re|prise**[2] (ri prīz′), *v.i.,* **-prised, -pris|ing.** to act in reprisal; pay back in kind; retaliate: *The foreign minister warns that ... his country can reprise better than ours can* (Wall Street Journal). [back formation < *reprisal*]

**re|pris|es** (ri prī′ziz), *n.pl. Law.* an annual deduction, duty, or payment out of a manor or an estate. [plural of *reprise*[1]]

**re|pris|ti|nate** (rē pris′tə nāt), *v.t.,* **-nat|ed, -nat|ing.** to restore to the original state.

**re|pris|ti|na|tion** (rē pris′tə nā′shən), *n.* a restoration to the original state.

**re|pro** (rē′prō), *n., pl.* **-pros.** *Informal.* a reproduction.

**re|proach** (ri prōch′), *n., v.* — ***n.*** **1** blame or censure: *to bring reproach on one's family. His conduct at work is above reproach.* **2** a cause of blame or disgrace: *A coward is a reproach to an army.* SYN: discredit. **3** an object of blame, censure, or disapproval. **4** words of blame; expression of blame, censure, or disapproval: *Mr. Travers ... overwhelmed him with reproaches* (Joseph Conrad).
— ***v.t.*** **1** to blame or censure; upbraid: *Father reproached me for being late.* SYN: reprove, rebuke. See syn. under **blame.** **2** to disgrace; shame: *to reproach one's life.*
[< Old French *reproche* < *reprocher* < Vulgar Latin *repropiāre* lay at the door of < Latin *re-* again + *prope* near] — **re|proach′a|ble,** *adj.* — **re|proach′a|bly,** *adv.* — **re|proach′er,** *n.* — **re|proach′ing|ly,** *adv.*

**re|proach|ful** (ri prōch′fəl), *adj.* **1** full of reproach; expressing reproach: *a reproachful expression.* **2** *Obsolete.* disgraceful; blameworthy. — **re|proach′ful|ly,** *adv.* — **re|proach′ful|ness,** *n.*

**rep|ro|ba|cy** (rep′rə bə sē), *n.* reprobate state.

**rep|ro|bance** (rep′rə bans), *n. Obsolete.* reprobate state; reprobacy: *... fall to reprobance* (Shakespeare).

**rep|ro|bate** (rep′rə bāt), *n., adj., v.,* **-bat|ed, -bat|ing.** — ***n.*** a very wicked or unprincipled person; scoundrel: *a penniless, drunken reprobate* (Theodore Watts-Dunton).
— ***adj.*** **1** very wicked; unprincipled. SYN: depraved, corrupt, dissolute, profligate. **2** condemned as worthless or inferior. **3** *Theology.* predestined to eternal punishment or death; beyond salvation.
— ***v.t.*** **1** to disapprove; condemn; censure. **2** to reject; refuse. **3** *Theology.* to exclude from the number of elect or from salvation; predestine to eternal punishment.
[< Late Latin *reprobātus,* past participle of *reprobāre* reprove, reject < Latin *re-* against, dis- + *probāre* approve < *probus* good] — **rep′ro|ba′tion,** *n.*

**rep|ro|ba|tive** (rep′rə bā′tiv), *adj.* reprobating; expressing disapproval. — **rep′ro|ba′tive|ly,** *adv.*

**rep|ro|ba|to|ry** (rep′rə bə tôr′ē, -tōr′-), *adj.* = reprobative.

**re|proc|ess** (rē pros′es; *especially British* rē prō′ses), *v.t.* to process again.

**re|proc|essed** (rē pros′est; *especially British* rē prō′sest), *adj.* salvaged and made over again into the same material, as wool that has been made into clothes, then unraveled, and remade into yarn.

**re|pro|duce** (rē′prə düs′, -dyüs′), *v.,* **-duced, -duc|ing.** — ***v.t.*** **1** to produce again: *A radio reproduces sounds. Some animals are able to reproduce lost parts or organs of their bodies. The exact conditions that existed ten years ago cannot be reproduced today.* **2** to produce (offspring): *One function of all animals is to reproduce their own kind.* **3** to make a copy of: *A phonograph will reproduce your voice. A camera will reproduce a picture.*
— ***v.i.*** **1** to produce offspring: *Most plants reproduce by seeds.* SYN: propagate, generate. **2** to be reproduced; make a copy; take copying: *This carbon paper reproduces badly.* — **re′pro|duc′er,** *n.*

**re|pro|duce|a|ble** (rē′prə dü′sə bəl, -dyü′-), *adj. Especially British.* = reproducible.

**re|pro|duc|i|bil|i|ty** (rē′prə dü′sə bil′ə tē, -dyü′-), *n.* the quality or condition of being reproducible.

**re|pro|duc|i|ble** (rē′prə dü′sə bəl, -dyü′-), *adj.* that can be reproduced. — **re′pro|duc′i|bly,** *adv.*

**re|pro|duc|tion** (rē′prə duk′shən), *n.* **1** a reproducing or being reproduced: *the reproduction of sounds.* **2** a copy: *That model is a fine reproduction of the original.* **3** the process by which animals and plants produce individuals like themselves: *Reproduction is one of the two essential features of life* (Scientific American).

**re|pro|duc|tive** (rē′prə duk′tiv), *adj., n.* — ***adj.*** **1** that reproduces. **2** for or concerned with reproduction.
— ***n.*** a reproductive organism, especially among the social insects: *At certain seasons winged male and female reproductives (future kings and queens) are also present* (Scientific American). — **re′pro|duc′tive|ly,** *adv.* — **re′pro|duc′tive|ness,** *n.*

**re|pro|duc|tiv|i|ty** (rē′prə duk tiv′ə tē), *n.* the quality or power of being reproductive: *Insects' tremendous reproductivity is one reason for the havoc they can cause* (Wall Street Journal).

**re|pro|gram** (rē prō′gram, -grəm), *v.t.,* **-grammed, -gram|ming** or **-gramed, -gram|ing.** **1** to program again: *NASA is obligated to tell the Congress how it will reprogram the money the Congress has appropriated for the agency* (San Francisco Chronicle). **2** to rewrite (a computer program).

**re|pro|graph|ic** (rē prə graf′ik), *adj.* of or having to do with reprography.

**re|prog|ra|phy** (ri prog′rə fē), *n.* the reproduction of graphic material, especially by electronic means: *Finally, there is reprography—which runs from simple ink and spirit duplicators through photocopying equipment to offset lithography* (London Times). [< French *reprographie* < *repro(duction)* + *-graphie* -graphy]

**re|proof** (ri prüf′), *n.* words of blame or disapproval; blame; rebuke: *Reproofs from authority ought to be grave, not taunting* (Francis Bacon). [< Middle French *reprove,* and *reprouve* < *reprover;* see etym. under **reprove**; form influenced by *proof*]

**re|prov|a|ble** (ri prü′və bəl), *adj.* deserving reproof.

**re|prov|al** (ri prü′vəl), *n.* the act of reproving.

**re|prove** (ri prüv′), *v.t.,* **-proved, -prov|ing.** to show disapproval of; find fault with; blame; scold: *She reproved the boy for teasing the cat.*
[< Old French *reprover,* learned borrowing from Late Latin *reprobāre* reprove; (originally) reject; see etym. under **reprobate**] — **re|prov′ing|ly,** *adv.*
— *Syn.* **Reprove, rebuke, reprimand** mean to criticize or blame someone for a fault. **Reprove** suggests expressing disapproval without scolding and with the purpose or hope of correcting the fault: *The principal reproved the students who had been smoking in the locker room.* **Rebuke** means to reprove sharply and sternly: *The doctor rebuked the nurse who had been neglecting her patients.* **Reprimand** implies severe and public reproof from an official source: *The careless captain was reprimanded and demoted.*

**re|prov|er** (ri prü′vər), *n.* a person or thing that reproves.

**reps** (reps), *n.* a heavy ribbed fabric; rep.

**rep|tant** (rep′tənt), *adj.* = repent[2]. [< Latin *rēptāns, -antis,* present participle of *rēptāre* to creep < *rēpere* to crawl]

**rep|tile** (rep′təl, -tīl), *n., adj.* — ***n.*** **1a** any one of a class of cold-blooded animals with a backbone which breathe by means of lungs and usually have skin covered with horny plates or scales. Reptiles creep or crawl. Snakes, turtles, lizards, alligators, and crocodiles are reptiles. Reptiles were the dominant form of life during the Mesozoic. **b** *Informal.* any creeping or crawling animal. **c** *Informal.* an amphibian. **2** *Figurative.* a low, mean, despicable person.
— ***adj.*** **1** of or like a reptile; crawling; creeping. **2** *Figurative.* low; mean; venal: *a reptile press.*
[< Late Latin *rēptile,* (originally) neuter of *rēptilis* crawling < Latin *rēpere* to crawl] — **rep′tile|like′,** *adj.*

**Rep|til|i|a** (rep til′ē ə), *n.pl.* the class of vertebrates comprising the reptiles.

**rep|til|i|an** (rep til′ē ən), *adj., n.* — ***adj.*** **1** of or having to do with reptiles. **2** like a reptile; base; mean: *a reptilian nature. This individual was ... an unmitigated villain—a reptilian villain!* (Theodore Dreiser).
— ***n.*** = reptile.

**Repub.,** **1** Republic. **2** Republican.

**re|pub|lic** (ri pub′lik), *n.* **1** a nation or state in which the citizens elect representatives to manage the government, which is usually headed by a president rather than a monarch. The United States and Mexico are republics. SYN: commonwealth. **2** the form of government existing in such a state. **3** any one of the major political divisions of the Soviet Union or of Yugoslavia: *the Latvian Republic, the Croatian Republic, the Republic of Turkmenistan.* **4** *Figurative.* any body of persons or things: *the republic of authors and scholars.*
[< Middle French *république,* learned borrowing from Latin *rēs pūblica* public interest; the state; *rēs* affair, matter(s); things; *pūblica,* feminine adjective, public]

**Re|pub|lic** (ri pub′lik), *n.,* **the.** *U.S.* the United States of America: *Rarely in the history of the Republic has the division been so deep ... over foreign policy* (Lester Markel).

**re|pub|li|can** (ri pub′lə kən), *adj., n.* — ***adj.*** **1** of a republic; like that of a republic: *republican institutions. Many countries have a republican form of government.* **2** favoring a republic. **3** (of birds) living in communities, as the cliff swallow does.
— ***n.*** a person who favors a republic: *The republicans fought with the king's supporters.*

**Re|pub|li|can** (ri pub′lə kən), *adj., n.* — ***adj.*** of or having to do with the Republican Party.
— ***n.*** a member of the Republican Party. *Abbr:* Rep.

**republican grosbeak,** a weaverbird of South Africa, many pairs of which build in common an enormous umbrellalike nest.

**re|pub|li|can|ism** (ri pub′lə kə niz′əm), *n.* **1** republican government. **2** republican principles; adherence to republican principles.

**Re|pub|li|can|ism** (ri pub′lə kə niz′əm), *n.* the principles or policies of the Republican Party.

**re|pub|li|can|ize** (ri pub′lə kə nīz), *v.,* **-ized, -iz|ing.** — ***v.t.*** to make republican.
— ***v.i.*** to show republican tendencies. — **re|pub′li|can|i|za′tion,** *n.*

**Republican Party,** **1** one of the two main political parties in the United States. The other is the Democratic Party. The Republican Party was formed in 1854 by opponents of slavery. **2** (originally) the Antifederal Party which later became the Democratic-Republican Party.

**re|pub|li|ca|tion** (rē′pub lə kā′shən), *n.* **1** publication anew. **2** a book or the like published again.

**republic of letters,** **1** all people engaged in literary or learned work. **2** the field of literature.

**re|pu|di|ate** (ri pyü′dē āt), *v.t.,* **-at|ed, -at|ing.** **1** to refuse to accept; reject: *to repudiate a doctrine. The old man shook his head, gently repudiating the imputation* (Dickens). SYN: disclaim.

2 to refuse to acknowledge or pay: *to repudiate a debt, to repudiate a claim.* **3** to cast off; disown: *to repudiate a son.* **4** to put away by divorce. [< Latin *repudiāre* (with English *-ate*[1]) < *repudium* divorce, rejection, perhaps < *re-* back, away + unrecorded *podium* a kicking, related to *pēs, pedis* foot] —**re|pu′di|a′tor,** *n.*

**re|pu|di|a|tion** (ri pyü′dē ā′shən), *n.* the act of repudiating, or fact or condition of being repudiated: *repudiation of a doctrine or public debt.*

**re|pu|di|a|tion|ist** (ri pyü′dē ā′shə nist), *n.* a person who favors repudiation, especially of a public debt.

**re|pu|di|a|tive** (ri pyü′dē ā′tiv), *adj.* characterized by repudiation.

**re|pugn** (ri pyün′), *v.t.* **1** to oppose; object to. **2** to cause repugnance in. —*v.i. Obsolete.* to be opposed. [< Old French *repugner,* learned borrowing from Latin *repūgnāre;* see etym. under **repugnant**]

**re|pug|nance** (ri pug′nəns), *n.* **1** a strong dislike, distaste, or aversion: *Some people feel a repugnance for snakes.* SYN: antipathy. **2** a contradiction; inconsistency: *repugnance between statements.*

**re|pug|nan|cy** (ri pug′nən sē), *n., pl.* **-cies.** = repugnance.

**re|pug|nant** (ri pug′nənt), *adj.* **1** disagreeable or offensive; distasteful: *Work is repugnant to lazy people.* SYN: objectionable. **2** objecting; averse; opposed: *We are repugnant to every sort of dishonesty.* **3** inconsistent; contrary (to): *a clause repugnant to the body of the act.* [< Latin *repūgnāns, -antis,* present participle of *repūgnāre* to resist < *re-* back + *pūgnāre* to fight < *pūgna* a fight, battle] —**re|pug′nant|ly,** *adv.*

**re|pulse** (ri puls′), *v.,* **-pulsed, -puls|ing,** *n.* —*v.t.* **1** to drive back; repel: *Our soldiers repulsed the enemy. Thy faithful dogs ... who ... will ... Repulse the prowling wolf* (John Dryden). **2** to refuse to accept; reject: *She coldly repulsed him.* —*n.* **1** the action of driving back or condition of being driven back: *After the second repulse, the enemy surrendered.* **2** refusal or rejection: *Her repulse was quite unexpected.*
[< Latin *repulsus,* past participle of *repellere* repel] —**re|puls′er,** *n.*

**re|pul|sion** (ri pul′shən), *n.* **1** strong dislike or aversion: *a look of repulsion.* SYN: repugnance. **2** the action of repelling or condition of being repelled; repulse. **3** *Physics.* the tendency of particles or forces to increase their distance from one another: *Protons exert forces of repulsion on other protons, electrons exert forces of repulsion on other electrons* (Sears and Zemansky).

**re|pul|sive** (ri pul′siv), *adj.* **1** causing disgust, strong dislike, or aversion: *Snakes are repulsive to some people.* SYN: revolting. **2** tending to drive back or repel. **3** *Physics.* of the nature of or characterized by repulsion. —**re|pul′sive|ly,** *adv.* —**re|pul′sive|ness,** *n.*

**rep|u|nit** (rep yü′nit), *n.* a number having one or more identical integers, such as 11, 111, and 1111. [< *rep*(eating) *unit*]

**re|pur|chase** (rē pėr′chəs), *v.,* **-chased, -chas|ing,** *n.* —*v.t.* to buy again; buy back.
—*n.* the act of buying back. —**re|pur′chas|er,** *n.*

**rep|u|ta|bil|i|ty** (rep′yə tə bil′ə tē), *n.* reputable quality.

**rep|u|ta|ble** (rep′yə tə bəl), *adj.* **1** having a good reputation; well thought of; in good repute, respectable: *a reputable citizen, a reputable newspaper.* SYN: estimable. **2** (of words) having acceptable usage. —**rep′u|ta|ble|ness,** *n.* —**rep′u|ta|bly,** *adv.*

**rep|u|ta|tion** (rep′yə tā′shən), *n.* **1** what people think and say the character of a person or thing is; character in the opinion of others; name; repute: *He had the reputation of being very bright. This store has an excellent reputation for fair dealing.* **2** a good name; good reputation: *Cheating at the game ruined that player's reputation.* **3** fame: *a man of some local reputation. The astronauts won an international reputation.*

**re|pute** (ri pyüt′), *n., v.,* **-put|ed, -put|ing.** —*n.* **1** reputation: *a generous man by repute. This is a district of bad repute because there are so many robberies here.* **2** good reputation; credit.
[< verb]
—*v.t.* to suppose to be; consider; suppose: *He is reputed the richest man in the city.*
[< Latin *reputāre* < *re-* back, again + *putāre* to think; cleanse, prune (a tree)]

**re|put|ed** (ri pyü′tid), *adj.* accounted or supposed to be such: *the reputed author of a book.*

**re|put|ed|ly** (ri pyü′tid lē), *adv.* by repute; supposedly.

**req.,** 1 required. 2 requisition.

**re|quest** (ri kwest′), *v., n.* —*v.t.* **1** to ask for; ask as a favor: *We requested a loan from the bank.* SYN: See syn. under **ask.** **2** to ask: *He requested her to go with him.* SYN: beg, beseech, entreat.
—*n.* **1** the act of asking: *a request for help. Your request for a ticket was made too late. She did it at our request.* **2** what is asked for: *He granted my request.* **3** the condition of being asked for or sought after: *She is such a good singer that she is in great request to give concerts.*
**by request,** in response to a request: *Records are played by request on some radio programs.*
[< Old French *requester* < *requeste* < Vulgar Latin *requaesita,* for Late Latin *requaesīta,* past participle of *requaerere* < Latin *re-* again, back + *quaerere* to ask, seek] —**re|quest′er,** *n.*

**Req|ui|em** or **req|ui|em** (rek′wē əm, rē′kwē-), *n.* **1a** a Mass for the dead; musical church service for the dead. **b** the music for it. **2** any musical service or hymn for the dead. **3** anything that suggests a service or hymn for the dead: *Every bird thy requiem sings* (Robert Burns). [< Latin *requiem,* accusative of *requiēs* rest < *re-* (intensive) + *quiēs, -ētis* quiet (*requiem* is the first word of the Mass for the dead)]

**re|qui|es|cat** (rek′wē es′kat), *n.* a wish or prayer for the repose of the dead. [< Latin *requiescat,* may he (or she) rest, ultimately < *re-* (intensive) + *quiēs, -ētis* quiet]

**re|qui|es|cat in pa|ce** (rek′wē es′kat in pā′sē), *Latin.* "May he (or she) rest in peace," a wish or prayer for the repose of the dead. *Abbr:* R.I.P.

**re|quir|a|ble** (ri kwīr′ə bəl), *adj.* that can be required.

**re|quire** (ri kwīr′), *v.,* **-quired, -quir|ing.** —*v.t.* **1** to have need for; need; want: *We shall require more spoons at our party.* **2** to demand; order; command: *The rules required us all to be present. That condition requires immediate attention.* SYN: See syn. under **demand.** **3** to put under an obligation or necessity: *Circumstances may require us to submit.* **4** *Archaic.* to ask for; seek.
—*v.i.* to make necessary: *to do as the law requires, ready to act if circumstances require.*
[< Latin *requīrere* < *re-* back, again + *quaerere* to ask, seek. See related etym. at **request.**]

**re|quired course** (ri kwīrd′), a course of study that all students of a school or department must take, usually to fulfill the requirements for a major or for graduation.

**required reading,** a book or books that all students of a class or school must read: *Stalin's Short History of the Communist Party, which was required reading for university students [in the USSR], was withdrawn* (London Times).

**re|quire|ment** (ri kwīr′mənt), *n.* **1** a need; thing needed: *Food is a requirement of life. Patience is a requirement in teaching.* SYN: essential. **2** a demand; thing demanded: *He has fulfilled all the requirements for graduation.*

**req|ui|site** (rek′wə zit), *adj., n.* —*adj.* required by circumstances; needed; necessary; essential; indispensable: *the qualities requisite for a leader, the number of votes requisite for election.* —*n.* a thing needed; requirement: *Food and air are requisites for life.* [< Latin *requisītus,* past participle of *requīrere;* see etym. under **require**] —**req′ui|site|ly,** *adv.* —**req′ui|site|ness,** *n.*

**req|ui|si|tion** (rek′wə zish′ən), *n., v.* —*n.* **1** the act of requiring: *His requisition of the car prevented others from using it.* **2** a demand made, especially a formal written demand: *The requisition of supplies for troops included new shoes, uniforms, and blankets.* **3** the condition of being required for use or called into service: *The car was in constant requisition for errands.* **4** an essential condition; requirement.
—*v.t.* **1** to demand or take by authority: *to requisition supplies, horses, or labor.* SYN: commandeer. **2** to make demands upon: *The hospital requisitioned the city for more funds.*

**re|quit|al** (ri kwī′təl), *n.* **1** repayment; payment; return: *What requital can we make for all his kindness to us?* SYN: recompense. **2** the act of requiting.

**re|quite** (ri kwīt′), *v.t.,* **-quit|ed, -quit|ing.** **1** to pay back; make return for: *to requite kindness with love. The Bible says to requite evil with good.* SYN: repay, reward. **2** to make return to; reward: *The knight requited the boy for his warning. My father will be glad to requite you for this night's hospitality* (Bret Harte). **3** to make retaliation for; avenge. [< *re-* back + *quite,* variant of *quit*] —**re|quit′a|ble,** *adj.* —**re|quit′er,** *n.*

**re|quite|ment** (ri kwīt′mənt), *n.* = requital.

**re|ra|di|ate** (rē rā′dē āt), *v.t., v.i.,* **-at|ed, -at|ing.** to send out (radio signals, light beams, electromagnetic waves or other electromagnetic waves) again into the surrounding area by reflection or transmission. —**re′ra|di|a′tion,** *n.*

**re|ra|di|a|tive** (rē rā′dē ā′tiv), *adj.* that reradiates; capable of reradiation.

**re|ran** (rē ran′), *v.* the past tense of **rerun.**

**re|read** (rē rēd′), *v.t.,* **-read** (-red′), **-read|ing.** to read again or anew: *to reread a good book. Rereading John Milton now, one cannot help realizing at once how close he is to us and how remote from us* (Thomas Merton).

**rere|brace** (rir′brās′), *n.* a piece of armor for the upper arm, from the shoulder to the elbow. [< unrecorded Anglo-French *rerebras* < *rere-* back, rear + *bras* arm. Compare French *arrièrebras* (literally) rear arm.]

**rere|dos** (rir′dos), *n.* **1** a screen or a decorated part of the wall behind an altar: *From the nave, the flat wall appears to be an apse behind the reredos, with the figures of Moses and Aaron standing out as clear as statues* (Manchester Guardian). **2** the back of a fireplace. [< Anglo-French *reredos,* short for *areredos* < Old French *a-* to + *rere* rear[1] (< Latin *retrum*) + *dos* back[1] < Latin *dossus,* variant of *dorsum*.]

**rere|mouse** (rir′mous′), *n., pl.* **-mice.** *Archaic.* a bat. [Old English *hreremūs* < *hrere* (uncertain meaning and origin) + *mūs* mouse]

**re|roll** (rē rōl′), *v.t.* to roll again. —**re|roll′er,** *n.*

**re|route** (rē rüt′, -rout′), *v.t.,* **-rout|ed, -rout|ing.** to send by a new or different route.

**re|run** (*v.* rē run′; *n.* rē′run′), *v.,* **-ran, -run, -run|ning,** *n.* —*v.t., v.i.* to run again.
—*n.* **1** the action or fact of running again: *the rerun of a race.* **2** a television program or motion-picture film that is shown again: *We even saw one TV program that was a rerun of a Summit review—which was taped to begin with—and the next day, ... there was a re-review of the review* (Saturday Review).

**res** (rēz), *n., pl.* **res** (rēz). *Latin.* **1** a matter. **2** a case in law.

**res.,** an abbreviation for the following:
1 research.
2 reserve.
3 residence.
4 resides.
5 resigned.
6 resistance.

**RES** (no periods), reticuloendothelial system.

**res ad|ju|di|ca|ta** (rēz ə jü′də kā′tə), *Latin.* **1** a case in which a final decision has been reached by a court of highest authority. **2** (literally) a case decided.

**re|said** (rē sed′), *v.* the past tense and past participle of **resay.**

**re|sail** (rē sāl′), *v.t., v.i.* **1** to sail again. **2** to sail back.

**re|sal|a|ble** (rē sā′lə bəl), *adj.* that can be resold; fit to be resold; easily resold.

**re|sale** (rē′sāl′, rē sāl′), *n.* **1** the act or practice of selling again: *the resale of a house.* **2** the act or practice of selling at retail: *This store has a 20 per cent markup over the wholesale price for resale.*

**resale price maintenance,** *Especially British.* fair trade.

**re|sa|lute** (rē′sə lüt′), *v.t.,* **-lut|ed, -lut|ing.** **1** to salute or greet anew. **2** to salute in return.

**re|say** (rē sā′), *v.t.,* **-said, -say|ing.** to say again; repeat.

**re|sched|ule** (rē skej′ül; *especially British or Canadian* rē shed′yül), *v.t.,* **-uled, -ul|ing.** **1** to schedule again or anew; set a new time for: *The conference has been rescheduled to begin here on October 28th* (New York Times). **2** to put on a new schedule: *Every student was rescheduled according to the degree of his past learning* (B. Frank Brown).

**re|scind** (ri sind′), *v.t.* to deprive of force; repeal; cancel: *to rescind a law, to rescind a treaty.* SYN: revoke. [< Latin *rēscindere* < *re-* back + *scindere* to cut, related to Greek *schízein.* Compare etym. under **schism.**] —**re|scind′er,** *n.*

**re|scind|a|ble** (ri sin′də bəl), *adj.* that can be rescinded.

**re|scind|ment** (ri sind′mənt), *n.* = rescission.

**res|cin|na|mine** (ri sin′ə mēn), *n.* a gray or whitish alkaloid obtained from rauwolfia, used as a sedative and tranquilizer. *Formula:* $C_{35}H_{42}N_2O_9$

**re|scis|sion** (ri sizh′ən), *n.* the act of rescinding. SYN: annulment. [< Latin *rēscissiō, -ōnis* < *rēscindere;* see etym. under **rescind**]

**re|scis|so|ry** (ri sis′ər ē, -siz′-), *adj.* serving to rescind.

**re|score** (rē skôr′, -skōr′), *v.t.,* **-scored, -scor|ing.** to score again or in a new way.

**re|screen** (rē skrēn′), *v.t.* to screen again.

**re|script** (rē′skript), *n.* **1** a written answer to a question or petition. **2** an official announcement; edict; decree. **3** the act or process of rewriting: *I wrote it three times—chastening and subduing the phrases at every rescript* (Charlotte Brontë). **4** an official answer from a pope or a Roman emperor on some question referred to them. [< Latin *rēscrīptum,* (originally) neuter past participle of *rēscrībere* to write in reply < *re-* back + *scrībere* to write]

**Pronunciation Key:** hat, āge, cãre, fär; let, ēqual, tėrm; it, īce; hot, ōpen, ôrder; oil, out; cup, pu̇t, rüle; child; long; thin; ᴛʜen; zh, measure; ə represents **a** in about, **e** in taken, **i** in pencil, **o** in lemon, **u** in circus.

**res|cue** (res′kyü), *v.*, **-cued, -cu|ing,** *n.* **—*v.t.*** **1** to save from danger, capture, or harm; free; deliver: *The firemen rescued the children from the burning house.* **2** *Law.* **a** to take (a person) forcibly or unlawfully from a jail, policeman, or other person or place of authority. **b** to take (property) from legal custody.
**—*n.*** **1** the act or fact of saving or freeing from danger, capture, or harm: *A dog was chasing our cat when your brother came to the rescue.*
**2** *Law.* the forcible or unlawful taking of a person or thing from the care of the law.
[< Old French *rescou-,* stem of *rescourre* < *re-* again + *escourre* to shake, stir < Latin *excutere* < *ex-* out + *quatere* to shake] **—res′cu|er,** *n.*
**—*Syn.*** *v.t.* **1 Rescue, deliver** mean to save or free from danger, harm, or restraint. **Rescue** means to save a person by quick and forceful action from immediate or threatened danger or harm, such as death, injury, attack, capture, or confinement: *Searchers rescued the campers lost in the mountains.* **Deliver** means to set someone free from something holding him in captivity or under its power or control, such as prison, slavery, oppression, suffering, temptation, or evil: *Moses delivered the Israelites from bondage.*

**rescue grass,** a variety of brome grass native to South America, grown for forage.

**rescue suit,** a fire-resistant suit coated with aluminum to reflect heat and protect the body completely, used especially by firemen to walk through flames.

**re|search** (ri sėrch′, rē′sėrch), *n., v.* **—*n.*** **1** hunting for facts or truth about a subject; inquiry; investigation: *The researches of men of science have done much to lessen disease.* **SYN:** study. **2** organized scientific investigation to solve problems, test hypotheses, or develop or invent new products: *atomic research, cancer research.*
**—*v.i.*** to make researches; do research: *On these three subjects he is directed to read and research—corn laws, finance, tithes* (Robert Southey). **—*v.t.*** to search into; investigate carefully: *He had employed himself ... in researching history* (Mrs. A. M. Bennett).
[< Middle French *recerche* < Old French *recercher* < *re-* again + *cercher,* later, *chercher* to seek for, search] **—re|search′a|ble,** *adj.*

**re-search** (rē sėrch′), *v.t., v.i.* to search again or repeatedly: *The lads searched and re-searched this place, but in vain* (Mark Twain).

**re|searched** (ri sėrcht′, rē′sėrcht), *adj.* based upon research: *Although the work is heavily researched, it does not get entangled with historical theories and countertheories* (Wall Street Journal).

**research engineer,** an engineer who applies findings of research to specific industrial uses, such as product improvement and processing.

**re|search|er** (ri sėr′chər, rē′sėr′-), *n.* a person who makes researches; investigator.

**re|search|ful** (ri sėrch′fəl), *adj.* characterized by research; inquisitive: *Pity that the researchful notary has not ... told us in what century ... he was a writer* (Samuel Taylor Coleridge).

**re|search|ist** (ri sėr′chist), *n.* = researcher.

**research reactor,** an atomic reactor for the study of fission and nuclear energy, or for research in radioactivity, medicine, biology, and the like.

**re|seat** (rē sēt′), *v.t.* **1** to seat again. **2** to put a new seat on. **3** to put in place again: *to reseat a valve.* **4** to restore parliamentary rights and privileges to.

**ré|seau** (rā zō′), *n.* **1** *Astronomy.* a crisscross of squares photographed on the same plate as a star for the purpose of measurement. **2** a sensitive filter screen used in making color films. **3** = network. **4** the mesh in lace. [< French *réseau,* probably < Old French *roisel* (diminutive) < *roiz* < Latin *rētēs,* plural of *rēte* net]

**re|sect** (ri sekt′), *v.t. Surgery.* to cut away or remove a part of. [< Latin *resectus,* past participle of *resecāre* to cut off < *re-* back + *secāre* to cut] **—re|sect′a|ble,** *adj.*

**re|sect|a|bil|i|ty** (ri sek′tə bil′ə tē), *n.* resectable condition.

**re|sec|tion** (ri sek′shən), *n.* the surgical removal of a portion of some structure, especially bone. [< Latin *resectiō, -ōnis* < *resecāre;* see etym. under **resect**]

**re|sec|tion|al** (ri sek′shə nəl), *adj.* of or having to do with a resection: *resectional surgery.*

**re|sec|to|scope** (ri sek′tə skōp), *n.* a thin, tubular, cutting instrument with a sliding knife, which allows a resection to be performed without any opening other than that made by the instrument itself.

**re|se|da** (ri sē′də), *n., adj.* **—*n.*** **1** = mignonette. **2** grayish green. **—*adj.*** grayish-green. [< Latin *resēda*]

**res|e|da|ceous** (res′ə dā′shəs), *adj.* belonging to a family of dicotyledonous, largely Mediterranean plants typified by the mignonette. [< New Latin *Resedaceae* the reseda family (< Latin *resēda*) + English *-ous*]

**re|see** (rē sē′), *v.t.,* **-saw, -seen, -see|ing.** to see again: *If I could see and resee a hundred times this Captain's shifty slow fox trot, ...* (Manchester Guardian Weekly).

**re|seed** (rē sēd′), *v.t., v.i.* to seed again: *A considerable acreage of damaged wheat was reseeded to barley* (Wayne Dexter).

**re|seg|men|ta|tion** (rē′seg mən tā′shən), *n.* **1** the act or process of dividing into segments. **2** the act or process of dividing segments into smaller segments.

**re|seg|re|gate** (rē seg′rə gāt), *v.t.,* **-gat|ed, -gat|ing.** **1** to segregate (a racial group) again or in a new way. **2** to renew segregation in: *In effect the schools have been resegregated on an overwhelmingly Negro basis* (Wall Street Journal). **—re|seg′re|ga′tion,** *n.*

**re|seize** (rē sēz′), *v.t.,* **-seized, -seiz|ing.** **1** to seize again; seize a second time. **2** to put into possession of; reinstate. **3** *Law.* to take possession of, as of lands and tenements which have been disseized.

**re|sei|zure** (rē sē′zhər), *n.* a second seizure; the act of seizing again.

**re|sell** (rē sel′), *v.t.,* **-sold, -sell|ing.** to sell again.

**re|sem|blance** (ri zem′bləns), *n.* **1** likeness; similar appearance: *Twins often show great resemblance. There are certain resemblances between the two cases.* **2** appearance: *under the resemblance of a mist.* **3** a copy; image. [< Anglo-French *resemblance* < Old French *resembler* to resemble]
**—*Syn.*** **1 Resemblance, similarity** mean a likeness between two persons or things. **Resemblance** emphasizes looking alike or having some of the same external features or superficial qualities: *There is some resemblance between the accounts of the fire, but all the important details are different.* **Similarity** suggests being of the same kind or nature or having some of the same essential qualities: *The similarity between the two reports suggests that one person wrote both.*

**re|sem|blant** (ri zem′blənt), *adj.* resembling; similar: *The yearling was surely the mare's son, because two homelier but more resemblant animals never lived* (New Yorker).

**re|sem|ble** (ri zem′bəl), *v.t.,* **-bled, -bling.** **1** to be like; be similar to; have likeness to in form, figure, or qualities: *An orange resembles a grapefruit.* **2** *Archaic.* to liken; compare: *Unto what is the kingdom of God like? and whereunto shall I resemble it?* (Luke 13:18). [< Old French *resembler* < *re-* again + *sembler* to appear < Latin *simulāre* (originally) to copy < *similis* similar]

**re|sem|bler** (ri zem′blər), *n.* a person or thing that resembles some other person or thing.

**re|send** (rē send′), *v.t.,* **-sent, -send|ing.** **1** to send again or in a new way. **2** to send back.

**re|sent** (ri zent′), *v.t.* **1** to feel injured and angry at; feel indignation at: *to resent criticism. She resented being called a baby. Our cat seems to resent having anyone sit in its chair. He naturally resented the promotion of his younger colleague to a rank above his own.* **2** to show such feeling by action or speech: *Putting his hand upon his sword, the knight threatened to resent this insult.* [< French *ressentir* < *re-* back + *sentir* < Latin *sentīre* to feel] **—re|sent′er,** *n.*

**re|sent|ful** (ri zent′fəl), *adj.* **1** feeling resentment; injured and angry: *a resentful child.* **2** showing resentment: *a resentful remark.* **—re|sent′ful|ly,** *adv.* **—re|sent′ful|ness,** *n.*

**re|sent|ment** (ri zent′mənt), *n.* **1** the feeling that one has at being injured or insulted; indignation: *Everyone feels resentment at being treated unfairly. Resentment is never an asset* (Atlantic). **SYN:** pique, umbrage. **2** the act of showing this feeling by action or speech.

**res|er|pine** (res′ər pin, -pēn; rə sėr′-), *n.* a powerful alkaloid obtained from the juices of the rauwolfia plant, used as a tranquilizer and sedative, in reducing high blood pressure, and in the treatment of mental illness. *Formula:* $C_{33}H_{40}N_2O_9$ [apparently < New Latin *R(auwolfia) serp(entina)* the rauwolfia plant + English *-ine*²]

**res|er|va|tion** (rez′ər vā′shən), *n.* **1** the act of keeping back; hiding in part; something not expressed: *She outwardly approved of the plan but with the mental reservation that she would change it to suit herself.* **2** a limiting condition: *The United States accepted the plan with reservations plainly stated.* **SYN:** limitation. **3** land set aside for a special purpose. The government has set apart Indian reservations. **SYN:** reserve. **4** an arrangement to keep a thing for a person; securing of accommodations in advance: *Please make reservations for rooms at a hotel in Portland and seats at the theater that night.* **5** something reserved.
**off the reservation,** away from the norm or from the expected way of acting or thinking: *Though some of them strayed off the reservation ... , most of New York's influential labor leaders are firmly in the Wagner-Screvane camp* (Harper's).

**re|serve** (ri zėrv′), *v.,* **-served, -serv|ing,** *n., adj.* **—*v.t.*** **1** to keep back; hold back for the present: *to reserve criticism. Mother reserved her complaint about my messy room until my friend left. Take each man's censure, but reserve thy judgment* (Shakespeare). **SYN:** retain. **2** to set apart: *time reserved for recreation. He reserves his evenings for reading to his son.* **3** to save for use later: *Reserve enough money for your fare home.* **4** to set aside for the use of a particular person or persons: *Reserve a table at a restaurant.*
**—*n.*** **1** the actual cash in a bank or assets that can be turned into cash quickly. Banks must keep a reserve of money. **2** a body of soldiers, sailors, ships, aircraft, or other military or police forces, kept ready to help the main force in battle: *A facet of the proposed program which is of interest to science and industry would be a continuous "screening" of men in the reserve* (Newsweek). **3** public land set apart for a special purpose: *a forest reserve.* **4** anything kept back for future use; store: *a reserve of food or energy.* **5** the act of keeping back or holding back; reservation: *You may speak before her without reserve.* **6** the fact or condition of being kept, set apart, or saved for use later: *to keep money in reserve.* **7** the act of keeping one's thoughts, feelings, and affairs to oneself; self-restraint in action or speech: *to maintain a polite reserve when talking about politics.* **8** a silent manner that keeps people from making friends easily: *The deaf man's reserve was mistaken for haughtiness.* **9** an exception or qualification to the acceptance of some idea, belief, or the like: *The scientists accepted the new theory with some reserves.* **10** an avoidance of excess, fads, or the like, in literary or artistic work.
**—*adj.*** kept in reserve; forming a reserve: *a reserve stock, a reserve force.*
**reserves,** soldiers, sailors, or other members of the armed forces who are not in active service but ready to serve if needed: *The reserves were quickly mobilized during the war.*
[< Latin *reservāre* < *re-* back + *servāre* to keep] **—re|serv′er,** *n.*

**reserve bank,** one of the twelve Federal Reserve Banks.

**reserve book,** a book held in reserve, usually one which cannot be taken from the library.

**re|served** (ri zėrvd′), *adj.* **1** kept in reserve; kept by special arrangement: *a reserved seat.* **SYN:** withheld, retained. **2** set apart: *a reserved section at the stadium.* **3** having or showing self-restraint: *reserved comment. As a statesman he was reserved, seldom showing his own thoughts* (James A. Froude). **SYN:** restrained, reticent. **4** disposed to keep to oneself: *A reserved boy does not make friends easily.*

**re|serv|ed|ly** (ri zėr′vid lē), *adv.* in a reserved manner; with reserve.

**re|serv|ed|ness** (ri zėr′vid nis), *n.* the character of being reserved.

**reserved powers,** *U.S.* the powers not granted by the Constitution to the Federal government but reserved for the states or the people.

**reserve officer,** an officer in the reserves.

**re|serves** (ri zėrvz′), *n.pl.* See under **reserve.**

**re|serv|ist** (ri zėr′vist), *n.* a member of the reserves; soldier, sailor, or other member of the armed forces who is not in active service but available if needed: *50,000 reservists were recalled to the colors* (Time).

**res|er|voir** (rez′ər vwär, -vwôr, -vôr), *n.* **1** a place where water is collected and stored for use, especially an artificial basin created by the damming of a river: *This reservoir supplies the entire city.* **2** anything to hold a liquid: *an oil reservoir for an engine. A fountain pen has an ink reservoir.* **3** *Figurative.* a place where anything is collected and stored: *Her mind was a reservoir of facts.* **4** *Figurative.* a great supply: *a reservoir of manpower. There exists in the world today a gigantic reservoir of good will toward us, the American people* (Wendell Willkie). **5** *Biology.* **a** a part of an animal or plant in which some fluid or secretion is collected or retained. **b** an organism that carries a disease germ or virus to which it is immune: *They hope that the laboratories will soon identify the animal carriers—the reservoirs—and the insects—vectors—that transmit the disease* (New York Times).
[< French *réservoir* < Old French *reserver* to reserve]

**re|set** (*v.* rē set′; *n.* rē′set′), *v.,* **-set, -set|ting,** *n.* **—*v.t.*** **1** to set again: *The diamond was reset in platinum. His broken arm had to be reset.* **2** to set (type) again.
**—*n.*** **1** the act of resetting. **2** a thing reset. **3** matter set in type again.

**re|set|ta|ble** (rē set′ə bəl), *adj.* that can be reset.
**re|set|tle** (rē set′əl), *v.t., v.i.,* **-tled, -tling.** to settle again; reestablish; relocate.
**re|set|tle|ment** (rē set′əl mənt), *n.* the act of settling again.
**res ges|tae** (rēz jes′tē), *Latin.* **1** deeds; achievements. **2** *Law.* facts; accompanying facts.
**resh** (rāsh), *n.* the twentieth letter of the Hebrew alphabet. [< Hebrew *resh* (literally) head]
**re|shape** (rē shāp′), *v.t.,* **-shaped, -shap|ing.** to shape anew; form into a new or different shape.
**re|ship** (rē ship′), *v.,* **-shipped, -ship|ping.** — *v.t.* **1** to ship again: *to reship merchandise to Chicago.* **2a** to put on board of a ship again. **b** to transfer to a different ship.
— *v.i.* (of men) to take ship again. — **re|ship′per,** *n.*
**re|ship|ment** (rē ship′mənt), *n.* **1** the act of shipping again. **2** that which is shipped again.
**re|shoot** (rē shüt′), *v.t., v.i.,* **-shot, -shoot|ing.** to shoot again or in a new way: *And then the scene was shot and reshot from the new angle* (New Yorker).
**re|shuf|fle** (rē shuf′əl), *v.,* **-fled, -fling,** *n.* — *v.t.* **1** to shuffle again: *It is like forever shuffling and reshuffling a pack of cards* (Maclean's). **2** *Figurative.* to arrange in a new or different way; reorganize completely: *The Premier, who delights in political intricacy, has appointed or reshuffled no fewer than 104 Cabinet ministers* (Time).
— *n.* a complete rearrangement or reorganization; shakeup. — **re|shuf′fle|ment,** *n.*
**re|side** (ri zīd′), *v.i.,* **-sid|ed, -sid|ing.** **1** to live (in or at a place) for a long time; dwell: *This family has resided in Richmond for 100 years.* **2** to be (in); exist (in): *Her charm resides in her happy smile. The power to declare war resides in Congress.* **SYN:** inhere. [< Latin *residēre* < *re-* back + *sedēre* to sit, settle]
**res|i|dence** (rez′ə dəns), *n.* **1** a house or home; place where a person lives; abode: *a fine residence. The President's residence is the White House in Washington, D.C. Many of these residences, which are among the most magnificent country homes on the face of the earth, are now going to solitary ruin* (Newsweek). **SYN:** dwelling, habitation. **2** the act or fact of residing; living; dwelling: *Long residence in France made him very fond of the French people.* **3** the period of residing in a place: *He spent a residence of ten years in France.* **4** the fact of living or staying regularly at or in some place for the discharge of special duties, or to comply with some regulation: *the residence of a rector in his benefice, a two-year requirement of residence for students.* **5** *Figurative.* the seat of some power, principle, activity, or the like.
**in residence,** living in a place while on duty or doing active work: *Many large resorts have a doctor in residence.*
**res|i|den|cy** (rez′ə dən sē), *n., pl.* **-cies.** **1** = residence. **2** the position of a doctor who continues practicing in a hospital after completing his internship. **3** *U.S.* advanced training or education in some field, similar to a medical residency: *The company instituted a series of "residencies" across the country—one- to three-week stands in Los Angeles, San Francisco, Chicago and at the University of Illinois—that combined performances with seminars and lecture-demonstrations* (Time). **4a** (formerly) the official residence of a representative of the British governor general of India at a native court. **b** the official residence of a diplomatic officer or governor general. **5** (formerly) an administrative division in the Dutch East Indies and in certain other areas under colonial rule.
**res|i|dent** (rez′ə dənt), *n., adj.* — *n.* **1** a person living in a place permanently, not a visitor; dweller: *The residents of the town are proud of its new library.* **2** a resident physician, especially one who has completed internship. **3** an official sent to live in a foreign land to represent his country. **4** (formerly) a representative of the British governor general of India at a native court. **5** (formerly) the governor of an administrative division of the Dutch East Indies.
— *adj.* **1** dwelling in a place; residing; staying: *A resident owner lives on his property. Grandmother wants a resident companion.* **2** living in a place while on duty or doing active work: *Doctor Jones is a resident physician at the hospital.* **3** not migratory: *English sparrows are resident birds.* **4** present, inherent, or established: *resident powers.*
[< Latin *residēns, -entis,* present participle of *residēre* reside]
**resident alien,** *U.S.* an alien who lives in a country on a permanent basis, enjoying the rights of citizens but not permitted to vote.
**resident commissioner,** *U.S.* an official representative of a territory or dependency in the House of Representatives, who has speaking rights but may not vote. Puerto Rico has a resident commissioner in the United States.
**res|i|dent|er** (rez′ə den′tər), *n. Scottish and U.S.* a resident; an inhabitant.
**res|i|den|tial** (rez′ə den′shəl), *adj.* **1** of, having to do with, or fitted for homes or residences: *They live in a good residential district outside the city.* **2** of or having to do with residence: *The city is considering the adoption of a residential requirement for all city employees to live within the city limits.* **3** serving or used as a residence: *a residential building.* — **res′i|den′tial|ly,** *adv.*
**res|i|den|ti|ar|y** (rez′ə den′shē er′ē, -shər-), *adj., n., pl.* **-ar|ies.** — *adj.* **1** residing in a place; resident. **2** involving official residence: *a residentiary canonry.*
— *n.* **1** = resident. **2** a clergyman who is bound to official residence.
**res|i|dent|ship** (rez′ə dənt ship), *n.* the condition or station of a resident.
**re|sid|er** (ri zī′dər), *n.* = resident.
**re|sid|u|a** (ri zij′ü ə), *n.* plural of **residuum.**
**re|sid|u|al** (ri zij′ü əl), *adj., n.* — *adj.* **1** of or forming a residue; remaining; left over: *Residual fuel oil is the thick, heavy oil left over after refining crude oil.* **2** left after subtraction. **3** *Geology.* resulting from the weathering of rock: *residual clay soil, a residual deposit.*
— *n.* **1** the amount left over; remainder. **2** = residual quantity. **3a** money earned from the resale of motion pictures, especially films sold to television: *Writers ... were threatening to walk out on the studios if they weren't cut in on a slice of the residuals* (Newsweek). **b** a fee paid to a performer or writer for each rerun of a television commercial or show in which he participated. — **re|sid′u|al|ly,** *adv.*
**residual oil,** a heavy liquid hydrocarbon obtained as a residual by-product of petroleum distillation, used mainly as an industrial fuel: *Residual oil is used by schools and factories as both a fuel and a heating oil* (Wall Street Journal).
**residual quantity,** *Mathematics.* a binomial having one of its terms negative, as 2a − b.
**re|sid|u|ar|y** (ri zij′ü er′ē), *adj.* **1** receiving or entitled to the remainder of an estate: *a residuary legatee.* **2** = residual.
**res|i|due** (rez′ə dü, -dyü), *n.* **1** what remains after a part is taken; remainder: *The syrup had dried up, leaving a sticky residue at the bottom of the jar. The solution of almost any problem in science leaves, as a residue, other unsolved questions* (Fred W. Emerson). **2** the part of an estate that is left after all debts, charges, and particular devises and bequests have been satisfied: *His will directed that after the payment of all debts and $10,000 to his brother, the residue of his property should go to his son.* **3** *Chemistry.* an atom or group of atoms considered as a radical or part of a molecule. [< Old French *residu,* learned borrowing from Latin *residuum* left over. See etym. of doublet **residuum.**]
**re|sid|u|um** (ri zij′ü əm), *n., pl.* **-sid|u|a.** **1** what is left at the end of any process; residue; remainder. **2** *Law.* the residue of an estate. [< Latin *residuum* < *re-* back + *sedēre* to sit. See etym. of doublet **residue.**]
**re|sign** (ri zīn′), *v.i.* **1** to give up a job, office, or position: *The manager of the football team resigned.* **2** to yield; submit: *resigned to one's fate.*
— *v.t.* to give up (as an office, position, or right): *to resign the presidency. The manager of the local newspaper resigned his position.*
**resign oneself,** to submit quietly; adapt oneself without complaint; yield: *He had to resign himself to a week in bed when he hurt his back.*
[< Old French *resigner* < Latin *resīgnāre* to unseal < *re-* back + *sīgnāre* to sign, seal < *sīgnum* a seal] — **re|sign′er,** *n.*
▶ **Resign** is often followed by *from,* though sometimes the object follows without the *from: He resigned from the editorship of the school paper.* Or: *He resigned the editorship of the school paper.*
**re-sign** (rē sīn′), *v.t.* to sign again.
**res|ig|na|tion** (rez′ig nā′shən), *n.* **1** the act of resigning: *There have been so many resignations from the committee that a new one must be formed.* **2** a written statement giving notice that one resigns. **3** patient acceptance; quiet submission: *She bore the pain with resignation.* **SYN:** acquiescence, meekness.
**re|signed** (ri zīnd′), *adj.* **1** accepting what comes without complaint: *resigned obedience.* **SYN:** submissive, acquiescent. **2** characterized by or showing resignation: *a resigned smile* (Joseph Conrad). — **re|sign′ed|ly,** *adv.* — **re|sign′ed|ness,** *n.*
**re|sile** (ri zīl′), *v.i.,* **-siled, -sil|ing.** **1** to spring back, as an elastic body does. **2** to draw back, as from an agreement or purpose. **3** to shrink back, as in fear or disgust. [< Middle French *resiler,* learned borrowing from Latin *resilīre* to recoil; see etym. under **resilient**]
**re|sil|i|ence** (ri zil′ē əns, -zil′yəns), *n.* **1** the power of springing back; resilient quality or nature; elasticity: *Rubber has resilience.* **2** *Figurative.* the power of recovering readily; buoyancy; cheerfulness: *a man of great resilience.*
**re|sil|i|en|cy** (ri zil′ē ən sē, -zil′yən-), *n.* = resilience.
**re|sil|i|ent** (ri zil′ē ənt, -zil′yənt), *adj.* **1** springing back; returning to the original form or position after being bent, compressed, or stretched: *resilient steel, resilient turf.* **2** *Figurative.* readily recovering; buoyant; cheeful: *a resilient nature that throws off trouble.* [< Latin *resiliēns, -entis,* present participle of *resilīre* to rebound, recoil < *re-* back + *salīre* to jump, leap] — **re|sil′i|ent|ly,** *adv.*
**res|in** (rez′ən), *n., v.* — *n.* **1** a sticky, yellow or brown substance that flows from certain plants and trees, especially the pine and fir. Resin is transparent or translucent, does not conduct electricity, and is used in medicine, varnish, plastics, inks, and adhesives. When pine resin is heated it yields turpentine; the hard yellow substance that remains is called rosin. Copal, rosin, and amber are types of resin. **2** any one of a large group of resinous substances that are made artificially and are used especially in making plastics: *Synthetic resins are made up of many simple molecules linked together to form large complex ones* [*called*] *high polymers* (W. Norton Jones, Jr.).
— *v.t.* to treat, rub, or coat with resin.
[< Latin *rēsīna* < *rasis* raw pitch] — **res′in|like′,** *adj.*
**res|in|ate** (rez′ə nāt), *n., v.,* **-at|ed, -at|ing.** — *n.* a mixture of certain acids in resin, such as used in making soap, or paints: *New uses already are being found for tung oil through the addition of zinc resinate* (E. G. Moore).
— *v.t.* to flavor or impregnate with resin.
**resin canal,** = resin duct.
**resin cyst,** a cyst or sac, in wood, containing resin.
**resin duct,** a canal in the wood of trees, especially conifers, through which resin is secreted and conducted.
**resin gnat,** a small dipterous insect whose larvae live in exuding masses of resin on pine trees and feed on the abraded bark.
**re|sin|ic** (re zin′ik), *adj.* of or having to do with resin.
**res|in|if|er|ous** (rez′ə nif′ər əs), *adj.* yielding resin: *a resiniferous tree.*
**res|in|i|fy** (rez′ə nə fī), *v.,* **-fied, -fy|ing.** — *v.t.* to make resinous.
— *v.i.* to become resinous.
**res|in|oid** (rez′ə noid), *adj., n.* — *adj.* = resinous (def. 2).
— *n.* a resinous substance, especially a thermosetting synthetic resin.
**res|i|no|sis** (rez′ə nō′sis), *n.* an abnormal outflow of resin from a coniferous tree.
**res|in|ous** (rez′ə nəs), *adj.* **1** of resin: *resinous materials.* **2** like resin. **3** containing resin; full of resin. [< Latin *rēsīnōsus* < *rēsīna;* see etym. under **resin**] — **res′in|ous|ly,** *adv.*
**resin passage,** = resin duct.
**res in|te|gra** (rēz in′tə grə), *n. Latin.* a matter not yet acted on, or a point of law not yet adjudicated.
**res in|ter a|li|os** (rēz in′tər ā′li ōs), *Latin.* **1** the acts of third parties, or strangers to a proceeding, not relevant to the case. **2** (literally) transactions between others.
**res|in|y** (rez′ə nē), *adj.* = resinous.
**res|i|pis|cence** (res′ə pis′əns), *n.* a change to a better frame of mind.
**res|i|pis|cent** (res′ə pis′ənt), *adj.* changing to a better frame of mind. [< Latin *resipiscens, -entis,* present participle of *resipiscere* recover one's senses < *re-* again + *sapere* be wise]
**res ip|sa lo|qui|tur** (rēz ip′sə lō′kwə tər), *Latin.* the thing itself speaks; the case speaks for itself.
**re|sist** (ri zist′), *v., n.* — *v.t.* **1** to act against; strive against; oppose: *to resist change. The window resisted all efforts to open it.* **SYN:** See syn. under **oppose.** **2** to strive successfully against; keep from: *I could not resist laughing.* **3** to withstand the action or effect of (as an acid or storm): *A healthy body resists disease.*
— *v.i.* to act against something; oppose something.
— *n.* **1** a coating put on a surface to make it withstand the action of weather, acid, etc. **2** a coating on parts of a fabric that are not to be colored, when the fabric is dyed.

**Pronunciation Key:** hat, āge, cãre, fär; let, ēqual, tėrm; it, īce; hot, ōpen, ôrder; **oil, out;** cup, pu̇t, rüle; **ch**ild; lo**ng**; **th**in; **ᴛʜ**en; **zh,** measure; ə represents **a** in about, **e** in taken, **i** in pencil, **o** in lemon, **u** in circus.

[< Latin *resistere* < *re-* back + *sistere* take a stand, stand < *stāre* stand] —**re|sist′ing|ly**, *adv.*

**re|sist|ance** (ri zis′təns), *n.* **1** the act of resisting: *The bank clerk made no resistance to the robbers.* **2** the power to resist: *She has little resistance to germs and so is often ill. Get enough sleep and eat well-balanced meals to help keep up resistance built up during the cold months* (Time). **3** a thing or act that resists; opposing force; opposition: *An airplane can overcome the resistance of the air and go in the desired direction, but an ordinary balloon just drifts.* **4** the property of a conductor that opposes the passage of an electric current and changes electric energy into heat. Copper has a low resistance. *Resistance is the electrical counterpart of friction, and can serve the same damping function* (Roy F. Allison). **5** a conductor, coil, etc., that offers resistance. **6** *Physics* an opposing force, especially one tending to prevent motion. [< Middle French *résistance*, alteration of earlier *résistence* < *résister* resist < Latin *resistere;* see etym. under **resist**]

**Re|sist|ance** (ri zis′təns), *n.* the people who secretly organize and fight for their freedom in a country occupied and controlled by a foreign power: *the French Resistance in World War II.*

**resistance coil**, a coil or wire made of metal that has a high resistance, used especially for measuring resistance, reducing voltage or amperage, and producing heat.

**re|sist|ance|less** (ri zis′təns lis), *adj.* lacking resistance: *At low temperature a resistanceless current can cross an insulating gap* (New Scientist).

**resistance meter**, an instrument used to measure the performance of the ignition coil and condenser in an internal-combustion engine.

**resistance thermometer**, an electric thermometer based on the variation in conductivity of metals as a result of changing temperature.

**resistance welding**, welding by heat from resistance to the flow of an electric current; electric welding.

**re|sist|ant** (ri zis′tənt), *adj., n.* —*adj.* resisting. —*n.* **1** = resister. **2** = resist (def. 2).

**ré|sis|tant** (rā zēs tän′), *n. French.* a member of the Resistance: *During the German occupation, he defended some of the French résistants in the special courts* (New Yorker).

**resist dyeing**, the process of dyeing in a pattern with a resist.

**re|sist|ent** (ri zis′tənt), *adj.* = resistant.

**re|sist|er** (ri zis′tər), *n.* **1** a person or thing that resists. **2** = resistor.

**re|sist|i|bil|i|ty** (ri zis′tə bil′ə tē), *n.* the quality or condition of being resistible.

**re|sist|i|ble** (ri zis′tə bəl), *adj.* that can be resisted: *earthquakes … the least resistible of natural violence* (Samuel Johnson).

**re|sis|tive** (ri zis′tiv), *adj.* resisting; capable of resisting or inclined to resist. —**re|sis′tive|ly**, *adv.* —**re|sis′tive|ness**, *n.*

**re|sis|tiv|i|ty** (rē′zis tiv′ə tē), *n., pl.* **-ties.** the electrical resistance of the equivalent of one cubic centimeter of a given substance.

**re|sist|less** (ri zist′lis), *adj.* **1** that cannot be resisted: *A resistless impulse made him wander over the earth.* **SYN:** irresistible. **2** that cannot resist. —**re|sist′less|ly**, *adv.* —**re|sist′less|ness**, *n.*

**re|sis|to|jet** (ri zis′tō jet′), *n.* a jet engine that uses electric resistance to heat a liquid propellant, used chiefly to keep an artificial satellite steady during orbit.

**re|sis|tor** (ri zis′tər), *n.* a conductor used to control voltage in an electric circuit, as of a radio or televison set, a tape recorder, a computer, or other electronic equipment, because of its resistance: *A resistor is simply a poor conductor of electricity* (John R. Pierce).

**re|sit** (*v.* rē sit′, rē′sit′; *n.* rē′sit′), *v.,* **-sat, -sit|ting,** *n. British.* —*v.t.* to take (a written examination) a second time: *So many students resit the engineering examination each year that an eventual pass rate of 80 per cent, as suggested by Mr. Alan Sim, may occur* (Sunday Times).
—*n.* the taking of a written examination a second time: *the September resit.*

**re-site** (rē sīt′), *v.t.,* **-sit|ed, -sit|ing.** to place on a new site.

**re|size** (rē sīz′), *v.t.,* **-sized, -siz|ing.** to size again or anew.

**res ju|di|ca|ta** (rēz jü′də kā′tə), *Latin.* res adjudicata.

**re|slant** (rē slant′, -slänt′), *v.t.* **1** to slant again. **2** to slant in a new direction.

**res|na|tron** (rez′nə tron), *n.* a vacuum tube for generating large amounts of high-frequency power, such as for jamming radar in warfare. [< *res*(o)*na*(tor) + (elec)*tron*]

**res nul|li|us** (rēz nul′ē əs), *Latin.* a thing belonging to no one: *The moon, however, is almost certainly res nullius, and therefore capable of appropriation through effective occupation* (Bulletin of Atomic Scientists).

**re|so|cial|ize** (rē sō′shə līz), *v.t.,* **-ized, -iz|ing.** to restore to an earlier social status; return to normal society; rehabilitate socially: *The U.S. Army … will attempt to educate, train, and resocialize many who are at present rejects of society* (London Times). —**re|so′cial|i|za′tion**, *n.*

**re|sod** (rē sod′), *v.t.,* **-sod|ded, -sod|ding.** to sod again: *to resod a lawn.*

**res|o|jet** (rez′ō jet′), *n.* = pulsejet. [< *reso*(nant) *jet*]

**re|sold** (rē sōld′), *v.* the past tense and past participle of **resell**.

**re|sole** (*v.* rē sōl′; *n.* rē′sōl′), *v.,* **-soled, -sol|ing,** *n.* —*v.t.* to put a new sole on (as a shoe or boot).
—*n.* a new sole, such as on a shoe or boot.

**re|sol|u|bil|i|ty** (ri zol′yə bil′ə tē, -sol′-), *n.* the quality of being resoluble.

**re|sol|u|ble**[1] (rə zol′yə bəl, rez′ə lə-), *adj.* that can be resolved; resolvable: *The distinctiveness of all that which we call brogue, accent, etc., is ultimately resoluble into a specialty of modulation* (John Earle). [< Late Latin *resolūbilis* < Latin *resolvere;* see etym. under **resolve**] —**re|sol′u|ble|ness**, *n.*

**re|sol|u|ble**[2] (rē sol′yə bəl), *adj.* that can be dissolved again: … *a precipitate partly resoluble in carbonate of ammonia* (Andrew Ure). [< *re-* + *soluble* (def. 1)]

**res|o|lute** (rez′ə lüt), *adj.* **1** having a fixed resolve; determined; firm: *He was resolute in his attempt to climb to the top of the mountain.* **2** constant in pursuing a purpose; bold: *A soldier must be resolute in battle. The risks will be greater in a few years, if we* [*the U.S.A.*] *dare not be resolute now* (Elmer Davis). **3** indicating or suggesting firmness and determination: *a resolute attitude, a resolute chin.* [< Latin *resolutus,* past participle of *resolvere;* see etym. under **resolve**] —**res′o|lute′ly**, *adv.* —**res′o|lute′ness**, *n.*

**res|o|lu|tion** (rez′ə lü′shən), *n.* **1** a thing decided on; thing determined: *I made a resolution to get up early.* **2** the act of resolving or determining. **3** the power of holding firmly to a purpose; determination: *Lincoln's resolution overcame his poverty and lack of schooling.* **4** a formal expression of opinion: *a joint resolution of the Congress. The club passed a resolution thanking the teacher for his help throughout the year. Strong resolutions were adopted* [*in Parliament*] *against the queen* (Macaulay). **5** the act of breaking into parts. **6** the act or result of solving; solution: *the resolution of a problem, the resolution of a plot in a novel. Of this question … we must be content to live without the resolution* (Samuel Johnson). **7** *Medicine.* the reduction or disappearance of inflammation without the formation of pus. **8** *Music.* **a** the progression of a voice part or of the harmony as a whole from a dissonance to a consonance. **b** the tone or chord by which this is effected. **9** *Optics.* the ability of a lens to produce separate images of objects that are very close together; resolving power: *Resolution is the capacity of a lens to show two close objects as two, rather than as a single fuzzy one* (Scientific American).

**res|o|lu|tion|er** (rez′ə lü′shə nər), *n.* a person making, accepting, or approving a resolution.

**re|solv|a|bil|i|ty** (ri zol′və bil′ə tē), *n.* the property of being resolvable; resolvableness.

**re|solv|a|ble** (ri zol′və bəl), *adj.* that can be resolved. —**re|solv′a|ble|ness**, *n.*

**re|solve** (ri zolv′), *v.,* **-solved, -solv|ing,** *n.* —*v.t.* **1** to make up one's mind; determine; decide: *He resolved to do better work in the future. Richard resolved to reform* (Newsweek). **SYN:** See syn. under **decide**. **2** to decide by vote; adopt or pass a resolution: *It was resolved that our school have a lunchroom.* **3** to clear away; dispel: *The letter resolved all our doubts.* **4** to clear up; answer and explain; solve: *The conviction … neither solves the mystery of Rémon's death nor resolves Panama's political problems* (Newsweek). **5** to break into parts; break up: *Some chemical compounds can be resolved by heat.* **6** to change: *The assembly resolved itself into a committee. Earth, that nourished thee, shall claim thy growth, to be resolved to earth again* (William Cullen Bryant). **7** to produce separate images of; make distinguishable, as by optical instruments or radar: *to resolve a cluster of stars with a high-powered telescope.* **8** *Music.* to cause (a voice part or harmony) to progress from a dissonance to a consonance. **9** *Medicine.* to cause (inflammation) to disappear without the formation of pus.
—*v.i.* **1** to come to a decision; decide (on): *consultations … in which much was proposed, but nothing resolved on* (Scott). **2** to break into parts: *This chemical resolves when distilled at a high temperature.* **3** *Music.* to progress from a dissonance to a consonance.
—*n.* **1** a thing determined on: *He kept his resolve to do better.* **2** firmness in carrying out a purpose; determination: *George Washington was a man of great resolve.*
[< Latin *resolvere* < *re-* back + *solvere* loosen] —**re|solv′er**, *n.*

**re|solved** (ri zolvd′), *adj.* determined; firm; resolute. —**re|solv′ed|ly**, *adv.* —**re|solv′ed|ness**, *n.*

**re|sol|vent** (ri zol′vənt), *adj., n.* —*adj.* resolving; solvent. —*n.* **1** a remedy that reduces swellings or inflammation. **2** = solvent.
[< Latin *resolvēns, -entis,* present participle of *resolvere;* see etym. under **resolve**]

**re|solv|ing power** (ri zol′ving), **1** the ability of a lens or optical system to produce separate images of objects that are very close together; resolution: *The device has a resolving power of 600,000 which means it can separate one part in 600,000* (Science News Letter). **2** the ability of electronic equipment, such as radar or a radio telescope, or of photographic equipment to produce distinguishable images: *The ability of a photographic material to record fine detail—its resolving power—is limited by its granular structure* (Hardy and Perrin).

**res|o|nance** (rez′ə nəns), *n.* **1** a resounding quality; being resonant: *the resonance of an organ.* **2** a reinforcing and prolonging of sound by reflection or by vibration of other objects. The sounding board of a piano gives it resonance. The hollow body of a guitar gives it resonance. **3** the condition of an electrical circuit adjusted to allow the greatest flow of current at a certain frequency: *A radio set must be in resonance to receive music or speech from a radio station.* **4** *Chemistry.* the oscillation of molecules between two or more structures, each possessing identical atoms but different arrangements of electrons. **5** *Nuclear Physics.* an unstable particle of extremely short duration; any one of a group of energy states that behave like elementary particles but may be temporary associations of unstable particles such as mesons and hyperons: *The rho meson is a particle in its own right although it is also frequently referred to as a resonance* (Thomas Groves).

**res|o|nant** (rez′ə nənt), *adj., n.* —*adj.* **1** continuing to sound; resounding; echoing: *The resonant sounds of the band filled the city streets.* **2** tending to increase or prolong sounds: *the resonant hollow body of a guitar.* **3** of or in resonance.
—*n. Phonetics.* a nasal consonant, such as *n* and *ng;* nasal.
[< Latin *resonāns, -antis,* present participle of *resonāre* < *re-* back + *sonāre* to sound, related to *sonus* sound] —**res′o|nant|ly**, *adv.*

**resonant jet**, = pulsejet.

**res|o|nate** (rez′ə nāt), *v.,* **-nat|ed, -nat|ing.** —*v.i.* **1** to exhibit resonance; resound. **2** to oscillate with the same frequency as the source: *The wavelength of the radio waves can be calculated from the measured size of the particular cavity in which they will "tune" or resonate* (Scientific American). —*v.t.* to cause to resonate.
[< Latin *resonāre* (with English *-ate*[1]); see etym. under **resonant**]

**res|o|na|tor** (rez′ə nā′tər), *n.* **1** something that produces resonance; appliance for increasing sound by resonance. **2** a device for detecting electromagnetic radiation, such as radiobroadcasting waves. **3** an additional muffler in an automobile exhaust system to reduce excessive exhaust noise. [< New Latin *resonator* < Latin *resonāre* to resonate]

**res|o|na|to|ry** (rez′ə nə tôr′ē, -tōr′-), *adj.* producing resonance.

**re|sorb** (ri sôrb′), *v.t., v.i.* to absorb again. [< Latin *resorbēre* < *re-* again + *sorbēre* drink in]

**re|sorb|ence** (ri sôr′bəns, -sōr′-), *n.* = reabsorption.

**re|sorb|ent** (ri sôr′bənt, -sōr′-), *adj.* absorbing again.

**res|or|cin** (rez ôr′sin), *n.* = resorcinol.

**res|or|cin|ol** (rez ôr′sə nol, -nōl), *n.* a crystalline compound used in medicine as an antiseptic and in making dyes and adhesives; metadihydroxybenzene. *Formula:* $C_6H_6O_2$ [< *res*(in) + *orcinol*]

**re|sorp|tion** (ri sôrp′shən), *n.* **1** the action or fact of resorbing. **2** the state of being resorbed. **3** the remelting and reabsorbing of a crystal by the molten magma in the formation of igneous rocks.

**re|sorp|tive** (ri sôrp′tiv), *adj.* having to do with or characterized by resorption.

**re|sort** (ri zôrt′), *v., n.* —*v.i.* **1** to go; go often: *Many people resort to the beaches in hot weather.* **2** to turn for help; have recourse (to): *to resort to violence. The mother resorted to punishment to make the child obey.*
—*n.* **1** an assembling; going to (a place, etc.) often: *A park is a place of popular resort in good weather.* **2** a place people go to, usually for recreation: *There are many summer resorts in the mountains.* **3** the act of turning for help; recourse: *The resort to force is forbidden in this*

*school.* **4** a person or thing turned to for help: *Books are her resort when she is lonely. Good friends are the best resort in trouble.*
[< Old French *resortir* < *re-* back + *sortir* go out] —**re|sort′er,** *n.*

**re|sound** (ri zound′), *v.i.* **1** go give back sound; echo: *The hills resounded when we shouted.* **2** to sound loudly: *Radios resound from every house.* **3** to be filled with sound: *The room resounded with the children's shouts.* **4** *Figurative.* to be much talked about: *The fame of the first flight across the Atlantic resounded all over the world.*
—*v.t.* **1** to give back (sound); echo: *The buildings resounded the siren's warning.* **2** *Figurative.* to repeat loudly; celebrate: *to resound a hero's praise.* [< Latin *resonāre;* see etym. under **resonate**] —**re|sound′er,** *n.*

**re-sound** (rē sound′), *v.t., v.i.* to sound again.

**re|sound|ing** (ri zoun′ding), *adj.* **1** that resounds; making an echoing sound; sounding loudly: *a resounding blow.* **2** ringing; sonorous: *resounding eloquence.* **3** impressive; striking: *a resounding victory.* —**re|sound′ing|ly,** *adv.*

**re|source** (ri sôrs′, -sōrs′; rē′sôrs, -sōrs), *n.* **1** any supply that will meet a need; stock or reserve upon which to draw when necessary. We have resources of money, of quick wit, or of strength. **2** any means of getting success or getting out of trouble: *Climbing a tree is a cat's resource when chased by a dog.* **3** skill in meeting difficulties or getting out of trouble: *Many of the early explorers were men of great resource.* **4** a possibility of aid or assistance.
**resources,** the actual and potential wealth of a country: *natural resources, human resources.*
[< French *resource,* earlier *resourse* < Old French *resourdre* to rally, to rise again < Latin *re-* again + *surgere* to rise]

**re|source|ful** (ri sôrs′fəl, -sōrs′-), *adj.* **1** good at thinking of ways to do things; quick-witted: *That resourceful boy mowed lawns all summer to earn enough money to buy a new bicycle.* **2** abounding in resources; rich: *The United States is a resourceful country.* —**re|source′ful|ly,** *adv.* —**re|source′ful|ness,** *n.*

**re|source|less** (ri sôrs′lis, -sōrs′; rē′sôrs-, -sōrs-), *adj.* without resource; lacking resources: *The creation of an artificial, resourceless, hapless, meaningless State—inexorably correcting itself* (Manchester Guardian). —**re|source′less|ly,** *adv.* —**re|source′less|ness,** *n.*

**re|sourc|es** (ri sôr′siz, -sōr′-; rē′sôr-, -sōr-), *n.pl.* See under **resource.**

**re|sow** (rē sō′), *v.t., v.i.,* **-sowed, -sown** or **-sowed, -sow|ing.** to sow again.

**resp.,** **1a** respective. **b** respectively. **2** respiration. **3** respondent.

**re|speak** (rē spēk′), *v.,* **-spoke, -spo|ken, -speak|ing.** *v.i.* to speak again: *I listened to the Prime Minister speak and respeak on subjects of which I have some knowledge* (Sunday Times). —*v.t.* to reecho; resound: *... the heavens shall bruit again, respeaking earthly thunder* (Shakespeare).

**re|spect** (ri spekt′), *n., v.* —*n.* **1** high regard; honor; esteem: *Children should show respect to those who are older and wiser.* SYN: reverence, veneration. **2** the condition of being esteemed or honored: *We hold the flag of our country in respect.* **3** care, consideration, or regard: *We should show respect for school buildings, parks, and other public property.* **4** a feature, point, matter, or detail: *This hasty plan is unwise in many respects.* SYN: particular. **5** relation; reference. **6** unfair consideration; partiality: *It is not good to have respect of persons in judgment* (Proverbs 24:23).
—*v.t.* **1** to feel or show honor or esteem for: *We respect an honest person.* **2** to care for; show consideration for: *Respect the ideas and feelings of others.* **3** to relate to; refer to; be connected with.
**in respect of,** with reference or comparison to: *The interest income ... will now in fact be equally free from tax in respect of approved contracts* (London Times).
**in respect that,** because of the fact that; since: *To a bad clergyman this may be an advantage, in respect that it allows him to remain bad* (William E. Gladstone).
**in respect to,** in relation, reference, or regard to (something): *It is generally agreed in Cambridge that Harvard would certainly not care to be in M.I.T.'s shoes in respect to involvement in government projects* (Christopher Rand).
**respects,** expressions of respect; regards: *Give her my respects. We must pay our respects to the governor.*
**with respect to,** with relation, reference, or regard to (something): *We must plan with respect to the future.*
[< Latin *respectus, -ūs* regard, (literally) a looking back < *respicere* look back, have regard for < *re-* back + *specere* to look. See etym. of doublet **respite.**] —**re|spect′er,** *n.*
—*Syn. n.* **3 Respect, regard** mean consideration for someone or something of recognized worth. **Respect** implies both recognition and esteem of worth with or without liking: *to treat an opponent with respect.* **Regard** implies recognition of worth, with the element of approval or disapproval specified: *It is difficult to respect someone for whose abilities one has small regard.*

**re|spect|a|bil|i|ty** (ri spek′tə bil′ə tē), *n., pl.* **-ties.** **1** the quality or condition of being respectable: *By maintaining a modicum of respectability ... they steer clear of harsher reprisals* (Newsweek). **2** respectable social standing. **3** respectable people, as a group: *Nearly the whole respectability of the town was either fussily marshalling processions or gazing down at them* (Arnold Bennett).

**re|spect|a|bil|ize** (ri spek′tə bə līz), *v.t.,* **-ized, -iz|ing.** to make respectable; consider or treat as respectable.

**re|spect|a|ble** (ri spek′tə bəl), *adj., n.* —*adj.* **1** worthy of respect; having a good reputation; honest and decent: *Respectable citizens obey the laws. His parents were poor but respectable people.* SYN: estimable. **2** fairly good; moderate in size or quality: *His record in school was always respectable but never brilliant.* **3** good enough to use; fit to be seen: *Though respectable, her clothes were certainly not stylish. That dirty dress is not respectable.*
—*n.* a respectable person: *Pleasance plays the husband as the abject dog beneath the good grey skin of a middle-aged respectable who has made his pile and lost his nerve* (Time). —**re|spect′a|ble|ness,** *n.*

**re|spect|a|bly** (ri spek′tə blē), *adv.* **1** in a respectable manner: *What a mother she was! ... Through what troubles she struggled to bring up her children respectably* (Mrs. J. H. Riddell). **2** moderately; pretty well.

**re|spect|ful** (ri spekt′fəl), *adj.* showing respect; considerate and polite: *He was always respectful to older people.* —**re|spect′ful|ly,** *adv.* —**re|spect′ful|ness,** *n.*

**re|spect|ing** (ri spek′ting), *prep.* regarding; about; concerning: *A discussion arose respecting the merits of different automobiles.*

**re|spec|tive** (ri spek′tiv), *adj.* belonging to each; particular; individual: *The classes went to their respective rooms.*

**re|spec|tive|ly** (ri spek′tiv lē), *adv.* as regards each one in his turn or in the order mentioned: *Bob, Dick, and Tom are 6, 8, and 10 years old respectively.*

**re|spects** (ri spekts′), *n.pl.* See under **respect.**

**re|spect|wor|thy** (ri spekt′wėr′ᴛʜē), *adj.,* **-thi|er, -thi|est.** worthy of respect; deserving respect.

**re|spell** (rē spel′), *v.t.* to spell over again, especially in another language or in a phonetic alphabet.

**re|spi|ce fi|nem** (res′pə sē fī′nem), *Latin.* consider the end; look to the end.

**re|spir|a|bil|i|ty** (rə spīr′ə bil′ə tē, res′pər-), *n.* the quality of being respirable.

**re|spir|a|ble** (ri spīr′ə bəl, res′pər-), *adj.* **1** that can be breathed. **2** able to breathe.

***res|pi|ra|tion** (res′pə rā′shən), *n.* **1** the act of inhaling and exhaling; breathing: *Her bad cold hinders her respiration. Of course, it is your breathing, or respiration, that gets the used air out of the air sacs in your lungs and takes in fresh air* (Beauchamp, Mayfield, and West). **2** *Biology.* the process by which an animal, plant, or living cell secures oxygen from the air or water, distributes it, combines it with food materials in the tissues to produce energy, and gives off carbon dioxide: *The remarkable thing about respiration is that it releases energy from food in living cells* (Heber W. Youngken).

**res|pi|ra|tor** (res′pə rā′tər), *n.* **1** a device, usually of gauze, worn over the nose and mouth to prevent inhaling harmful substances. **2** a device used to help a person breathe. Respirators are used by underwater swimmers and in giving artificial respiration.

**res|pi|ra|to|ry** (res′pər ə tôr′ē, -tōr′-; ri spīr′ə-), *adj.* having something to do with breathing or used for breathing. The lungs are respiratory organs.

**respiratory distress syndrome,** = hyaline membrane disease.

**respiratory enzyme,** an enzyme causing respiration in cells. Respiratory enzymes, such as oxidase, act on oxygen and the foods in the cells to produce energy.

**respiratory pigment,** any substance that carries oxygen in the blood, such as hemoglobin and hemocyanin: *It was further discovered that ... the respiratory pigment of blood is not identical with the haemoglobin in muscle cells that makes meat red* (H. Munro Fox).

**respiratory quotient,** the ratio of the volume of carbon dioxide released to that of oxygen consumed in a given period or interval.

**respiratory system,** the system of organs and passages by which air is taken into the body and carbon dioxide and oxygen are exchanged. In the human body the respiratory system includes the nasal cavities, pharynx, larynx, trachea, and the lungs.

**re|spire** (ri spīr′), *v.,* **-spired, -spir|ing.** —*v.i.* **1** to inhale and exhale; breathe. **2** *Figurative.* to breathe freely again, as after anxiety or trouble: *The Imperial City stands released From bondage threatened by the embattled East, and Christendom respires* (Wordsworth).
—*v.t.* to breathe in and out; inhale and exhale (as air or gas): (*Figurative.*) *I seemed to respire hope and comfort with the free air* (Washington Irving).
[< Latin *respīrāre* < *re-* back, again + *spīrāre* to breathe]

**res|pi|rom|e|ter** (res′pə rom′ə tər), *n.* a device for measuring the degree and nature of respiration.

**res|pi|ro|met|ric** (res′pə rō met′rik), *adj.* of or having to do with respirometry or the respirometer: *respirometric studies of fungi.*

**res|pi|rom|e|try** (res′pə rom′ə trē), *n.* **1** the measurement of the degree and nature of respiration. **2** the use of a respirometer.

***respiration**
definition 1

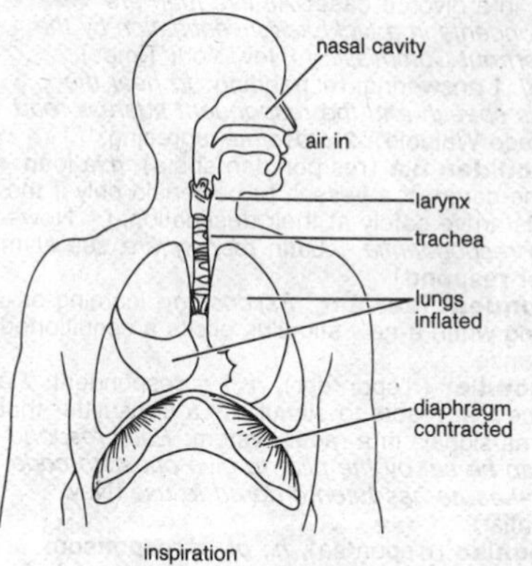

inspiration

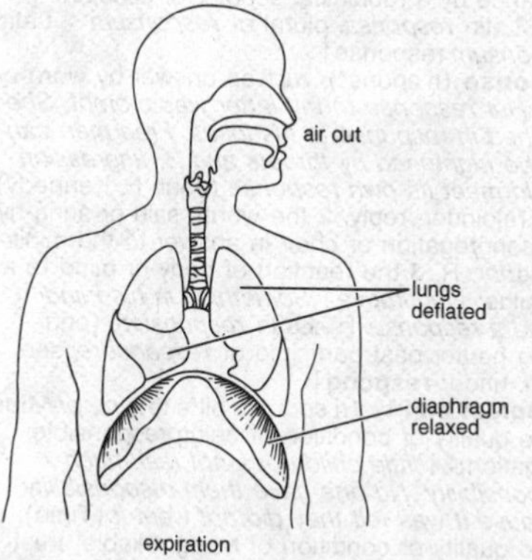

expiration

**res|pite** (res′pit), *n., v.,* **-pit|ed, -pit|ing.** —*n.* **1** a time of relief and rest; lull: *a respite from toil, a slight respite from the storm. A thick cloud brought a respite from the glare of the sun. The cold war goes on without respite.* **2** the act of putting off; delay, especially in carrying out a sentence of death; reprieve.
—*v.t.* **1** to give a respite to. **2** to put off; postpone.
[< Old French *respit* < Vulgar Latin *respectus* delay < Late Latin *respectus, -ūs* recourse, refuge < Latin, regard; (literally), a looking back. See etym. of doublet **respect.**]

**re|splend|ence** (ri splen′dəns), *n.* great brightness; gorgeous appearance; splendor.

**re|splend|en|cy** (ri splen′dən sē), *n.* = resplendence.

**re|splend|ent** (ri splen′dənt), *adj.* very bright; shining; splendid: *the resplendent rays of the sun, a face resplendent with joy. The queen was resplendent with jewels.* [< Latin *resplendēns,*

*-entis,* present participle of *resplendēre* to glitter < *re-* back + *splendēre* to shine] — **re|splend′ent|ly,** *adv.*

**re|spoke** (rē spōk′), *v.* the past tense of **respeak.**

**re|spo|ken** (rē spō′kən), *v.* the past participle of **respeak.**

**re|spond** (ri spond′), *v., n.* — ***v.i.*** **1** to answer; reply in words: *He responded briefly to the question.* SYN: See syn. under **answer. 2** to act in answer; react: *A dog responds to kind treatment by loving its master. She responded quickly to the medicine and was well in a few days.* **3** *U.S.* to give legal satisfaction.
— ***n.*** **1** a response made in church. *Abbr:* R. **2** a half pillar or the like engaged in a wall to support an arch.
[< Old French *respondre* < Latin *respondēre* < *re-* back + *spondēre* to promise]

**re|spon′de|at su|pe|ri|or** (ri spon′dē at sù pir′ē ôr), *Latin.* **1** a phrase used to express the doctrine that the principal is responsible for the acts of his agents when done within the scope of their employment. **2** (literally) let the principal answer.

**re|spond|ence** (ri spon′dəns), *n.* **1** = response. **2** *Obsolete.* an agreement.

**re|spond|en|cy** (ri spon′dən sē), *n., pl.* **-cies.** = respondence.

**re|spond|ent** (ri spon′dənt), *n., adj.* — ***n.*** **1** a person who responds. **2** *Law.* a defendant, especially in a divorce case: *All five men are respondents in a kickback investigation by the Waterfront Commission* (New York Times).
— ***adj.*** **1** answering; responding: *to hear the king's speech and the respondent address read* (Horace Walpole). **2** *Obsolete.* agreeing.

**res|pon|den|ti|a** (res′pon den′shē ə), *n.* a loan on the cargo of a vessel, to be repaid only if the goods arrive safely at their destination. [< New Latin *respondentia* < Latin *respondēre;* see etym. under **respond**]

**respondent learning,** *Psychology.* learning occurring when a new stimulus elicits a conditioned response.

**re|spond|er** (ri spon′dər), *n.* **1** = respondent. **2** a device that reacts to stimuli, as a transmitter that returns signals in a radar system: *Each responder can be set by the pilot to give out such code signal as he has been ordered to use* (New Scientist).

**re|spon|sa** (ri spon′sə), *n., pl. of* **responsum.** answers to questions involving Jewish law and observance by a rabbinical scholar or scholars. [< New Latin *responsa,* plural of *responsum* < Latin *respōnsum* response]

**re|sponse** (ri spons′), *n.* **1** an answer by word or act: *Her response to my letter was prompt. She laughed in response to his jokes. Free men cannot be frightened by threats and ... aggression would meet its own response* (John F. Kennedy). SYN: rejoinder, reply. **2** the words said or sung by the congregation or choir in answer to the minister. *Abbr:* R. **3** the reaction of body or mind to a stimulus: (*Figurative.*) *Something in his mind found a response.* [< Latin *respōnsum,* (originally) neuter past participle of *respondēre;* see etym. under **respond**]

**re|spon|si|bil|i|ty** (ri spon′sə bil′ə tē), *n., pl.* **-ties. 1** the quality or condition of being responsible; obligation: *A little child does not feel much responsibility. No one gave them responsibility because it was felt they did not want it* (Time). **2** the quality or condition of being reliable; trustworthiness. **3** a person or thing for which one is responsible: *Keeping house and caring for the children are the responsibilities of most mothers.*

**re|spon|si|ble** (ri spon′sə bəl), *adj., n.* — ***adj.*** **1** obliged or expected to account (for, to); accountable; answerable. *Each pupil is responsible for the care of the books given him. The people had given him his command, and to the people alone he was responsible* (James A. Froude). **2** deserving credit or blame: *The bad weather is responsible for the small attendance. Who is responsible for all these changes?* **3** trustworthy; reliable: *The club chose a responsible member to take care of its money.* **4** involving obligation or duties: *The President holds the most responsible position in our country.* **5** able to tell right from wrong; able to think and act reasonably: *Insane people are not responsible.* **6** able to discharge obligations or pay debts: *responsible tenants.*
— ***n.*** **1** a person of responsibility. **2** an actor who undertakes to play any part which may be temporarily required: *Hearing that one of their 'responsibles' had just left, I went straight to the manager ... and was accepted* (Jerome K. Jerome). — **re|spon′si|ble|ness,** *n.*

**re|spon|si|bly** (ri spon′sə blē), *adv.* in a responsible manner.

**re|spon|sion** (ri spon′shən), *n.* = response.

**responsions,** (at Oxford University) the first examination that candidates for the degree of B.A. are required to pass; smalls.
[< Latin *respōnsiō, -ōnis* < *respondēre;* see etym. under **respond**]

**re|spon|sive** (ri spon′siv), *adj.* **1** making answer; responding: *a responsive glance.* **2** easily moved; responding readily: *a very friendly person with a responsive nature, to be responsive to kindness.* **3** using or containing responses: *responsive reading in church in which minister and congregation read in turn.* **4** corresponding. — **re|spon′sive|ly,** *adv.* — **re|spon′sive|ness,** *n.*

**re|spon|so|ry** (ri spon′sər ē), *n., pl.* **-ries.** a response in church music, especially an anthem sung by a soloist and choir, following a reading from the Bible. [< Late Latin *respōnsōria* < Latin *respondēre;* see etym. under **respond**]

**re|spon|sum** (ri spon′səm), *n., pl.* **-sa.** one of the responsa: *A responsum ... consists of a judgment usually revolving around a concrete problem in the commercial, social, moral, or religious sphere* (New Scientist).

**re|spray** (rē sprā′), *v., n.* — ***v.t.*** to spray again, as with paint: *A motorist seldom gets his car resprayed just for the sake of changing the colour* (Sunday Telegraph).
— ***n.*** a respraying: *A motor car may need both a new camshaft and a respray* (New Scientist).

**res pu|bli|ca** (rēz pub′lə kə), *Latin.* the republic; the State.

**res|sen|ti|ment** (rə säɴ tē män′), *n. French.* **1** a generalized feeling of resentment held by a group of people against those of another group, usually of a higher economic level: *It is the position of the lower middle class: moralistic and punitive, filled with what Nietzsche called ressentiment* (Atlantic). **2** (literally) resentment.

***rest[1]** (rest), *n., v.* — ***n.*** **1** a state of quiet and ease; sleep; repose: *The children had a good night's rest.* **2** ease after work or effort; freedom from activity: *The workmen were allowed an hour for rest. The seventh day is the sabbath of rest ... ye shall do no work therein* (Leviticus 23:3). **3** freedom from anything that tires, troubles, disturbs, or pains; respite: *The medicine gave the sick man a short rest from pain.* **4a** an absence of motion; stillness: *The driver brought the car to a rest.* **b** inactivity of growth or development; dormant state or condition. **5** a support; something to lean on: *a headrest, a rest for a billiard cue.* **6** a place for resting: *a rest for sailors, a travelers' rest.* **7** *Music.* **a** a silence of definite length between tones. **b** a mark to show such a silence. **8** a short pause in reading; caesura. **9** death; the grave. [Old English *reste, ræste*]
— ***v.i.*** **1** to be still or quiet; sleep: *My mother rests for an hour every afternoon. Lie down and rest.* **2** to be free from work, effort, care, or trouble: *Schoolteachers can rest in the summer. And on the seventh day God ended his work ... and he rested on the seventh day from all his work* (Genesis 2:2). **3** to stop moving; come to rest; stop: *The ball rested at the bottom of the hill.* **4** to lie, recline, sit, or lean, for rest or ease: *He spent the whole day resting in a chair. The younger ones ... think that now the country is free, it can rest on its oars* (New Yorker). **5** to be supported; lean: *The ladder rests against the wall. The roof rests on columns.* **6** to look; be fixed: *Our eyes rested on the open book.* **7** to be at ease: *Don't let her rest until she promises to visit us.* **8** to be or become inactive: *Let the matter rest.* **9** to depend (on); rely (on); trust (in); be based: *Our hope rests on you.* **10** to be found; be present; lie: *In a democracy, government rests with the people. A smile rested on her lips.* **11** to be dead; lie in the grave: *The old man rests at last with his forefathers in the old village cemetery.* **12** *Law.* to end voluntarily the introduction of evidence in a case: *The state rests.* **13** (of agricultural land) to be unused for crops, especially in order to restore fertility.
— ***v.t.*** **1** to give rest to; refresh by rest: *Stop and rest your horse. It rests one's feet to take off one's shoes. Is my boy, God rest his soul, alive or dead?* (Shakespeare). **2** to cause to stop moving. **3** to let remain inactive: *Rest the matter there.* **4** to place for support; lay; lean: *to rest one's head on a pillow. He rested his rake against the fence. Straight he took his bow of ashtree, On the sand one end he rested* (Longfellow). **5** to cause to rely or depend; base: *We rest our hope on you.* **6** to fix (as the eyes): *She rested her eyes on him steadily* (Henry James). **7** to end voluntarily the introduction of evidence in (a case at law): *The lawyer rested his case.*
**at rest, a** asleep: *What Sir, not yet at rest? the king's abed* (Shakespeare). **b** not moving: *The lake was at rest.* **c** free, as from pain or trouble: *The injured man is now at rest.* **d** dead: *Welcome the hour, my aged limbs Are laid with thee at rest!* (Robert Burns).
**lay to rest,** to bury: *Lay his bones to rest.*
**rest up,** to get a thorough rest: *New Yorkers are all home or out of town today resting up for another week of the greatest city in the world* (New York Times).
[Old English *restan*]

***rest[1]**
definition 7b

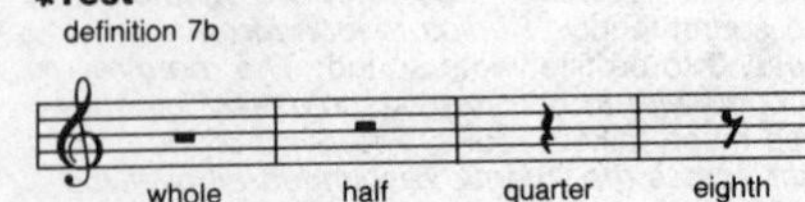


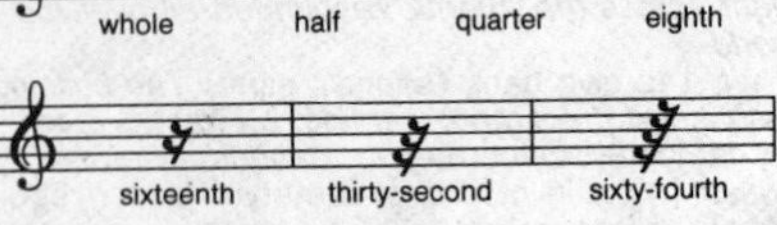


**rest[2]** (rest), *n., v.* — ***n.*** **1** what is left; those that are left; remainder: *The sun was out in the morning but it clouded over at noon and rained for the rest of the day. One horse was running ahead of the rest.* **2** *British.* the reserve or surplus funds of a bank, especially of the Bank of England.
— ***v.i.*** to continue to be; remain: *You may rest assured that I will keep my promise. The final decision rests with father.*
[< Middle French *reste* < *rester* to remain < Latin *restāre* be left < *re-* back + *stāre* to stand]

**rest[3]** (rest), *n.* a support for the butt of a lance attached to the breastplate or cuirass in medieval armor. A knight set his lance in rest as he prepared to charge the enemy: *Each ready lance is in the rest* (Scott). [short for Middle English *arest* arrest, noun; perhaps influenced by *rest[1]*]

**re|staff** (rē staf′, -stäf′), *v.t.* to staff again with new personnel.

**re|stage** (rē stāj′), *v.t.,* **-staged, -stag|ing. 1** to stage again or in a new way: *Antony Tudor ... consented to restage four of his most famous ballets for the Ballet Theatre* (New York Times). **2** to reenact (an event).

**re|start** (*v.* rē stärt′; *n.* rē′stärt′), *v., n.* — ***v.t., v.i.*** to start again; recommence: *The trial restarts on January 19* (Manchester Guardian Weekly).
— ***n.*** a fresh start; recommencement.

**re|start|a|ble** (rē stär′tə bəl), *adj.* that can be restarted: *a restartable rocket engine.*

**re|state** (rē stāt′), *v.t.,* **-stat|ed, -stat|ing. 1** to state again or anew. **2** to state in a new way.

**re|state|ment** (rē stāt′mənt), *n.* **1** the act of stating again. **2** a statement made again: *But once in a while there is a need for a summing up, or a restatement of belief* (Time). **3** a new statement.

**res|tau|rant** (res′tər ənt, -tə ränt), *n.* a place to buy and eat a meal. [American English < French *restaurant,* (originally) present participle of Old French *restaurer* to restore < Latin *restaurāre*]

**res|tau|ra|teur** (res′tə rə tėr′), *n.* the keeper of a restaurant. [< French *restaurateur* < Old French *restaurer;* see etym. under **restaurant**]

**rest cure,** a treatment for nervous disorders consisting of a complete rest, usually combined with systematic feeding, massage, and other regimen.

**re|ster|il|ize** (rē ster′ə līz), *v.t.,* **-lized, -liz|ing.** to sterilize again.

**res|tes** (res′tēz), *n.* plural of **restis.**

**rest|ful** (rest′fəl), *adj.* **1** full of rest; giving rest: *She had a restful nap.* **2** quiet; peaceful: *a restful view of the countryside.* — **rest′ful|ly,** *adv.* — **rest′ful|ness,** *n.*

**rest|har|row** (rest′har′ō), *n.* any one of a group of low European herbs or shrubs of the pea family, with pink, white, or yellow flowers and tough roots. [< *rest[3]* + *harrow*]

**rest home, 1** a place where old people are cared for; old-age home. **2** a convalescent or nursing home.

**rest|house** (rest′hous′), *n.* **1** a boarding house or inn for persons requiring rest and recreation. **2** (in India) a building in which travelers can obtain rest and shelter.

**res|tif** (res′tif), *adj. Archaic.* restive.

**res|ti|form** (res′tə fôrm), *adj.* cordlike. [< New Latin *restiformis* < Latin *restis* a cord + *forma* form]

**restiform body,** one of a pair of large, cordlike bundles of nerve fibers lying one on each side of the medulla oblongata and connecting it with the cerebellum.

**re|stim|u|late** (rē stim′yə lāt), *v.t.,* **-lat|ed, -lat|ing.** to stimulate anew. — **re|stim′u|la′tion,** *n.*

**rest|ing** (res′ting), *adj.* **1** dormant, as spores, especially of algae and fungi, that can germinate only after a period of dormancy. **2** (of cells) not dividing or preparing to divide: *When a cell is not dividing or preparing to divide it is said to be in the resting stage* (A. M. Winchester).

**res|tis** (res′tis), *n., pl.* **res|tes.** = restiform body.

**res|ti|tute** (res′tə tüt, -tyüt), *v.,* **-tut|ed, -tut|ing.** — ***v.t.*** **1** to give back (something lost or taken). **2** to make good (loss, damage, or injury).
— ***v.i.*** to make restitution: *If ... he acts to the detriment of someone's interest, he must be*

*compelled to restitute* (Westminster Gazette). [< Latin *restituere;* see etym. under **restitution**]

**res|ti|tu|ti|o in in|te|grum** (res tə tü′shē ō in in′ti grəm), *Latin.* restoration in its entirety to the previous condition (used in law when a court annuls a transaction or contract and orders the restoration of what has been received or given).

**res|ti|tu|tion** (res′tə tü′shən, -tyü′-), *n.* **1** the giving back of what has been lost or taken away: *Charlemagne tried to enforce the restitution of the Roman lands.* **SYN:** return, restoration. **2** the act of making good any loss, damage, or injury: *It is only fair that those who do the damage should make restitution.* **SYN:** reparation, amends. **3** *Physics.* the return of an elastic body to its original form or position when released from strain. [< Latin *restitūtiō, -ōnis* < *restituere* restore, rebuild, replace < *re-* again + *statuere* to set up < *stāre* to stand]

**res|ti|tu|tive** (res′tə tü′tiv, -tyü′-), *adj.* having to do with restitution.

**re|stit|u|to|ry** (ri stit′yə tôr′ē, -tōr′-), *adj.* = restitutive.

**res|tive** (res′tiv), *adj.* **1** restless; uneasy: *a restive audience. A restive, resurgent Germany, ten years after the abyss of total defeat ...* (Newsweek). **2** hard to manage: *a restive child.* **SYN:** intractable, refractory. **3** refusing to go ahead; balky: *a restive mule.* [< Old French *restif, restive* motionless < *rester* rest² < Latin *restāre*] —**res′tive|ly,** *adv.* —**res′tive|ness,** *n.*

**rest|less** (rest′lis), *adj.* **1** unable to rest; uneasy: *The dog seemed restless, as if he sensed some danger.* **2** without rest or sleep; not restful: *The sick child passed a restless night.* **3** rarely or never still or quiet; always moving: *That nervous boy is very restless.* **4** preventing rest: *Ease to the body some, none to the mind From restless thoughts* (Milton). —**rest′less|ly,** *adv.* —**rest′less-ness,** *n.*

**restless cavy,** the wild guinea pig.

**rest mass,** *Physics.* the mass, such as of an atom or electron, when it is at a low velocity or when regarded as not being in motion.

**re|stock** (rē stok′), *v.t., v.i.* to supply with a new stock; replenish.

**re|stor|a|ble** (ri stôr′ə bəl, -stōr′-), *adj.* that can be restored.

**re|stor|al** (ri stôr′əl, -stōr′-), *n.* the act or process of restoring; restoration.

**res|to|ra|tion** (res′tə rā′shən), *n.* **1** the act or process of restoring; bringing back to a former or normal condition: *the restoration of health, the restoration of a king, the restoration of peace after war.* **2** the fact or condition of being restored; recovery: *a restoration from sickness.* **3** something restored, such as a representation of the original form of an ancient structure or extinct animal: *The house we slept in was a restoration of a colonial mansion.*

**Res|to|ra|tion** (res′tə rā′shən), *n.* **1** the reestablishment of the monarchy in 1660 under Charles II of England. **2** the period from 1660 to 1688 in England, during which Charles II and James II reigned.

**Restoration comedy,** the comedy of manners, marked by wit and social satire, that flourished in England during the Restoration period.

**res|to|ra|tion|ism** (res′tə rā′shə niz əm), *n.* doctrines or belief of the restorationists.

**res|to|ra|tion|ist** (res′tə rā′shə nist), *n.* **1** a person who believes in the doctrine of the final restoration of all men to a state of happiness and the favor of God. **2** a person who restores old or dilapidated buildings.

**Res|to|ra|tion|ist** (res′tə rā′shə nist), *adj.* of or having to do with the English Restoration or with Restoration comedy.

**re|stor|a|tive** (ri stôr′ə tiv, -stōr′-), *adj., n.* —*adj.* capable of restoring; tending to restore health or strength: *a restorative medicine.*
—*n.* something that restores health, strength, or consciousness: *Ammonia is used as a restorative when a person has fainted.* —**re|stor′a|tive|ly,** *adv.* —**re|stor′a|tive|ness,** *n.*

**re|store** (ri stôr′, -stōr′), *v.t.,* **-stored, -stor|ing.** **1** to bring back; establish again: *The police restored order.* **2** to bring back to a former condition or to a normal condition: *to restore a painting, to restore a person to consciousness. The old house has been restored. He is restored to health. The Bishops were restored to their seats in the Upper House* (Macaulay). **SYN:** See syn. under **renew. 3** to give back; put back: *to restore a book to the proper shelf. The honest boy restored the money he had found to its owner.* **4** *Obsolete.* to compensate for: *But if the while I think on thee, dear friend, all losses are restored and sorrows end* (Shakespeare). [< Old French *restorer* < Latin *restaurāre*] —**re|stor′er,** *n.*

**re|stow** (rē stō′), *v.t.* to stow again; repack: *The two astronauts ... were busy restowing all of the gear in their cabin* (New York Times).

**rest period, 1** a short period during working hours for rest, relaxation, or amusement, as in a factory, school, or military base. **2** *Botany.* a period in which a plant is inactive or does not grow.

**restr.,** restaurant.

**re|strain** (ri strān′), *v.t.* **1** to hold back; keep down; keep in check; keep within limits: *She could not restrain her curiosity to see what was in the box. He restrained the excited dog when guests came. History shows that very few rulers restrained their powers of their own accord. We no longer have "disturbed wards" and it's a rare case when we have to restrain anyone* (Wall Street Journal). **SYN:** detain, repress, curb. See syn. under **check. 2** to keep in prison; confine. [< Old French *restreindre, restraindre* < Latin *restringere;* see etym. under **restrict**] —**re|strain′a|ble,** *adj.*

**re|strain|ed|ly** (ri strā′nid lē, -strānd′-), *adv.* in a restrained manner; with restraint: *These and the other like precepts of our Saviour, are not to be taken strictly, but restrainedly* (William Burkitt).

**re|strain|er** (ri strā′nər), *n.* **1** a person or thing that restrains. **2** a chemical, such as potassium bromide, added to a photographic developer to slow down its action.

**re|strain|ing circle** (ri strā′ning), a circle on a basketball court, having a diameter of 12 feet and containing the center circle.

**restraining order,** *U.S.* an order issued by a law court enjoining a person or group to stop all action or proceedings until an injunction applied for is granted or denied: *The Government's application for a temporary restraining order to prevent the merger was denied by the court* (Wall Street Journal).

**re|straint** (ri strānt′), *n.* **1** the act of restraining; holding back or hindering from action or motion: *Noisy children sometimes need restraint.* **SYN:** restriction, check, curb. **2** the condition of being restrained; confinement: *Restraint is for the savage, the rapacious, the violent: not for the just, the gentle, the benevolent* (Herbert Spencer). **3** a means of restraining: *They threw off all restraints, conventions, pretences* (Arnold Bennett). **4** a tendency to restrain natural feeling; reserve: *He was very angry but he spoke with restraint.* [< Old French *restrainte* < *restraindre;* see etym. under **restrain**]

**restraint of trade,** any limitation or prevention of free competition in business, as by creating a monopoly, fixing prices, or limiting markets.

**re|strict** (ri strikt′), *v.t.* **1** to keep within limits; confine: *Our club membership is restricted to twelve. His activities were restricted by old age.* **2** to put limitations on: *to restrict the meaning of a word.* [< Latin *restrictus,* past participle of *restringere* < *re-* back + *stringere* draw tight]

**re|strict|ed** (ri strik′tid), *adj.* **1** kept within limits; limited: *She is on a restricted diet and can have no sweets.* **2** having restrictions or limiting rules: *Factories may not be built in this restricted residential section. The restricted shares would be convertible into unrestricted parent company common* (Wall Street Journal). **3** limited to certain groups (a euphemism for a policy, especially of social discrimination on an ethnic or religious basis). —**re|strict′ed|ly,** *adv.*

**re|stric|tion** (ri strik′shən), *n.* **1** something that restricts; limiting condition or rule: *The restrictions on the use of the playground are: no fighting; no damaging property.* **2** the act or fact of restricting or the condition of being restricted: *This park is open to the public without restriction.*

**restriction enzyme** or **endonuclease,** an enzyme that cleaves the DNA strands of a species at a specific site which matches the DNA fragment of another species cut by the same enzyme, enabling segments of DNA from different sources to be joined in new combinations: *A recently discovered class of enzymes called "restriction enzymes" has made gene insertions possible, but ... has also created potential biohazards* (Science News).

**re|stric|tion|ism** (ri strik′shə niz əm), *n.* the practice or policy of setting up restrictions, especially on import trade.

**re|stric|tion|ist** (ri strik′shə nist), *n., adj.* —*n.* a person in favor of restrictions, especially one who advocates the limitation of imports.
—*adj.* having to do with restrictionism.

**re|stric|tive** (ri strik′tiv), *adj., n.* —*adj.* restricting; limiting: *Some laws are prohibitive; some are only restrictive.*
—*n.* a restrictive word or expression: *In English, what thickens the confusion, is the indeterminate character of the restrictives,* alone *and* only (Jeremy Bentham). —**re|stric′tive|ly,** *adv.* —**restric′tive|ness,** *n.*

**restrictive clause,** a subordinate clause that qualifies the noun it modifies so definitely that it cannot be left out without changing the meaning of the sentence. *Example:* All employees *who have been with this firm for five years* will receive bonuses.
▶Notice that the restrictive clause in the sentence above is not set off by commas; a nonrestrictive clause is: *John Jones, who has been with the firm for five years, will receive a Christmas bonus.*

**restrictive covenant,** *U.S.* an agreement among property owners in a given area to restrict the use of land or the kind of residents, especially as to ethnic origin or religion.

**restrictive endorsement,** *Commerce.* an endorsement limiting the transfer or negotiability of a check or other instrument. A check signed "Pay to ___ only" is a restrictive endorsement.

**re|strike** (*v.* rē strīk′; *n.* rē′strīk′), *v.,* **-struck, -strik|ing,** *n.* —*v.t.* **1** to strike again. **2** to stamp (a coin) again, especially with a different impression.
—*n.* an impression, such as of a coin, medal, woodcut, or etching, made from a plate, die, or similar source that has already been used; a second or subsequent impression: *I was studying the framed Cézanne etching, in an effort to determine, beneath its dusty glass, the vintage and source of the restrike* (Atlantic).

**re|string** (rē string′), *v.t.,* **-strung, -string|ing.** to put a new string or new strings on: *to restring beads on a necklace.*

**rest room,** *U.S.* a room in a public building with toilet facilities; lavatory.

**re|struc|ture** (rē struk′chər), *v.t., v.i.,* **-tured, -tur|ing.** to structure anew; rearrange; reorganize: *Thinking is a guided process of restructuring a problem situation until it takes on the configuration of a solution* (Scientific American).

**re|stud|y** (rē stud′ē), *n., pl.* **-stud|ies,** *v.t.,* **-stud-ied, -stud|y|ing.** —*n.* a new study: *Another part of the new program, he said, includes a restudy of merchandising techniques* (Wall Street Journal).
—*v.t.* to study anew.

**re|style** (rē stīl′), *v.t.,* **-styled, -styl|ing.** to change the style of; redesign.

**re|sub|ject** (rē′səb jekt′), *v.t.* to subdue again. —**re′sub|jec′tion,** *n.*

**re|sub|mit** (rē′səb mit′), *v.t.,* **-mit|ted, -mit|ting.** to submit again, as for consideration or judgment: *The President planned to resubmit other important proposals that the last Democratic Congress failed to adopt* (Newsweek).

**re|sult** (ri zult′), *n., v.* —*n.* **1** that which happens because of something; what is caused; outcome: *The result of the fall was a broken leg.* **SYN:** consequence. See syn. under **effect. 2** a good or useful result: *We want results, not talk.* **3** a quantity or value obtained by calculation. [< verb]
—*v.i.* **1** to be a result; follow as a consequence: *Sickness often results from eating too much.* **2** to have as a result; end: *Eating too much often results in sickness.*
[< Latin *resultāre* to rebound (frequentative) < *resilīre* rebound; see etym. under **resilient**] —**result′less,** *adj.*

✱**re|sult|ant** (ri zul′tənt), *adj., n.* —*adj.* that results; resulting.
—*n.* **1** = result. **2** *Physics.* a vector, representing force, velocity, or other factor, having the same effect as and being the sum of two or more vectors. —**re|sult′ant|ly,** *adv.*

**✱resultant**
definition 2

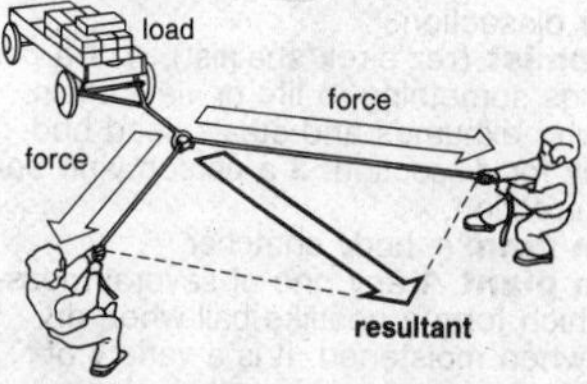


**re|sult|ful** (ri zult′fəl), *adj.* fruitful; effective. —**result′ful|ly,** *adv.*

**re|sume¹** (ri züm′), *v.,* **-sumed, -sum|ing.** —*v.t.* **1** to begin again; go on: *Resume reading where we left off.* **2** to get or take again: *Those standing may resume their seats.* **3** to take back: *concessions which the sovereign had freely made and might at his pleasure resume* (Macaulay). —*v.i.* to begin again; continue. [< Latin *resūmere* < *re-* again + *sūmere* take up]

**Pronunciation Key:** hat, āge, cãre, fär; let, ēqual, tėrm, it, īce, hot, ōpen, ôrder; **oil, out;** cup, pu̇t, rüle; **child;** long; thin, ᴛʜen; **zh,** measure; **ə** represents **a** in about, **e** in taken, **i** in pencil, **o** in lemon, **u** in circus.

—re|sum′a|ble, *adj.* —re|sum′er, *n.*

**rés|u|mé** or **res|u|me²** (rez′ù mā′, rez′ə mā), *n.* **1** a summary: *a résumé of a book.* **2** *U.S.* a biographical summary, especially of a person's education and professional career: *a résumé of a person's education.* [< French *résumé,* noun use of past participle of Middle French *résumer* to resume, learned borrowing from Latin *resūmere*]

**re|sump|tion** (ri zump′shən), *n.* **1** the act of resuming: *the resumption of duties after absence.* **2** *U.S. History.* the return to specie payments by the government: *The Resumption Act of 1875 provided for resumption on January 1, 1879.* [< Late Latin *resumptiō, -ōnis* < Latin *resūmere;* see etym. under **resume¹**]

**re|sump|tive** (ri zump′tiv), *adj.* **1** tending to resume. **2** that summarizes. —**re|sump′tive|ly,** *adv.*

**res u|ni|ver|si|ta|tis** (rēz yü′nə vėr′sə tā′tis), *Latin.* **1** places of common access, as the churches and parks of a city. **2** (literally) things of the community.

**re|su|pi|nate** (ri sü′pə nāt), *adj. Botany.* bent backward; inverted; appearing as if upside down. [< Latin *resupīnātus,* past participle of *resupīnāre* < *resupīnus;* see etym. under **resupine**]

**re|su|pi|na|tion** (ri sü′pə nā′shən), *n. Botany.* a resupinate condition; inversion of parts.

**re|su|pine** (rē′sü pīn′), *adj.* lying on the back; supine. [< Latin *resupīnus* < *re-* back + *supīnus* supine, lying on the back]

**re|sup|ply** (rē′sə plī′), *v.,* **-plied, -ply|ing,** *n., pl.* **-plies.** —*v.t.* to supply again or anew; provide with a fresh supply.
—*n.* a fresh supply.

**re|sur|face** (rē sėr′fis), *v.,* **-faced, -fac|ing.** —*v.t.* to provide with a new or different surface.
—*v.i.* to surface again; reappear: *One young woman resurfaced from the darkness ..., clutching her garments* (Time).

**re|sur|gam** (ri sėr′gam), *Latin.* I shall rise again.

**re|surge** (ri sėrj′), *v.i.,* **-surged, -surg|ing.** to rise again: *The reason Explorer I's apparently dead radio resurged to life ... was reported* (Science News Letter). [< Latin *resurgere* < *re-* again + *surgere* to rise]

**re|sur|gence** (ri sėr′jəns), *n.* a rising again: *a resurgence of interest, a resurgence of friendship.*

**re|sur|gent** (ri sėr′jənt), *adj., n.* —*adj.* rising or tending to rise again: *A restive, resurgent Germany, ten years after the abyss of total defeat ...* (Newsweek).
—*n.* a person who has risen again.

**res|ur|rect** (rez′ə rekt′), *v.t.* **1** to raise from the dead; bring back to life. **2** *Figurative.* to bring back to sight or into use: *to resurrect an old custom.* **3** to take out of a grave. [back formation < *resurrection*]

**res|ur|rec|tion** (rez′ə rek′shən), *n.* **1** the act or fact of coming to life again; rising from the dead. **2** the state of being alive again after death. **3** *Figurative.* a restoration, as from decay or disuse; revival. [< Latin *resurrēctiō, -ōnis* < *resurgere* < *re-* again + *surgere* to rise]

**Res|ur|rec|tion** (rez′ə rek′shən), *n.* the rising again of Christ after His death and burial.

**res|ur|rec|tion|al** (rez′ə rek′shə nəl), *adj.* of or having to do with resurrection.

**res|ur|rec|tion|ar|y** (rez′ə rek′shə ner′ē), *adj.* **1** having to do with or of the nature of resurrection. **2** having to do with resurrectionism.

**res|ur|rec|tion|ism** (rez′ə rek′shə niz əm), *n.* the practice of exhuming and stealing dead bodies, especially for dissection.

**res|ur|rec|tion|ist** (rez′ə rek′shə nist), *n.* **1** a person who brings something to life or view again. **2** a person who exhumes and steals dead bodies, especially for dissection. **3** a person who believes in resurrection.

**resurrection man,** = body snatcher.

**resurrection plant, 1** any one of several mosslike plants which form a nestlike ball when dry and expand when moistened. It is a variety of selaginella. **2** any one of various other plants having the same property, such as the rose of Jericho or one of the fig marigolds.

**res|ur|rec|tive** (rez′ə rek′tiv), *adj.* causing resurrection; bringing the dead to life.

**re|sur|vey** (*v.* rē′sər vā′; *n.* rē sėr′vā), *v., n.* —*v.t.* **1** to examine over again: *to resurvey a problem.* **2** to survey (as land) again.
—*n.* a new survey.

**re|sus|ci|ta|ble** (ri sus′ə tə bəl), *adj.* that can be resuscitated.

**re|sus|ci|tate** (ri sus′ə tāt), *v.,* **-tat|ed, -tat|ing.** —*v.t.* **1** to bring back to life or consciousness; revive: *The doctor resuscitated the man who was overcome by gas.* **2** *Figurative.* to renew or restore (a thing). —*v.i.* to come to life or consciousness again; revive. [< Latin *resuscitāre* (with English *-ate*[1]) < *re-* again + *sub-* (from) under + *citāre* to rouse (frequentative) < *ciēre* stir up]

**re|sus|ci|ta|tion** (ri sus′ə tā′shən), *n.* **1** restoration to life or consciousness. **2** *Figurative.* restoration.

**re|sus|ci|ta|tive** (ri sus′ə tā′tiv), *adj.* helping to resuscitate.

**re|sus|ci|ta|tor** (ri sus′ə tā′tər), *n.* **1** a device used to treat asphyxiation by forcing oxygen into the lungs: *It consists of a resuscitator which weighs only 28 lbs. and so can be taken to the scene of emergency* (New Scientist). **2** a person who resuscitates.

**ret** (ret), *v.t.,* **ret|ted, ret|ting.** to expose (as flax or hemp) to moisture or soak in water, in order to soften by partial rotting. [probably < Middle Dutch *reten*]

**ret., 1** retard. **2** retired. **3** returned.

**re|ta|ble** (ri tā′bəl), *n.* a shelf, as for lights or flowers, or the frame for a picture, or the like, above and behind an altar. [< French *rétable* < Spanish *retablo,* adaptation of Catalan *retaule,* earlier *reataula* < *rea-* behind (< Latin *retrō-*) + *taula* table < Latin *tabula* tablet]

**re|tail** (*n., adj., adv., v.t. 1, v.i.* rē′tāl; *v.t. 2* ri tāl′), *n., adj., adv., v.* —*n.* the sale of goods in small quantities at a time, directly to the consumer: *Our grocer buys at wholesale and sells at retail.*
—*adj.* **1** in small lots or quantities: *The wholesale price of this coat is $20; the retail price is $30.* **2** selling in small quantities: *a retail merchant, the retail trade.*
—*adv.* at a retail price: *to sell retail.*
—*v.t.* **1** to sell in small quantities: *to retail dresses.* **2** to tell over again; repeat the particulars of to others: *She retails everything she hears about her acquaintances.*
—*v.i.* to be sold in small quantities or at retail: *This radio retails for $14.95.*
[< Old French *retaille* scrap < *retaillier* cut up < *re-* back + *taillier* to cut < Late Latin *tāliāre* < Latin *tālea* rod]

**re|tail|er** (rē′tā lər), *n.* a retail merchant or dealer: *The task of holding thousands of retailers to the agreement that they will observe minimum list prices is well nigh impossible* (Newsweek).

**re|tail|ing** (rē′tā ling), *n.* the business of selling goods at retail.

**retail store,** *U.S.* a store selling items in small quantities directly to the consumer.

**re|tain** (ri tān′), *v.t.* **1** to continue to have or hold; keep: *China dishes retain heat longer than metal pans do. The old lady has retained all her interest in life.* SYN: See syn. under **keep. 2** to keep in mind; remember: *She retained the tune but not the words of the song.* **3** to employ by payment of a fee; secure the services of by payment of a retainer: *He retained the best lawyer in the state.* [< Old French *retenir* < Vulgar Latin *retenīre,* for Latin *retinēre* < *re-* back + *tenēre* to hold]

**re|tain|a|ble** (ri tā′nə bəl), *adj.* that can be retained.

**re|tained earnings** (ri tānd′), = earned surplus.

**retained object,** an object in a passive construction corresponding to the direct or indirect object in an active construction. *Example:* The boy was given a *nickel.* A nickel was given to the *boy.*

**re|tain|er¹** (ri tā′nər), *n.* **1** a person who serves someone of rank; vassal; attendant; follower: *The king had many retainers.* **2** a person kept in service; attendant: *that old retainer, Bridget the cook* (Winston Churchill). **3** a person who retains. [< *retain* + *-er*[1]]

**re|tain|er²** (ri tā′nər), *n.* **1** a fee paid to secure services, on a continuing basis or when necessary: *This lawyer receives a retainer before he begins work on a case.* **2** a retaining of a person's service. [< noun use of Old French *retenir;* see etym. under **retain**]

**re|tain|ing wall** (ri tā′ning), a wall built to hold back a mass of earth or, sometimes, water.

**re|tain|ment** (ri tān′mənt), *n.* the act of retaining; retention.

**re|take** (*v.* rē tāk′; *n.* rē′tāk′), *v.,* **-took, -tak|en, -tak|ing,** *n.* —*v.t.* **1** to take again. **2** to take back. **3** to make (a film sequence) over again.
—*n.* **1** the process of retaking: *a retake of a scene in a motion picture.* **2** the sequence or film obtained. —**re|tak′er,** *n.*

**re|tal|i|ate** (ri tal′ē āt), *v.,* **-at|ed, -at|ing.** —*v.i.* to pay back a wrong or injury; return like for like, usually to return evil for evil: *If we insult them, they will retaliate.*
—*v.t.* to return in kind: *He retaliated on the ... Huns of Pannonia the same calamities which they had inflicted on the nations* (Edward Gibbon).
[< Latin *retāliāre* (with English *-ate*[1]) < *re-* back + unrecorded *tāl-* payment; perhaps influenced by *tālis* such (a)]

**re|tal|i|a|tion** (ri tal′ē ā′shən), *n.* **1** a paying back of a wrong or injury; return of evil for evil. **2** an act of reprisal.

**re|tal|i|a|tive** (ri tal′ē ā′tiv), *adj.* disposed to retaliate; retaliatory.

**re|tal|i|a|tor** (ri tal′ē ā tər), *n.* a person who retaliates: *It is often difficult to tell offenders from retaliators* (London Times).

**re|tal|i|a|to|ry** (ri tal′ē ə tôr′ē, -tōr-), *adj.* returning like for like, especially evil for evil: *a retaliatory raid, retaliatory weapons.*

**re|tard** (*v., n. 1* ri tärd′; *n. 2* rē′tärd), *v., n.* —*v.t.* **1** to make slow; delay the progress of; keep back; hinder: *Lack of education retards progress. Bad roads retarded the car.* **2** to defer; postpone: *to advance or retard the hour of refection beyond the time* (Scott). **3** to adjust (the ignition system of a gasoline engine) so that the spark occurs at a later point in the cycle of movement of the piston.
—*v.i.* to be delayed or hindered.
—*n.* **1** delay; retardation. **2** *U.S. Slang.* a retarded person; retardate.
**in retard,** retarded; delayed: *I was far in retard ... in real knowledge* (John Ruskin).
[< Latin *retardāre* < *re-* back + *tardāre* to slow < *tardus* slow]

**re|tard|an|cy** (ri tär′dən sē), *n.* the quality or state of being retardant.

**re|tard|ant** (ri tär′dənt), *n., adj.* —*n.* something that delays an action, process, or effect, usually a chemical.
—*adj.* retarding; tending to hinder: *We know the retardant effect of society upon artists of exalted sensibility* (Edmund C. Stedman).

**re|tard|ate** (ri tär′dāt), *n.* a person who is retarded: *"Criminal" covers a broad span of lawbreakers from the psychopath to the mental retardate* (Science News Letter).

**re|tar|da|tion** (rē′tär dā′shən), *n.* **1** the act of retarding: *A gradual change ... would then effect the necessary retardation in the rate of increase* (Thomas Malthus). **2** the condition of being retarded: *The business slowdown ... was described as a "pause," a "retardation"* (M. A. Kriz). **3** = mental retardation. **4** that which retards; hindrance. **5** a decrease in velocity; negative acceleration. **6** *Music.* a discord similar to suspension, resolving upward instead of downward.

**re|tard|a|tive** (ri tär′də tiv), *adj.* tending to retard.

**re|tard|a|to|ry** (ri tär′də tôr′ē, -tōr′-), *adj.* tending to retard; of a retarding effect.

**re|tard|ed** (ri tär′did), *adj.* slow in mental development; backward: *Retarded children—I.Q. between 65 and 90—have the capacity to learn if properly taught* (Scientific American).

**re|tard|ee** (ri tär′dē), *n.* a retarded person; retardate.

**re|tard|er** (ri tär′dər), *n.* **1** a person or thing that retards. **2** a braking device built into the hump track of a railroad yard to regulate a car's speed as it rolls down the hump.

**re|tard|ment** (ri tärd′mənt), *n.* = retardation.

**retch** (rech), *v.i.* to make efforts to vomit; make straining movements like those of vomiting. —*v.t.* to throw up in retching; vomit. [Old English *hrǣcan* clear the throat]

**retd., 1** retained. **2** retired. **3** returned.

**ret'd.,** returned.

**re|te** (rē′tē), *n., pl.* **-ti|a** (-shē ə, -tē-). a network, such as of fibers, nerves, or blood vessels. [< Latin *rēte, -is* net, related to *rārus* thin, of loose texture]

**re|tell** (rē tel′), *v.t.,* **-told, -tell|ing.** to tell again. —**re|tell′a|ble,** *adj.*

**re|tem** (rē′tem), *n.* a desert shrub of the Near East with small, white flowers and rushlike branches. It is the juniper mentioned in the Old Testament. [< Arabic *ratam*]

**re|te mi|ra|bi|le** (rē′tē mi rab′ə lē), *pl.* **re|ti|a mi|ra|bi|li|a** (rē′shē ə mir′ə bil′ē ə, rē′tē ə). an elaborate network or plexus of small arteries and veins forming one unified system between two parts of a larger artery or vein, and usually found near the junction of an extremity and the main body. [< Latin *rēte, -is* net, *mīrābile* wonderful]

**re|tene** (rē′tēn, ret′ēn), *n.* a white, crystalline hydrocarbon obtained especially from the tar of resinous woods and certain fossil resins. *Formula:* $C_{18}H_{18}$ [< Greek *rhētīnē* (pine) resin + English *-ene*]

**re|ten|tion** (ri ten′shən), *n.* **1** a retaining. **2** a being retained. **3** the power to retain. **4** the ability to remember. [< Latin *retentiō, -ōnis* < *retinēre* retain]

**re|ten|tion|ist** (ri ten′shə nist), *adj., n.* —*adj.* favoring retention, as of a law or policy.
—*n.* a retentionist person or group.

**re|ten|tive** (ri ten′tiv), *adj.* **1** able to hold or keep: *a material retentive of moisture.* **2** able to remember easily: *a retentive memory.* —**re|ten′tive|ly,** *adv.* —**re|ten′tive|ness,** *n.*

**re|ten|tiv|i|ty** (rē′ten tiv′ə tē), *n.* **1** the power to retain; retentiveness. **2** the capacity of a substance to retain induced magnetic force after the source of the magnetization has been removed.

3 the power of resisting magnetization.

**re|te|pore** (rē′tə pôr, -pōr), *n.* any one of a group of bryozoans that form corallike colonies. [< New Latin *Retepora* the genus name < Latin *rēte, -is* net + *porus* pore²]

**re|test** (*v.* rē test′; *n.* rē′test′), *v., n.* —*v.t.* to test again: *to retest airplane pilots.*
—*n.* the act or process of retesting; repeated test: *We encourage members to take retests* (London Times).

**re|the** (re′the), *n.* one of the governing districts or provinces into which Albania is divided. [< Albanian *rethe* share, division]

**re|think** (*v.* rē thingk′; *n.* rē′thingk′), *v., n.,* **-thought, -think|ing.** —*v.t.* to think out, or think over, again; consider afresh: *Rahner believes that each generation must rethink the problems of theology* (London Times).
—*v.i.* to think again: *I cannot help thinking and rethinking of your going to the island so heroically* (Jane Austen).
—*n.* the act of rethinking; reconsideration: *Using the metal [titanium] to its best advantage calls for a thorough rethink of metal-working methods* (New Scientist).

**re|ti|ar|i|us** (rē′shē ãr′ē əs), *n., pl.* **-ar|i|i** (-ãr′ē ī). a gladiator equipped with a net and a trident. [< Latin *rētiārius* < *rēte, -is* net]

**re|ti|ar|y** (rē′shē er′ē), *adj.* **1** using a net or any entangling device. **2** making a web: *a retiary spider.* **3** netlike.

**ret|i|cence** (ret′ə səns), *n.* the tendency to be silent or say little; reserve in speech.

**ret|i|cen|cy** (ret′ə sən sē), *n., pl.* **-cies.** = reticence.

**ret|i|cent** (ret′ə sənt), *adj.* disposed to keep silent or say little; not speaking freely; reserved in speech: *She had been shy and reticent with me, and now ... she was telling me aloud the secrets of her inmost heart* (W. H. Hudson). **SYN:** reserved, taciturn. See syn. under **silent.** [< Latin *reticēns, -entis,* present participle of *reticēre* keep silent < *re-* back + *tacēre* be silent] —**ret′i|cent|ly,** *adv.*

**ret|i|cle** (ret′ə kəl), *n.* a line, or a network of fine lines, wires, or the like, placed in the focus of the objective of a telescope or other optical instrument to make accurate observation easier. [< Latin *rēticulum.* See etym. of doublets **reticule, reticulum.**]

**re|tic|u|lar** (ri tik′yə lər), *adj.* **1** having the form of a net; netlike: *reticular tissue, reticular fibers.* **2** intricate; entangled. [< New Latin *reticularis* < Latin *rēticulum;* see etym. under **reticulum**] —**re|tic′u|lar|ly,** *adv.*

**reticular formation,** a network of small nerve cells extending from the diencephalon downward through the spinal cord, with distinct formations in the medulla oblongata and mesencephalon. It exerts control over the body's motor activities. *The reticular formation is now often referred to as the "working centre" of the brain* (New Scientist).

***re|tic|u|late** (*adj.* ri tik′yə lit, -lāt; *v.* ri tik′yə lāt), *adj., v.,* **-lat|ed, -lat|ing.** —*adj.* covered with a network; netlike. Reticulate leaves have the veins arranged like the threads of a net.
—*v.t.* to cover or mark with a network.
—*v.i.* to form a network.
[< Latin *rēticulātus* < *rēticulum;* see etym. under **reticulum**] —**re|tic′u|late|ly,** *adv.*

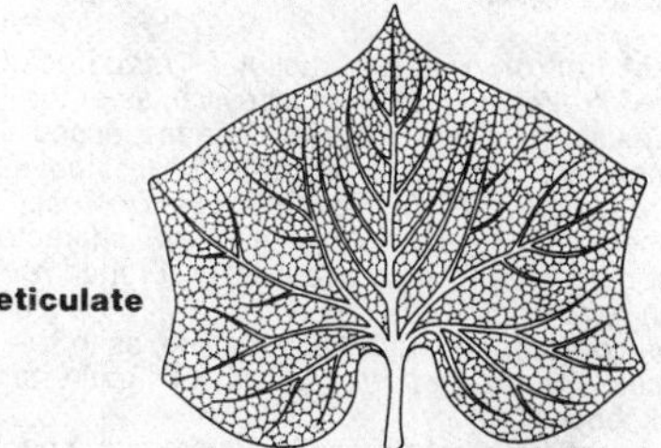
***reticulate**

**re|tic|u|lat|ed** (ri tik′yə lā′tid), *adj.* = reticulate.

**reticulate python,** a python of southeastern Asia and the East Indies that is among the world's largest snakes, growing up to 30 feet in length.

**re|tic|u|la|tion** (ri tik′yə lā′shən), *n.* **1** a reticulated formation, arrangement, or appearance; network. **2** one of the meshes of a network.

**ret|i|cule** (ret′ə kyül), *n.* **1** a woman's small handbag, especially one with a drawstring: *women in cloaks, bearing reticules and bundles* (Henry James). **2** = reticle. [< French *reticule,* learned borrowing from Latin *rēticulum* net. See etym. of doublets **reticle, reticulum.**]

**Re|tic|u|li** (ri tik′yə lī), *n.* genitive of **Reticulum.**

**re|tic|u|lo|cyte** (ri tik′yə lə sīt), *n.* a red blood cell that is not fully developed. Reticulocytes comprise from 0.1 to 1 per cent of the red blood cells. [< Latin *rēticulum* net + English *-cyte*]

**re|tic|u|lo|cy|to|sis** (ri tik′yə lə sī tō′sis), *n.* the presence of an unusually large number of reticulocytes in the blood.

**re|tic|u|lo|en|do|the|li|al** (ri tik′yə lō en′dō thē′lē əl), *adj.* of or having to do with the reticuloendothelial system: *a reticuloendothelial cell or tissue.* [< Latin *rēticulum* net + English *endothelial*]

**reticuloendothelial system,** a system of cells in the body, especially in the spleen, lymph nodes, bone marrow, and liver, that function in freeing the body of foreign matter and disease germs, in the formation of certain blood cells, and in the storing of fatty substances: *They found that cortisone depressed the activity of the blood cell forming reticuloendothelial system, particularly the spleen* (Science News Letter).

**re|tic|u|lose** (ri tik′yə lōs), *adj.* netlike; reticular.

**re|tic|u|lo|sis** (ri tik′yə lō′sis), *n., pl.* **-ses** (-sēz). = reticulocytosis.

**re|tic|u|lum** (ri tik′yə ləm), *n., pl.* **-la** (-lə). **1** any reticulated system or structure; network. **2** the second stomach of animals that chew the cud: *When first eaten the food passes into the rumen, later balls of this food, called the cud, are passed into the reticulum and up to the esophagus back into the mouth for thorough chewing* (A. M. Winchester). [< Latin *rēticulum* (diminutive) < *rēte, -is* net. See etym. of doublets **reticle, reticule.**]

**Re|tic|u|lum** (ri tik′yə ləm), *n., genitive* **Re|tic|u|li.** a southern constellation near Argo.

**re|tic|u|lum-cell sarcoma** (ri tik′yə ləm sel′), a cancer of the lymphatic tissue characterized by the formation of a network of malignant cells.

**re|ti|form** (rē′tə fôrm, ret′ə-), *adj.* netlike; reticulate. [< New Latin *retiformis* < Latin *rēte, -is* net + *forma* form]

**ret|i|na** (ret′ə nə), *n., pl.* **-nas, -nae** (-nē). a layer of cells at the back of the eyeball which is sensitive to light and receives the images of things looked at. The retina contains the rods and cones near its outer surface, and is continuous on its inner surface with the optic nerve. *Towards the periphery of the retina the proportion of rods increases. That is why a very faint star can often be seen only when one looks slightly to one side of it* (Science News). See diagram under **eye.** [< Medieval Latin *retina,* probably < Latin *rēte, -is* net]

**ret|i|nac|u|lar** (ret′ə nak′yə lər), *adj.* of or having to do with a retinaculum.

**ret|i|nac|u|lum** (ret′ə nak′yə ləm), *n., pl.* **-u|la** (-yə lə). **1** *Botany.* a viscid gland on the stigma of orchids and plants of the milkweed family for holding the pollen masses together. **2** *Anatomy.* a bridle or frenum; a fibrous structure binding down the tendons of muscles. **3** *Zoology.* **a** a small scale or plate which in some insects checks too much protrusion of the sting. **b** an arrangement of hooks, or of hooks and bristles, whereby the fore and hind wings of insects are interlocked when in flight. [< Latin *retinaculum* a band, halter < *retinēre* to hold back; see etym. under **retain**]

**ret|i|nal** (ret′ə nəl), *adj., n.* —*adj.* of or on the retina: *retinal images.* —*n.* = retinene.

**re|tin|a|lite** (ri tin′ə līt), *n.* a waxy, resinous variety of serpentine.

**re|tine** (ri tēn′), *n.* a chemical substance found in various body tissues which retards the growth of cells: *Theoreticians suggested that a cancerous condition may result if retine is not in balance with promine, a similar chemical which stimulates cancer growth* (Milton Golin). [< *ret*(ard) + *-ine*]

**ret|i|nene** (ret′ə nēn), *n.* a yellow pigment in the retina of the eye, an aldehyde of vitamin A, formed when rhodopsin in the rods of the eye is broken down by light: *The retinene, in the presence of the enzymes ... is changed to vitamin A* (Science News Letter). *Formula:* $C_{20}H_{28}O$ [< *retin*(a) + *-ene*]

**ret|i|nite** (ret′ə nīt), *n.* any one of various fossil resins, especially one of those derived from brown coal. [< French *rétinite* < Greek *rhētínē* resin + French *-ite* -ite¹]

**ret|i|ni|tis** (ret′ə nī′tis), *n.* inflammation of the retina. [< *retin*(a) + *-itis*]

**ret|i|no|blas|to|ma** (ret′ə nō blas tō′mə), *n.* cancer of the eye. It is very rare and can be inherited.

**ret|i|no|cer|e|bral** (ret′ə nō ser′ə brəl, -sə rē′brəl), *adj.* having to do with both the retina and the brain.

**ret|i|nol¹** (ret′ə nōl, -nol), *n.* a yellowish oil obtained by the distillation of rosin, used especially in printing inks and lubricants. [< Greek *rhētínē* resin + English *-ol*²]

**ret|i|nol²** (ret′ə nōl, -nol), *n.* = vitamin A.

**ret|i|nop|a|thy** (ret′ə nop′ə thē), *n.* a noninflammatory disorder of the retina. [< *retina* + *-pathy*]

**ret|i|no|scope** (ret′ə nə skōp), *n.* = ophthalmoscope.

**ret|i|no|scop|ic** (ret′ə nə skop′ik), *adj.* of or having to do with retinoscopy.

**ret|i|nos|co|pist** (ret′ə nos′kə pist), *n.* an optometrist or ophthalmologist who practices retinoscopy.

**ret|i|nos|co|py** (ret′ə nos′kə pē, ret′ə nə skō′-), *n.* examination of the retina with the aid of an ophthalmoscope to measure the amount of refraction of the eye.

**ret|i|nue** (ret′ə nü, -nyü), *n.* a group of attendants or followers; following: *The King's retinue accompanied him on the journey.* [< Old French *retinue,* (originally) feminine past participle of *retenir* to retain < Latin *retinēre*]

**ret|i|nued** (ret′ə nüd, -nyüd), *adj.* accompanied by a retinue: *Rickey arrived, heavily retinued* (New Yorker).

**re|tin|u|la** (re tin′yə lə), *n., pl.* **-lae** (-lē). a cluster of pigmented cells in the compound eyes of arthropods, from which the rhabdom arises: *Each retinula [of a nocturnal moth] is composed of seven or eight photoreceptor cells* (H. R. Steeves and J. S. VandeBerg).
[< New Latin *retinula* (diminutive) < Medieval Latin *retina* retina]

**re|tin|u|lar** (re tin′yə lər), *adj.* of or constituting a retinula: *retinular cells.*

**re|tir|a|cy** (ri tīr′ə sē), *n.* = retirement.

**re|tir|al** (ri tīr′əl), *n.* = retirement.

**re|tire** (ri tīr′), *v.,* **-tired, -tir|ing.** —*v.i.* **1** to give up an office or occupation, especially because of approaching old age: *Our teachers retire at 65. You and your wife ... look forward to the day when you can retire* (Newsweek). **2** to go away, especially to a place which is more quiet: *She retired to the country. The Roman senators still retired in the winter season to the warm sun, and the salubrious springs, of Baiæ* (Edward Gibbon). **SYN:** See syn. under **depart. 3** to go back; retreat: *The enemy retired before the advance of our troops.* **4** to go to bed: *We retire early.* **5** to recede or appear to recede: *Gradually the shore retired from view.*
—*v.t.* **1** to remove from an office or occupation. **2** to withdraw; draw back; send back: *The government retires worn or torn dollar bills from use.* **3** to withdraw from circulation and pay off (bonds, loans, or other securities). **4** to put out (a batter or side) in baseball and cricket.
[< Middle French *retirer* < *re-* back + *tirer* draw < Vulgar Latin *tirāre,* perhaps < a Germanic word] —**re|tir′er,** *n.*

**re|tired** (ri tīrd′), *adj., n.* —*adj.* **1** withdrawn from one's occupation: *a retired sea captain, a retired teacher.* **2** reserved; retiring: *She has a shy, retired nature.* **3** secluded; shut off; hidden: *a retired spot.*
—*n.* a retired person. —**re|tired′ly,** *adv.* —**re|tired′ness,** *n.*

**retired list,** a list of persons who have been retired from active service in the armed services.

**re|tir|ee** (ri tī′rē), *n.* a person who has retired from his occupation.

**re|tire|ment** (ri tīr′mənt), *n.* **1** the act of retiring or state of being retired; withdrawal: *The teacher's retirement from teaching was regretted by the school. He thus had a choice of prison in the U.S. or retirement in Italy* (Newsweek). **2** a quiet way or place of living: *A hermit lives in retirement, away from everyone.*

**re|tir|ing** (ri tīr′ing), *adj.* shrinking from society or publicity; reserved; shy; bashful: *The girl next door has a retiring nature.* —**re|tir′ing|ly,** *adv.* —**re|tir′ing|ness,** *n.*

**re|ti|trate** (rē tī′trāt, -tit′rāt), *v.t.,* **-trat|ed, -trat|ing.** to titrate (a solution) again after some change, as that caused by exposure to the air.

**re|told** (rē tōld′), *v.* the past tense and past participle of **retell:** *He then retold the story for the newcomers.*

**re|took** (rē tu̇k′), *v.* the past tense of **retake:** *The army retook the fort.*

**re|tool** (rē tül′), *v.i.* to change the tools, machinery, designs, or methods, in a plant to make new models or products. —*v.t.* to make over for this purpose.

**re|tor|sion** (ri tôr′shən), *n.* = retortion.

**re|tort¹** (ri tôrt′), *v., n.* —*v.i.* to reply quickly or sharply.
—*v.t.* **1** to say in sharp reply: *"It's none of your business," he retorted.* **2** to return in kind; turn back on: *to retort insult for insult or blow for blow.*
—*n.* **1** the act of retorting. **2** a sharp or witty reply, especially one that turns the first speaker's

---

**Pronunciation Key:** hat, āge, cãre, fär; let, ēqual, tėrm; it, īce; hot, ōpen, ôrder; **oil, out;** cup, pu̇t, rüle; **ch**ild; lo**ng**; **th**in; **ᴛʜ**en; **zh,** measure; **ə** represents **a** in about, **e** in taken, **i** in pencil, **o** in lemon, **u** in circus.

statement or argument against him: *"Why are your teeth so sharp?" asked Red Ridinghood. "The better to eat you with" was the wolf's retort.*
[<Latin *retortus,* past participle of *retorquēre* turn back <*re-* back + *torquēre* to twist]

**re|tort**[2] (ri tôrt′, rē′tôrt), *n., v.* —*n.* **1** a container used for distilling or decomposing substances by heat. **2** a container for heating an ore to separate the metal by distillation.
—*v.t.* to distill by heating in a retort: *Retorting of this mass of broken shale in place might release an additional 25 million barrels of petroleum products* (Scientific American).
[<Vulgar Latin *retorta,* (originally) feminine past participle of Latin *retorquēre;* see etym. under **retort**[1]]

**re|tort|er** (ri tôr′tər), *n.* a person who retorts metals.

**re|tort-gas tar** (ri tôrt′gas′), coal tar collected as a by-product at various points in the manufacture of gas from coal.

**re|tor|tion** (ri tôr′shən), *n.* **1** the act of turning or bending back. **2** *International Law.* a retaliation in kind by one state upon the citizens of another by imposing equivalent restrictions to those originally imposed on the citizens of the other state. [< Vulgar Latin *retortiō, -ōnis* <Latin *retorquēre;* see etym under **retort**[1]]

**re|touch** (rē tuch′, rē′tuch′), *v., n.* —*v.t.* to improve (as a photographic negative, painting, or composition) by new touches or slight changes: *Retouched and smoothed and prettified to please* (Berton Braley). —*v.i.* to give retouches: *retouch a little, here and there, before the paint dries.*
—*n.* a second or further touch given, as to a picture or composition, to improve it. —**re|touch′er,** *n.*

**re|tour** (re tür′), *v.i.* **1** to revert (to a person). **2** to return (to a place).

**re|trace** (ri trās′), *v.t.,* **-traced, -trac|ing. 1** to go or trace back over: *We retraced our steps to where we started. Slowly, hesitatingly, he retraced the route the doctor had taken, down the steps onto the tough rocky ground* (Graham Greene). **2** to trace again in memory; recall: *Shall one retrace his life?* (Ernest Dowson). **3** to go over again with the sight or attention. [<Middle French *retracer* <*re-* back + Old French *tracier* to trace[1]] —**re|trace′a|ble,** *adj.*

**re-trace** (rē trās′), *v.t.,* **-traced, -trac|ing.** to trace over again: *re-traced lines in a drawing.* [< *re-* + *trace*[1]]

**re|tract** (ri trakt′), *v.t.* **1** to draw back or in: *to retract a plane's landing gear. The kitten retracted her claws and purred when I petted her. The dog snarled and retracted his lips.* **2** to withdraw; take back: *to retract an offer or an opinion.* SYN: revoke, rescind, recall. —*v.i.* **1** to be able to draw back or in: *claws that retract.* **2** to make a withdrawal; be taken back. [<Latin *retractus,* past participle of *retrahere* <*re-* back + *trahere* to draw] —**re|tract′a|ble,** *adj.*

**re|tract|a|bil|i|ty** (ri trak′tə bil′ə tē), *n.* the property of being retractable.

**re|trac|ta|tion** (rē′trak tā′shən), *n.* the act of retracting a promise, statement, or the like.

**re|tract|ed** (ri trak′tid), *adj. Phonetics.* pronounced with the tongue drawn farther back than normal for a particular vowel.

**re|trac|tile** (ri trak′təl), *adj.* that can be drawn back or in.

**re|trac|til|i|ty** (rē′trak til′ə tē), *n.* the quality of being retractile.

**re|trac|tion** (ri trak′shən), *n.* **1** the act of drawing or condition of being drawn back or in. **2** the act of taking back; withdrawal of a promise, statement, or the like: *The boy who accused her of cheating made a retraction of the charge. The newspaper published a retraction of the erroneous report.* **3** retractile power.

**re|trac|tive** (ri trak′tiv), *adj.* tending or serving to retract.

**re|trac|tor** (ri trak′tər), *n.* **1** a person or thing that draws back something. **2** a muscle that retracts an organ, protruded part, or other process. **3** a surgical instrument for drawing back the edges of an incision or wound.

**re|train** (rē trān′), *v.t.* to train again, especially in order to teach a new skill or reinforce something already learned: *Every dancer in the company either has been trained by Balanchine from an early stage, or has been retrained according to Balanchine's principles of dance technique* (New Yorker). —*v.i.* to undergo retraining.

**re|train|a|ble** (rē trā′nə bəl), *adj.* that can be retrained: *retrainable workers.*

**re|tral** (rē′trəl), *adj.* at the back; posterior: *Beneath the retral ethmoidal spike is seen the olfactory groove* (Journal of Microscopic Sciences). [<Latin *retrō* back(wards) + English *-al*[1]] —**re′tral|ly,** *adv.*

**re|trans|fer** (*v.* rē′trans fėr′, -trans′fėr; *n.* rē-trans′fėr), *v.,* **-ferred, -fer|ring,** *n.* —*v.t.* **1** to transfer back to a former place or condition. **2** to transfer a second time.
—*n.* **1** a transfer back to a previous place or condition. **2** a second transfer.

**re|trans|form** (rē′trans fôrm′), *v.t.* to transform again or to a previous state. —**re′trans|for|ma′tion,** *n.*

**re|trans|late** (rē′trans lāt′, -tranz-; rē trans′lāt, -tranz′-), *v.t.,* **-lat|ed, -lat|ing.** to translate back into the original form or language: *Of Cicero . . . he had translated and retranslated every extant oration* (James Pycroft).

**re|trans|la|tion** (rē′trans lā′shən, -tranz-), *n.* **1** the act or process of retranslating. **2** what is retranslated.

**re|trans|mis|sion** (rē′trans mish′ən, -tranz-), *n.* transmission back to a source or to a new destination: *Six long panels of solar batteries ... supply electrical power to the satellite for retransmission of signals received from earth* (New York Times).

**re|trans|mit** (rē′trans mit′, -tranz-), *v.t.,* **-mit|ted, -mit|ting.** to transmit back again or further on: *The response is received by the satellite and again retransmitted at high power* (New Scientist).

**re|tread** (*v.* rē tred′; *n.* rē′tred′), *v.,* **-tread|ed, -tread|ing,** *n.* —*v.t.* to put a new tread on.
—*n.* **1** a tire that has been retreaded: *The exemption from the camelback tax would offset retreads for small and medium cars* (Wall Street Journal). **2** *Informal.* **a** a restoration or renewal, as of an old or worn thing, event, or idea: *[He] regards the issue of "bossism" as a retread of the successful Wagner campaign theme of four years ago* (New York Times). **b** the thing, event, idea, or the like, itself. **3** *Slang.* a person who rehashes old material.
[<*re-* + *tread,* noun]

**re-tread** (rē tred′), *v.t., v.i.,* **-trod, -trod|den** or **-trod, -tread|ing.** to tread back over. [<*re-* + *tread,* verb]

**re|treat** (ri trēt′), *v., n.* —*v.i.* **1** to go back; move or draw back; withdraw: *The enemy retreated before the advance of our soldiers. Seeing the big dog, the tramp retreated rapidly.* **2** to incline backward, as an airfoil or other part of an aircraft. —*v.t.* **1** to draw back; take away; remove. **2** *Chess.* to move (a piece) back. [probably < noun]
—*n.* **1** the act of going back or withdrawing: *The army's retreat was orderly.* SYN: withdrawal. **2** a signal for retreat: *The drums beat a retreat.* **3a** the ceremony at sunset during the lowering of the flag. **b** a signal on a bugle or drum during this ceremony. **4** a safe, quiet place; place of rest or refuge: *He went to his mountain retreat for the weekend.* **5** a retirement, or period of retirement, by a group of people for religious exercises and meditation: *The monks conducted a retreat.* **6** an asylum for insane people and for habitual drunkards. **7** the amount of curve or backward slope, as of an airfoil or other part of an aircraft.
**beat a retreat,** to run away; retreat: *We dropped the apples and beat a hasty retreat when the farmer chased us.*
[<Old French *retraite,* (originally) past participle of *retraire* <Latin *retrahere* retract <*re-* back + *trahere* to draw, pull. See related etym. at **retract.**]

**re-treat** (rē trēt′), *v.t.* to treat again: *The tissue residue is then re-treated with alcohol at 99°* (A. M. Brown).

**re|treat|ant** (ri trē′tənt), *n.* a person who takes part in a religious retreat: *A nun read spiritual writings to the retreatants at the lunch period* (Seattle Times Pictorial).

**re-treat|ment** (rē trēt′mənt), *n.* further or renewed treatment: *The quick re-treatment of the relapsing patient is one of the most satisfying aspects of current psychiatric treatment in England* (Atlantic).

**re|tree** (ri trē′), *n.* broken, wrinkled, or imperfect paper. [perhaps <French *retrait* <Middle French *retirer;* see etym. under **retire**]

**re|trench** (ri trench′), *v.t.* **1** to cut down or reduce (expenses). **2** *Military.* to protect by a retrenchment. —*v.i.* to reduce expenses: *In hard times, we must retrench to keep out of debt.* SYN: economize.
[<Old French *retrencher* <*re-* back + *trencher* to cut] —**re|trench′er,** *n.*

**re|trench|ment** (ri trench′mənt), *n.* **1** a cutting down or reduction of expenses: *Plant closing and retrenchment were the order of the day* (Wall Street Journal). **2** a cutting down; cutting off. **3** a second defense within an outer line of fortification.

**re|tri|al** (rē trī′əl, rē′trī-), *n.* a second trial; new trial.

**re|trib|al|ize** (rē trī′bə līz), *v.t.,* **-ized, -iz|ing.** to return to tribal status or to tribal ways and practices: *One of [Marshall] McLuhan's basic propositions is that we are crossing a technological frontier dividing the age of the collectivist from that of the individualist: We are being retribalized* (Saturday Review). —**re|trib′al|i|za′tion,** *n.*

**ret|ri|bu|tion** (ret′rə byü′shən), *n.* a deserved punishment; return for evil done, or sometimes for good done: *Accusation was preferred and retribution most singular was looked for* (Charles Lamb). [<Latin *retribūtiō, -ōnis* <*retribuere* < *re-* back + *tribuere* to assign, related to *tribus, -ūs* tribe]

**re|trib|u|tive** (ri trib′yə tiv), *adj.* paying back; bringing or inflicting punishment in return for some evil, wrong, etc.: *In death he suffered, with a kind of retributive justice* (Wall Street Journal). —**re|trib′u|tive|ly,** *adv.*

**re|trib|u|tiv|ism** (ri trib′yə tə viz′əm), *n.* belief in punishing criminals as retribution for the injury they have caused.

**re|trib|u|tiv|ist** (ri trib′yə tə vist), *adj.* of or characterized by retributivism: *retributivist theories of punishment.*

**re|trib|u|tor** (ri trib′yə tər), *n.* a person who makes retribution.

**re|trib|u|to|ry** (ri trib′yə tôr′ē, -tōr′-), *adj.* = retributive.

**re|triev|a|bil|i|ty** (ri trē′və bil′ə tē), *n.* retrievable condition or quality: *the retrievability of information from a computer.*

**re|triev|al** (ri trē′vəl), *n.* **1** the act of retrieving; recovery: *data storage and retrieval.* **2** the possibility of recovery.

**re|trieve** (ri trēv′), *v.,* **-trieved, -triev|ing,** *n.*
—*v.t.* **1** to get again; recover: *to retrieve a lost pocketbook, to retrieve information from the storage of a computer.* SYN: See syn. under **recover.** **2** to bring back to a former or better condition; restore: *to retrieve one's fortunes.* **3a** to make good; make amends for; repair: *to retrieve a mistake, to retrieve a loss or defeat.* **b** to rescue; save: *to retrieve the nations sitting in darkness from eternal perdition* (William H. Prescott). **4** to find and bring to a person: *Some dogs can be trained to retrieve game.* —*v.i.* to find and bring back killed or wounded game.
—*n.* the act of retrieving; recovery, or possibility of recovery.
[<Old French *retruev-,* stem of *retrouver* <*re-* again + *trouver* to find] —**re|triev′a|ble,** *adj.* —**re|triev′a|bly,** *adv.*

**re|trieve|ment** (ri trēv′mənt), *n.* **1** the act of retrieving. **2** the fact or condition of being retrieved.

***re|triev|er** (ri trē′vər), *n.* **1** a dog belonging to one of several powerfully built breeds trained to find killed or wounded game and bring it to a hunter: *A good retriever can be a big help to the hunter and to wildlife* (Science News Letter). **2** any dog trained to retrieve game. **3** a person or thing that retrieves.

***retriever**
definition 1

Labrador retriever

**ret|ro**[1] (ret′rō), *n.* = retrorocket. [<*retro* (rocket)]

**ret|ro**[2] (ret′rō), *n., adj.* —*n.* a revival, as of the fashion, music, or plays, of earlier decades, especially in France: *The Group TSE's productions . . . have been in the vanguard of the French vogue for "retro"* (Manchester Guardian Weekly). —*adj.* characteristic of or belonging to such a revival. [< French *rétro* < Latin *retrō* backward]

**retro-,** *prefix.* backward; back; behind, as in *retroactive, retrorocket, retrospection.* [<Latin *retrō* back, backward]

**ret|ro|act** (ret′rō akt′), *v.i.* **1** to operate in a backward direction; affect what is past. **2** to react.

**ret|ro|ac|tion** (ret′rō ak′shən), *n.* **1** a retroactive force. **2** an action in return; reaction.

**ret|ro|ac|tive** (ret′rō ak′tiv), *adj.* acting back; having an effect on what is past. A retroactive law applies to events that occurred before the law was passed. —**ret′ro|ac′tive|ly,** *adv.*

**retroactive inhibition,** *Psychology.* the act or fact of forgetting something, attributed to interference caused by learning something new that is similar to the thing learned first.

**ret|ro|ac|tiv|i|ty** (ret′rō ak tiv′ə tē), *n.* a being retroactive or retrospective.

**ret|ro|bron|chi|al** (ret′rə brong′kē əl), *adj.* situated or occurring behind the bronchi.

**ret|ro|car|di|ac** (ret′rə kär′dē ak), *adj.* situated behind the heart.

**ret|ro|cede**[1] (ret′rə sēd′), *v.i.,* **-ced|ed, -ced|ing.**

to go back; recede. [<Latin *retrōcēdere* <*retrō-* backward + *cēdere* go]

**ret|ro|cede**[2] (ret′rə sēd′), *v.t.*, **-ced|ed, -ced|ing.** to cede back (territory or privilege).

**ret|ro|ced|ent** (ret′rə sē′dənt), *adj.* going back.

**re|tro|ces|sion**[1] (ret′rə sesh′ən), *n.* the act of going back.

**ret|ro|ces|sion**[2] (ret′rə sesh′ən), *n.* the act of ceding back.

**ret|ro|ces|sive**[1] (ret′rə ses′iv), *adj.* going back.

**ret|ro|ces|sive**[2] (ret′rə ses′iv), *adj.* ceding back.

**ret|ro|choir** (ret′rə kwīr, rē′trə-), *n.* the space in a large church behind the choir or the main altar.

**re-trod** (rē trod′), *v.* the past tense and a past participle of **re-tread**.

**ret|ro|dis|placed** (ret′rə dis plāst′), *adj.* displaced backward.

**ret|ro|dis|place|ment** (ret′rə dis plās′mənt), *n.* displacement backward: *retrodisplacement of the uterus.*

**ret|ro|en|gine** (ret′rō en′jən), *n.* a rocket engine that produces thrust opposed to forward motion.

**ret|ro|fire** (ret′rō fīr′), *n., v.*, **-fired, -fir|ing.** **—*n.*** the act of firing a retrorocket: *When a . . . capsule is about to re-enter the atmosphere, it will be positioned for retrofire by computers on the ground* (Time). **—*v.i., v.t.*** to fire (a retrorocket).

**ret|ro|fit** (ret′rə fit′), *v.*, **-fit|ted, -fit|ting,** *n.* **—*v.t.*** to modify (something) to include new or improved materials or parts in an existing piece of equipment or a structure: *Cars. . .must be retrofitted with exhaust catalysts to remove pollutants* (Science News). **—*n.*** a retrofitting, as of an aircraft, motor vehicle, or building.

**ret|ro|flec|tion** (ret′rə flek′shən), *n.* = retroflexion.

**ret|ro|flex** (ret′rə fleks), *adj., v.* **—*adj.*** **1** bent backward. **2** having the tip raised and bent backward. **3** made by raising the tip of the tongue and bending it backward: *Most Americans have a retroflex vowel in "hurt."*

**—*v.t., v.i.*** **1** to raise and bend backward the tip of (the tongue). **2** to pronounce with the tip of the tongue raised and bent backward.

[<Latin *retrōflexus,* past participle of *retrōflectere* <*retrō-* back + *flectere* to bend]

**ret|ro|flexed** (ret′rə flekst), *adj.* = retroflex.

**ret|ro|flex|ion** (ret′rə flek′shən), *n.* **1** the act or fact of bending backward, especially of the uterus. **2** pronunciation with a bending backward and raising of the tip of the tongue.

**ret|ro|gra|da|tion** (ret′rə grā dā′shən), *n.* **1** a backward movement; retreat; decline; deterioration. **2** *Astronomy.* an apparent backward motion of a planet or asteroid from east to west.

**ret|ro|grade** (ret′rə grād), *adj., v.*, **-grad|ed, -grad|ing.** **—*adj.*** **1** moving backward; retreating. **2** becoming worse; declining; deteriorating. **3** inverse or reversed: *retrograde order. After the brilliant quantitative work of W. D. Wright, . . . it seems somewhat retrograde to examine one's sensations with little pieces of coloured paper* (Tansley and Weale). **4** *Astronomy.* characterized by retrogradation. **5** *Aerospace.* having negative acceleration; producing thrust opposed to forward motion: *To bring a satellite to earth, scientists use devices called retrograde rockets, or, in space jargon, retrorockets* (James J. Haggerty, Jr.). **6** *Obsolete.* opposed; contrary: *It is most retrograde to our desire* (Shakespeare).

**—*v.i.*** **1** to move or go backward. **2** to fall back toward a worse condition; grow worse; decline; deteriorate: *All that is human must retrograde if it do not advance* (Edward Gibbon). **3** *Astronomy.* (of a planet or asteroid) to appear to move backward from east to west: *Once during each synodic period the planet turns and moves westward, or retrogrades, for a time before resuming the eastward motion* (Robert H. Baker).

**—*v.t.*** to cause to go backward; turn back: *We see, now, events forced on, which seem to retard or retrograde the civility of ages* (Emerson).

[<Latin *retrōgradus* <*retrōgradī* to go back < *retrō-* backward + *gradī* to go, step] **—ret′ro|grade′ly,** *adv.*

**ret|ro|gress** (ret′rə gres, ret′rə gres′), *v.i.* **1** to move backward; go back, especially to an earlier or less advanced condition. **2** to become worse; decline; deteriorate. SYN: retrograde. [<Latin *retrōgressus,* past participle of *retrōgradī;* see etym. under **retrograde**]

**ret|ro|gres|sion** (ret′rə gresh′ən), *n.* **1** a backward movement. **2** the process of becoming worse; falling off; decline; deterioration; degeneration. **3** *Astronomy.* retrogradation.

**ret|ro|gres|sive** (ret′rə gres′iv), *adj.* **1** moving backward. **2** becoming worse; declining; deteriorating. **—ret′ro|gres′sive|ly,** *adv.*

**ret|ro|ject** (ret′rə jekt), *v.t.* to cast or throw back. **—ret′ro|jec′tion,** *n.*

**ret|ro|lent|al fi|bro|pla|sia** (ret′rə len′təl fī′brə plā′zhə), a growth of fibrous tissue behind the lens of the eye, occurring in premature infants and resulting in blindness. It is caused chiefly by administering too much oxygen to the premature child. [<*retro-* + Latin *lēns* (compare etym. under **lens**) + English *-al*[1]]

**ret|ro|pack** (ret′rō pak′), *n.* a retrograde rocket unit attached to a spacecraft to slow it down: *John Glenn . . . advised Cooper when to jettison the retropack* (Hugh Odishaw).

**ret|ro|per|i|to|ne|al** (ret′rō per′ə tə nē′əl), *adj.* occurring or situated behind the peritoneum: *a retroperitoneal hernia, retroperitoneal veins.*

**ret|ro|re|flec|tion** (ret′rō ri flek′shən), *n.* reflection of light back to its source.

**ret|ro|re|flec|tive** (ret′rō ri flek′tiv), *adj.* reflecting light back to its source: *In the case of light three reflecting surfaces, all at right angles to one another, form a corner with the same retroreflective property* (Scientific American).

**ret|ro|re|flec|tor** (ret′rō ri flek′tər), *n.* a prismlike device that reflects light back to its source, used as an aid in radar observations and in measuring the distance of the moon or other body in space from the earth.

**ret|ro|rock|et** (ret′rō rok′it), *n.* a small rocket at the front of a rocket or other spacecraft. It produces thrust opposite to the motion of the spacecraft in order to reduce speed for landing or for reentry. *The way to bring a satellite, manned or unmanned, down to the atmosphere is to fire a forward-pointing retrorocket to reduce its speed* (Time).

**re|trorse** (ri trôrs′), *adj.* turned backward; turned in a direction opposite to the usual one. [<Latin *retrōrsus,* contraction of *retrōversus;* see etym. under **retroversion**] **—re|trorse′ly,** *adv.*

**ret|ro|se|quence** (ret′rō sē′kwəns), *n.* the sequence of events before, during, and after a retrofiring: *John Glenn, aboard a command ship off the Japanese coast, provided the countdown for the retrosequence* (Hugh Odishaw).

**ret|ro|ser|rate** (ret′rō ser′āt, -it), *adj. Botany.* having retrorse teeth; serrate backwards.

**ret|ro|spect** (ret′rə spekt), *n., v.* **—*n.*** **1** a survey, as of past time or events; thinking about the past: *My retrospect of life recalls to my view many opportunities of good neglected* (Samuel Johnson). *We may be presenting, not simply retrospects of bygone episodes of this campaign year, but the two stories that will make the politics of 1952 memorable* (Harper's). **2** a looking back; reference: *He deprecated any invidious retrospect as to what had happened in former debates* (William E. H. Lecky).

**—*v.t.*** to think of (something past).

**—*v.i.*** **1** to look back in thought. **2** to refer (to).

**in retrospect,** when looking back: *He saw, in retrospect, that the battle could have been won.*

[<Latin *retrōspectus* <*retrōspicere* to look back <*retrō-* back + *specere* to look]

**ret|ro|spec|tion** (ret′rə spek′shən), *n.* **1** the act or fact of looking back on things past; survey of past events or experiences: *Old people often enjoy retrospection.* **2** a reference to something.

**ret|ro|spec|tive** (ret′rə spek′tiv), *adj., n.* **—*adj.*** **1** looking back on things past; surveying past events or experiences. **2** looking or directed backward: *Frequent retrospective glances . . . served to assure me that our retreat was not cut off* (Herman Melville). **3** applying to the past; retroactive.

**—*n.*** **1** = retrospective show. **2** any survey or review of past works: *Sy Oliver, the principal arranger for Jimmy Lunceford and Tommy Dorsey between 1933 and the late forties, is holding a retrospective of his work ... with the help of a nine-piece group that includes two trumpets, two trombones, two reeds, and three rhythm* (New Yorker). **—ret′ro|spec′tive|ly,** *adv.*

**retrospective show,** an exhibition of paintings reviewing the work of an artist or group of artists over a number of years: *the Picasso retrospective show at the Museum of Modern Art.*

**ret|ro|spec|tiv|ist** (ret′rō spek′tə vist), *n.* a person who surveys or reviews past events.

**ret|rous|sage** (ret′rü säzh′; *French* rə trü säzh′), *n.* a method used in the printing of etchings to produce effective tone, as in foregrounds or shadows, by skillfully bringing out the ink from the filled lines with a soft cloth. [<French *retroussage*]

**ret|rous|sé** (ret′rü sā′; *French* rə trü sā′), *adj.* turned up: *a retroussé nose.* [<French *retroussé,* past participle of Middle French *retrousser* <*re-* back + Old French *trousser* truss (up), load. Compare etym. under **trousseau.**]

**ret|ro|ver|sion** (ret′rə vėr′zhən, -shən), *n.* the act of turning or condition of being turned backward; displacement backwards: *a retroversion of the uterus.* [<Latin *retrōversus* (<*retrō-* back + *vertere* to turn) + English *-ion*]

**ret|ro|vert** (ret′rə vėrt), *v.t.* to turn backward; displace as by tipping backward, as the uterus.

**re|try** (rē trī′), *v.t.*, **-tried, -try|ing.** to try again.

**ret|si|na** (ret′sə nə), *n.* a Greek wine flavored with resin. [<New Greek *retsina*]

**ret|ting** (ret′ing), *n.* the process of wetting flax, hemp, or the like, and allowing it to decay until the fibers can be easily separated from the woody parts of the stalks. Also, **rotting.** [<present participle of *ret*]

**re|tube** (rē tüb′, -tyüb′), *v.t.*, **-tubed, -tub|ing.** to provide with a new tube or tubes: *to retube a boiler, to retube a gun.*

**re|tune** (rē tün′, -tyün′), *v.t.*, **-tuned, -tun|ing.** to tune (a musical instrument) again.

**re|turf** (rē tėrf′), *v.t.* to lay with new turf.

**re|turn** (ri tėrn′), *v., n., adj.* **—*v.i.*** **1** to go or come back: *to return this summer. Your mother will return in a moment. We will return to this hard example after doing the easy ones. And the spirit shall return unto God who gave it* (Ecclesiastes 12:7). **2** to make an answer or reply: *A plain-spoken ... critic might here perhaps return upon me with my own expressions* (Robert Louis Stevenson).

**—*v.t.*** **1** to bring back, give back, send back, hit back, put back, or pay back: *Return that book to the library. She admired my dress, and I returned the compliment. You took this cap; return it at once. Return good for evil.* **2** to yield: *The concert returned about $50 over expenses.* **3** to report or announce officially: *The jury returned a verdict of guilty.* **4** to reply; answer: *"No!" he returned crossly.* SYN: respond. **5** to elect or reelect to a lawmaking body: *Many Presidents have been returned to office for a second term.* **6** to lead (the suit led by one's partner in a card game). **7** to continue (as a wall or molding); turn at an angle. **8** to reflect (as light or sound).

**—*n.*** **1** the act of going or coming back; happening again: *a prompt return to work. We look forward all winter to our return to the country. We wish you many happy returns of your birthday.* SYN: recurrence. **2** a bringing back; giving back; sending back; hitting back; putting back; paying back: *The boy's bad behavior was a poor return for his uncle's kindness.* **3** a thing returned: *The bookstore would not accept returns, even ones in good condition.* **4a** Often, **returns.** profit; amount received: *The returns from the sale were more than $100. Return on investment is the product of two ratios: the margin of profit on sales, and the rate of turnover of capital* (Wall Street Journal). **b** a report; account: *to make out an income-tax return. The election returns are all in.* **5** a reply; answer. **6** a lead responding to the suit led by one's partner in a card game. **7** the ratio of the yield on a unit of a product to the cost of the unit. **8** *Sports.* the act of hitting or striking back the ball in play: *a return of a serve.* **9** a pipe, tubing, or other channel for the return of a liquid or gas to its origin. **10** a bend or turn, as in a river, part of a machine, or part of a building.

**—*adj.*** **1** having something to do with a return: *a return ticket to the point of starting.* **2** sent, given, or done in return: *a return game, a return cargo.* **3** repeated: *a return engagement.* **4** that bends or turns, often turning back on itself: *the return angle of the nave.* **5** causing or allowing the return of some part of a device to its normal or starting position: *a return spring, a return valve.*

**in return,** as a return; to return something: *thanks in return for aid. If you will loan me your skates now, I'll loan you my tennis racket next summer in return.*

[<Old French *retourner* <*re-* back + *tourner* to turn] **—re|turn′less,** *adj.*

**re|turn|a|ble** (ri tėr′nə bəl), *adj., n.* **—*adj.*** **1** that can be returned: *returnable merchandise.* **2** meant or required to be returned: *They hinted that returnable missiles from either of these planets could introduce something on the earth* (Science News Letter).

**—*n.*** *U.S.* an empty bottle or container that one may return to a store to collect a deposit included in its purchase price.

**return address,** the address of the sender on a letter or package.

**re|turn|ee** (ri tėr′nē′, -tėr′nē), *n.* **1** a person who comes back, especially one who has returned to his own country after capture or service abroad: *The total number of returnees rose at the appliance division plant* (Wall Street Journal). **2** a person who sends something back.

**re|turn|er** (ri tėr′nər), *n.* a person or thing that returns.

**re|turn|ing board** (ri tėr′ning), *U.S.* a board appointed in some states to determine the results of elections.

**Pronunciation Key:** hat, āge, cãre, fär; let, ēqual, tėrm; it, īce; hot, ōpen, ôrder; oil, out; cup, pu̇t, rüle; child; long; thin; ᴛʜen; zh, measure; ə represents **a** in about, **e** in taken, **i** in pencil, **o** in lemon, **u** in circus.

**returning officer**, *Especially British.* **1** the officer at an election who reports the returns to the proper authority. **2** the officer who returns writs or other documents to the issuing court.

**re|turns** (ri tėrnz′), *n.pl.* See under **return** (*n.* def. 4a).

**re|tuse** (ri tüs′, -tyüs′), *adj. Botany.* having an obtuse or rounded apex with a shallow notch in the center: *a retuse leaf.* [< Latin *retūsus,* past participle of *retundere* to blunt; beat back < *re-* back + *tundere* to beat]

**re|type** (rē tīp′), *v.,* **-typed, -typ|ing.** – ***v.t.*** **1** to typify anew. **2** to recopy with a typewriter.
– ***v.i.*** to acquire a stock of new type.

**Reu|ben**[1] (rü′bən), *n.* **1** the oldest son of Jacob (in the Bible, Genesis 29:32). **2** the tribe of Israel that was made up of his descendants (in the Bible, Numbers 32).

**Reu|ben**[2] (rü′bən), *n. U.S.* a trophy presented annually by the National Cartoonist Society to the outstanding cartoonist of the year. [< *Reuben* ("Rube") L. Goldberg, 1883-1970, an American cartoonist who designed the trophy and was one of the founders of the Society, in 1948]

**Reuben sandwich**, a combination of corned beef, Swiss cheese, and sauerkraut served hot. [probably < *Reuben's,* name of a former sandwich shop in the theatrical section of New York City]

**re|u|ni|fi|ca|tion** (rē′yü nə fə kā′shən, rē yü′-), *n.* **1** the action or process of reunifying: *reunification of the two sections of Germany.* **2** the condition of being reunified.

**re|u|ni|fy** (rē yü′nə fī), *v.t.,* **-fied, -fy|ing.** to bring back together again; unify again: *This includes preserving Berlin from eventual incorporation into the East German Regime, and ... reunifying her under a democratic process* (Sunday Times).

**re|un|ion** (rē yün′yən), *n.* **1** the act or process of coming together again: *the reunion of parted friends. We have a family reunion at Thanksgiving.* **2** the fact or state of being reunited. **3** a social gathering of persons who have been separated or who have interests in common: *a class reunion.*

**re|un|ion|ism** (rē yün′yə niz əm), *n.* the principles of reunionists; the belief in reunion.

**re|un|ion|ist** (rē yün′yə nist), *n.* a person who believes in or works for reunion, especially reunion of the Anglican Church with the Roman Catholic Church.

**re|un|ion|is|tic** (rē yün′yə nis′tik), *adj.* of or having to do with reunionism or reunionists.

**re|u|nite** (rē′yü nīt′), *v.,* **-nit|ed, -nit|ing.** – ***v.t.*** to bring together again: *to reunite a family. Mother and child were reunited after years of separation.*
– ***v.i.*** to come together again.
[< Medieval Latin *reunitus,* past participle of *reunire* < Latin *re-* again + *unīre* to unite] – **re′u|nit′er**, *n.*

**re-up** (rē up′), *v.i.,* **-upped, -up|ping.** *U.S. Slang.* to rejoin the army, navy, or other armed services; reenlist: *More cooks, truck drivers, and other practitioners of "soft skills" actually "re-up" ... than the services need* (Newsweek).

**re|up|hol|ster** (rē′up hōl′stər), *v.t.* to put new upholstery on.

**re|us|a|bil|i|ty** (rē yü′zə bil′ə tē), *n.* reusable condition or quality.

**re|us|a|ble** (rē yü′zə bəl), *adj.* that can be used again.

**re|use** (*v.* rē yüz′; *n.* rē yüs′), *v.,* **-used, -us|ing,** *n.* – ***v.t.*** to use again: *Almost all swimming pools built today are filtered, reusing the same water* (Newsweek).
– ***n.*** the act of using again.

**rev** (rev), *n., v.,* **revved, rev|ving.** *Informal.* – ***n.*** a revolution (of an engine or motor).
– ***v.t.*** **1** to increase the speed of (an engine or motor). **2** Usually **rev up.** *Figurative.* **a** to stimulate: *About the time I got out of college ... there were a bunch of idealistic youths who had been revved up by a bunch of articulate and persuasive politicians* (Carlton Gladder). **b** to increase in tempo; accelerate: *The New London Faust (stereo) ... offers lofty heights and deep lows ... And the symphonic postludes have been revved up rather than intensified* (Saturday Review). **c** to raise; step up: *In auto racing, purse money was revved up* (Bill Braddock).
– ***v.i.*** to increase, as in speed or action.

**rev.**, an abbreviation for the following:
**1** revenue.
**2** reverse.
**3** review.
**4a** revise. **b** revised. **c** revision.
**5** revolution.
**6** revolving.

**Rev.**, **1** Revelation (book of the Bible). **2** Reverend.

**re|vac|ci|nate** (rē vak′sə nāt), *v.t.,* **-nat|ed, -nat|ing.** to vaccinate again. – **re′vac|ci|na′tion**, *n.*

**re|val|i|date** (rē val′ə dāt), *v.t.,* **-dat|ed, -dat|ing.** to validate or confirm anew: *From July 1 to December 1, all citizens and aliens were required to revalidate their identity cards* (William S. Stokes). – **re|val′i|da′tion**, *n.*

**re|val|or|ize** (rē val′ə rīz), *v.t.,* **-ized, -iz|ing.** to assign a new value to (as a currency or price); valorize anew. – **re|val′or|i|za′tion**, *n.*

**re|val|u|ate** (rē val′yü āt), *v.t.,* **-at|ed, -at|ing.** **1** = revalue. **2** = revalorize.

**re|val|u|a|tion** (rē′val yü ā′shən), *n.* **1** a second or revised valuation: *The dollar suffered from rumors of Continental currency revaluations* (Wall Street Journal). **2** = reevaluation.

**re|val|ue** (rē val′yü), *v.t.,* **-ued, -u|ing.** **1** to value again or anew: *to revalue a property.* **2** = reevaluate: *to revalue a classic.*

**re|valve** (rē valv′), *v.t.,* **-valved, -valv|ing.** to put new valves in.

**re|vamp** (rē vamp′), *v., n.* – ***v.t.*** **1** to patch up; repair: *to revamp an old car.* **2** to take apart and put together in a new form: *to revamp a plan.*
– ***n.*** something revamped.
[American English]

**re|vanche** (rə vänsh′), *n.* = revenge. [< French *revanche,* Old French *revenge;* see etym. under **revenge**]

**re|vanch|ism** (rə vän′shiz əm), *n.* the beliefs or practices of the revanchists.

**re|vanch|ist** (rə vän′shist), *n., adj.* – ***n.*** a person who advocates taking up arms, as against a country or government, to recover territory lost in a war.
– ***adj.*** of or having to do with revanchists or revanchism: *a revanchist party.*

**re|vas|cu|lar|ize** (rē vas′kyə lə rīz), *v.t.,* **-ized, -iz|ing.** to place blood vessels in (an area of the heart or other parts of the body) to increase the blood supply: *Specialists at the meeting ... estimated that as many as 60 medical centers in the world might be doing operations to revascularize the hearts of gravely ill patients* (New York Times). – **re|vas′cu|lar|i|za′tion**, *n.*

**re|veal** (ri vēl′), *v., n.* – ***v.t.*** **1** to make known; divulge: *Promise never to reveal my secret. The wrath of God is revealed from heaven against all ungodliness and unrighteousness of men* (Romans 1:18). **2** to display; show: *to reveal a room by opening a door. Her smile revealed her even teeth.*
– ***n.*** **1** = jamb. **2** that part of a jamb between the face of a wall and that of the frame containing the door or window. **3** the border of an automobile window.
[< Latin *revēlāre* < *re-* back + *vēlāre* to cover, veil < *vēlum* veil] – **re|veal′a|ble**, *adj.* – **re|veal′er**, *n.*
– ***Syn.*** ***v.t.*** **1 Reveal, disclose** mean to make known something hidden or secret. **Reveal** applies especially when the thing has been unknown or unrecognized before: *At the new school he revealed an aptitude for science.* **Disclose** applies especially when the thing has been kept hidden on purpose: *She disclosed that she had been married for a month.*

**re|vealed theology** (ri vēld′), the study of theology from the standpoint of supernatural revelation, without the aid of natural reason.

**re|veal|ing** (ri vē′ling), *adj.* disclosing something not known before or not shown: *a revealing novel, speech, or dress.* – **re|veal′ing|ly**, *adv.*

**re|veal|ment** (ri vēl′mənt), *n.* = revelation.

**re|veg|e|tate** (rē vej′ə tāt), *v.i.,* **-tat|ed, -tat|ing.** **1** to grow again. **2** to grow plants again; become green with plants again. – **re′veg|e|ta′tion**, *n.*

**rev|e|hent** (rev′ə hənt), *adj. Anatomy.* conveying back: *revehent blood vessels.* [< Latin *revehens, -entis,* present participle of *revehere* carry back < *re-* back + *vehere* carry]

**rev|eil|le** (rev′ə lē; *British* ri val′ē), *n.* **1** a signal on a bugle, whistle, or drum to waken soldiers or sailors in the morning: *The bugler blew reveille.* **2** the first military formation of the day, at which the roll is usually taken. [< French *réveillez* awaken, imperative of *réveiller* < Old French < *re-* again + *eveiller* < Latin *ex-* out + *vigilāre* be awake < *vigil, -ilis* awake]

**rev|el** (rev′əl), *v.,* **-eled, -el|ing** or (*especially British*) **-elled, -el|ling,** *n.* – ***v.i.*** **1** to take very great pleasure (in): *The children revel in country life. Young boys who liked Enright's "Kinty" ... should revel in the excitement, color, and action of this little story* (Saturday Review). **2** to make merry.
– ***n.*** a noisy good time; merrymaking: *A parade and fireworks were planned for the Fourth of July revels. Christmas revels with feasting and dancing were common in England.*
[< Old French *reveler* be disorderly, make merry < Latin *rebellāre.* See etym. of doublet **rebel**, verb.]

**rev|e|la|tion** (rev′ə lā′shən), *n.* **1** the act of making known: *The revelation of the thieves' hiding place by one of them caused their capture. Revelation of serious unrest in the army has an added significance* (London Times). **2** the thing made known: *Her true nature was a revelation to me.* **3** God's disclosure of Himself and of His will to His creatures. [< Latin *revēlātiō, -ōnis* < *revēlāre* to reveal]

**Rev|e|la|tion** (rev′ə lā′shən), *n.* Also, **Revelations.** the last book of the New Testament, supposed to have been written by the Apostle John. Its full title in the Authorized Version (1611) is *The Revelation of Saint John the Divine. Abbr:* Rev.

**rev|e|la|tion|ist** (rev′ə lā′shə nist), *n.* **1** a person who believes in divine revelation. **2** a person who makes a revelation.

**rev|e|la|tor** (rev′ə lā′tər), *n.* = revealer.

**rev|e|la|to|ry** (rev′ə lə tôr′ē, -tōr′-), *adj.* **1** that makes known; revealing: *The novel is the most sincere, honest, and revelatory fictional treatment of the Soviet epoch to come out of Russia* (Atlantic). **2** of religious revelation.

**rev|el|er** (rev′ə lər), *n.* a person who revels or takes part in a revel.

**rev|el|ler** (rev′ə lər), *n. Especially British.* reveler.

**rev|el|ry** (rev′əl rē), *n., pl.* **-ries.** boisterous reveling or festivity; wild merrymaking.

**rev|e|nant** (rev′ə nənt), *n.* a person who returns, especially as a spirit after death; ghost. [< French *revenant,* present participle of Old French *revenir* to come back; see etym. under **revenue**]

**re|venge** (ri venj′), *n., v.,* **-venged, -veng|ing.**
– ***n.*** **1** harm done in return for a wrong; returning evil for evil; vengeance: *to get revenge, a blow struck in revenge.* **2** a desire for vengeance: *and we shall prevail against him, and we shall take our revenge on him* (Jeremiah 20:10). **3** a chance to win in a return game after losing a game.
– ***v.t.*** to do harm in return for: *I will revenge that insult. Every malcontent embraced the fair opportunity of revenging his private or imaginary wrongs* (Edward Gibbon).
– ***v.i.*** to take vengeance.
**be revenged**, to get revenge; have the person that hurt you get hurt in return: *She has ... a most decided desire to be revenged of him* (Scott).
**revenge oneself**, to pay back to a person the injury he did to one: *The cat revenged itself on the teasing boy by scratching him.*
[< Old French *revenge,* variant of *revenche* < *revenger* avenge < Latin *re-* back + *vindicāre* to avenge] – **re|veng′ing|ly**, *adv.*
– ***Syn.*** ***v.t.*** **Revenge, avenge** mean to punish someone in return for a wrong. **Revenge** applies when it is indulged in to get even: *Gangsters revenge the murder of one of their gang.* **Avenge** applies when the punishment seems just: *They fought to avenge the enemy's invasion of their country.*

**re|venge|ful** (ri venj′fəl), *adj.* feeling or showing a strong desire for revenge; vengeful; vindictive: *I had a keen, revengeful sense of the insult* (Hawthorne). – **re|venge′ful|ly**, *adv.* – **re|venge′ful|ness**, *n.*

**re|veng|er** (ri ven′jər), *n.* a person who revenges; avenger.

**re|ve|nons à nos mou|tons** (rəv nôɴ′ à nō mü tôɴ′), *French.* **1** let us return to our business. **2** (literally) let us return to our sheep.

**rev|e|noo|er** (rev′ə nü′ər), *n. U.S. Dialect.* revenuer.

**rev|e|nue** (rev′ə nü, -nyü), *n.* **1** money coming in; income: *The government got much revenue from taxes last year.* **2** a particular item of income. **3** a source of income. **4** the government department that collects taxes: *the Internal Revenue Service.* [< Middle French *revenue* < Old French, a return, feminine past participle of *revenir* come back < Latin *revenīre* < *re-* back + *venīre* come]

**revenue agent**, a government official who collects or enforces the collection of taxes, duties, and other revenue.

**revenue bond**, *U.S.* a bond issued by a city, state, or other government, payable out of its future income.

**revenue cutter**, a small, armed coastguard ship used especially to prevent smuggling.

**rev|e|nu|er** (rev′ə nü′ər, -nyü′-), *n. U.S. Informal.* **1** a revenue agent, especially one enforcing the laws against the illegal distilling or smuggling of alcoholic liquor. **2** an employee of the Internal Revenue Service: *Revenuers again urge taxpayers to pay closer heed to their arithmetic in filling out returns* (Wall Street Journal).

**revenue sharing**, *U.S.* the distribution among local governments, especially the state governments, of a part of the revenue from Federal taxes: [*His*] *dominant theme was ... "revenue sharing"—that government had to be returned to local control by way of sending the taxpayers' money back to the states, counties, cities, and towns* (New Yorker).

**revenue stamp**, a stamp to show that money

has been paid to the government as a tax on something.

**revenue unit,** *U.S.* a unit of revenue from postal services, equal to the average income which a post office receives annually for each 1000 pieces of mail it processes. A first-class post office is one that has 950 or more revenue units. A fourth-class post office has less than 36 revenue units.

**re|verb** (ri vėrb′), *v.t., v.i. Informal.* to reverberate: *The crowd has been around a discothèque before, and the records reverb* (New Yorker). [short for *reverberate*]

**re|ver|ber|ant** (ri vėr′bər ənt), *adj.* reverberating: *So reverberant* [*was*] *the air, they could hear the man's footsteps on the stony hillside* (Caine Hall).

**re|ver|ber|ate** (*v.* ri vėr′bə rāt; *adj.* ri vėr′bə rit), *v.,* **-at|ed, -at|ing,** *adj.* **—*v.i.*** to echo back: *His deep, rumbling voice reverberates from the high ceiling.* **2** to be cast back; be reflected a number of times, as light or heat. **3** to be deflected, as flame in a reverberatory furnace.
**—*v.t.*** **1** to reecho (a sound or noise). **2** to cast back; reflect (light or heat). **3** to deflect (flame or heat) on something, as in a reverberatory furnace.
**—*adj.*** that reverberates; reverberant.
[< Latin *reverberāre* (with English *-ate*[1]) beat back < *re-* back + *verberāre* to beat < *verber, -eris* (originally) whip, lash]

**re|ver|ber|a|tion** (ri vėr′bə rā′shən), *n.* **1** the act or fact of echoing back sound; echo: *Reverberations of the split were felt all over the country* (New Yorker). **2** the reflection of light or heat. **3** the fact of being reflected. **4** that which is reverberated; reechoed sound: *Shoutings and pistol-shots sent their hollow reverberations to the ear* (Mark Twain).

**reverberation time,** the time it takes for a sound made in a room, once its source is stopped, to decrease to one millionth of its initial value: *The changes will bring the hall's reverberation time, the acoustician's measure of echo, from 1.6 seconds to 2.1 seconds* (New York Times).

**re|ver|ber|a|tive** (ri vėr′bə rā′tiv), *adj.* reverberating.

**re|ver|ber|a|tor** (ri vėr′bə rā′tər), *n.* **1** a person or thing that reverberates. **2** a reflecting lamp.

**re|ver|ber|a|to|ry** (ri vėr′bər ə tôr′ē, -tōr′-), *adj., n., pl.* **-ries.** **—*adj.*** **1** characterized by or produced by reverberations; deflected. **2** built with a vaulted roof so that heat and flame are deflected onto the ore or metal but the fuel remains in a separate compartment: *a reverberatory furnace or kiln.*
**—*n.*** a reverberatory furnace or kiln.

**re|vere**[1] (ri vir′), *v.t.,* **-vered, -ver|ing.** to love and respect deeply; honor greatly; show reverence for: *We revere sacred things. People revered the great saint.* [< Latin *reverērī* < *re-* back + *verērī* to stand in awe of, to fear]
**—*Syn.*** **Revere, reverence** mean to feel deep respect for someone or something. **Revere** implies deep respect mixed with love, and applies especially to persons: *People revere a great statesman.* **Reverence** implies, in addition, wonder or awe, and applies especially to things: *We reverence the tomb of the Unknown Soldier.*

**re|vere**[2] (ri vir′), *n.* = revers.

**re|vere|a|ble** (ri vir′ə bəl), *adj.* worthy of being revered.

**rev|er|ence** (rev′ər əns, rev′rəns), *n., v.,* **-enced, -enc|ing.** **—*n.*** **1** a feeling of deep respect, mixed with wonder, fear, and love: *He had ... a sincere reverence for the laws of his country* (Macaulay). **SYN:** veneration, adoration. **2** a deep bow: *He made a profound reverence to the ladies* (Fanny Burney). **3** the condition of being greatly respected or venerated. **4** *Obsolete.* deference.
**—*v.t.*** to regard with reverence; revere: *We reverence men of noble lives. Ye shall keep my sabbaths, and reverence my sanctuary* (Leviticus 19:30). **SYN:** See syn. under **revere**[1].
[< Latin *reverentia* < *reverēns;* see etym. under **reverent**]

**Rev|er|ence** (rev′ər əns, rev′rəns), *n.* a title used in speaking of or to a clergyman: *Your Reverence, His Reverence.*

**rev|er|enc|er** (rev′ər ən sər, rev′rən-), *n.* a person who feels or shows reverence.

**rev|er|end** (rev′ər ənd, rev′rənd), *adj., n.* **—*adj.*** **1** worthy of great respect. **2** having to do with or characteristic of clergymen.
**—*n.*** *Informal.* a clergyman.
[< Latin *reverendus* (he who is) to be respected, gerundive of *reverērī* to revere]

**Rev|er|end** (rev′ər ənd, rev′rənd), *n.* a title for clergymen: *The Reverend Thomas A. Johnson. Abbr:* Rev.
► **Reverend,** in formal usage, is preceded by *the,* is not applied to the last name alone, and is usually not abbreviated: *the Reverend James Shaw, the Reverend J. T. Shaw, the Reverend Mr. Shaw.* The abbreviation (*Rev.*) is used in newspapers and in more or less informal writing: *Reverend James Shaw, Reverend J. T. Shaw, Rev. James Shaw, Rev. J. T. Shaw.* It is also used in addressing an envelope: *"The Rev. Allen Price."*

**rev|er|ent** (rev′ər ənt, rev′rənt), *adj.* feeling reverence; showing reverence: *He gave reverent attention to the sermon.* [< Latin *reverēns, -entis,* present participle of *reverērī* to revere] **—rev′er|ent|ly,** *adv.*

**rev|er|en|tial** (rev′ə ren′shəl), *adj.* = reverent. **—rev′er|en′tial|ly,** *adv.*

**rev|er|ie** (rev′ər ē), *n.* **1** dreamy thoughts; dreamy thinking of pleasant things: *She was so lost in reverie that she did not hear the doorbell ring. He loved to indulge in reveries about the future.* **2** the condition of being lost in dreamy thoughts. **3** a fantastic idea; ridiculous fancy. **4** *Music.* a composition suggesting a dreamy or musing mood. Also, **revery.** [< Old French *reverie* (originally) raving, delirium < *rever* to dream]

**re|vers** (rə vir′, -vãr′), *n., pl.* **-vers** (-virz′, -vãrz′). **1** a part of a garment, such as a lapel, turned back to show the lining, facing, or underside. **2** an imitation of such a part. **3** the material covering either of these. Also, **revere.** [< French *revers* < Old French, adjective *reverse* < Latin *reversus;* see etym. under **reverse**]

**re|ver|sal** (ri vėr′səl), *n.* **1** a change to the opposite; reversing or being reversed: *a reversal of attitude, a reversal in the weather. The high court's opinion was a reversal of the lower court's decision.* **2** *Photography.* a method of converting negatives into positives and positives into negatives by bleaching and redeveloping.

**re|verse** (ri vėrs′), *n., adj., v.,* **-versed, -vers|ing.** **—*n.*** **1** the opposite or contrary: *She did the reverse of what I ordered.* **2** the back: *His name is on the reverse of the medal.* **3** an opposite or contrary motion or direction: *a reverse in dancing, a locomotive moving in reverse.* **4a** the gear or gears that reverse the movement of machinery. **b** the arrangement of such a gear or gears: *Drive the automobile in reverse until you get out of the garage.* **c** the position of the control that moves such a gear or gears. **5** a change to bad fortune; check or defeat: *He used to be rich, but he met with reverses in his business. Caesar was never more calm than under a reverse* (James A. Froude). **SYN:** setback, failure.
**—*adj.*** **1** turned backward; opposite or contrary in position or direction: *Play the reverse side of that phonograph record.* **2** acting in a manner opposite or contrary to that which is usual: *reverse discrimination.* **3** causing an opposite or backward movement: *the reverse gear of an automobile.* **4** *Printing.* with black and white reversed: *reverse etching, reverse plates.* **5** *Military.* connected with or facing towards the rear: *a reverse battery, reverse fire.*
**—*v.t.*** **1** to turn the other way; turn inside out or upside down: *Reverse that hose; don't point it at me. Reverse your sweater or you will put it on wrong side out. If you reverse those two pieces, the puzzle will fit together.* **2** to work or revolve in the opposite direction. **3** to change to the opposite; repeal: *The court reversed its decree of imprisonment, and the man went free.* **4** to use or do in a way opposite to the usual method: *to reverse the usual order of conducting business.*
**—*v.i.*** **1** to put or work an engine or mechanism in the opposite direction: *Alternating current reverses from negative to positive about 60 times a second.* **2** to turn in a direction opposite to the usual one while dancing.
[< Latin *reversus,* past participle of *revertere* turn around; see etym. under **revert**] **—re|vers′er,** *n.*
**—*Syn.*** *v.t.* **1 Reverse, invert** mean to turn something the other way. **Reverse** is the more general in application, meaning to turn to the other side or in an opposite position, direction, order, or the like: *to reverse a phonograph record, reverse one's steps.* **Invert** means to turn upside down: *Invert the glasses to drain.*

**reverse** or **reversed fault,** *Geology.* a fault in which one side has moved above and over the other side, as in a thrust fault.

**re|verse|ly** (ri vėrs′lē), *adv.* **1** in a reverse position, direction, or order: *Stated reversely, the law of rent is necessarily the law of wages and interest taken together* (Henry George). **2** on the other hand; on the contrary.

**re|verse|ment** (ri vėrs′mənt), *n.* = reversal.

**reverse osmosis,** a process for desalting or purifying water, using a semipermeable membrane of cellulose acetate through which the water is forced by high pressure: *Reverse osmosis—the pressuring of solvent through a semipermeable membrane against the usual osmotic flow—has been considered for some time as a way of reclaiming water from industrial effluents* (New Scientist).

**reverse shell,** a spiral shell, as of a gastropod, in which the whorl rises from right to left, in the reverse of the usual direction; sinistral shell.

**reverse transcriptase,** = Temin enzyme.

**re|ver|si** (ri vėr′sē), *n.* a game for two played on a board, using counters that are differently colored on the opposite sides. The object is to surround the opponent's counters, giving one the right to reverse them to one's own color and thus capture them. [< French *reversi*]

**re|vers|i|bil|i|ty** (ri vėr′sə bil′ə tē), *n.* the fact or quality of being reversible.

**re|vers|i|ble** (ri vėr′sə bəl), *adj., n.* **—*adj.*** **1** that can be reversed; that can reverse: *reversible seats on a train.* **2** finished on both sides so that it can be worn with either side showing: *a reversible fabric. Men to whom life had appeared as a reversible coat—seamy on both sides* (O. Henry).
**—*n.*** **1** a garment, such as a raincoat, made so that either side may be worn exposed. **2** a reversible fabric.

**re|vers|i|ble-pitch propeller** (ri vėr′sə bəl pich′), a propeller that can reverse its pitch for reverse thrust to slow down an aircraft, especially while landing.

**reversible reaction,** a chemical reaction the progress of which may be halted and reversed or, after change has taken place, be caused to occur again in reverse, so as to leave the substances involved once again in their original state: *A reaction in which the products can interact to form the starting materials is known as a reversible reaction* (Parks and Steinbach).

**re|vers|i|bly** (ri vėr′sə blē), *adv.* in a reversible manner; so as to be reversible.

**re|vers|ing layer** (ri vėr′sing), the thin innermost layer of the atmosphere of the sun and other stars: *The reversing layer is a mass of vapors, entirely of the earthly elements, that stretches some 1200 miles above the photosphere* (Bernhard, Bennett, and Rice).

**re|ver|sion** (ri vėr′zhən, -shən), *n.* **1** a return, as to a former condition, practice, or belief: *It had become, by one of those periodic reversions to the ways of the eighteenth century ... a question of dominating importance* (Lytton Strachey). **2** the return of an estate to the person who makes the grant or his heirs after the grant expires. **3** an estate returning to the person who granted it or his heirs. **4** the right to future possession of a property, title, etc., under certain conditions. **5** *Biology.* a return to an earlier type; atavism. **6** the act or fact of turning or being turned the reverse way; reversal. **7** *Obsolete.* a remainder. [< Latin *reversiō, -ōnis* < *revertere* turn around; see etym. under **revert**]

**re|ver|sion|al** (ri vėr′zhə nəl, -shə-), *adj.* of, having to do with, or involving a reversion.

**re|ver|sion|ar|y** (ri vėr′zhə ner′ē, -shə-), *adj.* = reversional.

**re|ver|sion|er** (ri vėr′zhə nər, -shə-), *n. Law.* a person who possesses the reversion to an estate, office, or the like.

**re|vert** (ri vėrt′), *v., n.* **—*v.i.*** **1** to go back; return: *After the settlers left, the natives reverted to their savage customs. My thoughts reverted to the last time I had seen her.* **2** to go back to a former possessor or his heirs: *If a man dies without heirs, his property may revert to the state.* **3** *Biology.* to go back to an earlier stage of development.
**—*n.*** a person who returns to his original, or a previous, faith.
[< Old French *revertir* < Latin *revertere* < *re-* back + *vertere* to turn]

**re|vert|ant** (ri vėr′tənt), *n., adj. Genetics.* **—*n.*** a mutant that reverts to an earlier condition, usually by a second mutation.
**—*adj.*** that has reverted to an earlier condition: *revertant strains, revertant cells.*

**re|vert|er**[1] (ri vėr′tər), *n.* a person or thing that reverts. [< *revert* + *-er*[1]]

**re|vert|er**[2] (ri vėr′tər), *n. Law.* reversion, as of an estate. [< noun use of Anglo-French *reverter* to revert]

**re|vert|i|ble** (ri vėr′tə bəl), *adj.* that can revert.

**rev|er|y** (rev′ər ē), *n., pl.* **-er|ies.** = reverie.

**re|vest** (rē vest′), *v.t.* **1** to vest (a person) again, as with ownership, office, or power. **2** to vest (power, ownership, or office) again (in a person).
**—*v.i.*** to become vested again; revert to a former owner.
[< Old French *revestir,* learned borrowing from Latin *revestīre* < *re-* again + *vestīre* to clothe < *vestis* garment]

---

**Pronunciation Key:** hat, āge, cãre, fär; let, ēqual, tėrm; it, īce; hot, ōpen, ôrder; **oi**l, **ou**t; cup, pu̇t, rüle; **ch**ild; lo**ng**; **th**in; ᴛʜen; **zh**, measure; **ə** represents **a** in about, **e** in taken, **i** in pencil, **o** in lemon, **u** in circus.

**re|vet** (ri vet′), *v.t.*, **-vet|ted, -vet|ting.** to face (as a wall or embankment) with masonry or other material. [< French *revêtir* < Old French *revestir;* see etym. under **revest**]

**re|vet|ment** (ri vet′mənt), *n.* a retaining wall; facing, as of stone, brick, or cement, supporting or protecting a bank or embankment. [< French *revêtement* < Old French *revestir;* see etym. under **revest**]

**re|vi|brate** (rē vī′brāt), *v.*, **-brat|ed, -brat|ing.** — ***v.i.*** to vibrate again: *The chord once touched, every note revibrated* (Jane Porter).
— ***v.t.*** to cause to vibrate again. — **re′vi|bra′tion,** *n.*

**re|vict|ual** (rē vit′əl), *v.*, **-ualed, -ual|ing** or (*especially British*) **-ualled, -ual|ling.** — ***v.t.*** to victual again; furnish again with provisions: *The Roman fleet after it had been revictualled and repaired, stood right across the Mediterranean* (Bosworth Smith).
— ***v.i.*** to renew one's stock of provisions: *An invading army ... is therefore greatly harassed and cannot easily revictual* (Daily News).

**re|view** (ri vyü′), *v., n.* — ***v.t.*** **1** to study again; look at again: *Review today's lesson for tomorrow. He reviewed the scene of the crime.* **2** to look back on: *Before falling asleep, she reviewed the day's happenings. Now let's review the situation* (W. H. Hudson). **3** to look at with care; examine again; examine. **4** *Law.* to subject (a decision or proceedings) to examination or revision: *A superior court may review decisions of a lower court.* **5** to inspect formally: *The President reviewed the fleet.* **6** to examine to give an account of; write and publish, or read aloud to a television or radio audience, an account of a book, play, motion picture, concert, ballet, or exhibition, giving its merits and faults: *He reviews books for a living.*
— ***v.i.*** to review books, plays, motion pictures, concerts, ballets, or exhibitions. [partly < noun, partly earlier *re-view* < *re-* + *view,* verb]
— ***n.*** **1** the act or process of studying again: *Before the examinations we have a review of the term's work.* **2** the act or process of looking back; survey: *A review of the trip was pleasant. I have lived a life of which I do not like the review* (Samuel Johnson). **3** = reexamination. **4** *Law.* an examination or revision of the decision or proceedings of a lower court by a higher one. **5** an examination; inspection: *A review of the troops will be held during the general's visit to the camp.* **6** an account of a book, play, motion picture, concert, ballet, or exhibition, giving its merits and faults: *Reviews of new books, motion pictures, and plays appear in the newspapers. Her book is clever ... If it is put into capable hands for review! that's all it requires* (George Meredith). **7** a magazine containing articles on subjects of current interest, including accounts of books: *a law review, a financial review, a motion-picture review.* **8** = revue.
[< Middle French *reveüe,* feminine past participle of *revoir* < Old French *reveoir, reveeir* see again < Latin *revidēre* < *re-* again + *vidēre* to see]
— ***Syn.*** *n.* **6 Review, criticism** mean an account discussing and evaluating a book, play, motion picture, concert, ballet, or exhibition. **Review** applies particularly to an account of a current book, play, or other art form, giving some idea of what it is about, its good and bad points, and the reviewer's critical or personal opinion: *That magazine contains good reviews of current books. Have the reviews of that movie made you decide to see it?* **Criticism** applies particularly to an account giving a critical judgment, often of a number of related works, based on deep and thorough study and applying sound critical standards of what is good and bad in books, music, pictures, or any other art form: *I read a good criticism of Faulkner's works.*

**re-view** (rē vyü′), *v.t.* to view again or anew: *Certain performances seem to gain on re-viewing* (Saturday Review).

**re|view|a|ble** (ri vyü′ə bəl), *adj.* that can be reviewed.

**re|view|al** (ri vyü′əl), *n.* **1** the act or process of reviewing. **2** = review.

**re|view|er** (ri vyü′ər), *n.* **1** a person who reviews. **2** a person who writes articles discussing books, plays, motion pictures, concerts, ballets, or exhibitions: *After a fortnight of low ratings and blows from the reviewers, an emergency meeting of network bigwigs was held to try to pep up the show* (Newsweek).

**reviewing stand,** a grandstand from which a parade is reviewed.

**re|vile** (ri vīl′), *v.*, **-viled, -vil|ing.** — ***v.t.*** to call bad names; abuse with words: *The tramp reviled the man who drove him off.*
— ***v.i.*** to speak abusively.
[< Old French *reviler* despise < *re-* again + *vil* vile] — **re|vile′ment,** *n.* — **re|vil′er,** *n.* — **re|vil′ing|ly,** *adv.*

**re|vis|a|ble** (ri vī′zə bəl), *adj.* that can be revised.

**re|vis|al** (ri vī′zəl), *n.* **1** the act or process of revising. **2** = revision.

**re|vise** (ri vīz′), *v.*, **-vised, -vis|ing,** *n.* — ***v.t.*** **1** to read carefully in order to correct or make improvements; look over and change; examine and improve: *to revise a manuscript, to revise a textbook, to revise a local ordinance. She had revised the long story she wrote to make it shorter.* **2** to change; alter: *A stubborn person is slow to revise his opinion.*
— ***n.*** **1** the process of revising. **2** a revised form or version. **3** a proof sheet printed after corrections have been made.
[< Old French *reviser,* learned borrowing from Latin *revīsere,* probably < *re-* again + *vidēre* to see] — **re|vis′er,** *n.*

**Re|vised Standard Version** (ri vīzd′), an American Protestant revision of the New Testament, published in 1946; of the whole Bible, in 1952. *Abbr:* R.S.V.

**Revised Version,** the revised form of the Authorized (King James) Version of the Bible. The New Testament was published in 1881 and the Old Testament in 1885. *Abbr:* R.V.

**re|vi|sion** (ri vizh′ən), *n.* **1** the act or work of revising: *a very great work, the revision of my dictionary* (Samuel Johnson). *We'd rather wait for orderly, treaty-type revisions* (Newsweek). **2** a revised form or version: *A revision of that book will be published in June.* **3** *British.* a careful scrutiny or review of work: *The month before the final examination is given to careful revision of the subjects.*

**re|vi|sion|al** (ri vizh′ə nəl), *adj.* of or having to do with revision.

**re|vi|sion|ar|y** (ri vizh′ə ner′ē), *adj.* = revisional.

**re|vi|sion|ism** (ri vizh′ə niz əm), *n.* the beliefs or practices of the Communist revisionists.

**re|vi|sion|ist** (ri vizh′ə nist), *n., adj.* — ***n.*** **1** a person who favors or supports revision: *Martin Luther, a sixteenth century revisionist* (New Yorker). **2** a reviser, especially one of those who made the Revised Version of the Bible. **3** a Communist who tends to a somewhat flexible or nationalistic interpretation of Marxism, believing in the revision of doctrines according to changing national needs.
— ***adj.*** favoring revision or revisionism.

**re|vis|it** (rē viz′it), *v., n.* — ***v.t.*** to visit again; return to: *He revisited his birthplace and he traveled over again to places where he had been as a boy actor* (Atlantic).
— ***n.*** a repeated or second visit: *The proposed revisit of the Russian pianist ... has been abandoned* (London Daily News).

**re|vi|sor** (ri vī′zər), *n.* = reviser.

**re|vi|so|ry** (ri vī′zər ē), *adj.* of or having to do with revision: *a revisory committee.*

**re|vi|tal|ize** (rē vī′tə līz), *v.t.*, **-ized, -iz|ing.** to restore to vitality; put new life into: ... *to revitalize the Federal business-regulating agencies* (Wall Street Journal). — **re|vi′tal|i|za′tion,** *n.*

**re|viv|a|ble** (ri vī′və bəl), *adj.* that can be revived.

**re|viv|al** (ri vī′vəl), *n.* **1** the act or process of bringing or coming back to life or consciousness: *On his revival from the swoon ..., he recovered his speech and sight* (Edward Gibbon). **SYN:** reanimation, resuscitation. **2** a restoration to vigor or health: *He had an amazing revival after his operation.* **SYN:** reinvigoration. **3** the act of bringing or coming back to style, use, or activity: *the revival of a play performed years ago.* **4** something revived: *The most conspicuously important revivals were ... Chekhov's "Uncle Vanya" ... and James Joyce's "Exiles"* (Eric Shorter). **5** an awakening or increase of interest in religion. **6** special services or efforts made to awaken or increase interest in religion.

**re|viv|al|ism** (ri vī′və liz əm), *n.* **1** the spirit and practices of religious revivals and revivalists: *Revivalism, the archbishop admits, accomplishes some things for which God should be praised* (Newsweek). **2** a tendency to revive what belongs to the past.

**re|viv|al|ist** (ri vī′və list), *n., adj.* — ***n.*** a person who holds special services to awaken interest in religion, especially an evangelistic preacher: *His voice boomed like that of a camp-meeting revivalist when he talked to his audience* (Newsweek).
— ***adj.*** = revivalistic.

**re|viv|al|is|tic** (ri vī′və lis′tik), *adj.* of revivalism or revivalists: [*He*] *campaigned for his fourth term in the typical give-'em-hell, revivalistic style* (Time).

**Revival of Learning, Letters,** or **Literature,** the Renaissance in its relation to learning.

**re|vive** (ri vīv′), *v.*, **-vived, -viv|ing.** — ***v.t.*** **1** to bring back to life or consciousness: *He was nearly drowned, but we revived him.* **2** to bring back to a fresh, lively condition. **3** to make fresh; restore: *Hot coffee revived the cold, tired man.* **SYN:** refresh. **4** to bring back to notice, use, fashion, memory, or activity: *to revive an old song. An old play is sometimes revived on the stage. Petrarch ... indulged his fancy by deliberately reviving Latin words and constructions* (Simeon Potter). **5** *Chemistry.* to restore to its natural form; reduce to its uncombined state.
— ***v.i.*** **1** to come back to life or consciousness: *The half-drowned swimmer revived. Henry is dead and never shall revive* (Shakespeare). **2** to come back to a fresh, lively condition: *Flowers revive in water.* **3** to become fresh. **4** to come back to notice, use, fashion, memory, or activity: *The fine arts revived during the Renaissance.* **5** *Chemistry.* to recover its natural or uncombined state.
[< Latin *revīvere* < *re-* again + *vīvere* to live]
— **re|viv′er,** *n.*

**re|viv|i|fi|ca|tion** (rē viv′ə fə kā′shən), *n.* **1** restoration to life. **2** *Chemistry.* the reduction of a metal in combination to its metallic state.

**re|viv|i|fy** (rē viv′ə fī), *v.t., v.i.*, **-fied, -fy|ing.** to restore to life; give new life to. — **re|viv′i|fi′er,** *n.*

**rev|i|vis|cence** (rev′ə vis′əns), *n.* a return to life or vigor.

**rev|i|vis|cen|cy** (rev′ə vis′ən sē), *n.* = reviviscence.

**rev|i|vis|cent** (rev′ə vis′ənt), *adj.* returning to life or vigor. [< Latin *revīviscens, -entis,* present participle of *revīviscere* revive < *re-* again + *vīvere* to live]

**re|vi|vor** (ri vī′vər), *n.* an action, as to revive a lawsuit, interrupted by the death of one of the parties, or by some other circumstance.

**rev/min** (no periods), revolutions per minute: *a speed of 15,500 rev/min.*

**rev|o|ca|bil|i|ty** (rev′ə kə bil′ə tē, ri vō′-), *n.* the quality of being revocable.

**rev|o|ca|ble** (rev′ə kə bəl, ri vō′-), *adj.* that can be repealed, canceled, or withdrawn. — **rev′o|ca|ble|ness,** *n.* — **rev′o|ca|bly,** *adv.*

**rev|o|ca|tion** (rev′ə kā′shən), *n.* the act of revoking; repeal; canceling; withdrawal: *the revocation of a law.* **SYN:** revoking, rescinding, annulment. [< Latin *revocātiō, -ōnis* < *revocāre;* see etym. under **revoke**]

**rev|o|ca|to|ry** (rev′ə kə tôr′ē, -tōr′-), *adj.* revoking; recalling; repealing.

**re|voice** (rē vois′), *v.t.*, **-voiced, -voic|ing.** **1** to voice again; echo. **2** to readjust the tone of: *to revoice an organ pipe.*

**rev|o|ka|ble** (rev′ə kə bəl, ri vō′-), *adj.* = revocable.

**re|voke** (ri vōk′), *v.*, **-voked, -vok|ing,** *n.* — ***v.t.*** **1** to take back; repeal; cancel; withdraw: *to revoke a driver's license. The king revoked his decree.* **2** *Obsolete.* to call back.
— ***v.i.*** to fail to follow suit in playing cards when one can and should; renege.
— ***n.*** **1** a failure to follow suit in cards when one can and should; renege. **2** = revocation.
[< Latin *revocāre* < *re-* back + *vocāre* call, related to *vōx, vocis* voice] — **re|vok′er,** *n.*

**re|volt** (ri vōlt′), *n., v.* — ***n.*** the act or state of rebelling: *The town is in revolt against higher school taxes. It was not possible to think of such things without a revolt of his whole being* (Edith Wharton).
— ***v.i.*** **1** to turn away from and fight against a leader; rise against the government's authority: *The people revolted against the dictator.* **2** to turn away with disgust: *to revolt at a bad smell. Our whole hearts revolt against the way women have hitherto been treated* (William H. Mallock).
— ***v.t.*** to cause to feel disgust: *A dirty restaurant revolts even a hungry man. There were several ... whom this brutality revolted* (Robert Louis Stevenson). **SYN:** repel, sicken.
[< Middle French *révolte* < Italian *rivolta,* ultimately < Latin *revolvere;* see etym. under **revolve**] — **re|volt′er,** *n.*
— ***Syn.*** *n.* **Revolt, insurrection, rebellion** mean a rising up in active resistance against authority. **Revolt** emphasizes casting off allegiance and refusing to accept existing conditions or control: *The revolt of the American colonists developed into revolution.* **Insurrection** applies to an armed uprising of a group, often small, poorly organized, and selfishly motivated: *The insurrection was started by a few malcontents.* **Rebellion** applies to open armed resistance organized to overthrow the government or force it to do something: *A rebellion may become civil war.*

**re|volt|ing** (ri vōl′ting), *adj.* disgusting; repulsive: *a revolting odor.* — **re|volt′ing|ly,** *adv.*

**rev|o|lute** (rev′ə lüt), *adj. Botany.* rolled or curled backward or downward, as the tips or margins of some leaves and fronds. [< Latin *revolūtus,* past participle of *revolvere;* see etym. under **revolve**]

**rev|o|lu|tion** (rev′ə lü′shən), *n.* **1** a complete overthrow of an established government or political system: *The American Revolution from 1763 to 1783 gave independence to the colonies. Geria, after the Revolution, got free primary and secondary schooling* (Harper's). **2** a complete change: *The automobile caused a revolution in ways of traveling.* **3** movement around some point in a circle or curve: *One revolution of the earth around the sun takes a year.* **4a** the act or fact of turning around a center or axis; rotation: *The wheel of the motor turns at a rate of more than one thousand revolutions a minute. The revolution of the earth causes day and night.* **b** the time or distance of one revolution. **5** a complete cycle or series of events: *The revolution of the four seasons fills a year.* [< Latin *revolūtiō, -ōnis* < *revolvere;* see etym. under **revolve**]

**rev|o|lu|tion|ar|y** (rev′ə lü′shə ner′ē), *adj., n., pl.* **-ar|ies.** —*adj.* **1** of a revolution; connected with a revolution: *In considering the policy to be adopted for suppressing the insurrection, I have been anxious and careful that the inevitable conflict for this purpose shall not degenerate into a violent and remorseless revolutionary struggle* (Abraham Lincoln). **2** bringing or causing great changes: *Radio and television were two revolutionary inventions of this century. The antibiotics were a revolutionary advance in medical treatment.*

—*n.* = revolutionist.

**Revolutionary calendar**, a calendar introduced in France October 5, 1793, which gave new names to the months. It began counting time from September 22, 1792.

**rev|o|lu|tion|ise** (rev′ə lü′shə nīz), *v.t., v.i.,* **-ised, -is|ing.** *Especially British.* revolutionize.

**rev|o|lu|tion|ist** (rev′ə lü′shə nist), *n., adj.* —*n.* a person who advocates, or takes part in, a revolution: *There is nothing of the rebel or the revolutionist about him* (Harper's).

—*adj.* = revolutionary.

**rev|o|lu|tion|ize** (rev′ə lü′shə nīz), *v.,* **-ized, -iz|ing.** —*v.t.* **1** to change completely; produce a very great change in: *The automobile and radio have revolutionized country life. The new chief of police says he will revolutionize that department.* **2** to cause a revolution in the government of. **3** to indoctrinate with revolutionary ideas or principles.

—*v.i.* **1** to be revolutionized. **2** to make a revolution or revolutions. —**rev′o|lu′tion|iz′er,** *n.*

**re|volv|a|ble** (ri vol′və bəl), *adj.* that can be revolved.

**re|volve** (ri volv′), *v.,* **-volved, -volv|ing,** *n.* —*v.i.* **1** to move in a circle; move in a curve around a point: *The moon revolves around the earth.* **SYN:** See syn. under **turn. 2** to turn around a center or axis; rotate: *The wheels of a moving car revolve.* **3** to move in a complete cycle or series of events: *The seasons revolve.* **4** to be turned over in the mind.

—*v.t.* **1** to cause to move around. **2** to cause to move about a central point. **3** to turn over in the mind; consider from many points of view: *He wishes to revolve the problem before giving an answer. Long stood Sir Belevedere, revolving many memories* (Tennyson).

—*n. Especially British.* a revolving stage: *Sliding walls and revolves … realign themselves as street scenes and interiors, and accelerate like a merry-go-round for the police chase in the last act* (London Times).

[< Latin *revolvere* < *re-* back, again + *volvere* to roll]

**re|volv|er** (ri vol′vər), *n.* **1** a pistol that can be fired several times without reloading. It has a revolving cylinder in which the cartridges are contained. Revolvers with cylinders that have six chambers are called six-shooters. See picture under **pistol. 2** a person or thing that revolves.

**re|volv|ing** (ri vol′ving), *adj.* **1** that revolves: *The royal view would include a section of the tower's electric ad board and all of the revolving crane* (New Yorker). **2** of or having to do with an internal-combustion airplane engine whose cylinders revolve about a stationary crankshaft. **3** that is renewed automatically, as by regular payments; have to do with or based on revolving credit: *If they have a "revolving" charge account at a department store, they pay interest on the unpaid balance of money they owe the store* (L. T. Flatley).

**revolving credit**, credit that is automatically renewed on payment of debts, bills, or other obligations: *American Standard in January arranged with a group of banks a revolving credit of up to $50 million* (Wall Street Journal).

**revolving door**, a door set in a cylinder having an opening on two sides and four sections at right angles that revolve on a central axis.

**revolving fund**, **1** a fund used for loans. It is kept up by the repayment of past loans. **2** a fund established by the U.S. government from which money can be lent to organizations important to the general welfare, as utilities.

**revolving stage**, a stage with a circular platform that revolves to allow for quick scene changes: *The use of the revolving stage to provide swift vignettes of a carousing … London has merit* (Howard Taubman).

**re|vote** (rē vōt′), *v.,* **-vot|ed, -vot|ing,** *n.* —*v.t.* to grant, settle, or decree again by a new vote.

—*n.* a second or repeated vote; renewed grant.

**Revs.**, Reverends.

**Rev. Stat.**, Revised Statutes.

**re|vue** (ri vyü′), *n.* a theatrical entertainment with singing, dancing, parodies of recent movies and plays, humorous treatments of happenings and fads of the year, and the like: *One of those dismal … revues, that are neither comedies nor farces, nor anything but shambling, hugger-mugger contraptions into which you fling anything that comes handy* (Alfred G. Gardiner). [< French *revue* < Middle French *reveüe;* see etym. under **review**, noun]

**re|vulse** (ri vuls′), *v.t.,* **-vulsed, -vuls|ing.** to fill with repugnance; disgust: *The hippie community was revulsed by the massacre* (Lexington [Kentucky] Leader). [back formation < *revulsion*]

**re|vul|sion** (ri vul′shən), *n.* **1a** a sudden, violent change or reaction, especially of disgust: *My feeling for my new friend underwent a revulsion when I discovered his cruelty and dishonesty.* **b** a feeling of strong distaste or aversion created by such a change; repugnance: *The violence of the movie filled him with revulsion.* **2** the drawing of blood from one part of the body to another part, as by counterirritation. **3** a drawing or being drawn back or away, especially suddenly or violently: *the revulsion of capital from the woolen industry.* **4** the fact of being withdrawn. **5** a sudden reverse tendency, as in business: *to sustain the credit of the merchants under the revulsion consequent on peace* (George Bancroft). [< Latin *revulsiō, -ōnis* < *revellere* < *re-* back + *vellere* tear away]

**re|vul|sive** (ri vul′siv), *adj.* tending to produce revulsion.

**Rev. Ver.**, Revised Version.

**re|ward** (ri wôrd′), *n., v.* —*n.* **1** a return made for something done: *to give a reward for good behavior. Hanging was the reward of treason and desertion* (William Stubbs). **2** money given or offered. Rewards are given for the capture of criminals and the return of lost property. *Rewards totaling $150,000 attracted 5,000 letters with tips* (Newsweek).

—*v.t.* **1** to give a reward to: *Excellent results rewarded him for his efforts.* **SYN:** recompense, repay. **2** to give a reward for: *She rewarded his past services with liberality* (Lytton Strachey). [< Old North French *reward* < *rewarder,* variant of Old French *regarder,* earlier *reguarder* < *re-* back + *guarder* to guard, care for. See etym. of doublet **regard.**] —**re|ward′er,** *n.*

**re|ward|a|ble** (ri wôr′də bəl), *adj.* that can be rewarded; worthy of reward.

**re|ward|ful** (ri wôrd′fəl), *adj.* yielding a reward: *He was happy, because his labor of love was also rewardful.*

**re|ward|ing** (ri wôr′ding), *adj.* that rewards; useful; beneficial: *a rewarding experience. You will find this book very rewarding.* —**re|ward′ing|ly,** *adv.*

**re|ward|less** (ri wôrd′lis), *adj.* without reward.

**re|wa|ter** (rē wôt′ər, -wot′-), *v.t., v.i.* **1** to water again. **2** to place in water again.

**re|win** (rē win′), *v.t.,* **-won, -win|ning.** to win back or again; regain; recover.

**re|wind** (*v.* rē wīnd′; *n.* re′wīnd′), *v.,* **-wound, -wind|ing,** *n.* —*v.t., v.i.* to wind again: *to rewind the clock, to rewind a reel of tape. The film rewinds automatically.*

—*n.* **1** the process of rewinding: *The typewriter ribbon became tangled on the rewind.* **2** a thing that rewinds.

**re|wire** (rē wīr′), *v.t., v.i.,* **-wired, -wir|ing. 1** to put new wires on or in. **2** to telegraph again.

**re|word** (rē wėrd′), *v.t.* **1** to put in other words; rephrase. **2** to repeat exactly.

**re|work** (rē wėrk′), *v.t.* to work over again; reprocess; revise: *He had done most of the writing and rewriting himself, reworking key passages again and again* (Time).

**re|write** (*v.* rē rīt′; *n.* rē′rīt′), *v.,* **-wrote, -writ|ten, -writ|ing,** *n.* —*v.t., v.i.* **1** to write again; write in a different form; revise. **2** *U.S.* to write (a news story) from material supplied over the telephone or in a form that cannot be used as copy.

—*n.* **1** the act or process of rewriting. **2** *U.S.* a news story that has to be rewritten. —**re|writ′er,** *n.*

**rewrite man**, *U.S.* a newspaper reporter or editor skilled in rewriting.

**rewrite rule**, *Linguistics.* a rule indicating that a sentence, phrase, or clause, should be rewritten in terms of its components. *Example:* The rule VP → vt + NP means that a verb phrase, such as *face the music,* should be rewritten as consisting of a transitive verb plus a noun phrase.

**rex** or **Rex** (reks), *n., pl.* **re|ges** or **Re|ges.** *Latin.* king.

**Rex cat**, any one of a breed of short-haired cats with soft, closely curled coats and curly whiskers.

**Rex|ine** (rek′sēn), *n. Trademark.* an artificial leather used especially in upholstery and bindings for books.

**Reyn|ard** (ren′ərd, rā′närd), *n.* the name for the fox in stories and poems. Reynard the Fox is the main character in a group of medieval fables about animals. [earlier *Renard* < Old French *Renart,* or *Renard,* probably < Middle Flemish *Reinaert*]

**reyn|ard** (ren′ərd, rā′närd), *n.* = fox.

**Rey|nold's number** (ren′əldz), a mathematical factor used to express the relation between the velocity, viscosity, density, and dimensions of a fluid in any system of flow. It is used in aerodynamics to correct the results of tests of scale-model airplanes in wind tunnels. [< Osborne *Reynolds,* 1842-1912, a British scientist, who determined it]

**rez-de-chaus|sée** (rā′də shō sā′), *n. French.* the ground floor; first story.

**re|zone** (rē zōn′), *v.t.,* **-zoned, -zon|ing.** to zone again; change the present zoning of: *to rezone an area.*

**rf.**, *Baseball.* **1** right field. **2** right fielder.

**r.f.**, **1** radio frequency. **2** rapid-fire.

**RF** (no periods), **1** radio frequency. **2** releasing factor.

**R.F.**, an abbreviation for the following:
**1** French Republic (French, *République française*).
**2** radio frequency.
**3** rapid-fire.
**4** representative fraction.

**R.F.A.**, Royal Field Artillery.

**R factor**, a cytoplasmic component in various bacteria that gives them immunity or resistance to one or more antibiotics: *Bacteria that have survived exposure to an antibiotic by developing resistance to it pass on this resistance in the form of genetic material—the R factor—to other species or strains* (London Times). [< *R*(esistance) *factor*]

**RFC** (no periods), Reconstruction Finance Corporation.

**R.F.C.**, (formerly) Royal Flying Corps.

**R.F.D.**, Rural Free Delivery.

**RFE** (no periods) or **R.F.E.**, Radio Free Europe.

**r.g.**, right guard.

**R.G.A.**, Royal Garrison Artillery.

**R.G.G.**, Royal Grenadier Guards.

**R.G.S.**, Royal Geographical Society.

**r.h.**, **1** relative humidity. **2** *Music.* right hand.

**Rh** (no period), **1** Rh factor. **2** rhodium (chemical element).

**R.H.**, **1** Royal Highlanders. **2** Royal Highness.

**R.H.A.**, Royal Horse Artillery.

**Rhab|di|tis form** (rab dī′tis), a free-swimming sexual stage in the development of certain parasitic nematodes. [< New Latin *rhabditis* < Greek *rhábdos* rod]

**rhab|dom** (rab′dəm), *n.* any one of the rods supporting the crystalline lenses in a compound eye. [< Late Greek *rhabdōma* group of rods < Greek *rhábdos* rod]

**rhab|do|man|cy** (rab′də man′sē), *n.* **1** divination by means of a rod or wand. **2** the art of discovering water, ores, or the like, by means of a divining rod; dowsing.
[< Greek *rhabdomanteiā* < *rhábdos* rod + *manteiā* divination]

**rhab|do|man|tist** (rab′də man′tist), *n.* a person who divines by means of a rod or wand; dowser.

**rhab|do|mere** (rab′də mir), *n.* a unit or segment of a rhabdom.

**rhab|do|mer|ic** (rab′də mer′ik), *adj.* of or having to do with a rhabdomere.

**rhab|do|my|o|ma** (rab′dō mī ō′mə), *n., pl.* **-mas, -ma|ta** (-mə tə). a tumor that is usually benign and composed chiefly of striated muscle fiber. [< New Latin *rhabdomyoma* < Greek *rhábdos* rod + *mŷs, myós* muscle + *-ōma* a growth]

**rhab|do|my|o|sar|co|ma** (rab′dō mī′ō sär kō′mə), *n.* a malignant tumor or cancer of the skeletal muscles. [< Greek *rhábdos* rod + *mŷs, myós* muscle + English *sarcoma*]

**rhab|do|vi|rus** (rab′dō vī′rəs), *n.* any one of a group of viruses associated with various diseases transmitted by animal or insect bites: *One of the things which is known about rabies virus is that its genetic material is ribonucleic acid (RNA). Because of this property and its morphology it has been classified with the rhabdovirus group (from the Greek rhábdos meaning a rod)* (Science Journal).

---

**Pronunciation Key:** hat, āge, cãre, fär; let, ēqual, tėrm; it, īce; hot, ōpen, ôrder; oil, out; cup, pu̇t, rüle; child; long; thin; ᴛʜen; zh, measure; ə represents **a** in about, **e** in taken, **i** in pencil, **o** in lemon, **u** in circus.

**rha|chis** (rā′kis), *n., pl.* **rha|chis|es, rhach|i|des** (rak′ə dēz, rā′kə-). = rachis.

**rhach|i|tome** (rak′ə tōm), *n.* any one of an order of extinct reptiles of the Permian period, typified by the eryops. [< New Latin *Rhachitomi* the order name < Greek *rháchis* backbone + *-tomía* a cutting]

**Rhad|a|man|thine** (rad′ə man′thin), *adj.* **1** of or having to do with Rhadamanthus. **2** very strict.

**Rhad|a|man|thus** (rad′ə man′thəs), *n. Greek Mythology.* a son of Zeus and Europa, and brother of King Minos of Crete. Because he showed the spirit of justice in all his life, he was made a judge of the dead in Hades after he died.

**Rhae|tian** (rē′shən), *adj.* **1** of or having to do with Rhaetia, the ancient name for a district comprising southeastern Switzerland, part of the Tyrol, and adjoining regions. **2** = Rhaeto-Romanic.

**Rhae|tic** (rē′tik), *adj. Geology.* of or having to do with certain strata, extensively developed in the Rhaetian Alps, having features of both the Triassic and the Jurassic periods.

**Rhae|to-Ro|man|ic** (rē′tō rō man′ik), *adj., n.* — ***adj.*** of or having to do with a group of Romance dialects spoken in the Rhaetian Alps.
— ***n.*** the Rhaeto-Romanic dialects.

**rham|na|ceous** (ram nā′shəs), *adj. Botany.* belonging to the buckthorn family. [< New Latin *Rhamnaceae* the family name (< *Rhamnus* the typical genus < Late Latin *rhamnus* the buckthorn < Greek *rhámnos*) + English *-ous*]

**rham|nose** (ram′nōs), *n.* a sugar occurring in combination with a glycoside in many plants. *Formula:* $C_6H_{12}O_5$ [< Greek *rhámnos* the buckthorn (one of the plants in which it occurs)]

**rhap|sode** (rap′sōd), *n.* an ancient Greek rhapsodist. [< Greek *rhapsōidós* < *rháptein* sew + *ōidḗ* song, ode]

**rhap|sod|ic** (rap sod′ik), *adj.* = rhapsodical.

**rhap|sod|i|cal** (rap sod′ə kəl), *adj.* of, having to do with, or characteristic of rhapsody; extravagantly enthusiastic; ecstatic: *It is a powerful piece of work, long, elaborate, rhapsodical, and digressive* (Atlantic). — **rhap|sod′i|cal|ly,** *adv.*

**rhap|so|dist** (rap′sə dist), *n.* **1** a person who talks or writes with extravagant enthusiasm. **2** a professional reciter of epic poetry in ancient Greece. **3** any professional reciter or singer of poems.

**rhap|so|dis|tic** (rap′sə dis′tik), *adj.* = rhapsodical.

**rhap|so|dize** (rap′sə dīz), *v.,* **-dized, -diz|ing.**
— ***v.i.*** to talk or write with extravagant enthusiasm: *rhapsodising on this and that—poetry, politics, life, and death* (Maurice H. Hewlett).
— ***v.t.*** to recite as a rhapsody.

**rhap|so|dy** (rap′sə dē), *n., pl.* **-dies. 1** an utterance or writing marked by extravagant enthusiasm: *She went into rhapsodies over her garden.* **2** *Music.* an instrumental composition, irregular in form, resembling an improvisation: *Liszt's Hungarian rhapsodies.* **3** an epic poem, or a part of such a poem, suitable for recitation at one time. [< Latin *rhapsōdia* < Greek *rhapsōidía* verse composition < *rháptein* to stitch + *ōidḗ* song, ode]

**rhat|a|ny** (rat′ə nē), *n., pl.* **-nies. 1** a trailing South American shrub of the pea family whose dried root is used in tanning, in medicine as an astringent, and to color port wine. **2** a closely related plant, whose root is similarly used. **3** the root of either of these plants. [< Spanish *ratania* or *rataña* < Quechua (Peru) *rataña*]

**Rh disease,** = erythroblastosis.

**Rhe|a** (rē′ə), *n. Greek Mythology.* a daughter of Uranus and Gaea, the wife of Cronus, and mother of Zeus, Hera, Poseidon, Hades, Hestia, and Demeter. She was called the "Mother of the Gods."

**rhe|a** (rē′ə), *n.* any one of several large birds of South America that are much like the ostrich, but are smaller and have three toes instead of two. Rheas cannot fly. See picture under **ostrich.** [< New Latin *Rhea* the genus name < Latin *Rhea* Rhea]

**rhe|bok** (rē′bok; *Afrikaans* rā′bok), *n.* one of several varieties of comparatively small South African antelopes with slender, sharp horns: *The vaal rhebok is not among the fastest of antelopes* (C. S. Stokes). [< Dutch and Afrikaans *reebok* roe buck]

**rhe|in** (rē′in), *n.* a yellow, crystalline acid found in the leaves of the rhubarb and senna. *Formula:* $C_{15}H_8O_6$ [< Greek *rhéon* rhubarb + English *-in*]

**Rhein|gold** (rīn′gōld′), *n. German and Norse Mythology.* a magic hoard of gold owned by the Nibelungs and later by Siegfried. Also, **Rhinegold.** [< German *Rheingold* (literally) Rhine gold]

**rhe|mat|ic** (ri mat′ik), *adj.* **1** having to do with the formation of words. **2** having to do with or derived from a verb. [< Greek *rhēmatikós* < *rhêma, -atos* verb, word < *eirein* say, speak. See related etym. at **rhetor.**]

**rhe|nic** (rē′nik), *adj.* having to do with or containing rhenium. [< *rhen*(ium) + *-ic*]

**Rhen|ish** (ren′ish), *adj., n.* — ***adj.*** of the river Rhine or the regions near it.
— ***n.*** = Rhine wine.
[< Latin *Rhēnus* the Rhine + English *-ish*[1]]

***rhe|ni|um** (rē′nē əm), *n.* a rare, hard, heavy, grayish, metallic chemical element which occurs in molybdenum ore. It has chemical properties similar to those of manganese and a very high melting point (above 3,000 degrees centigrade). Rhenium is used in making alloys. *Aircraft metallurgists are excited about the rare element rhenium, which is found occasionally in copper ores* (Newsweek). [< New Latin *rhenium* < Latin *Rhēnus* Rhine + New Latin *-ium,* a suffix meaning "element"]

***rhenium**

| symbol | atomic number | atomic weight | oxidation state |
|---|---|---|---|
| Re | 75 | 186.2 | 4,6,7 |

**rheo-,** *combining form.* stream; electric current: *Rheostat = an instrument that regulates the strength of an electric current.* [< Greek *rhéos* a flowing, stream < *rheîn* to flow]

**rheo.,** rheostat or rheostats.

**rhe|o|log|i|cal** (rē′ə loj′ə kəl), *adj.* of or having to do with rheology. — **rhe′o|log′i|cal|ly,** *adv.*

**rhe|ol|o|gist** (rē ol′ə jist), *n.* an expert in rheology: *The fundamental task of the experimental rheologist is to measure viscosity and other flow problems* (New Scientist).

**rhe|ol|o|gy** (rē ol′ə jē), *n.* the science that deals with flow and alteration of form of matter.

**rhe|om|e|ter** (rē om′ə tər), *n.* **1** an instrument for measuring the flow of blood. **2** an instrument for measuring electric currents.

**rhe|o|scope** (rē′ə skōp), *n.* an instrument that indicates the presence of an electric current.

**rhe|o|scop|ic** (rē′ə skop′ik), *adj.* = electroscopic.

***rhe|o|stat** (rē′ə stat), *n.* an instrument for regulating the strength of an electric current by introducing different amounts of resistance into the circuit.

***rheostat**

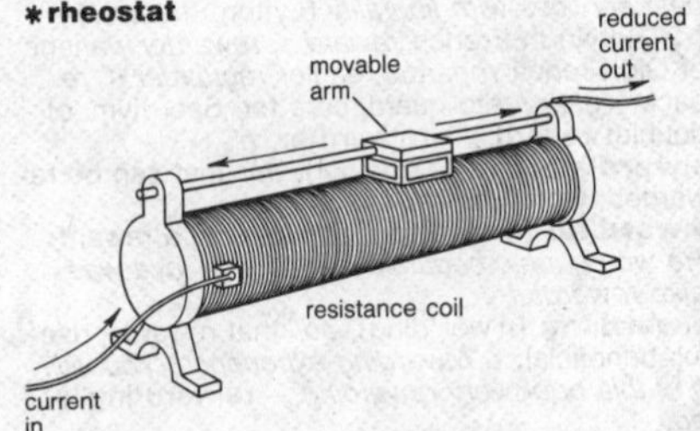


**rhe|o|stat|ic** (rē′ə stat′ik), *adj.* having to do with a rheostat.

**rhe|o|tac|tic** (rē ə tak′tik), *adj.* of or having to do with the movements of organisms in currents of liquid.

**rhe|o|tax|is** (rē′ə tak′sis), *n.* the movement of a cell or organism in response to the stimulus of a current of water or air. [< *rheo-* + Greek *táxis* arrangement]

**rhe|o|trope** (rē′ə trōp), *n.* a device for reversing the direction of an electric current.

**rhe|ot|ro|pism** (rē ot′rə piz əm), *n. Biology.* the orientation in growth of plants or sessile animals in response to a current of water or air.

**rhe|sis** (rē′sis), *n.* **1** a saying or speech, often one, or a passage from one, in a play, poem, or book. **2** a set speech or discourse. [< Greek *rhêsis*]

**rhe|sus** (rē′səs), *n.* a small, yellowish-brown monkey with a short tail, found in India. It is often used in medical research. The rhesus is a kind of macaque. [< New Latin *rhesus,* arbitrary use of Latin *Rhēsus* Rhesus]

**Rhe|sus** (rē′səs), *n. Greek Legend.* a Thracian ally of the Trojans, slain by Odysseus and Diomedes, because they knew that an oracle had said that Troy would not fall if Rhesus's horses drank from the Xanthus River.

**Rhesus factor,** = Rh factor.

**rhet.,** **1** rhetoric. **2** rhetorical.

**Rhe|tic** (rē′tik), *adj.* = Rhaetic.

**rhe|tor** (rē′tər), *n.* **1** a master or teacher of rhetoric. **2** an orator, especially a professional one. [< Latin *rhētor* < Greek *rhḗtōr, -oros* < *eirein* to say]

**rhet|o|ric** (ret′ər ik), *n.* **1** the art of using words in speaking or writing so as to persuade or influence others: *The communication of those thoughts to others falls under the consideration of rhetoric* (John Stuart Mill). **2** the language used: *Blifil suffered himself to be overpowered by the forcible rhetoric of the squire* (Henry Fielding). **3** a book on rhetoric: *Aristotle himself has given it a place in his Rhetoric among the beauties of that art* (Joseph Addison). **4** mere display in language: *the exaggerated rhetoric of presidential campaigns* (New York Times); *the limp loquacity of long-winded rhetoric, so natural to men and soldiers in an hour of emergency* (Algernon Charles Swinburne). [< Latin *rhētorica* < Greek *rhētorikḗ* (*téchnē*) (art) of an orator < *rhḗtōr;* see etym. under **rhetor**]

**rhe|tor|i|cal** (ri tôr′ə kəl, -tor′-), *adj.* **1** of or having to do with rhetoric. **2** using rhetoric. **3** intended especially for display; artificial: *a rhetorical style, rhetorical language.* **4** = oratorical. — **rhe|tor′i|cal|ness,** *n.*

**rhe|tor|i|cal|ly** (ri tôr′ə klē, -tor′-), *adv.* in a rhetorical manner; according to the rules of rhetoric: *to treat a subject rhetorically, a discourse rhetorically delivered.*

**rhetorical question,** a question asked only for effect, not for information. *Example:* "Who can tell whether or not life exists on other planets?"

**rhet|o|ri|cian** (ret′ə rish′ən), *n.* **1** a person skilled in rhetoric: *Her poetry is the diary or autobiography ... of an acute psychologist, a wonderful rhetorician, and one of the most wonderful writers who ever lived* (Harper's). **2** a person given to display in language. **3** a teacher of the art of rhetoric.

**rheum**[1] (rüm), *n.* **1** a watery discharge, such as mucus, tears, or saliva: *A few drops of women's rheum, which are As cheap as lies* (Shakespeare). **2** a cold; catarrh: *But he was brooding even more than usual on the frailty of the human body in general and his own aches and rheums in particular* (Atlantic). [< Old French *reume,* learned borrowing from Latin *rheuma* < Greek *rheûma, -atos* a flowing < *rheîn* to flow]

**rhe|um**[2] (rē′əm), *n.* = rhubarb. [< New Latin *Rheum* the genus name < Greek *rhêon*]

**rheu|mat|ic** (rü mat′ik), *adj., n.* — ***adj.*** **1** of or having to do with rheumatism: *rheumatic symptoms.* **2** having or liable to have rheumatism: *Silk mittens ... covered her rheumatic hands* (Edith Wharton). **3** causing rheumatism. **4** caused by rheumatism.
— ***n.*** a person who has or is liable to have rheumatism.

**rheumatics,** *Informal.* rheumatism: *a new cure for the rheumatics* (Robert Louis Stevenson). [< Latin *rheumaticus* < Greek *rheumatikós* < *rheûma;* see etym. under **rheum**[1]] — **rheu|mat′i|cal|ly,** *adv.*

**rheumatic fever,** a disease more common among children than among grown-ups, characterized by fever, pains in the joints, and often damage to the heart: *But iritis, a chronic eye ailment that was the residue of an earlier bout with rheumatic fever, ended his schooling* (Time).

**rheumatic heart disease,** inflammation or scarring of the heart muscle resulting from rheumatic fever.

**rheu|mat|ick|y** (rü mat′ə kē), *adj.* having rheumatism; affected by rheumatism: *rheumaticky limbs, a rheumaticky old horse.*

**rheu|ma|tism** (rü′mə tiz əm), *n.* **1** a disease with inflammation, swelling, and stiffness of the joints. **2** = rheumatic fever. **3** = rheumatoid arthritis. [< Latin *rheumatismus* < Greek *rheumatismós* < *rheumatízein* < *rheûma;* see etym. under **rheum**[1]]

**rheumatism weed, 1** = Indian hemp. **2** = pipsissewa.

**rheu|ma|toid** (rü′mə toid), *adj.* **1** resembling rheumatism: *rheumatoid diseases.* **2** having rheumatism. — **rheu′ma|toi′dal|ly,** *adv.*

**rheu|ma|toi|dal** (rü′mə toi′dəl), *adj.* = rheumatoid.

**rheumatoid arthritis,** a chronic disease characterized by inflammation and stiffness of the joints, often crippling in its effects: *Rheumatoid arthritis is a seasonal disease that is likely to begin or grow worse in the colder months* (Science News Letter).

**rheumatoid factor,** an antibody found especially in the blood serum of arthritics which reacts against globulins in the individual's own serum.

**rheu|ma|tol|o|gist** (rü′mə tol′ə jist), *n.* an expert in rheumatology.

**rheu|ma|tol|o|gy** (rü′mə tol′ə jē), *n.* the study and treatment of rheumatism and related diseases: *Medical science was a late starter in the field of rheumatology, which comprises the study of a group of diseases numbering 50 or more which kill infrequently but cripple greatly* (London Times).

**rheum|y** (rü′mē), *adj.,* **rheum|i|er, rheum|i|est. 1** full of rheum: *Nobody recognized the aging white-haired man who walked about Moscow,* *staring with rheumy eyes at the broad streets and tall buildings* (Time). **2** causing rheum; damp and cold.

**rhex|is** (rek′sis), *n.* rupture of a blood vessel or of any organ. [< Greek *rhêxis* < *rhegnýnai* break]

**Rh factor**, an antigen found in the red blood cells of most human beings and the higher mammals. Blood containing this substance is Rh positive and does not combine favorably with blood which is Rh negative and lacks this substance. *The presence or absence of the Rh factor is governed by a dominant gene, which means that when Rh-positive and Rh-negative genes are paired, the resulting children are always Rh-positive* (J. Randal). Also, **Rhesus factor.** [< *rh*(esus); it was first discovered in the blood of the rhesus monkey]

**R.H.G.**, Royal Horse Guards.

**RHI** (no periods), range-height indicator (a radarscope that shows the range and height of an aircraft).

**rhig|o|lene** (rig′ə lēn), *n.* an extremely volatile liquid obtained from petroleum. It is used to produce local anesthesia by freezing. [< Greek *rhîgos* cold + English *-ol*[2] + *-ene*]

**rhi|nal** (rī′nəl), *adj.* of or having to do with the nose; nasal. [< Greek *rhîs, rhīnós* nose + English *-al*[1]] **–rhi′nal|ly,** *adv.*

**rhi|nar|i|um** (rī nãr′ē əm), *n., pl.* **-nar|i|a** (-nãr′ē ə). **1** the front part of the clypeus, as of neuropteran insects and certain beetles. **2** the area of bare skin around the nostrils of ruminants; muffle. [< New Latin *rhinarium* < Greek *rhís, rhīnós* nose]

**Rhine|gold** (rīn′gōld′), *n.* = Rheingold.

**Rhine|land|er** (rīn′lan′dər), *n.* a native or inhabitant of the Rhineland region of West Germany.

**Rhine|maid|en** (rīn′mā′dən), *n.* any one of the maidens, in Wagner's version of the Nibelung legend, who guard the gold treasure of the Rhine.

**rhi|nen|ce|phal|ic** (rī′nen sə fal′ik), *adj.* having to do with the rhinencephalon.

**rhi|nen|ceph|a|lon** (rī′nen sef′ə lon), *n., pl.* **-la** (-lə). the part of the brain most closely connected with the olfactory nerves: *All the brain damage occurred in a region of the cerebrum known as the rhinencephalon* (Science News Letter). [< New Latin *rhinencephalon* < Greek *rhîs, rhīnós* nose + New Latin *encephalon* encephalon]

**rhine|stone** (rīn′stōn′), *n.* an imitation diamond, made of glass or paste. [translation of French *caillou du Rhin* Rhine pebble, originally made at Strasbourg]

**Rhine wine** (rīn), **1** wine produced in the valley of the Rhine. Most Rhine wines are light, dry, white wines. **2** a similar wine made elsewhere.

**rhi|ni|tis** (rī nī′tis), *n.* inflammation of the mucous membrane of the nose. [< New Latin *rhinitis* < Greek *rhîs, rhīnós* nose + New Latin *-itis* -itis]

**rhi|no**[1] (rī′nō), *n., pl.* **-nos** or **-no.** *Informal.* a rhinoceros: *We saw two rhino come down to the river to drink* (J. H. Patterson).

**rhi|no**[2] (rī′nō), *n. Slang.* money; cash: *ready rhino.* [origin unknown]

**rhino-**, *combining form.* nose; of the nose, as in *rhinology, rhinoscope.* [< Greek *rhîs, rhīnós* nose]

***rhi|noc|er|os** (rī nos′ər əs), *n., pl.* **-os|es** or (*collectively*) **-os.** a large animal with thick skin and one or two upright horns on the snout. Rhinoceroses are mammals of Africa and Asia and eat grass and other plants. There are five living species in the rhinoceros family. See picture below. [< Latin *rhīnoceros* < Greek *rhinókerōs* < *rhîs, rhīnós* nose + *kéras* horn]

***rhinoceros beetle**, any one of several large scarabaeid beetles of tropical regions. The male has a large horn on the head. See picture below.

**rhinoceros bird**, a small bird that perches on the back of the rhinoceros and feeds on the parasitic insects found there; oxpecker.

**rhinoceros hornbill**, a hornbill of Malaysia having a red and yellow growth that rises from its forehead like a horn.

***rhinoceros iguana**, a rare iguana lizard of the West Indies with three blunt horns on its snout. See picture below.

**rhinoceros viper**, a brilliantly colored viper of the rain forests of central Africa, having a pair of large, pointed growths at the tip of its snout.

**rhi|nog|e|nous** (rī noj′ə nəs), *adj.* of nasal origin.

**rhi|no|lar|yn|gol|o|gy** (rī′nō lar′ing gol′ə jē), *n.* the branch of medicine dealing with diseases of the nose and larynx. [< *rhino-* + *laryngology*]

**rhi|no|lith** (rī′nə lith), *n.* a calculus formed in the nasal cavities.

**rhi|no|log|i|cal** (rī′nə loj′ə kəl), *adj.* having to do with rhinology.

**rhi|nol|o|gist** (rī nol′ə jist), *n.* a specialist in diseases of the nose.

**rhi|nol|o|gy** (rī nol′ə jē), *n.* the branch of medicine dealing with the nose and its diseases.

**rhi|no|pha|ryn|ge|al** (rī′nō fə rin′jē əl, -far′in jē′-), *adj.* of or having to do with the nose and the pharynx.

**rhi|no|phar|yn|gi|tis** (rī′nō far′in jī′tis), *n.* inflammation of the mucous membrane of the nose and the pharynx. [< *rhino-* + *pharyngitis*]

**rhi|no|phar|ynx** (rī′nō far′ingks), *n.* = nasopharynx.

**rhi|no|plas|tic** (rī′nə plas′tik), *adj.* of or having to do with rhinoplasty.

**rhi|no|plas|ty** (rī′nə plas′tē), *n.* plastic surgery of the nose.

**rhi|nor|rhe|a** (rī′nə rē′ə), *n.* excessive secretion of mucus from the nose: *If the patient is allergic, the onset is frequently sudden, with profuse watery rhinorrhea, sneezing and nasal blockage* (Francis Loeffler Lederer). [< Greek *rhîs, rhīnós* nose + *rheîn* flow]

**rhi|no|scope** (rī′nə skōp), *n.* an instrument for examining the nasal passages.

**rhi|nos|co|py** (rī nos′kə pē), *n.* use of the rhinoscope.

**rhi|no|tra|che|i|tis** (rī′nə trā′kē ī′tis), *n.* a viral disease of cattle, characterized by inflammation of the mucous membrane of the nose and the windpipe. [< *rhino-* + *tracheitis*]

**rhi|no|vi|rus** (rī′nō vī′rəs), *n.* any one of a group of viruses associated with the common cold and other respiratory diseases: *This could pave the way ... for the development of killed and live virus vaccines, especially the rhinoviruses, which are a principal cause of the common cold and for which there is no specific control* (Science News Letter).

**rhip|i|dis|ti|an** (rip′ə dis′tē ən), *adj., n.* **–adj.** of or belonging to a group of crossopterygian fishes believed to be the direct ancestors of the first amphibians. **–n.** a rhipidistian fish.

[< New Latin *Rhipidistia* the order name < Greek *rhīpís, rhīpid* fan + *histion* tissue]

**R. Hist. S.**, Royal Historical Society.

**rhi|zo|bic** (rī zō′bik), *adj.* of or having to do with the rhizobia.

**rhi|zo|bi|um** (rī zō′bē əm), *n., pl.* **-bi|a** (-bē ə). any one of a group of rod-shaped, nitrogen-fixing bacteria that live symbiotically in nodules on the roots of leguminous plants. [< New Latin *rhizobium* < Greek *rhíza* root + *bíos* life]

**rhi|zo|car|pic** (rī′zə kär′pik), *adj.* = rhizocarpous.

**rhi|zo|car|pous** (rī′zə kär′pəs), *adj.* having the stem annual but the root perennial. The perennial herbs are rhizocarpous. [< Greek *rhíza* root + *karpós* fruit + English *-ous*]

**rhi|zo|caul** (rī′zə kôl), *n. Zoology.* the rootlike part of a polyp, used for attachment to some support. [< Greek *rhíza* root + *kaulós* stalk]

**rhi|zo|ceph|a|lan** (rī′zə sef′ə lən), *adj.* = rhizocephalous.

**rhi|zo|ceph|a|lous** (rī′zə sef′ə ləs), *adj.* of or belonging to a group of crustaceans that are parasitic on crabs, living within the host as a mass of modified cells resembling rootlike processes. [< New Latin *Rhizocephala* the order name (< Greek *rhíza* root + *kephalê* head) + English *-ous*]

**rhi|zoc|to|ni|a** (rī′zok tō′nē ə), *n.* a fungus that causes damping-off and various diseases in plants. [< New Latin *Rhizoctonia* the genus name < Greek *rhíza* root + *któnos* murder]

**rhi|zo|gen|ic** (rī′zə jen′ik), *adj.* producing roots: *rhizogenic cells or tissues.* [< Greek *rhíza* root + English *-gen* + *-ic*]

**rhi|zog|e|nous** (rī zoj′ə nəs), *adj.* = rhizogenic.

**rhi|zoid** (rī′zoid), *adj., n.* **–adj.** = rootlike. **–n.** one of the rootlike filaments by which a moss, fern, liverwort, or fungus is attached to the substratum. **–rhi′zoid|like′,** *adj.*

**rhi|zoi|dal** (rī zoi′dəl), *adj.* resembling a rhizoid.

**rhi|zo|mat|ic** (rī′zə mat′ik), *adj.* having to do with rhizomes; having the appearance of a rhizome.

**rhi|zom|a|tous** (rī zom′ə təs, -zō′mə-), *adj.* **1** of or having to do with a rhizome. **2** having rhizomes: *But if more plants of the rhizomatous type are wanted, a leaf is pulled off and inserted in regular soil* (New York Times).

***rhi|zome** (rī′zōm), *n.* a rootlike stem lying on or underneath the ground, which usually sends out roots below and leafy shoots above; rootstock. The rhizome stores food to be used by the new plant the following year. *In some underground stems, that is rhizomes, many of these leaves develop very poorly, taking the form of scales* (Fred W. Emerson). [< Greek *rhízōma* < *rhizoûn* cause to strike root < *rhíza* root]

***rhizome**

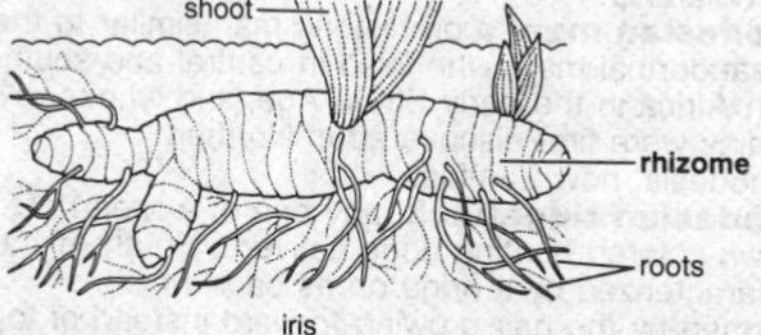


**rhi|zo|mic** (rī zō′mik, -zom′-), *adj.* belonging to or consisting of rhizomes.

**rhi|zo|morph** (rī′zə môrf), *n.* a rootlike filament of hypha in various fungi. [< Greek *rhíza* root + *morphê* form]

**rhi|zo|mor|phous** (rī′zə môr′fəs), *adj. Botany.* rootlike in form. [< Greek *rhíza* root + *morphê* form + English *-ous*]

**rhi|zoph|a|gous** (rī zof′ə gəs), *adj.* feeding on roots. [< Greek *rhíza* root + *phageîn* eat + English *-ous*]

**rhi|zoph|i|lous** (rī zof′ə ləs), *adj.* growing or parasitic upon roots.

**rhi|zo|pho|ra|ceous** (rī′zō fə rā′shəs), *adj.* belonging to a family of mostly tropical trees and shrubs typified by the mangrove. [< New Latin *Rhizophoraceae* the family name (< Greek *rhíza* root + *phérein* bear) + English *-ous*]

**rhi|zo|pod** (rī′zə pod), *n.* any one of a class of mostly marine protozoans that have pseudopods for moving about and taking in food; sarcodinian: *Amebas are rhizopods.* [< New Latin *Rhizopoda* the class name < Greek *rhíza* root + *poús, podós* foot]

**rhi|zop|o|dan** (rī zop′ə dən), *n., adj.* **–n.** = rhizopod. **–adj.** of or having to do with a rhizopod.

**rhi|zop|o|dous** (rī zop′ə dəs), *adj.* = rhizopodan.

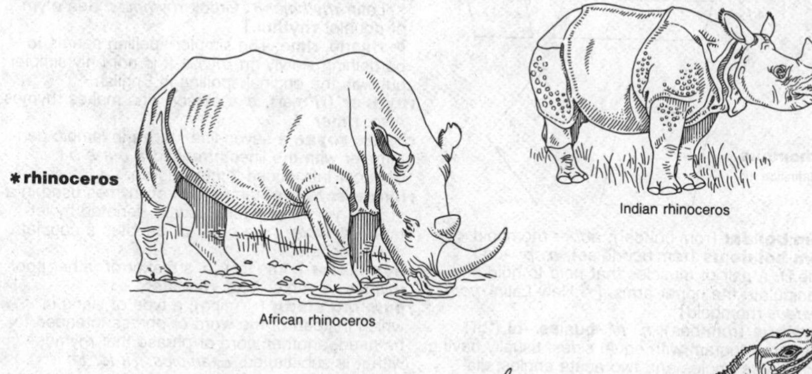

***rhinoceros**

African rhinoceros

Indian rhinoceros

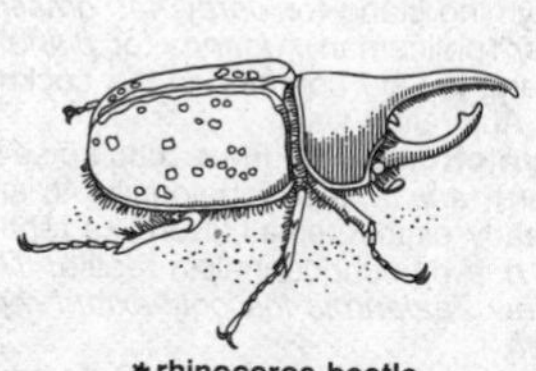

***rhinoceros beetle**

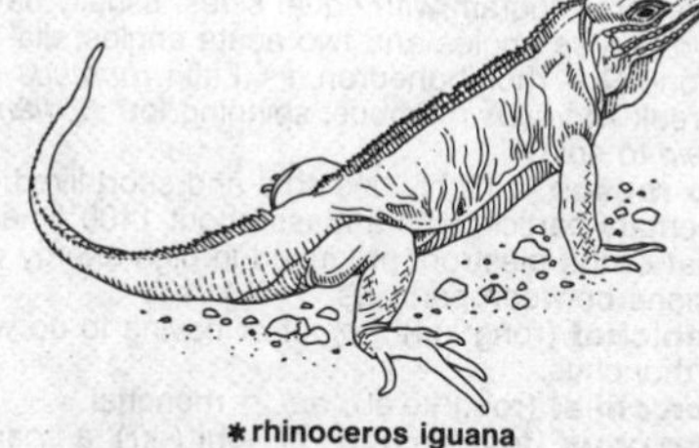

***rhinoceros iguana**

**Pronunciation Key:** hat, āge, cãre, fär; let, ēqual, tėrm; it, īce; hot, ōpen, ôrder; oil, out; cup, pu̇t, rüle; child; long; thin; ŦHen; zh, measure; ə represents **a** in about, **e** in taken, **i** in pencil, **o** in lemon, **u** in circus.

**rhi|zo|pus** (rī′zə pəs), *n.* any of a group of fungi that includes bread mold and potato rot. [< New Latin *Rhizopus* the genus name < Greek *rhíza* root + *poús, podós* foot]

**rhi|zo|sphere** (rī′zə sfir), *n.* the zone immediately surrounding the roots of a plant: *At the heart of soil-plant relationships are the events ... that occur on the surfaces of roots and in their immediate vicinity in the rhizosphere* (Science). [< Greek *rhíza* root + English *sphere*]

**rhi|zo|spher|ic** (rī′zə sfer′ik), *adj.* of or having to do with the rhizosphere: *rhizospheric compounds.*

**rhi|zot|o|mist** (rī zot′ə mist), *n.* a person who collects roots to use as medicine.

**rhi|zot|o|my** (rī zot′ə mē), *n., pl.* **-mies**. the surgical operation of cutting a spinal nerve root. [< Greek *rhíza* root + *-tomíā* a cutting]

**Rh negative**, lacking the Rh factor: *Rh negative blood.*

***rho** (rō), *n.* **1** the 17th letter of the Greek alphabet corresponding to English *R, r.* **2** = rho meson. [< Greek *rhô*]

***rho** definition 1

| Ρ | ρ |
|---|---|
| capital letter | lower-case letter |

**rho|da|min** (rō′də min), *n.* = rhodamine.

**rho|da|mine** (rō′də mēn, -min), *n.* **1** a red dye having brilliant fluorescent qualities, obtained by heating an amino derivative of phenol with phthalic anhydride and hydrochloric acid. *Formula:* $C_{23}H_{31}ClN_2O_3$ **2** any one of a group of related dyes. [< Greek *rhódon* rose + English *amine*]

**Rhode Island bent** (rōd), a variety of redtop, much valued as a lawn grass.

**Rhode Islander**, a native or inhabitant of Rhode Island.

**Rhode Island greening**, a green apple with an acid flavor, grown in the northeastern United States.

**Rhode Island Red**, any one of an American breed of chickens of medium weight that have reddish feathers and a black tail.

**Rhode Island White**, any of an American breed of chickens similar to the Rhode Island Red but having white plumage.

**Rhodes grass** (rōdz), a perennial South African grass, grown in warm regions for forage.

**Rho|de|sian** (rō dē′zhən), *adj., n.* **—*adj.*** of or having to do with Rhodesia.
**—*n.*** **1** a person born or living in Rhodesia. **2** a student attending Oxford University on a Rhodes Scholarship.

**Rhodesian man**, a prehistoric man similar to the Neanderthal man, who lived in central and southern Africa in the early Stone Age, and whose remains were first discovered in Northern Rhodesia, now Zambia.

**Rhodesian ridgeback**, any one of a breed of fawn-colored hunting dogs native to South Africa, characterized by a ridge on its back which is formed by the hair growing forward instead of toward the back like the rest of his coat.

**Rhodes scholar**, a holder of a Rhodes scholarship.

**Rhodes scholarship**, a two- or three-year scholarship at Oxford University, founded by Cecil Rhodes.

**Rho|di|an** (rō′dē ən), *adj., n.* **—*adj.*** of or having to do with the island of Rhodes.
**—*n.*** a native or inhabitant of Rhodes.

**rho|dic** (rō′dik), *adj.* **1** of or having to do with rhodium. **2** containing rhodium, especially with a high valence.

***rho|di|um** (rō′dē əm), *n.* a rare, silver-white metallic chemical element found chiefly in platinum ores. It is similar to aluminum, but harder, and forms salts that give rose-colored solutions. Rhodium has a very high melting point, is resistant to acid, and is used for plating silverware and jewelry. [< Greek *rhódon* rose + New Latin *-ium,* a suffix meaning "element" (from the rosy color of its salts)]

***rhodium**

| symbol | atomic number | atomic weight | oxidation state |
|---|---|---|---|
| Rh | 45 | 102.905 | 3 |

**rho|do|chro|site** (rō′dō krō′sīt), *n.* a mineral consisting essentially of manganese carbonate and usually occurring in rose-red crystals; dialogite. *Formula:* $MnCO_3$ [< German *Rhodochrosit* < Greek *rhodóchrōs, -chrōtos* rose-colored (< *rhódon* rose + *chrṓs, chrōtós* flesh-colored skin) + German *-it* -ite[1]]

**rho|do|den|dron** (rō′də den′drən), *n., pl.* **-drons, -dra** (-drə). **1** a shrub or tree with leathery leaves and beautiful large, pink, purple, or white flowers. Most rhododendrons are evergreen. There are many kinds, making up a genus of plants belonging to the heath family. **2** the flower. [< New Latin *Rhododendron* the genus name < Greek *rhodódendron* < *rhódon* rose + *déndron* tree, related to *drŷs* tree]

**rho|do|lite** (rō′də līt), *n.* a rose-red variety of garnet, sometimes used as a gem. [< Greek *rhódon* rose + English *-lite*]

**rhod|o|mon|tade** (rod′ə mon tād′, -täd′), *n., adj., v.i.,* **-tad|ed, -tad|ing.** = rodomontade.

**rho|do|nite** (rō′də nīt), *n.* a rose-red mineral, consisting essentially of manganese silicate. It is sometimes used as an ornamental stone. *Formula:* $MnSiO_3$ [< German *Rhodonit* < Greek *rhódon* rose + German *-it* -ite[1]]

**rho|do|plast** (rō′də plast), *n.* one of the chromatophores which bear the red coloring matter in the cells of the red algae. [< Greek *rhódon* rose + *plastós* something formed]

**rho|dop|sin** (rō dop′sin), *n.* a purplish-red protein pigment that is sensitive to light, found in the rods of the retina of the eye; visual purple: *Rhodopsin was found to be the visual pigment in all vertebrates from the primitive lamprey to man* (Science News Letter). [< Greek *rhódon* rose + *ópsis* sight + English *-in*]

**rho|do|ra** (rō dôr′ə, -dōr′-), *n.* a low deciduous species of rhododendron of Canada and the northeast United States, with purplish-rose flowers that appear before the leaves do. [< New Latin *Rhodora* the genus name < Latin *rodarum* < a Gaulish word]

**rhomb** (rom, romb), *n.* **1** = rhombus. **2** = rhombohedron. [< Middle French *rhombe,* learned borrowing from Latin *rhombus* < Greek *rhómbos;* see etym. under **rhombus**]

**rhom|ben|ce|phal|ic** (rom′ben sə fal′ik), *adj.* of or having to do with the hindbrain.

**rhom|ben|ceph|a|lon** (rom′ben sef′ə lon), *n.* = hindbrain. [< New Latin *rhombencephalon* < Greek *rhómbos* (see etym. under **rhombus**) + *en-* in + *kephalḗ* head]

**rhom|bic** (rom′bik), *adj.* **1** having the form of a rhombus. **2** having a rhombus as a base or cross section. **3** bounded by rhombuses. **4** *Chemistry.* having to do with a system of crystallization characterized by three unequal axes intersecting at right angles; orthorhombic.

**rhom|bi|cal** (rom′bə kəl), *adj.* = rhombic.

**rhom|bo|he|dral** (rom′bə hē′drəl), *adj.* of, or in the form of, a rhombohedron.

**rhom|bo|he|dron** (rom′bə hē′drən), *n., pl.* **-drons, -dra** (-drə). a solid bounded by six rhombic planes. [< Greek *rhómbos* (see etym. under **rhombus**) + *hédra* base]

***rhom|boid** (rom′boid), *n., adj.* **—*n.*** a parallelogram with equal opposite sides, unequal adjacent sides, and oblique angles.
**—*adj.*** shaped like a rhombus or rhomboid. [< Late Latin *rhomboīdes* < Greek *rhombo̱eidḗs* < *rhómbos* (see etym. under **rhombus**) + *eîdos* form]

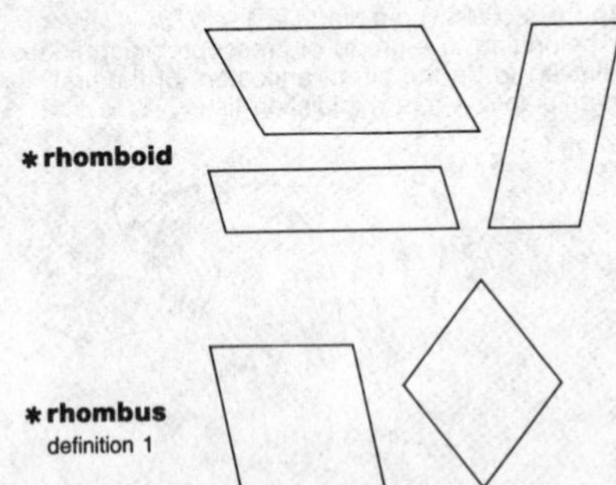

***rhomboid**

***rhombus** definition 1

**rhom|boi|dal** (rom boi′dəl), *adj.* = rhomboid.

**rhom|boi|de|us** (rom boi′dē əs), *n., pl.* **-de|i** (-dē ī). a pair of muscles that help to hold and manipulate the upper arms. [< New Latin *rhomboideus* rhomboid]

***rhom|bus** (rom′bəs), *n., pl.* **-bus|es, -bi** (-bī). **1** a parallelogram with equal sides, usually having two obtuse angles and two acute angles; diamond. **2** = rhombohedron. [< Latin *rhombus* < Greek *rhómbos* rhombus; spinning top < *rhémbein* to spin]

**rho meson**, a highly unstable and short-lived elementary particle with a mass about 1400 times that of the electron, produced in high-energy collisions between particles.

**rhon|chal** (rong′kəl), *adj.* of or having to do with a rhonchus.

**rhon|chi|al** (rong′kē əl), *adj.* = rhonchal.

**rhon|chus** (rong′kəs), *n., pl.* **-chi** (-kī). a coarse sound resembling a snore, caused by obstruction of the bronchial tubes or trachea with secretions. [< Latin *rhoncus* a snoring, croaking, perhaps related to Greek *rhénchos* < *rénkein,* or *rénchein* to snore]

**rho|ta|cism** (rō′tə siz əm), *n.* an excessive use, mispronunciation, or substitution of the sound represented by *r* in English. [< New Latin *rhotacismus* < Greek *rhōtakízein* overuse the letter *rhô* rho]

**Rh positive**, containing the Rh factor: *Rh positive blood.*

**rhu|barb** (rü′bärb), *n.* **1** a garden plant with very large leaves, whose thick, sour stalks are used for making sauce or pies; pieplant. It belongs to the buckwheat family. **2** its stalks. **3** the sauce made of them. **4** a purgative medicine made from a kind of dried rhubarb. **5** *Slang.* a violent argument or protest, usually marked by scornful comment: *a ball game filled with rhubarbs.* [< Old French *rheubarbe,* learned borrowing from Medieval Latin *rheubarbarum* < Greek *rhéon bárbaron* foreign rhubarb]

**rhu|barb|ing** (rü′bär bing), *adj., n. British.* **—*adj.*** (of actors) muttering sounds to simulate background noise of talk or conversation.
**—*n.*** noisy talk: *The players filed off the stage, and the silence dissolved in the rhubarbing of the multitude of spectators* (Manchester Guardian Weekly).
[< *rhubarb,* the theatrical direction and the word customarily repeated at different speeds by actors to give the impression of a general hubbub]

**rhumb** (rum, rumb), *n.* **1** any one of the 32 points of the compass. **2** = rhumb line. [< Latin *rhombus* < Greek *rhómbos;* see etym. under **rhombus**]

**rhum|ba** (rum′bə), *n., v.i.,* **-baed** (-bəd), **-ba|ing** (-bə ing). = rumba.

**rhum|ba|tron** (rum′bə tron), *n. Electronics.* **1** two hollow metal containers in a klystron for changing the flow of electrons into the ultra-high-frequency current. **2** = klystron. [< *rhumba* + (elec)*tron* (because of the dancing motion of the electrons)]

**rhumb line**, a line on the surface of a sphere cutting all meridians at the same oblique angle; loxodromic curve.

**rhumb sailing**, sailing on a rhumb line.

**rhus** (rüs), *n., pl.* **rhus** or **rhus|es**. a sumac, especially poison sumac or poison ivy. [< New Latin *Rhus* the genus name < Latin *rhūs* sumac < Greek *rhous*]

**rhyme** (rīm), *v.,* **rhymed, rhym|ing,** *n.* **—*v.i.*** **1** to sound alike, especially in the last part: *"Long" and "song" rhyme. "Go to bed" rhymes with "sleepyhead."* **2** to make rhymes.
**—*v.t.*** **1** to put or make into rhyme: *to rhyme a translation.* **2** to use (a word) with another that rhymes with it: *to rhyme "love" and "dove."*
[Middle English *rimen* < Old French *rimer* < *rime;* see the noun]
**—*n.*** **1** a word or line having the same last sound as another: *"Cat" is a rhyme for "mat." "Hey! diddle, diddle" and "The cat and the fiddle" are rhymes.* **2** verses or poetry with some of the lines ending in similar sounds. **3** an agreement in the final sounds of words or lines. Also, **rime**.
**without rhyme or reason**, having no system or sense: *On an irregular bare earth floor, machinery was strewn without apparent rhyme or reason* (New York Times).
[Middle English *rime* < Old French *rime,* probably < Latin *rhythmus* < Greek *rhythmós.* See etym. of doublet **rhythm**.]
▶ **rhyme, rime**. The simpler spelling seems to be gaining slowly on *rhyme.* It is not only simpler but was the original spelling in English.

**rhym|er** (rī′mər), *n.* a person who makes rhymes. Also, **rimer**.

**rhyme royal**, a seven-line stanza in iambic pentameter with the lines arranged *a b a b b c c.* Chaucer introduced it into English.

**rhyme scheme**, the pattern of rhymes used in a stanza, verse, or poem, usually denoted by letters. *Example: "a a b b c c"* denotes a couplet rhyme scheme.

**rhyme|ster** (rīm′stər), *n.* a maker of rather poor rhymes or verse. Also, **rimester**.

**rhym|ing slang** (rī′ming), a type of slang in which instead of the word or phrase intended to be used, another word or phrase that rhymes with it is substituted. *Examples: Tit for tat* is rhyming slang for *derby hat, grasshopper* for *copper* (policeman), *Joanna* for *piano.* Rhyming slang is very common in the cockney dialect and in Australian slang.

**rhyn|cho|ce|pha|li|an** (ring′kō sə fā′ lē ən, -fāl′-yən), *adj., n.* **—*adj.*** belonging to an order of nearly extinct, small, lizardlike reptiles.
**—*n.*** a rhynchocephalian reptile: *The tuatara of New Zealand is the only extant rhynchocephalian.*
[< New Latin *Rhynchocephala* the order name

(< Greek *rhýnchos* snout + *kephalḗ* head) + English *-ian*]

**rhyn|choph|o|ran** (ring kof′ər ən), *n.* any one of the beetles having the head prolonged into a snout; weevil. [< Greek *rhýnchos* snout + *phórein* to bear + English *-an*]

**rhyn|choph|o|rous** (ring kof′ər əs), *adj.* of or belonging to the rhynchophorans.

**rhy|o|lite** (rī′ə līt), *n.* a volcanic rock containing quartz with texture often showing the lines of flow. [< German *Rhyolit* < Greek *rhýāx, -ākos* lava flow; torrent (< *rhéin* to flow) + German *-it* -ite[1]]

**rhy|o|lit|ic** (rī′ə lit′ik), *adj.* of or resembling rhyolite.

**rhythm** (riᴛʜ′əm), *n.* **1** movement with a regular repetition of a beat, accent, rise and fall, or the like: *the rhythm of the tides, the rhythm of one's heartbeats.* **2** a repetition of musical beats; arrangement of recurring strong and weak accents: *A rhythm of One two three One two three is characteristic of waltz.* **3** arrangement of syllables or cadences in a line of poetry: *The rhythms of "The Lord's Prayer," "The Night Before Christmas" and "The Star-Spangled Banner" are different.* **4** a grouping by accents or beats: *triple rhythm, rumba rhythm.* **5** *Biology.* a pattern of involuntary behavior, action, etc., occurring regularly and periodically: *Furthermore, ants, which may be non-rhythmic, have been trained to feed at several time intervals, whereas bees, which have a marked rhythm and are active only in the daytime, cannot be trained on other than a 24-hour basis* (J. L. Cloudsley-Thompson). **6** = rhythm method. **7** *Fine Arts.* the proper relation of parts producing a harmonious whole, especially by repeating certain forms and colors. [< Latin *rhythmos* < Greek *rhythmós,* perhaps related to *rheîn* to flow. See etym. of doublet **rhyme**.]

**rhythm and blues**, *U.S.* rock'n'roll with blues as its melodic element.

**rhythm band**, a children's musical band of percussion instruments such as chimes, gongs, cymbals, wood blocks, sticks, and drums.

**rhythmed** (riᴛʜ′əmd), *adj.* = rhythmical.

**rhyth|mic** (riᴛʜ′mik), *adj., n.* —*adj.* = rhythmical: *Berto Lardera ... gets an almost musical sense of rhythmic movement in his pieces* (New Yorker).
—*n.* = rhythmics.

**rhyth|mi|cal** (riᴛʜ′mə kəl), *adj.* **1** having rhythm: *rhythmical speech.* **2** of or having to do with rhythm: *rhythmical sound in music.* —**rhyth′mi|cal|ly**, *adv.*

**rhyth|mic|i|ty** (riᴛʜ mis′ə tē), *n.* rhythmic character: *The rhythmicity of the heart is as much a built-in feature as the anatomical structure of its cells* (Scientific American).

**rhyth|mics** (riᴛʜ′miks), *n.* **1** the science of rhythm and rhythmical structures. **2** exercises done to music, especially as part of a physical education program.

**rhyth|mist** (riᴛʜ′mist), *n.* a person who is expert in, or has a fine sense of, rhythm.

**rhyth|mize** (riᴛʜ′mīz), *v.t.,* **-mized, -miz|ing.** to put into rhythm. —**rhyth′mi|za′tion**, *n.*

**rhythm|less** (riᴛʜ′əm lis), *adj.* having no rhythm.

**rhythm method**, a form of birth control involving a period of continence coordinated with the estimated period of ovulation.

**rhythm sticks**, a pair of wooden sticks struck together to beat time, especially in a rhythm band.

**rhyt|i|dome** (rit′ə dōm), *n. Botany.* the outer bark, consisting of alternating layers of cork and dead cortex. [< New Latin *rhytidoma* < Greek *rhytídōma* wrinkle < *rhytidoûn* to wrinkle]

**rhy|ton** (rī′ton), *n., pl.* **-ta** (-tə). a kind of drinking vessel used in ancient Greece, shaped like a horn and having the form of an animal's head at the lower end. [< Greek *rhytón* < *rheîn* to flow]

**RI** (no periods), **1** religious instruction. **2** respiratory infection (virus). **3** Rhode Island (with postal Zip Code).

**R.I.**, an abbreviation for the following:
**1a** King and Emperor (Latin, *Rex et Imperator*).
**b** Queen and Empress (Latin, *Regina et Imperatrix*).
**2** religious instruction.
**3** Rhode Island.
**4** Royal Institute.

**ri|a** (rē′ä), *n., pl.* **ri|as**. an arm of the sea that gradually becomes shallower inland, formed by a submerged valley. [< Spanish *ría* < *río* river.]

**R.I.A.**, Royal Irish Academy.

**ri|al** (rē ôl′, -äl′), *n.* **1** the unit of money of Iran, a coin or note. **2** the unit of money of Oman. **3** = riyal. [< Persian, Arabic *riyāl* < Spanish *real.* Compare etym. under **real**[2], **regal, royal**.]

**Ri|al|to** (rē al′tō), *n.* **1** a former business district of Venice, Italy. **2** a famous bridge in Venice, Italy, that crosses the Grand Canal. **3** a theater district.

**ri|al|to** (rē al′tō), *n., pl.* **-tos**. an exchange; market place. [< *Rialto*]

**ri|an|cy** (rī′ən sē), *n.* = gaiety.

**ri|ant** (rī′ənt; *French* rē äɴ′), *adj.* laughing; smiling; gay. [< Middle French *riant,* present participle of Old French *rire* < Vulgar Latin *rīdere,* for Latin *rīdēre* to laugh] —**ri′ant|ly**, *adv.*

**ri|a|ta** (rē ä′tə), *n.* = lariat. [< Spanish *reata*]

**rib** (rib), *n., v.,* **ribbed, rib|bing.** —*n.* **1** one of the curved bones extending around the chest from the backbone to the front of the body. They are joined to the spine in humans. Human beings and most vertebrates have ribs. *Furthermore, certain parts of the skeleton, such as the skull and ribs, protect the delicate parts of your body from injury* (Beauchamp, Mayfield, and West). See picture under **chest**. **2** anything like a rib; piece that forms a frame: **a** one of the curved members of a ship's frame which go out from the keel. **b** one of the metal strips supporting the fabric of an umbrella. **c** a thick vein of a leaf. **d** *Aeronautics.* a structural member within a wing, running from the front to the back edge. **e** *Architecture.* one of the arches forming the supports for a vault. **3** a ridge, as in cloth or knitting. **4** a cut of meat containing a rib: *a rib of beef.* **5** a wife (in humorous allusion to the creation of Eve). **6** *Informal.* **a** a joke. **b** a teasing or mocking; a satire on or parody of something: *All the stories are ... acted with a tongue-in-check seriousness that adds up to a rib of Hollywood costume pictures* (Time).
—*v.t.* **1** to furnish or strengthen with ribs. **2** to mark with riblike ridges. **3** *Informal.* to tease: *to rib a person about a mistake.*
**tickle the ribs**, to cause laughter: *a good joke to tickle the ribs.*
[Old English *ribb*] —**rib′ber**, *n.* —**rib′like′**, *adj.*

**R.I.B.A.**, Royal Institute of British Architects.

**rib|ald** (rib′əld), *adj., n.* —*adj.* offensive in speech; coarsely mocking; irreverent; indecent; obscene: *a ribald story, a ribald party.* **SYN**: indelicate, gross.
—*n.* a person who is ribald or given to ribaldry. [< Old French *ribauld,* perhaps < Germanic (compare Old High German *hrībā, hrīpā* prostitute)] —**rib′ald|ly**, *adv.*

**rib|ald|ry** (rib′əl drē), *n., pl.* **-ries**. **1** ribald quality or character. **2** ribald language: *He ducked and dodged as he exchanged ribaldries with anyone who attempted to hit him* (Sunday Times).

**rib|and**[1] (rib′ənd, -ən), *n.* = ribband.

**rib|and**[2] (rib′ənd), *n. Archaic.* ribbon.

**rib|band** (rib′band′, -ənd, -ən), *n.* a lengthwise timber or the like used to secure a ship's ribs in position while the outside planking or plating is being put on. [perhaps special use of a Middle English variant of *ribbon*]

**ribbed** (ribd), *adj.* having ribs or ridges: *a ribbed fabric.*

**ribbed vault**, *Architecture.* a vault with diagonal arches that project from the surface.

**rib|bing** (rib′ing), *n.* **1** ribs collectively; a group or arrangement of ribs: *the delicate ribbing of a leaf, the ribbing of corduroy.* **2** *Informal.* an act of mocking or teasing.

**rib|ble-rab|ble** (rib′əl rab′əl), *n.* **1** confused, meaningless jabber or sounds. **2** = rabble[1].

**rib|bon** (rib′ən), *n., v.* —*n.* **1** a strip or band of silk, satin, velvet, paper, or other material. Belts and badges are often made of ribbon. *She wrapped the gift in paper tying it in yards of yellow ribbon.* **2** anything like such a strip: *a typewriter ribbon, a ribbon of steel. I'll tell you how the sun rose—a ribbon at a time* (Emily Dickinson). **3** a small badge, especially of cloth worn in place of a decoration for bravery or as a sign of membership in an order: *the red ribbon of the French Legion of Honor.* **4** a lengthwise timber to hold a ship's ribs in position; ribband.
—*v.t.* **1** to adorn with or as if with ribbons: *I could see all the inland valleys ribboned with broad waters* (Richard Blackmore). **2** to separate into ribbons; tear into ribbons. —*v.i.* to take the shape of, or move in the winding manner of, a ribbon or ribbonlike strip: *Annecy boasts of a fourteenth-century castle and canals that ribbon through the old town* (Harper's).
**cut** (or **tear**) **to ribbons, a** to rip into small pieces; shred: *Her dress was torn to ribbons by the thorns and briers she had come through.* **b** to insult or disparage thoroughly: *How disconcerting then to find that William Barkley had been allowed to cut Lord Beaverbrook to ribbons* (Punch).
**ribbons, a** torn strips of anything; tatters; shreds: *The sails hung in ribbons from the yards* (Century Magazine). **b** = reins: *the coachman's ribbons.*
[Middle English *ryban,* earlier *reban* < Old French *riban,* variant of *ruban,* perhaps < Germanic (compare Dutch *ringband*)] —**rib′bon|like′**, *adj.*

***ribbon back**, a back of a piece of furniture decorated with a ribbon design carved in wood.

***ribbon back**

**ribbon building**, *British.* the building of a ribbon development.

**rib|bon|bush** (rib′ən bu̇sh′), *n.* a tall shrub of the buckwheat family of tropical Pacific islands, with flat, ribbonlike branches and red or purplish fruit.

**ribbon development**, *British.* **1** a row, as of houses or stores, along a main road, extending outward from a town into the countryside: *Look at the ribbon development of cafes, hotels, villas, and beach huts that stretch out of Athens along the coast to Sounion* (Manchester Guardian Weekly). **2** = ribbon building.

**rib|bon|fish** (rib′ən fish′), *n., pl.* **-fish|es** or (*collectively*) **-fish**. any one of several deep-sea fishes with a long, very slender, ribbonlike body, such as the dealfish and oarfish.

**ribbon grass**, a tall, white or yellowish striped grass of North America and Europe, sometimes grown for ornament.

**ribbon machine**, a glass-blowing machine for producing light bulbs from a ribbon of hot, flexible glass.

**rib|bons** (rib′ənz), *n.pl.* See under **ribbon**.

**ribbon seal**, a brown seal of the northern Pacific, the male of which has a band of yellowish white about the neck, rump, and each front flipper.

**ribbon snake**, a small, striped garter snake common in the central and eastern United States.

**ribbon work**, a decorative design of ribbons, often used in the Italian Renaissance.

**ribbon worm**, **1** any one of a phylum of soft, thin, contractile worms varying in length from less than an inch to over 80 feet and living chiefly in the sea; nemertean. **2** = tapeworm.

**rib|by** (rib′ē), *adj.,* **-bi|er, -bi|est**. full of ribs; having prominent ribs.

**rib|cage** (rib′kāj′), *n.* the barrel-shaped enclosure formed by the ribs of the chest; framework of the ribs. See picture under **skeleton**.

**ri|bes** (rī′bēz), *n., pl.* **-bes**. any one of a group of plants of the saxifrage family that includes the gooseberry and currant. [< New Latin *Ribes* the genus name < Medieval Latin *ribes* currant < Arabic *rībās* sorrel]

**rib eye steak**, a very tender boneless beefsteak cut from the tip of the loin.

**rib grass**, any plantain, especially the narrow-leaf plantain or ribwort.

**rib|let** (rib′lit), *n.* a little rib: *a veal riblet.*

**ri|bo|fla|vin** (rī′bō flā′vin), *n.* a constituent of the vitamin B complex, present in liver, eggs, milk, spinach, and certain other food; lactoflavin. Riboflavin is an orange-red crystalline substance. It is sometimes called vitamin G or $B_2$. Persons who lack riboflavin are retarded in growth. *Formula:* $C_{17}H_{20}N_4O_6$ [< *ribo*(se) + *flavin,* its earlier name in England]

**ri|bo|nu|cle|ase** (rī′bō nü′klē ās, -nyü′-), *n.* an enzyme that promotes the hydrolysis of ribonucleic acid.

**ri|bo|nu|cle|ic acid** (rī′bō nü klē′ik, -nyü-), a complex chemical compound, a nucleic acid, found in the cytoplasm and sometimes in the nuclei of all living cells. It consists of long chains of repeating units of ribose combined with phosphoric acid and several chemical bases; ribose nucleic acid. Ribonucleic acid plays an important part in making proteins and in genetic transmission. *A second type of large molecule, ribonucleic acid (RNA), carries the instructions from the genes to the building sites, where it directs the assembly of proteins* (Scientific American). *Abbr:* RNA (no periods).

**ri|bo|nu|cle|o|pro|tein** (rī′bō nü′klē ō prō′tēn,

**Pronunciation Key:** hat, āge, cãre, fär; let, ēqual, tėrm; it, īce; hot, ōpen, ôrder; **oi**l, **ou**t; cup, pu̇t, rüle; **ch**ild; lo**ng**; **th**in; ᴛʜen; **zh**, measure; ə represents **a** in about, **e** in taken, **i** in pencil, **o** in lemon, **u** in circus.

-tē in; -nyü′-), *n.* a nucleoprotein containing a portion of ribonucleic acid. *Abbr:* RNP (no periods).

**ri|bo|nu|cle|o|side** (rī′bō nü′klē ə sīd, -sid; -nyü′-), *n.* a nucleoside containing ribose as its sugar.

**ri|bo|nu|cle|o|tide** (rī′bō nü′klē ə tīd, -tid; -nyü′-), *n.* a nucleotide containing ribose as its sugar.

**ri|bose** (rī′bōs), *n.* a pentose sugar present in all plant and animal cells and obtained in the dextrorotatory form chiefly from nucleic acids contained in plants: *Ribose is a sugar formed of five carbon atoms to the molecule, instead of the six that make up the more familiar glucose* (Science News Letter). *Formula:* $C_5H_{10}O_5$ [< a German alteration of English *arabinose*]

**ribose nucleic acid,** = ribonucleic acid.

**ri|bo|so|mal** (rī′bə sō′məl), *adj.* of or having to do with a ribosome or ribosomes: *... the role of ribosomal nucleic acids in protein synthesis* (London Times).

**ribosomal RNA,** a ribonucleic acid that is a basic part of the structure of the ribosomes.

**ri|bo|some** (rī′bə sōm), *n.* any of the granular particles consisting largely of ribonucleic acid that are found in the cytoplasm of cells and carry out the synthesis of protein and enzymes. See picture under **cell.** [< *ribo*(nucleic acid) + *-some*[3]]

**rib roast,** a cut of beef including a part of one or more ribs, suitable for roasting.

**rib-tick|ler** (rib′tik′lər), *n. Informal.* a funny story or joke.

**rib-tick|ling** (rib′tik′ling), *adj. Informal.* funny; jocular.

**rib twist,** a twist formed in glassware, by cutting a stem and twisting it to form spiral grooves.

**rib-twist|ed** (rib′twis′tid), *adj.* formed with a rib twist.

**rib|wort** (rib′wėrt′), *n.,* or **ribwort plantain,** **1** a plantain having long, narrow leaves with prominent ribs; narrow-leaf plantain. **2** any one of certain similar plantains.

**Ri|car|di|an** (ri kär′dē ən), *adj., n.* —*adj.* of or having to do with the theories of the English political economist David Ricardo (1772-1823) or his followers.
—*n.* a follower of Ricardo.

***rice** (rīs), *n., v.,* **riced, ric|ing.** —*n.* **1** the starchy seeds or grain of a plant grown in warm climates. Rice is one of the most important foods of the world. **2** the plant itself. Rice is a kind of grass.
—*v.t.* to reduce to a form like rice: *to rice potatoes.*
[< Old French *ris* < Italian *riso* < Latin *orȳza* < Greek *óryza*]

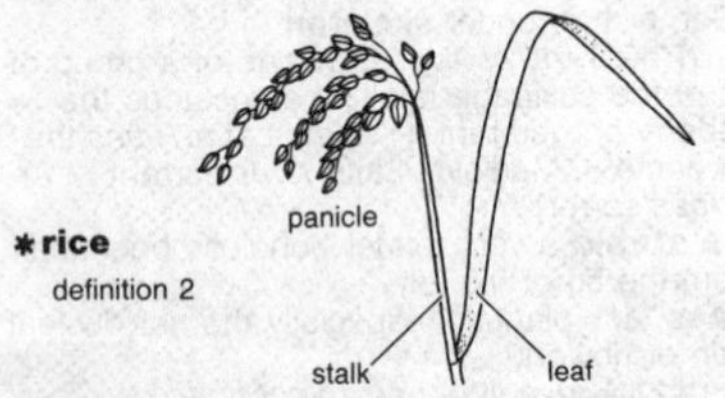


***rice**
definition 2

**rice|bird** (rīs′bėrd′), *n.* **1** *Southern U.S.* the bobolink. **2** = Java sparrow.

**rice bowl,** an area where rice is grown extensively: *French Indo-China was once known as the rice bowl of the world* (New Yorker).

**rice bran,** the separated cuticle of the rice grain.

**rice flour, 1** ground rice, used especially in making puddings, cakes, and face powder. **2** the layer of the rice kernel next to the cuticle, rubbed off as a powder in the processes of hulling and polishing.

**rice grub,** the larva of a scarabaeid beetle that damages the roots of upland rice in the southern United States.

**rice paper, 1** a thin paper made from the straw of rice. **2** a paper made from the pith of the rice-paper plant or of certain other plants.

**rice-pa|per plant** or **tree** (rīs′pā′pər), a small tree or shrub of Asia, belonging to the ginseng family, from whose pith rice paper is made. The rice-paper plant has greenish flowers and large, spreading leaves, for which it is often grown as an ornamental.

**ric|er** (rī′sər), *n.* a utensil for ricing cooked potatoes and other foods, by pressing them through small holes.

**rice rat,** a gray or brownish rat of the southern United States and Mexico, found especially in wet, grassy areas.

**ri|cer|car** (rē′chər kär′), *n.* = ricercare.

**ri|cer|ca|re** (rē′cher kä′rā), *n., pl.* **-ri** (-rē). *Music.* **1** a fugue using contrapuntal devices: *He had arranged the movements in an order which started with the three part ricercare on the royal theme* (London Times). **2** an early form of the fugue, somewhat similar to a motet, but instrumental. [< Italian *ricercare* (literally) seek out < Latin *re-* again + *cicāre* go about]

**rice weevil,** a beetle which feeds on rice and other grains. It is found in all parts of the world.

**rice wine,** an alcoholic beverage made from fermented rice, popular in Japan; sake.

**rich** (rich), *adj., n.* —*adj.* **1** having much money, land, goods, or other property: *Henry Ford and John D. Rockefeller were rich men.* **2** well supplied; abounding: *The United States is rich in oil and coal.* (*Figurative.*) *All this part of the river is rich in Indian history and traditions* (Mark Twain). **3** abundant: *a rich supply.* **4** producing or yielding much; fertile: *rich soil, a rich mine.* **SYN:** productive, fruitful, fecund. **5** having great worth; valuable: *a rich harvest, a rich virtue.* **6** costly; elegant: *rich dresses, rich jewels, rich carpets.* **SYN:** expensive, sumptuous, luxurious. **7a** containing plenty of butter, eggs, flavoring, sugar, and the like: *a rich fruit cake, rich milk.* **b** having many desirable elements or qualities. **8** deep; full; vivid: *a rich red, a rich tone.* **9** strong and finely flavored: *a rich, mellow sherry.* **10** containing more fuel and less air than is normally required: *a rich fuel mixture.* **11** *Informal.* **a** very amusing. **b** ridiculous; absurd. **12** great, thorough, or fine: *A couple of boys left to themselves will furnish richer fun than any troop of trained comedians* (George Meredith).
—*n.* **the rich,** rich people: *The rich ... do not, in general, require to be so much stimulated to benevolence* (Scott).
**strike it rich,** *U.S. Informal.* **a** to find rich ore, oil, or other mineral: *After three months of drilling in the desert, the prospectors struck it rich.* **b** *Figurative.* to have a sudden or unexpected great success: *The gaffer happens to be the head stableman on the opulent country estate of a former longshoreman who has struck it rich* (New Yorker).
[probably fusion of Middle English *riche* (< Old French < Germanic), and Old English *rīce*]
—**rich′ness,** *n.*
—*Syn. adj.* **1 Rich, wealthy** mean having much money or property. **Rich** implies having more than enough money, possessions, or resources for all normal needs and desires: *With a five-dollar bill in his pocket, Tom felt rich.* **Wealthy** suggests greater and more permanent resources: *Some of our greatest universities, libraries, and museums were established by wealthy people.*

**Rich.,** Richard.

**Rich|ard Roe** (rich′ərd rō′), a fictitious name used in legal forms or proceedings for the name of an unknown person.

**Rich|ard|son's goose** (rich′ərd sənz), = Hutchins' goose. [< Sir John *Richardson,* 1787-1865, a Scottish naturalist]

**Richardson's owl,** a small, brown and white owl resembling the saw-whet owl, occurring in Canada and occasionally during the winter in the northern United States. [< Sir John *Richardson*]

**rich|en** (rich′ən), *v.t., v.i.* to make or become rich or richer.

**rich|es** (rich′iz), *n.pl.* wealth; abundance of property; much money, land, or goods: *to rise from rags to riches.* **SYN:** affluence, opulence. [< Old French *richesse,* singular < *riche* rich]

**rich|ling** (rich′ling), *n.* a rich person.

**rich|ly** (rich′lē), *adv.* **1** in a rich manner: *storied windows richly light* (Milton). **2** fully: *a richly deserved punishment.*

**rich rhyme,** = perfect rhyme.

***Rich|ter scale** (rik′tər), a scale for indicating the magnitude of earthquakes, using numbers from 1 upwards, with 1.5 measuring slight seismic disturbances, 4.5 measuring potentially destructive eathquakes, and from 8.5 up measuring major earthquakes: *The record was broken when Aug. 19 passed without the recording of any tremor of magnitude eight or more on the Richter scale striking U.S. territory* (Science News). [< Charles Francis *Richter,* born 1900, an American seismologist]

**rich|weed** (rich′wēd′), *n.* **1** a common urticaceous herb of North America and Japan. **2** a plant of the mint family of eastern North America, used medicinally especially as a diuretic and tonic. **3** any one of several ragweeds.

**ri|cin** (rī′sin, ris′in), *n.* a poisonous albumin found in castor-oil seeds. [< New Latin *Ricinus;* see etym. under **ricinus**]

**ric|in|o|le|ate** (ris′ə nō′lē āt), *n.* a salt or ester of ricinoleic acid.

**ric|in|o|le|ic acid** (ris′ə nə lē′ik, -nō′lē-), an unsaturated, fatty hydroxy acid obtained from castor oil. *Formula:* $C_{18}H_{34}O_3$ [< *ricinus* + *oleic acid*]

**ric|in|o|le|in** (ris′ə nō′lē in), *n.* the glycerol ester of ricinoleic acid. It makes up about 80 per cent of castor oil. *Formula:* $C_{57}H_{104}O_9$ [< *ricinole*(ic acid) + *-in*]

**ric|i|nus** (ris′ə nəs), *n.* = castor-oil plant. [< New Latin *Ricinus* the genus name < Latin *ricinus* castor-oil plant, croton; (originally) a tick (from its tick-shaped seeds)]

**rick**[1] (rik), *n., v.* —*n.* an outdoor stack, such as of hay or straw, especially one made or covered so that the rain will run off it.
—*v.t.* to form into a rick or ricks.
[Old English *hrēac*] —**rick′er,** *n.*

**rick**[2] (rik), *v.t., n.* = wrick.

**rick|ets** (rik′its), *n.* a disease of childhood, caused by lack of vitamin D, which prevents the body from using calcium; rachitis. Rickets causes softening, and sometimes bending, of the bones, and can be prevented by providing the child plenty of sunlight and food rich in vitamin D and calcium. [apparently alteration of *rachitis*]

**rick|ett|si|a** (ri ket′sē ə), *n., pl.* **-si|as, -si|ae** (-sē ē). any one of a genus of microorganisms intermediate between the bacteria and viruses, living in the tissue of arthropods and sometimes transmitted to humans, causing such diseases as Rocky Mountain spotted fever, typhus, and Q fever. [American English < New Latin *Rickettsia* < Howard T. *Ricketts,* 1871-1910, an American pathologist, who investigated the microorganisms]

**rick|ett|si|al** (ri ket′sē əl), *adj.* of or having to do with the rickettsias.

**rick|et|y** (rik′ə tē), *adj.* **1** liable to fall or break down; shaky or weak: *a rickety old chair.* **SYN:** tottering. **2** having rickets; suffering from rickets. **3** feeble in the joints. —**rick′et|i|ness,** *n.*

**rick|ey** (rik′ē), *n., pl.* **-eys. 1** a drink made with limes, sugar, carbonated water, and gin or other alcoholic liquor. **2** a nonalcoholic carbonated drink made with lime juice. [American English, reputedly < a Colonel *Rickey*]

**rick|le** (rik′əl), *n. Scottish.* **1** a heap. **2** a small rick of hay or grain. [< *rick*[1] + *-le,* a diminutive suffix]

**rick|rack** (rik′rak′), *n.* a narrow, zigzag braid used as trimming. Also, **ricrac.** [American English, perhaps reduplication of *rack*[1], verb]

**rick|shaw** or **rick|sha** (rik′shô), *n.* = jinrikisha.

**rick|yard** (rik′yärd′), *n.* a farmyard containing ricks of hay or corn; stackyard.

**rick|y-tick** (rik′ē tik′), *adj., n. U.S. Slang.* —*adj.* **1** old-fashioned or trite; rinky-dink. **2** imitative of the sound of rapidly picked strings: *ricky-tick banjo music.*
—*n.* ricky-tick sound or beat, especially in jazz.
[compare **rinky-dink**]

**ric|o|chet** (rik′ə shā′; *especially British* rik′ə-shet′), *n., v.,* **-cheted** (-shād′), **-chet|ing** (-shā′-ing) or (*especially British*) **-chet|ted** (-shet′id), **-chet|ting** (-shet′ing). —*n.* the skipping or jumping motion of an object as it goes along a flat surface: *the ricochet of a flat stone thrown along*

***Richter scale**

| Richter scale magnitude | Characteristic effects | Mercalli scale intensity |
|---|---|---|
| | Registers only on a seismograph. | I |
| 3.0 to | Affects only sensitive people. | II |
| 3.9 | Feels like the rumble of a passing truck. | III |
| 4.0 to | Shakes dishes, windows, and standing objects. | IV |
| 4.9 | Breaks dishes and windows; wakes sleeping people. | V |
| 5.0 to | Affects everyone; moves heavy furniture. | VI |
| 5.9 | | |
| | Cracks walls; damages poorly-built buildings. | VII |
| 6.0 to | | |
| 6.9 | Tumbles chimneys; damages ordinary buildings. | VIII |
| 7.0 to | Breaks underground pipes; damages well-built buildings. | IX |
| 7.9 | Destroys most masonry and frame buildings. | X |
| 8.0 to | Destroys almost all buildings, damaging the rest. | XI |
| 8.9 | Destroys everything; makes the ground rise and fall in waves; tosses objects into the air. | XII |

the surface of water. SYN: carom.
—*v.i.* to move with a skipping or jumping motion; bounce: *The handball ricocheted all over the court. The cannon balls struck the ground and ricochetted through the tall grass* (Ulysses S. Grant). *Ricocheting along the street, like a witch who had lost her broom, I streaked for home* (Tallulah Bankhead).
[< French *ricochet;* origin uncertain]

**ri|cot|ta** (ri kot′ə), *n.* a soft Italian cottage cheese. [< Italian *ricotta* < Latin *recocta,* feminine of *recoctus,* past participle of *recoquere* to cook again < *re-* again + *coquere* to cook]

**ric|rac** (rik′rak′), *n.* = rickrack.

**ric|tal** (rik′təl), *adj.* of or having to do with the rictus.

**ric|tus** (rik′təs), *n.* **1** the cleft of the open mouth; gape. **2** an open mouth, as in a grin: *the teeth disclosed in a perpetual rictus* (Robert Louis Stevenson). [< Latin *rictus, -ūs* a mouth opened wide, for laughter or food < *ringī* to gape]

**rid[1]** (rid), *v.t.,* **rid** or **rid|ded, rid|ding. 1** to make free (of): *What will rid a house of mice?* **2** *Obsolete.* to expel: *I will rid evil beasts out of the land* (Leviticus 26:6). **3** *Obsolete.* to rescue.

**be rid of,** to be freed from: *Queen Victoria had called Gladstone a dreadful old man and longed to be rid of him* (Manchester Guardian Weekly).

**get rid of, a** to get free from: *I can't get rid of this cold.* **b** to do away with: *Poison will get rid of the rats in the barn.*

[probably fusion of Old English *āryddan,* or *geryddan* to strip, plunder and Middle English *rydan* < Scandinavian (compare Old Icelandic *rythja* to clear)] —**rid′der,** *n.*

**rid[2]** (rid), *v. Archaic.* a past tense and a past participle of **ride.**

**rid|a|ble** (rī′də bəl), *adj.* **1** that can be ridden. **2** that can be ridden over. Also, **rideable.**

**rid|dance** (rid′əns), *n.* **1** the act or fact of clearing away or out; removal: *He shall make even a speedy riddance of all them that dwell in the land* (Zephaniah 1:18). **2** deliverance or rescue (from something): *a riddance from sin.* SYN: liberation.

**good riddance,** an exclamation expressing relief that something or somebody has been removed: *Good riddance to bad rubbish.*

**rid|den** (rid′ən), *v.* a past participle of **ride**: *The horseman had ridden all day.*

**rid|dle[1]** (rid′əl), *n., v.,* **-dled, -dling.** —*n.* **1** a puzzling question, statement, or problem, usually presented as a game or pastime. *Example:* When is a door not a door? *Answer:* When it is ajar. SYN: enigma, puzzle, conundrum. **2** a person or thing that is hard to understand, explain, or predict: *All that Silver said was a riddle to him* (Robert Louis Stevenson). *Russia ... is a riddle wrapped in a mystery inside an enigma* (Sir Winston Churchill).
—*v.i.* **1** to speak in riddles. **2** to ask riddles.
—*v.t.* to solve (a riddle or question): *Riddle me this, and guess him if you can, who bears a nation in a single man?* (John Dryden).
[Middle English *redel* < earlier *redels,* taken as plural, Old English *rǣdels* < *rǣdan* to guess, explain] —**rid′dler,** *n.*

**rid|dle[2]** (rid′əl), *v.,* **-dled, -dling,** *n.* —*v.t.* **1** to make many holes in: *The door of the fort was riddled with bullets.* SYN: perforate. **2** to sift: *to riddle gravel.* **3** *Figurative.* to impair or weaken as if by making many holes in: *The witness's testimony was riddled with lies.* [< noun]
—*n.* a coarse sieve.
[Old English *hriddel* sieve]

**rid|dle|me|ree** (rid′əl me rē′), *n.* rigmarole; nonsense: *On the basis of some such riddlemeree, [he] has concocted a story about a man who loses himself in a fantasy* (New Yorker). [alteration of *riddle me a riddle, riddle my riddle*]

**rid|dling** (rid′ling), *adj.* presenting a riddle or riddles; enigmatic; puzzling; mysterious: *He [Merlin] laugh'd ... and answer'd me In riddling triplets* (Tennyson). —**rid′dling|ly,** *adv.*

**ride** (rīd), *v.,* **rode** or (*Archaic*) **rid, rid|den** or (*Archaic*) **rid, rid|ing,** *n.* —*v.i.* **1** to sit on a horse and make it go: *The messenger rode hard, changing horses often to carry the warning.* **2** to sit on a camel, bicycle, or other animal or mechanical device, and make it go: *The bicycle tipped over as he rode along paying no attention to where he was going.* **3** to be carried along as if on horseback; be carried along by anything: *to ride on a train, to ride in a car.* **4** to be capable of being ridden: *a horse that rides easily.* **5** to be carried along in any way: *The eagle rides on the wind.* (*Figurative.*) *Disdain and scorn ride sparkling in her eyes* (Shakespeare). **6** to move or float: *The ship rode into port.* (*Figurative.*) *The moon rode clear and high in heaven* (Scott). **7** to lie at anchor: *a windy, tossing anchorage where yawls and ketches ride* (John Masefield). **8** to rest or turn on something, such as a pivot or axle: *Strong as the axletree on which heaven rides* (Shakespeare). **9** to extend or project; overlap.
—*v.t.* **1** to sit on and manage: *to ride a camel, to ride a bicycle.* (*Figurative.*) *[The leader] and the ministers he has backed believe they can ride the Communist tiger* (Atlantic). **2** to ride over, along, or through: *to ride a hundred miles.* **3** to do or perform: *to ride a hundred miles.* **4** to be mounted on; be carried on: *The gull rides the winds.* **5** to move on; float along: *The ship rode the waves.* **6** to extend or project over; overlap (something). **7** to cause to ride or be carried: *He rode his little brother piggyback. The villagers had a strong desire to ... ride him on a rail for body-snatching* (Mark Twain). **8** *Figurative.* to control, dominate, or tyrannize over: *to be ridden by foolish fears. The tradesman ... is ridden by the routine of his craft* (Emerson). **9** *Informal.* to make fun of; tease; harass; nag: *Don't ride him for the blunder this time.* **10** to keep (a ship) moored.
—*n.* **1** a trip on horseback, in a carriage, car, train, or boat, or on any other thing that carries: *On Sunday we take a ride into the country. My brother enjoyed his ride on the merry-go-round.* **2** a path, trail, or road, made for riding. **3** any wrestling hold that limits the other wrestler's maneuverability, such as gripping the opponent's ankle. A wrestler can earn points by using a variety of rides.

**hitch a ride,** *U.S. Informal.* to get a free ride: *I had asked the Ambassador if I could hitch a ride back to Bad Godesberg with him* (New Yorker).

**let ride,** to leave undisturbed or inactive: *Let the matter ride until the next meeting.*

**ride down, a** to knock down: *He rode down anyone who got in his way.* **b** *Figurative.* to overcome: *The support of the Commons ... enabled Harley to ride down all resistance* (John R. Green). **c** to overtake by riding: *He ... was on the point of riding down a large old roomy family carriage* (Thackeray). **d** to exhaust by riding: *The Czar was very active ..., and rode down four horses* (London Gazette).

**ride for a fall.** See under **fall.**

**ride herd on.** See under **herd[1].**

**ride high,** to enjoy success; do very well: *The conservatives, from looking like a beaten party earlier this year, are beginning to feel as if they were riding high* (Manchester Guardian).

**ride out, a** to withstand (a gale or storm) without great damage: *The small boat rode out the storm without damage.* **b** *Figurative.* to endure successfully: *Such weapons could ride out an enemy attack and still hit back effectively* (Wall Street Journal).

**ride up,** to slide up out of place: *That coat rides up at the back.*

**take for a ride,** *Slang.* **a** to murder: *[He] was taken for a ride ... and dumped out dead near Contronl's Laurentian estate* (Maclean's). **b** to cheat: *The taxpayer is being taken for a ride* (New York Times).

[Old English *rīdan*]

—*Syn. n.* **1 Ride, drive** mean a trip by some means of transportation. **Ride** suggests being carried along in or by something, as on horseback, in a boat, train, bus, or in a car if one is going nowhere in particular or is strictly a passenger: *Let's go for a ride in my new car.* **Drive** suggests going in a particular direction, and applies particularly to a trip in a horse-drawn or motor vehicle one controls or operates himself or helps to direct: *Let's take a drive into the country.*

**ride|a|ble** (rī′də bəl), *adj.* = ridable.

**rid|er** (rī′dər), *n.* **1** a person who rides: *The West is famous for its riders. Riders objected to jammed Friday night trains* (Newsweek). **2** anything added to a record, document, legislative bill, or statement after it was supposed to be complete: *Now all the Council had to do was tack the rider on again and send the bill back to the Assembly* (Newsweek). SYN: addendum. **3** an object resting on another, usually with one part hanging down on each side, such as a strand of wire that can be moved back and forth on the beam of a balance as a minute weight.

**rid|er|less** (rī′dər lis), *adj.* without a rider.

**ridge** (rij), *n., v.* **ridged, ridg|ing.** —*n.* **1** the long and narrow upper part of something: *the ridge of an animal's back, the ridge of a hill.* **2** a line where two sloping surfaces meet: *the ridge of a roof.* **3** a long, narrow chain of hills or mountains: *the Blue Ridge of the Appalachian Mountains.* **4** a long, narrow elevation on the ocean floor: *the Mid-Atlantic Ridge.* **5** any raised narrow strip: *the ridges in plowed ground, the ridges on corduroy cloth.* **6** *Meteorology.* a trough of high barometric pressure: *A rather weak ridge of high pressure will extend from this high over the northern Mississippi Valley and the Northern Plains States* (New York Times).
—*v.t.* **1** to form or make into ridges. **2** to mark with ridges; cover with ridges. —*v.i.* to form ridges. [Old English *hrycg*]

**ridge|back** (rij′bak′), *n.* = Rhodesian ridgeback.

**ridge|board** (rij′bôrd′, -bōrd′), *n.* = ridgepole.

**ridge|ling** (rij′ling), *n.* **1** a male animal, especially a horse, bull, or ram, one or both of whose testicles have not descended to the scrotum. **2** an animal that has been imperfectly castrated. [probably < *ridge* + *-ling* (because the testicles were believed to have remained near the animal's back)]

**ridge|piece** (rij′pēs′), *n.* = ridgepole.

**ridge|plate** (rij′plāt′), *n.* = ridgepole.

**ridge|pole** (rij′pōl′), *n.* the horizontal timber along the top of a roof or tent; rooftree.

**ridg|er** (ri′jər), *n.* a cultivator for heaping loose soil against young plants planted in rows. Its two hinged moldboards are side by side on a wheel at the rear.

**ridge roof,** a raised or peaked roof.

**ridge|top** (rij′top′), *n.* the top of a ridge.

**ridge|way** (rij′wā′), *n.* a road along or following a ridge, especially the ridge of downs or low hills.

**ridg|ling** (rij′ling), *n.* = ridgeling.

**ridg|y** (rij′ē), *adj.,* **ridg|i|er, ridg|i|est.** rising in a ridge or ridges: *ridgy ground, ridgy cloth.*

**rid|i|cule** (rid′ə kyül), *v.,* **-culed, -cul|ing,** *n.* —*v.t.* to laugh at; make fun of; mock: *Sometimes boys ridicule their sisters' friends. My father discouraged me by ridiculing my performances* (Benjamin Franklin). [< noun]
—*n.* **1** laughter in mockery; words or actions that make fun of somebody or something: *Silly mistakes and odd clothes often invite ridicule.* SYN: derision. **2** *Archaic.* ridiculous quality or character: *to see the ridicule of this monstrous practice* (Joseph Addison). **3** *Archaic.* something ridiculous.
[< French *ridicule* < Middle French, adjective < Latin *rīdiculum,* neuter of *rīdiculus;* see etym. under **ridiculous**] —**rid′i|cul′er,** *n.*
—*Syn. v.t.* **Ridicule, deride, mock** mean to make fun of someone or something and cause him or it to be laughed at. **Ridicule** emphasizes making fun of a person or thing, in either a good-natured or an unkind way, with the intention of making him or it seem little and unimportant: *Boys ridicule their sisters' friends.* **Deride** emphasizes laughing in contempt and holding up to scorn: *Some people deride patriotic rallies and parades.* **Mock** means to ridicule or deride in a scornful way: *The impudent boys mocked the teacher.*

**ri|dic|u|lous** (ri dik′yə ləs), *adj.* deserving ridicule; absurd; laughable: *It would be ridiculous to walk backward all the time.* [< Latin *rīdiculōsus* < *rīdiculus* < *rīdēre* to laugh] —**ri|dic′u|lous|ly,** *adv.* —**ri|dic′u|lous|ness,** *n.*
—*Syn.* **Ridiculous, absurd, preposterous** mean not sensible or reasonable. **Ridiculous** emphasizes the laughable effect produced by something out of keeping with good sense: *His obvious attempts to be the life of the party were ridiculous.* **Absurd** emphasizes the contrast with what is true or sensible: *His belief that he was too clever to be caught in his wrongdoing was absurd.* **Preposterous** adds to *absurd* the idea of being contrary to nature: *The bandit made the preposterous suggestion that he would drop his gun if the policeman first dropped his.*

**rid|ing[1]** (rī′ding), *n., adj.* —*n.* **1** the act of a person or thing that rides. **2** a road for persons riding a bicycle or on horseback.
—*adj.* **1** that rides; traveling. **2** used for riding or when riding: *a riding whip. An average riding horse eats about 4 to 6 tons of hay a year* (Sunset).

**rid|ing[2]** (rī′ding), *n.* **1** one of the three administrative divisions of Yorkshire, England. **2** a similar division elsewhere, as in Canada or New Zealand. *He flew back to his own riding in Toronto just in time to watch the voters give him the greatest majority ever won by a candidate in the constituency's history* (Maclean's). [Middle English *thriding* < Scandinavian (compare Old Icelandic *thridjungr* one third); the *th-* was assimilated to a previous *-t* or *-th,* as in *East Thriding, North Thriding*]

**riding boot,** a high boot worn by horseback riders.

**riding crop,** a short whip with a loop on one end instead of a lash.

***riding habit**, a dress or suit worn by horseback riders.

***riding habit**

**riding light**, *Nautical.* a light hung on a ship riding at anchor.

**rid|ley** (rid′lē), *n.* = bastard turtle. [probably < *Ridley,* a proper name]

**ri|dot|to** (ri dot′ō), *n., pl.* **-tos**. a public ball, often in masquerade. [< Italian *ridotto,* earlier *ridotta* a resort, retreat. See etym. of doublet **redoubt**.]

**ri|el** (rē el′), *n.* the unit of money of Cambodia, equal to 100 sen. [perhaps alteration of *rial*]

**Rie|mann|i|an** (rē′män′ē ən), *adj.* of or having to do with Georg Riemann (1826-1866), German mathematician, or his mathematical theories and equations.

**Riemannian geometry**, = elliptic geometry.

**Ries|ling** (rēs′ling, rēz′-), *n.* **1** a dry, white wine. **2** the grape from which this wine is made, grown in the upper Rhine and in California. [< German *Riesling*]

**RIF** (no periods) or **R.I.F.**, *U.S.* Reduction In Force (a notice of dismissal of government employees).

**ri|fa|ci|men|to** (rē fä′chē men′tō), *n., pl.* **-ti** (-tē). a recast or adaptation, especially of a literary or musical work. [< Italian *rifacimento* refashioning < *rifac-,* stem of *rifare* to remake < *ri-* re- + *fare* make]

**ri|fam|pi|cin** (ri fam′pə sən, rī-), *n.* a semisynthetic antibiotic drug, derived from a rifamycin, which inhibits the growth of bacterial cells and the replication of viruses by interfering with the action of RNA polymerases in the synthesis of RNA. [alteration of *rifamycin*]

**rif|am|pin** (rif′am pən), *n.* = rifampicin.

**rif|a|my|cin** (rif′ə mī′sən), *n.* any one of a group of antibiotics derived from a species of streptomyces isolated from the soil in the pine forests of southern France. Several rifamycins and their derivatives have shown antimicrobial and antiviral properties. [< *rifa-* (of unknown origin) + (strepto)-*mycin*]

**rife** (rīf), *adj., adv.* **—*adj.*** **1** happening often; common; numerous; widespread: *all those noises so rife in a Portuguese inn* (George Borrow). **SYN**: prevalent. **2** well supplied; full; abounding: *The whole city was rife with rumors of political corruption.* **SYN**: replete.
**—*adv.*** in a rife manner; abundantly: *Wolfsbane ... grew rife in the Sierra Nevada* (W. H. Prescott). [probably Old English *rȳfe*] **—rife′ly,** *adv.*

**riff** (rif), *n., v.* **—*n.*** a melodic phrase in jazz, especially as a recurring statement of the theme.
**—*v.i.*** to perform riffs.
[origin uncertain]

**Riff** (rif), *n., pl.* **Riffs, Riff,** or **Riff|i** (rif′ē). a member of a Berber tribe living in the Rif in northern Africa.

**Riff|i|an** (rif′ē ən), *adj., n.* **—*adj.*** of or having to do with the Rif, in northern Africa, or its people.
**—*n.*** a native or inhabitant of the Rif.

**rif|fle**[1] (rif′əl), *n., v.,* **-fled, -fling.** **—*n.*** **1** a shoal or other object in a stream causing a stretch of choppy water. **2** such a stretch of water; rapid. **3** = ripple. **4** the act of shuffling cards by bending the edges slightly.
**—*v.t., v.i.*** **1** to shuffle (cards) by bending the edges slightly, so that the two divisions of the deck slide into each other. **2** to leaf through the pages of (a book or magazine) quickly as by bending the edges slightly and slipping the pages quickly out from under the thumb: *At home on East Street, he riffled through a 2-ft.-high stack of telegrams* (Time). **3** to make (water) flow in riffles; form a riffle. **4** to move or play with a rippling motion; ripple: *In "Love No. 2" he riffles the strings* (Time). **5** *Figurative.* to ruffle: *He permitted a slight smile to riffle his façade* (Harper's).
[American English, variant of *ripple*[1], or *ruffle*[1]]

**rif|fle**[2] (rif′əl), *n.* **1** an arrangement at the bottom of a sluice or the like, to catch and hold particles of a mineral, such as gold, platinum, or tin. **2** a slot or groove in such an arrangement. [perhaps < *riffle*[1]]

**rif|fler** (rif′lər), *n.* a file with a curved end, for smoothing or shaping a depression. [< French *rifloir* < Old French *rifler;* see etym. under **rifle**[1]]

**riff|raff** (rif′raf′), *n., adj.* **—*n.*** **1** worthless people: *Bourgeois ... is an epithet which the riffraff apply to what is respectable* (Anthony Hope). **SYN**: rabble. **2** trash. **SYN**: rubbish.
**—*adj.*** = worthless.
[Middle English *riffe and raff* < Old French *rif et raf,* and *rifle et rafle* every scrap < *rifler* to spoil, rifle[2] + *rafler* carry off]

***ri|fle**[1] (rī′fəl), *n., v.,* **-fled, -fling.** **—*n.*** **1** a gun with spiral grooves in its long barrel which spin or twist the bullet as it is shot. A rifle is usually fired from the shoulder. **2** one of the spiral grooves in the bore of a rifle. **3** a wooden block covered with emery to sharpen tools. [< verb]
**—*v.t.*** **1** to cut spiral grooves in (a gun barrel). **2** to shoot or drive (a ball) with great force or speed: *[He] rifled the 235-yard ... shot that carried the pond guarding the green* (New Yorker). **3** to shoot with a rifle.

**rifles**, a body of soldiers armed with rifles; riflemen: *The rifles, about 500 in all, lay behind the hill waiting for the order to fire.*
[probably < Old French *rifler* to scratch, groove, strip. Compare etym. under **rifle**[2].]

***rifle**[1]
definition 1

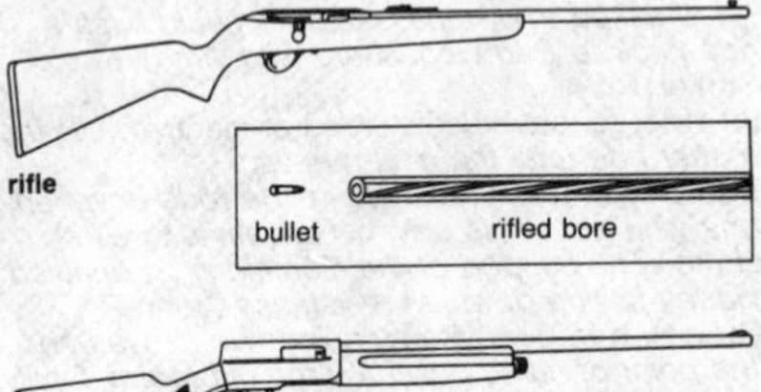


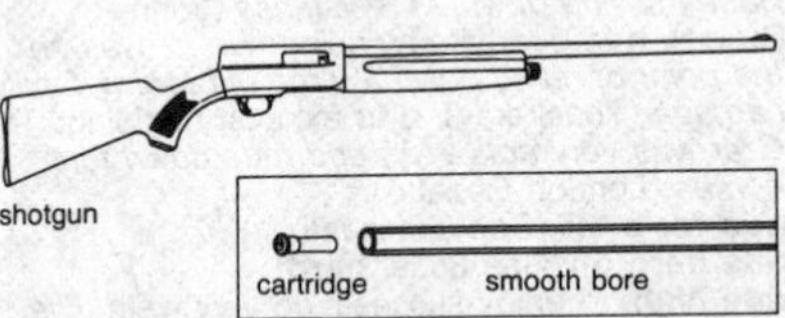


**ri|fle**[2] (rī′fəl), *v.,* **-fled, -fling.** **—*v.t.*** **1** to search and rob; ransack and rob: *The thieves rifled all the drawers in the house.* **SYN**: pillage, plunder. **2** to take away; steal: *The raccoons rifled all the food in the camp.* **3** to strip bare: *The boys rifled the apple tree.*
**—*v.i.*** to engage in ransacking and robbing: *The pirates rifled about the ship.* [< Old French *rifler* to scratch, groove, strip, perhaps < Germanic (compare Middle High German *riffeln* to comb, hackle thoroughly, Old High German *riffilōn* to comb flax)]

**ri|fle|bird** (rī′fəl bėrd′), *n.* any one of various birds of paradise.

**rifle grenade**, a grenade fired from the muzzle of a rifle.

**ri|fle|man** (rī′fəl mən), *n., pl.* **-men.** **1** a soldier armed with a rifle. **2** a man who uses a rifle: *The supply of fresh meat depends mainly on the skill of the riflemen* (Theodore Roosevelt).

**rifle pit**, a pit or short trench which shelters riflemen firing at an enemy.

**ri|fler** (rī′flər), *n.* **1** a person who rifles; robber. **2** *Falconry.* a hawk that does not return to the lure.

**rifle range**, **1** a place for practice in shooting with a rifle. **2** the distance that a rifle will shoot a bullet.

**ri|fle|ry** (rī′fəl rē), *n., pl.* **-ries.** **1** shooting with a rifle, especially in target practice: *Montana's Lones Wigger, Jr. won two medals in riflery at Tokyo* (Time). **2** firing from rifles: *Once before Shakespeare's cliff reverberated with the roar of riflery* (Punch).

**rifle salute**, a military salute given while shouldering or ordering arms.

**ri|fling** (rī′fling), *n.* **1** the act or process of cutting spiral grooves in a gun barrel. **2** the system of spiral grooves in a rifle.

**rift** (rift), *n., v.* **—*n.*** a cleft; break; crack: *a rift in the earth or a rock,* (*Figurative.*) *a rift in a friendship. The sun shone through a rift in the clouds.* **SYN**: fissure, fracture.
**—*v.t., v.i.*** to cause or form a rift; split; cleave.
[< Scandinavian (compare Old Icelandic *ript* breach < *rīfa* to tear, rive)]

**rift saw**, a saw for making boards, laths, and other long strips.

**rift-sawed** (rift′sôd′), *adj.* sawed lengthwise into quarters before being sawed into boards.

**rift valley**, a valley formed by the lowering of an area of land between two nearly parallel faults; graben. See picture under **fault**.

**Rift Valley fever**, a virus disease common in parts of Africa, affecting sheep, cattle, and sometimes man. [< *Rift Valley,* in Kenya, Africa]

**rift zone**, *Geology.* a large area of the earth in which a rift occurs when plates of the earth's crust move away from one another.

**rig**[1] (rig), *v.,* **rigged, rig|ging,** *n.* **—*v.t.*** **1** to fit (a ship) with masts, sails, and ropes: *The sailor rigged a toy boat for the little boy.* **2** to move (as a shroud, boom, or stay) to its proper place: *to rig a new mainmast.* **3** to equip; fit out. **4** *Informal.* to dress: *On Halloween the children rig themselves up in funny clothes.* **5** to get ready for use: *Forward there! rig the head-pump!* (Richard Henry Dana). **6** to put together in a hurry or by using odds and ends: *The boys rigged up a tent in the back yard with a rope and a blanket.*
**—*n.*** **1** the arrangement of masts, sails, and ropes on a ship. A schooner has a fore-and-aft rig; that is, the sails are set lengthwise on the ship. **2** *Informal.* a set of clothes; costume: *His rig consisted of a silk hat and overalls.* **3a** outfit; equipment: *a camper's rig.* **SYN**: accouterment, tackle. **b** heavy machinery, or elaborate tools, such as those required to drill a well: *an oil rig.* **4** *Informal.* **a** an automobile or truck: *A terrified truck driver rode his runaway five-ton rig through Winsted at eighty miles an hour this morning with no brakes* (New York Times). **b** a carriage with its horse or horses.

**rig out**, to fit out: *to rig out a football team with uniforms. The free trappers, being newly rigged out and supplied, were in high spirits* (Washington Irving).
[< Scandinavian (compare Danish *rigge,* perhaps < Low German *riggen,* variant of *rīgen* join together)]

**rig**[2] (rig), *n. Scottish.* a ridge. [variant of *ridge*]

**rig**[3] (rig), *v.,* **rigged, rig|ging,** *n.* **—*v.t.*** **1** to arrange in an unfair way: *The race was rigged. Other costs and prices are rigged and falsified* (London Times). **2** to arrange unfavorably: *The mathematical odds are rigged against the divorcee* (Life).
**—*n.*** **1** a prank; trick. **2** a fraudulent scheme; swindle.
[origin unknown]

**rig|a|doon** (rig′ə dün′), *n.* **1** a lively dance for one couple. **2** the quick, duple rhythm for this dance. **3** a piece of music in such time. [< French *rigodon, rigaudon;* origin uncertain; probably < *Rigaud,* a Marseilles dancing master, who invented it]

**rig|a|ma|role** (rig′ə mə rōl), *n.* = rigmarole.

**rig|a|to|ni** (rig′ə tō′nē), *n.* macaroni in the form of short, curved tubes with grooved sides. [< Italian *rigatoni* < *rigato* furrowed, past participle of *rigare* to furrow < *riga* line]

**Ri|gel** (rī′jəl, -gəl), *n.* a star of the first magnitude in the left foot of Orion. [< Arabic *rijl* foot]

**rigged** (rigd), *adj.* designed to deceive or defraud: *a rigged market.*

**-rigged**, *combining form.* having a ___ rig: *Full-rigged = having a full rig.*

**rig|ger** (rig′ər), *n.* **1** a person who rigs. **2** a person who rigs ships, or works with hoisting tackle, or cable of any kind. **3** a person who assembles airplanes or adjusts their controls. **4** a person who manipulates something fraudulently.

**rig|ging**[1] (rig′ing), *n.* **1** the ropes, chains, and cables used to support and work the masts, yards, and sails on a ship. **2** tackle; equipment: *Did you need all that rigging for a trip of only two days?*

**rig|ging**[2] (rig′ing), *n. Scottish.* **1** the roof of a house. **2** the ridge of a roof. [< *rig*[2]]

**Riggs' disease** (rigz), = periodontitis. [< John M. *Riggs,* 1810-1885, an American dentist]

**right** (rīt), *adj., adv., n., v.* **—*adj.*** **1** that is as it ought to be; agreeing with what is good, just, or lawful: *He did the right thing when he told the truth.* **SYN**: equitable, ethical. **2** correct; true: *the right answer. A fool must now and then be right, by chance* (William Cowper). **SYN**: accurate. **3** fitting; suitable; proper: *Learn to say the right thing at the right time.* **SYN**: fit, seemly, due, appropriate. **4** favorable: *If the weather is right, we'll go.* **SYN**: propitious. **5** healthy; normal: *to be in one's right mind. He was thin and pale last week, but he looks all right now.* **6** meant to be seen; most important: *the right side of cloth.* **SYN**: principal, front, upper. **7a** the opposite of left; belonging to or having something to do with the side of anything that is turned east when the main side is turned north. You have a right hand and a left hand. Most people eat, write, and work with the right hand. **b** on this side when viewed from the front: *the right wall of a room.* **c** toward this side: *Make a right turn.* **8** straight: *a right line.* **9** having a line or axis perpendicular to another line or surface: *a right angle, a right cone.* **10** often, **Right.** having conservative or reactionary ideas in politics. **11** *Archaic.* rightful; real: *the right owner.*
**—*adv.*** **1** in a way that is good, just, or lawful: *He acted right when he told the truth.* **SYN**: justly.

2 correctly; truly: *She guessed right.* 3 properly; well: *It is faster to do the job right the first time. It serves you right to lose if you cheat.* SYN: aptly. 4 favorably: *Such schemes don't always turn out right.* SYN: advantageously. 5 in a good or suitable condition: *Put things right. Don't mix up my papers; I shall never get them right again.* 6 on or to the right side: *to turn right.* 7 exactly; just; precisely: *Your cap is right where you left it.* 8 at once; immediately: *Stop playing right now.* 9 very (used in some titles): *the right honorable, the right reverend. It is with stinging memories ... that many people in the country who are not labourers come to the reading of the talk of right honourable gentlemen* (J. W. R. Scott). 10 *Dialect.* extremely: *I am right glad to see you. He commands a right good crew* (W. S. Gilbert). 11 in a straight line; directly: *Look me right in the eye.* 12 completely: *His hat was knocked right off.* SYN: altogether, quite.

—*n.* 1 that which is just, good, or true: *Do right, not wrong.* SYN: morality, virtue. 2 a just claim, title, or privilege; something that is due a person: *a property right. Each member of the club has a right to vote. He demanded his rights. The claimants submitted that the Japanese, ... acquired no belligerent rights under international law and could acquire no right to the property* (London Times). SYN: prerogative. 3 fair treatment; justice: *payment as a matter of simple right.* 4 a blow struck with the right hand: *a hard right to the jaw.* 5 the right side or what is on the right side: *to drive on the right, to turn to the right. Please sit on my right.* 6 Often, **Right**. **a** the part of a lawmaking body made up of conservative or reactionary political groups. It usually sits to the right of the presiding officer. **b** *Figurative.* the persons or parties holding conservative or reactionary views. 7**a** a privilege of subscribing for a stock or bond. **b** a certificate granting such a privilege.

—*v.t.* 1 to make correct; put in order; set right: *to right a wrong, to right one's accounts.* SYN: rectify, amend, adjust. 2 to do justice to: *to right the oppressed.* SYN: vindicate. 3 to put in the proper position: *to right an overturned car. The boys righted the capsized boat.* 4 to inform (a person) correctly: *He was in error but I righted him.*

—*v.i.* to get into proper position: *The ship righted after the big wave passed.*

**by right** or **rights**, justly; properly; correctly: *This book ought to be mine by rights.*

**in one's own right**, by inherent or personal right; independent of other conditions or qualifications: *The two-year college is an important educational institution in its own right, with its own special function and, hopefully, with its own distinguished future* (Harper's). *A novelist in her own right with a dozen books to her name* (Manchester Guardian Weekly).

**in the right**, right: *Which party is in the right?*

**right about!** turn in the opposite direction: *The command was given—right about!—and the troops marched back to the barracks.*

**right along**, **a** without stopping: *There was hardly any traffic and we drove right along till we got home.* **b** without trouble: *His business is going right along.*

**right and left**, **a** to the right and the left; on every side: *He would lay about him right and left, what havoc he would make!* (London Examiner). **b** continually; in great numbers; from all sides: *He is being robbed right and left* (Frank F. Moore). *The archaeologists ... left the actual labor to the "experts" who committed archaeological atrocities right and left* (Atlantic).

**right away** or **right off**, at once; immediately: *He promised to do it right away. He ... had a kind of fit this noon and died right off* (Harper's).

**right on**, *U.S. Slang.* absolutely right; entirely correct or true: *The phrase "Right on," which originated with the Black Panther Party, is* (or *was*) *an expression of affirmation on the revolutionary left, as in this colloquy: Speaker: Imperialism must be smashed! Audience: Right on!* (New Yorker).

**rights**, **a** *U.S. Informal.* civil rights: *a rights group, the rights movement, Commission on Rights.* **b** a share or interest in property: *With the rights to "Charley's Aunt" in hand, the fledgling producers could hardly be regarded as nonentities* (New Yorker).

**to rights**, *Informal.* in or into proper condition, order, or the like: *In my chamber, setting things and papers to rights* (Samuel Pepys).

[Old English *riht*] —**right'er**, *n.* —**right'ness**, *n.*

▶ **Right** in the sense of "very" or "extremely" (*He's a right friendly man*) is now a localism.

**Right** (rīt), *adv.* very (used in titles): *The Right Honorable Thomas Jones, Lord Mayor of London.*

**right|a|ble** (rī'tə bəl), *adj.* that can be righted.

**right|a|bout** (rīt'ə bout'), *n., adj., adv.* —*n.* 1 the direction opposite to that which one is facing. 2 a complete turn.

—*adj.* that is in the opposite direction: *a right-about turn.* —*adv.* in the opposite direction: *to turn rightabout.*

**right about-face**, 1 a turning in the opposite direction. 2 a turn in the opposite direction; reversal: *a right about-face in policy.*

**right angle**, an angle that is formed by a line perpendicular to another line; angle of 90 degrees. The angles in a square or in the capital letters F, L, and T are right angles. See picture under **angle**[1].

**right-an|gle** (rīt'ang'gəl), *adj.* = right-angled.

**right-an|gled** (rīt'ang'gəld), *adj.* 1 containing a right angle or right angles. 2 = rectangular.

**right ascension**, the arc of the celestial equator intercepted between the vernal equinox and the great circle of the celestial sphere passing through the celestial poles of a heavenly body whose position is being considered, reckoned toward the east and expressed in hours.

**right bower**, the jack of trumps in certain card games.

**right-cen|ter** (rīt'sen'tər), *adj., n.* —*adj.* of or belonging to the conservative or reactionary segment of a political party or group of the center.

—*n.* a right-center party, group, or position.

**right|eous** (rī'chəs), *adj.* 1 doing right; virtuous; behaving justly: *a righteous man.* SYN: upright, just. 2 proper, just, or right, especially morally right or justifiable: *righteous anger, a righteous cause. He was stirred by righteous wrath* (John Galsworthy). [Old English *rihtwīs* < *riht* right + *wīs* way, manner; altered by analogy with adjectives ending with *-eous*] —**right'eous|ly**, *adv.*

**right|eous|ness** (rī'chəs nis), *n.* 1 upright conduct; virtue: *Righteousness exalteth a nation* (Proverbs 14:34). SYN: rectitude. 2 the quality or condition of being right and just: *the righteousness of a claim.*

**right face**, a turn to the right.

**right field**, *Baseball.* 1 the part of the outfield from the first-base foul line to the center field. 2 the position of the player in this area. *Abbr:* rf.

**right fielder**, *Baseball.* a player stationed in right field.

**right|ful** (rīt'fəl), *adj.* 1 according to law; by rights; legal: *the rightful owner of this dog.* SYN: lawful, legitimate. 2 just and right; proper; fair: *rightful demands.* SYN: due. —**right'ful|ness**, *n.*

**right|ful|ly** (rīt'fə lē), *adv.* 1 according to right, law, or justice; in a rightful manner; legitimately: *a title rightfully vested.* 2 properly; fittingly.

**right hand**, 1 the hand on the right side of the body, normally the stronger and more used of the two. 2 *Figurative.* a person of great usefulness to someone; very efficient or indispensable helper. 3 the right side.

**right-hand** (rīt'hand'), *adj.* 1 on or to the right: *a right-hand turn.* 2 of, for, or with the right hand; right-handed: *a right-hand drive.* 3 *Figurative.* most helpful or useful: *a right-hand man.*

**right-hand|ed** (rīt'han'did), *adj., adv.* —*adj.* 1 using the right hand more easily and readily than the left: *So Uncle Bob started early to convert a naturally right-handed boy into a southpaw* (Time). 2 done with the right hand. 3 made to be used with the right hand. 4 turning from left to right: *a right-handed screw.* 5 having a spiral that winds from left to right: *a right-handed thread.*

—*adv.* toward the right; with the right hand.

—**right'-hand'ed|ly**, *adv.* —**right'-hand'ed|ness**, *n.*

**right-hand|er** (rīt'han'dər), *n.* 1 a right-handed person. 2 a right-handed baseball pitcher. 3 a blow given by the right hand.

**right-hand rule**, a rule used in electricity to show the relation between the direction of the current and the magnetic poles in an electric motor: *The right-hand rule ... states that if the forefinger of the right hand has the shape and direction of the current flow, the thumb of the right hand points to the north pole of the induced magnetic field* (Scientific American).

**right|ism** or **Right|ism** (rī'tiz əm), *n.* adherence or tendency to adhere to conservative or reactionary views in politics.

**right|ist** or **Right|ist** (rī'tist), *n., adj.* —*n.* 1 a person who has conservative or reactionary ideas in politics: *Angrily the extreme rightists strode from the Chamber* (Time). 2 a member of a conservative or reactionary political organization. —*adj.* having conservative or reactionary ideas in politics.

**right|ly** (rīt'lē), *adv.* 1 justly; fairly: *The decision was rightly made by a judge.* 2 correctly; exactly; accurately: *He rightly guessed that I was safe.* 3 properly; in a suitable manner: *We were rightly repaid for our expenses.* SYN: appropriately, suitably. [Old English *rihtlīce*]

**right-mind|ed** (rīt'mīn'did), *adj.* having right opinions or principles. SYN: honest, upright. —**right'-mind'ed|ness**, *n.*

**right|o** (rī'tō), *interj. Informal.* all right; O.K.

**right-of-cen|ter** (rīt'əv sen'tər), *adj.* occupying a position on the right side of those in the center; holding a rightist view in politics; right-wing: *a right-of-center party or regime.*

**right of search**, the searching of a vessel or the examining of its papers, cargo, or crew, by officers of a belligerent state to learn its nationality, whether it carries contraband, its destination, and other particulars.

**right of visit** or **right of visit and search**, *Especially British.* right of search.

**right of way**, *pl.* **rights of way** or **right of ways.** 1 the right to go first; precedence over all others, especially the right of a vehicle to cross in front of another. 2 the right to pass over another's property. 3 a strip of land: **a** on which others have the right to pass. **b** on which a public highway, power line, railroad, sewer line, or public utility or service is built.

**right-on** (rīt'on', -ôn'), *adj. U.S. Slang.* being right on; completely correct, true, or trustworthy: *In Boston,* [*he*] *is known as a "right-on lawyer"—he defends blacks, war protesters, and poor people* (Time).

**rights** (rīts), *n.pl.* See under **right**.

**Rights** (rīts), *n.pl.* **Bill of.** See **Bill of Rights**.

**right-to-die** (rīt'tə dī'), *adj.* opposed to the use of artificial measures or extreme treatment to prolong the life of a person who is incurably ill or injured: *The Quinlan case gave impetus to the so-called right-to-die movement, and California ... became the first state to enact a right-to-die law* (Michael Wheeler).

**right-to-life** (rīt'tə līf'), *adj.* advocating or supporting laws to make passive euthanasia or induced abortions illegal; opposed to abortion; pro-life: *He has drawn criticism from right-to-life groups for his refusal to support a constitutional amendment on abortion* (Time). —**right'-to-lif'er**, *n.*

**right-to-work** (rīt'tə wėrk'), *adj. U.S.* of or having to do with the right of a worker to get or keep a job whether he belongs or does not belong to a labor union: *a right-to-work policy. Right-to-work laws ban the union shop, which requires a worker to join the union at a plant to continue working at the plant* (Wall Street Journal).

***right triangle**, a triangle with one right angle.

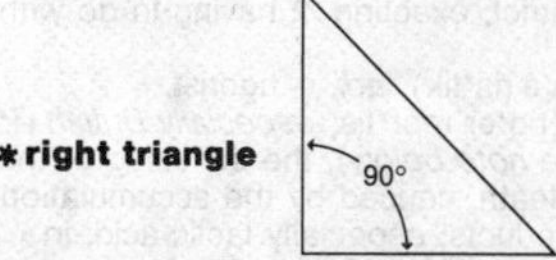

***right triangle**

**right|ward** (rīt'wərd), *adv., adj.* on or toward the right.

**right|wards** (rīt'wərdz), *adv., adj.* = rightward.

**right whale**, any one of several whales from which whalebone and oil are obtained. Right whales have very large heads, a bonnet on the snout, and about 350 long, toothlike whalebones on each side of the mouth to sieve food from the water which they gulp.

**right whale dolphin**, a small black dolphin of Pacific waters, with a white belly and without a dorsal fin.

**right wing**, 1 Often, **Right Wing.** the conservative or reactionary members, especially of a political party: *There is no sign that the right wing of the party will call off its crusade to drive him from the party* (New York Times). 2 persons or parties holding conservative or reactionary views.

**right-wing** (rīt'wing'), *adj.* belonging to or like the right wing.

**right-wing|er** (rīt'wing'ər), *n.* 1 a right-wing member of a political group. 2 a person who has conservative or reactionary ideas in politics.

**right-wing|ism** (rīt'wing'iz əm), *n.* the doctrines or practices of right-wingers.

**right|y** (rī'tē), *n., pl.* **right|ies.** 1 *U.S. Informal.* a right-handed person: *Switch-hitters traditionally do better against righties* (Newsweek). 2 *British Informal.* a conservative or reactionary; right-winger: *The frightening gulf of our day ... between lefties and righties* (Manchester Guardian Weekly).

**rig|id** (rij'id), *adj.* 1 stiff; firm; not bending: *a rigid support. Hold your arm rigid.* SYN: unyielding, un-

**Pronunciation Key:** **hat**, **āge**, **cãre**, **fär**; **let**, **ēqual**, **tėrm**; **it**, **īce**; **hot**, **ōpen**, **ôrder**; **oil**, **out**; **cup**, **pu̇t**, **rüle**; **child**; **long**; **thin**; **ᴛʜen**; **zh**, **measure**;
**ə** represents **a** in about, **e** in taken, **i** in pencil, **o** in lemon, **u** in circus.

bending. See syn. under **stiff**. **2** strict; not changing: *rigid discipline. In our home, it is a rigid rule to wash one's hands before eating. The young man is under the dictates of a rigid schoolmaster or instructor* (Sir Richard Steele). **3** severely exact; rigorous: *a rigid examination.* **SYN**: See syn. under **strict**. **4** having a framework within the envelope to maintain its shape: *a rigid airship.* [< Latin *rigidus* < *rigēre* be stiff, perhaps related to *frīgidus* frigid] —**rig′id|ly**, *adv.* —**rig′id|ness**, *n.*

**ri|gid|i|fi|ca|tion** (rə jid′ə fə kā′shən), *n.* **1** the act or process of rigidifying: *Confinement obviously makes for rigidification of behavior* (New Scientist). **2** the result of rigidifying; being rigidified: *personality rigidification.*

**ri|gid|i|fy** (rə jid′ə fī), *v.t., v.i.,* **-fied, -fy|ing.** to make or become rigid: *The proliferation of controls rigidifies the industry* (Wall Street Journal).

**ri|gid|i|ty** (rə jid′ə tē), *n., pl.* **-ties. 1** stiffness; firmness: *the rigidity of an iron bar.* **2** strictness; severity: *the rigidity of a school regulation.* **SYN**: stringency.

**ri|gid|ize** (ri′jə dīz), *v.t., v.i.,* **-ized, -iz|ing.** to rigidify: *Once inflated, the balloon is rigidized mechanically by stretching the skin beyond its elastic limit* (Science News Letter).

**rig|ma|role** (rig′mə rōl), *n.* foolish talk or activity; words or action without meaning; nonsense: *But was it not in order to cope with the situation … that the Government set up in recent years … the whole rigmarole of scheduling, listing, and building preservation orders?* (London Times). Also, **rigamarole.** [Middle English *ragman's roll* < *rageman* a list, catalog + *roll*]

**rig|o|lette** (rig′ə let′), *n.* a kind of knitted wool scarf, worn as a headcovering by women. [< French *rigolette*]

**rig|or** (rig′ər), *n.* **1** strictness; severity: *The sergeant trained the new recruits with great rigor.* **SYN**: inflexibility. **2** harshness: *the rigor of a long, cold winter. Let him have all the rigor of the law* (Shakespeare). **SYN**: inclemency. **3** logical exactness: *the rigor of scientific method.* **4** a chill caused by illness. [< Latin *rigor, -ōris* < *rigēre;* see etym. under **rigid**]

**rig|or|ism** (rig′ə riz əm), *n.* extreme strictness.

**rig|or|ist** (rig′ər ist), *n., adj.* —*n.* a person who believes in or supports extreme strictness, especially in matters of spiritual or moral conduct: *Even the moral rigorists who espouse suppression and try to enforce it are strong proponents of publicity* (Bulletin of Atomic Scientists).
—*adj.* **1** rigid; strict; exacting. **2** having to do with rigorism.

**rig|or|is|tic** (rig′ə ris′tik), *adj.* = rigorist.

**rig|or mor|tis** (rig′ər môr′tis; *especially British* rī′gôr môr′tis; *see note below*), the stiffening of the muscles after death, caused by the accumulation of metabolic products, especially lactic acid, in the muscles. [probably < Medieval Latin *rigor mortis* (literally) stiffness of death < Latin *rigor* rigor; *mortis,* genitive of *mors* death]
▶The pronunciation (rī′gôr), conforming to the older fashion of pronouncing Latin words in English, has lost currency in the United States, but survives in Great Britain.

**rig|or|ous** (rig′ər əs), *adj.* **1** very severe; strict: *the rigorous discipline in the army. The strike put the Administration's labor policy to a rigorous test* (New York Times). **SYN**: stern. See syn. under **strict**. **2** harsh: *a rigorous climate, a rigorous winter.* **3** thoroughly logical and scientific; exact: *the rigorous methods of science.* —**rig′or|ous|ly**, *adv.* —**rig′or|ous|ness**, *n.*

**rig|our** (rig′ər), *n. Especially British.* rigor.

**rig-out** (rig′out′), *n. Informal.* an outfit; costume: *This toggery of yours will never fit—you must have a new rig-out* (William T. Moncrieff).

**Rigs|dag** (rigz′däg′), *n.* the former parliament of Denmark. It was replaced in 1953 by the Folketing. [< Danish *Rigsdag* (literally) imperial diet]

**rigs|da|ler** (rigz′dä′lər), *n.* a former Danish silver coin, worth about 90 cents. [< Danish *rigsdaler* (literally) imperial dollar. Compare etym. under **dollar**.]

**Rig-Ve|da** (rig vā′də, -vē′-), *n.* the oldest and most important of the sacred books of the Hindus. [< Sanskrit *rigveda* < *ric-* praise + *veda* knowledge]

**R.I.I.A.,** Royal Institute of International Affairs.

**rijks|daal|der** (rīks′däl′dər; *informal* rīks′dä′lər), *n.* = rix-dollar. [< Dutch *rijksdaalder* (literally) imperial dollar. Compare etym. under **dollar**.]

**rijst|ta|fel** (rīst′tä′fəl), *n.* an elaborate meal consisting of rice with numerous side dishes of meats and vegetables, of Indonesian origin and popular in the Netherlands. [< Dutch *rijst* rice + *tafel* table]

**Riks|dag** (riks′däg′), *n.* the parliament of Sweden. [< Swedish *Riksdag* (literally) imperial diet]

**riks|da|ler** (riks′dä′lər), *n.* a former Swedish silver coin. [< Swedish *riksdaler* (literally) imperial dollar. Compare etym. under **dollar**.]

**rik|sha** (rik′shô), *n.* = jinrikisha.

**Riks|mål** (riks′môl), *n.* the older of the two varieties of standard, literary Norwegian (contrasted with *Landsmål*); Bokmål. It is a Norwegian form of Danish spoken in cities. [< Norwegian *Riksmål* < *riks,* genitive of *rik* empire, realm + *mål* language, speech]

**rile** (rīl), *v.t.,* **riled, ril|ing.** *Informal.* **1** to disturb; irritate; vex: *There ain't no sense In getting riled* (Bret Harte). **2** = roil (def. 1). [American English, variant of *roil*]

**ril|ey** (rī′lē), *adj. Especially U.S. Informal.* **1** angry; irritable; vexed. **2** roiled; turbid.

**ri|lie|vo** (rē lye′vō), *n., pl.* **-vi** (-vē). (in sculpture or painting) relief. [< Italian *rilievo*]

**rill**[1] (ril), *n., v.* —*n.* a tiny stream; little brook: *I love thy rocks and rills, Thy woods and templed hills* (Samuel F. Smith). **SYN**: rivulet, runnel.
—*v.i.* to flow in a small stream.
[compare Dutch *ril* groove, furrow]

**rill**[2] or **rille** (ril), *n.* a long, narrow valley on the surface of the moon: *There are many rills, or clefts—cracks of the order of half a mile wide and of unknown depth* (Robert H. Baker). [< German *Rille* a furrow]

**rill|et** (ril′it), *n.* a little rill.

**ril|letts** or **ril|lettes** (ri lets′, rē yet′), *n.pl.* a potted delicacy made principally of minced chicken, pork, and truffles, used in sandwiches or with salad. [< French *rillette* (diminutive) < *rille* piece of pork]

**rim** (rim), *n., v.,* **rimmed, rim|ming.** —*n.* an edge, border, or margin on or around anything: *the rim of a wheel, the rim of a cup, the south rim of the Grand Canyon. The basketball hit the rim of the basket and bounced off.*
—*v.t.* **1** to form a rim around; put a rim around: *Wild flowers and grasses rimmed the little pool.* **2** to roll around the rim of: *The golf ball rimmed the cup and fell into the hole.*
[Old English *rima*]

**ri|ma** (rī′mə), *n., pl.* **-mae** (-mē). *Biology.* a long, narrow opening; fissure; cleft. [< Latin *rīma* cleft]

**rime**[1] (rīm), *v.i., v.t.,* **rimed, rim|ing,** *n.* = rhyme: *Coleridge's "Rime of the Ancient Mariner."*
▶See **rhyme** for usage note.

**rime**[2] (rīm), *n., v.,* **rimed, rim|ing.** —*n.* white frost; hoarfrost, especially from the freezing of vapor in drifting fog: *Evening cloud and whitening sunrise rime told of the coming of the wintertime* (John Greenleaf Whittier).
—*v.t.* to cover with rime or something like rime: (*Figurative.*) *Years had rimed his once black hair.*
[Old English *hrīm*]

**rim|er** (rī′mər), *n.* = rhymer.

**rime|ster** (rīm′stər), *n.* = rhymester.

**rim-fire** (rim′fīr′), *adj.* **1** (of a cartridge) having its primer at the rim of its base. **2** (of a firearm) designed to fire rim-fire cartridges.

**rim|land** (rim′land′), *n.* the area or areas on or around the outer edges of a heartland.

**rim|less** (rim′lis), *adj.* having no rim or rims: *rimless glasses.*

**rimmed** (rimd), *adj.* having a rim or rims.

**rimmed steel**, steel which has been incompletely deoxidized, and whose outer edge forms a rim as it solidifies.

**ri|mose** (rī′mōs, rī mōs′), *adj.* full of chinks or cracks. [< Latin *rīmōsus* < *rīma* chink, cleft]

**rim|ous** (rī′məs), *adj.* = rimose.

**rim|ple** (rim′pəl), *n., v.i., v.t.,* **-pled, -pling.** *Dialect.* wrinkle; ripple. [Middle English *rymple*]

**rim|rock** (rim′rok′), *n.* rock rising like a rim from the bedrock of an elevated piece of land, as above a basin.

**rim saw**, a saw with a ringlike, toothed cutting part mounted on the rim of a disk.

**rim|y** (rī′mē), *adj.,* **rim|i|er, rim|i|est.** covered with rime or hoarfrost; frosty.

**rin** (rin), *n., pl.* **rin.** a former Japanese money of account, worth 1/10 sen. The rin was removed from circulation in 1954. [< Japanese *rin*]

**rin|ceau** (raɴ sō′), *n.pl.* **-ceaux** (-sō′). *French.* an ornamental scroll elaborated with acanthus leaves.

**rind**[1] (rīnd), *n., v.* —*n.* the firm outer covering of fruits such as oranges and melons, and of some cheeses. The bark of a tree or plant may be called the rind. **SYN**: peel, skin.
—*v.t.* to strip the rind from: *While the sap of the oak was rising … trees were most easily flayed, flawed, ripped, rinded or barked* (Punch).
[Old English *rinde*]

**rind**[2] (rīnd, rind), *n.* = rynd.

**rind|ed** (rīn′did), *adj.* having a rind (of a certain kind): *soft-rinded cheeses.*

**rin|der|pest** (rin′dər pest′), *n.* an acute and usually fatal, infectious virus disease especially of cattle and sheep. It is marked by fever, dysentery, and inflammation of the mucous membranes. *Rinderpest is the world's deadliest cattle disease, killing 90% to 100% of the cattle it infects* (Science News Letter). [< German *Rinderpest* cattle plague < *Rinder,* plural of *Rind* ox + *Pest* pestilence, plague]

**rind|less** (rīnd′lis), *adj.* having no rind.

**rin|for|zan|do** (rin′fôr tsän′dō), *adj. Music.* with sudden increased force, as a single phrase or voice part to be made prominent. [< Italian *rinforzando,* gerund of *rinforzare* strengthen, reinforce]

**ring**[1] (ring), *n., v.,* **ringed, ring|ing.** —*n.* **1** a circle: *The elves danced in a ring.* **2a** a thin circle of metal, usually gold or silver, or other material: *rings on her fingers, a wedding ring.* **b** a circle of metal, wood, plastic, or other material, used for attaching, hanging, or other purposes: *a curtain ring, a key ring, a napkin ring.* **3** persons or things arranged in a circle: *A cottage … close environ'd with a ring of branching elms* (William Cowper). **4** the outer edge or border of a coin, plate, wheel, or anything round. **5** the space between two circles having the same center. **6** a circular object, line, or bend. **7** an enclosed space for races, games, circus performances, or similar activities: *The ring for a prizefight is square.* **SYN**: arena. **8** prizefighting. **9** a space at a race track where bets are made. **10** competition; rivalry; contest: *in the ring for election to the Senate.* **11** a group of people combined for a selfish or bad purpose: *The police broke up a ring of smugglers operating in various ports. An alleged spy ring went on trial in London on charges of stealing naval secrets* (Wall Street Journal). **12** an exclusive group of people; circle; clique: *I had always understood that the theatrical "ring" was impenetrable to an outsider* (Arnold Bennett). **13** a circular layer of wood produced yearly in a tree trunk; annual ring: *You can tell the age of a tree by counting the number of rings in its wood; one ring grows every year.* **14** *Chemistry.* a closed chain of atoms linked by bonds that may be represented graphically in circular form. **15** *Mathematics.* a set of elements subject to the operations of addition and multiplication, in which the set is commutative under addition and associative under multiplication, and in which the two operations are related by distributive laws.
—*v.t.* **1** to put a ring around; enclose; form a circle around: *The cowboys ringed the herd before driving them into the pens. The circling sea that rings the earth* (William Morris). **SYN**: encircle. **2** to toss a horseshoe, quoit, or the like, around (a certain mark or post): *He ringed the post.* **3** to provide with a ring. **4** to put a ring in the nose of (an animal). **5** to cut away the bark in a ring around (a tree or branch).
—*v.i.* **1** to move in a ring. **2** (of a hawk or other bird that soars on air currents) to rise in circular flight. **3** to form a ring or rings.
**hold the ring,** *Especially British.* to keep a situation from getting out of hand; hold the line: *The Army is there … to hold the ring while statesmen make a further attempt to find a political framework that will accommodate in peace the two historic communities in the north of Ireland* (London Times).
**run rings around,** *Informal.* to surpass with great ease; beat easily: *It seems to be generally accepted that* [*he*] *is running rings around the Opposition* (London Times).
[Old English *hring*] —**ring′like′**, *adj.*

**ring**[2] (ring), *v.,* **rang** or (*now Dialect*) **rung, rung, ring|ing,** *n.* —*v.i.* **1** to give forth a clear sound, as a bell does: *Did the telephone ring?* **2** to cause a bell to sound: *Did you ring?* **3** to call, as to church or prayers, by ringing bells. **4** to sound loudly; resound: *The room rang with shouts of laughter.* **5** to echo; give back sound: *The mountains rang with the roll of thunder. The camp rang with the bugle's call for reveille.* **6** *Figurative.* to be filled with report or talk: *The whole town is ringing with the good news.* **7** *Figurative.* to sound; impress one as having a certain quality: *Your words rang true.* **8** to hear a sound like that of a bell ringing; hear inner ringing: *My ears are ringing.*
—*v.t.* **1** to cause to give forth a clear ringing sound: *Ring the bell. He rang his silver money upon the counter* (Owen Wister). **2** to make (a sound) by ringing: *The bells rang a joyous peal.* **3** to announce or proclaim by bells; usher; conduct: *to ring a fire alarm. Ring out the old year; ring in the new. Big Ben rang out the hour.* **4** *Figurative.* to proclaim or repeat loudly everywhere: *to ring a person's praises.* **5** to call on the telephone: *I'll ring you tomorrow.*
—*n.* **1** an act of ringing: *A ring of the bell called us to dinner.* **2** a sound of a bell: *Did you hear a ring?* **3** a sound like that of a bell: *On a cold night we can hear the ring of skates on ice. Tap the rim with your fingernail and the clear ring reveals the exquisite perfection of this crystal glassware* (Newsweek). **4** a characteristic sound or quality: *a ring of sincerity, a ring of scorn in*

*her voice.* **5** a call on the telephone: *If [he] were to give me a ring in half an hour's time he could have the inquiry* (London Times). **6** a set or peal of bells.
**ring a bell**. See under **bell**.
**ring down the curtain**. See under **curtain**.
**ring for**, to summon by a bell: *to ring for a porter.*
**ring in, a** *Informal.* to bring in dishonestly or trickily: *She can't be kept out of the case entirely, after all. We'll have to ring her in* (Theodore Dreiser). **b** to record one's arrival at work on a time clock: *The foreman rings in five minutes before the workers ring in.*
**ring off**, to end a telephone call: *She heard him ring off, hang up the receiver, and go out into the hall* (Munsey's Magazine).
**ring out**, to record one's leaving from work on a time clock: *The day shift at the mill rings out at 5 P.M.*
**ring the changes**. See under **change**.
**ring up, a** to record (a specific amount) on a cash register: *The continued increase in the amount of consumer debt rang up more sales for the merchant* (Harry M. Kelly). **b** to call on the telephone: *We did not look forward to the reproaches of Mrs. Slocum, who had already rung up the local policeman* (London Times).
**ring up the curtain**. See under **curtain**.
[Old English *hringan*]
▶ **Rung** as a past-tense form (*He rung the bell*), once standard and still widespread in nonstandard use, is now uncommon in cultivated English.

**ring-a-le|vi|o** (ring′ə lē′vē ō), *n.* a game in which one team must find hidden members of the opposing team, capture and imprison them, and prevent their being freed by their teammates. [origin uncertain]

**ring armor**, **1** armor made of chain mail. **2** armor made of metal rings fastened on leather or cloth.

**ring-a|round-a-ros|y** (ring′ə round′ə rō′zē), *n.* = ring-around-the-rosy.

**ring-a|round-the-ros|y** (ring′ə round′ᴛʜe rō′zē), *n.* a children's game in which the singing players skip around in a circle and drop to the floor on the song's last line.

**ring-bark** (ring′bärk′), *v.t.* to girdle (a tree or branch).

**ring|bill** (ring′bil′), *n.* = ring-necked duck.

**ring-billed gull** (ring′bild′), a North American gull almost identical to the herring gull but smaller, and with a black ring around the bill.

**ring binder**, a loose-leaf notebook with hinged metal rings for holding the sheets of paper in place.

**ring|bolt** (ring′bōlt′), *n.* a bolt with an eye in its head in which a ring is fitted.

**ring|bone** (ring′bōn′), *n.* an abnormal growth of bone on the pastern or coronet of a horse.

**ring buoy**, a ring-shaped life buoy.

**ring compound**, a compound of several atoms united to form a ring; cyclic compound; closed-chain compound.

**ring|craft** (ring′kraft′, -kräft′), *n.* knowledge of or special skill in boxing in the ring.

**ring dance**, a dance with dancers in a circle; round dance.

**ring|dove** (ring′duv′), *n.* **1** a wood pigeon of Europe, with a whitish patch on either side of the neck; cushat. **2** a pigeon of Europe and Asia, with a black half ring around its neck. It is related to the turtledove.

**ringed** (ringd), *adj.* **1** having or wearing a ring or rings. **2** marked or decorated with a ring or rings. **3** surrounded by a ring or rings. **SYN:** circled. **4** formed of or with rings; ringlike. **5** *Zoology.* composed of ringlike segments; annulated.

**ringed perch**, = yellow perch.

**ringed plover**, a plover of the Old World and eastern parts of arctic America, very similar to the semipalmated plover.

**ringed seal**, a common seal of arctic regions, brownish above and yellowish below with ringlike markings on the sides; floe rat.

**rin|gent** (rin′jənt), *adj.* **1** gaping. **2** having the lips widely opened: *a ringent labiate corolla.* [< Latin *ringēns, -entis,* present participle of *ringī* to gape; show the teeth]

**ring|er¹** (ring′ər), *n.* **1** a person or thing that encircles or surrounds with a ring. **2a** a horseshoe, quoit, or ring, thrown so as to fall over a peg. **b** the toss which does this. **3** a game of marbles in which the target marbles are placed on a cross drawn in the center of a circle usually 10 feet in diameter; ringtaw. **4** (in Australia) **a** a very fast or expert sheepshearer. **b** a cattle drover. [< *ring*¹ + *-er*¹]

**ring|er²** (ring′ər), *n.* **1** a person or thing that rings. **2** a device for ringing a bell. **3** *Slang.* a person or thing very much like another. **4** *Slang.* **a** a horse, athlete, or other contestant competing under a false name or some other device to conceal his identity, skill, or the like: *West appeared as a "ringer" for Nat (Killer) Jackson ... and was knocked out by Brown in the third round* (New York Times). **b** a player who is not a regular member of the team that he is playing on. **c** any person who pretends to be another; impostor: *Immigration screening has been tight, and few ringers have slipped past interrogators* (Time).
**be a (dead) ringer for**, to be the image of: *He was a ringer for a ship's carpenter named Andersen* (New Yorker).
[< *ring*² + *-er*¹]

**Ringer solution**, = Ringer's solution.

**Ring|er's solution** (ring′ərz), an aqueous solution of the chlorides of sodium, potassium, and calcium in the approximate proportion in which they are found in blood and tissue fluid. It is used to preserve mammalian tissue in experiments and as a synthetic body fluid especially to combat dehydration. [< Sydney *Ringer,* 1835-1910, an English physician]

**ring finger**, the finger next to the little finger, especially on the left hand.

**ring gear**, **1** the large circular gear in the differential of an automobile that engages the pinion gear. **2** a circular gear with teeth on the inside. See picture under **planetary**.

**ring|hals** (ring′hals′), *n., pl.* **-hals|es.** a South African species of cobra that spits its venom into the face and eyes of its victims, causing burning pain and sometimes blindness; spitting cobra. It has a narrow hood and a ring of color around its neck. [< Afrikaans *ringhals* < *ring* ring + *hals* neck]

**ring|ing** (ring′ing), *adj.* having the sound of a bell; resounding: *a ringing voice, ringing oratory.* —**ring′ing|ly**, *adv.*

**ring|lead** (ring′lēd′), *v.t.,* **-led, -lead|ing.** to conduct or manage as ringleader. [back formation < *ringleader*]

**ring|lead|er** (ring′lē′dər), *n.* a person who leads others in opposition to authority or law: *the ringleaders of the mutiny.* [< *to lead the ring,* that is, to be the first]

**ring|less** (ring′lis), *adj.* without rings: *her ringless hand.*

**ring|let** (ring′lit), *n.* **1** a curl: *She wears her hair in ringlets.* **2** a little ring: *Drops of rain made ringlets in the pond.*

**ring|let|ed** (ring′lə tid), *adj.* having ringlets; curled.

**ring|mas|ter** (ring′mas′tər, -mäs′-), *n., v.* —*n.* **1** a person in charge of the performances in the ring of a circus. **2** *Figurative: The directors miss a firm but genial ringmaster whose flexibility of body and mind puts many younger men to shame* (London Times).
—*v.t.* **1** to direct or manage as a circus ringmaster: *I saw the circus in action, ringmastered by Calder himself, back in the nineteen-forties* (New Yorker). **2** *Figurative: a convention so thoroughly ringmastered by the President that all the nonsurprises came out of his pouch or hat* (Time).

**ring nebula**, **1** a kind of planetary nebula that looks like a ring when viewed through a telescope or on a photographic plate. **2 Ring Nebula**, the ring nebula in the constellation Lyra.

**ring|neck** (ring′nek′), *n.* any one of various birds having the neck ringed with a band or bands of color, such as certain ducks, plovers, and pheasants.

**ring-necked** (ring′nekt′), *adj.* having the neck ringed with a band or bands of color: *a ring-necked bird.*

**ring-necked duck**, a North American duck, the male of which has a black head, back, and breast, and a faint chestnut ring about the neck.

**ring-necked pheasant**, a pheasant native to China, the male of which has bright-colored plumage, a long, pointed tail, and a white ring around the neck. It has become established in the central and northern United States and southern Canada.

**ring-necked plover**, = semipalmated plover.

**ringneck snake**, any one of several dark-colored North American snakes with yellow, orange or red bellies, and a yellow or orange ring about their necks.

**ring of fire**, a belt of volcanoes surrounding the Pacific Ocean and causing violent seismic activity; circle of fire.

**Ring of the Nibelung**, **1** *German Legend.* a magic ring made from the Rheingold by Alberich, a dwarf. **2** a cycle of four operas by Richard Wagner.

**ring ouzel**, a European thrush which is black with a white marking on the breast.

**ring plain**, one of the nearly level circular areas on the moon's surface which are surrounded by high ridges and which have no central crater.

**ring plover**, **1** = semipalmated plover. **2** = ringed plover.

**ring-po|rous** (ring′pôr′əs, -pōr′-), *adj.* having pores which differ in size and distribution, being larger and more numerous in the spring than in the summer, such as the wood of the oak, ash, and hackberry.

**ring post**, one of the four posts of a boxing or wrestling ring.

**ring-pull** (ring′pu̇l′), *adj.* having a scored metal top that comes off in one piece by pulling at a small ring attached to it: *a ring-pull can.*

**ring road**, *British.* a by-pass.

**ring rot**, a bacterial disease of potatoes characterized by the decay of the ring of vascular bundles in the plant's tubers.

**ring shake**, a crack in timber, usually caused by frost, in which the extremes of contraction and expansion tear apart the annular rings.

**ring|side** (ring′sīd′), *n., adj.* —*n.* **1** the place just outside a ring or arena, especially at a circus or prizefight: *The reporters sat at ringside writing a description of the fight.* **2** *Figurative: Through television the American public sat at ringside for the entire moon exploration program.*
—*adj.* of or at ringside: *a ringside view of the parade.*

**ring|sid|er** (ring′sī′dər), *n.* a person who sits or observes at the ringside: *Startled ringsiders heard that the official loser ... had been robbed* (New Yorker).

**ring snake**, = ringneck snake.

**ring|spot** (ring′spot′), *n.,* or **ring spot**, **1** a yellowish, necrotic discoloration in the form of spots or circles, symptomatic of a disease in plants. **2** any one of various plant diseases characterized by such discoloration: *tobacco ringspot.*

**ring|ster** (ring′stər), *n. U.S. Informal.* a member of a ring, especially a political ring.

**ring-straked** (ring′strākt′), *adj. Archaic.* ring-streaked.

**ring-streaked** (ring′strēkt′), *adj.* having streaks or bands of color around the body.

**ring|tail** (ring′tāl′), *n.* a small, squirrellike mammal with a pointed face and a long tail with black rings, found in the southwest United States and Mexico; cacomistle. It is sometimes kept as a pet for catching rats and mice.

**ring-tailed** (ring′tāld′), *adj.* **1** having the tail or the tail feathers marked with a ring or rings of a different color from the rest of the animal. **2** having the end of the tail curled into a ring.

**ring-tailed cat**, = ringtail.

**ring-tailed eagle**, = golden eagle.

**ring|taw** (ring′tô′), *n.* = ringer¹ (def. 3).

**ring|toss** (ring′tôs′, -tos′), *n.* quoits played with a ring of rope or plastic, especially on shipboard.

**ring vaccination**, the vaccination of all persons connected with a case of smallpox or similar contagious disease.

**ring|way** (ring′wā′), *n. British.* ring road; by-pass.

**ring|worm** (ring′wėrm′), *n.* any one of several contagious skin diseases caused by fungi. One kind appears in the form of ring-shaped patches on the skin. Ringworm of the feet is called athlete's foot. Ringworm of the scalp often occurs among schoolchildren.

**rink** (ringk), *n.* **1** a sheet of ice for skating, especially one that is artificially prepared. **2** a smooth floor for roller-skating. **3** a building for ice-skating or roller-skating. **4** ice marked off for curling. **5** a bowling green. **6** a team of players in bowls, curling, or the like. [originally Scottish, perhaps < Old French *renc, reng* course, rank¹]

**rink|side** (ringk′sīd′), *n.* the area beside a skating rink.

**rink|y-dink** (ring′kē dingk′), *n., adj. U.S. Slang.* —*n.* something that is old-fashioned or trite, often in a gaudy way: *Eighteen-nineties rinky-dink, complete with fire engine, but the banjo band is above average* (New Yorker).
—*adj.* old-fashioned or trite, often in a gaudy way: *But then came the new rocks—and the Supremes [a singing group] suddenly sounded a little rinky-dink.* (Time).
[probably originally formed in imitation of the sound of banjo music formerly played at parades]

**rinse** (rins), *v.,* **rinsed, rins|ing,** *n.* —*v.t.* **1** to wash with clean water: *Rinse all the soap out of your hair after you wash it.* **2** to wash lightly: *Rinse your mouth with warm water.* **3** to give a quick washing to, as by holding under a tap, without use of soap or other cleanser: *to rinse a glass before drinking.*
—*n.* **1** the act or process of rinsing: *Give the plate a final rinse in cold water.* **2** water used in rinsing. **3** a preparation used in water to add color or luster to the hair.
[< Old French *reïncier,* ultimately < Latin *recēns, -entis* fresh] —**rins′a|ble**, *adj.*

**rins|er** (rin′sər), *n.* a person who rinses.

**Pronunciation Key:** hat, āge, cãre, fär; let, ēqual, tėrm; it, īce; hot, ōpen, ôrder; **oi**l, **ou**t; cup, pu̇t, rüle; **ch**ild; lo**ng**; **th**in; ᴛʜen; **zh**, measure; ə represents **a** in about, **e** in taken, **i** in pencil, **o** in lemon, **u** in circus.

**rins|ing** (rin′sing), *n.* the act of one who rinses. **rinsings, a** the liquid or liquor with which anything has been rinsed out: ... *being drenched with the rinsings of an unclean imagination* (James Russell Lowell). **b** = dregs: *The beadle . . . washed down the greasy morsel with the last rinsings of the pot of ale* (Scott).

**ri|om|e|ter** (rī om′ə tər), *n.* an instrument for recording the strength of radio noise and the level of its absorption by the ionosphere. [< *r*(elative) *i*(onospheric) *o*(pacity) *meter*]

**ri|ot** (rī′ət), *n., v.* —*n.* **1** a disturbance; confusion; disorder; wild, violent public disturbance: *The guards stopped several riots in the prison.* **SYN:** outbreak, tumult. **2** *Law.* a tumultuous disturbance of the public peace by three or more persons who assemble for some private purpose and execute it to the terror of the people. **3** a loud outburst: *to break out in a riot of laughter.* **4** loose living; wild reveling. **5** *Figurative.* a bright display: *The garden was a riot of color.* **6** *Informal.* a very amusing person or performance: *He was a riot at the party.*
—*v.i.* **1** to behave in a wild, disorderly way: *In protest, the Marathas rioted* (Newsweek). **2** to revel. **3** to live in a loose way.
—*v.t.* to spend or waste (money, time, or health) in loose living: *He ... Had rioted his life out, and made an end* (Tennyson).
**run riot, a** to act or speak without restraint: *Sometimes he runs riot and doesn't know when he has said enough.* **b** to grow wildly or luxuriantly: (*Figurative.*) *The colors of the cliffs ... run riot on a bright day* (William O. Douglas).
[< Old French *riote* dispute < *rioter* to quarrel, ultimately < Latin *rūgīre* to roar] —**ri′ot|er,** *n.*

**Riot Act,** an English statute of 1715 providing that if twelve or more persons assemble unlawfully and riotously, to the disturbance of the public peace, and refuse to disperse within an hour upon proclamation of the statute by a competent authority they shall be considered guilty of felony.
**read the riot act, a** to give orders for disturbance to cease: *They find it necessary to enforce order, to read the riot act,* [*and*] *to issue an injunction to ensure respect for property* (Canadian Saturday Night). **b** *Figurative: Mr. Daly ... read the riot act ... and vanished into his den, leaving the naughty girls overwhelmed* (Dora Knowlton Ranous).

**riot gun,** a gun, especially a small shotgun, used in quelling riots: *The officers of the law, armed with tear gas and riot guns, cordoned off the area* (New Yorker).

**ri|ot|ous** (rī′ə təs), *adj.* **1** taking part in a riot: *Riotous students were jailed during the disturbance.* **2** characterized by or of the nature of a riot: *He was expelled from college for riotous conduct.* **3** boisterous; disorderly: (*Figurative.*) *Sounds of riotous glee came from the playhouse.* **SYN:** turbulent, tumultuous. —**ri′ot|ous|ly,** *adv.* —**ri′ot|ous|ness,** *n.*

**riot squad,** a body of police trained and equipped to deal with riots: *Riot squads and mounted police stood by in case of violence* (Wall Street Journal).

**rip[1]** (rip), *v.,* **ripped, rip|ping,** *n.* —*v.t.* **1** to cut roughly; tear apart; tear off: *Rip the cover off this box.* **SYN:** rend. See syn. under **tear. 2** to cut or pull out (the threads in the seams of a garment); take apart (a garment) by opening the seams: *The tailor ripped the hem and shortened the dress.* **3** to saw (wood) along the grain, not across the grain. **4** *Informal.* to speak or say with violence: *He ripped out an angry oath.*
—*v.i.* **1** to become torn apart. **2** to come apart or be taken apart at a seam. **3** *Informal.* to move fast or violently. **4** *Informal.* to burst out angrily or violently: *Captain Peleg ripped and swore astern in the most frightful manner* (Herman Melville).
—*n.* a torn place, especially a seam burst in a garment: *Please sew up this rip in my sleeve.*
**let her rip,** *U.S. Slang.* to let a thing run its course, or do its best or worst: *In "Medea," I just open my big mouth and let her rip* (Time).
**rip into,** *Informal.* to attack violently: *Mr. Baird ... rips into toadyism* (Orville Prescott).
**rip off,** *U.S. Slang.* **a** to steal: *to rip off an expensive camera. For extra, unanticipated personal needs, he "rips off"* (Time). **b** to exploit: *"Rock is the cultural part of politics, and it's not going to be segregated or ripped off anymore"* (New Yorker).
[Middle English *rippen*]

**rip[2]** (rip), *n.* **1** a stretch of rough water made by opposing currents meeting. **2** a swift current made by the tide. [American English, perhaps special use of *rip[1]*]

**rip[3]** (rip), *n. Informal.* **1** a worthless or dissolute person: *the old rip, bewigged and gouty, ornate and enormous, with his jewelled mistress at his side* (Lytton Strachey). **SYN:** rake, roué. **2** a worthless, worn-out horse. [origin uncertain]

**R.I.P.,** may he or she (they) rest in peace (Latin, *Requiescat* (*requiescant*) *in pace*).

**ri|par|i|al** (ri pãr′ē əl, rī-), *adj.* = riparian.

**ri|par|i|an** (ri pãr′ē ən, rī-), *adj., n.* —*adj.* of or on the bank of a river or other waterway, or sometimes, a lake: *riparian property.*
—*n.* a person or group that lives or owns property on the banks of a river or other waterway, or sometimes, a lake. [< Latin *rīpārius* (< *rīpa* riverbank) + English *-an*]

**riparian rights,** the legal rights of a person, business, or government to approach and use water and bordering land, especially as a holder of property lying on a waterway or lake.

**rip cord, 1** a cord that is pulled to open a parachute. **2** a cord on a balloon or airship which allows gas to escape when pulled, causing a rapid descent.

**rip current,** = riptide.

**ripe** (rīp), *adj.,* **rip|er, rip|est. 1** full-grown and ready to be gathered and eaten; mature: *ripe fruit, ripe grain, ripe vegetables.* **SYN:** mellow, matured. **2** resembling ripe fruit in ruddiness and fullness: *ripe lips.* **3** at the peak, as of flavor or bouquet; mellow: *ripe cheese.* **4** fully developed: *ripe in knowledge, ripe plans. I ... saw, beneath his jaunty air, true mettle, and ripe bravery* (Richard Blackmore). **SYN:** mature. **5** ready to break or be lanced: *a ripe boil.* **6** ready; fully prepared: *ripe for mischief. The country is ripe for revolt.* **7** far enough along; sufficiently advanced: *The hour is ripe to strike.* **8** advanced in years: *the ripe age of 85.* [Old English *rīpe*] —**ripe′ly,** *adv.* —**ripe′ness,** *n.*

**rip|en** (rī′pən), *v.i.* to become ripe: *Farmers need good weather so that their crops will grow and ripen* (James E. Miller). —*v.t.* to make ripe.

**rip|en|er** (rī′pə nər), *n.* **1** a person or thing that comes to ripeness. **2** a person or thing that causes ripening.

**ri|pid|o|lite** (ri pid′ə līt, rī-), *n.* a mineral, a variety of chlorite; clinochlore. [< German *Ripidolith* (with English *-lite*) < Greek *rhipis, -idis* fan + *lithos* stone]

**ri|pie|no** (rē pyā′nō), *adj., n., pl.* **-ni** (-nē), **-nos.** —*adj.* supplementary or reinforcing.
—*n.* a supplementary instrument or performer.
[< Italian *ripieno* < Latin *re-* again + *plēnus* full]

**rip|off** or **rip-off** (rip′ôf′, -of′), *n. U.S. Slang.* **1** a theft or robbery. **2** something that exploits a popular trend or interest.

**ri|poste** or **ri|post** (ri pōst′), *n., v.,* **-post|ed, -post|ing.** —*n.* **1** *Fencing.* a quick thrust given after parrying a lunge. **2** a quick, sharp reply or return. **SYN:** retort.
—*v.i.* to make a riposte; reply; retaliate.
[< French *riposte* < Italian *risposta* a reply < *rispondere* respond < Latin *respondēre*]

**rip-pan|el** (rip′pan′əl), *n.* a part in the bag of a balloon or airship that can be ripped to let gas escape for a quick descent.

**rip|per** (rip′ər), *n.* **1** a person who rips. **2** a tool for ripping. **3** Also, **ripper law, bill,** or **act.** *U.S.* a law taking away the power of appointment to office from its usual holders and conferring it on a chief executive, such as the President or a governor.

**rip|ping** (rip′ing), *adj., adv. Especially British Slang.* fine; splendid: *a ripping good business* (H. G. Wells). —**rip′ping|ly,** *adv.*

**ripping panel,** = rip-panel.

**rip|ple[1]** (rip′əl), *n., v.,* **-pled, -pling.** —*n.* **1** a very little wave: *Throw a stone into still water and watch the ripples spread in rings.* **SYN:** See syn. under **wave. 2** anything that seems like a tiny wave: *ripples in hair.* **3** a sound that reminds one of little waves: *a ripple of laughter in the crowd.*
—*v.i.* **1** to make a sound like rippling water. **2** to form or have ripples. **3** to flow with ripples on: *A breeze rippled the quiet waters.*
[origin uncertain]

**rip|ple[2]** (rip′əl), *n., v.,* **-pled, -pling.** —*n.* a tool with teeth to remove seeds, as from flax or hemp.
—*v.t.* to remove the seeds from (as flax or hemp) with a ripple.
[compare Middle English *ripplen* comb seeds from flax]

**ripple effect,** a spreading effect, result, or influence: *Supplies of automobiles were stacking up ... and the ripple effect of the auto-industry slowdown had not even been felt yet* (New Yorker).

**ripple mark,** one of the wavy lines made on sand or rock, as by waves or wind.

**rip|pler** (rip′lər), *n.* **1** a person who ripples. **2** = ripple.

**rip|plet** (rip′lit), *n.* a little ripple.

**rip|pling** (rip′ling), *adj.* that ripples; flowing in ripples: *rippling hair.* —**rip′pling|ly,** *adv.*

**rip|ply** (rip′lē), *adj.* characterized by ripples; rippling.

**rip|rap** (rip′rap′), *n., v.,* **-rapped, -rap|ping.** —*n.* **1** a wall or foundation of broken stones thrown together irregularly. **2** broken stones so used.
—*v.t.* to build or strengthen with loose, broken stones.
[American English, reduplication of *rap[1]*, or related to *ripple[1]*]

**rip|roar|ing** (rip′rôr′ing, -rōr′-), *adj. Informal.* hilarious; uproarious; lively: *a riproaring good time.* [American English]

**rip|roar|i|ous** (rip′rôr′ē əs, -rōr′-), *adj. Slang.* riproaring. [American English < *rip[1]*, patterned on *uproarious*]

**rip|saw** (rip′sô′), *n.* a saw with large, coarse teeth, used for cutting wood along the grain, not across the grain.

**rip|snort|er** (rip′snôr′tər), *n. Informal.* **1** a thing that is unusually violent: *The new quake has an intensity of five, which is termed as "destructive, but not a ripsnorter"* (Wall Street Journal). **2** a person who becomes violent or unusually angry. [American English, perhaps < *rip[1]* + *snort,* verb + *-er[1]*]

**rip|snort|ing** (rip′snôr′ting), *adj. Informal.* boisterous or wild: *ripsnorting frontier days.*

**rip|tide** (rip′tīd′), *n.* a strong, narrow surface current which flows rapidly away from the shore usually at a right angle to it; rip current. A riptide flows against another current, usually causing a violent disturbance.

**Rip|u|ar|i|an** (rip′yu̇ ãr′ē ən), *adj., n.* —*adj.* **1** of or having to do with the ancient Franks who lived along the Rhine in the area around Cologne. **2** of or having to do with the code of laws observed by them.
—*n.* a Ripuarian Frank.
[< Medieval Latin *Ripuarius* (origin uncertain) + English *-an*]

**Rip Van Win|kle** (rip′ van wing′kəl), **1** a story by Washington Irving. **2** its hero, who falls asleep and wakes 20 years later to find everything changed. **3** someone who is unaware of current events and conditions.

**ris de veau** (rē də vō′), *French.* calf's sweetbread.

**rise** (rīz), *v.,* **rose, ris|en, ris|ing,** *n.* —*v.i.* **1** to get up from a lying, sitting, or kneeling position; stand up; get up: *Please rise and remain standing during the salute to the flag.* **SYN:** arise, stand. **2** to get up from sleep or rest: *The farmer's wife rises at six every morning.* **3** to go up; come up; move up; ascend: *The kite rises in the air. Mercury rises in a thermometer on a hot day. The curtain rose on the first act of the play. The fog is rising from the river.* **4** to extend upward: *The tower rises to a height of 60 feet.* **5** to slope upward: *Hills rise in the distance. The road rises up and over the hill.* **6** to go higher; increase: *Butter rose five cents in price. The temperature is rising. During the spring thaw the river rises and often floods the valley. My anger rose at the remark.* **7a** to advance, as in importance or rank: *He rose from office boy to president of the company.* **b** to advance, as to a higher level of action, thought, feeling, or expression: *His books never rise above mediocrity.* **8** to become louder or of higher pitch: *Her voice rose in anger.* **9a** to come to the surface of the water or ground: *The submarine rose near shore. The fish rose and seized the bait.* **b** to come to the surface of the skin; develop on the skin: *A blister rose on his heel.* **10** to come above the horizon: *The sun rises in the morning.* **SYN:** appear, emerge. **11** to come into view: *Off in the distance the town rose before the travelers. A specter rose before his fevered mind.* **SYN:** appear, emerge. **12** to start; begin: *The river rises from a spring. Quarrels often rise from trifles.* **13** to come into being or action: *The wind rose rapidly.* **14** to be built up, erected, or constructed: *New houses are rising on the edge of town.* **15** *Figurative.* to become more cheerful or more animated: *Our spirits rose at the good news.* **16** to revolt; rebel: *to rise against the government. The slaves rose against their masters. At our heels all hell should rise With blackest insurrection* (Milton). **17** to grow larger and lighter: *Yeast makes bread dough rise.* **SYN:** swell, increase. **18** *Figurative.* to come to life again: *Christ is risen.* **19** to end a meeting or session: *The senate rose for summer recess.*
—*v.t.* **1a** to cause to rise: *The dogs ran ahead to rise the birds. At almost every cast he rose a fish. He walked so far he rose a blister on his heel.* **b** to cause to rise above the horizon by approaching nearer to it. **2** to ascend; mount: *The Americans had to descend into a little hollow and rise a hill on its opposite side* (James Fenimore Cooper). **3** *Dialect.* to increase; make higher: *to rise the price of provisions* (Lord Nelson).
—*n.* **1** an upward movement; ascent: *We watched the rise of the balloon.* **2** an upward slope: *a rise in a road. The rise of that hill is gradual.* **3** a piece of rising or high ground; hill: *The house is situated on a rise. Slatter's hill ... was a rise of ground covering perhaps, an acre and a quarter* (Thomas B. Aldrich). **4** the vertical

height, as of a slope, step, or arch. **5a** an increase: *The rise of the tide was four feet. There has been a great rise in prices since the war.* **b** *British.* an increase in wages or salary: *It is a shame his firm won't give him a rise, but money isn't everything* (Punch). **6** an advance, as in rank, power, or position: *Her rise in the company was swift.* **7** an increase in loudness or to a higher pitch. **8** a coming above the horizon. **9** origin; beginning; start: *the rise of a river, the rise of a storm, the rise of a new problem, the rise of industrialism.* **10** *U.S. Informal.* an emotional response or reaction, especially of anger: *to get a rise out of a person by teasing him.* **11** the act or fact of fish coming to the surface of the water, as to seize bait: *Mr. 'Ayward ... he has plenty of rises but he don't hook them salmon* (Atlantic).

**give rise to,** to bring about; start; begin; cause: *The circumstances of his disappearance gave rise to the suspicion that he may have been kidnaped. The gas shortage gave rise to many problems for car owners. The invention of the phonograph gave rise to the record industry.*

**rise to,** to be equal to; be able to deal with: *to rise to an emergency. They rose to the occasion.*

[Old English *rīsan*]

▶ In referring to people, **get up** is informal, **rise** is rather formal; **arise** is formal and poetic.

**ris|en** (riz′ən), *v.* the past participle of **rise**: *The sun had risen long before I woke up.*

**ris|er** (rī′zər), *n.* **1** a person or thing that rises: *an early riser.* **2** the vertical part of a step. See picture under **staircase. 3** a portable stage platform wider than a rostrom. **4** a special strap attached to the shoulder portion of the harness of a parachute. **5** an opening in a mold through which molten metal can flow.

**ri|shi** (rē′shē, rish′ē), *n.* an inspired Hindu poet, seer, or sage, especially one of several to whom the laws of the Vedas were revealed along the banks of the Indus and Ganges rivers. [< Sanskrit *ṛṣi*]

**ris|i|bil|i|ty** (riz′ə bil′ə tē), *n., pl.* **-ties.** the ability or inclination to laugh.

**risibilities,** the desire to laugh; sense of humor: *The articles are concerned ... with the writers' lives, sensibilities and risibilities* (Harper's).

[< Late Latin *rīsibilitās* < Latin *rīdēre* to laugh]

**ris|i|ble** (riz′ə bəl), *adj.* **1** able or inclined to laugh. **2** of laughter; used in laughter: *By and by something would be said to touch his risible faculties* (W. H. Hudson). **3** causing laughter; amusing; funny; comical: *a few wild blunders and risible absurdities* (Samuel Johnson). [< Late Latin *rīsibilis* < Latin *rīdēre* to laugh]

**ris|ing** (rī′zing), *n., adj., prep.* **—*n.*** **1** the act of a person or thing that rises: *the rising of the sun. Seven o'clock is my hour for rising.* **2** a fight against the government; rebellion; revolt: *There was a rising now in Kent, my Lord of Norwich being at the head of them* (John Evelyn). **SYN:** insurrection. **3** *U.S.* **a** a quantity of dough set to rise. **b** the time dough is let rise before baking: *a short rising.* **4** *Dialect.* an abnormal swelling, such as a boil, tumor, or abscess.

***—adj.*** **1** that rises: **a** having an upward slope: *rising ground.* **b** mounting: *a rising temperature, rising anger.* **c** appearing above the horizon: *the rising sun.* **d** increasing: *a rising wind.* **e** advancing in power, influence, etc.: *a rising young lawyer.* **f** growing: *the rising generation.* **2** *Prosody.* (of a foot or rhythm) increasing in stress; having the ictus at the end.

***—prep.*** **1** approaching; about: *a horse rising five years old. Now, rising sixty-seven, he gets to Yankee Stadium daily before the first eager rookie* (Saturday Review). **2** *U.S. Informal.* somewhat more than: *The enclosure contains something rising forty acres* (Outing Magazine).

**rising diphthong,** a diphthong having more stress on the second element than on the first, as the element *i* of the diphthong *wi* in the word *win.*

**risk** (risk), *n., v.* **—*n.*** **1** a chance of harm or loss; danger: *He rescued the dog at the risk of his own life. If you drive carefully, there is no risk of being fined.* **SYN:** hazard, peril, jeopardy. **2** a person or thing with reference to the chance of loss from insuring him or it: *Very fat men and drunkards are not good risks. Racing drivers are poor risks.* **3** the amount of possible loss. **4** an insurance obligation: *Our company has no risks in that city.*

***—v.t.*** **1** to expose to the chance of harm or loss: *to risk one's health. You risk your neck in trying to climb that tree. A soldier risks his life. To risk the certainty of little for the chance of much* (Samuel Johnson). **SYN:** hazard, endanger, imperil, jeopardize. **2** to take the risk of: *They risked getting wet. She risked defeat in running against the popular candidate.* **3** to bet; hazard: *to risk $85 on a horse race.*

**at risk,** *British.* **a** in danger; imperiled: *The dismissal of two senior ministers and the resignation of a third in the small hours of yesterday morning shows that that policy is now at risk* (London Times). **b** running the risk of becoming pregnant: *There must be at least 10 million married women "at risk" in this country* (New Scientist).

**run** (or **take**) **a risk,** to expose oneself to the chance of harm or loss: *In order to win the war we had to take the risk of offending neutral nations.*

[< French *risque* < earlier Italian *risco* < *risicare* to dare; (originally) skirt cliffs in sailing < Vulgar Latin *resecum* sharp cliff < Latin *resecāre* shorten, cut off < *re-* back + *secāre* cut] **—risk′er,** *n.* **—risk′less,** *adj.*

**risk capital,** capital not covered by collateral and invested at the risk of a loss in the hope of profit; venture capital: *It was risk capital from the United States which sparked many of Canada's major raw material development programs* (Wall Street Journal).

**risk|y** (ris′kē), *adj.,* **risk|i|er, risk|i|est. 1** full of risk; dangerous: *It's a risky thing getting mixed in any matters with the like of you* (John M. Synge). **SYN:** hazardous, perilous, precarious, unsafe. **2** somewhat improper; risqué. **—risk′i|ly,** *adv.* **—risk′i|ness,** *n.*

**Ri|sor|gi|men|to** (rē sôr′jē men′tō), *n., pl.* **-ti** (-tē). the revival of the political movement for the unification of Italy about 1815. [< Italian *risorgimento* < *risorgere* < Latin *resurgere* < *re-* back + *surgere* surge]

**ri|sot|to** (rē sôt′tō), *n.* a dish consisting of rice cooked in olive oil, then chicken broth, and served with the meat of the chicken, grated cheese, and a tomato sauce. [< Italian *risotto* < *riso* rice, learned borrowing from Late Latin *oryza*; see etym. under **rice**]

**ris|qué** (ris kā′), *adj.* suggestive of indecency; somewhat improper: *a risqué joke.* [< French *risqué,* past participle of *risquer* to risk < *risque;* see etym. under **risk**]

**Riss** (ris), *n. Geology.* the third glaciation of the Pleistocene in Europe. [< *Riss* River, in southwestern Germany, Alpine locality of the glaciation]

**ris|sole** (ris′ōl; *French* rē sôl′), *n. French.* a fried ball or cake of meat or fish mixed with breadcrumbs, egg, and seasoning.

**ris|so|lé** (rē sô lā′), *adj. French.* browned in hot fat (in the oven or on top of the stove).

**rit.** or **ritard.,** ritardando.

**Ri|ta|lin** (ri tā′lin), *n. Trademark.* = methylphenidate.

**ri|tard** (rē tärd′, rē′tärd), *n.* = ritardando. [< *ritardando*]

**ri|tar|dan|do** (rē′tär dän′dō), *adj., adv., n., pl.* **-dos, -di** (-dē). *Music.* ***—adj., adv.*** becoming gradually slower.

***—n.*** a gradual decrease of speed.

[< Italian *ritardando,* gerund of *ritardare* to retard < Latin *retardāre*]

**rite¹** (rīt), *n.* **1** a solemn ceremony; formal procedure or act in a religious or other observance. Most churches have rites for baptism, marriage, and burial. Secret societies have their special rites. **2** a particular form or system of ceremonies. The Roman Catholic Church uses a Latin rite. **SYN:** See syn. under **ceremony. 3** a part of the Christian church distinguished by its liturgy. **4** any customary ceremony or observance: *He omitted such empty rites as saying "Yes" or "Please"* (Arnold Bennett).

[< Latin *rītus, -ūs*] **—rite′less,** *adj.*

**ri|te²** (rī′tē), *adv.* (of an academic degree, as granted or obtained) in the proper or prescribed manner; not as an honorary distinction. [< Latin *rīte* < *rītus* rite]

**rite de pas|sage** (rēt′ də pä säzh′), *pl.* **rites de pas|sage** (rēt′ də pä säzh′). *French.* **1** a rite or ceremony that marks such occasions as birth, naming, puberty, and marriage, especially in primitive societies. **2** (literally) rite of passage.

**ri|te|nu|to** (rē′tə nü′tō), *adj., adv., n., pl.* **-tos, -ti** (-tē). *Music.* ***—adj., adv.*** becoming suddenly slower.

***—n.*** a sudden decrease of speed.

[< Italian *ritenuto,* past participle of *ritenere* to hold back, retain < Latin *retinēre*]

**rite of passage,** = rite de passage.

**ri|tor|nel|lo** (rē′tôr nel′lō), *n., pl.* **-li** (-lē), **-los, -loes.** *Music.* **1** an instrumental part in a piece of music written for solo or choral voice. **2** one of the orchestral parts in a concerto for a particular instrument. [< Italian *ritornello* (diminutive) < *ritorno* a return]

**Rit|ter** (rit′ər), *n., pl.* **Rit|ter.** *German.* **1** a knight. **2** a member of a low order of the nobility in Germany and Austria.

**rit|u|al** (rich′ù əl), *n., adj.* **—*n.*** **1** a form or system of rites. The rites of baptism, marriage, and burial are parts of the ritual of most churches. Secret societies have a ritual for initiating new members. **2** a book containing rites or ceremonies. **3** the carrying out of rites: *... hear the ritual of the dead* (Tennyson). *17 teenagers gravely went through a ritual familiar to Boy Scouts the world over* (Time).

***—adj.*** of or having to do with rites or rituals; done as a rite: *a ritual dance, ritual laws. As through a zodiac, moves the ritual year of England's Church* (Wordsworth).

[< Latin *rītuālis* (adjective) < *rītus, -ūs* rite]

**—rit′u|al|ly,** *adv.*

**rit|u|al|ism** (rich′ù ə liz′əm), *n.* **1** fondness for ritual; insistence upon ritual. **2** the study of ritual practices or religious rites.

**rit|u|al|ist** (rich′ù ə list), *n.* **1** a person who practices or advocates observance of ritual. **2** a person who studies or knows much about ritual practices or religious rites.

**rit|u|al|is|tic** (rich′ù ə lis′tik), *adj.* **1** having to do with ritual or ritualism. **2** fond of ritual. **—rit′u|al|is′ti|cal|ly,** *adv.*

**rit|u|al|ize** (rich′ù ə līz), *v.t., v.i.,* **-ized, -iz|ing.** to make into or be a ritual: *the ritualized gift-giving of the Kwakiutl, Haida, and other tribes of the Northwest Coast of North America* (Melville J. Herskovits). **—rit′u|al|i|za′tion,** *n.*

**ritual murder,** the killing of a human being as a sacrifice to a deity.

**ritz|y** (rit′sē), *adj.,* **ritz|i|er, ritz|i|est.** *Slang.* smart; stylish; gaudy; classy: *Baia, a few miles north of Naples, was Rome's ritziest seaside resort* (Time). [< *Ritz,* name of the palatial hotels in London, Paris, and New York City, founded by César Ritz, 1850-1918, a Swiss hotelier + English *-y¹*] **—ritz′i|ly,** *adv.* **—ritz′i|ness,** *n.*

**riv.,** river.

**riv|age** (riv′ij), *n. Archaic.* a bank; coast; shore. [< Old French *rivage* < *rive* a bank, seashore < Latin *rīpa.* Compare etym. under **river¹, riparian.**]

**ri|val** (rī′vəl), *n., adj., v.,* **-valed, -val|ing** or (*especially British*) **-valled, -val|ling. —*n.*** **1** a person who wants and tries to get the same thing as another, or who tries to equal or do better than another: *The two boys were rivals for the same class office. They were also rivals in sports. There were no rivals: I had no competitor, none to dispute sovereignty or command with me* (Daniel Defoe). **SYN:** competitor, contestant, antagonist. **2** a thing that will bear comparison with something else; equal; match. **3** *Obsolete.* a colleague; associate.

***—adj.*** wanting the same thing as another; trying to outdo or equal another; being a rival: *A rival store tried to get our grocer's trade.* **SYN:** competing.

***—v.t.*** **1** to try to equal or outdo; compete with: *The stores rival each other in beautiful window displays.* **2** to equal; match: *The sunset rivaled the sunrise in beauty. He soon rivaled the others in skill.*

***—v.i.*** to engage in rivalry; compete.

[< Latin *rīvālis* one who uses the same stream < *rīvus* stream] **—ri′val|less,** *adj.*

**ri|val|rous** (rī′vəl rəs), *adj.* causing rivalry; accompanied by rivalry; competitive: *Countries become threatened by disintegration and the rivalrous interventions of other powers* (Manfred Halpern).

**ri|val|ry** (rī′vəl rē), *n., pl.* **-ries.** an effort to obtain something another person wants; action, position, or relation of a rival or rivals; competition: *There is rivalry among business firms for trade.* **SYN:** contest.

**rive** (rīv), *v.t., v.i.,* **rived, rived** or **riv|en, riv|ing.** to tear apart; split; cleave: *the anguish and despair that are ... riving thousands of hearts* (Harriet Beecher Stowe). [< Scandinavian (compare Old Icelandic *rīfa*)]

**riv|en** (riv′ən), *adj., v.* ***—adj.*** torn apart; split: *It* [*a tree*] *stood up, black and riven: the trunk, split down the centre, gaped ghastly* (Charlotte Brontë).

***—v.*** rived; a past participle of **rive.**

**riv|er¹** (riv′ər), *n.* **1** a large natural stream of water that flows into a lake, an ocean, or another river. The Nile is the longest river in the world. The Amazon River in South America, the largest river in the world, flows into the Atlantic Ocean. **2** *Figurative: rivers of blood, a river of lava. The full-flowing river of speech* (Tennyson).

**sell down the river,** *Informal.* to hand over to an enemy; abandon in a cruel manner; betray: *Those African leaders ... have now fallen victims of neocolonialism and sold their fellow Africans down the river* (Manchester Guardian).

[< Old French *rivere* < Vulgar Latin *rīpāria,* noun use of feminine of Latin *rīpārius* of a riverbank <

---

**Pronunciation Key:** hat, āge, cãre, fär; let, ēqual, tėrm; it, īce; hot, ōpen, ôrder; **oi**l, **ou**t; cup, pu̇t, rüle; **ch**ild; lo**ng**; **th**in; **ᴛʜ**en; **zh**, measure; ə represents **a** in about, **e** in taken, **i** in pencil, **o** in lemon, **u** in circus.

*rīpa* bank, shore] —**riv′er\|less**, *adj.* —**riv′er-like′**, *adj.*

**riv\|er²** (rī′vər), *n.* a person or thing that rives.

**riv\|er\|bank** (riv′ər bangk′), *n.* the ground bordering a river.

**river basin**, the land that is drained by a river and its tributaries.

**riv\|er\|bed** (riv′ər bed′), *n.* the channel or bed in which a river flows.

**river birch**, a birch tree of the eastern United States with shiny, reddish-brown bark, that grows along riverbanks and in swamps; red birch.

**river blindness**, = onchocerciasis.

**riv\|er\|boat** (riv′ər bōt′), *n.* a boat for use on a river, usually having a flat bottom or very shallow draft.

**riv\|er\|boat\|man** (riv′ər bōt′mən), *n., pl.* **-men.** a man who works on a riverboat.

**river cow**, = manatee.

**river crab**, any one of various freshwater crabs living in the rivers and lakes of southern Europe.

**riv\|er\|front** (riv′ər frunt′), *n.* the part of a town or city on or near a river or a harbor area.

**riv\|er-god** (riv′ər god′), *n.* a river regarded as a deity; a god supposed to dwell in and to preside over a river.

**riv\|er\|head** (riv′ər hed′), *n.* the source of a river.

**river hog**, **1** any one of various African wild hogs. **2** = capybara.

**river horse**, = hippopotamus.

**riv\|er\|ine** (riv′ə rīn, -ər in), *adj.* **1** of or having to do with a river. **2** situated or living on the banks of a river.

**river otter**, **1** any one of various otters inhabiting rivers and lakes or the nearby land, having webbed feet and a thick, tapered tail; land otter. **2** its fur, used to make coats.

**riv\|er\|scape** (riv′ər skāp), *n.* **1** a scene on a river. **2** a picture representing such a scene. [< *river*¹ + *-scape*]

**riv\|er\|side** (riv′ər sīd′), *n., adj.* —*n.* the bank of a river: *We walked along the riverside.*
—*adj.* beside a river; on the bank of a river: *The riverside path is much used.*

**river trout**, a brown trout of Europe, introduced into the United States.

**river valley**, a valley eroded or followed by a river.

**riv\|er\|ward** (riv′ər wərd), *adv., adj.* toward a river: *to look riverward* (adv.); *a riverward look* (adj.).

**riv\|er\|wards** (riv′ər wərdz), *adv.* = riverward.

**riv\|er\|way** (riv′ər wā′), *n.* a way over a river; a river that boats or ships can go on: *the traffic across riverways to the sea.*

**riv\|er\|weed** (riv′ər wēd′), *n.* any one of various small, submerged, freshwater plants.

**riv\|er\|wor\|thy** (riv′ər wėr′ᴛʜē), *adj.,* **-thi\|er, -thi\|est.** suitable for use on a river: *An open, conventional canoe— aluminum, canvas, or birch-bark — will feel to me about as riverworthy as a rickshaw* (John McPhee).

**riv\|er\|y** (riv′ər ē), *adj.,* **-er\|i\|er, -er\|i\|est. 1** abounding in streams and rivers. **2** resembling a river; riverlike.

**riv\|et** (riv′it), *n., v.* —*n.* a metal bolt with a head at one end, the other end being hammered into a head after insertion. Rivets fasten heavy steel beams together.
—*v.t.* **1** to fasten with a rivet or rivets. **2** to flatten (the end of a bolt) so as to form a head. **3** *Figurative.* to fasten firmly; fix firmly: *Their eyes were riveted on the speaker. Equally unable to fly or to advance, he stood riveted to the spot* (James Fenimore Cooper). *That march riveted the attention of the world* (Bosworth Smith). **4** *Figurative.* to engross the attention of: *I ... was riveted by the book* (Mark Pattison).
[< Middle French, Old French *rivet* < *river* to fix, fasten < Vulgar Latin *rīpāre* come to shore < Latin *rīpa* bank] —**riv′et\|er**, *n.*

**riv\|et\|ing** (riv′it ing), *adj.* that rivets the attention; stunning; spellbinding: *Ouranopolis, where the sands are endless and the sunsets are riveting* (Manchester Guardian Weekly).

**riv\|i\|er\|a** (riv′ē ãr′ə), *n.* a pleasant shore or coastline used as a resort.
[< the *Riviera*, a section of the Mediterranean coast, famous as a resort]

**ri\|vière** (rē vyer′), *n. French.* a necklace of gems, especially in more than one string.

**Riv\|o\|li's hummingbird** (riv′ə lēz), a large hummingbird with green, bronze, and purple plumage, brilliantly iridescent in the male, found from Arizona and New Mexico south to Nicaragua. [< François Victor Masséna, the Duke of *Rivoli*, 1799-1863, a French ornithologist and friend of Audubon]

**riv\|u\|let** (riv′yə lit), *n.* a very small stream: *A fine stream, fed by rivulets and mountain springs, pours through the valley* (Washington Irving). [< Italian *rivoletto* (diminutive) < *rivolo* (diminutive) < *rivo* stream < Latin *rīvus* stream]

**rix-dol\|lar** (riks′dol′ər), *n.* any one of various silver coins, as of the Netherlands, Denmark, and Germany, now mostly out of use, which were worth about a dollar. [< earlier Dutch *rijcksdaler* (in Dutch, *rijksdaalder*), (literally) imperial dollar. Compare etym. under **rigsdaler.**]

**ri\|yal** (ri yôl′, -yäl′), *n.* **1** the unit of money of Saudi Arabia, a coin or note equal to 20 qurush; rial. **2** the unit of money of Yemen, a coin equal to 40 buqshas; rial. [< Arabic *riyāl*]

**Ri\|zal Day** (rē säl′), December 30, a legal holiday in the Philippines, the anniversary of the death of José Rizal at the hands of the Spanish.

**RJ** (no periods), road junction.

**RLF** (no periods), retrolental fibroplasia.

**rm.**, **1** ream (of paper). **2** room.

**r.m.**, reichsmark or reichsmarks.

**Rm.**, reichsmark or reichsmarks.

**RM.** or **RM** (no period), reichsmark or reichsmarks.

**R.M.A.**, Royal Military Academy (at Woolwich, England).

**R.M.C.**, Royal Military College (at Sandhurst, England).

**R meter**, = roentgenometer.

**R month**, any one of the months (September to April) in the name of which an *r* occurs and during which oysters are in season.

**rms.**, **1** reams (of paper). **2** rooms.

**r.m.s.**, *Statistics.* root-mean-square.

**R.M.S.**, **1** Royal Mail Service (of Great Britain). **2** Royal Mail Steamship (of Great Britain).

**Rn** (no period), radon (chemical element).

**RN** (no periods), Royal Navy.

**R.N.**, **1** registered nurse. **2** Royal Navy.

**RNA** or **rna** (no periods), ribonucleic acid.

**RNA\|ase** (är′en′ā′ās), *n.* = ribonuclease. [< *RNA* + *-ase*]

**RNA polymerase**, an enzyme that acts upon DNA to synthesize ribonucleic acid; replicase: *Scientists have wondered how this one enzyme, RNA polymerase, could catalyze the synthesis of such differing RNA molecules* (Earl A. Evans).

**RNAS** (no periods) or **R.N.A.S.**, Royal Naval Air Service (of Great Britain).

**RN\|ase** (är′en′ās′), *n.* = RNAase.

**R.N.C.**, Royal Naval College.

**RNP** (no periods), ribonucleoprotein.

**r.-'n'-r.**, rock'n'roll.

**R.N.R.**, or **RNR** (no periods), Royal Naval Reserve.

**R.N.V.R.** or **RNVR** (no periods), Royal Naval Volunteer Reserve.

**R.N.W.M.P.**, Royal North-West Mounted Police (of Canada).

**RNZAF** (no periods) or **R.N.Z.A.F.**, Royal New Zealand Air Force.

**ro.**, **1** recto. **2** roan. **3** rood.

**R.O.**, **1** radio operator. **2** recruiting officer.

**roach¹** (rōch), *n.* = cockroach. [American English; short for *cockroach*]

**roach²** (rōch), *n., pl.* **roach\|es** or (*collectively*) **roach. 1** a silvery European freshwater fish with a greenish back, related to the carp. **2** any one of various similar fishes, such as the golden shiner. **3** any one of various American sunfishes. [< Old French *roche;* origin uncertain]

**roach³** (rōch), *n., v., adj.* —*n.* **1** an upward curve along the bottom of a square sail to improve the foot of the sail. **2** the water thrown up behind a seaplane that is taking off or landing. **3** *Informal.* an upstanding curl or roll of hair over the forehead.
—*v.t.* **1** to cut (a sail) with a roach. **2** to cut short (a horse's mane) so that it stands up straight; hog. **3** *Informal.* to cause (hair) to form a roach: *His hair was roached up over his forehead.*
—*adj.* curved; arched: *a roach back.*
[origin unknown]

**roach⁴** (rōch), *n. U.S. Slang.* the butt of a marijuana cigarette. [probably < *roach*¹]

**roach\|back** (rōch′bak′), *n.* = grizzly bear.

**roach clip** or **holder**, *U.S. Slang.* a clip with a handle for holding the butt of a marijuana cigarette.

**road** (rōd), *n.* **1** a way between places; way made for automobiles, trucks, wagons, or other vehicles to travel on: *the road from New York to Boston. Our road went through the woods. You have to know every bump in the road* (Newsweek). *Abbr:* Rd. SYN: roadway, turnpike, thoroughfare. **2** *Figurative.* a way or course: *the road to ruin, the road to peace. Man ... shows formidable signs of taking the road of the dinosaurs, though by quite another track* (Loren Eiseley). SYN: channel, route. **3** a railroad: *The road stated that further considerations will be given at the September meeting* (Wall Street Journal). **4** Also, **roads**, a place near the shore where ships can ride at anchor; roadstead: *The ship continued a fortnight in the roads, repairing some damage which had been done her in the late storm* (Daniel Defoe).

**hold the road**, to drive or travel on a road easily, smoothly, and safely: *Larger and heavier cars usually hold the road better than small cars.*

**on the road**, **a** on tour, as in a theater company: *I was Blanche Wilmot, on the road for ten years, — never got a show in London* (Arnold Bennett). **b** traveling, especially as a salesman: *... his star salesman in from a good week on the road* (New York Times).

**take to the road**, **a** to go on the road; begin to travel: *To miss the holiday traffic, they took to the road before dawn.* **b** to become a highwayman: *So, I took to the road, and ... the first man I robbed was a parson* (Jonathan Swift).

**the road**, the tour of a theater company, or other show: *Since the death, or at least near-death, of "the road," local theatres have multiplied prodigiously* (New York Times).
[Old English *rād* a riding; journey < *rīdan* to ride]
—**road′less**, *adj.*

**road\|a\|bil\|i\|ty** (rō′də bil′ə tē), *n.* the ability of a vehicle to travel over roads of all kinds easily, smoothly, and safely.

**road agent**, *U.S.* a highwayman in the days of stagecoach travel in the West.

**road\|bed** (rōd′bed′), *n.* **1** the foundation of a road or railroad. **2** crushed stone and other materials used to form such a foundation.

**road\|block** (rōd′blok′), *n., v.* —*n.* **1** a barrier placed across a road to stop vehicles: *The soldiers threw up a roadblock to halt the enemy's advance.* **2** *Figurative: Legal roadblocks had been thrown in the way and finally sessions were deferred until next Monday* (Wall Street Journal).
—*v.t.* **1** to place a roadblock before; obstruct; block: *The police roadblocked all exits.* **2** *Figurative: Her refusal to sign the papers roadblocked the proceedings.*

**road\|build\|er** (rōd′bil′dər), *n.* a person who designs or builds roads.

**road\|build\|ing** (rōd′bil′ding), *n., adj.* —*n.* the designing or building of roads.
—*adj.* of or used in roadbuilding; having to do with roadbuilding: *roadbuilding equipment.*

**road company**, *U.S.* a traveling theatrical group: *The audition routine is the same for a road company as for a Broadway show* (Bruce Savan).

**road\|craft** (rōd′kraft′, -kräft′), *n. British.* knowledge or ability in driving a car; driving skills.

**road\|e\|o** (rō′dē ō), *n., pl.* **-e\|os.** *U.S.* a contest or exhibition of skill in driving automobiles, trucks, or other motor vehicles. [American English; blend of *road* and *rodeo*]

**road gang**, *U.S.* a group of prisoners assigned to work on roads.

**road hog**, *Informal.* a person who uses more of the road than is necessary, especially by driving in the center of the road: *Memorial Day road hogs trying to beat their neighbors to the beach* (Time).

**road\|hold\|ing** (rōd′hōl′ding), *n.* the ability of a vehicle to hold the road and be maneuvered at high speeds, especially when cornering.

**road\|house** (rōd′hous′), *n.* a restaurant on a highway outside of a city, where people can stop for refreshments and sometimes entertainment.

**road\|ie** (rō′dē), *n. Slang.* a person who looks after the needs of, and often manages, singers or other performers on tour: *The Rolling Stones and their roadies load up one of Al's Convairs. . .during the group's seven-week tour* (People). [< *road* (manager) + *-ie*]

**road map**, a map for automobile travel that shows the roads in a region and indicates distances between cities and towns.

**road metal**, broken stone, cinders, or the like, used to build and repair roads and roadbeds.

**road pen**, a steel pen with two parallel points to draw roads in mapmaking.

**road race**, a race between cars, bicycles, or the like, that takes place on a road instead of a track. The course in an automobile road race has all types of curves, including sharp corners, and often hills. —**road racer.**

**road racing**, the sport of racing on a road instead of a track, especially in automobiles. The Grand Prix is an international road racing event.

**road roller**, = steamroller.

**road runner**, or **road\|run\|ner** (rōd′run′ər), *n.* a long-tailed bird living in the dry regions of the southwestern United States and in northern Mexico; chaparral cock; ground cuckoo. Instead of flying, it usually runs at great speed. It is related to the cuckoo.

**road show**, *U.S.* a traveling theatrical show: *He reached the movies by way of theatrical stock companies and road shows* (Newsweek).

**road\|side** (rōd′sīd′), *n., adj.* —*n.* the side of a road: *Flowers grew along the roadside.*
—*adj.* beside a road: *roadside billboards.*

**road sign**, a sign along a road indicating speed limits, approaching curves, direction, distances, or other driving information: *[He] kept one eye. . . flashing between his speedometer and the road signs* (Maclean's).

**road|stead** (rōd′sted), *n.* a protected place near the shore where ships can anchor; road. [Middle English *radestede* < *rade* road + *stede* place]

*** road|ster** (rōd′stər), *n.* **1** an automobile having either no top or a collapsible fabric top, a single wide seat, and, often, a rumble seat, common in the 1920's and 1930's. **2** a horse for riding or driving on the roads. **3** (formerly) a bicycle for road use. **4** the driver of a coach. **5** a person accustomed to traveling on the roads.

*** roadster**
definition 1

**road test**, **1** a test of roadworthiness given to a vehicle: *The car's acceleration is only one of its many attractions, as I found out in a road test* (London Times). **2** a test of ability of a driver in actual driving conditions.

**road-test** (rōd′test′), *v.t.* to subject to a road test: *The vehicle has been road-tested at maximum speed and has presented no problems* (Science News Letter).

**road train**, a group of trailers pulled by a truck, used to transport cattle and merchandise in parts of Australia where there are no railroads.

**road|way** (rōd′wā′), *n.* **1** = road. **2** the part of a road used by wheeled vehicles: *Walk on the path, not in the roadway.*

**road|work** (rōd′wėrk′), *n.* running distances along a road or path, as a form of physical training, especially by boxers: *At five the next morning he is in Central Park, doing his roadwork—five miles in about forty-five minutes every day before breakfast* (New Yorker).

**road|wor|thy** (rōd′wėr′ᴛʜē), *adj.*, **-thi|er, -thi|est.** (of vehicles) in a suitable condition for use on the road: *Car owners who find that their cars have deteriorated to such an extent that they are no longer roadworthy dispose of them for what they can get* (London Times). —**road′wor′thiness**, *n.*

**roam** (rōm), *v., n.* —*v.i.* to go about with no special plan or aim; wander: *to roam through the fields. Herds of horses and cattle roamed at will over the plain* (George W. Cable). *Her eyes were roaming about the room* (Hawthorne).
—*v.t.* to wander over: *to roam the earth, to roam a city. Thunder clouds roamed the skies at Taunton yesterday* (London Times).
—*n.* a walk or trip with no special aim; wandering: *a roam through the house.*
[Middle English *romen;* origin uncertain] —**roam′er**, *n.*
—***Syn.*** *v.t., v.i.* **Roam, rove, ramble** mean to wander. **Roam** suggests going about as one pleases over a wide area, with no special plan or aim: *The photographer roamed about the world.* **Rove** usually adds the suggestion of a definite purpose, though not of a settled destination: *Submarines roved the ocean.* **Ramble** suggests straying from a regular path or plan and wandering about aimlessly for one's own pleasure: *The children rambled over the field stopping here and there to pick pretty wild flowers.*

**roan** (rōn), *adj., n.* —*adj.* **1** yellowish- or reddish-brown sprinkled with gray or white. **2** made of roan leather.
—*n.* **1** a roan horse or another animal of roan color: *Beaufort's ... brougham, drawn by a big roan* (Edith Wharton). **2** a soft, flexible leather made from sheepskin, used in bookbinding. **3** a roan color.
[< Middle French *roan* < Spanish *roano,* probably < Germanic (compare Gothic *raudan,* accusative, red)]

**roar** (rôr, rōr), *v., n.* —*v.i.* **1** to make a loud, deep sound; make a loud noise: *The lion roared. The bull roared with pain. The wind roared at the windows.* **SYN:** bellow, bawl, howl, yell. **2** to laugh loudly or without restraint: *The whole audience roared at the clown.* **3** to move with a roar: *The train roared past us.* **4** (of a horse) to make a loud sound in breathing. —*v.t.* **1** to utter loudly: *to roar out an order. The audience ... roared its amusement* (Arnold Bennett). **2** to make or put by roaring: *The crowd roared itself hoarse.*
—*n.* a loud, deep sound; loud noise: *the roar of the cannon, a roar of laughter, the roar of a lion, the roar of a jet engine. The roar of the surf breaking upon the beach* (Herman Melville).
[Old English *rārian*] —**roar′er**, *n.*

**roar|ing** (rôr′ing, rōr′-), *adj., adv., n.* —*adj.* **1** that roars; extremely loud: *a roaring lion, a roaring wind.* **2** characterized by noise or revelry; riotous: *a roaring party.* **3** *Informal.* brisk; successful: *a roaring trade.*
—*adv.* extremely; thoroughly: *roaring drunk.*
—*n.* **1** the act of a person or thing that roars. **2** a loud cry or sound. **3** a disease of horses that causes them to breathe loudly. —**roar′ing|ly**, *adv.*

**roaring forties**, **1** a rough part of the northern Atlantic Ocean, between 40 degrees and 50 degrees north latitude. **2** the region between 40 degrees and 50 degrees in the south latitude.

**Roaring Twenties**, = Jazz Age (def. 2).

**roast** (rōst), *v., n. adj.* —*v.t.* **1** to cook by dry heat; cook before a fire or in an oven; bake: *We roasted meat and potatoes.* **2** to prepare by heating: *to roast coffee, roast a metal ore.* **3** *Figurative.* to make very hot: *Making a roaring fire, I roasted myself for half an hour, turning like a duck on a spit* (Weir Mitchell). **4** *Informal, Figurative.* **a** to make fun of; ridicule: *Editorial writers roasted her (one decided she was "mentally retarded")* (Maclean's). **b** to reprove; criticize severely: *The Administration's high-level Business Advisory Council will be roasted by the House anti-monopoly subcommittee for refusing to produce its files for inspection* (Newsweek).
—*v.i.* **1** to be cooked by dry heat; be baked: *Put the meat in the oven to roast.* **2** to be prepared by heating. **3** *Figurative.* to become very hot: *I roasted before the fire.*
—*n.* **1** a piece of roasted meat, or a piece of meat to be roasted: *to buy a roast for Sunday dinner.* **2** the act or process of roasting. **3** an informal outdoor meal, at which some food is cooked over an open fire: *a hot dog roast.*
—*adj.* roasted: *roast beef, roast pork.*
**rule the roast**, to be master, especially master of affairs in the home: *He had it all his own way, and ruled the roast ... right royally* (Charles Kingsley).
[< Old French *rostir* < Germanic (compare Old High Germanic *rōstan*)]

**roast|er** (rōs′tər), *n.* **1** a pan used in roasting. **2** a chicken, a young pig, or something else fit to be roasted. **3** a person or thing that roasts.

**roast|ing** (rōs′ting), *adj., n.* —*adj.* **1** that roasts. **2** exceedingly hot; scorching.
—*n.* **1** the act or process of cooking by dry heat. **2** a type of extractive metallurgy which removes sulfur and other impurities from the ore.

**rob** (rob), *v.*, **robbed, rob|bing.** —*v.t.* **1** to take away from by force or threats; steal from; plunder; pillage: *Thieves robbed the bank of thousands of dollars. The tramps robbed the orchard.* **SYN:** loot. **2** to steal: *Some children robbed fruit from the orchard.* **3** *Figurative: The disease had robbed him of his strength. Laryngitis robbed me of my voice. The shock of the explosion had robbed him of speech and movement* (Joseph Conrad).
—*v.i.* to steal; commit robbery: *He said he would not rob again.*
**rob one blind**, *Slang.* to steal from someone who is unaware and, usually, trusting: *She [owned] the bar concession and the bartender was robbing her blind* (Atlantic).
**rob Peter to pay Paul**. See under **Peter**.
[< Old French *rober* < Germanic (compare Old High German *roubôn*). See related etym. at **reave**[1].]

**rob|a|lo** (rob′ə lō, rō′bə-), *n., pl.* **-los** or (*collectively*) **-lo.** any one of a family of carnivorous fishes. Some varieties, such as the snook, are esteemed as food. [< Spanish *róbalo,* or Portuguese *robalo* < Catalan, alteration of *llobarro,* ultimately < Latin *lupus* wolf]

**rob|and** (rob′ənd), *n.* a short piece of spun yarn or other material used to secure a sail to a yard, gaff, or the like. Also, **robbin.** [earlier Scottish *raband,* perhaps < Scandinavian (compare Old Icelandic *rābenda* bend a sail)]

**rob|ber** (rob′ər), *n.* a person who robs. **SYN:** See syn. under **thief.**

**robber baron**, **1** a noble of former times who took property unfairly, especially from travelers through his lands. **2** an American capitalist, in the late 1800's, who acquired wealth through ruthless business methods.

**robber crab**, = coconut crab.

**robber fly**, any one of a family of large, swift flies which prey upon other insects; bee killer.

**robber frog**, a large frog of Texas found among the rocks on riverbanks. It has a cry like the bark of a dog.

**rob|ber|y** (rob′ər ē, rob′rē), *n., pl.* **-ber|ies. 1** the act of robbing; theft; stealing: *a bank robbery.* **2** *Law.* the felonious taking of property of another from his person or from his immediate presence, against his will, by violence or threats. [< Old French *roberie* < *rober;* see etym. under **rob**]

**rob|bin** (rob′ən), *n.* = roband.

**robe** (rōb), *n., v.,* **robed, rob|ing.** —*n.* **1** a long, loose outer garment: *The priests wore robes. Many Arabs wear robes.* **2** a garment that shows a rank or office: *a judge's robe, the king's robes of state.* **3** a covering or wrap: *Put a robe over you when you go for a ride on a cold day.* **4** *U.S. and Canada.* (formerly) the dressed skin of a buffalo or other animal, used especially for protection against moisture and cold. **5** a bathrobe or dressing gown.
—*v.t., v.i.* to put a robe on; dress.
**the long robe, a** the legal profession: *The Houses ... have likewise appointed a committee of the long robe to declare how the King ought ... by the law to pass those ordinances* (Richard Montagu). **b** the clerical profession: *... the long-lived gentlemen of the surplice and the long robe* (Punch).
**the robe**, *Especially British.* the legal profession: *rich advocates and other gentlemen of the robe* (John L. Motley).
**the short robe**, the military profession: *The king's council was made up of both men of the short robe and of the long robe.*
[< Old French *robe* (originally) plunder, booty < Germanic (compare Old High German *rouba* spoils, booty, vestments. Compare etym. under **rob.**]

**robe de cham|bre** (rôb′ də shäɴ′brə), *French.* a dressing gown.

**robe de nuit** (rôb′ də nwē′), *French.* a nightgown.

**robe de style** (rôb′ də stēl′), *French.* a formal gown with tight-fitting bodice and a full skirt.

**Rob-gob|lin** (rob′gob′lən), *n.* = hobgoblin. [< *Rob,* a nickname for *Robert* or *Robin* + *goblin*]

**rob|in** (rob′ən), *n.* **1** a large thrush of North America, brownish-gray with a reddish breast and white on the lower abdomen and throat; redbreast. **2** a small, brownish European thrush with a yellowish-red breast. [< *Robin,* proper name < Old French (diminutive) < *Robert*]

**Robin Good|fel|low** (gůd′fel′ō), Puck, a mischievous fairy of English folklore: *That shrewd and knavish sprite call'd Robin Goodfellow* (Shakespeare).

**rob|ing room** (rō′bing), *British.* a room where ceremonial robes are put on.

**Robin Hood**, **1** the legendary leader of a band of outlaws in Sherwood Forest who robbed the rich and helped the poor. **2** any similar champion of the common people: *Mexicans have argued whether Villa was the Robin Hood he claimed to be or just an ordinary hood* (Time).

**Robin Hood hat**, a high-crowned hat with the brim turned up sharply at the back and turned down sharply at the front; a modern version of the hat worn by Robin Hood.

**ro|bin|i|a** (rō bin′ē ə), *n.* any one of a group of leguminous trees and shrubs of the central and southern United States, including the locust. [< New Latin *Robinia,* the genus name < Jean *Robin,* 1550-1629, a French botanist and royal gardener ar Paris, whose son introduced the genus into Europe in 1635]

**robin redbreast**, = robin.

**rob|in's-egg blue** (rob′ənz eg′), greenish blue.

**Rob|in|son Cru|soe** (rob′ən sən krü′sō), **1** the hero and narrator of Daniel Defoe's novel *Robinson Crusoe* (1719), a sailor shipwrecked on a desert island. **2** any solitary castaway who survives through his own efforts.

**ro|ble** (rō′blā), *n.* any one of several white oaks, especially a variety of California. [American English < American Spanish *roble* < Spanish, oak tree < Latin *rōbur, -oris* oak tree, heartwood]

**ro|bomb** (rō′bom′), *n.* = robot bomb. [< *ro*(bot) *bomb*]

**rob|o|rant** (rob′ər ənt), *adj., n.* —*adj.* strengthening.
—*n.* a roborant medicine; tonic.
[< Latin *rōborāns, -antis,* present participle of *rōborāre* to strengthen < *rōbur, -oris* strength; (originally) oak tree]

**ro|bot** (rō′bət, -bot; rob′ət), *n.* **1** a machine made in imitation of a human being; a mechanical device that does routine work in response to commands: *A mechanical robot ... walks, talks, and moves its arms at the touch of a button by its 14-year-old inventor* (Raymond F. Yates). *... robot explorers for neighboring planets* (Saturday Review). **2** *Figurative.* a person who acts or works in a dull, mechanical way. **3** any machine or mechanical device that operates automatically or by remote control. [< Czech *robot* (coined by

**Pronunciation Key:** hat, āge, cãre, fär; let, ēqual, tėrm; it, īce; hot, ōpen, ôrder; oil, out; cup, pu̇t, rüle; child; long; thin; ᴛʜen; zh, measure; ə represents **a** in about, **e** in taken, **i** in pencil, **o** in lemon, **u** in circus.

Karel Capek for his play, *R.U.R.*); suggested by Czech *robota* work, *robotnik* serf] —**ro′bot|like′**, *adj.*

**robot bomb**, a jet-propelled airplane, steered by a mechanical device, without a pilot, which carries a heavy charge of explosives; buzz bomb.

**ro|bot|ics** (rō bot′iks), *n.* the science or technology that deals with robots: *There has been some excellent progress in robotics—the study of computer-controlled robots ... programmed to "see" (some things), to "hear," and even to "speak" (some sounds)* (Alan J. Perlis).

**ro|bot|ism** (rō′bə tiz əm, rob′ə-), *n.* **1** the condition of being a robot. **2** *Figurative.* mechanical behavior or character: *It shows how we can avoid robotism and build a society in which the emphasis is on man and not upon things* (Saturday Review).

**ro|bot|is|tic** (rō′bə tis′tik, rob′ə-), *adj.* **1** of, having to do with, or like a robot. **2** *Figurative.* mechanical in behavior.

**ro|bot|ize** (rō′bə tīz, rob′ə-), *v.t.*, **-ized, -iz|ing.** **1** to make into a robot. **2** *Figurative.* to make mechanical or automatic; cause to function like a robot. —**ro′bot|i|za′tion**, *n.*

**ro|bot|o|mor|phic** (rō′bot ə môr′fik), *adj.* modeled on the behavior of robots: *robotomorphic views of Man* (New Scientist).

**ro|bot|ry** (rō′bə trē, rob′ə-), *n.* **1** the condition of being a robot. **2** robots as a group.

**Rob Roy** (rob′ roi′), a cocktail consisting of Scotch whisky, sweet vermouth, and a dash of bitters. [< *Rob Roy*, the nickname of Robert Macgregor, 1671-1734, a Scottish outlaw]

**ro|bur** (rō′bər), *n.* a species of oak common in England and much of Europe. Its hard, straight-grained wood, used for woodwork is pale when first cut, but on exposure gradually turns very dark. [< Latin *rōbur* oak]

**ro|bur|ite** (rō′bə rīt), *n.* a powerful, flameless explosive of very high power, consisting mostly of ammonium nitrate, used especially for blasting in mining. [< Latin *rōbur, -oris* strength; (originally) oak tree + English *-ite*[1]]

**ro|bust** (rō bust′, rō′bust), *adj.* **1** strong and healthy; sturdy: *a robust person, a robust mind.* **SYN:** hardy, stalwart, stout, sound. See syn. under **strong.** **2** suited to or requiring bodily strength: *robust exercises. Crowds in this country ... prefer a more robust game* (London Times). **3** rough; rude: *the robuster sorts of evangelism* (John Galsworthy). [< Latin *rōbustus* (originally) oaken < *rōbur, -oris* oak tree, strength] —**ro|bust′ly**, *adv.* —**ro|bust′ness**, *n.*

**ro|bus|ta** (rō bus′tə), *n.* **1** coffee made from the seeds of a variety of coffee shrub native to east central Africa. **2** the seeds from which it is made. [< New Latin (*Coffea*) *robusta*, the shrub]

**ro|bus|tious** (rō bus′chəs), *adj.* **1** rough; rude; boisterous: *Oh, it offends me to the soul to hear a robustious periwig-pated fellow tear a passion to tatters ...* (Shakespeare). **2** robust; strong; stout. —**ro|bus′tious|ly**, *adv.* —**ro|bus′tious-ness**, *n.*

**roc** (rok), *n.* a legendary bird having such enormous size and strength that it could seize and carry off an elephant, famous in such Arabian tales as *Sinbad.* [< Arabic *rukhkh*]

**ro|caille** (rō kī′; *French* rô kä′yə), *n.* **1** a style of decoration of the 1700's, based on the forms of water-worn rocks and shells. **2** rockwork in a garden that combines pebbles and shells in figures of sea gods, dolphins, and the like, used as decoration. [< French *rocaille* rockwork, shellwork; see etym. under **rococo**]

**roc|am|bole** (rok′əm bōl), *n.* a European plant closely related to the leek, used for flavoring in foods. [< French *rocambole* garlic; spice; origin uncertain]

**Roch|dale principles** or **system** (roch′dāl), a cooperative system in which profits are divided among the members in proportion to their purchases. [< *Rochdale*, England, the site of the first cooperative store in England]

**Roche limit** (rôsh, rōsh), a distance of 2.44 times a planet's radius, measured from the planet's center, within which any satellite or heavenly body would be in danger of disruption due to the gravitational force of the planet. [< Edouard *Roche*, a French mathematician of the 1800's]

**Ro|chelle powder** (rō shel′), = Seidlitz powder.

**Rochelle salt**, a colorless or white, crystalline compound, potassium sodium tartrate, used as a mild saline laxative, in the manufacture of cheese, in silvering mirrors, and as a piezoelectric crystal. *Formula:* $KNaC_4H_4O_6 \cdot 4H_2O$ [< *La Rochelle*, France (probably because it was exported from there)]

**roche mou|ton|née** (rôsh′ mü tô nā′), *French.* a moundlike piece of rock rounded and smoothed by glacial action; sheepback.

**Roche's limit** (rô′shiz, rō′-), = Roche limit.

**roch|et** (roch′it), *n.* a vestment of linen or lawn, resembling a surplice, worn by bishops and abbots. [< Old French *rochet* < *roc* cloak < Germanic (compare Old High German *roc, rokkes* coat)]

**Ro|ci|nan|te** (rō′sē nan′tē; *Spanish* rō thē nän′tā), *n.* the thin, worn-out horse ridden by Don Quixote. [< Spanish *Rocinante* < *rocín* a hack horse, jade]

**rock**[1] (rok), *n., adj.* —*n.* **1** a large mass of stone: *The ship was wrecked on the rocks.* **2** any piece of stone; a stone: *He threw a rock in the lake.* **3a** the mass of mineral matter of which the earth's crust is made up: *The three main kinds of rocks are igneous rocks, sedimentary rocks, and metamorphic rocks* (David E. Jensen). **b** a particular layer or kind of such matter. Granite, sandstone, and gneiss are rocks. **4** *Figurative.* something firm like a rock; support; defense: *Christ is called the Rock of Ages. The Lord is my rock* (II Samuel 22:2). **5** *Figurative.* something dangerous, as rocks are to ships. **6** *Figurative.* anything that suggests a rock: *The division of the profits was the rock on which the partners split.* **7** something hard and uneven. **8** = rock candy. **9** *Slang.* a precious stone, especially a diamond. **10** = striped bass. **11** = rock pigeon.
—*adj.* made of rock: *a rock cavern.*
**on the rocks, a** in or into a condition of ruin or failure; wrecked; ruined: *Her marriage ... went on the rocks in 1929* (Harper's). **b** *Informal.* bankrupt: *After a year of high costs and poor sales the business found itself on the rocks.* **c** *Informal.* (of alcoholic drinks) with ice but without water or mixes: *Here's where I discovered rum on the rocks* (New Yorker).
**rocks,** *Slang.* money: *Old man's piling up the rocks* (Rudyard Kipling).
**the Rock,** Gibraltar: *The apes have been on the Rock longer than the Spaniards* (Punch).
[< Old French *roque* < Vulgar Latin *rocca;* origin uncertain. Compare Old English *stānrocc.*]
—**rock′like′**, *adj.*

**rock**[2] (rok), *v., n.* —*v.i.* **1** to move backward or forward, or from side to side; sway: *My chair rocks.* **SYN:** roll. See syn. under **swing.** **2** *Figurative.* to be moved or swayed violently with emotion: *to rock with laughter.* **3** *Mining.* to use a cradle or rocker in gold digging.
—*v.t.* **1** to move back and forth; sway from side to side; tip up and down: *The waves rocked the boat. The earthquake rocked the house.* **SYN:** roll. See syn. under **swing.** **2** to put (to sleep, rest, or otherwise at ease) with swaying movements: *Mother rocked the baby to sleep.* **3** *Figurative.* **a** to move or sway powerfully with emotion: *The speaker's dramatic appeal rocked the audience.* **b** to throw off balance; upset: *The scandal rocked the government.* **4** *Engraving.* to prepare the surface of (a plate) for a mezzotint. **5** *Mining.* to wash in a cradle or rocker: *to rock gold-bearing gravel.*
—*n.* a rocking movement: *a sailor with a definite rock to his walk.*
[Old English *roccian*]

**rock**[3] (rok), *n., adj., v. Informal.* —*n.* a form of popular music with a strongly marked, regular beat; rock'n'roll: *Classical music is the foundation of our present-day jazz and rock* (Saturday Review).
—*adj.* of or having to do with rock'n'roll: *a rock singer. A rock score can have both variety and vitality* (Herbert Kupferberg).
—*v.i.* to dance to rock'n'roll: *Young people who . . . rock like mad on the dance floor* (New York Times).
[shortened from *rock'n'roll*]

**rock**[4] (rok), *n. Archaic.* a distaff. [Middle English *rokke*, or *rooke.* Compare Middle Dutch *rocke.*]

**rock|a|bil|ly** (rok′ə bil′ē), *n.* rock'n'roll with hillbilly music themes: *Rockabilly artists such as Elvis Presley (who combined country and R & R)* (Saturday Review). [< *rock*[3] + *-a-* (as in *rock-away*) + (hill)*billy*]

**rock-and-roll** (rok′ən rōl′), *n., adj., v.i.* = rock'n'roll.

**rock and rye**, an alcoholic drink sold in bottles, consisting of rye whiskey, rock candy, and slices of orange, lemon, and sometimes other fruits.

**rock|a|way** (rok′ə wā), *n.* a light four-wheeled carriage. [American English < *Rockaway*, New Jersey, where many were made]

**rock barnacle**, any barnacle that attaches itself to rocks by its base rather than a stalk. See picture under **barnacle**[1].

**rock bass**, **1** an olive-green fish of eastern North America, about 9 inches long with a dark red iris; redeye. **2** = striped bass. **3** = cabrilla.

**rock beauty**, an angelfish found along the Atlantic coast from Florida to Brazil. See picture under **angelfish.**

**rock bit**, a bit with jagged teeth, used for drilling through hard rock, especially in the petroleum industry.

**rock bottom**, the very bottom; lowest level.

**rock-bot|tom** (rok′bot′əm), *adj.* down to the very bottom; very lowest: *the rock-bottom price.* [American English < *rock* + *bottom*]

**rock-bound** (rok′bound′), *adj.* surrounded by rocks; rocky: *a rock-bound harbor.*

**rock brake**, any one of a group of low ferns of cool areas of the Northern Hemisphere.

**rock burst**, a sudden, violent bursting of masses of rock from a weakened wall, as in a quarry or mine: *The rock burst* [*may*] *... occur in any man-made excavation if the rock is sufficiently highly stressed before stress relief, in the form of tunnelling, can take place* (New Scientist).

**rock candy**, sugar in the form of large, hard crystals.

**rock cod**, **1** = rockfish (def. 2). **2** a small cod found on rocky sea-bottoms or ledges.

**Rock Cornish hen**, a small hybrid fowl bred by crossing a Cornish chicken with a white Plymouth Rock, eaten as a delicacy.

**rock crab**, any one of several different kinds of crab found on rocky sea-bottoms.

**rock|craft** (rok′kraft′, -kräft′), *n.* skill in climbing rocks and cliffs.

**rock crusher**, **1** a person or machine that crushes rocks and stones. **2** *Slang.* an overwhelmingly strong hand in cards.

**rock crystal**, a colorless, transparent variety of quartz that is often used for jewelry and ornaments.

**rock-cut** (rok′kut′), *adj.* excavated in solid rock, as many of the cave tombs in Egypt, Asia Minor, and India.

**rock dove**, a wild pigeon native to Europe and Asia, an ancestor of most common domestic breeds; rock pigeon.

**rock drill**, a machine for boring into rocks.

**rock|dust** (rok′dust′), *v.t., v.i.* to coat (the surfaces of a coal mine) with finely powdered limestone in order to blanket the highly explosive coal dust in the mine.

**rock eel**, = gunnel[2].

**rock elm**, **1** a large elm of eastern North America, with a corky bark and hard, heavy wood; cork elm. **2** its wood, used for furniture and woodenware.

**rock|er** (rok′ər), *n.* **1** one of the curved pieces on which a cradle, rocking chair, or rocking horse rocks. **2a** = rocking chair. **b** = rocking horse. **3** a person who rocks a cradle. **4** any one of various devices that operate with a rocking motion, such as: **a** a tool with a toothed edge, used to roughen the surface of a plate for an engraving. **b** *Mining.* a cradle. **c** an ice skate with a curved blade. **d** an armlike piece attached to a rockshaft. **5a** a framework to which hides being tanned are attached and which is made to rock back and forth in order to soak the hides evenly in the vat; cradle. **b** the tanning solution or liquors contained in the vat in which the hides are soaked; handler. **6** Also, **Rocker.** *British.* one of a group of teen-agers of the 1960's, wearing leather jackets and jeans and traveling in gangs on motorcycles: *A rocker, sun winking on his belt studs, slouched in* (Punch). **7** *Informal.* **a** a rock singer or musician: *a top rocker.* **b** a rock song or composition: *... Ringo Starr's hit rocker "Oh My My"* (Newsweek).
**off one's rocker,** *U.S. Slang.* crazy; mad: *"I felt uncertain about going ahead with such an unusual thing," he told me. "People might think I was off my Rocker if it ever got out"* (New Yorker).

**rocker arm**, an armlike piece attached to a rockshaft in machinery.

**rock|er|y** (rok′ər ē), *n., pl.* **-er|ies.** a pile of rough stones and soil on which to grow ferns and other plants; rock garden.

***rock|et**[1] (rok′it), *n., v.* —*n.* **1** a device consisting of a tube open at one end and filled with some substance that burns very rapidly as fuel. The burning fuel creates expanding gases which escape from the open end, moving the rocket rapidly upward or forward. Rockets are used to carry fireworks, signals, weapons, satellites and space capsules, and aerial targets. The larger rockets often carry oxygen required for combustion and are referred to as rocket engines. The rocket principle is used as the driving power of some aircraft. *It should be noted that a rocket does not depend on the atmosphere for its propulsion, but actually would perform better in the absence of an atmosphere because of lessened air resistance* (Sears and Zemansky). **2** a spacecraft, missile, firework, or distress signal, propelled by such a device: *to send a rocket to the moon.*
—*v.i.* **1** to go like a rocket; move very, very fast: *The racing car rocketed across the finish line to victory.* **2** to rise very fast; skyrocket: *The brilliant scientist rocketed to fame with his discoveries.* **3** to fly straight up rapidly: *Pheasants often rocket when disturbed.* **4** to be put into orbit with a rocket.
—*v.t.* **1** to send or launch with a rocket; put into

orbit with a rocket: *Russia rocketed a second satellite into space carrying a small dog* (Wall Street Journal). **2** to attack with rockets: *Rail and supply installations on both coasts were bombed and rocketed by naval ships and planes* (New York Times). **3a** to cause to rise very fast; cause to skyrocket: *His discoveries rocketed the scientist to fame.* **b** to send or throw as if it were a rocket: *During a game last year ... Hull rocketed a high, hard shot* (Time).
[< Italian *rocchetta,* probably (diminutive) < *rocca* distaff (from the similarity in shape) < a Germanic word]

***rocket¹**
definition 1

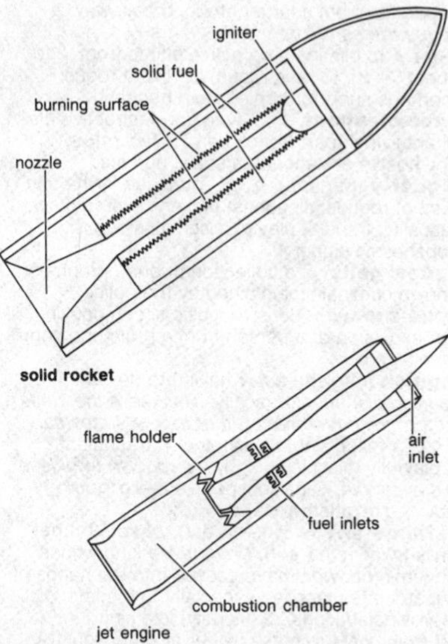


**rock|et²** (rok′it), *n.* **1** a garden plant of the mustard family with fragrant white or purplish flowers. **2** a European plant of the mustard family used as a salad; rocket salad. [< earlier Italian *rochetta,* variant of *rucchetta* < *ruca* < Latin *ērūca* colewort]
**rocket astronomy**, the collection and study of astronomical data from photographs and instrument readings taken at high altitude through instruments carried in a rocket.
**rocket belt**, a portable, rocket-powered device equipped with controls, used experimentally to propel a person through the air.
**rocket bomb**, a bomb propelled by a rocket.
**rocket booster**, a rocket engine used as a booster: *Ballistic missiles, once separated from their rocket boosters, can't be shifted to alternate targets or called back* (Wall Street Journal).
**rock|et|drome** (rok′it drōm), *n.* a place for launching rockets or rocket ships. [< *rocket* + *-drome*]
**rock|et|eer** (rok′ə tir′), *n.* a person who works with rockets, especially an expert in rocketry.
**rock|et|eer|ing** (rok′ə tir′ing), *n.* = rocketry.
**rocket engine**, = rocket¹ (*n.* def. 1).
**rock|et|er** (rok′ə tər), *n.* a bird that rockets.
**rocket gun**, = rocket launcher.
**rocket launcher**, a device consisting of a tube or cluster of tubes from which rockets are launched.
**rocket plane**, an airplane powered by a rocket engine.
**rock|et-pro|pelled** (rok′it prə peld′), *adj.* propelled by one or more rockets or rocket engines: *rocket-propelled missiles.*
**rocket propulsion**, propulsion by means of rockets or rocket engines: *Development of new methods of rocket propulsion ... will make interstellar travel more practical* (Science News Letter).
**rock|et|ry** (rok′ə trē), *n.* **1** the science of building, using, and firing rockets. **2** rockets collectively: *Small satellite spheres would be launched as test vehicles ... to check the rocketry, instrumentation, and ground stations* (Wall Street Journal).
**rocket salad**, = rocket² (def. 2).
**rocket ship**, a spacecraft using rocket propulsion for its chief or only source of power.
**rocket sled**, a sled with a rocket engine that operates on a rail and can be quickly accelerated to very high speeds, used especially in testing human tolerance, seat ejection, and parachute opening under simulated flight conditions.
**rock|et|sonde** (rok′it sond), *n.* a rocket used to gather information on that portion of the lower atmosphere which is inaccessible to balloons. [< *rocket* + (radio)*sonde*]
**rocket thrust**, the thrust of a rocket engine or motor, usually expressed in pounds.
**rocket vehicle**, a vehicle propelled by a rocket motor or engine, used to carry a missile, satellite, space capsules, or scientific equipment.
**rock|face** (rok′fās′), *n.* the face of a rock or cliff.
**rock|fall** (rok′fôl′), *n.* **1** the action of rock falling down a slope or in a mine or cave: *It was a rockfall in a cave in Iraq, probably caused by an earthquake, that killed the primitive man* (Science News Letter). **2** the fallen rock.
**Rock fever**, = undulant fever. [< the *Rock* of Gibraltar, where it is found]
**rock-fill dam** (rok′fil′), a dam built of coarse, heavy rocks and stones, graded in size to fit together compactly.
**rock|fish** (rok′fish′), *n., pl.* **-fish|es** or (*collectively*) **-fish.** **1** any one of various fishes found among rocks, especially the striped bass. **2** any one of various groupers of the Atlantic coast of the United States, such as the bonaci. **3** a killifish of the Atlantic coast of the United States. **4** any one of various edible fishes of the Pacific coast of the United States, such as the priestfish.
**rock flour**, = rock meal.
**rock flower**, any one of a group of early-flowering shrubs found in arid parts of the southwestern United States.
**rock garden**, a garden on rocky ground or among rocks for the growing of flowers, ornamental plants, and the like.
**rock hind**, a grouper found in tropical seas.
**rock hound**, *Slang.* a person who collects and studies rocks as a hobby.
**rock|i|ly** (rok′ə lē), *adv.* shakily; weakly: *The frightened boy walked down the street rockily.*
**rock|i|ness¹** (rok′ē nis), *n.* the condition of being rocky; being full of rocks.
**rock|i|ness²** (rok′ē nis), *n.* the condition of being shaky; unsteadiness; weakness.
**rock|ing chair** (rok′ing), a chair mounted on rockers, or on springs, so that it can rock back and forth; rocker.
**rocking horse**, a toy horse on rockers, or on springs, for children to ride; hobbyhorse.
**rocking stone**, = logan stone.
**rocking valve**, a cylindrical valve that opens and closes by rotating or oscillating.
**rock|let** (rok′lit), *n.* a small rock.
**rock|ling** (rok′ling), *n.* any one of various small gadoid fishes of the North Atlantic.
**rock lobster**, any one of a group of crayfish or lobsters common on the coast of Europe and South Africa; spiny lobster.
**rock|man** (rok′mən), *n., pl.* **-men.** **1** a man who splits slate in a quarry. **2** a man who operates a jackhammer. **3** = miner (def. 1).
**rock maple**, = sugar maple.
**rock meal**, a fine, mealy geological deposit that has been eaten in times of great scarcity; bergmehl.
**rock milk**, a powdery variety of calcium carbonate; agaric mineral.
**rock'n'roll** (rok′ən rōl′), *n., adj., v.* **—*n.*** **1** a kind of popular music with a strong beat and a simple, repetitious melody. It is played with two-beat rhythm that accents every second beat, usually with guitars and various other instruments for singing or dancing; rock. Rock'n'roll is derived from folk music, blues, and jazz. **2** a vigorous dance done to this music. The style of rock'n'roll is characterized by improvisation and exaggerated movements.
**—*adj.*** of or having to do with rock'n'roll: *rock'n'roll music, a rock'n'roll band.*
**—*v.i.*** to dance to rock'n'roll.
**rock'n'roll|er** (rok′ən rō′lər), *n.* a person who plays, sings, or dances rock'n'roll.
**rock oil**, = petroleum.
**rock|oon** (ro kün′), *n.* a solid-fuel rocket carried by a balloon into the upper atmosphere where it is released. The rockoon makes it possible for small rockets to reach high altitudes. [< *rock*(et) + (ball)*oon*]
**rock opera**, an opera with rock'n'roll music: *There are pitfalls aplenty ... in his screen translation of the ballyhooed Broadway rock opera* (Newsweek).
**rock pigeon**, **1** = rock dove. **2** = sand grouse.
**rock pool**, a pool of water remaining in a rocky or coral shore when the tide goes out: *the teeming life of rock pools.*
**rock ptarmigan**, a brown and white ptarmigan or grouse of arctic America which changes in winter to pure white with a black tail and a black stripe on each cheek.
**rock rabbit**, = pika.
**rock-ribbed** (rok′ribd′), *adj.* **1** having ridges of rock: *The hills rock-ribbed and ancient as the sun* (William Cullen Bryant). **2** *Figurative.* unyielding; rigid; inflexible: *rock-ribbed endurance, rock-ribbed determination. Jake is a rock-ribbed old die-hard* (Sinclair Lewis). **3** *Figurative.* not likely to fail; sound: *a rock-ribbed bank.*
**rock|rose** (rok′rōz′), *n.* **1** any one of a group of low shrubs of the Mediterranean region, grown in rock gardens for their showy flowers. **2** the flower.
**rocks** (roks), *n.pl.* See under **rock¹**.
**rock salt**, common salt as it occurs in the earth in large crystals; halite. Rock salt is often used to melt ice on roads and sidewalks.
**rock|shaft** (rok′shaft′, -shäft′), *n.* a shaft that rocks or oscillates on its journals instead of revolving, such as the shaft of a bell or a pendulum, or the shaft operating the valves of an engine.
**rock|slide** (rok′slīd′), *n.* **1** a sliding down of a mass of rock on a steep slope: *Huge rockslides at times bury bulldozers and other machines* (Wall Street Journal). **2** the mass that slides down.
**rock squirrel**, a large gray or blackish ground squirrel of the southwestern United States and Mexico.
**rock sturgeon**, = lake sturgeon.
**rock temple**, a temple cut out of solid rock, as in India.
**rock tripe**, a large, dark-brown, leafy lichen with a leathery appearance, found in northern regions. It is sometimes boiled and seasoned for use as an emergency ration.
**rock waste**, debris left by disintegration and decomposition of rock.
**rock|weed** (rok′wēd′), *n.* any one of various seaweeds common on the rocks exposed at low tide: *a wagon-load of live lobsters, packed in rockweed* (Hawthorne).
**rock wool**, woollike fibers made from rock or slag and used for insulation and soundproofing; mineral wool.
**rock|work** (rok′wėrk′), *n.* **1** a natural mass of rocks. **2** masonry made to imitate natural rock. **3** = rockery.
**rock wren**, a large, grayish-brown wren common in arid, rocky regions of western North America.
**rock|y¹** (rok′ē), *adj.,* **rock|i|er, rock|i|est.** **1** full of rocks: *a rocky shore, a rocky field.* **2** made of rock: *The waves cut pools in the barren rocky shore.* **3** *Figurative.* like rock; hard; firm; unyielding: *rocky determination, a rocky heart.*
**rock|y²** (rok′ē), *adj.,* **rock|i|er, rock|i|est.** **1** likely to rock; shaky: *That table is a bit rocky; put a piece of wood under the short leg.* **2** unpleasantly uncertain. **3** *Informal.* sickish; weak; dizzy.
**Rocky Mountain columbine**, a columbine with blue-and-white flowers that is the state flower of Colorado.
**Rocky Mountain goat**, a goatlike animal of the northern Rockies; mountain goat.
**Rocky Mountain jay**, a jay of the Rocky Mountains similar to the Canada jay.
**Rocky Mountain sheep**, = bighorn.
**Rocky Mountain spotted fever**, an infectious disease characterized by fever, pain, and a rash, caused by a rickettsia and transmitted by the bite of infected ticks. It was formerly believed to be prevalent chiefly in the Rocky Mountain area but is now known to occur throughout the Western Hemisphere.
**ro|co|co** (rō kō′kō, rō′kə kō′), *n., adj.* **—*n.*** a style of architecture and decoration with elaborate ornamentation, combining such effects as shellwork, scrolls, and foliage. It grew out of the baroque in the 1600's and reached its greatest popularity in France from 1720 to 1780.
**—*adj.*** **1** of or having to do with this style. **2** tasteless and florid: *... her unsophisticated intelligence gulped down his rococo allurements with peculiar zest* (Lytton Strachey). **3** = antiquated.
[< French *rococo,* apparently < *rocaille* shellwork < Middle French *roc* rock¹]
**rod** (rod), *n.* **1** a thin, straight bar of metal or wood. An atomic reactor is controlled by rods that trap atomic particles. *Pulling the rods through ... dies draws them out thin to form wire* (Walter R. Williams, Jr.) **2** a thin, straight stick, either growing or cut off: *Jacob took him rods of green poplar, and of the hazel and chestnut tree* (Genesis 30:37). **3** anything like a rod in shape. **4** a stick used to beat or punish: *I knew I was in trouble when I was taken to the garage with a rod.* **5** *Figurative.* punishment: *Spare the rod and spoil the child.* **6** a long, light pole; fishing rod: *The rod bent as he pulled in the fish.* **7** a measure of length; 5½ yards or 16½ feet or 5.0292 meters; perch. A square rod is 30¼ square yards or 272¼ square feet or 25.293 square meters.

**Pronunciation Key:** hat, āge, cãre, fär; let, ēqual, tėrm, it, īce, hot, ōpen, ôrder; oil, out; cup, pu̇t, rüle; child; long; thin, ᴛʜen; zh, measure; ə represents a in about, e in taken, i in pencil, o in lemon, u in circus.

8 a stick used to measure with. 9 *U.S. Slang.* a pistol: *He was a show-off when he first got his rod* (Saturday Review). 10 a branch of a family or tribe: *the rod of Jesse.* 11 a staff or wand carried as a symbol of one's position: *hands that the rod of empire might have sway'd* (Thomas Gray). 12 power; authority; tyranny. 13 = divining rod. 14 one of the microscopic sense organs in the retina of the eye that are sensitive to dim light: *The eye has two kinds of visual receptors, rods and cones* (Science News Letter). 15 a cylindrical or rod-shaped bacterium; bacillus.
**spare the rod**, to fail to punish: *"Spare the rod and spoil the child" is an old saying.*
[Old English *rodd*] **—rod′less**, *adj.* **—rod′like′**, *adj.*

**rod|der** (rod′ər), *n. U.S. Slang.* a hot-rodder.

**rode** (rōd), *v.* a past tense of **ride:** *We rode ten miles yesterday.*

***ro|dent** (rō′dənt), *n., adj.* **—*n.*** 1 any one of a group of mammals having two continually growing incisor teeth in each jaw especially suitable for gnawing wood and similar material. Rats, mice, squirrels, porcupines, and beavers are rodents. Rodents are an order of mammals. 2 *Figurative.* a low, mean person.
**—*adj.*** 1 gnawing. 2 of or like a rodent.
[<Latin *rōdēns, -entis,* present participle of *rōdere* to gnaw] **—ro′dent|like′**, *adj.*

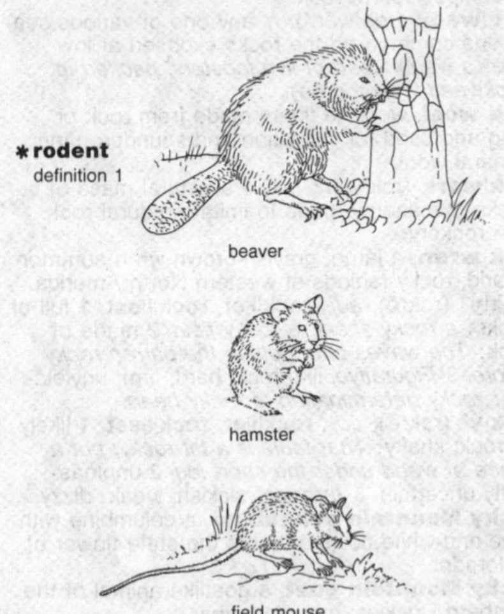

***rodent** definition 1

**ro|den|tial** (rō den′shəl), *adj.* of or having to do with rodents. [<New Latin *Rodentia* the order name (<Latin *rōdēns, -entis*) + English *-al*[1]] **—ro|den′tial|ly**, *adv.*

**ro|den|ti|cide** (rō den′tə sīd), *n.* a poison for rats and mice, or other rodents.

**rodent ulcer**, a malignant ulcer, usually of the face, which slowly works inward, destroying the deeper tissues and bone; noli-me-tangere.

**ro|de|o** (rō′dē ō, rō dā′-), *n., pl.* **-de|os**, *v.,* **-de|oed, -de|o|ing.** **—*n.*** 1 a contest or exhibition of skill in roping cattle, riding horses and steers, and other cowboy skills. 2 *Western U.S.* the driving together of cattle; roundup.
**—*v.i.*** to take part in a rodeo.
[American English <Spanish *rodeo* <*rodear* to go around <Latin *rotāre* <*rota* wheel]

**Ro|din|esque** (rō′də nesk′), *adj.* having to do with or characteristic of the French sculptor Auguste Rodin (1840-1917) or his work: *Rodinesque realism.*

**rod|let** (rod′lit), *n.* a tiny rod.

**rod|man** (rod′mən), *n., pl.* **-men.** the man who carries the leveling rod in surveying.

**rod mill**, 1 a machine containing metal rollers for forming steel rods. 2 the part of a plant containing such machines.

**rod|ney** (rod′nē), *n. British Dialect.* a vagrant; bum.

**rod|o|mon|tade** (rod′ə mon tād′, -täd′), *n., adj., v.,* **-tad|ed, -tad|ing.** **—*n.*** vain boasting; bragging; blustering talk: *A day it was of boast, swagger, and rodomontade* (Washington Irving).
**—*adj.*** bragging; boastful; ranting.
**—*v.i.*** to boast; brag. Also, **rhodomontade.**
[<French *rodomontade* <Italian *rodomontata* <*Rodomonte,* a braggart king in Ariosto's work <dialectal *rodare* roll away (<Latin *rotāre* rotate <*rota* wheel) + *monte* mountain <Latin *mōns, montis*]

**rod puppet**, a puppet moved by rods inserted into its trunk and limbs. Rod puppets are used in some puppet shows.

**roe**[1] (rō), *n.* 1 fish eggs, especially when contained in the ovarian membrane of the female fish. 2 the eggs or spawn of various crustaceans. [Middle English *rowe,* perhaps <*rown* (taken as a plural form) <Scandinavian (compare Old Icelandic *hrogn*)]

**roe**[2] (rō), *n., pl.* **roes** or (*collectively*) **roe.** 1 a small, agile deer of Europe and Asia, with forked antlers. 2 = hind. [<Old English *rā*]

**roe|buck** (rō′buk′), *n., pl.* **-bucks** or (*collectively*) **-buck.** a male roe deer.

**roe deer**, = roe[2] (def. 1). [Old English *rādēor* <*rā* roe + *dēor* deer]

**roent|gen** (rent′gən), *n., adj.* **—*n.*** the international unit of the intensity of X rays or gamma rays. It is equal to the quantity of radiation required to produce one electrostatic unit of electrical charge in one cubic centimeter of dry air under normal temperature and pressure. *Symbol:* r (no period).
**—*adj.*** having to do with X rays or gamma rays. Also, **röntgen.**
[<Wilhelm K. *Roentgen,* 1845-1923, a German physicist, who discovered X rays]

**roent|gen|ize** (rent′gə nīz), *v.t.,* **-ized, -iz|ing.** to expose to the action of X rays or gamma rays. Also, **röntgenize.**

**roentgeno-,** *combining form.* roentgen rays; X rays: *Roentgenogram* = *an X-ray photograph. Roentgenotherapy* = *therapy in which X rays are used.* [<*roentgen rays*]

**roent|gen|o|gram** (rent′gə nə gram), *n.* an X-ray photograph.

**roent|gen|o|graph** (rent′gə nə graf, -gräf), *n.* = roentgenogram.

**roent|gen|o|graph|ic** (rent′gə nə graf′ik), *adj.* of or having to do with roentgenography; radiographic. **—roent′gen|o|graph′i|cal|ly**, *adv.*

**roent|gen|og|ra|phy** (rent′gə nog′rə fē), *n.* X-ray photography; radiography.

**roent|gen|o|log|ic** (rent′gə nə loj′ik), *adj.* = roentgenological.

**roent|gen|o|log|i|cal** (rent′gə nə loj′ə kəl), *adj.* of or having to do with roentgenology. **—roent′gen|o|log′i|cal|ly**, *adv.*

**roent|gen|ol|o|gist** (rent′gə nol′ə jist), *n.* an expert in roentgenology.

**roent|gen|ol|o|gy** (rent′gə nol′ə jē), *n.* the branch of radiology having to do with X rays, especially as used in medical diagnosis and treatment.

**roent|gen|o|lu|cent** (rent′gə nə lü′sənt), *adj.* permitting X rays to pass through.

**roent|gen|om|e|ter** (rent′gə nom′ə tər), *n.* a device for measuring the intensity of X rays or gamma rays; R meter.

**roent|gen|o|paque** (rent′gə nō pāk′), *adj.* that cannot be penetrated by X rays.

**roent|gen|o|par|ent** (rent′gə nə pãr′ənt), *adj.* that can be seen with X rays. [<*roentgeno-* + (ap)*parent*]

**roent|gen|o|scope** (rent′gə nə skōp), *n.* = fluoroscope.

**roent|gen|o|scop|ic** (rent′gə nə skop′ik), *adj.* of or having to do with roentgenoscopy.

**roent|gen|os|co|py** (rent′gə nos′kə pē), *n.* direct examination with X rays.

**roent|gen|o|ther|a|pist** (rent′gə nə ther′ə pist), *n.* a person skilled in roentgenotherapy.

**roent|gen|o|ther|a|py** (rent′gə nə ther′ə pē), *n.* treatment of disease by means of X rays.

**roentgen** or **Roentgen ray**, = X ray.

**ROG** (no periods) or **R.O.G.**, receipt of goods.

**Ro|gal|list** (rō gal′ist), *n.* a person who engages in hang gliding.

**Ro|gal|lo** (rō gal′ō), *n., pl.* **-los.** 1 Rogallo wing. 2 = hang glider.

**Rogallo wing**, a kitelike, flexible wing supported by several metal poles or rods, used for soaring, gliding, parachuting, slowing down the descent of a spacecraft upon reentry, and the like. [<Francis M. *Rogallo,* an American engineer for the National Aeronautics and Space Administration, who invented it]

**ro|ga|tion** (rō gā′shən), *n.* 1 a solemn prayer or supplication, especially as chanted on the three days before Ascension Day. 2 in ancient Rome: **a** the proposal of a law by consuls or tribunes to be approved by the people. **b** a law so proposed. [<Latin *rogātiō, -ōnis* <*rogāre* to ask]

**Rogation Days**, the Monday, Tuesday, and Wednesday before Ascension Day, observed by solemn supplication.

**rog|a|to|ry** (rog′ə tôr′ē, -tōr′-), *adj.* that asks or requests: *a rogatory commission.* [<Latin *rogātus,* past participle of *rogāre* to ask + English *-ory*[1]]

**rog|er** (roj′ər), *interj. Informal.* O.K.; message received and understood. [<*roger,* signaler's word for the letter *r,* used as abbreviation for "received"]

**Rog|er** (roj′ər), *n.* = Jolly Roger.

**rogue** (rōg), *n., adj., v.,* **rogued, ro|guing.** **—*n.*** 1 a tricky, dishonest, or worthless person; rascal: *a rogue and cheat, hardened in crime.* **SYN:** knave, scoundrel. 2 a mischievous person: *The little rogue has his grandpa's glasses on.* **SYN:** scamp. 3 an animal with a savage nature that lives apart from the herd: *An elephant that is a rogue is very dangerous. The rogue ... is found among hippopotami, elk, deer, and other granivores as well as among ... the larger carnivores* (Richard F. Burton). 4 *Biology.* an individual, usually a plant, that varies from the standard. 5 *Archaic.* a vagrant; vagabond: *To hovel thee with swine, and rogues forlorn, in short and musty straw* (Shakespeare).
**—*adj.*** 1 wild; savage: *a rogue animal, a rogue hippopotamus.* 2 deviating from the standard; aberrant: *a rogue sapling.* 3 defective: *There is no way in which a rogue car can be turned into a race or rally winner* (London Times). 4 *British.* separated from a larger group; breakaway: *a rogue trades union.*
**—*v.t.*** 1 to eliminate defective plants from. 2 to cheat. **—*v.i.*** to be a rogue; act like a rogue.
[perhaps short for earlier *roger* beggar]

**rogue elephant**, 1 a savage or destructive elephant living apart from a herd. 2 *Figurative.* any hostile or dangerous social outcast.

**ro|guer|y** (rō′gər ē), *n., pl.* **-guer|ies.** 1 the conduct of rogues; dishonest trickery. **SYN:** knavery, rascality, fraud. 2 playful mischief. **SYN:** mischievousness, waggery.

**rogues' gallery**, a collection of photographs of known criminals maintained by the police.

**rogue's march**, derisive music accompanying the expulsion of a person from a regiment, community, etc.

**ro|guish** (rō′gish), *adj.* 1 having to do with rogues; dishonest; rascally: *These are the ideas of a roguish merchant rather than a statesman* (H. G. Wells). **SYN:** knavish, tricky, fraudulent. 2 playfully mischievous: *with a roguish twinkle in his eyes.* **SYN:** waggish, sportive. **—ro′guish|ly**, *adv.* **—ro′guish|ness**, *n.*

**roi fai|né|ant** (rwä′ fe nā äN′), *pl.* **rois fai|né|ants** (rwä′ fe nā äN′), *French.* 1 a king whose governing powers have passed into the hands of subordinates (applied especially to the later Merovingian kings). 2 (literally) idle king.

**roil** (roil), *v.t.* 1 to make (water or other liquid) muddy by stirring up sediment: *I had ... made a well of clear gray water, where I could dip up a pailful without roiling it* (Thoreau). 2 *Figurative.* to disturb; irritate; vex; rile: *Some people get roiled up over petty things.* [<Old French *rouiller* to rust, make muddy <*rouil,* and *rouille* mud, rust, ultimately <Latin *rōbīgō, -inis* rust]

**roil|y** (roi′lē), *adj.,* **roil|i|er, roil|i|est.** *U.S.* 1 muddy; turbid. 2 *Figurative.* riled; vexed.

**rois|ter** (rois′tər), *v., n.* **—*v.i.*** to be boisterous; revel noisily; swagger: *these genial, roistering dare-devils [soldiers] who ... are supposed to carry their lives in their hands* (George du Maurier). **—*n. Archaic.*** a boisterous fellow; noisy reveler. [<Old French *ruistre, ruiste* rude <Latin *rūsticus* rustic <*rūs, rūris* the country] **—rois′ter|er**, *n.* **—rois′ter|ing|ly**, *adv.*

**rois|ter|ous** (rois′tər əs, -trəs), *adj.* noisy; blustery; boisterous. **—rois′ter|ous|ly**, *adv.*

**ROK** (rok), *n.* 1 Republic of Korea. 2 a soldier in the South Korean army.

**ro|la|mite** (rō′lə mīt), *n.* a mechanical device consisting of a thin, flexible S-shaped band looped around two or more rollers so that the rollers turn almost without any sliding friction. [(coined by its inventor, Donald F. Wilkes, an American engineer) <*rol*(ler) + *-amite* (arbitrary ending, perhaps as in *dynamite*)]

**Ro|land** (rō′lənd), *n.* one of Charlemagne's legendary chiefs, famous for his prowess, who defeated the Saracens in Spain and was killed at the battle of Roncesvalles. He and another hero, Oliver, once fought for five days without either's gaining the advantage.
**a Roland for an Oliver**, one thing thought to be a full match for another: *[He was] comforted ... by the thought that he had given Mrs. Carr a Roland for her Oliver* (H. Rider Haggard).

**role** or **rôle** (rōl), *n.* 1 an actor's part, as in a play, motion picture, or opera: *She played the leading role in the school play.* 2 *Figurative.* a part played in real life; part or function assumed by any person or thing: *the role of a mediator in a dispute. A mother's role is to comfort and console.* 3 *Sociology.* the actions or behavior expected from an individual because of his position in a group. [<French *rôle* the roll (of paper) on which a part was written]

**role model**, a person whose behavior, especially that exhibited in a particular capacity, serves as a model or standard for another person to follow: *I am unclear what a "role model" is, but those who used the term seemed to be saying that teachers are people children tend to emulate* (Russell Baker).

**role-play|ing** (rōl′plā′ing), *n.* a method of instruction or rehabilitation in which the students or subjects act out real-life situations and discuss and study them. It is used especially in training people to handle problems or in rehabilitating mental patients.

**rolf|ing** (rol′fing), *n.* a method of correcting bodily deformities by manipulating the fascial tissue of the muscles in order to reorganize the body's natural orientation to the force of gravity: *Rolfing is a system of deep massage that stretches and rearranges the tissues surrounding the muscles* (New Yorker). [< Ida *Rolf,* an American biochemist and physiotherapist, who developed the method]

**roll** (rōl), *v., n.* — ***v.i.*** **1** to move along by turning over and over: *Wheels roll. The ball rolled away.* **2** to become wrapped around itself or some other thing: *The string rolled into a ball. This wire rolls easily.* **SYN:** curl, coil. **3** to move or be moved on wheels: *The car rolled along. He rolled onstage in a wheel chair* (Newsweek). **SYN:** wheel. **4** to move smoothly; sweep along: *Waves roll in on the beach.* (*Figurative.*) *The years roll on.* **5** to turn around; revolve: *His eyes rolled with fear.* **6** to perform a periodical revolution in an orbit: *The moon rolls about the earth.* **7** to move with a side-to-side motion: *The ship rolled in the waves.* **SYN:** rock, sway. **8** to turn over, or over and over: *The horse rolled in the dust.* **9** to walk with a swaying gait; swagger. **10** to rise and fall again and again: *Around me the prairie was rolling in steep swells and pitches* (Francis Parkman). **11** to make deep, loud sounds: *Thunder rolls.* **12** *Informal, Figurative.* to abound (in); wallow: *to be rolling in money. The authors roll in luxury on the devastation of mankind* (Benjamin H. Malkin). **13** (of a bird) to warble or trill in song. **14** (of an airplane) to sway or turn on an axis parallel to the direction of flight: *The rate at which the wing rises, causing the aircraft to roll, depends on several things* (G. N. Lance). **15** *Archaic.* to travel; wander; roam.
— ***v.t.*** **1** to cause to move along by turning over and over: *to roll a barrel. The child rolls a hoop.* **2** to turn around and around on itself or on something else; wrap: *Roll the string into a ball. The boy rolled himself up in a blanket.* **SYN:** curl, coil. **3** to move along on wheels or rollers: *to roll a bicycle.* **SYN:** wheel. **4** to sweep along: *The tide was coming in, rolling quite big waves on the rocks* (W. H. Hudson). **5** to cause to turn around; rotate: *to roll something between one's hands. The girl rolled her eyes.* **6** to cause to sway from side to side: *The huge waves rolled the ocean liner.* **7** to cause to lie or turn over, as on the back: *The dog rolled himself on the rug to scratch his back.* **8** to make flat or smooth with a roller, a rolling pin, or other device: *Rolling the grass helps to make a smooth lawn. Roll the dough thin for these cookies.* **9** to spread (out); spread (out) with something, such as a rolling pin: *to roll out dough to make a pie crust, to roll out a bolt of cloth.* **10** *Printing.* to put ink on (type, an engraving, or other plate) with a roller. **11** to beat (a drum) with rapid, continuous strokes. **12** to utter with full, flowing sound: *The organ rolled out the stirring hymn.* **13** to utter with a trill: *to roll one's r's.* **14a** to cast (dice). **b** to turn up (a number) on dice: *to roll a seven.* **15** *U.S. Slang.* to rob (a person who is drunk or helpless), especially by turning him over to search through his pockets.
[< Old French *roller* < Vulgar Latin *rotulāre* < Latin *rotula;* see the noun]
— ***n.*** **1a** something rolled up; cylinder formed by rolling (often forming a definite measure): *rolls of paper, a roll of carpet or film. A large, wrinkled roll of yellowish sea charts* (Herman Melville). *He pulled out a roll of bills as if to count them* (Rudyard Kipling). **b** = scroll. **2** a rounded or rolled-up mass: *a roll of butter. Her tiny hands, with … rolls of aged fat encircling the wrist like ivory bracelets* (Edith Wharton). **3** motion up and down, or from side to side: *The ship's roll made many people sick.* **4** a rapid, continuous beating on a drum. **5** a deep, loud sound: *the roll of thunder.* **6** the act of rolling. **7** motion like that of waves; undulation: *the roll of a meadow.* **8** a roller; revolving wheellike tool used by bookbinders. **9** a list of names; record; list: *to call the roll. Employment rolls in mid-October stood at 65.2 million* (Newsweek). (*Figurative.*) *Happy king, whose name The brightest shines in all the rolls of fame!* (Alexander Pope). **SYN:** roster, register. See syn. under **list. 10a** a small piece of dough which is cut, shaped, and often doubled or rolled over and then baked: *a dinner roll, a sweet roll.* **b** a cake rolled up after being spread with something: *jelly roll.* **c** any food prepared by being rolled up, such as meat. **11** *Informal.* paper money rolled up. **12** a part which is rolled and turned over: *the roll in a hem.* **13** a cylindrical piece of wood or metal used to help move something. **14** a rich or rhythmical flow of words: *the roll of a verse.* **15** a rolling gait; swagger: *to walk with a roll.* **16** a trill or warbling sound, especially of certain birds. **17** a complete turn made by an airplane about its longitudinal axis without changing the direction of flight.
**roll back, a** to cause (prices, wages, or interest rates) to return to a lower level: *The government ordered the farmers to roll back the prices of crops.* **b** *Informal.* to set back; cause to fall behind: *Their overrash campaign promises to … "roll back" the Soviet conquests* (Saturday Review).
**roll up,** to pile up or become piled up; increase: *Debts roll up fast. Bills roll up fast. The deeper his inquiries went, the stronger the evidence rolled up* (Edward Bok).
**strike off the rolls,** to expel from membership: *If I had … thrown over a client of mine by such carelessness as that, I'd—I'd stike my own name off the rolls* (Anthony Trollope).
[< Old French *rolle* and *roule,* learned borrowings from Latin *rotula* (diminutive) < *rota* a wheel]

**roll|a|ble** (rō′lə bəl), *adj.* that can be rolled.

**rol|la|ti|ne** (rō′lä tē′nā), *n., pl.* **-ni** (-nē). an Italian dish consisting of a slice of veal, beef, or other meat rolled around a seasoned filling and cooked. [< Italian *rollatine* < *rollare* to roll]

**roll|a|way** (rō′lə wā′), *n.* a bed that folds together and can be rolled away when not in use.

**roll|back** (rōl′bak′), *n.* a rolling back, especially of prices, wages, or interest rates, to a lower level: *An extreme case is the 8½ cent wage rollback recently imposed on Southern Massachusetts textile employes* (Newsweek).

**roll|bar** (rōl′bär′), *n.,* or **roll bar,** an overhead steel bar in an automobile or on a tractor or other vehicle, that protects passengers or an operator if the vehicle turns over.

**roll book,** a book in which a record of attendance or roll calls is kept.

**roll call, 1** the calling of a list of names, as of soldiers, students, or members of a legislature, to find out who is present: *Seventeen Congressmen were absent at the Congressional roll call.* **2** the time of day of such a calling. **3** a signal for such a calling, as by ringing a bell or sounding a bugle.

**roll-call vote** (rōl′kôl′), a voting or vote by a roll call, of the members of an assembled body, as in a legislature, society, union, etc.: *In 36 roll-call votes on domestic matters the majorities of both parties in the Senate agreed 18 times.*

**roll|er** (rō′lər), *n.* **1** a thing that rolls; cylinder on which something is rolled along or rolled up: *The roller for this window shade is broken. The men used logs as rollers to slide the heavy packing cases onto the truck. Many women use rollers to curl their hair.* **2** a cylinder of metal, stone, wood, or plastic, used for smoothing, pressing, or crushing. A heavy roller is used in making and repairing roads and tennis courts. *Wet clothes were put between the rollers of a clothes wringer to squeeze out the water in them.* **3** a long rolled bandage. **4** a long, swelling wave: *Huge rollers broke on the sandy beach.* **SYN:** billow. **5** a person who rolls something. **6a** a kind of canary that has a trilling voice. **b** a kind of tumbler pigeon. **c** any one of various jaylike Old World birds that roll about while flying, especially during courtship. **7** *Baseball.* a batted ball that rolls along the ground in fair or foul territory; grounder: *The relief pitcher caused the first batter to hit a weak roller permitting an out at the plate* (Atlantic).

*****roller bearing,** a bearing in which the shaft turns on rollers held between rings to lessen friction.

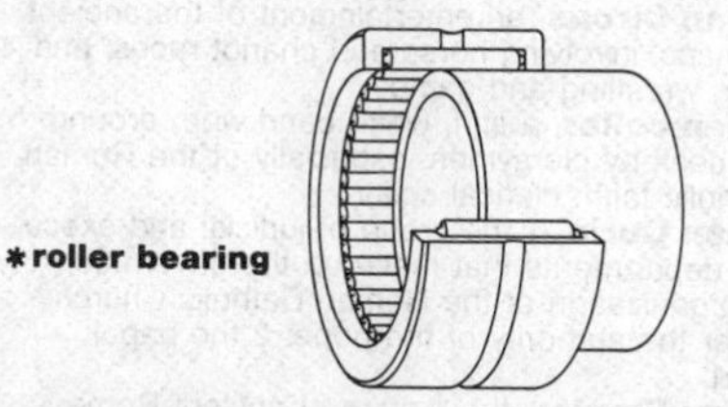

*****roller bearing**

**roller coaster,** a railway for amusement, consisting of inclined tracks along which small cars roll, abruptly dip, and turn.

**roller dam,** a dam with a roller gate.

**roller derby,** a roller-skating contest of speed between two teams, in which a player scores points by passing an opponent after skating one lap more than the opponent. Players are allowed to block each other and use other forms of rough play to prevent opponents from scoring.

**roll|ered** (rō′lərd), *adj.* having rollers; mounted on rollers.

**roller gate,** a cylindrical gate at the top of a dam that regulates water level by rolling up or down an inclined track.

**roller mill,** a mill that crushes or grinds materials such as wheat or other grain by pulling or pushing it between horizontal rolls of steel.

**roller skate,** a skate with small wheels instead of a runner, for use on a floor or sidewalk; skate.

**roll|er-skate** (rō′lər skāt′), *v.i.,* **-skat|ed, -skat|ing.** to move on roller skates: *The children roller-skated to the park.*

**roller skater,** a person who roller-skates.

**roll|er-skat|ing hockey** (rō′lər skā′ting), a sport similar to ice hockey in which the players wear roller skates. The rink on which it is played is much smaller than in ice hockey.

**roller towel,** a long towel sewed together at the ends and hung on a roller.

**roll film,** photographic film rolled on a spool.

**rol|lick** (rol′ik), *v., n.* — ***v.i.*** to enjoy oneself in a free, hearty way; be merry; frolic: *We rollicked along into Washington Street* (J. T. Fields).
— ***n.*** **1** a frolic: *Once my life was a child's rollick, half trick, half dream* (J. Parker). **2** gaiety; merriment: *a party filled with noisy rollick.*
[origin uncertain. Perhaps related to **frolic.**]
— **rol′lick|er,** *n.*

**rol|lick|ing** (rol′ə king), *adj.* frolicking; jolly; lively: *I had a rollicking good time at the picnic. A giddy and rollicking company were gathered at Judge Thatcher's* (Mark Twain). **SYN:** sportive. — **rol′licking|ly,** *adv.*

**rol|lick|some** (rol′ik səm), *adj.* = rollicking.

**roll|ing** (rō′ling), *n., adj.* — ***n.*** the action, motion, or sound of anything that rolls or is being rolled: *the rolling of a ball, the rolling of thunder.*
— ***adj.*** **1** moving forward by continuous rolls: *a rolling ball.* **2** that moves or runs on wheels: *a rolling cargo.* **3** rising and falling in gentle slopes: *rolling land, rolling hills.* **4** swaying from side to side: *a sailor's rolling gait.* **5** making deep, loud, or swelling sounds; resounding: *rolling thunder.* **6** continuously sounded; trilled. **7** heaving; surging: *a rolling wave, a rolling billow of smoke.* **8** *Figurative.* recurring: *the rolling seasons.* **9** turning or folding over: *a rolling collar.*

**rolling chair,** a wheeled chair, especially for outdoor use.

**rolling hitch,** a kind of hitch made round a spar, or the like, with the end of a rope, and which jams when the rope is pulled. See picture under **hitch.**

**rolling mill, 1** a factory where metal is rolled into sheets and bars. **2** a machine for doing this.

**rolling pin,** a cylinder of wood, plastic, or glass with a handle at each end, for rolling out dough.

**rolling stock,** the locomotives and cars of a railroad; wheeled vehicles generally.

**roll-neck** (rōl′nek′), *adj.* having a long turtle-neck collar made to be rolled over: *a turquoise roll-neck pullover.*

**roll-off** (rōl′ôf′, -of′), *n. U.S.* a play-off between bowlers or bowling leagues.

**roll-on** (rōl′on′, -ôn′), *adj., n.* — ***adj.*** **1** applied on the skin by a bottle or container fitted with a plastic roller that conveys the application without letting it spill or pour out: *a roll-on deodorant, a roll-on skin cream.* **2** equipped to carry cargo or freight loaded in trucks, trailers, or other vehicles that are driven aboard: *roll-on ships.*
— ***n.*** a woman's elastic girdle.

**roll-on-roll-off** (rōl′on′rōl′ôf′; -ôn′-; -of′), *adj.* carrying loaded trucks, trailers, or other vehicles that enter and leave under their own power for quick loading and unloading: *a roll-on-roll-off cargo ship.*

**roll-out** or **roll|out** (rōl′out′), *n.* **1** *Informal.* the first public showing of something new, as an aircraft or space vehicle. **2** *U.S. Football.* a play in which a quarterback runs out of the area formed by blockers before passing: *Duhon … was a left-handed quarterback at Tulane where he set records as a scrambling roll-out runner-passer for three years* (New York Times). **3** the part of a landing after touchdown when an airplane slows down on the runway before it taxis to the unloading ramp: *[The] plane was loaded with 128 passengers headed for Mexico City. It landed safely. But no sooner was it on the ground—still on roll-out—than all four engines quit again!* (Paul Harvey).

**roll|o|ver** (rōl′ō′vər), *n.* **1** a rolling over, especially of an automobile; overturn: *the impact of a 70-mph rollover.* **2** *Commerce.* **a** a deferment of payment, as of a tax or loan. **b** the period of such a deferment.

**roll sulfur,** a commercial form of sulfur made by melting sulfur and pouring it into cylindrical molds.

**Pronunciation Key:** hat, āge, cãre, fär; let, ēqual, tėrm; it, īce; hot, ōpen, ôrder; **oi**l, **ou**t; cup, pu̇t, rüle; **ch**ild; lo**ng**; **th**in; **ᴛʜ**en; **zh**, measure; **ə** represents **a** in about, **e** in taken, **i** in pencil, **o** in lemon, **u** in circus.

**roll-top** (rōl′top′), *adj.* having a top that rolls back: *a roll-top desk.*

**roll-up** (rōl′up′), *n. Australian Slang.* a meeting; a gathering of people.

**roll|way** (rōl′wā′), *n.* **1** a way or place where things are rolled or moved on rollers, especially a place where logs are rolled into a stream. **2** a pile of logs at the side of a stream ready to be moved.

**ro|ly-po|ly** (rō′lē pō′lē), *adj., n., pl.* **-lies.** **—*adj.*** short and plump: *a roly-poly child.* **SYN**: pudgy.
**—*n.*** **1** a short, plump person or animal. **2** a pudding made of jam or fruit spread on a rich dough, rolled up, and cooked. [< reduplication of *roll*]

**Rom** or **rom** (rom), *n.* a Gypsy man or boy. [< Romany *Rom*]

**rom.**, roman (type).

**Rom.**, an abbreviation for the following:
**1** Roman.
**2** Romance.
**3a** Romania. **b** Romanian.
**4** Romanic.
**5** Romans (a book of the New Testament).

**ROM** (no periods), read-only memory (a computer storage system for holding permanent data).

**Ro|ma|ic** (rō mā′ik), *n., adj.* **—*n.*** the everyday speech of modern Greece.
**—*adj.*** of or having to do with this speech.
[< Greek *Rhōmaïkós* (originally) of Rome, of the Roman Empire (in Late Greek, of the Eastern Empire)]

**ro|ma|i|ka** (rō mā′ə kə), *n.* a popular dance of modern Greece. [< New Greek *rhōmaïkê*]

**ro|maine** (rō mān′), *n.* a variety of lettuce having long, green leaves with crinkly edges, loosely joined at the base; cos. See picture under **lettuce.** [< French *romaine* < Old French, feminine adjective, Roman, learned borrowing from Latin *Rōmānus* (probably first introduced at Avignon in the days of the Avignon papacy)]

**Ro|man** (rō′mən), *adj., n.* **—*adj.*** **1** of or having to do with ancient or modern Rome or its people: *Augustus was the first Roman emperor.* **2** of or having to do with the Roman Catholic Church: *Many Roman missions preached to the Indians of South America.* **3** of or having to do with a style of architecture developed by the ancient Romans, characterized by massive walls and pillars, rounded arches and vaults, domes, and pediments. **4** = roman.
**—*n.*** **1** a person born or living in Rome: *So many Romans own cars that the streets are always clogged with traffic.* **2** a citizen of ancient Rome: *Under Caesar many Romans were officers in the legions.* **3** roman type. **4** a Roman Catholic (used in an unfriendly way). **5a** the Italian dialect of modern Rome. **b** the language of the ancient Romans; Latin.
[< Latin *Rōmānus* < *Rōma* Rome < Etruscan (compare *Rūmōn,* Etruscan name for the Tiber)]

***ro|man¹** (rō′mən), *n., adj.* **—*n.*** the style of type most used in printing and typewriting.
**—*adj.*** of or in roman. *Abbr:* rom.
[< *Roman* (because the style resembles that of Roman inscriptions)]

***roman¹**

The World Book Dictionary

**ro|man²** (rô mäN′), *n. French.* **1** a novel. **2** a romantic tale in verse in old French literature.

**ro|man à clef** (rô mäN′ à klā′), *French.* **1** a novel in which the characters and events represent real persons and events, but the story is told as if it were fictional: *He hints at parallels ... and, by introducing well-known persons, gives the impression that he is writing a roman à clef* (New York Times). **2** (literally) novel with a key (to the actual people and events portrayed).

**Roman alphabet**, the alphabet originally used by the Romans to write Latin. We use the Roman alphabet, with minor modifications, in writing English. *The early Roman alphabet had about 20 letters, and gradually gained 3 more* (I.J. Gelb).

**Roman arch**, a semicircular arch.

**Roman architecture**, the architecture of the ancient Romans, characterized by the development of the semicircular arch and vault, the dome, and the use of brick and concrete.

**ro|man à thèse** (rô mäN′ à tez′), *French.* a novel with a thesis; novel which expounds or illustrates an idea, doctrine, or theory.

**Roman calendar**, the calendar of the ancient Romans that had 12 months of irregular numbers of days. The modern calendar is a modification of it.

**Roman candle**, a kind of firework consisting of a tube that shoots out balls of fire: *But when carbon 14 is mentioned, he lights up like a Roman candle* (Time).

**Roman Catholic**, **1** of, having to do with, or belonging to the Christian church that recognizes the pope as the supreme head. **2** a member of this church.

**Roman Catholic Church**, the Christian church of which the pope, or Bishop of Rome, is the supreme head.

**Roman Catholicism**, the doctrines, faith, practices, and system of government of the Roman Catholic Church.

**ro|mance¹** (*n.* rō mans′, rō′mans; *v.* rō mans′), *n., v.,* **-manced, -manc|ing.** **—*n.*** **1** a love story: *She read a cheap romance in that magazine.* **SYN**: See syn. under **novel. 2** a story of adventure: *"The Arabian Nights" and "Treasure Island" are romances.* **SYN**: See syn. under **novel. 3** a medieval story or poem telling of heroes: *Have you read the romances about King Arthur and his Knights of the Round Table?* **4a** real happenings that are like stories of heroes and are full of love, excitement, or noble deeds: *The boy dreamed of traveling in search of romance. The explorer's life was filled with romance.* **b** the character or quality of such events or conditions: *Huge cloudy symbols of a high romance* (Keats). *This thing [lighting of the river] has knocked the romance out of piloting* (Mark Twain). **5** interest in adventure and love: *You have no romance in you* (George Bernard Shaw). **6** a love affair: *"Cinderella" is the story of the romance between a beautiful girl and a handsome prince. Miss Ailie had her romance* (James M. Barrie). **7** a made-up story; extravagant or wild exaggeration: *Nobody believes her romances about the wonderful things that have happened to her.* **SYN**: falsehood. **8** adventure stories, poems and stories of heroes, noble deeds, and the like, as a class of literature; romantic literature: *I soon found ... that the world in reality was very different from what it appeared in poetry and romance* (Richard Graves).
**—*v.i.*** **1** to make up romances: *Some children romance because of their lively imaginations.* **2** to think or talk in a romantic way: *Stop romancing and get down to work.* **3** to exaggerate; lie: *Now when, for the first time, they told the truth, they were supposed to be romancing* (Macaulay).
**—*v.t. Informal.*** to court as a lover; woo: *His mother wouldn't have him romancing the scrubbing girl* (Angela Carter).
[< Old French *romanz* verse narrative; vernacular, as in *romanz escrire* to write in the vernacular, "Roman" language < Vulgar Latin *rōmānicē scrībere* to write in Latin, instead of Frankish < Latin *Rōmānus* Roman < *Rōma* Rome]

**ro|mance²** (rō mans′), *n.* **1** *Music.* **a** a short, simple, sweet melody. **b** a short melodic piece for a solo instrument or group of instruments, usually in a slow or moderate tempo. **2** in Spanish literature: **a** a short narrative poem. **b** a short lyric. [< French *romance* < Spanish, a poem in stanzas < Old Provençal *romans.* Compare etym. under **romance¹.**]

**Ro|mance** (rō mans′, rō′mans), *n., adj.* **—*n.*** the group of Romance languages.
**—*adj.*** of or having to do with the Romance languages. *Abbr:* Rom.
[< obsolete French (*langue*) *romance* < Old French *romanz;* see etym. under **romance¹**]

**Romance languages**, French, Italian, Spanish, Portuguese, Romanian, Provençal, and other languages that came from Latin, the language of the Romans.

**ro|manc|er** (rō man′sər), *n.* **1** a writer of romance. **2** a person who makes up false or extravagant stories.

**Roman Circus**, an entertainment of the ancient Romans, involving horse and chariot races, and later, wrestling and games.

**Roman collar**, a stiff, white band worn around the neck by clergymen, especially of the Roman Catholic faith; clerical collar.

**Roman Curia**, **1** the group of judicial and executive departments that make up the governmental organization of the Roman Catholic Church, under the authority of the pope. **2** the papal court.

**Roman Empire**, the empire of ancient Rome that lasted from 27 B.C., when it was established by Augustus, to A.D. 395, when it was divided into the Eastern Roman Empire or Byzantine Empire (A.D. 395-1453) and the Western Roman Empire (A.D. 395-476).

**Ro|man|esque** (rō′mə nesk′), *n., adj.* **—*n.*** **1** a style of architecture using round arches and vaults, developed in Europe during the early Middle Ages, between the periods of Roman and Gothic architecture. **2** a Romance language, especially Provençal.
**—*adj.*** **1** of, in, or having to do with the Romanesque style of architecture. **2** of or having to do with a Romance language, especially Provençal.
[< French *romanesque* < *roman* a roman² (< *romanz* romance¹) + *-esque* -esque]

**Romanesque Revival**, a style of architecture of the 1870's and 1880's that imitated Romanesque.

**ro|man-fleuve** (rô mäN′flœv′), *n. French.* a saga novel.

**Roman holiday**, **1** a savage or barbaric spectacle suggesting the gladiatorial sports of the ancient Romans. **2** any public event or entertainment providing enjoyment to some at the expense or through the sufferings of others: *[The] overture ... was so fierce in its brilliance that one momentarily wondered if Berlioz was being butchered to make a Roman holiday* (London Times).

**Ro|ma|ni|an** (rō mā′nē ən, -mān′yən), *adj., n.* **—*adj.*** of or having to do with Romania, a country in southern Europe, its inhabitants, or their language.
**—*n.*** **1** a person born or living in Romania. **2** the Romance language of Romania. Also, **Roumanian, Rumanian.**

**Ro|man|ic** (rō man′ik), *adj., n.* **—*adj.*** **1** derived from Latin; Romance: *French, Italian, and Spanish are Romanic languages.* **2** derived from the Romans; Roman.
**—*n.*** the group of languages derived from Latin; Romance.
[< Latin *Rōmānicus* < *Rōmānus* Roman < *Rōma;* see etym. under **Roman**]

**Ro|man|ism** (rō′mə niz əm), *n.* **1** the spirit or institutions of ancient Rome. **2** Roman Catholicism (used in an unfriendly way).

**Ro|man|ist** (rō′mə nist), *n., adj.* **—*n.*** **1** a student of Roman law, institutions, etc. **2** a member of the Roman Catholic Church (used in an unfriendly way).
**—*adj.*** belonging to the Roman Catholic Church (used in an unfriendly way).

**Ro|man|is|tic** (rō′mə nis′tik), *adj.* **1** = Roman Catholic. **2** having to do with Roman law. **3** = Romance.

**Ro|man|i|za|tion** (rō′mə nə zā′shən), *n.* the act or process of Romanizing.

**Ro|man|ize** (rō′mə nīz), *v.t., v.i.,* **-ized, -iz|ing.** **1** to make or become Roman in character. **2** to make or become Roman Catholic. **3** to change or be changed into Roman characters.

**Roman law**, the system of laws of the ancient Romans. Roman law is the basis of civil law in many countries.

**Roman nose**, a nose that curves downward, having a prominent bridge.

**Roman numerals**, the system of numerals like XXIII, LVI, and MDCCLX, used by the ancient Romans in numbering.

**Ro|ma|no** (rō mä′nō), *n.* a hard Italian cheese with a dry, sharp, salty taste and a black, waxed rind, used grated for flavoring certain dishes. [< Italian *romano*]

**Roman punch**, lemon ice flavored with rum.

**Roman Revival**, a style of architecture and furnishings widespread during the first half of the 1800's, imitating classical Roman style and motifs.

**Roman rite**, the form of Roman Catholic ceremony used in celebrating Mass and in administering sacraments in the diocese of Rome; Latin Rite.

**Roman Rota**, = Sacred Roman Rota.

**Ro|mans** (rō′mənz), *n. pl., singular in use.* a book of the New Testament, an epistle by Saint Paul to the Christians of Rome. *Abbr:* Rom.

**Roman sandal**, a low-heeled or heelless sandal with the front consisting entirely of equally spaced straps.

**Ro|mansh** or **Ro|mansch** (rō mansh′, -mänsh′), *n.* a Rhaeto-Romanic dialect of Switzerland: *Rhaeto-Romanic comes directly from ancient Latin and has two distinct dialects,* Ladin *and* Romansh (F. C. Erickson). [< Rhaeto-Romanic *rumantsch* < Vulgar Latin *Rōmānicē;* see etym. under **romance¹**]

**Roman snail**, a European snail used for food. Once it was believed to have been introduced into Britain by the Romans.

**ro|man|tic** (rō man′tik), *adj., n.* **—*adj.*** **1** characteristic of romances or romance; appealing to fancy and the imagination: *a romantic life in exotic lands. She likes romantic tales of love and war. She thought it would be romantic to be an actress.* **SYN**: imaginative, fanciful. **2** having ideas or feelings suited to romance; interested in adventure and love: *The romantic schoolgirl's mind was full of handsome heroes, jewels, dances, and fine clothes.* **SYN**: sentimental. **3** suited to a romance: *soft, romantic music. What a romantic wood! Fairies might live here!* **4** fond of making up fanciful stories. **5** of or having to do with romanticism; representing life in literature or art as one pleases; not realistic and not classical. Romantic writing usually tells about the unusual and adventurous aspects of life, with particular freedom of form and expression. **6a** not based on fact; fanciful; imaginary; unreal. **b** not custom-

ary or practical; fantastic; extravagant; quixotic: *romantic illusions.* **SYN**: unrealistic. **7** Also, **Romantic. a** of or having to do with romanticism; belonging to the romantic movement in literature, art, and music, especially in the 1800's. **b** of or having to do with a group of English poets of the late 1700's and early 1800's whose verse is characterized by a great freedom of form, with special emphasis on the imaginative power of the mind. The Romantic poets include William Wordsworth, Samuel Taylor Coleridge, Percy Bysshe Shelley, Lord Byron, and John Keats.
**—*n.* 1** a romanticist: *His "The Midnight Meditation" is as fine an expression as I know of the romantic's irremediable disconsolation* (Poetry). **2** a romantic person.
**romantics, a** romantic ideas, ways, feelings, and the like: *There you are with your romantics again* (William Black). **b** Usually, **Romantics.** the Romantic poets of England: *The Romantics flourished in the late 1700's and early 1800's.*
[< French *romantique* (originally) romanesque < earlier *romant* a romance, variant of Old French *romanz;* see etym. under **romance**[1]]

**ro|man|ti|cal|ly** (rō man′tə klē), *adv.* in a romantic manner.

**ro|man|ti|cise** (rō man′tə sīz), *v.t., v.i.,* **-cised, -cis|ing.** *Especially British.* romanticize.

**ro|man|ti|cism** (rō man′tə siz əm), *n.* **1** the romantic tendency in literature and art; a style of literature, art, and music, especially widespread in the 1800's. Romanticism allows freedom of form and stresses strong feeling, imagination, love of nature, and often the unusual and supernatural. **2** romantic spirit or tendency: *You hope she has remained the same, that you may renew that piece of romanticism that has got into your head* (W. Black).

**ro|man|ti|cist** (rō man′tə sist), *n.* a follower of romanticism in literature, art, or music. Wordsworth, Constable, and Schubert were romanticists.

**ro|man|ti|cize** (rō man′tə sīz), *v.,* **-cized, -ciz|ing. —*v.t.*** to make romantic; give a romantic character to: *He romanticized his own asceticism* (Atlantic). *This is played in the original scoring ... and also is broadly romanticized* (Atlantic).
**—*v.i.*** to be romantic; act, talk, or write in a romantic manner. **—ro|man′ti|ci|za′tion,** *n.* **—ro|man′ti|ciz|er,** *n.*

**ro|man|tics** (rō man′tiks), *n. pl.* See under **romantic.**

**romantic vitalism,** a belief in the idea, held especially by the writer D. H. Lawrence, that man should bring his instincts and emotions into balance with his overdeveloped intellect.

**Roman tonsure,** a style of tonsure used by Roman Catholic priests, in which a ring of hair is left around the head to represent the crown of thorns worn by Jesus; St. Peter's tonsure.

**Rom|a|ny** (rom′ə nē), *n., pl.* **-nies,** *adj.* **—*n.* 1** a Gypsy. **2** the Gypsies as a group. **3** the Indic language of the Gypsies.
**—*adj.*** belonging or having to do with the Gypsies, their customs, or their language: *the wildest Romany beliefs and superstitions* (Walter T. Watts-Dunton). Also, **Rommany.**
[< Romany *Romani* plural of *Romano,* adjective < *Rom* a Gypsy; man, husband]

**Romany rye,** a person who associates closely with Gypsies. [< *Romany, rye*[2]]

**ro|man|za** (rō man′zə), *n.* = romance[2]. [< Italian *romanza*]

**ro|maunt** (rō mônt′, -mänt′), *n. Archaic.* a romantic poem or tale; romance. [< Old French *romaunt,* variant of *romant,* variant of *romanz;* see etym. under **romance**[1]]

**Rom. Cath.,** Roman Catholic.

**Rom. Cath. Ch.,** Roman Catholic Church.

**Rome** (rōm), *n.* the Roman Catholic Church.

**Rome Beauty,** a red cooking apple with yellow or green markings and a tart flavor.

**Rom|el|dale** (rom′əl dāl), *n.* any one of a breed of American sheep developed for fine wool and high-quality meat by crossing Romneys and Rambouillets. [probably irregular < *Rom*(ney) + (Corri)*edale*]

**Ro|me|o** (rō′mē ō), *n., pl.* **-os. 1** the hero of Shakespeare's play *Romeo and Juliet,* who died for love. **2** a passionate lover. **3** a lovesick young man. **4** *U.S.* a code name for the letter *r,* used in transmitting radio messages.

**Rome|ward** (rōm′wėrd), *adj., adv.* directed to, or tending toward, the Roman Catholic Church: *Romeward sympathies.*

**Rom|ish** (rō′mish), *adj.* = Roman Catholic (used in an unfriendly way). **—Rom′ish|ly,** *adv.* **—Rom′ish|ness,** *n.*

**Rom|ma|ny** (rom′ə nē), *n., pl.* **-nies,** *adj.* = Romany.

**Rom|ney** (rom′nē, rum′-), *n.* any one of a breed of sheep having long wool and originating in Romney Marsh, a tract of pastureland in southeastern England.

**romp** (romp), *v., n.* **—*v.i.* 1** to play in a rough, boisterous way; rush, tumble, and punch in play: *boys and girls romping together and running after one another* (Samuel Butler). **2a** to run or go rapidly and with little effort, as in racing. **b** to win easily: *The favorite horse romped in by four lengths.*
**—*n.* 1** rough, lively play or frolic: *A pillow fight is a romp.* **2** a girl or boy who likes to romp: *a brisk young creature of seventeen, who was of the order of romps or tomboys* (Thackeray). **3** a swift but effortless victory in which all others are left behind, as in racing: *to win in a romp.*
[perhaps ultimately a variant of *ramp*[2], verb]
**—romp′er,** *n.*

**romp|ers** (rom′pərz), *n. pl.* a loose outer garment, usually consisting of short bloomers and top, worn by young children at play; jumpers.

**romp|ing** (rom′ping), *adj.* that romps; rompish: *The air she gave herself was that of a romping girl* (Sir Richard Steele). **—romp′ing|ly,** *adv.*

**romp|ish** (rom′pish), *adj.* given to romping. **—romp′ish|ly,** *adv.* **—romp′ish|ness,** *n.*

**Rom|u|lus** (rom′yə ləs), *n. Roman Legend.* the founder and first king of Rome. He and his twin brother, Remus, abandoned as infants, were nourished by a wolf. The Romans identified him with the god Quirinus.

**ron|ca|dor** (rong′kə dôr′), *n., pl.* **-dors** or (*collectively*) **-dor.** any one of various carnivorous fishes of the Pacific coast of North America. [< Spanish *roncador* < *roncar* snore < Late Latin *rhoncāre*]

**ron|da|vel** (ron′də vəl), *n.* a round, native South African hut, usually with a single room. Modernized rondavels with two or more rooms are frequently annexes of hotels. [< Afrikaans *rondawel*]

**rond de jambe** (rôɴ də zhäɴb′), *pl.* **ronds de jambe** (rôɴ də zhäɴb′), *French.* a circular movement of the leg in ballet, with the moving foot on the floor or in the air.

**ron|deau** (ron′dō, ron dō′), *n., pl.* **rondeaux** (ron′dōz, ron dōz′). **1** a short poem with thirteen (or ten) lines; roundel. The opening words are used in two places as an unrhymed refrain. *The poem "In Flanders Fields" is a rondeau.* **2** *Music.* rondo (def. 1). [< Middle French *rondeau,* variant of *rondel* < Old French. See etym. of doublet **rondel.**]

**ron|del** (ron′dəl), *n.* a short poem, usually with fourteen lines and two rhymes. The initial couplet is repeated in the middle and at the end. [< Old French *rondel* (diminutive) < *ronde* round[1]. See etym. of doublet **rondeau.**]

**ron|de|let** (ron′də let), *n.* a short poem similar to the rondel. It has a stanza of five or seven lines on two rhymes, with the opening words or word used as an unrhymed refrain. [< Old French *rondelet* (diminutive) < *rondel* rondel]

**ron|di|no** (ron dē′nō), *n. Music.* a short, simple form of rondo. [< Italian *rondino* (diminutive) < *rondo;* see etym. under **rondo**]

**ron|do** (ron′dō, ron dō′), *n., pl.* **-dos. 1** *Music.* a work or movement having one principal theme which is repeated at least three times in the same key and to which return is made after the introduction of each subordinate theme. **2** = rondeau. [< Italian *rondo* < French *rondeau, rondel* < Old French; see etym. under **rondel**]

**ron|do|let|to** (ron′də let′ō), *n.* = rondino.

**ron|dure** (ron′jər), *n. Archaic.* **1** a circle; round space: *All things rare That heaven's air in this huge rondure hems* (Shakespeare). **2** = roundness. [< Middle French *rondeur* roundness < *ronde* round[1]]

**ron|geur** (rôɴ zhėr′), *n.* a surgical forceps for cutting and removing bone. [< French *rongeur* < Old French *ronger* to gnaw < *rougier* (< Vulgar Latin *rōdicāre* < Latin *rōdere*), blended with Old French *rungier* to ruminate < Latin *rūmigāre*]

**ron|quil** (rong′kəl), *n.* **1** a food fish of the northern Pacific Ocean. **2** any fish of the same group. [< Spanish *ronquillo* slightly hoarse (diminutive) < *ronco* hoarse]

**rönt|gen** (rent′gən), *n., adj.* = roentgen.

**rönt|gen|ize** (rent′gə nīz), *v.t.,* **-ized, -iz|ing.** = roentgenize.

**röntgen rays,** = X ray.

**ron|yon** (run′yən), *n. Archaic.* a scab (used in an unfriendly way of a woman). [< French *rogne* scab, mange]

**'roo** (rü), *n.* (in Australia) a kangaroo.

**rood** (rüd), *n.* **1a** 40 square rods; 1/4 of an acre or 10.117 ares. **b** 1 square rod or 25.293 square meters. **c** a varying unit of linear measure, equal to about 6 to 8 yards. **2** *Archaic.* the cross on which Christ suffered and died: *Socrates drinking the hemlock, and Jesus on the rood* (W. H. Carruth). **3** a representation of it; crucifix, such as a large crucifix at the entrance to the chancel of a medieval church. [Old English *rōd* (apparently originally) pole]

**rood beam,** a beam across the entrance to the choir or chancel of a church to support the rood, and usually forming the head of a rood screen.

**rood loft,** a gallery in a church over a rood screen.

**rood screen,** a screen, often of elaborate design and properly surmounted by a rood, separating the nave from the choir or chancel of a church.

**rood stair,** a stairway leading to the top of the rood screen or rood loft.

**rood steeple,** a steeple built over the rood or over the intersection of the nave and transepts.

**rood tower,** a tower in the position of a rood steeple.

**roof** (rüf, rủf), *n., pl.* **roofs,** *v.* **—*n.* 1** the top covering of a building: *Structural alterations are being made, and the gutters could not take the water from the temporary roof* (London Times). **2** *Figurative:* *the roof of a car, the roof of a cave, the roof of the mouth.* **3** *Figurative.* a house; home.
**—*v.t.*** to cover with a roof; form a roof over: *rude log cabins, roofed with bark* (George Bancroft). (*Figurative.*) *The trees roofed the glade where we camped.*
**raise the roof,** *Informal.* to make a disturbance; create an uproar or confusion: *She* [*would*] *raise the roof when people didn't do what she wanted them to do* (New York Times).
[Old English *hrōf*] **—roof′like′,** *adj.*

**roof|age** (rü′fij, rủf′ij), *n.* material for a roof; roofing.

**roof deck,** a flat roof or portion of a roof used for lounging or dining.

**roof|er** (rü′fər, rủf′ər), *n.* a person who makes or repairs roofs.

**roof garden, 1** a garden on the flat roof of a building: *She stayed at a "grand hotel" where there was a roof garden with an excellent view of the city* (New Yorker). **2** the roof or top story, as of a building, ornamented with plants or the like, and used for a restaurant, theater, etc.

**roof|ing** (rü′fing, rủf′ing), *n., adj.* **—*n.*** material used for roofs. Shingles are a common roofing for houses.
**—*adj.*** used for roofs: *roofing tile, roofing nails.*

**roof|less** (rüf′lis, rủf′-), *adj.* **1** having no roof. **2** having no home or shelter: *a roofless orphan.*

**roof|line** (rüf′līn′, rủf′-), *n.* shape or outline of a roof, as of a car: *The new hardtop has a thin roofline that overhangs wrap-around rear-windows* (Wall Street Journal).

**roof rat,** a long-tailed black rat found about buildings in Europe, southern North America, and South America; black rat.

**roof|top** (rüf′top′, rủf′-), *n., adj.* **—*n.*** the top of a building; roof: *The streets, balconies, and rooftops were packed with a clapping, shouting crowd* (Time).
**—*adj.*** on top of a building: *rooftop antennas, a rooftop restaurant.*

**roof|tree** (rüf′trē′, rủf′-), *n.* **1** the main horizontal timber along the top of a roof; ridgepole. **2** *Figurative.* a roof; home: ... *to seek shelter under a strange rooftree* (Anthony Trollope).

**roof truss,** a truss in the framework of a roof, as the triangular one formed by two principal rafters and a tie beam.

**roo|i|nek** (rō′i nek′, rü′-), *n.* an Englishman (used in an unfriendly way in South Africa). [< Afrikaans *rooinek* (literally) redneck < *rooi* red + *nek* neck]

**rook**[1] (rủk), *n., v.* **—*n.* 1** a common European bird like a crow, that often nests in large flocks in trees near buildings. The rook belongs to the same genus as the crow. *The rooks cawed peacefully in the old elms* (John Galsworthy). **2** a person who cheats, as at cards or dice.
**—*v.t.*** to cheat.
[Old English *hrōc*]

**rook**[2] (rủk), *n.* one of the pieces in the game of chess; castle. It is placed at the corners of the board to begin the game, and moves any number of unoccupied squares along a rank or file. See picture under **chess**[1]. [< Old French *roc* < Arabic *rukhkh.* Compare etym. under **roc.**]

**rook|er|y** (rủk′ər ē), *n., pl.* **-er|ies. 1** a breeding place of rooks; colony of rooks. **2** a breeding place or colony where other birds or animals are crowded together: *a rookery of seals.* [*He*] *led a small troop across 4 miles of unsettled ice to a huge penguin rookery* (Newsweek). **3** *Figurative.* a crowded, dirty, mean, and poor tenement house or group of such houses.

**rook|ie** or **rook|y**[1] (rủk′ē), *n., pl.* **rook|ies.** *Informal.* **1** an inexperienced recruit: *a police rookie, a rookie in the army.* **2** a beginner; novice. **3** a new

---

**Pronunciation Key:** hat, āge, cãre, fär; let, ēqual, tėrm; it, īce; hot, ōpen, ôrder; **oi**l, **ou**t; cup, pủt, rüle; **ch**ild; lo**ng**; **th**in; **ᴛʜ**en; **zh**, measure; ə represents **a** in about, **e** in taken, **i** in pencil, **o** in lemon, **u** in circus.

player on an athletic team, especially a professional baseball, football, basketball, or hockey player in his first season on a major-league team: *Last season he won twenty and was named rookie of the year in the American League* (New York Times). [perhaps alteration of *recruit*, influenced by *rook*[1], in earlier sense "simpleton"]

**Rook|wood** (ru̇k′wu̇d′), *adj.* of or having to do with a type of earthenware which uses tints of all colors and many types of ornamentation and glazes for bowls, vases, candlesticks, and dinnerware: *Rookwood pottery.*

**rook|y²** (ru̇k′ē), *adj.* full of rooks; visited often by rooks: *Light thickens and the crow Makes wing to the rooky wood* (Shakespeare).

**room** (rüm, ru̇m), *n., v.* —*n.* **1** a part of a house, or other building, with walls separating it from the rest of the building of which it is a part: *a dining room, a room in a school.* **2** the people in a room: *The whole room laughed. The room applauded vociferously* (Thackeray). **3** space occupied by, or available for, something: *The street was so crowded that the cars did not have room to move. There is little room to move in a crowd. I am pent up in frouzy lodgings, where there is not room enough to swing a cat* (Tobias Smollett). **4** *Figurative.* opportunity: *There is room for improvement in his work.* **5** *Archaic.* place; stead: *The inland countries had not been required to furnish ships, or money in the room of ships* (Macaulay). **6** *Obsolete.* a position; post; office.
—*v.i.* to occupy a room; live in a room; lodge: *He rooms in the gray house. Three girls from our town roomed together at college.*
—*v.t.* to provide with a room: *The door's open, and if they couldn't room any more guests they'd pretty soon close up, I guess* (Daily Telegraph).
**rooms,** lodgings: *He travelled ... to Islington, the locality of Mrs. Harper's latest "rooms"* (Leonard Merrick).
[Old English *rūm*]

**room|age** (rü′mij, ru̇m′ij), *n.* room or space afforded.

**room and board,** lodging and meals: *a hotel providing room and board, to pay for one's room and board.*

**room-and-pil|lar** (rüm′ən pil′ər, ru̇m′-), *adj.* of or designating a system of mining coal in which a series of rooms is cut into the coal bed, in each of which the miners leave columns of coal standing to help support the roof until they mine out a particular area. Most underground coal mines in the United States are room-and-pillar mines.

**room clerk,** *U.S.* an employee in a hotel, motel, or resort, who assigns rooms to guests.

**room divider,** a panel, screen, set of shelves, or other furniture, used as a partial partition: *The room divider ... has lately been debased into more or less trivial reproductions of the panels used in Japanese houses* (New Yorker).

**room|er** (rü′mər, ru̇m′ər), *n.* a person who lives in a rented room or rooms in another's house; lodger. [American English < *room* + *-er*[1]]

**room|ette** (rü met′, ru̇-), *n. U.S.* a small private bedroom on a railroad sleeping car, often furnished with toilet and washing facilities.

**room|ful** (rüm′fu̇l, ru̇m′-), *n., pl.* **-fuls. 1** enough to fill a room: *a roomful of books.* **2** the people or things in a room.

**room|i|ly** (rü′mə lē, ru̇m′ə-), *adv.* in a roomy manner.

**room|i|ness** (rü′mē nis, ru̇m′ē-), *n.* ample space; abundance of room; spaciousness.

**room|ing house** (rü′ming, ru̇m′ing), a house with rooms to rent.

**room|ing-in** (rü′ming in′, ru̇m′ing-), *n.* **1** the practice of living in a house in which one is employed as a domestic servant; living-in. **2** an arrangement in some hospitals whereby the mother of a newborn baby may keep it in her own room instead of in the nursery; lying-in.

**room|mate** (rüm′māt′, ru̇m′-), *n.* a person who shares a room with another or others.

**rooms** (rümz, ru̇mz), *n. pl.* See under **room.**

**room service,** a special service of a hotel or, sometimes, a motel or resort, whereby food and drinks may be ordered for delivery to one's room: *Entombed as he is, the playwright ... can count on room service to sustain the slender thread of life* (Harper's).

**room temperature,** the normal or average temperature of a room, from 65 to 75 degrees Fahrenheit.

**room|y** (rü′mē, ru̇m′ē), *adj.,* **room|i|er, room|i|est.** having plenty of room; large; spacious: *a roomy house.*

**roor|back** or **roor|bach** (ru̇r′bak), *n.* a false story or slander about a candidate for office, circulated for political effect. [American English; from a damaging statement about the character of James K. Polk, allegedly contained in *Roorback's Tour through the Western and Southern States, 1836,* a nonexistent travel book]

**roose** (rüz), *v.,* **roosed, roos|ing.** *Scottish.* —*v.t.* to praise; extol; flatter.
—*v.i.* to boast; be proud.
[< Scandinavian (compare Old Icelandic *hrōsa*)]

**Roo|se|velt|i|an** (rō′zə vel′tē ən), *adj.* of, having to do with, or characteristic of Franklin D. Roosevelt (1882-1945) or Theodore Roosevelt (1858-1919) or their policies as presidents of the United States: *Rooseveltian internationalism, a Rooseveltian New Deal.*

**roost** (rüst), *n., v.* —*n.* **1** a bar, pole, or perch on which birds rest or sleep: *the sudden rustling in the thicket of birds frightened from their roost* (Washington Irving). **2** a place for birds to roost in. **3** *Figurative: a robber's roost in the mountains. Sam Lawson ... continued to occupy his usual roost in the chimney-corner* (Harriet Beecher Stowe).
—*v.i.* **1** to sit as birds do on a roost. **2** to settle for the night. —*v.t.* to afford a resting place to; accommodate; harbor.
**come home to roost,** to come back so as to harm the doer or user; backfire; boomerang: *Curses are like young chickens, and still come home to roost* (Edward G. Bulwer-Lytton).
**rule the roost,** *Informal.* to be master: *CERN [European Council for Nuclear Research] will rule the roost in high-energy physics until the 30-Bev machine at Brookhaven National Laboratory goes into operation next year* (Time).
[Old English *hrōst*]

**roost|er** (rüs′tər), *n.* **1** the male of the common domestic bird kept for its eggs and meat; male chicken; cock. SYN: chanticleer. **2** *Figurative.* a cocky man or boy. [apparently < *roost* + *-er*[1]]

**roost|er|fish** (rüs′tər fish′), *n., pl.* **-fish|es** or (*collectively*) **-fish.** a colorful game and food fish found from southern California to Brazil.

***root¹**
definition 1

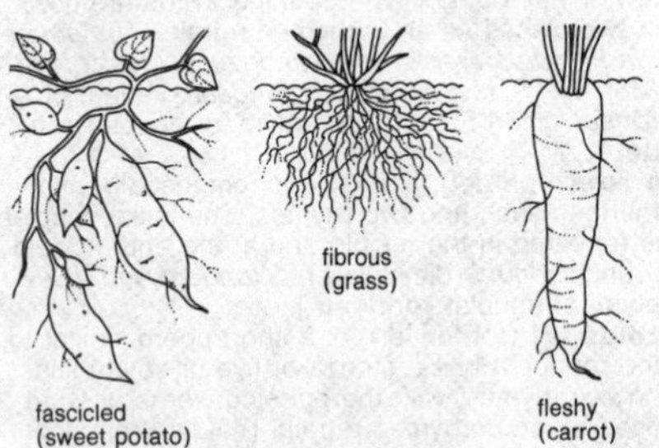


***root¹** (rüt, ru̇t), *n., v.* —*n.* **1** the part of a plant that grows downward, usually into the soil, holds it in place, absorbs water and mineral foods from the soil, and often stores food material. **2** any underground part of a plant, especially when fleshy, such as the carrot or turnip. **3a** something like a root in shape, position, or use: *the root of a tooth, the roots of the hair.* **b** the bottom of anything: *A burst of water driven as from the roots of the sea* (Shelley). **4** *Figurative.* a part from which other things grow and develop; cause; source: *For the love of money is the root of all evil* (1 Timothy 6:10). *There are a thousand hacking at the branches of evil to one who is striking at the root* (Thoreau). **5** *Figurative.* the essential part; base: *to get to the root of a problem.* **6** *Figurative.* **a** an ancestor: *myself should be the root and father Of many kings* (Shakespeare). **b** an offspring: *And in that day there shall be a root of Jesse, which shall stand for an ensign of the people* (Isaiah 11:10). **7a** a quantity that produces another quantity when multiplied by itself a certain number of times: *2 is the square root of 4 and the cube root of 8* ($2 \times 2 = 4, 2 \times 2 \times 2 = 8$). **b** a quantity that satisfies an equation when substituted for an unknown quantity: *In the equation* $x^2 + 2x - 3 = 0$, *1 and −3 are the roots.* **8a** a word from which other words are made. *Example: Room* is the root of *roominess, roomer, roommate,* and *roomy.* **b** the supposed ultimate element of language. **9** *Music.* the fundamental tone of a chord.
—*v.i.* **1** to become fixed in the ground; send out roots and begin to grow: *Some plants root more quickly than others.* **2** *Figurative.* to become firmly fixed.
—*v.t.* **1** to fix by the root. **2** *Figurative.* to fix firmly: *He was rooted to the spot by surprise. The principle ... was firmly rooted in the public mind* (Macaulay). **3** to pull, tear, or dig (up or out) by the roots; get rid of completely: (*Figurative.*) *to root out common errors and superstitions, to root out corruption in government.* SYN: extirpate, exterminate.
**take root, a** to send out roots and begin to grow: *Thou ... didst cause it [a vine] to take deep root, and it filled the land* (Psalms 80:9). **b** *Figurative.* to become firmly fixed: *One of the other secret organizations ... took root on the coast* (Graham Greene).
[< Scandinavian (compare Old Icelandic *rōt*)]
—**root′like′,** *adj.*

**root²** (rüt, ru̇t), *v.i.* **1** to dig with the snout. **2** *Figurative.* to poke; pry; search; rummage: *to root for an answer. She rooted through the closet looking for her old shoes.* —*v.t.* **1** to turn over or dig up with the snout: *The pigs rooted up the garden.* **2** *Figurative.* to search (out); hunt (up): *to root the truth out of the prisoner.* [Old English *wrōtan*]

**root³** (rüt, ru̇t), *v.i., v.t. Informal.* to cheer or support a team, a member of (a team, a contestant, or a candidate) enthusiastically: *to root our team on to victory. Who you rootin' for, for Republican candidate, Mr. Babbitt?* (Sinclair Lewis). [American English, probably < earlier sense "work hard" < *root*[2]]

**root|age** (rü′tij, ru̇t′ij), *n.* **1** the act of rooting. **2** a condition of being firmly fixed by means of roots.

**root and branch,** *Especially British.* **1** radical; drastic; extreme: *Our ... service is obsolete, requiring root and branch reform* (London Times). **2** completely; utterly: *Political circumstances have forced him to oppose the Marples programme root and branch* (Manchester Guardian Weekly).

**root beer,** a carbonated drink flavored with the juice of the roots of certain plants, such as sarsaparilla or sassafras. It contains no alcohol.

**root canal,** a passage in the root of a tooth through which nerves and vessels pass to the pulp.

**root cap,** a mass of cells at the tip of growing roots that protects the active growing point immediately behind it: *The root cap grows from the inside and its old collapsing outer cells wear off as it is pushed through the soil* (Fred W. Emerson).

**root cellar,** a cellar for storing root crops.

**root collar,** that place at the base of a tree where the swelling and spreading of the roots begin.

**root crop,** or **root|crop** (rüt′krop′, ru̇t′-), *n.* a crop of sweet potatoes, turnips, beets, or the like, grown for their edible roots.

**root|ed** (rü′tid, ru̇t′id), *adj.* **1** having roots. **2** *Figurative.* having taken root; firmly fixed: *a deeply rooted belief.* —**root′ed|ly,** *adv.* —**root′ed|ness,** *n.*

**root|er¹** (rü′tər, ru̇t′ər), *n.* **1** an uprooter. **2** a machine that roots out or uproots trees, stumps, and the like. **3** a thing or person that takes root. [< *root*[1] + *-er*[1]]

**root|er²** (rü′tər, ru̇t′ər), *n.* an animal that digs with its snout. [< *root*[2] + *-er*[1]]

**root|er³** (rü′tər, ru̇t′ər), *n.* a person who cheers or supports enthusiastically. [< *root*[3] + *-er*[1]]

**root fungus,** fungus growing in symbiotic association with the roots of plants.

**root graft, 1** the process of grafting scions directly onto a small part of a root. **2** a natural joining of the roots of nearby plants.

**root hair,** a hairlike outgrowth from a root of a plant. Root hairs absorb water and dissolved minerals from the soil.

**root|hold** (rüt′hōld′, ru̇t′-), *n.* **1** a place in the ground where plants may take firm root: *Erosion and its debris have provided roothold for hanging, scrubby woodland* (London Times). **2** a firm rooting of a plant or plants in the ground: *There is an accumulation of sand and mud sufficient to permit a roothold* (John and Mildred Teal).

**root|i|ness** (rü′tē nis, ru̇t′ē-), *n.* the quality of being rooty.

**root knot,** a disease of plants caused by nematode worms, in which knots form on the roots and the growth of the plant is stunted.

**root|less** (rüt′lis, ru̇t′-), *adj.* having no roots; not firmly fixed or established; not rooted. —**root′less|ness,** *n.*

**root|let** (rüt′lit, ru̇t′-), *n.* a little root; small branch of a root.

**root maggot,** one of several species of dipterous larvae which affect the roots of vegetables and other plants.

**root mass,** the lump of earth dug up when transplanting a plant, containing and protecting enough of the root system so that the plant can survive the shock of transplantation.

**root-mean-square deviation** (rüt′mēn′skwãr′), = standard deviation.

**root neck,** the line of union of the root and stem of a plant.

**root rot,** a disease which affects the roots of plants, causing decay and death. Fungi or bacteria are either the primary or the secondary cause of the disease. Unfavorable conditions of soil make plants more susceptible to it.

**root|stalk** (rüt′stôk′, ru̇t′-), *n.* = rootstock.

**root|stock** (rüt′stok′, růt′-), *n.* **1** = rhizome. **2** a root that serves as a stock for propagating plants. **3** *Figurative.* an earlier or original form; source.

**root symbiosis**, a symbiotic relation between certain bacteria and fungi and the roots of the higher plants.

**root tubercle**, *Botany.* one of the small rootlike growths or nodules produced on the roots of leguminous plants by nitrogen-fixing bacteria.

**root|worm** (rüt′wėrm′, růt′-), *n.* any one of various worms or insect larvae that feed on the roots of plants.

**root|y** (rü′tē, růt′ē), *adj.,* **root|i|er, root|i|est.** **1** having many roots. **2** like roots.

**R.O.P.**, run-of-paper.

**rop|a|ble** (rō′pə bəl), *adj.* = ropeable.

**rope** (rōp), *n., v.,* **roped, rop|ing.** —*n.* **1** a strong, thick line or cord, made by twisting smaller cords together: *Several strands of the rope broke as the ship strained at its anchor.* **2** *U.S.* a lasso. **3** a number of things twisted or strung together: *a rope of pearls.* **4** a cord or noose for hanging a person. **5** death by being hanged. **6** a sticky, stringy, mass: *Molasses candy forms a rope.* —*v.t.* **1** to tie, bind, or fasten with a rope. **2** to enclose or mark off with a rope. **3** *U.S.* to catch (a horse, calf, or other animal) with a lasso; lasso: *He dexterously roped a horse* (Owen Wister). **4** to attach (persons) to each other by a rope in mountaineering. —*v.i.* to form a sticky, stringy, mass; become ropy: *Cook the syrup until it ropes when you lift it with a spoon.*

**give one rope**, to let one act freely: *Give this man rope—he's doing our work splendidly* (Thomas A. Guthrie).

**know** (or **learn**) **the ropes, a** to know or learn the various ropes of a ship: *The captain, who ... knew the ropes, took the steering oar* (Richard Henry Dana). **b** *Informal.* to know or learn about a business or activity: *After spending five years at that state-supported institution, she thought she knew the ropes about teaching* (New York Times).

**on the ropes, a** driven against the ropes that enclose a boxing ring: *The champion had the contender on the ropes for most of the third round.* **b** *Informal, Figurative.* in trouble: *The Tories are on the ropes ... as an effective instrument of government* (John T. McLeod).

**rope in**, *Informal.* to get or lead in by tricking: *I knew the first house would keep mum and let the rest of the town get roped in* (Mark Twain).

**ropes**, the cords used to enclose a boxing ring or other space: *As he entered the ring, the champion leaped over the ropes.*

**the end of one's rope**, the end of one's resources, activities, or the like: *They have come to the end of their rope: their time is up* (Walter Besant).

[Old English *rāp*]

**rope|a|ble** (rō′pə bəl), *adj.* **1** *Australian.* uncontrollable; wild; untamable. **2** *Australian Slang.* (of a person) intractable; obstinate; violently angry. Also, **ropable.**

**rope|danc|er** (rōp′dan′sər, -dän′-), *n.* a person who dances or balances on a rope stretched high above the floor or ground.

**rope|danc|ing** (rōp′dan′sing, -dän′-), *n.* the performance of a ropedancer.

**rope hose tool**, a rope with an attached hook, used by firemen, especially to secure hose to a ladder and tie victims to firemen's backs.

**rope of sand**, something that cannot hold together; something that only looks like a bond, tie, or means of union.

**rop|er** (rō′pər), *n.* **1** a person who uses a lasso: *A good roper will hurl out the coil with marvelous accuracy and force* (Theodore Roosevelt). **2** a person who makes ropes.

**rope race**, the groove that a rope runs in, in a pulley block or similar device.

**rop|er|y** (rō′pər ē), *n., pl.* **-er|ies.** **1** a place where ropes are made; ropewalk. **2** *Archaic.* trickery; knavery; roguery.

**ropes** (rōps), *n.pl.* See under **rope.**

**rope tow**, an endless, moving belt of rope driven by a motor for towing skiers up a hill.

**rope|walk** (rōp′wôk′), *n.* a place where ropes are made. A ropewalk is usually a long, low shed.

**rope|walk|er** (rōp′wô′kər), *n.* **1** a person who walks on a rope stretched high above the floor or ground. **2** = ropedancer.

**rope|way** (rōp′wā′), *n.* an overhead stretch of rope or cable along which heavy objects are carried: *A 27-mile ropeway high in the Himalayas is being built to speed trade between Tibet and northern India* (Science News Letter).

**rope yarn**, the loosely twisted thread of hemp, or the like, which rope is made of.

**rop|ing** (rō′ping), *n.* **1** the act of one who ropes. **2** ropes collectively: *We had on board pretty good store of roping made of mats and flags* (Daniel Defoe). **3** a ropelike formation.

**rop|y** (rō′pē), *adj.,* **rop|i|er, rop|i|est.** **1** forming sticky threads; stringy: *ropy syrup.* **2** like a rope or ropes. —**rop′i|ly,** *adv.* —**rop′i|ness,** *n.*

**roque** (rōk), *n.* a form of croquet played on a hard-rolled court and modified so as to demand greater skill. [abstracted from *croquet*]

**Roque|fort** (rōk′fərt), *n.* **1** a strongly flavored French cheese made of sheep's or goat's milk, veined with mold. **2** a cheese of similar flavor, made from cow's milk. [< *Roquefort,* a town in France, where originally made]

**roq|ue|laure** (rok′ə lôr, -lōr; *French* rôk lōr′), *n.* a man's cloak reaching to the knee, worn during the 1700's and early 1800's. [< French *roquelaure* < the Duc de *Roquelaure,* 1656-1738, who popularized it]

**ro|quet** (rō kā′), *v.,* **-queted** (-kād′), **-quet|ing** (-kā′ing), *n.* in croquet and roque: —*v.t.* **1** to strike (another player's ball) with the ball being played. **2** (of a ball) to make contact with (another ball).

—*v.i.* to strike another ball with one's own ball in play.

—*n.* the act of roqueting.

[alteration of *croquet.* Compare etym. under **roque.**]

**ro|quette** (rō ket′), *n.* a plant of the mustard family; rocket; rocket salad.

**ro|ric** (rôr′ik, rōr′-), *adj.* dewlike. [< Latin *rōs, rōris* dew + English *-ic*]

**ro-ro ship** (rō′rō′), a freighter that can carry loaded trucks, trailers, or other vehicles which drive on it at one port and drive off of it at another: *Ro-ro ships and containerization have caused sea freight rates to fall by about 40 per cent* (Science Journal). [< *ro*(ll-on)-*ro*(ll-off) *ship*]

**ror|qual** (rôr′kwəl), *n.* any one of the whalebone whales having grooves in the throats and undersides and a small dorsal fin, especially a species of the Atlantic, Pacific, and Antarctic which grows 40 to 60 feet long; finback; razorback. [< French *rorqual* < Norwegian *røyrkval,* perhaps < Old Icelandic *reytharhvalr* < *reythr* rorqual + *hvalr* whale]

**Ror|schach** (rôr′shäk), *adj., n.* —*adj.* of or having to do with the Rorschach test: *a Rorschach inkblot. ... yellow and red Rorschach scrawls* (New Yorker).

—*n. Informal.* a Rorschach test.

***Rorschach test**, a psychological test which measures personality traits, general intelligence, etc., based on the subject's response to ten different standardized inkblot designs; inkblot test: *The Rorschach test ... can be considered a valid test of personality only as its results show positive correlations with the results of other personality tests* (Scientific American). [< Hermann *Rorschach,* 1884-1922, a Swiss psychiatrist]

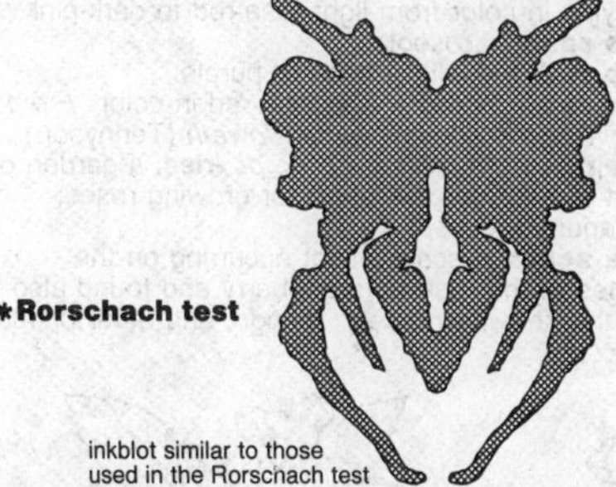

***Rorschach test**

inkblot similar to those used in the Rorschach test

**ro|sace** (rō′zās), *n.* a highly decorative circular ornament on a building, as a rondel filled with sculpture. [< Middle French *rosace* < *rose* rose]

**ro|sa|ceous** (rō zā′shəs), *adj.* **1** belonging to the rose family. **2** like a rose in form. **3** = rose-colored. **SYN:** roseate. [< Latin *rosāceus* (with English *-ous*) < *rosa* rose[1]]

**ro|sa|lia** (rō zāl′yə), *n. Music.* a form of melody in which a phrase or figure is repeated two or three times, each time a step or a half-step higher. [< Italian *rosalia* < *Rosalia, mia cara,* an old Italian popular song]

**Ros|a|lind** (roz′ə lind, -līnd), *n.* the heroine of Shakespeare's comedy *As You Like It.*

**ros|an|i|lin** (rō zan′ə lin), *n.* = rosaniline.

**ros|an|i|line** (rō zan′ə lēn, -lin, -līn), *n.* **1** a crystalline base derived from aniline, forming salts which yield red and other dyes. *Formula:* $C_{20}H_{21}N_3O$ **2** any one of the dyes obtained from this compound. [< *ros*(e) + *aniline*]

**ro|sar|i|an** (rō zãr′ē ən), *n.* a person who cultivates roses. [< Latin *rosārium* rose garden + English *-an*]

**ro|sar|i|um** (rō zãr′ē əm), *n., pl.* **-i|ums, -i|a** (-ē ə). a rose garden; rosery. [< Latin *rosārium* < *rosa* rose[1]]

***ro|sa|ry** (rō′zər ē), *n., pl.* **-ries.** **1** a string of beads for keeping count in saying a series of prayers: *The lama ... fingered his rosary awhile* (Rudyard Kipling). **2a** a series of prayers consisting of a specified number of Aves (salutations to the Virgin Mary), of paternosters (repetitions of the Lord's Prayer), and of Glorias (or doxologies). **b** a string of beads of various sizes representing the same number of Aves, paternosters, and Glorias respectively, used for marking off these prayers. **3** a garden of roses; bed of roses: *The rosary today displays a marvelous collection of 1,200 different roses* (New York Times). [< Medieval Latin *rosarium* < Latin *rosārium* rose garden < *rosa* rose[1]]

***rosary** definition 1

**rosary pea**, a tropical climbing shrub of the pea family whose seeds are used for beads and in rosaries; Indian licorice.

**rosary ribs**, = rachitic rosary.

**ros|coe** (ros′kō), *n. Slang.* a pistol: *No shamus worth his salt turns up for a job without his roscoe, and roscoes cost money* (Maclean's). [perhaps < *Roscoe,* a proper name]

**rose[1]** (rōz), *n., adj., v.,* **rosed, ros|ing.** —*n.* **1** a flower that grows on a bush usually with thorny stems. Roses are red, pink, white, or yellow and usually smell very sweet. Wild roses have one circle of petals; cultivated roses usually have more than one circle and are sometimes even cabbage-shaped in body. The rose is the state flower of Georgia, Iowa, New York, and North Dakota. *Red as a rose is she* (Samuel Taylor Coleridge). *That which we call a rose by any other name would smell as sweet* (Shakespeare). **2** the bush itself, any one of a genus belonging to the rose family. **3** any one of various related or similar plants or flowers. **4** a pinkish-red color: *shows in her cheek the roses of eighteen* (Alexander Pope). **5** a perfume made from roses. **6** something shaped like a rose or suggesting a rose, such as: **a** a rosette. **b** the sprinkling nozzle of a water pot. **c** a gem cut out with faceted top and flat base. See picture under **gem. d** *Heraldry.* a bearing in the form of a rose, usually consisting of five lobes or petals, used as the mark of cadency of the seventh son. **7** *Figurative.* a woman of great beauty, loveliness, or excellence. **8a** the compass card or the thirty-two-pointed figure on it showing the points of the compass. **b** a thirty-two- or three-hundred-and-sixty-pointed figure printed on a map showing compass directions. **9** = rose head (def. 2).

—*adj.* pinkish-red.

—*v.t.* **1** to make rosy: *Till all the sails were dark-en'd in the west, And rosed in the east* (Tennyson). **2** to scent or perfume with rose.

**come up roses**, to turn out well: *Disasters continually seem to impend but somehow—I touch wood earnestly—everything comes up roses* (Alfred Friendly).

**under the rose**, in secret; privately; sub rosa: *There was even a story told, with great mystery, and under the rose, of his having shot the devil with a silver bullet* (Washington Irving).

[Old English *rose, rōse* < Latin *rosa*] —**rose′like′,** *adj.*

**rose[2]** (rōz), *v.* the past tense of **rise:** *The cat rose and stretched itself.*

**ro|sé** or **Ro|sé** (rō zā′), *n.* a pink table wine. [< French *rosé* (originally) pink < Old French *rose* rose[1], learned borrowing from Latin *rosa*]

**rose acacia**, a shrub of the pea family, a variety of locust, with large, rose-colored flowers, growing in the mountains from Virginia to Georgia.

**ro|se|al** (rō′zē əl), *adj.* = rosy.

**ro|se|ate** (rō′zē it, -āt), *adj.* **1** = rose-colored. **2** *Figurative.* cheerful: *the roseate face of a happy child.* **3** *Figurative.* bright; optimistic: *roseate dreams of the future.* [< Latin *roseus* rosy (< *rosa* rose[1]) + English *-ate*[1]] —**ro′se|ate|ly,** *adv.*

**Pronunciation Key:** hat, āge, cãre, fär; let, ēqual, tėrm, it, īce, hot, ōpen, ôrder; oil, out; cup, pu̇t, rüle; child; long; thin, ᴛʜen; zh, measure; ə represents **a** in about, **e** in taken, **i** in pencil, **o** in lemon, **u** in circus.

**roseate spoonbill**, a spoonbill of warm or tropical parts of the Americas, with plumage chiefly pink deepening in parts to red.

**roseate tern**, a black-capped tern of the coasts of temperate and tropical regions, with a blackish bill and slightly pinkish underparts.

**rose|bay** (rōz′bā′), *n.* **1** = oleander. **2** = rhododendron. **3** = willow herb.

**rose beetle**, = rose bug.

**rose-breast|ed grosbeak** (rōz′bres′tid), a grosbeak of eastern North America, the male of which has a black head and back, white underparts, and a large triangle of rose on its breast.

**rose|bud** (rōz′bud′), *n.* the bud of a rose.

**rose bug**, a tan-colored bug destructive to roses, peonies, and certain other garden plants, especially by eating the blossoms.

**rose|bush** (rōz′bu̇sh′), *n.* a shrub or vine bearing roses.

**rose campion**, **1** = mullein pink. **2** the red corn cockle.

**rose chafer**, = rose bug.

**rose cold**, hay fever that occurs in the spring or early summer, thought to be caused by pollen from roses; rose fever.

**rose color**, a pinkish red.

**rose-col|ored** (rōz′kul′ərd), *adj.* **1** pinkish-red. **2** *Figurative.* bright; cheerful; optimistic: *The colonel was ... full of his rose-colored plans for the future* (Francis H. Smith).

**rose-colored glasses**, a cheerful attitude or disposition; an optimistic outlook: *to see life through rose-colored glasses.*

**rose comb**, a type of low comb on certain breeds of chickens, such as the Dominique, Wyandotte, and Hamburg, covered with rounded points and a spike extending to the rear.

**rose disease**, erysipelas in which reddish patches appear on the skin of swine.

**rose engine**, a lathe for making decorative combinations of curved lines, such as on watchcases and on plates for printing bank notes and bonds.

***rose family**, a large group of dicotyledonous trees, shrubs, and herbs, including the apple, pear, blackberry, spirea, hawthorn, and rose. Typical members of the rose family have alternate leaves, five-petaled flowers, and fruits with many seeds. See picture below.

**rose fever**, = rose cold.

**rose|fish** (rōz′fish′), *n., pl.* **-fish|es** or (*collectively*) **-fish.** a food fish of the North Atlantic, with a spiny head and mostly red color, now frozen and sold widely throughout the United States (under various names).

**rose geranium**, any geranium of a group with fragrant, narrowly divided leaves, and small, pinkish flowers.

**rose head**, **1** a sprinkler nozzle with many small openings for making a spray. **2a** the head on a nail or spike with corrugations or facets. **b** a nail having such a head.

**rose hip**, the fruit of the rose: *When the British were desperate for food during the early years of the war, a team of food experts ... discovered that rose bushes grown in cold climate contained more ascorbic acid (Vitamin C) in their ... hips than oranges ... and rose hip jam became important in the diet of British school children* (New York Times).

**rose leaf**, the petal of a rose.

**ro|se|lite** (rō′zə līt), *n.* a rose-colored mineral, an arsenate of calcium, cobalt, and magnesium.

**ro|sel|la** (rō zel′ə), *n.* any one of a group of colorful, medium-sized parrots of Australia. [alteration of *Rosehiller* < *Rosehill,* a district in southeastern Australia frequented by these birds]

**ro|selle** (rō zel′), *n.* a hibiscus native to tropical regions of the Old World, grown for its edible red calyx and involucre, and for a fiber made from its stem. [origin unknown]

**ro|se|ma|ling** (rō′zə mä′ling), *n.* a Scandinavian style of painting or carving floral designs on walls, furnishings, and utensils. [< Norwegian *rosemaling* (literally) rose painting]

**rose mallow**, **1** any one of a group of plants of the mallow family having large, rose-colored flowers; hibiscus; mallow rose. The muskmallow and okra are rose mallows. **2** = hollyhock.

**rose|mar|y** (rōz′mãr′ē), *n., pl.* **-mar|ies.** a fragrant, evergreen shrub native to southern Europe, whose leaves yield an oil used in making perfume, and are also much used in seasoning food. It belongs to the mint family. Rosemary is a symbol of remembrance. [earlier *rosmarine* < Latin *rōsmarīnus* (literally) dew of the sea < *rōs, rōris* dew + *marīnus* marine; influenced by *rose*[1] and *Mary*]

**rose moss**, a portulaca with broad leaves, native to Brazil and commonly grown as a garden plant in North America.

**rose noble**, an English gold coin bearing an imprint of a rose on its face, first issued by Edward IV and then worth ten shillings.

**rose of Jericho**, a small plant of the mustard family, native to the arid deserts of southwestern Asia and northeastern Africa; resurrection plant. It rolls up as it dries but will open again when kept wet.

**rose of Sharon**, **1** a shrub of the mallow family with pink, purple, or white flowers; althea. It is a species of hibiscus. **2** a plant mentioned in the Bible, a kind of St.-John's-wort having yellow flowers; Aaron's beard. **3** a flower, perhaps the autumn crocus (in the Revised Version of the Bible, Song of Solomon (Psalms) 2:1).

**rose oil**, = attar of roses.

**ro|se|o|la** (rō zē′ə lə), *n.* **1** any rosy rash that occurs with various fevers, especially that occurring with a mild disease of early infancy that resembles measles. **2** = German measles. [< New Latin *roseola* (diminutive) < Latin *roseus* rosy < *rosa* rose[1]]

**ro|se|o|lar** (rō zē′ə lər), *adj.* **1** of or having to do with roseola. **2** showing a roseola.

**rose pink**, a soft, light pink color; rose color. —**rose′-pink′**, *adj.*

**rose|point** (rōz′point′), *n.* a fine lace first made in Venice, with raised flowers in large patterns.

**rose quartz**, a translucent or transparent quartz, varying in color from light rose-red to dark-pink.

**rose rash**, = roseola.

**rose red**, red with a tinge of purple.

**rose-red** (rōz′red′), *adj.* rose red in color: *From thy rose-red lips my name Floweth* (Tennyson).

**rose|ry** (rōz′rē, rō′zər ē), *n., pl.* **-ries.** a garden or part of a garden set apart for growing roses; rosarium. [< *rose*[1] + *-ry*]

**rose scale**, a scale insect occurring on the canes of the rose and raspberry and found also on the strawberry, pear, mango, and other plants.

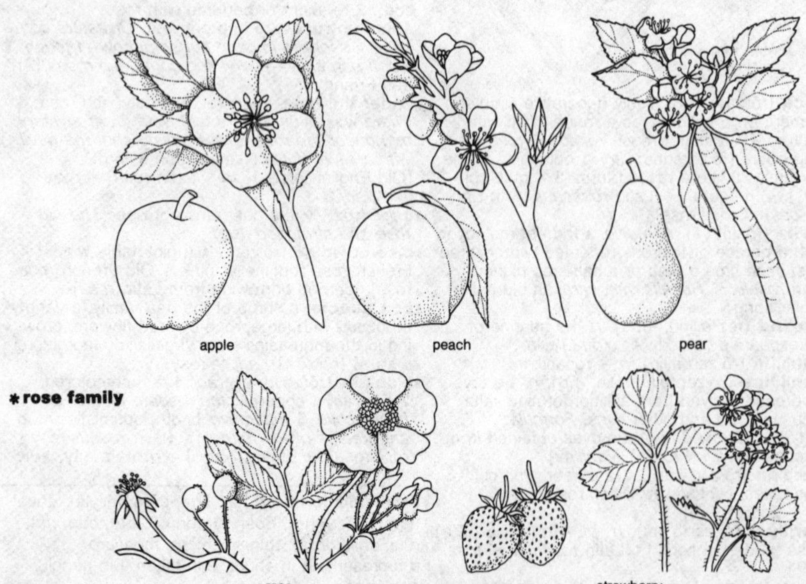


***rose family**

**rose slug**, the larva of a sawfly that feeds on the leaves of roses.

**ros|et** (roz′it), *n. Scottish.* resin.

**rose-tint|ed** (rōz′tin′tid), *adj.* rose-colored: **a** pinkish-red: *rose-tinted beiges.* **b** *Figurative.* cheerful; optimistic: *rose-tinted views.*

**rose-tinted spectacles**, = rose-colored glasses.

**Ro|set|ta stone** (rō zet′ə), **1** a slab of black basalt found in 1799 near the mouth of the Nile. A decree carved on it in hieroglyphic and demotic ancient Egyptian writing and in Greek provided the key to the deciphering of Egyptian hieroglyphics. **2** *Figurative. these meteorites retain their physical purity far better than the earth, and so are Rosetta stones to the history of the universe* (Newsweek). [< *Rosetta* (< Arabic *Rashid*), a town near one of the mouths of the Nile]

**ro|sette** (rō zet′), *n.* an ornament, object, or arrangement shaped like a rose. Rosettes are often made of ribbon. Carved or molded rosettes are used in architecture. Another kind of rosette is a cluster of leaves or other plant parts naturally arranged in a circle. *Before a rosette of microphones, the President ignored the raindrops streaming down his face* (Time). [< French *rosette* (diminutive) < Old French *rose,* learned borrowing from Latin *rosa* rose[1]]

**ro|set|ted** (rō zet′id), *adj.* **1** ornamented with rosettes: *The low-cut and rosetted shoe* (Atlantic). **2** formed into rosettes: *rosetted ribbons.*

**rosette plant**, a plant with clusters of leaves at the surface of the ground or at the summit of a caudex.

**rose water**, water made fragrant with oil of roses, used as a perfume and in some Oriental cooking.

**rose-wa|ter** (rōz′wô′tər, -wot′-), *adj.* **1** having the odor of rose water. **2** *Figurative.* affectedly delicate, nice, or fine: *rose-water philanthropy* (Thomas Carlyle).

***rose window**, an ornamental circular window, especially one with a pattern of small sections that radiate from a center (usually in churches).

***rose window**

**rose|wood** (rōz′wu̇d′), *n.* **1** a beautiful dark reddish wood used in fine furniture. **2** any one of various trees that it comes from, especially one of a group of tropical trees of the pea family.

**Rosh Ha|sha|nah** or **Ha|sha|na** (rosh hə shä′nə, rōsh), the Jewish New Year, celebrated as a solemn holiday on the first and second day of Tishri. Rosh Hashanah and Yom Kippur are the High Holidays and usually occur in September. [< Hebrew *rōsh* head + *hashānāh* the year]

**Rosh Ha|sho|na** (hə shô′nə), = Rosh Hashanah.

**Rosh Ho|desh** (hō′desh, ḥō′-), the first day (and, sometimes, the second day) of the new month in the Hebrew calendar beginning with the new moon, celebrated with special prayers. [< Hebrew *rōsh* head + *hodhesh* new moon]

**ro|shi** (rō′shē), *n.* a master or teacher of Zen Buddhism. [< Japanese *rōshi*]

**Ro|si|cru|cian** (rō′zə krü′shən), *n., adj.* —*n.* **1** a member of a secret society prominent in the 1600's and 1700's which claimed to have a special and secret knowledge of nature and religion. **2** a member of any one of various similar societies founded later.
—*adj.* of or having to do with the Rosicrucians. [< a Latinized form (< Latin *rosa* rose[1] + *crux, crucis* cross) of *Rosenkreuz,* the supposed founder in 1484 of the order + *-ian*]

**Ro|si|cru|cian|ism** (rō′zə krü′shə niz əm), *n.* the theories and practices of Rosicrucians.

**ros|i|ly** (rō′zə lē), *adv.* **1** with a rosy tinge or color. **2** *Figurative.* brightly; cheerfully.

**ros|in** (roz′ən), *n., v.* —*n.* a hard, yellow, brown, or black substance that remains when turpentine is evaporated from pine resin. Rosin is rubbed on violin bows, and on the shoes of acrobats and ballet dancers to keep them from slipping. It is also used in varnishes, in soap, and as a sizing for paper. *Rosin is made mainly from the gum of pine trees* (Wall Street Journal).
—*v.t.* to cover or rub rosin on: *rosin a violin bow.* [< Old French *rosine,* variant of *resine;* see etym. under **resin**]

**Ros|i|nan|te** (roz′ə nan′tē), *n.* a poor, worn-out horse. [< *Rocinante*]

**rosin bag**, *Baseball.* a small bag containing rosin used for drying the hands.

**ros|i|ness** (rō′zē nis), *n.* **1** a rosy state. **2** a rosy color.

**rosin oil**, a yellowish, oily liquid; retinol.

**ros|in|ous** (roz′ə nəs), *adj.* of, like, or containing rosin.

**ros|in|weed** (roz′ən wēd′), *n.* any one of various coarse North American plants of the composite family with resinous juice, especially the compass plant.

**ros|in|y** (roz′ə nē), *adj.* = rosinous.

**ro|so|lio** (rō zōl′yō), *n.* a cordial made especially from raisins, popular in southern Europe. [< Italian *rosolio* < Medieval Latin *ros solis* sundew, a plant; also, a liqueur < Latin *rōs, rōris* dew, *sōl, sōlis* sun]

**rosse** (rôs), *adj. French.* characterized by a brutal or cynical disregard of convention.

**ross|er** (rôs′ər, ros′-), *n.* a lumberjack who barks and smooths the side of a log to make it slide easier. [origin unknown]

**ros|se|rie** (rôs rē′), *n. French.* cynical disregard of convention.

**ros|so an|ti|co** (rō′sō an tē′kō), a hard, red, Wedgwood stoneware. [< Italian *rosso antico* red antique]

**Ross seal** (rôs, ros), a small, rather rare hair seal of antarctic regions. [< James C. *Ross,* 1800-1862, a British polar explorer]

**Ross's goose**, a white goose of arctic America with black primary feathers, similar to the snow goose, but smaller. [< Bernard R. *Ross,* 1827-1874, chief trader of the Hudson's Bay Company]

**ros|tel|lar** (ros tel′ər), *adj.* of, having to do with, or resembling a rostellum.

**ros|tel|late** (ros′tə lit, -lāt), *adj.* having a rostellum. [< New Latin *rostellatus* < Latin *rōstellum* (diminutive) < *rōstrum* beak; see etym. under **rostrum**]

**ros|tel|lum** (ros tel′əm), *n., pl.* **-tel|la** (-tel′ə). **1** any small part shaped like a beak, such as the stigma of many violets. **2** a modified stigma in many orchids that bears the glands to which the masses of pollen are attached. [< Latin *rōstellum* (diminutive) < *rōstrum;* see etym. under **rostrum**]

**ros|ter** (ros′tər), *n.* **1** a list giving each person's name and duties: *Many "servants" are mentioned in the roster of the Mayflower* (H. G. Wells). **2** any list of persons or things: *In spite of the unique requirements for membership, the Club roster grows* (Newsweek). [< Dutch *rooster* list; (originally) gridiron < *roosten* to roast; the shift of meaning is because the parallel lines on a list resemble a gridiron]

**ros|tral** (ros′trəl), *adj.* **1** of or having to do with a rostrum. **2** adorned with beaks of warships. [< Late Latin *rōstrālis* < *rōstrum;* see etym. under **rostrum**]

**ros|trate** (ros′trāt), *adj. Biology.* having a beaklike part.

**ros|trum** (ros′trəm), *n., pl.* **-trums, -tra** (-trə). **1** a platform for public speaking: *Mr. Tappertit mounted on an empty cask which stood by way of a rostrum in the room* (Dickens). *A brief discussion of colonial affairs brought a few left-wing delegates to the rostrum to criticize the Government's policy* (London Times). SYN: stage, dais. **2** the platform in the forum in ancient Rome from which public speakers delivered orations. **3** a portable stage platform, usually one that folds up. **4** the beak of an ancient war galley. **5** *Biology.* a part or structure resembling a beak, such as a snout. [< Latin *rōstrum* beak, prow of a ship, related to *rōdere* gnaw (referring to the speakers' platform in the Roman forum, which was decorated with the beaks of captured galleys)]

**ros|u|late** (roz′yə lit, -lāt), *adj. Botany.* arranged in a rosette: *rosulate leaves.* [< Late Latin *rosula* (diminutive) < *rosa* rose[1] + English *-ate*[1]]

**ros|y** (rō′zē), *adj.,* **ros|i|er, ros|i|est. 1a** like a rose; pinkish-red; rose-red: *a rosy cloud, the rosy tints of sunset.* **b** blushing. **2a** decorated with roses. **b** made of roses. **3** *Figurative.* bright; cheerful: *a rosy future. Two Labor Department reports pictured a generally rosy employment picture across the nation* (Wall Street Journal).

**rosy finch**, any one of several brownish finches with pinkish wings and rump and a gray patch on the back of the head, found in the mountains of western North America.

**rot** (rot), *v.,* **rot|ted, rot|ting,** *n., interj.* —*v.i.* **1** to become rotten; decay; spoil: *So much rain will make the fruit rot.* SYN: decompose, putrefy. See syn. under **decay. 2** to lose vigor. **3** *Figurative.* to decay morally or mentally; become corrupt; degenerate.
—*v.t.* **1** to cause to decay: *So much rain will rot the fruit.* **2** to moisten or soak (as flax) in order to soften; ret.
—*n.* **1** the process of rotting; decay: *In the damp cellar rot destroyed many of the beams of the house.* **2** rotten matter. **3** a liver disease of animals, especially of sheep, caused by a liver fluke and marked by anemia, weakness, and swollen jaws. **4** any one of various diseases of plants marked by decay and caused by bacteria or fungi, such as crown rot. **5** any wasting disease. **6** *Informal, Figurative.* nonsense; rubbish: *I wish you wouldn't talk such infernal rot* (Arnold Bennett).
—*interj.* nonsense! rubbish! *There were exclamations of "Rot" and "Rubbish"* (London Times). [Old English *rotian*]

**rot.**, **1** rotating. **2** rotation.

**ro|ta** (rō′tə), *n., pl.* **-tas. 1** = roster. **2** a round; routine; rotation: *They have organized rotas and there are always three in the cottage, cooking, cleaning and mending* (Punch). **3** Often, **Rota.** an ecclesiastical tribunal of the Roman Curia forming a court of final appeal; Sacred Roman Rota. [< Latin *rota* a wheel]

**ro|tam|e|ter** (rō tam′ə tər), *n.* an instrument for measuring the distance covered by a wheel, especially for measuring curved lines. [< Latin *rota* wheel + English *-meter*]

**Ro|tar|i|an** (rō tãr′ē ən), *n., adj.* —*n.* a member of a Rotary Club. —*adj.* belonging to or having to do with Rotary Clubs.

**Ro|tar|i|an|ism** (rō tãr′ē ə niz′əm), *n.* the theories and practices of Rotarians.

**ro|ta|ry** (rō′tər ē), *adj., n., pl.* **-ries.** —*adj.* **1** turning like a top or a wheel; rotating. **2** (of motion) circular: *In the windmills that operate pumps the rotary motion must be changed into reciprocating (back-and-forth) motion* (Beauchamp, Mayfield, and West). **3** having parts that rotate. **4** of or having to do with a rotary engine.
—*n.* **1** a rotary engine or machine. **2** = traffic circle. **3** *Electricity.* a synchronous converter.
[< Medieval Latin *rotarius* < Latin *rota* wheel]

**Rotary Club**, an association of business and professional men formed with the purpose of serving their community. All Rotary Clubs are united in an international organization.

**rotary engine**, **1** a turbine engine, electric motor, or internal-combustion engine, in which the pistons, blades, armature, or similar parts rotate instead of moving in a straight line, or in which a cylinder rotates upon a piston. **2** an internal-combustion engine in aircraft, having radially arranged cylinders that revolve around a common fixed crankshaft.

**rotary hoe**, any one of various tools that cultivate soil with rotating prongs or blades.

**rotary plow** or **tiller**, a tool with blades on a revolving horizontal shaft. The revolving blades rip up and break up the soil. It is also used to clear snowdrifts.

**rotary press**, a printing press using revolving cylinders for both the printing part and the surface to be printed.

**rotary table**, a heavy steel turntable which turns the bit in drilling for oil.

**rotary wing**, the lifting surface of a helicopter or autogiro.

**ro|tat|a|ble** (rō′tā tə bəl, rō tā′-), *adj.* that can be rotated.

**ro|tat|a|bly** (rō′tā tə blē, rō tā′-), *adv.* in a rotatable manner; so as to be rotated.

**ro|tate**[1] (rō′tāt), *v.,* **-tat|ed, -tat|ing.** —*v.i.* **1** to move around a center or axis; turn in a circle; revolve. Wheels, tops, and the earth rotate. SYN: See syn. under **turn. 2** to change in a regular order; take turns; alternate: *The officials will rotate in office.*
—*v.t.* **1** to cause to turn around. **2** to cause to take turns: *to rotate men in office. Farmers rotate crops in a field.*
[< Latin *rotāre* (with English *-ate*[1]) < *rota* a wheel]

**ro|tate**[2] (rō′tāt), *adj. Botany.* spreading out nearly flat like a wheel; wheel-shaped, as a corolla with a short tube and spreading limb. [< Latin *rota* wheel + English *-ate*[1]]

**ro|ta|tion** (rō tā′shən), *n.* **1a** the act or process of turning around a center or axis; turning in a circle; revolving: *the rotation of a top. The earth's rotation causes night and day.* **b** the time required for one such movement. **c** one such movement. **2** change in a regular order. **3** *Military.* the exchange of individuals or units in hazardous or uncomfortable areas with those more favorably located.
**in rotation**, in turn; in regular succession: *We all had a chance to recite in rotation. All being summoned in rotation, my own turn came at last* (Herman Melville).

**ro|ta|tion|al** (rō tā′shə nəl), *adj.* of or with rotation. —**ro|ta′tion|al|ly**, *adv.*

**rotation of crops**, the varying from year to year of the crops grown in the same field to keep the soil from losing its fertility; crop rotation.

**ro|ta|tive** (rō′tə tiv), *adj.* **1** rotating. **2** having to do with rotation. —**ro′ta|tive|ly**, *adv.*

**ro|ta|tor** (rō′tā tər), *n., pl.* **ro|ta|tors,** *also* **ro|ta|to|res** (rō′tə tôr′ēz, -tōr′-) *for 2.* **1** a person or thing that rotates. **2** a muscle that turns a part of the body: *Muscles that rotate a body part are called rotators, some of which move the structure clockwise and others move it counterclockwise* (A. M. Winchester). [< Latin *rotātor* < *rotāre;* see etym. under **rotate**[1]]

**ro|ta|to|ry** (rō′tə tôr′ē, -tōr′-), *adj.* **1** turning like a top or wheel; rotating; rotary: *rotatory motion.* **2** causing rotation: *a rotatory muscle.* **3** passing or following from one to another in succession: *a rotatory office in a club.*

**rotatory power**, the property possessed by certain substances and solutions of rotating the plane of polarization.

**ROTC** (no periods) or **R.O.T.C.**, Reserve Officers' Training Corps.

**rotche** or **rotch** (roch), *n.* = dovekie. [earlier *rotge;* origin uncertain]

**rote**[1] (rōt), *n.* a set, mechanical way of doing things: *The rote learning of rules once so universal* (James Grant).
**by rote**, by memory without thought of the meaning: *Most people learn the alphabet by rote. The hearers of such literature ... had to get it by rote* (Maurice Hewlett).
[Middle English *rote;* origin uncertain]

**rote**[2] (rōt), *n.* a kind of medieval stringed musical instrument resembling a lyre. [< Old French *rote* < Medieval Latin *rotta,* or < a Germanic word < Celtic (compare Welsh *crwth* crowd[2])]

**rote**[3] (rōt), *n.* the sound of the sea or surf: *The rote of the sea from its sandy coast ... Seemed the murmurous sound of the judgment host* (John Greenleaf Whittier). [origin uncertain. Compare Old Icelandic *rjōta,* Norwegian *rut.*]

**ro|te|none** (rō′tə nōn), *n.* a white, crystalline compound obtained from the roots of various plants, used as an insecticide and fish poison. It is relatively harmless to birds and mammals. *Formula:* $C_{23}H_{22}O_6$ [< Japanese *roten* derris (plant) + English *-one*]

**rot|gut** (rot′gut′), *n. U.S. Slang.* cheap whiskey; bad or adulterated liquor.

***ro|ti|fer** (rō′tə fər), *n.* any one of a phylum of complex, microscopic water animals that have one or more rings of cilia on a disk at the head of the body, which aid in locomotion and drawing in food: *Small ponds appear choked with gelatinous algae and microscopic animals such as rotifers* (Gabriele Rabel). [< New Latin *Rotifera* the phylum name < Latin *rota* wheel + *ferre* to carry]

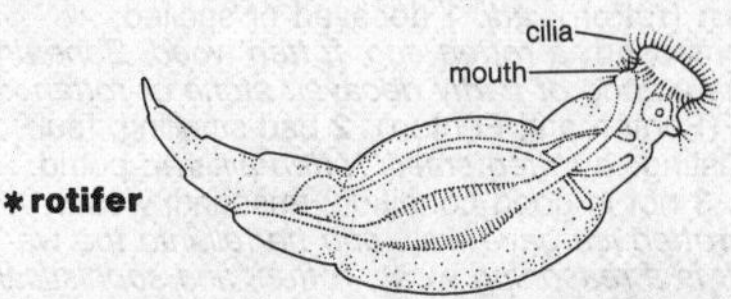

***rotifer**

**ro|tif|er|al** (rō tif′ər əl), *adj.* **1** of or having to do with the rotifers. **2** having a wheel or wheellike organ.

**ro|tif|er|ous** (rō tif′ər əs), *adj.* = rotiferal.

**ro|tis|se|rie** (rō tis′ər ē), *n.* **1** a spit for roasting food, often enclosed in a hood and turned by an electric motor. **2** a restaurant or shop that sells meats and poultry cooked on a spit. [< French *rotisserie* < *rôtir* roast]

**rot|l** (rot′əl), *n., pl.* **ar|tal. 1** a unit of weight used in North Africa and nearby parts of Europe and Asia. It corresponds roughly to the pound but varies according to place. **2** a dry measure, used in the same areas and also varying greatly. [< Arabic *raṭl* < Greek *lītrā,* or Latin *lībra* a pound[1]]

**ro|to**[1] (rō′tō), *n., pl.* **-tos.** = rotogravure. [shortened < *rotogravure*]

**ro|to**[2] (rō′tō), *n., pl.* **-tos.** (in Latin America) a person living in a slum or shantytown; very poor person. [< American Spanish *roto* (literally) tattered one]

**ro|to|chute** (rō′tə shüt), *n.* a parachute with freely turning blades, like the rotor of an autogiro, instead of a canopy to slow descent. [< *roto*(r) + (para)*chute*]

**ro|to|graph** (rō′tə graf, -gräf), *n.* a photograph printed by running a strip of sensitized paper under a negative, producing a succession of copies. [< Latin *rota* wheel + English *-graph*]

**ro|to|gra|vure** (rō′tə grə vyůr′, -grā′vyər), *n.* **1** a process of printing from an engraved copper cylinder on which the pictures, letters, or designs have been depressed instead of raised. **2** a print or picture made by this process. **3** a section of a newspaper having such pictures. **4** a kind of pa-

**Pronunciation Key:** hat, āge, cãre, fär; let, ēqual, tėrm; it, īce; hot, ōpen, ôrder; oil, out; cup, půt, rüle; child; long; thin; ᴛʜen; zh, measure; ə represents a in about, e in taken, i in pencil, o in lemon, u in circus.

per on which rotogravure and many picture sections and picture magazines are usually printed: *[They] changed the weekly from rough newsprint to slick rotogravure* (Newsweek). [American English < *roto*(graph) + *gravure*]

**ro|ton** (rō′ton), *n.* a quantum of energy involving the rotating motion of liquid helium atoms, analogous to the phonon: *A roton ... can form in superfluid helium at temperatures near absolute zero* (Science News). [< Latin *rotāre* rotate + English *-on*]

**ro|tor** (rō′tər), *n.* **1** the rotating part of a machine or apparatus: *the rotor of a centrifugal pump. The blades of the rotors are carefully curved and streamlined to make the turbine as efficient as possible* (Beauchamp, Mayfield, and West). **2** the system of rotating blades by which a helicopter is able to fly. **3** the armature or other rotating part of an electric motor or generator. [short for *rotator*]

**ro|tor|craft** (rō′tər kraft′, -kräft′), *n., pl.* **-craft.** a helicopter or other aircraft driven by a rotor: *Despite his enthusiasm for rotorcraft, he makes it clear that they will not be used by private fliers for commuting* (New York Times).

**rotor mast**, a rotating cylinder rising above the deck to propel a rotor ship.

**rotor ship**, a ship equipped with a rotor mast in place of sails.

**ro|to section** (rō′tō), the section of a newspaper printed by rotogravure.

**ro|to|till** (rō′tə til′), *v.t., v.i.* to break up the soil with a rotary plow or tiller: *In a mulched area, I never plow or rototill but simply open up a seed furrow with a hoe each spring* (New York Times).

**ro|to|till|er** (rō′tə til′ər), *n.* a rotary plow or tiller: *A power cultivator of the rototiller type is the most efficient tool for the job* (New York Times).

**ro|to|vate** (rō′tə vāt), *v.t., v.i.,* **-vat|ed, -vat|ing.** *British.* to rototill: *Not until the light soil was really dry in late April was the area rotovated twice, and set with sprouted seed* (London Times).

**ro|to|va|tor** (rō′tə vā′tər), *n. British.* a rototiller: *Mechanical rotovators and tillers will turn over the soil and applications of balanced fertilisers or composts will ensure fertility* (Sunday Times). [alteration of earlier *rotavator* < *rota*(ry culti)*vator*]

**rot|sy** or **rot|see** (rot′sē), *n. U.S. Slang.* the ROTC: *"Rotsee," as collegians call it, remains highly popular* (Time). [< pronunciation of *ROTC*]

**rot|ten** (rot′ən), *adj.* **1** decayed or spoiled; decomposed: *a rotten egg, rotten wood. Beneath this is a zone of partly decayed stone or rotten rock* (Fenton and Fenton). **2** bad-smelling; foul; disgusting: *a rotten smell, rotten air.* **SYN**: putrid, fetid. **3** not in good condition; unsound; weak: *The rotten ice gave way, and he fell into the water. It is a reasoning weak, rotten, and sophistical* (Edmund Burke). **4** *Figurative.* corrupt; dishonest: *rotten government. Something is rotten in the state of Denmark* (Shakespeare). **5** bad; nasty: *rotten luck, to feel rotten, a rotten joke, to have a rotten time. He said furiously, "You loved Scobie," and added quickly, "Sorry. Rotten thing to say"* (Graham Greene). [< Scandinavian (compare Old Icelandic *rotinn*)] **—rot′ten|ly,** *adv.* **—rot′ten|ness,** *n.*

**rotten borough, 1** a borough in England before 1832 that had only a few voters, but kept the privilege of sending a member to Parliament. **2** any electoral district having an insufficient number of voters to justify the representation it has.

**rot|ten|stone** (rot′ən stōn′), *n.* a decomposed limestone that resembles silica, used as a powder for polishing metals.

**rot|ter** (rot′ər), *n. British Slang.* a vile or objectionable person; scoundrel: *a thorough rotter. One does not feel a rotter For one is doing good* (Punch). [< *rot,* verb + *-er*[1]]

**rot|ting** (rot′ing), = retting.

**rott|weil|ler** (rot′wī′lər), *n.* any one of a breed of short-haired, black and tan working dogs developed from cattle dogs used by the Romans. Today they are trained for police work. [< German *Rottweiler* < *Rottweil,* a city in West Germany]

**ro|tund** (rō tund′), *adj.* **1** round or plump: *a rotund face.* **2** sounding rich and full; full-toned: *a rotund voice.* **SYN**: sonorous. [< Latin *rotundus,* related to *rota* wheel. See etym. of doublet **round**[1].] **—ro|tund′ly,** *adv.* **—ro|tund′ness,** *n.*

***ro|tun|da** (rō tun′də), *n.* **1** a round building or part of a building, especially one with a dome. **2** a large, high, circular room: *The Capitol at Washington has a large rotunda. The band played in the rotunda in honor of the minister of Militia as he was dining* (Calgary [Alberta, Canada] Eye Opener). See picture above. [< Italian *rotonda,* feminine of *rotondus,* learned borrowing from Latin *rotundus;* see etym. under **rotund**]

**ro|tun|di|ty** (rō tun′də tē), *n., pl.* **-ties. 1** roundness or plumpness. **SYN**: chubbiness. **2** something round. **SYN**: sphere. **3** rounded fullness of tone: *[His] language was unequaled, said Churchill, "in point, in rotundity, in antithesis or in comprehension"* (Time). **SYN**: sonority.

**ro|ture** (rô tyr′), *n.* **1** a low rank. **2** *French-Canadian Law.* rented possession without any privileges. [< French *roture* < Middle French, newly cleared field < Latin *ruptūra* a breaking; see etym. under **rupture**]

**ro|tu|rier** (rô ty ryā′), *n., pl.* **-riers** (-ryā′). a person of low rank. [< French *roturier* < *roture;* see etym. under **roture**]

**rou|ble** (rü′bəl), *n.* = ruble.

**rouche** (rüsh), *n.* = ruche.

**rou|é** (rü ā′, rü′ā), *n.* a dissipated man; rake: *I knew him for a young roué of a vicomte—a brainless and vicious youth* (Charlotte Brontë). **SYN**: profligate. [< French *roué,* (originally) past participle of Old French *rouer* break on the wheel < *roue* wheel < Latin *rota* (first applied around 1720 to a group of profligates, companions of the Duc d'Orléans)]

**Rou|en** (rü än′, -äN′), *n.* any one of a breed of large domestic ducks developed from and resembling mallards. [< *Rouen,* a city in northern France]

**rouge** (rüzh), *n., v.,* **rouged, roug|ing.** **—*n.*** **1** a red powder, paste, or liquid for coloring the cheeks or lips. **2** a red powder, chiefly an oxide of iron, used especially for polishing metal, jewels, and glass.

**—*v.t.*** to color with rouge: *She was admirably rouged and powdered* (Arnold Bennett).

**—*v.i.*** to use rouge on the face: *Fanny Minafer, who rouged a little* (Booth Tarkington).

[< French *rouge* < Old French *roge* red < Latin *rubeus* < *ruber* red]

**rouge et noir** (rüzh′ ā nwär′), a gambling game at cards, played on a table marked with two red and two black diamond-shaped spots that the players place their bets on. [< French *rouge et noir* red and black (see etym. under **rouge**); *noir* < Latin *niger*]

**rou|geot** (rü zhō′), *n.* a disease of grape leaves, causing them to turn red and die. [< French *rougeot* < *rouge* red]

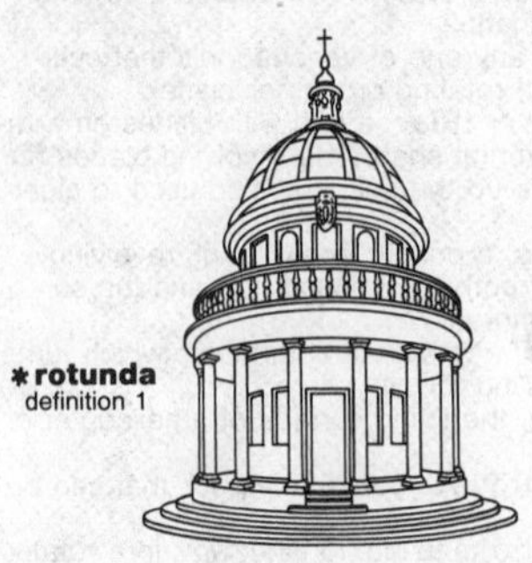

***rotunda**
definition 1

**rough** (ruf), *adj., n., v., adv.* **—*adj.*** **1** not smooth; not level; not even: *rough boards, the rough bark of oak trees, rough hilly country covered with rocks.* **2** stormy: *rough weather, a rough sea.* **SYN**: inclement. **3** likely to hurt others; not gentle; harsh; rude: *rough manners. My temper is rough, and will not be controlled* (William Godwin). **SYN**: discourteous, impolite, uncivil. **4a** without luxury and ease: *rough life in camp.* **SYN**: uncultivated, unpolished. **b** without culture or refinement: *a rough soldier with little education.* **5** without polish or fine finish: *rough diamonds.* **6** not completed or perfected; done as a first try; without details: *a rough drawing, a rough idea. It is impossible to make any but the roughest guess at the numbers of these Northwestern Indians* (Theodore Roosevelt). **SYN**: approximate, imperfect, incomplete, preliminary. **7** coarse and tangled: *rough fur, a dog with a rough coat of hair.* **SYN**: shaggy, bristly. **8** *Informal.* unpleasant; hard; severe: *I was in for a rough time. Being out of work is rough on a man with a wife and children. It was early to prophesy and conditions were still "pretty rough," yet a courageous start had been made* (London Times). **SYN**: drastic, rigorous. **9** disorderly; riotous: *a rough crowd.* **SYN**: boisterous, tumultuous. **10** requiring merely strength rather than intelligence or skill: *rough work.* **11a** harsh, sharp, or dry to the taste: *rough wines.* **b** harsh to the ear; grating; jarring: *rough sounds, a rough voice.* **12** *Phonetics.* pronounced with an aspirate; having the sound of *h.* **13** uneven in pulse or sound and operating improperly, as an internal-combustion engine that is misfiring: *The plane's Number 3 engine had backfired and had been rough* (New York Times).

**—*n.*** **1** a coarse, violent person: *Without an army Pompey could do little against the roughs in the streets* (James A. Froude). **2** ground that is rocky, filled with ravines and covered with underbrush and other natural debris. **3** a rough thing or condition; hard or unpleasant side or part: *to take the rough with the smooth.* **4** ground where there is long grass, etc., on a golf course, adjoining the fairways on either side: *He hooked his drive off the high tee into thick, impossible rough* (Time).

**—*v.t.*** **1** to make rough; roughen: *to rough the soles of new shoes to keep from slipping.* **2** to treat roughly: *The angry mob roughed up the suspected traitor.* **3** *Sports.* to subject (an opposing player) to unnecessary and intentional physical abuse. **4** to shape or sketch roughly: *to rough out a plan, to rough in the outlines of a face.*

**—*v.i.*** **1** to become rough. **2** to behave roughly.

**—*adv.*** in a rough manner; roughly: *Those older boys play too rough for me.*

**in the rough, a** not polished or refined; coarse; crude: *We must never forget that the truths of political economy are truths only in the rough* (John Stuart Mill). **b** in an untidy or informal state; in an everyday condition: *I wish you'd come with me, and take her in the rough, and judge her for yourself* (Dickens). **c** in an imperfect state; in a preliminary sketch or design: *Every kind of surface is first formed in the rough, and then finished by means of tools* (P. Nicholson).

**rough it,** to live without comforts and conveniences: *He has been roughing it in the woods this summer. He looked old ... as if he had roughed it all his life, and had found living a desperate long, hard grind* (George du Maurier).

[Middle English *rough,* Old English *rūh*]

**rough|age** (ruf′ij), *n.* **1** rough or coarse material. **2** the coarser parts or kinds of food. Bran, fruit skins, and straw are roughage. Roughage stimulates the movement of food and waste products through the intestines.

**rough-and-read|y** (ruf′ən red′ē), *adj.* **1** rough and crude, but good enough for the purpose; roughly effective: *Nor did he [Lincoln] make himself an exact lawyer; a rough-and-ready familiarity with practice ... contented him* (Baron Charnwood). **2** showing rough vigor rather than refinement: *He had a bluff, rough-and-ready face* (Robert Louis Stevenson).

**rough-and-tum|ble** (ruf′ən tum′bəl), *adj., n.*

**—*adj.*** showing confusion and violence; with little regard for rules; roughly vigorous; boisterous: *a rough-and-tumble football game, a rough-and-tumble campaign. This Grammick was no rough-and-tumble type but ... a college man, soft-spoken* (Saul Bellow). **SYN**: riotous.

**—*n.*** a rough-and-tumble fight or struggle: *the rough-and-tumble of popular debate* (Baron Charnwood).

**rough bluegrass,** a perennial European grass, naturalized in North America and grown for lawns or pasturage.

**rough breathing,** *Greek Grammar.* **1** the mark placed over an initial vowel or rho to indicate aspiration. **2** having the sound of *h;* aspirated. [translation of Latin *spīritus asper*]

**rough burning,** the rapid changes in pressure at the beginning of the firing of a ramjet or rocket.

**rough|cast** (ruf′kast′, -käst′), *n., v.,* **-cast, -cast|ing.** **—*n.*** **1** a coarse plaster for outside surfaces. **2** a rough form or model.

**—*v.t.*** **1** to cover or coat with coarse plaster. **2** to make, shape, or prepare in a rough form: *to roughcast a story.* **—rough′cast′er,** *n.*

**rough collie,** a collie with a long, thick, coat.

**rough cut, 1** a type of tobacco chopped into irregular, small pieces. **2** a selection of the most effective film shots assembled from the daily rushes by a film editor: *They recently screened a rough cut of the picture for a small group of ... friends* (New Yorker).

**rough-dry** (ruf′drī′), *v.,* **-dried, -dry|ing,** *adj.*

**—*v.t.*** to dry (clothes) after washing without ironing. **—*adj.*** dried after washing but not ironed.

**rough|en** (ruf′ən), *v.t.* to make rough. **—*v.i.*** to become rough: *The broken landscape, by degrees Ascending, roughens into rigid hills* (James Thomson).

**rough|er** (ruf′ər), *n.* a workman who makes something in the rough; one who carries out the less finished operations of a work.

**rough-hew** (ruf′hyü′), *v.t.,* **-hewed, -hewed** or **-hewn, -hew|ing. 1** to hew (timber, stone, or other material) roughly or without smoothing or finishing. **2** to shape roughly; give crude form to: (*Figurative.*) *There's a divinity that shapes our ends, Rough-hew them how we will* (Shakespeare). **—rough′-hew′er,** *n.*

**rough-hewn** (ruf′hyün′), *adj.* **1** roughly shaped: *His figures are rough-hewn, still bear the sculptor's chisel marks* (Time). **2** without refinement; crude: (*Figurative.*) ... *[a] rough-hewn, painfully serious ... Illinois stock and grain farmer* (Time).

**rough|house** (ruf′hous′), *n., v.,* **-housed, -hous|ing.** *Informal.* **—*n.*** rough play; rowdy conduct; disorderly behavior.

—*v.i.* to act in a rough or disorderly way: *One driver on Second Avenue put off a group of pupils for roughhousing* (New York Times).
—*v.t.* to disturb by such conduct.

**rough|ish** (ruf′ish), *adj.* rather rough.

**rough|leg** (ruf′leg′), *n.* = rough-legged hawk.

**rough-leg|ged hawk** (ruf′leg′id), a North American hawk with plumage which varies from brown and white to a melanistic phase.

**rough lumber**, lumber having straight sides and edges, but rough and splintery, as distinguished from fully dressed lumber.

**rough|ly** (ruf′lē), *adv.* **1** in a rough manner. **2** approximately: *From New York to Los Angeles is roughly three thousand miles.* **SYN**: about.

**rough|neck** (ruf′nek′), *n.* **1** *Informal.* a rough, coarse person. **2** *U.S.* a skilled worker on an oil-drilling rig.

**rough|ness** (ruf′nis), *n.* **1** the quality of being rough. **2** rough condition. **3** a rough part or place: *There were other breaks and roughnesses on that flat green expanse* (W. H. Hudson).

**rough|ride** (ruf′rīd′), *v.i., v.t.,* **-rode, -rid|den, -rid|ing. 1** to break in and ride (a rough, wild horse or horses). **2** to ride over or overcome by rough tactics: *Tough as they were, they were supposed to have a rough time with Army's roughriding halfbacks* (Time).

**rough|rid|er** (ruf′rī′dər), *n.* **1** a person used to rough, hard riding: *the roughrider of the plains, the hero of rope and revolver* (Theodore Roosevelt). **2** a person who breaks in and rides rough, wild horses.

**Rough|rid|ers** (ruf′rī′dərz), *n.pl.,* or **Rough Riders**, members of a volunteer cavalry regiment organized by Theodore Roosevelt and Leonard Wood during the Spanish-American War.

**rough|shod** (ruf′shod′), *adj.* having horseshoes with calks to prevent slipping.
**ride roughshod over**, to domineer over; show no consideration for; treat roughly: *He had a sensitive distaste for riding roughshod over anybody's feelings* (London Times).

**rough sledding**, *Informal.* unfavorable conditions; difficult going: *Many of these proposals could encounter rough sledding* (Wall Street Journal).

**rough-winged swallow** (ruf′wingd′), a grayish North American swallow with a brownish back, that nests in a hole which it digs in a bank.

**rou|lade** (rü läd′), *n., v.,* **-lad|ed, -lad|ing.** —*n.* **1** a slice of meat rolled about a filling, as of chopped meat, carrot, parsley, and seasonings, and cooked. **2** a rapid succession of tones sung to a single syllable: *Singers stepped out of character at will, indulging in barbarous cadenzas or improvised roulades* (Time). —*v.i. Music.* to sing roulades. [< French *roulade* < *rouler* to roll]

**rou|leau** (rü lō′), *n., pl.* **-leaux** or **-leaus** (-lōz′). **1** a roll of coins wrapped in paper. **2** a roll; coil. [< French *rouleau* < Middle French *rolel* < Old French *role* or *roule;* see etym. under **roll**]

**rou|lette** (rü let′), *n., v.,* **-let|ted, -let|ting.** —*n.* **1** a gambling game in which the players bet on the numbered or colored section of a revolving wheel into which a small ball will come to rest. **2** a small wheel with sharp teeth for making lines of marks, dots, or perforations: *a roulette for perforating sheets of postage stamps.* **3** *Philately.* one of the separations cut in a sheet of stamps.
—*v.t.* to cut, mark, or pierce with a roulette. [< French *roulette* < Old French (diminutive) < *rouel* wheel (diminutive) < *roue* < Latin *rota* wheel. Compare etym. under **rowel.**]

**roul|roul** (rül′rül), *n.* a partridgelike bird of Java, Sumatra, Borneo, and surrounding areas. The male has a rich-green body and a long, red crest.

**Roum.**, **1** Roumania. **2** Roumanian.

**Rou|ma|ni|an** (rü mā′nē ən, -mān′yən), *adj., n.* = Romanian.

**rounce** (rouns), *n. Printing.* a pulley on a hand printing press with bands turned by a handle to run the type bed in and out under the platen. [< Dutch *rondse, ronse.* Compare *rond* round.]

**round**[1] (round), *adj., n., v., adv., prep.* —*adj.* **1** shaped like a ball, a ring, the trunk of a tree, or the like; having a circular or curved outline or surface: *a round hoop, a round bowl, a round hatbox, a round tabletop. Oranges are round. Candles and columns are usually round.* **SYN**: cylindrical, spherical, globular. **2** plump: *Her figure was short and round.* **SYN**: stout. **3** by, with, or involving a circular movement: *round dancing.* **4** *Figurative.* **a** full; complete; entire: *a round dozen; ... a round score of muskets* (Robert Louis Stevenson). **b** large; considerable: *a good, round sum of money.* **5** *Figurative.* plain-spoken; plainly expressed; frank: *The boy's father scolded him in good round terms. I will a round unvarnish'd tale deliver* (Shakespeare). **6** *Figurative.* **a** with a full tone: *a mellow, round voice.* **b** full-bodied: *Fine beer, the experts say, should taste "round" ... no rough edges, a smooth harmony of flavors* (New Yorker). **7** vigorous; brisk; quick: *I rode at a round trot.* **8** *Phonetics.* spoken with the lips rounded: *"O" is a round vowel.* **9** stated in round numbers: *He returned me immediately an order on the paymaster for the round sum of one thousand pounds, leaving the remainder to the next account* (Benjamin Franklin). **10** rough; approximate: *a round estimate. I may form a round guess ...* (Scott).
—*n.* **1** anything shaped like a ball, circle, tree trunk, or the like. The rungs of a ladder are sometimes called rounds. **2** a fixed course ending where it begins: *The watchman makes his round of the building every hour.* **3a** movement in a circle or about an axis: *the earth's yearly round.* **b** a roundabout way or course: *You took them in a round, while they supposed themselves going forward* (Oliver Goldsmith). **4** a series (as of duties, events, or drinks); routine: *a round of pleasures, a round of duties. Serve out a round of brandy to all hands* (Robert Louis Stevenson). **5** the distance between any limits; range; circuit: *the round of human knowledge.* **6a** a section of a game or sport, such as in a boxing match or a number of shots in archery at specified distances allowed each archer: *the semifinal round in a tournament.* **b** a complete game or unit: *a round of golf.* **c** the number of holes in a game of golf, usually 18, or in a match, 18, 36, or more. **7a** a discharge, as of firearms or artillery, especially by a group of soldiers at the same time. **b** bullets, powder, or shells, for one such discharge, or for a single shot: *The sergeant had only three rounds of ammunition left in his rifle.* **8** an act that a number of people do together: *a round of applause, a round of cheers.* **9** a dance in which the dancers move in a circle; round dance. **10** a short song, sung by several persons or groups beginning one after the other. "Three Blind Mice" is a round. **11** a cut of beef just above the hind leg and below the rump.
—*v.t.* **1** to make round: *The carpenter rounded the corners of the table. We round our lips when we say "oo." The healthy air rounded her cheeks.* **2** to go wholly or partly around: *They rounded the island. The ship rounded Cape Horn. The car rounded the corner at high speed.* **3** to take a circular course about; make a complete or partial circuit of: *The spacecraft rounded the moon.* **4** *Figurative.* to fill; complete: *We are such stuff as dreams are made on; and out little life is rounded with a sleep* (Shakespeare). **5** to surround; encircle: *The hollow crown That rounds the mortal temples of a king* (Shakespeare). **6** to cause to turn round or move in a circle: *She rounded her face toward him.* **7** *Phonetics.* to utter (a vowel) with a small circular opening of the lips.
—*v.i.* **1** to become round: *The little boy's lips rounded when he tried to whistle.* **2** to turn around; wheel about: *The men who met him rounded on their heels And wonder'd after him* (Tennyson). **3** to take a circular or winding course; make a complete or partial circuit: *The road rounded about the mountain. The night watchman rounds every half hour.* **4** *Figurative.* to become finished or complete.
—*adv.* **1** in a circle; with a whirling motion: *Wheels go round. The bird flew round and round.* **2** on all sides; in every direction; around: *The travelers were compassed round by dangers. So twice five miles of fertile ground With walls and towers were girdled round* (Samuel Taylor Coleridge). **3** in circumference; in distance around: *The pumpkin measures 50 inches round.* **4** by a longer road or way: *We went round by the grocery store on our way home.* **5** from one to another: *A report is going round that the schools will close.* **6** through a round of time: *Summer will soon come round again. It fetched us a dollar a day apiece all the year round* (Mark Twain). **7** about; around: *He doesn't look fit to be round.* **8** here and there: *I am just looking round.* **9** for all: *There is just enough cake to go round.* **10** in the opposite direction or course: *to turn round. She continued to sit very still, without looking round* (John Galsworthy). **11** to the opposite opinion: *to coax someone round.*
—*prep.* **1** so as to make a turn to the other side of: *We walked round the corner.* **2** so as to surround or encircle: *They built a fence round the yard. He ... saw ghosts dancing round him* (Thomas Love Peacock). *The Government yesterday put a smoke screen round the preparations for a show of force in the eastern Mediterranean* (London Times). **3** in all directions from; to all parts of: *We took our cousins round the town.* **4** about; around: *She stood still and looked round her.* **5** on all sdies of: *Arrows struck round the riders, but they were not hit.* **6** here and there in: *There are boxes for mail all round the city.* **7** throughout (a period of time): *The ivy stays green round the year.* **8** so as to revolve or rotate about: *a wheel's motion round its axis.*

**come around** or **round**. See under **come**.
**get round**. See under **get**.
**go the round**, to be passed, told, shown, etc., by many people from one to another: *This celebrated epistle ... created quite a sensation ... as it went the round after tea* (Thomas Hughes).
**in the round, a** having seats all around a central stage: *a theater in the round.* **b** in a form of sculpture in which the figures are apart from any background: *The cow's right horn must have been carried in the round, only the tip being attached to the background of the relief* (Alexander S. Murray). **c** in the open; showing all sides or aspects: *The whole pavilion, in fact, is a huge museum of modern art in the round* (Manchester Guardian). (*Figurative.*) *The new material ... does not alter our conception of Byron in any essential way, but it does help us to see him more in the round, both as a physical and as a social being* (New Yorker).
**make** (or **go**) **the rounds**, to go about from place to place in a fixed course ending where it begins: *The watchman made the rounds of the building.*
**round down** (or **up**), to convert (currency) to the lower (or higher) value of the nearest round number: *The Decimal Currency Board have made some clear recommendations by which the new halfpenny conversion table will enable prices sometimes to be rounded down, although some may be rounded up* (London Times).
**round in**, *Nautical.* to haul in: *Ease off the lee brace and round the yard in* (Richard Henry Dana).
**round off, a** to make or become round: *The lower* [*stone*] *... is shorter and rounded off instead of being square at the corners* (Scott). **b** *Figurative.* to finish; complete: *A referendum held last month rounded off this period of anxiety* (Manchester Guardian Weekly). **c** to express the approximate value of (a number) to the nearest hundredth, tenth, ten, hundred, and so on. 75.38 rounded off to the nearest tenth would be 75.4.
**round on** (or **upon**) **a** to attack or assail, especially in words: *Now everyone rounds on them and tells them that they are a selfish, grasping lot* (Punch). **b** to turn informer against; betray: *The self-alienated man gives way to impulses to round upon his associates and accuse them* (Edmund Wilson).
**round out, a** to make or become round: *Working at the wheel, the ceramist rounded out the form, and the bowl appeared finished.* **b** *Figurative.* to finish; complete: *to round out a paragraph after much thought, to round out a career and retire.*
**rounds**, the ringing of a set of bells from the highest tone through the major scale to the lowest tone: *A man well practiced in all that pertained to bells, whether rounds* [*or*] *changes* (Frederic T. Jane).
**round to**, *Nautical.* to come head up to the wind: *We rounded to and let go our anchor* (Richard Henry Dana).
**round up, a** to drive or bring (cattle or horses) together: *The cowboys rounded up the cattle.* **b** to gather together; collect: *It took the young couple a long time to round up enough money for a trip to Europe.* See also **round down.**
[< Old French *rond, roont* < Latin *rotundus,* related to *rota* wheel. See etym. of doublet **rotund.**] —**round′ness**, *n.*
▶ **round, around.** In informal usage *round* and *around* are used interchangeably, with a definite tendency to use *round* (or to clip the *a* of *around* so short that it would be taken for *round*). In formal English there is some tendency to keep *around* to mean "here and there" or "in every direction" and *round* for "in a circular motion" or "in a reverse motion": *I have looked all around. There aren't any around here. He is going round the world. Everyone turned round.*

**round**[2] (round), *Archaic.* —*v.i.* to whisper: *to round in one's ear.* —*v.t.* **1** to whisper (something): *The "Ghosts of Life" rounded strange secrets in his ear* (Thomas Carlyle). **2** to whisper to. [< obsolete *roun,* Old English *rūnian*]

**round|a|bout** (round′ə bout′), *adj., n.* —*adj.* **1** not straight; indirect: *a roundabout route, in a roundabout way.* **SYN**: circuitous. **2** that surrounds or encircles. **3** cut round at the bottom: *a roundabout coat or jacket.*
—*n.* **1** an indirect way, course, or speech. **2** a short, tight jacket for men or boys: *His close-buttoned blue cloth roundabout was new and natty* (Mark Twain). **3** *British.* traffic circle: *Already a*

**Pronunciation Key:** hat, āge, cãre, fär; let, ēqual, tėrm; it, īce; hot, ōpen, ôrder; oil, out; cup, pu̇t, rüle; child; long; thin; ᴛʜen; zh, measure; ə represents **a** in about, **e** in taken, **i** in pencil, **o** in lemon, **u** in circus.

*roundabout has been built at the capital's one road junction* (London Times). **4** *Especially British.* a merry-go-round: *a steam "roundabout," where wooden horses revolved to the blare of an organ* (Eden Phillpotts). —**round′a|bout′ness**, *n.*

**round angle**, a complete circle; an angle of 360 degrees.

**round arch**, a semicircular arch.

**round|arm** (round′ärm′), *adj.* performed or executed with an outward, circular movement of the arm: *Taylor was frequently off the target with roundarm blows to the head* (London Times).

**round clam**, an almost circular, edible American clam; quahog.

**round dance**, **1** a dance performed by couples with circular or revolving movements. **2** a folk dance with dancers in a circle.

**round|ed** (roun′did), *adj.* **1** round: *rounded edges.* **2** *Phonetics.* spoken by rounding the lips: *a rounded vowel. The word "joke" has a rounded sound "o." One can learn to produce the rounded front vowels by practising lip-positions before a mirror* (Leonard Bloomfield). **3** expressed in round numbers, as in even tens, hundreds, thousands, and so on. —**round′ed-ness**, *n.*

**roun|del** (roun′dəl), *n.* **1** a small round ornament, window, panel, tablet, insigne, or the like: *... with freshly painted RAF roundels on its flanks and the red flaring tail of its rocket motor protruding from the back* (New Scientist). **2** *Heraldry.* a circular figure used as a bearing, distinguished by its tincture: *a roundel sable.* **3** = rondeau. **4** = roundelay (def. 2). [< Old French *rondel* (diminutive) < *rond;* see etym. under **round**[1]]

**roun|de|lay** (roun′də lā), *n.* **1** a song or poem in which a phrase or a line is repeated again and again. **2** a dance in which the dancers move in a circle; round dance; roundel. [< Old French *rondelet* (diminutive) < *rondel* rondel; influenced by *lay*[4]]

**round|er** (roun′dər), *n.* **1** a person or thing that rounds something. **2** *Slang.* a habitual drunkard or criminal: *A "square John" is a man who does honest work for a living; a "rounder" is one who doesn't* (Maclean's). **3** *U.S. Slang.* a person who makes the rounds of places of amusement, especially disreputable places.

**round|ers** (roun′dərz), *n. pl.* a game, somewhat like baseball, played with a bat, ball, and bases. It originated in England.

**round-eyed** (round′īd′), *adj.* having the eyes rounded or wide open, as with wakefulness or astonishment; wide-eyed: *round-eyed and alert as an owl.*

**round game**, a game for four or more players during which each player plays for himself and does not have a partner.

**round hand**, a style of handwriting in which the letters are round and full.

**Round|head** (round′hed′), *n.* a Puritan who supported the Parliament in England during the English civil wars from 1642 to 1652. The Roundheads wore their hair cut short in contrast to the long curls of their opponents, the Cavaliers. *When, in October, 1641, the Parliament reassembled ... two hostile parties ... appeared confronting each other. During some years they were designated as Cavaliers and Roundheads* (Macaulay).

**round|head|ed** (round′hed′id), *adj.* **1** having a round head or top: *a roundheaded screw. A brachycephalic person is roundheaded.* **2** with the hair on the head cut short: *The Roundheads were so called because they were roundheaded.* **3** *Architecture.* topped with a semicircular arch. —**round′head′ed|ness**, *n.*

**round|heel** (round′hēl′), *n. U.S. Slang.* **1** a person who is easily swayed or unable to resist a particular appeal. **2** a promiscuous woman.

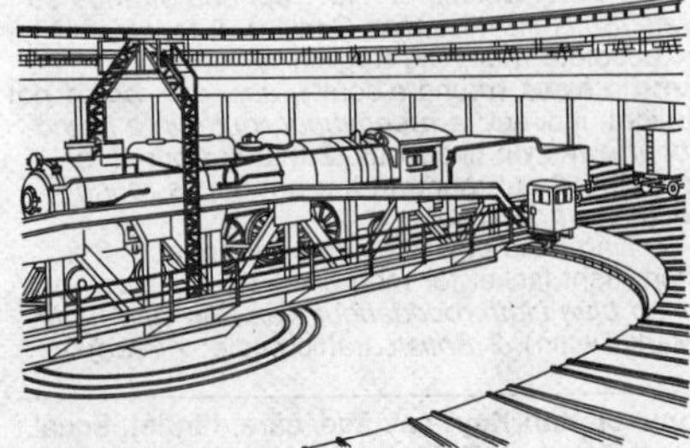

***roundhouse** definition 1

***round|house** (round′hous′), *n., adj.* —*n.* **1** a circular building for storing or repairing locomotives. It is built about a turntable. **2** a cabin on the after part of a ship's quarterdeck. **3** *Obsolete.* a jail. —*adj. Informal.* having or done with a sweeping or exaggerated curve, as a hook in boxing or a pitch in baseball: *Rocky crossed with a roundhouse right to the jaw* (Time).

**round|ing** (roun′ding), *adj.* that rounds; used in making something round: *a rounding tool, a rounding motion.*

**round|ish** (roun′dish), *adj.* somewhat round. —**round′ish|ness**, *n.*

**round-leaved sundew** (round′lēvd′), the commonest kind of sundew, found in moist, acid soil throughout most of the United States, and in parts of Canada, Europe, and Asia.

**round|let** (round′lit), *n.* **1** a small circle. **2** a small circular object. [< Old French *roundelet, rondelet;* see etym. under **rondelet**]

**round lot**, securities for trade, especially 100 shares of stock or $1,000 worth of bonds as a unit of exchange.

**round|ly** (round′lē), *adv.* **1** in a round manner; in a circle, curve, globe, or the like. **2** *Figurative.* plainly; bluntly; severely: *to refuse roundly, to scold roundly; ... roundly proclaimed himself at the end no theist but a thoroughgoing agnostic* (Scientific American). **3** *Figurative.* fully; completely.

**round number**, **1** a number in even tens, hundreds, thousands, and so on. 3874 in round numbers would be 3900 or 4000. **2** a whole number without a fraction.

**round of beef**, a cut of the thigh of beef through and across the bone.

**round pompano**, a species of pompano growing to about a foot in length and weighing about three pounds, found as far north as Cape Cod.

**round robin**, **1a** a petition, protest, or other document with the signatures written in a circle, so that it is impossible to tell who signed first. **b** any statement signed by a number of individuals. **2** a contest in which every player or team plays every other player or team.

**rounds** (roundz), *n.pl.* See under **round**[1].

**round-shoul|dered** (round′shōl′dərd), *adj.* having the shoulders bent forward.

**rounds|man** (roundz′mən), *n., pl.* **-men. 1** a person who makes rounds of inspection, especially a police inspector. **2** *British.* a deliveryman: *Between leaving school and going to the war, I was a milk roundsman* (Sunday Times).

**round steak**, a cut of beef just above the hind leg. See picture under **beef**.

**round|sters** (round′stərz), *n.* the act or right of selecting the best location outside the ring in the game of marbles; circling.

**Round Table**, **1** the table around which King Arthur and his knights sat. **2** King Arthur and his knights.

**round table**, a group of persons assembled, as for an informal discussion.

**round-ta|ble** (round′tā′bəl), *adj.* of or at a round table; informal: *a round-table discussion.*

**round-the-clock** (round′ᴛʜə klok′), *adj., adv.* —*adj.* continual; unceasing; around-the-clock: *round-the-clock protection.* [*He*] *told the Senate he hoped for a vote on his motion by the end of the week, even if he had to force round-the-clock sessions* (Wall Street Journal). —*adv.* throughout the day and night; without stopping: *to work round-the-clock.*

**round|tree** (round′trē′), *n.* the American mountain ash.

**round trip**, a trip to a place and back again. —**round′-trip′**, *adj.*

**round-trip|per** (round′trip′ər), *n. Slang.* a home run: [*He*] *slammed his third round-tripper of the day* (New York Times).

**round|up** (round′up′), *n.* **1a** the act of driving or bringing cattle together from long distances: *The missing ones* [*cattle*] *are generally recovered in the annual roundups, when the calves are branded* (Theodore Roosevelt). **b** the men and horses that do this. **2** *Figurative.* **a** a gathering: *a roundup of old friends. The answer from a roundup of scholars and business leaders is an enthusiastic affirmative* (Wall Street Journal). **b** a summing up; summary: *a roundup of late news.*

**roun|dure** (roun′jər, -dyůr), *n.* roundness; rounded form or space.

**round window**, an opening in the middle ear located below the oval window. It is covered with a membrane that serves as a secondary eardrum. See picture under **ear**[1].

**round|wood** (round′wůd′), *n.* = roundtree.

**round|worm** (round′wėrm′), *n.* any one of a group of worms that have long round bodies and live in soil or water or are parasitic in animals and plants; nematode. The hookworm, trichina, and filaria are roundworms. *There is hardly a spot on the earth that does not contain roundworms* (A. M. Winchester).

**round writing**, handwriting with strong curves and exaggerated shading, used especially in lettering and ornamental engraving.

**roup**[1] (rüp), *n.* **1** either of two diseases of poultry and pigeons characterized by hoarseness and a discharge of catarrh from the eyes, nostrils, and throat. One form of roup, caused by a protozoan, is contagious and is often fatal; the other is caused by a lack of vitamin A in the diet. **2** hoarseness or huskiness. [origin uncertain]

**roup**[2] (roup, rüp), *n., v. Scottish.* —*n.* an auction. —*v.i.* to cry or shout. —*v.t.* to auction: *An auctioneer ... rouped the kirk seats ... beginning by asking for a bid* (James M. Barrie). [< Scandinavian (compare Old Icelandic *raupa* boast)]

**roup|et** (rü′pit), *adj. Scottish.* roupy.

**roup|y** (rü′pē), *adj.,* **roup|i|er, roup|i|est. 1** affected with the disease roup. **2** hoarse or husky.

**rous|ant** (rou′zənt), *adj. Heraldry.* (of a bird) starting up as if about to fly.

**rouse**[1] (rouz), *v.,* **roused, rous|ing,** *n.* —*v.t.* **1** to wake up: *I was roused by the ring of the telephone.* **SYN:** awaken. **2** *Figurative.* **a** to stir up: *The dogs roused a deer from the bushes. Ethan, with a touch of his whip, roused the sorrel to a languid trot* (Edith Wharton). *The Franks forgot their first panic, roused themselves, rallied, resisted, overcame* (G. P. R. James). **b** to excite; arouse: *He was roused to anger by the insult. The ocean-going steamers ... roused in him wild and painful longings* (Arnold Bennett). **SYN:** provoke, stimulate, incite, inflame. **3** *Nautical.* to haul with great force: *You and the boy, rouse the cable up* (Frederick Marryat). —*v.i.* to become active; rise; wake: *Morpheus rouses from his bed* (Alexander Pope). —*n.* **1** the act of rousing. **2** a signal for rousing or action. [(originally, of a hawk) to shake the feathers; origin uncertain]

**rouse**[2] (rouz), *n. Archaic.* **1** a drinking party; carouse: *Fill the cup and fill the can. Have a rouse before the morn* (Tennyson). **2** a full draft of liquor; bumper. [perhaps short for *carouse*]

**rouse|a|bout** (rouz′ə bout′), *n. Australian.* a handyman, especially one on a sheep ranch. [< *rouse*[1] + *about*]

**rouse|ment** (rouz′mənt), *n. U.S.* **1** the act of rousing up, especially to religious fervor. **2** a noisy demonstration.

**rous|er** (rou′zər), *n.* **1** a person or thing that rouses to action. **2** *Informal.* something interesting or astonishing: *The candidate's speech was a rouser.*

**rous|ing** (rou′zing), *adj.* **1** that rouses; stirring; vigorous; brisk: *a rousing speech, to do a rousing business.* **2** *Informal.* outrageous; extraordinary: *a rousing lie.* —**rous′ing|ly**, *adv.*

**Rous sarcoma** (rous), a cancer of the connective tissue of poultry, caused by a virus containing ribonucleic acid. [< Francis P. *Rous,* 1879-1970, an American pathologist]

**Rous|seau|an** (rü sō′ən), *adj.* of, having to do with, or characteristic of the French author Jean Jacques Rousseau (1712-1778) or his views, as on religion, politics, and education: *The description of village conditions after the Revolution hardly encourages a Rousseauan view of peasant life* (Oscar Lewis).

**Rous|seau|ism** (rü sō′iz əm), *n.* the principles or doctrines of Jean Jacques Rousseau, especially in regard to social order and relations, or the social contract.

**Rous|seau|ist** (rü sō′ist), *n., adj.* —*n.* a follower of Rousseau or of his ideas. —*adj.* = Rousseauan.

**Rous|seau|is|tic** (rü′sō is′tik), *adj.* = Rousseauan.

**roust** (roust), *v.t. Informal.* to rout: **a** to move; stir: *to roust men out of their beds.* **b** to get; fetch. [perhaps alteration of *rouse*[1]]

**roust|a|bout** (roust′ə bout′), *n. U.S.* an unskilled laborer, as on wharves, ships, ranches, or in circuses or oil fields: *Roustabouts from the Clyde Beatty circus appeared to offer any manual labor needed* (Los Angeles Times). [American English < *roust* + *about*]

**roust|er** (rous′tər), *n. U.S.* a roustabout.

**rout**[1] (rout), *n., v.* —*n.* **1** the flight of a defeated army in disorder: *The enemy was in full rout. A retreat is painful enough; a rout borders on the unbearable* (New Yorker). **2** a complete defeat accompanied by disorderly retreat: *The enemy's defeat soon became a rout.* **3** a noisy, disorderly crowd; mob; rabble. **SYN:** riffraff. **4** a riot; disturbance. **5** a group of followers; train; retinue. **6** *Archaic.* a crowd; band: *a rout of roisterers* (Tennyson). **7** *Archaic.* a large evening party. —*v.t.* **1** to put to flight in disorder: *Our soldiers routed the enemy.* **2** *Figurative.* to defeat completely: *The baseball team routed its opponents by a score of ten to one.* **SYN:** vanquish. [< Old French *route* detachment, ultimately < Latin *rumpere* to break. See etym. of doublet **route**.]

**rout**[2] (rout), *v.t.* **1** to dig (out); get by searching: *Foraging about ... I routed out some biscuit ... and a piece of cheese* (Daniel Defoe). **2** to put (out); force (out, up): *The farmer routed his sons out of bed at five o'clock. From even this stronghold the unlucky Rip was at length routed by his termagant wife* (Washington Irving). **3** to root with the snout as pigs do. **4** to hollow out; scoop out; gouge. **—*v.i.*** **1** to dig with the snout: *The pigs were routing for nuts under the trees.* **2** to poke; search; rummage: *He had been routing among the piled newspapers under the kitchen dresser* (H. G. Wells). [variant of *root*[2]]

**rout**[3] (rout), *v.i. Dialect.* to snore. [Old English *hrūtan*]

**rout**[4] (rout, rüt), *v., n. Dialect.* **—*v.i.*** to roar; bellow.
**—*n.*** a roar; loud noise; uproar. Also, **rowt, rowte.** [< Scandinavian (compare Old Icelandic *rauta*)]

**rout cake** (rout), *British.* a kind of rich, sweet cake originally made for routs or evening parties. [< *rout*[1] (*n.* def. 7)]

**route** (rüt, rout), *n., v.,* **rout|ed, rout|ing.** **—*n.*** **1a** a way to go; road: *to take the shortest route. Will you go to the coast by the northern route? They ... arrived at the next inn upon the route of the stage-coach* (Henry Mackenzie). **SYN:** path. **b** a fixed, regular course or area, as of a person making deliveries or sales: *a newspaper route, a milk route. His route includes the south side of town.* **2** an order for soldiers to move from one place to another. **3** the course a kind of medicine takes through the body.
**—*v.t.*** **1** to arrange the route for: *The automobile club routed us on our vacation to Canada.* **2** to send by a certain route: *The signs routed us around the construction work and over a side road. Route this memo through the sales department.*
**go the route,** *Baseball.* to pitch a complete nine innings: *Paul Minner, a southpaw, went the route for the Cubs and gained his sixth victory* (New York Times).
[< French *route* < Old French < Latin *rupta* (*via*) (a way) opened up, (a passage) forced, feminine past participle of *rumpere* to break. See etym. of doublet **rout**[1].]
► **route.** The pronunciation *rüt* is general, but *rout* is in common use, especially in the Army and informally, as of newspaper and delivery routes.

**route|man** (rüt′man′, -mən; rout′-), *n., pl.* **-men.** **1** a man who makes deliveries of products or who sells goods over a particular route. **2** a man in charge of routing deliveries or work in a factory, office, or the like.

**route march,** a march of troops in route step.

**rout|er**[1] (rou′tər), *n., v.* **—*n.*** **1** any one of various tools or machines for hollowing out or furrowing. **2** a person who routs.
**—*v.t.*** to hollow out with a router.
[< *rout*[2] + *-er*[1]]

**rout|er**[2] (rü′tər, rou′-), *n.* **1** a person who arranges a route for someone or something. **2** a thing that sends by a certain route. [< *rout*(e) + *-er*[1]]

**route step,** **1** a way of marching in which troops maintain order but are permitted to break step and to talk. **2** a command to march in this manner: *The command "Route Step!" is given as troops approach a suspension bridge. When the soldiers break step, their weight is not thrown in the same direction at the same time* (Robert G. Hennes).

**routh** (rüth, routh), *n. Scottish.* plenty. [origin unknown]

**rou|tine** (rü tēn′), *n., adj.* **—*n.*** **1** a fixed, regular method of doing things; habitual doing of the same things in the same way: *Getting up and going to bed are parts of your daily routine. All this sort of thing was fresh and exciting at first, and then it began to fall into a routine and became habitual* (H. G. Wells). **2** an act or skit that is part of some entertainment: *The Marx brothers were famous for their comedy routines.* **3a** a set of coded instructions arranged in proper sequence to direct a computer to perform a sequence of operations. **b** the sequence of operations performed by a computer.
**—*adj.*** **1** using routine: *routine methods, a routine operation.* **2** average or ordinary; commonplace: *a routine day, routine regulations, a routine show with routine performances.*
[< French *routine* < *route* route] **—rou|tine′ness,** *n.*

**rou|tined** (rü tēnd′), *adj.* **1** subjected to or regulated by routine: *There we led a routined, rigorous existence in a residential community of over five hundred females* (Alison Adburgham). **2** disciplined in routine; practiced: [*He*] *is a thoroughly experienced and routined Heldentenor* (Atlantic).

**rou|ti|neer** (rü′tə nir′), *n.* a person who acts by, or adheres to a routine: *My poem "Flying Crooked" was written as a satire on the ingenious routineers of poetry, as also on the ingenious routineers of science ... who fail to understand that ... erratic flight provides a metaphor for all original and constructive thought* (Robert Graves).

**rou|tine|ly** (rü tēn′lē), *adv.* **1** as a matter of routine; regularly: *Routinely the youth squad checks bars for underage patrons* (Time). **2** in a routine manner; without varying: *The reactor has since been rebuilt and has operated routinely since 1957* (Scientific American).

**rout|ing plane** (rou′ting), a router used to plane molding or to plane the edge of a board into a particular shape.

**rou|ti|nier** (rü′tē nyā′), *n.* a very conservative or conventional orchestra conductor: *Heger, an experienced man, conducts with a firm grip on the music but in the fashion of a routinier, making little effort to achieve the dynamic scheme of the opera, letting the orchestra* (*a good one*) *play in a competent rather than inspired manner* (Harper's). [< French *routinier* (literally) routineer]

**rou|tin|ism** (rü tē′niz əm), *n.* adherence to routine.

**rou|tin|ist** (rü tē′nist), *n.* a person who believes in following or is dominated by routine.

**rou|tin|i|za|tion** (rü tē′nə zā′shən), *n.* **1** the act or process of routinizing: *Professor Brown is evidently horrified by the routinization of the imaginative which occurs in the contemporary academy* (Harper's). **2** the fact or state of being routinized: *Such routinization leaves little room for chance, luck, imagination, or excitement* (Science News Letter).

**rou|tin|ize** (rü tē′nīz), *v.t.,* **-ized, -iz|ing.** to cause to become a routine; make habitual: *to routinize a process or operation, to routinize religion.*

**rout seat** (rout), *British.* a light bench or chair rented for use at evening parties: *The waltz was over. He could see her now, on a rout seat against the wall* (John Galsworthy).

**roux** (rü), *n.* butter and flour cooked together to a stiff, brown paste, used to thicken and color sauces, soups, and other food. [< French (*beurre*) *roux* reddish-brown (butter) < Latin *russus* red]

**rove**[1] (rōv), *v.,* **roved, rov|ing,** *n.* **—*v.i.*** to wander; wander about; roam: *He loved to rove through the woods. For ten long years I roved about, living first in one capital, then another* (Charlotte Brontë). **SYN:** ramble, range. See syn. under **roam.**
**—*v.t.*** to wander over or through; cross; traverse: *to rove the woods. Their young men ... roved the spurs of the Alleghenies, in quest of marketable skins* (George Bancroft).
**—*n.*** the act of roving; ramble.
[Middle English *roven* to shoot (arrows) at random targets while moving; origin uncertain]

**rove**[2] (rōv), *v.* a past tense and a past participle of **reeve**[2].

**rove**[3] (rōv), *n., v.,* **roved, rov|ing.** **—*n.*** a sliver of wool, cotton, etc., drawn out and very slightly twisted in preparation for spinning.
**—*v.t.*** to form (as slivers of wool or cotton) into roves.
[origin uncertain]

**rove**[4] (rōv), *n.* a small ring of metal in which the point of a nail is flattened in building boats. [< Scandinavian (compare Old Icelandic *rō*)]

**rove beetle,** any long, thin beetle of a large group that run very fast and prey on other insects; staphylinid. Certain varieties live in decaying matter and in association with ants.

**rove-o|ver** (rōv′ō′vər), *adj.* of or having to do with a kind of poetic meter with a foot forming the end of one line and the first part of the next.

**rov|er**[1] (rō′vər), *n.* **1** a person who roves; wanderer: *The Indian of the west is a rover of the plain* (Washington Irving). **SYN:** roamer, rambler. **2** a mark selected at random in archery. **3** in croquet: **a** a ball that goes through all the arches. **b** the person playing this ball. **4** *British.* a senior Boy Scout, 18 years or older. **5** = lunar rover. [< *rov*(e)[1] + *-er*[1]]

**rov|er**[2] (rō′vər), *n.* **1** a pirate: *the rovers whom Scandinavia had sent forth to ravage Western Europe* (Macaulay). **2** a pirate ship: *Our ship ... was surprised ... by a Turkish rover of Sallee, who gave chase to us with all the sail she could make* (Daniel Defoe). [< Middle Dutch *roover opt zee* pirate, thief of the sea < *roven* to rob]

**rov|er**[3] (rō′vər), *n.* **1** a machine or frame for roving cotton, wool, or other fiber. **2** a person who operates a roving frame or machine. [< *rov*(e)[3] + *-er*[1]]

**rov|ing**[1] (rō′ving), *adj.* **1** wandering; roaming; nomadic: *the roving tribes of the desert, a roving band of robbers.* **2** inclined to wander or roam: *roving thoughts, a roving mind, a young lover with a roving eye.* **3** not limited to a particular place or sphere of activity: *a roving ambassador, a roving commission.* [< *rove*[1]]

**rov|ing**[2] (rō′ving), *n.* **1** the process of converting cotton, wool, or other fiber, into roves. **2** the soft, loose cord drawn out from a sliver by this process; a rove or roves. [< *rove*[3]]

**row**[1] (rō), *n., v.* **—*n.*** **1** a line of people or things, especially a straight line: *a row of houses. A row of children stood in front of the row of chairs. Corn is planted in rows.* **SYN:** file, series. **2** a street with a line of buildings on either side.
**—*v.t.*** to arrange in a row; place in rows.
**hard row to hoe,** a difficult thing to do: *The lecturer then set himself a hard row to hoe: the scholarly correction of everything his audience may have been taught at school about King John* (London Times).
**in a row, a** in line; in alignment: *three houses in a row.* **b** in succession; successively: *for the second day in a row.*
[Old English *rāw*]

**row**[2] (rō), *v., n.* **—*v.i.*** **1** to use oars to move a boat: *Row to the island. We rowed across the lake.* **2** (of a boat) to be moved by the use of oars.
**—*v.t.*** **1** to cause (a boat) to move by the use of oars. **2** to carry in a rowboat: *We were rowed to the shore.* **3** to perform (a race) by rowing. **4** to row against in a race. **5** to use (oars) for rowing. **6** to have (oars): *a boat rowing 8 oars.*
**—*n.*** **1** the act of using oars. **2** a trip in a rowboat: *It's only a short row to the island.*
[Old English *rōwan*] **—row′er,** *n.*

**row**[3] (rou), *n., v.* **—*n.*** **1** a noisy quarrel or disturbance; clamor; noise: *What's all this row about? It wasn't any ordinary difference of opinion; it was a "row"* (H. G. Wells). **SYN:** fracas, rumpus. **2** a squabble: *The children had a row over the bicycle.*
**—*v.i.*** to quarrel noisily; make noise; squabble.
**—*v.t.*** *Informal.* to scold.
[origin uncertain]

**row|an** (rō′ən, rou′-), *n.* **1** = European mountain ash. **2** its red, berrylike fruit. [< Scandinavian (compare Norwegian dialectal *raun*)]

**row|an|ber|ry** (rō′ən ber′ē, rou′-), *n., pl.* **-ries.** the berry of the rowan.

**rowan tree,** = European mountain ash.

**row|boat** (rō′bōt′), *n.* a boat moved by oars.

**row crop** (rō), a crop planted in rows, such as corn or cotton.

**row|de|dow** (rou′dē dou′), *n. Informal.* noise; uproar; disturbance. [probably < *row*[3]]

**row|dy** (rou′dē), *n., pl.* **-dies,** *adj.,* **-di|er, -di|est.** **—*n.*** a rough, disorderly, quarrelsome person. **SYN:** brawler.
**—*adj.*** rough; disorderly; quarrelsome.
[American English, probably < *row*[3]] **—row′di|ly,** *adv.* **—row′di|ness,** *n.*

**row|dy|dow** (rou′dē dou′), *n.* = rowdedow.

**row|dy|dow|dy** (rou′dē dou′dē), *adj. Informal.* characterized by noisy roughness. [probably < *rowdedow,* influenced by *rowdy*]

**row|dy|ish** (rou′dē ish), *adj.* like a rowdy; rough and disorderly; quarrelsome. **—row′dy|ish|ness,** *n.*

**row|dy|ism** (rou′dē iz əm), *n.* disorderly, quarrelsome conduct; rough, noisy behavior: *rowdyism at Halloween.*

**-rowed,** *combining form.* having ___ rows: *Six-rowed = having six rows.*

**row|el** (rou′əl), *n., v.,* **-eled, -el|ing** or (*especially British*) **-elled, -el|ling.** **—*n.*** **1** a small wheel with sharp points, attached to the end of a spur: *Striking his rowels into his horse, he was out of sight in an instant* (Jane Porter). **2** a piece of silk or other material inserted under the skin of an animal to cause a discharge of pus or fluid.
**—*v.t.*** **1** to spur (a horse) with a rowel; use a rowel on. **2** to insert a rowel in (an animal).
[< Old French *roel, rouelle* (diminutive) < *roue* wheel < Latin *rota.* Compare etym. under **roulette.**]

**row|en** (rou′ən), *n.* the second crop of grass or hay in a season; aftermath. [Middle English *rewayn,* apparently < unrecorded Old North French *rewain,* probably < Old French *re-* re- + *gaïn* gain[1]]

**row house** (rō), one of a row of attached houses of the same design, usually two floors high and occupied by one family.

**row|ing boat** (rō′ing), *British.* a rowboat.

**row|lock** (rō′lok′), *n.* a notch, metal support, or wooden pegs in which the oar rests in rowing; oarlock. [< *row*[2]; patterned on *oarlock*]

**rowt** or **rowte** (rout), *v.,* **rowt|ed, rowt|ing,** *n. Scottish.* roar; bellow; rout. [variant of *rout*[4]]

---

**Pronunciation Key:** hat, āge, cãre, fär; let, ēqual, tėrm; it, īce; hot, ōpen, ôrder; **oi**l, **ou**t; cup, pu̇t, rüle; **ch**ild; lo**ng**; **th**in; **ᴛʜ**en; **zh**, measure; ə represents **a** in about, **e** in taken, **i** in pencil, **o** in lemon, **u** in circus.

**rox|burghe** (roks′bėr′ō), *n.* a bookbinding of plain leather with cloth or paper boards and gilt leaves. [< the third Duke of *Roxburghe,* 1740-1804, a British collector of books]

**Roy.**, Royal.

**roy|al** (roi′əl), *adj., n.* —*adj.* **1a** of kings and queens: *the royal family.* **b** belonging to the family of a king or queen: *a royal prince.* **2** belonging to a king or queen: *royal power, a royal palace.* **3a** serving a king or queen: *the royal household.* **b** founded by, or under the patronage of, a king or queen: *the Royal Academy.* **4** from or by a king or queen: *a royal command.* **5** of a kingdom: *a royal army or navy.* **6** appropriate for a king or queen; splendid: *a royal welcome, a royal feast.* SYN: magnificent. **7** like a king; noble; majestic: *The lion is a royal beast.* SYN: august. **8** fine; excellent. **9** rich and bright: *royal red.* **10** chemically inert; noble: *royal metals.*
—*n.* **1** a small mast, sail, or yard, set above the topgallant. **2** a size of writing paper (19 X 24 inches). **3** a size of printing paper (20 X 25 inches). **4** *Informal.* a member of a royal family; royal personage: *The Swedish royals are French* (Time). *He thinks that his true parents are European royals* (Punch). **5** any one of various former coins, such as the ryal.
[< Old French *roial, real* < Latin *rēgālis* < *rēx, rēgis* king. See etym. of doublets **real²**, **regal.**]
—**roy′al|ly,** *adv.*
—*Syn. adj.* **1, 2 Royal, regal, kingly** mean of or belonging to a king or kings. **Royal** is the most general in application, describing people or things associated with or belonging to a king: *Sherwood Forest is a royal forest.* **Regal** emphasizes the majesty, pomp, and magnificence of the office, and is now used chiefly of people or things showing these qualities: *The general has a regal bearing.* **Kingly** emphasizes the personal character, actions, purposes, or feelings of or worthy of a king: *Tempering justice with mercy is a kingly virtue.*

**Royal Air Force**, the air force of Great Britain. *Abbr:* R.A.F.

**Royal Ann cherry**, a variety of sweet cherry having a pale yellow color, usually blotched with light red.

**royal antler**, the third branch of an antler.

**royal blue**, a bright purplish blue color.

**royal coachman**, a fishing fly with white wings, a greenish and red body, and a golden tail.

**royal commission**, in Canada: **a** a group of people commissioned by the Crown to conduct an inquiry into any matter that concerns the federal or provincial governments. **b** the inquiry conducted by such a group.

**royal demesne**, the private property of the Crown; crown lands.

**royal fern**, a fern with tall, upright fronds, growing in clumps.

**royal flush**, a straight flush in poker in which the highest card is an ace.

**roy|al|ism** (roi′ə liz əm), *n.* adherence to a king or to a monarchy.

**roy|al|ist** (roi′ə list), *n., adj.* —*n.* a supporter of a king or of a royal government, especially in times of evil war or rebellion.
—*adj.* of or having to do with royalists or royalism: *royalist principles, a royalist party.*

**Roy|al|ist** (roi′ə list), *n.* **1** a supporter of Charles I in England in his struggle with Parliament; Cavalier. **2** a supporter of the British in the American Revolution; Tory; Loyalist. **3** a supporter of the Bourbons in France since 1793.

**roy|al|is|tic** (roi′ə lis′tik), *adj.* = royalist.

**roy|al|ize** (roi′ə līz), *v.t.,* **-ized, -iz|ing.** to make royal.

**royal jelly**, a creamy, jellylike substance rich in vitamins and proteins, fed to the young larvae of honeybees and throughout the larval stage to queen bees to give the queen a longer life and greater fertility. A preparation containing royal jelly is used by women as a cosmetic. *The U.S. Government is inquiring whether the advertising and sale of royal jelly, the queen bee food, is a "racket"* (Science News Letter).

**royal mast**, the mast next above the topgallant.

**royal moth**, any large, hairy moth of a group, including the regal moth and imperial moth.

**royal palm**, a tall, graceful palm tree of tropical America that has a whitish trunk and is often planted for ornament.

**royal poinciana**, a tropical tree of the pea family often cultivated for its large spikes of scarlet and orange flowers; flamboyant.

**royal purple**, a dark bluish purple color.

**royal tennis**, = court tennis.

**royal tern**, a large tern, white with a grayish mantle. The royal tern is found along the coast in the warmer parts of North and South America.

**roy|al|ty** (roi′əl tē), *n., pl.* **-ties. 1** a royal person or royal persons. Kings, queens, princes, and princesses are royalty. **2** the rank or dignity of a king or queen; royal power: *The crown is a symbol of royalty.* **3** kingly nature; royal quality; nobility. SYN: kingliness. **4** a royal right or privilege. **5** a royal domain; realm. **6a** a share of the receipts or profits paid to an owner of a patent, copyright, or mineral right for the use of it. An author receives royalties from the publishers of his books. *He prevailed upon the management to pay a small royalty for the use of the fourth movement of Shostakovich's Fifth Symphony* (New Yorker). **b** a payment for the use of any one of various rights: *The joint enterprise will pay a royalty to the government, as the owner of the underground oil* (Time). [< Old French *roialte* < *roial;* see etym. under **royal**]

**royal water**, a mixture of nitric acid and hydrochloric acid; aqua regia: *It is termed royal water because of [its] action upon the noble, or royal, metals* (W. N. Jones).

**Roz|wi** (rōz′wē), *n., pl.* **-wi** or **-wis. 1** a member of a subgroup of the Mashona living in Rhodesia and western Mozambique. **2** the Bantu language of this group.

**roz|zer** (roz′ər), *n. British Slang.* a policeman or detective. [origin unknown]

**Rp.**, rupiah.

**R.P.**, **1** Reformed Presbyterian. **2** Regius Professor.

**R.P.E.**, Reformed Protestant Episcopal.

**RPG** (no periods), **1** report program generator (a computer language designed for programs involving analysis or tabulation of data). **2** rocket-propelled grenade.

**r.p.m.** or **rpm** (no periods), revolutions per minute.

**RPM** (no periods) or **R.P.M.**, resale price maintenance.

**R.P.O.** or **RPO** (no periods), **1** Railway Post Office. **2** Royal Philharmonic Orchestra.

**r.p.s.** or **rps** (no periods), revolutions per second.

**rpt.**, report.

**RPV** (no periods), remotely piloted vehicle (an unmanned aircraft controlled from the ground for use in aerial reconnaissance, target practice, bomb delivery, and the like): *The USAF has set up a new organization to manage RPV programmes, and is considering the use of RPVs fitted with warheads as "kamikaze" planes* (New Scientist).

**R.Q.** or **r.q.**, respiratory quotient.

**R.R.**, **1** railroad. **2** Right Reverend. **3** rural route.

**RRB** (no periods), Railroad Retirement Board.

**RR Lyrae star**, any variable star of a class with very short periods between fluctuations of brightness. Such fluctuations are usually less than a day.

**rRNA** (no periods), ribosomal RNA: *Then virtually everyone still believed that the templates were the RNA molecules (rRNA) found in the small cellular particles called ribosomes* (James D. Watson).

**rs.**, rupees.

**Rs** (no period), rupees.

**Rs.**, **1** reis. **2** rupees.

**R.S.**, **1** recording secretary. **2** Revised Statutes. **3** Royal Society.

**R.S.A.**, **1** Royal Scottish Academician. **2** Royal Scottish Academy.

**R.S.F.S.R.** or **RSFSR** (no periods), Russian Soviet Federated Socialist Republic.

**RSG** (no periods) or **R.S.G.**, regional seat of government.

**R.S.L.**, Royal Society of Literature.

**R.S.M.**, regimental sergeant major.

**R.S.P.C.A.** or **RSPCA** (no periods), *British.* The Royal Society for the Prevention of Cruelty to Animals.

**R.S.S.**, Fellow of the Royal Society (Latin, *Regiae Societatis Socius*).

**RSV** (no periods) or **R.S.V.**, **1** Revised Standard Version (of the Bible). **2** Rous sarcoma virus.

**R.S.V.P.** or **r.s.v.p.**, please answer (French, *répondez s'il vous plaît*).

**rt.**, right.

**r.t.**, reverberation time.

**RT** (no periods), **1** radiotelephone. **2** room temperature.

**rte.**, route.

**Rt. Hon.**, Right Honorable.

**RTO** (no periods), radiotelephone operator.

**Rt. Rev.**, Right Reverend.

**Rts.**, *Finance.* rights.

**r-t-w** (no periods), ready-to-wear: *The r-t-w suits will be around 40 gns.* (London Times).

**Ru**, ruthenium (chemical element).

**Ru.** **1** Rumanian. **2** runic.

**ru|a|na** (rü ä′nə), *n.* a square, heavy kind of poncho worn in Colombia and in parts of the Andes region. [< American Spanish *ruana*]

**ru|at coe|lum** (rü′at sē′ləm), *Latin.* though the heavens fall.

**rub** (rub), *v.,* **rubbed, rub|bing,** *n.* —*v.t.* **1** to move (one thing) back and forth (against another); move (two things) together: *Rub your hands to warm them. He rubbed soap on his hands. Solomon Gill rubbed his hands with an air of stealthy enjoyment* (Dickens). **2** to push and press along the surface of; move one's hand or an object over the surface of: *The nurse rubbed my lame back.* **3** to make or bring (to some condition) by rubbing: *to rub silver bright. Don't rub my skin off.* **4** to clean, smooth, or polish by moving one thing firmly against another: *to rub a table with steel wool.* **5** to irritate or make sore by rubbing: *The new shoe rubbed his heel, causing a blister. You rub the sore, when you should bring the plaster* (Shakespeare). SYN: chafe. **6** *Figurative.* to annoy; make angry: *His conceit rubbed her considerably.* —*v.i.* **1** to press as it moves: *That door rubs on the floor. Stray, homeless cats rubbed against his legs* (Winston Churchill). **2** to be capable of being rubbed; admit of rubbing. **3** *Figurative.* to keep going with difficulty: *Money is scarce, but we shall rub along.*
—*n.* **1** the act of rubbing: *Give the silver a rub with the polish.* **2** *Figurative.* something that hurts the feelings: *He didn't like her mean rub at his slowness.* **3** a rough spot due to rubbing. **4** *Figurative.* a difficulty: *The rub came when both boys wanted to sit with the driver. To sleep: perchance to dream: ay, there's the rub* (Shakespeare).

**rub down, a** to rub (the body); massage: *He went to the Turkish bath to have his aching back rubbed down.* **b** to clean (a horse) from dust and sweat by rubbing: *After the horses are rubbed down, the men proceed to the straw barn* (H. Stephens).

**rub elbows with.** See under **elbow**.

**rub (it) in,** *Informal.* to keep on mentioning something unpleasant: *to rub in a point. The sterile oscillation between home and pub is rubbed in hard* (Listener). *Ye needn't rub it in any more* (Rudyard Kipling).

**rub off, a** to remove by rubbing: *There's some dust on your sleeve; rub it off.* **b** to be removed by rubbing: *Ink rubs off easily with this eraser.*

**rub off on,** to cling to; become a part of; take hold of: *Possibly some of Wilson's devotion to style has rubbed off on him* (Saturday Review).

**rub out, a** to erase: *Rub out your error with an eraser.* **b** *U.S. Slang, Figurative.* to murder: *Shoveling the money back into the house, the frantic badmen realize that the little old lady must be rubbed out* (Time).

**rub shoulders with.** See under **shoulder**.

**rub the wrong** (or **right**) **way.** See under **way**.

**rub up,** *Especially British Informal.* to make better; improve: *The Earl of Chincham ... is rubbing him up a bit in Society ways* (Punch). *She told ... him to rub up his English or get out of her service* (New Yorker).
[Middle English *rubben.* Compare Low German *rubben,* Danish *rubbe.*]

**rub|a|boo** or **rub|ba|boo** (rub′ə bü′), *n. Canadian.* a soup made by boiling pemmican in water with flour and other ingredients. [< Canadian French *rababou* < Algonkian]

**rub-a-dub** (rub′ə dub′), *n., v.,* **-dubbed, -dub|bing.** —*n.* **1** the sound of a drum being beaten. **2** a similar sound. —*v.i.* to make such a sound. [probably imitative]

**ru|ba 'i** (rü bä′ē), *n., pl.* **ru|bái|yát** (rü′bī yät, -bē-) = quatrain. [< Arabic *rubā'i* having four]

**Ru|bái|yát** (rü′bī yät, -bē-), *n.pl.* a collection of poems in quatrains written in Persia in the 1100's by Omar Khayyám, translated into English by Edward FitzGerald, and published in 1859. [< Arabic *rubā'iyāt,* feminine plural of *rubā'īya* quatrain < *rubā'i* ruba'*i*]

**ru|basse** (rü bas′, -bäs′), *n.* quartz crystals containing particles of hematite which reflect a bright-red color, used as a gem. [< earlier French *rubace* < stem of *rubis* ruby]

**ru|ba|to** (rü bä′tō), *adj., n., pl.* **-tos, -ti** (-tē). *Music.* —*adj.* having certain notes of a measure or phrase lengthened or shortened for the purpose of expression or individual interpretation.
—*n.* a rubato tempo or passage: *He is acquainted with most of the traditional rubati of the Johann Strauss style* (Winthrop Sargeant).
[< Italian (*tempo*) *rubato* (literally) robbed (time), past participle of *rubare* to rob]

**rub|ber¹** (rub′ər), *n., adj., v.* —*n.* **1** an elastic substance obtained from the milky juice of certain tropical plants, or made synthetically by chemical processes; india rubber. Rubber will not let air or water through. Pure rubber is a whitish hydrocarbon that becomes black and more easily worked when vulcanized for commercial use in the manufacture of tires, erasers, etc. *Natural rubber is made up of long molecules consisting of simple hydrocarbons strung together end to end like beads in a necklace* (Edith Goldman). **2** any one of various synthetic products resembling rubber. **3** something made from rubber, such as a rubber band. Pencils often have rubbers for erasing pencil marks. **4** *Baseball.* **a** the rectangular piece of

rubber on the pitcher's mound. **b** home plate. **5a** a person or thing that rubs. **b** a person who gives a rubdown; masseur. **c** a person who makes brass rubbings: *an amateur rubber.* **6** *Slang.* a condom.
— ***adj.*** made of rubber: *a rubber tire. Since the 1930's when rubber foam first bounded into the auto industry, its use as a padding for seats has climbed* (Wall Street Journal).
— ***v.i.*** *Slang.* to stretch the neck or turn the head to look at something.
**rubbers**, rubber overshoes, especially low-cut ones.
[(def. 1) for *India rubber* (from its use originally as an eraser)] — **rub′ber\|like′**, *adj.*

**rub\|ber[2]** (rub′ər), *n.* **1** a series of two games out of three or three games out of five won by the same side in bridge, whist, and certain other card games. **2** the deciding game in such a series: *If each side has won two games, the fifth game will be the rubber.* **3** any game which breaks a tie. [origin uncertain]

**rubber band**, a circular strip of rubber, used to hold things together: *I keep a rubber band around the small cardboard tickets that I get with every purchase at the bakery* (Atlantic). **SYN:** elastic.

**rubber bridge**, a type of contract bridge in which players settle the score after each rubber.

**rubber cement**, an adhesive consisting of natural or synthetic rubber in a solvent, used to bond leather, paper, rubber, and some other light articles.

**rubber check**, *Slang.* a check refused by the bank on which it is drawn because of insufficient money on deposit to cover the amount; check that bounces.

**rubber game**, the deciding game or match in an odd-numbered series as in baseball or boxing.

**rub\|ber\|ise** (rub′ə rīz), *v.t.,* **-ised, -is\|ing.** *Especially British.* rubberize.

**rub\|ber\|ize** (rub′ə rīz), *v.t.,* **-ized, -iz\|ing.** to cover or treat with rubber: *rubberized cloth.*

**rubber latex**, latex used to make rubber balls, vulcanized rubber yarn, and other articles of rubber. The hevea tree, guayule, and milkweed plants produce rubber latex.

**rub\|ber\|neck** (rub′ər nek′), *n., v., adj. U.S. Slang.* — ***n.*** a sightseer, especially an unsophisticated one or any other person who stares and gapes: *A good-sized crowd of rubbernecks quickly gathered, anxious to see who had been bold enough to jaywalk when the heat was on* (New Yorker).
— ***v.i.*** **1** to stare or gape: *Everyone has gone ashore to buy, to drink, to rubberneck* (New Yorker). **2** to go sightseeing: *He rubbernecked through Cairo last week* (Time).
— ***adj.*** of or for sightseeing: *a rubberneck tour. She had flown through the Middle East with rubberneck stops at Beirut, Damascus, Amman, Jerusalem, and Tel Aviv* (Time). — **rub′ber\|neck′er**, *n.*

**rubber plant**, **1** any plant yielding rubber. **2** an ornamental house plant native to tropical Asia with oblong, shining, leathery leaves. It belongs to the same genus as the fig and to the mulberry family. See picture under **mulberry family**.

**rubber stamp**, **1** a stamp made of rubber, used with ink for printing dates, signatures, or special imprints. **2** *Informal, Figurative.* a person or group that approves or endorses something without thought or without power to refuse: *Russia charged that the General Assembly was merely a rubber stamp* (Newsweek).

**rub\|ber-stamp** (*v.* rub′ər stamp′; *adj.* rub′ər-stamp′), *v., adj.* — ***v.t.*** **1** to print or sign with a rubber stamp: *He read through my sheaf of papers and rubber-stamped each of them three or four times* (New Yorker). **2** *Informal, Figurative.* to approve or endorse (as a policy or bill) without thought or without power to refuse.
— ***adj.*** **1** using a rubber stamp. **2** *Informal, Figurative.* that approves or endorses without thought or without power to refuse.

**rubber tree**, a tree from which rubber is produced, such as the hevea.

**rub\|ber\|y** (rub′ər ē), *adj.* like rubber; elastic; tough.

***rub\|bing** (rub′ing), *n.* a reproduction of an engraved or sculptured design obtained by pressing a thin tough paper such as parchment, onto the surface and rubbing it with crayon, charcoal, or other solid coloring matter: *These rubbings from medieval English brass plates commemorate the contemporary nobility* (New York Times).

**rubbing alcohol**, a solution of denatured or isopropyl alcohol, usually slightly scented, used in massaging or as an antiseptic.

**rubbing table**, a table to massage a person on.

**rub\|bish** (rub′ish), *n.* **1** waste stuff of no use; trash: *Pick up the rubbish and burn it.* **SYN:** litter, debris, refuse. **2** *Figurative.* silly words and thoughts; nonsense: *Gossip is often a lot of rubbish. The jumbled rubbish of a dream* (Tennyson). *All this modern newspaper rubbish about a New York aristocracy* (Edith Wharton). [Middle English *robys, robbous;* origin uncertain]

**rub\|bish\|ing** (rub′i shing), *adj.* rubbishy; trashy: *rubbishing melodrama.*

**rub\|bish\|y** (rub′i shē), *adj.* **1** full of or covered with rubbish. **2** of or like rubbish: (*Figurative.*) *The doggerel expresses the rubbishy lives of the modern London sophisticates* (Time). **SYN:** trashy.

**rub\|ble** (rub′əl), *n., adj.* — ***n.*** **1** rough broken stones or bricks: *the rubble left by an explosion or an earthquake.* **2** coarse masonry made of this: *The house was built of rubble and plaster.*
— ***adj.*** made of or like rubble: *rubble masonry, rubble ballast.*
[Middle English *robel;* origin uncertain]

**rub\|ble\|work** (rub′əl wėrk′), *n.* masonry built of rubble or roughly dressed stones.

**rub\|bly** (rub′lē), *adj.* full of, consisting of, or like rubble: *These combined with the rubbly, half-demolished buildings in the older sections to give the whole city an air of impermanence* (New Yorker).

**rub\|down** (rub′doun′), *n.* the act or process of rubbing the body; massage.

**rube** (rüb), *n., adj. Slang.* — ***n.*** an unsophisticated person from the country; rustic: *Generations of comedians have vulgarized Peoria as the symbol of the rube and the boob* (Saturday Evening Post).
— ***adj.*** of a rube; like rubes: *a rube town. One of your rube detectives should come over to my cottage* (Charles Dutton).
[American English, earlier *reub,* abbreviation of *Reuben,* a proper name]

**ru\|be\|an\|ic acid** (rü′bē an′ik), a reddish powder made from hydrogen sulfide and cyanogen, used as a reagent. *Formula:* $C_2H_4N_2S_2$

**ru\|be\|fa\|cient** (rü′bə fā′shənt), *adj., n.* — ***adj.*** causing redness, especially of the skin: *a rubefacient liniment.*
— ***n.*** a rubefacient application, such as a mustard plaster.
[< Latin *rubefaciēns, -entis,* present participle of *rubefacere* < *rubeus* red + *facere* make]

**ru\|be\|fac\|tion** (rü′bə fak′shən), *n.* **1** a making red. **2** redness of the skin, especially as caused by a rubefacient.

**Rube Gold\|berg** (rüb′ gōld′bėrg), (of an invention, device, or scheme) ridiculously complicated: *He called the three-gun color tube used by present manufacturers, "a Rube Goldberg contraption if there ever was one"* (Wall Street Journal). [< *Rube Goldberg,* 1883-1970, an American cartoonist noted for a cartoon series depicting fantastically complicated mechanical inventions for performing the simplest tasks]

**ru\|bel\|la** (rü bel′ə), *n.* = German measles. [< New Latin *rubella,* neuter plural of Latin *rubellus* reddish (diminutive) < *rubeus* red]

**ru\|bel\|lite** (rü bel′īt), *n.* a pink or red variety of tourmaline, used as a gem. [< Latin *rubellus* (see etym. under **rubella**) + English *-ite*[1]]

**Ru\|ben** (rü′bən), *n.* (in the Douay Bible) Reuben[1].

**Ru\|ben\|esque** (rü′bə nesk′), *adj.* suggestive or characteristic of the paintings or style of Rubens: *The models of his choice are of rather Rubenesque fullness* (Observer). [< Peter Paul *Rubens,* 1577-1640, the Flemish painter + *-esque*]

**Ru\|ben\|si\|an** (rü ben′sē ən), *adj.* = Rubenesque.

**ru\|be\|o\|la** (rü bē′ə lə, rü′bē ō′-), *n.* = measles. [< New Latin *rubeola* < a diminutive form of Latin *rubeus* red]

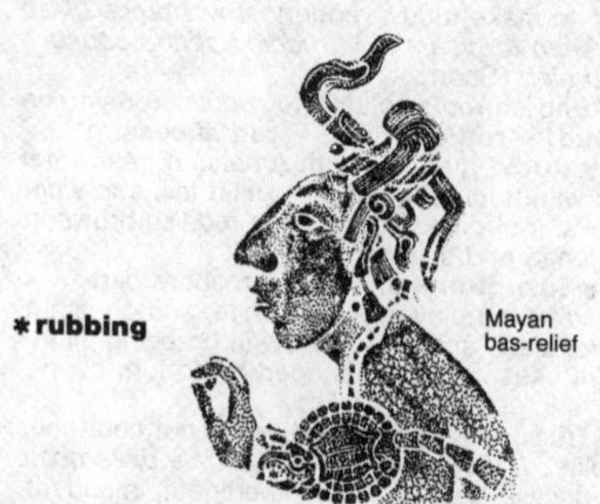


***rubbing**

**ru\|be\|o\|lar** (rü bē′ə lər, rü′bē ō′-), *adj.* of, having to do with, or like rubeola.

**ru\|bes\|cence** (rü bes′əns), *n.* the action of growing or condition of being red.

**ru\|bes\|cent** (rü bes′ənt), *adj.* becoming red; blushing. [< Latin *rubēscēns, -entis,* present participle of *rubēscere* become red < *rubēre* be red, related to *ruber* red]

**ru\|bi\|a\|ceous** (rü′bē ā′shəs), *adj.* belonging to the madder family: *The coffee plant, gardenia, and bluet are rubiaceous plants.* [< New Latin *Rubiaceae* the family name (< *Rubia* the madder genus < Latin *rubia* madder < *rubeus* red) + English *-ous*]

**ru\|bi\|celle** (rü′bə sel), *n.* a yellow or orange-red spinel. [< French *rubicelle,* (apparently diminutive) < earlier *rubace;* see etym. under **rubasse**]

**Ru\|bi\|con** (rü′bə kon), *n.* a limit to a course of action from which one cannot turn back.
**cross** (or **pass**) **the Rubicon,** to make an important decision from which one cannot turn back: [*Napoleon*] *would ... have crossed the Rubicon at the head of the popular party* (Scott). *A pause—in which I began to steady the palsy of my nerves, and to feel that the Rubicon was passed* (Charlotte Brontë).
[< *Rubicon,* a small river in eastern Italy that was part of the boundary between the Roman republic and its provinces. By crossing the Rubicon into Italy in 49 B.C., Julius Caesar started the civil war that made him master of Rome.]

**ru\|bi\|cund** (rü′bə kund), *adj.* reddish; ruddy: *The jolly captain had a ribicund face.* **SYN:** florid. [< Latin *rubicundus* < *rubeus* red]

**ru\|bi\|cun\|di\|ty** (rü′bə kun′də tē), *n.* rubicund quality or condition.

***ru\|bid\|i\|um** (rü bid′ē əm), *n.* a soft, silver-white metallic chemical element resembling potassium. It reacts violently in water and burns spontaneously when exposed to air. Rubidium is used in photoelectric cells. *Rubidium and cesium, like the other alkali metals, never occur free in nature* (W. N. Jones). [< New Latin *rubidium* < Latin *rubidus* red < *rubēre* be red (from the two red lines in its spectrum)]

***rubidium**

| symbol | atomic number | atomic weight | oxidation state |
|---|---|---|---|
| Rb | 37 | 85.47 | 1 |

**ru\|bied** (rü′bēd), *adj.* colored like the ruby.

**ru\|big\|i\|nose** (rü bij′ə nōs), *adj.* = rubiginous.

**ru\|big\|i\|nous** (rü bij′ə nəs), *adj.* **1** rusty; rust-colored. **2** (of plants) affected with rust or blight. [< Latin *rūbīginōsus* < *rūbīgō, -inis* rust, mold, related to *ruber* red]

**ru\|bi\|go** (rü bī′gō), *n.* a reddish ferric oxide, used as a pigment and in polishing compounds; rouge. [< Latin *rūbīgō*]

**ru\|bi\|ous** (rü′bē əs), *adj.* red; rubied.

**ru\|ble** (rü′bəl), *n.* the unit of money of the Soviet Union, a coin or note equal to 100 kopecks. *Abbr:* r. Also, **rouble.** [< Russian *rubl′*]

**ru\|bor** (rü′bər), *n.* redness of the skin. [< Latin *rubor* < *rubēre* be red]

**rub\|out** (rub′out′), *n. U.S. Slang.* a murder; gangland killing: *Frankie was the picture of innocence, said he ran because "I thought it was a rubout"* (Time).

**rub rail**, **1** a protective guard on the gunwale of a boat: *Then it came to me: ... get a leg hooked over the rub rail and onto the deck, and then pull up* (Harper's). **2** a metal projection on cars and trucks, as a bumper, to guard against scraping. **3** any raillike protection.

**ru\|bric** (rü′brik), *n., adj.* — ***n.*** **1** the title or heading, as of a chapter or a law, written or printed in red or in special lettering. **2** a direction for the conducting of religious services, inserted in a prayer book or ritual. **3** *Figurative.* any heading, rule, or guide: *I think that the rubrics of the materialist dialectic are useful aids to thought* (Scientific American). *I talked to him till I was black in the face, and all I got out of him was the law and the rubrics* (Frank O'Connor). **4** *Archaic.* **a** red ocher. **b** a red color.
— ***adj.*** = rubrical.
[< Old French *rubrique,* learned borrowing from Late Latin *rubrīca* rubric < Latin, red color, red coloring matter < *ruber* red]

**ru\|bri\|cal** (rü′brə kəl), *adj.* **1** red; marked with red; printed or written in red or in special lettering. **2** of, having to do with, or according to religious rubrics. — **ru′bri\|cal\|ly**, *adv.*

**ru\|bri\|cate** (rü′brə kāt), *v.t.,* **-cat\|ed, -cat\|ing.** **1** to mark or color with red. **2** to furnish with rubrics. **3** to regulate by rubrics. [< Latin *rubrīcāre* (with English *-ate*[1]) to color red < *rubrīca* red coloring matter; see etym. under **rubric**]

**ru\|bri\|ca\|tion** (rü′brə kā′shən), *n.* **1** the act of rubricating. **2** that colored red.

**ru\|bri\|ca\|tor** (rü′brə kā′tər), *n.* a person who inserts rubrics in a manuscript.

**ru\|bri\|cian** (rü brish′ən), *n.* a person who studies or is an expert in religious rubrics.

**Pronunciation Key:** hat, āge, cãre, fär; let, ēqual, tėrm; it, īce; hot, ōpen, ôrder; **oil**, **out**; cup, pu̇t, rüle; **ch**ild; lo**ng**; **th**in; **ᴛʜ**en; **zh**, measure; ə represents **a** in about, **e** in taken, **i** in pencil, **o** in lemon, **u** in circus.

**ru|bric|i|ty** (rü bris′ə tē), *n.* **1** the assumption of a red color: *the periodical ... rubricity of the Nile* (Auckland C. Geddes). **2** adherence to liturgical rubrics.

**ru|bus** (rü′bəs), *n., pl.* **-bus.** any bramble, such as the blackberry, raspberry, and dewberry. [< New Latin *Rubus* the genus name < Latin *rubus* blackberry, bramble]

**ru|by** (rü′bē), *n., pl.* **-bies,** *adj.* **—*n.*** **1** a clear, hard, red precious stone. It is a variety of corundum. Real rubies are very rare. *Formula:* $Al_2O_3$ **2** its color, a deep, glowing red: *the natural ruby of your cheek* (Shakespeare). **3** something made of ruby, especially a bearing in a watch. **4** red wine: *Still the Vine her ancient Ruby yields* (Edward FitzGerald). **5** *British.* a size of printing type; approximately 5½ points. In the United States it is called *agate.* **6** *British Slang.* blood.
**—*adj.*** deep, glowing red: *ruby lips, ruby wine.*
[< Old French *rubis,* plural of *rubi,* ultimately < Latin *rubeus* red] **—ru′by|like′,** *adj.*

**Ru|by** (rü′bē), *n., pl.* **-bies.** a red-fleshed variety of grapefruit developed from natural sports of other varieties.

**ru|by-crowned kinglet** (rü′bē kround′), a tiny, grayish, North American bird, the male of which has a bright ruby patch on the crown.

**ruby silver, 1** = pyrargyrite. **2** = proustite.

**ruby spaniel,** a chestnut red variety of the English toy spaniel.

**ruby spinel,** = spinel ruby.

**ru|by|tail** (rü′bē tāl′), *n.* any one of various small, solitary, stinging insects that are brilliantly colored and lay their eggs in the nests of other insects. One variety has a ruby-colored abdomen.

**ru|by|throat** (rü′bē thrōt′), *n.* = ruby-throated hummingbird.

**ru|by-throat|ed hummingbird** (rü′bē thrō′tid), a hummingbird of eastern North America with bright-green plumage above. The male also has a brilliant-red throat.

**R.U.C.,** Royal Ulster Constabulary.

**ru|cer|vine** (rü sėr′vīn, -vin), *adj.* of or having to do with a group of large East Indian deer that have branching antlers and long tines extending forward over the brow. [< New Latin *Rucervus* the genus name (< Malay *rūsa* deer + Latin *cervus* deer) + English *-ine*[1]]

**ruche** (rüsh), *n.* a full pleating or frill of lace, ribbon, net, or other decorative material, used as trimming, especially on the collars and cuffs of women's dresses. Also, **rouche.** [< French *ruche* (originally) beehive (from its shape)]

**ruched** (rüsht), *adj.* **1** made into a ruche or ruches: *The top and hem are ruched nylon and lace* (Sunday Times). **2** having a ruche or ruches: *a ruched collar, a ruched dress.*

**ruch|ing** (rü′shing), *n.* **1** trimming made of ruches. **2** material used to make ruches.

**ruck**[1] (ruk), *n., v.* **—*n.*** **1** a large group; crowd; throng: *a ruck of people, a ruck of horses.* **2** the great mass of common or inferior people or things. **3** the horses left behind in a race: *a brilliant young charioteer in the ruck of the race* (George Meredith). **4** *Rugby.* a group of players pressing aggressively for possession of the ball.
**—*v.i.*** *Rugby.* to form a ruck so as to gain possession of the ball: *As usual, the Oxford pack rucked exceedingly well* (Sunday Times).
[< Scandinavian (compare Norwegian *ruka* little heap)] **—ruck′er,** *n.*

**ruck**[2] (ruk), *n., v.* **—*n.*** **1** a crease; wrinkle. **2** = ridge.
**—*v.i.*** to become creased or wrinkled.
**—*v.t.*** **1** to crease; wrinkle. **2** to gather in folds. [apparently < Scandinavian (compare Norwegian *rukka,* Old Icelandic *hrukka*)]

**ruck|sack** (ruk′sak′, růk′-), *n.* a kind of knapsack, usually of canvas with two shoulder straps. [< German *Rucksack* < dialectal *Ruck,* variant of *Rücken* back + *Sack* sack]

**Rück|um|laut** (rʏk′üm′lout), *n. German.* the absence of umlaut.

**ruck|us** (ruk′əs), *n. Informal.* a noisy disturbance or uproar; row: *Like most old campaigners, [he] often likes to stir up a ruckus* (Newsweek). [American English, perhaps blend of *ruction* and *rumpus*]

**ruc|tion** (ruk′shən), *n. Informal.* a disturbance; quarrel; row: *when the racial ructions rise* (Rudyard Kipling). [perhaps alteration of *insurrection*]

**ruc|us** (ruk′əs), *n. U.S. Slang.* ruckus.

**rud** (rud), *n.* **1** *Archaic.* red or ruddy color. **2** *Dialect.* ruddle. **3** *Obsolete.* complexion. [Old English *rudu,* related to *rēad* red]

**rud|beck|i|a** (rud bek′ē ə), *n.* any one of various herbs of the composite family with showy flowers consisting of petals around a conical dark center; coneflower: *The yellow daisy or the black-eyed Susan is a common rudbeckia.* [< New Latin *Rudbeckia* the genus name < Olaus *Rudbeck,* 1630-1702, a Swedish botanist]

**rudd** (rud), *n.* a red-finned, European freshwater fish related to the carp. [earlier *rowde,* apparently a use of *rud* redness, Old English *rudu;* see etym. under **rud**]

***rud|der** (rud′ər), *n.* **1** a movable flat piece of wood or metal at the rear end of a boat or ship, by which it is steered. **2** a similar piece on an aircraft (for right-and-left steering). **3** *Figurative.* a person or thing that guides, directs, or controls. [Middle English *roder* < Old English *rōthor*]

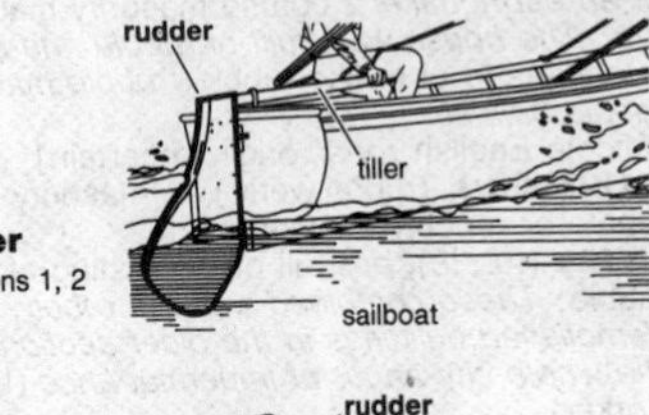

***rudder**
definitions 1, 2

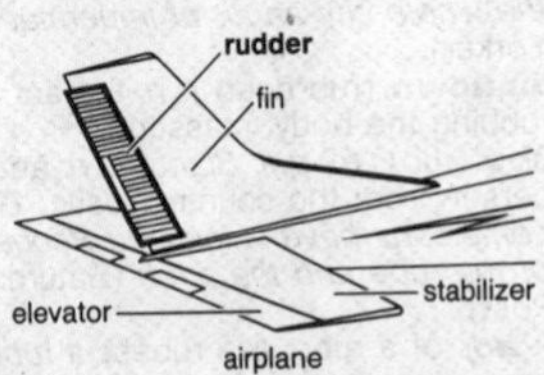


**rudder bar,** a foot-operated bar in the cockpit of certain light airplanes, to which the control cables leading to the rudder are attached.

**rud|dered** (rud′ərd), *adj.* having a rudder.

**rud|der|head** (rud′ər hed′), *n.* the upper end of the rudder, into which the tiller is fitted.

**rud|der|less** (rud′ər lis), *adj.* without a rudder or controls: *a rudderless boat.* (*Figurative.*) *Left rudderless, Pakistan drifted on the currents of opportunism, intrigue and corruption* (Atlantic). **SYN:** drifting, aimless.

**rud|der|post** (rud′ər pōst′), *n.* **1** an extension of the sternpost on which the rudder is hung. **2** = rudderstock.

**rud|der|stock** (rud′ər stok′), *n.* the part of a rudder by which it is connected to the ship.

**rud|dle** (rud′əl), *n., v.,* **-dled, -dling.** **—*n.*** = red ocher.
**—*v.t.*** to mark or color with ruddle.
[apparently < *rud*]

**rud|dle|man** (rud′əl mən), *n., pl.* **-men.** a dealer in ruddle.

**rud|dock** (rud′ək), *n., pl.* **-docks** or (*collectively*) **-dock.** the European robin: *The sweet And shrilly ruddock, with its bleeding breast* (Thomas Hood). [Old English *rudduc,* related to *rudu* red; see etym. under **rud**]

**rud|dy** (rud′ē), *adj.,* **-di|er, -di|est,** *adv., v.,* **-died, -dy|ing.** **—*adj.*** **1** red or reddish: *the ruddy glow of a fire. As dear to me as are the ruddy drops That visit my sad heart* (Shakespeare). **SYN:** rubicund, florid. **2a** of a fresh, healthy red: *ruddy cheeks.* **SYN:** rosy. **b** having such a color in the cheeks: *a short, stout, ruddy young fellow* (Herman Melville). **3** *British Slang.* bloody; blinking: *But one thinks the bad words—one says them back of one's teeth while one is nodding and smiling at the ruddy idiot* (Smith's London Journal).
**—*adv.*** *British Slang.* very; surely; extremely: *He was ruddy near right! We'll ruddy well see the admiral* (Maclean's).
**—*v.t.*** to make ruddy; redden: *A wondrous blaze was seen to gleam ... It ruddied all the copsewood glen* (Scott).
[Old English *rudig,* related to *rudu;* see etym. under **rud**] **—rud′di|ly,** *adv.* **—rud′di|ness,** *n.*

**ruddy duck,** a small North American freshwater duck with a long, broad bill, a stiff tail, and white cheeks; fool duck. The male is reddish-brown in the spring and summer.

**ruddy turnstone,** an American shore bird related to the plover, black, white, and chestnut above, black and white below in breeding plumage. It uses its wedge-shaped bill to turn over stones in search of food.

**rude** (rüd), *adj.,* **rud|er, rud|est.** **1** not courteous; impolite: *It is rude to stare at people or to point.* **SYN:** uncivil, discourteous, impertinent, impudent. **2** roughly made or done; without finish or polish; coarse; rough: *rude tools, a rude cabin, a rude sketch; ... a rude bed upon the floor* (Dickens). **SYN:** unwrought, raw, crude. **3** rough in manner or behavior; violent; harsh: *the rude winds of winter. Rude hands seized the dog and threw him into the car. He had a rude shock when the boys threw a pail of water on him. In far less polished days, A time when rough rude men had naughty ways* (Robert Burns). **4** harsh to the ear; unmusical. **5** not having learned much; rather wild; barbarous: *Life is rude in tribes that have few tools. ... the rude forefathers of the hamlet* (Thomas Gray). **SYN:** primitive. **6** belonging to the poor or to uncultured people; without luxury or elegance; simple: *a rude, primitive culture. The temple ... is of rude design and indifferent execution* (Amelia B. Edwards). **7** not fully or properly developed. **8** robust; sturdy; vigorous: *rude health, rude strength.* **9** *Archaic.* inexpert; unskilled. [< Latin *rudis*] **—rude′ly,** *adv.* **—rude′ness,** *n.*

**ru|der|al** (rü′dər əl), *adj., n.* **—*adj.*** growing in rubbish or waste places: *a ruderal plant, ruderal vegetation.*
**—*n.*** a ruderal weed: ... *ruderals of open ground* (New Scientist).
[< New Latin *ruderalis* < Latin *rūdera* (plural of *rūdus* broken stone) + *-ālis* al[1]]

**rudes|by** (rüdz′bē), *n., pl.* **-bies.** *Archaic.* a rude or unmannerly fellow: *Rudesby, be gone!* (Shakespeare). [< *rude* + *sby,* an ending of proper names, such as *Crosby, Hornsby*]

**Rü|des|heim|er** (rʏ′dəs hī′mər), *n.* a fine white Rhine wine. [< German *Rüdesheimer* < *Rüdesheim,* a town on the Rhine]

**ru|di|ment** (rü′də mənt), *n.* **1** a part to be learned first; beginning: *the rudiments of arithmetic. [He] received the first rudiments of his education at a little free-school* (Richard Graves). **2** something in an early stage; undeveloped or imperfect form: *a youth ... who apparently had not in him even the rudiments of worldly successfulness* (Arnold Bennett). **3** an organ or part incompletely developed in size or structure: *the rudiments of wings on a baby chick.* [< Latin *rudīmentum* < *rudis* rude, ignorant]

**ru|di|men|tal** (rü′də men′təl), *adj.* = rudimentary.

**ru|di|men|ta|ry** (rü′də men′tər ē, -trē), *adj.* **1** that is to be learned or studied first; elementary: *It is almost impossible to learn multiplication without knowing the rudimentary steps of addition.* **SYN:** See syn. under **elementary. 2** in an early stage of development; undeveloped: *rudimentary wings.* **SYN:** embryonic. **—ru′di|men′ta|ri|ly,** *adv.* **—ru′di|men′ta|ri|ness,** *n.*

**rue**[1] (rü), *v.,* **rued, ru|ing,** *n.* **—*v.t.*** to be sorry for; regret; repent: *She will rue the day she insulted your mother. Thou shalt rue this treason* (Shakespeare). *Was ever son so rued a father's death?* (Shakespeare). **SYN:** deplore.
**—*v.i.*** *Archaic.* to feel sorrow; lament.
**—*n.*** sorrow; regret; repentance: *With rue my heart is laden For golden friends I had* (A. E. Housman).
[Middle English *rewen,* Old English *hrēowan;* compare *ruth*]

**rue**[2] (rü), *n.* a plant with yellow flowers, and leaves that have a strong smell and a bitter taste. It grows in the Mediterranean region. Rue is a woody herb of the same family as the citrus. Its leaves were formerly much used in medicine. [< Old French *rue* < Latin *rūta,* perhaps < Greek *rhytē*]

**rue**[3] (rʏ), *n. French expression.* street: *Rue de Rivoli, Rue La Fayette.*

**rue anemone** (rü), a small North American perennial plant of the crowfoot family with white or pinkish flowers that bloom in the spring; windflower.

***rue family** (rü), a group of chiefly tropical or subtropical herbs, shrubs, and trees, many of which yield an aromatic oil. The family is dicotyledonous and includes the rue, citrus fruits, dittany, and hop tree.

***rue family**

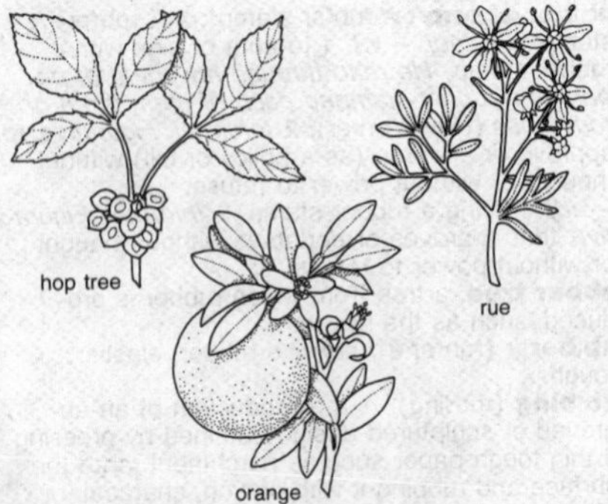


**rue|ful** (rü′fəl), *adj.* **1** sorrowful; unhappy; mournful: *a rueful expression.* **SYN:** doleful, woeful, lugubrious, melancholy. **2** causing sorrow or pity: *The lost child's distress was a rueful sight.*
**—rue′ful|ly,** *adv.* **—rue′ful|ness,** *n.*

**ru|er** (rü′ər), *n.* a person who rues.

**ru|fes|cence** (rü fes′əns), *n.* reddishness.

**ru|fes|cent** (rü fes′ənt), *adj.* = reddish. [< Latin *rūfēscēns, -entis,* present participle of *rūfēscere* become reddish < *rūfus* reddish, red-haired, related to *ruber* red]

***ruff**[1] (ruf), *n.* **1** a deep frill, stiff enough to stand out, worn around the neck by men and women in the 1500's and 1600's. **2** a collar of specially marked feathers or hairs on the neck of a bird or animal. **3** a sandpiper of Europe and Asia, the male of which has ear tufts and a ruff on the neck during the breeding season. The female ruff is called a reeve. [perhaps related to **ruffle**[1], perhaps < *rough*]

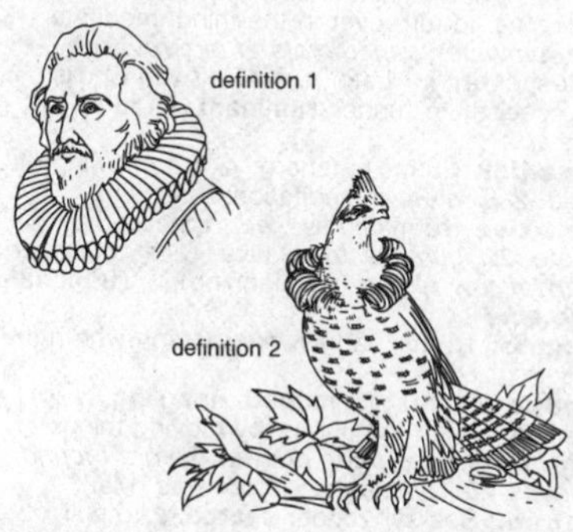


***ruff**[1]
definitions 1, 2

**ruff**[2] (ruf), *v., n.* —***v.t., v.i.*** to trump in a card game: *West had to ruff with a good trump and the prospective penalty was down to 100* (Observer).
—*n.* **1** the act of trumping. **2** *Obsolete.* a card game resembling whist.
[< Middle French *roffle* < Old French *ronfle, romfle*]

**ruff**[3] or **ruffe** (ruf), *n.* a small European freshwater fish similar to the perch. [perhaps < Middle English *roughe* rough (probably from its prickles)]

**ruffed** (ruft), *adj.* having a ruff.

**ruffed grouse**, a game bird of North America with a tuft of gleaming black feathers on each side of the neck and a fan-shaped tail. It is called a partridge in New England and a pheasant in the southern United States.

**ruffed lemur**, a black and white lemur with a woolly ruff of hair on the sides of its face.

**ruf|fi|an** (ruf′ē ən), *n., adj.* —*n.* a rough, brutal, or cruel person; hoodlum: ... *an abominable lot of lawless ruffians.* (Joseph Conrad). **SYN**: bully, rowdy, rough.
—***adj.*** rough; brutal; cruel: *He heard a ruffian voice in the alley and hurried along.*
[< Middle French *rufian* < Italian *ruffiano* a pander; meaning perhaps influenced by *rough*]

**ruf|fi|an|ism** (ruf′ē ə niz′əm), *n.* the conduct or character of a ruffian.

**ruf|fi|an|ly** (ruf′ē ən lē), *adj.* like a ruffian; rough, lawless, and violent.

**ruf|fle**[1] (ruf′əl), *v.,* **-fled, -fling,** *n.* —***v.t.*** **1a** to make rough or uneven; destroy the smoothness of; wrinkle; rumple: *A breeze ruffled the lake. He ruffled up his gray moustache with thumb and forefinger* (Booth Tarkington). **SYN**: roughen. **b** to cause to rise in anger or fear: *The hen ruffled her feathers at the sight of the dog.* **2a** to gather into a ruffle. **b** to trim with ruffles. **3** to disturb; annoy: *Nothing can ruffle her calm temper. He was not ruffled by the immense disappointment* (Arnold Bennett). **SYN**: disquiet, discompose. **4** to shuffle (playing cards). **5** to turn over (the pages of a book) rapidly; riffle.
—***v.i.*** to become ruffled: *The flag ruffled in the breeze. "Of course you consider it would have been so," sighed the lady, ruffling* (George Meredith).
—*n.* **1** roughness or unevenness in some surface; wrinkling. **2a** a strip of cloth, ribbon, or lace gathered along one edge and used for trimming. Women's dresses sometimes have ruffles; some men's shirts for evening wear have ruffles.
**b** something resembling this, such as the ruff on a bird. **3** disturbance; annoyance: *the ordinary rubs and ruffles which disturb even the most uniform life* (Scott). **4** disorder; confusion.
[Middle English *ruffelen.* Compare Low German *ruffelen* to rumple, Old Icelandic *hrufla* to stretch.]

**ruf|fle**[2] (ruf′əl), *n., v.,* **-fled, -fling.** —*n.* a low steady beating of a drum, softer than a roll.
—***v.t.*** to beat (a drum) in this way.
[perhaps imitative]

**ruf|fle**[3] (ruf′əl), *v.,* **-fled, -fling,** *n.* —***v.i.*** **1** to be violent or rough, as wind or waves. **2** to make a display; swagger: *Here he was, a provincial man of business, ruffling it with the best of them!* (Arnold Bennett). **3** *Archaic.* to struggle; contend.
—*n. Archaic.* a struggle; fight; brawl: *the ruffle betwixt the Scottish Archers and the provost-marshal's guard* (Scott).
[Middle English *ruffelyn;* origin uncertain]

**ruf|fler**[1] (ruf′lər), *n.* **1** a person or thing that ruffles or annoys: *that enemy of all repose and ruffler of even tempers—the mosquito* (Herman Melville). **2** an attachment for a sewing machine to gather cloth into ruffles. [< *ruffl(e)*[1] + *-er*[1]]

**ruf|fler**[2] (ruf′lər), *n.* **1** *Archaic.* a bully; ruffian. **2** *Obsolete.* one of a group of roving bullies in the 1500's. [< *ruffl(e)*[3] + *-er*[1]]

**ruf|fly** (ruf′lē), *adj.* having ruffles.

**ru|fous** (rü′fəs), *adj.* **1** reddish or reddish-brown: *rufous hair, rufous granite.* **2** red-faced; ruddy: *The rufous, foxy little dentist would give another turn of the screw to the instruments of torture I wore in my mouth* (New Yorker). [< Latin *rūfus* (with English *-ous*)]

**rufous hummingbird**, a hummingbird of western North America, the male of which has bright rufous upper parts and a bright scarlet throat.

**rug**[1] (rug), *n.* **1** a heavy floor covering usually covering only part of a room's floor: *a rag rug, a grass rug.* **2** a thick, warm cloth used as covering: *The Indian wrapped his woolen rug around him.*
**cut a rug**, *U.S. Slang.* to dance in a lively manner: *Shirley, who is an expert dancer, cut many a rug at the Stage Door Canteen* (Time).
**pull the rug (out) from under**, to upset the plans of: *Until the afternoon, there seemed some hope of a settlement. Then the Supreme Court pulled the rug out from under the President* (Newsweek).
**sweep under the rug**, *Informal.* to conceal (an error, scandal, problem, or difficulty), especially from the public: *For years this national scandal has been swept under the rug* (Harper's).
[< Scandinavian (compare Norwegian dialectal *rugga* coarse coverlet)]

**rug**[2] (rug), *v.,* **rugged, rug|ging,** *n. Scottish.*
—***v.t., v.i.*** to pull roughly; tug.
—*n.* a rough pull; jerk.
[< Scandinavian (compare Old Icelandic *rugga*)]

**ru|ga** (rü′gə), *n., pl.* **-gae** (-jē). a wrinkle; fold; ridge. [< Latin *rūga* a crease, wrinkle]

**ru|gate** (rü′gāt), *adj.* wrinkled; rugose.

**Rug|bei|an** (rug bē′ən), *adj., n.* —***adj.*** **1** of or having to do with Rugby, England, or its inhabitants. **2** of or having to do with the school for boys there.
—*n.* a man who has been educated at Rugby.

**Rug|by** or **rug|by** (rug′bē), *n.* an English game somewhat like football, played by teams of 15 or 13 men who kick or pass an oval ball to get it into the opposing team's goal. The forward pass is not allowed, and play is stopped only for penalties and injuries. [< *Rugby,* a famous school for boys in Rugby, England]

**Rugby** or **rugby football**, = Rugby.

**Rugby League** or **rugby league**, the variety of Rugby played by teams of 13 players each. Rugby League is played by both professional and amateur teams.

**Rugby Union** or **rugby union**, the variety of Rugby played by teams of 15 players each. Rugby Union is played by amateur teams, and is the best known form of Rugby.

**rug|ged** (rug′id), *adj.* **1** covered with rough edges; rough and uneven: *rugged ground. So onward, o'er the rugged way That runs through rocks and sand* (Oliver Wendell Holmes). **SYN**: craggy, scraggy, furrowed. **2** sturdy and vigorous; able to do and endure much; hardy: *a rugged figure in rawhide boots and coonskin cap* (Winston Churchill). *Pioneers were rugged people.* **3** strong and irregular: *rugged features.* **4** *Figurative.* harsh; stern; severe: *rugged times.* **5** rude; unpolished; unrefined: *rugged manners; ... rugged maxims hewn from life* (Tennyson). **6** stormy: *rugged weather.* **7** *Figurative.* harsh to the ear: *rugged sounds.* **SYN**: discordant. **8** *Obsolete.* rough; shaggy: ... *the rugged Russian bear* (Shakespeare). [< Scandinavian (compare Swedish *rugga* to roughen)] —**rug′ged|ly,** *adv.* —**rug′ged|ness,** *n.*

**rug|ged|i|za|tion** (rug′ə də zā′shən), *n.* the act or process of ruggedizing: *Part of this program is aimed at ruggedization and miniaturization of electronic components* (Newsweek).

**rug|ged|ize** (rug′ə dīz), *v.t.,* **-ized, -iz|ing.** to make (a piece of equipment) rugged enough for practical, everyday use.

**Rug|ger** or **rug|ger** (rug′ər), *n. British Informal.* Rugby: *I was subjected to so much compulsory chapel, rugger, bell training ... that I was too exhausted to absorb much of the excellent tuition* (Manchester Guardian).

**ru|go|sa** (rü gō′sə), *n.,* or **rugosa rose**, any one of various hybrid roses with flowers of different colors, used mainly for shrubbery. [< New Latin (*Rosa*) *rugosa* rugose (rose)]

**ru|gose** (rü′gōs, rü gōs′), *adj.* having rugae or wrinkles; wrinkled; ridged: *a rugose leaf.* [< Latin *rūgōsus* < *rūga* wrinkle] —**ru′gose|ly,** *adv.*

**ru|gos|i|ty** (rü gos′ə tē), *n., pl.* **-ties. 1** wrinkled condition. **2** = wrinkle.

**ru|gu|lose** (rü′gyə lōs), *adj.* having small wrinkles; slightly rugose.

**Ruhm|korff coil** (rüm′kôrf), = induction coil. [< H. D. *Ruhmkorff,* 1803-1877, a German inventor]

**ru|in** (rü′ən), *n., v.* —*n.* **1** something left after destruction, decay, or downfall, especially a building or wall that has fallen to pieces: *That ruin was once a famous castle.* (*Figurative.*) *A paralysis had ravaged his stately form, and left it a shaking ruin* (Washington Irving). **2** very great damage; destruction; decay; overthrow: *The ruin of property caused by the earthquake was enormous.* (*Figurative.*) *His enemies planned the duke's ruin.* **3** a fallen or decayed condition: *The house had gone to ruin from neglect.* **4** a cause of destruction, decay, or downfall: (*Figurative.*) *Gambling was his ruin.* **5** = bankruptcy. **6** the act or process of falling or tumbling down, as of a building. **7** the dishonor of a woman.
—***v.t.*** **1** to bring to ruin; destroy; spoil: *The rain has spotted my new dress and ruined it. Too much smoking and drinking will ruin your health.* **SYN**: demolish, wreck. See syn. under **spoil**. **2** to make bankrupt: *His father, a printer, has been ruined by Napoleon's suppression of the press* (Edmund Wilson). **SYN**: impoverish.
—***v.i.*** **1** to be destroyed; come to ruin. **2** *Archaic.* to fall with a crash: *Hell saw Heaven ruining from heaven* (Milton).
**ruins, a** that which is left after destruction, decay, or downfall, such as a building or wall that has fallen to pieces: *the ruins of an ancient city.* **b** injuries or damage done or received: *Till thy father hath made good The ruins done to Malta and to us* (Christopher Marlowe).
[< Old French *ruin,* learned borrowing from Latin *ruīna* a collapse < *ruere* to collapse] —**ru′in|able,** *adj.* —**ru′in|er,** *n.*
—***Syn.*** *n.* **2 Ruin, destruction** mean great damage. **Ruin** implies total or extensive damage caused by external force or especially by natural processes, such as decay: *Proper care protects property from ruin.* **Destruction** implies damage, extensive or not, caused by external forces, such as wind or explosion: *The storm caused widespread destruction.*

**ru|in|ate** (rü′ə nāt), *v.,* **-at|ed, -at|ing,** *adj. Archaic.* —***v.t., v.i.*** to ruin.
—***adj.*** ruined: *a famous city now ruinate* (Milton).

**ru|in|a|tion** (rü′ə nā′shən), *n.* ruin; destruction; downfall: (*Figurative.*) *Pride is the ruination of many a successful man.*

**ru|ined** (rü′ənd), *adj.* reduced to ruins; damaged beyond repair; destroyed.

**ru|in|ous** (rü′ə nəs), *adj.* **1** bringing ruin; causing destruction: *ruinous expense, a ruinous war. The heavy frost in late spring was ruinous to the crops. Of all those expensive and uncertain projects ... there is none perhaps more perfectly ruinous than the search after new silver and gold mines.* (Adam Smith). **SYN**: calamitous, disastrous. **2** fallen into ruins; in ruins; ruined: *a building in a ruinous condition; ... a ruinous wooden fence* (Hawthorne). **SYN**: dilapidated. **3** of ruins; made of ruins: *Damacus ... shall be a ruinous heap* (Isaiah 17:1). —**ru′in|ous|ly,** *adv.* —**ru′in|ous|ness,** *n.*

**ru|ins** (rü′ənz), *n. pl.* See under **ruin**.

**rule** (rül), *n., v.,* **ruled, rul|ing.** —*n.* **1** a statement of what to do and not to do; principle governing conduct, action, or arrangement; law: *the rules of a club, the rules of the road, the rules of grammar and spelling. Obey the rules of the game.* **SYN**: regulation, order, precept. **2** an order by a law court, based upon a principle of law. A special rule is limited to a particular case; a general rule regulates the procedure or decisions of a court. **3** a set of rules or code of discipline under which a religious order lives: *Different kinds of monks live under different rules, such as the rule of St. Benedict.* **4** control; government: *In a democracy the people have the rule. A wife's rule should only be over her husband's house, not over his mind* (John Ruskin). **SYN**: direction, authority, dominion, sway. **5** the period of power of a ruler; reign: *The Revolutionary War took place during the rule of George III.* **6** a regular method; thing that usually happens or is done; what is usually true: *Fair weather is the rule in Arizona.* **7** a straight strip used to measure or as a guide to drawing; ruler. **8** a thin, type-high strip of metal, for printing a line or lines. **9** *Obsolete.* conduct; behavior.
—***v.i.*** **1** to make a rule; decide: *Their father ruled against television on school nights.* **2** to make a

**Pronunciation Key:** hat, āge, cãre, fär; let, ēqual, tėrm; it, īce; hot, ōpen, ôrder; oil, out; cup, pu̇t, rüle; child; long; thin; ᴛʜen; zh, measure; ə represents **a** in about, **e** in taken, **i** in pencil, **o** in lemon, **u** in circus.

formal decision: *The judge ruled against them.* **3** to exercise highest authority; control; govern; manage: *The majority rules in a democracy. This love of life, which in our nature rules* (George Crabbe). *Let them obey that know not how to rule* (Shakespeare). SYN: direct. **4** to prevail; be current: *Prices of wheat and corn ruled high all the year.*
—*v.t.* **1** to declare (a rule); decide (something): *The umpire ruled that the ball was foul.* **2** to decide formally: *The judge ruled a mistrial.* **3** to exercise highest authority over; govern; control: *the evil influence that rules your fortunes* (Hawthorne). *To rule men, we must be men* (Benjamin Disraeli). **4** to prevail in; dominate: *Wit rules all his poems.* **5** to mark with lines: *I used a ruler to rule the paper.* **6** to mark off.
**as a rule,** normally; generally; usually: *As a rule, hail falls in summer* (Thomas H. Huxley). *As a rule it should not take more than an hour to reach areas of natural terrain from the center of a city* (Saturday Review).
**out of rule,** contrary to practice or custom: *Miss Portman ... blushes for you ... when you propose that she, who is not yet a married woman, should chaperon a young lady. It is quite out of rule* (Maria Edgeworth).
**rule out,** to decide against; exclude: *He did not rule out a possible camping trip this summer.*
**rules,** *British, Obsolete.* **a** an area near a prison, where certain prisoners were permitted to live: *He was permitted to live in the rules—consequently his punishment was merely nominal* (The Examiner). **b** the freedom of such an area: *Any prisoner for debt may ... enjoy the rules, or liberty to walk abroad* (John Entick).
[< Old French *riule, reule* < Latin *rēgula* straight stick, related to *regere* to rule, straighten, and to *rēx, rēgis* king. See etym. of doublet **rail**[1].] —**rul′a|ble,** *adj.*
—*Syn. v.i., v.t.* **3 Rule, govern** mean to control by the exercise of authority or power. **Rule** implies control over others through absolute power both to make laws and to force obedience: *He tries to rule his family as a dictator rules a nation.* **Govern** implies sensible control by the wise use of authority or power, usually for the good of the thing, person, or nation governed: *Parents govern a child until he develops the power to govern himself.*

**rule|book** (rül′bu̇k′), *n.,* or **rule book,** a book or collection of rules.

**ruled surface** (rüld), *Geometry.* a surface generated by the motion of a straight line so that the surface may be wholly covered by a group of lines. A cone or a cylinder is a ruled surface.

**rule joint,** a joint hinging two strips together end to end, each strip turning edgeways, used especially in folding rules.

**rule|less** (rül′lis), *adj.* **1** lawless; unruly; ungoverned: *ruleless tribes.* **2** without rules; irregular: *a seemingly ruleless language.*

**rule of law, 1** a recognized legal principle, usually in the form of a maxim, applied as a guide for decisions in doubtful cases. **2** a governing by law or laws: *As human society evolved from clans to nations, we have learned that rule of force is war, and rule of law is peace—the only peace possible* (Bulletin of Atomic Scientists).

**rule of the road, 1** any of the regulations of a country, state, or town, with regard to the movement of vehicles on a highway. **2** any of the regulations embodied in a code of rules for the safe handling of boats or ships meeting or passing each other: *If [a naval maneuvre] requires ships to pass starboard side to starboard side, the rule of the road is waived* (Listener).

**rule of three,** a method of finding the fourth term in a mathematical proportion when three are given. The product of the means equals the product of the extremes.

**rule of thumb** or **rule o' thumb, 1** a rule based on experience or practice rather than on scientific knowledge: *The practical men believed that the idol whom they worship—rule of thumb—has been the source of the past prosperity, and will suffice for the future* (Thomas H. Huxley). **2** a rough, practical method of procedure: *People were not so introspective then ... they lived more according to a rule of thumb* (Samuel Butler). *A rule of thumb for reviewing is that one must first discern the author's intention and then judge how well he carried it off* (Wall Street Journal). —**rule′-of-thumb′,** *adj.*

**rul|er** (rü′lər), *n.* **1** a person who rules or governs, such as a king: *All rulers should be subject to the will of the people.* SYN: sovereign. **2** a straight strip of wood, metal, or plastic used in drawing lines or in measuring. Rulers are usually marked in inches or centimeters. SYN: rule. **3** a person or machine that makes lines on paper.

**rul|er|ship** (rü′lər ship), *n.* the position or power of a ruler: *In the Kremlin, the rulership by committee will bring more jockeying for power* (Newsweek).

**rules** (rülz), *n.pl.* See under **rule.**

**rules of order,** = parliamentary law.

**rul|ing** (rü′ling), *n., adj.* —*n.* **1** a decision of a judge or court: *a ruling on a point of law.* **2** a ruled line or lines. **3** the act of making lines, as on paper or fabric. **4** government.
—*adj.* **1** that rules; governing; controlling: *a ruling body. The tiny principality would become French territory if the ruling prince had no male issue* (Newsweek). **2** predominating; prevalent; chief: *a ruling passion. Samuel Johnson was the ruling authority on English in the 1700's.* **3** used for marking lines: *a draftsman's ruling pen.* —**rul′ing|ly,** *adv.*

**ruling grade,** the steepest grade for a railroad to be built on, used as a standard for determining the size of the load that a freight train can pull: *Tunnels reduce the ruling grade and allow trains to haul more goods at less cost* (R. G. Hennes).

**ru|ly** (rü′lē), *adj.* = orderly.

**rum**[1] (rum), *n.* **1** an alcoholic liquor made from sugar cane or molasses. **2** any alcoholic liquor. [apparently short for obsolete *rumbullion* rum; origin unknown]

**rum**[2] (rum), *adj. Slang.* odd; queer; strange: *Deuced rum sensation!* (John Galsworthy). [perhaps < Romany *rom* male, husband]

**Rum.,** 1 Rumania. 2 Rumanian.

**Ru|man** (rü′mən, rü män′), *adj., n., pl.* **-mans.** = Rumanian.

**Ru|ma|ni|an** (rü mā′nē ən, -mān′yən), *adj., n.* = Romanian.

**Ru|mansh** (rü mansh′, -mänsh′), *adj., n.* = Rhaeto-Romanic.

**rum|ba** (rum′bə), *n., v.,* **-baed** (-bəd), **-ba|ing** (-bə ing). —*n.* **1** a lively ballroom dance that originated among the Cuban Negroes. It is in quadruple time. *For years he has been taking dancing lessons "for exercise," and his creditable rumba, flavored with Victorian courtliness, has won him several competitive awards* (New York Times). **2** music for this dance.
—*v.i.* to dance the rumba. Also, **rhumba.**
[< Cuban Spanish *rumba* (literally) spree]

**rum|ba|ba** (rum′bä′bə), *n.* = baba au rhum.

**rum|ble** (rum′bəl), *v.,* **-bled, -bling,** *n.* —*v.i.* **1** to make a deep, heavy, continuous sound: *The thunder rumbled overhead.* **2** to move with such a sound: *The train rumbled along over the tracks.*
—*v.t.* **1** to utter with a rumbling sound. **2** to cause to move with a rumbling sound. **3** to polish or mix in a tumbling box.
—*n.* **1** a deep, heavy, continuous sound: *We heard the far-off rumble of thunder. "Wouldn't you have thought," ... she ventured in her throaty military rumble* (Mary McCarthy). **2** *U.S. Slang.* a teen-age gang fight: *The Minotaurs, like many of the longer-established gangs, avoid "rumbles" (mass fights) if a sneak raid on an enemy will avenge an insult or settle a score* (New York Times). **3** the rear part of a carriage or old automobile containing an extra seat or a place for baggage. **4** = tumbling box.
[Middle English *romblen.* Compare Middle Dutch *rommelen.*] —**rum′bling|ly,** *adv.*

**rum|bler** (rum′blər), *n.* **1** a person or thing that rumbles. **2** a resounding line of poetry.

**rumble seat,** an extra, outside seat for two in the back of some older coupés and roadsters.

**rum|bly** (rum′blē), *adj.* **1** that rumbles. **2** causing rumbling. **3** accompanied by rumbling.

**rum|bus|tious** (rum bus′chəs), *adj. Informal.* boisterous; unruly: ... *a fortnightly newspaper, a rumbustious and gossipy affair ...* (Punch). *The sperm whales are such ... rumbustious fellows* (Charles Kingsley). [variant of *robustious*] —**rum-bus′tious|ly,** *adv.*

**ru|men** (rü′mən), *n., pl.* **-mi|na** (-mə nə). **1** the first stomach of an animal that chews the cud, in which most food collects immediately after being swallowed: *Sheep, as cattle and goats do, have an "extra stomach," the rumen, where rough feed is predigested with the help of bacteria* (Science News Letter). **2** the cud of such an animal. [< Latin *rūmen, -inis* gullet]

**ru|me|not|o|my** (rü′mə not′ə mē), *n.* the cutting into the rumen of a cud-chewing animal to permit the evacuation, as of gases or impacted food. [< *rumen* + *-tomy*]

**ru|mi|nal** (rü′mə nəl), *adj.* of the rumen: *Portions of the ruminal contents are regurgitated, thoroughly chewed ..., and returned to the rumen* (Science News).

**ru|mi|nant** (rü′mə nənt), *n., adj.* —*n.* an animal that chews the cud. Cows, sheep, and camels are ruminants. The ruminants comprise a suborder of even-toed, hoofed, herbivorous mammals, having a stomach with four or three separate cavities. The group also includes deer, goats, and giraffes.
—*adj.* **1** belonging to the group of ruminants. **2** chewing the cud; ruminating. **3** *Figurative.* meditative; reflective. SYN: contemplative, musing. [< Latin *rūmināns, -antis,* present participle of *rūmināre* to chew a cud < *rūmen, -inis* gullet] —**ru′mi|nant|ly,** *adv.*

**ru|mi|nate** (rü′mə nāt), *v.,* **-nat|ed, -nat|ing.** —*v.i.* **1** to chew the cud. **2** *Figurative.* to think or ponder; meditate; reflect: *I ruminated on the strange events of the past week. Mr. Wendover ... stood gloomily ruminating in front of the fire* (Mrs. Humphry Ward). SYN: cogitate.
—*v.t.* **1** to chew again: *A cow ruminates its food.* **2** *Figurative.* to turn over in the mind; meditate on: *to ruminate strange plots of dire revenge* (Shakespeare). [< Latin *rūmināre* (with English *-ate*[1]); see etym. under **ruminant**] —**ru′mi|nat′ing|ly,** *adv.*

**ru|mi|na|tion** (rü′mə nā′shən), *n.* **1** a chewing of the cud. **2** *Figurative.* meditation; reflection.

**ru|mi|na|tive** (rü′mə nā′tiv), *adj.* **1** inclined to ruminate. **2** *Figurative.* meditative: ... *a ruminative woman of few words* (A. Manning). —**ru′mi|na′tive|ly,** *adv.*

**ru|mi|na|tor** (rü′mə nā′tər), *n.* a person who ruminates.

**rum|mage** (rum′ij), *v.,* **-maged, -mag|ing,** *n.*
—*v.t.* **1** to search thoroughly by moving things about: *I rummaged three drawers before I found my gloves. He rummaged his pockets* (Mark Twain). SYN: See syn. under **search. 2** to pull from among other things; bring to light: *She rummaged change from the bottom of her purse. Theobald had rummaged up a conclusion from some odd corner of his soul* (Samuel Butler).
—*v.i.* to search in a disorderly way: *She rummaged in her purse for some change.* [< noun]
—*n.* **1** a thorough search in which things are moved about: *After a last rummage of the old trunk, he gave up the locket as lost.* **2** = rummage sale. **3** odds and ends. **4** *Obsolete.* a disturbance. **5** *Obsolete.* **a** the stowing or removing of cargo on a ship. **b** a ship's hold.
[earlier *romage* < Middle French *arrumage* < *arrumer* stow cargo < unrecorded *rum,* variant of *run* hold of a ship < Germanic (compare Dutch *ruim*)]

**rum|mag|er** (rum′ə jər), *n.* **1** a person who searches. **2** *Obsolete.* a person who arranges cargo in a ship.

**rummage sale,** a sale of odds and ends, or old clothing, usually held to raise money for charity.

**rum|mer** (rum′ər), *n.* **1** a large drinking glass, especially with a tall, stemless, cylindrical form. **2** a cupful of wine or other liquor. [probably < Dutch *romer, roemer* a fancy, show-off glass, (literally) boaster]

**rum|my**[1] (rum′ē), *adj.,* **-mi|er, -mi|est.** *Slang.* odd; strange: *There seemed to be some rummy mystery about his absence* (A. S. M. Hutchinson). [< *rum*[2] + *-y*[1]]

**rum|my**[2] (rum′ē), *n., v.,* **-mied, -my|ing.** —*n.* a card game in which points are scored by melding sets of three or four cards of the same rank or sequences of three or more cards of the same suit.
—*v.i.* to end the game by using or discarding the last card in one's hand.
[American English; origin uncertain]

**rum|my**[3] (rum′ē), *n., pl.* **-mies,** *adj.* —*n. U.S. Slang.* a drunkard.
—*adj.* of or like rum: *a rummy flavor.*
[American English < *rum*[1] + *-y*[1]]

**ru|mor** (rü′mər), *n., v.* —*n.* **1** a story or statement talked of as news without any proof that it is true: *The rumor spread that a new school would be built here. The rumor of what had happened ... had spread about the premises* (Arnold Bennett). SYN: report. **2** vague, general talk, not based on definite knowledge: *Rumor has it that the new girl went to school in France. According to the rumor of the times, she may have been a daughter of Lord Byron* (Time). **3** *Archaic.* reputation; fame: *Great is the rumour of this dreadful knight* (Shakespeare). **4** *Obsolete.* confused noise; din.
—*v.t.* to tell or spread by rumor: *It was rumored that the government was going to increase taxes.*
[< Old French *rumor* great uproar < Latin *rūmor, -ōris* rumor, noise] —**ru′mor|er,** *n.*

**ru|mor|mon|ger** (rü′mər mung′gər, -mong′-), *n.* a person who spreads rumors.

**ru|mour** (rü′mər), *n., v.t. British.* rumor.

**rump** (rump), *n., adj.* —*n.* **1** the hind part of the body of an animal, where the legs join the back. **2** a cut of beef from this part. **3** the corresponding part of the human body; buttocks. **4** *Figurative.* **a** an unimportant or inferior part; remnant. **b** a parliament, assembly, or other legislative body having only a remnant of its former membership because of the departure, expulsion, or resignation of a large number of its members.
—*adj.* small; unimportant; inferior, as of a splinter group: *Both were named by acclamation at a*

*rump convention of southern Democrats* (Milwaukee Journal).
[< Scandinavian (compare Swedish *rumpa* rump)]

**Rump** (rump), *n.* the Long Parliament in England after the exclusion, in December, 1648, of about 100 members who favored compromise with King Charles I: *The Rump alone was left to stand for the old tradition of Parliament* (Henry Morley).

**rump|bone** (rump′bōn′), *n.* the bone of the rump; sacrum.

**rum|ple** (rum′pəl), *v.*, **-pled, -pling,** *n.* —***v.t.*** **1** to crumple; crush; wrinkle: *a rumpled sheet of paper. Don't play in your best dress; you'll rumple it.* SYN: pucker, crease. **2** to tousle; disorder: *to rumple up hair.*
—***v.i.*** to become wrinkled, crumpled, or disordered. SYN: pucker, crease.
[apparently < noun]
—***n.*** a wrinkle; crease.
[< earlier Dutch *rompel*]

**rum|ply** (rum′plē), *adj.*, **-pli|er, -pli|est.** rumpled; disorderly; wrinkled: *rumply clothes, rumply hair.*

**rum|pot** (rum′pot′), *n. Slang.* a drunkard: *I had hysterical thoughts of Henry Fielding's wonderful rumpot, Squire Western, roaring in on the scene* (Maclean's).

**Rump Parliament,** = Rump.

**rum|pus** (rum′pəs), *n. Informal.* **1** a noisy disturbance; row: *He ... knocked down so many students and easels and drawingboards ... and made such a terrific rumpus* (George du Maurier). **2** noise; uproar: *The affair caused considerable rumpus.* [origin uncertain]

**rumpus room,** *U.S.* a room in a house, often in the basement, set apart for parties, games, or other recreation: *... a gaudy rumpus room, the ceilings decorated with Venetian carnival masks* (Saturday Review).

**rum|run|ner** (rum′run′ər), *n. U.S.* a person or ship that smuggles alcoholic liquor into a country.
[American English < *rum* + *runner*]

**rum|run|ning** (rum′run′ing), *n., adj.* —***n.*** the act of smuggling alcoholic liquor.
—***adj.*** that smuggles alcoholic liquor.

**run** (run), *v.*, **ran, run, run|ning,** *n., adj.* —***v.i.*** **1** to go by moving the legs quickly; go faster than walking: *A horse can run faster than a man.* SYN: sprint, gallop. **2a** to go in a hurry; hasten: *Run for help. What need a man ... run to meet what he would most avoid?* (Milton). SYN: hurry, rush, race, speed. **b** to make a quick trip: *to run up to the city. Let's run over to the lake for the weekend.* **3** to escape; flee: *Run for your life.* **4a** to keep going; go; move: *This bus runs between Chicago and St. Louis. Does your watch run well?* **b** to sail or be driven: *The ship ran aground on the rocks.* **c** to turn; revolve: *A wheel runs on an axle.* **5** to go on; proceed: *Prices of hats run as high as $50.* **6** to creep; trail; climb: *Vines run up the sides of the chimney.* **7** to pass quickly: *Time runs on.* (*Figurative.*) *The thought ran through his mind that he might forget his speech.* **8** to stretch; extend: *Shelves run along the walls. A fence runs around the house. The road runs south from New York to Atlanta.* **9** to flow: *Blood runs from a cut. But if ye will not hear it, my soul shall weep in secret places for your pride; and mine eye shall weep sore, and run down with tears, because the Lord's flock is carried away captive* (Jeremiah 13:17). **10** to discharge fluid, mucus, or pus: *My nose runs whenever I have a cold.* **11** *Figurative.* to get; become: *Never run into debt. The well ran dry.* **12** *Figurative.* to have a specified character, quality, form, or size: *These potatoes run large. Her hair runs to curls.* **13** to spread: *The color ran when the dress was washed. Ink runs on a blotter.* **14** *Figurative.* to continue; last: *a lease to run two years. The play ran for a whole season.* **15** to have currency or be current; occur: *The story runs that school will close early today. In haste I snatch up my pen ... to give you news as it runs* (Alexander Hamilton). **16** to have legal force. **17a** to take part in a race or contest. **b** to finish a race, contest, or project in a certain way: *The horse ran last.* **18** to be a candidate for election: *He will run for president.* **19** *Figurative.* to move easily, freely, or smoothly; keep operating: *A rope runs in a pulley. The engine ran all day without overheating.* **20** to be worded or expressed: *How does the first verse run?* **21** to go about without restraint: *The children were allowed to run about the streets.* **22** to drop stitches; ravel: *Nylon stockings often run.* **23** to soften; become liquid; melt: *The wax ran when the candles were lit.* **24** to pass to or from the sea; migrate, as for spawning: *The salmon are running.* **25** *Figurative.* to return often to the mind: *A tune kept running in my head.* **26a** to make many and urgent demands for money or payment: *to run on a bank.* **b** to collect, accumulate, or become payable in due course, as interest on a loan.
—***v.t.*** **1** to cause to run; cause to move: *The jockey ran the horse up and down the track.* **2a** to go by, or as if by, running: *to run a race, to run an errand.* **b** to cover by running: *to run ten miles.* **3** to go along (as a way or path): *to run the course until the end.* **4** to pursue; chase (game): *to run a fox. The chief difficulty in running buffalo ... is that of loading the gun ... at full gallop* (Francis Parkman). **5** to cause to pass quickly: *She ran her eyes over the old notes before discarding them. He ran his hand over the pipe to see if it was hot before grabbing it.* **6** to trace: *Run that report back to its source.* **7** to put; spread; lead: *to run a shelf along a wall.* **8** to drive; force; thrust: *He ran a splinter into his hand. I ... chanced to run my nose directly against a post* (Sir Richard Steele). **9a** to flow with: *The streets ran oil after an oil truck overturned. All the brooks ran gold* (A. E. Housman). **b** to cause to flow; give forth: *to run a fever or temperature.* **10a** to bring into a certain state by running: *to run oneself out of breath.* **b** *Figurative.* to lead or force into some state or action: *to run myself into trouble* (Scott). *He runs his father in debt* (Thoreau). **11** to expose oneself to: *to run a risk of catching a cold.* **12** *Figurative.* to cause to move easily, freely, or smoothly; cause to keep operating: *to run a machine.* SYN: operate. **13** *Figurative.* to conduct; manage: *to run a business. Was it not obvious ... that this was how the whole of society should be run?* (Edmund Wilson). SYN: operate. **14** to sew temporarily and quickly by pushing a needle in and out with even stitches in a line; baste: *to run a hem.* **15** to get past or through: *Enemy ships tried to run the blockade.* **16** to smuggle: *to run rum. The plan was to bargain with the slave to run him to Canada for a stipulated sum* (St. Louis Reveille). **17** to publish (as an advertisement, story, column, or picture) in a newspaper, magazine, or other publication: *He ran an ad in the evening paper.* **18** to shape by melting: *to run bullets through a mold, to run silver into bars.* **19a** to carry; take; transport: *Can you run this book over to the library for me?* **b** to discharge; be able to carry: *a drain that runs 10 gallons of water every hour.* **20** to put up as a candidate: *The Democrats ran him for the Presidency twice.* **21** to enter (a horse or other contestant) in a race. **22** *Football.* to run off (a play). **23** to contend with in a race: *I will run you a mile.* **24** to make an unbroken sequence of (shots or strokes), as in billiards or pool. **25** to draw or trace (as a line) on a surface.
—***n.*** **1** the act of running: *to set out at a run.* **2a** a spell or period of causing a machine, device, or operation to work: *During a run of eight hours the factory produced 100 cars.* **b** the amount of anything produced in such a period: *a run of 100 cars. Refinery runs averaged 975,874 barrels daily* (Wall Street Journal). **3** a spell of causing something liquid to run or flow, or the amount that runs: *the run of sap from maple trees.* **4a** a trip: *Through freight trains make the run from Chicago to New York in as little as 22 hours* (Newsweek). **b** a quick trip: *We took a run up to the country for the day.* **5a** a unit of score in baseball or cricket. In baseball a run is made by a runner touching home plate after having touched the bases in order. **b** an unbroken sequence of scoring plays, as billiards or pool. **6** *Figurative.* a continuous spell or course; continuous extent; time; period: *a run of bad luck, a run of fine weather.* **7a** a succession, as of performances or showings: *This play has had a run of two years.* **b** a sudden demand or series of demands: *There was a run on the bank to draw out money.* **c** a set of things following in consecutive order, such as a sequence of cards. **d** a spell of being in demand or favor: *A history of the Bloody Assizes ... was expected to have as great a run as the Pilgrim's Progress* (Macaulay). **8** *Figurative.* onward movement; progress; course; trend: *the run of events.* **9** *Music.* a rapid succession of tones. **10** *Figurative.* kind or class: *the common run of mankind. As for the usual run of concerts, he hated them* (Samuel Butler). **11** freedom to go over or through, or to use; free use: *The guests were given the run of the house.* **12** a flow or rush of water; small stream: *There is no ... Flat rich Land to be found—till one gets far enough from the River to head the little runs and drains* (George Washington). **13a** a number of fish moving together: *a run of salmon.* **b** the action or fact of fish moving up a river from the sea to spawn. **14** a way: **a** a track, as for skiing. **b** a trough or pipe. **15a** a stretch of ground or enclosed space for animals: *a dog run, a chicken run.* **b** (in Australia) a large area for grazing sheep. **16** a place where stitches have slipped out or become undone: *a run in a stocking.* **17** a landing of smuggled goods. **18** the extreme afterpart of a ship's bottom. **19** a track or support on which something can move. **20** the direction, line, or lie of anything: *the run of the grain of wood.*
—***adj.*** **1** melted: *run butter.* **2** melted and run into a mold; cast: *run steel.* **3** (of a fish) having ascended a stream from the sea. **4** smuggled: *The pirates brought in run goods at night.*

**a run for one's money, a** strong competition: *Determined to give the large chain a run for its money, he opened a discount store.* **b** satisfaction, as for one's expenditures or efforts: *The travel agent promised to give the tourists a run for their money.*

**in the long run,** on the whole; in the end: *A full investigation would, in the long run, do less harm than continued official silence* (David McReynolds).

**in the short run,** in the immediate present; for the moment: *In the short run, the mood of the investors is what counts* (New Yorker).

**on the** (or **a**) **dead run,** moving at full speed: *Mr. Nixon is on the dead run from the time he wakes up at 7:30 a.m. ... until 1:30 next morning* (Wall Street Journal).

**on the run, a** hurrying: *You could see the people tearing down on the run* (Mark Twain). **b** in retreat or rout; fleeing: *Since then Lahorie had been on the run for six years, hidden for part of that time by Hugo's mother* (New Yorker). **c** while running: *He caught the ball on the run.*

**run across,** to meet by chance; find: *I ran across an old freind in town today. Until two years ago I had never run across this deviation in my patients* (Maclean's).

**run afoul of.** See under **afoul.**

**run after, a** to pursue, especially with admiration or attentions: *She found that her daughter was being run after by all our idle young men* (Mary Charlton). **b** to follow eagerly; take up with: *... to prevent their running blindly after any doctrine* (John Keble).

**run against,** to clash with; oppose: *The second of my working conditions ... ran against supposed IBM tradition* (John Lear).

**run along,** to leave; go away: *Run along now, little boy.*

**run around,** *Informal.* to keep company; associate: *He has been running around with a bad crowd.*

**run away,** to escape by running; flee in a hurry: *When he saw the policeman, the thief ran away.*

**run away with, a** to win easily over others: *He ran away with every prize in the tournament.* **b** to elope with: *Dutton ... leaving Win in the lurch, ran away with another man's wife* (Tobias Smollett). **c** to overcome: *Don't let your passion run away with your senses* (John Gay).

**run down, a** to stop going or working: *The clock has run down. The toys that had been set in motion for the baby had all stopped and run down long ago* (Dickens). **b** to chase till caught or killed; hunt down: *The fox ran down the hare.* **c** to knock down by running against: *We stand a good chance of being run down by a car in this traffic.* **d** *Figurative.* to speak evil against; disparage: *He found himself run down as a superficial prating quack* (Joseph Addison). **e** to make tired or ill: *She is run down from working too hard.* **f** to fall off, diminish, or decrease; deteriorate: [*She*] *had let everything run down; she had, in truth, no money for repairs* (Harper's).

**run for it,** to run for safety: *As soon as they heard the siren, they ran for it.*

**run foul of.** See under **foul.**

**run in, a** *Slang.* to arrest and put in jail: *Yusef is a very bad man. Why don't the authorities run him in?* (Graham Greene). **b** to pay a short visit: *My neighbor runs in to see me when she pleases.* **c** to set (type or copy) without a break in the running text: *to run in indented lines.*

**run into, a** to meet by chance: *If you run into my friend this noon, be sure to tell him "hello" for me.* **b** to crash into; collide with: *A large steamship ran into the tugboat.*

**run off, a** to cause to be run or played: *On the theory that the more plays a team runs off the greater its chances of scoring, Wilkinson had Oklahoma running as many as three plays in 38 seconds* (Newsweek). **b** to print: *to run off 1000 copies for a first edition.* **c** to run away; flee: *They cast their arms to the ground, and ran off ... as fast as they could* (Henry Brooke). **d** to write or recite rapidly: *to run off an article. She ran off glibly a list of the places they would visit.* **e** to draw or drain off (a liquid); flow off or away: *The rainwater ran off the eaves.* **f** *U.S.* to steal: *He's down on tramps ever since they ran off his chickens* (Bret Harte).

---

**Pronunciation Key:** hat, āge, cãre, fär; let, ēqual, tėrm; it, īce; hot, ōpen, ôrder; **oi**l, **ou**t; cup, pu̇t, rüle; **ch**ild; lo**ng**; **th**in; **ꟈ**en; **zh**, measure; **ə** represents **a** in about, **e** in taken, **i** in pencil, **o** in lemon, **u** in circus.

**run off with**, **a** to steal: *The thief ran off with her ring and bracelet.* **b** to elope: *His daughter ran off with a soldier.*

**run on**, **a** to continue, as in operation or effect: *This abuse has been allowed to run on unchecked for too long.* **b** to elapse: *... as months ran on and rumour of battle grew* (Tennyson). **c** to continue speaking: *"I'm a fool—I always was," he ran on, hurriedly* (F. W. Robinson). **d** to expand; develop: *The proposed six lessons ran on into perhaps eight or nine* (John Ruskin). **e** to set (type or copy) without a break in the running text: *to run on paragraphs.* **f** to add (a run-on entry): *This dictionary runs on many words ending in -ly.*

**run out**, **a** to come to an end; become exhausted: *After three minutes his time ran out on the telephone call. Time was running out and no solution was in sight* (Maclean's). **b** *Cricket.* to put out (the batsman) before he completes a run by knocking off a bail with the ball.

**run out of**, to use up; have no more: *Mother ran out of eggs and had to borrow some from our neighbor. When we had run out of money, we had no living soul to befriend us* (Manchester Guardian).

**run out on**, *Informal.* **a** to leave suddenly; fail to help; desert: *Only a coward would run out on his best friend at a difficult time.* **b** to back out of; not be faithful to; renege on: *He ran out on his promise to help her.* **c** to run away from; escape: *He ran out on me without paying his rent.*

**run over**, **a** to ride or drive over: *The car ran over some glass.* **b** to overflow: *The waiter filled his cup too full and the coffee ran over onto the table. Now was my heart full of joy, ... and mine affections running over with love* (John Bunyan). **c** to go through quickly: *The particulars of his life have been often written, and therefore I shall run them over briefly* (Horace Walpole).

**run rings around**. See under **ring**[1].

**run riot**. See under **riot**.

**run scared**. See under **scared**.

**run short**. See under **short**.

**run through**, **a** to use up, spend, or consume rapidly and foolishly: *The foolish young man ran through his month's allowance in a week. Working women run through an average of 36 pairs of nylons a year* (Wall Street Journal). **b** *Figurative.* to review or rehearse: *The teacher ran through the homework assignment a second time. The players ran through the new football plays before the game.* **c** to pierce: *I ran one of the assassins through the body* (Henry Brooke).

**run up**, **a** to make quickly: *The team ran up a big lead in the first quarter.* **b** to collect; accumulate: *Don't run up a big bill.* **c** to amount: *The cost of the repair ran up to $50.* **d** to raise: *to run up a flag.* **e** to add up quickly: *to run up a column of numbers.* **f** to sew quickly: *I want you to run up a tear in my dress.*

**run up against**, **a** to meet by chance or casually: *The very man I've been hoping I'd run up against one of these days* (Beatrice Butt). **b** to come across (some difficulty): *This is one of the most puzzling cases I have ever run up against* (Theodore Dreiser). *Called in to investigate the killing ..., he immediately ran up against the usual barrier of silence* (New Yorker).

[Old English *rinnan;* the vowel may be from the Old English past participle *runnon*]

**run|a|bout** (run′ə bout′), *n.* **1** a light, open automobile or carriage with a single seat. **2** a small motorboat. **3** a person who runs about from place to place, such as a vagabond or peddler.

**run action**, *Football.* a play in which the quarterback fakes a running play and drops back to pass.

**run|a|gate** (run′ə gāt′), *n. Archaic.* **1** a runaway; fugitive. **2** a vagabond; wanderer. [alteration of Middle English *renegat* renegade; influenced by *run* + earlier *agate* away]

**run|a|round** (run′ə round′), *n.* **1** *Informal.* evasion or indefinite postponement of action, especially in regard to a request; avoidance: *Even those who would probably get visas hate to take the risk of getting a consular runaround* (Time). **2** type set less than the full measure to permit the insertion of an illustration or the like.

**run|a|way** (run′ə wā′), *n., adj.* —*n.* **1** a person or animal that runs away: *The runaway dragged the empty carriage behind him.* **2** the act of running away; eloping: *The young couple's runaway caused great sadness to their parents.*
—*adj.* **1** running with nobody to guide or stop it; out of control: *a runaway horse, a runaway car. Her knees bounced up and down like runaway jackhammers* (Time). **2** done by runaways: *a runaway marriage.* **3** easily won; one-sided: *a runaway victory. The book turned out to be a runaway best seller* (Time). **4** escaped; fugitive: *runaway slaves.*

**runaway shop**, a plant moved to another site by the employer to escape local union demands.

**run|back** (run′bak′), *n.* **1** *Football.* the run made by a player who has received the ball as a result of an opponent's kick or an intercepted pass: *His 86-yard run was a record for a Rose Bowl punt runback to a touchdown* (New York Times). **2** the area between the base line and the backstop on a tennis court or other playing area.

**run|ci|ble spoon** (run′sə bəl), a fork with three short, wide prongs, used as a spoon in eating ice cream and other semisolid food. [apparently < *runc*(inate) + *-ible*]

***run|ci|nate** (run′sə nit, -nāt), *adj.* having coarse, toothlike notches or lobes pointing backward. Dandelion leaves are runcinate. [< Latin *runcina* plane (but taken as "saw") < Greek *rhykánē;* influenced by Latin *runcāre* to clear (of thorns)]

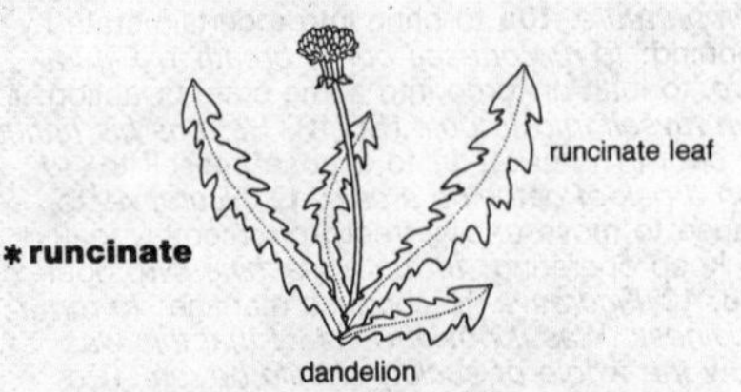

***runcinate**

**run|dle** (run′dəl), *n.* **1** a rung of a ladder. **2** a bar of a kind of pinion. **3** a wheel; rotating part. [Middle English *rundel,* variant of *roundel*]

**rund|let** (rund′lit), *n. Archaic.* **1** an old measure of liquid equal to about 18 gallons. **2** a cask; small barrel: *... twelve small rundlets of fine powder for our small-arms* (Daniel Defoe). Also, **runlet**. [Middle English *rowndelet, rondelet* < Old French (diminutive) < *rondelle* small tun < *rond* round]

**run|down** (run′doun′), *n. Informal.* an account; summary: *a rundown of the week's news. The speaker gave a brief rundown on his career.* [< *run* + *down*]

**run-down** (*adj.* run′doun′; *n.* run′doun′), *adj., n.* —*adj.* **1** tired; sick: *If you are generally "rundown," ask your doctor about preventive measures against respiratory infections* (Time). **2** falling to pieces; partly ruined: *a run-down building.* **3** that has stopped going or working.
—*n.* **1** *Baseball.* the attempt to tag out a base runner caught off base between two players. **2** decrease; decline: *... a run-down in the labor force due to rapid mechanization* (Wall Street Journal).
[< *run down,* idiom]

**rune**[1] (rün), *n.* **1** any letter of the Germanic alphabet used from about the 200's A.D. to about the 1200's. **2** a mark that looks like a rune and has some mysterious, magic meaning: *Wise he was, and many curious arts, Postures of runes, and healing herbs he knew* (Matthew Arnold). **3** a verse or sentence that has a magic meaning.
[Old English *rūn* < Scandinavian (compare Old Icelandic *rūn* secret, rune)]

**rune**[2] (rün), *n.* **1** an old Scandinavian poem or song: *Of the Troll of the Church they sing the rune By the Northern Sea in the harvest moon* (John Greenleaf Whittier). **2** a poem; song; verse. [< Finnish *runo* < Scandinavian (compare Old Icelandic *rūn*)]

**runed** (ründ), *adj.* inscribed with runes.

**rune stone**, a stone having runic inscriptions: *Professor Hagen, philologist, made an intensive study of the Kensington rune stone* (New York Times).

**rung**[1] (rung), *v.* a past tense and the past participle of **ring**[2]: *The bell has rung.*

**rung**[2] (rung), *n.* **1** a round rod or bar used as a step of a ladder: *The rung he was standing on broke leaving him dangling from the ladder.* (*Figurative.*) *Hard work and long hours are rungs in the ladder of success.* **2** a crosspiece set between the legs of a chair or stool or as part of the back or arm of a chair: *The clerks sat on high stools with feet twisted over the rungs.* **3** a spoke of a wheel. **4** a bar of wood having a similar shape and use. **5** *Scottish.* a stout staff; cudgel. [Old English *hrung*]

**ru|nic**[1] (rü′nik), *adj.* consisting of runes; written in runes; marked with runes. [< *run*(e)[1] + *-ic*]

**ru|nic**[2] (rü′nik), *adj.* like a rune. [< *run*(e)[2] + *-ic*]

**run|i|form** (rün′ə fôrm), *adj.* having the appearance of runes.

**run-in** (run′in′), *n., adj.* —*n.* **1** *Informal.* a sharp disagreement; argument; quarrel; row. **2** *Printing.* copy to be set starting on the same line and right after what comes before it.
—*adj. Printing.* that is a run-in.

**run|kle** (rung′kəl), *n., v.,* **-kled, -kling.** *Scottish.* wrinkle; crease.

**run|less** (run′lis), *adj.* without runs: *a runless inning, a runless game of cricket.*

**run|let**[1] (run′lit), *n.* a small stream. SYN: rivulet, runnel. [< *run,* noun + *-let*]

**run|let**[2] (run′lit), *n.* = rundlet.

**run|na|ble** (run′ə bəl), *adj.* suitable for the chase, as deer; warrantable: *His coat was in perfect condition, ... and he was a runnable deer, that is, of age and size sufficient for the chase* (Richard Jefferies).

**run|nel** (run′əl), *n.* **1** a small stream or brook; rivulet; runlet: *... hearing no sound except ... the various gurgling noises of innumerable runnels* (W. H. Hudson). **2** a small channel for water; gutter. [Old English *rynel,* related to *rinnan* run; probably influenced by Middle English *runnen* run]

**run|ner** (run′ər), *n.* **1** a person, animal, or thing that runs; racer: *A runner arrived out of breath. The world's fastest runners can cover 100 yards in less than 10 seconds* (Walter H. Gregg). **2a** *Baseball.* a base runner: *The game was close with two out and runners at first and third.* **b** *Football.* a player who carries the ball. **c** a messenger: *a runner for a bank or brokerage house.* SYN: courier. **3** a person who runs or works a machine, etc. **4** either of the long narrow pieces on which a sleigh or sled slides. **5** the blade of a skate. **6** a long, narrow strip: *We have a runner of carpet in our hall and runners of linen and lace on our dressers.* **7** a smuggler; person or ship that tries to evade somebody: *a blockade runner.* **8a** a slender stem that takes root along the ground, thus producing new plants. Strawberry plants spread by runners. *Many plants produce runners and rhizomes that effectively extend the area they occupy* (Fred W. Emerson). **b** a plant that spreads by such stems. **9** any one of various climbing bean plants: *the scarlet runner.* **10** a raveled place: *There was a runner in her stocking, an affecting thinness to her ankles* (New Yorker). **11** a support or groove along, on, or in which anything slides. **12** the rotating part of a turbine. **13** a jurel of the Atlantic coast of America. **14** a person who tries to get business, as for a hotel or tradesman. **15.** a collector, agent, or the like, as for a bank or brokerage house. **16** a channel along which molten metal runs from the furnace to the mold. **17** the millstone which turns against a fixed stone in a grinding mill.

**runner bean**, a climbing bean plant; runner.

**run|ner-up** (run′ər up′), *n., pl.* **run|ners-up.** a player or team that takes second place in a contest.

**run|ning** (run′ing), *n., adj.* —*n.* **1** the act of a person, animal, or thing that runs: *a running of a race, the running of a store.* **2** that which runs.
—*adj.* **1** discharging matter: *a running sore.* **2** flowing: *running water.* **3** liquid; fluid: *molten running iron.* **4** *Figurative.* going or carried on continuously: *a running commentary.* **5** current: *the running month.* **6** *Figurative.* repeated continuously: *a running pattern.* **7** *Figurative.* following in succession: *for three nights running.* **8** cursive: *Running handwriting joins all letters of a word together.* **9** prevalent: *Stores were advised to ... watch selling carefully to guide reorders on running styles* (New York Times). **10** moving or proceeding easily or smoothly. **11** *Figurative.* **a** moving when pulled or hauled: *a running rope.* **b** slipping or sliding easily: *a running knot or noose.* **12** (of plants) creeping or climbing; sending out runners. **13** that is measured in a straight line. **14** of the run of a train, bus, or other conveyance: *the running time between towns.* **15** performed with or during a run: *a running leap.* **16** *Figurative.* operating, as a machine; going; working. **17** of a horse: **a** trained to travel at a run. **b** traveling with speed at a run.

**in the running**, **a** having a chance to win; in the race or competition: *Although he is no longer the leading candidate, he is still in the running.* **b** among the leading competitors in a race or contest: *Experts place that horse in the running.*

**out of the running**, **a** having no chance to win; out of the race or competition: *The new British champion crashed and put himself out of the running* (London Times). **b** not among the leading competitors in a race or contest: *Out of the running for the second season, he is considered a poor bet.*

**running bale**, a finished bale of cotton as it comes from the gin and is ready for market: *Running bales ... usually vary somewhat in weight from the Agriculture Department's statistical 500-pound bale* (Wall Street Journal).

**running blackberry**, = dewberry.

**running board**, a metal or wood step or footboard attached below the door on some cars and trucks.

**running bond**, a method of bricklaying in which all layers of bricks are stretchers; stretcher bond.

**running bowline**, a bowline knot made round a part of the same rope to form a noose.

**running broad jump**, a broad jump in which the

broad-jumper takes a running start for the jump.

**running gear,** 1 the wheels and axles of an automobile, locomotive, or other vehicle. 2 ropes used to adjust a vessel's sails.

**running hand,** handwriting in which each word is formed without lifting the pen or pencil from the paper.

**running head,** 1 a heading printed at the top of each page of a book or other publication. 2 = running title.

**running high jump,** a high jump in which the high-jumper takes a running start for the jump, approaching the bar from any angle he chooses.

**running knot,** a knot so made as to slide along the rope; slipknot.

**running light,** a light required on a ship or aircraft while navigating at night.

**running mate,** 1a a candidate in an election running on the same ticket with another, but for a less important office, such as a candidate for vice-president. b *Figurative.* any companion or associate. 2 a horse that paces another in a race.

**running myrtle,** the common periwinkle, a low, creeping vine with blue flowers.

**running noose,** a noose with a running knot.

**running part,** part of a tackle that is free to slide, as between sheaves or pulleys.

**running rigging,** the ropes, chains, and other lines used to adjust the sails and movable spars.

**running shed,** *British.* a roundhouse for locomotives.

**running shoe,** = track shoe.

**running start,** 1 = flying start. 2 *Figurative: He designed the machines that later gave Renault a running start in the postwar period* (Wall Street Journal).

**running stitch,** several short, even stitches taken with the needle at one time.

**running title,** a title of a book or article printed at the top of the left-hand pages, or of all the pages.

**run|ny** (run′ē), *adj.,* **-ni|er, -ni|est.** that runs: *a runny nose. A runny faucet leaks.*

**run|off** (run′ôf′, -of′), *n., adj.* — *n.* 1 something that runs off, such as rain that flows off the land in streams: *The runoff of precipitation from northwestern America amounts to over 200 trillion gallons each year* (Ralph E. Lapp). 2 a final, deciding race or contest: *In the December 10 runoff, former Councilman Louie Welch was elected mayor by about 13,500 votes over Bob Hervey* (A. F. Muir). 3 *U.S.* a runoff primary: *In the Democratic gubernatorial primary, ... a segregationist squeezed toward a runoff with the favored candidate* (Time).

— *adj.* that decides a race or contest: *a runoff competition. If no candidate receives a clear majority in the first round, a runoff election is held a week later, when a single plurality suffices to elect* (John C. Cairns).

**runoff primary,** *U.S.* a second primary held between the two candidates polling the greatest number of votes in the first primary.

**run-of-mine** (run′əv mīn′), *adj.* = run-of-the-mine.

**run-of-pa|per** (run′əv pā′pər), *adj.* (of an advertisement) not requiring special or preferred placement in a newspaper; that may be placed on any page or in any section. *Abbr:* R.O.P.

**run-of-riv|er** (run′əv riv′ər), *adj.* = run-of-the-river.

**run-of-the-mill** (run′əv ᴛʜe mil′), *adj.* average or commonplace; ordinary; unselected: *a run-of-the-mill play.* [earlier *run of the mill* coarsely finished or unrefined mill products]

**run-of-the-mine** (run′əv ᴛʜe mīn′), *adj.* = run-of-the-mill. [earlier *run of the mine* crude, unsorted coal, or ores]

**run-of-the-riv|er** (run′əv ᴛʜə riv′ər), *adj.* (of a hydroelectric power plant) using the flow of a stream as it occurs; having no reservoir for storing power: *Kariba ... has ample long-term storage and can provide continuous firm power; Kafne, being virtually run-of-the-river, could not* (London Times).

**run-on** (run′on′, -ôn′), *adj., n.* — *adj.* 1 *Printing.* a continued or added without a break at the end: *Run-on chapters may begin anywhere on a page.* b = run-in. 2 *Prosody.* continuing without pause from one line of verse to another.

— *n.* 1 *Printing.* matter to be run on. 2 = run-on entry.

**run-on entry,** a dictionary entry which is not defined. It is usually formed by adding a common suffix to a simple root word and appears in heavy type at the end of the entry word from which it is formed. **Rurally** may be found as a run-on entry under **rural.**

**run-on sentence,** *Grammar.* a sentence in which a comma is mistakenly inserted between two main clauses instead of a period, semicolon, or conjunction. *Example:* We were early, the school was still closed.

**run|out** (run′out′), *n.* 1 *U.S. Slang.* the act of running out on someone; escape. 2 *Cricket.* an act or instance of running out the batsman.

**take a runout powder,** to run away; take a powder: *They [tenants in arrears] readily take a runout powder, and they do not even shrink from suicide* (New Yorker).

**run|o|ver** (run′ō′vər), *n. Printing.* matter that runs over the space assigned to it: *To avoid runover ... keep everything within a kind of rectangle* (New Yorker).

**run-o|ver** (run′ō′vər), *adj.* 1 = worn-out: *Even the shoes I wear are, despite run-over heels ... the same* (Harper's). 2 *Printing.* that runs over the assigned space: *run-over copy.*

**run sheep run,** a children's game similar to hide-and-seek but played with two sides. As one side hunts for the other side, the leader of the group in hiding remains at the base and warns his teammates with signals.

**runt** (runt), *n.* 1a an animal, person, or plant that is smaller than the usual size: *The runts were weak and had to be nursed by bottle rather than by the sow.* SYN: dwarf. b the smallest animal of a litter. 2 an ox or cow of a small breed. 3 *British Dialect.* an old or decayed stump of a tree. 4 *Scottish.* the stalk or stem of a plant. [perhaps unrecorded Old English *hrunta* (compare *Hrunting,* Beowulf's sword) < *hrung* rung[2]]

**run-through** (run′thrü′), *n.* 1 a brief review; summary: *He began with a run-through of Freud's ... speculations on telepathy as a ... means of human communication* (New Yorker). 2 a rehearsal of a play or other prepared entertainment: *a final run-through of a play before opening night.* 3 a railroad train operated over lines owned by other companies.

**runt|i|ness** (run′tē nis), *n.* runty quality or condition.

**runt|ish** (run′tish), *adj.* = runty.

**runt|y** (run′tē), *adj.,* **runt|i|er, runt|i|est.** unusually small; undersized; stunted; dwarfish.

**run-up** (run′up′), *n.* 1 an increase: *a run-up in prices.* 2 the preliminary run before the jump in the broad jump. 3 *British.* the act of sending a ball up to the goal or into a position for final play: *... to restrict a bowler's run-up to 20 yards* (London Times). 4 *British.* a period leading up to some event; prelude: *In the run-up to the Greater London Council elections, the capital may show few signs of urban malaise to the visitor* (Manchester Guardian Weekly). 5 the running or speeding up of an engine in order to test, check, or warm it.

**run|way** (run′wā′), *n.* 1 a smooth, level strip of land on which aircraft take off and land. It is usually paved. 2 an enclosed place for animals to run in: *When I got home with her, I unbridled her in the runway of the barn which was about twelve feet wide and fifty feet long* (Harper's). 3 the beaten track of deer or other animals. SYN: spoor. 4 a way, track, groove, trough, or the like, along which something moves or slides. 5 a stream bed. 6 a groove to return bowling balls to the head of the alley.

**ru|pee** (rü pē′), *n.* 1 the unit of money of India, Pakistan, Bhutan, and Nepal, equal to 100 paise. 2 the unit of money of Sri Lanka (Ceylon) and Mauritius, equal to 100 cents. 3 a nickel or cupronickel coin or piece of paper money worth one rupee. [< Hindi *rūpiyah* < Sanskrit *rūpya* wrought silver or gold]

**ru|pes|tri|an** (rü pes′trē ən), *adj.* found on rocks: *rupestrian inscriptions. This rupestrian art, which is of mysterious origin and said to be very beautiful, was an important find* (New Yorker). [< New Latin *rupestris* (< Latin *rūpes* rock) + English *-ian*]

**ru|pes|trine** (rü pes′trin), *adj. Biology.* living or growing among rocks.

**ru|pi|ah** (rü pē′ə), *n., pl.* **-ah** or **-ahs.** the unit of money of Indonesia, equal to 100 sen. [< Indonesian *rupiah* < Hindi *rūpiyah* rupee]

**ru|pic|o|line** (rü pik′ə līn), *adj.* = rupestrine. [< Latin *rūpes* rock + *colere* inhabit + English *-ine*[1]]

**ru|pic|o|lous** (rü pik′ə ləs), *adj.* = rupestrine.

**rup|tive marking** (rup′tiv), patterns of light and dark color that break up the outline of a bird to give it protective coloration. [*ruptive* < Latin *ruptus* (past participle of *rumpere* to break) + English *-ive*]

**rup|tur|a|ble** (rup′chər ə bəl), *adj.* that can be ruptured.

**rup|ture** (rup′chər), *n., v.,* **-tured, -tur|ing.** — *n.* 1 the act of breaking or state of being broken: *The rupture of a blood vessel usually causes the mark of a bruise. During the war it was found that in zones of secondary damage rupture of welding was rare* (London Times). 2 the act of breaking off friendly relations that threatens to become actual war: *The smothered dissensions among the emigrants suddenly broke into open rupture* (Francis Parkman). 3 the sticking out of some tissue or organ of the body through the wall of the cavity that should hold it in; hernia.

— *v.t.* 1 to break; burst; break off: *The earthquake ruptured water mains flooding the streets.* 2 to affect with hernia.

— *v.i.* 1 to suffer a break. 2 to suffer a hernia. [< Latin *ruptūra* < *rumpere* to break, burst]

**ru|ral** (rür′əl), *adj.* 1 in the country; belonging to the country; like that of the country: *Rural life is quiet. As cities grow, they spread farther and farther into what were once rural areas. The smell of grain, or tedded grass, or kine, Or dairy, each rural sight, each rural sound* (Milton). 2 of or having to do with agriculture: *rural economy.* [< Late Latin *rūrālis* < *rūs, rūris* country] — **ru′ral|ly,** *adv.* — **ru′ral|ness,** *n.*

— *Syn.* 1 **Rural, rustic, pastoral** mean of, relating to, or characteristic of the country as opposed to the city. **Rural** is the most objective term, implying neither favor nor disfavor (*rural roads*) or mild, general favor (*healthful rural life*). **Rustic** implies simplicity and roughness, regarded favorably (*rustic charm*) or unfavorably (*rustic speech*). **Pastoral** implies idyllic simplicity, suggesting shepherds, grazing flocks, green pastures, and serene peace: *He paints pastoral pictures.*

**rural dean,** a priest holding the first rank among the clergy of a district outside the cathedral city.

**ru|ra|les** (rü rä′läs), *n.pl.* mounted police in Mexico, originally made up largely of revolutionaries of President Diaz: *The rurales, I was told, prefer not to take prisoners* (New Yorker). [< Spanish (*guardias*) *rurales* rural (guards)]

**rural free delivery** or **rural delivery,** the free delivery of mail in country districts by regular carriers. *Abbr:* R.F.D., R.D.

**ru|ral|ism** (rür′ə liz əm), *n.* 1 rural character; rural life. 2 an expression, idiom, or custom peculiar to the country.

**ru|ral|ist** (rür′ə list), *n.* 1 a person who leads or advocates a rural life. 2 a person who lives or works in the country: *Then they drive the country roads, visiting ruralists in tobacco fields or strawberry patches* (Wall Street Journal). 3 a person skilled in the management of rural affairs or the cultivation or development of country regions.

**ru|ral|i|ty** (rü ral′ə tē), *n., pl.* **-ties.** 1 rural character. 2 a rural characteristic, matter, or scene.

**ru|ral|i|za|tion** (rür′ə lə zā′shən), *n.* the fact of ruralizing.

**ru|ral|ize** (rür′ə līz), *v.,* **-ized, -iz|ing.** — *v.t.* to cause to become rural.

— *v.i.* to spend time in the country.

**rural route,** a mail-delivery circuit in the country; route for rural free delivery: *Entrants will be accepted from Thamesville and surrounding rural routes* (Chatham, Ontario, Daily News). *Abbr:* R.R.

**rur|ban** (rėr′bən, rür′-), *adj. U.S.* of or having to do with a group or an area marked by both rural and urban features. [< *rur*(al) + (ur)*ban*]

**ru|ri|dec|a|nal** (rür′ə dek′ə nəl, -di kā′-), *adj.* of or having to do with a rural dean or deans: *As the basic unit of church synodal government, these ruridecanal synods will elect representatives to the diocesan synods and General Synod of the church* (Time).

**Ru|ri|ta|ni|an** (rür′ə tā′nē ən, -tān′yən), *adj.* 1 characteristic of an imaginary kingdom or land. 2 of or having to do with a romanticized, glamorous concept of royalty. [< *Ruritania,* the fictional kingdom in *The Prisoner of Zenda,* a novel by Anthony Hope, 1863-1933, a British novelist]

**rurp** (rėrp), *n.* a type of piton shaped somewhat like a picture hook: *Scott uses a number of American rurps ... whose blades are only 9¾ inches long* (Sunday Times). [< *r*(ealized) *u*(ltimate) *r*(eality) *p*(iton)]

**Rus.,** 1 Russia. 2 Russian.

**ru|sa** (rü′sə), *n.* any one of a group of large East Indian deer with a mane; sambar. [< New Latin *Rusa* the genus < Malay *rūsa* deer]

**ru|sal|ka** (rü säl′kə), *n. Russian Legend.* a water nymph. [< Russian *rusalka*]

**ruse** (rüz, rüs), *n.* a trick; scheme or device to mislead others; stratagem: *It was a ruse on the part of the governing authorities ... to get the rioters out of the city* (Cardinal Newman). SYN: artifice, dodge, wile. See syn. under **stratagem.** [< Old French *ruse* < *ruser* to dodge, get out of the way < Late Latin *refusāre* < Latin *recusāre* push back, deny]

**ru|sé** (rü zā′), *adj.* artful; cunning; sly. [< French *rusé,* past participle of *ruser;* see etym. under **ruse**]

---

**Pronunciation Key:** **h**at, **ā**ge, **c**ãre, **f**är; **l**et, **ē**qual, **t**ėrm; **i**t, **ī**ce; **h**ot, **ō**pen, **ô**rder; **oi**l, **ou**t; **c**up, **p**ůt, **r**üle; **ch**ild; lo**ng**; **th**in; **ᴛʜ**en; **zh**, measure; **ə** represents **a** in about, **e** in taken, **i** in pencil, **o** in lemon, **u** in circus.

**rush**[1] (rush), *v., n., adj.* —*v.i.* **1** to move with speed or force: *to rush from the room. The river rushed past. We rushed to the station. Our sail was now set, and, with the still rising wind, we rushed along* (Herman Melville). SYN: dash, hurry, speed. **2** to run forward to make an attack: *The crazed man rushed at the doctor who was trying to help him.* (*Figurative.*) *All his creditors would have come rushing on him in a body* (Thackeray). **3** to come, go, pass, or act with speed or haste: *color rushing to the face,* (*Figurative.*) *Thoughts rushing through the mind.* (*Figurative.*) *He rushes into things without knowing anything about them.*
—*v.t.* **1** to send, push, force, or carry with speed or haste: *Rush this order, please. We rushed him home before the rain began. The sick child was rushed to the hospital.* **2** to attack, overcome, or take with much speed and force: *They rushed the enemy.* **3** to urge to hurry: *Don't rush me.* **4** *U.S. Informal.* to give much attention to, especially to persuade to join a fraternity or sorority: *There were a lot of students who weren't rushed or pledged who found solace in the Y ... or musical clubs* (Eva Thompson). **5** to advance (a football) by running.
—*n.* **1** the act of rushing; dash: *The rush of the flood swept everything before it. The little girl told her sad story in a rush of tears. There was a general rush of the men towards the beach* (Herman Melville). **2** busy haste; hurry: *the rush of city life. So sorry to have kept you waiting, but we're rather in a rush to-day* (G. K. Chesterton). **3** the great or sudden effort of many people to go somewhere or get something: *the gold rush. The Christmas rush is hard on clerks.* **4** eager demand; pressure: *a rush for tickets to a play, a rush on steel stocks. A sudden rush of business kept everyone working hard.* **5** an attempt to carry the ball through the opposing line in football. **6** *U.S.* a scrimmage held as a form of sport between groups or classes of students. **7** an attack: *The infantry rush which followed captured them* (John Buchan). **8** *U.S. Informal.* a rushing, as for a fraternity or sorority.
—*adj.* **1** requiring speed: *A rush order must be filled at once.* **2** *U.S. Informal.* of or having to do with rushing: *Formal rush week for all sororities on the campus will be Oct. 1 to Oct. 6* (Denver Tribune).
**rushes,** the first filmed scenes of a part of a motion picture, projected especially for the approval of the director: *Doris Day always looks at the daily rushes of her pictures* (Maclean's). *Sometimes ... I'm not satisfied with the rushes and they let me dub in new lines* (Clifton Webb).
**with a rush,** suddenly; quickly: *The Confederate States perceive that they cannot carry all before them with a rush* (London Times).
[Middle English *ruschen* force out of place by violent impact, probably < Old French *russher,* variant of *ruser;* see etym. under **ruse**] —**rush'er,** *n.*

**rush**[2] (rush), *n.* **1** any one of a family of grasslike plants with pithy or hollow stems, that grow in wet ground or marshy places. Rushes comprise a family of plants. **2** a stem of such a plant, used for making chair seats, baskets, floor mats, and the like: *A heap of dried leaves and rushes ... for rest at night* (Cardinal Newman). **3** something of little or no value. [Old English *rysc*]

**rush|bear|ing** (rush'bãr'ing), *n.* an annual ceremony in northern districts of England, consisting of carrying rushes and garlands to the church and strewing the floor or decorating the walls with them, usually a general holiday.

**rush candle,** = rushlight.

**rush|ee** (rush ē'), *n. U.S. Informal.* a student undergoing rushing in a college.

**rush hour,** the time of day when traffic is heaviest or when trains, buses, and other means of transportation are most crowded.

**rush|ing** (rush'ing), *n., adj.* —*n. U.S. Informal.* **1** the act of paying special attention to someone, especially to persuade to join a fraternity or sorority: *Howard has a normally lively interest in extracurricular activities like ... fraternity and sorority rushing* (Life). **2** the period when fraternity rushing takes place.
—*adj.* **1** moving or going with speed; dashing. **2** proceeding with great activity: *a rushing business.* —**rush'ing|ly,** *adv.*

**rush|light** (rush'līt'), *n.* a candle with a wick made from a rush.

**rush|like** (rush'līk'), *adj.* like a rush or reed.

**rush line,** the forward line in football; line.

**rush|y** (rush'ē), *adj.,* **rush|i|er, rush|i|est.** **1** abounding with rushes; covered with rushes: *Artemis haunted streams and rushy pools* (Maurice Hewlett). **2** made of rushes: *my rushy couch* (Oliver Goldsmith). **3** like rushes: *rushy herbs.*

**ru|sine antler** (rü'sīn, -sin), an antler with a single brow tine and a simple fork at the end of the main stem. [< New Latin *Rusa* (see etym. under **rusa**) + English *-ine*[1]]

**rus in ur|be** (rus' in ėr'bē), *Latin.* the country in the city.

**rusk** (rusk), *n.* **1** a piece of bread or cake toasted in the oven. **2** a kind of light, soft, sweet biscuit. [< Spanish, Portuguese *rosca* roll, twist of bread; (literally) spiral; origin uncertain]

**Russ** (rus), *n., pl.* **Russ** or **Russ|es,** *adj.* —*n.* **1** a Russian (used in an unfriendly way). **2** *Rare.* the Russian language. —*adj. Rare.* Russian.
[< Russian *Rus'* the Russians, Russia, ultimately < *Ros*(lagen), in Sweden, where the founders of Russia came from]

**Russ.,** **1** Russia. **2** Russian.

**Rus|sell diagram** (rus'əl), *Astronomy.* a diagram of the relation between the brightness and temperature of stars; Hertzsprung-Russell diagram. [< Henry N. *Russell,* 1877-1957, an American astronomer]

**Rus|sell|ite** (rus'ə līt), *n.* a former name of a member of Jehovah's Witnesses. [< Charles T. *Russell,* 1852-1916, an American religious leader, founder of Jehovah's Witnesses + *-ite*[1]]

**Russell's viper,** a large, very poisonous snake with bright reddish-brown spots, common to southeastern Asia. [< Patrick *Russell,* 1727-1805, a British physician]

**rus|set** (rus'it), *adj., n.* —*adj.* **1** yellowish-brown or reddish-brown: *The leaves in the fall are scarlet, yellow, and russet.* **2** rustic; homely; simple. **3** made of russet (cloth). **4** made of leather that has not been blackened: *russet shoes.*
—*n.* **1** a yellowish brown or reddish brown. **2** a coarse, russet-colored cloth. The English peasants used to make and wear russet. **3** a kind of winter apple with a rough, brownish skin. **4** leather that is finished but not polished.
[< Old French *rousset* (diminutive) < *rous* < Latin *russus* red, related to *ruber* red]

**rus|set-backed thrush** (rus'it bakt'), the olive-backed thrush, especially the variety of the Pacific Coast of North America.

**rus|set|y** (rus'ə tē), *adj.* of a color like russet.

**rus|sia** (rush'ə), *n.* = Russia leather.

**Russia leather,** a fine, smooth leather, often dark-red, originally produced in Russia by tanning and dyeing and then rubbing with birch oil.

**Rus|sian** (rush'ən), *adj., n.* —*adj.* of or having to do with Russia (the Soviet Union), its people, or their language: *The Western world was treated to the first publication of general Soviet economic statistics, including the Russian census ... since 1939* (Newsweek).
—*n.* **1** a person born or living in Russia, especially a member of the dominant Slavic people of the Soviet Union. **2** a person of Russian descent. **3** the East Slavic language of Russia, the most widely used of the Slavic languages and the official language of the Soviet Union.

**Russian bath,** a bath similar to a Turkish bath except that only steam is used.

**Russian Blue cat,** any short-haired cat of a breed with thick, bluish-gray fur.

**Russian Church,** a self-governing branch of the Eastern or Orthodox Church, with its see at Moscow; Russian Orthodox Church. It was the national church of Russia before 1918.

**Russian cross,** a cross with one or two horizontal bars and one additional bar which slants to the right near the foot. It is used in the Eastern Orthodox Churches. See picture at **cross.**

**Russian desman,** the desman of the Soviet Union, the largest of all molelike mammals, having a length of about 14 inches, including the tail.

**Russian dressing,** mayonnaise with chili sauce or catchup, usually used as a salad dressing.

**Rus|sian|ism** (rush'ə niz'əm), *n.* **1** a tendency to favor Russia. **2** prevalence of Russian ideas or spirit: *Stravinsky ... abandoned his so-called Russianism and began to compose in a style that had sharp classical references* (John Brodbin Kennedy). **3** a word, phrase, or meaning typically Russian: *He accuses Mr. Nabokov of using Russianisms* (London Times).

**Rus|sian|i|za|tion** (rush'ə nə zā'shən), *n.* **1** the act of Russianizing. **2** the condition of being Russianized.

**Rus|sian|ize** (rush'ə nīz), *v.t., v.i.,* **-ized, -iz|ing.** to make or become like the Russians, as in customs or language.

**Russian mink,** = kolinsky.

**Russian olive,** = oleaster (def. 1).

**Russian Orthodox Church,** = Russian Church.

**Russian Revolution,** the revolution which overthrew the government of Nicholas II in 1917 and established the Soviet Union.
► **Russian Revolution.** The Russian Revolution has two parts: "the February Revolution," of March, 1917 (February, Old Style), establishing the Kerensky government, and "the October Revolution," of November, 1917 (October, Old Style), establishing the Lenin or Bolshevik government.

**Russian roulette** or **Roulette,** a game of chance played with a revolver loaded with one bullet. After spinning the chamber a player points the gun at his head and pulls the trigger. *A Frenchman was shooting up the German air force with a forward-firing machine gun that worked much on the principle of "Russian roulette"—you just fired and took a chance that the propeller would not be hit* (Wall Street Journal).

**Russian tea,** *Especially British.* tea flavored with lemon but not milk.

**Russian thistle,** a large weed of the goosefoot family with spiny branches, that develops into a troublesome tumbleweed.

**Russian turnip,** = rutabaga.

**Russian wolfhound,** any tall, slender, swift dog of a breed having silky hair; borzoi.

**Rus|si|fi|ca|tion** (rus'ə fə kā'shən), *n.* = Russianization.

**Rus|si|fy** (rus'ə fī), *v.t., v.i.,* **-fied, -fy|ing.** = Russianize.

**Russo-,** *combining form.* Russian: *Russophilia = great admiration for the Russians.* [< *Russia,* or *Russ*]

**Rus|so-Byz|an|tine** (rus'ō biz'ən tēn, -tīn; -bizan'tin), *adj.* both Russian and Byzantine; Russian, as developed from the Byzantine style: *Russo-Byzantine architecture.*

**Rus|so-Jap|a|nese** (rus'ō jap'ə nēz', -nēs'), *adj.* having to do with or between Russia and Japan: *the Russo-Japanese War of 1904-1905.*

**Rus|so|phile** (rus'ə fīl, -fil), *n.* a person who greatly admires or favors Russia or things Russian or associated with Russia.

**Rus|so|phil|i|a** (rus'ə fil'ē ə), *n.* great admiration of Russia or things Russian or associated with Russia.

**Rus|soph|i|lism** (rə sof'ə liz əm), *n.* the beliefs and theories of a Russophile.

**Rus|so|phobe** (rus'ə fōb), *n.* a person with an excessive fear or hatred of Russia or things Russian or associated with Russia.

**Rus|so|pho|bi|a** (rus'ə fō'bē ə), *n.* an excessive fear or hatred of Russia or things Russian or associated with Russia.

**rust** (rust), *n., v., adj.* —*n.* **1** the reddish-brown or orange coating that forms on iron or steel when exposed to air or moisture. Rust is formed by oxidation of the surface metal and is made up principally of hydrated ferric oxide. **2** any film or coating on any other metal due to oxidation or corrosion: *Aluminum has built-in protection against rust* (Newsweek). **3** *Figurative.* a harmful effect or influence, as on character or abilities, especially as a result of inactivity or lack of use. **4** Also, **rust fungus. a** a plant disease that spots leaves and stems. **b** any one of various fungi that produce this disease: *wheat rust.* **5** a reddish brown or orange.
—*v.i.* **1** to become covered with rust: *Don't let your tools rust by leaving them in the rain. From the practical standpoint, the most undesirable property of iron is its tendency to rust* (W. N. Jones). **2** *Figurative.* to become spoiled by not being used: *Don't let your mind rust during the vacation. Neglected talents rust into decay* (William Cowper). **3** to have the disease rust. **4** to become rust-colored.
—*v.t.* **1** to coat with rust: *The rain rusted his tools.* **2** *Figurative.* to spoil by not using. **3** to cause to have the disease rust.
—*adj.* reddish-brown or orange.
[Old English *rūst*]

**rust|a|ble** (rus'tə bəl), *adj.* that can become rusted or rusty.

**rust-col|ored** (rust'kul'ərd), *adj.* reddish-brown or orange.

**rust fungus,** = rust (*n.* def. 4).

**rus|tic** (rus'tik), *adj., n.* —*adj.* **1** belonging to the country; suitable for the country; rural: *a rustic lane in the quiet countryside. Some rustic phrases which I had learned at the farmer's house* (Jonathan Swift). SYN: See syn. under **rural. 2** simple; plain; like that or those of common people. *His rustic speech and ways made him uncomfortable in the city school.* **3** rough; awkward. **4** made of branches with the bark still on them: *rustic furniture, a rustic fence.* **5** having the surface rough or the joints deeply sunk or chamfered: *rustic masonry.*
—*n.* **1** a country person: *The rustics gathered at the country fair.* **2** a crude or boorish person considered as coming from the country.
[< Latin *rūsticus* < *rūs, rūris* country] —**rus'ti|cal|ly,** *adv.*

**rus|ti|cal** (rus'tə kəl), *adj., n. Archaic.* rustic.

**rus|ti|cate** (rus'tə kāt), *v.,* **-cat|ed -cat|ing.** —*v.i.* to go to the country; stay in the country: *Month after month, he rusticated in solitary grandeur in Pasadena* (New Yorker).
—*v.t.* **1** to send to the country. **2** *British.* to suspend (a student) from a university or college as a punishment. **3** to make (masonry) with a rough surface or sunken joints.

[<Latin *rūsticārī* (with English *-ate*[1]) <*rūsticus;* see etym. under **rustic**]

**rus|ti|ca|tion** (rus′tə kā′shən), *n.* **1a** the act of rusticating. **b** the condition of being rusticated. **2** residence in the country. **3** *British.* the temporary dismissal of a student from a college or university as a punishment.

**rus|ti|ca|tor** (rus′tə kā′tər), *n.* a person who rusticates.

**rus|tic|i|ty** (rus tis′ə tē), *n., pl.* **-ties. 1** a rustic quality, characteristic, or peculiarity: *a rusticity of manner.* **2** rural life. **3** awkwardness; ignorance.

**rust|i|ly** (rus′tə lē), *adv.* in a rusty state; in such a manner as to suggest rustiness.

**rust|i|ness** (rus′tē nis), *n.* the quality or condition of being rusty.

**rus|tle** (rus′əl), *n., v.,* **-tled, -tling.** —*n.* **1** a light, soft sound of things gently rubbing together, such as the sound that leaves make when moved by the wind. **2** *U.S. Informal.* hustle: *to get a rustle on.* [<verb]
—*v.i.* **1** to make a light, soft sound of things gently rubbing together: *The leaves rustled in the breeze.* **2** to move or stir, making such a sound: *the wind rustling through the woods.* **3** *U.S. Informal.* to move, work, or act with energy or speed. **4** *U.S. Informal.* to steal cattle, horses, or sheep; be a rustler.
—*v.t.* **1** to cause to make a light, soft sound of things gently rubbing together: *The wind rustled the papers.* (*Figurative.*) *Memory was turning over the leaves of her volume, rustling them to and fro* (Hawthorne). **2** *U.S. Informal.* to do or get with energy or speed: *I'll sure buy Pedro back . . . just as soon as ever I rustle some cash* (Owen Wister). **3** *Informal.* to steal (cattle, horses, etc.).
**rustle up, a** to gather; find: *If I am to go on the trip, I must rustle up some money.* **b** to get ready; prepare: *The cook rustled up some food.*
[Middle English *rustelen,* perhaps Old English *hrūxlian* make noise]

**rus|tler** (rus′lər), *n.* **1** *Informal.* a cattle thief: *The cattle thieves — the rustlers — were gaining in numbers and audacity* (Owen Wister). **2** *Informal.* an active, energetic person. **3** a person or thing that rustles; rustling leaf, bird, or the like. [American English <*rustl*(e) to steal cattle + *-er*[1]]

**rust|less** (rust′lis), *adj.* free from rust; resisting rust.

**rus|tling|ly** (rus′ling lē), *adv.* with a rustle.

**rust|proof** (rust′prüf′), *adj.* resisting rust.

**rus|tre** (rus′tər), *n. Heraldry.* a bearing in the form of a lozenge with a hole in the middle. [< French *rustre*]

**rust|y**[1] (rus′tē), *adj.,* **rust|i|er, rust|i|est. 1** covered with rust; rusted: *a rusty knife.* **2** made by rust: *a rusty spot, a rusty stain.* **3** colored like rust. **4** faded; shabby: *a rusty black, a rusty old coat; . . . a little rusty, musty old fellow, always groping among ruins* (Washington Irving).
**5** *Figurative.* **a** damaged by lack of use: *Mother's arithmetic. is rusty, she says. Editorial contacts were getting rusty* (Newsweek). **b** out of practice: *Hector . . . Who in this dull and continued truce Is rusty grown* (Shakespeare). **6** affected with the disease rust: *rusty wheat.*

**rust|y**[2] (rus′tē), *adj.,* **rust|i|er, rust|i|est.** stubborn; contrary; cross: *The people got rusty about it, and would not deal* (Scott).
**ride** (or **run**) **rusty,** to act in a stubborn, contrary, or disagreeable way: *How the devil am I to get the crew to obey me? Why, even Dick Fletcher rides rusty on me now and then* (Scott).
[perhaps alteration of *resty,* variant of *restive;* perhaps influenced by *rusty*[1] in sense "surly"]

**rusty blackbird,** a blackbird of northern and eastern North America, solid black in the spring and rusty in the fall.

**rut**[1] (rut), *n., v.,* **rut|ted, rut|ting.** —*n.* **1** a track made in the ground by wheels: *A sleepy land, where under the same wheel The same old rut would deepen year by year* (Tennyson). **SYN:** groove. **2** any furrow or track. **SYN:** groove.
**3** *Figurative.* a fixed or established way of acting, especially one that is boring or monotonous: *The old man was so set in his ways that everyone said he was in a rut. I was in a rut, so I decided to spend the summer traveling. It's time to pull out of the rut of earthbound traffic* (Newsweek). **SYN:** routine.
—*v.t.* to make a rut or ruts in: *The road was beaten into paste and rutted two feet deep by the artillery* (Sir Arthur Conan Doyle).
[perhaps variant of *route*]

**rut**[2] (rut), *n., v.,* **rut|ted, rut|ting.** —*n.* **1** sexual excitement of male deer, and, sometimes, of other male animals, such as goats or sheep, occurring at regular intervals, usually annually. **2** the period during which it lasts.
—*v.i.* to be in rut.
[<Old French *rut,* and *ruit* <Latin *rugītus, -ūs* a bellowing <*rūgīre* to bellow]

**ru|ta|ba|ga** (rü′tə bā′gə, -beg′ə), *n.* a kind of large, yellow or white turnip of the mustard family; Russian turnip; Swedish turnip. [<Swedish dialectal *rotabagge*]

**ru|ta|ceous** (rü tā′shəs), *adj.* **1** belonging to the rue family: *Orange and lemon trees are rutaceous plants.* **2** of or like rue. [<New Latin *Rutaceae* the rue family <Late Latin *rūtāceus* having to do with rue <Latin *rūta* a bitter herb <Greek *rhȳtē* rue]

**ruth** (rüth), *n. Archaic.* **1** pity; compassion: *I came back to her now with no other emotion than a sort of ruth for her great sufferings* (Charlotte Brontë). **2** sorrow; grief. **3** remorse. [Middle English *rewthe* <*rewen* to rue[1], Old English *hrēowan*]

**Ruth** (rüth), *n.* in the Bible: **1** the wife of Boaz. She is famous for her devotion to her mother-in-law, Naomi. Ruth left her native land of Moab to go with Naomi to Bethlehem. **2** the book of the Old Testament that tells about her.

**Ru|the|ni|an** (rü thē′nē ən), *adj., n.* —*adj.* of or having to do with Ruthenia, a part of the Soviet Union, or with its people or their language.
—*n.* **1** a native or inhabitant of Ruthenia. **2** the language of Ruthenia, a form of Ukrainian.

**ru|then|ic** (rü then′ik, -thē′nik), *adj.* of or having to do with ruthenium, especially with a high valence.

**ru|the|ni|ous** (rü thē′nē əs), *adj.* of or having to do with ruthenium, especially with a low valence.

***ru|the|ni|um** (rü thē′nē əm), *n.* a brittle, silver-white chemical element found in platinum ores and used in alloys. Ruthenium is a rare metal similar to platinum. [<New Latin *ruthenium* < Medieval Latin *Ruthenia* Russia (because it was discovered in platinum ores from the Urals)]

***ruthenium**

| symbol | atomic number | atomic weight | oxidation state |
|---|---|---|---|
| Ru | 44 | 101.07 | 3 |

**Ruth|er|ford atom** (ruᴛʜ′ər fərd), the atom as described in the atomic theory proposed by Lord Ernest Rutherford in 1911. The mass of this atom is located in its center, or nucleus, with electrons revolving about the nucleus much like planets revolve around the sun.

**ruth|er|for|di|um** (ruᴛʜ′ər fôr′dē əm), *n.* the American name for element 104. [<Lord Ernest *Rutherford,* 1871-1937, a British physicist]

**ruth|ful** (rüth′fəl), *adj.* **1** = compassionate. **2** sorrowful; rueful. —**ruth′ful|ly,** *adv.* —**ruth′ful|ness,** *n.*

**ruth|less** (rüth′lis), *adj.* having no pity; showing no mercy; cruel: *a ruthless dictator. What a ruthless thing is this . . . to take away the life of a man?* (Shakespeare). **SYN:** hard-hearted, relentless, merciless, pitiless. —**ruth′less|ly,** *adv.* —**ruth′less|ness,** *n.*

**ru|ti|lant** (rü′tə lənt), *adj.* shining; glowing; gleaming. [<Latin *rutilāns, -antis,* present participle of *rutilāre* glow with red-gold light <*rutilus;* see etym. under **rutile**]

**ru|ti|lat|ed** (rü′tə lā′tid), *adj.* containing needles of rutile: *rutilated quartz.*

**ru|tile** (rü′tēl, -tīl), *n.* a mineral consisting of titanium oxide, often with a little iron. It has a metallic or diamondlike luster and is usually red-dish-brown or black. Rutile is a common ore of titanium. *Formula:* $TiO_2$ [<French *rutile* <German *Rutil* <Latin *rutilus* red-gold, related to *ruber* red]

**ru|tin** (rü′tin), *n.* a substance found in the leaves of the buckwheat, pansy, tobacco, and other plants, that relaxes and expands blood vessels. It is effective in preventing small hemorrhages. *Formula:* $C_{27}H_{30}O_{16}$ [<Latin *rūta* rue + English *-in*]

**rut|ti|ness** (rut′ē nis), *n.* rutty quality.

**rut|tish** (rut′ish), *adj.* lustful; lascivious. —**rut′tish|ly,** *adv.* —**rut′tish|ness,** *n.*

**rut|ty** (rut′ē), *adj.,* **-ti|er, -ti|est. 1** full of ruts: *a rutty country road.* **2** = ruttish.

**RV** (no periods), **1** recreational vehicle. **2** reentry vehicle. **3** Revised Version (of the Bible).

**R.V.,** Revised Version (of the Bible).

**R.W., 1** Right Worshipful. **2** Right Worthy.

**Rwan|dan** (rü än′dən), *adj., n.* = Rwandese.

**Rwan|dese** (rü än′dēz′, -dēs′), *adj., n., pl.* **-dese.** —*adj.* of or having to do with the republic of Rwanda (formerly part of Ruanda-Urundi) in central Africa.
—*n.* a native or inhabitant of Rwanda.

**Rwy.,** railway.

**Rx** (är′eks′), *n., pl.* **Rx's. 1** a medical prescription: *More and more physicians are specifying by brand or manufacturers' names the products to be used in filling their "Rx's"* (New York Times). **2** *Figurative: Rx for a healthy summer* (Consumer Report). **SYN:** remedy, course, solution. [<*Rx,* symbol (short for Latin *recipe* take)]

**Rx** or **rx** (no periods), **1** (in medical prescriptions) take (Latin, *recipe*). **2** tens of rupees.

**-ry,** *suffix forming nouns from other nouns.* **1** occupation or work of a ___: *Dentistry = the occupation or work of a dentist. Chemistry = the occupation or work of a chemist.*
**2** act of a ___: *Mimicry = act of a mimic.*
**3** quality or condition of a ___: *Rivalry = the condition of a rival.*
**4** group or collection of ___s: *Jewelry = collection of jewels. Peasantry = group of peasants.*
[short for *-ery*]

**Ry.,** railway.

**ry|a** (rē′ə), *n.* **1** a colorful handwoven rug with a deep pile, originally made by Scandinavian peasants for use chiefly as bedcovers and wraps.
**2** the pattern or weave characteristic of this rug.
[<Swedish *rya* rug]

**ry|al** (rī′əl), *n.* **1** an old English gold coin; rose noble. **2** an old gold or silver coin of Scotland. [Middle English *ryal,* variant of *royal*]

**ry|a|ni|a** (rī ā′nē ə), *n.* the ground wood of a tropical American tree, used as an insecticide. [< New Latin *Ryania* genus name of the tree]

***rye**[1] (rī), *n., adj.* —*n.* **1** a hardy, annual plant widely grown in cold regions for its grain, and also to protect or improve the soil. Rye is a cereal grass. **2** its seeds or grain, used for making flour, as food for livestock, and in making whiskey. **3** the dark flour made from the grain of rye. Pumpernickel and rye bread are made from it. **4** = rye whiskey: *After a long day's work they often shared a bottle of rye and sang songs* (Maclean's).
—*adj.* made from the grain or flour of rye: *rye crisp.*
[Old English *ryge*]

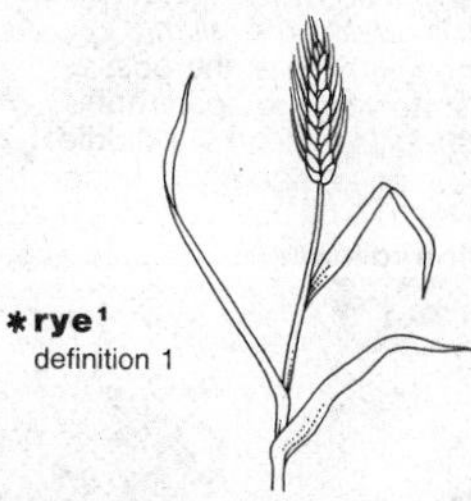

***rye**[1]
definition 1

**rye**[2] (rī), *n.* (among Gypsies) a gentleman. [< Gypsy *rei, rai* lord]

**rye bread,** bread made of the flour of rye, usually combined with wheat flour.

**rye|grass** (rī′gras′, -gräs′), *n.* any one of several grasses having spicules growing in a zigzag pattern along the stem, used for pastures and lawns.

**Rye|land** (rī′lənd), *n.* any one of a breed of sheep having medium wool, originating in the Ryeland district of Herefordshire, in western England.

**rye whiskey,** whiskey distilled partly or entirely from rye. Straight rye whiskey is distilled from a mash containing at least 51 percent rye grain.

**ryke** (rīk), *v.i.,* **ryked, ryk|ing.** *Scottish.* to reach.

**rynd** (rīnd, rind), *n.* a piece of iron fastened across the hole of an upper millstone, and serving to support the stone. Also, **rind.** [early variant of *rind*[2]]

**ry|o|kan** (rē ō′kən), *n.* a Japanese hotel or inn, especially one operated in a traditional style: *The most charming hotel I ever stayed at was a Japanese ryokan in the mountain spa of Kinugawa north of Tokyo* (Pierre Berton). [< Japanese *ryokan*]

**ry|ot** (rī′ət), *n.* a small farmer or peasant in India. [earlier *riat* <Hindustani *raiyat,* ultimately <Arabic *ra'āyyah* non-Moslem subjects of Moslem rulers]

**Ry|u|kyu|an** (rē yü′kyü ən), *n., adj.* —*n.* a native or inhabitant of the Ryukyu Islands, southwest of Japan.
—*adj.* of or having to do with the Ryukyu Islands.

**Pronunciation Key:** hat, āge, cãre, fär; let, ēqual, tėrm; it, īce; hot, ōpen, ôrder; **oil, out;** cup, pu̇t, rüle; **ch**ild; lo**ng**; **th**in; ᴛʜen; **zh,** measure; **ə** represents **a** in about, **e** in taken, **i** in pencil, **o** in lemon, **u** in circus.

***S**[1] or **s** (es), *n., pl.* **S's** or **Ss, s's** or **ss. 1** the 19th letter of the English alphabet. There are two *s*'s in *sister.* **2** any sound represented by this letter. **3** (used as a symbol for) the 19th, or more usually 18th (of an actual or possible series, either *I* or *J* being omitted).

**S**[2] (es), *n., pl.* **S's.** anything shaped like the letter S: *The road curved in a big S.*

**'s,** the shortened form of *is, has,* or *us,* added to the preceding word: *That's it* = *That is it. He's here* = *He is here. She's just gone* = *She has just gone. That's been done* = *That has been done. Let's eat* = *Let us eat.*

**-s**[1], a suffix used to form the plural of most nouns as in *boys, dogs, hats, houses.* It also forms the plural of noun substitutes, such as symbols. [Middle English *-es,* or *-s,* Old English *-as,* suffix denoting the nominative or accusative plural of certain masculine nouns]

**-s**[2], a suffix used to form the third person singular of verbs in the present indicative active, as in *lies, runs, rides, sees, asks, tells, bites, bluffs.* [Middle English *-es,* or *-s,* Old English, (originally) suffix denoting the second person singular]

**-s**[3], a suffix used to form some adverbs, as in *needs, unawares.* [Middle English, Old English *-es,* (originally) suffix denoting the genitive singular of masculine and neuter nouns and adjectives]

**-'s,** a suffix used to form the possessive case of nouns in the singular, as in *fellow's, man's, child's, book's, elf's,* and also of plural nouns not ending in *s,* as in *men's, children's, alumni's.* (When the singular ends with an *s,* the possessive is sometimes indicated by the apostrophe above, as *Jesus'* and *goodness' sake*) [Middle English, Old English *-es,* or *-s;* see etym. under **-s**[3]]

**s.,** an abbreviation for the following:
**1** half (Latin, *semi*).
**2** *Anatomy.* sacral.
**3** school.
**4** scribe.
**5** scruple (weight).
**6** second or seconds.
**7** section.
**8** see.
**9** series.
**10** set or sets.
**11** shilling or shillings.
**12a** sign. **b** signed.
**13** silver.
**14** singular.
**15** sire (in animal pedigrees).
**16** solo.
**17** son or sons.
**18** soprano.
**19a** south. **b** southern.
**20** steel.
**21** stem.
**22** stratus (cloud).
**23** substantive.
**24** sun.

**S** (no period), an abbreviation or symbol for the following:
**1** Saxon.
**2** *Linguistics.* sentence.
**3a** South. **b** Southern.
**4** specific heat.
**5** *Physics.* strangeness.
**6** sulfur (chemical element).
**7** Svedberg unit.

**S.,** an abbreviation for the following:
**1** fellow (as of a society; Latin, *socius*).
**2** page or pages (German, *Seite*).
**3** Sabbath.
**4** saint.
**5** Saturday.
**6** school.
**7** sea.
**8** Senate (bill; used with a number): *S. 1421.*
**9** September.
**10** signor.
**11** socialist.
**12** society.
**13** soprano.
**14a** south. **b** southern.
**15** Sunday.
**16** surplus.

**s.a.,** an abbreviation for the following:
**1** semiannual.
**2** subject to approval.
**3** undated (Latin, *sine anno,* without a year).
**4** under the year (Latin, *sub anno*).

**SA** (no periods), **1** seaman apprentice. **2** storm troops (German, *Sturmabteilung*). **3** surface-to-air.

**S.A.,** an abbreviation for the following:
**1** corporation (for French *Société Anonyme,* Spanish *Sociedad Anónima,* Italian *Società Anonima,* etc.).
**2** Salvation Army.
**3a** Saudi Arabia. **b** Saudi Arabian.
**4** Seventh Avenue.
**5a** South Africa. **b** South African.
**6a** South America. **b** South American.
**7a** South Australia. **b** South Australian.
**8** storm troops (German, *Sturmabteilung*).

**Saa|nen** (sä′nən), *n.* any one of a Swiss breed of short-haired goats raised for their milk. Saanens have been introduced into the United States. [< *Saanen,* a village in Switzerland]

**Saar|land|er** (sär′lan′dər), *n.* a native or inhabitant of the Saar (state in West Germany).

**Sab.,** Sabbath.

**sab|a|dil|la** (sab′ə dil′ə), *n.* **1** a Mexican and Central American plant of the lily family with long, grasslike leaves and bitter seeds. **2** the seeds, used in medicine as a source of veratrine, and in making an insecticide. [< New Latin *Sabadilla* the genus name < Spanish *cebadilla* (diminutive) < *cebada* barley; ultimately < Latin *cibus* food nourishment]

**Sa|bah|an** (sə bä′hən), *adj., n.* **—*adj.*** of or having to do with Sabah, the former British North Borneo or its people.
**—*n.*** a native or inhabitant of Sabah.

**Sa|ba|ism** (sā′bē iz əm), *n.* star worship. [< Hebrew *ṣābā* host (of heaven) + English *-ism.* Compare etym. under **Sabaoth.**]

**Sa|ba|ist** (sā′bē ist), *n.* a worshiper of stars.

**Sab|a|oth** (sab′ē oth, -ōth; sə bā′ōth), *n.pl.* armies; hosts: *The Lord of Sabaoth* (Romans 9:29).
[< Latin *Sabaōth* < Greek *Sabaôth* of hosts < Hebrew *ṣəbā'oth* armies]

**sab|a|ton** (sab′ə ton), *n.* **1** a shoe or half boot made especially of satin or cloth of gold, worn by persons of wealth in the 1400's. **2** an armed foot covering, broad and blunted at the toes, worn by warriors in armor in the 1500's. [< Old Provençal *sabaton* < *sabata* shoe. See related etym. at **sabot.**]

**Sab|bat** (sab′ət), *n.* a midnight meeting of demons, sorcerers, and witches, presided over by the Devil, supposed in medieval times to have been held annually as an orgy or festival; witches' Sabbath. [< French *Sabbat* (literally) Sabbath < Latin *sabbatum;* see etym. under **Sabbath.**]

**Sab|ba|tar|i|an** (sab′ə tãr′ē ən), *n., adj.* **—*n.*** **1** a person who observes Saturday, the seventh day of the week, as a day of worship and rest, as Jews and some Christians do. **2** a Christian who favors a very strict observance of Sunday.
**—*adj.*** of or having to do with the Sabbath, Sabbatarians, or Sabbath observance: *He was sharply criticized by strict Sabbatarian elements when he first began playing golf on Sundays* (Newsweek).
[< Late Latin *Sabbatārius* of the Sabbath (in Latin, plural, keepers of the Sabbath < *sabbatum* sabbath) + English *-an*]

**Sab|ba|tar|i|an|ism** (sab′ə tãr′ē ə niz′əm), *n.* the beliefs or practices of the Sabbatarians.

**Sab|bath** (sab′əth), *n., adj.* **—*n.*** **1** a day of the week used for rest and worship: **a** the seventh day of the week, observed by Jews and some Christians. **b** Sunday, observed by most Christians. **2** Also, **sabbath.** *Figurative.* a time or period of rest and quiet: *Those endless Sabbaths the blessed ones see* (John M. Neale).
**—*adj.*** of, belonging to, or suitable for the Sabbath: *a Sabbath meal, Sabbath rest.*
[< Latin *sabbatum* < Greek *sábbaton* < Hebrew *shabbāth* < *shābath* he rested]
► See **Sunday** for usage note.

**Sab|bath-day's journey** (sab′əth dāz′), the distance in ancient times that a Jew might lawfully travel on the Sabbath.

**Sab|bath|less** (sab′əth lis), *adj.* having or observing no Sabbath, or day of rest.

**Sabbath school, 1** = Sunday school. **2** a school for religious instruction held on Saturday by Seventh-day Adventists.

**sab|bat|ic** (sə bat′ik), *adj., n.* = sabbatical. [< Greek *sabbatikós* < *sábbaton;* see etym. under **Sabbath**]

**sab|bat|i|cal** (sə bat′ə kəl), *adj., n.* **—*adj.*** **1** of or suitable for the Sabbath. **2** *Figurative.* of or for a rest from work.
**—*n.*** **1** = sabbatical leave. **2** = sabbatical year.

**sabbatical leave,** a leave of absence for a year or half year given to school, college, and university teachers, commonly once in seven years, for study, travel, or rest: *John Wheeler from Princeton interrupted a well-deserved sabbatical leave in Europe* (Science).

**sab|bat|i|cal|ly** (sə bat′ə klē), *adv.* in a sabbatical manner.

**sabbatical year, 1** (among the ancient Jews and in modern Israel) every seventh year, during which fields are left untilled and debtors released (and, in former times, slaves set free); shemitta. **2** = sabbatical leave.

**Sab|ba|tism** (sab′ə tiz əm), *n.* observance of the Sabbath or of a sabbath. [< Late Latin *sabbatismus* < Greek *sabbatismós* < *sábbaton* Sabbath + *-ismos* -ism]

**Sa|be|an** (sə bē′ən), *adj., n.* **—*adj.*** **1** of or having to do with Sheba, an ancient kingdom of Arabia, noted for its trade in spices and gems. **2** *Figurative.* fragrant; rich: *Sabaean odours from the spicy shore of Araby the bless'd* (Milton).
**—*n.*** an inhabitant of Sheba.
[< Latin *Sabaeus* (< Greek *Sabaîos* < *Sába* an ancient name of Sheba, a city in Yemen) + English *-an*]

**Sa|bel|li|an** (sə bel′ē ən), *n., adj.* **—*n.*** **1** a member of a group of related peoples who inhabited parts of ancient Italy, comprising the Sabines, Samnites, and others. **2** a group of early Italic dialects spoken by these people.
**—*adj.*** of or having to do with the Sabellians or their language.
[< Latin *Sabellī,* for *Sabīnī* Sabines + English *-an*]

**sa|ber** (sā′bər), *n., v.* **—*n.*** **1** a heavy sword, usually slightly curved, having a single cutting edge. Sabers are often used by cavalry. **2** a soldier armed with a saber. **3a** a sword used in fencing, similar to the foil but with two cutting edges. **b** the sport or skill of fencing with a sword similar to the foil but with two cutting edges.
**—*v.t.*** to strike, cut, wound, or kill with a saber. Also, **sabre.**
[< French *sabre,* alteration of *sable* < earlier German *Sabel* (now *Säbel*) < Hungarian *szablya* < Slavic (compare Russian *sáblja*), perhaps < Semitic (compare Arabic *sajf,* Aramaic *sajpā*)]

**sa|bered** (sā′bərd), *adj.* armed or equipped with a saber: *sabered cavalry charging on horseback.* Also, **sabred.**

**sa|ber-legged** (sā′bər legd′, -leg′id), *adj.* (of a horse) having a congenital malformation of the hind leg that extends the foot forward in a curve like that of a saber.

**sa|ber|like** (sā′bər līk′), *adj.* shaped like a saber; curved; crescentic: *There is one extinct land family, the sabertooths, which had saberlike upper canine teeth* (William C. Beaver).

**saber rattling,** a bold or reckless exhibition of military power; threat of violent action in behalf of a cause.

**saber saw,** a kind of electric jigsaw: *A portable saber saw is needed to cut out the animals* (New York Times).

**sa|ber|tooth** (sā′bər tüth′), *n.* = saber-toothed tiger.

**sa|ber-toothed** (sā′bər tütht′), *adj.* having very long, curved, upper canine teeth.

**saber-toothed tiger,** a large, extinct, catlike carnivorous mammal whose upper canine teeth were very long and curved. There were several kinds.

**Sa|bi|an** (sā′bē ən), *n.* **1** a member of a religious sect in Babylonia classed in the Koran with the

***S**[1]
definition 1

Script letters look like examples of fine penmanship. They appear in many formal uses, such as invitations to social functions.

Handwritten letters, both manuscript or printed (left) and cursive (right), are easy for children to read and to write.

Roman letters have *serifs* (finishing strokes) adapted from the way Roman stonecutters carved their letters. This is *Times Roman* type.

Sans-serif letters are often called *gothic.* They have lines of even width and no serifs. This type face is called *Helvetica.*

Between roman and gothic, some letters have thick and thin lines with slight flares that suggest serifs. This type face is *Optima.*

Computer letters can be sensed by machines either from their shapes or from the magnetic ink with which they are printed.

Moslems, Jews, and Christians, as believers in the true God. **2** a member of a sect of star worshipers in Mesopotamia in the 800's A.D. [< Arabic *Ṣābi'* Sabian + English *-an*]

**Sa|bi|an|ism** (sā′bē ə niz′əm), *n.* star worship.

**sa|bin** (sā′bin), *n.* a unit to measure the sound absorption qualities of a surface. It is equivalent to one square foot of a completely absorptive surface. [< Wallace C. *Sabine,* 1868-1919, an American physicist]

**Sa|bine** (sā′bīn), *n., adj.* **—*n.* 1** a member of an ancient tribe in central Italy which was conquered by the Romans in the 200's B.C. **2** their Italic language.
**—*adj.*** of or belonging to the Sabines or their language.
[< Latin *Sabīnus*]

**Sabine's gull,** a small gull of arctic regions with a forked tail and black and white wings. [< Sir Edward *Sabine,* 1788-1883, a British scientist and arctic explorer]

**Sabin vaccine,** a vaccine for preventing the development of paralytic polio. It consists of living but attenuated polioviruses, and it is taken orally in a single dose. [< Albert B. *Sabin,* born 1906, an American virologist, who developed it]

**sa|ble** (sā′bəl), *n., pl.* **-bles** or (*collectively for 1 and 3*) **-ble,** *adj.* **—*n.* 1** a small, flesh-eating mammal valued for its soft, dark-brown glossy fur. It is related to the marten and is found in northern Europe and Asia. **2** its fur. Sable is one of the most costly furs. **3** the marten of North America; American sable. **4a** the color black: *clothes of sable.* **b** black clothing, especially as a symbol of mourning. **5** *Heraldry.* black, as one of the heraldic colors, in engraving represented by crossing horizontal and vertical lines.
**—*adj.*** black; dark: ... *did a sable cloud Turn forth her silver lining on the night?* (Milton).
**sables,** mourning garments: *Nay then let the Devil wear black, for I'll have a suit of sables* (Shakespeare).
[< Old French *sable,* probably < Medieval Latin *sabellum* < Slavic (compare Russian *sobol',* Polish *soból*)] **—sa′ble|ness,** *n.*

**sable antelope,** a large South and East African antelope with large, sickle-shaped horns. The male is black with white underparts.

**sa|ble|fish** (sā′bəl fish′), *n., pl.* **-fish|es** or (*collectively*) **-fish.** = beshow.

**sa|bles** (sā′bəlz), *n.pl.* See under **sable.**

***sab|ot** (sab′ō; *French* sà bō′), *n.* **1** a shoe hollowed out of a single piece of wood, worn by peasants in France, Belgium, and other European countries. **2** a coarse leather shoe with a thick wooden sole. **3** a cuplike cap fitted to the base of a shell or other projectile to position it correctly in the barrel, prevent the escape of gases, and make contact with the rifling. [< French *sabot* < Old French *çabot,* alteration of unrecorded *çavate* old shoe (influenced by *bot,* or *botte* boot), perhaps < Arabic *ṣabbāṭ* sandal, shoe]

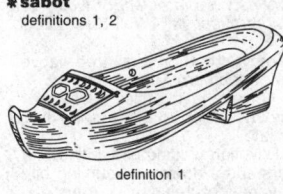

***sabot**
definitions 1, 2

definition 1

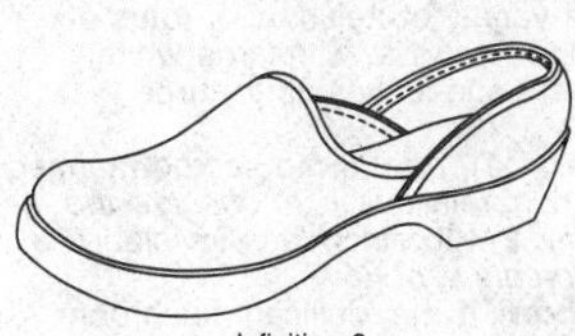

definition 2

**sab|o|tage** (sab′ə täzh), *n., v.,* **-taged, -tag|ing.** **—*n.* 1** damage done, as to work, tools, or machinery, by workmen as an attack or threat against an employer: *A part of the syndicalist's method is sabotage, which originally referred to throwing a shoe into a machine so as to stop production and to further revolution* (Emory S. Bogardus). **2** such damage done by civilians of a conquered nation to injure the conquering forces: *The jailed cardinal furnished a rallying cause for anti-Communist agitation and sabotage in Hungary* (Time). **3** damage done by enemy agents or sympathizers in an attempt to slow down a nation's war effort. **4** malicious attacking of or secret working against any cause to which cooperation is due.
**—*v.t.*** to damage or destroy by sabotage: *to sabotage an ammunition plant. Conservatives sabotaged the heavy spending program.*
[< French *sabotage* < *saboter* to bungle, walk noisily < *sabot* wooden shoe (possibly because wooden shoes were thrown into machinery to damage it); see etym. under **sabot**]

**sab|o|teur** (sab′ə tėr′), *n.* a person who engages in sabotage. [< French *saboteur,* ultimately < *sabot;* see etym. under **sabot**]

**sa|bra** (sä′brə), *n., pl.* **-bras.** a person born in Israel: *Only three of the authors are sabras, born in Palestine and accustomed to the language from infancy* (Time). [< Hebrew *ṣābrāh* cactus (because the person is thought of as tough on the outside and soft on the inside)]

**sa|bre** (sā′bər), *n., v.t.* **-bred, -bring.** = saber.

**sa|bred** (sā′bərd), *adj.* = sabered.

**sa|breur** (sà brœr′), *n. French.* a person, especially a cavalryman, who fights with a saber.

**Sa|bri|na** (sə brī′nə), *n.* the legendary daughter of Locrine and Estrildis. She was drowned in the river Severn and became its nymph.

**sab|u|los|i|ty** (sab′yə los′ə tē), *n.* sandiness; grittiness.

**sab|u|lous** (sab′yə ləs), *adj.* consisting of sand; full of sand; sandy; gritty. [< Latin *sabulōsus* < *sabulum* sand]

**sac** (sak), *n.* a part like a bag in an animal or plant, often containing a liquid. The human bladder is a sac. The honeybee carries honey in a honey sac. The octopus has an ink sac. SYN: cyst, vesicle. [< French, Old French *sac* < Latin *saccus;* see etym. under **sack**[1]] **—sac′like′,** *adj.*

**Sac** (sak, sôk), *n., pl.* **Sac** or **Sacs,** *adj.* = Sauk.

**SAC** (no periods), Strategic Air Command.

**sac|a|lait** (sak′ə lā), *n. U.S. Dialect.* any one of various small fishes, especially the crappie and the killifish. [< Louisiana French *sac à lait* (literally) sack of milk, alteration (by folk etymology) of Choctaw *sakli* trout]

**sac|a|ton** (sak′ə tōn′), *n.* any one of several coarse grasses of the dry regions of the southwestern United States, grown for pasture or hay; zacatón. [American English < Spanish *zacatón* zacatón]

**sac|cade** (sə käd′), *n.* an involuntary jerking of the eye as it moves from one position to another: *The most common major eye movement is the saccade. Saccades usually take less than a twentieth of a second, but they happen several times each second in reading* (Scientific American). [< French *saccade* jerk < Old French *saquer, sacher* pull, draw]

**sac|cad|ic** (sə kä′dik), *adj.* of or characterized by a saccade or saccades; jerky: *saccadic movement.*

**sac|cate** (sak′āt), *adj.* **1** having the form of a sac or pouch. **2** having a sac or pouch. [< Latin *saccus* a bag, sack + English *-ate*[1]]

**sac|cat|ed** (sak′ā tid), *adj.* = saccate.

**sac|cha|rase** (sak′ə rās), *n.* = invertase. [< *sacchar*(ic) + *-ase*]

**sac|cha|rate** (sak′ə rāt), *n.* **1** a salt of any saccharic acid. **2** a compound of a metallic oxide with a sugar: *calcium saccharate.* **3** = sucrate. [< *sacchar*(ic acid) + *-ate*[2]]

**sac|char|ic** (sə kar′ik), *adj.* having to do with or obtained from a sugar. [< Greek *sákcharis* (see etym. under **saccharin**) + English *-ic*]

**saccharic acid,** a dibasic acid, occurring in three optically different forms, produced by oxidizing glucose and various other hexose sugars. *Formula:* $C_6H_{10}O_8$

**sac|cha|ride** (sak′ə rīd, -ər id), *n.* **1** a compound consisting of one or more simple sugars; carbohydrate. **2** a compound of sugar with an organic base. **3** a compound of a metallic oxide with a sugar; saccharate.

**sac|cha|rif|er|ous** (sak′ə rif′ər əs), *adj.* yielding or containing sugar. [< Greek *sákcharis* (see etym. under **saccharin**) + English *-ferous*]

**sac|char|i|fi|ca|tion** (sə kar′ə fə kā′shən, sak′ər ə-), *n.* transformation into sugar.

**sac|char|i|fy** (sə kar′ə fī, sak′ər ə-), *v.t.,* **-fied, -fy|ing.** to change (as starch) into sugar; saccharize.

**sac|cha|rim|e|ter** (sak′ə rim′ə tər), *n.* a device for measuring the amount of sugar in a solution, especially a polarimeter. [< French *saccharimètre* < Greek *sákcharis* (see etym. under **saccharin**) + French *-mètre* -meter]

**sac|cha|rim|e|try** (sak′ə rim′ə trē), *n.* the use of a saccharimeter.

**sac|cha|rin** (sak′ər in), *n.* a very sweet substance used as a substitute for sugar. Saccharin is a white crystalline substance obtained from coal tar. A pellet of it has as much sweetening power as several hundred times its weight of cane sugar. *Saccharin ... has no food value but is used for sweetening foods, especially foods for diabetics* (Monroe K. Offner). *Formula:* $C_7H_5NO_3S$ [< Medieval Latin *saccharum* sugar (< Greek *sákcharon,* for *sákcharis* < Pali *sakkharā* < Sanskrit *ṣarkarā* candied sugar; originally, gravel, grit) + English *-in*[1]]

**sac|cha|rine** (sak′ər in, -ə rīn), *adj., n.* **—*adj.*** **1** very sweet; sugary: *a saccharine smile. He knew how to handle youngsters without being saccharine or patronizing* (Newsweek). SYN: honeyed. **2** of or like sugar.
**—*n.*** = saccharin. **—sac′cha|rine|ly,** *adv.*

**sac|cha|rin|i|ty** (sak′ə rin′ə tē), *n.* the quality of being saccharine.

**saccharin sodium,** a white, crystalline powder used as a substitute for sugar. It is a sodium salt of saccharin, up to 500 times as sweet as sugar; Crystallose. *Formula:* $C_7H_4NNaO_3S{\cdot}2H_2O$

**sac|cha|rize** (sak′ə rīz), *v.t.,* **-rized, -riz|ing.** to change into sugar; saccharify.

**sac|cha|roid** (sak′ə roid), *adj. Geology.* having a granular texture like that of loaf sugar.

**sac|cha|roi|dal** (sak′ə roi′dəl), *adj.* = saccharoid.

**sac|cha|ro|lyt|ic** (sak′ə rə lit′ik), *adj.* having the power of chemically splitting sugar.

**sac|cha|rom|e|ter** (sak′ə rom′ə tər), *n.* a device for measuring the amount of sugar in a solution, especially a kind of hydrometer.

**sac|cha|rom|e|try** (sak′ə rom′ə trē), *n.* the use of a saccharometer.

**sac|cha|ro|my|ces** (sak′ə rō mī′sēz), *n., pl.* **-ces.** any one of a group of ascomycetous fungi which produce alcoholic fermentation in saccharine fluids; yeast plant. [< Greek *sákcharon* sugar + *mýkēs, -ētos* fungus]

**sac|cha|rose** (sak′ə rōs), *n.* = sucrose. [< Greek *sákcharis* (see etym. under **saccharin**)]

**sac|ci|form** (sak′sə fôrm), *adj.* sac-shaped; saclike. [< Latin *saccus* sac + English *-form*]

**sac|cos** (sak′os), *n.* a short vestment corresponding to the Western dalmatic, worn in the Eastern Church by metropolitans. Also, **sakkos.** [< New Greek *sakkos* < Greek *sákkos* sack[1]]

**sac|cu|lar** (sak′yə lər), *adj.* having to do with or having the form of a saccule or sac.

**sac|cu|late** (sak′yə lāt), *adj.* formed of little sacs; divided into saclike dilations.

**sac|cu|lat|ed** (sak′yə lā′tid), *adj.* = sacculate.

**sac|cu|la|tion** (sak′yə lā′shən), *n.* **1** the formation of a saccule or saccules. **2** a sacculate part.

**sac|cule** (sak′yül), *n.* **1** a little sac. **2** the smaller of the two membranous sacs in the labyrinth of the internal ear. [< Latin *sacculus* (diminutive) < *saccus;* see etym. under **sack**[1]]

**sac|cu|lus** (sak′yə ləs), *n., pl.* **-li** (-lī). = saccule.

**sa|cer|do|cy** (sas′ər dō′sē), *n., pl.* **-cies.** **1** sacerdotal or priestly character or dignity. **2** a priestly office or system.

**sac|er|do|tal** (sas′ər dō′təl), *adj.* **1** of priests or the priesthood; priestly: *Régine took on the job of tending the church altar and the sacerdotal robes* (Time). **2** of, based on, or having to do with the doctrine that the priesthood is invested by ordination with supernatural powers. [< Latin *sacerdōtālis* < *sacerdōs, -ōtis* priest < *sacra* rites + a stem *dōt-* to put, set]

**sac|er|do|tal|ism** (sas′ər dō′tə liz əm), *n.* **1a** the sacerdotal system; spirit or methods of the priesthood. **b** priestcraft (in an unfavorable sense). **2** the theory that the priesthood is invested by ordination with supernatural powers.

**sac|er|do|tal|ist** (sas′ər dō′tə list), *n.* a person who advocates or supports sacerdotalism.

**sac|er|do|tal|ly** (sas′ər dō′tə lē), *adv.* in a sacerdotal manner.

**sac fungus,** = ascomycete.

**sa|chem** (sā′chəm), *n.* **1** the chief of a tribe or a confederation among some North American Indians: *Tammany was sachem of the Delaware Indians in the 1600's.* **2** *U.S.* one of a body of twelve high officials in the Tammany Society of New York: *a sachem of Tammany Hall.* [American English < Algonkian (Narragansett) *sâchimau* chief. See related etym. at **sagamore.**]

**sa|chem|ic** (sā chem′ik, sā′chə mik), *adj.* of or having to do with a sachem: *The sachemic office was hereditary.*

**sa|chem|ship** (sā′chəm ship), *n.* the office or position of a sachem.

**Sa|cher|tor|te** (zä′ᴋʜər tôr′tə), *n., pl.* **-tor|ten** (-tôr′tən), a rich layer cake filled with apricot jam and covered with chocolate frosting. [< *Sacher,* a hotel in Austria specializing in this cake + German *Torte* torte]

**sa|chet** (sa shā′; *especially British* sash′ā), *n.* **1** a small bag or pad containing perfumed powder, usually placed among articles of clothing. **2** perfumed powder. [< French, Old French *sachet* (diminutive) < *sac* sack, bag]

**sachet powder,** strongly perfumed powder used in sachets.

**sack**[1] (sak), *n., v.* **—*n.* 1** a large bag, usually made of coarse cloth. Sacks are used for storing

---

**Pronunciation Key:** hat, āge, cãre, fär; let, ēqual, tėrm; it, īce; hot, ōpen, ôrder; oil, out; cup, pu̇t, rüle; child; long; thin; ᴛʜen; zh, measure; ə represents **a** in about, **e** in taken, **i** in pencil, **o** in lemon, **u** in circus.

S

and carrying grain, flour, potatoes, charcoal, and the like. **SYN**: See syn. under **bag. 2** such a bag with what is in it: *He bought two sacks of corn.* **3** the amount that a sack will hold: *We burned two sacks of coal.* **4** *U.S.* any bag or what is in it: *a sack of candy.* **5** *U.S. Slang.* (in baseball) a base. **6** *Slang.* a bed. **7** dismissal from employment or office: *to give a person the sack.*
— ***v.t.* 1** to put into a sack or sacks: *to sack coal.* **2** to dismiss from employment or office; fire.
**hit the sack**, *Slang.* to go to bed: *I'm sleepy; let's hit the sack.*
**hold the sack**, *Informal.* to be left empty-handed; be left to suffer the consequences: *We will be holding the sack for an additional ... deficit of nearly $1000* (University of Kansas Graduate Magazine).
**sack out**, *Slang.* to go to bed: *It's still too early to sack out.*
[Middle English *sacke,* or *secke,* Old English *sacc* < Latin *saccus* < Greek *sákkos* < Semitic (compare Hebrew *shaq*)] — **sack′like′**, *adj.*

**sack[2]** (sak), *v., n.* — ***v.t.*** to plunder (a captured city); loot and despoil; pillage: *The soldiers sacked the town.* **SYN**: devastate. [< noun]
— *n.* the act of plundering (a captured city): *The city was sure to be delivered over to fire, sack, and outrage* (John L. Motley).
[< Middle French *sac* < Italian *sacco* < Vulgar Latin *saccāre* take by force; origin uncertain]

**sack[3]** (sak), *n.* **1** a loose jacket worn by women and children: *a knitted sack for a baby.* **2** a kind of loose gown formerly worn by women or a long back piece fastened to the gown at the shoulders and forming a train. Also, **sacque**. [apparently < *sack*[1]. Compare Dutch *zak,* German (*französischer*) *Sack.*]

**sack[4]** (sak), *n.* **1** = sherry. **2** any one of certain other strong, light-colored wines formerly exported from Spain and certain other parts of southern Europe. [< French (*vin*) *sec* dry (wine) < Latin *siccus*]

**sack bearer**, the larva of a North American moth, which feeds on oak leaves and protects itself with a case made of leaves.

**sack|but** (sak′but), *n.* **1** a bass trumpet with a slide like that of a trombone for altering the pitch. It was a form of the trombone in the Middle Ages. **2** an ancient stringed instrument mentioned in the Bible (Daniel 3). [< Middle French, Old French *saquebute,* Old North French *saqueboute* hooked lance for unhorsing an enemy; (literally) pull-push < *saquer* to pull (probably < *sac* < Latin *saccus;* see etym. under **sack**[1]) + *bouter* to push. Compare etym. under **butt**[3].]

**sack|cloth** (sak′klôth′, -kloth′), *n.* **1** a coarse cloth for making sacks; sacking. **2** a coarse fabric worn as a sign of mourning or penitence: *The sackcloth of the Bible was a dark fabric of goats' or camels' hair.*
**in sackcloth and ashes**, with grief, humiliation, or abject penitence: *The culprit's only proper course would seem to be repentance in sackcloth and ashes* (Arthur Krock).

**sack cloud**, a form of mammatocumulus in which the pocket hanging from the cloud becomes so deep as to resemble a sack or bag, sometimes seeming to reach to the ground.

**sack coat**, a man's short, loose-fitting coat for ordinary wear.

***sack dress**, a loose-fitting dress with straight lines.

***sack dress**

**sack|er[1]** (sak′ər), *n.* a person who sacks or plunders. [< *sack*[2] + *-er*[1]]

**sack|er[2]** (sak′ər), *n. Baseball Slang.* a baseman: *But Thompson, in his haste to make the throw, didn't wait for Davey Williams, Giant second sacker, to reach the bag* (New York Times). [< *sack*[1] + *-er*[2]]

**Pronunciation Key:** hat, āge, cãre, fär; let, ēqual, tėrm; it, īce; hot, ōpen, ôrder; oil, out; cup, pu̇t, rüle; child; long; thin; ᴛʜen; zh, measure; ə represents **a** in about, **e** in taken, **i** in pencil, **o** in lemon, **u** in circus.

**sack|ful** (sak′fu̇l), *n., pl.* **-fuls. 1** enough to fill a sack. **2** *Informal.* a great quantity; large amount.

**sack|ing** (sak′ing), *n.* a coarse cloth used for making sacks or bags. Sacking is closely woven of hemp, cotton, flax, or jute.

**sack|less** (sak′lis), *adj.* **1** *Scottish.* **a** harmless. **b** lacking energy, spirit, or sense. **c** feeble-minded. **2** *Obsolete.* **a** guiltless. **b** secure. [Old English *saclēas,* perhaps < *sacu* sake, behalf + *-lēas* -less or, perhaps < Scandinavian (compare Old Icelandic *saklauss*)]

**sack race**, a race in which each competitor is enveloped in a sack, the mouth of which is secured around his neck or waist.

**sacque** (sak), *n.* = sack[3]. [Gallicized variant of *sack*[3]]

**sa|cral[1]** (sā′krəl, sak′rəl), *adj.* of or having to do with sacred rites or observances. [< Latin *sacer, sacris* sacred + English *-al*[1]]

**sa|cral[2]** (sā′krəl), *adj.* of, having to do with, or in the region of the sacrum. [< New Latin *sacralis* < Latin (*os*) *sacrum* sacrum; (literally) sacred (bone), neuter of *sacer,* adjective, sacred]

**sa|cral|i|ty** (sā kral′ə tē, sak ral′-), *n.* sacred quality or state; sacredness; sanctity.

**sa|cral|i|za|tion** (sā′krə lə zā′shən, sak′rə-), *n.* the act or process of sacralizing; sanctification.

**sa|cral|ize** (sā′krə līz, sak′rə-), *v.t.,* **-ized, -iz|ing.** to make sacred; endow (an idea or institution) with sacredness; sanctify.

**sac|ra|ment** (sak′rə mənt), *n.* **1** a solemn religious ceremony of the Christian church. In Roman Catholic and Eastern Churches there are seven sacraments: Baptism, Confirmation, Eucharist, Penance, Extreme Unction or Anointing of the Sick, Holy Orders, and Matrimony. From the 1500's, Protestants generally have had two sacraments only—Baptism and Communion. **SYN**: rite. **2** Often, **Sacrament. a** Communion (the Eucharist or Lord's Supper). **b** the consecrated bread and wine. **c** the bread alone (the Host). **3** something especially sacred: *To the true mystic, life itself is a sacrament* (W. R. Inge). **4** a sign; token; symbol. **5** a solemn promise; oath. **SYN**: vow.
[< Old French *sacrement,* learned borrowing from Latin *sacrāmentum* a consecrating (usually an oath or surety) < *sacrāre* to consecrate < *sacer* holy, sacred]

**sac|ra|men|tal** (sak′rə men′təl), *adj., n.* — ***adj.*** **1** of or having to do with a sacrament; used in a sacrament: *sacramental wine.* **2** especially sacred: *The fulfillment of her father's lifelong ambition about this library was a sacramental obligation for Romola* (George Eliot). **SYN**: consecrated, hallowed, holy.
— *n.* a rite or ceremony of the Roman Catholic Church similar to but not included among the sacraments. The use of holy water or oil and the sign of the cross are sacramentals.

**sac|ra|men|tal|ism** (sak′rə men′tə liz əm), *n.* the doctrine that there is in the sacraments themselves by Christ's institution a direct spiritual power to confer grace upon the recipient.

**sac|ra|men|tal|ist** (sak′rə men′tə list), *n.* a person who holds the doctrine of sacramentalism.

**sac|ra|men|tal|i|ty** (sak′rə men tal′ə tē), *n.* sacramental quality or character: *the sacramentality of marriage.*

**sac|ra|men|tal|ly** (sak′rə men′tə lē), *adv.* after the manner of a sacrament.

**sac|ra|men|tar|i|an** (sak′rə men târ′ē ən), *adj.* of or having to do with the sacraments. [< *sacramentary,* adjective + *-an*]

**Sac|ra|men|tar|i|an** (sak′rə men târ′ē ən), *n., adj.* — *n.* **1** a person who believes that the bread and wine of Communion are the symbol of Christ's sacrifice, but not actually His flesh and blood. **2** a person who believes that the sacraments in themselves confer spiritual grace upon the recipient; a sacramentalist.
— *adj.* of or having to do with the Sacramentarians.
[< German *Sakramentarian* (coined by Martin Luther) < Medieval Latin *sacramentarius,* adjective, sacramentary]

**Sac|ra|men|tar|i|an|ism** (sak′rə men târ′ē ə niz′-əm), *n.* the doctrine or belief held by Sacramentarians; sacramentalism.

**sac|ra|men|ta|ry** (sak′rə men′tər ē), *adj., n., pl.* **-ries.** — ***adj.*** sacramental; sacramentarian.
— *n.* a book containing religious offices or services formerly in use in the Western Church, containing the rites and prayers connected with the sacraments and other ceremonies.
[< Medieval Latin *sacramentarium* < Latin *sacrāmentum;* see etym. under **sacrament**]

**sacrament cloth**, the veil or cloth which covers the pyx or vessel containing the reserved Eucharist.

**sacrament house**, the tabernacle for the reserved Eucharist.

**sa|crar|i|um** (sə krãr′ē əm), *n., pl.* **-i|a** (-ē ə). **1** the sanctuary of a church. **2** (in Roman Catholic use) a basin used to dispose of water after certain ablutions; piscina. **3** (in ancient Rome) a shrine or sanctuary. [< Latin *sacrārium* < *sacrāre* to consecrate < *sacer* sacred]

**Sa|cra Ro|ma|na Ro|ta** (sā′krə rō mā′nə rō′tə), the official Latin name of the Sacred Roman Rota.

**sa|cre** (sā′kər), *v.t.,* **-cred, -cring.** to consecrate; hallow (now only as in *sacred* and *sacring*). [< Old French *sacrer,* learned borrowing from Latin *sacrāre;* see etym. under **sacrarium**]

**sa|cré** (sà krā′), *adj.* **1** sacred. **2** damned; cursed; confounded. [< French *sacré,* past participle of *sacrer* to consecrate, learned borrowing from Latin *sacrāre;* see etym. under **sacrarium**]

**Sa|cré-Coeur** (sà′krā kœr′), *n.* Sacred Heart (of Jesus). [< French *Sacré-Cœur* (literally) sacred heart]

**sa|cred** (sā′krid), *adj.* **1** belonging to or dedicated to God or a god; holy: *the sacred altar. A church is a sacred building. This statement says that the people of Cyprus "will carry on their sacred struggle without fear of any repressive measures or prison cells"* (London Times). **SYN**: consecrated. See syn. under **holy. 2** connected with religion; religious: *sacred music, sacred writings. Prayer is a sacred duty. What is called sacred may be an object. Thus the thunderbird or the coyote may be sacred in one group but not in another ... the objects chosen to be sacred are those which are related to the unknown forces of mana, or other powers* (Ogburn and Nimkoff). **3** *Figurative.* worthy of reverence: *the sacred memory of a dead hero. To a feather-brained schoolgirl nothing is sacred* (Charlotte Brontë). **4** *Figurative.* set apart for or dedicated to some person, object, or purpose: *This monument is sacred to the memory of the Unknown Soldier.* **5** that must not be violated or disregarded: *He made a sacred promise. Their property would be held sacred* (Macaulay). **6** properly immune, as from violence or interference; sacrosanct; inviolable: *The persons of Saturninus and Glaucia were doubly sacred, for one was tribune and the other praetor* (James A. Froude). **7** *Rare.* accursed: *For sacred hunger of my Gold I die* (John Dryden). [(originally) past participle of *sacre*] — **sa′cred|ness**, *n.*

**sacred baboon**, the hamadryas baboon. It was revered in ancient Egypt.

**Sacred College**, the cardinals of the Roman Catholic Church collectively; College of Cardinals. The Sacred College elects and advises the Pope.

**sacred cow**, **1** a cow believed to be sacred in certain religions, as among the Hindus: *On the balcony of a dingy little flat in Old Delhi, looking down on a street that swarmed with sacred cows, bullock carts, peddlers and beggars ...* (Maclean's). **2** *Figurative: The need for widespread secrecy has become a sacred cow, a belief hedged by the deepest emotions and accepted without question by many Americans* (Bulletin of Atomic Scientists). *Is foreign policy a "sacred cow," an inscrutable object of worship to be accepted without question?* (Wall Street Journal).

**sacred earflower**, a shrub or small tree native to the mountains of southern Mexico and Guatemala, with flowers having thick fleshy petals that are sometimes used to add a spicy flavor to tea and chocolate.

**sacred ibis**, an Egyptian wading bird with white and black feathers and a downward-curving bill.

**sacred lotus**, a variety of nelumbo or lotus of southern Asia and Australia, with large white, pink or red flowers and leaves up to three feet wide.

**sa|cred|ly** (sā′krid lē), *adv.* **1** in a sacred manner; with due reverence; religiously: *to observe the Sabbath sacredly.* **2** with strict care; inviolably: *a secret to be sacredly kept.*

**sacred mushroom**, **1** the Mexican mushroom from which the hallucinogenic drug psilocybin is derived. Certain Indians of Mexico eat the mushroom in religious rites. **2** any other mushroom grown or used for its hallucinogenic effects.

**sacred orders**, = holy orders.

**Sacred Roman Rota** or **Sacred Rota**, the Rota, an ecclesiastical tribunal forming a court of final appeal in the Roman Catholic Church: *The Sacred Roman Rota* [*is*] *the Vatican court that considers marriage problems and grants annulment on rare occasions to Roman Catholic couples* (New York Times).

**sac|ri|fice** (sak′rə fīs), *n., v.,* **-ficed, -fic|ing.** — ***n.*** **1a** the act of offering to a god, especially for the purpose of propitiation or homage: *Sacrifices were invaluable features of early religions. By this method the relationships with the gods were renewed and strengthened* (Emory S. Bogardus). **SYN**: immolation. **b** the animal or other thing offered: *The ancient Hebrews killed animals on the altars as sacrifices to God.* **2a** the act of giving up one thing for another; destruction or surrender

of something valued or desired for the sake of a higher object or more pressing claim: *Our teacher does not approve of any sacrifice of studies to sports. Wisdom and sacrifices are demanded from all sides* (Science News Letter). **b** the thing so given up or destroyed. **3a** a loss brought about in selling something below its value: *He will sell his house at a sacrifice because he needs money.* **b** something that is sold below its value. **4** *Baseball.* a sacrifice hit: *The Phillies caused consternation by ... advancing a man to third on a sacrifice and an error* (Christopher "Christy" Mathewson).
*—v.t.* **1** to give or offer to a god: *They sacrificed oxen, sheep, and doves.* SYN: immolate. **2a** to give up (something) for some higher advantage or dearer object: *A mother will sacrifice her life for her children.* **b** to permit injury or disadvantage to, for the sake of something else: *to sacrifice business for pleasure.* **3** to sell at a loss: *He sacrificed his house when he moved to France to work.* **4** *Baseball.* to advance or score (a runner) by a sacrifice hit: *He sacrificed Mantle to second base.*
*—v.i.* **1** to offer or make a sacrifice. **2** *Baseball.* to make a sacrifice hit.
**make the supreme sacrifice**, to give one's life; die: *On Memorial Day we honor the men in our armed forces who made the supreme sacrifice for their country.*
[< Old French *sacrifice,* learned borrowing from Latin *sacrificum* < *sacrificāre* < *sacra* rites, neuter plural of *sacer* holy + *facere* to perform, do]

**sacrifice fly**, *Baseball.* a sacrifice hit in the form of a fly to the outfield.

**sacrifice hit**, *Baseball.* a bunt that advances a base runner or a fly ball that scores a base runner, although the batter is put out. It does not count as an official time at bat.

**sac|ri|fic|er** (sak′rə fī′sər), *n.* a person who sacrifices, especially a priest.

**sac|ri|fi|cial** (sak′rə fish′əl), *adj.* **1** having to do with or used in sacrifice: *sacrificial rites.* **2** involving sacrifice or loss to the seller: *a sacrificial sale of summer dresses.* —**sac′ri|fi′cial|ly**, *adv.*

**sacrificial lamb**, a person or thing sacrificed for some gain or advantage: *The firemen may have to be the "sacrificial lamb" in obtaining concessions from the carriers* (Wall Street Journal).

**sac|ri|lege** (sak′rə lij), *n.* an intentional injury to anything sacred or held sacred; disrespectful treatment of anyone or anything sacred: *Robbing the church was a sacrilege.* SYN: profanation. [< Old French *sacrilege,* learned borrowing from Latin *sacrilegium* temple robbery < *sacrum* sacred object; (originally) neuter of *sacer* sacred + *legere* to take; select]

**sac|ri|le|gious** (sak′rə lij′əs, -lē′jəs), *adj.* **1** injurious or insulting to sacred persons or things; involving sacrilege: *sacrilegious acts.* **2** committing sacrilege; guilty of sacrilege. SYN: impious, irreverent. —**sac′ri|le′gious|ly**, *adv.* —**sac′ri|le′gious|ness**, *n.*
▶ The more common pronunciation (sak′rə lij′əs) has arisen on the analogy of *sacrilege* (sak′rə lij) and of *religious.* It is a frequent cause of misspelling.

**sac|ri|le|gist** (sak′rə lē′jist), *n.* a person guilty of sacrilege.

**sa|cring** (sā′kring), *n.* a consecrating, especially that of the bread and wine in the Mass. [< *sacr*(e) + *-ing*[1]]

**sacring bell**, in the Roman Catholic Church: **1** a small bell rung at the elevation of the Host. **2** the ringing of the bell at the elevation of the Host.

**sa|crist** (sā′krist), *n.* = sacristan. [< Old French *sacriste,* learned borrowing from Latin *sacrista.* See etym. of doublets **sacristan, sexton.**]

**sac|ris|tan** (sak′rə stən), *n.* **1** a person in charge of the sacred vessels, robes, and other property used in ceremonies of a church or monastery. **2** *Obsolete.* a sexton. [< Medieval Latin *sacristanus* < Latin *sacrista* a sacristan < *sacer* holy. See etym. of doublets **sacrist, sexton.**]

**sac|ris|ty** (sak′rə stē), *n., pl.* **-ties.** the place where the sacred vessels, robes, and other property used in ceremonies of a church or monastery are kept. SYN: vestry. [< Medieval Latin *sacristia* < Latin *sacrista;* see etym. under **sacristan**]

**sa|crō|coc|cyx** (sā′krō kok′siks), *n.* the sacrum and coccyx regarded as one bone.

**sa|cro|il|i|ac** (sā′krō il′ē ak, sak′rō-), *adj., n.* *—adj.* **1** of or having to do with the sacrum and the ilium: *sacroiliac articulation.* **2** designating the joint between the sacrum and the ilium.
*—n.* the sacroiliac joint: *Strictly speaking, the sacroiliac is an area at the base of the spine; everybody has one* (Atlantic).
[< New Latin *sacrum* sacrum + English *iliac*]

**sac|ro|sanct** (sak′rō sangkt), *adj.* **1** very holy; very sacred; inviolable: *He reluctantly accepts the sacrosanct character of FBI files* (Scientific American). *Nowadays modernism is sacrosanct under the name of experimentation* (Harper's). **2** set apart as sacred; consecrated. [< Latin *sacrōsānctus* < *sacrō,* ablative of *sacer* sacred + *sānctus,* past participle of *sancīre* ordain, establish] —**sac′ro|sanct′ness**, *n.*

**sac|ro|sanc|ti|ty** (sak′rō sangk′tə tē), *n.* the condition of being sacrosanct; especial sacredness; inviolability: *[He] asked whether the basic, minimum civil liberties—"the sacrosanctity of the person"—could be infringed and even violated if the party leader so decided* (Atlantic).

**sa|cro|sci|at|ic** (sā′krō sī at′ik, sak′rō-), *adj.* of or having to do with the sacrum and the ischium: *the sacrosciatic notch.* [< New Latin *sacrum* sacrum + English *sciatic*]

**sa|crum** (sā′krəm), *n., pl.* **-cra** (-krə), **-crums.** a compound, triangular bone at the lower end of the spine, made by the joining of several vertebrae and forming the back of the pelvis: *In the sacral region the vertebrae in some animals are considerably thickened without great change while in others they are much flattened and more or less fused into a platelike structure, the sacrum* (A. Franklin Shull). [< Late Latin *(ōs) sacrum* sacred (bone), translation of Greek *hieròn ostéon* (probably because it was offered as a dainty in sacrifices)]

**sad** (sad), *adj.,* **sad|der, sad|dest.** **1** not happy: **a** full of sorrow; grieving: *You feel sad if your best friend goes away. I was very sad, I think sadder than at any one time in my life* (John Bunyan). **b** in low spirits: *She was sad because she lost her money.* **2** characterized by sorrow; sorrowful: *a sad life, a sad occasion.* **3** causing sorrow; distressing: *a sad accident. The death of a pet is a sad loss.* SYN: deplorable, lamentable, calamitous, disastrous. **4** expressing sorrow; gloomy; downcast: *sad looks, a sad countenance. Of all sad words of tongue or pen, the saddest are these: "It might have been!"* (John Greenleaf Whittier). **5** dull in color; not cheerful-looking; dark: *The general colouring was uniform and sad* (Robert Louis Stevenson). **6** extremely bad; shocking: *a sad state of affairs. In the present sad state of international distrust, there is only a faint hope of achieving such a step in political evolution* (Bulletin of Atomic Scientists). **7** *Dialect.* (of bread or pastry) that has not risen properly; heavy. [Old English *sæd* sated; later, weary] —**sad′ness**, *n.*
*—Syn.* **1 Sad, dejected, depressed** mean unhappy or in a state of low spirits. **Sad** is the general term, and implies nothing as to the degree, duration, or cause of the state: *Moonlight makes her sad.* **Dejected** implies a very low but usually temporary state of unhappiness due to some specific cause: *She is dejected over his leaving.* **Depressed** implies a temporary and usually not very low state of unhappiness due to some vague or general cause: *He is depressed by the state of the world.* However, in a more technical sense it can mean any of varying degrees of unhappiness endured for, sometimes, long periods of time: *The artist would become depressed suffering from such fits for long periods of time in which he accomplished nothing.*

**sad|den** (sad′ən), *v.t.* to make sad or sorrowful; depress in spirits: *The bad news saddened him. Her gloomy presence saddens all the scene* (Alexander Pope). *—v.i.* to become sad or gloomy: *Her face saddened at the news. Better be merry with the fruitful grape than sadden after none, or bitter, fruit* (Edward FitzGerald).

**sad|den|ing|ly** (sad′ə ning lē), *adv.* in a way that saddens.

**sad|dhu** (sä′dü), *n.* = sadhu.

***sad|dle** (sad′əl), *n., v.,* **-dled, -dling.** *—n.* **1** a seat for a rider on a horse's back, on a bicycle, or on other things. See picture below. **2** the part of a harness that holds the shafts, or to which a checkrein is attached. **3** something like a saddle in shape, position, or use: *The wide, curved end of a violin is called a saddle. The floorboards joined at the door where the carpenter covered them with a saddle.* **4** a ridge between two hills or mountain peaks: *The colors of the cliffs that rim this saddle run riot on a bright day* (William O. Douglas). **5** a cut of mutton, venison, or lamb consisting of both loins and the back portion between them, used as food. **6** the rear part of the back of a male fowl, extending to the tail. **7** the bearing on the axle of a railroad car. **8** the part of certain gun carriages which supports the trunnions. **9** *Bookbinding.* the center portion of the back of the binding; outer part of the spine.
*—v.t.* **1** to put a saddle on: *to saddle a horse.* **2** *Figurative.* to load with (something) as a burden; burden: *He is saddled with too many jobs.* SYN: encumber. **3** *Figurative.* to put as a burden on: *If you like not my company, you can saddle yourself on someone else* (Robert Louis Stevenson). **4** to train (a race horse).
*—v.i.* **1** to put a saddle on a horse: *It's time to saddle up and go home.* **2** to get into the saddle.
**in the saddle**, in a position of control or command: *[He] resigned in the belief that things would soon break down without him and he would be back in the saddle more firmly seated than before* (Observer).
[Old English *sadol*] —**sad′dle|like′**, *adj.*

**sad|dle|back** (sad′əl bak′), *n.* **1** a hill or summit shaped like a saddle. **2** = great black-backed gull. **3** = saddleback seal.

**saddleback caterpillar**, a green caterpillar having a brown mark shaped like a saddle on its back and stinging hairs which can cause severe irritation to the skin.

**sad|dle-backed** (sad′əl bakt′), *adj.* **1** having the back, upper surface, or edge curved like a saddle: *a saddle-backed hill, a saddle-backed horse.* **2** having saddlelike markings on the back: *a pinto horse with saddle-backed marking.*

**saddleback seal**, a gray or yellowish seal with a black face and a black or brown band along the back and sides, found in arctic regions south to the St. Lawrence River; harp seal.

**sad|dle|bag** (sad′əl bag′), *n.* one of a pair of bags laid across the back of a horse, mule, or other animal behind the saddle.

**sad|dle-billed stork** (sad′əl bild′), a large white and blackish stork of tropical Africa, with scarlet on the knees, feet, and bill.

**saddle blanket**, = saddlecloth.

**sad|dle|bow** (sad′əl bō′), *n.* the arched front part of a saddle or saddletree.

**sad|dle|cloth** (sad′əl klôth′, -kloth′), *n.* a cloth put between an animal's back and the saddle.

**saddle gall**, a raw area formed on a horse's back by uneven pressure of the saddle.

**saddle horse**, a horse for riding.

**saddle leather**, **1** hide of cattle specially prepared for making saddles. **2** leather made to resemble this, for use in clothing and accessories.

**sad|dle|mak|er** (sad′əl mā′kər), *n.* = saddler.

**saddle nose**, a nose considerably depressed at the bridge because of fracture or disease.

**sad|dler** (sad′lər), *n.* a person who makes, mends, or sells saddles and harness.

**saddle roof**, a ridged roof with two gables.

**sad|dler|y** (sad′lər ē), *n., pl.* **-dler|ies.** **1** the work of a saddler. **2** the shop of a saddler. **3** saddles, harness, and other equipment for horses.

**saddle shell**, **1** a shell suggesting a saddle in shape, as that of a bivalve mollusk of East Indian seas. **2** a mollusk with such a shell.

**saddle shoe**, a low shoe, usually white, with the instep crossed by a band of leather of a different color. Saddle shoes are worn especially for sports and casual wear. *The saddle shoes and the dark Shakerknit sweater ... gave him the air of a college athlete home for vacation* (New Yorker).

**saddle soap**, a substance, now usually consisting chiefly of a mild soap and neat's-foot oil, used for cleaning and conditioning saddles, harnesses, boots, and the like.

**sad|dle|sore** (sad′əl sôr′, -sōr′), *adj.* sore or stiff from riding horseback: *"Jorrocks," at the New Theatre, London, is an innocuous musical*

***saddle** definition 1

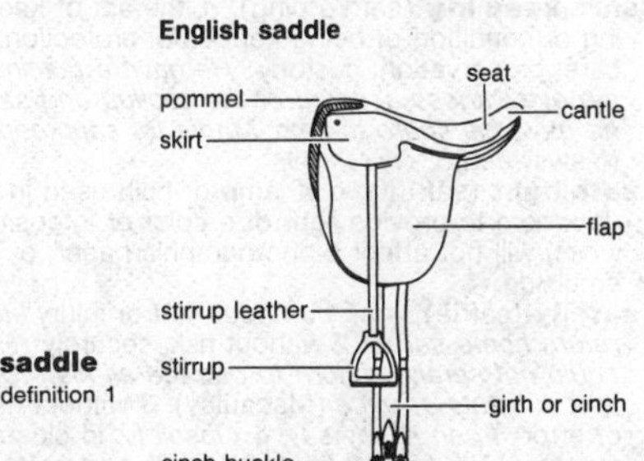


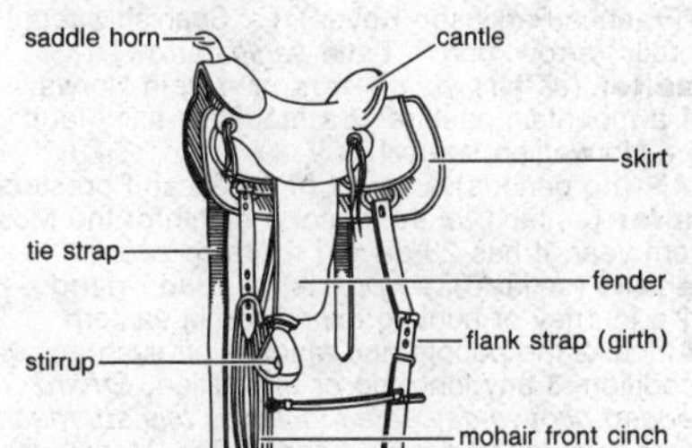

*derived from the Surtees novels about the saddlesore grocer among the grandees of the hunting field* (Manchester Guardian Weekly).

**sad|dle|tree** (sad′əl trē′), *n.* 1 the frame of a saddle. 2 *U.S.* the tulip tree.

**Sad|du|ce|an** or **Sad|du|cae|an** (saj′ə sē′ən, sad′yə-), *adj., n.* —*adj.* of or having to do with the Sadducees. —*n.* = Sadducee.

**Sad|du|cee** (saj′ə sē, sad′yə-), *n.* one of a Jewish sect, of the time of Christ, that rejected the oral law and denied the resurrection of the dead and the existence of angels. The sect stood for hereditary priestly authority. *Next to the Pharisees in power, but not quite so numerous, were the Sadducees* (Hendrik van Loon). [Old English *sadducēas,* plural < Latin *Saddūcaeus* of the *Saddūcaeī,* the Sadducees < Late Greek < *Saddoukaîoi* the Sadducees < Hebrew *ṣadduqi* < *ṣadduq* Zadok, apparently the Hebrew high priest in the time of David (II Samuel 8:17, Ezekiel 40:46)]

**Sad|du|cee|ism** (saj′ə sē iz′əm, sad′yə-), *n.* 1 the beliefs and practices of the Sadducees. 2 = skepticism.

**sa|dha|na** (sä′də nə), *n. Hinduism.* the spiritual training leading to the state of samadhi: *Ganja was there considered a beginning of sadhana* (Allen Ginsberg). [< Sanskrit *sādhana* < *sādhu* straight, virtuous]

**sa|dhe** (sä dā′, tsä′dē), *n.* the eighteenth letter of the Hebrew alphabet. Also, **tsadi.** [< Hebrew *ṣadhe*]

**sa|dhu** (sä′dü), *n.* a Hindu holy man. Also, **saddhu, sadu.** [< Sanskrit *sādhu* straight, virtuous]

**sad|i|ron** (sad′ī′ərn), *n.* a heavy flatiron for pressing clothes. [< *sad* in obsolete sense of "solid" + *iron*]

**sa|dism** (sā′diz əm, sad′iz-), *n.* 1 the practice of a person who gets pleasure from hurting someone else: *By his own principles he would stand convicted of various abnormalities, including masochism, sadism ...* (Harper's). 2 an unnatural love of cruelty. [< French *sadisme* < the Count or Marquis Donatien de *Sade,* 1740-1814, who wrote of it]

**sa|dist** (sā′dist, sad′ist), *n.* 1 a person who gets pleasure from hurting someone else. 2 a person having an unnatural love of cruelty.

**sa|dis|tic** (sə dis′tik, sā-), *adj.* of or relating to sadism or to sadists: *Those who torture others in mind or body in order to gain ego satisfaction are sadistic* (George Simpson). —**sa|dis′ti|cal|ly,** *adv.*

**sad|ly** (sad′lē), *adv.* 1 sorrowfully; mournfully. 2 in a manner to cause sadness; lamentably; deplorably: *Authors ... are sadly prone to quarrel* (William Cowper).

**sa|do|mas|och|ism** (sā′dō mas′ə kiz əm, -maz′-), *n.* a form of perversion marked by a love for both receiving and inflicting pain; masochism and sadism combined.

**sa|do|mas|och|ist** (sā′dō mas′ə kist, -maz′-), *n.* a person who exhibits sadomasochism.

**sa|do|mas|och|is|tic** (sā′dō mas′ə kis′tic, -maz′-), *adj.* of or having to do with sadomasochism; exhibiting both sadism and masochism.

**sad sack,** *Informal.* 1 a poor, bewildered soldier who blunders his way through the mazes of army life, constantly making mistakes and getting into trouble: *The Hemingway-type hero is no Jake, no Lieut. Henry, but the saddest of fictional sad sacks, called, of all things, Tyree Shelby* (Time). 2 any bewildered, blundering person: *[He] is a sort of egghead's sad sack* (Newsweek). [< *sad* + slang *sack* a sleepy, lazy, slovenly soldier; popularized in the comic strip drawn by Sergeant George Baker]

**sa|du** (sä′dü), *n.* = sadhu.

**sae** (sā), *adv., conj., interj., pron. Scottish.* so.

**s.a.e.,** self-addressed envelope; stamped addressed envelope.

**SAE number,** a number established by the Society of Automotive Engineers to designate the viscosity of a lubricant. SAE 10 is light oil; SAE 40 is heavy oil.

**sa|e|ta** (sä ā′tä), *n.* a Spanish song of mourning or penitence sung during the processions of Holy Week: *Seville is the sound of the saetas* (Frances Parkinson Keyes). [< Spanish *saeta* (literally) arrow, dart < Latin *sagitta* arrow]

**sae|ter** (sē′tər), *n., pl.* **-ters** or **-ter.** in Norway: 1 a mountain pasture. 2 a mountain dairy farm. [< Norwegian *saeter*]

**SAF** (no periods), Society of American Foresters.

**Sa|far** (sə fär′), *n.* the second month of the Moslem year. It has 29 days. [< Arabic *ṣafar*]

**sa|fa|ri** (sə fär′ē), *n., pl.* **-ris,** *v.,* **-ried, -ri|ing.** —*n.* 1 a journey or hunting expedition in eastern Africa. 2 the people and animals on such an expedition. 3 any long trip or expedition: *Erhard ended his two-day safari in Texas this afternoon with a clutch of double handshakes* (Manchester Guardian Weekly).

—*v.i.* to go on a safari: *Forsaking academe, he married three times, safaried in Africa ...* (Philip Kopper).

[< Swahili *safari* < Arabic *safar* journey, voyage]

**Sa|fa|vid** (sə fä′wēd), *n.* a member of a Moslem dynasty that ruled Persia from the 1500's until 1722. Under the Safavids, the Shiah sect of Islam became Persia's chief religion.

**safe** (sāf), *adj.,* **saf|er, saf|est,** *n.* —*adj.* 1 free from harm, danger, or loss: *safe from disease or enemies. Keep money in a safe place.* 2 having been kept from or escaped injury, damage, or danger; not harmed; uninjured: *to bring goods safe to land. He returned from war safe and sound.* 3 out of danger; secure: *We feel safe with the dog in the house.* 4 not causing harm or danger: *Is it safe to leave the house unlocked? A soft rubber ball is a safe plaything. The old building was pronounced safe.* 5 put beyond the power of doing harm; no longer dangerous: *a criminal safe in prison.* 6 not taking risks; careful; cautious: *a safe guess, a safe move, a safe driver.* 7 that can be depended on; reliable; trustworthy: *a safe guide, a safe bridge. A Manchester cloth firm got out a range of nearly forty colours—and the stores took less than a dozen of them, all in "safe" colours* (Observer). 8 *Baseball.* reaching a base or home plate without being put out: *safe on first.* 9 not likely to be lost to an opposing party in an election: *a safe state.*

—*n.* 1 a steel or iron box for money, jewels, papers, or other valuable things, often built into a wall. 2 a place made to keep things safe: *a meat safe.*

[< Old French *sauf,* earlier *salf* < Latin *salvus.* Compare etym. under **save**[1].] —**safe′ness,** *n.*

—*Syn. adj.* 1 **Safe, secure** mean free from danger, harm, or risk. **Safe** emphasizes being not exposed to danger, harm, or risk: *The children are safe in their own yard.* **Secure** emphasizes being protected or guarded against loss, attack, injury, or other anticipated or feared danger or harm and having no worry or fear: *A child feels secure with his mother.*

**safe-con|duct** (sāf′kon′dukt), *n.* 1 the privilege of passing safely through a region, especially in time of war: *The nurse was given safe-conduct through the enemy's camp.* 2 a paper granting this privilege. SYN: passport. 3 the act of conducting or convoying in safety.

**safe|crack|er** (sāf′krak′ər), *n.* a person who opens or is skilled at opening safes for purposes of robbery, by manipulation of the tumblers of the lock, removal of the door, or blowing it open with explosives: *A smash-and-grab epidemic cleaned out jewelers' windows in several Paris suburbs, and safe-crackers were busy all over the country* (Maclean's).

**safe|crack|ing** (sāf′krak′ing), *n.* the work or skill of a safecracker.

**safe deposit,** a place in which valuables may be stored in safety.

**safe-de|pos|it box** (sāf′di poz′it), a box for storing valuables, especially in the vault of a bank.

**safe|guard** (sāf′gärd′), *v., n.* —*v.t.* 1 to keep safe; guard against hurt, danger, or attack; protect: *to safeguard the country from surprise attack. Pure food laws safeguard our health.* 2 to guard; convoy. [< noun]

—*n.* 1 a protection; defense: *Keeping clean is a safeguard against disease. Personnel security programs can and should incorporate more of our traditional legal safeguards* (Bulletin of Atomic Scientists). SYN: security, shield. 2 a guard; convoy. SYN: escort.

[< Old French *sauvegarde* < *sauve,* feminine of *sauf* safe + *garde* guard]

**safe hit,** *Baseball.* a base hit.

**safe house,** a place made secure from wiretapping or other forms of surveillance, used for meetings or for concealment by intelligence agents, secret police, and the like: *Officials from the development company and from C.I.A. headquarters would meet to discuss the operation in one of two "safe houses," fashionable apartments leased in nearby Santa Monica and Long Beach* (Seymour M. Hersh).

**safe|keep|ing** (sāf′kē′ping), *n.* the act of keeping or condition of being kept safe; protection; care; preservation; custody: *He gave a fascinating eye-witness account of the stickup and said he gave his share to Jazz Maffie for safekeeping* (Newsweek).

**safe|light** (sāf′līt′), *n.* a lamp or bulb used in a darkroom to provide light of a color or intensity which will not affect a photographic paper, or emulsion.

**safe|ly** (sāf′lē), *adv.* 1 without hurt or injury: *to return home safely.* 2 without risk; securely: *He could not safely venture to outrage all his Protestant subjects at once* (Macaulay). 3 without risk of error: *I can safely say.* 4 *Obsolete.* in close custody: *Till then I'll keep him dark and safely lock'd* (Shakespeare).

**safe period,** the period in the female menstrual cycle when conception is least likely to take place.

**safe|ty** (sāf′tē), *n., pl.* **-ties,** *adj.* —*n.* 1 the quality or condition of being safe; freedom from harm or danger: *A bank assures safety for your money. You can cross the road in safety when the policeman holds up his hand to stop the cars.* SYN: security. 2 freedom from risk or possible damage or hurt; safeness: *I am very well satisfied of the safety of the experiment* (Lady Mary Wortley Montagu). 3 a device to prevent injury or accident. 4 a device that controls part of the firing mechanism and prevents a gun from being fired: *The hunters clicked off their safeties* (Harper's). 5 *Football.* a a play in which an offensive player downs the ball, or is downed, behind his own goal line when the impetus of the ball across the goal has come from his own team. A safety counts two points for the other team. *Iowa's Hawkeyes edged into a 2-to-0 lead with a safety in the second quarter* (New York Times). b the two points so scored. c = safety man. 6 *Baseball.* a base hit; hit.

—*adj.* giving safety; bringing no harm or danger; making harm unlikely: *One large market visualized for the process is steel-toed safety shoes for industry* (Wall Street Journal). SYN: protective.

**safety belt,** 1 a belt attached to the seat of an airplane, used to hold the passenger or pilot in the seat and so protect him from bumps; seat belt: *Just then the plane ... lurched and plunged at the same time, ... and I thought it better to get back to the reassurance of my safety belt* (Patricia Collinge). 2 a similar belt attached to the seat of an automobile or other vehicle; seat belt: *... a campaign to get drivers to fit and use safety belts in their cars* (New Scientist). 3 a strap, or pair of short straps, used by window washers, linemen, tree workers, and others who climb to prevent falling. 4 = life belt.

**safety bicycle,** the early name for a bicycle with two low wheels, as distinguished from the older type with one high and one small wheel and no gears or clutch.

**safety catch,** a catch or stop attached to a mechanical contrivance, used as a safeguard, as in firearms and hoisting apparatus.

**safety chain,** a chain used for additional security, such as on a door latch, a pocket watch, or the coupling of railway cars.

**safe|ty-de|pos|it box** (sāf′tē di poz′it), = safe-deposit box.

**safety factor,** 1 the proportion of the ultimate strength of a material to the maximum strains that can be brought upon it. 2 an element, condition, quality, or other factor that helps to bring about safety: *The unions claim the jobs not only are needed but are a vital safety factor* (Wall Street Journal).

**safety fuse,** 1 a fuse filled or saturated with a slow-burning composition. 2 *Electricity.* a fuse.

**safety glass,** glass that resists shattering, made of two or more layers of glass joined together by a layer of transparent plastic. Safety glass is used especially for automobile windows.

**safety harness,** 1 a combination of straps and belt attached to the frame of an automobile or other vehicle, used to hold a person in the seat while traveling. 2 any one of various other combinations of straps worn by a person to keep him from falling.

**safety island,** = safety zone.

✱**safety lamp,** 1 a miner's lamp in which the flame is kept from setting fire to explosive gases by a piece of wire gauze. 2 an electric lamp similarly protected.

**✱safety lamp**
definition 1

**safety man,** *Football.* a defensive back who usually lines up closest to his team's goal line: *There was no one between him and a touchdown except the safety man* (New Yorker).

**safety match,** a match that will ignite only when rubbed on a specially prepared surface.

**safety pin,** 1 a pin bent back on itself to form a spring and having a guard that covers the point and prevents accidental unfastening. 2 a pin on a grenade or mine that ignites the fuze when pulled; pin.

**safety razor**, a razor having the blade protected to prevent cutting the skin deeply.

**safety valve**, **1** a valve in a steam boiler or the like that opens and lets steam or fluid escape when the pressure becomes too great. **2** *Figurative: Free speech as a ... safety valve for public resentment cannot work when people get the idea that no one is listening* (Anthony Lewis).

**safety zone**, a part of a road set off by painted strips, a fence, or a curb, to protect people from traffic while they are waiting for a bus, or to cross a street, or the like.

**saf|fi|an** (saf′ē ən), *n.* a kind of leather made from goatskin or sheepskin tanned with sumac and dyed in various colors without a previous treating with fats. [< Russian *saf'jan* < Romanian *saftian* < Persian *sakhtijān*]

**saf|flow|er** (saf′lou′ər), *n.* **1** an herb like a thistle, with large, white to brilliant red flower heads. It is an Old-World composite plant, the seeds of which yield an oil used for cooking. **2** its dried petals, used in making certain red dyestuffs and in medicine as a substitute for saffron. **3** the red dyestuff. [earlier *safflore* (spelling influenced by *flower*), probably < Dutch *saflor* < earlier Italian *saffiore,* alteration of *zaffrole;* origin uncertain]

**safflower oil**, an oil derived from the seeds of the safflower, used for cooking and lighting, and in medicine as a possible agent to reduce the level of cholesterol in the blood.

**saf|fron** (saf′rən), *n., adj.* — *n.* **1** an autumn crocus with purple flowers having orange-yellow stigmas. **2** an orange-yellow coloring matter consisting of the dried stigmas of this crocus. Saffron is used to color and flavor food, candy, or drinks. **3** an orange yellow.
— *adj.* orange-yellow.
[Middle English *safran, safroun* < Old French *safran,* learned borrowing from Medieval Latin *safranum* < Arabic *za'farān;* influenced by Italian *zafferano*]

**saffron yellow**, orange yellow.

**S. Afr.**, **1** South Africa. **2** South African.

**saf|ra|nin** (saf′rə nin), *n.* = safranine.

**saf|ra|nine** (saf′rə nēn, -nin), *n.* any one of a class of organic synthetic dyes, chiefly red, derivatives of azonium compounds, used for dyeing wool, silk, or other fabric, and as a microscopic stain. *Formula:* $C_{18}H_{14}N_4$ [< German *Safranin* < Middle High German *safran* (< Old French *safran;* see etym. under **saffron**) + *-in* -ine[2]]

**S. Afr. D.**, South African Dutch.

**saf|rol** (saf′rōl, -rol), *n.* = safrole.

**saf|role** (saf′rōl), *n.* a colorless or faintly yellow, poisonous, oily liquid, obtained from oil of sassafras, used in making perfumes, soaps, and insecticides. *Formula:* $C_{10}H_{10}O_2$ [< German *Safrol,* short for *Sassafrol* < *Sassafras* sassafras (< Spanish *sasafras*) + *-ol* -ole]

**saft** (saft, säft), *adj., adv., n., interj. Scottish.* soft.

**sag** (sag), *v.*, **sagged, sag|ging**, *n.* — *v.i.* **1** to sink under weight or pressure; bend or curve down in the middle, as a rope, beam, cable, or plank: *As we walked across the plank over the brook it sagged in the water and we got our feet wet.* **2** to hang down unevenly: *Your dress sags in the back.* **3** *Figurative.* to become less firm or elastic; yield through weakness, weariness, or lack of effort; droop; sink: *The mind I sway by and the heart I bear, Shall never sag with doubt, nor shake with fear* (Shakespeare). **4** *Figurative.* to decline in price or value: *sagging cash incomes. Industrials sagged as a wave of selling began.* **5** (of a ship) to drift from her course: *We're sagging South on the Long Trail* (Rudyard Kipling).
— *v.t.* to cause to sag.
— *n.* **1** the act, condition, or degree of sagging: *Her voice is further let down by the sag of a large string orchestra* (New Yorker). **2** a place where anything sags. **3** *Figurative.* a decline in price. **4** the drift of a ship from her course.
[Middle English *saggen,* perhaps ultimately < Scandinavian (compare Old Icelandic *sekkva* to drift)]

**sa|ga** (sä′gə), *n.* **1** a medieval Icelandic story of heroic deeds, especially one embodying the traditional history of Icelandic families or of the kings of Norway. **2** any story of heroic deeds; narrative having the characteristics of such sagas: *The story of this American's business career in the Philippines is a ... saga that seems almost too overblown to be believed* (New Yorker). **SYN:** epic. [< Scandinavian (compare Old Icelandic *saga*). See related etym. at **saw**[3], **say**[1].]

**sa|ga|cious** (sə gā′shəs), *adj.* **1** wise in a keen, practical way; shrewd. **SYN:** astute, perspicacious. See syn. under **shrewd**. **2** resulting from or showing wisdom or sagacity: *He was observant and thoughtful, and given to asking sagacious questions* (John Galt). **3** (of animals) intelligent. [< Latin *sagāx, -ācis* (with English *-ous*), related to *sāgus* prophetic] — **sa|ga′cious|ly**, *adv.* — **sa|ga′cious|ness**, *n.*

**sa|gac|i|ty** (sə gas′ə tē), *n., pl.* **-ties**. keen, sound judgment; mental acuteness; shrewdness: ... *a mariner of infinite resource and sagacity* (Rudyard Kipling). **SYN:** acumen, perspicacity.

**sag|a|more** (sag′ə môr, -mōr), *n.* (among the Algonkian Indian tribes of New England) a chief or great man, sometimes below a sachem. [American English, earlier *sagamo* < Algonkian (Abnaki) *sa$^{n}$gma$^{n}$* chief, ruler. See related etym. at **sachem**.]

**saga novel**, a long, rambling novel dealing in some detail with the lives of the members of a large family, or group of families, over several generations.

**sage**[1] (sāj), *adj.*, **sag|er, sag|est**, *n.* — *adj.* **1** showing wisdom or good judgment: *a sage reply. The sage counsels of Lord Salisbury seemed to bring with them not only wealth and power, but security* (Lytton Strachey). **SYN:** judicious, prudent. See syn. under **wise. 2** wise; able to give good advice: *The President surrounded himself with sage advisers. Cousin of Buckingham, and you sage, grave men ...* (Shakespeare). **SYN:** judicious, prudent. See syn. under **wise**. **3** wise-looking; grave; solemn: *Owls are sage birds.*
— *n.* a very wise man: *The sage gave advice to his friends.*
[< Old French *sage* < Vulgar Latin *sapius,* for Latin *sapiēns -entis,* present participle of *sapere* be wise. Compare etym. under **sapient**.]
— **sage′ly**, *adv.* — **sage′ness**, *n.*

**sage**[2] (sāj), *n.* **1a** a plant whose grayish-green leaves are used as seasoning and in medicine. It is a small shrub, a species of salvia, that belongs to the mint family. **b** its dried leaves: *Turkey stuffing and sausages are seasoned with sage.* **2** any one of various other shrubs or herbs of the same genus; salvia. **3** = sagebrush. [< Old French *sauge* < Latin *salvia.* See etym. of doublet **salvia**.] — **sage′like′**, *adj.*

**SAGE** (no periods), Semi-Automatic Ground Environment (a ground-operated system of the United States Air Force to detect and intercept enemy aircraft and missiles).

**sage|brush** (sāj′brush′), *n.* a grayish-green bushy plant, common on the dry plains and mountains of western North America, that smells like sage. It is a shrub that belongs to the composite family. The sagebrush is the state flower of Nevada. *Some ranchers are reported as utilizing sagebrush to keep stock alive* (British Columbia Mining Journal).

**Sagebrush State**, a nickname for Nevada.

**sage cock**, a male sage grouse.

**sage green**, a dull grayish green.

**sage grouse**, the largest American grouse, common on the sagebrush plains of western North America.

**sage hen**, the sage grouse, especially the female.

**sage sparrow**, a grayish-brown sparrow of the arid regions of the southwestern United States and nearby Mexico.

**sage tea**, an infusion of sage leaves, used as a mild tonic or stimulant.

**sage thrasher**, a grayish-brown and white thrasher of arid regions of the western United States, similar to the mockingbird.

**sag|ger** or **sag|gar** (sag′ər), *n., v.* — *n.* **1** a case of fired clay in which procelain and other delicate wares are enclosed while firing. **2** the clay of which saggers are made.
— *v.t.* to place or fire in a sagger. Also, **seggar**.
[perhaps variant of dialectal *saggard,* perhaps contraction of *safeguard*]

**sag|gy** (sag′ē), *adj.*, **-gi|er, -gi|est**. sagging: *saggy trousers, saggy rubber.*

**Sa|git|ta** (sə jit′ə), *n., genitive* **Sa|git|tae**. a northern constellation south of Cygnus; the Arrow. [< Latin *Sagitta* < *sagitta* arrow]

**Sa|git|tae** (sə jit′ē), *n.* genitive of **Sagitta**.

**sag|it|tal** (saj′ə təl), *adj.* **1** naming or having to do with a suture between the parietal bones of the skull: ... *a sagittal crest running along the top of the skull* (New Scientist). **2** naming or situated in the vertical plane dividing an animal into equal halves, or a plane parallel to it. **3** of, like, or having to do with an arrow or arrowhead. [< New Latin *sagittalis* < Latin *sagitta* arrow (because of the suture's long and narrow shape)]
— **sag′it|tal|ly**, *adv.*

**Sag|it|tar|i|i** (saj′ə tãr′ē ī), *n.* genitive of **Sagittarius** (def. 1).

**Sag|it|tar|i|us** (saj′ə tãr′ē əs), *n., genitive* (def. 1) **Sag|it|tar|i|i**. **1** a southern constellation between Scorpio and Capricorn, seen by ancient astronomers as having the rough outline of a centaur drawing a bow; Archer: *The center of our galaxy lies in the direction of Sagittarius.* **2** the ninth sign of the zodiac. The sun enters Sagittarius about November 22. **3** a person born under the sign of Sagittarius. **4** *Heraldry.* a representation of an archer or centaur on a coat of arms. [< Latin *Sagittārius* (literally) the Archer < *sagitta* arrow]

**sag|it|tar|y** (saj′ə ter′ē), *n., pl.* **-tar|ies**. **1** = archer. **2** = centaur. [variant of *Sagittarius,* in the heraldic sense]

**sag|it|tate** (saj′ə tāt), *adj.* shaped like an arrowhead. Calla lilies have sagittate leaves. [< New Latin *sagittatus* < Latin *sagitta* arrow]

**sa|git|ti|form** (sə jit′ə fôrm, saj′ə tə-), *adj.* = sagittate.

**sa|go** (sā′gō), *n., pl.* **-gos**. **1** a starchy food obtained from the pith of various tropical palms, especially the sago palm, and made into sago flour: *The largest supply of sago comes from the East Indies* (Leone R. Carroll). **2** = sago palm. [< Malay *sagu*]

**sago flour**, flour made from sago, used mostly in making puddings and as a thickening for soups.

**sago palm**, an East Indian palm tree from whose pith a starchy food is made. There are several kinds.

**sa|gua|ro** (sə gwä′rō, -wä′-), *n., pl.* **-ros**. a very tall, branching cactus of Arizona and neighboring regions, from 25 to 50 feet high, bearing an edible fruit; giant cactus. Its white blossom is the state flower of Arizona. *The watchtower of the hawk ... was a giant saguaro cactus* (Atlantic). Also, **sahuaro**. See picture under **cactus family**. [American English < Mexican Spanish *saguaro*]

**sa|gum** (sā′gəm), *n., pl.* **-ga** (-gə). a kind of cloak worn by Roman soldiers and inferior officers. [< Latin *sagum,* or *sagus,* perhaps < a Celtic word]

**Sa|hap|tan** (sä hap′tən), *adj., n.* = Shahaptian.

**Sa|har|a** (sə hãr′ə, -här′-), *n.* **1** an arid place; desert. **2** *Figurative.* a place, environment, or enterprise lacking intellectual or spiritual stimulation: *the Sahara of contemporary verse.* [< *Sahara,* the great desert in northern Africa]

**Sa|har|an** (sə hãr′ən, -här′-), *adj., n.* — *adj.* of or having to do with the Sahara, the largest desert in the world, in northern Africa, or the people living there: *A young Scots surgeon, Mungo Park, rode through Saharan sand and thorn* (Atlantic).
— *n.* a native or inhabitant of the Sahara.

**Sa|hel|i|an** (sə hel′yən, -hē′lē ən), *adj.* **1** of or having to do with the group of countries below the Sahara Desert including Chad, Gambia, Mali, Mauritania, Senegal, Upper Volta, and Niger: *the Sahelian region, zone, or strip.* **2** (originally) of the Sahel, or coastal plain of Tunisia. [< Arabic *sāhel* coastal strip]

**sa|hib** (sä′ib), *n.* sir; master (used especially by natives in former British India when speaking to or of a European): *The sahibs have not all this world's wisdom* (Rudyard Kipling). [< Hindi *sāhib* < Arabic *ṣāḥib*]

**Sa|hi|wal** (sä′ē wäl), *n.* any one of a breed of zebus of India and Pakistan, raised as dairy cattle. [< *Sahiwal,* a city in Pakistan]

**sa|hua|ro** (sə wä′rō), *n., pl.* **-ros**. = saguaro.

**sa|ic** (sä ēk′), *n.* a kind of ketch very common in the Levant. [< French *saïque* < Turkish *şayka*]

**saice** (sīs), *n.* = syce.

**said** (sed), *v., adj.* — *v.* past tense and past participle of **say**[1]: *He said he would come. She has said "No" every time.*
— *adj.* named or mentioned before: *the said witness, the said sum of money.* **SYN:** aforesaid, aforementioned.
▶ **said.** As an adjective *said* is largely confined to legal language, and is usually regarded as inappropriate elsewhere.

**sai|ga** (sī′gə), *n.* an antelopelike animal of western Asia and eastern Russia with a peculiarly expanded nose which serves to filter dust and warm the air breathed in. [< Russian *sajga* < a Turkic word]

**Sai|gon|ese** (sī′gə nēz′, -nēs′), *adj., n., pl.* **-nese**.
— *adj.* of Saigon, the capital of South Vietnam, or its people.
— *n.* a native of Saigon.

***sail** (sāl), *n., v.* — *n.* **1** a piece of cloth attached to the rigging of a ship to catch the wind and make the ship move on the water. See the picture opposite at the bottom of the next page. **2** sails: *with all sail set.* **3** something like a sail, such as the part of an arm of a windmill that catches the wind: *Many recent submarines have a tall streamlined sail instead of a conning tower.* **4a** a ship having sails: *a fleet numbering 30 sail.* **b** such ships as a group: *To them the sinking only proved that the days of sail were done* (London Times). **5a** a trip or outing on a boat with sails: *Let's go for a sail.* **b** a trip or outing on any other vessel. **6** a bird's wing: *The mountain eagle ... spread her dark sails on the wind* (Scott).

**Pronunciation Key:** hat, āge, cãre, fär; let, ēqual, tėrm; it, īce; hot, ōpen, ôrder; **oi**l, **ou**t; cup, pu̇t, rüle; **ch**ild; lo**ng**; **th**in; **ᴛʜ**en; **zh**, measure; ə represents **a** in about, **e** in taken, **i** in pencil, **o** in lemon, **u** in circus.

—*v.i.* **1a** to travel or go on water in a boat by the action of wind on sails. **SYN**: navigate, cruise. **b** to travel or go in a boat propelled by any means, such as a steamship. **SYN**: navigate, cruise. **c** to travel through the air, as in an airplane, balloon, or glider. **SYN**: navigate, cruise. **2** to move on or through the water: *a schooner sailing for the Azores, two submarines sailing from New London to the Caribbean.* **3** *Figurative.* to move smoothly like a ship with sails: *The swans sailed along the lake. The eagle sailed by. The duchess sailed into the room. The necessary minimum of 76 votes was secured, and the measure ... soon sailed through the House* (New York Times). **4** to manage a ship or boat: *The children are learning to sail this summer.* **5** to begin a trip by water; set sail: *She sailed from New York.*

—*v.t.* **1** to sail upon, over, or through: *to sail the seas.* **2** to manage or navigate (a ship or boat).

**crowd sail**, to hoist an unusual number of sails on a ship; carry a press of sail for the purpose of speed: *They crowded all the sail they could* (London Gazette).

**make sail**, **a** to spread out the sails of a ship: *The men ... were making sail upon the yacht nimbly* (Clark Russell). **b** to begin a trip by water: *We will make sail on Friday.*

**sail into**, *Informal.* **a** to attack; beat: *He sailed into me for no reason and gave me a black eye.* **b** to criticize; scold: *The drama critics sailed into the new play.* **c** to rush into; go into boldly or spiritedly: *Though paralysed by fright ... I gritted my teeth and sailed into it* (Tallulah Bankhead).

**set sail**, to begin a trip by water: *We will set sail for Europe next week.*

**take in sail**, **a** to lower or lessen the sails of a ship: *The men took in sail when the storm approached.* **b** *Figurative.* to lessen, as one's hopes or ambitions: *It is time to be old, to take in sail* (Emerson).

**trim one's sails**, to modify one's views or principles so as to settle differences; compromise: *Some spend years in prison cells, ... others turn their coats or trim their sails* (Sunday Times).

**under sail**, having the sails spread out: *The ship is under sail, making toward the land.*

[Old English *segl*] —**sail′like′**, *adj.*

▶ **Sail**, noun, is used collectively when it means sails for a sailing vessel (def. 2): *Our ship had all sail spread.* **Sail** may also mean a ship or ships (def. 4a and 4b). When it means ships it is used collectively and often with a numeral: *a fleet of thirty sail.*

**sail|a|ble** (sā′lə bəl), *adj.* that can be sailed or navigated; navigable.

**sail|board** (sāl′bôrd′, -bōrd′), *n.* a small, very light sailboat, with one mast, a triangular sail, and a flat hull, usually without a cockpit.

***sail|boat** (sāl′bōt′), *n.* any boat that is moved by a sail or sails. Schooners and sloops are kinds of sailboats.

**sail|boat|er** (sāl′bō′tər), *n.* a person who engages in sailboating.

**sail|boat|ing** (sāl′bō′ting), *n.* the sport of navigating or riding in a sailboat: [*It*] *makes one think of summer sailboating with one's best girl* (New Yorker).

**sail|cloth** (sāl′klôth′, -kloth′), *n.* **1** canvas or other sturdy material used for making sails and tents. **2** = tarpaulin.

**-sailed**, *combining form.* having ____ sail or sails: *White-sailed = having white sails.*

**sail|er** (sā′lər), *n.* **1** a ship with reference to its sailing power: *the best sailer in the fleet, a fast sailer.* **2** a sailing vessel.

**sail|fish** (sāl′fish′), *n., pl.* **-fish|es** or (*collectively*) **-fish**. **1** a large saltwater fish that has a long, high fin on its back. There are a number of kinds, comprising a genus of fishes related to the swordfish and marlin. **2** = basking shark.

**sail hook**, a small hook used to hold sailcloth while it is being sewed.

**sail|ing** (sā′ling), *n.* **1** the act of a person or thing that sails. **2** the art of managing and maneuvering a ship; navigation; seamanship. **3a** the departure of a ship from port. **b** its occupancy or load: *Transatlantic steamship lines report capacity sailings for April* (Newsweek).

**sailing boat**, *British.* a sailboat.

**sailing vessel**, any vessel, ranging in size from a boat to a ship (but usually the latter), that is moved by a sail or sails.

**sail|less** (sāl′lis), *adj.* without sails.

**sail lizard**, a large lizard of the Moluccas, with a crested tail.

**sail|mak|er** (sāl′mā′kər), *n.* **1** a person who makes or repairs sails. **2** *U.S. Navy.* (formerly) a warrant officer in charge of maintaining sails, awnings, and the like.

**sail needle**, a large, three-sided needle used to sew canvas.

masthead
jib
boom
cockpit
tiller
rudder
centerboard

***sailboat**

**sail|or** (sā′lər), *n., adj.* —*n.* **1** a person whose work is handling a sailboat or other vessel. In these days most sailors are on ships that are driven by engines. **2** a member of a ship's crew. The men in a navy are called sailors if they are not officers. **3** = sailor hat.

—*adj.* like a sailor's: *The little boy wore a sailor cap.*

**good sailor**, a person who does not get seasick: *Some of the heartier passengers proved to be good sailors during the stormy voyage and aided those who were ill.*

**poor** (or **bad**) **sailor**, a person who readily becomes seasick: *He wished people who were bad sailors would not travel* (Mary Bridgman).

**talk sailor**, to use nautical language: *I ... could talk sailor like an "old salt"* (Century Magazine).

**sailor collar**, a large collar, broad and square across the back, with ends tapering to a point to meet on the breast.

**sailor hat**, a straight-brimmed straw hat with a flat crown.

**sail|or|ing** (sā′lər ing), *n.* the work or life of a sailor.

**sail|or|like** (sā′lər līk′), *adj.* like or resembling a sailor.

**sail|or|ly** (sā′lər lē), *adj.* like a sailor; suitable for a sailor.

**sail|or|man** (sā′lər man′), *n., pl.* **-men**. *Archaic.* a sailor; seaman.

**sail|or's-choice** (sā′lərz chois′), *n., pl.* **sail|or's-choic|es** or (*collectively*) **sail|or's-choice**. a local name of various American fishes: **a** = grunt. **b** = porgy. **c** = pigfish. **d** = pinfish.

***sailor suit**

***sailor suit**, a suit or outfit worn by children and women, with a sailor collar and middy blouse, modeled after the uniform worn by sailors: *... the little figure in trim sailor suit and knickerbockers* (Punch).

**sail|o|ver** (sāl′ō′vər), *n.* the action or fact of repeating a yacht run previously interrupted or inconclusive.

**sail plan**, the rig of a sailboat.

**sail|plane** (sāl′plān′), *n., v.,* **-planed, -plan|ing.** —*n.* a lightweight glider with especially long wings to take advantage of rising air currents so as to remain aloft, as distinguished from a heavy glider, designed to be towed by a powered aircraft; soaring plane: *Sailplanes are of course designed to meet rough weather, but it is quickly established that they need much too large a propulsive power to make them suitable as man-powered vehicles* (New Scientist). —*v.i.* to fly in a sailplane.

**sail|plan|er** (sāl′plā′nər), *n.* a person who flies in a sailplane: *To the sailplaner, the good things in*

*life are a cramped cockpit, a buoyant wing, the song of the wind, and unending miles of sky* (Time).

**sain** (sān), *v.t. Archaic.* **1a** to make the sign of the cross on. **b** to cross (oneself). **2** to protect, as by prayer, from evil influence. **3** to bless. [Old English *segnian,* ultimately < Latin *signāre* to mark, especially with the sign of the cross < *sīgnum* sign (in Late Latin, sign of the cross)]

**sain|foin** (sān′foin), *n.* a low, pink-flowered, Old World perennial herb of the pea family, grown for forage. [< French *sainfoin* < *sain* wholesome, healthy (< Latin *sānus*) + *foin* < Old French *fein* hay < Latin *fēnum*]

**saint** (sānt; *see note below*), *n., v., adj.* **—*n.*** **1a** a very holy person; one who is pure in heart and upright in life: *a Buddhist saint.* **b** *Figurative.* a person who is very humble, patient, or like a saint in other ways: *The deaf boy's teacher was a saint: always patient, never without a kind word.* **2** a person who has gone to heaven; one of the blessed dead in heaven (distinguished from the angels, who are superhuman beings): *We therefore pray thee, help thy servants ... Make them to be numbered with thy Saints in glory everlasting* (Book of Common Prayer). **3** a person declared to be a saint by the Roman Catholic Church and certain other churches. *Abbr:* St. **4** an angel: *The Lord came from Sinai ...; he shined forth from mount Paran, and he came with ten thousands of saints* (Deuteronomy 33:2). **5** Also, **Saint. a** a person belonging to any religious body whose members are called Saints. The Church of Latter-day Saints is the official name of the Mormon Church. **b** (in the New Testament) a member of any Christian church.

**—*v.t.*** **1** to make a saint of; canonize. **2** to give the name of saint to; call or consider a saint.

**—*v.i.*** to live or act like a saint.

**—*adj.*** holy; sacred (now only before proper names): *Saint John, Saint Paul.*

[< Old French *saint* < Latin *sānctus* holy, consecrated < *sancīre* consecrate, related to *sacer* holy, sacred]

▶ When it precedes a name, **Saint (St.)** is unstressed in British English and pronounced (sənt) or (sint); in present American use the word is ordinarily (sānt) in all contexts.

**Saint.** Names more commonly written in the abbreviated form, such as *St. Anthony's fire, St.-John's-wort,* will be found in their alphabetical places following **St.** For names of saints that appear in the Bible, look under the Christian name, such as *Andrew* or *John.*

**Saint Ag|nes's Eve** (ag′nə siz), the night of January 20. According to legend, any girl who performed certain ceremonies on this night would dream of her future husband.

**Saint Andrew's cross,** a cross shaped like the letter X. Also, **St. Andrew's cross.** See diagram under **cross.**

**Saint Andrew's Day,** November 30, a feast day commemorating the martyrdom of Saint Andrew, the patron saint of Scotland, in about A.D. 70; Andermass.

**Saint An|tho|ny's cross** (an′thə nēz, -tə-), a cross in which the transverse bar lies on the top of the upright, like the letter T; tau cross. See diagram under **cross.**

**Saint Anthony's fire,** = St. Anthony's fire.

**Saint Augustine grass,** = St. Augustine grass.

**Saint Bar|thol|o|mew's Day** (bär thol′ə myüz), August 24, especially this day in the year 1572, on which a great massacre of Huguenots was begun in Paris by order of King Charles IX at the instigation of Catherine de Medici.

**Saint Ber|nard** (bər närd′), one of a breed of big, red-and-white dogs with large heads. These intelligent, powerful dogs were first bred by the monks at the hospice of Great St. Bernard, a pass in the Swiss Alps, to rescue travelers lost in the snow. Also, **St. Bernard.**

**Saint David's Day,** a holiday in honor of the patron saint of Wales (Saint David), March 1.

**saint de bois** (saN′ də bwä′), *French.* **1** a hypocrite. **2** (literally) a saint of wood.

**saint|dom** (sānt′dəm), *n.* **1** saintliness. **2** saints as a group.

**Sainte** (sānt, saNt), *n.* the French feminine form of **Saint.** *Abbr:* Ste.

**saint|ed** (sān′tid), *adj.* **1** declared to be a saint; canonized. **2** thought of as a saint; gone to heaven; dead (an occasional euphemism). **3** sacred; very holy. **SYN:** consecrated, hallowed. **4** saintly.

**Saint Elmo's fire** or **light,** = St. Elmo's fire.

**Saint George's cross** (jôrj′iz), the Greek cross, red on a white ground, as used on the English flag. Also, **St. George's cross.**

**saint|hood** (sānt′hủd), *n.* **1** the character, status, or dignity of a saint. **2** saints collectively.

**Saint-John's-wort** (sānt jonz′wėrt′), = St.-John's-wort.

**Saint Lawrence skiff,** = St. Lawrence skiff.

**saint|like** (sānt′līk′), *adj.* like or befitting a saint; saintly.

**saint|li|ness** (sānt′lē nis), *n.* the quality or condition of being saintly; piety; holiness.

**Saint Louis encephalitis,** = St. Louis encephalitis.

**Saint Luke's summer,** = St. Luke's summer.

**saint|ly** (sānt′lē), *adj.,* **-li|er, -li|est. 1** like a saint; very holy: *I mention still Him whom thy wrongs, with saintly patience borne* (Milton). **SYN:** angelic, godly. **2** *Figurative.* very good, patient, humble, or possessing other qualities thought of as belonging to saints. **SYN:** virtuous.

**Saint Mar|tin's Lent** (mär′tənz), (in the Middle Ages) a period of religious fasting, from Martinmas to Christmas (November 11 to December 25).

**Saint Martin's summer,** = St. Martin's summer.

**Saint Pat|rick's Day** (pat′riks), March 17. It is an Irish national holiday, in honor of Saint Patrick, the patron saint of Ireland.

**saint's day,** a day set aside each year to honor the memory of a particular saint. It is usually the anniversary of his death.

**saint|ship** (sānt′ship), *n.* = sainthood.

**Saint Swith|in's Day** (swiᴛʜ′inz), the feast day of Saint Swithin, a bishop in ancient England, observed July 15.

**Saint Val|en|tine's Day** (val′ən tīnz), February 14, a day on which valentines are exchanged; Valentine's Day. It is the feast day of Saint Valentine.

**Saint Vi|tus's dance** (vī′tə siz), = St. Vitus's dance.

**Sa|iph** (sä ēf′), *n.* a star of the second magnitude that forms part of the great quadrilateral of the constellation Orion. [< Arabic *saif* sword. Compare etym. under **seif.**]

**sair** (sãr), *adj., n., adv. Scottish.* sore.

**sais** (sīs), *n.* = syce.

**Sa|ite** (sā′īt), *adj., n.* **—*adj.*** of or having to do with Sais, a city on the Nile Delta in ancient Egypt, or with an Egyptian dynasty centered upon Sais and lasting from 670 to 525 B.C.

**—*n.*** a native or inhabitant of Sais.

**saith** (seth), *v. Archaic.* says.

**saithe** (sāth), *n., pl.* **saithe.** the pollack, a saltwater food fish, especially when mature: *Those who think the epitome of the meal is smoked salmon may like to try smoked saithe* (London Times). [< Old Icelandic *seithr*]

**Sai|va** (sī′və), *n.* a person devoted to the worship of Siva; Sivaist. [< Sanskrit *śaiva* < *śiva* Siva]

**Sai|vism** (sī′viz əm), *n.* the worship of Siva; Sivaism.

**Sa|kai** (sä′kī), *n., pl.* **-kai.** a member of an aboriginal Malayan people or tribe.

**sake**[1] (sāk), *n.* **1** purpose; end: *She rattled on just talking for talking's sake.* **SYN:** reason. **2** cause; account; interest: *Put yourself to no trouble for our sake.*

**for old sake's sake,** for the sake of old times or old friendship: *I continue to take an interest in him for old sake's sake as they say* (Robert Louis Stevenson).

**for one's own sake,** on one's own account; in order to help oneself: *For my own sake as well as for yours, I will do my very best* (Benjamin Jowett).

**for the sake of, a** because of; on account of: *to move to the country for the sake of peace and quiet, to give up smoking for the sake of health. He does not differ from that opinion for the sake of difference, but for the sake of the values embodied in perception* (Manchester Guardian Weekly). **b** in order to help or please: *It is necessary for a father to exert himself for the sake of his family.*

[Old English *sacu* a cause at law]

**sa|ke**[2] (sä′kē), *n.* an alcoholic beverage made from a fermented mash of rice, popular in Japan. It somewhat resembles a still white wine and is drunk by the Japanese in slightly warmed porcelain cups. Also, **saki.** [< Japanese *sake*]

**sa|ker** (sā′kər), *n.* a large Old World falcon used in falconry. [< Old French *sacre* < Arabic *ṣaqr*]

**sa|ki**[1] (sak′ē, sä′kē), *n., pl.* **-kis.** a South American monkey with a bushy, nonprehensile tail and a long, thick coat of hair. There are several species. [< French *saki* < Tupi *saguī*]

**sa|ki**[2] (sä′kē), *n.* = sake[2].

**sak|i|eh** (sak′ē ä), *n.* a kind of water wheel powered by oxen or other draft animals, used for raising water in the Near East. [< Arabic *sāqiyah*]

**sak|kos** (sak′os), *n.* = saccos.

**Sak|ta** (sak′tə), *n.* = Shakta.

**Sak|ti** (sak′tē; *Sanskrit* shuk′tē), *n.* = Shakti.

**Sak|tism** (sak′tiz əm), *n.* = Shaktism.

**sal** (sal), *n.* salt (used especially in druggists' terms such as *sal ammoniac*). [< Latin *sāl, salis*]

**sa|la** (sä′lə), *n.* a large hall. [< Spanish *sala* hall, parlor < a Germanic word]

***sa|laam** (sə läm′), *n., v.* **—*n.*** **1** a greeting that means "Peace," used especially in Moslem countries or regions. **2** a very low bow, with the palm of the right hand placed on the forehead.

**—*v.t.*** to greet with a salaam.

**—*v.i.*** to make a salaam.

[< Arabic *salām* peace]

***salaam** definition 2

**sa|laam a|lei|kum** (sə läm′ ä lā′kủm), *Arabic.* peace be upon you (a greeting).

**sal|a|bil|i|ty** (sā′lə bil′ə tē), *n.* salable condition or quality. Also, **saleability.**

**sal|a|ble** (sā′lə bəl), *adj.* that can be sold; fit to be sold; easily sold: *Permit the new association ... to make its bonds more salable* (New York Times). **SYN:** marketable, merchantable, purchasable. Also, **saleable.**

**sal|a|bly** (sā′lə blē), *adv.* in a salable manner; so as to be salable. Also, **saleably.**

**sa|la|cious** (sə lā′shəs), *adj.* **1** obscene; indecent; smutty: *a salacious joke or book.* **2** lustful; lewd: *a salacious person.* **SYN:** lecherous, lascivious. [< Latin *salāx, -ācis* (with English *-ous*)] **—sa|la′cious|ly,** *adv.* **—sa|la′cious|ness,** *n.*

**sa|lac|i|ty** (sə las′ə tē), *n.* salacious quality.

**sal|ad** (sal′əd), *n.* **1** raw green vegetables, such as lettuce, cabbage, and celery, served with a dressing, usually of oil and vinegar or of mayonnaise. Often cold meat, fish, eggs, cooked vegetables, or fruits are used along with, or instead of, the raw green vegetables. **2** any green vegetable that can be eaten raw. **3** *Dialect.* lettuce. **4** *Figurative.* a mixture: *The old cathedral is an entertaining salad of style.* [< Old French *salade* < Old Provençal *salada* < Vulgar Latin *salāre* to salt < Latin *sāl, salis* salt]

**salad days,** days of youthful inexperience: *My salad days, when I was green in judgement* (Shakespeare).

**salad dressing,** a sauce used in or on a salad, such as oil and vinegar mixed with seasonings, or mayonnaise.

**salad oil, 1** olive oil, usually of superior quality, used in dressing salads and for other culinary purposes. **2** any oil used in salad dressing.

**sal|a|man|der** (sal′ə man′dər), *n.* **1** a cold-blooded animal shaped like a lizard but belonging to the same class as frogs and toads, such as the mud puppy of North America. Salamanders have moist, scaleless skin, four short legs, and usually a long tail. The larvae, as well as some adults, breathe by gills. Salamanders live in water or in damp places. See picture under **amphibian.** **2** a legendary lizard or reptile supposed to live in or be able to endure fire. **3** *Figurative.* a person who likes or can stand a great deal of heat. **4** a spirit or imaginary being supposed to live in fire (originally hypothesized by Paracelsus as inhabiting fire, one of the four elements). **5** any one of various articles formerly used in connection with fire or capable of withstanding great heat, such as an iron or poker formerly used for lighting a pipe or igniting gunpowder or a plate used for browning puddings: *Press them tight into shells or a dish, and brown them with a salamander* (Sunday Times). [< Old French *salamandre* < Latin *salamandra* < Greek *salamándra*]

**sal|a|man|drine** (sal′ə man′drin), *adj., n.* **—*adj.*** **1** *Zoology.* of, having to do with, resembling, or related to the salamanders. **2** resembling the legendary salamander in being able to live in or endure fire.

**—*n.*** *Zoology.* a salamander.

**sa|la|mi** (sə lä′mē), *n.* a kind of thick sausage, often flavored with garlic. It is usually sliced and eaten cold. [< Italian *salami,* plural of *salame* < Vulgar Latin *salāmen* < Latin *sāl, salis* salt]

**sal ammoniac,** = ammonium chloride.

**sa|lar|i|at** (sə lãr′ē at), *n.* the salaried class; the class of workers receiving a salary. [< French

**Pronunciation Key: h**a**t, ā**ge**, c**ã**re, f**ä**r; l**e**t, ē**qual**, t**ė**rm; **i**t, ī**ce**; h**o**t, ō**pen**, ô**rder**; **oi**l, **ou**t; c**u**p, p**ủ**t, r**ü**le; **ch**ild; lo**ng**; **th**in; **ᴛʜ**en; **zh**, measure; **ə** represents **a** in about, **e** in taken, **i** in pencil, **o** in lemon, **u** in circus.

*salariat.* Compare etym. under **proletariat.**]

**sal|a|ried** (sal′ər id, sal′rid), *adj.* **1** receiving a salary: *a salaried employee.* **2** having a salary attached to it: *a salaried position.*

**sal|a|ry** (sal′ər ē, sal′rē), *n., pl.* **-ries.** fixed pay for regular work. It is made periodically to a person, especially by the week or month. *Clerks in that store receive a salary of $100 a week. The fees annually paid to lawyers ... amount in every court, to a much greater sum than the salaries of the judges* (Adam Smith). **SYN:** stipend. [< Anglo-French *salarie,* learned borrowing from Latin *salārium* soldier's allowance for salt; pay < *sāl, salis* salt] —**sal′a|ry|less,** *adj.*

► **salary, wages.** Though these words are synonyms, *salary* generally refers to a fixed compensation for regular work (usually uninterrupted by weather, sales demands, or other outside influences) and often paid at longer intervals than *wages* (usually paid on an hourly basis).

**sa|lat** (sə lät′), *n.* the prayer recited by Moslems five times daily. [< Arabic *ṣalāt*]

**sal At|ti|cum** (sal at′ə kəm), *Latin.* sal Atticus.

**sal At|ti|cus** (sal at′ə kəs), *Latin.* pungent wit; Attic salt.

**sal|chow** (sal′kov), *n.* a jump in figure skating in which the skater leaps from the inside back edge of one skate, rotates in the air, and lands on the outside back edge of the other skate: *With all the confidence of a champion, long-legged Tenley glided out to begin her free skating—the difficult double loops and axels and double salchows of her own devising* (Time). [< Ulrich *Salchow,* a skater after whom the jump was named]

**sale** (sāl), *n.* **1** the act of selling; exchange of goods or property for money or some other valuable consideration: *no sale yet this morning. The sale of his old home made him sad.* **2** an amount sold: *a large sale of bonds.* See also **sales. 3** a chance to sell; demand; market: *There is almost no sale for washboards in these days.* **4** the act of selling at lower prices than usual: *This store is having a sale on suits.* **5** the act or fact of putting up goods to be sold at auction, especially a public auction; auction. **SYN:** vendue.

**for sale,** to be sold: *My car is for sale.*

**on sale, a** available at lower prices than usual: *The grocer has coffee on sale today. This ten-dollar hat is now on sale for five.* **b** at a reduced price: *I bought this dress on sale.* **c** to be sold: *There are many houses on sale but few for rent.*

**on sale or return,** *Especially British.* **a** on condition that the customer can decide after examining the item whether to buy it or return it; on approval: *The coat ... had been delivered to the defendants on sale or return* (London Times). **b** on condition that the retailer may return to the wholesaler any part of the goods that he fails to sell: *to buy a quantity of merchandise on sale or return.*

[Old English *sala,* perhaps < Scandinavian (compare Old Icelandic *sala*)]

**sale|a|bil|i|ty** (sā′lə bil′ə tē), *n.* = salability.

**sale|a|ble** (sā′lə bəl), *adj.* = salable.

**sale|a|bly** (sā′lə blē), *adv.* = salably.

**sale and leaseback,** an arrangement whereby a company sells all or part of its property to another organization and takes out a long-term lease on the property at the same time; leaseback. The original seller pays rent, which is considered a tax-deductible business expense.

**sale and return,** an arrangement whereby a retailer accepts goods from a wholesaler on condition that he may return any part of the goods that he fails to sell.

**sal|ep** (sal′ep), *n.* a starchy foodstuff consisting of the dried tubers of certain orchids, formerly also used as a drug. Also, **saloop.** [< French *salep,* or Spanish *salép* < Turkish *salep,* perhaps a contraction of Arabic *khaṣyu-ththa'lab* testicles of a fox. Compare etym. under **orchid.**]

**sal|e|ra|tus** (sal′ə rā′təs), *n. U.S., Archaic.* **1** sodium bicarbonate; baking soda. **2** potassium bicarbonate, a compound similar to sodium bicarbonate, used in cookery. [American English < New Latin *sal aeratus* aerated salt]

**sale|room** (sāl′rüm′, -rům′), *n. British.* salesroom.

**sales** (sālz), *n., adj.* —*n.pl.* **1** the amount sold; total volume of selling: *How are sales today?* **2** the business of selling; selling activity: *His first job was in sales.*

—*adj.* of or having to do with sales: *a sales manager, a sales plan.*

**sales|clerk** (sālz′klėrk′), *n.* a person whose work is selling in a store.

**sales engineer,** a salesman of mechanical, electrical, and other equipment who has had technical training and is familiar with the details of installation, operation, and maintenance of the equipment.

**sales|girl** (sālz′gėrl′), *n.* a girl whose work is selling in a store: *The salesgirl showed her nearly all the hats in the shop.* **SYN:** shopgirl.

**Sa|le|sian** (sə lē′zhən), *n., adj.* —*n.* a member of the Society of St. Francis de Sales, a Roman Catholic congregation of priests, clerics, and lay brothers, founded in the mid-1800's mainly for education of the young.

—*adj.* **1** of or having to do with St. Francis de Sales (1567-1622) or his writings on spiritual matters. **2** of or having to do with the Society of St. Francis de Sales.

**sales|la|dy** (sālz′lā′dē), *n., pl.* **-dies.** = saleswoman.

**sales|man** (sālz′mən), *n., pl.* **-men.** a man whose work is selling: *Four salesmen were showing people suits and sweaters.*

**sales|man|ship** (sālz′mən ship), *n.* **1** the work of a salesman. **2** ability at selling.

**sales|peo|ple** (sālz′pē′pəl), *n.pl.* salespersons.

**sales|per|son** (sālz′pėr′sən), *n.* a person whose work is selling, especially in a store. **SYN:** clerk.

**sales promotion,** the methods and activities involved in producing or selling a product or service, often in addition to direct selling and advertising. Sales promotion includes getting publicity through various media, distributing samples, providing displays in stores, and giving free demonstrations. *To increase exports one must spend freely on sales promotion of every kind* (London Times).

**sales resistance,** a customer's unwillingness to buy, because of price, class, nature, and appearance of goods, or other causes: *to overcome sales resistance.*

**sales|room** (sālz′rüm′, -rům′), *n.* a room where things are sold or shown for sale.

**sales talk, 1** a talk by a salesperson designed to sell something. **2** any talk to convince or persuade.

**sales tax,** a tax based on the amount received for articles sold: *Her coat cost $50 plus 5% sales tax of $2.50.*

**sales|wom|an** (sālz′wům′ən), *n., pl.* **-wom|en.** a woman whose work is selling, especially in a store; saleslady.

**sale|work** (sāl′wėrk′), *n.* **1** work that is made for sale rather than for home use. **2** work or things made in a perfunctory manner, and usually of inferior quality: *I see no more in you than in the ordinary of nature's salework* (Shakespeare).

**sale|yard** (sāl′yärd′), *n. Australian.* a yard where livestock is sold; stockyard.

**Sa|li|an** (sā′lē ən), *adj., n.* —*adj.* of or having to do with the Salii, a tribe of Franks who lived in the regions of the Rhine near the North Sea.

—*n.* a member of this tribe of Franks.

**Sal|ic** (sal′ik, sā′lik), *adj.* based on or contained in the code of the Salian Franks. Also, **Salique.** [< Medieval Latin *Salicus* < Late Latin *Saliī, -orum* the Salian Franks]

**sal|i|ca|ceous** (sal′ə kā′shəs), *adj.* belonging to the family of trees and shrubs containing the willows and poplars. [< New Latin *Salicaceae* the willow family (< Latin *salix, -icis* willow) + English *-ous*]

**sal|i|cin** (sal′ə sin), *n.* a bitter, colorless, crystalline compound of glucose, obtained from the bark and leaves of various willows and used in medicine as a tonic and to reduce fever. *Formula:* $C_{13}H_{18}O_7$ [< French *salicine* < Latin *salix, -icis* willow + French *-ine* -ine[2]]

**sal|i|ci|na plum** (sal′ə sī′nə, -sē′-), = Japanese plum. [< New Latin (*Prunus*) *salicina* the Japanese plum tree]

**sal|i|cine** (sal′ə sin, -sēn), *n.* = salicin.

**Salic law, 1** the code of laws of the Salian Franks. **2** a law believed to be based on this code, excluding women from succession to the crown.

**sal|i|cyl|al|de|hyde** (sal′ə sə lal′də hīd), *n.* a fragrant, colorless oil used in the manufacture of dyestuffs, odor bases, and petroleum additives, produced from phenol and chloroform. It is the aldehyde of salicylic acid. *Formula:* $C_7H_6O_2$ [< *salicyl*(ic) + *aldehyde*]

**sal|i|cyl|am|ide** (sal′ə sə lam′īd, -id), *n.* a yellowish, crystalline compound made by treating oil of wintergreen with concentrated ammonia. *Formula:* $C_7H_7NO_2$ [< *salicyl*(ic) + *amide*]

**sal|i|cyl|ate** (sal′ə sil′āt, sal′ə sil′-; sə lis′ə lāt), *n.* any salt or ester of salicylic acid.

**sal|i|cyl|ic** (sal′ə sil′ik), *adj.* of or having to do with salicin.

**salicylic acid,** a crystalline or powdery acid used as a mild antiseptic and preservative, and in making aspirin. Salicylic acid is prepared by treating sodium phenolate with carbon dioxide. *Formula:* $C_7H_6O_3$ [< *salic*(in), from which it was first obtained + *-yl* + *-ic*]

**sa|li|ence** (sā′lē əns, sāl′yəns), *n.* **1** the fact or condition of being salient. **2** a salient or projecting object, part, or feature.

**sa|li|en|cy** (sā′lē ən sē, sāl′yən-), *n., pl.* **-cies.** = salience.

✱**sa|li|ent** (sā′lē ənt, sāl′yənt), *adj., n.* —*adj.* **1** standing out; easily seen or noticed; prominent; striking: *the salient features in a landscape.* (*Figurative.*) *the salient points in a speech.* **SYN:** noticeable, conspicuous. **2** pointing outward; projecting: *a salient angle.* **3** *Archaic.* **a** leaping; jumping. A lion salient on a coat of arms is standing with forepaws raised as if jumping. **b** (of animals) saltatorial.

—*n.* **1** a salient angle or part; projection: *The Soviet Union has thrust a huge salient into the heart of Europe* (Wall Street Journal). **2** a part of a fortification or line of trenches that projects toward the enemy.

[< Latin *saliēns, -entis,* present participle of *salīre* to leap] —**sa′li|ent|ly,** *adv.*

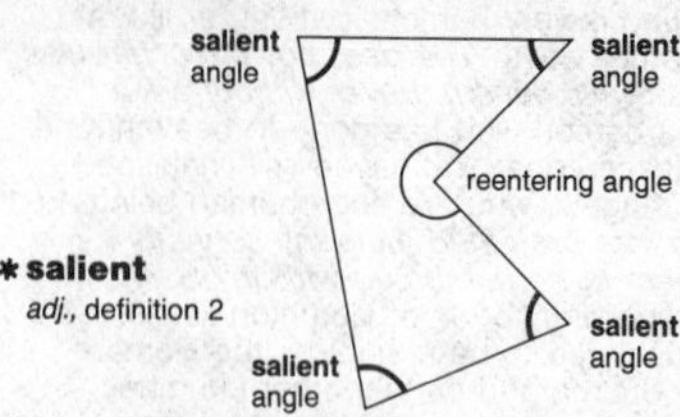


✱**salient** *adj., definition 2*

**sa|li|en|ti|an** (sā′lē en′shē ən, -shən), *adj., n.* —*adj.* of or belonging to an order of amphibians that includes the frogs and toads; anuran.

—*n.* a salientian animal.

[< New Latin *Salientia* the order name (< Latin *saliēns, -entis* leaping; see etym. under **salient**) + English *-an*]

**sa|lif|er|ous** (sə lif′ər əs), *adj.* containing salt; producing salt. [< Latin *sāl, salis* salt + English *-ferous*]

**sal|i|fi|a|ble** (sal′ə fī′ə bəl), *adj.* that can be salified.

**sal|i|fi|ca|tion** (sal′ə fə kā′shən), *n.* **1** the act of salifying. **2** the state of being salified.

**sal|i|fy** (sal′ə fī), *v.t.,* **-fied, -fy|ing. 1** to form into a salt, as by combination with an acid. **2** to combine with a salt or add a salt to. [< French *salifier* < Latin *sāl, salis* salt]

**sa|lim|e|ter** (sə lim′ə tər), *n.* = salinometer.

**sa|li|na** (sə lī′nə), *n.* **1** a salt marsh or spring. **2** = saltworks. [< Spanish *salina* < Latin *salīnae, -ārum,* plural, saltworks < *sāl, salis* salt]

**sal|i|na|tion** (sal′ə nā′shən), *n. Especially British.* salinization: *... the salination of the soil which makes it barren* (Listener).

**sa|line** (sā′līn, -lēn′), *adj., n.* —*adj.* **1a** of salt; like salt; salty: *a saline taste.* **b** consisting of or constituting common salt: *saline particles, saline substances.* **2** containing common salt or any other salts: *a saline solution.* **3a** of or having to do with chemical salts. **b** (of medicines) consisting of or based on salts of the alkaline metals or magnesium: *a saline laxative.*

—*n.* **1** a salt spring, well, or marsh; salina. **2** a salt of an alkali or magnesium, used as a cathartic. **3** a solution with a high concentration of salt, especially one with a concentration similar to that of the blood, used in medical examinations and treatment. **4** *Medicine.* the injection of a saline solution into the uterus to induce a miscarriage.

[< Latin *sāl, salis* salt + English *-ine*[1]]

**sal|i|nelle** (sal ə nel′), *n.* a mud volcano which pours out a saline product. [< French *salinelle* (diminutive) < *saline* saltworks < Latin *salīnae;* see etym. under **salina**]

**sa|lin|i|ty** (sə lin′ə tē), *n., pl.* **-ties. 1** saline quality or condition; saltness. **2** saline concentration: *At very low salinities the electrical resistance of the solutions becomes very high* (New Scientist).

**sa|lin|i|za|tion** (sā′lən ə zā′shən, -līn-), *n.* the accumulation of salt, especially in the soil: *salinization of sea-coast farmland.*

**sal|i|nom|e|ter** (sal′ə nom′ə tər), *n.* a hydrometer for measuring the percentage of salt present in a given solution. [< *salin*(ity) + *-meter*]

**Sa|lique** (sȧ lēk′, sal′ik, sā′lik), *adj.* = Salic.

**Salis|bur|y steak** (sôlz′ber′ē, -bər-; salz′-), chopped beef shaped before cooking into a patty about twice the size of a hamburger, usually served with a gravy.

**Sa|lish** (sā′lish), *n.* a Salishan Indian. [American English < Salishan *sälst* people]

**Sa|lish|an** (sā′li shən, sal′i-), *adj., n.* —*adj.* of or having to do with an American Indian linguistic stock of the northwestern United States and British Columbia, including Flathead and Coeur-d'Alêne.

—*n.* this linguistic stock.

**sa|li|va** (sə lī′və), *n.* the liquid produced by glands in the mouth and cheeks to keep the mouth moist, help in chewing and swallowing food, and start digestion of starch; spittle. Saliva is colorless and watery. **SYN:** spit. [< Latin *salīva*]

**sal|i|var|y** (sal′ə ver′ē), *adj.* of or producing saliva.

✱**salivary gland**, any one of various glands that empty their secretions into the mouth. The salivary glands of human beings and certain other vertebrates are digestive glands that secrete saliva containing the digestive enzyme ptyalin, salts, albumin, and mucus.

✱**salivary gland**

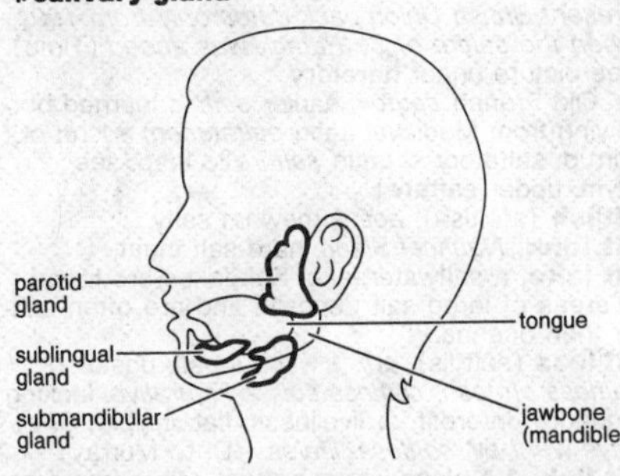


**sal|i|vate** (sal′ə vāt), *v.*, **-vat|ed, -vat|ing.** —*v.i.* to secrete saliva: [*Pavlov*] *found that ... dogs ... would quite quickly associate the sound of the bell with food and soon the bell alone would cause them to salivate* (J. A. V. Butler).
—*v.t.* to produce an unusually large secretion of saliva in, as by the use of mercury.
[< Latin *salīvāre* (with English *-ate*[1]) < *salīva* saliva]

**sal|i|va|tion** (sal′ə vā′shən), *n.* **1** the act or process of salivating: *It is supposed that in ... salivation the presence of food in the mouth activates a particular clump of nerve cells* (S. A. Barnett). **2** an abnormally large secretion of saliva, such as may be caused by mercury or nervous disorders; ptyalism.

**Salk vaccine** (sôk, sôlk), a vaccine containing dead polioviruses that cause the body to produce antibodies. These antibodies protect the central nervous system from infection by live polioviruses. Salk vaccine is given in a series of injections. [< Jonas E. *Salk*, born 1914, an American bacteriologist, who developed it]

**salle** (sal), *n.* a hall. [< French *salle.* See related etym. at **sala.**]

**salle à man|ger** (sål′ à mäɴ zhā′), *French.* dining room.

**sal|len|ders** (sal′ən dərz), *n.pl.* a dry, scabby condition of the hock of a horse, resembling psoriasis in humans. [< Middle French *solandres;* origin unknown]

**sal|let** (sal′it), *n.* a light rounded helmet, with or without a visor, worn as part of medieval armor. [< Middle French *salade* < Italian *celata* < Latin *caelāre* to chisel < *caelum* chisel, related to *caedere* to cut]

**sal|low**[1] (sal′ō), *adj., v.* —*adj.* having a sickly, yellowish color: *a sallow skin, a sallow complexion, a sallow person.*
—*v.t.* to make yellowish or sallow.
[Old English *sealwes*] —**sal′low|ness**, *n.*

**sal|low**[2] (sal′ō), *n.* **1** a willow, especially a small Old World tree used in making charcoal. **2** a willow twig. [Old English *sealh*]

**sal|low|ish** (sal′ō ish), *adj.* somewhat sallow.

**sal|low|y** (sal′ō ē), *adj.* full of sallows (willows).

**sal|ly** (sal′ē), *v.*, **-lied, -ly|ing**, *n., pl.* **-lies.** —*v.i.* **1** to go suddenly from a defensive position to attack an enemy. **2** to rush forth suddenly; go out; set out briskly: *We sallied forth at dawn.* **3** to set out briskly or boldly: (*Figurative.*) *I cannot praise a fugitive and cloistered virtue ... that never sallies out and sees her adversary* (Milton). **4** to go on an excursion or trip. **5** (of things) to issue forth, especially suddenly.
—*n.* **1** a sudden attack on an enemy made from a defensive position; sortie: *The men in the fort made a brave sally and returned with many prisoners.* **2** any sudden rushing forth: *I come from haunts of coot and hern, I make a sudden sally, And sparkle out among the fern, To bicker down a valley* (Tennyson). **3** the act of going forth; trip; excursion: (*Figurative.*) *I made my second sally into the world* (Daniel Defoe). **4** a sudden start into activity: *Nature goes by rule, not by sallies and saltations* (Emerson). **5** *Figurative.* **a** an outburst, as of anger, delight, or wit: *Sudden sallies and impetuosities of temper* (Cardinal Manning). **b** a witty remark; witticism; quip: *She continued her story undisturbed by the merry sallies of her hearers.*
[< Old French *saillie* a rushing forth, outrush, noun use of feminine past participle of *saillir* leap < Latin *salīre*]

**Sally Lunn** or **sally lunn** (lun′), a slightly sweetened tea cake, served hot with butter. [< *Sally Lunn,* supposedly a woman who sold such cakes in Bath, England, in the late 1700's]

**sally port**, a protected gate or underground passage in a fort through which troops may pass when making a sally.

**sal|ma|gun|di** (sal′mə gun′dē), *n.* **1** a dish of chopped meat, anchovies, eggs, onions, oil, and seasonings. **2** *Figurative.* any mixture, medley, or miscellany. **SYN:** jumble, hodgepodge. [< French *salmigondis* < Italian *salami conditi* pickled sausages (see etym. under **salami**); *conditi,* past participle of *condere* to flavor < Latin *condīre* to preserve]

**sal|mi** or **sal|mis** (sal′mē; *French* sål mē′), *n.* a highly seasoned stew, especially of game seared by roasting and then simmered in wine. [< French *salmi,* short for *salmigondis;* see etym. under **salmagundi**]

**salm|on** (sam′ən), *n., pl.* **-ons** or (*collectively*) **-on**, *adj.* —*n.* **1** a large marine and freshwater fish with silvery scales and yellowish-pink flesh. It is found in the North Atlantic near the mouths of large rivers which it swims up in order to spawn. The salmon is one of the chief food fishes. It belongs to the same genus as several species of trout. **2** any one of a genus of other fishes of the same family common in the northern Pacific and important as food fishes, such as the chinook salmon and sockeye salmon. **3** a variety of Atlantic or Pacific salmon that lives in lakes; landlocked salmon. **4** a yellowish pink like that of the flesh of the salmon; salmon pink: *More pastels, including pink and salmon, are crowding red as the traditional color for the humble building brick* (Wall Street Journal).
—*adj.* yellowish-pink.
[< Old French *salmun* < Latin *salmō, -ōnis*]

**salm|on|ber|ry** (sam′ən ber′ē), *n., pl.* **-ries. 1** the salmon-colored, edible fruit of a raspberry of the Pacific coast of North America. **2** the plant itself, bearing red flowers.

**salmon cloud**, a band of parallel cirrostratus clouds stretching almost entirely across the sky and appearing, by perspective, to taper at the ends, so that it resembles the outline of a salmon.

**salm|on-col|ored** (sam′ən kul′ərd), *adj.* = salmon.

**sal|mo|nel|la** (sal′mə nel′ə), *n., pl.* **-nel|las, -nel|lae** (-nel′ē), or **-nel|la.** any one of a genus of bacteria that cause food poisoning, typhoid and paratyphoid fever, and other infectious diseases. [< New Latin *Salmonella* the genus name < Daniel E. *Salmon,* 1850-1914, an American pathologist]

**sal|mo|nel|lo|sis** (sal′mə nə lō′sis), *n.* any infectious disease caused by salmonella, such as cholera in fowls or typhoid fever.

**salm|on|id** (sam′ə nid), *adj., n.* = salmonoid.

**sal|mo|noid** (sal′mə noid), *adj., n.* —*adj.* **1** of or belonging to a family of fishes including the salmon and trout. **2** resembling a fish of this family. —*n.* a salmonoid fish.

**salmon pike**, = Chautauqua muskellunge.

**salmon pink**, a yellowish pink; salmon. —**salm′-on-pink′**, *adj.*

**salmon trout**, **1** the sea trout of Europe. **2** = lake trout. **3** = steelhead. **4** any other large trout.

**salmon wheel**, a tall wheel, set in a rapid and turned by the current, which catches ascending salmon in scoop nets and throws them into a pen.

**sal|ol** (sal′ōl, -ol), *n.* a white, crystalline, aromatic powder, a salicylate of phenyl, prepared from phenol and salicylic acid. It is used as an antiseptic and to reduce fever. *Formula:* $C_{13}H_{10}O_3$ [< *sal*(icylic) + *-ol*[1]]

**Sa|lo|me** (sə lō′mē), *n.* the daughter of Herodias, whose dancing so pleased Herod that he granted her anything she would ask. Instructed by her mother, she demanded the head of John the Baptist, which she then presented to Herodias on a platter (in the Bible, Matthew 14:3-11). Her name is not given in the Bible.

**sa|lom|e|ter** (sə lom′ə tər), *n.* = salinometer.

**sa|lon** (sə lon′; *French* så lôɴ′), *n., pl.* **-lons** (-lonz′; *French* -lôɴ′). **1** a large room for receiving or entertaining guests: *The social and political elite of Paris ... filed into a cavernous salon in the Ministry of the Interior* (Newsweek). **2** a gathering of distinguished persons in such a room, usually one consisting of fashionable people: *Madame Steinheil ... presided over a salon of artists and men of letters until 1908* (Listener). **3a** a place used to exhibit works of art. **SYN:** gallery. **b** an exhibition of works of art. **4** a fashionable or stylish shop: *a fashion salon, a beauty salon.* [< French *salon* < Italian *salone* < *sala* hall < Germanic (compare Old High German *sal*). See related etym. at **saloon.**]

**Sa|lon** (sə lon′; *French* så lôɴ′), *n.* an annual exhibition, in Paris, of the works of living artists. [< French *Salon* (originally held in one of the *salons* of the Louvre)]

**sa|lon|ist** (sə lon′ist), *n.* = salonnard.

**sa|lon|nard** (sə lon′ärd; *French* så lô när′), *n.* a person who frequents fashionable salons. [< French *salonnard*]

**sa|loon** (sə lün′), *n.* **1** a place where alcoholic drinks are sold and drunk; tavern: *The majority of the citizens of this village are tired of the saloon and want it to go* (Cowansville [Quebec] Observer). **SYN:** bar. **2** a large room for general or public use: *The ship's passengers ate in the dining saloon.* **3** Also, **saloon car.** *British.* **a** a sedan. **b** a saloon carriage. **4** = salon (def. 1). [American English < French *salon.* See related etym. at **salon.**]

**saloon car**, = saloon (def. 3).

**saloon carriage**, *British.* a railroad parlor car.

**sa|loon|keep|er** (sə lün′kē′pər), *n. U.S.* a man who keeps a saloon where alcoholic drinks are sold and drunk.

**sa|loop** (sə lüp′), *n.* **1** a hot beverage made from salep or (later) sassafras, milk, and sugar, popular in England, especially in London, during the late 1700's and early 1800's. **2** = salep. [< earlier *salop,* variant of *salep*]

**Sa|lo|pi|an** (sə lō′pē ən), *adj., n.* —*adj.* of Shropshire, county in England. —*n.* a native of Shropshire.
[< *Salop,* another name for Shropshire + *-ian*]

**sal|pa** (sal′pə), *n.* any one of a group of transparent, spindle-shaped, free-swimming tunicates, reproducing asexually in one generation, sexually in the next. [< New Latin *Salpa* the genus name < Latin *salpa* a stockfish < Greek *salpê*]

**sal|pi|con** (sal′pə kon), *n.* cooked meat, mushrooms, and truffles, cut into small pieces and mixed with a rich sauce, used as a filling, especially for patés, or served separately. [< French *salpicon* < Spanish *salpicón* < *salpicar* sprinkle < *sal* salt + *picar* to pick]

**sal|pi|form** (sal′pə fôrm), *adj.* of or having the form or structure of a salpa; fusiform. [< New Latin *Salpa* salpa + English *-form*]

**sal|pi|glos|sis** (sal′pə glos′is), *n.* **1** any of a group of Chilean herbs of the nightshade family, having funnel-shaped flowers in rich colors, often variegated. **2** the flower of any one of these plants; painted tongue. [< New Latin *Salpiglossis* the genus name < Greek *sálpinx, -pingos* trumpet + *glôssa* tongue (the shape of the stigma)]

**sal|pin|gec|to|my** (sal′pin jek′tə mē), *n., pl.* **-mies.** the surgical removal of a salpinx.

**sal|pin|gi|an** (sal pin′jē ən), *adj.* of or having to do with a salpinx or salpinges.

**sal|pin|gi|tis** (sal′pin jī′tis), *n.* inflammation of the Fallopian or the Eustachian tubes. [< New Latin *salpinx, -pingos* Fallopian or Eustachian tube]

**sal|pinx** (sal′pingks), *n., pl.* **sal|pin|ges** (sal pin′jēz). *Anatomy.* **1** = Eustachian tube. **2** = Fallopian tube. [< New Latin *salpinx, -pingos* < Greek *sálpinx, -pingos* trumpet]

**sal|sa** (säl′sä), *n.* a kind of popular music of Caribbean origin, similar to mambo: *At the moment, the dance is the hustle and the Latin music is salsa, which ... is either a brand new sound or a brand new name for music that has been around for years* (New York Times). **2** a dance performed to this music. [< Spanish *salsa* (literally) sauce]

**sal|si|fy** (sal′sə fī), *n.* **1** a plant with purple flowers and a long root like a parsnip whose flavor is thought to be like that of an oyster; oyster plant; vegetable oyster; oysterroot; goatsbeard. Salsify is a biennial belonging to the composite family. Its flowers remain open only in the morning. **2** its root, eaten as a vegetable. [< French *salsifis* < Italian *sassefrica* < Latin *saxifraga.* See etym. of doublet **saxifrage.**]

**sal|sil|la** (sal sil′ə), *n.* any one of a group of usually twining herbs of the amaryllis family of tropical America, that yield edible tubers. [< Spanish *salsilla* (diminutive) < *salsa* sauce < Latin; see etym. under **sauce**]

**sal soda**, = sodium carbonate. [< Latin *sal* salt]

**sal|su|gi|nous** (sal sü′jə nəs), *adj.* growing in salty soil: *a salsuginous plant.* [< Latin *salsūgō, -inis* saltness (< *salīre* to salt < *sāl salis* salt)]

**salt**[1] (sôlt), *n., adj., v.* —*n.* **1** a white substance found in the earth and in seawater; sodium chloride; table salt. Salt is used to season and preserve food and in many industrial processes. *Formula:* NaCl **2** a chemical compound derived from an acid by replacing the hydrogen wholly or partly with a metal or a radical. A salt is formed when an acid and a base neutralize each other. Baking soda is a salt. See the usage note below. **3** *Figurative.* anything that gives liveliness, freshness, piquancy, or pungency to anything: *His character has the salt of honesty about it* (William Hazlitt). *Though we are justices and doctors*

**Pronunciation Key:** hat, āge, cãre, fär; let, ēqual, tėrm; it, īce; hot, ōpen, ôrder; oil, out; cup, pu̇t, rüle; child; long; thin; ᴛʜen; zh, measure; ə represents **a** in about, **e** in taken, **i** in pencil, **o** in lemon, **u** in circus.

*and churchmen, Master Page, we have some salt of our youth in us* (Shakespeare). **SYN**: flavor. **4** = saltcellar. **5** *Informal.* a sailor, especially an experienced one: *Nor, though I am something of a salt, do I ever go to sea as a Commodore, or a Captain or a Cook* (Herman Melville). **SYN**: tar.
—***adj.*** **1** containing salt: *salt water.* **2** tasting like salt; salty; saline: *food that is too salt.* **3** flooded with or growing in salt water: *salt soil, salt weeds.* **4** cured or preserved with salt: *salt beef, salt cod.* **5** *Figurative.* sharp; pungent; to the point; lively: *salt speech.* **SYN**: piquant.
—***v.t.*** **1** to mix or sprinkle with salt: *These [curds] are salted, adding about an ounce of salt to every three pounds of curd* (J. A. Barnett). **2** to cure or preserve with salt, either in solid form or as brine. **3** to provide with salt: *to salt cattle.* **4** *Figurative.* to make pungent; season: *conversation salted with wit.* **5** *Chemistry.* **a** to treat or impregnate with a salt. **b** to add a salt to (a solution) in order to precipitate a dissolved substance. **c** Usually, **salt out.** to precipitate (a dissolved substance) in this manner. **6** to make (a mine, an account, or a venture) appear more prosperous or productive than it actually is by fraudulent or illegal means: *At the gold diggings of Australia, miners sometimes salt an unproductive hole by sprinkling a few grains of gold dust over it* (John C. Hotten).
**eat one's salt**, to be one's guest: *He who abuses my hospitality shall never again eat my salt.*
**rub salt in** (or **into**) **the wound**, to aggravate a person or situation further: *As if to rub salt in the wound, a special report to Parliament by the Iron and Steel Board ... takes a gloomy view of the industry's chances in export markets* (London Times).
**salt away** (or **down**), **a** to pack with salt to preserve: *The fish were salted down in a barrel.* **b** *Informal, Figurative: I can't help thinking he must be salting a lot of money away* (Booth Tarkington).
**salts, a** a medicine that causes movement of the bowels: *Epsom salts, Rochelle Salts.* **b** smelling salts: *Virginia had run for the salts as soon as she perceived that her mother was unwell* (Frederick Marryat).
**with a grain** (or **pinch**) **of salt**, with some reservation or allowance: *His claims must be taken with a grain of salt until they are established.*
**worth one's salt**, worth one's support, wages, or the like; capable or efficient: *It was plain from every line of his body that our new hand was worth his salt* (Robert Louis Stevenson).
[Old English *sealt*] —**salt'like'**, *adj.*
▶ **salt.** The nomenclature of chemical salts has reference to the acids from which they are derived. For example, sulfates, nitrates, and carbonates imply salts of sulfuric, nitric, and carbonic acids. The suffix *-ate* implies the maximum of oxygen in the acids; the suffix *-ite* implies the minimum.

**salt**[2] (sôlt), *adj. Obsolete.* **1** lewd; lecherous: *Whose salt imagination yet hath wrong'd Your well defended honor* (Shakespeare). **2** excessive; inordinate: *It is no salt desire Of seeing countries ... hath brought me out* (Ben Jonson). **3** (of a female animal) in heat. [< Middle French *(a) saut* (on the) jump, ultimately < Latin *saltus, -ūs* a leaping, jump < *salīre* to leap]

**SALT** (sôlt), *n.* Strategic Arms Limitation Talks (a series of conferences between the United States and the Soviet Union to limit nuclear armament, begun in Helsinki, Finland, on November 17, 1969). The first round of meetings, *SALT I*, ended in December, 1972; the second round, *SALT II*, began in March, 1973.

**sal|ta** (sal'tə), *n.* a game similar to halma, and somewhat like Chinese checkers. [ultimately < Latin *saltāre* leap]

**salt-and-pep|per** (sôlt'ən pep'ər), *adj.* = pepper-and-salt.

**sal|tant** (sal'tənt), *adj.* leaping, jumping, or dancing. [< Latin *saltāns, -antis,* present participle of *saltāre;* see etym. under **saltate**]

**sal|ta|rel|lo** (sal'tə rel'ō), *n., pl.* **-los. 1** an animated Italian and Spanish dance in triple time, sometimes classed as a galliard or a jig and containing numerous skips or jumps. **2** the music for it. [< Italian *saltarello* (diminutive) < *salto* a leap, jump < Latin *saltāre;* see etym. under **saltate**]

**sal|tate** (sal'tāt), *v.i.,* **-tat|ed, -tat|ing.** to leap; jump; dance. [< Latin *saltāre* (with English *-ate*[1]) (frequentative) < *salīre*]

**sal|ta|tion** (sal tā'shən), *n.* **1a** the act of leaping, bounding, or jumping: *Locusts ... being ordained for saltation, their hinder legs do far exceed the other* (Thomas Browne). **b** a leap. **2** *Figurative.* an abrupt movement, change, or transition. **3** *Biology.* a mutation. **4** the process by which material too heavy to remain in suspension is moved along by a current of water or air in a series of jumping movements. [< Latin *saltātiō, -ōnis* < *saltāre;* see etym. under **saltate**]

**sal|ta|to** (säl tä'tō), *n., pl.* **-tos.** *Music.* a technique of bowing a stringed instrument in which the bow is allowed to spring back from the string by its own elasticity. [< Italian *saltato* < *saltare* to spring < Latin *saltāre;* see etym. under **saltate**]

**sal|ta|to|ri|al** (sal'tə tôr'ē əl, -tōr'-), *adj.* **1** of, having to do with, or characterized by leaping, jumping, or dancing. **2** fitted or adapted for leaping.

**sal|ta|to|ry** (sal'tə tôr'ē, -tōr'-), *adj.* **1** characterized by or adapted for leaping: *Nature hates calculators; her methods are saltatory and impulsive* (Emerson). **2** having to do with or adapted for dancing. **3** *Figurative.* proceeding by abrupt movements.

**salt|box** (sôlt'boks'), *n. U.S.* an old-style, square-shaped, two-story house with a lean-to kitchen in the rear, originally built in Connecticut in the 1700's.

**salt|bush** (sôlt'bu̇sh'), *n.* any one of a widely distributed group of grayish herbs or shrubs of the goosefoot family, especially common in poor soils of Australia and North America.

**salt cake**, crude sodium sulfate that occurs as a by-product in the manufacture of hydrochloric acid from sodium chloride.

**salt cedar**, a variety of tamarisk native to southeastern Europe and western Asia, now naturalized in parts of the United States.

**salt|cel|lar** (sôlt'sel'ər), *n.* a shaker or small dish for holding salt, used on the table during meals. [< *salt*[1] + obsolete *saler* saltcellar < Old French *salier* < Latin *salārius* of salt < *sāl, salis* salt; influenced by *cellar*]

**salt dome**, *Geology.* a circular structure of sedimentary rocks resulting from the upward movement of a subterranean mass of salt: *In the northeastern area of the Caspian Sea, salt domes and subsalt formations have been discovered* (New Scientist).

**salt|ed** (sôl'tid), *adj.* **1** seasoned, cured, or preserved with salt: *salted peanuts.* **2** *Figurative.* experienced; hardened: *An expert and thoroughly "salted" journalist* (Westminster Gazette). **3** making a mine, account, or venture appear more prosperous or productive than it actually is, by fraudulent or illegal means. **4** treated so as to produce a large amount of radioactive fallout: *The technical feasibility of "salted" weapons ... had been studied ... but the Defense Department had never been asked by the AEC to produce these weapons* (Bulletin of Atomic Scientists). **5** *Archaic or Dialect.* (of animals) immune to a disease from having had it.

**salt|er** (sôl'tər), *n.* **1** a person who makes or sells salt. **2** a person who salts meat, fish, hides, and the like.

**salt|ern** (sôl'tərn), *n.* = saltworks. [Old English *sealtern, sealtærn* < *sealt* salt + *ærn* building]

**salt|er|y** (sôl'tər ē), *n., pl.* **-er|ies.** a factory that prepares salted fish for market.

**salt flat**, **1** a large, level area of flat land containing salt deposits: *It had come a very long way ... across salt flats abandoned ten million years ago by the shingling off of waters* (Ray Bradbury). **2** the basin of a playa.

**salt-free** (sôlt'frē'), *adj.* containing no salt or very little salt; low in sodium chloride: *Doctors prescribe a salt-free diet for patients with certain types of heart or kidney disease.*

**salt gland**, a gland found in various animals, especially aquatic birds, that secretes the excess salt taken into the bloodstream by drinking seawater and eating marine animals.

**salt|glaze** (sôlt'glāz'), *n., adj.* —***n.*** a glaze produced on ceramic ware by putting salt in the kilns during firing.
—***adj.*** having a saltglaze: *... a pair of saltglaze plates painted with two scenes of a gallant and a young woman in a garden* (London Times).

**salt grass**, any one of various grasses that grow in land having large salt or alkali deposits. Some kinds are used for fodder and hay.

**salt hay**, hay consisting of salt grass, used for food and bedding, and as a mulch.

**salt horse**, *Nautical Slang.* salted beef: *There is nothing left us but salt horse and sea-biscuit* (Herman Melville).

**sal|tier** (sal'tir), *n.* = saltire.

**sal|ti|grade** (sal'tə grād), *adj.* having limbs modified for leaping, as certain insects and spiders. [< New Latin *Saltigradae* group name < Latin *saltus, -ūs* a leap (< *salīre* to leap) + *gradī* go]

**salt|i|ly** (sôl'tə lē), *adv.* in a salty manner.

**sal|tim|ban|co** (sal'tim bang'kō), *n.* a mountebank; quack. [< Italian *saltimbanco* < *saltare* to leap + *in* on + *banco* bench. Compare etym. under **mountebank.**]

**sal|tim|banque** (sal'tim bangk), *n.* = saltimbanco. [< French *saltimbanque*]

**salt|ine** (sôl tēn'), *n.* a thin, crisp, salted cracker.

**salt|i|ness** (sôl'tē nis), *n.* salty condition.

**salt|ing** (sôl'ting), *n.* **1** the act of a person or thing that salts. **2** *British.* a tract of land overflowed at times by the sea: *At the bridge of the lower saltings the cattle gather and blare* (Rudyard Kipling).

**sal|tire** (sal'tir), *n. Heraldry.* an ordinary in the form of a Saint Andrew's cross, formed by the crossing of a bend and a bend sinister: *The present British Union Jack dates only from 1801, when the saltire of St. Patrick was added* (Time). See picture under **heraldry**.
[< Old French *sautoir,* earlier *saltoir,* learned borrowing from Medieval Latin *saltatorium* a kind of stirrup; saltatory < Latin *saltāre* to leap; see etym. under **saltate**]

**salt|ish** (sôl'tish), *adj.* somewhat salty.

**salt junk**, *Nautical Slang.* hard salt meat.

**salt lake**, a saltwater lake. Salt lakes are found in areas of large salt deposits and are often saltier than oceans.

**salt|less** (sôlt'lis), *adj.* **1** without salt; unsalted: *saltless cheese, saltless soil.* **2** *Figurative.* lacking piquancy, interest, or liveliness; flat; insipid: *The days went by, saltless, lifeless* (D. C. Murray).

**salt lick**, **1** a place where natural salt is found on the surface of the ground and where animals go to lick it up; lick: *[Moose] also like to roll in mud holes and eat the salty earth or salt licks* (Victor H. Cahalane). **2** a block of salt set out, especially in a pasture, for animals to lick, in order to provide necessary salt in the diet.

**salt|ly** (sôlt'lē), *adv.* with a salt taste or smell.

**salt marsh**, a marsh regularly overflowed or flooded by salt water, as by the action of winds or tides: *Most types of environment are to be found ... an exposed cliff-beach, salt marsh and tidal mud, and a shingle spit* (Science News).

**salt-marsh caterpillar** (sôlt'märsh'), the hairy larva of an arctiid moth that feeds on various grasses, especially the salt grasses of the New England seacoast.

**salt mine**, **1** a mine from which salt is extracted. **2** a place or situation of drudgery or enslavement: *This is not a prep school for the industry salt mine* (Harper's).

**salt|mouth** (sôlt'mouth'), *n.* a wide-mouthed bottle suitable for holding solid chemicals.

**salt|ness** (sôlt'nis), *n.* = saltiness.

**salt of the earth**, the best people: *He has been driven to imagining that his sole solidarity lies with a small number of superior persons who have been appointed as the salt of the earth* (Edmund Wilson).

**salt pan**, **1** a large, shallow vessel in which salt water is evaporated to yield salt. **2** a shallow depression in the ground in which salt water is evaporated in salt making. **3** any dried-up salt lake or marsh, especially in Africa: *The waterholes of the salt pans are almost permanently ringed by zebra and wildebeest* (New Scientist).

**salt|pans** (sôlt'panz'), *n.pl.* = saltworks.

**salt|pe|ter** or **salt|pe|tre** (sôlt'pē'tər), *n.* **1** a salty, white mineral, used in making gunpowder, in preserving meat, and in medicine; naturally occurring potassium nitrate; niter. *Formula:* $KNO_3$ **2** a naturally occurring form of sodium nitrate, used as a source of nitrogen in fertilizing soil; Chile saltpeter. *Formula:* $NaNO_3$ **3** = calcium nitrate. [< Old French *salpetre,* learned borrowing from Medieval Latin *sal petrae* salt of rock < Latin *sāl, salis* salt, *petrae,* genitive of *petra* rock < Greek *pétrā*]

**salt pit**, a pit where salt is mined.

**salt pork**, the fatty back or middle parts of a pig, cured with salt or in brine. Salt pork is used to flavor many dishes.

**salt rheum**, *Informal.* a skin eruption, as eczema: *Salt rheum ... has long baffled the art of the most experienced physicians* (Canadian Courant).

**salts** (sôlts), *n.pl.* See under **salt**.

**salt sage**, = shadscale.

**salt|shak|er** (sôlt'shā'kər), *n.* a container for salt, with a perforated top through which the salt is sprinkled.

**salt spoon**, a small spoon, usually having a round, deep bowl, used in taking salt at the table.

**salt tree**, **1** a leguminous tree with white, pinnate leaves, growing in central Asia. **2** (in India) a species of tamarisk, the twigs of which are frequently covered with a slight efflorescence of salt.

**sal|tus** (sal'təs), *n., pl.* **-tus.** a breach of continuity, as in a process of reasoning; leap from premises to conclusion. [< Latin *saltus, -ūs* a leap < *salīre* to leap]

**salt|wa|ter** (sôlt'wôt'ər, -wot'-), *adj.* **1** consisting of or containing salt water: *a saltwater solution.* **2** living in the sea or in water like seawater: *a saltwater fish.* **3** taking place or working on the sea: *a saltwater fisherman, a saltwater sport.*

**saltwater crocodile**, a crocodile of Southeast Asia, the East Indies, and Australia, averaging a length of 12 to 14 feet.

**saltwater taffy**, *U.S.* a kind of taffy sold at seaside resorts, originally containing a very small amount of salt water as an ingredient.

**salt well**, a well sunk, usually by boring, in order to procure brine.

**salt|works** (sôlt′wėrks′), *n.pl. or sing.* an establishment for obtaining salt in commercial quantities by evaporation of naturally salty water, as that in the sea.

**salt|wort** (sôlt′wėrt′), *n.* any one of several plants that grow on beaches, in salt marshes, or in regions of alkaline soil: **1** any one of various plants of the goosefoot family, especially a prickly plant used in making soda ash (barilla). **2** any one of several glassworts.

**salt|y** (sôl′tē), *adj.*, **salt|i|er, salt|i|est. 1** containing salt; tasting of salt. Sweat and tears are salty. *What there is* [*of underground water*] *proves mostly too salty for human use continuously* (R. N. Elston). **SYN**: saline, briny. **2** *Figurative.* **a** to the point; terse, witty, and a bit improper: *a salty remark.* **SYN**: racy. **b** that manifests itself in salty language: *a salty sense of humor.* **3** of or suggestive of the sea or life at sea.

**sa|lu|bri|ous** (sə lü′brē əs), *adj.* favorable or conducive to good health; healthful: *a salubrious diet. Their salubrious effects, which include the relief of pain ... are seldom more than palliative and almost never permanent* (New Yorker). **SYN**: wholesome, salutary. [< Latin *salūbris* (with English *-ous*), related to *salūs, -ūtis* good health]
—**sa|lu′bri|ous|ly**, *adv.* —**sa|lu′bri|ous|ness**, *n.*

**sa|lu|bri|ty** (sə lü′brə tē), *n.* salubrious quality or condition; healthfulness: *The salubrity of their walk is sadly tinctured by carbon monoxide* (New Yorker).

**sa|lu|ki** (sə lü′kē), *n.* any hunting dog of what is probably the oldest known breed of dogs, familiar to the ancient Egyptians and Arabs and the "dog" of the Bible; gazelle hound. It resembles the greyhound in build and has short, silky hair and fringed ears and tail. *Excavation of the Sumerian Empire of 7,000 to 6,000 B.C. has found evidence of ... the saluki* (Cape Times). [< Arabic *salūqi* of *Salūq*, an ancient city of Arabia]

**Sa|lus** (sā′ləs), *n. Roman Mythology.* the goddess of health and prosperity, identified with the Greek Hygeia. [< Latin *Salūs, -ūtis* (originally) health]

**sa|lus po|pu|li su|pre|ma lex es|to** (sā′ləs pop′yə lī sə prē′mə leks es′tō), *Latin.* let the people's welfare be the supreme law (the motto of Missouri).

**sal|u|tar|y** (sal′yə ter′ē), *adj.* **1** promoting or contributing to a more satisfactory condition; beneficial: *The teacher gave the discouraged student salutary advice. Through a wise and salutary neglect* [*of the colonies*], *a generous nature has been suffered to take her own way to perfection* (Edmund Burke). **SYN**: profitable, useful. **2** good for the health; wholesome: *Walking is a salutary exercise.* [< Latin *salūtāris* < *salūs, -ūtis* good health] —**sal′u|tar′i|ly**, *adv.* —**sal′u|tar′i|ness**, *n.*

**sal|u|ta|tion** (sal′yə tā′shən), *n.* **1** the act of greeting; saluting: *The man raised his hat in salutation. Out into the yard sallied mine host himself also, to do fitting salutation to his new guests* (Scott). **2a** something uttered, written, or done to salute: *A formal bow was her parting salutation.* **b** any one of the various conventional forms of address with which a letter is begun, such as "Dear Sir" or "My Dear Mrs. Jones."

**sal|u|ta|tion|al** (sal′yə tā′shə nəl), *adj.* of or having to do with a salutation.

**sa|lu|ta|to|ri|an** (sə lü′tə tôr′ē ən, -tōr′-), *n.* the student who delivers the address of welcome at the graduation of a class. The salutatorian is often the student who ranks second in the class. [American English < *salutator(y)* + *-ian*]

**sa|lu|ta|to|ry** (sə lü′tə tôr′ē, -tōr′-), *adj., n., pl.* **-ries.** —*adj.* **1** expressing greeting; welcoming. **2** *U.S.* designating the address by the salutatorian at graduation exercises in a college or school.
—*n.* **1** an address of greeting. **2** an opening address welcoming guests at the graduation of a class.
[American English < Latin *salūtātōrius* < *salūtāre*; see etym. under **salute**]

**✱sa|lute** (sə lüt′), *v.*, **-lut|ed, -lut|ing,** *n.* —*v.t.* **1** to honor in a formal manner as by raising the hand to the head, by firing guns, or by dipping flags: *We salute the flag every day at school. The soldier saluted the officer.* **SYN**: welcome, hail. **2** to meet with kind words, a bow, clasp of the hand, kiss, or other greeting; greet: *The old gentleman walked along the avenue saluting his friends.* **3** to make a bow, gesture, or the like, to. **4** *Figurative.* to come to (the eye or ear); strike; meet: *Shouts of welcome saluted their ears.*
—*v.i.* **1** to make a salute. **2** to perform a salutation.
—*n.* **1** an act of saluting; sign of welcome, farewell, or honor: *The queen gracefully acknowledged the salutes of the crowd.* **2a** the act or gesture by which a person or thing, such as a superior officer or national flag, is honored or shown respect. **b** the position, such as of the hand, rifle, or sword, in saluting.
[< Latin *salūtāre* to greet (wish health to) < *salūs, -ūtis* good health] —**sa|lut′er**, *n.*

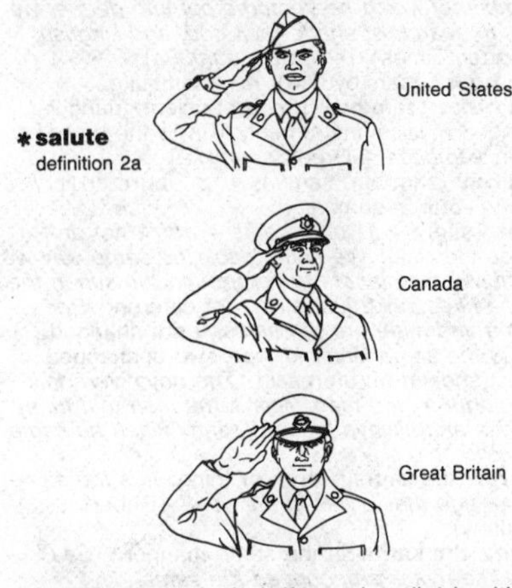

**✱salute** definition 2a

**sal|u|tif|er|ous** (sal′yu̇ tif′ər əs), *adj.* **1** healthful; salubrious. **2** *Figurative.* conducive to well-being, safety, or salvation. [< Latin *salūtifer* (< *salūs, -ūtis* good health + *ferre* to bear) + English *-ous*]

**Salv.**, Salvador.

**sal|va|ble** (sal′və bəl), *adj.* **1** (of a ship, cargo, or the like) = salvageable. **2** *Theology.* admitting of salvation. [< Late Latin *salvāre* to save (< Latin *salvus* safe) + English *-able*]

**Sal|va|do|ran** (sal′və dôr′ən, -dōr′-), *adj., n.* —*adj.* of or having to do with El Salvador, a country in western Central America, or its people. —*n.* a person born or living in El Salvador.

**Sal|va|do|re|an** or **Sal|va|do|ri|an** (sal′və dôr′ē-ən, -dōr′-), *adj., n.* = Salvadoran.

**sal|vage** (sal′vij), *n., v.*, **-vaged, -vag|ing.** —*n.* **1** the act of saving a ship or its cargo from wreck or capture: *After the ship sank, salvage of its cargo was impossible.* **2** a payment for saving it: *The owners paid a high salvage to recover the ship's cargo.* **3** the rescue of property from fire, flood, shipwreck, or other danger: *Salvage of the furniture was hampered by the heat of the flames.* **4a** the property salvaged or saved: *the salvage from a shipwreck or a fire.* **b** the value of this property, or the proceeds from its sale. **5** *Figurative.* **a** any saving from ruin: *the salvage of one's dignity.* **b** anything saved thus.
—*v.t.* **1** to save from fire, flood, shipwreck, or capture: *The passengers and crew ... were evacuated ... except for the captain and six of his men, who are remaining, trusting that the ship ... may be salvaged* (London Times). **2** *Figurative: to salvage one's reputation.*
[< Middle French *salvage* < Medieval Latin *salvagium* < Late Latin *salvāre* < Latin *salvus* safe]

**sal|vage|a|bil|i|ty** (sal′və jə bil′ə tē), *n.* the quality or condition of being salvageable.

**sal|vage|a|ble** (sal′və jə bəl), *adj.* that can be salvaged: *Submarines preyed particularly on tankers during the war, but there is little hope that oil cargoes are salvageable* (Wall Street Journal).

**salvage archaeology**, the hasty excavation of sites about to be ruined or made inaccessible by a construction project, flooding, or other man-made destruction, in order to salvage archaeological remains: *The site was discovered in the course of salvage archaeology in an area that will soon be flooded by a hydroelectric project* (Scientific American).

**Sal|var|san** (sal′vər san), *n. Trademark.* arsphenamine. [< German *Salvarsan* < Latin *salvus* safe + German *Arsenik* arsenic]

**sal|va|tion** (sal vā′shən), *n.* **1** the act of saving or state of being saved; preservation from destruction, ruin, loss, or calamity: *Many a Burgoyne has capitulated because the means of salvation were not ... put into his hands* (Archibald Alison). **2** a person or thing that saves. Christians believe that Christ is the salvation of the world. (*Figurative.*) *Sleep is the salvation of the nervous system* (M. L. Holbrook). **3** the act of saving the soul; deliverance from sin and from punishment for sin. **SYN**: redemption. [< Late Latin *salvātiō, -ōnis* < *salvāre* save < Latin *salvus* safe]

**sal|va|tion|al** (sal vā′shə nəl), *adj.* having to do with or concerned with salvation. —**sal|va′tion|al|ly**, *adv.*

**Salvation Army**, an international organization to spread the Christian religion and help the poor, founded in England in 1865 by William Booth.

**sal|va|tion|ism** (sal vā′shə niz əm), *n.* religious teaching which lays prime stress on the saving of the soul. [< *salvation* + *-ism*]

**Sal|va|tion|ism** (sal vā′shə niz əm), *n.* the principles or methods of the Salvation Army. [< *salvationism*]

**sal|va|tion|ist** (sal vā′shə nist), *n.* a teacher or disciple of salvationism: *They were rich ... and were both internationally famous as applied salvationists* (New Yorker).

**Sal|va|tion|ist** (sal vā′shə nist), *n., adj.* —*n.* a member of the Salvation Army: *She was the daughter of Salvationists.*
—*adj.* having to do with Salvationists or Salvationism: *Salvationist leaders from many countries met in London* (Norman S. Marshall).

**salve**[1] (sav, säv), *n., v.*, **salved, salv|ing.** —*n.* **1** a soft, greasy substance put on wounds and sores; healing ointment: *Is this salve good for burns?* **SYN**: unguent. **2** *Figurative.* **a** *The kind words were a salve to my hurt feelings. Ronald had this salve for his conscience* (Charles Kingsley). **SYN**: balm. **b** *Slang.* praise; flattery.
—*v.t.* **1** to put salve on: *The nurse salved the burns with ointment.* **2** *Figurative: He salved his conscience by the thought that his lie harmed no one.* **SYN**: soothe.
[Old English *sealf*]

**salve**[2] (salv), *v.t.*, **salved, salv|ing.** to save from loss or destruction; salvage. [back formation < *salvage*]

**sal|ve**[3] (sal′vē), *interj.* hail! *"Salve Regina, mater misericordiae," he prayed* (Edgar Maass). [< Latin *salvē!* be in good health! probably imperative of *salvēre* < *salvus* safe, well]

**sal|ver** (sal′vər), *n.* a tray, especially one for food or drinks or a small one, such as for letters or calling cards. [< French *salve* < Spanish *salva* (literally) a foretasting < *salvar* in the sense of "safeguard (a superior) by pretasting food" < Late Latin *salvāre* save < Latin *salvus* safe]

**sal|ver|form** (sal′vər fôrm), *adj. Botany.* (of a corolla) shaped like a tube, with the limb spreading out flat.

**sal|ver-shaped** (sal′vər shāpt′), *adj.* = salverform.

**sal|vi|a** (sal′vē ə), *n.* any one of a genus of herbs and shrubs of the mint family, especially the scarlet sage and the common garden sage; sage. *Salvia* is commonly used to refer to the ornamental varieties of sage. [< Latin *salvia*, probably < *salvus* healthy, safe (because of its supposed healing properties). See etym. of doublet **sage**[2].]

**sal|vif|ic** (sal vif′ik), *adj.* tending to save; providing or causing salvation: *A number of liberal Catholic thinkers have suggested that unbaptized children may get to heaven after all because of God's "salvific will"—his desire that all mankind be saved* (Time). [< Late Latin *salvificus* < Latin *salvus* safe + *facere* to make]

**sal|vo**[1] (sal′vō), *n., pl.* **-vos** or **-voes**, *v.*, **-voed, -vo|ing.** —*n.* **1a** the discharge of several guns at the same time as a broadside or as a salute. **b** the dropping by an aircraft of a complete rack of bombs at the same time over a target. **c** the launching at the same time of every rocket in a group of rockets: *It could briefly match the firepower of a modern cruiser with its close-in salvos of rockets* (Time). **d** the projectiles or bombs thus discharged, dropped, or fired. **2** *Figurative: a salvo of rocks, a salvo of insults. Britain's electioneering war will begin with a salvo of statistics tomorrow* (Wall Street Journal). **3** a round of cheers or applause.
—*v.t., v.i.* to discharge a salvo (of).
[< Italian *salva* < Latin *salvē* hail!; see etym. under **salve**[3]]

**sal|vo**[2] (sal′vō), *n., pl.* **-vos. 1** a reservation (as of a right); saving clause; proviso. **2** a quibbling evasion. **3** an expedient for saving a person's reputation or soothing offended pride or conscience. [< Medieval Latin *salvo jure* (literally) with a right being saved or reserved; ablative forms of Latin *salvus* safe, saved, and *jūs, jūris* law, a right]

**sal vo|la|ti|le** (vō lat′ə lē), **1** a colorless or white crystalline salt of ammonium; ammonium carbonate; volatile salt. **2** an aromatic solution of this, used especially to relieve faintness and headaches. [< New Latin *sal volatile* < Latin *sāl, salis* salt, and *volātile* volatile]

**sal|vor** (sal′vər), *n.* **1** a person who salvages or attempts to salvage vessels, cargo, or other endangered, damaged, or abandoned property. **2** a ship used in salvage.

**sal|war** (säl′wär), *n.* = shalwar.

**Pronunciation Key:** hat, āge, cãre, fär; let, ēqual, tėrm; it, īce; hot, ōpen, ôrder; oil, out; cup, pu̇t, rüle; child; long; thin; ᴛʜen; zh, measure; ə represents **a** in about, **e** in taken, **i** in pencil, **o** in lemon, **u** in circus.

**Sam.**, Samuel (two books of the Old Testament, usually distinguished as I Sam. or 1 Sam.; II Sam. or 2 Sam.).

**SAM** (sam), *n.* a surface-to-air missile: *The North's air-defense system continually grows stronger with SAMs* (Time).

**S. Am.**, **1** South America. **2** South American.

**sam** (sam), *v.t.*, **sammed, sam|ming.** = sammy.

**sa|madh** (sə mäd′), *n.* a place of immolation or burial, especially the tomb of a Hindu yogi supposed to be lying in a state of trance. [< Hindustani *samādh* < Sanskrit *samādhi* (literally) deep meditation]

**sa|ma|dhi** (sə mä′dē), *n. Hinduism.* a state of mystical contemplation in which distinctions between the self and the outer world disappear: *Of samadhi it is said, "If a man goes into it a fool he comes out a sage"* (Manchester Guardian Weekly). [< Sanskrit *samādhi* deep meditation]

***sam|a|ra** (sam′ər ə, sə mär′-), *n.* any dry fruit that has a winglike extension and does not split open when ripe; a key or key fruit. The fruit of the maple tree is a double samara with one seed in each half. [< Latin *samara* elm seed]

***samara**

**Sa|mar|i|tan** (sə mar′ə tən), *n., adj.* —*n.* **1** a native or inhabitant of Samaria, a region and ancient kingdom of northern Palestine. **2** *Figurative.* a person who helps another in trouble or distress; Good Samaritan; unselfish person.
—*adj.* **1** of or having to do with Samaria or its people. **2** *Figurative.* characteristic of a Good Samaritan; unselfish; charitable: *a Samaritan society.*

**sa|mar|i|tan|ism** (sə mar′ə tə niz′əm), *n.* **1** the religious doctrine of the Samaritans, a modification of Sadduceeism. **2** a word, phrase, or expression peculiar to the Hebrew dialect of the Samaritans. **3** *Figurative.* charitableness or benevolence like that of the Good Samaritan: *Samaritanism today means courage* (Maclean's).

***sa|mar|i|um** (sə mãr′ē əm), *n.* a hard, brittle, grayish-white, metallic chemical element of the cerium group, discovered in 1879 in samarskite. Samarium is one of the rare-earth elements. It is used in control rods in nuclear reactors. [< *samar*(skite) + New Latin *-ium*, a suffix meaning "element"]

***samarium**

| symbol | atomic number | atomic weight | oxidation state |
|---|---|---|---|
| Sm | 62 | 150.35 | 2,3 |

**Sam|ar|kand** (sam′ər kand, sä′mər känd), *n.* a Turkmen rug usually having three medallions in its center and a border of foamy waves. [< *Samarkand*, a city in the Soviet Union, in the Uzbek SSR]

**sa|mar|skite** (sə mär′skīt), *n.* a black mineral, containing niobium, uranium, cerium, samarium, and the like. [< German *Samarskit* < a Colonel *Samarski*, a Russian official in the 1800's + German *-it* -ite[1]]

**sam|ba** (sam′bə), *n., pl.* **-bas,** *v.,* **-baed, -ba|ing.** —*n.* **1** an African dance adapted and modified in Brazil as a ballroom dance, in syncopated duple time. **2** music for this dance. —*v.i.* to dance the samba. [< Portuguese *samba*, probably < an African word]

**sam|bal** (säm′bäl), *n.* a condiment of Malaya and Indonesia made of peppers, fruits, herbs, or fish foods, usually eaten with curry and rice. [< Malay]

**sam|ba|qui** (säm bä′kē), *n.* any pile of shell and refuse found along the Brazilian coast, containing items deposited by prehistoric man. [< Portuguese *śambaquí* < a Tupi word]

**sam|bar** (sam′bər, säm′-), *n., pl.* **-bars** or (*collectively*) **-bar.** any one of certain large, maned deer of Asia, especially a kind with massive, rusine antlers, found in India. [< Hindi *sāmbar* < Sanskrit *sambara* kind of deer]

**sam|bo**[1] (sam′bō), *n., pl.* **-bos. 1** the child of a Negro and an Indian, or of a Negro and a mulatto (used in an unfriendly way). **2** any Negro (used in an unfriendly way). Also, **zambo.** [< Spanish *zambo*]

**sam|bo**[2] (sam′bō), *n.* a type of wrestling similar to judo, popular in international competitions. [< Russian *sambo*, acronym for *sam*(ooborona) *b*(ez) *o*(rushia) self-defense without weapons]

**Sam Browne belt** (sam′ broun′), a leather belt supported by a light strap passing over the shoulder, worn by British and American army officers, especially in World War I, and by policemen and others. [< Sir *Samuel Browne*, 1824-1901, a British general, who invented it]

**sam|buk** (sam′bük), *n.* a kind of small ship, similar to a dhow, used off western India and the Arabian coast: *He is also part owner of a leaky sambuk in which he ventures out into deeper waters in search of shark, rock cod, and kingfish* (London Times). [< Arabic *sambūq*]

**sam|bu|ka** (sam byü′kə), *n.* = sambuke.

**sam|buke** (sam′byük), *n.* an ancient, triangular, stringed musical instrument, akin to the harp. [< Latin *sambūca* < Greek *sambykē*]

**sam|bur** (sam′bər, säm′-), *n., pl.* **-burs** or (*collectively*) **-bur.** = sambar.

**same** (sām), *adj., pron., adv.* —*adj.* **1** not another; identical: *We came back the same way we went. All the planets travel around the sun in the same direction.* **2** just alike; not different: *Her name and mine are the same.* **3** not changed: *He is the same kind old man.* SYN: unchanged. **4** just spoken of; aforesaid: *The boys were talking about a nice man. This same man told funny stories and always brought candy when he came to visit.*
—*pron.* the same person or thing: *It is the same in our age that it was in our youth* (Robert Southey).
—*adv.* **the same,** in the same manner: *"Sea" and "see" are pronounced the same.*
**all the same, a** notwithstanding; regardless; nevertheless: *All the same, I'm glad to be home again.* **b** of little importance: *Whether or not it rains is all the same to me.*
**just the same, a** in the same manner: *The stairs creaked just the same as ever.* **b** nevertheless: *Just the same, I am planning to go. My mother was a lady ... but just the same she ate boiled cabbage with a knife except when company came* (Hugh McHugh).
[probably < Scandinavian (compare Old Icelandic *samr*)]
—*Syn. adj.* **1, 2 Same, identical** mean not different from something else or each other. When referring to something or someone already mentioned, either word applies: *That is the same* (or *identical*) *man I saw yesterday.* When describing two or more people or things, **same** implies likeness of some kind or degree; **identical** implies absolute likeness: *He always has the same lunch. Their cars are identical.*
▶ **Same,** the adjective, is always preceded by the definite article (*the*) or by a demonstrative pronoun (*this, that,* etc.).
▶ **Same** as a substitute for *it* or other pronouns is largely confined to legal usage and is generally regarded as unnecessarily cumbersome: *The committee has completed its report and will present same* (standard: *it*) *at the next meeting.*

**sa|mekh** or **sa|mech** (sä′mekh, -mek), *n.* the fifteenth letter of the Hebrew alphabet. [< Hebrew *sāmeh*]

**same|ness** (sām′nis), *n.* **1** the condition or quality of being the same; exact likeness. **2** lack of variety; tiresomeness: *It seems that giants in industry are taking refuge in sameness* (Atlantic). SYN: uniformity, monotony.

**S. Amer.**, **1** South America. **2** South American.

**Sa|mhain** (sä′win), *n.* **1** an autumn festival of the Druids marking the end of the harvest season. **2** the period of this festival, coinciding with the time of All Saints' Day; Allhallowtide. [< Irish Gaelic *samhain*]

**Sa|mi|an** (sā′mē ən), *adj., n.* —*adj.* of or having to do with the island of Samos, an island in the Aegean Sea, west of Asia Minor.
—*n.* a native or inhabitant of Samos.

**sam|iel** (sam′yel), *n.* a hot, dry, sand-laden desert wind of Arabia and northern Africa; simoom: *the samiel or mortifying wind of the desert near Bagdad* (James Smith). [< Turkish *samyel* < *sam* poisonous (< Arabic *samm* poison) + *yel* wind]

***samisen**

***sam|i|sen** (sam′ə sen), *n.* a Japanese musical instrument somewhat like a guitar, with a long neck and almost square body, and three strings played by plucking: *After dinner we listened to the strange music of the samisen* (New York Times). Also, **shamisen.** [< Japanese *samisen* < Chinese roots *som* three + *sien* string]

**sam|ite** (sam′īt, sā′mīt), *n.* a heavy, rich silk fabric, sometimes interwoven with gold or silver, worn in the Middle Ages: *Clothed in white samite, mystic, wonderful* (Tennyson). [< Old French *samit*, short for Medieval Greek *hexamiton* (literally) six-threaded < Greek *héx* six + *mítos* thread]

**sam|iz|dat** (säm′iz dät′), *n.* **1** the practice of writers in the Soviet Union of secretly publishing and distributing literature banned by the government: *By samizdat, Russians endlessly retype and clandestinely circulate the work of such banned writers as Alexander Solzhenitsyn* (Time). **2** the literature or writings produced this way: *In an "Epilogue to the Russian Edition Abroad," Mr. Solzhenitsyn writes: "This book cannot be published now in our country except in samizdat because of censorship"* (New York Times). [< Russian *samizdat* < *sam* self + *izdat*(*el'stvo*) publishing, probably coined as a pun on *Gosizdat* the State Publishing House]

**Sam|khya** (säng′kyə), *n.* = Sankhya.

**Saml.**, Samuel (two books of the Old Testament, usually distinguished as I Saml. or 1 Saml.; II Saml. or 2 Saml.).

**sam|let** (sam′lit), *n.* a young or small salmon. [< *sa*(l)*m*(on) + *-let*]

**sam|lor** (sam′lər), *n.* = pedicab. [< Thai *samlor*]

**sam|my** (sam′ē), *v.t.*, **-mied, -my|ing. 1** to dampen (skins) in dressing leather. **2** to season (skins) to a uniform temper. [origin unknown]

**Sam|nite** (sam′nīt), *n., adj.* —*n.* one of a people of ancient Italy, believed to be an offshoot of the Sabines.
—*adj.* of or having to do with the Samnites or Samnium, an ancient country of central Italy.

**Sa|mo|an** (sə mō′ən), *adj., n.* —*adj.* of or having to do with Samoa, a group of islands in the South Pacific, or its people.
—*n.* **1** a native or inhabitant of Samoa. **2** the Polynesian language of the Samoans.

**sa|mo|gon** (sä′mə gon), *n.* a Russian vodka illegally distilled from various elements, such as sugar beets, potatoes, or grain. [< Russian *samogon*]

**Sam|o|thra|cian** (sam′ə thrā′shən), *adj., n.* —*adj.* of or having to do with the island of Samothrace, in the northern Aegean Sea.
—*n.* a native or inhabitant of Samothrace.

***sam|o|var** (sam′ə vär, sam′ə vär′), *n.* a metal urn used for heating water for tea: *Tea was brewing in a big Kashmiri samovar nearby* (New Yorker). [< Russian *samovar* (literally) self-boiler < *sam* self + *varit'* boil]

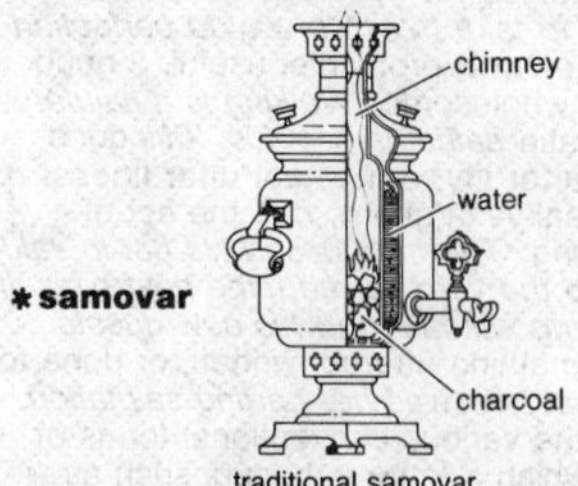


***samovar**

**Sam|o|yed** or **Sam|o|yede** (sam′ə yed′), *n., adj.* —*n.* **1** one of a Mongoloid people living in northern Siberia and northeastern Russia. **2** a group of Ural-Altaic languages spoken by these people. **3** any one of a Siberian breed of large working dogs having a long-haired, white or cream-colored coat, used in arctic regions to guard reindeer herds and pull sleds. They were originally bred by the Samoyeds.
—*adj.* of or having to do with the Samoyeds or their languages. [< Russian *samoyed*]

**Sam|o|yed|ic** (sam′ə yed′ik), *adj., n.* —*adj.* of or having to do with the Samoyeds or their languages. —*n.* their languages.

**samp** (samp), *n. U.S.* coarsely ground corn, boiled and eaten, usually with milk and sugar. [American English < Algonkian (Narraganset) *nasaump* porridge of meal]

**sam|pa|gui|ta** (sam′pə gē′tə), *n.* the fragrant white flower of an East Indian jasmine. It is the national flower of the Philippines. [< Tagalog *sampaga* + Spanish *-ita* (diminutive suffix)]

***sam|pan** (sam′pan), *n.* any one of various small boats of the rivers and coastal waters of China and nearby regions. A sampan is sculled by one or more oars at the stern; it usually has a single sail and a cabin made of mats. See picture opposite on the next page. [< Chinese *san pan* (literally) three boards, planks < Portuguese *champão*; origin uncertain]

**sam|phire** (sam′fīr), *n.* **1** a European plant of the parsley family, growing in clefts of rocks by the sea. Its aromatic, saline, fleshy leaves are used in pickles. **2** = glasswort. [earlier *sampere* < French (*herbe de*) *Saint Pierre* St. Peter's (herb)]

**sam|ple** (sam′pəl, säm′-), *n., adj., v.,* **-pled, -pling.** —*n.* a part to show what the rest is like; one thing to show what the others are like: *Get samples of blue silk for a new dress.* (*Figurative.*) *Pushing people aside to get on a bus is a sample of his bad manners.* **SYN**: specimen. See syn. under **example.**

—*adj.* serving as a sample: *a sample copy, sample ores.*

—*v.t.* to take a part of; test a part of: *We sampled the cake and found it very good.* (*Figurative.*) *Each of us ... seems to have sampled all the different varieties of human experience* (Mark Twain).

[short for *essample,* variant of *example* < Old French *essample*]

**sam|pler** (sam′plər, säm′-), *n.* **1** a person who samples. **2** a piece of cloth embroidered to show skill in needlework. **3** something containing typical samples: *a sampler of Poe's work.* **4** a mechanism for collecting samplings. [short for Old French *essamplaire* < Latin *exemplārium* model pattern, original < Latin *exemplum* example]

**sample room,** *U.S.* **1** a room where samples, especially of merchandise, are kept or shown. **2** *Informal.* a barroom; saloon.

**sam|pling** (sam′pling, säm′-), *n.* **1** an act or process of taking samples; a testing or trying of anything by means of samples, especially in order to determine its quality or nature: *A second requirement in prospecting in any area is to find the constitution of the surface layers of the sea bed by direct sampling* (Gaskell and Hill). **2** something taken or serving as a sample: *Samplings were ... tested out by a physician on eight military patients* (Newsweek).

**Samp|son** (samp′sən), *n.* a variety of tangelo grown in the United States.

**sam|sa|ra** (səm sä′rə), *n. Hinduism.* the endless repetition of births, deaths, and rebirths to which man is subject. [< Sanskrit *samsāra*]

**sam|shu** (sam′shü), *n.* **1** a Chinese alcoholic beverage made from fermented rice or millet. **2** alcoholic or intoxicating liquor generally. [< Cantonese *sam-shiu* (literally) three times distilled]

**Sam|son** (sam′sən), *n.* **1** a man of very great strength who was one of the judges of Israel (in the Bible, Judges 13-16). **2** any very strong man.

**Sam|so|ni|an** (sam sō′nē ən), *adj.* of, having to do with, or resembling Samson; showing great strength: [*He*] *gave a faintly Samsonian performance, for one had the odd impression that some of his prodigious strength left him after a capital loss* (London Times).

**Sam|u|el** (sam′yu̇ əl), *n.* **1** a Hebrew leader, judge, and prophet of the 1000's B.C. He anointed Saul, the first king of Israel, and later, David. **2** either of two books of the Old Testament, I Samuel and II Samuel, coming after Judges and named after Samuel. In the Douay Bible, these books are called I Kings and II Kings. *Abbr:* Sam.

**sam|u|rai** (sam′u̇ rī), *n., pl.* **-rai. 1** the military class in feudal Japan, consisting of the retainers of the great nobles. **2** a member of this class. [< Japanese *samurai* warrior, knight]

**san** (san), *n. Informal.* a sanitorium.

**San** (sän), *adj. Spanish and Italian.* Saint.

**san|a|tive** (san′ə tiv), *adj.* having the power to cure or heal; healing; curative. **SYN**: therapeutic, sanatory, remedial. [< Late Latin *sānātīvus* < Latin *sānāre* to heal < *sānus* healthy]

**san|a|to|ri|um** (san′ə tôr′ē əm, -tōr′-), *n., pl.* **-to-ri|ums, -to|ri|a** (-tôr′ē ə, -tōr′-). **1** = sanitarium. **2** a health resort, especially one in the hills or mountains of hot countries such as India, for summer use. [< New Latin *sanatorium,* neuter of Late Latin *sānātōrius* health-giving < Latin *sānāre* to heal < *sānus* healthy]

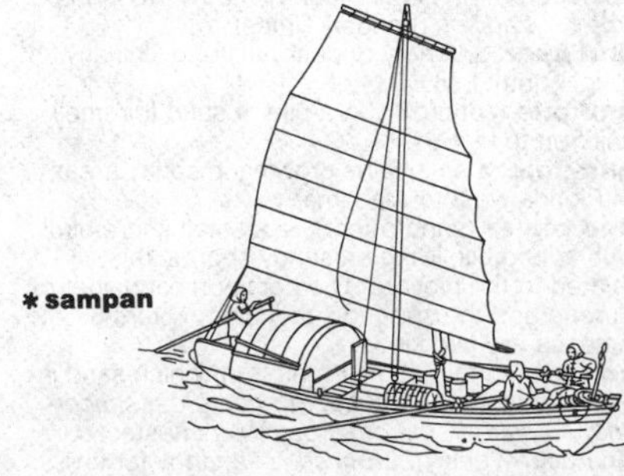

*** sampan**

**san|a|to|ry** (san′ə tôr′ē, -tōr′-), *adj.* **1** favorable to health; healing; curing. **2** of or having to do with healing. [< Late Latin *sānātōrius;* see etym. under **sanatorium**]

**san|be|ni|to** (san′bə nē′tō), *n., pl.* **-tos. 1** a yellow penitential garment with a red Saint Andrew's cross before and behind, worn by a confessed heretic under trial by the Inquisition. **2** a black garment ornamented with flames, devils, and other symbols of magic worn by a condemned heretic at an auto-da-fé. [< Spanish *sanbenito* < *San Benito* Saint Benedict (because he introduced the scapular)]

**San Blas** (san blas′), **1** a group of four tribes of American Indians living on the San Blas Islands off the eastern coast of Panama. **2** the Chibchan language of these tribes.

**San|cho Pan|za** (san′chō pan′zə), the squire of Don Quixote, whose simplicity and common sense contrast sharply with Don Quixote's visionary heroics.

**sanc|ti|fi|ca|tion** (sangk′tə fə kā′shən), *n.* the act of sanctifying or state of being sanctified; consecration; purification from sin: *God hath from the beginning chosen you to salvation through sanctification of the Spirit and belief of the truth* (II Thessalonians 2:13).

**sanc|ti|fied** (sangk′tə fīd), *adj.* **1** made holy; set apart for sacred services; consecrated; sacred. **2** sanctimonious: *a sanctified whine.*

**sanc|ti|fi|er** (sangk′tə fī′ər), *n.* a person who sanctifies or makes holy.

**sanc|ti|fy** (sangk′tə fī), *v.t.,* **-fied, -fy|ing. 1** to make holy; make legitimate or binding by a religious sanction: *to sanctify a marriage. We will our youth lead on to higher fields, And draw no swords, but what are sanctify'd* (Shakespeare). **2** to set apart as sacred; observe as holy; consecrate: *"Lord, sanctify this our offering to thy use." And God blessed the seventh day, and sanctified it* (Genesis 2:3). **3** to make (a person) free from sin: *He prayed to God to sanctify his heart.* **SYN**: redeem. **4** to make right; justify or sanction: *a custom sanctified by law.* (*Figurative.*) *Does the end sanctify the means?* (W. H. Hudson). [< Latin *sānctificāre* < *sānctus* holy (see etym. under **saint**) + *facere* make]

**sanc|ti|fy|ing|ly** (sangk′tə fī′ing lē), *adv.* in a manner or degree tending to sanctify or make holy.

**sanc|ti|mo|ni|ous** (sangk′tə mō′nē əs), *adj.* **1** making a show of holiness; putting on airs of sanctity: *a sanctimonious hypocrite. The sanctimonious pirate, that went to sea with the ten Commandments, but scraped one out of the Table* (Shakespeare). **SYN**: pharisaic. **2** *Obsolete.* consecrated; sacred; holy. —**sanc′ti|mo′ni|ous-ly,** *adv.* —**sanc′ti|mo′ni|ous|ness,** *n.*

**sanc|ti|mo|ny** (sangk′tə mō′nē), *n.* **1** a show of holiness; affected or hypocritical devoutness; airs of sanctity. **2** *Obsolete.* holiness; sanctity. [< Old French *sainctimonie,* learned borrowing from Latin *sānctimōnia* < *sānctus* holy; see etym. under **saint**]

**sanc|tion** (sangk′shən), *n., v.* —*n.* **1a** permission with authority; support; approval: *We have the sanction of the recreation department to play ball in this park. Plans are also being prepared for the building of nine others, for which all necessary sanctions from various interested authorities have been obtained* (London Times). **SYN**: approbation. **b** *Figurative.* encouragement given to an opinion or practice, as by an influential person or by custom or public opinion: *Religion gave her sanction to that intense and unquenchable animosity* (Macaulay). **2** the act of making legally authoritative or binding; solemn ratification or confirmation: *The day on which the royal sanction was ... solemnly given to this great Act* (Macaulay). **3a** a provision of a law stating a penalty for disobedience to it or a reward for obedience. **b** the penalty or reward. **4** an action by several nations toward another nation, such as a blockade, restrictions on trade, or withholding loans, intended to force it to obey international law: *to apply economic sanctions, rather than to threaten with military ones.* **5** a consideration that leads one to obey a rule of conduct. **6** binding force: *This word* [*honor*] *is often made the sanction of an oath* (Jonathan Swift).

—*v.t.* **1** to approve; allow: *Her conscience does not sanction stealing. The use of a site in Hyde Park, selected by the Prince, was sanctioned by the Government* (Lytton Strachey). **SYN**: authorize. See syn. under **approve. 2** to make valid or binding; confirm.

[< Latin *sānctiō, -ōnis* < *sānctus* holy; see etym. under **saint**] —**sanc′tion|er,** *n.*

**sanc|ti|tude** (sangk′tə tüd), *n.* sanctity; holiness. [< Latin *sānctitūdō* < *sānctus* holy; see etym. under **saint**]

**sanc|ti|ty** (sangk′tə tē), *n., pl.* **-ties. 1** holiness of life; saintliness; godliness: *the sanctity of a saint.* **2** holy character; sacredness: *the sanctity of a church.* (*Figurative.*) *the sanctity of the home. His affirmations have the sanctity of an oath* (Charles Lamb). **SYN**: inviolability.

**sanctities, a** sacred obligations, feelings, or the like: *the sanctities of obedience and faith* (Emerson). **b** sacred things: *the flower of olden sanctities* (Coventry Patmore).

[< Latin *sānctitās* < *sānctus* holy; see etym. under **saint**]

**sanc|tu|a|rize** (sangk′chu̇ ə rīz), *v.t.,* **-rized, -riz-ing.** to shelter by means of a sanctuary or sacred privileges.

**sanc|tu|ar|y** (sangk′chu̇ er′ē), *n., pl.* **-ar|ies. 1** a sacred place; holy spot; place where sacred things are kept. A church is a sanctuary; so was the ancient Hebrew temple at Jerusalem. **2a** the part of a church around the altar. **b** the most sacred part of any place of worship. **c** the sacred place where the Ark of the Covenant was kept in the temple at Jerusalem. **3** a place of refuge or protection: *a wildlife sanctuary.* **4** refuge or protection: *The escaped prisoner found sanctuary in the temple.* (*Figurative.*) *The cabin provided sanctuary from the rain.* [< Latin *sānctuārium* < *sānctus* holy; see etym. under **saint**]

**sanc|tum** (sangk′təm), *n., pl.* **-tums,** (*Rare*) **-ta** (-tə). **1** a sacred place. **2** a private room or office where a person can be undisturbed. **SYN**: study. **3** *Figurative.* anything set apart as sacred. [< Latin *sānctum* originally adjective, neuter of *sānctus* holy; see etym. under **saint**]

**sanc|tum sanc|to|rum** (sangk′təm sangk tôr′-əm, -tōr′-), **1** the holy of holies. **2** an especially private place; inner sanctum (often humorous in use): ... *When she expressed an interest in bebop he had unearthed the inner sanctum sanctorum of that art in Harlem and taken her there* (William Ard). [< Latin *sānctum sānctōrum* < Greek translation of Hebrew *godhesh haqqodhåshim*]

**Sanc|tus** (sangk′təs, sängk′tu̇s), *n.* **1** a hymn beginning "Sanctus, Sanctus, Sanctus" in Latin and "Holy, holy, holy, Lord God of hosts" in English, ending the preface of the Mass or Eucharistic service. **2** a musical setting of this. [< Latin *sānctus* holy; see etym. under **saint** (because it is the first word of the hymn)]

**Sanctus bell,** the bell rung to signal the more solemn portions of the Mass in the Roman Catholic Church, usually first rung at the Sanctus.

**sand** (sand), *n., v., adj.* —*n.* **1** tiny grains of worn-down or disintegrated rock, mainly siliceous, finer than gravel: *the sand of the seashore.* **2a** the sand in an hourglass. **b** a grain of this: (*Figurative.*) *The sands of time are running out for all of us.* **3** *U.S. Slang.* courage; pluck; grit: *She had more sand in her than any girl I ever see* (Mark Twain). **4** a yellowish red.

—*v.t.* **1** to sprinkle with or as if with sand. People used to sand the kitchen floor; they also sanded letters to dry the ink. **2** to spread sand over: *The highway department sanded the icy road.* **3** to scrape, smooth, polish, or clean with sand or sandpaper: *to sand the edges of a piece of wood.* **4** to fill up (a harbor) with sand. **5** to add sand to: *to sand sugar.* **6** to cover with sand; bury under sand.

—*adj.* yellowish-red.

**build on sand,** to have a weak foundation or basis; have little support: *Their ... material wellbeing is built on sand* (Manchester Guardian Weekly).

**run into the sands,** to become bogged down or reach a dead end: *The short novels of this middle period are much better than most of his longer ones, which are likely to start off invitingly but in the second volume to run into the sands* (New Yorker).

**sands, a** a tract or region composed mainly of sand: *the sands of the desert; ... the principal sands in the estuary of the Thames* (Thomas H. Huxley). **b** moments, minutes, or small portions of time (in allusion to the sand in the hourglass for measuring time); lifetime: *Now there were voices in France, too, which called for compromise and reform before the sands ran out* (Newsweek).

[Old English *sand*] —**sand′like′,** *adj.*

**san|dal**[1] (san′dəl), *n., v.,* **-daled, -dal|ing** or (*especially British*) **-dalled, -dal|ling.** —*n.* **1** a kind of shoe made of a sole fastened to the foot by straps: *Our hero proudly strutting along the promenade, shod in sandals, wearing a short sleeved multicoloured shirt ...* (London Times). **2** any one of various kinds of low-cut shoes or slippers. **3** a light, low, rubber overshoe that has no heel.

---

**Pronunciation Key:** hat, āge, cãre, fär; let, ēqual, tėrm; it, īce; hot, ōpen, ôrder; oil, out; cup, pu̇t, rüle; child; long; thin; ᴛʜen; zh, measure; ə represents **a** in about, **e** in taken, **i** in pencil, **o** in lemon, **u** in circus.

—*v.t.* to furnish with sandals.
[< Old French *sandale,* learned borrowing < Latin *sandalium* < Greek *sandálion* (diminutive) < *sándalon*]

**san|dal²** (san′dəl), *n.* = sandalwood. [< Medieval Latin *sandalum* < Greek *sántalon* < Arabic *ṣandal* < Persian *chandal,* ultimately < Sanskrit *candana*]

**san|daled** (san′dəld), *adj.* wearing sandals.

**san|dalled** (san′dəld), *adj. Especially British.* sandaled.

**sandal tree, 1** = white sandalwood. **2** an East Indian evergreen tree of the mahogany family, having edible fruit and a red, close-grained heartwood that takes a fine polish.

**san|dal|wood** (san′dəl wu̇d′), *n.* **1** the fragrant heartwood of certain trees of Asia, especially the white sandalwood. It is a hard, close-grained yellowish wood used for carving, making ornamental boxes and fans, and is also burned as incense. **2** any one of the trees that it comes from. **3** any one of several other trees or their similar wood, especially the red sandalwood, an East Indian tree of the pea family. [< *sandal²* + *wood¹*]

**sandalwood oil,** a fragrant oil extracted from the heartwood and roots of the sandalwood tree, used in incense and perfumes.

**san|da|rac** (san′də rak), *n.* **1** a brittle, pale-yellow, translucent, slightly aromatic resin yielded by the bark of the sandarac tree, used as incense and in making varnish. **2** = sandarac tree. **3** red arsenic sulfide; realgar. [< Latin *sandaraca* < Greek *sandarákē*]

**sandarac tree,** a tree of northwest Africa of the cypress family, whose fragrant, hard wood is much used in building. It is the source of the resin sandarac.

**sand|bag** (sand′bag′), *n., v.,* **-bagged, -bag|ging.** —*n.* **1** a bag filled with sand. Sandbags are used to protect trenches, as ballast on a balloon, and to reinforce a levee or dike. **2** a small bag of sand used as a club.
—*v.t.* **1** to furnish with sandbags: *There was no flood here; nothing had been damaged; no one was sandbagging streets or houses* (Harper's). **2** to hit or stun with a sandbag: (*Figurative.*) *to be sandbagged by creditors,* (*Figurative.*) *sandbagging tactics.* —**sand′bag′ger,** *n.*

**sand bank** (sand′bangk′), *n.* a ridge of sand forming a shoal or hillside: *But many ships have foundered and lives have been lost on what must be one of the best known sandbanks in the world* (New Scientist).

**sand bar,** or **sand|bar** (sand′bär′), *n.* a ridge of sand formed in a river or along a shore by the action of tides or currents: *Many heavily-laden streams deposit sand bars in their channels thus making their courses shallower and rendering them more likely to flood their valleys* (White and Renner).

**sand bath, 1** a receptacle containing hot sand, in which a chemical retort or the like is heated. **2** a therapeutic treatment in which the body is covered with warm sand. **3** the shaking of the body and feathers in sand or dry dirt, a method by which birds clean and rid themselves of lice.

**sand belt, 1** a belt coated with sand or other abrasives, used in wood-polishing, surfacing, and finishing machines. **2** an arid ridge of sand, often extending many miles.

**sand binder,** any plant which serves to bind or fix shifting sands.

**sand|blast** (sand′blast′, -bläst′), *n., v.* —*n.* **1** a blast of air or steam containing sand, used to clean, grind, cut, or decorate hard surfaces, such as glass, stone, or metal. **2** the apparatus used to apply such a blast. A sandblast is often used in cleaning the outside of buildings faced with stone.
—*v.t., v.i.* to use a sandblast on; clean, grind, cut, or decorate by a sandblast: *The accumulated grime was removed by sandblasting* (New York Times).

**sand|blast|er** (sand′blas′tər), *n.* **1** a person who sandblasts. **2** an apparatus that sandblasts.

**sand-blind** (sand′blīnd′), *adj. Archaic.* half-blind; dim-sighted; purblind. [perhaps alteration of unrecorded Old English *samblind* < *sām-* part, half + *blind* blind] —**sand′-blind′ness,** *n.*

**sand|box** (sand′boks′), *n.* **1** a box for holding sand, especially for children to play in. **2** a place in a locomotive to hold sand for use when the wheels slip. **3** = sandbox tree.

**sandbox tree,** a tropical American tree of the spurge family, whose fruit (a woody capsule) bursts with a sharp report when ripe and dry, scattering the seeds.

**sand|boy** (sand′boi′), *n. British Informal.* **as happy (jolly, merry,** or the like) **as a sandboy,** completely happy; very glad or cheerful: *"Happy as a sandboy" about my deposit account* (London Times).

**sand|bur** or **sand|burr** (sand′bėr′), *n.* **1** any one of various weeds growing in sandy or waste places and bearing a small, burlike fruit. **2** = bur grass.

**sand-cast** (sand′kast′, -käst′), *v.t., v.i.,* **-cast, -cast|ing.** to cast (metal) by pouring it in a sand mold.

**sand-cast|ing** (sand′kas′ting, -käs′-), *n.* **1** the process of making a casting by pouring metal in a sand mold. **2** the casting so made.

**sand cherry,** a shrub bearing small, bitter, black cherries, that grows on the sand dunes of the Great Lakes and in sandy areas elsewhere in the Middle West and Canada.

**sand clock,** = sandglass: *One child turned over the sand clock, another struck the ship's bell* (New Scientist).

**sand cone,** a low, conical projection of glacial ice the rapid melting of which is prevented by a covering of sand.

**sand crab,** any terrestrial American crab of a group living in burrows high up on sandy beaches; beach crab.

**sand crack,** a disease that causes cracks in the wall of a horse's hoof, often resulting in lameness.

**sand|cul|ture** (sand′kul′chər), *n.* a method of growing plants in wet sand, nutrients and moisture being supplied by means of regular feeding with a weak solution of the necessary chemicals.

**sand dab,** = flatfish.

**san|dek** (sän′dek), *n.* the person who holds a Jewish infant during the ceremony of circumcision and acts the part of a godfather. [< Yiddish *sandik* < Hebrew *sandīqōs*]

***sand dollar,** any one of certain small, flat, round sea urchins that live on sandy bottoms of coastal waters from New England to Brazil, from California to Japan, and along eastern Africa. *Heart urchins and sand dollars, lying in saturated sand, keep on sorting out bits of food* (New Yorker). [because its shape resembles that of a silver dollar]

***sand dollar**

living sand dollar

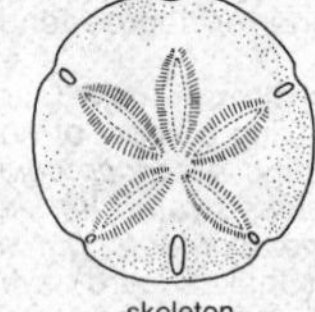
skeleton

**sand dune,** = dune.

**sand|ed** (san′did), *adj.* **1** covered or sprinkled with sand: *a sanded floor.* **2** adulterated with sand: *sanded sugar.* **3** *Obsolete.* of a sandy color.

**sand eel,** = sand launce.

**sand|er** (san′dər), *n.* **1** a person or apparatus that sands: *a road sander.* **2** a person or apparatus that sandpapers: *a floor sander.*

**sand|er|ling** (san′dər ling), *n.* a small, gray and white shore bird of worldwide distribution, which follows the retreating waves along beaches in search of food.

**sand|fish** (sand′fish′), *n., pl.* **-fish|es** or (*collectively*) **-fish. 1** any scaleless fish of a small family of the northern Pacific with oddly fringed lips. They commonly bury themselves in the ocean bottom with only their head exposed. **2** a small edible sea bass of Atlantic waters with a striped gray or tan body.

**sand flea, 1** any flea found in sandy places. **2** = chigoe. **3** = beach flea.

**sand fly, 1** a small, bloodsucking, two-winged fly that transmits certain diseases, such as kala-azar. **2** any one of certain similar flies.

**sand|glass** (sand′glas′, -gläs′), *n.* a device for measuring time by the flow of sand from one glass enclosure to another, especially an hourglass.

**sand grass,** any grass that grows on sandy soil, as by the seashore.

**sand-grop|er** (sand′grō′pər), *n. Australian Slang.* a native of Western Australia. [< *sand* + *groper* (because the original settlers were gold prospectors)]

**sand grouse,** any bird of a family, similar to a pigeon, found in sandy regions of southern Europe, western Asia, and northern Africa.

**san|dhi** (san′dē, sän′-), *n.* the changes or differences in speech sounds, stress, or juncture that may occur when a word or phrase is used as part of a construction rather than spoken independently. The assimilation of sounds in the constructions *I'm ready, He's got it,* and *That'll do* are examples of sandhi. [< Sanskrit *saṁdhi* a placing together]

**sandhi form,** *Phonetics.* the form of a word or phrase used within a construction when it differs from the form used independently. The sentence *It's raining* has the sandhi form *'s* rather than the absolute form *is.*

**sand hill,** a hill or bank of sand; dune.

**sand|hill crane** (sand′hil′), a crane of North America with gray plumage and a bare, red forehead, that stands about four feet tall.

**sand|hog** (sand′hog′, -hôg′), *n. U.S.* a person who works under air pressure much higher than that of the atmosphere either underground, as in a boring for a tunnel, or underwater, as in a caisson.

**sand hopper,** a small crustacean found along beaches; beach flea.

**sand|i|ness** (san′dē nis), *n.* sandy character: *the sandiness of the soil.*

**San|di|nis|ta** (san′də nēs′tə), *n.* a member of a guerrilla organization of Nicaragua: *In October the Sandinistas ... launched a major offensive with the declared intention of overthrowing the Somoza regime and establishing a broadly based democracy* (Henry Webb, Jr.). [< Spanish *Sandinista* < Augusto César *Sandino,* Nicaraguan nationalist leader murdered in 1933 + *-ista* -ist]

**san|di|ver** (san′də vər), *n.* a scum that rises upon melted glass in the furnace. [Middle English *sandyver* < Old French *suin de verre; suin* suint, *de* of, *verre* glass]

**sand jack,** a device for lowering into place a heavy weight, such as the span of a bridge, by having it supported on sand which can be allowed to run out as desired.

**sand launce** or **lance,** any one of various small, elongate, marine fishes which burrow into the sand along beaches when the tide goes out; sand eel. [< *sand* + *launce,* variant of *lance* (because of its shape)]

**sand leaf,** one of the lowest, poor leaves on a tobacco plant, small and often sandy.

**sand|less** (sand′lis), *adj.* having little or no sand: *a sandless desert.*

**sand lily,** a low, stemless, white-flowered plant of the lily family, found in the western United States.

**sand|ling** (sand′ling), *n.* = sanderling.

**sand lizard,** a common European lizard found in sandy areas.

**sand|lot** (sand′lot′), *adj. U.S.* of or having to do with games, especially baseball, played between informally organized teams, as on undeveloped city lots and small fields: *a sandlot second baseman.*

**sand|lot|ter** (sand′lot′ər), *n. U.S.* a person who plays sandlot baseball or, sometimes, some other informally arranged team sport.

**sand|man** (sand′man′), *n.* a fabled man who is said to make children sleepy by sprinkling sand on their eyes. [< *sand* + *man.* Compare German *Sandmann.*]

**sand martin,** = bank swallow.

**sand mole, 1** a large South African mole rat that burrows in the sand. **2** a smaller related species of South Africa, very troublesome in gardens.

**sand painter,** a person who makes sand paintings.

**sand painting,** a design made by pouring various colored sands, powdered rock, charcoal, or other granules, on a flat, sandy surface; dry painting. Sand paintings are used by some American Indian tribes in healing ceremonies and other rituals. *Taken together, the Navaho sand paintings are symbolic of an enormously complex myth cycle, recounting the creation of the universe, the preparation of the world for habitation by man, and the origins of most rituals and ceremonies* (Beals and Hoijer).

**sand|pa|per** (sand′pā′pər), *n., v.* —*n.* a strong paper with a layer of sand or similar substance that rubs and scrapes glued on one side, used for smoothing, cleaning, or polishing, especially wood.
—*v.t.* to smooth, clean, or polish with sandpaper.

**sand|pa|per|y** (sand′pā′pər ē), *adj.* like sandpaper; rough; grating: [*His*] *sandpapery tones and aptitude on the stage made him a Ko-Ko in the true ... tradition* (London Times).

**sand pear,** a variety of pear native to China, with rough, gritty fruit.

**sand|pile** (sand′pīl′), *n.* a pile of sand for small children to play in.

**sand pine,** a small pine growing in sandy areas of Florida west to Alabama.

**sand|pip|er** (sand′pī′pər), *n.* a small shore bird with a long bill, living on sandy shores. It is related to the plovers. The common sandpiper of Europe and the spotted sandpiper of North America are two kinds.

**sand|pit** (sand′pit′), *n.* **1** a pit from which sand is excavated: *I stood on the rim of a great saucer-shaped sandpit the other day* (Manchester Guardian Weekly). **2** *British.* a sandbox for children: *She said swings were no longer enough, and regretted that in Birmingham water and sandpits were not allowed* (London Times).

**sand plain**, a small sandy plain, usually a flat-topped hill originally formed as a delta by water running out of a glacier.

**sand|plov|er** (sand′pluv′ər, -plō′vər), *n., pl.* **-ers** or (*collectively*) **-er.** a ringed plover or ringneck that frequents sandy beaches: *Sandplovers were breed ing 2,000 miles outside their known range* (London Times).

**sand rat, 1** a pocket gopher found in sandy areas on the western coast of North America. **2** any one of several rodents found in sandy areas, such as the gerbil.

**sand reef**, a strip of low, sandy land, or barrier beach, built by the action of waves on a shallow sea floor not far from the coast and often enclosing a narrow lagoon.

**sand ripple**, alternate ridge and hollow formed in sand through the influence of waves, wind, or currents.

**sands** (sandz), *n.pl.* See under **sand**.

**S. and s.c.**, sized and supercalendered.

**sand sea**, a large stretch of desert consisting of barchans: *A sand sea, with small crescentic dunes* [*that*] *migrate as entities across the desert floor* (Robert M. Garrels).

**sand shark**, a variety of shark common along the Atlantic coast, which attains a length of almost eleven feet but is not known to attack humans.

**sand sink**, a method of removing oil spilled at sea by spraying the oil with a mixture of chemically treated sand and water which sticks to the oil causing it to sink.

**sand smelt**, a silversides, especially a common British species.

**sand|soap** (sand′sōp′), *n.* a soap mixed with fine sand, used to remove roughness and stains in washing.

**sand-spit** (sand′spit′), *n.* a low, sandy area jutting out into a lake or sea: *Many Northerners maintain palatial winter homes on this sand-spit 70 miles north of Miami Beach* (Wall Street Journal).

**sand|spout** (sand′spout′), *n.* a pillar of sand similar to a waterspout, produced by a whirlwind, as on a desert.

**sand star, 1** = starfish. **2** = ophiuran.

**sand|stone** (sand′stōn′), *n.* a kind of sedimentary rock formed mostly of sand, the grains being held together by a natural cement of silica, calcite, iron oxide, or the like. *Before the use of Portland cement and reinforced concrete, sandstone was widely used to build large buildings* (Richard M. Pearl).

**sand|storm** (sand′stôrm′), *n.* a storm of wind that carries along clouds of sand: *The latest explosion had come in Jordan with the suddenness of a desert sandstorm* (Newsweek).

**sand sucker, 1** a pump that removes wet sand, silt, or mud from an area: *Both expeditions made feverish plans to go after the copper lode with sand suckers and . . . power shovels* (Newsweek). **2** = flatfish.

**sand table**, a table with a rim, on which sand is spread for children's play or for modeling terrain for military study, projected land use, or engineering problems: *At three or four; the children go to a preprimary school, where they learn to run, hop, skip, play at sand tables, and even fingerpaint* (Time).

**sand trap**, a shallow pit filled with sand on a golf course, usually near a green and serving as a hazard: *Great Britain's Prime Minister Harold Macmillan* (*in the low 80s*) *. . . can be reduced to hopeless and despairing silence when three tries fail to get him out of a sand trap* (Newsweek). See picture under **golf course**.

**sand tube**, a tube of fused or sintered sand which has been melted together along the path of a stroke of lightning.

**san|dun|ga** (sän düng′gä), *n.* a Mexican folk dance in which couples face each other in two lines and each woman dances before her partner, who follows her around. [< Mexican Spanish *sandunga*, probably related to colloquial Spanish *sandunga* gracefulness]

**sand verbena**, any one of a group of low herbs of the four-o'clock family with verbenalike flowers, found in western North America.

**sand-vine** (sand′vīn′), *n.* a vine of the milkweed family growing in the southeastern United States, having deeply cordate, ovate leaves, small whitish flowers in axillary cymes, and large follicles.

**sand viper, 1** = hognose. **2** = horned viper.

**sand wasp**, a solitary wasp that nests in the sand.

**sand wedge**, a special golf club used for hitting out of sand traps: *He pulled out his sand wedge, swung— and blasted the ball straight into the cup* (Time).

**sand|wich** (sand′wich), *n., v.* **—*n.* 1** two or more slices of bread with meat, jelly, cheese, or some other filling between them. **2** *Figurative: When used as the outer leaf of an insulating sandwich, it provides a membrane which gives fairly good control of light and heat* (Scientific American).
**—*v.t.* 1** to put or squeeze in (between): *He was sandwiched between two fat women.* [*He*] *also lived in Paris from around 1924 to 1927, but . . . this visit was sandwiched between visits to his native Japan* (New Yorker). **2** to put in a sandwich.
[< John Montagu, the fourth Earl of *Sandwich*, 1718-1792, supposedly the inventor]

**sandwich bar**, a restaurant specializing in sandwiches, usually served at a counter.

***sandwich board**, a board carried by a sandwich man.

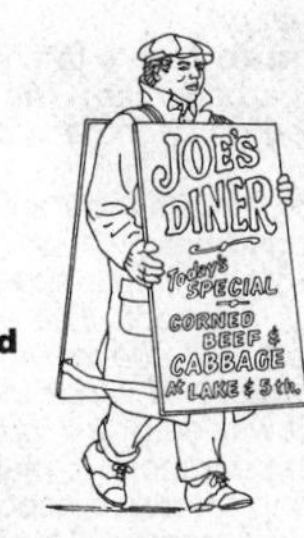


***sandwich board**

**sandwich coin**, a coin made of layers of metal bonded together; clad coin.

**sandwich course**, *British.* a course in an industrial school that combines classroom study with practical experience in factories: *"Sandwich" courses— alternate periods of industrial and academic study— are being run in co-operation with technical colleges* (Punch).

**Sandwich glass**, glassware manufactured by the Boston and Sandwich Glass Company at Sandwich, Massachusetts, from 1825 to 1888. Sandwich glass often has elaborate designs to give a complex, lacelike effect.

**sandwich man**, a man carrying two advertising boards hung from his shoulders, one before him and one behind: *Walking on rosy clouds, he passed a sandwich man who handed him an advertising circular* (Time).

**sandwich panel**, a panel used in construction, made by bonding together several layers of material, such as aluminum, steel, or plastic, so that one layer is sandwiched between two other layers: *Built of aluminum sandwich panels, it would weigh about half as much as a comparable conventional car* (Wall Street Journal).

**sand|worm** (sand′wėrm′), *n.* = lugworm.

**sand|wort** (sand′wėrt′), *n.* any one of a genus of low, scrubby herbs of the pink family that grow in sandy soil and bear very small, white flowers.

**sand|y** (san′dē), *adj.,* **sand|i|er, sand|i|est. 1** containing sand; consisting of sand: *sandy soil.* **2** covered with sand: *Most of the shore is rocky, but there is a sandy beach.* **3a** yellowish-red: *She has sandy hair.* **b** having such hair: *The ladies Fitz-Warene were sandy girls* (Benjamin Disraeli). **4** *Figurative.* shifting like sand; not stable: *But mark how sandy is your own pretence* (John Dryden).

**sand yacht**, a vehicle on three wheels with a mast and small sails, for racing before the wind on a beach or other sandy area; land yacht: *The first attempt to cross the Sahara by sand yacht ended in success . . . when eight of the fragile craft arrived at the finish line* (New York Times).

**sand yachting**, the sport of racing with a sand yacht.

**sand yachtsman**, a person who engages in sand yachting.

**sane** (sān), *adj.,* **san|er, san|est. 1a** having a healthy mind; not crazy; sound: *Their doctrine could be held by no sane man* (Robert Browning). **b** not diseased or disordered: *a sane mind.* **2a** having or showing good sense or sound judgment; sensible: *She has a sane attitude toward driving and never goes too fast.* **b** regulated by reason; rational: *It is the American woman who is primarily responsible for the safe and sane Fourth* [*of July*] (Edward Bok). [< Lātin *sānus* healthy] **—sane′ly,** *adv.* **—sane′ness,** *n.*

**SANE** (sān), *n.* National Committee for a Sane Nuclear Policy.

**San|for|ize** (san′fə rīz), *v.t.,* **-ized, -iz|ing.** *Trademark.* to shrink (cotton, linen, or rayon fabric) by a patented process before it is made into a garment, that is then guaranteed a maximum shrinkage of one per cent. [American English < *Sanfor*(d) L. Cluett, born 1874, the inventor + *-ize*]

**San Fran|cis|can** (san′ fran sis′kən), a native or inhabitant of San Francisco, California.

**sang** (sang), *v.* the past tense of **sing:** *The bird sang for us yesterday.*

**Sang|a|mon** (sang′ə mən), *adj. Geology.* of or having to do with the third interglacial stage in the topographical development of North America, beginning about 175,000 years ago. [< *Sangamon*, a river in Illinois]

**san|gar** (sung′gər), *n.* a breastwork of stone. Also, **sungar.** [< Hindustani *sangar*]

**san|ga|ree** (sang′gə rē′), *n.* a tropical drink consisting of wine (usually red), water, sugar, spice, and sometimes brandy. [< Spanish *sangría* (literally) bleeding (because of its color) < *sangre* blood < Latin *sanguīs*]

**säng|er|bund** (zeng′ər bùnt), *n.* a German male singing society. [< German *Sängerbund* < *Sänger* (literally) singers + *Bund* group, federation]

**säng|er|fest** (zeng′ər fest), *n.* a German song festival, especially a gathering of German singing societies for competition: *The town's newest, and just about its best, triad, are half in earnest, half in fun during their up-tempo sängerfest* (New Yorker). [< German *Sängerfest* < *Sänger* (literally) singers + *Fest* festival, festivities]

**sang-froid** or **sang|froid** (sän frwá′), *n.* coolness of mind; calmness; composure: *The Canadian bush pilots, on the other hand, tended to call it "pretty much routine, so long as you look where you are going"— a view which may be an overemphasis of their professional sangfroid* (Harper's). **SYN:** equanimity, imperturbability. [< French *sang froid* (literally) cold blood, ultimately < Latin *sanguīs* blood, *frīgidus* frigid]

**san|gha** (sang′gə), *n.* the Buddhist monastic community; Buddhist monks and nuns collectively: . . . *the hundred thousand monks who wear the saffron robe of the Buddhist sangha* (Atlantic). [< Sanskrit *sangha*]

**San|go** (säng′gō), *n.* a Niger-Congo language spoken in the Central African Empire, Chad, Gabon, and adjacent areas.

**San|graal** (sang grāl′), *n.* = Holy Grail. [< Old French *Saint Graal; Saint* holy (see etym. under **saint**), *Graal* Grail]

**San|gre|al** (sang′grē əl), *n.* = Holy Grail.

**san|gri|a** or **san|grí|a** (sang grē′ə), *n.* a Spanish drink made of red or white wine mixed with fruit juice and club soda or water, and often fruit slices: *Along with the flamenco comes sangria* (Atlantic). [< Spanish *sangria* < *sangre* blood]

**san|guic|o|lous** (sang gwik′ə ləs), *adj.* inhabiting the blood, as a parasite. [< Latin *sanguīs* blood + *colere* inhabit + English *-ous*]

**san|guif|er|ous** (sang gwif′ər əs), *adj.* bearing or conveying blood, as a vein. [< Latin *sanguīs* blood + English *-ferous*]

**san|gui|fi|ca|tion** (sang′gwə fə kā′shən), *n.* the production of blood.

**san|gui|mo|tor** (sang′gwə mō′tər), *adj.* of or having to do with the circulation of the blood. [< Latin *sanguis* blood + *mōtor* mover]

**san|gui|nar|i|a** (sang′gwə när′ē ə), *n.* = bloodroot. [American English < New Latin *sanguinaria* (because of its color) < Latin (*herba*) *sanguināria*, (originally) a kind of plant, probably polygonum; (literally) (herb) for stanching blood < *sanguīs, -inis* blood]

**san|gui|nar|i|ly** (sang′gwə ner′ə lē), *adv.* in a sanguinary manner; bloodthirstily.

**san|guin|a|rine** (sang gwin′ə rēn), *n.* an alkaloid obtained from the roots of the sanguinaria. *Formula:* $C_{20}H_{15}NO_5$

**san|gui|nar|i|ness** (sang′gwə ner′ē nis), *n.* sanguinary quality; bloodthirsty disposition.

**san|gui|nar|y** (sang′gwə ner′ē), *adj.* **1** with much blood or bloodshed; bloody: *a sanguinary battle. We may not propagate Religion by wars or by sanguinary persecutions to force consciences* (Francis Bacon). **2** delighting in bloodshed; bloodthirsty: *a sanguinary rebel. The sanguinary and ferocious conversation of his captor— the list of slain that his arm had sent to their long account . . . made him tremble* (G. P. R. James). **3** imposing the death penalty freely; *sanguinary laws.* **4** of blood. [< Latin *sanguinārius* < *sanguīs, -inis* blood]

**san|guine** (sang′gwin), *adj., n.* **—*adj.* 1** naturally cheerful and hopeful: *a sanguine disposition. The invincible hopefulness of his sanguine temperament had now got Mr. Britling well out of the pessimistic pit again* (H. G. Wells). **SYN:** optimistic. **2** confident; hopeful: *sanguine of success. I was not too sanguine of seeing an epic when I took my seat in the Garden on the night of the fight* (New Yorker). **SYN:** optimistic. **3** having a healthy red color; ruddy: *a sanguine complexion.* **4** (in ancient and medieval physiology) having blood as the predominant humor, indicated by a ruddy complexion and a cheerful and ardent disposi-

**Pronunciation Key:** hat, āge, cãre, fär; let, ēqual, tėrm; it, īce; hot, ōpen, ôrder; **oi**l, **ou**t; cup, pu̇t, rüle; **ch**ild; lo**ng**; **th**in; **ᴛʜ**en; **zh**, measure; **ə** represents **a** in about, **e** in taken, **i** in pencil, **o** in lemon, **u** in circus.

tion. 5 = sanguinary.
— *n.* 1 *Heraldry.* the blood-red color in coats of arms, in engravings represented by intersecting diagonal lines; murrey. 2a a crayon colored red with iron oxide. b a drawing executed with red chalks.
[< Middle French *sanguin,* learned borrowing from Latin *sanguineus* < *sanguīs, -inis* blood]
— **san′guine|ly,** *adv.* — **san′guine|ness,** *n.*

**san|guin|e|ous** (sang gwin′ē əs), *adj.* 1 of blood; like blood; bloody. 2 red like blood. 3 abounding with blood; full-blooded. 4 sanguine; hopeful. 5 bloodthirsty; sanguinary: *His passion, cruel grown, took on a hue fierce and sanguineous* (Keats).

**san|guin|i|ty** (sang gwin′ə tē), *n.* 1 the quality of being sanguine: *But I distrust your sanguinity* (Jonathan Swift). 2 = consanguinity.

**san|guin|o|lent** (sang gwin′ə lənt), *adj.* = bloody. [< Middle French *sanguinolent,* learned borrowing from Latin *sanguinolentus* < *sanguīs, -inis* blood + *-olentus* full of]

**san|guiv|o|rous** (sang gwiv′ər əs), *adj.* feeding on blood. [< Latin *sanguīs* blood + Latin *vorāre* to devour + English *-ous*]

**San|he|drim** (san′hi drim), *n.* = Sanhedrin.

**San|he|drin** (san′hi drin), *n.* 1 Also, **Great Sanhedrin.** the supreme council and highest religious and legal authority of the ancient Jewish nation, consisting of 70 members. 2 a lower court of justice, of 23 members, with lesser or local jurisdiction. [< Hebrew *sanhedrīn* < Greek *synédrion* council, (literally) a sitting together < *syn-* together + *hédra* a seat]

**san|i|cle** (san′ə kəl), *n.* any herb of a group of the parsley family, once credited with great medicinal value; selfheal. [< Old French *sanicle,* learned borrowing from Medieval Latin *sanicula,* perhaps < Latin *sānus* healthy]

**san|i|dine** (san′ə dēn), *n.* a glassy form of orthoclase occurring in volcanic rocks. [< Greek *sanís, -idos* plank + English *-in* (because of its flat crystals)]

**sa|ni|es** (sā′nē ēz), *n.* a thin, greenish fluid containing pus mixed with serum or blood, discharged, as from ulcers or wounds. [< Latin *saniēs* diseased blood]

**san|i|fi|ca|tion** (san′ə fə kā′shən), *n.* the process of rendering sanitary; the putting and keeping (something) in a sanitary condition.

**san|i|fy** (san′ə fī), *v.t.,* **-fied, -fy|ing.** to make healthy; improve the sanitary conditions of (a city or other place). [< Latin *sānus* healthy + English *-fy*]

**sa|ni|ous** (sā′nē əs), *adj.* of, consisting of, or discharging sanies. [< Latin *saniōsus* < *saniēs* sanies]

**san|i|tar|i|an** (san′ə tãr′ē ən), *n., adj.* — *n.* a person who studies sanitation or favors sanitary reform.
— *adj.* = sanitary.

**san|i|tar|i|ly** (san′ə ter′ə lē), *adv.* as regards health or its preservation.

**san|i|tar|i|ness** (san′ə ter′ē nis), *n.* the state or condition of being sanitary.

**san|i|tar|i|um** (san′ə tãr′ē əm), *n., pl.* **-i|ums, -i|a** (-ē ə). 1 a place, especially in a good climate, for treatment of the sick or those recovering from illness. Those suffering from a long, slow disease like tuberculosis often go to sanitariums. *Once these were the houses of the rich; today they are sanitaria for the proletariat* (John Gunther). 2 = health resort. Also, **sanatorium.** [< Latin *sānitas* health (< *sānus* healthy) + *-ārium* place for]

**san|i|tar|y** (san′ə ter′ē), *adj., n., pl.* **-tar|ies.**
— *adj.* 1a of or having to do with health: *sanitary regulations in a hospital. He worked to improve the sanitary conditions of slums.* b favorable to health; preventing disease; healthful: *sanitary soap, sanitary gloves. Sanitary landfill is defined ... as a method of disposing of refuse on land without creating nuisances or hazards to public health* (Richard D. Vaughan). SYN: hygienic. 2 free from dirt and filth: *Food should be kept in a sanitary place.*
— *n.* a public toilet or urinal.
[< French *sanitaire* < Latin *sānitās* (< *sānus* healthy) + French *-aire* -ary]

**sanitary belt,** a belt or band, usually elastic, for holding a sanitary napkin in place.

**sanitary cordon,** = cordon sanitaire.

**sanitary engineering,** a branch of engineering dealing with water supply and sewage systems, and air pollution and radiation controls, as in the construction of dams, pipelines, incinerators, and the like.

**sanitary napkin,** a soft, absorbent pad used to absorb the uterine discharge during menstruation.

**sanitary ware,** coarse glazed earthenware used for drainage, sewer pipes, and lavatory fittings.

**san|i|tate** (san′ə tāt), *v.,* **-tat|ed, -tat|ing.** — *v.t.* to subject to sanitation; make sanitary: *It seems incomprehensible that man can progress very far in sanitating the lowlands against malaria because of the staggering cost* (White and Renner).
— *v.i.* to introduce sanitation. [back formation < *sanitation*]

**san|i|ta|tion** (san′ə tā′shən), *n.* the act, fact, or process of working out ways to improve health conditions; practical application of sanitary measures: *When people gathered together and built large cities, many problems were raised concerning a proper water supply, a safe food supply, disposal of garbage and human wastes, keeping the city clean, and preventing the spread of disease. Most of these problems are related to sanitation* (Beauchamp, Mayfield, and West). [< *sanit*(ary) + *-ation*]

**san|i|ta|tion|man** (san′ə tā′shən mən), *n., pl.* **men.** *U.S.* a garbageman: *The sanitationmen left, emptying three garbage cans on their way out* (New Yorker).

**san|i|ti|za|tion** (san′ə tə zā′shən), *n.* the act or process of sanitizing.

**san|i|tize** (san′ə tīz), *v.t.,* **-tized, -tiz|ing.** 1 to make sanitary; disinfect: *The unit is intended to keep the water well above 145 degrees, "the lowest temperature at which clothes still could be sanitized"* (Newsweek). 2 *Figurative.* to give a wholesome appearance to; make more acceptable by removing offensive aspects or elements: *The House Un-American Activities Committee has tried to sanitize its image. It changed its name to the House Internal Security Committee in 1969 and made abortive attempts to revive its lost vigor* (Time).

**san|i|tiz|er** (san′ə tī′zər), *n.* a sanitizing substance or product: *We are also concerned with the hygiene of the operators and machinery in the factory, and we test manufacturers' claims for sanitizers* (New Scientist).

**san|i|ty** (san′ə tē), *n.* 1 soundness of mind; mental health: *His sanity was in question once they found out he was the one going around starting fires.* 2 soundness of judgment; sensibleness; reasonableness: *Many people question the sanity of huge amounts of money spent for defense.* [< Latin *sānitās* < *sānus* healthy]

**San Ja|cin|to Day** (san jə sin′tō), April 21, a legal holiday in Texas commemorating the Battle of San Jacinto, in which General Sam Houston defeated the Mexican Army in 1836.

**san|jak** (san′jak), *n.* a former Turkish administrative district, a subdivision of a vilayet. [< Turkish *sancak* (literally) flag]

**San Jo|se scale** (san hō zā′), a scale insect very injurious especially to fruit trees and shrubs, first discovered in the United States at San Jose, California.

**sank** (sangk), *v.* the past tense of **sink:** *The ship sank in forty fathoms of water.*

**San|khya** (säng′kyə), *n.* one of the six principal systems of Hindu philosophy, based on the dualism of spirit and matter, with the latter deriving from the former. [< Sanskrit *sāṁkhya*]

**san|nup** (san′up), *n.* a married man among North American Indians. [American English < Algonkian (Penobscot, Passamaquoddy) *sana$^{n}$ba, seena$^{n}$be* man]

**sann|ya|si** (sun yä′sē), *n.* a Hindu hermit or holy man who lives from alms. [< Hindi *sannyāsī* < Sanskrit *sannyāsin* casting away]

**sann|ya|sin** (sun yä′sin), *n.* = sannyasi.

**S-A node,** = sinoatrial node.

**sans**[1] (sanz; *French* säɴ), *prep.* without: *a wallet sans cash, to print a letter sans comment; ... sans teeth, sans eyes, sans taste, sans everything* (Shakespeare). [< Old French *sans* < Latin *absentiā,* ablative, in the absence (of) < *abesse* to be away; Old French influenced by Latin *sine* without]

**sans**[2] (sanz), *n.* = sans-serif.

**Sans.,** Sanskrit.

**san|sa** (san′sə), *n.* an African musical instrument consisting of a wooden box having at the top tongues of bamboo or iron which the performer vibrates with his thumbs. Also, **zanza.** [< Arabic *ṣinj* cymbals]

**San|scrit** (san′skrit), *n., adj.* = Sanskrit.

**sans-cu|lotte** (sanz′kyů lot′), *n.* 1 a contemptuous term used during the French Revolution for a republican of the poorer classes in Paris, adopted by the revolutionists as a designation of honor. 2 any extreme republican or revolutionary: *The scientists of today ... are the sans-culottes of a second scientific revolution in which the prime methods of the laboratory are being conquered by a new and more thoroughgoing empiricism* (Scientific American).
[< French *sansculotte* (literally) without knee breeches (because the republicans substituted pantaloons for knee breeches); *sans* without, *culotte* knee breeches. Compare etym. under **culottes.**]

**sans-cu|lot|te|rie** (sanz′kyů lot′ə rē), *n.* = sansculottism.

**sans-cu|lot|tic** (sanz′kyů lot′ik), *adj.* of the sans-culottes or sans-culottism.

**sans-cu|lot|tid** (sanz′kyů lot′id), *n.* = sans-culottide.

**sans-cu|lot|tide** (sanz′kyů lot′id; *French* säɴ kü-lô tēd′), *n.* (in the French Revolutionary calendar) one of the 5 (in leap year 6) complementary days resulting from the division of the year into 12 months of 30 days each. They were added as festival days at the end of the month Fructidor. [< French *sans-culottide* < *sans-culotte* sans-culotte]

**sans-cu|lot|tish** (sanz′kyů lot′ish), *adj.* = sans-culottic.

**sans-cu|lot|tism** (sanz′kyů lot′iz əm), *n.* the principles or practices of sans-culottes.

**sans doute** (säɴ düt′), *French.* without doubt; beyond question.

**San|sei** or **san|sei** (sän′sā′), *n., pl.* **-sei** or **-seis.** a native-born American or Canadian citizen whose grandparents were Japanese immigrants: *The Nisei and their Sansei children have rapidly adopted American ways of life* (Felix M. Keesing). [< Japanese *san* third + *sei* generation]

**san|se|vie|ri|a** (san′sə vir′ē ə), *n.* any one of a group of Asiatic and African herbs of the agave family, various species of which are grown for their mottled, sword-shaped leaves; bowstring hemp. [< New Latin *Sansevieria* the genus name < the Prince of *Sanseviero,* 1710-1771, an Italian patron of learning]

**sans gêne** (säɴ zhen′), *French.* without constraint or embarrassment; without ceremony; free and easy: ... *a love affair with a beautiful waif who is also decidedly sans gêne* (Atlantic).

**Sansk.,** Sanskrit.

***San|skrit** (san′skrit), *n., adj.* — *n.* 1 the ancient sacred and literary language of India. It is of importance in the study of Indo-European: *Sanskrit is of great interest to linguists because of the ... stimulus which the introduction of Sanskrit to Western scholarship gave to the development of modern linguistic science* (H. A. Gleason, Jr.). 2 the classical literary form of this language, as distinguished from the earlier Vedic.
— *adj.* of or having to do with Sanskrit; Sanskritic. Also, **Sanscrit.** [< Sanskrit *saṁskṛta* prepared, cultivated (applied to the literary language as contrasted with the vernacular language). Compare etym. under **Prakrit.**]

***Sanskrit** definition 1

किं करोमि

What shall I do?

**San|skrit|ic** (san skrit′ik), *adj., n.* — *adj.* having to do with, derived from, or resembling Sanskrit: *The Sanskritic languages include Hindi, Urdu, and related languages.*
— *n.* the group of languages derived from Sanskrit.

**San|skrit|ist** (san′skrit ist), *n.* an expert in Sanskrit language or literature.

**San|skrit|i|za|tion** (san′skrit ə zā′shən), *n.* 1a the act or process of Sanskritizing. b the fact or result of being Sanskritized. 2 the adoption of the customs, attitudes, and status symbols of a Hindu upper caste by a caste below it: *There is still a hierarchy, but castes can make their way upward within it by ... Sanskritization* (London Times).

**San|skrit|ize** (san′skrit īz), *v.t.,* **-ized, -iz|ing.** 1 to translate into Sanskrit. 2 to render similar to Sanskrit; modify by Sanskritic influences.

**sans pa|reil** (säɴ pà re′yə), *French.* 1 unequaled. 2 (literally) without equal.

**sans peur et sans re|proche** (säɴ pœr′ ā säɴ rə prôsh′), *French.* without fear and without reproach; fearless and blameless.

***sans-ser|if** (sanz′ser′if), *n.,* or **sans serif,** *Printing.* any one of various styles of type without serifs: *The type was a very readable sans-serif, all upper case* (Atlantic). [< French *sans* without (< Old French; see etym. under **sans**) + English *serif*]

***sans-serif**

**The World Book Dictionary**

**sans sou|ci** (säɴ sü sē′), *French.* without care or worry.

**San|ta**[1] (san′tə), *n.* = Santa Claus. [American English, short for *Santa Claus*]

**San|ta**[2] (san′tə, sän′tä), *adj.* a Spanish or an Italian word meaning *holy* or *saint,* used in combinations, as in *Santa Maria, Santa Lucia.* [< Spanish, or Italian *santa,* feminine of *santo* < Latin *sānctus* holy. Compare etym. under **saint**]

**San|ta An|a** (san′tə an′ə), a strong, hot, dry wind occurring in southern California usually in the winter: *Santa Anas are not strangers to the Los Angeles area* (Time). [< *Santa Ana,* a city and mountain range in southern California]

**San|ta Bar|bar|a** (san′tə bär′bər ə), **1** a variety of English walnut grown along the coastal plains and the valleys of southern California. **2** its edible nut. [< *Santa Barbara,* coastal city and chain of islands in southwestern California]

**San|ta Claus** (san′tə klôz′), Saint Nicholas, the saint of Christmas giving. He is pictured as a fat, jolly old man with a white beard, dressed in a fur-trimmed red suit. [American English < dialectal Dutch *Sante Klaas* Saint Nicholas, a bishop of Asia Minor who lived in the 300's A.D. and a patron saint especially of children]

**San|ta Fe|an** (san′tə fā′ən), a native or inhabitant of Santa Fe, New Mexico.

**San|ta Ger|tru|dis** (san′tə gėr trü′dis), a breed of cattle developed in the United States, that is a cross between a shorthorn and a Brahma. It is able to withstand the humid heat of the South and Southwest. *Santa Gertrudis cattle are a deep cherry red, a color that is supposed to discourage flies and other stinging insects* (New Yorker). [< *Santa Gertrudis,* the name of a section of a very large ranch in Texas]

**san|tal** (san′təl), *n.* = sandalwood. [< Middle French *santal* < Medieval Latin *santalum,* variant of *sandalum.* See related etym. at **sandal²**.]

**san|ta|la|ceous** (san′tə lā′shəs), *adj.* belonging to a family of dicotyledonous plants typified by the sandalwood. [< New Latin *Santalaceae* the family name (< Medieval Latin *santalum,* variant of *sandalum;* see etym. under **sandal²**) + *-ous*]

**San|ta|li** (sun tä′lē), *n.* a Munda language of central India.

**san|ta|lin** (san′tə lin), *n. Chemistry.* the coloring matter of red sandalwood, that forms minute red crystals. *Formula:* $C_{15}H_{14}O_5$ [< French *santaline* < Middle French *santal* santal]

**San|tee** (san tē′), *n., pl.* **-tee** or **tees**. **1** a member of a North American Indian tribe living chiefly in South Carolina and closely related to the Dakota. **2** the Siouan language of this tribe. **3** a division of the Dakota.

**San|te|rí|a** (san′tə rē′ə; *Spanish* sän′te rē′ä), *n.* an Afro-Cuban religion that combines Roman Catholic and African tribal ceremonies. Followers of Santería believe that Catholic saints represent African gods. [< Cuban Spanish *Santería* < Spanish *santo* saint + *-ería* -ery]

**san|tir** (sän tir′, san-), *n.* a kind of dulcimer of the Arabs and Persians. Also, **santoor, santour, santur**. [< Arabic *santīr,* Persian *sāntūr,* alteration of Greek *psaltērion*]

**San|to|brite** (san′tə brīt), *n. Trademark.* a sodium salt used for the eradication of algae and slime. *Formula:* $C_6Cl_5ONa$

**san|tol** (sän tōl′), *n.* an evergreen tree of the mahogany family, having axillary panicles of small sweet-scented flowers, and bearing a fleshy, acid fruit eaten especially in preserves. [< Tagalog *santól*]

**san|to|li|na** (san′tō lē′nə), *n.* a fragrant shrub, related to the camomile, that grows in the Mediterranean region: *A thick hedge of green santolina is on each side of the planting* (New York Times). [< Italian *santolina* < Latin *sānctus* holy + *līnum* flax]

**san|ton¹** (san′tən), *n.* a Moslem holy man or ascetic; marabout: *He was* (*say the Arabian historians*) *one of those ... santons, who pass their lives in hermitages, in fasting, meditation, and prayer, until they attain to the purity of saints and the foresight of prophets* (Washington Irving). [< French *santon* < Spanish *santón* (augmentative) holy man < *santo* saint; see etym. under **Santa²**]

**san|ton²** (sän tôN′), *n.* a clay figurine of a religious nature, usually associated with the nativity scene, made in southern France: *Pierre ... longed to enter the contest for shaping clay into santons ... but his uncle wouldn't hear of it* (Atlantic). [< French *santon* < Provençal *santoun* (diminutive) little saint < *sant* saint < Latin *sānctus* holy; see etym. under **saint**]

**san|ton|i|ca** (san ton′ə kə), *n.* **1** a European wormwood. **2** its dried unexpanded flower heads, used as a vermifuge. [< New Latin *santonica* < Latin (*herba*) *santonica* < *Santoni* a Gaulish people in Aquitaine]

**san|to|nin** or **san|to|nine** (san′tə nin), *n.* a bitter, colorless, crystalline compound, obtained from santonica and used to destroy or expel intestinal worms. *Formula:* $C_{15}H_{18}O_3$ [< *santon*(ica) + *-in.* Compare French *santonine.*]

**san|toor, san|tour,** or **san|tur** (sän tůr′, san-), *n.* = santir.

**Saor|stat Eir|eann** (sãr′stôt ãr′ən), Irish Free State (so designated in Irish Gaelic). [< Irish *Saorstat Eireann* < *saor* free + *stát* state (< English *state*) + *Eireann* having to do with Erin (Ireland)]

**sap¹** (sap), *n., v.,* **sapped, sap|ping.** — *n.* **1a** the liquid that circulates through a plant, consisting of water and food, as blood does in animals. Rising sap carries water and minerals from the roots; sap going downward carries sugar, gums, and resins. Maple sugar is made from the sap of some maple trees. *The trees of the Lord also are full of sap* (English Book of Common Prayer). **b** *Figurative: The world's whole sap is sunk* (John Donne). **2** = sapwood. **3** *Slang.* a silly, stupid person; fool: *He would talk all the way back from school about what a sap she was* (Atlantic). **4** *Slang.* a short club or blackjack; billy.
— *v.t.* **1** to remove sap from (wood or a tree). **2** *Slang.* to strike or knock out with a sap.
[Old English *sæp*]

**sap²** (sap), *v.,* **sapped, sap|ping,** *n.* — *v.t.* **1** to dig under or wear away the foundation of; undermine: *The walls of the boathouse had been sapped by the waves.* **2** *Figurative.* to weaken; use up: *The extreme heat sapped our strength. New York's public school system is being harassed and sapped by increasing problems of discipline and delinquency* (New York Times). *Sapping a solemn creed with solemn sneer ...* (Byron). **3a** to approach or undermine (an enemy's position) by means of protected trenches or tunnels. **b** to dig through (ground, an area, or fortification) in constructing trenches or tunnels.
— *v.i.* to dig or use protected trenches or tunnels.
— *n.* **1** a long, deep trench, protected by the earth dug up; trench dug to approach the enemy's position when a besieged place is within range of fire: *They were now pushing forward saps into No Man's Land, linking them across, and so continually creeping nearer to the enemy and a practicable jumping-off place for attack* (H. G. Wells). **2** the making of trenches or tunnels to approach or mine an enemy position.
[< Middle French *sapper* < *sappe* spade, or Italian *zappare* < *zappa* spade, hoe; goat (because of the resemblance of the handle to a goat's horns), perhaps < Late Latin *sappa*]

**sap|a|jou** (sap′ə jü; *French* sȧ pȧ zhü′), *n.* any one of a group of South and Central American monkeys; capuchin. [< French *sapajou,* probably < a Tupi word]

**sa|pan|wood** (sə pan′wůd′), *n.* = sappanwood.

**sap chafer**, any one of various beetles that feed on the nectar of flowers or exuding sap of trees.

**sa|pe|le** (sä pā′lā), *n.* a large mahogany tree of western and central Africa whose very strong close-grained wood is much used for furniture frames. [< the native name in western Africa]

**sap green**, **1** a green pigment prepared from the juice of buckthorn berries. **2** the yellowish green color of this pigment.

**sap|head** (sap′hed′), *n. Slang.* a silly, stupid person: *You don't seem to know anything, somehow—perfect saphead* (Mark Twain).

**sap|head|ed** (sap′hed′id), *adj. Slang.* silly; stupid.

**sa|phe|na** (sə fē′nə), *n., pl.* **-nae** (-nē). either of two large superficial veins of the leg, one extending along the inner side of the leg from the foot to the groin, and the other extending along the outer and posterior side from the foot to the knee. [< Medieval Latin *saphena* < Arabic *aṣ-ṣāfin* the hidden one; perhaps influenced by Greek *saphēnēs* clear (intellectually)]

**sa|phe|nous** (sə fē′nəs), *adj.* of, designating, or having to do with a saphena.

**sa|phir d'eau** (sȧ fēr′ dō′), *French.* water sapphire.

**sap|id** (sap′id), *adj.* **1** having taste or flavor. **2** having a pleasant taste or flavor; savory; palatable. **3** *Figurative.* pleasing to the mind or mental taste; agreeable. [< Late Latin *sapidus* savory, tasty < Latin *sapere* (originally) to have a taste]

**sa|pid|i|ty** (sə pid′ə tē), *n.* sapid quality; tastefulness; savor; relish.

**sa|pi|ence** (sā′pē əns), *n.* wisdom; insight and judgment such as are gained from much experience or study; sagacity: *She was timeless, with a beauty that comes with sapience, valiant, artistic, and incredibly vital* (Atlantic).

**sa|pi|en|cy** (sā′pē ən sē), *n.* = sapience.

**sa|pi|ens** (sā′pē ənz), *adj.* of, resembling, or having to do with modern man or Homo sapiens: *Beginning with the sapiens races of the late Pleistocene, we find well-developed chins* (Beals and Hoijer). [< (Homo) *sapiens*]

**sa|pi|ent** (sā′pē ənt), *adj., n.* — *adj.* having or showing sapience; wise; sage: *Nor bring ... some doctor ... To shake his sapient head and give the ill he cannot cure a name* (Matthew Arnold).
— *n.* **1** an early member of the species Homo sapiens; a prehistoric man: *New finds from the Omo region, and East Rudolf, North Kenya, have put the age of both large and small Australopithecines back to the 2-3 million year mark, while African sapients from the Upper Middle Pleistocene are now known from the same region* (Science Journal). **2** *Archaic.* a wise person; sage.
[< Latin *sapiēns, -entis* present participle of *sapere* be wise; (originally) to have a taste] — **sa′pi|ent|ly,** *adv.*

**sa|pi|en|tial** (sā′pē en′shəl), *adj.* belonging to or characterized by wisdom. [< Latin *sapientiālis* < *sapiēns;* see etym. under **sapient**]

**sap|in|da|ceous** (sap′in dā′shəs), *adj.* belonging to the soapberry family of plants. [< New Latin *Sapindaceae* the family name (< *Sapindus* the typical genus < Latin *sāpō, -ōnis* soap + *Indicus* Indian) + English *-ous*]

**sap|less** (sap′lis), *adj.* **1** without sap; withered; dry. **2** *Figurative.* without energy or vigor; insipid; trivial: *Now sapless on the verge of death he stands* (John Dryden). — **sap′less|ness,** *n.*

**sap|ling** (sap′ling), *n.* **1** a young tree, especially a young forest tree with a trunk from one to four inches in diameter. **2** *Figurative.* a young or inexperienced person.

**sap|o|dil|la** (sap′ə dil′ə), *n.* **1** a large evergreen tree of tropical America that yields chicle and bears large, brownish berries that taste like pears; mammee; sapota; naseberry. **2** its fruit. [< Mexican Spanish *zapotilla* (diminutive) < *zapote;* see etym. under **sapota**]

**sapodilla family**, a group of (chiefly) tropical, dicotyledonous trees and shrubs, with a milky juice. The fruit of certain species, as the sapodilla, star apple, and marmalade tree, is edible; other species are valued for their hard timber; and others yield gutta-percha and gums.

**sap|o|na|ceous** (sap′ə nā′shəs), *adj.* of the nature of or like soap; soapy. [< Medieval Latin *saponaceus* (with English *-ous*) < Latin *sāpō, -ōnis* soap] — **sap′o|na′ceous|ness,** *n.*

**sa|pon|i|fi|a|ble** (sə pon′ə fī′ə bəl), *adj.* that can be saponified.

**sa|pon|i|fi|ca|tion** (sə pon′ə fə kā′shən), *n.* **1** the act or process of saponifying: *The process for making a Fortisan rayon yarn from an acetate base* (*called saponification by the chemists*) *was perfected by Celanese researchers back in 1937* (Wall Street Journal). **2** the condition of being saponified. **3** *Chemistry.* **a** alkaline hydrolysis of any ester to form an alcohol and a salt or acid. **b** any hydrolysis.

**sa|pon|i|fi|er** (sə pon′ə fī′ər), *n.* **1** an apparatus for the manufacture of glycerin and soap by the decomposition of fats and oils. **2** a substance that produces saponification, such as caustic soda or potash.

**sa|pon|i|fy** (sə pon′ə fī), *v.,* **-fied, -fy|ing.** — *v.t.* **1** to make (a fat or an oil) into soap by treating with an alkali: *Considerable preliminary concentration can be effected by saponifying the oil, that is by turning the glycerides of fatty acids which constitute the bulk of the oil into soaps, which are sodium salts of the fatty acids* (Science News). **2** to decompose (an ester of an acid) into an alcohol and a salt of the acid by treating with an alkali.
— *v.i.* to become soap.
[< New Latin *sāpōnificāre* < Latin *sāpō, -ōnis* soap + *facere* to make]

**sap|o|nin** (sap′ə nin), *n.* any one of the glucosides obtained from the soapwort, soapbark, soapberry, and many other plants, and forming (in solution) a soapy lather when shaken. The commercial substance, a mixture of saponins, is used to produce foam in beverages, as a detergent, and in fire extinguishers. [< French *saponine* < Latin *sāpō, -ōnis* soap + French *-ine* -ine²]

**sap|o|nine** (sap′ə nin, -nēn), *n.* = saponin.

**sap|o|nite** (sap′ə nīt), *n.* a mineral having a soapy feel, occurring in soft, amorphous masses, filling veins and cavities, as in serpentine and traprock. It is a hydrous silicate of aluminum and magnesium. [< Swedish *saponit* (translation of German *Seifenstein*) < Latin *sāpō, -ōnis* soap + *-it* -ite¹]

**sa|por** (sā′pôr, -pər), *n.* that quality in a substance which is perceived by the sense of taste, as sweetness, bitterness, or sourness; taste; savor. [< Latin *sapor, -ōris* flavor, savor, related to *sapere* to taste, be wise]

**sap|o|rif|ic** (sap′ə rif′ik), *adj.* producing or imparting taste or flavor.

**sap|o|rous** (sap′ər əs), *adj.* having flavor or taste.

**sa|po|ta** (sə pō′tə), *n.* **1** = sapodilla. **2** a general term in tropical America for any one of various different sapotaceous fruits or the trees that these fruits grow on. [< New Latin *sapota* < Mexican Spanish, variant of *sapote,* or *zapote,* short for Nahuatl *cuauhtzapotl* zapote tree]

**sap|o|ta|ceous** (sap′ə tā′shəs), *adj.* belonging to the sapodilla family.

**sa|po|te** (sə pō′tā), *n.* a tropical American tree with edible fruit; marmalade tree. [< Mexican

---

**Pronunciation Key:** hat, āge, cãre, fär; let, ēqual, tėrm; it, īce; hot, ōpen, ôrder; oil, out; cup, pu̇t, rüle; child; long; thin; ᴛʜen; zh, measure; ə represents a in about, e in taken, i in pencil, o in lemon, u in circus.

Spanish *sapote;* see etym. under **sapota**]

**sa|pour** (sā′pôr, -pər), *n. Especially British.* sapor.

**sap|pan|wood** (sə pan′wu̇d′), *n.* **1** a wood yielding a red dye, obtained from an East Indian tree of the pea family. **2** the tree itself. Also, **sapan-wood.** [half-translation of Dutch *sapanhout; sapan* < Malay *sapan*]

**sap|per¹** (sap′ər), *n.* **1** a soldier employed in the construction of trenches, fortifications, and the like. **2** a person employed to detect and disarm mines, bombs, and other explosive devices: *The sappers had not yet examined the rubble and blasted buildings for ... booby traps* (New York Times). **3** *Figurative.* a person or thing that saps or undermines: *The bastions will stand ... however much the sappers of successful integration burrow away* (Elspeth Huxley). [< *sap²* + *-er¹*; patterned on Middle French *sappeur*]

**sap|per²** (sap′ər), *n.* **1** a person who removes the sap from wood or trees: *a maple syrup sapper.* **2** a tool for cutting away sapwood. [< *sap¹* + *-er¹*]

**Sap|phic** (saf′ik), *adj., n.* **—*adj.*** **1** of or having to do with Sappho, a Greek lyric poetess who lived about 600 B.C. **2** having to do with certain meters, or a four-line stanza form, used by or named after her: *We send our thanks to you ... in scattered Sapphic lines* (Atlantic). **—*n.*** a Sapphic stanza, strophe, or line of verse.

**Sap|phi|ra** (sə fī′rə), *n.* a woman who, with her husband Ananias, was struck dead for lying (in the Bible, Acts 5:1-10).

**sap|phire** (saf′īr), *n., adj.* **—*n.*** **1a** a bright-blue precious stone that is hard and clear like a diamond. It is a variety of corundum. **b** *Figurative: Orselli considered the stars, each shining with a separate glory: golden Dubhe, blue Denebola, Vega the pale sapphire* (Henry Morton Robinson). **2** the color of the sapphire; bright blue. **3** a gem-quality corundum of any other color except red (commonly prefixed by the color): *a pink sapphire.*

**—*adj.*** **1** bright-blue: *a sapphire gown, a sapphire sky.* **2** made or consisting of a sapphire or sapphires: *a sapphire brooch.*

[< Old French *safir,* learned borrowing from Latin *saphīrus* < Greek *sáppheiros* < Semitic (compare Hebrew *sappīr*) < Sanskrit *sani-priya* sapphire; dear to the planet Saturn]

**sap|phire|ber|ry** (saf′īr ber′ē), *n., pl.* **-ries.** a small tree native to Japan and China with fragrant white flowers and bright blue fruit.

**sapphire blue, 1** a bright blue, the color of the gem. **2** *Poetic.* any clear or deep blue.

**sapphire quartz,** a dark-blue variety of quartz.

**sap|phir|ine** (saf′ər in, -ə rīn), *adj., n.* **—*adj.*** of or like sapphire: *a sapphirine sky.*

**—*n.*** **1** a pale-blue or greenish mineral consisting of a silicate of aluminum and magnesium.
**2** *Especially British.* a blue variety of spinel.

**Sap|phism** (saf′iz əm), *n.* female homosexuality; Lesbianism. [< *Sappho,* a Greek lyric poetess of the 600's B.C. + *-ism* (because of her reputed homosexuality)]

**sap|pi|ness** (sap′ē nis), *n.* the quality or state of being sappy.

**sap|py** (sap′ē), *adj.,* **-pi|er, -pi|est. 1** full of sap; juicy. **2** *Figurative.* vigorous; energetic. **3** *Slang.* silly; foolish: *... a committee of sappy women* (Mark Twain).

**sa|pre|mi|a** or **sa|prae|mi|a** (sə prē′mē ə), *n.* a form of blood poisoning due to the absorption of toxins produced by bacteria. [< Greek *saprós* rotten + English *-emia*]

**sa|pre|mic** or **sa|prae|mic** (sə prē′mik), *adj.* having to do with or affected with sapremia.

**sap|ro|gen|ic** (sap′rə jen′ik), *adj.* **1** producing decay: *saprogenic bacteria.* **2** formed by putrefaction. [< Greek *saprós* rotten + English *-gen* + *-ic*]

**sa|prog|e|nous** (sə proj′ə nəs), *adj.* = saprogenic.

**sap|ro|lite** (sap′rə līt), *n.* soft, partly decomposed rock remaining in its original place. [< Greek *saprós* rotten + English *-lite*]

**sap|ro|lit|ic** (sap rə lit′ik), *adj.* of, having to do with, or like saprolite.

**sa|proph|a|gous** (sə prof′ə gəs), *adj.* living on decomposing matter; saprophytic. [< New Latin *saprophagus* (with English *-ous*) < Greek *saprós* rotten + *phageîn* devour]

**sap|ro|phyte** (sap′rə fīt), *n.* any vegetable organism that lives on decaying organic matter: *The best-known saprophytes ... include mushrooms, molds, mildew, bacteria, rusts, and smuts* (William C. Beaver). [< Greek *saprós* rotten + English *-phyte*]

**sap|ro|phyt|ic** (sap′rə fit′ik), *adj.* of or like a saprophyte; living on decaying organic matter. **—sap′ro|phyt′i|cal|ly,** *adv.*

**sap|sa|go** (sap′sə gō), *n.* a hard, greenish cheese flavored with melilot, originally made in Switzerland. [< alteration of German *Schabzieger* < *schaben* to shave, grate + Swiss German *Zieger* whey cheese, whey]

**sap|suck|er** (sap′suk′ər), *n.* a small North American woodpecker that feeds on the sap and sapwood of trees. The common or yellow-bellied sapsucker drills rows of small holes in trees and eats the inner bark, and later the sap and insects that gather in the holes. [American English < *sap¹* + *sucker*]

**sap|u|ca|ia** (sap′ə kä′yə), *n.* **1** a South American tree related to the monkeypot that yields an edible nut. **2** the hard wood of this tree, used in building. [< Portuguese (Brazil) *sapucaia* < Tupi]

**sapucaia nut,** the nut of the sapucaia, similar to the Brazil nut, and yielding a valuable oil; paradise nut.

**sap|wood** (sap′wu̇d′), *n.* the soft, new, living wood between the bark and the hard, inner wood of most trees; alburnum.

**Sar., 1** Sardinia. **2** Sardinian.

**Sar|a** (sär′ə), *n.* a Negro tribe living near the Ubangi River in the Central African Republic. The female members of this tribe are called Ubangis.

**sar|a|band** (sar′ə band), *n.* **1** a slow and stately dance of Spanish origin, popular in the 1600's and 1700's. The saraband was originally for a single dancer, but was later performed by couples. **2** music for it. [< French *sarabande* < Spanish *zarabanda,* perhaps < Persian *serbend* a kind of dance]

**Sar|a|cen** (sar′ə sən), *n., adj.* **—*n.*** **1** an Arab. **2** a Moslem at the time of the Crusades. **3** a member of the nomadic peoples of the Syrian and Arabian deserts at the time of the later Greeks and of the Roman Empire.

**—*adj.*** of or having to do with the Saracens. [partly Old English *Saracene,* plural < Late Latin *Saracēnī,* partly < Old French *sarrazin,* learned borrowing from Late Latin < Greek *Sarakēnós*]

**Sar|a|cen|ic** (sar′ə sen′ik), *adj.* of, having to do with, or characteristic of the Saracens.

**Sar|a|cen|i|cal** (sar′ə sen′ə kəl), *adj.* = Saracenic.

**Sar|ah** (sär′ə), *n.* the wife of Abraham and the mother of Isaac (in the Bible, Genesis 17:15).

**SARAH** (no periods), Search and Rescue and Homing (a radio and radar beam device used in locating people lost at sea): *SARAH ... weighs only about 3 lb. and can be carried in a Mae West* (London Times).

**Sa|ra|ko|le** (sär′ə kō′lā, -kōl), *n., pl.* **-le** or **-les. 1** a member of a chiefly Moslem Negro people of Mali and Gambia descended from the Soninkes, who established the empire of Ghana. The Sarakole are mainly farmers, cattle raisers, and merchants. **2** the Mandingo language of this people. Also, **Serahuli.**

**sa|ran** (sə ran′), *n.* a thermoplastic resin produced as a fiber, film, or molded form and highly resistant to damage and soiling. It is used to package food, in automobile seat covers, in clothing, and for other commercial purposes. [< *Saran,* a trademark]

**sa|ran|gi** (sä′rang gē), *n.* a stringed musical instrument of India resembling a violin: *... the sarangi, a chunky instrument fitted with 29 strings* (Time). [< Sanskrit *sāraṅgī*]

**sa|ra|pe** (sə rä′pē), *n.* = serape.

**Sa|ras|va|ti** (sə räs′və tē), *n.* the Hindu goddess of learning, and patroness of the arts and music.

**Sa|ras|wa|ti** (sə räs′wə tē), *n.* = Sarasvati.

**Sar|a|to|ga trunk** (sar′ə tō′gə), a kind of large trunk formerly much used by women. [American English < *Saratoga Springs,* New York]

**sar|casm** (sär′kaz əm), *n.* **1** the act of making fun of a person to hurt his feelings; harsh or bitter irony: *"How unselfish you are!" said the girl in sarcasm as her brother took the biggest piece of cake. Sarcasm, I now see to be, in general, the language of the Devil* (Thomas Carlyle). **2** a sneering or cutting remark; ironical taunt: *Blows are sarcasms turned stupid* (George Eliot). **3** the substance of such a remark or remarks. [< Late Latin *sarcasmus* < Greek *sarkasmós* < *sarkázein* to sneer; (literally) strip of flesh < *sárx, sarkós* flesh]

▶ See **irony** for usage note.

**sar|cas|tic** (sär kas′tik), *adj.* using sarcasm; sneering; bitterly cutting; ironical; taunting; caustic: *"Don't hurry!" was her father's sarcastic comment as she slowly dressed.* **—sar|cas′ti|cal|ly,** *adv.*

**—*Syn.*** **Sarcastic, sardonic, satirical** mean scornful or contemptuous. **Sarcastic** implies exhibiting scorn in such a way as to hurt someone's feelings: *The teacher's sarcastic comment about the girl's essay made her cry.* **Sardonic** implies exhibiting scorn in a cold, aloof manner but not directed at anything or anyone in particular: *Our efforts to cheer him up produced only a sardonic smile.* **Satirical** implies exhibiting something in a scornful light but not necessarily so as to hurt anyone: *We were all amused by the satirical comparison of life at college and in the army.*

**Sar|cee** (sär′sē), *n., pl.* **-cee** or **-cees. 1** a member of an Athapascan people of Alberta, Canada. Most of the Sarcee are now living on a reservation near Calgary. **2** the Athapascan dialect of this people. Also, **Sarsi.**

**sarce|net** (särs′net), *n.* a soft, thin silk fabric, either plain or twilled, used especially for linings. Also, **sarsenet.** [< Anglo-French *sarzinett,* probably (diminutive) < *Sarzin,* Old French *sarrazin* Saracen (because of its resemblance to the garb of the Saracens)]

**Sar|ci** (sär′sē), *n., pl.* **-ci** or **-cis.** = Sarcee.

**sarco-,** *combining form.* **1** flesh; fleshy, as in *sarcology.*
**2** muscle tissue, as in *sarcosome.*
[< Greek *sárx, sarkós* flesh]

**sar|co|carp** (sär′kō kärp), *n.* **1** the fleshy mesocarp of certain fruits, such as the peach and plum. It is the part usually eaten. **2** any fruit that is fleshy. [< Greek *sárx, sarkós* flesh + *karpós* fruit]

**sar|code** (sär′kōd), *n.* the protoplasm of a one-celled animal: *Two years later, in 1835, Dujardin, a French protozoologist, described the semifluid substance in unicellular animals and coined the term sarcode* (Hegner and Stiles). [< French *sarcode* < Greek *sarkṓdēs* fleshy < *sárx, sarkós* flesh + *eîdos* form]

**sar|co|din|i|an** (sär′kō din′ē ən), *adj., n.* **—*adj.*** of or belonging to a large group of amebalike protozoans that move and take in food by means of pseudopodia. The rhizopods are sarcodinian organisms.

**—*n.*** a protozoan belonging to this group; rhizopod.

[< New Latin *Sarcodina* the class name (< Greek *sarkṓdēs* fleshy) + English *-ian*]

**sar|co|gen|ic** (sär′kō jen′ik), *adj.* producing muscle or flesh. [< *sarco-* + *-gen* + *-ic*]

**sar|cog|e|nous** (sär koj′ə nəs), *adj.* = sarcogenic.

**sar|coid** (sär′koid), *n.* = sarcoidosis.

**sar|coi|do|sis** (sär′koi dō′sis), *n.* a chronic disease in which tumorlike lesions develop in many parts of the body. Its cause is undetermined. *This disease was sarcoidosis, a chronic infectious disease affecting the eyes and face* (Science News Letter). *A mysterious and sometimes fatal tuberculosislike disease, sarcoidosis is linked to the Eastern pine tree* (Science News Letter). [< New Latin *sarcoidosis* < Greek *sarkoeidês* fleshy (< *sárx, sarkós* flesh + *eîdos* form) + New Latin *-osis* -osis]

**sar|co|lac|tic acid** (sär′kō lak′tik), the dextrorotatory form of lactic acid found in the blood and muscles as a result of the metabolism of glucose: *Sarcolactic acid ... has been called the "acid of fatigue" ... because a greater amount of sarcolactic acid is present in the muscles when a person is tired* (George L. Bush). [< *sarco-* + *lactic acid*]

**sar|co|lem|ma** (sär′kō lem′ə), *n.* an elastic transparent membrane enclosing each of the fibers of striated muscle tissue, excepting that of the heart. [< Greek *sárx, sarkós* flesh + *lémma* husk]

**sar|co|lem|mal** (sär′kō lem′əl), *adj.* of or having to do with a sarcolemma or sarcolemmas: *Each giant fiber is surrounded by a stout sarcolemmal complex with associated nuclei* (Graham Hoyle).

**sar|col|o|gy** (sär kol′ə jē), *n.* the branch of anatomy that has to do with the fleshy parts of the body. [< *sarco-* + *-logy*]

**sar|col|y|sin** (sär kol′ə sin), *n.* a nitrogen mustard used in treating malignant tumors. *Formula:* $C_{13}H_{18}Cl_2N_2O_2$

**sar|co|ma** (sär kō′mə), *n., pl.* **-mas, -ma|ta** (-mə tə). any one of a class of cancers originating in tissue that is not epithelial, chiefly connective tissue: *It is possible to have tumors of the mesoderm, these being usually known as sarcomata* (Science News). [< New Latin *sarcoma* < Greek *sárkōma, -atos* < *sarkôn* to produce flesh; grow fleshy < *sárx, sarkós* flesh]

**sar|co|ma|toid** (sär kō′mə toid), *adj.* = sarcomatous.

**sar|co|ma|to|sis** (sär kō′mə tō′sis), *n.* a condition characterized by the formation of sarcomas in many parts of the body. [< New Latin *sarcomatosis* < *sarcoma, -atos* sarcoma + *-osis* -osis]

**sar|com|a|tous** (sär kom′ə təs), *adj.* having to do with or of the nature of a sarcoma.

**sar|co|mere** (sär′kə mir), *n.* one of the segments or pieces of a sarcostyle. [< *sarco-* + *-mere*]

**sar|co|phag|ic** (sär′kō faj′ik), *adj.* = sarcophagous.

**sar|coph|a|gid** (sär kof′ə jid), *n.* a flesh-eating fly; flesh fly. [< New Latin *Sarcophagidae* the family name of such flies < Greek *sárx, sarkós* flesh + *phageîn* to eat]

**sar|coph|a|gous** (sär kof′ə gəs), *adj.* flesh-eating; carnivorous. [< Latin *sarcophagus* + English *ous*]

**sar|coph|a|gus** (sär kof′ə gəs), *n., pl.* **-gi** (-gī), **-gus|es. 1** a stone coffin, especially one ornamented with sculptures or bearing inscriptions: *The early doges had themselves buried, in St. Mark's porch, in sarcophagi that did not belong to them, displacing the bones of old pagans and Paleo-Christians* (New Yorker). **2** a kind of limestone that the ancient Greeks used for coffins because they supposed it quickly consumed the flesh of corpses placed in it. [< Latin *sarcophagus* (originally) flesh-eating (stone) < Greek *sarkophágos* < *sárx, sarkós* flesh + *phageîn* to eat]

**sar|co|phile** (sär′kə fīl), *n.* = Tasmanian devil. [< *sarco-* + *-phile*]

**sar|co|plasm** (sär′kō plaz əm), *n.* the clear protoplasmic substance which separates the fibrillae, or sarcostyles, in a striated muscle fiber.

**sar|co|plas|mic** (sär′kō plaz′mik), *adj.* having to do with or of the nature of sarcoplasm: *Inside muscle fibres, calcium ions are stored in the sarcoplasmic reticulum—an intracellular network of fine tubules responsible for transmitting stimuli from the cell surface to the centre of the fibre* (New Scientist).

**sar|cop|tic** (sär kop′tik), *adj.* of, having to do with, or caused by itch mites. [< New Latin *Sarcoptes,* genus of parasites including the itch mite < Greek *sárx, sarkós* flesh + *kóptein* to cut]

**sarcoptic mange**, a mange caused by the burrowing of itch mites into the skin: *Sarcoptic mange in a puppy could infect the whole household* (London Times).

**sar|co|some** (sär′kō sōm), *n.* any one of the very small cell inclusions found in muscle tissue, believed to be a principal factor in keeping the heart muscle strong and active. [< *sarco-* + *-some*[3]]

**sar|co|spo|ri|di|o|sis** (sär′kō spô rid′ē ō′sis, -spō-), *n.* a disease of animals caused by a parasite, believed to be a protozoan or fungus, which invades the muscles, especially the striated muscles. It is encountered frequently in ducks, sheep, swine, horses, reptiles, and birds. [< New Latin *Sarcosporidia* the order name of the parasite (< Greek *sárx, sarkós* flesh + *sporá* spore) + *-osis* -osis]

**sar|co|style** (sär′kō stīl), *n.* one of the delicate fibrillae which make up the fiber of a striated muscle.

**sar|cous** (sär′kəs), *adj.* having to do with or consisting of flesh or muscle. [< Greek *sárx, sarkós* flesh + English *-ous*]

**sard** (särd), *n.* a mineral, a variety of chalcedony, varying in color from brown to deep red, used in jewelry. [< Latin *sarda.* Compare etym. under **sardius.**]

**sar|da|na** (sär dä′nə), *n.* a dance of Catalonia, danced in a large ring with much twirling and hand-clapping to the rhythm of a flute and drum. [< Catalan *sardana*]

**Sar|da|na|pa|li|an** (sär′də nə pā′lē ən), *adj.* inordinately luxurious and effeminate. [< *Sardanapalus,* an Assyrian king, proverbial for his wealth and splendor + *-ian*]

**sar|dar** (sär′där, sər där′), *n.* = sirdar.

**Sar|di|an** (sär′dē ən), *adj., n.* —*adj.* of or having to do with Sardis, the ancient capital of Lydia in Asia Minor: *His monument ... [was] erected near Sardis by the joint efforts of the whole Sardian population* (George Grote).
—*n.* a native or inhabitant of Sardis: *You have condemned and noted Lucius Pella for taking bribes here of the Sardians* (Shakespeare).

**sar|dine**[1] (sär dēn′), *n., pl.* **-dines** or (*collectively*) **-dine,** *v.,* **-dined, -din|ing.** —*n.* **1** a young or small, saltwater fish related to the herring, preserved in oil for food. Sardines are young pilchards. **2** any one of certain similar small fishes prepared in a similar way: *The 40-odd canneries in Maine provide all the domestic supply of small snack-type sardines* (Wall Street Journal).
—*v.t.* to pack closely; crowd: *Hundreds of thousands of people ... will be sardined into the famous amusement park area and on the littered beach* (New York Times).
**packed like sardines**, very much crowded: *We rode on the subway at rush hour, packed like sardines.*
[< Old French *sardine* < Italian *sardina* < Latin *sardīna* < *sarda* sardine, probably (literally) Sardinian fish]

**sar|dine**[2] (sär′din, -dīn), *n.* = sard. [< Late Latin *sardīnus,* apparently < Latin *sarda* sard]

**Sar|din|i|an** (sär din′ē ən), *adj., n.* —*adj.* of or having to do with Sardinia, a large island near Italy, its people, or their dialect.
—*n.* **1** a native or inhabitant of Sardinia. **2** the Romance dialect spoken in Sardinia: *Sardinian is quite distinct from Italian* (H. A. Gleason, Jr.).

**sar|di|us** (sär′dē əs), *n.* **1** = sard. **2** (in the Bible) one of the precious stones in the breastplate of the Jewish high priest, thought to have been a ruby. [< Late Latin (*lapis*) *sardius,* for Greek (*líthos*) *sárdios* (stone) of *Sardis,* a city in Lydia]

**sar|don|ic** (sär don′ik), *adj.* bitterly contemptuous; coldly scornful; mocking: *a fiend's sardonic laugh, a sardonic outlook. I well remember his sardonic amusement over the hoopla occasioned in this country by the first Kinsey report* (Atlantic). **SYN:** derisive. See syn. under **sarcastic**. [< French *sardonique* < Latin *sardonius* (< Greek *sardónios* of bitter or scornful smiles or laughter < *sardónion* a supposed Sardinian plant that produced hysterical convulsions + French *-ique* -ic]
—**sar|don′i|cal|ly**, *adv.*

**sar|don|i|cism** (sär don′ə siz əm), *n.* the quality of being sardonic.

**sar|do|nyx** (sär′də niks), *n.* a variety of onyx containing layers of sard: *The engraved carnelian and sardonyx rings that fashionable Greeks wore on their toes ... had swivel mountings, so that the center was reversible* (New Yorker). [< Latin *sardonyx* < Greek *sardónyx,* probably < *sárdios,* or *sárdion* sardius + *ónyx* onyx]

**sa|ree** (sä′rē), *n., pl.* **-rees.** = sari.

**sar|gas|so** (sär gas′ō), *n., pl.* **-sos**, or **sargasso weed**, any one of a group of brown seaweeds that have berrylike air bladders and float in large masses; sargassum. [< Portuguese *sargasso,* or *sargaço,* perhaps < *sarga* a type of grape (because of the berrylike air sacs on the seaweed) or, perhaps < Latin *sargus* a kind of sea fish]

**sar|gas|sum** (sär gas′əm), *n.* any one of a group of brown seaweeds that inhabit the warmer waters of the globe, especially an area of the Atlantic off southern North America; gulfweed: *It is commonly supposed that this area [the Sargasso Sea] of the Atlantic is so thick with seaweed that ships cannot penetrate it. Although it is indeed strewn with floating sargassum, it is actually a biological desert* (J. H. Ryther). [< New Latin *Sargassum* the genus name < Portuguese *sargasso;* see etym. under **sargasso**]

**sargassum fish**, any one of the frogfishes often found among floating masses of sargassum, common in warm parts of the Atlantic: *If you have trouble seeing the sargassum fish ... hidden among the tropic and semi-tropic sargassum sea weed ... so do his natural enemies* (Science News Letter).

**sarge** (särj), *n. U.S. Informal.* sergeant.

**sar|go** (sär′gō), *n.* a small, edible, silvery fish with dark spots on the body and yellow fins, a variety of grunt found off the Pacific coast of North America. [< Spanish *sargo* < Latin *sargus;* see etym. under **sargasso**]

***sa|ri** (sä′rē), *n., pl.* **-ris.** a long piece of cotton or silk worn around the body with one end falling nearly to the feet and the other end thrown over the head or shoulder. It is the principal outer garment of Hindu women and is sometimes brightly colored. *The sari, which has come a long way since it left Delhi, now makes its influence felt in two-piece dacron-and-cotton dresses* (New Yorker). [< Hindi *sārī* < Prakrit *sāḍī* < Sanskrit *śāṭī* garment, petticoat]

***sari**

**sar|in** or **Sar|in** (sar′in), *n.* a highly lethal nerve gas that is a compound of phosphorus: *A protecting antidote for the nerve gas called sarin has been developed* (Science News Letter). *Formula:* $C_4H_{10}FPO_2$ [< German *Sarin*]

**sa|rin|da** (sə rin′də), *n.* a stringed musical instrument of India, played with a bow, of the class characterized by the rebab. [< Hindustani *sārindā*]

**sark** (särk), *n. Scottish.* shirt. [Old English *serc*]

**sar|ky** (sär′kē), *adj. British Slang.* sarcastic: *Some do get a bit sarky* (Sunday Times).

**Sar|ma|tian** (sär mā′shən), *adj., n.* —*adj.* of or having to do with Sarmatia, an ancient region in Europe extending from the Vistula to the Volga, sometimes poetically identified with Poland or with the inhabitants of this region.
—*n.* a native or inhabitant of Sarmatia.

**sar|ment** (sär′mənt), *n. Obsolete.* **1** sarmentum. **2** a cutting. [< Latin *sarmentum* twig]

**sar|men|to|gen|in** (sär men′tō jen′in), *n.* a glycoside obtained from the seeds of a tropical African vine of the dogbane family, used in the production of cortisone. *Formula:* $C_{23}H_{34}O_5$

**sar|men|tose** (sär men′tōs), *adj. Botany.* **1** having runners. **2** of or like a runner. [< Latin *sarmentōsus* < *sarmentum* twig]

**sar|men|tous** (sär men′təs), *adj.* = sarmentose.

**sar|men|tum** (sär men′təm), *n., pl.* **-ta** (-tə). *Botany.* a runner (stem), as that of the strawberry. [< Latin *sarmentum* twig, related to *sarpere* to prune, trim]

**sa|rod** (sə rōd′), *n.* an ancient stringed instrument of India. It has twenty-five strings, ten of which are plucked, the other fifteen providing resonance. *[He] is a performer on the sarod, a stringed instrument of beautiful design that is plucked according to a highly intricate technique* (New Yorker). [< Hindi *sarod* < Persian *si* three + *rōd* string]

**sa|rod|ist** (sə rō′dist), *n.* a player of the sarod.

***sa|rong** (sə rông′, -rong′), *n.* **1** a rectangular piece of cloth, usually a brightly colored printed material, worn as a skirt by men and women in the Malay Archipelago, East Indies, and certain other islands of the Pacific: *The shop has a selection of filmy and transparent saris from India and hand-painted Javanese sarongs* (New York Times). **2** a fabric used to make this garment. [< Malay *sarong,* perhaps ultimately < Sanskrit *śāṭa* cloth, garment]

***sarong**
definition 1

**sa|ros** (sār′os), *n. Astronomy.* a cycle of 18 years and 11⅓ days, in which solar and lunar eclipses repeat themselves. If the interval contains five leap years instead of four, it is 18 years and 10⅓ days. It was discovered by the ancient Chaldeans. [< Greek *sáros* < Semitic (compare Assyrian *shāru*)]

**Sa|rouk** (sə rük′), *n.* a Persian rug, usually dark blue and red, with a fine-grained weave and short, velvety pile. [< *Sarouk,* a village in Iran]

**Sar|pe|don** (sär pē′dən), *n. Greek Legend.* **1** a son of Zeus and Europa, king of the Lycians, to whom Zeus granted the privilege of living for three generations. **2** (in another account) a son of Zeus and Laodamia, leader of the Lycians in the Trojan War and an ally of the Trojans, killed by Patroclus.

**sar|ra|ce|ni|a** (sar′ə sē′nē ə), *n.* a bog plant with pitcher-shaped leaves and a more or less arching hood at the top, usually partly filled with rain water and decomposing insects on which the plant subsists; pitcher plant. [< New Latin *Sarracenia* the genus name < Dr. D. *Sarrazin,* a Canadian botanist of the 1600's who sent the first samples to Europe]

**sar|ra|ce|ni|a|ceous** (sar′ə sē′nē ā′shəs), *adj.* belonging to a family of American dicotyledonous bog herbs typified by the sarracenia.

**sar|sa|pa|ril|la** (sas′pə ril′ə, sär′sə-), *n.* **1** a tropical American climbing or trailing plant of the lily family; any one of several species of greenbrier. **2** its dried root, used for flavoring and formerly used in medicine. **3** a cooling drink flavored with this root. It is nonalcoholic and usually carbonated. [< Spanish *zarzaparrilla* < *zarza* bramble (perhaps < Basque *sartzia*) + *parrilla* (diminutive) < *parra* vine (origin uncertain)]
▶ The second pronunciation, although it agrees with the spelling, is rare in the United States.

**sar|sar** (sär′sər), *n.* a killingly cold wind. [< Arabic *ṣarṣar*]

**sar|sen** (sär′sən), *n.* any number of large boulders or blocks of sandstone found as parts or remnants of prehistoric buildings. The sarsens of Stonehenge, in England, are the most famous stones of this kind. *Those that first catch the attention are the immense sarsens, great monoliths of sandstone* (Scientific American). [apparently variant of *Saracen* (because they were originally thought to have built the buildings)]

**sarse|net** (särs′net), *n.* = sarcenet.

**Sar|si** (sär′sē), *n., pl.* **-si** or **-sis.** = Sarcee.

**sar|tor** (sär′tər, -tôr), *n.* a tailor (in humorously pedantic use). [< Latin *sartor*]

**sar|to|ri|al** (sär tôr′ē əl, -tōr′-), *adj.* **1** of tailors or their work: *His clothes were a sartorial triumph.*

**Pronunciation Key:** hat, āge, cãre, fär; let, ēqual, tėrm; it, īce; hot, ōpen, ôrder; oil, out; cup, pu̇t, rüle; child; long; thin; ᴛʜen; zh, measure; ə represents **a** in about, **e** in taken, **i** in pencil, **o** in lemon, **u** in circus.

*His sartorial taste runs to loud candy-striped shirts* (Newsweek). **2** *Anatomy.* of or having to do with the sartorius. [< Latin *sartōrius* of a tailor (< *sarcīre* to patch) + English *-al*[1]] —**sar|to′ri|al|ly,** *adv.*

**sar|to|ri|us** (sär tôr′ē əs, -tōr′-), *n., pl.* **-to|ri|i** (-tôr′ē ī, -tōr′-). a flat, narrow muscle, the longest in the human body, running from the ilium to the top of the tibia, and crossing the thigh obliquely in front. [< New Latin *sartorius* < Latin *sartor, -ōris* tailor, patcher < *sarcīre* to patch]

**Sar|tri|an** or **Sar|tre|an** (sär′trē ən), *adj.* of, having to do with, or characteristic of the French existentialist philosopher and writer Jean-Paul Sartre (born 1905), his writings, or his ideas: *Honesty, objectivity, compassion and acceptance of total personal responsibility is the Sartrian prescription* (Sunday Times).

**Sar|um** (sãr′əm), *adj.* of or having to do with the order of divine service and the liturgy used in the diocese of Salisbury, England, from the late Middle Ages to the Reformation: *the Sarum use or rite, a Sarum missal.* [< Medieval Latin *Sarum,* for *Sarisburia* Salisbury]

**sar|us crane** (sãr′əs), a large crane of India, Malaya, and the Philippines: *... the first Sarus crane ever to hatch in the United States* (Science News Letter). [< Hindi *sāras* < Sanskrit *sārasa* of a lake]

**SAS**, Special Air Services (a special strike force and peacekeeping unit of the British Army).

**Sa|sa|ni|an** (sa sā′nē ən), *n., adj.* = Sassanid.

**sash**[1] (sash), *n., v.* —*n.* **1** a long, broad strip of cloth or ribbon, worn as an ornament or belt around the waist, especially by women and children: *She wore a white dress with a blue sash around her waist.* **2** a similar ornamental strip, often fringed, worn over one shoulder or around the waist as part of a uniform or as an emblem of rank: *Acting President Nereu Ramos took off the green-and-gold sash of office and draped it across the incoming President's breast* (Time).
—*v.t.* to dress or adorn with a sash: *Her lace dress was sashed in satin.* [earlier *shash* < Arabic *shāsh* muslin cloth (worn in turbans)]

**sash**[2] (sash), *n., v.* —*n.* **1** the frame for the glass in a window or door: *A pane of glass, broken out of the sash, lay in splinters on the floor.* **2** such frames collectively. **3** the part or parts of a window that can be moved to open or close it.
—*v.t.* to provide with a sash or sashes.
[earlier *shashes,* taken as plural < French *châssis,* or *châsse* frame or sash. Compare etym. under **chassis.**]

**sa|shay** (sa shā′), *v., n.* —*v.i.* **1** *Informal.* to glide, move, or go about, especially lightly or casually: *When they passed the Wade Hampton Inn, they less walked than sashayed* (New Yorker). **2** to do a chassé, especially in folk dancing.
—*n.* **1** a chassé, especially in folk dancing. **2** *Informal, Figurative.* a short trip or excursion: *From time to time, he also permits himself cautious sashays into such subjects as history, education, politics ...* (New Yorker).
[American English, alteration of *chassé* a gliding step]

**sash cord, 1** rope which runs over a pulley and connects a window sash with its counterbalancing weight. **2** the rope made for this purpose.

**sa|shi|mi** (sä shē′mē), *n.pl.* thin slices of raw fish, eaten as an appetizer in Japan. [< Japanese *sashimi*]

**sash weight,** a slender, metal weight hung within the frame of a window by a sash cord, and used to counterbalance the weight of the sash.

**sa|sin** (sā′sin), *n.* the common Indian antelope; the black buck. It is brown or black on the upper parts with a white abdomen and breast, and straight corkscrew horns. [origin uncertain. Compare Sanskrit *śaśin* of or having to do with a hare or deer.]

**Sask.,** Saskatchewan.

**sas|ka|toon** (sas′kə tün′), *n. Canadian.* **1** any one of various shadbushes, especially the serviceberry and a species with purple fruit. **2** the berry of any one of these plants. [American English, apparently < Algonkian (Cree) *misâskwatomin* fruit of the *misâskwat* tree of many branches]

**Sas|quatch** (sas′kwach, -kwôch), *n.* a big-footed hairy beast supposed to live in the Pacific Northwest. [probably < an Athapascan name]

**sass** (sas, säs), *n., v.* —*n.* **1** *Informal.* rudeness; back talk; impudence. **2** *U.S. Dialect.* vegetables, especially those used in making sauces; sauce.
—*v.t. Informal.* to be saucy to; sauce: *He'd come to me and sass me sumthin' dreadful, naggin' me to let him play* (New York Times). —*v.i. Informal.* to talk or act rudely or impudently.
[< a variant pronunciation of *sauce*]

**sas|sa|by** (sas′ə bē), *n., pl.* **-bies** or (*collectively*) **-by.** a large, dark-red, South African antelope. [< dialectal Bantu *tsessébe*]

**sas|sa|fras** (sas′ə fras), *n.* **1** a slender tree of eastern North America that has fragrant, yellow flowers, bluish-black fruit, and light, soft, yellowish wood. It belongs to the laurel family. **2** the aromatic dried bark of its root, used in medicine and to flavor candy, soft drinks, and tea. It yields an aromatic volatile oil used in making perfume. [American English < Spanish *sasafrás,* perhaps < an American Indian language, and later influenced by Spanish *sassifragia,* earlier *saxifragia;* see etym. under **saxifrage**]

**sassafras tea,** a tea made by boiling the dried root bark of the sassafras, formerly much used as a tonic.

**Sas|sa|ni|an** (sa sā′nē ən), *n., adj.* = Sassanid.

**Sas|sa|nid** or **Sas|sa|nide** (sas′ə nid), *n., adj.* —*n.* one of the Sassanidae.
—*adj.* of or having to do with the Sassanidae.

**Sas|san|i|dae** (sa san′ə dē), *n.pl.* the dynasty that ruled Persia from A.D. 226 to 651. [< Medieval Latin *Sassanidae,* ultimately < Persian *Sāsān,* grandfather of Ardashir, the first king of the dynasty]

**Sas|se|nach** (sas′ə naʜ), *n. Scottish and Irish.* **1** an Englishman: *It had been hoped that a special commemorative stamp would be issued ... but the Sassenachs in Parliament in London would not agree* (Cape Times). **2** the English; Englishmen collectively. [< Irish *sasanach* (literally) Saxon < Medieval Latin *Saxonicus.* See related etym. at **Saxon.**]

**sas|si|ly** (sas′ə lē), *adv. Informal.* saucily: *All that viewers saw or heard was Elsa Maxwell sassily telling Host Jack Paar that Walter Winchell had never voted* (Time).

**sas|si|ness** (sas′ē nis), *n. Informal.* sauciness.

**sas|sy**[1] (sas′ē), *adj.,* **-si|er, -si|est.** *Informal.* saucy: *Also on the bill are Bobbi Wright, a Harlem miss with a sassy voice and great ebullience* (New Yorker). [< *sass* + *-y*[1]]

**sas|sy**[2] (sas′ē), *n.* **1** = sassy bark. **2** a large African tree of the pea family, whose poisonous bark is used by the natives as a poison to test a person at an ordeal, and for capturing fish; sassywood. [origin uncertain; perhaps < a West African word, or perhaps < English *sassy*[1]]

**sassy bark, 1** the bark of the sassy tree. **2** = sassy[2] (def. 2).

**sas|sy|wood** (sas′ē wu̇d′), *n.* = sassy[2] (def. 2).

**sas|tra** (säs′trə), *n.* **1** (in Hindu use) any of certain sacred books constituting the sources of Hindu law. **2** *Figurative.* any of various authoritative books for instruction in some science or art. Also, **shastra.** [< Hindi *ṣāstr* < Sanskrit *śāstra*]

**sas|tru|ga** (sas trü′gə), *n., pl.* **-gi** (-gē). a windblown ridge of snow and ice; zastruga. [< Russian *zastruga*]

**sat** (sat), *v.* a past tense and a past participle of **sit**: *Yesterday I sat in the train all day. The cat has sat at that mouse's hole for hours.*

**SAT** (no periods) or **S.A.T.,** Scholastic Aptitude Test.

**Sat., 1** Saturday. **2** Saturn.

**Sa|tan** (sā′tən), *n.* the evil spirit; the enemy of goodness; the Devil. Satan is the great adversary of God and mankind, especially in Christian theology. *Satan finds some mischief still for idle hands to do* (Isaac Watts). *And he laid hold on the dragon, that old serpent, which is the Devil, and Satan, and bound him a thousand years* (Revelation 20:2). [Old English *Satan* < Latin *Satān* < Greek *satanâs,* adapted from *satân* < Hebrew *shāṭān* adversary]

**sa|tang** (sä tang′), *n., pl.* **-tang.** a Thai bronze coin and money of account, equal to 1/100 of a baht. [< Thai *satāṅ* (literally) having one hundred < *sata* hundred < Sanskrit *śata*]

**sa|tan|ic** or **Sa|tan|ic** (sā tan′ik, sə-), *adj.* **1** of Satan. **2** like that of Satan; very wicked: *Though he is capable of satanic mockery ... the mocker cannot jeer at such a doom without breaking ... his own neck as well* (Edmund Wilson). **SYN:** diabolical, devilish, infernal.

**sa|tan|i|cal** (sā tan′ə kəl, sə-), *adj.* = satanic.

**sa|tan|i|cal|ly** (sā tan′ə klē, sə-), *adv.* in a satanic manner; with the wicked and malicious spirit of Satan; devilishly.

**Sa|tan|ism** (sā′tə niz əm), *n.* **1** the worship of Satan. Satanism had a vogue in France during the 1800's. It was mostly a form of decadence rather than actual belief in Satan. **2** the principles of or rites used in this worship. **3** devilishness, as a satanic or diabolical disposition or doctrine: *With such a mixture of ... loyalty, mysterious Satanism, and reputation for conquests over her sex ... Bothwell must have fascinated the Queen* (Andrew Lang).

**sa|tan|ist** (sā′tə nist), *n.* a very wicked person.

**Sa|tan|ist** (sā′tə nist), *n.* a believer in Satanism.

**sa|tan|oph|a|ny** (sā′tə nof′ə nē), *n., pl.* **-nies. 1** an appearance of Satan. **2** the condition of being possessed by a devil. [< *Satan;* patterned on *theophany*]

**Sa|tan|o|pho|bi|a** (sā′tə nə fō′bē ə), *n. Rare.* fear of the Devil. [< Greek *Satanâs* (see etym. under **Satan**) + English *-phobia*]

**Satan's mushroom,** a large mushroom, a boletus, that is poisonous to some people and not to others. It grows on the ground in wooded areas.

**S.A.T.B.,** soprano, alto, tenor, bass: *Standard carol books still more or less automatically gear their arrangements to the S.A.T.B. church choir* (London Times).

**satch|el** (sach′əl), *n.* a small bag, especially one for carrying clothes or books; handbag: *The whining schoolboy, with his satchel and shining morning face* (Shakespeare). [< Old French *sachel* < Latin *saccellus* money bag, purse, (diminutive) < *sacculus* (diminutive) < *saccus;* see etym. under **sack**[1]]

**satchel charge,** an explosive charge that can be carried and set off either by one person or a small group: *The satchel charges would replace the unwieldy TNT charges used heretofore by engineers ... to demolish bridges* (New York Herald Tribune).

**sat|com** (sat′kom), *n.* a station or center for tracking and monitoring communications satellites: *The difficulty of having large and small stations working through the same transponder has been circumvented by a novel technique, now adopted for the planned NATO satcom* (Science Journal). [< *sat*(ellite) *com*(munications)]

**sate**[1] (sāt), *v.t.,* **sat|ed, sat|ing. 1** to satisfy fully (any appetite or desire): *A long drink sated my thirst.* **2** to supply with more than enough, so as to disgust or weary; glut. **SYN:** See syn. under **satiate.** [alteration of earlier *sade,* Old English *sadian* to glut (compare etym. under **sad**); influenced by Latin *satiāre* satiate]

**sate**[2] (sat, sāt), *v. Archaic.* sat; a past tense and a past participle of **sit.**

**sa|teen** (sa tēn′), *n.* a cotton cloth made to imitate satin. It is often used for lining sleeves. [variant of *satin;* probably influenced by *velveteen*]

**sate|less** (sāt′lis), *adj. Archaic.* that cannot be sated; insatiable.

**sat|el|lite** (sat′ə līt), *n., adj.* —*n.* **1a** a heavenly body that revolves around a planet, especially around one of the nine major planets of the solar system. The moon is a satellite of the earth. *The number of known satellites in the solar system, including the earth's moon, rose to 32* (Newsweek). **b** a man-made object launched by rocket into an orbit around the earth or other heavenly body; artificial satellite. Such satellites are used to send weather or other scientific information back to earth; they also transmit television programs across the earth. *Far up in outer space, U.S. satellites derive their radio voices from the Transistor* (New Yorker). *The magnetic field of the Earth induces sufficiently large eddy currents in the metal hull of a satellite to slow down its rotation* (New Scientist). **2** *Figurative.* **a** a follower or attendant upon a person of importance: *Three thousand armed satellites escorted his steps* (John L. Motley). **b** a subservient follower: *Legree encouraged his two black satellites to a kind of coarse familiarity with him* (Harriet Beecher Stowe). **3** *Figurative.* **a** a country that claims to be independent but is actually under the control of another, especially such a country under the control of the Soviet Union: *South Africa produces ... as much uranium as the U.S.S.R. and her satellites put together* (Economist). **b** *U.S.* a suburban community; suburb: *DeKalb County, Ga.* [*is*] *a white-collar, upper-middle-class satellite of Atlanta* (New York Times).
—*adj.* of, having to do with, or of the nature of a satellite: **a** secondary; minor: *a satellite group, party, or regime.* **b** allied; associated: *Percival maintains that Canada's supremacy in hockey is being lost because coaching and conditioning in the NHL and its satellite leagues hasn't advanced* (Eric Hutton).
[< Middle French *satellite,* learned borrowing from Latin *satelles, -itis* attendant]

**satellite city,** = new town.

**satellite DNA,** a form of DNA in animal cells which is of a different density than other DNA and consists of repeating sequences of nucleotide pairs. Its specific function is not known.

**satellite town,** = new town.

**sat|el|lit|ic** (sat′ə lit′ik), *adj.* of, having to do with, or of the nature of a satellite: *With a directed booster at the end, this rocket could have been fired into a satellitic orbit* (Scientific American).

**sat|el|lit|ism** (sat′ə lī tiz′əm), *n.* the policy or practice of seeking political satellites: *The nationalism learned from the West makes the new nations sensitive to Communist satellitism* (American Scholar).

**sat|el|li|za|tion** (sat′ə lə zā′shən), *n.* the turning of a country into a satellite: *Understanding of a wider world would help Canadians resist American satellization* (Canadian Saturday Night).

**sat|el|loid** (sat′ə loid), *n.* **1** a space vehicle that travels at less than the speed required for it to remain long in orbit: *The glider is now a satelloid ... travelling 1,000 mph less than the velocity needed to make it an orbiting space fixture* (Newsweek). **2** a manned and rocket-powered space vehicle that is part airplane and part satellite, made to orbit the earth for a short time and return intact: *Pilots of experimental rocket aircraft ... are only a few years before pilots of "satelloids," a class of semi-space ships now being developed* (Newsweek).

**sa|tem language** (sä′tem, sā′-), one of the languages of the eastern division of the Indo-European languages, including Indo-Iranian, Armenian, Balto-Slavic, and Albanian. The satem languages are characterized by their use of sibilant sounds instead of the velar sounds found in corresponding words of the centum languages. [< Avestan *satəm* hundred (because the initial letter of this word in satem languages represents the sound of *c* in *cent,* as distinguished from centum languages, in which the initial letter represents the sound of *c* in *cat*)]

**sa|ti** (su tē′, sut′ē), *n.* = suttee.

**sa|ti|a|bil|i|ty** (sā′shē ə bil′ə tē, -shə bil′-), *n.* capability of being satiated.

**sa|ti|a|ble** (sā′shē ə bəl, -shə bəl), *adj.* that can be satiated. —**sa′ti|a|ble|ness,** *n.*

**sa|ti|a|bly** (sā′shē ə blē, -shə blē), *adv.* so as to satiate.

**sa|ti|ate** (*v.* sā′shē āt; *adj.* sā′shē it, -āt), *v.,* **-at|ed, -at|ing,** *adj.* —*v.t.* **1** to feed fully; satisfy fully. **2** to weary or disgust with too much; supply with too much; glut; cloy: *She was so satiated with bananas that she would not even look at one.*
—*adj.* filled to satiety; satiated: *In life's cool evening, satiate of applause* (Alexander Pope). [< Latin *satiāre* (with English *-ate*[1]) < *satis* enough]
—*Syn. v.t.* **1 Satiate, sate, surfeit** mean to fill with more than enough to satisfy. **Satiate** means to feed, literally or figuratively, as a person or mind, to the point where something that did please or was wanted no longer gives pleasure: *Children who are given every toy they see become satiated.* **Sate** usually means to satisfy a desire or appetite so fully that it dies: *Will nothing sate his lust for power?* **Surfeit** means to eat or supply to the point of being sick or disgusted: *He surfeited them with candy and sodas.*

**sa|ti|a|tion** (sā′shē ā′shən), *n.* **1** the act of satiating. **2** the state of being satiated.

**sa|ti|e|ty** (sə tī′ə tē), *n.* the feeling of having had too much; disgust or weariness caused by excess; satiated condition: *Of knowledge there is no satiety* (Francis Bacon). [< Latin *satietās* < *satis* enough]

**sat|in** (sat′ən), *n., adj.* —*n.* a silk, rayon, nylon, or cotton cloth with one very smooth, glossy side.
—*adj.* **1** made of satin. **2** of satin; like satin in texture or surface; smooth and glossy: *The color finish—of semi-gloss or satin appearance—is said to be permanent* (Wall Street Journal).
[< Old French *satin,* also *zatanin,* perhaps < Spanish *aceituní* < Arabic *zaitūnī* having to do with or from *Zaitūn,* adaptation of Chinese *Tzu-t'ing* Chuanchow]

**satin bowerbird,** a bowerbird of Australia having a glossy, blue-black color and china-blue eyes.

**sat|i|net** or **sat|i|nette** (sat′ə net′), *n.* **1** a cloth woven with a cotton warp and woolen woof and having a satiny surface. **2** a thin satin. **3** an imitation satin cloth, especially of silk mixed with cotton.

**sat|in|flow|er** (sat′ən flou′ər), *n.* = honesty (def. 3).

**satin glass,** white opaque glass flashed with a color and treated with hydrofluoric acid to produce a satiny finish: *In England, Thomas Webb and Sons of Stourbridge produced much coloured glass including satin glass* (London Times).

**sat|in|pod** (sat′ən pod′), *n.* = honesty (def. 3).

**satin spar,** a fibrous variety of calcite or gypsum.

**satin stitch,** an embroidery stitch made by filling in a design with straight or slanting, parallel stitches, close enough together to look satiny and to look nearly the same on the reverse side.

**satin weave,** a basic weave in which the threads of the warp are caught and looped by the weft only at certain intervals, producing the smooth, unbroken surface of satin: *Satin weave is really a broken twill in which the twill lines do not show* (Elizabeth C. Baity).

**sat|in|wood** (sat′ən wu̇d′), *n.* **1** the smooth, yellowish-brown wood of an East Indian tree, used especially to ornament furniture: *This wardrobe is made of stinkwood with satinwood panels* (Cape Times). **2** the tree itself. It belongs to the mahogany family. **3** a small West Indian tree of the rue family, having hard, fine-grained, orange-colored wood, used especially for cabinetwork.

**sat|in|y** (sat′ə nē), *adj.* like satin in smoothness and gloss: *The wood is a satiny hand-rubbed and hand-waxed cypress, almost impervious to the elements* (New Yorker).

**sat|ire** (sat′īr), *n.* **1** the use of mockery, irony, or wit to attack or ridicule something, such as a habit, idea, or custom that is, or is considered to be, foolish or wrong: *Satire ... to tell men freely of their foulest faults, to laugh at their vain deeds and vainer thoughts* (John Dryden). *Satire should, like a polished razor keen, wound with a touch that's scarcely felt or seen* (Lady Mary Wortley Montagu). **2** a poem, essay, story, or other literary or artistic form, that attacks or ridicules in this way: *Jonathan Swift's "Gulliver's Travels," in prose, is one of the greatest satires* (J. N. Hook). [< Middle French *satire,* learned borrowing from Latin *satira,* variant of (*lanx*) *satura* medley; (literally) mixed (dish) < *satis* enough]
▶ See **irony** for usage note.

**sa|tir|ic** (sə tir′ik), *adj.* **1** of or containing satire: *a satiric novel or poem.* **2** fond of using satire: *a satiric poet.*

**sa|tir|i|cal** (sə tir′ə kəl), *adj.* **1** fond of using satire. **SYN:** ironical. See syn. under **sarcastic.** **2** satiric; of or containing satire. —**sa|tir′i|cal|ly,** *adv.* —**sa|tir′i|cal|ness,** *n.*

**sat|i|rise** (sat′ə rīz), *v.t.* **-rised, -ris|ing.** *Especially British.* satirize.

**sat|i|rist** (sat′ər ist), *n.* **1** a person who uses satire, especially a writer of satires. The follies and vices of their own times are the chief subjects of satirists.

**sat|i|rize** (sat′ə rīz), *v.t.,* **-rized, -riz|ing.** to attack with satire; criticize with mockery; seek to improve by ridicule.

**sat|i|riz|er** (sat′ə rī′zər), *n.* a person who satirizes.

**sat|is|fac|tion** (sat′is fak′shən), *n.* **1** the act of satisfying; fully supplying or gratifying wants or wishes; fulfillment of conditions or desires: *The satisfaction of hunger requires food. The problem has been settled to the satisfaction of all concerned.* **SYN:** gratification. **2** the condition of being satisfied, or pleased and contented: *She felt satisfaction at winning a prize. Jones expressed the utmost satisfaction at the account* (Henry Fielding). **SYN:** contentment, complacency. **3** anything that makes a person feel pleased or contented: *It is a great satisfaction to have things turn out just the way you want. I cannot express what a satisfaction it was to me, to come into my old hutch* (Daniel Defoe). **4** a response, such as information, that fully meets doubts, objections, or demands. **5** the payment of debt; discharge of an obligation or claim; making up for a wrong or injury done. **SYN:** reparation, atonement, expiation, amends. **6** the performance by a penitent, especially as part of the sacrament of penance, of the expiatory act set forth by Church authority.
**give satisfaction, a** to satisfy: *If this product does not give satisfaction, your money will be refunded.* **b** to fight a duel because of an insult: *It is called "giving a man satisfaction" to urge your offence against him with your sword* (Sir Richard Steele).
[< Latin *satisfactiō, -ōnis* < *satisfacere;* see etym. under **satisfy**]

**sat|is|fac|to|ri|ly** (sat′is fak′tər ə lē, -trə-), *adv.* in a satisfactory manner; so as to give satisfaction.

**sat|is|fac|to|ri|ness** (sat′is fak′tər ē nis, -trē-), *n.* satisfactory character or state; the power of satisfying or contenting.

**sat|is|fac|to|ry** (sat′is fak′tər ē, -trē), *adj.* **1** good enough to satisfy; satisfying; pleasing or adequate: *He did satisfactory work in third grade and will pass to fourth grade next fall.* **SYN:** gratifying, sufficient. **2** *Theology.* expiatory; making reparation.

**sat|is|fi|a|ble** (sat′is fī′ə bəl), *adj.* that can be satisfied: *a satisfiable condition or demand.*

**sat|is|fi|er** (sat′is fī′ər), *n.* a person or thing that satisfies.

**sat|is|fy** (sat′is fī), *v.,* **-fied, -fy|ing.** —*v.t.* **1** to give enough to (a person); meet or fulfill (as desires, hopes, or demands); put an end to (needs or wants): *to satisfy one's curiosity. He satisfied his hunger with a sandwich and milk. What do you suppose will satisfy the soul, except to walk free and own no superior?* (Walt Whitman). **2** to make contented; please: *Are you satisfied now?* **3** to pay; make right: *After the accident he satisfied all claims for the damage he had caused.* **4** to set free from doubt or uncertainty; convince: *He was satisfied that it was an accident.* **5** to fulfill the conditions of: *to satisfy an algebraic equation.*
—*v.i.* **1** to give satisfaction; please. **2** to make up for a wrong or injury.
[< Middle French *satisfier,* learned borrowing from Latin *satisfacere* < *satis* enough + *facere* do]
—*Syn. v.t.* **1 Satisfy, content** mean to meet, wholly or partly, a person's desires and wants. **Satisfy** means to give enough to fulfill a person's desires, hopes, or needs: *The little mongrel satisfied the boy's desire for a dog.* **Content** means to give enough to please a person and keep him from being unhappy because he does not have everything he wants: *A letter from her daughter once a week contented her.*

**sat|is|fy|ing|ly** (sat′is fī′ing lē), *adv.* so as to satisfy; satisfactorily.

**sa|to|ri** (sä tôr′ē, -tōr′-), *n.* spiritual enlightenment, the goal of Zen Buddhism: *His meditations may lead him to a mental crisis that produces a flash of intuitive insight known as satori* (New Yorker). [< Japanese *satori*]

**sa|trap** (sā′trap, sat′rap), *n.* **1** a ruler, often a tyrant, who is subordinate to a higher ruler. **2** a governor of a province under the ancient Persian monarchy. [< Latin *satrapes* < Greek *satrápēs* < Old Persian *xšathra-pāvan* guardian of the realm]

**sa|trap|y** (sā′trə pē, sat′rə-), *n., pl.* **-trap|ies.** the province, position, or authority of a satrap: *Eventually, the three sects ... developed huge financial and territorial satrapies in return for their subservience to colonialism* (Newsweek).

**sat|su|ma** (sat sü′mə), *n.* **1** a Japanese variety of mandarin orange. **2** a kind of fine Japanese pottery made on the island of Kyushu since the 1600's. [< *Satsuma,* a region of southern Japan or the people who live there]

**sat|u|ra|ble** (sach′ər ə bəl), *adj.* that can be saturated; capable of saturation.

**saturable reactor,** = magnetic amplifier.

**sat|u|rant** (sach′ər ənt), *adj., n.* —*adj.* saturating. —*n.* any substance that charges, impregnates, or neutralizes completely.

**sat|u|rate** (sach′ə rāt), *v.,* **-rat|ed, -rat|ing,** *adj.* —*v.t.* **1** to soak thoroughly; fill full: *During the fog, the air was saturated with moisture. The rain had saturated us by the time we had walked all the way home. Saturate the moss with water before planting the bulbs in it.* (*Figurative.*) *The whole spiritual atmosphere was saturated with cant* (James A. Froude). **SYN:** steep, drench, imbue. **2** to cause (a substance) to unite with the greatest possible amount of another substance. A saturated solution of sugar is one that cannot dissolve any more sugar. **3** *Physics.* to magnetize (a substance) so that the intensity of its magnetization reaches its maximum value. **4** to cover with or concentrate bombs on (a target) so as to destroy completely.
—*adj.* **1** (of colors) intense; deep. **2** = saturated. [< Latin *saturāre* (with English *-ate*[1]) to glut, sate < *satur* full < *satis* enough]

**sat|u|rat|ed** (sach′ə rā′tid), *adj.* **1** soaked thoroughly; wet. **2** (of colors) containing no white; of the greatest intensity. **3** *Chemistry.* **a** that has combined with or taken up in solution the largest possible proportion of some other substance: *When the relative humidity reaches 100 per cent the air is saturated.* **b** (of an organic compound) lacking double or triple bonds and having no free valence, as methane, ethane, and propane: *The members of the Methane Series do not form addition products and are therefore said to be saturated* (Parks and Steinbach). **4** *Physics.* charged to the full extent of its capacity: *Further increase of plate potential does not increase the plate current, which is then said to become saturated* (Sears and Zemansky). **5** (of minerals) containing the greatest proportion of silica possible.

**saturated fat,** solid or semisolid animal fat, such as butter and lard, that contains mainly saturated fatty acids. A diet high in such fat is believed to raise the cholesterol level in the blood, and is associated with certain heart diseases. *The degree of saturation depends on the number of hydrogen atoms on the fat molecule. Saturated fats can accommodate no more hydrogens* (Time).

**sat|u|rat|er** (sach′ə rā′tər), *n.* = saturator.

**sat|u|ra|tion** (sach′ə rā′shən), *n.* **1** the act or process of saturating: *The process of saturation is employed in changing liquid fats into solid fats* (Harbaugh and Goodrich). **2** the fact of being saturated; saturated condition. The saturation of a color increases as the amount of white in it is decreased. *The body is first magnetized to saturation ... the field reduced to zero and it remains permanently magnetized* (Science News).

**saturation bombing,** a method of bombing in which the heaviest possible tonnage or largest possible number of bombs is concentrated on a target so as to destroy it completely: *They used a new strategy of saturation bombing, aimed at stopping the Communist rail supply to the front so that it stayed stopped* (New York Times).

**saturation dive,** a dive made by saturation diving.

---

**Pronunciation Key:** hat, āge, cãre, fär; let, ēqual, tėrm; it, īce; hot, ōpen, ôrder; **oi**l, **ou**t; cup, pu̇t, rüle; **ch**ild; lo**ng**; **th**in; **ŦH**en; **zh**, measure; ə represents **a** in about, **e** in taken, **i** in pencil, **o** in lemon, **u** in circus.

**saturation diver**, a diver who uses saturation diving.

**saturation diving**, a method of diving used to shorten the time and frequency of decompression by remaining at a given depth until the body becomes saturated with the synthetic gas mixture used for breathing: *Saturation diving will allow the divers to stay at depth for as long as desired* (Science News).

**saturation point**, **1** the point at which a substance will combine with or take up in solution no more of another substance. **2** *Figurative.* the condition in which a person can endure no more: *The meeting was filled almost to the saturation point with upsets* (New Yorker).

**sat|u|ra|tor** (sach′ə rā′tər), *n.* a person or thing that saturates: *a saturator for supplying air saturated with water vapor.*

**Sat|ur|day** (sat′ər dē, -dā), *n.* the seventh day of the week; day after Friday; day of worship among Jews and some Christians. *Abbr:* Sat. [Old English *Sæterdæg,* also *Sæterndæg,* half-translation of Latin *Sāturnī diēs* day of Saturn]

**Saturday night special**, *U.S.* a kind of inexpensive, widely sold, handgun: *A Senate subcommittee on juvenile delinquency voted ... a proposal that would outlaw the public sale of "Saturday night specials," cheap and ubiquitous pistols* (Time).

***Sat|urn** (sat′ərn), *n.* **1** the ancient Roman god of agriculture and the harvest. The Greeks called him Cronus. Saturn was believed to have ruled during a golden age and to have been deposed by his son Jupiter. **2** the second largest planet in the solar system, and the sixth in distance from the sun. Its orbit lies between those of Jupiter and Uranus and takes 29.46 years to complete, at a mean distance from the sun of 887,500,000 miles. Saturn is encircled by a system of three rings made up of tiny particles of matter. *Saturn, the only planet easily visible on July evenings, shines toward the south* (Science News Letter). See diagram under **solar system.** **3** the metal lead (in alchemy and old chemistry). [< Latin *Sāturnus;* associated by the Romans with *satiō* sowing < *serere* to sow]

*** Saturn**
definition 2
♄
symbol

**Sat|ur|na|le** (sat′ər nā′lē), *n.* singular of **Saturnalia.**

**Sat|ur|na|li|a** (sat′ər nā′lē ə, -nāl′yə), *n.pl.* the ancient Roman festival of Saturn, celebrated in December with much feasting and merrymaking. [< Latin *Sāturnālia* < *Sāturnus* Saturn]

**sat|ur|na|li|a** (sat′ər nā′lē ə, -nāl′yə), *n.pl.* any period of unrestrained revelry and license. [< *Saturnalia*]

**Sat|ur|na|li|an** (sat′ər nā′lē ən, -nāl′yən), *adj.* of or having to do with the Roman Saturnalia.

**sat|ur|na|li|an** (sat′ər nā′lē ən, -nāl′yən), *adj.* riotously merry; reveling without restraint. [< *Saturnalian*]

**Sa|tur|ni|an** (sə tėr′nē ən), *adj.* **1** of or having to do with the god Saturn or his reign, referred to as "the golden age." **2** *Figurative.* prosperous, happy, or peaceful. **3** of or having to do with a form of verse used in early Roman poetry. **4** of or having to do with the planet Saturn.

**sa|tur|ni|id** (sə tėr′nē id), *n., adj.* —*n.* any one of a family of thick-bodied, giant silkworm moths, as the Cecropia moth, the luna moth, and the Polyphemus moth.
—*adj.* of or belonging to this family of moths.
[< New Latin *Saturniidae* the family name < *Saturnia* the typical genus < Latin *Sāturnius* having to do with Saturn (because of its titanic size)]

**sat|ur|nine** (sat′ər nīn), *adj.* **1** gloomy; grave; taciturn: *The saturnine young man returned to France as the dashing hero of a cause célèbre* (Time). **SYN**: cheerless, glum. **2** *Astrology.* born under or affected by the influence of the planet Saturn. **3** suffering from or caused by lead poisoning. **4** of, having to do with, or like lead (in old chemistry). [< *Saturn,* the planet (because it was supposed to make those born under its sign morose) + *-ine*[1]] —**sat′ur|nine′ly**, *adv.*

**sat|ur|nism** (sat′ər niz əm), *n.* chronic lead poisoning.

**Sat|ya|gra|ha** (sut′yə gru′hə), *n.* a policy of passive resistance and withdrawal of cooperation with the state, begun by Gandhi and his followers in India in 1919 as a protest against certain abuses: *... as Gandhi conceived it—not only as a technique but as a soul force, Satyagraha* (Atlantic). [< Sanskrit *satyāgraha* justified obstinacy < *satya* truth + *ā-graha* a hanging on < *grah* to grasp]

**Sat|ya|gra|hi** (sut′yə gru′hē), *n.* one who favors the policy of Satyagraha.

**sat|yr** (sat′ər, sā′tər), *n.* **1** an ancient Greek deity of the woods, who was part man and part goat or horse. The satyrs were merry, riotous followers of Bacchus, the god of wine. **2** *Figurative: From forty to fifty a man is at heart either a stoic or a satyr* (Arthur Wing Pinero). **3** a man having satyriasis. **4** any one of a family of brown or grayish butterflies that have eyespots on the wings. [< Latin *satyrus* < Greek *sátyros*]

**sat|y|ri|a|sis** (sat′ə rī′ə sis), *n.* a morbid and uncontrollable sexual desire in a man. [< New Latin *satyriasis* < Greek *satyríāsis* < *sátyros* satyr]

**sa|tyr|ic** (sə tir′ik), *adj.* of or having to do with a satyr or satyrs.

**sa|tyr|i|cal** (sə tir′ə kəl), *adj.* of or like a satyr; satyric: *Boasting the most improbable plot since the satyrical heyday of Thorne Smith ...* (Time).

**satyr play**, a ribald drama of ancient Greece, with a chorus of satyrs or satyr-like characters, written to be performed following a trilogy of tragedies at the springtime Dionysian Festival: *The Athenians ... would sit through three tragedies and a satyr play in one morning* (London Times).

**satyr tragopan**, a tragopan of the Himalayas with brilliant orange and scarlet feathers, a black head, and white spots.

**sau** (sou), *n., pl.* **sau.** a coin of Vietnam equal to 1/100 of a dong. [< Vietnamese *sau* < French *sou* sou]

**sauce** (sôs), *n., v.,* **sauced, sauc|ing.** —*n.* **1** something, usually a liquid, served with a food to make it taste better. We eat cranberry sauce with turkey, mint sauce with lamb, egg sauce with fish, and many different sauces with puddings. **2** *U.S.* stewed fruit or the like: *rhubarb sauce.* **3** *Figurative.* something that adds interest or relish: *Fame is only one of the sauces of life* (A. C. Benson). **4** *Informal.* sauciness; impertinence: *I don't like your sauce. Jaunty girls gave sailors sauce* (Atlantic). **SYN**: pertness, flippancy. **5** *U.S. Dialect.* garden sass. **6** *U.S. Slang.* alcoholic liquor: *Vowing that he was off the sauce for life, Sammy insisted that he had not been an alcoholic* (Time).
—*v.t.* **1** to prepare with sauce; season: *to sauce meat with pepper. Now the shish kebab, sauced in Burgundy ...* (New Yorker). **2** *Figurative.* to give interest or flavor to. **3** *Informal.* to be saucy to. **4** to reduce the harshness of: *to sauce criticism with flattery.*
[< Old French *sauce,* earlier *saulse* < Latin *salsa,* feminine adjective, salted, ultimately < *sāl, salis* salt]

**sauce Béarnaise**, *French.* béarnaise sauce.

**sauce|boat** (sôs′bōt′), *n.* a dish for serving sauce, usually with a lip.

**sauce|box** (sôs′boks′), *n. Informal.* a saucy person, especially a girl or young child.

**sauce di|a|ble** (dē ä′blə), a meat or fish sauce thickened with browned flour and butter and flavored with wine, vinegar, and various spices and herbs. [< French *diable* devil]

**sauce|pan** (sôs′pan′), *n.* **1** a metal dish with a handle and usually a lid, used for boiling, stewing, and other like things: *Hotplates have special "glide-over" tops that remove the danger of tipping saucepans* (London Times). **2** a small skillet with a long handle formerly used for boiling sauces and other small things.

**sau|cer** (sô′sər), *n.* **1** a small, shallow dish to set a cup on. **2** a small, round dish with its edge curved up: *to give a cat a saucer of cream.* **3** something round and shallow like a saucer. [< Old French *saucier* sauce dish < *sauce;* see etym. under **sauce**] —**sau′cer|like′**, *adj.*

**saucer eye**, a large, round eye.

**sau|cer-eyed** (sô′sər īd′), *adj.* having very large, round eyes: *Saucer-eyed children sat watching the circus performers.*

**sau|cer|ful** (sô′sər fu̇l), *n., pl.* **-fuls.** enough to fill a saucer.

**sau|cer|man** (sô′sər man′), *n., pl.* **-men.** a creature from outer space; someone who travels by flying saucer: *Visiting saucermen from Mars might well report back to base that all our gods must be hard of hearing* (New Scientist).

**sauce suprême**, a velouté made from chicken stock; suprême.

**sau|cier** (sō syā′), *n. French.* a cook who specializes in preparing sauces.

**sau|ci|ly** (sô′sə lē), *adv.* in a saucy manner; impudently; pertly.

**sau|ci|ness** (sô′sē nis), *n.* pertness; impudence; rudeness.

**sau|cis|son** (sō sē sôN′), *n. French.* a long pipe or bag made waterproof and filled with powder to serve as a fuze.

**sau|cy** (sô′sē), *adj.,* **-ci|er, -ci|est.** **1** showing lack of respect; rude; impudent: *saucy language, saucy conduct.* **SYN**: See syn. under **impertinent.** **2** pert; smart: *She wore a saucy new hat.* **3** *Obsolete.* scornful; disdainful: *In saucy state the griping broker sits* (John Gay).

**Sa|u|di** (sä ü′dē, sou′-), *adj., n.* —*adj.* = Saudi Arabian.
—*n.* **1** a native or inhabitant of Saudi Arabia; Saudi Arabian. **2** a member or supporter of the royal dynasty of Saudi Arabia.

**Saudi Arabian**, **1** of or having to do with the kingdom of Saudi Arabia, its people, or their language. **2** a native or inhabitant of Saudi Arabia. Also, **Saudi.**

**sau|er|bra|ten** (sou′ər brä′tən), *n.* a pot roast marinated in vinegar and herbs before cooking. [< German *Sauerbraten* < *sauer* sour + *Braten* roast meat]

**sauer|kraut** (sour′krout′), *n.* cabbage cut fine, salted, and allowed to sour or ferment. [< German *Sauerkraut* < *sauer* sour + *Kraut* vegetable, cabbage]

**sau|ger** (sô′gər), *n.* a North American pike perch smaller than a walleye. [American English; origin uncertain]

**saugh** (sôH, souH, säH), *n. Scottish.* a willow; sallow. [Old English *salh,* variant of *sealh* sallow[2]]

**Sauk** (sak, sôk), *n., pl.* **Sauk** or **Sauks,** *adj.* —*n.* a member of a tribe of North American Indians of Algonkian stock who formerly lived in Michigan and Wisconsin, west of Lake Michigan. They now live in Oklahoma, Iowa, and Kansas. **2** the language of this tribe, closely related to Fox.
—*adj.* of or having to do with this tribe. Also, **Sac.**

**Saul** (sôl), *n.* **1** the first king of Israel (in the Bible, I Samuel 9-31). **2** the original name of the Apostle Paul. He was also known, prior to his conversion, as Saul of Tarsus (in the Bible, Acts 9:1-31).

**sault** (sü), *n.* a rapid in a river: *Sault Sainte Marie.* [< Canadian French *sault,* variant of Old French *saut* < Latin *saltus, -ūs* a leap < *salīre* leap. Compare etym. under **assault.**]

**Saul|teaux** (sôl tō′), *n., pl.* **-teaux** (-tō′, -tōz′), *adj.* —*n.* **1** a member of a tribe of Ojibwa Indians inhabiting the woodlands of western Ontario, north of Lake Huron and Lake Superior. **2** the language of this tribe.
—*adj.* of or having to do with this tribe or its language.
[< French *Saulteaux* < *sault* falls, rapids + *eaux,* plural of *eau* water; because the tribe annually met at the rapids of Sault Ste. Marie in Ontario]

**sau|na** (sou′nä), *n.* **1** a steam bath in which the steam is produced by throwing water on hot stones. It originated in Finland. **2** a building or room used for such steam baths: *And a $20,000 sauna (steam) bath had to be constructed* (Wall Street Journal). [< Finnish *sauna*]

**saun|ter** (sôn′tər, sän′-), *v., n.* —*v.i.* to walk along slowly, happily, and aimlessly; stroll: *People sauntered through the park on summer evenings.*
—*n.* **1** a leisurely or careless gait: *The other ... walked slowly, with a sort of saunter, towards Adam* (George Eliot). **2** a stroll: *a weekday saunter through the less busy parts of the metropolis* (Charles Lamb).
[origin uncertain] —**saun′ter|er**, *n.* —**saun′ter|ing|ly**, *adv.*

**sau|rel** (sôr′əl), *n., pl.* **-rels** or (*collectively*) **-rel.** any one of various carangoid saltwater fishes common off the Atlantic coasts of Europe and America; scad; horse mackerel. Saurels are fusiform in shape with vertical plates arming the entire lateral line. [< French *saurel* < Old French *saur, sor* herring < a Germanic word]

**sau|ri|an** (sôr′ē ən), *n., adj.* —*n.* **1** = lizard. **2** any similar reptile, such as a crocodile or dinosaur.
—*adj.* **1** belonging to or having to do with the saurians. **2** of or like a lizard.
[< New Latin *Sauria* an earlier order name (< Greek *saûros* lizard) + English *-an*]

**saur|is|chi|an** (sô ris′kē ən), *n., adj.* —*n.* any one of an order of carnivorous and herbivorous dinosaurs of the Mesozoic, having a hip structure similar to that of modern lizards, including members of the sauropod and theropod suborders.
—*adj.* of or belonging to this order.
[< New Latin *Sauria* an earlier order name (< Greek *saûros* lizard) + Greek *ischíon* hip + English *-ian*]

**sau|ro|pod** (sôr′ə pod), *n., adj.* —*n.* any one of a suborder of herbivorous dinosaurs with a small head, long neck and tail, and limbs with five toes, comprising the largest land animals known.
—*adj.* of or belonging to the sauropods.
[< New Latin *Sauropoda* the suborder name < Greek *saûros* lizard + *poús, podós* foot]

**sau|rop|o|dous** (sô rop′ə dəs), *adj.* of or having to do with the sauropods.

**sau|ry** (sôr′ē), *n., pl.* **-ries** or (*collectively*) **-ry.** any one of various small, slender, long-snouted fish related to the needlefishes and flying fishes. [apparently < New Latin *saurus* the species name < Greek *saûros* lizard]

**sau|sage** (sô′sij), *n.* chopped pork, beef, or other meats, seasoned and usually stuffed into a thin tube: *The frankfurter ... is the most popular sausage in the world* (John C. Ayres). [< Old North French *saussiche,* Old French *saucisse* < Vulgar Latin *salcīcia* < Latin *salere* to salt < *sāl, salis* salt. Compare etym. under **sauce**.]

**sausage tree**, any African tree of a group of the bignonia family with panicles of orange or reddish flowers, especially a variety grown for its long, edible fruit.

**saus|su|rite** (sôs′yə rīt, sô sůr′īt), *n.* a very compact mineral formed by the alternation of feldspar, composed chiefly of zoisite. [< Professor Horace B. de *Saussure,* 1740-1799, a Swiss naturalist, who described it first]

**sau|té** (sō tā′, sô-), *adj., n., v.,* **-téed, -té|ing**. **—*adj.*** cooked or browned in a little fat, usually quickly and over a hot fire. **—*n.*** a dish of food cooked or browned in a little fat. **—*v.t.*** to fry quickly in a little fat: *crabmeat sautéed with butter.* [< French *sauté,* past participle of *sauter* to jump < Latin *saltāre* hop, dance (frequentative) < *salīre* to leap]

**sau|terne** or **Sau|terne** (sō tėrn′, sô-), *n.* **1** Also, **sauternes** or **Sauternes**. a sweet white wine made in the region south of Bordeaux, France. **2** a similar wine made elsewhere. [< *Sauternes,* a town in France near where the grapes are grown]

**sau|toir** (sō twär′), *n.* **1** a long ribbon, chain, or the like, worn about the neck, and drawn together some distance above the lower ends, often used to hold eyeglasses. **2** *Heraldry.* saltire. [< French *sautoir;* see etym. under **saltire**]

**sauve qui peut** (sōv′ kē pœ′), *French.* **1** a general rout; hasty flight. **2** (literally) let whoever can, save (himself).

**sav|a|ble** (sā′və bəl), *adj.* that can be saved. Also, **saveable**.

**sav|age** (sav′ij), *adj., n., v.,* **-aged, -ag|ing.** **—*adj.*** **1** not civilized; barbarous: *savage customs. Gaudy colors please a savage taste. ... the barriers, which had so long separated the savage and the civilized nations of the earth* (Edward Gibbon). **SYN**: primitive. **2** fierce; cruel; ready to fight; brutal: *a savage temper. The savage lion attacked the hunter.* **SYN**: ferocious. See syn. under **fierce**. **3** wild or rugged; uncultivated: *He likes savage mountain scenery.* **4** undomesticated; untamed. **5a** furiously angry; enraged: *Come, Jasper, you need not look so savage* (W. S. Hayward). **b** rough or unsparing in speech: *He turned and gave a short savage order to one of his men* (Graham Greene). **6** *Archaic.* (of a plant) uncultivated: *St. Foin ... grows naturally savage without sowing or tillage* (Jethro Tull). **7** *Archaic.* rude; unpolished: *To savage music, wilder as it grows* (Shelley).

**—*n.*** **1** a member of a people in the lowest stage of development or civilization; uncivilized person: *nations of savages ... barbarous and brutish to the last degree* (Daniel Defoe). **2** a fierce, brutal, or cruel person: *Witness the patient ox ... Driv'n to the slaughter ... while the savage at his heels Laughs at the frantic suff'rer's fury* (William Cowper). **3** a person ignorant or neglectful of the rules of good manners. **4** *Obsolete.* a wild animal: *When the grim savage* [*the lion*], *to his rifled den Too late returning, snuffs the track of men* (Alexander Pope).

**—*v.t.*** **1** (of an animal) to attack viciously, especially with the teeth. **2** to assail in a ferocious manner; subject to savage attack: *The current vogue in satire ... is to savage every father figure in sight* (Manchester Guardian)

[< Old French *sauvage* < Late Latin *salvāticus,* for Latin *silvāticus* < *silva* forest] **—sav′age|ly,** *adv.* **—sav′age|ness,** *n.*

**sav|age|ry** (sav′ij rē), *n., pl.* **-ries**. **1** fierceness; cruelty; brutality: *What they could not get by borrowing or adapting, they went after with a savagery that bloodied history* (Time). **SYN**: ferocity. **2** wildness: *The appearance of the rock-bound coast is one of unrelieved savagery* (George Augustus Sala). **3** an uncivilized condition: *to live in savagery.* **4** savage persons or beasts as a group: *That the white settlers were not entirely overwhelmed in the first mad, blood-thirsting rush of relentless savagery is a matter for marvel* (Robert S. S. Baden-Powell).

**sav|ag|ism** (sav′ə jiz əm), *n.* = savagery.

**Savak** or **SAVAK** (sä vak′), *n.* the National Intelligence and Security Organization of Iran: *Since its establishment 19 years ago, Savak—the name is an acronym for Persian words ... has become probably the most powerful and dreaded police force in the Moslem Middle East* (Eric Pace).

**sa|van|na** or **sa|van|nah** (sə van′ə), *n.* **1** a grassy plain with few or no trees, especially one in the southeastern United States or near the tropics. **2** a region of grassland with scattered trees lying between the equatorial forest and the hot deserts in either hemisphere. [< Spanish *sabana* < earlier *zavana* < Arawak (Haiti)]

**sa|vant** (sə vänt′, sav′ənt; *French* sȧ väɴ′), *n., pl.* **-vants** (*French* -väɴ′). a man of learning: *This seemed to make him a savant on subjects political* (Atlantic). *Saint-Simon divided mankind into three classes: the savants, the propertied, and the unpropertied* (Edmund Wilson). **SYN**: sage, scholar. [< Old French *savant,* present participle of *savoir* know < Vulgar Latin *sapēre,* for Latin *sapere* be wise]

**sa|vate** (sȧ vȧt′), *n.* a French style of boxing in which the feet and head are used as well as fists. [< French *savate* (literally) old shoe; origin uncertain. Compare etym. under **sabot**.]

**save**[1] (sāv), *v.,* **saved, sav|ing,** *n.* **—*v.t.*** **1** to make safe from harm, danger, hurt, or loss; rescue: *The dog saved the boy's life. The woman saved her jewels from the fire.* **SYN**: deliver, redeem. **2** to keep safe from harm, danger, hurt, or loss; protect: *to save one's honor. The loan saved my credit, and made my fortune* (Edward G. Bulwer-Lytton). **SYN**: safeguard, shield, preserve. **3** to lay aside; store up: *to save rubber bands. The father is saving money for his son's education.* **SYN**: hoard, reserve. **4** to keep from spending or wasting: *Save your strength.* **5** to prevent; make less: *to save work, to save trouble, to save expense. A stitch in time saves nine.* **6** to treat carefully to lessen wear or weariness: *Large print saves one's eyes.* **7** to prevent the loss of: *Another goal will save the game.* **8** to set free from sin and its results: *The Christian religion teaches that Christ came to save the world.* **SYN**: deliver, redeem. **9** *Especially British.* to avoid missing: *The note must go this instant to save the post* (Thackeray).

**—*v.i.*** **1** to keep a person or thing from harm, danger, hurt, or loss. **2** to lay up money; add to one's property. **3** to avoid expense or waste; be economical: *She saves in every way she can.*

**—*n.*** the act of saving, especially a play that keeps an opponent from scoring or winning in a game: *The ... goalie ... had a comparatively easy time of it. He had to make only three saves in the first period* (New York Times).

[< Old French *sauver,* earlier *salver* < Late Latin *salvāre* < Latin *salvus* safe] **—sav′er,** *n.*

**save**[2] (sāv), *prep., conj.* **—*prep.*** except; but: *He works every day save Sundays. He heard no other sound save ... his own breathing* (James M. Barrie). **—*conj.*** **1** excepting. **2** *Archaic.* unless. [variant of *safe,* in sense of "not being involved"; probably patterned on French *sauf* safe, used in an absolute construction]

**save|a|ble** (sā′və bəl), *adj.* that can be saved. Also, **savable**.

**save-all** (sāv′ôl′), *n.* **1** a means for preventing loss or waste, especially a receptacle for collecting things that would otherwise be lost or not used. **2** = penny bank. **3** *Dialect.* a pinafore or overall.

**sav|e|loy** (sav′ə loi), *n. British.* a highly seasoned, dried pork sausage. [< French *cervelas,* earlier *cervelat.* Compare etym. under **cervelat**.]

**Sav|ile Row** (sav′il), a street in London, England, noted as a center of fashions in men's clothing.

**sav|in or sav|ine** (sav′in), *n.* **1** a juniper shrub whose tops yield an oily drug used in medicine. **2** this drug. **3** any one of various junipers, such as the red cedar. [Old English *safīne* < Vulgar Latin *savina* < Latin (*herba*) *sabīna* Sabine herb]

**sav|ing** (sā′ving), *adj., n., prep., conj.* **—*adj.*** **1** that saves; preserving: *Her saving ways forced her to keep all kinds of things she would never use.* **2** tending to save up money; avoiding waste; economical: *Old-fashioned housewives were usually very saving.* **SYN**: thrifty, provident, sparing, frugal. **3** making a reservation: *a saving clause.* **4** *Theology.* delivering from sin: *Good works may exist without saving principles ...; but saving principles ... never can exist without good works* (Samuel Taylor Coleridge). **5** compensating; redeeming: *Rich in saving common sense* (Tennyson).

**—*n.*** **1** an act or way of saving money or time: *It will be a saving to take this short cut.* **2** the act of preserving, or rescuing. **3** that which is saved, especially a sum of money: *The discount gave me a saving of $25.* **4** *Law.* a reservation; exception.

**—*prep.*** **1** with the exception of; save; except: *Saving a few crusts, we had eaten nothing all day.* **2** with all due respect to or for: *saving your presence.*

**—*conj.*** with the exception of: *And what pleasure more has he that possesses them, saving that he may look upon them with his eyes?* (Miles Coverdale).

**savings**, money saved: *With our policyholder dividends your total savings can be really surprising* (Newsweek).

**—sav′ing|ly,** *adv.* **—sav′ing|ness,** *n.*

**saving grace**, **1** a redeeming feature. **2** *Theology.* God's grace that gives salvation.

**sav|ings account** (sā′vingz), an account in a savings bank or a similar account in a regular bank.

**savings and loan association**, a bank that uses the savings deposits of its members to make loans, usually for the purchase and building of homes, paying the members dividends from the profits; building and loan association; cooperative bank.

**savings bank**, a bank which accepts money only for savings and investment and which pays interest on all deposits. It does not transfer money to other banks or persons on checks written by the depositors.

**savings bond**, a bond issued by the U.S. Government to help pay its expenses and encourage personal saving. Savings bonds can be cashed with interest after a certain time and have been used in wartime to help curb inflation by absorbing excess private funds.

**sav|ior** (sāv′yər), *n.* a person who saves or rescues: *He was extolled as the savior of the country* (Washington Irving). **SYN**: deliverer. [< Old French *sauveour,* adaptation of Late Latin *salvātor* < *salvāre* to save]

**sav|iour** (sāv′yər), *n. Especially British.* savior.

**Sav|iour** or **Sav|ior** (sāv′yər), *n.* = Jesus Christ.

**sa|voir-faire** (sav′wär fãr′), *n.* knowledge of just what to do and how to do it; social grace; tact: *It was typical of the confusion—the absence of savoir-faire—that he had expected from Earline* (New Yorker). [< French *savoir-faire* (literally) knowing how to act]

**sa|voir-vi|vre** (sav′wär vē′vrə), *n.* knowledge of the world and of the usages of polite society; good breeding: *Our society is to have the utmost polish, ease, and grace of manner, and the completest savoir-vivre* (William H. Mallock). **SYN**: urbanity. [< French *savoir-vivre* (literally) knowing how to live]

**sa|vor** (sā′vər), *n., v.,* **—*n.*** **1** a taste or smell; flavor: *This soup has a savor of onion.* **SYN**: smack. **2** *Figurative.* a distinctive quality; noticeable trace: *There is a savor of conceit in everything he says. The savor of death from all things there that live ...* (Milton). **3** a pleasing flavor; interesting quality: (*Figurative.*) *a dull life, quite without savor.* **4** *Archaic, Figurative.* repute; estimation.

**—*v.t.*** **1** to enjoy the savor of; perceive or appreciate by taste or smell: *We savored the soup with pleasure.* (*Figurative.*) *In his youth the cavalier had savored life to the full.* **2** to give flavor to; season. **3** *Figurative.* to show traces of the presence or influence of: *Bad manners savor a bad education. Willful barrenness, that ... savors only rancor and pride ...* (Milton). **5** *Obsolete.* to discern; note; perceive.

**—*v.i.*** **1** to taste or smell (of): *That sauce savors of lemon.* **2** *Figurative.* to have the quality or nature (of): *a request that savors of a command. The plot savored of treason.* **SYN**: smack.

[< Old French *savour, savur* < Latin *sapor, -ōris,* related to *sapere* taste, be wise] **—sa′vor|er,** *n.*

**sa|vor|i|ly** (sā′vər ə lē), *adv.* in a savory manner; with a pleasing taste or smell.

**sa|vor|i|ness** (sā′vər ē nis), *n.* savory quality; pleasing taste or smell.

**sa|vor|less** (sā′vər lis), *adj.* without flavor; insipid.

**sa|vor|ous** (sā′vər əs), *adj.* = savory.

**sa|vor|y**[1] (sā′vər ē), *adj., n.,* **-vor|i|er, -vor|i|est,** *n., pl.* **-vor|ies.** **—*adj.*** **1** pleasing in taste or smell: *The savory smell of roasting turkey greeted us as we entered the house.* **SYN**: appetizing, palatable, tasty, toothsome. **2** giving a relish; salty or piquant and not sweet. **3** *Figurative.* morally pleasing; agreeable.

**—*n.*** a small portion of highly seasoned food served at the beginning or end of a dinner to stimulate the appetite or digestion: *Later over soup, steak and savory, served by several maids, there were painful attempts at conversation* (New Yorker).

[< Old French *savouré,* past participle of *savourer* to taste < *savour;* see etym. under **savor**]

**sa|vor|y**[2] (sā′vər ē), *n., pl.* **-vor|ies**. any one of several fragrant, often woody herbs and small shrubs of the mint family, used for seasoning food. [Middle English *saverey* < Old French *savoreie,* alteration of Latin *saturēia*]

**sa|vour** (sā′vər), *n., v.i., v.t. Especially British.* savor.

**sa|vour|y**[1] (sā′vər ē), *adj.,* **-vour|i|er, -vour|i|est,** *n., pl.* **-vour|ies**. *Especially British.* savory[1].

**sa|vour|y**[2] (sā′vər ē), *n., pl.* **-vour|ies**. *Especially British.* savory[2].

---

**Pronunciation Key:** hat, āge, cãre, fär; let, ēqual, tėrm; it, īce; hot, ōpen, ôrder; **oil**, **out**; cup, pủt, rüle; **ch**ild; lo**ng**; **th**in; **ᴛʜ**en; **zh**, measure; **ə** represents **a** in about, **e** in taken, **i** in pencil, **o** in lemon, **u** in circus.

**sa|voy** (sə voi′), *n.*, or **savoy cabbage**, a variety of cabbage with a compact head and wrinkled leaves. [< French (*chou de*) *Savoie* (cabbage of) Savoy < *Savoie* Savoy, a region in France]

**Sa|voy|ard** (sə voi′ərd), *n., adj.* —*n.* **1** an actor, producer, or warm admirer of Gilbert and Sullivan's operas, many of which were first produced at the Savoy Theatre, London. **2** a native or inhabitant of Savoy, a region in southeastern France.
—*adj.* **1** of Savoy or its people. **2** of or having to do with Gilbert and Sullivan's operas or their admirers.

**Savoy cake**, = ladyfinger.

**Savoy medlar**, a European shrub or tree, related to the shadbush.

**sav|vi|ness** (sav′ē nis), *n. Slang.* understanding; savvy.

**sav|vy** (sav′ē), *v.*, **-vied, -vy|ing**, *n., adj. Slang.* —*v.t., v.i.* to know; understand: *You think you are wise, but there's a lot of things you don't savvy* (Owen Wister).
—*n.* understanding; intelligence; sense: *I said he had savvy enough to find the index in "Gray's Anatomy"* (Sinclair Lewis). *Author Laing shows enough savvy about supermarkets to have been born and bred in one* (Time).
—*adj.* intelligent; sensible; knowing: *a savvy farm spokesman and Ike's campaign adviser on agriculture* (Time).
[partly < French *savez*(*-vous*)? do you know? partly < Spanish *sabe* (*usted*) (or *sabes*) you know, both < Vulgar Latin *sapēre*, for Latin *sapere* be wise, be knowing; have taste]

***saw¹** (sô), *n., v.*, **sawed, sawed** or **sawn, saw|ing.** —*n.* **1** a tool for cutting, made of a thin blade with sharp teeth on the edge: *Workmen use saws to cut wood, stone, metal, plastics, and other material* (Arthur C. Ansley). **2** a machine with such a tool for cutting. **3** a tool without teeth that wears its way, as through stone.
—*v.t.* **1** to cut with a saw: *The man sawed wood for the fireplace.* **2** to make with a saw: *Boards are sawed from logs.* **3** *Figurative: Do not saw the air too much with your hand* (Shakespeare). **4** to work (something) from side to side like a saw. —*v.i.* **1** to use a saw: *Can you saw straight?* **2** to be sawed: *Pine wood saws more easily than oak.* **3** *Figurative.* to cut as a saw does.
[Old English *sagu, saga*] —**saw′er**, *n.* —**saw′-like′**, *adj.*

***saw¹**
definition 1

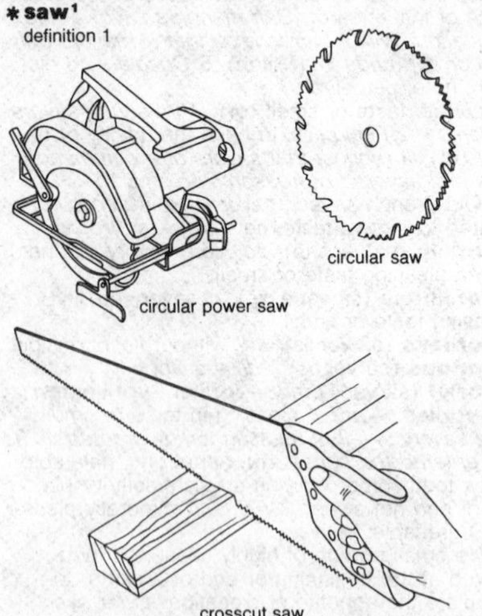

circular saw

circular power saw

crosscut saw

**saw²** (sô), *v.* the past tense of **see¹**: *I saw a robin yesterday.*

**saw³** (sô), *n.* a wise saying; proverb: *"A stitch in time saves nine" is a familiar saw. It is an old Wall Street saw that "the market never discounts anything twice"* (Newsweek). SYN: maxim, adage. [Old English *sagu*, related to *secgan* to say]

**saw|back** (sô′bak′), *n.* a regularly serrate ridge or mountain.

**saw|bill** (sô′bil′), *n.* any one of various birds with a serrate bill, such as the motmot.

**saw|bones** (sô′bōnz′), *n., pl.* **-bones** or **-bones-es.** *Slang.* a doctor; surgeon.

**saw|buck** (sô′buk′), *n. U.S.* **1** a sawhorse. **2** *Slang.* **a** a ten-dollar bill. **b** a twenty-dollar bill. **3** *Slang.* a ten-year prison sentence. [American English, probably < Dutch *zaagbok*]

**saw|der** (sô′dər), *n. Informal.* flattery; blarney. [variant of *solder*]

**saw|dust** (sô′dust′), *n., adj., v.* —*n.* tiny particles of wood made by sawing: *We prefer hardwood sawdust, like birch, maple, and oak* (New Yorker).
—*adj.* **1** filled or covered with sawdust: *a sawdust doll, a sawdust floor.* **2** of or having to do with a tent show or tent meeting at which the floor is covered with sawdust: *a sawdust star, a sawdust preacher.* **3** *Figurative.* unsubstantial; insignificant: [*Mussolini*] *knew himself to be a sawdust Caesar* (Punch).
—*v.t.* to cover, sprinkle, or strew with sawdust.

**sawdust trail**, *U.S.* **1** the trail of revivalists; the round of repentance or revival meetings and activities. **2** the road of repentance or conversion: *to hit the sawdust trail.* [because repentant sinners at a tent meeting go down the sawdust-covered aisle to the altar]

**saw-edged** (sô′ejd′), *adj.* = saw-toothed.

**sawed-off** (sôd′ôf′, -of′), *adj.* **1** having one end sawed or cut off: *a sawed-off shotgun.* **2** *U.S. Slang.* small in size; short: *An amiable, sawed-off little man, with a manner as unobtrusive as his ... crew haircut* (Newsweek).

**saw|fish** (sô′fish′), *n., pl.* **-fish|es** or (*collectively*) **-fish.** any one of a family of rays resembling sharks, having a long, flat snout with a row of sharp teeth on each edge. The sawfish grows to about 20 feet long and bears live young.

**saw|fly** (sô′flī′), *n., pl.* **-flies.** any one of two families of hymenopterous insects. The female sawfly has a sawlike organ for cutting slits in plants to hold her eggs.

**saw grass**, *U.S.* any one of various plants of the sedge family having long, slender, saw-toothed leaves: *The saw grass is not grass but an abrasive sedge, and a man trying to bull through it would soon be stripped of clothing* (Philip Wylie).

**saw|horse** (sô′hôrs′), *n.* a frame for holding wood that is being sawed.

**saw log**, or **saw|log** (sô′lôg′, -log′), *n.* a log fit for sawing into boards: *Crooked and diseased trees can be sold as pulpwood, while straight, healthy trees grow into valuable saw logs* (Science News Letter).

**saw|man** (sô′mən), *n., pl.* **-men.** a man who works with a saw: *The sawman in a steel mill ... tries to calculate how to divide up billets hundreds of feet in length* (New Scientist).

**saw|mill** (sô′mil′), *n.* **1** a building or place where machines saw timber into planks or boards. **2** a machine for such sawing.

**saw|mill|er** (sô′mil′ər), *n.* the proprietor or manager of a sawmill.

**saw|mill|ing** (sô′mil′ing), *n.* the business or work of sawing wood in a sawmill.

**sawn** (sôn), *v.* sawed; a past participle of **saw¹**.

**saw|ney** (sô′nē), *n., pl.* **-neys**, *adj., v. Especially British Informal.* —*n.* a fool or simpleton.
—*adj.* foolish; foolishly sentimental.
—*v.i.* to act the sawney; fool.
[perhaps alteration of *zany*]

**Saw|ney** (sô′nē), *n., pl.* **-neys.** *Informal.* a nickname for a Scotsman. [variant of *Sandy*, short for *Alexander*]

**sawn|wood** (sôn′wu̇d′), *n.* wood cut up for lumber.

**saw|ny** (sô′nē), *n., pl.* **-nies**, *adj., v.* = sawney.

**Saw|ny** (sô′nē), *n., pl.* **-nies.** = Sawney.

**saw palmetto**, a shrublike palmetto with leafstalks with spiny teeth, found in the southern United States and the West Indies.

**saw|pit** (sô′pit′), *n.* a pit over which a log is sawed into planks by two men, the pit allowing room for the blade and for the bottom sawyer to work.

**saw set**, an instrument used to set the teeth of a saw.

**saw shark**, any one of a family of small sharks that resemble sawfish but have their gill openings on the side of the neck.

**saw|tim|ber** (sô′tim′bər), *n.* trees large enough to be cut for lumber: *The growth of new sawtimber at last almost matches the amount cut down* (Time).

**saw|tooth** (sô′tüth′), *n., pl.* **-teeth** or **-tooths**, *adj.* —*n.* **1** a tooth of a saw. **2** a notched tooth of an animal or machine: *a snake's sawteeth.* **3** *Figurative.* anything shaped like the tooth of a saw: *dazzling sawtooths of rock and ice* (Manchester Guardian Weekly).
—*adj.* having or resembling sawteeth; saw-toothed; serrate: *sawtooth waves. They found that during a dream the eyeballs move rapidly and brain waves take on a sawtooth pattern quite different from the long, rolling waves of dreamless sleep* (Scientific American).

**saw-toothed** (sô′tütht′), *adj.* **1** having teeth on the edge, like a saw. **2** notched like teeth on a saw; serrate.

**saw-whet owl** (sô′hwet′), a small, brown and white owl of North America, which has an extremely harsh and rasping call: *But we almost missed the tiny saw-whet owl, motionless on a dead limb just out of arm's reach* (Atlantic). [because the owl's call sounds like the filing of a saw]

**saw|yer** (sô′yər), *n.* **1** a man whose work is sawing timber into planks or boards. **2** any one of various beetles whose larvae bore large holes in wood. **3** *U.S.* a tree with one end caught in the bed of a stream and the other swaying with the current: *... abundance of water from shore to shore, and no bars, snags, sawyers, or wrecks in his road* (Mark Twain). [< *saw¹* + *-yer*, as in *lawyer*]

**sax¹** (saks), *n.* a tool for trimming slate roof tiles and for making nail holes in them. [Old English *seax* knife, dagger]

**sax²** (saks), *n., pl.* **sax|es.** *Informal.* **1** a saxophone: [*He*] *turned down an offer to play his sax on a U.S. vaudeville circuit* (Maclean's). **2** a saxophone player: *The five saxes play with savage bite or else hum in their eerie, split harmonies behind a pagan trumpet solo* (Time). [short for *saxophone*]

**Sax.**, **1** Saxon. **2** Saxony.

**sax|a|tile** (sak′sə təl), *adj. Biology.* saxicoline. [< Latin *saxātilis* < *saxum* rock, stone]

**sax|horn** (saks′hôrn′), *n.* one of a group of brass musical instruments like a trumpet, having valves, a cup-shaped mouthpiece, a loud, full tone, and a wide range. A tuba is a large saxhorn with a bass tone. [< Adolphe *Sax*, 1814-1894, a Belgian inventor. Compare etym. under **saxophone.**]

**sax|ic|a|vous** (sak sik′ə vəs), *adj.* rock-boring, as certain mollusks. [< New Latin *saxicavus* (with English *-ous*) < Latin *saxum* rock + *cavāre* to hollow]

**sax|ic|o|line** (sak sik′ə līn, -lin), *adj. Biology.* living on or among rocks; saxatile. [< Latin *saxum* rock, stone + *colere* inhabit + English *-ine¹*]

**sax|ic|o|lous** (sak sik′ə ləs), *adj.* = saxicoline.

**sax|i|fra|ga|ceous** (sak′sə frə gā′shəs), *adj.* belonging to the saxifrage family. [< New Latin *Saxifragaceae* the family name (< *Saxifraga* the typical genus, saxifrage) + English *-ous*]

**sax|i|frage** (sak′sə frij), *n.* **1** a low, spreading plant with white, pink, purple, or yellow flowers. Most saxifrages have rosettes of thick leaves with silvery, toothed edges. Saxifrages are often grown in rock gardens. *Saxifrage leaves resemble cacti in their adaptation to dry climate* (Scientific American). **2** the flower. [< Old French *saxifrage, sassifrage* < Latin *saxifraga* < *saxum* rock + a root of *frangere* to break. See etym. of doublet **salsify.**]

**saxifrage family**, a group of dicotyledonous herbs, shrubs, and small trees found chiefly in temperate and frigid regions. The family includes the saxifrage, gooseberry, currant, hydrangea, syringa, and miterwort.

**sax|ist** (sak′sist), *n. Informal.* a saxophonist. [< *sax²* + *-ist*]

**sax|i|tox|in** (sak′sə tok′sən), *n.* a very poisonous substance that attacks the central nervous system and causes paralysis, secreted by a species of dinoflagellate which is ingested by various edible shellfish: *Saxitoxin ... is responsible for "paralytic shellfish poisoning"* (Scientific American). *Formula:* $C_{10}H_{17}N_7O_4 \cdot 2HCl$ [< New Latin *Saxi*(*domus*) the genus name of a clam from which the poison was isolated + English *toxin*]

**Sax|on** (sak′sən), *n., adj.* —*n.* **1** a member of a Germanic tribe that, with the Angles and Jutes, conquered Britain in the 400's and 500's A.D. **2** the language of the Saxons. **3** = Anglo-Saxon. **4** a native or inhabitant of Saxony, a region in East Germany, formerly a state of Germany.
—*adj.* **1** of or having to do with the early Saxons or their language. **2** = Anglo-Saxon. **3** = English. **4** of or having to do with Saxony in modern Germany.
[probably < Old French *Saxon*, learned borrowing from Latin *Saxo, Saxonēs*, plural < Germanic (compare Old High German *Sahso*)]

**Saxon architecture**, a rough, unrefined variety of Romanesque architecture common in England before the Norman Conquest.

**Sax|o|ni|an** (sak sō′nē ən), *adj.* **1** of or having to do with Saxony in modern Germany; Saxon. **2** of or having to do with a division of the Permian period at the end of the Paleozoic era.

**Sax|on|ism** (sak′sə niz əm), *n.* **1** Saxon or Anglo-Saxon character. **2** an attachment for what is Anglo-Saxon. **3** an Anglo-Saxon idiom.

**Sax|on|ize** (sak′sə nīz), *v.t.*, **-ized, -iz|ing.** to make Saxon or Anglo-Saxon: *Other invaders ... poured in ... till the island was Saxonized* (Charles H. Pearson).

**Sax|o|ny** or **sax|o|ny** (sak′sə nē), *n., pl.* **-nies.** **1** a woolen fabric of high quality with a glossy surface. **2** a fine knitting yarn with a close twist.

***sax|o|phone** (sak′sə fōn), *n.* a brass musical wind instrument with a curved body, keys for the fingers, and a mouthpiece with a single reed, like that of a clarinet. See picture on the opposite page. [< Adolphe *Sax*, 1814-1894, a Belgian inventor + *-phone*]

**sax|o|phon|ic** (sak′sə fon′ik), *adj.* of or for the saxophone.

**sax|o|phon|ist** (sak′sə fō′nist), *n.* a saxophone player.

**sax|tu|ba** (saks′tü′bə, -tyü′-), *n.* a large saxhorn having a deep tone. [< *sax*[2] + *tuba*]

**say** (sā), *v.*, **said, say|ing,** *adv., n.* —*v.t.* **1** to speak: *What did you say? Mother has taught me always to say "please" and "thank you." And Enid could not say one tender word* (Tennyson). **SYN:** utter, articulate, enunciate. **2** to put into words; declare; express; state: *Say what you think. We hear it said that men go down before your spear* (Tennyson). **SYN:** tell, announce, assert, allege. **3** to recite; repeat: *to say grace. Say your prayers.* **SYN:** recount. **4** to take as an estimate; suppose or guess: *The bookcase contains, I would say, about 100 books.* **SYN:** assume. **5** to express an opinion: *It is hard to say which dress is prettier. Can anyone really say he is wrong?*
—*v.i.* **1** to say words; talk: *So he says.* **2** to express an opinion.
—*adv.* **1** about; approximately: *You can learn to dance in, say, ten lessons.* **2** such as; for example: *Pick any card, say the ten of diamonds.*
—*n.* **1** what a person says or has to say: *I said my say and sat down.* **2** a turn or chance to say something: *Has everyone had his say? If so, let's vote on the matter.* **3** the right, power, or authority to make or help to make a decision: *To guard the security of its loan, the bank wants a say in any future Egyptian borrowings* (Newsweek). *The landscape architect has a say not only in the development but in the planning and siting of these roads* (Observer).
**not to say,** to use a more moderate word or statement than: *His language was irreverent, not to say blasphemous.*
**that is to say,** that is; in other words: *She invited us to her birthday party on Labor Day; that is to say, next Monday.*
**to say nothing of,** without mentioning: *She is a beautiful young woman, to say nothing of her kindness and generosity.*
**when all is said and done,** in the end; in the last analysis; ultimately: *When all is said and done, a person's most important possession is his health.*
**You can say that again!** or **You said it!,** *Slang.* I agree with you completely: *"That was a terrific game, wasn't it?" "You can say that again!"*
**You don't say,** *Informal.* really; indeed; I am surprised: *"Our service is the best in the world," the hotel manager said. "You don't say," I replied.*
[Middle English *seien,* Old English *secgan*]
—**say′er,** *n.*
—*Syn.* **Say, talk, state. Say** is the general word for speaking: *Please say when you have had enough.* **Talk** implies a series of sayings, a conversation: *They talked all evening about old times.* **State** implies a formal saying or, as the word itself suggests, a statement: *Would you please state your frank opinion of the plan?*

**sa|ya** (sä′yä), *n., pl.* **-yas.** a skirt worn in the Philippines in the manner of a sarong. [< Tagalog *saya*]

**say|a|ble** (sā′ə bəl), *adj.* that can be said: *Browning has said all that was sayable concerning the celebrated cause* (F. M. Wilson).

**say|est** (sā′ist), *v. Archaic.* say. "Thou sayest" means "you say."

*** saxophone**

**sa|yid** (sī′id, sä′yid), *n.* the title given in Moslem countries to a person supposed to be descended from Mohammed through his daughter Fatima: *A young sayid, or holy man, presented himself for employment the first day* (Atlantic). Also, **sayyid.** [< Arabic *sayyid* lord]

**say|ing** (sā′ing), *n.* **1** something said; statement. **SYN:** utterance, declaration, assertion. **2** a proverb: *"Haste makes waste" is a saying.* **SYN:** adage, saw, maxim. **3** making a statement: *Saying and doing are two things, we say* (Thomas Heywood).
**go without saying,** to be too obvious to need mention: *It goes without saying that you are always welcome at our house.*

**say|nète** (se net′), *n.* **1** (in Spain) a short, amusing dramatic piece with few characters. **2** (in France) a somewhat similar short dramatic piece. [< French *saynète* < Spanish *sainete* (literally) a delicacy < *sain* fat]

**sa|yo|na|ra** (sä′yō nä′rä), *n. Japanese.* goodbye; farewell: *Michener's novel concludes with the lovers forlornly bidding each other sayonara* (New Yorker).

**says** (sez), *v.* the third person singular, present indicative of **say**[1]: *He says "No" to everything.*

**Say's law** (sāz), *Economics.* the theory that in a system of free enterprise the goods produced represent demand as well as supply, so that total supply and total demand are equal, and overproduction is impossible. [< Jean Baptiste *Say,* 1767-1832, a French economist who formulated the theory]

**say-so** (sā′sō′), *n. Informal.* **1** one's mere word; an unsupported statement: *Do you believe that, just on his say-so? They'd grab a bright idea right away, just on the say-so of somebody they trusted* (New Yorker). **2** authority or power to decide: *We would want the say-so on where the buildings are put up and what kind of buildings* (Wall Street Journal).

**sayst** (sāst), *v. Archaic.* sayest; say. "Thou sayst" means "You say."

**say|yid** (sī′id), *n.* = sayid.

**Saz|e|rac** (saz′ə rak), *n.* a cocktail made with bourbon, absinthe, bitters, and sugar, and served with ice and a twist of lemon peel. [probably < a French proper name]

**sb.,** substantive.

**s.b.** or **sb** (no periods), stolen base or stolen bases.

**Sb** (no period), antimony (chemical element; Latin, *stibium*).

**S.B.,** **1** Bachelor of Science (Latin, *Scientiae Baccalaureus*). **2** simultaneous broadcast. **3** South Britain (England and Wales).

**SBA** (no periods) or **S.B.A.,** *U.S.* Small Business Administration: *SBA lends to small business, helps it get government contracts, provides information ...* (Newsweek).

**S-band** (es′band′), *n.* a band of ultrahigh radio frequencies ranging between 1550 and 5200 megahertz: *The Jet Propulsion Laboratory in Pasadena will use the S-band to study the near-surface gravitational profile of the moon and the subsurface gravity anomalies such as mascons and impact craters* (Science News).

**sbir|ro** (zbir′rō), *n., pl.* **-ri** (-rē). (in Italy) a policeman. [< Italian *sbirro,* variant of *birro* < Late Latin *birrus* a cloak (because they are worn by policemen)]

**'sblood** (zblud), *interj. Archaic.* "God's blood," used as an oath.

**SBR** (no periods), styrene-butadiene rubber.

**sc** (no periods), small capitals.

**sc.,** an abbreviation for the following:
1 he or she engraved or carved it (Latin, *sculpsit*).
2 namely (Latin, *scilicet*).
3 scale.
4 scene.
5a science. b scientific.
6 screw.
7 scruple or scruples (in apothecaries' weight).

**s.c.,** **1** (of paper) sized and calendered. **2** small capitals. **3** (of paper) supercalendered.

**Sc** (no period), **1** scandium (chemical element). **2** strato-cumulus (cloud).

**Sc.,** **1** science. **2** Scotch. **3** Scots. **4** Scottish.

**SC** (no periods), South Carolina (with postal Zip Code).

**S.C.,** an abbreviation for the following:
1 Sanitary Corps.
2 Signal Corps.
3 South Carolina.
4 Staff College.
5 Staff Corps.
6 Supreme Court.

**SCA** (no periods), Standard Consolidated Area (the official name in the United States for two or more adjacent metropolitan areas and additional counties, such as Greater Chicago).

**scab** (skab), *n., v.,* **scabbed, scab|bing.** —*n.* **1** a crust that forms over a sore or wound as it heals: *A scab formed on the spot where he was vaccinated.* **2** a skin disease in animals, especially sheep; scabies or mange. **3a** any one of several fungous or bacterial diseases of plants, usually producing dark, crustlike spots. **b** one of these spots. **4** *Informal.* a workman who will not join a labor union or who takes a striker's place: *Thousands of workers poured through picket lines amid shouts of "scabs," "blacklegs" and "traitors" and into auto making factories* (Wall Street Journal). **5** *Slang.* a rascal; scoundrel.
—*v.i.* **1** to become covered with a scab. **2** *Informal.* to act or work as a scab.
[< Scandinavian (compare Danish *skab*)]

**scab|bard** (skab′ərd), *n., v.* —*n.* a sheath or case for the blade of a sword, dagger, or knife.
—*v.t.* to put into a scabbard; sheathe.
[alteration (perhaps influenced by *halberd*) of Middle English *scauberc* < Anglo-French *escaubers,* plural, Old French *escalberc,* perhaps < Germanic]

**scabbard fish,** any one of various fishes with a long, thin, silvery body and a long dorsal fin, such as a variety found in the Pacific off North America.

**scabbed** (skabd), *adj.* **1** having scab or mange. **2** covered with scabs. **3** *Obsolete, Figurative.* mean; contemptible.

**scab|ble** (skab′əl), *v.t.,* **-bled, -bling.** to shape or dress (stone) roughly. [variant of *scapple* < Old French *escapeler, eschapeler* to dress timber]

**scab|bling** (skab′ling), *n.* a chip of stone.

**scab|by** (skab′ē), *adj.,* **-bi|er, -bi|est. 1** covered with scabs. **2** consisting of scabs. **3** having the skin disease scab. **4** *Informal, Figurative.* low; mean; contemptible. —**scab′bi|ly,** *adv.* —**scab′biness,** *n.*

**sca|bies** (skā′bēz, -bē ēz), *n.* a disease of the skin caused by mites that live as parasites under the skin and cause itching; the itch. [< Latin *scabiēs,* related to *scabere* to scratch]

**sca|bi|et|ic** (skā′bē et′ik), *adj.* of or having scabies or mange.

**sca|bi|o|sa** (skā′bē ō′sə), *n.* = scabious[2]. [< New Latin *Scabiosa* the genus name < Medieval Latin *scabiosa;* see etym. under **scabious**[2]]

**sca|bi|ous**[1] (skā′bē əs), *adj.* **1** = scabby. **2** of or like scabies or mange. [< Latin *scabiōsus* mangy, rough < *scabiēs;* see etym. under **scabies**]

**sca|bi|ous**[2] (skā′bē əs), *n.* any one of a group of herbs with long, tough stems and dense flower heads of various colors. [< Medieval Latin *scabiosa* (literally) having to do with the itch, noun use of feminine of Latin *scabiōsus* scabious[1]]

**scab|land** (skab′land′), *n.* an area stripped of topsoil by floodwaters, leaving low hills of bare rock, as in the Pacific Northwest.

**scab|rin** (skab′rin), *n.* a potent insecticide obtained as an oily yellow liquid from the roots of various plants of the composite family. *Formula:* $C_{22}H_{35}NO$ [< New Latin *scabra* species name of a plant that yields it + English *-in*]

**sca|brous** (skā′brəs), *adj.* **1** rough with very small points or projections: *scabrous skin.* **SYN:** scraggly. **2** full of difficulties; harsh; thorny: *scabrous questions, a scabrous situation.* **3** hard to treat with decency; indelicate; risqué: *The inhabitants mix, mate, and mismate in a series of scabrous sexual exercises* (Time). [< Late Latin *scabrōsus* < Latin *scaber* scaly, related to *scabere* to scratch, scrape] —**sca′brous|ly,** *adv.* —**sca′brous|ness,** *n.*

**scad** (skad), *n.* = saurel. [origin uncertain; perhaps < Scandinavian (compare Norwegian dialectal *skad.* Compare etym. under **shad.**]

**scads** (skadz), *n.pl. Informal.* a large quantity or number: *scads of trouble, scads of people.* [American English; origin uncertain]

*** scaffold**
definition 1

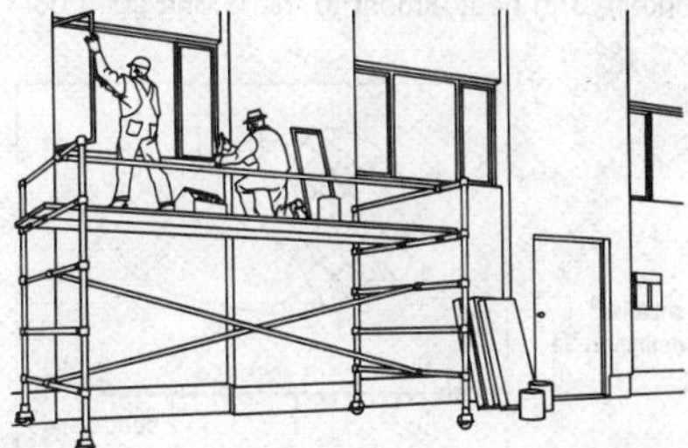

*** scaf|fold** (skaf′əld), *n., v.* —*n.* **1** a temporary structure for holding workmen and materials dur-

**Pronunciation Key:** hat, āge, cãre, fär; let, ēqual, tėrm; it, īce; hot, ōpen, ôrder; oil, out; cup, pu̇t, rüle; child; long; thin; ᴛʜen; zh, measure; ə represents a in about, e in taken, i in pencil, o in lemon, u in circus.

ing the construction, repair, or decoration of a building. **2** a raised platform on which criminals are put to death, especially by hanging: *Truth forever on the scaffold, wrong forever on the throne* (Lowell). **3** a platform, stage, or stand for exhibiting shows, seating spectators, or the like. **4** any raised framework. **5** scaffolding material.
— ***v.t.*** to furnish with a scaffold; support with a scaffold: *The walls were scaffolded for the use of firearms* (Scott).
[Middle English *scafald* < Old French *eschaffault,* also *escadafaut*]

**scaf|fold|er** (skafʹəl dər), *n. British.* a person who erects scaffolding.

**scaf|fold|ing** (skafʹəl ding), *n.* **1** a scaffold or a system of scaffolds: *A fire which broke out in scaffolding that had been erected round it during repair work …* (London Times). **2** materials for scaffolds.

**scag** (skag), *n. U.S. Slang.* heroin. [origin unknown]

**scagl|ia** (skalʹyə), *n.* an Italian limestone, similar to the chalk of England. [< Italian *scaglia* < a Germanic word. Compare etym. under **shale.**]

**scagl|io|la** (skal yōʹlə), *n.* plasterwork that imitates marble, granite, or the like, used especially in decorating interior walls. [< Italian *scagliuola* (diminutive) < *scaglia;* see etym. under **scaglia**]

**scal|a|ble** (skāʹlə bəl), *adj.* that can be scaled or climbed.

**sca|lade** (skə lādʹ), *n. Obsolete.* escalade.

**scal|age** (skāʹlij), *n.* **1a** an amount deducted, as from the listed weight or price, to allow for moisture, leakage, or the like. **b** the act of making such an allowance or deduction. **2** the estimated board feet of lumber obtainable from a log, tree, stand of timber, or the like.

**sca|lar** (skāʹlər), *adj., n.* — ***adj.*** **1** *Mathematics.* having or indicating magnitude, but no direction; capable of being described by a real number. Scalar quantities or measurements specify length, mass, time, temperature, and the like. **2** capable of being represented by a point on a scale. **3** of or resembling a musical or other scale: *a dozen choruses full of double-stops, immense scalar leaps …* (New Yorker).
— ***n.*** *Mathematics.* a scalar number or quantity, as distinguished from a vector.
[< Latin *scālāris* like a ladder < *scālae* ladder; see etym. under **scale³**]

**sca|lar|e** (skə lärʹē, -läʹrē), *n.* a small South American angelfish that has a silvery body with black bars and large fins, commonly raised in aquariums. See picture under **angelfish.** [< New Latin *scalare,* noun use of neuter of Latin *scālāris* like a ladder; see etym. under **scalar**]

**sca|lar|i|form** (skə larʹə fôrm), *adj.* ladderlike: *scalariform plant cells.* [< Latin *scālāris* like a ladder; see etym. under **scalar**]

**scalar product,** *Mathematics.* dot product.

**sca|lar-ten|sor theory** (skāʹlər tenʹsər, -sôr), = Brans-Dicke theory.

**sca|la|tion** (skā lāʹshən), *n.* the nature and form of the scales, as in fishes or snakes.

**scal|a|wag** (skalʹə wag), *n.* **1** *Informal.* a good-for-nothing person; scamp; rascal: *They are mostly crooks and scalawags* (Time). **2** a white Southerner who acted with the Republican Party after the Civil War (an unfriendly term used by Southern Democrats). Also, **scallawag, scallywag.**
[American English; origin uncertain]

**scald¹** (skôld), *v., n., adj.* — ***v.t.*** **1** to burn with hot liquid or steam: *She scalded herself with hot grease.* **2** to pour boiling liquid over; use boiling liquid on: *Scald the dishes before drying them. You scald a pig after you slaughter it* (New Yorker). **3** to heat almost to the boiling point but not quite: *Scald the milk for the bread dough.* **4** *Figurative: The tears that scald the cheek …* (William Cullen Bryant). **5** *Obsolete.* to inflame; irritate: *Would not a secret … scald you to keep it?* (Philip Massinger).
— ***v.i.*** **1** to be heated almost to boiling, but not quite. **2** to become burned by hot liquid or steam.
— ***n.*** **1** a burn caused by hot liquid or steam: *The scald on her hand came from carelessly lifting a pot cover.* **2** a browning of foliage by very hot weather. **3** any one of several parasitic plant diseases, especially of cranberries.
— ***adj.*** heated almost to the boiling point; scalded: *scald milk.*
[< Old North French *escalder* < Late Latin *excaldāre* bathe (off) in hot water < Latin *ex-* off + *calidus* hot]

**scald²** (skôld, skäld), *n.* = skald. [older spelling of *skald*]

**scald³** (skôld), *adj., n. Obsolete.* — ***adj.*** **1** scabby. **2** *Figurative.* mean; contemptible.
— ***n.*** a scab; scruff. Also, **scalled.**
[< *scalled,* adjective < *scall;* see etym. under **scall**]

**scald|ic** (skôlʹdik, skälʹ-), *adj.* = skaldic.

**scald|ing** (skôlʹding), *adj.* **1** that scalds; hot enough to scald: *scalding water. He … drinks his tea scalding* (Scott). **2** *Figurative: scalding tears. Our venomous and scalding words … burn like coals* (John Jackson). — **scaldʹing|ly,** *adv.*

**scal|di|no** (skäl dēʹnō), *n., pl.* **-ni** (-nē). a small earthenware brazier used in Italy. [< Italian *scaldino* < *scaldare* to heat]

**scale¹** (skāl), *n., v.,* **scaled, scal|ing.** — ***n.*** **1a** one of the thin, flat, hard plates forming the outer covering of many fishes, snakes, and lizards. **b** a part like this in other animals, such as one of the very small plates covering the wings of moths and butterflies or one of the plates covering the tails of certain mammals. **c** such scales collectively: *And fishes which were isles of living scale* (Shelley). **2** a thin layer like a scale: *Scales of skin peeled off after she had scarlet fever.* **3** a thin piece of metal or other material: *the scales of a scale armor. The handle of the pocketknife has an ivory scale on each side.* **4a** a mineral coating formed on the inside of something, such as a boiler or kettle, by water during heating. **b** an oxide formed on metals when heated. **5a** one of the parts that unite to cover a bud in winter. Scales are modified rudimentary leaves found on the leaf buds of most perennial deciduous plants. **b** a part like those of the leaf bud, such as one of the layers of an onion bulb, or one of the scalelike leaves of a rhizome or pine cone. **6** an insect that has a shieldlike covering under which it hides and feeds; scale insect.
— ***v.t.*** **1** to remove scales from: *He scaled the fish with a sharp knife.* **2** to remove in thin layers. **3** to cover with scales. **4** to throw (a thin flat object) so that it moves edgewise: *to scale a paper plate.* **5** *Scottish.* to cause to separate; disperse; scatter: *to scale a crowd.*
— ***v.i.*** **1** to come off in scales: *The paint is scaling off the house.* **2** to become coated with scale.
[< Old North French *escale* < Germanic (compare Old High German *scāla* shell, husk). Compare etym. under **scale².**] — **scaleʹlikeʹ,** *adj.*

**scale²** (skāl), *n., v.,* **scaled, scal|ing.** — ***n.*** **1** the dish or pan of a balance. **2** Usually, **scales,** a balance; instrument for weighing: *bathroom scales. The butcher weighed the turkey on the scales. The baby scale helps record the growth of tiny infants* (E. A. Fessenden).
— ***v.t.*** **1** to weigh: *He scales 180 pounds. Thousands of trout fishermen have never seen a brook trout that scaled six pounds* (New York Times). **2** to weigh in scales; measure: (*Figurative.*) *You have found, scaling his present bearing with his past, that he's your fixed enemy* (Shakespeare). **SYN:** compare.
— ***v.i.*** **1** to be weighed. **2** to have weight.
**tip the scales, a** to have as one's weight: *Quarterback Joseph Weiss … stands 6 ft. 4 in. and tips the scales at an even 200 lbs.* (Time). **b** *Figurative.* to overbalance one for another: *He also believes that the scales have been unduly tipped in favor of ambitious, power-hungry labor bosses by … legislation of the New Deal period* (Wall Street Journal).
**turn the scale** (or **scales**), **a** to weigh slightly more than: *He had weighed it carefully … and it turned the scale at thirty-four pounds* (J. K. Jerome). **b** *Figurative.* to determine the success or superiority of one of two opposing actions or sides; preponderate; decide: *The scale was turned in favour of strong measures by the voice of the native troops* (William Stubbs).
[< Scandinavian (compare Old Icelandic *skāl*). Compare etym. under **shale, shell, scall.**]

***scale³** (skāl), *n., v.,* **scaled, scal|ing,** *adj.* — ***n.*** **1** a series of steps or degrees; scheme of graded amounts, especially from the lowest to the highest: *The scale of wages in this factory ranges from ten dollars to twenty dollars a day. He was not at all certain that it did not sometimes happen lower down the scale* (London Times). **2a** a series of marks made along a line or curve at regular distances to use in measuring. A thermometer has a scale. **b** an instrument marked in this way, used for measuring. **3a** the size of a plan, map, drawing, or model compared with what it represents: *This map is drawn to a scale of one inch for each 100 miles.* See picture below. **b** the equally divided line, as on a map, plan, or chart, that indicates this relationship. **4** *Figurative.* relative size or extent: *The rich woman entertains on a large scale.* **5** a system of numbering: *The decimal scale counts by tens, as in cents, dimes, dollars.* **6** *Music.* a series of tones ascending or descending in pitch: *She practices scales on the piano. Abbr:* sc. **7** a graded series of tests or problems used to measure something, such as intelligence, learning, or adjustment. **8** an estimate of the number of board feet in logs or trees. **9** *Obsolete.* **a** a ladder or staircase or other means of ascent: (*Figurative.*) *A scale by which the soul ascends from mighty means to more important ends* (William Cowper). **b** a rung of a ladder.
— ***v.t.*** **1** to reduce or increase by a certain amount in relation to other amounts: *To draw this map, mileage was scaled down to one inch for each 100 miles. The 22 striking unions—which had scaled down their wage demands to an 18½-cent-an-hour boost …* (Newsweek). *Their figures must be scaled up to contemporary levels* (London Times). **2** to climb up or over: *They scaled the wall by ladders.* **SYN:** ascend, mount. **3** to make according to a scale. **4** to measure by, or as if by, a scale. **5** to estimate the number of board feet in (logs or trees).
— ***v.i.*** **1** to go upward; climb. **SYN:** ascend, mount. **2** to form a graduated series.
— ***adj.*** based upon or using a scale: *a scale drawing, scale singing.*
[< Latin *scālae,* ladder, steps < *scandere* to climb]

**scale armor,** armor consisting of small, overlapping scales of metal, horn, or leather.

**scale|board** (skālʹbôrdʹ, -bōrdʹ; skabʹərd), *n.* **1** a very thin board used for the back of a picture, veneer, or the like. **2** a thin strip of wood used in aligning hand-set type. [< *scale¹* + *board*]

**scale carp,** any fish of a variety of carp, covered evenly with scales, having a long dorsal fin and growing up to four feet in length.

**scaled-down** (skāldʹdounʹ), *adj.* = scale-down.

**scale dove,** any one of various small doves or

***scale³**
definition 3a

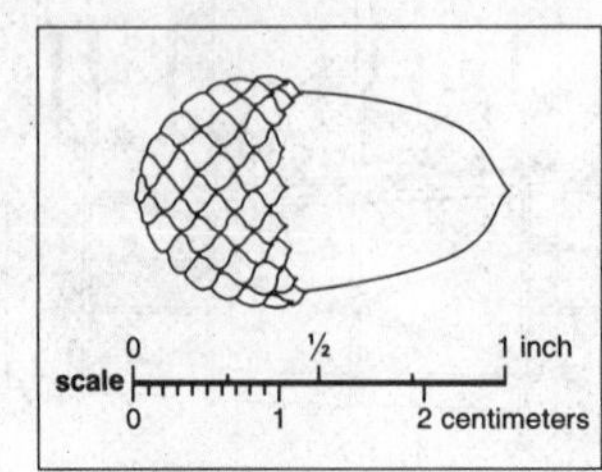

life-size drawing of an acorn

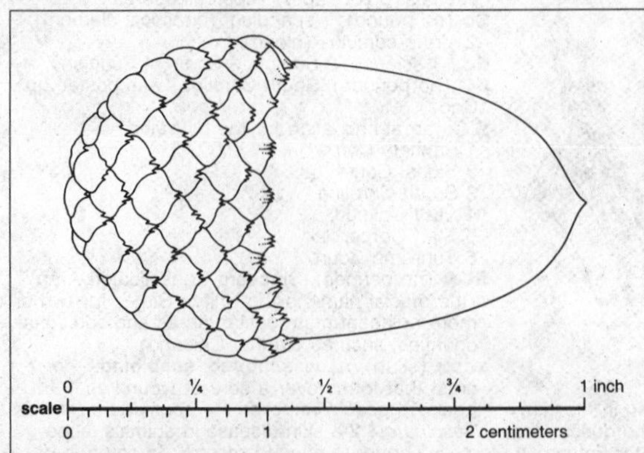

large-scale drawing of an acorn

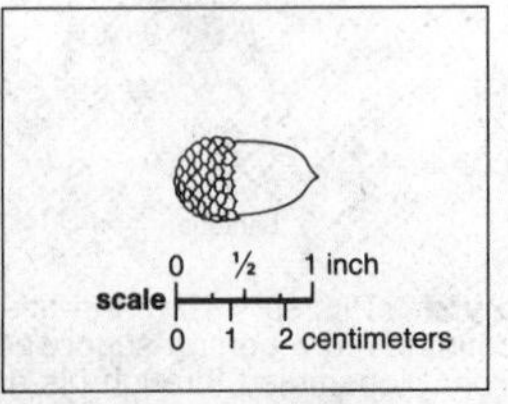

small-scale drawing of an acorn

pigeons of tropical America having feathers that look like scales.

**scale-down** (skāl′doun′), *adj., n.* — ***adj.*** being reduced by a certain proportion: *Mill buying was scale-down in nature with the cotton textile market currently in a lull* (Wall Street Journal).
— ***n.*** a proportional reduction: *They're buying a little on a scale-down in the stocks they like* (New York Times).

**scaled quail** (skāld), a quail of the western and southwestern United States, having a crest and slate-blue feathers.

**scaled-up** (skāld′up′), *adj.* = scale-up.

**scale hopper**, a device in the cupola of a grain elevator for weighing the grain.

**scale insect**, any one of various small insects that feed on and often destroy plants by piercing them and sucking the sap. The females have the body and eggs covered by a waxy scale or shield formed by a secretion from the body. Certain kinds are a source of lac or dye.

**scale leaf**, one of the parts that unite to cover a bud in winter; scale.

**scale|less** (skāl′lis), *adj.* **1** without scales: *The catfish is scaleless.* **2** not done to scale: *a scaleless drawing or sculpture.*

**scale model**, a model of something with all parts proportional: *a scale model of the new hospital.*

**scale moss**, any one of various liverworts with small, overlapping, scalelike leaves.

**sca|lene** (skā lēn′, skā′lēn), *adj.* **1** (of a triangle) having three unequal sides. See diagram under **triangle**. **2** (of a cone or other solid figure) having the axis inclined to the base. [< Late Latin *scalēnus* < Greek *skalēnós* uneven < *skélos* leg]

**scalene muscle**, any one of several triangular muscles that connect the upper ribs with vertebrae.

**scale|pan** (skāl′pan′), *n.* either one of the dishes or pans of a balance: *... naughty mice who won't stay on the scalepan while their food intake is being measured* (New Scientist).

**scal|er** (skā′lər), *n.* **1** a person or thing that scales: *We are soul-probers, star-mappers, wood-walkers, scalers of Everests, pursuers of tomorrow and tomorrow and tomorrow* (Atlantic). **2** an instrument for removing scales from fish. **3** a device that records impulses electronically by selecting them in groups when the impulses run through a circuit too rapidly to be measured by the metering equipment: *A scaler unit counts the scatter or impulses for one or two minutes* (New Scientist). **4** an instrument used by dentists to remove tartar from the teeth.

**scales** (skālz), *n.pl.* See under **scale²** (*n.* def. 2).

**Scales** (skālz), *n.pl.* = Libra. [translation of Latin *Lībra*]

**scale-up** (skāl′up′), *adj., n.* — ***adj.*** increased by a certain proportion: *Trading was slow but mill and commission house buying met mostly scale-up hedging and liquidation* (Wall Street Journal).
— ***n.*** a proportional increase: *The scale-up from pilot plant to full production was a billion to one, surely the greatest in technological history* (Scientific American).

**scal|ic** (skā′lik), *adj.* of or having to do with a musical scale or scales: *The music doggedly pursues repetitive triadic or scalic patterns* (London Times).

**scal|i|ness** (skā′lē nis), *n.* scaly quality or condition.

**scal|ing** (skā′ling), *n.* **1** scales, as of a fish. **2** the arrangement of scales, such as on a fish.

***scaling ladder**, a ladder for climbing walls.

***scaling ladder**

**scall** (skôl), *n.* a scabby eruption, especially on the scalp. [probably < Scandinavian (compare Old Icelandic *skalle* a bald head)]

**scal|la|wag** (skal′ə wag), *n.* = scalawag.

**scalled** (skôld), *adj. Obsolete.* scald³.

**scal|lion** (skal′yən), *n.* **1** a kind of onion that does not form a large, distinct bulb. **2** = shallot. **3** = leek. [< Anglo-French *scaloun* < Latin (*caepa*) *Ascalōnia* (onion) from Ascalon, in Palestine]

***scal|lop** (skol′əp, skal′-), *n., v.* — ***n.*** **1a** a shellfish somewhat like a clam. In some kinds the large muscle that opens and closes the shell is good to eat. **b** this muscle, used as food. **c** one of the two rounded, fanlike, ribbed parts of the shell: *Pilgrims returning from Palestine formerly wore scallops as a sign of their pilgrimage.* **2** a small dish or scallop shell, in which fish or other food is baked and served. **3** one of a series of curves on an edge of anything: *This cuff has scallops.*
— ***v.t.*** **1** to bake with sauce and breadcrumbs in a dish; escallop: *scalloped oysters, scalloped potatoes.* **2** to make with a series of curves on: *She scalloped the edges of the paper with which she covered the shelves.* Also, **scollop**.
[earlier, short for *escallop*¹]

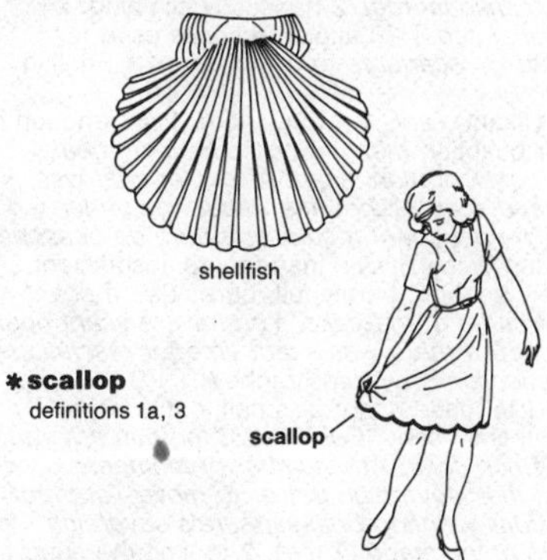

***scallop**
definitions 1a, 3

**scal|lop|er** (skol′ə pər, skal′-) *n.* **1** a person or thing that scallops. **2** a boat used to gather scallops. Also, **scolloper**.

**scal|lop|ing** (skol′ə ping, skal′-), *n.* **1** an ornamental edging. **2** the embroidery stitch used in making a variety of such edging.

**scal|lop|pi|ne** or **scal|lop|pi|ni** (skal′ə pē′nē), *n.pl.* thin slices of veal pounded flat and cooked in Marsala wine, sometimes with mushrooms, cheese, or tomato paste. [alteration of Italian *scaloppine*, plural of *scaloppina* small thin slice]

**scal|ly|wag** (skal′ē wag), *n.* = scalawag.

**sca|lo|gram** (skā′lə gram), *n.* a graded series of related questions or problems which become progressively more difficult to answer. Scalograms are used in psychological and other tests to measure the uniformity and consistency of responses. [< *scale*³ + *-gram*¹]

**scalp** (skalp), *n., v.* — ***n.*** **1** the skin and hair on the top and back of the head. **2a** a part of this skin and hair cut off as a token of victory. Some Indians of North America used to collect the scalps of their enemies. **b** *Figurative: The angry Chancellor made no bones of the fact he was out to get Dehler's political scalp* (Newsweek). **3** *Informal.* a small profit made by quickly buying and selling.
— ***v.t.*** **1** to cut or tear the scalp from: *A party of St. Francis Indians ... scalped one of his companions* (George Bancroft). **2** *Informal.* **a** to buy and sell to make small, quick profits. **b** to trade in (as theater tickets or stocks), especially buying at face value and selling at higher prices.
— ***v.i.*** *Informal.* to buy and sell, as theater tickets or stocks, to make small, quick profits: *A corporation like the Pennsylvania Railroad must protect itself against loss through scalping* (Nation).
[perhaps < Scandinavian (compare Old Icelandic *skālpr* sheath)] — **scalp′er**, *n.*

**scalp dance**, a ceremonial dance of the American Indians in which the scalps of enemies were used in celebrating a victory.

**scal|pel** (skal′pəl), *n.* a small, straight knife used in surgery and in dissections. [< Latin *scalpellum* (diminutive) < *scalprum* knife, related to *scalpere* to carve]

**scalp lock**, a long lock or tuft of hair left on the head (the rest being shaved) by certain North American Indians to show their status as warriors and as a challenge to their enemies.

**scal|prum** (skal′prəm), *n., pl.* **-pra** (-prə). the cutting edge of an incisor tooth. [< Latin *scalprum* knife]

**scal|y** (skā′lē), *adj.,* **scal|i|er, scal|i|est.** **1** covered with scales; having scales like a fish: *The iron pipe is scaly with rust.* **2** suggesting scales. **3** consisting of scales or scale. **4** that comes off in scabs. **5** having scale insects; infested with scale. **6** *Slang, Figurative.* mean; shabby; stingy. [< *scal(e)*¹ + *-y*¹]

**scaly anteater** or **lizard**, = pangolin.

**scam** (skam), *n. U.S. Slang.* a dishonest scheme; swindle. [origin unknown]

**scam|ble** (skam′bəl), *v.i., v.t.,* **-bled, -bling,** *n. Archaic.* scramble. [origin uncertain; perhaps related to *scramble*]

**scam|mon|ic** (skə mon′ik), *adj.* derived from scammony: *a scammonic medicine.*

**scam|mo|ny** (skam′ə nē), *n., pl.* **-nies.** **1** a twining Asiatic plant of the morning-glory family, a variety of convolvulus. **2** a gum resin obtained from its root, used as a purgative. [Old English *scammonie* < Latin *scammōnia* < Greek *skammōniā*]

**scamp** (skamp), *n., v.* — ***n.*** a worthless or unprincipled person; rascal; rogue: *Old Dodd had a scamp of a son who had run away from school* (Margaret Kennedy).
— ***v.t.*** to do (work) in a hasty, careless manner: *I will undertake to say he never scamped a job in the whole course of his life* (Samuel Butler). *The motivations of the novel are scamped in the film* (Newsweek).
— ***v.i.*** *U.S.* to be stingy; skimp.
[perhaps < dialectal *scamp* to roam, probably < *scamper*] — **scamp′er**, *n.*

**scam|per** (skam′pər), *v., n.* — ***v.i.*** **1** to run quickly; go hastily: *The mice scampered when the cat came.* **2** to run away or decamp: *The wagoners took each a horse out of his team and scampered* (Benjamin Franklin).
— ***n.*** a quick run: *Let the dog out for a scamper.*
[< Old French *escamper* to run away, ultimately < Latin *ex-* out of + *campus* field]

**scam|pi** (skäm′pē), *n.pl. Italian.* shrimps.

**scamp|ish** (skam′pish), *adj.* like a scamp; rascally.

**scan** (skan), *v.,* **scanned, scan|ning,** *n.* — ***v.t.*** **1** to look at closely; examine with care: *His mother scanned his face to see if he was telling the truth.* **SYN**: scrutinize. **2** to glance at; look over hastily. **SYN**: skim. **3a** to mark off (lines of poetry) into feet. *Example:* Sing′ a/ song′ of/ six′-pence. **b** to read or recite (poetry), marking off the lines into feet. **4** to expose (bits of a surface) in rapid succession to beams of electrons in order to transmit a picture by television. The electron beam moves in successive horizontal lines from top to bottom analyzing the light values of the object. **5** to search (an area) with radar. **6** to examine (a part of the body) for abnormalities by tracing or recording the distribution of an administered radioactive substance: *to scan the brain for tumors.*
— ***v.i.*** **1a** to conform to rules for marking off lines of poetry into feet: *The new poets scan* (Time). **b** to scan verse. **2** to scan a surface in transmitting a picture by television.
— ***n.*** **1** the act or fact of scanning: *Radio astronomers began an intensive radio scan of the sun* (Scientific American). **2** the area of vision in television or radar. **3** a picture of the distribution of a radioactive substance in the body: *A side-view brain scan ... reveals a brain tumor* (Henry N. Wagner, Jr.).
[< Latin *scandere* to scan; (originally) to climb, related to *scālae* ladder]

**Scan.**, **1** Scandinavia. **2** Scandinavian.

**Scand.**, **1** Scandinavia. **2** Scandinavian.

**scan|dal** (skan′dəl), *n., v.,* **-daled, -dal|ing** or (*especially British*) **-dalled, -dal|ling.** — ***n.*** **1** a shameful action, condition, or event that brings disgrace or shocks public opinion: *It was a scandal for the city treasurer to take tax money for his own use. The state-government scandals of 1939-1940 retired him to private life when he first was governor* (Newsweek). **2** damage to reputation; disgrace: *to avoid scandal at all costs. O the disgrace of it! The scandal, the incredible come-down* (Max Beerbohm). **SYN**: discredit, disrepute, dishonor. **3** public talk about a person that will hurt his reputation; evil gossip; slander; defamation: *You'll have no scandal while you dine, but honest talk and wholesome wine* (Tennyson). **SYN**: calumny. **4** discredit to religion caused by irreligious conduct or moral lapse.
— ***v.t.*** **1** *Archaic.* to spread scandal about (a person); defame. **2** *Obsolete.* to disgrace.
**be the scandal of**, to scandalize: *The visiting dignitaries who got into a public brawl were the scandal of the town.*
[< Latin *scandalum* (cause for) offense, temptation < Greek *skándalon* scandal, offense; (originally) trap with a springing device. See etym. of doublet **slander**.]

**scan|dal|ise** (skan′də līz), *v.t.,* **-ised, -is|ing.** *Especially British.* scandalize.

**scan|dal|i|za|tion** (skan′də lə zā′shən), *n.* **1** the act of scandalizing. **2** the condition or fact of being scandalized: *The Prince and his wife, to the amusement of some and the scandalization of others, indulged in a violent bout of fisticuffs in*

**Pronunciation Key:** hat, āge, cãre, fär; let, ēqual, tėrm; it, īce; hot, ōpen, ôrder; oil, out; cup, pu̇t, rüle; child; long; thin; ᴛʜen; zh, measure; ə represents **a** in about, **e** in taken, **i** in pencil, **o** in lemon, **u** in circus.

*open court* (Daily Telegram).

**scan|dal|ize** (skan′də līz), *v.t.*, **-ized, -iz|ing.** to offend or horrify by doing something thought to be wrong or improper; shock: *She scandalized her grandmother by smoking cigarettes.* —**scan′dal|iz′er,** *n.*

**scan|dal|mon|ger** (skan′dəl mung′gər, -mong′-), *n.* a person who spreads scandal and evil gossip: *Political scandalmongers were even tossed a surprising and piquant new morsel* (Newsweek).

**scan|dal|ous** (skan′də ləs), *adj.* **1** disgraceful; shameful; shocking: *a scandalous crime.* SYN: disreputable, infamous. **2a** spreading scandal or slander; slandering: *a scandalous piece of gossip.* SYN: slanderous, defamatory, libelous. **b** fond of scandal. —**scan′dal|ous|ly,** *adv.* —**scan′dal|ous|ness,** *n.*

**scandal sheet,** a newspaper or magazine devoted primarily to items of a notorious, scandalous, or gossipy nature.

**scan|da|roon** (skan də rün′), *n.* a variety of homing pigeon, with a long head and body, long legs, wide shoulders, and a long curved bill. [< *Scanderoon,* variant of *Iskenderon,* a seaport in southern Turkey]

**scan|dent** (skan′dənt), *adj.* climbing: *a scandent vine.* [< Latin *scandēns, -entis,* present participle of *scandere* to climb]

**scan|di|a** (skan′dē ə), *n.* a white, infusible powder, an oxide of scandium. *Formula:* $Sc_2O_3$ [< New Latin *scandia* < *scandium;* see etym. under **scandium**]

**Scan|di|an** (skan′dē ən), *adj., n.* = Scandinavian. [< Latin *Scandia* Scandinavia + English *-an*]

**scan|dic** (skan′dik), *adj.* of or having to do with scandium.

**Scan|di|na|vi|an** (skan′də nā′vē ən, -nāv′yən), *adj., n.* —*adj.* of or having to do with Scandinavia, its people, or their languages.
—*n.* **1** a person born or living in Scandinavia. **2** the languages of Scandinavia and Iceland, both modern and historical; North Germanic. Scandinavian includes Danish, Icelandic, Norwegian, and Swedish.

***scan|di|um** (skan′dē əm), *n.* a rare, gray, metallic chemical element, found in many minerals in Scandinavia: *Observations show that scandium is rather abundant in some of the stars* (Scientific American). [< New Latin *scandium* < Latin *Scandia* Scandinavia]

***scandium**

| symbol | atomic number | atomic weight | oxidation state |
|---|---|---|---|
| Sc | 21 | 44.956 | 3 |

**scan|na|ble** (skan′ə bəl), *adj.* that can be scanned.

**scan|ner** (skan′ər), *n.* **1** a person or thing that scans. **2** = scanning disk. **3** the rotating antenna that sends out and receives radar signals: *The scanner is mounted in the nose of the aircraft and must be capable of operating under all conditions of pressure and temperature encountered in flight* (New Scientist). **4** a photoelectric cell that scans printed data and converts it into the electric impulses fed into a computer or data-processing machine.

**scan|ning** (skan′ing), *n., adj.* —*n.* **1** close investigation or consideration; critical examination or judgment. **2** = scansion. **3** the process in which an electron beam scans the television picture area. **4** a method of detecting abnormalities in the body by the use of special photographic instruments that record the movement of an administered radioactive substance as it passes through the organs, body fluids, and the like: *In scanning, a radioactivity compound is administered to the patient, after which the compound's distribution is mapped out by a scintillation camera that detects gamma rays coming from the child* (Science News).
—*adj.* **1** that scans or examines closely; critical; searching: *When his eyes fell again they glanced round with a scanning coolness* (George Eliot). **2** spoken in a measured manner, with more or less regular pauses between syllables, characteristic of certain nervous diseases, as multiple sclerosis: *scanning speech.*

**scanning disk, 1** a filter disk made up of sections of red, blue, and green, placed in front of the camera lens and the receiver in one type of color television. **2** a mechanical device used for scanning in early television.

**scanning electron microscope,** an electron microscope that uses a very fine moving beam of electrons to scan a specimen and project a three-dimensional image of it on a television screen. The image obtained, though not as sharp as that provided by the standard electron microscope, contains much more detail. *Abbr:* SEM

**scanning radar,** a radar with a large, stationary antenna which points the radar beam in different vertical directions by shifting the frequency of the radar waves.

**scan|sion** (skan′shən), *n.* the marking off of lines of poetry into feet; scanning. The marks for scansion are - or ′ for a long or stressed syllable, ⌣ for a short syllable, / for a foot division, and ^ for a pause. *Example:* And fíréd / thĕ shót / heărd roúnd / thĕ wórld /. In the oral scansion of poetry, a reader stresses the accented syllables heavily. [< Latin *scānsiō, -ōnis* < *scandere* to scan]

**scan|sion|ist** (skan′shə nist), *n.* a person skilled in scansion.

**scan|so|ri|al** (skan sôr′ē əl, -sōr′-), *adj.* **1** having to do with or adapted for climbing: *Woodpeckers have scansorial feet.* **2** habitually climbing: *a scansorial bird.* [< Latin *scānsōrius* used for climbing (< *scandere* to climb; scan) + English *-al*[1]]

**scant** (skant), *adj., v., adv.* —*adj.* **1** not enough in size or quantity; meager; poor: *a scant meal, scant consideration, scant help. Her coat was short and scant. When the canal was undertaken, he got scant recognition from de Lesseps* (Edmund Wilson). SYN: inadequate, insufficient. **2** barely enough; barely full; bare: *Use a scant cup of butter in the cake. You have a scant hour to pack. But there was scant time for resolutions and reflections* (Lytton Strachey).
—*v.t.* **1** to make scant or small; cut down in amount; limit; stint: *Don't scant the butter if you want a rich cake. Any number of moments lacked their sovereign power to move—and not least from scanting Shakespeare's sovereign powers of language* (Time). **2** to limit the supply of; withhold: *You have obedience scanted* (Shakespeare).
—*adv. Dialect.* scarcely; barely; hardly: *His manner was scant civil* (Robert Louis Stevenson).
**scant of,** having not enough: *She was scant of breath.*
[< Scandinavian (compare Old Icelandic *skamt* short)] —**scant′ness,** *n.*

**scant|ies** (skan′tēz), *n.pl.* very short, snug-fitting panties for women. [blend of *scanty* and *panties*]

**scant|i|ly** (skan′tə lē), *adv.* in a scanty manner; insufficiently; inadequately.

**scant|i|ness** (skan′tē nis), *n.* too small an amount; scanty quality or condition.

**scant|ling** (skant′ling), *n.* **1a** a small beam or piece of timber, often used as an upright piece in the frame of a building. **b** such beams or timbers collectively. **2** the width and thickness of a board, beam, cut stone, or other building material, used as a measure of size. **3** the dimensions of the various parts of a vessel in shipbuilding. **4** a small quantity or amount; modicum. **5** *Archaic.* a portion; share; allowance: *The muleteer … thought not of tomorrow … provided he got but his scantling of Burgundy* (Laurence Sterne). [variant of earlier *scantillon* < Old French *escantillon* splinter, ultimately < Vulgar Latin *cantus.* Compare etym. under **cant**[2].]

**scant|ly** (skant′lē), *adv.* **1** scantily; in a scant manner or degree; slightly: *A grace but scantly thine* (Tennyson). **2** *Archaic.* scarcely; hardly; barely.

**scant|y** (skan′tē), *adj.,* **scant|i|er, scant|i|est.** **1** existing or present in small or insufficient quantity; not enough; not abundant: *His scanty clothing did not keep out the cold. My paper is scanty and time more so* (William Penn). **2** not ample or copious; barely enough; meager: *a scanty meal. Drought caused a scanty harvest. Congregations were scanty* (Andrew Lang). **3** deficient in extent, compass, or size: *Our minds are narrow and scanty in their capacities* (Isaac Watts). [perhaps a back formation < *scantiness* or perhaps *scant* + *-y*[3]]
—*Syn.* **1, 2 Scanty, sparse, meager** mean less than is needed or normal. **Scanty** implies falling short of the needed or standard amount: *The scanty rainfall is causing a water shortage.* **Sparse** implies a thin scattering of what there is, particularly of numbers or units: *He carefully combs his sparse hair.* **Meager** implies thinness, a lack of something necessary, as for fullness, completeness, richness, or strength: *Meager soil produces meager crops.*

**SCAP** (no periods), Supreme Commander for the Allied Powers (in Japan).

**scape**[1] (skāp), *n., v.t., v.i.,* **scaped, scap|ing.** *Archaic.* escape.

**scape**[2] (skāp), *n.* **1** *Botany.* a leafless flower stalk rising from the ground, such as that of the narcissus, dandelion, or hyacinth. **2** something like a stalk, such as the shaft of a feather or the shaft of a column. [< Latin *scāpus* stalk]

**scape**[3] (skāp), *n.* a view of scenery of any kind: *to sketch a scape in pencil.* [abstracted from *landscape*]

**'scape** (skāp), *n., v.t., v.i.,* **'scaped, 'scap|ing.** *Archaic.* escape. [short for *escape*]

**-scape,** *combining form.* a scenic picture or view of, as in *seascape.* [< (land)*scape*]

**scape|goat** (skāp′gōt′), *n., v.* —*n.* **1** a person or thing made to bear the blame for the mistakes or sins of others: *He has been made the scapegoat for many of the sins … of other individuals* (Edward A. Freeman). **2** a goat on which the sins of the people were laid by the ancient Jewish high priests on the Day of Atonement. The goat was then driven into the wilderness (in the Bible, Leviticus 16:5-22).
—*v.t.* to make a scapegoat of: *This suggests that witches did not simply exist in nature in the form of demented women—but that the Inquisition created them by scapegoating innocent women* (New York Times).
[< *scape*[1], variant of *escape* + *goat*]

**scape|goat|ism** (skāp′gō′tiz əm), *n.* the act or practice of seeking out a scapegoat to lay blame on: *Much of the anti-American feeling that does exist in Europe can be charged to scapegoatism* (Newsweek).

**scape|grace** (skāp′grās′), *n.* a reckless, good-for-nothing person; scamp: *He … was the most charming young scapegrace in the army* (Thackeray). [short for (person who e)*scape*(s) *grace*]

**scape|ment** (skāp′mənt), *n.* an escapement in a clock or watch.

**scape wheel,** the toothed wheel in the escapement of a watch or clock that actuates the pendulum or balance. [< *scape*[1], variant of *escape* + *wheel*]

**scaph|o|ce|phal|ic** (skaf′ō sə fal′ik), *adj.* (of a skull) boat-shaped; very long and narrow. [< Greek *skáphē* boat + English *cephalic*]

**scaph|oid** (skaf′oid), *adj., n.* —*adj.* **1** boat-shaped. **2** = navicular.
—*n.* = navicular.
[< Greek *skaphoidês* < *skáphē* boat, tub, trough (< *skáptein* to dig, carve) + *eîdos* form]

**scaph|o|pod** (skaf′ə pod), *n.* any one of a class of marine mollusks with a long, tubular shell open at both ends, and delicate tentacles; tooth shell. Scaphopod shells were used as money by Pacific coast Indians. [< New Latin *Scaphopoda* the class name < Greek *skáphē* boat, trough + *poús, podós* foot]

**scap|o|lite** (skap′ə līt), *n.* any one of a group of minerals of variable composition, essentially silicates of aluminum, calcium, and sodium, occurring in tetragonal crystals and also massive, such as wernerite. [< German *Skapolith* < Greek *skâpos* shaft (with English *-lite*)]

**sca|pose** (skā′pōs), *adj. Botany.* **1** having scapes. **2** consisting of or like a scape. [< *scap*(e)[2] + *-ose*[1]]

**scap|ple** (skap′əl), *v.t.,* **-pled, -pling.** = scabble.

**s.caps.,** small capitals.

**scap|u|la** (skap′yə lə), *n., pl.* **-lae** (-lē), **-las.** **1** = shoulder blade. **2** one of the other bones of the pectoral arch of some vertebrates. [< New Latin *scapula* shoulder blade < Late Latin, shoulder < Latin *scapulae,* plural, shoulders]

**scap|u|lar** (skap′yə lər), *adj., n.* —*adj.* of the shoulder or shoulder blade.
—*n.* **1** a loose, sleeveless garment hanging from the shoulders, worn by members of certain religious orders in the Roman Catholic Church: *She knelt once more before him to be formally clothed with the girdle, scapular, and white veil betokening Sister Laurentia's official reception into the thirteen-centuries-old Order of St. Benedict* (Atlantic). **2** two small pieces of cloth joined by string passed over the shoulders, worn under the ordinary clothing by Roman Catholics as a mark of religious devotion: *He hastily muttered a Hail Mary to the Blessed Virgin, asking her protection, and promising always to … wear her scapular* (James T. Farrell). **3** a bird's feather growing in the shoulder region where the wing joins the body. **4** a bandage that goes over the shoulder. **5** = scapula.
[< New Latin *scapularis* < Late Latin *scapulāre* scapular, tippet < *scapula* shoulder, scapula]

**scapular medal,** a medal worn by Roman Catholics instead of the cloth scapular.

**scap|u|lar|y** (skap′yə ler′ē), *adj., n., pl.* **-lar|ies.** = scapular.

**scap|u|li|man|cy** (skap′yə lə man′sē), *n.* divination by means of the cracks in an animal's shoulder blade scorched in a fire. [< Latin *scapula* shoulder + Greek *manteíā* divination]

**scar**[1] (skär), *n., v.,* **scarred, scar|ring.** —*n.* **1** a mark left by a healed cut, wound, burn, or sore: *My vaccination scar is small. He jests at scars that never felt a wound* (Shakespeare). **2** any mark like this: *See the scars your shoes have made on the chair.* (*Figurative.*) *War leaves many deep scars on the minds of those who endure it.* **3a** a mark where a leaf has formerly joined the stem. **b** *Zoology.* a cicatrix.
—*v.t.* to mark with a scar: *He scarred the door with a hammer. Yet I'll not shed her blood, Nor*

*scar that whiter skin of hers than Snow* (Shakespeare).
—*v.i.* to form a scar; heal: *Her wound is scarring well.*
[< Old French *escarre* < Late Latin *eschara* scab < Greek *eschárā* scab; hearth. See etym. of doublet **eschar.**]

**scar**[2] (skär), *n.* **1** a steep, rocky place on the side of a mountain; precipice; cliff. **2** a low rock in the sea. Also, **scaur.** [< Scandinavian (compare Old Icelandic *sker* reef). See related etym. at **skerry.**]

***scar|ab** (skar′əb), *n.* **1a** a beetle, especially the sacred beetle of the ancient Egyptians; a broad, black dung beetle. The scarabs comprise a large family of insects. **b** an image of this beetle. Scarabs were much used in ancient Egypt as charms or ornaments. **2** a gem cut in the form of a beetle. **3** = dung beetle. [< Middle French *scarabée,* learned borrowing from Latin *scarabaeus* < Greek *kárabos* beetle; crayfish]

***scarab**
definitions 1a, 1b

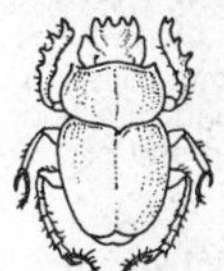

definition 1a    definition 1b

**scar|a|bae|an** (skar′ə bē′ən), *adj., n.* = scarabaeid.

**scar|a|bae|id** (skar′ə bē′id), *adj., n.* —*adj.* of or having to do with a large group of broad, thick-bodied beetles with antennae ending in flattened segments. Scarabaeid beetles include the chafers, June bugs, and Japanese beetles.
—*n.* a scarabaeid beetle.
[< New Latin *Scarabaeidae* the family name < Latin *scarabaeus;* see etym. under **scarab**]

**scar|a|bae|oid** (skar′ə bē′oid), *adj., n.* —*adj.* **1** of, having to do with, or like a scarabaeid. **2** resembling a scarab (image or gem).
—*n.* a scarab, either much conventionalized or an imitation.

**scar|a|bae|us** (skar′ə bē′əs), *n., pl.* **-bae|us|es, -bae|i** (-bē′ī). = scarab. [< New Latin *scarabaeus* < Latin, beetle; see etym. under **scarab**]

**Scar|a|mouch** (skar′ə müsh), *n.* a cowardly braggart in traditional Italian comedy. [< French *Scaramouche* < Italian *Scaramuccia* (literally) skirmish. Compare etym. under **skirmish.**]

**scar|a|mouch** or **scar|a|mouche** (skar′ə-mouch, -müsh), *n.* **1** a cowardly braggart: *The habit of this greasy Don was very proper for a scaramouch ... being a dirty calico, with all the tawdry and trapping of a fool's coat* (Daniel Defoe). **2** a rascal; scamp: *He swore that no scaramouch of an Italian robber would dare to meddle with an Englishman* (Washington Irving). [< *Scaramouch*]

**scarce** (skãrs), *adj.,* **scarc|er, scarc|est,** *adv.* —*adj.* hard to get; rare: *Very old stamps are scarce. Good cooks are scarce. Milk was scarce during the strike. Craftsmanship is increasingly scarce in our mechanized society.* **SYN:** See syn. under **rare.**
—*adv.* = scarcely: *I scarce kept myself from shedding tears* (George Gissing).
**make oneself scarce,** *Informal.* **a** to go away: *Please do make yourself scarce. You are in my way, and I'm very busy* (Arnold Bennett). **b** to stay away: *My liberty was granted only on condition of making myself scarce in the two Castilles* (Benjamin Malkin).
**scarce as hen's teeth,** *Informal.* very scarce: *Now good comedians are as scarce as hen's teeth* (Newsweek).
[< Old North French *escars* < Vulgar Latin *excarpsus,* for Latin *excerpsus* extracted, past participle of *excerpere* select, excerpt < Latin *ex-* out + *carpere* to pluck] —**scarce′ness,** *n.*

**scarce|ly** (skãrs′lē), *adv.* **1** not quite; barely: *I can scarcely hear your voice. We could scarcely see the ship through the thick fog.* **SYN:** See syn. under **hardly.** **2** decidedly not: *He can scarcely have said that.* **3** very probably not: *I will scarcely pay that much.*
► **scarcely.** Since its negative force is weak, *scarcely* readily lends itself to use in a concealed double negative: *For a while we couldn't scarcely see a thing.* In standard English this would be: *For a while we could scarcely see a thing.*

**scarce|ment** (skãrs′mənt), *n.* in building: **1** a setoff in the face of a wall or in a bank of earth. **2** a footing or ledge formed by a setoff in a wall.

**scar|ci|ty** (skãr′sə tē), *n., pl.* **-ties.** too small a supply; lack; rarity: *There is a scarcity of nurses.*
—***Syn.* Scarcity, dearth** mean a shortage or lack of something. **Scarcity** implies a supply inadequate to meet the demand or satisfy the need: *There was a scarcity of heating fuel last winter.* **Dearth,** used of anything thought of as wanted or needed, means an extreme scarcity amounting almost to a famine: *a dearth of information.*

**scare**[1] (skãr), *v.,* **scared, scar|ing,** *n., adj.* —*v.t.* **1** to frighten; make afraid; strike with sudden fear or terror: *Scaring a child is wrong. We were scared and ran away. The play [is] a plausible melodrama that is likely to scare the living daylights out of you* (New York Times). *"Wasn't the rabbit scared, Uncle Remus?" asked the little boy* (Joel Chandler Harris). *The noise of thy crossbow Will scare the herd* (Shakespeare). **SYN:** terrify, alarm. See syn. under **frighten. 2** to frighten (away); drive off: *The watchdog scared away the robber by barking. ... the poet must pull down the shade so that they may not scare off his fancies* (Edmund Wilson).
—*v.i.* to become frightened; be scared: *Courageous people don't scare easily.*
—*n.* **1** a fright, especially sudden fright: *I had a sudden scare when I saw a dog running toward me. Peyrol actually laughed at this momentary scare* (Joseph Conrad). **2** a frightened condition.
—*adj. U.S. Informal.* **1** causing fear; frightening; alarming: *scare headlines, scare statistics.* **2** designed to frighten or alarm: *scare tactics, scare propaganda.*
**scare up,** *Informal.* to get; raise, locate, or prepare: *to scare up a few extra blankets on a cold night.*
[alteration of Middle English *skerre* < Scandinavian (compare Old Icelandic *skirra* < *skjarr* timid)] —**scar′er,** *n.* —**scar′ing|ly,** *adv.*

**scare**[2] (skãr), *n.* the part of a golf club where the head joins the shaft. [originally Scottish < Scandinavian (compare Old Icelandic *skör* joint)]

**scare buying,** buying more than one needs in fear of threatened or alleged shortage.

**scare|crow** (skãr′krō′), *n.* **1** a figure dressed in old clothes, set in a field to frighten birds away from crops: *The farmer decided to build a scarecrow so terrifying it would scare the hateful crows to death when they got a good look at it* (New Yorker). **2** a person, usually skinny, dressed in ragged clothes: *There ranged themselves in front of the schoolmaster's desk, half-a-dozen scarecrows, out at knees and elbows* (Dickens). **3** *Figurative.* anything that fools people into being frightened; bugbear; bugaboo.

**scared** (skãrd), *adj.* frightened; afraid; terrified: *Don't be scared, the dog won't bite you. We were scared and ran away.*
**run scared, a** to run a political campaign as if in fear of losing: *Though confident, Republicans run scared* (Wall Street Journal). **b** to run fast or hard, as if in fear: *I don't like to say that the Nashua stable, warming up here in Saratoga, will run scared* (Newsweek).

**scared|y cat** (skãr′dē), = fraidy cat.

**scare|head** (skãr′hed′), *n.* a newspaper headline in very large type, and usually of a sensational nature.

**scare|mon|ger** (skãr′mung′gər, -mong′-), *n.* a person who spreads alarming reports; alarmist: *He declared "scaremongers" are at work attempting to frighten automobile workers with the "bogeyman of automation"* (Wall Street Journal).

**scare|mon|ger|ing** (skãr′mung′gər ing, -mong′-), *n.* the spreading of alarming reports: *No incidents were reported from the disturbed areas today, but ... the atmosphere in the affected areas was still tense owing to "sporadic attempts at scaremongering"* (Times of India).

**scarf**[1] (skärf), *n., pl.* **scarfs** or **scarves,** *v.* —*n.* **1a** a long, broad strip of silk, lace, or other material, worn about the neck, shoulders, head, or waist. **b** = muffler (def. 2). **2** a long strip of linen, etc., used as a cover for a bureau, table, piano, etc. **3** a necktie with hanging ends. **4** a sash worn across the chest to indicate membership in some ceremonial order.
—*v.t.* **1** to clothe, cover, or wrap with, or as if with, a scarf. **2** to wrap about or around a person in the manner of a scarf. **3** *Archaic.* to deck with flags: *The scarfed bark puts from her native bay* (Shakespeare).
[< Old North French *escarpe* < Germanic (compare Old High German *scharpe* bag, pocket)]

**scarf**[2] (skärf), *n., pl.* **scarfs,** *v.* —*n.* **1a** a joint in which the ends of beams are cut so that they lap over and join firmly. **b** an end cut in this way. **2** a cut made in the body of a whale.
—*v.t.* **1** to join by a scarf. **2** to form a scarf on (a beam). **3** to remove the skin and blubber from (a whale). **4** *Metallurgy.* to remove surface blemishes from (steel ingots) by spraying with oxygen before rolling: *There is increasing demand for oxygen in the "scarfing" ... of steel ingots or billets* (Wall Street Journal). Also, **scarph.**
[perhaps < Scandinavian (compare Swedish *skarv*)] —**scarf′er,** *n.*

**scar-faced** (skär′fāst′), *adj.* having a scarred face; with scars on the face.

**scarfed** (skärft), *adj.* wearing a scarf or scarfs; decorated with or as if with a scarf: *The scarfed bark puts from her native bay* (Shakespeare). Also, **scarved.**

**scarf joint,** a scarf, such as in a beam.

**scarf|pin** (skärf′pin′), *n.* an ornamental pin worn in a scarf or necktie.

**scarf|skin** (skärf′skin′), *n.* the outer layer of skin; epidermis. [< *scarf*[1], in the sense of "light outer covering" + *skin*]

**scar|i|fi|ca|tion** (skar′ə fə kā′shən), *n.* **1** the act of scarifying. **2** a scratch or scratches: *scarification in elaborate geometrical patterns* (Atlantic).

**scar|i|fi|er** (skar′ə fī′ər), *n.* **1** a person or thing that scarifies. **2** *Agriculture.* a cultivator with prongs for loosening the soil without turning it over.

**scar|i|fy** (skar′ə fī), *v.t.,* **-fied, -fy|ing. 1a** to make scratches or cuts in the surface of (as the skin). **b** to cover with scratches: *These ... could be stamped out of plastic or Fiberglas with a scarified top* (New Yorker). *Fixing her nails in his antagonist's face, she scarified all one side of his nose* (Tobias Smollett). **2** *Figurative.* to criticize severely; hurt the feelings of; wound; harrow: *He ... cut up a rising genius or scarified some unhappy wretch* (Benjamin Disraeli). **3** to loosen (soil) without turning it over. **4** to slit the coats of (seeds) to hasten sprouting. **5** to make cuts in the bark of (a tree) as a treatment or to tap the sap. [< Old French *scarifier,* learned borrowing from Late Latin *scarīficāre* < Latin *scarīfāre* < Greek *skarīphâsthai* to scratch < *skarîphos* stylus] —**scar′i|fy′ing|ly,** *adv.*

**scar|i|ly** (skãr′ə lē), *adv. Informal.* in a scary manner.

**scar|i|ness** (skãr′ē nis), *n. Informal.* scary feeling or condition.

**scar|i|ous** (skãr′ē əs), *adj.* **1** *Botany.* thin, dry, and membranous: *the scarious bracts of many composites.* **2** *Zoology.* scabby; scurfy. [< New Latin *scariosus;* origin uncertain]

**scar|la|ti|na** (skär′lə tē′nə), *n.* = scarlet fever. [< New Latin *scarlatina* < Italian *scarlattina,* feminine of *scarlattino* (diminutive) < *scarlatto* scarlet]

**scar|la|ti|nal** (skär′lə tē′nəl), *adj.* like or resulting from scarlatina.

**scar|less** (skär′lis), *adj.* **1** having no scar; unscarred. **2** leaving no scar.

**scar|let** (skär′lit), *n., adj.* —*n.* **1** a very bright red, much lighter than crimson. **2** cloth or clothing having this color: *Alas, alas, that great city, that was clothed in fine linen, and purple, and scarlet* (Revelation 18:16).
—*adj.* **1** very bright red. **2** red, as with shame: *Embarrassed, her face turned scarlet.* **3** *Figurative.* glaring; flagrant; notorious: *scarlet sins, a scarlet crime.*
[short for Old French *escarlate* < Medieval Latin *scarlatum,* perhaps ultimately < Persian *saqlāt* rich cloth]

**scar|let|ber|ry** (skär′lit ber′ē), *n., pl.* **-ries. 1** = bittersweet (def. 1). **2** its berry.

**scarlet clover,** = crimson clover.

**scarlet cross,** = scarlet lychnis.

**scarlet fever,** a very contagious disease that affects chiefly children, characterized by a scarlet rash, sore throat, and fever. It is caused by a form of streptococcus.

**scarlet haw,** any variety of hawthorn with bright red fruit.

**scarlet ibis,** an ibis of tropical South America, about two feet long, with completely scarlet plumage except for black primary feathers.

**scarlet letter,** a scarlet letter "A" worn as punishment for adultery, as by Hester Prynne in Nathaniel Hawthorne's *The Scarlet Letter.*

**scarlet lychnis,** a common garden plant of the pink family with showy, red or white flowers; Maltese cross.

**scarlet macaw,** a red, blue, and yellow macaw found from Mexico to Bolivia.

**scarlet maple,** = red maple.

**scarlet oak,** a kind of oak of eastern North America whose leaves turn a brilliant scarlet in fall.

**scarlet pimpernel,** an herb of the primrose family with bright-scarlet flowers that close in cloudy or rainy weather.

**scarlet plume,** a shrubby variety of spurge native to Mexico, with scarlet appendages extending from between the lobes of the involucre.

**scarlet runner,** a tall, twining bean of tropical America that has showy scarlet flowers and long pods with large, black, edible seeds.

**scarlet sage**, a common garden plant of the mint family with racemes of bright-red flowers that bloom in the autumn. It is a species of salvia.

**scarlet tanager**, the common tanager of eastern North America; redbird. The male has black wings and tail and a scarlet body.

**Scarlet Woman**, the woman described in Revelation 17, variously interpreted as representing pagan Rome, papal Rome, or the spirit of worldliness and evil.

**scarlet woman**, a harlot; whore.

**scarp** (skärp), *n., v.* —*n.* **1** a steep slope: *sheer scarps of grey rock* (Henry Kingsley). **2** the inner slope or side of a ditch surrounding a fortification; escarp.
—*v.t.* to make into a steep slope; slope steeply: *The rock on which this fort stands was scarped towards the city* (Garnet J. W. Wolseley).
[< Italian *scarpa* slope. Compare etym. under **escarp.**]

**scarp|er** (skär′pər), *v.i. British Slang.* to run away; go away; leave in a hurry: *A raft of people got the wind up and scarpered for foreign climes* (Punch). [apparently < Italian *scappare* escape] —**scarp′er|er**, *n.*

**scarph** (skärf), *n., pl.* **scarphs**, *v.* = scarf².

**scar|ry¹** (skär′ē), *adj.,* **-ri|er, -ri|est.** marked with scars: *scarry skin, a scarry face.* [< *scar*¹ + *-y*¹]

**scar|ry²** (skär′ē), *adj.* precipitous; rocky: *a high, steep, scarry bank.* [< *scar*² + *-y*¹]

**scart** (skärt), *n., v. Scottish.* —*n.* **1** a scratch. **2** a mark made by a pen.
—*v.t., v.i.* to scratch or scrape.
[alteration of *scrat;* see etym. under **scratch**]

**scar tissue**, the new connective tissue that forms when a wound, sore, or ulcer heals. Scar tissue forms after granulation. *A grafting technique ... could eliminate scar tissue in wounds that are healing* (Science News Letter).

**scarved** (skärvd), *adj.* = scarfed.

**scarves** (skärvz), *n.* scarfs; a plural of **scarf**.

**scar|y** (skãr′ē), *adj.,* **scar|i|er, scar|i|est.** *Informal.* **1** causing fright or alarm: *a scary ghost story. Maxwell Anderson's scary melodrama dealing with a winsome little girl who is also homicidal ...* (New Yorker). **2** easily frightened: *A scary comrade in the woods is apt to make a short path long* (James Fenimore Cooper). **SYN:** timorous.

**scat¹** (skat), *interj., v.,* **scat|ted, scat|ting.** *Informal.* —**interj.** an exclamation used to drive away an animal.
—*v.i.* to go away, especially in a hurry.
[perhaps < *hiss* + *cat*]

**scat²** (skat), *n.* a tax; tribute. Also, **scatt**. [originally Scottish < Scandinavian (compare Old Icelandic *skattr*). See related etym. at **scot**, tax.]

**scat³** (skat), *n., v.,* **scat|ted, scat|ting,** *adj. Jazz, Slang.* —*n.* nonsense chatter and sounds, usually sung or spoken rapidly to jazz music: ... *a mirthful and really quite pretty collection of fugues and preludes sung in scat ("dooby do, papa-dah")* (Time).
—*v.i., v.t.* to sing or speak scat: *Miss Fitzgerald, in the space of four records, sings, scats, hums, and noodles her way through thirty-seven ... tunes* (New Yorker).
—*adj.* of or having to do with scat: *a scat session, a scat singer.*
[probably imitative]

**SCAT** (no periods), supersonic commercial air transport.

**scat|back** (skat′bak′), *n. U.S. Football.* a swift, agile back, usually of relatively small stature. [< *scat*¹ + *back*¹]

**scath** (skath), *v.t., n. Dialect.* scathe.

**scathe** (skāᴛʜ), *v.,* **scathed, scath|ing,** *n.* —*v.t.* **1** to blast or sear with abuse or invective; wither with satire: *His satire flashed about, ... scathing especially his old enemies the monks* (James A. Froude). **2** to injure or destroy, as by fire or lightning; sear; scorch: ... *a place where the tree had been scathed by lightning* (Washington Irving). **3** *Archaic.* to injure; damage.
—*n.* **1** *Archaic.* a hurt; harm. **2** *Archaic.* a matter for sorrow or regret. **3** *Obsolete.* an injury.
[< Scandinavian (compare Old Icelandic *skathi,* noun; *skatha,* verb)]

**scathe|ful** (skāᴛʜ′fəl), *adj. Archaic.* hurtful; harmful; injurious.

**scathe|less** (skāᴛʜ′lis), *adj.* without harm; unhurt: *It is a game from which you will come out scatheless, but I have been scalded* (Anthony Trollope). **SYN:** uninjured, unharmed.

**scath|ing** (skā′ᴛʜing), *adj.* bitterly severe; withering: *a scathing remark, scathing criticism.* **SYN:** stinging. —**scath′ing|ly**, *adv.*

**scat|o|log|ic** (skat′ə loj′ik), *adj.* = scatological.

**scat|o|log|i|cal** (skat′ə loj′ə kəl), *adj.* of or having to do with scatology. —**scat′o|log′i|cal|ly**, *adv.*

**sca|tol|o|gist** (skə tol′ə jist), *n.* a writer of obscene literature.

**sca|tol|o|gy** (skə tol′ə jē), *n.* **1a** the study of or an interest in obscenity, especially in literature. **b** obscene literature: *especially in the light of this year's Broadway scatology* (Time). **2a** the study of fossil excrement to learn about animals. **b** the branch of medicine that deals with diagnosis by means of the feces. [< Greek *skôr, skatós* excrement + English *-logy*]

**sca|toph|a|gous** (skə tof′ə gəs), *adj.* feeding upon dung. [< Greek *skôr, skatós* excrement + *phageîn* eat + English *-ous*]

**sca|tos|co|py** (skə tos′kə pē), *n.* examination of the feces for the purpose of diagnosis or divination. [< Greek *skôr, skatós* excrement + English *-scopy*]

**scat-sing** (skat′sing′), *v.,* **-sang, -sung, -sing|ing.** —*v.i.* to sing scat: *The Swingles either hum or scat-sing* (New Yorker).
—*v.t.* to sing in scat: *She ... sizzlingly scat-sang a duet with Clayton's trumpet* (Sunday Times).
[< *scat*³ + *sing*]

**scatt** (skat), *n.* = scat².

**scat|ter** (skat′ər), *v., n.* —*v.t.* **1** to throw here and there; sprinkle: *The farmer scattered corn for the chickens. Scatter ashes on the icy sidewalk.* **SYN:** strew, sow. **2** to distribute here and there: *So long as works of art are scattered through the nation, no universal destruction of them is possible* (John Ruskin). **3** to separate and drive off in different directions: *The police scattered the disorderly crowd.* **4** *Physics.* to throw back or deflect (as rays of light or radioactive particles) in all directions: *There would be no lens surfaces to scatter light, and the working distance could be quite large* (J. G. Thomas).
—*v.i.* to separate and go in different directions: *The hens scattered in fright when the truck honked at them.*
—*n.* **1** the act or fact of scattering: *There was a general scatter of the party who had come to see the duel* (Samuel Lover). **2** anything that is scattered: *significant rock formations on the scatter of islands west of Ellesmere* (New Scientist). **3** *Slang.* an apartment; room: *The Grand Duke hurries straightway to Marian's scatter, where she tenderly awaits Orloff* (New Yorker).
[perhaps unrecorded Old English *sceaterian.* Compare etym. under **shatter.**] —**scat′ter|er**, *n.*
—*Syn. v.t.* **3 Scatter, dispel, disperse** mean to separate and drive away so that an original form or arrangement is lost. **Scatter** means to separate and drive off in different directions a group or mass of people or objects: *The wind scattered my papers.* **Dispel** applies only to things that cannot be touched, such as clouds and feelings, and means to drive them completely away: *The pilot's confidence dispelled my doubts about the bad weather.* **Disperse** means to scatter thoroughly the individuals of a compact body or mass but not so that they cannot come together again: *Storms dispersed the convoy.*

**scat|ter|a|tion** (skat′ə rā′shən), *n.* **1** the act of scattering. **2** the fact of being scattered: *The scatteration of economic authority in Washington is notorious* (Harper's). **3** the policy of spreading grants of money over many small projects instead of concentrating them on a few of greater value.

**scat|ter|brain** (skat′ər brān′), *n.* a thoughtless, flighty person: *The scatterbrains ... are deeply involved in personal problems while behind the wheel of a car and are inclined to daydream* (New York Times).

**scat|ter|brained** (skat′ər brānd′), *adj.* not able to think steadily; thoughtless; flighty. **SYN:** heedless.

**scat|ter|brains** (skat′ər brānz′), *n.* = scatterbrain.

**scatter communication**, long-distance communication using the troposphere or other areas of atmospheric ionization to deflect radio waves over a long distance.

**scatter diagram**, *Statistics.* a graph showing the relationship between two variables, in which one variable is marked off on the x-axis and the other on the y-axis, and points representing the values of the variables in a distribution are plotted along the lines of the graph. When the relationship is close, the points tend to form a diagonal line or a curve.

**scat|tered** (skat′ərd), *adj.* **1** disunited or dispersed; disorganized: *He ... began to collect his scattered forces* (Macaulay). **2** occurring at wide intervals; placed here and there; spread over a wide area: *scattered clouds. Ye scattered birds that faintly sing* (Robert Burns). —**scat′tered|ly**, *adv.* —**scat′tered|ness**, *n.*

**scat|ter|good** (scat′ər gůd′), *n.* a person who is very wasteful; a spendthrift.

**scat|ter|gram** (skat′ər gram), *n.* = scatter diagram.

**scat|ter|gun** (skat′ər gun′), *n. U.S. Informal.* a shotgun.

**scat|ter|ing** (skat′ər ing), *adj., n.* —*adj.* **1** widely separated; occurring here and there: *scattering drops of rain.* **SYN:** sporadic. **2** divided in small numbers among several candidates: *scattering votes.*
—*n.* a small amount or number scattered or interspersed: *There seldom were more than a half-dozen senators on the floor at one time and only a scattering of people in the Senate galleries* (Newsweek). —**scat′ter|ing|ly**, *adv.*

**scattering layer**, a layer of plankton or other organisms in the ocean that reflects and scatters sound waves.

**scat|ter|om|e|ter** (skat′ə rom′ə tər), *n.* a radar-like instrument equipped with several aerials for directing microwaves over a wide area and recording the returned signal at all angles: *The ... scatterometer will use radar techniques to penetrate cloud cover* (Science News). [< *scatter* + *-ometer,* as in *thermometer*]

**scatter pins**, small ornamental pins worn in groups on the clothing by women and girls: *Scatter pins ... come in three graduated sizes, to twinkle on the lapel of your new spring suit* (New York Times).

**scatter propagation**, = scatter communication.

**scatter rug**, a small rug, covering part of a floor.

**scatter shot**, **1** = buckshot. **2** the spread of small shot from a shotgun.

**scat|ter|shot** (skat′ər shot′), *adj., n.* —*adj.* spreading widely like the burst of shot from a shotgun.
—*n.* = scatter shot.

**scat|ter|site housing** (skat′ər sīt′), *U.S.* government-sponsored public housing designed to disperse low-income groups outside of a ghetto or inner city; housing provided in scattered sites throughout a city.

**scatter transmission**, = scatter communication.

**scat|ti|ness** (skat′ē nis), *n. Especially British Informal.* the quality or state of being scatter-brained; flightiness.

**scat|ty** (skat′ē), *adj.,* **-ti|er, -ti|est.** *Especially British Informal.* scatterbrained: *"I went quite scatty," she says. "Fortunately, I was playing a scatty part in a play, so nobody noticed"* (Time).

**sca|tu|ri|ent** (skə tůr′ē ənt, -tyůr′-), *adj.* streaming or flowing out; gushing forth. [< Latin *scatūriēns, -entis,* present participle of *scatūrīre* stream forth < *scatēre* gush]

**scaup duck** (skôp), either of two broad-billed wild diving ducks related to the canvasback. The males have glossy black heads and necks. [perhaps variant of dialectal *scalp* bank that provides a bed for shellfish]

**scaur¹** (skôr), *n.* = scar². [variant of *scar*²]

**scaur²** (skôr), *v.t., v.i. Scottish.* scare¹.

**scav|enge** (skav′ənj), *v.,* **-enged, -eng|ing.** —*v.t.* **1a** to pick over (discarded objects) for things to use or sell. **b** to remove dirt and rubbish from (a street, surface of a river, etc). **2** to expel burned gases from (the cylinder of an internal-combustion engine). **3** to clean (molten metal) by chemically removing its impurities.
—*v.i.* **1** to be a scavenger. **2** to undergo scavenging.
[back formation < *scavenger*]

**scav|en|ger** (skav′ən jər), *n.* **1** an animal that feeds on decaying matter. Vultures, jackals, and some snails and beetles are scavengers. *Turkey buzzards ... their services as scavengers are invaluable* (Frank M. Chapman). **2** a person who searches through discarded objects for something of value. **3** a person who cleans streets or other public areas of dirt and filth: *An army of scavengers ... was cleansing the asphalt roadway* (George du Maurier). [alteration of Middle English *skavager* inspector < Anglo-French *scawager* < *scawage* a toll < Old North French *escauwage* < *escauwer* to inspect < Flemish *scauwen.* Compare etym. under **passenger, messenger.**]

**scavenger fish**, = small wrasse.

**scavenger hunt**, a game played at parties, in which the players are told to obtain, without buying, various things that are usually hard to find, the winner being the one returning first with all the things by a given time.

**Sc. B.**, Bachelor of Science (Latin, *Scientiae Baccalaureus*).

**SCCA** (no periods) or **S.C.C.A.**, Sports Car Club of America.

**Sc. D.**, Doctor of Science (Latin, *Scientiae Doctor*).

**sceat** (shat), *n.* a small Old English silver coin, about 15 grains in weight, used in the 600's and 700's A.D. Also, **sceatta**. [Old English *sceat, scætt*]

**sceat|ta** (shat′ə), *n.* = sceat.

**sce|na** (shā′nə), *n.* **1** a scene in an opera: *The big scena of madness in the second act ... brought out her most affecting and colorful tone* (Manchester Guardian Weekly). **2** a composition consisting largely of recitative of a dramatic and impassioned character, for one or more voices and accompaniment, either forming part of an opera or composed separately for the concert room. [< Italian *scena* < Latin *scēna* scene]

**sce|nar|i|o** (si nãr′ē ō, -när′-), *n., pl.* **-i|os. 1** the outline of a motion picture, giving the main facts about the scenes, persons, and acting. **2** the outline of any play, opera, or theatrical work: *The two men met, and the scenario for "La Chambre" is the result* (New Yorker). **3** *Figurative: The new style strategists ... construct "scenarios" in which hypothetical opponents engage in various levels of violence over unstated political objectives* (New Yorker). [< Italian *scenario* < *scena* scene < Latin *scēna*]

**sce|nar|ist** (si nãr′ist, -när′-), *n.* a person who writes scenarios.

**scend** (send), *v., n.* **—*v.i.*** (of a ship) to lurch upward on the swell of a wave.
**—*n.*** a sudden upward heave on the swell of a wave. Also, **send.**
[spelling variant of *send*]

**scene** (sēn), *n.* **1a** the time, place, and circumstances of a play or story: *The scene of the book is laid in Boston in the year 1775.* **b** the place where anything is carried on or takes place: *the scene of an accident, the scene of my childhood.* **2** the painted screens or hangings used on the stage to represent places: *The scene represents a city street.* **3** a part of an act of a play: *The king comes to the castle in Act I, Scene 2.* **4** a particular incident of a play or story: *the balcony scene in "Romeo and Juliet." The trial scene is the most exciting one in "The Merchant of Venice."* **5** an action, incident, or situation occurring in reality or represented in literature or art: *He painted a series of pictures called "Scenes of My Boyhood."* **6** a view; picture: *The white sailboats on the blue water made a pretty scene.* **SYN:** See syn. under **view.**
**7** *Figurative.* a show of strong feeling in front of others; exhibition; display: *The child kicked and screamed and made such a scene on the bus that his mother was ashamed of him.* **8** *Slang, Figurative.* any place or area of activity: *Besides the hipster scene at the club, there were two other scenes where pot was common* (Maclean's). **9** *Archaic.* the stage of a theater.
**behind the scenes, a** out of sight of the audience: *Things happening in the action of the play, and supposed to be done behind the scenes* (John Dryden). **b** *Figurative.* privately; secretly; not publicly: *Important conferences were held behind the scenes.* **c** *Figurative.* privy to what is going on; in a capacity to be in on or to influence matters privately decided: *Miss Pratt ... had obtained the entrée to a number of great houses, and was behind the scenes in many fashionable families* (Maria Edgeworth).
**make the scene,** *Slang.* **a** to appear or be present, especially at a fashionable place or event: *A slim, elegantly dressed character ... used to make the jazz scene at the club* (Maclean's).
**b** to be popular or successful: *These days the girl who can't perform a mean frug ... will never make the scene* (Time).
[< Middle French *scene,* learned borrowing from Latin *scēna* < Greek *skēnḗ* (originally) tent, in the theater, where actors changed costumes]

**scene dock,** the place in which scenery is stored in a theater; dock. It is usually at the back or side of the stage.

**scene|let** (sēn′lit), *n.* a short scene in a play, motion picture, or the like.

**scen|er|y** (sē′nər ē, sēn′rē), *n., pl.* **-er|ies. 1** the general appearance of a place; natural features of a landscape: *She enjoys mountain scenery.*
**2** the painted hangings or screens used in a theater to represent places: *The scenery pictures a garden in the moonlight.*
**chew the scenery,** to act in an exaggerated fashion; overact: *a family unabashedly given to chewing the scenery* (New Yorker).
**—scen′er|y|less,** *adj.*

**scene|shift|er** (sēn′shif′tər), *n.* a person who shifts and arranges the scenes in a theater.

**scene-steal|er** (sēn′stē′lər), *n.* an actor who seizes all the attention of an audience with his performance.

**sce|nic** (sē′nik, sen′ik), *adj., n.* **—*adj.* 1a** of or having to do with natural scenery: *The scenic splendors of Yellowstone Park are famous.*
**b** having much fine scenery; picturesque: *a scenic highway.* **2** of or having to do with stage scenery or stage effects: *The production of the musical comedy was a scenic triumph.* **3** representing an action, incident, or situation, in art: *There is far less antagonism between what is decorative and what is scenic in painting than is sometimes supposed* (C. H. Moore).
**—*n.*** a moving picture of natural scenes. **—sce′ni|cal|ly,** *adv.*

**sce|ni|cal** (sē′nə kəl, sen′ə-), *adj.* = scenic.

**scenic dome,** a glass or plastic dome on top of a railroad car through which passengers can view the passing scenery.

**scenic railway,** a small railroad at an amusement park, fair, or the like, which provides short trips through attractive, usually artificial scenery.

**sce|no|graph** (sē′nə graf, -gräf), *n.* a perspective drawing of some object, such as a building.

**sce|no|graph|ic** (sē′nə graf′ik, sen′ə-), *adj.* of or having to do with scenography. **—sce′no|graph′i|cal|ly,** *adv.*

**sce|no|graph|i|cal** (sē′nə graf′ə kəl, sen′ə-), *adj.* = scenographic.

**sce|nog|ra|phy** (sē nog′rə fē), *n.* **1** the representing of objects according to the rules of perspective. **2** scene painting, especially for the ancient Greek stage. [< Latin *scēnographia* < Greek *skēnographiā* < *skēnḗ* scene, stage + *-graphiā* description of < *gráphein* to draw, write]

**scent** (sent), *n., v.* **—*n.* 1** smell; distinctive or characteristic odor, especially when pleasing: *The scent of roses filled the air. Several drops of a strong flower scent ... were added* (Scientific American). **2** the sense of smell: *Bloodhounds have a keen scent.* **3a** the smell left in passing: *The dogs followed the fox by scent.* **b** the trail of such a smell: *to lose or recover the scent.*
**4** *Figurative: The police are on the scent of the thieves.* **5** the paper scraps left as a trail in the game of hare and hounds. **6** perfume: *She uses too much scent.* [< verb]
**—*v.t.* 1a** to smell; recognize by the sense of smell: *The dog scented a rabbit and ran off after it.* **b** *Figurative.* to have a suspicion of; be aware of: *I scent a trick in their offer. The Tory rank and file, scenting Labor blood, are convinced that they can sweep the country* (Time). **2** to fill with odor. **3** to perfume: *scented writing paper. She scented the room to rid it of the fish smell.*
**—*v.i.*** to hunt by using the sense of smell: *The dog scented about till he found the trail of the rabbit.*
[< Old French *sentir* to smell, sense < Latin *sentīre* to sense, feel]

**-scented,** *combining form.* **1** having scent, or the sense of smell: *Keen-scented = having a keen sense of smell.*
**2** having a scent or odor: *Sweet-scented = having a sweet scent.*

**scent gland,** a gland which secretes an odoriferous substance: *the scent glands of ... female moths* (New Scientist).

**scent hound,** a hunting dog that chases by scent rather than sight. Beagles and bloodhounds are scent hounds.

**scent|less** (sent′lis), *adj.* having no smell. **SYN:** odorless.

**scent|om|e|ter** (sen tom′ə tər), *n.* an instrument that analyzes the content of breath and records the extent of dust or pollutants in it.

**scep|sis** (skep′sis), *n.* = skepsis.

***scep|ter** (sep′tər), *n., v.* **—*n.* 1** the rod or staff carried by a ruler as a symbol of royal power or authority. **2** *Figurative: The Persian conqueror governed his new subjects with an iron scepter* (Edward Gibbon). **SYN:** sovereignty.
**—*v.t.* 1** to furnish with a scepter. **2** to touch with a scepter as a sign of royal assent.
[< Old French *sceptre,* learned borrowing from Latin *scēptrum* < Greek *skēptron* staff]

orb

***scepter**
definition 1

**scep|tered** (sep′tərd), *adj.* **1** furnished with or bearing a scepter. **2** *Figurative.* invested with regal authority; regal.

**scep|tic** (skep′tik), *n., adj.* = skeptic.

**Scep|tic** (skep′tik), *n.* = Skeptic.

**scep|ti|cal** (skep′tə kəl), *adj.* = skeptical.

**scep|ti|cism** (skep′tə siz əm), *n.* = skepticism.

**scep|ti|cize** (skep′tə sīz), *v.i.,* **-cized, -ciz|ing.** = skepticize.

**scep|tre** (sep′tər), *n., v.t.,* **-tred, -tring.** = scepter.

**sch.,** **1** school. **2** schooner.

**Schab|zie|ger** (shäp′tsē gər), *n. German.* sapsago.

**Scha|den|freu|de** (shä′dən froi′də), *n. German.* malicious joy or pleasure.

**schanz** (skäns), *n.* (in South Africa) a small fort or barricade, as of stones or earth. [< Afrikaans *schanz* < Dutch *schans*]

**schat|chen** (shät′ʜən), *n., pl.* **-cho|nim** (-ʜô′nim). *Yiddish.* shadchan.

**sched|u|lar** (skej′u̇ lər; *especially British or Canadian* shed′yu̇ lər), *adj.* of, by, or according to a schedule.

**sched|ule** (skej′u̇l; *especially British or Canadian* shed′yül), *n., v.,* **-uled, -ul|ing. —*n.* 1** a written or printed statement of details; list: *A timetable is a schedule of the coming and going of airplanes, trains, or buses. The teacher posted the schedule of classes.* **2** the time fixed as for the doing of something or arrival at a place: *The plane was an hour behind schedule.* **3a** a blank form on which to fill out particulars under several headings: *List the expenditures under schedule B of this income-tax form.* **b** an official statement arranged under prescribed headings, such as assets and liabilities, particulars liable to income tax, or the like. **4** an appendix to a legislative act or a legal document containing a statement of details not included in the body of the main document. **5** *Obsolete.* a scroll of parchment or paper containing a writing; document.
**—*v.t.* 1** to make a schedule of; enter in a schedule: *The city scheduled buses to leave the park every half hour.* **2** to plan or arrange (something) for a definite time or date: *to schedule a convention for the fall.*
[< Old French *cedule,* learned borrowing from Late Latin *schedula* (diminutive) < Latin *scheda* < Greek *schédē* sheet of papyrus < *skízein* to split] **—sched′ul|er,** *n.*

**sched|uled airline** (skej′u̇ld; *especially British or Canadian* shed′yüld), = certificated airline.

**Scheduled Caste,** a name for the untouchables of India.

**Schee|le's green** (shā′ləz; shē′-; -lēz), a yellowish-green poisonous powder, used as a pigment and as an insecticide; copper arsenite. *Formula:* $CuHAsO_3$ [< Karl W. *Scheele,* 1742-1786, a Swedish chemist, who discovered it]

**schee|lite** (shā′līt, shē′-), *n.* a mineral, calcium tungstate, an ore of tungsten, found chiefly in brilliant crystals of various colors. *Formula:* $CaWO_4$ [< Karl W. *Scheele,* 1742-1786, a Swedish chemist, who discovered tungstic acid in it + *-ite*[1]]

**schef|fer|ite** (shef′ə rīt), *n.* a mineral, a variety of pyroxene, usually of yellowish or reddish-brown color, containing manganese and often iron. [< H. T. *Scheffer,* 1710-1759, a Swedish chemist + *-ite*[1]]

**schef|fler|a** (shef lir′ə), *n.* any one of a group of showy tropical plants of the Ginseng family, an Australian species of which is grown as a house plant. [< New Latin *Schefflera,* genus name < J. C. *Scheffler,* German botanist of the 1700's]

**Sche|her|a|za|de** (shə her′ə zä′də, -hir′-), *n.* the young bride of the Sultan in *The Arabian Nights* who related tales nightly to him to save her life.

**sche|ma** (skē′mə), *n., pl.* **-ma|ta** (-mə tə). **1** a diagram, plan, or scheme: *What Dr. Donaldson found was a perfectly good schema which ... put the arbitrary zero at body temperature, with "warm" as its label* (New Yorker). **2** a draft of decrees to be issued by an ecumenical council: *This schema consisted of ... such topics as the principles of liturgical renewal, the eucharistic mystery, the sacraments and sacramentals* (New Yorker). **3** (in Kantian philosophy) any one of certain forms or rules of the "productive imagination" through which the understanding is able to apply its "categories" to the manifold of sense perception in the process of realizing knowledge or experience. [< Latin *schēma* < Greek *schêma, -atos* figure, appearance. See etym. of doublet **scheme.**]

**sche|mat|ic** (skē mat′ik), *adj., n.* **—*adj.* 1** having to do with or like a diagram, plan, or scheme; diagrammatic: *My representations became even more schematic and abstract* (Time). **2** suggested or modified by a preconceived system.
**—*n.*** a diagrammatic presentation or arrangement.

**sche|mat|i|cal|ly** (skē mat′ə klē), *adv.* **1** by means of or using a schematic diagram. **2** in a definite pattern; according to a symmetrical plan.

**sche|mat|i|cism** (skē mat′ə siz əm), *n.* = schematism.

**sche|ma|tise** (skē′mə tīz), *v.t., v.i.,* **-tised, -tis|ing.** *Especially British.* schematize.

**sche|ma|tism** (skē′mə tiz əm), *n.* **1** an arrangement, as by diagrams or outlines. **2** a schematic presentation. **3** an arrangement; structure.

**sche|ma|ti|za|tion** (skē′mə tə zā′shən), *n.* reduc-

**Pronunciation Key:** hat, āge, cãre, fär; let, ēqual, tėrm; it, īce; hot, ōpen, ôrder; oil, out; cup, pu̇t, rüle; child; long; thin; ᴛʜen; zh, measure; ə represents **a** in about, **e** in taken, **i** in pencil, **o** in lemon, **u** in circus.

tion to a scheme or formula; arrangement according to a scheme or formula.

**sche|ma|tize** (skē′mə tīz), *v.t., v.i.*, **-tized, -tiz|ing.** to reduce to or arrange according to a scheme or formula. [< Greek *schēmatízein* assume a form < *schêma, -atos* a form; see etym. under **scheme**]

**scheme** (skēm), *n., v.*, **schemed, schem|ing.** — ***n.*** **1** a program of action; plan: *He has a scheme for extracting salt from seawater. It forms no part of our scheme to tell what became of the remainder* (Thackeray). **SYN:** design, project. **2** a self-seeking or underhanded project; plot: *a scheme to cheat the government.* **3** a system of connected things, parts, or thoughts: *a scheme of theology. The color scheme of the room is blue and gold.* **4** a diagram; outline; table: *a scheme of postal rates.* **5** a visionary plan; foolish project. **6** *Obsolete.* an astrological diagram of the heavens.
— ***v.i.*** to devise plans, especially underhanded or evil ones; plot: *Those men were scheming to cheat the government by bringing the jewels into the country without paying duty.* **SYN:** See syn. under **plot.**
— ***v.t.*** to devise (a plan or scheme); plan; plot. **SYN:** See syn. under **plot.**
[< Latin *schēma* < Greek *schêma, -atos* figure, appearance < *échein* to have. See etym. of doublet **schema.**] — **schem′er,** *n.*

**schem|ing** (skē′ming), *adj.* making tricky schemes; crafty. **SYN:** plotting, intriguing, contriving, designing, wily. — **schem′ing|ly,** *adv.*

**sche|moz|zle** (shə moz′əl), *n. Especially British Slang.* **1** a mix-up; mess; confusion: *Nobody knows ... how fearsome a schemozzle will develop at the Motorway's terminal points* (Punch). **2** a fight; quarrel: *[He had] to leave the field with a cut forehead after a schemozzle* (Listener). Also, **shemozzle.** [probably alteration of Yiddish *shlemazl* an unlucky person or thing]

**schenk beer** (shengk), a mild German beer brewed for immediate use, and not stored like lager. [< German *Schenkbier* < *schenken* pour out; retail + *Bier* beer]

**scher|zan|do** (sker tsän′dō), *adj., adv., n., pl.* **-dos, -di** (-dē). *Music.* — ***adj., adv.*** lively; playful; sportive (used as a direction).
— ***n.*** a scherzando movement or passage.
[< Italian *scherzando* < *scherzare* to play, sport < *scherzo;* see etym. under **scherzo**]

**scher|zo** (sker′tsō), *n., pl.* **-zos, -zi** (-tsē). *Music.* a light or playful piece, or movement of a sonata or symphony. It developed from the minuet. [< Italian *scherzo* < German *Scherz* a joke]

**Schick test** (shik), a test to determine if a person is immune to diphtheria, made by injecting a very small amount of diphtheria toxin under the skin. Reddening of the skin shows lack of immunity. [< Béla *Schick,* 1877-1967, an American pediatrician born in Hungary, who developed it]

**Schie|dam** (skē dam′), *n.* = Hollands (gin). [< *Schiedam,* a town in Holland, where it is distilled]

**Schiff reagent** (shif), a solution of fuchsin in water, decolored by reaction with sulfur dioxide. It is used as a test for aldehydes, the presence of which produces a purplish-red color. [< Hugo *Schiff,* 1834-1915, a German chemist]

**Schiff's reagent** (shifs), = Schiff reagent.

**schil|ler** (shil′ər), *n.* a peculiar, almost metallic luster, sometimes with iridescence, occurring on certain minerals, such as hypersthene. [< German *Schiller* play of colors]

**schil|ler|i|za|tion** (shil′ər ə zā′shən), *n.* a process of change in crystals giving rise to a schiller, appearing when the crystal is turned in various directions.

**schil|ler|ize** (shil′ə rīz), *v.t.*, **-ized, -iz|ing.** to give a schiller to (a crystal) by rearranging tiny particles within the crystal along certain planes.

**schil|ling** (shil′ing), *n.* **1** a copper and nickel coin and unit of money of Austria, equal to 100 groschen. **2** a former German coin worth 12 pfennigs. [< German *Schilling*]

**schip|per|ke** (skip′ər kē), *n.* any dog of a small, sturdy breed with erect ears and a rather rough, black coat. [< Dutch dialectal *schipperke* (literally) little boatman < Dutch *schipper* skipper[1] (from its use as a watchdog on canal boats)]

**schism** (siz′əm, skiz′-), *n.* **1** a division into hostile groups: ... *the possibility of a serious schism in the ranks of one of the two big British parties* (Wall Street Journal). **2** a discord or breach between persons or things. **3a** the division, either of the whole Church or of some portion of it, into separate and hostile organizations, because of some difference of opinion about religion. **b** the offense of causing or trying to cause such a schism. **c** a sect or group formed by a schism within a church. [< Latin *schisma* < Greek *schísma, -atos* < *schízein* to split]

**schis|mat|ic** (siz mat′ik, skiz-), *adj., n.* — ***adj.*** **1** causing or likely to cause schism. **2** inclined toward, or guilty of, schism. **3** of, having to do with, or of the nature of a schism.
— ***n.*** a person who tries to cause a schism or takes part in a schism.

**schis|mat|i|cal** (siz mat′ə kəl, skiz-), *adj.* = schismatic.

**schis|mat|i|cal|ly** (siz mat′ə klē, skiz-), *adv.* in a schismatic manner; by schism.

**schis|ma|tist** (siz′mə tist, skiz′-), *n. Rare.* = schismatic.

**schis|ma|tize** (siz′mə tīz, skiz′-), *v.i.*, **-tized, -tiz|ing. 1** to act as a schismatic. **2** to belong to a schismatic body.

**schist** (shist), *n.* a kind of crystalline metamorphic rock that splits easily into layers. It is usually composed mainly of mica. *In a few places the rocks are less coarsely crystalline, and are varieties of green slate and schist* (E. F. Roots). [< French *schiste,* learned borrowing from Latin *schistos* < Greek *schistós* cleft, separated < *schízein* to split]

**schis|to|cyte** (skis′tə sīt), *n.* a segmenting red blood cell. [< Greek *schistós* cleft + English *-cyte* hollow body < Greek *kytos*]

**schis|to|cy|to|sis** (skis′tə sī tō′sis), *n.* division of a red blood cell. [< New Latin *schistocytosis* < Greek *schistós* cleft + *kýtos* hollow body + English *-osis*]

**schis|to|glos|si|a** (skis′tə glos′ē ə), *n.* a congenitally cleft tongue.

**schist|oid** (shis′toid), *adj.* somewhat like schist.

**schis|tor|rha|chis** (skis tor′ə kis), *n.* = spina bifida. [< New Latin *schistorrhachis* < Greek *schistós* cleft + *rhachis* spine]

**schist|ose** (shis′tōs), *adj.* of or like schist; having the structure of schist; laminated.

**schis|tos|i|ty** (shis tos′ə tē), *n.* schistose structure or formation.

**schis|to|some** (shis′tə sōm), *n.* any one of a genus of trematode worms that are parasitic in the blood vessels of mammals in tropical countries, causing schistosomiasis; blood fluke. [< New Latin *Schistosoma* the genus name < Greek *schistós* divided (see etym. under **schist**) + *sôma, -atos* body]

**schis|to|so|mi|a|sis** (shis′tə sō mī′ə sis), *n.* a disease prevalent in Africa and other tropical areas, occurring in human beings and animals, and caused by schistosomes infesting the blood; bilharziasis. [< *schistosom*(e) + *-iasis*]

**schist|ous** (shis′təs), *adj.* **1** = schistose. **2** formed of schist.

**schiz-,** *combining form.* the form of **schizo-** before vowels, as in *schizoid.*

**schi|zan|thus** (ski zan′thəs), *n.* any plant of a group of variously colored annual and biennial herbs, native to Chile, that are often cultivated, especially in greenhouses, for their showy and abundant flowers. [< Greek *schízein* to split + *ánthos* flower]

**schiz|o** (skit′sō, skiz′ō), *n., pl.* **-os.** *Informal.* a schizophrenic: *Treatment turns out to be only palliative at best; the truth is they are schizos, whose psychic split is too wide ever to be healed* (Harper's).

**schizo-,** *combining form.* split; divided; a cleavage: *Schizocarp = a fruit that divides when ripe. Schizogenesis = reproduction by dividing.* Also, **schiz-** before vowels. [< Greek *schízein* to divide, split]

**schiz|o|carp** (skiz′ə kärp), *n. Botany.* any dry fruit that divides, when ripe, into two or more one-seeded seed vessels that do not split open, as in the carrot and celery. [< *schizo-* + Greek *karpós* fruit]

**schiz|o|car|pous** (skiz′ə kär′pəs), *adj. Botany.* of or like a schizocarp.

**schi|zog|a|my** (ski zog′ə mē), *n. Biology.* reproduction in which a sexual form is produced by fission or by budding from a sexless one, as in some worms.

**schiz|o|gen|e|sis** (skiz′ə jen′ə sis), *n. Biology.* reproduction by fission, such as in the schizophytes. [< New Latin *schizogenesis* < Greek *schízein* divide + *génesis* reproduction]

**schi|zog|e|nous** (ski zoj′ə nəs), *adj.* reproducing by schizogenesis.

**schiz|o|go|ni|a** (skiz′ə gō′nē ə), *n.* = schizogony.

**schiz|o|gon|ic** (skiz′ə gon′ik), *adj.* having to do with or exhibiting schizogony.

**schi|zog|o|nous** (ski zog′ə nəs), *adj.* = schizogonic.

**schi|zog|o|ny** (ski zog′ə nē), *n.* = schizogenesis.

**schiz|oid** (skit′soid, skiz′oid), *adj., n.* — ***adj.*** **1** having schizophrenia. **2** like or tending toward schizophrenia: *A journalist writing of a visit to Revéron's thatched hut some time after his first schizoid crisis in 1945 describes the artist's bizarre method of painting* (Newsweek).
— ***n.*** a person who has, or tends toward, schizophrenia; schizophrenic.

**schiz|o|my|cete** (skiz′ō mī sēt′), *n.* = bacterium. [< *schizo-* + Greek *mýkēs, -ētos* fungus]

**schiz|o|my|ce|tous** (skiz′ō mī sē′təs), *adj.* of or belonging to bacteria.

**schiz|o|my|co|sis** (skiz′ō mī kō′sis), *n.* any disease caused by bacteria.

**schiz|ont** (skiz′ont), *n.* (in sporozoans) a fully developed trophozoite that divides by fission into a number of new cells. [< *schiz-* + Greek *ôn, óntos* being]

**schiz|o|pel|mous** (skiz′ə pel′məs), *adj.* (of birds) having two flexor tendons for the toes. [< *schizo-* + Greek *pélma* sole of the foot + English *-ous*]

**schiz|o|phrene** (skit′sə frēn, skiz′ə-), *n.* a person suffering from schizophrenia.

**schiz|o|phre|ni|a** (skit′sə frē′nē ə, -frēn′yə; skiz′ə-), *n.* **1** a form of psychosis in which the patient dissociates himself from his environment and deteriorates in character and personality: *She was a victim of the most common form of mental illness, schizophrenia—a loss of touch with reality, a disintegration of personality* (Wall Street Journal). **2** the condition of having or showing markedly inconsistent or contradictory qualities; split personality: *He finds America suffering from schizophrenia, pulled in opposite directions between an idealism ... and a realism that is not consistently followed through* (Wall Street Journal). [< New Latin *schizophrenia* < Greek *schízein* to split + *phrên, phrenós* mind]

**schiz|o|phren|ic** (skit′sə fren′ik, skiz′ə-), *adj., n.* — ***adj.*** **1** of or having to do with schizophrenia. **2** having schizophrenia: *It has long been known that schizophrenic patients show biological and chemical changes as well as mental changes* (Wall Street Journal).
— ***n.*** a person who has schizophrenia: *About half of all hospital beds are occupied by mental patients and about half of the latter are schizophrenics* (Wall Street Journal). — **schiz′o|phren′i|cal|ly,** *adv.*

**schiz|o|phren|i|form** (skit′sə fren′ə fôrm, skiz′ə-), *adj.* taking on the form of schizophrenia; like schizophrenia.

**schiz|o|phy|ceous** (skiz′ə fī′shəs, -fish′əs), *adj.* of or belonging to a group of marine and freshwater blue-green algae that often pollute reservoirs, ponds, and the like. [< New Latin *Schizophyceae* the class name (< Greek *schízein* to split + *phýkos* seaweed)]

**schiz|o|phyte** (skiz′ə fīt), *n.* any one of the bacteria and blue-green algae, reproducing by simple fission or by spores, that are sometimes classified as a group. [< *schizo-* + Greek *phytón* plant]

**schiz|o|phyt|ic** (skiz′ə fit′ik), *adj.* of or belonging to the schizophytes.

**schiz|o|pod** (skiz′ə pod), *adj., n.* — ***adj.*** of or belonging to the soft-shelled, shrimplike crustaceans with branched limbs that were formerly classified as a group.
— ***n.*** a schizopod crustacean.
[< New Latin *Schizopoda* the former order name < Greek *schizópous, -podos* with parted toes < *schízein* split + *poús, podós* foot]

**schiz|o|thy|mi|a** (skit′sə thī′mē ə, skiz′ə-), *n.* a condition bordering on schizophrenia. [< New Latin *schizothymia* < Greek *schízein* split + *thȳmós* spirit]

**schiz|o|thy|mic** (skit′sə thī′mik, skiz′ə-), *adj.* of or having to do with schizothymia.

**schiz|o|zo|ite** (skiz′ə zō′īt), *n.* an organism reproduced by schizogamy. [< *schizo-* + Greek *zôion* animal + English *-ite*]

**schle|miel** or **schle|mihl** (shlə mēl′), *n. Slang.* a clumsy person; bungler; gullible fool. Also, **shlemiel.** [American English < Yiddish *shlumiel* < the Hebrew name *Shelumiel* (compare Numbers 7:36)]

**schlepp** or **schlep** (shlep), *v.*, **schlepped, schlep|ping,** *n. Slang.* — ***v.t., v.i.*** to move slowly, with difficulty, or unwillingly; drag: *He slaved for years like a dog, schlepped through rain and snow to put bread in his children's mouths* (New Yorker).
— ***n.*** a stupid, awkward, or dull person. Also, **shlep.**
[< Yiddish *shlepen* to drag and *shlep* drag, bore]

**schlie|ren** (shlir′ən), *n., adj.* — ***n.pl.*** **1** irregular, dark or light streaks occurring in igneous rock because of varying proportions of the minerals present. **2** *Physics.* **a** areas in a medium where refraction varies as a result of differences in density. **b** the shadows cast on a screen when light is refracted by these areas so that it cannot hit the screen.
— ***adj.*** **1** of or having to do with schlieren: *Focused shadowgraphs were taken through windows. They are known as schlieren photographs and show the shock waves about the model* (Science News Letter). **2** using schlieren to study substances or their behavior in motion, to indicate irregularities, as in glass, heat convection, or shock wave patterns: *This schlieren system is probably best known from its use in photographing the shock waves formed by air passing at great speeds over airplane models in wind tun-*

nels (Science News Letter).
[< German *Schlieren* < *Schlier* marl, or perhaps < *Schliere* slime]

**schlie|ric** (shlir′ik), *adj.* of or having to do with schlieren.

**schlock** (shlok), *n., adj. Slang.* —***n.*** something cheap or inferior; junk: *What might have been at least an amusing trifle becomes merely another piece of schlock* (Russell Baker).
—***adj.*** cheap; inferior; junky: *The dealers were guilty of schlock, sleazy, bargain-basement, fast-buck advertising* (New York Times). Also, **shlock**.
[< Yiddish *shlak* junk, trash; a curse, blow]

**schlock|meis|ter** (shlok′mīs′tər), *n. U.S. Slang.* **1** a person who supplies giveaway shows, celebrities, or other promoters, with various products in exchange for free advertisement of those products: *A schlockmeister [is] defined in the radio-TV lexicon as "somebody in the business of giving away somebody else's merchandise"* (Time). **2** a dealer of cheap or second-hand merchandise. [< *schlock* + German *Meister* master]

**schlock|y** (shlok′ē), *adj.*, **schlock|i|er**, **schlock|i|est**. *Slang.* cheap; inferior; schlock. Also, **shlocky**.

**schloss** (shlôs), *n.* = castle. [< German *Schloss*]

**schmaltz** or **schmalz** (shmälts), *n.* **1** *Slang.* **a** a cloying sentimentalism, as in music, art, or literature: *Here were no treacly saxophone sections, no "crooners"—none of the cloying, fake romanticism which made our dance halls misty with schmaltz* (Punch). **b** anything characterized by such sentimentalism. **2** chicken fat. [< German *Schmalz* (literally) rendered fat]

**schmaltz|y** (shmält′sē), *adj.*, **schmaltz|i|er**, **schmaltz|i|est**. *Slang.* of or characterized by schmaltz; cloyingly sentimental: *Big, schmaltzy dance bands* (Wall Street Journal).

**schmalz|y** (shmält′sē), *adj.*, **schmalz|i|er**, **schmalz|i|est**. = schmaltzy.

**schmear** (shmir), *n. Slang.* matter; affair; business: *We never learned to sit a horse; we missed out on the whole chivalry schmear* (Gilbert Rogin). [< Yiddish *shmir* spread]

**Schmidt camera** (shmit), a camera with a concave spherical mirror to converge light rays to a focal point, together with a thin correcting plate or lens to overcome spherical aberration. [< Bernhard *Schmidt*, 1879-1935, a German optics specialist]

**Schmidt telescope**, a telescope with an objective that uses an optical system like that of the Schmidt camera.

**schmier|kä|se** (shmir′kā′zə), *n.* = cottage cheese. [< German *Schmierkäse* (literally) smear cheese]

**schmo** or **schmoe** (shmō), *n., pl.* **schmoes**. *Slang.* a silly person; fool: *He's no schmo. He's a brilliant guy that needs editing* (Newsweek). Also, **shmo**. [probably alteration of Yiddish *shmok*]

**schmoos** or **schmoose** (shmüz), *n., v.*, **schmoosed**, **schmoos|ing**. *Slang.* —***n.*** chatter; gossip; idle talk. —***v.i.*** to gossip; talk idly.
[< Yiddish *shmues* < Hebrew *shemuoth* news]

**schmuck** (shmuk), *n. Slang.* a very stupid person; jerk. [< Yiddish *shmok*]

**schna|bel** (shnä′bəl), *n.* a whitefish of Europe.
[< German *Schnabel* beak]

**schna|bel|kan|ne** (shnä′bəl kän′ə), *n.* a jug or vessel with a long spout. [< German *Schnabelkanne* (literally) beak can]

**schnap|per** (shnap′ər, snap′-), *n.* a reddish food fish of Australia and New Zealand. [perhaps < German *Schnapper* kind of fish]

**schnapps** or **schnaps** (shnäps), *n.* **1** = Hollands. **2** any alcoholic liquor: *But the city did have a splendid period of song and schnapps, of beer gardens and opera and theater* (Newsweek). [< German *Schnapps* (originally) a mouthful, gulp < *schnappen* gulp, gasp]

**schnau|zer** (shnou′zər), *n.* any of three breeds or varieties of wire-haired German terriers, typically with a long head, small ears, and heavy eyebrows, mustache, and beard. The three breeds or varieties are the miniature, standard, and giant schnauzers. [< German *Schnauzer*, also *Schnauze* snout]

**schneck|en** (shnek′ən), *n.pl.* snail-shaped rolls made from a sweet dough, with yeast, butter, cinnamon or other spices, and nuts. [< German *Schnecken* (literally) snails]

**schnei|der** (schnī′dər), *v., n.* —***v.t.*** (in various card games) to beat (an opponent) by a decisive margin, usually by taking all possible points: *I'm going to schneider you* (New Yorker).
—***n.*** the act or fact of schneidering: *Australia frankly anticipates that the challenge round will be a rout, a schneider, a kick in the pants* (Newsweek).
[< German *Schneider* tailor]

**schnell** (shnel), *adj., adv. Music.* fast; quick. [< German *schnell*]

**schnit|zel** (shnit′səl), *n.* a veal cutlet, usually seasoned with lemon juice, parsley, capers, and sardines. [American English < German *Schnitzel* cutlet < *schnitzen* carve (frequentative) < *schneiden* to cut]

**schnook** (shnůk), *n. Slang.* a simple or stupid person. [origin unknown]

**schnor|kle** or **schnor|kel** (shnôr′kəl), *n.* = snorkel.

**schnor|rer** (shnôr′ər, shnōr′-), *n. Slang.* a beggar; sponger: *A real schnorrer, but sort of likable* (New Yorker). [< Yiddish *shnorer* < *shnoren* beg < Middle High German]

**schnoz|zo|la** (shnə zō′lə), *n. U.S. Slang.* a nose, especially a large nose. [probably < Yiddish *shnoits* snout + English *-ola*, a slang suffix of Italian origin]

**Schoen|berg|i|an** (shœn bėr′gē ən), *adj., n.* —***adj.*** of or having to do with the Austrian composer Arnold Schoenberg (1874-1951), his music, or his musical style.
—***n.*** an admirer of Schoenberg's musical style or theories.

**schol.**, scholium.

**scho|la can|to|rum** (skō′lə kan tôr′əm, -tōr′-), **1** a choir school or choir associated with a cathedral or monastery. **2** the part of a church reserved for the use of the choir. [< Latin *schola cantōrum* school of singers]

**schol|ar** (skol′ər), *n.* **1** a learned person; person having much knowledge: *The professor was a famous Latin scholar. To talk in public, to think in private, to read and to hear, to inquire and answer inquiries, is the business of a scholar* (Harper's). **SYN:** savant, sage. **2** a pupil at school; student; learner: *a poor scholar, failing in every course.* **SYN:** See syn. under **student**. **3** a student who is given a scholarship. **4** a person who is able to read and write (usually in illiterate use).
[< Late Latin *scholāris* < Latin *schola;* see etym. under **school**[1]]

**schol|arch** (skol′ärk), *n.* the head of a school, especially of a school of philosophy in ancient Athens. [< Greek *scholárchēs* < *scholē̂* (see etym. under **school**[1]) + *árchein* to lead]

**schol|ar|li|ness** (skol′ər lē nis), *n.* scholarly quality or character.

**schol|ar|ly** (skol′ər lē), *adj., adv.* —***adj.*** **1** of a scholar; like that of a scholar: *scholarly habits. Spectacles gave her a scholarly look.* **2** fit for a scholar: *the scholarly retreat of one's study.* **3** having much knowledge; learned; erudite: *The scholarly old man knew so much about bugs that experts came for his advice.* **4** fond of learning; studious: *a scholarly student.* **5** thorough and orderly in methods of study.
—***adv.*** in a scholarly manner: *Speak scholarly and wisely* (Shakespeare).

**schol|ar|ship** (skol′ər ship), *n.* **1a** the possession of knowledge gained by study; quality of learning and knowledge: *Good scholarship is more important than athletics. Scholarship, ... education, in a country like ours, is a branch of statesmanship* (Newsweek). **SYN:** erudition. **b** the collective attainments of scholars; sphere of learning: *modern French scholarship.* **2a** money or other aid given to help a student continue his studies: *He had such high marks that the college offered him a scholarship.* **b** a fund to provide this money. **c** the position or status of a student thus aided.

**scho|las|tic** (skə las′tik), *adj., n.* —***adj.*** **1** of schools, scholars, or education; academic: *scholastic life, scholastic methods.* **2** of or like scholasticism. **3** pedantic or formal.
—***n.*** **1** Also, **Scholastic.** a person who favors scholasticism. **2** a theologian and philosopher of the Middle Ages. **3** a man who is studying to become a Jesuit priest.
[< Latin *scholasticus* < Greek *scholastikós* < *schológein* be a scholar, devote one's leisure to learning < *scholē̂;* see etym. under **school**[1]]

**scho|las|ti|cal** (skə las′tə kəl), *adj.* = scholastic.

**scho|las|ti|cal|ly** (skə las′tə klē), *adv.* in a scholastic way or manner; in scholastic respects: *scholastically qualified.*

**Scholastic Aptitude Test**, *U.S.* a test prepared and supervised by the College Entrance Examination Board to test the general intelligence and academic aptitude of a prospective applicant to a college. *Abbr:* SAT (no periods).

**scho|las|ti|cate** (skə las′tə kāt, -kit), *n.* a house of study for Jesuits before ordination. [< New Latin *scholasticatus* < Latin *scholasticus;* see etym. under **scholastic**]

**scho|las|ti|cism** (skə las′tə siz əm), *n.* **1** Also, **Scholasticism.** the system of theological and philosophical teaching in the Middle Ages, based chiefly on the authority of the church fathers and of Aristotle, and characterized by a formal method of discussion. **2** adherence to the teachings of the schools or to traditional doctrines and methods.

**scho|li|a** (skō′lē ə), *n.* a plural of **scholium**.

**scho|li|ast** (skō′lē ast), *n.* **1** a commentator upon the ancient classics: *From their seats ... arose the gentler and graver ghosts ...—of Grecian or of Roman lore—to crown ... the ... love labours of their unwearied scholiast* (Charles Lamb). **2** a commentator upon the works of an author. [< Medieval Greek *scholiástēs* < *schólion;* see etym. under **scholium**]

**scho|li|as|tic** (skō′lē as′tik), *adj.* of or having to do with a scholiast or his work.

**scho|li|um** (skō′lē əm), *n., pl.* **-li|a** or **-li|ums**. **1** an explanatory note or comment, especially upon a passage in the Greek or Latin classics. **2** a note added by way of illustration or amplification. [< Medieval Latin *scholium* < Greek *schólion* (diminutive) < *scholē̂* discussion; see etym. under **school**[1]]

**school**[1] (skül), *n., v., adj.* —***n.*** **1a** a place for teaching and learning: *an elementary or high school, public or private schools, a dancing school.* **SYN:** academy. **b** learning in school; education received at school; instruction: *to enjoy school. Most children start school when they are about 5 years old.* **c** regular meetings of teachers and pupils for teaching and learning: *summer school.* **d** the time or period of such meetings: *to stay after school.* **e** pupils who are taught and their teachers: *Our school will be in a new building next fall.* **2** *Figurative.* any place, situation, or experience, as a source of instruction or training: *the school of adversity. The men of 1776 were trained in the strictest school of ... discipline* (E. Everett). **3** a place of training or discipline. **4** *Figurative.* **a** a group of people holding the same beliefs or opinions: *a gentleman of the old school.* **b** a group of people taught by the same person or united by a general similarity of principles and methods: *the Dutch school of painting.* **5a** a particular department or group in a university, specializing in a particular branch of learning: *a medical school, a law school, a school of music.* **b** a room, rooms, building, or group of buildings in a university, set apart for the use of one department: *The art school is across the street from the main campus.* **6** *Military, Naval.* **a** special drill regulations or drill applying as to the individual, squad, or other unit: *the school of the squad.* **b** the performance of a drill in accordance with such regulations. **7** (in the Middle Ages) a place where lectures were given in logic, metaphysics, and theology.
—***v.t.*** **1** to teach; educate in a school. **2** to train; discipline: *School yourself to control your temper.* **3** to instruct (a person) how to act: *Herodias schooled Salome in the part she was to play* (H. R. Reynolds).
—***adj.*** of or having to do with a school or schools: *a school semester, the school curriculum, the state school system.*
[Old English *scōl* < Latin *schola* < Greek *scholē̂* discussion; (originally) leisure, related to *échein* to have]

**school**[2] (skül), *n., v.* —***n.*** a large group of the same kind of fish or water animals swimming together: *a school of mackerel.*
—***v.i.*** to swim together in a school.
[< Dutch *school.* See related etym. at **shoal**[2].]

**school age**, **1** the age at which a child begins to go to school. **2** the years during which going to school is compulsory or customary.

**school-a|ger** (skül′ā′jər), *n.* a young person of school age.

**school|bag** (skül′bag′), *n.* briefcase, knapsack, or other bag used to carry books and papers to and from school.

**school board**, a local board or committee managing the public schools.

**school|book** (skül′bůk′), *n., adj.* —***n.*** a book for study in schools.
—***adj.*** *Especially U.S.* characteristic of schoolbooks; oversimplified: *Film enthusiasts find it simpler to explain movies in terms of the genius-artist-director, the schoolbook hero—the man who did it all* (Pauline Kael).

**school|boy** (skül′boi′), *n.* a boy attending school.

**school|boy|ish** (skül′boi′ish), *adj.* like or characteristic of a schoolboy: *His prose style, though lucid, is awkward and repetitious—it has a schoolboyish ring* (Atlantic).

**school bus**, a bus that carries children to and from school.

**school|child** (skül′chīld′), *n., pl.* **-chil|dren**. a schoolboy or schoolgirl.

**school|craft** (skül′kraft′, -kräft′), *n. Archaic.* knowledge taught in the schools.

**school day**, **1** a day on which school is in session. **2** the time of such a session.

---

**Pronunciation Key:** hat, āge, cãre, fär; let, ēqual, tėrm; it, īce; hot, ōpen, ôrder; oil, out; cup, pu̇t, rüle; child; long; thin; ᴛʜen; zh, measure; ə represents a in about, e in taken, i in pencil, o in lemon, u in circus.

**school district**, an area, such as that of a town or county, having its own school or schools. The school district usually serves as a unit of local taxation.

**school edition**, the form of a book published for use in the classroom: *Many novels are published in paperback school editions with notes and glossaries in the back.*

**school|er** (skü′lər), *n.* = schoolchild.

**school|fel|low** (skül′fel′ō), *n.* a companion at school.

**school figure**, one of a required set of figures or movements in a skating competition: *School figures . . . include turns like threes, double threes, brackets, and loops, and combinations thereof* (New Yorker).

**school|girl** (skül′gėrl′), *n., adj.* **—*n.*** a girl attending school.
**—*adj.*** of or like that of a young girl: *a schoolgirl figure.*

**school|girl|ish** (skül′gėr′lish), *adj.* like or characteristic of a schoolgirl.

**school|house** (skül′hous′), *n.* a building used as a school.

**school|ing** (skü′ling), *n.* **1** instruction in school; education received at school. **2** training: *At a riding academy both horses and riders receive schooling.* **3** the cost of instruction. **4** *Archaic.* a reprimand; reproof.

**school|kid** (skül′kid′), *n. Informal.* a child of school age.

**school land**, *U.S.* land set apart for the maintenance of a school.

**school-leav|er** (skül′lē′vər), *n. British.* a person who leaves or quits school before he completes his course of study: *The chief works of literature, in particular those of our century, are unknown to most school-leavers* (Manchester Guardian).

**school-leav|ing** (skül′lē′ving), *n. British.* a leaving or quitting of school before completion of the course of study.

**school|less** (skül′lis), *adj.* without a school; deprived of a school or schooling: *It thus appeared that Little Rock's high-school students might as well settle down to a long schoolless winter* (Time).

**school|ma'am** (skül′mam′), *n. Informal or Dialect.* a woman teacher; schoolmistress.

**school|maid** (skül′mād′), *n. Archaic.* a schoolgirl.

**school|man** (skül′mən), *n., pl.* **-men. 1** a man engaged in teaching or in managing a school. **2** Also, **Schoolman.** a teacher in a university of the Middle Ages; medieval theologian. **3** an expert in traditional learning, formal logic, and the like.

**school|marm** (skül′märm′), *n. Informal or Dialect.* a woman teacher; schoolmistress.

**school|marm|ish** (skül′mär′mish), *adj. Informal.* like or characteristic of a schoolmarm.

**school|mas|ter** (skül′mas′tər, -mäs′-), *n., v.* **—*n.*** **1** a man who teaches in a school, or is its principal. **2** *Figurative.* any person or thing that teaches or disciplines. **3** a snapper of the West Indies and adjacent waters.
**—*v.t.*** to supervise or instruct as a schoolmaster.
**—*v.i.*** to be a schoolmaster.

**school|mas|ter|ing** (skül′mas′tər ing, -mäs′-), *n.* the occupation or profession of a schoolmaster.

**school|mas|ter|ish** (skül′mas′tər ish, -mäs′-), *adj.* like or characteristic of a schoolmaster: *schoolmasterish jokes.* **—school′mas′ter|ish|ly,** *adv.*

**school|mas|ter|ly** (skül′mas′tər lē, -mäs′-), *adj.* like or characteristic of a schoolmaster: *schoolmasterly tones.*

**school|mate** (skül′māt′), *n.* a companion at school.

**school|mis|tress** (skül′mis′tris), *n.* a woman who teaches in a school, or is its principal.

**school|room** (skül′rüm′, -rům′), *n.* a room in which pupils are taught.

**school section**, *Canadian.* a section of government land given to a local government by the federal government for the support of public schools.

**school|ship** (skül′ship′), *n.* a seagoing vessel used as a school for practical instruction in seamanship.

**school|teach|er** (skül′tē′chər), *n.* a person who teaches in a school. SYN: instructor.

**school|teach|er|ish** (skül′tē′chər ish), *adj.* like or characteristic of a schoolteacher: *Her hair is short, gray, curly, and parted in the middle, giving her a slightly schoolteacherish look, which is often intensified by a pair of rimless spectacles* (New Yorker).

**school|teach|er|ly** (skül′tē′chər lē), *adj.* like or characteristic of a schoolteacher: *He gave us . . . a thoughtful, schoolteacherly talk on how clean the election was going to be* (Christopher Rand).

**school|teach|ing** (skül′tē′ching), *n.* the occupation or profession of a schoolteacher.

**school|time** (skül′tīm′), *n.* **1** the time at which school begins or during which school continues. **2** the period of life which is passed at school.

**school tuna**, a tuna fish ranging from 20 to 100 pounds.

**school|ward** (skül′wərd), *adv., adj.* toward school: *They reluctantly trudged schoolward* (adv.). *They found many distractions on their schoolward journey* (adj.).

**school|work** (skül′wėrk′), *n.* a student's work in school.

**school|yard** (skül′yärd′), *n.* a piece of ground around or near a school, used for play or games.

**school year**, the part of the year during which school is in session. A school year usually begins in September of one year and ends in May or June of the following year.

***schoon|er** (skü′nər), *n.* **1** a ship with two or more masts and fore-and-aft sails. **2** = prairie schooner. **3a** *U.S. Informal.* a large glass for beer: *He ordered a schooner of beer and knocked it off with unaffected enthusiasm* (New Yorker). **b** *British.* a customary measure of beer. [American English, probably < dialectal *scoon* to skim]

***schooner**
definition 1

**schooner rig**, = fore-and-aft rig.

**schoon|er-rigged** (skü′nər rigd′), *adj.* having fore-and-aft sails.

**Scho|pen|hau|er|i|an** (shō′pən hou′ə rē ən), *adj., n.* **—*adj.*** of, having to do with, or characteristic of the German philosopher Arthur Schopenhauer (1788-1860) or his doctrines.
**—*n.*** a believer in or supporter of the philosophical doctrines of Schopenhauer.

**Scho|pen|hau|er|ism** (shō′pən hou′ə riz əm), *n.* the philosophy of Arthur Schopenhauer, German philosopher; belief that life is evil, and cannot be made good.

**schorl** (shôrl), *n.* a mineral, tourmaline, especially black tourmaline. [< German *Schörl*]

**schor|la|ceous** (shôr lā′shəs), *adj.* of the nature of, resembling, or containing schorl.

**schot|tische** or **schot|tish** (shot′ish), *n.* **1** a dance in 2/4 time, somewhat like the polka but slower, popular in the 1800's. **2** music for it. [< German *Schottische* (originally) Scottish]

**schr.** or **Schr.**, schooner: *The Schr. Rival.*

**schrei|ber|site** (shrī′bər sīt, -zīt), *n.* a phosphide of iron and nickel occurring only in meteoric iron. *Formula:* $(Fe,Ni)_3P$ [< German *Schreibersit* < Carl von *Schreibers,* an Austrian museum director + *-it* -ite]

**schrik** (skrik), *n. Afrikaans.* sudden terror.

**Schrö|ding|er (wave) equation** (shrœ′ding ər), a general equation of wave mechanics describing the behavior of atomic particles passing through a field of force. [< Erwin *Schrödinger,* 1887-1961, an Austrian physicist, who formulated this equation in 1926]

**schtik** (shtik), *n. Slang.* an act, routine, gimmick, or trick, especially thought of as characteristic of a particular entertainer: *John Barber's schtik is to flay his native land* (Maclean's). Also, **shtick.** [< Yiddish *shtik* piece, slice]

**Schu|bert|i|an** (shü bėr′tē ən), *adj., n.* **—*adj.*** of, having to do with, or characteristic of Franz Schubert (1797-1828), Austrian musical composer: *Schubertian beauty and expressiveness* (New York Times).
**—*n.*** an admirer of Franz Schubert's style or theory of music.

**schuh|platt|ler** (shü′plät′lər), *n.* a Bavarian folk dance for couples, in which the woman turns slowly in place, while her partner dances around her slapping his thighs and the soles of his shoes. [< German *Schuhplattler* < *Schuh* shoe + dialectal *Plattler* one who strikes]

**schuit** (skoit), *n.* a short, somewhat bargelike ship used on the rivers and canals of the Netherlands. It has a sloop rigging but is now powered by motor. Also, **schuyt.** [< Dutch *schuit*]

**Schu|man Plan** (shü′mən), a plan providing for the pooling of the coal and steel resources of France, Italy, West Germany, Belgium, the Netherlands, and Luxembourg, with production supervised by a joint authority. [< Robert *Schuman,* 1886-1963, a French political figure, who devised it]

**schuss** (shůs), *n., v.,* **schussed, schuss|ing.** in skiing: **—*n.*** **1** a fast run down a straight course. **2** the course itself.
**—*v.i.*** to make a run at top speed over a straight course: *He was schussing down Hahnenkamm at something like 50 miles an hour when he hit a bare spot* (Newsweek).
[< German *Schuss* (literally) shot] **—schuss′er,** *n.*

**schuss|boom** (shůs′büm′), *v.i. Slang.* to ski at high speed, especially downhill.

**schuss|boom|er** (shůs′bü′mər), *n. Slang.* a skier who schussbooms; high-speed skier.

**Schutz|staf|fel** (shůts′shtä′fəl), *n.* the SS Troops, especially those of the German army during World War II. [< German *Schutzstaffel* (literally) protective staff]

**schuyt** (skoit), *n.* = schuit.

***schwa** (shwä), *n.* **1** an unstressed vowel sound such as *a* in *about* or *u* in *circus,* represented by the symbol ə; a neutral vowel. **2** the symbol ə. [< German *Schwa* < Hebrew *shəwa*]

***schwa**
definition 2

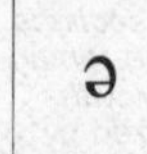

taken = tā′kən
pencil = pen′səl

**Schwann cell** (shwän, shvän), any one of the cells that form a myelin sheath around the nerve fibers or axons in the peripheral nervous system. [< Theodor *Schwann,* 1810-1882, a German anatomist]

**Schwär|me|rei** or **schwär|me|rei** (shver′mə-rī′), *n. German.* enthusiasm; devotion: *We had a great schwärmerei for Frank which would come like measles and go as completely* (New Yorker).

**Schwarz|schild radius** (shvärts′shilt, shwôrts′-shild), the size at which the gravitational forces of a collapsing body in space become so strong that they prevent the escape of any matter or radiation: *Eventually an object whose collapse continues reaches a limiting size that depends on its mass. The size is called the Schwarzschild radius. For the sun, it is about three kilometers. When the object shrinks to less than its Schwarzschild radius, it becomes a black hole* (Science News). [< Martin *Schwarzschild,* born 1912, an American astrophysicist]

**Schwed|ler maple** (shved′lər), a variety of Norway maple with bright red leaves that turn dark green in summer.

**Schweit|zer's reagent** (shvīt′sərz), a reagent used to test for the presence of wool, consisting of an hydroxide of copper combined with ammonia. [< Matthias *Schweitzer,* 1818-1860, a German chemist]

**Schwei|zer|kä|se** or **schwei|zer|kä|se** (shvīt′-sər kā′zə), *n. German.* Swiss cheese.

**Schwenk|fel|der** (shvengk′fel′dər), *n.* a member of a Protestant church originating with immigrants from Silesia who settled in Pennsylvania in the 1730's. The Schwenkfelders have simple church services. [< Kaspar *Schwenkfeld,* 1489-1561, a German religious reformer]

**Schwer|punkt** (shvār′půngkt′), *n. German.* **1** the point of main thrust of a military attack: *On the insistence of Manstein . . . the Schwerpunkt was redirected to the Ardennes and Sedan* (Observer). **2** (literally) center of gravity.

**Schwyz|er|dütsch** (shvēt′sər dych′), *n.* the German dialect of Switzerland. [< Schwyzerdütsch *Schwyzerdütsch* Swiss German < *Schwyz* Switzerland + *dütsch* German]

**sci.**, **1** science. **2** scientific.

**SCI** (no periods), Ship Controlled Interception (a radar system used by warships to direct fighter planes against enemy bombers).

**sci|ae|nid** (sī ē′nid), *adj., n.* = sciaenoid.

**sci|ae|noid** (sī ē′noid), *adj., n.* **—*adj.*** of or belonging to a large group of spiny-finned carnivorous fishes usually with air bladders that make a drumming sound. It includes the drumfishes and some kingfishes.
**—*n.*** a sciaenoid fish.
[< Latin *sciaena* kind of fish (< Greek *skiaina)* + English *-oid*]

**sci|a|gram** (sī′ə gram), *n.* = skiagram.

**sci|a|graph** (sī′ə graf, -gräf), *n., v.t.* = skiagraph.

**sci|a|graph|ic** (sī′ə graf′ik), *adj.* = skiagraphic.

**sci|ag|ra|phy** (sī ag′rə fē), *n.* = skiagraphy.

**sci|am|a|chy** (sī am′ə kē), *n., pl.* **-chies. 1** fighting with a shadow; futile combat with an imaginary enemy. **2** a sham combat. Also, **sciomachy.** [< Greek *skiāmachiā* < *skiāmachein* fight against a shadow < *skiā, -âs* shadow + *machē* battle < *máchesthai* to fight]

**sci|at|ic** (sī at′ik), *adj.* **1** of or in the region of the hip: *the sciatic artery.* **2** affecting the sciatic nerve: *sciatic neuralgia.* [< Medieval Latin *sciaticus,* alteration of Latin *ischiadicus* < Greek *ischiadikós* < *ischíon* hip joint]

**sci|at|i|ca** (sī at′ə kə), *n.* pain in a sciatic nerve and its branches, felt in the hip, thigh, and leg: *In severe cases, sciatica can cause loss of leg reflexes or the wasting of muscles in one or both calves* (Louis D. Boshes). [< Medieval Latin *sciatica* (*passio*) sciatic (disease), feminine of *sciaticus;* see etym. under **sciatic**]

**sci|at|i|cal** (sī at′ə kəl), *adj.* of sciatica; affected with sciatica. —**sci|at′i|cal|ly,** *adv.*

**sciatic nerve,** a large, branching nerve which extends from the lower back down the back part of the thigh and leg to the foot.

**sci|ence** (sī′əns), *n.* **1a** knowledge based on observed facts and tested truths arranged in an orderly system: *the laws of science, pure science. Science is verified knowledge; that is, knowledge that can be validated and communicated to other people* (George Simpson). **b** a branch of such knowledge. Biology, chemistry, physics, and astronomy are natural sciences. Economics and sociology are social sciences. Agriculture and engineering are applied sciences. **2** a branch of such knowledge dealing with the phenomena of the universe and their laws; a physical or natural science: *Geology, botany, and zoology are sciences.* **3** skill based on training and practice; technique: *the science of judo, the science of sailing, to have housework down to a fine science.* **SYN:** proficiency. **4** a particular branch of knowledge or study, especially as distinguished from art: *the science of perspective.* **5** the search for truth: *a martyr to science. Be love my youth's pursuit, and science crown my age* (Thomas Gray). [< Old French *science,* learned borrowing from Latin *scientia* knowledge < *sciēns, -entis,* present participle of *scīre* to know]

**Sci|ence** (sī′əns), *n.* = Christian Science.

**science court,** a proposed panel of scientists appointed to review scientific issues of national concern and advise the government on their practicability: *The term "science court," [Margaret Mead] says, conjures up visions of yet another expensive Washington institution with an entrenched bureaucracy and bad architecture* (Science News).

**science fair,** a group of exhibits, each demonstrating a scientific principle, process, development, etc.

**science fiction,** a novel, short story, play, or the like, that combines science and fantasy. Science fiction deals with life in the future, in other galaxies, or in other fantastic situations, usually making much use of recent discoveries of technology and advances in science. *Science fiction is as old as the myth of Icarus and Daedalus* (New York Times).

**science fictioneer,** a writer of science fiction.

**sci|en|ter** (sī en′tər), *n. Law.* **1** a clause in a complaint or indictment charging that the defendant has knowledge which makes him responsible or guilty. **2** the fact that the defendant has such knowledge. [< Latin *scienter* knowingly]

**sci|en|tial** (sī en′shəl), *adj.* **1** of or having to do with science or knowledge. **2** having knowledge.

**sci|en|tif|ic** (sī′ən tif′ik), *adj.* **1a** based on, regulated by, or done according to the facts and laws of science: *a scientific arrangement of fossils, scientific farming.* **b** using the facts and laws of science: *scientific research, a scientific farmer.* **2** of or having to do with science; used in science: *scientific books, scientific laws, scientific instruments.* **3a** systematic; accurate; exact: *a scientific survey.* **b** trained in skill or technique: *a scientific boxer, a scientific engraver.* [< Late Latin *scientificus* < *scientia* knowledge (see etym. under **science**) + *facere* to make]

**sci|en|tif|i|cal|ly** (sī′ən tif′ə klē), *adv.* **1** in a scientific manner: *Einstein and Edison thought scientifically.* **2** according to the facts and laws of science: *A perpetual motion machine is scientifically impossible. It is easier to believe than to be scientifically instructed* (John Locke).

**scientific method,** an orderly method used in scientific research, generally consisting in identifying a problem, gathering all the pertinent data, formulating a hypothesis, performing experiments, interpreting results, and drawing a conclusion.

**scientific notation,** a method used in scientific work to express a number as the product of a number from 1 to 10 and a power of 10. *Examples:* The scientific notation for 500 is $5 \times 10^2$. The scientific notation for 800,000,000 is $8 \times 10^8$.

**sci|en|tism** (sī′ən tiz′əm), *n.* **1** the habit of thought and manner of expression characteristic of scientists: *The lingo of scientism is still used by businessmen* (Wall Street Journal). **2** the tendency to reduce all reality and experience to mathematical descriptions of physical and chemical phenomena: *Those of us who think that scientific method is applicable to political problems are apt to be told, rather sharply, that we are talking "Scientism"* (Saturday Review).

**sci|en|tist** (sī′ən tist), *n.* a person who has expert knowledge of some branch of science. Persons specially trained in and familiar with the facts and laws of such fields as biology, chemistry, mathematics, physics, geology, and astronomy are scientists.

**Sci|en|tist** (sī′ən tist), *n.* = Christian Scientist.

**sci|en|tis|tic** (sī′ən tis′tik), *adj.* of or like the methods of a scientist; scientific. —**sci′en|tis′ti|cal|ly,** *adv.*

**sci|en|tize** (sī′ən tīz), *v.,* **-tized, -tiz|ing.** —*v.t.* to treat in a scientific manner; organize scientifically: *to scientize raw data.*
—*v.i.* to lay down scientific propositions; theorize.

**sci-fi** (sī′fī′), *n., adj. Informal.* —*n.* science fiction. —*adj. Especially U.S.* of or having to do with science fiction: *a sci-fi thriller.* [< *sci*(ence) *fi*(ction), patterned after *hi-fi* (high-fidelity)]

**scil.,** scilicet; namely.

**scil|i|cet** (sil′ə set), *adv.* to wit; namely. *Abbr.:* sc. [< Latin *scīlicet* < *scīre* to know + *licet* it is allowed]

**scil|la** (sil′ə), *n.* any one of a group of early-blooming, ornamental plants of the lily family with bluish or white flowers; squill. [< Latin *scilla* < Greek *skílla*]

**Scil|la** (sil′ə; *Italian* shēl′lä), *n.* = Scylla.

**Scil|lo|ni|an** (si lō′nē ən), *n., adj.* —*n.* a native or inhabitant of the Scilly Isles, a group of islands southwest of England. —*adj.* of or having to do with the Scilly Isles or the Scillonians.

**scim|i|tar** or **scim|i|ter** (sim′ə tər), *n.* a short, curved sword used by Turks, Persians, Arabs, and other Oriental peoples. Also, **simitar.** See picture under **sword.** [< Italian *scimitarra,* perhaps < Persian *shimshīr*]

**scin|coid** (sing′koid), *adj., n.* —*adj.* **1** belonging to the same group of reptiles as the skinks. **2** resembling the skinks. —*n.* a skink. [< Latin *scincus* skink[1] + English *-oid*]

**scin|tig|ra|phy** (sin tig′rə fē), *n.* a means of obtaining diagnostic pictures of internal organs by administering radioisotopes to the patient and subsequently recording their distribution with a device related to the scintillation counter. [< *scinti*(llation) + *-graphy*]

**scin|til|la** (sin til′ə), *n.* a spark; particle; trace: *not a scintilla of truth. There was approval in the lady's gaze. There was, however, not a scintilla of recognition in it* (Leonard Merrick). **SYN:** jot, mite. [< Latin *scintilla* spark. See etym. of doublets **stencil, tinsel.**]

**scin|til|lant** (sin′tə lənt), *adj.* scintillating; sparkling. —**scin′til|lant|ly,** *adv.*

**scin|til|late** (sin′tə lāt), *v.,* **-lat|ed, -lat|ing.** —*v.i.* to sparkle; flash; twinkle: *The snow scintillates in the sun like diamonds.* (*Figurative.*) *Brilliant wit scintillates.* **SYN:** glitter, glisten.
—*v.t.* to flash with; shower like sparks: *That this globe was originally a globe of liquid fire, scintillated from the body of the sun, by the percussion of a comet* (Washington Irving).
[< Latin *scintillāre* < *scintilla* a spark]

**scin|til|lat|ing** (sin′tə lā′ting), *adj.* that scintillates; sparkling: *The Berlin Philharmonic may not be the most scintillating orchestra in the world, but it is ... magnificent* (New Yorker). —**scin′til|lat′ing|ly,** *adv.*

**scin|til|la|tion** (sin′tə lā′shən), *n.* **1** the act of sparkling; flashing. **2** a spark; flash: (*Figurative.*) *Let the scintillations of your wit be like ... summer lightning, lambent but innocuous* (Edward M. Goulburn). **3** the twinkling of the stars. **4** *Physics.* a flash or spark produced by ions in a phosphor, as when an alpha particle impinges on certain solid materials, especially zinc sulfide.

**scintillation camera,** a photographic camera which records the scintillations of radiation, used especially to trace the distribution of radioactive substances in the body.

**scintillation counter,** a device which detects and counts radioactive particles by counting the number of scintillations when radiation strikes a luminescent liquid, crystal, or gas. It is sensitive to gamma rays.

**scintillation plastic,** a plastic that gives off flashes of light when exposed to radioactive energy, used to detect nuclear and cosmic radiation.

**scin|til|la|tor** (sin′tə lā′tər), *n.* **1** a scintillating star. **2** the liquid, crystal, or gas used as the source of scintillations in a scintillation counter.

**scin|til|les|cent** (sin′tə les′ənt), *adj.* = scintillating.

**scin|til|lom|e|ter** (sin′tə lom′ə tər), *n.* **1** = scintillation counter. **2** an instrument for measuring the intensity of the scintillation of the stars.

**scin|til|lo|scope** (sin til′ə skōp), *n.* = spinthariscope.

**sci|o|graph** (sī′ə graf, -gräf), *n., v.* = skiagraph.

**sci|o|graph|ic** (sī′ə graf′ik), *adj.* = skiagraphic.

**sci|o|lism** (sī′ə liz′əm), *n.* superficial knowledge: *The sciolism of literary or political adventurers* (George Eliot). [< Late Latin *sciolus* one who knows a little (< *scius* knowing < *scīre* to know) + English *-ism*]

**sci|o|list** (sī′ə list), *n.* a person who pretends to have more knowledge than he really has. **SYN:** charlatan, quack.

**sci|o|lis|tic** (sī′ə lis′tik), *adj.* of, or like sciolism or sciolists.

**sci|o|lous** (sī′ə ləs), *adj.* having only superficial knowledge; shallow. [< Late Latin *sciolus* one who knows a little (diminutive) < Latin *scīre* to know; + English *-ous*]

**sci|om|a|chy** (sī om′ə kē), *n., pl.* **-chies.** = sciamachy.

**sci|o|man|cy** (sī′ə man′sē), *n.* divination by means of the shades of the dead. [< Greek *skiā́* shadow, shade + *manteiā́* divination]

**sci|on** (sī′ən), *n.* **1** a bud or branch cut for grafting or planting; cutting; slip. Also, **cion. 2** a descendant; heir: *the scion of a wealthy family. ... it became more obvious that Bertie [Prince Albert] was a true scion of the House of Brunswick* (Lytton Strachey). *The present Mr. Chadwick was a worthy scion of a worthy stock* (Anthony Trollope). **SYN:** offspring. [< Old French *cion,* perhaps < Latin *sectiō, -ōnis* a cutting, section]
▶ See **cion** for usage note.

**sci|oph|i|lous** (sī of′ə ləs), *adj. Botany.* growing or living by preference in the shade; shade-loving. [< Greek *skiā́* shadow + English *-phil* + *-ous*]

**sci|o|phyte** (sī′ə fīt), *n.* a sciophilous plant. [< Greek *skiā́* shadow + English *-phyte*]

**sci|re fa|ci|as** (sī′rē fā′shē as), *Law.* **1** a writ requiring the party against whom it is brought to show cause why a judgment, letters patent, or the like, should not be executed, vacated, or annulled. **2** a proceeding based on such a writ. [< Latin *scīre faciās* you must make known]

**scir|rhoid** (skir′oid, sir′-), *adj.* resembling a scirrhus.

**scir|rho|ma** (ski rō′mə, si-), *n., pl.* **-ma|ta** (-mə tə). = scirrhus. [< New Latin *scirrhoma.*]

**scir|rhos|i|ty** (ski ros′ə tē, si-), *n., pl.* **-ties.** scirrhous condition; a morbid hardness.

**scir|rhous** (skir′əs, sir′-), *adj.* **1** of or like a scirrhus. **2** hard or hardened with fibrous tissue.

**scir|rhus** (skir′əs, sir′-), *n., pl.* **scir|rhi** (skir′ī, sir′-), **scir|rhus|es. 1** a hard, fibrous cancer. **2** a hard tumor. [< New Latin *scirrhus* < Latin *scirros* < Greek *skirrhós* hard]

**scis|sel** (sis′əl), *n.* metal scrap from some process, such as that left after cutting blanks for coins. [< French *cisaille* < *cisailler* clip with shears]

**scis|sile** (sis′əl), *adj.* that can be easily cut, divided, or split: *Slate is a scissile rock.* [< Latin *scissilis* < *scindere* to cut]

**scis|sion** (sizh′ən, sish′-), *n.* the act of cutting, dividing, or splitting; division; separation. [< Late Latin *scissiō, -ōnis* < Latin *scindere* to split]

**scis|sor** (siz′ər), *v., n.* —*v.t., v.i.* **1** to cut with scissors: *Each folio being scissored into half a dozen pieces* (D. C. Murray). (*Figurative.*) *The author does not scissor the story neatly out of whole cloth to a preconceived pattern* (Time). **2** to move (the legs) in vaulting, swimming, or other sports, like the movements of scissors blades: *High hurdlers leap over the final hurdle ... Outstretched arms maintain balance and help the runners to "scissor" their legs over the 3½-foot bars* (Ed Chay).
—*n. Informal.* scissors: *Lend me your scissor.* [< *scissors*] —**scis′sor|er,** *n.*

**scis|sor|a|ble** (siz′ər ə bəl), *adj.* that can be cut with scissors.

**scis|sor|bill** (siz′ər bil′), *n.* = skimmer (def. 3).

**scis|sor|like** (siz′ər līk′), *adj.* similar to scissors.

***scissors** definition 1

***scis|sors** (siz′ərz), *n.pl. or sing.* **1** a tool or instrument for cutting that has two sharp blades with

**Pronunciation Key:** hat, āge, cãre, fär; let, ēqual, tėrm; it, īce; hot, ōpen, ôrder; oil, out; cup, pu̇t, rüle; child; long; thin; ᴛʜen; zh, measure; ə represents **a** in about, **e** in taken, **i** in pencil, **o** in lemon, **u** in circus.

handles, so fastened that their edges slide against each other: *a pair of scissors. Give me the scissors to cut the cloth.* SYN: shears. **2a** a wrestling hold with the legs clasped around an opponent. **b** a movement of the legs while vaulting or high jumping that is like the movement of scissors blades. **c** = scissors kick. [< Old French *cisoires,* plural < Late Latin *cīsōria,* plural of *cīsōrium* tool for cutting < Latin *caedere* to cut; confused with Latin *scissōr* a cutter < *scindere* to cleave, split]

▶ **scissors.** In the sense of a cutting instrument, scissors is usually plural: *The scissors aren't sharp.* The word is singular in the sense of a movement of the legs: *The wrestler got a scissors around his opponent's body.*

**scis|sors-and-paste** (siz′ərz ən pāst′), *adj.* put together like a scrapbook; derivative; superficial: *His latest book is a scissors-and-paste affair, consisting mostly of anecdotes* (New Yorker).

**scissors gait,** a gait characteristic of spastic paralysis, in which a person walks on his toes with his feet turned inward, his knees together, and with one leg crossing over in front of the other.

**scissors hold,** = scissors (def. 2a.)

**scissors kick,** a movement of the legs in swimming like the movement of scissors blades.

**scis|sor|tail** (siz′ər tāl′), *n.* a grayish flycatcher of the southern United States, Mexico, and Central America, with a very long, deeply forked tail that opens and closes as it flies.

**scis|sor-tailed flycatcher** (siz′ər tāld′), = scissortail.

**scis|sure** (sizh′ər, sish′-), *n.* **1** a longitudinal opening cut in a body. **2** *Figurative.* a division or schism; split. **3** *Anatomy.* a natural opening in an organ or part. [< Latin *scissūra* < *scindere* cut]

**sci|u|rine** (sī′yu̇ rīn, -yu̇r in), *adj., n.* —*adj.* of or belonging to a group that includes the squirrels, chipmunks, and certain related rodents.
—*n.* a squirrel or other sciurine animal.
[< Latin *sciūrus* squirrel (< Greek *skíouros* < *skiā́* shadow + *ourā́* tail) + English *-ine*[1]]

**sci|u|roid** (sī yu̇r′oid), *adj.* **1** = sciurine. **2** like a squirrel's tail; curved and bushy: *the sciuroid spikes of certain grasses.* [< Latin *sciūrus* (see etym. under **sciurine**) + English *-oid*]

**sclaff** (sklaf, skläf), *v., n.* —*v.t., v.i. Golf.* **1** to scrape (the ground) with a golf club before hitting the ball. **2** to hit (a golf ball) after scraping the ground with the club.
—*n.* **1** *Golf.* a sclaffing stroke. **2** *Scottish.* the noise made by a slight, glancing blow.
[probably imitative] —**sclaff′er,** *n.*

**SCLC** (no periods) or **S.C.L.C.,** Southern Christian Leadership Conference (an American organization, consisting chiefly of Southern churches, formed in 1957 to campaign for Negro civil rights).

**scler-,** *combining form.* the form of **sclero-** sometimes used before vowels, as in *scleroid.*

**scle|ra** (sklir′ə), *n.* = sclerotic coat. [< New Latin *sclera* < Greek *sklērós* hard < *skéllein* to dry up]

**scler|al** (sklir′əl), *adj.* of or having to do with the sclerotic coat of the eyeball.

**scle|re|id** (sklir′ē id), *n. Botany.* a thickened, sclerotic cell; stone cell.

**scle|ren|chy|ma** (skli reng′kə mə), *n. Botany.* nonliving plant tissue composed of thickened and hardened cells from which the protoplasm has disappeared. It is found chiefly as a strengthening and protecting tissue in the stem and in such hard parts of plants as nutshells. [< New Latin *sclerenchyma* < Greek *sklērós* hard (see etym. under **sclera**) + New Latin *enchyma* enchyma]

**scle|ren|chym|a|tous** (sklir′eng kim′ə təs), *adj.* of or like sclerenchyma: *sclerenchymatous tissue, a sclerenchymatous polyp.*

**scle|ri|a|sis** (skli rī′ə sis), *n.* **1** a hardening of body tissue. **2** = scleroderma. [< New Latin *scleriasis* < Greek *sklēríāsis* < *sklērós* hard; see etym. under **sclera**]

**scle|rite** (sklir′īt), *n. Zoology.* a chitinous or calcareous plate, spicule, or the like, of an invertebrate animal, especially one of the plates of the exoskeleton of a grasshopper or similar arthropod. [< Greek *sklērós* hard + English *-ite*[1]]

**scle|rit|ic** (skli rit′ik), *adj.* **1** of or like a sclerite; hardened or chitinized. **2** of or having to do with scleritis.

**scle|ri|tis** (skli rī′tis), *n.* inflammation of the sclerotic coat of the eyeball.

**sclero-,** *combining form.* **1** hard: *Sclerodermatous = having a hard body covering.*
**2** having to do with the sclerotic coat of the eyeball: *Scleroiritis = inflammation of the sclerotic coat and iris of the eye.* Also, **scler-** before vowels. [< Greek *sklērós*]

**scle|ro|cau|ly** (sklir′ə kô′lē), *n.* a condition of plant stems in which they become slender, hard, and dry. [< Greek *sklēros* hard + *kaulos* stem + English *-y*[3]]

**scle|ro|dac|tyl|i|a** (sklir′ə dak til′ē ə), *n.* atrophy and deformity of the fingers, with thickening and hardening of the skin covering them. [< New Latin *sclerodactylia* < *sclero-* + Greek *dáktylos* finger]

**scle|ro|der|ma** (sklir′ə dėr′mə), *n.* a disease in which the skin becomes hard and rigid. [< New Latin *scleroderma* < Greek *sklērós* hard + *dérma* skin]

**scle|ro|der|ma|tous** (sklir′ə dėr′mə təs), *adj. Zoology.* having a hard body covering, as of plates or scales.

**scle|roid** (sklir′oid), *adj. Biology.* hard; indurated. [< *scler-* + *-oid*]

**scle|ro|i|ri|tis** (sklir′ō ī rī′tis), *n.* inflammation of the sclerotic coat and iris of the eye. [< *sclero-* + *ir*(is) + *-itis*]

**scle|ro|ma** (skli rō′mə), *n., pl.* **-ma|ta** (-mə tə). a hardening of body tissue. [< New Latin *scleroma* < Greek *sklērōma* < *sklērós* hard (see etym. under **sclera**) + *-ōma* a growth]

**scle|rom|e|ter** (skli rom′ə tər), *n.* an instrument for measuring the hardness of a substance, especially a mineral. [< *sclero-* + *-meter*]

**scle|ro|phyll** (sklir′ə fil), *n.* a plant with small, leathery leaves that reduce evaporation, making the plant adaptable to dry conditions. [< *sclero-* + Greek *phýllon* leaf]

**scle|ro|phyl|lous** (sklir′ə fil′əs), *adj. Botany.* **1** having leathery leaves which resist easy loss of moisture. **2** made up of sclerophylls.

**scle|ro|phyl|ly** (sklir′ə fil′ē), *n.* a thickened and hardened condition of foliage due to sclerenchyma.

**scle|ro|pro|tein** (sklir′ə prō′tēn, -tē in), *n.* = albuminoid.

**scle|ro|sal** (skli rō′səl), *adj.* having to do with sclerosis.

**scle|ro|scope** (sklir′ə skōp), *n.* an instrument for testing the hardness of metal. [< *sclero-* + *-scope*]

**scle|rose** (skli rōs′), *v.t., v.i.,* **-rosed, -ros|ing.** to harden; affect with sclerosis. [back formation < *sclerosed*]

**scle|rosed** (skli rōst′, sklir′ōst), *adj.* affected with sclerosis: *sclerosed tissue.* [< *scleros*(is) + *-ed*[2]]

**scle|ro|sis** (skli rō′sis), *n., pl.* **-ses** (-sēz). **1** a hardening of a tissue or part of the body by an increase of connective tissue or the deposition of salts at the expense of more active tissue. **2** a hardening of a tissue or cell wall of a plant by thickening or the formation of wood. [< New Latin *sclerosis* a hardness, hard tumor < Greek *sklērōsis* hardening < *sklērós* hard; see etym. under **sclera**]

**scle|ro|tial** (skli rō′shəl), *adj.* of or having to do with a sclerotium or sclerotia.

**scle|rot|ic** (skli rot′ik), *n., adj.* —*n.* = sclerotic coat.
—*adj.* **1** of or having to do with the sclerotic coat. **2** of, with, or having sclerosis. **3** *Botany.* hardened; stony in texture.
[< New Latin *scleroticus* < Greek *sklērós* hard; see etym. under **sclera**]

**scle|rot|i|ca** (skli rot′ə kə), *n.* the sclerotic coat of the eyeball. [< New Latin *sclerotica*]

**sclerotic coat,** the tough, white outer membrane which covers the eyeball, except for the part covered by the cornea; sclera; sclerotic.

**scle|ro|ti|oid** (skli rō′shē oid), *adj.* having to do with or resembling a sclerotium.

**scle|ro|tit|ic** (sklir′ō tit′ik), *adj.* affected with sclerotitis or scleritis.

**scle|ro|ti|tis** (sklir′ō tī′tis), *n.* = scleritis.

**scle|ro|ti|um** (skli rō′shē əm), *n., pl.* **-ti|a** (-shē ə). *Botany.* a tuberlike body of reserve food material that forms the mycelium of certain fungi. [< New Latin *sclerotium* < Greek *sklērótēs* hardness < *sklērós* hard]

**sclerotium rot,** a fungous disease of plants that causes yellowing and wilting.

**scle|ro|ti|za|tion** (sklir′ə tə zā′shən), *n.* = sclerosis.

**scle|ro|tize** (sklir′ə tīz), *v.t., v.i.,* **-tized, -tiz|ing.** = sclerose.

**scle|ro|toid** (sklir′ə toid), *adj.* = sclerotioid.

**scle|rot|o|my** (skli rot′ə mē), *n., pl.* **-mies.** a surgical incision into the sclerotic coat of the eyeball, as for the extraction of foreign bodies. [< *sclero-* + Greek *-tomiā* a cutting]

**scle|rous** (sklir′əs), *adj.* hardened; hard; bony. [< *scler-* + *-ous*]

**Sc.M.,** Master of Science (Latin, *Scientiae Magister*).

**sco|bi|form** (skō′bə fôrm), *adj.* having the form of or resembling sawdust: *scobiform seeds.* [< Latin *scobis* (or *scobs*) sawdust, filings + English *-form*]

**sco|del|la** (skō del′ə), *n.* a majolica vessel in the form of a shallow bowl on a footed stem. Also, **scudella.** [< Italian *scodella* < Latin *scutella* platter; see etym. under **scuttle**[1]]

**scoff**[1] (skôf, skof), *v., n.* —*v.i.* to make fun to show one does not believe something; mock: *We scoffed at the idea of drowning in three inches of water. Fools, who came to scoff, remain'd to pray* (Oliver Goldsmith).
—*v.t.* to jeer at; deride: *He ... scoff'd their easy fears* (Robert Southey). [< noun]
—*n.* **1** mocking words or acts: *With scoffs and scorns and contumelious taunts* (Shakespeare). **2** something ridiculed or mocked: *The principles of liberty were the scoff of every grinning courtier* (Macaulay).
[< Scandinavian (compare Danish *skuffe* to deceive, earlier, to mock, ridicule, fool < Middle Low German *schoven* deceive)] —**scoff′er,** *n.* —**scoff′ing|ly,** *adv.*
—*Syn. v.i.* **Scoff, jeer, sneer** mean to show scorn or contempt for someone or something. **Scoff** implies scornful irreverence or cynicism: *He scoffs at religion.* **Jeer** implies mocking laughter: *The mob jeered when the speaker got up to talk.* **Sneer** means to express ill-natured contempt or disparagement by look, tone, or manner of speech: *He sneers at everything sentimental.*

**scoff**[2] (skôf, skof), *n., v. Slang.* —*n.* food; a meal.
—*v.t., v.i.* to eat heavily.
[< Afrikaans *scoff* < Dutch *schoft* a meal]

**scoff|law** (skôf′lô′, skof′-), *n. U.S. Informal.* a person with little regard for the law; person who regularly flouts the law: *One of the twins was named the city's champion scofflaw, with eighty-six traffic and parking violations dating from 1947* (New York Times).

**scoke** (skōk), *n.* = pokeweed.

**scold** (skōld), *v., n.* —*v.t.* to find fault with; blame with angry words: *His brother scolded him for breaking the baseball bat.*
—*v.i.* **1** to find fault; talk angrily: *Don't scold so much.* **2** *Obsolete.* to quarrel noisily; brawl.
[< noun]
—*n.* a person who scolds, especially a noisy, scolding woman: *In older times, scolds were punished by being ducked in ponds.*
[probably < Scandinavian (compare Old Icelandic *skāld* poet, in sense of "lampooner")] —**scold′er,** *n.*
—*Syn. v.t.* **Scold, upbraid, chide** mean to find fault with someone. **Scold** particularly suggests reproval of someone younger or subordinate, often without good reason: *That woman is always scolding the children in our neighborhood.* **Upbraid** suggests sharp and severe censure for a definite fault: *The judge upbraided the argumentative lawyers and threatened to cite them for contempt.* **Chide** means to censure mildly in the hope of improvement: *The foreman chided several of the workers for carelessness and lack of safety on the job.*

**scold|ing** (skōl′ding), *adj., n.* —*adj.* that scolds: *I have seen tempests, when the scolding winds have riv'd the knotty oaks* (Shakespeare).
—*n.* the act of a person who scolds: *Was not mamma often in an ill-humor; and were they not all used to her scoldings?* (Thackeray). —**scold′ing|ly,** *adv.*

**scold's bit** or **bridle,** = branks.

**scol|e|cite** (skol′ə sīt, skō′lə-), *n.* a mineral, a hydrous silicate of calcium and aluminum, found in needle-shaped crystals and fibrous or radiated masses. *Formula:* $CaAl_2Si_3O_{10}\cdot 3H_2O$ [< German *Scolezit* < Greek *skṓlēx, -ēkos* worm + German *-it* -ite[1]]

**sco|lex** (skō′leks), *n., pl.* **sco|le|ces** (skō lē′sēz), **scol|i|ces** (skol′ə sēz, skō′lə-). **1** the larva of a tapeworm or similar parasitic worm. **2** the head of the adult form. [< New Latin *scolex* < Greek *skṓlēx, -ēkos* worm, grub]

**sco|li|id** (skō′lē id), *adj., n.* —*adj.* of or having to do with a family of hairy wasps whose larvae are parasitic on the larvae of certain beetles.
—*n.* a scoliid wasp.
[< New Latin *Scoliidae* the family name]

**sco|line** (skō lēn′), *n.,* or **scoline chloride,** = succinylcholine. [< *s*(uccinyl)*c*(h)*oline*]

**sco|li|on** (skō′lē on), *n., pl.* **-li|a** (-lē ə). a short song sung in turn by the guests at an ancient Greek banquet. [< Greek *skólion* < *skoliós* curved]

**sco|li|o|sis** (skō′lē ō′sis, skol′ē-), *n.* a lateral curvature of the spine. [< New Latin *scoliosis* < Greek *skolíōsis* curvature, crookedness < *skoliós* crooked]

**sco|li|ot|ic** (skō′lē ot′ik, skol′ē-), *adj.* of or having to do with scoliosis.

**scol|lop** (skol′əp), *n., v.t.* = scallop. —**scol′lop|er,** *n.*

**scol|o|pen|drid** (skol′ə pen′drid), *n., adj.* —*n.* any one of a group of chilopods including many large and poisonous centipedes.
—*adj.* of or belonging to this group.
[< New Latin *Scolopendridae* the centipede family < Latin *scolopendra* a kind of multiped < Greek *skolópendra*]

**scol|o|pen|drine** (skol′ə pen′drīn, -drin), *adj.* of or having to do with the scolopendrids.

**sco|lyt|id** (skə lit′id), *n.* any one of a group of

bark beetles, one variety of which carries the fungus of Dutch elm disease. [< New Latin *Scolytidae* the family name < *Scolytus* the typical genus < Greek *skolýptein* to peel, strip]

**scom|bri|form** (skom′brə fôrm), *adj.* = scombroid.

**scom|brin** (skom′brin), *n.* a protamine found in the testicles of the mackerel. [< Greek *skómbros* mackerel]

**scom|broid** (skom′broid), *adj., n.* —*adj.* **1** of or belonging to a group of fishes including the mackerels and tunas. **2** resembling the mackerel.
—*n.* a mackerel or mackerellike fish.
[< New Latin *Scombroidea* the group name < Latin *scomber* mackerel < Greek *skómbros*]

**sconce**[1] (skons), *n.* a bracket projecting from a wall, used to hold a candle or other light, often with a reflector. [perhaps < Old French *esconse* lantern, hiding place < Medieval Latin *sconsa* < Latin *abscondere* to hide < *ab-* away + *condere* place, put]

**sconce**[2] (skons), *n. Informal.* **1** the head, especially, the top of the head: *Peter Stuyvesant dealt him a thwack over the sconce with his wooden leg* (Washington Irving). **SYN**: skull. **2** sense; wit. **SYN**: brains. [perhaps special use of *sconce*[3]]

**sconce**[3] (skons), *n., v.,* **sconced, sconc|ing.** —*n.* **1** a small detached fort or earthwork. **2** a shelter; screen; protection.
—*v.t.* to fortify; shelter; ensconce.
[< Dutch *schans* earthwork; brushwood (used as a protective screen)]

**sconce**[4] (skons), *v.,* **sconced, sconc|ing,** *n.* —*v.t.* to mulct; fine for some breach of conventional usage.
—*n.* the fine imposed.

**scone** (skōn, skon), *n.* **1a** a thick, flat cake cooked on a griddle. **b** a similar cake baked in an oven. Some scones taste much like bread; some are like buns. **2** one of the four pieces into which such a cake is often cut. [originally Scottish, probably < Middle Dutch *schoon(brot)* fine (bread)]

**S. Con. Res.,** Senate concurrent resolution (used with a number).

**scoop** (sküp), *n., v.* —*n.* **1** a tool like a shovel, but having a short handle and a deep hollow part for dipping out or shoveling up and carrying loose materials: **a** a kitchen utensil to take up flour, sugar, and the like. **b** a large ladle. **c** a utensil for dishing out a portion of ice cream, mashed potatoes, or other semisolids. **2** the part of a dredge or power shovel that takes up the coal, sand, or other like things. **3** the act of taking up with, or as if with, a scoop. **4a** the amount taken up at one time by a scoop; scoopful: *She used two scoops of flour and one of sugar.* **b** *Informal.* a big haul, as of money made in speculation. **5** a place scooped or hollowed out; hollow: *The rabbit hid in the scoop it had made in the earth.* **SYN**: cavity. **6** *Informal.* **a** the publishing of a piece of news before a rival newspaper does. **SYN**: beat. **b** the piece of news. **7** a spoon-shaped surgical instrument used to extract matter from cavities.
—*v.t.* **1a** to take up or out with a scoop, or as a scoop does: *Scoop out a quart of grain. The boys scooped up the snow with their hands to make snowballs.* **b** *Informal.* to gather up or in as if with a scoop: *Werner was with us when father scooped us all up and took us to the concert at the Stadium* (Harper's). **2** to hollow out; dig out; make by scooping: *The children scooped holes in the sand.* **SYN**: excavate. **3** to empty with a scoop. **4** *Informal.* to publish a piece of news before (a rival newspaper). **5** *Informal.* to sing (a note or phrase) by sliding to the correct pitch from a note below: *She is given to scooping her notes and is unable to produce convincing chest tones* (New Yorker).
[< Middle Dutch *schœpe* bucket, and *schoppe* shovel] —**scoop′er,** *n.*

**scoop|ful** (sküp′fu̇l), *n., pl.* **-fuls.** enough to fill a scoop.

**scoop neck** or **neckline,** a rounded, fairly low-cut neck, as on a dress or blouse.

**scoop-necked** (sküp′nekt′), *adj.* having a scoop neck.

**scoop net,** a net to scoop something out of the water, as a person in a rescue operation: *The pilot ... was rescued within a few minutes by a scoop net attached to a helicopter* (London Times).

**scoot** (sküt), *v., n., interj. Informal.* —*v.i.* to go quickly; dart: *The cat scooted out the door.*
—*n.* the act of scooting.
—*interj.* be off with you! scat!
[(originally) Scottish, to squirt, gush, eject, perhaps < a Scandinavian word. See related etym. at **shoot.**]

**scoot|er**[1] (skü′tər), *n., v.* —*n.* **1** a child's vehicle consisting of a board for the feet between two wheels, one in front of the other, steered by a handlebar and propelled by pushing against the ground with one foot. **2** a similar vehicle run by a motor; motor scooter. **3** *U.S.* a sailboat with runners, for use on either water or ice.
—*v.i.* to sail or go in or on a scooter.
[< *scoot,* verb]

**scoot|er**[2] (skü′tər), *n.* = scoter.

**scoot|er|ist** (skü′tər ist), *n.* a person who rides a motor scooter.

**scop** (skop, skōp), *n.* an Anglo-Saxon poet or minstrel; bard. [Old English *scop*]

**sco|pal|a|mine** (skō pə lam′ēn, -in), *n.* = scopolamine.

**scope**[1] (skōp), *n.* **1a** the distance the mind can reach; extent of view: *Very hard words are not within the scope of a child's understanding.* **SYN**: compass. See syn. under **range. b** the area over which any activity operates or is effective; range of application: *This subject is not within the scope of our investigation. Beyond the scope of all speculation* (Edmund Burke). **SYN**: compass. See syn. under **range. 2** room to range; space; opportunity: *Football gives scope for courage and quick thinking. I gave full scope to my imagination* (Laurence Sterne). **3** the range or length of flight of an arrow or other missile. **4a** extent; length; sweep: *The yacht's gig was towing easily at the end of a long scope of line* (Joseph Conrad). **b** the length of cable at which a ship rides when at anchor. **5** *Archaic.* an aim; purpose; ultimate object. [< Italian *scopo,* learned borrowing from Late Latin *scopus* < Greek *skopós* aim, object < *skopeîn* behold, consider]

**scope**[2] (skōp), *n. Informal.* **1** an instrument for viewing, such as a microscope, telescope, or radarscope. **2** a telescopic sight for a rifle: *All were equipped with 20-power scopes* (New York Times). [back formation < *telescope, radarscope*]

**-scope,** *combining form.* an instrument for viewing, examining, or observing: *Telescope = an instrument for viewing distant objects. Stethoscope = an instrument for examining the chest.* [< New Latin *-scopium* < Greek *-skopion* < *skopeîn* look at, examine]

**sco|po|la** (skō′pə lə), *n.* the dried rhizome and larger roots of a plant of the nightshade family, used as a source of atropine and scopolamine.

**sco|pol|a|mine** (skō pol′ə mēn, -min; skō′pə lam′ēn, -in), *n.* an alkaloid drug that has a depressant effect on the central nervous system, and is used to dilate the pupils of eyes, to produce a partial stupor known as "twilight sleep," and as a truth serum. *Formula:* $C_{17}H_{21}NO_4$
[< New Latin *Scopola canicola* a plant of the nightshade family that yields this drug (< Giacomo *Scopoli,* 1723-1788, an Italian naturalist) + English *-amine*]

**sco|po|line** (skō′pə lēn, -lin), *n.* a crystalline, narcotic compound obtained from scopolamine by decomposition. *Formula:* $C_8H_{13}NO_2$

**scop|u|la** (skop′yə lə), *n., pl.* **-las** or **-lae** (-lē). a small brushlike pad of stiff hairs on the tarsi of bees and spiders. [< New Latin *scopula* < Latin *scōpula;* see etym. under **scopulate**]

**scop|u|late** (skop′yə lāt, -lit), *adj. Zoology.* shaped like a broom or brush; brushlike. [< New Latin *scopulatus* < Latin *scōpula* broom twig (diminutive) < *scōpa* twig]

**-scopy,** *combining form.* observation; examination: *Cranioscopy = examination of the cranium.* [< Greek *skopiā* watchtower < *skopeîn* look at]

**scor|bu|tic** (skôr byü′tik), *adj.* **1** of, having to do with, or like scurvy. **2** affected with scurvy. [< New Latin *scorbuticus* < *scorbutus* scurvy < French *scorbut* < a Germanic word]

**scor|bu|ti|cal** (skôr byü′tə kəl), *adj.* = scorbutic.

**scor|bu|tus** (skôr byü′təs), *n.* = scurvy. [< New Latin *scorbutus;* origin uncertain]

**scorch**[1] (skôrch), *v., n.* —*v.t.* **1** to burn slightly; burn on the outside: *The cake tastes scorched. I scorched the shirt in ironing it.* **2** to dry up; wither: *The grass is scorched by so much hot sunshine.* **3** *Figurative.* to criticize with burning words. —*v.i.* **1** to be or become scorched. **2** *Informal, Figurative.* to drive or ride very fast.
—*n.* a slight burn.
[origin uncertain]

**scorch**[2] (skôrch), *v.t. Obsolete.* to slash with a knife. [alteration of *score*]

**scorched earth** (skôrcht), destruction by government orders of all things useful to an invading army.

**scorch|er** (skôr′chər), *n.* **1** a person or thing that scorches. **2** *Informal.* a very hot day. **3** *Informal, Figurative.* a person who drives or rides very fast. **4** *Informal, Figurative.* a scathing rebuke; withering criticism.

**scorch|ing** (skôr′ching), *adj.* that scorches; burning; withering. —**scorch′ing|ly,** *adv.*

**scor|da|to** (skôr dä′tō), *adj. Music.* put out of tune; tuned in an unusual manner for the purpose of producing particular effects. [< Italian *scordato,* past participle of *scordare* put out of tune]

**scor|da|tu|ra** (skôr′dä tü′rä), *n., pl.* **-tu|re** (-tü′rā), **-tu|ras.** *Music.* an intentional deviation from the usual tuning of a stringed instrument for some particular effect. [< Italian *scordatura*]

**score** (skôr, skōr), *n., v.,* **scored, scor|ing.** —*n.* **1** the record of points made in a game, contest, or test: *to keep score. The score was 9 to 2 in favor of our school. He had nearly a perfect score on the history exam.* **2a** an amount owed; debt; account: *He paid his score at the inn.* **b** *Archaic.* a record of this kept by notches or marks. **c** *Archaic.* a notch, cut, or mark made in keeping an account or a record. **3** a group or set of twenty; twenty: *A score or more were present at the party.* **4** a written or printed piece of music arranged for different instruments or voices: *the score of an opera. She was studying the score of the piece she was learning to play.* **5** a cut; scratch; stroke; mark; line: *scores made on a tree for its sap. The carpenter used a nail to make a score on the board.* **6** *Sports.* a line to show the beginning or end as of a course or range, such as the line at which a marksman stands to shoot. **7** *Figurative.* the act of making or winning a point; successful stroke, rejoinder, or the like. **8** *Figurative.* an account; reason; ground: *Don't worry on that score. She was excused on the score of illness. The chemical industry is not alone in entertaining doubts on that score* (London Times).
—*v.t.* **1a** to make as points in a game, contest, or test: *to score two runs in the second inning. He scored 85 per cent on the final exam.* **b** to keep a record of (the number of points made in a game, contest, or test). **c** to be counted as in the score: *In American football, a touchdown scores six points.* **d** to make as an addition to the score: *He scored 35 points in the last basketball game.* **e** *Baseball.* to cause (a base runner) to score: *Maury Wills singled off Pete Richert to score McCarver with the winning run* (Les Woodcock). **2** *Figurative.* to gain; win; achieve: *The new play scored a great success with the critics.* **3** to record; set down; mark: *The innkeeper scored on a slate the number of meals each person had.* **4a** to arrange (a piece of music) for different instruments or voices: *to score a sonata for piano and strings.* **b** to write out (music) in score. **5a** to cut; scratch; stroke; mark; line: *He scored the board with a pencil and ruler before sawing it. Mistakes are scored in red ink. Moving the furniture across the floor scores the polish. Passages had been scored in his favourite books* (Thackeray). **b** to make long cuts in the surface of, before cooking: *to score a ham before baking.* **6** *Figurative.* to blame or scold severely; berate: *The President scored the newspapers for their warmongering reporting.* **7** *Slang.* to obtain (narcotic drugs) illegally: *He had a runner who plied back and forth ... scoring dope for him* (Atlantic).
—*v.i.* **1a** to make points in a game, contest, or on a test: *to be in a position to score. In baseball, only the side at bat can score.* **b** to keep a record of the number of points in a game, contest, or test: *The teacher will appoint some pupil to score for both sides.* **2** *Figurative.* to achieve an advantage or success; succeed: *to score with a new idea. The pressures to "score" with girls ...* (New York Times). **3** to make notches, cuts, or lines: *Scoring first makes it easy to cut glass.* **4** *Slang.* to obtain narcotic drugs illegally: *Once he walked from Mill Hill to Earls Court with cramps, trying to score for opium* (Sunday Times). *"She told me she'd just 'scored' and asked if I wanted some kicks"* (Maclean's). **5** *Obsolete.* to run up a score (debt).

**pay off** (or **settle**) **a score,** to get even for an injury or wrong: *Paying for damages did not really settle the score for the slander inflicted upon the merchant's good name.*

**scores,** a large number; great numbers: *Scores died in the epidemic.*

**the score,** *Informal.* the truth about anything or things in general; the facts: *The new man doesn't know the score yet. Time and again [he] demonstrated that he knew the score, but either he did not act at all upon it or he acted ineffectually* (New Yorker).
[Old English *scoru* < Scandinavian (compare Old Icelandic *skor* notch, tally stick; score)]

**score|board** (skôr′bôrd′, skōr′bōrd′), *n.* **1** a board on which the scores of a sporting event are posted. **2** a record, as of any contest, situation, or business undertaking: (*Figurative.*) *The*

---

**Pronunciation Key:** hat, āge, cãre, fär; let, ēqual, tėrm; it, īce; hot, ōpen, ôrder; oil, out; cup, pu̇t, rüle; child; long; thin; ᴛʜen; zh, measure; ə represents **a** in about, **e** in taken, **i** in pencil, **o** in lemon, **u** in circus.

*earnings scoreboard for the first ... quarter is not yet complete* (Newsweek).

**score|book** (skôr′bu̇k′, skōr′-), *n.* a book for recording the scores of games and, sometimes, the performance of the players.

**score|card** (skôr′kärd′, skōr′-), *n.*, or **score card**, a card on which to keep the score of a game, especially while it is being played: *He strolled through the final 36 holes with a steady 141; came home with an overall scorecard that showed 283 strokes* (Time).

**score|keep|er** (skôr′kē′pər, skōr′-), *n.* a person who keeps score: *In a baseball game, the umpire is the official scorekeeper.* (*Figurative.*) *Dun and Bradstreet, the master scorekeeper of business failures, has found that more than nine out of ten business failures were caused by lack of experience or incompetence* (Harper's).

**score|keep|ing** (skôr′kē′ping, skōr′-), *n.* the act or process of keeping score; scoring.

**score|less** (skôr′lis, skōr′-), *adj.* **1** having no score: *The game ended in a scoreless tie.* **2** making no score or mark.

**scor|er** (skôr′ər, skōr′-), *n.* **1** = scorekeeper. **2** a person who makes a score in a game, contest, or test. **3** a person or thing that scores or notches.

**scores** (skôrz, skōrz), *n.pl.* See under **score**.

**score|sheet** (skôr′shēt, skōr′-), *n.* a sheet of paper upon which a record, as of the tallies or runs in baseball or cricket, may be written.

**sco|ri|a** (skôr′ē ə, skōr′-), *n., pl.* **sco|ri|ae** (skôr′ē ē, skōr′-). **1** the slag or refuse left from ore after the metal has been melted out; dross. **2** porous, cinderlike fragments of lava; slag. [< Latin *scōria* < Greek *skōriā* < *skôr, skatós* dung]

**sco|ri|ac** (skôr′ē ak, skōr′-), *adj.* = scoriaceous.

**sco|ri|a|ceous** (skôr′ē ā′shəs, skōr′-), *adj.* **1** like slag or clinkers. **2** consisting of slag, clinkers, or the like. [< Greek *skōriā* dross (see etym. under **scoria**) + English *-aceous*]

**sco|ri|fi|ca|tion** (skôr′ə fə kā′shən, skōr′-), *n.* **1** the act of scorifying. **2** (in assaying) a process by which gold or silver is separated from its ore by heating with lead, the impurities being removed as a slag.

**sco|ri|fi|er** (skôr′ə fī′ər, skōr′-), *n.* a thing that scorifies.

**sco|ri|form** (skôr′ə fôrm, skōr′-), *adj.* in the form of scoria; like scoria.

**sco|ri|fy** (skô′rə fī, skō′-), *v.t.*, **-fied, -fy|ing.** to reduce to scoria. [< *scori*(a) + *-fy*]

**scor|ing** (skôr′ing, skōr′-), *n., adj.* —*n.* **1** the act of making a score. **2** a score made. **3a** the act or process of arranging a piece of music for different instruments, or voices. **b** the result of this: *... little song-like snatches that rise to the surface of his complex and highly original scoring* (New Yorker).
—*adj.* resulting in a score: *Leggett threw a 21-yard scoring pass* (New York Times).

**scorn** (skôrn), *v., n.* —*v.t.* **1** to look down upon; think of as mean or low; despise: *Honest boys scorn sneaks and liars. Death had he seen ... knew all his shapes, and scorn'd them all* (Scott). **SYN:** disdain, spurn. **2** to reject or refuse as low or wrong: *The judge scorned to take a bribe. I scorn the counterfeit sentiment you offer* (Charlotte Brontë). **3** *Obsolete.* to mock; deride.
—*v.i. Obsolete.* to mock; scoff.
—*n.* **1** a feeling that a person, animal, or act is mean or low; contempt: *Most pupils feel scorn for those who cheat. The red glow of scorn and proud disdain* (Shakespeare). **2** a person, animal, or thing that is scorned or despised: *That bully is the scorn of the school. Oh! aren't you the scorn of women?* (J. M. Synge). **3** mockery; derision. **4** *Archaic.* an expression of contempt; taunt; insult.
[Middle English *schornen* < Old French *escarnir* < Germanic (compare Old High German *skernôn*)] —**scorn′er**, *n.*
—*Syn.* *n.* **1 Scorn, contempt, disdain** mean a strong feeling that a person or thing is unworthy of respect. **Scorn** implies angry dislike or disapproval of what is considered worthless or evil: *He attacked their proposals in words of bitter scorn.* **Contempt** implies disgust combined with strong disapproval: *We feel contempt for a coward.* **Disdain** implies feeling oneself above a person or thing considered mean or low: *We feel disdain for a person who cheats.*

**scorn|ful** (skôrn′fəl), *adj.* showing contempt; mocking; full of scorn: *He spoke of our old car in a scornful voice.* **SYN:** disdainful, derisive, contemptuous. —**scorn′ful|ly**, *adv.* —**scorn′ful-ness**, *n.*

**scor|o|dite** (skôr′ə dīt, skor′-), *n.* a mineral, a hydrous ferric arsenate, occurring in orthorhombic crystals and in earthy form, and usually of a greenish or brown color. *Formula:* $FeAsO_4 \cdot 2H_2O$ [< German *Skorodit* < Greek *skórodon* garlic (because of its smell when heated) + German *-it* -ite[1]]

**scor|pae|nid** (skôr pē′nid), *n.* = scorpaenoid.

**scor|pae|noid** (skôr pē′noid), *adj., n.* —*adj.* of or belonging to a family of marine fishes that have spiny fins, including the scorpionfishes.
—*n.* a scorpaenoid fish.
[< Latin *scorpaena* a kind of fish (< Greek *skórpaina*) + English *-oid*]

**Scor|pi|i** (skôr′pē ī), *n.* genitive of **Scorpius**.

**Scor|pi|o** (skôr′pē ō), *n., genitive* (def. 1) **Scor|pi-o|nis.** **1** a southern constellation between Libra and Sagittarius, seen by ancient astronomers as having the rough outline of a scorpion; Scorpius. **2** the eighth sign of the zodiac; Scorpion. The sun enters Scorpio about October 24. **3** a person born under this sign. [< Latin *Scorpiō, -ōnis* (literally) scorpion < Greek *skorpíōn, -ōnos* Scorpio; scorpion]

**scor|pi|oid** (skôr′pē oid), *adj.* **1a** of or belonging to a group of animals including the scorpions. **b** like a scorpion. **2** *Botany.* curved at the end like the tail of a scorpion. [< Greek *skorpioeidês* < *skórpios* scorpion + *eîdos* form]

*__scor|pi|on__ (skôr′pē ən), *n.* **1** a small animal belonging to the same group as the spider and having a poisonous sting at the end of its tail. Scorpions make up an order of arachnids. **2** a kind of whip made of knotted cords or with lead or steel spikes (in the Bible, I Kings 12:11). [< Old French *scorpion*, learned borrowing from Latin *scorpiō, -ōnis* < Greek *skorpíōn, -ōnos*] —**scor′pi|on|like′**, *adj.*

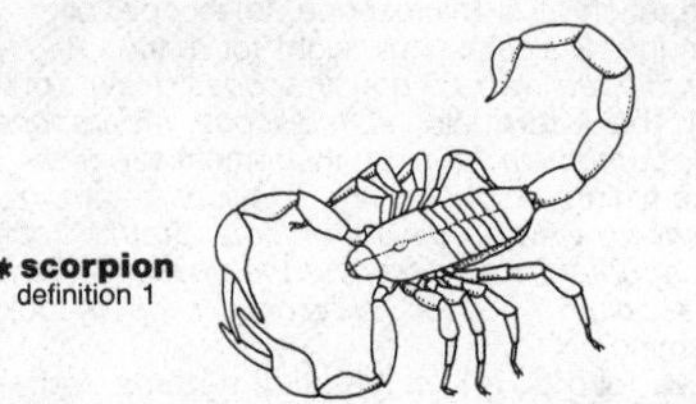

***scorpion**
definition 1

**Scor|pi|on** (skôr′pē ən), *n.* = Scorpio (def. 2).

**scor|pi|on|fish** (skôr′pē ən fish′), *n., pl.* **-fish|es** or (*collectively*) **-fish.** any marine fish of a group having spines on the head and fins.

**scorpion fly**, any insect of a group, the male of which has an extension of the abdomen resembling the stinger of a scorpion.

**scor|pi|on|ic** (skôr′pē on′ik), *adj.* of or having to do with the scorpion.

**Scor|pi|o|nis** (skôr pē ō′nis), *n.* genitive of **Scorpio.**

**Scor|pi|us** (skôr′pē əs), *n., genitive* **Scor|pi|i.** = Scorpio (def. 1).

**scor|za|lite** (skôr′zə līt), *n.* a blue mineral, a phosphate of iron and aluminum, occurring in crystalline or massive form.

**scot** (skot), *n.* one's share of a payment; payment; tax. **SYN:** assessment. [probably fusion of Old English *gescot* with Scandinavian (compare Old Icelandic *skot*). See related etym. at **shot.**]

**Scot** (skot), *n.* **1** a person born or living in Scotland; Scotchman. **2** one of an ancient Gaelic-speaking people living especially in Ireland and Scotland. Scotland is named after them. [Old English *Scottas* the Irish, the Scotch < Late Latin *Scottus*]
► See **Scotchman** for a usage note.

**Scot.**, **1** Scotch. **2** Scotland. **3** Scottish.

**scot and lot**, a municipal tax formerly assessed proportionately upon members of a community.
**pay off scot and lot**, to pay off completely; settle with: *I'll pay you off scot and lot by and by* (Dickens).

**scotch** (skoch), *v., n.* —*v.t.* **1a** to make (something thought of as dangerous) harmless for a time: *We have scotched the snake, not killed it* (Shakespeare). **SYN:** disable, cripple. **b** to stamp on or stamp out (something dangerous); crush: *to scotch a rumor.* **2** to cut or gash; score. **3** to block or wedge (a wheel, log, or other round object) so as to prevent moving or slipping.
—*n.* **1** a cut; score; gash. **2** a line drawn on the ground, as in hopscotch. **3** a block placed under a wheel, log, or other round object, to prevent moving or slipping.
[origin uncertain; perhaps < Anglo-French *escoche*, Old French *coche* notch, nick, ultimately < Latin *coccum* berry of scarlet oak (notchlike in appearance)]

**Scotch** (skoch), *adj., n.* —*adj.* **1** of or having to do with Scotland, its people, or their language; Scottish. **2** *Informal.* stingy; mean; parsimonious.
—*n.* **1** the people of Scotland as a group. **2** English as it is spoken by the people of Scotland; Scottish. **3** = Scotch whisky. **4** a dry snuff. **5** a style of modern printing type developed by Scottish type founders in the 1700's.
► **Scotch, Scots, Scottish** have the same literal meaning but are only in part interchangeable. *Scotch* is a familiar form before certain nouns (*Scotch whisky, Scotch broth*); in Scotland itself, this form does not have wide usage. *Scots* is used outside of Scotland in a few collocations (*Middle Scots, Scots law, Scots Guards*). *Scottish* is used widely in Scotland, and is elsewhere rapidly gaining in currency (*Scottish history, the Scottish character*).

**Scotch blessing**, *Informal.* a stern rebuke.

**Scotch broom**, a hardy European broom with bright yellow flowers that has become common in the United States, growing wild in Virginia and California.

**Scotch broth**, a soup containing pearl barley, meat, and small pieces of vegetables.

**Scotch cap**, any one of various brimless caps worn in Scotland, as the glengarry or the Balmoral.

**Scotch elm**, = wych-elm.

**Scotch foursome**, a game of golf in which two players play against two others, with each side playing alternate strokes on one ball.

**Scotch-Gael|ic** (skoch′gā′lik), *n.* = Scottish Gaelic.

**Scotch|gard** (skoch′gärd′), *n. Trademark.* a fluorochemical substance used for making textiles resistant to water, oils, and other staining elements.

**Scotch heath**, = twisted heath.

**Scotch heather**, the heather commonly found on moors in Scotland and England.

**Scotch-I|rish** (skoch′ī′rish), *adj., n.* —*adj.* **1** of or having to do with a part of the population of Northern Ireland descended from Scottish settlers. **2** of both Scottish and Irish descent.
—*n.* a person of both Scottish and Irish descent.

**Scotch laburnum**, a hardy variety of laburnum with long flower clusters, native to southern Europe.

**Scotch|man** (skoch′mən), *n., pl.* **-men.** a person born or living in Scotland; Scotsman.
► **Scotchman, Scotsman, Scot.** In Scotland, *Scotsman* is the preferred and current form; *Scot* is an occasional, somewhat literary, and inoffensive variant, especially in the plural: *Scots! wha hae wi' Wallace bled ...* (Robert Burns). *Scotchman,* probably still the common term in most other parts of the English-speaking world, is virtually never used by natives of the country.

**Scotch mist**, **1** a very dense, wet, penetrating mist like that common in the Highlands of Scotland. **2** a steady, soaking rain.

**Scotch pine**, a European and Asian pine with reddish-tinged wood, used for lumber, as a source of tar, and as a Christmas tree. It has become naturalized in areas of eastern North America.

**Scotch tape**, **1** a very thin, transparent or opaque adhesive tape for mending, patching, and sealing. **2** *Trademark.* any one of several kinds of transparent or opaque adhesive tapes.

**scotch-tape** (skoch′tāp′), *v.t.*, **-taped, -tap|ing.** to mend, patch, or seal with Scotch tape: *Scotch-taping the family's finger painting on the kitchen walls ...* (New York Times).

**Scotch terrier**, = Scottish terrier.

**Scotch verdict**, an inconclusive verdict.

**Scotch whisky**, a whiskey distilled in Scotland from barley malt, having a slightly smoky flavor.
► See **whiskey** for usage note.

**Scotch|wom|an** (skoch′wu̇m′ən), *n., pl.* **-wom-en.** = Scotswoman.
► See **Scotchman** for a usage note.

**Scotch woodcock**, cooked eggs served on toast with anchovy paste.

**Scotch|y** (skoch′ē), *adj.*, **Scotch|i|er, Scotch|i-est.** having the characteristics of what is Scotch; suggesting Scotch people or ways.

**sco|ter** (skō′tər), *n.* any one of several large, black sea ducks, native to arctic regions and common in northern seas, usually called coot in the United States; surf duck. Also, **scooter.** [origin uncertain]

**scot-free** (skot′frē′), *adj.* **1** free from punishment, loss, or injury; unharmed: *The driver was fined for speeding, but his passengers got off scot-free.* **2** *Obsolete.* free from payment of scot (tax), tavern score, fine, or the like.

**sco|tia** (skō′shə), *n.* a concave molding, as at the base of a column. [< Latin *scotia* < Greek *skotiā* a shadowed (because sunken or hollowed) molding at the base of a pillar; (originally) darkness < *skótos* the dark]

**Sco|tia** (skō′shə), *n.* the Latin name of Scotland. [< Medieval Latin *Scotia* < Late Latin *Scōtus*, variant of *Scottus* a Scot]

**Scot|ic** (skot′ik), *adj.* of or relating to the Scots.

**Sco|tism** (skō′tiz əm), *n.* the doctrines of the scholastic theologian John Duns Scotus (about 1265 to about 1308) or his followers. Its fundamental doctrine is that distinctions of the mind are real, although they exist only in their relation to mind.

**Sco|tist** (skō′tist), *n.* a follower of John Duns Scotus or of Scotism.

**Scot|land Yard** (skot′lənd), **1** the headquarters of the London police. **2** the London police, especially the department that does detective work. [< the name of the building in London where it was located]

**scot|o|din|i|a** (skot′ə din′ē ə), *n.* a dizziness combined with dimness of vision. [< New Latin *scotodinia* < Greek *skótos* darkness + *dī́nos* a whirling]

**sco|to|ma** (skə tō′mə), *n., pl.* **-ma|ta** (-mə tə). a loss of vision in a part of the visual field. [< Late Latin *scotōma* dimness of vision < Greek *skótōma, -atos* dizziness, vertigo < *skótos* darkness]

**sco|tom|a|tous** (skə tom′ə təs), *adj.* having to do with or affected with a scotoma.

**sco|to|pho|bi|a** (skō′tə fō′bē ə, skot′ə-), *n.* an abnormal fear of the dark; nyctophobia. [< Greek *skótos* darkness + English *-phobia*]

**sco|to|pho|bic** (skō′tə fō′bik, skot′ə-), *adj.* **1** of or having to do with scotophobin: *The scotophobic effect seems to be very specific for this structure ... Very probably some rigorous stereospecificity is involved in the scotophobic mechanism* (New Scientist and Science Journal). **2** of or having scotophobia.

**sco|to|pho|bin** (skō′tə fō′bən, skot′ə-), *n.* a chemical compound that is believed to be the basis of a specific conditioned response, fear of the dark, isolated from the brain tissue of rodents conditioned to fear darkness. [< Greek *skótos* darkness + *phóbos* fear + English *-in*]

**sco|to|pi|a** (skō tō′pē ə), *n.* **1** adaptation to darkness. **2** the ability to see in darkness. [< New Latin *scotopia* < Greek *skótos* darkness + *ōps, ōpós* eye]

**sco|top|ic** (skō top′ik, -tō′pik), *adj.* **1** that can adapt to darkness. **2** that can see in darkness.

**Scots** (skots), *adj., n.* **—*adj.*** **1** of Scotland; Scottish. **2a** in the older Scottish currency: *two pounds Scots.* **b** in the older Scottish weights and measures: *one Scots pint.*
**—*n.*** **1** (*pl.*) the people of Scotland. **2** (*sing.*) the dialect of English spoken by the people of Scotland.
[Scottish short form of earlier *Scottis* < Late Latin *Scottus* a Scot]
▶ See **Scotch** for a usage note.

**Scots|man** (skots′mən), *n., pl.* **-men.** a person born or living in Scotland; Scot.
▶ See **Scotchman** for a usage note.

**Scots pine,** = Scotch pine.

**Scots|wom|an** (skots′wu̇m′ən), *n., pl.* **-wom|en.** a woman who is a native or inhabitant of Scotland. Also, **Scotchwoman.**

**Scot|ti|cism** (skot′ə siz əm), *n.* a word, phrase, or meaning used in Scotland, but not in widespread use in other English-speaking countries.

**Scot|tie** or **scot|tie** (skot′ē), *n. Informal.* **1** a Scottish terrier. **2** a nickname for a Scotsman. Also, **Scotty.**

**Scot|tish** (skot′ish), *adj., n.* **—*adj.*** of or having to do with Scotland, its people, or their language: *Scottish lakes. "Laird" is a Scottish word.*
**—*n.*** **1** *pl. in use.* the people of Scotland. **2** English as it is spoken by the people of Scotland.
*Abbr:* Sc. **—Scot′tish|ness,** *n.*
▶ See **Scotch** for a usage note.

**Scottish Blackface,** any one of a breed of blackfaced sheep of Scotland whose coarse wool is valuable for tweeds, carpets, and mattresses. In the United States it is called *Blackface Highland.*

**Scottish deerhound,** = deerhound.

**Scottish Gaelic,** the Celtic language of the Scottish Highlanders; Erse.

**Scottish Rite,** one of the two advanced branches of membership in the Freemasons (the other being the York Rite).

**Scottish terrier,** one of a breed of short-legged terriers with rough, wiry hair and pointed, standing ears; Scotch terrier. Its short coat can range from black or gray to a sandy color.

**Scott's oriole,** an oriole of Mexico and the southwestern United States, the male of which is light yellow with black head, throat, back, wings, and tail. [< General Winfield *Scott,* 1786-1866, an American army officer and hero of the Mexican War]

**Scot|ty** or **scot|ty** (skot′ē), *n., pl.* **-ties.** = Scottie.

**scoun|drel** (skoun′drəl), *n., adj.* **—*n.*** a very bad person without honor or good principles; villain; rascal: *The scoundrels who set fire to the barn have been caught.* **SYN:** blackguard, scamp.
**—*adj.*** scoundrelly; villainous; unprincipled; base: *these scoundrel Doones* (Richard D. Blackmore).

**scoun|drel|dom** (skoun′drəl dəm), *n.* scoundrels, or their ways or habits.

**scoun|drel|ism** (skoun′drə liz əm), *n.* **1** the character or conduct of a scoundrel. **2** a scoundrelly action.

**scoun|drel|ly** (skoun′drə lē), *adj.* **1** having the character of a scoundrel. **2** having to do with or characteristic of a scoundrel.

**scour**[1] (skour), *v., n.* **—*v.t.*** **1** to clean or polish by hard rubbing: *to scour the floor with a brush and soapsuds. Mother scours the frying pan with cleanser.* **2** to remove dirt or grease from (anything) by rubbing: *to scour soiled clothing, scour woolens.* **3** to make clear by flowing through or over: *The stream had scoured a channel.* **4** to clean; cleanse; purge, as an animal. **5** *Figurative.* to rid or clear of what is undesirable: *to scour the sea of the pirates* (Sir Philip Sidney). **6** *Figurative.* to beat; scourge; punish: *But I will pay the dog, I will scour him* (Henry Fielding).
**—*v.i.*** **1** to rub something vigorously to clean or polish it. **2** to remove dirt or grease, as from clothing.
**—*n.*** **1** the act of scouring. **2** the cleansing substance used in scouring woolens and the like. **3** a place in a river where the bottom is scoured by the stream.
**scours,** *U.S.* diarrhea in cattle, horses, and other animals, especially newborn ones: *His calves will very likely take the "scours"* (D. G. Mitchell).
[probably < Middle Dutch *schuren,* perhaps ultimately < Latin *ex-* completely + *cūra* care]

**scour**[2] (skour), *v.t.* **1** to move quickly over: *Men scoured the country round about looking for the lost child.* **2** to look into every part of; search: (*Figurative.*) *to scour one's memory for a forgotten date. He cannibalized damaged machinery to get spare parts to get other machines running, repaired buildings, put into production lines, scoured Germany for raw materials* (Wall Street Journal). **SYN:** comb. **—*v.i.*** to go swiftly in search or pursuit: *The horsemen ... gave reins to their steeds and scoured for the frontier* (Washington Irving).
[perhaps < Scandinavian (compare Old Icelandic *skura* rush violently), or perhaps < Old French *escourre* run forth < Latin *excurrere.* Compare etym. under **excursion.**]

**scour|er** (skour′ər), *n.* **1** a person who scours. **2** a thing for scouring or scrubbing: *Brushes and sponges are household scourers.* **3** a purgative agent; cathartic. [< *scour*[1] + *-er*[1]]

**scour|fish** (skour′fish′), *n., pl.* **-fish|es** or (*collectively*) **-fish.** = escolar. [because of its rough skin]

**scourge** (skėrj), *n., v.,* **scourged, scourg|ing.**
**—*n.*** **1** a whip; lash. **2** any means of punishment. **3** *Figurative.* some thing or person that causes great trouble or misfortune, such as an outbreak of disease or a war: *Malaria, an old scourge, is now confined to the far jungles* (Time).
**—*v.t.*** **1** to punish severely; whip; flog; chastise: *the waves ... scourged with the wind's invisible tyranny* (Shelley). **2** *Figurative.* to trouble very much; afflict; torment.
[< Anglo-French *escorge,* and *escurge,* Old French *escorgiee,* ultimately < Latin *ex-* + *corrigia* strap, latchet < *corium* a hide]

**scourg|er** (skėr′jər), *n.* a person who scourges or punishes; flagellant.

**scour|ing cinder** (skour′ing), a slag low in silica which wears out the lining of a furnace.

**scouring pad,** a soft mass of steel wool or plastic mesh used for cleansing and polishing.

**scouring rush,** any one of various horsetail plants formerly used to scour and polish.

**scour|ings** (skour′ingz), *n.pl.* **1** dirt, refuse, or other material, removed by scouring; dregs: (*Figurative.*) *a gang built up from the scourings of the slums.* **2** refuse removed from grain before milling.

**scours** (skourz), *n.pl.* See under **scour**[1].

**scour|way** (skour′wā′), *n.* a channel eroded by a stream, especially by a former glacial stream.

**scour|wort** (skour′wėrt′), *n.* = soapwort.

**scouse**[1] (skous), *n.* = lobscouse. [short for *lobscouse*]

**Scouse** or **scouse**[2] (skous), *n., adj. British Slang.* **—*n.*** **1** the dialect of Liverpool, England: *substituting scouse for Etonian slang* (Punch). **2** a native of Liverpool, England; Scouser.
**—*adj.*** of Liverpool: *a Scouse accent.*
[< earlier *Scouseland,* slang name for Liverpool, because of the popularity of *lobscouse* or *scouse* in Liverpool]

**scouse kettle,** *Nautical.* an iron kettle for cooking.

**Scous|er** or **scous|er** (skou′sər), *n. British Slang.* a native of Liverpool, England.

**Scous|i|an** (skou′sē ən), *adj. British Slang.* Scouse.

**scout**[1] (skout), *n., v.* **—*n.*** **1a** a person sent to find out what the enemy is doing. A scout wears a uniform; a spy does not. **b** a warship, airplane, or other thing used to find out what the enemy is doing. **2** a person who is sent out to get information. **3** a person sent out to get information about athletes or athletic teams. **4** the act of scouting: *on scout, to the scout.* **5** a person belonging to the Boy Scouts or Girl Scouts. **6** *Informal.* a fellow; person: *He's a good scout. George, old scout, you were sore-headed about something* (Sinclair Lewis). **7** *British.* a college servant at Oxford University.
**—*v.i.*** to act as a scout; hunt around to find something: *Go and scout for firewood for the picnic.*
**—*v.t.*** to observe or examine to get information; reconnoiter.
[< Old French *escoute* act of listening, listener < *escouter* listen, ultimately < Latin *auscultāre*]
**—scout′er,** *n.* **—scout′ing|ly,** *adv.*

**scout**[2] (skout), *v.t.* to refuse to believe in; reject with scorn: *He scouted the idea of a dog with two tails. A large, looming man, Wenning is alleged to have been a significant athlete at college ... although he scouts the idea* (Newsweek).
**—*v.i.*** = scoff.
[< Scandinavian (compare Old Icelandic *skūta* to taunt)]

**scout car,** any one of various fast, open-top vehicles designed for military reconnaissance.

**scout|craft** (skout′kraft′, -kräft′), *n.* knowledge and skill in activities required to be a good boy or girl scout.

**scouth** (sküth), *n. Scottish.* **1** opportunity; scope. **2** abundance; plenty.

**scout|ing** (skou′ting), *n.* the activities of scouts.

**scout|mas|ter** (skout′mas′tər, -mäs′-), *n.* **1** the man in charge of a troop of boy scouts. **2** the leader of a band of scouts.

***scow** (skou), *n.* a large, rectangular boat with a flat bottom, used to carry freight, coal, sand, or other like things. [American English < Dutch *schouw*]

***scow**

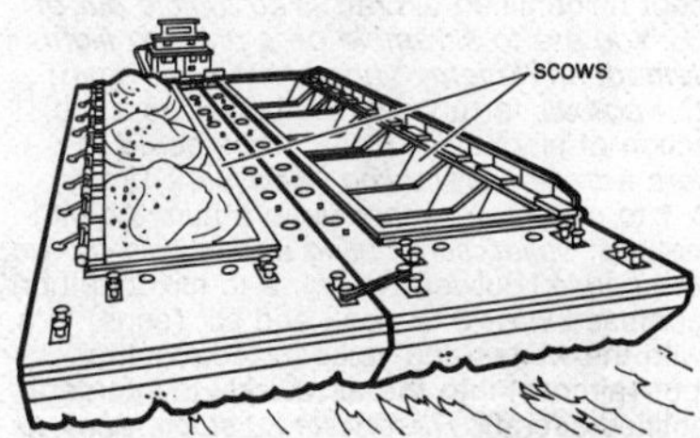


**scowl** (skoul), *v., n.* **—*v.i.*** **1** to look angry or sullen by lowering the eyebrows; frown: *The angry man scowled at his son. She scowls dreadfully ... out of pure ugliness of temper* (Hawthorne). **SYN:** See syn. under **frown.** **2** *Figurative.* to have a gloomy or threatening aspect. **SYN:** See syn. under **frown.**
**—*v.t.*** **1** to affect by scowling. **2** to express with a scowl: *to scowl one's disapproval.*
**—*n.*** **1** an angry, sullen look; frown. **2** *Figurative.* a gloomy or threatening aspect.
[Middle English *scoulen.* Compare Danish *skule* cast down the eyes.] **—scowl′er,** *n.* **—scowl′ing|ly,** *adv.*

**SCP** (no periods), single-cell protein.

**scr.,** scruple or scruples.

**scrab|ble** (skrab′əl), *v.,* **-bled, -bling,** *n.* **—*v.i.*** **1** to scratch or scrape about, as with hands or claws; scramble: *to scrabble up a sandbank. She scrabbled among the papers* (H. G. Wells). **2** to struggle or scramble feverishly or desperately: *to scrabble for scraps of food,* (*Figurative.*) *to scrabble for a living.* (*Figurative.*) *Similar cars driven by other men scream and scrabble for a footing on the roadway* (Atlantic). **3** to scrawl; scribble.
**—*v.t.*** **1** to scratch; scrape: *But Tubal got him a pointed rod, and scrabbled the earth for corn* (Rudyard Kipling). **2** to scratch or rake hurriedly; obtain by scratching or raking about. **3** to scrawl (something) or upon (something).
**—*n.*** **1** a scrabbling; scraping; scramble. **2** a scrawling character, writing, etc.
[< Dutch *schrabbelen* (frequentative) < *schrabben* to scratch]

**Scrab|ble** (skrab′əl), *n. Trademark.* a game played on a board with small tiles having printed letters which the players try to fit together to spell words.

**scrab|bly** (skrab′lē), *adj.* minor; unimportant: *They are writing about ... scrabbly little social problems* (Harper's).

**scrag**[1] (skrag), *n., v.,* **scragged, scrag|ging.** **—*n.*** **1** a lean, skinny person or animal. An old bony

---

**Pronunciation Key:** hat, āge, cãre, fär; let, ēqual, tėrm; it, īce; hot, ōpen, ôrder; **oi**l, **ou**t; cup, pu̇t, rüle; **ch**ild; lo**ng**; **th**in; **ᴛʜ**en; **zh,** measure; **ə** represents **a** in about, **e** in taken, **i** in pencil, **o** in lemon, **u** in circus.

horse is a scrag. **2** the lean, bony end of a neck of veal or mutton. **3** *Slang.* the neck.
—***v.t.*** *Slang.* **1a** to wring the neck of. **b** to strangle. **2** to hang on the gallows.
[< Scandinavian (compare Swedish dialectal *skragge* old and torn thing)]

**scrag$^2$** (skrag), *n. British Dialect.* **1** a stump of a tree. **2** a rough projection on a pole, trunk, tree, rock, or the like. **3** rough, rocky, or barren ground. [compare Scottish *scrog* stunted bush; origin uncertain]

**scrag|gi|ness** (skrag′ē nis), *n.* scraggy quality or condition.

**scrag|gling** (skrag′ling), *adj.* irregular in outline or distribution; straggling.

**scrag|gly** (skrag′lē), *adj.*, **-gli|er, -gli|est.** rough or irregular; ragged: *a scraggly growth of trees or hair.*

**scrag|gy$^1$** (skrag′ē), *adj.*, **-gi|er, -gi|est. 1** having little flesh; lean; thin; bony: *... his sinewy, scraggy neck* (Scott). **SYN:** scrawny. **2** *Figurative.* meager; scanty. [< *scrag$^1$* + *-y$^1$*]

**scrag|gy$^2$** (skrag′ē), *adj.*, **-gi|er, -gi|est.** rough in surface; broken in line; jagged; irregular; scraggly: *old scraggy bushes, scraggy and irregular handwriting.* [< *scrag$^2$* + *-y$^1$*]

**scram** (skram), *v.*, **scrammed, scram|ming,** *interj. Slang.* —***v.i.*** to go at once; leave immediately.
—***interj.*** begone! scat!
[American English; perhaps short for *scramble*]

**scram|ble** (skram′bəl), *v.*, **-bled, -bling,** *n.* —***v.i.*** **1** to make one's way by climbing, crawling, or jumping: *We scrambled up the steep, rocky hill.* **2** to struggle with others for something: *The boys scrambled to get the football.* (*Figurative.*) *All those commuters rush to town to scramble for a living.* **3** to get an aircraft into the air quickly to intercept unidentified aircraft: *You tumble out of bed ... You are to scramble on a practice flight to intercept an "enemy" bomber* (H. L. Hogan). **4** *U.S. Football.* to run with the ball without the protection of blockers: [*He*] *... bewildered the Packers with his scrambling* (New York Times).
—***v.t.*** **1** to collect or gather up in a hurry or without method: *Juliet, scrambling up her hair, darted into the house* (Bulwer-Lytton). **2** to mix together in a confused way. **3** to cook and stir (eggs) in a pan with the whites and yolks mixed together. **4** to put (aircraft) into the air quickly to intercept unidentified aircraft: *Reservists ... stood ready to scramble fighters aloft to intercept any unidentified planes* (Time). **5** to break up or mix (a message, radio or television signal, or telephone message) so that it cannot be received and understood without special equipment: *The broadcasting is done by coding or scrambling the pictures so that the general public can't receive them unless they pay for a special device to unscramble the broadcast on their sets* (Wall Street Journal).
—***n.*** **1** a climb or walk over rough ground: *It was a long scramble through bushes and over rocks to the top of the hill.* **2** a struggle to possess: (*Figurative.*) *the scramble for wealth and power.* (*Figurative.*) *Politics is sometimes nothing but a scramble for office.* **3** any disorderly struggle or activity; scrambling: *The pile of boys on the football seemed a wild scramble of arms and legs.* **4** (in the Air Force) the act or process of scrambling: *If there's a scramble, you fly, regardless of weather* (New Yorker).
[perhaps variant of *scrabble*]

**scram|bler** (skram′blər), *n.* **1** a person who scrambles **2** a device for breaking up a telephone, radio, or television signal. **3** *U.S. Football.* a quarterback who scrambles: [*He*] *is known in the trade as a "scrambler," who would just as soon run as throw, who can turn a potential 10-yd. loss into a 50-yd. gain* (Time).

**scram|bling|ly** (skram′bling lē), *adv.* in a scrambling or haphazard manner.

**scram|bly** (skram′blē), *adj.*, **-bli|er, -bli|est.** scrambled; disorganized: *I find the lovers' climatic quarrel in Act II a scratchy, scrambly business* (Punch).

**scram|jet** (skram′jet′), *n.* **1** a ramjet which produces thrust by burning fuel in an airstream moving at supersonic speeds: *Scramjets theoretically could extend flight speeds to at least Mach 14* (New Scientist). **2** an aircraft powered by a scramjet. [< *s*(upersonic) *c*(ombustion) *ramjet*]

**scran** (skran), *n.* **1** *Dialect.* scraps of food; provision; fare. **2** *Irish Slang.* luck: *bad scran.* [origin uncertain]

**scran|nel** (skran′əl), *adj. Archaic.* **1** thin; slight. **2** squeaky and harsh. [< Scandinavian (compare Norwegian dialectal *skran* lean, shriveled)]

**scrap$^1$** (skrap), *n.*, *v.*, **scrapped, scrap|ping,** *adj.* —***n.*** **1** a small piece; little bit; small part left over: *I gave some scraps of meat to the dog. Put the scraps of paper in the wastebasket.* (*Figurative.*) *The girls haven't a scrap of imagination* (John Galsworthy). **SYN:** remnant. **2** a bit of something written or printed; short extract: *She read aloud scraps from the letter.* **3** old or discarded metal fit only to be melted and used again: *About half of all our new steel is old steel, otherwise known as scrap* (New Yorker).
—***v.t.*** **1** to make into scraps; break up. **2** to throw aside as useless or worn out; discard: *Existing plans could be scrapped and fresh ones made* (London Times).
—***adj.*** **1** in the form of scraps: *scrap metal.* **2** made of scraps or fragments; useful only as scrap.
**scraps,** the remains of animal fat after the oil has been tried out: *We had codfish and pork scraps for dinner.*
[< Scandinavian (compare Old Icelandic *skrap* scraps, trifles)]

**scrap$^2$** (skrap), *n.*, *v.i.*, **scrapped, scrap|ping.** *Slang.* fight, quarrel, or struggle: *Let's not have a scrap about it. Those two dogs are always scrapping.* [probably variant of *scrape*, noun, def. 4]

**scrap|book** (skrap′bu̇k′), *n.* a book in which pictures or clippings are mounted and kept.

**scrape** (skrāp), *v.*, **scraped, scrap|ing,** *n.* —***v.t.*** **1** to rub with something sharp or rough; make smooth or clean by doing this: *Scrape your muddy shoes with this knife.* **2a** to remove by rubbing with something sharp or rough: *to scrape mud off shoes. The man scraped some paint off the table when he pushed it through the doorway.* **b** to scratch or graze by rubbing against something rough: *She fell and scraped her knee on the sidewalk.* **3** to rub with a harsh sound: *to scrape the floor with one's chair. Don't scrape your feet on the floor.* **4** to dig: *The child scraped a hole in the sand.* **5** to collect by scraping or with difficulty: *The hungry boy scraped up the last crumbs from his plate.* (*Figurative.*) *He has scraped together enough money to buy a bicycle.* **6** to smooth the surface of (an unpaved road), as with a bulldozer.
—***v.i.*** **1** to rub harshly: *The branch of the tree scraped against a window.* **2** to give a harsh sound; grate. **3** to gather with labor and difficulty; hoard up: (*Figurative.*) *He scraped long and hard to earn a living for his family.* **4** *Figurative.* to manage with difficulty: *That family can just scrape along but never asks for charity.* **5** *Figurative.* to bow with a drawing back of the foot: *Bowing and scraping and rubbing his hands together* (Anthony Trollope).
—***n.*** **1** the act of scraping. **2** a scraped place. **3** a harsh, grating sound: *the scrape of the bow of a violin.* **4** *Figurative.* a position hard to get out of; difficulty; predicament: *Boys often get into scrapes.* **5** *Figurative.* a bow with a drawing back of the foot.
**scrape through,** to get through with difficulty: *to scrape through a narrow opening. He barely scraped through the examination.*
[perhaps alteration of Old English *scrapian*, influenced by Scandinavian (compare Old Icelandic *skrapa*)]

**scrap|er** (skrā′pər), *n.* **1** an instrument or tool for scraping: *We removed the loose paint with a scraper.* **2** a person who scrapes: **a** *Figurative.* a person who scrapes together money meanly; miser. **b** a fiddler, as a person who scrapes the strings (used in an unfriendly way). **c** a barber, as a person who scrapes the skin in shaving. **3** a two-wheeled, tractor-drawn machine for excavation and hauling, used especially on fairly dry ground and in wide areas that are not too hilly.

**scrap|heap** (skrap′hēp′), *n.*, *v.* —***n.*** **1** a pile of scraps. **2** a place for useless or worn-out things.
—***v.t.*** **1** to consign to a scrapheap. **2** *Figurative.* to discard as useless or worthless.

**scrap|ie** (skrā′pē), *n.* a virus disease of sheep which attacks the nervous system, usually causing death: *Scrapie is ... so named because bleating victims rub themselves against posts or wire to relieve the itching* (Time).

**scrap|ing** (skrā′ping), *n.* **1** the act of a person or thing that scrapes. **2** the sound produced by this.
**scrapings,** that which is scraped off, up, or together: *An apprentice ... thinking of ... the miseries of the milk and water, and thick bread and scrapings* (Dickens).

**scrap iron,** broken or waste pieces of old iron to be melted and used again.

**scrap|man** (skrap′man′), *n.*, *pl.* **-men.** a junkman who deals in old or discarded metal: *The affluent society only wants new cars and the scrapman has lost interest in old ones* (New Scientist).

**scrap|page** (skrap′ij), *n.* **1** the act of scrapping, especially old cars. **2** what is scrapped; amount scrapped.

**scrap|per** (skrap′ər), *n. Slang.* **1** a person who scraps or fights; boxer: *a good lightweight scrapper.* **2** *Figurative.* a person given to fighting: *He's a real scrapper for a little boy.*

**scrap|ple** (skrap′əl), *n.* scraps of pork or other meat boiled with corn meal or flour, made into cakes, sliced, and fried. [American English; diminutive of *scrap$^1$*]

**scrap|py$^1$** (skrap′ē), *adj.*, **-pi|er, -pi|est. 1** made up of odds and ends: *a scrappy meal of leftovers.* **2** fragmentary; disconnected; disjointed: *a scrappy conversation.* [< *scrap$^1$* + *-y$^1$*] —**scrap′pi|ly,** *adv.* —**scrap′pi|ness,** *n.*

**scrap|py$^2$** (skrap′ē), *adj.*, **-pi|er, -pi|est.** *Slang.* fond of fighting; pugnacious. **SYN:** quarrelsome. [< *scrap$^2$* + *-y$^1$*]

**scraps** (skraps), *n.pl.* See under **scrap$^1$**.

**scrap|yard** (skrap′yärd′), *n.* the place where a scrapman stores his items and carries on his business: *Most cars will reach the scrapyard by their tenth birthday* (London Times).

**scratch** (skrach), *v.*, *n.*, *adj.* —***v.t.*** **1** to break, mark, or cut slightly with something sharp or rough: *Your shoes have scratched the chair.* **2** to tear or dig with the claws or nails: *The cat scratched me.* **3** to rub or scrape to relieve itching, to give pleasure, or from force of habit: *Don't scratch your mosquito bites. He scratched his head.* **4** to rub with a harsh noise; rub: *He scratched a match on the wall.* **5** to write or draw in a hurry or carelessly; scribble: *I also scratched down another ballad* (Scott). **6** to scrape out; strike out; draw a line through: *I have often scratched out passages from papers and pamphlets* (Jonathan Swift). **7** to withdraw (as a horse or candidate) from a race or contest: *High Gun, a good horse in America who has been difficult to train this season, was officially scratched yesterday* (London Times). **8** *Figurative.* to gather by effort; scrape: *The oil wealth has yet to trickle down to many thousands of half-nomadic rural Venezuelans, who scratch subsistence diets out of jungle clearings* (Time). **9** *U.S.* **a** to split (one's ballot) but still support most of the members of one's party. **b** to fail to support part of (a party ticket). **c** to erase the name of (a candidate) on a party ticket.
—***v.i.*** **1** to use the claws, nails, or the like, as for tearing a surface or digging. **2** to rub some part of one's body to relieve itching, to give pleasure, or from force of habit. **3** to rub with a slight grating noise: *This pen scratches.* **4** *Figurative.* to get along with difficulty. **5** to withdraw from a race or contest. **6** to make a miss or fluke in billiards or pool.
—***n.*** **1** a mark made by scratching: *There are deep scratches on this desk.* **2** a very slight cut: *He escaped with only a scratch on his face.* **3** a rough mark made as by a pencil or pen; hasty scrawl; scribble. **4** the sound of scratching: *the scratch of a pen, the scratch of a match.* **5** any act of scratching. **6a** the line marking the starting place of a race or contest. **b** the starting place, time, or status of a competitor who has neither allowance nor penalty. **c** such a competitor. **7** (formerly) a line at which boxers met and began to fight. **8** in billiards or pool: **a** a miss. **b** a fluke. **9** = scratch wig.
—***adj.*** **1** for quick notes, a first draft, or the like: *scratch paper.* **2** collected or prepared by chance or hastily and often of poor quality: *a scratch football team, a scratch crew, a scratch meal.* **3** done by chance; dependent on chance: *a scratch shot.* **4** without a handicap in a race.
**from scratch,** with no advantage; from the beginning: *He had to borrow money and start his business from scratch. Its rulers are virtually starting from scratch, not only in industrialization but in administration* (Manchester Guardian Weekly).
**up to scratch,** up to standard; in good condition: *"The Lost Princess" is ... a shepherd's daughter, who has also been taken in hand by the wise woman but who fails to come up to scratch* (New Yorker).
[perhaps alteration of earlier *scrat* scratch; influenced by obsolete *cratch* scratch; origin uncertain] —**scratch′er,** *n.*

**Scratch** (skrach), *n.* the Devil.

**scratch|board** (skrach′bôrd′, -bōrd′), *n.* a kind of cardboard covered with chalk, used for drawings, as in pen and ink or crayon. Its prepared surface can also be scratched out with a cutting tool to achieve certain effects of lighting.

**scratch gage** or **gauge,** a tool for marking on metal, having a hard steel point.

**scratch hit,** a weakly hit ground ball to the infield in baseball, that enables a fast base runner to reach first base before the throw.

**scratch line, 1** a line which marks the start of a race. **2** a line which may not be crossed in performing the broad jump, javelin throw, or other field event.

**scratch pad,** a pad of paper for hurried notes or first-draft writing.

**scratch sheet,** *U.S. Slang.* a publication that lists the horses scratched from a race and other racing information; form sheet.

**scratch test,** a test for allergy to a particular

substance, made by scratching the skin with a dose of the substance.

**scratch wig**, a wig covering only part of the head.

**scratch|y** (skrach′ē), *adj.*, **scratch|i|er, scratch|i|est. 1** that scratches, scrapes, or grates: *a scratchy pen.* **2** consisting of mere scratches: *scratchy writing. A child's first drawings are scratchy.* **3** scanty; straggling: *scratchy hair.* —**scratch′i|ly**, *adv.* —**scratch′i|ness**, *n.*

**scrawl** (skrôl), *v., n.* —*v.t., v.i.* to write or draw poorly or carelessly.
—*n.* **1** poor, careless handwriting. **2** something scrawled, such as a hastily or badly written letter or note.
[perhaps < obsolete *scrawl* spread out the limbs, sprawl; gesticulate; perhaps alteration of *crawl*, influenced by *sprawl*] —**scrawl′er**, *n.*

**scrawl|y** (skrô′lē), *adj.*, **scrawl|i|er, scrawl|i|est.** awkwardly written or drawn.

**scraw|ni|ness** (skrô′nē nis), *n.* scrawny quality or appearance.

**scraw|ny** (skrô′nē), *adj.*, **-ni|er, -ni|est.** *Informal.* lean; thin; skinny: *Turkeys have scrawny necks.* [American English, perhaps variant of dialectal *scranny.* Compare etym. under **scrannel**.]

**screak** (skrēk), *v., n.* —*v.i.* **1** to screech; scream. **2** = creak.
—*n.* a shrill cry; screech.
[apparently < Scandinavian (compare Swedish *skrika*)]

**scream** (skrēm), *v., n.* —*v.i.* **1** to make a loud, sharp, piercing cry. People scream in fright, in anger, or in sudden pain. *She screamed when she saw the child fall.* **2** to give forth a characteristic shrill cry, as certain birds and animals do or a whistle does: *I heard the owl scream and the crickets cry* (Shakespeare). **3** *Figurative.* to laugh loudly. **4a** to speak loudly: *Stop screaming! we can hear you.* **b** to write excitedly. **5** *Figurative.* to produce a vivid impression or startling effect: *The colors of her pink sweater and orange blouse screamed at each other.*
—*v.t.* **1** to utter loudly: *It was so noisy in the room that I had to scream my name.* **2** to bring about by screaming: *Bugles ... to scream us out of bed* (Scott).
—*n.* **1** a loud, sharp, piercing cry, as of fright, anger, or sudden pain: (*Figurative.*) *loud screams of laughter* (W. H. Hudson). **2** a shrill sound like a scream: *The screams of the engines announced that the day was done* (Leonard Merrick). **3** something extremely funny: *Ted observed that her friends were "a scream of a bunch"* (Sinclair Lewis).
[perhaps unrecorded Old English *scrǣman*]
—*Syn. v.i.* **1 Scream, shriek** mean to make a loud, sharp, piercing sound. **Scream** suggests a loud, high-pitched, piercing cry expressing fear, pain, or almost hysterical anger or joy: *She screamed when the bees attacked her. The little girl screamed with rage in a temper tantrum.* **Shriek** suggests a more high-pitched, wild, hair-raising and back-tingling cry, expressing extreme terror, horror, agony, or uncontrolled rage or laughter: *The prisoner shrieked when he was tortured.*

**scream|er** (skrē′mər), *n.* **1** a person or thing that screams. **2** any one of a group of aquatic South American birds that are about the size of a swan and have a loud cry. Screamers have long unwebbed toes, sharp spurs on the wings, and a layer of air-filled cells under the skin. **3a** a headline in very large type across the page. **b** an exclamation point. **4** *Slang.* **a** an exceptional person, animal, or thing: *[Her] whirlwind tour of the dress racks was punctuated by such remarks as "That's a screamer" ... while she discarded the dresses of overbold and too-subtle patterns* (New York Times). **b** a very thrilling or funny story. **5** *Slang.* **a** a very long shot in golf. **b** a hard-hit ball in baseball: *to hit a screamer deep to the outfield.*

**scream|ing** (skrē′ming), *adj.* **1** that screams; sounding shrilly: *High the screaming fife replies* (A. E. Housman). **2** *Figurative.* calling forth screams of laughter: *a screaming farce, a screaming joke.* **3** *Figurative.* startling: *screaming headlines, screaming colors.* —**scream′ing|ly**, *adv.*

**screaming mee|mies** (mē′mēz), *U.S. Slang.* extreme nervousness or hysteria; jitters. [*meemies*, probably reduplication and alteration of *screaming*]

**scream|y** (skrē′mē), *adj.*, **scream|i|er, scream|i|est.** *Informal.* **1** inclined to scream: *The crew ... will have been selected with meticulous care to exclude screamy or jittery types* (Time). **2** screaming: (*Figurative.*) *screamy songs,* (*Figurative.*) *screamy coloring.*

**scree** (skrē), *n.* a steep mass of loose rocky fragments lying at the base of a cliff or on the side of a mountain; talus. [< *screes*, plural, probably spelling for earlier *screthes* < Scandinavian (compare Old Icelandic *skrithna* landslide, related to *skrītha* to slide)]

**screech** (skrēch), *v., n.* —*v.i., v.t.* to cry out sharply in a high voice; scream; shriek: *"Help! help!" she screeched.*
—*n.* a shrill, harsh scream: *The woman's screeches brought the police.*
[apparently alteration of Middle English *scritchen*; perhaps imitative] —**screech′er**, *n.* —**screech′ing|ly**, *adv.*

**screech owl**, **1** a small, usually gray or reddish-brown owl with hornlike tufts of feathers and a long, wavering cry rather than a hoot. Screech owls occur in several color phases and varieties. **2** any owl that screeches, as distinguished from one that hoots. **3** *British.* the barn owl. It has a very shrill, explosive cry.

**screech|y** (skrē′chē), *adj.*, **screech|i|er, screech|i|est. 1** screeching: ... *a shrill, screechy voice* (W. H. Hudson). **2** given to screeching: *a screechy woman.*

**screed** (skrēd), *n., v.* —*n.* **1a** a long speech or writing; harangue; tirade. **b** a long roll or list. **2** a strip of plaster (or wood) of the proper thickness, applied to a wall as a guide in plastering. **3** *Dialect.* **a** a fragment; shred. **b** a torn piece of some cloth. **c** a bordering strip; edging. **4** *Scottish.* **a** a sound as of the tearing of cloth. **b** a rent; tear. **5** *Obsolete.* a drinking bout.
—*v.t., v.i. Dialect.* to shred; tear; rip.
[< variant of Old English *scrēade* shred; influenced by Scandinavian words beginning with *sk-*]

**screen** (skrēn), *n., v.* —*n.* **1a** a covered frame that hides, protects, or separates: *a fire screen, a folding screen, to hide a trunk behind a screen.* **SYN:** shield, protection, fender. **b** wires woven together with small openings in between, used as a protection: *We have screens on our windows to keep out the flies.* **c** an ornamental partition. **2** *Figurative: A screen of trees hides our house from the road. An impenetrable screen of secrecy ...* (William De Morgan). **3** a surface on which motion pictures, television or radar images, or slides appear or are shown. **4** motion-picture films; motion-picture industry; films. **5** a sieve for sifting sand, gravel, coal, seed, or other like things. **6** a body of soldiers detached toward the enemy to protect an army. **7** an escort of destroyers, or other attack ships, to protect battleships, aircraft carriers, or merchant convoys, as against submarine attack. **8** *Physics.* a barrier against some special form of energy. **9** a transparent plate with fine lines that cross at right angles, used in photoengraving to produce the minute dots in half-tones.
—*v.t.* **1a** to shelter, protect, or hide with or as if a screen: *We have screened our porch to keep out flies. She screened her face from the fire with a fan.* **b** *Figurative.* to save from danger, punishment, or exposure; shield: *The mother tried to screen her guilty son. Great exertions were made to screen him from justice, but in vain* (Washington Irving). **2a** to show (a motion picture) on a screen: *See the film of this adventurous journey, now being screened at main cinemas throughout South Africa* (Cape Times). **b** to adapt (a story, play, or other literary work) for reproduction as a motion picture. **c** to photograph with a motion-picture camera. **3a** to sift with a screen: *to screen sand.* **b** *Figurative: Many government agencies screen their employees for loyalty. He said that the Government should have screened vaccine batches more carefully* (New York Times). **4** to print with a screen or in the silk-screen process: *[It] is perhaps the handsomest paper of the lot, and certainly the most meticulously screened* (New Yorker).
—*v.i.* to be suitable for reproducing on a motion-picture screen.
[< Old French *escren*; origin uncertain]
—**screen′er**, *n.* —**screen′like′**, *adj.*

**screen|a|ble** (skrē′nə bəl), *adj.* that can be screened.

**screen grid**, an electrode placed between the control grid and the plate of certain vacuum tubes to reduce capacitance between the electrodes.

**screen|ing** (skrē′ning), *n.* a fine wire mesh for making screens, filters, or other devices.
**screenings**, a matter separated out by sifting through a sieve or screen. **b** the finely broken pieces of rice used in flour mixes and in distilling and brewing.

**screen|land** (skrēn′land′), *n.* = filmland.

**screen memory**, *Psychoanalysis.* a minor or trivial memory of childhood which conceals and helps to keep repressed a more important and disturbing recollection.

**screen|o** (skrē′nō), *n.* a form of bingo originally played in movie houses.

**screen pass**, *Football.* a forward pass in which the offensive linemen form a protective screen in front of the receiver.

**screen|play** (skrēn′plā′), *n.* a motion-picture story in manuscript form, including the dialogue, descriptions of scenes, action, and camera directions; scenario with dialogue.

**screen-print** (skrēn′print′), *v.t.* to print with a screen or in the silk-screen process: *These designs ... can also be screen-printed on ... any of several fabrics* (New Yorker).

**screen test**, a filmed scene to test how an actor performs or looks in a motion picture.

**screen-test** (skrēn′test′), *v.t.* to put (an actor) to a screen test: *The producer screen-tested her and gave her a small romantic role* (Newsweek).

**screen|wash** (skrēn′wosh′, -wôsh′), *n. British.* the washing done by a screenwasher.

**screen|wash|er** (skrēn′wosh′ər, -wôsh′-), *n. British.* an automatic windshield washer.

**screen|wip|er** (skrēn′wī′pər), *n. British.* windshield wiper.

**screen|writ|er** (skrēn′rī′tər), *n.* a person who writes screenplays.

**machine screws:**

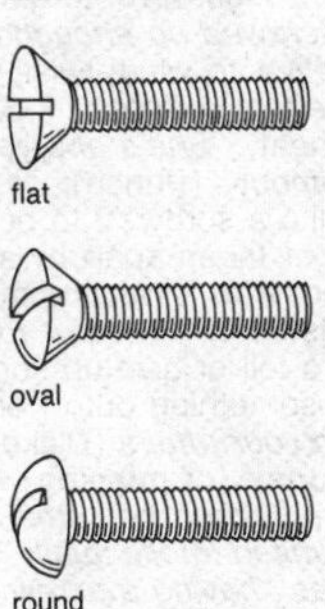

flat

oval

round

***screw** definition 1

**setscrews:**

headless slotted

square

**wood screws:**

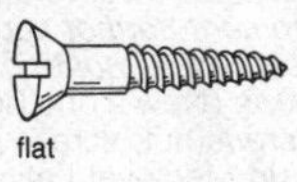

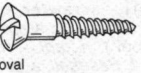

flat

oval

round

**thumbscrew**

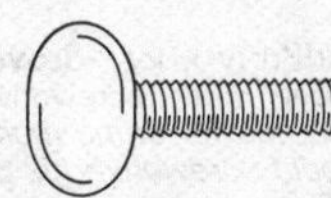

***screw** (skrü), *n., v.* —*n.* **1** a kind of nail, with a ridge twisted evenly around its length and usually a groove across the head: *Turn the screw to the right to tighten it.* **2a** a cylinder with a ridge winding around it; external screw. It is a simple machine. Screws are used in jacks to lift heavy loads. **b** the part, a threaded cylindrical hole, into which this cylinder fits and advances; internal screw. **3** anything that turns like a screw or looks like one, such as a corkscrew or the boring part of a gimlet. **4a** a turn of a screw; screwing motion. **b** a twist or turn such as that applied to a screw: (*Figurative.*) *Strained to the last screw he can bear ...* (William Cowper). **5** *Figurative.* a contortion, as of the body or face: *The Englishman ... listened to them all with a certain screw*

**Pronunciation Key:** hat, āge, cãre, fär; let, ēqual, tėrm; it, īce; hot, ōpen, ôrder; oil, out; cup, pu̇t, rüle; child; long; thin; ᴛʜen; zh, measure; ə represents a in about, e in taken, i in pencil, o in lemon, u in circus.

*of the mouth, expressive of incredulity* (Washington Irving). **6** a propeller that moves a boat or ship; screw propeller. **7** *Figurative.* **a** a very stingy person; miser. **b** a person who drives a sharp bargain: *He's a terrible screw at a bargain* (Harriet Beecher Stowe). **8** *Slang.* an odd or crazy person. **9** *Especially British.* a small amount, as of tobacco, snuff, or salt, wrapped up in a twist of paper. **10** a former instrument of torture for compressing the thumbs; thumbscrew. **11** a broken-down horse. **12** *Especially British Slang.* salary; wages: *I shall have something left out of this week's screw* (Leonard Merrick). **13** *Slang.* a guard in a prison.

*–**v.t.*** **1** to turn as one turns a screw; twist: *Screw the lid on the jar.* **2a** to fasten or tighten with a screw or screws: *The carpenter screwed the hinges to the door.* **b** to work (a screw) by turning. **3** to force, press, or stretch tight by using screws, pegs, or the like: *to screw the strings of a guitar.* **4** *Figurative.* **a** to force to do something. **b** to force (prices) down. **c** to force (a seller) to lower his price. **d** to force someone to tell or give up (something): *to screw information or money out of a person.* **5** *Figurative.* to gather for an effort: *He finally screwed up enough courage to try to dive.* **6** *Figurative.* to wind; twist; contort: *His face was screwed up with fear.* **7** *Slang.* to take advantage of; cheat: *"She's always ... trying to screw me on alimony"* (Punch).

*–**v.i.*** **1** to turn like a screw. **2** to be fitted for being put together or taken apart by a screw or screws. **3a** to turn with a twisting motion; wind. **b** to become twisted or turned. **4** *Figurative.* to force a person to tell or give up something.

**a screw loose**, something out of order: *There's a screw loose in your affairs* (Dickens).

**have a screw loose** (or **missing**), *Slang.* to be crazy or eccentric: *When he came across a person who was "limited intellectually" he normally referred to him as "having a screw loose"* (London Times). *The musicians had a theory that a man had to have a few screws missing to take up the bass fiddle in the first place* (John O'Hara).

**put the screws on**, to use pressure or force to get something: *Love strains the heartstrings of the human race, and not unfrequently puts the screws on so hard as to snap them asunder* (E. G. Paige).

**screw up**, *Slang.* to make a mess of; do or get all wrong; foul up: *The film, like the play, is a heavyweight contest with a couple of bantamweights thrown into the ring to screw things up* (Manchester Guardian Weekly).

**tighten** (or **turn**) **the screws**, to apply increased pressure: *A government cannot suppress freedom in a foreign country without tightening the screws on its citizens* (New York Times).

[< Old French *escroue* nut, screw, perhaps < Latin *scrōfa* sow[2] (in Medieval Latin, engine for undermining walls)] –**screw′er**, *n.*

**screw auger**, an auger with a spiral shank.

**screw|ball** (skrü′bôl′), *n., adj.* *–**n.*** **1** *Slang.* an eccentric person. **2** *Baseball.* a pitch thrown with a break or spin opposite to that of a curve.

*–**adj.*** *Slang.* eccentric; erratic: *screwball arguments that don't make sense.*

**screw bean**, **1** a tree of the pea family, growing in the southwestern United States and in Mexico, and having twisted pods that are used as fodder; tornillo. **2** the pod.

**screw cap**, a threaded cap or cover, as for a jar or pipe.

**screw|drive** (skrü′drīv′), *v.t.*, **-drove, -driv|en, -driv|ing.** to drive in with a screwdriver: (*Figurative.*) *He stared at me for some moments fixedly as though he would screwdrive his gaze through my brain* (Clark Russell).

**screw|driv|en** (skrü′driv′ən), *adj.* driven by a screw propeller: *The "Great Britain" ... was then the largest ship afloat, the first iron-built screw-driven ship to cross the Atlantic* (London Times).

**screw-drive nail** (skrü′drīv′), a nail with a body like a screw.

**screw|driv|er** (skrü′drī′vər), *n.* **1** a tool for putting in or taking out screws by turning them. **2** a drink made of vodka and orange juice.

**screwed** (skrüd), *adj.* **1** fastened or furnished with screws. **2** having threads, like those of a screw. **3a** Also, **screwed-up.** twisted round; contorted: *screwed-up features.* **b screwed up.** *Slang.* messed up; fouled up: *He lost his money and his wife left him and now he's all screwed up.* **4** *Especially British Slang.* drunk; intoxicated.

**screw eye**, a screw with a head shaped like a loop.

**screw|head** (skrü′hed′), *n.* the upper end of a screw, into which the screwdriver is fitted for turning.

**screw hook**, a screw with a head shaped like a hook.

**screw|i|ness** (skrü′ē nis), *n. Slang.* screwy quality; oddness; craziness.

**screw jack**, = jackscrew.

**screw|loose** (skrü′lüs′), *adj., n.* *–**adj.*** very eccentric.

*–**n.*** a screwloose person.

**screw|man** (skrü′man′), *n., pl.* **-men.** *U.S.* a stevedore who stows compressed cotton bales in the hold of a vessel.

**screw pine**, any one of a genus of tropical plants found chiefly in the Malay Archipelago and Pacific islands, having a palmlike or branched stem, tufts or crowns of long, tough, prickly leaves, strong aerial roots, and a roundish, edible fruit; pandanus.

**screw propeller**, a revolving hub with radiating blades for propelling a ship or aircraft: *Screw propellers ... were first used on ocean-going ships in 1839* (Beauchamp, Mayfield, and West). See picture under **propeller**.

**screw thread**, **1** the spiral ridge of a screw. **2** one complete turn of the thread of a screw as a unit of length of a screw's axis.

**screw|up** (skrü′up′), *n. U.S. Slang.* something botched up; foul-up.

**screw|worm** (skrü′wėrm′), *n.* the larva of the screwworm fly.

**screwworm fly**, a blowfly that deposits its eggs in the sores of animals, the eggs developing into tiny larvae which eat into the wound. The screwworm fly injures and kills cattle and other livestock in southern and southwestern United States.

**screw|y** (skrü′ē), *adj.*, **screw|i|er, screw|i|est.** *Slang.* **1** very odd or peculiar: *a screwy person, screwy weather.* **2** crazy; mad: *He's screwy enough to jump into the pool with all his clothes on.*

**scrib|al** (skrī′bəl), *adj.* **1** of or having to do with a scribe. **2** made by a scribe or copyist: *a scribal error.*

**scrib|ble[1]** (skrib′əl), *v.*, **-bled, -bling,** *n.* *–**v.t.*** **1** to write or draw carelessly or hastily: *to scribble verses.* **2** to write in an untidy or illegible hand: *to scribble a note.* **3** to cover or fill with meaningless scrawls, sloppy writing, worthless matter, or the like: *walls scribbled over with names.*

*–**v.i.*** **1** to write or draw carelessly or hastily: *some poor devil in Grub Street scribbling for his dinner* (Robert Louis Stevenson). *Another damned thick square book! Always scribble, scribble, scribble! Eh, Mr. Gibbon?* (William Henry, Duke of Gloucester). **2** to make marks that do not mean anything.

*–**n.*** **1** something scribbled. **2** hurried or irregular marks: *Did you ever behold such a vile scribble as I write?* (Hawthorne).

[< Medieval Latin *scribillare,* ultimately < Latin *scrībere* to write]

**scrib|ble[2]** (skrib′əl), *v.t.*, **-bled, -bling.** to comb or tease coarsely, as wool. [probably < Low German (compare German *schrubbeln*)]

**scrib|bler** (skrib′lər), *n.* **1** a person who scribbles. **2** *Figurative.* an author who has little or no importance.

**scrib|bling** (skrib′ling), *n.* **1** the act of a person who scribbles. **2** a scribble; scrawl.

**scribe** (skrīb), *n., v.*, **scribed, scrib|ing.** *–**n.*** **1** a person whose occupation is writing, especially copying manuscripts. Before printing was invented, there were many scribes. In many parts of the world people who do not know how to read or write use scribes to write letters or documents for them. **2** (in ancient times) a teacher of the Jewish law: *Ezra was a scribe.* **3** a writer; author (often used humorously). **4** any one of various officials of ancient or former times who performed clerical or secretarial duties. **5** a marking tool; scriber. **6** *Archaic.* a person skilled in penmanship.

*–**v.t.*** **1** to mark or cut with something sharp. **2** *Archaic.* to write down; inscribe.

*–**v.i.*** **1** to use a scriber to mark lines. **2** to write.

[< Latin *scrība* < *scrībere* to write]

**scrib|er** (skrī′bər), *n.* **1** a pointed tool for marking or cutting lines, as on wood, stone, or metal. **2** a person who scribes.

**scrieve** (skrēv), *v.i.*, **scrieved, scriev|ing.** *Scottish.* to move or glide along swiftly. [apparently < Scandinavian (compare Old Icelandic *skrefa* to stride)]

**scrim** (skrim), *n.* **1** a thin, loosely woven cotton or linen material, much used for curtains. **2** a curtain made of this or a similar material, used in a theater for special effects. A scrim looks transparent when lighted from behind. [origin unknown]

**scrim|mage** (skrim′ij), *n., v.* **-maged, -mag|ing.** *–**n.*** **1** a rough fight or struggle: *... one of those chums that stand up for a fellow in a scrimmage and look after him should he be hurt* (Joseph Conrad). **2a** the play in football that takes place when the two teams are lined up and the ball is snapped back. **b** football playing for practice: *an hour of scrimmage between the first and second teams.*

*–**v.i.*** **1** to take part in a rough fight or struggle. **2** to take part in a scrimmage in football. **3** to bustle about, especially in search of something.

*–**v.t.*** to oppose in football practice: *to scrimmage the second team.* Also, *especially British,* **scrummage.**

[variant of *skirmish*] –**scrim′mag|er**, *n.*

**scrimmage line**, *Football.* an imaginary line through the forward end of the football and running across the field; line of scrimmage. A player cannot cross the line of scrimmage before a play starts.

**scrimp** (skrimp), *v., adj., n.* *–**v.t.*** **1** to be sparing of; use too little of. **2** to treat stingily or very economically. *–**v.i.*** to be very economical; stint; skimp: *Many parents have to scrimp to keep their children in college.*

*–**adj.*** scanty; meager; deficient.

*–**n.*** *Informal.* a miser.

[origin uncertain]

**scrimp|y** (skrim′pē), *adj.*, **scrimp|i|er, scrimp|i|est.** too small; too little; scanty; meager. –**scrimp′i|ly**, *adv.* –**scrimp′i|ness**, *n.*

**scrim|shank** (skrim′shangk′), *v.i. British Military Slang.* to shirk duty. [origin unknown] –**scrim′shank′er**, *n.*

***scrim|shaw** (skrim′shô′), *n., v.* *–**n.*** **1** the art or craft of carving fanciful designs on shells, whales' teeth, walrus tusks, and the like, practiced by sailors during long whaling or other voyages: *In an art form known as scrimshaw, a nineteenth century whaler has carved his memories on a horn cup* (Maclean's). **2** a shell, piece of ivory, or the like, so carved or engraved. **3** such articles or products collectively.

*–**v.t.*** to decorate or produce as scrimshaw.

*–**v.i.*** to do scrimshaw work.

[American English; origin unknown]

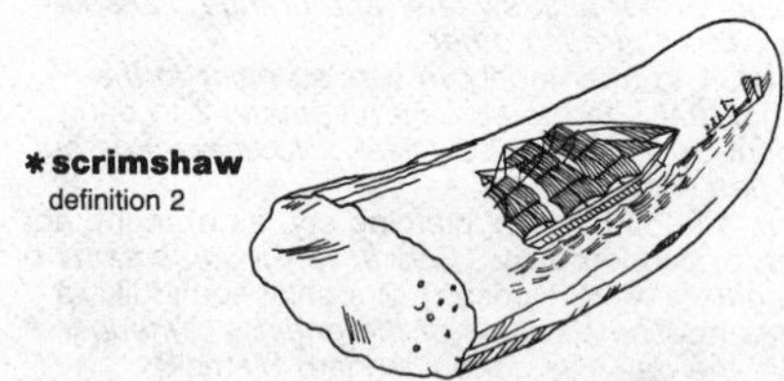

***scrimshaw**
definition 2

**scrip[1]** (skrip), *n.* **1a** paper money in denominations of less than a dollar, formerly issued in the United States. **b** any one of various paper currencies, such as those issued by an occupying power during or after a war, or by a government in time of emergency: *... the mine companies began paying the miners half in gold and half in scrip, or checks with no redemption date* (Lucius M. Beebe). **c** a piece of such currency. **2a** a receipt, certificate, or other document showing a right to something, especially a certificate entitling the holder to a fraction of a share of stock. **b** Also, **scrip dividend.** a stock dividend in the form of a note payable at a later date. **3** a small scrap of writing; writing. [variant of *script*]

**scrip[2]** (skrip), *n. Archaic.* a small bag, wallet, or satchel. [probably < Scandinavian (compare Old Icelandic *skreppa*)]

**Scrip.**, Scripture.

**script** (skript), *n., v.* *–**n.*** **1a** written letters, figures, signs, or characters; handwriting. **b** a kind of writing; system of alphabetical or other written characters: *Russian script.* **2** a style of printing that looks like handwriting. **3a** the manuscript of a play or actor's part: *... to work over a script that some lonely playwright has put together* (New Yorker). **b** a manuscript used in making a motion picture; screenplay. **c** a manuscript used in broadcasting. **4** *Law.* an original or principal document, as distinguished from a copy or duplicate. **5** *Archaic.* something written; a piece of writing.

*–**v.t.*** **1** to write a script for. **2** to turn into a script: *Famous and familiar stories are being scripted for some major TV shows* (Maclean's).

*–**v.i.*** to write radio or television programs or screenplays.

[< Latin *scrīptum,* (originally) neuter past participle of *scrībere* write. Compare etym. under **shrift.**]

**Script.**, Scripture.

**script editor**, an editor who corrects and prepares scripts for radio or television.

**script|er** (skrip′tər), *n. U.S. Informal.* a scriptwriter. [< *script* + *-er*[1]]

**scrip|to|ri|al** (skrip tôr′ē əl, -tōr′-), *adj.* of, having to do with, or using script.

**scrip|to|ri|um** (skrip tôr′ē əm, -tōr′-), *n., pl.* **-to|ri|ums, -to|ri|a** (-tôr′ē ə, -tōr′-). a writing room, especially a room in a monastery set apart for writing or copying manuscripts. [< Late Latin *scriptorium,* (originally) neuter adjective < Latin *scrībere* write]

**scrip|tur|al** (skrip′chər əl), *adj.* **1** Also, **Scriptural.** **a** of, in, or from the Scriptures. **b** according to the Scriptures; based on the Scriptures. **2** of or having to do with writing. —**scrip′tur|al|ness,** *n.*

**scrip|tur|al|ism** (skrip′chər ə liz′əm), *n.* literal adherence to the Scriptures.

**scrip|tur|al|ist** (skrip′chər ə list), *n.* **1** a person who adheres literally to the Scriptures. **2** a person well acquainted with the Scriptures.

**scrip|tur|al|ly** (skrip′chər ə lē), *adv.* in a scriptural manner; in accordance with the Scriptures.

**Scrip|ture** (skrip′chər), *n.* **1** = Bible. **2** a particular passage or text of the Bible. *Abbr:* Script.

**the (Holy) Scriptures,** the Bible: *I would teach the knowledge of the Scriptures only* (Joseph Priestley).

[< Late Latin *Scrīptūra* < Latin *scrīptūra* a writing < *scrībere* write]

**scrip|ture** (skrip′chər), *n.* **1** any sacred writing: *Most men do not know that any nation but the Hebrews have had a scripture* (Thoreau). **2** *Archaic.* an inscription or superscription. **3** *Archaic.* a written record; writing. [< *Scripture*]

**scrip|tured** (skrip′chərd), *adj.* **1** covered with writing. **2** *Obsolete.* **a** well acquainted with the Scriptures. **b** decreed by the Scriptures.

**script|writ|er** (skript′rī′tər), *n.* a person who writes scripts.

**scri|vel|lo** (skri vel′ō), *n., pl.* **-vel|loes** or **-vel|los.** a small elephant's tusk, used for making billiard balls. [< Portuguese *escrevelho*]

**scriv|en** (skriv′ən), *v.t., v.i. Archaic.* to write or work as a scrivener. [back formation < *scrivener*]

**scrive|ner** (skriv′nər), *n.* **1** any professional writer (used in an unfriendly way). **2** *Archaic.* **a** a public writer of letters or documents for others; clerk. **b** a notary. [< obsolete *scrivein* scrivener < Old French *escrivein* < Vulgar Latin *scrībānus* < Latin *scrība* scribe < *scrībere* write]

**scrod** (skrod), *n. U.S.* **1** a young cod or haddock, especially one that is cut into strips across the grain for cooking. **2** a piece of such a cod: *to order broiled scrod.* [American English; origin unknown]

**scrof|u|la** (skrof′yə lə), *n.* a form of tuberculosis characterized by the enlargement of the lymphatic glands, especially those in the neck, and inflammation of the joints: *... sufferers applying to be touched by King Charles II for scrofula—"king's evil"* (London Times). [< Medieval Latin *scrofula* < Latin *scrōfulae,* plural < *scrōfa* a sow (reason for use is unknown)]

**scrof|u|la|root** (skrof′yə lə rüt′, -rut′), *n.* = dogtooth violet.

**scrof|u|la|weed** (skrof′yə lə wēd′), *n.* = rattlesnake plantain.

**scrof|u|lism** (skrof′yə liz əm), *n.* the state of being scrofulous.

**scrof|u|lo|sis** (skrof′yə lō′sis), *n.* = scrofulism.

**scrof|u|lous** (skrof′yə ləs), *adj.* **1** of or having to do with scrofula: *He suffered from a scrofulous ear complaint* (Newsweek). **2** like scrofula. **3** having scrofula. **4** *Figurative.* (of literature) morally corrupt. —**scrof′u|lous|ly,** *adv.* —**scrof′u|lous|ness,** *n.*

**scrog** (skrog), *n. Scottish.* **1** a stunted bush. **2** a branch broken from a tree.

**scrogs,** thicket; underbrush: *I have gathered nuts from the scrogs of Tynron* (Blackwood's Magazine).

[compare dialectal *scrag* tree stump; origin uncertain]

**scrog|gy** (skrog′ē), *adj.,* **-gi|er, -gi|est.** *Scottish.* **1** full of scrogs. **2** = stunted.

**scroll** (skrōl), *n., v.* —*n.* **1a** a roll of parchment, paper or other material, especially one with writing on it: *He slowly unrolled the scroll as he read from it.* **b** a list, as of names or events; roll; schedule: (*Figurative.*) *to be entered in the scrolls of history.* **2** an ornament resembling a partly unrolled sheet of paper, or having a spiral or coiled form, such as the spiral ornaments in the Ionic and Corinthian capitals or the curved head of a violin or cello. **3** *Obsolete.* **a** a piece of writing, such as a letter. **b** a draft or copy, as of a letter.

—*v.t.* **1** to write down on a scroll; inscribe. **2** to form into a scroll. **3** to ornament with scrolls.

[alteration (influenced by *roll*) of Middle English *scrow* < Anglo-French *escrowe,* Old French *escroue* a scrap, perhaps < Germanic (compare Old High German *scrōt*)] —**scroll′-like′,** *adj.*

**scroll|er|y** (skrō′lər ē, skrōl′rē), *n.* = scrollwork.

**scroll painting, 1** the ancient Chinese and Japanese art of painting figures and scenes on scrolls, usually telling a story. **2** a painting of this kind: *Japanese scroll paintings are done on long strips of paper, usually about 12 inches high, which are rolled from one spindle to another* (Atlantic).

**scroll saw,** a very narrow saw for cutting thin wood in curved or ornamental patterns.

**scroll|work** (skrōl′wėrk′), *n.* **1** decorative work in which scrolls are much used. **2** ornamental work cut with a scroll saw.

**scrooch** (skrüch), *v.i. Dialect.* to crouch; cower: *Scrooch down and see if you can't wriggle down underneath* (J. C. Lincoln).

**scrooge** (skrüj), *v.t., v.i.,* **scrooged, scroog|ing,** *n.* = scrouge.

**Scrooge** (skrüj), *n.* **1** the embittered old miser in Charles Dickens' story *A Christmas Carol.* **2** Usually, **scrooge.** any greedy and stingy person; miser.

**scroop** (skrüp), *v., n. Dialect.* —*v.i.* to grate; creak; squeak. —*n.* a grating, creaking, or squeaking noise. [probably imitative]

**scroph|u|lar|i|a|ceous** (skrof′yə lãr′ē ā′shəs), *adj.* belonging to the figwort family: *Snapdragon and foxglove are scrophulariaceous plants.* [< New Latin *Scrophularia* the typical genus (< *scrophula* < Medieval Latin *scrofula;* see etym. under **scrofula**) + English *-aceous*]

**scro|tal** (skrō′təl), *adj.* of or having to do with the scrotum.

**scro|tum** (skrō′təm), *n., pl.* **-ta** (-tə), **-tums.** the pouch that contains the testicles. [< Latin *scrōtum*]

**scrouge** (skrüj, skrouj), *v.,* **scrouged, scroug|ing,** *n. Informal.* —*v.t., v.i.* to squeeze; press; crowd. —*n.* a crowd. Also, **scrooge.** [apparently alteration of earlier *scruze* squeeze, press together; origin uncertain]

**scroug|er** (skrü′jər), *n. U.S. Slang.* **1** a person who scrouges. **2** anything exceptional, as in size or capacity; whopper.

**scrounge** (skrounj), *v.,* **scrounged, scroung|ing.** *Slang.* —*v.i.* **1** to search about for what one can find: *He scrounged around in junk shops and acquired ... the French mantel clock* (Atlantic). **2** to sponge (on). —*v.t.* **1** to beg; get by begging: *to scrounge a meal. I scrounged an umbrella and Margaret and I walked home together in the rain* (Al Schacht). **2** to take dishonestly; pilfer. [apparently alteration of dialectal *scrunge* pilfer, steal] —**scroung′er,** *n.*

**scroyle** (skroil), *n. Obsolete.* a rascal.

**scrub**[1] (skrub), *v.,* **scrubbed, scrub|bing,** *n.* —*v.t.* **1** to rub hard; wash or clean by rubbing: *to scrub dirty clothes. She scrubbed the floor with a brush and soapsuds.* **2** to remove impurities from (a gas). **3** *U.S. Slang, Figurative.* to cancel: *The design was scrubbed at the drawingboard stage as being impractical.* —*v.i.* to wash.

—*n.* the act of scrubbing: *Give your hands a good scrub before dinner.*

[perhaps < Middle Dutch *schrubben* or < Scandinavian (compare Norwegian dialectal *skrubba*)]

**scrub**[2] (skrub), *n., adj.* —*n.* **1a** low, stunted trees or shrubs: *Sometimes the Colonel and I would go wandering through the trenches, which are gradually disappearing under a tangle of scrub* (New Yorker). **b** land overgrown with stunted trees or shrubs, such as the Australian bush. **2** *Figurative.* **a** anything small, or below the usual size: *He is a little scrub of a man.* **b** a steer, horse, or other animal, of mixed stock, often inferior in size or disposition to the purebred. **c** a mean, insignificant person. **3** *Figurative.* a person who has to work hard or do menial work to make a living; drudge. **4** a player not on the regular or varsity team.

—*adj.* **1** small; poor; inferior: *A scrub wagon team of four ... unkempt, dejected, and vicious-looking broncos* (Theodore Roosevelt). **2** *Sports.* of or for players not on the regular or varsity team: *a scrub ball team, a scrub game, scrub practice.*

**scrubs,** a team of inferior or substitute players: *His brother made the varsity, but he played with the scrubs.*

[< Scandinavian (compare Middle Danish *skrubbe* brushwood)]

**scrub|ba|ble** (skrub′ə bəl), *adj.* that can be scrubbed or will not be injured by scrubbing.

**scrub|bed** (skrub′id), *adj. Archaic.* scrubby.

**scrub|ber** (skrub′ər), *n.* **1** a person who scrubs. **2** a scrubbing brush: *a back scrubber.* **3** an apparatus for washing gas or removing pollutants from a gaseous mixture: *Sulfur can also be removed from coal smoke by special chemical catalysts called "scrubbers" before the smoke goes up the stack* (Time).

**scrub|bi|ness** (skrub′ē nis), *n.* scrubby quality or condition.

**scrub|bing brush** (skrub′ing), a brush with hard bristles for scrubbing.

**scrub|bird** (skrub′bėrd′), *n.* either of two wrenlike perching birds that live in the dense scrub of Australia. One kind is nearly extinct.

**scrub brush,** = scrubbing brush.

**scrub|by** (skrub′ē), *adj.,* **-bi|er, -bi|est.** **1** below the usual size; low; stunted; small: *a scrubby tree.* SYN: undersized. **2** covered with scrub: *scrubby land.* **3** *Figurative.* shabby; mean: *... a scrubby loft in the West Thirties full of noise and commotion* (New Yorker).

**scrub fowl,** = scrub hen.

**scrub hen,** the Australian mound builder or megapode, which lives in the thick underbrush or scrub.

**scrub jay,** = Florida jay.

**scrub|land** (skrub′land′), *n.* land overgrown with scrub: *Tractors have been used to clear scrubland for cultivation* (London Times).

**scrub nurse,** a nurse in charge of the instruments in the operating room of a hospital: *The senior scrub nurse knew the senior surgeon's methods so well that he rarely had to ask for an instrument* (Time).

**scrub oak,** any one of various small, scrubby oaks growing in sandy or barren soil, such as the bur oak.

**scrub pine,** any one of various low pines that commonly grow in poor or sandy soil, especially: **a** a pine found from New York to Georgia, usually small and straggly but reaching a height of 100 feet in the western part of its range. **b** the Pacific coast variety of the lodgepole pine.

**scrubs** (skrubz), *n.pl.* See under **scrub**[2].

**scrub typhus,** a disease with fever, inflammation of the lymph glands, and neuritis, caused by a rickettsia that is transmitted by certain chiggers; Japanese river fever; tsutsugamushi disease.

**scrub|wom|an** (skrub′wům′ən), *n., pl.* **-wom|en.** = cleaning woman.

**scrub wren,** a small, insect-eating passerine bird related to the thrush, common in parts of Australia.

**scruff** (skruf), *n.* the skin at the back of the neck; back of the neck: *to pick up a cat by the scruff.* Also, **scuff.** [perhaps alteration of *scuff;* origin uncertain]

► See **nape** for usage note.

**scruf|fi|ness** (skruf′ē nis), *n.* **1** scruffy quality or condition; scaliness. **2** *Figurative.* meanness; shabbiness.

**scruf|fle** (skruf′əl), *v.i., v.t.,* **-fled, -fling,** *n. British Dialect.* scuffle.

**scruf|fler** (skruf′lər), *n. British Dialect.* scuffler.

**scruf|fy** (skruf′ē), *adj.,* **-fi|er, -fi|est.** **1** *Especially British.* covered with dandruff; scaly: *A scruffy, somewhat aggressively-inclined individual, aged sixteen ...* (Punch). **2** *Figurative.* mean; shabby: *a scruffy lie. In all this ancient pomp, there was one concession to scruffy present reality* (Time).

**scrum** (skrum), *n. British.* a scrummage in Rugby football: *Sykes went over for a try from a scrum five yards from the Rhodesian line* (London Times). [short for *scrummage*]

**scrum-half** (skrum′haf′, -häf′), *n., pl.* **-halves.** *Rugby.* the halfback who throws the ball into scrummage.

**scrum|mage** (skrum′ij), *n., v.,* **-maged, -mag|ing.** *British.* —*n.* **1** a formation in Rugby used to begin play again after it has been stopped, in which the ball is thrown between two lines of no more than three players each, each of whom tries to kick the ball to other players lined up in back of him: *The early play was mainly a hard slog of scrummage, lineout, and maul* (London Times). **2** = scrimmage.

—*v.i.* to take part in a scrummage or scrimmage.

—*v.t.* **1** to begin play by rolling (the ball) in a scrummage. **2** = scrimmage.

[variant of *scrimmage*] —**scrum′mag|er,** *n.*

**scrump|tious** (skrump′shəs), *adj. Informal.* elegant; splendid; first-rate: *Probably the lumberyard isn't as scrumptious as all these Greek temples* (Sinclair Lewis). [American English; apparently alteration of *sumptuous*] —**scrump′tious|ly,** *adv.* —**scrump′tious|ness,** *n.*

**scrunch** (skrunch), *v., n.* —*v.t., v.i.* to crunch; crush; crumple; squeeze: *Every part of it ... may be profitably scrunched between molars* (New Yorker). *Don't scrunch up like that, Huckleberry—set up straight* (Mark Twain).

—*n.* **1** the noise made by scrunching. **2** an act of scrunching.

[perhaps < *crunch*]

**scru|ple** (skrü′pəl), *n., v.,* **-pled, -pling.** —*n.* **1a** a feeling of doubt about what one ought to do; hesitation to do something: *No scruple of caution ever holds him back from prompt action.* **b** a feeling of uneasiness that keeps a person from doing something; uneasiness affecting the conscience: *He has scruples about playing cards for money.* **2** a measure of apothecaries' weight equal to 20 grains or 1.296 grams. Three scruples make 1 dram. **3a** an ancient Roman weight equal to 1/24 ounce. **b** an ancient Roman coin. Its

---

**Pronunciation Key:** hat, āge, cãre, fär; let, ēqual, tėrm; it, īce; hot, ōpen, ôrder; oil, out; cup, půt, rüle; child; long; thin; ᴛʜen; zh, measure; ə represents **a** in about, **e** in taken, **i** in pencil, **o** in lemon, **u** in circus.

weight in gold determined its value. **4** *Figurative.* a very small amount: *... the smallest scruple of her excellence* (Shakespeare).
—***v.i.*** **1** to hesitate or be unwilling (to do something): *A dishonest man does not scruple to deceive others. As a Parliamentarian he has never scrupled to use any weapon which comes to hand* (Harper's). **2** to have scruples.
—***v.t.*** to have or make scruples about.
**make scruple,** to hesitate or be reluctant, especially because of conscientiousness: *She made no scruple of oversetting all human institutions* (Hawthorne).
[< Latin *scrūpulus* a feeling of uneasiness (diminutive) < *scrūpus* uneasiness, anxiety such as the pricking of conscience like the pricking of a sharp stone; (originally) sharp stone]

**scru|pu|los|i|ty** (skrü'pyə los'ə tē), *n., pl.* **-ties.** **1** the fact or condition of being scrupulous; strict regard for what is right; scrupulous care: *Albert, with characteristic scrupulosity, attempted to thread his way through the complicated labyrinth of European diplomacy* (Lytton Strachey). **2** an instance of this.

**scru|pu|lous** (skrü'pyə ləs), *adj.* **1** very careful to do what is right: *a scrupulous man, scrupulous honesty.* **SYN:** conscientious. **2** attending thoroughly to details; very careful: *A soldier must pay scrupulous attention to orders.* [< Latin *scrūpulus* (see etym. under **scruple**) + English *-ous*] —**scru'pu|lous|ly,** *adv.* —**scru'pu|lous|ness,** *n.*
—*Syn.* **2 Scrupulous, punctilious** mean very careful and exact. **Scrupulous** implies conscientious care in following what is considered correct, exact, or the like: *a scholar's scrupulous regard for accuracy. She takes scrupulous care of the children's health.* **Punctilious** emphasizes strict and often excessive attention to an observance of fine points of laws, rules of conduct, or performance of duties: *He is punctilious in returning borrowed books.*

**scru|ta|ble** (skrü'tə bəl), *adj.* that can be penetrated or understood by investigation. [< Latin *scrūtārī* examine + English *-able*]

**scru|ta|tor** (skrü tā'tər), *n. British.* a person who examines or investigates, especially a scrutineer. [< Latin *scrūtātor* < *scrūtārī* examine]

**scru|ti|neer** (skrü'tə nir'), *n. British.* a person who inspects and counts election ballots.

**scru|ti|nise** (skrü'tə nīz), *v.,* **-nised, -nis|ing.** *Especially British.* scrutinize.

**scru|ti|nize** (skrü'tə nīz), *v.t.,* **-nized, -niz|ing.** to examine closely; inspect carefully: *The jeweler scrutinized the diamond for flaws. But never before have so many citizens been scrutinized with suspicion* (Scientific American). —**scru'ti|niz'er,** *n.* —**scru'ti|niz'ing|ly,** *adv.*

**scru|ti|nous** (skrü'tə nəs), *adj.* scrutinizing; searching; critical. —**scru'ti|nous|ly,** *adv.*

**scru|ti|ny** (skrü'tə nē), *n., pl.* **-nies.** **1** a close examination; careful inspection: *His work looks all right, but it will not bear scrutiny.* **2** a looking searchingly at something or someone; searching gaze: *I observed him throwing a glance of scrutiny over all the passengers* (Charlotte Brontë). **3** an official examination of the votes cast at an election. **4** a ballot cast by a cardinal during the election of a new pope: *If a pope is elected, the scrutinies are burned alone, and the waiting crowd sees white smoke* (Fulton J. Sheen). [< Late Latin *scrūtinium* < Latin *scrūtārī* to examine, investigate]

**scru|to** (skrü'tō), *n. Theater.* a trap door or doorway which springs into place after being used for quick appearances and disappearances. [origin unknown]

**scru|toire** (skrü twär'), *n.* = escritoire.

**scry** (skrī), *v.,* **scried, scry|ing.** —***v.i.*** to see images revealing remote future events by looking into a crystal or the like; descry. —***v.t.*** *British Dialect.* to descry; see; perceive. —**scry'er,** *n.*

**SCS** (no periods), Soil Conservation Service.

**S. Cu.,** strato-cumulus.

**scu|ba** (skü'bə), *n., adj.* —***n.*** the portable breathing equipment, including one or more tanks of compressed air, used by underwater swimmers and divers: *Skindivers who use scuba favor contact [lenses] because spectacles ... are cumbersome inside a watertight face mask* (Time).
—***adj.*** having to do with, comprising, or using underwater breathing equipment: *scuba diving, scuba gear, a scuba diver.*
[< *s*(elf)-*c*(ontained) *u*(nderwater) *b*(reathing) *a*(pparatus)]

**scud[1]** (skud), *v.,* **scud|ded, scud|ding,** *n.* —***v.i.*** **1** to run or move swiftly: *Clouds scudded across the sky driven by high winds. [His] turbojet speedboat, Bluebird, has scudded through a series of trial runs* (Newsweek). **2** *Nautical.* to run before a storm with little or no sail set: *We were scudding before a heavy gale, under bare poles* (Frederick Marryat).
—***n.*** **1** the act of scudding. **2** clouds or spray driven by the wind, as in a storm at sea: *At 500 feet [altitude] you break out under the dark scud, into a rainy but fairly clear area* (Atlantic). **3** *Dialect.* **a** a brief, driving shower of rain or fall of snow. **b** a sudden gust of wind. **4** *Scottish.* a slap.
[perhaps < Scandinavian (compare Danish *skyde* shoot, glide)]

**scud[2]** (skud), *v.,* **scud|ded, scud|ding,** *n.* —***v.t.*** to scrape (hide) to remove dirt, bits of flesh, and hair roots.
—***n.*** the dirt and other matter removed by scudding.
[< obsolete *scud* dirt; origin uncertain]

**scud|der** (skud'ər), *n.* a person or thing that scuds.

**scu|del|la** (skü del'ə), *n.* = scodella.

**scu|do** (skü'dō), *n., pl.* **-di** (-dē). **1** a former Italian silver coin and money of account, worth about a dollar. **2** a former gold coin of the same value. [< Italian *scudo* coin marked with a shield; (literally) a shield < Latin *scūtum* shield]

**scuff[1]** (skuf), *v., n.* —***v.i.*** to walk without lifting the feet; shuffle: *to scuff through sand, to scuff into a room.*
—***v.t.*** to wear or injure the surface of by hard use: *to scuff one's shoes.*
—***n.*** **1a** the act of scuffing. **b** the noise made by scuffing. **2** a slipper with only a sole and toe piece: *Travel scuffs of the softest glove leather ...* (New Yorker). **3** a scar made by scuffing. **4** *Scottish.* a glancing blow.
[perhaps variant of *scuffle,* or perhaps < Scandinavian (compare Swedish *skuffa* shove, push)]

**scuff[2]** (skuf), *n.* = scruff.

**scuf|fle** (skuf'əl), *v.,* **-fled, -fling,** *n.* —***v.i.*** **1** to struggle or fight in a rough, confused manner: *The two boys fell as they scuffled. Somewhere in the darkness two rats scuffled* (Graham Greene). **2** to go or move in hurried confusion: *Drive the populace headlong past it as fast as they can scuffle* (John Ruskin). **3** = shuffle.
—***v.t.*** to stir the surface of (land), hoe (a crop), or cut up (weeds) by means of a scuffle hoe: *This land was ploughed deep and ... harrowed and scuffled till there was tilth enough for planting* (London Times).
—***n.*** **1** a confused, rough struggle or fight: *The boy lost his hat in the scuffle. The mob followed ... a scuffle ensued* (Cardinal Newman). **SYN:** tussle, scrimmage. **2** the act of shuffling: *They could hear a scuffle of feet* (George J. Whyte-Melville). **3** = scuffle hoe.
[apparently a frequentative form of *scuff*]

**scuffle hoe,** a hoe which is pushed instead of pulled.

**scuf|fler** (skuf'lər), *n.* a person or thing that scuffles.

**scuff|proof** (skuf'prüf'), *adj.* resistant to scuffing: *scuffproof leather.*

**scug** (skug), *n. British Slang.* an ill-favored, untalented, and unpopular schoolboy.

**scul|dud|der|y** (skul dud'ər ē), *n. Archaic.* **1** *U.S.* skulduggery. **2** *Scottish.* obscenity.

**sculk** (skulk), *v.i., n.* = skulk. —**sculk'er,** *n.*

**scull[1]** (skul), *n., v.* —***n.*** **1** an oar worked with a side twist over the end of a boat to make it go. **2** one of a pair of oars used, one on each side, by a single rower. **3** the act of propelling by sculls. **4** a light racing boat for one or more rowers. In a scull each rower uses two oars. **5** any boat propelled by a scull or sculls.
—***v.t.*** to make (a boat) go by a scull or sculls.
—***v.i.*** to scull a boat.
[origin unknown]

**scull[2]** (skul), *n. Scottish.* a large, shallow basket. [< a Scandinavian word]

**scull|er** (skul'ər), *n.* **1** a person who sculls. **2** a boat propelled by sculling.

**scul|ler|y** (skul'ər ē, skul'rē), *n., pl.* **-ler|ies,** *adj.* —***n.*** **1** a small room where the dirty, rough work of a kitchen is done. **2** *Obsolete.* **a** the department of a household that cares for the plates, dishes, and kitchen utensils. **b** the room or rooms for this department.
—***adj.*** of or having to do with a scullery: *a scullery maid, scullery work.*
[< Old French *escuelerie* < *escuelle* dish < Vulgar Latin *scūtella,* for Latin *scutella* (diminutive) < *scutra* platter]

**scull|ing** (skul'ing), *n.* the sport of rowing with sculls.

**scul|lion** (skul'yən), *n. Archaic.* **1** a servant who does the dirty, rough work in a kitchen: *... to hear the clinking of the plates ... as the scullion rinsed them and put them by* (Samuel Butler). **2** a low, contemptible person. [< Old French *escouillon, escouvillon* a swab, cloth < *escouve* broom < Latin *scōpa*]

**sculp** (skulp), *v.t., v.i. Informal.* to sculpture: *There's some bohemians up that dirt road there. They all sculp or weave or something* (New Yorker). [< Latin *sculpere* carve]

**sculp.,** an abbreviation for the following:
1 sculpsit.
2 sculptor.
3 sculptural.
4 sculpture.

**scul|pin** (skul'pin), *n.* **1** any one of a family of small fishes with large pectoral fins, eyes near the top of a big, spiny head, and a wide mouth. Sculpins are found in salt and fresh water and are not considered edible by most people. **2** a scorpionfish or rockfish of the southern Californian coast. [perhaps alteration of French *scorpène*]

**sculps.** or **sculpt.,** sculpsit.

**sculp|sit** (skulp'sit), *Latin.* he or she carved it.

**sculpt** (skulpt), *Informal.* —***v.t.*** to sculpture: *[He] sculpted an abstract seagull in brilliantly clear crystal* (New York Times). —***v.i.*** to make sculptures: *Parents painted, drew and sculpted alongside their grade-school-age children* (Time). [< French *sculpter* < Latin *sculpere* carve]

**sculpt.,** an abbreviation for the following:
1 sculpsit.
2 sculptor.
3 sculptural.
4 sculpture.

**sculp|tor** (skulp'tər), *n.* a person who makes figures, as by carving, modeling, or casting; artist in sculpture. Sculptors usually make statues of marble or other stone, wood, bronze, clay, wax, or a substance like any of these. [< Latin *sculptor, -ōris,* variant of *scalptor* < *scalpere* to carve]

**Sculp|tor** (skulp'tər), *n., genitive* **Sculp|to|ris.** a southern constellation near Phoenix. [short for New Latin *(Apparatus) Sculptoris*]

**Sculp|to|ris** (skulp tôr'is, -tōr'-), *n.* genitive of **Sculptor.**

**sculp|tress** (skulp'tris), *n.* a woman sculptor.

**sculp|tur|al** (skulp'chər əl), *adj.* of or having to do with sculpture; like sculpture: *... one rolled-up sleeve baring a sculptural forearm* (Joseph Conrad). —**sculp'tur|al|ly,** *adv.*

**sculp|ture** (skulp'chər), *n., v.,* **-tured, -tur|ing.** —***n.*** **1** the art of carving or modeling figures. Sculpture includes the cutting of statues from blocks of marble or other stone or wood, casting in bronze or other material, and making metal statues by welding, and modeling in clay or wax: *Sculpture gives expression to the most prized personality traits* (Emory S. Bogardus). **2** sculptured work: *temples adorned with sculpture.* **3** a piece of such work: *There are many famous sculptures in the museum. Most of Stankiewicz's sculptures are extremely funny* (Newsweek).
—***v.t.*** **1** to make (figures) by carving, modeling, welding, or casting: *to sculpture a horse in bronze.* **2** to cover or ornament with sculpture. **3** *Geology.* to alter the contour of by erosion.
[< Latin *sculptūra,* variant of *scalptūra* < *scalpere* to carve]

**sculp|tured** (skulp'chərd), *adj.* **1** covered or ornamented with sculpture. **2** carved or molded in sculpture: *Hood and fenders of the highly-styled car are sculptured* (Wall Street Journal).

**sculp|tur|esque** (skulp'chə resk'), *adj.* resembling or suggesting sculpture. —**sculp'tur|esque'ly,** *adv.* —**sculp'tur|esque'ness,** *n.*

**scum** (skum), *n., v.,* **scummed, scum|ming.** —***n.*** **1a** a thin layer that rises to the top of a liquid: *When Mother makes jelly, she skims off the scum. Green scum floated on top of the pond. The idea is prevalent that algae, especially those which form a scum on the water, are loathsome or filthy. This is far from the truth* (Fred W. Emerson). **b** the refuse that rises to the surface of metals in a molten state. **2** *Figurative.* undesirable or disreputable people; dregs: *The saloon was filled with the scum of the town.*
—***v.i.*** to form scum; become covered with a scum. —***v.t.*** **1** to remove scum from; skim. **2** to form scum on; cover with scum: *A thick mist scummed the windshields* (Time).
[perhaps < Middle Dutch *schuum,* Danish *skum*]

**scum|ble** (skum'bəl), *v.,* **-bled, -bling,** *n. Painting and Drawing.* —***v.t.*** **1** to soften the effect of (colors or the harder lines), as by overlaying with a thin coat of opaque or semiopaque color, or by spreading the lines. **2** to produce (an effect) by either or both of these processes.
—***n.*** **1** the act or technique of overlaying paint or color. **2** the effect produced. **3** the paint or color used.
[perhaps a frequentative form of *scum,* verb]

**scum|my** (skum'ē), *adj.,* **-mi|er, -mi|est.** **1** consisting of or containing scum: *a scummy pond.* **2** *Figurative.* low; mean; worthless: *a scummy fellow, a scummy trick.*

**scun|gy** (skun'jē), *adj.,* **-gi|er, -gi|est.** *Slang.* **1** (in Australia) dirty. **2** (in South Africa) dark; murky. [origin uncertain; perhaps related to Scottish *scuge* to slink about]

**scun|ner** (skun'ər), *n., v.* —***n.*** **1** a feeling of disgust or loathing. **2** an object of disgust.
—***v.i., v.t.*** to sicken; disgust. [origin unknown]

**scup** (skup), *n., pl.* **scups** or (*collectively*) **scup.** a narrow, high-backed sea fish used for food, common on the eastern coast of the United States; a variety of porgy. [American English, short for earlier *scuppaug* < Algonkian (Narraganset) *mishcuppauog,* plural of *mishcup*]

**scup|per** (skup′ər), *n., v.* —*n.* an opening in the side of a ship to let water run off the deck: *The fruit fell from his hand. Before it had rolled to the scupper, Able was rising from his chair* (Atlantic).
—*v.t. Slang.* to catch by surprise and kill or destroy; overwhelm: *The greater part of our tank force has recently been scuppered* (Atlantic). [origin uncertain]

**scup|per|nong** (skup′ər nông, -nong), *n.* **1** a large, yellowish-green grape grown in the southern United States. It is a variety of the muscadine or fox grape. **2** a wine made from these grapes. [American English < *Scuppernong* River, North Carolina, near which the grape was first cultivated]

**scupper shoots,** tubes which carry overboard the water from the spar deck.

**scup|seat** (skup′sēt′), *n.* a wooden seat on which a sailor sits while working aloft where he can obtain no foothold.

**scur** (skėr), *v., n.* = skirr.

**scurf** (skėrf), *n.* **1** small scales of dead skin. Dandruff is a kind of scurf. **2** any scaly matter on a surface. **3** *Figurative.* something no longer useful or essential, that can be sloughed off. [Old English *scurf* < Scandinavian (compare Old Swedish *skurf*)]

**scurf|i|ness** (skėr′fē nis), *n.* a being scurfy; scurfy condition.

**scurf|y** (skėr′fē), *adj.,* **scurf|i|er, scurf|i|est. 1** covered with scurf. **2** of or like scurf.

**scur|rile** or **scur|ril** (skėr′əl), *adj. Archaic.* scurrilous. [< Latin *scurrīlus;* see etym. under **scurrilous**]

**scur|ril|i|ty** (skə ril′ə tē), *n., pl.* **-ties. 1** coarse joking: ... *based on the proposition that millions like to wallow in scurrility* (Time). **2** indecent abuse. **3** an indecent or coarse remark: *abusive speech filled with scurrilities.*

**scur|ri|lous** (skėr′ə ləs), *adj.* **1** coarsely joking; using abusive or derisive language: *a scurrilous political writer.* **2** abusive in an indecent way; foul: *scurrilous language;* ... *so indiscreet as to print scurrilous reflections on the government of neighbouring states* (Benjamin Franklin). [< Latin *scurrīlis* (with English *-ous*) < *scurra* buffoon] —**scur′ri|lous|ly,** *adv.* —**scur′ri|lous|ness,** *n.*

**scur|ry** (skėr′ē), *v.,* **-ried, -ry|ing,** *n., pl.* **-ries.**
—*v.i.* to run quickly; scamper; hurry: *We could hear mice scurrying about in the walls.*
—*n.* **1** a hasty running; hurrying: *With much fuss and scurry, she at last got started.* **2** a short, quick run or race on horseback.
[short for *hurry-scurry*]

**S-curve** (es′kėrv′), *n.* a curve shaped like the capital letter S.

**scur|vied** (skėr′vēd), *adj.* affected with scurvy; scorbutic.

**scur|vish** (skėr′vish), *n.* = evening primrose. [alteration of *scabious*[2]]

**scur|vy** (skėr′vē), *n., adj.,* **-vi|er, -vi|est.** —*n.* a disease caused by lack of vitamin C in the diet. It is characterized by swollen and bleeding gums, extreme weakness, and livid spots on the skin. Scurvy used to be common among sailors when they ate too much bread and salt meat and not enough vegetables and fruits. [< adjective]
—*adj.* **1** mean; contemptible; base: *a scurvy fellow, a scurvy trick. A wooden tenement known as the Old Brewery ... had the reputation of being the scurviest hovel in town* (New Yorker). SYN: low. **2** *Obsolete.* scurfy; scabby.
[variant of *scurfy*] —**scur′vi|ly,** *adv.* —**scur′vi|ness,** *n.*

**scurvy grass,** a plant of the mustard family, found in the arctic and northern regions, formerly used as a remedy for scurvy.

**scut** (skut), *n.* **1** an erect, short tail, especially that of a hare, rabbit, or deer. **2** *Slang.* a mean fellow. [origin uncertain. Compare Old Icelandic *skutr* stern.]

**scu|ta** (skyü′tə), *n.* plural of **scutum.**

**scu|tage** (skyü′tij), *n.* a payment exacted in lieu of military service in the feudal system. [< Medieval Latin *scutagium* < Latin *scūtum* a shield]

**scu|tate** (skyü′tāt), *adj.* **1** *Zoology.* having shieldlike parts or large scales of bone, shell, etc. **2** *Botany.* shaped like a round shield: *Nasturtiums have scutate leaves.* [< Latin *scūtātus* having a shield < *scūtum* shield]

**scutch** (skuch), *v., n.* —*v.t.* **1** to free (flax or hemp fiber) from woody parts by beating. **2** to separate (cotton fibers) after loosening and cleansing.
—*n.* **1** = scutcher. **2** a tool with perpendicular double edges to trim brick.

**scutch|eon** (skuch′ən), *n.* **1** = escutcheon. **2** *Zoology.* a scutum.

**scutch|eoned** (skuch′ənd), *adj.* having scutcheons.

**scutch|er** (skuch′ər), *n.* **1** a tool for scutching flax, cotton, or other fiber. **2** a person or thing that scutches.

**scute** (skyüt), *n.* = scutum (def. 1). [< Latin *scūtum* shield]

**scu|tel|la** (skyü tel′ə), *n.* plural of **scutellum.**

**scu|tel|lar** (skyü tel′ər), *adj.* of or having to do with a scutellum.

**scu|tel|late** (skyü′tə lāt, skyü tel′it), *adj. Biology.* **1** having scutella. **2** formed into a scutellum. **3** hollow like a shield; platter-shaped. [< New Latin *scutellātus* < Latin *scutella* platter < *scutra* dish, but taken as < New Latin *scutellum;* see etym. under **scutellum**]

**scu|tel|lat|ed** (skyü′tə lā′tid), *adj.* = scutellate.

**scu|tel|la|tion** (skyü′tə lā′shən), *n.* **1** arrangement of scales. **2** a scaly covering, as on a bird's leg.

**scu|tel|lum** (skyü tel′əm), *n., pl.* **-la.** *Biology.* a small plate, scale, or other shieldlike part, as on the feet of certain birds, the bodies of insects, or a cotyledon of some grasses. [< New Latin *scutellum* (diminutive) < Latin *scūtum* shield]

**Scu|ti** (skyü′tī), *n.* genitive of **Scutum.**

**scu|ti|form** (skyü′tə fôrm), *adj.* = shield-shaped. [< Latin *scūtum,* shield]

**scu|to bo|nae vo|lun|ta|tis tu|ae co|ro|nas|ti nos** (skyü′tō bō′nē vol′ən tā′tis tyü′ē kor′ə nas′tī nōs), *Latin.* with the shield of Thy favor Thou hast encompassed us (motto on the state seal of Maryland, in Psalms 5:12).

**scut|ter** (skut′ər), *v., n. Dialect.* —*v.i.* to scurry.
—*n.* a scuttering; scurrying.

**scut|tle**[1] (skut′əl), *n.* **1** a kind of bucket for holding or carrying coal. SYN: hod. **2** *Obsolete.* a broad, shallow basket, as for carrying grain or vegetables. [Old English *scutel* < Latin *scutella* platter (diminutive) < *scutra* dish]

**scut|tle**[2] (skut′əl), *v.,* **-tled, -tling,** *n.* —*v.i.* to run with quick, hurried steps; scamper; scurry: *The dogs scuttled off into the woods. The women had grasped the peril of their position and were scuttling away* (New Yorker).
—*n.* a short, hurried run.
[variant of earlier *scuddle,* frequentative of *scud*]

**scut|tle**[3] (skut′əl), *n., v.,* **-tled, -tling.** —*n.* **1** an opening in the deck or side of a ship, with a lid or cover. **2** an opening in a wall or roof, with a lid or cover. **3** the lid or cover for any such opening.
—*v.t.* **1a** to cut a hole or holes through the bottom or sides of (a ship) to sink it: *After the pirates captured the ship, they scuttled it. His Black Sea fleet had been scuttled* (London Times). **b** to open the seacocks or valves of (a ship) to sink it. **2** to cut a hole or holes in the deck of (a ship) to salvage the cargo. **3** *Figurative.* **a** to give up; let go: *The West was willing to scuttle the present ... government in favor of a truly neutralist one* (Time). **b** to undermine; destroy: *His weakness for the rash remark eventually would scuttle him* (New Yorker).
[perhaps < Middle French *escoutille* < Spanish, or directly < Spanish *escotilla* hatchway, perhaps < a Germanic word]

**scut|tle|butt** (skut′əl but′), *n.* **1** *U.S. Informal.* rumor and stories not based on fact; gossip: *Moscow scuttlebutt says Ekaterina is now a sports car buff* (Time). **2a** a water cask for drinking, with a hole in the top for a cup or dipper, kept on the deck of a ship. **b** a drinking fountain. [< *scuttle*[3] + *butt*[4] (def. 1, because the scuttle was a place to gossip)]

**scut|tler**[1] (skut′lər), *n.* a person who hurries off, usually in an undignified manner.

**scut|tler**[2] (skut′lər), *n.* a person who scuttles a ship, especially with the design of "losing" her and claiming the insurance money.

**scu|tum** (skyü′təm), *n., pl.* **-ta. 1** *Zoology.* a shieldlike part, as of a bone or shell, such as is on a turtle or armadillo; scute. **2** a large, oblong Roman shield. [< Latin *scūtum* shield]

**Scu|tum** (skyü′təm), *n., genitive* **Scu|ti.** a southern constellation near Sagittarius. [< New Latin *Scutum* < Latin *scūtum* shield]

**S.C.V.,** *U.S.* Sons of Confederate Veterans.

**scye** (sī), *n.* the armhole of a garment, into which the sleeve is set. [origin unknown]

**Scyl|la** (sil′ə), *n.* **1** a dangerous rock opposite the whirlpool Charybdis at the extreme southwestern tip of Italy. **2** *Greek Mythology.* a female monster that snatched sailors from ships. Also, **Scilla.**
**between Scylla and Charybdis,** between two evils or dangers, both of which must be avoided: *to guide the ship of state between the Scylla of provocation and the Charybdis of appeasement* (New York Herald Tribune).

**scy|phi** (sī′fī), *n.* plural of **scyphus.**

**scy|phi|form** (sī′fə fôrm), *adj. Botany.* cup-shaped.

**scy|phis|to|ma** (sī fis′tə mə), *n., pl.* **-ma|ta** (-mə tə). a scyphozoan embryo that multiplies by budding, and gives rise to permanent colonies of scyphozoans. See diagram under **alternation of generations.** [< New Latin *scyphistoma* < *scyphus* + *stoma* < Greek *stóma* mouth]

**scy|phis|tome** (sī fis′tōm), *n.* = scyphistoma.

**scy|pho|zo|an** (sī′fə zō′ən), *n., adj.* —*n.* any one of a class of marine coelenterates, including many of the large jellyfishes, having a bell-shaped, gelatinous body and long, trailing tentacles, and lacking a true polyp stage.
—*adj.* of or belonging to the scyphozoans.
[< New Latin *scyphus* (see etym. under **scyphus**) + Greek *zōion* animal + English *-an*]

**scy|phus** (sī′fəs), *n., pl.* **-phi. 1** *Botany.* a cup-shaped part, such as the end of a lichen's fruit stalk or the corolla of a flower. **2** an ancient Greek cup. [< New Latin *scyphus* < Latin, a large drinking cup < Greek *skýphos*]

**scyt|a|le** (sit′ə lē), *n.* **1** a method of secret writing used by the ancient Spartans, in which the message was written on a strip of parchment wound spirally around a cylindrical stick, so that it became illegible when the parchment was unrolled, and could be read only by someone who rewound the parchment on a stick of the same form and size. **2** the stick and parchment used in this method. **3** a secret message conveyed by this method. [< Greek *skytálē* (literally) stick, staff; message]

***scythe** (sīᴛʜ), *n., v.,* **scythed, scyth|ing.** —*n.* a long, slightly curved blade on a long handle, for cutting grass or the like.
—*v.t.* to cut or mow with a scythe.
—*v.i.* to use a scythe: *Far away ... men were scything* (John Galsworthy).
[Old English *sīthe;* spelling later influenced by Latin *scindere* to cut]

***scythe**

**scythed** (sīᴛʜd), *adj.* having scythes or sharp blades attached to the wheels, as ancient war chariots did.

**scythe|man** (sīᴛʜ′mən), *n., pl.* **-men. 1** a man who uses a scythe: *It suggested the simple, ancient grace of a good scytheman or sower* (New Yorker). **2** *Figurative.* time and death.

**Scyth|i|an** (sith′ē ən), *adj., n.* —*adj.* of or having to do with ancient Scythia, its people, or their language.
—*n.* **1** a native or inhabitant of ancient Scythia. **2** the Iranian language of these people.

**s.d.,** **1** sight draft. **2** sine die. **3** standard deviation.

**SD** (no periods), **1** the security service of the Schutzstaffel in Nazi Germany (German, *Sicherheitsdienst*). **2** South Dakota (with postal Zip Code).

**S.D.,** **1** Doctor of Science (Latin, *Scientiae Doctor*). **2** South Dakota. **3** standard deviation.

**S. Dak.,** South Dakota.

**'sdeath** (zdeth), *interj. Archaic.* "God's death," used as an oath: *'Sdeath! sir, do you question my understanding?* (Thomas Love Peacock).

**SDI** (no periods) or **S.D.I.,** Selective Dissemination of Information (a computerized system for providing scientists with data on published technical literature).

**S. Doc.,** Senate document (used with a number): *S. Doc. 23764.*

**S.D.R.** or **S.D.R.s,** Special Drawing Rights.

**SDS** (no periods) or **S.D.S.,** Students for a Democratic Society (any one of several political organizations of radical college students, especially an American national organization formed in 1962 and split thereafter into various factions representing leftist, New Leftist, and anarchist views).

**S-dump** (es′dump′), *n.* a chute curved or bent resembling the letter S.

**s.e.,** **1** southeast. **2** southeastern.

**Se** (no period), selenium (chemical element).

**Pronunciation Key:** hat, **ā**ge, c**ã**re, f**ä**r; let, **ē**qual, t**ė**rm; it, **ī**ce; h**o**t, **ō**pen, **ô**rder; **oi**l, **ou**t; cup, p**ů**t, r**ü**le; **ch**ild; lo**ng**; **th**in; **ᴛʜ**en; **zh**, measure; **ə** represents **a** in about, **e** in taken, **i** in pencil, **o** in lemon, **u** in circus.

**SE** (no periods) or **S.E.**, an abbreviation for the following:
1 southeast.
2 southeastern.
3 *Football.* split end.
4 Stock Exchange.
5 systems engineer.

**sea** (sē), *n., adj.* —*n.* **1** the great body of salt water that covers almost three fourths of the earth's surface; the ocean. **2** any large body of salt water, smaller than an ocean, partly or wholly enclosed by land: *the North Sea, the Mediterranean Sea, the Dead Sea. The seas that surround Antarctica are notably stormy* (Paul A. Siple). **3** a large lake of fresh water: *the Sea of Galilee.* **4a** a large, heavy wave: *A high sea swept over the ship's deck.* **b** the swell of the ocean: *a heavy sea. Some ship in distress, that cannot live in such an angry sea* (Longfellow). **5** *Figurative.* an overwhelming amount or number: *a sea of troubles.* **6** *Figurative.* a broad expanse: *a sea of faces.* **7** Often, **Sea**. one of the dark, flat plains on the moon once thought to be seas; mare: *the Sea of Tranquility. The dark markings which are called "seas," even though they are entirely dry, make up the surface of the "man in the moon"* (Science News Letter).
—*adj.* of, on, or from the sea; marine: *a sea animal, a sea route, a sea breeze.*
**at sea, a** out on the sea; on shipboard: *We were at sea out of sight of land for ten days.* **b** *Figurative.* puzzled; confused: *I can't understand this problem; I'm all at sea.* **c** *Figurative.* in error; astray; quite wrong: *Your're altogether at sea in your guesses.*
**follow the sea**, to be a sailor: *As a boy, Columbus dreamed of following the sea.*
**go to sea, a** to become a sailor: *The captain had gone to sea when he was barely seventeen.* **b** to begin a sea voyage: *The family went to sea last month.*
**put to sea**, to begin a sea voyage: *Our fleet put to sea from Boston.*
**take to sea**, to start a voyage; embark: *The ships of the Spanish Armada took to sea in 1588.*
[Old English *sǣ*]

***sea anchor**, **1** a drag used in a gale to prevent a ship from drifting and to keep its head to the wind. It usually consists of a floating framed cone of canvas with its large, open base toward the ship. **2** any one of various somewhat similar devices by which a seaplane or amphibious aircraft may be held more or less stationary with its hull pointed into the wind, used especially after a forced landing at sea.

***sea anchor**
definition 1

**sea anemone**, a flowerlike polyp with a fleshy, cylindrical body and a mouth surrounded by many brightly colored tentacles. There are numerous kinds.

**sea arrow**, any one of various fast-swimming squids that dart in the water to catch fish.

**sea bag**, a large canvas bag that seamen use to carry clothing and other articles to and from a ship.

**sea bass**, **1** a common food and game fish of the northeastern coast of the United States with a peculiar tail fin. **2** any one of various similar fishes.

**sea bat**, = batfish.

**sea|beach** (sē′bēch′), *n.* = seashore.

**sea bean**, **1** the large, hard, beanlike edible seed of a tropical, leguminous climbing plant often carried by ocean currents to distant shores. **2** the plant producing this seed. **3** any one of various small univalve shells somewhat resembling coffee beans.

**sea bear**, **1** = polar bear. **2** any one of various fur seals, especially the northern fur seal.

**sea|bed** (sē′bed′), *n.* the bottom of the sea; ocean bed; sea-bottom.

**Sea|bee** (sē′bē′), *n.* a member of the construction battalion of the United States Navy, composed of mechanics, carpenters, welders, and other construction personnel, who normally take no part in combat. [< pronunciation of the initials *C.B.* of Construction Battalion]

**sea beef**, the flesh of the porpoise or the whale.

**sea bird**, any bird that lives on or near the sea. The petrels, gannets, and jaegers are sea birds. SYN: seafowl.

**sea biscuit**, a hard biscuit prepared for long keeping; hardtack; ship biscuit.

**sea bladder**, = Portuguese man-of-war.

**sea|board** (sē′bôrd′, -bōrd′), *n., adj.* —*n.* land near the sea; seacoast; seashore: *New York City is on the Atlantic seaboard.*
—*adj.* bordering on the sea.
[earlier *sea-bord,* adjective < *sea* + *bord, board* side, border < Old French *bord*]

**sea boat**, a vessel considered with reference to her behavior at sea.

**sea boots**, high, waterproof boots for use at sea.

**sea|born** (sē′bôrn′), *adj.* **1** born in or of the sea. **2** produced in or by the sea.

**sea|borne** (sē′bôrn′, -bōrn′), *adj.* **1** conveyed by sea; carried on the sea: *Authorities reported today that tens of thousands of penguins were dying on islands off the Cape coast because their feathers were clogged with seaborne oil* (New York Times). **2** carried or floating on the sea: *a seaborne ship.*

**sea-bot|tom** (sē′bot′əm), *n.* the bottom or lowest depth of the sea.

**sea|bound** (sē′bound′), *adj.* **1** bounded by the sea: *a seabound castle.* **2** bound for the sea; on the way to the sea or seashore: *a seabound train, a seabound voyage.*

**sea bread**, = hardtack.

**sea bream**, **1** any one of certain edible marine fishes belonging to the same family as the porgies, especially a common European species. **2** any fish belonging to this family.

**sea breeze**, a breeze blowing from the sea toward the land: *Late every afternoon, practically the year round, a stiff sea breeze blows in from the Pacific, carrying with it on many days fog heavy enough to require windshield wipers and headlights* (Harper's).

**sea buckthorn**, a thorny shrub growing on the coasts and Alpine rivers of Europe, having silvery leaves and abundant orange or yellow berries with an acid flavor.

**SEAC** (no periods), Standard Eastern Automatic Computer (a high-speed, electronic computing machine used by the National Bureau of Standards).

**sea calf**, the common hair seal of the North American coasts; harbor seal.

**sea canary**, the beluga whale, in reference to the trilling sound it makes.

**sea captain**, the master (captain) of a seagoing vessel, especially a merchant vessel; man whose profession is to command at sea.

**sea cave**, a cave formed by the action of waves against a rocky shore.

**sea change**, **1** a change brought about by the sea: *Nothing of him that doth fade but doth suffer a sea change into something rich and strange* (Shakespeare). **2** *Figurative.* any radical or complete change; transformation: *In its transition to the screen ... Shaw's novel ... has undergone quite a sea change* (New Yorker).

**sea-change** (sē′chānj′), *v.i.*, **-changed**, **-changing.** to undergo a sea change; be completely transformed: *... living bones that had sea-changed into pearls and coral* (Hannah Arendt).

**sea chest**, **1** a seaman's chest or box for his clothing and other belongings. **2** = seacock.

**sea cliff**, a cliff facing the sea, usually formed by the erosive action of waves at its base. See picture under **peninsula**.

**sea coal**, *British Archaic.* coal dug from the earth and formerly carried to London by sea, as distinguished from charcoal.

**sea|coast** (sē′kōst′), *n.* the land along the sea; coast: *the seacoast of North America.*

**sea|cock** (sē′kok′), *n.* **1** (in a marine steam engine) a cock or valve in the injection water pipe which passes from the sea to the condenser. It is supplementary to the ordinary cock at the condenser and is intended to serve in case this should be damaged. **2** any cock or valve forming a connecting passage from a ship's hull to the sea: *Tuckfield opened a seacock, and the forward escape hatch began to fill with water* (Time).

**sea|cop|ter** (sē′kop′tər), *n.* a helicopter with a floating hull, that can operate from land or water. [< *sea* + (heli)*copter*]

**sea cow**, **1** any one of several large, fishlike, plant-eating mammals living in the sea. The manatee and dugong are two kinds of sea cow. **2** = walrus. **3** *Obsolete.* a hippopotamus.

**sea|craft** (sē′kraft′; -kräft′), *n., pl.* **-craft. 1** a seagoing vessel. **2** skill in navigation.

**sea crayfish** or **crawfish**, = spiny lobster.

**sea crow**, **1** = coot (def. 1). **2** = oyster catcher.

***sea cucumber**, any one of a group of small, spiny sea animals related to the starfishes, most of which have flexible bodies that look somewhat like cucumbers; holothurian.

***sea cucumber**

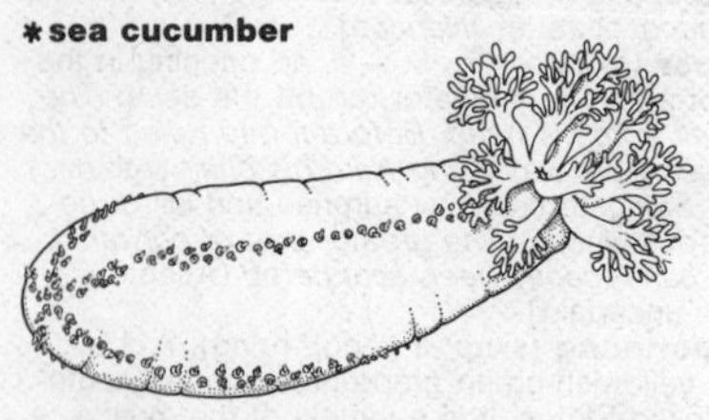

**sea devil**, **1** a large fish related to the shark; devilfish. **2** a shark having large, winglike fins; angelshark.

**sea dog**, **1** a sailor, especially one who has had long experience. **2** a privateer or pirate. **3a** the common or harbor seal. **b** = dogfish. **4** = fogdog.

**sea|drome** (sē′drōm′), *n.* a large floating structure providing a landing place at sea for aircraft (such as was projected during the 1920's for transoceanic flights). [< *sea* + (air)*drome*]

**sea duck**, any duck of a group including the scoters and eiders, members of which dive for their food, have a lobate hind toe and are found chiefly on salt water.

**sea dust**, *Geology.* dust of deserts, usually of brick-red color, borne away by the wind and descending at a long distance.

**Sea Dyak**, = Iban.

**sea eagle**, **1** any one of several eagles that feed mainly on fish, especially a species of northern Europe, and the Steller's sea eagle, found on islands off the Alaskan and Siberian coasts. **2** = osprey.

**sea-ear** (sē′ir′), *n.* = abalone.

**sea elephant**, either of two very large seals, the male of which has a trunklike snout; elephant seal.

**sea fan**, any one of a genus of fan-shaped corals, especially of the Caribbean and the Gulf of Mexico; gorgonia.

**sea|far|er** (sē′fãr′ər), *n.* **1** a sailor: *The people of Scandinavia have a long tradition as seafarers* (Lionel Casson). SYN: mariner, seaman. **2** a traveler on the sea.

**sea|far|ing** (sē′fãr′ing), *adj., n.* —*adj.* going, traveling, or working on the sea: *Sailors are seafaring men.* —*n.* **1** the business or calling of a sailor. **2** the act or fact of traveling by sea: *His novel is salt-encrusted in the best tradition of literary seafaring* (Newsweek).

**sea farmer**, = mariculturist.

**sea farming**, = mariculture.

**sea feather**, = sea pen.

**sea fight**, a fight between ships at sea; naval battle.

**sea fire**, phosphorescence at sea, such as that produced by noctilucae.

**sea floor**, the floor or bottom of a sea or ocean; seabed.

**sea-floor spreading** (sē′flôr′, -flōr′), the process by which the sea floor is being continuously formed and spread by upwellings from the earth's mantle along the mid-ocean ridges when crustal plates move apart, and continuously destroyed by the sinking of the sea floor into the mantle when plates push against each other: *In the study of sea-floor spreading and plate tectonics, continental margins assume special significance, for it is there that plate interactions or early stages of spreading occur* (Science News).

**sea|flow|er** (sē′flou′ər), *n.* a sea anemone or related organism.

**sea foam**, **1** foam of the sea. **2** = meerschaum.

**sea|food** (sē′füd′), *n.* saltwater fish and shellfish that are good to eat.

**sea|fowl** (sē′foul′), *n., pl.* **-fowls** or (*collectively*) **-fowl.** = sea bird.

**sea|front** (sē′frunt′), *n.* **1** land fronting the sea; oceanfront. **2** that portion or side of a building, piece of property, or the like, facing the sea.

**sea gate**, an entrance from the sea into a bay, harbor, or the like.

**sea|girt** (sē′gėrt′), *adj.* surrounded by the sea.

**sea god**, a god of the sea, such as Neptune or Nereus: *Proteus, that sea god who can change his shape at will ...* (Time).

**sea goddess**, a goddess of the sea, such as Amphitrite, wife of Poseidon.

**sea|go|ing** (sē′gō′ing), *adj., n.* —*adj.* **1** going by sea; seafaring. **2** fit for going to sea: *a powerful seagoing tug.* **3** = catadromous.
—*n.* a going or traveling by sea.

**sea gooseberry**, any radially symmetrical marine organism of a group resembling jellyfish, such as certain ctenophore.

**sea grant college** or **university**, *U.S.* an institution that receives a grant of money from the government to engage in oceanographic study and research. [patterned after *land grant college* or *university*]

**sea grape**, a tropical American shrub or small tree of the buckwheat family, having white flowers and attractive autumn foliage, and bearing bunches of grapelike fruit that are made into jelly and a beverage.

**sea grass**, any one of various grasses or grasslike plants that grow in the sea, such as the glasswort and eelgrass.

**sea green**, a light bluish green. SYN: aquamarine. —**sea-green′**, *adj.*

**sea gull**, any gull, especially one living on or near the sea.

**sea hare**, any one of a group of gastropod mollusks with a vestigial shell and four tentacles, the front pair of which resemble somewhat the ears of a hare.

**sea heath**, a heathlike shrub of European coasts.

**sea hedgehog**, = sea urchin.

**sea hog**, = porpoise.

**sea holly**, a coarse European herb of the parsley family, a variety of eryngo, with toothed or spiny leaves whose root was formerly candied for use as a sweetmeat.

**sea horizon**, the circle which bounds the view of the observer at sea.

***sea horse**, **1** a kind of small fish with a head suggesting that of a horse, and a prehensile tail, living in warm waters; hippocampus. The sea horses belong to the same family as the pipefish. **2** = walrus. **3** a sea animal in old stories with the foreparts of a horse and the hind parts of a fish. The Nereids are fabled to have used sea horses for riding, and Neptune to have used them for drawing his chariot. *Notice Neptune, though, taming a sea horse ... cast in bronze for me!* (Robert Browning). **4** a large, white-crested wave.

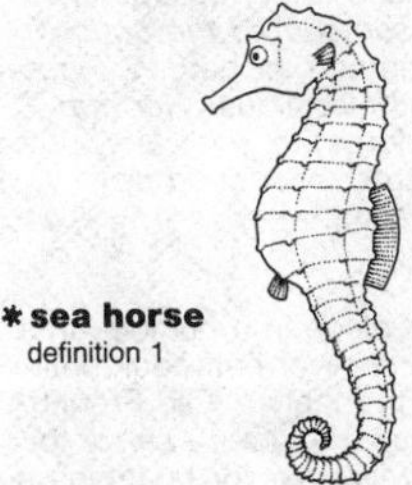

***sea horse**
definition 1

**sea ice**, frozen seawater. Sea ice has many saltwater pockets. *Both the theory and tests disprove the long-held rule that sea ice is only one-third as strong as fresh-water ice* (Science News Letter).

**sea-is|land cotton** (sē′ī′lənd), **1** a long-staple variety of cotton formerly grown on the islands off the coast of South Carolina and Georgia and now grown especially in the West Indies. **2** the plant producing it.

**sea kale**, a plant of the mustard family, growing near the sea, with large cabbagelike leaves; crambe. The leaf stems are blanched and eaten as a vegetable in certain countries of Europe.

**sea|kind|ly** (sē′kīnd′lē), *adj.* easy to handle at sea: *The ship proved seakindly.*

**sea king**, a Scandinavian pirate chief of the Middle Ages. [translation of Old Icelandic *sǣkonungr*]

**seal**[1] (sēl), *n., v.* —*n.* **1** a design stamped on a piece of wax or other soft material, used to show ownership or authenticity. The seal of the United States is attached to important government papers. **2** a stamp for marking things with such a design: *She has a seal with her initials on it, with which she stamps sealing wax to fasten her letters securely.* **3** a piece of wax, paper, or metal on which the design is stamped. **4** a thing that fastens or closes something tightly. **5** *Figurative.* something that secures; pledge: *under seal of secrecy.* **6** *Figurative.* something that settles or determines: *the seal of authority.* **7** *Figurative.* a mark; sign: *Sea sands are made beautiful by their bearing the seal of the motion of the waters* (John Ruskin). *The haughty ... passions that set their seal upon her brow ...* (Dickens). **8** a special kind of stamp: *Christmas seals, Easter seals.* **9** a small quantity of water left in a trap to prevent the escape of foul air from a sewer or drain. —*v.t.* **1** to mark (a document) with a seal; make binding by affixing seals; authenticate: *The treaty was signed and sealed by both governments.* **2** to stamp as an evidence of standard measure or quality or legal size: *to seal weights and measures.* **3** to close tightly; fasten; shut: *Seal the letter before mailing it. She sealed the jars of fruit. Every train passing through on the mainline ... had its windows sealed with steel shutters* (Newsweek). (*Figurative.*) *Her promise sealed her lips.* (*Figurative.*) *His eyes were sealed with sleep.* **4** to close up the cracks of: *They sealed the log cabin with clay.* **5** *Figurative.* to fix firmly: *But ah, she gave me never a look for her eyes were seal'd to the holy book* (Matthew Arnold). **6** *Figurative.* to settle; determine: *The judge's words sealed the prisoner's fate.* **7** *Figurative.* to give a sign that (a thing) is true: *to seal a promise with a kiss. They sealed their bargain by shaking hands.* **8** to set apart; decide beyond recall; destine: (*Figurative.*) *the God ... who had watched over the growth of a family into a nation, who had sealed that family for Himself ...* (Sir John R. Seeley). **9** (in Mormon use) to set apart and bind spiritually forever by a solemn ceremony, as in marriage. **10** *Electricity.* to bring into position so that the circuit is complete: *to seal a plug and jack.*

**seal off** (or **up**), to shut up within impenetrable barriers; make inaccessible: *a ship sealed up in ice. Zoo officials ... put the sad little ape in quarantine in a sealed-off room* (Time).

**set one's seal to**, **a** to put one's seal on: *The king set his seal to the decree.* **b** *Figurative.* to approve: *To this truth Mr. Hobbs sets his seal with all willingness imaginable* (Henry More).

**the seals**, *British.* the symbols of public office: *The King sent him to the Earl of Jersey, with a peremptory order to return the seals* (Philip Henry Stanhope).

**under seal**, authenticated or confirmed by affixing a seal: *If the agreement of the grantee is considered as under seal, ... it falls within the settled rule of the common law* (Supreme Court Reporter).

[< Old French *seel* < Vulgar Latin *sigellum* < Latin *sigillum* (diminutive), related to *sīgnum* a sign]

***seal**[2]
definition 1

fur seal

harbor seal

sea lion

related to seal

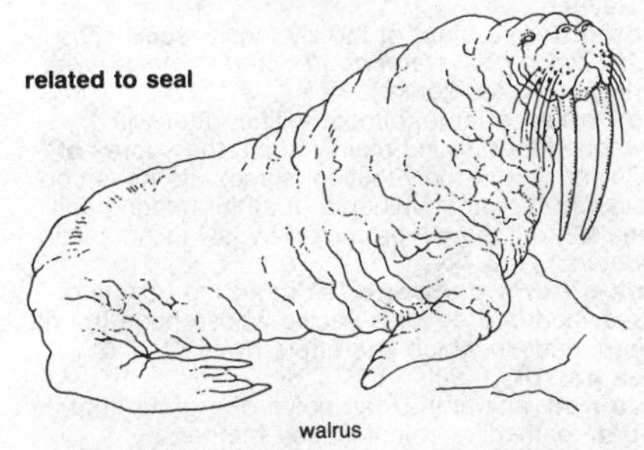

walrus

***seal**[2] (sēl), *n., pl.* **seals** or (*collectively for 1*) **seal**, *v.* —*n.* **1** a kind of sea animal with large flippers, usually living in cold regions. Seals are flesh-eating mammals with long bodies covered with thick fur or bristle. Some kinds are hunted only for their valuable fur, but the Eskimos use the blubber of seals for food and as a source of oil. Seals include the family of eared seals, such as the northern fur seal of the Bering Sea, and the family of earless or hair seals, such as the harbor seal of North American coasts. **2** the fur of the fur seal; sealskin. **3** some other fur used as a substitute for sealskin: *Hudson seal is obtained from the muskrat.* **4** leather made from the skin of a seal. **5** = seal brown.
—*v.i.* to hunt or take seals.
[Old English *sēolwes,* genitive of *seolh*] —**seal′like′**, *adj.*

**seal**[3] (sēl), *v.t.* = seel.

**Sea|lab** (sē′lab′), *n.* any one of several underwater vessels of the U.S. Navy designed to serve as habitats for aquanauts: *The goal of the Sealabs is to develop techniques whereby men can operate on the ocean floor* (New York Times). [< *Sea* + *lab*(oratory)]

**seal|a|ble** (sē′lə bəl), *adj.* that can be sealed: *a sealable paper bag.*

**sea ladder**, **1** a ladder made up of metal rungs fixed to a ship's side above the water line. **2** = Jacob's ladder (def. 2).

**sea lamprey**, a marine lamprey of the Atlantic coasts of Europe and North America which spawns in fresh water. It has become landlocked in the Great Lakes and certain other waters, where it is highly destructive of lake trout and other fish.

**sea lane**, a particular course or route regularly used by most ships when crossing an ocean or large area of water.

**seal|ant** (sē′lənt), *n.* a compound for sealing: *a paint sealant.*

**sea lavender**, any one of a group of mostly perennial herbs with many tiny, lavender, yellow, or multicolored flowers that retain their color long after being cut and dried; statice.

**sea lawyer**, *Informal.* a sailor inclined to find fault and to argue.

**seal brown**, a rich, dark-brown color. —**seal′-brown′**, *adj.*

**sea leather**, the skin, as of sharks, porpoises, or dogfishes, prepared to be used for the same purposes as ordinary leather.

**sealed** (sēld), *adj.* **1** authenticated or ratified by a seal. **2** guaranteed as to exactness, measure, quality, or the like, by a seal. **3** fastened with a seal. **4** *Figurative.* closed to knowledge; unknown.

**sealed-beam headlight** (sēld′bēm′), an automobile headlight in which filament, lens, and reflector form a single unit, insuring the correct focus of the filament and the constant reflecting power of the lens.

**sealed bid**, a confidential bid, as for a contract, usually submitted in a sealed envelope.

**sealed book**, something unknown or undiscoverable: *The young generation was always something of a sealed book to him* (John Galsworthy).

**sealed orders**, sealed written orders to be opened after leaving port, instructing the commander of a ship where to proceed on a voyage.

**sea legs**, *Informal.* legs accustomed to walking steadily on a rolling or pitching ship: *Michel, who had good sea legs, kept his balance to the movements of the craft* (Joseph Conrad).

**get one's sea legs**, to become accustomed to the motion of a ship, especially after an initial period of seasickness: *In addition to all this, I had not got my sea legs* (Richard Henry Dana).

**sea leopard**, a large, spotted seal of the southern and antarctic seas, that attacks little seals and penguins; leopard seal.

**seal|er**[1] (sē′lər), *n.* **1** a person or thing that seals. **2** a local or municipal official, appointed to examine and test weights and measures, scales, and other measuring devices for accuracy.

**seal|er**[2] (sē′lər), *n.* **1** a person who hunts seals. **2** a ship used for hunting seals.

**seal|er|y** (sē′lər ē), *n., pl.* **-er|ies**. **1** the act or occupation of hunting seals; sealing. **2** a place where seals are hunted.

**sea letter**, a document formerly issued by the civil authorities of a port in which a vessel was fitted out, certifying her nationality, and specifying the kind, quantity, ownership, and destination of her cargo.

**sea lettuce**, any one of a genus of green seaweeds whose fronds look like strips of lettuce. They are sometimes eaten.

**sea level**, the surface of the sea, especially when halfway between mean high and low water. Mountains, plains, and ocean beds are measured as so many feet or meters above or below sea level.

**sea|lift** (sē′lift′), *n.* a system of using ships for transportation of military personnel and equipment to places where land approaches are closed or inadequate.

**sea lily**, = crinoid.

**sea line**, **1** the horizon at sea; line where sea and sky seem to meet. **2** a long line for fishing in deep water.

**seal|ing** (sē′ling), *n.* the hunting and taking of seals, as an occupation or commercial undertaking.

**Pronunciation Key:** hat, āge, cãre, fär; let, ēqual, tėrm; it, īce; hot, ōpen, ôrder; **oi**l, **ou**t; cup, pu̇t, rüle; **ch**ild; lo**ng**; **th**in; **ᴛʜ**en; **zh**, measure;
**ə** represents **a** in about, **e** in taken, **i** in pencil, **o** in lemon, **u** in circus.

**sealing wax**, a hard, brittle substance made of resin and shellac which becomes soft when heated, used for sealing letters, packages, or other containers.

**sea lion**, a large, eared seal, especially of the northern Pacific coast. There are several kinds. Sea lions are sometimes trained for use in circus and carnival acts. See picture under **seal**[2].

**seal limb** or **limbs**, = phocomelia.

**sea loch**, *Scottish.* loch (def. 2).

**seal point**, a variety of Siamese cat having a cream-colored body and dark-brown points (ears, face, feet, and tail). [< *seal* (brown) + *point* (def. 8)]

**seal ring**, a finger ring engraved with a seal design so that it can be used as a signet ring.

**seals** (sēlz), *n.pl.* See under **seal**[1].

**seal|skin** (sēl′skin′), *n., adj.* —*n.* **1** the skin of a fur seal, prepared for use: *a coat of brown sealskin.* **2** a garment or article made of this fur. —*adj.* made of sealskin.

**sea lungwort**, a fleshy herb of the borage family, growing along the northern coasts of North America, Europe, and Asia; oyster plant; oyster leaf.

**Sea|ly|ham terrier**, or **Sea|ly|ham** (sē′lē ham, -əm), *n.* any small Welsh dog of a breed with short legs, a square jaw, and a rough, shaggy, white coat, sometimes marked with lemon, tan, or brown on the head and ears. It resembles the Scottish terrier but regularly has the tail docked. [< *Sealyham,* an estate in Pembrokeshire, Wales, where the breed was originated]

**seam**[1] (sēm), *n., v.* —*n.* **1** the line formed by sewing together the edges of two pieces of cloth, canvas, leather, or the like: *the seams of a coat, the seams of a sail.* **2** any line where edges join: *The seams of the boat must be filled in or they will leak.* **3** any mark or line like a seam. **4** *Geology.* a layer or stratum, especially of a mineral; bed: *a seam of coal.* **5** a line of purled stitches in knitting. **6** *Dialect.* sewing; needlework.
—*v.t.* **1** to sew the seam or seams of; join with a seam or seams. **2** to mark (a surface, such as the face) with lines or indentations; furrow, scar, or wrinkle: *Marshes, seamed and crossed with narrow creeks ...* (John Greenleaf Whittier). **3** (in knitting) to make a seam or apparent seam in; purl.
—*v.i.* **1** to crack open. **2** to form a seam in knitting; purl. **3** *Dialect.* to sew.
**burst at the seams**, to be too full or crowded: *With the highest birth rate in the world ... the island, which is only twenty-six miles long and fourteen miles wide, was bursting at the seams* (Atlantic).
**come apart at the seams**, to fall apart; break up: *If he fails, the party might come apart at the seams* (Harper's).
[Old English *sēam.* See related etym. at **sew**.]

**seam**[2] (sēm), *n. Dialect.* fat; grease; lard. [< Old French *saim* < Vulgar Latin *sagīmen* < Latin *sagīna*]

**sea maid**, **1** = mermaid. **2** a goddess or nymph of the sea.

**sea maiden**, = sea maid.

**sea|man** (sē′mən), *n., pl.* **-men. 1** a sailor; mariner: *a fine seaman.* **2a** a sailor who is not an officer. **b** *U.S. Navy and Coast Guard.* an enlisted man ranking below a petty officer.

**seaman apprentice**, an enlisted man in the U.S. Navy or Coast Guard who ranks next below a seaman.

**sea|man|like** (sē′mən līk′), *adj., adv.* —*adj.* like a seaman; having or showing the skill of a good seaman: *seamanlike skill in tying knots. Seamanlike precautions were taken to safeguard the lives of passengers.*
—*adv.* in a seamanlike manner.

**sea|man|ly** (sē′mən lē), *adj., adv.* = seamanlike.

**seaman recruit**, the lowest ranking seaman in the U.S. Navy or Coast Guard, below a seaman apprentice.

**sea|man|ship** (sē′mən ship), *n.* **1** skill in navigating or managing a ship at sea. **2** the skill of a good seaman.

**sea|mark** (sē′märk′), *n.* **1** a lighthouse, beacon, or other landmark that can be seen from the sea, used as a guide for a ship's course. **2** a line on the shore that shows the upper limit of the tide.

**sea mat**, a bryozoan that forms colonies resembling flat, matted seaweed.

**seam bowler**, a bowler in cricket who uses the seam of the ball so as to make it swerve in flight.

**seamed** (sēmd), *adj.* **1** joined with a seam or seams, as by sewing. **2** cleft, furrowed, or marked with seams: *a seamed face. A great ship, an East Indiaman, with rusty, seamed, blistered sides ...* (George W. Curtis).

**sea|men** (sē′mən), *n.pl.* sailors.

**seam|er** (sē′mər), *n.* **1** a person or thing that seams. **2** a kind of sewing machine for seaming fabrics together. **3** a machine for bending two pieces of sheet metal to unite them in a seam or joint. **4** *Cricket.* a seam bowler.

**sea mew**, a sea gull, especially the common gull of Europe.

**sea mile**, = nautical mile.

**sea milkwort**, a plant of the primrose family, common on the seacoast; milkwort.

**seam|i|ness** (sē′mē nis), *n.* seamy state or quality.

**seam|less** (sēm′lis), *adj.* without a seam or seams: *seamless stockings.* —**seam′less|ly**, *adv.* —**seam′less|ness**, *n.*

**sea monster**, **1** a fabulous marine animal of terrifying proportions and shape. **2** a huge fish, cetacean, or the like.

**sea moss**, **1** = bryozoan. **2** a seaweed, such as carrageen.

**sea|mount** (sē′mount′), *n.* a tall, cone-shaped hill or mountain arising from the sea-bottom with its summit beneath the surface of the sea, and often having a flat top, as a guyot does.

**sea mouse**, any large polychaete sea worm of a group covered with long, fine, hairlike setae, that give it a mouselike appearance.

**seam|ster** (sēm′stər), *n.* a person whose occupation is sewing (originally applied to a woman, but now only to a man); tailor. Also, **sempster**. [Old English *sēamestre* (originally), feminine of *sēamere* tailor < *sēam* seam[1]]

**seam|ster|ing** (sēm′stər ing), *n.* the work of a seamstress.

**seam|stress** (sēm′stris), *n.* **1** a woman whose work is sewing. **2** a girl or woman who sews; needlewoman: *an excellent seamstress, a born seamstress.* Also, **sempstress**.

**seam|y** (sē′mē), *adj.,* **seam|i|er, seam|i|est. 1** having or showing a seam or seams: *the seamy side of a garment.* **2** *Figurative.* least pleasant; worst: *A policeman sees much of the seamy side of life.*

**Sean|ad Eir|eann** (shan′əᴛʜ ãr′ən), or **Sean-ad**, *n.* the upper house of the legislature (Oireachtas) of the Irish Republic. [< Irish *Seanad Eireann*]

**sé|ance** (sā′äns), *n.* **1** a meeting of people trying to communicate with spirits of the dead by the help of a medium: *... attending spiritual lectures and séances, whenever a noted medium visited the place* (John Hay). **2** a sitting or session, as of a learned society or other body of persons. [< French *séance* a sitting < *seoir* to sit < Latin *sedēre*]

**sea necklace**, a chain of egg cases of certain conchs that look like leathery wafers strung on a cord.

**sea nettle**, a jellyfish, so called because of the stinging organs (nematocysts) in its tentacles.

**sea nymph**, a nymph supposed to inhabit the sea; Nereid.

**sea oats**, a tall grass with oatlike panicles, growing along the southern coast of the United States.

**sea onion**, a plant of the lily family; squill: *The sea onion grows around the Mediterranean Sea* (Harold N. Moldenke).

**sea otter**, a large, almost extinct otter with webbed feet, found mainly along the shores of California and the Aleutian Islands. Its fur is considered the most valuable of all fur-bearing animals, but it is now protected by law in American waters.

**sea-ot|ter's cabbage** (sē′ot′ərz), a very large seaweed of the North Pacific whose huge fronds form beds in which sea otters dwell.

**sea|parrot**, = puffin.

**sea pen**, any anthozoan polyp of a group that form featherlike colonies; sea feather.

**sea|perch** (sē′pėrch′), *n.* any small, mostly marine fish of a family that bears live young; surf fish.

**sea pie**[1], a sailors' dish made of meat, vegetables, and dumpling, baked with a crust.

**sea pie**[2], *Especially British.* the oyster catcher (so called from its pied coloration).

**sea|piece** (sē′pēs′), *n.* a picture representing a scene at sea: *... a piece representing Sir F. Drake's action in the year 1580, an excellent seapiece* (John Evelyn).

**sea pigeon**, a black guillemot having the size of a small duck and a plump, dovelike appearance; pigeon guillemot.

**sea pink**, any one of a group of low evergreen plants of temperate regions bearing usually pink flowers; thrift.

**sea plain**, a plain produced by erosive action, as of waves, currents, or tides.

**sea|plane** (sē′plān′), *n.* **1** an airplane that can rise from and alight on water, especially one which has floats; hydroplane. **2** an airplane that can take off from or land on either land or water; amphibian.

**sea|poose** (sē′püs, -pu̇s), *n.* = sea puss.

**sea porcupine**, any one of various globefishes with skin covered with spiny processes; burrfish; porcupine fish.

**sea|port** (sē′pôrt′, -pōrt′), *n.* a port or harbor on the seacoast; city or town with a harbor that ships can reach from the sea: *San Francisco and New Orleans are seaports. Seaports, the termini of ocean trade routes, are both the creations and creators of such routes* (White and Renner).

**sea post**, the postal service conducted at sea, concerned with the sorting of mail on ocean steamers so as to be in readiness for prompt transmission to the various destinations on arrival in port.

**sea power**, **1** a nation having a strong navy. **2** naval strength.

**sea purse**, the horny case or pouch that skates, rays, or certain sharks secrete around their eggs to protect them and anchor them especially to rocks or weeds.

**sea puss**, *U.S.* a swirl of the undertow, making a small whirlpool on the surface of the water, which is dangerous to bathers. [American English, alteration (by folk etymology) of earlier *seapoose* < Algonkian (Delaware) *sepuus, sipus* brook, small river]

**sea|quake** (sē′kwāk′), *n.* a sudden agitation of the sea caused by a volcanic eruption or earthquake at the bottom of the sea.

**sear**[1] (sir), *v., n., adj.* —*v.t.* **1a** to burn or char the surface of: *The hot iron seared the cloth. The trees were seared by lightning.* **b** to brown (meat) very quickly in a hot oven or pan: *to sear a roast.* **SYN:** See syn. under **burn**. **2** *Figurative.* to make hard and unfeeling: *a more seared and callous conscience than even Nero himself* (Henry Fielding). **3** to cause to dry up; wither; blight: *The hot summer sun seared the grain.*
—*v.i.* **1** to become dry, burned, or hard. **2** *Figurative.* to become hardened or callous: *Her conscience sears* (William Morris).
[Old English *sēarian,* verb < *sēar* dried up]
—*n.* a mark made by searing.
—*adj.* dried up; sere.
[Old English *sēar*]

**sear**[2] (sir), *n.* the pivoted piece in a gunlock that holds the hammer at full cock or half cock until released by the trigger. [probably < Old French *serre* something that grasps; a lock < *serrer* to grasp, ultimately < Latin *sera* bar for fastening a door]

**sea raven**, a large fish with a long, spiny dorsal fin, a variety of sculpin common on the North Atlantic coast of America.

**search** (sėrch), *v., n.* —*v.i.* to try to find by looking; seek: *We searched all day for the lost kitten.*
—*v.t.* **1** to go over carefully in trying to find something. **2** to examine, especially for something concealed: *to search one's baggage. The boys searched the entire cave for the hidden treasure.* **3** to look through (as writings or records) in order to discover if certain things are there: *Search the scriptures* (John 5:39). **4** to examine by probing: *The doctor searched the wound for the bullet.* **5** to pierce; penetrate, as of wind, cold, or firearms. **6** *Archaic.* to look for; try to find: *My fancy ranging thro' and thro', to search a meaning for the song* (Tennyson).
—*n.* **1** the act of searching; examination: *to give up the search, the search after knowledge. I found my book after a long search.* **2** the act of stopping and examining a neutral vessel on the high seas in time of war to discover if it is violating neutrality.
**in search of**, trying to find; looking for: *The boys went in search of their lost dog. [He] has been voyaging lately in search of fresh talent* (Manchester Guardian Weekly).
**search me**, *U.S. Slang.* **a** I don't have it: *"Where is my book?" "Search me."* **b** I don't know: *"Why does he act so strangely?" "Search me."*
**search out**, **a** to find by searching: *He searched out all the facts of the case.* **b** to look for: *His primary object is to search out the truth* (Weekly Times).
[< Old French *cerchier* < Late Latin *circāre* go about, wander < Latin *circus* circle] —**search′a|ble**, *adj.* —**search′er**, *n.*
—*Syn. v.i., v.t.* **1, 2, 3 Search, explore, rummage** mean to look through a place for something. **Search** implies looking for something known or thought to be there: *We searched the woods for the lost child.* **Explore** implies looking for whatever may be there: *Geologists explored the newly discovered mineral deposit.* **Rummage** suggests searching among the contents and moving them about: *He rummaged through the drawers looking for a map.*

**search coil**, a small coil of insulated wire used for measuring the strength of magnetic fields by means of the currents induced in the coil.

**search|ing** (sėr′ching), *adj.* **1** examining carefully; thorough: *a searching investigation.* **2** keenly observant; penetrating: *a searching gaze or look; ... the searching eye of heaven* (Shakespeare). **3** piercing; sharp; keen: *a searching wind.* —**search′ing|ly**, *adv.* —**search′ing|ness**, *n.*

**search|light** (sėrch′līt′), *n.* **1** a powerful light that can throw a very bright beam of light in any direction. **2** the beam of light so thrown: *The searchlights had begun their nightly wanderings* (John Galsworthy).

**search party**, a group of persons searching for someone or something lost or hiding.

**search warrant**, a written court order authorizing the search of a house or building, as for stolen goods, criminals, and illegal narcotics.

**sear|ing** (sir′ing), *adj.* that sears; burning; scorching. —**sear′ing|ly**, *adv.*

**searing iron**, an iron which is heated for use as in cauterizing or branding.

**sea risk**, risk or hazard at sea; danger of injury or destruction by the sea.

**sea robber**, a pirate. **SYN**: corsair, buccaneer.

**sea robin**, **1** any fish of a group of marine gurnards with a large head, mailed cheeks, and separate pectoral rays, especially certain reddish or brown American species. **2** = red-breasted merganser.

**sea room**, space at sea free from obstruction, in which a ship can easily and safely sail, tack, or turn around: *The sloop ... at length ... recovered sea room enough to weather the Point of Warroch* (Scott).

**sea route**, **1** a path or course followed by or mapped out for ships: *Whenever it is decided that a sea-route is "essential to the trade and economy of the nation," ships using the route are entitled to a subsidy* (Atlantic). **2** markings on a chart giving point of departure, course, and destination for a ship's voyage.

**sea rover**, **1** = pirate. **2** a pirate ship.

**sea salt**, salt (sodium chloride) obtained by the evaporation of seawater.

**sea|scape** (sē′skāp), *n.* **1** a picture of a scene or scenery at sea: *The work in the current showing consists principally of landscapes, seascapes, and still lifes* (New Yorker). **SYN**: marine. **2** a view of scenery on the sea: *The landing ... offers a large, beautiful seascape* (Atlantic). [< *sea* + *scape*[3]]

**sea scorpion**, **1** = eurypterid. **2** = sculpin. **3** = scorpionfish.

**sea scout**, a boy trained in seamanship by the Boy Scout organization.

**sea scouting**, training in seamanship by the Boy Scout organization.

**sea serpent**, **1** a huge, snakelike animal said to have been repeatedly seen at sea. **2** = sea snake (def. 1).

**Sea Serpent**, the southern constellation Hydra.

**sea shell**, or **sea|shell** (sē′shel′), *n.* the shell of any sea animal, especially a mollusk, such as an oyster, conch, or abalone.

**sea|shore** (sē′shôr′, -shōr′), *n., adj.* —*n.* **1** the land at the edge of a sea; shore; coast: *The waves broke over the seashore damaging the coastal road and many houses.* **SYN**: seacoast. **2** the area between the lines of ordinary high tide and ordinary low tide.
—*adj.* of or at the seashore: *a seashore resort.*

**sea|sick** (sē′sik′), *adj.* sick because of a ship's motion.

**sea|sick|ness** (sē′sik′nis), *n.* sickness caused by a ship's motion.

**sea|side** (sē′sīd′), *n., adj.* —*n.* the land along the sea; seacoast; seashore: *a hotel at the seaside.*
—*adj.* of or at the seaside: *a seaside hotel.*

**seaside plantain**, any one of various rushlike plantains found especially on beaches and cliffs, at the seashore. The leaves of some have been used in medicine to lessen inflammation.

**seaside sparrow**, a dingy, grayish sparrow with a yellow mark in front of the eye, found in saltwater marshes from Massachusetts to Florida and Texas.

**sea slug**, **1** any marine gastropod of a group lacking shells in the adult state, and somewhat resembling land slugs; nudibranch. **2** = sea cucumber.

**sea snail**, a marine gastropod with a spiral shell resembling a helix, such as the periwinkle.

**sea snake**, **1** any one of a family of poisonous snakes with finlike tails that live in tropical seas: *The true sea snakes have a poison as deadly as that of the cobra* (Science News Letter). **2** = sea serpent (def. 1).

**sea soldier**, = marine.

***sea|son** (sē′zən), *n., v.* —*n.* **1** one of the four periods of the year; spring, summer, autumn, or winter. Each season begins astronomically at an equinox or solstice, but popularly at various dates in different climates. See diagram below. **2** a period of the year with reference to the particular conditions, as of weather or temperature, that characterize it: *a most extraordinary wet and cold season* (John Evelyn). **3** any period of time marked by something special or characteristic: *the holiday season, the harvest season, a season of peace.* **4** the time when something is occurring, active, at its best, or in fashion: *the hunting, fishing, or baseball season, the theatrical season, the oyster season, the London or Florida season.* **5** *Figurative.* **a** period or time: *at a certain season of our life ...* (Thoreau). **b** a suitable or fit time: *But that was no season for internal dissensions* (Macaulay).
—*v.t.* **1** to add salt, pepper, spices, herbs, or other flavoring to (food); improve the flavor of: *to season soup with salt.* **2** *Figurative.* to give interest or character to: *to season conversation with wit.* **3** to make fit for use by a period of keeping or treatment: *Wood is seasoned for building by drying and hardening it.* (*Figurative.*) *Knowledge and timber shouldn't be much used till they are seasoned* (Oliver Wendell Holmes). **SYN**: age, mature, ripen. **4a** to make fit physically: *an extremely vigorous person ... tanned and seasoned by the life of his class, by the yachting, hunting, and shooting* (Mrs. Humphry Ward). **SYN**: harden. **b** *Figurative: Soldiers are seasoned to battle by experience in war.* **SYN**: accustom, train, inure, habituate, acclimate. **5** *Figurative.* to make less severe; soften; moderate; temper: *Season justice with mercy.* **SYN**: alleviate.
—*v.i.* **1** to become fit for use. **2** to become hardened or inured.
**for a season**, for a time; for an indefinite period: *Thou shalt be blind, not seeing the sun for a season* (Acts 13:11).
**in good season**, early enough: *The two young men desired to get back again in good season* (Dickens).
**in season**, **a** at the right or proper time: *Mr. March has to be home by a certain day; and we shall just get back in season* (William Dean Howells). **b** in the time or condition, as for eating or hunting: *Winter apples are in season now.* **c** early enough: *News of this intention reached him in season to effect his escape* (W. Walker).
**in season and out of season**, at all times: *He will be repeating his folly in season and out of season, until at last it has a hearing* (Arthur Helps).
**out of season**, not in season: *Oysters are considered out of season from May through August. So spake the fervent Angel, but his zeal none seconded, as out of season judg'd* (Milton).
[Middle English *sesun* < Old French *seison* < Latin *satiō, -ōnis* a sowing < *serere* to sow]
► **seasons**. *Winter, spring, summer, fall,* and *autumn* are not capitalized except for stylistic emphasis, as sometimes in poetry.

**sea|son|a|ble** (sē′zə nə bəl, sēz′nə-), *adj.* **1** suitable to the season: *Hot weather is seasonable in July.* **2** coming at the right or proper time: *The Red Cross brought seasonable aid to the flood victims.* **SYN**: opportune, timely. **3** in good season; early: *to leave at a seasonable hour.* —**sea′son|a|ble|ness**, *n.*

**sea|son|a|bly** (sē′zə nə blē, sēz′nə-), *adv.* in due time or season; at the right moment; sufficiently early: *to sow or plant seasonably.*

**sea|son|al** (sē′zə nəl), *adj.* **1** having to do with the seasons: *seasonal variations in the weather.* **2a** depending on a season: *a seasonal business.* **b** employed only during a certain season: *a seasonal worker.* **3** happening at regular intervals; periodical: *Monsoon rains are seasonal in Asia and Africa.*

**sea|son|al|i|ty** (sē′zə nal′ə tē), *n.* the quality or condition of being seasonal; periodicity: *This masterly analysis of the agricultural implications of seasonality deserves serious study* (New Scientist).

**sea|son|al|ly** (sē′zə nə lē), *adv.* according to season; periodically.

**sea|soned** (sē′zənd), *adj.* **1a** matured, hardened, or accustomed by some process of seasoning: *seasoned timber, seasoned troops.* **b** *Figurative: This was the finding last week of the seasoned political observers* (Newsweek). **SYN**: experienced, trained. **2** flavored with seasoning.

**sea|son|er** (sē′zə nər), *n.* **1** a person or thing that seasons. **2** *U.S.* a fisherman who hires for the season. **3** *U.S. Informal.* a loafer; beachcomber.

**sea|son|ing** (sē′zə ning, sēz′ning), *n.* **1** something that gives a better flavor to food. Salt, pepper, spices, and herbs are seasonings. **SYN**: condiment. **2** *Figurative.* something that gives interest or character: *We like conversation with a seasoning of humor.*

**season ticket**, a ticket or pass that gives its holder certain privileges for the season or for a specified period, such as the right to attend a series of games or entertainments, or to make a daily trip on a railroad for a stated period of time.

**sea spider**, **1** any one of a group of tiny spiderlike marine arthropods. **2** = spider crab.

**sea squirt**, **1** any one of a class of small, soft-bodied marine animals of the tunicate subphylum that squirt water when they contract; a simple ascidian: *The salient contradiction here is between the adult sea squirt, which is anchored to a rock, and its free-swimming and seemingly much more advanced and go-ahead larvae* (Observer). **2** = tunicate.

**sea stack**, a sharp, isolated hill rising from the sea-bottom.

**sea star**, **1** = starfish. **2** any star which guides mariners at sea.

**sea step**, one of a set of narrow steps on the side of a ship, used in going on board from a boat when the side ladders are unshipped.

**sea swallow**, = tern.

**sea swell**, a wave of symmetrical form which has outrun the wind which produced it.

**seat**[1] (sēt), *n., v.* —*n.* **1** something to sit on. Chairs, stools, benches, and sofas are seats. *Take a seat, please.* **2** a place to sit: *Can you find a seat on the train?* **3a** a place in which one has the right to sit: *Our seats are in the fifth row of the first balcony. Please reserve a seat on the next airplane for me.* **b** *Figurative.* a right to sit as a member, or the position of being a member: *a seat on the stock exchange, a seat in Congress.* **4** that part of a chair, stool, bench, or the like, on which one sits: *This bench has a broken seat.* **5** that part of the body on which one sits, or the clothing covering it: *The seat of his trousers was patched.* **6** manner of sitting on horseback: *That rider has a good seat.* **7** that on which anything rests or appears to rest; base.
—*v.t.* **1** to set or place on a seat or seats; cause to sit down: *to seat oneself at the piano. He seated himself in the most comfortable chair.* **2** to have seats for (a specified number): *Our school auditorium seats one thousand pupils.* **3a** to provide with a seat or seats: *to seat a delegation at a convention.* **b** *Figurative.* to establish or give the right to sit: *He was ... opposed to seating the Chinese Communists in the United Nations* (New York Times). **4** to put a seat on (as a chair or trousers).

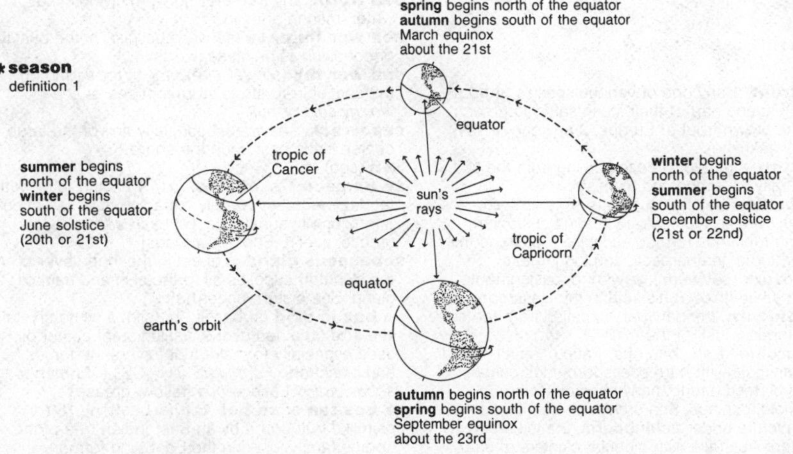

**be seated**, **a** to sit down: *Please be seated.* **b** to be sitting: *He was seated in A Chariot of an inestimable value* (Shakespeare).
[< Scandinavian (compare Old Icelandic *sǣti*)]
—**seat′less**, *adj.*

**seat**² (sēt), *n., v.* —*n.* **1** an established place or center: *A university is a seat of learning.* **2** a city or place in which a government, throne, or the like is established; capital: *Our county seat has a large high school. The seat of our government is in Washington, D.C.* **3a** the throne of a king, bishop, or the like. **b** *Figurative.* the authority or dignity of a king, bishop, or the like. **4** a residence; home: *The family seat of the Howards is in Sussex, England.* SYN: abode. **5** location; situation; site: *the seat of a disease. The seat of ethics is in our hearts, not in our minds* (Atlantic).
—*v.t.* to fix in a particular or proper place; locate. **be seated**, to be situated in a certain position or place; be located: *London ... is seated on clay* (Thomas Henry Huxley).
[probably extended use of *seat*¹; influenced by uses of Latin *sēdes*]

**sea tangle**, any one of various brown seaweeds.

**seat belt**, a strap attached to the seat of an automobile or airplane, and buckled across the occupant's lap to hold him in the seat in the event of a crash, jolt, or bump; safety belt.

**-seated**, *combining form.* having a ___ seat or seats: *Two-seated = having two seats.*

**seat er** (sē′tər), *n.* **1** a person who seats. **2** *U.S. Historical.* a person who assigned seats at a meeting of settlers or citizens.

**seat ing** (sē′ting), *n.* **1** the act of providing with a seat or seats. **2a** the arrangement of seats, as in a building or for a party. **b** the seats themselves. **3** material for the seats, as of chairs. **4a** a support. **b** a part resting on a support.

**seat mate** (sēt′māt′), *n.* a person sitting next to one on a bus, train, aircraft, or the like.

**seat-mile** (sēt′mīl′), *n.* one mile multiplied by the number of seats in a plane, used as a unit in determining costs, profits, or the like, in air transportation: *A fifty-seat plane flying a 1,000 mile trip flies 50,000 seat-miles.*

**SEATO** or **Sea to** (sē′tō), *n.* Southeast Asia Treaty Organization (group of seven nations, consisting of Australia, France, Great Britain, New Zealand, the Philippines, Thailand, and the United States, that signed a treaty in 1954 for common defense in southeastern Asia; it was abolished in 1977).

**seat-of-the-pants** (sēt′əv ŦHə pants′), *adj. Slang.* **1** experienced in navigating without instruments: *a seat-of-the-pants bush flier.* **2** based upon accumulated experience: *The architect ... must still have the capacity for a fair measure of seat-of-the-pants design* (New Scientist).

**seat pack**, a parachute attached to the wearer's seat instead of his back or chest.

***sea train**, a seagoing vessel, with tracks on its deck, for the transport of railroad cars, used especially in coastal traffic.

***sea train**

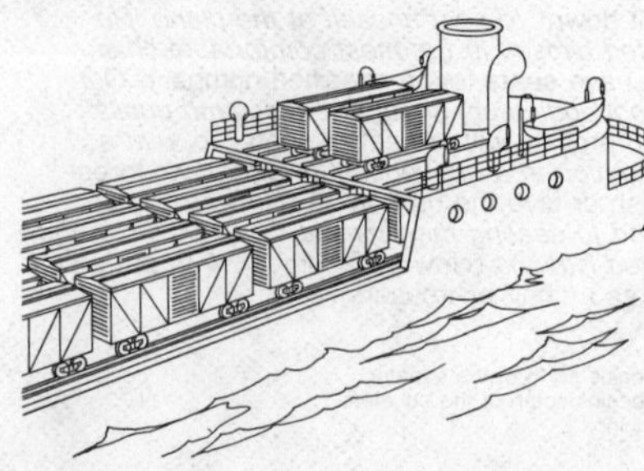

**sea trout**, **1** any one of various species of trout which spend part of their life in salt water, such as the brown trout of Europe. **2** any one of several weakfishes.

**sea turn**, a gale or breeze coming from the sea, generally accompanied by mists.

**sea turtle**, any one of various large turtles or tortoises living in the sea; any marine chelonian, having the limbs formed as flippers, such as the green turtle, leatherback, and loggerhead.

**seat work** (sēt′wėrk′), *n.* work or assignments that a child does at his seat in the classroom.

**sea unicorn**, the narwhal, so called from the single hornlike tusk of the male.

**sea urchin**, **1** any one of a group of small, round sea animals with hard shells formed of calcareous plates bearing many movable spines; echinoid; echinus. Sea urchins are echinoderms. See picture under **echinoderm**. **2** a tall shrub of western Australia with globular clusters of crimson flowers whose yellow styles project beyond the perianth.

**sea view** (sē′vyü′), *n.* **1** a view or prospect of the sea, or at sea: *a room with a seaview.* **2** a picture representing a scene at sea; seascape.

**sea wall**, a strong wall or embankment made especially to keep the waves from wearing away the shore or to act as a breakwater: *Sea walls to protect the Netherlands against flooding from the sea were the unanimous recommendation of the Government's Delta Commission* (Warren E. Howland).

**sea walnut**, any one of various ctenophores resembling a walnut in shape.

**sea wan** (sē′wən), *n.* loose or unstrung beads made from shells, once used by certain tribes of North American Indians as money. Also, **sewan**. [earlier *sewan* < Algonkian (Narragansett) *siwan* scattered, (literally) unstrung <*siwen* he scatters]

**sea want** (sē′wənt), *n.* = seawan.

**sea ward** (sē′wərd), *adv., adj., n.* —*adv., adj.* toward the sea: *a seaward breeze* (adj.). *Our house faces seaward. The river glided seaward* (Robert Louis Stevenson) (adv.).
—*n.* the direction toward the sea or away from land: *The island lies a mile to seaward.*

**sea wards** (sē′wərdz), *adv.* = seaward.

**sea ware** (sē′wãr′), *n.* seaweed, especially coarse seaweed used as manure. [Old English *sǣwār* < *sǣ* sea + *wār* alga]

**sea wasp**, a large jellyfish of the South Pacific and Indian oceans whose sting is very painful and often fatal.

**sea wa ter** (sē′wôt′ər, -wot′-), *n.* the salt water of the sea or ocean: *Seawater can get as cold as 28 degrees without freezing because of the salt in solution* (Science News Letter).

**sea way** (sē′wā′), *n.* **1** an inland waterway that connects with the open sea and is deep enough to permit ocean shipping: *Ocean-going freighters reach Detroit and Chicago by passing through the St. Lawrence Seaway.* **2** a way over the sea, especially a regular shipping lane. **3** the sea as a means of communication; the open sea. **4** the progress of a ship through the waves; headway: *to lose seaway.* **5** a rough sea: *a very safe boat ... buoyant and clever in a seaway* (Robert Louis Stevenson).

***sea weed** (sē′wēd′), *n.* any plant or plants growing in the sea, especially any one of various algae growing in the sea.

***seaweed**

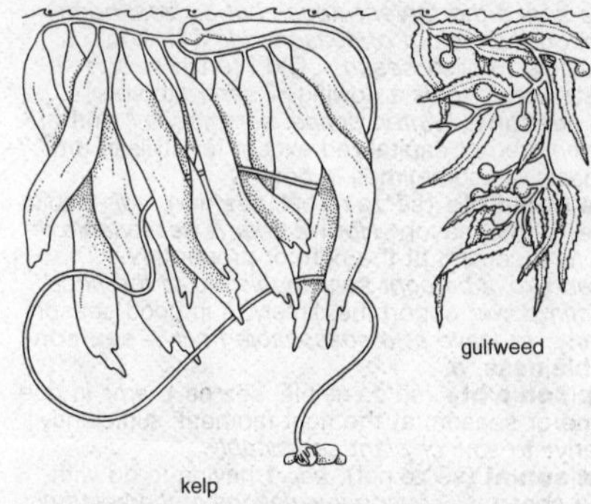


**sea whip**, a gorgonian coral of slender, straight, or spiral shape that has small branches or is branchless.

**sea wind**, a wind blowing from the sea toward the land.

**sea wolf**, **1** = pirate. **2** a privateering vessel.

**sea worm**, any free-moving worm living in salt water; marine annelid.

**sea wor thi ness** (sē′wėr′ŦHē nis), *n.* the quality or condition of being seaworthy.

**sea wor thy** (sē′wėr′ŦHē), *adj.* fit for sailing on the sea; able to stand storms at sea: *a seaworthy ship or hull.*

**sea wrack**, seaweed, especially any of the large, coarse kinds cast upon the shore.

**Seb** (seb), *n.* = Geb.

**se ba ceous** (si bā′shəs), *adj.* **1** having to do with fat; fatty; greasy. SYN: oily, oleaginous. **2** secreting a fatty or oily substance. [< Latin *sēbum* tallow, grease, suet + English *-aceous*]

**sebaceous gland**, a gland in the inner layer of the skin that supplies oil to the skin and hair; oil gland. See picture under **hair**.

**se bac ic acid** (si bas′ik, -bā′sik), a white crystalline acid obtained by the distillation of castor oil, used especially to make fruit flavors, perfumes, and lubricants. *Formula:* $C_{10}H_{18}O_4$ [< French *sébacique* < Latin *sēbum* tallow, grease]

**se bes ten** or **se bes tan** (si bes′tən), *n.* **1** a plumlike fruit borne by an East Indian tree of the borage family, used in the East, and formerly in Europe, for medicinal purposes. **2** the tree it grows on. **3** the fruit of a related species or the tree it grows on. [< Arabic *sabastān* < Persian *sapistān*]

**se bif er ous** (si bif′ər əs), *adj.* **1** producing or secreting fat, as certain glands. **2** *Botany.* producing vegetable wax or tallow. [< Latin *sēbum* tallow, grease + *ferre* to carry + English *-ous*]

**seb or rhe a** or **seb or rhoe a** (seb′ə rē′ə), *n.* an abnormal discharge from the sebaceous glands, forming an oily coating on the skin. [< New Latin *sebum* tallow, grease + Greek *rheîn* to flow]

**seb or rhe ic** or **seb or rhoe ic** (seb′ə rē′ik), *adj.* of or having to do with seborrhea.

**se bum** (sē′bəm), *n.* the fatty secretion of the sebaceous glands. [< New Latin *sebum* < Latin *sēbum* tallow, grease]

**sec** (sek), *adj.* dry; not sweet (applied originally and still especially to champagne). [< French *sec* (literally) dry < Latin *siccus*]

**sec** (no period), secant.

**sec.**, an abbreviation for the following:
**1** according to (*Latin,* secundum).
**2** secant.
**3** second or seconds.
**4** secondary.
**5** secretary.
**6** section or sections.
**7** sector.

**SEC** (no periods) or **S.E.C.**, Securities and Exchange Commission.

**se cant** (sē′kənt, -kant), *n., adj.* —*n.* **1** *Geometry.* a straight line that intersects a curve at two or more points. See picture under **circle**. **2** *Trigonometry.* **a** the ratio of the length of a hypotenuse of a right-angled triangle to the length of the side adjacent to an acute angle. It is the reciprocal of the cosine. **b** a straight line drawn from the center of a circle through one extremity of an arc to the tangent from the other extremity of the same arc. **c** the ratio of the length of this line to the length of the radius of the circle. *Abbr:* sec (no period).
—*adj. Geometry.* intersecting: *a secant plane.* [< Latin *secāns, -antis,* present participle of *secāre* to cut]

**sec a teurs** (sek′ə tėrz), *n.pl. Especially British.* pruning shears: *She snipped at the roses with her secateurs* (Punch). [< French *sécateur* (singular) < Latin *secāre* to cut]

**sec co** (sek′ō), *adj., n.* —*adj. Music.* dry; unaccompanied; plain.
—*n.* = secco painting.
[< Italian *secco* < Latin *siccus* dry]

**secco painting**, painting on dry plaster with water colors.

**se cede** (si sēd′), *v.i.,* **-ced ed, -ced ing.** to withdraw formally from an organization: *[President] Buchanan reiterated that the South had no right to secede* (Herbert Agar). [< Latin *sēcēdere* < *sē-* apart + *cēdere* go]

**se ced er** (si sē′dər), *n.* one who withdraws formally from association with an organization.

**se cern** (si sėrn′), *v.t., v.i.* **1** = discriminate. **2** *Physiology.* to secrete. [< Latin *sēcernere* < *sē-* aside, apart + *cernere* distinguish]

**se cern ent** (si sėr′nənt), *adj. Physiology.* that secretes.

**se cern ment** (si sėrn′mənt), *n. Physiology.* secretion.

**se ces sion** (si sesh′ən), *n.* **1** the act of formally withdrawing from an organization; seceding. **2** Also, **Secession**. the seceding of the eleven Southern states from the Union in 1860-61, which resulted in the Civil War. [<Latin *sēcessiō, -ōnis* < *sēcēdere;* see etym. under **secede**]

**se ces sion al** (si sesh′ə nəl), *adj.* of or having to do with secession.

**se ces sion ism** (si sesh′ə niz əm), *n.* the principles of those in favor of secession.

**se ces sion ist** (si sesh′ə nist), *n., adj.* —*n.* **1** a person or group that favors secession. **2** a person who secedes. SYN: seceder. **3** Also, **Secessionist**. a person who supported or participated in the secession of the Southern states from the Union in 1860-61.
—*adj.* favoring or taking part in secession; separatist: *... still another attempt to force the secessionist province of Katanga back under the authority of the central government* (Time).

**sec.-ft.**, second-foot.

**sech** (no periods), hyperbolic secant.

**seck** (sek), *adj.* not returning a profit: *a seck rent.* [< Anglo-French *(rente) secque* dry (rent), ultimately < Latin *siccus* dry]

**Seck el** or **seck el** (sek′əl, sik′-), *n.* an American variety of small, sweet, reddish-brown pear. Also, **Sickle**. [American English < *Seckel,* a Philadelphian, who introduced the variety]

**sec. leg.**, secundum legem.

**se clude** (si klüd′), *v.t.,* **-clud ed, -clud ing. 1** to keep apart from company; shut off from others: *He secludes himself and sees only his close* friends. SYN: withdraw, isolate, sequester. **2** *Obsolete.* to shut or keep out; exclude: *He has the doors and windows open in the hardest frosts, secluding only the snow* (John Evelyn). [< Latin *sēclūdere* < *sē-* apart + *claudere* shut]

**se|clud|ed** (si klü′did), *adj.* shut off from others; undisturbed; remote: *The author wanted to be alone while he was writing and rented a secluded cottage in the woods for the summer.* SYN: withdrawn, isolated. —**se|clud′ed|ly**, *adv.* —**se|clud′ed|ness**, *n.*

**se|clu|sion** (si klü′zhən), *n.* **1** the act of secluding: *His seclusion of the rabbit in the barn kept it a secret from everyone else.* **2** the state of being secluded; retirement: *She lives in seclusion apart from her friends.* **3** a secluded place: *Sweet seclusions for holy thoughts and prayers* (Longfellow).
[< Medieval Latin *seclusio, -onis* < Latin *sēclūdere;* see etym. under **seclude**]

**se|clu|sion|ist** (si klü′zhə nist), *n.* a person who favors or advocates seclusion, such as a supporter of monasticism or one who opposes the admission of foreigners to his country.

**se|clu|sive** (si klü′siv), *adj.* **1** fond of seclusion. **2** tending to seclude. —**se|clu′sive|ly**, *adv.* —**se|clu′sive|ness**, *n.*

**sec|o|bar|bi|tal** (sek′ə bär′bə tôl, -tal; sē′kō-), *n.* a white barbiturate used (usually in the form of secobarbital sodium) as a sedative for nervousness and sleeplessness. *Formula:* $C_{12}H_{18}N_2O_3$

**secobarbital sodium**, the form of secobarbital commonly used in medicine. *Formula:* $C_{12}H_{17}N_2O_3Na$

**Sec|o|nal** (sek′ə nəl, -nôl, -nol; sē′kə-), *n. Trademark.* secobarbital.

**sec|ond**[1] (sek′ənd), *adj., adv., n., v.* —*adj.* **1** next after the first: *the second seat from the front, second prize, the second volume of a book.* **2** below the first; subordinate: *second in command, the second officer on a ship.* **3** inferior to the first; next to the best: *She did not want to buy cloth of second quality to make her party dress.* **4** another; other: *to take a second sheet of paper. Napoleon has been called a second Caesar.* **5** *Music.* **a** lower in pitch. **b** rendering a part lower in pitch: *second soprano.* **6** designating the gear ratio of a standard automobile transmission between that of low and high.
—*adv.* in the second group, division, rank, etc.; secondly: *to speak second.*
—*n.* **1** a person or thing that is second: *One sock is here; the second is on the floor.* **2a** a person who supports or aids another; backer: *Both explorers were assisted by a second who did the work of keeping up the camp.* **b** a person who attends a boxer or duelist: *Seated in his corner, Cockell was closely examined by his seconds, who did their best to close a deep cut between the eyes* (London Times). **3** *Music.* **a** a tone on the next degree from a given tone. **b** the interval between two consecutive tones of the scale. **c** the harmonic combination of such tones. **d** the second part in a concerted piece. **e** a voice or instrument rendering such a part. **f** the second tone in any scale. **g** the subordinate part in a duet; secondo. **4** the forward gear or speed of an automobile or similar machine, having a ratio to the engine speed between that of low and high.
—*v.t.* **1a** to support; back up; assist (a person or his aims or actions): *Deeds must second words when needful* (Thomas Arnold). **b** to attend (a boxer or duelist). **2** to express approval or support of (a motion, amendment, proposal, or the one who makes it): *One member made a motion to adjourn the meeting, and another seconded it.* **3** *British.* to transfer temporarily to another assignment, by secondment. **4** *Obsolete.* to repeat, as an action.
**seconds**, **a** articles below first quality: *These stockings are seconds and have some slight defects.* **b** an inferior, coarse flour: *Some millers sell only seconds.* **c** the bread made from it: *His bread was much cheaper and many went to buy seconds at the baker's.*
[< Old French *seconde,* learned borrowing from Latin *secundus* (literally) following, second (of a series), present participle of *sequī* follow. See etym. of doublet **secund**.] —**sec′ond|er**, *n.*

**✱second²** definition 1

He finished in 4′37″.
symbol

**✱sec|ond²** (sek′ənd), *n.* **1** one of the 60 very short, equal periods of time that make up a minute; 1/60 of a minute; 1/3600 of an hour. The time between the ticks of some clocks is a second. **2** *Figurative.* a very short time; instant; moment. **3** 1/3600 of a degree of an angle. 12°10′30″ means 12 degrees, 10 minutes, 30 seconds. *Abbr:* sec.
[< Old French *seconde* < Medieval Latin *secundum* second; division of time; also *secunda* (*minuta*) second (minute), that is, the result of the second division of the hour by sixty]

**Second Advent**, the second coming of Christ at the Last Judgment; Advent.

**Second Adventist**, a person who believes in the Second Advent; millenarian or premillenarian.

**sec|ond|ar|i|ly** (sek′ən der′ə lē), *adv.* **1** indirectly. **2** subordinately. **3** *Obsolete.* secondly.

**sec|ond|ar|i|ness** (sek′ən der′ē nis), *n.* **1** subordinate character or position. **2** secondary quality or condition.

**sec|ond|ar|y** (sek′ən der′ē), *adj., n., pl.* **-ar|ies.**
—*adj.* **1** next after the first in order, place, time, or importance: *a secondary layer of tissue. Other industries, especially the lighter ones, are called secondary because they employ the products of previous manufacture as their raw materials* (Finch and Trewartha). **2** having less importance; not main or chief: *Reading fast is secondary to reading well.* SYN: subordinate, subsidiary, auxiliary, inferior, minor. **3** not original; derived: *a secondary source of a report.* SYN: derivative. **4** *Electricity.* of or having to do with a coil or circuit in which a current is produced by induction. **5** *Chemistry.* involving the substitution of two atoms or groups. **6** *Geology.* produced from another mineral by decay, alteration, or the like. **7** (of suffixes, derivation, and the like) added to or based on a form which is itself a derivative.
—*n.* **1** a person or thing that is secondary, second in importance, or subordinate. **2** the defensive backfield in football. **3** = secondary accent. **4** = secondary coil. **5** = secondary feather. **6** a heavenly body that revolves around another, especially a satellite of a planet: *The moon is a secondary that revolves in an orbit around the earth, a primary. The earth, in turn, is a secondary that travels in an orbit around the sun* (Eric D. Carlson).
[< Latin *secundārius* of the second class or quality < *secundus;* see etym. under **second**[1]]

**secondary accent**, **1** an accent that is weaker than the strongest stress in a word (primary accent), but stronger than no stress. The second syllable of *ab/bre′vi/a′tion* has a secondary accent. **2** the mark (′) used to show a weaker accent.

**secondary boycott**, the practice of combining to prevent the handling of goods of one manufacturer, employer, or union, as a means of intimidating or coercing a second manufacturer, employer, or group of workers.

**secondary cell**, = storage battery.

**secondary coil**, a coil in which an electric current is produced by induction, as in a transformer.

**secondary color**, = binary color.

**secondary consumer**, *Ecology.* an animal, such as a fox or a hawk, that feeds on smaller, plant-eating animals. See diagram under **food chain**.

**secondary crusher**, a machine in which rock broken down by a primary crusher is reduced to pieces about ¾ of an inch wide.

**secondary distribution**, = secondary offering.

**secondary electron**, an electron given off by secondary emission. An anode struck by electrons flowing from a cathode will give off secondary electrons.

**secondary emission**, the freeing of electrons from the surface of a metal or other substance by bombardment with other electrons or ions.

**secondary feather**, one of the flight feathers on the forearm of a bird's wing.

**secondary group**, *Sociology.* a specialized, often formal, group whose members have less intimate contact with each other than those of a primary group.

**secondary metal**, metal obtained from scrap or as a by-product in producing other metal.

**secondary offering**, the act of putting up for sale a large block of stock that has been held by a stockholder or corporation, often to settle an estate or liquidate holdings.

**secondary rainbow**, an outer and fainter rainbow parallel with the primary bow, formed by rays reflected twice within each raindrop.

**secondary recovery**, any method designed to take oil from a well that has nearly or completely stopped producing. Oilmen may inject gas or water into the reservoir to force the oil to a well where it is pumped to the surface.

**secondary root**, *Botany.* a branch of a primary root.

**secondary school**, a school attended after the elementary school; a high school or (in England) a public school.

**secondary seventh chord**, *Music.* a seventh chord constructed upon any tone other than the dominant.

**secondary sex** (or **sexual**) **characteristic**, any one of the characteristics which appear in both sexes at puberty, such as the growth of breasts and pubic hair in females, and the growth of the genitals and facial hair in males. They are called secondary because these characteristics are not directly involved with reproduction.

**secondary shock**, *Medicine.* a condition following the onset of shock caused by severe wounds or operations, in which the symptoms of shock become intensified. In secondary shock a person's blood pressure falls, breathing becomes shallow and weak, perspiration turns cold, and blood vessels near the surface of the skin collapse.

**secondary stress**, = secondary accent.

**secondary syphilis**, syphilis in its second stage, characterized by anemia, skin disease, inflammation of mucous membranes, and swelling of lymph glands.

**secondary wave**, an earthquake wave in which rock particles vibrate at right angles to the direction of travel.

**se|con|da vol|ta** (sā kōn′dä vôl′tä), *Music.* the second time. [< Italian *seconda vōlta*]

**second ballot**, **1** an electoral method in which a second or supplementary election is held when no candidate has secured a majority of the votes cast. **2** the second poll itself.

**second banana**, *Slang.* **1** a comedian who supports the leading comic actor: *[He] has emerged as one of the best known second bananas in television, but he has no desire to be a top banana such as his boss* (New York Times). **2** the person next below a leader in any field; second-in-command.

**second base**, *Baseball.* **1** the base opposite home plate on the diamond, that must be touched second by a runner. **2** the position of the fielder covering the area near this base. —**second baseman**.

**sec|ond-best** (sek′ənd best′), *adj., n., adv.*
—*adj.* next in quality to the first: *In that case the second-best solution would be for Britain and France to put their nuclear forces under some form of joint control* (Manchester Guardian Weekly).
—*n.* Usually, **second best**. a person or thing inferior to the best: *Most people must be contented with second bests in this world* (Illustrated London News).
—*adv.* **come off second-best**, to be defeated in a contest: *I am glad to hear of fighting, even though we come off second-best* (Abigail Adams).

**second childhood**, a foolish or childish condition caused by old age; dotage: *The silly old man acted as if he were in his second childhood.*

**second class**, **1** the class of passenger or living accomodations next after first class in quality and cost. **2** the class of mail that includes newspapers, magazines, and other periodicals sent regularly from the office of publication and not sealed against inspection.

**sec|ond-class** (sek′ənd klas′, -kläs′), *adj., adv.*
—*adj.* **1** of or belonging to the class next after the first: *second-class mail.* **2** of or having to do with second class: *a second-class car, a second-class ticket.* **3** of inferior grade or quality; second-rate: *to be treated as a second-class citizen, a noisy second-class hotel.*
—*adv.* on or in second-class passenger or living accommodations: *We could afford only to travel second-class.*

**second-class matter**, (in the U.S. postal system) newspapers and other periodicals sent regularly from the office of publication and not sealed against inspection.

**Second Coming**, = Second Advent.

**second cousin**, **1** a child of one's first cousin. **2** a grandchild of one's great-aunt or great-uncle. See picture under **family tree**.

**sec|ond-de|gree burn** (sek′ənd di grē′), a burn in which blisters are formed.

**second-degree murder**, *Law.* homicide committed unintentionally but without justification.

**sec|ond-drawer** (sek′ənd drôr′), *adj. Informal.* of lesser importance; secondary; second-rate: *the second-drawer leaders of the party.*

**se|conde** (si kond′; *French* sə gôɴd′), *n. Fencing.* the second in a series of eight defensive positions or parries. [< French *seconde,* feminine of *second* second[1]]

**Pronunciation Key:** **h**a**t**, **ā**ge, c**ã**re, f**ä**r; **l**e**t**, **ē**qual, t**ė**rm; **i**t, **ī**ce; h**o**t, **ō**pen, **ô**rder; **oi**l, **ou**t; c**u**p, p**u̇**t, r**ü**le; **ch**ild; lo**ng**; **th**in; **ᵺ**en; **zh**, measure; **ə** represents **a** in about, **e** in taken, **i** in pencil, **o** in lemon, **u** in circus.

*** Second Empire**, of or having to do with a style, as of dress or furniture, derived from the Empire style and in fashion during the second French Empire (1852-1870).

*** Second Empire**

**second estate** or **Second Estate**, the nobility, as distinguished from the clergy and the common people, especially in French history.

**second fiddle**, a secondary part.

**be** (or **play**) **second fiddle** (**to**), to take a lesser part or position; play a secondary role: *In any case, the Navy is playing second fiddle to the Air Force* (New York Times).

**sec|ond-foot** (sek′ənd fu̇t′), *n., pl.* **-feet**. = foot-second. *Abbr:* sec.-ft.

**second gear**, an intermediate speed gear of an automobile; second.

**second growth**, a growth or crop of vegetation replacing one previously cut or destroyed.

**sec|ond-guess** (sek′ənd ges′), *v.t.* **1** to say afterwards what someone ought to have said; use hindsight to correct: *Armed with ... their most involved charts and theories, the economists are out in force to second-guess the President and his own economic advisers* (Newsweek). **2** = outguess. — **sec′ond-guess′er**, *n.*

**sec|ond-hand** (sek′ənd hand′), *adj., adv.* — ***adj.*** **1** not original; obtained from another: *second-hand information.* **2** not new; used or worn already by someone else: *a second-hand car, second-hand clothes, second-hand books.*
**3** dealing in used goods: *a second-hand bookstore, a second-hand dealer.*
— ***adv.*** from other than the original source; not directly; not firsthand: *Babylonian culture could continue to reach Canaan second-hand* (S. Cook).

**second hand**, **1** the hand on a clock or watch pointing to the seconds. It moves around the whole dial once in a minute. **2** *Obsolete.* an intermediary; middleman.

**second head rice**, a grade of rice consisting of perfect kernels mixed with large broken pieces.

**sec|ond-in-com|mand** (sek′ənd in kə mand′), *n., pl.* **sec|onds-in-com|mand**. a person ranking in authority next to the one in charge.

**second intention**, the healing of a wound by the formation of granulated tissue in the wound cavity.

**second lieutenant**, a commissioned officer of the air force, army, or marines having the lowest rank, next below a first lieutenant, often having command of a platoon.

**sec|ond|ly** (sek′ənd lē), *adv.* in the second place; second.

**sec|ond|ment** (sek′ənd mənt), *n. British.* temporary transfer to another position or staff, usually without loss of position or seniority in the organization from which the transfer takes place.

**second mortgage**, a mortgage second in point of claim to a first mortgage.

**second nature**, a habit, quality, or knowledge that a person has acquired and had for so long that it seems to be almost a part of his nature.

**se|con|do** (sā kōn′dō), *n., pl.* **-di** (-dē). *Music.* **1** the subordinate part, as in a duet. **2** the performer of this part. [< Italian *secondo* < Latin *secundus;* see etym. under **second**[1]]

**second person**, **1** the form of a pronoun which refers to the person spoken to. *You* and *your* are pronouns of the second person. **2** the form of a verb which has *you* as its subject.

**second pilot**, = copilot.

**second quarter**, **1** the period between the first half moon and full moon. **2** the phase of the moon when it has revolved far enough to reveal its entire face; full moon.

**sec|ond-rate** (sek′ənd rāt′), *adj.* **1** rated as second-class. **2** inferior: *a very second-rate performance.* **SYN**: middling. — **sec′ond-rate′ness**, *n.*

**sec|ond-rat|er** (sek′ənd rā′tər), *n.* a second-rate person or thing.

**Second Reich**, the German Empire begun by Otto von Bismarck in 1871 and terminated in 1918 by the defeat of the Germans in World War I.

**Second Republic**, the government of France from 1848 to 1852.

**sec|ond-run** (sek′ənd run′), *adj.* **1** (of a new motion picture) not shown for the first time; shown after its general release; not first-run: *The movies were second-run and six a day* (Atlantic). **2** (of a theater) featuring second-run motion pictures.

**sec|onds** (sek′əndz), *n.pl.* See under **second**[1].

**second sight**, the supposed power of seeing distant objects or future events as if they were present. **SYN**: clairvoyance.

**sec|ond-sight|ed** (sek′ənd sī′tid), *adj.* having second sight.

**second sound**, *Physics.* the rapid heat transfer of helium at very low temperatures by a motion like that of sound waves.

**second speed**, = second gear.

**sec|ond-sto|ry man** (sek′ənd stôr′ē, -stōr′-), *U.S.* a burglar who gets into a house through an upstairs window; cat burglar.

**sec|ond-strike** (sek′ənd strīk′), *adj.* **1** (of a nuclear weapon or force) able to retaliate or strike back after a nuclear attack: *a second-strike nuclear weapon or force.* **2** of retaliation; retaliatory: *second-strike capability.*

**sec|ond-string** (sek′ənd string′), *adj.* **1** *Sports.* not of the first or regular team: *a second-string quarterback.* **2** second-rate; secondary; subordinate: *second-string executives, a second-string college.*

**sec|ond-string|er** (sek′ənd string′ər), *n. Informal.* a second-string person; subordinate.

**second summer**, = Indian summer.

**second thought**, a thought or idea occurring later.

**on second thought**, upon further consideration: *On second thought, how can we be sure?*

**second wind**, **1** a renewal of regular breathing and energy while continuing the activity that brought about the original loss of breath or fatigue. **2** *Figurative.* any renewal of energy: *Packaging workers seem to go faster when they get their second wind after a cup of coffee* (Wall Street Journal).

**Second World War**, the world war, 1939-1945, that ended with the defeat of the Axis powers, Germany, Italy, Japan, and their allies; World War II.

**sec|par** (sek′pär′), *n.* = parsec.

**se|cre|cy** (sē′krə sē), *n., pl.* **-cies**. **1** the condition of being secret or of being kept secret: *to carry out a plan in secrecy, to observe the strictest secrecy.* **2** the ability to keep things secret: *to give a promise of secrecy.* **3** a tendency to conceal; lack of frankness: *to maintain secrecy as to one's plans.* [alteration of Middle English *secretie* < *secre* secret + *-tie* -ty]

**se|cret** (sē′krit), *adj., n.* — ***adj.*** **1** kept from the knowledge of others: *a secret marriage, a secret errand, a secret weapon.* **2** keeping to oneself what one knows: *He is as secret as a mouse.* **SYN**: uncommunicative, secretive. **3** known only to a few: *a secret sign, a secret password, a secret society.* **4** kept from sight; hidden: *a secret drawer, a secret passage.* **SYN**: concealed, covered. **5** retired; secluded: *a secret place.* **6** working or acting without the knowledge of others: *a secret messenger.* **7** very hard to understand or discover: *secret influences.* **SYN**: obscure, recondite, esoteric.
— ***n.*** **1** something secret or hidden; mystery: *Can you keep a secret?* **2** a thing known only to a few: *The secret of the authorship was known to only one man* (Edward Bok). *Each cherished a secret, which she did not confide to the other* (Longfellow). **3** a hidden cause or reason: *the secret of his success.*

**in secret**, in private; not openly or publicly; secretly: *I have said nothing in secret that I would not say openly.*

[< Old French *secret,* learned borrowing from Latin *sēcrētus,* past participle of *sēcernere* set apart < *sē-* apart + *cernere* to separate. See etym. of doublet **secrete**.] — **se′cret|ly**, *adv.* — **se′cret|ness**, *n.*

— *Syn. adj.* **1 Secret, covert, clandestine** mean done, made, or carried on without the knowledge of others. **Secret** is the general word and applies to concealment of any kind and for any purpose: *They have a secret business agreement.* **Covert**, a more formal word, suggests partial concealment, and applies to anything kept under cover, disguised, or not openly revealed: *A hint is a covert suggestion.* **Clandestine**, also formal, suggests concealment for an unlawful or improper purpose: *He feared someone would learn of his clandestine trips.*

**Se|cret** (sē′krit), *n.* a prayer or prayers following the Offertory and before the Preface of the Mass, recited inaudibly, except for the last phrase, by the celebrant.

**se|cre|ta** (si krē′tə), *n.pl.* the products of secretion. [< New Latin *secreta,* neuter plural of Latin *sēcrētus;* see etym. under **secret**]

**se|cre|tage** (sē′krə tij), *n.* a process in preparing furs, using mercury or some of its salts to impart the property of felting to the fur. [< French *secrétage*]

**secret agent**, an agent of a government secret service; spy: *Soviet technicians who were actually secret agents* (Newsweek).

**se|cre|ta|gogue** (si krē′tə gôg, -gog), *n.* a substance that promotes secretion: *These secretagogues are distinct from the irritant substances contained in many tear gases that induce reflex tearing* (Scientific American). [< New Latin *secreta* secreta + Greek *agōgós* leading < *ágein* to lead]

**sec|re|taire** (sek′rə tãr′), *n.* a high desk shaped like a cabinet, with drawers and pigeonholes. [< French *secrétaire*]

**sec|re|tar|i|al** (sek′rə tãr′ē əl), *adj.* of a secretary; having to do with a secretary: *She learned to do stenography, typewriting, and other secretarial work.*

**sec|re|tar|i|at** (sek′rə tãr′ē it, -at), *n.* **1a** the office or position of secretary or secretary-general. **b** the department, including staff, buildings, etc., controlled by a secretary or secretary-general: *Coordinating the labors of these far-flung agencies and linking them to the U.N. proper is the job of the Secretariat* (Time). **2** a group of secretaries, as within a government or department. **3** the place where a secretary transacts business. [< French *secrétariat* < Old French *secretaire* secretary, learned borrowing from Late Latin *sēcrētārius*]

**sec|re|tar|i|ate** (sek′rə tãr′ē it), *n.* = secretariat.

*** sec|re|tar|y** (sek′rə ter′ē), *n., pl.* **-tar|ies**. **1** a person who writes letters and keeps records for a person, company, club, committee, or the like: *a private secretary. Our club has a secretary who keeps the minutes of the meetings.* **SYN**: clerk. **2** an official who has charge of a department of the government or similar organization. The Secretary of the Treasury is the head of the Treasury Department. **3** a diplomatic agent, usually of a lower rank in an embassy or legation, often designated as first secretary, second secretary, and so on. *Abbr:* sec. **4** a writing desk with a set of drawers and often with shelves for books. [< Late Latin *sēcrētārius* confidential officer < Latin *sēcrētum* a secret, neuter of *sēcrētus;* see etym. under **secret**]

*** secretary**
definition 4

**secretary bird**, a large, long-legged African bird of prey that feeds on reptiles and other vertebrates, so called because its crest suggests pens stuck behind the ear; snake killer.

**sec|re|tar|y-gen|er|al** (sek′rə ter′ē jen′ər əl, -jen′rəl), *n., pl.* **sec|re|tar|ies-gen|er|al**. the chief secretary; administrative head of a secretariat: *the secretary-general of the United Nations.*

**Secretary of State**, **1** *U.S.* **a** the head of the State Department and principal advisor to the President on foreign affairs. **b** an officer of a state government in charge of making and keeping records. **2** *British.* the head of any one of various government departments.

**sec|re|tar|y|ship** (sek′rə ter′ē ship), *n.* the position or duties of a secretary.

**secret ballot**, voting in secret, usually on a voting machine or on printed or written ballots that are put in a ballot box.

**se|crete**[1] (si krēt′), *v.t.,* **-cret|ed, -cret|ing**. **1** to keep secret; hide: *A certain French lady ... had secreted herself on board the vessel* (John Leland). **SYN**: conceal, ensconce. **2** to remove secretly; appropriate in a secret manner: *He was delivering back to the Company money of their own, which he had secreted from them* (Edmund Burke). [< Latin *sēcrētus.* See etym. of doublet **secret.**]

**se|crete**[2] (si krēt′), *v.t.,* **-cret|ed, -cret|ing**. to produce and discharge; make; prepare: *Glands in the mouth secrete saliva. Most people secrete the appropriate blood group substances* (*antigens*) *in bodily secretions such as saliva and* *tears* (Science News). [back formation < *secretion*]

**se|cre|tin** (si krē′tin), *n.* an intestinal hormone that stimulates secretion of the pancreatic juice by the pancreas.

**se|cre|tion** (si krē′shən), *n.* **1** a substance that is secreted by some part of an animal or plant: *Bile is the secretion of the liver.* **2** the act or process of producing and discharging such a substance: *The secretion from his infection continued until it was completely healed.* **3** the act of concealing; hiding. [< Latin *sēcrētiō, -ōnis* < *sēcrētus;* see etym. under **secret**]

**se|cre|tion|al** (si krē′shə nəl), *adj.* of or having to do with secretion; secretory.

**se|cre|tion|ar|y** (si krē′shə ner′ē), *adj.* = secretional.

**se|cre|tive** (si krē′tiv), *adj.* **1** having the habit of secrecy; not frank and open: *There was certainly nothing secretive or hidden in the Poujadists' campaign, animated as it was by shouting hecklers ... that echoed in every corner of France* (New Yorker). **SYN**: reticent. **2** causing or aiding secretion. — **se|cre′tive|ly**, *adv.* — **se|cre′tive-ness**, *n.*

**se|cre|tor** (si krē′tər), *n.* a person or thing that secretes: *the silk secretor of a spider.*

**se|cre|to|ry** (si krē′tər ē), *adj., n., pl.* **-ries.** — ***adj.*** of or causing secretion; secreting.
— ***n.*** an organ of the body that secretes.

**secret partner**, a partner who may take an active part in the business's affairs but is not publicly known as a partner.

**secret police**, a governmental police force working to control and spy on persons considered dangerous or subversive, as in certain dictatorial governments.

**secret service**, **1** a branch of a government that makes secret investigations. **2** official service of a secret nature. **3** = Secret Service. — **se′cret-serv′ice**, *adj.*

**Secret Service**, the branch of the United States Treasury Department concerned with discovering and preventing counterfeiting, with protecting the President, and, in wartime, with espionage.

**secret society**, an organization to promote some cause by secret methods, its members being sworn to observe secrecy.

**secs.**, **1** seconds. **2** sections.

**sect** (sekt), *n.* **1** a group of persons having the same principles, beliefs, or opinions: *a philosophical sect. Each religious sect in the town had its own church.* **SYN**: denomination. **2** a religious group separated from an established church. **3** *Obsolete.* a class or kind (of persons). [< Latin *secta* party, school, probably < *sectārī* keep following < *sequī* to follow]

**sect.**, section.

**sec|ta** (sek′tə), *n.* in Old English law: **1** a case in court; suit. **2** the witnesses brought to court by a plaintiff to prove his arguments. [< Latin *secta* party, school]

**sec|tar|i|al** (sek tãr′ē əl), *adj.* = sectarian.

**sec|tar|i|an** (sek tãr′ē ən), *adj., n.* — ***adj.*** **1** of or having to do with a sect; denominational. **2** characteristic of one sect only; strongly prejudiced in favor of a certain sect.
— ***n.*** **1** a devoted member of a sect, especially a narrow-minded or strongly prejudiced member. **2** a member of a religious group separated from an established church; nonconformist. **SYN**: dissenter.

**sec|tar|i|an|ism** (sek tãr′ē ə niz′əm), *n.* the spirit or tendencies of sectarians; adherence or too great devotion to a particular sect, especially a religious sect.

**sec|tar|i|an|ize** (sek tãr′ē ə nīz), *v.t.,* **-ized, -izing.** to make sectarian.

**sec|ta|ry** (sek′tər ē), *n., pl.* **-ries,** *adj.* — ***n.*** a member of a particular sect, especially a member of a religious group separated from an established church.
— ***adj.*** = sectarian.
[< Medieval Latin *sectarius* < Latin *secta;* see etym. under **sect**]

**sec|tile** (sek′təl), *adj.* that can be cut smoothly by a knife but cannot withstand pulverization: *a sectile mineral. If the specimen can be cut by a knife, like a piece of hard tar, and yet shatters under a sharp blow, it is sectile* (Scientific American). [< Latin *sectilis* < *secāre* to cut]

**sec|til|i|ty** (sek til′ə tē), *n.* the property of being easily cut; sectile character.

**sec|tion** (sek′shən), *n., v.* — ***n.*** **1** a part cut off; part; division; slice: *Mother cut the pie into eight equal sections. His section of the family estate was larger than his brother's.* **2a** a division of a book, a law, or the like: *Our arithmetic book has several sections on fractions. Chapter X has seven sections.* **b** a division of an orchestra, band, or chorus: *the string section, the rhythm section, the alto section.* **c** any division of an organization; department: *the biography section of the library, the tube section of a television factory.* **d** a specialized military unit or subdivision. **3** a region or district; part of a country, city, community, or group: *The city has a business section and a residential section.* **4** a district one mile square; 640 acres. A township usually contains 36 sections. **5** one of the parts of something that is built of a number of similar parts: *the sections of a bookcase.* **6** the act of cutting or dividing. **7** a representation of a thing as it would appear if cut straight through. **8** a thin slice of a tissue, mineral, or the like, cut off for microscopic examination. **9** the part of a railroad line maintained by one group of workmen: *The front coach was crowded with Galicians going down the line to work on the section* (Calgary [Canada] Eye Opener). **10** *U.S.* a part of a sleeping car containing an upper and a lower berth. **11** *U.S.* one of two or more trains operating on the same schedule. **12** *Bookbinding.* a sheet of paper folded together to form a unit; signature. **13** a symbol used to introduce a subdivision or as a mark of reference; section mark. *Abbr:* sect.
— ***v.t.*** **1** to cut into sections; divide into sections: *to section an orange.* **2** to cut through so as to present a section.
[< Latin *sectiō, -ōnis* < *secāre* to cut]

**sec|tion|al** (sek′shə nəl), *adj., n.* — ***adj.*** **1** of or having to do with a particular section; regional or local: *sectional interests, sectional prejudices, sectional legislation.* **2** made of sections or parts: *a sectional bookcase.*
— ***n.*** a sectional couch, bookcase, or other piece of furniture. — **sec′tion|al|ly**, *adv.*

**sec|tion|al|ism** (sek′shə nə liz′əm), *n.* too great regard for sectional interests; sectional prejudice or hatred: *When the people of a region become self-centered and neglect their relation to the larger national unity, they suffer from sectionalism or provincialism* (Emory S. Bogardus). **SYN**: parochialism.

**sec|tion|al|ist** (sek′shə nə list), *n.* a person who advocates sectional aims or interests.

**sec|tion|al|ize** (sek′shə nə līz), *v.t.,* **-ized, -iz|ing.** **1** to make sectional in scope or spirit: *The principal results of the struggle were to sectionalize parties.* **2** to divide into sections; divide (land or an area) into plots or districts. — **sec′tion|al|i|za′tion**, *n.*

**section boss**, *U.S.* section foreman.

**Section Eight**, **1** discharge of a soldier from the U.S. Army because of unfitness for military service. **2** a soldier who is given such a discharge. [< *Section 8* of an Army Regulation specifying this form of discharge, in effect from 1922 to 1944]

**section foreman**, *U.S.* the foreman of a section gang.

**section gang** or **crew**, *U.S.* a group of workmen who maintain a single railroad section.

**section hand** or **man**, *U.S.* a worker on a section gang.

**section mark**, *Printing.* the mark used to indicate a section in a book, a law, or the like, or as a mark of reference to notes in the margin or at the foot of a page.

**sec|tor** (sek′tər), *n., v.* — ***n.*** **1** the part of a circle, ellipse, or the like, between two radii and the included arc. **2** a clearly defined military area which a given military unit protects or covers with fire; part of a front held by a unit. **3** any clearly defined section or division; segment: *the consumer-oriented sector of the economy* (Atlantic). *Direct mail is the fastest growing sector in the advertising industry* (London Times). **SYN**: zone, quarter. **4** an instrument consisting of two rulers connected by a joint, used in measuring or drawing angles.
— ***v.t.*** to divide into sectors; provide with sectors.
[< Late Latin *sector, -ōris* (in Latin, a cutter) < *secāre* to cut]

**sec|tor|al** (sek′tər əl), *adj.* of or having to do with a sector: *sectoral spaces.*

**sec|to|ri|al** (sek tôr′ē əl, -tōr′-), *adj.* **1** of, having to do with, or resembling a sector. **2** adapted for cutting, as certain teeth are; carnassial.

**sector scan**, a radar scan through a limited angle to provide a continuous surveillance of a particular area or airspace.

**Sect Shinto**, Shintoism revolving around the teachings of a particular leader or group, with individual sects carrying out programs of religious education and worship. Sect Shinto evolved after the abolition of Shintoism as a state religion in Japan following World War II.

**sec|u|lar** (sek′yə lər), *adj., n.* — ***adj.*** **1** connected with the world and its affairs; of things not religious or sacred; worldly: *secular music, a secular education. Bishops now were great secular magistrates, and ... were involved in secular occupations* (Cardinal Newman). **2** living in the world; not belonging to a religious order: *a secular clergy, a secular priest.* **3** occurring once in an age or century: *When Augustus celebrated the secular year, which was kept but once in a century ...* (Joseph Addison). **4** lasting through long ages; going on from age to age: *the secular cooling or refrigeration of the globe.*
— ***n.*** **1** a secular priest; clergyman living among the laity and not in a monastery: *While the Danish wars had been fatal to the monks—the "regular clergy" as they were called—they had also dealt heavy blows at the seculars, or parish priests* (J. R. Green). **2** = layman.
[< Latin *saeculāris* < *saeculum* age, span of time; later, the present age or world, the world]

**sec|u|lar|ise** (sek′yə lə rīz), *v.t.,* **-ised, -is|ing.** *Especially British.* secularize.

**sec|u|lar|ism** (sek′yə lə riz′əm), *n.* **1** skepticism in regard to religion; the ignoring or exclusion of religious duties, instruction, or considerations: *Caught between secularism and militant Hindu fanaticism, the missionaries themselves are gloomy* (Newsweek). **SYN**: worldliness. **2** opposition to the introduction of religion into public schools and other public affairs.

**sec|u|lar|ist** (sek′yə lər ist), *n., adj.* — ***n.*** a believer in secularism.
— ***adj.*** = secularistic.

**sec|u|lar|is|tic** (sek′yə lə ris′tik), *adj.* of or characterized by secularism.

**sec|u|lar|i|ty** (sek′yə lar′ə tē), *n., pl.* **-ties.** **1** secular spirit or quality; worldliness. **2** a secular matter.

**sec|u|lar|i|za|tion** (sek′yə lər ə zā′shən), *n.* the act or process of secularizing or state of being secularized.

**sec|u|lar|ize** (sek′yə lə rīz), *v.t.,* **-ized, -iz|ing.** **1** to make secular or worldly; separate from religious connection or influence: *to secularize Sunday, to secularize the schools.* **2** to transfer (property) from the possession of the church to that of the government. **3** to transfer (clergy) from regular or monastic to secular: *to secularize a monk.* — **sec′u|lar|iz′er**, *n.*

**sec|u|lar|ly** (sek′yə lər lē), *adv.* in a secular or worldly manner.

**se|cund** (sē′kund, sek′und), *adj. Botany.* arranged on one side only; unilateral: *The flowers of the lily of the valley and the false wintergreen are secund.* [< Latin *secundus* following. See etym. of doublet **second**[1].]

**sec|un|dine** (sek′ən dīn, -din), *n. Botany.* the second or inner coat or integument of an ovule.
**secundines**, the afterbirth: *to deliver the baby and the secundines.*
[< Late Latin *secundīnae*, plural < Latin *secundus;* see etym. under **second**[1]]

**se|cun|dum** (si kun′dəm), *prep. Latin.* according to; in accordance with.

**se|cun|dum le|gem** (si kun′dəm lē′jəm), *Latin.* according to law.

**se|cur|a|ble** (si kyůr′ə bəl), *adj.* that can be secured.

**se|cure** (si kyůr′), *adj., v.,* **-cured, -cur|ing.** — ***adj.*** **1** safe against loss, attack, escape, or danger: *Keep the prisoner secure within his cell. This is a secure hiding place. Land in a growing city is a secure investment.* **SYN**: See syn. under **safe**. **2** that can be counted on; sure; certain: *We know in advance that our victory is secure.* **3** free from care, fear, or worry: *He hoped for a secure old age.* **4** firmly fastened; not liable to break or fall: *The boards of this bridge do not look secure.* **SYN**: fast, firm, stable, immovable.
— ***v.t.*** **1** to make safe; protect: *You cannot secure yourself against all risks and dangers. Every loan was secured by bonds or mortgages.* **SYN**: guard, defend, shield. **2** to make (something) sure or certain: *Their manner of building secured a certain air of solidity and grandeur* (P. H. Hunter). **SYN**: assure, ensure. **3** to make firm or fast: *Secure the locks on the windows. Having secured by boat, I took my gun and went on shore* (Daniel Defoe). **SYN**: fasten, tie. **4** to get by effort; obtain: *to secure the attention of an audience, to secure a hearing at court. We have secured our tickets for the school play.* **SYN**: gain. **5** to seize and confine: *They ... formed a conspiracy to seize the ship and secure me* (Jonathan Swift).
— ***v.i.*** to make oneself safe; be safe: *We must secure against the dangers of the coming storm.*
[< Latin *sēcūrus* < *sē-* free from + *cūra* care. See etym. of doublets **sure, sicker.**] — **se|cure′ly**, *adv.* — **se|cure′ness**, *n.* — **se|cur′er**, *n.*

**se|cure|ment** (si kyůr′mənt), *n.* the act of securing.

**se|cu|ri|ties** (si kyůr′ə tēz), *n.pl.* See under **security**.

**se|cu|ri|ty** (si kyůr′ə tē), *n., pl.* **-ties,** *adj.* — ***n.***

---

**Pronunciation Key:** hat, āge, cãre, fär; let, ēqual, tėrm; it, īce; hot, ōpen, ôrder; **oi**l, **ou**t; cup, půt, rüle; **ch**ild; lo**ng**; **th**in; **ᴛʜ**en; **zh**, measure; **ə** represents **a** in about, **e** in taken, **i** in pencil, **o** in lemon, **u** in circus.

1 freedom from danger, care, or fear; feeling or condition of being safe: *You may cross the street in security when a policeman holds up his hand. Insurance is the modern Aladdin's lamp from which flows the power to protect the possessions of man—give security and peace of mind* (Newsweek). **SYN**: confidence. **2** freedom from doubt; certainty. **3** overconfidence; carelessness. **4** something that secures or makes safe: *My watchdog is a security against burglars. Rubber soles are a security against slipping.* **SYN**: safety, protection, defense. **5** something given as a pledge that a person will fulfill some duty or promise: *A life-insurance policy may serve as security for a loan.* **6** a person who agrees to be responsible for another; surety: *Father was security for his partner.*
—***adj.*** of or having to do with the security, as of a country or business: *a security agent, a security agreement, some security procedure.*
**securities**, an evidence of debt or of property ownership; bond or stock certificates: *These public securities can be sold for $5,000.*

**security analyst**, a person who analyzes and evaluates stock and bonds: *The job of a security analyst is not to report facts, but to evaluate them* (New York Times).

**security blanket**, **1** a blanket or similar cloth which a child carries for a feeling of security: *Pails which are distributed to passengers ... contain such items as a handkerchief-size child's security blanket, which the stewardess demonstrates by rubbing it against her cheek* (Time). **2** the censoring of information in order to protect some person or thing.

**security clearance**, **1** permission given to a person or group, after official investigation, to enter or work in classified areas, deal with confidential or secret material, or meet with high government officials. **2** the investigation conducted before giving such clearance or permission: *Although not strictly Government employees, the contract experts have been required ... to undergo security clearance* (New York Times).

**Security Council**, a body in the United Nations consisting of five permanent member nations and ten rotating members, concerned primarily with preserving world peace. The Security Council can investigate any situation that might cause international friction, and may ask member nations to furnish troops and order them into areas of international conflict.

**security police**, = secret police.

**security risk**, **1** a person; especially an employee or prospective employee of the Federal government, who is regarded as unreliable or dangerous in positions involving national security, especially because of weakness of character, criminal record, or affiliation with subversive organizations. **2** any condition or development regarded as a risk to national security.

**security system**, any system for maintaining or safeguarding national or international security.

**se|cu|tor** (si kyü′tər), *n.* a light-armed gladiator with a square shield and a sword who opposed the retiarius in the gladiatorial contests of ancient Rome. [< Latin *secūtor* (literally) pursuer < *sequī* to follow, pursue]

**secy.** or **sec'y.**, secretary.

**se|dan** (si dan′), *n.* **1** a type of closed automobile having a front and a rear seat and seating four or more persons. **2** = sedan chair. [origin uncertain]

***sedan chair**, a covered chair for one person, carried on poles by two men. Sedan chairs were much used during the 1600's, 1700's, and early 1800's.

***sedan chair**

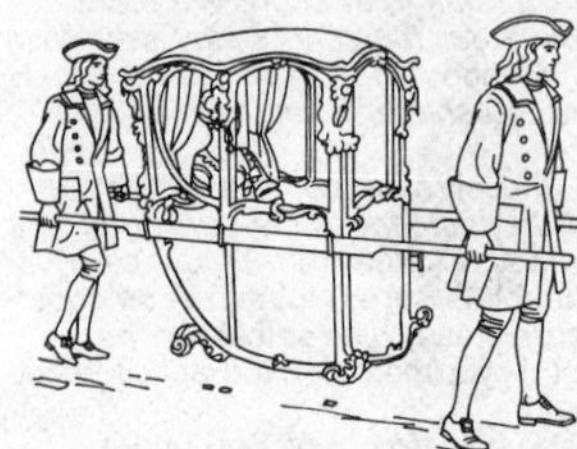

**se|date¹** (si dāt′), *adj.* quiet, calm, and composed; serious; undisturbed by passion or excitement: *She is very sedate for a child and would rather read and sew than play. One of those calm, quiet, sedate natures, to whom the temptations of turbulent nerves or vehement passions are things utterly incomprehensible* (Harriet Beecher Stowe). **SYN**: placid, staid, sober, collected, unruffled. [< Latin *sēdātus,* past participle of *sēdāre* to calm; (originally) to seat, related to *sedēre* to sit] —**se|date′ly**, *adv.* —**se|date′ness**, *n.*

**se|date²** (si dāt′), *v.t.,* **-dat|ed, -dat|ing.** to treat or calm with sedatives: *They tried ... to sedate her, and take care of her—and she would not let them* (Theodore H. White). [back formation < *sedation*]

**se|da|tion** (si dā′shən), *n. Medicine.* **1** the act of producing a calm or relaxed state, especially through a diminishing of the rate of functional activity; treatment with sedatives. **2** the calm or relaxed state induced by such treatment.

**sed|a|tive** (sed′ə tiv), *n., adj.* —*n.* **1** a medicine that lessens nervousness, pain, or excitement: *Drugs called barbiturates and bromides are commonly used sedatives* (Solomon Garb). **2** anything soothing or calming. **SYN**: salve.
—***adj.*** **1** lessening nervousness, pain, or excitement; lowering functional activity; calmative: *a sedative drug.* **2** soothing; calming: ... *soothing the cares of Polynesian life in the sedative fumes of tobacco* (Herman Melville).

**se de|fen|den|do** (sē def′en den′dō), *Law.* in self-defense (a plea offered to justify homicide). [< Latin *sē dēfendendō* (literally) in defending himself; *sē* oneself, *dēfendendō,* ablative of the gerund of *dēfendere* defend]

**sed|en|tar|i|ly** (sed′ən ter′ə lē), *adv.* in a sedentary manner.

**sed|en|tar|i|ness** (sed′ən ter′ē nis), *n.* the state or habit of being sedentary.

**sed|en|tar|y** (sed′ən ter′ē), *adj.* **1** used to sitting still much of the time; inactive: *Sedentary people get little physical exercise.* **2** that keeps one sitting still much of the time: *Bookkeeping is a sedentary occupation.* **3** moving little and rarely. **4** *Zoology.* **a** living in one place, as English sparrows do; not migratory or moving far: *Pigeons are sedentary birds.* **b** attached to one spot; not moving: *a sedentary mollusk.* **c** spinning a web and lying in wait: *I discovered that this was no web-spinning, sedentary spider, but a wandering hunter* (W. H. Hudson). [< Latin *sedentārius* ultimately < *sedēre* to sit]

**sed|en|ta|tion** (sed′ən tā′shən), *n.* the state of having become sedentary.

**Se|der** (sā′dər), *n., pl.* **Se|ders, Se|dar|im** (sedär′im). the religious service and feast held in Jewish homes on the first two nights (or first night only) of Passover. [< Hebrew *sēder* (literally) order, arrangement]

**sedge** (sej), *n.* **1** a grasslike plant that grows in wet places. The sedges comprise a large family of monocotyledonous herbs, resembling grasses but having solid, three-sided stems and small, inconspicuous flowers usually in spikes or heads. **2** any one of various coarse, grassy, rushlike or flaglike plants growing in wet places. [Old English *secg*]

**sedged** (sejd), *adj.* **1** bordered with sedge: *sedged brooks.* **2** *Obsolete.* made of sedge.

**sedge family**, a large group of monocotyledonous herbs resembling grasses but having solid, three-sided stems and small, inconspicuous flowers usually in spikes or heads. The family includes the sedge, papyrus, chufa, and bulrush.

**sedge hen**, = clapper rail.

**sedge|land** (sej′land′), *n.* land between high and low watermarks.

**sedge warbler**, any one of a group of small, Old World birds commonly found in marshy areas.

**sedg|y** (sej′ē), *adj.,* **sedg|i|er, sedg|i|est.** **1** abounding in or covered with sedge; bordered with sedge: *a sedgy brook.* **2** like sedge: *a sedgy growth of reeds.*

**se|di|le** (si dī′lē), *n., pl.* **-dil|i|a** (-dil′ē ə). one of the three seats in the chancel for the use of the clergy officiating in the Eucharist. [< Latin *sedīle* seat < *sedēre* to sit]

**sed|i|ment** (sed′ə mənt), *n., v.* —*n.* **1** any matter that settles to the bottom of a liquid; dregs. **SYN**: lees. **2** *Geology.* earth, stones, or other matter suspended in or deposited by water, wind, or ice: *When the Nile overflows, it deposits sediment on the land it covers.*
—***v.t., v.i.*** to deposit as or form sediment.
[< Latin *sedimentum* < *sedēre* to settle; sit]

**sed|i|men|tal** (sed′ə men′təl), *adj.* = sedimentary.

**sed|i|men|ta|ri|ly** (sed′ə men′tər ə lē), *adv.* in the form of a sedimentary deposit.

**sed|i|men|ta|ry** (sed′ə men′tər ē), *adj.* **1** of sediment; having to do with sediment. **2** *Geology.* formed from sediment. Shale is a sedimentary rock. *Sedimentary rocks—the hardened remnants of sediments laid down by ancient rivers and seas ...* (Scientific American). *Sedimentary rocks are derived not only from rock fragments but also from plant and animal remains* (Frederick H. Pough).

**sed|i|men|ta|tion** (sed′ə men tā′shən), *n.* the action or fact of depositing sediment.

**sed|i|men|to|log|ic** (sed′ə men′tə loj′ik), *adj.* = sedimentological.

**sed|i|men|to|log|i|cal** (sed′ə men′tə loj′ə kəl), *adj.* of or having to do with sedimentology. —**sed′i|men′to|log′i|cal|ly**, *adv.*

**sed|i|men|tol|o|gist** (sed′ə men tol′ə jist), *n.* a specialist in sedimentology: *Sedimentologists are trying to acquire a deeper physical, chemical and biological insight into modern sediments and apply this knowledge to interpreting sediments of the past* (New Scientist).

**sed|i|men|tol|o|gy** (sed′ə men tol′ə jē), *n.* the branch of geology that deals with the formation and structure of sediments.

**se|di|tion** (si dish′ən), *n.* **1** speech or action causing discontent or rebellion against the government; incitement to discontent or rebellion: *Sedition against the Federal Government, the Court held, is a field in which Congress alone has jurisdiction to enact laws* (Wall Street Journal). **2** *Archaic.* a revolt; rebellion. [< Old French *sedicion,* learned borrowing from Latin *sēditiō, -ōnis* < *sē-* apart + *īre* to go]

**se|di|tion|ar|y** (si dish′ə ner′ē), *adj., n., pl.* **-ar|ies.** —***adj.*** having to do with or involving sedition; seditious.
—*n.* a person who promotes or is guilty of sedition.

**se|di|tious** (si dish′əs), *adj.* **1** stirring up discontent or rebellion: *a seditious speech.* **2** taking part in sedition; guilty of sedition: *a seditious person, a seditious faction.* **3** having to do with sedition; arising from sedition: *seditious strife.* —**se|di′tious|ly**, *adv.* —**se|di′tious|ness**, *n.*

**Sed|litz powder** or **powders** (sed′lits), = Seidlitz powder.

**Se|dor|mid** (si dôr′mid), *n. Trademark.* a synthetic drug used as a sedative and hypnotic. *Formula:* $C_9H_{16}N_2O_2$

**sed|ra** (sed′rə), *n., pl.* **-ras, -rath** (-rōth). *Judaism.* a weekly section of the Pentateuch which is read in the synagogue on the Sabbath. [< Aramaic *sedrah* order, arrangement. Compare Hebrew *sēder* Seder.]

**se|duce** (si düs′, -dyüs′), *v.t.,* **-duced, -duc|ing.** **1** to tempt to wrongdoing; persuade to do wrong: *Benedict Arnold, was seduced by the offer of great wealth and betrayed his country to the enemy.* **SYN**: corrupt. **2** to lead away from virtue; lead astray: *Caelius ... tried to seduce Caesar's garrison and was put to death for his treachery* (James A. Froude). **SYN**: mislead. **3** to win over; beguile; entice: *Pandora was seduced by curiosity. ... Or if not drive, seduce them to our party* (Milton). **4** to persuade or entice to have sexual intercourse; cause to surrender chastity. **SYN**: betray.
[< Latin *sēdūcere* < *sē-* aside, away + *dūcere* to lead] —**se|duc′ing|ly**, *adv.*

**se|duc|ee** (si dü′sē′, -dyü′-), *n.* a person who is seduced.

**se|duce|ment** (si düs′mənt, -dyüs′-), *n.* = seduction.

**se|duc|er** (si dü′sər, -dyü′-), *n.* a person, especially a man, who seduces.

**se|duc|i|ble** (si dü′sə bəl, -dyü′-), *adj.* that can be seduced; corruptible.

**se|duc|tion** (si duk′shən), *n.* **1** the act of seducing. **2** the condition of being seduced. **3** something that seduces; temptation; attraction. **SYN**: enticement. [< Latin *sēductiō, -ōnis* < *sēdūcere;* see etym. under **seduce**]

**se|duc|tive** (si duk′tiv), *adj.* **1** that tempts or entices; alluring: *a very seductive offer.* **2** captivating; charming: *a seductive smile.* **3** arousing physical desire: *a woman with a seductive figure.* —**se|duc′tive|ly**, *adv.* —**se|duc′tive|ness**, *n.*

**se|duc|tress** (si duk′tris), *n.* a woman who seduces.

**se|du|li|ty** (si dü′lə tē, -dyü′-), *n.* sedulous quality; sedulous application or care.

**sed|u|lous** (sej′ů ləs), *adj.* hard-working; diligent; painstaking: *The most sedulous friend of union ... was Benjamin Franklin* (George Bancroft). *The laziest will be sedulous and active where he is in pursuit of what he has much at heart* (Jonathan Swift). **SYN**: industrious, assiduous, persevering, untiring. [< Latin *sēdulus* (with English *-ous*) < *sē dolō* diligently; (literally) without deception; *sē,* for *sine* without, *dolō,* ablative of *dolus* guilt, deceit] —**sed′u|lous|ly**, *adv.* —**sed′u|lous|ness**, *n.*

**se|dum** (sē′dəm), *n.* any one of a large genus of fleshy herbs and small shrubs of the orpine family, most of which have clusters of yellow, white, or pink flowers; stonecrop. [< Latin *sedum* houseleek]

**see¹** (sē), *v.,* **saw, seen, see|ing.** —***v.t.*** **1** to look at; be aware of by using the eyes: *See that black cloud.* **2** to use the eyes to see (things): *to see a tennis match or a play.* **SYN**: watch, witness, regard, view. **3** *Figurative.* to be aware of with the mind; understand: *I see what you mean. I did not immediately see the purpose of his lordship's question* (Scott). *She sees only his good qualities. He sees his father in the child's character.* **SYN**: recognize, notice, perceive, apprehend, discern. **4** to find out; learn: *I will see what needs to be done. Please see who is at the door.* **SYN**: ascertain. **5** to take care; make sure: *See that the work is done properly. See that the records are brought up to date.* **6** to think; consider: *You may go if you see fit to do so.* **SYN**: judge, deem. **7** to like or find likeable, useful, valuable, or worthy: *What she sees in him is beyond me.* **8** to foresee; anticipate: *I don't see myself living anywhere but here* (Shirley Hazzard). **SYN**: envision, imagine. **9** to have knowledge or experience of: *to see service in two wars. That coat has seen hard wear. The wisest men whom the world has seen* (Scott). **10** to go with; attend; escort: *to see a girl home.* **11a** to have a talk with; meet: *He wishes to see you alone.* **b** to call on: *I went to see a friend.* **c** to receive a visit from: *She is too ill to see anyone.* **d** to visit; attend: *We plan to see the Rose Bowl game.* **12** to meet (a bet in a card game) by staking an equal sum; call.

*—v.i.* **1** to perceive objects with the eyes: *I write and read till I can't see, and then I walk* (Lady Mary Wortley Montague). **2** to have the power of sight: *The blind do not see.* **3** *Figurative.* to perceive with the mind; understand: *I have explained it very carefully. Do you see now?* **4** to find out: *Ah, something terrible has happened! I must run and see!* (Hawthorne). **5** to look; behold: *But, see, the evening star comes forth* (Tennyson).

**see after**, to take care of: *Here Tom, Tom, see after the luggage* (Henry Kingsley).

**see into**, to understand the real character or hidden purpose of: *Well hath your Highness seen into this Duke* (Shakespeare).

**see off**, to go with to the starting place of a journey: *Escorted by a multitude of relatives and friends, who all went down ... to see them off* (Washington Irving).

**see out**, **a** to go through with; finish: *He evidently meant to see this thing out* (J. K. Jerome). **b** to survive: *Dev is in his eighties and may not see out his second Presidential term* (Manchester Guardian Weekly).

**see through**, **a** to understand the real character or hidden purpose of: *I saw through her dodge.* **b** to go through with (a matter) to the end; finish: *I mean to see this job through. I'm responsible and I'll see it through the only way I can* (Graham Greene). *Mr. Brown ... will remain at the Department of Economic Affairs to see the prices and incomes policy through* (Manchester Guardian Weekly). **c** to watch over or help (a person) through difficulty: *Her mother saw her through the measles. We will see him through if he were to burn the college down* (Henry Kingsley).

**see to (it)**, to look after; take care of; make sure: *He saw to it that his son went to college. Inflation has seen to it that the £20,000 ... is no longer the "fortune" it used to be* (Manchester Guardian Weekly).

[Old English *sēon*]

*—Syn. v.t.* **1 See, perceive, observe** mean to become aware of something through sight. **See**, the general word, implies awareness but not necessarily conscious effort or recognition: *We saw someone standing in the doorway.* **Perceive**, often a formal substitute for *see*, can also imply conscious notice or recognition of what is seen: *We perceived the figure to be your mother.* **Observe** implies conscious effort and attention: *We observed a change in her.*

► Nonstandard forms of the past tense are *see, seen,* and *seed: Jack seen him drive away,* etc. In the eastern states, for which evidence is available, *see* is the predominant dialectal form in New England, most of New York State, and northern Pennsylvania, and also occurs in parts of the coastal South; *seen* predominates in central and southern Pennsylvania, New Jersey, Delaware, Maryland, West Virginia, and South Carolina, and occurs at least sporadically everywhere else; *seed* is restricted to the South.

**see²** (sē), *n.* **1** the position or authority of a bishop. **2** the district under a bishop's authority; diocese; bishopric. **3** the seat of a bishop in his diocese. [< Old French *sie,* or *sied* < Latin *sēdēs* abode < *sedēre* to sit]

**see·a·ble** (sē′ə bəl), *adj.* that can be seen; visible.

**See·beck effect** (zā′bek, sē′-), the production of a current in a circuit composed of two different metals when the junctions between these metals are maintained at different temperatures. [< Thomas J. *Seebeck,* 1770-1831, a German physicist, who discovered it]

**see·catch** (sē′kach′), *n., pl.* **-catch·ie** (-kach′ē). the adult male of the fur seal. [< Russian *sekach*]

**seed** (sēd), *n., pl.* **seeds** or **seed**, *adj., v.* *—n.* **1a** the part of a plant from which a flower, vegetable, or other plant grows. A seed consists of a protective outer skin or coat enclosing the embryo that will become the new plant and a supply of food for its growth. *We planted seeds in the garden. Part of every crop is saved for seed.* **b** any seedlike part of certain plants, such as the fruit of the strawberry. **2** a bulb, sprout, or any part of a plant from which a new plant will grow. **3** *Figurative.* the source or beginning of anything: *the seeds of trouble. Every guilty deed holds in itself the seed of retribution and undying pain* (Longfellow). **4** *Figurative.* children; descendants: *The Jews are the seed of Abraham.* **5** semen; sperm. **6** very young oysters; seed oysters. **7** a minute bubble arising in glass during fusion. **8** *Sports.* a player whose name has been seeded in the draw of a tournament.

*—adj.* of or containing seeds; used for seeds.

*—v.t.* **1** to sow with seed; scatter seeds over: *The farmer seeded his field with corn.* **2** to sow (seeds): *Dandelions seed themselves.* **3** to remove the seeds from: *She seeded the grapes.* **4** *Sports.* to scatter or distribute (the names of players) so that the best players do not meet in the early part of a tournament. **5** to scatter dry ice or other chemicals into (clouds) from an airplane in an effort to produce rain: *Rainfall can be increased by 9 to 17 per cent or more by seeding clouds with silver iodide smoke* (Newsweek).

*—v.i.* **1** to sow seed. **2** to produce seed; shed seeds; grow to maturity: *Some plants will not seed in a cold climate.*

**go** (or **run**) **to seed**, **a** to come to the time of yielding seeds: *Dandelions go to seed when their heads turn white.* **b** *Figurative.* to come to the end, as of vigor, usefulness, or prosperity: *After the mines closed, the miners left and the town went to seed.*

[Old English *sǣd*] *—***seed′like′**, *adj.*

**seed·age** (sē′dij), *n.* the propagation of plants by means of seeds and spores.

**seed·ball** (sēd′bôl′), *n.* **1** a capsule containing seeds. **2** a mass of utricles or other one-seeded fruits.

**seed·bed** (sēd′bed′), *n.* **1** a piece of ground prepared for planting seed: *For a good seedbed, topsoil is needed ... about eight inches deep after it has settled* (New York Times). **2** *Figurative: The Middle East provides 80 per cent of the oil required by the European economy ... and could be the seedbed of a war* (Atlantic).

**seed bud**, *Botany.* **1** the part of a plant that develops into a seed; ovule. **2** the bud of a plant still in the seed; plumule.

**seed·cake** (sēd′kāk′), *n.* **1** a cake or cooky flavored with caraway or other spicy seeds. **2** the cake left after the oil has been pressed from cottonseeds.

**seed capsule**, = seed vessel.

**seed·case** (sēd′kās′), *n.* any pod, capsule, or other dry, hollow fruit that contains seeds; seed vessel; pericarp.

**seed coat**, the outer covering of a seed.

**seed coral**, coral in tiny pieces, used to make jewelry.

**seed corn**, or **seed·corn** (sēd′kôrn′), *n.* corn grown or saved for use as seed.

**seed·eat·er** (sēd′ē′tər), *n.* **1** = grassquit. **2** any granivorous bird.

**seed·ed** (sē′did), *adj.* modified, placed, or fixed by seeding, as at tennis.

**-seeded**, *combining form.* having ___ seed or seeds: *One-seeded = having one seed.*

**seed·er** (sē′dər), *n.* **1** a person who seeds. **2** a machine or device for planting seeds. **3** a machine or device for removing seeds.

**seed fern**, = pteridosperm.

**seed·i·ly** (sē′də lē), *adv.* shabbily: *The poor artist was seedily dressed.*

**seed·i·ness** (sē′dē nis), *n.* seedy condition.

**seed·ing** (sē′ding), *n.* **1** a sowing of seed; sowing with seed. **2** the production of seed. **3** the distribution of players in a tournament. **4** the dropping of dry ice or other chemicals into clouds.

**seed lac**, an especially pure form of lac.

**seed leaf**, the embryo leaf in the seed of a plant; cotyledon.

**seed·less** (sēd′lis), *adj.* without seeds: *seedless grapefruit.* *—***seed′less·ness**, *n.*

**seed·ling** (sēd′ling), *n., adj.* *—n.* **1** a young plant grown from a seed. **2** a young tree less than three feet high.

*—adj.* **1** developed or raised from seed. **2** like a small seed; existing in a rudimentary state. **3** (of oysters) hatched from seed.

**seed·man** (sēd′mən), *n., pl.* **-men.** = seedsman.

**seed money**, money used as initial capital to begin a new operation or project: *The bonds would have enabled the state to gain $17 million, to be used as seed money to set up the loan guarantee rotary fund* (New York Times).

**seed·ness** (sēd′nis), *n. Dialect.* seedtime.

**seed oyster**, a very young oyster ready for planting.

**seed pearl**, a very small pearl, often imperfect.

**seed plant**, any plant that bears seeds. Most seed plants have flowers and produce seeds enclosed in fruits; some, such as the pines, form seeds on cones.

**seed pod**, or **seed·pod** (sēd′pod′), *n.* a pod containing seeds, such as a legume or silique.

**seeds·man** (sēdz′mən), *n., pl.* **-men. 1** a dealer in seed. **2** a sower of seed.

**seed snipe**, any short-legged bird of a group resembling the quail and plover, found on rocky and barren ground of South America.

**seed stock**, or **seed·stock** (sēd′stok′), *n.* **1** a stock of seed kept for sowing. **2** a stock of animals, such as cattle, kept only for breeding purposes.

**seed tick**, a young or small tick, especially the young of a cattle tick.

**seed·time** (sēd′tīm′), *n.* the season for sowing seeds.

**seed tree**, **1** any tree which bears seed. **2** *Forestry.* a tree which provides the seed for natural reproduction.

**seed vessel**, any pod, capsule, or other hollow fruit that contains seeds; pericarp.

**seed weevil**, any one of various small weevils that feed on the seeds of beans, peas, and similar plants.

**seed·y** (sē′dē), *adj.,* **seed·i·er, seed·i·est. 1** full of seed. **2** gone to seed. **3** *Figurative.* **a** shabby; no longer fresh or new: *seedy clothes. ... a seedy man who had evidently spent the night in a doorway* (Thomas Bailey Aldrich). **SYN**: threadbare. **b** *Informal.* somewhat ill: *He had felt seedy all day and had taken no food* (George du Maurier).

**seed year**, *Forestry.* a year in which a given species of tree bears seed, especially one in which it bears abundantly.

**see·ing** (sē′ing), *conj., n., adj.* *—conj.* in view of the fact; considering; since: *Seeing that it is 10 o'clock, we will wait no longer. Deep harm to disobey, seeing obedience is the bond of rule* (Tennyson). **SYN**: because.

*—n.* **1** the act of a person or thing that sees: *a play worth seeing.* **2** ability to see; sight; vision. **3** the degree to which the atmosphere remains still and steady with respect to observation of heavenly bodies through a telescope: *Seeing is the scientists' term for the same effect that causes stars to "twinkle"* (Science News Letter).

*—adj.* that sees.

**seeing eye**, a device that detects an object and often activates some mechanism to which it is connected: *The photoelectric cell has become familiar in the form of ... the "seeing eye" for opening doors* (Scientific American).

**Seeing Eye**, an organization that breeds and trains dogs as guides for blind people.

**seeing eye dog**, a dog trained as a guide for the blind; guide dog: *Most seeing eye dogs are German shepherds* (George Werntz, Jr.).

**seek** (sēk), *v.,* **sought, seek·ing.** *—v.t.* **1** to try to find; look for; search for; hunt: *to seek something lost. The boys are seeking a good camping place.* **2** to try to get: *to seek relief from pain, to seek someone's friendship. Most men seek wealth; all men seek happiness. Friends sought his advice.* **3** to try; attempt; endeavor: *to seek to right a wrong. He seeks to make peace with his enemies. The schools seek to be laboratories where moral action is encouraged and practiced* (Atlantic). **4** to go to: *Being sleepy, he sought his bed.*

*—v.i.* **1** to make a search: *to seek for something lost. Seek, and ye shall find* (Matthew 7:7). **2** *Archaic.* to go: *Wisdom's self oft seeks to sweet retired solitude* (Milton).

**be sought after**, to be desired or in demand: *His company is greatly sought after.*

**to seek**, **a** to be sought; to be found: *The reason is not far to seek.* **b** absent; lacking: *Intelligence is sadly to seek among them.* **c** *Archaic.* at a loss; puzzled: *For the details of our itinerary, I am all to seek* (Robert Louis Stevenson).

[Old English *sēcan.* Compare etym. under **beseech.**] *—***seek′er**, *n.*

**seek·ing** (sē′king), *n., adj.* *—n.* the act of trying to find something: *a seeking after riches.*

*—adj.* that seeks; searching: *a seeking intellect.*

**of one's (own) seeking**, due to one's own fault: *The misfortune is entirely of my own seeking* (T. Hook).

*—***seek′ing·ly**, *adv.*

**seel** (sēl), *v.t.* **1** *Falconry.* **a** to stitch together the eyelids of (a hawk while being trained). **b** to stitch up (a bird's eyes). **2** *Archaic, Figurative.* to make blind: *She that, so young, could give out such a seeming, to seel her father's eyes up close as oak* (Shakespeare). Also, **seal**. [Middle English *silen* < Old French *ciller*, or *siller* < *cil* eyelash < Latin *cilium*]

**see|ly** (sē′lē), *adj. Dialect.* **1** insignificant; trifling. **2** mean; poor. **3** feeble; frail. [earlier form of *silly*]

**seem** (sēm), *v.i.* **1** to look like; appear to be: *This apple seemed good but was rotten inside. Does this room seem hot to you? He seemed a very old man. He seemed very strong for his age.* **2** to appear to oneself: *I still seem to hear the music.* **3** to appear to exist: *There seems no need to wait longer.* **4** to appear to be true or to be the case: *The dog seems to like that bone. It seems likely to rain. This, it seems, is your idea of cleaning a room.* [< Scandinavian (compare Old Icelandic *sœma* conform to)] —**seem′er**, *n.*
—***Syn.*** **1 Seem, appear** mean to give the impression or have the outward look of being something that it may or may not be in fact or reality. **Seem** emphasizes the impression created; **appear** emphasizes the outward looks: *He appears pale but he seems not to be sick.*

**seem|ing** (sē′ming), *adj., n.* —***adj.*** that appears to be; apparent: *a seeming advantage.* **SYN**: ostensible.
—***n.*** appearance; likeness: *It was worse in its seeming than in reality.* **SYN**: semblance. —**seem′ing|ly**, *adv.* —**seem′ing|ness**, *n.*

**seem|li|ness** (sēm′lē nis), *n.* **1** fitness; suitability; propriety; decorum; decency: *England is the country, so we have always been taught to believe, for seemliness and moderation* (London Times). **2** pleasing appearance; attractiveness.

**seem|ly** (sēm′lē), *adj.,* **-li|er, -li|est,** *adv.* —***adj.*** **1** fitting or becoming with respect to good taste; suitable; proper: *Some old people do not consider modern dances seemly.* **SYN**: See syn. under **fitting**. **2** *Archaic.* having a pleasing appearance: *... a seemly Georgian residence* (Arnold Bennett).
—***adv.*** properly; becomingly; fittingly: *Try to behave seemly. Nor is it seemly or piously attributed to the justice of God* (Milton).
[< Scandinavian (compare Old Icelandic *sœmiligr*)]

**seen** (sēn), *v., adj.* —***v.*** the past participle of **see**[1]: *Have you seen my brother?*
—***adj.*** skilled; versed; experienced: *A schoolmaster well seen in music* (Shakespeare).

**See of Rome**, = Holy See.

**seep** (sēp), *v., n.* —***v.i.*** to leak slowly; ooze; trickle: *Water seeps through sand. The independence seeped out of him* (Sinclair Lewis).
—***n.*** **1** moisture that seeps out. **2** a small spring. [apparently variant of *sipe* leak, Old English *sīpian* to sink low. Compare etym. under **sip**.]

**seep|age** (sē′pij), *n.* **1** the action of seeping; slow leakage; oozing. **2** moisture or liquid that seeps: *two feet of seepage in the cellar.*

**seep|y** (sē′pē), *adj.,* **seep|i|er, seep|i|est.** **1** full of moisture. **2** poorly drained: *seepy land.*

**seer**[1] (sir *for 1;* sē′ər *for 2*), *n.* **1** a person who foresees or foretells future events; prophet: *Seers ... are ... ever with us, whether they call themselves oracles, shamans, soothsayers, psychical mediums, or, in up-to-date parlance, "sensitives"* (New Yorker). **SYN**: augur, prognosticator. **2** a person who sees.

**seer**[2] (sir), *n.* = ser.

**seer|ess** (sir′is), *n.* a woman seer; prophetess.

**seer|suck|er** (sir′suk′ər), *n.* a cloth with alternate stripes of plain and crinkled material. It is made of cotton or a synthetic, or both, and is used especially for clothing worn during hot weather. [earlier *sirsaka* < Hindustani < Persian *shīr o shakkar* (literally) milk and sugar (in allusion to the stripes)]

**see|saw** (sē′sô′), *n., v., adj.* —***n.*** **1** a plank resting on a support near its middle so that the ends can move up and down; teeter-totter. **2** a children's game in which the children sit at opposite ends of such a plank and move alternately up and down or back and forth. **3** a movement up and down or back and forth: *the seesaw of a storm-tossed ship.* (*Figurative.*) *With uncanny skill he has managed to place himself at the exact dead center of the seesaw of French politics* (Atlantic). **4** = crossruff (in whist).
—***v.i., v.t.*** **1** to move up and down on a balanced plank: *The two boys seesawed on the old plank for some time.* **2** to move up and down or back and forth: *The ancient inn ... whose flapping sign these fifty years has seesawed to and fro* (Oliver Wendell Holmes).
—***adj.*** moving up and down or back and forth: (*Figurative.*) *I don't remember ever being seesaw ... when I'd made my mind up* (George Eliot).
[apparently varied reduplication of *saw*[1]]

**seethe** (sēᴛʜ), *v.,* **seethed** or (*Obsolete*) **sod, seethed** or (*Obsolete*) **sod|den, seeth|ing,** *n.*
—***v.i.*** **1a** to bubble and foam: *Water seethed under the falls.* **b** *Archaic.* to boil. **2** *Figurative.* to be excited; be disturbed; be agitated: *The pirate crew was seething with discontent and ready to mutiny.* **SYN**: See syn. under **boil**.
—***v.t.*** **1** to soak; steep: *They drown their wits, seethe their brains in ale* (Robert Burton). **2** *Archaic.* to boil: *The cook seethed the mutton.*
—***n.*** a state of agitation.
[Old English *sēothan*]

**seeth|ing** (sē′ᴛʜing), *adj.* ebullient; tumultuous: *seething foam,* (*Figurative.*) *seething rage.* —**seeth′ing|ly**, *adv.*

**see-through** (sē′thrü′), *adj., n.* —***adj.*** **1** transparent; permitting inspection of the inside or contents of something: *a see-through computer, a see-through model of the human body. The housewife ... was talking about prepackaged meat wrapped with see-through tops but with cardboard on the bottom* (New York Times). **2** so thin in texture that it can be seen through; very sheer: *The waitress ... was wearing enormous false eyelashes and black knitted see-through pants suit* (New Yorker).
—***n.*** a see-through dress, blouse, or other garment: *The resulting dresses are practically see-throughs* (Time).

**seg** (seg), *n. U.S. Slang.* a segregationist.

**seg.**, segment.

**se|gar** (si gär′), *n.* = cigar.

**seg|gar** (seg′ər), *n., v.t.* = sagger.

✱**seg|ment** (seg′mənt), *n., v.* —***n.*** **1** a piece or part cut off, marked off, or broken off; division; section: *An orange is easily pulled apart into its segments. There is a solid segment of educated citizens in the Latin American countries as well as in the United States* (Newsweek). **SYN**: portion. **2** *Geometry.* **a** a part of a circle cut off by a line, especially a part bounded by an arc and its chord. **b** a part of a sphere cut off by two parallel planes. **c** any finite section between two points on a line. **3** *Biology.* one of a series of parts having a more or less similar structure: *a segment of a tapeworm.*
—***v.t., v.i.*** to divide into segments: *The body of a vertebrate is segmented according to the number of vertebrae, whether any actual division of parts may be evident or not.*
[< Latin *segmentum* < *secāre* to cut]

✱**segment**
definitions 2a,2c

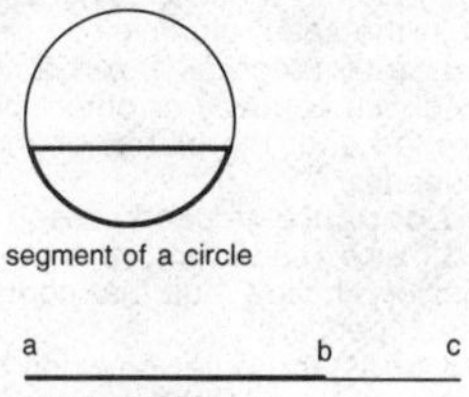

segment of a circle

a b c

segment of line, a c

**seg|men|tal** (seg men′təl), *adj.* **1** composed of segments. **2** of or having to do with segments. **3** having the form of a segment of a circle: *a segmental arch.* —**seg|men′tal|ly**, *adv.*

**segmental apparatus**, the brain exclusive of the cerebrum and the cerebellum; brain stem.

**seg|men|tar|y** (seg′mən ter′ē), *adj.* = segmental.

**seg|men|ta|tion** (seg′mən tā′shən), *n.* **1** division into segments. **2** the growth and division of a cell into two, four, eight cells, and so on.

**segmentation cavity**, the cavity of the blastula.

**se|gno** (sā′nyō), *n., pl.* **-gni** (-nyē). *Music.* a sign used to indicate the beginning or (rarely) the end of repetitions. [< Italian *segno* (literally) sign < Latin *sīgnum*. See etym. of doublet **sign**.]

**se|go** (sē′gō), *n., pl.* **-gos.** = sego lily. [American English < Shoshonean (Paiute) *sego*]

**sego lily**, **1** a perennial herb of the lily family, native to the western United States, with showy, white, trumpet-shaped flowers and an edible bulb. Its blossom is the floral emblem of Utah. **2** its bulb.

**seg|re|ant** (seg′rē ənt), *adj. Heraldry.* (of a griffin) rising on the hind legs, with the wings raised. [origin uncertain]

**seg|re|ga|ble** (seg′rə gə bəl), *adj. Genetics.* able to undergo segregation.

**seg|re|gant** (seg′rə gənt), *n.* **1** a person or thing that is or has been segregated. **2** *Genetics.* an organism resulting from segregation: *After prolonged growth and division in culture, the scientists isolated segregants that contained the single parental number of chromosomes* (Frank B. Rothman).

**seg|re|gate** (*v.* seg′rə gāt; *adj., n.* seg′re git, -gāt), *v.,* **-gat|ed, -gat|ing,** *adj., n.* —***v.t.*** **1** to separate from others; set apart; isolate: *The doctor segregated the child who was sick with mumps to protect the other patients.* **2** to separate or keep apart (one racial group) from another or from the rest of society by maintaining separate schools, separate public facilities, etc.
—***v.i.*** **1** to separate from the rest and collect in one place. **2** *Genetics.* to undergo segregation.
—***adj.*** segregated.
—***n.*** = segregant.
[< Latin *sēgregāre* (with English *-ate*[1]) < *sē-* apart (from) + *grex, gregis* herd]

**seg|re|ga|tion** (seg′rə gā′shən), *n.* **1** a separation from others; setting apart; isolation: *the segregation of lepers.* **2** the separation of one racial group from another or from the rest of society, especially in schools, theaters, restaurants, and other public places and private places of meeting, especially social gathering: *The United States Supreme Court ruled in 1954 that segregation in public schools is unconstitutional.* **3** a thing separated or set apart; isolated part, group, etc. **4** *Genetics.* the separation of opposing (allelomorphic) pairs of genes or characters, occurring during meiosis, in the gametes formed by a hybrid organism.

**seg|re|ga|tion|ist** (seg′rə gā′shə nist), *n., adj.* —***n.*** a person who believes in or practices racial segregation.
—***adj.*** of or having to do with segregationists or segregation.

**seg|re|ga|tive** (seg′rə gā′tiv), *adj.* **1** tending to segregate. **2** keeping apart from others; unsociable.

**seg|re|ga|tor** (seg′rə gā′tər), *n.* a person or thing that segregates.

**se|gue** (sā′gwā), *n., v.,* **-gued, -gue|ing.** —***n.*** a musical direction at the end of a movement to proceed with the following movement immediately.
—***v.i.*** **1** *Music.* to proceed immediately with the following movement; attacca. **2** *Figurative.* to proceed immediately; follow without a pause: *The main course ended ... and we segued into the dessert* (New Yorker).
[< Italian *segue,* third person singular of *seguire* follow < Latin *sequī*]

**se|gui|dil|la** (sā′gē ᴛʜēl′yä), *n.* **1** a Spanish dance in triple rhythm for two persons. **2** the music (instrumental or vocal) for such a dance. [< Spanish *seguidilla* < *seguida* sequence; (literally) a following < *seguir* to follow < Latin *sequī*]

**sei** (sā), *n.* = sei whale.

**sei|cen|to** (sā chen′tō), *n.* the 1600's (used especially in Italian art and literature of that period). [< Italian *seicento,* short for *mille seicento* one thousand and six hundred (that is, after 1600)]

**seiche** (sāsh), *n.* an occasional rhythmical movement from side to side of the water of a lake, with fluctuation of water level, thought to be caused by sudden local variations in atmospheric pressure. [< Swiss French *seiche*]

**sei|chom|e|ter** (sā shom′ə tər), *n.* an instrument measuring the fluctuations of the level of the water in lakes.

**sei|del** (zī′dəl), *n.* a mug for beer. [< German *Seidel* < Latin *situla* bucket]

**Seid|litz powder** or **powders** (sed′lits), a saline laxative consisting of two powders, one tartaric acid and the other a mixture of sodium bicarbonate and Rochelle salt (potassium sodium tartrate); Rochelle powder. These are dissolved separately, and the solutions are mixed and drunk while effervescing. Also, **Sedlitz powder**. [patterned on earlier *Seidlitz salt* (because of the similarity in use) < *Seidlitz,* a village in Czechoslovakia, the site of a mineral spring]

**seif** (sīf), *n.* a long dune found in sandy deserts in which the winds are variable. [< Arabic *saif* sword (because of its shape)]

**sei|gneur** (sēn yėr′; *French* se nyœr′), *n.* **1** a feudal lord or landowner; seignior. A grand seigneur was a person of high rank or one who behaved as a person of high rank should. **SYN**: liege. **2** (formerly, in Canada) the holder of a landed estate the title to which had its origin in a feudal grant from the king of France. [< French *seigneur* < Old French *seignor* seignior < Latin *seniōrem,* accusative of *senior.* See etym. of doublets **seignior, sieur**.]

**sei|gneur|i|al** (sēn yůr′ē əl), *adj.* of or having to do with a seigneur or seigniory: *seigneurial rights.*

**sei|gneur|ie** (sēn′yər ē; *French* se nyœ rē′), *n.* = seigneury.

**sei|gneur|y** (sēn′yər ē), *n., pl.* **-gneur|ies.** formerly, in Canada: **1** a landed estate held by feudal tenure. **2** the mansion of a seigneur. [< French *seigneurie* seigniory < Old French *seignorie* < *seignor* seignior]

**seign|ior** (sēn′yər), *n.* **1a** a feudal lord; nobleman who held his lands by feudal grant. **b** any lord (holder) of a manor; gentleman. **2** a title of respect, formerly corresponding (especially in France) approximately to *Sir.* [< Old French *seignor,* or *seignior* < Latin *senior.* See etym. of doublets **seigneur, sieur**.]

**seign|ior|age** (sēn′yər ij), *n.* **1** something claimed by a sovereign or superior as a prerogative. **2** a charge for coining gold or silver. **3** the difference between the face value of a coin and the cost of the bullion and the minting of it.

**seign|ior|al** (sēn′yər əl), *adj.* = seigniorial.

**seign|ior|i|al** (sēn yôr′ē əl, -yōr′-), *adj.* of or having to do with a seignior.

**seign|ior|y** (sēn′yər ē), *n., pl.* **-ior|ies.** **1** the power, authority, rights, or privileges of a seignior. **2** a feudal lord's domain. **3** a group of feudal lords. **4** = seigneury. [< Old French *seignorie* < *seignor;* see etym. under **seignior**]

**seign|or|age** (sēn′yər ij), *n.* = seigniorage.

**seign|or|i|al** (sēn yôr′ē əl), *adj.* = seigniorial.

***seine** (sān), *n., v.,* **seined, sein|ing.** **—*n.*** a fishing net that hangs straight down in the water. A seine has floats at the top and weights at the bottom.

**—*v.i.*** to fish or catch fish with a seine.

**—*v.t.*** **1** to catch (fish) with a seine. **2** to fish (a body of water) with a seine or seines.

[Old English *segne* < Latin *sagēna* < Greek *sagēnē*]

***seine**

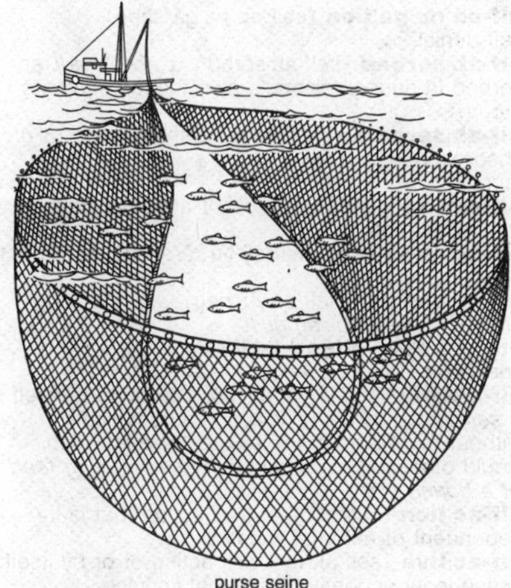

purse seine

**seine boat**, a boat for carrying and paying out a seine.

**sein|er** (sā′nər), *n.* a boat used in fishing with a seine.

**seise** (sēz), *v.t.,* **seised, seis|ing.** *Archaic or Law.* seize. [spelling variant of *seize*]

**seised** (sēzd), *adj. Law.* having ownership and right of possession, as of a freehold estate.

**sei|sin** (sē′zin), *n.* = seizin.

**seism** (sī′zəm, -səm), *n.* = earthquake.

**seis|mal** (sīz′məl, sīs′-), *adj.* = seismic.

**seis|met|ic** (sīz met′ik, sīs-), *adj.* = seismic.

**seis|mic** (sīz′mik, sīs′-), *adj.* **1** of or having to do with earthquakes or other movements of the earth's crust: *Seismic waves radiate through the earth.* **2** caused by an earthquake or other movement of the earth's crust: *a seismic catastrophe.* [< Greek *seismós* earthquake (< *seíein* shake) + English *-ic*]

**seis|mi|cal** (sīz′mə kəl, sīs′-), *adj.* = seismic. **—seis′mi|cal|ly,** *adv.*

**seis|mic|i|ty** (sīz mis′ə tē, sīs-), *n.* **1** liability to earthquakes. **2** the relative frequency of earthquakes in a given area: *One involves finding the number of earthquakes of this size in two places of well-measured seismicity, Southern California and New Zealand* (Bulletin of Atomic Scientists).

**seis|mism** (sīz′miz əm, sīs′-), *n.* the phenomena of earthquakes, collectively.

**seismo-**, *combining form.* earthquake: *Seismology = the scientific study of earthquakes.* [< Greek *seismós* < *seíein* shake]

**seis|mo|gram** (sīz′mə gram, sīs′-), *n.* the record made by a seismograph.

**seis|mo|graph** (sīz′mə graf, -gräf; sīs′-), *n.* an instrument for recording the direction, intensity, and duration of earthquakes or other movements of the earth's crust.

**seis|mog|ra|pher** (sīz mog′rə fər, sīs-), *n.* a person skilled in seismography.

**seis|mo|graph|ic** (sīz′mə graf′ik, sīs′-), *adj.* **1** of a seismograph. **2** of seismography.

**seis|mo|graph|i|cal** (sīz′mə graf′ə kəl, sīs′-), *adj.* = seismographic.

**seis|mog|ra|phy** (sīz mog′rə fē, sīs-), *n.* **1** the art of using the seismograph. **2** the branch of seismology dealing especially with the mapping and description of earthquakes.

**seismol.**, **1** seismological. **2** seismology.

**seis|mo|log|i|cal** (sīz′mə loj′ə kəl, sīs′-), *adj.* of or having to do with seismology. **—seis′mo|log′i|cal|ly,** *adv.*

**seis|mol|o|gist** (sīz mol′ə jist, sīs-), *n.* an expert in seismology.

**seis|mol|o|gy** (sīz mol′ə jē, sīs-), *n.* the scientific study of earthquakes and other movements of the earth's crust: *Seismology has lifted our notions about the interior of our planet from the realm of wild speculation to the stage of scientific measurement and well-reasoned inferences* (Scientific American).

**seis|mom|e|ter** (sīz mom′ə tər, sīs-), *n.* = seismograph.

**seis|mo|met|ric** (sīz′mə met′rik, sīs′-), *adj.* of or having to do with seismometry.

**seis|mo|met|ri|cal** (sīz′mə met′rə kəl, sīs′-), *adj.* = seismometric.

**seis|mom|e|try** (sīz mom′ə trē, sīs-), *n.* the scientific recording and study of earthquake phenomena, especially by means of the seismometer.

**seis|mo|scope** (sīz′mə skōp, sīs′-), *n.* a simple form of seismograph; instrument for indicating the occurrence of earthquake shocks.

**seis|mo|scop|ic** (sīz′mə skop′ik, sīs′-), *adj.* relating to or furnished by the seismoscope.

**seis|mo|tec|ton|ic** (sīz′mə tek ton′ik, sīs′-), *adj. Geology.* having to do with the structure of the earth's crust that is connected with earthquakes.

**seis|mot|ic** (sīz mot′ik, sīs-), *adj.* of or having to do with earthquakes; seismic.

**sei whale**, a very common rorqual of a bluish-black color; sei. [partial translation of Norwegian *seihval* < *sei* coalfish + *val* whale]

**seiz|a|ble** (sē′zə bəl), *adj.* that can be seized: *rich foreign lands, full of seizable wealth* (H. G. Wells).

**seize** (sēz), *v.,* **seized, seiz|ing.** **—*v.t.*** **1** to take hold of suddenly; clutch; grasp: *In fright she seized his arm.* **2** *Figurative.* to grasp with the mind; apprehend: *to seize an idea, to seize the point. He was confronted with what was really the more difficult task of seizing the trend of contemporary events* (Edmund Wilson). **3a** to take possession of by force; capture: *The soldiers seized the city.* **b** to take prisoner; arrest; catch: *to seize a man wanted for murder.* **4** *Figurative.* to take possession of or come upon suddenly: *to be seized with terror. A fever seized him.* **5** to take possession of (goods) by legal authority: *to seize smuggled goods.* **6** *Law.* to put in legal possession of (as a feudal holding or property); establish in (an office or dignity). **7** *Nautical.* to bind, lash, or join by winding around cord, wire, etc.: *to seize one rope to another.*

**—*v.i.*** *Metallurgy.* to cohere.

**seize on** (or **upon**) **a** to take hold of suddenly: *The snake seized on its prey.* **b** *Figurative.* to take possession of: *Victoria seized upon the idea with avidity* (Lytton Strachey). **c** *Figurative.* to take advantage of; make use of: *That group ... seized upon the day of his burial to bring out ... a fierce manifesto against him* (Edmund Wilson).

**seize up, a** (of bearings, joints, or the like) to cohere; become jammed: *Human hip bones seize up due to arthritis or have to be removed because of tumours* (New Scientist). **b** *British Informal, Figurative.* to become deadlocked; break down: *There is at present a real risk that the negotiations ... will seize up* (Listener).

[< Old French *seisir* < Late Latin *sacīre,* perhaps < Germanic (compare Old High German *satjan* put in possession)]

**—*Syn.*** ***v.t.*** **1, 2 Seize, grasp, clutch** mean to take hold of something, literally or figuratively. **Seize** suggests taking hold suddenly and with force, or (used figuratively of the mind) understanding something hard to get the meaning of: *The dog seized the sausages.* (*Figurative.*) *He seized the theme of the story after reading it only once.* **Grasp** suggests seizing and holding firmly, as with the fingers, claws, or talons closed around the object, or to understand fully: *The eagle grasped the snake.* (*Figurative.*) *She grasped the seriousness of his remarks.* **Clutch** suggests grasping eagerly, even desperately, and sometimes ineffectively: *A drowning man will clutch a straw.*

**seiz|er** (sē′zər), *n.* a person or thing that seizes.

**seize-up** (sēz′up′), *n.* **1** the state of bearings, etc., being seized up. **2** *British Informal.* a jam-up; breakdown.

**sei|zin** (sē′zin), *n. Law.* the possession of a freehold estate; possession of land under rightful title. Also, **seisin.** [< Old French *saisine* < *saisir,* or *seisir;* see etym. under **seize**]

***seiz|ing** (sē′zing), *n.* **1** the act of binding, lashing, or fastening together with several turns, as of a small rope or cord. **2** a fastening made in this way. See picture above in next column. **3** a small rope, cord, or wire used for this.

**sei|zor** (sē′zər, -zôr), *n. Law.* a person who seizes or is authorized to seize.

**sei|zure** (sē′zhər), *n.* **1** the act of seizing: *Seizure of the powers of government is illegal in the United States.* **2** the condition of being seized: *The fort's seizure by rebels caused the defenders to surrender.* **3** a sudden attack of disease: *an epileptic seizure. The seizure was, I think, not apoplectical* (Samuel Johnson). **4** a sudden onset of some emotion or of panic.

**se|jant** or **se|jeant** (sē′jənt), *adj. Heraldry.* (of animals) sitting with the forelegs upright. [Middle English *seiaunte,* and *seand* < Old French *seiant,* and *seant,* present participles of *seier,* or *seoir* to sit < Latin *sedēre*]

**Sejm** (sām), *n.* **1** the constituent assembly of the Polish Republic from 1918 to 1922. **2** (later) the lower house of the Polish parliament. **3** (currently) the Polish parliament. [< Polish *sejm* assembly]

**sel** (sel), *n. Scottish.* self.

**sel.**, **1** selected. **2** selection or selections.

**se|la|chi|an** (si lā′kē ən), *adj., n.* **—*adj.*** of or belonging to a group of fishes, including the sharks, skates, and rays. **—*n.*** a shark, dogfish, or other selachian fish. [< New Latin *Selachii* the group name (< Greek *seláchē,* plural of *sélachos* shark, ray < *sélas* light, flame) (because of their phosphorescence) + English *-an*]

**sel|a|choid** (sel′ə koid), *adj.* sharklike; of the group comprising the sharks.

**se|la|dang** (sə lä′däng), *n.* = gaur. [< Malay *seladang*]

**sel|a|gi|nel|la** (sel′ə jə nel′ə), *n.* any mosslike plant of a group related to the ferns, having delicate, low stems. [< New Latin *selaginella* (diminutive) < Latin *selāgo, -inis* club moss]

**se|lah** (sē′lə), *n.* a Hebrew word occurring frequently in the Psalms, perhaps a musical direction meaning "Pause here." [< Hebrew *selāh*]

**se|la|ma|tan** (se lä′mə tän), *n.* a religious ceremonial feast in Indonesia. [< Indonesian *selamatan* < *selamat* welfare, happiness]

**se|lam|lik** (se läm′lik), *n.* the part of a Turkish house reserved for men. [< Turkish *selâmlık* < Arabic *salām* peace + Turkish *-lık,* a noun suffix]

**sel|couth** (sel′küth), *adj. Obsolete.* rarely or little known; unusual; strange; wonderful. [Old English *seldcūth* < *seldan* seldom + *cūth* known, familiar]

**sel|dom** (sel′dəm), *adv., adj.* **—*adv.*** rarely; not often: *I am seldom ill. Seldom is advice given, seldomer still is the advice worth anything* (Harper's).

**—*adj.*** rare; infrequent: *Blunting the fine point of seldom pleasure* (Shakespeare).

[Old English *seldum,* alteration of *seldan,* on the analogy of adverbial dative plurals ending in *-um*]

► **Seldom ever** (*I seldom ever do that*) is regarded as nonstandard. *Seldom if ever* is the standard form: *In Bengal to move at all is seldom if ever done* (Noel Coward).

***seizing**
definition 2

first winding

finish

**se|lect** (si lekt′), *v., adj., n.* **—*v.t.*** to pick out from a number; choose: *Select the book you want. The soul selects her own society, then shuts the door* (Emily Dickinson). SYN: See syn. under **choose.** **—*v.i.*** to make a selection: *to select on the basis of quality.*

**—*adj.*** **1** picked as best; chosen specially: *The captain needs a select crew for this dangerous job. A few select officials were admitted into his confidence.* **2** choice; superior: *That store carries a very select line of merchandise.* **3** careful in choosing; particular as to friends, company, or associates; exclusive: *She belongs to a very select club.*

**—*n.*** **1** a person or thing that is selected. **2** something select or choice.

**select out**, to remove or isolate from a selection; weed out: *In order to select out all pairs of atoms that are close to each other, we have developed a procedure* (Scientific American). *The psychiatrists were ... to select out Peace Corps applicants who were emotionally unstable* (Manchester Guardian Weekly).

[< Latin *sēlectus,* past participle of *sēligere* < *sē-* apart + *legere* choose] **—se|lect′ly,** *adv.* **—se|lect′ness,** *n.*

**Pronunciation Key:** hat, āge, cãre, fär; let, ēqual, tėrm; it, īce; hot, ōpen, ôrder; oil, out; cup, pu̇t, rüle; child; long; thin; ᴛʜen; zh, measure; ə represents **a** in about, **e** in taken, **i** in pencil, **o** in lemon, **u** in circus.

**se|lect|a|ble** (si lek′tə bəl), *adj.* that can be selected.

**select committee**, a small committee of a legislative body appointed to consider and report on a special matter.

**select council**, the higher branch of the local legislative body in certain cities of the United States.

**se|lect|ee** (si lek′tē′), *n.* **1** a person drafted for military service; draftee. **2** a person who has been selected for any purpose: *There, spread out across the stage, were the selectees, ... fat men, spinsters, and devout-looking young girls* (Harper's).

**se|lec|tion** (si lek′shən), *n.* **1** the act of choosing; choice: *Her selection of a hat took a long time.* **2** the condition of being chosen: *His selection as a candidate was assured.* **3** a person, thing, or group chosen: *The plain blue hat was her selection.* **4** a quantity or variety to choose from: *The shop offered a very good selection of hats.* **5** a passage or piece, or a number of passages or pieces, selected from one or more books: *a volume of prose or poetical selections, a book containing a selection from an author's works.* **6** any process by which certain animals or plants survive and reproduce their kind, while other less suitable ones die or are prevented from breeding: *I have called this principle, by which each slight variation, if useful, is preserved, by the term Natural Selection* (Charles Darwin). **7a** the act of choosing a piece of land under the Australian land laws. **b** the land so chosen.

**se|lec|tive** (si lek′tiv), *adj.* **1** having the power to select; selecting. **2** having to do with selection. **3** responding to oscillations of a certain frequency only. When a selective radio is tuned to one station, those on other wave lengths are excluded. —**se|lec′tive|ly**, *adv.* —**se|lec′tive|ness**, *n.*

**selective buying**, *U.S.* a boycott: *Brazier ... threatened today "a massive wave of sit-ins, picketing, and selective buying campaigns" if integration demands are not met* (New York Times).

**selective service**, compulsory military service; draft; conscription.

**Selective Service System**, an agency of the United States government responsible for the selection of persons from the total manpower of the United States for compulsory military service, as established by Federal law. *Abbr:* SSS (no periods).

**se|lec|tiv|i|ty** (si lek′tiv′ə tē), *n.* **1** the quality of being selective: *Caution in the financial district ... has made for great selectivity in buying of securities* (Wall Street Journal). **2** the property of a circuit, instrument, or the like, by virtue of which it responds to electric oscillations of a particular frequency to the exclusion of others.

**se|lect|man** (si lekt′mən), *n., pl.* **-men.** a member of a board of town officers in New England (exclusive of Rhode Island), chosen each year to manage the town's public affairs. [American English]

**se|lec|tor** (si lek′tər), *n.* **1** a person who selects or chooses. **2** a mechanical or electrical device that selects: *Cars with automatic transmissions have selectors with which the driver may choose the gear he wishes.* **3** a settler in Australia who acquires land cheaply from the government.

**sel|e|nate** (sel′ə nāt), *n.* a salt of selenic acid. [< *selen*(ic acid) + *-ate*[2]]

**Se|le|ne** (si lē′nē), *n. Greek Mythology.* the goddess of the moon, daughter of Hyperion and Thea, and later identified with Artemis. The Romans called her Luna. [< Greek *Selḗnē* (literally) moon < *sélas* light, flame]

**se|le|nic** (si lē′nik, -len′ik), *adj.* **1** of selenium. **2** containing selenium, especially with a valence of six.

**selenic acid**, a strong, corrosive dibasic acid resembling sulfuric acid. In a water solution, selenic acid can dissolve gold and copper. *Formula:* $H_2SeO_4$

**sel|e|nide** (sel′ə nīd, -nid), *n.* a compound of selenium with a more electropositive element or radical.

**sel|e|nif|er|ous** (sel′ə nif′ər əs), *adj.* containing or yielding selenium, as ore.

**se|le|ni|ous** (si lē′nē əs), *adj.* **1** of selenium. **2** containing selenium, especially with a valence of four.

**selenious acid**, a dibasic acid formed from selenium and nitric acid, used as a chemical reagent. *Formula:* $H_2SeO_3$

**sel|e|nite**[1] (sel′ə nīt, si lē′-), *n.* a salt of selenious acid. [< *selen*(ious acid) + *-ite*[2]]

**sel|e|nite**[2] (sel′ə nīt, si lē′-), *n.* a variety of gypsum found in transparent crystals and foliated masses. [< Latin *selēnītēs* < Greek *selēnī́tēs* (*líthos*) moon (stone) < *selḗnē* moon < *sélas* light (because its brightness was supposed to wax and wane with the moon)]

***se|le|ni|um** (si lē′nē əm), *n.* a rare, nonmetallic chemical element found with sulfur in various ores. Selenium exists in several allotropic forms. Because its electrical conductivity increases with the intensity of light striking it, it is used in photoelectric cells. [< New Latin *selenium* < Greek *selḗnē* moon (because its properties follow those of tellurium)]

***selenium**

| symbol | atomic number | atomic weight | oxidation state |
|---|---|---|---|
| Se | 34 | 78.96 | -2,+4,+6 |

**selenium cell**, a photoelectric cell consisting of selenium placed between electrodes, valued for certain optical experiments because of the property of selenium of varying in electrical resistance under the action of light.

**se|le|no|cen|tric** (si lē′nō sen′trik), *adj.* **1** having to do with the center of the moon. **2** with the moon as center: *a selenocentric orbit.*

**sel|e|nod|e|sist** (sel′ə nod′ə sist), *n.* an expert in selenodesy: *The Lunar Orbiter also carried a micrometeorite detector and enabled selenodesists to obtain more accurate data on the Moon's shape and gravitational field from precise tracking of the artificial satellite's orbit* (N. J. Trask and H. E. Holt).

**sel|e|nod|e|sy** (sel′ə nod′ə sē), *n.* the study of the dimensions, gravity, and other physical characteristics of the moon: *A rapidly developing field appears to be lunar geodesy, a specialty the geodesists call "selenodesy"* (Science). [< Greek *selḗnē* moon + English (geo)*desy*]

**sel|e|nog|ra|pher** (sel′ə nog′rə fər), *n.* a person who studies selenography: *When a telescope user ceases to look at the moon in a merely desultory manner and begins to observe it, he has begun to be a selenographer* (Scientific American).

**se|le|no|graph|ic** (si lē′nə graf′ik), *adj.* of or having to do with selenography.

**selenographic chart**, a map of the moon.

**sel|e|nog|ra|phist** (sel′ə nog′rə fist), *n.* = selenographer.

**sel|e|nog|ra|phy** (sel′ə nog′rə fē), *n.* the science dealing with the moon, especially its physical features. [< New Latin *selenographia* < Greek *selḗnē* moon + *-graphiā* -graphy]

**se|le|no|log|i|cal** (si lē′nə loj′ə kəl), *adj.* of or having to do with selenology.

**sel|e|nol|o|gist** (sel′ə nol′ə jist), *n.* a person who studies selenology.

**sel|e|nol|o|gy** (sel′ə nol′ə jē), *n.* the science dealing with the moon, especially its astronomical features.

**se|le|no|trop|ic** (si lē′nə trop′ik), *adj. Botany.* turning toward the moon; taking a particular direction under the influence of the moon's light. [< Greek *selḗnē* moon + *-tropos* a turning + English *-ic*]

**sel|e|not|ro|pism** (sel′ə not′rə piz əm), *n.* selenotropic tendency or movement.

**se|le|nous** (si lē′nəs), *adj.* = selenious.

**Se|leu|cid** (sə lü′sid), *n., adj.* —*n.* one of the Seleucidae.
—*adj.* of or having to do with the Seleucidae.
[< Latin *Seleucidēs* < Greek *Seleukidēs* < *Séleukos* Seleucus I, founder of the Seleucidae]

**Se|leu|ci|dae** (sə lü′sə dē), *n.pl.* a dynasty that reigned in Syria, Persia, Bactria, and elsewhere in western Asia from 312 to about 64 B.C. It was founded by Seleucus I, one of the generals of Alexander the Great.

**self** (self), *n., pl.* **selves,** *adj., pron., pl.* **selves,** *v.*
—*n.* **1** one's own person: *his very self, her sweet self.* **2** one's own welfare or interests: *It is a good thing to think more of others and less of self. A selfish person puts self first.* **3** the character of a person; nature of a thing: *She does not seem like her former self. It seemed ... as if he had two distinct yet kindred selves* (H. G. Wells). **4** *Philosophy.* the individual consciousness of a being in its relationship to its own self. **5** a flower that is the same color throughout.
—*adj.* being the same throughout; all of one kind, quality, color, or material. SYN: uniform, unmixed.
—*pron.* myself; himself; herself; yourself: *a check made payable to self.*
—*v.t., v.i.* to fertilize (a flower) with its own pollen: *Several inbred lines from a parent rose are being produced by "selfing." Each of these lines will be further selfed* (Science News Letter).
[Old English *self*]
▶ **Self** as a suffix forms the reflexive and intensive pronouns: *myself, yourself, himself, herself, itself, oneself, ourselves, yourselves, themselves.* These are used chiefly for emphasis (*I can do that myself*) or as reflexive objects (*I couldn't help myself*).
▶ The pronominal use of **self** (*payable to self, a room for self and wife*) is largely confined to commercial English, and is not regarded as standard.

**self-**, *prefix.* **1** of or over oneself: *Self-conscious = conscious of oneself. Self-control = control over oneself.*
**2** by or in oneself or itself; without outside aid: *Self-inflicted = inflicted by oneself. Self-evident = evident in itself.*
**3** to or for oneself: *Self-addressed = addressed to oneself. Self-respect = respect for oneself.*
**4** oneself (as object): *Self-defeating = defeating oneself.*
**5** automatic or automatically: *Self-winding = winding automatically.*
[Old English *self-* < *self*]

**self-a|ban|don|ment** (self′ə ban′dən mənt), *n.* disregard of self or of self-interest.

**self-a|base|ment** (self′ə bās′mənt), *n.* abasement of self; humiliation of oneself.

**self-ab|hor|rence** (self′ab hôr′əns, -hor′-), *n.* abhorrence or detestation of oneself.

**self-ab|ne|gat|ing** (self′ab′nə gā′ting), *adj.* = self-denying.

**self-ab|ne|ga|tion** (self′ab′nə gā′shən), *n.* = self-denial.

**self-ab|sorbed** (self′ab sôrbd′, -zôrbd′), *adj.* absorbed in oneself or one's own thoughts, affairs, etc.

**self-ab|sorp|tion** (self′ab sôrp′shən, -zôrp′-), *n.* absorption in oneself or one's own thoughts, affairs, etc.

**self-a|buse** (self′ə byüs′), *n.* **1** abuse of oneself. **2** = masturbation.

**self-ac|cu|sa|tion** (self′ak′yü zā′shən), *n.* the act of accusing oneself.

**self-ac|cus|ing** (self′ə kyü′zing), *adj.* accusing oneself: *self-accusing guilt.*

**self-ac|knowl|edged** (self′ak nol′ijd), *adj.* acknowledged by oneself.

**self-act|ing** (self′ak′ting), *adj.* **1** working of itself: *a self-acting machine.* **2** acting automatically without the manipulation or mechanism which would otherwise be required: *the self-acting feed of a boring mill.*

**self-ac|tion** (self′ak′shən), *n.* action that is independent of external impulse.

**self-ac|tive** (self′ak′tiv), *adj.* acting of or by itself; acting independently of external impulse.

**self-ac|tiv|i|ty** (self′ak tiv′ə tē), *n.* inherent or intrinsic power of acting or moving.

**self-ac|tor** (self′ak′tər), *n.* a self-acting machine or part of a machine.

**self-ac|tu|al|i|za|tion** (self′ak′chü ə lə zā′shən, -chə lə-), *n.* = self-realization.

**self-ad|ap|ta|tion** (self′ad ap tā′shən), *n.* the adaptation of an organism in response to new conditions.

**self-ad|dressed** (self′ə drest′), *adj.* addressed to oneself: *He sent a self-addressed envelope along with his order.*

**self-ad|he|sive** (self′ad hē′siv, -ziv), *adj.* that sticks to a surface without glue, paste, or the like: *self-adhesive cellulose tape, self-adhesive plastic wallpaper, self-adhesive labels.*

**self-ad|just|ing** (self′ə jus′ting), *adj.* adjusting itself; requiring no external adjustment: *The system is self-adjusting and finds a new balance when it is disturbed* (New Scientist).

**self-ad|just|ment** (self′ə just′mənt), *n.* adjustment of oneself or itself: *Justice Oliver Wendell Holmes sagely commented that when competent men engage in speculation, it is "the self-adjustment of society to the probable"* (Time).

**self-ad|min|is|tered** (self′ad min′ə stərd), *adj.* administered by oneself.

**self-ad|mi|ra|tion** (self′ad′mə rā′shən), *n.* admiration of oneself; self-conceit.

**self-ad|mir|ing** (self′ad mī′ring), *adj.* full of admiration for oneself. —**self′-ad|mir′ing|ly**, *adv.*

**self-ad|mit|ted** (self′ad mit′id), *adj.* admitted by oneself; self-confessed: *a self-admitted gambler, self-admitted guilt.*

**self-ad|vance|ment** (self′ad vans′mənt, -väns′-), *n.* advancement of oneself by one's own effort: *... fabulous opportunities for self-advancement* (Time).

**self-ad|van|tage** (self′ad van′tij, -vän′-), *n.* one's own advantage.

**self-ad|van|ta|geous** (self′ad′vən tā′jəs), *adj.* advantageous to or for oneself.

**self-ad|ver|tise|ment** (self′ad′vər tīz′mənt; -ad vėr′tis-, -tiz-; self′ad′vər tīz′-), *n.* advertisement of oneself; showing off oneself in a deliberate manner.

**self-ag|gran|dize|ment** (self′ə gran′diz mənt), *n.* aggrandizement of oneself.

**self-ag|gran|di|zing** (self′ag′rən dī zing, -ə gran′-), *adj.* aggrandizing oneself; seeking to aggrandize oneself: *a self-aggrandizing official, self-aggrandizing schemes.*

**self-a|lign|ing** or **self-a|lin|ing** (self′ə lī′ning),

*adj.* aligning automatically.

**self-a|nal|y|sis** (self′ə nal′ə sis), *n., pl.* **-ses** (-sēz). **1** = self-examination. **2** = autoanalysis (def. 1).

**self-an|ni|hi|la|tion** (self′ə nī′ə lā′shən), *n.* destruction or obliteration of self.

**self-ap|par|ent** (self′ə par′ənt), *adj.* apparent to oneself, or in itself.

**self-ap|plause** (self′ə plôz′), *n.* approval or commendation of oneself.

**self-ap|pli|ca|tion** (self′ap′lə kā′shən), *n.* application of oneself or itself.

**self-ap|point|ed** (self′ə poin′tid), *adj.* appointed by oneself, not by anyone else: *Leigh Hunt himself was, as Mr. Colvin has observed, a kind of self-appointed poet laureate of Hampstead* (Athenaeum).

**self-ap|prais|al** (self′ə prā′zəl), *n.* appraisal of oneself.

**self-ap|prov|al** (self′ə prü′vəl), *n.* approval of oneself.

**self-ap|prov|ing** (self′ə prü′ving), *adj.* **1** implying approval of one's own conduct or character. **2** justifying such approval.

**self-as|ser|tion** (self′ə sėr′shən), *n.* insistence on one's own wishes, opinions, claims, or the like.

**self-as|ser|tive** (self′ə sėr′tiv), *adj.* putting oneself forward; insisting on one's own wishes, opinions, claims, or the like. —**self′-as|ser′tive|ly,** *adv.* —**self′-as|ser′tive|ness,** *n.*

**self-as|sumed** (self′ə sümd′), *adj.* assumed by one's own act or authority: *a self-assumed title.*

**self-as|sur|ance** (self′ə shůr′əns), *n.* = self-confidence.

**self-as|sured** (self′ə shůrd′), *adj.* = self-confident.

**self-at|tach|ment** (self′ə tach′mənt), *n.* attachment to oneself or itself.

**self-au|thor|ized** (self′ô′thə rīzd), *adj.* authorized by oneself.

**self-a|ware** (self′ə wãr′), *adj.* **1** having self-awareness. **2** = self-conscious.

**self-a|ware|ness** (self′ə wãr′nis), *n.* awareness of oneself; self-realization: *There are a few glints of self-awareness, such as his realization that his diary had taken a political-literary rather than a personal form* (New Yorker).

**self-bal|anc|ing** (self′bal′ən sing), *adj.* automatically balancing oneself or itself.

**self-belt** (self′belt′), *n.* a belt attached to and made of the same material as a garment: *It would consist of a blouse of green-brown with a self-belt* (New York Times).

**self-be|tray|al** (self′bi trā′əl), *n.* betraying of oneself; self-deception.

**self-bind|er** (self′bīn′dər), *n.* **1** a machine that gathers cut grain and ties it into sheaves. **2** a reaper or harvester with such an attachment; binder.

**self-born** (self′bôrn′), *adj.* originating from oneself or itself: *String quartets are not made; they are self-born* (Alexander Moskowski).

**self-bow** (self′bō′), *n. Archery.* a bow made of a single piece of wood, or of two pieces spliced endwise at the handle.

**self-can|cel|ling** (self′kan′sə ling), *adj. Especially British.* canceling itself out: *The dialogue shows a brilliant talent for extending cant and clichés into spirals of self-cancelling logic* (London Times).

**self-care** (self′kãr′), *n.* care of oneself.

**self-cen|sor|ship** (self′sen′sər ship), *n.* censorship of oneself or itself: *I foresee that self-censorship in television programs will be severe* (Lee De Forest).

**self-cen|tered** (self′sen′tərd), *adj.* **1** occupied with one's own interests and affairs. **2** = selfish. **3** being a fixed point around which other things move. —**self′-cen′tered|ly,** *adv.* —**self′-cen′tered|ness,** *n.*

**self-cen|tred** (self′sen′tərd), *adj. Especially British.* self-centered.

**self-charg|ing** (self′chär′jing), *adj.* automatically charging itself.

**self-cho|sen** (self′chō′zən), *adj.* chosen by oneself; not imposed; voluntary: *Freedom of religious practice can be observed in homes and churches under ... self-chosen guidance* (New York Times).

**self-clean|ing** (self′klē′ning), *adj.* cleaning itself by mechanical or electrical means, or by gas: *a self-cleaning oven.*

**self-cleans|ing** (self′klen′zing), *adj.* = self-cleaning.

**self-clos|ing** (self′klō′zing), *adj.* closing of itself; closing or shutting automatically: *a self-closing bridge, a self-closing door.*

**self-cock|ing** (self′kok′ing), *adj.* (of a gun) cocking automatically; having the hammer cocked and released by simply pulling the trigger.

**self-col|or** (self′kul′ər), *n.* **1** one uniform color, as of a dyed fabric. **2** natural (undyed) color.

**self-col|ored** (self′kul′ərd), *adj.* **1** of one uniform color. **2** of the natural color.

**self-com|mand** (self′kə mand′, -mänd′), *n.* control of one's actions or feelings; self-control.

**self-com|ment** (self′kom′ent), *n.* comment of or over oneself.

**self-com|mun|ion** (self′kə myün′yən), *n.* communion with oneself: *The scholar was in his study locked deep in self-communion.*

**self-com|pas|sion** (self′kəm pash′ən), *n.* compassion for oneself; self-pity.

**self-com|pla|cence** (self′kəm plā′səns), *n.* = self-complacency.

**self-com|pla|cen|cy** (self′kəm plā′sən sē), *n.* the condition of being self-satisfied; complacency.

**self-com|pla|cent** (self′kəm plā′sənt), *adj.* pleased with oneself; self-satisfied; complacent. —**self′-com|pla′cent|ly,** *adv.*

**self-com|plete** (self′kəm plēt′), *adj.* complete in oneself or itself.

**self-com|posed** (self′kəm pōzd′), *adj.* calm; composed.

**self-con|ceit** (self′kən sēt′), *n.* too much pride in oneself or one's ability; conceit. SYN: egotism.

**self-con|ceit|ed** (self′kən sē′tid), *adj.* having or showing self-conceit.

**self-con|cen|trat|ed** (self′kon′sən trā′tid), *adj.* concentrated on or over oneself.

**self-con|cen|tra|tion** (self′kon′sən trā′shən), *n.* concentration over oneself.

**self-con|cept** (self′kon′sept), *n.* = self-conception.

**self-con|cep|tion** (self′kən sep′shən), *n.* conception of oneself; view of oneself: *An individual's self-conception often differs from the conception others have of him.*

**self-con|cern** (self′kən sėrn′), *n.* = self-interest.

**self-con|dem|na|tion** (self′kon′dem nā′shən), *n.* condemnation by oneself of one's own action.

**self-con|demned** (self′kən demd′), *adj.* condemned by one's own conscience or confession.

**self-con|fessed** (self′kən fest′), *adj.* confessed by oneself; self-admitted: *a self-confessed failure, a self-confessed baseball fan.* —**self′-con|fess′ed|ly,** *adv.*

**self-con|fi|dence** (self′kon′fə dəns), *n.* belief in one's own ability, power, or judgment; confidence in oneself.

**self-con|fi|dent** (self′kon′fə dənt), *adj.* believing in one's own ability, power, or judgment. —**self′-con′fi|dent|ly,** *adv.*

**self-con|grat|u|la|tion** (self′kən grach′ə lā′shən), *n.* congratulation of oneself: *Her* [*his wife's*] *practical capacity was for him a matter for continual self-congratulation* (H. G. Wells).

**self-con|grat|u|la|to|ry** (self′kən grach′ə lə tôr′ē, -tōr′-), *adj.* congratulating oneself: *a self-congratulatory mood.*

**self-con|scious** (self′kon′shəs), *adj.* **1** embarrassed, especially by the presence or the thought of other people and their attitude toward one; made conscious of how one is appearing to others; shy: *self-conscious of a world looking on* (Thomas Carlyle). **2** *Philosophy.* having consciousness, as of oneself, one's actions, or sensations. —**self′-con′scious|ly,** *adv.* —**self′-con′scious|ness,** *n.*

**self-con|se|quence** (self′kon′sə kwens, -kwəns), *n.* a sense of one's own importance; self-importance.

**self-con|sist|en|cy** (self′kən sis′tən sē), *n.* the quality or state of being self-consistent.

**self-con|sist|ent** (self′kən sis′tənt), *adj.* consistent with oneself or itself; having its parts or elements in agreement.

**self-con|sti|tut|ed** (self′kon′stə tü′tid, -tyü′-), *adj.* constituted by oneself or itself: *a self-constituted board of inquiry.*

**self-con|tained** (self′kən tānd′), *adj.* **1** saying little; reserved: *They are rather silent, self-contained men when with strangers* (Theodore Roosevelt). **2** containing in oneself or itself all that is necessary; independent of what is external: *When London was smaller, and the parts of London more self-contained and parochial ...* (G. K. Chesterton). **3** having all its working parts contained in one case, cover, or framework: *A watch is self-contained.* **4** *British.* having approaches, entrances, and apartments restricted to the use of a single household: *a self-contained house.* —**self′-con|tain′ed|ness,** *n.*

**self-con|tain|ment** (self′kən tān′mənt), *n.* the condition of being self-contained.

**self-con|tem|pla|tion** (self′kon′təm plā′shən), *n.* contemplation of oneself or of one's own conduct, motives, and the like.

**self-con|tempt** (self′kən tempt′), *n.* contempt for oneself: *Perish in thy self-contempt!* (Tennyson).

**self-con|tent** (self′kən tent′), *n.* = self-satisfaction.

**self-con|tent|ed** (self′kən ten′tid), *adj.* = self-satisifed. —**self′-con|tent′ed|ly,** *adv.* —**self′-con|tent′ed|ness,** *n.*

**self-con|tent|ment** (self′kən tent′mənt), *n.* = self-satisfaction.

**self-con|tra|dic|tion** (self′kon′trə dik′shən), *n.* **1** contradiction of oneself or itself. **2** a statement containing elements that are contradictory.

**self-con|tra|dic|to|ry** (self′kon′trə dik′tər ē), *adj.* contradicting oneself or itself.

**self-con|trol** (self′kən trōl′), *n.* control of one's actions or feelings: *His handsome face had all the tranquillity of Indian self-control; a self-control which prevents the exhibition of emotion* (Francis Parkman).

**self-con|trolled** (self′kən trōld′), *adj.* having or showing self-control.

**self-con|vict|ed** (self′kən vik′tid), *adj.* convicted by one's own consciousness, knowledge, or avowal: *Guilt stands self-convicted when arraign'd* (Richard Savage).

**self-cor|rect|ing** (self′kə rek′ting), *adj.* correcting oneself or itself automatically: *a self-correcting mechanism.*

**self-cor|rec|tion** (self′kə rek′shən), *n.* automatic correction of oneself or itself.

**self-cor|rec|tive** (self′kə rek′tiv), *adj., n.* —*adj.* = self-correcting.
—*n.* a corrective of oneself or itself: *Democracy's great self-corrective is reasonable dissent and debate* (Time).

**self-cor|rupt|ed** (self′kə rup′tid), *adj.* corrupted by oneself or itself.

**self-cre|at|ed** (self′krē ā′tid), *adj.* created, brought into existence, or constituted by oneself: *The particular, partly self-created, character of Gibbon's mind ...* (R. H. Hutton).

**self-crit|i|cal** (self′krit′ə kəl), *adj.* critical of oneself.

**self-crit|i|cism** (self′krit′ə siz əm), *n.* criticism of a person by himself.

**self-cul|ti|va|tion** (self′kul′tə vā′shən), *n.* cultivation of oneself; self-culture.

**self-cul|ture** (self′kul′chər), *n.* the cultivation or development by one's own efforts, of one's mind, faculties, manners, and the like.

**self-deal|ing** (self′dē′ling), *n.* **1** the use of a charitable foundation to grant loans or other financial benefits to contributors or to protect the founders' private income. **2** any similar use of a company's or organization's funds.

**self-de|ceit** (self′di sēt′), *n.* = self-deception.

**self-de|ceit|ful** (self′di sēt′fəl), *adj.* = self-deceptive.

**self-de|ceived** (self′di sēvd′), *adj.* deceived by oneself.

**self-de|ceiv|er** (self′di sē′vər), *n.* a person who practices self-deception.

**self-de|ceiv|ing** (self′di sē′ving), *adj.* = self-deceptive.

**self-de|cep|tion** (self′di sep′shən), *n.* the act or fact of deceiving oneself; self-delusion; self-deceit.

**self-de|cep|tive** (self′di sep′tiv), *adj.* deceiving oneself.

**self-de|clared** (self′di klãrd′), *adj.* declared by oneself; self-proclaimed: *a self-declared conservative, self-declared limitations.*

**self-ded|i|ca|tion** (self′ded′ə kā′shən), *n.* dedication of oneself to some person or purpose.

**self-de|feat|ing** (self′di fē′ting), *adj.* defeating oneself or itself; contrary to one's own purpose or interests: *U.S. taxation on foreign business activity is self-defeating* (Time). *In the long run, it is self-defeating to allocate aid only to known political allies* (Manchester Guardian).

**self-de|fence** (self′di fens′), *n. Especially British.* self-defense.

**self-de|fense** (self′di fens′), *n.* defense of one's own person, property, or reputation.

**self-de|fen|sive** (self′di fen′siv), *adj.* tending to defend oneself; of the nature of self-defense.

**self-de|fined** (self′di fīnd′), *adj.* defined by oneself or itself.

**self-de|fin|ing** (self′di fī′ning), *adj.* defining by oneself or itself; self-explanatory.

**self-def|i|ni|tion** (self′def′ə nish′ən), *n.* definition of one's own character, identity, or the like: *Africa's central problem is political self-definition* (New York Times).

**self-de|lud|ed** (self′di lü′did), *adj.* deluded by oneself.

**self-de|lu|sion** (self′di lü′zhən), *n.* the act or fact of deluding oneself; self-deception.

**self-de|ni|al** (self′di nī′əl), *n.* sacrifice of one's own desires and interests; going without things one wants; austerity. SYN: self-sacrifice, abstemiousness.

**self-den|i|gra|tion** (self′den′ə grā′shən), *n.* = self-deprecation.

**Pronunciation Key:** hat, āge, cãre, fär; let, ēqual, tėrm; it, īce; hot, ōpen, ôrder; oil, out; cup, pu̇t, rüle; child; long; thin; ᴛʜen; zh, measure; ə represents a in about, e in taken, i in pencil, o in lemon, u in circus.

**self-de|ny|ing** (self′di nī′ing), *adj.* sacrificing one's own wishes and interests; unselfish. —**self′-de|ny′ing|ly**, *adv.*

**self-de|pend|ence** (self′di pen′dəns), *n.* reliance on oneself with a feeling of independence of others; self-reliance.

**self-de|pend|ent** (self′di pen′dənt), *adj.* depending on oneself, or on one's own efforts; self-reliant: *Left early to his own guidance, he had begun to be self-dependent while yet a boy* (Hawthorne). —**self′-de|pend′ent|ly**, *adv.*

**self-dep|re|cat|ing** (self′dep′rə kā′ting), *adj.* deprecating of oneself. —**self′-dep′re|cat′ing|ly**, *adv.*

**self-dep|re|ca|tion** (self′dep′rə kā′shən), *n.* deprecation of oneself; self-disparagement.

**self-dep|re|ca|to|ry** (self′dep′rə kə tôr′ē, -tōr′-), *adj.* = self-deprecating.

**self-de|rived** (self′di rīvd′), *adj.* derived from oneself or from itself.

**self-de|sir|a|ble** (self′di zīr′ə bəl), *adj.* desirable in or of oneself or itself.

**self-de|spair** (self′di spãr′), *n.* despair of oneself; a despairing view, as of one's character or prospects.

**self-de|stroy|ing** (self′di stroi′ing), *adj.* = self-destructive.

**self-de|struct** (self′di strukt′), *v.i.* to destroy oneself or itself: *An international team of scientists ... has designed a plastic that Guillet claims will self-destruct when exposed to sunlight, but will remain intact if it is kept indoors* (Time).

**self-de|struc|tion** (self′di struk′shən), *n.* the destruction of oneself or itself.

**self-de|struc|tive** (self′di struk′tiv), *adj.* **1** tending to destroy oneself or itself: *Suicide is a self-destructive urge or act. The Nationalists, like many Americans, believe in the self-destructive attributes of Communism* (Manchester Guardian). **2** causing its own destruction: *Each balloon has a self-destructive device to release the gas if anything goes wrong* (Newsweek). —**self′-de-struc′tive|ly**, *adv.* —**self′-de|struc′tive|ness**, *n.*

**self-de|ter|mi|na|tion** (self′di tėr′mə nā′shən), *n.* **1** direction from within only, without influence or force from without. **2** the deciding by the people of a nation what form of government they shall have, without reference to the wishes of any other nation, especially one to which it has been subject.

**self-de|ter|mined** (self′di tėr′mənd), *adj.* determined by oneself or itself; having the power of self-determination.

**self-de|ter|min|ing** (self′di tėr′mə ning), *adj.* determining one's own acts; having the power of self-determination.

**self-de|vel|op|ment** (self′di vel′əp mənt), *n.* **1** development of oneself: *The secret of true happiness consists of self-discovery* [*and*] *self-development* (Atlantic). **2** spontaneous development.

**self-de|vo|tion** (self′di vō′shən), *n.* = self-sacrifice.

**self-de|vo|tion|al** (self′di vō′shə nəl), *adj.* characterized by self-devotion.

**self-di|ag|no|sis** (self′dī′əg nō′sis), *n.* diagnosis of one's own disease: *"Self-diagnosis" of venereal disease is impossible, and medical advice should always be sought* (London Times).

**self-dif|fer|en|ti|a|tion** (self′dif′ə ren′shē ā′-shən), *n. Biology.* the differentiation shown in organs, tissues, and the like, that are relatively independent of neighboring structures in their development.

**self-dif|fu|sion** (self′di fyü′zhən), *n.* the diffusion of atoms within a metal that is composed of chemically identical atoms, especially at high temperature.

**self-di|ges|tion** (self′də jes′chən, -dī-), *n. Physiology.* digestion or breakdown of cells or tissue by enzymes produced by these cells; autolysis.

**self-di|rect|ed** (self′də rek′tid, -dī-), *adj.* directed by oneself.

**self-di|rec|tion** (self′də rek′shən, -dī-), *n.* control or management of oneself; self-guidance.

**self-dis|ci|pline** (self′dis′ə plin), *n.* careful control and training of oneself.

**self-dis|ci|plined** (self′dis′ə plind), *adj.* having self-discipline.

**self-dis|clo|sure** (self′dis klō′zhər), *n.* disclosure of oneself; self-revelation.

**self-dis|con|tent|ed** (self′dis′kən ten′tid), *adj.* discontented with or over oneself.

**self-dis|cov|er|y** (self′dis kuv′ər ē, -kuv′rē), *n.* discovery of one's identity, position in society, or the like.

**self-dis|gust** (self′dis gust′), *n.* disgust with oneself; self-hatred: *Some of their self-disgust may stem from not having been rebellious enough* (Time).

**self-dis|par|age|ment** (self′dis par′ij mənt), *n.* disparagement of oneself.

**self-dis|sat|is|fac|tion** (self′dis sat′is fak′shən), *n.* dissatisfaction with or over oneself.

**self-dis|trust** (self′dis trust′), *n.* distrust of oneself; lack of confidence in one's own abilities.

**self-dis|trust|ful** (self′dis trust′fəl), *adj.* distrustful of oneself or one's own abilities.

**self-doubt** (self′dout′), *n.* doubt of oneself; doubt of one's own abilities, worth, decisions, motives, or the like.

**self-doubt|ing** (self′dou′ting), *adj.* characterized by self-doubt.

**self-dram|a|ti|za|tion** (self′dram′ə tə zā′shən, -drä′mə-), *n.* dramatization of oneself.

**self-dram|a|tize** (self′dram′ə tīz, -drä′mə-), *v.i.,* **-tized, -tiz|ing.** to dramatize oneself. —**self′-dram′a|tiz′er**, *n.*

**self-drive car** (self′drīv′), *British.* a car for rent, driven by the renter: *Now, you can hire a ... self-drive car and leave it at your destination at no extra charge* (Sunday Times).

**self-driv|en** (self′driv′ən), *adj.* driven by itself; automatic.

**self-ed|u|cat|ed** (self′ej′u̇ kā′tid), *adj.* self-taught; educated by one's own efforts.

**self-ed|u|ca|tion** (self′ej′u̇ kā′shən), *n.* education by or through one's own efforts.

**self-ef|face|ment** (self′ə fās′mənt), *n.* the act or habit of modestly keeping oneself in the background: *Self-effacement in a generation of self-salesmanship ...* (Hugh R. Orr).

**self-ef|fac|ing** (self′ə fā′sing), *adj.* effacing oneself; keeping oneself in the background. —**self′-ef|fac′ing|ly**, *adv.*

**self-e|lec|ted** (self′i lek′tid), *adj.* **1** elected by oneself; self-appointed. **2** (of a body) elected by its members: *Self-elected Town Councils* (Macaulay).

**self-em|ployed** (self′em ploid′), *adj.* earning one's livelihood from one's own business or by offering one's services to the public; not employed by others; working for oneself: *The Senate Finance Committee decided to make social security voluntary for physicians, dentists, lawyers, farmers, and other self-employed persons* (Time).

**self-em|ploy|ment** (self′em ploi′mənt), *n.* the condition of being self-employed: *After a spell of self-employment he applied for jobs in Wolverhampton* (London Times).

**self-en|am|ored** (self′en am′ərd), *adj.* enamored of or over oneself.

**self-en|er|giz|ing** (self′en′ər jī′zing), *adj.* energizing oneself or itself; generating energy or power automatically: *a self-energizing dynamo.*

**self-en|forc|ing** (self′en fôr′sing, -fōr′-), *adj.* enforcing by oneself or itself.

**self-es|teem** (self′es tēm′), *n.* **1** the thinking well of oneself; self-respect. **2** the thinking too well of oneself; conceit.

**self-e|val|u|a|tion** (self′i val′yu̇ ā′shən), *n.* evaluation of oneself.

**self-ev|i|dence** (self′ev′ə dəns), *n.* **1** the quality or condition of being self-evident: *the self-evidence of natural law.* **2** something that is self-evident: *The author shows enormous erudition, but much of it is devoted to expressing self-evidences* (Manchester Guardian Weekly).

**self-ev|i|dent** (self′ev′ə dənt), *adj.* evident by itself; needing no proof; axiomatic: *We hold these truths to be self-evident* (Declaration of Independence). *The self-evident fact that growth is the result of eating and drinking ...* (Benjamin Jowett). —**self′-ev′i|dent|ly**, *adv.*

**self-ex|al|ta|tion** (self′eg′zôl tā′shən), *n.* exaltation of oneself; self-glorification.

**self-ex|am|i|na|tion** (self′eg zam′ə nā′shən), *n.* an examination into one's own state, conduct, motives, and the like.

**self-ex|ci|ta|tion** (self′ek′sī tā′shən), *n.* the excitation of the field of a generator by currents taken from its own armature.

**self-ex|cit|ed** (self′ek sī′tid), *adj.* (of a generator) excited by the current of its own armature.

**self-ex|cit|ing** (self′ek sī′ting), *adj.* capable of self-excitation: *a self-exciting dynamo.*

**self-ex|cus|ing** (self′ek skyü′zing), *adj.* excusing oneself.

**self-ex|e|cut|ing** (self′ek′sə kyü′ting), *adj.* becoming effective automatically under circumstances or at a time as specified, and needing no legislation to enforce it: *a self-executing clause in a treaty or contract.*

**self-ex|ile** (self′eg′zīl, -ek′sīl), *n.* **1** voluntary exile: *to live in self-exile.* **2** a self-exiled person.

**self-ex|iled** (self′eg′zīld, -ek′sīld), *adj.* voluntarily exiled; absent by choice from one's native land.

**self-ex|ist|ence** (self′eg zis′təns), *n.* the property or fact of being self-existent.

**self-ex|ist|ent** (self′eg zis′tənt), *adj.* **1** existing independently of any other cause. **2** having an independent existence.

**self-ex|plain|ing** (self′ek splā′ning), *adj.* = self-explanatory.

**self-ex|plan|a|to|ry** (self′ek splan′ə tôr′ē, -tōr′-), *adj.* explaining itself; that needs no explanation; obvious.

**self-ex|plo|ra|tion** (self′eks′plə rā′shən), *n.* exploration of one's own motives or actions; self-examination.

**self-ex|po|sure** (self′ek spō′zhər), *n.* exposure of oneself.

**self-ex|pres|sion** (self′ek spresh′ən), *n.* the expression of one's personality.

**self-ex|pres|sive** (self′ek spres′iv), *adj.* expressive of one's personality: *a self-expressive art created by the imagination, tastes, and desires of the artist* (New Yorker).

**self-feed** (self′fēd′), *v.t.,* **-fed, -feed|ing.** *Agriculture.* to supply (animals) with enough food so that they may eat whenever and as much as they want to.

**self-feed|er** (self′fē′dər), *n.* **1** a machine that feeds itself automatically, such as a printing press. **2** a machine that supplies food to animals automatically.

**self-feed|ing** (self′fē′ding), *adj.* that feeds itself automatically: *a self-feeding press.*

**self-feel|ing** (self′fē′ling), *n. Psychology.* selfish feeling or emotion.

**self-fer|tile** (self′fėr′təl), *adj. Botany.* capable of self-fertilization.

**self-fer|til|i|ty** (self′fėr til′ə tē), *n. Botany.* the ability to fertilize itself.

**self-fer|ti|li|za|tion** (self′fėr′tə lə zā′shən), *n.* **1** *Botany.* the fertilization of the ovules of a flower by pollen from the same flower; autogamy. **2** *Zoology.* the fertilization of two gametes from the same animal among some hermaphrodites.

**self-fer|ti|lized** (self′fėr′tə līzd), *adj.* fertilized by its own pollen; autogamous: *a self-fertilized flower.*

**self-fer|ti|liz|ing** (self′fėr′tə lī′zing), *adj.* **1** fertilizing by the pollen of its own flowers alone: *Tobacco is normally a self-fertilizing species* (Science News). **2** breeding from closely related individuals; inbreeding: *populations of self-fertilizing organisms.*

**self-fig|ured** (self′fig′yərd), *adj.* woven with figures in its own color: *a self-figured fabric.*

**self-fill|er** (self′fil′ər), *n.* any one of various types of fountain pen that can be filled by operating some mechanism while the lower part of the pen is dipped in ink.

**self-fill|ing** (self′fil′ing), *adj.* that can fill itself.

**self-fi|nanced** (self′fə nanst′, -fī-; -fī′nanst), *adj.* financed by oneself or itself: *a self-financed project or investment.*

**self-flag|el|la|tion** (self′flaj′ə lā′shən), *n.* flagellation of oneself; punishment of oneself.

**self-flat|ter|ing** (self′flat′ər ing), *adj.* too favorable to oneself; involving too high an idea of one's own qualities or achievements.

**self-flat|ter|y** (self′flat′ər ē), *n.* flattery of oneself; indulgence in self-flattering ideas: *sentimental self-flattery.*

**self-for|get|ful** (self′fər get′fəl), *adj.* forgetful of oneself or one's own individuality; showing no thought of one's own advantage or interest. —**self′-for|get′ful|ly**, *adv.* —**self′-for|get′ful-ness**, *n.*

**self-for|get|ting** (self′fər get′ing), *adj.* = self-forgetful.

**self-ful|fill|ing** (self′fu̇l fil′ing), *adj.* becoming fulfilled or realized by the very fact that it is predicted or believed inevitable: *Responsible ... leaders characterize the sensationalist reporting of several of the newspapers as self-fulfilling prophecy* (Atlantic). *There is now a potentially self-fulfilling state of economic alarm* (London Times).

**self-ful|fill|ment** or **self-ful|fil|ment** (self′fu̇l-fil′mənt), *n.* achievement of one's true needs, aspirations, or the like, by one's own efforts or actions; self-realization.

**self-gen|er|at|ed** (self′jen′ə rā′tid), *adj.* generated by oneself or itself, independently of any external agency.

**self-gen|er|at|ing** (self′jen′ə rā′ting), *adj.* automatically generating.

**self-giv|ing** (self′giv′ing), *adj.* giving of oneself for others; self-sacrificing.

**self-glo|ri|fi|ca|tion** (self′glôr′ə fə kā′shən, -glōr′-), *n.* glorification or exaltation of oneself: *The unconscious Captain walked out in a state of self-glorification* (Dickens).

**self-glo|ri|fy|ing** (self′glôr′ə fī′ing, -glōr′-), *adj.* glorifying or exalting oneself.

**self-glo|ry** (self′glôr′ē, -glōr′-), *n.* vainglory; boasting: *... narcissuslike in its self-glory* (Time).

**self-gov|erned** (self′guv′ərnd), *adj.* **1** having self-government: *a self-governed state.* **2** governing one's own actions or affairs; independent. **3** marked by or exercising self-control.

**self-gov|ern|ing** (self′guv′ər ning), *adj.* that governs itself; having self-government; autonomous: *a self-governing territory.*

**self-gov|ern|ment** (self′guv′ərn mənt, -ər-), *n.* **1a** government of a group by its own members:

*We have self-government through our elected representatives.* **b** the state of having such a government. **2** government, as of one's actions or affairs, by oneself or independently of others. **3** self-control; self-command: *Virtuous self-government ... improves the inward constitution or character* (Joseph Butler).

**self-grat|i|fi|ca|tion** (self′grat′ə fə kā′shən), *n.* the gratification of oneself or one's desires, vanity, or the like.

**self-grat|u|la|tion** (self′grach′ə lā′shən), *n.* = self-congratulation.

**self-grat|u|la|to|ry** (self′grach′ə lə tôr′ē, -tōr′-), *adj.* = self-congratulatory.

**self-guid|ance** (self′gī′dəns), *n.* guidance of oneself in one's own course, action, or the like.

**self-guid|ed** (self′gī′dəd), *adj.* **1** directed along a course by self-contained devices, such as a homing mechanism: *a self-guided missile.* **2** guided by one's own course, action, or the like.

**self-hard|en** (self′här′dən), *v.i.* (of steel) to harden without the usual quenching process.

**self-hard|en|ing** (self′här′də ning), *adj.* hardening without the usual quenching process: *self-hardening steel.*

**self-hate** (self′hāt′), *n.* = self-hatred.

**self-hat|ing** (self′hā′ting), *adj.* characterized by self-hatred.

**self-ha|tred** (self′hā′trid), *n.* a very strong dislike of oneself; hate of oneself.

**self|heal** (self′hēl′), *n.* **1** an herb of the mint family, with purple, pink, or white flowers, formerly supposed to heal wounds; allheal. **2** any one of various other plants formerly supposed to possess healing powers, such as the sanicle.

**self-heal|ing** (self′hē′ling), *adj.* healing by itself without external application: *a self-healing wound.*

**self-help** (self′help′), *n.* **1** a helping oneself; getting along without assistance from others: *The first lesson the backwoodsmen learned was the necessity of self-help* (Theodore Roosevelt). **2** *Law.* the act or right of redressing or preventing wrongs by one's own actions, without recourse to legal process.

**self-help|ful** (self′help′fəl), *adj.* helping oneself. —**self′-help′ful|ness**, *n.*

**self|hood** (self′hu̇d), *n.* **1** the quality by virtue of which one is oneself; personal individuality. **2** devotion to self; self-centeredness. **3** one's personal interests or character; one's personality: *In cultivating manhood we develop selfhood* (Century Magazine).

**self-hyp|no|sis** (self′hip nō′sis), *n.* self-induced hypnosis; autohypnosis.

**self-i|den|ti|cal** (self′ī den′tə kəl), *adj.* identical with itself.

**self-i|den|ti|fi|ca|tion** (self′ī den′tə fə kā′shən), *n.* identification of oneself with another or others: *Hogarth had a sympathy for Trump almost amounting to self-identification, as the dog was allowed to steal the foreground of the artist's self-portrait* (London Times).

**self-i|den|ti|ty** (self′ī den′tə tē), *n.* **1** the identity of a thing with itself. **2** a person's own identity.

**self-ig|nite** (self′ig nīt′), *v.i.*, **-nit|ed, -nit|ing.** to ignite by itself; begin to burn without being fired.

**self-ig|ni|tion** (self′ig nish′ən), *n.* the act or process of self-igniting.

**self-im|age** (self′im′ij), *n.* = self-conception.

**self-im|mo|la|tion** (self′im′ə lā′shən), *n.* the act of sacrificing oneself; self-sacrifice: *It was not mere sorrow that kept her so strangely sequestered; it was devotion, it was self-immolation; it was the laborious legacy of love* (Lytton Strachey).

**self-im|por|tance** (self′im pôr′təns), *n.* a having or showing too high an opinion of one's own importance; conceit, or behavior showing conceit.

**self-im|por|tant** (self′im pôr′tənt), *adj.* having or showing too high an opinion of one's own importance. —**self′-im|por′tant|ly**, *adv.*

**self-im|posed** (self′im pōzd′), *adj.* imposed on oneself by oneself: *a self-imposed task.*

**self-im|prove|ment** (self′im prüv′mənt), *n.* improvement of one's character, mind, or the like, by one's own efforts.

**self-im|prov|ing** (self′im prü′ving), *adj.* improving oneself by one's own efforts.

**self-in|clu|sive** (self′in klü′siv), *adj.* inclusive of oneself or itself.

**self-in|crim|i|nat|ing** (self′in krim′ə nā′ting), *adj.* incriminating oneself.

**self-in|crim|i|na|tion** (self′in krim′ə nā′shən), *n.* the incriminating of oneself through one's own testimony: *He pleaded his privilege against self-incrimination under the fifth amendment of the Constitution* (Wall Street Journal).

**self-in|curred** (self′in kėrd′), *adj.* incurred by oneself.

**self-in|duced** (self′in düst′, -dyüst′), *adj.* **1** induced by oneself or itself. **2** *Electricity.* produced by self-induction.

**self-in|duct|ance** (self′in duk′təns), *n. Electricity.* the property by which an electromotive force is induced in one circuit by a varying current in the same circuit.

**self-in|duc|tion** (self′in duk′shən), *n. Electricity.* the inducing of an electromotive force in a circuit by a varying current in that circuit.

**self-in|dul|gence** (self′in dul′jəns), *n.* the gratification of one's own desires, passions, or the like, with too little regard for the welfare of others.

**self-in|dul|gent** (self′in dul′jənt), *adj.* characterized by self-indulgence. —**self′-in|dul′gent|ly**, *adv.*

**self-in|fec|tion** (self′in fek′shən), *n. Medicine.* autoinfection.

**self-in|flict|ed** (self′in flik′tid), *adj.* inflicted on oneself by oneself: *a self-inflicted wound.*

**self-i|ni|ti|at|ed** (self′i nish′ē ā′tid), *adj.* begun by oneself or itself.

**self-i|ni|ti|at|ing** (self′i nish′ē ā′ting), *adj.* initiating by itself; occurring spontaneously or automatically.

**self-in|ju|ri|ous** (self′in ju̇r′ē əs), *adj.* injurious to or for oneself.

**self-in|ju|ry** (self′in′jər ē), *n., pl.* **-ries.** injury to or for oneself.

**self-in|oc|u|la|tion** (self′i nok′yə lā′shən), *n. Medicine.* autoinoculation.

**self-in|struct|ed** (self′in struk′tid), *adj.* self-educated; self-taught.

**self-in|struc|tion** (self′in struk′shən), *n.* self-education; self-schooling.

**self-in|struc|tion|al** (self′in struk′shə nəl), *adj.* of or for self-instruction: *A teaching machine is a self-instructional device.*

**self-in|sur|ance** (self′in shu̇r′əns), *n.* the insuring of oneself, one's own property, or the like, through oneself rather than through an insurance company, as by setting aside a fund for the purpose.

**self-in|sured** (self′in shu̇rd′), *adj.* insured by oneself rather than through an insurance company.

**self-in|sur|er** (self′in shu̇r′ər), *n.* a person or company that is self-insured.

**self-in|tel|li|gi|ble** (self′in tel′ə jə bəl), *adj.* intelligible of oneself or itself.

**self-in|ter|est** (self′in′tər ist, -trist), *n.* **1** interest in one's own welfare or advantage with too little care for the welfare of others; selfishness: ... *the self-interest of the calculating statesman* (Henry Morley). **2** personal interest or advantage.

**self-in|ter|est|ed** (self′in′tər ə stid, -trəs-; -tə res′-tid), *adj.* motivated solely by regard for one's own welfare or advantage; showing self-interest. —**self′-in′ter|est|ed|ness**, *n.*

**self-in|vit|ed** (self′in vī′tid), *adj.* **1** not waiting for an invitation; invited by oneself. **2** occasioned, encouraged, or incited by oneself.

**self-in|volved** (self′in volvd′), *adj.* wrapped up in oneself or one's own thoughts: *He was not self-involved—at times ... he could forget himself* (C. P. Snow).

**self|ish** (sel′fish), *adj.* **1** caring too much for oneself and too little for others. A selfish person puts his own interests first. *This selfish, well-fed and supremely indifferent old man ...* (Edith Wharton). **2** showing care solely or chiefly for oneself: *selfish motives. Want makes almost every man selfish* (Samuel Johnson). —**self′ish|ly**, *adv.* —**self′ish|ness**, *n.*

**self-jus|ti|fi|ca|tion** (self′jus′tə fə kā′shən), *n.* justification of oneself.

**self-jus|ti|fy|ing** (self′jus′tə fī′ing), *adj.* **1** justifying oneself; excusing oneself. **2** *Printing.* justifying lines of type automatically: *a self-justifying typesetter.*

**self-know|ing** (self′nō′ing), *adj.* knowing oneself; having self-knowledge.

**self-knowl|edge** (self′nol′ij), *n.* knowledge of one's own character, ability, or the like.

**self-lac|er|a|tion** (self′las′ə rā′shən), *n.* a laceration of oneself; self-inflicted injury.

**self|less** (self′lis), *adj.* having no regard or thought for self; unselfish. —**self′less|ly**, *adv.* —**self′less|ness**, *n.*

**self-lim|i|ta|tion** (self′lim′ə tā′shən), *n.* limitation of oneself, one's nature, or one's capacities: *Commitment always involves choice, discipline, and self-limitation* (Daniel Jenkins).

**self-lim|it|ed** (self′lim′ə tid), *adj.* **1** limited by oneself or itself. **2** (of a disease) that runs a definite course, being little modified by treatment: *Influenza is self-limited, usually lasting three or four days* (Science News Letter).

**self-lim|it|ing** (self′lim′ə ting), *adj.* **1** limiting or controlling oneself or itself; self-regulating. **2** = self-limited.

**self-liq|ui|dat|ing** (self′lik′wə dā′ting), *adj.* that will convert goods into cash quickly.

**self-load|er** (self′lō′dər), *n.* a firearm that loads itself; an automatic or semiautomatic firearm.

**self-load|ing** (self′lō′ding), *adj.* that loads itself; automatic or semiautomatic: *a self-loading firearm or gun.*

**self-loath|ing** (self′lō′ᴛʜing), *n.* = self-hatred.

**self-lock|ing** (self′lok′ing), *adj.* locking automatically.

**self-love** (self′luv′), *n.* **1** love of oneself; selfishness. **2** = conceit. **3** *Philosophy.* the regard for one's own well-being or happiness, considered as a natural and proper relation of a man to himself. **4** = narcissism.

**self-lov|ing** (self′luv′ing), *adj.* loving oneself too much.

**self-lu|bri|cat|ing** (self′lü′brə kā′ting), *adj.* lubricating automatically.

**self-lu|mi|nos|i|ty** (self′lü′mə nos′ə tē), *n.* the property or condition of being self-luminous; luminosity caused by the spontaneous vibratory motions of the particles of the luminous body: *Bodies like radium that exhibit self-luminosity in the dark ...* (Nature).

**self-lu|mi|nous** (self′lü′mə nəs), *adj.* having in itself the property of giving off light, as the sun or flames: *The necessity for an outward flow of energy explains why a star must be self-luminous* (Scientific American).

**self-made** (self′mād′), *adj.* **1** made by oneself. **2** successful through one's own efforts, especially without material aid from one's family. A self-made man is one who succeeds in business, or other endeavor, without much help from others.

**self-mail|er** (self′mā′lər), *n.* a leaflet that can be addressed, sealed, and mailed without an envelope. Self-mailers are often used in direct-mail advertising.

**self-man|age|ment** (self′man′ij mənt), *n.* the management of a factory, farm, or business by the workers or employees, as in some socialist or communist countries: ... *Yugoslavia's workers' self-management* (New York Times).

**self-mas|ter|y** (self′mas′tər ē, -mäs′-), *n.* the mastery of oneself; self-control.

**self-mate** (self′māt′), *n.* a checkmate produced in chess by the side that is mated; suimate.

**self-med|i|ca|tion** (self′med′ə kā′shən), *n.* **1** the act of taking medicines without the advice of a doctor: *Many compounded the mischief by harmful self-medication, especially with laxatives* (Time). **2** the proper medical treatment of oneself, in the absence of doctors: *Space men and women ... should be trained in self-medication and, particularly, the use of antibiotics* (New Yorker).

**self-mock|er|y** (self′mok′ər ē), *n.* mockery of oneself; scoffing at one's own talents, personality, appearance, accomplishments, or the like: *Success seems to have cost them their capacity for self-mockery* (New Yorker).

**self-mor|ti|fi|ca|tion** (self′môr′tə fə kā′shən), *n.* mortification of oneself, one's passions, etc.

**self-mor|ti|fied** (self′môr′tə fīd), *adj.* mortified of oneself.

**self-moved** (self′müvd′), *adj.* moved of itself, without external agency.

**self-mov|ing** (self′mü′ving), *adj.* that can move by itself; moving spontaneously or automatically.

**self-mur|der** (self′mėr′dər), *n.* the taking of one's own life; suicide.

**self-mur|der|er** (self′mėr′dər ər), *n.* a person who kills himself; suicide.

**self-mu|ti|la|tion** (self′myü′tə lā′shən), *n.* injury inflicted upon oneself.

**self-ne|glect** (self′ni glekt′), *n.* neglect of oneself.

**self-noise** (self′noiz′), *n.* noise produced by a ship itself as it passes through water, as distinguished from the noise caused by the water's turbulence.

**self-ob|sessed** (self′əb sest′), *adj.* obsessed of or over oneself; self-concentrated.

**self-ob|ses|sion** (self′əb sesh′ən), *n.* obsession of or over oneself; self-concentration.

**self-oc|cu|pied** (self′ok′yə pīd), *adj.* **1** occupied with oneself; self-absorbed. **2** = self-employed.

**self-op|er|at|ing** (self′op′ə rā′ting), *adj.* operating automatically.

**self-o|pin|ion** (self′ə pin′yən), *n.* **1** opinion of oneself. **2** = conceit. **3** obstinacy in one's own opinion.

**self-o|pin|ion|at|ed** (self′ə pin′yə nā′tid), *adj.* **1** having an exaggerated opinion of oneself; conceited. **2** = stubborn.

**self-o|pin|ioned** (self′ə pin′yənd), *adj.* = self-opinionated.

**self-op|posed** (self′ə pōzd′), *adj.* opposed to oneself or itself; having parts or elements that are opposed one to another.

---

**Pronunciation Key:** hat, āge, cãre, fär; let, ēqual, tėrm; it, īce; hot, ōpen, ôrder; oil, out; cup, pu̇t, rüle; child; long; thin; ᴛʜen; zh, measure; ə represents **a** in about, **e** in taken, **i** in pencil, **o** in lemon, **u** in circus.

**self-or|dained** (self′ôr dānd′), *adj.* ordained by oneself or itself.

**self-or|gan|ized** (self′ôr′gə nīzd), *adj.* organized of or by oneself.

**self-out|lawed** (self′out′lôd′), *adj.* outlawed by oneself.

**self-par|o|dy** (self′par′ə dē), *n., pl.* **-dies.** a parody of oneself; a ridiculous exaggeration of one's own characteristics.

**self-per|cep|tion** (self′pər sep′shən), *n.* perception of or by oneself.

**self-per|fect** (self′pėr′fikt), *adj.* perfect in oneself or itself.

**self-per|pet|u|at|ing** (self′pər pech′ů ā′ting), *adj.* perpetuating oneself or itself: *The largest single block of stock is owned by a charitable foundation whose trustees are self-perpetuating* (Wall Street Journal).

**self-per|pet|u|a|tion** (self′pər pech′ů ā′shən), *n.* perpetuation of oneself or itself: *Self-perpetuation of the organization is assured* (Harper's).

**self-pi|lot|ing** (self′pī′lə ting), *n.* a ramjet ignition system which uses part of the fuel-air mixture as a pilot flame to ignite the rest of the fuel-air mixture.

**self-pit|y** (self′pit′ē), *n.* pity for oneself, especially to excess: *Honesty rare as a man without self-pity ...* (Stephen Vincent Benét).

**self-pit|y|ing** (self′pit′ē ing), *adj.* characterized by self-pity: *sharply pathetic, but not self-pitying ...* (Manchester Guardian). **—self′-pit′y|ing|ly,** *adv.*

**self-pleased** (self′plēzd′), *adj.* pleased with oneself; self-complacent.

**self-poised** (self′poizd′), *adj.* **1** poised or balanced of itself or without external aid: *Thy form self-poised as if it floated on the air* (Longfellow). **2** having or showing mental poise, steadiness, or self-possession, regardless of external circumstances: *Decorous and self-poised, he was only passionate before the enemy* (John L. Motley).

**self-po|lic|ing** (self′pə lē′sing), *adj., n.* **—*adj.*** policing of oneself or itself.
**—*n.*** the act or process of policing oneself or itself: *He favored self-policing by the industry* (New York Times).

**self-pol|li|nate** (self′pol′ə nāt), *v.t., v.i.,* **-nat|ed, -nat|ing.** to fertilize with pollen from the same flower or plant; undergo or cause to undergo self-pollination: *Inbred lines [are] produced by continually self-pollinating the offspring originating from a single plant* (London Times). *These new plants are allowed to self-pollinate* (Lester R. Brown).

**self-pol|li|na|tion** (self′pol′ə nā′shən), *n.* the transfer of pollen from a stamen to a stigma of the same flower, or to a stigma of another flower or clone of the same plant. See diagram under **pollination.**

**self-pol|lu|tion** (self′pə lü′shən), *n.* = masturbation.

**self-por|trait** (self′pôr′trit, -trāt; -pōr′-), *n.* a portrait made by a person of himself.

**self-pos|sessed** (self′pə zest′), *adj.* having or showing control of one's feelings and actions; not excited, embarrassed, or confused; calm: *... as impenitent and self-possessed a young lady as one would desire to see* (George Bernard Shaw). *In a moment he recovered his usual self-possessed manner* (W. H. Hudson). **SYN:** composed, collected, poised, assured, unruffled.

**self-pos|ses|sion** (self′pə zesh′ən), *n.* control of one's feelings and actions; self-command; composure; calmness: *Their quiet self-possession and dignified ease impressed me pleasurably* (Samuel Butler). **SYN:** equanimity, imperturbability.

**self-pow|ered** (self′pou′ərd), *adj.* powered automatically.

**self-praise** (self′prāz′), *n.* praise of oneself by oneself.

**self-pre|oc|cu|pa|tion** (self′prē ok′yə pā′shən), *n.* preoccupation with oneself.

**self-prep|a|ra|tion** (self′prep′ə rā′shən), *n.* preparation of or by oneself.

**self-pres|er|va|tion** (self′prez′ər vā′shən), *n.* preservation of oneself from harm or destruction: *the instinct of self-preservation.*

**self-pride** (self′prīd′), *n.* pride in oneself, one's achievements, or one's position; personal pride: *But it is also true that most people have independence and self-pride enough to prefer work to unemployment* (Wall Street Journal).

**self-prim|ing** (self′prī′ming), *adj.* priming automatically.

**self-pro|claimed** (self′prə klāmd′), *adj.* made known by oneself about oneself; self-declared: *a self-proclaimed art critic.*

**self-pro|duced** (self′prə düst′, -dyüst′), *adj.* produced by or from within oneself or itself.

**self-prof|it** (self′prof′it), *n.* a person's own profit or advantage; self-interest: *... unbias'd by self-profit* (Tennyson).

**self-pro|pelled** (self′prə peld′), *adj.* propelled by an engine or motor within itself: *a self-propelled missile.*

**self-pro|pel|ling** (self′prə pel′ing), *adj.* that moves under its own power, as an automobile.

**self-pro|pul|sion** (self′prə pul′shən), *n.* movement forward or onward by one's own power: *The charter contains no instrument of self-propulsion* (New York Times).

**self-pro|tec|tion** (self′prə tek′shən), *n.* protection of oneself; self-defense.

**self-pro|tec|tive** (self′prə tek′tiv), *adj.* protecting of or over oneself or itself. **—self′-pro|tec′tive|ly,** *adv.* **—self′-pro|tec′tive|ness,** *n.*

**self-pu|ri|fi|ca|tion** (self′pyůr′ə fə kā′shən), *n.* a purification of oneself.

**self-ques|tion|ing** (self′kwes′chə ning), *adj.* questioning of oneself.

**self-rais|ing** (self′rā′zing), *adj.* = self-rising.

**self-rat|ing scale** (self′rā′ting), a rating scale on which a person evaluates himself in various areas, as personality, character, or ability.

**self-re|al|i|za|tion** (self′rē′ə lə zā′shən), *n.* the fulfillment by one's own efforts of the possibilities of development of the self.

**self-re|cord|ing** (self′ri kôr′ding), *adj.* that makes a record of its own operations; recording automatically; self-registering: *a self-recording thermometer.*

**self-re|crim|i|na|tion** (self′ri krim′ə nā′shən), *n.* self-accusation; self-reproach: *She mixed self-recrimination with self-justification until it was enough to make a man's head swim* (New Yorker).

**self-re|gard** (self′ri gärd′), *n.* **1** regard of or consideration for oneself. **2** = self-respect.

**self-re|gard|ing** (self′ri gär′ding), *adj.* looking towards or centering upon oneself; self-serving: *The pleasures and pains of amity and enmity are of the self-regarding cast* (Jeremy Bentham).

**self-reg|is|ter|ing** (self′rej′ə stər ing), *adj.* registering automatically.

**self-reg|u|lat|ing** (self′reg′yə lā′ting), *adj.* regulating oneself or itself. Automatic devices are self-regulating.

**self-reg|u|la|tion** (self′reg′yə lā′shən), *n.* regulation by or of oneself or itself.

**self-reg|u|la|tive** (self′reg′yə lā′tiv), *adj.* tending or serving to regulate oneself or itself.

**self-reg|u|la|to|ry** (self′reg′yə lə tôr′ē, -tōr′-), *adj.* = self-regulative.

**self-re|la|tion** (self′ri lā′shən), *n.* the identity of a thing with itself.

**self-re|li|ance** (self′ri lī′əns), *n.* reliance on one's own acts, abilities, or the like: *A greater self-reliance must work a revolution in all the offices and relations of men* (Emerson).

**self-re|li|ant** (self′ri lī′ənt), *adj.* having or showing self-reliance. **—self′-re|li′ant|ly,** *adv.*

**self-re|nun|ci|a|tion** (self′ri nun′sē ā′shən), *n.* renunciation of one's own will, interests, or the like; self-sacrifice.

**self-re|nun|ci|a|to|ry** (self′ri nun′sē ə tôr′ē, -tōr′-), *adj.* = self-sacrificing.

**self-re|pair** (self′ri pãr′), *n.* repair by itself without external application.

**self-rep|li|cat|ing** (self′rep′lə kā′ting), *adj.* replicating oneself or itself: *Every molecular biologist believes that DNA is a self-replicating molecule* (New Scientist).

**self-rep|li|ca|tion** (self′rep′lə kā′shən), *n.* replication of itself or by itself: *These organisms [pleuropneumonia-like organisms] which are even smaller than some viruses, are thought to possess only the minimum number of structures needed for self-replication and independent existence* (Scientific American).

**self-re|pressed** (self′ri prest′), *adj.* repressed by oneself.

**self-re|pres|sion** (self′ri presh′ən), *n.* repression of oneself or one's own impulses, desires, or the like.

**self-re|proach** (self′ri prōch′), *n.* blame by one's own conscience.

**self-re|proach|ful** (self′ri prōch′fəl), *adj.* reproaching oneself.

**self-re|pro|duc|ing** (self′rē′prə dü′sing, -dyü′-), *adj.* reproducing of oneself or itself.

**self-re|pro|duc|tion** (self′rē′prə duk′shən), *n.* reproduction or copy of oneself or itself.

**self-re|proof** (self′ri prüf′), *n.* reproof of oneself by oneself.

**self-re|spect** (self′ri spekt′), *n.* respect for oneself; proper regard for the dignity of one's character or position, with recognition of its obligations of worthy conduct; proper pride: *With shame and repentance ... had come a strange new feeling—that of a dawning self-respect* (George du Maurier).

**self-re|spect|ing** (self′ri spek′ting), *adj.* having self-respect; properly proud: *... the shame of boasting that shuts the mouths of self-respecting Scots* (Ian Maclaren).

**self-re|spon|si|bil|i|ty** (self′ri spon′sə bil′ə tē), *n., pl.* **-ties.** responsibility to or for oneself.

**self-re|strained** (self′ri strānd′), *adj.* restrained by oneself or itself; showing self-control.

**self-re|straint** (self′ri strānt′), *n.* restraint imposed by oneself on one's actions, or desires; self-control.

**self-re|veal|ing** (self′ri vē′ling), *adj.* revealing of oneself or of one's real self: *The essays ... represent not Camus's finest work, but his most self-revealing* (Saturday Review).

**self-rev|e|la|tion** (self′rev′ə lā′shən), *n.* revelation of oneself; disclosure of one's real self.

**self-right|eous** (self′rī′chəs), *adj.* thinking that one is more moral than others; thinking that one is very good and pleasing to God: *She's narrow and self-righteous* (Eden Phillpotts). **—self′-right′eous|ly,** *adv.* **—self′-right′eous|ness,** *n.*

**self-right|ing** (self′rī′ting), *adj.* that can right itself after being upset: *a self-righting life raft.*

**self-ris|ing** (self′rī′zing), *adj.* that has a leavening agent mixed with it during its manufacture; self-raising: *self-rising flour.*

**self-rule** (self′rül′), *n.* = self-government.

**self-rul|ing** (self′rü′ling), *adj.* = self-governing.

**self-sac|ri|fice** (self′sak′rə fīs), *n.* sacrifice of one's own interests and desires for the sake of one's duty or the welfare of others.

**self-sac|ri|fic|ing** (self′sak′rə fī′sing), *adj.* giving up things for someone else; unselfish: *self-sacrificing love.* **—self′-sac′ri|fic′ing|ly,** *adv.*

**self-sales|man|ship** (self′sālz′mən ship), *n.* ability at selling oneself to others.

**self|same** (self′sām′), *adj.* very same; identical: *We study the selfsame books that you do. A bird sings the selfsame song, with never a fault in its flow* (Thomas Hardy). **—self′same′ness,** *n.*

**self-sat|is|fac|tion** (self′sat′is fak′shən), *n.* satisfaction with oneself; complacency.

**self-sat|is|fied** (self′sat′is fīd), *adj.* pleased with oneself, one's achievements, position, or the like; complacent.

**self-sat|is|fy|ing** (self′sat′is fī′ing), *adj.* that satisfies oneself; giving self-satisfaction.

**self-schooled** (self′sküld′), *adj.* **1** schooled by oneself; self-educated. **2** disciplined by oneself.

**self-school|ing** (self′skü′ling), *n.* **1** schooling of oneself. **2** disciplining of or by oneself.

**self-scru|ti|ny** (self′skrü′tə nē), *n., pl.* **-nies.** scrutiny of oneself or itself.

**self-seal|ing** (self′sē′ling), *adj.* closing tightly or fastening by itself.

**self-search|ing** (self′sėr′ching), *adj., n.* **—*adj.*** examining one's actions or motives carefully.
**—*n.*** careful examination of one's motives or actions.

**self-seek|er** (self′sē′kər), *n.* a person who seeks his own interests, welfare, advancement, or the like, without regard for that of others: *So the three self-seekers banded and beset the one unselfish* (Charlotte Brontë).

**self-seek|ing** (self′sē′king), *adj., n.* **—*adj.*** = selfish.
**—*n.*** = selfishness.

**self-se|lec|tion** (self′si lek′shən), *n.* **1** selection by oneself. **2** the selection of merchandise in a retail store by customers without the help of salespeople.

**self-serv|ice** (self′sėr′vis), *n., adj.* **—*n.*** the act or process of serving oneself, as in a restaurant or store.
**—*adj.*** of or for self-service.

**self-serv|ing** (self′sėr′ving), *adj.* serving one's own interests; seeking advantage for oneself: *Often he is a self-serving schemer, intent on discrediting those who stand between him and the presidency of the great corporation* (Atlantic). **—self′-serv′ing|ly,** *adv.*

**self-slaugh|ter** (self′slô′tər), *n.* the killing of oneself; suicide.

**self-so|lic|i|tude** (self′sə lis′ə tüd, -tyüd), *n.* anxiety for oneself.

**self-sown** (self′sōn′), *adj.* **1** sown by itself: *flowers self-sown by last year's plants.* **2** sown by any agency other than man, as by the wind or by birds.

**self-sta|bi|liz|ing** (self′stā′bə lī′zing), *adj.* automatically stabilizing of oneself or itself.

**self-start|er** (self′stär′tər), *n.* **1** an electric motor or other device used to start an engine automatically; starter. **2** an automobile whose engine is equipped with such a device. **3** *U.S. Informal.* a person who initiates work, projects, or the like, by himself, not by the urging of others.

**self-steer|ing** (self′stir′ing), *adj.* designed to keep a boat or aircraft on a fixed course: *self-steering gear.*

**self-ster|ile** (self′ster′əl), *adj.* unable to fertilize itself, as certain flowers or plants.

**self-ste|ril|i|ty** (self′stə ril′ə tē), *n.* the inability of a flower or plant to fertilize itself.

**self-striped** (self′strīpt′), *adj.* woven with stripes in its own color, as a self-colored fabric.

**self-stud|y** (self′stud′ē), *n., pl.* **-stud|ies.** = self-examination.

**self-styled** (self′stīld′), *adj.* so called by oneself:

*a self-styled leader whom no one follows, the self-styled party of progress.*

**self-sub|sist|ence** (self′səb sis′təns), *n.* subsistence by oneself without dependence on anything external.

**self-sub|sist|ent** (self′səb sis′tənt), *adj.* subsisting alone without dependence on or support of anything external.

**self-suf|fi|cien|cy** (self′sə fish′ən sē), *n.* **1** the ability to supply one's own needs. **2** conceit; self-assurance.

**self-suf|fi|cient** (self′sə fish′ənt), *adj.* **1** asking or needing no help; independent: *a grave and self-sufficient child.* **2** having too much confidence in one's own resources, powers, or the like; conceited.

**self-suf|fic|ing** (self′sə fī′sing), *adj.* sufficing in or for oneself or itself; self-sufficient.

**self-suf|fic|ing|ness** (self′sə fī′sing nis), *n.* = self-sufficiency.

**self-sug|gest|ed** (self′səg jes′tid), *adj.* suggested to or by oneself; caused by self-suggestion.

**self-sug|ges|tion** (self′səg jes′chən), *n.* **1** suggestion to oneself; autosuggestion. **2** a suggestion arising of itself.

**self-sup|port** (self′sə pôrt′, -pōrt′), *n.* unaided support of oneself or itself.

**self-sup|port|ed** (self′sə pôr′tid, -pōr′-), *adj.* supported by oneself or itself without outside aid.

**self-sup|port|ing** (self′sə pôr′ting, -pōr′-), *adj.* supporting oneself or itself without outside aid; earning one's expenses; getting along without help: *a self-supporting private college. The children would soon become self-supporting and independent* (Samuel Butler).

**self-sur|ren|der** (self′sə ren′dər), *n.* a complete yielding, as to another person, to emotion, or to religion.

**self-sus|tained** (self′sə stānd′), *adj.* sustained by oneself or itself without outside aid.

**self-sus|tain|ing** (self′sə stā′ning), *adj.* **1** = self-supporting. **2** proceeding automatically once it has been started: *a self-sustaining chain reaction.*

**self-tap|ping screw** (self′tap′ing), a screw that cuts its own internal screw thread in metal: *The three-cornered screws are self-tapping* (New York Times).

**self-taught** (self′tôt′), *adj.* **1** taught by oneself without aid from others; self-educated: *a self-taught cook. That egotism ... characteristic of self-taught men* (William Hazlitt). **2** acquired by one's own unaided efforts: *self-taught knowledge.*

**self-teach|ing** (self′tē′ching), *n.* teaching of oneself; self-instruction.

**self-think|ing** (self′thing′king), *adj.* thinking for oneself; forming one's own opinions and not borrowing them ready-made from others, or merely following prevalent fashions of thought.

**self-thread|ing** (self′thred′ing), *adj.* threading of itself; threading automatically.

**self-tim|er** (self′tī′mər), *n.* a device on a camera that opens and closes the shutter automatically after a certain lapse of time. A self-timer enables the photographer to take his own picture.

**self-tor|ment** (self′tôr′ment), *n.* the action of tormenting oneself.

**self-tor|ture** (self′tôr′chər), *n.* torture inflicted on one by oneself.

**self-tran|scen|dence** (self′tran sen′dəns), *n.* the quality of transcending or going beyond one's own self: *Man's highest capacity, Koestler says, is self-transcendence, or unselfishness* (Time).

**self-treat|ment** (self′trēt′mənt), *n.* the treatment of one's own ailments without medical advice; self-medication; autotherapy.

**self-un|der|stand|ing** (self′un′dər stand′ing), *n.* understanding of oneself; self-knowledge.

**self-un|load|er** (self′un lōd′ər), *n.* a cargo ship with self-contained handling machinery which can unload bulk cargo without help from shore conveniences: *The self-unloader ... [in which] a discharge arm carrying a conveyor belt extends from the ship, and the cargo pours off its end in a smooth stream* (New Scientist).

**self-vin|di|ca|tion** (self′vin′də kā′shən), *n.* vindication of oneself.

**self-whole** (self′hōl′), *adj.* complete in or of oneself or itself.

**self-will** (self′wil′), *n.* an insistence on having one's own way; obstinacy.

**self-willed** (self′wild′), *adj.* insisting on having one's own way; objecting to doing what others ask or command: *The children ... were young and self-willed and rude, and would not learn to do as they were bid* (George MacDonald). —**self′-willed′ness**, *n.*

**self-wind|er** (self′wīn′dər), *n.* a self-winding timepiece: *The new 15-jewel clock is a self-winder, deriving its power from the driver's turning of the wheel and from the vibration of the car* (Wall Street Journal).

**self-wind|ing** (self′wīn′ding), *adj.* that is wound automatically. A self-winding watch winds itself by the movements of the person wearing it.

**self-worth** (self′wėrth′), *n.* a favorable estimate or opinion of oneself; self-esteem.

**se|li|ha** (sə lē′hä), *n., pl.* **-hes** (-hes), **-hoth** (-hōth). *Judaism.* pentitential prayers recited on fast days, on the week preceding Rosh Hashanah, and on the ten days between Rosh Hashanah and Yom Kippur. [< Hebrew *seliḥah* < *sā-laḥ*, forgive, pardon]

**Sel|juk** (sel jük′), *adj., n.* —*adj.* of or having to do with certain Turkish dynasties, or the tribes to which they belonged, that ruled over large parts of Asia from the 1000's to the 1200's.
—*n.* a member of a Seljuk dynasty or tribe.
[< Turkish *Selçuk*, the name of the legendary leader]

**Sel|juk|i|an** (sel jü′kē ən), *adj., n.* = Seljuk.

**sell¹** (sel), *v.*, **sold, sell|ing,** *n.* —*v.t.* **1** to exchange for money or other payment: *He will sell his house.* **SYN:** barter, trade, vend. **2** to keep regularly for sale; deal in: *A butcher sells meat.* **3** to give up or betray: *to sell one's soul. The traitor sold his country for money.* (*Figurative.*) *You would have sold your king to slaughter* (Shakespeare). **4** to take money or a reward for, or make profit or gain of (something not a proper object for such action): *to sell one's vote. When perjury ... Sells oaths by tale, and at the lowest price ...* (William Cowper). **5** *Informal, Figurative.* **a** to cause to be accepted, approved, or adopted by representations and methods characteristic of salesmanship: *to sell an idea to the public.* **b** to cause to accept, approve, or adopt thus: *to sell the public an idea.* **6** to promote the sale of: *Advertisements sold many new cars.* **7** *Slang, Figurative.* to cheat; trick; hoax.
—*v.i.* **1** to dispose of something for money or other payment; engage in selling. **2** to be in demand as an article of sale; find purchasers; be on sale; be sold: *This article sells well. Strawberries sell at a high price in January.* **3** *Informal, Figurative.* to win acceptance, approval, or adoption: *an idea that will sell.*
—*n.* **1** *U.S. Informal.* **a** an act or method of selling; selling activity. **b** sales quality; salability: *He has shrewdly applied his promotion sense to get "sell" out of it [the magazine]* (Harper's). **2** *Slang, Figurative.* a cheat; trick; hoax. **3** *British Slang.* a letdown; disappointment.
**sell off,** to dispose of by sale: *Reynolds Metals sold off ... a new stock* (Wall Street Journal).
**sell on,** *U.S.* **a** to inspire with the desire to buy or possess something: *I was sold on the house the minute I saw it.* **b** *Informal, Figurative.* to show or convince of the value, truth, or the like, of something: *They failed to sell the Supreme Court on this argument* (Wall Street Journal).
**sell out, a** to sell all that one has of; get rid of by selling: *All the tickets have been sold out. A couple of years from now you'll kick yourself around the block for selling out cheap* (New York Times). **b** *Informal, Figurative.* to betray by a secret bargain: *The self-alienated man gives way to impulses to round upon his associates and accuse them of selling out the cause* (Edmund Wilson). **c** (1) to sell at the market price (stock or commodities held on margin where the nominal owner fails to meet his margin requirements): *I wrote ... a power of attorney to him [the broker] to sell out the stock* (Frederick Marryat). (2) to sell thus the stocks or commodities of (an individual or other investor): *When margins went up, several of the investors were sold out at a loss.*
**sell short, a** to sell stocks or commodities not in one's possession at the time of sale, hoping to buy them at a lower rate before the time of delivery and make a profit: *People sell short when they expect the market to decline. It is risky to sell short.* **b** *U.S. Informal, Figurative.* to have a low opinion of; belittle; downgrade: *Nobody but nobody was selling him short on this occasion* (New York Times).
**sell up,** *Especially British.* **a** to dispose of the whole of (as one's stock or property) by sale: *Soon afterwards he sold up his English home and settled abroad permanently* (London Times). **b** to dispose of the whole or a portion of a bankrupt person's goods for the benefit of creditors: *He ... would ... drink his glass with a tenant and sell him up the next day* (Thackeray).
[Old English *sellan* sell; give]

**sell²** (sel), *n. Scottish.* self.

**sell³** (sel), *n. Archaic.* **1** a seat. **2** a saddle. [< Old French *selle* < Latin *sella* seat, related to *sēdes* seat]

**sell|a|ble** (sel′ə bəl), *adj.* that can be sold; salable.

**sel|lan|ders** (sel′ən dərz), *n.pl.* = sallenders.

**sell|er** (sel′ər), *n.* **1** a person who sells: *A druggist is a seller of drugs and medicines. The stock exchange was filled with buyers and sellers of stocks.* **2** a thing considered with reference to its sale: *This book is a steady seller. Our new product turned out to be a very good seller.*

**seller's market,** an economic condition in which the demand for goods exceeds the supply of them, and prices are usually high.

**sell|ing** (sel′ing), *adj., n.* —*adj.* **1a** that is sold: *a steadily selling item.* **b** *Archaic.* easily salable. **2** at which sale is or can be accomplished: *a low selling price.* **3** that is engaged in selling.
—*n.* the act of one who sells.

**selling plate,** = selling race.

**sell|ing-plat|er** (sel′ing plā′tər), *n.* a horse that competes in a selling race.

**selling point,** a good point or desirable feature to be stressed in selling a product or service: *The £50 allowance is currently the neatest selling point for cruising* (London Times).

**selling price,** the price at which something is sold or at which it is offered for sale.

**selling race,** a race for horses which are to be offered for sale after the race at prices stated when they are entered.

**sell-off** (sel′ôf′, -of′), *n.* a widespread selling, as of stocks or securities.

**sell|out** (sel′out′), *n.* **1** a selling of all that one has: *a near sellout of their first issue.* **2** a performance, as of a play or sports event, for which no unsold seats are left. **3** *U.S. Informal, Figurative.* a selling out; betrayal.

**sel|syn** (sel′sin), *n.* **1** a synchro unit designed for various purposes, such as for synchronizing gunfire with a radar scanner or the projectors of a three-dimensional motion picture with each other. **2** Selsyn. a trademark for such a unit. [< *sel*(f)-*syn*(chronous)]

**Selt|zer** (selt′sər), *n.,* or **Seltzer water, 1** a bubbling mineral water containing salt and calcium and magnesium carbonates. **2a** an artificial mineral water of similar composition. **b** any carbonated water. [alteration of earlier *Selters* < German *Selterser* < *Selters,* a village in Germany, where it is found]

**sel|va** (sel′və), *n., pl.* **-vas.** a tract of densely wooded country, such as that lying in the basin of the Amazon River in South America. [< Portuguese *selva* < Latin *silva* wood]

**sel|vage** or **sel|vedge** (sel′vij), *n.* **1** the edge of a woven fabric finished off to prevent raveling. **2** any similar strip or surplus section of material, especially wallpaper. **3** the edge plate of a lock, through which the bolt shoots. **4** *Figurative.* a border; edge: *Ducks gobble at the selvage of the brook* (John Masefield). [probably < earlier Flemish *selfegghe* self-edge (because it serves as an edge for itself)]

**selves** (selvz), *n., pron.* plural of self: *He had two selves—a friendly self and a shy self.*

**sem.,** semicolon.

**Sem.,** **1** seminary. **2** Semitic.

**SEM** (no periods), scanning electron microscope: *SEM's advantage over other microscopic techniques is the ability to present a three-dimensional image more realistically* (Walter Clark).

**se|mai|nier** (sə men′yā), *n.* a tall, narrow chest, having seven drawers, one for each day of the week.
[< French *semainier* < *semaine* week < Late Latin *septimāna,* feminine of Latin *septimānus* of seven < *septem* seven]

**se|man|teme** (sə man′tēm), *n. Linguistics.* a morpheme that has lexical rather than mere grammatical meaning. [< French *sémantème* < *sémantique* semantics + *-ème*, as in *phonème* phoneme]

**se|man|tic** (sə man′tik), *adj.* **1** having to do with meanings of words and other linguistic forms and expressions: *There is a semantic difference between bear (animal) and bear (carry), though the two words are identical in sound and spelling.* **2** having to do with semantics. —**se|man′ti|cal|ly,** *adv.*

**se|man|ti|cist** (sə man′tə sist), *n.* a person skilled in or who studies semantics.

**se|man|tics** (sə man′tiks), *n.* **1** the scientific study of the meanings, and the development of meanings, of words. **2** the scientific study of symbols as denotative units, of their relationship to each other, and of their impact on society. **3** any explanation of meaning or use of interpretation: *We are getting so technical with your semantics it is impossible for us to understand* (William J. Fulbright).
[< Late Latin *sēmanticus* < Greek *sēmantikós* significant < *sēmaínein* signify, show < *sêma, -atos* sign]

---

**Pronunciation Key:** hat, āge, cãre, fär; let, ēqual, tėrm; it, īce; hot, ōpen, ôrder; oil, out; cup, pu̇t, rüle; child; long; thin; ᴛʜen; zh, measure; ə represents **a** in about, **e** in taken, **i** in pencil, **o** in lemon, **u** in circus.

**✱sem|a|phore** (sem′ə fôr, -fōr), *n., v.,* **-phored, -phor|ing.** **—*n.*** **1** an upright post or structure with movable arms, or an arrangement of colored lights, lanterns, or flags, used in railroad signaling. **2** a system of signals for sending messages by using different positions of the arms or flags, or by using lanterns or other mechanical devices. See picture below.
**—*v.t., v.i.*** to signal by semaphore.
[< Greek *sêma, -atos* signal + English *-phore*]

**sem|a|phor|ic** (sem′ə fôr′ik, -fōr′-), *adj.* of, having to do with, or by means of a semaphore: *They flash a semaphoric SOS* (Time).

**se|ma|si|o|log|i|cal** (sə mā′sē ə loj′ə kəl), *adj.* having to do with semasiology.

**se|ma|si|ol|o|gist** (sə mā′sē ol′ə jist), *n.* = semanticist.

**se|ma|si|ol|o|gy** (sə mā′sē ol′ə jē), *n.* = semantics (def. 1). [< Greek *sēmasiā* meaning < *sēmaínein* (see etym. under **semantic**) + *-logy*]

**se|mat|ic** (si mat′ik), *adj. Biology.* serving as a sign or warning of danger: *The conspicuous colors or markings of various poisonous animals may be sematic.* [< Greek *sêma, -atos* sign + English *-ic*]

**sem|bla|ble** (sem′blə bəl), *adj., n. Archaic.* **—*adj.*** **1** like; similar (to). **2** suitable. **3** seeming.
**—*n.*** something similar; likeness.
[< Old French *semblable* < *sembler;* see etym. under **semblance**]

**sem|bla|bly** (sem′blə blē), *adv. Archaic.* similarly.

**sem|blance** (sem′bləns), *n.* **1a** outward appearance: *Their story had the semblance of truth, but was really false.* **b** an assumed or unreal appearance of something; mere show: *He was convicted without even the semblance of a trial.* **2a** a likeness; image or copy of something: *These clouds have the semblance of a huge head.* **b** the fact or quality of being like something; resemblance: *I see there was some semblance betwixt this good Man and me* (John Bunyan). **3** *Archaic.* the appearance or outward aspect of a person or thing: *Mine outward semblance doth deceive the truth* (Milton). [< Old French *semblance* < *sembler* to seem, resemble < Latin *similāre* < *similis* similar]

**sem|blant** (sem′blənt), *adj. Archaic.* **1** like; similar. **2** seeming.

**sem|ble** (sem′bəl), *v.i.* "it seems," a legal term used impersonally in judicial utterances to precede an incidental statement of opinion on a point of law which it is not necessary to decide in the case. [< French *semble* it seems]

**sem|bling** (sem′bling), *n.* the attraction of male insects to a captive female. [obsolete *semble* to come together, assemble + *-ing*[1]]

**se|mé** or **se|mée** (sə mā′), *adj. Heraldry.* strewn, as with small stars or flowers. [< Old French *semee,* feminine past participle of *semer* to sow < Latin *sēmināre* < *sēmen, -inis* seed]

**se|mei|o|log|i|cal** (sē′mī ə loj′ə kəl), *adj.* of or having to do with semeiology. Also, **semiological.**

**se|mei|ol|o|gist** (sē′mī ol′ə jist), *n.* an expert in semeiology. Also, **semiologist.**

**se|mei|ol|o|gy** (sē′mī ol′ə jē), *n.* **1** the science of signs. **2** = sign language. **3** the branch of medicine dealing with symptoms; symptomatology. Also, **semiology.** [< Greek *sēmeîon* sign + English *-logy*]

**se|mei|ot|ic** (sē′mī ot′ik), *adj., n.* **—*adj.*** **1** of or having to do with the general theory of signs. **2** relating to symptoms; symptomatic.
**—*n.*** = semiotics. Also, **semiotic.**
[< Greek *sēmeiōtikós* significant < *sēmioûn* interpret as a sign < *sēmeîon* sign]

**se|mei|ot|i|cal** (sē′mī ot′ə kəl), *adj.* = semeiotic.

**se|mei|ot|ics** (sē′mī ot′iks), *n.* = semiotics.

**Sem|e|le** (sem′ə lē), *n. Greek Mythology.* the daughter of Cadmus and Harmonia, mother by Zeus of Dionysus. Insisting upon seeing Zeus as he appeared among the gods, Semele was consumed by lightning, but her unborn child was rescued by Zeus.

**sem|el|in|ci|dent** (sem′əl in′sə dənt), *adj.* (of a disease) occurring only once; providing immunity against future infection. [< Latin *semel* once + English *incident*]

**sem|eme** (sem′ēm), *n. Linguistics.* the meaning of a morpheme: *We find the sememe 'female of such-and-such male' expressed not only by the suffix -ess, but also by composition, as in elephant cow, she-elephant, nanny goat, and by suppletion, as in ram: ewe* (Leonard Bloomfield). [(coined in 1933 by Leonard Bloomfield) < Greek *sêma* sign + English (morph)*eme*]

**se|men** (sē′mən), *n., pl.* **sem|i|na.** the fluid containing the male reproductive cells (spermatozoa) that fertilize the ova. It is produced in the male reproductive organs. [< Latin *sēmen, -inis,* related to *serere* to sow. Compare etym. under **season.**]

**se|mes|ter** (sə mes′tər), *n.* **1** a division, often one half, of a school year; term of instruction lasting usually from 15 to 18 weeks. **2** a period or term of six months in German universities, including the vacation periods. [American English < German *Semester* < Latin (*cursus*) *sēmēstris* (period) of six months < *sēmēstris* semiannual < *sex* six + *mēnsis* month]

**se|mes|tral** (sə mes′trəl), *adj.* relating to a semester; half-yearly; semiannual.

**se|mes|tri|al** (sə mes′trē əl), *adj.* = semestral.

**sem|i** (sem′ē), *n. Informal.* **1** a semitrailer. **2** a semifinal. **3** *British.* a semi-detached house.

**semi-,** *prefix.* **1** exactly half: *Semicircle = a half circle. Semirevolution = one half revolution. Semitone = one half tone.*
**2** about half; partly; incompletely: *Semiskilled = incompletely skilled. Semicivilized = partly civilized. Semibarbarian = partly barbarian. Semisecret = not completely secret.*
**3** half a (period of time); twice. Semi_____ly means in each half of a _____, or twice in a _____: *Semiannually = every half year, or twice a year.*
[< Latin *sēmi-*]
▶ **a Semi-** is not usually hyphened except before proper names (*semi-Christian*) or words beginning with *i* (*semi-invalid*). In British use the hyphen tends to be retained in words formed in English by adding the prefix to an existing form (*semi-detached*), as distinguished from words derived from forms without the hyphen in Latin, French, etc. **b Semi-** is usually pronounced (sem′ē-) before both vowels and consonants, sometimes (sem′ə-) before consonants, and occasionally (sem′ī-).

**sem|i|ab|stract** (sem′ē ab strakt′, -ab′strakt), *adj.* of or having to do with an abstract style of painting and sculpture in which the subject can be recognized or identified; partly abstract: *... twenty semiabstract oils in which are glimpses of factories, harbors, and airports* (New Yorker). **—sem′i|ab|stract′ly,** *adv.*

**sem|i|ab|strac|tion** (sem′ē ab strak′shən), *n.* a work of semiabstract art: *... brightly colored semiabstractions that owe more to the world of toys than to Matisse* (Time).

**sem|i|ab|strac|tion|ist** (sem′ē ab strak′shə nist), *n.* an artist who produces semiabstractions.

**sem|i|ad|her|ent** (sem′ē ad hir′ənt), *adj. Botany.* having the lower half adherent, as a seed or stamen.

**sem|i|ag|ri|cul|tur|al** (sem′ē ag′rə kul′chər əl), *adj.* not completely agricultural.

**sem|i|air-cooled** (sem′ē ãr′küld), *adj.* partially but not entirely air-cooled.

**sem|i|an|gle** (sem′ē ang′gəl), *n.* the half of a given or measuring angle.

**sem|i|an|nu|al** (sem′ē an′yü əl), *adj.* **1** occurring every half year. **2** lasting a half year: *a semiannual plant.* **—sem′i|an′nu|al|ly,** *adv.*

**sem|i|an|nu|lar** (sem′ē an′yə lər), *adj.* forming a half circle; semicircular.

**sem|i|an|thra|cite** (sem′ē an′thrə sīt), *n.* a coal intermediate between anthracite and bituminous coal. It is softer and more volatile than anthracite.

**sem|i|a|quat|ic** (sem′ē ə kwat′ik, -kwot′-), *adj.* partly aquatic; growing or living close to water, and sometimes found in water.

**sem|i|arc** (sem′ē ärk′), *n.* half an arc.

**sem|i|arch** (sem′ē ärch′), *n. Architecture.* half an arch: *to determine the center of gravity of a semiarch.*

**sem|i|ar|id** (sem′ē ar′id), *adj.* having very little rainfall.

**sem|i|a|rid|i|ty** (sem′ē ə rid′ə tē), *n.* semiarid nature or condition.

**sem|i|a|the|ist** (sem′ē ā′thē ist), *n.* a partial adherent of the tenets or theories of atheism; part atheist.

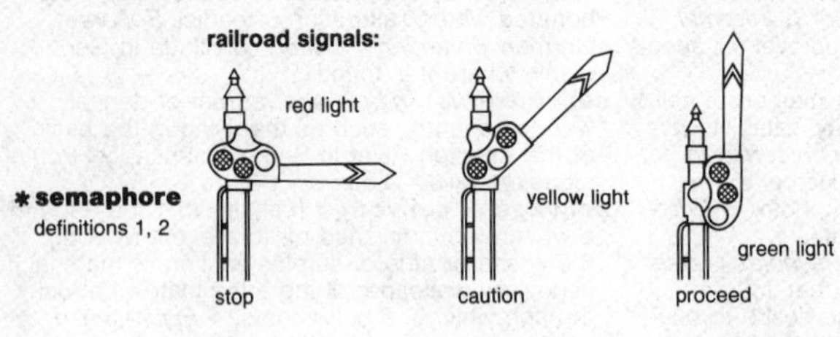


**✱semaphore**
definitions 1, 2

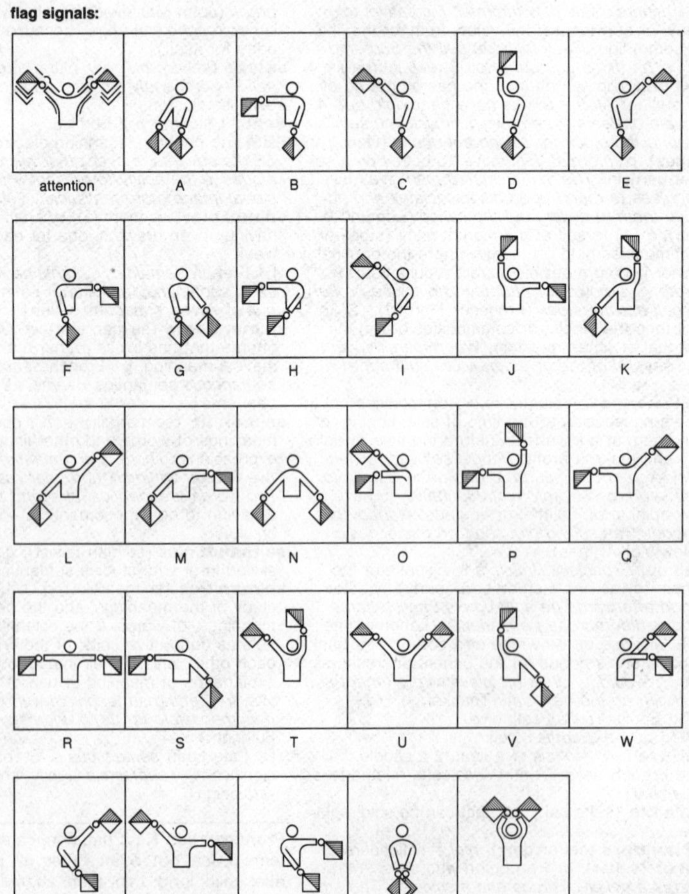

**sem|i|at|tached** (sem′ē ə tacht′), *adj.* **1** partially attached or united: *a semiattached house.* **2** partially bound by affection, interest, or special preference of any kind.

**sem|i|au|to|bi|o|graph|i|cal** (sem′ē ô′tə bī′ə-graf′ə kəl), *adj.* partly autobiographic.

**sem|i|au|to|mat|ic** (sem′ē ô′tə mat′ik), *adj., n.* —*adj.* **1** partly automatic; self-acting in some part of its operation. **2** capable of or designed for ejecting the empty cartridge and loading the next cartridge by an automatic mechanism, but requiring a press of the trigger to fire each shot; self-loading: *a semiautomatic firearm.*
—*n.* a semiautomatic firearm. —**sem′i|au′to|mat′i|cal|ly**, *adv.*

**sem|i|au|ton|o|mous** (sem′ē ô ton′ə məs), *adj.* not completely self-governing.

**sem|i|au|ton|o|my** (sem′ē ô ton′ə mē), *n.* partial self-government.

**sem|i|ax|is** (sem′ē ak′sis), *n.* half an axis, as of a hyperbola.

**sem|i|bar|bar|ic** (sem′ē bär bar′ik), *adj.* not completely barbaric; partly civilized: *a semibarbaric people.*

**sem|i|bar|ba|rism** (sem′ē bär′bə riz əm), *n.* the condition or state of being semibarbaric.

**sem|i|bar|ba|rous** (sem′ē bär′bər əs), *adj.* = semibarbaric.

**sem|i|bay** (sem′ē bā′), *n. Architecture.* half a bay.

**sem|i|blind** (sem′ē blīnd′), *adj.* partly blind: (*Figurative.*) *Once it happ'd that, semiblind, he* [*love*] *met thee on a summer day* (Thomas Hood).

**sem|i|breve** (sem′ē brēv′), *n. Especially British.* whole note.

**sem|i|cal|car|e|ous** (sem′ē kal kãr′ē əs), *adj.* **1** partly chalky. **2** approaching chalk in substance or appearance.

**sem|i|car|ti|lag|i|nous** (sem′ē kär′tə laj′ə nəs), *adj.* gristly; imperfectly cartilaginous.

**sem|i|cell** (sem′ē sel′), *n.* (in a certain green algae) one of the halves of a desmid cell.

**sem|i|cen|te|nar|y** (sem′ē sen′tə ner′ē, -sen ten′ər-; *especially British* sem′ē sen tē′nər ē), *n., pl.* **-nar|ies**, *adj.* —*n.* a fiftieth anniversary.
—*adj.* having to do with a period of fifty years.

**sem|i|cen|ten|ni|al** (sem′ē sen ten′ē əl), *adj., n.* —*adj.* occurring at the end of fifty years; celebrating the completion of fifty years, or half a century: *a semicentennial celebration.*
—*n.* a fiftieth anniversary or the celebration of this.

**sem|i|cen|tu|ry** (sem′ē sen′chər ē), *n., pl.* **-ries.** half a century; fifty years.

**se|mi|cha** (sə mē′ʜə), *n., pl.* **-chas** (-ʜəs), **-choth** (-ʜōth). *Judaism.* **1** ordination into the rabbinate. **2** the certificate or diploma of an ordained rabbi. [< Hebrew *semiḥāh,* literally, leaning upon someone < *sāmaḥ* to lean]

**sem|i|chem|i|cal** (sem′ē kem′ə kəl), *adj.* partly chemical.

**sem|i|cho|ric** (sem′ē kôr′ik, -kōr′-, -kor′-), *adj.* having to do with or of the nature of a semichorus.

**sem|i|cho|rus** (sem′ē kôr′əs, -kōr′-), *n. Music.* **1** a half chorus; a number of voices chosen from a full chorus, whether from all or from some of the parts. **2** a passage or piece to be sung by such a selection of voices.

**sem|i-Chris|tian** (sem′ē kris′chən), *adj.* partly Christian; incompletely Christian.

**sem|i|cir|cle** (sem′ē sėr′kəl), *n.* **1** the half of a circle: **a** either of the two identical figures formed by bisection of a circle. **b** the arc formed by half the circumference of a circle. **2** anything having, or arranged in, the form of half a circle: *We sat in a semicircle around the fire.*

**sem|i|cir|cu|lar** (sem′ē sėr′kyə lər), *adj.* having the form of half a circle. —**sem′i|cir′cu|lar|ly**, *adv.*

**semicircular canal,** any one of three curved, tubelike canals in the inner ear that help to maintain balance. See diagram under **ear**[1].

**sem|i|cir|cum|fer|ence** (sem′ē sər kum′fər əns), *n.* the half of a circumference.

**sem|i|cirque** (sem′ē sėrk′), *n. Poetic.* a semicircular formation or arrangement; semicircle: *Upon a semicirque of turf-clad ground* (Wordsworth).

**sem|i|civ|i|li|za|tion** (sem′ē siv′ə lə zā′shən), *n.* the state of being partly civilized.

**sem|i|civ|i|lized** (sem′ē siv′ə līzd), *adj.* partly civilized.

**sem|i|clas|sic** (sem′ē klas′ik), *adj., n.* —*adj.* = semiclassical.
—*n.* an artistic work based on classical motives; a semiclassical book, musical composition, or the like.

**sem|i|clas|si|cal** (sem′ē klas′ə kəl), *adj.* partly classical.

**sem|i|clo|sure** (sem′ē klō′zhər), *n.* half or partial closure.

**sem|i|co|ag|u|lat|ed** (sem′ē kō ag′yə lā′tid), *adj.* incompletely coagulated; partly thickened.

***sem|i|co|lon** (sem′ē kō′lən), *n.* a mark of punctuation that shows a separation not so complete as that shown by a period but more so than that shown by a comma. A semicolon is used in ordinary prose, especially: **a** between coordinate clauses not connected by a coordinating conjunction and for clarity: *A teacher affects eternity; he can never tell where his influence stops* (Henry Brooks Adams). **b** between sentence elements that are rather long or are subdivided by commas: *A fundamental, and as many believe, the most essential part of Christianity, is its doctrine of reward and punishment in the world beyond; and a religion which had nothing at all to say about this great enigma we should hardly feel to be a religion at all* (G. Lowes Dickinson).

* **semicolon**

;  Double, double toil and trouble;
Fire burn; and cauldron bubble.

**sem|i|co|lo|ni|al** (sem′ē kə lō′nē əl), *adj.* partly colonial.

**sem|i|col|umn** (sem′ē kol′əm), *n.* the half of a column (taken lengthwise); an engaged column of which one half projects from the wall.

**sem|i|co|lum|nar** (sem′ē kə lum′nər), *adj.* of or like a semicolumn; flat on one side and rounded on the other, as a stem, leaf, or petiole.

**sem|i|co|ma** (sem′ē kō′mə), *n., pl.* **-mas.** a partial coma.

**sem|i|co|ma|tose** (sem′ē kō′mə tōs, -kom′ə-), *adj.* partly unconscious: *She complained of … headache, became semicomatose …* (A. M. Hamilton).

**sem|i|com|ic** (sem′ē kom′ik), *adj.* partly comical: *He looked semitragic, semicomic, like a mask with two sides* (Lady Morgan).

**sem|i|com|mer|cial** (sem′ē kə mėr′shəl), *adj.* partly commercial.

**sem|i|con|duct|ing** (sem′ē kən duk′ting), *adj.* of, being, or designating a semiconductor: *Transistors and solar batteries are semiconducting devices.*

**sem|i|con|duc|tion** (sem′ē kən duk′shən), *n.* the transmission of electricity by a semiconductor.

**sem|i|con|duc|tive** (sem′ē kən duk′tiv), *adj.* = semiconducting.

**sem|i|con|duc|tor** (sem′ē kən duk′tər), *n.* a mineral substance, such as germanium or silicon, that conducts electricity with an efficiency between that of metals and insulators. Semiconductors can convert alternating current into direct current and sunlight into electricity. They are also used as amplifiers replacing vacuum tubes in radios, and in certain electronic instruments.

**semiconductor laser** = injection laser.

**sem|i|con|ic** (sem′ē kon′ik), *adj.* = semiconical.

**sem|i|con|i|cal** (sem′ē kon′ə kəl), *adj.* having the form of half a cone.

**sem|i|con|scious** (sem′ē kon′shəs), *adj.* partly conscious; not fully conscious. —**sem′i|con′scious|ly**, *adv.* —**sem′i|con′scious|ness**, *n.*

**sem|i|con|ser|va|tive** (sem′ē kən sėr′və tiv), *adj. Genetics.* designating a form of replication in which the original molecular strands are conserved individually rather than together.

**sem|i|con|so|nant** (sem′ē kon′sə nənt), *n.* **1** a sound having a partly consonantal character, as *y* in *you;* a semivowel viewed as a consonant. **2** a letter or character representing such a sound.

**sem|i|con|tin|u|ous** (sem′ē kən tin′yu̇ əs), *adj.* partly continuous.

**sem|i|con|tin|u|um** (sem′ē kən tin′yu̇ əm), *n., pl.* **-tin|u|a** (-tin′yu̇ ə). a cohesive but not perfect mathematical series; continuum with its ends cut off.

**sem|i|con|ver|sion** (sem′ē kən vėr′zhən, -shən), *n.* an incomplete conversion.

**sem|i|crys|tal|line** (sem′ē kris′tə lin, -līn), *adj.* partly or imperfectly crystallized: *Primitive limestone of a … semicrystalline grain* (Edinburgh Review).

**sem|i|cyl|in|der** (sem′ē sil′ən dər), *n.* the half of a cylinder (taken lengthwise).

**sem|i|cy|lin|dric** (sem′ē sə lin′drik), *adj.* shaped like or resembling a cylinder divided lengthwise.

**sem|i|cy|lin|dri|cal** (sem′ē sə lin′drə kəl), *adj.* = semicylindric.

**sem|i|dai|ly** (sem′ē dā′lē), *adv., adj.* twice a day.

**sem|i|dark|ness** (sem′ē därk′nis), *n.* partial darkness.

**sem|i|deaf** (sem′ē def′), *adj.* not entirely deaf; able to hear a little.

**sem|i|de|pend|ent** (sem′ē di pen′dənt), *adj.* half dependent or depending.

**sem|i|des|ert** (sem′ē dez′ərt), *adj., n.* —*adj.* partly desert; mostly barren, with a sparse vegetation.
—*n.* a semidesert area or region.

**sem|i|de|tached** (sem′ē di tacht′), *adj.* **1** partly detached. **2** *Especially British.* joined to another house by a common wall but separated from other buildings.

**sem|i|de|vel|oped** (sem′ē di vel′əpt), *adj.* not fully developed.

**sem|i|di|am|e|ter** (sem′ē dī am′ə tər), *n.* the half of a diameter; radius.

**sem|i|di|gest|ed** (sem′ē də jes′tid, -dī-), *adj.* partly digested.

**sem|i|di|lap|i|da|tion** (sem′ē də lap′ə dā′shən), *n.* the condition or state of being partly ruined; incomplete dilapidation.

**sem|i|di|ur|nal** (sem′ē dī ėr′nəl), *adj.* **1** occurring every twelve hours. **2** accomplished in half a day; continuing half a day. **3** *Astronomy.* of or having to do with the arc described by a heavenly body in half the time between its rising and setting. **4** *Entomology.* partly diurnal; flying at twilight: *semidiurnal moths.*

**sem|i|di|vine** (sem′ē də vīn′), *adj.* partly divine.

**sem|i|doc|u|men|ta|ry** (sem′ē dok′yə men′tər ē, -trē), *adj., n., pl.* **-ries.** —*adj.* partly documentary; presenting or dramatizing factual information but using fictional details, settings, or characters: *a semidocumentary film.*
—*n.* a semidocumentary book, motion picture, television program, or the like.

**sem|i|dome** (sem′ē dōm′), *n.* half a dome, especially one formed by a vertical section: *There is an apse at each end of the building … covered by a semidome* (G. H. Moore).

**sem|i|do|mes|tic** (sem′ē də mes′tik), *adj.* partly domestic: *some semidomestic breeds* (Charles Darwin).

**sem|i|do|mes|ti|cat|ed** (sem′ē də mes′tə kā′tid), *adj.* partly domesticated: *the semidomesticated buffalo* (W. C. L. Martin).

**sem|i|do|mes|ti|ca|tion** (sem′ē də mes′tə kā′shən), *n.* a partly domesticated condition.

**sem|i|dor|mant** (sem′ē dôr′mənt), *adj.* partly or almost asleep.

**sem|i|dou|ble** (sem′ē dub′əl), *adj. Botany.* having the outermost stamens converted into petals, while the inner ones remain perfect: *semidouble roses or poppies.*

**sem|i|dry** (sem′ē drī′), *adj.* partly dry: *a semidry photographic process.*

**sem|i|dry|ing** (sem′ē drī′ing), *adj.* partly drying; becoming very thick but not hard: *Cottonseed, corn, and sesame oils are of the semidrying type.*

**sem|i|ed|u|cat|ed** (sem′ē ej′u̇ kā′tid), *adj.* partly educated.

**sem|i|el|lipse** (sem′ē i lips′), *n.* the half of an ellipse bisected by one of its diameters, especially the transverse.

**sem|i|el|lip|tic** (sem′ē i lip′tik), *adj.* = semielliptical.

**sem|i|el|lip|ti|cal** (sem′ē i lip′tə kəl), *adj.* shaped like half of an ellipse, especially one that is cut transversely.

**sem|i|em|pir|i|cal** (sem′ē em pir′ə kəl), *adj.* partly empirical.

**sem|i|e|rect** (sem′ē i rekt′), *adj.* partly erect: *a semierect posture.*

**sem|i|farm|ing** (sem′ē fär′ming), *n.* unselective or uncontrolled farming of livestock or crops: *Because natural phenomena are controlled, the modern chicken farm is true farming, while the keeping of chickens in the farmyard is semifarming. In a similar way, sea farming is a case of semifarming* (Pieter Korringa).

**sem|i|fas|cist** (sem′ē fash′ist), *adj.* partly fascist.

**sem|i|fer|al** (sem′ē fir′əl), *adj.* partly wild; feral to some extent.

**sem|i|feu|dal** (sem′ē fyü′dəl), *adj.* partly feudal.

**sem|i|fic|tion|al** (sem′ē fik′shə nəl), *adj.* partly imaginative.

**sem|i|fi|nal** (sem′ē fī′nəl), *n., adj.* —*n.* one of the two rounds or matches that settle who will play in the final one, which follows: *The team that will face the state champions defeated our team in the semifinal.*
—*adj.* designating or having to do with such a round or match: *Our team lost in the semifinal game.*

**sem|i|fi|nal|ist** (sem′ē fī′nə list), *n.* a contestant in a semifinal round.

**sem|i|fin|ished** (sem′ē fin′isht), *adj.* partly finished.

**sem|i|fit|ted** (sem′ē fit′id), *adj.* partly fitted.

**sem|i|fit|ting** (sem′ē fit′ing), *adj.* partly or loosely fitting, as a garment.

**sem|i|fixed** (sem′ē fikst′), *adj.* partly fixed.

**sem|i|flex|ion** (sem′ē flek′shən), *n.* the posture of a limb or joint halfway between extension and complete flexion.

**Pronunciation Key:** hat, āge, cãre, fär; let, ēqual, tėrm; it, īce; hot, ōpen, ôrder; oil, out; cup, pu̇t, rüle; child; long; thin; ᴛʜen; zh, measure; ə represents **a** in about, **e** in taken, **i** in pencil, **o** in lemon, **u** in circus.

**sem|i|fluc|tu|at|ing** (sem′ē fluk′chü ā′ting), *adj.* *Medicine.* (of a tumor or other process) giving a sensation of elasticity when tapped.

**sem|i|flu|id** (sem′ē flü′id), *adj., n.* —*adj.* partly fluid; extremely viscous.
—*n.* a substance that flows but is very thick; partly liquid substance: *A soft-boiled egg is a semifluid.*

**sem|i|flu|id|i|ty** (sem′ē flü id′ə tē), *n.* the state of being semifluid.

**sem|i|for|mal** (sem′ē fôr′məl), *adj.* partly or moderately formal: *semiformal dress.*

**sem|i|fused** (sem′ē fyüzd′), *adj.* partly fused.

**sem|i|glazed** (sem′ē glāzd′), *adj.* slightly glazed; covered with a thin gloss.

**sem|i|globe** (sem′ē glōb′), *n.* the half of a globe; a hemisphere or hemispherical form or structure.

**sem|i|glob|u|lar** (sem′ē glob′yə lər), *adj.* of the form of a semiglobe or hemisphere.

**sem|i|gov|ern|men|tal** (sem′ē guv′ərn men′təl, -ər-), *adj.* partly governmental.

**sem|i|group** (sem′ē grüp′), *n.* *Mathematics.* a closed set under an associative binary operation.

**sem|i|har|dy** (sem′ē här′dē), *adj.* partly hardy.

**sem|i|hex|ag|o|nal** (sem′ē hek sag′ə nəl), *adj.* having the form of half a hexagon.

**sem|i|hol|i|day** (sem′ē hol′ə dā), *n.* a partial holiday; half holiday.

**sem|i|ho|ral** (sem′ē hôr′əl, -hōr′-), *adj.* half-hourly.

**sem|i|hu|man** (sem′ē hyü′mən), *adj.* partly human: *a semihuman prehistoric creature.*

**sem|i|hy|a|line** (sem′ē hī′ə lin, -līn), *adj.* partly hyaline or glassy; semitransparent.

**sem|i-im|mersed** (sem′ē i mėrst′), *adj.* partially immersed.

**sem|i-in|de|pend|ence** (sem′ē in′di pen′dəns), *n.* partial freedom, as from control; incomplete independence.

**sem|i-in|de|pend|ent** (sem′ē in′di pen′dənt), *adj.* not fully independent; half or partly dependent.

**sem|i-in|dus|tri|al|ized** (sem′ē in dus′trē ə līzd), *adj.* not fully industrialized.

**sem|i-in|tox|i|ca|tion** (sem′ē in tok′sə kā′shən), *n.* partial intoxication.

**sem|i-in|va|lid** (sem′ē in′və lid), *adj., n.* —*adj.* not completely well; partly invalid.
—*n.* a semi-invalid person.

**sem|i|lan|ce|o|late** (sem′ē lan′sē ə lāt, -lit), *adj.* lanceolate on one side only; partly lanceolate.

**sem|i|leg|end|ar|y** (sem′ē lej′ən der′ē), *adj.* partly legendary: *a semilegendary story.*

**sem|i|le|thal** (sem′ē lē′thəl), *adj.* partly lethal.

**sem|i|liq|uid** (sem′ē lik′wid), *adj., n.* = semifluid.

**sem|i|li|quid|i|ty** (sem′ē li kwid′ə tē), *n.* = semifluidity.

**sem|i|lit|er|a|cy** (sem′ē lit′ər ə sē), *n.* the quality or condition of being semiliterate.

**sem|i|lit|er|ate** (sem′ē lit′ər it), *adj., n.* —*adj.* partly literate; semieducated.
—*n.* a person who is semiliterate.

**sem|i|log** (sem′ē lôg′, -log′), *adj.* = semilogarithmic.

**sem|i|log|a|rith|mic** (sem′ē lôg′ə riᴛʜ′mik, -log′-), *adj.* having or using a logarithmic scale or coordinates on one axis and a standard scale on the other: *a semilogarithmic graph.*

**sem|i|loy|al|ty** (sem′ē loi′əl tē), *n., pl.* **-ties.** partial loyalty.

**sem|i|lu|nar** (sem′ē lü′nər), *adj., n.* —*adj.* shaped like a half moon; crescent-shaped.
—*n.* something of semilunar shape.

**semilunar bone,** the second bone of the proximal row of the carpus, counting from the thumb side; lunate bone.

**semilunar valve, 1** one of a set of three crescent-shaped flaps or valves at the opening of the aorta that prevent the blood from flowing back into the ventricle. See diagram under **heart.**
**2** one of a similar set of valves at the opening of the pulmonary artery. See diagram under **heart.**

**sem|i|ma|jor axis** (sem′ē mā′jər), **1** *Mathematics.* one half of the length or major axis of an ellipse or ellipsoid. **2** *Astronomy.* the mean distance of a planet from the sun.

**sem|i|man|u|fac|ture** (sem′ē man′yə fak′chər), *n.* a partly manufactured product, used in making end products. Steel and yarn are semimanufactures.

**sem|i|man|u|fac|tured** (sem′ē man′yə fak′chərd), *adj.* partly or incompletely manufactured: *semimanufactured materials.*

**sem|i|matte** or **sem|i|mat** (sem′ē mat′), *adj.* slightly shiny; partly matte or dull: *Most photographers use either glossy or semimatte paper for prints.*

**sem|i|me|chan|i|cal** (sem′ē mə kan′ə kəl), *adj.* partly mechanical.

**sem|i|mem|bra|no|sus** (sem′ē mem′brə nō′səs), *n., pl.* **-si** (-sī). a long, membranous muscle of the back of the thigh, arising from the ischiadic tuberosity, and inserted chiefly into the upper end of the tibia. It flexes and rotates the leg and extends the thigh.

**sem|i|mem|bra|nous** (sem′ē mem′brə nəs, -mem brā′-), *adj.* *Anatomy.* partly membranous; intersected by several broad, flat tendinous intervals, as the semimembranosus.

**sem|i|met|al** (sem′ē met′əl), *n.* an element that is nonmalleable and only partly metallic, as arsenic or tellurium.

**sem|i|me|tal|lic** (sem′ē mə tal′ik), *adj.* partly metallic: *A compound of zinc and the semimetallic element germanium* (Harper's).

**sem|i|mi|cro** (sem′ē mī′krō), *adj.* of, having to do with, or used in semimicrochemistry: *a semimicro centrifuge.*

**sem|i|mi|cro|chem|is|try** (sem′ē mī′krō kem′ə strē), *n.* microchemistry that deals with centigram quantities.

**sem|i|mil|i|tar|y** (sem′ē mil′ə ter′ē), *adj.* partly military: *a semimilitary costume.*

**sem|i|mil|le|nar|y** (sem′ē mil′ə ner′ē), *adj.* lasting 500 years.

**sem|i|mi|nor axis** (sem′ē mī′nər), *Mathematics.* one half of the minor axis of an ellipse or ellipsoid.

**sem|i|mo|bile** (sem′ē mō′bəl), *adj.* partly mobile.

**sem|i|month|ly** (sem′ē munth′lē), *adj., adv., n., pl.* **-lies.** —*adj.* occurring or appearing twice a month.
—*adv.* twice a month.
—*n.* something that occurs or appears twice a month, especially a magazine, newspaper, or other periodical published twice a month.

**sem|i|mute** (sem′ē myüt′), *adj.* nearly mute; almost unable to speak.

**sem|i|mys|ti|cal** (sem′ē mis′tə kəl), *adj.* partly mystical.

**sem|i|myth|i|cal** (sem′ē mith′ə kəl), *adj.* partly mythical; imaginary in part.

**sem|i|na** (sem′ə nə), *n.* plural of **semen.**

**sem|i|nal** (sem′ə nəl), *adj.* **1** of or having to do with the semen of men and animals: *a seminal vessel or gland, a seminal secretion.* **2** of seed or of the nature of seed. **3** containing or conveying semen or seed: *the seminal duct.* **4** having to do with reproduction: *the seminal or generative powers.* **5** *Figurative.* like seed; having the possibility of future development: *a seminal idea. There appeared other prophets who were trying to create by themselves small seminal new worlds inside the old* (Edmund Wilson). [< Middle French *séminal,* learned borrowing from Latin *sēminālis* < *sēmen, -inis* seed, related to *serere* to sow] —**sem′i|nal|ly,** *adv.*

**seminal fluid,** = semen.

**seminal vesicle,** either one of two receptacles for holding semen, situated on each side of the base of the bladder.

**sem|i|nar** (sem′ə när), *n.* **1** a group of college or university students engaged in discussion and original research under the guidance of a professor. **2** the meeting in class of such a group. **3** the course of study or work for such a group. **4** the room or other place in which such a group meets. **5** a course of study, discussion, or work undertaken by any group of people; workshop: *Some companies send their staffs to "secretaries' seminars"* (New York Times). [American English < German *Seminar* < Latin *sēminārium* plant nursery, hotbed < *sēmen, -inis* seed. See etym. of doublet **seminary.**]

**sem|i|nar|i|an** (sem′ə nãr′ē ən), *n.* a student at a seminary, now especially a religious seminary: *... nuns in white cotton habit, priests and Catholic seminarians in black* (Time).

**sem|i|nar|ist** (sem′ə ner′ist), *n.* = seminarian.

**sem|i|nar|y** (sem′ə ner′ē), *n., pl.* **-nar|ies. 1** a school or college for training students to be priests, ministers, or rabbis. **2** an academy or boarding school, especially for young women. **3** a school, especially one beyond high school. **4** a place for instruction, training, or development. **5** *Figurative.* a place of origin and early development: *a nursery and seminary of blunder* (James Russell Lowell). **6** *Obsolete.* a seminar. [earlier, a seedbed < Latin *sēminārium.* See etym. of doublet **seminar.**]

**sem|i|nate** (sem′ə nāt), *v.t.,* **-nat|ed, -nat|ing.** to sow; propagate; disseminate. [< Latin *sēmināre* (with English *-ate*[1]) to sow < *sēmen, -inis* seed]

**sem|i|na|tion** (sem′ə nā′shən), *n.* the act or process of sowing; propagation; dissemination.

**sem|i|nat|u|ral** (sem′ē nach′ər əl, -nach′rəl), *adj.* not completely natural; partly natural.

**sem|i|nif|er|ous** (sem′ə nif′ər əs), *adj.* **1** bearing or producing seed. **2** conveying, containing, or producing semen: *Spermatozoa are produced ... inside the long coiled seminiferous tubules of the testis* (Richard J. Goss). [< Latin *sēmen, -inis* seed + English *-ferous*]

**sem|i|niv|o|rous** (sem′ə niv′ər əs), *adj.* eating or feeding on seeds: *seminivorous birds.* [< Latin *sēmen, -inis* seed + *vorāre* devour + English *-ous*]

**Sem|i|nole** (sem′ə nōl), *n., pl.* **-nole** or **-noles,** *adj.* —*n.* a member of a tribe of North American Indians that left the Creek Confederacy and settled in Florida. Most Seminoles now live in Oklahoma; the remainder are in Florida.
—*adj.* of or having to do with this tribe.
[American English < Muskhogean (Creek) *simanóle* one who has camped away from the regular towns, perhaps < Spanish *cimarrón* wild]

**sem|i|no|ma** (sem′ə nō′mə), *n., pl.* **-mas, -ma|ta** (-mə tə). a tumor in a seminal passage or organ. [< Latin *sēmen, -inis* semen + English *-oma*]

**sem|i|no|mad|ic** (sem′ē nō mad′ik), *adj.* partly nomadic.

**sem|i|nude** (sem′ē nüd′, -nyüd′), *adj.* partly naked.

**sem|i|ob|scu|ri|ty** (sem′ē əb skyůr′ə tē), *n., pl.* **-ties.** the condition of being half concealed; partial obscurity.

**sem|i|oc|ca|sion|al** (sem′ē ə kā′zhə nəl), *adj.* occurring once in a while. —**sem′i|oc|ca′sion|al|ly,** *adv.*

**sem|i|oc|tag|o|nal** (sem′ē ok tag′ə nəl), *adj.* having the form of half an octagon.

**sem|i|of|fi|cial** (sem′ē ə fish′əl), *adj.* partly official; having some degree of official authority or knowledge. —**sem′i|of|fi′cial|ly,** *adv.*

**se|mi|o|log|i|cal** (sē′mē ə loj′ə kəl), *adj.* = semeiological.

**se|mi|ol|o|gist** (sē′mē ol′ə jist), *n.* = semeiologist.

**se|mi|ol|o|gy** (sē′mē ol′ə jē), *n.* = semeiology.

**sem|i|o|paque** (sem′ē ō pāk′), *adj.* imperfectly opaque; only partially transparent.

**sem|i|or|bic|u|lar** (sem′ē ôr bik′yə lər), *adj.* having the form of half a sphere.

**se|mi|ot|ic** (sē′mē ot′ik), *adj., n.* —*adj.* having to do with signs or symptoms; semeiotic.
—*n.* = semiotics.

**se|mi|ot|ics** (sē′mē ot′iks), *n.* **1** the study or science of signs and symbols. Semiotics is divided into pragmatics, syntactics, and semantics. **2** the branch of medicine concerned with the study of symptoms; symptomatology. Also, **semeiotics.** [< Greek *sēmeiōtikós* (see etym. under **semeiotic**) + English *-ics*]

**sem|i|o|val** (sem′ē ō′vəl), *adj.* having the form of half an oval; semielliptical.

**sem|i|o|vate** (sem′ē ō′vāt), *adj.* *Zoology.* having the form of half an ovate surface or plane.

**sem|i|o|vip|a|rous** (sem′ē ō vip′ər əs), *adj.* bearing living young so incompletely developed that they remain within the mother's pouch for a time. Kangaroos are semioviparous. [< *semi-* + *oviparous*]

**sem|i|o|void** (sem′ē ō′void), *adj.* having the form of half an ovoid solid.

**sem|i|pal|mate** (sem′ē pal′māt), *adj.* incompletely webbed; with the toes webbed only partway, as the feet of certain birds.

**sem|i|pal|mat|ed** (sem′ē pal′mā tid), *adj.* = semipalmate.

**semipalmated plover,** a small brown and white plover with a single black ring about the neck, that breeds in arctic regions and winters in South America.

**semipalmated sandpiper,** a small, common, brown and white American sandpiper with partially webbed toes; oxeye.

**sem|i|pa|ral|y|sis** (sem′ē pə ral′ə sis), *n., pl.* **-ses** (-sēz). a partially crippled condition; incomplete paralysis.

**sem|i|pa|ram|e|ter** (sem′ē pə ram′ə tər), *n.* half a parameter.

**sem|i|par|a|sit|ic** (sem′ē par′ə sit′ik), *adj.* **1** *Biology.* usually living on a host but able to live on decaying or dead organic matter. **2** *Botany.* living on a host, but containing chlorophyll and therefore able to manufacture carbohydrates from the air, as mistletoe.

**sem|i|par|a|sit|ism** (sem′ē par′ə sī tiz′əm), *n.* incomplete or partial parasitism.

**Sem|i-Pe|la|gi|an** (sem′ē pə lā′jē ən), *n., adj.* —*n.* a follower of Semi-Pelagianism. —*adj.* of or having to do with Semi-Pelagianism.

**Sem|i-Pe|la|gi|an|ism** (sem′ē pə lā′jē ə niz′əm), *n.* a modified form of Pelagianism which maintained that divine grace is not necessary for man to begin a supernatural conversion to God.

**sem|i|per|ma|nent** (sem′ē pėr′mə nənt), *adj.* not made to last; temporary: *a semipermanent residence, semipermanent telegraph lines.* —**sem′i-per′ma|nent|ly,** *adv.*

**sem|i|per|me|a|ble** (sem′ē pėr′mē ə bəl), *adj.* partly permeable; permeable to some substances but not to others. A semipermeable membrane allows the solvent, but usually not the dissolved substance, to pass through. *If salt water and fresh water are separated in a chamber by a semipermeable membrane, the fresh water will flow through the membrane into the salt water* (Luna B. Leopold).

**sem|i|pet|ri|fied** (sem′ē pet′rə fīd), *adj.* partly petrified.

**sem|i|plas|tic** (sem′ē plas′tik), *adj.* imperfectly plastic; in a state between plasticity and rigidity.

**sem|i|po|lit|i|cal** (sem′ē pə lit′ə kəl), *adj.* partly political: *a semipolitical, semisacerdotal fraternity* (Thomas Hughes).

**sem|i|pop|u|lar** (sem′ē pop′yə lər), *adj.* partly popular.

**sem|i|por|ce|lain** (sem′ē pôr′sə lin, -pōr′-; -pôrs′lən, -pōrs′-), *n.* **1** an inferior grade of porcelain. **2** earthenware made to resemble porcelain.

**sem|i|po|rous** (sem′ē pôr′əs, -pōr′-), *adj.* partly porous.

**sem|i|post|al** (sem′ē pōs′təl), *adj., n.* **—*adj.*** (of a postage stamp) valued at more than the face amount.
**—*n.*** a semipostal stamp.

**sem|i|pre|cious** (sem′ē presh′əs), *adj.* having value, but not sufficient value to rank as precious. Amethysts and garnets are semiprecious stones; diamonds and rubies are precious stones.

**sem|i|pri|vate** (sem′ē prī′vit), *adj.* partly private: *a semiprivate thoroughfare, semiprivate conferences.*

**sem|i|pro** (sem′ē prō′), *adj., n., pl.* **-pros.** = semiprofessional: *a semipro baseball team.*

**sem|i|pro|fes|sion|al** (sem′ē prə fesh′ə nəl, -fesh′nəl), *adj., n.* **—*adj.* 1a** playing a sport for money but on a part-time basis: *a semiprofessional baseball player or team.* **b** engaged in by semiprofessional players: *semiprofessional sports.* **2** partly professional: *semiprofessional activities.*
**—*n.*** a person who plays a sport for money but on a part-time basis. **—sem′i|pro|fes′sion|al|ly,** *adv.*

**sem|i|prone** (sem′ē prōn′), *adj.* partly prone.

**sem|i|pub|lic** (sem′ē pub′lik), *adj.* partly or to some degree public.

**sem|i|py|ram|i|dal** (sem′ē pə ram′ə dəl), *adj.* having the form of a pyramid of three, four, or more sides, vertically bisected.

**sem|i|quan|ti|ta|tive** (sem′ē kwon′tə tā′tiv), *adj.* partly or incompletely quantitative.

**sem|i|qua|ver** (sem′ē kwā′vər), *n. British.* a sixteenth note.

**Se|mir|a|mis** (si mir′ə mis), *n.* an Assyrian queen who in ancient legend was famous for her beauty, wisdom, and sensuality, and was said to have founded Babylon.

**sem|i|re|cum|bent** (sem′ē ri kum′bənt), *adj.* semiprone; partly recumbent.

**sem|i|reg|u|lar** (sem′ē reg′yə lər), *adj.* having to do with or containing a quadrilateral which has four equal sides, but only pairs of equal angles.

**sem|i|re|lief** (sem′ē ri lēf′), *n.* = mezzo-relievo.

**sem|i|re|li|gious** (sem′ē ri lij′əs), *adj.* partly religious: *on subjects semireligious and semischolastic* (Cardinal Newman).

**sem|i|re|tired** (sem′ē ri tīrd′), *adj.* not completely retired.

**sem|i|re|tire|ment** (sem′ē ri tīr′mənt), *n.* the condition of being retired.

**sem|i|re|trac|tile** (sem′ē ri trak′təl), *adj.* partly retractile.

**sem|i|rev|o|lu|tion** (sem′ē rev′ə lü′shən), *n.* half a revolution.

**sem|i|rig|id** (sem′ē rij′id), *adj.* **1** partly rigid. **2** having a rigid keel at the base, to which the gondola and engine are attached: *a semirigid airship. A dirigible is semirigid.*

**sem|i-Ro|man|ized** (sem′ē rō′mə nīzd), *adj.* partly Romanized: *the semi-Romanized Britons* (Westminster Review).

**sem|i|round** (sem′ē round′), *adj., n.* **—*adj.*** having one curved and one flat side.
**—*n.*** a thing that is semiround.

**sem|i|ru|ral** (sem′ē rür′əl), *adj.* partly rural: *a semirural suburb.*

**sem|i|sac|er|do|tal** (sem′ē sas′ər dō′təl), *adj.* partly priestly.

**sem|i|sa|cred** (sem′ē sā′krid), *adj.* partly sacred: *His eulogy of Latin as if it were a semisacred language ...* (Manchester Guardian Weekly).

**sem|i|sav|age** (sem′ē sav′ij), *adj., n.* **—*adj.*** semibarbaric; half civilized.
**—*n.*** a semisavage person.

**sem|i|scho|las|tic** (sem′ē skə las′tik), *adj.* partly scholastic.

**sem|i|sci|en|tif|ic** (sem′ē sī′ən tif′ik), *adj.* partly scientific: *semiscientific observations.*

**sem|i|se|cre|cy** (sem′ē sē′krə sē), *n., pl.* **-cies.** the condition of partial or incomplete secrecy: *working in semisecrecy.*

**sem|i|se|cret** (sem′ē sē′krit), *adj.* partly secret.

**sem|i|sed|en|tar|y** (sem′ē sed′ən ter′ē), *adj.* partly sedentary.

**sem|i|se|ri|ous** (sem′ē sir′ē əs), *adj.* partly serious.

**sem|i|skilled** (sem′ē skild′), *adj.* partly skilled: *a semiskilled laborer.*

**sem|i|smile** (sem′ē smīl′), *n.* a faint smile; a suppressed or forced smile.

**sem|i|so|cial|ist** (sem′ē sō′shə list), *n., adj.* **—*n.*** a partly socialistic person.
**—*adj.*** not completely socialistic.

**sem|i|soft** (sem′ē sôft′, -soft′), *adj.* of medium softness: *semisoft cheese.*

**sem|i|sol|id** (sem′ē sol′id), *adj., n.* **—*adj.*** partly solid.
**—*n.*** a partly solid substance.

**sem|i|so|phis|ti|cat|ed** (sem′ē sə fis′tə kā′tid), *adj.* not completely sophisticated.

**sem|i|spher|i|cal** (sem′ē sfer′ə kəl), *adj.* = hemispherical.

**sem|i|stag|na|tion** (sem′ē stag nā′shən), *n.* the condition of being partly stagnated.

**sem|i|star|va|tion** (sem′ē stär vā′shən), *n.* the condition of being nearly starved.

**sem|i|starved** (sem′ē stärvd′), *adj.* nearly starved.

**sem|i|sub|mers|i|ble** (sem′ē səb mėr′sə bəl), *adj., n.* **—*adj.*** partly submersible; fixed so that it floats on water: *a semisubmersible oil-drilling rig.*
**—*n.*** a semisubmersible vessel, rig, or other structure.

**sem|i|sub|ter|ra|ne|an** (sem′ē sub′tə rā′nē ən), *adj.* partly underground: *The semisubterranean house was in excellent state of preservation* (Science News Letter).

**sem|i|su|per|nat|u|ral** (sem′ē sü′pər nach′ər əl, -nach′rəl), *adj.* partly divine and partly human; demigodlike: *The Greeks ... were surrounded with a world of semisupernatural beings* (R. S. Perrin).

**sem|i|sweet** (sem′ē swēt′), *adj.* not too sweet; partially or moderately sweetened: *semisweet wine.*

**sem|i|syn|thet|ic** (sem′ē sin thet′ik), *adj.* partly artificial or synthetic.

**Sem|ite** (sem′īt, sē′mīt), *n.* **1** a member of the ancient and modern peoples speaking any of the Semitic languages. The ancient Hebrews, Phoenicians, and Assyrians were Semites. Arabs and Jews are sometimes called Semites. **2** a descendant of Shem.
[< New Latin *Semita* < Late Latin *Sēm* Shem < Greek *Sēm*]

**sem|i|ter|res|tri|al** (sem′ē tə res′trē əl), *adj.* partly terrestrial: *Gorillas, equally semiterrestrial ...* (Atlantic).

**Se|mit|ic** (sə mit′ik), *adj., n.* **—*adj.*** of or having to do with the Semites or their languages: *a Semitic nation.*
**—*n.*** the Semitic family of languages, including Hebrew, Arabic, Aramaic, Phoenician, and Assyrian.

**Se|mit|ics** (sə mit′iks), *n.* the study of the Semitic languages and literature.

**Sem|i|tism** (sem′ə tiz əm, sē′mə-), *n.* **1** Semitic character, especially the ways, ideas, and influence of the Jews. **2** a Semitic word or idiom.

**Sem|i|tist** (sem′ə tist, sē′mə-), *n.* a person skilled in Semitic languages and literature.

**Sem|i|tize** (sem′ə tīz, sē′mə-), *v.t.,* **-tized, -tiz|ing.** to make Semitic, as in character or language.

**sem|i|ton|al** (sem′ē tō′nəl), *adj.* = semitonic. **—sem′i|ton′al|ly,** *adv.*

**sem|i|tone** (sem′ē tōn′), *n. Music.* **1** an interval equal to half a tone on the scale; half step; half tone. **2** a tone at such an interval from another tone.

**sem|i|ton|ic** (sem′ē ton′ik), *adj.* having to do with or consisting of a semitone or semitones. **—sem′i|ton′i|cal|ly,** *adv.*

**sem|i|to|tal|i|tar|i|an** (sem′ē tō tal′ə tãr′ē ən), *adj.* partly totalitarian.

**sem|i|trag|ic** (sem′ē traj′ik), *adj.* partly tragic.

**sem|i|trail|er** (sem′ē trā′lər), *n.* a type of truck trailer that is supported at its forward end on the same wheels as the rear of the tractor and engine (tractor) unit.

**sem|i|trans|lu|cent** (sem′ē trans lü′sənt), *adj.* imperfectly translucent.

**sem|i|trans|par|en|cy** (sem′ē trans pãr′ən sē), *n., pl.* **-cies.** imperfect transparency; partial opaqueness.

**sem|i|trans|par|ent** (sem′ē trans pãr′ənt, -par′-), *adj.* imperfectly transparent.

**sem|i|trop|ic** (sem′ē trop′ik), *adj.* = semitropical.

**sem|i|trop|i|cal** (sem′ē trop′ə kəl), *adj.* halfway between tropical and temperate; partly tropical: *Florida is a semitropical state.*

**sem|i|trop|ics** (sem′ē trop′iks), *n.pl.* a semitropical region or regions; subtropics.

**sem|i|tu|bu|lar** (sem′ē tü′byə lər, -tyü′-), *adj.* like the half of a tube divided longitudinally; elongate, with parallel margins, one surface being strongly convex and the other strongly concave.

**sem|i|ur|ban** (sem′ē ėr′bən), *adj.* partly urban: *The swamping of the agricultural labourers by the semiurban population ...* (Manchester Examiner).

**sem|i|vi|bra|tion** (sem′ē vī brā′shən), *n.* a half vibration.

**sem|i|vit|re|ous** (sem′ē vit′rē əs), *adj.* partially vitreous, as mineral constituents of volcanic rocks.

**sem|i|vit|ri|fied** (sem′ē vit′rə fīd), *adj.* imperfectly vitrified; partially converted into glass.

**sem|i|vol|a|tile** (sem′ē vol′ə təl), *adj.* partly volatile.

**sem|i|vol|can|ic** (sem′ē vol kan′ik), *adj.* characterized by volcanic outbreaks without the emission of lava.

**sem|i|vol|un|tar|y** (sem′ē vol′ən ter′ē), *adj.* partly voluntary.

**sem|i|vow|el** (sem′ē vou′əl), *n.* **1** a sound that is acoustically like a vowel but functions like a consonant, such as the English sounds represented by *y* in *yes* and *w* in *well.* **2** a letter or character representing such a sound. *W* in *win* and *now* or *y* in *yes* and *boy* are semivowels.

**sem|i|week|ly** (sem′ē wēk′lē), *adj., adv., n., pl.* **-lies. —*adj.*** occurring or appearing twice a week.
**—*adv.*** twice a week.
**—*n.*** something that occurs or appears twice a week, especially a magazine, newspaper, or other periodical published twice a week.

**sem|i|year|ly** (sem′ē yir′lē), *adj., adv., n., pl.* **-lies. —*adj.*** occurring or appearing twice a year.
**—*adv.*** twice a year.
**—*n.*** something that occurs or appears twice a year.

**sem|o|li|na** (sem′ə lē′nə), *n.* the coarsely ground hard parts of wheat remaining after the fine flour has been sifted through, used in making puddings, macaroni, and the like. [alteration of Italian *semolino* (diminutive) < *semola* bran < Latin *simila* the finest flour]

**sem|per e|a|dem** (sem′pər ē′ə dem), *Latin.* always the same (motto of Queen Elizabeth I of England, 1533-1603).

**sem|per fi|de|lis** (sem′pər fi dē′lis, -del′is), *Latin.* always faithful (motto of the U.S. Marine Corps).

**sem|per i|dem** (sem′pər ī′dem), *Latin.* always the same.

**sem|per pa|ra|tus** (sem′pər pə rā′təs), *Latin.* always prepared; always ready (motto of the U.S. Coast Guard).

**sem|per|vi|rent** (sem′pər vī′rənt), *adj.* evergreen, as plants. [< Latin *semper* always + *virēns, -entis,* present participle of *virēre* be green]

**sem|per|vi|vum** (sem′pər vī′vəm), *n.* any crassulaceous plant of a genus that includes the houseleek and many other species. [< Latin *semper* always + *vīvus* alive]

**sem|pi|ter|nal** (sem′pi tėr′nəl), *adj.* everlasting; eternal: *All truth is from the sempiternal source of light divine* (William Cowper). [< Late Latin *sempiternalis* < Latin *sempiternus* everlasting < *semper* forever] **—sem′pi|ter′nal|ly,** *adv.*

**sem|pi|ter|ni|ty** (sem′pi tėr′nə tē), *n.* sempiternal quality or condition; everlasting duration.

**sem|pli|ce** (sem′plē chā), *adj. Music.* unaffected; simple; to be played in an unadorned and unpretentious manner in both tempo and expression (a direction). [< Italian *semplice* < Latin *simplex, -icis* simple]

**sem|pre** (sem′prā), *adv. Music.* always; in the same (or the designated) style throughout. [< Italian *sempre* < Vulgar Latin < Latin *semper* always]

**semp|ster** (sem′stər, semp′-), *n.* = seamster.

**semp|stress** (sem′stris, semp′-), *n.* = seamstress.

**sen** (sen), *n., pl.* **sen. 1** a former Japanese money of account, a copper or bronze coin worth 1/100 of a yen. **2** a Cambodian coin worth 1/100 of a riel. **3** an Indonesian coin worth 1/100 of a rupiah. [< Japanese *sen*]

**Sen.** or **sen., 1a** Senate. **b** senator. **2** senior.

**se|nar|i|us** (sə nãr′ē əs), *n., pl.* **-nar|i|i** (-nãr′ē ī). a verse of six feet in Greek and Latin poetry; an iambic trimeter. [< Latin *sēnārius* of six each; see etym. under **senary**]

**sen|a|ry** (sen′ər ē), *adj.* **1** of or having to do with the number six. **2** *Mathematics.* having six for the base: *the senary scale.* [earlier, six <Latin *sēnārius* of six each < *sēnī* six each]

**sen|ate** (sen′it), *n.* **1a** a governing or lawmaking assembly of a state or nation. **b** the upper and smaller branch of an assembly that makes laws. **2** the highest council of state in ancient Rome, whose membership and functions varied at different periods. **3** an assembly or council of citizens having the highest deliberative functions in the government of a state. **4** a governing or disciplinary body in certain universities. [< Old French *senat,* learned borrowing from Latin *senātus, -ūs* < *senex, senis* old man]

**Sen|ate** (sen′it), *n.* **1** the upper house of Congress (of the United States of America) or of a

---

**Pronunciation Key: hat, āge, cãre, fär; let, ēqual, tėrm; it, īce; hot, ōpen, ôrder; oil, out; cup, pu̇t, rüle; child; long; thin; ᴛʜen; zh,** measure;
**ə** represents **a** in about, **e** in taken, **i** in pencil, **o** in lemon, **u** in circus.

state legislature. **2** the upper house of the legislature of certain other countries, such as Canada and Australia.

**sen|a|tor** (sen′ə tər), *n.* a member of a senate. [< Latin *senātor, -ōris* < *senātus;* see etym. under **senate**]

**sen|a|to|ri|al** (sen′ə tôr′ē əl, -tōr′-), *adj.* **1** of or befitting a senator or senators: *a senatorial election.* **2** consisting of senators: *a senatorial subcommittee.* **3** entitled to elect a senator: *a senatorial district.* —**sen′a|to′ri|al|ly,** *adv.*

**senatorial courtesy,** *U.S.* the custom of the Senate of not confirming nominations for office made by the President without the approval of the senators from the state where the nominee lives.

**sen|a|to|ri|an** (sen′ə tôr′ē ən, -tōr′-), *adj.* senatorial (used chiefly with reference to the senators of ancient Rome).

**sen|a|tor|ship** (sen′ə tər ship), *n.* the position, duties, or authority of a senator.

**se|na|tus con|sul|tum** (sə nā′təs kən sul′təm), *pl.* **se|na|tus con|sul|ta** (sə nā′təs kən sul′tə). *Latin.* a decree of the senate of ancient Rome.

**send** (send), *v.,* **sent, send|ing,** *n.* —*v.t.* **1** to cause to go from one place to another: *to send someone for a doctor. Mother sends my brother on errands.* **SYN:** dispatch. **2** to cause to be carried: *to send good news, to send one's compliments. We sent the letter by airmail.* **3** to cause to come, occur, or be: *Send help at once. May God send peace. Ah, spring was sent for lass and lad* (A. E. Housman). **SYN:** bestow. **4** to compel or force to go; drive, impel, or throw: *to send a ball or an arrow. The blow sent him staggering to a chair. The arrival of the police sent the rioters flying in all directions. The volcano sent clouds of smoke into the air.* **5** to cause (a person) to live in a certain place, engage in certain employment, or the like, for a period of time: *to send a boy to college, to send a man to Congress.* **6** to refer (a reader) to some author or authority: *to send a reader to the dictionary.* **7** to cause (something) to go (down, up, or in some other condition): *The news sent the stock market up.* **8a** to transmit (as radio signals). **b** to transmit (as a current or electromagnetic wave) by means of pulsation. **9** *Slang.* to excite greatly or inspire, especially by jazz: *Two pumas snarled savagely at an Irish Jig but Home Sweet Home and Annie Laurie sent them* (Cape Times). **10** *Archaic.* to cause to be or become: *God send him well!* (Shakespeare). **SYN:** grant.

—*v.i.* **1** to send a message or messenger: *to send for a doctor, to send for a taxi. I have sent every half hour to know how she does* (Samuel Richardson). **2** of a ship: **a** to lurch forward into the trough of a wave. **b** = scend.

—*n.* **1** the driving impulse or force of a wave or waves on a ship: *The Mayflower ... stood for the open Atlantic, borne on the send of the sea* (Longfellow). **2** a sudden lurch forward of a ship into the trough of a wave.

**send down,** *British.* to expel from a university: *Another told us that he had been sent down from Oxford before coming to Exeter* (Listener).

**send packing,** to send away in a hurry; dismiss without delay or formality: *Sure as fate, we'll send you packing* (Robert Browning).

**send up, a** *U.S. Informal.* to send to prison: *They sent that fellow Sparser up for a year* (Theodore Dreiser). **b** *British Slang.* to make a parody on; ridicule; caricature: *Like Carson, he performs many of the commercials himself, sending many of them up. The harder he attacks a product, the more it is likely to sell the next morning* (Listener).

[Old English *sendan*]

**Sen|dai virus** (sen′dī), a paramyxovirus that induces rapid fusion of different types of cells. [< *Sendai,* a city in Japan, where the virus was first detected]

**sen|dal** (sen′dəl), *n.* **1** a thin, rich silk fabric used during the Middle Ages. **2** a garment made of it. [< Old French *cendal,* perhaps ultimately < Greek *sindṓn, -ónos* fine cloth]

**send|er** (sen′dər), *n.* **1** a person or thing that sends. **2** a transmitter, as in telegraphy.

**send-off** (send′ôf′, -of′), *n.* **1** a friendly demonstration in honor of a person setting out on a journey, course, career, etc. **2** *Informal.* a start (favorable or unfavorable) given to a person or thing: *Each of these groups sent representatives today to a press conference ... to give the new bill a send-off* (New York Times).

**send-up** (send′up′), *n. British Slang.* a parody or caricature; burlesque; take-off: *It [the book] is a splendidly detached send-up of the brainy female* (Punch). [< the British slang phrase *send up* to scoff at, mock, originally public-school slang meaning to send a boy to the headmaster to be punished]

**Sen|e|ca** (sen′ə kə), *n., pl.* **-cas** or **-ca. 1** a member of the largest tribe of the Iroquois Confederacy of American Indians, living mainly in western New York State. **2** the Iroquoian language of this tribe. [American English < Dutch *Sennacaas* the Five Nations < Algonkian (Mohegan) *A'sinnika* a place name < *ahsinni* stone, rock + *-ika* place of]

**Sen|e|can** (sen′ə kən), *adj.* of or having to do with Seneca (4 B.C.?-A.D. 65), a Roman Stoic philosopher, and the tragedies written by him and his imitators.

**Seneca snakeroot,** = senega.

**se|ne|ci|o** (sə nē′sē ō, -shē-), *n., pl.* **-os.** groundsel; ragwort. [< New Latin *Senecio* the genus name < Latin *senecio, -onis* groundsel; (literally) old man < *senex, senis* old]

**sen|e|ga** (sen′ə gə), *n.* **1** the dried root of a milkwort of eastern North America, used medicinally as an expectorant; rattlesnake root. **2** the plant itself. [American English < New Latin *senega* the species name, alteration of *Seneca* (because the Senecas used it to treat snakebites)]

**Sen|e|gal|ese** (sen′ə gô lēz′, -lēs′), *adj., n., pl.* **-ese.** —*adj.* of or having to do with Senegal, a republic in western Africa, its people, or their language.

—*n.* **1** a native or inhabitant of Senegal. **2** their language.

**Sen|e|gam|bi|an** (sen′ə gam′bē ən), *adj.* **1** of or having to do with both Senegal and Gambia. **2** of or having to do with Senegambia, a region in western Africa between the Senegal and Gambia rivers.

**se|nes|cence** (sə nes′əns), *n.* the fact or condition of growing old: *Senescence begins, and middle age ends, the day your descendants outnumber your friends* (New Yorker).

**se|nes|cent** (sə nes′ənt), *adj.* growing old; beginning to show old age. [< Latin *senēscēns, -entis,* present participle of *senēscere* grow old, related to *senex, senis* old]

**sen|es|chal** (sen′ə shəl), *n.* a steward in charge of a royal palace or a nobleman's estate in the Middle Ages. Seneschals often had the powers of judges or generals. [< Old French *seneschal,* ultimately < Germanic (compare Gothic *sinista* oldest, *skalks* servant)]

**sen|es|chal|ship** (sen′ə shəl ship), *n.* the office of seneschal.

**sen|gi** or **sen|ghi** (seng′gē), *n., pl.* **-gi** or **-ghi.** a unit of money in the Zaire Republic (the former Democratic Republic of the Congo) worth 1/100 of a likuta.

**se|nhor** (sā nyōr′), *n., pl.* **se|nho|res** (sā nyō′rās). *Portuguese.* **1** Mr. or sir. **2** a gentleman.

**se|nho|ra** (sā nyō′rə), *n. Portuguese.* **1** Mrs. or Madam. **2** a lady.

**se|nho|ri|ta** (sā′nyō rē′tə), *n. Portuguese.* **1** Miss. **2** a young lady.

**se|nile** (sē′nīl, -nəl), *adj., n.* —*adj.* **1** of or belonging to old age. **2** showing the weakness often characteristic of old age; characterized by senility: *a senile condition.* **3** caused by old age: *senile diseases.* **4** *Geology.* having reached an advanced stage of erosion; made flat or level, as by the action of water or wind: *a senile valley.*

—*n.* a senile person.

[< Latin *senīlis* < *senex, senis* old] —**se′nile|ly,** *adv.*

**senile psychosis** or **dementia,** a mental disorder caused by atrophy of the brain due to old age, characterized by loss of memory, depression, confusion, delusions, and irrational behavior.

**se|nil|i|ty** (sə nil′ə tē), *n.* **1** the mental and physical weakness often characteristic of old age; dotage. **2** old age: *He is yet in green and vigorous senility* (Charles Lamb).

**sen|ior** (sēn′yər), *adj., n.* —*adj.* **1** the older (used of a father whose son has the same given name): *John Parker, Senior, is the father of John Parker, Junior. Abbr:* Sr. **2** older or elder: *a senior citizen, senior children.* **3** higher in rank or longer in service: *a senior officer, a senior editor. Mr. Jones is the senior member of the firm of Jones and Brown. Thus, usually a more senior person such as a professor or reader finds it much easier to get assistance than does a young lecturer with a bright idea* (Listener). **4** of or having to do with the students of a graduating class: *the senior class, the senior year.*

—*n.* **1** an older person: *He is his brother's senior by two years.* **2** a person of higher rank or longer service. **3** a student who is a member of the graduating class of a high school or college. **4** a graduate or faculty member in an English university who assists in the college government.

[< Latin *senior, -ōris,* comparative of *senex, senis* old. See etym. of doublet **sire.**]

**senior high school,** a school attended after junior high school. It usually has grades 10, 11, and 12.

**sen|ior|i|ty** (sēn yôr′ə tē, -yor′-), *n., pl.* **-ties. 1** the condition or fact of being older; superiority in age or standing: *He felt that two years' seniority gave him the right to advise his brother.* **2** priority or precedence in office or service. **3** *British.* the body of seniors of a college or public school.

**senior master sergeant,** a noncommissioned officer in the U.S. Air Force ranking next below a chief master sergeant and next above a master sergeant.

**senior optime,** *British.* an optime placed in the second class.

**senior school,** (in Great Britain) a school for pupils from 14 to 17 years of age.

**sen|i|ti** (sen′ə tē), *n., pl.* **-ti.** a unit of money in Tonga worth 1/100 of a pa'anga. [< Tongan *seniti,* alteration of English *cent*]

**sen|na** (sen′ə), *n.* **1** a laxative extracted from the dried leaves or pods of any of several cassia plants. **2** the dried leaves of any of these plants. **3** any one of a group of plants of the pea family; cassia, or a plant of the same genus which is similar to it. [< New Latin *senna* < Arabic *sanā*]

**senna family,** a former grouping of plants now classified as a subfamily of the pea family.

**sen|net**[1] (sen′it), *n.* a particular set of notes played on a trumpet or cornet as a signal for an important entrance or exit. The word occurs chiefly in the stage directions of Elizabethan plays. [variant of *signet*]

**sen|net**[2] (sen′it), *n.* any one of several barracudas of Atlantic waters.

**sen|night** (sen′īt, -it), *n. Archaic.* seven nights and days; week: *She shall never have happy hour, unless she marry within this sennight* (Ben Jonson). [Old English *seofon nihta* seven nights]

**sen|nit** (sen′it), *n.* **1** a kind of flat, braided cordage used on shipboard, formed by plaiting strands of rope yarn or other fiber. **2** plaited straw or palm leaves for making hats.

**se|no|pi|a** (sə nō′pē ə), *n.* a condition of old people in which persons formerly having myopic vision acquire apparently normal sight. [< New Latin *senopia* < Latin *senex* old + Greek *ôps* eye]

**se|ñor** (sā nyōr′), *n., pl.* **-ño|res** (-nyō′res). *Spanish.* **1** Mr. or sir. *Abbr:* Sr. **2** a gentleman.

**se|ño|ra** (sā nyō′rä), *n. Spanish.* **1** Mrs. or Madam. **2** a lady.

**se|ño|ri|ta** (sā′nyō rē′tä), *n. Spanish.* **1** Miss. **2** a young lady.

**sen|ryu** (sen′ryü, -rē ü), *n.* a Japanese poem or verse similar in structure to the haiku but humorous or satiric in content. [< Japanese *senryū*]

**sen|sate**[1] (sen′sāt), *adj. Obsolete.* **1** endowed with sense or sensation. **2** perceived by the senses. [< Late Latin *sensātus* < *sēnsus, -ūs;* see etym. under **sense**]

**sen|sate**[2] (sen′sāt), *v.t.,* **-sat|ed, -sat|ing.** to perceive by a sense or the senses; have a sensation of. [< Latin *sēnsus, -ūs* (see etym. under **sense**) + English *-ate*[1]]

**sen|sa|tion** (sen sā′shən), *n.* **1** the action of the senses; power to see, hear, feel, taste, or smell: *A dead body is without sensation. Blindness is loss of the sensation of sight.* **SYN:** See syn. under **sense. 2** a particular mental condition produced by the stimulation of a sense organ or nerves; feelings: *Ice gives a sensation of coldness; polished wood, of smoothness; sugar, of sweetness. He has a sensation of dizziness when he walks along cliffs.* **3** a vague, generalized feeling: *a sensation of tiredness or of apprehension. The moviegoer is thus left with the highly unpleasant sensation ...* (Time). **4a** a state of strong or excited feeling: *The announcement of peace caused a sensation throughout the nation.* **b** a cause of such feeling: *Atomic developments are the greatest sensations of the present age. Man's first landing on the moon was a great sensation.* **5** *Psychology.* experience received directly through the sense organs.

[< Late Latin *sēnsātiō, -ōnis* < *sensātus* having feelings, sense < Latin *sēnsus, -ūs;* see etym. under **sense**]

**sen|sa|tion|al** (sen sā′shə nəl, -sāsh′nəl), *adj.* **1** arousing strong or excited feeling: *The outfielder's sensational catch made the crowd cheer wildly. There were sensational developments in the murder case.* **SYN:** exciting, thrilling, dramatic, startling. **2** trying to arouse strong or excited feeling: *a sensational novel, a sensational newspaper story.* **3** of the senses; having to do with sensation. **4** of, based on, or adhering to sensationalism in philosophy. —**sen|sa′tion|al|ly,** *adv.*

**sen|sa|tion|al|ism** (sen sā′shə nə liz′əm, -sāsh′nə-), *n.* **1** sensational methods; writing, language, photography, art, or music aimed at arousing strong or excited feeling. **2** the philosophical theory or doctrine that all ideas are derived solely through sensation. **3** *Ethics.* sensualism. **4** *Psychology.* sensationism.

**sen|sa|tion|al|ist** (sen sā′shə nə list, -sāsh′nə-), *n., adj.* —*n.* **1** a sensational writer, speaker, artist, musician, or photographer or motion-picture director, or other promoter; one who tries to

make a sensation. **2** a believer in philosophical sensationalism.
—*adj.* sensationalistic: *It could be exploited by sensationalist managers* (London Times).

**sen|sa|tion|al|is|tic** (sen sā′shə nə lis′tik,-sāsh′nə-), *adj.* of or having to do with sensationalism or sensationalists.

**sen|sa|tion|al|ize** (sen sā′shə nə līz), *v.t.,* **-ized, -iz|ing.** to make sensational; exaggerate in a sensational manner: *Certainly juvenile delinquency is a problem today. But it will not help to have it misrepresented and sensationalized* (New York Times).

**sen|sa|tion|ism** (sen sā′shə niz əm), *n. Psychology.* the doctrine that all states of consciousness are derived from sensations.

**sen|sa|tion|ist** (sen sā′shə nist), *n.* a psychologist who believes in sensationism.

**sen|sa|to|ry** (sen′sə tôr′ē, -tōr′-), *adj.* of or having to do with sensation; sensory.

**sense** (sens), *n., v.,* **sensed, sens|ing.** —*n.* **1a** the power of the mind to know what happens outside itself. Sight, hearing, touch, taste, and smell are the five senses. *A dog has a keen sense of smell.* **b** a receptor, or group of receptors, whereby an animal receives and responds to external or internal stimuli. **2** a feeling: *a sense of warmth, a sense of incompleteness. The extra lock on the door gave him a sense of security. He seems to have no sense of shame. Duty well done brings a sense of pleasure.* **3** a faculty, perception, or sensation not based on the five senses: *a sixth sense.* **4a** the five senses viewed collectively as a faculty. **b** the exercise or function of this faculty; sensation. **5** the faculties of the mind or soul, compared or contrasted with the bodily senses: *moral sense.* **6** understanding; appreciation: *She has a poor sense of duty.* **7** an instinctive or acquired faculty of perception or accurate estimation: *a sense of direction, a sense of beauty.* **8** Often, **senses.** a clear or sound state of mind: *He must be out of his senses to act so. Has he taken leave of his senses? He must be brought back to his senses. We hope that he will soon come to his senses.* **9** judgment; intelligence: *She had the good sense to keep out of foolish quarrels. Common sense would have prevented the accident.* **10** the recognition (as of a duty or virtue) as incumbent upon one or as fitting and proper: *a sense of justice. Will his words carry this sense of American responsibility for freedom attained through regard for the eternal rules of order?* (Time). **11** meaning: *He was a gentleman in every sense of the word.* **SYN**: See syn. under **meaning.** **12** discourse that has a satisfactory or intelligible meaning: *to speak or write sense.* **13** the general opinion: *The sense of the assembly was clear even before the vote.* **14** *Mathematics.* either of two opposite directions in which motion takes place.
—*v.t.* **1** to be aware of; feel: *Mother sensed that Father was tired. The herd of deer sensed the danger and made off into the woods.* **2** to understand; grasp: *I cannot sense your meaning sometimes* (Thomas Hardy). **3** to detect or react to (signals, stimuli, coded data, or the like) automatically: *A photoelectric cell senses objects that a person cannot see.*
—*v.i.* **1** to sense something; act as a sense organ, sensor, or sensing device: *Two more wires, one to "sense" and one to "inhibit," are separately threaded through all cores in each plane* (Scientific American). **2** to experience sensations: *We may sense in dreams ... as intensively as we sense under ... actual sensory stimuli* (Edward B. Titchener).
**in a sense,** in some respects; to some degree: *The consciousness of the body is of course, in a sense, its inner nature* (A. Barratt).
**make sense,** to be understandable; have a meaning; be reasonable: *We all agreed that the plan made sense.*
[< Latin *sēnsus, -ūs* < *sentīre* perceive, know, feel]
—*Syn. n.* **1a, 2 Sense, sensation, sensibility** mean the power or act of feeling or perceiving. **Sense** applies to the power of the mind to respond to stimulation: *An eagle's sense of sight enables it to recognize a mouse even from a great height.* **Sensation** applies particularly to the response to stimulation of a bodily organ like the eyes or nerves: *He has no sensation in his feet.* **Sensibility** applies particularly to emotional or esthetic response: *He lacks the sensibility of a true poet. Nothing is little to him that feels it with great sensibility* (Samuel Johnson).

**sense datum,** a fact of experience resulting directly from the stimulation of one of the senses.

**sense|ful** (sens′fəl), *adj.* full of sense; meaningful; sensible.

**sen|sei** (sen sā′), *n. Japanese.* master; teacher: *It was most startling, also, to observe the respect for the sensei, or teacher, in Japan* (Atlantic).

**sense|less** (sens′lis), *adj.* **1** unconscious: *A hard blow on the head knocked him senseless.* **2** foolish; stupid: *a senseless fellow, a senseless idea.* **3** meaningless: *senseless words.* **4** lacking mental perception or appreciation: *I am senseless of your wrath* (Shakespeare). —**sense′less|ly,** *adv.* —**sense′less|ness,** *n.*

**sense of humor,** the ability to understand a joke, or to appreciate and state the amusing side of things: *Everyone thinks he has a sense of humor. Nothing spoils a romance so much as a sense of humour in the woman* (Oscar Wilde).

**sense organ,** an eye, ear, taste bud, or other part of the body, by which a person or an animal receives sensations, as of heat, colors, sounds, or smells; receptor.

**sense perception,** perception by the senses.

**sense stress,** the stress pattern of a phrase or sentence; sentence stress.

**sen|si|bil|i|ty** (sen′sə bil′ə tē), *n., pl.* **-ties. 1** the ability to feel or perceive: *Some drugs lessen a person's sensibilities.* **SYN**: See syn. under **sense. 2** the quality of being easily and strongly affected by emotional influences; sensitiveness: *a sensibility to the beauties of nature.* **SYN**: impressibility. **3** a fineness of feeling; delicate sensitiveness of taste: *The painter has an unusual sensibility for colors. ... the admiration of every traveller of sensibility and taste* (William Prescott). **4** a tendency to feel hurt or offended too easily; susceptibility. **5** keen awareness; consciousness: *a person's sensibility of his own good fortune. ... Expressed great sensibility of your loss* (Samuel Johnson). **6** *Figurative.* the property, as in plants or certain instruments, of being readily affected by external influences.
**sensibilities,** sensitive feelings; emotional capacities: *Something intensely human, narrow, and definite pierces to the seat of our sensibilities more readily than huge occurrences and catastrophes* (Oliver Wendell Holmes).

**sen|si|bi|lize** (sen′sə bə līz), *v.t.,* **-lized, -liz|ing.** to make sensitive; sensitize. —**sen′si|bi|liz′er,** *n.*

**sen|si|ble** (sen′sə bəl), *adj., n.* —*adj.* **1** having good sense; showing good judgment; wise: *She is too sensible to do anything foolish. Now do be sensible. One hears very sensible things said on opposite sides* (George Eliot). **2** aware; conscious: *I am sensible of your kindness. [He] said how deeply sensible he was of the great honour done him by his appointment as chairman of the board* (London Times). **SYN**: sentient, cognizant. **3** that can be noticed; considerable: *a sensible reduction in expenses. There is a sensible difference between yellow and orange.* **SYN**: perceptible, appreciable. **4** that can be perceived by the senses: *the sensible horizon.* **5** capable of feeling or perceiving, as organs, tissues, or parts of the body. **6** sensitive: *sensible of shame.* **7** sensitive to external influences, as a balance or thermometer.
—*n.* **1** that which produces sensation; an object of sense. **2** a person who shows sensibility.
[< Latin *sēnsibilis* < *sēnsus, -ūs;* see etym. under **sense**] —**sen′si|ble|ness,** *n.*
—*Syn. adj.* **1 Sensible, practical** mean having or showing good sense. **Sensible** applies particularly to the common sense shown in acting and speaking, and implies both natural intelligence and good judgment: *He is too sensible to be worried by silly rumors.* **Practical** applies particularly to the common sense used in the performance of everyday tasks, and implies the ability to see what must or can be done and to use the best means at hand to accomplish it: *She is a practical woman and does not understand people who dream, speculate, or theorize.*

**sen|si|bly** (sen′sə blē), *adv.* **1** in a sensible manner; with good sense. **SYN**: judiciously, reasonably. **2** so as to be felt. **SYN**: perceptibly.

**sen|sil|lum** (sen sil′əm), *n., pl.* **-la** (-lə). an elementary sense organ, as a single epithelial cell at the end of a sensory nerve fiber. [< New Latin *sensillum* (diminutive) < Latin *sēnsus* sense]

**sens|ing device** or **instrument** (sen′sing), a device or instrument, such as an antenna, gyroscope, or photocell, that reacts in some way when acted upon by electronic or other waves coming from an object.

**sen|si|tive** (sen′sə tiv), *adj., n.* —*adj.* **1** receiving impressions readily: *The eye is sensitive to light.* **2a** easily affected or influenced: *The mercury in the thermometer is sensitive to changes in temperature.* **b** easily affected by certain agents: *paper sensitive to white light.* **c** (of a radio receiving set) readily affected by incoming radio waves. **d** fluctuating or tending to fluctuate rapidly: *sensitive prices or stocks.* **3** easily hurt or offended: *to be sensitive to criticism. She is sensitive when scolded. He was keenly sensitive about his failure.* **4** of, having to do with, or connected with the senses or sensation: *the sensitive perception of objects.* **5** *Medicine.* unusually susceptible: *sensitive to a serum.* **6** *Biology.* able to respond to stimulation by various external agents, such as light or gravity. **7** *Botany.* responding to external stimuli by moving, as the leaves of the sensitive plant. **8** having or involving access to secret or classified documents or data: *employees occupying sensitive positions in the government.*
—*n.* **1** a person who is sensitive to psychic, hypnotic, or spiritualistic influences; medium. **2** a person having a highly developed sensitive faculty: *He was a sublime emotional Englishman, who lived by atmosphere. He was a great sensitive* (G. K. Chesterton).
[< Old French *sensitif, sensitive,* learned borrowing from Medieval Latin *sensitivus* < Latin *sēnsus, -ūs;* see etym. under **sense**] —**sen′si|tive|ly,** *adv.* —**sen′si|tive|ness,** *n.*
—*Syn. adj.* **2a Sensitive, susceptible** mean easily affected or influenced. **Sensitive** suggests having, by nature or because of a physical or emotional condition, a specially keen or delicate capacity for feeling or for responding to an external influence: *Sensitive people are quickly touched by something beautiful or sad. The insecure student is sensitive to all criticism.* **Susceptible** suggests a nature or character easily acted on because of inability to resist some influence: *Susceptible people are easily tricked.*

**sensitive brier,** a perennial American plant of the pea family, having rose-colored flowers and many leaflets that fold together when touched. It is closely related to the sensitive plant.

**sensitive fern,** a North American fern in which the segments of the fronds tend to fold together after being detached.

**sensitive pea,** = partridge pea.

*** sensitive plant, 1** a tropical American mimosa often grown in greenhouses, whose leaflets fold together at the slightest touch. It belongs to the pea family. **2** any one of various other plants sensitive to touch.

*** sensitive plant**
definition 1

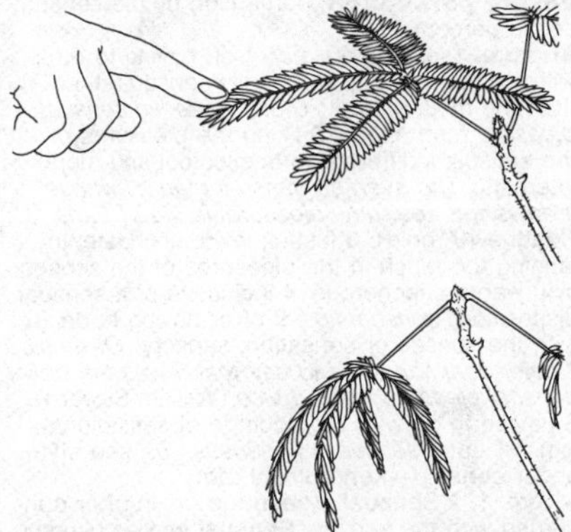

**sen|si|tiv|i|ty** (sen′sə tiv′ə tē), *n., pl.* **-ties. 1** the condition or quality of being sensitive: *Sentimentality and sensitivity, not in the maudlin but in the highest sense, are perhaps the greatest and most important qualities in a good mother* (New York Times). **2a** the capacity of an organism or part to respond to stimuli; irritability. **b** the degree of this. **3** the degree of responsiveness of an electrical or electronic device, as to a signal.

**sensitivity group,** = encounter group.

**sensitivity training,** training by a group of people, under the guidance of a leader, to develop self-awareness and sensitivity to the feelings of others, as in an encounter group or T-group.

**sen|si|ti|za|tion** (sen′sə tə zā′shən), *n.* the act, process, or result of sensitizing or making sensitive.

**sen|si|tize** (sen′sə tīz), *v.t.,* **-tized, -tiz|ing. 1** to make sensitive. Camera films have been sensitized to light. **2** *Immunology.* to make unusually sensitive to a protein or other substance by repeated injections.

**sen|si|tiz|er** (sen′sə tī′zər), *n.* **1** a person or thing that sensitizes. **2** *Photography.* the chemical agent or bath by which films or substances are made sensitive to light.

**sen|si|tom|e|ter** (sen′sə tom′ə tər), *n.* a device or apparatus for determining degree of sensitiveness, especially to light, of the eye, or of photographic plates or films.

**sen|si|to|met|ric** (sen′sə tə met′rik), *adj.* of or

**Pronunciation Key:** hat, āge, cãre, fär; let, ēqual, tėrm; it, īce; hot, ōpen, ôrder; oil, out; cup, pu̇t, rüle; child; long; thin; ᴛʜen; zh, measure;
ə represents **a** in about, **e** in taken, **i** in pencil, **o** in lemon, **u** in circus.

having to do with sensitometry.
**sen|si|tom|e|try** (sen′sə tom′ə trē), *n.* the determination of the degree of sensitivity of photographic materials.
**sen|sor** (sen′sər, -sôr), *n.* **1** any one of various devices that react to changes in temperature, radiation, motion, or the like, by generating or transmitting signals that may be used to measure an output or control an automatic operation: *Feedback in automation depends on sensors to transmit data to the controlling computer.* **2** any sensing device, such as a radar system, photoelectric cell, or remote sensor. **3** an instrument for recording and transmitting data about physiological changes; biosensor: *Scientists on the ground received electrocardiograms direct from sensors attached to the spacemen's bodies* (Time). **4** any sensory structure; sense organ: *the sensors of an insect.* [apparently back formation < *sensory*]
**sen|so|ri|al** (sen sôr′ē əl, -sōr′-), *adj.* = sensory.
**sen|so|ri|mo|tor** (sen′sər ē mō′tər), *adj.* of or having to do with both sensory and motor activity in the body.
**sen|so|ri|um** (sen sôr′ē əm, -sōr′-), *n., pl.* **-so|ri-ums, -so|ri|a** (-sôr′ē ə, -sōr′-). **1** the supposed seat of sensation in the brain, usually taken as the cortex or gray matter. **2** the whole sensory apparatus of the body. **3** the brain or mind (an unscientific use of the word). [< Late Latin *sēnsōrium* < Latin *sēnsus, -ūs;* see etym. under **sense**]
**sen|so|ry** (sen′sər ē), *adj.* **1** of or having to do with sensation or the senses. The eyes and ears are sensory organs. **2** conveying an impulse from the sense organs to a nerve center: *sensory nerves, sensory ganglia. Thus we see that some of the nerves are sensory and pick up sensations from sense organs to carry them to the main cords and brain, while others are motor and carry impulses from the brain and main nerves to the muscles in order to produce the proper response to the stimulation* (A. M. Winchester).
**sensory perception**, perception by the senses; sense perception.
**sen|su|al** (sen′shu̇ əl), *adj.* **1** of, having to do with, or appealing to the bodily senses rather than the mind or soul: *Gluttons derive sensual pleasure from eating.* **2** liking the pleasures of the senses; indifferent to intellectual and moral interests: *The average sensual man ... whose ideal is the free, gay, pleasurable life of Paris* (Matthew Arnold). **3** lustful; lewd; unchaste; indulging too much in the pleasures of the senses. **SYN**: wanton, lecherous. **4** indicative of a sensual disposition: *sensual lips.* **5** of or having to do with the senses or sensation; sensory: *Of music Doctor Johnson used to say that it was the only sensual pleasure without vice* (William Seward). **6** having to do with the doctrine of sensationalism. [< Latin *sēnsuālis* < *sēnsus, -ūs;* see etym. under **sense**] — **sen′su|al|ly**, *adv.*
— *Syn.* **1, 2 Sensual, sensuous** mean of or concerned with the senses. **Sensual** implies pleasurable satisfaction to the bodily appetites and often suggests baseness or excess: *the sensual delight in a hot bath after hard work. Profligates are basically sensual people.* **Sensuous**, always favorable, implies a high sensitivity to beauty and the pleasures of the senses and feelings: *She derives sensuous delight from traditional church music.*
**sen|su|al|ism** (sen′shu̇ ə liz′əm), *n.* **1** = sensuality. **2** the ethical doctrine that gratification of the senses is the main object of life.
**sen|su|al|ist** (sen′shu̇ ə list), *n.* **1** a person who likes, pursues, or indulges too much in the pleasures of the senses. **2** a believer in the ethical doctrine of sensualism.
**sen|su|al|is|tic** (sen′shu̇ ə lis′tik), *adj.* having to do with sensualism.
**sen|su|al|i|ty** (sen′shu̇ al′ə tē), *n., pl.* **-ties. 1** sensual nature: *Claude's agonizing longing for purity struggles against a sensuality that is wholly animal* (Saturday Review). **2** a liking for the pleasures of the senses. **3** excessive indulgence in the pleasures of the senses. **4** lewdness; lasciviousness.
**sen|su|al|ize** (sen′shu̇ ə līz), *v.t.,* **-ized, -iz|ing.** to make sensual. — **sen′su|al|i|za′tion**, *n.*
**sen|su|os|i|ty** (sen′shu̇ os′ə tē), *n.* sensuous quality; sensuousness.
**sen|su|ous** (sen′shu̇ əs), *adj.* **1** of or derived from the senses; having an effect on the senses; perceived by the senses: *the sensuous thrill of a warm bath, a sensuous love of color. The sensuous joy from all things fair his strenuous bent of soul repressed* (John Greenleaf Whittier). **SYN**: See syn. under **sensual. 2** enjoying the pleasures of the senses. **SYN**: See syn. under **sensual.** [< Latin *sēnsus, -ūs* (see etym. under **sense**) + English *-ous*] — **sen′su|ous|ly**, *adv.* — **sen′su-ous|ness**, *n.*

**sent** (sent), *v.* the past tense and past participle of **send**: *They sent the trunks last week. She was sent on an errand.*
**sent.**, sentence.
***sen|tence** (sen′təns), *n., v.,* **-tenced, -tenc|ing.** — *n.* **1** a group of words (or sometimes a single word) that is grammatically complete and expresses a statement, request, command, question, or exclamation. A sentence normally contains a subject and predicate. "Boys and girls" is not a sentence. "The boys are here" is a sentence. *Examples: He is good* (declarative sentence); *Is he good?* (interrogative sentence); *Be good!* (imperative sentence); *Good boy!* (exclamatory sentence). **2** *Mathematics.* a group of symbols that expresses a complete idea or a requirement. *Examples:* $4+2=6$ is a closed sentence expressing a complete idea; $x+2=6$ is an open sentence expressing a requirement. **3** an opinion pronounced on some particular question; decision: *My sentence is for open war* (Milton). **4a** a decision by a judge or court, especially on the punishment of a criminal. **b** the punishment itself: *The remaining two months of his sentence slipped by ... rapidly* (Samuel Butler). **5** *Music.* a phrase or (sometimes) a period. **6** *Archaic.* a short, wise saying; proverb: *Who fears a sentence or an old man's saw shall by a painted cloth be kept in awe* (Shakespeare).
— *v.t.* to pronounce punishment on: *The judge sentenced the thief to five years in prison.*
[< Old French *sentence,* learned borrowing from Latin *sententia* (originally) opinion < *sentīre* to feel, perceive]

***sentence**
definitions 1, 2

**in grammar:**

He read the sentence slowly.
subject — predicate

**in mathematics:**

$3^2 + 4^2 = 25$
closed sentence

$3^2 + y = 16$
open sentence

**sen|tenc|er** (sen′tən sər), *n.* a person who pronounces sentence; judge.
**sentence stress** or **accent**, the varying emphasis given to words that affects the meaning of a sentence. *Example:* "*He* killed the dog, not his brother," as compared with, "He killed the *dog,* not his *brother.*"
**sen|ten|ti|a** (sen ten′shē ə), *n., pl.* **-ti|ae** (-shē ē). a pithy or pointed statement; aphorism or epigram. [< Latin *sententia* opinion; see etym. under **sentence**]
**sen|ten|tial** (sen ten′shəl), *adj.* **1** having to do with or of the nature of a judicial sentence or decree. **2** having to do with a grammatical sentence.
**sentential calculus**, = propositional calculus.
**sentential function**, = propositional function (def. 2).
**sen|ten|tious** (sen ten′shəs), *adj.* **1** full of meaning; saying much in few words: *grave reflections and sententious maxims.* **SYN**: pithy. **2** speaking as if one were a judge settling a question. **3** inclined to make wise sayings; abounding in proverbs: *a long, sententious letter, full of Latin quotations* (Charles Kingsley). **SYN**: epigrammatic. [< Latin *sententiōsus* < *sententia;* see etym. under **sentence**] — **sen|ten′tious|ly**, *adv.* — **sen|ten′-tious|ness**, *n.*
**sen|tience** (sen′shəns), *n.* **1** capacity for feeling: *Some people believe in the sentience of flowers.* **2** mere responsiveness to sensory stimuli; sensory capacity, as of the skin to pain.
**sen|tien|cy** (sen′shən sē), *n.* = sentience.
**sen|tient** (sen′shənt), *adj., n.* — *adj.* that can feel; having feeling: *Poets are very apt to credit inanimate objects with being sentient.*
— *n.* a person or thing that feels.
[< Latin *sentiēns, -entis,* present participle of *sentīre* to feel] — **sen′tient|ly**, *adv.*
**sen|ti|ment** (sen′tə mənt), *n.* **1a** a mixture of thought and feeling. Admiration, patriotism, and loyalty are sentiments. **b** Often, **sentiments.** a mental attitude or personal opinion: *What are his sentiments in the matter?* **SYN**: view, thought. **2** feeling, especially tender feeling: *a sentiment of pity.* **3a** emotional regard to ideal considerations as a principle of action or judgment: *a man completely without sentiment.* **b** such regard carried to or possessed in an excessive degree, especially to the degree of maudlin sentimentality: *She thinks clearly but her sister is full of sentiment.* **4** a thought or saying that expresses feeling: *a very charming sentiment. "Now, here is a little girl who wants my autograph and a 'sentiment'"* (Longfellow). **SYN**: maxim, epigram. [< Medieval Latin *sentimentum* < Latin *sentīre* to feel]
— *Syn.* **2 Sentiment, sentimentality** mean refined or tender feeling, or a quality or characteristic showing or produced by feeling. **Sentiment** suggests sincere, tender, or noble feeling: *Birthdays are times for sentiment.* **Sentimentality** suggests affected or false, excessive or exaggerated feeling: *The sentimentality of the usual soap opera bores many people.*
**sen|ti|men|tal** (sen′tə men′təl), *adj.* **1** having or showing much tender feeling: *sentimental poetry, a touchingly sentimental letter.* **2** likely to act from feelings rather than from logical thinking: *a sentimental schoolgirl.* **3** of sentiment; dependent on sentiment: *She values her mother's gift for sentimental reasons.* **4** having too much sentiment. **SYN**: emotional, gushing. — **sen′ti|men′tal-ly**, *adv.*
**sen|ti|men|tal|ise** (sen′tə men′tə līz), *v.i., v.t.,* **-ised, -is|ing.** *Especially British.* sentimentalize.
**sen|ti|men|tal|ism** (sen′tə men′tə liz əm), *n.* **1** a tendency to be influenced by sentiment rather than reason. **2** excessive indulgence in sentiment. **3** a display of sentimentality; feeling expressed too openly or commonly or sentimentally.
**sen|ti|men|tal|ist** (sen′tə men′tə list), *n.* a sentimental person; person who indulges in sentimentality.
**sen|ti|men|tal|i|ty** (sen′tə men tal′ə tē), *n., pl.* **-ties. 1** a tendency to be influenced by sentiment rather than reason; sentimental quality, disposition, or behavior. **SYN**: See syn. under **sentiment. 2** excessive indulgence in sentiment. **3** a sentimental notion or the like; feeling expressed too openly or sentimentally.
**sen|ti|men|tal|i|za|tion** (sen′tə men′tə lə zā′shən), *n.* the act or process of sentimentalizing.
**sen|ti|men|tal|ize** (sen′tə men′tə līz), *v.,* **-ized, -iz|ing.** — *v.i.* to indulge in sentiment; affect sentiment: *He had left his father tearfully sentimentalizing about the Queen* (Arnold Bennett).
— *v.t.* **1** to make sentimental: *Coming away from New England has sentimentalized us all* (Harriet Beecher Stowe). **2** to be sentimental about: *to sentimentalize one's college days.*
**sen|ti|nel** (sen′tə nəl), *n., v.,* **-neled, -nel|ing** or (*especially British*) **-nelled, -nel|ling.** — *n.* **1** a person stationed to keep watch and guard against surprises; sentry: *The party now approached the sentinels on guard at the castle* (Scott). **2** *Figurative.* a person or thing that watches, or stands as if watching: *The tree stood by itself, a lonely sentinel against the sky.*
— *v.t.* **1** to stand guard over; watch as a sentinel: (*Figurative.*) *when the watches of the night were set, and the band on deck sentinelled the slumbers of the band below* (Herman Melville). **2** to furnish with or as if with a sentinel or sentinels. **3** to post as a sentinel.
**stand sentinel**, to act as a sentinel; keep watch: *One of the campers stood sentinel while the others slept.*
[< Middle French *sentinelle* < Italian *sentinella* < Late Latin *sentīnāre* pump out the bilge water from a ship; to be in difficulty or danger < Latin *sentīna* bilge water]
**sen|try** (sen′trē), *n., pl.* **-tries,** *v.,* **-tried, -try|ing.** — *n.* **1** a soldier stationed at a post to watch and guard against surprises; guard; sentinel. **2** *Figurative.* a person or thing that keeps guard. **3** the occupation, duty, or service of a sentry: watch kept by a sentry.
— *v.t.* to guard as a sentry does.
**stand sentry**, to keep watch; guard: *We stood sentry over the sleepers.*
[perhaps short for earlier *centrinel,* variant of *sentinel*]
**sentry box**, a small building for sheltering a sentry on a post or watch.
**sen|try-go** (sen′trē gō′), *n. Especially British.* the patrol or duties of a sentry.
**sentry radar**, a type of radar used by ground troops to detect the movement of enemy troops and vehicles. The indicator makes a different sound for each type of target detected.
**Se|nu|fo** (sə nü′fō), *n., pl.* **-fo** or **-fos. 1** a member of a West African people living in the Ivory Coast Republic, Upper Volta, and Mali. The Senufo are noted for their statuettes and figures carved from wood. **2** the Mandingo language of this people.
**Se|nu|si** or **Se|nus|si** (se nü′sē), *n., pl.* **-si.** a North African of a fanatical and warlike Moslem sect.
**Se|nu|si|an** (se nü′sē ən), *adj.* of or having to do with the Senusi.
**sep.**, **1** sepal. **2** separate.
**Sep.**, **1** September. **2** Septuagint.
**se|pal** (sē′pəl), *n.* one of the leaflike divisions of the calyx, or outer covering, of a flower. In a carnation, the sepals make a green cup at the base of the flower. In a tulip, the sepals are bright, just

like the petals. An unopened bud is covered by the sepals. ... *the calyx consists of sepals, distinct as in the tomato, or united as in the Easter lily* (Harbaugh and Goodrich). See picture under **carpel**. [< French *sépale* < New Latin *sepalum*, apparently coined from Greek *sképē* covering]

**-sepaled**, *combining form.* having ___ sepals: *Four-sepaled = having four sepals.*

**sep|al|ine** (sep′ə lin, -līn), *adj.* of or belonging to the sepal of a flower.

**sep|al|o|dy** (sep′ə lō′dē), *n.* the change in form of petals or other flower organs into sepals or organs resembling sepals.

**sep|al|oid** (sep′ə loid), *adj.* of or like a sepal.

**sep|al|ous** (sep′ə ləs), *adj.* having sepals.

**sep|a|ra|bil|i|ty** (sep′ər ə bil′ə tē, sep′rə-), *n.* the quality of being separable.

**sep|a|ra|ble** (sep′ər ə bəl, sep′rə-), *adj.* that can be separated; divisible. —**sep′a|ra|ble|ness**, *n.*

**sep|a|ra|bly** (sep′ər ə blē, sep′rə-), *adv.* in a separable manner; so as to be separable.

**sep|a|ra|ta** (sep′ə rā′tə), *n.* plural of **separatum**.

**sep|a|rate** (*v.* sep′ə rāt; *adj., n.* sep′ər it, sep′rit), *v.*, **-rat|ed, -rat|ing,** *adj., n.* —***v.t.*** **1** to be between; keep apart; divide: *The Atlantic Ocean separates America from Europe.* **2** to take apart; part; disjoin: *to separate church and state.* **3** to cause to live apart. A husband and wife may be separated by agreement or by order of a court. **4** to divide into parts or groups; divide or part (a mass, compound, or whole) into elements, sizes, or kinds: *to separate a tangle of string.* **5a** to put apart; take away: *Separate your books from mine.* **b** to set apart for a special purpose; segregate. **6** *U.S.* to discharge, as from an office, service, or school; dismiss.

—***v.i.*** **1** to go, draw, or come apart; become disconnected or disunited: *The rope separated under the strain.* **2** to part company: *After school, the children separated in all directions.* **3** to live apart: *The husband and wife separated several years ago and don't see each other anymore.* **4** to become parted from a mass or compound, as crystals.

—***adj.*** **1** apart from others; without access; shut off from others: *in a separate part of the house. He leads a separate life away from the community. He sought them both, but wish'd his hap might find Eve separate* (Milton). **2** divided; not joined: *separate seats, separate questions. Our teeth are separate.* **3** individual; single: *the separate parts of a machine; ... a hundred trifles too insignificant for separate notice* (Arnold Bennett). **4** belonging to one; not shared with others: *separate rooms. Those twins have separate problems in school—one cannot read well and the other is poor at arithmetic.* **5** existing independently; distinct: *to keep private matters separate from official business.*

—***n.*** something separate, especially an article or document issued separately.

**separates**, women's blouses, skirts, sweaters, and other articles of outer clothing, not usually part of a suit. Separates are sold individually and worn interchangeably to make various coordinated outfits. *Among the cotton-knit separates from Italy are cardigans ... teamed with pullovers that have wide square necks and no sleeves* (New Yorker).

[< Latin *sēparāre* (with English *-ate*[1]) < *sē-* apart + *parāre* make equal < *pār, paris* equal]

—**sep′a|rate|ness**, *n.*

—***Syn.*** *v.t.* **2 Separate, divide** mean to put apart what has been together. **Separate** implies that the parts have formerly been together: *The brothers had been separated by the war.* **Divide** implies a cutting or breaking into parts according to some plan or measure: *I divided the cake in two, saving half for the next meal. The teacher divides the class for field trips.*

**separate but equal**, *U.S.* of or having to do with a policy of racial segregation between Negroes and whites, as in education, employment, or transportation, while providing ostensibly equal facilities for all: *In the South, the "separate but equal" doctrine, which was struck down by the 1954 Supreme Court ruling, had led to the establishment of dual school systems* (New York Times).

**sep|a|rate|ly** (sep′ər it lē, sep′rit-), *adv.* in a separate manner; one by one; one at a time.

**separate school**, in Canada: **1** a Roman Catholic parochial school. **2** any school that is not part of the public-school system.

**sep|a|ra|tion** (sep′ə rā′shən), *n.* **1** the act of separating; dividing; taking apart: *Three groups of unit operations exist, concerned respectively with size reduction, mixing, and physical separation of materials* (J. F. Pearson). **2** the condition of being separated: *The friends were glad to meet after so long a separation. The apparent separation of two stars depends not only on the distance between them, but also on their distance from us* (W. H. Marshall). **3** a line or point of separating; place where two or more objects separate: *We have come upstream to the separation of the two branches of the river.* **4** the living apart of husband and wife by agreement or by order of a court. **5** *U.S.* discharge, as from an office, service, or school; dismissal.

**separation center**, *U.S.* a military base where men in the armed forces are released from service.

**sep|a|ra|tion|ist** (sep′ə rā′shə nist), *n., adj.* = separatist.

**separation negative**, a negative made in color printing for each separate color by photographing the original copy through a filter to eliminate all colors from the negative except the color desired.

**separation pay**, = severance pay.

**sep|a|ra|tism** (sep′ər ə tiz′əm, sep′rə-), *n.* the principle or policy of separation; opposition to ecclesiastical, political, or ethnic union.

**sep|a|ra|tist** (sep′ər ə tist, sep′rə-), *n., adj.* —***n.*** **1** a member of a group that separates or withdraws from a larger group. **2** a person who favors separation from a church or state.

—***adj.*** of or characteristic of separatists or separatism: *The report accuses [him] of aiding the separatist tendency of the services* (Wall Street Journal).

**Sep|a|ra|tist** (sep′ə rā′tist, -ər ə-; sep′rə-), *n.* any one of the Puritans who broke from the Church of England during the reign of James I.

**sep|a|ra|tis|tic** (sep′ə rə tis′tik), *adj.* = separatist.

**sep|a|ra|tive** (sep′ə rā′tiv), *adj.* tending to separate; causing separation.

**sep|a|ra|tor** (sep′ə rā′tər), *n.* **1** a person or thing that separates, especially a machine for separating, as the cream from milk, or wheat from chaff or dirt: *The pieces that sift through are then dumped into a separator—a large vat shaped like an inverted cone* (New Yorker). **2** any one of various devices used for dressing ore. [< Latin *sēparātor* < *sēparāre;* see etym. under **separate**]

**sep|a|ra|to|ry** (sep′ər ə tôr′ē, -tōr′-), *adj.* that separates; separative.

**sep|a|ra|tum** (sep′ə rā′təm), *n., pl.* **-ta**. a copy of an article read at a meeting, or printed in the journal, of a learned society or the like; separate. [< New Latin *separatum* < Latin *sēparāre;* see etym. under **separate**]

**Se|phar|di** (si fär′dē), *adj.* = Sephardic.

**Se|phar|dic** (si fär′dik), *adj.* of or descended from the Sephardim: *the daughter of a rich Sephardic family—educated by private tutors, a friend of Emerson* (New Yorker).

**Se|phar|dim** (si fär′dim), *n.pl.* Spanish-Portuguese Jews and their descendants, as contrasted with the Ashkenazim and their descendants: *They have encountered in the less traveled quarters of Greater New York ... the Hasidim and Sephardim* (New Yorker). [< Hebrew *səfardīm*, plural of *səfardī* < *səfārāth*, a country mentioned in Obadiah 20, perhaps Spain]

**se|pi|a** (sē′pē ə), *n., pl.* **-pi|as, -pi|ae** (-pē ē), *adj.* —***n.*** **1** a dark-brown paint or ink prepared from the inky secretion of cuttlefish. **2** a dark brown. **3** a drawing, photograph, lithograph, or the like, in tones of brown. **4** any one of a group of cuttlefish having an internal shell.

—***adj.*** **1** dark-brown. **2** done in sepia: *a sepia print.*

[< Latin *sēpia* < Greek *sēpiā* cuttlefish < *sēpein* make foul; to rot, related to *sápros* rotten]

**se|pi|o|lite** (sē′pē ə līt), *n.* native hydrous silicate of magnesium; meerschaum. [< German *Sepiolith* (with English *-lite*) < Greek *sēpion* cuttlebone (< *sēpiā;* see etym. under **sepia**) + *lithos* stone]

**se|poy** (sē′poi), *n.* (formerly) a native of India who was a soldier in the British army, or a member of the army of the British East India Company in the 1700's and early 1800's. [probably < Portuguese *sipae* < Hindustani *sipāhī* soldier, horseman < Persian < *sipāh* army. Compare etym. under **spahi**.]

**sep|pu|ku** (sep′pü′kü), *n. Japanese.* hara-kiri.

**sep|sine** (sep′sēn, -sin), *n.* any one of certain poisonous ptomaines formed as by decaying yeast or blood. [< *seps*(is) + *-ine*[2]]

**sep|sis** (sep′sis), *n.* **1a** a poisoning of the system by disease-producing bacteria and their toxins absorbed into the bloodstream, as from festering wounds; blood poisoning. **b** the condition of being infected with such bacteria as streptococci or staphylococci. **2** = putrefaction. [< New Latin *sepsis* < Greek *sēpsis* putrefaction < *sēpein* to rot, related to *sápros* foul, rotten]

**sept** (sept), *n.* **1** a clan, especially of descendants of a common ancestor. **2** an ancient Irish clan. [probably early variant of *sect;* influenced by Latin *sēptum* enclosure; see etym. under **septum**]

**sept-**, *combining form.* seven: *Septangular = having seven angles.* Also, **septem-, septi-** before consonants. [< Latin *septem*]

**Sept** (no period), September.

**Sept.**, **1** September. **2** Septuagint.

**sep|ta** (sep′tə), *n.* plural of **septum**.

**sep|tal** (sep′təl), *adj.* of or having to do with a septum: *a septal filament.*

**sep|tan|gu|lar** (sep tang′gyə lər), *adj.* having seven angles.

**sep|tar|i|an** (sep tãr′ē ən), *adj.* **1** of or having to do with a septarium. **2** containing a septarium.

**sep|tar|i|um** (sep tãr′ē əm), *n., pl.* **-i|a** (-ē ə). *Geology.* a rounded lump of minerals occurring in layers, as in sand or clay. A septarium is usually of calcium carbonate or carbonate of iron, having a network of cracks filled with calcite and other minerals. [(originally) a septate object < New Latin *septarium* < Latin *sēptum* septum, a divider]

**sep|tate** (sep′tāt), *adj.* divided by a septum or septa: ... *all other filamentous fungi are more or less completely septate (that is, the cells are separated from each other by cross walls)* ... (Fred W. Emerson). [< New Latin *septatus* < Latin *sēptum* septum]

**sep|tat|ed** (sep′tā tid), *adj.* = septate.

**sep|ta|tion** (sep tā′shən), *n.* septate condition.

**sep|ta|va|lent** (sep′tə vā′lənt, sep tav′ə-), *adj.* = septivalent.

**sep|tec|to|my** (sep tek′tə mē), *n., pl.* **-mies**. surgical removal of part of the nasal septum. [< *sept*(um) + Greek *ektomē* a cutting out]

**septem-**, *combining form.* a form of **sept-**, as in *septemvirate.*

**Sep|tem|ber** (sep tem′bər), *n.* the ninth month of the year. It has 30 days. *Abbr:* Sept. [< Latin *September, -bris* < *septem* seven (because of its position in the early Roman calendar)]

**Sep|tem|brism** (sep tem′briz əm), *n.* the principles and actions of the Septembrists.

**Sep|tem|brist** (sep tem′brist), *n.* (in French history) a person who instigated or took part in the massacre of the royalists and political prisoners in Paris, September 2-6, 1792.

**sep|te|mi|a** (sep tē′mē ə), *n.* = septicemia.

**sep|tem|par|tite** (sep′tem pär′tīt), *adj. Botany.* divided nearly to the base into seven parts.

**sep|tem|vir** (sep tem′vər), *n., pl.* **-vi|ri** (-və rī), **-virs**. one of seven men who hold some office or authority. [< Latin *septemviri*, plural < *septem* seven + *viri*, plural of *vir* man]

**sep|tem|vi|rate** (sep tem′və rāt), *n.* **1** the office of a septemvir. **2** government by septemviri. **3** a group of seven men in office or authority. **4** any group of seven.

**sep|te|nar|i|us** (sep′tə ner′ē əs), *n.* a line of seven feet or seven accented syllables, especially in Latin poetry. [< Latin *septēnārius* septenary]

**sep|te|nar|y** (sep′tə ner′ē), *adj., n., pl.* **-nar|ies**.

—***adj.*** **1** of or having to do with the number seven. **2** forming a group of seven. **3** = septennial.

—***n.*** **1** the number seven. **2** a group or set of seven things. **3** a period of seven years. **4** *Prosody.* = septenarius.

[< Latin *septēnārius* < *septēnī* seven each < *septem* seven]

**sep|ten|de|cil|lion** (sep′ten də sil′yən), *n.* **1** (in the U.S., Canada, and France) 1 followed by 54 zeros. **2** (in Great Britain and Germany) 1 followed by 102 zeros. [< Latin *septendecim* seventeen (< *septem* seven + *decem* ten) + English *-illion*, as in *million*]

**sep|ten|nate** (sep ten′āt), *n.* a period of seven years. [< French *septennat* < Latin *septennis*]

**sep|ten|ni|al** (sep ten′ē əl), *adj.* **1** lasting seven years. **2** occurring every seven years. [< Latin *septennium* seven-year period (< *septem* seven + *annus* year) + English *-al*[1]] —**sep|ten′ni|al|ly**, *adv.*

**sep|ten|ni|um** (sep ten′ē əm), *n., pl.* **-ten|ni|ums, -ten|ni|a** (-ten′ē ə). a period of seven years. [< Latin *septennium;* see etym. under **septennial**]

**sep|ten|tri|on** (sep ten′trē ən), *n., adj.* —***n.*** *Archaic.* **1** the north: *Thou art as opposite to every good ... as the south to the septentrion* (Shakespeare). **2** a northerner.

—***adj.*** = septentrional.

[< Latin *septentriō, -ōnis*]

**sep|ten|tri|o|nal** (sep ten′trē ə nəl), *adj.* **1** = northern. **2** of or from the north: *For Paris, this has been the longest, coldest stretch of septentrional weather known since ... 1940* (New Yorker).

**Sep|ten|tri|ons** (sep ten′trē ənz), *n.pl. Archaic.* the constellation of the Great Bear. [< Latin *septentriōnēs* (literally) the seven oxen that circle the polestar, singular of *septentriō, -ōnis* the north]

**Pronunciation Key:** hat, āge, cãre, fär; let, ēqual, tėrm; it, īce; hot, ōpen, ôrder; oil, out; cup, pu̇t, rüle; child; long; thin; ᴛʜen; zh, measure; ə represents **a** in about, **e** in taken, **i** in pencil, **o** in lemon, **u** in circus.

**sep|tet** or **sep|tette** (sep tet′), *n.* **1** a musical composition for seven voices or instruments. **2** a group of seven singers or players performing together. **3** any group of seven. [< German *Septett* < Latin *septem* seven; patterned on German *Duett* duet]

**sept|foil** (sept′foil′), *n. Architecture.* an ornament with seven cusps or points. [< Late Latin *septifolium* < Latin *septem* seven + *folium* leaf]

**septi-**, *combining form.* a form of **sept-** before consonants, as in *septivalent.*

**sep|tic** (sep′tik), *adj., n.* —*adj.* **1** causing infection or putrefaction: *We did, of course, practice rigid asepsis (avoidance of infection) but septic surgery could be a nightmare* (Harper's). **2** caused by infection or putrefaction.
—*n.* a substance that causes or promotes sepsis.
[< Latin *sēpticus* < Greek *sēptikós* < *sēpein* to rot, related to *sápros* foul, rotten]

**sep|ti|ce|mi|a** or **sep|ti|cae|mi|a** (sep′tə sē′mē ə), *n.* blood poisoning, especially in which microorganisms and their toxins enter the bloodstream. [< New Latin *septicemia* < Greek *sēptikós* septic + *haîma* blood]

**sep|ti|ce|mic** or **sep|ti|cae|mic** (sep′tə sē′mik), *adj.* **1** causing septicemia. **2** caused by or having septicemia.

**septicemic plague**, a virulent form of plague that infects the bloodstream directly, causing death before there is time for the formation of buboes.

**sep|ti|cid|al** (sep′tə sī′dəl), *adj. Botany.* (of dehiscent seed capsules) bursting along the septa: *There are three kinds of valvular dehiscence: septicidal, loculicidal, and septifragal* (Heber W. Youngken). [< *septum* + Latin *caedere* to cut + *-al*[1]] —**sep′ti|cid′al|ly**, *adv.*

**sep|tic|i|ty** (sep tis′ə tē), *n.* septic character or quality: *septicity in sewage* (New Scientist).

**sep|ti|cize** (sep′tə sīz), *v.t.,* **-cized, -ciz|ing.** to make septic.

**sep|ti|co|py|e|mi|a** or **sep|ti|co|py|ae|mi|a** (sep′tə kō pī ē′mē ə), *n.* = pyemia.

**septic sore throat**, a throat condition caused by a streptococcic infection.

**septic tank**, a tank in which sewage is decomposed by anaerobic bacteria: *Septic tanks meant for open areas were installed among patches of homes because sewers could not be built fast enough* (Wall Street Journal).

**sep|ti|form** (sep′tə fôrm), *adj.* = sevenfold.

**sep|tif|ra|gal** (sep tif′rə gəl), *adj. Botany.* characterized by the breaking away of the valves from the septa in dehiscence. [< *septum* + Latin *frag-*, stem of *frangere* to break + English *-al*[1]]

**sep|til|lion** (sep til′yən), *n., adj.* **1** (in the U.S., Canada, and France) 1 followed by 24 zeros; 1,000 to the eighth power. **2** (in Great Britain and Germany) 1 followed by 42 zeros; 1,000,000 to the seventh power. [< French *septillion* < Latin *septem* seven; patterned on *million* million]

**sep|til|lionth** (sep til′yənth), *adj., n.* **1** last in a series of a septillion. **2** one (or being one) of a septillion equal parts.

**sep|ti|mal** (sep′tə məl), *adj.* having to do with or based on the number seven. [< Latin *septimus* seventh (< *septem* seven) + English *-al*[1]]

**sep|time** (sep′tēm), *n. Fencing.* the seventh in a series of eight defensive positions or parries. [< Latin *septimus* < *septem* seven]

**sep|ti|par|tite** (sep′tə pär′tīt), *adj.* consisting of seven parts.

**sep|ti|syl|la|ble** (sep′tə sil′ə bəl), *n.* a word of seven syllables.

**sep|ti|va|lent** (sep′tə vā′lənt, sep tiv′ə-), *adj. Chemistry.* having a valence of 7. Also, **septavalent.**

**sep|tu|a|ge|nar|i|an** (sep′chů ə jə nãr′ē ən, -tyů-), *n., adj.* —*n.* a person who is 70 years old or between 70 and 80 years old.
—*adj.* 70 years old or between 70 and 80 years old.
[< Latin *septuāgēnārius* septuagenary + English *-an*]

**sep|tu|ag|e|nar|y** (sep′chů aj′ə ner′ē, -tyů-), *n., pl.* **-nar|ies,** *adj.* —*n.* = septuagenarian.
—*adj.* **1** = septuagenarian. **2** consisting of 70.
[< Latin *septuāgēnārius* < *septuāgēnī* seventy each < *septem* seven]

**Sep|tu|a|ges|i|ma** (sep′chů ə jes′ə mə, -tyů-), *n.,* or **Septuagesima Sunday**, the third Sunday before Lent. [< Late Latin *septuāgēsima* (literally) seventieth]

**Sep|tu|a|gint** (sep′chů ə jint, -tyů-), *n.* the Greek translation of the Old Testament that was made before the time of Christ. According to tradition, the first part of the Old Testament, the Pentateuch, was translated from Hebrew to Greek by seventy Jewish scholars brought for this purpose to Alexandria by Ptolemy II of Egypt. *Abbr:* LXX (no periods). [earlier, the seventy translators < Late Latin *septuāgintā* (*interpretes*) seventy (interpreters) < Latin]

**Sep|tu|a|gin|tal** (sep′chů ə jin′təl, -tyů-), *adj.* of or having to do with the Septuagint.

**sep|tum** (sep′təm), *n., pl.* **-ta.** a dividing wall, as of membrane, bone, or cartilage; partition. There is a septum of bone and cartilage between the nostrils. The ventricles of the heart are separated by a septum. The inside of a green pepper is divided into chambers by septa. [< Latin *sēptum,* variant of *saeptum* a fence < *saepīre* to hedge in < *saepēs, -is* a hedge, fence]

**sep|tu|or** (sep′chů ôr, -tyů-), *n.* = septet.

**sep|tu|ple** (sep′tů pəl, -tyů-; sep tü′-, -tyü′-), *adj., n., v.,* **-pled, -pling.** —*adj.* **1** seven times as great; sevenfold. **2** *Music.* characterized by seven beats to the measure.
—*n.* a number or amount seven times as great as another.
—*v.t.* to make seven times as great.
—*v.i.* to become seven times as great.
[< Late Latin *septuplus* < Latin *septem* seven + *-plus* -fold]

**sep|tu|plet** (sep′tů plit, -tyů-; sep tü′-, -tyü′-), *n.* **1** one of seven offspring born to the same mother at the same time. **2** any group or combination of seven. **3** *Music.* a group of seven notes of the same time value that are performed in the time usually taken for a different number of notes.

**sep|ul|cher** (sep′əl kər), *n., v.* —*n.* **1** a place for putting the bodies of persons who have died; tomb; grave. **2** a structure or recess in old churches in which sacred relics were deposited on the Thursday or Friday before Easter to be taken out at Easter.
—*v.t.* to bury (a dead body) in a sepulcher.
[< Old French *sepulcre,* learned borrowing from Latin *sepulcrum* < *sepelīre* to bury]

**se|pul|chral** (sə pul′krəl), *adj.* **1** of sepulchers or tombs: *They are more than sepulchral effigies: they exist in their own right as an embodiment of worldly power* (Atlantic). **2** of burial: *sepulchral ceremonies.* **SYN:** funeral. **3** *Figurative.* deep and gloomy; dismal; suggesting a tomb: *sepulchral darkness. He heard his own name spoken in the hollow, sepulchral tones of death* (James Fenimore Cooper). **SYN:** funereal. —**se|pul′chral|ly,** *adv.*

**sep|ul|chre** (sep′əl kər), *n., v.t.,* **-chred, -chring.** = sepulcher.

**sep|ul|ture** (sep′əl chər), *n.* **1** = burial. **2** *Archaic.* a place of burial; sepulcher. [< Old French *sepulture,* learned borrowing from Latin *sepultūra* < *sepelīre* to bury]

**seq.,** **1** sequel. **2** the following (Latin, *sequens*).

**seqq.,** the following (items) (Latin, *sequentia*).

**se|qua|cious** (si kwā′shəs), *adj.* **1** proceeding smoothly and regularly: *a sequacious argument.* **2** disposed to follow, especially in a slavish or unreasoning manner. **3** following. [< Latin *sequāx, -ācis* a follower, one following (< *sequī* to follow) + English *-ous*] —**se|qua′cious|ly,** *adv.* —**se|qua′cious|ness,** *n.*

**se|quac|i|ty** (si kwas′ə tē), *n.* **1** the quality or condition of being sequacious. **2** *Obsolete.* ductility; pliability (of matter).

**se|quel** (sē′kwəl), *n.* **1** that which follows; continuation: *She referred to the expected decease of her mother, and the gloomy sequel of funeral rites* (Charlotte Brontë). **2** something that follows as a result of some earlier happening; result of something; outcome: *Among the sequels of the party were many stomachaches. Our dreams are the sequel of our waking knowledge* (Emerson). **SYN:** consequence. **3** a complete story continuing an earlier one about the same people: *Robert Louis Stevenson's "David Balfour" is a sequel to his "Kidnapped."* **4** *Obsolete.* an inference. [< Old French *sequelle,* learned borrowing from Latin *sequēla* < *sequī* to follow]

**se|que|la** (si kwē′lə), *n., pl.* **-lae** (-lē). **1** a thing following or resulting: *I was just getting into the inevitable simmering sequelae of ripostes to the editor* (New Yorker). **2** a disease or abnormal condition which is the result of a previous disease. [< Latin *sequēla* sequel]

**se|quence** (sē′kwəns), *n., v.,* **-quenced, -quenc|ing.** —*n.* **1** the act or fact of coming one after another; succession; order of succession: *Arrange the names in alphabetical sequence. By using the method of priority and sequence a good deal can be learned about how much mechanical invention influences social change* (Ogburn and Nimkoff). **SYN:** See syn. under **series.** **2** a connected series: *a sequence of lessons on one subject.* **3** something that follows; result: *Crime has its sequence of misery.* **4** a set of three or more playing cards of the same suit following one after another in order of value. **5a** part of a motion picture consisting of an episode without breaks. **b** any group of scenes of a motion picture taken as a unit. **6** *Music.* a series of melodic or harmonic phrases repeated three or more times at successive pitches upward or downward. **7** *Mathematics.* a set of quantities or elements whose order corresponds to the natural order of whole numbers. *Example:* ½, ¼, ⅛, 1/16 ... **8** Also, **Sequence.** a hymn sung after the Gradual and before the Gospel in the Roman Catholic Church.
—*v.t.* to work out the sequence of; arrange in order or sequence: *to sequence computer data. The techniques for sequencing nucleic acids are now available* (New Scientist).
[< Late Latin *sequentia* < Latin *sequēns;* see etym. under **sequent**]

**se|quenc|er** (sē′kwən sər), *n.* a device that determines or regulates a sequence, such as an electronic device on a space vehicle.

**se|quen|cy** (sē′kwən sē), *n.* consecutiveness: *a want of sequency in the narrative of events* (J. W. Donaldson).

**se|quent** (sē′kwənt), *adj., n.* —*adj.* **1** following; subsequent: *a sequent king.* **2** following in order; consecutive: *The galleys have sent a dozen sequent messengers ... at one another's heels* (Shakespeare). **SYN:** successive. **3** following as a result; consequent.
—*n.* that which follows; result; consequence. **SYN:** sequel.
[< Latin *sequēns, -entis,* present participle of *sequī* to follow]

**se|quen|tial** (si kwen′shəl), *adj., n.* —*adj.* **1** forming a sequence or connected series; characterized by a regular sequence of parts. **2** = sequent. **3** (of contraceptive pills) taken in a particular sequence to eliminate side effects.
—*n.* **sequentials,** *pl.* sequential pills: *Some are combinations in which both the estrogen and the progestin are taken for 21 days a month; others are "sequentials," in which the estrogen alone is taken for 14 to 16 days, and estrogen with progestin for five or six* (Time).
—**se|quen′tial|ly,** *adv.*

**se|ques|ter** (si kwes′tər), *v., n.* —*v.t.* **1a** to remove or withdraw from public use or from public view; seclude: *The shy old lady sequestred herself from all strangers.* **b** to keep (something or someone) apart from all others; isolate: *The virtue of art lies in detachment, in sequestering one object from the embarrassing variety* (Emerson). **2** to take away (property) for a time from an owner until a debt is paid or some claim is satisfied. **3** to seize by authority; take and keep: *The soldiers sequestered food from the people they conquered.* **SYN:** confiscate. **4** *Chemistry.* to prevent precipitation of (metallic ions) in solution by the addition of a chemical compound.
—*n. Obsolete.* a withdrawal or separation; sequestration: *This hand of yours requires A sequester from liberty* (Shakespeare).
[< Latin *sequestrāre* place in safekeeping < *sequester, -trī* trustee, mediator; (originally) following, interposing, related to *sequī* to follow]

**se|ques|tered** (si kwes′tərd), *adj.* **1** withdrawn; secluded. **2** living in retirement or seclusion.

**se|ques|tra|ble** (si kwes′trə bəl), *adj.* that can be sequestered; separable.

**se|ques|trant** (si kwes′trənt), *n.* a chemical compound that takes away or prevents the usual precipitation reactions of metallic ions in solution: *Many of the most common and most easily obtainable sequestrants are designed to soften water by pre-empting calcium and magnesium salts* (Newsweek).

**se|ques|trate** (si kwes′trāt), *v.t.,* **-trat|ed, -trat|ing.** **1** = confiscate. **2** *Archaic.* to sequester.

**se|ques|tra|tion** (sē′kwes trā′shən, si kwes′-), *n.* **1a** the act of seizing and holding property until a debt is paid or legal claims are satisfied. **b** a writ authorizing this. **2** forcible or authorized seizure; confiscation: *His former delinquencies ... were severely punished by fine and sequestration* (Scott). **3** separation or withdrawal from others; seclusion.

**se|ques|tra|tor** (sē′kwes trā′tər, si kwes′trā-), *n.* **1** a person who holds property in trust when there are outstanding claims. **2** a person authorized to collect and administer the income of a sequestrated estate. **3** a person who sets apart; separator.

**se|ques|trum** (si kwes′trəm), *n., pl.* **-tra** (-trə). a dead part of bone separated from the living part, as in necrosis. [< New Latin *sequestrum* < Latin, a separation, neuter of *sequester;* see etym. under **sequester**]

**se|quin** (sē′kwin), *n.* **1** a small spangle used to ornament dresses, scarfs, or other clothing: *An evening sheath of black marquisette, whose skirt is spangled with black sequins* (New Yorker). **2** a former Italian and Turkish gold coin, worth about $2.25. [< French *sequin* < Italian *zecchino* < *zecca* a mint < Arabic *sikka* a die used in minting]

**se|quined** or **se|quinned** (sē′kwind), *adj.* ornamented with sequins: *a sequined dress.*

**se|qui|tur** (sek′wə tər), *n.* an inference or conclusion that follows from the premises: ... *a mad rhetorician of many words and few sequiturs* (New Yorker). [abstracted from *non sequitur*]

**se|quoi|a** (si kwoiʹə), *n.* either of two kinds of very tall evergreen trees of California that belong to the taxodium family: **a** = redwood (def. 1a). **b** = giant sequoia. [American English < New Latin *Sequoia* the genus name < *Sequoya* < Muskogean (Cherokee) *Sikwayi*, the Cherokee Indian who invented the Cherokee system of writing]

**ser** (sir), *n.* a weight of India, officially about 2 pounds but varying according to locality. Also, **seer.** [earlier *seer* < Hindi *ser* (in Prakrit, a kind of measure), probably ultimately < Sanskrit *kṣetra* field]

**ser.,** 1 series. 2 sermon.

**se|ra** (sirʹə), *n.* serums; a plural of **serum**: *Future work ... will also be directed towards the production of immune sera* (New Scientist).

**se|rac** (sā rakʹ), *n.* a large block or pinnaclelike mass of ice on a glacier, formed by the intersection of two or more crevasses. [< Swiss French *sérac*]

**se|ra|glio** (sə ralʹyō, -rälʹ-), *n., pl.* **-glios.** 1 the women's quarters of a Moslem house or palace; harem. SYN: zenana. 2 a Turkish palace. [< Italian *serraglio* (influenced by *serrare* to close, lock up, ultimately < Latin *sera* bar, bolt) < Turkish *saray*; see etym. under **serai**]

**Ser|a|hu|li** (serʹə hüʹlē, -wüʹ-), *n., pl.* **-li** or **-lis.** = Sarakole.

**se|rai** (sə rīʹ, -räʹē), *n.* 1 (in Eastern countries) a hotel for caravans or an inn for travelers. 2 = seraglio. [< Turkish *saray* palace, lodging < Persian *serāī*]

**se|rail** (sə rālʹ), *n.* = seraglio.

**ser|al** (sirʹəl), *adj.* of or having to do with an ecological sere. [< *sere*[2] + *al*[1]]

**se|rang** (sə rangʹ), *n.* an Indian or Pakistani head of a lascar crew, similar to a boatswain in status and duties or sometimes employed in an engine room. [Anglo-Indian < Persian *sarhang* commander]

***se|ra|pe** (sə räʹpē), *n.* a shawl or blanket, often striped in bright colors, worn by Spanish Americans. Also, **sarape.** [American English < Mexican Spanish *serape*, or *sarape*]

***serape**

**ser|aph** (serʹəf), *n., pl.* **-aphs** or **-a|phim.** 1 one of the highest order of angels, of a warm, loving nature: *With a love that the winged seraphs of Heaven coveted her and me ...* (Edgar Allan Poe). 2 one of the six-winged celestial beings seen hovering above the throne of God in Isaiah's vision (in the Bible, Isaiah 6:2). [new singular < *seraphim*, plural, Old English *seraphim* < Late Latin *seraphīm* < Greek *serapheím* < Hebrew *såråfim*]

**se|raph|ic** (sə rafʹik), *adj.* 1 of seraphs. 2 *Figurative: At the royal palace, his fingertips pressed together in the customary seraphic greeting, [he] played benign host* (Time) SYN: angelic. — **se-raphʹi|cal|ly,** *adv.*

**se|raph|i|cal** (sə rafʹə kəl), *adj.* = seraphic.

**ser|a|phim** (serʹə fim), *n.* seraphs; a plural of **seraph.**

**Se|rap|ic** (sə rapʹik), *adj.* of or having to do with Serapis.

**Se|ra|pis** (sə rāʹpis), *n.* an Egyptian god of the lower world, whose worship was a combination of Egyptian and Greek cults.

**ser|as|kier** (serʹə skirʹ), *n.* a Turkish general, especially the commander in chief. [< Turkish *seraskier* < Persian *ser* head + Arabic *'askar* army]

**ser|a|weel** (serʹə wēlʹ), *n.* loose, wide trousers tied at the waist with a sash, worn by men and women in northern Africa. [< Arabic *sarāwīl*, *sirwīl* trousers]

**Serb** (sėrb), *n., adj.* — *n.* 1 a person born or living in Serbia. 2 the language of Serbia; Serbo-Croatian.
— ***adj.*** of Serbia, its people, or their language. [< Serbian *srb*]

**Serb.,** 1 Serbia. 2 Serbian.

**Ser|bi|an** (sėrʹbē ən), *adj., n.* — ***adj.*** of Serbia, its people, or their language.
— *n.* = Serb.

**Ser|bo-Cro|at** (sėrʹbō krōʹat), *adj., n.* = Serbo-Croatian.

**Ser|bo-Cro|a|tian** (sėrʹbō krō āʹshən), *adj., n.* — ***adj.*** 1 both Serbian and Croatian. 2 of or having to do with Serbo-Croatian or the Serbo-Croatians.
— *n.* 1 the branch of the Slavic language spoken by Serbs and Croats of Yugoslavia, usually written in the Cyrillic alphabet in Serbia and in the Roman alphabet in Croatia. 2 a person whose native language is Serbo-Croatian.

**Ser|bo|ni|an bog** (sər bōʹnē ən), any difficult or embarrassing situation from which it is almost impossible to free oneself; distracting state of affairs. [< Greek *Serbōnis* (*límnē*) (lake) Serbonis, in Egypt, in which armies are said to have been swallowed up + English *-ian*]

**ser|dab** (sėrʹdab, sėr dabʹ), *n.* 1 (in western Asia) a cellar or underground chamber. 2 (formerly in Egypt) a narrow chamber in a tomb, holding a statue of the dead person. [< Arabic *serdāb* < Persian]

**sere**[1] (sir), *adj.* dried up; withered; sear: *the sere valleys of eastern Kentucky* (Atlantic). ... *sere, withered little men* (New Yorker). [variant of *sear*[1]]

**sere**[2] (sir), *n.* the complete series of ecological communities occupying a given area over a period of hundreds or thousands of years from the initial to the final or climax stage. [< *series*; perhaps influenced by Latin *serere* join, connect]

**se|reh** (sēʹre), *n.* a serious disease of sugar cane which attacks and destroys the entire grass. It is especially common in India and the Malay Archipelago. [< a native name]

**se|rein** (sə raɴʹ), *n.* a fine rain falling from an apparently clear sky, especially after sunset. The clouds may be too thin to be seen, or may be to the windward side. [< French *serein*, ultimately < Latin *sērum* evening, neuter of *sērus* late]

**ser|e|nade** (serʹə nādʹ), *n., v.,* **-nad|ed, -nad|ing.** — *n.* 1 music played or sung outdoors at night, especially by a lover under his sweetheart's window. 2 a piece of music suitable for such a performance. 3 *Music.* a work of four to eight connected instrumental movements, usually written for a small orchestra.
— *v.t.* to sing or play a serenade to.
— *v.i.* to sing or play a serenade.
[< French *sérénade* < Italian *serenata* < Latin *serēnus* serene; influenced by Italian *sera* evening < Latin *sērus* late]

**ser|e|nad|er** (serʹə nāʹdər), *n.* a person who serenades.

**ser|e|na|ta** (serʹə näʹtə), *n., pl.* **-tas, -te** (-tā). 1 a cantata, usually pastoral or dramatic. 2 a serenade for a small orchestra. [< Italian *serenata*; see etym. under **serenade**]

**ser|en|dip|i|tist** (serʹən dipʹə tist), *n.* 1 a person who believes in or hopes to find things by serendipity. 2 = serendipper.

**ser|en|dip|i|tous** (serʹən dipʹə təs), *adj.* having to do with, resulting from, or characterized by serendipity: *As a serendipitous by-product of volcano research, scientists have found new fresh-water sources* (Time). — **serʹen|dipʹi|tous|ly,** *adv.*

**ser|en|dip|i|ty** (serʹən dipʹə tē), *n.* 1 *no pl.* the ability to make fortunate discoveries by accident, such as finding interesting items of information or unexpected proof of one's theories, while looking for something else; discovery of things not sought. 2 *pl.* **-ties.** something found by a lucky accident; a chance discovery: *We look forward ... to Christmas serendipities of the kind the city has brought us in the past* (New Yorker). [(coined by Horace Walpole) < "The Three Princes of *Serendip*" (old name of Ceylon), a fairy tale whose heroes made such discoveries]

**ser|en|dip|per** (serʹən dipʹər), *n.* a person who has the gift of serendipity or who finds things unsought. [probably back formation < *serendipity*]

**se|rene** (sə rēnʹ), *adj., n.* — ***adj.*** 1 peaceful; calm; tranquil: *serene happiness, a serene smile. He kept serene and calm, by ... knowing nothing of the dangers which surrounded him* (Daniel Defoe). SYN: placid, untroubled. See syn. under **peaceful.** 2 not cloudy; clear and pleasant: *a serene sky. One serene and moonlight night, when all the waves rolled by like scrolls of silver ...* (Herman Melville). 3 bright; clear and fine: *Full many a gem of purest ray serene ...* (Thomas Gray).
— *n. Poetic.* 1 an expanse of clear sky or calm sea: *The bark that plows the deep serene ...* (William Cowper). 2 serene condition; serenity: *that unhoped serene, That men call age* (Rupert Brooke).
[< Latin *serēnus*] — **se|reneʹly,** *adv.* — **se|reneʹness,** *n.*

**Se|rene** (sə rēnʹ), *adj.* having the title of Serenity: *His Serene Highness, His Serene Majesty, Charles II.*

**se|ren|i|ty** (sə renʹə tē), *n., pl.* **-ties.** 1 quiet peace; peacefulness; calmness: *He was always a cool man; nothing could disturb his serenity* (Mark Twain). SYN: tranquillity, placidity. 2 clearness; brightness.

**Se|ren|i|ty** (sə renʹə tē), *n., pl.* **-ties.** a title of honor given to reigning princes and other dignitaries: *His Serenity, the Pope.*

**Se|rer** (sā rārʹ), *n., pl.* **-rer** or **-rers.** 1 a member of a native tribe of Senegal, consisting mainly of farmers. 2 the West Atlantic language of this tribe.

**serf** (sėrf), *n.* 1 a peasant in the feudal system midway between a freeman and a slave: *The serf was a bondman, generally bound to the soil, and required to provide certain payments and services to his lord ... but by custom, the serf enjoyed certain rights* (Bryce Lyon). 2 *Figurative.* a person treated almost like a slave; person who is mistreated or underpaid. A serf has little or no hope of advancement, change, or the like. 3 *Obsolete.* a slave. [< Old French *serf* < Latin *servus* slave] — **serfʹlikeʹ,** *adj.*

**serf|age** (sėrʹfij), *n.* 1 the condition of a serf. 2 the serf system. 3 the serf class.

**serf|dom** (sėrfʹdəm), *n.* 1 the condition of a serf: *Break up ere long The serfdom of this world!* (Elizabeth Barrett Browning). 2 the custom of having serfs or people treated almost like slaves. Serfdom existed all over Europe in the Middle Ages and lasted in Russia until the middle 1800's. (*Figurative.*) *The Soviet rulers are learning from experience that serfdom is not a profitable method of production* (Wall Street Journal).

**serf|hood** (sėrfʹhůd), *n.* the condition of a serf.

**serg.** or **Serg.,** sergeant.

**serge** (sėrj), *n.* a kind of cloth woven with slanting lines or ridges in it. Worsted serge is used for coats and suits. Silk serge is used for linings. [Old French *serge* < Vulgar Latin *sārica*, variant of Latin *sērica* (*vestis*) silken (garment), feminine of *sēricus* < Greek *sērikós* silken; Chinese < *Sēres* the Chinese (because they are thought to be the originators of silk)]

**ser|gean|cy** (särʹjən sē), *n., pl.* **-cies.** the position, rank, or duties of a sergeant.

**ser|geant** (särʹjənt), *n.* 1 a noncommissioned military officer of a grade higher than corporal or an equivalent rank, especially: **a** (in the U.S. Army and Marine Corps) a noncommissioned officer ranking next above a corporal and next below a staff sergeant. **b** (in the U.S. Air Force) a noncommissioned officer ranking next above an airman first class and next below a staff sergeant. 2 a police officer ranking next above a patrolman, constable, trooper, or other ordinary policeman. A sergeant ranks next below a lieutenant or captain. *Abbr:* Sgt. 3 = sergeant at arms. 4 = sergeant-at-law. 5 *Obsolete.* an attendant; servant, as of a soldier. 6 *Obsolete.* an officer of the court who arrested offenders, issued summonses, and enforced court orders: *This fell sergeant, death, Is strict in his arrest* (Shakespeare). 7 *Especially British, Obsolete.* a person below a knight, and holding land in return for military service. Also, *British,* **serjeant.** [Middle English *sergeaunte* < Old French *sergent, serjent* < Latin *serviēns, -entis* serving (in Late Latin, a public official), present participle of *servīre* to serve < *servus* slave]

**sergeant at arms,** or **ser|geant-at-arms** (särʹjənt ət ärmzʹ), *n., pl.* **sergeants at arms, sergeants-at-arms.** an officer who keeps order, as in a legislature or law court.

**ser|geant-at-law** (särʹjənt ət lôʹ), *n., pl.* **sergeants-at-law.** (formerly) a barrister of superior rank in England.

**sergeant first class,** a noncommissioned officer in the U.S. Army, ranking next below a master sergeant and next above a staff sergeant. *Abbr:* Sfc.

**sergeant fish,** 1 a large, semitropical marine fish with spiny fins and a black stripe along its side, similar to a mackerel; cobia. 2 = robalo.

**sergeant major,** *pl.* **sergeants major.** 1 the highest-ranking noncommissioned officer in the U.S. Army and Marine Corps. *Abbr:* Sgt. Maj. 2 a sergeant who assists an adjutant at an army or air force headquarters: *A former commando sergeant major ... He looked too lawless for any policeman* (Geoffrey Household). *Abbr:* Sgt. Maj. 3 a damselfish of tropical American waters; pintano.

**ser|geant|ship** (särʹjənt ship), *n.* the position, rank, or duties of a sergeant.

**Pronunciation Key:** hat, āge, cãre, fär; let, ēqual, tėrm; it, īce; hot, ōpen, ôrder; oil, out; cup, pu̇t, rüle; child; long; thin; ᴛʜen; zh, measure; ə represents a in about, e in taken, i in pencil, o in lemon, u in circus.

**ser|geant|y** (sär′jən tē), *n., pl.* **-geant|ies.** a form of feudal tenure in England for some personal service to the king. Also, *British,* **serjeanty.** [< Old French *sergentie* < *sergent;* see etym. under **sergeant**]

**sergt.** or **Sergt.**, sergeant.

**se|ri|al** (sir′ē əl), *n., adj.* — *n.* **1** a story published, broadcast, or televised one part at a time: *The film is an extension of the popular television serial* (Sunday Times). **2** a report published like a serial, especially at long intervals; periodical.
— *adj.* **1** published, broadcast, or televised one part at a time: *a serial publication, a serial story.* **2** of a series; arranged in a series; making a series: *Place volumes 1 to 5 on the shelf in serial order.* **3** of serials; having to do with a serial: *the serial rights of a novel.* **4** *Music.* twelve-tone.
[< New Latin *serialis* < Latin *seriēs* series]

**se|ri|al|ise** (sir′ē ə līz), *v.t.,* **-ised, -is|ing.** *Especially British.* serialize.

**se|ri|al|ism** (sir′ē əl iz əm), *n.* the twelve-tone system or technique of atonal music.

**se|ri|al|ist** (sir′ē ə list), *n., adj.* — *n.* **1** a writer of serials. **2** a composer or musician who uses the serial technique. — *adj.* = serialistic.

**se|ri|al|is|tic** (sir′ē ə lis′tik), *adj.* of serialism; twelve-tone.

**se|ri|al|i|ty** (sir′ē al′ə tē), *n.* serial character; occurrence or arrangement in a series.

**se|ri|al|i|za|tion** (sir′ē ə lə zā′shən), *n.* publication in serial form.

**se|ri|al|ize** (sir′ē ə līz), *v.t.,* **-ized, -iz|ing. 1** to publish, broadcast, or televise in a series of installments: *Gordon's Monthly was serializing the novel in America* (Arnold Bennett). **2** to arrange in a series.

**se|ri|al|ly** (sir′ē ə lē), *adv.* in a series; as a serial.

**serial number,** a number given to one of a series of persons or things, as a means of identification. Every dollar bill has a serial number.

**serial position effect,** *Psychology.* the effect which the position of an item has on the learning or remembering of a list of items. An item near the beginning or end of a list will be remembered with greater ease than one that is near the middle.

**se|ri|ar|y** (sir′ē er′ē), *adj.* of, having to do with, or belonging in a series.

**se|ri|ate** (*adj.* sir′ē it, -āt; *v.* sir′ē āt), *adj., v.,* **-at|ed, -at|ing.** — *adj.* arranged or occurring in one or more series or rows. — *v.t.* to put into the form of a series. — **se′ri|ate|ly,** *adv.*

**se|ri|a|tim** (sir′ē ā′tim, ser′-), *adv., adj.* — *adv.* in a series; one after the other: *This question subdivides into several questions, which we will consider seriatim* (Herbert Spencer).
— *adj.* following one after the other; arranged in a series: *There are places where force would be lost by dividing it into two or three successive and seriatim sentences* (John Earle).
[< Medieval Latin *seriatim* < Latin *seriēs* series]

**se|ri|a|tion** (sir′ē ā′shən, ser′-), *n.* **1** formation of or into a series. **2** *Archaeology.* a method of arranging artifacts from a particular civilization in a sequence to show the changes in style that reflect the cultural change: *Behind the fragments is a seriation diagram, in which the relative abundance of each kind of pottery is plotted against time* (Scientific American).

**se|ri|ceous** (sə rish′əs), *adj.* **1a** made of silk. **b** like silk. **2** covered with fine, silky hairs. [< Late Latin *sēriceus* (with English *-ous*) < Latin *sēricus* silken; see etym. under **serge**]

**ser|i|ci|cul|tur|al** (ser′ə si kul′chər əl), *adj.* = sericultural.

**ser|i|ci|cul|ture** (ser′ə si kul′chər), *n.* = sericulture.

**ser|i|ci|cul|tur|ist** (ser′ə si kul′chər ist), *n.* = sericulturist.

**ser|i|cin** (ser′ə sin), *n.* the gelatinous element of raw silk. [< Latin *sēricum* silk, neuter of *sēricus* (see etym. under **serge**) + English *-in*]

**ser|i|cite** (ser′ə sīt), *n.* a variety of muscovite with a silky luster, occurring in fine scales of greenish- or yellowish-white color. [< Latin *sēricum* silk + English *-ite*[1]]

**ser|i|cit|i|za|tion** (ser′ə sī′tə zā′shən), *n.* the alteration of a mineral or rock to sericite.

**ser|ic|te|ri|um** (ser′ik tir′ē əm), *n., pl.* **-te|ri|a** (-tir′ē ə). a glandular apparatus in insects, especially silkworms, for the secretion of silk. [< New Latin *serícterium* < Latin *sēricum* silk]

**se|ric|ter|y** (sə rik′tər ē), *n., pl.* **-ter|ies.** = sericterium.

**ser|i|cul|tur|al** (ser′ə kul′chər əl), *adj.* **1** of or having to do with sericulture. **2** engaged in sericulture.

**ser|i|cul|ture** (ser′ə kul′chər), *n.* the breeding and care of silkworms for the production of raw silk. [short for French *sériciculture* < Latin *sēricum* silk (see etym. under **serge**) + *cultūra* culture]

**ser|i|cul|tur|ist** (ser′ə kul′chər ist), *n.* a person who raises silkworms or who studies them.

**ser|i|e|ma** (ser′ē ē′mə, -ā′-), *n.* **1** a large, long-legged, crested screamer (bird), found especially in Brazil. **2** a somewhat smaller related bird, found especially in Argentina. [earlier *çariama* < New Latin *Cariama* the genus name < Tupi (Brazil) *sarīa* the native name]

**se|ries** (sir′ēz), *n., pl.* **-ries,** *adj.* — *n.* **1** a number of things alike in a row: *A series of rooms opened off the hall.* **2** a number of things placed one after another: *names in alphabetical series. There were a series of strange objects on the teacher's desk.* **3** a number of things or events coming one after the other; succession: *a series of experiments. A series of rainy days spoiled their vacation. He wrote a series of books about Eskimo life. My favorite television series is a weekly show called "The Robot Squad."* **4** coins, stamps, or the like, as of a particular issue, ruler, or country. **5** written or artistic works that are produced one after another, usually having a common subject or purpose, and often by a single author, artist, or composer: *The so-called "series books" are often helpful in breaking the ice for the reluctant reader* (Sidonie M. Gruenberg). **6** an electrical arrangement in which a number of batteries, capacitors, or other devices are connected so that a current flows in turn through each one: *wires connecting batteries in series, magnets placed in series.* **7** *Mathematics.* **a** a succession of terms related by some law, and consequently predictable. 2 + 4 + 6 + 8 + 10 is an arithmetic series; each term of the series is formed by adding 2 to the preceding term. **b** the summing of the terms of a sequence. *Example:* ½ + ¼ + ⅛ + 1⁄16 + .... **8** *Geology.* a division of rocks ranking below a system, containing the rocks formed during a geological epoch. **9** *Chemistry.* a number of elements or compounds having common properties or relations. **10** a group of elements of a sentence written one after another. **11** *Sports.* a group or set of consecutive games. *Abbr:* ser.
— *adj.* having the components joined so that electric current flows in turn through one component of a circuit to the next, each component completing a part of the circuit: *a series circuit.*

**the Series,** *U.S. Informal.* the world series: *People have been known to smuggle radios onto the [stock exchange] floor during the Series* (Wall Street Journal).
[< Latin *seriēs* < *serere* to join]
— *Syn. n.* **1 Series, sequence, succession** mean a number of things, events, or people, arranged or coming one after another in some order. **Series** applies to a number of similar things with the same purpose or relation to each other: *She gave a series of lectures on Mexico.* **Sequence** implies a closer or unbroken connection in thought, between cause and effect, or in numerical or alphabetical order: *He reviewed the sequence of events leading to the discovery.* **Succession** emphasizes following in order of time, sometimes of place, usually without interruption: *He had a succession of illnesses.*
▶ **series.** Commas are used between the items of a series of three or more short items. Usage generally favors omitting a comma before *and* preceding the last item of the series: *pen, ink and paper* or *pen, ink, and paper.*

**series dynamo** or **generator,** a series-wound generator.

**series motor,** a series-wound motor.

**series turn,** any one of the ampere turns in a series winding.

**series winding,** *Electricity.* the act or process of winding a motor or generator whereby the field magnet coils are connected in series with the armature and carry the same current.

**se|ries-wound** (sir′ēz wound′), *adj. Electricity.* that has series winding: *a series-wound motor.*

***ser|if** (ser′if), *n.* a thin or smaller line used to finish off a main stroke of a letter, as at the top and bottom of *I* and *M,* or ending the cross stroke in *T.* [probably < Dutch *schreef* line, stroke]

*** serif**

**se|rif|ic** (sə rif′ik), *adj.* having to do with the making of silk threads: *the serific glands of a silkworm.* [< Latin *sēri*(cum) + English *-fic*]

**ser|i|graph** (ser′ə graf, -gräf), *n.* a color print made by serigraphy.

**se|rig|ra|pher** (sə rig′rə fər), *n.* a person who makes serigraphs; one who uses serigraphy.

**ser|i|graph|ic** (ser ə graf′ik), *adj.* of or having to do with serigraphy; silk-screen.

**se|rig|ra|phy** (sə rig′rə fē), *n.* the art of producing handmade prints in several colors by pressing oil paint or similar pigment through a series of silk screens. [< Latin *sēricum* silk, neuter of *sēricus* (see etym. under **serge**) + English *-graphy*]

**ser|in**[1] (ser′in), *n.* a small finch of central and southern Europe, closely related to the canary. [< French *serin* canary; origin uncertain]

**ser|in**[2] (ser′in, sir′-), *n.* = serine.

**ser|ine** (ser′ēn, -in; sir′-), *n.* a colorless, crystalline compound, an amino acid, present in many proteins or produced synthetically. *Formula:* $C_3H_7NO_3$ [< *ser*(um) + *-ine*[2]]

**se|rin|ga** (sə ring′gə), *n.* **1** any one of a group of Brazilian trees of the spurge family, which yield rubber. **2** = syringa (def. 1). [< French *seringa* < New Latin *syringa* syringa]

**se|ri|o|com|e|dy** (sir′ē ō kom′ə dē), *n., pl.* **-dies.** a seriocomic play or incident.

**se|ri|o|com|ic** (sir′ē ō kom′ik), *adj.* partly serious and partly comic: *Irony ... assumes that man is a seriocomic animal* (James Harvey Robinson). [< *serio*(us) + *comic*] — **se′ri|o|com′i|cal|ly,** *adv.*

**se|ri|o|com|i|cal** (sir′ē ō kom′ə kəl), *adj.* = seriocomic.

**se|ri|ous** (sir′ē əs), *adj.* **1a** showing deep thought or purpose; thoughtful; grave: *a serious manner, a serious face.* **SYN:** solemn, sober. See syn. under **grave. b** thought-provoking; not superficial: *a serious style of writing. The symphonic upswing reflects to some extent a general increase in interest in serious music* (Wall Street Journal). **2** in earnest; not fooling; sincere: *Are you joking or serious?* **3a** needing thought; important: *Choice of one's lifework is a serious matter.* **SYN:** weighty, momentous. **b** significant; large; considerable: *to take a serious part in the negotiations.* **4** important because it may do much harm; dangerous: *a serious illness. The badly injured man was in serious condition. We live in serious times* (James Fenimore Cooper). **SYN:** critical, alarming. [< Late Latin *sēriōsus* < Latin *sērius* earnest] — **se′ri|ous|ly,** *adv.* — **se′ri|ous|ness,** *n.*

**se|ri|ous-mind|ed** (sir′ē əs mīn′did), *adj.* earnest; having serious intentions. — **se′ri|ous-mind′ed|ly,** *adv.* — **se′ri|ous-mind′ed|ness,** *n.*

**ser|jeant** (sär′jənt), *n. British.* sergeant.

**ser|jeant|y** (sär′jən tē), *n., pl.* **-jeant|ies.** *British.* sergeanty.

**ser|mon** (sėr′mən), *n., v.* — *n.* **1** a public talk on religion or something connected with religion. Ministers preach sermons in church. *A sermon requires meditation, leisure, and a certain loneliness* (J. W. R. Scott). **2** *Figurative.* **a** a serious talk about morals, conduct, or duty: *After the guests left, the boy got a sermon on table manners from his father.* **b** a long, tiresome speech; harangue.
— *v.t.* to preach to; sermonize: *Come, sermon me no further* (Shakespeare). *Black-flagged orators ... sermoned me through to guilt and the Irish Trinity* (John Ciardi).
[< Latin *sermō, -ōnis* a talk; (originally) a stringing together of words, perhaps < *serere* join]
— **ser′mon|like′,** *adj.*

**ser|mon|ette** or **ser|mon|et** (sėr′mə net′), *n.* a short sermon: (*Figurative.*) *His conversations also ranged far and wide, including a sermonette on the hazards of jaywalking* (Time).

**ser|mon|ic** (sėr mon′ik), *adj.* of, having to do with, or like a sermon. — **ser|mon′i|cal|ly,** *adv.*

**ser|mon|i|cal** (sėr mon′ə kəl), *adj.* = sermonic.

**ser|mon|ise** (sėr′mə nīz), *v.i., v.t.,* **-ised, -is|ing.** *Especially British.* sermonize.

**ser|mon|ize** (sėr′mə nīz), *v.,* **-ized, -iz|ing.** — *v.i.* to give a sermon; preach: *... recalling a time when preachers sermonized against jazz in the churches* (Harper's).
— *v.t.* to preach to: (*Figurative.*) *I see no right you have to sermonize me* (Charlotte Brontë). **SYN:** lecture. — **ser′mon|iz′er,** *n.*

**ser|mon|ol|o|gy** (sėr′mə nol′ə jē), *n.* the art of writing and preaching sermons; homiletics.

**Sermon on the Mount,** Christ's sermon to His disciples which presents His basic teachings, as reported in the Bible in Matthew 5-7 and Luke 6: 20-49.

**sero-,** *combining form.* **1** serum: *Serodiagnosis = diagnosis by means of serums.* **2** serum and ___: *Seromucous = containing serum and mucus.*
[< Latin *serum* whey, liquid]

**se|ro|di|ag|no|sis** (sir′ō dī′əg nō′sis), *n., pl.* **-ses** (-sēz). a diagnosis by means of serums.

**se|ro|log|ic** (sir′ə loj′ik), *adj.* = serological.

**se|ro|log|i|cal** (sir′ə loj′ə kəl), *adj.* of or having to do with serology: *Serological tests and examination by electron microscope have established that the two viruses are distinct* (New Scientist).

**se|ro|log|i|cal|ly** (sir′ə loj′ə klē), *adv.* **1** in a serologic manner. **2** from the point of view of serology: *one of approximately 80 serologically* *different coatings that surround the bacteria* (Science News Letter).

**se|rol|o|gist** (si rol′ə jist), *n.* an expert in serology.

**se|rol|o|gy** (si rol′ə jē), *n.* the scientific study of the use of serums in curing or preventing disease. [< *sero-* + *-logy*]

**se|ro|mu|cous** (sir′ō myü′kəs), *adj.* **1** containing both serum and mucus. **2** of the nature of both serum and mucus.

**se|ro|mus|cu|lar** (sir′ō mus′kyə lər), *adj.* having to do with both the serous and muscular coats of the intestine.

**Se|ro|my|cin** (sir′ō mī′sin), *n. Trademark.* cycloserine.

**se|root** (sə rüt′), *n.,* or **seroot fly,** a fly of the upper Nile region whose female sucks much blood and often transmits diseases. It is related to the horsefly. [< an African word]

**se|ro|pu|ru|lent** (sir′ō pyůr′ə lənt, -yə-), *adj.* composed of serum mixed with pus.

**se|ro|sa** (si rō′sə), *n.* = serous membrane. [< New Latin *serosa* < Latin *serum* whey, liquid]

**se|ro|sal** (si rō′səl), *adj.* of or having to do with a serous membrane.

**se|ro|si|tis** (sir′ə sī′tis), *n.* inflammation of a serous membrane. [< New Latin *serositis* < *serosus* serous + English *-itis*]

**se|ros|i|ty** (si ros′ə tē), *n., pl.* **-ties. 1** a serous condition. **2** = serous fluid. [< New Latin *serositas* < *serosus* serous < Latin *serum* whey, liquid]

**se|ro|ther|a|pist** (sir′ō ther′ə pist), *n.* a person skilled in serum-therapy.

**se|ro|ther|a|py** (sir′ō ther′ə pē), *n.* = serum-therapy.

**se|rot|i|nal** (si rot′ə nəl), *adj.* = serotine[1].

**ser|o|tine[1]** (ser′ə tin, -tīn), *adj.* late blooming, developing, or appearing: *a serotine plant.* [< Latin *sērōtinus* < *sērō,* adverb < *sērus* late]

**ser|o|tine[2]** (ser′ə tin, -tīn), *n.* a small European bat that flies late in the evening. [< French *sérotine* < feminine of Latin *sērōtinus;* see etym. under **serotine[1]**]

**se|rot|i|nous** (si rot′ə nəs), *adj.* = serotine[1].

**se|ro|to|nin** (sir′ō tō′nən), *n.* a substance in the blood that causes blood vessels to constrict and aids in blood clotting; hydroxytriptamine. It is an indole, chemically related to adrenalin and hallucinogenic drugs, that also occurs in the brain and in smooth muscles of the intestines and functions in brain chemistry. *Formula:* $C_{10}H_{12}N_2O$

**se|ro|type** (ser′ə tīp), *n., v.,* **-typed, -typ|ing.** —*n.* a group of bacteria or other microorganisms that have the same combination of antigens.
—*v.i.* to type microorganisms by the set of antigens they have in common; classify according to serotype: [*Of*] *331 human cases of a particular Salmonella infection ... 271 have been traced by serotyping through the abattoir and back to the farm* (Manchester Guardian Weekly).

**se|rous** (sir′əs), *adj.* **1** of or having to do with serum. **2** like serum; watery. Tears are drops of a serous fluid. **3** producing or carrying serum. [< Middle French *séreux* (with English *-ous*) < Latin *serum* whey, liquid]

**serous fluid,** any one of various animal liquids resembling blood serum, such as the fluids of the serous membranes.

**serous membrane,** any one of various thin membranes of connective tissue, such as the peritoneum and pericardium, lining certain cavities of the body and moistened with a serous fluid.

**ser|ow** (ser′ō), *n.* any one of a group of sturdy, dark-colored, goatlike antelopes of eastern Asia. [< the native name]

**Ser|pens** (sėr′penz), *n., genitive* **Ser|pen|tis.** a long, narrow constellation on the celestial equator near Scorpio. [< Latin *Serpēns,* (originally) present participle of *serpere;* see etym. under **serpent**]

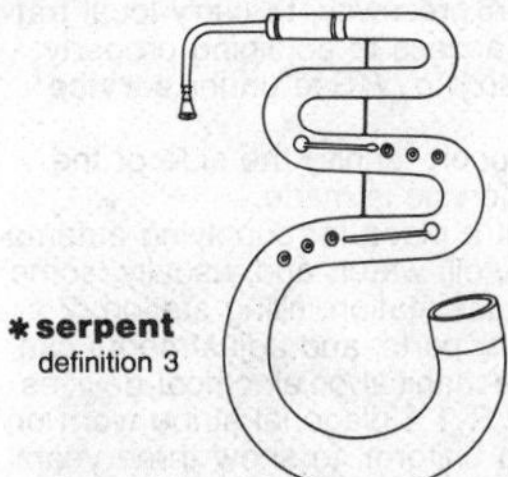

***serpent**
definition 3

***ser|pent** (sėr′pənt), *n.* **1a** a snake, especially a big snake. **b** any one of various animals in legend supposed to be like a snake in shape but usually of enormous size and often living in the sea or a lake. **2** *Figurative.* a sly, treacherous person. **3** a bass wood-wind instrument with three U-shaped turns, used especially in the 1700's and 1800's: *The fiddles finished off with a screech, and the serpent emitted a last note that nearly lifted the roof* (Thomas Hardy). **4** a firework that whizzes up with a snaky twist. **5** *Archaic.* any one of various animals thought of as creeping and dangerous, such as crocodiles or spiders. [< Latin *serpēns, -entis,* (originally) present participle of *serpere* to creep]

**Ser|pent** (sėr′pənt), *n.* the Devil; Satan (in the Bible, Genesis 3:1-13).

**ser|pen|tar|i|a** (sėr′pən tãr′ē ə), *n.* **1** the root of the Virginia snakeroot. **2** the plant itself. [< Late Latin *serpentāria* < Latin *serpēns;* see etym. under **serpent**]

**ser|pen|tar|i|um** (sėr′pən tãr′ē əm), *n., pl.* **-i|ums, -i|a** (-ē ə). a place where serpents are kept for safety or for exhibition. [New Latin *serpentarium* < Latin *serpēns, -entis* serpent]

**Serpent Bearer,** = Ophiuchus.

**serpent eagle,** a tropical hawk of Asia that lives in the tops of forest trees and lives chiefly on snakes.

**ser|pen|ti|form** (sər pen′tə fôrm), *adj.* having the form of a serpent; serpentlike.

**ser|pen|tine** (*adj., v.* sėr′pən tēn, -tīn; *n.* sėr′pəntēn), *adj., n., v.,* **-tined, -tin|ing.** —*adj.* **1** of or like a serpent. **2** twisting; winding: *the serpentine course of a creek.* **3** *Figurative.* **a** cunning; sly; treacherous: *a serpentine plot.* **b** diabolical; Satanic: *serpentine cunning.*
—*n.* **1** a greenish mineral with an oily luster, consisting chiefly of magnesium. It is sometimes spotted like a serpent's skin. Serpentine is a soft, waxy substance. *Formula:* $Mg_3Si_2O_5(OH)_4$
**2** *Figurative.* anything twisted or winding like a snake: ... *entangled in a serpentine of military red tape* (Science). *The road winds up in serpentines through woods* (London Times).
—*v.i., v.t.* to wind like a snake: *the electronic safari that serpentined through French Equatorial Africa* (Time).
[< Late Latin *serpentīnus* < Latin *serpēns;* see etym. under **serpent**] —**ser′pen|tine|ly,** *adv.*

**ser|pen|tined** (sėr′pən tēnd, -tīnd), *adj.* **1** having serpents; infested with snakes: ... *the disappearance of two other woodsmen in the alligatored and serpentined gloom* (Newsweek). **2** *Figurative.* twisted or winding like a snake: *serpentined mountain roads.*

**serpentine marble,** = verd antique (def. 1).

**ser|pen|tin|ite** (sėr′pən tē′nīt), *n.* a rock made up chiefly of the mineral serpentine.

**ser|pen|tin|ize** (sėr′pən tē′nīz), *v.t.,* **-ized, -iz|ing.** to convert into serpentine: *They* [*the rocks*] *are made of so-called serpentinite and serpentinized peridotite* (New Scientist).

**ser|pen|ti|nous** (sėr′pən tī′nəs), *adj.* of, having to do with, or like the mineral serpentine.

**Ser|pen|tis** (sėr pen′tis), *n.* genitive of **Serpens.**

**ser|pent|ry** (sėr′pən trē), *n.* serpents as a group.

**serpent star,** = brittle star.

**ser|pig|i|nous** (sər pij′ə nəs), *adj.* of or having to do with serpigo. [< Medieval Latin *serpigo, -inis* serpigo + English *-ous*] —**ser|pig′i|nous|ly,** *adv.*

**ser|pi|go** (sər pī′gō), *n.* ringworm or a similar spreading skin disease. [< Medieval Latin *serpigo, -inis* < Latin *serpere* to creep]

**ser|ra|nid** (ser′ə nid), *adj., n.* = serranoid.

**ser|ra|noid** (ser′ə noid), *adj., n.* —*adj.* of or belonging to a group of fishes with spiny fins, including the sea basses, jewfishes, and groupers.
—*n.* a serranoid fish.
[< New Latin *Serranus* the typical genus (< Latin *serra* a saw, sawfish) + English *-oid*]

***ser|rate** (ser′āt, -it), *adj., v.,* **-rat|ed, -rat|ing.** —*adj.* notched like the edge of a saw; toothed: *a serrate leaf.*
—*v.t.* to make serrate; notch like a saw.
[< Latin *serrātus* < *serra* a saw]

***serrate**

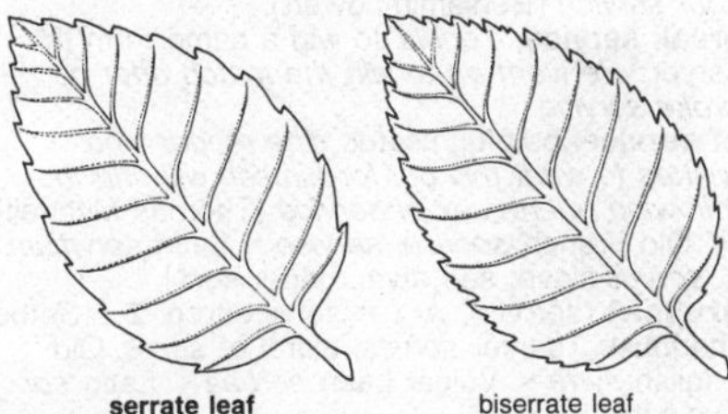

serrate leaf — biserrate leaf

**ser|rat|ed** (ser′ā tid), *adj.* = serrate.

**ser|ra|tion** (se rā′shən), *n.* **1** a serrate edge or formation. **2** one of its series of notches. **3** a serrate condition.

**ser|ra|ture** (ser′ə chər), *n.* = serration.

**ser|re|file** (ser′ə fīl), *n. Military.* any one of the men forming a line behind the last regular rank at the rear of a body of troops. [< French *serre-file* < *serrer* close up + *file* file[1]]

**serre-fine** (sãr′fēn′), *n.* a small forceps used for closing a blood vessel during an operation. [< French *serre-fine* < *serre* clamp (< *serrer* to close) + *fine* fine]

**ser|ri|corn** (ser′ə kôrn), *adj., n.* —*adj.* **1** having serrate antennae. **2** belonging to a group of beetles whose antennae are usually serrate, such as the firefly.
—*n.* a serricorn beetle.
[< New Latin *serricornis* < Latin *serra* saw + *cornū* horn]

**ser|ried[1]** (ser′ēd), *adj.* crowded closely together: *On every side rose up the serried ranks of pine trees* (Bret Harte). **SYN:** compact, dense. [adjectival use of past participle of *serry*]

**ser|ried[2]** (ser′ēd), *adj.* jagged or notched like a saw; serrate: *the serried coast.* [alteration of *serrate*]

**ser|ri|form** (ser′ə fôrm), *adj.* toothed like a saw; serrate. [< Latin *serra* saw + English *-form*]

**ser|ru|la** (ser′yə lə, ser′ə-), *n., pl.* **-lae** (-lē). *Biology.* a comblike ridge found on the appendages of arachnids, such as spiders, scorpions, and mites. [< Latin *serrula* (diminutive) < *serra* saw]

**ser|ru|late** (ser′yə lit, -lāt; ser′ə-), *adj.* very finely notched: *a serrulate leaf.* [< New Latin *serrulatus* < Latin *serrula* (diminutive) < *serra* a saw]

**ser|ru|lat|ed** (ser′yə lā′tid, ser′ə-), *adj.* = serrulate.

**ser|ru|la|tion** (ser′yə lā′shən, ser′ə-), *n.* **1** serrulate condition or form. **2** serration; one of a series of minute notches.

**ser|ry** (ser′ē), *v.,* **-ried, -ry|ing.** —*v.i.* to stand or press close: *High shoulders, low shoulders, broad shoulders, narrow ones, Round, square and angular serry and shove* (William E. Henley).
—*v.t.* to close up, especially troops in ranks: *The little band of devoted cavaliers about the king serried their forces* (Washington Irving).
[< French *serré,* past participle of *serrer* press close; fasten < Vulgar Latin *serrāre* to bar, fasten, for Latin *serāre* < *sera* a bar, bolt of a door]

**ser|tão** (ser toun′), *n. Portuguese.* back country; hinterland: *brush-covered sertão.*

**Ser|to|ma club** (sėr tō′mə), a club or association for serving the community. All Sertoma clubs are united in an international organization. [< *Ser*(vice) *to Ma*(nkind), the motto of Sertoma International]

**ser|tu|lar|i|an** (sėr′chů lãr′ē ən), *n., adj.* —*n.* any very simple invertebrate water animal or coelenterate of a group growing in branching colonies: *On what, I wondered, were these sertularians —carnivorous, like all hydroids—feeding?* (New Yorker).
—*adj.* of or having to do with a sertularian.
[< New Latin *Sertularia* the genus name < Latin *sertula* (diminutive) < *serta* garland; + English *-an*]

**ser|tu|lum** (sėr′chə ləm), *n., pl.* **-la** (-lə). selection of plants scientifically studied or described. [< New Latin *sertulum,* diminutive of Latin *sertula,* see etym. under **sertularian**]

**ser|tum** (sėr′təm), *n., pl.* **-ta** (-tə). a report or dissertation upon a collection of plants. [< unrecorded Latin *sertum,* assumed singular of *serta* garland]

**se|rum** (sir′əm), *n., pl.* **-rums** or **-ra. 1** the clear, pale-yellow liquid of the blood that separates from the clot when blood coagulates. **2** a liquid used to prevent or cure a disease, usually obtained from the blood of an animal that has been made immune to the disease. Polio vaccine and diphtheria antitoxin are serums. *Such serums, containing substances that will fight the particular diseases, are used for immunization* (Sidonie M. Gruenberg). **3** any watery liquid in animals. Lymph is a serum. **4** the watery substance of plants. **5** *Obsolete.* whey. [< Latin *serum* whey, liquid]

**se|rum|al** (sir′ə məl) *adj.* of, having to do with, or like a serum.

**serum albumin,** the albumin found in blood serum. It is the largest component of blood plasma and is a substitute for plasma.

**serum disease,** = serum sickness.

**serum globulin,** the globulin found in blood serum.

**serum hepatitis,** hepatitis caused by a virus that is carried by human blood, often accompanied by jaundice: *During World War II ... serum hepatitis was transmitted through plasma to many persons in the armed forces* (Scientific American).

**serum sickness,** illness from an abnormal sen-

**Pronunciation Key:** hat, āge, cãre, fär; let, ēqual, tėrm; it, īce; hot, ōpen, ôrder; **oi**l, **ou**t; cup, půt, rüle; **ch**ild; lo**ng**; **th**in; **ᴛʜ**en; **zh**, measure; ə represents **a** in about, **e** in taken, **i** in pencil, **o** in lemon, **u** in circus.

sitivity to an injection of animal serum.

**se|rum|ther|a|py** (sir′əm ther′ə pē), *n.* the treatment of disease by the injection of the serum of immunized animals.

**serv.**, **1** servant. **2** service.

**serv|a|ble** (sėr′və bəl), *adj.* that can be served.

**ser|val** (sėr′vəl), *n.* an African wildcat that has a brownish-yellow coat with black spots, long legs, large ears, and a ringed tail. [< New Latin *serval* the species name < French < Portuguese (*lobo*) *cerval* lynx < Latin *cervārius* (*lupus*) lynx; wolf that attacks a stag < *cervus* stag]

**serv|ant** (sėr′vənt), *n.* **1** a person employed in a household. Cooks and nursemaids are servants. SYN: domestic. **2** a person employed by another or others. Policemen and firemen are public servants. SYN: employee. **3** a person devoted to any service. Ministers are called the servants of God. (*Figurative.*) *Fire and water be good servants, but bad masters* (John Clarke). **4** (formerly) a slave: *Why don't we teach our servants to read?* (Harriet Beecher Stowe). [< Old French *servant,* present participle of *servir* serve]

**serv|ant|less** (sėr′vənt lis), *adj.* having no servant: ... *with all the mechanised comfort of the servantless American way of life* (Manchester Guardian).

**serv|ant|ship** (sėr′vənt ship), *n.* the condition of being a servant.

**serve** (sėrv), *v.,* **served, serv|ing,** *n.* **—*v.i.*** **1** to be a servant; give service; work; perform duties: *He served as butler.* **2** to perform official or public duties: *to serve in Congress. My father left work for three weeks to serve on a jury. He had served three years in the army.* **3** to wait at table; bring food or drink to guests. **4** *Figurative.* to be useful; be what is needed; be of use: *Boxes served as seats. A flat stone served as a table. Short greeting serves in time of strife* (Scott). **5** *Figurative.* to be favorable or suitable, as wind, weather, or an occasion: *The ship will sail when the time and tide serve. We must take the current when it serves, Or lose our ventures* (Shakespeare). **5** to start play by hitting the ball in tennis and similar games. **6** to act as server at Mass.

**—*v.t.*** **1** to be a servant of; give service to; work for or in: *to serve customers in a store. The slave served his master. Good citizens serve their country. In the soul Are many lesser faculties that serve Reason as chief* (Milton). **2** to honor and obey; worship: *to serve God.* **3a** to wait on at table; bring food or drink to: *The waiter served us.* **b** to put (food or drink) on the table: *The waiter served the soup. Dinner is served. They did not expect to sleep in hammocks, clean their messes ... or serve up their meals* (London Times). **4a** to supply with something needed; supply; furnish: *The dairy serves us with milk. The pump ... that serves water to his garden* (John Evelyn). **b** to supply enough for: *One pie will serve six persons.* **5** to help; aid: *Let me know if I can serve you in any way.* **6** *Figurative.* to be favorable or suitable to; satisfy; answer the requirements of: *If fortune serve me, I'll requite this kindness* (Shakespeare). **7** *Figurative.* to be useful to; fulfill: *This will serve my purpose. My stomach serves me instead of a clock* (Jonathan Swift). **8** to treat; reward: *They served me unfairly. I could ... deprive him of all his possessions and serve him as he served me* (W. H. Hudson). **9** to pass; spend; go through: *He served a term as ambassador.* [*She*] *will be released from the Federal Reformatory ... her ten-year sentence served* (Newsweek). **10a** to deliver (an order from a court, a writ, or the like). **b** to present (with an order, as from a court): *He was served with a notice to appear in court.* **11** to put (the ball) in play by hitting it in tennis and similar games. **12** to operate or be a member of the crew that operates (a cannon, machine gun, or other such mechanism). **13** *Nautical.* to bind or wind (a rope or cable) with small cord to strengthen or protect it. **14** to mate with (a female animal); cover: *Female buffaloes can be served during April, May, and June and will calve during February to April* (Science Journal).

**—*n.*** in tennis, badminton, and similar games: **1** the act or way of serving: *And an innovation this year was a so-called tennis clinic to give the spectators a better idea of ... different types of serves, volleys, lobs* (New Yorker). **2** a player's turn to serve. **3** the ball, shuttlecock, or other object served: *The serve fell over the line and was out of play.*

**serve one right,** to be just what one deserves: *Workhouse funeral—serve him right!* (Dickens). *As far as I am concerned, that will only serve the brats right* (Saturday Review).

[< Old French *servir* < Latin *servīre* (originally) be a slave < *servus* slave]

**serv|er** (sėr′vər), *n.* **1** a person who serves. **2** a tray for dishes and the like, such as a salver. **3** any one of various pieces of tableware for serving food, usually a spatula: *a cake or pie server.* **4** an attendant who serves the celebrant at low Mass: *The interview was like a ritual between priest and server* (Graham Greene). **5** the player who puts the ball in play in tennis and similar games.

**serv|er|y** (sėrv′ər ē), *n., pl.* **-er|ies.** = butler's pantry.

**Ser|vi|an** (sėr′vē ən), *adj., n.* (formerly) Serbian.

**serv|ice**[1] (sėr′vis), *n., adj., v.,* **-iced, -ic|ing.** **—*n.*** **1** a helpful act or acts; aid; being useful to others: *a neighborly service. George Washington performed many services for his country. Myriads of souls were born again to ideas of service and sacrifice in those tremendous days* (H. G. Wells). **2** arrangements for supplying something useful or necessary: *Bus service was good. A big snowstorm interrupted telephone service in the town.* **3** occupation or employment as a servant: *She is in service to a wealthy family.* **4** Usually, **services. a** a performance of duties: *She no longer needs the services of a doctor.* **b** work in the service of others; useful labor: *We pay for such services as repairs, maintenance, and utilities.* **5** advantage, benefit; use: *This coat has given me great service. Every available vehicle was pressed into service.* **6a** a department of government or public employment: *the diplomatic service.* **b** the persons working in it: *The foreign service is having a banquet tonight.* **7** the armed forces: *My brother was in the service during the last war. All the services use machines to reveal on paper the performance of guided missiles, rockets, and other new "hardware"* (Newsweek). **8** duty in the armed forces: *He was on active service during the war.* **9** Often, **services. a** a religious meeting, ritual, or ceremony, especially as worship in a prescribed form: *The marriage service was performed at the home of the bride. We attend church services twice a week.* **b** the music for those parts of a liturgy that are sung: *When the English Church became completely separate from the Roman Catholic Church, composers wrote new services and anthems for English words* (Marion Eugénie). **10** regard; respect; devotion: *Sir, my service to you* (Oliver Goldsmith). **11a** the manner of serving food: *The service in this restaurant is excellent.* **b** the food served. **12** a number of things to be used together at the table: *She has a solid silver tea service.* **13** *Law.* the serving of a process or writ upon a person. **14** in tennis and similar games: **a** the act or manner of putting the ball, shuttlecock, or other object in play: *Knight won that game and settled the set and match on his service in the next* (London Times). **b** the ball, shuttlecock, or other object, as put into play. **c** a turn at starting the ball in play. **15** *Nautical.* a small cord wound about a rope or cable, to strengthen or protect it. **16** the loading and firing of a cannon, machine gun, or other weapon, by a gun crew. **17** *Archaic.* the devotion of a lover: *So well he wooed her ... with humble service, and with daily suit* (Edmund Spenser).

**—*adj.*** **1** for use as by household servants or tradespeople: *a service pantry, a service entrance.* **2** of or belonging to a branch of the armed forces: *service insignia, a pilot's service number.* **3** used for ordinary occasions: *a service uniform.*

**—*v.t.*** **1** to make fit for service; keep fit for service: *The mechanic serviced our automobile.* **2** to provide with a service of any kind: *Only two trains a day serviced the town.* **3** to mate with (a female animal); serve.

**at one's service, a** ready to do what one wants: *My name is Matthew Bramble, at your service* (Tobias Smollett). **b** ready or available for one to use: *My means, which are certainly ample, are at your service* (Benjamin Jowett).

**break service,** *Tennis.* to win a game from the server: *He went on to win the match after he broke service.*

**of service,** helpful; useful: *The reader who wishes to work this out for himself will find the following references of service* (Thomas Mitchell).

[< Old French *service, servise* < Latin *servitium* < *servus* slave; see etym. under **serf**]

**serv|ice**[2] (sėr′vis), *n.* **1** = service tree. **2** *U.S.* the shadbush. [earlier *serves,* plural of *serve,* Old English *syrfe* < Vulgar Latin *sorbea* < Latin *sorbus* sorb]

**serv|ice|a|bil|i|ty** (sėr′vi sə bil′ə tē), *n.* the quality of being serviceable; usefulness: *One of the admirable things about ... crystal is its serviceability* (New Yorker).

**serv|ice|a|ble** (sėr′vi sə bəl), *adj.* **1** useful for a long time; able to stand much use: *a sturdy, serviceable coat. He bought a serviceable used car.* SYN: durable. **2** capable of giving good service; useful: *You are useful to Mrs. Gradgrind, and ... you are serviceable in the family also* (Dickens). SYN: helpful. **3** *Archaic.* willing to be useful: *The footmen might be aptly compared to the waiters of a tavern, if they were more serviceable* (Tobias Smollett). **—serv′ice|a|ble|ness,** *n.*

**serv|ice|a|bly** (sėr′vi sə blē), *adv.* in a serviceable manner; so as to be serviceable.

**serv|ice|ber|ry** (sėr′vis ber′ē), *n., pl.* **-ries. 1** the fruit of a service tree. **2** = shadbush.

**service board,** *Nautical.* a small grooved, flat board with a handle, used in place of a serving mallet for winding a service on small rope; serving board.

**service book,** a book containing forms for divine service, as the Book of Common Prayer of the Anglican churches.

**service box,** (in handball, rackets, squash, and other enclosed court games) the designated area in which the server must stand when putting the ball in play.

**service cap,** a military cap with a flat top and a visor, forming a standard part of the uniform of a serviceman.

**service ceiling,** the height above sea level at which an airplane is unable to climb faster than 100 feet per minute.

**service charge,** a charge made for services given, such as delivery or extension of credit: *Revolving credit plans generally involve a service charge which is based on the monthly unpaid balance* (Wall Street Journal).

**service club, 1** a club formed to promote the interests of its members and of the community, such as Rotary or Kiwanis. **2** *Especially U.S.* a recreation center for soldiers and sailors. **3** *Especially British.* a men's club of members or retired members of the armed forces.

**service command,** an administrative and tactical division of the U.S. Army corresponding to an area of the world or a section of the United States in which troops are located.

**service court,** (in tennis, handball, or other court games) the space of an opponent's court into which the ball must be served.

**service engineer,** an engineer employed by a company to install, service, and repair equipment which the company makes or sells.

**service flag,** a flag with a star for each member of a family, school, organization, or other group, serving in the U.S. Armed Forces. Service flags with blue stars for soldiers in the service and gold stars for those who died in service were frequently displayed during World War II.

**service line, 1** a line drawn across a tennis court parallel to the net and 21 feet away from it to mark off the service court. **2** a corresponding line in handball, jai alai, or other court games, drawn parallel to the wall or board.

**serv|ice|man** (sėr′vis man′, -mən), *n., pl.* **-men. 1** a member of the armed forces. **2** a person who maintains or repairs machinery or some kind of equipment: *an automobile serviceman.*

**service mark,** a mark or symbol used by a business or organization to distinguish its services from the services of others: *Service marks are to services what trademarks are to goods* (New York Times).

**service medal,** *U.S.* a medal for military service in a particular campaign or for a period of service.

**service module,** the unit or section of a spacecraft which contains the propulsion system and supplies most of the spacecraft's consumable elements, such as oxygen, water, and propellants: *The service module contains the main propulsion system that maneuvers the modules so that they can rendezvous and dock with the space station* (W. G. Holder and W. D. Siuru, Jr.). *Abbr:* SM (no periods).

**service plate,** a large dinner plate to hold another plate of food during a course, or several courses, of the meal.

**service road, 1** = access road. **2** a road, generally paralleling an expressway, to carry local traffic and to provide access to adjoining property.

**serv|ic|es** (sėr′vi siz), *n.pl.* See under **service**[1] (*n.* def. 4).

**service side,** (in court tennis) the side of the court from which service is made.

**service station, 1** a place for supplying automobiles with gasoline, oil, water, and, usually, some parts and repairs; gas station; filling station. **2** a place where repairs, parts, and adjustments can be obtained for mechanical or electrical devices.

**service stripe,** *U.S.* **1** a diagonal stripe worn on the left sleeve of a uniform, to show three years of service in the Army or four in the Navy. **2** a small stripe or bar worn on the sleeve of railroad conductors or other uniformed employees to show the number of years of service.

**service tree, 1** a European, Asian, and African mountain ash tree bearing a small, pear-shaped or round fruit called the serviceberry, sorb, or sorb apple, that is edible when overripe. The service tree belongs to the rose family. **2** a closely related bush or small tree, the wild service tree, bearing harsh, bitter fruit; checker tree or sorb. 3 = shadbush.

**serv|ice|wom|an** (sėr′vis wům′ən), *n., pl.* **-women.** a female member of the armed forces.

**ser|vi|ent** (sėr′vē ənt), *adj. Especially Law.* subordinate. [< Latin *serviēns, -entis,* present participle of *servīre* serve]

**servient tenement,** *Law.* a tenement which is subject to an easement in favor of a dominant tenement.

**ser|vi|ette** (sėr′vē et′), *n. Especially British.* a table napkin: *His serviette was tucked under his chin* (Arnold Bennett). [< Middle French *serviette* < Old French *servir* serve]

**ser|vile** (sėr′vəl), *adj.* **1** like that of slaves; mean; base: *servile flattery. I did not ... aim at gaining his favor by paying any servile respect to him* (Benjamin Franklin). **SYN:** slavish, cringing, fawning, groveling. **2** of slaves; having to do with slaves: *a servile revolt, servile work.* **3** fit for a slave. **4** yielding, as through fear or lack of spirit: *An honest judge cannot be servile to public opinion.* **5** *Obsolete.* (of a people or state) politically enslaved. [< Latin *servīlis* < *servus* a slave]
— **ser′vile|ly,** *adv.* — **ser′vile|ness,** *n.*

**ser|vil|i|ty** (sėr vil′ə tē), *n., pl.* **-ties.** attitude or behavior fit for a slave; servile yielding: *Arrogance and servility, the common products of ignorance* (J. W. R. Scott).

**serv|ing** (sėr′ving), *n.* **1** the act of a person or thing that serves. **2** a portion of food or drink served to a person at one time; helping. **3** *Nautical.* a material used for serving a rope or cable.

**serving board,** *Nautical.* service board.

**serving mallet,** *Nautical.* a mallet-shaped piece of wood, used for serving ropes. It has a groove on one side to fit a rope.

**serving man,** a male servant.

**Ser|vite** (sėr′vīt), *n.* a mendicant friar or nun of a religious order founded in Italy in the 1200's, and following the rule of Saint Augustine. [< Medieval Latin *Servitae,* plural < Latin *servus* slave, servant]

**ser|vi|tial** (sėr vish′əl), *adj.* having to do with service, as that between servant and master or child and parent. [< Latin *servitium* service + English *-al*[1]]

**ser|vi|tor** (sėr′və tər), *n.* **1** a servant; attendant: *My noble queen ... henceforth I am thy true servitor* (Shakespeare). **2** a person in a shop of glass blowers who shapes the stem and base of a goblet. [< Old French *servitor,* learned borrowing from Late Latin *servitor* < Latin *servīre* serve]

**ser|vi|to|ri|al** (sėr′və tôr′ē əl, -tōr′-), *adj.* of or having to do with a servitor.

**ser|vi|tor|ship** (sėr′və tər ship), *n.* the position of a servitor.

**ser|vi|tress** (sėr′və tris), *n.* a woman servant or attendant.

**ser|vi|tude** (sėr′və tüd, -tyüd), *n.* **1** the condition of being a slave; slavery; bondage: *A disturbed liberty is better than a quiet servitude* (Joseph Addison). (*Figurative.*) *The Arabians ... tamely adopted the intellectual servitude of the nation which they conquered by their arms* (William Whewell). **SYN:** enslavement, subjection. **2** forced labor as a punishment: *The criminal was sentenced to five years' servitude.* **3** *Law.* **a** the condition of property subject to a right of enjoyment possessed by some person other than its owner, or attaching to some other property. **b** such a right of enjoyment. [< Old French *servitude,* learned borrowing from Latin *servitūdō, -inis* < *servus* a slave]

**ser|vo** (sėr′vō), *n., pl.* **-vos,** *adj., v.,* **-voed, -voing.** — *n.* **1** = servomechanism. **2** = servomotor. **3** = servosystem.
— *adj.* of or belonging to a servomechanism, servomotor, or servosystem: *a servo component, servo feedback.*
— *v.t.* to control or assist with a servomechanism: *Their ingenious double-sided vacuum servo ... servos the brakes on and servos them (and the driver's foot) off* (New Scientist and Science Journal).
[short for *servomechanism*]

**ser|vo-as|sist|ed brake** (sėr′vō ə sis′tid), *British.* power brake.

**servo brake, 1** an automobile brake with shoes so connected that one shoe passes on the force exerted on it by the rotating drum to increase the action of the other. **2** = power brake.

**ser|vo|con|trol** (sėr′vō kən trōl′), *n.* **1** the control of a process or operation by means of a servomechanism. **2** = servomechanism.

**ser|vo|con|trolled** (sėr′vō kən trōld′), *adj.* controlled or activated by a servomechanism or servosystem.

**Ser|vo-Cro|a|tian** (sėr′vō krō ā′shən), *adj., n.* = Serbo-Croatian.

**ser|vo|de|vice** (sėr′vō di vīs′), *n.* = servomechanism.

**ser|vo|mech|a|nism** (sėr′vō mek′ə niz əm), *n.* any one of various devices by which a supplementary source of power is activated to assist in the movement, manipulation, or guidance of some equipment. A servomechanism operates by automatically detecting and correcting errors in position, speed, output, and the like, according to a predetermined setting.

**ser|vo|mo|tor** (sėr′vō mō′tər), *n.* an auxiliary motor to supplement the primary source of power in the movement, manipulation, or guidance of a heavy or complex device: *The company's commercial items include various servomotors and other airborne components used in private and commercial aircraft* (Wall Street Journal). [< French *servo-moteur* < Latin *servus* slave + *mōtor* a mover]

**ser|vo|sys|tem** (sėr′vō sis′təm), *n.* a system of servomechanisms or servomotors to move or guide a heavy or complex device.

**Ser|vus ser|vo|rum De|i** (sėr′vəs sėr vôr′əm dē′ī, -vōr′-), *Latin.* servant of the servants of God (a title used by the Popes).

**ses|a|me** (ses′ə mē), *n.* **1a** Also, **sesame seed.** the small seeds of an East Indian plant, used to flavor bread, candy, and other foods, and in making an oil used in cooking. **b** = sesame oil. **2** the plant that produces these seeds. It is an annual herb with oblong leaves and tiny flowers, cultivated in tropical regions. **3** a magic password; open sesame: *No Tory, however wise, ... could have obtained the sesame to those apartments* (Edward R. Bulwer-Lytton). [< Latin *sēsama, sēsamum* < Greek *sēsamon* < Semitic (compare Syriac *shushmå*)]

**sesame oil,** a bland, yellow oil extracted from sesame seeds, used in cooking, salads, medicine, and cosmetics.

**ses|a|moid** (ses′ə moid), *adj., n.* — *adj.* of or having to do with certain small, oval, nodular bones or cartilages, as in the kneecap.
— *n.* a sesamoid bone or cartilage. See picture under **bone.**
[< Greek *sēsamoeidēs* < *sēsamon* (see etym. under **sesame**) + *eîdos* form]

**Se|so|tho** (se sō′thō), *n.* the Bantu language of the Basuto. It is one of the official languages of Lesotho. Also, **Sesuto, Sotho.**

**ses|qui|car|bon|ate** (ses′kwi kär′bə nāt, -nit), *n.* a salt whose composition is between a carbonate and a bicarbonate: *sodium sesquicarbonate.* [< Latin *sēsqui-* one and a half + English *carbonate*]

**ses|qui|cen|ten|ar|y** (ses′kwi sen ten′ər ē, -sen′tə ner′-), *n., pl.* **-ar|ies,** *adj.* = sesquicentennial.

**ses|qui|cen|ten|ni|al** (ses′kwi sen ten′ē əl), *adj., n.* — *adj.* of or having to do with 150 years or a 150th anniversary.
— *n.* **1** a 150th anniversary. **2** a celebration of a 150th anniversary: *The sesquicentennial of the Declaration of Independence was held in 1926.*
[American English < Latin *sēsqui-* one and a half + English *centennial*]

**ses|qui|ox|ide** (ses′kwi ok′sīd), *n.* a compound of oxygen and another element in the proportion of three atoms of oxygen to two of the other. [< Latin *sēsqui-* one and a half + English *oxide*]

**ses|quip|e|dal** (ses kwip′ə dəl, ses′kwi pē′-), *adj.* = sesquipedalian.

**ses|qui|pe|da|li|an** (ses′kwi pə dā′lē ən), *adj., n.* — *adj.* **1** very long; containing many syllables. **2** using or given to using long words: *The words gathered size like snowballs, and towards the end of her letter Miss Jenkyns used to become quite sesquipedalian* (Elizabeth Gaskell). **3** measuring a foot and a half.
— *n.* a very long word.
[< Latin *sēsquipedālis* a foot and a half long (< *sēsqui-* one and a half + *pēs, pedis* foot) + English *-ian*]

**ses|qui|pe|da|li|an|ism** (ses′kwi pə dā′lē ə niz′əm), *n.* the practice of using long words.

**ses|qui|ter|pene** (ses′kwi tėr′pēn), *n.* a terpene having one and a half times as many atoms in the molecule as a normal terpene. Farnesol is a sesquiterpene. *Formula:* $C_{15}H_{24}$

**sess.,** session.

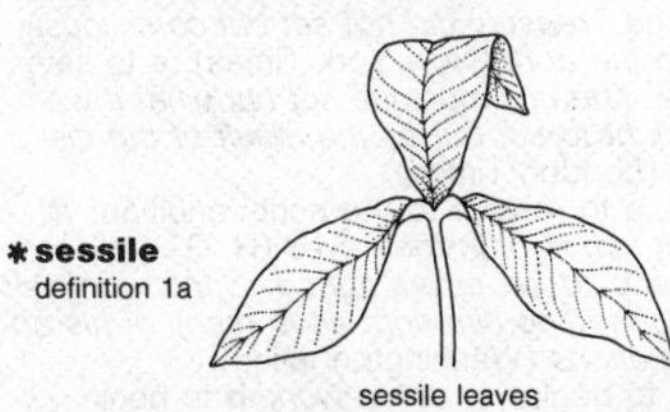

***sessile** definition 1a

sessile leaves

***ses|sile** (ses′əl), *adj.* **1a** *Botany.* attached by the base instead of by a stem. A leaf having no petiole or a flower having no peduncle or pedicel is sessile. *If no style intervenes between the ovary and stigma, the stigma is said to be sessile, as in the poppy* (Heber W. Youngken). **b** *Zoology.* attached by the base and having no connecting neck, as certain organs or animals. Some barnacles are sessile. **2** *Zoology.* sedentary; fixed to one spot; not able to move around: *A small group of about a dozen species of sessile, marine, wormlike animals ... secrete a hard tube in which they dwell* (A. M. Winchester). **3** static; immobile: *a sessile droplet of water, a sessile dislocation.* [< Latin *sessilis* sitting < *sedēre* to sit]

**ses|sil|i|ty** (se sil′ə tē), *n.* the condition of being sessile.

**ses|sion** (sesh′ən), *n.* **1a** a sitting or meeting of a court, council, or legislature. **b** a series of such sittings: *... the Administration's hopes and plans for the next session of Congress* (Time). **c** the term or period of such sittings: *This year's session of Congress was unusually long.* **2** any meeting: *an important session with some businessmen. After 100 sessions, the entire group is better in health and better adjusted* (Newsweek). **3** a single, continuous course or period of lessons and study into which a school day or year is divided: *the afternoon session, the summer session.* **4** *Archaic.* any sitting or being seated: *Vivien ... Leapt from her session on his lap* (Tennyson).
**in session,** meeting: *Congress is now in session. The teachers were in session all Saturday morning.*
**sessions, a** (in the United States) local courts dealing especially with lesser criminal offenses: *He was brought before the town court of sessions on a charge of petty larceny.* **b** Also, **sessions of the peace.** (in Great Britain) periodic sittings held by justices of the peace: *A favourite at the Old Bailey, and eke at the sessions* (Dickens).
[< Latin *sessiō, -ōnis* < *sedēre* to sit]

**ses|sion|al** (sesh′ə nəl), *adj.* **1** of a session; having to do with sessions. **2** occurring every session.

**ses|terce** (ses′tėrs), *n.* an ancient Roman silver or brass coin of small value, worth ¼ of a denarius. [< Latin *sēstertius* (originally) adjective, two and a half < *sēmis* half (< *sēmi-* half + *as* monetary unit) + *tertius* third]

**ses|ter|ti|um** (ses tėr′shē əm), *n., pl.* **-ti|a** (-shē ə). an ancient Roman unit of money equal to a thousand sesterces. [(erroneously formed as a neuter singular to Latin *sēstertia*) short for *mīlia sēstertium* thousands of sesterces]

**ses|tet** (ses tet′), *n.* **1** a musical sextet. **2** the last six lines of a sonnet, especially of an Italian or Petrarchan sonnet. **3** a poem or stanza of six lines. [< Italian *sestetto* (diminutive) < *sesto* sixth < Latin *sextus* < *sex* six]

**ses|ti|na** (ses tē′nə), *n., pl.* **-nas, -ne** (-nā). a poem of six six-line stanzas and a concluding triplet. The last words of the first stanza are repeated in the other five stanzas in different order, and in the concluding triplet. [< Italian *sestina* < *sesto;* see etym. under **sestet**]

**Se|su|to** (se sü′tō), *n.* = Sesotho.

**set** (set), *v.,* **set, set|ting,** *adj., n.* — *v.t.* **1** to put in some place; put; place: *to set a chair upright, to set a person on a throne, to set a lamp on the table. Set the box on its end.* **SYN:** See syn. under **put. 2a** to put in the right place, position, or condition for use; put in proper order; arrange: *The doctor set my broken leg. The hunter sets his traps. Set the table for dinner.* **b** to arrange (the hair) when damp to make it wave or take a certain position. **c** to raise or adjust (sails) to catch the wind. **3** to adjust according to a standard: *to set a clock.* **4** to put in some condition or relation; cause to be: *to set someone at ease. A spark set the woods on fire. The slaves were set free. ... the subtle strings that set the wheels of the whole world in motion* (Lytton Strachey). **SYN:** See syn. under **put. 5a** to put (a price); fix the value of at a certain amount or rate: *She set the value of the watch at $500.* **b** to put (a sum) down as a stake; bet: *to set $5 on a horse to win.* **6** *Figurative.* to put as the measure of esteem of a person or thing: *to set more by action than by talk.* **7** to post, appoint, or station for the purpose of performing some duty: *to set an investigator on a case.* **8a** to fix; arrange; appoint: *to set the rules for a contest, to set the stage for a scene in a play, to set the scene for negotiations. The teacher set a time limit for taking the examination.* **b** to allot or assign: *to set a difficult job for oneself.* **SYN:** prescribe. **9** to provide for others to follow: *to set a good example, to set a*

**Pronunciation Key:** hat, āge, cãre, fär; let, ēqual, tėrm; it, īce; hot, ōpen, ôrder; oil, out; cup, pu̇t, rüle; child; long; thin; ᴛʜen; zh, measure;
ə represents **a** in about, **e** in taken, **i** in pencil, **o** in lemon, **u** in circus.

*pace, to set the fashion.* **10a** to make firm or hard: *to set mortar, to set the white of an egg by boiling it.* **b** *Figurative.* to put in a fixed, rigid, or settled state; fix: *to set one's teeth, to set one's heart on something. If he sets his mind on it, he will do it.* **11** to put in a frame or other thing that holds: *The windows were set in stone. The jeweler set a diamond in gold.* **12** to adorn; ornament: *to set a bracelet with diamonds.* **13a** to put (a hen) to sit on eggs to hatch them. **b** to place (eggs) under a hen or in an incubator, to be hatched. **14** to encourage to attack; cause to be hostile: *They set the dogs upon the prowler.* **15** to turn in a particular direction; direct: *to set one's feet homeward.* **16** (of a dog) to mark the position of (game) by stopping and pointing the muzzle. **17** *Music.* **a** to adapt; fit: *to set words to music.* **b** to arrange (music) for certain voices or instruments. **18** *Printing.* to put (type) in the order required: *Walt Whitman set the type himself for his "Leaves of Grass."* **19** to make (a color, as of a fabric) fast. **20** to adjust (a machine, instrument, or one of the parts) to work properly or maintain a certain position: *to set the focus of a microscope, to set a wheel.* **21** to give a sharp edge to (a blade): *to set a razor.* **22** to change into curd; curdle: *to set milk.* **23** to mix (batter or dough containing yeast) and leave it to rise. **24** to remove the wrinkles from (an animal hide or leather) by pressing: *The hides are set or put through a machine which presses out the wrinkles and in general smooths the leather to a uniform evenness* (August C. Orthmann). **25** to put down or defeat (a contract in cards): *West was able to set the contract with his two aces and long trump.*

—*v.i.* **1** to become fixed; become firm or hard: *Jelly sets as it cools.* **2** to go down; sink; wane: *The sun sets in the west. His power has begun to set.* **SYN**: decline. **3** to have a direction; tend: *The current sets to the south.* **4** to hang or fit in a particular manner: *That coat sets well.* **5** to begin to move; start: *He set across the river.* **6** (of a hen) to sit on eggs. **7** *Figurative.* to be arranged; be fixed: *His face is set in stern lines.* **8** (of color) to become fast and permanent. **9** to form fruit in the blossom: *The blossoms were abundant, but they failed to set.* **10** (of a dog) to indicate the position of game by standing stiffly and pointing with the nose.

—*adj.* **1a** fixed or appointed beforehand; established: *a set time, set rules, a set speech.* **SYN**: determined, prescribed. **b** prepared; ready: *He is set to try again.* **2** fixed; rigid: *a set smile.* **3a** firm; hard. **b** *Figurative.* resolved; determined: *I am set on going today.* **4** *Informal, Figurative.* stubbornly fixed; obstinate: *to be set in one's ways.* **5** (of a kind of weather) persistent: *set snows.* **6** having a specified build or look: *deep-set eyes.*

—*n.* **1a** a number of things belonging together; outfit: *a set of dishes, a set of teeth, a set of furniture, a set of tools.* **SYN**: collection. **b** a set of furniture: *a dining-room set.* **c** a number of books by the same author, or covering the same subject, or of the same kind: *a set of Dickens, a set of plays.* **2** a number of people with similar habits, interests, or occupations; group: *a golfing set, a fast set. And this, at least according to Spens's translation, is how the Socrates set talked at meals* (Atlantic). **3a** the scenery of a play or scene; setting: *The set ... shows an impoverished attic room, with a mean bed and table, a telephone, and a huge curtained window* (New Yorker). **b** the scenery for a motion picture: *With all its championship furnishings Cortina, a popular resort ... took on the freshly built look of a Hollywood set* (Newsweek). **4** a device for receiving or sending by radio, telephone, telegraph, or television. **5** the way a thing or person is put or placed; form; shape: *a man of heavy set. There was a stubborn set to his jaw.* **6** a direction; tendency; course; drift: *The set of opinion was toward building a new bridge.* **7** the arrangement of the hair after it has been dampened. **8** a warp; bend; displacement: *a set to the right. The specimen does not return to its original length but retains a permanent strain or a set* (Sears and Zemansky). **9a** a slip or shoot for planting: *cucumber sets.* **b** a bulb, tuber, or part of a tuber for planting: *onion sets.* **10** a young fruit just formed from a blossom. **11** the act or manner of setting. **12** a group of games in tennis. One side must win six games and at least two more than the other side. *It was decided that the match would be for the best seven of thirteen sets* (New Yorker). **13** the way in which anything fits: *the set of a coat.* **14** the direction in which a current flows or a wind blows. **15** a dog's pointing in the presence of game: *Brownie got her set. She held it and we hurried* (New Yorker). **16a** the number of couples required for a square dance. **b** the figures of a square dance. **17** a clutch of eggs. **18** the lateral bending of the teeth of a saw. **19** *Mathematics.* a group of numbers, points, objects, or other elements which are distinguished from all other elements by specific common properties. The numbers from 0 to 10 form a set, and any number in this set is a member of the set. *The number 3 belongs to the set of prime numbers.* **20** *Psychology.* a temporary condition of an organism making a certain type of response or activity easier. **21** *Philately.* stamps of similar subject matter: *"I've brought you some stamps ... And here's a complete set of Liberians"* (Graham Greene). **22** *Basketball.* a set shot. **23** *British Informal.* a class in a school: *an English set, a maths set.*

**all set**, *Informal.* fully prepared; ready: *She is all set to leave for Europe.*

**set about**, to start work upon; begin: *to set about one's business. Set about your washing.*

**set against**, **a** to make unfriendly toward; cause to be hostile: *They set his friends against him.* **b** to balance; compare: *Setting the probabilities of the story against the credit of the witnesses* (Henry Brougham).

**set apart**, to reserve: *to set some food apart for winter.*

**set aside**, **a** to put to one side: *Set this aside, till I call for it* (Jehan Palsgrave). **b** to put by for later use; reserve: *to set money aside for one's education.* **c** to discard, dismiss, or leave out; reject; annul: *Sometimes a higher court sets aside the decision in a lawsuit.*

**set at**, to attack: *His enemies set at him from every side.*

**set back**, **a** to stop; hinder; check: *All his efforts were set back.* **b** *U.S. Informal.* to cost (a person) so much: *The new car set him back a lot of money.*

**set by**, to put away for future use: *She set by in the pantry what was left after meals.*

**set down**, **a** to deposit or let alight; put down: *to set down a suitcase. The bus set him down near town.* **b** to put down in writing or printing: *to set down a story.* **c** *Figurative.* to consider; regard: *to set a person down as a gossip.* **d** *Figurative.* to ascribe; attribute: *to set someone's actions down to ignorance. Your failure in the test can be set down to too much haste.*

**set forth**, **a** to make known; express; declare: *to set forth one's opinions on a subject.* **b** to start to go: *to set forth on a trip around the world.*

**set forward**, to start to go; set out: *He ... set forward at last in his own carriage* (Jane Austen).

**set in**, **a** to begin: *Winter set in early.* **b** to blow or flow toward the shore: *The current set in close to the shore.* **c** to sew in as a separate piece: *The sleeves of her dress were set in and without cuffs.*

**set loose**, to release; let go; set free: *The horses were set loose from the stables to graze and roam in the fields.*

**set off**, **a** to cause to go off; explode: *He set off the firecrackers.* **b** to start to go: *to set off for home. Sir Robert set off on a week's tour of his new domain* (Manchester Guardian Weekly). **c** *Figurative.* to touch off; instigate: *The war against Red guerrilla units ... set off the heaviest fighting in many months* (Wall Street Journal). **d** to increase by contrast; enhance: *The green dress set off her red hair.* **e** to balance; counterbalance; compensate: *Our losses were set off by some gains.* **f** to mark off; separate from others: *One sentence was set off from the rest by quotation marks.* **g** to allot or assign, especially for some special purpose away from the rest: *A part of the hospital was set off for the care of contagious disease.*

**set on**, **a** to attack: *The dog set on him.* **b** to urge to attack: *Prospero and Ariel setting them on* (Shakespeare).

**set out**, **a** to start to go: *He set out to cross the river. They set out on the hike with plenty of water.* **b** to spread out to show, sell, or use: *to set out a flag, to set out goods for sale.* **c** to plant: *to set out tomato plants in the spring.* **d** to plan; intend (to do something): *to set out to reform the courts. The Treasury did not set out consciously to reduce the debt* (New York Times). **e** to say; tell; state: *The communiqué set out what it was thought right to set out as the result of the discussions* (London Times).

**set right**, **a** to restore to the right condition: *It would set him right in their eyes* (H. G. Wells). **b** to correct: *to set errors right. I ... found myself capable of setting him right as to many of his antiquated notions* (Washington Irving).

**set to**, **a** to begin: *to set to work.* **b** to begin fighting: *The two boys set to.*

**set up**, **a** to build; erect: *to set up a monument.* **b** to begin; start: *He sold his business and set up a new one. Scholarships should be set up by the local colleges to enable the Southern teachers to obtain ... additional credits* (New York Times). **c** to assemble: *Flemish weavers set up their looms and taught the English to weave cloth* (M. J. Guest). **d** to put up; raise in place, position, power, or pride: *They set him up above his rivals.* **e** to raise; utter: *to set up a cry.* **f** to claim; pretend: *to set up to be honest.* **g** to plan, prepare, or establish: *to set up a business deal.*

**set upon**, to fall upon a person or enemy without warning; attack: *The marines were set upon by snipers* (New York Times).

[Old English *settan.* See related etym. at **sit**.]

▶ **set, sit.** People and things sit (past, *sat*) or they are *set* (past, *set*), meaning placed: *I like to sit in a hotel lobby. I have sat in this same seat for a long time. She set the soup down with a flourish. The post was set three feet in the ground.* A hen, however *sets* (on her eggs).

**Set** (set), *n.* the ancient Egyptian god of evil, brother of Osiris. Set oppressed souls after death. He was represented as having an animal's head with a pointed snout. Also, **Seth**.

**se|ta** (sē′tə), *n., pl.* **-tae** (-tē). *Biology.* a slender, stiff, bristlelike organ or part of an animal or plant. Earthworms have four pairs of setae on each segment. [< Latin *sēta, saeta* bristle]

**se|ta|ceous** (si tā′shəs), *adj. Biology.* **1** bristlelike; bristle-shaped. **2** furnished with bristles; bristly. [< New Latin *setaceus* (with English *-ous*) < Latin *sēta* bristle] —**se|ta′ceous|ly**, *adv.*

**se|tal** (sē′təl), *adj.* of or having to do with setae.

**set-a|side** (set′ə sīd′), *n. U.S.* **1** raw materials, food, or other supplies reserved by federal order, especially for the use of the armed forces. **2** anything put in reserve.

**set|back** (set′bak′), *n.* **1** a check to progress; reverse: *a temporary setback in one's fortunes, an unexpected setback in a patient's recovery.* **SYN**: relapse, retardation. **2** a steplike setting back of the outside wall of a tall building to give better light and air in the street. **3** a lessening in the thickness of a wall. **4** a flat, plain projection of a wall.

**set chisel**, a chisel used to cut off the heads of rivets and bolts.

**set|down** (set′doun′), *n.* a humiliating rebuke or rebuff: *I wish you had been there ... to have given him one of your setdowns* (Jane Austen).

**Seth** (seth), *n.* **1** the third son of Adam (in the Bible, Genesis 4:25). **2** = Set.

**se|tif|er|ous** (si tif′ər əs), *adj.* having setae. [< Latin *sēta* bristle + English *-ferous*]

**se|ti|form** (sē′tə fôrm), *adj.* shaped like setae: *The antennae of a dragonfly are setiform.* [< Latin *sēta* bristle]

**se|tig|er|ous** (si tij′ər əs), *adj. Zoology.* setaceous: *the setigerous growth on the skin of pigs.* [< Latin *sētiger* (< *sēta* bristle + *gerere* to bear) + English *-ous*]

**set-in** (set′in′), *adj.* **1** sewn into a garment as a separate piece: *set-in sleeves, a set-in belt.* **2** made to be placed within a larger unit: *The ... plant manufactures gas and electric set-in ranges and built-in ovens* (Wall Street Journal).

**se|tip|a|rous** (si tip′ər əs), *adj.* producing setae. [< Latin *sēta* bristle + *parere* give birth + English *-ous*]

**set|line** (set′līn′), *n.* **1** a long fish line having short lines and baited hooks attached, laid on the bottom, its ends anchored. **2** = trotline.

**set|off** (set′ôf′, -of′), *n.* **1** a thing used to set off or adorn; ornament; decoration. **SYN**: trimming. **2** something that counterbalances or makes up for something else; compensation; offset. **3a** the settlement of a debt by means of a claim in the debtor's favor. **b** a claim so used. **4** the act of setting off on a trip; start; departure. **5** a setback on a building.

**se|tose** (sē′tōs, si tōs′), *adj.* bristly; setaceous. [< Latin *sētōsus* < *sēta* bristle]

**set|out** (set′out′), *n.* **1** a start; outset: *The parties were pretty equal at the setout* (Byron). **2a** a display, as of a set of china. **b** a spread of food; buffet. **3** an entertainment for a group of people; party: *This was a very different setout, a children-and-parents party with a puppet show* (New Yorker). **4** a person's costume or get-up. **5** a turnout, such as a carriage with its horses and harness. **6** outfit; equipment.

**set piece**, **1** a usually formal or stylized scene in a painting, story, play, motion picture, or other work, often written or painted to tell a story of its own. **2** = set scene.

**set point**, **1** the established point that determines a set of variables or frame of reference for the quantity being controlled: *The control engineer ... would expect the body's temperature control system to have a "set point," but this cannot easily be established physiologically* (New Scientist). **2** the concluding point that is needed to win a set in tennis.

**set scene**, *Theater.* a stage set not painted on a flat or drop.

**set|screw** (set′skrü′), *n.* a machine screw used to fasten gears, pulleys, etc., to a shaft: *Three* *setscrews permit accurate adjustment in level* (Herman J. Shea).

**set shot,** *Basketball.* a long shot at the basket, usually from beyond the foul line or from a corner with the player standing still.

*** set square,** a flat triangular instrument, with one right angle and the other angles of either 60° and 30° or both of 45°, used in mechanical or architectural drawing.

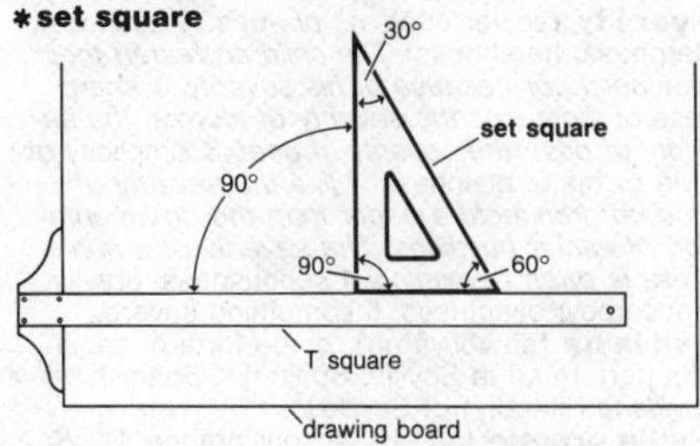

*** set square**

**Set|swa|na** (set swä′nə, sə tswä′-), *n.* the Bantu language of the Batswana; Tswana.

**sett** (set), *n. Especially British.* **1** a small, square stone used for paving: *Setts were designed to give a smooth surface for motor traffic* (Scotsman). **2a** each of the squares in the pattern of a tartan. **b** the pattern itself. **3** the adjustment of the reeds of a loom for making a particular pattern in the fabric. **4** the figures that make up a country-dance or square dance: *These "fancy figures" ... became popular as the last dance in a "sett"* (New Yorker). **5** the earth or burrow of a badger: *Badgers emerge from their setts in the evening* (London Times). [variant of *set*]

**set|ta|ble** (set′ə bəl), *adj.* that can be set.

**set|te|cen|to** (set′tä chen′tō), *n.* the 1700's (used especially in connection with a period of Italian art and literature). [< Italian *settecento* seven hundred, short for *millesettecento* one thousand and seven hundred]

**set|tee** (se tē′), *n.* a sofa or long bench with a back and, usually, arms: *Over against one wall was ... not a davenport, not a settee, but simply a battered old leather couch* (Robert Traver). [perhaps a variant of *settle*[2]]

**set|ter** (set′ər), *n.* **1** a person or thing that sets: *a setter of type, a setter of jewels.* **2** a long-haired hunting dog, often trained to stand motionless and point its nose toward the game that it scents: *There are three recognized breeds in the setter family: English, Gordon, and Irish* (Maxwell Riddle). See picture under **dog**.

**set theory,** the branch of mathematics that deals with sets, their properties, and their relationships: *Set theory is widely used in teaching to demonstrate how things can be grouped and how groups are related to one another* (Scientific American).

**set|ting** (set′ing), *n., v.* —*n.* **1** a frame or other thing in which something is set. The mounting of a jewel is its setting. **2a** the scenery of a play, including the lighting and other things that contribute to the play. **b** a single scene or set. **3** the place and time of a play or story. **4** *Figurative.* surroundings; background: *a fashionable setting, a scenic mountain setting.* **5a** music composed to go with certain words. **b** music composed or arranged for particular instruments: *a symphonic setting.* **6** the eggs that a hen sets on for hatching: *He had been given the hen while she was broody and had bought a setting of New Hampshire eggs to put under her* (George Johnston). **SYN:** clutch. **7** the act of a person or thing that sets. **8** dishes or cutlery required to set one place at a table: *He bought his wife six settings of fine china.*
—*v.* the present participle of **set**: *She was setting the table.*

**setting hammer, 1** a tinsmith's hammer, having a square head and a chisel-shaped peen. **2** a specially shaped light hammer to swage the teeth of saws in setting them.

**setting point,** the place or point at which an adjustment or setting can be made in a mechanism.

**setting screw, 1** a screw by which cams or timing devices may be adjusted to work as desired. **2** = setscrew.

**set|ting-up exercises** (set′ing up′), exercises that require no equipment, such as pushups and sit-ups; calisthenics.

**set|tle**[1] (set′əl), *v.,* **-tled, -tling.** —*v.t.* **1a** to make a decision on; determine; decide: *Children bring their disputes to Mother to settle. The lama waved a hand to show that the matter was finally settled in his mind* (Rudyard Kipling). **b** to agree upon (as a time, place, or plan); fix beforehand: *to settle a course of action, Thus, the preliminaries settled ...* (William Cowper). **SYN:** set. See syn. under **fix.** **2** to put in order; arrange: *I must settle all my affairs before going away for the winter.* **SYN:** set. See syn. under **fix.** **3** to pay; arrange payment of: *He settled all his bills before leaving town.* **4** to cause to take up residence in a place, especially a new country, town, or area: *to settle one's family in the country.* **5** to establish colonies in; colonize: *The English settled New England.* **6** to set in a fairly permanent position, place, or way of life: *to settle one's son in business. We quickly settled ourselves in our new house.* **7** to place in a desired or comfortable position; adjust: *to settle one's feet in the stirrups. The cat settled herself in the chair for a nap.* **8** *Figurative.* to make quiet; calm; soothe: *A vacation will settle your nerves. He took some medicine to settle his stomach.* **9** to cause to sink down. **10** to make (a liquid) clear: *A beaten egg or cold water will settle coffee.* **11** to cause (dregs or other impurities) to sink to the bottom. **12** to make firm and compact; cause to subside into a solid or more compact mass: *to settle the contents of a barrel, to settle soil by watering it.* **13** *Law.* to decide (a case) by arrangement between the parties.
—*v.i.* **1a** to come to a conclusion; resolve; decide; determine: *Have you settled on a day for the picnic?* **b** to arrange matters in dispute; come to terms or agreement (with): *to settle with a union.* **2** to be put in order, especially by closing an account (with). **3** to take up residence (in a new country or place): *Our cousin intends to settle in New York.* **4** (of a bird or insect) to alight: *Flies everywhere settled in clouds, and the hospital was full of malaria patients* (Graham Greene). **5** to be set in a fairly permanent position, place, or way of life: *He settled into his new position at the company very quickly.* **6a** to come to rest in a particular place; lodge: *My cold settled in my chest.* (*Figurative.*) *A heavy fog settled over the airport.* **b** to come to a definite condition: *The elements of war are often gradually accumulating before they settle into an open rupture* (Benjamin Disraeli). **7** to come to a desired or comfortable position. **8** *Figurative.* to become quiet or composed: *The children were too excited with their Christmas presents to settle at once.* **9** to go down; sink gradually, especially by its own weight: *Our house has settled several inches since it was built.* **10** (of a liquid) to become clear by depositing dregs or impurities. **11** (of dregs) to sink to the bottom. **12** to become firm and compact, as soil.

**settle down, a** to live a more regular life: *Botanizing, music, writing the first chapters of his Confessions, Rousseau seemed to be settling down at Wootton* (Listener). **b** to direct steady effort or attention: *When he finally settled down to his work he managed to complete it in two hours.* **c** *Figurative.* to calm down; become quiet: *The baby kept crying and refused to settle down.*

**settle for,** to be content with; agree upon; accept, often less than one wanted: *But neither the star nor the composer was willing to settle for that kind of routine triumph* (Henry Hewes).

**settle on** (or **upon**), to give (property, a right, or a sum) to by law: *He settled one thousand dollars a year upon his old servant.*

[Old English *setlan* < *setl;* see etym. under **settle**[2]]

*** set|tle**[2] (set′əl), *n.* a long bench, usually with arms and a high back: *The man on the settle waited a minute, and then got up and passed the length of the bar* (Geoffrey Household). [Old English *setl* a sitting place; an abode]

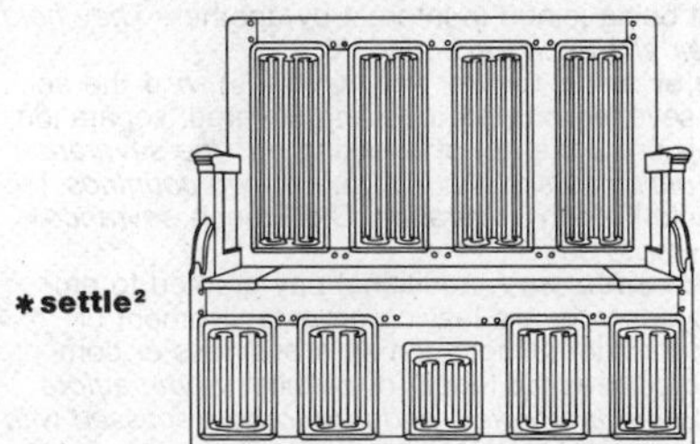
*** settle**[2]

**set|tled** (set′əld), *adj.* **1** fixed in place or position; having a fixed home: *Becoming a settled ... instead of a nomadic people ...* (Arthur P. Stanley). **2** populated: *a densely settled region.* **3** fixed or established: *... the settled course of things* (Joseph Butler). **4** placed on a permanent basis, as government. **5** maintained or continuing without change: *settled fair weather.* **6** fixed; firmly seated; unchanging: (*Figurative.*) *His old buoyancy and confidence gave way to something like settled gloom* (Edmund Wilson). **7** *Figurative.* **a** steadfast, staid, or sober, as the character or mind. **b** indicating such a character, as the countenance. **8a** established in a regular way of life, or in fixed ways: *a settled married man, a settled old woman.* **b** steady or orderly: *the settled life of an old man.* **9** established, as in an office or charge. **10** secured to a person by a legal act or process, as an estate or property. **11a** appointed or fixed definitely, as a time. **b** decided definitely, as a question or a matter in doubt. **12** adjusted or closed, as an account by payment. —**set′tled|ness,** *n.*

**set|tle|ment** (set′əl mənt), *n.* **1** the act of settling or state of being settled: *With a settlement of their debts came a settlement of the dispute.* **2** the establishment of a person in life, in marriage, in employment, or in another situation, or of oneself, as in a fixed place or a permanent residence. **3** the act of deciding or determining, as a time, question, or dispute: *the settlement of a date. Until a compromise settlement was achieved, that issue alone prolonged the strike for almost a month* (Newsweek). **4a** the act or process of putting in order; arrangement: [*The Secretary of State*] *publicly "dissociated" the U.S. from the settlement* (Newsweek). **b** the resulting condition of affairs; established order of things. **5** the payment of an account: *Settlement of all claims against the company will be made shortly.* **6** the act or process of settling persons in a new country or area; colonization: *The settlement of the English along the Atlantic coast gave England claim to that section.* **7** a colony: *England had many settlements along the Atlantic coast.* **8** a group of buildings and the people living in them: *Indians often attacked the little settlements of the colonists. The explorers spent the night in an Indian settlement.* **9** a place in a poor, neglected neighborhood where work for its improvement is carried on; settlement house: *Hull House is a famous settlement on the west side of Chicago.* **10a** the act or process of settling property upon someone: *She received $200,000 by a marriage settlement.* **b** the amount so given: *As to his own settlement, the Duke observed that he would expect the Duke of York's marriage to be considered the precedent* (Lytton Strachey). **11** legal residence. **12** a gradual sinking or subsidence, as of a structure.

**settlements,** breaks or other damage caused by the settlement of a building or structure: *They complained to the builder about the extent of the house's settlements.*

**settlement house,** an establishment to improve conditions in a poor neighborhood, as by providing educational and social services and activities; social settlement.

**set|tle|ment-work|er** (set′əl mənt wėr′kər), *n.* a person who gives his time to help in the work of a neighborhood settlement.

**set|tler** (set′lər), *n.* **1** a person who settles in a new country, an undeveloped region, or the like: *The settlers of Plymouth Colony invited the Indians to their first Thanksgiving feast.* **SYN:** colonist. **2** a person who settles: *a settler of disputes.* **3** *Law.* a person who settles property on someone.

**settler's twine,** a grasslike plant of the arum family, used by pioneers in New South Wales and Queensland as cord or string.

**set|tling** (set′ling), *n.* **1a** the act of a thing that settles; sinking down: *As the new house begins to age, its parts begin to shrink, stretch, bend, shift, and crack. This natural process is called "settling"* (New York Times). **b** the result of this. **2** the act of a person who settles.

**settlings,** things in a liquid which settle to the bottom; sediment; dregs: *Yet 'tis but the lees and settlings of a melancholy blood* (Milton).

**settling clerk,** a bank employee sent to a clearinghouse to settle accounts.

**settling tank,** a tank for holding a liquid until the suspended matter or sediment settles.

**set|tlor** (set′lər), *n. Law.* a person who settles property on someone. Also, **settler.**

**set-to** (set′tü′), *n., pl.* **-tos.** *Informal.* **1** a fight; dispute: *a sudden set-to between two children.* **2** a contest; match; bout: *Such bi-weekly set-tos are a "reformed" remnant of medieval tournaments* (Time). [< *set to,* idiom]

**set|up** (set′up′), *n.* **1a** an arrangement, such as of apparatus or machinery: *But before Chicago can reap the benefits ... of increased trade, it must practically rebuild its entire port setup* (Newsweek). **b** the arrangement of an organization: *an efficient setup, to learn the setup of a company.* **2** *U.S. Informal.* **a** a glass and ice cubes, often with carbonated water, ginger ale,

**Pronunciation Key:** hat, āge, cãre, fär; let, ēqual, tėrm; it, īce; hot, ōpen, ôrder; oil, out; cup, pu̇t, rüle; child; long; thin; ᴛʜen; zh, measure; ə represents **a** in about, **e** in taken, **i** in pencil, **o** in lemon, **u** in circus.

or the like, for a person to mix an alcoholic drink for himself. **b** a place setting for a customer in a restaurant. **3** *Slang.* **a** a contest or match where the outcome is assured. **b** anything that is very easy to do or whose outcome is readily predictable: *That job would be a setup for any good carpenter. This release from ... obligatory reading has resulted in a euphoria that makes me a setup for a book* (Harper's). **4** *U.S. Archaic.* the manner of holding the head and body; carriage.

**sève** (sev), *n. French.* the special flavor and aroma of a wine.

**sev|en** (sev′ən), *adj., n.* —***adj.*** being one more than six.
—***n.*** **1** one more than six; 7: *Seven is the number of days in the week.* **2** a playing card, throw of the dice, domino, billiard ball, or other part of a game with seven spots or a "7" on it.
[Old English *seofon*]

**Seven against Thebes**, *Greek Legend.* the seven heroes who made an expedition against Thebes to put Polynices on the throne.

**sev|en-a-side** (sev′ən ə sīd′), *n. Rugby.* a game or match played with seven men on each side.

**seven deadly sins**, pride, covetousness, lust, anger, gluttony, envy, sloth.

**sev|en|fold** (sev′ən fōld′), *adv., adj.* —***adv.*** **1** seven times as much or as many. **2** seven times as much or as often; in the proportion of seven to one.
—***adj.*** **1** seven times as much or as many: *Last year's total was ... about a sevenfold increase* (Newsweek). **2** having seven parts.

**sev|en|gill** (sev′ən gil′), *n.,* or **sevengill shark**, a shark of the Pacific and Atlantic Oceans having seven gill slits along each side of the head instead of the usual five.

**sev|en-league boots** (sev′ən lēg′), the magical boots in the fairy tale of Hop o'my Thumb, which enabled the wearer to cover seven leagues at each stride.

**seven seas** or **Seven Seas**, all the seas and oceans of the world, traditionally believed to be the Arctic, Antarctic, North Atlantic, South Atlantic, North Pacific, South Pacific, and Indian oceans: *to sail the seven seas.*

**Seven Sisters**, = Pleiades.

**sev|en|teen** (sev′ən tēn′), *n., adj.* seven more than ten; 17. [Old English *seofontēne*]

**sev|en|teenth** (sev′ən tēnth′), *adj., n.* **1** next after the 16th; last in a series of 17. **2** one, or being one, of 17 equal parts.

**sev|en|teen-year locust** (sev′ən tēn′yir′), a cicada of the United States that requires from thirteen to seventeen years to develop from egg to adult; periodical cicada. The larva burrows underground and feeds on roots, emerging to live a short time as an adult. *Seventeen-year locusts ... climb trees in the summer and produce a lonesome continuous singing* (A. M. Winchester).

**sev|enth** (sev′ənth), *adj., n.* —***adj.*** **1** next after the sixth; last in a series of 7: *Saturday is the seventh day of the week.* **2** being one of 7 equal parts.
—***n.*** **1** next after the sixth; last in a series of 7. **2** one of 7 equal parts: *A day is one seventh of a week.* **3** *Music.* **a** the interval between two tones that are seven degrees apart. **b** the harmonic combination of two such tones. **c** the seventh tone of a scale.

**Seventh Avenue**, a street in New York City that is the center of the American fashion and garment industry: *These hats are doing for the hat industry what the chemise has done for Seventh Avenue* (New Yorker).

**seventh chord**, *Music.* a chord consisting of a fundamental tone together with its third, fifth, and seventh.

**sev|enth-day** or **Sev|enth-day** (sev′ənth dā′), *adj.* **1** of, having to do with, or belonging to any of several Christian denominations observing Saturday, the seventh day of the week, as the principal day of rest and religious observance. **2** of or having to do with the seventh day, especially as the Sabbath.

**Seventh-day Adventist**, a member of a seventh-day Protestant denomination that emphasizes the doctrine of the second coming of Christ.

**seventh heaven**, **1** the highest place or condition of joy and happiness: *"What a surprise they'll have in the morning when they see Cousin Augie! ... Anna will be in seventh heaven"* (Saul Bellow). **2** the highest part of heaven.

**sev|enth|ly** (sev′ənth lē), *adv.* in the seventh place.

**sev|en|ti|eth** (sev′ən tē ith), *adj., n.* **1** next after the 69th; last in a series of 70. **2** one, or being one, of 70 equal parts.

**sev|en|ty** (sev′ən tē), *n., pl.* **-ties**, *adj.* —***n.*** seven times ten; 70.
—***adj.*** seven times ten; 70.

**the Seventy**, **a** the scholars who translated the Septuagint into Greek: *The Seventy render it ... "ta glyptá," by which they understand graven images* (Edward Stillingfleet). **b** the disciples appointed by Jesus to preach the gospel (in the Bible, Luke 10:1-20): *Matthias ... was one of the Seventy that was chosen and ordained by the other Apostles to succeed Judas in the Apostolate* (John Scott). **c** the Great Sanhedrin: *The thief was brought before the Seventy for trial.* See under **Sanhedrin**.
[Old English *seofontig*, short for *hundseofontig*]

**sev|en|ty-eight** or **78** (sev′ən tē āt′), *n.* a phonograph record which revolves at 78 revolutions per minute.

**sev|en|ty-five** (sev′ən tē fīv′), *n.* a 75-millimeter gun, especially the standard artillery piece of the French in World War I.

**sev|en|ty|fold** (sev′ən tē fōld′), *adj., adv.* **1** 70 times as many. **2** 70 times as much.

**sev|en-up** (sev′ən up′), *n.* a card game for two or more players, to each of whom six cards are dealt, in which there are four special chances of scoring a point, seven points constituting a game.

**sev|er** (sev′ər), *v.t.* **1** to cut apart; cut off: *The sailor severed the rope with a knife. The ax severed the branch from the trunk.* **2** to break off: *The two countries severed friendly relations.*
—***v.i.*** to part; divide; separate: *The frayed rope suddenly severed and the swing fell down. The church severed into two factions. Ae fond kiss, and then we sever* (Robert Burns).
[< Anglo-French *severer,* Old French *sevrer* < Vulgar Latin *sēperāre,* for Latin *sēparāre* to separate]

**sev|er|a|bil|i|ty** (sev′ər ə bil′ə tē, sev′rə-), *n.* the quality or condition of being severable.

**sev|er|a|ble** (sev′ər ə bəl, sev′rə-), *adj.* **1** that can be severed or separated. **2** *Law.* that can be separated into distinct rights or obligations.

**sev|er|al** (sev′ər əl, sev′rəl), *adj., n.* —***adj.*** **1** being more than two or three but not many; some; a few: *to gain several pounds. Some of the men ... remembered ... to have seen several strangers on the road* (Robert Louis Stevenson). **2** different; individual; respective: *The boys went their several ways, each minding his own business.* **3** considered separately as distinct or single: *The several steps in the process of making paper were shown in a movie.* **4** *Law.* binding or bound separately or distinctly. **5** *Archaic.* different: *... three several times astonished* (George Eliot). **6** *Archaic.* single.
—***n.*** more than two or three but not many; some; a few: *Several have given their consent.*
[< Anglo-French *several* < Medieval Latin *seperalis, separalis* < Latin *sēpar, -aris* distinct < *sēparāre* to separate]

**sev|er|al-fold** (sev′ər əl fōld′, sev′rəl-), *adv., adj.* several times as much or as many: *It is possible to reduce those effects several-fold* (Scientific American) (adv.). *It has led to a several-fold increase in yields since 1910* (New Scientist) (adj.).

**sev|er|al|ly** (sev′ər ə lē, sev′rə-), *adv.* **1** separately; singly; individually: *Consider these points, first severally and then collectively. He turned severally to each for their opinion* (Oliver Goldsmith). **2** respectively. **3** *Archaic.* apart from others; independently.

**sev|er|al|ty** (sev′ər əl tē, sev′rəl-), *n., pl.* **-ties**. **1** the state of being separate or distinct. **2** *Law.* **a** the condition of being held or owned by separate or individual rights. **b** land so held.
**in severalty**, *Law.* in a person's own right without being joined in interest by another: *They hold their shares in severalty.*

**sev|er|ance** (sev′ər əns, sev′rəns), *n.* **1** the act of severing or state of being severed; separation; division. **2** the act of breaking off: *the severance of diplomatic relations between two countries.* [< Anglo-French *severance,* Old French *sevrance* < *sevrer* to sever]

**severance pay**, additional pay granted to employees who are leaving an establishment or other undertaking, such as a business or company, based on length of service: *Some actors didn't fit their roles, and had to be dismissed with severance pay* (Newsweek).

**severance tax**, *U.S.* a tax on the amount of ore, oil, timber, or the like processed during a certain period, levied on producers in certain states.

**se|vere** (sə vir′), *adj.,* **-ver|er, -ver|est**. **1** very strict; stern; harsh: *a severe reprimand, severe self-denial. The judge imposed a severe sentence on the criminal.* **2** sharp or violent: *severe criticism, a severe winter. I have a severe headache. That was a severe storm.* **3** serious; dangerous; grave: *a severe illness.* **4** very plain or simple; without ornament: *She wore a severe black dress.* SYN: chaste, unadorned. **5** difficult; taxing: *The new gun had to pass a series of severe tests.* SYN: exacting. **6** rigidly exact, accurate, or methodical: *severe reasoning.* SYN: precise, rigid. [< Latin *sevērus*] —**se|vere′ly**, *adv.* —**se|vere′ness**, *n.*
—*Syn.* **1 Severe, stern** mean having or showing strictness. **Severe** implies uncompromising strictness and the absence of any mildness or indulgence: *a severe critic, severe punishment.* **Stern** implies rigid firmness of manner or appearance, sometimes assumed only for the occasion: *a stern look of disapproval. The coach is stern when boys break training.*

**se|ver|i|ty** (sə ver′ə tē), *n., pl.* **-ties**. **1** strictness; sternness; harshness: *The children feared their new neighbor because of his severity.* **2** sharpness or violence: *the severity of storms, the severity of pain, the severity of grief.* **3** simplicity of style or taste; plainness: *I like the severity of modern architecture better than the ornamentation of earlier buildings. The severity of a nun's dress is often becoming.* **4** seriousness; gravity. **5** accuracy; exactness. **6** something severe.

**se|vil|la|na** (sā′vēl yä′nä), *n.* the form of seguidilla performed in Seville, Spain. [< Spanish *sevillana* (literally) of Seville]

**Se|ville orange** (sə vil′), = sour orange. [< *Seville,* a city in Spain]

**Sev|in** (sev′in), *n. Trademark.* carbaryl.

**Sè|vres** (sev′rə), *n., adj.* —***n.*** a choice and costly kind of porcelain made in Sèvres, France. —***adj.*** of or designating this porcelain: *a Sèvres vase.* [< *Sèvres,* a town in France]

**sew** (sō), *v.,* **sewed, sewed** or **sewn, sew|ing**.
—***v.i.*** to work with a needle and thread. You can sew by hand or with a machine.
—***v.t.*** **1** to fasten with stitches: *to sew on a button.* **2** to use a needle and thread to make or mend.
**sew up**, **a** to close with stitches: *The doctor sewed up the wound.* **b** *U.S. Informal.* to make certain: *Betsy Davison had a job sewed up at an uptown private nursery school* (Mary McCarthy).
[Old English *seowian*]

**sew|age** (sü′ij), *n.* the waste matter carried off in sewers and drains.

**sewage farm**, a farm which disposes of sewage by using it to irrigate and fertilize the fields.

**se|wan** (sē′wən), *n.* loose shell beads used as money by American Indians; seawan.

**se|wel|lel** (sə wel′əl), *n. U.S.* a mountain beaver. [American English < Chinook *shewalal* a robe or blanket made from the skins of mountain beaver < *ogwulal* mountain beaver]

**sew|er**[1] (sü′ər), *n.* an underground drain to carry off waste water and refuse. SYN: conduit. [< Old French *sewiere* sluice from a pond, ultimately < Latin *ex* out + *aquāria* (water) vessel < *aqua* water]

**sew|er**[2] (sō′ər), *n.* a person or thing that sews. [< *sew* + *-er*[1]]

**sew|er**[3] (sü′ər), *n.* (formerly) a head servant in charge of arranging the table and serving the meals: *The sewer with savoury meats Dish after dish served them* (William Cowper). [short for Anglo-French *assoeur* (literally) seater < Vulgar Latin *assedēre,* for Latin *assidēre* to sit by < *ad-* by + *sedēre* to sit]

**sew|er|age** (sü′ər ij), *n.* **1** the removal of waste matter by sewers. **2** a system of sewers. **3** = sewage.

**sew|ing** (sō′ing), *n., adj.* —***n.*** **1** work done with a needle and thread: *The fine even stitching was a beautiful piece of sewing.* SYN: needlework. **2** something to be sewed: *He took his sewing to the tailor.*
—***adj.*** for sewing; used in sewing: *a sewing room.*

**sewing circle**, a group of women who meet regularly to sew, as for their church or for charity: *Her sewing circle was to meet at her house ... and most of the members were too decrepit to climb the stairs* (New Yorker).

**sewing machine**, a machine for sewing or stitching cloth.

**sewing silk**, silk thread.

**sewn** (sōn), *v.* sewed; a past participle of **sew**: *Mother has sewn a new button on your shirt.*

**sex** (seks), *n., adj., v.* —***n.*** **1** one of the two divisions of human beings and animals. Men, bulls, and roosters are of the male sex; women, cows, and hens are of the female sex. **2a** the character of being male or female: *People were admitted without regard to age or sex.* **b** the physical quality in plants of having male or female functions. **3** the differences in structure and function between male and female: *The young need ... to be told ... all we know of three fundamental things; the first of which is God ... and the third Sex* (H. G. Wells). **4** the attraction of one sex for the other: *the subject of sex in literature.* **5** behavior between the sexes; sexual matters: *Freud brought sex out from its mid-Victorian cloak* (Alfred B. Heilbrun, Jr.). **6** *Informal.* sexual intercourse.
—***adj.*** of sex; having to do with sex: *sex distinctions, sex education, the sex organs, the sex*

*drive, a person's sex life, the sex attractant of an insect.*
—*v.t.* **1** to determine the sex of: *"We can sex infants before birth* (Donald Gould). *Crocodiles are very hard to sex* (New Scientist). **2** Usually, **sex up.** *Informal.* to make sexy; give sex appeal to: *to sex up a play or movie.*
**the sex,** *Archaic.* women: *The sex of Venice are undoubtedly of a distinguished beauty* (Arthur Young).
[< Latin *sexus, -ūs*]

**sex-,** *combining form.* six: *Sexangular = having six angles.* Also, **sexi-.** [< Latin *sex* six]

**sex|a|ge|nar|i|an** (sek′sə jə nãr′ē ən), *n., adj.*
—*n.* a person who is 60 years old or between 60 and 70 years old.
—*adj.* 60 years old or between 60 and 70 years old.
[< Latin *sexāgēnārius* sexagenary + English *-an*]

**sex|ag|e|nar|y** (sek saj′ə ner′ē), *adj., n., pl.* **-nar|ies.** —*adj.* **1** of or having to do with the number 60. **2** composed of or going by sixties. **3** = sexagenarian.
—*n.* = sexagenarian.
[< Latin *sexāgēnārius* < *sexāgēnī* sixty each < *sexāgintā* sixty]

**Sex|a|ges|i|ma** (sek′sə jes′ə mə), *n.,* or **Sexagesima Sunday,** the second Sunday before Lent. [< Latin *sexāgēsima* (literally) sixtieth < *sexāgintā* sixty]

**sex|a|ges|i|mal** (sek′sə jes′ə məl), *adj., n.* —*adj.* having to do with or based upon the number 60. A sexagesimal fraction is one whose denominator is 60 or a power of 60. *Each table is transcribed in the now standard adaptation of Hindu-Arabic numerals to the sexagesimal notation of the Babylonians* (Science).
—*n.* a sexagesimal fraction.
[< Medieval Latin *sexagesimalis* < Latin *sexāgēsimus* sixtieth < *sexāgintā* sixty]

**sex|an|gu|lar** (seks ang′gyə lər), *adj.* = hexagonal. [< *sex-* + *angular*]

**sex appeal, 1** attraction for the opposite sex: *She has a large endowment of the "plus" quality of femininity, the unexplainable but unmistakable flair called "sex appeal"* (Sunday Express). **2** popular attraction or appeal: *The expression "fiscal responsibility" ... has had little political sex appeal* (Canada Month).

**sex|a|va|lent** (sek′sə vā′lənt, sek sav′ə-), *adj.* = sexivalent.

**sex bomb,** *Slang.* a sexpot.

**sex cell,** an egg cell or sperm cell; germ cell.

**sex|cen|te|nar|y** (seks sen′tə ner′ē, -sen ten′ər-), *adj., n., pl.* **-nar|ies.** —*adj.* having to do with the number 600.
—*n.* **1** a period of 600 years. **2** a 600th anniversary.
[< Latin *sexcentēnī* 600 each (< *sexcentī* 600 < *sex* six + *centum* 100) + English *-ary*]

**sex chromatin,** = Barr body.

**sex chromosome,** either of a pair of chromosomes which in combination with each other determine sex and sex-linked characteristics.

**sex|de|cil|lion** (seks′də sil′yən), *n.* **1** (in the U.S., Canada, and France) 1 followed by 51 zeros. **2** (in Great Britain and Germany) 1 followed by 96 zeros. [< Latin *sexdecim* sixteen (< *sex* six + *decem* ten) + English *-illion,* as in *million*]

**sexed** (sekst), *adj.* having sex or the characteristics of sex.

**sex|en|ni|al** (seks en′ē əl), *adj., n.* —*adj.* **1** of or for six years. **2** occurring every six years.
—*n.* a sexennial celebration or other event.
[< Latin *sexennium* period of six years (< *sex* six + *annus* year) + English *-al*¹] —**sex|en′ni|al|ly,** *adv.*

**sex|en|ni|um** (seks en′ē əm), *n., pl.* **-en|ni|ums, -en|ni|a** (-en′ē ə). a period of six years. [< Latin *sexennium;* see etym. under **sexennial**]

**sex gland,** a gland that produces sex hormones. The gonads are sex glands.

**sex hormone,** a hormone which influences the development or stimulates the function of reproductive organs and other sexual characteristics: *Scientists call the female sex hormones estrogens and the male hormones androgens* (Science News Letter).

**sex hygiene,** the hygiene of sex and sexual activity.

**sexi-,** *combining form.* a form of **sex-,** as in *sexivalent.*

**sex|i|ly** (sek′sə lē), *adv. Informal.* in a sexy manner.

**sex|i|ness** (sek′sē nis), *n. Informal.* the quality of being sexy.

**sex|i|po|lar** (sek′si pō′lər), *adj.* having six poles.

**sex|ism** (sek′siz əm), *n.* discrimination or prejudice based on a person's sex; sexual prejudice, especially against women, as in business or politics: *Our dominant economic classes and institutions ... find declamations against "sexism" less troublesome than having to raise the wages of women workers* (Irving Howe).

**sex|ist** (sek′sist), *n., adj.* —*n.* a person who favors or practices sexism.
—*adj.* of or having to do with sexism; based on or characterized by sexism: *sexist attitudes, a sexist society, sexist laws.*
[patterned after *racist*]

**sex|i|va|lent** (sek′si vā′lənt), *adj.* having a valence of six.

**sex kitten,** *Slang.* a sexy girl or woman.

**sex|less** (seks′lis), *adj.* without sex or the characteristics of sex; asexual. —**sex′less|ly,** *adv.* —**sex′less|ness,** *n.*

**sex-lim|it|ed** (seks′lim′ə tid), *adj. Biology.* capable of phenotypic expression in one sex but not in the other: *Sex-limited characters are sometimes classed as secondary sexual characters. Examples are: beard in man; bright-colored plumage in certain male birds ...; broody tendency of female chickens* (Harbaugh and Goodrich).

**sex-link|age** (seks′ling′kij), *n. Biology.* the state or condition of being sex-linked.

**sex-linked** (seks′lingkt′), *adj. Biology.* of or having to do with a characteristic, such as hemophilia, that is transmitted by genes located in the sex chromosomes: *Traits such as color blindness are said to be sex-linked* (Hegner and Stiles).

**sex|o|log|i|cal** (sek′sə loj′ə kəl), *adj.* of or having to do with sexology.

**sex|ol|o|gist** (sek sol′ə jist), *n.* a person who studies or is an expert in sexology.

**sex|ol|o|gy** (sek sol′ə jē), *n.* the science dealing with sex and sexual conduct.

**sex|par|tite** (seks pär′tīt), *adj.* divided into or consisting of six parts. [< New Latin *sexpartitus* < Latin *sex* six + *partītus* partite, past participle of *partīre* to divide]

**sex|ploi|ta|tion** (seks′ploi tā′shən), *n.* the exploitation of sex in the arts, especially in motion pictures. [blend of *sex* and *exploitation*]

**sex|ploit|er** (seks′ploi tər), *n. Informal.* a motion picture produced for sexploitation.

**sex|pot** (seks′pot′), *n. Slang.* a very sexy or seductive woman.

**sex ratio,** the proportion of males to females in a given population, usually stated as the number of males per 100 females. In man, the sex ratio is 103 to 107 (that is, 103 to 107 males are born to every 100 females born).

**sext** or **Sext** (sekst), *n.* **1** the fourth of the seven canonical hours set aside for prayer and meditation. **2** the office or service for this hour, originally fixed for noon, the sixth hour after sunrise. [< Latin *sexta* (*hōra*) sixth (hour) < *sex* six. See etym. of doublet **siesta.**]

**sex|tain** (seks′tān), *n.* a stanza of six lines. [perhaps alteration of obsolete French *sestine;* patterned on *quatrain*]

**sex|tan** (seks′tən), *n., adj.* —*n.* a fever or ague characterized by paroxysms that recur every sixth day, both days of consecutive occurrence being counted.
—*adj.* **1** of such a fever or ague. **2** recurring every sixth day.
[< New Latin *sextana* (*febris*) sextan (fever) < Latin *sex* six]

**Sex|tans** (seks′tənz), *n., genitive* **Sex|tan|tis.** a constellation south of Leo; the Sextant. [< New Latin *Sextans;* see etym. under **sextant**]

*****sex|tant** (seks′tənt), *n.* **1** an instrument used especially by navigators and surveyors for measuring the angular distance between two objects. Sextants are used at sea to measure the altitude of the sun or a star in order to determine latitude and longitude. *Scientific research has produced another device to make aircraft navigation easier and safer—an automatic celestial sextant* (New York World Telegram). **2** one sixth of a circle. [< New Latin *sextans* (apparently coined by Tycho Brahe) sextant < Latin *sextāns, -antis* a sixth < *sex* six]

*** sextant**
definition 1

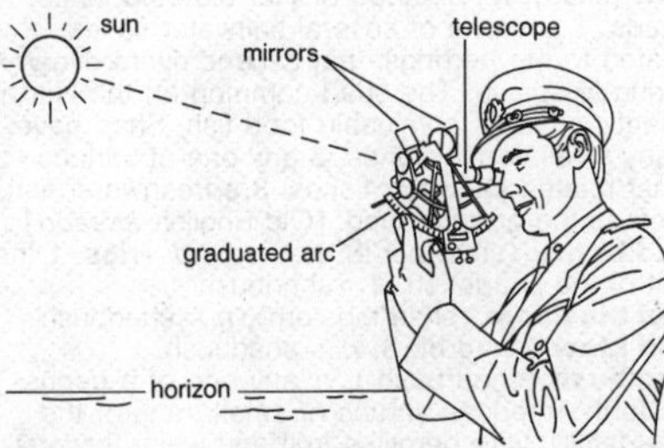


**Sex|tant** (seks′tənt), *n.* = Sextans. [< *sextant*]

**Sex|tan|tis** (sek stan′tis), *n.* genitive of **Sextans.**

**sex|tet** or **sex|tette** (seks tet′), *n.* **1a** a piece of music for six voices or instruments. **b** a group of six singers or players performing together. **2** any group of six. [partly < German *Sextett,* partly alteration of *sestet;* influenced by Latin *sex* six]

**sex|tile** (seks′təl), *adj., n. Astrology.* —*adj.* of or having to do with the aspect of two heavenly bodies 60 degrees distant from each other.
—*n.* a sextile aspect.
[earlier, one sixth of the zodiac < Latin *sextīlis* (*mēnsis*) old name of August; (literally) pertaining to the sixth month < *sex* six]

**sex|til|lion** (seks til′yən), *n., adj.* **1** (in the U.S., Canada, and France) 1 followed by 21 zeros; 1,000 to the seventh power. **2** (in Great Britain and Germany) 1 followed by 36 zeros; 1,000,000 to the sixth power. [< French *sextillion* < Latin *sextus* sixth; patterned on *million* million]

**sex|til|lionth** (seks til′yənth), *adj., n.* **1** last in a series of a sextillion. **2** one, or being one, of a sextillion equal parts.

**sex|to|dec|i|mo** (seks′tō des′ə mō), *n., pl.* **-mos,** *adj.* —*n.* **1** a size of a book, or of its pages, made by folding a sheet of paper into sixteen parts to form leaves about 4½ × 6¾ inches. **2** a book with pages this size.
—*adj.* of this size; having pages this size.
[< Latin *sextō,* ablative of *sextus* sixth (< *sex* six) + *decimō,* ablative of *decimus* tenth < *decem* ten]

**sex|tole** (seks′tōl), *n.* = sextolet.

**sex|to|let** (seks′tə let′), *n. Music.* a group of six notes to be played in the time of four. [< Latin *sextus* sixth + English *-let*]

**sex|ton** (seks′tən), *n.* **1** a man who takes care of a church. A sexton's duties, in addition to acting as janitor, sometimes include ringing the bell and digging graves. **2** the caretaker of a synagogue or Jewish temple. [< Old French *segrestein* and *secrestein,* learned borrowing from Medieval Latin *sacristanus.* See etym. of doublet **sacristan.**]

**sexton beetle,** any one of certain beetles that bury small dead animals in which they have deposited their eggs; burying beetle. Their larvae eat the decaying flesh.

**sex|tu|ple** (seks′tů pəl, -tyů-; seks tü′-, -tyü′-), *adj., n., v.,* **-pled, -pling.** —*adj.* **1** consisting of six parts; sixfold. **2** six times as great. **3** *Music.* characterized by six beats to the measure: *sextuple rhythm.*
—*n.* a number or amount six times as great as another.
—*v.t., v.i.* to make or become six times as great.
[< Latin *sextus* sixth; patterned on *quadruple*]

**sex|tu|plet** (seks′tů plit, -tyů-; seks tü′-, -tyü′-), *n.* **1** one of six offspring born of the same mother at the same time. **2** any group or combination of six. [< *sextuple,* patterned on *quadruplet*]

**sex|tu|plex** (seks′tů pleks, -tyů-), *adj.* **1** = sixfold. **2** of or having to do with a system of telegraphy by which six messages may be transmitted simultaneously over one wire. [< Medieval Latin *sextuplex* sixfold < Latin *sex* six; patterned on *quadruplex*]

**sex|tu|pli|cate** (*adj., n.* seks tü′plə kit, -tyü′-; *v.* seks tü′plə kāt, -tyü′-), *adj., v.,* **-cat|ed, -cat|ing,** *n.* —*adj.* **1** sixfold; sextuple. **2** *Mathematics.* raised to the sixth power.
—*v.t.* to make sixfold; sextuple.
—*n.* one of six things, especially six copies of a document, exactly alike.
**in sextuplicate,** in six copies, exactly alike: [*She*] *took down the ... testimony in sextuplicate* (Newsweek).
[< Medieval Latin *sextuplicatus,* past participle of *sextuplicāre* < *sextuplex;* see etym. under **sextuplex**]

**sex|u|al** (sek′shů əl), *adj.* **1** of or having to do with sex. In sexual reproduction, animals and plants reproduce their own kind by the union of the male and female germ cells or gametes. **2** of or between the sexes: *sexual love. Her very frankness suggested a perfect sexual equality* (Bret Harte). **3** having to do with the relations between the sexes: *sexual morality, sexual excess.* **4** having sex; separated into two sexes. [< Late Latin *sexuālis* < Latin *sexus, -ūs* sex]

**sexual generation,** the sexual phase in the alternation of generations. See picture under **alternation of generations.**

**sex|u|a|li|a** (sek′shů ā′lē ə), *n.pl.* books or writings dealing with sex: *a library of sexualia.* [< New Latin *sexualia* < Late Latin *sexuālis* sexual]

**sexual intercourse,** the uniting or joining of sexual organs, usually with ejaculation of semen; coitus; copulation.

**sex|u|al|ism** (sek′shů ə liz′əm), *n.* **1** sexuality as

**Pronunciation Key:** hat, āge, cãre, fär; let, ēqual, tėrm; it, īce; hot, ōpen, ôrder; **oi**l, **ou**t; cup, půt, rüle; **ch**ild; lo**ng**; **th**in; **ᴛʜ**en; **zh**, measure; ə represents **a** in about, **e** in taken, **i** in pencil, **o** in lemon, **u** in circus.

a principle of action or thought. **2** = sexuality.
**sex|u|al|i|ty** (sek′shü al′ə tē), *n.* **1** sexual character; possession of sex. **2** the possession of sexual powers or capability of sexual feelings. **3** attention to sexual matters.
**sex|u|al|i|za|tion** (sek′shü ə lə zā′shən), *n.* the act or fact of sexualizing.
**sex|u|al|ize** (sek′shü ə līz), *v.t.,* **-ized, -iz|ing.** to give sexual meaning or character to; make sexual: *to sexualize an object or a relationship.*
**sex|u|al|ly** (sek′shü ə lē), *adv.* **1** by means of sex. **2** in regard to sex.
**sexual relations,** = sexual intercourse.
**sexual selection,** *Biology.* natural selection perpetuating certain characteristics that attract one sex to the other, such as bright feathers in birds: *I conclude that of all the causes which have led to the differences in external appearance between the races of men ... sexual selection has been by far the most efficient* (Charles Darwin).
**sex|u|pa|ra** (sek sü′pə rə), *n.pl.* parthenogenetic female organisms which give birth to males and to females that lay fertilized eggs. [< New Latin *sexupara* < Latin *sexus, -ūs* sex + *parere* to bring forth]
**sex|u|pa|rous** (sek sü′pə rəs), *adj.* having to do with sexupara.
**sex|y** (sek′sē), *adj.,* **sex|i|er, sex|i|est.** *Informal.* sexually appealing or stimulating; having sex appeal: *sexy photographs, sexy beauties. With words and music just simple, sad and sexy enough to make it sound like a hit* (Time).
**Sey|chell|ois** (sā shel′wä), *n., pl.* **-ois,** *adj.* —*n.* a native or inhabitant of Seychelles (a country of many islands in the Indian Ocean). —*adj.* of or from the Seychelles.
**Sey|fert** (sē′fərt), *n.,* or **Seyfert galaxy,** any one of a group of spiral galaxies having very small, starlike centers which exhibit broad emission lines indicative of a high state of atomic excitation: *A possible link between normal galaxies and quasars may be provided by the Seyfert galaxies, which have unusually bright nuclei similar in many ways to the sharply defined quasars* (Science Journal). [< Carl K. *Seyfert,* 1911-1960, an American astronomer, who listed and described ten of these galaxies in the 1940's]
**Seym** (sām), *n.* = Sejm.
**sf.,** sforzando.
**SF** (no periods), science fiction: *Long ago the SF writer was deprived of his Bug-eyed Monsters and compelled to use jargon that bore at least a superficial patina of conviction to the student of physics* (Punch).
**Sfc.,** sergeant first class.
**sfer|ics** (sfer′iks), *n.* **1** = atmospherics. **2** the study of atmospherics; spherics. **3** an electronic detector of atmospheric disturbances. [variant of *spherics*[2]]
**sfor|zan|do** (sfôr tsän′dō), *adj., adv., n., pl.* **-dos, -di** (-dē). *Music.* —*adj.* with special, usually sudden, emphasis (used as a direction). —*adv.* in a sforzando manner.
—*n.* a tone or chord played with special emphasis or rendered louder than the rest: *In Beethoven his sforzandi were often hard and ugly* (London Times). *Abbr:* sfz.
[< Italian *sforzando,* present participle of *sforzare* to force]
**sfor|za|to** (sfôr tsä′tō), *adj.* = sforzando. [< Italian *sforzato,* past participle of *sforzare* to force]
**sfu|ma|to** (sfü mä′tō), *n.* a misty or indistinct effect in a painting caused by blending the tints so that the outlines cannot be perceived. [< Italian *sfumato* (literally) smoked]
**sfz.,** sforzando.
**s.g.,** specific gravity.
**S.G.,** solicitor general.
**S.-G.,** Secretary-General (of the United Nations).
**sgd.,** signed.
**sgraf|fi|to** (zgraf fē′tō), *n., pl.* **-ti** (-tē). a type of decoration scratched through a layer as of paint, plaster, or clay; graffito: *... embellished with sgraffito designs of foliage on a slightly ridged surface* (New Yorker). [< Italian *sgraffito.* Compare etym. under **graffito.**]
**Sgt.** or **sgt.,** sergeant.
**Sgt. Maj.,** sergeant major.
**sh** or **'sh** (sh), *interj.* a shortened form of **hush,** used in urging silence: *"Sh!" she whispered. "Never mind what you make"* (Leonard Merrick).
**sh.,** an abbreviation for the following:
**1** share.
**2** *Bookbinding.* sheep.
**3** sheet.
**4** shilling or shillings.
**5** short.
**SH** (no period), sulfhydryl.
**SHA** (no periods), sidereal hour angle.
**Sha|ban** (shə bän′), *n.* the eighth month of the Moslem year. It has 29 days. [< Arabic *sha'bān*]
**Shab|bat** (shə bät′), *n. Hebrew.* the Jewish Sabbath.
**shab|bi|ly** (shab′ə lē), *adv.* in a shabby manner: (*Figurative.*) *Schumann's exacting Toccata was also rather shabbily treated* (London Times).
**shab|bi|ness** (shab′ē nis), *n.* shabby condition or quality.
**shab|ble** (shab′əl), *n. Archaic.* **1** a saber. **2** a curved sword. [< Italian *sciabola.* Ultimately related to **saber.**]
**Shab|bos** (shä′bəs), *n. Yiddish.* the Jewish Sabbath.
**shab|by** (shab′ē), *adj.,* **-bi|er, -bi|est. 1** much worn: *His old suit looks shabby. The other had his hand bound up with shabby strips of a tropical shirt* (Graham Greene). **2** wearing old or much worn clothes; poorly dressed: *She is always shabby.* **3** poor or neglected; run-down: *a shabby old house.* **4** *Figurative.* not generous; mean; unfair: *It is shabby not to speak to an old friend because he is poor. Strangers get such shabby treatment in this town that they never want to visit it again.*
**shab|by-gen|teel** (shab′ē jen tēl′), *adj.* shabby but genteel; making or showing an effort to keep up appearances.
**shab|by-gen|til|i|ty** (shab′ē jen til′ə tē), *n.* the condition of being shabby-genteel.
**shab|le** (shab′əl), *n.* = shabble.
**shab|rack** (shab′rak), *n.* a saddlecloth used in European armies. [< French *schabraque* < German *Schabracke,* perhaps < Turkish *chaprak*]
**Sha|bu|oth** or **Sha|bu|ot** (shä vü′ōth, -ōt), *n.* a Jewish festival, seven weeks after the beginning of Passover, celebrating the harvest and the giving of the Torah to Moses; Pentecost; Feast of Weeks. Also, **Shavuos.** [< Hebrew *shabuoth* (literally) weeks, plural of *shabuā*]
**shack**[1] (shak), *n., v.* —*n.* **1** a roughly built hut or cabin: *The boys made a shack out of old boards in the backyard. The Caney Creek Community Center was born in a one-room shack* (Newsweek). SYN: shanty. **2** *Informal.* **a** a house in bad condition: *There are a lot of shacks in the rundown part of town near the railroad.* **b** a house that is poorly built or designed.
—*v.i. Slang.* **1** to live at a place; dwell: *He shacks in a boarding house.* **2** Usually, **shack up. a** to stay in a place: *I was going to shack up in a hotel for a couple of days* (J. D. Salinger). **b** to live together as husband and wife though not legally married; cohabit.
[American English; origin uncertain; perhaps back formation < *ramshackle*]
**shack**[2] (shak), *v.t.* = shag[2].
**shack|le** (shak′əl), *n., v.,* **-led, -ling.** —*n.* **1** a metal band fastened around the ankle or wrist of a prisoner or slave. Shackles are usually fastened to each other, the wall, or the floor by chains. **2** the link fastening together the two rings for the ankles and wrists of a prisoner. **3** Also, **shackles.** *Figurative.* anything that prevents freedom of action or thought: *Superstition and fear of change are two great shackles on men's minds. ... the bars and shackles of civilization* (Mark Twain). *He frequently writes of the shackles imposed by the Japanese family system* (Atlantic). SYN: impediment, obstacle. **4** a thing for fastening or coupling, leaving some freedom of movement: *The springs of a car are secured on each end by shackles.*
—*v.t.* **1** to put shackles on. **2** *Figurative.* to restrain; hamper. SYN: obstruct, restrict. **3** to fasten or couple with a shackle: (*Figurative.*) *... who were not shackled to the past in their thinking* (New York Times). [Old English *sceacel*]
**shack|le-bone** (shak′əl bōn′), *n. Scottish.* the wrist.
**shack|ler** (shak′lər), *n.* a person or thing that shackles.
**shack|town** (shak′toun′), *n. U.S. and Canada.* a group or settlement of makeshift shacks; shantytown.
**shad** (shad), *n., pl.* **shad** or (*for different kinds*) **shads. 1** any one of several saltwater fishes, related to the herrings, that ascend rivers every spring to spawn. The shad common on the North Atlantic coast is a valuable food fish. Shad have many small, loose bones. **2** any one of various other related saltwater fishes. **3** a freshwater fish, such as the gizzard shad. [Old English *sceadd*]
**shad|ber|ry** (shad′ber′ē, -bər-), *n., pl.* **-ries. 1** the fruit of the shadbush. **2** = shadbush.
**shad|blos|som** (shad′blos′əm), *n.* = shadbush.
**shad|blow** (shad′blō′), *n.* = shadbush.
**shad|bush** (shad′bùsh′), *n.* any one of a genus of North American shrubs or small trees of the rose family, with berrylike fruit and white flowers which blossom about the time when shad appear in the rivers; Juneberry; serviceberry.
**shad|chan** (shäd′ʜən), *n., pl.* **shad|cho|nim** (shäd′ʜō′nim). *Yiddish.* a professional matchmaker or marriage broker. Also, **schatchen.**
**shad|dock** (shad′ək), *n.* **1** the pear-shaped citrus fruit of a tree of the rue family, like a coarse, dry, inferior grapefruit. **2** the tree that it grows on. [< a Captain *Shaddock,* who introduced the fruit into the West Indies in the 1600's]
**shade** (shād), *n., v.,* **shad|ed, shad|ing.** —*n.* **1** a partly dark place, not in the sunshine: *We sat in the shade of a big tree.* **2** a slight darkness or coolness given by something that cuts off light: *Leafy trees cast shade.* **3** *Figurative.* a place or condition of comparative obscurity or seclusion. **4** something that shuts out light: *Pull down the shades of the windows.* **5** lightness or darkness of color: *I want to see silks in all shades of blue.* SYN: See syn. under **color. 6a** the dark part of a picture. **b** = shading. **7** *Figurative.* a very small difference, amount, or degree; little bit: *a shade of meaning, a shade too long, many shades of opinion. Your coat is a shade longer than your dress.* **8** *Figurative.* a darkening look, feeling, or the like; shadow; cloud: *A shade of doubt troubled her.* **9a** a ghost; spirit: *the shades of departed heroes. This woman had been a dissolute creature in life and she was certainly no less so as a shade* (New Yorker). **b** *Figurative.* something that has only a momentary existence, or that has become reduced almost to nothing.
—*v.t.* **1** to keep light from; darken: *A big hat shades the eyes.* **2** to make darker than the rest, especially to use black or color to give the effect of shade in a picture. **3** *Figurative.* to make dark or gloomy. **4** *Figurative.* to lessen slightly: *to shade prices.*
—*v.i.* to show very small differences; change little by little: *This scarf shades from deep rose to pale pink.*
**in** (or **into**) **the shade, a** out of the light: *Two maximum thermometers are issued—one to observe the greatest heat in the sun, the other in the shade* (Edmund Parkes). **b** *Figurative.* in or into a condition of being unknown or unnoticed: *Bacon still remained in the shade* (Richard W. Church).
**shades,** *Slang.* sunglasses: *Your teen-age daughter asks what you think of her shades, which you are canny enough to know are her sunglasses* (New York Times).
**shades of,** reminiscent of: *... a shimmering silk velvet in oyster white* (*shades of Jean Harlow*) (New York Times). *Shades of the thirties! Then the recruits in the Civilian Conservation Camps were planting trees on our plains to save them from the elements* (Murray L. Silberstein).
**(the) shades, a** the darkness of evening or night: *The shades ... had by this time fallen upon the quiet city* (Thackeray). **b** the inhabitants of hell, as a group: *A journey after death to reach the home of shades* (Charles Keary).
**c** hell: *See! on one Greek three Trojan ghosts attend, This, my third victim, to the shades I send* (Alexander Pope).
[Old English *sceadu.* Compare etym. under **shadow.**] —**shad′er,** *n.*
**shad|ed** (shā′did), *adj.* **1a** protected from light or heat: *There are shaded walks for study and contemplation* (Margaret Calderwood). **b** covered with a shade: *The shaded lamps were lighted* (Iza Duffus Hardy). **2** covered with shadow: *O'er the shaded billows rushed the night* (Alexander Pope). **3** having colors gradually passing into one another; marked with gradations of color. **4** (in painting and drawing) furnished with colors or markings to indicate shade.
**shade|less** (shād′lis), *adj.* having or affording no shade.
**shade tree, 1** any tree that gives shade. **2** any one of certain species of trees, as most maples, that provide good shade.
**shad|fly** (shad′flī′), *n., pl.* **-flies,** or **shad fly,** a May fly or similar insect that appears at or near the time when shad start up the river.
**shad|ing** (shā′ding), *n.* **1** a covering from the light. **2** the use of black or color to give the effect of shade or depth in a picture. **3** *Figurative.* a slight variation or difference of color, character, or quality.
**sha|doof** (shä düf′), *n.* a long rod with a bucket on one end and a weight on the other, used for raising water in the Near East. [< Arabic *shādūf*]
**shad|ow** (shad′ō), *n., v., adj.* —*n.* **1** shade made by some person, animal, or thing; darkness which something casts on a surface by intercepting direct rays of light. Sometimes a person's shadow is much longer than he is, and sometimes much shorter. **2** shade, darkness, or partial shade: *Don't turn on the light; we like to sit in the shadow.* **3** the dark part of a place or picture. **4** *Figurative.* a little bit; small degree; slight suggestion: *There's not a shadow of a doubt about their guilt.* **5** a ghost; specter: *There sat the Shadow fear'd of man* (Tennyson). **6** *Figurative.* **a** faint image: *She was worn to a shadow of her usual self.* **b** anything that is unreal or imaginary even though it seems real: *Titles are shadows, Crowns are empty things* (Daniel Defoe).

*What shadows we are, and what shadows we pursue* (Edmund Burke). **7** a reflected image: *And on the bay the moonlight lay, And the shadow of the Moon* (Samuel Taylor Coleridge). **8** *Figurative.* protection; shelter: *Hide me under the shadow of thy wings* (Psalms 17:8). **9** a person who follows another closely and secretly, such as a detective. **10** a constant companion; follower. **11** *Figurative.* **a** sadness; gloom. **b** something that causes gloom: *Love is sunshine, hate is shadow* (Longfellow). **12** *Figurative.* a gloomy or troubled look or expression. **13** *Figurative.* a temporary interruption: *A shadow came over their friendship.* **14** *Figurative.* something that obscures, such as the luster of fame or glory: *There is a shadow over his reputation.* **15** *Figurative.* obscurity.
— ***v.t.*** **1** to protect from light; shade: *The grass is shadowed by huge oaks.* **2** to cast a shadow on. **3** *Figurative.* to represent faintly. **4** to follow closely and secretly: *The detective shadowed the suspected burglar.* **5** *Figurative.* to make sad or gloomy. **6** to represent in a prophetic way.
— ***adj.*** **1** of or belonging to a shadow cabinet: *Labour's principal speaker was ... the shadow Chancellor of the Exchequer* (Manchester Guardian Weekly). **2** unofficial: *a shadow legislature, a shadow organization, a shadow Presidential campaign. He has formed a sort of shadow government that is said to be busy drafting bills without reference to the wishes of the President* (Tom Buckley).
**be afraid of one's own shadow,** to be unreasonably timorous; be extremely frightened: *One gets the impression that the whole back line [of people] are afraid of their own shadows* (Vivian Jenkins).
**cast a long shadow,** to wield great influence or power: [*She*] *is always driven by the need for self-assertion, whether it involves ... meddling with politics and art, or merely casting a long shadow over all the people she encounters* (Atlantic).
**shadow forth,** to represent faintly: *By the same four* [*creatures*], *in the opinion of many of the Fathers, are shadowed forth the four Evangelists* (Thomas Godwin).
**(the) shadows,** the darkness after sunset: *Shadows of the evening Steal across the sky* (Sabine Baring-Gould).
**under** (or **in**) **the shadow of,** very near to: *The friends met in a little cafe under the shadow of St. Peter's.*
[< Old English *sceadwe,* oblique case of *sceadu* shade. Compare etym. under **shade.**] — **shad′ow·er,** *n.* — **shad′ow·like′,** *adj.*

**shadow band,** one of a series of roughly parallel broken bands, alternately bright and dark, and moving with an irregular, flickering motion over every light-colored surface during a solar eclipse. It is seen just before and after the period of total eclipse. *The fact that shadow bands are not visible at all eclipses proves satisfactorily their atmospheric origin* (New Scientist).

**shadow bird,** = umbrette.

**shad|ow|box** (shad′ō boks′), *v.i.* to engage in shadowboxing: *Then he shadowboxed, and imagined that he was beating up some hard guy* (James T. Farrell).

**shadow box,** **1** a box or boxlike structure with artificial lighting to draw attention to and highlight certain features of an object or painting displayed in it: *There was a great framed shadow box containing a representation of the coronation of Czar Alexander II* (New Yorker). **2** a device to shield a projection surface for viewing a film in daylight.

**shad|ow|box|ing** (shad′ō bok′sing), *n.* **1** boxing with an imaginary opponent for exercise or training: *In the morning he did fifteen minutes' shadowboxing before going down to breakfast* (Atlantic). **2** *Figurative.* fighting with imaginary opponents: *political shadowboxing. The Administration is in no mood for the usual diplomatic shadowboxing* (London Times).

**shadow cabinet,** **1** a group of influential advisers chosen by the head of a government; kitchen cabinet: *Some back-benchers are commenting bitterly on the judgment of the shadow cabinet* (Sunday Times). **2** a similar group of advisers forming the governing body of a minority or opposition party: *Labor's shadow cabinet ... men who would be Cabinet ministers if their party returned to power* (Time).

**shadow dance,** a dance in which the shadows of the performers (who are invisible) are thrown on a screen.

**shadow figure,** a flat figure or silhouette used in puppetry to cast black or colored shadows on a screen.

**shad|ow|graph** (shad′ō graf, -gräf), *n.* **1** a picture produced by throwing a shadow on a lighted screen. **2** an X-ray picture; radiograph. **3** = shadow play.

**shad|ow|graph|ist** (shad′ō graf′ist, -gräf′-), *n.* a person who is skilled or trained in shadowgraphy.

**shad|ow|graph|y** (shad′ō graf′ē, -gräf′-), *n.* the producing of shadowgraphs.

**shad|ow|land** (shad′ō land′), *n.* a region of shadows, phantoms, unrealities, or uncertainties: *Congress ... has a responsibility to watch carefully over an agency it created to stand watch in that shadowland between peace and war* (Wall Street Journal).

**shad|ow|less** (shad′ō lis), *adj.* having or casting no shadow. — **shad′ow|less|ly,** *adv.*

**shadow of death,** the darkness or gloom of death, especially approaching or imminent death: *Before I go whence I shall not return, even to the land of darkness and the shadow of death* (Job 10:21).

**shadow pantomime,** = shadow play.

**shadow play,** an entertainment in which the shadows of actors, puppets, or other forms are cast upon a screen placed between the stage and the auditorium: *In these shadow plays, the figures are made of cardboard with translucent paper for the eyes and mouth* (Atlantic).

**shad|ow|y** (shad′ō ē), *adj.* **1** having much shadow or shade; shady: *We are glad to leave the hot sun and come into the cool, shadowy room.* SYN: dark, obscure. **2** like a shadow; dim, faint, or slight: *a shadowy figure. We saw a shadowy outline on the window curtain.* (*Figurative.*) *But as for who the shadowy seller of the forgeries was, no one had the slightest idea* (New Yorker). SYN: fleeting, vague, indistinct. **3** *Figurative.* not real; ghostly; imaginary. **4** *Obsolete.* symbolic. — **shad′ow|i|ly,** *adv.* — **shad′ow|i|ness,** *n.*

**Sha|drach** (shā′drak, shad′rak), *n.* a companion of Daniel, one of the three young Hebrews who remained unharmed in Nebuchadnezzar's fiery furnace (in the Bible, Daniel 2:49-3:30): *The oil that calked the walls of Babylon and may have fired the furnace through which Shadrach, Meshach and Abednego walked unscathed now bubbles through huge pipelines to the Mediterranean* (Time).

**shad|scale** (shad′skāl′), *n.* a low scaly shrub of the goosefoot family growing in dry, salty areas of the western United States: *Commonest of the uranium-indicating plants are rabbit brush, shadscale ...* (Science News Letter).

**sha|duf** (shä düf′), *n.* = shadoof.

**shad-wait|er** (shad′wā′tər), *n.* a whitefish of lakes of Siberia and North America from New England to Alaska.

**shad|y** (shā′dē), *adj.,* **shad|i|er, shad|i|est.** **1** in the shade; shaded. SYN: shadowy. **2** giving shade. **3** *Informal, Figurative.* of doubtful honesty or character: *That man is a shady character, if not an actual criminal. He has engaged in rather shady occupations.* SYN: dubious, questionable. — **shad′i|ly,** *adv.* — **shad′i|ness,** *n.*

**SHAEF** (shāf), *n.* Supreme Headquarters, Allied Expeditionary Forces.

**Sha|fi'i** (shä′fē ē), *n.* a member of a large sect of Sunnites or orthodox Moslems in Yemen. [< (*al-*) *Shafi'i,* A.D. 767-820, the Arab founder of a school of Islamic law to whose tenets this sect adheres]

**shaft** (shaft, shäft), *n., v.* — ***n.*** **1** a bar to support parts of a machine that turn, or to help move parts such as gears or pulleys, or to transmit power from one part of a machine to another, such as the drive shaft of an automobile. **2** a deep passage sunk in the earth. The entrance to a mine is called a shaft. *He had been caught by a landslide in a tiny shaft of the cave* (Newsweek). **3** a passage that is like a well; long, narrow space: *an elevator shaft.* **4** the long, slender stem of an arrow, spear, or lance. **5** an arrow, spear, or lance. **6** *Figurative.* something aimed at a person like an arrow or spear: *shafts of ridicule. A shield against its shafts of doubt* (John Greenleaf Whittier). *The shaft of love ... had struck me* (Arnold Bennett). **7a** a ray or beam of light. **b** *Figurative:* [*His*] *observations are a refreshing and badly needed shaft of common sense* (Wall Street Journal). **8** one of the two wooden poles between which a horse is harnessed to a carriage or other vehicle. **9** the main part of a column or pillar. See picture under **Corinthian.** **10a** a column. **b** a column or obelisk erected as a memorial. **c** = flagpole. **d** the part of a candlestick that supports the branches. **11** the long, straight handle as of a hammer, ax, or golf club: *the shaft of an umbrella.* **12** a stem; stalk: *... the symmetrical shaft of the cocoanut tree* (Herman Melville). **13** the rib of a feather. **14** a fiber of human hair. **15** the long part of a bone.
— ***v.t.*** **1** to fit (an arrowhead, weapon, or tool) with a shaft. **2** to propel (a barge or the like) with a pole. **3** *Slang.* to take unfair advantage of; victimize: *"If you shaft somebody who is down ... then other people know they're going to get shafted, too"* (New Yorker).
[Old English *sceaft*] — **shaft′like′,** *adj.*

**shaft|ed** (shaf′tid, shäf′-), *adj.* having a shaft or shafts.

**shaft horsepower,** the horsepower delivered by the drive shaft of an engine. *Abbr:* s.hp.

**shaft house,** a heavy framework at the top of a mine shaft, to support the hoisting machinery, sometimes enclosed.

**shaft|ing** (shaf′ting, shäf′-), *n.* **1** shafts. **2** a system of shafts, especially for transmitting power to machinery. **3** material for shafts.

**shaft|man** (shaft′man′, -mən; shäft′-), *n., pl.* **-men.** a man employed to sink shafts or to keep shafts in repair: *a colliery shaftman.*

**shaft|ment** (shaft′mənt), *n.* the feathered or back part of an arrow.

**shaft tug,** one of a pair of long leather straps in a horse's harness to which the shafts of a carriage or wagon are attached.

**shag**[1] (shag), *n., v.,* **shagged, shag|ging,** *adj.*
— ***n.*** **1a** rough, matted hair, wool, or the like. **b** a mass of this: *the shag of a dog.* **2a** the long, rough nap of some kinds of cloth, especially a layer of woven loops, longer and coarser than pile. **b** cloth having such a nap, especially a fabric of worsted or silk. **3** a tangled mass, such as of shrubs, trees, or foliage. **4** a coarse tobacco cut into shreds. **5** a cormorant, especially a European species which in the breeding season has a short, upright crest.
— ***v.t.*** **1** to make rough or shaggy (with a growth of trees or the like). **2** *Obsolete.* to make a long or rough nap or pile on (a fabric).
— ***adj.*** having a shag; shaggy: *a shag dog, a shag rug.*
[perhaps Old English *sceacga* matted hair, wool]
▶ See **pile**[3] for usage note.

**shag**[2] (shag), *v.,* **shagged, shag|ging.** — ***v.t.*** *Informal.* **1** to catch or retrieve and throw back (a ball): *At ten, he was shagging flies at the Toronto Maple Leaf baseball practices* (Maclean's). **2** to run after; chase: *He hastened in ... and shagged away the kids who played on the furniture* (Saul Bellow).
— ***v.i.*** **1** *Informal.* to catch or retrieve balls for a player: *During a warmup on the practice range, he had driven a ball that hit a caddie who was shagging for Bill Collins* (New York Times).
**2** *U.S. Slang.* to go away; leave at once; get out: *Time to shag. Let's shag off.*
[origin unknown]

**shag**[3] (shag), *n., v.,* **shagged, shag|ging.** — ***n.*** a hopping dance popular in the 1930's: *As they swoop and leap to the remembered acrobatics of the Lindy, the Shag ... time is, in a sense, expunged* (New Yorker).
— ***v.i.*** to dance the shag.
[< earlier *shag* to shake. See related etym. at **shake.**]

*** shag|bark** (shag′bärk′), *n.* **1** a kind of hickory tree of eastern North America whose rough outer bark peels off in long strips. **2** the nut of this tree. Shagbarks have fairly thin shells and are considered the best hickory nuts. **3** its wood. **4** = shellbark (def. 2). **5** a cotton fabric of rough texture somewhat like the bark of the shagbark: *Sun dresses of pink or orchid shagbark, a cotton into which raised pin dots and stripes are woven ...* (New Yorker). [American English < *shag*[1] + *bark*]

*** shagbark** definition 1

**shag-eared** (shag′ird′), *adj.* having hairy ears: *a shag-eared pony.*

**shag|ged** (shag′id), *adj.* **1a** covered with shaggy hair. **b** like shaggy hair. **2** covered with a rough

---

**Pronunciation Key:** hat, āge, cãre, fär; let, ēqual, tėrm; it, īce; hot, ōpen, ôrder; oil, out; cup, pu̇t, rüle; child; long; thin; ᴛʜen; zh, measure; ə represents **a** in about, **e** in taken, **i** in pencil, **o** in lemon, **u** in circus.

growth of vegetation: *a deep mountain glen, wild, lonely, and shagged* (Washington Irving). **3** having a jagged or broken surface.

**shag|ger** (shag′ər), *n.* a person who catches or retrieves balls and throws them back. [< *shag*² + *-er*¹]

**shag|gy** (shag′ē), *adj.,* **-gi|er, -gi|est. 1** covered with a thick, rough mass of hair or wool, or something resembling them: *a shaggy dog.* **2** long, thick, and rough: *shaggy eyebrows, a shaggy mustache.* **3** unkempt in appearance, especially needing a haircut or shave. **4** covered with a rough, tangled growth of plants. **5** having a long, rough nap; of coarse texture: *a shaggy felt hat, a shaggy rug.* — **shag′gi|ly,** *adv.* — **shag′gi|ness,** *n.*

**shaggy dog story,** a story which relates, usually at great length, a number of unimportant incidents in building up to an unexpected or ridiculous climax. [< an original story of this type in which a *shaggy dog* appeared]

**shag|gy-mane** (shag′ē mān′), *n.* a fungus having a white top that is good to eat.

**sha|green** (shə grēn′), *n., adj.* — *n.* **1** a kind of untanned leather with a granular surface made from the skin of the horse, ass, shark, seal, or other animals. It is usually dyed green. **2** the rough skin of certain sharks and rays, used especially for polishing.
— ***adj.*** made of shagreen: *a shagreen case.*
[< French *chagrin* < Turkish *sağri* rump of a horse. Compare etym. under **chagrin.**]

**Shah** or **shah** (shä), *n.* **1** the title of the ruler of Iran. **2** a title of local chiefs in various Asian countries, especially India. [< Persian *shāh* king]

**Sha|hap|ti|an** (shä hap′tē ən), *adj., n., pl.* **-ans** or **-an.** — ***adj.*** of or having to do with an American Indian linguistic family that includes the language of the Nez Percés.
— ***n.*** **1** an Indian of this linguistic family. Shahaptians lived in the northern part of the valley of the Columbia River. **2** this linguistic family. Also, **Sahaptan.**
[American English < Salishan *Saháptini,* plural of *Sáptini* a Salishan name for the Nez Percé Indians]

**Shah|dom** or **shah|dom** (shä′dəm), *n.* the territory under the rule of a Shah.

**shah|rith** (shäʜ′ris, -rith), *n. Judaism.* the daily morning prayer or service. [< Hebrew *shaḥarith* < *shaḥar* morning]

**shaikh** (shēk; *especially British* shāk), *n. Especially British.* sheik.

**shaikh|dom** (shēk′dəm; *especially British* shāk′-), *n. Especially British.* sheikdom.

**shai|tan** (shī tän′), *n.* **1** in Moslem usage: **a** Often, **Shaitan.** Satan; the Devil. **b** an evil spirit, especially one of an order of the jinn. **2** a vicious person or animal. Also, **sheitan.** [< Arabic *shaiṭān* < Hebrew *sāṭān* adversary]

**Shak.,** Shakespeare.

**shak|a|ble** (shā′kə bəl), *adj.* that can be shaken.

**shake** (shāk), *v.,* **shook, shak|en, shak|ing,** *n.*
— ***v.t.*** **1** to cause to move quickly backwards and forwards, up and down, or from side to side: *to shake a rug, to shake one's head. The baby shook the rattle.* **2** to bring, throw, force, rouse, or scatter by or as if by movement: *to shake dust from a rug. He shook the snow off his clothes.* **3** to clasp (a hand or hands) in greeting or congratulating another: *The businessmen shook hands after signing the contract.* **4** to make tremble: *The explosion shook the building.* **5** *Figurative.* to cause to totter or waver: *to shake the very foundations of society.* **6** *Figurative.* to disturb; make less firm or sure; upset: *His lie shook my faith in his honesty. I'd jump up abruptly, in the middle of a word, but I still couldn't shake them* (New Yorker). **7** *Slang, Figurative.* to get rid of (a person); give up (a habit): *Can't you shake him?* **8** *Music.* to execute with a trill; trill. **9** to mix (dice) before throwing.
— ***v.i.*** **1** to move quickly backwards and forwards, up and down, or from side to side: *The branches of the old tree shook in the wind.* **2** to be shaken: *Sand shakes off easily.* **3** to tremble: *He is shaking with cold. The house shook in the storm. The boy shook with fear at the sound of the howling dog.* **4** *Figurative.* to become weakened or unsteady; totter; waver: *My courage began to shake.* **5** to clasp hands: *Let's shake and make up.* **6** *Music.* to trill.
— ***n.*** **1** the act or fact of shaking: *A shake of her head was the answer.* **2** *Informal.* an earthquake. **3** a drink made by shaking ingredients together: *a milk shake.* **4** *Slang.* a moment: *I'll be there in two shakes.* **5** *Informal.* treatment; deal: *Both Pyongyang and Hanoi felt ... that the [New York] Times men were likely to give them a favorable shake* (Time). **6** *Music.* a rapid alternation of a note with the note above it or below it; trill. **7a** a crack in a growing tree; fissure. **b** such cracks as a group. **8** a fissure, as in rock or mineral strata. **9** a rough shingle used to cover cabins, barns, and the like.

**no great shakes,** *Informal.* not unusual, extraordinary, or important: *Her early novels were no great shakes, as she herself fully realized* (New York Times).

**shake down, a** to bring or throw down by shaking: *Parts of two monasteries had been shaken down by earthquakes* (Henry F. Tozer). **b** to settle down or cause to settle down: *The Gemini 5 astronauts worked through a busy day ... shaking down for a long voyage* (Evert Clark). *It now appears that Korea, communism and foreign policy in particular have been fairly well shaken down as issues* (New York Times). **c** to bring into working order: *He finally managed to shake down the troublesome motor and get on his way.* **d** *Slang.* to get money from dishonestly: ... *a fantastic story of how two men had tried to shake him down for $500,000* (Time).

**shake off,** to get rid of: *I am glad I have wholly shaken off that family* (Jonathan Swift).

**shake out, a** to shake thoroughly or vigorously: *Let's shake out that dusty rug.* **b** to take out or spread out by shaking: *to shake out a blanket for a picnic.* **c** (1) to remove water from (a canoe) by rocking it: *We shook out the canoe and got back in.* (2) to allow the removal of water: *This canoe does not shake out easily.*

**shake up, a** to shake hard: *She shook up a mixture of oil and vinegar to make salad dressing.* **b** to stir up: *Bob ... hollers to his horses, and shakes 'em up, and away we goes* (Thomas Hughes). **c** *Figurative.* to jar in body or nerves: *He was much shaken up by his frightening experience.*

**the shakes,** *Informal.* **a** any disease characterized by a trembling of the muscles and limbs: *Anxiety symptoms were relieved, he revealed, and the "shakes" lessened* (Newsweek).
**b** *Figurative.* nervousness caused by fear or horror: *The Administration is not planning any action now toward a blockade of Red China, a possibility British and French leaders have had the shakes over* (Wall Street Journal).
[Old English *sceacan* to vibrate, make vibrate; move (away)]
— *Syn. v.i.* **3 Shake, tremble, quiver** mean to move with an agitated, vibrating motion. **Shake** is the general word: *He shook with laughter.* **Tremble,** used chiefly of people or animals, suggests an uncontrollable shaking caused by fear or other strong feeling, cold, or weakness: *In his excitement his hands trembled.* **Quiver** suggests a slight trembling motion: *The dog's nostrils quivered at the scent.*

**shake|a|ble** (shā′kə bəl), *adj.* = shakable.

**shake-down**¹ or **shake|down**¹ (shāk′doun′), *n., adj.* — *n.* **1** *Informal.* a bringing into proper condition or working order, as by use or practice: *The new ocean liner was given a shakedown by a trial voyage.* **2** a makeshift bed: *We made a shakedown of straw and blankets on the floor.* **3** the process of shaking down: *Now give the bed a shake-down* (Thomas Hardy). **4** a thorough search of a place or person.
— ***adj.*** *Informal.* having to do with a trial and adjustment of new equipment, sometimes to permit a crew to become familiar with it: *a shakedown cruise.*

**shake-down**² or **shake|down**² (shāk′doun′), *n. Slang.* an exaction, as of money, by compulsion, especially in various forms of graft: ... *letters alleging pay-offs, graft and shake-downs in military clothing contracts* (New York Times). [< *shake down* (slang) to get money from dishonestly, translation of Italian *riscuotere* to collect, shake down (e.g., fruit from a tree)]

**shake|fork** (shāk′fôrk′), *n.* **1** a large wooden fork, used especially for lifting and shaking threshed straw to separate the grain. **2** a bearing on a coat of arms having the shape of a Y with blunted ends that do not reach the edge of the shield.

**shak|en** (shā′kən), *v.* the past participle of **shake.**

**shake|out** (shāk′out′), *n. Informal.* **1a** a recession in a particular type of business, industry, trade, or other area of the economy, especially when accompanied by a disappearance of small competitors, marginal enterprises, and the like: *A shakeout already is under way that will end with six or eight producers dominating the field* (Wall Street Journal). *So far, unemployment hasn't approached the level of the last business shakeout* (Wall Street Journal). **b** a similar decline in the stock market, resulting in widespread sellout of securities: *The stock market last week saw its sharpest shakeout since May* (Time). **2** a drastic reorganization, as of policy or personnel, usually resulting in the dismissal of some employees; shakeup: ... *a possible shakeout of leading personalities associated with the succession* (Birmingham Post-Herald). **3a** the act of shaking something out. **b** the act of removing water from a canoe by rocking it.

**shak|er** (shā′kər), *n.* **1** a person who shakes something. **2** a machine or utensil used in shaking. **3** a container, such as for pepper or salt, having a perforated top.

***Shak|er** (shā′kər), *n., adj.* — ***n.*** a member of an American religious sect that originated in England in the 1700's as an offshoot of the Quakers, so called from movements of the body that formed part of their worship. Shakers did not marry and owned all property in common.
— ***adj.*** **1** of or having to do with the Shakers: *Shaker customs, Shaker communities.* **2** made by or in the style of the Shakers: *Shaker furniture, Shaker stitch. Shaker flannel is napped on both sides.*

***Shaker**
adj., definition 2

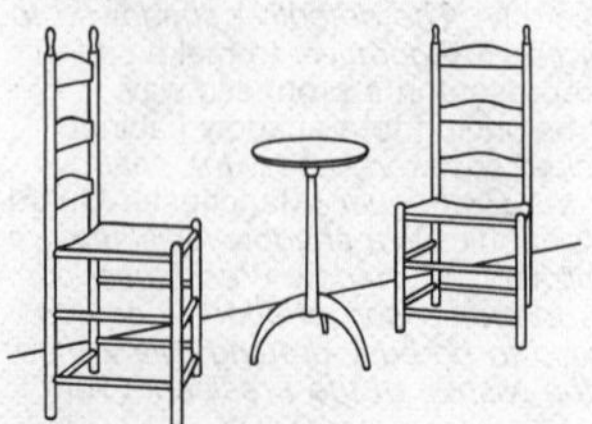

**Shak|er|ism** (shā′kə riz əm), *n.* the principles and practices of the Shakers.

**Shak|er|knit** (shā kər nit′), *adj.* (of a sweater, scarf, or the like) knitted in a plain stitch with coarse yarn, like some of the garments worn by the Shakers.

**shakes** (shāks), *n.pl.* See under **shake.**

**Shake|spear|e|an** (shāk spir′ē ən), *adj., n.* = Shakespearian.

**Shake|spear|e|a|na** (shāk′spir ē ä′nə, -an′ə, -ā′nə), *n.pl.* = Shakespeariana.

**Shake|speare garden** (shāk′spir), a garden designed to include the plants, statuary, and other features of gardens mentioned in the plays and poems of Shakespeare or used in Shakespeare's time. Many public parks in the United States have Shakespeare gardens.

**Shake|spear|i|an** (shāk spir′ē ən), *adj., n.* — ***adj.*** of, having to do with, or suggestive of William Shakespeare (1564-1616) or his works: *Sarah Siddons was probably the most noted of all Shakespearian actresses* (G. E. Bentley).
— ***n.*** an expert on Shakespeare or his works.

**Shake|spear|i|a|na** (shāk′spir ē ä′nə, -an′ə, -ā′nə), *n.pl.* things written about or by Shakespeare or associated with him.

**Shake|spear|i|an|ism** (shāk spir′ē ə niz′əm), *n.* **1** the form of expression peculiar to Shakespeare. **2** devotion to Shakespeare. **3** the influence of Shakespeare.

**Shakespearian sonnet,** = Elizabethan sonnet.

**Shake|sper|i|an** (shāk spir′ē ən), *adj., n.* = Shakespearian.

**shake|up** or **shake-up** (shāk′up′), *n. Informal.* a sudden and complete change; drastic rearrangement, as of policy or personnel: *The mayor resigned during a shakeup in the government. Shakeups are under way in Russia's Far Eastern embassies* (Newsweek).

**shak|i|ly** (shā′kə lē), *adv.* in a shaky manner.

**shak|i|ness** (shā′kē nis), *n.* shaky condition.

**shak|ing** (shā′king), *n., adj.* — ***n.*** **1** the act of a person or thing that shakes. **2** that which is shaken down. **3** = ague.
— ***adj.*** that shakes.
**shakings,** bits, such as of cordage or canvas, used in making oakum: *The sailors swept up the shakings from the deck.*
— **shak′ing|ly,** *adv.*

**shaking palsy,** = Parkinson's disease.

***shak|o** (shak′ō), *n., pl.* **shak|os** or **shak|oes.** a high, stiff military hat with a plume or other ornament: *His hat was a giant, moth-eaten bearskin shako* (New Yorker). [< French *schako* < Hungarian *csákó* peaked cap; (originally) point of a cow's horn]

***shako**

**Shak|sper|i|an** or **Shak|sper|e|an** (shāk spir′ē ən), *adj., n.* = Shakespearian.

**Shak|ta** (shuk′tə), *n.* a worshiper of Shakti. Also, **Sakta.**

**shak|ti** (shuk′tē), *n.* creative energy; vital force (in Hinduism). [< Sanskrit *śakti* power, force]

**Shak|ti** (shuk′tē), *n.* in Hinduism: **1** the female principle: *As Shakti, or Female Energy, she symbolizes the whole universe* (New York Times). **2** a goddess, Devi, the consort of Shiva. Also, **Sakti.** [< Sanskrit *śakti* power, force]

**Shak|tism** (shuk′tiz əm), *n.* the worship of Shakti. Also, **Saktism.**

**sha|ku** (shä′kü), *n.* a Japanese measure of length, equal to about 11¾ inches. [< Japanese *shaku* foot]

**sha|ku|do** (shä′kü dō′), *n.* a Japanese alloy of copper with from one to ten per cent of gold, much used for ornamental metalwork. It is often subjected to a chemical process which produces a blue patina and exposes a thin film of gold. [< Japanese *shakŭdō* red copper]

**sha|ku|ha|chi** (shä′kü hä′chē), *n.* a Japanese bamboo flute with five holes. [< Japanese *shakuhachi*]

**shak|y** (shā′kē), *adj.,* **shak|i|er, shak|i|est.** **1** shaking: *a shaky voice, shaky handwriting.* **2** liable to break down or give way; not firm or solid; weak: *a shaky porch, a shaky ladder.* (*Figurative.*) *The movement made a start, if a somewhat shaky one, on the tasks of reshaping its organization and attitudes to meet the needs of the times* (London Times). **3** *Figurative.* not to be depended on; not reliable: *a shaky bank, a shaky supporter of reform, a shaky knowledge of history.*

**Sha|la|ko** (shä lä′kō), *n., pl.* **-kos.** **1** a ceremony of the Zuñi Indians celebrating the arrival of supernatural spirits representing ancestors. **2** a masked dancer who personifies one of these spirits during this ceremony. [American English < Zuñi *shalako*]

**shale** (shāl), *n.* a fine-grained rock, formed from hardened clay or mud, that splits easily into thin layers: *In the United States and elsewhere, large supplies of oil-yielding organic matter are contained in compact shales* (Gilluly, Waters, and Woodford). [Old English *scealu*]

**shale oil,** petroleum obtained by the destructive distillation of shale.

**shall** (shal; *unstressed* shəl), *auxiliary v., pres.* **shall,** *2nd sing. also* (*Poetic*) **shalt;** *past* **should,** *2nd sing. also* (*Archaic*) **shouldst** or **should|est.** *Shall* is used to express future time, determination, command, obligation, necessity, or uncertainty. **1** in general, *shall* in the first person expresses simple futurity, in the second and third, determination or obligation: *We shall come soon. I shall miss you. You shall hear from us. You shall go to the party, I promise you. He shall not do it.* **2** In questions, *shall* is used for all persons if *shall* is expected in the answer: *Shall I drink the milk? Shall you come? Yes, I shall.* **3** In an indirect quotation, *shall* is used if it would properly be used in a direct form of the quotation: *She says I shall go. He says you shall wait.* **4** In subordinate clauses introduced by *if, when,* etc., *shall* is used rather than *will* for all persons to express future time: *When I shall see her, I shall give her your message. If he shall come, we shall be saved.* [Old English *sceal* (infinitive *sculan*)]

► See **will**[1] for usage note.

**shal|loon** (sha lün′), *n.* a twilled woolen cloth used chiefly for linings. [Middle English *chaloun* (material used as) a coverlet < Old French *chalon* < *Châlons-sur-Marne,* a city in France]

**shal|lop** (shal′əp), *n.* **1** any one of various small, light, open boats with sail or oars, or both, often like a dinghy: ... *a shallop flitteth, silken sailed* (Tennyson). **2** any one of various small, sloop-rigged vessels used as vessels of war. [< Middle French *chaloupe* < Dutch *sloep,* perhaps < *sloepen* to guide. See etym. of doublet **sloop.**]

**shal|lot** (shə lot′, shal′ət), *n.* **1** a small plant much like an onion, but with a bulb composed of sections or cloves; eschalot. It belongs to the amaryllis family and to the same genus as the onion. **2** a bulb or clove of this plant. Shallots are often used for seasoning cooked foods. [short for *eschalot* < Middle French *eschalotte,* alteration of Old French *eschaloigne* scallion]

**shal|low** (shal′ō), *adj., n., v.* **—adj.** **1** not deep: *shallow water, a shallow dish. Scobie dropped asleep—into one of those shallow sleeps that last a few seconds* (Graham Greene). **2** *Figurative.* lacking depth, such as of thought, knowledge, or feeling; superficial: *a shallow mind, a shallow person.*

**—*n.*** Usually, **shallows.** a shallow place: *The boys splashed in the shallows of the pond.* (*Figurative.*) *Here was something beyond the shallows of ladies'-school literature* (George Eliot).

**—*v.i.*** to become less deep. **—*v.t.*** to make less deep.

[Middle English *shalowe,* perhaps related to Old English *sceald* shallow, adjective. Compare etym. under **shoal**[1].] **—shal′low|ly,** *adv.* **—shal′low|ness,** *n.*

**shal|ly** (shal′ē), *v.i.,* **-lied, -ly|ing.** = shilly-shally.

**shalm** (shôm), *n.* = shawm.

**sha|lom** (shä lōm′, shō-), *n., interj. Hebrew.* **1a** hello. **b** good-by. **2** (literally) peace.

**sha|lom a|lei|chem** (shä lōm′ ä lā′ᴛʜəm, shô′ləm ə lā′ᴛʜəm), *Hebrew.* peace be upon you (a greeting).

**shalt** (shalt), *v. Archaic.* 2nd person singular present of **shall.** "Thou shalt" means "You shall": *Thou shalt not kill.*

**shal|war** (shäl′wär), *n.* loose, trousers worn in Pakistan, Bangladesh, and parts of India, especially by women and girls. Also, **salwar.** [< Hindi and Urdu *shalwār* < Persian]

**shal|y** (shā′lē), *adj.* **1** of or containing shale: *shaly sandstone.* **2** like shale.

**sham** (sham), *n., adj., v.,* **shammed, sham|ming.** **—*n.*** **1** fraud; pretense: *His goodness is all a sham. If peace is sought to be defended or preserved for the safety of the luxurious and the timid, it is a sham* (Emerson). *But when it comes to sham—either academic or political—he could be merciless* (Time). SYN: hypocrisy. **2** counterfeit; imitation. SYN: forgery. **3** a person who is not what he pretends to be. **4** a cover or the like to give a thing a different outward appearance: *a pillow sham.* **5** *Obsolete.* a hoax.

**—*adj.*** **1** false; pretended; feigned: *The soldiers fought a sham battle for practice.* **2** counterfeit; imitation: *sham diamonds.*

**—*v.t.*** **1** to assume the appearance of; feign: pretend: *He shammed sickness so he wouldn't have to work.* **2** to create a false imitation of: ... *tawdry frescoes shamming stonework* (J. A. Symonds). **3** *Obsolete.* to trick.

**—*v.i.*** to make false pretenses; pretend: *The boy is not really angry but only shamming.*

[(originally) dialectal variant of *shame*]

**sha|mal** (shə mäl′), *n.* a cold northwest wind that periodically blows across parts of central Asia and the Persian Gulf. [< Arabic *shamāl* left hand; north; north wind]

**sha|man** (shä′mən, sham′ən), *n.* a priest with magic powers, as over diseases or evil spirits: **a** a priest or medicine man of certain Ural-Altaic tribes of northern Asia: *The province of the shaman is the world of ideas, especially about the unknown* (Ogburn and Nimkoff). **b** a medicine man among certain American Indians: *Some tribes believe that shamans, or medicine men, can communicate directly with spirits* (H. C. Smith). [< Russian *shamán* < Tungus *šaman* < Pali *samaṇa* < Sanskrit *śramaṇa* Buddhist monk; (literally) self-tormentor < *śramati* he tires, fatigues]

**sha|man|ism** (shä′mə niz əm, sham′ə-), *n.* **1** the primitive religion of the Ural-Altaic peoples of northern Asia, based on a belief in controlling spirits who can be influenced only by shamans. **2** any similar religion, such as that of certain American Indians: *Though these practitioners are paid for their services, there are none who devote full time to shamanism* (Beals and Hoijer).

**sha|man|ist** (shä′mə nist, sham′ə-), *n.* a believer in shamanism.

**sha|man|is|tic** (shä′mə nis′tik, sham′ə-), *adj.* of or having to do with shamans or shamanism: *According to traditional beliefs, the spirits of the departed can be called back to this world—usually by shamanistic rites* (Atlantic).

**Sha|mash** (shä′mäsh), *n.* the sun god of Babylonian and Assyrian mythology.

**sham|a|teur** (sham′ə chůr, -chər, -tůr, -tər), *n. Slang.* a player classed as an amateur even though he is paid like a professional. [blend of *sham* and *amateur*]

**sham|a|teur|ism** (sham′ə chə riz′əm, -tə-), *n. Slang.* **1** the use of shamateurs in sports. **2** the condition of being a shamateur.

**sham|ba** (sham′bə), *n.* (in East Africa) a piece of cultivated land: *At dawn, parties form up to draw water, to drive cattle, and to work on the shambas* (London Times). [< Swahili *shamba*]

**sham|ble** (sham′bəl), *v.,* **-bled, -bling,** *n.* **—*v.i.*** to walk awkwardly or unsteadily: *The tired old man shambles. He shambled around the floor like a lost kid* (Time).

**—*n.*** a shambling walk.

[probably special use of *shamble,* singular of obsolete *shambles* tables, benches (from the straddling legs of a bench)] **—sham′bling|ly,** *adv.*

**sham|bles** (sham′bəlz), *n.pl. or sing.* **1** a confusion; mess; general disorder: *to make a shambles of a clean room. He left his affairs in a complete shambles when he died. The voice radio was a shambles of several different operators speaking at once* (New Yorker). **2a** = slaughterhouse. **b** *Figurative.* a place of butchery or of great bloodshed: *the gloomy bigot ... who ... converted all these gay cities into shambles* (John L. Motley). **3** *British.* **a** tables or stalls for the sale of meat, especially in a public market. **b** a butcher's shop. **c** *Obsolete.* tables or counters for displaying goods, etc. [Old English *scēamel* counter in a market, bench, ultimately < Latin *scamellum* (diminutive) < *scamnum* bench, stool]

**sham|bling** (sham′bling), *adj.* = shambly.

**sham|bly** (sham′blē), *adj.,* **-bli|er, -bli|est.** characterized by an awkward, irregular gait or motion; ungainly.

**sham|bol|ic** (sham bol′ik), *adj. British Slang.* disorderly; in a shambles. [irregularly derived < *shambles,* probably after such pairs as *symbol, symbolic*]

**shame** (shām), *n., v.,* **shamed, sham|ing.** **—*n.*** **1** a painful feeling of having done something wrong, improper, or silly: *The child blushed with shame when he was caught stealing candy.* SYN: humiliation, mortification. **2** a loss of reputation; disgrace; dishonor: *That young man's arrest has brought shame to a fine family.* **3** a fact to be sorry about; circumstance that brings disgrace, dishonor, or regret; pity: *It is a shame to be so wasteful. What a shame you can't come to the party.* **4** a person or thing to be ashamed of; cause of disgrace. **5** a sense of what is decent or proper.

**—*v.t.*** **1** to cause to feel shame; make ashamed: *My silly mistakes shamed me.* SYN: humiliate, mortify. **2** to drive or force by shame or fear of shame: *He was shamed into combing his hair.* **3** to bring disgrace upon: *He has shamed his parents.* **4** to surpass; make dim by comparison; outshine: *She'll shame 'em with her good looks, yet* (Dickens).

**for shame!** shame on you!: *At which remark ... Miss Caroline very properly said, "For shame, Becky!"* (Thackeray).

**put to shame, a** to disgrace; make ashamed: *The drunkard put to shame his wife and children.* **b** to surpass; make dim by comparison: *His careful work put all the rest to shame. Every ship from the New World came freighted with marvels which put the fictions of chivalry to shame* (Francis Parkman).

[Old English *sceamu*]

**sha|me|a|nah** (shä′mē ä′nə), *n.* = shamiana.

**shame|faced** (shām′fāst′), *adj.* **1** showing shame and embarrassment: *It was pitiful to see his confusion and hear his awkward and shamefaced apologies* (Mark Twain). SYN: abashed. **2** bashful; shy. SYN: diffident. [earlier, *shamefast;* later taken as if from *shame* + *face*] **—shame′fac′ed|ly,** *adv.* **—shame′fac′ed|ness,** *n.*

**shame|fast** (shām′fast, -fäst), *adj. Obsolete.* shamefaced. [Old English *sceamfæst* firm in modesty, shame] **—shame′fast|ly,** *adv.* **—shame′fast|ness,** *n.*

**shame|ful** (shām′fəl), *adj.* causing shame; bringing disgrace. SYN: dishonorable. **—shame′ful|ly,** *adv.* **—shame′ful|ness,** *n.*

**shame|less** (shām′lis), *adj.* **1** without shame; improper: *a shameless woman.* **2** not modest: *shameless boldness;* ... *this shameless falsehood* (Edmund Burke). SYN: impudent, brazen. **—shame′less|ly,** *adv.* **—shame′less|ness,** *n.*

**sha|mes** (shä′məs), *n., pl.* **sha|mos|im** (shä mos′im), **1** a person who takes care of a synagogue; synagogue sexton or caretaker. **2** an extra candle used to light the candles in the menorah on each of the eight nights of Hanukkah. Also, **shammes, shammash.** [< Yiddish *shames* < Hebrew *shāmmāsh*]

**sha|mi|a|na** (shä′mē ä′nə), *n.* (in India) an awning set on poles, often with open sides. [< Hindustani *shamiyāna* < Persian]

**sham|i|sen** (sham′ə sən), *n.* = samisen.

**sham|mash** (shä mäsh′, shä′məs), *n., pl.* **shamma|shim** (shä mä shēm′, shä mos′im). = shames.

**sham|mer** (sham′ər), *n.* a person who shams.

**sham|mes** (shä′məs), *n., pl.* **sham|mo|sim** (shä-mos′im). = shames.

**sham|my** (sham′ē), *n., pl.* **-mies,** or **shammy leather,** = chamois.

**sham|ois** or **sham|oy** (sham′oi), *n.* = chamois.

**sham|poo** (sham pü′), *v.,* **-pooed, -poo|ing,** *n.* **—*v.t.*** **1** to wash (the hair, the scalp, or a rug) with a soapy or other cleansing preparation. **2** to wash the hair or scalp of (a person). **3** *Archaic.* to massage.

**—*n.*** **1** the act of washing the hair, the scalp, or a rug, with a soapy or other cleansing preparation. **2** a preparation used for shampooing: *a liquid shampoo.* **3** *Archaic.* a massage.

**Pronunciation Key:** hat, āge, cãre, fär; let, ēqual, tėrm; it, īce; hot, ōpen, ôrder; oil, out; cup, pu̇t, rüle; child; long; thin; ᴛʜen; zh, measure; ə represents **a** in about, **e** in taken, **i** in pencil, **o** in lemon, **u** in circus.

[Anglo-Indian < Hindustani *chāmpō,* imperative (literally) press, knead < Sanskrit *cap* knead] — **sham|poo'er,** *n.*

***sham|rock** (sham'rok), *n.* **1** a bright-green leaf composed of three parts like clover. The shamrock is the national emblem of Ireland. *A son of the Ould Sod who still sports a blackthorn stick, shamrock tie pin, shamrock cuff links, and heavy brogue* (Newsweek). **2** any one of various plants that have leaves like this, such as white clover and the wood sorrel. The name is now most commonly applied to a yellow-flowered clover. [< Irish *seamrōg* (diminutive) < *seamar* clover]

***shamrock**
definition 1

**sha|mus** (shā'məs), *n. U.S. Slang.* a detective. [< Yiddish *shames* sexton, caretaker; see etym. under **shames**]

**Shan** (shän, shan), *n., pl.* **Shan** or **Shans. 1** a member of certain tribes of southeastern Asia, especially in the Shan state of Upper Burma. **2** the Thai language of these people.

**shan|a|chy** or **shan|a|chie** (shan'ə kē), *n., pl.* **-chies.** a traveling minstrel or storyteller who tells of ancient times and traditions in Ireland: *Fortunately for the readers of this handsome volume, artist-shanachie Reynolds sidestepped in time* (Saturday Review). [< Irish Gaelic *seanchaidhe*]

**Shan|de|an** (shan'dē ən), *adj.* of, having to do with, or characteristic of the novel *Tristram Shandy,* by the English novelist Laurence Sterne (1713-1768), or the Shandy family portrayed in the novel: *I write a careless kind of a civil, nonsensical, good-humoured Shandean book* (Laurence Sterne). *He affects a Shandean fabrication of words* (Thomas Jefferson).

**shan|dry|dan** (shan'drē daŋ), *n.* **1** a light two-wheeled cart or gig. **2** any old-fashioned, rickety conveyance. [compare dialectal *shandry* a light cart on springs; origin unknown]

**shan|dy** (shan'dē), *n., pl.* **-dies. 1** = shandygaff. **2** beer and lemonade mixed.

**shan|dy|gaff** (shan'dē gaf), *n.* beer and ginger ale or ginger beer mixed. [perhaps < dialectal *shandy* wild, half crazy + *gaff*[2] in the sense "vociferous joking"]

**Shang** (shäng), *n.* the ruling Chinese dynasty from about 1500 to 1027 B.C., known for weapons and other instruments of bronze and for its oracle bones.

**Shan|gaan** (shän gän'), *n.* a member of a Bantu people in the northern Transvaal in South Africa. [< Bantu *Shangana*]

**shang|hai** (shang'hī, shang hī'), *v.t.,* **-haied, -hai|ing. 1** to make unconscious, as by drugs or liquor, and put on a ship to serve as a sailor. **2** *Informal, Figurative.* to bring or get by trickery or force: *Thirteen bewildered strollers in Foley Square were legally "shanghaied" ... to complete a trial jury* (New York Times). [American English (from the practice of securing sailors by illicit means for long voyages, often to *Shanghai,* China)]

**Shang|hai** (shang'hī, shang hī'), *n.* one of a long-legged breed of chicken. [< *Shanghai,* a seaport in China]

**Shan|gri-la** or **Shan|gri-La** (shang'gri lä'), *n.* an idyllic earthly paradise: *The austere serenity of Shangri-La. Its ... pale pavilions shimmered in repose from which all the fret of existence had ebbed away* (James Hilton). [< the name of an inaccessible land in the remote Himalayas in *Lost Horizon,* 1933, a novel by James Hilton]

**shank** (shangk), *n., v.* —*n.* **1** the part of the leg between the knee and the ankle. **2a** the corresponding part in animals. **b** a cut of meat from the upper part of the leg of an animal. **3** the whole leg: *to stir one's shanks.* **4** any part like a leg, stem, or shaft. The shank of a fishhook is the straight part between the hook and the loop. **5** the body of a printing type. **6** that part of an instrument, tool, or other device, which connects the acting part with the handle. **7a** the narrow part of a shoe, connecting the broad part of the sole with the heel. **b** the piece of metal, fiber, or other material, used to shape this part. **8** the eye or loop of a button. **9** the latter end or part of anything: *the shank of the day.* **10** *Music.* a crook.
—*v.t.* to strike (a golf ball) with the heel of an iron club: *He had a quick snatch at the ball, shanked it and took five* (London Times).
**shank it,** to walk: *Let him shank it! We're in no hurry to have him home* (George Douglas).
**shank off,** to rot at the stem: *Entire beds [of pansies] have been known to shank off during a very hot summer* (J. Turner).
[Old English *sceanca*]

**shank|bone** (shangk'bōn'), *n.* the shinbone of an animal.

**shanked** (shangkt), *adj.* having or furnished with a shank or shanks: *a shanked button.*

**shank's mare** or **pony,** *Informal.* one's own feet; walking: *Pilgrims had converged from all over India—by train, by cart and by shank's mare* (Scientific American).
**ride on shank's mare** (or **pony**), *Informal.* to go on foot; walk: *I'd rather ... ride on shank's mare* (S. Bishop).

**shan|ny** (shan'ē), *n., pl.* **-nies** or (*collectively*) **-ny.** the smooth blenny of Europe [origin uncertain]

**shan't** (shant, shänt), shall not.

**shant|ey** (shan'tē), *n., pl.* **-eys.** = chantey.

**shan|tih** or **shan|ti** (shän'tē), *n. Hinduism.* peace. [< Sanskrit *śantih*]

**shan|tung** or **Shan|tung** (shan'tung, shantung'), *n.* **1** a rayon or cotton fabric similar to pongee and having a rough, uneven surface. **2** a heavy pongee, a kind of soft silk. [< *Shantung,* a province in China]

**shan|ty**[1] (shan'tē), *n., pl.* **-ties.** a roughly built hut or cabin; shack: *Her childhood was spent in a succession of Florida and Georgia cracker shanties, in dreary sawmill towns* (Time). [American English, perhaps < Canadian French *chantier* lumberjack's headquarters, in French, timber yard, dock < Latin *canthērius* framework, rafter; beast of burden]

**shan|ty**[2] (shan'tē), *n., pl.* **-ties.** = chantey. [variant of *chantey*]

**shanty boat,** a rude houseboat used especially on the Mississippi River and in logging areas.

**shan|ty|man** (shan'tē man', -mən), *n., pl.* **-men. 1** = lumberman. **2** = backwoodsman.

**shan|ty|town** (shan'tē toun'), *n.,* or **shanty town,** *U.S.* **1** a poor, run-down section of a city or a town: *Rural workers flock to oilfields and cities, only to sit idle in shantytowns* (Time). **2** a settlement of makeshift shacks, tents, or other living quarters, usually near a new military installation or factory: *Shantytowns spring up overnight on the outskirts of Lima and other cities* (Atlantic).

**shap|a|ble** (shā'pə bəl), *adj.* that can be shaped.

**shape** (shāp), *n., v.,* **shaped, shap|ing.** —*n.* **1** the outward contour or outline; form; figure: *An apple is different in shape from a banana. All circles have the same shape; rectangles have different shapes. A white shape stood at his bedside.* SYN: cast, build. See syn. under **form. 2** an assumed appearance; guise; disguise: *A witch was supposed to take the shape of a cat or bat.* **3** condition: *The athlete exercised to keep himself in good shape.* **4** a definite form; proper arrangement; order: *Take time to get your thoughts into shape. He collected his cut of the surplus value in the shape of the rent which was paid him* (Edmund Wilson). **5** a kind; sort: *dangers of every shape.* **6** a mold or pattern for giving shape to something. **7** something shaped, such as jelly or pudding in a mold or metal: *But the English firmly entrenched behind impenetrable ramparts of ... cold shape and suet pudding, have gone right on boiling their Brussels sprouts* (Time). [Old English *gesceap*]
—*v.t.* **1** to form; make into a form; mold: *The child shapes clay into balls.* **2** to adapt in form: *That hat is shaped to her head.* **3** to give definite form or character to: *events that shape people's lives.* **4** to plan; devise; direct; aim: *to shape one's course in life.* **5** to express in words: *to shape a question or a reply. She had a way of idiomatically shaping a musical phrase that cannot be taught* (New York Times). **6** to mold; pattern. **7** *Obsolete.* to appoint; decree; determine.
—*v.i.* **1** to take shape; assume form; develop: *Clay shapes easily. Our plan is shaping well.* **2** to turn out; happen.
**in shape,** *Informal.* in good condition or health: *All he needs is a week's rest and he'll be back in shape.*
**lick into shape,** *Informal.* to make presentable or usable: *to lick a story into shape. They ... promised their cooperation in licking it into shape* (London Times).
**shape up, a** to take on a certain form or appearance; develop: *The plans for the new building are shaping up nicely.* **b** to show a certain tendency: *What had shaped up as a Democratic cat-and-dog fight became ... a "high-level" debate* (Newsweek). **c** to get into shape; ready oneself: *Gina Hawthorn, fourth in the 1968 Olympic slalom, [is] shaping up for one more attempt on a British medal* (Manchester Guardian Weekly). **d** *U.S. Informal.* to fall into line; behave properly; conform: *The apparent presidential-vice-presidential view [is] that the economy can be saved ... or civil peace restored if only Harriet Van Horne [a daily columnist] will shape up* (Washington Post).
**take shape,** to have or take on a definite form: *The general outline of the novel began to take shape.*
[Middle English *shapen,* Old English *sceapen,* past participle of *scieppan* to create]

**SHAPE** (shāp), *n.* Supreme Headquarters Allied Powers in Europe.

**shaped** (shāpt), *adj.* formed by shaping; made into a particular shape: *a shaped mirror, a shaped wooden bowl.*

**-shaped,** *combining form.* having a ___ shape or shapes: *Cone-shaped = having a cone shape. Many-shaped = having many shapes.*

**shaped charge,** a cone-shaped explosive charge used especially in armor-piercing shells, such as those of a bazooka.

**shape|less** (shāp'lis), *adj.* **1** without definite shape: *He wore a shapeless old hat.* SYN: formless. **2** having a shape which is not attractive; not shapely: *a fat, shapeless figure.* SYN: unshapely. —**shape'less|ly,** *adv.* —**shape'less-ness,** *n.*

**shape|li|ness** (shāp'lē nis), *n.* shapely condition.

**shape|ly** (shāp'lē), *adj.,* **-li|er, -li|est.** having a pleasing shape; well-formed: ... *a delicate shapely little hand* (W. H. Hudson).

**shap|en** (shā'pən), *adj., v.* —*adj.* **1** having a certain shape: *She was a good-looking woman ..., well shapen* (George Eliot). **2** = shaped: *a shapen oar.*
—*v.t.* to shape; give a shape to: *The creature has ... shapened itself into the form of a cottage loaf* (Westminster Gazette).
[< *shapen,* obsolete past participle of *shape*]

**shap|er** (shā'pər), *n.* **1** a person who makes, forms, or shapes. **2** (in metalwork) a combined lathe and planer, which can be used, with attachments, for doing a great variety of work. **3** a stamp or press for cutting and molding sheet metal or certain plastics. **4** (in woodworking) a planer, such as for cutting moldings or panels which have irregular forms.

**shape-up** (shāp'up'), *n. U.S.* a system of hiring longshoremen whereby the men line up each workday to be selected for work by the foreman.

**sha|poo** (shä'pü), *n.* a mountain sheep of central Asia which resembles the bighorn of North America. [< Tibetan *sha-pho*]

**shar|a|ble** (shãr'ə bəl), *adj.* = shareable.

**shard**[1] (shärd), *n.* **1** a piece of broken earthenware or pottery. **2** a broken piece; fragment. **3** the hard case that covers a beetle's wing; elytron. Also, **sherd.** [Old English *sceard* fragment]

**shard**[2] (shärd), *n. British Dialect.* excrement; a mass of cow dung. [origin uncertain]

**shard beetle,** any one of various dung beetles.

**shard-born** (shärd'bôrn'), *adj.* **1** born or generated in shards or dung: ... *The shard-born beetle* ... (Shakespeare). **2** borne on shards or elytra (due to a misinterpretation of Shakespeare).

**shard|ed** (shär'did), *adj.* having shards or elytra, as a beetle; coleopterous: *Sharded insects ... vastly outnumber all the other forms of active life we see* (New York Times).

**share**[1] (shãr), *n., v.,* **shared, shar|ing.** —*n.* **1** the part belonging to one person; part; portion: *to take little share in a conversation. He left each child an equal share of his property. He does more than his share of the work.* SYN: allotment, quota. **2** a part of anything owned in common with others: *One of the boys offered to sell his share in the boat.* **3** each of the equal parts into which the ownership of a company or corporation is divided. Shares are usually in the form of transferable certificates of stock. *The ownership of this railroad is divided into several million shares. With borrowed money, they bought 59,-100 shares ... then agreed to resell the block* (Newsweek). *Abbr:* sh.
—*v.t.* **1** to use together; enjoy together; have in common: *Since one tent leaked, all the boys shared the other one.* **2** to divide into parts, each taking a part: *The child shared his candy with his sister.* **3** to divide: ... *a thin oaten cake, shared into fragments* (Charlotte Brontë).
—*v.i.* to have a share; take part: *to share in the expenses. Everyone shared in making the picnic a success.*
**go shares,** to share in something: *If you find the treasure we will go shares* (H. Rider Haggard).
**on shares,** sharing in the risks and profits: *Men can always be had to go on shares, which is by far the most profitable method, both to the employers and the fishermen* (Jeremy Belknap).
**share and share alike, a** to share alike in; have equal shares, such as in a will or insurance policy: *I bequeath to my nephews and nieces ... the whole of my ... personal effects, share and share alike* (Frederick Marryat). **b** to share everything with others: *Children should not fight about*

*who is to have a toy, but should share and share alike.*
[Old English *scearu* a cutting, shaving, division, related to *scieran* to cut, shear]
—*Syn.* *v.t.* 1 **Share, participate, partake** mean to use, enjoy, or have something in common with another. **Share** emphasizes the idea of common possession, enjoyment, or use: *The sisters share the same room.* **Participate,** followed by *in,* implies joining with others in some activity or undertaking: *Only a few club members participated in the discussion.* **Partake,** usually followed by *of,* and somewhat formal, means to take one's (own) share of food, pleasure, or qualities: *to partake of refreshments.*
**share²** (shãr), *n.* = plowshare. [Old English *scear,* related to *scieran* to cut, divide]
**share|a|ble** (shãr′ə bəl), *adj.* that can be shared. Also, **sharable.**
**share|crop** (shãr′krop′), *v.i., v.t.,* **-cropped, -crop|ping.** to farm as a sharecropper: *Later they sharecropped, saved money, bought their own land, grew cotton, corn and rice* (Time).
**share|crop|per** (shãr′krop′ər), *n.* a person who farms land for the owner in return for part of the crops: *Sharecroppers and tenant farmers left the farm and turned to the rapidly growing opportunities in industry* (Time). [American English < earlier *share-crop,* adjective]
**share|hold|er** (shãr′hōl′dər), *n.* a person owning shares of stock; stockholder: *This railroad has many thousands of shareholders.*
**share|hold|ing** (shãr′hōl′ding), *n.* stockholding; shareownership: *Chase Manhattan plans to acquire ... an important shareholding in an overseas banking corporation* (New York Times).
**share|out** (shãr′out′), *n.* distribution (as of prizes, shares, or commodities) in shares: *In the shareout of decorations which had accompanied victory his name had been noticeably absent* (Sunday Times).
**share|own|er** (shãr′ō′nər), *n.* = shareholder.
**share|own|er|ship** (shãr′ō′nər ship), *n.* ownership of shares of stock: *Without stock markets this free exchange of shareownership obviously would be extremely difficult, if not totally impossible* (Alfred L. Malabre, Jr.).
**shar|er** (shãr′ər), *n.* a person or thing that shares.
**Sha|ri|a** or **Sha|ri|ah** (shə rē′ə), *n.* the religious law of the Moslems, consisting of the Koran and the traditional sayings of Mohammed: *They urge the enforcement of a modified Sharia law and propagate the principle of a theocratic state* (Atlantic). Also, **Sheria.** [< Arabic *sharī'a* road to the watering place, law]
**sha|rif** (shə rēf′), *n.* = sherif.
***shark¹** (shärk), *n.* any one of a group of fishes, mostly marine, certain kinds of which are large and ferocious and eat other fishes. Certain kinds are sometimes dangerous to man. Sharks have streamlined, spindlelike bodies, with gill slits on the sides and thick, dull-colored skin, and swim by movements of the tail. [origin uncertain]
—**shark′like′,** *adj.*

***shark¹**

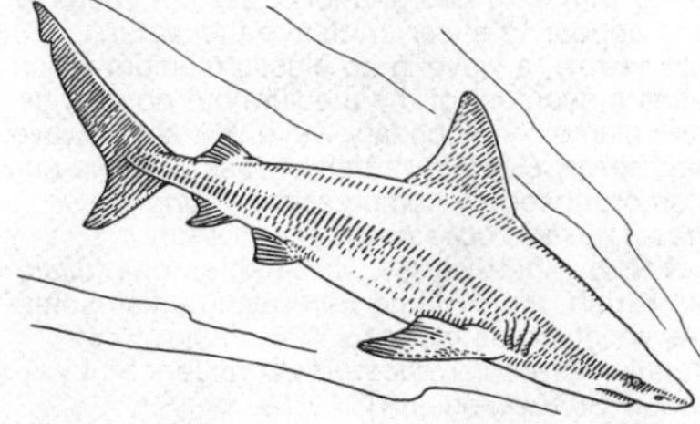

**shark²** (shärk), *n., v.* —*n.* 1 a dishonest person who preys on others. 2 *Slang.* a person unusually good at something; expert: *a shark at bridge.*
—*v.i.* 1 to act or live by preying on others; live by trickery. 2 to be a cardsharp.
—*v.t.* 1 to obtain by trickery, fraud, or theft. 2 *Archaic.* to collect quickly.
[probably < *shark¹*]
**shark-liv|er oil** (shärk′liv′ər), oil extracted from the liver of sharks, used as a source of vitamin A and as a preservative.
**shark|proof** (shärk′prüf′), *adj.* able to withstand an attack by a shark; protected against sharks: *The sharkproof cage, made of chicken wire and supported by empty gasoline drums ...* (New Yorker).
**shark|skin** (shärk′skin′), *n.* 1 a fabric made from fine threads of wool, rayon, or cotton, used in suits: *... dapper, aromatic men in sharkskin and effulgent neckties* (New Yorker). 2a the skin of a shark. b leather made from the skin of a shark.
**shark sucker,** a fish, widely distributed over warm seas, that attaches itself by means of a sucker to large fish without regard to their species; remora.
***sharp** (shärp), *adj., adv., n., v.* —*adj.* 1 having a thin cutting edge or a fine point: *a sharp knife, a sharp pin, a sharp pencil.* 2 having or coming to a point; not rounded: *a sharp nose, a sharp corner on a box.* SYN: angular, pointed. 3 with a sudden change of direction; abrupt: *a sharp turn in the road.* 4 very cold; nippy: *sharp weather, a sharp morning.* 5 *Figurative.* severe; biting: *sharp words, a sharp note of reproof. The coal industry urged Congress to place sharp curbs on imports of residual fuel oil* (Wall Street Journal). SYN: sarcastic, tart, caustic. 6 feeling somewhat like a cut or prick; acting keenly on the senses: *a sharp taste, a sharp noise, a sharp pain.* SYN: piercing, intense, painful. 7 clear; distinct: *the sharp contrast between black and white.* 8 quick in movement; brisk: *a sharp walk or run.* 9 fierce; violent: *a sharp attack or struggle.* 10 keen; eager: *a sharp desire, a sharp appetite.* 11 being aware of things quickly: *sharp ears. Their lack of immediate concern ... doesn't mean bankers and economists aren't following it with a sharp eye* (Wall Street Journal). SYN: quick, discerning, perspicacious. 12 wide-awake; watchful; vigilant: *The sentry kept a sharp watch for the enemy.*
13 *Figurative.* quick in mind; shrewd; clever: *a sharp lawyer, a sharp critic, sharp at a bargain. With their own sharp and realistic minds, they had lopped off the sentimentality and fantasy* (Edmund Wilson). 14 *Figurative.* dishonest; unscrupulous: *Fear of having displeased God by sharp practice in business ...* (Listener). *Would it not have been better ... to prevent "sharp operators" from cashing in at their expense?* (London Times). 15 high in pitch; shrill: *a sharp voice, a sharp cry of fear.* 16 *Music.* a above the true pitch; too high in pitch. b raised a half step or half tone above natural pitch: *music written in the key of F sharp.* c having sharps in the signature. 17 *Phonetics.* pronounced with breath and not with voice; voiceless: *a sharp consonant.*
18 *U.S. Slang.* attractive; stylish: *a sharp dresser.*
—*adv.* 1 promptly; exactly: *Come at one o'clock sharp.* 2 in a sharp manner; in an alert manner; keenly: *Look sharp!* 3 suddenly; abruptly: *to pull a horse up sharp.* 4 *Music.* above the true pitch: *to sing sharp.*
—*n.* 1 *Music.* a a tone one half step above natural pitch. b the sign that shows this. 2 a swindler; sharper: *... chiseling tactics on the part of back-alley sharps* (Wall Street Journal). 3 *Informal.* an expert: *What the sales manager was about to say would seem painfully old-hat to a personnel sharp* (Atlantic).
—*v.t. Music.* to raise (a note) in pitch, especially by one half step.
—*v.i. Music.* to sound a note above the true pitch.
**sharps,** a the hard part of grain, requiring a second grinding: *These sharps were ground a second time, ... and the produce was 46 lb. of ... barley* (Farmer's Magazine). b long needles with very sharp points: *The sharps are those usually called "sewing needles"* (Michael Morrall).
[Old English *scearp*] —**sharp′ly,** *adv.* —**sharp′ness,** *n.*
—*Syn. adj.* 13 **Sharp, keen, acute,** used to describe a person or the mind, mean penetrating. **Sharp** implies cleverness, shrewdness, and quickness to see and take advantage, sometimes dishonestly: *He is a sharp salesman.* **Keen** implies clearness and quickness of perception and thinking: *a keen mind.* **Acute** implies penetrating perception, insight, or understanding: *an acute interpreter of current events.*

***sharp**
*n.,* definition 1

**sharp-cut** (shärp′kut′), *adj.* 1 cut sharply to give a clear outline. 2 sharply defined; distinct; clear.
**sharp-edged** (shärp′ejd′), *adj.* 1 having a sharp edge or edges. 2 *Figurative.* a trenchant; incisive: *Instead of the ... sharp-edged direction that Herman Shumlin brought to the play, there is in the film a sluggish, confused manipulation of ideas and players* (Time). b caustic; sarcastic: *Harold Talburt is a veteran political cartoonist, known for his sharp-edged lampoons* (Newsweek).
**sharp|en** (shär′pən), *v.t.* to make sharp or sharper: *Sharpen the pencil.* (*Figurative.*) *sharpen your wits.* —*v.i.* to become sharp or sharper.
—**sharp′en|er,** *n.*
**sharp|er** (shär′pər), *n.* 1 a swindler; cheat. 2 a gambler who makes a living, as by cheating at cards: *a cardsharper.*
**sharp-eyed** (shärp′īd′), *adj.* 1 having keen sight: *a sharp-eyed person, sharp-eyed mice.* 2 watchful; vigilant: *The top candidates were counting the early returns, like sharp-eyed pineapple sorters in a canning factory* (Time).
**sharp-fanged** (shärp′fangd′), *adj.* 1 having sharp teeth. 2 *Figurative.* biting; caustic; sarcastic.
**sharp-freeze** (shärp′frēz′), *v.t.,* **-froze, -fro|zen, -freez|ing.** = quick-freeze.
**sharp|ie** (shär′pē), *n.* 1 a long, flat-bottomed boat with a centerboard and one or two masts, each rigged with a triangular sail. 2 *Slang.* an unusually keen, alert, or clever person. 3 *U.S. Slang.* a sharper; cheat: *We hear of a girl who was loaded with furs and automobiles by a sharpie using absconded funds* (Alistair Cooke).
**sharp|ish** (shär′pish), *adj.* somewhat sharp.
**sharp-nosed** (shärp′nōzd′), *adj.* 1 having a pointed nose or end: *sharp-nosed pliers.*
2 *Figurative.* having a keen scent: *sharp-nosed dogs.*
**sharps** (shärps), *n.pl.* See under **sharp.**
**sharp-set** (shärp′set′), *adj.* 1 keen; eager. 2 very hungry: *Being sharp-set, we told him to get breakfast* (Herman Melville).
**sharp-shinned** (shärp′shind′), *adj.* having slender shanks.
**sharp-shinned hawk,** a small North American hawk with short wings, long tail, and a white breast barred with reddish-brown.
**sharp|shoot|er** (shärp′shü′tər), *n.* 1 a person who shoots very well, especially with a rifle. 2 a soldier chosen to do accurate shooting: *The absence of a sharpshooter ... blunted the sharp edge of their attack and minimised their chances of victory* (Times of India).
**sharp|shoot|ing** (shärp′shü′ting), *n., adj.* —*n.* the act of a sharpshooter.
—*adj.* that acts as a sharpshooter.
**sharp-sight|ed** (shärp′sī′tid), *adj.* 1 having sharp sight: *He is as sharp-sighted as a hawk* (Scott).
2 *Figurative.* sharp-witted: *a sharp-sighted move.*
—**sharp′-sight′ed|ly,** *adv.* —**sharp′-sight′ed|ness,** *n.*
**sharp|ster** (shärp′stər), *n.* a swindler; sharper.
**sharp-tailed** (shärp′tāld′), *adj.* having a sharp-pointed tail or tail feathers.
**sharp-tailed grouse,** a grouse of the northwestern United States and Canada with a short, pointed tail; pintail.
**sharp-tailed sandpiper,** a sandpiper of Asia that is seen along the Pacific coast of North America during migration.
**sharp-tailed sparrow,** a sparrow found in marshes of the eastern United States and Canada.
**sharp-tongued** (shärp′tungd′), *adj.* sharp or bitter of speech; severely critical; cutting; biting: *They were oblivious of the scornful comments of their sharp-tongued neighbors* (New Yorker).
**sharp-wit|ted** (shärp′wit′id), *adj.* having or showing a quick, keen mind. SYN: bright, clever.
**sharp|y** (shär′pē), *n., pl.* **sharp|ies.** *U.S. Slang.* sharpie (def. 2,3).
**shash|lik** (shäs lik′), *n.* = shish kebab.
**Shas|ta daisy** (shas′tə), 1 a cultivated variety of daisy having large flowers with white rays. 2 its flower. [American English < Mount *Shasta,* a mountain in California]
**Shas|tan** (shas′tən), *adj., n. Geology.* Comanchean.
**shas|tra** (shäs′trə), *n.* = sastra.
**shat|ranj** (shät ränj′), *n.* = chaturanga.
**shat|ter** (shat′ər), *v., n.* —*v.t.* 1 to break into pieces: *A stone shattered the window.* SYN: smash, splinter. See syn. under **break.** 2 *Figurative.* to disturb greatly; destroy: *Our hopes for a picnic were shattered by the rain. The great mental strain and overwork shattered his mind. A great postwar illusion ... was shattered decisively last week by the people of France themselves* (Newsweek). 3 *Obsolete.* to scatter; disperse.
—*v.i.* to be shattered: *The glass shattered.* SYN: smash, splinter. See syn. under **break.**
—*n.* 1 the act or fact of shattering: *The stone hit the window and a shatter of glass fell on their heads.* 2 a shattering quality or condition: *Only superior audio equipment can begin to play back a brilliantly recorded piano disc without shatter or distortion* (Harper's).
**shatters,** fragments: *If ever the heart come to be sensible of its blows, it will break all to shatters* (William Fenner).
[Middle English *schater(en)* cause (leaves, etc.) to fall; to disperse. Perhaps related to **scatter.**]

**Pronunciation Key:** hat, āge, cãre, fär; let, ēqual, tėrm; it, īce; hot, ōpen, ôrder; **oi**l, **ou**t; cup, pu̇t, rüle; **ch**ild; lo**ng**; **th**in; ᴛʜen; **zh,** measure; ə represents **a** in about, **e** in taken, **i** in pencil, **o** in lemon, **u** in circus.

**shatter cone**, a cone-shaped rock fragment with distinctive ridges, produced by intense shock forces: *It would be necessary to see in more detail the occurrence of tektites in relation to that of shatter cones before the two could be linked in one theory. Perhaps a search for shatter cones in areas where only tektites have so far been found would be rewarding* (New Scientist).

**shat|ter-coned** (shat′ər kōnd′), *adj.* having or characterized by shatter cones.

**shat|ter|er** (shat′ər ər), *n.* a person or thing that shatters or makes a shatter.

**shat|ter|ing** (shat′ər ing), *adj., n.* —*adj.* **1** that shatters; destructive: *We felt the shattering impact as the ship hit the rocks.* **2** *Figurative.* startling; emotionally overpowering: *To see this play is to undergo a shattering experience. Her answer ... was as shattering as it was rapid* (Thomas De Quincey). **3** (of sound) earsplitting; very loud: *The shattering trumpet shrilleth high* (Tennyson).
—*n.* **1** a breaking into pieces. **2** the broken pieces; shatters. —**shat′ter|ing|ly,** *adv.*

**shat|ter|proof** (shat′ər prüf′), *adj.* that will not shatter; resistant to shattering: *The door ... is said to be weather-resistant, shatterproof, and warp-proof* (Science News Letter).

**shat|ters** (shat′ərz), *n.pl.* See under **shatter**.

**shat|ter|y** (shat′ər ē), *adj.* **1** liable to be shattered. **2** easily crumbled, as rock or soil.

**Sha|van|te** (shə van′tē), *n., pl.* **-tes** or **-te.** **1** a member of a Brazilian tribe of the Ge linguistic family living along the Tocantins River in Brazil. **2** the language of this tribe.

**shave** (shāv), *v.,* **shaved, shaved** or **shav|en, shav|ing,** *n.* —*v.t.* **1** to cut hair from (the face, chin, or other part of the body) with a razor: *The actor shaved his head in order to portray a bald man.* **2** to cut off (hair) with a razor. **3** to cut off in thin slices; cut in thin slices: *She shaved the chocolate.* **4** to cut very close. **5** *Figurative.* to come very close to; graze: *The car shaved the corner.* **6** *U.S. Informal.* to discount (a promissory note) at a very high rate of interest. **7** *Informal.* to reduce: *Mondolini, sentenced in absentia ... had his term shaved to two years* (Maclean's).
—*v.i.* **1** to remove hair with a razor: *Father shaves every day.* **2** to be hard or extortionate in bargains.
—*n.* **1** the act of cutting off hair with a razor: *The barber gave him a shave and a haircut.* **2** any one of various tools for shaving, scraping, or removing thin slices. **3** a thin slice; shaving. **4** *Figurative.* a narrow miss or escape: *The shot missed him, but it was a close shave. The racing cars passed each other by a shave.*
[Old English *sceafan* to shave]

**shave|ling** (shāv′ling), *n.* **1** a tonsured monk, friar, or priest (an unfriendly use). **2** a youth.

**shav|en** (shā′vən), *adj., v.* —*adj.* **1** shaved: *a shaven face.* **2** closely cut: *the shaven lawns of village streets.* **3** = tonsured.
—*v.* shaved; a past participle of **shave**: *The man with the beard had not shaven for years.*

**shav|er** (shā′vər), *n.* **1** a person who shaves. **2** an instrument for shaving. **3** *Informal.* a youngster; small boy: *Young shavers like you don't have pipes* (William De Morgan).

**shave|tail** (shāv′tāl′), *n. U.S. Slang.* a second lieutenant, especially one who has recently been commissioned: *Every military type is represented—the good soldier, the coward, the goldbrick, the rank-happy shavetail* (Time). [American English; earlier, an army mule (because of the appearance of their tails)]

**Sha|vi|an** (shā′vē ən), *adj., n.* —*adj.* **1** of or having to do with George Bernard Shaw (1856-1950). **2** characteristic of George Bernard Shaw: *Shavian wit. He is a dapper and well-to-do gentleman who sports a Shavian beard* (Time).
—*n.* an admirer of George Bernard Shaw, his works, or his theories.

**shav|ie** (shā′vē), *n. Scottish.* a trick or prank. [perhaps < Scandinavian (compare Old Icelandic *skeifr* wry, crooked, oblique)]

**shav|ing** (shā′ving), *n.* **1** Often, **shavings.** a very thin piece or slice taken off a surface: *shavings of cheese. Shavings of wood are cut off by a plane.* **2** the act or process of cutting hair from the face, chin, or some other part of the body with a razor: *He washed his face after shaving.* **3** the act of scraping or cutting a thin slice off a surface.

**shaving brush**, a brush used to put on the lather before shaving.

**shaving cream**, a creamy preparation put on the face for shaving.

**shaving lotion**, a fragrant lotion usually containing alcohol, applied to the face before or after shaving to soothe the skin.

**shaving mug**, a mug used to hold soap or lather for shaving.

**Sha|vu|os** (shä vü′ōth, shə vü′əs), *n.* = Shabuoth.

**shaw** (shô), *n.* **1** *Archaic.* a thicket; small wood. **2** *Scottish.* the stalks and leaves of potatoes, turnips, etc. [Old English *sceaga.* See related etym. at **shag**¹.]

**shawl** (shôl), *n.* a square or oblong piece of cloth to be worn about the shoulders or head. **SYN:** scarf. [< Persian *shāl*]

* **shawl collar**, a yokelike collar and lapel reaching from the neck to the chest or waistline: ... *a wrapped cocoon coat with a wide shawl collar* (New Yorker).

* **shawl collar**

**shawled** (shôld), *adj.* wearing or covered with a shawl.

**shawl pattern**, a pattern on cloth, resembling patterns on Oriental shawls.

**shawm** (shôm), *n.* any one of certain wood-wind musical instruments like the oboe or clarinet, used especially in the Middle Ages: *The instrument had a sweet, thin, flutelike tone, comparable to that of a shepherd's shawm* (New Yorker). [apparent new singular < Middle English *shalmys* (taken as plural) < Old French *chalemie,* variant of *chalemel.* See etym. of doublet **chalumeau.**]

**Shaw|nee** (shô nē′), *n., pl.* **-nee** or **-nees,** *adj.* —*n.* **1** a member of a tribe of American Indians formerly living in Ohio and Tennessee, and now living mainly in Oklahoma. **2** the Algonkian language of this tribe.
—*adj.* of or belonging to this tribe.
[American English < Algonkian (Shawnee) *Shawunogi* southerners]

**Shaw|nee|wood** (shô nē′wu̇d′), *n.* = western catalpa.

**Shaw|wal** (shô wäl′), *n.* the tenth month of the Moslem year. It has 29 days. [< Arabic *Shawwāl*]

* **shay** (shā), *n. Informal.* a light carriage with two wheels and one seat; chaise. [< *chaise* (taken as plural). See etym. of doublets **chaise, chair, cathedra.**]

* **shay**

**she** (shē), *pron., sing. nom.* **she,** *poss.* **her** or **hers,** *obj.* **her;** *pl. nom.* **they,** *poss.* **their** or **theirs,** *obj.* **them;** *n., pl.* **shes.** —*pron.* **1** the girl, woman, or female animal spoken about or mentioned before: *My sister says she likes to read.* **2** anything thought of as female and spoken about or mentioned before: *She was a fine old ship.*
—*n.* a girl; woman; female animal: *Is the baby a he or a she?*
[probably Old English *sēo,* or *sīe,* demonstrative pronoun]

**she-**, *combining form.* a female ____: *She-goat = a female goat.*

**shea** (shē), *n.* an African tree of the sapodilla family, whose seeds yield shea butter; butter tree. [< Mandingo *si, sye*]

**shea butter**, a fat obtained from the seeds of the shea, used as food and in Europe especially for the manufacture of soap.

**shead|ing** (shē′ding), *n.* a civil division on the Isle of Man. [variant of earlier *shedding,* verbal noun < *shed,* in early meaning "to divide"]

**sheaf** (shēf), *n., pl.* **sheaves,** *v.* —*n.* **1** one of the bundles in which grain is bound after reaping. **2** a bundle of things of the same sort bound together or so arranged that they can be bound together: *a sheaf of papers, a sheaf of arrows.*
—*v.t.* to bind into a sheaf or sheaves: *Anyone with a patch of land worth talking about was out cutting hay or sheafing corn* (New Yorker).
[Old English *scēaf*]

**sheal** (shēl), *v.t. British Dialect.* to shell (peas or the like).

**sheal|ing** (shē′ling), *n. Scottish.* shieling.

**shear** (shir), *v.,* **sheared** or (*Archaic*) **shore, sheared** or **shorn, shear|ing,** *n.* —*v.t.* **1** to cut with shears or scissors, especially in order to remove (wool or fleece): *to shear wool from sheep.* **2** to cut the wool or fleece from: *The farmer sheared his sheep.* **3** to cut close; cut off; cut: *The storm drove the ship forward shearing its anchor line and setting it adrift.* **4** to break by a force causing two parts or pieces to slide on each other in opposite directions: *Too much pressure on the handles of the scissors sheared off the rivet holding the blades together.* **5** *Figurative.* to strip or deprive as if by cutting: *The assembly had been shorn of its legislative powers.* **6** *Dialect.* to reap with a sickle.
—*v.i.* **1** to break by shearing force: *Several bolts sheared, causing the floor to sag dangerously.* **2** *Dialect.* to use a sickle on crops. **3** *Archaic.* to cut through something with the aid of a weapon.
—*n.* **1** the act or process of shearing. **2** that which is taken off by shearing. **3** one blade of a pair of shears. **4** a pair of shears. **5** any one of various machines for cutting metal, especially sheet metal. **6a** a force causing two parts or pieces to slide on each other in opposite directions. **b** the strain or deformation resulting from this; shearing stress.
[Old English *sceran.* Compare etym. under **share**¹, **share**².] —**shear′er,** *n.*

**shear boom**, (in lumbering) a boom fixed to guide floating logs in the desired direction.

**sheared** (shird), *adj.* **1** that has undergone shearing; shorn. **2** with the fur trimmed to make it even or prevent curling: *sheared beaver, sheared raccoon.*

**shear flocks**, the part of the nap which is cut from cloth while it is being sheared.

**shear|ing** (shir′ing), *n.* **1** the act of a person or thing that shears. **2** an instance of shearing.
**shearings,** something cut off with shears or some other sharp instrument: *Put the shearings of scarlet cloth upon the coals* (G. Smith).

**shearing plane**, *Geology.* the plane along which rupture from shearing stress takes place in rocks.

**shearing stress**, the stress in a body caused by shear.

**shear legs**, a hoist for heavy weights; shears.

**shear|ling** (shir′ling), *n.* **1** a sheep that has been shorn once. **2** the fleece of such a sheep.

**shear|man** (shir′mən), *n., pl.* **-men.** a person who shears cloth.

**shear pin**, a pin designed to be sheared off in order to disconnect the moving parts of a machine before they are damaged.

**shear plane**, *Geology.* shearing plane.

**shears** (shirz), *n.pl.* **1** large scissors: *barber's shears.* **2** any cutting instrument resembling scissors: *grass shears, tin shears.* **3** an apparatus for hoisting heavy weights, consisting of two or more poles fastened together at the top to support a block and tackle. [Old English *scēara,* plural of *scēar.* Compare etym. under **share**².]

**shear|wa|ter** (shir′wôt′ər, -wot′-), *n.* any one of a genus of sea birds of the same family as the petrels, with long bills and long, slender wings which appear to shear or cleave the water.

**shear wave**, a wave in an elastic medium which causes movement of the medium but no change in its volume. A secondary wave is a shear wave.

**shear zone**, *Geology.* a belt of rock crushed and metamorphosed by compression: *Along shear zones massive rocks become schists.*

**sheat|fish** (shēt′fish′), *n., pl.* **-fish|es** or (*collectively*) **-fish.** a very large European catfish sometimes weighing as much as 400 pounds. [alteration of earlier *sheath-fish;* influenced by German *Scheide* sheath]

* **sheath** (shēth), *n., pl.* **sheaths** (shēᴛʜz), *v.* —*n.* **1** a case or covering for the blade of a sword, dagger, or knife: *He drew his sword from its sheath.* **2** any similar covering, especially on an animal or plant: **a** *Botany.* the part of an organ rolled around a stem or other body to form a tube: *In the grasses, the blade arises, not from a petiole, but from a sheath* (Fred W. Emerson). **b** *Zoology.* the elytron of a beetle. **3** a narrow, tight-fitting dress with straight lines. See the picture on the opposite page.
—*v.t.* = sheathe.
[Old English *scēath*]

**sheath|bill** (shēth′bil′), *n.* either of two white, pigeonlike sea birds related to the plovers, with a horny case partly covering the bill. It lives in cold regions of the Southern Hemisphere.

**sheathe** (shēᴛʜ), *v.t.,* **sheathed, sheath|ing.** **1** to put (a sword or other instrument or tool) into a sheath or scabbard: *The sabre is sheathed and the battle is o'er* (Byron). (*Figurative.*) *Not I, till I have sheathed my rapier in his bosom* (Shakespeare). **2** to enclose in a case or covering: *a mummy sheathed in linen, doors sheathed in* *metal. He is a motorboat fancier, and his latest vessel ... is sheathed in teak* (New Yorker). SYN: encase. **3** to retract (claws).

**sheath|er** (shē'ᴛʜər), *n.* a person who sheathes.

**sheath|ing** (shē'ᴛʜing), *n.* **1** a casing; covering. The first covering of boards on a house, nailed to the rafters, is sheathing. The thin protective covering of copper on the hull of a vessel is sheathing. **2** the material used for either of these, especially boards such as plywood. **3** the act of putting on or into a sheath.

**sheath knife**, a knife carried in a sheath.

**sheath-winged** (shēth'wingd'), *adj.* having the wings sheathed in elytra, as a beetle.

**shea tree**, = shea.

**sheave[1]** (shēv), *v.t.*, **sheaved, sheav|ing.** to gather and tie into a sheaf or sheaves: *to sheave wheat.* [< *sheaf,* by analogy to plural *sheaves*]

**sheave[2]** (shēv, shiv), *n.* a wheel with a grooved rim, such as the wheel of a pulley. [Middle English *sheeve,* variant of *schive*]

**sheaves** (shēvz; *for 2 also* shivz), *n.* **1** plural of **sheaf. 2** plural of **sheave[2]**.

**She|ba** (shē'bə), *n.* **Queen of,** a queen who visited Solomon to learn of his great wisdom (in the Bible, I Kings 10:1-13).

**she-bal|sam** (shē'bôl'səm), *n.* = Fraser fir.

**she|bang** (shə bang'), *n. U.S. Slang.* **1** an outfit; concern: *A single skilled button pusher can run the whole shebang* (New Yorker). **2** an affair; event: *They went to a big shebang last night and slept late this morning.* [American English; earlier, dilapidated shelter or conveyance; perhaps alteration of French *char à bancs* car with benches]

**She|bat** (shə bät'), *n.* the fifth month of the Jewish civil year, and the eleventh month of the ecclesiastical year, beginning in January. [< Hebrew *shəbāṭ*]

**she|been** (shi bēn'), *n., v.* chiefly in Ireland and Scotland: **—*n.*** a place where alcoholic liquor is sold without a license: *But after winning a big fight he goes to a shebeen ... to celebrate* (Cape Times).

**—*v.i.*** to operate a shebeen.

[< Irish *séibín* a small mug < *séibe* a mug or bottle; liquid measure]

**she|chi|ta** or **she|chi|tah** (shə ʜē'tə), *n.* the Jewish method of slaughtering animals according to rabbinical law. [< Hebrew *shəḥīṭāh*] Also, **shehita, shehitah.**

**shed[1]** (shed), *n., v.,* **shed|ded, shed|ding. —*n.*** **1** a building used for shelter or storage of goods or vehicles, usually having only one story and often open at the front or sides: *a wagon shed, a tool shed, a train shed.* **2** a hut; cottage: *To shame the meanness of his humble shed* (Oliver Goldsmith). **3** any covering, such as the lair of an animal.

**—*v.t.*** to place in a shed: *to shed sheep, to shed cotton bolls.*

[Middle English *shadde* apparently variant of *shade,* Old English *scead* shelter] **—shed'like',** *adj.*

***sheath**
definitions 1, 2a, 3

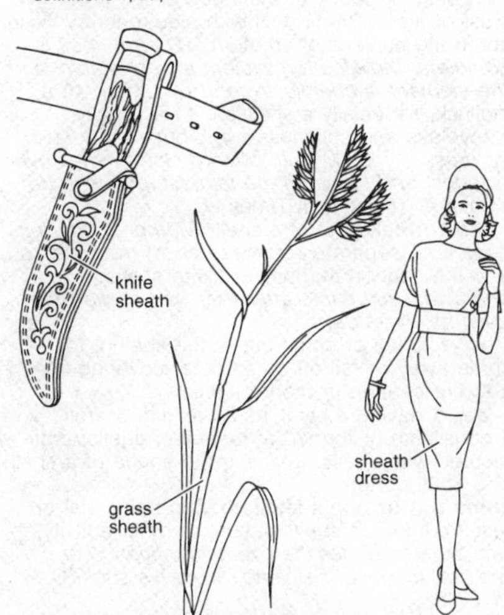


**shed[2]** (shed), *v.,* **shed, shed|ding,** *n.* **—*v.t.*** **1** to pour out; cause to flow; let fall: *The girl shed tears. A man who is good enough to shed his blood for his country is good enough to be given a square deal afterward* (Theodore Roosevelt). **2** to throw off; cast off; let drop or fall: *The umbrella sheds water. The snake sheds its skin. The duke shed his coat* (Mark Twain). SYN: molt, discard. **3** to scatter abroad; give forth: *The sun sheds light. Flowers shed perfume.* (*Figurative.*) *They* [*the reports*] *were aimed at shedding light on the need for additional power* (New York Times). SYN: emit, diffuse. **4** *Figurative.* to get rid of: *to shed one's worries, to shed inhibitions. "I'm going to lose ten pounds," she said, causing Studs to think, pleased, that she could shed that weight without hurting her figure* (James T. Farrell). **5** *Informal.* to divorce: *She* [*had*] *shed a nice, well-heeled Yale man a few years before on the ambiguous grounds of mental cruelty* (Harper's).

**—*v.i.*** **1** to throw off a covering, hair, etc.: *That snake has just shed. The cats are shedding.* **2** to drop or fall, as leaves or grain from the ear.

**—*n.*** **1** something that is or has been shed. **2** a watershed or ridge of high ground.

[Old English *scēadan*]

**shed[3]** (shād), *n., pl.* **she|dim.** (in Jewish folklore) an evil spirit or demon. [< Hebrew *shēdh* < Assyrian *shēdu*]

**she'd** (shēd; *unstressed* shid), **1** she had. **2** she would.

**shed|der** (shed'ər), *n.* **1** a person or thing that sheds. **2a** a crab or lobster beginning to shed its shell. **b** a lobster that has just grown its new shell. **c** = soft-shell crab.

**she-dev|il** (shē'dev'əl), *n.* a woman or girl who is like a devil in character or actions.

**she|dim[1]** (shā'dim), *n.* plural of **shed[3]**.

**she|dim[2]** (shā'dim), *n.* plural of **shedu.**

**shed roof,** = pent roof.

**she|du** (shā'dü), *n., pl.* **-dim.** an Assyrian protective spirit or demigod. [< Assyrian *shēdu*]

**shee** (shē), *n., pl.* **shee** or **shees.** a fairy in Irish folklore. Also, **sidhe.** [< Irish *sīdhe* fairies, plural of *sīd* mound or hill (because fairies were supposed to live in them). Compare etym. under **banshee.**]

**sheen** (shēn), *n., v., adj.* **—*n.*** **1** gleaming brightness; luster: *the sheen of satin or polished silver.* SYN: See syn. under **polish. 2** gorgeous attire: *In costly sheen ... arrayed* (Byron).

**—*v.i.*** *Poetic.* to glisten.

**—*adj.*** *Poetic.* bright; shining; resplendent.

[Old English *scēne, scīene* bright]

**sheen|y** (shē'nē), *adj.,* **sheen|i|er, sheen|i|est.** bright; lustrous: *The silken sheeny woof* (Tennyson).

**sheep** (shēp), *n., pl.* **sheep. 1** an animal raised for wool, meat, or skin. Sheep are cud-chewing mammals related to goats and cattle, and sometimes have horns. The various kinds comprise a genus of animals. **2** *Figurative.* a person who is weak, timid, or stupid: *"Are you men or are you sheep?" cried the captain.* **3** leather made from the skin of a sheep; sheepskin.

**make sheep's eyes at,** to give a longing, loving look at: *The horrid old Colonel ... was making sheep's eyes at a half-caste girl* (Thackeray).

**separate the sheep from the goats,** *Especially British.* to separate what is good from what is bad (originally in allusion to the division into "sheep" and "goats," those saved or lost at the Last Judgment): *One sad consequence of the massive output of television and radio is that it is virtually impossible to separate the sheep from the goats* (London Times).

[Old English *scēap*]

**sheep|back** (shēp'bak'), *n.* a moundlike piece of rock rounded and smoothed by glacial action.

**sheep|ber|ry** (shēp'ber'ē, -bər-), *n., pl.* **-ries. 1** a tall North American shrub of the honeysuckle family, bearing clusters of small white flowers and edible, black, berrylike fruit. **2** the fruit itself. **3** the black haw or its fruit.

**sheep|bine** (shēp'bīn'), *n.* a small species of bindweed that grows as a weed in fields of Europe and North America.

**sheep botfly,** a botfly whose larvae are deposited in the nostrils of sheep, from which they crawl into the cavities of the nose and the head sinuses.

**sheep bug,** = sheep ked.

**sheep|bur** (shēp'bėr'), *n.* = cocklebur.

**sheep|cot** (shēp'kot'), *n.* = sheepcote.

**sheep|cote** (shēp'kōt'), *n.* a shelter for sheep; sheepfold. SYN: fold.

**sheep|dip** or **sheep-dip** (shēp'dip'), *n.* a disinfecting mixture into which sheep are dipped.

**sheep|dog** (shēp'dôg', -dog'), *n.,* or **sheep dog.** a collie or other dog trained to help a shepherd watch and tend sheep.

**sheep fescue,** a low, tufted fescue grass with fine leaves and culms, native in many mountain regions, and forming the bulk of the sheep pasturage in the Scottish Highlands. Also, **sheep's fescue.**

**sheep fly,** a European fly related to the screwworm fly of the United States. Its larvae infest the bodies of live sheep, especially in Great Britain and Ireland.

**sheep|fold** (shēp'fōld'), *n.* a pen or covered shelter for sheep.

**sheep|herd|er** (shēp'hėr'dər), *n.* a person who watches and tends large numbers of sheep while they are grazing on unfenced land.

**sheep|herd|ing** (shēp'hėr'ding), *n., adj.* **—*n.*** the herding of sheep in large numbers on unfenced land.

**—*adj.*** of or having to do with sheepherding.

**sheep|hook** (shēp'hůk'), *n.* a shepherd's staff. Its upper end is usually curved or bent into a hook.

**sheep|ish** (shē'pish), *adj.* **1** awkwardly bashful or embarrassed: *a sheepish smile.* SYN: diffident. **2** like a sheep; timid, weak, or stupid: ... *saying the downright things that the sheepish society around her is afraid to utter* (Alexander Kinglake). SYN: timorous. **—sheep'ish|ly,** *adv.* **—sheep'ish|ness,** *n.*

**sheep ked,** a small bloodsucking fly that is a harmful parasite on sheep; sheep tick.

**sheep laurel,** a low North American shrub of the heath family, similar to the mountain laurel but lower and with purple or red flowers; lambkill. It is said to be poisonous to sheep.

**sheep|like** (shēp'līk'), *adj., adv.* **—*adj.*** meek; submissive; sheepish: *sheeplike conformity.*

**—*adv.*** meekly; submissively: ... *stoops your pride And leads your glories sheeplike to the sword* (Christopher Marlowe).

**sheep|man** (shēp'man'), *n., pl.* **-men. 1** a person who owns and raises sheep: *Veritable dynasties were built up by cattlemen and sheepmen* (Harper's). **2** = sheepherder.

**sheep range,** a tract of land on which sheep are pastured; sheepwalk.

**sheep scab,** a contagious disease of sheep due to mites which live on the skin and cause the formation of scabs with the fall of the wool; acariasis of sheep.

**sheep's fescue,** = sheep fescue.

**sheep|shank** (shēp'shangk'), *n.* **1** a leg of a sheep. **2** something lank, slender, or weak. **3** a kind of knot, hitch, or bend made on a rope to shorten it temporarily.

**sheeps|head** (shēps'hed'), *n., pl.* **-heads** or (*collectively for 1 and 2*) **-head. 1** a large saltwater food fish related to the porgies, common on the Atlantic coast of the United States. **2** the freshwater drumfish of the Mississippi River and the Great Lakes. **3** the head of a sheep, especially as food. **4** a fool; simpleton.

**sheep|shear|er** (shēp'shir'ər), *n.* **1** a person who shears sheep. **2** a machine for shearing sheep.

**sheep|shear|ing** (shēp'shir'ing), *n.* **1** the act of shearing sheep. **2** the time of year for shearing sheep. **3** the feast held at that time.

**sheep-sick** (shēp'sik'), *adj.* (of pastureland) exhausted or diseased by excessive sheep-pasturing and no longer fit for this use.

**sheep|skin** (shēp'skin'), *n.* **1** the skin of a sheep, especially with the wool on it. **2** leather or parchment made from the skin of a sheep. **3a** *Informal.* a diploma. **b** a person holding a diploma: *The accumulation of sheepskins has helped give the city good government, good schools ...* (Wall Street Journal).

**sheep sorrel,** the common American sorrel, a low-growing plant with three-lobed, arrow-shaped leaves, and spikes of small flowers, common as a weed on poor soil; red sorrel; sour dock.

**sheeps|wool** (shēps'wůl'), *n.,* or **sheepswool sponge,** a tough, flexible horse sponge found along the coasts of Florida, Honduras, and in the West Indies; wool sponge.

**sheep tick,** = sheep ked: *Sheep ticks are properly not ticks at all, but wingless flies* (Science News Letter).

**sheep|walk** (shēp'wôk'), *n.* = sheep range.

**sheep|weed** (shēp'wēd'), *n.* **1** = soapwort. **2** = butterwort. **3** = velvetleaf.

**sheep|y** (shē'pē), *adj.,* **sheep|i|er, sheep|i|est.** characteristic of or resembling sheep; sheeplike; sheepish: *He called the social English the most sheepy of sheep* (George Meredith).

**sheer[1]** (shir), *adj., adv., n.* **—*adj.*** **1** very thin; almost transparent: *Sheer white curtains hung at the little windows to let in as much light as possible.* **2** unmixed with anything else; complete: *sheer nonsense. She fainted from sheer weariness.* SYN: unadulterated, pure, absolute, utter. **3** straight up and down; very steep: *From the top of the wall there was a sheer drop of 100 feet to the water below.* **4** *Obsolete.* bright; shining; shiny.

**—*adv.*** **1** completely; quite: *He fell sheer to the bottom of the cliff.* **2** straight up and down; very

---

**Pronunciation Key:** hat, āge, cãre, fär; let, ēqual, tėrm; it, īce; hot, ōpen, ôrder; **oi**l, **ou**t; cup, půt, rüle; **ch**ild; lo**ng**; **th**in; **ᴛʜ**en; **zh**, measure; **ə** represents **a** in about, **e** in taken, **i** in pencil, **o** in lemon, **u** in circus.

steeply: *The cliff rose sheer from the river's edge.*
—*n.* **1** a thin, fine, almost transparent cloth. **2** a dress made of this: *She wore a billowing pink sheer to the Junior Prom.*
[Middle English *scere* clear, free, partly Old English *scīr* bright; vowel influenced by Old Icelandic *skǣrr* bright] —**sheer′ness**, *n.*

**sheer**[2] (shir), *v., n.* —*v.i.* to turn from a course; turn aside; swerve: *Birds perching on the surrounding roofs took to flight immediately, while those passing over on the wing sheered off* (New Scientist).
—*v.t.* to cause to sheer.
—*n.* **1** the act of turning a ship from its course. SYN: deviation. **2** the upward curve of a ship's deck or lines from the middle toward each end. **3** the position in which a vessel at anchor is placed to keep her clear of the anchor.
[probably < Dutch *scheren.* Compare etym. under **shear**, verb, in the sense of "to form two parts or pieces by cutting or breaking."]

**sheer|hulk** (shir′hulk′), *n.* an old ship with hoists mounted on it, used especially for loading.

**sheer legs**, a hoist for heavy weights; shears.

**sheer|ly** (shir′lē), *adv.* absolutely; thoroughly; quite: *Some of the audience may have come sheerly out of curiosity* (Newsweek).

**sheet**[1] (shēt), *n., adj., v.* —*n.* **1** a large piece of cloth, usually of linen or cotton, used to sleep on or under: *He drew the sheet up over his head as he trembled in bed while the lightning crackled and the thunder boomed.* **2** a broad, thin piece of anything: *a sheet of glass, a sheet of iron.* **3a** a single piece of paper: *She tore a sheet from the pad and scribbled a note.* **b** a piece of paper printed and folded to page size; unbound page of a book: *He checks the paper itself for finish ... examines sheets for cleanliness* (Newsweek). **c** a piece of paper printed with rows of postage stamps. **4** a newspaper. **5** a broad, flat surface: *a sheet of ice, a sheet of flame. The rain came down in sheets.* **6** a nearly horizontal, thin layer of rock or gravel.
—*adj.* rolled out in a sheet during the manufacturing process: *sheet steel.*
—*v.t.* to furnish or cover with a sheet or layer: *a sheeted ghost* (Longfellow). *The river was sheeted with ice* (Washington Irving).
—*v.i.* to spread or flow in a sheet or layer: *The water sheeted down* (Observer).
[Old English *scēte, scīete* a cloth, covering]
—**sheet′less**, *adj.* —**sheet′like′**, *adj.*

**sheet**[2] (shēt), *n., v. Nautical.* —*n.* a rope or chain that controls the angle at which a sail is set. It is attached to a lower or after corner of the sail. *Better change to heavy jib sheets* (Newsweek).
—*v.t.* **sheet home**, to stretch (a square sail) as flat as possible by pulling hard on the sheets fastened to it: *The topsails were let fall and sheeted home* (Michael Scott).
**a sheet in the wind** (or **wind's eye**), *Informal.* tipsy; drunk: *Maybe you think we were all a sheet in the wind's eye. But ... I was sober* (Robert Louis Stevenson).
**sheets**, the space not occupied by thwarts at the bow or stern of an open boat: *The sheets are usually called either foresheets or sternsheets.*
**three sheets in the wind**, *Informal.* very drunk: *He ... seldom went up to the town without coming down three sheets in the wind* (Richard Henry Dana).
[Old English *scēata* lower part of sail, piece of cloth. See related etym. at **sheet**[1].]

**sheet anchor**, **1** a large anchor formerly carried in the waist of a ship for use in emergencies. **2** *Figurative.* a final reliance or resource: *The United States Supreme Court ... has been called the sheet anchor of our governmental system* (Harper's). [earlier *sheat-*, variant of Middle English *shutte* (*anker*); origin uncertain]

**sheet bend**, a kind of knot used to fasten two ropes together; becket bend; hawser bend.

**sheet erosion**, the washing away of soil in layers from barren, sloping land by rainfall.

**sheet-fed** (shēt′fed′), *adj.* (of a printing press) having the paper fed in single sheets instead of from a continuous roll.

**sheet glass**, glass made into large, flat sheets before cooling.

**sheet ice**, ice formed on the surface of a body of water.

**sheet|ing** (shē′ting), *n.* **1** a cotton or linen cloth, as for bedsheets: *heavy industrial cloth, such as "sheetings" used in cloth bags, auto upholstery and other industrial products* (Wall Street Journal). **2** a lining or covering of timber or metal, used to protect a surface: *plywood sheeting.* **3** the act or process of making into or covering with sheets.

**sheet iron**, iron in sheets or thin plates.

**sheet lightning**, lightning in broad flashes. Sheet lightning often occurs without a thunderstorm in the summer. It is actually a reflection of lightning that occurs beyond the horizon.

**sheet metal**, metal in thin pieces or plates.
—**sheet′-met′al**, *adj.*

**sheet music**, music printed on unbound sheets of paper: *Sheet music doesn't sell the way it did in the old days* (Atlantic).

**sheet|pile** (shēt′pīl′), *n.* a piling formed of thick planks driven between the main piles of a cofferdam or other hydraulic work to retain or to exclude water: *The cofferdams are basically a series of interlocking cells filled with sand and walled by steel sheetpile* (William W. Jacobus).

**sheet|pil|ing** (shēt′pī′ling), *n.* = sheetpile.

**Sheet|rock** (shēt′rok′), *n. Trademark.* a plasterboard with a core of gypsum between two sheets of heavy paper, used as a building material.

**sheets** (shēts), *n.pl.* See under **sheet**[2].

**sheet web**, the web spun by a sheet-web weaver.

**sheet-web weaver** (shēt′web′), any one of various spiders that spin webs in the form of flat sheets or nets of crisscrossed threads between blades of grass or branches of shrubs and trees.

**sheet|y** (shē′tē), *adj.* **1** consisting of or resembling sheets. **2** (of rocks) showing a tendency to break up into thin tabular masses.

**Shef|field plate** (shef′ēld), an especially durable silver plate made by rolling out sheets of copper and silver fused together. [< *Sheffield,* a city in England, where the process was perfected]

**she|hi|ta** or **she|hi|tah** (shə ʜē′tə), *n.* = shechita.

**sheik** or **sheikh** (shēk; *especially British* shāk), *n.* **1** an Arab chief or head of a family, village, or tribe: *One by one, the tribal sheiks who had strayed to the Saudi side ... led their camel-riding followers into the Sultan's camp to beg forgiveness* (Newsweek). **2** a Moslem religious leader. **3** a title of respect used by Moslems. **4** *Slang.* a man supposed to be irresistibly fascinating to women; great lover. [< Arabic *shaikh* (originally) old man < *shākha* he grew (or was) old] Also, *especially British,* **shaikh**.

**sheik|dom** or **sheikh|dom** (shēk′dəm; *especially British* shāk′dəm), *n.* the territory ruled by a sheik.

**sheik|ly** or **sheikh|ly** (shēk′lē; *especially British* shāk′lē), *adj.* of, having to do with, or characteristic of a sheik.

**shei|la** (shē′lə), *n. Australian Slang.* a young woman. [< *Sheila,* a proper name]

**sheil|ing** (shē′ling), *n. Scottish.* shieling.

**shei|tan** (shī tän′), *n.* = shaitan.

**shek|el** (shek′əl), *n., pl.* **shek|els, she|ka|lim** (shə kä′lim). **1** an ancient silver coin of the Hebrews that weighed about half an ounce. **2** an ancient unit of weight originating in Babylonia, equal to about half an ounce.
**shekels**, *Slang.* coins; money: *Ordinary degrees in technology were bringing in the shekels* (Economist).
[< Hebrew *sheqel* < *shāqal* he weighed (it)]

**She|ki|nah** (shi kē′nə, -hē′nə, -kī′nə), *n.* (in Jewish theology) the divine presence, or a visible symbol of it, as the glory of light or the cloud resting over the mercy seat. [< Hebrew *shəkīnāh* < *shākan* he rested, dwelt]

**shel|drake** (shel′drāk′), *n., pl.* **-drakes** or (*collectively*) **-drake**. **1** any one of a group of large ducks of Europe and Asia, many of which resemble geese and have variegated plumage. Sheldrakes comprise a genus of birds. **2** = merganser. [< obsolete *sheld* variegated + *drake*]

**shel|duck** (shel′duk′), *n.* = sheldrake (def. 1).

**shelf** (shelf), *n., pl.* **shelves**. **1a** a thin, flat piece of wood, metal, stone, or other material, fastened to a wall or frame to hold things, such as books or dishes: *The books sat on a shelf above the fireplace.* **b** the contents of a shelf: *to read a whole shelf in a week.* **2** anything like a shelf, such as a ledge of land or rock, especially a submerged ledge or bedrock: *The ship hit a shelf of coral. In the Gulf the shelf—the offshore sea bottom—is muddy* (Scientific American). **3** *Archery.* the part of the hand that the arrow rests on as the bow is drawn.
**off the shelf**, directly from stock on hand; without requiring special preparation or modification: [*When*] *aircraft themselves could almost be purchased off the shelf, it was not difficult for a company to obtain new aircraft to meet unexpected needs* (London Times).
(**put**) **on the shelf**, put aside as no longer useful or desirable; in a state of inactivity or uselessness: *The trouble is that the Americans obsessed with their purity of purpose, stubbornly cling to an idea that should either be dropped or at least put on the shelf* (Canadian Forum).
[perhaps < Middle Low German *schelf*] —**shelf′-like′**, *adj.*

**shelf|ful** (shelf′fu̇l′), *n., pl.* **-fuls**. the amount a shelf can hold; a full shelf.

**shelf fungus**, = bracket fungus.

**shelf ice**, a ledge of ice sticking out into the sea from an ice sheet: *Some species of marine plants even manage to thrive in the lightless waters beneath the shelf ice* (Scientific American).

**shelf life**, the length of time a product may be shelved or stored without becoming spoiled or useless: *the shelf life of a drug.*

**shelf list**, a list of the books in a library in the order of their location.

**shelf sea**, the part of the sea that covers a continental shelf.

***shell**
definitions 7, 9

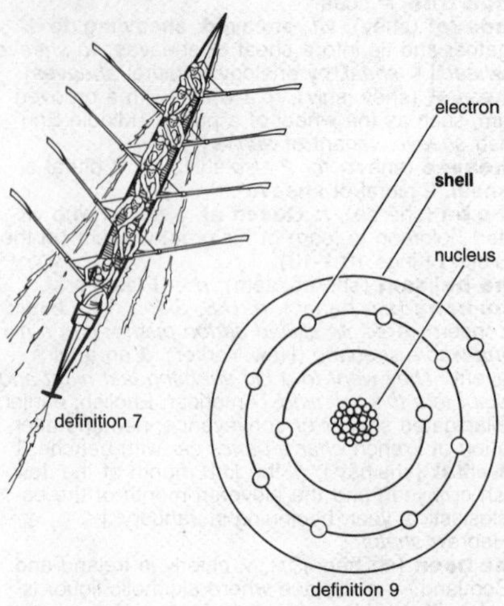


***shell** (shel), *n., v., adj.* —*n.* **1** the hard outer covering of certain animals. Oysters and other mollusks, beetles and some other insects, and turtles have shells. *The largest shell is that of the giant clam of the South Pacific Ocean* (R. Tucker Abbott). SYN: carapace. **2** the hard outside covering of an egg: *The cook cracked the egg on the side of the pan to break the shell.* **3** the hard outside covering of a nut, seed, or fruit. **4** tortoise shell, once widely used in combs or ornaments. **5a** something like a shell, such as the framework of a house. **b** *Figurative.* outward show; outer part or appearance: *Going to church is the mere shell of religion. The shell of party polemics, that convention which is in itself an abrogation of peacetime relations and an obstacle to serious discussions ...* (Edmund Wilson). **6a** a cartridge used in a rifle or a shotgun. **b** a hollow metal case filled with explosives, and sometimes chemicals or gas, that is fired by artillery and explodes on impact or over the target. **c** a cartridgelike firework that explodes in the air. **7** a long, narrow racing boat of light wood, rowed by a crew or by a single oarsman. **8** a hollow case especially of pastry or meringue or the lower crust of a pie. **9** any orbit with electrons revolving about the nucleus of an atom: *When a shell is complete, the electron system is very stable, and the element is chemically inert* (J. Little). **10** a mollusk, especially a shellfish. **11** a usually sleeveless and collarless overblouse: *"My favorite dress ... has a multi-colored chiffon shell over culottes, and I haven't the faintest idea who designed it"* (New York Times).
—*v.t.* **1** to take out of a shell: *Mother is shelling peas.* **2** to separate (grains of corn) from the cob. **3** to fire cannon at; bombard with shells: *The enemy assault came after they had shelled the town for three days.*
—*v.i.* **1** to fall or come out of the shell. **2** to come away or fall off as an outer covering does. **3** to fire cannon or mortar shells.
—*adj.* **1** having a shell, as an animal or fruit. **2** consisting or formed of a shell or shells; ornamented with shells. **3** having the shape of a shell or a shell pattern.
**come out of one's shell**, to stop being shy or reserved; join in conversation, or other activity, with others: *Under the soothing influence of coffee and tobacco, he came out of his shell* (C. F. M. Bell).
**go** (or **retire**) **into one's shell**, to become shy and reserved; refuse to join in conversation, or other activity, with others: [*He*] *rarely spoke unless personally appealed to, and speedily retired into his shell again* (Henry Vizetelly).
**shell out**, *Informal.* **a** to give (something) away: *to shell out candy at Halloween.* **b** to hand over (money); pay out: *He shelled out five dollars for the broken window. The U.S. will keep shelling out aid abroad as long as the menace of Communism persists* (Wall Street Journal).
**shells**, burnt limestone before it is slaked: *He*

*brings his lime from the kiln, lays it in small heaps, about a firlot of shells in each heap* (John Sinclair).
[Old English *scell, sciell.* Perhaps related to **shale.**] —**shell′-like′,** *adj.*

**she'll** (shēl; *unstressed* shil), **1** she shall. **2** she will.

**shel|lac** (shə lak′), *n., v.,* **-lacked, -lack|ing.** —*n.* **1** a varnish made with alcohol that gives a smooth, shiny appearance to wood, metal, or the like. Shellac is made from refined lac. **2** refined lac, used in sealing wax and, formerly, on phonograph records.
—*v.t.* **1** to put shellac on; cover or fasten with shellac: *to shellac a floor.* **2** *Informal.* to defeat completely: *The cool-headed squad that shellacked Italy last week operated with precision and brutal efficiency* (Time).
[< *shell* + *lac*¹; translation of French *laque en écailles* lac in thin plates] —**shel|lack′er,** *n.*

**shel|lack** (shə lak′), *n., v.t.* = shellac.

**shell|back** (shel′bak′), *n.* **1** an experienced sailor. **2** a person who has crossed the equator on shipboard.

**shell|bark** (shel′bärk′), *n.* **1** = shagbark (defs. 1, 2, 3). **2** a hickory tree similar to the shagbark but having a larger nut.

**shell bean, 1** any one of various beans that are shelled before cooking and only the seeds are being eaten; field bean. **2** the plant bearing such beans.

**shell|burst** (shel′bėrst′), *n.* the explosion of a shell.

**shell concrete,** reinforced concrete in the form of very thin, curved slabs resembling the shape of sea shells, used especially to build domelike roofs or buildings spanning large spaces.

**-shelled,** *combining form.* having a ____ shell: *A hard-shelled crab = a crab having a hard shell.*

**shell|er** (shel′ər), *n.* **1** a person who shells something, as peas or clams. **2** a tool or machine used in shelling.

**Shel|ley|an** (shel′ē ən), *adj.* of or having to do with the English poet Percy Bysshe Shelley (1792-1822) or his works.

**shell eye,** a primitive organ of sight found on the shells of various univalve and bivalve mollusks.

**shell|fire** (shel′fīr′), *n.* the firing of explosive shells; artillery fire.

**shell|fish** (shel′fish′), *n., pl.* **-fish|es** or (*collectively*) **-fish.** a water animal with a shell, especially a mollusk or a crustacean that is used for food. Clams, oysters, crabs, and lobsters are shellfish. Shellfish are not true fish; they lack a backbone and look very different from regular fish. [Old English *scielfisc*]

**shell-fish|er|y** (shel′fish′ər ē), *n., pl.* **-er|ies.** the business or industry of gathering oysters, clams, and other shellfish.

**shell game, 1** a gambling game in which a pea or other object is placed under one of several walnut shells that are rapidly rearranged, after which bets are made on the shell concealing the pea. **2** a swindling form of this, in which the person arranging the shells conceals the pea in his hand. **3** anything regarded as a game of chance and especially as a swindle or fraud.

**shell|heap** (shel′hēp′), *n.* = kitchen midden.

**shell hole,** a hole in the ground formed by the explosion of a mine or shell.

**shell house** or **home,** a house that is unfinished on the inside, the remaining work being done by the purchaser.

**shell jacket,** a mess jacket, especially one worn in place of a tuxedo jacket.

**shell-lac** (shə lak′), *n., v.t.,* **-lacked, -lack|ing.** = shellac.

**shell-less** (shel′lis), *adj.* having no shell, as some mollusks.

**shell marl,** a variety of marl having a high content of shells.

**shell molding,** a casting process for making thin, shell-like products, in which a mixture of fine sand and phenolic resin is placed on a preheated metal pattern, causing the resin to flow and form a thin shell on the pattern; solvent molding.

**shell number,** the number of shells of a given atom.

**shell parakeet,** = budgerigar.

**shell pink,** a soft, delicate pink with a tinge of yellow.

**shell|proof** (shel′prüf′), *adj.* able to withstand the impact and explosive force, as of shells or bombs.

**shell road,** a road surface composed of sea shells.

**shells** (shelz), *n.pl.* See under **shell.**

**shell shock,** any nervous or mental disorder resulting from the strain of combat in war; combat neurosis.

**shell|shocked** (shel′shokt′), *adj.* suffering from shell shock: *a shellshocked war veteran.*

**shell|work** (shel′wėrk′), *n.* decorative work made of or made to look like sea shells.

**shell|y** (shel′ē), *adj.,* **shell|i|er, shell|i|est.** **1** abounding in shells. **2** consisting of a shell or shells. **3** shell-like.

**shel|ter** (shel′tər), *n., v.* —*n.* **1** something that covers or protects from weather, danger, or attack: *Trees are a shelter from the sun. Only people who were secure in strong blast-proof shelters would have any chance of survival* (Bulletin of Atomic Scientists). *They pull some of the flotsam from the sea and make a pathetic shelter* (Time). SYN: safeguard, defense, shield. **2** protection; refuge: *We took shelter from the storm in a barn.* (*Figurative.*) *The tribunals ought to be sacred places of refuge, where ... the innocent of all parties may find shelter* (Macaulay). **3** a place of temporary lodging for the homeless poor.
—*v.t.* to protect; shield; hide; be or provide a shelter for: *to shelter runaway slaves. It is a serious crime to shelter a known criminal from the police.* (*Figurative.*) *The parents sheltered their daughter from life to such an extent that she had no friends.* SYN: screen, harbor.
—*v.i.* to find or take shelter: *The sheep sheltered from the hot sun in the shade of the haystack. This is a night when polecats and rabbits would shelter together in peace* (Henry Kingsley).
[origin uncertain] —**shel′ter|er,** *n.*

**shelter belt,** trees planted in a row to prevent soil erosion from water or wind; tree belt.

**shelter half,** *pl.* **shelter halves.** a rectangular piece of canvas that is half of a shelter tent.

**shel|ter|ing|ly** (shel′tər ing lē), *adv.* in a sheltering position or manner; so as to shelter.

**shel|ter|less** (shel′tər lis), *adj.* **1** giving no shelter: *The wind blew across the shelterless beach.* **2** having no shelter: *a shelterless roadstead.*

**shelter tent,** a small tent, usually made of pieces of waterproof cloth that fasten together.

**shelter trench,** a trench hastily excavated to obtain shelter from enemy fire.

**shelter wood,** = shelter belt.

**shel|ter|y** (shel′tər ē), *adj.* giving shelter: ... *the warm and sheltery shores of Gibraltar and Barbary* (Gilbert White).

**shel|ty** or **shel|tie** (shel′tē), *n., pl.* **-ties.** **1** = Shetland pony. **2** = Shetland sheep dog. [probably < the Orkney-Shetland pronunciation of Old Icelandic *Hjalti* Shetlander]

**shelve¹** (shelv), *v.t.,* **shelved, shelv|ing.** **1** to put on a shelf. **2** *Figurative.* to lay aside by failing to consider (a question or request) or removing (a person) from active service: *Let us shelve that argument.* **3** to furnish with shelves. [apparently < *shelf;* -v-, as in *sheave,* verb]

**shelve²** (shelv), *v.i.,* **shelved, shelv|ing.** to slope gradually: ... *a shelving part of the shore* (Thomas Love Peacock). SYN: incline, slant. [origin uncertain; perhaps a figurative use of *shelf* in sense of "ledge"]

**shelves** (shelvz), *n.* plural of **shelf.**

**shelv|ing** (shel′ving), *n.* **1** wood, metal, or other material used for shelves: *The carpenter ordered 40 feet of pine shelving.* **2** shelves collectively. **3** the act of laying aside.

**shelv|y** (shel′vē), *adj.* sloping gradually: *I had been drowned but that the shore was shelvy and shallow* (Shakespeare).

**Shem** (shem), *n.* the oldest of the three sons of Noah, regarded as the ancestor of the Semitic peoples (in the Bible, Genesis 10:21-31).

**She|ma** (shə mä′, shmä), *n.* the name given to the verse "Hear, O Israel: the Lord our God is one Lord," recited by Jews as a confession or reiteration of faith. Deuteronomy 6:4. [< Hebrew *shəma'* hear, imperative]

**She|mi|ni A|tze|reth** or **She|mi|ni A|tze|ret** (shə mē′nē ät ser′əs, -ser′ət), the eighth day of the Jewish festival of Sukkoth, observed as a separate holiday. A special prayer for rain is recited this day. [< Hebrew *shəmini 'aṣereth* (literally) eighth (day of) convocation]

**Shem|ite** (shem′īt), *n.* = Semite.

**She|mit|ic** (she mit′ik), *adj.* = Semitic.

**she|mit|ta** or **she|mit|tah** (shə mē′tə), *n.* the Jewish sabbatical year: *A year of shemitta, when the land must lie fallow and all loans must be canceled* (J. B. Agus). [< Hebrew *shəmittāh* (literally) release]

**she|moz|zle** (shə moz′əl), *n.* = schemozzle.

**she|nan|i|gan** (shə nan′ə gən), *n. Informal.* **shenanigans,** mischief or trickery: *Their predecessors could be bluffed by students marking all answers to a multiple-choice question; not these: they reject an exam paper at the first sign of shenanigans* (Maclean's). [American English; origin uncertain]

**shend** (shend), *v.t.,* **shent, shend|ing.** *Archaic.* **1** to put to shame or confusion. **2** to blame; reproach. **3** to defeat; destroy. **4** to damage. [Middle English *shenden* revile, Old English *scendan*]

**sheng** (sheng), *n.* a small hand organ first used in China around 1250, the forerunner of the modern accordion, harmonica, and concertina: *Sir Thomas Beecham ... soothed himself by trying to make music on a sheng* (Time). [< Chinese *shêng*]

**shent** (shent), *adj., v. Archaic.* —*adj.* **1** shamed. **2** blamed; scolded. **3** defeated. **4** ruined. **5** damaged.
—*v.* the past tense and past participle of **shend.**

**she oak, 1** any one of the casuarina trees of Australia. **2** *Australian Slang.* beer.

**She|ol** (shē′ōl), *n.* a Hebrew name for the abode of the dead. [< Hebrew *she'ol*]

**she|ol** (shē′ōl), *n. Informal.* hell.

**shep|herd** (shep′ərd), *n., v.* —*n.* **1** a man who takes care of sheep. **2** a person who cares for and protects. **3** *Figurative.* a spiritual guide; pastor. SYN: clergyman.
—*v.t.* **1** to take care of: *He will shepherd his flock.* SYN: tend. **2** to guide; direct: *The teacher shepherded the children safely out of the burning building.*
**the Shepherd,** Jesus Christ; Good Shepherd (in the Bible, John 10:11-16).
[Old English *scēaphierde* < *scēap* sheep + *hierde* herder < *heord* a herd]

**shepherd dog,** = sheep dog.

**shep|herd|ess** (shep′ər dis), *n.* a woman who takes care of sheep.

**shepherd god,** a god worshiped especially by shepherds.

**Shepherd Kings,** the Hyksos, a succession or dynasty of kings of Egypt. [translation of Greek *basileîs poiménes*]

**shepherd's check, 1** a black-and-white pattern of small checks. **2** a fabric, usually woolen, with this pattern.

**shepherd's pie,** a meat pie covered with mashed potatoes rather than pastry.

**shep|herd's-purse** (shep′ərdz pėrs′), *n.* a weed of the mustard family that has small, white flowers and purselike pods. [< the resemblance of its pods to shepherds' purses or pouches]

**Shep|pard's adjustment** (shep′ərdz), an adjustment to correct certain statistical errors caused by assuming that all cases in one class interval have the same value exactly, whereas they actually may have any value within the class interval. [< William F. *Sheppard,* a British statistician of the 1900's]

**sher|ard|ize** (sher′ər dīz), *v.t.,* **-ized, -iz|ing.** to coat (iron articles) with zinc. [< *Sherard* Cowper-Coles, a British scientist, died 1936, who invented the process + *-ize*]

***Sher|a|ton** (sher′ə tən), *adj.* in or having to do with the style of light, graceful furniture designed by Thomas Sheraton. It is marked especially by straightness of line, simplicity of form, and little use of ornament. [< Thomas *Sheraton,* 1751-1806, an English cabinetmaker and furniture designer]

***Sheraton**

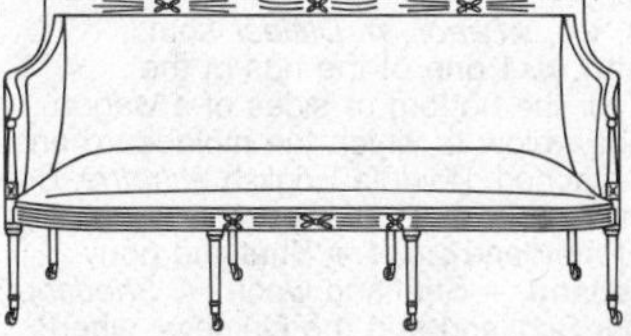

**sher|bet** (shėr′bət), *n.* **1** a frozen dessert made of fruit juice, sugar, and water, milk, or whites of eggs. **2** a cooling drink made of fruit juice, sugar, and water, popular in the Orient. **3** a dish, usually with a long stem, to hold frozen sherbet. [< Turkish *şerbet* < Arabic *sharbat* a drink]

**sherd** (shėrd), *n.* = shard¹: *a few fragmentary sherds of Aegean painted pottery* (Scientific American).

**She|ri|a** (shə rē′ə), *n.* = Sharia.

**she|rif** or **she|reef** (shə rēf′), *n.* **1** a descendant of Mohammed through his daughter Fatima. **2** an Arab prince or ruler, especially the chief magistrate of Mecca or (formerly) the sovereign of Morocco. **3** *Archaic.* a Moslem priest. Also, **sharif.** [< Arabic *sharīf exalted* < *sharafa* he was exalted]

**sher|iff** (sher′if), *n.* the most important law-enforcing officer of a county, in most states of the United States elected by popular vote. A sheriff aids the courts and appoints deputies to help him keep order in the county. [Old English *scīrgerēfa* < *scīr* shire + *gerēfa* reeve¹]

**Pronunciation Key:** hat, āge, cãre, fär; let, ēqual, tėrm; it, īce; hot, ōpen, ôrder; oil, out; cup, pu̇t, rüle; child; long; thin; ᴛʜen; zh, measure;
ə represents **a** in about, **e** in taken, **i** in pencil, **o** in lemon, **u** in circus.

**sher|iff|al|ty** (sher′ə fəl tē), *n., pl.* **-ties.** = shrievalty.

**sher|iff|dom** (sher′if dəm), *n.* **1** the district or territory under a sheriff's jurisdiction. **2** the office of sheriff.

**sher|iff|ship** (sher′if ship), *n.* = sheriffdom.

**she|ris|ta|dar** (she ris′tə där′), *n., pl.* **-dars.** (in India) an officer or clerk, as of a court, who keeps records.

**sher|lock** (shėr′lok), *n. Informal.* a private detective. [< *Sherlock* Holmes]

**Sher|lock Holmes** (shėr′lok hōmz′), a fictional English detective with remarkable powers of observation and reasoning, created by Sir Arthur Conan Doyle (1859-1930) in 1887.

**Sher|lock|i|an** (shėr lok′ē ən), *adj., n.* —*adj.* of or having to do with Sherlock Holmes; Holmesian.
—*n.* an admirer or devotee of Sherlock Holmes: *The excisions ... will nevertheless be annoying to many a good Sherlockian* (Atlantic).

**Sher|pa** (shėr′pə), *n.* **1** a member of a Mongoloid people of Nepal. Sherpas have served as guides and porters for most of the expeditions to climb Mount Everest. *Foot over foot for five weeks, the 13 Britons and the 35 Sherpas ... drive up a jagged icefall of 3,000 feet* (Time). **2 sherpa.** *British Slang.* a porter.

**sher|ris** (sher′is), *n. Archaic.* sherry.

**sher|ry** (sher′ē), *n., pl.* **-ries. 1** a strong wine originally made in southern Spain. Its color varies from pale yellow to brown. **2** any similar wine: *This week we can offer our Golden Cyprus Sherry in a medium sweet or medium dry* (London Times). [new singular < *sherris* (taken as plural) wine from (earlier name) *Sherries* < earlier Spanish (*vino de*) *Xeres*, a Spanish town (modern *Jerez*)]

**sherry cobbler**, a drink of sherry, sugar, lemon, and water.

***sher|wa|ni** (shər wä′nē), *n.* a long, tight, buttoned coat with a high collar, worn in India as a man's formal dress. [< Hindi *shērwānī*]

***sherwani**

**she's** (shēz; *unstressed* shiz), **1** she is: *She's going home tomorrow.* **2** she has: *She's already gone home.*

**shet** (shet), *v.t., v.i., adj., n. Dialect.* shut.

**sheth** (sheth), *n.* **1** one of the ribs of the framework for the bottom or sides of a wagon. **2** the part of a plow to which the moldboard and share are attached. [Middle English *schethe.* See related etym. at **shed**¹.]

**Shet|land** (shet′lənd), *n.* **1** = Shetland pony. **2** Also, **shetland.** = Shetland wool. [< *Shetland* Islands, near Scotland and the Orkneys, where the breed originated, and the wool was spun]

**Shetland pony**, a small, sturdy, rough-coated pony, originally from the Shetland Islands, from 9 to 11½ hands high and weighing from 300 to 500 pounds.

**Shetland sheep**, one of a breed of sheep native to the Shetland Islands.

**Shetland sheepdog**, a long-haired working dog resembling a small collie, of a breed originated in the Shetland Islands. It has a black or brown coat with white or tan markings.

**Shetland wool**, a fine, hairy, strong worsted spun from the wool of Shetland sheep, widely used in knitting fine shawls, sweaters, and other garments.

**sheugh** or **sheuch** (shyüH), *n. Scottish.* a furrow; ditch; gully. [Middle English *sough*]

**shew** (shō), *v.t., v.i.,* **shewed, shewn, shew|ing,** *n., adj. Especially British or Archaic.* show.

**shew|bread** (shō′bred′), *n.* the unleavened bread placed near the altar every Sabbath by the ancient Jewish priests as an offering to God (in the Bible, Leviticus 24:5-9). Also, **showbread.** [< *shew* + *bread;* influenced by German *Schaubrot* (coined by Luther), translation of Hebrew *lechem pānīm* (literally) face bread (because it was shown, not eaten)]

**SHF** (no periods), superhigh frequency.

**Shi|ah** or **Shi|a** (shē′ə), *n.* **1** one of the two great Moslem sects, centered in Iran, which regards Ali, the son-in-law of Mohammed, as the true successor of Mohammed and rejects the first three caliphs and the Sunnite book of tradition handed down under their protection. **2** = Shiite. [< Arabic *shī'ah* sect]

**shib|bo|leth** (shib′ə lith), *n.* **1** any test word, watchword, or pet phrase of a political party, a class, a sect, or other group. **2** *Figurative.* any use of language, habit, or custom, considered distinctive of a particular group or class. [< Hebrew *shibbōleth* stream; used as a password by the Gileadites to distinguish the fleeing Ephraimites, because the Ephraimites could not pronounce *sh.* Judges 12:4-6.]

**shi|bu|i|chi** (shē′bü ē′chē), *n.* an alloy widely used in Japanese decorative art. It is made of three parts copper to one part silver. [< Japanese *shibuichi* < *shi* four + *bu* part + *ichi* one]

**shick|er** (shik′ər), *adj., n. Australian Slang.* —*adj.* drunk.
—*n.* drunkard. [< Yiddish *shiker* < Hebrew *shikkūr*]

**shied** (shīd), *v.* a past tense and past participle of **shy**: *The horse shied and threw the rider. He had never shied like that before.*

**shiel** (shēl), *n. Scottish.* **1** a hut; shanty. **2** a shepherd's summer hut. [Middle English *shale, schele;* origin uncertain]

***shield** (shēld), *n., v.* —*n.* **1** a piece of armor carried on the arm or in the hand to protect the body in battle, used in ancient and medieval warfare. **2** anything used to protect: *He turned up his collar as a shield against the cold wind. A heavy face shield protects a welder's face and eyes from being burned.* (*Figurative.*) *Active French forces in the Allied "shield" in Europe now stand officially at four divisions* (New York Times). **3** something shaped like a shield. **4** a covering for moving parts of machinery. **5a** any substance to protect against exposure to radiation, especially in nuclear reactors, such as lead or water. **b** a barrier built out of one of these substances. **6a** a framework pushed ahead in a tunnel to prevent the earth from caving in while the tunnel is being lined. **b** a movable framework protecting a miner at his work. **7** a steel screen or plate, such as that attached to a cannon or howitzer, to protect something, such as a crew or a mechanism. **8a** a policeman's badge. **b** = escutcheon. **9** a piece of fabric, often rubberized, worn inside a dress at the armpit. **10** *Zoology.* a protective plate covering a part on the body of an animal, such as a scute, carapace, or plastron.
—*v.t.* **1** to be a shield to; protect; defend; shelter: *to shield the child from attack by the savage watchdog, to shield a criminal. Her hat shielded her eyes from the sun.* (*Figurative.*) *His mother shielded him from punishment.* **2** *Obsolete.* to avert; prevent.
—*v.i.* to act or serve as a shield.
[Old English *sceld, scield*] —**shield′er**, *n.* —**shield′like′**, *adj.*

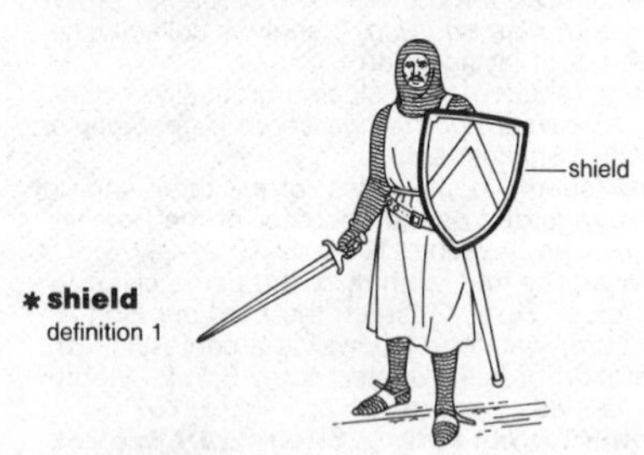

***shield**
definition 1

***shield-back** (shēld′bak′), *n.* a chair with a back whose center resembles a shield, a design much used by George Hepplewhite in England in the 1700's.

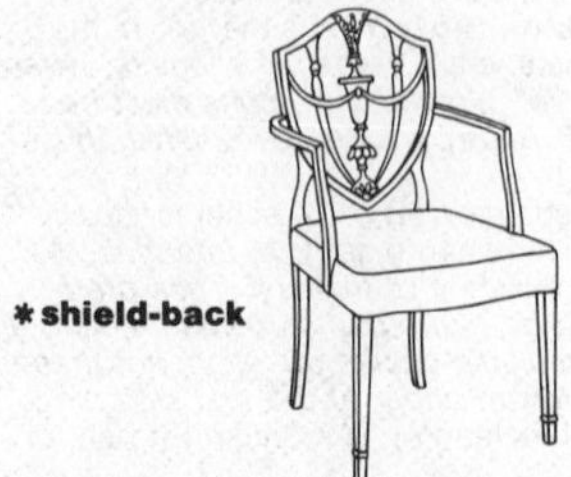
***shield-back**

**shield-bear|er** (shēld′bãr′ər), *n.* (formerly) a soldier who carried his chief's shield.

**shield fern**, = wood fern.

**shield|ing** (shēl′ding), *n.* a substance that shields against radiation; shield.

**shield law**, *U.S.* a law that permits a member of the press to protect his confidential sources: *Under "shield laws" in twelve States, newsmen can refuse to reveal their sources* (Time).

**shield|less** (shēld′lis), *adj.* without a shield; unprotected.

**Shield of So|bies|ki** (sō byes′kē, sô-), *Astronomy.* a constellation over the bow of Sagittarius, represented as a shield having a cross. [< John *Sobieski,* 1624-1696, a king of Poland]

**shield pigeon**, one of a breed of domesticated pigeons of small size, having a white head and body, parti-colored wings, and no crest.

**shield-shaped** (shēld′shāpt′), *adj.* like a shield in shape.

**shield volcano**, a low, flat, dome-shaped volcano, built up of coalescing and overlapping lava streams with almost no explosive activity and with relatively little pyroclastic material: *Most shield volcanoes are composed of basalt, though a few are andesite* (Gilluly, Waters, and Woodford).

**shiel|ing** (shē′ling), *n. Scottish.* **1** a shiel. **2** a piece of pasture: *... sone ... she and her colleagues may have chanted on the lone shieling* (Punch). Also, **shealing, sheiling.**

**shi|er**¹ (shī′ər), *n.* a horse that shies. Also, **shyer.**

**shi|er**² (shī′ər), *n.* a person who shies (throws). Also, **shyer.**

**shi|er**³ (shī′ər), *adj.* a comparative of **shy**¹.

**shi|est** (shī′ist), *adj.* a superlative of **shy**¹.

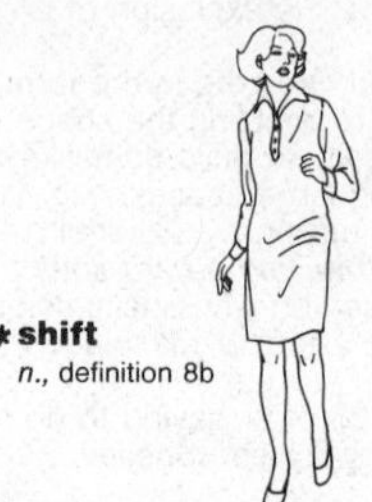
***shift**
*n.,* definition 8b

***shift** (shift), *v., n.* —*v.t.* **1** to move or change (something) from one place, position, person, or sound to another: *I shifted the heavy bag from one hand to the other. He always tries to shift the blame to someone else. The Administration is only shifting its stance a little to meet the old challenger in the continuation of the old bout* (Observer). **SYN:** transfer. **2** to remove and replace with another or others; change: *to shift the scenes on a stage. But nothing would shift the General Staff's blind belief in the Maginot Line and static warfare* (Observer). **3** to change the position of (the gears of an automobile, truck, or mechanism). **4** *Archaic.* to change the clothes of. **5** to get rid of. **6** *Obsolete.* to divide; distribute.
—*v.i.* **1** to move from one place, position, person, or sound to another: *The wind shifted to the southeast. Scobie shifted uncomfortably in his chair* (Graham Greene). **SYN:** transfer. **2** to manage to get along; contrive: *When his parents died, he had to shift for himself.* **3** to be rather dishonest; scheme. **4** *Archaic.* to change one's clothing. **5** to connect the motor to a different set of gears in an automobile: *He had to shift as he drove around the corner and up the hill.* **6** *Obsolete.* to make a distribution.
—*n.* **1** a change of position, direction, or attitude; a substituting in the place of another person or thing; change: *a shift of the wind, a shift in policy. There are two shifts of work at the factory.* **2** a group of workmen who work during the same period of time; group: *This man is on the night shift.* **SYN:** crew, gang. **3** the time during which such a group works: *He works a day shift.* **4** a way of getting on; scheme; trick; artifice: *The lazy man tried every shift to avoid doing his work.* **SYN:** expedient. **5** a change in the arrangement of players before a football is put into play. **6** *Geology.* a slight fault or dislocation in a seam or stratum. **7** *Linguistics.* sound change that affects the phonetic and phonemic system of a language or language group. **8a** *Archaic.* a woman's chemise. **b** a loosely fitting dress like a chemise, but with straighter lines: *The shift is nothing more than an easy-fitting sheath, ... street-length or to the floor* (Time). **9** *Music.* **a** a change of the hand's position on the finger board of a string instrument. **b** one of the positions thus reached. **c** a moving of the trombone slide to vary the pitch. **10** *Archaic or Dialect.* a change of clothing.
**make shift, a** to manage to get along: *He made shift pretty well till he got to low land, and then had to drop upon his hands and knees and crawl* (Arthur Quiller-Couch). **b** to manage with effort or difficulty: *When she first came here she could speak no English; now she can make shift to talk it a little* (Charlotte Brontë). **c** to do as well as one can: *Act then as persons ... who accord-*

ingly make shift and put up with anything that comes to hand* (Cardinal Newman).
[Old English *sciftan* arrange] —**shift′er**, *n.*

**shif|ta** or **Shif|ta** (shif′tə), *n., pl.* **-ta** or **-tas.** a member of a nomadic band of Somalis engaged in terrorist and guerrilla activities in Somalia, Kenya, and Ethiopia. [< Amharic *shifta* (literally) bandit]

**shift|a|ble** (shift′tə bəl), *adj.* that can be shifted: *shiftable scenery.*

**shift|ed tax** (shif′tid), a tax whose cost is passed on to someone else. An indirect tax is a shifted tax.

**shift|er fork** (shif′tər), a forklike device used in machinery to shift moving parts. Shifter forks are used to guide belts from a tight to a loose pulley or vice versa.

**shift|i|ly** (shif′tə lē), *adv.* in a shifty manner; cowardly; underhandedly.

**shift|i|ness** (shif′tē nis), *n.* the character or quality of being shifty; sneakiness.

**shift joint,** in masonry: **1** the placing of a stone or brick so that the vertical joints will come over the solid members of the course below. **2** the stone or brick so placed.

**shift key,** a typewriter key that shifts the type to print upper-case letters.

**shift|less** (shift′lis), *adj.* lazy; inefficient: *Going to hunt up her shiftless husband at the inn* (Thomas Hardy). —**shift′less|ly,** *adv.* —**shift′less|ness,** *n.*

**shift register,** a computer mechanism for storing data in which it is possible to shift or manipulate the stored information in various ways: *The device in question is a single 64-bit dynamic shift register which will work at frequencies of more than 20 megahertz against the 10 megahertz or so of the fastest shift registers available today* (New Scientist).

**shift|work** (shift′wėrk′), *n.* work done by those working in shifts: *In nursing, for example, shiftwork and weekend work may cause difficulty* (London Times).

**shift|y** (shif′tē), *adj.,* **shift|i|er, shift|i|est. 1** not straightforward; tricky: *shifty eyes, a shifty fellow.* **2** full of shifts; quick-witted; inventive.

**shift|y-eyed** (shif′tē īd′), *adj.* having shifty eyes: *a shifty-eyed gambler.*

**shi|gel|la** (shi gel′ə), *n., pl.* **-gel|lae** (-gel′ē), **-gel|las.** any one of a group of Gram-negative, rod-shaped bacteria that cause bacillary dysentery: *The proportion of resistant strains of shigellae, the organisms responsible, has been growing steadily* (New Scientist). [< New Latin *Shigella* the genus name < Kiyoshi *Shiga,* 1870-1957, a Japanese bacteriologist, who discovered the bacteria in 1898]

**shi|gel|lo|sis** (shi′gə lō′sis), *n., pl.* **-ses** (-sēz). = bacillary dysentery. [< *shigella* + *-osis*]

**Shih Tzu** (shē′ dzü′), a toy dog of Chinese and Tibetan origin, with a long, thick black-and-white coat, a broad head, a short, square snout, and large black eyes. [< Chinese (Peking) *shi tzu*]

**Shi|ism** (shē′iz əm), *n.* the principles or doctrines of the Shiites.

**Shi|ite** (shē′īt), *n., adj* —*n.* a member of the Shiah sect of the Moslem religion.
—*adj.* of or having to do with the Shiah or Shiites: *A Shiite imam.*
[< *Shi*(ah) (see etym. under **Shiah**) + English *-ite*[1]]

**Shi|it|ic** (shē it′ik), *adj.* of or having to do with the Shiites.

**shi|kar** (shi kär′), *n., v.* in India: —*n.* hunting; sport: *His service in the Indian Army and his periods of leave ... were almost invariably spent on shikar* (London Times).
—*v.t.* to hunt.
[< Hindi *shikār* < Persian]

**shi|ka|ra** (shē′kər ə), *n.* a long, narrow boat with a peak at each end, used in Kashmir: *Shikaras ... are used for quick trips around the city or for romantic outings on moonlit nights* (New Yorker). [< Kashmiri *shikhara*]

**shi|ka|ri** or **shi|ka|ree** (shi kä′rē), *n.* in India: **1** a hunter, especially a native hunter: *These became a professional group, the European shikaris, the White Hunters of song and story* (Harper's). **2** a native guide or assistant to a European sportsman. [< Hindi *shikāri* < Persian < *shikār* shikar]

**shik|sa** or **shik|se** (shik′sə), *n. Yiddish.* **1** a non-Jewish girl. **2** an unobservant or irreligious Jewish girl.

**shill**[1] (shil), *n., v. U.S. Slang.* —*n.* a person hired, as by a gambler or auctioneer, to pose as a bystander and decoy others to bet, buy, bid, or otherwise enter the proceedings: *An almost universal characteristic of booms is the sprouting of fast operators, shills and suckers* (Wall Street Journal).
—*v.t.* to be a shill for: *I certainly could use a character like you just to sit alongside me on the show and shill my pitch* (Harper's).
—*v.i.* to work as a shill; act as a lure: *to shill for a gambler.* (*Figurative.*) *This is ... the fish that shills for a poisonous anemone, luring other fish to their destruction* (Time).
[< earlier *shillaber;* origin uncertain]

**shill**[2] (shil), *adj. Obsolete.* shrill. [Middle English *schille,* Old English *scyl*]

**shil|la|la** or **shil|la|lah** (shə lā′lē, -lə), *n.* = shillelagh.

**shil|le|lagh** or **shil|le|lah** (shə lā′lē, -lə), *n. Irish.* a stick to hit with; cudgel: (*Figurative.*) *Meanwhile, Teddy Roosevelt was taking after the big trusts, wielding the shillelagh of the Sherman Act* (Harper's). [< *Shillelagh,* a town and barony in Ireland]

**shil|ling** (shil′ing), *n.* **1a** a former British unit of money equal to 12 pence or 1/20 of a pound sterling. The shilling was replaced in 1971 by a coin of equal value worth 5 new pence. **b** a former silver or cupronickel coin equal to one shilling. *Abbr:* s. **2** a similar unit of money in any of various countries such as Somalia, Tanzania, and Uganda, equal to 100 cents or 1/20 of a pound. **3** a corresponding piece of money of one of the thirteen American colonies. **4** a former Scottish coin and money of account, worth one English penny in the 1600's. [Old English *scilling*]

**shilling mark, 1** the mark used to divide shillings and pence. *Example:* The hat was cheap at 16/4d. **2** this mark used for other purposes in writing and printing; virgule; slash.

**shilling shocker,** *British.* a short, sensational novel, originally sold for a shilling: *She wanted to prove that she could write rather better than the fair young ladies of London society whose shilling shockers littered the shelves of circulating libraries up and down the country* (Listener).

**shil|lings|worth** (shil′ingz wėrth′), *n. British.* as much as can be bought for a shilling: *A good shillingsworth of dry fino was jerked out of the glass* (Punch).

**Shil|luk** (shi lük′), *n., pl.* **-luks** or **luk. 1** a member of a Nilotic people of the Sudan, occupying a region on the left bank of the White Nile: *The stately Shilluks still spear lion and crocodile, still stand for hours, cranelike, on one foot* (Time). **2** the language of this people.

**shil|ly-shal|ly** (shil′ē shal′ē), *adj., adv., v.,* **-lied, -ly|ing,** *n.* —*adj.* vacillating; wavering; hesitating; undecided: *I'm not going to be stopped by any shilly-shally nonsense* (Anthony Trollope). **SYN:** irresolute.
—*adv.* in a vacillating or hesitating manner: *I see no good that comes of standing shilly-shally* (Thomas De Quincey).
—*v.i.* to be undecided; vacillate; hesitate: *Bruce had been for a long time shilly-shallying as to the side he should take* (Thackeray).
—*n.* inability to decide; hesitation; vacillation: *What I wished to point out to you was, that there can be no shilly-shally now* (George Eliot).
[< earlier *shill I, shall I,* varied reduplication of *shall I?*]

**shilp|it** (shil′pit), *adj. Scottish.* **1** sickly; feeble; puny. **2** (of drink) weak; insipid. [origin unknown]

**shi|ly** (shī′lē), *adv.* = shyly.

**shim** (shim), *n., v.,* **shimmed, shim|ming.** —*n.* a thin strip of metal, wood, or the like, used to raise a part, make it fill some other part, or fill up a space.
—*v.t.* to put a shim or shims in.
[American English; origin uncertain]

**shim|mer** (shim′ər), *v., n.* —*v.i.* to shine with a flickering light; gleam faintly: *The satin shimmers.*
—*n.* a faint gleam or shine: *The pearls have a beautiful shimmer.*
[Old English *scimerian*]

**shim|mer|ing** (shim′ər ing), *adj.* softly bright or gleaming; lambent: (*Figurative.*) *He directed without quite the verve needed to give Richard Strauss' shimmering music its best display* (Wall Street Journal). —**shim′mer|ing|ly,** *adv.*

**shim|mer|y** (shim′ər ē), *adj.* shimmering; gleaming softly: *The moon, full last night, will be up soon, casting a shimmery reflection in the pond* (New York Times).

**shim|mey** (shim′ē), *n., v.i.* = shimmy.

**shim|my**[1] (shim′ē), *n., pl.* **-mies,** *v.,* **-mied, -my|ing.** —*n.* **1** an unusual shaking or vibration: *a dangerous shimmy of a ladder. The basic causes of dangerous nosewheel shimmy in aircraft have been uncovered* (Science News Letter). **2** a jazz dance popular in the early 1920's, a fox trot with much shaking of the body.
—*v.i.* **1** to shake; vibrate: *The front wheels of the car shimmied.* **2** to dance the shimmy.
[American English; origin uncertain]

**shim|my**[2] (shim′ē), *n., pl.* **-mies.** *Informal.* chemise. [variant of *chemise*]

**shi|mo|se** (shi mō′se), *n.* a Japanese explosive consisting largely of picric acid. [< Masachika *Shimose,* 1859-1911, a Japanese engineer, who invented it]

**Shim|pa** or **shim|pa** (shim′pä), *n.* a realistic form of Japanese theater, influenced by Western drama, which developed in the late 1800's: *The Shimpa ... was designed to free the stage from the rigid conventions of the Kabuki* (Donald Richie). [< Japanese *shinpa* new school]

**shin**[1] (shin), *n., v.,* **shinned, shin|ning.** —*n.* **1** the front part of the leg from the knee to the ankle. **2** the lower part of the leg in beef cattle. **3** = shinbone.
—*v.i., v.t.* to climb by holding fast with the hands or arms and legs and drawing oneself up: *He shinned up a tree.*
[Old English *scinu*]

**shin**[2] (shēn), *n.* the twenty-first letter of the Hebrew alphabet. Also, **sin.** [< Hebrew *shin* (literally) tooth]

**Shin** (shin), *n.* a Japanese Buddhist sect that practices Amidism. [< Japanese *Shin*(*shū*) < *Shin* Faith + *shū* sect]

**Shi|nar** (shī′när), *n.* a name in the Bible for Sumer or Babylonia as a whole.

**shin|bone** (shin′bōn′), *n.* the inner and thicker of the two bones between the knee and the ankle; tibia. See picture under **leg.**

**shin|dig** (shin′dig), *n. Informal.* a merry or noisy dance, party, or other gathering: *... rented an airport hangar to toss a shindig at which an estimated ton of food was served* (New York Times). [American English, perhaps < *shindy;* influenced by *shin*[1] + earlier *dig* a blow]

**shin|dy** (shin′dē), *n., pl.* **-dies.** *Informal.* **1** a disturbance; rumpus: *to kick up a shindy. The tension is increased by the fact that the marshal in a recent shindy ... has lost the use of his trigger finger* (Newsweek). **2** = shindig. [origin uncertain]

**shine** (shīn), *v.,* **shone** or (*especially for v.t. 1*) **shined, shin|ing,** *n.* —*v.i.* **1** to send out light; be bright with light; reflect light; glow: *The sun shines by day, the moon by night. His face is shining with soap and water. Wax makes the floors shine.* (*Figurative.*) *What fun shone in his eyes* (Charlotte Brontë). **SYN:** beam, gleam. **2** *Figurative.* to do very well; be brilliant; be conspicuous in ability, character, achievement, or position; excel: *to shine in conversation. She shines in school. He is a shining athlete.*
—*v.t.* **1** to make bright; polish: *to shine shoes. After roughing up one side of the ball, pitchers used to shine ... the other side on a part of their uniform heavily dosed with paraffin* (Time). **2** to cause to shine: *to shine a light in someone's face.*
—*n.* **1** light; brightness: *the shine of a lamp.* **SYN:** radiance, gleam. **2** luster; polish; gloss; sheer: *Silk has a shine.* **3** fair weather; sunshine: *He goes to work rain or shine.* **4a** a polish put on shoes. **b** the act of putting on such a polish. **5** *Slang.* a fancy; liking.
**shines,** *Slang.* tricks; pranks: *He's up to his old shines again.*
**shine up to,** *Slang.* to try to please and get the friendship of: *Mother was always hectorin' me about getting married, and wantin' I should shine up to this likely girl and that* (Congregationalist).
**take a shine to,** *Slang.* to become fond of; like: *He took a shine to you that night you saw him* (Winston Churchill).
**take the shine out of** (or **off,** or **off of**), *Informal.* **a** to take the brightness or cheer from: *... enough to take more of the shine out of things than church-going on Sundays could put in again* (George MacDonald). **b** to outshine: *I am only sorry I didn't bring Seth Sprague along with me, with his pitch pipe, just to take the shine off of them there singers* (Seba Smith).
[Old English *scīnan*]

**shin|er** (shī′nər), *n.* **1** a person or thing that shines. **2** a small American freshwater fish with glistening scales. There are various kinds, related to the carp and dace. **3** *Slang.* a black eye. **4** *British Slang.* a guinea or a sovereign.

**Shin|ge|ki** or **shin|ge|ki** (shin′gə kē), *n.* the contemporary form of Japanese theater, which developed after World War II and uses the styles and techniques of popular and avant-garde Western plays. [< Japanese *shingeki* < *shin* new + *geki* drama]

***shin|gle**[1] (shing′gəl), *n., v.,* **gled, -gling.** —*n.* **1** a thin piece of wood or other material, used to cover roofs, walls, or the like. Shingles are laid in overlapping rows with the thicker ends showing. **2** *U.S. Informal.* a small signboard, especially one outside a doctor's or lawyer's office. **3** a woman's short haircut in which the hair is made to taper from the back of the head to the nape of the neck.

---

**Pronunciation Key:** hat, āge, cãre, fär; let, ēqual, tėrm; it, īce; hot, ōpen, ôrder; oil, out; cup, pu̇t, rüle; child; long; thin; ᴛʜen; zh, measure;
ə represents **a** in about, **e** in taken, **i** in pencil, **o** in lemon, **u** in circus.

*—v.t.* **1** to cover with shingles: *to shingle a roof.* **2** to cut (the hair) in a shingle.
**hang out one's shingle**, *Informal.* to open an office (used only of professional people): *He studied law ... and hung out his shingle* (Albion W. Tourgee).
[Middle English *schingel, scingel,* apparently by alteration < Latin *scindula*]

***shingle[1]**
definitions 1, 3

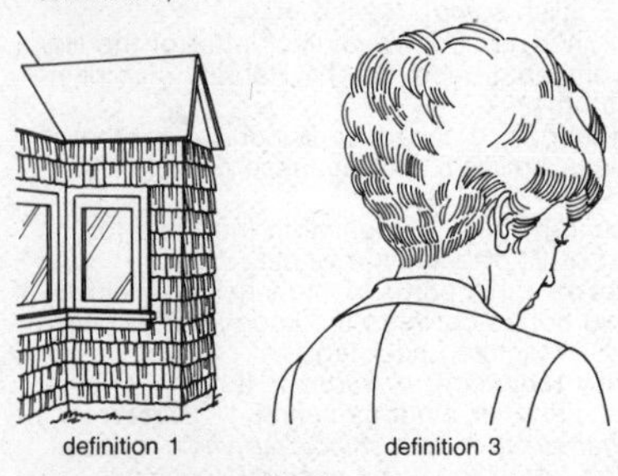

definition 1 definition 3

**shin|gle[2]** (shing′gəl), *n. Especially British.* **1** loose stones or pebbles such as lie on the seashore; coarse gravel. **2** a beach or other place covered with this. [earlier *chingle;* origin uncertain. Compare Norwegian *singling* small round pebble.]
**shin|gle[3]** (shing′gəl), *v.t.,* **-gled, -gling.** to hammer or squeeze (a mass of iron taken from a puddling furnace) to press out the slag and impurities. [< French *cingler* < German *zängeln* < *Zange* tongs]
**shingle bolt**, a block of wood ready to be cut into shingles.
**shin|gled** (shing′gəld), *adj.* covered with loose pebbles: *I was content to rove the shingled beach* (Walter de la Mare).
**shingle nail**, a nail used to fix shingles in building. [Middle English *schingelneil*]
**shin|gler[1]** (shing′glər), *n.* **1** a person who shingles houses. **2** a person or a machine that cuts and prepares shingles.
**shin|gler[2]** (shing′glər), *n.* a person or thing that shingles iron.
**shin|gles** (shing′gəlz), *n. sing. or pl.* a virus disease that causes pain in certain nerves and an outbreak of itching spots or blisters on the skin in the area of the affected nerves. The commonest location is on the chest or lower part of the back. [< Medieval Latin *cingulus,* variant of Latin *cingulum* (translation of Greek *zōstḗr* girdle, shingles; see etym. under **zoster**) girdle < *cingere* to gird]
**shin|gling** (shing′gling), *n. Geology.* the arrangement of flat pebbles or boulders by streams in such a manner that they overlap like shingles.
**shin|gly** (shing′glē), *adj.* consisting of or covered with small, loose stones or pebbles: *a shingly beach.*
**Shin|gon** (shin′gon), *n.* a mystical Buddhist sect in Japan, teaching that truth is inherent in all living beings and may be developed by special rituals.
**shin guard**, or **shin|guard** (shin′gärd′), *n.* a pad such as that worn by baseball catchers or ice hockey players to protect the leg.
**shin|i|ly** (shī′nə lē), *adv.* in a shiny manner; glossily.
**shin|i|ness** (shī′nē nis), *n.* shiny or glossy character or condition; glossiness; sheen.
**shin|ing** (shī′ning), *adj.* **1** that shines; bright. **SYN:** glowing, radiant, glistening. **2** *Figurative.* brilliant; outstanding: ... *a man of shining talents* (Benjamin Disraeli). **SYN:** distinguished, eminent. —**shin′ing|ly,** *adv.* —**shin′ing|ness,** *n.*
**shining light**, a person conspicuous for some excellence (after John 5:35): *Pavlov, ... however brilliant his methodological innovations and experimental contributions, was no shining light as a theorist* (Bulletin of Atomic Scientists).
**shin|leaf** (shin′lēf′), *n.* any one of a group of low perennial herbs of the Northern Hemisphere, related to the pipsissewa and pinedrops, with creeping underground stems, evergreen leaves, and racemes of white, greenish, or purplish flowers; wintergreen. [< the use of this plant as a shinplaster]
**shin|ner|y** (shin′ər ē), *n., pl.* **-ner|ies.** = cheniere.
**shin|ney** (shin′ē), *n., v.i.* = shinny[1].
**shin|ny[1]** (shin′ē), *n., pl.* **-nies,** *v.,* **-nied, -ny|ing.** *—n.* **1** a simple kind of field hockey, played with a ball or the like and sticks curved at one end. **2** the stick used in this game.
*—v.i.* **1** to play shinny. **2** to drive the ball in shinny. Also, **shinty.**
[origin uncertain]
**shin|ny[2]** (shin′ē), *v.i., v.t.,* **-nied, -ny|ing.** *Informal.* to shin; climb. [< *shin*[1]]
**shin|plas|ter** (shin′plas′tər, -pläs′-), *n.* **1** a plaster for a sore leg, often paper wet with vinegar. **2** *Informal.* a piece of paper money that has depreciated greatly in value, especially one issued by private bankers.
**shin splints**, inflammation and soreness of the shins commonly affecting track-and-field athletes, especially runners.
**Shin|to** (shin′tō), *n., pl.* **-tos,** *adj. —n.* **1** the native religion of Japan, primarily the worship of nature deities and of ancestors: *The result was Shinto, the Way of the Gods—a lock step of temporal rule and religion, more efficient perhaps than any since ancient Sparta* (Time). **2** an adherent of this religion.
*—adj.* of or having to do with Shinto: *Shinto girls worship the Sun Goddess, but ecumenically they also believe that sincerity binds God and man* (Saturday Review).
[< Japanese *shintō* < Chinese *shên tao* way of the gods]
**Shin|to|ism** (shin′tō iz əm), *n.* the Shinto religion.
**Shin|to|ist** (shin′tō ist), *n., adj. —n.* a believer in the Shinto religion.
*—adj.* of Shintoism or Shintoists.
**Shin|to|is|tic** (shin′tō is′tik), *adj.* of or having to do with Shinto or Shintoism.
**shin|ty** (shin′tē), *n., pl.* **-ties.** = shinny[1].
**shin|y** (shī′nē), *adj.,* **shin|i|er, shin|i|est.** **1** reflecting light; shining; bright: *A new penny is shiny.* **2** worn to a glossy smoothness: *a coat shiny from hard wear.*
***ship** (ship), *n., v.,* **shipped, ship|ping.** *—n.* **1** a large vessel for traveling on water, especially a seagoing vessel such as a steamship, a frigate, or a galley. Ships are propelled by engines or sails: *a cargo ship, a passenger ship.* See picture below. **2** a large sailing vessel, especially one with three square-rigged masts and a bowsprit. **3** a large vessel for traveling in air or in space, such as an airship, airplane, or spacecraft: *"No decision has been made whether the crew will*

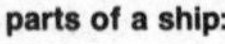
**parts of a ship:**

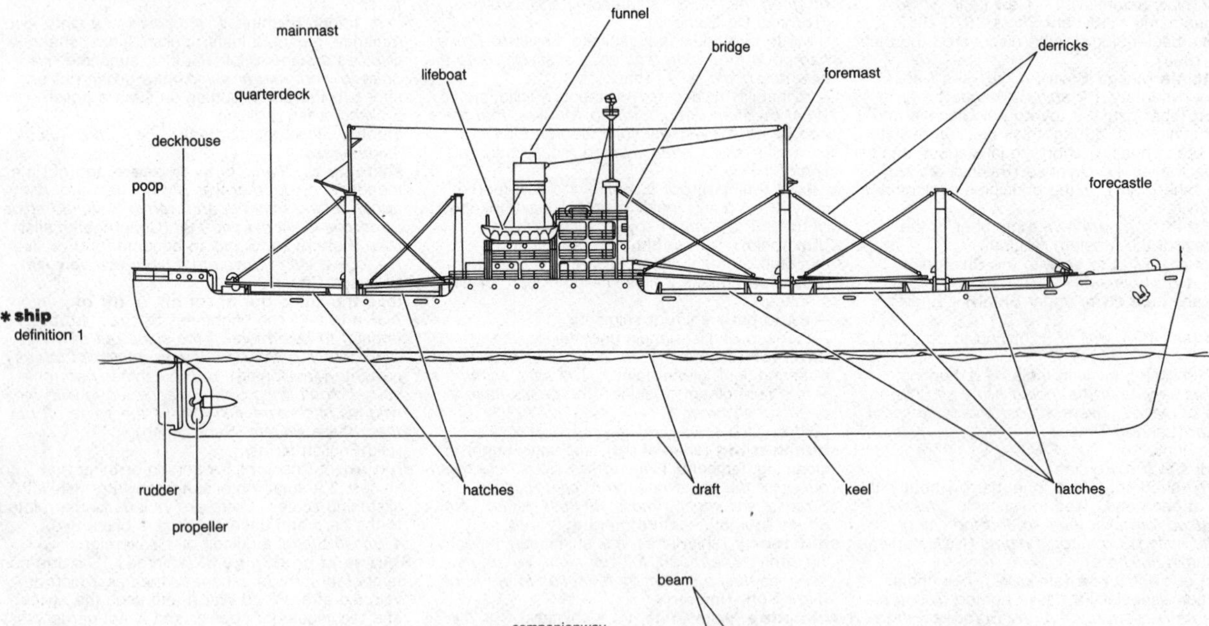


***ship**
definition 1

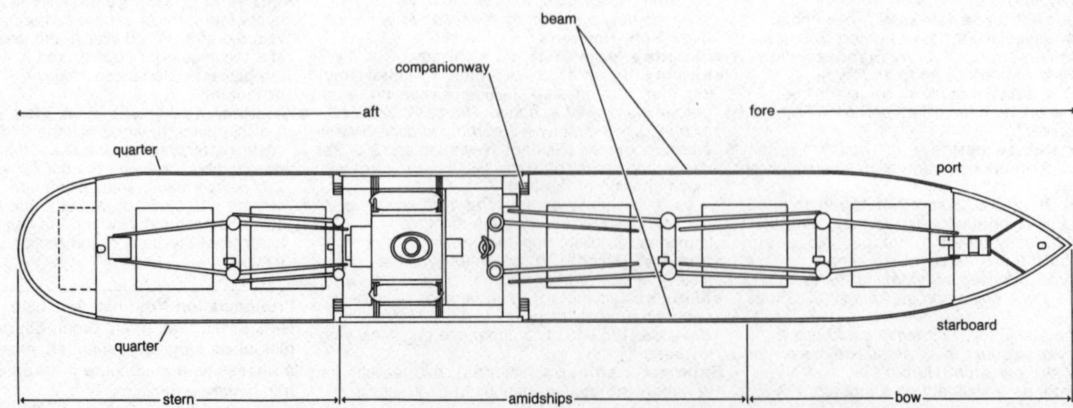

*engage in extravehicular activity"—the official term for movement outside the ship* (New York Times). **4** the officers and crew of a vessel.
*—v.t.* **1** to put, take, or receive (persons or goods) on board a ship: *During the war in Europe, the Army shipped thousands of men.* **2** to send or carry from one place to another by a ship, train, truck, or airplane: *Did you ship it by express or by freight?* SYN: convey, transport. **3** *Informal, Figurative.* to send off; get rid of: *When I start using that sextant in the nose I have to unstrap myself, ship my parachute ... take off my helmet* (Harper's). **4** to take in (water) over the side as a boat does when the waves break over it: *We shipped a sea that drenched us all to the skin* (Tobias Smollett). **5** to engage for service on a ship: *The captain is shipping a new crew.* **6** to fix in a ship or boat in its proper place for use: *to ship a rudder.*
*—v.i.* **1** to go on board a ship: *People wishing to cross the Atlantic by boat must now ship at New York.* SYN: embark. **2** to travel on a ship; sail: *to ship across the sea.* **3** to take a job on a ship: *He shipped as cook.*
**about ship!** a command to turn a ship so it will be on the other tack: *The cry of "about ship!" rang out, and the men scrambled to reset the sails.*
**dress ship, a** to run flags on a line across the mastheads the full length of the ship as a decoration: *The crew dressed ship on docking and on sailing.* **b** *U.S. Navy.* to hoist and fly ensigns on each masthead and on the flagstaff: *The captain gave the order to dress ship as soon as they came in sight of the fleet.*
**give up the ship,** to abandon some one or thing; fail to complete or continue to support: *My exhortation would rather be "not to give up the ship"* (Thomas Jefferson). *Nobody ever gives up the ship in parlor or veranda debate* (George W. Cable).
**jump ship, a** to desert a ship: *The convicts who had been impressed as sailors jumped ship at the first opportunity.* **b** to leave any place or cause suddenly and without notice: *In a crisis, he will jump ship rather than face danger.*
**one's ship comes in** (or **home**), one's fortune is made; one gets money: *I'll take a long vacation when my ship comes in. One also forgets how many lean years ... the big winners experienced before their ships came in* (Saturday Review).
**run a tight** (or **taut**) **ship,** to be in full control; run a well-disciplined organization: *Mr. Lyons was considered to run a taut ship in his Borough President's office* (New York Times).
**ship oars.** See under **oar**.
**ship out, a** to leave; depart: *My father never shipped out ...* (Harry Brown). **b** to send away: *State troopers, brought in to help curb protests, were shipped out* (Time).
[Old English *scip*]
► The distinction between **ship** and **boat** is primarily one of size, the former designating larger and the latter smaller vessels. *Boat* is applied, however, to some vessels of large size, such as ferryboats, that operate in harbors and narrow waters, and (loosely, chiefly in landsmen's use) to what are technically and officially ships, for example river steamships and even ocean liners.

**-ship,** *suffix forming nouns from other nouns.* **1** office, position, or occupation of ___: *Governorship = the office of governor. Authorship = the occupation of an author.* **2** the quality or condition of being ___: *Partnership = the condition of being a partner.* **3** the act, power, or skill of ___: *Workmanship = skill of a workman. Dictatorship = power of a dictator.* **4** relation between ___s: *Fellowship = relation between fellows.* **5** the number of ___s: *Readership = the number of readers.*
[Middle English *-ship*, Old English *-scipe.* See related etym. at **shape**.]

**ship biscuit,** = hardtack.

**ship|board** (ship′bôrd′, -bōrd′), *n., adj.* *—n.* **1** = ship. **2** *Archaic.* the side of a ship.
*—adj.* aboard ship; at sea: *shipboard life.*
**on shipboard,** on or inside a ship; aboard ship: *Being then on shipboard, bound for Bengal* (Dickens).

**ship|borne** (ship′bôrn′, -bōrn′), *adj.* carried in a ship: *a shipborne wave recorder.*

**ship bread,** = hardtack.

**ship|break|er** (ship′brā′kər), *n.* **1** a person who deals in old, unfit ships that are broken up for sale. **2** a person whose work is breaking up such ships.

**ship|break|ing** (ship′brā′king), *n.* the work or occupation of a shipbreaker.

**ship|build|er** (ship′bil′dər), *n.* a person who designs or constructs ships.

**ship|build|ing** (ship′bil′ding), *n., adj.* *—n.* **1** the designing or building of ships. **2** the art of building ships.
*—adj.* of or used in shipbuilding; having to do with shipbuilding: *shipbuilding employers.*

**ship canal,** a canal wide and deep enough for ships.

**ship chandler,** a dealer who supplies ships with necessary stores.

**ship chandlery,** the business of, or goods dealt in by, a ship chandler.

**ship|en|tine** (ship′ən tēn), *n.* a four-masted vessel having the first three masts square-rigged and the last one fore-and-aft-rigged. [< *ship;* patterned on *barkentine*]

**ship fever,** typhus as occurring on overcrowded ships.

**ship|fit|ter** (ship′fit′ər), *n.* a person who fits together parts of ships.

**ship|ful** (ship′fu̇l), *n., pl.* **-fuls.** a quantity or number sufficient to fill a ship.

**ship|lap** (ship′lap′), *n., adj.* *—n.* **1** a flush, overlapping joint between boards, formed by cutting corresponding rabbets in the adjoining edges and lapping the boards to the depth of the rabbets. **2** boards so rabbeted.
*—adj.* **1** having such rabbets: *shiplap siding.* **2** utilizing lumber so milled: *shiplap construction.*

**ship|less** (ship′lis), *adj.* **1** unoccupied by ships. **2** possessing no ships; deprived of one's ship or ships.

**ship|load** (ship′lōd′), *n.* a full load for a ship: *shiploads of military equipment.* SYN: cargo.

**ship|man** (ship′mən), *n., pl.* **-men.** **1** the master of a ship; shipmaster. **2** *Archaic.* a sailor.

**ship|mas|ter** (ship′mas′tər, -mäs′-), *n.* the master, commander, or captain of a ship, especially a merchant ship.

**ship|mate** (ship′māt′), *n.* **1** a fellow sailor on a ship: *Members of the catering staff walked off the ship in protest against the threatened dismissal of two of their shipmates* (London Times). **2** a person who sails on the same ship; fellow passenger: *He also told of catching 75-pound groupers ... from the crash boat he and a shipmate were* [*on*] (Newsweek).

**ship|ment** (ship′mənt), *n.* **1** the act of shipping goods: *A thousand boxes of oranges are ready for shipment.* **2** the goods sent at one time to a person or company: *a shipment to Europe, a large shipment of nails. We received two shipments of boxes from the factory.* SYN: consignment.

**ship money,** an old English tax to provide money to build ships in time of war. It was abolished by an act of Parliament in 1640.

**ship of state,** the government: *... sail on, O Ship of State! Sail on, O Union strong and great!* (Longfellow).

**ship of the desert,** = camel.

***ship of the line,** a sailing warship of the largest class, carrying 74 or more guns, big enough to be part of the line of battle of a fleet.

***ship of the line**

**ship-of-war** (ship′əv wôr′), *n.* = *warship.*

**ship|own|er** (ship′ō′nər), *n.* a person who owns a ship or ships.

**ship|own|ing** (ship′ō′ning), *n., adj.* *—n.* ownership in a ship or ships.
*—adj.* that owns a ship.

**ship|pa|ble** (ship′ə bəl), *adj.* that can be shipped.

**ship|per** (ship′ər), *n.* a person or company that ships goods: *shippers of bulk cargo.*

**shipper fork,** a two-pronged device for guiding a belt from one pulley to another on a machine.

**ship|ping** (ship′ing), *n.* **1** the act or business of sending goods by water, rail, truck, or air: *Mr. Hecht brought his own kind of jet propulsion into shipping long before the airplane people even dreamed of it* (New York Times). **2a** ships collectively: *Much of the world's shipping passes through the Panama Canal.* **b** the ships of a nation, city, or business: *British merchant shipping.* **c** their total tonnage: *an increase of 250,000 deadweight tons in merchant shipping.* **3** *Obsolete.* a voyage: *God send 'em good shipping* (Shakespeare).

**shipping clerk, 1** a person whose work is to see to the packing and shipment of goods. **2** any person who works in a shipping room.

**shipping fever,** a disease similar to influenza, attacking animals, such as cattle and horses, that are being shipped. The exhaustion of travel and changes in climate, water, and feed cause them to lose appetite, and to develop fever and a cough and red, watery eyes.

**shipping lane,** a regular route for ships, usually provided with aids to navigation; lane.

**shipping line,** a company that has ships for transporting goods or passengers.

**shipping room,** a room in a business house, factory, or warehouse, where consignments of goods are made up and packed, and from which they are sent.

**shipping ton,** a unit of measure of the carrying capacity of a ship, equal to 40 cubic feet or 1.13 cubic meters; measurement ton; freight ton.

**ship|pon** (ship′ən), *n.* Scottish. a cattle barn. [Old English *scypen.* See related etym. at **shop**.]

**ship-rigged** (ship′rigd′), *adj.* **1** rigged with square sails on all three masts. **2** carrying square sails; square-rigged: *a ship-rigged mast.*

**ship's bell,** the bell on a ship that is struck every half hour to tell time, indicate the time of the watch, etc.

**ship's boat,** a rowboat, launch, or the like, carried on or towed by a ship for use in landing passengers, as a lifeboat, and for other purposes.

**ship|shape** (ship′shāp′), *adj., adv.* *—adj.* in good order; trim: *We finally got the rocket shipshape just before the admiral in charge of aviation policy arrived* (Atlantic). SYN: tidy.
*—adv.* in a trim, neat manner.

**ship's husband,** a man who has the care of a ship while in port; a person who oversees the general interests of a ship, such as berthing, provisioning, repairing, and entering and clearing.

**ship|side** (ship′sīd′), *n.* the area alongside which a ship is docked: *Cargo has to be moved to shipside* (Harper's).

**ship's papers,** the documents giving information, especially as to the ship's nationality, owner, crew, equipment, and cargo, which every ship must carry.

**ship's store,** a general store for a ship's personnel; a Navy Exchange afloat.

**ship-to-ship** (ship′tu̇ ship′), *adj.* passing from one ship to another; aimed at another ship: *a ship-to-ship rocket or missile.*

**ship-to-shore** (ship′tu̇ shôr′, -shōr′), *adj., adv.* *—adj.* passing from a ship to the shore; working between a ship and shore: *In a ship-to-shore call she urged her husband not to waste his time meeting her at the pier* (Harper's). *—adv.* from a ship to the shore: *to radio ship-to-shore.*

**ship|way** (ship′wā′), *n.* **1** the structure on which a ship is built; ways: *The entire assembly is hoisted into the spider-web of girders that make up the shipway, for quick insertion* (Wall Street Journal). **2** = ship canal.

**ship|worm** (ship′wėrm′), *n.* any one of various clams, having small valves and long, wormlike bodies, which burrow into the timbers, especially of ships and docks; teredo; copperworm.

**ship|wreck** (ship′rek′), *n., v.* *—n.* **1** the destruction or loss of a ship by foundering, by striking a rock or shoal, etc.: *Only two people were saved from the shipwreck.* **2** a wrecked ship or what remains of it; wreckage. **3** *Figurative.* a total loss or ruin; destruction: *The shipwreck of his plans discouraged him.*
*—v.t.* **1a** to cause (a person) to suffer shipwreck: *shipwrecked by a hurricane.* **b** to cause the loss of (goods) by shipwreck. **2** *Figurative.* to wreck, ruin, or destroy: *a career shipwrecked by war.*
*—v.i.* to suffer shipwreck.

**ship|wright** (ship′rīt′), *n.* a person who builds or repairs ships.

**ship|yard** (ship′yärd′), *n.* a place near the water where ships are built or repaired.

**shir|a|lee** (shir′ə lē), *n.* *Australian Slang.* a bundle of personal belongings; swag.

**Shi|ra|zi** (shi rä′zē), *n.* a Zanzibari of mixed African and Persian descent. [< *Shiraz*, a city in southwestern Iran]

**shire** (shīr), *n.* **1** one of the counties into which Great Britain is divided: *They mean to live to themselves more than ever in the shires* (J. W. R.

Scott). **2** one of the larger divisions of a state local administration in Australia. **3** *Obsolete.* a province; district; region. [Old English *scīr*]
▶ **Shire** (def. 1) is now restricted chiefly to literary use and applied mainly to counties with names ending in *-shire: Yorkshire;* **county** is the usual official term.

**Shire** (shīr), *n.* = shire horse. [< *the Shires,* a section of England, where they are raised]

**shire horse**, any large, strong draft horse of a breed with long hair on the back of the legs from the knees and hocks down, bred for a time in the midland counties of England.

**shire town**, the town where the business of a shire is transacted.

**shirk** (shėrk), *v., n.* — ***v.t., v.i*** to avoid or get out of doing (work or a duty): *He lost his job because he shirked his work. Common men cannot shirk world politics and at the same time enjoy private freedom* (H. G. Wells). **SYN**: evade, shun, neglect.
— ***n.*** a person who shirks or does not do his share; person who avoids work, duty, obligations, or the like: *You think we're all a lot of shirks* (Edith Wharton). [origin uncertain. Compare etym. under **shark[2]**.] — **shirk′er**, *n.*

**Shir|ley poppy** (shėr′lē), a showy variety of corn poppy, usually with a single flower and white base, widely grown in flower gardens. [< *Shirley* Vicarage, near London, England, where it was developed in the 1880's]

**shirr** (shėr), *v., n.* — ***v.t.*** **1** to draw up or gather (cloth) on parallel threads, especially to trim (a garment) with shirring. **2** to bake (eggs) in a shallow dish, or in individual dishes, with butter, and (sometimes) cream, and breadcrumbs.
— ***n.*** a shirred arrangement of cloth.
[American English; origin unknown]

***shirr|ing** (shėr′ing), *n.* a gathering of cloth by sewing with parallel threads and pulling on the threads.

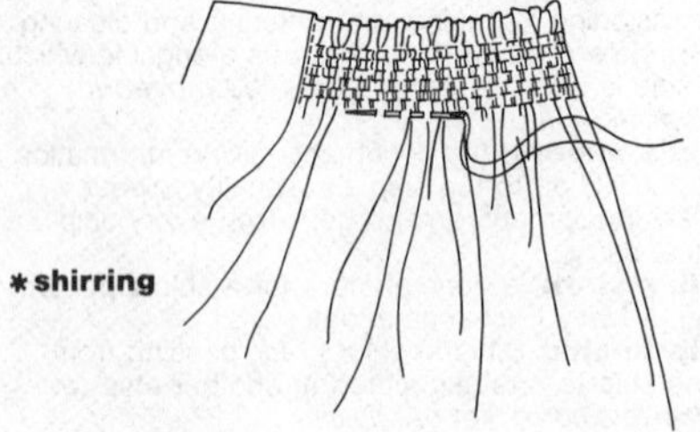

***shirring**

**shirt** (shėrt), *n., v.* — ***n.*** **1** a garment for the upper part of a man's or boy's body. It is usually of cotton, linen, or other washable fabric and is commonly buttoned down the front. A shirt has long or short sleeves and usually a collar and is worn as an outer garment or under a vest or jacket. **2a** any one of various women's or girls' garments patterned on this. **b** = shirtwaist. **3** an undergarment for the upper part of the body; undershirt. **4** = nightshirt.
— ***v.t.*** to clothe with or as if with a shirt.
**keep one's shirt on**, *U.S. Slang.* to stay calm; keep one's temper: *It don't make any difference ... so you can just keep your shirt on* (R. D. Saunders).
**lose one's shirt**, *U.S. Slang.* to lose everything one owns: *The same people who hopefully predicted that my father would lose his shirt now say that he had the Midas touch* (New Yorker).
[Old English *scyrte.* See related etym. at **skirt**.]
— **shirt′like′**, *adj.*

**shirt|band** (shėrt′band′), *n.* the neckband, collar, or other band of a shirt.

**shirt dress**, a shirtwaist dress; shirtwaister: ... *pale blue Osmaline shirt dress, the bib front hand-embroidered in silk, the collar, cuffs, and sleeves silk-stitched* (Sunday Times).

**shirt front**, **1** the part of a shirt covering the chest. **2** = dickey.

**shirt|ing** (shėr′ting), *n.* cloth for shirts: *He is also one of the most brilliant designers of shirting alive today* (New Yorker).

**shirt|less** (shėrt′lis), *adj.* without a shirt or shirts: *barefooted and shirtless boys.*

**shirt|mak|er** (shėrt′mā′kər), *n.* a person whose work is making or altering shirts.

**shirt|sleeve** or **shirt-sleeve** (shėrt′slēv′), *n., adj.* — ***n.*** a sleeve of a shirt.
— ***adj.*** **1** informal; direct: *a shirtsleeve conference, shirtsleeve diplomacy.* **2** plainspoken; homespun; folksy: *He was the local shirtsleeve philosopher* (New Yorker).
**in (one's) shirtsleeves**, with one's jacket or coat off; wearing one's shirt: *Lincoln thought it friendly to open the door himself in his shirtsleeves when two most elegant ladies came to call* (Baron Charnwood). *Working in shirtsleeves, Jake and Roy eschewed the usual trappings of executive life* (Time).
[American English < *shirt sleeve*]

**shirt|sleeved** or **shirt-sleeved** (shėrt′slēvd′), *adj.* in shirtsleeves; wearing a shirt without a coat: *shirt-sleeved men watering their lawns in the gentle half-light* (Time).

**shirt|tail** (shėrt′tāl′), *n., adj.* — ***n.*** the divided lower part of a shirt, especially the back part: *His dress, however, has improved ... and although he occasionally wears his shirttails out they are more often neatly tucked in* (New Yorker).
— ***adj.*** casual; informal: *a shirttail conference.*
**hang onto one's shirttails**, to depend completely upon one: *The Tunisian newspaper L'Action ... said "the hard reality teaches us every day that hanging onto the shirttails of the West brings us only insults and humiliation"* (Wall Street Journal).

***shirt|waist** (shėrt′wāst′), *n., adj.* — ***n.*** **1** a woman's or girl's tailored blouse, usually with a collar and cuffs, worn with a separate skirt. **2** a one-piece dress with a shirtlike top.
— ***adj.*** having a bodice that resembles a shirt: *a trim shirtwaist dress.*
[American English < *shirt* + *waist*]

***shirtwaist**
definition 2

**shirt|waist|er** (shėrt′wās′tər), *n.* a one-piece dress with a shirtwaist top: *Of these charming shirtwaisters, some printed, others in woven cotton, the best are high waisted, slim* (Observer).

**shirt|y** (shėr′tē), *adj.,* **shirt|i|er, shirt|i|est.** *British Slang.* ill-tempered; ill-natured.

**shish|ka|bob** (shish′kə bob′), *n.* = shish kebab.

**shish ke|bab** (shish′ kə bob′), square pieces of lamb or beef roasted or broiled on skewers or a spit with tomatoes, peppers, onion slices, etc. [< Armenian *shish kabab*]

**shit|tah** (shit′ə), *n., pl.* **shit|tahs, shit|tim** (shit′im), or **shittah tree**, a tree from which shittim was obtained, probably a species of acacia with a hard, durable wood (in the Bible, Isaiah 41:19). [< Hebrew *shiṭṭāh*]

**shit|tim** (shit′im), *n.,* or **shittim wood**, **1** the tough, durable wood of the shittah tree, from which the Ark of the Covenant and various parts of the Jewish tabernacle were built (in the Bible, Exodus 25:10-27:6). **2** any one of various buckthorns of the United States, especially the cascara. [< Hebrew *shiṭṭīm,* plural of *shiṭṭāh* shittah]

**shiv** (shiv), *n. U.S. Slang.* a knife or razor. [perhaps earlier *chiv, chive* knife, file < a Romany word]

**shiv|a** or **shiv|ah** (shiv′ə), *n., pl.* **shiv|as, shiv-ahs.** *Judaism.* the initial seven days of mourning for a parent, brother, sister, husband, or wife, beginning immediately after burial. [< Hebrew *shib'ah* seven]

**Shi|va** (shē′və), *n.* = Siva.

**shiv|a|ree** (shiv′ə rē′), *n., v.,* **-reed, -ree|ing.** *U.S.* — ***n.*** a mock serenade to a newly married couple, made by beating as on kettles or pans, especially one performed by neighbors and friends outside the couple's bedroom; charivari.
— ***v.t.*** to greet or serenade with a shivaree: *A crowd started out to shivaree the bride and groom* [American English; spelling of a pronunciation of *charivari*]

**shive[1]** (shīv), *n.* **1** a thin, flat cork for stopping a wide-mouthed bottle. **2** *British Dialect.* a slice, especially of bread. [origin uncertain. Compare Middle Dutch *scheve.*]

**shive[2]** (shīv), *n.* **1** a particle of husk. **2** a piece of thread or fluff, as on the surface of cloth.
**shives**, the refuse of hemp or flax: *Chipboard can also be made from peanut shells, flax shives and bagasse* (Wall Street Journal).
[Middle English *schive.* Compare Middle Low German *schīve.*]

**shiv|er[1]** (shiv′ər), *v., n.* — ***v.i.*** **1** to shake as with cold, fear, or excitement; tremble; quiver: *A sudden gust of cold wind made me shiver. The leaves shivered in the breeze. He shivered as with an ague* (Hawthorne). *As a dog withheld a moment ... shivers ere he springs* (Tennyson). **2** to sound or resound vibrantly: *a cry that shiver'd to the tingling stars* (Tennyson).
— ***v.t.*** to cause (a sail or sails) to flutter through the action of the wind on the edge or edges, as by luffing the helm.
— ***n.*** the act or condition of shaking from cold, fear, or excitement: *Cold shivers went down Trilby's back as she listened* (George du Maurier).
**the shivers**, a fit of shivering; ague; chills: *It gives me the cold shivers when I think what might have become of me* (Century Magazine).
[Middle English *schiveren;* origin uncertain]
— **shiv′er|er**, *n.* — **shiv′er|ing|ly**, *adv.*
— ***Syn.*** *v.i.* **1 Shiver, shudder, quake** mean to shake or tremble. **Shiver**, used chiefly of people and animals, suggests a quivering of the flesh: *I crept shivering into bed.* **Shudder** suggests sudden, sharp shivering of the whole body in horror or extreme disgust: *He shuddered at the ghastly sight.* **Quake** suggests violent trembling with fear or cold, or shaking and rocking from a violent disturbance: *The house quaked to its foundations.*

**shiv|er[2]** (shiv′ər), *v., n.* — ***v.t.*** to break into small pieces; shatter or split into fragments or pieces: *a tree shivered by lightning. He shivered the mirror with a hammer.*
— ***v.i.*** to be shattered or split; fly into small pieces: *His statue fell, and shivered on the stones* (James A. Froude).
— ***n.*** a small piece; splinter: *thorns of the crown and shivers of the cross* (Tennyson).

**shiv|ers** (shiv′ərz), *n.pl.* See under **shiver[1]**.

**shiv|er|some** (shiv′ər səm), *adj.* **1** causing shivers. **2** = shuddersome.

**shiv|er|y[1]** (shiv′ər ē, shiv′rē), *adj.* **1** quivering from or as if from cold, fear, or excitement; shivering: *Shivery, we had another drink; climbed into the car, and moved on* (Atlantic). **2** inclined to shiver, especially from cold: ... *the frail, shivery ... little being, enveloped in a tangle of black silk wraps* (Harriet Beecher Stowe). **3** chilly: *shivery weather.* **4** causing shivers, especially from fear: *a shivery experience.* [< *shiver*[1] + *-y*[1]]

**shiv|er|y[2]** (shiv′ər ē, shiv′rē), *adj.* apt to shatter or split; brittle. [< *shiver*[2] + *-y*[1]]

**shives** (shīvz), *n.pl.* See under **shive[2]**.

**shi|voo** (shi vü′), *n. Australian Slang.* a noisy party or celebration.

**shi|vy** or **shi|vey** (shī′vē), *adj.* containing shives, as of wool or hair.

**shle|miel** (shlə mēl′), *n.* = schlemiel.

**shlep** (shlep), *v.t., v.i.,* **shlepped, shlep|ping,** *n.* = schlepp.

**shlock** (shlok), *n., adj.* = schlock.

**shlock|y** (shlok′ē), *adj.,* **shlock|i|er, shlock|i|est.** = schlocky.

**shlo|ka** (shlō′kə), *n.* = sloka.

**shmo** (shmō), *n., pl.* **shmos, shmoes.** *Slang.* schmo.

**shnook** (shnu̇k), *n.* = schnook.

**shoal[1]** (shōl), *n., adj., v.* — ***n.*** **1** a place in a sea, lake, or stream where the water is shallow: *The water at the treacherous shoal looked as dark and deep as the rest of the river.* **2a** a sandbank, sand bar, or ledge of rock, coral, or the like, that makes the water shallow, especially one that can be seen at low tide: *The ship was wrecked on the shoals.* **b** *Figurative:* *caught on the shoals of poor financial planning.* **SYN**: pitfall, danger. **3** *Nautical.* a bank, mound, or ridge, of sand or muck, that is never more than 36 feet beneath the surface of the sea.
— ***adj.*** not deep; shallow: *shoal water, a shoal channel.*
— ***v.i.*** to become shallow or more shallow: *He anchored where the river shoaled.*
— ***v.t.*** **1** to cause (a piece of water) to become shallow. **2** to obstruct by shoals. **3** to proceed from a greater to a lesser depth of (water): *There was no apparent change in colour to indicate that they shoaled their water* (Frederick Marryat).
[Old English *sceald* shallow, adjective]

**shoal[2]** (shōl), *n., v.* — ***n.*** a large number; crowd: *a shoal of tourists, a shoal of troubles. We saw a shoal of fish in the water. The letters which followed her in shoals from Berlin flattered her to the skies* (Mrs. Humphry Ward).
— ***v.i.*** to form into a shoal or shoals; crowd together.
[perhaps Old English *scolu* host (of people), school of fish, or perhaps < Middle Dutch *schole* a host, flock, shoal. See related etym. at **school[2]**.]

**shoal|i|ness** (shō′lē nis), *n.* shoaly condition.

**shoal|y** (shō′lē), *adj.* full of shoals or shallow places: *a shoaly channel.*

**shoat[1]** (shōt), *n.* a young pig that no longer suckles but feeds itself: *The hood was thin and narrow, like a shoat's nose—you remember the way all Model-T Fords were built* (Marjorie Kinnan Rawlings). Also, **shote.** [origin uncertain]

**shoat[2]** (shōt), *n.* = geep. [blend of *sheep* and *goat*]

**sho|chet** (shō′ḥət), *n., pl.* **sho|chets, sho|che-**

tim (shō′ʜə tim). = shohet.

**shock¹** (shok), *n., v.* —*n.* **1a** a sudden and violent shake, blow, or crash: *Earthquake shocks are often felt in Japan. The two trains crashed head-on with a terrible shock.* **SYN**: concussion, jolt, impact. **b** the effect of such a shake, blow, or crash: *The shock broke the windows.* **2** *Figurative.* a sudden, violent, or upsetting disturbance: *His death was a great shock to his family. A shock, chill and painful, deprived me of speech* (Owen Wister). **3** a condition of physical collapse or depression, together with a sudden drop in blood pressure, often resulting in unconsciousness. Shock may set in after a severe injury, a great loss of blood, or a sudden emotional disturbance. *The operation was successful, but the patient suffered from shock.* **4** the disturbance produced by an electric current passing through the body. **5** *U.S. Informal.* a shock absorber, especially of an automobile.
—*v.t.* **1** to cause to feel surprise, horror, or disgust: *That child's bad language shocks everyone. Ernest was terribly shocked when he heard of the loss of his money* (Samuel Butler). **SYN**: horrify, startle. **2** to give an electric shock to. **3** to cause (a person or part of the body) to suffer a physical, especially a nervous, shock. **4a** to strike together violently; jar; jolt. **SYN**: collide. **b** to shake or weaken by sudden collision.
—*v.i.* to collide with a shock: *All at fiery speed the two shock'd on the central bridge* (Tennyson).
[probably < French *choc,* noun, and *choquer,* verb, perhaps < a Germanic word]

***shock²** (shok), *n., v.* —*n.* **1** a group of stalks of corn or bundles of grain set up on end together in the field in order to dry or to await harvesting. **2** a large collection of various things; heap: *Lilacs, wind-beaten, staggering under a lopsided shock of bloom* (Amy Lowell).
—*v.t.* to make into a shock or shocks: *to shock corn.*
—*v.i.* to make shocks: *If you will shock, I will tie.*
[origin uncertain]

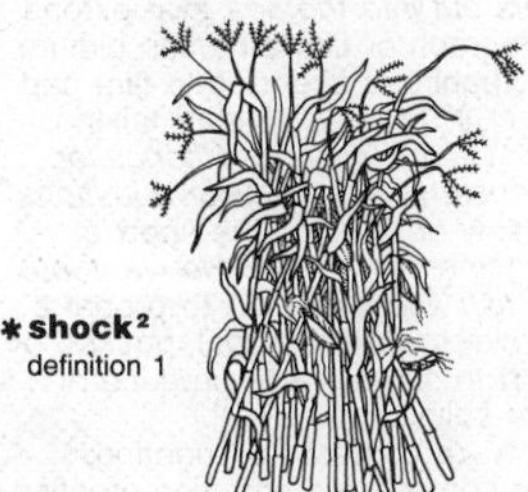
***shock²** definition 1

**shock³** (shok), *n., adj.* —*n.* **1** a thick, bushy mass: *He has a shock of red hair.* **2** a dog having long, shaggy hair, especially a poodle.
—*adj.* (of hair) rough and thick; shaggy.
[origin uncertain]

**shock|a|bil|i|ty** (shok′ə bil′ə tē), *n.* the state or quality of being shockable.

**shock|a|ble** (shok′ə bəl), *adj.* that can be shocked; easily shocked.

***shock absorber**, **1** anything that absorbs or lessens a shock or shocks. **2** a device consisting of springs, hydraulic pistons, or the like, on automobiles to absorb the force of sudden impacts caused by rough roads. **3** a hydraulic device in the landing gear of airplanes to absorb the shock of the wheels striking the ground in landing.

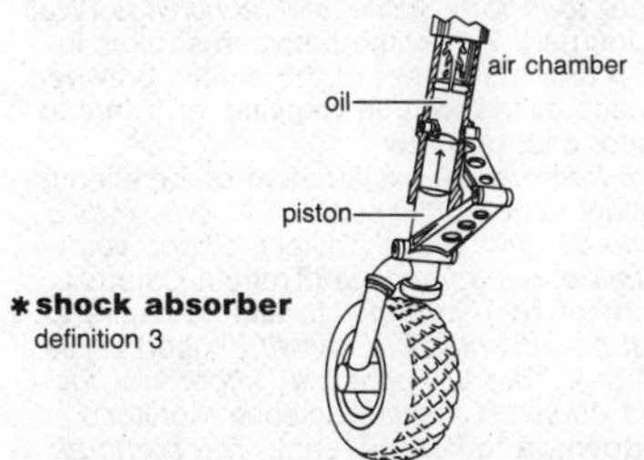

***shock absorber** definition 3

**shock action**, a mass attack; attack by an overwhelming force on a limited front, such as by an armored unit or units given close tactical support by artillery or aircraft, or both.

**shock cord**, a cord consisting of a bundle of rubber strands that permit stretching, used as a shock absorber: *an airplane shock cord.*

**shock dog**, a dog with long, shaggy hair.

**shock|er¹** (shok′ər), *n.* **1** *Informal.* a highly sensational written work, especially a story: *That young man loves to read shockers.* **2** *Slang.* a person or thing that shocks: *You never know what he'll do next—a real shocker, isn't he?*

**shock|er²** (shok′ər), *n.* a person or device that shocks cornstalks and grain.

**shock front**, the outer part of a shock wave, at which pressure reaches the highest point: *By spreading out the shock front ... it should be possible not only to make the bang less intense, but also to reduce drag and frictional heating of the aircraft's skin* (New Scientist).

**shock-head** (shok′hed′), *n., adj.* —*n.* **1** a head covered with a thick, bushy mass of hair. **2** a shock-headed person.
—*adj.* = shock-headed.
[< *shock³* + *head*]

**shock-head|ed** (shok′hed′id), *adj.* having a thick, bushy mass of hair.

**shock|ing** (shok′ing), *adj.* **1a** causing intense and painful surprise: *shocking news.* **SYN**: appalling. **b** offensive; disgusting; revolting: *a shocking sight.* **SYN**: outrageous, scandalous. **c** *Informal.* very bad: *shocking manners.* **2** that shocks: *Mice soon learn to avoid the shocking current, which occurs at about 5-minute intervals* (Science).
—**shock′ing|ly**, *adv.* —**shock′ing|ness**, *n.*

**shocking pink**, **1** a very strong, bright pink color: *... dresses of shocking pink, blue, and cerise* (Manchester Guardian Weekly). **2** of such a color; intensely pink: *... shocking pink and lavender flowers* (New Yorker).

**shock|proof** (shok′prüf′), *adj.* **1** capable of withstanding or resisting shock: *a shockproof watch.* **2** safe from electric shock: *The heating pad is waterproof, shockproof ... and will not overheat* (Newsweek).

**shock-re|sist|ant** (shok′ri zis′tənt), *adj.* capable of resisting shock; shockproof: *Plastic mirrors, unlike those of glass, do not shatter, are shock-resistant, and do not steam or cloud* (Science News Letter).

**shock-rock** (shok′rok′), *n.* rock'n'roll music with shocking sounds or lyrics, such as hard rock or acid rock.

**shock stall**, the stall of an aircraft traveling near the speed of sound, in which the separation of the airflow to the rear of the shock wave causes an increase in drag and a decrease in lift.

**shock tactics**, the use of masses of troops, heavy artillery, armored units, and other forces, to break through an enemy line.

**shock therapy**, the treatment of mental disorder through shock induced by chemical or electrical means.

**shock treatment**, **1** = shock therapy. **2** any act that is deliberately intended to shock: *In 1861 he [William Henry Seward] had been willing to provoke war with England and Spain in the rash hope that the shock treatment of trouble abroad would draw the seceded states back into the Union* (Atlantic).

**shock troops**, troops chosen and specially trained for making attacks.

**shock tube**, a long, gas-filled tube for testing the effects of shock waves upon scale models, such as of airplanes, missiles, and satellites. The tube is usually divided into two compartments, separated by a diaphragm; one, containing the model to be tested has low pressure, and the other, high. An explosion in the high-pressure compartment breaks the diaphragm and creates a shock wave of very high speed and temperature in the other.

**shock wave**, **1** a disturbance of the atmosphere created by the movement of an aircraft, rocket, or any missile at velocities greater than that of sound: *The shock wave created in the atmosphere by a reentering 5000-mile missile has a temperature in the tens of thousands of degrees Centigrade* (Atlantic). **2** a similar effect caused by the expansion of gases away from an explosion; blast: *There was an enormous explosion ashore, and the small boat, gathering way, rocked as the hot shock wave reached them* (Nicholas Monsarrat). **3** *Figurative.* a violent or explosive reaction: *A series of defaults could have spread financial shock waves throughout the U.S. business community* (Time).

**shod** (shod), *v.* the past tense and past participle of **shoe**: *The blacksmith shod the horses. They had never been shod before.*

**shod|di|ly** (shod′ə lē), *adv.* in a shoddy manner.

**shod|di|ness** (shod′ē nis), *n.* shoddy quality or condition.

**shod|dy** (shod′ē), *adj.,* **-di|er, -di|est,** *n., pl.* **-dies.** —*adj.* **1** pretending to be better than it is; of inferior quality; poorly made or designed: *a shoddy necklace, shoddy merchandise. It [painting] was all false, insincere, shoddy* (W. Somerset Maugham). **2** mean; shabby: *shoddy treatment, a shoddy trick.* **3** made of woolen waste.
—*n.* **1** anything inferior made to look like what is better; pretense, sham: *They have no taste for the shoddy in art.* **2a** an inferior kind of wool made of woolen waste, old rags, yarn, etc. **b** a cloth made of woolen waste and some new wool.
[origin uncertain]

***shoe** (shü), *n., pl.* **shoes** or (*Archaic*) **shoon**, *v.,* **shod, shoe|ing.** —*n.* **1** an outer covering for a person's foot. Shoes are usually made of leather and normally consist of a stiff, durable sole and heel and a lighter upper part. **2** something like a shoe in shape, position, or use. **3** = horseshoe. **4** a metal rim, ferrule, band, or casing to protect the end of a staff, cane, spear, or other pole. **5** the part of a brake that presses on a wheel or brake drum to slow down or stop a vehicle: *In bonding brake lining ... a cement is used between the shoes and lining* (Automotive Encyclopedia). **6** the outer casing of a pneumatic tire, enclosing the inner tube or air chamber. **7** a metal strip on the bottom of a runner of a sleigh or sled. **8** a metal plate upon which a moving part of a mechanism bears. **9** a sliding plate or contact by which an electric locomotive or car takes current from the third rail.
—*v.t.* to put shoes or boots on; furnish with a shoe or shoes: *A blacksmith shoes horses. Her feet were shod in big hiking boots.* **2** to protect or arm at the point; edge or face with metal: *a stick shod with steel.*
**drop the other shoe**, to finish or complete what one has started (said especially of something unpleasant): *The Rhodesian Front, by threatening unilateral independence, has kept the issue hot, but so far ... has been unwilling to drop the other shoe* (Atlantic).
**fill one's shoes**, to take a person's place; fill another's position: *[He] has now put an end to the buzz of speculation about who was going to fill his shoes* (Mollie Panter-Downes).
**in another's shoes**, in another's place, situation, or circumstances: *I judge I should put more to risk if I were in his shoes* (John Adams).
**the shoe is on the other foot**, the situation is reversed: *All of us have a chance to help, as we would want to be helped if the shoe were on the other foot* (New York Times).
**where the shoe pinches**, where the real trouble or difficulty lies: *Oh, is that where the shoe pinches?* (Charles Reade).
[Old English *scōh*]
► **shoe.** In the United States, *shoe, n.,* normally applies to footwear ending below, at, or just above the ankle, as distinguished from *boot,* which applies to footwear reaching to the middle of the calf. In British use, *shoe* is commonly applied to oxfords, opera pumps, and other low-cut footwear, while *boot* applies to footgear covering the whole foot including the ankle.

***shoe** definition 1

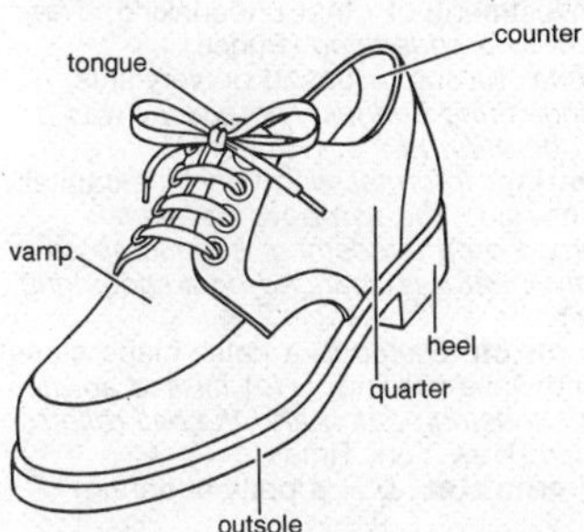


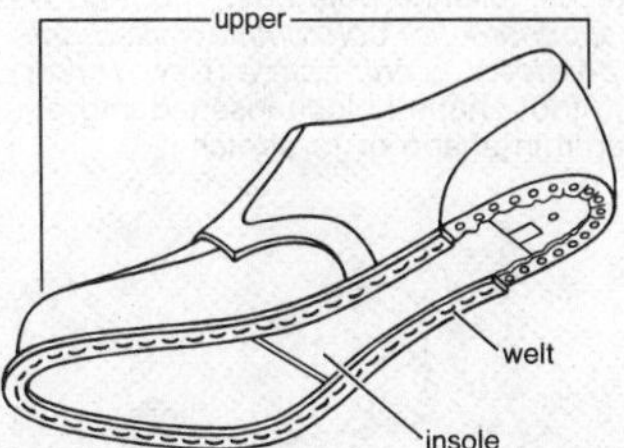


**shoe|bill** (shü′bil′), *n.* a large, grayish wading bird of central Africa, especially along the White Nile, that has a broad bill shaped somewhat like a shoe, and is related to the herons and storks.

**shoe|black** (shü′blak′), *n.* a person who cleans

**Pronunciation Key:** hat, āge, cãre, fär; let, ēqual, tėrm; it, īce; hot, ōpen, ôrder; **oi**l, **ou**t; cup, pu̇t, rüle; **ch**ild; lo**ng**; **th**in; **ᴛʜ**en; **zh**, measure; ə represents **a** in about, **e** in taken, **i** in pencil, **o** in lemon, **u** in circus.

and polishes shoes to earn money; bootblack.
**shoe board**, a kind of hard cardboard used for making shoe soles and heels.
**shoe boil**, a flabby growth over the elbow of a horse, caused by lying on hard floors or with the front feet doubled under the body.
**shoe|box** (shü′boks′), *n.* **1** a thin cardboard box, usually of a standard size, used for holding shoes: *The instrument weighs less than 20 pounds and is only slightly larger than a shoebox* (Science News Letter). **2** *Informal.* something that resembles a shoebox, especially a building: *He has been nurturing his company in a glorified Manhattan shoebox called City Center* (Time).
**shoe|brush** (shü′brush′), *n.* a brush for cleaning and polishing shoes.
**shoe|horn** (shü′hôrn′), *n., v.* —*n.* a curved piece of metal, horn, or plastic, used to help slip a shoe more easily over the heel.
—*v.t.* to put or force (into) as if with a shoehorn: *The new buildings will shoehorn another 125,000 to 150,000 office workers into one of the world's most congested areas* (New York Times).
**shoe|lace** (shü′lās′), *n.* a cord, braid, or leather strip for fastening a shoe.
**shoe|less** (shü′lis), *adj.* without a shoe or shoes: *a shoeless horse. Why do you roam about shoeless and in rags?* (Wall Street Journal).
**shoe|mak|er** (shü′mā′kər), *n.* a person who makes or mends shoes. **SYN:** cobbler.
**shoe|mak|ing** (shü′mā′king), *n.* the business of making or mending shoes.
**shoe|pack** or **shoe|pac** (shü′pak′), *n. U.S.* **1** a waterproof boot with laces, for wear in cold weather: [*He*] *got back the day before wearing regular boots, not the shoepacks that we had for the cold* (Ward Just). **2** a kind of high moccasin that covered the ankles and was made without a separate sole, worn by North American Indians and early pioneers. [American English, alteration (by folk etymology) of Algonkian (Delaware) *shipak*]
**sho|er** (shü′ər), *n.* a person who shoes horses or mules.
**shoe|shine** (shü′shīn′), *n.* **1** the act of shining or polishing the shoes. **2** the condition or appearance of shoes after being shined. **3** = shoeshine boy.
**shoeshine boy**, *U.S.* a boy who shines shoes to earn money; shoeblack: *The other day a high-ranking, nattily-dressed official ... stopped to bawl out a ragged group of shoeshine boys on a busy street corner* (Wall Street Journal).
**shoe|shop** (shü′shop′), *n.* = shoe store.
**shoe store**, an establishment that sells shoes at retail.
**shoe|string** (shü′string′), *n., adj.* —*n.* **1** = shoelace. **2** *Informal, Figurative.* a very small amount of money used especially to start or carry on a business, investment, or other undertaking: *They don't amount to a shoestring* (Punch).
—*adj. Informal.* having or based on very little capital: *a shoestring budget. The agency was a shoestring operation at first* (Harper's).
**on a shoestring**, *Informal.* with very little capital; on a small margin: *The two boys traveled through Europe on a shoestring. In general, an off-Broadway theater is financed on a shoestring* (Newsweek).
**shoestring catch**, *Baseball.* a catch made close to the ground while running: [*He*] *missed an attempt for a shoestring catch and the ball rolled to the bullpen* (New York Times).
**shoestring gambler**, *U.S.* a petty or tinhorn gambler.
**shoestring potatoes**, *U.S.* potatoes cut in long, stringlike pieces; julienne potatoes: *The food was simple but superior—hot consommé, mixed grill, shoestring potatoes ... and coffee* (New Yorker).
**shoe tree**, a foot-shaped block inserted into a shoe to keep it in shape or to stretch it.

*** shofar**

***sho|far** (shō′fär, -fər), *n., pl.* **sho|froth** (shō′frōs, shō frōt′), **sho|fars.** an ancient Hebrew musical instrument made of a curved ram's horn, still used in Jewish religious services, especially on Rosh Hashanah and Yom Kippur: *The ancient Hebrews decreed that a warning blast should be sounded on the shofar to mark the third case of an infectious disease in the community* (Time). Also, **shophar.** [< Hebrew *shōphār*]
**shog** (shog), *v.,* **shogged, shog|ging,** *n. Dialect.* —*v.t.* to shake (something) from side to side; jolt; jog.
—*v.i.* to shake to and fro; rock.
—*n.* **1** a shake, jerk, or jog. **2** a shogging gait. [Middle English *shogge;* origin uncertain]
**sho|gi** (shō′gē), *n.* the game of chess as played in Japan: *Shogi ... where the captured piece becomes the property of the capturing side to be used for that side's offensive* (Science News Letter). [< Japanese *shōgi* chess]
**sho|gun** (shō′gun, -gün), *n.* the former hereditary commander in chief of the Japanese army. The shoguns were the real rulers of Japan for hundreds of years until 1867. [< Japanese *shōgun* < Chinese *chiang chün* army leader]
**sho|gun|ate** (shō′gun it, -āt; -gün-), *n.* **1** the position, rank, or rule of a shogun. **2** government by shoguns: *... the arrival of Commodore Matthew C. Perry in 1853 with both the shogunate and feudalism ending shortly thereafter* (Atlantic).
**sho|het** (shō′ʜət), *n., pl.* **sho|hets, sho|he|tim** (shō′ʜə tim). a Jewish slaughterer who is learned in the rabbinical laws of slaughtering animals. Also, **shochet.** [< Hebrew *shōḥeṭ*]
**sho|ji** (shō′jē), *n., pl.* **-ji** or **-jis,** or **shoji screen,** a sliding screen of translucent paper used to make up the partitions or walls of a Japanese house: *Shoji screens slide in front of a glass bedroom wall* (Sunset). [< Japanese *shōji*]
**Sho|na** (shō′nə), *n., pl.* **-na** or **-nas.** = Mashona.
**shone** (shōn), *v.* a past tense and past participle of **shine**: *The sun shone all last week. It has not shone since.*
**shoo** (shü), *interj., v.,* **shooed, shoo|ing.** —*interj.* **1** an exclamation used to scare away cats, hens, birds, and other animals. **2** scat! go away!
—*v.t.* to scare or drive away by or as if by calling "Shoo!": *Shoo those flies away from the sugar. If a cow came into this farmyard everybody in the place would be shooing it out again* (H. G. Wells).
—*v.i.* **1** to call "Shoo!" **2** to hurry away in obedience to a call of "Shoo."
[probably imitative. Compare Low German *schu,* French *shou.*]
**shoo|fly** (shü′flī′), *n., pl.* **-flies.** = wild indigo. [from the belief that attaching the plant to a harness will keep away horseflies]
**shoo-fly pie**, a pie or cake made of flour, crumbs, brown sugar, and molasses: *Shoo-fly pie ... is a breakfast cake, he insists, and it's perfectly permissible to dunk it* (Wall Street Journal). [from the sweetness of the pie, which attracts flies that have to be shooed away]
**shoo-in** (shü′in′), *n. U.S. Informal.* **1** an easy or sure winner: *He had been considered a shoo-in, but now the strategists are not so sure* (Newsweek). **2** an easy race or contest to win; sure thing: *The election will be no shoo-in for the Republicans* (New York Daily News). [< *shoo* + *in*]
**shook¹** (shu̇k), *n.* **1** a set of staves and pieces for top and bottom sufficient for a single barrel or keg, ready to be put together. **2** a set of the parts of a box or article of furniture, ready to be put together. [American English, apparently special use of *shook,* old past participle of *shake*]
**shook²** (shu̇k), *v., adj.* —*v.* the past tense of **shake**: *They shook hands. They shook with laughter. The solitary monk* [*Martin Luther*] *who shook the world* (Robert Montgomery).
—*adj. Slang.* shaken; shook-up: *"We had one guy so shook he couldn't speak when he came for an interview"* (New York Times).
**shook³** (shu̇k), *n. Especially British.* a shock of corn or bundles of grain. [variant of **shock²**]
**S-hook** (es′hu̇k′), *n.* a double-pointed hook with the points turned in opposite directions.
**shook-up** (shu̇k′up′), *adj.,* or **shook up,** *Slang.* shaken; disturbed; upset: *I can't get particularly shook-up about a couple of days' delay* (The Nation).
**shool** (shül), *n., v.t., v.i. Dialect.* shovel.
**shoon** (shün), *n. Archaic.* shoes; a plural of **shoe.**
**shoot** (shüt), *v.,* **shot, shoot|ing,** *n., interj.* —*v.t.* **1** to hit, wound, or kill with a bullet, arrow, or other missile: *The hunter shot a rabbit.* **2** to send forth or let fly (a bullet, arrow, or other missile) from a firearm, bow, or the like. **3** *Figurative.* to send forth like a shot or an arrow; send swiftly: *The reporters shot question after question at the mayor.* **4** to fire or use (a gun or other shooting weapon); discharge (a bow, catapult, or other device): *to shoot a rifle.* **5** to kill game in or on (an area): *He shot the east side of the mountain.* **6** *Figurative.* to move suddenly and swiftly: *I shot back the bolt.* **7** *Figurative.* to pass quickly along, through, under, or over: *to shoot a bridge, to shoot Niagara Falls in a barrel. Only a shallow boat can shoot this stretch of the rapids.* **8** *Figurative.* to send out (rays, flames, or the like) swiftly and forcibly; dart: *The sun obliquely shoots his burning ray* (Alexander Pope). **9** to put forth (buds, leaves, branches, or flowers). **10a** to send (a ball, puck, or other playing piece) toward the goal, pocket, or basket in attempting to score. **b** to score (a goal or points) by doing this: *He shot two goals.* **11** to propel (a marble), as from the thumb and forefinger: *He taught them to fly kites and shoot marbles* (Washington Irving). **12a** to play (craps, pool, or golf). **b** to cast or toss (the dice) in playing craps. **13a** to take (a picture or pictures) with a camera. **b** to take a picture of (a scene, person, or object) with a camera; photograph; film: *A television outfit went there to shoot the story of George Voskovec, a Czech actor* (New Yorker). **14** to measure the altitude of: *to shoot the sun.* **15** to vary, as with some different color: *Her dress was shot with threads of gold. The river lay in pools of the most enchanting sea green shot with watery browns* (Robert Louis Stevenson). **16** to dump; empty out. **17** to straighten or fit the boards of (a joint) by planing. **18** to open, loosen, or remove by setting off a charge of an explosive: *to shoot an oil well.* **19** to pull (one's cuffs) out so that they project beyond the sleeves of one's coat. **20** *Slang.* to inject into the vein: *to shoot heroin.*
—*v.i.* **1** to send forth a bullet, arrow, or other missile from a firearm, bow, or the like: *The boys shot at the mark. Who's there? ... speak quickly, or I shoot* (Shakespeare). **2** to send a bullet; go off; fire: *This gun shoots straight.* **3** *Figurative.* to move suddenly and swiftly; go: *A car shot by us. Flames shot up from the burning house.* **4** *Figurative.* to go sharply through part of the body, especially from time to time: *Pain shot up his arm from his hurt finger.* **5** to come forth from the ground; grow rapidly: *Buds shoot forth in the spring.* (*Figurative.*) *To rear the tender thought, To teach the young idea how to shoot* (James Thomson). **6** to put forth buds or shoots, as a plant does; germinate: *Always cut close, not leaving any stump to shoot again* (James Abercrombie). **7** *Figurative.* to project sharply; jut out: *a cape that shoots out into the sea.* **SYN:** extend. **8a** to take a photograph or film a motion picture. **b** to begin photographing a scene. **c** to film part of a motion picture. **9** *Informal.* to start talking; go ahead; begin: *"Okay," said the Chancellor, "shoot. I'll do my best to answer your questions"* (Punch). **10** to follow or practice the sport of hunting or killing game with a gun: *He went into the mountains to fish and shoot.* **11** to propel a ball, puck, or marble, toward the goal, pocket, or basket, in an effort to score. **12** to produce or form crystals, as a solution, or a salt.
—*n.* **1a** a trip, party, or contest for shooting; shooting match or contest. **b** a shooting practice. **c** a game-shooting expedition: *What a grand shoot it was in those far-off days ... there were pheasants, partridges, grouse, and blackgame* (London Times). **2a** a new part growing out, such as a young bud or stem; offshoot: *See the new shoots on that rosebush. These changes in volume and consequent pressures may in part serve the germinating seed by eventually permitting the emergence of the delicate root and shoot from the seed coat without damage* (A. M. Mayer). **b** the act of sprouting or growing. **c** the amount of growth in a certain period. **3** a short, sharp twinge of pain. **4** a sloping trough, as for conveying coal, grain, or water to a lower level; chute. **5** a swift or sudden movement of something as though shooting or being shot in a particular direction. **6** the launching of a missile or rocket: *Since its first shoot early in 1957, it has had more than forty successful launchings* (Wall Street Journal). **7** the time between strokes in rowing. **8** one movement of the shuttle between the threads of the warp in weaving, or a thread so placed; cast or throw.
—*interj. Informal.* an exclamation of impatience or irritation; shucks: *"Oh, shoot, Noona, Paul's the same as any"* (Anne Taylor). *Shoot, you've got to talk about something* (Truman Capote).
**shoot at** (or **for**), *Informal.* to aim at; aspire to: *I shoot at no advantage to myself* (Robert Louis Stevenson). *The Air Force will "shoot" for the moon in August* (Christian Science Monitor).
**shoot down, a** to kill by a shot: *The corporal was shot down by a sniper.* **b** to cause (an airplane or bird) to fall down by shooting: *The ace was credited with having shot down more than twenty enemy aircraft.*
**shoot it out,** *U.S.* to shoot until one side wins; fight it out with guns: *He shot it out with the gunman ...* [*who*] *was wounded in the head* (New York Times).
**shoot off,** to discharge; fire: *A bonfire was lighted, the pipes were played, and guns were shot off* (Lytton Strachey).
**shoot one's bolt.** See under **bolt¹**.
**shoot the breeze.** See under **breeze¹**.

**shoot the works.** See under **works.**
**shoot up, a** to grow tall or large quickly, as a plant or young person: *The corn is shooting up in the warm weather.* **b** to go up quickly; rise fast. *New buildings have shot up recently in Detroit* (Listener). *A score of impatient hands shot up* (New York Times). **c** *U.S.* to shoot at in a reckless way: *The rival hoodlums shot each other up.* **d** *U.S. Informal.* to rush through (a place) shooting wildly in all directions: *The angry cowboys went on a rampage and shot up the town.* **e** *Slang.* to inject (a liquefied narcotic drug) into the vein: *to shoot up amphetamines. After the high ends, there is the frantic scramble for a new supply in order to shoot up again* (Time). [Middle English *schoten,* Old English *scēotan*]
**shoot|a|ble** (shü′tə bəl), *adj.* that can be shot; fit for shooting.
**shoot-'em-up** (shüt′əm up′), *n. U.S. Informal.* **1** a motion picture or television program filled with gunfighting and shoot-outs: *A real old-fashioned shoot-'em-up, with enough good guys and bad guys to populate the entire Western frontier* (Time). **2** a shoot-out.
**shoot|er** (shü′tər), *n.* **1** a person who shoots: *Most shooters interested in the future of their sport refrain from hunting until the end of May* (New York Times). **2** something that shoots or is used for shooting: *Each player uses a larger marble, the shooter, to knock, or "shoot," the small marbles out of the ring* (Carl A. Troester, Jr.). *Then Jack drew his shooter out and shot Billy Bill through the head* (William Black). **3** a person who shoots oil wells with nitroglycerin.
**shoot|ing** (shü′ting), *n.* **1** the act of a person or thing that shoots. **2** a shoot or sprout. **3** the exclusive right to kill game on a particular tract: *Gentlemen ... combine and lease the shooting over wide areas* (Richard Jefferie). **4** the tract itself.
**shooting box,** *Especially British.* a small house used by hunters during the shooting season; hunting lodge.
**shooting brake,** *British.* a station wagon.
**shooting gallery, 1** a long room or a deep booth fitted with targets for practice in shooting. **2** *U.S. Slang.* a place where narcotic addicts meet to inject themselves with heroin or other drugs.
**shooting iron,** *Informal.* a gun, especially a rifle or pistol; firearm: *What he called "shooting irons" were his weapons* (Joseph Conrad).
**shooting lodge,** *British.* a shooting box; hunting lodge.
**shooting script,** a motion-picture or television script indicating the order or sequence of camera shots.
**shooting star, 1** a meteor resembling a star seen falling or darting through the sky at night: *A knowledge of the constellations is a great help in reporting these shooting stars* (Bernhard, Bennett, and Rice). **2** a North American perennial herb of the primrose family with a cluster of nodding, rose, purple, or white flowers whose petals and sepals turn backward.
***shooting stick, 1** an implement used by printers to tighten or loosen the quoins in a chase by striking with a mallet. **2** a walking stick with a small, hinged seat: *The Oklahoma oil broker rested on a shooting stick between each stroke* (Time).

***shooting stick**
definition 2

**shooting war,** a war in which military weapons are used; hot war.
**shoot-off** (shüt′ôf′, -of′), *n.* a supplementary contest to decide a tie in a shooting match or contest.
**shoot-out** (shüt′out′), *n. U.S. Informal.* a duel with guns; gunfight.
**shoot-the-chute** (shüt′ᴛʜə shüt′), *n. U.S.* chute-the-chute.
**shoot-up** (shüt′up′), *n. Slang.* the act of shooting up a drug: *But the most dramatic technique is the "shoot-up" where the more serious addicts inject themselves or each other with a nausea-producing liquid* (Time).
**shop** (shop), *n., v.,* **shopped, shop|ping.** —*n.* **1** a place where things are sold at retail; store, especially one dealing in a single type or limited range of commodities: *a small dress shop.* **2** a place where things are made or repaired; workshop: *He works in a carpenter's shop.* **3** a place where a certain kind of work is done: *tailor's shop.* **4a** a course given in schools in certain trades, such as carpentry and metalwork. **b** the classroom for such a course. **5** *Informal.* a person's place of business or occupation. **6** *British Slang.* an engagement or job in the theatrical business: *You'll be able to get me a shop! If Ross takes the piece ...* (Leonard Merrick).
—*v.i.* to visit stores to look at or to buy things: *We shopped all morning for a coat. I thought Joan was going with you, and that you would be shopping* (Benjamin Disraeli).
—*v.t.* **1** to visit (a store or stores) to examine merchandise or compare prices, especially as a shopper. **2** to do one's shopping in: *In older times most people shopped the general store.* **3** *U.S. Slang.* to dismiss from a job or position. **4** *British Slang.* **a** to give a job to, especially in the theatrical business: *I can't shop everybody; there aren't enough parts to go around* (Leonard Merrick). **b** to shut up or cause to be shut up in prison.
**set up shop, a** to start work or business: *Every morning the fruit and vegetable man sets up shop at the corner.* **b** to start a business: *He set up shop in the fur trade.*
**shop around,** *U.S.* to make a search; try to find and acquire something: *to shop around for an apartment. People aren't shopping around for jobs the way they used to* (Wall Street Journal).
**shut up shop, a** to end work or business: *The grocer shuts up shop at six.* **b** to give up work or business: *With another loss as large as this one, we will have to shut up shop.*
**talk shop,** to talk about one's work or occupation: *There is a coffee break in the afternoon, or tea in the library, when the associates gather with the partners and talk shop* (Harper's).
[Old English *sceoppa* a (lean-to) booth. See related etym. at **shippon.**]
**shop assistant,** *British.* a salesclerk; salesman or saleswoman.
**shop|break|ing** (shop′brā′king), *n.* the act of breaking into and entering a store to steal or commit some other crime.
**shop|craft** (shop′kraft′, -kräft′), *n.* the occupation or skill of a shopworker.
**shopcraft union,** a craft union of shopworkers.
**Shope virus** (shōp), a virus which causes papillomas: *The Shope virus, which induces warts on the skin of rabbits, has no symptomatic effects on mice, rats, dogs, or monkeys* (New Scientist). [< Richard E. *Shope,* 1901-1966, an American physician, who discovered the virus]
**shop|front** (shop′frunt′), *n.* the front or front room of a store.
**shop|girl** (shop′gėrl′), *n.* a girl who works in a shop or store.
**sho|phar** (shō′fär, -fər), *n., pl.* **sho|phroth** (shō′frōs, shō frōt′), **sho|phars.** = shofar.
**shop|keep|er** (shop′kē′pər), *n.* a person who owns or manages a shop or store. **SYN:** tradesman.
**shop|keep|ing** (shop′kē′ping), *n.* the keeping of a shop; business of a shopkeeper.
**shop|lift** (shop′lift′), *v.t., v.i.* to steal goods from a store while pretending to be a customer. [back formation < *shoplifting*]
**shop|lift|er** (shop′lif′tər), *n.* a person who steals goods from a store while pretending to be a customer. [< *shop* + *lifter* thief < *lift* to steal, take away]
**shop|lift|ing** (shop′lif′ting), *n.* the act of stealing goods from a store while pretending to be a customer: *From shoplifting and petty thievery, the addict quickly graduates to major crimes* (New York Times).
**shop|man** (shop′mən), *n., pl.* **-men. 1** = shopkeeper. **2** *Especially British.* a salesman in a shop.
**shoppe** (shop), *n.* = shop.
▶ This archaic spelling is used sometimes for a quaint, old-world effect, especially in names of small specialty shops and similar establishments: *His ferryboat was beached ... and turned into a gift shoppe* (Time).
**shop|per** (shop′ər), *n.* **1** a person who visits stores to look at or buy things: *bargain basement shoppers* (Newsweek). **2** a person hired to buy goods at retail for another, especially one hired by a retail store to buy items from competitors in order to compare prices or quality of merchandise; comparison shopper. **3** *U.S.* a newspaper filled with advertisements for local shops and businesses, freely distributed to attract customers.
**shop|ping** (shop′ing), *n.* the act of visiting stores to look at or to buy things: *Mother does her shopping on Wednesdays and Saturdays.*
**go shopping,** to go to a store or stores in order to buy: *We go shopping every Thursday at the shopping center.*
**shopping bag,** a bag with handles for carrying packages obtained while shopping.
**shopping cart,** a small, four-wheeled cart, used by customers in a supermarket or other self-service store to carry goods from the shelves to the clerk at the cash register or checkout counter.
**shopping center,** a group of retail stores and shops, especially in a suburban or new community. Most shopping centers have large areas for parking automobiles.
**shopping list,** a list of items to be bought: *Ground-to-air missiles were on the "shopping list" of defence equipment* (London Times).
**shopping mall,** an area of retail stores and shops, sometimes with shaded walks, where people can shop around without hindrance by vehicular traffic.
**shop|py** (shop′ē), *adj.* **1** having to do with or characteristic of shops. **2** consisting of many shops. **3** having to do with a person's interest, as in his occupation, hobby, or trade; talking shop.
**shop|soiled** (shop′soild′), *adj. British.* shopworn: *For those who could not afford quite the best there were a couple of shopsoiled bargains* (London Times).
**shop steward,** a union worker in a factory or company elected by fellow workers to represent them in dealing with management and maintaining union regulations.
**shop|talk** (shop′tôk′), *n.* **1** talk about one's work or occupation, especially outside of working hours; talking shop: *Mere shoptalk, while of course it is heard, is not encouraged or admired for its own sake* (New York Times). **2** the informal language of an occupation: *the shoptalk of lawyers, the shoptalk of actors.*
▶ **shoptalk.** For the most part shoptalk consists of the necessary names, as for materials, processes, and tools—for everything that is commonly referred to in the line of work. While many of these words are in good standing, they are not often needed outside of the vocation.
**shop|walk|er** (shop′wô′kər), *n. Especially British.* a floorwalker.
**shop|win|dow** (shop′win′dō), *n.* a window of a shop or store in which goods are displayed for sale; show window.
**shop|wom|an** (shop′wu̇m′ən), *n., pl.* **-wom|en.** a woman who works in a shop or store; shopgirl.
**shop|work|er** (shop′wėr′kər), *n.* a person who works in a shop or workshop.
**shop|worn** (shop′wôrn′, -wōrn′), *adj.* **1** soiled or frayed by being displayed and handled in a shop or store. **2** *Figurative.* old and worn; threadbare: *After all these years and books, another factual account of the crucial European battles of World War II may sound like pretty shopworn fare* (Wall Street Journal).
**sho|ran** (shôr′an, shōr′-), *n.* a method of navigation in which radar signals are sent out from a craft to two ground stations and retransmitted by the stations. The time interval between sending and receiving the signals is used to determine the craft's exact position. *Surveys over water generally depend on radio navigation aids such as shoran* (Scientific American). [< *sho*(rt) *ra*(nge) *n*(avigation)]
**shore¹** (shôr, shōr), *n., v.,* **shored, shor|ing.** —*n.* **1** land at the edge of a sea, lake, river, or other body of water: *The* [*Mississippi*] *River cuts at the shores to give itself man-size room; past Memphis and Vicksburg and New Orleans* (Newsweek). **SYN:** strand. **2** land near a sea; coast: *I have seen the kingly ocean gain advantage on the kingdom of the shore* (Shakespeare). **SYN:** seaboard. **3** the land (as contrasted with the sea): *Our marines serve on both the sea and the shore.* **4** *Law.* the ground lying between the ordinary high-water and low-water marks; foreshore. **5** *U.S.* the seashore as a place of vacation resort: *to go to the shore for the summer.*
—*v.t.* to put or set ashore: *to shore goods or passengers. The boat was temporarily shored on the beach* (J. Spence).
**in shore,** in or on the water, but near to the shore or nearer to the shore: *Steer in shore of them* (Frederick Marryat).
**off shore,** in or on the water, but not far from the shore: *The yacht was anchored off shore opposite Sandy Point.*
**shores,** land: *As one who long detain'd on foreign shores pants to return* (William Cowper).
[Middle English *schore,* perhaps < Low German, or Middle Dutch]

---

**Pronunciation Key:** hat, āge, cãre, fär; let, ēqual, tėrm; it, īce; hot, ōpen, ôrder; **oi**l, **ou**t; cup, pu̇t, rüle; **ch**ild; lo**ng**; **th**in; **ᴛʜ**en; **zh,** measure; ə represents **a** in about, **e** in taken, **i** in pencil, **o** in lemon, **u** in circus.

**shore**[2] (shôr, shōr), *n., v.,* **shored, shor|ing.** *—n.* a prop placed against or beneath something to support it; strut.
*—v.t.* Usually, **shore up.** to prop up or support with shores: *We laid the ship aground ... and shored her up on each side* (Daniel Defoe). *The hydraulic mechanism also has been shored up by inserting metal filters in place of paper ones* (Wall Street Journal). (*Figurative.*) *The Europeans have been helping shore up the dollar* (Harper's). [Middle English *schore,* perhaps < Middle Dutch, a prop]

**shore**[3] (shôr, shōr), *v. Archaic.* a past tense of **shear.**

**shore**[4] (shôr, shōr), *v.t.,* **shored, shor|ing.** *Scottish.* **1** to threaten. **2** to scold. **3** to offer. [origin unknown]

**shore-based** (shôr′bāst′, shōr′-), *adj.* having its base of operations on or near the shore; land-based: *shore-based radar.*

**shore bird,** any bird that frequents the shores of seas, inlets, lakes, or other bodies of water. Plovers, snipes, and sandpipers are shore birds.

**shore crab,** the green crab of Europe and the Atlantic coast of America.

**shore dinner,** *U.S.* a dinner featuring various seafoods.

**shore fast,** the length of cable which secures a ship to the dock; hawser.

**shore|front** (shôr′frunt′, shōr′-), *n., adj. —n.* the area near to or on a shore; an oceanfront, lakefront, riverfront, or the like.
*—adj.* of a shorefront; fronting a shore: *shorefront hotels in a seaside resort, a shorefront park.*

**shore-go|ing** (shôr′gō′ing, shōr′-), *n., adj. —n.* the act or fact of going, staying, or living on shore.
*—adj.* going or living on shore; having to do with life on shore.

**shore leave,** leave for a member or members of a ship's crew to go ashore: *Though we made two ports in Australia, no shore leave was granted* (Harper's).

**shore|less** (shôr′lis, shōr′-), *adj.* **1** having no shore; having no low land adjacent to the water: *a rocky, shoreless island.* **2** *Figurative.* boundless: *He was adrift on the shoreless tides of delirium* (Rudyard Kipling).

**shore|line** (shôr′līn′, shōr′-), *n.* the line where shore and water meet: *The lake has several miles of shoreline.*

**shore patrol,** a detail or detachment of two or more enlisted men of the United States Navy or Coast Guard assigned to maintain order among personnel of their own branch of the service while ashore, as in a particular city or district.

**Shore Patrol,** the policing branch of the United States Navy and Coast Guard, as a distinct division of the service. *Abbr:* SP (no periods), S.P.

**shor|er** (shôr′ər, shōr′-), *n.* **1** a person whose work it is to prop up structures, as during construction operations. **2** something that shores; a prop.

**shores** (shôrz, shōrz), *n.pl.* See under **shore**[1].

**shore|scape** (shôr′skāp′, shōr′-), *n.* **1** a view of scenery on a shore: *Morning showed shorescapes of a most inviting aspect; fields ... thick forests ... with ash trees at the riverbanks* (Wall Street Journal). **2** a picture or painting showing a scene on a shore. [< *shore* + *-scape*]

**shore|side** (shôr′sīd′, shōr′-), *adj., n. —adj.* of, on, or toward the shore; along the shore.
*—n.* the land along the shore.

**shore wall,** an accumulation of sand and gravel pushed up into mounds by the expansion and contraction of ice formed on rivers or lakes.

**shore|ward** (shôr′wərd, shōr′-), *adv., adj.* toward the shore: *The winds blew shoreward* (adv.). *We felt the shoreward breeze* (adj.).

**shore|wards** (shôr′wərdz, shōr′-), *adv.* = shoreward.

**shor|ing** (shôr′ing, shōr′-), *n.* **1** a system of shores or props, as for supporting a building, ship, or dock. **2** the act of building or providing with shores.

**shorn** (shôrn, shōrn), *v., adj. —v.* a past participle of **shear**: *The sheep was shorn of its wool.*
*—adj.* **1** sheared: *Early in the period choice 102-pound shorn lambs sold for $21.50* (Wall Street Journal). **2** *Figurative.* deprived: *a man newly shorn of his wealth.*

**short** (shôrt), *adj., adv., n., v. —adj.* **1a** not long; of small extent from end to end: *a short distance, a short time, a short street. The life so short, the craft so long to learn* (Chaucer). **b** not long for its kind: *a short tail.* **2** not tall; having little height: *a short man, short grass.* **3** *Figurative.* extending or reaching but a little way: *a short memory.* **4a** not coming up to the right amount, measure, or standard: *short weight. The cashier is short in his accounts.* **b** not having enough; scanty: *a short supply of money. The prisoners were kept on short allowance of food. He was short with his rent for the approaching quarter day* (H. G. Wells). **5** so brief as to be rude: *She was so short with me that I felt hurt.* SYN: abrupt, curt, sharp. **6** not long-winded; concise: *Let me pray you to be short and explicit in what you have to say* (Scott). **7** (of vowels or syllables) taking a relatively short time to speak. The vowels are short in *fat, net, pin, not, up.* **8** breaking or crumbling easily; crisp or crumbly. Pastry is made short with butter or other shortening. **9** not ductile; brittle: *short metals, short iron.* **10** not owning at the time of sale the stocks, securities, or commodities that one sells: *A trader is short when he sells something he does not have, usually in the expectation that the price will go down before he must deliver* (New York Times). **11** of, noting, or having to do with sales of stocks, securities, or commodities that the seller does not possess; having to do with a short sale or short selling. **12** depending for profit on a decline in prices. **13** (of a bill, note, or other security) that is to be paid within a short time, as within ten days.
*—adv.* **1** so as to be or make short: *to throw short.* **2** in a short manner; suddenly; abruptly: *The horse pulled up short.* **3** briefly. **4** without possessing at the time of sale the stocks, securities, or commodities sold.
*—n.* **1a** something short: *Stories range from 20-line shorts to two-page essays* (Time). **b** what is deficient or lacking. **2** = short circuit. **3** a short motion picture, such as a cartoon or newsreel, especially one shown on the same program with a full-length picture (feature); short subject. **4** a short sound or syllable. **5** a size of garment for men who are shorter than average. **6** *Baseball.* the position of shortstop: *to play short.* **7a** a fish too small to be worth keeping, or to keep legally. **b** *Especially Northeastern U.S.* a lobster with a body measurement below that required for keeping legally. **8** a shot that strikes in front of the target, as while firing to adjust the range. **9** *Commerce.* **a** a person who has sold or is selling short: *This not only put the company in effective competition with the shorts as bidders for the stock ...* (Wall Street Journal). **b** a short sale: *to cover one's shorts.* **c** stock or other securities sold short: *The biggest gains were made in shorts where the 4½ per cent ... stock ... gained ¾* (Economist). **10** *Informal.* an unmixed drink of liquor.
*—v.t.* **1** = short-circuit. **2** to cheat out of something: *He shorted the house a mixed case of scotch and rye on the initial inventory and bribed hotel workmen to scrub and paint for him* (Atlantic). *—v.i.* = short-circuit.

**be caught short.** See under **caught.**

**cut short.** See under **cut.**

**fall short.** See under **fall.**

**for short,** in order to make shorter; by way of abbreviation; as a nickname: *Robert was called Rob for short.*

**in short,** briefly: *The twins no longer are fed from the bottle; in short, they are weaned.*

**run short, a** not have enough: *Let me know if you run short of money before then.* **b** not be enough: *The hunter's supply of food ran short at the end of the long winter.*

**sell short.** See under **sell**[1].

**short for,** a shortened form of: *The word "phone" is short for "telephone."*

**short of, a** not up to; less than: *Nothing short of your best work will satisfy me. Fine seasoned regiments were short of half their strength* (Baron Charnwood). **b** not having enough of; in want of; lacking: *He is short of funds right now. Allow me to take your hat—we are rather short of pegs* (Dickens). **c** on the near side of (an intended or particular point): *to stop short of actual crime. He halted ... at Malmesbury, twenty miles short of Bath* (John F. Kirk). **d** other than: *Short of the President himself, probably no one could have put the American case more persuasively* (Manchester Guardian Weekly).

**short on,** poorly furnished with; having little of; lacking: *U.S. housewives, long on gadgets and short on help, often look enviously to the Old World as a place where ... willing hands are plentiful* (Time).

**short out,** to short-circuit: *The resulting short circuit shorted out the power supplies which fed each grid* (New Scientist).

**shorts, a** short, loose trousers usually reaching to above the knees. Shorts are worn by men, women, or children in hot weather or when playing tennis, running races, or taking part in other sports. *I ... stood outside in football shorts, nailed boots, and sweater* (Blackwood's Magazine). **b** similar short trousers, worn as an undergarment by men or boys: *a set of undershirt and shorts.* **c** a baby's short clothes: *Six months passed ... and then he* [*the baby*] *was put into shorts* (Frederick Marryat). **d** knee breeches; smallclothes: *The little old gentleman ... follows him, in black shorts and white silk stockings* (Walter Besant). **e** a mixture of bran and coarse meal: *The farmers ate middlings, shorts, or corn meal at least once a day.*

**squeeze the shorts,** to demand and get higher prices (for securities) from short sellers at the time they must make delivery: *Firms that squeeze the shorts compel short sellers to buy back the stocks at a heavy loss to themselves.*
[Old English *sceort*] *—***short′ness,** *n.*
*—Syn. adj.* **1 Short, brief** mean of small extent. **Short** may refer to either space or time, and often suggests being curtailed or unfinished: *Because he was late he could take only a short walk today.* **Brief** usually refers to time and means coming to an end quickly. When applied to speeches or writings, it is more likely to suggest leaving out unnecessary details than cutting off the end: *A brief essay is short but to the point.*

**short account, 1** the account of a person who sells stocks or commodities short. **2** all short sales of one stock or commodity, or of an entire market at a given time.

**short|age** (shôr′tij), *n.* **1** too small an amount; lack; deficiency: *a shortage of rain. There is a shortage of grain because of poor crops. There is still an acute shortage of housing facilities in the large cities of this country* (Andrew W. Mellon). **2** the amount by which something is deficient: *The total shortage was $500.*

**short and,** = ampersand.

**short-arm** (shôrt′ärm′), *adj.* = short-armed.

**short-armed** (shôrt′ärmd′), *adj.* **1** that has short arms; not long of arm or reach. **2** that travels a short distance and is delivered with the arm not fully straight: *a short-armed jab to the chin.*

**short ballot,** *U.S.* a simplified ballot having only the principal offices filled through election.

**short-billed marsh wren** (shôrt′bild′), a wren of eastern North America with white streaks on the crown that nests in wet, grassy marshes and meadows.

**short bit,** *U.S. Dialect.* 10 cents; a dime.

**short|bread** (shôrt′bred′), *n.* a rich cake or cookie that crumbles easily, made with much butter or other shortening.

**short-breathed** (shôrt′bretht′), *adj.* **1** short of breath; short-winded: *Being short-breathed and unable to go up even a gentle hill without panting and puffing ...* (Blackwood's Magazine). **2** lacking prolonged effort; fleeting; short-lived: *a short-breathed attempt.*

**short|cake** (shôrt′kāk′), *n.* **1a** a cake made of rich biscuit dough and shortening, usually slightly sweetened, covered or filled with berries or other fruit. **b** a sweet cake filled with fruit. **2** any one of various rich cookies or small cakes resembling shortbread, but unsweetened. **3** *Archaic.* shortbread.

**short-change** (shôrt′chānj′), *v.t.,* **-changed, -chang|ing. 1** to give less than the right change to (a person), especially intentionally. **2** to give less than is considered a proper return or full share; cheat: *to short-change the public.*
*—***short′-chang′er,** *n.*

**short circuit,** a side circuit of electricity that is formed when insulation wears off a wire or wires that touch each other or some connecting conductor, so that the main circuit is by-passed. A short circuit usually blows a fuse and may cause a fire by heating wires.

**short-cir|cuit** (shôrt′sėr′kit), *v.t.* **1** to make a short circuit in (an electric system). **2** (of a conductor) to carry (a current) by acting as a short circuit. **3** to cut off the current from (part of an apparatus) by making a short circuit. **4** *Surgery.* to make a direct passage from (an organ) into some other part when the normal passage is obstructed. **5** *Informal, Figurative.* to get around; avoid; by-pass: *It was he who ... contrived to short-circuit the ... defense order* (Harper's).
*—v.i.* to make a short circuit.

**short|com|ing** (shôrt′kum′ing), *n.* a flaw in one's character or conduct; fault; defect: *Rudeness is a serious shortcoming.* SYN: failing.

**short commons,** little to eat: *In a word, the Army is on short commons and the lack of funds is apparent everywhere* (London Times).

**short covering,** the buying of securities to cover a short sale.

**short cut,** or **short|cut** (shôrt′kut′), *n.* **1** a less distant or quicker way between two places. **2** *Figurative.* a quick or quicker way: *There are no short cuts to wisdom and learning.*

**short-cut** (shôrt′kut′), *v.,* **-cut, -cut|ting.** *—v.i.* to use a short cut.
*—v.t.* to avoid by using a short cut: *to short-cut a city. One reason for short-cutting the legal order ... is the unwillingness some judges are showing now to sign such orders* (New York Times).

**short-dat|ed** (shôrt′dā′tid), *adj.* **1** falling due at an early date: *short-dated bills, bonds, or notes.* **2** having little time to run: *a short-dated life or career.*

**short-day plant** (shôrt′dā′), a plant that blooms only when its daily exposure to light is relatively short, as in the spring or late fall when the days are short and the nights are long. Sugar cane, wild strawberries, violets, and poinsettias are some short-day plants.

**short division**, a method of dividing numbers in which the various steps of the division are worked out mentally. It is used to divide small numbers. See picture under **division**.

**short-eared owl** (shôrt′ird′), an owl about 15½ inches long that frequents open, marshy areas and often hunts during the day; hawk owl.

**short|en** (shôr′tən), *v.t.* **1** to make shorter; cut off: *to shorten the working day. The new highway shortens the trip. She has had all her dresses shortened. Envy and wrath shorten the life* (Ecclesiasticus 30:24). **2** to make seem shorter: *Thus were the hours of labour shortened ... by shrewd remarks and bits of local gossip* (Joseph Conrad). **3** to make rich, as with butter or lard; add shortening to: *She used butter to shorten her cakes.* **4** to lessen the area of (a vessel's sails) by reefing or furling; take in (sail). **5** (in the Bible) to reduce the reach or power of: *Behold, the Lord's hand is not shortened, that it cannot save* (Isaiah 59:1). **6** to treat or pronounce (a vowel or syllable) as short. **–*v.i.*** **1** to become shorter; dwindle in size: *The days shorten in November in this country.* **2** (of odds or prices) to decrease. **–short′en|er**, *n.*

**–*Syn.*** *v.t.* **1 Shorten, curtail, abbreviate** mean to make shorter. **Shorten** is the general word meaning to reduce the length or extent of something: *The new highway shortens the trip.* **Curtail**, more formal, means to cut something short by taking away or cutting off a part, and suggests causing loss or incompleteness: *Bad news made us curtail our trip.* **Abbreviate** most commonly means to shorten the written form of a word or phrase by leaving out syllables or letters or by substitution, without impairing meaning: *Abbreviate "pound" to "lb." after numerals. Abbreviate* may also be used more generally, closer in meaning to *shorten* than to *curtail.*

**short-end|er** (shôrt′en′dər), *n. U.S. Informal.* a contestant who is not favored to win; underdog.

**short|en|ing** (shôr′tə ning, shôrt′ning), *n.* **1** butter, lard, or other fat, used to make pastry or cake crisp or easily crumbling: *Shortening, like salad oil, starts out as roughly refined "summer oil"* (Wall Street Journal). **2** the act of a person or thing that shortens.

**short|fall** (shôrt′fôl′), *n.* the act or fact of falling short; failure to reach an expected amount; decrease: *a shortfall in purchasing.*

**short-fired** (shôrt′fīrd′), *adj.* (of china and pottery) not sufficiently baked.

**short fuse**, *U.S.* a quick temper: *While Darwin the writer was the soul of serenity and balance, Darwin the golfer had one of the shortest fuses in history* (New Yorker).

**short|hair cat**, or **short|hair** (shôrt′hãr′), *n.* any one of a breed of medium-sized, domestic cats having long, slender bodies and short hair: *Shorthair of the Year was ... a black Manx male* (Theodore M. O'Leary).

*** shorthand**
definition 2

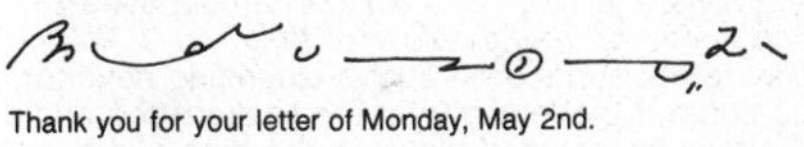

Thank you for your letter of Monday, May 2nd.

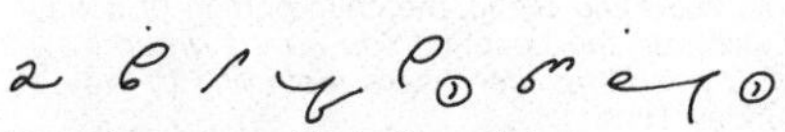

We are happy to report that, with your help,

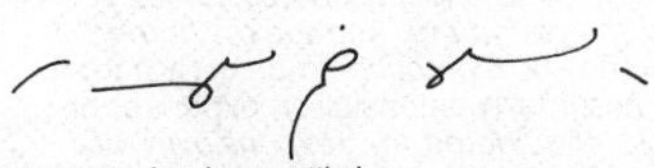

the matter has been settled.

Gregg method (Diamond Jubilee edition)

***short|hand** (shôrt′hand′), *n., adj.* **–*n.*** **1** a method of rapid writing that uses symbols or abbreviations in place of letters, sounds, syllables, words, and phrases; stenography: *Sometimes it is possible to make actual notes in shorthand or longhand, and occasionally a simultaneous electrical recording may be made of the interview* (Anthony H. Richmond). **2** writing in such symbols. **3** *Figurative.* any shortened form or system of communicating: *Sociologists all have their own shorthand or jargon* (Listener).

**–*adj.*** **1** written in shorthand: *shorthand notes.* **2** using shorthand: *a shorthand clerk or stenographer.*

**short-hand|ed** (shôrt′han′did), *adj.* not having enough workmen or helpers; undermanned; understaffed: *The post office is always short-handed in the Christmas season.* **–short′-hand′ed|ness**, *n.*

**shorthand machine**, a machine for recording speech rapidly by means of lettered keys like those on a typewriter. Shorthand machines have 21 keys, any number of which may be struck at one time. They are often used for recording speeches and court testimony.

**short|hand-typ|ist** (shôrt′hand′tī′pist), *n. British.* a stenographer.

**short|hand-writ|er** (shôrt′hand′rī′tər), *n. British.* a shorthand-typist.

**short-haul** (shôrt′hôl′), *adj.* of or having to do with transportation over relatively short distances: *a short-haul airline.*

**short-head|ed** (shôrt′hed′id), *adj.* having a short head; brachycephalic. **–short′-head′ed|ness**, *n.*

**short|horn** or **Short|horn** (shôrt′hôrn′), *n.* one of a breed of cattle with short horns, raised chiefly for beef; Durham. Shorthorns are white, red, or roan. The breed originated in northern England. *The Shorthorn is generally considered a dual-purpose breed, though different strains have been selected primarily for meat or for milk production* (Ralph W. Phillips).

**short-horned** (shôrt′hôrnd′), *adj.* having short horns: *a short-horned cow or bull.*

**short-horned grasshopper**, any grasshopper of a family having short antennae and commonly migrating in great swarms; locust.

**short hundredweight**, the American hundredweight, equal to 100 pounds.

**shor|ti|a** (shôr′tē ə), *n.* any perennial plant of a group of the mountains of North and South Carolina and of Japan, with evergreen leaves and nodding white or rose flowers. Shortia, prized in cultivation, was long thought the rarest of North American plants. [American English < New Latin *Shortia* the genus name < Charles W. *Short,* 1794-1863, an American botanist]

**short|ie** (shôr′tē), *n., adj.* **–*n.*** **1** a garment of short length: *Trousers ... tapering elegantly from under my new camel shortie* (Basil Boothroyd). **2** *Informal.* a short person.

**–*adj.*** (of a garment) of short length: *a blue shortie raincoat.* Also, **shorty**.

**short interest**, a quantity of borrowed stock sold in a short sale; number of shares sold short.

**short iron**, a golf club with an iron or steel head inclined at a relatively large angle to its short shaft, suitable for shots close to the green.

**short|ish** (shôr′tish), *adj.* rather short: *a shortish run, visit or speech.*

**short|jaw chub** (shôrt′jô′), a common American freshwater chub having a short lower jaw.

**short-joint|ed** (shôrt′join′tid), *adj.* **1** (of plants) having short gaps between the joints. **2** (of a horse) having a short pastern.

**short|leaf pine** (shôrt′lēf′), a pine tree of the southern and eastern United States having short needles and small cones.

**short-leg|ged** (shôrt′leg′id, -legd′), *adj.* having short legs.

**short line**, **1** a railroad or bus line covering short routes, usually less than 200 miles. **2** the center line across the width of a handball court.

**short-list** (shôrt′list′), *v.t. British.* to include in a list of chosen applicants or candidates, from which a final selection will be made: *Candidates short-listed will be interviewed on 27th July* (London Times).

**short-lived** (shôrt′līvd′, -livd′), *adj.* **1** living only a short time; having a short life: *a short-lived plant.* **2** lasting only a short time; fleeting; brief: *a short-lived improvement, short-lived hope.*

► The first and more common pronunciation also accords better with the derivation, since the underlying form is the noun *life,* not the verb *live.* The second pronunciation is nevertheless an established variant, and the prevailing one in British English. An exactly parallel situation exists with regard to *long-lived.*

**short loin**, **1** the front part of the loin of beef, extending from the ribs to the sirloin. **2** a tender cut of beef from this part.

**short|ly** (shôrt′lē), *adv.* **1** in a short time; before long; soon: *I will be with you shortly.* **SYN:** presently. **2** a short time (after or before): *He went shortly before they came.* **3** in a few words; briefly; concisely: *"The business of America is business," said Calvin Coolidge shortly.* **SYN:** tersely. **4** briefly and rudely; abruptly; curtly: *"I think very differently," answered Elizabeth shortly* (Jane Austen).

**short|nose gar** (shôrt′nōz′), a North American gar ranging from the Great Lakes to the Gulf coast, that grows up to three feet in length.

**short-or|der** (shôrt′ôr′dər), *adj. U.S.* preparing or selling meals, sandwiches, or other food, that can be quickly cooked or made on order: *a short-order cook, a short-order diner.*

**short-pe|ri|od variable** (shôrt′pir′ē əd), a variable star whose period from one peak of brightness to the next is less than 100 days.

**short position**, = short interest.

**short-range** (shôrt′rānj′), *adj.* not reaching far in time or distance; having a limited use or application; not long-range: *a short-range view, a short-range forecast.*

**short ribs**, a thin cut of beef from the lower end of the ribs, between the rib roast and plate.

**short-run** (shôrt′run′), *adj.* for or lasting a brief time: *Four steps—one a short-run corrective measure and three for the long pull—should be promptly taken* (Harper's).

**shorts** (shôrts), *n.pl.* See under **short**.

**short sale**, the sale of what a person does not have but hopes to buy at a lower price before the time of delivery.

**short seller**, a person who sells stocks or commodities short.

**short selling**, the act of selling stocks or commodities short.

**short shrift**, **1** little or no consideration, mercy, or delay in dealing with a person or problem: *Flagrant violators will get short shrift, the chief said* (New York Times). **2** a short time for confession and absolution.

**make short shrift of**, to give little consideration to: *The unification of Germany ... led to making short shrift of the claims of non-German neighbors in regions where Germans, too, were involved* (Edmund Wilson).

**short-sight|ed** (shôrt′sī′tid), *adj.* **1** not able to see far; near-sighted; myopic: *He was very short-sighted, and this early encouraged his preference for reading rather than sport* (Manchester Guardian). **2** *Figurative.* **a** lacking in foresight; not prudent: *It is short-sighted and self-deluding to ascribe more than a small part of Russian success to efficient espionage* (Bulletin of Atomic Scientists). **b** characterized by or proceeding from lack of foresight: *a short-sighted strategy. Heaven mocks the short-sighted views of man* (Horace Walpole). **–short′-sight′ed|ly**, *adv.* **–short′-sight′ed|ness**, *n.*

**short snort|er** (snôr′tər), *Slang, especially in the 1930's and 1940's.* **1** a dollar bill or other piece of paper currency autographed by some or all of those who have shared in a transoceanic flight with its owner. **2** a person who shared in such a flight and had to buy drinks for others who made the flight if he could not produce his autographed bill on demand.

**short-spo|ken** (shôrt′spō′kən), *adj.* **1** speaking in a short or brief manner; concise. **2** curt of speech or manner; abrupt.

**short-sta|ple** (shôrt′stā′pəl), *adj.* (of cotton or other fiber) having the fiber short.

**short|stop** (shôrt′stop′), *n.* **1** a baseball player stationed between second base and third base. **2** an acid solution used to halt the developing process in photography; stop bath.

**short story**, a prose story which usually describes a single main event, has a limited number of characters, and is much shorter than a novel: [*He*] *is a novelist, and in short stories he tends to take an episode and fine it down* (Punch). **–short′-sto′ry**, *adj.*

**short subject**, a short motion picture running from 7 to 20 minutes between feature films. Cartoons, newsreels, and travelogues are short subjects.

**short sweetening**, *U.S. Dialect.* sugar.

**short-swing** (shôrt′swing′), *adj. U.S. Finance.* based on or covering a six-month or shorter period in which a transaction is concluded: *short-swing trading.*

**short-tailed hawk** (shôrt′tāld′), a small hawk of light and dark color phases, found from Florida and Mexico south to Argentina.

**short-tailed shrew**, a large, very common shrew found throughout the eastern half of the United States and into southern Canada; blarina.

**short-tailed weasel**, a brown weasel of North America with white feet, throat, and belly. In winter it turns white except for a black tip on the tail.

**short-tem|pered** (shôrt′tem′pərd), *adj.* easily made angry; quick-tempered.

**short-term** (shôrt′tėrm′), *adj.* **1** for a short period: *short-term plans, short-term training.* **2** falling due in a short time: *a short-term loan, short-term interest.*

---

**Pronunciation Key:** hat, āge, cãre, fär; let, ēqual, tėrm; it, īce; hot, ōpen, ôrder; oil, out; cup, pu̇t, rüle; child; long; thin; ᴛʜen; zh, measure; ə represents **a** in about, **e** in taken, **i** in pencil, **o** in lemon, **u** in circus.

**short-time** (shôrt′tīm′), *adj.* of or for a short time; temporary: *short-time housing.*
**short-tim|er** (shôrt′tī′mər), *n.* a person who serves or works for a short time: *Soldiers near the end of their enlistment or draft period describe themselves as short-timers, an old prison term* (David Boroff).
**short-toed eagle** (shôrt′tōd′), a hawk of Europe, Asia, and Africa that lives mainly on snakes, hunting for them by hovering over forest and grassland hillsides.
**short ton**, 2,000 pounds avoirdupois or 907.18 kilograms; net ton.
**short-waist|ed** (shôrt′wās′tid), *adj.* having a short waist; short from neck to waistline.
**short wave**, a radio wave having a wave length of 100 meters or less. Short waves range from high-frequency to superhigh-frequency bands and are used to broadcast to foreign countries, in frequency-modulation broadcasting, in television programs, and for transoceanic telephone calls and other long-distance communications.
**short-wave** or **short|wave** (shôrt′wāv′), *n., v.,* **-waved, -wav|ing,** *adj.* —*n.* = short wave.
—*v.t., v.i.* to transmit by short waves.
—*adj.* of or using short waves: *short-wave radio.*
**short|weight** or **short-weight** (shôrt′wāt′), *n., v.* —*n.* a weight that is short of the weight charged for by the seller: ... *the evil perpetrated by some stores of defrauding the public by short-weights in items they prepackage for sale* (New York Times).
—*v.t., v.i.* to defraud by giving shortweight: *Ship's pursers ... short-weighted ... rancid salt pork* (Maclean's).
**short-wind|ed** (shôrt′win′did), *adj.* getting out of breath very easily or too quickly; having difficulty in breathing. —**short′-wind′ed|ness**, *n.*
**short|y** (shôr′tē), *n., pl.* **-ties**, *adj.* = shortie.
**Sho|sho|ne** (shō shō′nē), *n., pl.* **-nes** or **-ne**, *adj.* —*n.* **1** a member of a tribe of North American Indians originally ranging from Wyoming to California and now found chiefly in Wyoming, Idaho, and Nevada. **2** the Shoshonean language of this tribe.
—*adj.* of or having to do with this tribe or language. Also, **Shoshoni, Shoshonee.**
**Sho|sho|ne|an** (shō shō′nē ən), *adj.* belonging to or constituting a widely extended linguistic stock of North American Indians of the western United States including the Shoshone, Comanche, Ute, Hopi, and other tribes.
**Sho|sho|nee** (shō shō′nē), *n., pl.* **-nees** or **-nee**, *adj.* = Shoshone.
**Sho|sho|ni** (shō shō′nē), *n., pl.* **-nis** or **-ni**, *adj.* = Shoshone.
**shot**[1] (shot), *n., pl.* **shots** or (*for 2*) **shot** or **shots**, *v.,* **shot|ted, shot|ting.** —*n.* **1a** the discharge as of a gun, cannon, or bow: *to fire a shot. He heard two shots.* **b** the act of shooting: ... *taken without shot or slaughter* (Charles Kingsley). **2** what is discharged in shooting: **a** tiny balls of lead or steel; bullets: *Storm'd at with shot and shell* (Tennyson). **b** a single ball of lead or steel for a gun or cannon. **c** tiny balls or pellets of lead, of which a number are combined in one charge, used chiefly in shotguns. **d** one such ball or pellet. **3a** an attempt to hit by shooting: *That was a good shot, and it hit the mark.* **b** *Figurative.* a remark aimed at some person or thing: *The speaker ... presently delivered a shot which went home, and silence and attention resulted* (Mark Twain). *Porter's article about Utica's political aberration ... contains one omission and two cheap shots which call for a response* (New York Times). **4a** the distance a weapon can shoot, or to which a missile will go; range: *We were within rifle shot of the fort.* **b** the range or reach of anything like a shot: *Beyond the shot of tyranny* (Shelley). *Out of the shot and danger of desire* (Shakespeare). **5** a person who shoots, especially with a firearm: *He is a good shot.* **SYN**: marksman. **6** an aimed stroke or throw, or a scoring attempt in billiards, hockey, or various other games. **7** anything like a shot; something emitted, cast, launched or set off, such as a nuclear bomb or spacecraft: *After the fourteenth shot, no more Nevada tests are contemplated* (New York Times). **8** *Informal.* **a** a dose of a drug in the form of an injection: *a typhoid shot. A polio shot is an injection of vaccine to protect against getting polio.* **b** a dose, as of medicine. **9** *Informal.* one drink, usually a jigger, of alcoholic liquor: *a shot of whiskey.* **10a** an attempt or try: *to take a shot at the job.* **b** a random guess. **SYN**: conjecture. **c** a bet; chance: *A 34-1 shot named Sky Clipper beat Bally Ache in a photo finish* (New Yorker). **11a** a picture taken with a camera; photograph; snapshot: *Last week, a visitor ... took a shot of a squirrel, a close-up with a tiny Japanese camera* (New Yorker). **b** the motion-picture or television record of a scene: *For the final shot [the director] said: "I want you with your eyes staring open as ... your dead hand beckons the man"* (Newsweek). **c** the taking of a picture. **12** a heavy metal ball, usually weighing 16 pounds, used in the shot-put. **13** in mining: **a** a blast. **b** the charge of powder sufficient for a blast. **14** an amount due or to be paid, especially at a tavern, or one's share in such payment.
—*v.t.* **1** to load with shot; furnish with shot: *Her [a ship's] shotted guns were discharging* (Scott). **2** to weigh by attaching a shot or shots. **3** to attempt; try.
**call the shots** (or **one's shot**), *Informal.* **a** to control the proceedings or outcome; direct; manage: *He let the Republicans call the shots, but when the hearings opened ... he put the responsibility on their shoulders* (Atlantic). **b** to state what will happen or is happening: *Southern editors who ... call their shots as they see them* (Time).
**like a shot**, at once; with great rapidity: *If anybody can suggest to me anything else that I can do—I'll do it like a shot* (Arnold Bennett).
**not by a long shot**. See under **long shot**.
**put the shot**, to send a heavy metal ball as far as one can with one push: *to put the shot in an athletic contest.*
**shot in the arm**, *Informal.* something that stimulates or revives; incentive; spur: *As a shot in the arm for industry, there could be generous investment allowances* (Sunday Times).
**shot in the dark**, *Informal.* a guess based upon little or no evidence; wild guess: *[He] really had no facts of any substance. ... His innuendos about "covering up" were mere shots in the dark* (Blair Fraser).
**stand shot**, to meet the expense; pay the bill: *Are you going to stand shot to all this good liquor?* (Scott).
[Old English *sceot* < *sceōtan* shoot]
**shot**[2] (shot), *v., adj.* —*v.* the past tense and past participle of **shoot**: *Many years ago he shot a rival and was himself shot in revenge.*
—*adj.* **1a** woven or dyed so as to show a play of colors: *blue silk shot with gold.* **b** variable, as a color; changeable. **2** that has grown or sprouted, as a stalk or blade. **3** *Slang, Figurative.* that has been used up, worn out, or ruined: *The game was shot for the Brooks in the third [inning]* (New York Times).
**shot through with**, full of: *a composition shot through with errors, speeches shot through with wit. It was an immense ... rabbit warren shot through with a network of narrow paths* (New Yorker).
**shot borer**, a small beetle which bores many minute holes in trees; pin borer.
**shot cartridge**, a cartridge containing shot instead of a bullet.
**shote** (shōt), *n.* **1** a young weaned pig; shoat. **2** *Dialect.* a thriftless, worthless person.
**shot|fire** (shot′fīr′), *v.i.,* **-fired, -fir|ing.** *Mining.* to fire a blasting charge: *As detonator and high-explosive are embedded in the borehole, shotfiring can be done entirely by electrical means* (New Scientist).
**shot|fir|er** (shot′fīr′ər), *n.* a miner who fires blasting charges.
**shot glass**, = jigger.
**shot|gun** (shot′gun′), *n., adj., v.,* **-gunned, -gun|ning.** —*n.* a gun with no grooves in its barrel, for firing cartridges filled with bird shot or buckshot. It is used for killing birds and small mammals. See picture under **rifle**[1].
—*adj.* **1** *Informal.* random; haphazard; hit-or-miss: *shotgun recommendations. The Virgin Lands campaign was a shotgun attempt to grow wheat on the cheap* (Time). **2** *U.S.* long; boxlike: *a shotgun house, building, or cabin. The typical "shotgun" shack is made of unpainted board* (New York Times).
—*v.t.* **1** to shoot with a shotgun: (*Figurative.*) *The destroyer hunted back and forth, shotgunning depth charges left and right* (Time). **2** *U.S. Informal.* to force, as into a shotgun marriage: *We distinguish between grooms who marry brides of their own choice and those who are shotgunned into marriage* (Scientific American).
**ride shotgun**, **a** to ride on a vehicle as an armed guard or escort: *I saw an Australian soldier and I asked him to jump in with me and ride shotgun until we got to the American military police* (Frank Palmos). **b** *Slang.* to accompany as a passenger in a vehicle, especially in a car or truck: *The driver picked up a hitchhiker who rode shotgun clear across the country.*
[American English]
**shotgun marriage** or **wedding**, *U.S. Informal.* a forced marriage or wedding, as to save honor or reputation.
**shotgun microphone**, a microphone that can pick up and amplify very faint sounds.
**shot hole**, **1** a hole made by a gunshot. **2** *Mining.* a hole drilled in rock to insert an explosive charge.
**shot metal**, an impure form of lead containing two percent of arsenic, used for making shot for cartridges.
**shot-proof** (shot′prüf′), *adj.* proof against shot: *An enormous vessel, with shot-proof bulwarks* (John L. Motley).
✱**shot-put** (shot′pu̇t′), *n.* an athletic contest in which a person sends a heavy metal ball through the air as far as he can with one push.

✱**shot-put**

**shot-put|ter** (shot′pu̇t′ər), *n.* a person who puts the shot in athletic contests.
**shott** (shot), *n.* a shallow, saline lake or marsh in northern Africa, usually dry in the summer and filled with deposits of salt, gypsum, and sand. Also, **chott.** [< Arabic *shaṭṭ*]
**shot|ten** (shot′ən), *adj.* **1** that has recently spawned: *a shotten herring.* **2** *Figurative.* exhausted; worthless. [apparently Old English *sceoten,* past participle of *scēotan* shoot]
**shot tower**, a high tower for making small shot by dropping molten lead from the top into water at the bottom.
**should** (shu̇d; *unstressed* shəd), *v., past tense of* **shall.** **1** See **shall** for ordinary uses. **2 Should** has special uses as an auxiliary: **a** to express duty, obligation, or propriety: *You should try to make fewer mistakes. Conquest, lady, should soften the heart* (Scott). **b** to make statements, requests, or the like less direct or blunt: *I should not call her beautiful.* **c** to express uncertainty: *If it should rain, I will not go. If I should win the prize, how happy I would be.* **d** to make statements about something that might have happened but did not: *I should have gone if you had asked me.* **e** to express a condition or reason for something: *He was pardoned on the condition that he should leave the country.* **f** to imply that something is unreasonable, unbelievable, or unjustifiable (in questions introduced by *why*): *Why should you think that I did not like the book?* [Old English *sceolde*]
► The frequent misspelling **should of** for *should have* arises out of the fact that *have* and *of,* when completely unstressed, are pronounced identically.
**shoul|der** (shōl′dər), *n., v.* —*n.* **1** the part of the body to which an arm, foreleg, or wing is attached. **2** the joint by which the arm or the foreleg is connected to the trunk. **3** the part of a garment that covers a shoulder. **4** the cut of meat consisting of the upper foreleg and its adjoining parts of a slaughtered animal. **5** something that sticks out like a shoulder: *the shoulder of a hill.* **6** the edge of a road, often unpaved: *Don't drive on the shoulder of the road.* **7** *Printing.* the flat surface on a type extending beyond the base of the letter. **8** (in fortification) the angle of a bastion included between the face and a flank. **9** *Surfing Slang.* the calm portion of a wave breaking on the beach: *"You want a green wave with a good shoulder," says a stripling to me* (Sunday Times).
—*v.t.* **1** to take upon or support with the shoulder or shoulders: *to shoulder a tray. Caleb ... shouldered the round box and took a hurried leave* (Dickens). **2** *Figurative.* to bear (a burden or blame); assume (responsibility, expense, or the like): *He shouldered the responsibility of sending his nephew to college.* **3** to push or thrust with the shoulder, especially energetically or with violence: *to shoulder someone aside. He shouldered his way through the crowd.* (*Figurative.*) *Custom and prejudice ... shouldering aside the meek and modest truth* (William Cowper). **4** to furnish with one or more shoulderlike parts or projections.
—*v.i.* to push with the shoulders: *to shoulder through a crowd.*
**put one's shoulder to the wheel**, to set to work vigorously; make a great effort: *Instead of putting their shoulders to the wheel, the lazy workers stood idling in the shop.*
**rub shoulders with**, to mingle with; rub elbows

with: *Never have we rubbed shoulders with as many ranking celebrities* (Vladimir Nabokov).
**shoulder arms**. See under **arms**.
**shoulders, a** the two shoulders and the upper part of the back, where burdens are sometimes carried: *The man carried a trunk on his shoulders.* **b** *Figurative.* the strength to support burdens; sustaining power: *to take the work or blame on one's own shoulders.*
**shoulder to shoulder, a** side by side; together: *... that band of heroes who died shoulder to shoulder* (Michael Donovan). **b** *Figurative.* with united effort: *We are ... strongest when we are labouring shoulder to shoulder for some common object* (Augustus Jessopp).
**square one's shoulders**, to bring the shoulders smartly back, so as to be at right angles with the vertical axis of the body: *The troops squared their shoulders and stood at attention while the general reviewed them.*
**straight from the shoulder, a** with the fist brought to the shoulder and then swiftly sent forward: *No! Give me a chap that hits straight from the shoulder* (Charles Reade). **b** *Figurative.* frankly; directly: *The first speaker was evasive, but the second spoke straight from the shoulder about the college's financial difficulties.*
**turn** (or **give**) **a cold shoulder (to)**. See under **cold shoulder**.
[Old English *sculdor*] — **shoul'der|like'**, *adj.*

**shoulder bag**, a handbag with a long strap worn over the shoulder.

**shoulder belt**, **1** *Military.* a belt worn over the shoulder and across the breast. **2** = shoulder harness (def. 1).

**shoulder blade**, the flat, triangular bone of either shoulder, in the upper back; scapula. See picture under **skeleton**.

**shoulder block**, *Nautical.* a block with a projection on the shell to prevent the rope that is rove through it from becoming jammed.

**shoulder board**, a stiff cloth piece bearing insignia of rank, worn on each shoulder of an officer's uniform: *... a grey, Soviet-style topcoat with red lapels and huge shoulder boards* (Time).

**shoulder bone**, **1** = humerus. **2** = shoulder blade.

**shoulder brace**, an appliance for correcting or preventing round shoulders.

**-shouldered**, *combining form.* having ___ shoulders: *Round-shouldered = having round shoulders.*

**shoulder harness**, **1** an anchored strap inside an automobile, to be worn across the shoulder and chest together with a seat belt: *Padded roll bars and shoulder harnesses are standard on the* [*car*] (Time). **2** a harness strapped to a person's shoulders for carrying a young child or infant: *... offering shoulder harnesses to mothers so that they can carry their babies with them while they shop* (London Times).

**shoul|der-high** (shōl'dər hī'), *adj., adv.* so high as to reach the shoulders.

**shoul|der-hit|ter** (shōl'dər hit'ər), *n. U.S. Informal.* a person who hits from the shoulder; bully.

**shoulder knot**, a knot of ribbon or lace worn on the shoulder, especially by fashionable men in the 1600's and 1700's.

**shoulder loop**, a narrow strap of cloth extending on each shoulder of a uniform coat from the sleeve to the collar, for wearing insignia of rank.

**shoulder pad**, **1** a padded piece sewn inside the shoulder of a jacket or coat to give it form. **2** a piece of equipment worn under the jersey to protect the shoulders and collarbone in football and certain other sports.

**shoulder patch**, a cloth insigne worn on the upper sleeve of a uniform or other garment, just below the shoulder.

**shoulder piece**, = shoulder strap.

**shoulder rest**, a device placed between the back of a violin and the player's shoulder to prevent the instrument from slipping off.

**shoul|ders** (shōl'dərz), *n.pl.* See under **shoulder**.

**shoulder screw**, an external screw having a shoulder which limits the distance to which it can be screwed in.

**shoulder steak**, a steak of beef cut from the forequarter through the shoulder.

**shoulder strap**, **1** a strap (usually one of a pair) worn over the shoulder to hold a garment up. **2a** an ornamental strip fastened on the shoulder of an officer's uniform to show rank. **b** any one of various strips of fabric sewn on the shoulders as of a shirt or coat, to attach insignia of rank.

**should|est** (shůd'əst), *v. Archaic.* shouldst.

**should|na** (shůd'nə), *Scottish.* should not.

**should|n't** (shůd'ənt), should not.

**shouldst** (shůdst), *v. Archaic.* second person singular of **should**. "Thou shouldst" means "you should."

**shout** (shout), *v., n.* — *v.i.* **1** to call or cry loudly and vigorously: *The drowning boy shouted for help.* **SYN**: See syn. under **cry**. **2** to talk or laugh very loudly: *The crowd shouted with laughter.* **3** (in Australia) to treat, especially to a drink.
— *v.t.* **1** to express by a shout or shouts; utter (something) by shouting: *Somebody shouted: "Fire!" The crowd shouted its approval.* **2** (in Australia) to treat to (a drink or other refreshment).
— *n.* **1** a loud, vigorous call or cry: *Shouts of joy rang through the halls.* **2** a loud outburst of laughter. **3** in Australia: **a** a free drink for everyone present. **b** a turn in buying free drinks for everyone present.
**shout down**, to silence, as by very loud talk or shouts of disapproval: *When he got up to speak at the meeting, his opponents shouted him down.*
[Middle English *shout;* origin uncertain. Perhaps ultimately related to **scout**[2].] — **shout'er**, *n.*

**shout|ing** (shou'ting), *n., adj.* — *n.* uproar; clamor: *Dobbin ... kept up a great shouting* (Thackeray).
— *adj.* that shouts; clamorous; vociferous: *shouting spectators.* (*Figurative.*) *The shouting seas drive by* (Rudyard Kipling).
**all over but the shouting**, nearly completed, finished, or decided, with the result appearing certain: *Canadians who hoped that the various Medicare battles were all over but the shouting had better reach for their tranquilizers* (Jeff Holmes). — **shout'ing|ly**, *adv.*

**shouting distance**, a short distance; a stone's throw: *The beach is within shouting distance of our cabin.*

**shouting match**, a loud argument; noisy quarrel: *... only if there is a real dialogue and not a shouting match that the real issues can be brought out* (London Times).

**shove** (shuv), *v.,* **shoved, shov|ing**, *n.* — *v.t.* **1** to move (something) forward or along by the application of force from behind; push: *We shoved the bookcase into place.* **SYN**: thrust. See syn. under **push**. **2** to push roughly or rudely against; jostle (a person): *The bully shoved me out of the room.* **3a** to put or thrust (carelessly or hastily) into a place or receptacle. **b** to thrust (aside or away). — *v.i.* **1** to push; apply force against something in order to move it. **2** to push or jostle in a crowd; make one's way by jostling or elbowing.
— *n.* **1** an act of shoving; push: *He gave the boat a shove which sent it far out into the water. A minor shove by the government from time to time ...* (Edmond Taylor). **2** a rough or careless push or thrust: *Someone in the crowd gave me a shove that sent me flying.*
**shove off, a** to push a boat away from the shore; row away: *Into the boat he sprang, and in haste shoved off to his vessel* (Longfellow). **b** *Slang, Figurative.* to leave a place; start on one's way: *The older boys told him to shove off and find some friends his own age.*
[Old English *scūfan*]

**shove-half|pen|ny** or **shove-ha'pen|ny** (shuv'hā'pə nē, -hāp'nē), *n. British.* **1** shuffleboard. **2** a gambling game similar to shuffleboard.

**shov|el** (shuv'əl), *n., v.,* **-eled, -el|ing** or (*especially British*) **-elled, -el|ling**. — *n.* **1** a tool with a broad blade or scoop attached to a handle, used to lift and throw loose matter: *a coal shovel, a snow shovel.* **2** = shovelful. **3** = shovel hat.
— *v.t.* **1a** to lift and throw with a shovel: *to shovel snow from the sidewalk. The men shoveled the sand into a cart.* **b** *Figurative: The hungry man shoveled the food into his mouth.* **2** to make with a shovel: *They shoveled a path through the snow.* — *v.i.* to use a shovel.
[Old English *scofl.* See related etym. at **shuffle, scuffle**.] — **shov'el|like'**, *adj.*

**shov|el|bill** (shuv'əl bil'), *n.* = shoveler (def. 2).

**shov|el|board** (shuv'əl bôrd', -bōrd'), *n.* = shuffleboard.

**shov|el|er** (shuv'ə lər, shuv'lər), *n.* **1** a person or thing that shovels. **2** a kind of freshwater duck with a broad, flat bill, especially a species found widely in the Northern Hemisphere.

**shov|el|fish** (shuv'əl fish'), *n., pl.* **-fish|es** or (*collectively*) **-fish**. = shovelhead.

**shov|el|ful** (shuv'əl fůl), *n., pl.* **-fuls**. as much as a shovel can hold.

***shovel hat**

***shovel hat**, a hat with a broad brim turned up at the sides and projecting with shovellike curves in front and behind. Some clergymen of the Church of England formerly wore shovel hats.

**shov|el|head** (shuv'əl hed'), *n.* **1** a shark with a flattish head, similar and related to the hammerhead. **2** = shovel-nosed sturgeon.

**shov|el-head|ed** (shuv'əl hed'id), *adj.* having a broad, flat snout, like a shovel.

**shov|el|ler** (shuv'ə lər, shuv'lər), *n. Especially British.* shoveler.

**shov|el|nose** (shuv'əl nōz'), *n.* **1** any animal with the head or part of the head shaped like a shovel. **2** = hammerhead shark. **3** = shovel-nosed sturgeon.

**shov|el-nosed** (shuv'əl nōzd'), *adj.* having a wide, flat snout or beak: *a shovel-nosed snake.*

**shovel-nosed sturgeon**, a small sturgeon of the Mississippi valley, that has a wide, blunt snout.

**shovel plow**, a plow with a simple triangular blade, used for cultivating the ground between growing crops.

**shov|el-tusk|er** (shuv'əl tus'kər), *n.* a species of mastodon with great, flat lower tusks, sometimes broadening to a width of two feet.

**shov|el|weed** (shuv'əl wēd'), *n.* = shepherd's-purse. [from its shovel-shaped pods]

**shov|er** (shuv'ər), *n.* a person or thing that shoves.

**show** (shō), *v.,* **showed, shown** or **showed, show|ing**, *n., adj.* — *v.t.* **1a** to let be seen; put in sight; display: *The little girl showed her dolls to us. The dog showed his teeth.* **b** to exhibit (as animals or flowers) publicly: *to show one's dog.* **c** to display (as goods or wares) for sale or exhibition: *to show the newest fashions.* **2** to reveal; manifest; disclose: *to show great energy, to show one's good manners, to show signs of fear. He showed himself a generous man by giving to charity. The tendency was one which showed itself in various ... directions* (James Bryce). **3** to have visibly or in an exposed position: *a house showing signs of neglect, a dress showing coffee stains.* **4** to point out: *to show someone the sights of a town. The boy showed us the way to town.* **5** to guide or conduct; direct; usher: *to show someone to his room. Show him out.* **6** *Figurative.* **a** to make known, evident, or clear; explain: *Only time will show the results of the experiment.* **b** to make clear to; explain to: *Show us how to do the problem.* **7** *Figurative.* **a** to prove or demonstrate (as a fact or statement): *He showed that it was true. Many arguments are used to show that motion is the source of life* (Benjamin Jowett). **b** (of a thing) to be a proof, evidence, sign, or indication of: *All of it goes to show how little we know of each other* (Sir Arthur Helps). **8** to grant; give: *to show mercy, to show favor, to show gratitude to a friend.* **9** (of a list, record, recording instrument) to indicate: *a watch showing twelve o'clock.* **10** *Especially Law.* **a** to state, allege, or plead (as a cause or reason). **b** to produce (as a document) for inspection.
— *v.i.* **1** to be in sight; appear; be seen: *The hole in your sock shows above your shoe. Anger showed in his face.* **2** to present an appearance; make a display: *Her imperfect and unequal gait, which showed to peculiar disadvantage* (Scott). **3** to be evident or noticeable: *a stain that shows.* **4** *Informal.* to appear in or present a theatrical performance: *We are showing at the Orpheum.* **5** *Sports.* **a** to finish third in a race (contrasted with *win* and *place*). **b** to finish among the first three in a race.
— *n.* **1** a display; sight; spectacle: *The jewels made a fine show.* **2** a display for effect; ostentatious display; parade; pomp: *He made a show of learning to impress us.* **3** any kind of public exhibition or display, especially a temporary one: *an art show, a horse show. We are going to the flower show and to the automobile show.* **4** a play, motion picture, television program, or similar entertainment, or a performance of one of these: *We saw a good show on television last night. The new show is a western. The late show starts at 11:00.* **5** a showing: *The club voted by a show of hands.* **6** an appearance: *a bed which made a poor show of comfort. There is some show of truth in her excuse.* **7** *Figurative.* a trace; indication, as of the presence of metal in a mine or of oil in a well. **8** *Figurative.* a false appearance; pretense: *He hid his treachery by a show of friendship.* **SYN**: pretext. **9** an object of scorn; something odd; queer sight: *Don't make a show of yourself.* **10** a demonstration or display of military strength or of intention to take severe measures. **11** *Informal.* a chance; opportunity: *He hasn't a ghost of a show.* **12** *Sports.* third place,

**Pronunciation Key:** hat, āge, cãre, fär; let, ēqual, tėrm; it, īce; hot, ōpen, ôrder; oil, out; cup, půt, rüle; child; long; thin; ᴛʜen; zh, measure; ə represents **a** in about, **e** in taken, **i** in pencil, **o** in lemon, **u** in circus.

as in a horse race: *win, place, and show.*
—*adj.* **1** fitted or used for show or display: *a show dog.* **2** of or having to do with a theatrical show or shows. Also, *especially British or Archaic,* **shew.**
**for show**, for effect; to attract attention: *A fine pair of organs, which I could not find they made use of in divine service, ... but only for show* (John Evelyn).
**run the show**, *Informal.* to take complete charge of an operation or situation; assume control over something: *He is running the whole show.*
**show off, a** to act or talk for show; make a display of: *It is true that many of these boys try to show off and are irresponsible* (New York Times). **b** to display; exhibit: *Most girls like to show off fine clothes. Instead of hiring models to show off the new uniforms, Amtrak used its own personnel* (Saturday Review).
**show one's colors**. See under **color**.
**show one's face**. See under **face**.
**show one's hand**. See under **hand**.
**show the door**. See under **door**.
**show up, a** to hold up for ridicule or contempt; expose: *The pompous student was shown up by the professor.* **b** to stand out; be or become prominent: *[His face] showed up in the illumination of the dashboard, wide, pasty, untrustworthy* (Graham Greene). **c** to put in an appearance; turn up (at an appointed time or place): *The golfer showed up one hour late for his match.*
**stand a show**, *Informal.* to stand a chance; have a favorable prospect: *He stood no show of securing the nomination for the legislature* (Lisbon, North Dakota, Star).
**steal the show, a** to attract the most attention, applause, or favor: *The Stravinsky [piece] stole the show, as it always has* (Howard Klein). **b** to take away, as credit or applause (from someone): *Two relatively unknown American designers have stolen the show from older and better-established names* (Barbara Plumb).
[Old English *scēawian* look at]
—*Syn. n.* **1, 2, 3 Show, display** mean an offering or exhibiting to view or notice. **Show** applies to anything exposed to public view, and sometimes has unfavorable connotations: *The show at the planetarium is well worth seeing. That was a disgraceful show of temper.* **Display** applied particularly to something carefully arranged so as to call attention to its fineness, beauty, strength, or other admirable qualities: *That florist has the most beautiful displays in the city.*

**show|a|ble** (shō′ə bəl), *adj.* that can be shown.
**show and tell**, *U.S.* a period or activity in primary school in which the children discuss objects they have brought into the classroom.
**show bill**, a poster, placard, or the like, advertising a show.
**show biz**, *Slang.* show business: *... has brought the flair of show biz to the often-dull realm of televised talks and public affairs* (Maclean's).
**show|boat** (shō′bōt′), *n., v.* —*n.* **1** a steamboat with a theater for plays, especially one traveling on a river. Showboats carry their own actors and make frequent stops to give performances. *The showboat had a band of sixteen pieces, the majority of them trombones* (New Yorker). **2** *U.S. Slang.* a person who shows off or is shown off: *National chairmen rarely serve as showboats, and when a party controls the White House, its public image lives there* (Time).
—*v.i., v.t. U.S. Slang.* to show off; make a display (of): *They denounced him because he didn't showboat when Junior Stephens hit a home run* (Birmingham News). *The 98-year-old ballet is traditionally noted for ... the opportunity it affords a ballerina to showboat her versatility* (Time).
[American English < *show* + *boat*]
**show box**, a box in which objects of interest or curiosity are exhibited; a box containing a peep show.
**show|bread** (shō′bred′), *n.* = shewbread.
**show business**, the industry or world of entertainment or of professional entertainers: *There's no business like show business* (Irving Berlin).
—**show′-busi′ness**, *adj.*
**show|case** (shō′kās′), *n., v.,* **-cased, -cas|ing.**
—*n.* **1** a glass case in which to display and protect articles, as in a store or museum. **2** *Figurative: An editorial page column has been developed as a showcase for good writing on any subject* (Harper's).
—*v.t. Informal.* to display or present as if in a showcase: *This week's [program] ... showcased the first of five plays on Lincoln* (Newsweek).
**show cause order**, an order of court requiring a person to present a reason why a judgment should not be executed or confirmed.
**show|down** (shō′doun′), *n. Informal.* **1** a forced disclosure, as of facts, purposes, or methods, bringing a conflict, dispute, or the like to a decisive outcome: *to have a showdown with one's employer, to force a showdown with one's allies.* **2** the displaying of the hands of the players at the end of a round in card games, especially in poker, by which the winner of the round is revealed. [American English < *show* + *down*]
**show|er¹** (shou′ər), *n., v.* —*n.* **1a** a short fall of rain: *a hard shower.* **b** a short fall of moisture in any form: *Snow showers are predicted.* **2** *Figurative: a shower of tears, a shower of sparks from an engine.* **3** a party for giving presents to a woman about to be married or have a baby, or on some other special occasion, especially presents of a similar kind: *a kitchen shower, a linen shower.* **4a** a bath in which water pours down on the body from above in small jets: *to take a shower.* **b** an apparatus for producing such a bath: *to install a shower.* **c** an enclosure containing such an apparatus: *a tiled shower.*
—*v.i.* **1** to rain for a short time. **2** to come in a shower: (*Figurative.*) *The withered leaves came showering down* (Dickens). **3** to take a bath in which water pours on the body from above in small jets.
—*v.t.* **1** to wet with a shower; spray; sprinkle. **2a** *Figurative.* to send in a shower or showers; pour down: *to shower leaflets on a city. The women, from the roofs and windows, showered stones on the heads of the soldiers* (Edward Gibbon). **b** *Figurative.* to heap lavishly upon: *Her rich aunt showered gifts upon her.* **c** *U.S.* to hold a shower for: *to shower a bride.*
**send to the showers**, *U.S. Informal.* to remove (a ballplayer, especially a pitcher) from a game: *Sparked by another ... home run, the Pirates sent McNally to the showers in the fifth inning* (Time).
[Old English *scūr*]
**show|er²** (shō′ər), *n.* **1** a person who shows, points out, or exhibits. **2** an animal that shows well or makes a (good or bad) display of its qualities: *He is a smart shower and a well-made dog* (Kennel Gazette). [< *show* + *-er¹*]
**shower bath**, **1** a bath in which water pours on the body from an overhead nozzle in small jets. **2** the apparatus for such a bath.
**shower cap**, a rubber or plastic cap worn to keep the hair dry when taking a shower.
**show|er|i|ness** (shou′ər ē nis), *n.* the state of being showery.
**show|er-proof** (shou′ər prüf′), *adj. British.* water repellent, as a garment or fabric.
**shower stall**, = stall shower.
**show|er|y** (shou′ər ē), *adj.* **1** raining or falling in showers. **2** having many showers: *a showery summer afternoon* (Henry Morley). **3** like a shower.
**show|folk** (shō′fōk′), *n.pl.* people in show business; entertainers as a group.
**show|girl** (shō′gėrl′), *n.* = chorus girl.
**show|ground** (shō′ground′), *n.* an area set aside for exhibitions: *The showground, extending over 166 acres, is the largest that the Royal Agricultural Society has ever laid out* (London Times).
**show|i|ly** (shō′ə lē), *adv.* in a showy manner; with display.
**show|i|ness** (shō′ē nis), *n.* the quality of being showy; display; pompousness.
**show|ing** (shō′ing), *n.* **1** a show; display; exhibition: *a current showing of paintings. Out they [the programs] go to 150 television stations for immediate showing* (Newsweek). **2** *Especially U.S.* **a** manner of appearance or performance: *to make a good showing.* **b** a statement or presentation of figures, accounts, or the like: *He is wrong by his own showing.*
**show jumper**, a horse trained for and used in show jumping.
**show jumping**, an exhibition of skill in riding a horse over or between various hurdles: *Show jumping, as opposed to steeple-chasing, is entirely artificial* (London Times).
**show|man** (shō′mən), *n., pl.* **-men. 1** a man who manages a show. **2** a person skilled in presenting things in a dramatic and exciting way.
**show|man|ly** (shō′mən lē), *adj.,* **-li|er, -li|est.** like that of a showman; suitable for a showman: *The famous blues are played and sung in showmanly style* (Time).
**show|man|ship** (shō′mən ship), *n.* the skill or practice of a showman.
**show-me** (shō′mē′), *adj. U.S. Informal.* demanding demonstration; believing only on clear evidence: *a show-me attitude. The full house was in a show-me mood* (Time).
**Show Me State**, a nickname for Missouri.
**shown** (shōn), *v.* a past participle of **show**: *The clerk has shown the lady many hats. We were shown many tricks.*
**show-off** (shō′ôf′, -of′), *n.* **1** *Informal.* a person who shows off by always calling attention to himself: *He is a very good baseball player, but he's a terrible show-off. ... under the leader's or the group's influence the show-off or aggressive youngster often learns to channel his tendencies toward the common goal* (Sidonie M. Gruenberg). **2** the act of showing off.
**show|piece** (shō′pēs′), *n.* anything displayed as an outstanding example of its kind.
**show|place** (shō′plās′), *n.* a place that attracts visitors, as for its beauty or interest.
**show|room** (shō′rüm′, -rům′), *n.* a room used for the display of goods or merchandise, often of items that are samples of what may be bought, but not offered for sale themselves.
**show|stop|per** (shō′stop′ər), *n.* an act or performer so outstanding that the audience's spontaneous response or applause delays the continuation of the show: *A lampoon on infant prodigies was a showstopper* (Wall Street Journal).
**show|time** (shō′tīm′), *n.* the time at which a show is scheduled to begin.
**show trial**, a public trial conducted solely for purposes of propaganda, especially in a totalitarian state: *... a show trial that featured abject confessions in old Stalinist tradition* (Time).
**show window**, a window in the front of a store, where things are shown for sale; shopwindow.
**show|y** (shō′ē), *adj.,* **show|i|er, show|i|est. 1** making a display; likely to attract attention; striking; conspicuous: *A peony is a showy flower. She's showier and better-looking than they are* (Booth Tarkington). **SYN:** See syn. under **gaudy. 2** too bright and gay to be in good taste: *a showy red dress.* **SYN:** garish. **3** ostentatious: *They want to do vulgar, showy things* (H. G. Wells).
**showy goldenrod**, a goldenrod with hairy branches and a thick stem, found in open woods and prairies of the eastern and Midwestern United States.
**showy lady's-slipper**, an American orchid having large white flowers and a lip tinged with brilliant pinkish purple. It is the state flower of Minnesota.
**showy orchis**, a common North American species of orchid bearing a spike of pink-purple flowers with a white lip.
**sho|yu** (shō′yü), *n.* = soy (def. 1). [< Japanese *shōyu* < Chinese (Peking) *chiang-yu*]
**s. hp.**, shaft horsepower.
**shpt.**, shipment.
**shr.**, share or shares.
**shrad|dha** (shrä′də), *n.* = sradha.
**shrank** (shrangk), *v.* a past tense of **shrink**: *The shirt shrank in the wash.*
**shrap|nel** (shrap′nəl), *n.* **1** an artillery shell filled with pellets and powder, set to explode in the air and scatter pellets or shell fragments over a wide area. **2** such shells collectively: *to fire a barrage of shrapnel.* **3** one or more of the pellets or fragments scattered by the explosion of such a shell: *to be wounded by shrapnel.* [< Henry *Shrapnel*, 1761-1842, a British army officer, who invented it]
**shred** (shred), *n., v.,* **shred|ded** or **shred, shred|ding.** —*n.* **1** a very small piece torn off or cut off; very narrow strip; scrap: *The wind tore the sail to shreds.* **2** *Figurative.* a fragment; particle; bit: *There's not a shred of evidence that the missing papers were stolen.* **SYN:** iota, whit.
—*v.t.* to tear or cut into small pieces; reduce to shreds: *Paper is often shredded for use in packing dishes and the like.*
—*v.i.* to be reduced to shreds.
[Old English *scrēade*. Apparently related to **shroud.**]
**shred|ded wheat** (shred′id), a dry breakfast food made by shredding wheat and baking it in the form of biscuits.
**shred|der** (shred′ər), *n.* an instrument for shredding: *a cabbage shredder, a paper shredder.*
***shrew** (shrü), *n.* **1** a small mammal like a mouse, that has a long snout, tiny eyes and ears, and brownish fur. Shrews eat insects and worms. **2** *Figurative.* a bad-tempered, quarrelsome woman: *Once the marriage contract is signed, the sweet little bride turns into an extravagant shrew* (Time). **SYN:** vixen, termagant.
[Middle English *schrewe* a rascal, villain; later, a scold, Old English *scrēawa* the animal] —**shrew′-like′**, *adj.*

***shrew**
definition 1

**shrewd** (shrüd), *adj.* **1** having a sharp mind; showing a keen wit; clever: *a shrewd argument.*

*He is a shrewd businessman. He was too shrewd to go along with them upon a road which could lead only to their overthrow* (James Froude). **2a** effective; sharp; hard: *a shrewd thrust, a shrewd blow.* **b** *Archaic.* keen; piercing: *The night was shrewd and windy* (Irving). **3** *Archaic or Dialect.* malicious; mischievous: *That shrewd and knavish sprite Call'd Robin Goodfellow* (Shakespeare). **4** *Obsolete.* **a** cunning; artful. **b** dangerous; injurious: *That is a shrewd loss* (Scott). **c** shrewish: *Thou wilt never get thee a husband if thou be so shrewd of thy tongue* (Shakespeare). [earlier *shrewed* malignant, ill-disposed, past participle of *shrew,* verb, in sense of "to scold, curse"] —**shrewd′ly,** *adv.* —**shrewd′ness,** *n.*

—*Syn.* **1 Shrewd, sagacious, astute** mean having a sharp or keen mind and good judgment. **Shrewd** suggests natural cleverness in practical affairs or, sometimes, craftiness: *She is a shrewd lawyer.* **Sagacious** implies a wise and far-seeing understanding of practical affairs: *Lincoln was a sagacious man.* **Astute** implies shrewdness and sagacity plus the ability of being hard to fool: *an astute diplomat.*

**shrewd|ie** (shrü′dē), *n. Informal.* a shrewd person.

**shrew|ish** (shrü′ish), *adj.* that is, resembles, or is characteristic of a shrew; scolding or bad-tempered: *a shrewish remark.* —**shrew′ish|ly,** *adv.* —**shrew′ish|ness,** *n.*

**shrew mole,** a small mole of the humid Pacific coast of the United States and British Columbia.

**shrew|mouse** (shrü′mous′), *n., pl.* **-mice.** = shrew (def. 1).

**shriek** (shrēk), *n., v.* —*n.* **1** a loud, sharp, shrill sound: *a shriek of terror. We heard the shriek of an engine's whistle.* **2** a loud, shrill laugh.

—*v.i.* to make a loud, sharp, shrill sound. People sometimes shriek because of terror, anger, pain, or amusement. *Ghosts did shriek and squeal about the streets* (Shakespeare). SYN: See syn. under **scream.**

—*v.t.* to utter (words) loudly and shrilly: *In ... the confusion and uproar ... Cicero could only shriek that he had saved his country* (James A. Froude). [perhaps related to **screak**] —**shriek′er,** *n.*

**shriev|al** (shrē′vəl), *adj.* of or having to do with a sheriff.

**shriev|al|ty** (shrē′vəl tē), *n., pl.* **-ties.** the office, term or jurisdiction of a sheriff.

**shrieve**[1] (shrēv), *n. Obsolete.* sheriff. [variant of *sheriff*]

**shrieve**[2] (shrēv), *v.t., v.i.,* **shrieved, shriev|ing.** *Archaic.* shrive.

**shrift** (shrift), *n. Archaic.* **1** confession to a priest, followed by the imposing of penance and the granting of absolution. **2** the act of shriving. [Old English *scrift* < Latin *scrīptus* written, past participle of *scrībere* write. Compare etym. under **shrive.**]

**shrike** (shrīk), *n.* **1** a bird with a strong, hooked and toothed beak that feeds on large insects, frogs, mice, and sometimes other birds; butcherbird. There are several kinds, comprising a family of birds. Shrikes have a habit of impaling their food on thorns, barbs, or sharp twigs. **2** *Figurative.* a woman who attempts to destroy the man she loves. [Old English *scrīc* a thrush]

**shrill** (shril), *adj., v., n., adv.* —*adj.* **1** having a high pitch; high and sharp in sound; piercing: *a shrill cry or voice. Crickets, locusts, and katydids make shrill noises.* SYN: strident. **2a** full of shrill sounds: *a gym shrill with young fans.* **b** characterized or accompanied by sharp, high-pitched sounds: *the shrill merriment of children.* **3** *Archaic.* **a** keen; sharp: *The northern summer air is shrill and cold* (William E. Henley). **b** pungent. **c** poignant.

—*v.i.* to speak, cry, or sing with a shrill voice; make a shrill sound; sound sharply: *A wind that shrills All night in a waste land* (Tennyson).

—*v.t.* to utter or give forth (as a sound, cry, or words) in shrill tones; exclaim or proclaim with a shrill voice: *The locust shrills his song of heat* (John Greenleaf Whittier).

—*n.* a shrill sound or cry: *You may ... almost fancy you hear the shrill of the midsummer cricket* (Henry James).

—*adv.* with a shrill sound; shrilly: *The hounds and horn Through the high wood echoing shrill* (Milton).

[Middle English *shrille*] —**shrill′ness,** *n.*

**shrill|ish** (shril′ish), *adj.* somewhat shrill.

**shril|ly**[1] (shril′lē), *adv.* in shrill tones; with a shrill voice. [< *shrill* + *-ly*[1]]

**shril|ly**[2] (shril′ē), *adj.* somewhat shrill. [< *shrill* + *-y*[1]]

***shrimp** (shrimp), *n., pl.* **shrimps** or (*for 1, especially collectively*) **shrimp,** *v.* —*n.* **1** a small shellfish with a long tail, long feelers, and five pairs of delicate legs. There are various kinds. Some shrimps are used for food. *Shrimps vary in color from white to a brilliant red* (George A. Rounsefell). **2** *Figurative.* a small or insignificant person or thing: *Could she possibly care for a shrimp like himself* (George du Maurier).

—*v.i.* to fish for or catch shrimp: *Captain Davey ... has been shrimping for 50 years* (Newsweek). [Middle English *shrimpe.* Compare Middle High German *schrimpen* shrink up.] —**shrimp′like′,** *adj.*

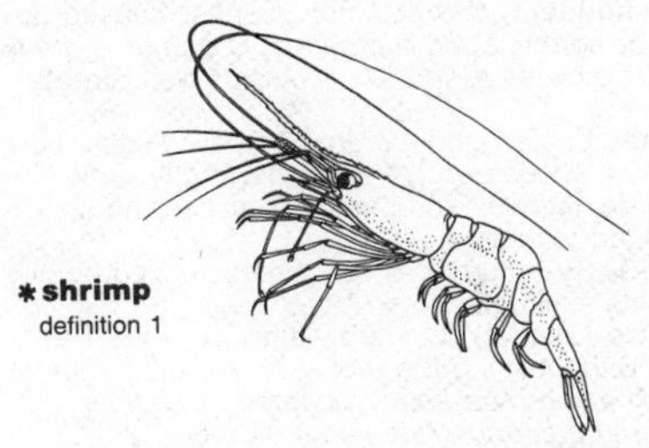

***shrimp** definition 1

**shrimp boat,** **1** a fishing boat used in catching shrimp. **2** a small plastic strip used in air traffic control as an identification marker by being placed next to a blip on a radarscope to keep track of the movement of an aircraft: *As the jet streaks across the sky, the blip moves across the radarscope, and the controller moves the shrimp boat along the blip's course* (Howard Bierman).

**shrimp|er** (shrim′pər), *n.* **1** a person whose business or work is catching or selling shrimp. **2** a shrimp boat.

**shrimp|ing** (shrim′ping), *n.* the catching of shrimp for a living or for pleasure.

**shrimp|y** (shrim′pē), *adj.* **1** of or like shrimp: *a shrimpy smell.* **2** filled with shrimp; full of shrimp: *shrimpy waters, a shrimpy gulf.* **3** *Figurative.* small or insignificant; puny: *a shrimpy young man.*

**shrine** (shrīn), *n., v.,* **shrined, shrin|ing.** —*n.* **1** a casket or box holding a holy object; reliquary. **2a** the tomb of a saint. **b** a place where sacred relics are kept. **3** an altar, small chapel, or other object or place of worship: *A very old priest in charge of the shrine tottered out to have a chat with the traveller* (London Times). SYN: temple. **4** *Figurative.* any place or object sacred because of its history; something sacred because of memories connected with it: *Shakespeare's birthplace is visited as a shrine. America is sometimes called freedom's shrine. Shrines are now built for national heroes as they once were for saints* (Ogburn and Nimkoff).

—*v.t.* to enclose in a shrine or something like a shrine; enshrine.

[Old English *scrīn* < Latin *scrīnium* case or box for keeping papers. Compare etym. under **screen.**]

**Shrin|er** (shrī′nər), *n.* a member of a fraternal organization of high-ranking Masons, founded in 1872. [< Ancient Arabic Order of Nobles of the Mystic *Shrine,* the organization's full name + *-er*[1]]

**shrink**[1] (shringk), *v.,* **shrank** or **shrunk, shrunk** or **shrunk|en, shrink|ing,** *n.* —*v.i.* **1** to draw back; recoil: *The dog shrank from the whip. That shy girl shrinks from meeting strangers.* **2a** to become smaller: *His wool sweater shrank when it was washed in hot water.* **2** to become less: *When his influence began to shrink, his wealth also decreased.*

—*v.t.* to make smaller or less; cause to shrink: *Hot water shrinks wool. Are all thy conquests, glories, triumphs, spoils, Shrunk to this little measure?* (Shakespeare).

—*n.* a shrinking.

[Old English *scrincan*] —**shrink′a|ble,** *adj.* —**shrink′ing|ly,** *adv.*

—*Syn. v.i.* **1 Shrink, flinch** mean to draw back from something painful, unpleasant, or the like. **Shrink** suggests drawing back physically or mentally because of instinctive fear, horror, or aversion: *to shrink at the sight of blood. He shrank from admitting his guilt.* **Flinch** suggests drawing back from danger, an unpleasant duty, or, especially, pain, because of weakness or lack of courage: *Spartans could bear torture without flinching. He flinched from adult responsibilities.*

▶ **Shrunken** is still sometimes used as a past participle (*It had shrunken*), but is chiefly used as an adjective (*a shrunken face*).

**shrink**[2] (shringk), *n. U.S. Slang.* a psychiatrist: *Afflicted with chronic depression leading occasionally to acute paranoia, ... he visits the shrink at the university health center* (Harper's). [< (head)-*shrink*(er)]

**shrink|age** (shring′kij), *n.* **1** the act or process of shrinking. **2a** the amount or degree of shrinking: *a shrinkage of two inches in the length of a sleeve.* **b** a depreciation or decrease, as in value or power: *the shrinkage of a fortune or a nation's influence. This divine ... was vindictively economical because of some shrinkage of his tithes* (H. G. Wells). **3** the part of the total weight, as of a steer or hog, lost in its shipment, butchering, and the subsequent curing of the meat: *You get away from that shrinkage ... that you have when the cattle are hauled around first by the trader* (Wall Street Journal).

**shrink|er** (shring′kər), *n.* **1** a device or agent used in shrinking. **2** a person who draws away from something, such as duty or social contact. **3** *U.S. Slang.* a psychiatrist.

**shrink|ing violet** (shring′king), a person who is shy, timid, or self-effacing: *We expect our rulers to be reasonably ambitious; shrinking violets are unfit for the harsh experience of power* (John Grigg).

**shrink|proof** (shringk′prüf′), *adj., v.* —*adj.* that will not shrink; resistant to shrinking: *Orlon, Dacron and nylon also are more easily washable, more shrinkproof, and more spot-resistant than the others* (Wall Street Journal).

—*v.t.* to make shrinkproof: *... experiments to find a way to shrinkproof and permanently crease wool* (Time).

**shrink wrap,** a protective plastic cover made by shrink wrapping.

**shrink wrapping,** the wrapping of goods in a plastic film that shrinks over the package to conform to its shape when the package is subjected to heat.

**shrive** (shrīv), *v.,* **shrove** or **shrived, shriv|en** or **shrived, shriv|ing.** *Archaic.* —*v.t.* to hear the confession of, impose penance on, and grant absolution to.

—*v.i.* **1** to make confession: *And who art thou, thou Gray Brother, That I should shrive to thee?* (Scott). **2** to hear confession, impose penance, and grant absolution.

**shrive oneself,** to confess to a priest and do penance: *Let me shrive me clean, and die* (Tennyson). Also, *Archaic,* **shrieve.**

[Old English *scrīfan* < Latin *scrībere* write. Compare etym. under **shrift, screed.**]

**shriv|el** (shriv′əl), *v.,* **-eled, -el|ing** or (*especially British*) **-elled, -el|ling.** —*v.t.* **1a** to dry up; wither: *The hot sunshine shriveled the grass.* **b** to shrink and wrinkle: *skin shriveled by age.* **2** to make helpless or useless.

—*v.i.* **1** to become contracted and wrinkled or curled (up), as from heat, cold, or age; wither: *The fruit shriveled up.* (*Figurative.*) *The men shriveled under the fierce blast of the captain's angry words.* **2** to waste away; become useless. SYN: atrophy. [origin uncertain]

**shriv|en** (shriv′ən), *v. Archaic.* a past participle of **shrive:** *The penitent was shriven by the priest.*

**shroff** (shrof), *n., v.* —*n.* **1** (in India) a banker or moneychanger. **2** (in China and other countries of the Far East) a native expert employed to test coins.

—*v.t., v.i.* to test (coins) to separate the genuine from the false.

[earlier *sheroff* < Arabic *sharrāf* < *sharafa* he exchanged]

**shrof|fage** (shrof′ij), *n.* **1** the act or practice of shroffing coins. **2** the charge for shroffing coins.

**Shrop|shire** (shrop′shir, -shər), *n.* any one of an English breed of blackfaced, hornless sheep, raised especially for meat. [< *Shropshire,* a county in England, where they were developed]

**shroud** (shroud), *n., v.* —*n.* **1** a cloth or garment in which a dead person is wrapped for burial; winding sheet. **2** something that covers, conceals, or veils: *The fog was a shroud over the city.* **3** Usually, **shrouds,** any one of a series of ropes, from a masthead to the side of a ship or a lower masthead, that help support the mast: *In an instant everyone sprung into the rigging, up the shrouds and out on the yards* (Richard H. Dana). **4** one of the lines attached to the canopy of a parachute. See picture under **parachute.**

—*v.t.* **1** to wrap for burial. **2** to bury. **3** to cover; conceal; veil: *The earth is shrouded in darkness. Their plans are shrouded in secrecy.* **4** *Archaic.* to shelter.

—*v.i. Archaic.* to seek or find shelter; take refuge: *I will here shroud till the dregs of the storm be past* (Shakespeare).

[Old English *scrūd* a garment, clothing. See related etym. at **shred.**]

**shroud knot,** *Nautical.* a knot joining the two parts of a broken or severed shroud.

**shroud-laid** (shroud′lād′), *adj.* (of a rope) made with four strands woven from left to right or

---

**Pronunciation Key:** hat, āge, cãre, fär; let, ēqual, tėrm; it, īce; hot, ōpen, ôrder; oil, out; cup, pu̇t, rüle; child; long; thin; ᴛʜen; zh, measure; ə represents **a** in about, **e** in taken, **i** in pencil, **o** in lemon, **u** in circus.

clockwise, usually around a central core.

**shroud|less** (shroud′lis), *adj.* **1** without a shroud or winding sheet: *Shroudless and tombless they sunk to their rest* (Oliver Wendell Holmes). **2** unshrouded; unobscured.

**shrove** (shrōv), *v. Archaic.* a past tense of **shrive**.

**Shrove Monday**, the Monday before Ash Wednesday.

**Shrove Sunday**, the Sunday before Ash Wednesday; Quinquagesima Sunday.

**Shrove|tide** (shrōv′tīd′), *n.* the three days before Ash Wednesday, the first day of Lent. Shrovetide is a time for confession and absolution in preparation for the solemn Lenten period, and of rejoicing and feasting.

**Shrove Tuesday**, the day before Ash Wednesday; the last day before Lent.

**shrub**[1] (shrub), *n.* a woody plant smaller than a tree, usually with many separate stems starting from or near the ground; bush. Shrubs are perennial plants. A lilac bush is a shrub. Rhododendrons, viburnums, and the box are shrubs. *Shrubs are much like trees, but are smaller, more profusely branched and often have several main small stems* (Fred W. Emerson). [Old English *scrybb* brush(wood), shrubbery] — **shrub′like′**, *adj.*

**shrub**[2] (shrub), *n.* a drink made from fruit juice (especially lemon or orange juice), sugar, and, usually, rum or brandy. [< Arabic *shurb* a drink. Compare etym. under **sherbet**.]

**shrub|ber|y** (shrub′ər ē, shrub′rē), *n., pl.* **-ber-ies**. **1** shrubs collectively or in a mass. **2** a place planted with shrubs.

**shrub|by** (shrub′ē), *adj.,* **-bi|er, -bi|est. 1** like shrubs. **2** covered with shrubs. **3** consisting of shrubs.

**shrubby althea**, = rose of Sharon.

**shrug** (shrug), *v.,* **shrugged, shrug|ging**, *n.* — ***v.t., v.i.*** to raise (the shoulders) as an expression of dislike, doubt, indifference, or impatience: *He merely shrugged his shoulders in answer to our request for help* (v.t.). *He shrugged and walked away* (v.i.).
— ***n.*** **1** the act of raising the shoulders as an expression of dislike, doubt, indifference, or impatience: *The deaf man's only answer was a shrug. He is a lively man, full of chat, and foreign shrugs and gestures* (Fanny Burney). **2** a woman's short sweater or jacket.
**shrug off**, to dismiss with indifference or contempt: *The foreman shrugged off his injury and went about his business.*
[Middle English *schruggen;* origin uncertain]

**shrunk** (shrungk), *v.* a past tense and past participle of **shrink**: *My wool socks have shrunk so that I can't get them on.*

**shrunk|en** (shrung′kən), *adj., v.* — ***adj.*** grown smaller; shriveled: *a shrunken face, a shrunken fortune.*
— *v.* shrunk; a past participle of **shrink**.
▶ See **shrink** for usage note.

**shtetl** (shtet′əl), *n., pl.* **shtetls, shtet|lach** (shtet′läн). a small Jewish community in any of the towns or villages of eastern Europe, especially before World War II. [< Yiddish *shtetl* (literally) small town < Middle High German *stetel* (diminutive) < *stat* town]

**shtg.**, shortage.

**shtick** (shtik), *n.* = schtik.

**Shu** (shü), *n.* the ancient Egyptian god of the air, typically represented with outstretched arms supporting the arched body of the sky goddess Nut.

**shu|ba** (shü′bə), *n. Russian.* a long fur coat or outer garment.

**shuck** (shuk), *n., v.* — ***n.*** **1** a husk, pod, or shell, especially the outer covering or strippings, as of corn (maize), chestnuts, or hickory nuts. **2** the shell of an oyster or clam. **3** *U.S. Slang.* fake; bluff: *Everybody with a brain in his head knew that this was the usual bureaucratic shuck* (Harper's).
— ***v.t.*** **1** to remove the husk, pod, or shell from: *to shuck ten ears of corn.* **2** to open the shells of (oysters or clams). **3** *Informal, Figurative.* Also, **shuck off, a** to take off; remove: *I like to shuck my shoes when I'm indoors.* **b** to get rid of: *We must shuck off the habits of the past* (Harper's). [origin uncertain] — **shuck′er**, *n.*

**shuck-bot|tom** (shuk′bot′əm), *adj., n.* — ***adj.*** *U.S.* (of a chair) having a seat made of the shucks or husks of corn.
— ***n.*** a shuck-bottom chair.

**shuck-bot|tomed** (shuk′bot′əmd), *adj.* = shuck-bottom.

**shucks** (shuks), *interj., n. Informal.* — ***interj.*** an exclamation of impatience or irritation: *"Oh, shucks," replied Clyde ... "What nonsense, Roberta"* (Theodore Dreiser).
— ***n.*** a type of something valueless (used especially in negative phrases); *not worth shucks. He was no great shucks as an outfielder.* [American English, perhaps < *shuck*]

**shud|der** (shud′ər), *v., n.* — ***v.i.*** to tremble or shiver suddenly and sharply with horror, fear, or cold: *She starts, like one that spies an adder ... the fear whereof doth make him shake and shudder* (Shakespeare). **SYN**: See syn. under **shiver**.
— ***n.*** the act or state of trembling; quivering.
**shudder at**, to feel dismay, horror, or fear, at: *She shudders at the sight of a snake.*
**the shudders**, *Informal.* nervousness caused by fear or horror: *Such a prospect is giving ... many wheat growers alike the shudders* (Wall Street Journal).
[Middle English *shodderen.* Compare Middle Low German *schôderen.*] — **shud′der|ing|ly**, *adv.*

**shud|der|some** (shud′ər səm), *n.* causing a shudder; fearsome.

**shud|der|y** (shud′ər ē), *adj.* characterized by or causing shudders.

**shuf|fle** (shuf′əl), *v.,* **-fled, -fling**, *n.* — ***v.i.*** **1** to walk without lifting the feet: *The old man shuffles feebly along. The bear ... comes ... shuffling along at a strange rate* (Daniel Defoe). **2** to dance with scraping motions of the feet.
**3** *Figurative.* to act or answer in a tricky way: *He said and unsaid, sighed, sobbed, beat his breast, shuffled, implored, threatened* (James A. Froude). **SYN**: dodge, equivocate, quibble. **4** to get (through) somehow; do hurriedly or perfunctorily: *to shuffle through one's lessons.* **5** to get (into clothing) in a clumsy or fumbling manner. **6** to divide a deck of cards and, by distributing one half into the other, to mix them into random order: *They draw, they sit, they shuffle, cut and deal* (George Crabbe).
— ***v.t.*** **1** to scrape or drag (the feet). **2** to perform (a dance or dance step) with such motions. **3** to mix (a deck of cards) so as to change the order. **4** to put or throw (together) in a mass indiscriminately, incongruously, or without order; huddle or jumble together: *Good days, bad days so shuffled together* (Charles Lamb). **5** to push about; thrust or throw with clumsy haste: *He shuffled on his clothes and ran out of the house.* **6** to move about this way and that; shift about: *to shuffle a stack of papers on one's desk.* **7** *Figurative.* to put or bring in a tricky way.
— ***n.*** **1** a scraping or dragging movement of the feet: *When the hobble had a second life from 1908 to 1914 skirts appeared to clip the ankles, walking became a kind of shuffle or glide* (London Times). **2** a dance or dance step with a shuffle: ... *a powerhouse rhythm section which divides itself between a two-beat calypso and a hot-blooded shuffle* (Time). **3a** a shuffling of a deck of cards. **b** the right or turn to shuffle (cards). **4** a movement this way and that: *After a hasty shuffle of his papers, the speaker began to talk.* **5** *Figurative.* an unfair act; trick; evasion: *Through some legal shuffle he secured a new trial.* **SYN**: subterfuge.
**shuffle off, a** to get rid of: *When we have shuffled off this mortal coil* ... (Shakespeare). [*They*] *are obliged for propriety's sake to shuffle off the anxious inquiries of the public* (Thackeray). **b** to proceed to go to: *to shuffle off to the seashore.* **c** *Figurative.* to die: *I mean in plain English that I am likely to shuffle off long before you kick the bucket* (Atlantic).
[perhaps < Low German *schuffeln.* See related etym. at **shovel**.]

*** shuf|fle|board** (shuf′əl bôrd′, -bōrd′), *n.* **1a** a game in which players use long wooden sticks to push large wooden or iron disks so that they slide along a flat surface into various numbered spaces. Shuffleboard is often played on the deck of a ship. **b** the surface on which it is played. **2a** a former game in which pieces of money or counters were driven by the hand toward certain compartments or lines marked on a table; shovehalfpenny. **b** the board or table used in this game. Also, **shovelboard**.

*** shuffleboard**
definition 1a

**shuf|fler** (shuf′lər), *n.* **1** a person or thing that shuffles. **2** *Figurative.* an evasive person. **3** = scaup duck.

**shuf|fling** (shuf′ling), *adj.* **1** moving the feet over the ground or floor without lifting them, or characterized by such movement: *Sounds like the shuffling steps of those that bear Some heavy thing* (William Morris). **2** *Figurative.* shifty or evasive, as persons or their actions: *her shuffling excuses* (Jane Austen). — **shuf′fling|ly**, *adv.*

**shul** or **shule** (shül), *n. Yiddish.* a synagogue: *"You mean church, Sergeant." "I mean shul, Grossbart!"* (Philip Roth).

**Shu|lam|ite** or **Shu|lam|mite** (shü′lə mīt), *n.* the epithet of the woman beloved in the Song of Solomon 6:13.

**Shu|man process** (shü′mən), a process of making wire glass, invented by Frank Shuman of Philadelphia. It consists of rolling one sheet of glass, into which a wire mesh or netting is pressed and rolled.

**shun** (shun), *v.t.,* **shunned, shun|ning**. to keep away from because of dislike; avoid: *to shun a person. She was lazy and shunned work. He shunned uttering a direct falsehood, but did not scruple to equivocate* (George Bancroft). **SYN**: See syn. under **avoid**. [Old English *scunian*] — **shun′ner**, *n.*

**Shu|nam|mite** (shü′nə mīt), *n.* an inhabitant of the town of Shunem in ancient Palestine (in the Bible, I Kings 1:3).

**shun|less** (shun′lis), *adj.* that cannot be shunned; inevitable.

**shun|pike** (shun′pīk′), *n., v.,* **-piked, -pik|ing**. *Especially U.S. Informal.* — ***n.*** a road taken by travelers, originally, to avoid paying the toll on a turnpike, but now more frequently, to avoid major highways.
— ***v.i.*** to travel by shunpike: *Besides making long trips at high speed, motorists could ... "shunpike" on quiet back roads* (Stacy V. Jones). [American English < *shun* + *pike*[4]]

**shun|pik|er** (shun′pī′kər), *n. Especially U.S. Informal.* a person who shunpikes: *Smooth roads, signposts, beautiful scenery—what more could a shunpiker want?* (Saturday Review).

**shunt** (shunt), *v., n.* — ***v.t.*** **1a** to switch (a train) from one track to another: *The car was uncoupled from the rest of the train and shunted into a siding* (London Times). **SYN**: deflection. **b** to switch (anything) to another route or place: *After the mixture ... is ground, a small blower shunts the feed to the top of the crib* (Wall Street Journal). **SYN**: deflection. **2** *Figurative.* **a** to push aside or out of the way; sidetrack: *My mind has been shunted off upon the track of other duties* (James Russell Lowell). **b** to get rid of. **3** *Electricity.* to carry (a part of a current) by means of a shunt. **4** *Medicine.* to divert (blood) by using a shunt.
— ***v.i.*** **1** (of a train) to move from one line of rails to another. **2** to move out of the way; turn aside: *Trucks shunt ... unceasingly, the drivers ... displaying something like wizardry in maneuvering them through perennial traffic jams* (Bulletin of Atomic Scientists).
— ***n.*** **1** the act of turning aside; shift. **2** a railroad switch. **3** a wire or other conductor, joining two points in an electric circuit and forming a path through which a part of the current may pass; bypass. It is usually of relatively low resistance. Shunts are used to regulate the amount of current passing through the main circuit. *However, by inserting a low resistance shunt in parallel with the pivoted coil ... any galvanometer may be modified to serve as an ammeter or voltmeter* (Sears and Zemansky). **4** *Medicine.* a communication between blood vessels; anastomosis: *Shunts ... had previously been detected by having the patient breathe a mixture of the gas nitrous oxide and tracing its course through the circulatory system* (Science News Letter). **b** an artificial pathway or connection formed to divert the blood from its normal channels: *In the new use of this arteriovenous shunt for radiation treatment, the permanent tubes in the arm are simply connected to a length of plastic tubing that leads the blood beyond the body to the radiation source and back* (New York Times). **5** *U.S. Slang.* a crash between cars in an automobile race.
[origin uncertain] — **shunt′er**, *n.*

**shunt dynamo** or **generator**, a shunt-wound generator.

**shunt motor**, a shunt-wound motor: *If the armature and the field windings are connected in series we have a series motor; if they are connected in parallel, a shunt motor* (Sears and Zemansky).

**shunt winding**, *Electricity.* a winding of a motor or generator whereby the field magnet coils are connected in parallel with the armature.

**shunt-wound** (shunt′wound′), *adj. Electricity.* that has shunt winding: *a shunt-wound motor.*

**shure** (shyr), *v. Scottish.* sheared; a past tense of **shear**.

**shush** (shush, shúsh), *v.t., v.i., n., interj.* = hush.

**shut** (shut), *v.,* **shut, shut|ting**, *adj., n.* — ***v.t.*** **1** to close (a container or opening) by pushing or pulling a lid, door, or some part into place: *to shut a*

*box, to shut a window, to shut a gate.* **SYN**: See syn. under **close**[1]. **2** to bring together the parts of: *to shut a knife. Shut your eyes. Shut the book.* **3** to close tightly; close securely; close doors or other openings of: *When our house was shut up for the summer we locked all the doors and windows.* **4** to enclose; confine; keep (from going out): *Shut the kitten in the basket. The criminal was shut in prison.* **5** *Figurative.* to close (as the mind) to something as if to deny its existence: *We should shut our ears to gossip.*
— ***v.i.*** to become closed; be closed: *The great gates slowly shut.* **SYN**: See syn. under **close**[1].
— ***adj.*** **1** closed; fastened up; enclosed. **2** *Phonetics.* **a** formed by completely checking the outgoing breath. **b** having sound stopped by a consonant at the end of a syllable.
— ***n.*** **1** the act or time of shutting or closing. **2** the line of junction of two pieces of welded metal.
**shut down, a** to close by lowering: *We shut down all the windows when the storm began.* **b** to close (a factory, mine, or the like) for a time; stop work: *We've got to shut down until there is a demand for our product.* **c** to settle down so as to cover or envelop: *Night shut down on the settlement* (Bret Harte). **d** to put a stop or check (on); suppress: *The military junta shut down the radio and the press.*
**shut in, a** to keep from going out, as by closing a door or receptacle: *The recluse shut himself in and refused to leave the house.* **b** to enclose with a barrier; hem in: *Wooded hills ... shut in the view on every side* (Edward A. Freeman).
**shut off, a** to prevent the passage of (steam, water, gas, or other fluid), as by closing a valve or tap: *The motion of the piston was equalized by shutting off the steam sooner or later from the cylinder* (Robert Stuart). **b** to turn off; check; obstruct: *Shut off the radio.* **c** to cut off; separate (from): *a lake shut off from the sea by a dike.*
**shut out, a** to keep from coming in; deny right of entry to a place; exclude: *The curtains shut out the light. Shut the dog out of this room.* **b** to beat (a team) without allowing it to score: *The pitcher shut out the other team, limiting them to three hits.*
**shut up, a** to close the doors and windows of: *Noah, you shut up the shop* (Dickens). **b** to keep from going out; enclose; confine: *She shuts her cats up during the day, but lets them roam the neighborhood at night.* **c** *Informal.* to stop, or stop from, talking: *... the boy would be torn between anger and a desire to shut the man up* (Edmund Wilson).
[Old English *scyttan* to bolt up]

**shut-down** or **shut|down** (shut′doun′), *n.* a shutting down; closing of a factory, mine, or the like, for a time: *The permanent shut-down was caused by an increase in use of oil and other domestic fuels* (Wall Street Journal).

**shut-eye** (shut′ī′), *n. Slang.* sleep.

**shut-in** (shut′in′), *adj., n.* — ***adj.*** **1a** not allowed or able to go out; kept in, as by illness or weakness. **b** held in; confined: *How can you stand the shut-in feeling those mountains give? They scare me* (New York Times). **2** *Psychiatry.* reluctant to associate or communicate with others; solitary.
— ***n.*** a person who is kept from going out by sickness or weakness.
[American English < *shut in,* idiom]

**shut-off** or **shut|off** (shut′ôf′, -of′), *n.* **1** something that shuts off, as a valve or switch: *an automatic shut-off.* **2** the state of being shut off: *a temporary shut-off of electricity.*

**shut-out** or **shut|out** (shut′out′), *n.* **1a** a game in which one side is kept from scoring: *to pitch a shut-out.* **b** the act of preventing the opposite side from scoring: *The home team won by a shut-out.* **c** *Cards.* a preemptive bid. **2** = lockout.

**shut|ter** (shut′ər), *n., v.* — ***n.*** **1** a movable cover, usually one of a pair, for a window; blind: *When we shut up our cottage for the winter, we put shutters on all the windows.* **2a** a movable cover or slide for closing any opening: *Every train ... had its windows sealed with steel shutters* (Newsweek). **b** a device that opens and closes in front of the film in a camera in order to regulate the length of an exposure. **3** a person or thing that shuts.
— ***v.t.*** to put a shutter or shutters on or over; close up; shut down: *We shuttered our windows before the storm. Shop owners shuttered their stores* (Wall Street Journal). — **shut′ter|less,** *adj.*

**shut|ter|bug** (shut′ər bug′), *n. U.S. Slang.* a devotee of photography; camera bug.

***shut|tle** (shut′əl), *n., v.,* **-tled, -tling,** *adj.* — ***n.*** **1a** the device that carries the thread from one side of the web to the other in weaving: *My days are swifter than a weaver's shuttle* (Job 7:6). **b** a similar device on which thread is wound, used in tatting and certain kinds of knitting and embroidery. **c** the sliding holder for the lower thread in a sewing machine, which moves back and forth once for each stitch. **2** any one of various things, not connected with weaving or sewing, characterized by a back-and-forth motion. **3** a bus, train, or airplane that runs back and forth regularly over a short distance. **4** = space shuttle.
— ***v.i., v.t.*** **1** to move quickly to and fro: [*He*] *shuttles between Lucerne and the Bürgenstock in a speedboat, making the run in seven minutes* (New Yorker). *A face of ... extreme mobility, which he shuttles about ... in a very singular manner while speaking* (Thomas Carlyle). **2** to transport or be transported by or as if by shuttle.
— ***adj.*** **1** that shuttles; shuttling: *a shuttle bus, a shuttle flight, a shuttle service.* **2** that is traversed by a shuttle: *a shuttle route.*
[Old English *scytel* a dart < *scēotan* to shoot]

***shuttle***
definition 1a

**shut|tle|cock** (shut′əl kok′), *n., v.* — ***n.*** **1** a cork or piece of rubber with feathers or a plastic webbing stuck in one end, used in the game of badminton; bird. **2a** a cork with feathers stuck in one end, that is hit back and forth by a small racket, called a battledore, in the old game of battledore and shuttlecock. **b** = battledore and shuttlecock.
— ***v.t.*** to throw or send backward and forward.
— ***v.i.*** to move to and fro; shuttle: *The hot, tired, apologetic traveler shuttlecocks between one uniformed official ... and another, getting more hot, more tired, more apologetic* (Mary Goldring).

**shuttle diplomacy,** diplomatic relations between belligerents conducted by a third party who moves between the belligerents conducting personal negotiations with their government leaders: *A remarkable performance in shuttle diplomacy by Secretary of State Henry Kissinger brought about a cease-fire and a disengagement accord that was widely hailed as a major American diplomatic achievement* (Robert J. Huckshorn).

**shuttle shell, 1** the elongated fusiform shell of a marine gastropod, so called from the resemblance to a weaver's shuttle. **2** the gastropod itself.

**shuttle train,** a train that runs back and forth over a short distance; shuttle.

**shy**[1] (shī), *adj.,* **shy|er, shy|est** or **shi|er, shi|est,** *v.,* **shied, shy|ing,** *n., pl.* **shies.** — ***adj.*** **1a** uncomfortable in company; bashful; retiring: *He is shy and dislikes parties.* **b** showing or resulting from bashfulness: *shy looks.* **2** easily frightened away; timid: *A deer is a shy animal.* **3** cautious; wary: *shy of an interview, shy of using a new tool.* **SYN**: suspicious, distrustful. **4** not bearing well; unprolific, as plants or trees. **5** not having enough; short; scant: *The store is shy on children's clothing.* **6** *Informal.* owing, as one's ante in poker; in arrears.
— ***v.i.*** **1** to start back or aside suddenly: *The horse shied at the newspaper blowing along the ground.* **2** to draw back; shrink: *He would shy in pretended fright at every shadow* (New Yorker).
— ***n.*** a sudden start to one side.
**fight shy of.** See under **fight.**
**shy away from,** to avoid out of shyness or fear; shrink from: *Some parents who shy away from a discussion group will feel more free to chat in a sewing class or furniture repair project* (New York Times).
**shy of, a** having little; short of: *I am shy of cash this week.* **b** not coming up to; lacking: *My brother is two months shy of being of voting age.*
[Old English *scēoh.* Compare etym. under **eschew, skew.**] — **shy′ness,** *n.*
— *Syn. adj.* **1 Shy, bashful** mean uncomfortable in the presence or company of others. **Shy** suggests a lack of self-confidence and is shown by a reserved or timid manner: *People who appear unfriendly are often really shy.* **Bashful** suggests shrinking by nature from being noticed, and is shown by awkward and embarrassed behavior in the presence of others: *The boy was so bashful that he blushed when he asked her to dance.*

**shy**[2] (shī), *v.,* **shied, shy|ing,** *n., pl.* **shies.** — ***v.t., v.i.*** to throw; fling: *to shy a stone at a tree.*
— ***n.*** **1** a throw; fling: *Jack-in-the-box—three shies a penny* (Dickens). **2** *Informal.* a verbal attack; sarcastic or taunting remark: *He wasn't above taking a few shies at his fellow school-board members.* **3** *Informal.* a try; fling. [origin uncertain]

**shy|er**[1] (shī′ər), *n.* a horse that shies. Also, **shier.**

**shy|er**[2] (shī′ər), *n.* a person who shies (throws). Also, **shier.**

**Shy|lock** (shī′lok), *n.* **1** the relentless and vengeful moneylender in Shakespeare's play *The Merchant of Venice.* **2** a greedy moneylender. **3** any moneylender.

**shy|lock** (shī′lok), *v.i.* to lend money at an excessively high or unlawful rate of interest: *His income derived from illicit activities—bookmaking, gambling, shylocking, and questionable union activities* (New York Times). [< *Shylock*]

**shy|ly** (shī′lē), *adv.* in a shy manner. Also, **shily.**

**shy|ster** (shīs′tər), *n. Informal.* a lawyer or other person who uses improper or questionable methods in his business or profession: *They all set up some crazy foundation under the control of ... the little shyster who drew the will* (New Yorker). [American English; origin uncertain]

**shy|ster|ism** (shī′stə riz əm), *n.* the practices of a shyster.

**si** (sē), *n. Music.* the seventh tone of the scale in solmization; B; ti. [see etym. under **gamut**]

**Si** (no period), silicon (chemical element).

**SI** (no periods), **1** Smithsonian Institution. **2** Système International d'Unités (the international meter-kilogram-second system of units). See **SI unit.**

**S.I., 1** Sandwich Islands. **2** Staten Island (in New York).

**si|al** (sī′al), *n.* a granitelike rock rich in silica and aluminum. Sial is the chief rock underlying the land masses, as distinct from the ocean basins. [< *si*(lica) + *al*(uminum)]

**si|al|a|gog|ic** (sī′ al′ə goj′ik), *adj., n.* = sialogogic.

**si|al|a|gogue** (sī al′ə gog, -gôg), *adj., n.* = sialogogue.

**si|al|ic** (sī al′ik), *adj.* **1** composed largely or chiefly of silica and aluminum: *Sial and granite are sialic rocks.* **2** consisting largely of sial: *a sialic land basin.*

**si|a|lid** (sī′ə lid), *adj., n.* — ***adj.*** of or belonging to a family of insects that includes the hellgrammite.
— ***n.*** a sialid insect.
[< New Latin *Sialidae* the family name < *Sialis* the typical genus < Greek *sialis* a type of bird]

**si|al|i|dan** (sī al′ə dən), *adj., n.* = sialid.

**si|al|o|gog|ic** (sī al′ə goj′ik), *adj., n.* — ***adj.*** stimulating or provoking an increased flow of saliva.
— ***n.*** = sialogogue.

**si|al|o|gogue** (sī al′ə gog, -gôg), *adj., n.* — ***adj.*** producing a flow of saliva.
— ***n.*** a drug that produces a flow of saliva.
[< New Latin *sialagogus* < Greek *síalon* saliva + *agōgós* leading < *ágein* to lead]

**si|a|loid** (sī′ə loid), *adj.* resembling saliva. [< Greek *síalon* saliva + English *-oid*]

**si|al|or|rhe|a** or **si|al|or|rhoe|a** (sī al′ə rē′ə), *n.* excessive flow of saliva. [< New Latin *sialorrhea, sialorrhoea* < Greek *síalon* saliva + *rhoia* flow < *rheîn* to flow]

**si|a|mang** (sē′ə mang, syä′mang), *n.* the largest of the gibbons, black, and having the second and third digits united to some extent. It inhabits Sumatra and the Malay Peninsula. [< Malay *siāmang* < *āmang* black]

**Si|a|mese**[1] (sī′ə mēz′, -mēs′), *adj., n., pl.* **-mese.**
— ***adj.*** of or having to do with Siam (Thailand), a country in southeastern Asia, its people, or their language; Thai.
— ***n.*** **1** a native or inhabitant of Siam (Thailand), especially a member of its dominant Thai-speaking people; Thai. **2** the official language of Siam (Thailand), belonging to the Thai linguistic family; Thai.

**si|a|mese** or **Si|a|mese**[2] (sī′ə mēz′, -mēs′), *v.t.,* **-mesed, -mes|ing.** to join; unite; couple: *The other pipes are siamesed together in pairs* (Science News Letter). [< *Siamese* twins]

**Siamese cat,** any one of a breed of short-haired, blue-eyed cats. The best-known varieties are one with light tan body and dark face, ears, feet, and tail (seal point), or one with bluish-white body and bluish face, ears, feet, and tail (blue point). The breed came originally from Siam (Thailand).

**Siamese connection, coupling,** or **joint,** (in fire apparatus) a Y-shaped device by which two or more pipes or hoses discharge into one hose.

**Siamese crocodile,** a crocodile of Java, Thailand, and nearby parts of Asia, having a broad snout and growing to 10 or 12 feet in length.

**Siamese fighting fish,** = fighting fish.

**Siamese twins,** twins who are born joined together. [< twin Siamese boys, Eng and Chang, 1811-1874, who were born joined together by a band of flesh between their chests]

**sib**[1] (sib), *adj., n.* — ***adj.*** related by blood; closely

**Pronunciation Key:** hat, āge, cãre, fär; let, ēqual, tėrm; it, īce; hot, ōpen, ôrder; oil, out; cup, pu̇t, rüle; child; long; thin; ᴛʜen; zh, measure; ə represents **a** in about, **e** in taken, **i** in pencil, **o** in lemon, **u** in circus.

related; akin. SYN: consanguineous.
—*n.* **1** a kinsman or kinswoman; relative: *the disease can be detected earlier if the children or sibs of patients are examined* (J.B.S. Haldane). **2** one's kin; kinsfolk; relatives. **3** a brother or sister; sibling.
[Old English *sibb*]
**sib²** (sib), *n. U.S. Anthropology.* a group or clan whose members trace their descent from a common ancestor through one line only. [perhaps a special use of *sib¹*, or perhaps short for *sibling*]
**Sib.**, 1 Siberia. 2 Siberian.
**Si|be|li|an** (sə bā′lē ən), *adj., n.* —*adj.* of, having to do with, or characteristic of the Finnish composer Jean Sibelius (1865-1957) or his music: *The first two movements are intensely Sibelian* (Harold C. Schonberg).
—*n.* a student or admirer of Sibelius or his works.
**Si|be|ri|a** (sī bir′ē ə), *n.* a place of exile or imprisonment; remote assignment (often used in a humorous way). [< *Siberia,* in Asia (traditional place of exile for Russian criminals)]
**Si|be|ri|an** (sī bir′ē ən), *adj., n.* —*adj.* of or having to do with Siberia, a large part of the Soviet Union extending across northern Asia.
—*n.* a native or inhabitant of Siberia.
**Siberian husky**, a strong, medium-sized sled dog of a breed that originated in Siberia; husky. It has a thick coat of medium length and a brush tail, and is black, tan, or gray with white markings.
**Siberian iris**, a tall iris with a wide, hollow stem and small, beardless, lilac flowers, native to Europe and Asia. It is the parent species of many hybrid irises.
**Siberian waxwing**, a waxwing of southeastern Siberia and Japan, somewhat larger and more colorful than the cedar waxwing.
**sib|i|lance** (sib′ə ləns), *n.* **1** the character of being sibilant. **2** a hissing sound.
**sib|i|lan|cy** (sib′ə lən sē), *n., pl.* **-cies.** = sibilance.
**sib|i|lant** (sib′ə lənt), *adj., n.* —*adj.* **1** hissing: *When he spoke, his voice was usually low and sibilant* (New Yorker). **2** *Phonetics.* articulated by forcing the breath stream through a very narrow passage, so that it makes a hissing sound, as English *ch* in *machine, s* in *so, z* in *zero, sh* in *show,* and *z* in *azure.*
—*n.* a hissing sound, or a letter or symbol for it. *S* and *sh* are sibilants. *The voices are picked up at close range ... without the unpleasant exaggerations of sibilants* (Harper's).
[< Latin *sībilāns, -antis,* present participle of *sībilāre* to hiss] —**sib′i|lant|ly,** *adv.*
**sib|i|late** (sib′ə lāt), *v.,* **-lat|ed, -lat|ing.** —*v.i.* to hiss; utter a hissing sound.
—*v.t.* **1** to make sibilant. **2** to pronounce with a hissing sound.
[< Latin *sībilāre* (with English *-ate¹*) to hiss]
**sib|i|la|tion** (sib′ə lā′shən), *n.* **1** the act of sibilating or hissing. **2** a hissing sound.
**sib|i|la|to|ry** (sib′ə lə tôr′ē, -tōr′-), *adj.* producing a hissing or sibilant effect.
**Si|bir|ic** (sī bir′ik), *adj.* of or having to do with the Asian peoples of Siberia, such as the Tungusic, Mongolian, Tartarian, Finnic, and Japanese groups. [< Russian *Sibirĭ* of Siberia + English *-ic*]
**sib|ling** (sib′ling), *n.* a brother or sister. An only child has no siblings. A sibling may be: **a** each or any one of two or more individuals born to the same parents but not at the same birth: *Siblings in a family group have special social relationships, not possessed by an only child* (Emory S. Bogardus). **b** each or any one of two or more individuals born to the same parents, including twins, triplets, and the like. **c** each or any one of two or more individuals having one parent in common. **d** any brother or sister adopted into a family. [< *sib¹* + *-ling*]
**sibling species**, any one of several species of animals that appear to be morphologically identical but that do not interbreed with one another.
**sib|ship** (sib′ship), *n.* the condition of being a sibling.
**sib|yl** (sib′əl), *n.* **1** any one of several prophetesses that the ancient Greeks and Romans consulted about the future. **2a** a prophetess; fortuneteller. **b** a witch, especially one with prophetic powers. [< Old French *sibile,* learned borrowing from Latin *Sibylla* < Greek *Sibylla*]
**si|byl|ic** or **si|byl|lic** (sə bil′ik), *adj.* = sibylline.
**sib|yl|line** (sib′ə lēn, -līn, -lin), *adj.* **1** of or like a sibyl; prophetic; mysterious: *... a numerical code ... [that] seemed to be a row of sibylline figures* (New Yorker). **2** said or written by a sibyl: *the Sibylline books, a sibylline oracle.*
**sib|yl|list** (sib′ə list), *n.* a believer in sibylline prophecies or in the oracles of the Sibylline books.
**sic¹** (sik), *adv. Latin.* so; thus.
► **Sic** is used to show or emphasize the fact that something has been copied just as it is in the original. *Sic,* italicized and set in brackets, is used to mark an error in quoted matter: *The letter was headed "Danbury, Conneticut [sic], Jan. 2."*
**sic²** (sik), *v.t.,* **sicked, sick|ing** or **sicced, sic|cing.** **1** to set upon or attack (chiefly used as a command to a dog). **2** to incite to set upon or attack: *to sic a dog on a stranger.* [American English, spelling variant of *sick²*]
**sic³** (sik), *adj., pron. Dialect.* such. [Scottish variant of *such*]
**Sic.**, 1 Sicilian. 2 Sicily.
**Si|ca|ni|an** (si kā′nē ən), *adj., n.* = Sicilian.
**Si|car|i|us** (si kãr′ē əs), *n., pl.* **-i|i** (-ē ī). one of an extremist group of Zealots in the later years of Nero's reign who used murder and other forms of violence against the Romans. [< Latin *Sicārius* (literally) assassin < *sīca* dagger]
**sic|ca** (sik′ə), *n., pl.* **-cas.** a newly coined rupee. [< Hindi *sikkā* < Arabic *sikkah* a die for coining]
**sic|ca|tive** (sik′ə tiv), *n., adj.* —*n.* a substance that hastens drying, especially one used in paint, such as linseed oil.
—*adj.* drying.[< Late Latin *siccātīvus* < Latin *siccāre* make dry < *siccus* dry]
**sice¹** (sīs), *n.* the number six at dice. [< Old French *sis* < Latin *sex* six]
**sice²** (sīs), *n.* = syce.
**Si|cil|ian** (si sil′yən), *adj., n.* —*adj.* of or having to do with Sicily, the largest island in the Mediterranean, near the southwestern tip of Italy, its people, or their dialect.
—*n.* **1** a person born or living in Sicily. **2** the dialect of Italian spoken in Sicily.
**si|cil|i|a|no** (si sil′ē ä′nō), *n.* **1** a slow, pastoral dance of the peasants of Sicily, accompanied with singing. **2** the music for this dance, in sextuple and moderately slow time, resembling the pastoral. [< Italian *siciliano* Sicilian]
**si|cil|i|enne** (si sil′ē en′), *n.* a heavy variety of mohair (fabric). [< French *sicilienne,* feminine of *sicilien* Sicilian]
**sick¹** (sik), *adj., n., v.* —*adj.* **1** in poor health; having some disease; ill. SYN: unwell, ailing, indisposed. **2** vomiting or inclined to vomit; feeling nausea: *O lend me a basin, I am sick, I am sick* (Ben Jonson). **3a** of, for, or connected with a sick person. **b** of, showing, or characterized by sickness: *a sick look.* **4** thoroughly tired; weary: *to be sick of drudgery. He is sick of school.* SYN: satiated. **5** disgusted; mortified; chagrined: *I am sick and tired of his complaints.* **6** affected with sorrow, longing, or some other strong feeling: *to be sick for old friends at home, sick with hate. She is sick at heart. Hope deferred maketh the heart sick* (Proverbs 13:12). **7** *Figurative.* not in the proper condition; impaired; unsound: *The enterprise is sick* (Shakespeare). **8** pale; wan. **9** mentally ill: *People tend to believe that it is wrong and "sick" to feel anxious or guilty* (Time). **10** *Figurative.* grisly; sadistic; cruel: *a sick joke, sick humor. I've produced every type of picture except sick ones* (Walt Disney). **11** *Agriculture.* **a** (of soil) not producing a sufficient yield of a crop: *cotton-sick.* **b** infested with destructive microorganisms.
—*n.* **the sick,** sick people collectively: *The sick need special care.*
—*v.i.* to vomit: *Gertrude [was] sicking up the contents of the poisoned cup on to the floor* (Jeremy Kingston).
[Old English *sēoc*]
► In England, **sick** meaning "unwell" survives chiefly in attributive use: *a sick man.* As a predicate adjective (*to be* or *feel sick*), it has been narrowed to mean "nauseated, about to vomit" or "vomiting" and in the general sense has been replaced by *ill.* In America, *sick* may have this restricted meaning, but it is also regularly used in the older general sense: *He was violently sick behind the hedge. He was sick all last year.*
**sick²** (sik), *v.t.* to set upon or incite to attack; sic²: *Sick him, Towser.* [American English, perhaps < dialectal variant of *seek*]
**sick bag**, *Especially British.* a bag for vomiting into.
**sick bay**, the part of a ship in which drugs are kept and medical treatment is given; ship's hospital, infirmary, or dispensary.
**sick|bed** (sik′bed′), *n.* the bed of a sick person: *She would get up from a sickbed to go shopping* (New Yorker).
**sick benefit**, money given to employees who cannot work because of illness, as arranged in a labor or insurance contract.
**sick berth**, = sick bay.
**sick call**, **1** a summons, such as to a doctor or clergyman, to visit a sick person. **2** *Military.* **a** a call sounded, as by a bugle or trumpet, as a signal to those who are sick to report to the hospital or medical officer. **b** the assembling of those who are sick in answer to this call.
**sick|en** (sik′ən), *v.i.* **1** to become sick: *to sicken with typhus. The bird sickened when kept in the cage.* **2a** to feel horror or nausea; experience revulsion (at something). **b** to grow weary or tired (of a thing). **c** to long eagerly.
—*v.t.* **1** to make sick: *The sight of blood sickened him.* **2** to make weary or tired of something: *He was sickened by too much luxury.*
**sick|en|er** (sik′ə nər), *n.* something that sickens, especially something that nauseates or disgusts.
**sick|en|ing** (sik′ə ning, sik′ning), *adj.* **1** making sick; causing nausea, faintness, disgust, or loathing: *a sickening sight; ... with monstrous head and sickening cry [the donkey]* (G. K. Chesterton). SYN: repulsive, offensive. **2** becoming sick; falling ill. —**sick′en|ing|ly,** *adv.*
**sick|er** (sik′ər), *adj. Scottish.* **1** that may be depended on; certain; sure. **2** free from danger or harm; secure; safe. Also, **siker.** [Old English *sicor* < Latin *sēcūrus.* See etym. of doublets **secure, sure.**] —**sick′er|ly,** *adv.*
**sick flag**, a yellow flag indicating the presence of disease, displayed, as at a quarantined building or ship, to prevent unauthorized communication.
**sick headache**, **1** a headache accompanied by nausea and stomach disorders. **2** = migraine.
**sick|ie** (sik′ē), *n.* **1** *U.S. Slang.* a sick person, especially one who is mentally ill. **2** *Australian Slang.* a sick leave.
**sick|ish** (sik′ish), *adj.* **1** somewhat sick; indisposed. **2** somewhat sickening. —**sick′ish|ly,** *adv.* —**sick′ish|ness,** *n.*
**sick|le** (sik′əl), *n., v.,* **-led, -ling.** —*n.* a tool with a short, curved blade on a short handle, used for cutting grass, reaping grain, and the like.
—*v.i.* to take the shape of a sickle: *The tendency of red blood cells from such people to sickle can be readily demonstrated* (New Scientist).
[Old English *sicol, sicel* < Latin *secula,* related to *secāre* to cut]
**Sick|le¹** (sik′əl), *n.* a group of stars shaped like a sickle in the northern constellation Leo. [< *sickle*]
**Sick|le²** (sik′əl), *n.* = Seckel.
**sick leave**, **1** a leave of absence given to a worker because of illness, usually a certain number of days and with pay. **2** a number of days allowed for this each year without loss of pay.
**sick|le|bill** (sik′əl bil′), *n.* **1** a curlew, or any one of various other birds with a curved bill. **2** any one of several kinds of birds of paradise of New Guinea.
**sickle cell**, a red blood cell that is sickle-shaped instead of round because of an abnormality in the hemoglobin: *The sickle cell is a genetic mutation that occurred long ago in malarial regions of Africa* (Scientific American). —**sick′le-cell′,** *adj.*
**sickle cell anemia**, a hereditary form of anemia in which the normally round red blood cells become sickle-shaped, are ineffective in carrying oxygen, and are easily destroyed: *Sickle cell anemia ... affects the Negro population almost exclusively* (New York Times). *The hemoglobin molecule in the cell ... and not the cell itself is the diseased factor in sickle cell anemia* (Science News Letter).
**sickle cell trait**, a hereditary condition in which a person has one gene for normal hemoglobin and one gene for the abnormal hemoglobin that produces sickle cells: *The sickle cell trait (which does not necessarily lead to sickle cell anemia) is appreciably more common in Negroes than in members of other populations* (Scientific American).
**sick|led** (sik′əld), *adj.* furnished with a sickle.
**sickle feather**, one of the long, curved feathers of a rooster's tail.
**sick|le|man** (sik′əl man′), *n., pl.* **-men.** a man who uses a sickle; reaper.
**sick|le|mi|a** (sik lē′mē ə), *n.* **1** = sickle cell anemia. **2** = sickle cell trait.
**sick|le|pod** (sik′əl pod′), *n.* a North American cress with long, curved pods.
**sick|ler** (sik′lər), *n.* a reaper or sickleman.
**sick|le-shaped** (sik′əl shāpt′), *adj.* shaped like a sickle; having a curved, hooklike form; falcate.
**sick|li|ly** (sik′lə lē), *adv.* in a sickly manner; sickly.
**sick|li|ness** (sik′lē nis), *n.* the condition or fact of being sickly; ill health.
**sick|ling** (sik′ling), *n.* a changing in the shape of red blood cells from round to convex, as in sickle cell anemia: *Sickling is not dangerous unless it affects most of the hemoglobin, in which case it can cause fatal anemia* (Scientific American).
**sick list**, a list of workers, military personnel, students, or others who are part of a group who are sick.
**sick-list|ed** (sik′lis′tid), *adj.* entered on the sick list; reported sick.
**sick|ly** (sik′lē), *adj., adv., v.,* **-li|er, -li|est,** *adv., v.,* **-lied, -ly|ing.** —*adj.* **1** often sick; not strong and healthy. SYN: ailing, indisposed. **2** of or having to do with sickness; suggesting sickness: *Her skin is a sickly yellow.* **3a** causing sickness: *That*

place has a sickly climate. **b** marked by the presence of sickness. **4** faint, weak; pale: *a sickly glow.* **5** *Figurative.* weak; mawkish: *sickly sentimentality.*
*—adv.* in a sick manner: (*Figurative.*) *to smile sickly.*
*—v.t.* **1** to cover with a sickly hue: *Thus the native hue of resolution Is sicklied o'er with the pale cast of thought* (Shakespeare). **2** to make sickly or pale.

**sick|ness** (sik′nis), *n.* **1a** the condition of being sick; poor health; illness; disease. **b** a particular disease as the cause of this; ailment; malady. **2** nausea; vomiting. SYN: queasiness, squeamishness.

**sick nurse**, a nurse for sick persons.

**sick-out** (sik′out′), *n.* an organized absence of employees from their work on the pretext of being sick, to avoid the legal penalties that may result from a formal strike: *The postal strike had barely ended when a sick-out by air traffic controllers continued the communications snarl* (Paul T. Hartman).

**sick parade**, an inspection of those who are sick, as in the armed forces.

**sick pay**, = sick benefit.

**sick|room** (sik′rüm′, -rům′), *n.* a room in which a sick person is cared for.

**sic pas|sim** (sik pas′im), *Latin.* so in various places.

**sic sem|per ty|ran|nis** (sik sem′pər tə ran′is), *Latin.* thus always to tyrants (the motto of Virginia; known also as the utterance of John Wilkes Booth to the audience at Ford's Theatre just after his shooting of Lincoln).

**sic tran|sit glo|ri|a mun|di** (sik tran′sit glôr′ē ə mun′dī, glōr′-), *Latin.* so passes away the glory of this world.

**sic|ut pa|tri|bus, sit De|us no|bis** (sik′ət pā′trə bəs sit dē′əs nō′bis), *Latin.* May God be with us, as with our fathers (motto of Boston).

**SID** (no periods), sudden ionospheric disturbance (usually caused by the sun).

**si|da** (sī′də), *n.* any plant of a group of herbs and shrubs of the mallow family, found mostly in warm climates and usually having small yellow or white flowers, such as Queensland hemp. [< New Latin *Sida* the typical genus < Greek *sidē* a water plant]

**sid|dur** (sid′ůr), *n., pl.* **sid|durs, sid|du|rim** (si′dů-rēm′). a Jewish prayer book, containing the daily, Sabbath, and festival prayers. It is written in Hebrew and Aramaic. [< Hebrew *siddūr* (literally) order]

**side**[1] (sīd), *n., adj., v.,* **sid|ed, sid|ing.** *—n.* **1** a surface or line bounding a thing: *the sides of a square, a side of a box.* **2** one of the two surfaces of an object that are not the front, back, top, or bottom: *a door at the side of a house, the sides of a bed, a table, or a wagon.* **3** one of the two surfaces, as of paper, cloth, or a phonograph record: *Write only on one side of the paper. Play both sides of the record.* **4a** a particular surface: *the outer and inner sides of a hollow ball, the side of the moon toward the earth.* **b** *Figurative.* an aspect or view of someone or something: *the better side of one's nature, the bright side of a difficulty, to hear all sides of an argument.* **5** the slope of a hill or bank, especially one extending for a considerable distance. **6** the bank or shore of a river or water, or the land bordering a river or water. **7** either the right or left part of a thing; either part or region beyond a central line, or extending in any direction from a certain place or point: *a region on both sides of a river, the east side of a city, our side of the street, to turn to one side.* **8** either the right or left part of the body of a person or animal: *The man was wounded in the side.* **9a** a group of persons who stand up for their beliefs, opinions, or ways of doing things against another group: *Both sides are ready for the contest.* **b** a sports team: *The two boys chose sides for a game of softball. The present Australian side is, on good pitches, a very powerful one* (Sunday Times). **10** *Figurative.* the position, course, attitude, or part of one person or party against another: *faults on both sides. It is pleasant to be on the winning side.* **11** *Figurative.* the line of descent; part of a family: *He is English on his mother's side.* **12** *British Slang.* pretentious airs; arrogance: *remarkable for his want of anything like "side"* (Samuel Butler). **13** either part of a ship's hull extending from stem to stern, above the water line. **14** *British.* a spinning motion given a billiard ball by striking it at a point not directly in the middle; english. **15** one page of an actor's lines.
*—adj.* **1** at one side; on one side: *side streets, the side aisles of a theater.* **2a** from one side: *a side view.* **b** toward one side; indirect: *a side glance.* **3** *Figurative.* less important; subsidiary: *a side issue.*
*—v.t.* **1** to provide with sides, as a building. **2** to put aside: *Mrs. Wilson was "siding" the dinner things* (Elizabeth Gaskell). *—v.i.* to take a side: *The Nobility are vexed, whom we see have sided In his behalf* (Shakespeare).
**by one's side**, near one: *His mother was by his side all during his illness.*
**off side**, not in a position, according to the rules of the game, to participate in a play: *One of the ends was off side, having started to go out for the pass a second before the ball was put into play.*
**on side**, in position, according to the rules of the game, to participate in a play: *All players were on side for the kickoff.*
**on the shady side of**, older than; beyond the age of: *From looking at his face one would not think he was on the shady side of fifty.*
**on the side, a** *Informal.* in addition to one's regular or ordinary duties: *Many producers of long-run shows are lenient about letting members of their casts earn money on the side* (New Yorker). **b** served as a side dish: *a hamburger with French fries on the side.*
**on the windy side of**, so as not to be scented and attacked by and therefore out of reach of; away from; clear of: *Still you keep o'th windy side of the Law* (Shakespeare).
**shiver my sides**, a mock oath attributed to sailors: *If fairer can be said by mortal seaman, shiver my sides!* (Robert Louis Stevenson).
**side against**, to oppose: *Most of the smaller boys sided against the bully and gave him a licking.*
**side by side, a** beside one another: *They walked side by side like a couple of policemen.* **b** equally: *In the hourly earning of its employees ... it ranked side by side with petroleum refining, an industry with a much higher profit margin* (New York Times).
**side with**, to take the part of; favor (one among opposing or differing groups or persons); take sides with: *The twins always side with each other when the older children quarrel. Scotchmen who sided alternately with the French and English interests* (Theodore Roosevelt).
**split one's sides**, to laugh or cause one to laugh very hard: *Unlike Mr. Milligan, who is forever trying to split our sides, he is content with inducing the wry chuckle, and this he does supremely well* (Manchester Guardian Weekly).
**take sides**, to place oneself with one person or group against another: *The bystander refused to take sides in the quarrel.*
**this side of**, short of; not spilling over into: *Its lean harmonies and themes keep the work this side of sentimentality* (Raymond Ericson).
[Old English *sīde*]

**side**[2] (sīd), *adj. Scottish.* reaching or hanging far down on the person; long. [Old English *sīd*]

**side|arm** (sīd′ärm′), *adj., adv. —adj. Sports.* throwing or thrown from the side with the arm swung nearly parallel to the ground; not overhand or underhand: *a sidearm pitcher, a sidearm pitch.*
*—adv.* in a sidearm manner.

**side arms**, a sword, dagger, revolver, or bayonet, carried at the side or in the belt.

**side-ax** (sīd′aks′), *n.* an ax with the handle slightly bent to one side to guard the hand.

**side|band** (sīd′band′), *n.* one of the bands comprising the frequencies on either side of the carrier frequency of a modulated wave when the carrier frequency is higher than the modulating frequency: *From this point of view existing plans in the United States for a Medical Radio System utilizing unused sidebands of existing FM broadcasting stations are of special interest* (New Scientist).

**side|bar** (sīd′bär′), *n.* **1** a latitudinal bar or longitudinal sidepiece as in a carriage or saddle. **2** a news report or feature which supplements a major news story.

**side bet**, an additional bet, secondary to the main bet or betting.

***sideboard**
definition 1

***side|board** (sīd′bôrd′, -bōrd′), *n.* **1** a cabinet with drawers and shelves, especially for holding silver or linen, and usually a flat top for dishes; buffet. **2** an additional and removable board placed on the side of a truck, wagon, or the like, as in slotted uprights, so as to increase the height of, or form, a side.
**sideboards, a** the fence surrounding a hockey rink; the boards. **b** *Slang.* side whiskers; sideburns: *to shave off one's sideboards.*

**side-boy** (sīd′boi′), *n.* a boy assigned to the gangway of a ship to wait on an officer who is coming aboard or leaving.

**side|burned** (sīd′bėrnd′), *adj. U.S.* wearing sideburns: *A sideburned youth beats out an insolent rhythm on a resonant fantail deck* (New Yorker).

***side|burns** (sīd′bėrnz′), *n.pl.* whiskers in front of the ears, especially when worn long and when the chin is shaved. [American English, alteration of *burnsides* < Ambrose E. *Burnside,* 1824-1881, a Union general]
► **Sideburns—burnsides** are related etymologically but have rarely, if ever, been exactly synonymous. *Burnsides,* now chiefly historical in use, designates relatively long, heavy whiskers, patterned on those worn by General Burnside (1824-1881). *Sideburns,* especially in current use, designates any hairy growth extending downward from a point just in front of the upper base of the ear, with length and closeness of cut being a matter of individual taste.

***sideburns**

burnsides

**side|car** (sīd′kär′), *n.* **1** a car for a passenger or baggage, attached to the side of a motorcycle: *Mercury ... bought an aged and decrepit motorcycle, with a sidecar* (New Yorker). **2** *U.S.* a cocktail made with an orange-flavored liqueur, brandy, and lemon juice in approximately equal parts.

**side chain**, **1** a chain of atoms attached to the principal chain in the structure of a molecule: *One possible line of research ... would be the production ... of a basic penicillin nucleus and the attachment to it of different side chains* (London Times). **2** a chain at the side of a vehicle, especially either of two chains that transmit motion from the engine to the driving wheels in some motor vehicles.

**side chair**, **1** an armless chair. **2** one of a set of chairs, with or without arms, placed at the side of a table or room: *A matching side chair, low-armed and inviting, is $55* (New Yorker).

**side chapel**, a chapel in an aisle or at the side of a church.

**side|check** (sīd′chek′), *n.* a checkrein in a horse's harness, placed at the side of the horse's head.

**side comb**, a comb used in a woman's hair to retain a curl or lock on the side of the head.

**side|curl** (sīd′kėrl′), *n.* = earlock.

**-sided**, *combining form.* having ___ sides: *Many-sided = having many sides.*

**side dish**, **1** an item of food served in addition to the main dish of a course or meal: *to have peas as a side dish.* **2** a dish, especially a small dish, for a serving of such an item of food.

**side door**, a door at the side of a house or building, used as a secondary entrance.

**side-dress** (sīd′dres′), *v.t.* to fertilize (a plant or plants) with something as a side dressing: *to side-dress corn with nitrates.*

**side dressing**, a fertilizer scattered on or worked shallowly into the soil near the base of a plant, especially as a supplement to that placed in the soil at planting or to overcome some nutritional deficiency.

**side drum**, a snare drum, especially for a marching band: *So we got a battered old saxophone, a second-hand side drum, a string-bass ...* (Harper's).

**side effect**, a secondary effect or reaction, usually undesirable or unpleasant: *The doctor cites* *the dangers of tranquilizers, among which were their side effects, drug dependency, habituation and addiction* (Science News Letter).

**side entrance**, a subsidiary entrance, such as on the side into a building or vehicle.

**side-glance** (sīd′glans′, -gläns′), *n.* a glance directed sideways; sidelong glance: *We got the drift, and our side-glances to each other said simply, "He stinks"* (Edward Weeks).

**side|head** (sīd′hed′), *n.* a subhead in the margin, such as in the left-hand margin of a left-hand page, aligned with the first line of the paragraph or context to which it applies.

**side|hill** (sīd′hil′), *n. Canadian and U.S.* a hillside: *Horseherds ranged the valleys and sidehills* (Canadian Geographic Journal).

**side horse**, a gymnasium apparatus for jumping or vaulting exercises.

**side issue**, a matter not connected with the subject under discussion.

**side|kick** or **side-kick** (sīd′kik′), *n. Informal.* a partner or close friend; crony: *He spent his spare time playing gin with his sidekicks* (Time).

**side|lamp** (sīd′lamp′), *n. Especially British.* the lamp on either side of a motor vehicle.

**side|less** (sīd′lis), *adj.* without sides; open at the sides.

**side|light** (sīd′līt′), *n.* **1** light coming from the side. **2** incidental information about a subject: *amusing sidelights in a biography. Such information may throw sidelight upon my story* (Herman Melville). **3** either of two lights required to be carried by a moving ship at night, a red one on the port side and a green one on the starboard. **4** a window or other opening for light, such as in the side of a building or ship. **5** a window at the side of a door or (sometimes) a larger window, used especially with a solid door to permit daylight to enter a hall that would otherwise be dark.

**side|line** (sīd′līn′), *n., v.,* **-lined, -lin|ing.** —*n.* **1** a line at the side of something. **2** a line that marks the limit of play, as in football, soccer, or tennis. **3a** an additional line of goods, of trade, or of business. **b** *Figurative.* any enterprise carried on apart from that in which one is chiefly or officially employed. **4** a branch line (of a railroad).

—*v.t.* to put on the sidelines; make inactive: *One was a right wing ... who was sidelined for two weeks with an ankle injury* (New York Times).

**sidelines, a** the area just outside the lines marking the limits of play: *The spectators watched the game from the sidelines.* **b** the position or status of those not actively taking part in a game: *In spite of Morgan's professed intention of retiring from competition after the Olympics, it was hardly to be expected that anyone so tireless and ambitious could remain on the sidelines for long* (London Times).

**—side′lin′er,** *n.*

**side|ling** (sīd′ling), *adv., adj.* —*adv.* with a sideward movement; sideways; obliquely.

—*adj.* **1** moving sideways; oblique: *a sideling motion, a sideling blow.* **2** sloping; steep: *a sideling hill.*

**side|lock** (sīd′lok′), *n.* = earlock.

**side|long** (sīd′lông′, -long′), *adj., adv.* to one side; toward the side: *a sidelong glance* (adj.). *He glanced sidelong at me* (adv.).

**side-look|ing** (sīd′lůk′ing), *adj.* directed or pointing sideways: *Side-looking sonar ... gives a profile of objects on the bottom* (New York Times).

**side-looking radar**, radar used in an aircraft to transmit a microwave signal at an acute angle sufficient to reflect a profile image. Such an image recorded on film is used to substitute for aerial photography over obscured terrain. *The acute grazing angle of the microwave illumination of side-looking radar emphasizes the form of the land* (Scientific American).

**side|man** (sīd′man′), *n., pl.* **-men.** *U.S.* a musician in a jazz ensemble other than the leader.

**side meat**, *U.S. Dialect.* **1** salt pork. **2** bacon.

**side|note** (sīd′nōt′), *n.* a note at the side of a written or printed page; a marginal note, as distinguished from a footnote.

**side oats**, a kind of oat whose spikelets grow all on one side of the stem instead of spreading out from all sides; horsemane oats.

**side-oats grama** (sīd′ōts′), a grama grass ranging from New Jersey to the Rocky Mountains and southward, bearing many short spikes along one side of the stem, used for forage.

**side out**, the loss of a team's or player's right to serve in volleyball and some other games, occurring when the serving side fails to win a point or play the ball legally.

**side partner**, a person who works alongside or alternately with another person.

**side|piece** (sīd′pēs′), *n.* a piece forming a side or part of a side, or fixed by the side, of something.

**side play**, motion which is not in the direction of the desired motion but at an angle to it, as in the parts of an automobile or other vehicle.

**sid|er** (sī′dər), *n.* a person who sides with a person, party, or cause; partisan; adherent.

**-sider**, *combining form.* a person born or living in ___: *Sydneysider = person born or living in Sydney, Australia. West-sider = person born or living on the West Side.* [abstracted from *outsider, hillsider,* etc.]

**sid|er|al** (sid′ər əl), *adj.* **1** = sidereal. **2** due to the stars.

**si|de|re|al** (sī dir′ē əl), *adj.* **1** of or having to do with the stars or constellations: *our sidereal system.* **SYN**: astral, stellar. **2** measured by the apparent daily motion of the stars: *A sidereal day is shorter than a mean solar day by 3 minutes and 56 seconds* (Eric D. Carlson). *A sidereal month—27⅓ days—is the time the moon takes to make one trip around the earth in relation to the stars* (Eugene M. Shoemaker). See also **sidereal time**. [< Latin *sīdereus* astral (< *sīdus, -eris* star) + English *-al*[1]]

***sidereal time**, time measured by the stars, or the hour angle of the vernal equinox. A sidereal day is one rotation of the earth in reference to any star or the vernal equinox at the meridian, and is about 4 minutes shorter than a mean solar day. A sidereal day consists of 23 hours, 56 minutes, and 4.09 seconds of mean solar time. It is divided into hours, minutes, and seconds, the same way that a regular day is.

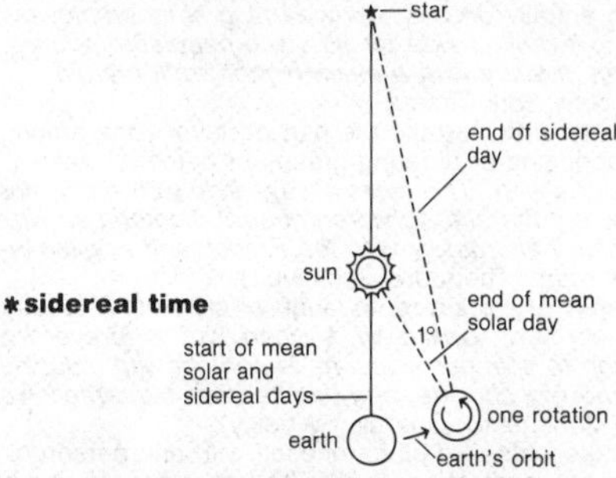


***sidereal time**

**sid|er|ite** (sid′ə rīt), *n.* **1** an iron ore occurring in various forms and colors and crystallizing with perfect rhombohedral cleavage; chalybite. *Formula:* $FeCO_3$ **2** a meteorite consisting mainly of iron. **3** *Obsolete.* loadstone. [< Latin *sidērītes* loadstone < Greek *sidērītēs* < *sídēros* iron]

**sid|er|it|ic** (sid′ə rit′ik), *adj.* of the nature of siderite.

**side road**, a secondary road alongside or turning off a main road.

**sid|er|o|graph|ic** (sid′ər ə graf′ik), having to do with or produced by siderography.

**sid|er|og|ra|phy** (sid′ə rog′rə fē), *n.* the art of engraving on steel, especially a process in which the design is subsequently transferred by pressure to other steel surfaces. [< Greek *sídēros* iron + English *-graphy*]

**sid|er|o|lite** (sid′ər ə līt), *n.* a meteorite composed of a mixed mass of iron and stone. [< Greek *sídēros* iron + English *-lite*]

**sid|er|o|na|trite** (sid′ər ə nā′trīt), *n.* a hydrated sulfate of iron and sodium occurring in crystalline masses of a dark-yellow color.

**sid|er|o|phile** (sid′ər ə fīl), *adj. Geology.* having an affinity for metallic iron. [< Greek *sídēros* iron + English *-phile*]

**sid|er|o|sis** (sid′ə rō′sis), *n.* a chronic inflammatory disease of the lungs caused by inhalation of iron particles. [< New Latin *siderosis* < Greek *sídēros* iron + *-ōsis* condition]

**sid|er|o|stat** (sid′ər ə stat), *n. Astronomy.* a device for keeping the direction of the reflected light of a star constant, usually consisting of a plane mirror carried on an axis parallel to the earth's axis and rotating once every 48 hours. [< Latin *sīdus, -eris* star + English *-stat*]

**sid|er|o|stat|ic** (sid′ə rə stat′ik), *adj.* of or having to do with a siderostat.

**sid|er|ur|gi|cal** (sid′ər ėr′jə kəl), *adj.* having to do with siderurgy.

**sid|er|ur|gy** (sid′ər ėr′jē), *n.* the art of working in iron and steel. [< Greek *sidērourgiā* < *sidērourgós* ironworker < *sídēros* iron + *érgon* work]

***side|sad|dle** (sīd′sad′əl), *n., adv.* —*n.* a woman's saddle so made that both of the rider's legs are on the same side of a horse, now especially one with knoblike protuberances to support the knees of the rider, who sits facing forward with the right knee slightly raised above the left.

—*adv.* with both legs on the same side of the horse: *to ride sidesaddle.*

**sidesaddle flower**, the common species of pitcher plant of the eastern United States.

**side sewing**, a method of fastening the signatures of a book by sewing them together through the side with strong thread of nylon or cotton.

**side show**, or **side|show** (sīd′shō′), *n.* **1** a small show in connection with a main one: *the side shows of a circus.* **2** *Figurative.* any minor proceeding or affair connected with a more important one.

**side|slip** (sīd′slip′), *n., v.,* **-slipped, -slip|ping.** —*n.* **1** a slip to one side, as in skiing; skid. **2** the slipping to one side and downward of an aircraft in flight; loss of altitude by a sliding sideward and downward, as along the plane of a bank.

—*v.i.* to slip to one side; do a sideslip: *The car sideslipped as it rounded the curve.*

**sides|man** (sīdz′mən), *n., pl.* **-men.** *British.* **1** an assistant to the churchwarden of a parish. **2** *Obsolete.* a person who takes sides; partisan.

**side|spin** (sīd′spin′), *n.* a rotary motion given to a ball to make it revolve horizontally in flight.

**side|split|ter** (sīd′split′ər), *n.* **1** an extremely funny joke or happening. **2** a spell of very loud and hearty laughter: *The audience broke into a hysterical orgy of laughter that ran 3 min. 45 sec. on the tape—probably the longest sidesplitter in television history* (Time).

**side|split|ting** (sīd′split′ing), *adj.* **1** extremely funny: *a sidesplitting joke.* **2** loud and hearty: *sidesplitting laughter.* —**side′split′ting|ly**, *adv.*

**side step**, **1** a step or stepping to one side. **2** a step at the side, as of a ship or vehicle.

**side-step** (sīd′step′), *v.t., v.i.,* **-stepped, -step|ping.** **1** to step aside: *to side-step in order to avoid a blow.* **2** *Figurative.* to avoid by or as if by stepping aside; evade: *to side-step a punch, to side-step a responsibility.* —**side′-step′per**, *n.*

**side|stroke** (sīd′strōk′), *n.,* or **side stroke**, a swimming stroke in which the swimmer lies on his side in the water, pulling alternately with his arms while performing a scissors kick: *The side stroke is a restful stroke and is not used for racing* (Adolph Kiefer).

**side|swipe** (sīd′swīp′), *v.,* **-swiped, -swip|ing,** *n.* —*v.t., v.i.* to hit with a sweeping blow along the side: *A chartered German plane en route to New York sideswiped a building and crashed in flames* (Wall Street Journal).

—*n.* a sweeping blow along the side or indirectly: (*Figurative.*) *The author takes some well-aimed sideswipes at our foreign policy* (New Yorker). [earlier *sidewipe*]

**side table**, **1** a table placed near the wall of a room, especially a dining room. **2** a table smaller than a dining table, placed to one side of it, and used in serving.

**side tool**, a tool with a cutting edge at the side.

**side|track** (sīd′trak′), *n., v.* —*n.* **1** a short railroad track to which a train may be switched from a main track; siding. **2** *Figurative.* the state of being diverted or turned aside: *to stick to the business at hand and avoid sidetracks.*

—*v.t.* **1** to switch (a train or car) to a sidetrack; move off the main track. **2** *Figurative.* to put aside; turn aside: *The teacher refused to be sidetracked by questions on other subjects.*

**side trip**, a short trip away from the main or direct route of a journey: *You can go straight up Highway 8A, making side trips to the ghost towns* (Sunset).

**side|view mirror** (sīd′vyü′), **1** a movable mirror attached at eye level outside an automobile or truck to give the driver a view of vehicles moving alongside him. **2** a mirror designed to show a side view or profile of a person.

*** sidesaddle**

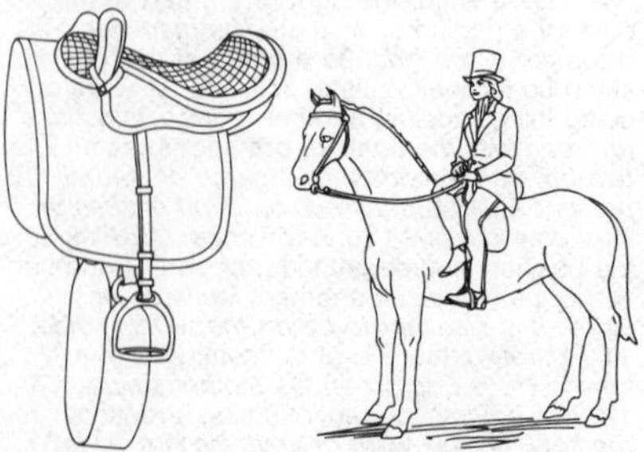

**side|walk** (sīd′wôk′), *n., adj.* —*n.* a place to walk at the side of a street, usually paved. **SYN**: footway, footpath.

—*adj.* **1** working on a sidewalk instead of in a shop, studio, or the like: *a sidewalk mechanic, a sidewalk artist.* **2** that views a subject from the outside; dilettante; armchair: *a sidewalk critic. She described the educators as "sidewalk diplomats who don't know and have no right to express an opinion on diplomacy"* (Manchester Guardian Weekly).

**sidewalk superintendent**, *Informal.* a person who stops on the street to observe the work of a construction or repair project: *Sidewalk superintendents can be a terrible nuisance, getting in the way of trucks, gear, and workmen* (New Yorker).

**side wall**, 1 either of the two side portions of an automobile tire, between the tread and the rim: *One of them is located in its normal rim position and the other in the side wall* (Wall Street Journal). 2 the outer surface of one of these: *to buy tires with white side walls.*

**side|wall** (sīd′wôl′), *n.* 1 a wall forming the side of a structure, room, or enclosure. 2 = side wall.

**side|ward** (sīd′wərd), *adj., adv.* toward one side.

**side|wards** (sīd′wərdz), *adv.* = sideward.

**side|way** (sīd′wā′), *adv., adj., n.* —**adv., adj.** = sideways.
—*n.* 1 a side street, as distinguished from a main road; byway. 2 = sidewalk.

**side|ways** (sīd′wāz′), *adv., adj.* 1 to one side; toward one side: *to walk sideways. Backwards and forwards and sideways did she pass* (Rudyard Kipling). 2 from one side: *a sideways glimpse.* 3 with one side toward the front; with a side other than the usual side facing upward or outward: *to stand sideways, to place a book sideways on a shelf.* 4 at one side of a place.

**side-wheel** (sīd′hwēl′), *adj.* having a paddle wheel on each side: *A leisurely trip up the Volga in a side-wheel steamer left over from Czarist days* (Time).

**side-wheel|er** (sīd′hwē′lər), *n.* a side-wheel steamer: *in 1839, twenty years after the "side-wheeler" Savannah made the first steamship crossing of the Atlantic Ocean* (Beauchamp, Mayfield, and West). See picture under **paddle-wheeler**.

**side whisker**, a hair growing long on the side of the face.
**side whiskers**, the whiskers that grow on the cheek or side of the face: *Pale young men with larded hair and Valentino-black side whiskers* (Atlantic).

**side-whisk|ered** (sīd′hwis′kərd), *adj.* having side whiskers.

**side wind**, a wind blowing from or on a side of an aircraft or ship: *The airplane is usually drifting sideways under the influence of side winds but the 67 determines the drift and allows for it* (Time).

**side|wind|er** (sīd′wīn′dər), *n.* 1 a small rattlesnake of the southwestern United States that travels in a sideways direction by looping its body. 2 a heavy blow delivered from the side, in which the fist is swung at or near the level of the shoulder through an arc of approximately 45 degrees.

**side|wipe** (sīd′wīp′), *v.,* **-wiped, -wip|ing,** *n.* = sideswipe.

**side|wise** (sīd′wīz′), *adv., adj.* = sideways.

**sidhe** (shē), *n., pl.* **sidhe** or **sidhes**. = shee.

**sid|ing** (sī′ding), *n.* 1 a short railroad track to which cars may be switched from a main track. SYN: sidetrack. 2 the boards, shingles, or other material forming the outside wall of certain types of frame buildings, nailed to a house over the sheathing or directly to the studs of a barn: *The personnel building now under construction is using aluminum siding and roofing.*

**si|dle** (sī′dəl), *v.,* **-dled, -dling,** *n.* —*v.i.* 1 to move sideways: *"I can't bear those things," Wilson said, sidling through the door* (Graham Greene). 2 to move sideways slowly so as not to attract attention: *The little boy shyly sidled up to the visitor.*
—*v.t.* to move, turn, or direct sideways: *The rider sidled his horse towards the tree and picked off an apple.*
—*n.* a movement sideways.
[probably back formation < *sideling*]

**SIDS** (no periods), sudden infant death syndrome.

**siè|cle** (sye′klə), *n. French.* century; age; epoch (especially in English contexts in certain phrases, as *fin de siècle*).

**siege** (sēj), *n., v.,* **sieged, sieg|ing.** —*n.* 1 the act of surrounding a fortified place by an army trying to capture it; besieging or being besieged: *Troy was under siege for ten years. The country was in a state of siege, and tanks were lined up in front of the Presidential palace* (Newsweek). 2 *Figurative.* any long or persistent effort to overcome resistance; any long-continued attack: *a siege of illness.* 3 *Obsolete.* a seat, especially one used by a person of rank or distinction. 4 *Obsolete.* a place in which one has his seat or residence; seat of rule, empire, etc.
—*v.t.* = besiege.
**lay siege to, a** to besiege: *He [Frederick the Great] laid siege to Prague, but was defeated in the battle of Kolin* (Robert G. L. Waite). **b** *Figurative.* to attempt to win or get by long and persistent effort: *His great ambition made him lay siege to all those who could help him achieve it.*
[Middle English *sege* seat < Old French *siege* < Vulgar Latin *sedium* < Latin *sedēre* to sit]
—*Syn. n.* 1 **Siege, blockade** mean a military operation to cut off normal communications and supplies of a place. **Siege**, chiefly applied to a land operation, means surrounding a city or fortified place, cutting off all movement to and from it, and usually assaulting it: *The Japanese laid siege to Corregidor.* **Blockade** applies to an operation, chiefly but not always naval, to close a harbor, coast, or city and cut off its supplies, but does not suggest attacking it: *In the struggle against Napoleon the British proclaimed a blockade of the northern coast of Europe. In 1948-1949, the airlift defeated the Russian blockade of Berlin.*

**siege|craft** (sēj′kraft′, -kräft′), *n.* the military science or art of besieging a city or fortified place.

**Siege Perilous**, the vacant seat at King Arthur's Round Table, that could be occupied only by the knight who was destined to find the Holy Grail. [< Middle French *siege perilous*]

**siege piece**, a coin, commonly of unusual shape and rude workmanship, struck and issued in a place during a siege, when the operations of the ordinary mints are suspended or their issues are not available.

**siege train**, the equipment of guns, carriages, ammunition, and the like, carried with an army for the purpose of besieging.

**Sieg|fried** (sēg′frēd), *n. German Legend.* a hero who killed a dragon, won the treasure of the Nibelungs, acquired a magic sword, and rescued Brunhild from an enchanted sleep. [< German *Siegfried* (literally) peace of victory]

**Siegfried Line**, an elaborate network of German fortifications facing the French Maginot Line, built shortly before World War II.

**Si|en|ese** (sē′ə nēz′, -nēs′), *adj., n., pl.* **-ese**.
—*adj.* of or having to do with Siena, a city and province of central Italy.
—*n.* a native or inhabitant of Siena.

**si|e|nite** (sī′ə nīt), *n.* = syenite.

**si|en|na** (sē en′ə), *n.* 1 any one of various mixtures of clay and oxides of iron and manganese, used as a pigment. In its natural state it is yellowish-brown (raw sienna). After heating, it becomes reddish-brown (burnt sienna). 2 a yellowish brown or reddish brown. [< Italian *sienna* short for *terra di Sienna* earth from Siena, a city in Italy]

**sie|ro|zem** (syer′ə zem), *n.* a grayish soil found in temperate or cool arid regions, supporting sparse, shrubby vegetation. It is low in humus and its lime is near or on the surface. [< Russian *serozëm* < *seryj* gray + *zemlja* land, soil]

**si|er|ra** (sē er′ə), *n.* 1 a chain of hills or mountains whose peaks suggest the teeth of a saw: *The road wound up the bold sierra which separates the great plateaus of Mexico and Puebla* (William H. Prescott). 2 any one of certain Spanish mackerels, such as the cero. [American English < Spanish *sierra* (literally) a saw < Latin *serra*]

**Si|er|ra** (sē er′ə), *n. U.S.* a code name for the letter *s*, used in transmitting radio messages.

**Si|er|ra Le|o|ne|an** (sē er′ə lē ō′nē ən, sir′ə), 1 a native or inhabitant of Sierra Leone, a country on the western coast of Africa: *Many distinguished Sierra Leoneans … have professional and family ties of long standing with Britain* (London Times). 2 of or having to do with Sierra Leone or its people.

**si|er|ran** (sē er′ən), *adj.* of or having to do with a sierra.

**sierra redwood**, = giant sequoia.

**si|es|ta** (sē es′tə), *n., v.,* **-taed, -ta|ing.** —*n.* a nap or rest taken at noon or in the afternoon. It is commonly taken during the hottest hours of the day in Spanish-speaking countries of the tropics or subtropics.
—*v.i.* to rest or take a nap; indulge in a siesta.
[< Spanish *siesta* < Latin *sexta* (*hōra*) sixth (hour) of the Roman day (that is midday). See etym. of doublet **sext**.]

**sieur** (syœr), *n.* a former French title of respect for a man; Sir. [< Old French *sieur* < Vulgar Latin *seiōrem* < Latin *seniōrem,* accusative of *senior* senior. See etym. of doublets **seigneur, seignior**.]

**Sie|va bean** (sē′və), a twining species of bean related to the Lima bean, with broad and curved pods containing flat seeds.

**sieve** (siv), *n., v.,* **sieved, siev|ing.** —*n.* a utensil shaped like a bowl or cup and having holes that let liquids and smaller pieces pass through, but not the larger pieces: *Shaking flour through a sieve removes lumps. We use a sieve to strain soup.* SYN: strainer, colander.
—*v.t., v.i.* to put or pass through a sieve.
[Old English *sife*] —**sieve′like′**, *adj.*

**sieve cell**, *Botany.* an elongated cell whose thin walls have perforations, usually at each end, which allow communication between adjacent cells of a similar nature. Sieve cells form the essential element of the phloem of lower vascular plants.

**sieve of Er|a|tos|the|nes** (er′ə tos′thə nēz′), a method for finding prime numbers by writing down a series of whole numbers, beginning with 2, then crossing out all the second numbers except 2, all the third except 3, and so on until all but the prime numbers remain. The method was invented by Eratosthenes, 276?-194? B.C., a Greek mathematician.

**sieve plate**, *Botany.* one of the thin walls of a sieve cell.

**sieve tissue**, *Botany.* tissue composed of sieve cells or sieve tubes.

**sieve tube**, *Botany.* 1 a tubelike structure composed of thin, elongated cells connected through perforations in their end walls, forming the essential element of the phloem of higher vascular plants: *The thin-walled sieve tubes are often filled with colloidal material and have the appearance of containing live protoplasm* (Fred W. Emerson). 2 one of the cells that make up this structure; sieve cell.

**Sif** (sif), *n. Norse Mythology.* the blond-haired wife of Thor.

**sif|fle** (sif′əl), *n. Medicine.* a sibilant rale. [earlier, verb, blow, whistle < Old French *siffler* < Latin *sīfilāre*, variant of *sībilāre* whistle]

**sif|flöt** (sē flœt′), *n.* 1 a whistle flute. 2 a flute stop in an organ having a whistling tone. [< German *Sifflöte* < French *siffloter* whistle < Old French *siffler;* see etym. under **siffle**]

**sift** (sift), *v.t.* 1 to separate large pieces from small by shaking in a sieve: *to sift ashes. Sift the gravel and put the larger stones in another pile.* 2 to put through a sieve: *Sift sugar on the top of the cake.* 3 *Figurative.* to examine very carefully: *The jury sifted the evidence to decide if the man was guilty.* SYN: scrutinize. 4 *Figurative.* to subject (a person) to close questioning.
—*v.i.* 1 to use a sieve. 2 to fall through a sieve: (*Figurative.*) *The snow sifted softly down.* [Old English *siftan,* related to *sife* sieve]

**sift|er** (sif′tər), *n.* a utensil or device for sifting: *a flour sifter.*

**sift|ing** (sif′ting), *n.* the act of a person or thing that sifts.
**siftings**, the parts of matter sifted out: *I would recommend to add to it … either sand, lime rubbish, or lime siftings* (Beck's Florist Journal).

**sig.**, 1 mark (Latin, *signa*). 2 signal. 3 signature.

**Sig.**, 1 (in pharmacy) signature. 2 Signor. 3 Signore. 4 Signori.

**sigh** (sī), *v., n.* —*v.i.* 1 to let out a very long, deep breath because one is sad, tired, or relieved: *We heard her sigh with relief.* 2 to make a sound like a sigh: *The wind sighed in the treetops. Nought but a lovely sighing of the wind* (Keats). 3 to wish very much; long: *She sighed for home and friends.* SYN: yearn. 4 to lament with sighing: *to sigh over one's unhappy fate.*
—*v.t.* 1 to say or express with a sigh. 2 to lament (an event or circumstance) with sighing.
—*n.* the act or sound of sighing: *a sigh of relief.*
[Middle English *sighen,* probably back formation < *sighte,* preterit of Old English *sīcan*] —**sigh′er**, *n.* —**sigh′ing|ly**, *adv.*

**sight** (sīt), *n., v.* —*n.* 1a the power of seeing; eyesight; vision: *Birds have better sight than dogs.* **b** mental or spiritual vision. 2a the act or fact of seeing; look: *One sight of the house was enough to make him want to buy it.* SYN: glance, gaze. **b** examination; inspection; scrutiny: *a bill of sight.* 3 the range of seeing: *to lose sight of a plane. Land was in sight.* 4 a thing seen; view; glimpse (of something): *I caught a sight of him running around a corner.* 5a something worth seeing: *to see the sights of the city. Niagara Falls is one of the sights of the world.* **b** something that looks bad or odd: *She is a sight in that ugly dress.* 6 *Figurative.* a way of looking or thinking; regard; estimation; judgment; opinion: *Dolls are very precious in a little girl's sight.* 7 *Informal.* a great number or quantity: *a sight of people; … an awful sight of money* (Mark Twain). 8 an observation taken with a telescope or other instrument. 9 a device, as on a gun or surveying instrument, to guide the eye in taking aim or observing: *the sights on a rifle.* 10 the aim or observation taken by such devices.
—*v.t.* 1 to see: *At last Columbus sighted land.* 2 to look at through sights; point to; aim at: *to sight a star.* 3 to adjust the sight or align the

**Pronunciation Key:** hat, āge, cãre, fär; let, ēqual, tėrm; it, īce; hot, ōpen, ôrder; oil, out; cup, pu̇t, rüle; child; long; thin; ᴛʜen; zh, measure; ə represents **a** in about, **e** in taken, **i** in pencil, **o** in lemon, **u** in circus.

sights of (a gun or instrument). **4** to provide with a sight or sights.
—***v.i.*** to take aim or observation by means of a sight or sights: *The hunter sighted carefully before firing his gun.*
**a sight for sore eyes**, a welcome or pleasing sight: *Elizabeth in the saddle must have been a sight for sore eyes* (London Times).
**at first sight, a** as soon as seen; upon the first look: *He fell in love with her at first sight.* **b** on a first or quick estimate: *At first sight the events of 1066 ... seem to offer an ideal subject for a writer* (Listener).
**at sight, a** as soon as seen: *She reads music at sight.* **b** as soon as presented; on demand: *Some banks will cash a check at sight.*
**catch sight of**, to see: *I caught sight of them. As we drove by the harbor we caught sight of a large steamship.*
**heave in sight**, to come into view as though rising above the horizon: *The great Spanish ships heave in sight, and a furious struggle begins* (John R. Green).
**in sight of**, where one can see or be seen by: *We live in sight of the school. After the long voyage, we were at last in sight of land. We are not yet in possession of ... peace, but for the first time we are fairly in sight of it* (Spectator).
**know by sight**, to know sufficiently to recognize when seen: *I know her by sight, but we have never spoken to each other.*
**lose sight of**, to forget; overlook: *He never loses sight of the obstacles still to be overcome* (Saturday Review).
**on sight**, as soon as seen; at sight: *The fugitive lived in fear of being shot on sight.*
**out of sight**, *Informal.* out of this world; wonderful: *Bibi thinks he's out of sight* (F. P. Tullius).
**out of sight of, a** where one cannot see: *Columbus was out of sight of land for several weeks.* **b** where one cannot be seen by: *out of sight of the neighbors.*
**sights**, goals; objectives: *to raise or lower one's sights. The countries of these regions have set their sights on full schooling by 1980* (New Scientist).
**sight unseen**, without seeing or examining (a person or thing) in advance: *She ordered the dress over the phone, sight unseen.*
[Old English *gesiht.* See related etym. at **see**[1].]

**sight bill**, a bill payable at sight or on presentation.

**sight|board** (sīt′bôrd′, -bōrd′), *n.* a white screen at the end of a cricket field for making the ball more easily visible to the batsman.

**sight draft**, a written order from one bank to another, requiring a certain amount of money to be paid on demand. *Abbr:* s.d.

**sight|ed** (sī′tid), *adj., n.* —***adj.*** **1** having sight or vision. **2** having a sight or sights, as a firearm.
—***n.*** a person who has sight or vision.

**-sighted**, *combining form.* having ___ sight: *Dim-sighted = having dim sight.*

**sight gag**, *U.S. Informal.* a wordless joke or prank that must be seen to be understood.

**sight|hole** (sīt′hōl′), *n.* a hole to see through in a surveying or other instrument.

**sight hound**, = gazehound.

**sight|ing** (sī′ting), *n.* **1** an act or instance of seeing: *Sea-serpent sightings have diminished of late* (Time). **2** the act of adjusting the sight or aligning the sights of a gun or instrument: *The rotation of the earth moves objects out of the field of vision before a sighting can be made and the camera put in place on a telescope* (Science News Letter).

**sight|less** (sīt′lis), *adj.* **1** unable to see; blind: *the sightless mole.* **2** unable to be seen; invisible.
—**sight′less|ly**, *adv.* —**sight′less|ness**, *n.*

**sight|line** (sīt′līn′), *n.* a straight line from the eye to the object looked at; line of sight.

**sight|li|ness** (sīt′lē nis), *n.* the state of being sightly; pleasing appearance; comeliness.

**sight|ly** (sīt′lē), *adj.,* **-li|er, -li|est.** **1** pleasing to the sight. SYN: fair, handsome. **2a** affording a fine view. **b** that can be seen from a distance.

**sight-read** (sīt′rēd′), *v.t., v.i.* to read (music or a passage, usually in a foreign language) at first sight; engage or be skilled in sight reading: *Candidates must sight-read in addition to playing ... orchestral passages* (Newsweek). [back formation < *sight reading*]

**sight reader**, a person who is skilled in or capable of sight-reading music or a passage, especially one in a foreign language.

**sight reading**, a reading of a piece of music or passage in a foreign language at first sight.

**sight rhyme**, = eye rhyme.

**sight|screen** (sīt′skrēn′), *n. Cricket.* a structure of canvas or wood behind the bowler, serving as a white background that enables the batsman to have a clear sight of the ball.

**sight|see** (sīt′sē′), *v.i., v.t.,* **-saw, -seen, -see|ing.** to go around to see objects or places of interest: *We all swam, ... sailed a little, sightsaw, and constructed castles in the sand* (Moira Keenan). *Eight tour buses a day visit the town, although there is little to sightsee besides a bank and a supermarket* (Time). [back formation < *sightseeing*]

**sight|see|ing** (sīt′sē′ing), *n., adj.* —***n.*** the action of going around to see objects or places of interest: *a weekend of sightseeing.*
—***adj.*** that goes around to see or show objects or places of interest: *a sightseeing tour, a sightseeing bus.*

**sight|se|er** (sīt′sē′ər), *n.* a person who goes around to see objects or places of interest.

**sight|wor|thy** (sīt′wėr′ᴛʜē), *adj.,* **-thi|er, -thi|est.** worthy of being seen, or of being visited as a sight.

**sig|il** (sij′il), *n.* **1** an occult mark or sign, as in astrology or magic: *Sign and sigil, word of power, From the earth raised keep and tower* (Scott). **2** a seal or signet. [< Late Latin *sigillum* < Latin *sigilla,* plural < *sīgnum* mark, sign. See etym. of doublet **seal**[1].]

**sigill.**, seal (Latin, *sigillum*).

**sig|il|lar|y** (sij′ə ler′ē), *adj.* having to do with seals or signets.

**sig|il|late** (sij′ə lāt), *v.t.,* **-lat|ed, -lat|ing.** **1** to mark with or as with impressions of a seal. **2** to close by or as by sealing. [< Late Latin *sigillāre* (with English *-ate*[1]) to seal < *sigillum;* see etym. under **sigil**]

**sig|il|lat|ed earth** (sij′ə lā′tid), Lemnian earth, so called because it is made into cakes stamped with a seal.

**sig|il|la|tion** (sij′ə lā′shən), *n.* **1** the act of marking or the state of being marked with or as with a seal. **2** a mark or marking so made.

**sig|il|log|ra|pher** (sij′ə log′rə fər), *n.* a person who is skilled in sigillography.

**sig|il|log|ra|phy** (sij′ə log′rə fē), *n.* the science or study of seals or signets. [< Late Latin *sigillum* (see etym. under **sigil**) + English *-graphy*]

*** sig|ma** (sig′mə), *n.* **1** the 18th letter of the Greek alphabet, corresponding to the English *S, s.* **2** something shaped like the letter S. **3** something shaped like the letter C (from the shape of the Greek letter in its uncial form). **4** = sigma factor. **5** = sigma particle. [< Greek *sígma*]

| ***sigma** definition 1 | Σ capital letter | σ, ς lower-case letters |
|---|---|---|

**sigma factor**, a protein that stimulates the synthesis of chains of ribonucleic acid: *The function of the sigma factor is to give the core enzyme its specificity to transcribing from a fixed point on a strand of DNA and producing RNA of defined length* (Science Journal).

**sigma particle**, an unstable elementary particle having a mass approximately 2400 times that of the electron: *The heavy sigma particle and the antiproton are produced by allowing beams from the CERN 28-GeV proton accelerator to strike metal targets* (New Scientist).

**sig|mate** (sig′mit, -māt), *adj., v.,* **-mat|ed, -mat|ing.** —***adj.*** **1** S-shaped; having the form of a sigma. **2** shaped like a C.
—***v.t.*** to add a sigma or *s* to; change by the addition of an *s* at the end, as *upward* into *upwards.*

**sig|ma|tion** (sig mā′shən), *n.* the adding of a sigma or *s* at the end of a word or a syllable.

**sig|ma|tism** (sig′mə tiz əm), *n.* **1** the use or presence of sigma or *s;* repetition or recurrence of *s* or of the *s*-sound. **2** difficult or defective pronunciation of the sound *s.*

**sig|mic** (sig′mik), *adj.* of or containing sigma particles: *Kaonic and sigmic atoms tend to go together, since experiments aimed at making kaonic atoms make sigmic ones too* (Science News).

**sig|moid** (sig′moid), *adj.* **1** shaped like the letter S: *P. F. Verhulst showed in 1838 that the growth of human population followed an S-shaped or sigmoid curve* (F. S. Bodenheimer). **2** *Anatomy.* having to do with the sigmoid flexure of the colon. **3** shaped like the letter C. [< Greek *sigmoeidḗs* < *sígma* sigma + *eîdos* form]

**sig|moi|dal** (sig moi′dəl), *adj.* = sigmoid.

**sigmoid flexure**, **1** *Anatomy.* the S-shaped bend of the colon just above the rectum. **2** *Zoology.* an S-shaped curve.

**sig|moid|o|scope** (sig moi′də skōp), *n.* a tube about 10 inches long which is inserted through the anus for the purpose of examining the colon: *... the use of the sigmoidoscope in routine physical examination to spot cancer of the colon* (Frank P. Matthews).

**sign** (sīn), *n., v.* —***n.*** **1** an inscribed board, plate, or space serving for advertisement, guidance, or information: *See the sign over the door. The sign reads, "Keep off the grass." The names of streets are on signs at the corners.* **2a** an indication: *There are no signs of life about the house. Careful scrutiny revealed signs that someone had broken in. The ruin is a sign of past grandeur.* SYN: See syn. under **mark**. **b** an indication of a disease: *Fever is often a sign of infection.* **3** an indication of a coming event: *Dawn is the first sign of a new day. The coming of robins is a sign of spring. The star in the east was a sign of Christ's coming.* **4** a trace: *The hunter found signs of deer.* **5a** any mark or thing used to mean, represent, or point out something: *to use an equal sign. Three balls are the sign of a pawnbroker. We lunched at the sign of the Red Lion.* **b** *Mathematics.* a mark or symbol used especially to indicate an operation to be performed on a quantity or number or a relation of quantities or numbers: *The four signs of the arithmetic operations are addition* (+), *subtraction* (−), *multiplication* (×), *division* (÷). *The sign* (=) *means "equals." The signs* (+) *and* (−) *in algebra and higher mathematics define positive and negative numbers.* **c** *Music.* a flat, sharp, or other symbol used in notation to give directions, indicate tonality, etc. **6** a motion or gesture used to mean, represent, or point out something: *The priest made the sign of the cross. A nod is a sign of agreement. We talked to the deaf man by signs.* **7** any one of the twelve divisions of the zodiac, each named for a constellation and each denoted by a special symbol. **8** a miraculous occurrence.
—***v.t.*** **1** to put one's name on: *Sign this letter. He signed the check.* **2** to write: *Sign your initials here.* **3** to designate (oneself) in a signature or signatures: *He signed himself "a constant reader."* **4** to hire by a written agreement: *to sign a new ballplayer, to sign on a new crew.* **5** to mark with a sign. **6** to mark, protect, or consecrate with the sign of the cross. **7** to give a signal to; communicate by gesture: *to sign someone to enter, to sign assent.* **8** to indicate; signify; betoken.
—***v.i.*** **1** to write one's name to show authority, agreement, or obligation. We sign for telegrams or parcels. *Sign on the dotted line.* **2** to accept employment: *They signed for three years.* **3** to make a sign or signal.
**sign away**, to give by signing one's name: *to sign away one's inheritance. "I promise," he said, with a sense of despair, as though he were signing away the whole future* (Graham Greene).
**sign in**, to register one's arrival by signing; check in: *The convention delegates were asked to sign in at the door.*
**sign off, a** to stop broadcasting after announcing the end of a program: *The show signs off at midnight.* **b** to quit, as a job or service: *I shipped out in a tanker, signed off six months later in Honolulu, and went to work in a junkyard* (Peter Throckmorton).
**sign on, a** to join or enlist by written agreement; sign up: *He signed on as first mate.* **b** to begin broadcasting: *The station signs on with the playing of the National Anthem.*
**sign out**, to register one's departure by signing: *She had to leave work early and was the first to sign out that day.*
**sign over**, to hand over by signing one's name: *He has signed over one of his houses to his brother.*
**sign up**, to enlist or join by written agreement: *The new boy in school has signed up as a member of our club.*
[< Old French *signe,* learned borrowing from Latin *sīgnum*]
—***Syn.*** ***n.*** **3 Sign, omen** mean an indication of a coming event. **Sign** applies to something which provides objective evidence that the event can reasonably be expected: *Those big, black clouds are signs of a storm.* **Omen** applies to something which, particularly from a religious or superstitious point of view, is regarded as extraordinary and as a promise of something good or bad to come: *He believed his dream was an omen of success.*

**sign|a|ble** (sī′nə bəl), *adj.* **1** that can be signed; requiring a signature. **2** that can sign.

**sig|nal** (sig′nəl), *n., v.,* **-naled, -nal|ing** or (*especially British*) **-nalled, -nal|ling,** *adj.* —***n.*** **1** a sign, object, light, sound, or the like, giving notice, warning, or pointing out something: *A red light is a signal of danger. A bell is often used as a signal that a train is approaching a crossing. A siren is used as a fire signal.* **2a** a sign agreed upon or understood as the occasion of concerted action: *The raising of the flag was a signal to advance.* **b** an inciting action or movement; exciting cause; occasion: *This tyrannous act was the signal for insurrection.* **3** a token; indication: *His wave was* *a signal of recognition.* **4a** a wave, current, impulse, or picture component, serving to convey sound and images in communications, as by radio or television: *Signals describing the condition of the air are transmitted to the ground station by the radio sonde* (Herz and Tennent). **b** the communication or effect thus conveyed. **c** the wave serving to modulate the carrier wave. **5** a bid or play in card games that gives certain information to one's partner.

*—v.t.* **1** to make a signal or signals to (as a person or ship); summon, direct, or invite by signal: *He signaled the car to stop by raising his hand.* **2** to make known by a signal or signals: *A bell signals the end of a school period.*

*—v.i.* to give notice, warning, or information, by signal.

*—adj.* **1a** used as a signal or in signaling: *a signal light.* **b** designating a place or thing from which signals are given or worked. **c** of or having to do with signaling: *a signal officer.* **2** remarkable; striking; notable: *a signal success. The airplane was a signal invention.* SYN: conspicuous.

**signals,** the numbers called by an offensive back in football, usually the quarterback, designating a particular play, or by a member of the defensive team to direct the positions of the players: *to call the signals.*

[alteration of Old French *seignal* < Medieval Latin *signale,* noun < Late Latin *sīgnalis,* adjective < Latin *sīgnum* sign] —**sig′nal|er,** *especially British,* **sig′nal|ler,** *n.*

**signal box, 1** a small house or tower in which railway signals are worked. **2** the alarm box of a police or fire-alarm system.

**Signal Corps,** the branch of the United States Army in charge of communications and communication equipment, members of which are usually attached to units of other branches in tactical operations.

**signal fire,** a fire used in giving a signal.

**signal flag,** a flag used in giving a signal.

**sig|nal|ing** (sig′nə ling), *n.* the act of using, controlling, or transmitting signals.

**sig|nal|i|za|tion** (sig′nə lə zā′shən), *n.* the act or process of signalizing.

**sig|nal|ize** (sig′nə līz), *v.t.,* **-ized, -iz|ing. 1** to make stand out; make notable: *Many great inventions signalize the last 150 years. The year 1969 was signalized by man's first landing on the moon.* **2** to point out; mention specially; draw attention to: *Need we have waited for Sweden to signalize the discovery?* (New York Times). **3a** to make signals to; communicate with by signal. **b** to announce by a signal or signals.

**sig|nal|ling** (sig′nə ling), *n. Especially British.* signaling.

**sig|nal|ly** (sig′nə lē), *adv.* in a remarkable manner; strikingly; notably: *a signally imprudent policy.* SYN: remarkably.

**sig|nal|man** (sig′nəl mən), *n., pl.* **-men. 1** a man in charge of the signals on a railroad, especially one who sets the signals controlling the flow of traffic over a specified part of the line. **2** a man who sends or receives messages by signaling in the army or navy.

**sig|nal|ment** (sig′nəl mənt), *n.* **1** a description of a person wanted by the police. **2** a distinguishing mark.

**sig|nals** (sig′nəlz), *n.pl.* See under **signal.**

**signal service, 1** an organized system of service concerned with communicating by means of signals, especially in the military service. **2** the organization or body having charge of such a system.

**signal tower,** a tower from which signals are sent or displayed, as by a semaphore.

**sig|na|ry** (sig′nər ē), *n., pl.* **-ries.** a list of the characters or signs of an ancient language, such as the hieroglyphic signs of ancient Egypt.

**sig|na|tar|y** (sig′nə ter′ē), *n., pl.* **-tar|ies,** *adj.* = signatory.

**sig|nate** (sig′nāt), *adj.* **1** distinguished in some way. **2** *Zoology.* having spots or marks resembling letters.

**sig|na|to|ry** (sig′nə tôr′ē, -tōr′-), *n., pl.* **-ries,** *adj.* *—n.* **1** any one of the signers of a document: *Most of the signatories of the Declaration of Independence were intellectuals* (Harper's). **2** a country, company, or other institution or group, on whose behalf a person signs a document.

*—adj.* signing: *signatory delegates, signatory nations.*

***sig|na|ture** (sig′nə chər, -chůr), *n.* **1a** a person's name written by himself: *His signature was signed at the bottom of the letter in a bright green ink.* SYN: autograph. **b** the act of writing one's name, especially authenticating a document by doing so. **2** a set of signs, usually placed at the beginning of a staff immediately after the clef, to show the pitch, key, and time of a piece of music; key signature or time signature. **3** *Printing, Bookbinding.* **a** a sheet folded together to form a unit of a book; section. A signature often consists of from 4 to 64 different pages printed on a single sheet. **b** a letter or number on such a sheet to show how it is to be folded; signature mark. **4** music, sound effects, or announcement, used to identify a particular radio or television program; theme. **5** *Pharmacy.* the part of a prescription that is to be copied on the label, giving directions for taking the medicine. *Abbr:* S (no period), Sig. **6** *Nuclear Physics.* a characteristic track of bubbles or sparks made by a subatomic particle in a bubble or spark chamber, by means of which it may be identified. **7** *Figurative.* any characteristic or distinctive mark of identification: *The ... seismic "signatures" of different earthquakes can be deciphered only after information is accumulated for many years* (Robert W. Decker). *Visconti's signature is on every shot* [*of the motion picture*] (New Yorker).

[< Late Latin *signātūra* marking (of sheep) < Latin *sīgnum* sign]

***signature**
definition 2

**key signatures:**

C major G major G minor

**time signatures:**

four-four three-four six-eight

**signature mark,** a letter or number printed at the bottom of the first page of every sheet in a book, to show how it is to be folded and arranged in pages.

**signature tune,** = theme song.

**sign|board** (sīn′bôrd′, -bōrd′), *n.* a board having a sign, notice, advertisement, or inscription on it; billboard.

**signed number** (sīnd), a number with a plus sign or minus sign in front; positive or negative number. *Example:* The equation (+5) + (−8) = (−3) consists of three signed numbers.

**sign|er** (sī′nər), *n.* **1** a person who signs. **2** a person who writes his name in token of authority, agreement, or obligation: *the signers of the Declaration of Independence.*

**sig|net** (sig′nit), *n., v.* *—n.* **1a** a small seal, usually one fixed in a finger ring. **b** a small seal of this kind in formal or official use, especially as employed to give authentication or authority to a document: *The order was sealed with the king's signet.* **2a** the stamp or impression made by a signet, as in soft sealing wax. **b** a mark, sign, or stamp. *—v.t.* to stamp with a signet.

[< Old French *signet* (diminutive) < *signe* sign < Latin *sīgnum* seal]

**signet ring,** a finger ring set with a signet or seal.

**sig|ni|fi|a|ble** (sig′nə fī′ə bəl), *adj.* that can be signified.

**sig|nif|i|cance** (sig nif′ə kəns), *n.* **1** importance; consequence: *The President wanted to see him on a matter of great significance.* SYN: moment, weight, gravity. **2** the meaning of something; what is meant: *She did not understand the significance of my nod. What is the significance of $H_2SO_4$?* SYN: import, sense. **3** significant quality; expressiveness: *the significance of her smile.*

**sig|nif|i|can|cy** (sig nif′ə kən sē), *n.* = significance.

**sig|nif|i|cant** (sig nif′ə kənt), *adj., n.* *—adj.* **1** full of meaning; important; of consequence: *July 4, 1776, is a significant date for Americans.* SYN: momentous. **2** having a meaning; expressive: *Smiles are significant of pleasure.* SYN: See syn. under **expressive. 3** having or expressing a hidden meaning: *A significant nod from my friend warned me to stop talking.* *—n.* something that expresses or conveys a meaning.

[< Latin *sīgnificāns, -antis,* present participle of *sīgnificāre;* see etym. under **signify**] —**sig|nif′i|cant|ly,** *adv.*

**sig|ni|fi|ca|tion** (sig′nə fə kā′shən), *n.* **1** meaning; sense; import: *The signification of a proposition is the sum total of the contextual senses of its parts* (Simeon Potter). SYN: significance. **2** the act or process of signifying: *Signification relies largely upon words and gestures.*

**sig|nif|i|ca|tive** (sig nif′ə kā′tiv), *adj.* **1** serving to signify; having a meaning. **2** significant or suggestive. —**sig|nif′i|ca′tive|ly,** *adv.* —**sig|nif′i|ca′tive|ness,** *n.*

**sig|nif|i|ca|tor** (sig nif′ə kā′tər), *n.* **1** a person or thing that signifies or indicates something. **2** *Astrology.* the planet that rules a house.

**sig|nif|i|ca|to|ry** (sig nif′ə kə tôr′ē, -tōr′-), *adj.* serving to signify; significative.

**sig|nif|ics** (sig nif′iks), *n.* the science or the systematic study of the exact significance of terms in any department of education or learning: *Modern semantics originated in the early 1900's in what an English philosopher ... called significs* (S. I. Hayakawa). [< *signif*(icance) + *-ics*]

**sig|ni|fi|er** (sig′nə fī′ər), *n.* a person or thing that signifies.

**sig|ni|fy** (sig′nə fī), *v.,* **-fied, -fy|ing.** *—v.t.* **1** to be a sign of; mean: *"Oh!" signifies surprise.* SYN: represent, denote, imply, suggest. **2** to make known by signs, words, or actions: *to signify consent with a nod.* SYN: indicate, intimate. *—v.i.* to have importance; be of consequence; have significance; matter: *What a fool says does not signify. What does it signify how we dress on a camping trip?* [< Latin *sīgnificāre* < *sīgnum* sign + *facere* to make]

**sig|ni|fy|ing** (sig′nə fī ing, -in), *n. U.S.* a verbal game or contest among black youths, in which a series of insults are exchanged to test the participants' restraint and ability with words: *Girls are also the objects of much signifyin' by male students. The signifyin' may relate to a girl's looks or ... her boyfriend* (Today's Education).

**sign-in** (sīn′in′), *n.* the collecting of people's signatures in support of a petition or demand addressed to any authoritative body.

**si|gnior** (sēn′yôr), *n.* = signor.

**sign language, 1** a system of communication in which motions, especially of the hands, stand for letters, words, ideas, or actions. **2** a system of gestures used by some American Indians for communicating between tribes.

**sign|less** (sīn′ləs), *adj.* **1** making no sign or manifestation; quiet; passive. **2** having no algebraic sign, or being essentially positive, like the modulus of an imaginary or a tensor.

**sign manual, 1** a person's signature, especially that of a sovereign or magistrate, that authenticates an official document. **2** a distinctively individual sign, stamp, or quality.

**sign-off** (sīn′ôf′, -of′), *n.* **1** an act or instance of signing off; a going off the air. **2** a word or phrase used in signing off: [*Her*] *television sign-off is "Have a Happy"* (New York Times).

**sign of the cross,** the movement of the right hand from the forehead to the breast and to the shoulders which Catholics and members of the Eastern Orthodox Churches perform as a sacramental.

**sign of the zodiac,** any one of the 12 zodiacal divisions: *The signs of the zodiac no longer agree with the constellations of the same name* (Robert H. Baker).

**si|gnor** (sē nyōr′), *n. Italian.* **1** Mr. or sir. **2** a gentleman.

**si|gno|ra** (sē nyō′rä), *n., pl.* **-re** (-rā). *Italian.* **1** Mrs. or Madam. **2** a lady.

**si|gno|re** (sē nyō′rā), *n., pl.* **-ri** (-rē). *Italian.* **1** sir. **2** a gentleman.

▶ **Signore** becomes **signor** when it is used before a person's name.

**si|gno|ri|a** (sē′nyô rē′ä), *n., pl.* **-ri|as.** a governing body in old Italian republics, especially Venice. [< Italian *signoria*]

**si|gno|ri|na** (sē′nyô rē′nä), *n., pl.* **-ne** (-nā). *Italian.* **1** Miss. **2** a young lady.

**si|gno|ri|no** (sē′nyô rē′nō), *n., pl.* **-ni** (-nē). *Italian.* **1** Master (as used to a boy or youth). **2** a young gentleman.

**si|gno|ry** (sēn′yər ē), *n., pl.* **-ries. 1** = seigniory. **2** a governing body, especially that by which Venice was ruled as a republic. [< Old French *signorie,* variant of *seignorie* (see etym. under **seigniory**); influenced by Italian *signoria*]

**sign painter,** a person who paints signs, as for tradesmen.

**sign|post** (sīn′pōst′), *n., v.* *—n.* **1** a post having signs, notices, or directions on it; guidepost. **2** *Figurative.* anything that marks, points, guides, or from which bearings may be taken or conclusions drawn.

*—v.t. British.* to equip or provide with signposts.

**sign-up** (sīn′up′), *n.* act or instance of signing up.

**Sig|urd** (sig′ėrd), *n.* a hero in Norse legends who slays a dragon, identified with the German Siegfried.

**si jeu|nesse sa|vait, si vieil|lesse pou|vait** (sē zhœ nes′ sȧ ve′ sē vye yes′ pü ve′), *French.* if youth but knew, if age but could.

**si|ka** (sē′kə), *n.* a small deer native to Japan and China, having a brown coat that is spotted with white in the summer. [< Japanese *shika* deer]

**sike** (sīk), *n. Scottish.* **1** a small stream of water; rill; streamlet. **2** a ditch or channel through which such a stream flows. [Old English *sīc*]

**Pronunciation Key:** hat, āge, cãre, fär; let, ēqual, tėrm; it, īce; hot, ōpen, ôrder; oil, out; cup, pu̇t, rüle; child; long; thin; ᴛʜen; zh, measure; ə represents **a** in about, **e** in taken, **i** in pencil, **o** in lemon, **u** in circus.

**sik|er** (sik′ər), *adj. Scottish.* safe; sure; dependable; sicker. [Old English *sicor*]

**Sikh** (sēk), *n., adj.* —*n.* a member of a religious sect of northwestern India, founded in the early 1500's as an offshoot of Hinduism, from which it differs sharply, especially in being monotheistic and in denying caste. Sikhs are famous as soldiers.
—*adj.* of or having to do with the Sikhs.
[< Hindi *sikh* disciple]

**Sikh|ism** (sē′kiz əm), *n.* the religious system and practices of the Sikhs: *Sikhism is a monotheistic religion incorporating elements of Hinduism, Islam and other religions* (New York Times).

**Sik|kim|ese** (sik′ə mēz′, -mēs′), *adj., n., pl.* **-ese.** —*adj.* of or having to do with Sikkim, a small state in the Himalayas, or its people: *Sikkimese customs.*
—*n.* a native or inhabitant of Sikkim: ... *the Bhutias, people from Tibet and Bhutan who have been Sikkimese for centuries* (London Times).

**si|lage** (sī′lij), *n.* green fodder for winter feeding of livestock, stored in a silo or other airtight chamber and preserved by partial fermentation; ensilage. Silage is usually chopped stalks of slightly immature corn. [alteration of *ensilage*, probably influenced by *silo*]

**sil|ane** (sil′ān), *n.* a compound of silicon and hydrogen. It is a colorless gas that burns spontaneously with a brilliant white flame when exposed to air. *Formula:* $SiH_4$

**si|lat** (sē′lät), *n.* a formal system of fencing practiced in Indonesia. [< Indonesian *silat*]

**sild** (sild), *n., pl.* **silds** or (*collectively*) **sild.** an immature herring similar to a brisling, canned in Norway. [< Norwegian *sild*]

**si|le|na|ceous** (sī′lə nā′shəs), *adj.* belonging to the pink family of plants; caryophyllaceous. [< New Latin *Silene* (< Latin *Sīlēnus* Silenus) + English *-aceous*]

**si|lence** (sī′ləns), *n., v.,* **-lenced, -lenc|ing,** *interj.* —*n.* **1** an absence of all sound or noise; stillness; noiselessness: *The teacher asked for silence. And silence, like a poultice, comes to heal the blows of sound* (Oliver Wendell Holmes). **SYN**: hush, quiet. **2** the state of being or keeping silent; not talking: *to keep or break silence, to listen in silence. Silence gives consent* (Oliver Goldsmith). **SYN**: reticence, reserve. **3** a failure to mention; omission of mention or notice in a narrative, or omission or neglect to write, communicate, or reply (about something); secrecy: *Mother passed over our foolish remarks in silence. Silence in matters of public interest is intolerable in a free society.*
—*v.t.* **1** to stop the speech or noise of; make silent; quiet: *The nurse silenced the baby's crying. To silence envious tongues* (Shakespeare). **2** to make silent by restraint or prohibition; repress: *to silence the press, to silence an uprising.* **3** *Figurative.* to put at rest; stop the activity of: *to silence doubts, one's conscience, or scruples.* **4** to stop (enemy guns) from firing by destroying or disabling them: *Fighter-bombers ripped rails, knocked out rolling stock and silenced gun positions in attacks deep in North Korea* (New York Times).
—*interj.* keep still!; be still!
[< Old French *silence* < Latin *silentium* < *silēre* be silent]

**silence cloth,** a sheet of thick cotton cloth or the like placed under the linen cloth on a dining table.

**si|lenc|er** (sī′lən sər), *n.* **1** a person or thing that silences. **2** a device which muffles the sound of a gun. It usually fits over and extends slightly forward of the barrel. **3** *British.* a muffler on an internal-combustion engine.

**si|lent** (sī′lənt), *adj., n.* —*adj.* **1** quiet; still; noiseless: *a silent house, the silent hills.* **SYN**: hushed. **2** not speaking; saying little or nothing: *Pupils must be silent in the study hour. He was silent about his early life. Ulysses ... was the most eloquent and the most silent of men* (William Broome). **3** performed, made, suffered, or otherwise done or endured, in silence or without speaking; not spoken; not said out loud: *a silent prayer, silent agony, silent opposition, a silent movie.* **SYN**: unspoken, unsounded. **4** *Figurative.* not active or operative; quiescent: *a silent volcano.* **5** omitting mention of something, as in a narrative: *An event has happened, upon which it is difficult to speak, and impossible to be silent* (Edmund Burke). **6** (of a letter in spelling) not representing a sound: *The "b" in "dumb" is silent.*
—*n.* **silents,** motion pictures without recorded and synchronized sounds: *He confined his moviegoing to Charlie Chaplin silents* (Atlantic).
[< Latin *silēns, -entis,* present participle of *silēre* be silent] —**si′lent|ly,** *adv.* —**si′lent|ness,** *n.*
—*Syn. adj.* **2 Silent, taciturn, reticent** mean saying little or nothing. **Silent** especially means not talkative, characteristically speaking only when necessary or saying very little: *He is a silent, thoughtful boy.* **Taciturn** means not fond of talking, being by nature inclined to be silent and avoid conversation: *He is a taciturn man who dislikes parties.* **Reticent** means not saying all one knows, disposed to keep silent, especially about private affairs: *He is reticent about his early life.*

**silent butler,** a boxlike or bowllike container with a handle and hinged top, into which crumbs may be brushed, ashtrays emptied, or the like.

**si|len|ti|ar|y** (sī len′shē er′ē), *n., pl.* **-ar|ies. 1** a person who practices or advocates silence, especially from religious motives. **2** an official appointed to enforce silence, as in a public assembly. [< Late Latin *silentiārius* < Latin *silentium* silence]

**si|lent le|ges in|ter ar|ma** (sī′lənt lē′jēz in′tər är′mə), *Latin.* laws are silent in the midst of war.

**Silent Ma|jor|i|tar|i|an** (mə jôr′ə tãr′ē ən, -jor′-), a member of the Silent Majority.

**Silent Majority** or **silent majority, 1** *Especially U.S.* the politically nonvocal section of the population that is believed to constitute the majority of Americans: *One political columnist saw the typical member of this silent majority as a suburbanite or small-town dweller who was deeply disturbed by high prices and taxes, crime in the streets, political demonstrations and violence* (Steven V. Roberts). **2** any nonvocal majority: *I detect a feeling among the silent majority of MPs on both sides ... that the government has done the right thing* (Tam Dalyell). [< a phrase used by President Richard M. Nixon in an address to the nation on November 3, 1969: "And so—to you, the great silent majority of my fellow Americans—I ask for your support."]

**silent partner,** a partner in a business who has no share in managing the business.

**silent service,** *U.S.* submarines and their crews, as a part of the U.S. Navy or sometimes any navy. [because of their characteristic mode of operation]

**silent system,** a system of prison discipline that imposes complete silence on the prisoners.

**silent treatment,** a deliberate attitude of silence and unfriendliness toward a person as a way of showing disapproval or scorn: *The class decided to give the bully the silent treatment.*

**silent vote, 1** the collective vote of those who take no avowed part in a campaign. **2** the vote represented by the number of persons qualified to vote, but who do not vote.

**Si|le|nus** (sī lē′nəs), *n. Greek Mythology.* a minor woodland deity, the foster father and companion of Dionysus and leader of the satyrs. He is represented as a short, stout, bald, drunken old man.

**si|le|nus** (sī lē′nəs), *n., pl.* **-ni** (-nī). *Greek Mythology.* **1** any of various minor deities of the forests, resembling the satyrs. **2** = satyr. [< Latin *Sīlēnus* < Greek *Seilēnós* Silenus]

**si|le|sia** (sə lē′shə, -zhə; sī-), *n.* a fine, light, smooth cotton or linen cloth used for lining. [< *Silesia*, where it was first made]

**Si|le|sian** (sə lē′shən, -zhən; sī-), *adj., n.* —*adj.* of or having to do with Silesia, a region of central Europe, now included in Czechoslovakia and Poland.
—*n.* a native or inhabitant of Silesia.

**si|lex** (sī′leks), *n.* **1** flint; silica. **2** a strong glass that is mostly quartz and resists heat. [< Latin *silex, -icis* flint]

**Si|lex** (sī′leks), *n. Trademark.* a coffee maker made of silex glass.

***silhouette**
definition 1

***sil|hou|ette** (sil′ü et′), *n., v.,* **-et|ted, -et|ting.** —*n.* **1** an outline portrait cut out of a black paper or drawn and filled in with some single color. **2** a dark image outlined against a lighter background: *the cat's dark silhouette on the wall* (John Greenleaf Whittier). **3** the contour, as of a garment or figure: *The slim silhouette gained over the full-skirted silhouette in women's daytime clothes* (Helen C. Wells).
—*v.t.* to show in outline: *The mountain was silhouetted against the sky.*
**in silhouette,** in outline or profile, especially in black against a white background: *This framing of the trees, which stand out in silhouette against a bright blue sky* (Harper's).
[< French *silhouette* < Étienne de *Silhouette,* 1709-1767, French minister of finance in 1759]

**sil|hou|et|tist** (sil′ü et′ist), *n.* a maker of silhouettes.

**sil|i|ca** (sil′ə kə), *n.* a common mineral, silicon dioxide, a hard, white or colorless substance. In the form of quartz, it enters into the composition of many rocks and is contained in sponges and certain plants. Flint, sand, opal, and chalcedony are forms of silica. *Formula:* $SiO_2$ [< New Latin *silica* < Latin *silex, -icis* flint]

**silica gel,** a type of colloidal silica, resembling coarse sand, used as an adsorbent in air conditioners and petroleum refining.

**silica glass,** = quartz glass.

**sil|i|cate** (sil′ə kit, -kāt), *n.* a compound containing silicon with oxygen and a metal; a salt of silicic acid. Silicates constitute the greater number of the minerals that compose the crust of the earth. Mica, garnet, talc, asbestos, and feldspar are silicates.

**sil|i|cat|ed** (sil′ə kā′təd), *adj.* coated, mixed, combined, or impregnated with silica: *silicated complexion soap.*

**sil|i|ca|ti|za|tion** (sil′ə kə tə zā′shən), *n.* the process of combining with silica so as to change to a silicate.

**si|li|ceous** or **si|li|cious** (sə lish′əs), *adj.* **1** containing or consisting of silica; resembling silica: *Paleolithic stone tools were made by chipping or flaking hard siliceous* (*glasslike*) *materials like flint, quartzite, and obsidian* (Beals and Hoijer). **2** growing best or solely in soil containing much silica. [< Latin *siliceus* (with English *-ous*) of flint < *silex, -icis* flint]

**si|lic|ic** (sə lis′ik), *adj.* **1** containing silicon or silica: *The more volatile or acidic or silicic constituents of the fluid rock beneath the surface may have concentrated in the original uplifts* (Scientific American). **2** of or obtained from silicon or silica.

**silicic acid,** any one of various weak acids obtained from silicon. The formula of a common kind is $H_4SiO_4$

**sil|i|cide** (sil′ə sīd, -sid), *n.* a compound of silicon and another element or radical.

**sil|i|cif|er|ous** (sil′ə sif′ər əs), *adj.* yielding or containing silica; united with silica. [< Latin *silex, -icis* flint + English *-ferous*]

**si|lic|i|fi|ca|tion** (sə lis′ə fə kā′shən), *n.* conversion into silica.

**si|lic|i|fied wood** (sə lis′ə fīd), wood so impregnated or replaced by silica that it has become quartz or opal.

**si|lic|i|fy** (sə lis′ə fī), *v.,* **-fied, -fy|ing.** —*v.t.* to convert into or impregnate with silica: *The walnut kernels are ... a golden brown in color and perfectly silicified* (Scientific American).
—*v.i.* to become siliceous.

**si|li|ci|um** (sə lish′ē əm, -lis′-), *n.* = silicon. [< New Latin *silicium* < Latin *silex, -icis* flint]

**sil|i|cle** (sil′ə kəl), *n. Botany.* a short, broad silique, as in shepherd's-purse. [probably < French *silicule,* learned borrowing from Latin *silicula* (diminutive) < *siliqua* seed pod]

***sil|i|con** (sil′ə kən), *n.* a nonmetallic chemical element found only combined with other elements, chiefly with oxygen in silica. Next to oxygen, silicon is the most abundant element in nature and occurs in amorphous and crystalline forms. The crystalline form is much used in the manufacture of steel as a deoxidizing and hardening agent. [< *silica*]

***silicon**

| symbol | atomic number | atomic weight | oxidation state |
|---|---|---|---|
| Si | 14 | 28.086 | 2,±4 |

**silicon carbide,** a substance that is almost as hard as diamond, used in grinding metals, beveling glass, in polishing powders and other abrasives, and as a semiconductor in transistors. *Formula:* SiC

**silicon dioxide,** = silica.

**sil|i|cone** (sil′ə kōn), *n.* an organic compound in which silicon has replaced some of the carbon. Noted for their stability and their ability to resist extremes of heat and cold, silicones are used for lubricants, varnishes, and insulators. *Silicones are fluids and resins that keep clothes and shoes and brick walls dry in the rain* (Scientific American). [< *silic*(on) + *-one*]

**silicone rubber,** a rubber made of oxygen and silicon that can keep its rubberlike properties at much higher and lower temperatures than natural rubber or any other type of synthetic rubber. Silicone rubber is used in such products as seals, gaskets, and other parts of machinery exposed to high temperatures.

**sil|i|con|ize** (sil′ə kə nīz), *v.t., v.i.,* **-ized, -iz|ing.** to combine, or cause to combine, with silicon.

**sil|i|co|sis** (sil′ə kō′sis), *n.* a disease of the lungs caused by continually breathing air filled with dust from quartz or silicates, formerly common among certain types of workers, such as stonecutters. [< *silic*(on) + *-osis*]

**sil|i|cot|ic** (sil′ə kot′ik), *adj., n.* —***adj.*** having to do with, causing, or suffering from silicosis.
—***n.*** a person having silicosis.

**si|lic|u|la** (sə lik′yə lə), *n., pl.* **-lae** (-lē). = silicle. [< Latin *silicula,* a little husk or pod; see etym. under **silicle**]

**si|lic|u|lar** (sə lik′yə lər), *adj. Botany.* having the shape or appearance of a silicula or silicle.

**sil|i|cule** (sil′ə kyül), *n. Botany.* silicle.

**si|lic|u|lose** (sə lik′yə lōs), *adj. Botany.* **1** bearing silicles. **2** having the shape or appearance of a silicle.

**si|lique** (sə lēk′, sil′ik), *n. Botany.* the characteristic podlike fruit of plants of the mustard family, a long, narrow, two-valved capsule which splits open from the bottom upward, exposing the seeds attached to two placentae. [< Latin *siliqua* seed pod]

**silk** (silk), *n., adj., v.* —***n.*** **1** the lustrous, fine, soft, strong fiber spun by silkworms to form their cocoons: *Raw silk that comes from Hong Kong ... is much heavier* (New Yorker). **2** a thread made of this. **3** a cloth made of silk fiber: *Japanese silks, imported silks.* **4** a garment of such material: *The little lady ... had on ... rather an old black silk* (Elizabeth Gaskell). **5** a fiber like silk, produced especially by spiders and moths, or made artificially. **6** anything like silk: *corn silk.* **7** *British.* the gown of silk which a king's or queen's counsel is entitled to wear.
—***adj.*** **1** of, made of, or having to do with silk; like silk; silken: *She sewed the silk dress with silk thread. Conventional balloons of light rubberised silk fabric can take payloads of half a ton or more* (New Scientist). **2** = silky.
—***v.i.*** *U.S.* (of corn) to produce silk.
**hit the silk,** *Slang.* to parachute from a plane: *The rookie pilots soon learned how to hit the silk.*
**silks,** the blouses and caps worn by jockeys and harness race drivers and the coverings sometimes draped over their horses which, by their coloring, identify the owner of these horses; colors: *Citation raced under the silks of Calumet Farm.*
**take silk,** *British.* to become a king's or queen's counsel: *After he ... had taken silk ... he became at least as redoubtable a leader as his father had been* (London Times).
[Old English *sioloc,* or *seolc* < Latin *sēricus* < *Sērēs* the Chinese < Greek *Sêres*] —**silk′like′,** *adj.*

**silk|a|line** or **silk|a|lene** (sil′kə lēn′), *n.* a soft, thin, cotton fabric resembling silk. [American English < *silk*]

**silk cotton,** **1** the silky, elastic down or fiber covering the seeds of certain tropical trees of the bombax family, used for packing, and for stuffing pillows and cushions. **2** = kapok.

**silk-cot|ton family** (silk′kot′ən), = bombax family.

**silk-cotton tree,** any one of a genus of trees of tropical America, the East Indies, and Africa, that bear large pods from which kapok or silk cotton is obtained; kapok tree.

**silk cup sponge,** a sponge found off the coasts of Egypt and Greece that is the most valuable of all commercial animal sponges.

**silk|en** (sil′kən), *adj., v.* —***adj.*** **1a** made of silk: *a silken dress. The king wore silken robes.* **b** of or having to do with silk stuffs or goods. **2** like silk; soft, smooth, and glossy: *She has silken hair.* **3a** resembling silk in being soft and smooth; silky: *a silken manner, a silken voice.* **b** balmy; gentle: *a silken climate.* **4** wearing silk clothes. **5** elegant; luxurious.
—***v.t.*** to make smooth and glossy like silk; give a silky luster to: [*A cream*] *to soften and silken your skin while you sleep* (New Yorker). —**silk′en|ly,** *adv.*

**silk|er** (sil′kər), *n.* **1** a person or thing that embroiders (as the back of a glove) in silk. **2** a person or thing that extracts silk from the cut kernels of corn.

**silk fowl,** = silky.

**silk gland,** any gland which secretes the substance of silk, as in the silkworm or silk spider; sericterium.

**silk grass,** **1** = Adam's-needle. **2a** any of various agaves and related plants that yield strong fibers. **b** the fibers of any of these plants.

**silk grower,** a person who produces silk cocoons by raising silkworms, and the mulberries or other plants on which they feed.

**silk hat,** **1** = top hat. **2** = opera hat.

**silk|i|ly** (sil′kə lē), *adv.* in a silky manner: *Each garment whispered silkily to the floor* (Harper's).

**silk|i|ness** (sil′kē nis), *n.* silky condition or quality.

**silk|man** (silk′man′), *n., pl.* **-men. 1** a dealer in silk fabrics. **2** a person employed in the manufacture of silks. **3** the manufacturer or director of a silk mill.

**silk moth,** a bombycid moth whose larva is a silkworm.

**silk oak,** = silky oak.

**silk|o|line** (sil′kə lēn′), *n.* = silkaline.

**silk paper,** a paper containing tiny pieces of colored silk, used especially for making postage stamps.

**Silk Road,** an ancient trade route between the Middle East and China. [because *silk* was a chief trade item]

**silks** (silks), *n.pl.* See under **silk**.

✱**silk-screen** (silk′skrēn′), *adj., n., v.* —***adj.*** of or having to do with the process of printing colors on a variety of surfaces, especially cloth, paper, and linoleum, by means of a stencil put on silk or other fine cloth stretched over a frame: *The studio also contains equipment for making silk-screen or serigraphic prints* (Wall Street Journal).
—***n.*** this process.
—***v.t.*** to print or apply by the silk-screen process: [*He*] *painstakingly silk-screens oil on canvas* (Time).

✱**silk-screen**

squeegee

stencil

ink

**silk spider,** any spider which spins a kind of silk, especially an orb weaver of the southern United States, which spins copiously, and is also notable for the unusual disparity of the sexes in size.

**silk-stock|ing** (silk′stok′ing), *adj., n.* —***adj.*** **1** made up of or populated by people of wealth and social prominence (who alone, in an earlier day, could afford to wear silk stockings): *a silk-stocking clientele, a silk-stocking district.* **2** *Figurative.* elegant; aristocratic: *a silk-stocking manner.*
—***n.*** **1** a well-to-do, elegant man or woman. **2** *U.S.* a member of the Federalist or (later) Whig parties (to which, in the early 1800's, most well-to-do people belonged).

**silk thrower,** a person who produces or manufactures thrown silk, or organzine.

**silk|weed** (silk′wēd′), *n. U.S.* milkweed.

**silk|worm** (silk′wėrm′), *n.* any caterpillar that spins silk to form a cocoon, especially the larva of a moth that feeds on mulberry leaves. It is usually a domesticated moth, originally of Asia. *Two glands near the silkworm's lower jaw give off a fluid that hardens into fine silk threads as it hits the air* (Hans Vaterlaus). [Old English *seolcwyrm*]

**silkworm moth,** any one of a family of large moths whose larvae spin cocoons of silk, such as the luna moth and Polyphemus moth; saturniid.

**silk|y** (sil′kē), *adj.,* **silk|i|er, silk|i|est,** *n., pl.* **silkies.** —***adj.*** **1** of or like silk; smooth, soft, and glossy; silken: *A kitten has silky fur.* **2** made or consisting of silk. **3** *Botany.* covered with fine, soft, closely set hairs having a silklike gloss, as a leaf.
—***n.*** any one of a breed of crested chickens with white, webless feathers of a peculiarly fluffy, silky texture; silk fowl. The silky weighs two to three pounds and has a purplish face and comb, small wings, and short tail.

**silky oak,** any one of several Australian trees whose wood is used for ornament.

**silky terrier,** any dog of a breed of small terrier with long, silky, blue and tan hair, erect ears, and docked tail, weighing from eight to ten pounds.

**sill** (sil), *n.* **1** a piece of wood, stone, or metal across the bottom of a door, window, or house frame: *a cat sunning itself on a window sill.* **2** a large beam, as of wood or metal, or an equivalent structure of masonry, on which an outside wall of a building rests. **3** any one of various beams, blocks, or combinations of these serving a purpose similar to this, such as one at the base of an arch of a bridge. **4** *Geology.* an intrusive sheet of igneous rock of approximately horizontal attitude, found between older rock beds. See picture under **valley**. [Old English *syll*]

**sil|la|bub** (sil′ə bub), *n.* **1** a dessert made of a mixture of whole milk or cream with wine or cider, usually slightly sweetened, and often including eggs, nutmeg, and cinnamon. **2** *Figurative.* something unsubstantial and frothy, especially floridly vapid discourse or writing. Also, **syllabub**. [origin unknown]

**sill cock,** a faucet or valve for use at the sill of a house or building to allow a hose connection.

**sill course,** *Architecture.* a continual horizontal course closely connected with the sills of a row of windows, either immediately below the sills, or more properly with its lower bed on a line with the lower beds of the sills so that the sills form part of it.

**sil|ler** (sil′ər), *n., adj., v. Scottish.* silver.

**sil|li|ly** (sil′ə lē), *adv.* in a silly manner; foolishly.

**sil|li|man|ite** (sil′ə mə nīt), *n.* a mineral consisting of a silicate of aluminum, and occurring in long, slender, crystalline needles or compact, fibrous masses; fibrolite. It is valuable commercially as a refractory or fire-resisting material. *Formula:* $Al_2SiO_5$ [< Benjamin *Silliman,* 1779-1864, an American scientist + *-ite*[1]]

**sil|li|ness** (sil′ē nis), *n.* **1** the quality of being silly; foolishness; senselessness. **2** any instance of this; silly act or thing.

**sil|ly** (sil′ē), *adj.,* **-li|er, -li|est,** *n., pl.* **-lies.** —***adj.*** **1** without sense or reason; foolish; ridiculous: *Baby talk is silly. Mamma says that she* [*Jane Austen*] *was then the prettiest, silliest, most affected ... butterfly she ever remembers* (Mary R. Mitford). **SYN:** senseless, nonsensical. See syn. under **foolish**. **2** of or characteristic of a silly person: *silly behavior, a silly remark.* **3** *Informal.* stunned; dazed: *I was knocked silly by the news.* **4** *Archaic or Scottish.* **a** harmless; simple; innocent: *His silly sheep, what wonder if they stray?* (William Cowper). **b** feeble-minded; imbecile: *William IV of England was called Silly Billy.* **c** weak, feeble, or frail; sickly; ailing: *She was but of a silly constitution* (John Galt). **5** *Obsolete.* unsophisticated; rustic.
—***n.*** a silly or foolish person.
[Middle English *syly* defenseless, weak, pitiable; variant of earlier *sely* seely, Old English *sǣlig* happy < *sǣl* happiness]

**silly billy,** *Informal.* a foolish person.

**silly season,** *Informal.* a season when there is little news and the editors of newspapers are supposed to be obliged to use any material, however foolish, that comes to hand.

✱**si|lo** (sī′lō), *n., pl.* **-los,** *v.,* **-loed, -lo|ing.** —***n.*** **1** an airtight building or pit in which green fodder for livestock is preserved and stored. A silo is often a cylindrical tower of wood or metal. **2** a vertical shaft built underground with facilities for housing and launching a guided missile.
—***v.t.*** to put into or store in a silo; turn into silage; ensile.
[< Spanish *silo* < Latin *sīrus* < Greek *sīrós* grain cellar]

farm silo

✱**silo**
definitions 1, 2

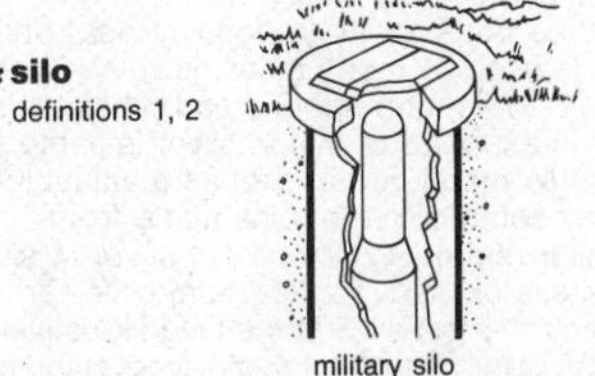

military silo

**sil|ox|ane** (sil ok′sān), *n.* any hydride of silicon in which silicon atoms alternate with atoms of oxygen. Siloxanes are very water-repellent and cannot be dissolved except by strong acids and alkalis. [< *sil*(icon) + *ox*(ygen) + *-ane*]

**sil|phid** (sil′fid), *n., adj.* —***n.*** any clavicorn beetle of a family that live mainly on carrion, as the sexton beetle.
—***adj.*** belonging to or having to do with this family.
[< New Latin *Silphidae* the family name < Greek *sílphē* cockroach]

**silt** (silt), *n., v.* —***n.*** **1a** very fine particles of earth,

**Pronunciation Key:** hat, āge, cãre, fär; let, ēqual, tėrm; it, īce; hot, ōpen, ôrder; oil, out; cup, pu̇t, rüle; child; long; thin; ᴛʜen; zh, measure; ə represents **a** in about, **e** in taken, **i** in pencil, **o** in lemon, **u** in circus.

sand, clay, or similar matter, carried by moving water: *a river brown with silt. Silt is made up of tiny particles which are anywhere from .01 to .1 mm. (.0004 to .004 inches) in diameter.* **b** such particles deposited as sediment: *The harbor is being choked up with silt.* **2** a deposit of sediment occurring as a stratum in soil.
—*v.t., v.i.* to fill or choke up with or as if with silt: *At the same time, the harbor of Palaeopolis was silting up, so that its merchant ships could no longer bring in grain* (Harper's).
[probably < earlier Flemish *sulte* salt marsh, perhaps < a Scandinavian word]

**sil|ta|tion** (sil tā′shən), *n.* the formation or deposition of silt.

**silt|stone** (silt′stōn′), *n.* a fine-grained rock formed of consolidated silt.

**silt|y** (sil′tē), *adj.* of silt; like silt; full of silt.

**si|lun|dum** (si lun′dəm), *n.* a very hard, insoluble substance consisting partly or entirely of silicon carbide, used as an abrasive and for electrical resistors. [< *sil*(icon) + (carbor)*undum*]

**Sil|u|res** (sil′yə rēz), *n.pl.* an ancient British tribe in southeastern Wales at the time of the Roman conquest. [< Latin *Silures*]

**Si|lu|ri|an** (sə lu̇r′ē ən, sī-), *n., adj.* —*n.* **1** the third geological period of the Paleozoic era, after the Ordovician and before the Devonian, characterized by the development of early land invertebrate animals and land plants. The Silurian formerly included what is now Ordovician and what is now Silurian. *In Europe … the close of the Silurian witnessed the rise of the majestic Caledonian Mountains, which ranged northeastward across the British Isles and Scandinavia* (Carl O. Dunbar). **2** the rocks formed during this period.
—*adj.* **1** of or having to do with this period or its rocks: *The total vegetation of the earth by the end of the Silurian period … appears to have been mostly algae floating in water and growing on wet soil* (Fred W. Emerson). **2** of or belonging to the ancient Silures, or to the district inhabited by them.
[< *Silures* + *-ian* (because such rock deposits were found on the site where the Silures formerly lived)]

**si|lu|rid** (sə lu̇r′id, sī-), *adj., n.* —*adj.* of or belonging to a family of freshwater catfish with long anal fins, found in Europe, Africa, and parts of Asia.
—*n.* a silurid fish.
[< New Latin *Siluridae* the family name < *Silurus* the typical genus < Latin *silūrus* < Greek *silouros* a kind of river fish]

**si|lu|roid** (sə lu̇r′oid), *adj., n.* —*adj.* of the silurid fishes; catfishlike.
—*n.* a siluroid fish.

**sil|va** (sil′və), *n.* **1** the trees of a particular region or period collectively. **2** a treatise on forest trees, or a descriptive list or catalog of trees. Also, **sylva**. [< Latin *silva,* or *sylva* forest]

**sil|van** (sil′vən), *adj., n.* = sylvan.

**Sil|va|nus** (sil vā′nəs), *n.* an ancient Italian god of woods, fields, and herds. [< Latin *Sylvānus* (originally) sylvan]

***sil|ver** (sil′vər), *n., adj., v.* —*n.* **1** a shining, metallic chemical element that can be hammered into very thin sheets or drawn into very fine wire. It is a whitish precious metal that occurs both native and in combination. Silver is superior to any other substance in its ability to conduct heat and electricity. It is used to make coins, jewelry, dishes, knives, forks, and spoons and other table utensils. If it is exposed to sulfur, silver is liable to tarnish. **2** this metal considered as a valuable possession or commodity. **3** coins made from this or a similar metal: *a pocketful of silver.* **4** silverware; utensils or dishes made from silver or plated with it: *table silver.* **5** something like silver, as in luster or color. **6** the color of silver; shining whitish gray. **7** *Photography.* a salt of silver, especially silver nitrate.
—*adj.* **1** made of silver or covered with a layer of silver: *a silver spoon.* **2** of or having to do with silver: *silver ore.* **3** producing, yielding, or selling silver: *a silver mine.* **4** having the color of silver: *silver hair, a silver slipper. There's a silver lining to every cloud* (William S. Gilbert). **5** *Figurative.* **a** having a clear, ringing sound like that of silver dropped on a hard surface; melodious: *But, there, the silver answer rang* (Elizabeth Barrett Browning). **b** eloquent; persuasive: *a silver tongue.* **6** of or advocating the use of silver as a standard of money: *the silver wing of the party.* **7** having to do with the 25th anniversary of an event: *The children gave a party to celebrate their parents' silver wedding anniversary.*
—*v.t.* **1** to cover or coat with silver: *A completely enclosed evacuated cylinder which was silvered on its inner surfaces to give the highest possible conductivity* (W. C. Vaughn). **2** to coat at the back with something like silver: *to silver glass to make a mirror.* **3** to make the color of silver: (*Figurative.*) *Moonlight silvered the lake.*
—*v.i.* to become the color of silver: *The old lady's hair had silvered.*
[Old English *siolfor*] —**sil′ver|er**, *n.* —**sil′ver|like′**, *adj.*

***silver**
definition 1

| symbol | atomic number | atomic weight | oxidation state |
|---|---|---|---|
| Ag | 47 | 107.868 | 1 |

**Silver Age**, **1** *Greek and Roman Mythology.* the second age of the world, in which Zeus, or Jupiter, ruled and the state of mankind was inferior to that of the earlier Golden Age of noble grandeur and ideal innocence, but superior to that of any age that followed. **2** the period in the literature of ancient Rome from the death of Augustus in A.D. 14 to about 180, in which writing is traditionally considered to have slipped from the peak of grandeur and grace of the immediately preceding Augustan age; age of Martial, Pliny, Juvenal, and Tacitus. [translation of Latin *argentea prōlēs* (used by Ovid), (literally) silver offspring]

**silver age**, any period following and inferior to that considered to have been the greatest or most brilliant in achievement.

**silver bass**, = white bass.

**silver bath**, **1** *Photography.* a solution of silver nitrate, used especially for sensitizing collodion plates or paper for printing. **2** a dish or tray for the use of such a solution.

**silver bell**, or **sil|ver-bell tree** (sil′vər bel′), a small North American tree, related to the storax, often grown for its white, bell-shaped flowers.

**sil|ver|ber|ry** (sil′vər ber′ē), *n., pl.* **-ries.** a North American shrub related to the oleaster, having silvery leaves, flowers, and berries.

**silver birch**, **1** = paper birch. **2** = yellow birch. **3** a birch of northern Europe and of Asia having white bark and often used for ornamental purposes.

**silver bromide**, a compound noted for its sensitivity to light, formed by the action of a bromide on an aqueous solution of silver nitrate. It is much used in photography. *Formula:* AgBr

**silver certificate**, paper money formerly issued by the United States Government, bearing a promise to pay for its face value in silver coin on demand: *The silver dollars … were inconvenient to carry, and so the government began issuing paper money called silver certificates* (Charles L. Prather).

**silver chloride**, a compound noted for its sensitivity to light, used especially in photography for sensitizing paper. *Formula:* AgCl

**silver chub**, = fallfish.

**silver crescent**, an American nymphalid butterfly, dark brown in color, with a band of orange across both wings, the undersides being marked with silvery lunules. It is of wide distribution, and its larvae feed on the foliage of a variety of composite plants.

**silver doctor**, an artificial fly with brown, green, blue, red, and yellow wings, a body of silver-colored tinsel, a yellow, red, blue, and green tail, and blue hackle, used especially in trout and salmon fishing.

**silver dollar**, a silver coin of the United States and Canada worth one dollar.

**sil|vered glass** (sil′vərd), = mercury glass.

**sil|ver|eye** (sil′vər ī′), *n.* a bird whose leading common color mark is a white eye ring; white-eye.

**silver fern**, one of numerous ferns in which the under surface of the frond is covered with a white or silvery powder.

**silver fir**, a tall fir tree, a native of Europe, with leaves that are dark green on top and have white bands below.

**sil|ver|fish** (sil′vər fish′), *n., pl.* **-fish|es** or (*collectively*) **-fish.** **1a** a silvery or white variety of goldfish. **b** any one of certain other silvery fishes, such as the tarpon and silversides. **2** any one of a group of small, wingless insects with silvery scales on the body and three bristles extending from the tip of the abdomen, especially a species that is injurious to books, wallpaper, and certain fabrics: *Silverfish are among the most primitive insects, according to the classification schemes of naturalists* (Science News Letter).

**silver foil**, = silver leaf.

**silver fox**, **1** any red fox in the color phase during which its fur is composed of black hairs with white bands near the tips. **2** this fur.

**silver fulminate**, a crystalline compound, the silver salt of fulminic acid, exploding violently when heated, used in making detonators. *Formula:* $Ag_2C_2N_2O_2$

**sil|ver-gilt** (sil′vər gilt′), *n.* **1** silver covered with gilding. **2** gilded articles of silver.

**silver glance**, a variety of silver ore; argentite.

**sil|ver-haired** (sil′vər hãrd′), *adj.* having white or lustrous gray hair: *a silver-haired man of sixty-five.*

**silver hake**, an edible hake common off the coast of New England; whiting.

**sil|ver|i|ness** (sil′vər ē nis), *n.* the state or character of being silvery.

**sil|ver|ing** (sil′vər ing), *n.* **1** the act of a person or thing that silvers. **2** silver plating.

**silver iodide**, a yellow compound of silver and iodine used in treating venereal diseases, in making photographic film, and in cloud seeding. *Formula:* AgI

**sil|ver|ite** (sil′və rīt), *n.* **1** a person who favors the free use of silver as money equally with gold; bimetallist. **2** *U.S.* a person who advocates the free coinage of silver, particularly one who desires free coinage at a particular ratio with gold.

**sil|ver|ize** (sil′və rīz), *v.t.,* **-ized, -iz|ing.** = silver.

**silver lace**, a silver braid used for trimming uniforms, and the like.

**sil|ver-lace vine** (sil′vər lās′), a hardy, twining, perennial vine of western China and Tibet, having fragrant, greenish-white flowers and long lanceolate leaves. It belongs to the buckwheat family.

**silver leaf**, silver beaten into very thin sheets.

**sil|ver|less** (sil′vər lis), *adj.* having no silver; made without silver: *silverless coins.*

**sil|ver|ling** (sil′vər ling), *n.* **1** an old standard of value in silver. **2** a piece of silver money.

**silver lining**, the brighter side of a sad or unfortunate situation.

**sil|ver|ly** (sil′vər lē), *adv. Poetic.* with a silvery appearance or sound: *the dinn'd air vibrating silverly* (Keats).

**silver maple**, **1** a large maple of eastern North America, having leaves that are light green on top and silvery white below. **2** its wood.

**sil|vern** (sil′vərn), *adj. Archaic.* made of, consisting of, or resembling silver.

**silver nitrate**, a colorless, crystalline, poisonous salt that becomes gray or black in the presence of light and organic matter, obtained by treating silver with nitric acid. It is used as a reagent in photography, in dyeing, to silver mirrors, as an antiseptic, etc. *Formula:* $AgNO_3$

**silver owl**, = barn owl.

**silver paper**, **1** a fine, white tissue paper. **2** = silver leaf. **3** *Especially British.* tin foil, as for wrapping candy.

**silver perch**, = white perch.

**silver plate**, **1** articles covered with a thin layer of silver or similar material. **2** a plating of silver or an alloy of silver.

**sil|ver-plat|ed** (sil′vər plā′tid), *adj.* covered with a thin layer of silver or similar material.

**sil|ver|point** (sil′vər point′), *n.* **1** the process of making a drawing with a point or pencil of silver on specially prepared paper: *Fifty drawings in silverpoint, ink, tempera, and wax encaustic by a facile, delicate draftsman* (Time). **2** a drawing made in this way.

**silver print**, a photographic positive made on paper sensitized by a silver salt.

**silver protein**, a compound of silver and protein used as a germicide.

**silver salmon**, = coho.

**silver screen**, **1** a screen with a silverlike coating on which motion pictures are shown. **2** motion pictures: *Yet if he orated on the silver screen he would be faintly ridiculous* (Maclean's).

**sil|ver|side** (sil′vər sīd′), *n.* **1** = silversides. **2** *British.* the upper and choicer part of a round of beef: *I had kippers, finnan haddock, roast beef and boiled silverside* (Manchester Guardian).

**sil|ver|sides** (sil′vər sīdz′), *n., pl.* **-sides.** **1** any one of a family of small, chiefly marine fishes having a silvery stripe along the body, such as the grunion. **2** any one of certain freshwater minnows related to the carps. **3** = coho.

**sil|ver|smith** (sil′vər smith′), *n.* a person who makes articles of silver.

**silver standard**, the use of silver as the standard of value for the money of a country, with all types of currency redeemable in silver coin or bullion.

**Silver Star**, a decoration awarded by the United States for gallantry in action against an armed enemy, consisting of a five-pointed bronze star set at the center with a silver star, conferring a greater degree of honor than the Bronze Star but less than the Distinguished Service Cross: [*He*] *won the DFC and Silver Star for combat missions over the Mediterranean* (Time).

**Silver State**, a nickname for Nevada.

**silver stick**, *British.* an officer of the royal palace, so called from the silvered wand which is his badge.

**silver thaw**, the phenomenon of rain freezing as it falls and forming a glassy coating on the ground, trees, and other objects.

**sil|ver|tip** (sil′vər tip′), *n.* a grizzly bear, so called because its fur is white at the tip.

**sil|ver-tongued** (sil′vər tungd′), *adj.* = eloquent.

**sil|ver|tree** (sil′vər trē′), *n.* a small, evergreen tree with silvery, lance-shaped leaves, native to South Africa.

***sil|ver|ware** (sil′vər wãr′), *n.* **1a** eating utensils, serving dishes, and the like, made of or plated with silver; silver tableware. **b** metal eating utensils as distinguished from plates and glasses. **2** things made of silver; ware of a silversmith.

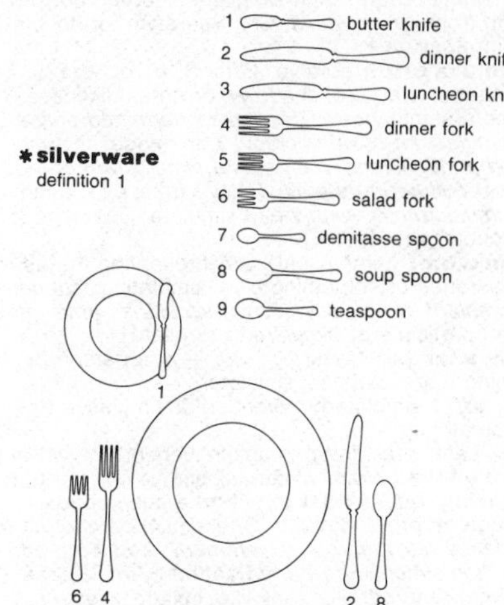

***silverware** definition 1

**silver wedding**, the 25th anniversary of a wedding.

**sil|ver|weed** (sil′vər wēd′), *n.* **1** an herb of the rose family, a variety of cinquefoil whose pinnate leaves are silvery on the underside. **2** a closely related short-stemmed plant, naturalized in North America from Europe, whose palmate leaves are silvery on the underside.

**silver work**, **1** ornamental work in silver. **2** vessels and utensils made of silver.

**sil|ver|y** (sil′vər ē), *adj.*, **-ver|i|er**, **-ver|i|est**. **1** like silver: *silvery hair.* **2** like that of silver: *a silvery gleam, silvery moonbeams.* **3** having a clear, gentle resonance, somewhat like that of pieces of silver dropped on a hard surface; melodious: *silvery laughter, a silvery voice.* **4** producing silver; containing silver.

**sil|vi|cal** (sil′vi kəl), *adj.* of or having to do with silvics.

**sil|vi|chem|i|cal** (sil′və kem′ə kəl), *n.* any chemical substance derived from trees. [< Latin *silva* forest + English *chemical*]

**sil|vic|o|lous** (sil vik′ə ləs), *adj.* living or growing in woodlands. [< Latin *silvicola* inhabiting woods + English *-ous*]

**sil|vics** (sil′viks), *n.* **1** the science dealing with the life of trees in a forest. **2** the characteristics of a forest tree. Also, **sylvics**. [< Latin *silva* forest + English *-ics*]

**sil|vi|cul|tur|al** (sil′və kul′chər əl), *adj.* of or having to do with silviculture. Also, **sylvicultural**. **— sil′vi|cul′tur|al|ly**, *adv.*

**sil|vi|cul|ture** (sil′və kul′chər), *n.* the cultivation of woods or forests; the growing and tending of trees as a branch of forestry: *Silviculture is ... the systematic growing of timber on a crop basis* (White and Renner). Also, **sylviculture**. [< Latin *silva* forest + *cultūra* culture]

**sil|vi|cul|tur|ist** (sil′və kul′chər ist), *n.* a person skilled in silviculture. Also, **sylviculturist**.

**s'il vous plaît** (sēl vü ple′), *French.* if you please.

**sil|y** (sil′ē), *n., pl.* **sil|y** or **sil|ys**. the unit of money of Guinea. It replaced the franc in 1972. Also, **syli**. [< a native name]

**si|ma** (sī′mə), *n.* a basaltic rock rich in silica and magnesium. Sima is the chief constituent of the ocean floors. [< *si*(lica) + *ma*(gnesium)]

**si|mar** (si mär′), *n.* a loose, light robe with a train formerly worn by women. Also, **cymar**. [< French *simarre* < Italian *zimarra*, variant of *cimarra*. See etym. of doublets **chimere**, **cymar**.]

**sim|a|rou|ba** (sim′ə rü′bə), *n.* **1** any one of a group of tropical American trees, having pinnate leaves and a plumlike fruit. **2** the bark of the root, used as a tonic or astringent. [< French *simarouba* < Carib *simaruba*]

**si|mat|ic** (sī mat′ik), *adj.* **1** composed largely of silica and magnesium. **2** consisting of sima: *a simatic ocean basin.*

**si|ma|zin** (sī′mə zən), *n.* = simazine.

**si|ma|zine** (sī′mə zēn), *n.* a moderately toxic chemical widely used as a weed killer. [< *sim-* (perhaps for *simple*) + (tri)*azine*]

**Sim|ba** (sim′bə), *n., pl.* **-bas**. a member of a Congolese group of leftist rebels in the Zaire Republic. [< Swahili *simba* lion]

**sim|bil** (sim′bəl), *n.* an African stork having a greenish and brownish-purple plumage with white underparts. [< a native name]

**Sim|chas Torah** (sim′ʜäs, sim ʜäth′), = Simhath Torah.

**Sim|e|on** (sim′ē ən), *n.* **1** in the Old Testament: **a** the second son of Jacob and Leah (Genesis 29:33). **b** one of the twelve tribes of Israel, that claimed him as ancestor (Numbers 26:12-14). **2** (in the New Testament) a pious old man who saw the child Jesus in the temple at Jerusalem and recognized him as the promised Messiah (Luke 2:25-35).

**Sim|hath Torah** (sim′ʜäs, sim ʜäth′), a Jewish holiday on the ninth and last day of the festival of Sukkoth, celebrating the end of the complete annual reading of the Pentateuch and the start of a new cycle with the beginning of Genesis. [< Hebrew *simḥath tōrāh* (literally) rejoicing of the law]

**sim|i|an** (sim′ē ən), *adj., n.* **— *adj.*** **1** like or characteristic of an ape or monkey; apelike or monkeylike: *The teeth were not forward-jutting ... and had no simian gap* (Time). **2** having to do with an ape or monkey.
**— *n.*** an ape or monkey (often applied to an anthropoid ape).
[< Latin *sīmia, sīmius* ape (< *sīmus* snub-nosed < Greek *sīmós*) + English *-an*]

**simian line** or **crease**, a single deep line or crease running across part of the palm of the hand nearest the fingers instead of the two separate lines found normally: *The so-called simian crease ... is normally rare but occurs frequently in Down's syndrome, or mongolism* (Scientific American). [so called from its being typical of the palms of simians]

**simian shelf**, a bony shelf along the inside of the lower jawbone of anthropoid apes: *The reduction of the jaw, especially the elimination of the "simian shelf," gave the tongue freer movement and thus helped create the potentiality for speech* (Julian H. Steward).

**sim|i|lar** (sim′ə lər), *adj.* **1** much the same; alike; like: *A creek and a brook are similar.* **2** *Geometry.* having the same shape but varying in size or position or both; having corresponding angles equal and corresponding sides proportional: *similar triangles.* [< French *similaire* < Latin *similis* like] **— sim′i|lar|ly**, *adv.*

**sim|i|lar|i|ty** (sim′ə lar′ə tē), *n., pl.* **-ties**. the condition of being similar; likeness; resemblance: *The parallel does not end there, for both pieces had points of similarity* (New York Times). **SYN:** See syn. under **resemblance**.
**similarities**, points of resemblance: *There are many curious similarities between the inhabitants of Europe and North America* (Saturday Review).

**similar motion**, *Music.* two parts or voices sounded together and moving in the same direction, both either ascending or descending in pitch, but not in the same intervals.

**sim|i|la|tive** (sim′ə lā tiv), *adj., n.* **— *adj.*** **1** expressing similarity. **2** *Grammar.* denoting the case which expresses similarity.
**— *n.*** a similative word or expression.

**sim|i|le** (sim′ə lē), *n.* a statement that one thing is like another, especially as a figure of speech for some effect. *Examples:* a face like marble, as hard as nails, as brave as a lion. [< Latin *simile*, neuter adjective, like]

**simile mark**, *Music.* an abbreviation mark signifying that the contents of the last measure that was written out are to be repeated.

**si|mil|i|a si|mil|i|bus cu|ran|tur** (sə mil′ē ə sə mil′ə bus kyù ran′tər), *Latin.* like things are cured by like things; like cures like (the basic formula of homeopathy).

**si|mil|i|ter** (sə mil′ə tər), *adv. Law.* in like manner; the technical designation of the common-law form by which, when the pleading of one party, tendering an issue, demands trial, the other accepts the issue by saying, "and the (defendant) doeth the like." [< Latin *similiter* < *similis* like, resembling]

**si|mil|i|tude** (sə mil′ə tüd, -tyüd), *n.* **1** a being similar; likeness; resemblance: *A striking similitude between the brother and sister now first arrested my attention* (Edgar Allan Poe). **SYN:** similarity. **2** a comparison drawn between two things or facts: *She could think of no similitude to describe the sunset.* **SYN:** simile. **3** a copy; image. **SYN:** counterpart. **4** a parable or allegory (chiefly in Biblical use). [< Latin *similitūdō, -inis* < *similis* like]

**sim|i|lize** (sim′ə līz), *v.t.*, **-lized**, **-liz|ing**. to liken; compare. [< Latin *similis* like + English *-ize*]

**sim|i|ous** (sim′ē əs), *adj.* = simian.

**sim|i|tar** (sim′ə tər), *n.* = scimitar.

**sim|mer** (sim′ər), *v., n.* **— *v.i.*** **1a** to make a murmuring sound while boiling gently: *The kettle simmered on the stove.* **b** to be at or just below the boiling point; boil gently: *The soup should simmer for a few hours to improve its taste.* **2** *Figurative.* to be on the point of just breaking out: *a simmering rebellion. He simmered with indignation, but said nothing.* **SYN:** See syn. under **boil**.
**— *v.t.*** to keep at or just below the boiling point: *Simmer the milk; do not boil it.*
**— *n.*** the process of cooking or being cooked at or just below the boiling point: *Do not let the soup cook faster than at a simmer.*
**simmer down**, **a** to calm down from an angry or excited state; cool off: *The owner of the house was enraged, but he simmered down when the boys promised to pay for the broken window.* **b** (of a liquid) to be reduced in quantity through continued simmering: *He left the brew on the fire for so long that it simmered down to almost nothing.*
[earlier *simper*; probably imitative]

**sim|nel** (sim′nəl), *n.* **1** a rich currant cake eaten on the Sunday in the middle of Lent in some parts of England. **2** any one of various breads or buns eaten in England until the late 1700's, made of fine flour and cooked partially or completely by boiling. [< Old French *simenel*]

**si|mo|le|on** (sə mō′lē ən), *n. Slang.* a dollar. [American English, apparently < earlier *simon* a dollar; perhaps on analogy of French *napoleon*, a former gold coin]

**Si|mon** (sī′mən), *n.* in the Bible: **1** the Apostle Peter's original name (Mark 3:16). **2** one of the disciples chosen by Jesus as His Apostles; Simon Zelotes (Luke 6:15). **3** a brother or relative of Jesus (Matthew 13:55). **4** a Samaritan sorcerer; Simon Magus. He was converted to Christianity by Philip and incurred the Apostle Peter's anger by trying to buy from Peter and John the power of imparting the Holy Ghost (Acts 8:9-24). **5** a tanner with whom the Apostle Peter stayed at Joppa (Acts 9:43).

**si|mo|ni|ac** (si mō′nē ak), *n.* a person who practices simony.

**si|mo|ni|a|cal** (sī′mə nī′ə kəl, sim′ə-), *adj.* **1** guilty of simony. **2** of, having to do with, or involving simony. **— si′mo|ni′a|cal|ly**, *adv.*

**si|mo|nism** (sī′mə niz əm, sim′ə-), *n.* the practice or advocacy of simony.

**si|mo|nist** (sī′mə nist, sim′ə-), *n.* a person who practices or advocates simony.

**si|mo|nize** (sī′mə nīz), *v.t.*, **-nized**, **-niz|ing**. to polish, especially with wax: *to simonize a car.* [< *Simoniz*, a trademark]

**Simon Le|gree** (li grē′), a harsh, cruel, or demanding person in authority, such as an employer or officer that is this way. [< *Simon Legree*, a brutal slave overseer in Harriet Beecher Stowe's *Uncle Tom's Cabin*]

**Simon Magus**, = Simon (def. 4).

**Simon Peter**, = Peter (def. 1).

**si|mon-pure** (sī′mən pyùr′), *adj. Informal.* **1** real; genuine; authentic; true: *simon-pure maple sugar.* **2** that is morally pure: *He's not as simon-pure as he pretends.* [American English < *Simon Pure*, a Quaker, whose identity is questioned but proven genuine, in the comedy *A Bold Stroke for a Wife* (1718), by Susanna Centlivre, 1667?-1723, an English dramatist]

**si mo|nu|men|tum re|qui|ris, cir|cum|spi|ce** (sī mon′yù men′təm ri kwī′ris sər kum′spə sē), *Latin.* if you would see his monument, look around (Sir Christopher Wren's epitaph in St. Paul's Cathedral, London).

**si|mo|ny** (sī′mə nē, sim′ə-), *n., pl.* **-nies**. **1** the act of buying and selling sacred things. **2** the sin of buying or selling positions or promotions in the church. [< Old French *simonie*, learned borrowing from Latin *simōnia* < *Simōn Magus*, who tried to buy the power of conferring the Holy Spirit. See Acts 8:9-24.]

**Simon Ze|lo|tes** (zə lō′tēz), = Simon (def. 2).

**si|moom** (sə müm′), *n.* a hot, dry, suffocating, sand-laden wind that sweeps across the deserts of Arabia, Syria, and northern Africa during the spring and summer; samiel. [< Arabic *simūm* < *samma* he poisoned]

**si|moon** (sə mün′), *n.* = simoom.

**simp** (simp), *n. U.S. Slang.* a simpleton; fool. [American English, short for *simpleton*]

**sim|pai** (sim′pī), *n.* the black-crested monkey of Sumatra, having a long, slender body, tail, and limbs, and highly variegated coloration. [< Malay *simpai*]

**sim|pa|ti|ca** (sim pä′ti kə), *adj.* feminine of **simpatico**: *To hear her say anyone was not sim-*

**Pronunciation Key:** **hat**, **āge**, **cãre**, **fär**; **let**, **ēqual**, **tėrm**; **it**, **īce**; **hot**, **ōpen**, **ôrder**; **oil**, **out**; **cup**, **pùt**, **rüle**; **child**; **long**; **thin**; **ᴛʜen**; **zh**, measure; **ə** represents **a** in about, **e** in taken, **i** in pencil, **o** in lemon, **u** in circus.

*patica gave me a turn* (Atlantic). [< Spanish *simpática*]

**sim|pa|ti|co** (sim pä′ti kō), *adj.* **1** arousing a sympathetic response; agreeable: *It is important to find the simpatico agent who will give the traveler what he wants and not what the agent thinks he ought to want* (Atlantic). **2** in agreement; in harmony; compatible: *If he goes, it won't be because the two are simpatico, ... but because his business interests are at stake.* (Wall Street Journal). [< Spanish *simpático* < *simpatía* sympathy < Latin *sympathīa*]

**sim|per** (sim′pər), *v., n.* **—v.i.** to smile in a silly, affected way; smirk: *She stood before the mirror ... simpering to her own image* (Hawthorne).
**—v.t.** to express by a simper; say with a simper.
**—n.** a silly, affected smile.
[perhaps < Scandinavian (compare Norwegian *semper* smart)] **—sim′per|er,** *n.* **—sim′per|ing|ly,** *adv.*

**sim|ple** (sim′pəl), *adj.*, **-pler, -plest,** *n.* **—adj.** **1** easy to do, understand, use, solve, or the like: *a simple problem, a simple explanation, a simple task. This book is in simple language.* **SYN:** See syn. under **easy. 2** not divided into parts; not compound; single: *a simple substance, a simple concept.* See also **simple leaf. 3** having few parts; not complex; not involved; elementary: *a simple pattern or design, a simple one-celled animal. A simple curve does not cross itself.* **4** considered or taken by itself; with nothing added; mere; bare: *a simple majority. My answer is the simple truth.* **SYN:** pure, absolute. **5a** without ornament; not rich or showy: *He eats simple food and wears simple clothing.* **b** unaffected; plain: *a simple tale, to write in a simple style.* **6** free from pride, ostentation, or display; not showing off; unaffected; natural: *a simple life. She has a pleasant, simple manner. Arthur ... neither wore on helm or shield the golden symbol of his kinglihood, But rode a simple knight among his knights* (Tennyson). **SYN:** unassuming, unpretentious. **7** free from duplicity or guile; undesigning; honest; sincere: *a simple heart. The short and simple annals of the poor* (Thomas Gray). **SYN:** open, straightforward. **8** not subtle; not sophisticated; innocent; artless: *a simple child.* **SYN:** naive, ingenuous. **9** common; ordinary: *a simple citizen, a simple private.* **10** of humble birth or position; lowly; undistinguished: *His parents were simple people.* **11** weak in mind; dull or stupid; foolish or silly: *Simple Simon met a pieman* (Nursery Rhyme). *Thou art as simple, I see, in this world's knowledge as ever* (Scott). **12** of little value or importance; insignificant; trifling; slight: *Great floods have flown from simple sources* (Shakespeare).
**—n.** **1** a foolish, stupid person. **2** something unmixed or uncompounded. **3** a medicine or food, composed of only one constituent. **4** *Archaic.* **a** a plant or herb used in medicine: *Saphira read his medical library, added herbs and simples she knew from her childhood, plus other remedies* (Harper's). **b** a medicine made from it. **5** *Archaic.* a person of poor or humble birth or position.
[< Old French *simple* < Latin *simplex, -icis.* See etym. of doublet **simplex.**] **—sim′ple|ness,** *n.*

**simple closed curve,** = Jordan curve.

**simple contract,** *Law.* a contract or agreement not under seal.

**simple equation,** = linear equation.

**sim|ple-faced** (sim′pəl fāst′), *adj.* (of bats) having no foliaceous appendages on the snout.

**simple fraction,** a fraction having a whole number in both the numerator and the denominator. *Examples:* $1/3$, $3/4$, $219/125$.

**simple fracture,** a fracture in which a broken bone does not penetrate the skin; closed fracture. See diagram under **fracture.**

**simple fruit,** a fruit developed from a single matured ovary, as the tomato, apple, and acorn. Simple fruits are classified as either fleshy or dry.

**sim|ple-heart|ed** (sim′pəl här′tid), *adj.* **1** having or showing a simple, unaffected nature: *The average simple-hearted lover of Westerns will be quite happy to see some of the familiar situations without bothering to understand exactly how they came about* (Punch). **2** guileless; sincere.

**simple honors,** a bare majority of honors in auction bridge; three trump honors or three aces at no trump, held by one side.

**simple interest,** interest that is paid only on the principal of a loan, mortgage, or other obligation and not on accrued interest.

**simple leaf,** a leaf consisting of a single blade. An oak leaf is a simple leaf.

**simple machine,** any one of the basic mechanical devices which multiply or change the direction of force and on which more complex machines are based. The lever, wedge, pulley, wheel and axle, inclined plane, and screw are the six simple machines.

**sim|ple-mind|ed** (sim′pəl mīn′did), *adj.* **1** without awareness of conventions; artless; inexperienced. **SYN:** unsophisticated. **2** ignorant; foolish; stupid. **3** = feeble-minded. **—sim′ple-mind′ed|ly,** *adv.* **—sim′ple-mind′ed|ness,** *n.*

**simple past,** the past tense without reference to the duration of action; past absolute.

**sim|pler** (sim′plər), *n. Archaic.* a person who gathers simples or medicinal herbs, or is skilled in their uses; herbalist.

**simple sentence,** a sentence consisting of one main clause. *Examples:* The whistle blows. John called his dog.

**Simple Simon,** = simpleton.

**simple sugar,** any monosaccharide, such as dextrose.

**simple time** or **measure,** *Music.* a rhythm or time having two or three beats to a measure.

**sim|ple|ton** (sim′pəl tən), *n.* a silly person; fool. [< *simple*]

**simple vow,** a public vow taken by a Roman Catholic religious under which ownership of property is retained and marriage is considered valid, though illicit. Simple vows may be temporary or perpetual.

**sim|plex** (sim′pleks), *adj., n., pl.* **sim|plex|es, sim|pli|ces** (sim′plə sēz), **sim|pli|ci|a** (sim plish′ē ə). **—adj.** **1** consisting of or characterized by a single part or structure; not compound. **2** of or having to do with a system for sending telegraphic messages in only one direction at a time.
**—n.** **1** a simple, uncompounded word. **2** *Mathematics.* a figure or element having the minimum number of boundary points in a Euclidean space of a specified number of dimensions. The simplex of one-dimensional space is the line segment, of two-dimensional space the triangle, and of three-dimensional space the tetrahedron.
[< Latin *simplex* single < *sem-* one- (for *semel* once) + *-plex* -fold. See etym. of doublet **simple.**]

**sim|pli|ci|den|tate** (sim′plə sə den′tāt), *adj., n.* **—adj.** of or belonging to a former suborder containing all those animals now classified as rodents, and characterized by only one pair of upper incisor teeth.
**—n.** a simplicidentate animal.
[< Latin *simplex, -icis* single + English *dentate*]

**sim|pli|cism** (sim′plə siz əm), *n.* = simplism.

**sim|pli|cist** (sim′plə sist), *n., adj.* **—n.** a person who advocates or cultivates simplicity: *In music he is a simplicist* (Harper's).
**—adj.** = simplistic.

**sim|pli|cis|tic** (sim′plə sis′tik), *adj.* = simplistic.

**sim|plic|i|ty** (sim plis′ə tē), *n., pl.* **-ties. 1** the condition or quality of being simple: *simplicity of structure.* **2** freedom from difficulty; clearness: *The simplicity of the book makes it suitable for children. Simplicity is become a very rare quality in a writer* (William Cowper). **3** an absence of ornament or freedom from useless accessories; plainness: *Hospital rooms are furnished with simplicity.* **4** an absence of or freedom from luxury; plainness, especially rustic plainness, of life: *The simplicities of cottage life* (Wordsworth). **5** an absence of show or pretense; sincerity; straightforwardness. **6** a lack of shrewdness; dullness: *His simplicity made him easily fooled.* **7** something simple or simple-minded: *The ... policy is to go on talking simplicities about defending freedom* (Anthony Lewis). [< Latin *simplicitās* < *simplex, -icis* simple]

**sim|pli|fi|ca|tion** (sim′plə fə kā′shən), *n.* **1** the act of simplifying: *The simplification ... is aimed ... at lightening unnecessary and unintended burdens on trade* (Wall Street Journal). **2** the condition of being simplified. **3** a change to a simpler form or condition: *Mounted above it was a large, multicolored simplification of the atom* (New Yorker).

**sim|pli|fi|ca|tive** (sim′plə fə kā′tiv), *adj.* tending to simplify.

**sim|pli|fi|ca|tor** (sim′plə fə kā′tər), *n.* = simplifier.

**sim|pli|fi|er** (sim′plə fī′ər), *n.* a person or thing that simplifies.

**sim|pli|fy** (sim′plə fī), *v.t.*, **-fied, -fy|ing.** to make plainer or easier; make simple or simpler: *"Tho" is a simplified spelling of "though." The program has been modified, but not simplified, for their benefit* (Time). [< French, Old French *simplifier,* adaptation of Medieval Latin *simplificari* < Late Latin *simplus,* variant of Latin *simplex, -icis* simple + *facere* to make]

**sim|plism** (sim′pliz əm), *n.* **1** the advocacy or cultivation of simplicity. **2** an affected or labored simplicity.

**sim|plis|tic** (sim plis′tik), *adj.* trying to explain everything, or too much, by a single principle: *The facts of nature and of life are more apt to be complex than simple. Simplistic theories are generally one-sided and partial* (James Freeman Clarke). **—sim|plis′ti|cal|ly,** *adv.*

**sim|ply** (sim′plē), *adv.* **1** in a simple manner: *The problem can be solved very simply by arithmetic.* **2** without much ornament; without pretense or affectation; plainly: *The nurse was simply dressed.* **3** in simple language; clearly. **4** merely; only: *The baby did not simply cry, he yelled.* **5** foolishly: *He acted as simply as an idiot.* **6** absolutely: *simply perfect, simply hopeless.*

**sim|u|la|cra** (sim′yə lā′krə), *n.* a plural of **simulacrum:** *We see why the greater part of the work done on the mechanical simulacra of the brain has been on machines which are more or less on a digital basis* (Norbert Wiener).

**sim|u|la|cre** (sim′yə lā′kər), *n. Archaic.* a material or mental representation; image of a person or thing. [< Old French *simulacre,* learned borrowing from Latin *simulācrum.* See etym. of doublet **simulacrum.**]

**sim|u|la|crum** (sim′yə lā′krəm), *n., pl.* **-cra** or **-crums. 1** a faint, shadowy, or unreal likeness; mere semblance: *The dictator permitted only a simulacrum of democracy.* **2** an image: *It exists on a little island in time as a simulacrum of Moslem culture in its purity* (New Yorker). [< Latin *simulācrum* < *simulāre* to simulate. See etym. of doublet **simulacre.**]

**sim|u|lant** (sim′yə lənt), *adj.* presenting the appearance of something else; simulating: *stamens simulant of petals.* [< Latin *simulāns, -antis,* present participle of *simulāre* to simulate]

**sim|u|lar** (sim′yə lər), *n., adj.* **—n.** a person or thing that simulates; simulator.
**—adj.** **1** simulated; pretended. **2** simulative of something.
[< Latin *simulāre;* perhaps influenced by *similar*]

**sim|u|late** (*v.* sim′yə lāt; *adj.* sim′yə lit), *v.*, **-lat|ed, -lat|ing,** *adj.* **—v.t.** **1** to put on a false appearance of; pretend; feign: *She simulated interest to please her friend. A government ... in word and action simulating reform* (Matthew Arnold). **SYN:** sham. **2** to act like; look like; imitate: *Certain insects simulate flowers or leaves.* **3** to imitate or represent (a physical or social system or its activity); make a simulation of: *What the computer did is called simulation. Working from data given it, the computer calculated, or simulated, the satellite's position at various instants and produced the picture on microfilm* (Atlantic).
**—adj.** pretended; feigned.
[< Latin *simulāre* (with English *-ate*[1]) < *similis* like]

**sim|u|la|tion** (sim′yə lā′shən), *n.* **1** the act or practice of simulating: **a** pretense; feigning: *Simulation is a pretence of what is not, and Dissimulation a concealment of what is* (Sir Richard Steele). **b** imitation: *a harmless insect's simulation of a poisonous one.* **2a** the representation or imitation of a physical or social system or its activity by a computer for the purpose of predicting the behavior of that system under certain conditions. **b** one such representation or model: *These methods, known collectively as simulations, involve the making of numerical models of large scale systems and solving them on high-speed computers for all imaginable configurations* (New York Times).

**sim|u|la|tive** (sim′yə lā′tiv), *adj.* characterized by simulation; simulating. **—sim′u|la′tive|ly,** *adv.*

**sim|u|la|tor** (sim′yə lā′tər), *n.* **1** a person who simulates or pretends. **2** a thing that simulates, such as an apparatus that duplicates airplane or missile flight conditions: [*The airline*] *has installed half a dozen new simulators within the past year to train pilots to land when visibility is bad* (Wall Street Journal).

**si|mul|cast** (sī′məl kast′, -käst′), *v.*, **-cast** or **-cast|ed, -cast|ing,** *n.* **—v.t., v.i.** to transmit (a program) over radio and television simultaneously: *The Firestone Hour ... is "simulcast" at 8:30* (New York Times).
**—n.** **1** a program transmitted over radio and television simultaneously: *The audience will get the usual feature and, in addition, the simulcast* (Newsweek). **2** transmission of a program over radio and television simultaneously.
[< *simul*(taneous) + (broad)*cast*]

**si|mu|li|um fly** (sə myü′lē əm), any one of a group of small flies or gnats found near rivers and streams throughout the world, as the black fly. Several varieties are the carriers of onchocerciasis. [< New Latin *Simulium* the genus name < Latin *simulāre* to simulate]

**si|mul|ta|ne|ism** (sī′məl tā′nē iz′əm, sim′əl-), *n.* = synthetic cubism.

**si|mul|ta|ne|i|ty** (sī′məl tə nē′ə tē, sim′əl-), *n.* the quality or fact of being simultaneous; occurrence at the same time: *It is this simultaneity of the end of history as we knew it in the Western world, and the beginning of history in Asia and Africa, which makes the present world situation so confused and unpredictable* (Bulletin of Atomic Scientists).

**si|mul|ta|ne|ous** (sī′məl tā′nē əs, sim′əl-), *adj.* done, existing, operating, or happening at the same time: *The two simultaneous shots sounded like one. Everyone in the audience burst into simultaneous applause.* **SYN:** coincident, contemporaneous. [< Medieval Latin *simultaneus* (with English *-ous*) simulated < Latin *similis* like; confused in sense with Latin *simul* at the same time] —**si'mul|ta'ne|ous|ness**, *n.*

**simultaneous equations**, two or more equations or inequalities, with two or more unknowns, for which a set of values of the unknowns is sought that is a solution of all the equations or inequalities.

**si|mul|ta|ne|ous|ly** (sī'məl tā'nē əs lē, sim'əl-), *adv.* at once; at the same time; together.

**si|murgh** (sē mürg'), *n.* a monstrous bird of Persian mythology, corresponding to the Arabian roc. [< Persian *sīmurgh* < Pahlavi *sīn* eagle + *murgh* bird]

**sin**[1] (sin), *n., v.,* **sinned, sin|ning.** —***n.*** **1a** a breaking of the law of God on purpose: *human sin. Men have dulled their eyes with sin* (Henry Van Dyke). **b** the state or condition resulting from this: *born and raised in sin.* **2** wrongdoing of any kind; immoral act. Lying, stealing, dishonesty, and cruelty are all sins. **3** a violation of any rule or standard, as of taste or propriety.
—***v.i.*** **1** to break the law of God; be a sinner: *That the saint sinned is not believable. The tempter, or the tempted, who sins most?* (Shakespeare). **2** to offend (against some principle, standard, person, or group); do wrong or be wrong: *more sinned against than sinning* (Shakespeare). *Faces sinning against all proportion* (Byron).
—***v.t.*** **1** to do, perform, or perpetrate sinfully; commit (a sin): *A man ... who had sinned all the sins* (H. G. Wells). **2a** to bring (oneself into a state, or beyond something) by sinning. **b** to drive (away) by sinning: *Souls which have sinned away the grace of God and are beyond its reach* (Edward B. Pusey).
**live in sin,** to live as man and wife without being married: ... *the peculiarities of income tax laws which can make living in sin a better financial proposition for working couples than respectable marriage* (Sunday Times).
[Old English *synn* wrongdoing, injury, hostility]

**sin**[2] or **sin'** (sin), *prep., conj., adv. Scottish.* since.

**sin**[3] (sēn), *n.* the twenty-first letter of the Hebrew alphabet; shin. [< Hebrew *sin*]

**Sin** (sin), *n.* = Nannar.

**sin** (no period), the mathematical notation for sine, used in formulas and equations.

**Si|nae|an** (si nē'ən, sī-), *adj.* = Chinese. [< Latin *Sīnae* the Chinese (< Greek *Sînai*) + English *-an*]

**Si|nai** (sī'nī), *n.* **Mount,** the mountain, often identified with several on the Sinai Peninsula, on which Moses received the Law and the Ten Commandments; Horeb (in the Bible, Exodus 19, 20, 34).

**Si|na|ic** (sī nā'ik), *adj.* = Sinaitic.

**Si|na|it|ic** (sī'nā it'ik), *adj.* having to do with Mount Sinai.

**sin|al|bin** (sin al'bin), *n.* a crystalline glucoside present in the seeds of the white mustard. *Formula:* $C_{30}H_{42}N_2O_{15}S_2$ [< Latin *sināpis* mustard + *alba* white + English *-in*]

**Si|nan|thro|pine** (sin'an thrō'pēn, si nan'thrə-pēn), *adj., n.* —***adj.*** of, having to do with, or resembling Peking man.
—***n.*** a Sinanthropine individual.

**Si|nan|thro|pus** (sin'an thrō'pəs, si nan'thrə pəs), *n.* = Sinanthropus pekinensis.

**Sinanthropus pe|ki|nen|sis** (pē'kə nen'sis), = Peking man. [< New Latin *Sinanthropus pekinensis* < Greek *Sînai* the Chinese + *ánthrōpos* man; *pekinensis* of Peking]

**sin|a|pin** (sin'ə pin), *n.* = sinapine.

**sin|a|pine** (sin'ə pēn, -pin), *n.* an alkaloid present in the seeds of the black mustard. *Formula:* $C_{16}H_{25}NO_6$ [< Latin *sināpis* + English *-ine*[2]]

**sin|a|pism** (sin'ə piz əm), *n.* = mustard plaster. [< Latin *sināpismus* < Greek *sināpismós* (use of) a mustard plaster < *sínāpi* mustard < *nâpy*]

**Sin|bad** (sin'bad), *n.* **1** a sailor in *The Arabian Nights* who had seven extraordinary voyages. **2** any sailor. Also, **Sindbad.**

**since** (sins), *prep., conj., adv.* —***prep.*** **1** from a past time till now: *The package has been ready since noon. The sun has been up since five.* **2** at any time between (some past time or event and the present): *We have not seen him since Saturday.*
—***conj.*** **1** after the time that; from the time when: *She has been home only once since she went to New York.* **2** after: *He has worked hard since he left school.* **3** because; seeing that; inasmuch as: *Since you feel tired, you should rest.*
—***adv.*** **1** from then till now; continually afterward: *He caught cold on Saturday and has been in bed ever since.* **2** at some time between then and now; subsequently; later: *She at first refused the position, but has since accepted it.* **3** before now; ago: *I heard that old joke long since.*
[Middle English *sinnes,* Old English *siththan* then later < *sīth* late, preposition]
► See **because** for usage note.

**sin|cere** (sin sir'), *adj.,* **-cer|er, -cer|est.** **1** free from pretense or deceit; genuine; real; honest: *sincere thanks, a sincere person, to be sincere in one's apologies. He made a sincere effort to pass his exams.* **SYN:** true, heartfelt, straightforward. **2** *Obsolete.* free from adulterants; pure; unadulterated: *As newborn babes, desire the sincere milk of the word, that ye may grow thereby* (I Peter 2:2). **3** *Obsolete.* free from hurt; uninjured. [< Latin *sincērus*] —**sin|cere'ly,** *adv.* —**sin|cere'ness,** *n.*

**sin|cer|i|ty** (sin ser'ə tē), *n., pl.* **-ties.** the character, quality, or state of being sincere; freedom from pretense or deceit; honesty; straightforwardness: *No one doubts the sincerity of Abraham Lincoln.*
**sincerities,** *Archaic.* sincere feelings or actions.

**sin|cip|i|tal** (sin sip'ə təl), *adj.* of or having to do with the sinciput.

**sin|ci|put** (sin'sə put, -pət), *n., pl.* **sin|ci|puts, sin|cip|i|ta** (sin sip'ə tə). **1** the front part of the head. **2** the upper part of the skull. [< Latin *sinciput* < *sēmi* half + *caput, -itis* head]

**Sind|bad** (sin'bad), *n.* = Sinbad.

**Sin|dhi** (sin'dē), *n., pl.* **-dhis** or **-dhi,** *adj.* —***n.*** **1** a native or inhabitant of Sind, a province of Pakistan. **2** the Indic language spoken in Sind.
—***adj.*** of or having to do with Sind, its people, or their language.

**sine**[1] (sīn), *n.* **1** the length of the side opposite an acute angle in a right triangle divided by the length of the hypotenuse. The sine, secant, and tangent are the three fundamental trigonometric functions. *Abbr:* sin (no period). **2** (originally) a perpendicular drawn from one extremity of an arc of a circle to the diameter which intersects its other extremity. [< Latin *sinus, -ūs* bend; fold in a garment, bosom (in Medieval Latin, a translation of Arabic *jaib* sine; (originally) bosom of a garment)]

**si|ne**[2] (sī'nē), *prep. Latin.* without.

**si|ne|cure** (sī'nə kyůr, sin'ə-), *n.* **1** an extremely easy job; position requiring little or no work and usually paying well: *His job has become a profession instead of a drowsy sinecure, as it was in the eighteenth century* (New Yorker). **2** an ecclesiastical benefice without parish duties. [< Medieval Latin (*beneficium*) *sine cura* (benefice) without cure (of souls) < Latin *sine,* preposition; *cūrā,* ablative singular of *cūra* care]

**si|ne|cur|ism** (sī'nə kyů riz'əm, sin'ə-), *n.* the practice of holding or permitting sinecures.

**si|ne|cur|ist** (sī'nə kyůr'ist, sin'ə-), *n.* a person who holds or seeks to obtain a sinecure.

***sine curve,** a curve showing the relationship between the size of an angle and its sine, plotted by using the successive values as coordinates.

***sine curve**

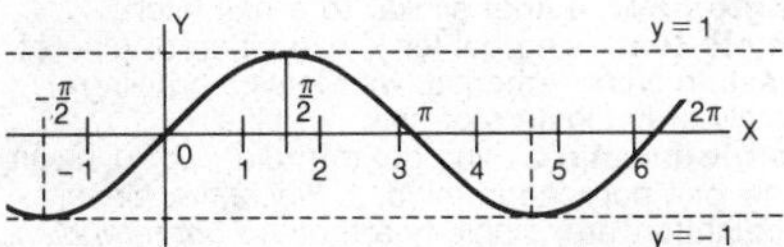


**si|ne di|e** (sī'nē dī'ē, sī'nə), without a day specified, as for another meeting or trial; indefinitely: *The committee adjourned sine die. Abbr:* s.d. [< Medieval Latin *sine die* without a day (being set)]

**si|ne qua non** (sī'nē kwā non', sī'nə), something essential; indispensable condition: *The most obvious quality, the sine qua non indeed, of a director is competence in professional matters* (Saturday Review). *The free exchange of ideas* [*is*] *a sine qua non of any distinguished scholarly activity* (New York Times). [< Late Latin *sine quā non* (literally) without which not]

**sin|ew** (sin'yü), *n., v.* —***n.*** **1** a tough, strong band or cord that joins muscle to bone; tendon: *You can see the sinews between the muscle and bone in a cooked chicken leg.* **2** *Figurative.* **a** strength; energy; force: *He is well liked, but as a leader he lacks sinew.* **b** a means of strength; source of power: *Men and money are the sinews of war.* **3** *Obsolete.* a nerve.
—***v.t.*** to furnish or strengthen with sinews: (*Figurative.*) *Ourselves well sinewed to our defence* (Shakespeare).
[Old English *sionu*]

**sine wave,** a simple wave, such as an electromagnetic or sound wave, that can be graphically represented as a sine curve.

**sin|ew|i|ness** (sin'yü ē nis), *n.* the state or character of being sinewy: *They are a deplorable lot, having ... the predatory sinewiness of hunting leopards* (Manchester Guardian).

**sin|ew|less** (sin'yü lis), *adj.* **1** lacking sinews. **2** *Figurative.* lacking vigor; feeble; weak; powerless.

**sin|ew|y** (sin'yü ē), *adj.* **1** having strong or well-developed sinews; strong; powerful: *A wrestler has sinewy arms.* **2** *Figurative.* vigorous; forcible: *a sinewy mind.* **3a** like sinews; tough; stringy. **b** furnished with or full of sinews.

**sin|fo|ni|a** (sin'fə nē'ə; *Italian* sēn'fô nē'ä), *n., pl.* **-ni|e** (-nē'ā). *Music.* **1** a symphony. **2** (originally) any one of various instrumental pieces, such as a sonata, or an overture or interlude in an opera or oratorio: *Haydn and Mozart wrote classic symphonies developed from the earlier sinfonia* (Grant Fletcher).
[< Italian *sinfonia* symphony]
► The Italian **sinfonia** in the 1600's and 1700's was an instrumental piece in an opera or oratorio, later usually the overture, especially the Italian allegro overture from which the symphony developed. In Italian the word *sinfonia* still means both "overture" and "symphony."

**sin|fo|niet|ta** (sin'fən yet'ə), *n.* **1** any one of various short instrumental pieces patterned on the symphony: *The stirring sinfoniettas from the double pianos ... begin at eight-thirty* (New Yorker). **2** a small orchestra, especially one consisting entirely or chiefly of strings: [*He*] *led the New York Sinfonietta in all-Vivaldi programs* (New Yorker). [< Italian *sinfonietta* (diminutive) < *sinfonia* symphony]

**sin|ful** (sin'fəl), *adj.* full of sin or sins; wicked; wrong; immoral; evil: *a sinful act. The sinful man repented.* **SYN:** depraved. —**sin'ful|ly,** *adv.* —**sin'ful|ness,** *n.*

**sing** (sing), *v.,* **sang** or (sometimes) **sung, sung, sing|ing,** *n.* —***v.i.*** **1** to make music with the voice: *to sing in a choir, to sing while working. He sings on the radio.* **SYN:** carol, warble, croon. **2** to make pleasant musical sounds: *Birds sing.* **3** to tell in song or poetry: *The poet sang of heroes. Homer sang of Troy. Thus have I sung of fields, and flocks, and trees* (John Dryden). **4** to admit of being sung: *The words of the verse sing well.* **5a** to make a ringing, murmuring, whistling, humming, or buzzing sound: *The teakettle sang on the stove.* **b** to move with such a sound: *The stone sang past my head* (Sir Arthur Conan Doyle). **6** to have a sensation of a ringing, buzzing, or humming sound; tingle: *A bad cold made my ears sing.* **7** *Slang, Figurative.* to inform; tell all: [*He*] *hopes to get consideration on his twelve-year jail sentence in return for singing in public* (Newsweek).
—***v.t.*** **1** to utter musically: *to sing a song. He almost seemed to sing his lines from the play.* **2** to chant; intone: *The priest sings Mass.* **3** to tell of in song or poetry: *The poet sang the deeds of heroes.* **4** *Figurative.* to proclaim: *to sing a person's praises.* **5a** to bring, send, or put with or by singing: *Sing the baby to sleep.* **b** to escort or wait upon with singing: *to sing the old year out and the new year in.*
—***n.*** **1** a singing, ringing, or whistling sound: *the sing of a bullet in flight.* **2** the act of singing, especially in a group.
**sing out,** to call loudly; shout: *Suddenly a scout sang out that a party was in sight* (Benjamin Disraeli).
**sing small,** to change to a humble tone or manner: *Sir R. Peel endorsed the remonstrance and I had to sing small* (William E. Gladstone).
[Old English *singan*] —**sing'a|ble,** *adj.*
► **Sung** as the past tense form was once common but is now rare in standard English.

**sing.,** singular.

**sing-a|long** (sing'ə lông', -long'), *n. U.S.* **1** an entertainment in which the audience joins in the singing of familiar songs: ... *a sing-along with a trio of Texas folk singers* (Time). **2** a phonograph recording of such an act or of songs used in such an act.

**singe** (sinj), *v.,* **singed, singe|ing,** *n.* —***v.t.*** **1** to burn a little: *The chicken was singed to remove the fine hairs.* **2** to burn the ends or edges of: *The barber singed my hair after he cut it.* **3** to remove by slight burning: *Mother singed the feathers from the chicken.* **4** *Figurative.* to injure slightly; harm: *A scandal singed the mayor's reputation.*
—***n.*** a slight burn; scorch.
[Old English *sengan*]

**sing|er**[1] (sing'ər), *n.* **1** a person who sings: *You can hear famous singers on the radio.* **SYN:** chorister, vocalist, songster. **2** a bird that sings; songbird: *Our canary is a fine singer.*

**sing|er**[2] (sin'jər), *n.* a person or thing that singes.

**Sin|gha|lese** (sing'gə lēz', -lēs'), *n., pl.* **-lese,** *adj.* —***n.*** **1** a member of the principal native people of Ceylon (Sri Lanka), an island country in the In-

**Pronunciation Key:** hat, āge, cãre, fär; let, ēqual, tėrm; it, īce; hot, ōpen, ôrder; **oil, out;** cup, půt, rüle; **ch**ild; lo**ng**; **th**in; **ᴛʜ**en; **zh**, measure; **ə** represents **a** in about, **e** in taken, **i** in pencil, **o** in lemon, **u** in circus.

dian Ocean. **2** the Indic language of this people; Sinhala. **—*adj.*** having to do with Ceylon (Sri Lanka), its principal native people, or their language. Also, **Sinhalese.** [< Sanskrit *Siṅhala* Ceylon + English *-ese*]

**Sing|ha|ra nut** (sing hä′rə), the large, sweet nut of a tree related and similar to the water chestnut, native to India and Ceylon (Sri Lanka). [< *Singhara,* probably alteration of Sanskrit *Siṅhala* Ceylon]

**sing-in** (sing′in′), *n. U.S.* a musical act or event in which the audience serves as a chorus or joins in the singing.

**sing|ing** (sing′ing), *n., adj.* **—*n.* 1** the sound made by one that sings: *Her singing was wildly applauded.* **2** a ringing in the ears.
**—*adj.* 1** that sings. **2** of or like singing; musical.

**singing bird,** a songbird; oscine bird.

**singing flame,** a flame, such as a gas jet, which, when burned in a tube of proper length, produces a clear, musical note.

**singing school,** a school in which singing and the fundamentals of music are taught.

**singing voice,** the voice as used in singing: *Her singing voice was small, but true and clear* (Harper's).

**sin|gle** (sing′gəl), *adj., n., v.,* **-gled, -gling. —*adj.* 1** one and no more; only one: *The spider hung by a single thread. Please give me a single piece of paper.* **2** of or for only one; individual: *a single room in a hotel. The girls share one room with two single beds in it.* **3** without others; alone: *Behold her, single in the field* (Wordsworth). **SYN:** solitary. **4a** not married: *They rent rooms to single men.* **SYN:** unmarried. **b** of or in the unmarried state: *single life.* **SYN:** celibate. **5** having only one on each side; between two persons: *The knights engaged in single combat.* **6** having only one set of petals. Most cultivated roses have double flowers with many petals; wild roses have single flowers with five petals. **7** consisting of one part, element, or member; not double; not multiple: *single houses.* **8** sincere; honest; genuine: *She showed single devotion to her work. To those whose views are single and direct, it is a great comfort to have to do business with frank and honorable minds* (Thomas Jefferson). **9** unique; singular; unmatched; unusual: *Favor your country with your counsels on such an important and single occasion* (John Jay). **10** seeing rightly or justly; without defect: *If ... thine eye be single, thy whole body shall be full of light* (Matthew 6:22).
**—*n.* 1a** a single thing or person; individual. **b** an unmarried person: *a party for singles.* **c** *Informal.* a single performer; soloist: *[She] is dickering with one of the networks for a TV show next fall as a result of her successful stand as a "single" in Las Vegas* (Newsweek). **2** a hit in baseball that allows the batter to reach first base only. **3** a hit in cricket for which one run is scored. **4** a game for two people only. **5** a phonograph record having only one song or tune on a side: *Victor ... has let these two ladies share a new long-playing record made up of old singles* (New Yorker). **6** a form of change in bell ringing.
**—*v.t.* 1** to pick from among others: *The teacher singled us out for praise. Romance had singled Jim for its own* (Joseph Conrad). **2** to advance or score (a runner) in baseball with a single.
**—*v.i.* 1** to make a hit in baseball that allows the batter to reach first base only. **2** = single-foot.
**singles,** a match game, especially in tennis, played with only one player on each side: *He likes to play singles rather than doubles.*
[< Old French *sengle, single* < Latin *singulus*]
**—*Syn.*** *adj.* **1 Single, sole, only** mean one alone. **Single** emphasizes one and no more: *She buys a single new dress each year.* **Sole** emphasizes being by itself, the only one there is: *My sole purpose is to help you.* **Only** emphasizes being one of a class of which it is the best or the single representative: *She is the only girl in the world for me. Of all the possible suggestions, her plan is the only solution to our problems. I am my parents' only child.*

**sin|gle-act|ing** (sing′gəl ak′ting), *adj.* that acts in one direction only: *A single-acting engine exerts force on the piston or pistons only on one end.*

**sin|gle-ac|tion** (sing′gəl ak′shən), *adj.* **1** = single-acting. **2** cocked and fired in separate motions: *In a single-action revolver, the user pulls back the hammer by hand; he then pulls the trigger to fire.*

**single blessedness,** the condition of being unmarried; celibacy.

**single bowknot,** a type of knot forming only one loop.

**sin|gle-breast|ed** (sing′gəl bres′tid), *adj.* overlapping across the breast just enough to fasten with only one row of buttons: *a suit with a single-breasted jacket.*

**sin|gle-cell protein** (sing′gəl sel′), a protein produced from liquid or gaseous petroleum fractions that are fermented by specially treated yeast cells or other microorganisms: *Single-cell protein is designed to be used as a food supplement in those areas of the world where protein is lacking in the diet. It can be added to bread or soft drinks or introduced into the diet in other ways* (Science News). *Abbr:* SCP (no periods).

**sin|gle-chan|nel** (sing′gəl chan′əl), *adj.* = monophonic.

**single combat,** combat with one on each side.

**single cross,** the hybrid produced by a single crossing of two inbred lines; single-cross hybrid.

**sin|gle-cross** (sing′gəl krôs′, -kros′), *adj. Genetics.* that is of the first generation produced by crossing two inbred lines: *a single-cross hybrid.*

**sin|gle-deck|er** (sing′gəl dek′ər), *adj.* having only one deck or level: *a single-decker bus, a single-decker grandstand.*

**single entry,** a simple system of bookkeeping in which there is one account to which all items are debited or credited. **—sin′gle-en′try,** *adj.*

**sin|gle-eyed** (sing′gəl īd′), *adj.* **1** having but one eye. **2** *Figurative.* seeing rightly; just; honest; straightforward: *He was single-eyed in all his dealings.*

**single file, 1** a line of persons or things arranged one behind another; Indian file: *to march in single file.* **2** by forming such a line: *to march single file.*

**sin|gle-foot** (sing′gəl fu̇t′), *n., v.* **—*n.*** a gait of a horse in which one foot is put down at a time; rack. First there is one foot ahead on the ground, then two, then one, then two, and so on.
**—*v.i.*** to go or move at a single-foot: *The easy-gaited little cutting horses single-footing in their wake made the police geldings look like draft stock* (New Yorker).

**sin|gle-hand|ed** (sing′gəl han′did), *adj., adv.* **—*adj.* 1** without help from others; working alone; unassisted; unaided: *Single-handed ... she performed all the labors of Mr. Jonathan Rossiter's little establishment* (Harriet Beecher Stowe). **2** using, requiring, or managed by only one hand or only one person: *a single-handed catch, a single-handed saw.*
**—*adv.*** without help from others; single-handedly: *In the end he had to man the ship single-handed to save himself* (New York Times). **—sin′gle-hand′ed|ly,** *adv.* **—sin′gle-hand′ed|ness,** *n.*

**sin|gle-hand|er** (sing′gəl han′dər), *n.* **1** a person who sails a racing or sailing vessel single-handedly. **2** a vessel manned by such a person.

**sin|gle-heart|ed** (sing′gəl här′tid), *adj.* **1** free from deceit; sincere; straightforward. **SYN:** ingenuous. **2** having only one purpose: *He was single-hearted in his aim* (W. Somerset Maugham). **—sin′gle-heart′ed|ly,** *adv.* **—sin′gle-heart′edness,** *n.*

**single knot,** a knot similar to a half hitch.

**sin|gle-leaf** (sing′gəl lēf′), *n.* a piñon or pine of western North America, with leaves growing singly or in clusters of two; nut pine.

**sin|gle-mind|ed** (sing′gəl mīn′did), *adj.* **1** having only one purpose in mind. **2** *Figurative.* sincere; straightforward; single-hearted: *An unpretending, single-minded, artless girl—infinitely to be preferred by any man of sense and taste* (Jane Austen). **SYN:** guileless. **—sin′gle-mind′ed|ly,** *adv.* **—sin′gle-mind′ed|ness,** *n.*

**sin|gle-name paper** (sing′gəl nām′), *Banking.* a promissory note endorsed only by the maker.

**sin|gle|ness** (sing′gəl nis), *n.* **1** state or quality of being single; oneness. **2** the unmarried state; celibacy. **3** *Figurative.* freedom from deceit; sincerity; honesty; integrity: *That we may do the work which Thou givest us to do ... with singleness of heart* (Book of Common Prayer). **SYN:** uprightness.

**sin|gle-phase** (sing′gəl fāz′), *adj.* **1** of or having to do with an alternating current having one phase; monophase: *a single-phase circuit.* **2** being in the same phase throughout; not differing in composition in any part: *Copper and nickel in any proportion form a single-phase alloy.*

**single phaser,** *Electricity.* a single-phase alternating-current generator.

**sin|gles** (sing′gəlz), *n.pl.* See under **single.**

**singles bar,** *U.S.* = dating bar.

**sin|gle-seat|er** (sing′gəl sē′tər), *n.* an aircraft or other vehicle that seats only one person.

**single sideband,** *Radio.* a transmitter or system that uses only one of the two sidebands of a frequency, eliminating the carrier signal completely. A single sideband permits more frequencies to exist and requires less space between them.

**sin|gle-space** (sing′gəl spās′), *v.t., v.i.,* **-spaced, -spac|ing.** to leave no blank line between lines in typing.

**sin|gle-stage** (sing′gəl stāj′), *adj.* having a propulsive force of only one charge and thus capable of reaching only one level of ascent: *a single-stage rocket or missile.*

**single standard, 1** a monetary standard or system based upon a single metal only as the circulating medium, usually gold; monometallism. **2** a standard of moral behavior that is the same for any group, as for men and women alike.

**single stem,** a skiing maneuver involving stemming with one ski.

**sin|gle|stick** (sing′gəl stik′), *n.* **1** a stick held in one hand, used in fencing and striking. **2** fencing with such a stick. **3** any short stick for striking; cudgel.

**sin|gle|stick|er** (sing′gəl stik′ər), *n. Informal.* a one-masted vessel, especially a sloop.

**sin|glet** (sing′glit), *n.* **1** a man's short-sleeved undershirt or jersey: *They were dressed in tattered singlets and equally tattered trousers* (New Yorker). **2** any undershirt for men. **3** *Nuclear Physics.* a resonance with a spin of zero.

**single tax, 1** a tax on one kind of property only, especially a tax on land. **2** a system of public revenue based on such a tax, such as one urged by Henry George, 1839-1897, American political economist, and his followers. **—sin′gle-tax′,** *adj.*

**sin|gle-tax|er** (sing′gəl tak′sər), *n.* an advocate of a single tax.

**single ticket,** *British.* a one-way ticket.

**sin|gle|ton** (sing′gəl tən), *n.* **1** something occurring singly or apart from others. **2** a playing card that is the only one of a suit in a player's hand. [< *single* + *-ton,* as in *simpleton*]

**sin|gle-track** (sing′gəl trak′), *adj.* = one-track.

**sin|gle|tree** (sing′gəl trē′), *n.* = whiffletree. [American English, variant of *swingletree*]

**single wingback formation** or **single wing formation,** *Football.* an offensive formation with one back behind and outside an end.

**sin|glings** (sing′glingz), *n.* (in distilling) the crude spirit which is the first to come over.

**sin|glo** (sing′glō), *n.* a kind of fine tea, consisting of large, flat leaves, not much rolled. [< *Sung-lo,* a range of hills in China]

**sin|gly** (sing′glē), *adv.* **1** by itself; separately; individually: *Let us consider each point singly.* **2** one by one; one at a time: *Misfortunes never seem to come singly.* **3** by one's own efforts; without help; unaided; unassisted; single-handed.

**sing-sing** (sing′sing′), *n.* a West African kob antelope. [< a native word]

**sing|song** (sing′sông′, -song′), *n., adj., v.* **—*n.* 1** a monotonous, up-and-down rhythm: *In childhood singsong is not a defect; it is simply the first form of rhythmical sensibility* (C. S. Lewis). **2** a monotonous tone or sound in speaking: *... the rapt singsong of the wayside fortuneteller* (Rudyard Kipling). **3** a monotonous or jingling verse. **4** an informal gathering for singing; gathering for community singing.
**—*adj.*** monotonous in tone or rhythm: *a singsong recitation of the multiplication table.*
**—*v.t., v.i.*** to recite or speak in a singsong way: *A group of children go singsonging along the road nearby* (Time).

**Sing|spiel** (zing′shpēl), *n. German.* **1** a semi-dramatic work or performance presenting a story in song, and subordinating instrumental accompaniment to the vocal parts. **2** (literally) a song play.

**sin|gu|lar** (sing′gyə lər), *adj., n.* **—*adj.* 1** extraordinary; unusual: *"Treasure Island" is a story of singular interest to boys. Einstein and Da Vinci were men of singular ability.* **SYN:** exceptional, uncommon, remarkable. **2** strange; queer; odd; peculiar: *The detectives were greatly puzzled by the singular nature of the crime. He was called strange and singular long before he was acknowledged to be great* (Walter S. Landor). **SYN:** curious, eccentric. **3** being the only one of the kind: *an event singular in history.* **SYN:** unique. **4** *Grammar.* **a** signifying or implying only one person or thing: *the singular number, a singular verb form.* **b** one in number. *Boy* is singular; *boys* is plural. **5** separate; individual; private: *a singular matter.* **6** *Logic.* of or having to do with some single thing, person, or instance; not general.
**—*n.* 1** *Grammar.* **a** the singular number. *Ox* is the singular of *oxen.* **b** a word in the singular number. *Book* is a singular; *books* is a plural. *Abbr:* sing. **2** *Logic.* a thing, person, or instance considered by itself; that which is not general. [< Latin *singulāris* < *singulus* single] **—sin′gu|lar|ly,** *adv.* **—sin′gu|lar|ness,** *n.*

**sin|gu|lar|i|ty** (sing′gyə lar′ə tē), *n., pl.* **-ties. 1** the condition or quality of being singular; peculiarity; oddness; strangeness; unusualness: *The singularity of the man's appearance attracted much attention. Singularity is almost invariably a clue* (Sir Arthur Conan Doyle). **2** something singular; peculiarity; oddity: *The giraffe's chief singularity is the length of its neck.* **3** individual character or property; individuality; distinctiveness.

**sin|gu|lar|ize** (sing′gyə lə rīz), *v.t.,* **-ized, -iz|ing. 1** to distinguish; signalize: *[She] reports to the Mother Superior that she fears Sister Luke is* *showing off—singularizing herself* (New Yorker). **2** to make singular or single; individualize. —**sin′gu|lar|i|za′tion**, *n.*

**sin|gu|lar|y** (sing′gyə lər ē), *adj.* consisting of one part or element only: *Glottalization and nasality could ... be regarded as singulary, not binary features, either present or absent in a particular case* (Wallace L. Chafe). [patterned after *binary*]

**sinh** (no periods), hyperbolic sine.

**Sin|ha|la** (sin′hə lə), *n.* the Indic language of Ceylon (Sri Lanka); Singhalese. [< Sanskrit *Siṅhala* Ceylon]

**Sin|ha|lese** (sin′hə lēz′, -lēs′), *n., pl.* **-lese**, *adj.* = Singhalese.

**Sin|ic** (sin′ik), *adj.* = Chinese. [< Late Latin *Sīnae* the Chinese + English *-ic*]

**Sin|i|cism** (sin′ə siz əm), *n.* **1** a Chinese mannerism, method, or custom; Chinese usage. **2** affectation or adoption of what is Chinese.

**Sin|i|cize** or **sin|i|cize** (sin′ə sīz), *v.t.,* **-cized, -ciz|ing.** to make Chinese in character.

**Sin|i|fy** (sin′ə fī), *v.t.,* **-fied, -fy|ing.** = Sinicize.

**sin|i|grin** (sin′ə grin), *n.* a colorless, crystalline glucoside present in the seeds of the black mustard. *Formula:* $C_{10}H_{16}KNO_9S_2 \cdot H_2O$ [< New Latin *Si(napis) nigr(a)* black mustard (< Latin *sināpis* mustard, *niger, -gra* black) + English *-in*]

**sin|is|ter** (sin′ə stər), *adj.* **1** showing ill will; threatening: *a sinister rumor, a sinister look.* **SYN:** ominous, inauspicious. **2** bad; evil; dishonest: *a sinister plan. I hope ... that you'll ... not impute to me any impertinence or sinister design* (Oliver Goldsmith). **SYN:** base. **3** bringing evil; disastrous; unfortunate: *Such a life was sinister to the intellect, and sinister to the heart* (Hawthorne). **SYN:** unlucky. **4** on the left; left: *My mother's blood runs in my dexter cheek and this sinister bounds in my father's* (Shakespeare). **5** *Heraldry.* situated to the right of the one looking at the escutcheon: *sinister base, sinister chief.* [< Latin *sinister* left (from the belief that omens seen on the left side were unlucky)] —**sin′is|ter|ly**, *adv.* —**sin′is|ter|ness**, *n.*

**si|ni|stra** (sē nēs′trä), *adv. Music. Italian.* with the left hand (used in marking a note or passage that is to be performed with the left hand in preference to the right).

**sin|is|trad** (sin′ə strad), *adv.* to the left. [< Latin *sinistra* the left hand + *ad* to]

**sin|is|tral** (sin′ə strəl), *adj., n.* —*adj.* **1** of or having to do with the left side; left; left-handed: *Two per cent of mankind are naturally sinistral* (Westminster Gazette). **2** having the spire or whorl rising from right to left as viewed from the outside: *In most species the shell is right-handed (dextral), being coiled clockwise as seen from the spire, but some are left-handed (sinistral)* (Tracy I. Storer). **3** having what is properly the left side converted into the upper one: *sinistral flatfish.*

—*n.* a left-handed person: *[He] claims there is at least some evidence that Alexander the Great was a sinistral* (London Times). —**sin′is|tral|ly**, *adv.*

**sin|is|tral|i|ty** (sin′ə stral′ə tē), *n.* the condition or quality of being sinistral.

**sin|is|troc|u|lar** (sin′ə strok′yə lər), *adj.* using the left eye more than the right. [< Latin *sinister* left hand + English *ocular*]

**sin|is|tro|dex|tral** (sin′ə strō deks′trəl), *adj.* **1** = left-handed. **2** moving from left to right: *sinistrodextral calligraphy.* [< Latin *sinister* left hand + *dexter* right hand + English *-al*]

**sin|is|tror|sal** (sin′ə strôr′səl), *adj.* = sinistrorse. —**sin′is|tror′sal|ly**, *adv.*

**sin|is|trorse** (sin′ə strôrs, sin′ə strôrs′), *adj.* **1** rising spirally from right to left: *the sinistrorse stem of a vine.* **2** = sinistral. [< Latin *sinistrōrsus* < *sinister* left (see etym. under **sinister**) + *versus*, past participle of *vertere* to turn] —**sin′is|trorse′|ly**, *adv.*

**sin|is|trous** (sin′ə strəs), *adj.* **1** sinister; disastrous; unlucky. **2** = sinistral (def. 3). —**sin′is|trous|ly**, *adv.*

**Si|nit|ic** (si nit′ik), *adj.* of or having to do with China or the various Chinese dialects; Sinic: *The Sinitic languages are used in eastern and parts of southeastern Asia* (John Whitney Hall). [< Late Latin *Sīnae* the Chinese + English *-ite*[1] + *-ic*]

**sink** (singk), *v.,* **sank** or (sometimes) **sunk, sunk** or (now chiefly used as an adjective) **sunk|en, sink|ing,** *n.* —*v.i.* **1** to go down; fall slowly; go lower and lower: *to sink into a chair. She sank to the floor in a faint. The sun is sinking in the west.* **SYN:** subside, descend, fall, settle, decline. **2** to go under: *The ship is sinking.* **SYN:** submerge. **3** to become lower or weaker: *The wind has sunk down.* **4** *Figurative.* to pass gradually (to or into a state as of sleep, silence, or oblivion): *to sink to rest, to sink into corruption.* **5** to go deeply; penetrate: *The ink sank into the blotting paper.* **6** *Figurative.* to become worse in health, morals, reputation, or social status: *Her spirits sank. It is indeed possible for men to sink into machines* (John Ruskin). *He had sunk by this time to the very worst reputation* (Thackeray). **7** to fall in; become hollow: *The sick man's cheeks have sunk.*

—*v.t.* **1** to make go down; make fall: *Lack of rain sank the reservoirs.* **2** to make go under: *The submarine sank two ships.* **3** to make lower or weaker; reduce: *Sink your voice to a whisper.* **SYN:** diminish. **4** to make go deep; dig: *The men are sinking a well.* **5** to insert or fasten into something, such as a concavity or hollow space: *a stone sunk into the wall.* **6** *Figurative.* to keep quiet about; conceal: *to sink evidence. By merely ... bestowing a rich aunt, and sinking half the children he was able to represent the whole family ... in a most respectable light* (Jane Austen). **7** *Figurative.* to invest (money), especially unprofitably: *We sank twenty dollars in a machine that we never used.* **8a** to score in basketball: *[He] sank three baskets and eight of his ten foul attempts* (New York Times). **b** to hit (a golf ball) into a hole; score thus with (a stroke): *He sank a 20-foot putt for a birdie.*

—*n.* **1** a shallow basin or tub with a drainpipe: *The dishes are in the kitchen sink.* **2** a drain; sewer. **3** a place where dirty water or any filth collects. **4** *Figurative.* a place of vice or corruption: *That roadhouse is a sink of iniquity.* **5** a low-lying inland area where waters collect or where they disappear by sinking downward or by evaporation: *Some sinks are many feet deep, are steep-sided, and have obvious openings through which the surface drainage runs underground* (Finch and Trewartha). **6** any natural or artificial means of absorbing or removing a substance from the atmosphere: *Gases spend varying periods there [in the troposphere] depending on the "sinks" by which each is removed from the atmosphere: incorporation into cloud droplets, reactions with other gases, loss to finely divided liquid or solid particles or the earth's surface and so on* (Scientific American). **7** *Printing.* **a** the extra space left at the top of a page for the beginning of a chapter or the like. **b** the amount of this space. **8** = sinking speed.

**sink in,** to be understood or grasped: *The warning failed to sink in, and he got into trouble as a consequence.*

**sink into,** to be understood or grasped by: *Let the lesson sink into your mind.*

**sink or swim,** to succeed or fail depending on one's own efforts: *Both groups recognize that they must sink or swim together and that they have to solve their own problems* (Theodore W. Kheel).

[Old English *sincan*]

**sink|a|ble** (sing′kə bəl), *adj.* that can be sunk.

**sink|age** (sing′kij), *n.* **1a** the act or process of sinking; subsidence. **b** an instance of this. **2** the amount of sinking. **3** something that sinks or has sunk. **4** *Printing.* = sink.

**sink|er** (sing′kər), *n.* **1** a person or thing that sinks. **2** a weight as of lead or stone for sinking a fishing line or net in the water. **3** *U.S. Slang.* a doughnut: *Sinkers and coffee, folks, get your doughnuts here* (Los Angeles Times). **4** a pitch in baseball that drops suddenly as it approaches the batter.

**sink|hole** (singk′hōl′), *n.* **1** a hole that drains surface water. **2a** a hole where water collects. **b** a funnel-shaped cavity formed in limestone regions by the removal of the rock through action of rain or running water, or both: *As the caverns enlarge, their roofs become incapable of supporting themselves and collapse, forming sinkholes at the surface* (Robert M. Garrels). **3** the hole in a sink; hole for waste to pass through. **4** *Figurative.* a place of vice and corruption: *Company towns and company stores were a polite expression for economic serfdom. We eliminated these sinkholes* (Atlantic).

**sink|ing fund** (sing′king), a fund formed by a government, corporation, or the like, usually by periodically setting aside certain amounts of money to accumulate at interest, for the paying off of a debt: *The new shares will have a sinking fund of $15,000 a year* (Wall Street Journal).

**sinking speed,** the speed at which an airplane, bird, or other flying object descends vertically while gliding.

**sinking spell, 1** a period when an ill person takes a turn for the worse; decline; relapse. **2** any period of decline: *With higher rates ahead, U.S. bonds had another sinking spell last week* (Time).

**sin|less** (sin′lis), *adj.* without sin. —**sin′less|ly**, *adv.* —**sin′less|ness**, *n.*

**sin|ner** (sin′ər), *n.* **1** a person who sins; person who disobeys divine law: *The sinner who repented was forgiven. God be merciful to me a sinner* (Luke 18:13). **SYN:** evildoer. **2** a person who does wrong, fails in any duty, or violates some rule or custom.

**Sinn Fein** (shin′ fān′), a political organization in Ireland, founded about 1905, demanding complete political separation of all Ireland from Great Britain. [< Irish *Sinn Fein* (literally) we ourselves]

**Sinn Fein|er** (fā′nər), a member or supporter of the Sinn Fein.

**Sinn Fein|ism** (fā′niz əm), adherence to Sinn Fein.

**Sino-,** *combining form.* **1** of China; Chinese ____: *Sinology = the study of Chinese history, customs, etc.*
**2** China (Chinese) and ____: *Sino-Japanese War = the war between China and Japan.*
[< Late Latin *Sīnae* the Chinese]

**si|no|a|tri|al** (sī′nō ā′trē əl), *adj.* of or having to do with the area between the sinus venosus and the right auricle of the heart: *a sinoatrial heart block, the sinoatrial pacemaker.* [< *sinus* (venosus) + *atrium* + *-al*[1]]

**sinoatrial node,** a mass of tissue in the right auricle of the heart near the point where the major veins enter, that originates the heartbeat; pacemaker: *In the case of long and lingering illnesses ... the heart is the last organ to fail, and the pacemaker of the heart—the sinoatrial node—is the last to die* (Paul Dudley White). *Abbr:* S-A node

**si|no|au|ric|u|lar node** (sī′nō ô rik′yə lər), = sinoatrial node.

**sin offering,** a sacrifice or other offering made to atone for sin. Exodus 29:14.

**Si|no-Jap|a|nese** (sī′nō jap′ə nēz′, -nēs′; sin′ō-), *adj.* of both China and Japan: *Sino-Japanese design is almost exclusively an art of contours* (Bernard Berenson).

**Si|no|log|i|cal** (sī′nə loj′ə kəl, sin′ə-), *adj.* of or having to do with Sinology.

**Si|nol|o|gist** (sī nol′ə jist, si-), *n.* a student of Chinese language, customs, or other elements of Chinese culture; person skilled in Sinology.

**Si|no|logue** (sī′nə lôg, -log; sin′ə-), *n.* = Sinologist.

**Si|nol|o|gy** (sī nol′ə jē, si-), *n.* the study of Chinese history, customs, institutions, language, and literature.

**Si|non** (sī′nən), *n.* a treacherous or perfidious betrayer. [< *Sinon,* a Greek character in Homer's *Iliad,* who induced the Trojans to bring the wooden horse into Troy]

**Si|no|phil** (sī′nə fil, sin′ə-), *adj., n.* = Sinophile.

**Si|no|phile** (sī′nə fīl, -fil; sin′ə-), *adj., n.* —*adj.* friendly to the Chinese; fond of Chinese ways, customs, literature, and the like.
—*n.* a friend or admirer of the Chinese.

**si|no|pi|a** (si nō′pē ə), *n., pl.* **-pi|e** (-pē ā) or **-pi|as. 1** a preliminary drawing or sketch made with the pigment sinopis on the cement underlying the final surface of a fresco: *Numerous sinopie ... have been revealed by the removal of the final frescoes that covered them* (John Canaday). **2** = sinopis. [< Italian *sinopia* < Latin *Sinōpis;* see etym. under **sinople**]

**si|no|pis** (si nō′pəs), *n.* a pigment of a fine red color, prepared from the earth sinople. [< Latin *Sinōpis;* see etym. under **sinople**]

**sin|o|pite** (sin′ə pīt), *n.* = sinople.

**sin|o|ple** (sin′ə pəl), *n.* **1** a ferruginous clay, sometimes used as a pigment. Also, **sinopite.** **2** a kind of ferruginous quartz found in Hungary. [< Old French *Sinople* < Latin *Sinōpis* < Greek *Sinōpís* < *Sinṓpē,* a colony]

**Si|no-So|vi|et** (sī′nō sō′vē et, sin′ō-; -it; -sov′ē-), *adj.* of or between China and the Soviet Union: *The Sino-Soviet ideological dispute centers around Peking's demand for a much stronger stand against the West* (Wall Street Journal).

**Si|no-Ti|bet|an** (sī′nō ti bet′ən, sin′ō-), *n., adj.* —*n.* a linguistic grouping including the Chinese, Tibeto-Burman, and Thai language families.
—*adj.* of or having to do with the people or the languages of this linguistic grouping.

**SINS** (no periods), Ship's Inertial Navigation System (used in nuclear-powered submarines).

**sin|syne** (sin′sīn), *adv. Scottish.* since then.

**sin tax,** *U.S. Informal.* a tax on alcoholic liquor, cigarettes, sweepstakes tickets, and the like: *The state's antiquated tax structure ... relies heavily on revenue from so-called "sin taxes"* (Joseph P. Ford).

**sin|ter** (sin′tər), *v., n.* —*v.t.* to fuse (metal particles or grains) to form larger particles or masses by heating, or by heat and pressure, but without melting.
—*v.i.* to be sintered.
—*n.* **1** something produced by sintering. **2** a hard incrustation or deposit formed on rocks or similar objects by evaporation of mineral waters.

**Pronunciation Key:** hat, āge, cãre, fär; let, ēqual, tėrm; it, īce; hot, ōpen, ôrder; oil, out; cup, pu̇t, rüle; child; long; thin; ᴛʜen; zh, measure;
ə represents **a** in about, **e** in taken, **i** in pencil, **o** in lemon, **u** in circus.

[< German *Sinter* dross, slag; origin uncertain]

***sin|u|ate** (sin′yù āt, -it), *adj.* **1** bent in and out; winding; sinuous. SYN: tortuous. **2** *Botany.* having the margin strongly or distinctly wavy: *a sinuate leaf.* [< Latin *sinuātus,* past participle of *sinuāre* bend, wind < *sinus, -ūs* a curve] — **sin′u|ate|ly,** *adv.*

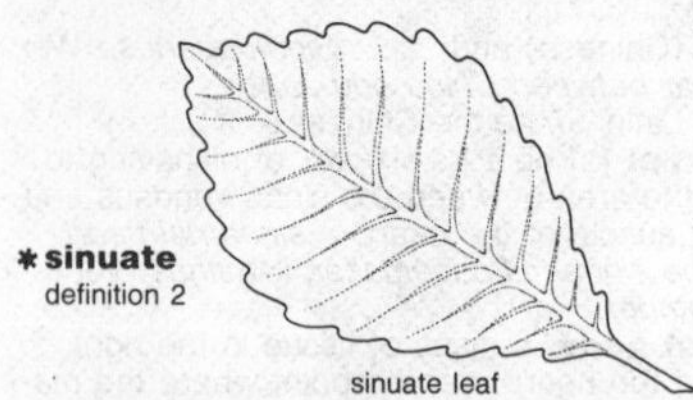

***sinuate** definition 2

**sin|u|at|ed** (sin′yù ā′tid), *adj.* = sinuate.

**sin|u|a|tion** (sin′yù ā′shən), *n.* = sinuosity.

**sin|u|os|i|ty** (sin′yù os′ə tē), *n., pl.* **-ties. 1** sinuous form or character; winding: *A snake has sinuosity. Meander is a river ... famous for the sinuosity and often returning thereof* (Michael Drayton). **2** a curve; bend; turn: *the endless sinuosities of the mountain road.*

**sin|u|ous** (sin′yù əs), *adj.* **1** having many curves or turns; winding: *The motion of a snake is sinuous. I have sinuous shells of pearly hue* (Walter S. Landor). SYN: serpentine. **2** indirect; devious; roundabout. **3** *Figurative.* morally crooked. **4** *Botany.* = sinuate. [< Latin *sinuōsus* < *sinus, -ūs* a curve] — **sin′u|ous|ly,** *adv.* — **sin′u|ous|ness,** *n.*

***si|nus** (sī′nəs), *n.* **1** a cavity in a bone, especially one of the air cavities lined with mucous membrane in the bones of the skull that connect with the nasal cavity: *The sinuses lighten the skull, and make it easier to hold up the head and to balance it on the neck* (William V. Mayer). **2** a long, narrow abscess with a small opening. **3** a reservoir or channel for venous blood. **4** a curved hollow; cavity. **5** a curve or bend, especially a curve between two projecting lobes of a leaf. [< Latin *sinus, -ūs* any bend or curve]

***sinus** definition 1

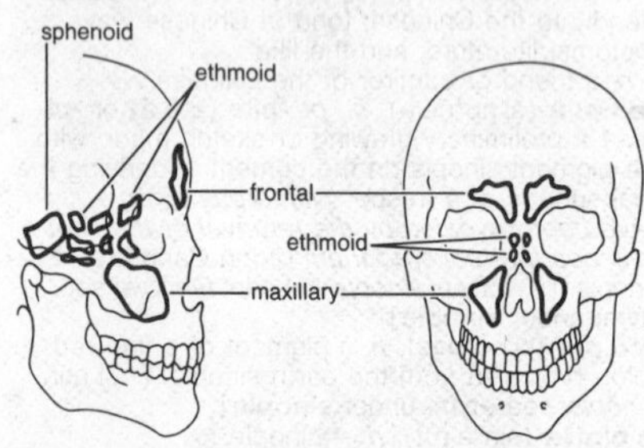


**si|nus|i|tis** (sī′nə sī′tis), *n.* inflammation of one of the sinuses of the head, especially a nasal sinus.

**sinus node,** = sinoatrial node.

**si|nus|oid** (sī′nə soid), *n.* **1** *Mathematics.* sine curve. **2** *Anatomy.* one of the spaces or tubes through which blood passes in various organs, such as the suprarenal gland and the liver.

**si|nus|oi|dal** (sī′nə soi′dəl), *adj.* **1** of or having to do with a sine curve. **2** of or having to do with a sinus. — **si′nus|oi′dal|ly,** *adv.*

***sinusoidal projection,** a type of map projection in which the central meridian and the equator are shown as straight lines, but the other meridians are shown as curved lines.

***sinusoidal projection**

**sinus ve|no|sus** (vi nō′səs), **1** the chamber in the heart of lower vertebrates to which the blood is returned by the veins: *The heart [of the alligator] lies in the anteroventral part of the thorax; it comprises a small sinus venosus, two auricles, and two ventricles* (Tracy I. Storer). **2** the cavity in the embryonic auricle of mammals in which the various venous systems are joined. [< New Latin *sinus venosus* < Latin *sinus, -ūs* (see etym. under **sinus**), *vēnōsus* venose]

**Si|on** (sī′ən), *n.* = Zion.

**Siou|an** (sü′ən), *n., adj.* — *n.* **1** the group of North American Indian tribes that includes the Sioux (Dakota), Osage, and Crow. **2** the family of languages spoken by them.
— *adj.* having to do with these tribes or their languages.

**Sioux** (sü), *n., pl.* **Sioux** (sü, süz), *adj.* — *n.* **1** a member of a tribe of American Indians living on the plains of northern United States and southern Canada; Dakota. **2** the Siouan language of this tribe.
— *adj.* of or having to do with the Sioux.
[American English, apparently < earlier French *Nadowes(sioux),* alteration of Algonkian (Ojibwa) *nadoweisiw* (diminutive) < *nadowe* snake; enemy]

**Sioux State,** a nickname of North Dakota.

**sip** (sip), *v.,* **sipped, sip|ping,** *n.* — *v.t., v.i.* **1** to drink little by little: *She sipped her tea.* SYN: See syn. under **drink. 2** *Figurative.* to take a mere taste of (something).
— *n.* **1** a very small drink: *She took a sip of water. It [beer] can't be tasted in a sip* (Dickens). **2** the act of sipping: *His first sip brought an exclamation of disgust.* **3** *Figurative.* a mere taste: *A sip is all that the public ... ever care to take from reservoirs of abstract philosophy* (Thomas De Quincey).
[Middle English *sippen;* origin uncertain]

**sipe¹** (sīp), *v.i.,* **siped, sip|ing.** *Scottish.* to trickle slowly; ooze. [Old English *sypian.* See related etym. at **seep.**]

**sipe²** (sīp), *n.* any one of the small grooves that make up the tread pattern of an automobile tire. [probably special use of dialectal *sipe,* noun, water that seeps or trickles through < *sipe¹*, verb]

**si|phon** (sī′fən), *n., v.* — *n.* **1** a bent tube through which liquid can be drawn over the edge of one container into another at a lower level by air pressure. **2** a bottle for soda water with a tube through which the liquid is forced out by the pressure of the gas in the bottle. **3** a tube-shaped organ of a clam, oyster, or certain other shellfish for drawing in and expelling water.
— *v.t.* **1** to draw off by means of a siphon: *The farmer siphoned water from the cellar into the ditch.* **2** *Figurative: The voters will decide whether to permit the state to siphon off surplus ... revenues to help solve the state's transportation problem* (Wall Street Journal).
— *v.i.* to pass through a siphon. Also, **syphon.**
[< Latin *sīphō, -ōnis* < Greek *sīphōn, -ōnos* pipe] — **si′phon|er,** *n.*

**si|phon|age** (sī′fə nij), *n.* the action of a siphon.

**si|phon|al** (sī′fə nəl), *adj.* of or having to do with a siphon.

**si|phon|ate** (sī′fə nāt), *adj.* having a siphon or siphons.

**siphon barometer,** a barometer with the lower end of the tube bent in the form of a siphon.

**siphon bottle,** = siphon (def. 2).

**si|phon|ic** (sī fon′ik), *adj.* **1** = siphonal. **2** working by means of or on the principle of a siphon.

**si|pho|no|phore** (sī′fə nə fôr, -fōr; sī fon′ə-), *n.* any one of a group of pelagic, free-swimming hydrozoans that form colonies made up of different types of polyps, such as the Portuguese man-of-war: *A siphonophore is not a single animal but a composite, or colony, of inseparably associated individuals—the multiple offspring of a single fertilized egg* (New Yorker). [< Greek *sīphōn, -ōnos* siphon + English *-phore*]

**si|pho|no|stele** (sī′fə nə stēl′, -stē′lē), *n. Botany.* vascular tissue in the form of a hollow tube with the pith in the center. [< Greek *sīphōn, -ōnos* siphon + English *stele*]

**si|pho|no|ste|lic** (sī′fə nə stē′lik), *adj.* of or having to do with siphonostele.

**si|phun|cle** (sī′fung kəl), *n.* **1** *Zoology.* a small tube passing through the partitions in the shell of certain cephalopods: *The siphuncle, a coiled fleshy tube enclosed in a limy covering, extends through all the chambers, connecting them with the body of the nautilus* (William J. Clench). **2** *Entomology.* either of two small tubular organs on the abdomen of an aphid, through which a waxy secretion is exuded. [< Latin *sīphunculus* (diminutive) < *sīphō;* see etym. under **siphon**]

**si|phun|cu|lar** (sī fung′kyə lər), *adj.* of, having to do with, or like a siphuncle.

**si|phun|cu|late** (sī fung′kyə lāt, -lit), *adj.* having a siphuncle.

**si|phun|cu|lat|ed** (sī fung′kyə lā′tid), *adj.* = siphunculate.

**sip|id** (sip′id), *adj.* **1** having a pleasing taste or flavor. **2** of agreeably distinctive character. [back formation < *insipid*]

**sip|per** (sip′ər), *n.* **1** a person who sips or drinks. **2** a straw for sipping liquid from a glass or bottle.

**sip|pet** (sip′it), *n.* **1** a bit of toast or fried bread, such as is served in soup, as a garnish, etc. **2** a bit; fragment. [< *sip* + *-et*]

**sip|pi|o** (sip′ē ō), *n.* a game like bagatelle, played with eight balls, driven into numbered holes or pockets by means of a cue ball struck with an ordinary cue.

**Sip|py diet** (sip′ē), a diet for the treatment of peptic ulcer by frequent feedings of small amounts of milk, cream, alkaline powders, cereal, eggs, and some other bland foods. [< Bertram W. *Sippy,* 1886-1924, an American physician]

**si|pun|cu|lid** (sī pung′kyə lid), *n.* any one of a group of elongated, tentacled marine worms that live in sand or mud, either within snail shells or free. [< New Latin *Sipunculus* the genus name < Latin *sīpunculus,* variant of *sīphunculus;* see etym. under **siphuncle**]

**si quae|ris pen|in|su|lam a|moe|nam, cir-cum|spi|ce** (sē kwī′ris pə nin′sù läm ä mē′näm sėr′kəm spē′sä), *Latin.* if you seek a pleasant pennisula, look about you (the motto of Michigan).

**sir** (sėr; *unstressed* sər), *n., v.,* **sirred, sir|ring.**
— *n.* **1** a title of respect or honor used to a man. A boy calls an older man "sir." *It's very kind of you, sir.* **2** Mr. or Master (often used in scorn, contempt, or indignation): *You, sir, have no business here; get out.* **3** a title of respect formerly used before a man's name or a noun designating his profession: *I am one that would rather go with sir Priest than sir Knight* (Shakespeare). **4** a lord or gentleman. In olden times, *sir* was equivalent to *sire.*
— *v.t., v.i.* to address as sir: *You mustn't sir me* (Graham Greene).
[probably unstressed variant of *sire*]

**Sir** (sėr; *unstressed* sər), *n.* **1** a form of salutation in a letter addressed to a man. We begin business letters with "Dear Sir." **2** the title of a knight or baronet: *Sir Walter Scott. Abbr:* Sr. **3** a title of respect or honor, used to a man.
► **Sir** is usually used with one given name plus the surname or with the given name alone, but not with the surname only. Thus *Sir William Craigie* might be addressed or referred to as *Sir William,* but not as *Sir Craigie.*

**SIR** (no periods), Submarine Intermediate Reactor (a nuclear reactor used in nuclear-powered submarines, utilizing liquid sodium metal as the heat exchanger).

**sir|car** (sėr′kär, sər kär′), *n.* = sirkar.

**sir|dar** (sėr′där, sər där′), *n.* **1** a military chief or leader in India. **2** a chief or headman in India. **3** the British commander of the Egyptian army in former times. **4** an Indian valet or servant. [< Anglo-Indian < Hindustani *sardār* chief < Persian *sar* head + *dār* having]

**sire** (sīr), *n., v.,* **sired, sir|ing.** — *n.* **1a** a male ancestor; forefather: *Strike—for the green graves of your sires!* (Fitz-Greene Halleck). **b** a male parent; father: *No children run to lisp their sire's return* (Thomas Gray). **2** the male parent: *Lightning was the sire of the race horse Danger.* **3** a title of respect used formerly to a great noble and now to a king: *"I am killed, Sire," said the messenger to Napoleon.* **4** *Obsolete.* a lord; master.
— *v.t.* to be the father of; beget: *Lightning sired the race horse Danger.*
[< Old French *sire* < Vulgar Latin *seior* < Latin *senior* older. See etym. of doublet **senior.**]

**si|re|don** (sī rē′dən), *n.* a salamander in its larval state, especially an axolotl. [< New Latin *Siredon* the genus name < Greek *seirēdōn,* earlier *seirēn* siren]

**sir|ee** (sə rē′), *n.* = sirree.

**sire|less** (sīr′lis), *adj. Archaic.* without a sire; fatherless.

**si|ren** (sī′rən), *n., adj.* — *n.* **1** a kind of whistle that makes a loud, piercing sound: *a police siren, an air-raid siren. We heard the sirens of the fire engines.* **2** Also, **Siren.** *Greek and Roman Legend.* any one of a group of nymphs who, by their sweet singing, lured sailors to destruction upon the rocks. **3** *Figurative.* any woman who lures, tempts, or entices: *... that pretty little girl who used to live just around the corner, has returned to town ... a full-fledged siren* (New Yorker). **4** any one of a genus of aquatic, eellike amphibians with small forelimbs, no hindlimbs, and three pairs of external gills that remain even after the lungs are formed.
— *adj.* of or like a siren; tempting; charming: *siren words, siren charms. The siren call of alleged panaceas* (New York Times). SYN: bewitching, alluring.
[< Latin *sīrēn* < Greek *seirēn, -ēnos*] — **si′ren-like′,** *adj.*

**si|re|ni|an** (sī rē′nē ən), *n., adj.* — *n.* any one of a small order of herbivorous sea mammals with forelimbs shaped like paddles and no hindlimbs. They are distinguished from whales by their rounded, unnotched tails. Manatees and dugongs are sirenians.
— *adj.* of or having to do with this order.

[< New Latin *Sirenia* the order name (< *Siren* the typical genus < Latin *sīrēn;* see etym. under **siren**) + English *-an*]

**si|ren|ic** (sī ren′ik), *adj.* **1** seductive; alluring; sirenlike. **2** = melodious.

**siren song,** a call or song of enticement; something which attracts a person irresistibly: *Africa's siren song to aluminum manufacturers isn't emanating from the Belgian Congo alone, by any means* (Wall Street Journal).

**siren suit,** *British.* coveralls.

**sir|gang** (sėr′gang), *n.* a crested, crowlike bird of southern Asia, with light-green to blue feathers. [< a native word]

**Sir|i|an** (sir′ē ən), *adj.* of or having to do with Sirius.

**si|ri|a|sis** (si rī′ə sis), *n.* **1** = sunstroke. **2** exposure to the sun for medical purposes; sun bath; insolation. [< New Latin *siriasis* < Greek *seiriásis* < *seiriân* to be scorching]

**Sir|i|us** (sir′ē əs), *n.* the brightest (fixed) star in the sky, in the constellation Canis Major; Dog Star. [< Latin *Sīrius* < Greek *Seírios*]

**sir|kar** (sėr′kär, sėr kär′), *n.* (in India) the government; the state. Also, **sircar.** [Anglo-Indian < Hindustani *sarkār* < Persian, < *sar* head + *-kār,* an agential suffix]

**sir|loin** (sėr′loin), *n.* **1** a cut of beef from the part of the loin in front of the rump and round. **2** a beefsteak cut from the portion of the loin immediately in front of this, beginning at the hip joint. Also, **surloin.** [< variant of Old French *surlonge* < *sur* over + *longe* loin]

**si|roc** (sə rok′, sī′rok), *n. Archaic.* sirocco.

**si|roc|co** (sə rok′ō), *n., pl.* **-cos. 1** a very hot, dry, and dust-laden wind blowing from the northern coast of Africa across the Mediterranean and parts of southern Europe: *Rain is followed usually by the sirocco—the hot wind from Africa —and the ground is quickly parched and cracked* (Atlantic). **2** a moist, warm, south or southeast wind in these same regions: *Sometimes the sirocco extends to the northern shore of the Mediterranean where it becomes a warm and moist wind* (Thomas A. Blair). **3** any hot, unpleasant wind: *The slow self-service elevator was an asphyxiating chamber with a fan that blew a withering sirocco* (New Yorker). [< Italian *scirocco* < Arabic *sharqī* east wind]

**sir|rah** (sir′ə), *n. Archaic.* fellow, used to address men and boys when speaking contemptuously, angrily, or impatiently: *"Silence, sirrah," said the prince to the stableboy.* [apparently < *sir* + *ha*]

**sir|ree** (sə rē′), *n. Informal.* sir (emphasized). Also, **siree.**

**sir-rev|er|ence** (sėr′rev′ər əns), *n. Obsolete.* saving your reverence, an apology: *A very reverent body; ay, such a one as a man may not speak of, without he says sir-reverence* (Shakespeare). [alteration of *s'r reverence,* shortened pronunciation of *save your reverence,* translation of Latin *salva reverentia*]

**Sir Rog|er de Cov|er|ley** (sėr roj′ər dē kuv′ər-lē), an old-fashioned English country-dance, something like the Virginia reel; Coverley. [see the entry **Coverley**]

**sir|ta|ki** (sir tä′kē), *n.* a Greek folk dance performed in a circle with locked arms and with sideways, alternately crossing steps, often with improvisations by individual dancers. [< New Greek *syrtaki* < Greek *syrtós* a kind of dance]

**sir|up** (sir′əp, sėr′-), *n.* = syrup.

**sir|up|y** (sir′ə pē, sėr′-), *adj.* = syrupy.

**sir|vente** (sir vänt′), *n.* a king of satirical song of the medieval troubadours, usually about the faults and vices of society. [< French *sirvente* < Old Provençal *sirventes,* or *serventes,* probably < *servir* serve]

**sir|ventes** (sir vänt′, -vents′), *n.* = sirvente.

**sis** (sis), *n. Informal.* sister. [American English; short for *sister*]

**sis|al** (sis′əl, sī′səl), *n.,* or **sisal hemp, 1** a strong fiber obtained from the leaves of a species of agave, used for making rope and twine. **2** the plant that it comes from; sisalana: *Careful where you sit, bub; those blasted sisal plants are needle-sharp* (New Yorker). **3** any related plant yielding a similar fiber, such as henequen. [< *Sisal,* a port in Yucatán, from which it was exported]

**sis|a|la|na** (sis′ə lä′nə, sī′sə-), *n.* the agave that yields sisal, native to the West Indies but raised in Brazil, Java, eastern Africa, and elsewhere. [< New Latin (*Agave*) *sisalana* the species name]

**sis-boom-bah** (sis′büm′bä′), *n. U.S. Slang.* spectator sports, especially football: *For the next 2½ years it was girls, flasks and sis-boom-bah* (Time). [< syllables commonly occurring in school cheers]

**sis|co|wet** (sis′kə wet), *n.* a very fat, thick-skinned variety of lake trout found in Lake Superior. [< Canadian French *siscowet,* alteration of Chippewa *pemitewiskawet* that which has oily flesh]

**Sis|er|a** (sis′ər ə), *n.* a commander of the Canaanites against the Israelites, slain by Jael after his defeat in battle (in the Bible, Judges 4 and 5).

**si sic om|ni|a** (sī sik om′nē ə), *Latin.* if all had been thus.

**sis|kin** (sis′kin), *n.* any one of a group of small finches, such as a green-and-yellow European finch related to the goldfinch, and the pine siskin of North America. [probably < Middle Dutch *sijsken* < Slavic (compare Czech *čížek*)]

**sis|mo|gram** (sis′mə gram), *n.* = seismogram.

**sis|mo|graph** (sis′mə graf, -gräf), *n.* = seismograph.

**sis|mo|graph|ic** (sis′mə graf′ik), *adj.* = seismographic.

**siss** (sis), *v.i., n.* = hiss. [imitative]

**Sis|se|ton** (sis′ə tən), *n., pl.* **-ton** or **-tons. 1** a member of a Siouan tribe living along the Mississippi and Minnesota rivers. **2** the language of this tribe.

**sis|si|fied** (sis′ə fīd), *adj. Informal.* effeminate.

**sis|soo** (sis′ü), *n.* **1** a large, deciduous tree of the pea family, common in India, having durable, dark-brown wood used extensively for boats and furniture. **2** its wood. [< Hindi *sīsū*]

**sis|sy** (sis′ē), *n., pl.* **-sies,** *adj.,* **-si|er, -si|est.** *Informal.* —*n.* **1** a boy or man who behaves too much like a girl: *I could not for a moment tolerate the idea of being thought of as a "kid" or a sissy* (John Masters). **2** a weak or cowardly person. **3** sister.
—*adj.* of or like a sissy; effeminate: *The feeling that it is sissy for a boy to take an interest in the arts has probably always existed among the middle class and is yet not extinct* (New Yorker). Also, *British,* **cissy.**
[probably diminutive form of *sis*]

**sissy bar,** *U.S.* a curved metal piece attached to the back of a bicycle seat to support or protect the rider's back.

**sissy britches,** *U.S. Slang.* **1** a sissy. **2** a coward.

**sis|sy|ish** (sis′ē ish), *adj. Informal.* of, like, or characteristic of a sissy.

**sis|ter** (sis′tər), *n., adj.* —*n.* **1a** a daughter of the same parents or parent. A girl is a sister to the other children of her parents or parent. **b** a half sister or stepsister. **2** a close friend or companion. **3** *Figurative.* a person or thing resembling or closely connected with another: *Its smaller sister, the IRBM* (*intermediate range ballistic missile*)*, could, at ranges of 600 to 1,500 miles, bombard many of the cities and airfields of Western Europe* (Hanson W. Baldwin). *Happiness and Intelligence are seldom sisters* (Thomas Love Peacock). **4** a woman member of the same church, society, or other group: *a sorority sister.* **5** a member of a religious sisterhood or order of women; nun. *Abbr:* Sr. **6** *British.* **a** a head nurse. **b** a nurse.
—*adj.* being a sister; related as if by sisterhood: *a sister ship.*
[< Scandinavian (compare Old Icelandic *systir*)]
▶ **Sister** is sometimes used alone as a word of address in very informal or nonstandard English as a substitute for "Miss" or "Madam": *Look, sister, I've told you the price three times now; it won't be less next time you ask.*

**sister block,** *Nautical.* a block with two sheaves in it, one above the other, used for various purposes.

**sis|ter|hood** (sis′tər hůd), *n.* **1** the bond between sisters; feeling of sister for sister. **2** an association of women with some common aim or characteristic: *the great sisterhood of mothers.* **3** the members of such an association; persons joined as sisters: *I'll dispose of thee, Among a sisterhood of holy nuns* (Shakespeare).

**sister hook,** *Nautical.* one of a pair of hooks working on the same axis and fitting closely together, much used about a ship's rigging.

**sis|ter-in-law** (sis′tər in lô′), *n., pl.* **sisters-in-law. 1** the sister of one's husband or wife: *She asked her sister-in-law to come to her brother's birthday.* **2** the wife of one's brother: *She called her brother to see how her sister-in-law was.* **3** the wife of one's brother-in-law.

**sis|ter|less** (sis′tər lis), *adj.* having no sister.

**sis|ter|li|ness** (sis′tər lē nis), *n.* sisterly affection or sympathy.

**sis|ter|ly** (sis′tər lē), *adj., adv.* —*adj.* **1** of or suitable for a sister: *sisterly traits.* **2** like a sister's; kindly: *sisterly interest, sisterly love.* **SYN:** affectionate. **3** of or having to do with a (religious) sisterhood: *a sisterly life.*
—*adv.* like a sister: *She spoke coolly and sisterly now* (F. W. Robinson).

**sis|tern** (sis′tərn), *n.pl. Dialect.* sisters.

**Sister of Charity,** a member of a sisterhood, especially a Roman Catholic sisterhood, devoted to work among the poor and to nursing the sick.

**Sister of Mercy,** a member of a Roman Catholic sisterhood devoted to nursing the sick and to the education and care of the poor.

**sis|te vi|a|tor** (sis′tē vī ā′tər), *Latin.* stop, traveler.

**Sis|tine** (sis′tēn, -tīn, -tin), *adj.* **1** of or having to do with any one of the five popes named Sixtus. **2** of or having to do with the Sistine Chapel in the Vatican. Also, **Sixtine.** [< Italian *sistino* < *Sisto* (Pope Sixtus IV) < Latin *sextus* sixth]

**sis|troid** (sis′troid), *adj. Geometry.* contained between the convex sides of two curves that intersect each other.

✱**sis|trum** (sis′trəm), *n., pl.* **-trums, -tra** (-trə). an ancient metal musical instrument or rattle, having an oval frame with loosely fitting transverse rods, used especially in Egypt in the worship of Isis. [< Latin *sīstrum* < Greek *seîstron* < *seíein* to shake]

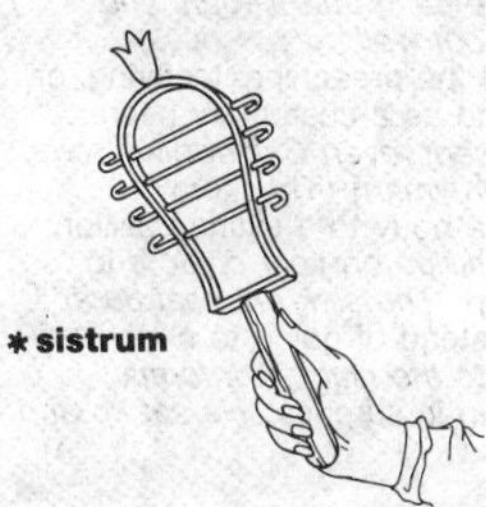
✱**sistrum**

**si|Swa|ti** (sə swä′tē), *n.* the Bantu language of the Swazi, closely related to Zulu.

**Sis|y|phe|an** or **Sis|y|phi|an** (sis′ə fē′ən), *adj.* of or having to do with Sisyphus.

**Sis|y|phus** (sis′ə fəs), *n. Greek Mythology.* a king of Corinth condemned forever to roll a heavy stone up a steep hill in Hades, only to have it always roll down again when he neared the top.

**sit** (sit), *v.,* **sat** or (*Archaic*) **sate, sat** or (*Obsolete*) **sit|ten, sit|ting,** *n.* —*v.i.* **1a** to rest on the lower part of the body, with the weight off the feet: *She sat in a chair.* **b** to do this in a certain way: *to sit cross-legged, to sit close to a fire.* **2** to be placed; be; have place or position: *The clock has sat on that shelf for years. We came upon a little village sitting in the hills.* **3** to have a seat in an assembly; be a member of a council: *to sit in Congress.* **4** to hold a session: *The court sits next month.* **5** to place oneself in a position for having one's picture made; pose: *to sit for a portrait.* **6** to be in a state of rest; remain inactive: *He did not join in the game; he just sat on the sidelines. Shall your brethren go to war, and shall ye sit here?* (Numbers 32:6). **7** *Figurative.* to press or weigh: *Care sat heavily on his brow.* **8** to perch; roost: *The birds were sitting on the fence rail.* **9** to cover eggs so that they will hatch; brood: *The hen will sit until the eggs are ready to hatch.* **10** = baby-sit: *My sister sits for the woman next door when she goes shopping.* **11** = fit: *Her coat sits well.*
—*v.t.* **1** to cause to sit; seat: *The woman sat the little boy in his chair.* **2** to seat (oneself): *He boldly sat himself down at my fireside.* **3** to sit on: *He sat his horse well.* **4** *British.* to take (an examination).
—*n.* **1** the way in which an article of clothing fits. **2** the act of stopping at a place for a short while; sojourn; stay: *The day before it was a trip round the Island and a sit in the arboretum* (Punch).
**sit down,** to take a seat; put oneself in a sitting position: *We sat down by the roadside to have our picnic.*
**sit in, a** to be present as a spectator or observer: *He was invited to sit in at the lecture.* **b** to take part (as in a game or conference): *to sit in with a musical group, sit in at a game.* **c** *U.S.* to take part in a sit-in: *... Negro pupils sitting in at the nearly all-white school* (New York Times).
**sit in on,** to be present at, as a spectator or observer: *The Senate Finance and Assembly Ways and Means Committees now have a legal right to sit in on the budget-making process* (New York Times).
**sit on** (or **upon**), **a** to sit in judgment or council on; deliberate on: *A committee of ... friends ... sat upon our affairs* (Harper's). **b** to have a seat on (a jury, committee, commission, or council): *He sat on the State Hospital Commission.* **c** *Informal.* to check, rebuke, or snub: *My lady felt rebuked, and, as she afterward expressed it, sat upon* (Lynn Linton).

**Pronunciation Key:** hat, āge, cãre, fär; let, ēqual, tėrm; it, īce; hot, ōpen, ôrder; **oi**l, **ou**t; cup, půt, rüle; **ch**ild; lo**ng**; **th**in; **ᴛʜ**en; **zh**, measure; **ə** represents **a** in about, **e** in taken, **i** in pencil, **o** in lemon, **u** in circus.

**sit out**, **a** to remain seated during (a dance): *She refused him a dance only once when she wanted to sit it out with her girl friend.* **b** to stay through (a performance or other event): *This is the only meeting which I have sat out.* **c** to stay later than (another): *I thought I would sit the other visitors out* (W. E. Norris). **d** *Informal, Figurative.* to do nothing about; stay out of: *He's prudently sitting out the scandal* (Maclean's).

**sit through**, to remain seated during; be present or in attendance at: *to sit through a dull concert, to sit through a lecture.*

**sit tight**, *Informal.* **a** to keep the same position or opinion: *When a company's business is down, it's far more inclined to sit tight and take a strike than when things are booming* (Wall Street Journal). **b** to let matters take their own course; refrain from action: *Be calm and sit tight and everything will turn out well.*

**sit under**, to attend the preaching, lecturing, or speaking, of; listen to as a customary hearer: *Members of Parliament, even Cabinet Ministers, sit under him* [*a clergyman*] (Thackeray).

**sit up**, **a** to raise the body to a sitting position: *Stop slumping and sit up on your chair.* **b** to keep such a position: *The sick man sat up at last.* **c** to stay up instead of going to bed: *They sat up talking far into the night.* **d** *Informal, Figurative.* to start up in surprise: *He sat up and took notice in a hurry.*

[Old English *sittan*]

▶ See **set** for usage note.

**Si|ta** (sē′tä), *n. Hindu Mythology.* the wife of Rama, and heroine of the Ramayana.

***si|tar** (si tär′), *n.* a musical instrument of India, having a long, fretted neck and body usually made from a gourd. It has 6 or 7 strings that are played with a plectrum and a larger number of strings, beneath the others, that vibrate sympathetically. [< Hindi *sitār*]

***sitar**

**si|tar|ist** (si tär′ist), *n.* a player of the sitar.

**sit|a|tun|ga** (sit′ə tu̇ng′gə), *n.* an antelope of central and eastern Africa which inhabits swampy, forested regions. [< a native name]

**sitch|com** (sich′kom), *n. U.S. Informal.* a situation comedy.

**sit|com** (sit′kom). *n.* = sitchcom.

**sit-down**[1] (sit′doun′), *adj.* served to persons seated at a table: *a sit-down lunch.*

**sit-down strike**, or **sit-down**[2] (sit′doun′), *n.* **1** a strike in which the workers stay in the factory, store, or offices, without working until their demands are met or an agreement is reached: *Three thousand workers staged a sit-down strike ... at the Bremen Goliath Automobile works* (New York Times). **2** a demonstration in which participants sit down in a public place and refuse to move as a form of protest against discrimination, the use of nuclear weapons, or other social or personal injustices: *He was ready to call a sit-down strike in Congress against funds for the Congo* (Manchester Guardian Weekly).

**site** (sīt), *n., v.,* **sit|ed, sit|ing.** —*n.* **1** the position or place (of a building, town, or the like): *The big house on the hill has one of the best sites in town.* SYN: location. **2** the ground or area upon which something has been, is being, may be, or will be built, done, or made to happen: *the site of a pioneer settlement, of a steel mill, or of a battle. A new school is to be built on the site of the old town hall. The chapel ... stands on the site of the ancient church burnt not long ago* (William Dean Howells).

—*v.t.* to place in a site; locate; situate: *There is also much to be said for siting industry so that the minimum fetching and carrying is required* (Sunday Times).

[< Latin *situs, -ūs*]

**sit|fast** (sit′fast′, -fäst′), *n.* = saddle gall.

**sith** (sith), *prep., conj., adv. Archaic.* since. [Old English *sīth* after (in time)]

**sith|en** (sith′ən), *prep., conj., adv. Archaic.* sith; since.

**sit-in** (sit′in′), *n.* a form of protest in which a group of people enter and remain seated for a long period of time in a public place. Sit-ins are organized to protest racial discrimination, government policies, etc.

**Sit|ka spruce** (sit′kə), a tall spruce tree of the Pacific Coast region from Alaska to California, valued for its lumber: *The arches are made from thinnings of Sitka spruce* (New Science). [< *Sitka,* a town in Alaska]

**si|tol|o|gy** (sī tol′ə jē), *n.* the science of food or diet; dietetics. [< Greek *sîtos* food, grain + English *-logy*]

**si|to|ma|ni|a** (sī′tō mā′nē ə), *n.* an abnormal craving for food. [< Greek *sîtos* food, grain + English *mania*]

**si|to|pho|bi|a** (sī′tō fō′bē ə), *n.* an abnormal dislike for food. [< Greek *sîtos* food, grain + English *-phobia*]

**si|tos|ter|ol** (sī tos′tə rōl, -rol), *n.* any one of several crystalline alcohols or sterols, similar to cholesterol, present in wheat, corn, bran, Calabar beans, and other plants. [< Greek *sîtos* grain, food + English (chole)*sterol*]

**si|to|tox|in** (sī′tō tok′sin), *n.* a toxin or poison generated by a microorganism in vegetable food. [< Greek *sîtos* grain, food + English *toxin*]

**sit-out** (sit′out′), *n.* a defensive maneuver in wrestling in which the wrestler on the bottom goes into a sitting position to escape a hold or assume the offensive.

**sit|rep** (sit′rep′), *n.* a report on military activities and operations. [< *sit*(uation) *rep*(ort)]

**sit spin**, (in figure skating) a spin on one leg with a gradual sinking into a sitting position in which the other leg is extended.

**sit|ter** (sit′ər), *n.* **1** a person who sits: *The number of sitters in the pine pews of the chapels and the oak pews of the churches falls ever lower* (J. E. R. Scott). **2** = baby sitter. **3** a bird sitting on its eggs, especially a hen. **4** anything easy or certain of performance: *In the last chukka, Hanut missed three shots running that normally would have been sitters for him* (London Times).

**sit|ter-in** (sit′ər in′), *n.* **1** a person who sits in or participates. **2** *British.* a baby sitter.

**sit|ting** (sit′ing), *n., adj.* —*n.* **1a** a meeting or session of a court, legislature, commission, or anything like it: *The hearing lasted for six sittings of the court.* **b** the period of time occupied by this. **2a** a time of remaining seated: *She read five chapters at one sitting.* **b** a period of posing: *to do a portrait in three sittings.* **3** the act of one that sits. **4a** the act of a bird, especially a hen, in setting; brooding. **b** the number of eggs on which a bird sits; clutch. **5** a seat for one person in a church or other place of worship: *The church is enlarged by at least five hundred sittings* (George Eliot).

—*adj.* **1** that sits; seated: *a sitting dog.* **2** that sets; setting: *a sitting hen.* **3** that has a seat, as in a legislative body or on a committee: *a sitting magistrate.* **4a** of or having to do with sitting: *to be in bed in a sitting position.* **b** used for sitting; in which one sits or may sit: *the sitting area of an auditorium, to find sitting space.* **c** used in sitting: *the sitting muscles.*

**sitting duck**, *Informal.* an easy target or mark: *Air Force doctrine holds that any aircraft carrier would be a sitting duck in a war of missiles* (Time).

**sitting room**, a room to sit in, entertain guests in, or the like; living room or parlor.

**sit|u|ate** (sich′u̇ āt), *v.,* **-at|ed, -at|ing,** *adj.* —*v.t.* to place or locate: *The firehouse is situated so that the firemen can easily reach all parts of town. They situated themselves in three separate chambers* (Thomas Paine). —*adj. Archaic except Law.* having its location; placed; situated. [< Medieval Latin *situare* (with English *-ate*[1]) < Latin *situs, -ūs* location]

**sit|u|at|ed** (sich′u̇ ā′tid), *adj.* **1** placed; located: *New York is a favorably situated city.* **2** in a certain financial or social position: *The doctor was quite well situated.*

▶ **Situated**, when followed by a preposition, is often an unnecessary sentence element: *He traveled to a small town in Canada called Picton,* [*situated*] *in Ontario.*

**sit|u|a|tion** (sich′u̇ ā′shən), *n.* **1a** a combination of circumstances; case; condition: *Act reasonably in all situations.* **b** position with regard to circumstances: *It is a very disagreeable situation to be alone and without money in a strange city.* **2** a place to work; job or position: *She is trying to find a situation.* SYN: post. See syn. under **position**. **3** a site; location; place: *Our house has a beautiful situation on a hill.* SYN: station, spot. **4** a state of affairs, series of events, or circumstance, in a play, novel, or other literary or dramatic work: *a good opening situation. The play turned upon a typical French situation* (Mrs. Humphry Ward).

**sit|u|a|tion|al** (sich′u̇ ā′shə nəl), *adj.* of or having to do with situations: *We must recognize that people are not just driven by situational pressures; they are also pulled by the ideals and goals of their cultures* (Scientific American). —**sit′u|a′tion|al|ly**, *adv.*

**situation comedy**, comedy which depends for its humor upon contrived situations built around a character or group of characters, as in a radio or television series: *A number of able comedians have been forced to rely on the artificial support of quiz-show routines, or of so-called situation comedy, which is far from being the same thing as pure, or "straight," comedy* (John Lardner).

**situation ethics**, a theory of ethics that rejects moral absolutes and maintains that ethical decisions must arise spontaneously from the demands of specific situations and contexts.

**sit|u|a|tion|ism** (sich′u̇ ā′shə niz′əm), *n.* **1** a psychological theory which emphasizes the influence of a person's present situation in determining his behavior. **2** = situation ethics.

**sit|u|a|tion|ist** (sich′u̇ ā′shə nist), *n.* a person who favors or advocates situationism: *To be a situationist is to have no ideology and to weigh each proposition as it arises* (Lloyd Garrison).

**situation room**, a room, usually at a military headquarters, where reports are given on the current status of any action or operation.

**sit|u|la** (sich′u̇ lə), *n., pl.* **-lae** (-lē). a deep, bucketlike vessel, vase, or urn used by the ancient Greeks and Romans. [< Latin *situla* bucket, urn]

**sit-up** (sit′up′), *n.* an exercise in which a person lies on the back with hands behind the head, legs extended, and then sits up without raising the feet.

**sit-up|on** (sit′ə pon′, -pôn′), *n. Slang.* the buttocks.

**si|tus** (sī′təs), *n.* position, situation, or location, especially the proper or original position of a part or organ. [< Latin *situs, -ūs*]

**si|tus in|ver|sus** (sī′təs in vėr′səs), a congenital defect of the human anatomy in which the organs of the right and left side are reversed. [< New Latin *situs inversus* < Latin *situs, -ūs* situs and *inversus* inverse]

**sit|u|tun|ga** (sit′ə tu̇ng′gə), *n.* = sitatunga.

**sit ve|ni|a ver|bo** (sit vē′nē ə vėr′bō), *Latin.* pardon the expression.

**sitz bath** (sits), **1** a tub to bathe in, in which the user sits so that only the hips and the lower part of the body are submerged. **2** the bath so taken, especially a hot bath for easing muscular pain. [half-translation of German *Sitzbad* < *Sitz* seat, sitting position (< *sitzen* to sit) + *Bad* bath]

**Sitz|fleisch** (zits′flīsh), *n. German.* **1** patience; perseverance. **2** (literally) seat flesh; buttocks.

**sitz|krieg** (sits′krēg′; *German* zits′krēk′), *n.* a war with little or no actual fighting; static warfare. [< German *Sitzkrieg* (literally) sitting war. Compare etym. under **blitzkrieg.**]

**sitz|mark** (sits′märk′; *German* zits′märk′), *n.* a hole in the snow made by a skier who falls backward and comes to rest approximately in a sitting position: *Thousands left their sitzmarks on the deep powder slopes of California's Sierras and Washington's Cascade range* (Time). [half-translation of German *Sitzmarke* < *Sitz* a sitting, seat + *Marke* sign]

**SIU** (no periods) or **S.I.U.**, Seafarers' International Union.

**SI unit**, any one of the units of measurement in the international meter-kilogram-second system. [*SI,* abbreviation of French *Système International* (*d'Unités*) International System (of Units)]

**Si|va** (sē′və, shē′-), *n.* one of the three chief Hindu divinities, known as "the Destroyer," the others being Brahma and Vishnu. Those who worship Siva as the primary Hindu divinity consider him to be the creative and reproductive force. Also, **Shiva.** [< Hindustani *Shiva* < Sanskrit *śiva* (literally) auspicious]

**Si|va|ism** (sē′və iz əm, shē′-), *n.* the worship of Siva.

**Si|va|ist** (sē′və ist, shē′-), *n.* a worshiper of Siva.

**Si|va|is|tic** (sē′və is′tik, shē′-), *adj.* of or having to do with Sivaism or Sivaists.

**Si|va|ite** (sē′və īt, shē′-), *n.* a person who worships Siva; an adherent of the worship of Siva.

**Si|van** (sē vän′, siv′ən), *n.* the ninth month of the Jewish civil year or the third of the ecclesiastical year, corresponding to May and sometimes part of June. [< Hebrew *siwān*]

**si|va snake** (sē′və), = king cobra.

**siv|a|there** (siv′ə thir), *n.* = sivatherium.

**siv|a|the|ri|um** or **Siv|a|the|ri|um** (siv′ə thir′ē əm), *n.* a large, extinct mammal, a forebear of the modern giraffe but having a shorter neck and legs, a skull as large as an elephant's, and two pairs of horns, the posterior pair attaining six-foot spread. Its fossil remains were found in the Tertiary strata of India. [< New Latin *Sivatherium* the genus name < *Siva* + Greek *thērion* beast]

**si|ver** (sī′vər), *n. Scottish.* a gutter, drain, or sewer. [perhaps < Old French *sewiere* sewer]

**Si|wan** (sē vän′, siv′ən), *n.* = Sivan.

**Si|wash** (sī′wosh), *n.* **1** a North American Indian of the northern Pacific coast (used in an unfriendly way). **2** *U.S. Slang.* a small or inferior college. [< Chinook jargon < French *sauvage* savage]

**six** (siks), *n., adj.* —*n.* **1** one more than five; 6: *Six of anything is the same as half a dozen.* **2** a set of six persons or things. **3** the number six. **4** a playing card or die with six spots. **5** anything identified as being or having six units, especially a six-cylinder automobile.
—*adj.* being one more than five: *Six apples are half a dozen apples.*
**at sixes and sevens, a** in confusion: *As usual, things were also at sixes and sevens in the stake races for fillies* (New Yorker). **b** in disagreement: *With the Democratic party at sixes and sevens since the Minnesota primary there will be a whole stable of dark horses in the background this year* (Wall Street Journal).
**knock** (or **hit**) **for six,** *British Slang.* to beat soundly; defeat; destroy: *Declaring that the Bill is a "serious infringement on the rights of women," they proceed to knock it for six* (London Times).
[Old English *siex, six*]

**six-by-six** (siks′bī siks′), *n.* a motor truck with six wheels: *Engineers banging down the road in six-by-sixes, raising red dust* (New Yorker).

**six|fold** (siks′fōld′), *adj., adv.* —*adj.* **1** six times as much or as many; sextuple. **2** having six parts.
—*adv.* six times as much or as many.

**six-foot** (siks′fu̇t′), *adj.* six feet long or tall.

**six-foot|er** (siks′fu̇t′ər), *n.* a person who is six feet tall.

**six-gun** (siks′gun′), *n. U.S.* a six-shooter.

**Six Nations,** a federation of Iroquois Indian tribes. The Tuscarora tribe of Iroquois in 1722 joined the original federation of Iroquois tribes called the Five Nations.

**606,** the original name of arsphenamine. [so called because it was the 606th compound tested by its discoverer]

**six-pack** (siks′pak′), *n.* a container holding six bottles, cans, or other items sold as a unit: *a six-pack of beer.*

**six|pence** (siks′pəns), *n.* **1** a sum of six British pennies; six pence. **2** a former British coin worth six pence or ½ of a shilling. The sixpence was discontinued in 1971.

**six|pen|ny** (siks′pen′ē, -pə nē), *adj.* **1** worth, costing, or amounting to sixpence. **2** *British.* of little worth; cheap. **3** two inches long; two-inch: *sixpenny nails.*

**six|score** (siks′skôr′, -skōr′), *adj. Archaic.* six times twenty; 120.

**six-shoot|er** (siks′shü′tər), *n. Informal.* **1** a revolver that can fire six shots without being loaded again. Six-shooters are of large caliber (.44 or .45; never less than .38). **2** any revolver.

**six|some** (sik′səm), *n.* **1** a group of six people. **2** a game played by six people. **3** the players.

**sixte** (sikst), *n. Fencing.* the sixth in a series of eight defensive positions or parries. [< Old French *sixte,* variant of *siste* < *sis* six < Latin *sex*]

**six|teen** (siks′tēn′), *n., adj.* six more than ten; 16: *There are sixteen ounces in a pound.* [Old English *sixtēne*]

**six|teen|mo** (siks′tēn′mō), *n., pl.* **-mos,** *adj.* = sextodecimo.

**six|teenth** (siks′tēnth′), *adj., n.* —*adj.* **1** next after the 15th; last in a series of 16: *a sixteenth birthday.* **2** being one of 16 equal parts: *An ounce is a sixteenth part of a pound.*
—*n.* **1** the next after the 15th; last in a series of 16. **2** one of 16 equal parts: *An ounce is one sixteenth of a pound.* **3** *Music.* a sixteenth note.

***sixteenth note,** *Music.* a note played for one sixteenth as long a time as a whole note; semiquaver.

***sixteenth note**
***sixteenth rest**

***sixteenth rest,** *Music.* a rest as long as a sixteenth note.

**sixth** (siksth), *adj., n.* —*adj.* **1** next after the fifth; last in a series of 6: *a sixth birthday.* **2** being one of 6 equal parts: *Ten minutes is a sixth part of an hour.*
—*n.* **1** the next after the fifth; last in a series of 6: *School starts on the sixth.* **2** one of 6 equal parts: *Two inches is a sixth of a foot.* **3** *Music.* **a** a tone or note six steps apart in the diatonic scale, or the sixth step of a diatonic scale, from a given tone or note. **b** the interval between such tones or notes. **c** the harmonic combination of such tones. **d** the sixth note or tone of a scale, six diatonic degrees above the tonic.

***sixth chord,** *Music.* a chord consisting of a note or tone, its third, and its sixth (symbol $^6_3$ or simply 6); the first inversion of a triad, with its original third in the bass; chord of the sixth.

***sixth chord**

**sixth|ly** (siksth′lē), *adv.* in the sixth place.

**sixth sense,** an unusual power of perception; intuition: *It was not a do-nothing Congress, but its political sixth sense may have helped to keep it from doing many things the country can well do without* (Wall Street Journal).

**six|ti|eth** (siks′tē ith), *adj., n.* —*adj.* **1** next after the 59th; last in a series of 60: *a sixtieth birthday.* **2** being one of 60 equal parts: *A minute is a sixtieth part of an hour.*
—*n.* **1** the next after the 59th; last in a series of 60: *That car is the sixtieth to drive by today.* **2** one of 60 equal parts: *a sixtieth of one's income.*

**Six|tine** (siks′tin), *adj.* = Sistine.

**six|ty** (siks′tē), *n., pl.* **-ties,** *adj.* six times ten; 60.
**like sixty,** *Informal.* very fast: *to go like sixty.*
[Old English *siextig, sixtig*]

**six|ty|fold** (siks′tē fōld′), *adj., adv.* sixty times as much or as many.

**sixty-four-dollar** or **$64 question,** *U.S.* the key question; the final and most important question: *The answer to the $64 question has thus far been given by the politicians, with woefully inadequate consideration of the scientist's point of view* (Science News Letter). [< the name of a radio quiz program of the 1940's, which offered a prize of *$64*]

***six|ty-fourth note** (siks′tē fôrth′, -fōrth′), *Music.* a note played for one sixty-fourth as long a time as a whole note; hemidemisemiquaver.

***sixty-fourth note**
***sixty-fourth rest**

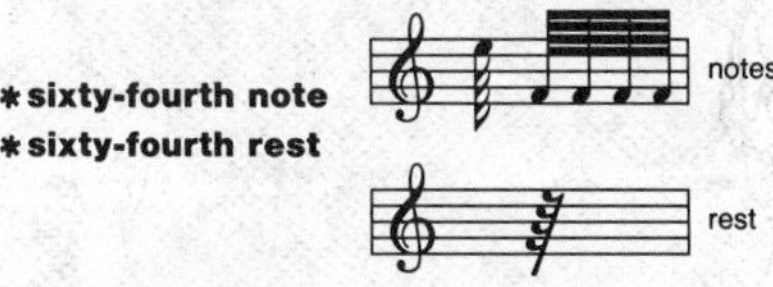


***sixty-fourth rest,** *Music.* a rest as long as a sixty-fourth note.

**siz|a|ble** (sī′zə bəl), *adj.* **1** fairly large: *a sizable sum.* **2** *Archaic.* of suitable or convenient size. Also, **sizeable.** —**siz′a|ble|ness,** *n.*

**siz|a|bly** (sī′zə blē), *adv.* to a sizable extent or degree. Also, **sizeably.**

**siz|ar** (sī′zər), *n.* a student who pays reduced rates in the colleges of Cambridge University in Cambridge, England, and of Trinity College in Dublin, Ireland. Also, **sizer.** [< *siz*(e)¹ + *-ar,* variant of *-er*²]

**siz|ar|ship** (sī′zər ship), *n.* the position, rank, or privileges of a sizar.

**size¹** (sīz), *n., v.,* **sized, siz|ing,** *adj.* —*n.* **1** the amount of surface or space a thing takes up: *The two boys are of the same size. The library has books of all sizes. We need a house of larger size.* **2** extent; amount; magnitude: *the size of an industry, the size of an undertaking.* **3** one of a series of measures: *The size of card I want is 3 by 5 inches. His collar is size fourteen.* **4** *Informal, Figurative.* the actual condition; true description: *That's about the size of it.* **5** *Obsolete.* a ration, allowance, or standard of food or drink: *'Tis not in thee To grudge my pleasures ... to scant my sizes* (Shakespeare).
—*v.t.* **1** to arrange or classify according to size or in sizes: *Will you size these nails? Why should a man's shirt be sized by his neck but his pyjamas by his chest?* (Observer). **2** to make of a certain size. **3** *Obsolete.* to regulate or control according to a fixed standard: *... to size weights and measures* (Francis Bacon).
—*adj.* having size; sized.
**cut down to size, a** to reduce to (a specified size or number) by or as if by cutting: *to cut a plant down to size. Sportswriters had named his team the best in the country, and he was determined to cut his players down to fighting size* (Time). **b** to diminish the sense of importance or ego of: *to cut a bully down to size.*
**of a size,** of the same size: *There are large and small pears, but the apples are all of a size.*
**size up,** *Informal.* **a** to form an opinion of; estimate: *A fellow ought to ... look 'em* [*candidates*] *all over and size 'em up, and then decide carefully* (Sinclair Lewis). **b** to come up to some size or grade: *It was a letter ... which sized up very well with the letters written in my part of the United States* (Owen Wister).
**try for size,** to try out or test for fit or appropriateness: *A British Railways liner train was tried for size at the first special depot* (London Times).
[Middle English *syse* an ordinance setting a fixed amount; also, assizes of justice; (perhaps originally) short for *assize*]
—*Syn. n.* **1, 2 Size, volume, bulk** mean the spatial measure of something. **Size** applies to the dimensions (length, width, and height or depth) of something, to the extent of surface occupied, or to the number of individuals included: *the size of a box. What is the size of your herd?* **Volume** is used of something measured by the cubic inches, feet, etc., it occupies: *The volume of water confined by Hoover Dam is tremendous.* **Bulk** means size or quantity measured in three dimensions, and often suggests largeness: *Let the dough double in bulk.*

**size²** (sīz), *n., v.,* **sized, siz|ing.** —*n.* a preparation made from glue, starch, or other sticky material; sizing. It is used to cover paper, plaster, or other material, or stiffen cloth, and glaze paper.
—*v.t.* to coat, treat, fill, or glaze with size.
[< Old French *assise* a sitting, fixing, layer]

**-size,** *combining form.* a variant of **-sized,** as in *life-size, an average-size man.*

**size|a|ble** (sī′zə bəl), *adj.* = sizable. —**size′a|ble|ness,** *n.*

**size|a|bly** (sī′zə blē), *adv.* = sizably.

**size copy,** *British, Printing.* a dummy.

**sized** (sīzd), *adj.* having size, especially as specified: *variously sized garments.*

**-sized,** *combining form.* having or of a ___ size: *Fair-sized = having a fair size. Large-sized = of a large size.* Also, **-size.**

**siz|er¹** (sī′zər), *n.* a device for testing the size of articles, or for separating them according to size.

**siz|er²** (sī′zər), *n.* = sizar.

**size-up** (sīz′up′), *n. Informal.* an estimate; opinion; consideration: *The United States is evolving a new defense policy, based on a new size-up of the world situation and a new concept of warfare* (Newsweek).

**siz|ing** (sī′zing), *n.* **1** a preparation made from such material as glue or starch; size. **2** the act or process of coating or treating with size.

**siz|y** (sī′zē), *adj.* of or like size; thick; viscous; glutinous. [< *siz*(e)² + *-y*¹]

**sizz** (siz), *v.i.* to hiss; sizzle; make a hiss somewhat resembling a buzz. [imitative]

**siz|zle** (siz′əl), *v.,* **-zled, -zling,** *n.* —*v.i.* **1** to make a hissing sound, as fat does when it is frying or scorching. **2** to be very hot: *to sizzle in a heat wave, to sizzle with anger.* —*v.t.* **1** to fry or scorch so as to produce a hissing sound. **2** to burn up with intense heat: *A gas ... ionizes into a hot, high-speed jet that sizzles the surface of the two metals and joins them* (Science).
—*n.* a hissing sound; sizzling.
[imitative]

**siz|zler** (siz′lər), *n.* **1** *Informal.* a very hot day: *Tuesday was really a sizzler.* **2** *Slang.* something outstanding, exciting, or dangerous: *But his Curnonsky folder was a sizzler: "Dangerous anarchist, without a fixed domicile since 1912"* (Atlantic).

**siz|zling** (siz′ling), *adj.* **1** that sizzles: *a sizzling steak, sizzling anger.* **2** very hot: *sizzling weather.* —**siz′zling|ly,** *adv.*

**S.J.,** Society of Jesus (the official name of the Jesuit order).

**sjam|bok** (sham′bok), *n., v.* —*n.* a strong, heavy whip made from thick, tough hide, such as that of the rhinoceros or hippopotamus, used in South Africa for driving cattle.
—*v.t.* to strike or drive with a sjambok.
[< earlier Afrikaans *sjambok* < Malay *sambok* < Persian *chābuk.* Compare etym. under **chabouk.**]

**S.J.D.,** Doctor of Juridical Science (Latin, *Scientiae Juridicae Doctor*).

**S.J. Res.,** *U.S.* Senate Joint Resolution (used with a number).

**sk.,** sack.

**skald** (skôld, skäld), *n.* a Scandinavian poet and singer of ancient times. Also, **scald.** [< Scandinavian (compare Old Icelandic *skāld*)]

**skald|ic** (skôl′dik, skäl′-), *adj.* of or having to do with the skalds or their poetry and songs. Also, **scaldic.**

**skat** (skät), *n.* **1** a card game for three players. Cards won in tricks are counted for points. **2** the widow dealt in this game. [< German *Skat* (origi-

**Pronunciation Key:** hat, āge, cãre, fär; let, ēqual, tėrm; it, īce; hot, ōpen, ôrder; oil, out; cup, pu̇t, rüle; child; long; thin; ᴛʜen; zh, measure; ə represents **a** in about, **e** in taken, **i** in pencil, **o** in lemon, **u** in circus.

nally) two cards for discard < Italian *scarto* a discard < *scartare* discard < Latin *ex-* out of + *charta* chart. Compare etym. under **card**[1].]

**skate**[1] (skāt), *n., v.,* **skat|ed, skat|ing.** *—n.* **1** a frame with a blade fixed to a shoe so that a person can glide over ice; ice skate. **2** a similar frame or shoe with small wheels for use on any smooth, hard surface; roller skate.
*—v.i.* **1** to glide or move along on skates. **2** to slide or glide along: *Insects skated on the water* (Longfellow). (*Figurative.*) *Many other savings institutions are skating close to their break-even points* (Wall Street Journal). *—v.t.* **1** to glide or move over (a surface) on skates. **2** to take part in (a contest or the like) by skating.
**skate on thin ice,** to take a risky or dangerous course: *A handful of savings and loan associations in the state are also known to be skating on thin ice* (Wall Street Journal).
[< Dutch *schaats* (taken as plural) < Old French *escache* stilt < a Germanic word]

***skate**[2]

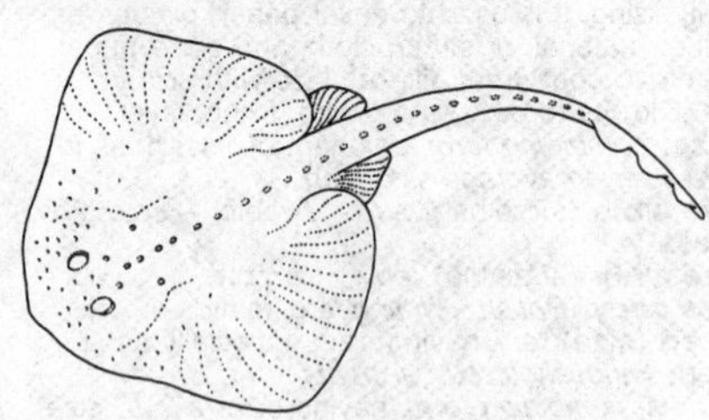

***skate**[2] (skāt), *n., pl.* **skates** or (*collectively*) **skate.** any one of several broad, flat fishes, usually having a pointed snout. A skate is a kind of ray. The barn-door skate and the thornback are two kinds. [< Scandinavian (compare Old Icelandic *skata*)]

**skate**[3] (skāt), *n. U.S. Slang.* **1** a term of contempt for an old, worn-out horse. **2** a fellow: *He's a good skate. Dave's a cheap skate, all right* (Sinclair Lewis). [origin uncertain]

**skate|bar|row** (skāt′bar′ō), *n.* the egg case of a skate, ray, or other elasmobranch fish, often called a mermaid's purse. Its shape suggests a handbarrow.

**skate|board** (skāt′bôrd′, -bōrd′), *n.* a narrow board resembling a surfboard, with roller-skate wheels attached to each end, used for gliding or moving on any hard surface. **—skate′board′er,** *n.*

**skate|board|ing** (skāt′bôr′ding, -bōr′-), *n.* the act or sport of riding a skateboard.

**skat|er** (skā′tər), *n.* **1** a person who skates. **2** any one of various long-legged insects that glide over water.

**skat|ing rink** (skā′ting), **1** a smooth sheet of ice for skating. **2** a smooth floor for roller skating.

**skat|ol** (skat′ōl, -ol), *n.* = skatole.

**skat|ole** (skat′ōl), *n.* a bad-smelling substance produced by the decomposition of albuminous matter in the intestinal canal, and present in feces. *Formula:* $C_9H_9N$ [< Greek *skôr, skatós* excrement + English *-ole*]

**skean** (shkēn, skēn), *n.* a type of dagger formerly used by foot soldiers in Ireland and Scotland. Also, **skene.** [< Irish Gaelic, Scottish Gaelic *sgian*]

**skean dhu** (ᴛʜü), a small dagger carried by Scottish Highlanders as an ornament, usually in a stocking: *He is armed with a claymore* (*broadsword*), *a dirk* (*dagger*), *and a skean dhu* (*a knife tucked in his sock*) (New York). [< *skean* + Scottish Gaelic *dubh* black]

**sked** (sked), *n. Informal.* schedule.

**ske|dad|dle** (ski dad′əl), *v.,* **-dled, -dling,** *n. Informal. —v.i.* to run away; leave suddenly and quickly; scatter in flight: *Meant to tame him* [*a gopher*] *but he got out of his box and skedaddled* (Atlantic).
*—n.* a hasty flight or scattering.
[origin uncertain] **—ske|dad|dler,** *n.*

**skee** (skē), *n., pl.* **skees** or **skee,** *v.i.,* **skeed, skee|ing.** = ski.

**skeet** (skēt), *n.* a kind of trapshooting in which the clay pigeons are flung into the air at angles similar to those taken by a bird in flight: *The riding trails, skeet fields and trout streams are waiting* (New Yorker). [compare Old Icelandic *skjōta* shoot]

**skeet|er** (skē′tər), *n.* **1** *U.S. Informal.* a mosquito. **2** a small sailboat for riding on ice; iceboat. [alteration of *mosquito*]

**skeet|shoot** (skēt′shüt′), *v.i.,* **-shot, -shoot|ing.** to shoot at clay pigeons in the sport of skeet; engage in skeet. **—skeet′shoot′er,** *n.*

**skee|zicks** or **skee|sicks** (skē′ziks), *n. U.S. Slang.* **1** a worthless fellow; chap. **2** a mischievous child (usually applied playfully). [American English; origin unknown]

**skeg** (skeg), *n.* **1** the part of a ship's keel nearest the stern. **2** a projection of the afterpart of a ship's keel for the support of a rudder. **3** a fin or rudder on a surfboard. [< Dutch *schegge,* perhaps < Scandinavian (compare Old Icelandic *skegg* a beak, beard)]

**skeg|ger** (skeg′ər), *n.* a salmon of the first year; a smolt. [origin uncertain]

**skeigh** (skēʜ), *adj. Scottish.* **1** (of horses) skittish; mettlesome; spirited. **2** (of persons) not easily approached or mastered; disdainful or proud. [compare Old English *scēoh* shy]

**skein** (skān), *n., v. —n.* **1** a small, coiled bundle of yarn or thread. There are 120 yards in a skein of cotton yarn. **2** *Figurative.* a confused tangle: *Freights entering the yard are pushed up an ar-*

***skeleton**
definition 1a

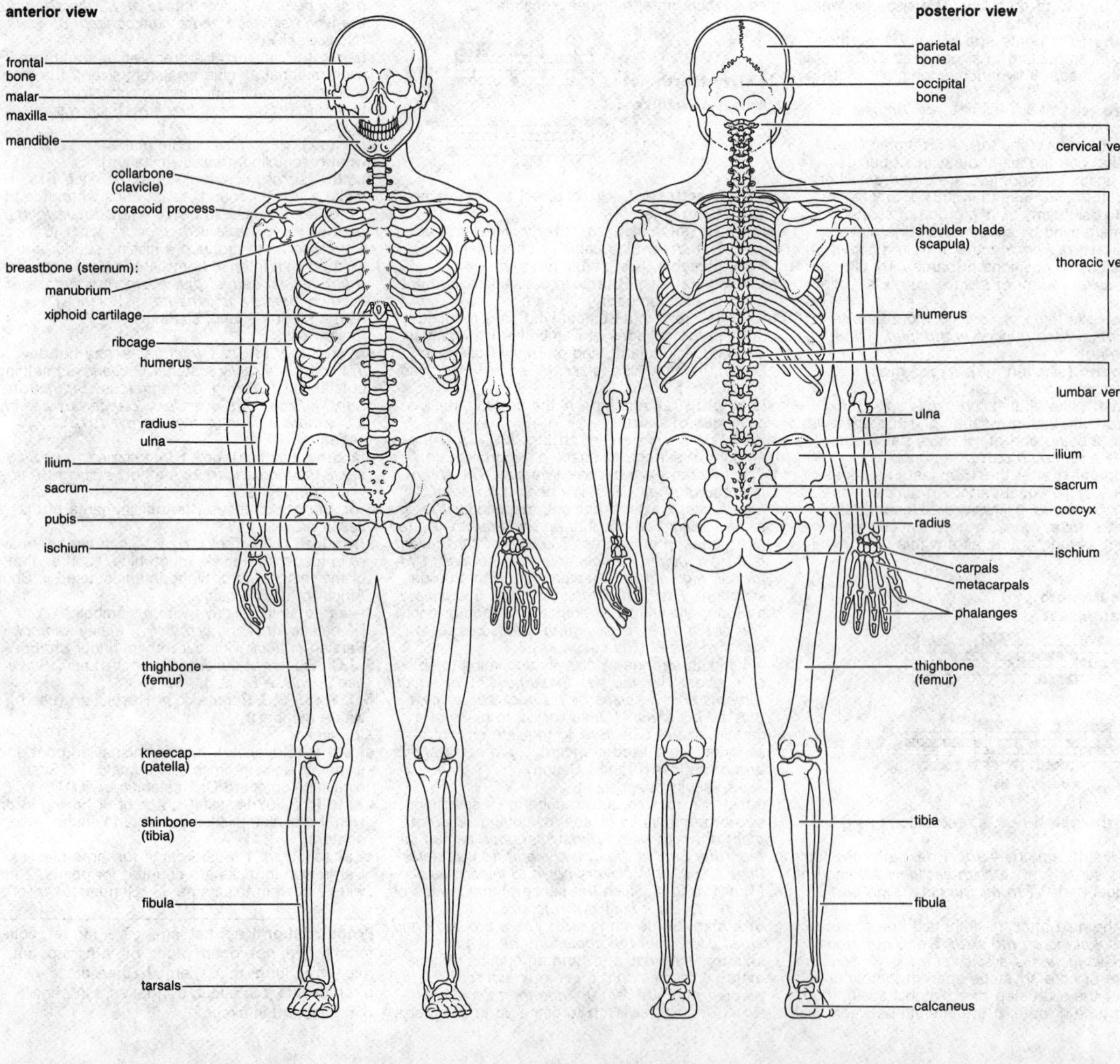

**anterior view**

frontal bone
malar
maxilla
mandible
collarbone (clavicle)
coracoid process
breastbone (sternum):
manubrium
xiphoid cartilage
ribcage
humerus
radius
ulna
ilium
sacrum
pubis
ischium
thighbone (femur)
kneecap (patella)
shinbone (tibia)
fibula
tarsals

**posterior view**

parietal bone
occipital bone
cervical vertebrae
shoulder blade (scapula)
thoracic vertebrae
humerus
lumbar vertebrae
ulna
ilium
sacrum
coccyx
radius
ischium
carpals
metacarpals
phalanges
thighbone (femur)
tibia
fibula
calcaneus

tificial "hump," uncoupled, then allowed to roll into a skein of classification tracks* (Newsweek). **3** a small cluster or arrangement like a skein. **4** a flight or group of wild geese or ducks. **5** *Figurative.* an unbroken string or series: *Constance's unbeaten skein in this country was stopped at six* (New York Times).

*—v.t.* to make into skeins: *to skein thread.*

[< Old French *escaigne*]

**skein|er** (skā′nər), *n.* a person or machine that winds yarn into skeins.

**skel|e|tal** (skel′ə təl), *adj.* **1** of or like a skeleton. **2** attached to, forming, or formed by a skeleton; *The movement of your body is made possible by the skeletal muscles; that is, the muscles that are attached to the bones* (Beauchamp, Mayfield, and West).

**skel|e|tal|ly** (skel′ə tə lē), *adv.* with reference to skeletal structure.

**skel|e|tog|e|nous** (skel ə toj′ə nəs), *adj.* producing a skeleton; giving rise to a skeleton; osteogenetic: *skeletogenous tissue.*

***skel|e|ton** (skel′ə tən), *n., adj.* *—n.* **1a** the bones of a body, fitted together in their natural places. The skeleton is a frame that supports the muscles and organs of the body and protects the soft internal organs. *By looking at a human skeleton ... you quickly see that there is a central column of bones to which the ribs and the bones of our arms and legs are attached* (Beauchamp, Mayfield, and West). See the picture on the opposite page. **b** the hard supporting or covering part of an invertebrate animal, such as the shell of a mollusk or crustacean. **2** a very thin person or animal: *A long illness made a skeleton out of him.* **3** a frame: *the steel skeleton of a building.* **SYN**: framework. **4** *Figurative.* the basic features or elements; outline: *the skeleton of a poem.* **SYN**: sketch, draft.

*—adj.* **1** of, like, or consisting of a skeleton. **2** *Figurative.* greatly reduced in numbers; fractional: *Only a skeleton crew was needed while the ship was tied up in dock.*

**skeleton at the feast**, a reminder of gloomy or depressing things in the midst of pleasure (because the Egyptians used to have a skeleton or mummy at feasts as a reminder of death): *With her constant complaints, she was always the skeleton at the feast.*

**skeleton in the closet** (**cupboard**, or **house**), a secret source of embarrassment, grief, or shame, especially to a family; hidden domestic trouble: *Some particulars regarding the Newcome family, which will show us that they have a skeleton or two in their closets, as well as their neighbours* (Thackeray).

[< New Latin *sceleton* < Greek *skeletón* (*sôma*) dried up (body) < *skéllein* dry out (up)] **—skel′e|ton|less**, *adj.* **—skel′e|ton|like′**, *adj.*

**skeleton clock**, a clock that has no case, so that the interior wheelwork is visible.

**skeleton construction**, a type of construction, used especially for skyscrapers, in which all loads are transmitted to the foundation by a rigidly constructed framework of beams, girders, and columns.

**skel|e|ton|ic** (skel′ə ton′ik), *adj.* **1** of a skeleton; like that of a skeleton. **2** skeletonlike; meager: *A young Italian painter whose skeletonic works ... are currently having a big success in the U.S.* (Life).

**skel|e|ton|ize** (skel′ə tə nīz), *v.*, **-ized**, **-iz|ing**. *—v.t.* **1** to make a skeleton of; reduce to a skeleton. **2** *Figurative.* to draw up in outline; sketch out; outline: *a skeletonized report.* **3** *Figurative.* to reduce greatly in numbers: *Lack of money forced the country to maintain only a skeletonized air force.* *—v.i.* to become a skeleton.

**skel|e|ton|iz|er** (skel′ə tə nī′zər), *n.* an insect which reduces leaves to skeletons.

**skeleton key**, a key made to open many locks. A skeleton key is often a thin, light key with most of the bit filed away.

**skel|lum** (skel′əm), *n. Archaic.* a rascal; scamp. [< Dutch *schelm* < German *Schelm*]

**skelp**[1] (skelp), *n., v. Scottish.* *—n.* a slapping blow or noise; smack.

*—v.t.* to slap; smack: *In the year you refer to ... I was getting skelped in the parish school* (Robert Louis Stevenson).

*—v.i.* to hurry: *Skelping about here, destroying the few deer that are left* (Scott).

[probably imitative]

**skelp**[2] (skelp), *n.* a strip of steel or iron used to make a pipe or tube.

**skel|ter** (skel′tər), *v.i.* to dash along; rush; hurry. [< short for *helter-skelter*]

**Skel|ton|ic** (skel ton′ik), *adj.* of, having to do with, or characteristic of John Skelton, the English poet, 1460?-1529, or his writings: *Skeltonic verse.*

**Skel|ton|ics** (skel ton′iks), *n.pl.* short, irregular lines of verse with frequent recurrence of the same rhyme.

**ske|ne**[1] (skē′nē), *n., pl.* **-nai** (-nī). the stage of an ancient Greek theater. [< Greek *skēnē* stage; scene]

**skene**[2] (shkēn, skēn), *n.* = skean.

**skep** (skep), *n.* **1** = beehive. **2** a large, deep basket; hamper. **3** the quantity of coal, grain, or other loose material held by a container of a certain size.

[Middle English *sceppe* < Scandinavian (compare Old Icelandic *skeppa* basket)]

**skep|sis** (skep′sis), *n.* philosophic doubt; skeptical philosophy. Also, **scepsis**. [< Greek *sképsis* < *sképtesthai* reflect]

**Skep|tic** (skep′tik), *n.* a member or adherent of an ancient Greek school of philosophy that maintained that real knowledge of things is impossible. Also, **Sceptic**. [< Latin *Sceptici*, plural < Greek *sképtikoi* < *skeptikós* reflective < *sképtesthai* reflect]

**skep|tic** (skep′tik), *n., adj.* *—n.* **1** a person who questions the truth of theories or apparent facts; doubter: *The skeptic doth neither affirm, neither deny, any position; but doubteth of it* (Sir Walter Raleigh). **2** a person who doubts or questions the possibility or certainty of our knowledge of anything. **3** a person who doubts the truth of religious doctrines, or of religion in general: *The smugness has gone out of cynicism and the skeptics are asking the questions which will lead at length to affirmation of some kind* (Atlantic). **SYN**: unbeliever, disbeliever, agnostic.

*—adj.* doubting; skeptical. Also, **sceptic**.

[< *Skeptic*]

**skep|ti|cal** (skep′tə kəl), *adj.* **1** of or like a skeptic; inclined to doubt; not believing easily: *a skeptical person.* **SYN**: doubting, incredulous, disbelieving, distrustful. **2** questioning the truth of theories or apparent facts: *a skeptical remark, a skeptical approach.* Also, **sceptical**. **—skep′ti|cal|ly**, *adv.* **—skep′ti|cal|ness**, *n.*

**skep|ti|cism** (skep′tə siz əm), *n.* **1** skeptical attitude; doubt; unbelief: *A wise skepticism is the first attribute of a good critic* (Lowell). *His skepticism made him distrustful of dreamy meddlers* (Atlantic). **SYN**: incredulity, mistrust, distrust. **2** doubt or disbelief with regard to religion: *Since skepticism was current, even during the Middle Ages, there were those who scoffed* (Newsweek). **3** the philosophical doctrine that nothing can be proved absolutely, and thus real knowledge of any kind is impossible. Also, **scepticism**.

**skep|ti|cize** (skep′tə sīz), *v.i.*, **-cized**, **-ciz|ing**. to act the skeptic; doubt; profess to doubt of everything. Also, **scepticize**.

**sker|rick** (sker′ik), *n. Australian.* the least possible amount; smallest piece: *There isn't a skerrick of meat in the pot.* [origin uncertain]

**sker|ry** (sker′ē), *n., pl.* **-ries**. *Scottish.* an isolated rock, a rocky island, or a reef. [< Old Icelandic *sker* reef]

**sketch** (skech), *n., v.* *—n.* **1** a rough, quickly done drawing, painting, clay model, or design: *The artist made many sketches in pencil before painting the portrait.* **2** an outline; plan: *Give me a sketch of his career.* **SYN**: draft, brief. **3** a short description, story, or account: *He gave us a sketch of the accident leaving out the gory details.* **4** a short play or performance, usually of light or comic nature.

*—v.t.* **1** to make a sketch of; draw roughly: *He sketched the mountains many times before making a painting of them.* **SYN**: outline, delineate. **2** to describe briefly, generally, or in outline: *Montesquieu sketched a government which should make liberty its end* (George Bancroft).

*—v.i.* to make a sketch; draw, paint, or model sketches: *She sketched for several hours before drawing the final plans.*

[< Dutch *schets* < Italian *schizzo* < Latin *schedium* extemporaneous poem < Greek *schédios* impromptu] **—sketch′er**, *n.*

**sketch|a|ble** (skech′ə bəl), *adj.* suitable for being sketched.

**sketch|block** (skech′blok′), *n.* a pad of paper for sketching on.

**sketch|book** (skech′bůk′), *n.*, or **sketch book**, **1** a book to draw or paint sketches in: *In the sketchbook were 35 exquisite drawings no bigger than his hand* (Time). **2** a book of short descriptions, stories, or plays: *Washington Irving's "Sketch Book."*

**sketch|i|ly** (skech′ə lē), *adv.* in a sketchy manner: (*Figurative.*) *a sketchily planned trip.* **SYN**: incompletely, slightly, imperfectly.

**sketch|i|ness** (skech′ē nis), *n.* the condition or quality of being sketchy.

**sketch map**, a map prepared without accurate measurement.

**sketch plan**, the first plan of a building, design; etc., suggesting matter to be developed in later detailed drawings.

**sketch|y** (skech′ē), *adj.*, **sketch|i|er**, **sketch|i|est**. **1** like a sketch; having or giving only outlines or main features. **2** *Figurative.* incomplete; done very roughly; slight; imperfect: *a sketchy recollection of an event, a sketchy costume. In his hurry he had only a sketchy meal.* **SYN**: unfinished, crude.

**skete** (skēt), *n.* a community of monks or hermits of the Greek Church. [< New Greek *skêtos* < Greek *askêtês* monk, ascetic]

**skew** (skyü), *adj., n., v.* *—adj.* **1** twisted to one side; slanting. **SYN**: askew, awry. **2** *Geometry.* not included in the same plane: *Skew lines do not intersect and are not parallel.* **3** having a part that deviates from a straight line, right angle, or the like: *a skew chisel, a skew facet.* **SYN**: crooked, bent. **4** not symmetrical. [< verb]

*—n.* **1** a slant; twist: *As alignment is lost, flutter and skew set in* (Scientific American). **2** a sideward movement.

[< verb or adjective]

*—v.i.* **1** to slant; twist. **2** to turn aside; swerve. **3** *Figurative.* to look suspiciously or slightingly.

*—v.t.* **1** to give a slanting form, position or direction, to. **2** *Figurative.* to represent unfairly; distort. **3** *Statistics.* to cause (a normal curve or distribution) to taper off to the right or left.

**on the** (or **a**) **skew**, on the slant; slantwise: *Over the Lune, which is crossed on the skew, the span is 350 ft.* (London Times).

[< Old North French *eskiuer* shy away from, eschew < Germanic (compare Old High German *sciuhen*)]

**skew arch**, an arch whose axis is not perpendicular to the face of the wall or member against which it abuts.

**skew|back** (skyü′bak′), *n.* **1** a sloping surface against which the end of an arch rests: *This skewback bearing is intended to support the end reactions of a road bridge ...* (New Science). **2** a stone, course of masonry, iron plate, or the like, with such a surface.

**skew|bald** (skyü′bôld′), *adj., n.* *—adj.* (of horses) irregularly marked with patches of white, brown, or red.

*—n.* a skewbald horse: *Crompton, on his skewbald, was the only scorer* (London Times).

[Middle English *skewed*. Compare etym. under **piebald**.]

**skew curve**, a curve in three dimensions.

**skew|er** (skyü′ər), *n., v.* *—n.* **1** a long pin of wood or metal stuck through meat to hold it together while it is cooking. **2** something shaped or used like a long pin.

*—v.t.* **1** to fasten with a skewer or skewers: *I ... jammed the hat on my head and skewered it savagely with the pins* (Arnold Bennett). **2** to pierce with a skewer: *Whole new fields are opening up for free divers, who, like Cousteau, soon tire of skewering fish as too easy* (Time).

[earlier *skiver;* origin uncertain]

**skew|er|wood** (skyü′ər wůd′), *n.* = spindle tree.

**skew-gee** (skyü′jē′), *adv., adj. Informal.* *—adv.* crookedly; askew.

*—adj.* crooked; skew; squint.

**skew|ness** (skyü′nis), *n.* **1** the quality of being skew; one-sidedness; distortion. **2** *Statistics.* asymmetry, especially of a frequency distribution: *Skewness is the degree that a group of items varies from a normal frequency curve* (Emory S. Bogardus).

**skew|whiff** (skyü′hwif′), *adj., adv. British Dialect.* askew; awry.

**ski** (skē; *Norwegian* shē), *n., pl.* **skis** or **ski**, *v.*, **skied**, **ski|ing**. *—n.* **1** one of a pair of long, flat, slender pieces of hard wood, plastic, or light metal curved upward at the front and fastened by straps or special harness to the shoes to enable a person to glide over snow: *With a pair of skis, a skilled traveler may keep up with a herd of reindeer and travel as many as seventy miles a day with a heavy pack* (Beals and Hoijer). **2** a skilike device fastened to the undercarriage of an airplane and used in place of wheels for landings on snow, mud, sand, or the like: *A Navy R4D (a modified DC-3) ... [made] a tricky ski landing—the first landing ever made at the South Pole* (Time). **3** = water ski.

*—v.i.* **1** to glide over snow on skis: *to learn to ski. They tramped, they skated, they skied* (Sinclair Lewis). **2** = water-ski.

*—v.t.* **1** to go or travel over on skis: *Ski Vermont!* (Harper's). **2** to put skis on; supply with skis: *When you are properly booted and skied, you must take the next big step* (Saturday Review). Also, **skee**.

[< Norwegian *ski*. Compare Old Icelandic *skīth* snowshoe] **—ski′like′**, *adj.*

**Pronunciation Key:** hat, āge, cãre, fär; let, ēqual, tėrm; it, īce; hot, ōpen, ôrder; oil, out; cup, půt, rüle; child; long; thin; ᴛʜen; zh, measure; ə represents **a** in about, **e** in taken, **i** in pencil, **o** in lemon, **u** in circus.

**ski|a|ble** (skē′ə bəl), *adj.* that can be skied on: *a skiable mountain.*

**ski|a|gram** (skī′ə gram), *n.* **1** = skiagraph. **2** an outline of the shadow of an object filled in with black.

**ski|a|gram|mat|ic** (skī′ə grə mat′ik), *adj.* = radiographic. — **ski′a|gram|mat′i|cal|ly**, *adv.*

**ski|a|graph** (skī′ə graf, -gräf), *n., v.* — ***n.*** a radiograph; X-ray picture.
— ***v.t.*** to take an X-ray photograph of. Also, **skiograph**.
[< Greek *skiâ* shadow + English *-graph*]

**ski|ag|ra|pher** (skī ag′rə fər), *n.* **1** = radiographer. **2** anyone concerned with skiagraphy. Also, **skiographer**.

**ski|a|graph|ic** (skī′ə graf′ik), *adj.* having to do with skiagraphy. Also, **skiographic**.

**ski|ag|ra|phy** (skī ag′rə fē), *n.* **1** = radiography. **2** the drawing of shadows or skiagrams.

**ski|a|scope** (skī′ə skōp), *n.* an instrument used in testing the refractive condition of the eye; retinoscope. [< Greek *skiâ* shadow + English *-scope*]

**ski|as|co|py** (skī as′kə pē), *n.* a method of testing the refractive condition of the eye; retinoscopy.

**ski bob**, a vehicle for sliding downhill on snow, consisting of a metal frame with handle bars connected to a short pivoting ski in front, and a seat attached to a longer fixed ski in the back. The rider usually wears small skis for balance.

**ski bobber**, a person who rides a ski bob.

**ski bobbing**, the act or sport of riding a ski bob.

**ski boot**, a boot of sturdy leather, specially made for protecting the foot, worn for skiing.

**ski bum** *U.S. Slang.* a skiing enthusiast, especially one who drifts from job to job so that he may travel around to be near ski slopes and skiers.

**skice** (skīs), *v.i.,* **skiced, skic|ing.** *British Dialect.* to run fast; move quickly; scurry. [origin unknown]

**skid**[1] (skid), *v.,* **skid|ded, skid|ding,** *n.* — ***v.i.*** **1** to slip or slide sideways while moving: *The car skidded on the slippery road.* **2** to slide along without turning, as a wheel does when held by a skid or brake. **3** (of an aircraft) to slide or be carried sideways, as when not banked enough while turning.
— ***v.t.*** **1** to slide along on a skid or skids. **2** to prevent (a wheel) from turning by means of a skid. **3** to cause (a vehicle or its wheels) to slide sideways while moving. **4** to haul (logs) from the cutting area to the landing or mill.
— ***n.*** **1** a sideways slip or slide while moving: *She had a skid running around the corner and fell on the wet floor.* **2** a piece of wood or metal to prevent a wheel from turning, as when going down a hill. **3** a timber, frame, or the like, on which something rests, or on which something heavy may slide. **4** a runner on the bottom of an airplane to enable the airplane to slide along the ground when landing. **5** a slightly raised wooden platform for carrying loads: *I was working for a florist back in the shambling thirties when iced skids of 250 roses sold for $2 at Faneuil Hall* (Atlantic).
**on the skids**, *Slang.* **a** headed for dismissal, failure, or other disaster; failing; slipping: *[He] is said to suspect that pro-French Americans are trying to withhold further U.S. aid and thus put him on the skids* (Newsweek). **b** on the way down; on the downgrade: *The aging boxer was plainly on the skids.*
**put the skids under**, *Informal.* to cause (someone or something) to head for failure or disaster; cause the ruin or downfall of: *This has really put the skids under Pearson. This is the knockout blow* (Time).
[origin uncertain. Compare Old Frisian *skīd* stick of wood. See related etym. at **ski**.]

**skid**[2] (skid), *v.i.,* **skid|ded, skid|ding.** to run or go quickly; scud. [variant of *scud*]

**skid|der** (skid′ər), *n.* **1** a person or thing that skids. **2** a person who uses a skid.

**skid|doo** (ski dü′), *v.i. Slang.* to be off; depart; vamoose. [American English, perhaps < *skedaddle,* or < *skid*[2]]

**skid|dy** (skid′ē), *adj.* liable to cause skidding.

**skid fin**, a finlike vertical plane set across the upper wing of some early aircraft to increase lateral stability.

**ski|doo** (ski dü′, skē′dü), *n.* **1** a motorized sledge, usually seating two, moving on endless tracks in the back and movable skis in front, used for travel on snow or ice. **2 Ski-Doo.** a trademark for this vehicle.

**skid|pan** (skid′pan′), *n.* **1** a water- or oil-covered circular course that simulates skidding conditions, used to test automobile tires or to train motorists to control cars on slippery surfaces: *The skidpan gives a maximum diameter turning circle of more than 400 feet* (London Times). **2** a device for slowing down the rotation of the wheels of a vehicle; drag.

**skid|proof** (skid′prüf′), *adj.* that prevents skidding or slipping: *skidproof soles on shoes, a skidproof surface on a bridge.*

**skid road**, (in lumbering) **1** a road over which logs are dragged, usually with heavy skids partly sunk in the ground. **2** Often, **Skid Road.** = skid row.

**skid row**, a slum street or section full of cheap saloons, rooming houses, and the like, frequented by derelict men: *Many management men still stereotype an alcoholic as a red-nosed skid row bum* (Wall Street Journal).

**skid|way** (skid′wā′), *n.* **1a** two logs or timbers laid parallel at right angles to a road, on which to pile a tier of logs for loading. **b** a way or path down which logs can slide as on a skid. **2** a wide, sloping tunnel in the rear of a whaling factory ship, leading from water level up to the work deck, used to drag the whale out of the water.

**skied**[1] (skēd), *v.* the past tense and past participle of **ski**.

**skied**[2] (skīd), *v.* a past tense and past participle of **sky**.

**ski|er** (skē′ər), *n.* a person who uses or travels on skis: *an expert skier.*

**skies** (skīz), *n.* the plural of **sky**: *cloudy skies.*

***skiff** (skif), *n.* **1** a small, light rowboat with a rounded bottom and flat stern. **2** a small, light boat with a mast for a single triangular sail. [< French *esquif* < Italian *schifo* < Germanic (compare Old High German *schif*). See related etym. at **ship**.]

***skiff** definition 1

**skif|fle** (skif′əl), *n., v.,* **-fled, -fling.** *Especially British.* — ***n.*** a type of Dixieland jazz in which folk or popular songs are rendered to a rapid beat by small groups playing guitars and improvised instruments such as washboards, bottles, and jugs: *U.S. rock 'n' roll, commercial hillbilly and folk music, warmed over and juiced up in a mishmash called skiffle* (Time).
— ***v.i.*** to play skiffle.

**skif|fler** (skif′lər), *n. Especially British.* a person who plays skiffle.

**ski flying**, the sport of jumping on skis to cover as much ground as possible: *In ski flying, only distance counts, with no marks for form* (James O. Dunaway).

**ski|ing** (skē′ing), *n.* the act or sport of gliding over snow on skis: *to be skillful at skiing.*

***ski|jor|ing** (skē jôr′ing, -jōr′-), *n.* a sport in which a person is towed on skis over snow or ice by a horse or vehicle. [American English < Norwegian *skijøring* < *ski* ski + *kjøring* driving]

***skijoring**

**ski jump**, **1** a jump made by a person on skis off the end of an elevated runway. **2** an elevated runway for making such a jump.

**ski-jump** (skē′jump′), *v.i.* to make a ski jump or jumps: *The ... photo editor wanted a picture of him ski-jumping* (Maclean's).

**skil|ful** (skil′fəl), *adj.* = skillful. — **skil′ful|ly**, *adv.* — **skil′ful|ness**, *n.*

***ski lift**, any one of various mechanisms for transporting skiers to the top of a slope, such as a chair running on a suspended cable: *Liechtenstein has no ski lifts; the husky young Olympians must hike up the steep Alpine slopes on foot* (Time).

**skill**[1] (skil), *n.* **1** ability gained by practice or knowledge; expertness: *to drive a car with skill. The trained teacher managed the children with skill. He had conducted an important negotiation with skill and tact* (Lytton Strachey). **SYN**: facility, proficiency. **2** ability to do things well with one's body or with tools: *It takes great skill to tune a piano. Not everyone has the skill to become a watchmaker.* **SYN**: dexterity, deftness, adroitness. **3** work that requires expert ability; art or craft: *to master the carpenter's skill, a lawyer's skill.* **4** *Obsolete.* cause; reason: *I think you have as little skill to fear as I have purpose to put you to't* (Shakespeare). [< Scandinavian (compare Old Icelandic *skil* discernment < *skilja* distinguish, separate, part)]

**skill**[2] (skil), *v.i. Archaic.* **1** to make a difference; matter: *Whate'er he be, it skills not much, we'll fit him to our turn* (Shakespeare). **2** to avail; help: *Whatever we say skills but little.* [Middle English *skilen* cause a distinction; earlier, to separate < Scandinavian (compare Old Icelandic *skilja*)]

**skilled** (skild), *adj.* **1** having skill; trained; experienced: *A carpenter is a skilled workman.* **SYN**: See syn. under **expert**. **2** showing skill; requiring skill: *a skilled piece of work. Plastering is skilled labor.*

**skil|less** (skil′lis), *adj.* lacking skill; unskilled; unskillful: *Let me see the wound; I am not quite skilless* (Byron). — **skil′less|ness**, *n.*

**skil|let** (skil′it), *n.* **1** a shallow pan with a long handle, used for frying. **2** a saucepan with a long handle. [origin uncertain]

**skill|ful** (skil′fəl), *adj.* **1** having skill; expert: *He is a very skillful surgeon.* **SYN**: dexterous, deft, adroit, proficient. **2** showing skill: *That is a skillful piece of bricklaying.* **SYN**: dexterous, deft, adroit, proficient. Also, **skilful**. — **skill′ful|ness**, *n.*

**skill|ful|ly** (skil′fə lē), *adv.* with skill; expertly.

**skil|ling** (skil′ing), *n.* a copper coin and money of account formerly used in Scandinavian countries, having a value of less than one cent. [< Danish *skilling.* Compare etym. under **shilling**.]

**skil|lion** (skil′yən), *n. Australian.* a lean-to or shed. [alteration of dialectal English *skilling,* Middle English *skelyng,* probably of Scandinavian origin]

**skill-less** (skil′lis), *adj.* = skilless. — **skill′-less|ness**, *n.*

**skil|ly** (skil′ē), *n. British.* **1** a thin, watery soup or gruel formerly fed to prisoners and paupers. **2** a drink made of oatmeal, sugar, and water formerly served to sailors in the British navy. [shortened < *skilligalee,* probably a fanciful formation]

**skim** (skim), *v.,* **skimmed, skim|ming,** *n., adj.*
— ***v.t.*** **1** to remove from the top: *Mother skims the fat from her homemade soup.* **2** to take something from the top of: *She skims the soup to remove most of the fat.* **3** to move lightly over: *gulls skimming the water. The pebble I threw skimmed the little waves. The skaters skimmed the ice.* **4** to cause to fly lightly; send skimming: *You can skim a flat stone over the water.* **5** to read hastily; read with omissions: *It took me an hour to skim the book.* **6** to cover with a thin layer such as of ice or scum.
— ***v.i.*** **1** to move lightly (over or through): *skaters skimming over the ice, to skim through the newspaper headlines.* **2** to glide along: *The swallows were skimming by.* **3** to become covered as with a thin layer of ice or scum: *The pond skimmed over with ice during the night.*
— ***n.*** **1** something which is skimmed off. **2** = skim milk. **3** a skimming or moving lightly.
— ***adj.*** skimmed.
[perhaps variant of *scum,* or < Old French *escumer* < *escume* scum < Germanic (compare Old High German *scûm*)]

**ski mask**, a head covering of knitted material, with holes for the eyes and mouth, used by skiers to protect the face from the wind and cold.

***ski lift**

**skim|ble-skam|ble** or **skim|ble-scam|ble** (skim′bəl skam′bəl, skim′əl skam′əl), *adj., n. Archaic.* — ***adj.*** rambling; confused; silly: *Such a deal of skimble-scamble stuff, as puts me from my faith* (Shakespeare).
— ***n.*** nonsense; gabble.
[varied reduplication of earlier *scamble* to struggle in an undignified manner, scramble for; origin uncertain]

**skimmed milk**, = skim milk.

**skim|mer** (skim′ər), *n.* **1** a person or thing that skims. **2** a shallow ladle, full of holes, with a long handle. It is used in skimming liquids. **3** a kind of sea bird that skims the surface of the water to get food; scissorbill. The skimmers comprise a family of birds, related to the gulls. **4** a man's or woman's straw hat with a flat crown and wide brim: *Not since the heyday of the Homburg and the skimmer have hat makers had so much to be happy about* (Wall Street Journal). **5** *U.S.* a simply cut dress with straight lines, often sleeveless and with a round neck: *A dress that could be all things to all women is a skimmer ... of flannel with small sleeves* (New York Times). **6** any one of various clams or scallops: *We ... watched Olaf [the walrus] munch some skimmer clams and herring out of a pail* (New Yorker).

**skim milk**, milk from which the cream has been removed.

**skim|ming** (skim′ing), *n.* **1** the act of one that skims. **2** that which is skimmed off: *greasy skimmings from soup.* **3** the practice of concealing a part of the winnings of a gambling casino to avoid paying taxes.

**skimmings**, *Metallurgy.* dross.

**skimming dish**, **1a** a shallow dish used in skimming liquids; skimmer. **b** *Figurative: The adherents of the inexplicable ... hinted that their antagonists were mere skimming dishes in point of depth* (George Eliot). **2** a kind of shallow sailboat or speedboat.

**skim|ming|ton** (skim′ing tən), *n.* **1** a burlesque procession or serenade formerly held in ridicule of a henpecked husband, common in villages and country districts of England. **2** *U.S. Dialect.* a mock serenade for newly married persons; shivaree.

**Ski|mo** (skē′mō), *n. Canadian Slang.* an Eskimo (used in an unfriendly way).

**ski|mo|bile** (skē′mə bēl), *n.* a small automobile running on tracks, for carrying skiers to the top of a slope.

**skimp** (skimp), *v., adj.* —*v.t.* **1** to supply in too small an amount: *Don't skimp the butter in making a cake.* **2** to do imperfectly: *The lazy boy skimped his job.*

—*v.i.* **1** to be very saving or economical: *She had to skimp to send her daughter to college.* **2** to do something imperfectly: *He was always skimping on his assignments.*

—*adj.* scanty; skimpy.

[origin uncertain. Compare etym. under **scrimp**.] —**skimp′ing|ly**, *adv.*

**skimp|y** (skim′pē), *adj.*, **skimp|i|er, skimp|i|est.** **1** not enough; scanty: *a skimpy bathing suit. He got hungry in the afternoon after a skimpy lunch.* **SYN:** meager. **2** too saving or economical. **SYN:** parsimonious. —**skimp′i|ly**, *adv.* —**skimp′i|ness**, *n.*

★**skin** (skin), *n., adj., v.*, **skinned, skin|ning.** —*n.* **1** the covering of the body in persons, animals, and plants, especially when soft and flexible: *Cows have thick skins. He slipped on a banana skin. The skin is the largest organ of the body and, next to the brain, the most complicated* (Science News Letter). **2a** the covering of an animal when stripped from the body to be dressed or tanned; hide; pelt: *The skin of a calf makes soft leather. The numbers of rabbits also fluctuate with the seasons, as can be seen from figures for exports of carcasses and skins* (Fenner and Day). **b** a container made of the hide of an animal for holding liquids: *a waterskin, a wineskin.* **3a** the planking or iron plating covering the ribs or frame of a ship. **b** the outside covering or casing of an aircraft, rocket, or spacecraft: *... heat-resistant alloys for use in the skins of missiles* (Time). **c** an outside covering, especially a metal covering, as of a trailer truck, freight container, or Quonset hut. **d** *Architecture.* a curtain wall, especially of lightweight metal or glass: *The outer skin of the building ... is composed of two-story aluminum frames* (Wall Street Journal). **4** *Slang.* a cheat; swindler. **5** *Slang.* a skinflint. **6** *Slang.* a dollar: *We get only the 75 skins a month ... And we can prove it* (Time). **7** *Slang.* a drum: *He beats the skins with a fine, off-beat flavor* (New York Times).

—*adj.* **1** of the skin; having to do with skin: *skin care, skin cream, skin cancer, a skin graft.* **2** *Slang.* having to do with nudity and sex; pornographic: *skin magazines, skin films, a skin book.*

—*v.t.* **1** to strip, rub, or scrape the skin off: *He skinned his knees when he fell. The hunter skinned the deer.* **2** to cover with or as if with skin: *It will but skin and film the ulcerous place* (Shakespeare). **3** *Slang.* to swindle, especially of money; cheat; defraud. **4** *U.S. Slang.* to skin-pop: *He quickly goes from "snorting" to "skinning" to "mainlining" heroin* (Science News).

—*v.i.* **1** to become covered with skin; form a new skin: *The wound gradually skinned over.* **2** to shed skin. **3** *Figurative.* to pass barely; slip by narrowly: *We skinned past a seething snag* (New Yorker). **4** *U.S. Slang.* to skin-pop.

**beneath the skin**, = under the skin.

**by** (or **with**) **the skin of one's teeth**, with nothing to spare; by a very narrow margin; barely: *About half way through I began to fear that the joke could not be sustained, but it was—by the skin of its teeth* (Listener). *His eldest son was implicated in the robbery ..., and came off by the skin of his teeth* (Nation).

**get under one's skin, a** to make one overly sensitive; irritate or annoy: *Don't let your opponents and what they say about you get under your skin* (Hubert H. Humphrey). **b** to affect emotionally; stimulate or excite: *Venice gets under your skin, all right, and it stays there. Once you've been a part of it, ... Venice will always be a part of you* (New Yorker).

**give** (or **get**) **skin**, *U.S. Slang.* to touch or shake hands in greeting: *The black expression "Give me some skin" has now become ... common among characters asking for a handshake* (New Yorker).

**have a thick** (or **thin**) **skin**, to be insensitive (or too sensitive) to criticism, reproach, or the like: *Don't worry about hurting his feelings; he has a thick skin.*

**in** (or **with**) **a whole skin**, safe and sound: *He was besides in a very great fright, For a whole skin he liked to be in* (Robert Southey).

**jump out of one's skin**, to jump with extreme delight, excitement, high spirits, or surprise: *Scipio ... was ready to jump out of his skin for joy at the sight of me* (Benjamin H. Malkin).

**no skin off one's nose** (**back, teeth**, or other part of the body), *Slang.* not one's concern; of no consequence or interest to one: *If Mr. Horvitz doesn't come into the service, it's no skin off my nose* (Jon C. Suggs).

**save one's skin**, to escape without harm: *He was taken prisoner ... and had to turn Dervish to save his skin* (Sir Arthur Conan Doyle).

**skin alive**, *Informal.* **a** to torture; flay: *They may skin me alive, if they please* (Benjamin Jowett). **b** *Figurative.* to scold severely: *His father will skin him alive if he comes home late.* **c** *Figurative.* to defeat completely: *Any amateur would be skinned alive competing against the world champion.*

**skin out**, *Slang.* to slip away, especially hastily; make off; escape: *I used to skin out of the old Sunday School ... every chance I got* (Sinclair Lewis).

**under the skin**, below the surface; basically: *The Dart and Plymouth [two cars] are "brothers under the skin." They are structurally alike, but somewhat different in appearance* (Wall Street Journal).

[< Scandinavian (compare Old Icelandic *skinn*)] —**skin′like′**, *adj.*

—*Syn. n.* **2a Skin, hide, pelt** mean the outer covering of the body of an animal. **Skin** is the general word, applying to the covering of a person or animal: *The skin of a baby is very soft.* **Hide** applies particularly to the tough skin of a large animal, commercially raw or tanned: *The hide of an elephant is tough.* **Pelt** applies particularly to the skin of a fur- or wool-bearing animal before dressing or tanning: *Trappers sell pelts of foxes; stores sell dressed skins.*

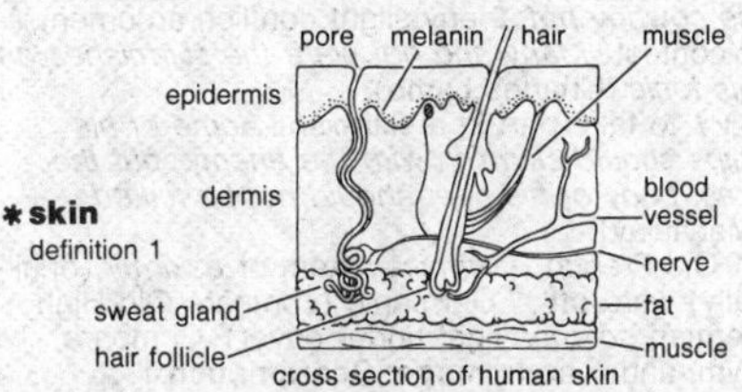

★**skin** definition 1

cross section of human skin

**skin and bones**, **1** extreme thinness or emaciation: *She languished and pined away to skin and bones* (Edward Herbert). **2** a very thin person: *"I like to eat," said Otto. "Not like ... skin and bones here"* (New Yorker).

**skin boat**, a boat made from animal skins extended over a frame: *Seals, walruses, and whales are used for the making of skin boats* (John C. Reed).

**skin-bound** (skin′bound′), *adj.* having the skin drawn tightly over the flesh.

**skin-deep** (skin′dēp′), *adj., adv.* —*adj.* no deeper than the skin; shallow; slight: *a skin-deep wound, beauty that is only skin-deep.*

—*adv.* in a superficial manner; slightly: (*Figurative.*) *Stings that have penetrated more than skin-deep into my mind* (Edmund Burke).

**skin disease**, a disease affecting the skin. Acne and eczema are skin diseases.

**skin-dive** (skin′dīv′), *v.i.*, **-dived, -div|ing.** to engage in skin diving: *Fish, skin-dive, or water-ski at ... Boca Chica lagoon* (New Yorker).

**skin diver**, a person engaged in skin diving as his work or as a sport; free diver.

**skin diving**, swimming about under water, sometimes at considerable depth and for long periods of time, usually equipped with a face mask, rubber flippers for the feet, and a portable breathing device; free diving: *As an ultimate in sports gear, an underwater camera has now been developed for the benefit of skin diving enthusiasts* (Newsweek).

**skin effect**, *Electricity.* a concentration of current density at the surface of a conductor, increasing with frequency and producing an increase in resistance.

**skin flick**, *Slang.* a pornographic motion picture.

**skin|flint** (skin′flint′), *n.* a mean, stingy person; miser: *And let him question such a thing as an appropriation for foreign aid to education; he is a skinflint without regard for the welfare of the world or even our own children* (Wall Street Journal).

**skin friction**, the friction developed between a solid and a fluid, especially the friction that occurs in the thin layer of air (boundary layer) over the surface of an aircraft moving at very high speeds, causing a sharp rise in temperature.

**skin|ful** (skin′fůl), *n., pl.* **-fuls. 1** as much as a skin for liquids can hold. **2a** *Informal.* as much as a person or animal can hold or drink. **b** *Slang.* as much as, or more than, one should drink at one time of alcoholic liquor.

**skin game**, *Informal.* a game or proceeding in which one is fleeced, cheated, or swindled: *The satellites fell victims to an incredible Soviet skin game. Poland was forced to buy Russian wheat at prices higher than Argentina's* (Newsweek).

**skin graft**, **1** a portion of skin surgically transferred from one part of a body to another or from one person to another person: *A thin skin graft is about one-thousandths of an inch thick and includes all of the epidermis ... and a little of the dermis* (William B. Youmans). **2** the act or fact of making such a graft.

**skin graft|ing** (graf′ting, gräf′-), the surgical transfer of healthy skin from one part of a body to another, or from one person to another, to replace skin destroyed by a burn or other injury.

**skin|head** (skin′hed′), *n.* a type of young British working-class tough who wears closely cropped hair, work clothes, and hobnailed boots, and engages in street fighting: *The skinheads ... specialize in terrorizing such menacing types as hippies and homosexuals, Pakistani immigrants and little old ladies* (Time).

**skin|head|ism** (skin′hed′iz əm), *n.* the practices of skinheads, especially the use of violence against members of minority groups.

**skink**[1] (skingk), *n.* any one of a family of small, smooth-scaled lizards, with no legs or with short, weak legs: *Many lizards that live on the ground can get along without any legs. Many kinds of skinks, for example, have no legs* (Clifford H. Pope). [< Latin *scincus* < Greek *skínkos*]

**skink**[2] (skingk), *v.t. Archaic.* to pour out or draw (liquor). [probably < Middle Dutch *schenken*]

**skink|er** (sking′kər), *n. Dialect.* a bartender; tapster: *If the skinker can't make your Dry Martini dry enough ...* (New Yorker).

**skin|less** (skin′lis), *adj.* having no skin or having a very thin skin: *skinless frankfurters.*

**skinned** (skind), *adj.* **1** stripped of the skin: *a skinned rabbit.* **2** *British.* peeled; alert: *"Her boy brought me a letter. You see I asked him to keep his eyes—skinned—is that the right word?"* (Graham Greene).

**-skinned**, *combining form.* having a ____ skin: *Dark-skinned = having a dark skin.*

**skin|ner** (skin′ər), *n.* **1** a person who skins animals. **2** a person who prepares or deals in skins and furs: *When the skinners got through with the forests, fireweed, scrub jack-pine, blueberries, and aspen took over the ravaged land* (Harper's). **3** = teamster. **4** = fleecer.

**Skinner box**, a box or cage, used in experiments with animal conditioning, in which an animal must learn to operate correctly a lever or other mechanism in order to escape punishment or obtain a reward. [< B. F. *Skinner*, born 1904, an American psychologist]

**Skin|ner|i|an** (ski nir′ē ən), *adj., n.* —*adj.* of or having to do with the ideas and theories of the American psychologist B. F. Skinner, especially his studies on controlling behavior through a system of rewards and reinforcements as practiced in operant conditioning and behavior therapy.

**Pronunciation Key:** hat, āge, cãre, fär; let, ēqual, tėrm; it, īce; hot, ōpen, ôrder; oil, out; cup, půt, rüle; child; long; thin; ᴛʜen; zh, measure; ə represents **a** in about, **e** in taken, **i** in pencil, **o** in lemon, **u** in circus.

—*n.* a supporter of B. F. Skinner or his theories.

**skin|ner|y** (skin′ər ē), *n., pl.* **-ner|ies.** 1 a place where skins are prepared, as for market. 2 *Obsolete.* skins or furs.

**skin|ni|ness** (skin′ē nis), *n.* skinny quality or condition.

**skin|ny** (skin′ē), *adj.,* **-ni|er, -ni|est.** 1 very thin; very lean: *The skinny boy didn't eat much.* SYN: gaunt, lank. 2 like skin.

**skin|ny-dip** (skin′ē dip′), *v.,* **-dipped, -dip|ping,** *n. U.S. Slang.* —*v.i.* to swim in the nude.
—*n.* a swim in the nude.

**skin|ny-dip|per** (skin′ē dip′ər), *n. U.S. Slang.* a person who swims in the nude.

**skin-pop** (skin′pop′), *v.t., v.i.,* **-popped, -popping.** *U.S. Slang.* to inject (a liquefied narcotic) just beneath the skin.

**skint** (skint), *adj. British Slang.* without money; penniless. [variant of *skinned*]

**skin test,** any test made on the skin, such as the Schick test or patch test, to determine susceptibility to a disease or allergic reaction to a substance.

**skin-tight** or **skin|tight** (skin′tīt′), *adj.* fitting closely to the skin; close-fitting.

**ski|o|gram** (skī′ə gram), *n.* = skiagram.

**ski|o|graph** (skī′ə graf, -gräf), *n., v.t.* = skiagraph.

**ski|og|ra|pher** (skī og′rə fər), *n.* = skiagrapher.

**ski|o|graph|ic** (skī′ə graf′ik), *adj.* = skiagraphic.

**skip**[1] (skip), *v.,* **skipped, skip|ping,** *n.* —*v.i.* **1a** to leap lightly; spring; jump: *Lambs skipped in the fields.* **b** to go along with light, springing movements: *The little girl skipped down the street.* 2 to go bounding along a surface. 3 to omit parts; pass from one thing to another, disregarding what is between: *Answer the questions in order without skipping. The art of reading is to skip judiciously* (Philip G. Hamerton). 4 *Figurative.* to change quickly, as from one task, pleasure, or subject, to another. 5 *Informal.* to leave in a hurry: *The revolutionary Polish officers, whom Bakúnin had been to pains to procure, gave the situation up and skipped out* (Edmund Wilson). 6 to advance in school by being promoted past the next regular grade or grades.
—*v.t.* 1 to spring or leap lightly over: *The girls skipped rope.* 2 to send bounding along a surface: *We like to skip stones on the lake.* **3a** to pass over; fail to notice; omit: *She skips the hard words when she reads.* SYN: disregard. **b** to advance past in being promoted in school: *I skipped a grade last year.* 4 *Informal, Figurative.* to dodge, avoid, or stay away from: *to skip school, to skip rehearsals.* 5 *Informal.* to leave (a place) in a hurry; flee: *The swindler has skipped town.*
—*n.* 1 a light leap, spring, or jump: *The child gave a skip of joy.* 2 a gait, especially of children, in which hops and steps are alternated. 3 the act or fact of passing over; omission. 4 that which is or may be skipped: *In his books there are scarcely any of those passages which, in our school days, we used to call skip* (Macaulay). 5 *Music.* a passing from one note to another more than one step away.
[compare Middle Swedish *skuppa,* Old Icelandic *skipa* undergo a change]

**skip**[2] (skip), *n., v.,* **skipped, skip|ping.** —*n.* the captain of a team at curling or bowling.
—*v.t.* to command or direct (a team) as skip.
[probably short for *skipper*[1]]

**skip**[3] (skip), *n.* 1 a bucket, box, basket, cage, or wagon in which mining or quarrying materials or men are drawn up or let down: ... *and then spewed out as a kind of gravel into immense containers, or skips, that hold twelve tons of the stuff each* (New Yorker). 2 = skip car (def. 1). [variant of *skep*]

**ski pants,** lightweight, close-fitting pants with tapering trouser legs, worn by skiers.

**ski patrol,** a rescue and first-aid unit that patrols skiing areas.

**skip-bomb** (skip′bom′), *v.t., v.i.* to attack by skip bombing.

**skip bombing,** a method of precision bombing in which an airplane flies just above the water toward a ship, dam, or other target, releasing its bombs so that they strike the target at or just below the level of the water, somewhat like a torpedo.

**skip car,** 1 a car used in iron- and steelmaking to carry coke, iron ore, and limestone on a track up an incline or ramp to be deposited into a blast furnace. 2 = skip[3] (def. 1). [< *skip*[3]]

**skip distance,** the minimum distance over which high-frequency radio waves must travel to make radio communication or broadcasting possible.

**Skip|e|tar** (skip′ə tär), *n.* 1 an Albanian. 2 the language of the Albanians. [< Albanian *Shqiptarë* (literally) mountaineer < *shqip* mountain]

**skip hoist,** the incline or ramp on which skip cars carry their loads up to the blast furnace, to the head of a mine shaft, or to the top of a quarry.

**skip|jack** (skip′jak), *n., pl.* **-jacks** or (*collectively for 1*) **-jack.** 1 any one of various fishes that sometimes leap out of the water, such as a variety of tuna. 2 = click beetle. 3 *Archaic.* a pert, lively, conceited fellow.

**ski|plane** (skē′plān′), *n.* an airplane equipped with skis for landing and taking off on snow.

**ski pole,** either one of the two metal, cane, or fiberglass poles used by skiers to maintain balance and help climb uphill and make turns.

**skip|pa|ble** (skip′ə bəl), *adj.* that may be skipped or passed over: *The second half of the book makes skippable reading* (New Scientist).

**skip|per**[1] (skip′ər), *n., v.* —*n.* 1 the captain of a ship, especially of a yacht or a small trading or fishing boat: *A new skipper had been piped aboard* (Newsweek). 2 any captain or leader: *the skipper of a baseball team.*
—*v.t.* to be the skipper of; captain; command: *He skippered one of the first paddle-wheel steamers on the upper Mississippi* (Atlantic).
[< Middle Dutch *schipper* < *schip* ship]

**skip|per**[2] (skip′ər), *n.* 1 a person or thing that skips. 2 any one of certain insects that make skipping movements, such as a maggot that lives in cheese. 3 any one of a group of small, mothlike insects that fly with a darting, hopping motion. 4 = saury. [< *skip*[1] + *-er*[1]]

**skipper's daughters,** tall white-crested waves; whitecaps.

**skip|pet** (skip′it), *n.* a small, round wooden box, enclosing and protecting a seal attached, usually by a ribbon, to a document. [origin uncertain]

**skip|ping rope** (skip′ing), a length of rope, often with a handle at each end, for jumping or skipping over.

**skip rope,** = skipping rope.

**skip tracer,** *Informal.* an investigator whose job it is to locate persons who run off without paying their bills, debts, or other obligations.

**skip-trac|ing** (skip′trā′sing), *n. Informal.* the work of a skip tracer: *Practically every store, financial institution and doctor's office does a certain amount of its own skip-tracing* (Wall Street Journal).

**skip vehicle,** a space vehicle that is propelled into outer space at such trajectory and speed that, on its return to the upper atmosphere, it bounces back one or more times in the manner of a stone skipping across the surface of water.

**skirl** (skėrl), *v., n.* —*v.t., v.i.,* **1a** (of bagpipes) to sound loudly and shrilly. **b** to play a bagpipe: *An imposing 6-footer, the chief of Clan Fraser, he charged into battle in a green bonnet ... flanked by two skirling pipers* (Newsweek). 2 to cry out shrilly; scream: *The womenfolk fair skirled wi' fear* (James M. Barrie). 3 to sing or play in loud, shrill tones: *The grunting horns and syncopated strings, the skirling clarinets ... made a classical tour de force* (Harper's).
—*n.* the sound of bagpipes or one like it: *the skirl of the grey sea-birds* (Elizabeth C. Gaskell).
[Middle English *skrillen* < Scandinavian (compare Norwegian dialectal *skrylla*)]

**skir|mish** (skėr′mish), *n., v.* —*n.* 1 a brief fight between small groups: *The scouts of our army had a skirmish with a small group of the enemy. The boys had a skirmish over who would wear the cowboy hat.* 2 any slight conflict, argument, or contest: *Many and hot were the skirmishes on this topic* (Charles Lamb).
—*v.i.* to take part in a skirmish: *Some of his ships should skirmish with the enemy: but the great body of his fleet should not be risked* (Macaulay).
[< Old French *eskirmiss-,* stem of *eskirmir* (originally) ward off < Germanic (compare Old High German *scirman* fight under cover). Compare etym. under **scrimmage, Scaramouch.**]

**skir|mish|er** (skėr′mi shər), *n.* 1 a person who skirmishes: *Round its front played a crowd of skirmishers ... flying, reforming, shrieking insults* (Rudyard Kipling). 2 one of the soldiers sent out in advance of an army, as to clear the way for the main attack or prevent a surprise attack by the enemy: *Despite his vigilance, small details of skirmishers now and then infiltrate his prepared position successfully* (New Yorker).

**skirmish line,** a line of skirmishers, thrown out, as to feel the enemy or protect the main body from unexpected attack.

**skirr** (skėr), *v., n.* —*v.i.* to go or move rapidly; rush; fly; scurry: *And make them skirr away as swift as stones enforced from the old Assyrian slings* (Shakespeare). *The willow trees skirr and waver* (Julian Symons).
—*v.t.* 1 to go rapidly over; scour: *Mount ye, spur ye, skirr the plain, That the fugitive may flee in vain* (Byron). 2 to throw with a rapid skimming motion.
—*n.* a grating, rasping, or whirring sound.
[origin uncertain. Compare etym. under **scurry.**]

**skir|ret** (skir′it), *n.* a plant of the parsley family, formerly much cultivated in Europe for its edible tubers that taste somewhat like turnips. [Middle English *skirwhit,* alteration by folk etymology (< obsolete *skire* pure + *white*) of Old French *eschervis,* variant of *carvi* caraway]

**skirt** (skėrt), *n., v.* —*n.* 1 a woman's or girl's outer garment that hangs from the waist: *The triangle flare skirt is fully lined ... to give it a majestic sweep from a tiny waist to the billowed hem* (New Yorker). 2 the part of a dress that hangs from the waist. 3 = petticoat. 4 something like a skirt: *the skirts of a man's long coat.* 5 *Slang.* a woman or girl: *She's as nice a looking skirt as there is in town* (Sinclair Lewis). 6 *Figurative.* a border; edge: *The rabbits fed on the skirts of the field. ... a few heavy drops from the skirt of the passing cloud* (Francis Parkman). 7 *Figurative.* the outer part of a place, group of people, or anything like it; outskirts: *The school is ... built right on the summer colony's skirts* (Wall Street Journal). 8 one of the flaps hanging from the sides of a saddle. 9 *British.* a cut of beef from the flank.
—*v.t.* 1 to border; edge: *Those vast and trackless forests that skirted the settlements ...* (Washington Irving). 2 to pass along the border, edge, or side of: *to skirt a swamp. The boys skirted the forest instead of going through it.* 3 to be, lie, or live, along the border of: (*Figurative.*) *So is man's narrow path By strength and terror skirted* (Emerson).
—*v.i.* 1 to pass along the border or edge: *to skirt around a swamp. Then I set off up the valley, skirting along one side of it* (Richard D. Blackmore). 2 to be, lie, or live, along the border, as of a place: *A sandy desert ... skirts along the doubtful confine of Syria* (Edward Gibbon).
[< Scandinavian (compare Old Icelandic *skyrta* shirt, skirt, kirtle). Compare etym. under **shirt.**]
—**skirt′er,** *n.* —**skirt′like′,** *adj.*

**skirt dancer,** a woman who does skirt dancing.

**skirt dancing,** a form of ballet dancing in which the effect is produced by graceful movements of a long, full skirt, often manipulated by the hands of the dancer.

**-skirted,** *combining form.* having a ____ skirt: *Short-skirted = having a short skirt.*

**skirt|ing** (skėr′ting), *n.* 1 cloth for making skirts. 2 *British.* a strip of masonry, wood, or other material, placed along the base of a wall; baseboard. 3 the process of trimming the inferior parts of a fleece in wool manufacturing.

**skirtings,** the trimmings or inferior parts of a fleece: *to separate skirtings.*

**skirting board,** *British.* skirting (def. 2).

**skirt|less** (skėrt′lis), *adj.* 1 having no skirt: *a skirtless coat.* 2 wearing no skirt: *Trousers, such as skirtless feminine bicyclists adopt* (London Daily News).

**ski run,** a snow-covered slope or steep runway used by skiers: *Several ski runs cut through the forest* (Atlantic).

**ski-scoot|er** (skē′skü′tər), *n. British.* skidoo.

**skish** (skish), *n.* a fisherman's game or sport in which bait-casting or fly-casting equipment is used to cast a plug or weight at a ring or other target from various distances. [a coined word; perhaps a blend of *skip*[1] and *fish*]

**skit**[1] (skit), *n.* a short sketch that contains humor or satire: *a television skit. When we graduated the school newspaper had skits about each one of us.* SYN: squib. [perhaps < *skit*[2]]

**skit**[2] (skit), *v.i.,* **skit|ted, skit|ting.** *Scottish.* to dart; skip; leap. [perhaps back formation < *skittish*]

**skite**[1] (skīt), *n. Scottish.* 1 a sudden, slapping blow at an angle. 2 a slight shower; sprinkle. [perhaps < Scandinavian (compare Old Icelandic *skȳt;* see etym. under **skittish**)]

**skite**[2] (skīt), *v.,* **skit|ed, skit|ing,** *n. Australian.*
—*v.i.* to boast.
—*n.* a boaster.
[probably special use of *skite*[1]]

**ski touring,** cross-country skiing: *Ski touring represents a return to the way people skied before skiing got fancy* (Time).

**ski tow,** a continuous rope on pulleys, kept moving by a motor, for pulling skiers to the top of a slope: *The city maintains two rinks, a toboggan run and a two-for-a-nickel ski tow* (Maclean's).

**ski train,** a special train for skiers traveling to skiing resorts.

**ski troops,** soldiers specially trained to fight and maneuver on skis, especially in northern or arctic areas: *The entire region surrounding the plant was patrolled by a regiment of ski troops* (Maclean's).

**skit|ter** (skit′ər), *v., n.* —*v.i.* 1 to move lightly or quickly; hurry about: *Motorscooters, ridden by sport-shirted youths, skittered among primitive horsemen in burnooses* (Time). 2 to skim or skip along a surface: ... *the Concepcion was skittering downstream at about fifteen knots* (Atlantic).

3 *U.S.* (in fishing) to draw a spoon or baited hook over the surface of the water with a skipping motion.
—*v.t.* 1 to cause to skitter. 2 *U.S.* (in fishing) to draw in (a spoon or baited hook) over the surface of the water with a skipping motion.
—*n.* a light skipping movement or the sound caused by this: *The slim shell trailed with dying headway to the skitter of the resting oars* (Scribner's Magazine).
[see related etym. at **skittish**]

**skit|ter|ish** (skit′ər ish), *adj.* moving lightly and quickly; skimming; skipping.

**skit|ter|y** (skit′ər ē), *adj.* 1 sliding; skidding; slippery. 2 *Figurative.* frightened; nervous; skittish: *He had an exercise boy take Hill Gail out to the track so that his admittedly skittery horse could get accustomed to all the noise* (Newsweek).

**skit|tish** (skit′ish), *adj.* 1 apt to start, jump, or run; easily frightened: *a skittish horse.* **SYN**: excitable. 2 fickle; changeable: *a skittish wind.* **SYN**: capricious, volatile. 3 difficult to manage; tricky: *a light, skittish boat.* 4 shy and timid; coy: *a skittish young girl.* **SYN**: bashful, demure. [perhaps < Scandinavian (compare Old Icelandic *skȳt-*, stem of *skjōta* shoot) + English *-ish*] —**skit′tish|ly**, *adv.* —**skit′tish|ness**, *n.*

✱**skit|tle** (skit′əl), *n., v.,* **-tled, -tling.** —*n.* one of the pins used in the game of skittles.
—*v.t. Cricket.* to get (batsmen) out rapidly in succession: *Jim Laker of England set a significant mark among bowlers when he skittled out nineteen Australians in two innings* (Newsweek).
**skittles**, a game in which each player tries to knock down nine wooden pins by rolling balls or throwing wooden disks at them: *Skittles resembles bowling.*
[probably < Scandinavian (compare Danish *skyttel* shuttle)]

skittles

✱**skittle**

**skittle alley**, an alley used in the game of skittles.

**skittle ball**, a heavy disk, usually of hard wood, for throwing or sliding at the pins in the game of skittles.

**skive¹** (skīv), *v.t.,* **skived, skiv|ing.** 1 to slice or split (leather or rubber) into layers. 2 to shave (hides). 3 to pare off. [perhaps < Scandinavian (compare Old Icelandic *skīfa*)]

**skive²** (skīv), *v.i.,* **skived, skiv|ing.** *Dialect.* 1 to move lightly and quickly; dart. 2 to go; depart: *He ... skived off to church* (Observer).

**skiv|er** (skī′vər), *n.* 1a a person who skives. b a tool that skives; knife for skiving. 2 a thin, soft leather sliced from the grain side of sheepskin, used for bookbinding and sweatbands in hats.

**skiv|ey** (skiv′ē), *n., pl.* **-eys.** *British Slang.* skivvy.

**skiv|vies** (skiv′ēz), *n.pl. U.S. Nautical Slang.* men's underwear: *Officers were in shirt sleeves; some of the crew lounged in their skivvies* (Newsweek). [origin unknown]

**skiv|vie shirt** (skiv′ē), *U.S. Nautical Slang.* an undershirt.

**skiv|vy** (skiv′ē), *n., pl.* **-vies,** *v.,* **-vied, -vy|ing.** *British Slang.* —*n.* a woman servant of low status, such as a scullery maid.
—*v.i.* to work as a skivvy; do domestic or menial work: *There are now better jobs than skivvying to look for, and wages sometimes comparable with what the job-seeking housewife herself might be earning* (Punch).

**ski|wear** (skē′wãr′), *n.* clothes worn for skiing.

**sklent** (sklent), *v., n., adj. Scottish.* —*v.i.* 1 to slant. 2 to deviate from the truth.
—*n.* 1 a slant. 2 a lie; fib.
—*adj.* slanting.
[variant of earlier *slent* < Scandinavian (compare Norwegian *slenta*)]

**skoal** (skōl), *n., interj., v.* —*n., interj.* a Scandinavian word used in drinking a health. It means "Hail" or "May you prosper."
—*v.i.* to drink healths.
[< Danish *skaal,* Norwegian *skål* < Old Icelandic *skāl* bowl, shell]

**sko|ki|aan** (skō′kē än), *n.* (in South Africa) illegally distilled whiskey; moonshine. [< Afrikaans *skokiaan*]

**skol|ly** (skol′ē), *n., pl.* **-lies.** (in South Africa) a young native rascal or hoodlum: *There has always been an element of skolly crime in the Peninsula* (Cape Argus). [< Afrikaans *skollie*]

**skoo|kum** (skü′kəm), *adj. Dialect.* strong; fine; excellent; good. [American English < Chinook jargon *skookum*]

**Skr.**, Sanskrit.

**Skry|mir** (skrē′mir), *n. Norse Mythology.* the king of the giants dwelling in Jotunheim.

**Skt.**, Sanskrit.

**sku|a** (skyü′ə), *n.,* or **skua gull**, any one of several large brown sea birds that are related to the gulls and jaegers: *The skua gull though rarely abundant, is ubiquitous; it appears to be the only scavenger in inland Antarctica* (E. F. Roots). [alteration of Faroese *skūgvur*]

**Skuld** (skuld), *n. Norse Mythology.* one of the three Norns or goddesses of fate, a dwarf representing the future.

**skul|dug|ger|y** (skul dug′ər ē, -dug′rē), *n. Informal.* trickery; dishonesty: *That was the season when the Cobb-Lajoie duel for the batting championship brought angry charges of skulduggery and complicity* (New York Times). Also, **skullduggery.** [American English; origin uncertain]

**skulk** (skulk), *v., n.* —*v.i.* 1 to keep out of sight to avoid danger, work, or duty; hide for a bad purpose; lurk in a cowardly way; sneak: *On Saturdays several boys could be seen skulking about behind the garage avoiding their chores.* **SYN**: See syn. under **lurk.** 2 to move in a stealthy, sneaking way: *The wolf was skulking in the woods near the sheep. It is a poor thing for a fellow to get drunk at night and skulk to bed* (Samuel Johnson).
—*n.* 1 a person who skulks: *You are certainly no skulk when duty is to be done* (James Fenimore Cooper). 2a a group or collection of animals which skulk: *We say a flight of doves ... a skulk of foxes* (Washington Irving). b a group of other animals or persons: *a skulk of thieves.*
[< Scandinavian (compare Danish *skulke*)]
—**skulk′er**, *n.* —**skulk′ing|ly**, *adv.*

✱**skull** (skul), *n., v.* —*n.* 1 the bony framework of the head, face, and lower jaw in man and other animals with backbones; bones of the head; cranium. The skull encloses and protects the brain. *The human skull may conveniently be divided into three principal portions: the cranium or cranial vault, the face, and the lower jaw or mandible* (Beals and Hoijer). 2 the head; brain: *Skulls that cannot teach and will not learn* (William Cowper). 3 a crust which is formed by the cooling of molten metal on the sides of a ladle or other vessel.
—*v.t. Slang.* to hit on the skull: *I've seen more guys skulled by warm-up throwers on the sidelines than I've ever seen hit in a ball game* (New York Times).
[< Scandinavian (compare Norwegian dialectal *skul* shell)]

✱**skull**
definition 1

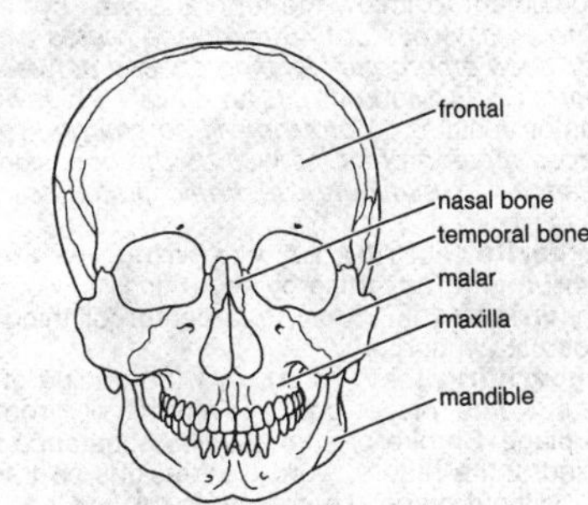


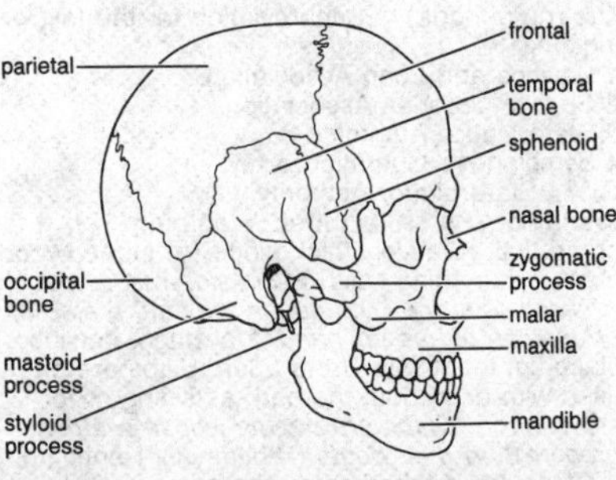


**skull and crossbones**, a picture of a human skull above two crossed bones. It was often used on pirates' flags as a symbol of death, and is now used on the labels of poisons.

**skull|cap** (skul′kap′), *n.* 1 a close-fitting cap without a brim: ... *a Presbyterian clergyman wearing a black silk skullcap, covering his short hair* (Scott). 2 any one of various plants of the mint family in which the calyx looks like a bowl-shaped helmet. 3 the upper, caplike part of the skull; top or roof of the head: *The extinct Solo man was inferred from eleven skullcaps found in Java.*

**skull|dug|ger|y** (skul dug′ər ē, -dug′rē), *n.* = skulduggery.

**skulled** (skuld), *adj.* having a skull.

**-skulled**, *combining form.* having a ______ skull: *Thick-skulled* = *having a thick skull.*

**skull|fish** (skul′fish′), *n., pl.* **-fish|es** or (*collectively*) **-fish.** an old whale, or one more than two years of age.

**skull practice**, *U.S. Sports Slang.* a lesson or drill in which diagrams are used to explain the tactics of a game: *Skull practice ... held by a football coach and his players* (New Yorker).

**skunk** (skungk), *n., pl.* **skunks** or (*collectively for 1*) **skunk,** *v.* —*n.* 1 a black, bushy-tailed animal of North and South America, usually with white markings on the back and tail; polecat. It is a burrowing mammal about the size of a cat. When frightened or attacked, a skunk squirts a spray of liquid with a very strong, unpleasant smell from a pair of glands near its tail. There are several kinds of skunks. They belong to the same family as the weasel. 2 the fur of this animal, used especially in making coats. 3 *Informal, Figurative.* a mean, contemptible person: *He must think me the most awful skunk* (John Galsworthy).
—*v.t. U.S. Slang.* to defeat utterly, as in an unequal contest where one side is held scoreless: *He had got 292 votes in New Orleans, and had been skunked in only two parishes out of sixty-three* (New Yorker).
[American English < Algonkian (probably Abnaki) *seganku*] —**skunk′like′**, *adj.*

**skunk bear**, = wolverine.

**skunk blackbird**, the male bobolink in full plumage. [because of the resemblance of the black and white coloration to that of the skunk]

**skunk cabbage**, 1 a low, broad-leaved, ill-smelling North American perennial plant of the arum family, growing commonly in moist ground. See picture under **arum family.** 2 a similar and related plant of the Pacific coast.

**skunk|er|y** (skung′kər ē), *n., pl.* **-er|ies.** a place where skunks are kept and raised, as for fur.

**skunk|weed** (skungk′wēd′), *n.* = skunk cabbage.

**skunk|y** (skungk′ē), *adj.,* **skunk|i|er, skunk|i|est.** 1 of a skunk; like that of a skunk: *People describe the odor as skunky* (New Yorker). 2 befitting a skunk; nasty: *You try to shove him into any skunky corner ... and he lets you know* (Richard D. Blackmore).

**Skup|shti|na** (sku̇p′shti nä), *n.* 1 the national assembly of Yugoslavia, consisting of a single chamber. 2 the former national assembly of Serbia or of Montenegro, likewise consisting in each case of a single chamber.
[< Serbian (*Narodna*) *Skupshtina* (National) Assembly]

**skurf** (skėrf), *v.i. Slang.* to ride on a skateboard: *Hundreds of vacationing teen-agers chanting "we want to skurf" wheeled to City Hall ... on their skateboards* (Toronto Globe and Mail). [blend of *skate* and *surf*] —**skurf′er**, *n.*

**skurf|ing** (skėr′fing), *n.* = skateboarding.

**sky** (skī), *n., pl.* **skies,** *v.,* **skied** or **skyed, sky|ing.** —*n.* 1 Often, **skies.** the covering over the world; the region of the clouds or the upper air; the heavens: *a blue sky, a cloudy sky, to open the sky to aircraft of all nations.* **SYN**: firmament. 2a the place where many people believe God and His angels live; heaven. b the heavenly power; the Deity. 3 weather or climate: *I seek a warmer sky* (Tennyson). 4 *Obsolete.* a cloud.
—*v.t.* 1 to hit, throw, or raise high into the air, as in golf or cricket: *to sky a ball.* 2 to hang (a picture or other piece of art) high up on the wall or near the ceiling, as at an exhibition.
**out of a clear (blue) sky**, suddenly; unexpectedly: *He dropped upon me ... out of a clear sky and began asking questions which I had to answer* (W. E. Norris).
**the sky is the limit**, there is no limit; everything is possible or achievable: *For a girl of real talent the sky is the limit* (London Times).
**to the skies** (or **sky**), to the highest possible degree; very highly: *to praise to the skies.*
[Middle English *skei* a cloud; the upper air < Scandinavian (compare Old Icelandic *skȳ* cloud)]

**Pronunciation Key:** hat, āge, cãre, fär; let, ēqual, tėrm; it, īce; hot, ōpen, ôrder; oil, out; cup, pu̇t, rüle; child; long; thin; ŦHen; zh, measure; ə represents **a** in about, **e** in taken, **i** in pencil, **o** in lemon, **u** in circus.

**sky blue**, a clear, soft blue; azure. **SYN**: cerulean. —**sky-′blue′**, *adj.*

**sky|borne** (skī′bôrn′, -bōrn′), *adj.* = airborne.

**sky|cap** (skī′kap′), *n. U.S.* a porter at an airport. [< *sky* + *-cap*, as in *redcap*]

**sky|dive** (skī′dīv′), *v.i.*, **-dived, -div|ing.** to engage in sky diving. [back formation < *sky diving*]

**sky diver**, a person who engages in sky diving: *Canada's sky divers are steadily gaining new converts to their sport—free-falling thousands of feet from an aircraft* (Maclean's).

**sky diving**, or **sky|div|ing** (skī′dī′ving), *n.* the sport, or military tactic, of diving from an airplane and dropping in a free fall for a great distance, controlling one's course by changing body positions, before releasing the parachute.

**sky|er** (skī′ər), *n.* a lofty hit at cricket: *He fell to a well-judged, running catch off a skyer* (London Times).

**Skye terrier**, or **Skye** (skī), *n.* any dog of an old Scottish breed of terriers having a long, low body with short, strong legs and long, shaggy hair. [< the Isle of *Skye*, near Scotland]

**sky|ey** (skī′ē), *adj.* **1** of or from the sky: *A breath thou art, servile to all the skyey influences* (Shakespeare). **2** *Figurative.* very high; lofty. **3** like the sky in color; sky-blue; azure.

**sky|glow** (skī′glō′), *n.* a shaft of light on the night sky, reflecting the lighting patterns of a city: *... to reduce skyglow, which could give navigational aid to enemy aircraft in an attack on principal U.S. target cities* (Bulletin of Atomic Scientists).

**sky-high** (skī′hī′), *adv., adj.* very high: *One firm in the advertising game that is not doing sky-high business is a skywriter here* (Wall Street Journal).

**sky|hook** (skī′hůk′), *n.* a flattish device that spirals slowly to earth when dropped from a plane, used to drop supplies, as of medicine.

**skyhook balloon**, a large, open-necked plastic balloon used to carry scientific instruments for making meteorological studies or observing cosmic rays, the sun's spectrum, etc.: *A different method of taking a hurricane's picture is also a Navy project: a giant skyhook balloon carrying a camera gondola* (Science News Letter).

**sky|ish** (skī′ish), *adj. Poetic.* skyey; lofty.

**sky|jack** (skī′jak′), *v., n.* —*v.t.* to take over (an aircraft) by force, causing it to fly to a place other than its original destination.
—*n.* **1** the act or fact of hijacking an aircraft: *World attention focused on the drama of a quadruple skyjack* (Time). **2** = skyjacker.
[back formation < *skyjacker*]

**sky|jack|er** (skī′jak′ər), *n.* a person who hijacks an aircraft; air pirate. [< *sky* + (hi)*jacker*]

**sky|jack|ing** (skī′jak′ing), *n.* the hijacking of an aircraft; air piracy.

**Sky|lab** (skī′lab′), *n.* any one of several earth-orbiting space stations of the United States, the first of which was launched in 1973.

**sky|lark** (skī′lärk′), *n., v.* —*n.* a small bird of Europe and Asia that sings very sweetly as it flies toward the sky: *A more inexhaustible singer than the skylark does not exist* (W. H. Hudson).
—*v.i.* to play pranks; frolic: *The children were skylarking in the orchard.* —**sky′lark′er**, *n.*

**sky|less** (skī′lis), *adj.* without visible sky; cloudy; dark; thick: *a skyless day.*

**sky|light** (skī′līt′), *n., v.*, **-light|ed** or **-lit**, **-light|ing.** —*n.* a window in a roof or ceiling.
—*v.t.* to furnish with or light by a skylight or skylights: *All the inside rooms were skylighted.*

**sky|line** (skī′līn′), *n.* **1** the line at which earth and sky seem to meet; horizon: *Often I had to crawl on all-fours to avoid appearing against the skyline on the ridge* (Theodore Roosevelt). **2** the outline of mountains, trees, or buildings, as seen against the sky: *The tall buildings and towers of New York City make a remarkable skyline.*

**sky|lin|er** (skī′lī′nər), *n.* a large, usually luxurious, commercial passenger airplane.

**sky|lit** (skī′lit′), *adj., v.* —*adj.* skylighted: *The long skylit corridor ... leads to the ten consulting rooms* (Time).
—*v.* skylighted; a past tense and a past participle of **skylight.**

**sky|lounge** (skī′lounj′), *n.* a surface vehicle for collecting air passengers at various locations, that is then flown by helicopter directly to the airport.

**sky|man** (skī′man′), *n., pl.* **-men.** *Informal.* an aviator.

**sky map**, = star map.

**sky marshal**, an armed law-enforcement officer, usually in plain clothes, assigned to protect aircraft and passengers from skyjackings.

**sky|mo|tel** (skī′mō tel′), *n.* a motel for air travelers, usually at or near an airport.

**sky parlor**, *Slang.* a garret or attic.

**sky|phos** (skī′fos′), *n., pl.* **-phoi** (-foi). an ancient Greek cup; scyphus: *... the pendant semicircle skyphos, which are found throughout the Aegean* (London Times). [< Greek *skýphos*]

**sky pilot**, **1** *Slang.* a clergyman; chaplain. **2** *Informal.* an aviator: *The present bishop ... flies his own plane ... to visit his far-flung missions, literally as well as figuratively a "sky pilot"* (Ernest Gruening).

**sky|port** (skī′pôrt′, -pōrt′), *n.* an airport for helicopters, built on top of a building.

**skyr** (skir), *n.* an Icelandic dessert made from curds that is much like yogurt, and is usually served with sugar and cream. [< Old Icelandic *skyr* sour milk]

**sky|rock|et** (skī′rok′it), *n., v.* —*n.* a firework that goes up high into the air and (usually) bursts into a shower of stars and sparks; rocket.
—*v.i., v.t.* to rise or cuase to rise very rapidly or suddenly, often with great display or notice; shoot up: *The price of gasoline skyrocketed during the shortage. "The Virginian" ... won instant success and skyrocketed its author to fame* (Atlantic).

**sky|sail** (skī′sāl′; *Nautical* skī′səl), *n.* a light sail set at the top of a mast above the royal on a square-rigged ship.

**sky|scape** (skī′skāp′), *n.* **1** a view of the sky: *It was the unbroken horizon which impressed me ... and the skyscapes which it afforded* (Robert Southey). **2** a picture or representation of part of the sky: *The landscape and skyscape in the background are an oil painting stretched on canvas over a built-in frame* (New Yorker). [*sky* + *-scape*]

**sky|scrap|er** (skī′skrā′pər), *n.* a very tall building: *New York is famous for its skyscrapers. Where did the skyscraper get its name? From the topmost sail of the clipper ships, according to Lewis Mumford* (New York Times).

**sky|scrap|ing** (skī′skrā′ping), *adj.* very high; lofty: *skyscraping towers.*

**sky sign**, *British.* an advertisement, announcement, or direction, set up so as to be visible against the sky, as on the top of a building: *If you drive round London at night you keep coming across illuminated sky signs suspended eerily in places where memory tells you there aren't any buildings* (Punch).

**Sky|sweep|er** (skī′swē′pər), *n. Trademark.* an automatic antiaircraft gun with radar and computer that tracks the target and aims the gun on the same carriage.

**sky|ward** (skī′wərd), *adv., adj.* toward the sky: *to move skyward* (adv.), *a skyward movement* (adj.).

**sky|wards** (skī′wərdz), *adv.* = skyward.

**sky wave**, a radio wave sent from a transmitter into the atmosphere and sometimes reflected back to earth by the ionosphere: *This zone of intense auroral activity, floating above the Iceland-Greenland-Labrador axis, can so disorganize the ionosphere that sky waves are not bent back to the earth* (Newsweek).

**sky|way** (skī′wā′), *n.* **1a** an air lane; airway. **b** a route for small private airplanes that lack the equipment to follow the federal airway system: *The 24 skyways are 40-mile wide routes picked for good emergency landing spaces between airports* (H. E. Mehrens). **2** an elevated highway for motor vehicles: *Motorists will be charged tolls to cross these arches, as well as the new skyway planned to eliminate the traffic bottleneck* (Maclean's).

**sky|write** (skī′rīt′), *v.t., v.i.*, **-wrote, -writ|ten, -writ|ing.** to advertise by skywriting.

**sky|writ|er** (skī′rī′tər), *n.* a person or thing that does skywriting.

**sky|writ|ing** (skī′rī′ting), *n.* **1** the tracing of letters, words, or designs, against the sky from an airplane. Smoke or some similar substance is used. **2** the letters, words, or designs so traced.

**s.l.**, without place (Latin, *sine loco*).

**S.L.**, **1** sergeant-at-law. **2** solicitor at law. **3** south latitude.

**SLA** (no periods), an abbreviation for the following:
**1** Savings and Loan Association.
**2** Special Libraries Association.
**3** State Liquor Authority.
**4** Symbionese Liberation Army.

**S.L.A.**, State Liquor Authority.

**slab**[1] (slab), *n., v.*, **slabbed, slab|bing.** —*n.* **1** a broad, flat, relatively thick piece (of stone, wood, meat, or anything solid): *This sidewalk is made of slabs of stone. The hungry boy ate a slab of cheese as big as my hand.* **2** a rough, outside piece cut lengthwise from a log. Slabs are often used with or without the bark as siding or for stove wood. *Slabs are beams whose width is greater than their depth* (Whitney C. Huntington). **3** *Slang.* the pitcher's plate on a baseball diamond; rubber.
—*v.t.* **1** to make into slabs. **2** to cut the outside pieces from (a log). **3** to lay with slabs; cover with slabs.
[Middle English *slabbe;* origin uncertain]

**slab**[2] (slab), *adj. Archaic.* semisolid; viscid: *Make the gruel thick and slab* (Shakespeare). [< Scandinavian (compare Danish *slab* slippery; mire)]

**slab|ber** (slab′ər), *v.i., v.t., n.* = slobber.

**slab|ber|er** (slab′ər ər), *n.* a person or animal that slabbers; driveler.

**slab|ber|y** (slab′ər ē), *adj.* covered with slobber; wet; sloppy.

**slab|bing mill** (slab′ing), a mill that rolls steel ingots into slabs for further processing.

**slab|by** (slab′ē), *adj.*, **-bi|er, -bi|est.** **1** thick; viscous: (*Figurative.*) *The writing is largely slabby and indigestible* (Punch). **2** *Archaic.* muddy; slimy; sloppy: *Bad slabby weather today* (Jonathan Swift).

**slab|like** (slab′līk′), *adj.* like a slab; broad, flat, and thick: *the bare slablike surfaces that are transforming Park Avenue* (New Yorker).

**slab-sid|ed** (slab′sī′did), *adj.* **1** having long, flat sides: *a slab-sided, fourteen-storey block still at the skeletal stage* (Manchester Guardian). **2** *Informal.* tall and lank: *long-legged, slab-sided, lean, sunburnt ... lads* (Henry Kingsley).

**slab|stone** (slab′stōn′), *n.* rock which splits readily into slabs or flags; flagstone.

**slack**[1] (slak), *adj., n., v., adv.* —*adj.* **1** not tight or firm; loose: *slack rigging, a slack bandage. The rope hung slack.* **2** careless: *She is a slack housekeeper. He was slack in fulfilling his promises and responsibilities.* **SYN**: lax, indolent, negligent, remiss. **3** slow; sluggish: *The horse was moving at a slack pace. Then he took advantage of the change from ebb to slack tide to bring her alongside the bulkhead* (New York Times). **4** not active; not brisk; dull: *Business is slack at this season.* **5** gentle or moderate.
—*n.* **1** a part that hangs loose: *He pulled in the slack of the rope.* **2** a dull season; quiet period; lull. **3** a stopping of a strong flow of the tide or a current of water.
—*v.t.* **1** to make less tight or firm; let up on; loosen; slacken. **2** to make less active; moderate; abate: *He ... without slacking his pace for an instant, stalked on* (Robert Louis Stevenson). **3** to leave undone; neglect; shirk. **4** = slake (def. 3).
—*v.i.* **1** to become less tight or firm. **2** to be or become slack; let up: *The breeze slacked. Still she went ... slacking not, pausing not* (Harriet Beecher Stowe). **3** (of lime) to become slaked.
—*adv.* in a slack manner.
**slack off, a** to loosen : *Slack off the halyards a little so the sails will billow.* **b** to lessen one's efforts: *The American artillery slacked off in its firing ... and this tactical error undoubtedly allowed a lot of fleeing troops to make their way through Chambois* (Harper's).
**slack up**, to slow down; go more slowly: *One expected to see the locomotive pause, or slack up a little* (Mark Twain).
[Old English *slæc*] —**slack′ly**, *adv.* —**slack′ness**, *n.*

**slack**[2] (slak), *n.* dirt, dust, and small pieces left after coal is screened; small or refuse coal. [probably < Middle Dutch *slacke*]

**slack**[3] (slak, släk), *n. Scottish.* **1** a hollow between hills. **2** a soft or boggy hollow. [< Scandinavian (compare Old Icelandic *slakki*)]

**slack|age** (slak′ij), *n.* the amount allowed for the droop or sag of a rope or cable when not fully strained; slack.

**slack-baked** (slak′bākt′), *adj.* **1** not baked enough. **2** *Figurative.* poorly designed, made, or contrived: *down to the slack-baked buckles in his shoes* (Dickens). [< *slack*[1], adverb + *baked*]

**slack|en** (slak′ən), *v.t.* **1** to make slower: *Don't slacken your efforts till the work is done.* **SYN**: retard. **2** to make looser: *Slacken the rope. Slackening the reins, I let my horse take his own course* (Francis Parkman). —*v.i.* **1** to become slower; become less active, vigorous, or brisk: *His business always slackens in the winter. Work slackens on a hot day.* **2** to become loose: *The rope slackened as the wave sent the boat toward the pier.* —**slack′en|er**, *n.*

**slack|en|ing** (slak′ə ning), *n.* the action of making or becoming slack; diminution; lessening: *Zinc demand continues strong, with no indications of immediate slackening* (Wall Street Journal).

**slack|er** (slak′ər), *n.* a person who shirks work or evades his duty, especially an able-bodied man who evades military service in time of war: *Every shirker, every coward and slacker ... decided at once to be a conscientious objector* (H. G. Wells).

**slack|er|ism** (slak′ə riz əm), *n.* the conduct of a slacker; attitude of shirkers: [*The*] *chairman of the Government shipbuilding agency called "illegitimate absenteeism a first cousin to slackerism"* (Baltimore Sun).

**slack-fill** (slak′fil′), *v.t.* to fill loosely so that there is room for more: *When a manufacturer slack-fills his cereal box, he makes a few extra pennies on each sale* (Harper's).

**slack-jawed** (slak′jôd′), *adj.* with the jaw or mouth partly open and loose: *slack-jawed admiration.*
**slack-mouthed** (slak′mouᴛʜd′, -moutht′), *adj.* = slack-jawed.
**slack-off** (slak′ôf′, -of′), *n. Informal.* a slowing down; a lessening; letup: *He explained that orders have been filled and an industry-wide slack-off exists* (Wall Street Journal).
**slacks** (slaks), *n.pl.* trousers for casual wear.
**slack suit,** a two-piece, informal suit consisting of a jacket or shirt and slacks, worn by both men and women.
**slack tide,** = slack water.
**slack water,** the time between tides when the water does not move either way: *These four dams when finished will provide slack water navigation from Astoria to Pasco, a distance of 328 miles* (Newsweek).
**slack wire,** a loosely stretched wire on which an acrobat performs: *A man twirling hoops while balancing on a slack wire* (New York Times).
**slade** (slād), *n. British Dialect.* **1** a little valley; dell. **2** an open space of green grass in a wood or between two woods. [Old English *slæd*]
**slag** (slag), *n., v.,* **slagged, slag|ging.** —*n.* **1** the rough, hard waste left after metal is separated from ore by melting: *Some 357 million tons of stone, sand, gravel, and slag now go into building roads each year* (Newsweek). **syn:** dross. **2** a light, spongy lava; the scoria from a volcano.
—*v.t.* **1** to change into slag. **2** to free from slag.
—*v.i.* to form slag; become a slaglike mass.
[probably < Scandinavian (compare Swedish *slagg,* Norwegian *slagga* dross < Middle Low German *slagge*)]
**slag furnace,** a furnace for the extraction of lead from slags, and from ores which contain little lead.
**slag|gy** (slag′ē), *adj.,* **-gi|er, -gi|est.** of, like, or having to do with slag.
**slag|less|ness** (slag′lis nis), *n.* the fact of having no slag or cinder.
**slag wool,** = mineral wool.
**slain** (slān), *v.* the past participle of **slay:** *The sheep were slain by wolves.*
**slain|te** (slān′chə), *interj.* a Gaelic word used in drinking a health: *They all took the whiskey straight ... "Slainte," said Willie-John, and they murmured it after him* (Joanna Ostrow). [< Irish and Scottish Gaelic *sláinte* health]
**slake** (slāk; *also* slak, *especially for v.t. 3, v.i. 1*), *v.,* **slaked, slak|ing.** —*v.t.* **1** to satisfy (as thirst, revenge, or wrath): *We slaked our thirst at the spring.* **syn:** assuage. **2** to put out (a fire). **syn:** extinguish. **3** to change (lime) to slaked lime by leaving it in the moist air or putting water on it. **4** *Archaic.* to make less painful: *Wake thou ... and slake ... A wound more fierce than his* (Shelley).
—*v.i.* **1** (of lime) to become slaked lime. **2** to become less active, vigorous, or intense.
[Middle English *slaken,* Old English *slacian* slacken < *slæc* slack]
**slaked lime** (slākt, slakt), a white powder obtained by exposing lime to moistened air or by putting water on lime; calcium hydroxide. Plaster contains slaked lime and sand. *Formula:* $Ca(OH)_2$
**slake|less** (slāk′lis), *adj.* that cannot be satisfied; insatiable: *a slakeless thirst.*
***sla|lom** (slä′ləm, -lōm; slal′əm), *n., v.* —*n.* **1** a skiing race downhill. The skiers race zigzag through pairs of poles placed in various combinations on the course and complete the run in turns, the winner being the one who does it fastest without error. **2** any similar race zigzagging between obstacles, as in water-skiing, canoeing, and automobile racing.
—*v.i.* to move as in a slalom; zigzag skillfully between objects: *I slalomed around cloverleafs trying to get turned the right way* (Maclean's).
[< Norwegian *slalom* (literally) track that slopes]

***slalom**
definition 1

**slalom canoe,** a canoe, usually with a deck, used in a canoe slalom.
**sla|lom|er** (slä′lə mər, slal′ə-), *n.* a person who takes part in a slalom.
**sla|lom|ist** (slä′lə mist, slal′ə-), *n.* = slalomer.
**slam¹** (slam), *v.,* **slammed, slam|ming,** *n.* —*v.t.* **1** to shut with force and noise; close with a bang: *She slammed the window down.* **2** to throw, push, hit, or move hard with force: *He slammed himself down on his bed. Why, he'd have slammed you through the window* (Mark Twain). **3** *U.S. Informal, Figurative.* to criticize harshly: *His habit of slamming friends made him unpopular.* —*v.i.* **1** to shut with force and noise; close with a bang: *The door slammed.* **2** to move hard with force: *My car slammed into the truck.*
—*n.* **1** a violent and noisy closing or striking; bang: *He threw his books down with a slam.* **2** *U.S. Informal, Figurative.* harsh criticism.
**slam²** (slam), *n.* **1** the winning of 12 tricks (little, or small, slam) or all 13 tricks (grand slam) in the game of bridge. **2** a hand of whist in which one side wins all the tricks. **3** a game of cards like ruff, played in the 1600's. [origin uncertain]
**slam|bang** (slam′bang′), *adv., adj., v. Informal.*
—***adv.*** with a slam and a bang; with noisy or headlong violence: *The car went slambang into a fence.* —***adj.*** violent and noisy; unrestrained: *... the slambang, profane hit play, "The Front Page"* (Newsweek).
—*v.i.* to go with a slam and a bang; go noisily: *Zooey's razor, new blade and all slambanged down into the metal wastebasket* (J. D. Salinger).
**slam|mer** (slam′ər), *n. Slang.* Usually, **the slammer.** prison; jail: *The judge is mulling how long he's going to give you in the slammer* (Newsweek).
**slan|der** (slan′dər, slän′-), *n., v.* —*n.* **1a** a false report meant to do harm to the good name and reputation of another: *Do not listen to slander.* **syn:** defamation, calumny. **b** *Law.* a spoken statement tending to damage a person's reputation. **2** the spreading of false reports about persons: *The mayor sued the television station for slander when it accused him of dishonest use of city funds. The worthiest people are the most injured by slander* (Jonathan Swift).
—*v.t.* to talk falsely about. **syn:** defame, calumniate. —*v.i.* to speak or spread slander.
[< Anglo-French *esclandre* scandal, adapted from Latin *scandalum.* See etym. of doublet **scandal.**] —**slan′der|er,** *n.*
▶ **Slander** and **libel** are sharply distinguished from each other in modern United States law. *Slander* applies only to what is spoken; *libel* applies only to what is written or printed.
**slander of title,** *Law.* defamatory and false statements injuring one's property, real or personal, or one's title thereto.
**slan|der|ous** (slan′dər əs, -drəs; slän′-), *adj.* **1** of, containing, or involving slander or a slander: *slanderous words.* **syn:** calumnious, defamatory. **2** speaking or spreading slanders: *Done to death by slanderous tongues* (Shakespeare). —**slan′der|ous|ly,** *adv.* —**slan′der|ous|ness,** *n.*
**slang** (slang), *n., v.* —*n.* **1** words, phrases, or meanings that are new, flashy, and popular, usually for only a short time. Slang is often very vivid and expressive and is used in familiar talk between friends but is not accepted as good English when speaking or writing formal English. *Slob* and *on the skids* are slang. *The central characteristic of slang comes from the motive for its use: a desire for novelty, for vivid emphasis, for being in the know, up with the times or a little ahead ... Many slang words have short lives—skiddoo, twenty-three, vamoose, beat it, scram, hit the trail, take a powder, drag out, shag out—have succeeded each other almost within a generation ... The chief objections to slang, aside from its possible conspicuousness, are to its overuse, and to its use in place of more exact expressions* (Porter G. Perrin). *All slang is metaphor, and all metaphor is poetry* (G. K. Chesterton). **2** the special talk or language of a particular class of people: *"Crib" often means "cheat" in students' slang. A "contract" is underworld slang for an "order to kill someone."* **3** the special language of tramps or thieves, or of some sport or, sometimes, an occupation; cant: *"Slang" in the sense of the cant language of thieves appears in print certainly as early as the middle of the last century* [*1700's*] (The Nation).
—*v.t.* **1** to attack with abusive language; rail at; scold. **2** to address in slang.
—*v.i.* **1** to use abusive language: *They slanged away at each other* (Atlantic). **2** to use slang.
[origin unknown]
**slang|i|ly** (slang′ə lē), *adv.* in a slangy manner.
**slang|i|ness** (slang′ē nis), *n.* slangy quality: [*The play*] *drew many a brickbat from critics ... for its slanginess* (Newsweek).
**slang|ing match** (slang′ging), *British.* a quarrel in which abusive language is used; violent dispute: *Their main fear is that the conference will be reduced to an unholy slanging match between pro and anti-Europeans* (London Times).
**slan|guage** (slang′gwij), *n.* slangy language: *It is also best to avoid attempts to talk teen slanguage* (Time). [blend of *slang* and *language*]
**slang|y** (slang′ē), *adj.,* **slang|i|er, slang|i|est.** **1** containing slang; full of slang: *Trilby's French was ... droll, slangy, piquant* (George du Maurier). **2** using much slang: *She's slangy, and she'd shock your sort of woman out of her wits* (Leonard Merrick). *You'd always thought of them before as being jazzy—you know, hep cats, slangy* (New York Times).
**slank** (slangk), *v. Archaic.* a past tense of **slink¹.**
**slant** (slant, slänt), *v., n., adj.* —*v.i.* to slope; go off at an angle; have or take an oblique direction or position: *Most handwriting slants to the right.* **syn:** See syn. under **slope.**
—*v.t.* **1** to cause to slant; slope: *The carpenter slanted the roof to allow water to run off.* **2** *U.S., Figurative.* to make (a story, news account, or report) biased by choosing or emphasizing certain facts: *Almost a third of them think that newspaper stories on their activities are "slanted"* (Time). [variant of Middle English *slenten* to slant, slip sideways < Scandinavian (compare Norwegian *slenta*)]
—*n.* **1** a slanting direction or position; slope: *Has your roof a sharp slant?* **syn:** incline. **2** *Figurative.* a way of regarding something; mental attitude; point of view: *Then the matter was given an entirely new slant by discoveries from another quarter* (Scientific American). *I have yet to see a piece of writing, political or nonpolitical, that doesn't have a slant* (New Yorker). **3** *U.S.* a glance; look. **4** *U.S. Slang.* an Asian; Oriental (used in an unfriendly way). **5** *Bacteriology.* a culture medium placed in a test tube slanted at a 30° angle to give larger growing area for a mold.
—***adj.*** sloping; oblique: *A lean-to has a slant roof. The ship sailed in a slant direction.*
[short for Middle English *aslante,* probably < *a-* on + *slant,* or *slent* a slope]
**slant board,** a reclining board, usually equipped with straps to prevent slipping, on which a person can lie head down and perform various exercises.
**slant drilling,** = slant-hole drilling.
**slan|ten|dic|u|lar** (slan′tən dik′yə lər, slän′-), *adj.* = slantindicular. —**slan′ten|dic′u|lar|ly,** *adv.*
**slant-eyed** (slant′īd′, slänt′-), *adj.* having eyes that slant, as certain Oriental people.
**slant-hole drilling** (slant′hōl′, slänt′-), the drilling of oil wells in a slanting instead of a vertical direction, especially with the unlawful purpose of tapping oil belonging to adjacent properties.
**slan|tin|dic|u|lar** (slan′tən dik′yə lər, slän′-), *adj. Humorous.* slanting; oblique. [< *slantin*(g) + (per-pen)*dicular*] —**slan′tin|dic′u|lar|ly,** *adv.*
**slant|ing** (slan′ting, slän′-), *adj.* that slants; sloping; oblique: *a slanting roof; ... slanting sunlight* (Winston Churchill). —**slant′ing|ly,** *adv.*
**slant|ly** (slant′lē, slänt′-), *adv.* in a slant or slanting direction.
**slant|ways** (slant′wāz′, slänt′-), *adv.* = slantwise.
**slant|wise** (slant′wīz′, slänt′-), *adv., adj.* —***adv.*** in a slanting manner; obliquely: *A crab scuttles slantwise.*
—***adj.*** slanting; oblique: *The slantwise rain Of light through the leaves* (John Greenleaf Whittier).
**slap¹** (slap), *n., v.,* **slapped, slap|ping,** *adv.* —*n.* **1** a blow with the open hand or with something flat; smack. **2** a sound made by slapping. **3** *Figurative.* sharp words of blame; direct insult or rebuff. **syn:** rebuke, reproval.
—*v.t.* **1** to strike with the open hand or with something flat; smack: *to slap a child for disobedience. I slapped the table with my hand.* **2** to put or throw with force: *She slapped the book down on the table.* **3** *Informal, Figurative.* **a** to hit by issuing (a restraint, summons, or the like): *The cop at Main and Scandinavia was going to slap me with a summons* (John O'Hara). [*His*] *California outfit ... was likely to be slapped with an injunction for violating U.S. anti-trust laws* (Canada Month). **b** to put flatly; exact or require: *He sent to Parliament a bill that would slap a 25% tax on the yield of German bonds* (Time).
—*v.i.* **1** to strike with the open hand or with something flat: *He slapped at the fly with a folded newspaper.* **2** to beat or hit with a slapping sound: *waves slapping against the dock. The piston was slapping in the cylinder.*
—***adv.*** **1** straight; directly: *The thief ran slap into a policeman.* **2** quickly; suddenly. **syn:** abruptly.
**slap down,** *Informal.* to put down; reject; squash:

**Pronunciation Key:** hat, āge, cãre, fär; let, ēqual, tėrm; it, īce; hot, ōpen, ôrder; **oi**l, **ou**t; cup, pu̇t, rüle; **ch**ild; lo**ng**; **th**in; ᴛʜen; **zh,** measure; ə represents **a** in about, **e** in taken, **i** in pencil, **o** in lemon, **u** in circus.

*The Senate Finance Committee slapped down a motion ... to end the panel's public hearings* (Wall Street Journal).
**slap in the face**, *Informal.* a humiliating insult or rebuff: *His decision to recognize Red China was a slap in the face because he had given contrary assurances* (Atlantic).
**slap on the wrist**, *Informal.* a light scolding: *NASA received a slap on the wrist for the way it has handled project Surveyor* (New Scientist).
**slap together**, to put together in a slapdash manner: *Ira Levin has slapped together a busy lampoon of a yarn* (New York Times).
[< Low German *slappe*]

**slap**[2] (slap, släp), *n. Scottish.* **1** an opening, as in a wall or hedge. **2** narrow pass, between hills. [< Flemish *slop* opening, passage]

**slap|bang** (slap′bang′), *adv., adj.* —*adv.* **1** without delay; immediately. **2** without due consideration or regard to the consequences: *He was bent on getting the Army slapbang into the Air Force's business of long-range strategic attack* (Time).
—*adj.* = slapdash.

**slap|dash** (slap′dash′), *adv., adj., n.* —*adv.* without much thought or care; hastily and carelessly: *I talked ... and said a thousand silly things, slapdash* (Washington Irving). **SYN:** precipitately.
—*adj.* hasty and careless: *Slapdash buildings were going up everywhere* (Time).
—*n.* **1** hasty, careless action, methods, or work: *The rest is swashbuckle and slapdash, jousting and broadsword, banqueting and jesting, and a fine siege of a beleaguered castle* (Newsweek). **SYN:** scramble. **2** rough plastering.

**slap-hap|py** or **slap|hap|py** (slap′hap′ē), *adj. Slang.* **1** dizzy and uncoordinated because of too many blows to the head; befuddled. **2** silly; giddy; senseless: *Two years has been long enough to inure the President against all slap-happy impulses* (Manchester Guardian Weekly).

**slap|jack** (slap′jak′), *n.* **1** *U.S. Dialect.* a flapjack; griddlecake or pancake. **2** a children's card game. [American English]

**slap|per** (slap′ər), *n.* a person or thing that slaps.

**slap|py** (slap′ē), *adj.,* **-pi|er, -pi|est.** smacking; spanking: *a slappy breeze, a slappy blow.*

**slap shot**, a quick shot made in ice hockey with a short, hard swing at the puck.

**slap|stick** (slap′stik′), *n., adj.* —*n.* **1** comedy full of rough play, pranks, and much contrived or unrelated humor: *Behind all this slapstick there is a serious question waiting in the wings* (Wall Street Journal). **2** a device consisting of two long, narrow sticks fastened so as to slap together loudly when a clown or actor hits somebody with it.
—*adj.* full of rough play, pranks, and much contrived or unrelated humor. In slapstick comedy, the actors knock each other around, throw pies, use other stage properties against each other, and often make jokes about the others' lines to make people laugh.
[American English < *slap*[1] + *stick*[1]]

**slap-up** (slap′up′), *adj. British Slang.* of superior quality; first-rate: *a slap-up hotel, a slap-up dinner for two.*

**slash**[1] (slash), *v., n.* —*v.t.* **1** to cut with a sweeping stroke of a sword, knife, ax, or whip; gash: *to slash a tree, to slash a person's face. He slashed the bark off the tree with his knife.* **2** to cut or slit (a garment) to let a different cloth or color show through. **3** to whip severely; lash. **4** *Figurative.* to criticize sharply, severely, or unkindly: *The critics slashed the new play in the next morning's papers.* **5** *Figurative.* to cut down severely; reduce a great deal: *to slash expenses. His salary was slashed when business became bad.* **6** to cut out parts of (as a book); change greatly (a book, article, motion picture, scene, or other written or motion-picture piece).
—*v.i.* **1** to make a sweeping stroke or strokes: *The hunter wounded the bear as he slashed at it with his knife. We ... came slashing down with the mad current into the narrow passage between the dykes* (Mark Twain). **2** *Figurative.* to criticize sharply, severely, or unkindly: *The writer slashed out against his critics.*
—*n.* **1** a sweeping, slashing stroke: *the slash of a sword; ... the slash of the rain* (Hamlin Garland); *rough slashes of sarcasm* (Thomas Carlyle). **2** a cut or wound made by such a stroke; gash: *The sword made a slash across his arm.* **3** an ornamental slit in a garment that lets a different cloth or color show through. **4a** a clearing in a forest, usually littered with felled trees, broken branches and the like, allowed to lie as they fell, as a result of storm, fire, or logging. **b** the tangle of fallen trees or branches: *Another change equally important, results from a more careful scientific disposal of slash and forest leftovers* (Atlantic). **5** *Figurative.* the act or fact of cutting down sharply; great reduction: *a slash in prices. Cotton has come down despite a drastic slash in plantings* (Wall Street Journal). **6** *U.S.* the slanting line used in writing and printing; virgule.
[Middle English *slaschen,* perhaps < Old French *esclachier* to break, variant of *esclater.* Compare etym. under **éclat.**]

**slash**[2] (slash), *n.* wet or swampy ground overgrown with bushes or trees. [American English; origin uncertain. Compare dialectal English *slashy* wet, miry.]

**slash-and-burn** (slash′ən bėrn′), *adj.* having to do with or designating a method of agriculture used by primitive peoples, in which trees were felled, and the land burned over just before planting season. The slash-and-burn method was wasteful because it used up the nutrients of the soil very quickly. *Indians of the South American tropics used slash-and-burn agriculture* (Clifford Evans).

**slash|er** (slash′ər), *n.* **1** a person who slashes; fighter; bully. **2** a machine that sizes warp yarns before weaving in textile manufacturing.

**slash|ing** (slash′ing), *adj., n.* —*adj.* **1** dashing; reckless. **2** that slashes; cutting: (*Figurative.*) *slashing criticism.*
—*n.* **1** the act of a person or thing that slashes. **2** a slash. —**slash′ing|ly,** *adv.*

**slash pine**, **1** a pine common in swamps of the southeastern United States: *The greatest proportion of forest and shelterbelt tree planting during the year was devoted to slash pine in the South* (Science News Letter). **2** its hard, durable wood. **3** = loblolly.

**slash pocket**, a diagonal pocket in an outer garment, with no flap on the outside.

**slat**[1] (slat), *n., v.,* **slat|ted, slat|ting.** —*n.* **1** a long, thin, narrow piece of wood or metal: *All the houses of the village were covered with slats or tiles* (J. Davies). **2** a hinged airfoil on the leading edge of an airplane's wing tip. It slants forward at low speeds to help the wing provide lift.
—*v.t.* to provide or build with slats: *to slat a porch or roof.*
**slats**, *Slang.* the ribs: *to take a stiff punch in the slats.*
[ultimately < Old French *esclat* split piece < *esclater* to splinter, burst. Compare etym. under **éclat.**]

**slat**[2] (slat), *v.,* **slat|ted, slat|ting,** *n. Archaic.*
—*v.t.* **1** to flap, cast, or dash. **2** to strike or beat; knock.
—*v.i.* to flap violently: *The mainsail was blowing and slatting with a noise like thunder* (Richard Henry Dana).
—*n.* a slap.
[origin uncertain. Compare Old Icelandic *sletta* to slap, splash, etc.]

**S. Lat.** or **S. lat.**, south latitude.

**slate**[1] (slāt), *n., adj., v.,* **slat|ed, slat|ing.** —*n.* **1** a fine-grained, usually bluish-gray rock that splits easily into thin, smooth layers. Slate is used to cover roofs and for blackboards. **2** a thin piece of this rock. Some children used to write on slates, but now they use paper. **3** a dark, bluish gray. **4** a list of candidates, officers, or others, to be considered, as for appointment, nomination, or election: *Apprehensions of Administration leaders that the Republican right wing will try to put up a rival slate are declining* (Newsweek).
—*adj.* dark bluish-gray.
—*v.t.* **1** to cover with slate. **2** to list on or as if on a slate: *He is slated for nomination to the office of club president.*
**clean slate**. See under **clean slate**.
**on the slate**, on credit: *Old-age pensioners would not be able to pop into the corner shop for a quarter pound on the slate* (Punch).
**wipe the slate clean**, to remove past errors or wrongdoings from one's record: *Germany ... has now wiped the slate clean. It is clearly in Britain's interest to reciprocate* (Manchester Guardian Weekly).
[Middle English *sclate* < Old French *esclate,* variant of *esclat;* see etym. under **slat**[1]] —**slate′like′,** *adj.*

**slate**[2] (slāt), *v.t.,* **slat|ed, slat|ing.** **1** to thrash severely. **2** *Figurative:* *The reviewers slated his book.* [perhaps variant of *slat*[2]]

**slate black**, a slate color having less than one tenth the luminosity of white.

**slate blue**, a dull blue with a grayish tinge.

**slate-col|ored junco** (slāt′kul′ərd), a grayish North American junco with white belly and outer tail feathers; snowbird.

**slate gray**, a relatively luminous slate color.

**slate pencil**, a pencil of soft slate or similar material, used for writing on a slate.

**slat|er**[1] (slā′tər), *n.* **1** a person who covers roofs with slates. **2** *Scottish.* a wood louse.

**slat|er**[2] (slā′tər), *n.* a violent critic.

**slate writer**, a person who practices slate writing.

**slate writing**, a sleight-of-hand trick in which a slate is written on apparently while tied or sealed face to face with another.

**slath|er** (slaᴛʜ′ər), *v., n. U.S. Informal.* —*v.t.* to spread or pour lavishly: *to slather butter on toast, to slather cream in coffee. He even smells stylish, slathering on ... cologne so liberally that it lingers on long after he leaves the room* (Time).
—*n.* Usually, **slathers**, a large amount: *They get slathers of money—most a dollar a day, Ben Rogers says* (Mark Twain).
[American English; origin unknown]

**slat|ing** (slā′ting), *n.* **1** slates: *to buy slating for a barn.* **2** the work or business of a slater.

**slat|ted** (slat′id), *adj.* furnished with, made of, or covered with slats: *a slatted frame.*

**slat|ter** (slat′ər), *v.t. British.* to spill; slop; scatter carelessly; waste. [origin uncertain]

**slat|tern** (slat′ərn), *n., adj.* —*n.* a woman or girl who is dirty, careless, or untidy, as in her dress, her ways, or her housekeeping. **SYN:** sloven.
—*adj.* slovenly; untidy: *a slattern wife, slattern manners.*
[related to **slatter**; origin uncertain. Compare Low German *slattje* slatterly woman.]

**slat|tern|ly** (slat′ərn lē), *adj.* like a slattern; slovenly; untidy: *a slatternly girl, in shoes down at heel* (Dickens). *A slatternly calico wrapper hung from her shoulders* (Edith Wharton). —**slat′tern|li|ness,** *n.*

**slat|y** (slā′tē), *adj.,* **slat|i|er, slat|i|est.** **1** of, like, or having to do with slate. **2** slate-colored: *The sun had disappeared under a cloud, and the sea had turned a little slaty* (G. Macdonald).

**slat|y|head|ed parakeet** (slā′tē hed′id), a large parakeet found from northwestern India to Thailand and Laos. It is about 15 inches long.

**slaugh|ter** (slô′tər), *n., v.* —*n.* **1** the killing of an animal or animals for food; butchering: *the slaughter of a steer, to fatten hogs for slaughter. They [passenger pigeons] were wiped out by one of the most relentless and perverse slaughters in history, exceeding in ruthlessness the better-known butchery of the buffalo* (Newsweek).
**2** brutal killing; much or needless killing: *The battle resulted in a frightful slaughter. Today Fourth of July slaughter on the American highways replaces marginal injury from fireworks.* **SYN:** murder, massacre.
—*v.t., v.i.* **1** to kill an animal or animals for food; butcher: *Millions of cattle are slaughtered every year in the stockyards.* **2** to kill brutally; massacre.
[Middle English *slahter* < Scandinavian (compare Old Icelandic *slātr* butcher meat)] —**slaugh′ter|er,** *n.*

**slaugh|ter|house** (slô′tər hous′), *n.* a place where animals are killed for food and other products. **SYN:** abattoir.

**slaugh|ter|man** (slô′tər mən), *n., pl.* **-men.** **1** a man whose work is to slaughter animals for food. **2** = executioner.

**slaugh|ter|ous** (slô′tər əs), *adj.* murderous; destructive: *Direness, familiar to my slaughterous thoughts, cannot once start me* (Shakespeare).
—**slaugh′ter|ous|ly,** *adv.*

**Slav** (släv, slav), *n., adj.* —*n.* a member of a group of peoples in eastern, southeastern, and central Europe whose languages are related. Russians, Ukrainians, Poles, Czechs, Slovaks, Moravians, Serbs, and Bulgarians are Slavs.
—*adj.* of or having to do with Slavs; Slavic. [< Medieval Latin *Slavus* Slav; slave, ultimately < Slavic (compare Russian *slovo* word); original meaning was member of a single speech community]

**Slav.**, **1** Slavic. **2** Slavonian. **3** Slavonic.

**Slav|dom** (släv′dəm, slav′-), *n.* the group or race of people called Slavs; Slavs collectively: *the civilization of Slavdom.*

**slave** (slāv), *n., v.,* **slaved, slav|ing,** *adj.* —*n.* **1** a person who is the property of another. Slaves were once bought and sold like horses in the United States. *We'll visit Caliban, my slave* (Shakespeare). **2** *Figurative.* **a** a person who is controlled or ruled by some desire, habit, or influence: *A drunkard is a slave of drink. Give me that man That is not passion's slave* (Shakespeare). **b** a person who submits to or follows another: *The head of a party and, consequently ... the slave of a party* (Macaulay). **3** a person who works like a slave. **4** = slave ant. **5a** an electronic device that receives and relays radio signals transmitted by a master control, as in loran navigation. **b** a mechanical or electric device, usually a kind of servomechanism, for manipulating objects by remote control, as in handling dangerous radioactive materials from outside a closed system.
—*v.i.* to work like a slave; work hard and long: *Many mothers slave for their children.*
—*v.t.* to make a slave of; enslave.
—*adj.* **1** of slaves; for slaves; done by slaves: *a slave dealer, a slave hunt, slave labor.* **2** of or having to do with an apparatus or device which duplicates an action or transmits back a signal in

the same form as sent: *The signal from the master goes directly to the navigator and also to the slave station, which, after synchronizing properly, retransmits the pulse* (James P. Baxter). [< Old French *esclave* < Medieval Latin *Sclavus,* later *Slavus* Slav; slave < Late Greek *Sklábos* (first applied to enslaved Slavs)] —**slave′like′**, *adj.*

**slave ant**, an ant that is captured and forced to work for other ants in a way that suggests slavery.

**slave bracelet**, an identification bracelet worn around the ankle.

**slave driver**, **1** an overseer of slaves. **2** a person who makes others work very hard; exacting taskmaster.

**slave fork**, a long, heavy piece of wood with a forked end formerly used in Africa for securing a slave, as when on the march, the forked end being made fast about the neck of the slave.

**slave|hold|er** (slāv′hōl′dər), *n.* an owner of slaves.

**slave|hold|ing** (slāv′hōl′ding), *adj., n.* —*adj.* owning slaves.
—*n.* the owning of slaves: *Secession was rebellion and revolution; but rebellion and revolution might be right, if only slaveholding was right* (New Yorker).

**slave|less** (slāv′lis), *adj.* without slaves: *a slaveless land* (John Greenleaf Whittier).

**slave|ling** (slāv′ling), *n.* a submissive or servile person or thing.

**slave maker**, an ant that captures and forces other ants to work for it.

**slave-mak|ing ant** (slāv′mā′king), = slave maker.

**slave market**, **1** a market where slaves are sold. **2** *Figurative: in the slave markets where teachers are hired* (Time).

**slave|own|er** (slāv′ō′nər), *n.* an owner of slaves.

**slav|er¹** (slā′vər), *n.* **1** a dealer in slaves. **2** a ship used in the slave trade. **3** = white slaver. [< *slave* + *-er*¹]

**slav|er²** (slav′ər), *v., n.* —*v.i.* to let saliva run from the mouth; drool: (*Figurative.*) *Beneath [Tammany's] shaky perch slavered a whole litter of lesser tigers* (Time).
—*v.t.* to wet with saliva; slobber.
—*n.* **1** saliva running from the mouth. **2** drivel; nonsense. **3** gross flattery.
[< Scandinavian (compare Old Icelandic *slafra*). Compare etym. under **slobber**.]

**slav|er|y** (slā′vər ē, slāv′rē), *n.* **1** the condition or fact of being a slave. Many African Negroes were captured and sold into slavery. SYN: bondage, serfdom, thralldom, servitude. **2** the custom of owning slaves. Where slavery is permitted, certain men own others. *Slavery is but half-abolished, emancipation is but half completed, while millions of freemen with votes in their hands are left without education* (Robert C. Winthrop). **3** *Figurative.* a condition like that of a slave: *The extreme slavery and subjection that courtiers live in* (John Evelyn). **4** hard work like that of a slave; drudgery.

**slave state**, **1** one of the Slave States. **2** a country ruled by absolute authority; dictatorship.

**Slave States**, the 15 states of the United States in which slavery was legal before and during the Civil War: Virginia, North Carolina, South Carolina, Georgia, Florida, Alabama, Mississippi, Louisiana, Texas, Arkansas, and Tennessee; Missouri, Kentucky, Maryland, and Delaware. The last four states did not join the Confederacy.

**slave trade**, the business of procuring, transporting, and selling slaves, especially Negro slaves: *For 250 years, Bristol and Liverpool merchants grew fat on the profits of the Nigerian slave trade, shipping tens of thousands of blacks yearly to the U.S.* (Newsweek).

**slave trader**, a person who buys and sells slaves as a business; slaver.

**slav|ey** (slā′vē), *n., pl.* **-eys**. *Especially British Informal.* a maid of all work.

**Slav|ic** (slä′vik, slav′-), *adj., n.* —*adj.* of or having to do with the Slavs or their languages; Slavonic: *Slavic origin, Slavic heritage, Slavic music.* —*n.* a language or the group of languages spoken by the Slavs, including West Slavic (Polish, Czech, Slovak, Serbian, and the extinct Polabian), East Slavic (Russian, Ruthenian), and South Slavic (Bulgarian, Serbo-Croatian, and Slovene).

**Slav|i|cism** (slä′və siz əm, slav′ə-), *n.* = Slavism.

**Slav|i|cist** (slä′və sist, slav′ə-), *n.* a person who studies Slavic languages and culture.

**Slav|i|cize** (slä′və sīz, slav′ə-), *v.t.,* **-cized, -ciz|ing**. to make Slavic in character, language, or culture: *to Slavicize a people, to Slavicize a name.*

**slav|ish** (slā′vish), *adj.* **1** of or having something to do with a slave or slaves. **2** like a slave; mean; base: *slavish fears.* **3** *Figurative.* weakly submitting: *the thoughtless, slavish victim of inclination.* SYN: servile. **4** like that of slaves; fit for slaves: *a slavish people.* **5** *Figurative.* lacking originality and independence: *a slavish copy.* —**slav′ish|ly**, *adv.* —**slav′ish|ness**, *n.*

**Slav|ism** (slä′viz əm, slav′iz-), *n.* the culture, languages, and spirit of the Slavs.

**Slav|ist** (slä′vist, slav′-), *n.* = Slavicist.

**Slavo-**, *combining form.* Slav or Slavs: *Slavophile = one who admires the Slavs.* [< Medieval Latin *Slavus;* see etym. under **Slav**]

**slav|oc|ra|cy** (slāv ok′rə sē), *n.* **1** domination by slaveholders. **2** the dominating body of slaveholders. [American English < *slave* + *-ocracy,* as in *democracy*]

**slav|o|crat** (slāv′ə krat), *n.* a member of a slavocracy.

**slav|o|crat|ic** (slāv′ə krat′ik), *adj.* of or having to do with slavocracy or slavocrats.

**Sla|vo|ni|an** (slə vō′nē ən), *adj., n.* —*adj.* **1** of or having to do with Slavonia, a region in northern Yugoslavia, or its people. **2** = Slavic.
—*n.* **1** a native of Slavonia. **2** = Slav. **3** the Slavic language or languages; Slavic.

**Sla|von|ic** (slə von′ik), *adj., n.* —*adj.* **1** = Slavic. **2** = Slavonian.
—*n.* **1** = Slav. **2** = Slavonian. **3** the Slavic language or languages.

**Slav|o|ni|za|tion** (slä′və nə zā′shən, slav′ə-), *n.* **1** the act of Slavonizing. **2** the state of being Slavonized.

**Slav|o|nize** (slä′və nīz, slav′ə-), *v.t.,* **-nized, -niz|ing**. to make Slavonian or Slavic in character, sentiment, language, or culture.

**Slav|o|phil** (slä′və fil, slav′ə-), *n.* = Slavophile.

**Slav|o|phile** (slä′və fīl, -fil; slav′ə-), *n.* an admirer or friend of the Slavs or their culture.

**Slav|o|phil|ic** (slä′və fil′ik, slav′ə-), *adj.* admiring the Slavs; favoring Slavic interests.

**Sla|voph|i|lism** (slə vof′ə liz əm; slä′və fə liz′-, slav′ə-), *n.* admiration for the Slavs or their culture.

**Slav|o|phobe** (slä′və fōb, slav′ə-), *n.* a person who fears or hates the Slavs or their policies.

**slaw** (slô), *n.* **1** finely sliced or chopped cabbage, raw or cooked, served with dressing; coleslaw. **2** a salad like coleslaw, made of cooked cabbage and served with a hot dressing. [American English, apparently short for *coleslaw*]

**slay** (slā), *v.t.,* **slew, slain, slay|ing**. **1** to kill with violence: *A hunter slays wild animals. Jack slew the giant. Saul hath slain his thousands, and David his ten thousands* (I Samuel 18:7). SYN: See syn. under **kill**. **2** *U.S. Slang, Figurative.* to amuse greatly: *That comedian just slays me.* **3** *Obsolete.* to smite; strike. [fusion of Old English *slēan* to strike, and Middle English *slayen* to kill, Old English *slægen*] —**slay′er**, *n.*
► **Slay** not regularly has as its principal parts *slay, slew, slain.* In its slang sense, however, *slayed* (instead of *slew* or *slain*) is usual: *Our act simply slayed them in Las Vegas.*

**SLBM** (no periods), submarine-launched ballistic missile.

**sld.**, **1** sailed. **2** sealed.

**SLD** (no periods), Specific Language Disability (inability to decode and reproduce the written symbols of language due to physical or neurological causes).

**SLE** (no periods), St. Louis encephalitis.

**sleave** (slēv), *n., v.,* **sleaved, sleav|ing**. —*n.* **1a** a small silk thread made by separating a thicker thread. **b** silk in the form of such threads; floss. **2** *Archaic.* anything confused and troublesome: *Sleep that knits up the ravel'd sleave of care* (Shakespeare).
—*v.t.* to divide or separate (silk or other thread) into smaller threads.
[Old English *-slǣfan,* as in *tōslǣfan* to divide]

**sleaze** (slēz), *n.* sleaziness; shoddiness: *For all its brazen sleaze, Soho is a pretty fair working model of … a city neighborhood* (Listener). [back formation < *sleazy*]

**slea|zi|ly** (slē′zə lē), *adv.* in a sleazy manner.

**slea|zi|ness** (slē′zē nis), *n.* sleazy quality.

**slea|zy** (slē′zē), *adj.,* **-zi|er, -zi|est**. **1** flimsy and poor; shoddy: *sleazy cloth, a sleazy dress. Wise pulled down the sleazy window shades* (Sinclair Lewis). (*Figurative.*) *It is a stammered, sleazy chronicle, told by fits and starts in bits and pieces, and constantly interrupted by the director and actors* (Time). **2** disreputable: *a sleazy neighborhood.* [origin uncertain]

***sled** (sled), *n., v.,* **sled|ded, sled|ding**. —*n.* **1a** a framework of boards mounted on runners for use on snow or ice. Sleds pulled by dogs are in common use in the Arctic. **b** *British.* a toboggan. **2** = sleigh. **3** a framework that moves on rails at controlled speeds, for testing effects, as of acceleration, deceleration, heat, or shock, produced on a vehicle or person.
—*v.i.* to ride on or in a sled.
—*v.t.* to carry (something) on a sled: *to sled logs out of the forest.*
[< Middle Dutch *sledde*] —**sled′like′**, *adj.*

**sled|der** (sled′ər), *n.* **1** a person who drives, rides on, or guides a sled. **2** a horse, dog, or other animal that pulls a sled.

**sled|ding** (sled′ing), *n.* **1** the action of riding or coasting on a sled. **2** the condition of the snow for the use of sleds: *two months of good sledding.*
**hard** (or **tough**) **sledding**, *Informal.* unfavorable conditions; difficult going: *With the loss of business the little grocery store was in for some hard sledding.*

**sled dog**, a dog used to draw a sled in arctic regions.

***sledge¹** (slej), *n., v.,* **sledged, sledg|ing**. —*n.* **1** a heavy sled or sleigh, usually pulled by horses: *Travelling is impossible by sledge because the ice is unsafe* (Gabriele Rabel). **2** *British.* a sleigh.
—*v.t.* to carry (something) on a sledge.
—*v.i.* to ride on or in a sledge: *On the shelf ice of this sound one can sledge without great difficulty* (Gabriele Rabel).
[< Middle Dutch *sleedse;* influenced by *sled*]

**sledge²** (slej), *n., v.* —*n.* = sledge hammer.
—*v.t., v.i.* to sledge-hammer: *to sledge a rock to pieces.*
[Old English *slecg*]

**sledge dog**, = sled dog.

**sledge hammer**, or **sledge|ham|mer¹** (slej′ham′ər), *n.* **1** a large, heavy hammer, usually swung with both hands. **2** *Figurative: Sarcasm can become a sledge hammer in a debate.*

**sledge-ham|mer** or **sledge|ham|mer²** (slej′ham′ər), *v., adj.* —*v.t., v.i.* **1** to hit with a sledge hammer. **2** *Figurative: I grant a sledge-hammering sort of merit in him* (Dickens).
—*adj.* powerful; crushing: *a sledge-hammer attack. In the past, the Russians have always used sledge-hammer tactics in trying to take over Iran* (Newsweek).

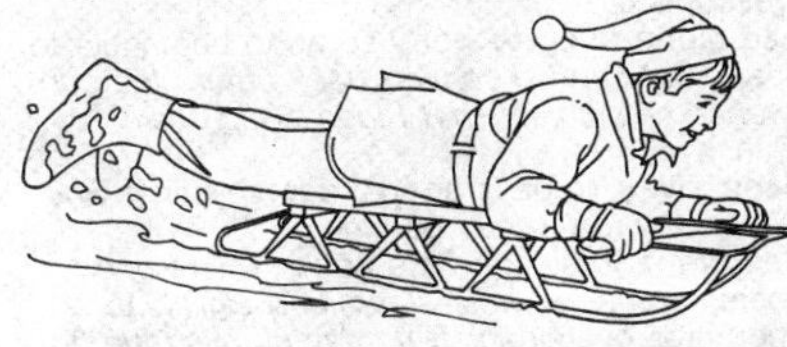
***sled** definition 1a

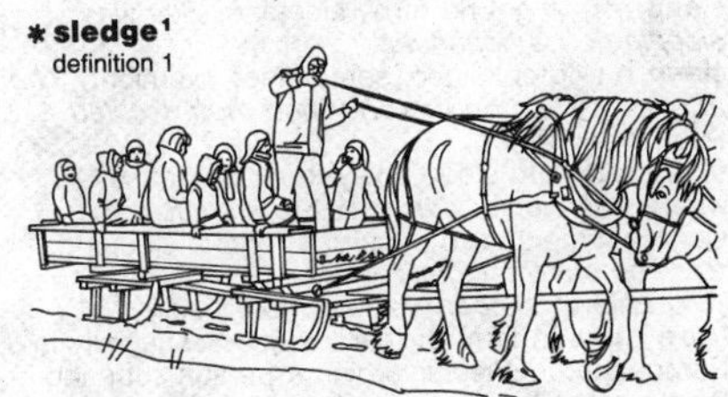
***sledge¹** definition 1

***sleigh** definition 1

**sleek** (slēk), *adj., v.* —*adj.* **1** soft and glossy; smooth: *sleek hair.* **2** having smooth, soft skin, hair, or fur: *a sleek cat.* **3** *Figurative.* smooth of speech and manners: *a sleek salesman. He had a look of sleek intelligence* (Graham Greene). **4** having clean lines; trim; smooth: *a sleek jet plane.*
—*v.t.* **1** to smooth; remove roughness from. **2** to make smooth and glossy: (*Figurative.*) *To sleek her ruffled peace of mind* (Tennyson). **3** to make tidy: *to sleek up a room.*
[Middle English *slike;* see etym. under **slick**]

**Pronunciation Key:** hat, āge, cãre, fär; let, ēqual, tėrm; it, īce; hot, ōpen, ôrder; oil, out; cup, pu̇t, rüle; child; long; thin; ᴛʜen; zh, measure; ə represents **a** in about, **e** in taken, **i** in pencil, **o** in lemon, **u** in circus.

—**sleek′ly**, *adv.* —**sleek′ness**, *n.*

**sleek|en** (slē′kən), *v.t.* to make sleek; smooth.

**sleek|er** (slē′kər), *n.* a person or a tool that sleeks leather.

**sleek|it** (slē′kit), *adj. Scottish.* **1** sleek: *Wee, sleekit, cow'rin', timrous beastie ...* (Robert Burns). **2** plausible; deceitful; sly. [variant of *sleeked,* past participle of *sleek*]

**sleek|y** (slē′kē), *adj.,* **sleek|i|er, sleek|i|est.** **1** sleek; smooth. **2** *Figurative.* plausible; artful; sly.

**sleep** (slēp), *v.,* **slept, sleep|ing,** *n.* —*v.i.* **1** to rest body and mind; be without ordinary thought or movement: *We sleep at night. Most animals sleep.* **SYN**: slumber, doze, drowse, nap, snooze. **2** *Figurative.* to be in a condition like sleep: *The seeds sleep in the ground all winter. How sweet the moonlight sleeps upon this bank!* (Shakespeare). **3** *Figurative.* to rest, as in the grave; lie buried: *So David slept with his fathers, and was buried in the city of David* (I Kings 2:10). **4** to have sexual relations (with). **5** *Informal.* to give sleep: *The new sofa did sleep much better than the old one* (Louise Meriwether). **6** *Botany.* to close petals or leaves, especially at night.
—*v.t.* **1** to provide with or offer sleeping accommodation for: *a hotel that sleeps 500 people.* **2** to pass in sleeping. **3** to take rest in (sleep): *He slept the sleep of exhaustion.*
—*n.* **1** rest of body and mind occurring naturally and regularly in animals: *Most people need eight hours of sleep a day. Tired nature's sweet restorer, balmy sleep!* (Edward Young). *The biological object of sleep seems to be recuperation, its psychological characteristic the suspension of interest in the outer world* (Sigmund Freud). **SYN**: slumber, doze, drowse, snooze, nap. **2** a period of sleep: *a short sleep. Have a good sleep.* **3** *Figurative.* a condition like sleep: *to put one's doubts to sleep.* **4** *Botany.* a movement of plants in which they assume at nightfall positions unlike those which they have maintained during the day; nyctitropism.
**lose sleep over**, to worry so as to be unable to sleep: *But can we convert back before the conference season, is what I lose sleep over* (Punch).
**sleep away**, to pass or spend in sleeping: *She slept away the whole morning.*
**sleep in, a** to sleep in the house where one works: *Some servants sleep in.* **b** *British.* to sleep late; oversleep: *Saturday morning the boys and I let Merna and Willa sleep in* (Maclean's).
**sleep off**, to get rid of by sleeping: *She was sleeping off a headache.*
**sleep on**, to consider (something) overnight: *The attendant slept on the offer and then decided* (New York Times).
**sleep out, a** to sleep away from the house where one works: *Our maid sleeps out.* **b** to sleep outdoors. **c** to pass or spend in sleeping: *to sleep out the night.*
[Old English *slǣpan*] —**sleep′like′**, *adj.*

**sleep cure**, a form of therapy used especially in European countries, in which a person suffering from insomnia, nervousness, depression, and the like is administered large doses of tranquilizers and barbiturates to keep him temporarily in a sleeping or dozing state: *The psychiatrist will order a sleep cure of about eight days, on the average. This is supposed to break the tension and get him out of his environment* (New Yorker).

**sleep|er** (slē′pər), *n.* **1** a person or thing that sleeps: *The noise woke the sleepers.* **2** a railroad car with berths for passengers to sleep in; sleeping car. **3a** a heavy horizontal beam used as a support. **b** one of the substantial strips of wood laid over concrete to enable wood floors to be nailed to it. **4** *British.* a tie to support a railroad track: *The steel rail, prised from the sleepers, had tilted over to one side* (Maclean's). **5** *Informal, Figurative.* a person or thing that makes an unexpected success, such as an athletic team, a motion picture, or a book: *I was in the peculiar spot of negotiating for a book that I hadn't read—but the deal went through in fine shape, and I think we've got a real sleeper* (Saturday Review). **6** *Informal.* a sleeping pill.
**sleepers**, one-piece pajamas for little children, extending from the neck and covering the feet: *winter sleepers.*

**sleep|er|ette** (slē′pə ret′), *n. Especially British.* a sleeping compartment on a train or boat.

**sleeper plane**, an airplane with sleeping accommodations for passengers.

**sleep|ful** (slēp′fəl), *adj.* marked by sleep; restful through sleep: *sleepful nights.*

**sleep|ful|ness** (slēp′fəl nis), *n.* = sleepiness.

**sleep|i|ly** (slē′pə lē), *adv.* in a sleepy manner.

**sleep-in** (slēp′in′), *adj., n.* —*adj.* sleeping in the place where one works: *Her mother was a sleep-in domestic servant who worked in another suburb of Cape Town* (New Yorker).
—*n.* the act of occupying a public place by a group of people to spend the night or to sleep there as a form of protest, demonstration, or indication of ownership rights.

**sleep|i|ness** (slē′pē nis), *n.* sleepy quality or condition; drowsiness.

**sleep|ing** (slē′ping), *n., adj.* —*n.* sleep.
—*adj.* **1** that sleeps: *a sleeping child.* **2** used for sleeping on or in: *sleeping quarters.*

**sleeping bag**, a canvas or waterproof bag, usually warmly lined, to sleep in outdoors.

**Sleeping Beauty**, **1** a fairy-tale princess shut up in a castle and put to sleep by enchantment for a hundred years. The kiss of a young prince awakens her. **2** *Figurative: A modern Sleeping Beauty held in ... imprisonment by order of her husband* (Atlantic).

**sleeping car**, a railroad car with berths for passengers to sleep in; Pullman.

**sleeping partner**, a partner who takes no active part in managing the business.

**sleeping pill**, a pill or capsule containing a drug that causes sleep.

**sleeping porch**, *U.S.* a room with open sides, or with walls of screen or glass; room open to the outside air: *Years ago, up-to-date Scarsdale families slept on sleeping porches, to get the benefit of the village's country air* (New York Times).

**sleeping powder**, a drug that causes sleep.

**sleeping sickness**, **1** a disease common in Africa carried by the tsetse fly, causing fever, inflammation of the brain, sleepiness and increasing weakness, and usually death; African sleeping sickness. It is caused by either of two trypanosomes. **2** a kind of epidemic encephalitis characterized by extreme drowsiness and muscular weakness, believed to be caused by a virus; lethargic encephalitis: *Sleeping sickness, the dread encephalitis, is not a strange disease afflicting only peoples in distant Africa or Asia* (Science News Letter).

**sleep-learn|ing** (slēp′lėr′ning), *n.* instruction obtained by or given to one who is asleep, usually by means of recordings, on the theory that the sleeper's unconscious is capable of absorbing the information; hypnopedia: *"Sleep-learning" is big business in the Soviet Union, where an increasing number of civil and military establishments are setting up dormitory facilities for pumping into trainees dull but necessary information—such as foreign language vocabularies—during the time "wasted" asleep* (New Scientist).

**sleep|less** (slēp′lis), *adj.* **1** without sleep; not sleeping; restless: *a hot, sleepless night.* **2** watchful; wide-awake: *sleepless vigilance.* **3** *Figurative: the sleepless tides. Winds are rude in Biscay's sleepless bay* (Byron). —**sleep′less|ly**, *adv.* —**sleep′less|ness**, *n.*

**sleep-teach|ing** (slēp′tē′ching), *n.* = sleep-learning.

**sleep|walk** (slēp′wôk′), *v., n.* —*v.i.* to walk about while asleep.
—*n.* a walk during sleep: *[a] sleepwalk that brought her near to the roofedge and death ...* (Punch).

**sleep|walk|er** (slēp′wô′kər), *n.* a person who walks about while asleep; somnambulist.

**sleep|walk|ing** (slēp′wô′king), *n., adj.* —*n.* the act of walking while asleep; somnambulism.
—*adj.* **1** that walks about while asleep. **2** having to do with someone who walks while asleep: *... superb in the sleepwalking scene* (Time).

**sleep|wear** (slēp′wãr′), *n.* pajamas, nightgowns, or other garments to be worn for sleeping: *children's sleepwear.*

**sleep|y** (slē′pē), *adj.,* **sleep|i|er, sleep|i|est.** **1** ready to go to sleep; inclined to sleep: *He never gets enough rest and is always sleepy.* **2** *Figurative.* not active; quiet: *a sleepy little mountain town.* **3** inducing sleep; soporific: *a warm, sleepy day. The sleepy sound of the chanting and the sleepier sound of the bells made her feel still more pressed* (Atlantic).
—*Syn.* **1 Sleepy, drowsy** mean ready or inclined to sleep. **Sleepy** suggests being ready to fall asleep or having a tendency to sleep: *After a long day out in the open air, we were all sleepy.* **Drowsy** suggests being heavy or dull with sleepiness: *After lying in the sun, she became drowsy.*

**sleep|y-eyed** (slē′pē īd′), *adj.* looking as if ready to fall asleep: *A sleepy-eyed girl opened the door for us.*

**sleepy grass**, a stout bunch grass of the Rocky Mountains which, when eaten, has a narcotic effect on livestock lasting several days.

**sleep|y|head** (slē′pē hed′), *n.* a sleepy, drowsy, or lazy person: *... small travelling alarm clocks, packed in miniature leather suitcases and designed to wake the sleepyhead in time* (New Yorker).

**sleet** (slēt), *n., v.* —*n.* **1** partly frozen rain; snow or hail mixed with rain. Sleet forms when rain falls through a layer of cold air. *In Texas, snow and sleet in near freezing temperatures iced over highways and closed schools* (Newsweek). **2** a thin coating of ice formed when rain falls on a very cold surface; glaze.
—*v.i.* to come down in sleet: *It sleeted; then it snowed; then it rained.*
—*v.t.* **1** to send down like sleet. **2** to beat or cover with sleet.
[Middle English *slete*]

**sleet|i|ness** (slē′tē nis), *n.* sleety quality or condition.

**sleet|y** (slē′tē), *adj.,* **sleet|i|er, sleet|i|est.** **1** of or like sleet: *sleety showers.* **2** characterized by sleet: *a dismal and sleety morning. The weather was cold, wet, and sleety.*

**sleeve** (slēv), *n., v.,* **sleeved, sleev|ing.** —*n.* **1** the part of a garment that covers the arm or the upper part of the arm: *The sleeves of his coat were too long and hung down over his hands. The scooped neckline blouse has a soft bow and short sleeves* (New Yorker). **2** a tube into which a rod or another tube fits: *a cylinder sleeve.* **3** the cover or jacket enclosing a phonograph record.
—*v.t.* **1** to fix, fasten, or couple by means of a sleeve or tube. **2** to provide (a garment) with sleeves; fashion: *the drifting peignoir sleeved with puffs, steeped in lace* (New Yorker).
**laugh in** (or **up**) **one's sleeve**, to be amused but not show it; laugh inwardly: *His shrewd nephew was laughing at him in his sleeve* (Henry Kingsley).
**roll up one's sleeves**, to get down to work; begin a task or job. *Citizens of Wells collectively rolled up their sleeves to raise $43,000 for a modern, well-equipped clinic* (Wall Street Journal).
**up one's sleeve**, in reserve; ready for use when needed: *Barrett had considerably more up his sleeve than the three lengths with which he finished* (London Daily News).
**wear on one's sleeve**, to show openly or publicly: *He does not wear competitive intensity on his sleeve* (London Times). *McCarthy [was] scornful of feelings worn on the sleeve* (Harper's).
[Old English *slēfe, slīefe*]

**sleeve bearing**, a bearing that fits around a journal or revolving pivot like a sleeve.

**sleeve board**, a shaped board on which sleeves are ironed or pressed.

**sleeved** (slēvd), *adj.* having sleeves.

**-sleeved**, *combining form.* having ___ sleeves: *Long-sleeved = having long sleeves.*

**sleeve dog**, a dog small enough to be carried in the sleeve, as among the Chinese and Japanese.

**sleeve|less** (slēv′lis), *adj.* **1** without sleeves: *a sleeveless summer dress.* **2** *Archaic.* futile; fruitless; useless: *... a sleeveless errand* (Shakespeare). —**sleeve′less|ness**, *n.*

**sleeve|let** (slēv′lit), *n.* **1** a covering worn over the forearm to protect the sleeve from dirt or wear. **2** a small sleeve.

**sleeve-note** (slēv′nōt′), *n.* a description or explanatory note on the jacket of a phonograph record or album.

**sleeve nut**, a double nut which has right-hand and left-hand threads for joining the ends of rods or tubes; union.

**sleeve Pekingese**, a very small Pekingese; a sleeve dog of the Pekingese breed.

**sleeve valve**, a sliding, cylindrical sleeve within an automobile's cylinder, having holes which its motion brings over ports in the cylinder for intake and exhaust.

**sleigh** (slā), *n., v.* —*n.* **1** a carriage or cart mounted on runners for use on snow or ice, pulled by one or more horses. In northern countries people once commonly used sleighs in the winter. *To grandfather's house we'll go; The horse knows the way To carry the sleigh Through the white and drifted snow* (Lydia Maria Child). See picture under **sled**. **2** = sled.
—*v.i.* to travel or ride in a sleigh.
[American English, earlier *slee* < Dutch, variant of *slede* sled]

**sleigh bed**, a type of bed of the early 1800's, having the ends curved upward and outward in the form of an elongated scroll, like the front of some sleighs.

**sleigh bell**, a small bell, usually a hollow ball of metal pierced by a slit and containing a loose pellet of metal, several of which are often attached to the harness of a horse drawing a sleigh: *But now the sleigh bells are jingling on the carriage outside, so heigh-ho, let's be away to the toy stores!* (New Yorker).

**sleigh|ing** (slā′ing), *n.* **1** the act or fact of riding in a sleigh. **2** the condition of the roads for using a sleigh: *a week of good sleighing. Hard-packed snow makes good sleighing.*

**sleight** (slīt), *n.* **1** skill; dexterity: *The squaw with a peculiar sleight threw her papoose over her* *shoulder* (Susannah Moodie). **2** a clever trick: *Unpractised in the sleights and artifices of controversy* (Benjamin Franklin). **3** craft or cunning, used to deceive: *Every interest did, by right, or might, or sleight, get represented* (Emerson). [alteration of Middle English *slethe* < Scandinavian (compare Old Icelandic *slǣgth* < *slǣgr* sly)]

**sleight of hand**, **1** skill and quickness in moving the hands: *A magician must practice for many hours to gain sleight of hand.* **2** the tricks or skill of a modern magician; juggling: *a magician's mastery of the usual sleight of hand (Figurative.) music that is free of self-conscious formulas and tricks of stylistic sleight of hand* (New Yorker). **SYN**: legerdemain.

**slen|der** (slen′dər), *adj.* **1** long and thin; not big around; slim: *A boy 6 feet tall and weighing 130 pounds is very slender. A pencil is a slender piece of wood.* **2** slight; small; scanty: *a slender meal, a slender income, a slender hope of success.* **3** *Phonetics.* (of vowels) high. [Middle English *slendre*, and *sclendre*, origin uncertain]
— **slen′der|ly**, *adv.* — **slen′der|ness**, *n.*
— *Syn.* **1 Slender, slim** mean thin, not big around. **Slender** suggests pleasing, graceful thinness: *Most girls want to be slender. The legs of those chairs are slender.* **Slim** suggests lack of flesh and lightness of frame or build: *He is a slim boy, but he may fill out as he becomes older.*

**slen|der|i|za|tion** (slen′dər ə zā′shən), *n.* **1** a slenderizing. **2** a being slenderized.

**slen|der|ize** (slen′də rīz), *v.*, **-ized, -iz|ing.** — ***v.t.*** **1** to make slender or more slender; cause to lose weight: *... ideal for men and women who want to keep fit and aid their slenderizing campaign easily* (Wall Street Journal). **2** to make appear less stout: *a slenderizing dress. Vertical lines in dress design tend to slenderize the matronly figure.*
— ***v.i.*** to become slender; lose weight; reduce.

**slender loris**, a tailless, nocturnal lemur of India and Ceylon (Sri Lanka), about 5 inches long with very large eyes.

**slen|tan|do** (slen tän′dō), *adj. Music.* lentando; slackening; becoming slower. [< Italian *slentando*, present participle of *slentare* slacken]

**slept** (slept), *v.* the past tense and past participle of **sleep**: *The baby slept soundly. I have not slept well for weeks.*

**sleugh** (slü), *n.* slough; soft, muddy ground.

**sleuth** (slüth), *n., v.* — ***n.*** **1** *Informal.* a detective: *He remains the most reluctant of sleuths throughout the book* (Newsweek). **2** = bloodhound.
— ***v.i.*** *Informal.* to be or act like a detective.
[< Scandinavian (compare Old Icelandic *slōth*) a trail] — **sleuth′er**, *n.*

**sleuth|hound** (slüth′hound′), *n.* **1** = bloodhound. **2** *U.S. Informal.* a detective.

**S level**, *British.* scholarship level, the level of examination given to secondary students who have passed the A level.

**slew**[1] (slü), *v.* the past tense of **slay**: *Jack slew the giant.*

**slew**[2] (slü), *v., n.* — ***v.t., v.i.*** to turn; swing; twist: *He slewed the front wheels sharply to avoid hitting the dog. The car slewed to the left when he put the brakes on hard.*
— ***n.*** a turn; swing; twist. Also, **slue**.
[origin unknown]

**slew**[3] (slü), *n.* a swampy place; marshy inlet: *A slew is often covered with reeds and marsh grass.* Also, **slough, slue.** [American English, spelling for pronunciation of *slough*[1]]

**slew**[4] (slü), *n. Informal.* a large number or amount; lot: *The new boy already has a slew of friends. Mulligan has been on the payroll of a slew of big-name companies himself* (Newsweek). Also, **slue.** [American English, perhaps through Anglo-Irish < Irish *sluagh* host, crowd]

**slg.**, sailing.

**slice** (slīs), *n., v.*, **sliced, slic|ing.** — ***n.*** **1** a thin, flat, broad piece cut from something: *a slice of bread, a slice of meat, a slice of cake.* **2** *Figurative.* a part; share: *Each partner receives his slice of the profits.* **3** a knife or spatula with a thin, broad blade, as for serving food or turning meat while frying: *a fish slice.* **4** a small spade-shaped tool used for taking up printing ink. **5** *Sports.* **a** a hit or stroke made in such a way that the ball curves in flight or after falling on the ground, as in golf, tennis, and baseball; slicing hit: [*She*] *employs heavy slice on the forehand side and considerable underspin on her backhand drive* (Sunday Observer). **b** the course of the ball so hit: *The ball spun away in a wicked slice.*
— ***v.t.*** **1** to cut into slices: *Slice the bread. We ate sliced peaches.* **2** to cut (off) as a slice or slices: *One side of the hill had been sliced off.* **3** to cut through or across; divide: *The boat sliced the waves.* **4** *Figurative.* to divide into parts or shares: *The estate was sliced up into very small bequests.* **5** to remove or take up, with a slice or slice bar. **6** *Sports.* to hit (a ball) so that it curves or spins to one's right if hit right-handed: [*He*] *cannot be fooled consistently by even the smartest pitchers, is as likely to slice the ball as pull it* (New York Times). *He sliced his forehand unmercifully* (New Yorker).
— ***v.i.*** **1a** to admit of being sliced: *Firm tomatoes slice well.* **b** to cut; cross: *The Pan American Highway links the countries of South America, often slicing through miles of thick forests or swamps* (Preston E. James). **2** *Sports.* to slice a ball, as in golf or tennis.
[probably short for Old French *esclice* thin chip < a Germanic word]

**slice|a|ble** (slī′sə bəl), *adj.* that can be sliced; easily sliced: *Hot cake is often not sliceable.*

**slice bar**, a long iron bar with a broad, flat end, used in a coal furnace to break up or clear away clinkers and ashes.

**slice-of-life** (slīs′əv līf′), *adj.* describing or presenting an actual segment of life without modification by selection or arrangement of material: *The Czechs blend the understated documentary techniques with a slice-of-life narrative style* (Time).

**slic|er** (slī′sər), *n.* **1** a tool or machine that slices: *a bread slicer, a meat slicer.* **2** a person who slices.

**slick** (slik), *adj., v., n., adv.* — ***adj.*** **1** soft and glossy; sleek; smooth: *slick hair.* **2** slippery; greasy: *a road slick with ice or mud.* **3** *Informal, Figurative.* **a** clever; ingenious; skillful; deft: *a slick barber, a slick shortstop.* **b** sly; tricky: *a slick operator.* **c** smooth of speech or manners but superficial; glib: *They were suspicious of* [*his*] *advertising, which they thought "slick" and American* (New York Times). **4** *Informal, Figurative.* of or like that of a smooth, tricky person; cunningly made up: *a slick excuse.*
— ***v.t.*** **1** to make sleek or smooth: *Rain slicked the winding mountain roads* (Time). **2** *U.S. History.* to punish by authority of a vigilance committee.
— ***v.i.*** to move in a smooth manner; glide; sweep: *Slowly, slowly, he slicked out* (Maclean's).
— ***n.*** **1** a smooth place or spot. Oil makes a slick on the surface of water. *There is a slick of mud on the road.* **2** *U.S. Informal.* a magazine printed on heavy, glossy paper: *He had spent nearly twenty years writing mostly wilderness-adventure serials, first for the pulps and then for the "slicks"* (Newsweek). **3a** a tool used for scraping and smoothing leather. **b** a trowel for smoothing the top of a mold in founding. **4** *U.S.* a large tire without a tread, made for hot rods.
— ***adv.*** **1** *Informal.* smoothly; slyly; cleverly. **2** directly.
[Middle English *slike*, related to Old English *-slician* make smooth] — **slick′ly**, *adv.* — **slick′ness**, *n.*

**slick chick**, *U.S. Slang.* a good-looking, well-groomed girl.

**slicked-up** (slikt′up′), *adj. Slang.* **1** made tidy; cleaned up: *a slicked-up living room. The result is an artificial slicked-up version of real life* (Observer). **2** sleek; attractive: *slicked-up utilitarian gadgets.*

**slick|en** (slik′ən), *adj. British Dialect.* smooth; polished.

**slick|ens** (slik′ənz), *n.pl.* fine or powdered ore, debris, or the like, as from a stamping mill. [perhaps < German *Schlich*]

**slick|en|side** (slick′ən sīd′), *n. Geology.* a rock surface that has become more or less polished and striated from the sliding or grinding motion of an adjacent mass of rock.

**slick|en|sid|ed** (slik′ən sī′did), *adj.* of or like slickenside; having slickensides.

**slick|er** (slik′ər), *n., v.* — ***n.*** *U.S.* **1a** a long, loose waterproof coat, made of oilskin or the like: *Fishermen used to wear slickers.* **b** any raincoat: *The rain dripped from my slicker as I waited in the shop for the ... chrysanthemum* (Milton White). **2** *Informal.* a sly, tricky person: *One of those city slickers sold him worthless shares.*
— ***v.t.*** *Slang.* to fool; trick: *to be slickered out of a month's wages.*

**slick-pa|per** (slik′pā′pər), *adj.* printed on heavy, glossy paper: *A slick-paper magazine, entirely for sportscar buffs, will make its debut this summer* (Maclean's).

**slick|ster** (slik′stər), *n.* a sly, tricky person; slick or smooth operator: *to negotiate such political shoals without giving the appearance of being a political slickster* (Wall Street Journal).

**slid** (slid), *v.* the past tense and a past participle of **slide**: *The minutes slid rapidly by. He has slid back into his old habits.*

**slid|a|ble** (slī′də bəl), *adj.* that can slide.

**slid|den** (slid′ən), *v.* a past participle of **slide**: *He has slidden back into his old habits.*

**slide** (slīd), *v.*, **slid, slid** or **slid|den, slid|ing**, *n.* — ***v.i.*** **1** to move smoothly along on a surface or in a groove, as a sled moves on snow or ice: *The bureau drawers slide in and out.* **2** to glide over the surface of ice or snow on the feet, or on a sled, toboggan, or the like: *When the snowstorm stops, let's go sliding down the hill.* **3** to move or go easily, quietly, or secretly: *The thief quickly slid behind the curtains.* **4** to slip as when losing one's foothold: *The car slid into the ditch.* **5** to pass by degrees; slip: *The car slid by us.* (*Figurative.*) *He has slid into bad habits.* **6** *Figurative.* to pass quietly and secretly; go unregarded: *Alack, how good men, and the good turns they do us, slide out of memory* (Charles Lamb). **7** *Music.* to pass or progress from tone to tone without perceptible step or break. **8** *Baseball.* to launch a slide for a base or home plate.
— ***v.t.*** **1** to cause to move smoothly along on a surface or in a groove: *Slide the door back into the wall.* **2** to put quietly or secretly: *He slid a pistol into his pocket.*
— ***n.*** **1** the act of sliding: *The children each take a slide in turn.* **2a** a smooth surface for sliding on: *The frozen brook makes a good slide.* **b** a kind of sloping surface or chute down which children slide: *The small playground had a slide, a seesaw, and two swings.* **3** a track, rail, groove, or smooth channel on or in which something slides. **4a** something that slides or that works by sliding. **b** = sliding seat. **5** the U-shaped tube of a trumpet or trombone that is pushed in or out to change the pitch of the tones. **6a** a mass of snow and ice or dirt and rocks sliding down; landslide; avalanche: *The slide cut off the valley from the rest of the world.* **b** the sliding down of such a mass: *The slide was felt at the other end of the valley.* **c** the place where this has occurred. **7** *Figurative.* a downward movement; downswing; decline: *a price slide. Steel operations normally head into a seasonal slide after October* (Wall Street Journal). **8** a small thin sheet of glass on which objects are placed in order to look at them under the microscope. **9** a small transparent photograph made of glass or film. Slides are put in a projector and shown on a screen. **10** *Music.* **a** a rapid ascending or descending series of three or more notes, composed of grace notes which ornament the last or principal note. **b** a passing from tone to tone without perceptible step or break; portamento. **11** *Baseball.* the act of throwing the body, usually feet first, along the ground in running to a base, so as to avoid being tagged. **12** a framed opening in a wall between two rooms for passing things through: *The cook put the dishes through the slide, and the maid, waiting in the china closet, received them and took them into the diningroom* (Harper's).
**let slide**, to not bother about; neglect: *Don't let your studies slide. He let his business slide until he was bankrupt.*
[Old English *slīdan*]
— *Syn. v.i.* **1 Slide, slip, glide** mean to move along smoothly, over a surface. **Slide** emphasizes continuous contact with a smooth or slippery surface: *The boat slid down the bank into the water.* **Slip** emphasizes a sudden, involuntary movement caused by a very smooth or slippery surface: *One of the climbers slipped on the rocks.* **Glide** emphasizes a continuous, easy, graceful movement, without reference to the surface: *The swans glide gracefully on the lake. The stream glides through the forest.*

**slide bar**, **1** a sliding bar in a machine or other device, as for opening or closing an aperture. **2** a bar that serves as a guide or track for a sliding or reciprocating part.

**slide calipers**, = caliper rule.

**slide fastener**, = zipper.

**slide knot**, a slipknot tied with two half hitches.

**slide projector**, an instrument for projecting onto a viewing screen the pictures on photographic slides.

**slid|er** (slī′dər), *n.* **1a** a person who slides. **b** a sliding thing or part. **2** a fast pitch in baseball with a sideways spin that makes the ball curve slightly: *You throw the slider like you throw a football* (Newsweek). **3** the toothed portion of a zipper: *... manufacturers of zipper hardware, including sliders, chain pulls and stops* (Wall Street Journal). **4** = red-bellied terrapin.

**slide rest**, an appliance for holding tools in turning, enabling them to be held in different ways in relation to the material worked on: *Control of the cutting tool was taken from the skilled hands of the turner and put into a ... slide rest* (Scientific American).

---

**Pronunciation Key:** hat, āge, cãre, fär; let, ēqual, tėrm; it, īce; hot, ōpen, ôrder; oil, out; cup, pu̇t, rüle; child; long; thin; ᴛʜen; zh, measure; ə represents **a** in about, **e** in taken, **i** in pencil, **o** in lemon, **u** in circus.

***slide rule**, a rule with a sliding section in the center, both parts marked with logarithmic scales, used for making rapid mathematical calculations.

***slide rule**

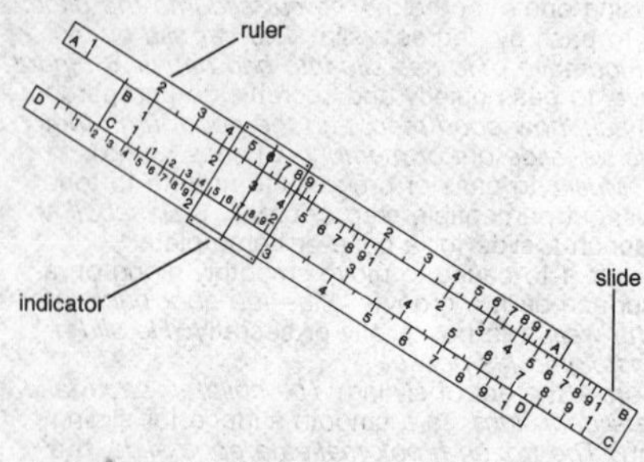


**slide trombone**, a trombone with a U-shaped bend near the cup mouthpiece, in which double telescoping tubes slide one upon the other to vary the length of the sounding tube and thus produce different tones.
**slide valve**, an engine valve that slides (without lifting) to open or close an aperture.
**slide|way** (slīd′wā′), *n.* a guideway on which some part of a machine moves.
**slid|ing** (slī′ding), *adj.* **1** that slides: *a sliding reptile, a sliding avalanche, a sliding panel.* **2** having a part that slides; adjustable; changing: *a sliding bar, a sliding joint.*
**sliding door**, a door, usually in two leaves, that slides in grooves or along a track.
**sliding scale**, **1** a scale of wages, prices, taxes, customs duties, or the like, that can be adjusted according to certain conditions: *The sliding scale tax formula for lead and zinc imports was proposed by the Administration as part of its long-range program for the mineral industry* (Wall Street Journal). **2** = slide rule.
**sliding seat**, **1** a seat, as in an outrigger, which moves backwards and forwards with the action of the rower. **2** a seat which can be slid out beyond the gunwale of a yacht.
**sli|er** (slī′ər), *adj.* a comparative of **sly**.
**sli|est** (slī′ist), *adj.* a superlative of **sly**.
**slight** (slīt), *adj., v., n.* —*adj.* **1** not much; not important; small: *I have a slight headache. One slice of bread is a slight lunch. I hardly felt that slight scratch. Therefore I am glad to take this slight occasion—this trifling occasion ...* (Dickens). **SYN**: inconsiderable, trivial, trifling. **2** not big around; slender; slim: *She is a slight girl.* **SYN**: thin. **3** flimsy; frail: *a slight structure, slight clothing, a slight excuse.*
—*v.t.* to pay too little attention to; treat as of little value or importance; neglect: *This maid slights her work. She felt slighted because she was not asked to the party.*
—*n.* an act showing neglect or lack of respect; slighting treatment shown to one who expects courtesy and friendliness: *Cinderella suffered many slights from her sisters. ... thwarted or stung by a fancied slight* (Bret Harte).
[Middle English *slight,* perhaps Old English *-sliht* level, as in *eorthslihtes* level with the ground]
—**slight′ness**, *n.*
—*Syn. v.t.* **Slight, overlook, neglect** mean to pay too little attention to someone or something needing or deserving it. **Slight** emphasizes intentionally doing so: *to slight one's homework.* **Overlook** emphasizes unintentionally doing so: *While reviewing our budget, we overlooked the telephone bill.* **Neglect** emphasizes doing so because of indifference, distaste, or laziness: *He regularly neglects brushing his teeth before going to bed.*
**slight breeze**, *Meteorology.* a breeze having a velocity of 4-7 miles per hour; light breeze.
**slight|ing** (slī′ting), *adj.* that slights; contemptuous; disdainful: *a slighting remark.* **SYN**: disparaging. —**slight′ing|ly**, *adv.*
**slight|ly** (slīt′lē), *adv.* **1** in a slight manner. **2** to a slight degree; a little; somewhat: *I know him slightly.* **3** in a slighting manner; disdainfully.
**sli|ly** (slī′lē), *adv.* = slyly.
**slim** (slim), *adj.,* **slim|mer, slim|mest**, *v.,* **slimmed, slim|ming**. —*adj.* **1** thin; slender: *He was very slim, being six feet tall and weighing only 130 pounds.* **SYN**: See syn. under **slender**. **2** *Figurative.* **a** small or slight; weak: *a slim victory. The invalid's chances for getting well were very slim.* **b** meager; scanty: *a slim meal. We had a slim attendance at the football game because of the rain.*
—*v.t., v.i.* to make or become slim or slender: *The girl slimmed her figure with a rigid diet* (v.t.). *You'll love your new, lively, lissom self when you've slimmed with Formula 21* (Sunday Times) (v.i.).
**slim down**, to reduce in size or number: *... the Marine Corps began slimming down under budget restrictions* (J. H. Thompson).
[< Dutch *slim* bad] —**slim′ly**, *adv.* —**slim′ness**, *n.*
**slime** (slīm), *n., v.,* **slimed, slim|ing**. —*n.* **1** soft, sticky mud or something like it: *His shoes were covered with slime from the swamp. At present, the most important commercial source of selenium is the anode mud or slime produced in the electrolytic refining of blister copper* (Wall Street Journal). **2** a sticky, slippery, substance given off by certain animals, such as snails, slugs, and fish. **3** *Figurative.* disgusting filth: *An honest man he is, and hates the slime That sticks on filthy deeds* (Shakespeare).
—*v.t.* **1** to cover or smear with, or as if with, slime. **2** to clear of slimy matter by scraping.
—*v.i.* to become covered with slime; turn slimy.
[Old English *slīm*]
**slime mold** or **fungus**, any one of a group of primitive organisms consisting of a thin mass of naked protoplasm and occurring in slimy masses, as on damp soil and decaying logs.
**slime pit**, **1** a tank or reservoir in which slimes are settled or stored. **2** *Archaic.* a pit yielding liquid bitumen.
**slim|i|cide** (slī′mə sīd), *n.* a chemical substance used to destroy slime molds: *The sources of Sweden's lake poisoning—mercurial slimicides and fungicides in the pulp industry—were banned some time ago* (Manchester Guardian Weekly).
[< *slime* + *-cide*[1]; influenced in form as by *fungicide* and *insecticide*]
**slim|i|ly** (slī′mə lē), *adv.* in a slimy manner.
**slim|i|ness** (slī′mē nis), *n.* slimy quality or condition.
**slim-jim** (slim′jim′), *adj., n. Slang.* —*adj.* very slim: *a coal shed full of slim-jim bottles* (Punch).
—*n.* a very slim person.
**slim|line** (slim′līn′), *adj.* having slim lines; long and slender: *New slimline model does more jobs in less space than any other copying machine* (Wall Street Journal).
**slim|ming** (slim′ing), *adj., n.* —*adj.* making one slim or slimmer: *Slimming diets, other than a sensible limitation of sweets and starches, are frowned upon for teenagers* (Sunday Times).
—*n.* the act or fact of making or becoming slim or slimmer; reducing: *Whenever women get together, sooner or later, the question of slimming arises* (Cape Times).
**slim|mish** (slim′ish), *adj.* somewhat slim.
**slimp|sy** (slimp′sē), *adj.,* **-si|er, -si|est**. *U.S. Informal.* slimsy.
**slim|sy** (slim′zē), *adj.,* **-si|er, -si|est**. *U.S. Informal.* flimsy; frail. [American English, apparently < *slim;* patterned on *flimsy*]
**slim|y** (slī′mē), *adj.,* **slim|i|er, slim|i|est**. **1** covered with slime: *The pond is too slimy to swim in. Yea, slimy things did crawl with legs upon the slimy sea* (Samuel Taylor Coleridge). **2** of slime; like slime: *a slimy secretion, the slimy sediment in a drain.* **3** *Figurative.* disgusting; vile; filthy.
***sling[1]** (sling), *n., v.,* **slung, sling|ing**. —*n.* **1** a strip of leather with a string fastened to each end, for throwing stones: *David put a stone in his sling and casting it so true slew Goliath.* **2** = slingshot. **3** a throw; hurling or casting. **4** a hanging loop of cloth, usually fastened around the neck, to support an injured arm or hand: *First of the walking cases to come on shore was an elderly man with an arm in a sling* (Graham Greene). **5** a loop of rope, band, or chain by which heavy objects are lifted, carried, or held: *The men lowered the boxes into the cellar by a sling. Rifles have slings to carry them over the shoulder.* [Middle English *slynge.* Compare Swedish *slinga.*]
—*v.t.* **1** to throw with a sling: *David slung a stone at Goliath, killing the giant.* **2** to throw; cast; hurl; fling: *The cruel boy slung stones at the cat.* **3** to raise, lower, or move, with a sling or slings: *By using a hoist the movers were able to sling the piano to the third floor.* **4** to hang in a sling; hang so as to swing loosely: *to sling a pack on one's back.* **5** to hang up or suspend (as a hammock), from one part to another. **6** *Slang.* to mix; serve.
**slings**, *Nautical.* **a** a rope or chain at the center of a yard connecting it to a mast. **b** a rope at the bow or stern, as for attaching a barrel or bale, to be hoisted or lowered.
[< Scandinavian (compare Old Icelandic *slyngva*)]
**sling[2]** (sling), *n. U.S.* a drink consisting of an alcoholic liquor, usually gin, lemon or lime juice, sugar, and water. [compare earlier British *sling* a drink, "pull" from a bottle, and German *schlingen* to swallow]
**sling|back** (sling′bak′), *n.* a woman's shoe with an upper that tapers off to become a strap instead of a closed back around the heel of the wearer.
**sling cart**, a two-wheeled cart used for transporting cannon or other heavy objects, by slinging them by a chain from the axletree.
**sling|er** (sling′ər), *n.* **1** a fighter armed with a sling. **2** a worker in charge of slings used in hoisting. **3** a person who slings.
**slinger ring**, a tubular ring around the hub of the propeller of an airplane, through which deicing fluid is sprayed over the propeller blades.
**sling|man** (sling′mən), *n., pl.* **-men**. a soldier armed with a sling; slinger.
**sling psychrometer**, a pair of thermometers, one wet-bulb and the other dry-bulb suspended by a chain and whirled about to bring the wet-bulb to a standard temperature for measuring the relative humidity.
**sling pump**, = slingback.
***sling|shot** (sling′shot′), *n.* a Y-shaped stick with a rubber band fastened between its prongs, used to shoot pebbles, or the like.
**sling|stone** (sling′stōn′), *n.* a stone used as a missile to be hurled by a sling.
**slink[1]** (slingk), *v.i.,* **slunk** or (*Archaic*) **slank, slunk, slink|ing**. to move in a secret, guilty manner; sneak: *After stealing the meat, the dog slunk away.* [Old English *slincan*] —**slink′ing|ly**, *adv.*

***sling[1]**
definitions 1, 4, 5

definition 1

definition 4

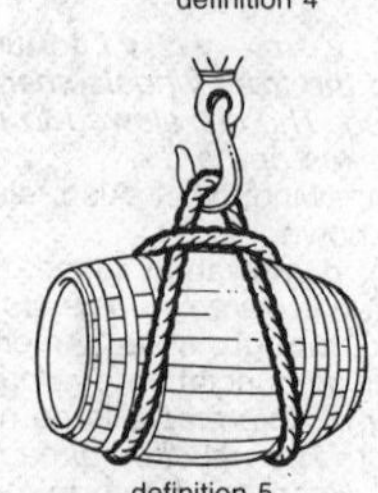

definition 5

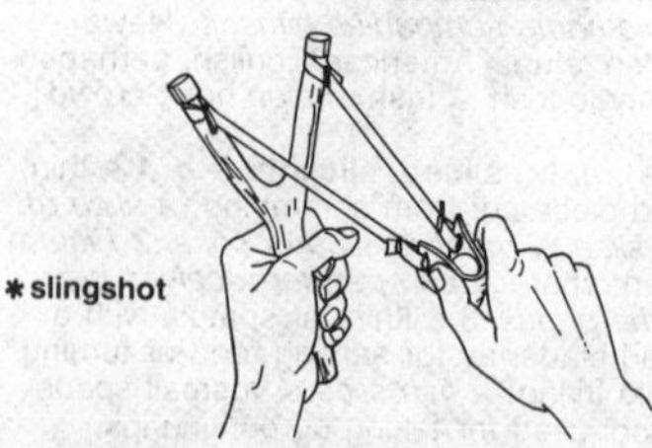

***slingshot**

**slink[2]** (slingk), *v.,* **slinked** or **slunk, slink|ing**, *n., adj.* —*v.t.* (of domestic animals) to bring forth (young) prematurely.
—*n.* **1** a calf or other young animal born prematurely. **2** the skin of such an animal; slinkskin: *I believe slink will be leading for fall ... The coat will sell for $895* (New York Times).
—*adj.* born prematurely.
[< *slink*[1]]
**slink|i|ly** (sling′kə lē), *adv.* in a slinky manner: *slinkily attired ... actresses* (Punch).
**slink|i|ness** (sling′kē nis), *n.* **1** sneakiness; furtiveness; stealthiness. **2** the allure given by slinky clothes.

**slink|skin** (slingk′skin′), *n.* the skin of a slink, or leather made from such skin.
**slink|weed** (slingk′wēd′), *n.* = swamp loosestrife.
**slink|y** (sling′kē), *adj.,* **slink|i|er, slink|i|est.** **1** sneaky; furtive; stealthy. **2a** closefitting, as if molded to the figure: *a slinky dress, a slinky negligee.* **b** wearing, or as if wearing, such clothes; sexy: *Her parody of the slinky and tarnished redhead whom the American colonel seeks to save ... is a particularly engaging bit* (Wall Street Journal).
**slip¹** (slip), *v.,* **slipped** or (*Archaic*) **slipt, slipped, slip|ping,** *n.* — ***v.i.*** **1** to go or move smoothly, quietly, easily, or quickly: *She slipped out of the room. Time slips by. The ship slips through the waves. The drawer slips into place. He slipped into a clean shirt.* **SYN**: See syn. under **slide. 2** to move out of place; slide: *The knife slipped and cut my finger. My axe slipped out of my hand.* **3** to slide suddenly without wanting to: *He slipped and fell on the icy sidewalk.* **4** *Figurative.* to make a mistake or error: *He slipped when he misspelled his own name.* **5** *Figurative.* to pass without notice; pass through neglect; escape: *Don't let this opportunity slip. The point seems to have slipped from the old man's mind. Wealth or power slips from one.* **6** *Figurative.* to fall off; decline; deteriorate: *The market for cotton continues to slip. New car sales have slipped.*
— ***v.t.*** **1** to cause to slip; put, push, or draw with a smooth or sliding motion: *to slip a shell into a rifle. She slipped the ring from her finger. Slip the note into your hand. He slipped the bolt of the lock.* **2** to put (on) or take (off) quickly and easily: *Slip on your coat. Slip off your shoes.* **3** *Figurative.* to get loose from; get away from; escape from: *The dog has slipped his collar. Your name has slipped my mind.* **4** to let go from a leash or slip; release: *He slipped the hound.* **5a** to allow (especially an anchor cable) to run out entirely, frequently with a buoy attached, often leaving an anchorage hastily. **b** to drop or disengage (an anchor) in this way: *The ship has slipped anchor and is off.* **6** *Figurative.* to untie (a knot); undo: *The bonds of heaven are slipt, dissolved and loosed* (Shakespeare). **7** (of animals) to bear (young) prematurely; slink. **8** *Archaic.* to let pass; neglect.
— ***n.*** **1** the act or fact of slipping: *His broken leg was caused by a slip on the ice.* **2a** a thing that covers and can be slipped on or off; covering: *Pillows are covered by slips. Slips are often put on furniture for the summer.* **b** a sleeveless garment worn under a dress or gown: *She wore a pink slip under her party dress.* **c** a child's pinafore or frock. **3** *Figurative.* a mistake; error; blunder: *He makes slips in pronouncing words. That remark was a slip of the tongue. There has been a bad slip somewhere* (New York Times). **4** *U.S.* a space for ships between two wharves or in a dock. **5a** an inclined platform alongside of the water, on which ships are built or repaired. **b** a similar platform, used as a landing place for ferries, small craft, amphibious aircraft, and the like: *They sent a boat up to tow us down here to the slip* (Atlantic). **6** a leash for one or two dogs, designed for quick release. **7** *Cricket.* **a** a position behind and to the side of the wicketkeeper: *Nor is his a one-stroke mind, for he varied his lustier blows with deft glances through the slips and clean cover drives* (London Times). **b** a player in this position. **8** the difference between the actual speed of a ship or boat in water and the speed it would attain if the propeller, paddle wheel, or air draft, were working in a solid or less mobile substance. **9** *Geology.* **a** a fault in rock due to the sinking of one section. **b** a movement producing such a fault. **c** the amount of such movement, measured by the amount of displacement along the fault plane.
**give one the slip,** *Informal.* to escape or get away from one; evade or elude one: *One of the principal officers of finance ... had given the slip to his guards* (James Mill).
**let slip,** to tell without meaning to: *She talked too much and let the secret slip. I will not let his name slip ... if I can help it* (Tennyson). *Lest ... he should let anything slip that might give a clue to the place or people* (G. Macdonald).
**slip one over on,** *Informal.* to get the advantage of, especially by trickery; outwit: *The fox slipped one over on the hounds and got away.*
**slip out,** to become known; leak out: *When one side or the other had written any particularly spicy dispatch, news of it was sure to slip out* (Thackeray).
**slips,** the slipping of a shooting marble from a player's hand: *If the player calls "slips" before the marble moves more than ten inches, he may shoot again.*
**slip up,** *Informal.* to make a mistake or error: *Slip up in my vernacular! How could I? I talked it when I was a boy* (Century Magazine).
[perhaps < Middle Low German *slippen.* Compare Old English *slip-,* as in *slipor* slipper², *slipig* slimy.]
**slip²** (slip), *n., v.,* **slipped** or (*Archaic*) **slipt, slipped, slip|ping.** — ***n.*** **1a** a small, narrow piece of paper on which a record is made: *a laundry slip.* **b** a narrow strip, such as of wood or land. **2** a young, slender person: *She is just a slip of a girl.* **3** a small branch or twig cut from a plant, used to grow a new plant: *She has promised us slips from her rosebushes.* **4** *British.* a galley proof. **5** *U.S.* an ordinary church pew that is long, narrow, and open on the aisle.
— ***v.t.*** to cut branches from (a plant) to grow new plants; take (a part) from a plant.
[probably < Middle Dutch, Middle Low German *slippen* to cut, slit]
**slip³** (slip), *n.* potter's clay made semifluid with water. It is used for coating or decorating pottery, cementing handles and other pieces; barbotine. [apparently Middle English *slyppe* mud, Old English *slypa* a semiliquid mass]
**slip|board** (slip′bôrd′, -bōrd′), *n.* a board sliding in grooves.
**slip|case** (slip′kās′), *n.* a box or covering designed to protect one or more books or records, usually so that only their backs or edges are exposed: *Four miniature books, in a decorated slipcase to match ... are sheer delight to view and read* (Atlantic).
**slip casting,** a method of making pottery by pouring semifluid clay into plaster casts, used especially in the manufacture of whiteware with intricate shapes.
**slip|cov|er** (slip′kuv′ər), *n., v.* — ***n.*** **1** a removable cloth cover for a chair, sofa, or footstool: *an armchair adorned with a gay print slipcover* (New Yorker). **2** a dust jacket for a book.
— ***v.t.*** to cover with a slipcover: *books to be bound, rebound or slipcovered* (New York Times).
**slipe** (slīp), *v., n. Dialect.* — ***v.t.*** to strip (off); peel. — ***n.*** **1** a slip or slice. **2** a sledge or sleigh. [origin uncertain]
**slip-form** (slip′fôrm′), *n., v.* — ***n.*** a steel form that is raised or moved in building or paving at the same time as concrete is added.
— ***v.t.*** to build or pave by means of a slip-form: *to slip-form a bridge pier, to slip-form a road.*
**slip glaze,** a liquid glaze of clay mixed with ground minerals.
**slip|horn** (slip′hôrn′), *n. Informal.* trombone.
**slip|knot** (slip′not′), *n.* **1** a knot made to slip along the rope or cord around which it is made; running knot. **2** a knot that can be undone by pulling the end. See picture under **knot¹.**
**slip noose,** a noose with a slipknot. It is made larger or smaller by sliding the knot on the cord, as on a lasso.
**slip-on** (slip′on′, -ôn′), *adj., n.* — ***adj.*** **1** that can be put on or taken off easily or quickly: *slip-on gloves with corduroy palms and plastic-leather backs* (New Yorker). **2** that must be put on or taken off over the head.
— ***n.*** a slip-on glove, blouse, sweater, or other article of clothing.
**slip|o|ver** (slip′ō′vər), *adj., n.* — ***adj.*** designed to be slipped on over the head: *a slipover sweater.* — ***n.*** = slip-on.
**slip|page** (slip′ij), *n.* **1** the act of slipping: *There were indications the profit margin slippage ... could well bring total fourth-quarter profits below year-ago levels* (Wall Street Journal). **2** the amount or extent of slipping, as in loss of working power in machinery.
**slipped disk** or **disc** (slipt), the loosening of an intervertebral disk, causing painful pressure on the spinal nerves: *Slipped disc ... is the most common of all types of rheumatism* (Science News Letter).
**slip|per¹** (slip′ər), *n., v.* — ***n.*** **1** a light, low shoe that is slipped on easily: *She has pretty dancing slippers and comfortable bedroom slippers.* **2** a person or thing that slips.
— ***v.t.*** to hit or beat with a slipper.
[< *slip*¹, verb + *-er*¹]
**slip|per²** (slip′ər), *adj. Obsolete except Dialect.* slippery: *a slipper road, a slipper tongue. A slipper and subtle knave, a finder of occasion* (Shakespeare). [Old English *slipor.* See related etym. at **slip¹.**]
**slipper animalcule,** = paramecium.
**slip|pered** (slip′ərd), *adj.* **1** wearing slippers. **2** *Figurative: His benign presence, slippered airs, and general good humour ...* (London Times).
**slip|per|i|ly** (slip′ər ə lē, slip′rə-), *adv.* in a slippery manner.
**slip|per|i|ness** (slip′ər ē nis, slip′rē-), *n.* slippery quality or condition: *the slipperiness of graphite.*
**slip|per|ing** (slip′ər ing), *n.* a beating with a slipper: *... to give me a good slippering for my misbehavior* (Herman Melville).
**slip|per|less** (slip′ər lis), *adj.* without slippers: *His feet were slipperless, Eastern fashion* (F. Marion Crawford).
**slipper limpet,** a gastropod with a convex oval shell, containing a shelflike partition: *Starfish are destroyers of one oyster pest, the slipper limpet* (New Scientist).
**slipper sock,** a wool sock with a leather sole, usually worn for lounging indoors; muckluck: *The girls appeared ... with scarfs bound around their pin curls, and wearing quilted robes and slipper socks* (Harper's).
**slip|per|wort** (slip′ər wėrt′), *n.* a tropical American plant of the figwort family; calceolaria.
**slip|per|y** (slip′ər ē, slip′rē), *adj.,* **-per|i|er, -per|i|est. 1** causing or likely to cause slipping: *A wet street is slippery. The steps are slippery with ice.* **2** slipping away easily; difficult to catch or hold: *Wet soap is slippery.* **3** *Figurative.* not to be depended on; shifty; tricky: *The traditional con man was a slippery customer.* **4** *Archaic.* licentious; wanton; unchaste: *Ha' not you seen Camillo? ... or heard? ... or thought? ... My wife is slippery?* (Shakespeare). [< *slipper*² + *-y*¹]
**slippery elm, 1** an elm tree of eastern North America with a hard wood and a fragrant inner bark that becomes slimy or slippery when moistened, or in early spring. **2** the inner bark.
**slip|pi|ness** (slip′ē nis), *n.* = slipperiness.
**slip proof,** *British.* a galley proof.
**slip|py** (slip′ē), *adj.,* **-pi|er, -pi|est. 1** *Informal.* slippery: *steep, slippy-feeling rocks* (John M. Synge). **2** *British Informal.* nimble, quick, or sharp: *Bring us two liqueur brandies, miss ... And look slippy, if ye please* (Arnold Bennett).
**slip|rail** (slip′rāl′), *n.* (in Australia) a fence rail or section that can be removed to serve as a gate.
**slip ring,** one of two or more rings with which the brushes make connection in a dynamo or motor: *The alternating current dynamo is a device by which mechanical energy is converted into electrical energy. Slip rings help the electrons surge back and forth* (Louis T. Masson).
**slip road,** *British.* a road leading into an express highway: *Signs should also be erected ... in positions where they can be seen by drivers before entering the motorway on the slip roads* (London Times).
**slip rope,** a rope so arranged that it may be readily let go.
**slip seat,** an upholstered seat which can be easily removed from a chair, stool, or bench.
**slip|sheet** (slip′shēt′), *v., n.* — ***v.t., v.i.*** to place blank sheets of paper between (printed sheets) to prevent the offset of wet ink.
— ***n.*** a blank sheet used for this.
**slip|shod** (slip′shod′), *adj.* **1** careless, as in dress, habits, or speech; untidy; slovenly: *a slipshod performance, slipshod work. Slipshod handling once the packages reach the grocery can reduce even the finest brand to a sorry and sometimes dangerous mess* (Wall Street Journal). **2** shuffling: *a slipshod gait.* **3** wearing slippers or shoes worn down at the heel. — **slip′shod′ness,** *n.*
**slip|slop** (slip′slop′), *n., adj.* — ***n.*** **1** sloppy food or drink. **2** sloppy talk or writing. **3** a blunder in the use of words.
— ***adj.*** sloppy; trifling.
**slip|sole** (slip′sōl′), *n.* a thin piece of leather placed between the outsole and insole of a shoe to make the bottom thicker.
**slip|stick** (slip′stik′), *n. Slang.* a slide rule: *Mr. Crane has done his homework, including much hot labor with his slipstick* (Saturday Review).
**slip stitch,** a stitch hidden between the fold of a cloth, such as on the bottom of a skirt, where stitches should not be seen.
**slip-stitch** (slip′stich′), *v.t.* to make a slip stitch or stitches in (a hem, facing, or the like).
**slip|stream** (slip′strēm′), *n., v.* — ***n.*** **1** Also, **slip stream.** a current of air produced by the propeller of an aircraft. **2** the current of air left behind a moving vehicle: *Cars that whip by rock your bike a little in their slipstream* (Canadian Saturday Night). **3** a pocket of greatly lowered air pressure directly behind a racing automobile: *Lund was letting the other drivers burn up valuable fuel while he rode in their slipstream* (Hot Rod).
— ***v.i., v.t.*** to drive very closely behind another (racing car) so as to use its slipstream and conserve fuel and tires: *Down the shimmering pit straight they tore at 150 m.p.h., wheel to wheel, slipstreaming and pulling out every ounce of power* (London Times).
**slipt** (slipt), *v. Archaic.* a past tense of **slip¹** and **slip².**

**Pronunciation Key:** hat, āge, cãre, fär; let, ēqual, tėrm; it, īce; hot, ōpen, ôrder; **oil, out;** cup, pu̇t, rüle; **ch**ild; lo**ng; th**in; **ᴛʜ**en; **zh,** measure; **ə** represents **a** in about, **e** in taken, **i** in pencil, **o** in lemon, **u** in circus.

**slip-up** (slip′up′), *n. Informal.* a mistake; error; failure: *I want this job done right, with no slip-ups.*

**slip|ware** (slip′wãr′), *n.* earthenware which is coated with slip, or thinly diluted clay.

**slip|way** (slip′wā′), *n.* a platform sloping from a dock into the water, on which ships are built or repaired; slip: *On the slipway beside the basin there towered a tanker* (Punch).

**slit** (slit), *v.,* **slit, slit|ting,** *n., adj.* —*v.t.* **1a** to cut or tear in a straight line: *to slit cloth into strips.* **b** to make a long, straight cut or tear in: *to slit a skirt to make a pocket.* **2** *Archaic.* to cut off; sever: *Comes the blind Fury with the abhorred shears And slits the thin-spun life* (Milton).
—*n.* a straight, narrow cut, tear, or opening: *a slit in a bag, the slit in a letter box.*
—*adj.* having a slit; divided: *a slit skirt, the slit tongue of a snake.*
[Middle English *slitten,* related to Old English *slītan* to slit] —**slit′like′,** *adj.*

**slit-eyed** (slit′īd′), *adj.* having long and narrow eyes: *... scars on his simple, slit-eyed face* (New Yorker).

**slith|er** (sliᴛʜ′ər), *v., n.* —*v.i.* **1** to slide down or along a surface, especially unsteadily or with noise: *Rocks slithered down the side of the cliff.* **2** to go with a sliding motion: *to slither into a room. The snake slithered into the weeds. Soon the cars would start slithering across the square like a funeral cortege* (New Yorker).
—*v.t.* to cause to slither or slide.
—*n.* a slithering movement; slide.
[variant of dialectal *slidder,* Old English *slidrian*]

**slith|er|y** (sliᴛʜ′ər ē), *adj.* slippery; crawly.

**slit lamp,** a lamp that projects a thin beam of light through a narrow slit, used in eye examinations.

**slit|less** (slit′lis), *n.* having no slit: *a slitless skirt.*

**slit|ter** (slit′ər), *n.* one that slits.

**slit|tered** (slit′ərd), *adj.* cut into strips with square ends, as the edge of a sleeve or garment.

**slit trench, 1** a narrow trench for one person or a small group, used as a shelter against shelling or bombing: *I was lucky, the going was good, and I rolled over into a shallow slit trench* (Cape Times). **2** a similar trench in front or on the flank of a military position, as for an observation post, often in the shape of an L or V, so as to protect against enfilading fire.

**sliv|er** (sliv′ər), *n., v.* —*n.* **1** a long, thin piece that has been split off, broken off, or cut off; splinter. **2** a loose fiber, such as of wool, cotton, or flax: *The tangled fibers are straightened out and ... rolled over and over one another to form slivers, which look like loose ropes of soft cotton yarn* (Elizabeth Chesley Baity).
—*v.t., v.i.* to split or break into slivers.
[Middle English *slivere,* related to Old English *-slīfan* to split, cleave]

**sliv|o|vitz** (sliv′ə vits), *n.* a strong brandy made from plums. [< Serbo-Croatian *sljivovica* < *sljiva* plum]

**slob** (slob), *n.* **1** *Informal.* a stupid, untidy, or clumsy person: *... and instead of asking, like some slobs, "Where do you want to go?" I say, "What is your pleasure, Madame?"* (New Yorker). **2** *Irish.* **a** mud or ooze. **b** a stretch of it, especially along a seashore. **3** in Newfoundland: **a** slushy ice and snow. **b** disintegrating pack ice. [probably < Irish *slab* mud]

**slob|ber** (slob′ər), *v., n.* —*v.i.* **1** to let saliva or other liquid run out from the mouth; slaver; drivel; drool. **2** *Figurative.* to speak in a silly, sentimental way: *Why is it that most Americans are always ready to slobber ecstatically over anything French?* (Time).
—*v.t.* to wet or smear with saliva.
—*n.* **1** saliva or other liquid running out from the mouth; slaver. **2** *Figurative.* silly, sentimental talk or emotion. Also, **slabber.**
[probably ultimately < Middle Flemish *slobberen*] —**slob′ber|er,** *n.*

**slob|ber|i|ness** (slob′ər ē nis), *n.* slobbering quality; sloppiness.

**slob|ber|y** (slob′ər ē), *adj.* **1** slobbering. **2** disagreeably wet; somewhat slimy; sloppy.

**slob|bish** (slob′ish), *adj.* boorish; slovenly. [< *slob* + *-ish*] —**slob′bish|ness,** *n.*

**slob ice,** disintegrating pack ice.

**slock|en** (slok′ən), *v.t. Scottish.* to quench. Also, **sloken.** [< Scandinavian (compare Old Icelandic *slokna* < *slökkva* go out, be slack)]

**sloe** (slō), *n.* **1** a small, black or dark-purple, plumlike stone fruit with a sharp, sour taste. **2** the thorny shrub of the rose family that it grows on; blackthorn. **3** any one of several related shrubs or trees that bear dark-purple fruit. [Old English *slāh*]

**sloe-eyed** (slō′īd′), *adj.* **1** having very dark eyes; black-eyed: *a sloe-eyed maiden.* **2** having slanted eyes.

**sloe gin,** an alcoholic liquor like ordinary gin, but flavored with sloes instead of juniper berries: *Sloe gin is not a true gin, but a liqueur* (J. Bernard Robb).

**sloe plum,** the fruit of the sloe.

**slog** (slog), *v.,* **slogged, slog|ging,** *n. Informal.* —*v.t.* to hit hard; slug.
—*v.i.* **1** to plod heavily. **2** to work hard (at something).
—*n.* **1** a hard blow. **2** a spell of difficult, steady work: *The early play was mainly a hard slog of scrummage, lineout, and maul* (London Times). [variant of *slug*[2]]

**slo|gan** (slō′gən), *n.* **1** a word or phrase used by a business, club, political party, or the like, to advertise its purpose; motto: *"Safety first" is our slogan. "Service with a smile" was the store's slogan.* **2** a war cry; battle cry: *Sound the fife and cry the slogan—Let pibroch shake the air* (William E. Aytoun).
[< Scottish Gaelic *sluagh-ghairm* < *sluagh* army, host + *gairm* a cry]

**slo|gan|eer** (slō′gə nir′), *n., v.* —*n.* a person who makes up or uses slogans: *a sloganeer, a master of rhetoric and exhortation* (New York Times).
—*v.i.* to make up or use slogans.
—*v.t.* = sloganize.

**slo|gan|eer|ing** (slō′gə nir′ing), *n.* the making up or use of slogans, as in advertising or political propaganda: *Some people seem to have accepted that epitome of simplified sloganeering—that foreign aid is like "pouring money down a rathole"* (Christian Science Monitor).

**slo|gan|i|za|tion** (slō′gə nə zā′shən), *n.* the act or process of sloganizing.

**slo|gan|ize** (slō′gə nīz), *v.t.,* **-ized, -iz|ing. 1** to express or use as a slogan: *We must have the courage to experiment with ideas among ourselves and within each of us—ideas which cannot be immediately sloganized or sold* (Bulletin of Atomic Scientists). **2** to influence or persuade by slogans: *He ... found the American people "sloganized" and the students "stereotyped"* (Newsweek). —**slo′gan|iz′er,** *n.*

**slog|ger** (slog′ər), *n. Informal.* a person who slogs.

**sloid** or **slojd** (sloid), *n.* = sloyd.

**slo|ka** (slō′kə), *n.* a couplet or distich of Sanskrit verse, each line containing sixteen syllables. Also, **shloka.** [< Sanskrit *śloka* sound, noise, hymn, stanza]

**slok|en** (slok′ən), *v.t. Scottish.* slocken.

***sloop** (slüp), *n.* a sailboat having one mast, a mainsail, a jib, and sometimes other sails. A sloop has fore-and-aft rigging. [< Dutch *sloep,* earlier *sloepe.* See etym. of doublet **shallop.**]

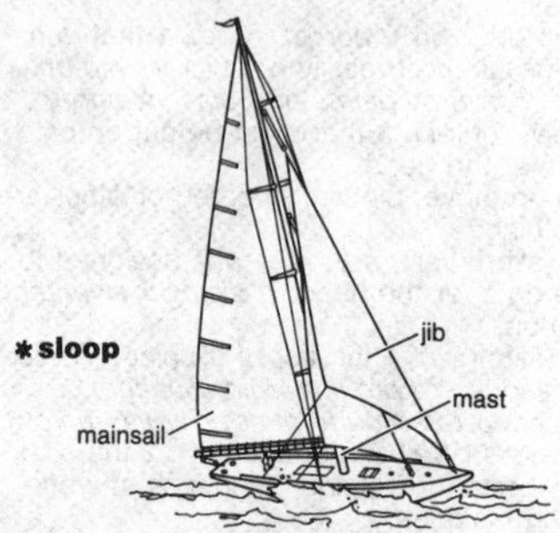

***sloop**

**sloop of war,** (formerly) a small warship having guns on the upper deck only.

**sloosh** (slüsh), *n. Dialect.* **1** a wash. **2** the sound, as of washing. **3** corn meal dough fried in bacon fat. [variant of *slosh*]

**slop**[1] (slop), *v.,* **slopped, slop|ping,** *n.* —*v.t.* **1** to spill (liquid); splash: *He slopped water on me.* **2** to spill liquid upon: *a table slopped with milk.* **3** to give slop or slops to: *The farmer slopped the pigs.*
—*v.i.* **1** to run over in spilling: *I poured the milk from the bottle so fast that it slopped over the sides of the cup.* **2** to splash through mud, slush, or water: *Then he slopped right along* (Mark Twain). *Beside the docks were the lees of the population, evidently much as they are today, slopping about among the pigs and the dogs* (Edmund Wilson).
—*n.* **1** liquid carelessly spilled or splashed about. **2** a thin, liquid mud or slush. **3** *Figurative.* weak sentiment; gush.
**slop over,** *Slang.* to show too much feeling, enthusiasm, or other sentiment; gush: *The "Herald" has slopped over this time, but it will steady itself as soon as it gets the facts* (New York Daily News).
**slops, a** dirty water; liquid garbage; dregs; swill: *kitchen slops.* **b** weak liquid or semiliquid food, such as gruel: *... please consider that you are steeping your poor original tea leaves in their fifth wash of hot water, and are drinking slops* (Atlantic). **c** what is left of grain, etc., after distilling out the alcohol, used to make food for animals: *Farmers use slops to make food for their stock.*
[Middle English *sloppe* a mud hole; origin uncertain]

**slop**[2] (slop), *n.* a loose outer garment, such as a jacket, gown, or smock.
**slops, a** cheap, ready-made clothing: *I bought an oilskin hat and a second-hand suit of slops* (W. S. Gilbert). **b** clothes, bedding, and other personal articles, supplied to sailors on a ship: *A young sailor, with a face innocent of everything but a pride in his slops* (Leigh Hunt). **c** loose trousers; wide, baggy breeches: *... two pair black silk slops, with hanging garters of carnation silk* (Scott).
[Middle English *sloppe* loose outer garment, later, loose trousers, apparently < Middle Dutch *slop*]

**slop basin, bowl,** or **bucket,** a container for holding slops or swill.

**slop book,** (in the British navy) a register of clothing and small stores issued.

**slop chest,** *Nautical Slang.* a ship's store that sells clothing, tobacco, and personal articles, to the crew during a voyage.

**slope** (slōp), *v.,* **sloped, slop|ing,** *n.* —*v.i.* **1** to go up or down at an angle: *The land slopes toward the sea.* **2** *Especially British Informal.* to go or move: *... layabouts who only saw the light of day when they sloped up to the pub* (Punch). *Dozens of MPs had sloped home, rather than vote* (Manchester Guardian Weekly).
—*v.t.* to cause to go up or down at an angle: *As the enemy climbed the opposite cliff, we sloped our firing to follow them.*
—*n.* **1a** any line or surface that goes up or down from a level: *the slope of a person's forehead.* **b** a stretch of rising or falling ground: *to climb a steep slope. If you roll a ball up a slope, it will roll down again.* **2** the amount of slope: *The floor of the theater has a slope of four feet from the back seats to the front seats.* **3** a passageway dug at a slant to reach coal that lies near the surface of a mine. **4** an economic recession. **5** *Mathematics.* the tangent of the angle formed by the intersection of a straight line with the horizontal axis of a pair of Cartesian coordinates. **6** *U.S. Slang.* an Asian; Oriental (used in an unfriendly way).
**slope off,** *Especially British Informal.* to go away or leave, especially in a stealthy manner: *He had failed to tend the machine of a man who had sloped off somewhere when he shouldn't have* (New Yorker).
[perhaps misdivision of *aslope,* adverb < Old English *āslopen,* past participle, slipped away] —**slop′er,** *n.*
—*Syn. v.i.* **Slope, slant** mean to go off at an angle from the horizontal or vertical. **Slope** usually suggests an angle more nearly horizontal; **slant,** an angle more nearly vertical: *The fields slope up to the foothills. That picture slants to the left.*

**slop|ing** (slō′ping), *adj.* that slopes: *That house has a sloping roof.* —**slop′ing|ly,** *adv.* —**slop′ing|ness,** *n.*

**slop jar** or **pail,** = slop basin.

**slop|pi|ly** (slop′ə lē), *adv.* in a sloppy manner.

**slop|pi|ness** (slop′ē nis), *n.* sloppy quality or condition.

**slop|py** (slop′ē), *adj.,* **-pi|er, -pi|est. 1** very wet; slushy: *sloppy ground, sloppy weather.* **2** splashed or soiled with liquid: *a sloppy table, a floor sloppy with suds.* **3** *Informal, Figurative.* careless; slovenly: *to do sloppy work, to use sloppy English. By returning to Freud's original work, Trilling suggests, we can clear up some of our own sloppy thinking on the subject* (Newsweek). **4** *Informal, Figurative.* weak; silly; weakly sentimental: *sloppy sentiment.* **5** loose or baggy; ill-fitting: *sloppy trousers.* **6** watery; unappetizing: *a sloppy pudding.* [< *slop*[1] + *-y*[1]]

**sloppy Joe,** *U.S.* **1** a large, loose or baggy sweater. **2** Often, **sloppy joe.** ground beef fried or broiled with tomato sauce, onions, and spices, and served on half of a bun or roll.

**slops** (slops), *n.pl.* See under **slop**[1] and **slop**[2].

**slop|sell|er** (slop′sel′ər), *n.* a person who sells ready-made, cheap, or inferior clothes.

**slop|shop** (slop′shop′), *n.* a store where cheap, ready-made clothing is sold.

**slop|work** (slop′wėrk′), *n.* **1** the manufacture of cheap clothing. **2** cheap clothing. **3** any work done cheaply or poorly.

**slop|work|er** (slop′wėr′kər), *n.* a person who does slopwork.

**slop|y** (slō′pē), *adj.,* **slop|i|er, slop|i|est.** sloping; inclined; oblique.

**slosh** (slosh), *v., n.* —*v.i.* **1** to splash in or through slush, mud, or water: *He sloshed around in the tub and got the floor wet.* **2** to go about idly; move aimlessly: *Devils don't slosh around*

*much of a Sunday, I don't reckon* (Mark Twain).
—*v.t.* **1** to cause (a liquid) to splash around in a container by shaking or stirring: *He nervously sloshed the liquor around in his glass.* **2** to pour or dash liquid upon: *He bangs his thumb, sloshes paint in his hair* (New York Times). **3** to beat; thrash.
—*n.* **1** = slush. **2** *Informal.* a watery or weak drink.
[perhaps blend of *slop*[1] and *slush*]

**sloshed** (slosht), *adj. Especially British Slang.* intoxicated; drunk.

**slosh|y** (slosh′ē), *adj.,* **slosh|i|er, slosh|i|est.** = slushy.

**slot**[1] (slot), *n., v.,* **slot|ted, slot|ting.** —*n.* **1** a small, narrow opening or depression, especially a groove or notch into which something can be pushed or fitted: *Put a penny in the slot to get a stick of gum from this machine.* **2** a narrow opening on the leading edge of an airplane wing, formed by the wing and a movable auxiliary airfoil, designed to create a smooth flow over the wing and thus increase the lift, especially at relatively low speeds. **3** a place or position in a schedule, list, or series: *The program premiers next week in the 9:30-to-10:30 slot on Saturday evening* (Wall Street Journal).
—*v.t.* **1** to make a slot or slots in. **2** *U.S. Informal, Figurative.* to put into a slot; schedule; slate: *The network slotted the new program for Sunday afternoon.*
[< Old French *esclot* the hollow between the breasts]

**slot**[2] (slot), *n., v.,* **slot|ted, slot|ting.** —*n.* a track; trail: *They followed the slot made by the deer's footprints in the mud.*
—*v.t.* to track by the slot: *They slotted the deer into the forest.*
[< Old French *esclot,* probably < Scandinavian (compare Old Icelandic *slōth* track). Compare etym. under **sleuth.**]

**slot car,** a toy racing car that is powered electrically to run on a slotted track while manipulated by remote control.

***sloth** (slôth, slōth), *n.* **1** a very slow-moving mammal of South and Central America that lives in trees. Sloths hang upside down from tree branches. There are two principal kinds in the sloth family. One kind has three toes on the forefeet and another has two. **2** unwillingness to work or exert oneself; laziness; idleness: *His sloth keeps him from taking part in sports.* SYN: sluggishness, indolence. **3** *Archaic.* slowness.
[Old English *slǣwth* < *slāw* slow]

***sloth**
definition 1

two-toed sloth

**sloth bear,** a long-haired bear of India and Ceylon (Sri Lanka). See picture under **bear**[1].

**sloth|ful** (slôth′fəl, slōth′-), *adj.* **1** unwilling to work or exert oneself; lazy; sluggish; idle: *He is the true slothful man that does no good* (Thomas Dekker). **2** characterized by sloth: *slothful habits.* SYN: sluggish. —**sloth′ful|ly,** *adv.* —**sloth′ful-ness,** *n.*

**sloth|hound** (slôth′hound′), *n.* a sleuthhound; bloodhound.

**sloth monkey,** = slow lemur.

**slot machine,** a machine that is worked by dropping money, usually a coin, into a slot. Some slot machines sell peanuts, sticks of gum, and other merchandise; others are used for gambling.

**slot man,** *U.S.* the news editor of a newspaper in charge of the copy desk.

**slot mining,** a method of mining diamonds in which slots are cut into the blue ground, causing the ground to settle and break into small pieces which then go to lower tunnels for processing.

**slot racer,** = slot car.

**slot racing,** the sport or hobby of racing slot cars.

**slot|ter** (slot′ər), *n.* a person or a machine that makes slots: *In a slotter, or vertical shaper, the cutting tool moves up and down instead of back and forth* (Ludlow King).

**slouch** (slouch), *v., n.* —*v.i.* **1** to stand, sit, walk, or move in an awkward, drooping manner: *The weary man slouched along. Don't slouch, sit up straight.* **2** to droop or bend downward: *The old hat slouched backward on his head.*
—*v.t.* to cause to droop or bend down: *He slouched his shoulders.*
—*n.* **1** a stooping or bending forward of the head and shoulders; awkward, drooping way of standing, sitting, or walking: *The tall man's slouch made his clothes look as if they didn't fit.* **2** a drooping or bending downward, as of a hat brim. **3** *Informal.* **a** an awkward or inefficient person: *He's no slouch when it comes to playing baseball.* **b** a lazy, idle, or slovenly person: *Don't be a slouch and get busy on your homework.*
[origin uncertain. Compare Old Icelandic *slōkr* a slouch, *slōka* to droop.]

**slouch|er** (slou′chər), *n.* a person who slouches, or walks with a slouching gait.

**slouch hat,** a soft hat, usually with a broad brim that bends down easily.

**slouch|i|ly** (slou′chə lē), *adv.* in a slouchy manner.

**slouch|i|ness** (slou′chē nis), *n.* slouchy quality or condition.

**slouch|ing** (slou′ching), *adj.* **1** that slouches; carrying oneself with a slouch: *a tall, slouching fellow* (Francis Parkman). **2** characterized by a slouch: *I adopted, along with my beggar's attire, a peculiar slouching and clownish gait* (William Godwin). —**slouch′ing|ly,** *adv.*

**slouch|y** (slou′chē), *adj.,* **slouch|i|er, slouch|i|est.** slouching awkwardly; carelessly untidy; slovenly.

**slough**[1] (*n.* slou *for 1 and 3,* slü *for 2; v.* slou), *n., v.* —*n.* **1** a soft, deep, muddy place; mud hole: *We visited sloughs that always have water, no matter the severity of the drought* (William O. Douglas). **2** a swampy place; marshy inlet; slew; slue. **3** *Figurative.* hopeless discouragement; degradation; decline: *Otto Kahn, the suave, music-loving-man-about-town, was … the man who rescued the Metropolitan Opera from a financial and artistic slough* (Newsweek).
—*v.i.* to plod heavily; slog: *They're here in Toronto and not sloughing through some Vietnamese rice paddy* (Canadian Saturday Night).
—*v.t.* to swallow up in a slough: *Somebody … got nearly sloughed up in one of the great marsh ditches* (Eleanor Ormerod).
[Old English *slōh*]

**slough**[2] (sluf), *n., v.* —*n.* **1** the old dead skin shed or cast off by a snake. **2** a layer of dead skin or tissue that drops or falls off as a wound or sore heals. **3** *Figurative.* anything that has been or can be shed or cast off: *As people became civilized, they cast off the slough of primitive ways and beliefs.* **4** a discard in a card game that might otherwise be a losing card.
—*v.t.* **1** to drop off; throw off; shed: *Through the processes of excision and sloughing of certain structures which contain wastes, plants get rid of wastes* (Harbaugh and Goodrich). (*Figurative.*) *The former thief sloughed his bad ways and became an honest man.* (*Figurative.*) *She could slough off a sadness and replace it by a hope* (Thomas Hardy). **2** to discard (a losing card) on a trick.
—*v.i.* to be shed or cast; drop or fall: *A scab sloughs off when new skin takes its place.* Also, **sluff.**
[Middle English *slouh;* origin uncertain]

**slough of despond** (slou), hopeless dejection; deep despondency: *What saves me from the slough of despond and keeps me going is a delight in the senses, all five of them* (Louis Untermeyer). [< the *Slough of Despond,* in *Pilgrim's Progress,* by John Bunyan, 1628-1688, an English minister and religious writer]

**slough|y**[1] (slou′ē), *adj.,* **slough|i|er, slough|i|est.** soft and muddy; full of soft, deep mud; miry: *sloughy creeks.*

**slough|y**[2] (sluf′ē), *adj.* of dead skin; covered with dead skin or tissue.

**Slo|vak** (slō′väk, -vak), *n., adj.* —*n.* **1** a member of a Slavic people living in Slovakia. The Slovaks are closely related to the Bohemians and the Moravians. **2** their language. It is a West Slavic language, related to Czech and Moravian.
—*adj.* of or having to do with Slovakia, a province in eastern Czechoslovakia, its people, or their language.
[< Czech, and Slovak *Slovák*]

**Slo|va|ki|an** (slō vä′kē ən, -vak′ē-), *n., adj.* = Slovak.

**slov|en** (sluv′ən), *n., adj.* —*n.* a person who is untidy, dirty, or careless in dress, appearance, habits, or work: *Since he had never taken any care of his personal appearance, he became every known variety of sloven* (Rudyard Kipling).
—*adj.* untidy; dirty; careless; slovenly.
[perhaps ultimately < Flemish *sloef* dirty, or Dutch *slof* careless]

**Slo|vene** (slō′vēn), *n., adj.* —*n.* **1** a member of a Slavic people living in Slovenia, a region in northwestern Yugoslavia. The Slovenes are closely related to the Croats, Serbians, and other southern Slavs. **2** their language. It is a South Slavic language, closely related to Serbo-Croatian.
—*adj.* of or having to do with Slovenia, its people, or their language.
[< German *Slovene* < Slovenian *slovenec*]

**Slo|ve|ni|an** (slō vē′nē ən, -vēn′yən), *adj., n.* = Slovene.

**slov|en|li|ness** (sluv′ən lē nis), *n.* lack of neatness; dirtiness; carelessness in appearance, dress, habits, or work: *Slovenliness is no part of religion* (John Wesley).

**slov|en|ly** (sluv′ən lē), *adj.,* **-li|er, -li|est,** *adv.*
—*adj.* untidy, dirty, or careless in dress, appearance, habits, or work: *A thin elderly man, rather threadbare and slovenly* (Washington Irving). SYN: unkempt, slatternly, slipshod, negligent.
—*adv.* in a slovenly manner.

**slov|en|ry** (sluv′ən rē), *n. Archaic.* slovenly character, condition, or procedure.

**slow** (slō), *adj., adv., v.* —*adj.* **1** taking a long time; taking longer than usual; not fast or quick: *a slow journey, a slow messenger.* **2** behind time; running at less than proper speed: *The fat man is a slow runner. Seldom readers are slow readers* (Charles Lamb). **3** showing a time earlier than the correct time: *The clock was slow and I was late for school.* **4** causing a low or lower rate of speed; retarding: *slow ground, a slow track.* **5** burning or heating slowly or gently: *a slow flame.* **6a** inactive; sluggish; slack: *Business is slow.* SYN: phlegmatic. **b** not quick to understand; dull: *a slow learner.* **7** not interesting; not lively; boring; dull: *a slow party.* SYN: wearisome, tiresome. **8** not fast or hurried; leisurely: *music in a slow tempo; … to proceed by slow marches and frequent halts* (Scott). **9a** not readily stirred or moved; not hasty: *slow to anger, slow to take offense.* **b** not ready or willing: *slow to answer, slow in or of speech.* **10** behind the times; not smart or up-to-date: *a slow town.* **11** (of time) passing slowly or heavily: *As slow years pass …* (Shelley).
—*adv.* in a slow manner or way; slowly: *Drive slow past a school. In front the sun climbs slow, how slowly!* (Arthur Hugh Clough).
—*v.t.* to make slow or slower; reduce the speed of: *to slow down a car.*
—*v.i.* to become slow; go slower: *Slow up when you drive through a town. Slow down, you're walking too fast for me.*
[Old English *slāw*] —**slow′ly,** *adv.* —**slow′ness,** *n.*
—*Syn. adj.* **1 Slow, leisurely, deliberate** mean taking a long time to do something or to happen. **Slow,** the general term, suggests taking longer than usual or necessary: *We took the slow train.* **Leisurely** suggests slowness because of having plenty of time: *I like leisurely meals.* **Deliberate,** describing people or their acts, suggests slowness due to care, thought, or self-control: *His speech is deliberate.*
▶ **Slow, slowly.** In standard English *slowly* is now the usual form of the adverb except in set phrases (*go slow, drive slow*) and in the comparative or superlative (where *slower* or *slowest* are often used instead of *more* or *most slowly*).

**slow burn,** a gradually increasing exasperation turning by degrees into intense, but still controlled, anger, used as a comic device by actors: *Jack Carson [was] master of the double-take and the slow burn* (Time).

**slow coach,** *Informal.* **1** a slowpoke. **2** an idle, inactive person. **3** an old-fashioned person; fogy.

**slow|down** (slō′doun′), *n.* the act or fact of slowing down, as in rate of production or pace of work: *Most concerns [are] expecting the traditional midsummer month slowdown* (Wall Street Journal).

**slow-foot|ed** (slō′fu̇t′id), *adj.* advancing slowly; slow-moving; slow-paced: (*Figurative.*) *get slow-footed members of Congress off and running early* (Harper's).

**slow|go|ing** (slō′gō′ing), *adj.* slow in moving, proceeding, or acting; leisurely: *a calm, slowgoing Arkansan* (Time).

**slow|hound** (slō′hound′), *n.* = sleuthhound.

**slow|ish** (slō′ish), *adj.* somewhat slow or dull: *a slowish waltz.*

**slow loris,** a small nocturnal lemur of India and the East Indies, noted for the extreme slowness of its movements.

**slow match,** a fuze that burns very slowly, used to set fire to gunpowder, dynamite, or other powerful explosives.

**slow-mo|tion** (slō′mō′shən), *adj.* **1** showing action at much less than its actual speed: *slow-motion photography.* **2** moving at less than

**Pronunciation Key:** hat, āge, cãre, fär; let, ēqual, tėrm; it, īce; hot, ōpen, ôrder; **oi**l, **ou**t; cup, pu̇t, rüle; **ch**ild; lo**ng**; **th**in; **ᵺ**en; **zh**, measure; ə represents **a** in about, **e** in taken, **i** in pencil, **o** in lemon, **u** in circus.

normal speed: *Lewisohn is at his narrative best as he puts a slow-motion technique to work* (New York Times).

**slow-mov|ing** (slō′mü′ving), *adj.* **1** that moves or goes slowly; slowgoing: *Large droves of patient, slow-moving cattle arrived* (Rolf Boldrewood). **2** making slow progress; advancing or acting slowly: *... overloads himself with slow-moving stock* (Harper's).

**slow neutron**, a neutron of relatively low energy, as compared with a fast neutron: *When $U^{238}$ atoms capture slow neutrons, they form atoms of $U^{239}$, but these atoms do not fission* (Robert L. Thornton).

**slow|paced** (slō′pāst′), *adj.* moving or advancing slowly: (*Figurative.*) *He has written a slowpaced, leisurely, rambling and discursive novel about several of the most important issues of our time* (New York Times).

**slow|poke** (slō′pōk′), *n. Informal.* a very slow person or thing.

**slow-spo|ken** (slō′spō′kən), *adj.* speaking at a slow pace: *a slow-spoken man with a brooding look* (New Yorker).

**slow|up** (slō′up′), *n.* = slowdown.

**slow virus**, a virus that may remain in the body of an infected individual for most or all of his life, believed to be the cause of many chronic diseases of man: *Evidence recently came to light that implicated slow viruses in such neurological disorders of humans as multiple sclerosis and polyneuritis as well as in rheumatoid arthritis* (Robert G. Eagon).

**slow-wit|ted** (slō′wit′id), *adj.* slow at thinking; dull; stupid.

**slow|worm** (slō′wėrm′), *n.* = blindworm.

**sloyd** (sloid), *n.* a system of manual training for children in work with the hands and simple tools, as for woodworking and other crafts, originally developed and taught in Sweden. Also **sloid, slojd.** [< Swedish *slöjd* skill, dexterity]

**SLR** (no periods), single-lens reflex (camera).

**slub** (slub), *v.,* **slubbed, slub|bing,** *n.* —*v.t.* to twist (wool, yarn, or other fiber) slightly after carding, to prepare for spinning: *Stripes, checks and other fancy patterns, are formed in prominent looped or slubbed yarns against a flat ground* (London Times).
—*n.* **1** a partially twisted silk, wool, or cotton fiber or cloth made from such a fiber. **2** a lump on a fiber that becomes attached to the yarn in spinning.
[origin uncertain. Compare earlier *slub* a lump on a thread.]

**slub|ber** (slub′ər), *v.t. Dialect.* **1** to stain; smear; daub; soil. **2** to do or make in a hurried and careless manner. [probably < Low German *slubbern;* perhaps variant of *slobber*]

**sludge** (sluj), *n., v.,* **sludged, sludg|ing.** —*n.* **1** soft mud; mire; ooze; slush. **2** a soft, thick, muddy mixture, deposit, or sediment. **3** small broken pieces of floating ice: *In winter there is sludge on the sea near the shore.*
—*v.t.* **1** to convert into sludge. **2** to stop up with liquid mud. **3** to clear from sludge or mud.
—*v.i.* to form sludge: *Unanswered is the question of what causes the blood to be over-viscous or to sludge* (Science News Letter).
[earlier *slutch;* origin uncertain]

**sludg|er** (sluj′ər), *n.* a pump or other apparatus for removing sludge from a bore.

**sludg|y** (sluj′ē), *adj.* consisting of sludge; miry; slushy.

**slue**[1] (slü), *v.t., v.i.,* **slued, slu|ing,** *n.* = slew[2].

**slue**[2] (slü), *n.* = slew[3].

**slue**[3] (slü), *n.* = slew[4].

**sluff** (sluf), *n., v.* = slough[2].

***slug**[1] (slug), *n., v.,* **slugged, slug|ging.** —*n.* **1** a slow-moving, slimy animal like a snail, without a shell or with only a very small shell. Slugs live mostly in forests, gardens, and damp places, feeding on plants. They are mollusks. There are various kinds. *A study of the embryonic development of the slug reveals that a shell is formed in the embryo just as it is in the snail, but fails to continue its development to a functional size* (A. M. Winchester). **2** a caterpillar or other insect larva that looks like a slug. **3** anything slow-moving or sluggish, such as a person, animal, or wagon. **4** a piece of lead or other metal for firing from a gun: *a slug from a .45-caliber revolver.* **5** a round metal piece or counterfeit coin inserted in a coin-operated machine instead of a genuine coin. **6a** a strip of metal used to space lines of type. A slug is more than 1/16 of an inch in thickness. Slugs are also used to fill out missing lines in page proofs and for printing temporary marks of identification. **b** a line of type cast in one piece by a linotype machine. **7** *Physics.* a unit of mass, equal to about 32.17 pounds, which has an acceleration of one foot per second per second when acted upon by a force of one pound. **8** *U.S. Slang.* a drink; shot: *a slug of whiskey.*
—*v.t.* **1** *Printing.* to insert slugs between lines of (type). **2** to load (a gun) with slugs.
—*v.i. Archaic.* **1** to be inactive or slothful. **2** to move slowly.
[Middle English *slugge* a slow person, perhaps < Scandinavian (compare Swedish dialectal *slogga* be sluggish)] —**slug′like′,** *adj.*

***slug**[1]
definition 1

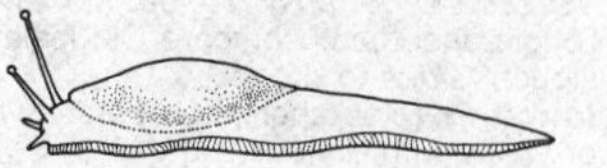

**slug**[2] (slug), *v.,* **slugged, slug|ging,** *n. Informal.* —*v.t., v.i.* **1** to hit hard with the fist: *to slug a person on the chin.* **2** to hit hard: *to slug a ball. He slugged two home runs in the deciding game of the series.*
—*n.* a hard blow, especially with the fist.
**slug it out,** *U.S. Informal.* to fight or compete until one side wins; fight it out: *Retail casualties mount as St. Louis merchants slug it out with discount houses* (Wall Street Journal).
[origin uncertain]

**slug|a|bed** (slug′ə bed′), *n.* a lazy, idle person who likes to lie in bed.

**slug|fest** (slug′fest′), *n. U.S. Slang.* **1** an occasion of much vigorous battling or contesting; fight; free-for-all: (*Figurative.*) *The backslapping camaraderie soon degenerated into a verbal slugfest* (Newsweek). **2** a baseball game dominated by heavy hitting: *Last night's anticipated pitching duel ... turned into a slugfest* (New York Times).

**slug|gard** (slug′ərd), *n., adj.* —*n.* a lazy, idle person: *Go to the ant, thou sluggard; consider her ways, and be wise* (Proverbs 6:6).
—*adj.* lazy; idle. **SYN:** sluggish, slothful.
[< *slug*[1], verb + Old French *-ard,* a suffix meaning "one who does"]

**slug|gard|ly** (slug′ərd lē), *adj.* lazy; indolent; slothful: *It failed ... to rouse me from a sluggardly half-sleep* (London Times).

**slug|gard|ness** (slug′ərd nis), *n.* laziness; indolence.

**slug|ger** (slug′ər), *n. Informal.* **1** a person who slugs or hits hard. **2** a boxer; pugilist. **3** a baseball player who hits balls that go far, especially one that gets many extra-base hits: *In ... a year when the sluggers controlled the game, 18 players batted .300 or better* (Time).

**slug|ging** (slug′ing), *n. Informal.* the act of a person who slugs or hits hard; hard hitting; beating.

**slugging average,** a percentage showing the effectiveness of a baseball player in making extra-base hits. It is obtained by dividing the total number of bases reached by the number of times at bat.

**slugging match,** **1** a boxing match or fistfight involving hard hits. **2** *Informal, Figurative.* a sharp or forceful dispute: *The Pentagon vs. Congress slugging match over the choice ...* (Wall Street Journal).

**slug|gish** (slug′ish), *adj.* **1** not active; slow-moving; lacking energy or vigor: *He has a sluggish mind and shows little interest in anything.* **SYN:** dull, inert. **2** lazy; idle. **3** moving very slowly; having little motion: *The stream was so sluggish that I could hardly tell which way it flowed.* **4** slow; tardy: *a sluggish digestion. Climbing again into his car, pushing at the sluggish starter* (Graham Greene). [< *slug*[1] + *-ish*] —**slug′gish|ly,** *adv.* —**slug′gish|ness,** *n.*

**slug|horn** (slug′hôrn′), *n.* a kind of trumpet. [variant of *slogan* battle cry]

**slug|worm** (slug′wėrm′), *n.* the slimy sluglike larva of any one of various sawflies.

**sluice** (slüs), *n., v.,* **sluiced, sluic|ing.** —*n.* **1** a structure with a gate or gates for holding back or controlling the water of a canal, river, or lake: *A big sluice has been constructed on the Austrian bank of the Danube and shipping can proceed through locks on the Bavarian side* (Wall Street Journal). **2a** a gate that holds back or controls the flow of water. When the water behind a dam gets too high, the sluices are opened. **b** *Figurative: War opens the sluices of hatred and bloodshed.* **3** the water held back or controlled by such a gate. **4** a valve, pipe, or other device that regulates the flow of water into or out of some receptacle. **5** a long, sloping trough through which water flows, used to wash gold from sand, dirt, or gravel: *The sluice consists of an inclined channel through which runs a stream of water and into which the gold-bearing earth is shoveled* (White and Renner). **6** a channel for carrying off overflow or surplus water.
—*v.t.* **1** to let out or draw off (water or other fluid) by opening a sluice: *The farmers watered their crops by sluicing water into the fields once a week.* **2** to flush or cleanse with a rush of water; pour or throw water over; slush: *Mud brought by the flooding was sluiced from the street by fire hoses.* **3** to wash (gold) from sand, dirt, or gravel in a sluice. **4** to carry or send (logs) along a channel of water.
—*v.i.* to flow or pour in a stream; rush: *Water sluiced down the channel.*
[< Old French *escluse* < Late Latin *exclūsa* a barrier to shut out water < Latin *exclūdere* shut out < *ex-* out + *claudere* close, shut]

**sluice gate,** a gate to control the flow of water in a sluice.

**sluice|way** (slüs′wā′), *n.* **1** a channel controlled or fed by a sluice. **2** any small, artificial channel for running water.

**sluic|y** (slü′sē), *adj. Archaic.* **1** pouring abundantly: *And oft whole sheets descend of sluicy rain* (John Dryden). **2** wet: *the cool and sluicy sands* (Keats).

**sluit** (slüt), *n.* (in South Africa) a gully made by heavy rains. [< Afrikaans *sloot*]

**slum** (slum), *n., v.,* **slummed, slum|ming.** —*n.* **1** Often, **slums.** a street, alley, or building in a crowded, run-down, dirty part of a city or town, where the poorest people live. Poverty and disease are common in the slums. *We hear stories now and then of some boy from a slum who makes good and winds up with a fortune. If* [*his*] *philosophy prevails, we shall have taken a long step backward toward the sweatshop and the slums* (Time). **2** extreme poverty and low social class, as in the slums: *to rise from the slums to power and wealth.*
—*v.i.* **1** to go into or visit a slum or slums. **2** to go into or visit any place thought of as greatly inferior to one's own.
[earlier, a room; origin uncertain]

**slum|ber** (slum′bər), *v., n.* —*v.i.* **1** to sleep; sleep lightly; doze. **2** *Figurative.* **a** to be like a person asleep; be inactive: *slumbering anger. The volcano had slumbered for years.* **b** to be negligently inactive: *to slumber while one's enemies arm themselves.*
—*v.t.* to pass in slumber: *The baby slumbers away the hours.*
—*n.* **1** a sleep; light sleep; doze: *He awoke from his slumber.* **2** *Figurative.* an inactive state or condition.
[Middle English *slumberen, slumeren* (frequentative) < Old English *slūma* sleep, noun] —**slum′ber|er,** *n.*

**slum|ber|land** (slum′bər land′), *n.* the imaginary country of slumber.

**slum|ber|less** (slum′bər lis), *adj.* without slumber; sleepless.

**slum|ber|ous** (slum′bər əs, -brəs), *adj.* **1** sleepy; heavy with drowsiness: *slumberous eyelids.* **2** causing or inducing sleep. **3** having to do with, characterized by, or suggestive of sleep. **4** *Figurative.* inactive; sluggish. **5** calm; quiet. —**slum′ber|ous|ly,** *adv.*

**slumber party,** *U.S.* a gathering of young girls in a home to spend the night together; pajama party: *They had been to a slumber party ... and had not slept at all* (New Yorker).

**slum|ber|y** (slum′bər ē), *adj.* **1** slumberous; sleepy. **2** of or like slumber.

**slum|brous** (slum′brəs), *adj.* = slumberous. —**slum′brous|ly,** *adv.*

**slum clearance,** the clearing away of slums in connection with a program of housing and redevelopment: *The largest efforts will be directed at slum clearance and improvement of blighted homes* (New York Times).

**slum|dom** (slum′dəm), *n.* **1** the condition of being a slum: *Neglected, this property will slip by degrees into slumdom* (London Times). **2** the people living in a slum.

**slum|dwell|er** (slum′dwel′ər), *n.* a person who lives in a slum.

**slum|gul|lion** (slum gul′yən), *n.* **1** a stew of meat and vegetables, usually potatoes and onions. **2** *Mining.* the thick and sticky refuse of the sluice boxes, generally of red, iron-bearing clay and water. **3** *Slang.* a low, worthless fellow. [perhaps < *slum* + *gullion,* alteration of *cullion*]

**slum|gum** (slum′gum), *n.* the impurities that remain as a residue after the wax is extracted from honeycombs.

**slum|ism** (slum′iz əm), *n. U.S.* the existence or proliferation of city slums: *We must show the same unhesitating commitment to fighting slumism, poverty, ignorance, prejudice, and unemployment* (Harper's).

**slum|lord** (slum′lôrd′), *n. U.S.* the owner of a run-down tenement house, usually in the slums: *The number of housing violations we have found* [*shows*] *how strongly we are attacking the slumlords* (Robert F. Wagner).

**slum|lord|ship** (slum′lôrd′ship), *n. U.S.* the condition of being a slumlord.

**slum|mer** (slum′ər), *n.* a person who visits slums for charitable purposes, curiosity, or study.

**slum|mi|ness** (slum′ē nis), *n.* the quality or condition of being slummy.

**slum|ming** (slum′ing), *n.* the visiting of slums, as for charitable purposes or from curiosity.

**slum|my** (slum′ē), *adj.*, **-mi|er, -mi|est.** **1** characteristic of a slum or of people living there: *a slummy street, accent, or manner.* **2** full of slums.

**slump** (slump), *v., n.* —*v.i.* **1** to drop heavily; fall suddenly: *Our feet slumped repeatedly through the melting ice. She slumped into a chair and gasped with the heat* (Sinclair Lewis). **2** to move, walk, sit, or otherwise behave or carry oneself in a drooping manner; slouch: *The bored students slumped in their seats.* **3** *Figurative.* to fall off; decline: *The stock market slumped. New England... put its brains to work and found new research and electronics industries after textiles slumped* (Time).
—*n.* **1** a heavy drop or sudden fall; collapse. **2** a great or sudden decline: *a slump in prices. In 1929, in the great slump, disaster fell* (Atlantic). **3** a drooping posture or stance.
[perhaps imitative]

**slump|fla|tion** (slump flā′shən), *n. Economics.* inflation accompanied by a steady decline in business and employment; inflump: *The $16 billion in rebates and tax credits might be too weak to jolt the economy out of its alarming slumpflation* (Time). *Stagflation changed into the still more unspeakable slumpflation* (Manchester Guardian Weekly). [blend of *slump* and *inflation*]

**slung** (slung), *v.* the past tense and past participle of **sling**[1]: *They slung some stones and ran away. The boy had slung his books over his shoulder.*

**slung shot**, a piece of metal or stone fastened to a short strap or chain, used as a weapon.

**slunk**[1] (slungk), *v.* a past tense and past participle of **slink**[1]: *The dog slunk away ashamed.*

**slunk**[2] (slungk), *v.* a past tense and a past participle of **slink**[2].

***slur** (slėr), *v.*, **slurred, slur|ring,** *n.* —*v.t.* **1** to pass lightly over; go through hurriedly or in a careless way: *Biographers have slurred a few facts in their hurry to carry out their theory of favourites* (Charles Kingsley). *The little word, as, which is always slurred over* (Richard Brinsley Sheridan). **2** to pronounce in an incomplete or indistinct way: *Many persons slur "ing" and "How do you do."* **3** *Music.* **a** to to sing or play (two or more tones of different pitch) without a break; run together in a smooth, connected manner. **b** to mark with a slur. **4** to harm the reputation of; insult; slight: *Hardly anything was so likely to be of advantage to the Lancastrians as to slur the descent of the House of York* (Scott). **5** *Printing.* to smudge or blur; mackle. **6** *Dialect.* to smear; stain; sully.
—*v.i.* **1** to speak or write sounds, letters, etc., so indistinctly that they run into each other. **2** to move heavily; shuffle. **3** *Dialect.* to slide.
—*n.* **1** a slurred pronunciation, sound, or word. **2** *Music.* **a** a slurring of tones. **b** a curved mark indicating this. **3** a blot or stain (upon reputation); insulting or slighting remark: *a slur on a person's good name.* **4** a mark; stain; blot. **5** *Printing.* a smudged or blurred place; mackle.
[origin uncertain; perhaps related to Low German *slurrn* drag the feet, shuffle]

***slur**
definition 2b

**slurb** (slėrb), *n.* an unsightly area on the outskirts of a large city, characterized by cheap housing, gas stations, used-car lots, diners, and the like: *These are the people who are existing in... cities so choked and "slurbs" so ugly that by comparison the New York-Washington corridor looks almost like a planned development* (John B. Oakes). [< *sl*(um sub) *urb*]

**slurp** (slėrp), *v., n. U.S. Slang.* —*v.i.* to eat or drink something with a noisy gurgling sound: *I never slurp, nor gobble as if I'm starving* (Wall Street Journal). —*v.t.* to eat or drink in this manner.
—*n.* a slurping or gurgling sound: *... the last whirling slurp of water down a drain* (Harper's).
[perhaps imitative] —**slurp′er,** *n.*

**slur|ry** (slėr′ē), *n., pl.* **-ries,** *v.,* **-ried, -ry|ing.** —*n.* a semifluid substance, such as a thin mixture of powdered coal, ore, clay, mud, slush, cement, or mortar with water: *In the wet process, water is added during the grinding, until a soupy mixture called a slurry forms* (Richard G. Knox).
—*v.t.* to make or convert into a slurry: *to slurry uranium ore or radioactive waste.*
[see related etym. at **slur**]

**slush** (slush), *n., v.* —*n.* **1** partly melted snow; snow and water mixed: *There was no traffic to turn the snow to slush* (James Barrie). **2** soft mud; mire. **3** *Figurative.* silly, sentimental talk, writing, or other expression; drivel. **4a** a mixture of grease and other materials for lubricating. **b** a mixture of white lead and lime, used for painting parts of machinery to prevent them from rusting. **5** used or spoiled fat from a ship's galley.
—*v.t.* **1** to splash or soak with slush or mud. **2** to grease, polish, or cover with slush: *The officer... ordered me to slush the mainmast... So I took my bucket of grease and climbed up* (Richard Henry Dana). **3** to fill up or cover with mortar or cement. **4** to wash with much water.
—*v.i.* **1** to go or walk through slush or mud: *The horses slushed in and out of the drenched courtyard.* **2** to move with a splashing sound: *The water slushed on the pavement.*
[origin uncertain. Perhaps related to **sludge.**]

**slush fund**, **1** money collected or set aside for dishonest purposes, such as bribery, or for political campaigning or the like: [*He*] *has rapidly sized up the situation and is using his slush funds for an all-out financing of the leftist groups inside the party* (Harper's). **2** a fund of money obtained from the sale of waste fat on ship or in camp.

**slush|i|ness** (slush′ē nis), *n.* **1** slushy quality or condition. **2** *Figurative.* sickening sentimentality: *Aside from their slushiness, the romantic epistles are historically interesting in graphically demonstrating the young prince's fickle ways* (Time).

**slush lamp**, a crude lamp that burns slush or refuse fat, often made from an old tin can with a rag as a wick.

**slush|y** (slush′ē), *adj.*, **slush|i|er, slush|i|est,** *n.* —*adj.* **1** having much slush; covered with slush: *slushy roads.* **2** of or like slush.
—*n.* **1** *Slang.* a ship's cook. **2** a cook's assistant on a sheep station in Australia during shearing time.

**slut** (slut), *n.* **1** a dirty, untidy woman or girl; slattern. **2** a woman or girl of loose morals. **3** a female dog; bitch. [Middle English *slutte* a slovenly person]

**slut|ter|y** (slut′ər ē), *n.* the character or practices of a slut; sluttishness.

**slut|tish** (slut′ish), *adj.* **1** dirty; untidy. **2** loose in morals. —**slut′tish|ly,** *adv.* —**slut′tish|ness,** *n.*

**sly** (slī), *adj.*, **sly|er** or **sli|er, sly|est** or **sli|est,** *n.* —*adj.* **1** able to fool, trick, or deceive; cunning; crafty; tricky; wily: *That boy is as sly as a fox. The sly cat stole the meat while the cook's back was turned.* **2** such as a sly person would use: *She asked sly questions.* **3** playfully mischievous or knowing; roguish: *Waiting for the surprise party to begin, the children exchanged many sly looks and smiles.* **4** acting secretly or stealthily. SYN: surreptitious, stealthy, furtive. **5** *Obsolete.* skilled; wise.
—*n.* **on the sly,** in a sly way; secretly; stealthily: *He read his comic book on the sly when he was supposed to be studying. Prominent politicians came to seek favors from him on the sly* (James Bryce).
[< Scandinavian (compare Old Icelandic *slægr*)]
—**sly′ness,** *n.*
—*Syn. adj.* **1 Sly, cunning** mean able to get what one wants by secret, wily, or indirect means. **Sly** emphasizes lack of frankness and straightforwardness, and suggests stealthy actions or secrecy and deceit in dealing with others: *That sly girl managed to get her best friend's job.* **Cunning** emphasizes cleverness in getting the better of others by tricks or schemes, unfair dealing, or cheating: *A fox is cunning enough to cross a stream so that dogs cannot follow its scent. He showed a cunning ability to manipulate his customers into spending more than they intended.*

**sly|boots** (slī′büts′), *n.* a sly, cunning, or crafty person.

**sly|ly** (slī′lē), *adv.* in a sly manner; secretly. Also, **slily.**

**slype** (slīp), *n.* a covered passage, especially from the transept of a cathedral to the chapter house. [origin uncertain]

**sm.,** small.

**Sm** (no period), samarium (chemical element).

**SM** (no periods), **1** service module. **2** speed midget (flashbulb).

**S.M.,** an abbreviation for the following:
**1** Master of Science (Latin, *Scientiae Magister*).
**2** Saint Mary.
**3** Sergeant Major.
**4** Soldier's Medal.
**5** State Militia.

**S-M** or **s-m** (no periods), sadomasochism or sadomasochistic: *S-M fiction brings the reader out of his down by making a spectacle of his own cruelty and vulnerability* (Harper's).

**SMA** (no periods), Standard Metropolitan Area. See also **SMSA** (no periods).

**smack**[1] (smak), *n., v.* —*n.* **1** a slight taste or flavor: *This sauce has a smack of lemon.* **2** a trace; touch; suggestion: *The old sailor still had a smack of the sea about him.* SYN: dash, tinge. **3** a small quantity; taste; mouthful.
—*v.i.* to have a taste, trace, or touch (of): *The speech of the man from Ireland smacked of the old country.* [Old English *smæcc*]

**smack**[2] (smak), *v., n., adv.* —*v.t.* **1** to open (the lips) quickly so as to make a sharp sound: *He smacked his lips over the thought of cake.* **2** to kiss loudly: *The little boy smacked his father on the cheek.* **3** to slap: *to smack someone in the face.* **4** to bring, put, throw, or send with a sharp blow or smack: *to smack a ball, to smack a home run.* **5** to crack (as a whip).
—*v.i.* to make or give out a smacking sound.
—*n.* **1** a smacking movement of the lips: *Tasting the wine with a judicious smack* (Sir Richard Steele). **2** the sharp sound made in this way: *Everybody turned at the smack of his lips and stared as the King ate his pudding.* **3** a loud kiss: *a big wet smack on the cheek.* **4** a slap: *a smack in the nose.* **5** a crack (as of a whip): *The loud, resounding smack of its* [*beaver's*] *tail on the water was at first as startling as gunfire* (William O. Douglas).
—*adv. Informal.* **1** directly; squarely; completely: *I fell smack on my face.* **2** suddenly and sharply; with or as with a smack: *He ran smack into the very man he was trying to avoid.*
[ultimately imitative. Compare Dutch *smacken.*]

***smack**[3] (smak), *n.* **1** a small sailboat with one mast rigged like a sloop or cutter, generally used as a coaster or for fishing. **2** a similar fishing boat with a well for keeping fish alive. [probably < Dutch *smak*]

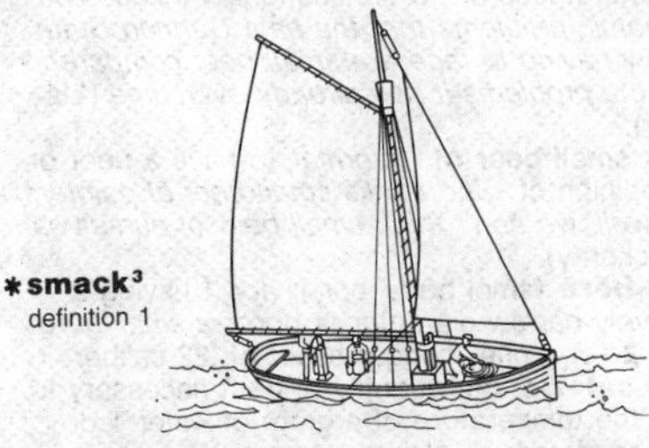

***smack**[3]
definition 1

**smack**[4] (smak), *n. U.S. Slang.* heroin. [origin uncertain]

**smack-dab** (smak′dab′), *adv. U.S. Informal.* directly; squarely; smack: *Then he zagged to his right and ran smack-dab through a fence* (New York Times).

**smack|er** (smak′ər), *n.* **1** a person or thing that smacks. **2** *Informal.* a loud kiss; smack. **3** a resounding blow. **4** *U.S. Slang.* a dollar: *The price will be somewhere around ten thousand smackers* (Harper's).

**smack|ing** (smak′ing), *adj.* **1** lively, brisk, or strong; spanking: *a smacking breeze.* **2** given with a smack or the sound of a smack: *a smacking blow, a smacking kiss.*

**smacks|man** (smaks′mən), *n., pl.* **-men.** a person who owns or works on a smack.

**small** (smôl), *adj., n., adv.* —*adj.* **1** not large or great; little in size; not large as compared with other things of the same kind: *a small country or city. A cottage is a small house.* SYN: diminutive, undersized, tiny, minute. See syn. under **little.** **2** not fully grown or developed; young: *small boys, small plants.* **3** not great in amount, degree, extent, duration, value, or strength: *a small dose, small hope of success. The cent is our smallest coin.* SYN: slight, inconsiderable. **4** having low value or rank; low: *to play a small trump.* **5** not important; of little interest: *Don't bother Mother with that small matter.* SYN: trifling, insignificant, trivial. **6** not prominent; humble; modest: *to make a small start. Both great and small people mourned the President's death. A small author, and smaller wit* (Benjamin Disraeli). **7** having little land or capital; doing business on a limited scale: *a small farmer. A man who keeps a little shop is a small dealer.* **8** having or showing littleness of mind or character; mean; ungenerous: *A person with a small nature is not generous.* SYN: selfish, illiberal, stingy. **9** having little strength; gentle; soft; low: *a small voice, a small crumbling sound.* **10** diluted; weak. **11** (of letters) not capital; lower-case.
—*n.* **1** that part which is small; small, slender, or narrow part: *the small of the back.* **2** a small person, animal, or thing.
—*adv.* **1** into small pieces. **2** in low tones. **3** in a small manner.

**Pronunciation Key:** hat, āge, cãre, fär; let, ēqual, tėrm; it, īce; hot, ōpen, ôrder; **oil, out;** cup, pu̇t, rüle; **ch**ild; lo**ng**; **th**in; **ᴛʜ**en; **zh**, measure; **ə** represents **a** in about, **e** in taken, **i** in pencil, **o** in lemon, **u** in circus.

**feel small**, to be ashamed or humiliated: *Her kindness to me after I had broken her window made me feel small.*

**no small**, great; considerable: *a man of no small curiosity.*

**sing small**. See under **sing**.

**smalls, a** parcels, commodities, or consignments of little size or weight: *Hitherto in Birmingham "smalls" had been defined to be quantities less than 2 cwt.* (London Times). **b** knee breeches; smallclothes: *He whisked away our smalls and washed them with loving care* (Punch). **c** *British Informal.* the first of three examinations which candidates for the degree of B.A. at Oxford University are required to pass; responsions: *I ought to be going up for smalls myself next term* (Thomas Hughes).

[Old English *smæl* slender, narrow] —**small′ness**, *n.*

**small|age** (smô′lij), *n.* celery, especially in its wild state, growing in marshy places, with the leafstalks little developed and having a sharp scent and bitter taste. [earlier *smalege,* Middle English *smale ache* < *smal* small + *ache* smallage; any celery or parsley < Old French *ache* < Latin *apium* parsley, or a related plant]

**small ale**, ale of low alcoholic strength, often made without hops; weak or light ale.

**small arms**, firearms that can be easily carried and used by a single person, such as rifles, revolvers, or submachine guns.

**small beer**, **1** weak beer. **2** *Figurative.* matters or persons of little or no consequence; trifles: *The economic problems that the east German State is now having to face are small beer compared with the problems it has already overcome* (Listener).

**think small beer of**, *Informal.* to have a poor or low opinion of: *She thinks small beer of painters, ...—well, we don't think small beer of ourselves* (Thackeray).

**small-bore** (smôl′bôr′, -bōr′), *adj.* **1** having a relatively narrow diameter or bore: *a small-bore pipe.* **2** (of a rifle) firing a bullet of .22 caliber.

**small calorie**, the quantity of heat necessary to raise the temperature of a gram of water 1 degree centigrade (Celsius); gram calorie.

**small capital**, a capital letter that is slightly smaller than the regular capital letter. *Abbr.:* s.c.

**small change**, **1** coins of small value, such as nickels and dimes. **2** *Figurative.* anything small and unimportant: *We must teach our students to manipulate the small change of language, the common coinage of everyday talk* (Donald J. Lloyd).

**small circle**, a circle on the surface of a sphere whose plane does not pass through the center of the sphere.

**small-claims court** (smôl′klāmz′), *U.S.* a state or municipal court that deals with claims involving small amounts of money: *... turning over to nonjudges such relatively minor responsibilities as running small-claims and traffic courts* (Time).

**small|clothes** (smôl′klōz′, -klōᴛʜz′), *n.pl.* knee breeches, especially close-fitting ones, worn by men in the 1700's.

**Small Cloud**, the smaller of the two Magellanic Clouds: *It has been possible to determine that the Small Cloud has basically the same spiral pattern as the Large Cloud* (Scientific American).

**small coal**, **1** slack; coal of small size. **2** *Obsolete.* charcoal.

**small craft warning**, a display along a seacoast or lakeshore predicting weather dangerous to small boats. It consists of a red pennant during the day or of a red light over a white light at night.

**small cranberry**, a small cranberry of Europe, Asia, and North America; European cranberry.

**small end**, the upper part of an automobile engine's connecting rod at its point of attachment to the piston.

**small fry**, **1** babies or children; small or young creatures: *Small fry and their mothers may share similar creative art experiences at the People's Art Center* (New York Times). **2** small fish. **3** *Figurative.* people or things having little importance: *The forest giants among the trees do not kill the small fry under them* (Scientific American).

**small game**, the smaller animals hunted by sportsmen, as distinguished from big game. Birds, squirrels, rabbits, and coyotes are small game.

**small|hold|er** (smôl′hōl′dər), *n.* a farmer who works a smallholding: *An aristocracy of planters ... and a multitude of smallholders, grew cotton for the world by slavelabour* (Sir Winston Churchill).

**small|hold|ing** (smôl′hōl′ding), *n.* **1** a piece of land smaller than an ordinary farm: *The workers each had their own smallholding of about an acre and had their own live stock—chickens, pigs, and cows* (Manchester Guardian). **2** the practice or occupation of working such a piece of land.

**small hours**, the early hours of the morning just after midnight: *Parliament adjourned in the small hours yesterday after both Chambers had sat late to deal with outstanding bills* (London Times).

**small intestine**, the slender part of the intestines, extending from the stomach to the large intestine. It is a long, winding tube that receives partly digested food from the stomach. The small intestine completes the digestion of the food and sends it into the blood. The human small intestine is about 20 feet long and consists of the duodenum, the jejunum, and the ileum. *The lower end of the small intestine opens into the side of the large intestine* (Beauchamp and West). See diagram under **intestine**.

**small|ish** (smô′lish), *adj.* rather small; somewhat small.

**small letter**, an ordinary letter, not a capital; lower-case letter.

**small-mind|ed** (smôl′mīn′did), *adj.* narrow-minded; petty; mean. —**small′-mind′ed|ly**, *adv.* —**small′-mind′ed|ness**, *n.*

**small|mouth** (smôl′mouth′), *n.* = smallmouth bass.

**smallmouth bass**, a North American freshwater game fish similar to the largemouth bass, but with a shorter upper jaw and a weight of up to about 11 pounds; black bass.

**small-mouthed black bass** (smôl′mouᴛʜd′, -moutht′), = smallmouth bass.

**small of the back**, the narrowest part of the back.

**small pastern bone**, the lower of two pastern bones between the fetlock and the hoof as of a horse, donkey, or mule.

**small pica**, 11-point type.

**small potatoes**, *U.S. Informal.* an unimportant person or thing; unimportant persons or things: *Against these increases, the cuts in spending looked like very small potatoes* (Newsweek).

**small|pox** (smôl′poks′), *n.* a very contagious disease with a fever and blisters on the skin that often leave permanent scars shaped like little pits; variola. *Smallpox is a viral disease that has been brought under control by the use of vaccine ...* (Sidonie M. Gruenberg). [< *small* + *pox,* for *pocks,* plural of *pock*]

**smalls** (smôlz), *n.pl.* See under **small**.

**small saphenous vein**, a large vein of the leg extending along the outer and posterior side.

**small-scale** (smôl′skāl′), *adj.* **1** involving few persons or things; limited: *a small-scale offensive, operation, or business. Syria's own resources are adequate for only small-scale projects* (Wall Street Journal). **2** made or drawn to a small scale: *a small-scale model. A small-scale map leaves out many details and covers a much larger area, such as the world* (E. B. Espenshade, Jr.).

**small screen**, *Especially British.* television: *Medical men ... are now no strangers either to the small screen or, for that matter, to the lay press* (New Scientist).

**small slam**, = little slam.

**small stores**, (in the U.S. Navy) articles for personal use such as tobacco, soap, and needles and thread, for which the men pay.

**small stuff**, spun yarn, marline, houseline, and other small ropes on a ship.

**small|sword** (smôl′sôrd′, -sōrd′), *n.* a light sword tapering from the hilt to the point and designed for thrusting, used in fencing.

**small talk**, talk about matters having little importance; chit-chat: *He mingled freely with other delegates, trying to make small talk and little jokes* (New York Times).

**small-time** (smôl′tīm′), *adj. Informal.* not first-rate; of lesser importance or consequence; mediocre: *It's a private-eye novel but you've not met (in fiction) an eye like small-time operative Barney Harris, who never had a criminal case before* (New York Times).

**small-tim|er** (smôl′tī′mər), *n. Slang.* a person who is small-time, especially a small-time hoodlum.

**small-town** (smôl′toun′), *adj. Especially U.S.* **1** of or from a small town: *The father of the present editor was a wonderful small-town newspaperman* (New Yorker). **2** as a small town is supposed to be; narrow; provincial: *Cosmopolitans, they do not sink into the ruts of a small-town life* (Harper's).

**small-town|er** (smôl′tou′nər), *n. Especially U.S.* a small-town person: *... the small-towners wearing their set, starched faces, all fever and suspicion, and proud to be there* (Atlantic).

**small wrasse**, a wrasse of tropical oceans, noted for picking bits of food from the lips of other fishes, such as the parrot fish; scavenger fish.

**smalt** (smôlt), *n.* **1** common glass colored a deep-blue by an oxide of cobalt and, after cooling, finely pulverized for use as a pigment: *Cobalt compounds, such as cobalt blue, ceruleum, new blue, smalt ... are used as pigments by artists and interior decorators, and in ceramics* (John R. Koch). **2** the pigment prepared from this glass. [< Middle French *smalt,* or Italian *smalto* < Medieval Latin *smaltum,* apparently < a Germanic word]

**smalt|ine** (smôl′tin, -tēn), *n.* = smaltite.

**smalt|ite** (smôl′tīt), *n.* a tin-white to steel-gray mineral consisting essentially of an arsenide of cobalt, but usually containing also nickel, and occurring in crystals or in compact or granular masses.

**smal|to** (zmäl′tō), *n., pl.* **-ti** (-tē). *Italian.* **1** a colored glass or enamel used in mosaics. **2** a piece of it.

**smar|agd** (smar′agd), *n.* = emerald. [< Old French *smaragde* < Latin *smaragdus* < Greek *smáragdos*]

**sma|rag|dine** (smə rag′din), *adj., n.* —*adj.* of an emerald color. —*n.* = emerald.

**sma|rag|dite** (smə rag′dīt), *n.* a brilliant grass-green or emerald-green variety of amphibole. [< French *smaragdite* < Greek *smáragdos* smaragd + French *-ite* -ite[1]]

**smarm** (smärm), *v., n. Informal.* —*v.i.* to behave in an offensively flattering or toadying manner: *Her way of smarming up to the rich was disgusting.*

—*v.t. Especially British.* to smooth down or slick (the hair) with oil or the like: *Tony's hair was ... smarmed down as I had never seen before* (Manchester Guardian Weekly).

—*n.* gushiness; slobber: *... a public conditioned by the melodic froth and smarm of the Viennese school* (Punch).

[variant of dialectal *smalm;* origin unknown]

**smarm|y** (smär′mē), *adj.,* **smarm|i|er, smarm|i|est.** *Informal.* offensively flattering or ingratiating: *a smarmy smugness.*

**smart** (smärt), *v., n., adj., adv.* —*v.i.* **1** to feel sharp pain: *My eyes smarted from the smoke.* **2** to cause sharp pain: *The cut smarts.* **3** to feel distress or irritation: *She smarted from the scolding.* **4** to suffer severely: *He shall smart for this.*

—*v.t.* to cause sharp pain to or in.

—*n.* **1** a sharp pain, especially a local pain: *The smart of the wound kept him awake.* **2** keen mental suffering; grief; sorrow; remorse. [< verb]

—*adj.* **1** sharp and severe; stinging: *He gave the horse a smart blow.* **2** keen; active; lively: *They walked at a smart pace.* **3a** quick at learning; clever; bright: *He is a smart student.* **b** sharp and shrewd in dealing with others: *a smart businessman.* **c** witty, superficial, and often somewhat impertinent: *a smart reply.* **4a** fresh and neat in appearance; in good order: *a smart uniform.* **b** stylish; fashionable: *a smart hat, a smart hotel. She has a smart new dress.* **5** *Informal or Dialect.* fairly large; considerable: *to walk a right smart distance. Madame ... left a smart legacy to the ... children* (Thackeray). **6** *Archaic.* causing sharp pain. [Old English *smeart*]

—*adv.* in a smart manner; cleverly. [< adjective]

**smarts**, *U.S. Informal.* intelligence; brains: *"I knew I had the smarts—the business smarts —even then"* (New Yorker).

[Old English *smeortan*] —**smart′ly**, *adv.* —**smart′ness**, *n.*

**smart al|eck** (al′ik), *U.S. Informal.* a conceited, obnoxious person.

**smart-al|eck** (smärt′al′ik), *adj. U.S. Informal.* smart-alecky: *Hugh was fond of ... saying in his best smart-aleck voice, "They don't make 'em like that any more"* (New Yorker).

**smart-al|eck|ism** (smärt′al′ə kiz əm), *n. U.S. Informal.* behavior or language characteristic of a smart aleck: *The critic who depends on smart-aleckism to gain readership can damage reputations and spread false imputations* (Thomas H. Creighton).

**smart-al|eck|y** (smärt′al′ə kē), *adj. U.S. Informal.* like that of a smart aleck; cocky; pretentious; conceited: *The writing verges on the smart-alecky, but it is certainly entertaining* (Harper's).

**smart bomb**, *U.S.* a bomb released from an aircraft and guided to a specific target by laser and television beams: *The Air Force now uses the term "precision-guided munitions" instead of "smart bombs," so that the public won't think other Air Force weapons are stupid* (Reader's Digest).

**smart|en** (smär′tən), *v.t., v.i.* **1** to improve in appearance; brighten: *The Council of Industrial Design felt sufficiently encouraged to open a souvenir section of its Design Index, with the object of smartening up tourist souvenirs* (Punch). **2** to make or become brisker: *He choreographed three new ballets for the company and smartened up its dancing in general* (New Yorker). **3** to make or become more alert, clever, or intelligent.

**smart money**, 1 *U.S. Informal.* **a** money for betting or investing by persons with special knowledge or experience, as on sporting events or the stock market: *The first game, at Yankee Stadium, made the smart money seem safe* (Time). **b** the informed speculators or betters. 2 *British.* **a** money allowed to soldiers and sailors for injuries received while on service. **b** money paid to obtain the discharge of a recruit. **c** any compensation for injury. 3 legal damages in excess of the injury done, as for gross misconduct on the part of the defendant. 4 money paid to escape an unpleasant engagement or situation.

**smarts** (smärts), *n.pl.* See under **smart**.

**smart set**, the most sophisticated and fashionable section of society.

**smart|weed** (smärt′wēd′), *n.* any one of various weeds of the buckwheat family growing in low or wet places, such as the water pepper. Smartweed causes an irritation when brought into contact with the skin.

**smart|y** (smär′tē), *n., pl.* **smart|ies**, *adj.*, **smart|i|er, smart|i|est.** *Informal.* — *n.* a would-be smart, clever, or witty person; smart aleck.
— *adj.* cocky; pretentious: *Not a bad line, either, he conceded, except there were no smarty lawyers around to bring in a writ of habeas corpus* (Margery Allingham).

**smart|y-pants** (smär′tē pants′), *n. U.S. Slang.* a person who acts as if he knows everything; an intellectual snob; wiseacre.

**smash** (smash), *v., n., adj.* — *v.t.* **1a** to break into pieces with violence and noise; shatter: *The boy smashed a window with a stone. The boat was smashed on the rocks.* SYN: See syn. under **break**. **b** to flatten by a crushing force: *to smash a hat.* SYN: crush. **c** to break, beat, or dash with violence: *to smash a cup against a wall, to smash a door in, to smash a lock off.* SYN: batter. 2 to destroy; ruin: *to smash a person's hopes, to smash an argument.* SYN: overcome, overwhelm, wreck. 3 to crush; defeat: *to smash an attack.* 4 *Informal.* to cause to fail financially; bankrupt. 5 to hit (a tennis ball) with a hard, fast overhand stroke; kill. 6 to hit (a person or thing) with a hard blow.
— *v.i.* 1 to be broken to pieces: *The dishes smashed on the floor as the tray upset.* 2 to rush violently; crash: *The car smashed into a tree.* 3 to become ruined; fail financially; become bankrupt: *Many small businesses are forced to take loans and give credit on which they smash beyond recovery.*
— *n.* **1a** a violent breaking; shattering; crash: *the smash of two automobiles.* **b** the sound of a smash or crash: *the smash of broken glass. We heard a smash in the kitchen.* 2 a crushing defeat; disaster; overthrow. 3 a business failure; bankruptcy. 4 a hard blow. 5 a hard, fast overhand stroke in tennis. 6 a drink made of water, mint, sugar, and brandy or other alcoholic liquor, served with ice: *I had a couple of smashes and marched in* (Maclean's). 7 *Informal.* a smash hit: *a theatrical smash. "Guys and Dolls"—Broadway's musical smash* (Newsweek).
— *adj. Informal.* highly successful; very profitable: *a smash Broadway musical.*
**to smash**, **a** into broken pieces; into bits: *to break, fly, or go to smash.* **b** to ruin: *The ... arrangements all went to smash* (Thomas Henry Huxley).
[origin uncertain. Compare Norwegian *smaske* smash to bits] — **smash′er**, *n.*

**smash|a|ble** (smash′ə bəl), *adj.* that can be smashed.

**smash-and-grab** (smash′and grab′, -ən-), *adj. Especially British.* of or having to do with a robbery committed by smashing a shopwindow and snatching the goods displayed inside: *Thieves made five smash-and-grab raids during dense fog in Nottingham last night* (London Times).

**smashed** (smasht), *adj. Slang.* intoxicated; drunk.

**smash|er|oo** (smash′ə rü′), *n. Slang.* a smash hit: *Even the best-laid plans tend to bend before a runaway box office smasheroo* (Punch).

**smash hit**, a highly successful performance or production of a play, motion picture, or the like; great hit: *It is a truism that Broadway critics are dangerously omnipotent, able to create a smash hit overnight or to kill a play stone dead* (Manchester Guardian Weekly).

**smash|ing** (smash′ing), *adj.* 1 that smashes; shattering; crushing: *a smashing blow.* 2 *Especially British Slang.* fine; excellent; splendid: *"Smashing" and "wizard" ... seem to have replaced the "ripping" of earlier days* (Holiday). — **smash′ing|ly**, *adv.*

**smashing machine**, a machine that compresses books between two steel blocks and gives each book a uniform thickness.

**smash-up** (smash′up′), *n.* 1 a bad collision; wreck: *But few people know the Air Force loses more personnel in auto smash-ups than in air accidents (83 killed in cars in two years; 72 in airplanes)* (Maclean's). 2 a business failure; bankruptcy. 3 a great misfortune; disaster. 4 a failure in health; crack-up.

**smatch** (smach), *n. Archaic.* 1 a smack, taste, or flavor. 2 a trace or touch: *Thy life hath had some smatch of honour in it* (Shakespeare). 3 a smattering: *... some Latin, and a smatch of Greek* (William Cowper). [Middle English *smach,* alteration of Old English *smæc* smack[1]]

**smat|ter** (smat′ər), *n., v.* — *n.* slight knowledge; smattering.
— *v.t.* 1 to speak (a language) with only slight knowledge of it: *She could read, and write, and dance, and sing ... and smatter French* (Tobias Smollett). 2 to study or learn superficially.
— *v.i.* to have a slight or superficial knowledge.

**smat|ter|er** (smat′ər ər), *n.* a person who smatters; dabbler.

**smat|ter|ing** (smat′ər ing), *n., adj.* — *n.* 1 slight or superficial knowledge: *a smattering of French.* 2 a small amount or number: *Today some 15 firms offer on tape over 200 selections, most of them classical or semi-classical, compared with only a smattering two years ago* (Wall Street Journal).
— *adj.* slight; superficial; imperfect: *a smattering knowledge of Russian.* — **smat′ter|ing|ly**, *adv.*

**smaze** (smāz), *n.* a combination of smoke and haze in the air. [blend of *smoke* and *haze*]

**sm. c.** or **sm. caps.**, small capitals.

**smear** (smir), *v., n., adj.* — *v.t.* 1 to cover or stain with anything sticky, greasy, or dirty: *She smeared her fingers with jam.* 2 to rub or spread (oil, grease, or paint): *to smear paint on one's hands.* 3 to rub or wipe (a brush, hand, or cloth) so as to make a mark or stain: *... smearing his sleeve across his mouth* (Dickens). 4 *Figurative.* to mark; soil; spoil: *to smear a person's good reputation.* SYN: sully. 5 *U.S. Slang, Figurative.* to defeat or rout decisively; overwhelm.
— *v.i.* to receive a mark or stain; be smeared: *Wet paint smears easily.* [Old English *smerian* rub with oil]
— *n.* 1 a mark or stain left by smearing; daub or blotch: *There are smears of paint on the wallpaper. She put her lips to the bandage and left a little smear of orange lipstick* (Graham Greene). 2 a small amount of something spread on a slide for microscopic examination, or on the surface of a culture medium. 3 a mixture for glazing pottery by evaporating salt or other substances. 4 *Figurative.* the act of smearing someone's reputation; slander: *Criticism, as an instrument not of inquiry and reform, but of power, quickly degenerates into the techniques of deceit and smear* (Harper's).
— *adj.* intended as a smear; slanderous; defamatory: *a smear campaign, smear tactics.*
[Old English *smeoru* grease] — **smear′er**, *n.*

**smear|case** (smir′kās), *n. U.S. Dialect.* cottage cheese. Also, **smiercase**. [< German *Schmierkäse* < *schmieren* to smear + *Käse* cheese]

**smear test**, = Pap test.

**smear|y** (smir′ē), *adj.*, **smear|i|er, smear|i|est.** 1 marked by a smear or smears; smeared. 2 tending to smear. — **smear′i|ness**, *n.*

**smec|tic** (smek′tik), *adj.* 1 cleansing; abstergent; detergent. 2 (of liquid crystals) consisting of a series of layers in which the molecules are arranged either in rows or at random. [< Latin *smēcticus* < Greek *smēktikós* < *smêchein* to wipe; cleanse]

**smeek** (smēk), *n., v. Scottish.* smoke.

**smeg|ma** (smeg′mə), *n.* a sebaceous secretion, especially that found under the prepuce. [< Latin *smēgma* < Greek *smêgma* a detergent, soap or unguent < *smêchein* to wipe; cleanse]

**smell** (smel), *v.,* **smelled** or **smelt, smell|ing,** *n.*
— *v.t.* 1 to detect or recognize by breathing in through the nose; perceive (an odor or scent) with the nose by means of the olfactory nerves: *Can you smell the smoke in the air?* 2 to sniff at; use the sense of smell on (something): *She picked up a rose and smelled it. The dog smelled the strange man's legs.* 3 *Figurative.* to find a trace or suggestion of; detect or discover by shrewdness or instinct; suspect: *to smell danger. We smelled trouble.*
— *v.i.* 1 to use the sense of smelling; perceive or be able to perceive odors: *We smell with our noses.* 2 to give out a smell; have a scent: *The garden smelled of roses.* 3 to give out a bad smell; have a bad smell; stink: *That dirty, wet dog smells. Garbage smells.* 4 *Figurative.* to have the smell (of); have the trace (of); show a touch or suggestion (of): *The plan smells of trickery.*
— *n.* 1 the sense of smelling: *Smell is keener in dogs than in humans.* 2 the quality in a thing that affects the sense of smell; odor: *The smell of burning rubber is not pleasant.* 3 *Figurative.* a trace, tinge, or suggestion (of): *the smell of injustice.* 4 an act of smelling; sniff: *Have a smell of this rose.*
**smell out**, to hunt or find by smelling: *A dog will smell out a thief.* (*Figurative.*) *Her sister smelled out a secret.*
**smell up**, *Informal.* to cause to have a bad smell: *to smell up the house cooking onions.*
[Middle English *smellen*]
— *Syn. n.* 2 **Smell, odor** have to do with that property or quality of a thing that affects the sense organs of the nose. **Smell** is the general word, used especially when the effect on the sense organs is emphasized: *There was a strong smell of gas in the room. I like the smells in the country after a rain.* **Odor** applies particularly to the actual property or quality itself, as belonging to and coming from what is smelled: *the odors of cooking. I find the odor of hay especially pleasing.*

**smell|a|bil|i|ty** (smel′ə bil′ə tē), *n.* the quality or condition of being smellable.

**smell|a|ble** (smel′ə bəl), *adj.* that can be smelled: *To be smellable, a substance must be soluble in fat or water—preferably both* (Scientific American).

**smell|er** (smel′ər), *n.* 1 a person or thing that smells. 2 a person who tests by smelling. 3 *Slang.* the nose or sense of smell. 4 a sensitive hair or process such as one of a cat's whiskers; feeler.

**smell|ie** (smel′ē), *n. Informal.* a motion picture in which odors are adapted to appropriate scenes.

**smell|ing salts** (smel′ing), a solution of a salt of ammonia, ammonium hydroxide, and some scent, inhaled to relieve such conditions as faintness or headache.

**smell-less** (smel′lis), *adj.* 1 having no sense of smell. 2 having no smell; odorless.

**smell|y** (smel′ē), *adj.*, **smell|i|er, smell|i|est.** having or giving out a strong or unpleasant smell: *I wonder what makes the sea so smelly. I don't like it* (Rudyard Kipling). SYN: noisome, rank.

**smelt**[1] (smelt), *v.t.* 1 to melt (ore) in order to get the metal out of it. 2 to obtain (metal) from ore by melting: *It also smelts some high grade tin from ores* (Wall Street Journal). 3 to refine (impure metal) by melting. — *v.i.* 1 to melt ore to extract metal, or melt metal to refine it. 2 to be subjected to smelting. [probably < Middle Low German *smelten* (originally) to melt]

**smelt**[2] (smelt), *n., pl.* **smelts** or (*collectively*) **smelt.** a small food fish with silvery scales. Smelts comprise a family of fishes, related to the salmon. Smelts live in cool oceans of the Northern Hemisphere, though some species swim up rivers to spawn and stay permanently in fresh water. [Old English *smelt*]

**smelt**[3] (smelt) *v.* smelled; a past tense and a past participle of **smell**.

**smelt|er** (smel′tər), *n.* 1 a person whose work or business is smelting ores or metals. 2 a place where ores or metals are smelted. 3 a furnace for smelting ores.

**smet|a|na** (smet′ə nə), *n. Russian, Yiddish.* sour cream.

**smew** (smyü), *n.* a small, crested, mostly white merganser of northern Europe and Asia. [origin uncertain]

**smice** (smīs), *n.* a combination of fog and ice crystals in the air; ice-fog: *Smice rears its misty head during the night, sharply reducing visibility but is otherwise unharmful* (New York Times). [blend of *smoke* and *ice*]

**smidge** (smij), *n.* = smidgen.

**smidg|en** or **smidg|eon** (smij′ən), *n. Informal.* a tiny bit; small piece or quantity: *There isn't a smidgen of truth in this rumor.* [origin uncertain]

**smidg|in** (smij′ən), *n.* = smidgen.

**smier|case** (smir′kās), *n.* = smearcase.

**smi|la|ca|ceous** (smī′lə kā′shəs), *adj.* belonging to a group of plants of the lily family, as the smilax. [< New Latin *Smilaceae* the lily family (< Latin *smīlax;* see etym. under **smilax**) + English *-ous*]

**smi|lax** (smī′laks), *n.* 1 a twining, trailing, African plant or vine of the lily family, much used by florists in decoration. Smilax belongs to the same genus as asparagus. 2 any one of a large group of tropical and temperate woody vines of the lily family, with prickly stems, umbrella-shaped clusters of small, greenish flowers, and small blackish or red berries, such as the sarsaparilla plant; greenbrier. [< Latin *smīlax, -acis* < Greek *smîlax, -akos* bindweed]

**smile** (smīl), *v.*, **smiled, smil|ing,** *n.* — *v.i.* 1 to look pleased or amused; show pleasure, favor, amusement, or kindness, by an upward curve of the mouth: *to smile at a friend. Why do you smile*

**Pronunciation Key:** hat, āge, cãre, fär; let, ēqual, tėrm; it, īce; hot, ōpen, ôrder; oil, out; cup, pu̇t, rüle; child; long; thin; ᴛʜen; zh, measure; ə represents **a** in about, **e** in taken, **i** in pencil, **o** in lemon, **u** in circus.

*at what I say? One may smile, and smile, and be a villain* (Shakespeare). **2** to look or be pleasant; be agreeable; look (upon) or regard with favor: *A sea that could not cease to smile* (Wordsworth). *The music does not really smile, and, indeed, is of the reserved kind that demands very many hearings* (London Times). (*Figurative.*) *Good fortune always smiled upon him.* **3** to show scorn or disdain by a curve of the mouth: *She smiled bitterly.*
—*v.t.* **1** to bring, put, or drive by smiling: *Smile your tears away.* **2** to give (a smile): *She smiled a sunny smile.* **3** to express by a smile: *to smile a welcome. She smiled consent.*
—*n.* **1** an act of smiling: *a friendly smile, a smile of pity. She met his eye with her sweet hospitable smile* (Henry James). **2** a favoring look or regard; pleasant look or aspect: (*Figurative.*) *the smile of fortune* (Joseph Conrad).
[Middle English *smilen*]

**smile|less** (smīl′lis), *adj.* without a smile; serious; gloomy; cheerless. —**smile′less|ly**, *adv.*

**smil|er** (smī′lər), *n.* **1** one who smiles. **2** one who looks smilingly, as from pleasure, derision, or real or affected agreeableness.

**smil|ey** (smī′lē), *adj.* smiling; cheerful.

**smil|ing** (smī′ling), *adj.* that smiles; bright; cheerful; pleasant: *The April countryside is fresh and smiling* (Atlantic). —**smil′ing|ly**, *adv.* —**smil′ingness**, *n.*

**smi|lo|don** (smī′lə don), *n.* any one of a group of the largest saber-toothed tigers, that became extinct in the Ice Age. [< New Latin *Smilodon* the genus name < Greek *smī́lē* knife + *odoús, odóntos* tooth]

**smil|y** (smī′lē), *adj.* = smiley.

**smirch** (smėrch), *v., n.* —*v.t.* **1** to make dirty; soil as with soot, dirt, or dust. **2** *Figurative: This is an attempt by the Attorney General to smirch the union* (James Hoffa). **SYN**: dishonor, disgrace, taint, tarnish, sully.
—*n.* **1** a dirty mark; blot; stain. **2** *Figurative.* a blot on a person's reputation.
[Middle English *smorchen* to discolor] —**smirch′er**, *n.*

**smirk** (smėrk), *v., n.* —*v.i.* to smile in an affected, silly, or self-satisfied way.
—*n.* an affected, silly, or self-satisfied smile: *Studs stood, posing ... with a smirk of superiority on his face* (James T. Farrell).
[compare Old English *smearcian* to smile]
—**smirk′ing|ly**, *adv.*

**smirk|y** (smėr′kē), *adj.*, **smirk|i|er, smirk|i|est.** of the nature of a smirk; simpering: *a smirky smile.*

**smit** (smit), *v.* **1** smitten; a past participle of **smite**. **2** *Obsolete.* smote; a past tense of **smite**.

**smitch** (smich), *n. Informal.* a particle; bit: *They didn't increase the visibility a smitch* (New Yorker). [origin uncertain]

**smite** (smīt), *v.*, **smote** or (*Obsolete*) **smit, smitten** or **smit, smit|ing.** —*v.t.* **1** to strike; strike hard; hit hard: *The hero smote the giant with his sword. ... those strange-looking instruments* [*golf clubs*] *which are used for smiting the little white ball* (Wall Street Journal). **2** to give or strike (as a blow or stroke). **3** to strike as with a weapon, so as to cause serious injury or death. **4** to affect, as with a sudden pain, disease, or remorse: *a city smitten with pestilence.* (*Figurative.*) *The thief's conscience smote him.* **5** to impress suddenly, as with a strong feeling or sentiment: *She was smitten with curiosity about the forbidden room. A grief that smites my very heart at root* (Shakespeare). **6** to strike down; punish severely; chasten or destroy: *The Lord shall smite the proud* (John Greenleaf Whittier).
—*v.i.* **1** to deliver, as a blow or blows or a stroke, with a stick or other weapon; strike. **2** to come or be overcome, as with pain or disease. **3** to come (together) forcibly or in conflict; strike or dash (on or against something): *His heart turned within him and his knees smote together* (Washington Irving). **4** to come with force (upon): *The sound of a blacksmith's hammer smote upon their ears.*
[Old English *smītan*]

**smit|er** (smī′tər), *n.* **1** a person or thing that smites or strikes. **2** *Obsolete.* a sword; scimitar.

**smith** (smith), *n., v.* —*n.* **1** a person who makes or shapes things out of metal, especially iron. **SYN**: metalworker. **2** = blacksmith.
—*v.t.* to make or shape by forging; forge: *to smith the blade of a penknife.*
—*v.i.* to work in metals; practice smithwork.
[Old English *smith*]

**smith|er|eens** (smiᴛʜ′ə rēnz′), *n.pl. Informal.* small pieces; bits: *to smash a chair to smithereens.* [apparently < Irish *smidirin*]

**smith|ers** (smiᴛʜ′ərz), *n.pl.* = smithereens.

**smith|er|y** (smith′ər ē), *n., pl.* **-er|ies.** **1** the work or craft of a smith. **2** = smithy.

**smith|son|ite** (smith′sə nīt), *n.* **1** native carbonate of zinc. *Formula:* $ZnCO_3$ **2** *British.* calamine (def. 2a). [< James *Smithson*, an English chemist and mineralogist + *-ite*[1]]

**smith|work** (smith′wėrk′), *n.* the work of a smith; work in metals.

**smith|y** (smith′ē, smiᴛʜ′-), *n., pl.* **smith|ies**, *v.*, **smith|ied, smith|y|ing.** —*n.* the workshop of a smith, especially a blacksmith; forge: *Under a spreading chestnut tree The village smithy stands* (Longfellow).
—*v.t.* to make or shape by smithing; forge or smith.

**smit|ten** (smit′ən), *v., adj.* —*v.* a past participle of **smite**: *The giant was smitten by the sword of the knight.*
—*adj.* **1** hard hit; struck: *sudden sparks from smitten steel.* **2** suddenly and strongly affected: *Sammy was smitten with show business about as soon as he could take a few dance steps* (Time). **3** very much in love. **SYN**: enamored.

**smock** (smok), *n., v.* —*n.* **1** a loose outer garment worn to protect clothing. **2** *Archaic or Dialect.* a woman's shift or chemise.
—*v.t.* **1** to ornament (a dress or other clothing) with a honeycomb pattern made of lines of stitches crossing each other diagonally: *Friede, that beloved niece for whom her aunt had smocked frocks and embellished the collars with forget-me-nots ...* (New Yorker). **2** to clothe in a smock.
[Old English *smoc*]

**smock frock**, a smock reaching to the middle of the leg, worn especially by laborers in Europe.

**smock|ing** (smok′ing), *n.* a honeycomb pattern made of lines of stitches crossing each other diagonally and gathering the material, used to ornament dresses or other clothing: *I wore brown holland smocks for everyday ... blue serge with scarlet smocking for winter* (New Yorker).

**smock mill**, a type of windmill in which the mill house is fixed and only the top revolves with the wind: *The smock mill—the name taken from a fancied resemblance to the countryman's dress—was introduced from Holland* (London Times).

**smog** (smog), *n., v.*, **smogged, smog|ging.** —*n.* a combination of smoke and fog in the air: *Automobile exhaust fumes are one of the major causes of smog.*
—*v.t.* to envelop in smog; cover with smog: *When we hear that ... Los Angeles residents are smogged in, then we get worried* (Saturday Review).
[blend of *smoke* and *fog*]

**smog|bound** (smog′bound′), *adj.* enveloped in smog; covered with smog. [patterned after *fogbound, snowbound*, etc.]

**smog|gy** (smog′ē), *adj.*, **-gi|er, -gi|est.** full of smog: *There was a virus in the ... smoky, smoggy air* (Newsweek).

**smog|out** (smog′out′), *n.* a condition of being completely enveloped by smog.

**smok|a|ble** (smō′kə bəl), *adj., n.* —*adj.* fit to be smoked: *The cigarette was bent in a couple of places, but it was smokable* (John O'Hara).
—*n.* **smokables**, tobacco, especially in the form of cigars or cigarettes: *A fiendish consumer of cigars, the man had smokables bulging in his every jacket pocket.* Also, **smokeable**.

**smoke** (smōk), *n., v.*, **smoked, smok|ing.** —*n.* **1a** a mixture of gases and carbon that can be seen rising in a cloud from anything burning: *The smoke from the burning home could be seen many blocks away.* **b** a mass, cloud, or column caused by anything burning, especially one serving as a signal, sign of encampment, or the like. **2** something like this, such as a mist or fog: *A heavy smoke blew in across the bay.* **SYN**: fume, reek. **3** *Figurative.* **a** something unsubstantial, quickly passing, or without value or result: *The affair ended in smoke.* **b** something that clouds or is meant to confuse or hide an issue. **4** that which is smoked; cigar, cigarette, or pipe. **5** an act or period of smoking tobacco: *The soldiers stopped about ten minutes for a smoke.* **6** *Physics and Chemistry.* a dispersion of solid particles in a gas.
—*v.i.* **1** to give off smoke or steam, or something like it: *The fireplace smokes. The turkey was brought smoking hot to the table.* **2** to move with great speed. **3** to draw in and puff out the smoke of burning tobacco. —*v.t.* **1** to draw the smoke from (a pipe, cigar, or cigarette) into the mouth and puff it out again: *Father smokes several cigars each day.* **2** to expose to the action of smoke. **3** to cure (as meat or fish) by exposing to smoke. People smoke fish to preserve them. **4** to color, darken, or stain with smoke. **5** to make, bring, or pass by smoking. **6** *Archaic.* to find out; suspect; notice. **7** *Archaic.* to make fun of; ridicule.
**go up in smoke**, to come to nothing; be unrealized; be without results: *Cardiff City's brave achievement, which won its full hour of praise, has gone up in smoke* (London Times).
**smoke out**, **a** to drive out with smoke, as an animal from its hole: *to smoke bees out of a nest in an old tree.* **b** *Figurative.* to find out and make known: *to smoke out a plot; a set of traitors, who ... will be smoked out like a nest of wasps* (Cardinal Newman).
**watch one's smoke**, *U.S. Slang.* to observe one's actions: *Out come the brandy, the long johns, the parka, and the racing goggles—and Lordy, watch his smoke* (Time).
[Old English *smoca*] —**smoke′like′**, *adj.*

**smoke|a|ble** (smō′kə bəl), *adj., n.* = smokable.

**smoke ball**, a spherical case filled with a composition which, while burning, emits a great quantity of smoke, used for concealment or for annoying an enemy's workmen in siege operations.

**smoke-blue** (smōk′blü′), *n., adj.* bluish gray: *A smoke-blue haze hangs over the mountains* (Atlantic).

**smoke bomb**, a bomb that gives off a dense cloud of smoke, used especially to conceal military movements.

**smoke|box** (smōk′boks′), *n.* a chamber in a steam boiler, between the flues and the chimney stack.

**smoke bush**, = smoke tree.

**smoke-col|ored** (smōk′kul′ərd), *adj.* of a dull-gray or brownish-gray color.

**smoked** (smōkt), *adj.* **1** treated or cured with smoke: *smoked meat.* **2** darkened by smoke: *smoked glass.* **3** gray: *smoked pearl.*

**smoke detector**, a photoelectric or ionization device that is sensitive to smoke from a fire. It is usually enclosed in a plastic case which can be attached to a wall or ceiling and sounds an alarm when smoke passes through it.

**smoke-dry** (smōk′drī′), *v.t.*, **-dried, -dry|ing.** to dry or cure by exposing to smoke: *He cut up and smoke-dried the flesh* (W. H. Hudson).

**smoke-eat|er** (smōk′ē′tər), *n. U.S. Slang.* a fireman, especially of the U.S. Forest Service.

**smoke-filled room** (smōk′fild′), *U.S.* a room in which influential politicians meet in private, especially at a political convention, to plan strategy or to negotiate: *The campaign for the Democratic nomination may well be decided in a smoke-filled room* (Newsweek). [in allusion to a hotel room in Chicago at which the decision to nominate Warren G. Harding as the Republican presidential candidate in 1920 was supposed to have been reached]

**smoke|house** (smōk′hous′), *n.* a building or place in which meat or fish is treated with smoke to keep it from spoiling. [American English < *smoke* + *house*]

**smoke-in** (smōk′in′), *n.* **1** an informal gathering for smoking tobacco and socializing; smoker. **2** a gathering to smoke marijuana or hashish, sometimes as a demonstration for legalizing their use: *Gone are the big smoke-ins punctuated by acid rock and strobe lights* (Time).

**smoke|jack** (smōk′jak′), *n.* an apparatus for turning a roasting spit, set in motion by the current of rising gases in a chimney.

**smoke jumper**, a member of a unit of the U.S. Forest Service trained to parachute into remote areas to fight forest fires.

**smoke|less** (smōk′lis), *adj.* **1** making or giving off little or no smoke: *smokeless fuel.* **2** having little or no smoke. —**smoke′less|ly**, *adv.* —**smoke′less|ness**, *n.*

**smokeless powder**, a substitute for ordinary gunpowder that gives off little or no smoke when it explodes.

**smoke-o** or **smoke-oh** (smō′kō), *n.* = smoko.

**smoke pipe**, the pipe that connects a furnace to the chimney.

**smoke|pot** (smōk′pot′), *n.* a pot for burning a mixture of fuels in order to produce a smoke screen.

**smoke|proof** (smōk′prüf′), *adj.* that will not let smoke through: *smokeproof equipment.*

**smok|er** (smō′kər), *n.* **1** a person who smokes tobacco. **2a** a railroad car or a part of it where smoking is allowed. **b** a similar area in a building. **3** an informal gathering of people for smoking, conversation, and entertainment. **4** a person who smokes meat, fish, or other foods. **5** something which throws out much smoke, such as a smoky locomotive or a device for smoking out bees: *After a piece of burlap has been ignited and stuffed into the tin, the bellows of the smoker is pumped* (*not too hard lest flames come out and scorch the bees' wings*) (New York Times).

**smoke ring**, smoke forced out between the lips of a smoker in the shape of a ring.

**smoke room**, = smoking room.

**smok|er|y** (smō′kə rē), *n., pl.* **-er|ies.** a place in which to smoke; a smoking room.

**smoke screen**, **1** a mass of thick smoke used to hide troops, ships, airplanes, or other equipment or maneuvers from the enemy. **2** *Figurative: Seasoned observers of the Irish scene believe that the Partition provides an ideological smoke* *screen for a policy embarrassing to most Irishmen* (Newsweek).

**smoke|shade** (smōk′shād′), *n.* the particles of dirt that can be seen in the air.

**smoke signal**, **1** a signal made with smoke, usually by covering and uncovering a fire, used especially by American Indians. **2** *Figurative: The nation's purchasing agents are a tough-minded down-to-earth group of businessmen who keep their eyes peeled for every economic smoke signal* (Newsweek). SYN: sign, trend.

**smoke|stack** (smōk′stak′), *n.* **1** a tall chimney: *... the broad expanse of roofs, the long, slanting conveyor belts, and the dark smokestacks characteristic of mines all over the world* (New Yorker). **2** a pipe that discharges smoke, heat, or gas, such as the funnel of a steamship.

**smoke tree**, a small tree or shrub of the cashew family, with flower clusters that look somewhat like tiny puffs of smoke; feather tree. It is related to the sumac.

**Smok|ey** or **smok|ey** (smō′kē), *n., pl.* **-eys.** *U.S. Slang.* a state trooper: *C.B.ers with their colorful pseudonyms and jargon may warn of Smokey's presence—but in hundreds of instances they have helped the police catch drunken and hit-and-run drivers* (Ernest Dickinson). [because of the resemblance of state troopers' wide-brimmed hats to that worn by *Smokey* Bear, an animal character in signs warning against forest fires]

**smok|ing** (smō′king), *n.* **1** the act of a person or thing that smokes. **2** the act or practice of smoking tobacco: *Captain Nutter gradually gave up smoking, which is an untidy, injurious ... and highly pleasant habit* (Thomas B. Aldrich).

**smoking car**, a smoker on a train.

**smoking gun**, evidence that is very incriminating; indisputable evidence of a crime: *The committee did not claim to have found a "smoking gun," in the form of a kill order ringing down ... through the C.I.A. chain of command* (New York Times).

***smoking jacket**, a lounging jacket to be worn while smoking, originally to protect the clothing.

***smoking jacket**

**smoking room**, a room set apart for smoking, as in a hotel or clubhouse.

**smo|ko** (smō′kō), *n. Australian Slang.* a short period of rest, especially for workers. Also, **smoke-o, smoke-oh.**

**smok|y** (smō′kē), *adj.,* **smok|i|er, smok|i|est.** **1a** giving off much smoke: *a smoky fire.* **b** tending to send smoke out into the room: *a smoky fireplace.* **2** full of smoke: *a smoky room.* **3** darkened or stained with smoke: *the smoky buildings of a great industrial city.* SYN: sooty. **4** like smoke or suggesting smoke: *a smoky gray, a smoky taste.* —**smok′i|ly,** *adv.* —**smok′i|ness,** *n.*

**smoky quartz** or **topaz**, a brownish-yellow quartz; cairngorm.

**smol|der** (smōl′dər), *v., n.* —*v.i.* **1** to burn and smoke without flame: *The campfire smoldered for hours after the blaze died down.* **2** *Figurative.* to exist or continue in a suppressed condition: *The people's discontent smoldered for years before it broke out into open rebellion.* **3** *Figurative.* to show suppressed feeling: *His eyes smoldered with anger.* [< noun]
—*n.* **1** a slow, smoky burning without flame; smoldering fire. **2** *Figurative.* a feeling of heated emotion: *a smolder of indignation.*
[Middle English *smolder;* origin uncertain]

**smolt** (smōlt), *n.* a young salmon with silvery scales, that is no longer a parr and is ready to descend, or has descended, to the sea for the first time. [Middle English *smolt.* Probably related to **smelt**².]

**smooch**¹ (smüch), *v.t., n.* = smudge. [variant of *smutch*]

**smooch**² (smüch), *v.i., v.t., n. Slang.* kiss. [alteration of *smouch*]

**smooch|y** (smü′chē), *adj.,* **smooch|i|er, smooch|i|est.** = smudgy. —**smooch′i|ly,** *adv.* —**smooch′i|ness,** *n.*

**smoodge** (smüj), *v.i. Australian Slang.* **1** to curry favor. **2** to kiss.

**smooth** (smüᴛʜ), *adj., adv., v., n.* —*adj.* **1** having an even surface, like glass, silk, or still water; flat; level: *smooth stones, a smooth tire, a smooth road or path.* SYN: plain, sleek, glossy. See syn. under **level.** **2** free from unevenness or roughness; proceeding evenly, calmly, or gently: *smooth sailing, a smooth voyage, a smooth landing, the smooth operation of a well-oiled machine.* **3** without lumps: *smooth gravy.* **4** without hair: *a smooth face, smooth leaves.* **5** *Figurative.* without trouble or difficulty; easy: *a smooth course of affairs.* **6** *Figurative.* calm; serene: *a smooth temper.* SYN: placid, unruffled. **7** *Figurative.* **a** polished; pleasant; polite: *That salesman has a friendly way about him and very smooth manners.* **b** too polished, pleasant, or polite to be sincere: *That smooth talker could sell you the Brooklyn Bridge with his smooth sales pitch.* **8** not harsh in sound or taste: *smooth verses, a smooth wine.* **9** (in Greek grammar) unaspirated.
—*adv.* in a smooth manner: (*Figurative.*) *The course of true love never did run smooth* (Shakespeare).
—*v.t.* **1** to make smooth or smoother; give a flat, even, level, or glossy surface to: *Smooth this dress with a hot iron. Smooth the board with sandpaper before you paint it. He smoothed out the ball of crushed paper and read it.* **2** to make easy; free from difficulty: (*Figurative.*) *Her tact smoothed the way to an agreement.* **3** *Figurative.* to make less harsh or crude; polish or refine (writing, manners, or other expression or behavior). **4** *Figurative.* to make calm or tranquil; soothe.
—*n.* **1** an act of smoothing: *She ... gave one smooth to her hair, and ... let in her visitor* (Thackeray). **2** something smooth; a smooth part or place.
**smooth away**, to get rid of (troubles or difficulties); iron out: *Our problems were minor and were soon smoothed away. He smoothed away all objections to the plan.*
**smooth down**, **a** to make smooth by pressing down: *She had an infant in one arm, and with the other she smoothed down her apron* (Scott). **b** *Figurative.* to calm; soothe: *She smoothed down her father's temper.*
**smooth over**, to make (something) seem less wrong, unpleasant, or noticeable: *The teacher tried to smooth over the differences between the two boys who were always quarreling.*
[Old English *smōth*] —**smooth′er,** *n.* —**smooth′ly,** *adv.* —**smooth′ness,** *n.*

**smooth-billed ani** (smüᴛʜ′bild′), a gregarious black tickbird, commonly found in the warmer parts of America.

**smooth blenny**, a European blenny with a smooth skin and no filaments or appendages on the head, found chiefly under stones and in seaweed along the coast; shanny.

**smooth|bore** (smüᴛʜ′bôr′, -bōr′), *adj., n.* —*adj.* not rifled. A smoothbore gun has no grooves in its barrel. —*n.* a smoothbore gun.
[American English < *smooth* + *bore*¹]

**smooth breathing**, *Greek Grammar.* **1** the absence of aspiration of an initial vowel. **2** the mark placed over a vowel or diphthong to indicate this. [translation of Latin *spīritus lēnis,* a translation of Greek *pneûma psilón*]

**smooth brome**, a beardless species of brome grass that was introduced from Europe, much valued as a hay and pasture grass.

**smooth-coat|ed terrier** (smüᴛʜ′kō′tid), a fox terrier with a short, smooth coat.

**smooth collie**, a kind of collie with a short, smooth coat.

**smooth dogfish**, a small shark of the Atlantic Ocean.

**smooth|en** (smü′ᴛʜən), *v.t.* to make smooth or smoother. —*v.i.* to become smooth or smoother.

**smooth-faced** (smüᴛʜ′fāst′), *adj.* **1** having a smooth face; beardless; clean-shaven. **2** having a smooth surface. **3** *Figurative.* agreeable in speech and manner, often insincerely; blandly ingratiating: *a smooth-faced hypocrite.*

**smooth|ie** (smü′ᴛʜē), *n. Slang.* a man who speaks or behaves in a polished manner, often insincerely, especially in trying to impress or court a woman.

**smooth muscle**, a type of muscle not contracted by voluntary action, with fibers in smooth layers or sheets; involuntary muscle. The muscles of the stomach, intestine, and other viscera (except the heart) are smooth muscles.

**smooth skate**, a skate of the Atlantic Ocean.

**smooth-spo|ken** (smüᴛʜ′spō′kən), *adj.* speaking easily and pleasantly; blandly gracious or polished in speech: *a smooth-spoken young lady.*

**smooth sumac**, a species of sumac that is entirely without hair, commonly found east of the Rocky Mountains, from Arizona to British Columbia.

**smooth-talk|ing** (smüᴛʜ′tô′king), *adj.* speaking smoothly and persuasively; trying to convince or persuade: *a smooth-talking salesman.* SYN: glib.

**smooth-tongued** (smüᴛʜ′tungd′), *adj.* speaking smoothly; blandly agreeable, flattering, and persuasive; suave.

**smooth|y** (smü′ᴛʜē), *n., pl.* **smooth|ies.** = smoothie.

**smor|gas|bord** or **smör|gås|bord** (smôr′gəs bôrd, -bōrd; *Swedish* smœr′gōs bürd), *n.* **1a** an elaborate Scandinavian luncheon or supper, with a large variety of meats, salads, fish, hors d'oeuvres, and the like, served from a buffet. **b** any buffet meal with an elaborate variety of food. **2** *Figurative: But to combat the accompanying inflation it has served up a regular smorgasbord of economic schemes* (Wall Street Journal). [American English < Swedish *smörgåsbord* < *smörgås* open-faced sandwich + *bord* table]

**smør|re|brød** or **smor|re|brod** (smor′ə brôd; *Danish* smœr′ə brœᴛʜ′), *n.* an open-face sandwich served as an hors d'oeuvre. [< Danish *smørrebrød* < *smør* butter + *brød* bread]

**smote** (smōt), *v.* a past tense of **smite**: *God smote the wicked city with fire from heaven.*

**smoth|er** (smuᴛʜ′ər), *v., n.* —*v.t.* **1** to make unable to get air; kill by depriving of air; suffocate: *The gas almost smothered the coal miners but they got out in time.* **2** to cover thickly: *In the fall the grass is smothered with leaves.* **3** to deaden or put out by covering thickly: *The fire is smothered by ashes.* **4** *Figurative.* **a** to keep back; check; suppress: *to smother one's fears, to smother a committee's report. I smothered a sharp reply.* **b** to cover up; conceal: *He smothered a yawn behind his hand.* **5** to cook in a covered pot or baking dish: *smothered chicken.*
—*v.i.* **1** to be unable to breathe freely; suffocate: *We are smothering in this stuffy room. The miners almost smothered when the shaft collapsed.* **2** *Figurative.* to be suppressed, concealed, or stifled. **3** *Dialect.* to smolder; burn slowly.
[Middle English *smortheren* suffocate with smoke < *smorther* smother, noun]
—*n.* **1** a cloud of dust, smoke, spray, or the like: *The distant building rose above the smother of traffic and industrial smog.* **2** anything that smothers or appears to smother. **3** *Figurative.* an excess of disorder; confusion: *a perfect smother of letters and papers.* **4** the condition of being smothered. **5** a smoking or smoldering condition.
[Middle English *smorther,* noun < Old English *smorian* to suffocate] —**smoth′er|er,** *n.*

**smoth|er|a|tion** (smuᴛʜ′ə rā′shən), *n.* the act of smothering, or the state of being smothered; suffocation.

**smoth|er|ing|ly** (smuᴛʜ′ər ing lē), *adv.* **1** suffocatingly. **2** *Figurative.* so as to suppress.

**smoth|er|y** (smuᴛʜ′ər ē), *adj.* tending to smother; full of dust, smoke, spray, or the like; stifling.

**smouch** (smouch, smüch), *v.i., v.t., n. Archaic.* kiss. [compare German *Schmatz*]

**smoul|der** (smōl′dər), *v.i., n.* = smolder.

**s.m.p.**, without male offspring (Latin, *sine mascula prole*).

**SMSA** (no periods), Standard Metropolitan Statistical Area (the official name of a metropolitan area in the United States).

**smudge** (smuj), *n., v.,* **smudged, smudg|ing.**
—*n.* **1** a dirty mark, especially one caused by smearing or by trying to rub out a previous mark; smear: *Erasing only made a smudge and she had to copy the note over.* **2a** a smoky fire made to drive away insects or to protect fruit and plants from frost. **b** any suffocating smoke. **3** a dirty or smeared condition.
—*v.t.* **1** to mark with dirty streaks; smear: *The picture was smudged by wet paint.* SYN: stain, blacken, smirch. **2** to smoke (an orchard) with a smudge or smudges to fumigate or protect from frost. —*v.i.* **1** to make or leave a stain. SYN: stain, blacken, smirch. **2** to be smudged.
[origin uncertain. Probably related to **smutch.**]

**smudge pot**, a pot or stove in which oil or other fuel is burned to produce smudge: *Florida's citrus growing belt reported 30 degrees, but smudge pots and burning piles of wood saved most of the crop* (Wall Street Journal).

**smudg|y** (smuj′ē), *adj.,* **smudg|i|er, smudg|i|est.** **1** smudged; marked with smudges: *smudgy fingermarks all around the light switch.* **2** smoky. **3** *British Dialect.* close or sultry: *smudgy air.* —**smudg′i|ly,** *adv.* —**smudg′i|ness,** *n.*

**smug** (smug), *adj.,* **smug|ger, smug|gest.** **1** too pleased with one's own goodness, cleverness, respectability, or accomplishments; self-satisfied; complacent: *Nothing disturbs the smug beliefs of some prim, narrow-minded people.* **2** sleek; neat; trim. SYN: spruce. [earlier, trim, neat, perhaps < Dutch, Low German *smuk* trim, neat] —**smug′ly,** *adv.* —**smug′ness,** *n.*

---

**Pronunciation Key:** hat, āge, cãre, fär; let, ēqual, tėrm; it, īce; hot, ōpen, ôrder; oil, out; cup, pu̇t, rüle; child; long; thin; ᴛʜen; zh, measure; ə represents **a** in about, **e** in taken, **i** in pencil, **o** in lemon, **u** in circus.

**smug|ger|y** (smug′ər ē), *n.* a smug attitude or condition.

**smug|gle** (smug′əl), *v.*, **-gled, -gling.** — *v.t.* **1** to bring into or take out of a country secretly and against the law, especially without the payment of legal duties: *It is a crime to smuggle goods into the United States.* **2** *Figurative.* to bring, take, or put secretly: *to smuggle presents into the attic. He tried to smuggle his snake into the house.*
— *v.i.* to engage in smuggling.
[earlier *smuckle,* apparently < Low German *smuggeln, smukkeln*]

**smug|gler** (smug′lər), *n.* **1** a person who smuggles. **2** a ship used in smuggling.

**smut** (smut), *n., v.,* **smut|ted, smut|ting.** — *n.* **1** indecent, obscene talk or writing: *Smut Held Cause of Delinquency* (New York Times). SYN: obscenity, ribaldry. **2a** a plant disease, especially of cereals, in which the ears of grain are replaced by black, dustlike spores. **b** any parasitic fungus producing this disease. **3a** soot, dirt, or the like. **b** a bit of this: *The controversial aft-placed funnel has been an unqualified success; not a smut, it is claimed, has yet besmirched her virgin decks* (London Times). **4** a dirty mark; smudge.
— *v.t.* **1** to soil with smut; smudge; blacken: *to smut one's hands with coal.* **2** to affect (a plant) with the disease smut.
— *v.i.* **1** to be soiled with smut. **2** (of a plant) to become affected by smut.
[perhaps variant of Middle English *smotten,* related to Middle High German *smotzen.* Compare Old English *smitte.*]

**smut ball, 1** the ball of black powder into which an ear of grain is changed by the smut fungus. **2** = puffball.

**smutch** (smutch), *v., n.* — *v.t.* to blacken with soot or dirt; smudge: *Let light forbear those lids; I have forbidden the feathery ash to smutch them* (Elinor Wylie).
— *n.* a dirty mark; smudge.
[origin uncertain. Probably related to **smudge.**]

**smutch|y** (smuch′ē), *adj.,* **smutch|i|er, smutch|i|est.** marked with smutches; dirty.

**smut grass,** a rushy grass growing in warm regions, with spikes usually blackened by a smut.

**smut|ty** (smut′ē), *adj.,* **-ti|er, -ti|est. 1** indecent; nasty; obscene: *"Let us not be smutty," appeals Lady Fidget, in the line Dame Edith Evans made famous* (London Times). SYN: pornographic, salacious. **2** having the plant disease smut. **3** soiled with smut, soot, or the like; dirty or sooty. SYN: grimy. **4** of the color of smut; dusky; dark.
— **smut′ti|ly,** *adv.* — **smut′ti|ness,** *n.*

**SMV** (no periods), slow-moving vehicle.

**Smyr|na fig** (smėr′nə), a large pulpy fig that has only female flowers which must be pollinated by the pollen from caprifigs before the fruit will grow. [< *Smyrna* (now Izmir), Turkey, where it was originally grown]

**Smyr|ne|an** (smėr′nē ən), *adj., n.* — *adj.* of or having to do with Smyrna (now Izmir), a seaport in western Turkey, on the Aegean Sea, or its people.
— *n.* a native or inhabitant of Smyrna.

**Smyr|ni|ot** (smėr′nē ot) or **Smyr|ni|ote** (smėr′nē ōt), *adj., n.* = Smyrnean.

**Smyth sewing** (smith), a method of stitching the sections of a book on the back of the fold to produce a rounded back so that the book opens flat. [< David *Smyth,* an American inventor of the 1800's, who invented a machine for this kind of bookbinding]

**s.n.,** without name (Latin, *sine nomine*).

**Sn** (no period), tin (chemical element).

**Sn.,** Sanitary.

**snack** (snak), *n., v.* — *n.* **1** a light meal, especially one eaten between regular meals: *He eats a snack before going to bed. We bought a snack at a roadside stand.* **2** a share; portion. SYN: allotment. [< verb]
— *v.i.* to have a little bit to eat between meals: *He's forever snacking and will always be overweight.*
**go snacks,** to have a share (in something): *The Princesses ... were mean enough to go snacks in the profits* (Temple Bar).
[Middle English *snaken* to snap (as a dog), perhaps < Middle Low German *snacken.* Compare etym. under **snatch.**]

**snack bar,** a lunch counter at which snacks are served: *Lunch is often a sandwich and a piece of pie at the cloakroom snack bar* (Time).

**snack|e|te|ri|a** (snak′ə tir′ē ə), *n. U.S.* a restaurant or cafeteria which serves snacks. [American English < *snack* + *-eteria,* as in *cafeteria*]

**snack table,** a tray or small top on folding legs upon which a helping of food or refreshments may be placed.

***snaf|fle¹** (snaf′əl), *n., v.,* **-fled, -fling.** — *n.* a slender, jointed bit used on a bridle; snaffle bit.
— *v.t.* **1** to control or manage by a snaffle. **2** to put a snaffle on.
[compare Dutch *snavel,* Frisian *snaffel* beak, mouth]

***snaffle¹**

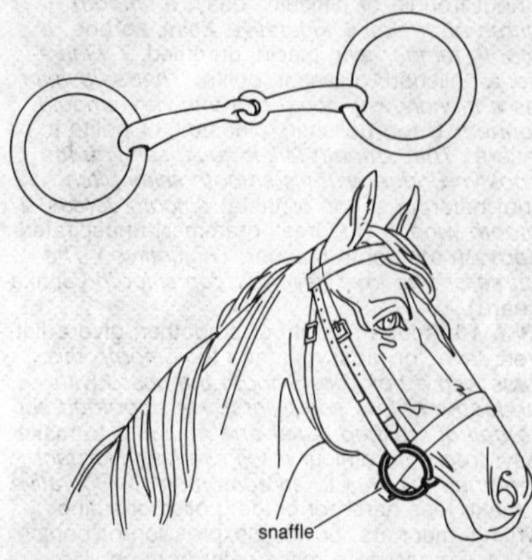


**snaf|fle²** (snaf′əl), *v.t.,* **-fled, -fling.** *Especially British Dialect.* to steal: *He returned to find that some had snaffled a few groceries* (Manchester Guardian Weekly). [origin uncertain]

**snaffle bit,** = snaffle.

**snaffle bridle,** a single-reined bridle having a snaffle bit.

**sna|fu** (sna fü′), *n., adj., v.,* **-fued, -fu|ing.** *Slang.* — *n.* **1** a condition of great disorder; chaotic state of affairs: *There were a few inevitable snafus* (*an unscheduled tornado raised hob at Richmond, Va., and communication lines went dead*) (Newsweek). **2** anything hopelessly mishandled; botched piece of work: *The former Ambassador ... left in July and snafus over political clearance held up another appointment* (Newsweek).
— *adj.* being in great disorder; snarled; confused.
— *v.t.* **1** to put in disorder or a chaotic state: *Shipments of the same drugs to our most severely hurt allies are snafued in bureaucracy* (Birmingham News). **2** to mishandle; botch. [< the initial letters of "situation normal—all fouled up"]

**snag** (snag), *n., v.,* **snagged, snag|ging.** — *n.* **1a** a tree or branch held fast in a river or lake, especially below the surface. Snags are dangerous to boats. *It required all his attention and skill ... to pilot her clear of sand bars and snags, or sunken trees* (Washington Irving). **b** the stump of a burned or dead tree. **2** any sharp or rough projecting point, such as the broken end of a branch or the point of a nail: *I tore my shirt on a snag in the rafters of the barn.* **3** the stump of a tooth; projecting tooth. **4** a tear made by snagging. **5** *Figurative.* a hidden or unexpected obstacle: *Our plans hit a snag. The treaty might be signed at the end of this week if no last-minute snags appeared* (New York Times). SYN: obstruction, impediment. **6** an imperfectly developed branch of an antler.
— *v.t.* **1** to run or catch on a snag: *He snagged his sweater on a nail.* **2** *Figurative.* to hinder; block as if with a snag: *The refugee issue had snagged treaty discussions* (New York Times). SYN: clog, obstruct. **3** to clear of snags.
— *v.i.* to run into a snag: (*Figurative.*) *Talks snagged on fringe issues* (Wall Street Journal).
**be snagged,** to be caught, pierced, or damaged by a snag: (*Figurative.*) *His project is snagged by failure to get approval first.*
[perhaps < Scandinavian (compare Norwegian dialectal *snage* point of land, *snag* stump, spike)]

**snagged** (snagd), *adj.* having snags; jagged.

**snag|gle|tooth** (snag′əl tüth′), *n., pl.* **-teeth.** an uneven, broken, or projecting tooth. [perhaps < a diminutive form of *snag* + *tooth*]

**snag|gle-toothed** (snag′əl tütht′), *adj.* having snaggleteeth: *a snaggle-toothed grin.*

**snag|gly** (snag′lē), *adj.,* **-gli|er, -gli|est.** uneven, broken, or projecting: *His laugh was enormous while his teeth were snaggly* (Saul Bellow).

**snag|gy** (snag′ē), *adj.,* **-gi|er, -gi|est. 1** having snags: *a snaggy tree, a snaggy river.* **2** projecting sharply or roughly.

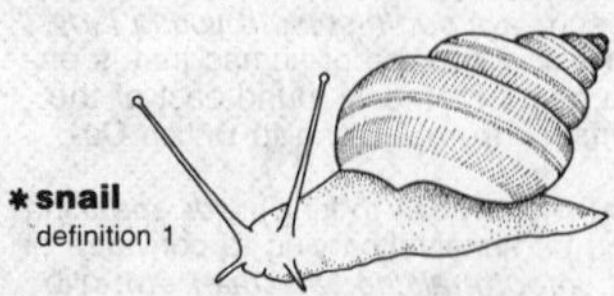

***snail**
definition 1

***snail** (snāl), *n.* **1** a small, soft-bodied mollusk that crawls very slowly. Most snails have spiral shells on their backs into which they can pull back for protection. There are land snails, freshwater snails, and marine snails. Snails are gastropods. **2** *Figurative.* a lazy, slow-moving person: *That janitor is a snail who never gets things done.* SYN: sluggard. [Old English *snægel*] — **snail′like′,** *adj.*

**snail bore,** a gastropod, such as a whelk, which bores and injures oysters.

**snail fever,** = schistosomiasis. [so called because it is caused by parasitic flatworms whose intermediate hosts are snails]

**snail|flow|er** (snāl′flou′ər), *n.* a twining bean, often cultivated in tropical gardens and in greenhouses for its showy white and purple fragrant flowers.

**snail-paced** (snāl′pāst′), *adj.* very slow in pace or progress; sluggish.

**snail's pace,** a very slow pace: ... *to accelerate our lunar research from a mere snail's pace to a speed which should reveal many new discoveries* ... (Gilbert Fielder).

**snake** (snāk), *n., v.,* **snaked, snak|ing.** — *n.* **1** a long, slender, crawling reptile without limbs and with a scaly skin and narrow, forked tongue. Some snakes are poisonous. These have poison glands connected with a pair of fangs which inject prey with poison when the snake bites. The snakes comprise a suborder of reptiles. *Snakes have tails, which is not to say they are all tail* (Scientific American). **2** *Figurative.* a sly, treacherous person: *I am not ... a snake, to bite when I have learned to love* (Rudyard Kipling). **3** anything resembling a snake in form or movement. **4** a long, flexible, metal tool used by plumbers to clean out a drain. **5** *Military.* a long pipe filled with explosives, used for blowing up all the mines in a field. **6** *Finance.* a joint-float system of currencies allowed to fluctuate within narrowly defined limits: *The so-called European snake ... bound France, West Germany, the Benelux countries, Sweden, Norway and Denmark to hold their currencies within a 4.5% range of fluctuation against each other* (Time).
— *v.i.* **1** to move, wind, or curve like a snake: *The narrow road snaked through the mountains. Since the train was snaking along at a brisk clip, the diner swayed from side to side* (New Yorker). **2** to creep along stealthily like a snake.
— *v.t.* **1** *U.S. Informal.* to drag; haul, especially along the ground with chains or ropes: *Old Sam cut down most of the virgin timber on his farm, snaked it out by mules to his own sawmills ...* (Time). **2** *U.S. Informal.* to yank; jerk: *to snake a car out of a ditch.* **3** to clean out (a drain) with a plumber's snake.
[Old English *snaca*] — **snake′like′,** *adj.*

**snake|bird** (snāk′bėrd′), *n.* **1** any one of certain swimming birds with a long, snaky neck, such as the water turkey of America; darter. **2** *British Dialect.* the wryneck.

**snake|bite** (snāk′bīt′), *n.* the bite of a snake, especially a poisonous snake: *Snakebite causes thousands of deaths in tropical regions every year* (Scientific American).

**snake charmer,** a person who is supposed to charm snakes, especially with music.

**snake dance, 1** *U.S.* an informal parade of persons dancing in a zigzag line in celebration, as of a victory or event: *There were victory rallies and ... snake dances on the Missouri campus* (New Yorker). **2** a ceremonial dance of the Hopi Indians, in which the dancers carry live snakes as an offering to the rain gods.

**snake-dance** (snāk′dans′, -däns′), *v.i.,* **-danced, -danc|ing.** to do a snake dance. — **snake′-danc′er,** *n.*

**snake doctor, 1** a doctor who treats snakebites. **2** = dragonfly.

**snake eater, 1** = secretary bird. **2** = markhor.

**snake eyes,** *Slang.* two ones on a roll of dice.

**snake feeder,** = dragonfly.

**snake fence,** a zigzag fence made of rails resting across one another at an angle.

**snake|fish** (snāk′fish′), *n., pl.* **-fish|es** or (*collectively*) **-fish.** any one of various fishes more or less resembling a snake, such as the lizard fish and the oarfish.

**snake|head** (snāk′hed′), *n.* **1** = turtlehead. **2** any one of a group of elongated labyrinth fish.

**snake killer, 1** = road runner. **2** = secretary bird.

**snake|let** (snāk′lit), *n.* a small snake.

**snake moss,** the common club moss.

**snake|mouth** (snāk′mouth′), *n.* a North American swamp orchid with a slender stem bearing a single, fragrant, rose-colored, nodding flower and a single leaf.

**snake|neck** (snāk′nek′), *n.* = snakebird.

**snake oil,** *U.S.* any one of various preparations advertised as medicine supposed to cure certain ailments, such as rheumatism, colds, or baldness, formerly sold by peddlers posing as scientists, doctors, or the like.

**snake pit, 1** a pit filled with snakes. **2** *Informal.* a backward or overcrowded mental institution, prison, or other such facility, especially one where outmoded theories and practices are perpetuated. **3** *Figurative.* any frightening or oppressive place or condition: *It's difficult to orient one's way in the snake pit we're living in* (Arthur Miller).

**snake plant**, = sansevieria.

**snake|root** (snāk′rüt′, -rủt′), *n.* **1** any one of various plants whose roots have been regarded as a remedy for snakebites, such as the Virginia snakeroot, the Seneca snakeroot, the white snakeroot, the button snakeroot, or a kind of bugbane: *Rauwolfia, also known as the snakeroot plant, is the source of reserpine,* [*a*] *relaxing drug* (Science News Letter). **2** the root of such plants.

**snake|skin** (snāk′skin′), *n.* **1** the skin of a snake. **2** leather made from it.

**snake|stone** (snāk′stōn′), *n.* **1** = ammonite. **2** a porous substance supposed to extract the venom from snakebites.

**snake|weed** (snāk′wēd′), *n.* **1** = bistort. **2** any one of the weedy plants among which snakes are supposed to abound. **3** any herb of a group of the composite family with small yellow flower heads.

**snake|wood** (snāk′wủd′), *n.* **1a** any one of certain East Indian shrubs or trees whose wood is supposed to cure snakebites. **b** the wood itself. **2a** a South American tree of the mulberry family with a mottled wood used especially for veneering. **b** the wood itself; letterwood.

**snak|y** (snā′kē), *adj.,* **snak|i|er, snak|i|est.** **1** of a snake or snakes. **2** like a snake; like the curving and turning of a snake; twisting; winding: *doing a snaky dance in front of a white statue* (New Yorker). **3** having many snakes. **4** *Figurative.* sly; venomous; treacherous. **5** formed with or composed of snakes. —**snak′i|ly,** *adv.* —**snak′i|ness,** *n.*

**snap** (snap), *v.,* **snapped, snap|ping,** *n., adj., adv.* —*v.i.* **1** to make a sudden, sharp sound: *Most pine snaps as it burns.* **2** to move, shut, catch, or otherwise come together, with a snap: *The door snapped shut behind me.* **3** to break suddenly or sharply, especially with a snapping sound: *The violin string snapped because it was fastened too tight.* **4** to become suddenly unable to endure a strain: (*Figurative.*) *His nerve snapped.* **5** to make a sudden, quick bite or snatch: *The turtle snapped at the child's hand.* **6** *Figurative.* to seize suddenly: *She snapped at the chance to go to Europe.* **7** to speak quickly and sharply: *to snap impatiently at a person who is slow.* **8** *Figurative.* to move quickly and sharply: *The soldiers snapped to attention. Her eyes snapped with anger.* **9** to take snapshots.
—*v.t.* **1a** to cause to make a sudden, sharp sound: *The teacher snapped her fingers to get our attention.* **b** to crack (a whip). **2** to cause to move, close, catch, or otherwise come together, with a snap: *to snap a door shut, to snap the jaws together, to snap a bolt into place.* **3** to break (something) suddenly or sharply: *to snap a stick in two.* (*Figurative.*) *It seemed for a moment as if the tradition of generations might be snapped.* (Lytton Strachey). **4** to snatch quickly with the mouth; bite suddenly: *The dog snapped up the meat.* **5** *Figurative.* to seize suddenly: *to snap up a bargain.* **6** to say quickly and sharply: *"Silence!" snapped the captain. The sergeant snapped out an order.* **7** *Figurative.* to move quickly and sharply: *You'd better snap it up or you will never get the job done.* **8** to take a snapshot of. **9** *Football.* to pass (the ball) back from the center with a quick motion to start a play; center: *To start a play, the offensive team's center snaps the ball to a teammate in the backfield* (Forest Evashevski). **10** *Baseball.* to throw (the ball) quickly: *to snap the ball to first base.*
—*n.* **1** a quick, sharp sound: *The box shut with a snap.* **2** a sudden, sharp breaking or the sound of breaking: *One snap made the knife useless.* **3** a quick, sudden bite or snatch: *The dog made a snap at the fly.* **4** a quick, sharp speech: *When she was tired, she sometimes answered with a snap.* **5** *Informal, Figurative.* **a** a quick, sharp way: *She moves with snap and energy.* **b** liveliness or crispness in writing: *a delightful little tale, full of romance, snap, and brightness.* **6** a short spell of cold weather. **7** a fastener; clasp: *One of the snaps of your dress is unfastened.* **8** the act of snapping the fingers, especially as a sign of disregard or contempt. **9** a thin, crisp cookie: *a chocolate snap, a ginger snap.* **10** *Informal.* a snapshot. **11** *Informal.* a snapdragon. **12** *Slang.* an easy job, piece of work, or the like. **13** *Football.* **a** the act of snapping the ball. **b** the center who does this; snapback.
—*adj.* **1** made or done quickly or suddenly: *A snap judgment is likely to be wrong.* **2** closing or fastening by action of a spring: *a snap bolt, a snap lock.* **3** *Slang.* very easy: *a snap course at college.*
—*adv.* **1** with a snap. **2** without a delay or hesitation.
**not a snap**, not at all: *I cared not a snap that he didn't write.*
**snap back**, *U.S. Informal.* to bounce back; recover suddenly: *Whitey Ford ... snapped back into his best pitching form* (New York Times).
**snap into**, to throw oneself into (an action): *Oh, snap into it! We want to get this done* (F. A. Pottle).
**snap out of it**, *Informal.* to change one's attitude or habit suddenly: *He was in a bad mood one minute, but then he snapped out of it and started to laugh.*
[earlier, to bite < earlier Dutch *snappen*]

**snap|back** (snap′bak′), *n.* **1** *U.S. Informal.* a snapping back to a former or normal condition; bounceback. **2** *Football.* **a** the passing back of the ball which puts it in play; snap. **b** center.

**snap bean**, **1** any one of several varieties of the common bean, whose unripe pods are used for food. **2** the pod itself.

**snap-brim** (snap′brim′), *n.* = snap-brim hat.

**snap-brim hat**, a hat with a brim that can be turned down, especially in front.

**snap|drag|on** (snap′drag′ən), *n.* **1** a common garden plant with spikes of showy flowers, chiefly of crimson, purple, white, and yellow. Snapdragons are herbs that belong to the figwort family and comprise a genus of plants. See picture under **figwort family.** **2** an old game in which people try to snatch raisins from burning brandy. [< *snap* + *dragon;* because the blossom's lips open like (dragon's) jaws when they are pressed, then snap shut again]

**snap fastener**, a metal fastening device in two pieces, one with a projection and the other with a hole or socket, which are fitted together to close up parts of a garment, fabric, or other article.

**snap|hance** (snap′hans), *n.* **1** an early flintlock worked by a spring. **2** a gun or pistol having such a lock. [< Dutch *snaphaan* < *snappen* snap + *haan* hammer]

**snap|haunce** (snap′hôns), *n.* = snaphance.

**snap link**, an open link closed by a spring or hinged part of a link used to connect chains or parts of a harness, and in mountain climbing where it is called a *karabiner.*

**snap-on** (snap′on′, -ôn′), *adj.* that is or can be snapped into place: *Snap-on sunglasses that double as safety glasses come with adjustable parts* (Science News Letter).

**snap|per** (snap′ər), *n., pl.* **-pers** or (*collective for 3*) **-per.** **1** a fastener; snap. **2** any person or thing that snaps. **3** = snapping turtle. **4a** any one of several large, mostly red or yellowish fish of tropical seas used for food, especially the red snapper of the Gulf of Mexico. The snappers comprise a family of fishes. **b** any one of certain similar fishes. **5** = snapping beetle.

**snap|per-back** (snap′ər bak′), *n. Football.* the center.

**snap|per-up** (snap′ər up′), *n.* one that snaps up or seizes upon a thing quickly.

**snap|ping** (snap′ing), *adj.* **1** making quick attempts to bite, as an animal. **2** snappish: *to talk in a snapping tone.* **3** making a sharp, cracking or clicking sound: *a snapping, clicker toy.* **4** flashing, as eyes. —**snap′ping|ly,** *adv.*

**snapping beetle**, any one of several beetles that jump with a snapping or clicking sound when turned on the back; click beetle.

**snapping turtle**, a large, savage turtle of American rivers and lakes that has powerful jaws with which it snaps at its prey. Snapping turtles comprise a family of reptiles.

**snap|pish** (snap′ish), *adj.* **1** apt to snap: *a snappish dog.* **2** quick and sharp in speech or manner; impatient: *a snappish person.* **SYN:** testy, crabbed, cross, irascible, petulant. **3** characteristic of a snappish person: *a snappish reply.* —**snap′pish|ly,** *adv.* —**snap′pish|ness,** *n.*

**snap|py** (snap′ē), *adj.,* **-pi|er, -pi|est.** **1** snappish; sharp: *a snappy answer.* **2** quick; hasty: *to walk at a snappy pace. The issues are too complex ... for snappy popular judgments* (James Reston). **3** snapping or crackling in sound: *a snappy fire.* **4** *Informal.* having snap, crispness, smartness, pungency, etc.; lively: *a snappy cheese, a snappy new suit.*
**make it snappy**, *Informal.* to hurry up: *All right, we'll wait for you, but make it snappy!*
—**snap′pi|ly,** *adv.* —**snap′pi|ness,** *n.*

**snap ring**, = piston ring.

**snap roll**, (of an airplane) a fast barrel roll, especially as a maneuver in stunting.

**snap|shoot** (snap′shüt′), *v.t.,* **-shot, -shoot|ing.** to take a snapshot of or at: *to snapshoot a duck. Tourist Janet Dulles ... was snapshot as she snapshot Geneva's lighter side* (Time). —**snap′-shoot′er,** *n.*

**snap|shot** (snap′shot′), *n., v.,* **-shot|ted, -shot|ting.** —*n.* **1** a photograph taken in an instant with a small camera. **2** a quick shot taken without time for careful aim, usually at game that has just been flushed.
—*v.t., v.i.* to take a snapshot (of): (*Figurative.*) *As domestic comedy, "The Male Animal" snapshots some familiar poses, strikes some reminiscent chords* (Time).

**snare[1]** (snãr), *n., v.,* **snared, snar|ing.** —*n.* **1** a noose for catching small animals and birds: *The boys made snares to catch rabbits.* **SYN:** See syn. under **trap.** **2** a trap; anything that entraps: (*Figurative.*) *Popularity is a snare in which fools are caught.* **SYN:** pitfall. **3** a loop of wire used especially to remove tonsils or tumors.
—*v.t.* **1** to catch with a snare: *One day the boys snared a skunk instead of a rabbit.* **2** to trap: (*Figurative.*) *Russia is greatly expanding ... its competitive ability to snare underdeveloped lands into its trade orbit* (Newsweek). **SYN:** entangle, ensnare, entrap.
[probably < Scandinavian (compare Old Icelandic *snara*)]

**snare[2]** (snãr), *n.* one of the strings of wire or gut stretched across the bottom of a snare drum. [probably < Middle Dutch *snare*]

**snare drum**, a small drum with strings of wire or gut stretched across the bottom to make a rattling sound. See picture under **drum[1]**.

**snar|er** (snãr′ər), *n.* **1** a person who entangles, or lays snares. **2** a person who catches animals with snares.

**snar|ing** (snãr′ing), *n.* **1** the act or practice of using a snare. **2** the method of catching fish by entangling them in nets.

**snark** (snärk), *n.* an animal imagined by Lewis Carroll as the object of the expedition described in his nonsense poem *The Hunting of the Snark* (1876). [blend of *snake* and *shark[1]*]

**snarl[1]** (snärl), *v., n.* —*v.i.* **1** to growl sharply and show one's teeth: *The dog snarled at the stranger.* **2** to speak harshly in a sharp, angry tone. —*v.t.* to say or express with a snarl: *The bully snarled out an angry threat.*
—*n.* **1** a sharp, angry, growl. **2** sharp, angry words: *A snarl was his only reply.*
[earlier *snar.* Compare Middle Dutch *snarren* to rattle. See related etym. at **snore, sneer.**]

**snarl[2]** (snärl), *n., v.* —*n.* **1** a tangled or knotted mass or tuft; tangle: *She combed the snarls out of her hair.* **2** *Figurative.* a tangled condition; confusion: *His legal affairs were in a snarl.*
—*v.t.* **1** to tangle: *The kitten snarled the yarn by playing with it.* **2** *Figurative.* to confuse.
—*v.i.* to become snarled: *Her hair snarls easily.*
[perhaps frequentative form of *snare[1]*]

**snarl[3]** (snärl), *v.t.* to raise or emboss (metal) by hammering on a tool held against the opposite surface. [perhaps special use of *snarl[2]* knot]

**snarl|er** (snär′lər), *n.* an animal or person that snarls.

**snarl|ing** (snär′ling), *adj.* **1** that growls angrily. **2** speaking or complaining in a sharp, bad-tempered manner: *The silver snarling trumpets 'gan to chide* (Keats).

**snarl|ing|ly** (snär′ling lē), *adv.* in a bad-tempered or growling manner.

**snarl-up** (snärl′up′), *n. Informal.* a confusion; mix-up: *a snarl-up in a recording session* (Time).

**snarl|y[1]** (snär′lē), *adj.,* **snarl|i|er, snarl|i|est.** inclined to snarl or growl; bad-tempered; cross. **SYN:** peevish, irritable. [< *snarl[1]* + *-y[1]*]

**snarl|y[2]** (snär′lē), *adj.,* **snarl|i|er, snarl|i|est.** tangled; full of snarls: *You're still within a snarly wood where angels and the devil wait for you to prove the advocate of good or evil* (New Yorker). **SYN:** jumbled. [< *snarl[2]* + *-y[1]*]

**snash** (snash), *n., v.i. Scottish.* insult.

**snatch** (snach), *v., n.* —*v.t.* **1** to seize suddenly, eagerly, or violently; grasp hastily; grab: *to snatch up one's hat and coat and run for a train. The hawk snatched the chicken and flew away. A thief snatched her purse in the crowd.* **SYN:** catch, snap. **2** to pull or take (off) suddenly: *He snatched off his hat and bowed.* **SYN:** pluck. **3** *Figurative.* to take or get hastily, suddenly, or improperly: *At half past four he had snatched a cup of tea* (John Galsworthy). **4** *Figurative.* to save or attain by quick action: *They snatched victory from what seemed to be sure defeat.* **SYN:** wrest. **5** *Slang.* to kidnap.
—*n.* **1** the act of snatching; sudden grab: *The boy made a snatch at the ball.* (*Figurative.*) *Here and there he made guesses and snatches at the truth* (Matthew Arnold). **2** a short time: *He had a snatch of sleep sitting in his chair.* **3** a small

**Pronunciation Key:** hat, āge, cãre, fär; let, ēqual, tėrm; it, īce; hot, ōpen, ôrder; oil, out; cup, pủt, rüle; child; long; thin; ᴛʜen; zh, measure; ə represents **a** in about, **e** in taken, **i** in pencil, **o** in lemon, **u** in circus.

amount; bit; scrap: *We heard snatches of their conversation as they raised their voices from time to time.* **4** an exercise in weight lifting in which the weight is raised from the floor to above the head in one continuous motion. **5** *Slang.* the act of kidnapping.
**by** (or **in**) **snatches,** by fits and starts; intermittently: *I have begun two or three letters to you by snatches, and been prevented from finishing them* (Alexander Pope).
**snatch at, a** to try to seize or grasp; seize; grasp: *He snatched at the railing as he began to fall down the stairs.* **b** *Figurative.* to take advantage of eagerly: *He snatched at the chance to travel.*
[perhaps < Middle Dutch *snakken;* perhaps influenced by *latch, catch*] —**snatch′a|ble,** *adj.* —**snatch′er,** *n.*

**snatch block,** a block with an opening in one side to receive the bight of a rope.

**snatch squad,** *British.* a special detachment of soldiers assigned to help quell a riot or disturbance by seizing the most conspicuous offenders: *After two hours the Army sent snatch squads into the area to bring out troublemakers* (London Times).

**snatch|y** (snach′ē), *adj.* done or occurring in snatches; disconnected; irregular. —**snatch′i|ly,** *adv.*

**snath** (snath), *n.* the long wooden handle of a scythe. [variant of *snead,* Old English *snǣd*]

**snathe** (snāᴛʜ), *n.* = snath.

**snav|el** (snav′əl), *v.t. Australian.* to steal; rob; snatch.

**snaz|zy** (snaz′ē), *adj.,* **-zi|er, -zi|est.** *U.S. Slang.* fancy; flashy; elegant: *With a great gold World Series ring on his finger, and wearing a snazzy blue suit with plaid socks, he looks as sharp as he feels* (Time). [origin unknown]

**SNCC** (snik), *n.,* or **S.N.C.C.,** Student National Coordinating Committee (a militant organization advocating Black Power, originally formed by Southern students in 1960 under the name Student Nonviolent Coordinating Committee to promote civil rights).

**snead** (snēd), *n. Dialect.* snath. [Old English *snǣd*]

**sneak** (snēk), *v., n., adj.* —*v.i.* **1** to move in a stealthy, sly way: *The man sneaked about the barn watching for a chance to steal the cow.* **SYN:** slink, skulk, lurk. **2** to act like a thief or a person who is ashamed to be seen: *He sneaked in by the back way. See how he cowers and sneaks* (Thoreau).
—*v.t.* **1** to get, put, or pass in a stealthy, sly way: *The children sneaked the snake into the house.* **2** *Informal.* to steal: *He sneaked all the cookies he could.*
—*n.* **1** a person who sneaks; sneaking, cowardly, or contemptible person. **2a** the act of sneaking. **b** *Informal.* a going quietly away; departure: *How about taking a sneak?* (Sinclair Lewis). **3** *U.S. Informal.* a sneak preview: *For the producer sweating out audience reaction, the sneak is the most fiendish torture* (Wall Street Journal).
—*adj.* sneaking; stealthy: *The steel magnates were so foolish as to try a sneak play* (Atlantic). *Sophisticated electronics systems are patrolling the skies to detect sneak nuclear explosions* (New York Times).
**on** (or **upon**) **the sneak,** sneakily: *A thief* [*was*] *detected in a house which he has entered, upon the sneak, for the purpose of robbing it* (J. H. Vaux).
**sneak out of,** to avoid by slyness: *He tried to sneak out of paying the fine by using every trick he could think of.*
**sneaks,** *U.S. Informal.* sneakers: *a pair of old sneaks.*
[origin uncertain. Compare Old English *snīcan.*]

**sneak attack,** a surprise attack made before a declaration of war: *In ... the age of supersonic planes and nuclear weapons, a sneak attack could wipe out the nation* (Newsweek).

**sneak boat,** *U.S.* a small, flat, shallow boat used for hunting wild fowl, usually covered with brush or weeds as camouflage.

**sneak|box** (snēk′boks′), *n. U.S.* sneak boat.

**sneak|er** (snē′kər), *n.* **1** a light canvas shoe with a soft rubber sole, used for games and sports. **2** a person who sneaks; sneak.

**sneak|ered** (snē′kərd), *adj.* having or wearing sneakers.

**sneak|ing** (snē′king), *adj.* **1** meanly or deceitfully underhand; cowardly or contemptible; concealed. **SYN:** skulking, slinking. **2** that one cannot justify or does not like to confess: *He had a sneaking suspicion that his mother knew about the window he had broken.* —**sneak′ing|ly,** *adv.*

**sneak preview,** *U.S. Informal.* the showing of a new motion picture without announcement beforehand or to a private audience before the film is released for the general public.

**sneaks** (snēks), *n.pl.* See under **sneak.**

**sneaks|by** (snēks′bē), *n., pl.* **-bies.** a paltry, sneaking fellow; a sneak.

**sneak shooting,** the act or practice of shooting wild fowl from a sneak boat.

**sneak thief,** a person who takes advantage of open doors, windows, or other easy opportunities to steal.

**sneak|y** (snē′kē), *adj.,* **sneak|i|er, sneak|i|est.** cowardly, mean, or contemptible: *They dropped their eyes and looked sneaky* (Mark Twain). —**sneak′i|ly,** *adv.* —**sneak′i|ness,** *n.*

**sneap** (snēp), *v., n. Archaic.* —*v.t.* **1** to nip or pinch: *An envious sneaping frost ...* (Shakespeare). **2** to check, reprove, or snub: *She had a tongue for the sneaping of too casual boys* (Arnold Bennett).
—*n.* a check; reproof; snub: *My lord, I will not undergo this sneap without reply* (Shakespeare). [< Scandinavian (compare Old Icelandic *sneypa* disgrace)]

**sneck** (snek), *n., v.t., v.i. Scottish.* latch; catch. [origin uncertain]

**sneck|draw** (snek′drô′), *n. Scottish.* **1** a thief; burglar. **2** a crafty, greedy person.

**sned** (sned), *v.t.,* **sned|ded, sned|ding.** *Scottish.* **1** to cut off (branches). **2** to prune (trees). [Old English *snǣdan*]

**sneer** (snir), *v., n.* —*v.i.* to show scorn or contempt by looks or words: *The mean girls sneered at the poor girl's cheap clothes. Damn with faint praise, assent with civil leer, And without sneering teach the rest to sneer* (Alexander Pope). **SYN:** jeer, gibe, flout, mock. See syn. under **scoff.**
—*v.t.* **1** to say or write with scorn or contempt: *"Bah!" he sneered with a curl of his lip.* **2** to bring, put, force, or otherwise move by sneering: *to sneer down all who disagree.*
—*n.* an act of sneering; look or words expressing scorn or contempt: *He fears sneers more than blows.*
[earlier *snere;* origin uncertain] —**sneer′er,** *n.*

**sneer|ful** (snir′fəl), *adj.* given to sneering.

**sneer|y** (snir′ē), *adj.* of a sneering or scornful character.

**sneesh** (snēsh), *n.* = sneeshing.

**sneesh|ing** (snē′shing), *n. Scottish.* **1** snuff. **2** a pinch of snuff. [perhaps < Scottish Gaelic *snaoisín,* Irish *snaoisean,* alterations of English *sneezing*]

**sneeze** (snēz), *v.,* **sneezed, sneez|ing,** *n.* —*v.i.* to expel air suddenly and violently through the nose and mouth, by an involuntary spasm. A person sneezes when he has a cold. *The pepper made her sneeze.*
—*n.* a sudden, violent expelling of air through the nose and mouth.
**sneeze at,** *Informal.* to treat with contempt; despise; scorn: *Ten dollars is not a sum to be sneezed at.*
[misreading of Middle English *fnesen,* Old English *fnēosan*]

**sneeze gas,** a gas, especially a derivative of arsine, used in warfare to produce nasal irritation, sneezing, and nausea.

**sneez|er** (snē′zər), *n.* **1** one who sneezes. **2** *British Dialect.* a violent blow; a blow that knocks the breath out.

**sneeze|weed** (snēz′wēd′), *n.* **1** any one of a group of American composite herbs with yellow flower heads that cause sneezing. **2** = sneezewort.

**sneeze|wort** (snēz′wėrt′), *n.* **1** a composite herb of Europe and Asia, closely related to the yarrow, that causes sneezing. **2** = sneezeweed.

**sneez|ing gas** (snē′zing), = sneeze gas.

**sneez|y** (snē′zē), *adj.* sneezing; accompanied by sneezes.

**snell**[1] (snel), *n., v.* —*n.* **1** a short piece of gut, or other leader, by which a fishhook is fastened to a longer line. **2** a short, light leader.
—*v.t.* to tie or fasten (a hook) to a line with a snell: *... makes it easy for a fisherman to snell hooks anywhere* (Science News Letter). [American English; origin uncertain]

**snell**[2] (snel), *adj., adv. Scottish.* —*adj.* **1** quick-moving. **2** smart; clever. **3** harsh; severe; unsparing: *Bleak December's winds ... Baith snell an' keen* (Robert Burns).
—*adv.* quickly; smartly; severely.
[Old English *snell*]

**Snell's law** (snelz), *Optics.* a fundamental law of the refraction of light, which states that the ratio of the sine of the angle of incidence to the sine of the angle of refraction is a constant that is independent of the angle of incidence. This constant is known as the index of refraction. [< Willebrord *Snell* van Royen, 1591-1626, a Dutch mathematician, who formulated this law]

**snick**[1] (snik), *v., n.* —*v.t.* **1** to cut, snip, or nick. **2** to strike sharply. **3** to give (a cricket ball) a light glancing blow.
—*n.* **1** a small cut; nick. **2** *Cricket.* **a** a light glancing blow given to the ball by the batsman. **b** a ball so hit.

**snick**[2] (snik), *n., v.* —*n.* a slight sharp sound; click.
—*v.i.* to make a clicking sound: *And ye may hear a breech bolt snick where never a man is seen* (Rudyard Kipling).
—*v.t.* to cause to make a clicking sound: [*He*] *was snicking BBs off the blackboard* (New Yorker).
[perhaps imitative]

**snick-a-snee** (snik′ə snē′), *n.* **1** = snickersnee. **2** a fight with swords or heavy knives. [alteration of earlier *snick and snee, stick or snee* < Dutch *steken* to thrust, stick + *snijen* to cut]

**snick|er** (snik′ər), *n., v.* —*n.* a half-suppressed and often disrespectful laugh; sly or silly laugh; giggle: *a self-conscious snicker.*
—*v.i.* **1** to laugh in this way. **2** (of horses) to neigh.
—*v.t.* to utter with a snicker. Also, **snigger.** [probably imitative] —**snick′er|er,** *n.* —**snick′er|ing|ly,** *adv.*

**snick|er|snee** (snik′ər snē′), *n.* a short sword or heavy knife: *As I gnashed my teeth, When from its sheath I drew my snickersnee* (W. S. Gilbert). [alteration of earlier *stick or snee;* see etym. under **snick-a-snee**]

**snick|er|y** (snik′ər ē), *adj.* characterized by snickers; snickering: *snickery laughter, snickery jokes.*

**snide** (snīd), *adj., n.* —*adj.* **1** mean or spiteful in a sly way; slyly insinuating; derogatory: *a snide remark.* **SYN:** disparaging. **2** dishonest: *a snide trickster.*
—*n.* **1** a dishonest person; cheat. **2** something done dishonestly. **3** a counterfeit; sham.
[origin uncertain] —**snide′ly,** *adv.*

**snid|er|y** (snī′də rē), *n., pl.* **-er|ies.** **1** snide quality or character. **2** a snide remark: *... those sardonic snideries which come too readily to one's lips* (Kenneth Allsop).

**sniff** (snif), *v., n.* —*v.i.* **1** to draw air through the nose in short, quick breaths that can be heard: *The man who had a cold was sniffing.* **2** to smell with sniffs: *The dog sniffed suspiciously at the stranger.* **3** to show or express contempt or scorn by sniffing.
—*v.t.* **1** to try the smell of; test by sniffing: *I sniffed the medicine before taking a spoonful of it.* **2** to draw in through the nose with the breath: *He sniffed steam to clear his head.* **3** *Figurative.* to suspect; detect: *to sniff danger. The police sniffed a plot and broke up the meeting.*
—*n.* **1** the act or sound of sniffing: *He cleared his nose with a loud sniff.* **2** a single breathing in of something; breath. **3** a smell; odor.
**sniff at,** to scorn; show contempt of by sniffing: *She sniffed at the present he gave her. Though this French aid can scarcely do much to carry the enormous burden of investment which the Alliance for Progress set itself, there is no need to sniff at it* (Manchester Guardian Weekly).
[see related etym. at **snivel**] —**sniff′er,** *n.*

**sniff|ish** (snif′ish), *adj.* = sniffy. —**sniff′ish|ly,** *adv.* —**sniff′ish|ness,** *n.*

**snif|fle** (snif′əl), *v.,* **-fled, -fling,** *n.* —*v.i.* **1** to sniff again and again as one does from a cold in the head: *The child stopped crying but kept on sniffling.* **2** to breathe audibly through a partly clogged nose.
—*n.* the act or sound of sniffling; loud sniff.
**the sniffles, a** a slight cold in the head; stuffy condition of the nose caused by a cold or hay fever: *The President ... has a slight case of the sniffles* (New York Times). **b** a fit of sniffling; tendency to sniffle: *He suffers from hay fever and is very prone to the sniffles.*
[apparently frequentative form of *sniff*] —**snif′fler,** *n.*

**sniff|y** (snif′ē), *adj.,* **sniff|i|er, sniff|i|est.** *Informal.* **1** inclined to sniff, especially in contempt, scorn, etc. **2** contemptuous; scornful; disdainful: *... whether the expression on Mr. Coolidge's face was his natural one or whether it was a shade more sniffy than usual* (New Yorker). **SYN:** supercilious. —**sniff′i|ly,** *adv.* —**sniff′i|ness,** *n.*

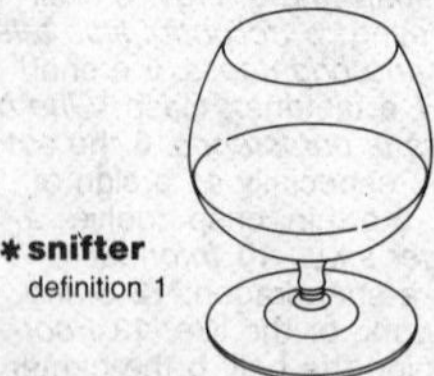

*** snifter**
definition 1

*** snif|ter** (snif′tər), *n.* **1** a stemmed glass for brandy or other aromatic alcoholic liquor, with a broad bottom and a narrow lip to prevent the aroma from escaping: *swirling his brandy around in a snifter* (New Yorker). **2** a small drink of alcoholic liquor. [apparently < dialectal *snift* to sniff]

**snig** (snig), *n. Dialect.* a young or small eel. [origin unknown]

**snig|ger** (snig′ər), *n., v.i., v.t.* = snicker. – **snig′-ger|er**, *n.*

**snig|ger|y** (snig′ər ē), *adj.* that sniggers; snickering: *Teachers everywhere seem to have kids as sniggery as those of Miss Barrett's* (Time).

**snig|gle** (snig′əl), *v.,* **-gled, -gling.** – ***v.i.*** to fish for eels by dropping a baited hook into their lurking place.
– ***v.t.*** to catch (eels) in this way.
[apparently related to **snig**]

**snip** (snip), *v.,* **snipped, snip|ping,** *n.* – ***v.t.*** **1** to cut with a small, quick stroke or series of strokes with scissors or something similar: *She snipped the thread. His mother was snipping dead leaves from the window plants* (Thomas Hardy). **2** *Figurative: The critics snipped the play into little pieces.*
– ***v.i.*** to make a cut or cuts with scissors or as if with scissors.
– ***n.*** **1** an act of snipping: *With a few snips she cut out a paper doll.* **2a** a small piece cut off: *Pick up the snips of thread from the floor.* **b** a small cut made by scissors. **3** any small piece; bit; fragment. **4** *Informal.* a small or unimportant person: *a snip of a girl.* **5** *British Slang.* a bargain. **6** a white or light mark, spot, or patch near the muzzle of a horse.
**snips, a** hand shears for cutting metal: *Hand shears ... are often called snips, to distinguish them from bench shears* ((Holtzapffel and Holtzapffel). **b** *Slang.* handcuffs: *The accused did not offer to go quietly till the police had the "snips" on him* (Newcastle Evening Chronicle).
[compare Low German *snippen*] – **snip′per,** *n.*

**snipe** (snīp), *n., pl.* **snipes** or (*collectively for 1 and 2*) **snipe,** *v.,* **sniped, snip|ing.** – ***n.*** **1** a marsh bird with a long bill, frequently hunted as game. Snipes are related to the sandpipers. The common or whole snipe of Europe and the American or Wilson's snipe are two kinds of snipe. **2** any one of certain similar shore birds, such as the jacksnipe of Europe and the dowitcher. **3** a shot made by or as if by a sniper. **4** *U.S. Slang.* a cigarette or cigar butt.
– ***v.i.*** **1** to shoot from a hidden place at an enemy one at a time, usually at long range. **2** to hunt snipe.
– ***v.t.*** to shoot at (soldiers) one at a time as a sportsman shoots at game; shoot from a concealed place.
**snipe at,** to attack suddenly or unexpectedly, especially by words: *In a series of barbed "Sunday speeches" he sniped at the ill-starred plan to "internationalize" the industrially opulent Saar border enclave* (Newsweek).
[< Scandinavian (compare Old Icelandic *snīpa*)]

**Snipe** (snīp), *n.* a popular type of racing sailboat that is about 15½ feet long and has a Marconi rig and movable keel. [< *snipe*]

**snipe eel,** a slender, eellike, marine fish, up to 3 feet long, with a speckled, pale back, and blackish belly and anal fin.

**snipe fish, 1** any one of various fish having long, tubular snouts resembling a snipe's beak. **2** = snipe eel.

**snipe fly,** a two-winged fly with a long proboscis and long, thin legs; deer fly.

**snipe|hunt** (snīp′hunt′), *n. U.S.* a prank played on a person by inviting him to a desolate place to hunt snipe with a group, none of whom turns up to join him.

**snipe|hunt|er** (snīp′hun′tər), *n.* a person who hunts snipe.

**snip|er** (snī′pər), *n.* a hidden sharpshooter.

**snip|er|scope** (snī′pər skōp), *n. U.S.* a device using infrared rays that can be mounted on a rifle and used to spot targets at night. [< *sniper* + (tele)*scope*]

**snip|pers** (snip′ərs), *n.* a pair of shears or scissors shaped for short or small cuts.

**snip|per-snap|per** (snip′ər snap′ər), *n.* an insignificant fellow; whipper-snapper.

**snip|pet** (snip′it), *n.* **1** a small piece snipped off; bit; scrap; fragment: *That is a poor snippet of malicious gossip* (Robert Louis Stevenson). *A narrow band runs low around the hips; below this is a mere snippet of a flounced skirt* (New York Times). **2** *Informal.* a small or unimportant person: *Do you suppose these snippets would treat Alice the way they do if she could afford to entertain?* (Booth Tarkington). [< *snip* + *-et*]

**snip|pet|y** (snip′ə tē), *adj.* = scrappy.

**snip|py** (snip′ē), *adj.,* **-pi|er, -pi|est. 1** *Informal.* sharp; curt. **2** *Informal.* haughty; disdainful. **3** made up of scraps or fragments. – **snip′pi-ness,** *n.*

**snips** (snips), *n.pl.* See under **snip.**

**snip-snap** (snip′snap′), *n.* a smart remark or reply; sharp repartee. [varied reduplication of *snip*]

**snip|y** (snī′pē), *adj.* having a long, pointed nose like a snipe's bill; resembling a snipe.

**snit** (snit), *n. Slang.* a state or condition of unrest or excitement; dither: *It [the broadcast] sent the British into a snit, for the 16 member nations ... had agreed not to broadcast any "entertainment" during the initial tests* (Time). [origin uncertain]

**snitch¹** (snich), *v.t. Slang.* to snatch; steal: *They had snitched too many carrots from the big piles of vegetables that were strewn around there* (New Yorker). **SYN:** filch. [perhaps variant of *snatch*] – **snitch′er,** *n.*

**snitch²** (snich), *v., n. Slang.* – ***v.i.*** to be an informer; tell tales; peach: *He was afraid the younger boy would snitch about a burglary they perpetrated* (Tuscaloosa News).
– ***n.*** an informer.
[originally, nose; origin unknown] – **snitch′er,** *n.*

**sniv|el** (sniv′əl), *v.,* **-eled, -el|ing** or (*especially British*) **-elled, -el|ling,** *n.* – ***v.i.*** **1** to cry with sniffling; whimper. **2** to put on a show of grief; whine: *sniveling sentiment.* **3** to run at the nose; sniffle.
– ***n.*** **1** pretended grief or crying; whining. **2** running from the nose; sniffling.
**the snivels,** the sniffles: *to take nose drops for the snivels.*
[Middle English *snevelen,* related to Old English *snyflung,* verbal noun, and *snofl* mucus] – **sniv′-el|er,** *especially British,* **sniv′el|ler,** *n.*

**sniv|el|y** (sniv′ə lē), *adj.* **1** running at the nose; snotty. **2** whining; sniveling.

**snob** (snob), *n.* **1a** a person who cares too much for rank, wealth, position, and the like, and too little for real merit: *a man of a fine old family, brave and loyal, but a dreadful snob.* **b** a person who tries too hard to please those above him and ignores those below him. **2** a person who is contemptuous of the popular taste in some field and is attracted to esoteric or learned things for their own sake: *a literary snob.* **3** *Archaic.* a shoemaker or his apprentice. **4** *Obsolete.* one of the common people who were supposed to have no breeding. [origin uncertain]

**snob appeal,** appeal directed to snobbishness; attraction possessed by something because it is expensive, rare, superior, exotic, or otherwise exclusive: *The factor of snob appeal operates in the world of books, but not to the extent ... that it does in the other arts* (New York Times).

**snob|ber|y** (snob′ər ē, snob′rē), *n., pl.* **-ber|ies.** the character or conduct of a snob; snobbishness: *A potent source of snobbery is the conviction that you know all the answers* (Punch).

**snob|bish** (snob′ish), *adj.* of or like a snob; looking down on those in a lower position: *a snobbish person, a snobbish remark. Some writers, even American writers ... display a snobbish shame of something homespun about these makers of America* (H. G. Wells). – **snob′bish|ly,** *adv.* – **snob′bish|ness,** *n.*

**snob|bism** (snob′iz əm), *n.* the quality of being a snob; snobbery; snobbishness: *I have no prejudice against tourists—I consider that a low form of snobbism* (Katherine Anne Porter). *The crowds interpret his detachment as snobbism* (Newsweek).

**snob|by** (snob′ē), *adj.,* **-bi|er, -bi|est.** of or having to do with a snob; snobbish.

**Sno-cat** (snō′kat′), *n.* **1** *Trademark.* a tractor that can travel over deep, soft snow on its four broad caterpillar treads or on large balloon tires that distribute its weight over a large area: *The weather was mostly frightful, as Antarctic weather usually is ... the Sno-cats ... kept falling into treacherous crevasses* (Scientific American). **2 sno-cat,** any vehicle of this kind; snow-cat.

**snoek** (snük), *n.* an edible fish found off the coasts of Australia, South Africa, and South America, having a narrow body and small scales: *Old Cape Town just the same as ever. Malays and snoek fish everywhere* (R. S. Baden-Powell). [< Afrikaans *snoek* < Dutch]

**sno|fa|ri** (snō fär′ē), *n., pl.,* **-ris.** an expedition into a snow- or ice-covered area, usually in ski-doos: *Tourists are invited to take a 20-mile guided snofari for £15* (London Times). [< *sno*(w) + (sa)*fari*]

**snol|ly|gos|ter** (snol′ē gos′tər), *n. Slang.* an ambitious, boastful, talkative, unprincipled fellow: *We are not going to let the special interests and the snollygosters take over this country and run it as their private property* (Harry S Truman).

***snood** (snüd), *n., v.* – ***n.*** **1** a net or bag worn over a woman's hair. A snood may be part of a hat. **2** a baglike hat. **3** a band or ribbon formerly worn around the hair by young unmarried women in Scotland and northern England. **4** = dewbill.
– ***v.t.*** to bind (hair) with a snood.
[Old English *snōd*]

**snood|ed** (snü′did), *adj.* **1** wearing a snood. **2** bound with a snood.

**snook¹** (snük), *v., n.* – ***v.i.*** *Scottish.* to pry around.
– ***n.*** **cock a** (or **one's**) **snook,** *Especially British Slang.* to thumb one's nose: *One feels that if the need arose they would defy Washington and Moscow as dauntlessly as they have already cocked their snook at London* (Manchester Guardian).
[variant of Middle English *snoken* snuff about, smell, probably < a Scandinavian word (compare Norwegian dialectal *snōka*)]

**snook²** (snük), *n.* any one of a group of edible fishes, such as a robalo of the Atlantic with a long body, long lower jaw, and prominent lateral line. [< Dutch *snoek.* Compare etym. under **snoek.**]

**snook|er** (snůk′ər), *n., v.* – ***n.*** a variation of pool played with 15 red balls, each counting 1, and 6 of other colors, counting 2 to 7.
– ***v.t.*** **1** to block (a player) in snooker from shooting in a straight line at a ball. **2** *Especially British Informal.* to block; hinder: *At the long 15th she was almost snookered by a tree from her tee shot* (London Times).
[origin uncertain]

**snool** (snül), *Scottish.* – ***v.i.*** **1** to snivel. **2** to submit tamely. – ***v.t.*** to keep in subjection. [origin uncertain]

**snoop** (snüp), *v., n. Informal.* – ***v.i.*** to go about in a sneaking, prying way; pry; prowl: *The old lady snooped into everybody's business. He did not remain ... where he belonged, but snooped all over the island* (Sinclair Lewis).
– ***n.*** a person who snoops.
[American English (originally) take food on the sly < Dutch *snoepen* eat in secret] – **snoop′er,** *n.*

**snoop|er|scope** (snü′pər skōp), *n. U.S.* an infrared device used especially by soldiers in World War II to see the enemy in the dark.

**snoop|er|y** (snü′pər ē), *n.* the practice of snooping: *It is a scandalous state of affairs when the snoopery of private wiretapping becomes so well established* (Newsweek).

**snoop|y** (snü′pē), *adj.,* **snoop|i|er, snoop|i|est.** *Informal.* inclined to snoop; nosy; prying; snooping: *Dogs are faithful, watchful, quick, loud, and dependable, and, while undeniably snoopy, keep their secrets to themselves* (New Yorker).
– **snoop′i|ly,** *adv.* – **snoop′i|ness,** *n.*

**snoot** (snüt), *n., v. Slang.* – ***n.*** **1** the nose. **2** the face. **3** a grimace, especially one of contempt.
– ***v.t.*** to snub or treat with contempt: *Without meaning to snoot the poor old demoded ice tray, I must say that the basket full of pieces of ice, as easy to pick up as marbles, is quite a sight* (New Yorker).
[originally Scottish variant of *snout*]

**snoot|ful** (snüt′fůl), *n., pl.* **-fuls.** *U.S. Slang.* **1** a large portion of alcoholic beverage, usually sufficient to cause drunkenness: *It may be a foggy mind controlling careless hands and feet ... or the too relaxing effects of a snootful* (Birmingham News). **2** *Figurative: He took it out on me. The chrome was rusty, I drove too slow, ...—nag, nag, nag. I finally got a snootful* (S. J. Perelman).

**snoot|y** (snü′tē), *adj.,* **snoot|i|er, snoot|i|est.** *Informal.* snobbish; conceited. – **snoot′i|ly,** *adv.* – **snoot′i|ness,** *n.*

**snooze** (snüz), *v.,* **snoozed, snooz|ing,** *n. Informal.* – ***v.i.*** to take a nap; sleep; doze: *The dog snoozed on the porch in the sun. ... solemn, whiskered gentlemen snoozing in deep black-leather armchairs under copies of "The Times"* (Atlantic).
– ***n.*** a nap; doze.
[origin uncertain] – **snooz′er,** *n.*

***snood** definition 1

**snoo|zle** (snü′zəl), *v.t.,* **-zled, -zling.** to nestle; snuggle: *A dog ... snoozled its nose overforwardly into her face* (Emily Brontë).

**Snopes** (snōps), *n., pl.* **Snopes|es.** *U.S.* an unscrupulous type of businessman or politician. [<

**Pronunciation Key:** hat, āge, cãre, fär; let, ēqual, tėrm; it, īce; hot, ōpen, ôrder; **oi**l, **ou**t; cup, pu̇t, rüle; **ch**ild; lo**ng**; **th**in; **ᴛʜ**en; **zh**, measure; **ə** represents **a** in about, **e** in taken, **i** in pencil, **o** in lemon, **u** in circus.

*Snopes,* the name of a family of such types in the novels of William Faulkner]

**Snopes|i|an** (snōp′sē ən), *adj.* characteristic of a Snopes; mean; unscrupulous: *Dehumanized by his property ... he is congenitally and irredeemably ... Snopesian* (Marshall Frady).

**snore** (snôr, snōr), *v.,* **snored, snor|ing,** *n.* —*v.i.* to breathe during sleep with a harsh, rough sound: *The child with a cold in his nose snored all night.*
—*v.t.* to pass in sleeping, especially while snoring: *The man snored away the afternoon.*
—*n.* the sound made in snoring.
[Middle English *snoren;* perhaps imitative]
—**snor′er,** *n.*

∗**snor|kel** (snôr′kəl), *n., v.* —*n.* **1** a shaft for taking in air and discharging gases, which allows submarines to remain under water for a very long period of time. It is like a periscope in shape. **2** a curved tube often attached to a face mask which enables swimmers to breathe under water while swimming near the surface: *They prepared to submerge, some with tanks strapped on their backs, and others equipped, less heavily, with a snorkel* (New Yorker).
—*v.i.* to travel or swim under water using a snorkel: *Reportedly, the scent of a snorkeling sub can be picked up several miles away and ... for as long as one hour after the sub has glided by under water* (Newsweek).
[< German navy slang *Schnorchel* nose (compare German *schnarchen* snore) (because the *snorkel* is the nose of the submarine, and because the intake valve produces a snoring sound)] —**snor′kel|er,** *n.*

∗**snorkel**
definition 2

**snor|kle** (snôr′kəl), *n., v.i.,* **-kled, -kling.** = snorkel. —**snor′kler,** *n.*

**snort** (snôrt), *v., n.* —*v.i.* **1** to force the breath violently through the nose with a loud, harsh sound: *The horse snorted.* **2** to make a sound like this: *The engine snorted.* **3a** to show contempt, defiance, anger, or other feeling by snorting. **b** to laugh loudly or roughly in contempt. **4** *U.S. Slang.* to snuff or inhale a narcotic: *There are "shooting galleries" where men can snort or mainline in comfort* (Time).
—*v.t.* **1** to say or express with a snort: *"Nonsense!" snorted the old man.* **2** to force out by, or as if by, snorting. **3** *U.S. Slang.* to snuff or inhale (a narcotic): *to snort powdered heroin.*
—*n.* **1** an act of snorting. **2** the sound made by snorting: *a loud snort of contempt.* **3** *Slang.* a drink (of liquor), especially one taken in a gulp: *a snort of whiskey.*
[perhaps < Low German *snorten*] —**snort′er,** *n.*

**snot** (snot), *n.* **1** *Vulgar or Dialect.* nasal mucus. **2** *Slang.* a snotty person or remark. [Middle English *snotte,* probably Old English *gesnot*]

**snot|ter** (snot′ər), *n. Nautical.* **1** a rope attached to a yardarm, to pull off the lift and brace. **2** a becket on a mast to hold the lower end of a sprit. [origin unknown]

**snot|ty** (snot′ē), *adj.,* **-ti|er, -ti|est,** *n., pl.* **-ties.** —*adj.* **1** *Informal.* saucy; impudent; conceited; snooty: *a snotty remark.* **2** *Vulgar or Dialect.* foul with snot.
—*n. British Slang.* **1** *Nautical.* a midshipman. **2** any very small, insignificant person. —**snot′ti|ly,** *adv.* —**snot′ti|ness,** *n.*

**snot|ty-nosed** (snot′ē nōzd′), *adj. Informal.* snotty: *Let snotty-nosed fellows ... approve what I write, or let them flout and fleer* (John Selden).

**snout** (snout), *n., v.* —*n.* **1a** the part of an animal's head that extends forward and contains the nose, mouth, and jaws. Pigs, dogs, and crocodiles have snouts. **b** a similar projection in certain insects; rostrum. **2** anything like an animal's snout, such as a nozzle. **3** *Informal.* **a** a large or ugly nose. **b** any nose.
—*v.t., v.i.* to root with, or as if with, the snout: *They snout the bushes and stones aside* (Rudyard Kipling).
[Middle English *snoute;* origin uncertain]

**snout beetle,** any one of a large family of small beetles that have the head prolonged to form a snout; weevil.

**snout butterfly,** any one of a small group of butterflies having long, beaklike mouthparts.

**snout|ed** (snou′tid), *adj.* having a snout: *A group of snouted, slit-eyed, sinister, and yet beautifully modelled Crusaders' helmets ...* (New Yorker).

**snout|y** (snou′tē), *adj.,* **snout|i|er, snout|i|est.** **1** resembling a snout or muzzle; having a pronounced or prominent snout: *The nose was ugly, long and big, Broad and snouty like a pig* (Thomas Otway). **2** overbearing; insolent; snooty: *Her manner was perfectly snouty* (London Times).

**snow** (snō), *n., v.* —*n.* **1** frozen water vapor in the form of crystals that fall to earth in soft, white flakes and usually spread upon it as a white layer. Snow falls in winter. *To watch his woods fill up with snow* (Robert Frost). **2** a fall of snow: *There was a heavy snow early in December.* **3** *Archaic.* pure whiteness. **4** something resembling or suggesting snow, such as the white hair of old age. **5** *Chemistry.* any one of various substances having a snowlike appearance: *carbon-dioxide snow.* **6** a pattern of dots on a television screen caused by atmospheric interference with the signal. **7** *Slang.* cocaine or heroin.
—*v.i.* **1** to fall as snow: *to snow all day.* **2** to come down like snow.
—*v.t.* **1** to let fall or scatter as snow. **2** to cover, block up, or otherwise obscure or obstruct, with snow, or as if with snow. **3** *U.S. Slang.* to deceive by artful talk.
**snow in,** to shut in by snow: *The mountain village was snowed in for a whole week after the blizzard.*
**snow under, a** to cover with snow: *The sidewalks and streets were snowed under by the storm.* **b** *Informal, Figurative.* to overwhelm: *He is snowed under with work. By margins of more than 3-1, Parliament snowed under motions of nonconfidence* (Wall Street Journal).
[Old English *snāw*] —**snow′like′,** *adj.*

**snow apple,** a red winter apple with very white flesh; Fameuse.

**snow|ball** (snō′bôl′), *n., v.* —*n.* **1** a ball made of snow pressed together. **2** a shrub with white flowers in large clusters like balls, especially the guelder-rose. It is a species of viburnum and belongs to the honeysuckle family.
—*v.t.* to throw balls of snow at: *The children snowballed each other.*
—*v.i.* **1** to increase rapidly by additions like a rolling snowball: *The number of signers of the petition for a new school snowballed. African nationalism and the drive for self-government are snowballing* (Atlantic). **2** to throw snowballs.

**snow|bank** (snō′bangk′), *n.* a large mass or drift of snow, especially at the side of a road.

**snow|bell** (snō′bel′), *n.* any one of a group of shrubs or small trees grown for their white flowers; storax.

**snow|belt** (snō′belt′), *n.* a region of heavy snowfall.

**snow|ber|ry** (snō′ber′ē, -bər-), *n., pl.* **-ries.** **1** a North American shrub of the honeysuckle family, with pink flowers and clusters of white berries. Its berries mature in the fall and last through the winter. **2** the berry. **3** any one of various other plants with white berries. [American English]

**snow|bird** (snō′bėrd′), *n.* **1** = slate-colored junco. **2** = snow bunting. **3** *U.S. Slang.* a person addicted to the use of heroin or cocaine.

**snow-blind** (snō′blīnd′), *adj.* affected with snow blindness.

**snow blindness,** temporary or partial blindness caused by the reflection of sunlight from snow or ice.

**snow|blink** (snō′blingk′), *n.* the reflection that arises from fields of snow or ice.

**snow blower,** a machine to clear an area of snow usually by throwing the snow out of its path with paddles or a screw device that feeds snow into a fan.

**snow|bound** or **snow-bound** (snō′bound′), *adj.* shut in by snow; snowed in.

**snow|break** (snō′brāk′), *n.* **1** a melting of snow; thaw. **2** a rush of loose or melting snow. **3** a narrow strip of forest or other barrier as a protection against snow.

**snow-broth** (snō′brôth′, -broth′), *n.* melting or melted snow.

**snow bunny,** *U.S. Slang.* **1** a person who is learning to ski. **2** a girl skier.

**snow bunting,** a small, white finch with black and brownish markings, that lives in cold northern regions; snowbird; snowflake.

**snow|bush** (snō′bu̇sh′), *n.* any one of various shrubs bearing many white flowers.

**snow|cap** (snō′kap′), *n.* a cap or covering of snow, especially on a mountaintop.

**snow-capped** or **snow|capped** (snō′kapt′), *adj.* having its top covered with snow: *Lebanon's mountains, usually snow-capped all winter, are nearly bare today* (New York Times).

**snow-cat** (snō′kat′), *n.* = Sno-cat.

**snow-clad** (snō′klad′), *adj.* covered with snow.

**snow|craft** (snō′kraft′, -kräft′), *n.* a knowledge of the behavior of snow and the best methods of combating it, especially in mountaineering.

**snow|drift** (snō′drift′), *n.* **1** a mass or bank of snow piled up by the wind. **2** snow driven before the wind.

**snow|drop** (snō′drop′), *n.* **1** a small European plant with drooping white flowers that blooms early in the spring. It belongs to the amaryllis family. See picture under **amaryllis family. 2** its bulb or flower. **3** the common anemone. [American English]

**snow dust,** fine particles of snow raised from the ground by the wind.

**snow|fall** (snō′fôl′), *n.* **1** a fall of snow: *Our car got stuck in the snowfall last night.* **2** the amount of snow falling within a certain time and area: *The snowfall in that one storm was 16 inches.*

∗**snow fence,** a fence put up to break the force of the wind in snowstorms and to prevent the drifting of snow.

∗**snow fence**
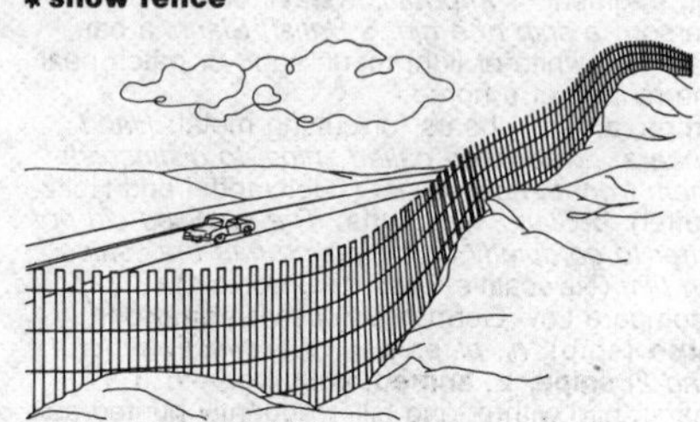

**snow|field** (snō′fēld′), *n.* a wide expanse of snow, especially in arctic regions.

**snow finch,** a sparrow of mountainous regions of southern Europe and Asia, resembling the snow bunting but having a brown back, gray head, and black chin.

**snow|flake** (snō′flāk′), *n.* **1** a small, feathery piece of snow. Snowflakes are crystals of frozen water vapor. **2** any one of a group of European plants of the amaryllis family, resembling the snowdrop but larger. **3** = snow bunting.

**snow flea,** any one of a group of adult springtails that often gather in great numbers on the surface of snow in early spring.

**snow fly, 1** a kind of stone fly which appears on the snow. **2** = snow flea.

**snow goose,** a white goose with black wing tips that nests in arctic regions and migrates to the southern United States in winter.

**snow|grass** (snō′gras′, -gräs′), *n.* a coarse, tall grass of New Zealand.

**snow gum,** a gum tree of Australia that grows on mountain ridges. Snow gums are often stunted by the effects of cold and wind and take on a distorted shape.

**snow|hole** (snō′hōl′), *n.* a deep hole dug in the snow by mountaineers for use as a temporary shelter.

**snow|house** (snō′hous′), *n.* a house built of snow; igloo.

**snow ice,** white, opaque ice formed by the freezing of slush.

**snow-in-sum|mer** (snō′in sum′ər), *n.* a perennial with white, tomentose stems, leaves, and calyx, grown in rock gardens and borders or found in the wild.

**snow job,** *U.S. Slang.* something designed to snow under or overwhelm a person or his efforts, especially a great deal of fast, persuasive talk: *You described* [*the*] *defense of his tax program as "sophisticated rhetoric." I call it a snow job* (Time).

**snowk** (snouk, snōk, snük), *v.i. Scottish.* snook[1].

**snow knife,** a knife of bone, formerly used by Eskimos for cutting blocks of snow in making igloos and for other purposes.

**snow leopard,** a wild cat of the mountains of central Asia; ounce. See picture under **leopard.**

**snow|less** (snō′lis), *adj.* free of snow: *Their houses were built with pitched roofs, rare in the snowless East* (Science News Letter).

**snow lily,** a yellow dogtooth violet of the Rocky Mountains.

**snow line 1** the line on mountains above which there is always snow. **2** the limit of distance from the equator beyond which snow never completely melts off.

**snow|mak|er** (snō′mā′kər), *n.* a snowmaking machine: *With enough piping, twelve nozzles, and suitable terrain, the snowmaker can produce an 8-in.-deep ski slope 250 ft. by 1,000 ft. overnight* (Time).

**snow|mak|ing** (snō′mā′king), *n., adj.* —*n.* the act or process of producing snow artificially, as by means of chemicals such as silver iodide or dry ice.
—*adj.* of or for producing snow artificially: *snowmaking systems.*
**snow|man** (snō′man′), *n., pl.* **-men.** a mass of snow made into a figure somewhat like that of a man.
**snow|melt** (snō′melt′), *n.* the water resulting from melted snow.
✱ **snow|mo|bile** (snō′mə bēl), *n.* a tractor or other vehicle for use in snow, some having skis or runners in front: *We took fifty men and ten snowmobiles, and in two months drove thirty-four hundred miles ... along the Arctic coast, and down the Alaska Highway to Edmonton* (New Yorker).

✱ **snowmobile**

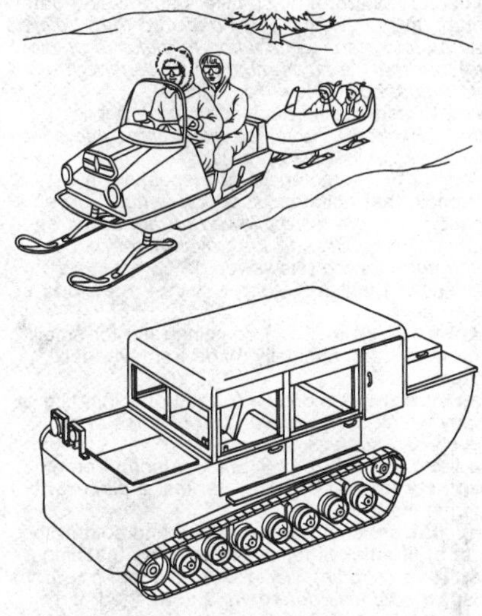

**snow|mo|bil|er** (snō′mə bē′lər), *n. U.S.* a person who drives a snowmobile, especially as a sport: *Snowmobilers have been accused of everything from terrorizing wildlife to vandalizing hunters' cabins* (Time).
**snow|mo|bil|ing** (snō′mə bē′ling), *n. U.S.* the act or sport of riding a snowmobile.
**snow mold, 1** a fungous growth that appears on wheat, rye, and other grasses in the late winter and early spring, especially under melting snow. **2** the disease caused by this growth.
**snow-on-the-moun|tain** (snō′on ᴛʜə moun′tən, -ôn-), *n.* a spurge of the western United States, having showy flowers with white bracts and leaves with white edges, often grown as an ornamental.
**snow owl,** = snowy owl.
**snow|pack** (snō′pak′), *n.* a large accumulation of snow, as on a mountainside.
**snow pea,** a variety of small, green pea in a tender pod, much used in Chinese cookery. Cooked snow peas are eaten together with the pods.
**snow pellets,** pellets of granular snow; soft hail.
**snow plant,** a bright-red saprophytic plant related to the shinleaf, that grows in high altitudes in the western United States, often appearing while snow is still on the ground.
**snow|plow** (snō′plou′), *n., v.* —*n.* **1** a machine for clearing away snow from streets, railroad tracks, and roads. It is often a broad, plowlike blade mounted on a truck or tractor. **2** *Skiing.* a double stem.
—*v.i.* **1** to clear streets with a snowplow. **2** *Skiing.* to execute a snowplow (double stem).
[American English < *snow* + *plow*]
**snow pudding,** a dessert made of beaten whites of eggs stiffened with gelatin or cornstarch, usually flavored with lemon.
**snow|scape** (snō′skāp′), *n.* a snow-covered landscape. [< *snow* + *-scape*]
**snow|shed** (snō′shed′), *n.* a long shed built over a railroad track to protect it from snowslides. [American English < *snow* + *shed*[1]]
✱ **snow|shoe** (snō′shü′), *n., v.,* **-shoed, -shoe|ing.** —*n.* a light, wooden frame with strips of leather stretched across it. Trappers, hunters, and others in the far North wear snowshoes on their feet to keep from sinking in deep, soft snow.
—*v.i.* to walk or travel on snowshoes.
[American English < *snow* + *shoe*]
**snowshoe hare,** a brownish hare of northern and mountainous areas of North America that turns white in winter; varying hare.
**snow|shoe|ing** (snō′shü′ing), *n.* travel on snowshoes.
**snow|sho|er** (snō′shü′ər), *n.* a person who walks or travels on snowshoes.
**snowshoe rabbit,** = snowshoe hare.
**snowshoe sickness,** a painful swelling of the feet occurring after long journeys on snowshoes.
**snow|slide** (snō′slīd′), *n.* **1** the sliding down of a mass of snow on a steep slope. **2** the mass of snow that slides. [American English < *snow* + *slide*]
**snow|slip** (snō′slip′), *n.* = snowslide.
**snow|storm** (snō′stôrm′), *n.* a storm with much snow. [American English < *snow* + *storm*]
**snow|suit** (snō′süt′), *n.* a warm, winter coat and leggings for a child: *Everybody's hollering for snowsuits and ski pants* (Wall Street Journal).
**snow|swept** (snō′swept′), *adj.* strewn or covered with blowing snow: *the snowswept plains of below-zero Alberta* (Time).
**snow tire,** an automobile tire with heavy treads to give extra traction on surfaces made slippery by snow or ice: *City council made it law today that—snow or no snow—drivers must have snow tires or chains on their vehicles from Jan. 1 to April 1 each year* (Montreal Star).
**snow train,** *U.S.* a ski train or similar train going to a winter resort.
**snow-white** (snō′hwīt′), *adj.* white as snow.
**snow|y** (snō′ē), *adj.,* **snow|i|er, snow|i|est.**
**1** having snow: *a snowy day.* **2** covered with snow: *a snowy roof.* **3** like snow; white as snow: *The old lady has snowy hair.* **4** having a blurred and dotted pattern: *The TV picture is snowy.*
—**snow′i|ly,** *adv.* —**snow′i|ness,** *n.*
**snowy egret,** a white heron or egret of temperate and tropical America with black legs and yellow feet.
**snowy owl,** a large owl of arctic and northern regions of both hemispheres, having white plumage usually with dusky markings; arctic owl.
**snowy plover,** a small white and light-brown plover of the western and southern United States and South America.
**SNP** (no periods) or **S.N.P.,** Scottish National Party.
**snub** (snub), *v.,* **snubbed, snub|bing,** *n., adj.*
—*v.t.* **1a** to treat coldly, scornfully, or with contempt: *The unfriendly woman snubbed her neighbors by refusing to speak to them.* **b** to rebuke or reprove in a sharp or cutting manner. **c** to treat this way in order to force a result: *to snub a person into silence.* **2** to check or stop (as a boat or horse) suddenly. **3** to check or stop (a rope or cable running out) suddenly.
—*n.* **1** cold, scornful, or disdainful treatment; affront: *Anatole France was a man of superior abilities who had taken some disagreeable snubs* (Edmund Wilson). **2** a sharp rebuke. **3** a sudden check or stop.
—*adj.* short and turned up at the tip: *a snub nose.*
[< Scandinavian (compare Old Icelandic *snubba,* snub, reprove, and *snubbōttr* stumpy, cutoff)]
**snub|ber** (snub′ər), *n.* **1** a person who snubs. **2** a device for snubbing a rope or cable. **3** an early type of automobile shock absorber.
**snub|by** (snub′ē), *adj.,* **-bi|er, -bi|est. 1** short and turned up at the tip; snub: *a snubby nose.* **2** short and thick; stubby: *a snubby pencil point.* —**snub′bi|ness,** *n.*
**snub-nosed** (snub′nōzd′), *adj.* having a snub nose; pug-nosed.
**snuck** (snuk), *v. Informal.* sneaked; a past tense and past participle of **sneak**: *The presidents of Smith and Vassar promptly snuck across the border* (Newsweek).

✱ **snowshoe**

**snudge** (snuj), *v.i.,* **snudged, snudg|ing.** *Dialect.* **1** to walk in a stooping or meditative attitude. **2** to remain snug and quiet; nestle. [origin uncertain]
**snuff**[1] (snuf), *v., n.* —*v.t.* **1** to draw in through the nose; draw up into the nose: *He snuffs up steam to relieve a cold.* **2** to smell at; examine by smelling: *The dog snuffed the track of the fox.* **SYN:** scent.
—*v.i.* **1** to draw air or other vapor up or in through the nose: (*Figurative.*) *The adventurer snuffed at the sweet smell of danger, inhaling it with excitement.* **2** to sniff, especially curiously as a dog would: *the dog snuffed at the tracks of the fox.* **3** to take powdered tobacco into the nose by snuffing; use snuff. **4** *Obsolete.* to express scorn, disdain, or contempt by snuffing.
—*n.* **1a** powdered tobacco, often scented, taken into the nose, chewed, or placed against the gums to be sucked. **b** a pinch of this, taken at one time. **2** the act of snuffing. **3** a smell; odor; scent.
**up to snuff, a** *Informal.* in good order or condition; as good as expected: *The performance was not up to snuff.* **b** *Slang.* not easily deceived: *You American ladies are so up to snuff, as you say* (William D. Howells).
[< earlier Flemish *snuffen*]
**snuff**[2] (snuf), *v., n.* —*v.t.* **1** to put out (a candle or other light); extinguish: *We snuffed the lights and went to bed.* **2** to cut or pinch off the burned wick of (a candle).
—*n.* **1** the burned part of a candlewick. **2** anything that is faint, feeble, or of no value.
**snuff it,** *Especially British Slang.* to die: *Josh Heckett isn't going to snuff it just for a crack on the head* (George R. Sims).
**snuff out, a** to put out; extinguish: *to snuff out the lights.* **b** *Figurative.* to put an end to suddenly and completely; wipe out: *The dictator snuffed out the people's hopes for freedom.*
[origin uncertain. Compare Middle Dutch *snuffen* blow the nose.]
**snuff bottle,** a bottle designed or used to contain snuff.
**snuff|box** (snuf′boks′), *n.* a very small box for holding snuff.
**snuff color,** a dark yellowish brown.
**snuff|col|ored** (snuf′kul′ərd), *adj.* dark yellowish-brown.
**snuff|er**[1] (snuf′ər), *n.* a person who snuffs, especially in disdain.
✱ **snuff|er**[2] (snuf′ər), *n.* **1** a person who snuffs (a light). **2a** = snuffers. **b** a small cup, often cone-shaped, with a long handle, used for putting out the light of a candle.
✱ **snuff|ers** (snuf′ərz), *n.pl.* small tongs for taking off burned wick or putting out the light of a candle.

✱ **snuffer**[2]
definition 2b

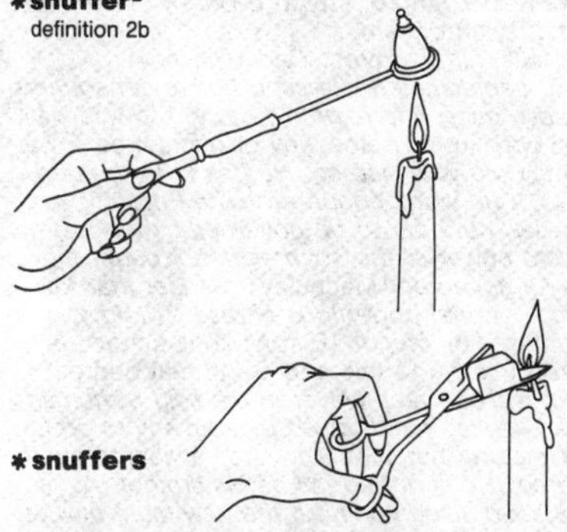

✱ **snuffers**

**snuf|fle** (snuf′əl), *v.,* **-fled, -fling,** *n.* —*v.i.* **1** to breathe nosily through the nose like a person with a cold in the head. **2** to snuff or smell; sniff: *Throughout its halls four-footed things lumber and snuffle, scratch and lurk* (Atlantic). **3a** to speak or sing, through the nose or with a nasal tone. **b** to speak or act like a hypocrite.
—*n.* **1** the act or sound of snuffling: *With snuffle and sniff and handkerchief* (Rupert Brooke). **2** the nasal tone of voice of a person who snuffles: *With a hypocritical snuffle and a sly twinkle of his eye ...* (Scott). **3** whining hypocrisy; sanctimoniousness.
**the snuffles, a** a fit of snuffling; a cold in the head or a similar condition caused by hay fever: *First the Queen deserts us; then Princess Royal beings coughing; then Princess Augusta gets the snuffles* (Frances Burney). **b** a respiratory disease of animals: *swine afflicted with the snuffles.*
[probably < Dutch or Flemish *snuffelen*] —**snuf′fler,** *n.* —**snuf′fling|ly,** *adv.*
**snuff|y** (snuf′ē), *adj.,* **snuff|i|er, snuff|i|est. 1** like

**Pronunciation Key:** hat, āge, cãre, fär; let, ēqual, tėrm; it, īce; hot, ōpen, ôrder; **oi**l, **ou**t; cup, pu̇t, rüle; **ch**ild; lo**ng**; **th**in; ᴛʜen; **zh**, measure; ə represents **a** in about, **e** in taken, **i** in pencil, **o** in lemon, **u** in circus.

snuff. 2 soiled or stained with snuff. 3 having the habit of using snuff. 4 disagreeable; cross. **SYN**: cranky. —**snuff′i|ly**, *adv.* —**snuff′i|ness**, *n.*

**snug** (snug), *adj.*, **snug|ger, snug|gest**, *adv., v.*, **snugged, snug|ging**, *n.* —*adj.* 1 comfortable and warm; sheltered: *The cat has found a snug cover behind the stove. The children were nestled all snug in their beds* (Clement Clarke Moore). **2a** compact, neat, and trim: *The cabins on the boat are snug.* **b** well-built; seaworthy: *a snug ship.* 3 fitting closely: *That coat is a little too snug.* 4 small but sufficient: *A snug income enables him to live in comfort.* 5 hidden; concealed: *The fox lay snug until the hunters passed by.* 6 agreeable, especially because of the absence of unpleasant persons or things: *They did occasionally give snug dinners to three or four literary men at a time* (Washington Irving).
—***adv.*** in a snug manner.
—***v.t.*** 1 to make snug. 2 to make (a ship) ready for a storm.
—***v.i.*** to nestle; snuggle.
—***n.*** a barroom, especially in an inn.
[originally, trim, well prepared (of a ship) probably < Low German] —**snug′ly**, *adv.* —**snug′ness**, *n.*
—*Syn. adj.* 1 **Snug, cozy** mean comfortable. **Snug** emphasizes the comfort and security of a small space, warm and sheltered from the weather: *The young foxes were snug in their den.* **Cozy** emphasizes warmth, shelter, and ease, often affection or friendliness, making for comfort and contentment: *The lonely man looked through the window at the cozy family.*

**snug|ger|y** (snug′ər ē), *n., pl.* **-ger|ies.** a snug place, position, or room.

**snug|gle** (snug′əl), *v.*, **-gled, -gling**, *n.* —***v.i.*** to lie, press, or draw closely for warmth or comfort or from affection; nestle; cuddle: *to snuggle up in a chair, to snuggle down in bed.* **SYN**: nuzzle.
—***v.t.*** 1 to draw or press closely to for warmth or comfort or from affection. 2 to draw closely.
—***n.*** an act of snuggling.
[< *snug*, verb + *-le*, frequentative]

**snuz|zle** (snuz′əl), *v.i.*, **-zled, -zling.** *Dialect.* to thrust the nose against; rub closely with the nose; nuzzle.

**sny**[1] (snī), *n., pl.* **snies.** *U.S. and Canada.* a river channel. [American English; apparently < French (colonial America) *chenail*, variant of *chenal* channel]

**sny**[2] (snī), *n.* the upward curve of the planking at the bow or stern of a ship. [perhaps < Scandinavian (compare Old Icelandic *snúa*)]

**sny**[3] (snī), *v.i.*, **snied, sny|ing.** *British Dialect.* to abound; swarm; teem.

**snye** (snī), *n., pl.* **snyes.** *Canadian.* sny[1].

**so**[1] (sō; *sometimes unstressed before consonants* sə), *adv., conj., interj., pron.* —***adv.*** 1 in this way; in that way; in the same way or degree; as shown: *Hold your pen so. He has to be treated just so or he won't cooperate. The English people ... will not bear to be governed by the unchecked power of the sovereign, nor ought they to be so governed* (Macaulay). *Sadder than owl songs ... is that portentous phrase, "I told you so," uttered by friends* (Byron). 2 as stated: *Is that really so?* 3 to this degree; to that degree: *Do not walk so fast. Never in the field of human conflict was so much owed by so many to so few* (Sir Winston Churchill). 4 in such a way; to such a degree: *He is not so tall as his brother. As in the arts, so also in politics, the new must always prevail over the old* (Benjamin Jowett). 5 very: *You are so kind.* 6 very much: *My head aches so!* 7 for this reason; for that reason; accordingly; therefore: *The dog was hungry; so we fed it. We leave at daybreak for Pekin, so I will wish you goodbye now* (Guy Boothby). 8 likewise; also: *She likes dogs; so does he.*
—***conj.*** 1 with the result that; in order that: *Go away so I can rest.* 2 with the purpose or intention that: *I did the work so you would not need to.* 3 on the condition that; if: *So it be done, I care not who does it.*
—***interj.*** 1 well!: *So! Late again!* 2 let it be that way! all right!: *The train is late! So!* 3 is that true?
—***pron.*** 1 the same: *A miser usually remains so.* 2 whatever has been or is going to be said; this; that.

**and so, a** likewise; also: *She is here and so is he. So it is, and so it will be* (Edna St. Vincent Millay). **b** accordingly: *I said I would go, and so I shall. The bill was signed by the President and so became a law.*

**and so forth.** See under **forth.**

**and so on,** and more of the same; et cetera: *Surrounded by cumbersome furniture, assorted mementos, an ancestral portrait, and so on, he is left literally and figuratively boxed in* (Robert Mazzocco).

**in so far.** See under **insofar.**

**or so,** more or less; approximately that: *a pound or so, a day or so ago. It cost a dollar or so.*

**so as (to),** in order (to); with the result or purpose: *to run so as to escape capture. He goes to bed early so as to get plenty of sleep.*

**so be it.** See under **be.**

**so far, a** to this or that point: *I can walk with you just so far.* **b** until now or then: *There's a lot of fever about, but I've only had one dose, and E. Wilson has so far escaped altogether* (Graham Greene).

**so far as,** to the extent that: *So far as you broke the rules, you will be punished.*

**so far so good,** up to this time all is well: *Concerning the weather, so far so good but it may rain this afternoon.*

**so much.** See under **much.**

**so that, a** with the result or consequence that: *He studies hard so that he will get high marks.* **b** with the purpose that: *These measures were taken so that he might escape.* **c** provided that; if: *To M. it was ... indifferent who was found guilty, so that he could recover his money* (Maria Edgeworth).

**so what?,** *Informal.* what about it? what difference does it make?: *So they lost the first inning; so what?*

[Old English *swā*]

▶ In comparison, **so ... as** is often used instead of **as ... as** after a negative: *It's not so large as the other. It's as large as the other.* Even in literary English, however, *as* frequently occurs in sentences of the first type, and in the spoken language it predominates.

**so**[2] (sō), *n.* the fifth tone of the musical scale; sol. [variant of *sol*[1]; see etym under **gamut**]

**s.o.,** seller's option.

**So.,** 1 South. 2 Southern.

**S.O.,** 1 Special Order or Special Orders. 2 Staff Officer.

**soak** (sōk), *v., n.* —***v.i.*** 1 to become very wet; remain until wet clear through: *The clothes soaked all night before she washed them* **2a** to make its way; enter; go: *Water will soak through the soil.* **b** *Figurative: The magnitude of the problem finally soaked into their minds.* **SYN**: penetrate. 3 *Informal.* to drink heavily: *You do nothing but soak with the guests all day long* (Oliver Goldsmith). —***v.t.*** 1 to let remain in water or other liquid until wet clear through: *Soak the clothes all night before you wash them.* 2 to make very wet; wet through: *The rain soaked my clothes. It rained very hard all day; I was thoroughly soaked* (Benjamin Franklin). **SYN**: See syn. under **wet.** **3a** to take in by absorption; suck: *The sponge soaked in the water.* **b** *U.S. Slang.* to draw or suck (out): *to soak out a stain.* 4 *U.S. Slang.* to punish severely; strike hard. 5 *Informal.* to make pay too much; charge or tax heavily: *He admitted he had been soaked in the deal.* 6 to drink too much.
—***n.*** 1 the act or process of soaking: *Give the clothes a long soak.* 2 the state of being soaked. 3 the liquid in which anything is soaked. 4 *Slang.* a heavy drinker; sot. 5 (in Australia) **a** a depression in the ground which holds water, especially after rain. **b** any temporary marsh or swampy spot.

**in soak,** *Slang.* in pawn: *to put one's rings in soak.*

**soak up, a** to take up; suck up; absorb: *to soak up sunshine. The towel soaked up the water.* **b** *Figurative: to soak up knowledge. Though they soaked up a basic vocabulary of about 1,500 words, they found it an exhausting experience* (Maclean's).

[Old English *socian*] —**soak′er**, *n.* —**soak′ing|ly**, *adv.*

**soak|age** (sō′kij), *n.* 1 the act of soaking. 2 the condition of being soaked. 3 the liquid which has filtered or oozed up; seepage. 4 the liquid soaked up; moisture absorbed.

**soak|a|way** (sōk′ə wā′), *n. British.* a place through which water soaks or drains away, as a cesspool.

**soak|ing pit** (sō′king), a furnace where steel ingots are put to give them an even temperature before rolling.

**so-and-so** (sō′ən sō′), *n., pl.* **-sos.** some person or thing not named: *I can't stand that old so-and-so. The president ... remarked that it would be a fine gift for so-and-so* (Time).

**soap** (sōp), *n., v.* —***n.*** 1 a substance used for washing, usually made of a fat and lye: *It's hard to hold a wet bar of soap because it's so slippery.* 2 *Chemistry.* any metallic salt of an acid derived from a fat. 3 *U.S. Slang.* money, especially money for bribery. 4 = soap opera: *Strangely, none of the catastrophes on soaps—and nearly every soap event is a catastrophe—are set up with much sentiment* (New Yorker).
—***v.t.*** to rub with soap: *to soap one's face. Soap the dirty shirts well.*

**no soap,** *U.S. Slang.* **a** no; nothing doing: *He wanted me to lend him another two dollars, but I told him "no soap."* **b** no results; nothing accomplished: *The chief negotiator summed up the meeting by saying "no soap."*

[Old English *sāpe*]

**soap|bark** (sōp′bärk′), *n.* 1 a bark that can be used like soap, especially that of a tree of Chile. 2 Also, **soapbark tree.** any tree or shrub bearing this bark, as a Chilean tree of the rose family or some tropical American shrubs of the pea family.

**soap|ber|ry** (sōp′ber′ē, -bər-), *n., pl.* **-ries.** 1 a fruit or nut that can be used like soap. 2 Also, **soapberry tree.** any of the tropical or subtropical trees bearing such fruit, such as the chinaberry.

**soapberry family,** a group of tropical, dicotyledonous trees and shrubs, with mostly alternate, pinnate leaves and small, odorless flowers. The family includes the soapberry, litchi, balloon vine, and inkwood.

**soap|box** (sōp′boks′), *n., pl.* **-box|es**, *v., adj.* —***n.*** 1 a box, especially of wood, in which soap is or used to be packed. 2 an empty box used as a temporary platform by speakers addressing gatherings on the streets: *[He] declared that "religion has an important contribution to make to political life" but that "a pulpit must never degenerate into a soapbox"* (New York Times).
—***v.i.*** to address an audience on the public street: *Excitedly, he joined picket lines and soapboxed at bread lines* (Time).
—***adj.*** of or characteristic of a speaker on a soapbox; that agitates: *soapbox oratory. Here soapbox orators were allowed to rant about everything from politics to the government ban on betel-nut chewing* (Newsweek).
[American English < *soap* + *box*] —**soap′box′er**, *n.*

**soapbox derby,** *U.S.* a coasting race for small motorless cars, originally made from wooden soapboxes.

**soap bubble,** 1 a bubble formed of a thin film of soapy water. 2 *Figurative: The talk has been mere soap bubbles* (Emerson).

**soap|er** (sō′pər), *n. U.S. Slang.* a soap opera.

**soap|er|y** (sō′pər ē), *n., pl.* **-er|ies.** a place where soap is made.

**soap flakes,** soap manufactured and sold in the form of fine flakes for use in washing machines.

**soap|less** (sōp′lis), *adj.* 1 lacking soap; free from soap: *a soapless detergent.* 2 unwashed; dirty.

**soap|mak|er** (sōp′mā′kər), *n.* a soap manufacturer.

**soap|mak|ing** (sōp′mā′king), *n.* the manufacture of soap.

**soap opera,** *U.S.* a daytime radio or television drama presented in serial form, usually featuring emotional domestic situations.

**soap-op|er|at|ic** (sōp′op′ə rat′ik), *adj. U.S.* of or like a soap opera.

**soap pad,** a pad of steel wool with a filling of soap, used for scouring pots and pans, and for other things that are difficult to clean.

**soap plant,** any one of various plants, some part or parts of which can be used like soap.

**soap powder,** powdered soap and alkaline salts, used as a cleansing agent or detergent.

**soap|root** (sōp′rüt′, -rů t′), *n.* any one of certain European herbs of the pink family whose roots are used like soap.

**soap sculpture,** the art of carving figures from soap.

**soap|stone** (sōp′stōn′), *n.* a soft rock that feels somewhat like soap, used for laboratory tabletops, sinks, some chemical equipment, and also as an electric insulator; steatite. It is a kind of talc.

**soap|suds** (sōp′sudz′), *n.pl.* bubbles and foam made with soap and water; suds.

**soap|weed** (sōp′wēd′), *n.* any soap plant, especially a yucca whose roots and stems are used like soap.

**soap|wort** (sōp′wėrt′), *n.* any one of a genus of Old World herbs of the pink family, with white, rose, or pink flowers. Some species have leaves and roots containing a juice that can be used as soap.

**soap|y** (sō′pē), *adj.*, **soap|i|er, soap|i|est.** 1 covered with soap or soapsuds. 2 containing soap: *soapy water.* 3 of or like soap; smooth; greasy: *to feel soapy. The water has a soapy taste.* (*Figurative.*) *soapy manners.* 4 *Slang.* soap-operatic; sudsy: *a soapy melodrama.* —**soap′i|ly**, *adv.* —**soap′i|ness**, *n.*

**soar** (sôr, sōr), *v., n.* —***v.i.*** 1 to fly at a great height; fly upward: *to soar over the ocean. The hawk soared without flapping its wings.* **2a** to rise up to a great height; tower above that which is near: *a soaring skyscraper or mountain.* **b** to rise beyond what is common and ordinary: *Prices are soaring.* (*Figurative.*) *His hope soared when he heard that there were some survivors in the shipwreck.* **c** *Figurative.* to aspire: *soaring ambition. Life ... soars high above the skies* (Richard F. Burton). 3 to fly or move through the air by means of rising air currents. A glider can soar for many miles.

—*v.t.* **1** to reach in soaring. **2** to fly or move upward through.
—*n.* **1** the act of soaring. **2** the height attained in soaring.
[< Old French *essorer* < Vulgar Latin *exaurāre* < Latin *ex-* out + *aura* breeze] —**soar′er**, *n.*

**soar|ing** (sô′ring, sō′-), *n.* the sport of flying in a sailplane.

**soaring plane**, = sailplane.

**so|a|ve** (sō ä′vā), *adv., adj. Italian.* with sweetness or tenderness (used as a direction in music).

**So|a|ve** (sō ä′vā), *n.* an Italian dry white wine.

**So|ay** (sō′ā), *n.*, or **Soay sheep**, a wild sheep native to the island of Soay in the Outer Hebrides: *These apparently wild Soay sheep have bred on the island for centuries, virtually untended by man* (New Scientist).

**sob** (sob), *v.*, **sobbed, sob|bing,** *n., adj.* —*v.i.* **1** to cry or sigh with short, quick breaths: *sobbing and crying ... as if her heart would break* (Laurence Sterne). **2** to make a sound like a sob: *The wind sobbed in the trees.*
—*v.t.* **1** to put, send, or become, by sobbing: *She sobbed herself to sleep.* **2** to utter with sobs: *"I have lost my penny," the child sobbed. She sobbed out her sad story.*
—*n.* **1** the act of catching short, quick breaths because of grief or some other emotion; act of sobbing. **2** the sound of sobbing or a sound like a sob: *The anchor came up with a sob* (Rudyard Kipling).
—*adj. U.S. Informal.* intended to arouse feelings of pity, sadness, or sympathy.
[Middle English *sobben;* perhaps ultimately imitative] —**sob′bing|ly**, *adv.*

**sob|by** (sob′ē), *adj.,* **-bi|er, -bi|est.** = soppy.

**so|be|it** (sō bē′it), *conj.* if it be so; provided that.

**so|ber** (sō′bər), *adj., v.* —*adj.* **1** not drunk: *Many accidents are caused by drivers who are not completely sober.* SYN: unintoxicated. **2a** temperate; moderate: *The minister led a sober, hard-working life.* **b** avoiding the use of alcoholic liquor altogether. **3** quiet; serious; solemn; dignified: *a sober expression, sober joy, as sober as a judge. He looked sober at the thought of missing the picnic.* SYN: See syn. under **grave**. **4** calm; sensible: *The judge's sober opinion was not influenced by prejudice or strong feeling. If we read Engel's letters of the nineties ... we get an old man's soberest effort to state his notion of the nature of things* (Edmund Wilson). **5** free from exaggeration or distortion: *sober facts.* **6** quiet in color; plain or simple; somber: *dressed in sober gray. The skies were ashen and sober* (Edgar Allan Poe).
—*v.t.* to make sober: *Seeing the car accident sobered us all.*
—*v.i.* to become sober: *The class sobered as the teacher came into the room.*
**sober down**, to make or become quiet, serious, or solemn: *At times ... solemn speeches sober down a dinner* (Oliver Wendell Holmes).
**sober up** (or **off**), to recover from too much alcoholic drink: *He will sober up after a nap.*
[< Old French *sobre,* learned borrowing from Latin *sōbrius*] —**so′ber|ly**, *adv.* —**so′ber|ness**, *n.*

**so|ber|ize** (sō′bə rīz), *v.t.,* **-ized, -iz|ing.** to make sober.

**so|ber-mind|ed** (sō′bər mīn′did), *adj.* having or showing a sober mind; self-controlled; sensible. SYN: reasonable. —**so′ber-mind′ed|ness**, *n.*

**so|ber|sid|ed** (sō′bər sī′did), *adj.* having or showing a serious disposition; serious; staid; sedate: *Since I had known them as sobersided and sensible fellows.* (Bulletin of Atomic Scientists). —**so′ber|sid′ed|ness**, *n.*

**so|ber|sides** (sō′bər sīdz′), *n., pl.* **-sides.** a sedate or serious person: *The movie is sure to give all but the sobersides in the audience some pleasant moments* (Newsweek).

**So|bran|je** or **So|bran|ye** (sō brän′ye), *n.* the national assembly of Bulgaria, consisting of a single chamber of elected deputies. [< Bulgarian *sŭbranie* (literally) assembly]

**so|bri|e|ty** (sə brī′ə tē), *n., pl.* **-ties. 1** soberness. **2a** temperance in the use of strong drink. SYN: abstemiousness. **b** avoidance of alcoholic beverages. SYN: abstinence. **3** = moderation. **4** quietness; seriousness. SYN: sedateness. [< Old French *sobriete,* learned borrowing from Latin *sōbrietās, -ātis* < *sōbrius;* see etym. under **sober**]

**so|bri|quet** (sō′brə kā), *n.* a nickname: *Because of his daring, energetic research methods, he acquired, and still wears, the sobriquet "Wild Bill"* (Time). Also, **soubriquet**. [< Middle French *sobriquet*]

**sob sister**, *U.S. Informal.* **1** a woman reporter who writes with undue sentiment, usually about stories of personal hardship: *The sob sisters of the sentimental magazines are familiar figures of fun, and I do not wish to join their ranks* (Sunday Times). **2** a person given to telling sob stories.

**sob story**, *U.S. Informal.* an overly sentimental story or pathetic account, especially of one's own hardship.

**soc.**, society.

**Soc.**, **1** Socialist. **2** Society.

**soc|age** or **soc|cage** (sok′ij), *n.* a former way of holding land by which the tenant paid a definite rent or did a definite amount of work, but gave no military service to his lord. [< Anglo-French *socage* < *soc* < Medieval Latin *soca* < Old English *sōcn* jurisdiction, inquiry, (originally) a seeking, hostile visitation]

**soc|ag|er** or **soc|cag|er** (sok′ə jər), *n.* a person who held land by socage.

**so-called** (sō′kôld′), *adj.* **1** called so, but really not so; called so improperly or incorrectly: *Her so-called friend hasn't even written to her.* SYN: pseudo, pretended. **2** called thus.
► **so-called**. *So-called* is usually hyphenated when it precedes the word or phrase which it modifies, but not when it follows the latter: *Their so-called liberal views were merely an echo of the conservative attitude. Their justice, so called, smacked of partiality.*

***soc|cer** (sok′ər), *n.* a game played between two teams of eleven players each, using a round ball; association football. The ball may be struck with any part of the body except the hands and arms. Only the goalkeeper may touch the ball with the hands and arms. [short for *assoc.,* abbreviation of *association*]
► **soccer, football**. In American use, these terms are not synonymous and refer to two completely different games. In British use, *soccer* is usually called either "football" or "association football," while "Rugby" or "Rugby football" is the name for *football* as played in Great Britain.

***soccer**

**so|cia|bil|i|ty** (sō′shə bil′ə tē), *n., pl.* **-ties.** social disposition; friendly behavior. SYN: sociableness, sociality.

**so|cia|ble** (sō′shə bəl), *adj., n.* —*adj.* **1** liking company; friendly: *They are a sociable family and entertain a great deal. Man is said to be a sociable animal* (Joseph Addison). SYN: See syn. under **social**. **2** marked by conversation and companionship: *We had a sociable afternoon together.* **3** naturally inclined to be in company with others of the same species; social: *sociable animals or plants.*
—*n.* an informal social gathering: *You'll see her settled down one of these days, and teaching Sunday School and helping at sociables* (Sinclair Lewis).
[< Latin *sociābilis* < *sociāre* to associate < *socius;* see etym. under **social**] —**so′cia|ble|ness**, *n.*

**sociable weaverbird** or **grosbeak**, = republican grosbeak.

**so|cia|bly** (sō′shə blē), *adv.* in a sociable manner; conversably; familiarly.

**so|cial** (sō′shəl), *adj., n.* —*adj.* **1** concerned with human beings in their relations to each other: *social justice. A great social and economic experiment, noble in motive and far-reaching in purpose* (Herbert Hoover). *The social state is ... so natural, so necessary, and so habitual to man* (John Stuart Mill). **2** of or dealing with the living conditions, health, or other aspects of the lives of human beings: *social problems, social work.* **3** living or liking to live with others: *Man is a social being.* **4** for companionship or friendliness; having to do with companionship or friendliness: *a social engagement. Ten of us girls have formed a social club.* **5** liking company: *a social nature; ... his own friendly and social disposition* (Jane Austen). **6** connected with fashionable society: *The mayor's wife is the social leader in our town. Others avoid her company because she has no social grace.* **7a** living together in organized communities. Ants and bees are social insects. **b** growing in patches or clumps: *social plants.* **8** = socialistic.
—*n.* a social gathering or party: *a church social.*
[< Latin *sociālis* < *socius* companion; (originally, adjective) mutual, sharing in, related to *sequī* to follow] —**so′cial|ness**, *n.*
—*Syn. adj.* **4, 5 Social, sociable** mean friendly or companionable. In this sense, **social** is now rarely applied to persons and, when it is, suggests fondness for group association rather than personal friendliness: *A man may be social but not at all sociable.* **Sociable**, the term usually ascribed to persons, means liking company and being inclined to seek and enjoy companionship and friendly relations even with strangers: *He is a likable, sociable person.*

**social action**, **1** *Sociology.* the behavior of an individual in response to his subjective evaluation of the motives of others and the values and goals of the society in which he lives. **2** organized action taken by a group to improve social conditions.

**social anthropology**, the branch of anthropology that deals with the social customs, beliefs, and practices of man, especially in primitive and isolated societies.

**social climber**, a person who tries to gain acceptance or improve his standing in fashionable society by associating with people having more wealth or influence than he has.

**social climbing**, the actions or conduct of a social climber.

**social contract**, **1** an agreement to regulate the relations of citizens with one another and with government. **2** an understanding between government and labor unions of a country in which the unions agree to limit wage demands in return for legislation and fiscal planning to create conditions favorable to workers: *The relative labor peace has been achieved only because the Labor government's "social contract" with the all-powerful unions is still holding* (Wall Street Journal).

**social control**, **1** control of individual behavior by society. **2** control of social institutions in the interest of the whole society.

**social credit**, an economic philosophy that believes in industrial cooperatives in which the consumers share the profits of industry as dividends.

**Social Cred|i|ter** (kred′ə tər), a member of the Social Credit Party, a Canadian political party, founded in the 1930's, advocating social credit; Socred.

**social Darwinism**, the application of the Darwinian theory of evolution to the origin, growth, and development of human society: *Social Darwinism ... held that human races evolve like animal species and that the nonwhite races were at the bottom of the evolutionary scale* (Time).

**social democracy**, **1** the principles of any one of various political parties advocating a gradual transition to socialism by democratic processes. **2** = socialism.

**social democrat**, an advocate of social democracy.

**social democratic**, characterized by or founded on the principles of social democracy.

**social disease**, **1** = venereal disease. **2** any disease that is spread, or is believed to be spread, through direct contact between people, such as infectious mononucleosis.

**social engineer**, a specialist in social engineering.

**social engineering**, the application of the principles of the social sciences to practical social problems: *Colonial administration making use of sociological knowledge about [primitive] peoples is an illustration of social engineering* (Ogburn and Nimkoff).

**social evil**, **1** anything that is a danger to the welfare of people or opposed to the values of society: *Rat-infested slums and drunkenness are social evils.* **2** = prostitution.

**social gospel** or **Social Gospel**, an American Protestant movement of the early 1900's that sought to apply the Christian gospel to social problems and issues: *The problem in industrialization, with bitter conflicts between capital and labor ... led the churches into preaching the optimistic "Social Gospel" of the early 1900's* (Time).

**so|cial-gos|pel|er** (sō′shəl gos′pə lər), *n.* a follower or supporter of the social gospel.

**social insurance**, insurance of a person against unemployment or illness, through government action: *There are several types of social insurance, such as accident insurance or workman's compensation, sickness and old-age insurance, and unemployment insurance* (Emory S. Bogardus).

**Pronunciation Key:** hat, āge, cãre, fär; let, ēqual, tėrm; it, īce; hot, ōpen, ôrder; oil, out; cup, pu̇t, rüle; child; long; thin; ᴛʜen; zh, measure; ə represents **a** in about, **e** in taken, **i** in pencil, **o** in lemon, **u** in circus.

**so|cial|ism** (sō′shə liz əm), *n.* **1** a theory or system of social organization by which the major means of production and distribution are owned, managed, or controlled by the government (state socialism), by associations of workers (guild socialism), or by the community as a whole. **SYN**: collectivism. **2** a political movement advocating or associated with this system. **3** the practice of such a system.

▶ See **communism** for usage note.

**so|cial|ist** (sō′shə list), *n., adj.* —*n.* a person who favors or supports socialism.
—*adj.* = socialistic.

**So|cial|ist** (sō′shə list), *n., adj.* —*n.* a member of a Socialist Party.
—*adj.* of or having to do with a Socialist Party.

**so|cial|is|tic** (sō′shə lis′tik), *adj.* **1** of or having to do with socialism or socialists. **2** favoring or supporting socialism. —**so′cial|is′ti|cal|ly**, *adv.*

**Socialist Party**, a political party that favors and supports socialism.

**socialist realism**, **1** the official aesthetic doctrine of the Soviet Union maintaining that art, literature, and music are to foster development of a socialist society. **2** the style of art, literature, and music that follows this doctrine: *The slender young Soviet poet ... has reportedly emerged as the new leader in innovations that have sprung up outside the persistent dogmatic socialist realism of Stalinist poetry* (New Yorker).

**so|cial|ite** (sō′shə līt), *n.* **1** a member of the fashionable society of a community. **2** a person active in the social life of a community.

**so|ci|al|i|ty** (sō′shē al′ə tē), *n., pl.* **-ties. 1** social activity; social intercourse. **2** social nature or tendencies: *The congregating of people in cities and towns shows sociality.*

**so|cial|i|za|tion** (sō′shə lə zā′shən), *n.* **1** the act of socializing: *Socialization is a genuine and wholesome identification of a person with the welfare of other persons, of his own group and of other groups* (Emory S. Bogardus). **2** the condition of being socialized. **3** the act of placing or establishing something on a socialistic basis.

**so|cial|ize** (sō′shə līz), *v.,* **-ized, -iz|ing.** —*v.i.* to be social or sociable; enter social relationships with others: *He has never learned to socialize with his fellow workers.*
—*v.t.* **1** to establish or regulate in accordance with socialism: *to socialize transportation.* **2** to make social: *to socialize a discussion.* **3** to make fit for living with others; adapt to life as a social animal. **4** to adapt to community needs. —**so′cial|iz′er**, *n.*

**so|cial|ized medicine** (sō′shə līzd), the providing of medical care and hospital services for all persons, either free or at nominal cost, especially through government subsidization and administration.

**social ladder**, the levels of society, from lowest to highest: *As an aggressive climber, he rose rapidly on the social ladder.*

**so|cial|ly** (sō′shə lē), *adv.* **1** in a social way or manner; in relation to other people: *to be highly developed socially.* **2** as a member of society or of a social group: *He is an able man, but socially he is a failure.*

**so|cial-mind|ed** (sō′shəl mīn′did), *adj.* aware of and concerned with social problems and conditions: *In a Communist-riddled see, this active, social-minded cardinal is loved for his generosity and simplicity* (Newsweek). —**so′cial-mind′ed|ness**, *n.*

**social pathology**, **1** the study of the problems and ills of human society, such as poverty, unemployment, crime, and divorce, considered as analogous to bodily disease. **2** these problems and ills themselves.

**social pressure**, the force of a group on an individual to make him behave more like the members of the group.

**social psychiatrist**, a person who studies or is skilled in social psychiatry.

**social psychiatry**, the branch of psychiatry that deals with the social influences that cause mental disorders and with the application of psychiatry to social problems.

**social psychologist**, a person who studies or is skilled in social psychology.

**social psychology**, the branch of psychology concerned with human beings in their relations to each other.

**Social Realism**, an anti-Romantic movement in art and literature primarily concerned with depicting and commenting upon the social, economic, and political problems of the times. The novels of Upton Sinclair and the paintings of the Ashcan School are examples of American Social Realism.

**Social Realist**, a follower or supporter of Social Realism.

**social register**, a list of people who are prominent in fashionable society.

**social reg|is|ter|ite** (rej′ə stər īt), a person listed in the social register; socially prominent person.

**social science**, the study of people, their activities, their customs, and their institutions in relationship to others. History, sociology, anthropology, economics, geography, and civics are social sciences.

**social scientist**, a person skilled in one or more of the social sciences.

**social secretary**, a secretary who makes arrangements for and keeps track of the social activities of a person or group.

**social security**, **1** *U.S.* a system of Federal old-age pensions and medical care for retired persons and their dependents, begun in 1935. The program is financed by compulsory contributions from the government, the employee, and the employer. **2** any similar system in countries other than the United States.

**social service**, = social work.

**social settlement**, an establishment to improve conditions in a poor neighborhood; settlement house.

**social studies**, a course of study in elementary and high schools that includes history, civics, economics, anthropology, geography, and other related fields.

**social unit**, **1** a person or any grouping of people considered as a unit in social organization: *An individual and a family are two different kinds of social units.* **2** the group of residents in a given area of a community which is being redeveloped.

**social wasp**, any one of various wasps, including hornets and yellow jackets, that live together, usually in large paperlike nests.

**social welfare**, = social work.

**social work**, work directed toward the betterment of social conditions in a community. Child welfare bureaus, district nursing organizations, free medical clinics, family counseling services, and recreational activities for underprivileged children are forms of social work.

**social worker**, a person who does social work.

**so|ci|e|tal** (sə sī′ə təl), *adj.* of or having to do with society: *Many of the interrelated societal factors ... have gone into the making of our modern American culture* (Hugh M. Hefner). —**so|ci′e|tal|ly**, *adv.*

**so|ci|e|tar|i|an** (sə sī′ə tãr′ē ən), *adj.* = societal.

**so|ci|e|tar|y** (sə sī′ə ter′ē), *adj.* = societal.

**so|cié|té a|no|nyme** (sô syā tā′ à nô nēm′), a business firm in which the liability of each partner or member is limited to the amount of his investment. *Abbr:* S.A. [< French (literally) anonymous society; because originally the members were silent and anonymous]

**so|ci|e|ty** (sə sī′ə tē), *n., pl.* **-ties,** *adj.* —*n.* **1** a group of persons joined together for a common purpose or by a common interest. A club, a fraternity, a lodge, or an association may be called a society: *a debating society, a legal society.* *Abbr:* Soc. **2a** all the people; human beings living together as a group: *Society must work hard for world peace. The good of society demands that all wrongdoing be punished. Gun-control and drug-control laws are enacted for the good of society.* **b** the people of any particular time or place: *American society, twentieth-century society. No political society can be, nor subsist without having in itself the power to preserve the property ... of all those of that society* (John Locke). *A culture is the way of life of a people; while a society is the organized aggregate of individuals who follow a given way of life* (Melville J. Herskovits). **c** those people thought of as a group because of common economic position, similar interest or vocation, or other form of similarity in identification: *in cultivated society; the lower, middle, or upper classes of society.* **d** their activities and customs: *Magic plays an important part in primitive society.* **3** company; companionship: *I enjoy his society. The soul selects her own society, Then shuts the door* (Emily Dickinson). **4** fashionable people or their doings: *high society, the café society, to be excluded from society. Her mother is a leader of local society.* **SYN**: elite. **5a** an organized community of animals or insects: *a society of wasps.* **b** an assemblage of plants of the same species forming a unit in an ecological community. **6** *U.S.* the corporation in Congregational churches that administers the church property, employs the minister, and superintends other church business.
—*adj.* of, having to do with, or belonging to fashionable or socially prominent people: *society gossip, a society debutante. The wedding was social history rather than society-page fare* (Time).
[< Middle French *société* < Old French *societe*, learned borrowing from Latin *societās* < *socius;* see etym. under **social**]

**society column**, *U.S.* a newspaper column about socially prominent people.

**Society of Friends**, the Quakers.

**Society of Jesus**, a Roman Catholic religious order, founded by Saint Ignatius Loyola in 1534. Its members are called Jesuits. *Abbr:* S.J.

**society verse**, light, graceful poetry. [translation of French *vers de société*]

**So|cin|i|an** (sō sin′ē ən), *n., adj.* —*n.* a person who believes in Socinianism. —*adj.* having to do with Socinianism or its followers.

**So|cin|i|an|ism** (sō sin′ē ə niz′əm), *n.* the doctrines of Laelius Socinus and his nephew Faustus, Italian theologians of the 1500's. They denied the divinity of Christ.

**so|ci|o|bi|o|log|i|cal** (sō′sē ō bī′ə loj′ə kəl, -shē-), *adj.* **1** of, having to do with, or involving sociobiology. **2** = biosocial.

**so|ci|o|bi|ol|o|gy** (sō′sē ō bī ol′ə jē, -shē-), *n.* the study of the biological basis of social behavior in animals and man. Sociobiology deals with the basic principles and mechanisms of animal societies. —**so′ci|o|bi|ol′o|gist**, *n.*

**so|ci|o|cul|tur|al** (sō′sē ō kul′chər əl, -shē-), *adj.* of or having to do with both society and culture; social and cultural at the same time: *The question of development is being more and more often treated as a complex sociocultural change where economic development is only one result to be obtained* (Bulletin of Atomic Scientists).

**so|ci|o|dra|ma** (sō′sē ō drä′mə, -shē-; -dram′ə), *n.* the acting out of real-life situations by a group as a method of instruction or rehabilitation; role-playing.

**so|ci|o|e|co|nom|ic** (sō′sē ō ē′kə nom′ik, -shē-; -ek′ə-), *adj.* **1** having to do with or involving factors that are both social and economic. **2** having to do with or involving a person's social and financial status: *By all the evidence, Americans will soon consider at least two years of college a socioeconomic necessity* (Time).

**so|ci|o|ge|net|ic** (sō′sē ō jə net′ik, -shē-), *adj.* of or having to do with the forces and conditions which create and mold society.

**so|ci|og|ra|phy** (sō′sē og′rə fē, -shē-), *n.* the observing and descriptive stage or branch of sociology.

**sociol.**, **1** sociological. **2** sociology.

**so|ci|o|lin|guist** (sō′sē ō ling′gwist, -shē-), *n.* a person who studies or is skilled in sociolinguistics.

**so|ci|o|lin|guis|tic** (sō′sē ō ling gwis′tik, -shē-), *adj.* of or having to do with sociolinguistics: *The basic sociolinguistic method is that of correlating social with linguistic variables* (Walter A. Wolfram). —**so′ci|o|lin|guis′ti|cal|ly**, *adv.*

**so|ci|o|lin|guis|tics** (sō′sē ō ling gwis′tiks, -shē-), *n.* a branch of linguistics that deals with the social aspects of language and speech, such as cultural influence on speech.

**so|ci|ol|o|gese** (sō′sē ol′ə jēz′, -shē-; -jēs′), *n.* sociological jargon: *The outcome is about 200 tables, some of them positive cadenzas of sociologese, e.g.: "Attitudes towards university expansion by degree of apprehension, within categories of political position per cent"* (Manchester Guardian Weekly). [< *sociolog*(y) + *-ese*]

**so|ci|o|log|ic** (sō′sē ə loj′ik, -shē-), *adj.* = sociological.

**so|ci|o|log|i|cal** (sō′sē ə loj′ə kəl, -shē-), *adj.* **1** of or having to do with human society or problems relating to it: *The care of the poor is a sociological concern. ... the sociological problem of a changing neighborhood* (New York Times). **2** of sociology: *Sociological concepts already mount upward into the hundreds* (Emory S. Bogardus). —**so′ci|o|log′i|cal|ly**, *adv.*

**so|ci|ol|o|gist** (sō′sē ol′ə jist, -shē-), *n.* a student of human society and its problems; an expert in sociology.

**so|ci|ol|o|gy** (sō′sē ol′ə jē, -shē-), *n.* the study of the nature, origin, and development of human society and community life; science of society that deals with the facts of crime, poverty, marriage, divorce, the church, the school, and other human institutions: *sociology, which deals with the relationship of man to his fellowman* (Harbaugh and Goodrich). *Sociology as the science of human association in groups has had a century-long history* (Emory S. Bogardus). *Abbr:* sociol. [< French *sociologie* < Latin *socius* companion + French *-logie* -logy]

**so|ci|o|met|ric** (sō′sē ō met′rik, -shē-), *adj.* **1** of or having to do with sociometry. **2** measuring or indicating the existence, extent, or quality of social relationships: *sociometric tests.*

**so|ci|om|e|try** (sō′sē om′ə trē, -shē-), *n.* the branch of sociology that measures human relationships.

**so|ci|o|path** (sō′sē ə path, -shē-), *n.* a person who lacks any sense of social or moral responsibility because of mental illness; antisocial person: *The sociopath is a person who knows that what he is doing is wrong, but doesn't care* (New York Times). [< *social;* patterned on *psychopath*]

**so|ci|o|path|ic** (sō′sē ə path′ik, -shē-), *adj.* of a

sociopath; like that of a sociopath: *a sociopathic personality.*

**so|ci|o|pol|it|i|cal** (sō′sē ō pə lit′ə kəl, -shē-), *adj.* of or having to do with both society and politics; social and political at the same time: *the constantly increasing sociopolitical pressure on all men to conform* (New Yorker).

**so|ci|o|psy|cho|log|i|cal** (sō′sē ō sī′kə loj′ə kəl, -shē-), *adj.* **1** social and psychological: *The major focus of our social policies on drug use should be on prevention by eliminating the sociopsychological roots* (New York Times). **2** of or having to do with social psychology. **3** = psychosocial.

**so|ci|o|re|li|gious** (sō′sē ō ri lij′əs, -shē-), *adj.* of or having to do with both society and religion; social and religious at the same time: *Religious circles emphasize ... the importance which should be given to socioreligious values such as ... indissolubility of the family, conjugal love, and responsible parenthood* (New York Times).

**so|ci|o|sex|u|al** (sō′sē ō sek′shü əl, -shē-), *adj.* of or having to do with relations between a group of people that involve sexual matters: *... a best-seller describing the sociosexual goings-on behind the traditional facade of a quiet New England town* (Philip Kopper).

**so|ci|o|tech|no|log|i|cal** (sō′sē ō tek′nə loj′ə kəl, -shē-), *adj.* having to do with or combining social and technological elements: *The concatenation linking monocultures, pests, pesticides, and all the complex procedures to control the toxicity of pesticides constitutes another obvious example of the sociotechnological failure* (Saturday Review).

**so|ci|us** (sō′sē əs), *n. Latin.* a fellow; associate; member.

**so|ci|us crim|i|nis** (sō′sē us krim′ə nis), *Law.* an accomplice or associate in the commission of a crime. [< Latin *socius* associate; *crīminis,* genitive of *crīmen* crime]

**sock**[1] (sok), *n., v.* **—*n.*** **1a** a short, close-fitting, knitted covering of wool, cotton, or other fabric for the foot and leg, especially one that reaches about halfway to the knee. **b** any article or covering similar to this. **2** a light, low shoe worn by actors in comedy in ancient Greece and Rome. **3** comedy. **4** the comic muse. **5** *Informal.* a wind sock.
**—*v.t.*** to provide with socks; put socks on.
**sock away,** *Slang.* to save or hoard (money), as by putting it away in a sock: *Most Americans still aren't convinced the recession is over, so they're still trying to sock a little money away—just in case* (Wall Street Journal).
**sock in,** *Slang.* to close or restrict because of poor visibility or bad weather: *Fog and drizzle had socked in the runways* (Time).
[Old English *socc* a light slipper < Latin *soccus*]

**sock**[2] (sok), *v., n., adv. Slang.* **—*v.t.*** **1** to strike or hit hard; punch: *to sock a person in the nose.* **2** to send by hitting: *to sock a ball over a fence.*
**—*n.*** a hard blow.
**—*adv.*** squarely; right.
**sock it to one,** *Slang.* to hit or attack in a vigorous, outspoken, or direct way; let one have it: *The sight of the politicians still socking it to each other was like a Punch and Judy show* (Manchester Guardian Weekly). *Each issue really socks it to you with uproarious satire* (Harper's).
[originally dialectal, probably related to *sockdolager*]

**sock|dol|a|ger** (sok dol′ə jər, -gər), *n. U.S. Slang.* **1** something unusual, exceptional, or outstanding of its kind: *The forthcoming safari into Tanganyika ... was destined to be a sockdolager* (New Yorker). **2** a decisive or finishing blow. [American English; perhaps alteration of *doxology;* influenced by *sock*[2]]

**sock|er|oo** (sok′ə rü′), *n. U.S. Slang.* a smash hit; smasheroo; socko.

**sock|et** (sok′it), *n., v.* **—*n.*** **1** a hollow part or piece for receiving and holding something. A candlestick has a socket in which to set a candle. A light bulb is screwed into a socket. **2** a connecting place for electric wires and plugs: *Please plug the lamp into the socket on the wall.* **3** a hollow place in some part of the body in which another part moves. A person's eyes are set in sockets. **4** the part of an iron golf club where the shaft is fitted into the head.
**—*v.t.*** to put in a socket; fit with a socket.
[< Anglo-French *soket* < Old French *soc* plowshare < Vulgar Latin *soccus,* probably < a Gaulish word]

**socket chisel,** a chisel having a hollow tang in which the handle is inserted.

**socket wrench,** a wrench having a socket fitted to a particular size and shape of nut or bolthead to be turned or held.

**sock|eye salmon** (sok′ī′), a salmon of the northern Pacific from Japan to California that ascends rivers to spawn; red salmon; blueback salmon. [American English, alteration of Salishan *sukkegh*]

**sock|less** (sok′lis), *adj.* lacking socks: *His sockless feet blistered in the wet boots.*

**sock|o** (sok′ō), *n., adj. U.S. Slang.* **—*n.*** a very successful venture or effect, especially in the theater: *It became a sweet socko, an experience that Wodehouse is probably more familiar with than any other humorist* (Newsweek).
**—*adj.*** very successful; wonderful; terrific, especially in reference to a theatrical hit: *For writers, too, the Private Eye shows make a socko source of income* (Time).
[< *sock*[2]]

**so|cle** (sok′əl, sō′kəl), *n.* a low, plain block supporting a wall, a pedestal, or the like: *I paused in front of a bust of Alfred de Musset to read again on its socle one of my favorite cheer-up bits of literature* (New Yorker). [< French *socle* < Italian *zoccolo* (originally) a wooden shoe < Latin *socculus* (diminutive) < *soccus* slipper; see etym. under **sock**[1]]

**soc|man** (sok′mən), *n., pl.* **-men.** a person who held land in socage.

**soc|man|ry** (sok′mən rē), *n., pl.* **-ries.** tenure by socage. [< Medieval Latin *socmanaria* < *socmannus* feudal tenant < Old English *sōcman*]

**So|crat|ic** (sō krat′ik), *adj., n.* **—*adj.*** of or having to do with Socrates, his philosophy or his followers: *My role was a Socratic one, to question them persistently and fairly ruthlessly to force them to consider important problems* (Technology).
**—*n.*** a follower of Socrates. **—So|crat′i|cal|ly,** *adv.*

**Socratic irony,** pretended ignorance in discussion.

**So|crat|i|cism** (sō krat′ə siz əm), *n.* **1** = Socratism. **2** a Socratic peculiarity or trait.

**Socratic method,** the use of a series of questions, especially to lead a pupil to think or to make an opponent contradict himself. It is based on the assumption that truth is never incompatible with reason.

**Soc|ra|tism** (sok′rə tiz əm), *n.* the doctrines or philosophy of Socrates.

**Soc|red** (sok′red), *n.* = Social Crediter.

**sod**[1] (sod), *n., v.,* **sod|ded, sod|ding.** **—*n.*** **1** ground covered with grass: *Scores of species of smaller grasses and of colorful wildflowers, all knit together into a deep, tough sod* (Fred W. Emerson). **2** a piece or layer of this containing the grass and its roots: *Some pioneers on the western prairies built houses of sods.*
**—*v.t.*** to cover with sods: *We must have the bare spots of our lawn sodded.*
**the old sod,** *Informal.* one's native country or district: *And did ye see old Ireland lately? And how's the poor old sod?* (E. Roper).
**under the sod,** buried: *I've heard the boys say that he would be under the sod that day* (Anthony Trollope).
[compare Middle Low German *sode*]

**sod**[2] (sod), *n., v.,* **sod|ded, sod|ding.** *British Slang.* **—*n.*** **1** a sodomite. **2** a contemptible or low person. **3** a chap; fellow.
**—*v.t.*** to curse; damn: *"Sod the shareholders and let's get at the assets"* (Sunday Times).
**sod off,** to go away; bugger off: *"Sod off, or I'll call the fuzz," said a pair of ... lips through a crack* (Alan Brien).
[< *sod*(omite)]

**sod**[3] (sod), *v. Obsolete.* a past tense of **seethe.**

**so|da** (sō′də), *n.* **1** any one of several chemical substances containing sodium, such as sodium carbonate (washing soda or sal soda), sodium bicarbonate (baking soda), and sodium hydroxide (caustic soda). **2** = soda water. **3** soda water flavored with fruit juice or syrup, and usually containing ice cream: *a chocolate soda.* **4** the top card, shown face up in the dealing box, as play begins in the game of faro. [< Medieval Latin, Italian, or Spanish *soda* < Italian *sodo* firm < Latin *solidus* solid]

**soda ash,** partly purified sodium carbonate: *Soda ash is used largely by glass makers* (Wall Street Journal).

**soda biscuit,** **1** a biscuit made with baking soda and sour milk. **2** = soda cracker.

**soda bread,** bread made with baking soda and sour milk.

**soda cracker,** a simple, light, thin cracker made with little or no sugar or shortening.

**soda fountain,** **1** an apparatus, often, with faucets for holding and for drawing off soda water and syrups. **2** a counter with places for holding soda water, flavored syrups, ice cream, and soft drinks. **3** a store having such a counter.

**soda jerk** or **jerker,** *Slang.* a person who works behind a soda fountain: *A jumbo-sized banana split Which, when the soda jerk was through, Looked like the Taj Mahal in goo* (Wall Street Journal).

**so|da-lead glass** (sō′də led′), an expensive glass made of lead oxide, widely used for fine tableware and art objects because it is soft and easy to melt; lead glass.

**soda lime,** a mixture of sodium hydroxide (caustic soda) and calcium hydroxide (slaked lime), used as a reagent and to absorb gases, especially carbon dioxide, and moisture.

**so|da-lime glass** (sō′də līm′), a strong inexpensive glass made of silica, sodium oxide, and calcium oxide, used for window glass, containers, and electric light bulbs.

**so|da|lite** (sō′də līt), *n.* a silicate of sodium and aluminum with chlorine. It occurs in crystals and also massively, is usually blue, and is found in igneous rocks. *Princess marble or sodalite is used for ornamental purposes* (A. Pabst). *Formula:* $Na_4(AlCl)Al_2(SiO_4)_3$ [< *soda* + *-lite*]

**so|dal|i|ty** (sō dal′ə tē), *n., pl.* **-ties.** **1** fellowship; friendship. **2** an association, society, or fraternity: *There were ... military sodalities of musketeers, cross-bowmen, archers, swordsmen in every town* (John L. Motley). **3** a lay society of the Roman Catholic Church with religious or charitable purposes. [< Latin *sodālitās* < *sodālis* companion; (literally) sociable]

**so|da|mide** (sō′də mīd), *n.* = sodium amide.

**soda pop,** a sweet-flavored, nonalcoholic carbonated drink.

**soda water,** water charged with carbon dioxide to make it bubble and fizz, often served with the addition of syrup and ice cream, or mixed with an alcoholic drink; carbonated water.

**sod|bust|er** (sod′bus′tər), *n. Western U.S. Slang.* a farmer: *Its tune was familiar to the lonely "sodbuster"* (Carl Sandburg).

**sod|den** (sod′ən), *adj., v.* **—*adj.*** **1** soaked through; saturated: *My clothes were sodden with rain.* **2** heavy and moist; soggy: *This bread is sodden because it was not baked well.* **3** dull-looking; stupid: *a sodden face, a head sodden with whiskey.* **4** *Obsolete.* boiled; seethed.
**—*v.t., v.i.*** **1** to make or become sodden. **2** *Obsolete.* a past participle of **seethe.** **—sod′den|ly,** *adv.* **—sod′den|ness,** *n.*

**sod|ding** (sod′ing), *adj. British Slang.* cursed; confounded; bloody. [< *sod*[2]]

**sod|dy** (sod′ē), *adj.,* **-di|er, -di|est,** *n., pl.* **-dies.** **—*adj.*** of or like sod; made of sods.
**—*n.*** a house made of sods: *Later, settlers often improved their soddies by whitewashing the walls and hauling in lumber for doors and ceilings* (Charlton Laird).

**sod house,** a house made of sods, especially houses that were built by early plains settlers who had no trees to supply lumber.

**so|dic** (sō′dik), *adj.* **1** of sodium. **2** containing sodium. [< *sod*(ium) + *-ic*]

***so|di|um** (sō′dē əm), *n.* a soft, silver-white, chemical element found only in combination with other elements. Salt and soda contain sodium. Sodium is one of the alkali metals which oxidize rapidly in the presence of air and react violently with water. *Sodium is made by distillation and in New York any still—sodium or bourbon—must be okayed by the liquor board* (Wall Street Journal). [< *sod*(a) + New Latin *-ium* element]

***sodium**

| symbol | atomic number | atomic weight | oxidation state |
|---|---|---|---|
| Na | 11 | 22.9898 | 1 |

**sodium acetate,** a colorless crystalline or white granular salt of acetic acid, used in dyeing and as a reagent in photography. *Formula:* $C_2H_3NaO_2$

**sodium alginate,** a cream-colored, powdery salt of algin obtained from kelp, used in making hand lotions and reducing pills, as a food preservative, and to thicken buttermilk and ice cream.

**sodium amide,** a white, crystalline, flammable powder used in making sodium cyanide and in organic synthesis; sodamide. *Formula:* $NaNH_2$

**sodium arsenite,** a very poisonous, white or grayish-white powdery salt, used as an insecticide against termites and scale insects and as an antiseptic. *Formula:* $NaAsO_2$

**sodium benzoate,** a white crystalline or powdery salt of benzoic acid, used especially to preserve food and in medicine as an antiseptic. *Formula:* $C_7H_5NaO_2$

**sodium bicarbonate,** a powdery, white, crystalline salt, with a somewhat alkaline taste, used in cooking, baking powder, medicine, and manufacturing; baking soda; bicarbonate of soda. Sodium bicarbonate soothes irritations of the skin and is a source of carbon dioxide. *Formula:* $NaHCO_3$

---

**Pronunciation Key:** h**a**t, **ā**ge, c**ã**re, f**ä**r; l**e**t, **ē**qual, t**ė**rm; **i**t, **ī**ce; h**o**t, **ō**pen, **ô**rder; **oi**l, **ou**t; c**u**p, p**u̇**t, r**ü**le; **ch**ild; lo**ng**; **th**in; **ᴛʜ**en; **zh**, measure; **ə** represents **a** in about, **e** in taken, **i** in pencil, **o** in lemon, **u** in circus.

**sodium bisulfate**, a crystalline or white granular salt, used as a strong acid in dyeing, in the manufacture of paper, glue, soap, and perfume, as a disinfectant, and as a flux for decomposing metals. *Formula:* $NaHSO_4$

**sodium borate**, = borax.

**sodium bo|ro|hy|dride** (bôr′ō hī′drīd, -drid; bōr′-), a crystalline salt, used to reduce aldehydes, ketones, and acid halides, and in making fuels for jet airplanes and guided missiles. *Formula:* $NaBH_4$

**sodium bromide**, a white, crystalline, granular or powdery salt with a somewhat bitter taste, used in photography and in medicine as a sedative. *Formula:* NaBr

**sodium carbonate**, **1** a salt that occurs in a powdery white form called soda ash and in a crystalline form called sal soda or washing soda. It is used for softening water, making soap and glass, neutralizing acids, as a reagent, and in medicine and photography. *Formula:* $Na_2CO_3$ **2** = sodium bicarbonate.

**sodium chlorate**, a colorless crystalline salt, used as an oxidizing agent, in fireworks and explosives, in dyeing, and as an antiseptic in toothpaste and mouthwash. *Formula:* $NaClO_3$

**sodium chloride**, a white, crystalline substance, the chloride of sodium, that is the ordinary salt used at the table; table salt. *Formula:* NaCl

**sodium citrate**, a white, odorless, crystalline, granular or powdery salt, used in photography, in medicine as a diuretic and expectorant and to prevent stored blood from clotting, and in preserving foods. *Formula:* $C_6H_5Na_3O_7{\cdot}2H_2O$

**sodium cyanide**, a very poisonous, white, crystalline salt, used in the cyanide process for extracting gold and silver from ores, and in fumigating. *Formula:* NaCN

**sodium dichromate**, an orange crystalline salt, used as an oxidizing agent, as a reagent, and as an antiseptic. *Formula:* $Na_2Cr_2O_7{\cdot}2H_2O$

**sodium fluoride**, a crystalline salt, used as an insecticide, a disinfectant, in the fluoridation of water, and in treating certain forms of tooth decay. *Formula:* NaF

**sodium fluoroacetate**, a white, odorless, poisonous powder used as a rodenticide; ten-eighty.

**sodium hydroxide**, a white solid that is a strong, corrosive alkali; caustic soda. It is used in making hard soaps and rayon, in the paper industry, in tanning, and as a bleaching agent. *Formula:* NaOH

**sodium hypochlorite**, a crystalline salt, used as an antiseptic and disinfectant. Most household bleaches contain a solution of 5 or 6 per cent sodium hypochlorite in water. *Formula:* $NaClO{\cdot}5H_2O$

**sodium hyposulfite**, **1** a crystalline salt, used as a bleaching and reducing agent. *Formula:* $Na_2S_2O_4$ **2** = sodium thiosulfate.

**sodium iodide**, a white, odorless, crystalline or granular salt, used in photography, animal feeds, and in treating respiratory and nervous disorders. *Formula:* NaI

**sodium lamp**, = sodium-vapor lamp.

**sodium met|a|bi|sul|fite** (met′ə bī sul′fīt), a white, crystalline compound, used especially as a reducing agent and food preservative. *Formula:* $Na_2S_2O_5$

**sodium met|a|sil|i|cate** (met′ə sil′ə kit, -kāt), a crystalline silicate, a form of water glass. *Formula:* $Na_2SiO_3$

**sodium nitrate**, a colorless, crystalline compound, used to produce other nitrates, such as potassium nitrate, and in making fertilizers and explosives; niter; Chile saltpeter. *Formula:* $NaNO_3$

**sodium nitrite**, a white or pale-yellow granular or powdery salt, used in making dyes and organic chemicals, and to treat cyanide poisoning in animals. *Formula:* $NaNO_2$

**sodium oxide**, a white powder that becomes sodium hydroxide by reaction with water, used especially as a dehydrating agent.

**sodium pentothal**, = thiopental sodium.

**sodium perborate**, = perborax.

**sodium phosphate**, any one of various colorless crystalline or white granular salts of sodium and phosphorous occurring in hydrous and anhydrous forms, and used as laxatives, in textile printing, photography, and in water softeners. *Formula:* $Na_2HPO_4$

**sodium pump**, the cellular mechanism or means by which sodium ions are moved out of the nerve cells and replaced with potassium ions: *The sodium pump ... gets hold of any sodium that gets into the cell and turns it out again* (Listener). *The "sodium pump" ... uses metabolic energy in the form of ATP to extrude sodium ions from the axon* (Scientific American).

**sodium silicate**, any one of various colorless, white or grayish-white crystallike substances used in preserving eggs, in soap powders, and as adhesives in paper and cardboard products; water glass.

**sodium sulfate**, an odorless, colorless crystalline or white granular salt, used in making glass, dyeing textiles, and in medicine as a strong laxative; Glauber's salt. *Formula:* $Na_2SO_4$

**sodium tet|ra|bo|rate** (tet′rə bôr′āt, -it; -bōr′-), = borax.

**sodium thiosulfate**, a colorless or white crystalline salt, used as a fixative in photography, in dyeing, and in bleaching; hypo. *Formula:* $Na_2S_2O_3$

**so|di|um-va|por lamp** (sō′dē əm vā′pər), an electric street light with two electrodes that cause the sodium vapor in the light to glow when electricity passes through them.

**Sod|om** (sod′əm), *n.* **1** an ancient, wicked city near the Dead Sea which was destroyed together with Gomorrah, by fire from heaven (in the Bible, Genesis 18 and 19). **2** any extremely wicked or corrupt place.

**sod|om|ite** (sod′ə mīt), *n.* a person who practices sodomy. [< *sodom*(y) + *-ite*[1]]

**sod|o|mit|i|cal** (sod′ə mit′ə kəl), *adj.* **1** of, having to do with, or involving sodomy. **2** grossly wicked.

**sod|om|ize** (sod′ə mīz), *v.t.*, **-ized, -iz|ing.** to commit sodomy upon.

**sod|om|y** (sod′ə mē), *n.* unnatural sexual intercourse, especially of one man with another or of a human being with an animal. [< Old French *sodomie* < *Sodom*]

**so|ev|er** (sō ev′ər), *adv.* **1** in any case; in any way; in any degree: *to persist no matter how long soever the task may take.* **2** of any kind; at all: *a poor beggar with no home soever.*

**-soever**, *suffix.* in any way; of any kind; at all; ever, as in *whosoever, whatsoever, whensoever, wheresoever, howsoever.*

**so|fa** (sō′fə), *n.* a long, upholstered seat or couch having a back and arms. **SYN**: settee, davenport. [perhaps < French *sofa* < Arabic *suffah*]

**sofa bed**, a sofa that can be made into a bed, usually by removing the cushions and pulling the seat forward.

**so|far** (sō′fär), *n.* a method of locating the position of an underwater explosion by measuring the difference in the time the vibrations of the sound reach three or more distant points. [< *so*(und) *f*(ixing) *a*(nd) *r*(anging)]

**so-fa syllables** (sō′fä′), syllables used in reading music; sol-fa syllables.

**sofa table**, a table designed to be placed near the side, back, or front of a sofa.

**sof|fio|ni** (sōf fyō′nē), *n.pl.* vents from which steam, sulfurous fumes, and other exhalations issue in the dying stages of volcanic action. [< Italian *soffioni* < *soffio* a blowing < *soffiare* to blow upwardly < Latin *sufflāre;* see etym. under **sufflate**]

*__sof|fit__ (sof′it), *n.* the undersurface or face of an architrave, arch, or the like. [< Italian *soffitta,* also *soffitto* ceiling, ultimately < Latin *suffīgere* < *sub-* under + *fīgere* to fix, fasten]

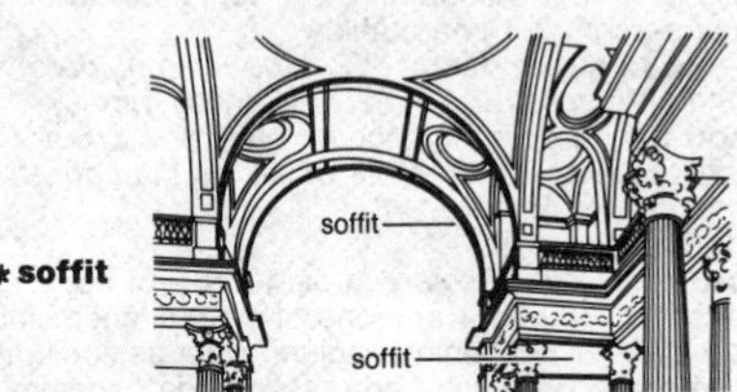


*__soffit__

**soft** (sôft, soft), *adj., adv., n., interj.* —*adj.* **1a** not hard; yielding readily to touch or pressure: *a soft tomato, soft ground, a soft bed.* **b** easily bent without breaking; not stiff; flexible: *Oil keeps leather soft.* **SYN**: pliable. **c** capable of being hammered or pressed into various shapes without being broken; malleable: *soft iron. Copper and lead are softer than steel.* **2** not hard compared with other things of the same kind: *Pine wood is softer than oak. Chalk is much softer than granite.* **3** *Figurative.* not hard or sharp; graceful: *soft shadows, soft outlines.* **4** fine in texture; pleasant to the touch; not rough or coarse; smooth: *a soft skin, the soft hair of a kitten, soft silk.* **5** not loud; quiet; subdued: *a soft tap on the door, to speak in a soft voice, to play soft music. The soft rustle of a maiden's gown* (Keats). **SYN**: low. **6** quietly pleasant; calm; mild: *a soft breeze. The soft airs that o'er the meadows play* (William Cullen Bryant). **7** *Figurative.* not glaring or harsh: *soft colors, a soft light.* **8** *Figurative.* gentle; kind; tender: *a soft heart. He ... was very soft and gentle with the children* (Thackeray). *He was fond of saying soft things which were intended to have no meaning* (Anthony Trollope). **SYN**: sympathetic, compassionate. **9** *Figurative.* not strong or robust; weak; unmanly: *muscles which have grown soft from lack of use. He became soft from idleness and luxury.* **10** *Figurative.* silly: *soft in the head.* **11** easy; easygoing: *a soft job, to lead a soft life.* **12** comparatively free from certain mineral salts that prevent soap from forming suds: *Soft water is easy to wash with. Rain water contains no dissolved solid matter and so is soft* (Clifford Cook Furnas). **13** *Phonetics.* **a** having a more or less hissing sound; pronounced as a fricative or an affricate, rather than as a stop. *Example: C is soft in city and hard in corn; g is soft in gentle and hard in get.* **b** (of Slavic consonants) palatalized. **c** = lenis. **d** = voiced. **14** *Physics.* of or having to do with radiation that has low powers of penetration, such as X rays. **15** of or having to do with soft goods: *For many years the chain sold soft lines—clothing—only on a limited basis* (Wall Street Journal). **16** having to do with or characteristic of soft art: *... half a dozen "soft" (i.e., psychologically or technically tentative) paintings, those by Rivers, Copley, Kitaj, Rosenquist, Dine, Oldenburg* (Harold Rosenberg). **17** having little contrast between light and shade: *a soft photographic print or negative.* **18** (of wheat) containing little gluten: *soft wheat.* **19** *Military.* not protected against missiles or bombs: *Hardened silos require a huge weight of explosives for their destruction. By contrast, our Minuteman is designed ... for retaliatory strikes on "soft" targets* (Time).
—***adv.*** in a soft manner; quietly; gently: *The wanderer ... Halts on the bridge to hearken How soft the poplar sighs* (A. E. Housman).
—***n.*** that which is soft; soft part.
—***interj.*** *Archaic.* hush! stop!
[Old English *sōfte*] —**soft′ly**, *adv.*

**sof|ta** (sof′tə), *n.* in Turkey: **1** a student at a secondary school. **2** a student of Moslem theology and sacred law. [< Turkish *softa* < Persian *sūkhtah* afire (with zeal for study)]

**soft art**, a form of art that makes use of pliable material, as in soft sculpture.

**soft|back** (sôft′bak′, soft′-), *adj., n.* = paperback.

*__soft|ball__ (sôft′bôl′, soft′-), *n.* **1** a kind of baseball. A larger and softer ball, lighter bats, and a smaller field are used in softball than in baseball. The ball is pitched underhand only. **2** the ball used in this game. [American English < *soft* + *ball*]

*__softball__
definitions 1, 2

**soft-bod|ied** (sôft′bod′ēd, soft′-), *adj.* having a soft body, as the mollusks.

**soft-boiled** (sôft′boild′, soft′-), *adj.* boiled only a little so that the yolk is still soft: *a soft-boiled egg.*

**soft|bound** (sôft′bound′, soft′-), *adj.* bound in flexible paper; not hard-bound: *Paperbacks are softbound books.*

**soft chancre**, = chancroid.

**soft clam**, an edible kind of clam with a long thin shell, found along both coasts of North America; soft-shell clam.

**soft coal**, coal that burns with a yellow, smoky flame; bituminous coal.

**soft-coat|ed wheaten terrier** (sôft′kō′tid, soft′-), any one of a breed of terriers originating in Ireland, having a wheat-colored coat of shaggy hair and a docked tail. It stands 18 or 19 inches high and weighs from 35 to 45 pounds.

**soft-core** (sôft′kôr′, soft′-; -kōr′), *adj.* not graphic or explicit; not hard-core: *soft-core pornography.*

**soft corn**, **1** a corn between the toes. **2** = flour corn.

**soft-cov|er** (sôft′kuv′ər, soft′-), *adj., n.* = paperback.

**soft currency**, a currency backed by government credit, but not entirely by gold or silver. Soft currency cannot be readily converted into other currencies without discount.

**soft detergent**, a detergent that can be decomposed by bacteria in sewage.

**soft drink**, a drink that does not contain alcohol. Soft drinks are sweetened, flavored, and usually carbonated.

**soft drug**, any drug that is not considered physically addictive, such as marijuana, mescaline, and various amphetamines: *Although there was no doubt about the deleterious effects of hard drugs (heroin, morphine, etc.), there was much debate concerning the harmful effects of the soft drugs, such as marijuana* (Donn L. Smith).

**soft|en** (sôf′ən, sof′-), *v.t.* to make soft or softer: *Lotion softens the skin.* **—*v.i.*** **1** to become soft or softer: *Soap softens in water.* **2** *U.S. Figurative.* to decrease; decline: *business was strong until the middle of September, then began softening* (Wall Street Journal).
**soften up, a** to weaken: *Did they in fact lose ... because they had been softened up by the good life?* (Saturday Review). **b** *Figurative.* to placate: *I thought, in short, that I was softening up the citizens, and they thought they were softening me up, at least to the point where a dialogue becomes possible* (Atlantic). **c** to ease: *The Governor hoped the stringent Guard regulations might soften up the stubborn resistance of merchants and restaurateurs, who have been adamant in opposing any integration* (New York Times). **d** to lessen the ability of (a country or region) to resist invasion or attack through preliminary bombing, shelling, etc., or through propaganda, or both: *In the Indian softening up operations several places in East Pakistan were bombed and saboteurs dropped to prepare for the actual invasion* (London Times).
**—soft′en|er,** *n.*

**soft|en|ing of the brain** (sôf′ə ning, sof′-), **1** a degenerative disease of the brain in which the tissues become soft and fatty, caused by a deficient blood supply. **2** = general paresis. **3** *Informal.* a weakening of the mental processes.

**soft-finned** (sôft′find′, soft′-), *adj.* (of fish) not having spines in the fins.

**soft focus,** intentional diffusion of the light in a photograph or motion-picture film to lessen the sharpness of detail, obtained either by a special lens or attachment on the camera, or by certain methods in processing.

**soft-fo|cus** (sôft′fō′kəs, soft′-), *adj.* having, characterized by, or causing a soft focus.

**soft goods,** textiles, clothing, and other dry goods.

**soft hail,** snow pellets.

**soft|head** (sôft′hed′, soft′-), *n.* a simpleton; fool.

**soft-head|ed** or **soft|head|ed** (sôft′hed′id, soft′-), *adj.* foolish; silly: *He would adopt a middle ground between ... panicked retreat ... and ... soft-headed submission* (New York Times).
**—soft′-head′ed|ly, soft′head′ed|ly,** *adv.* **—soft′-head′ed|ness, soft′head′ed|ness,** *n.*

**soft-heart|ed** or **soft|heart|ed** (sôft′här′tid, soft′-), *adj.* gentle; kind; tender: *My grandmother was ... soft-hearted to children* (Harriet Beecher Stowe). **—soft′-heart′ed|ly, soft′heart′ed|ly,** *adv.* **—soft′-heart′ed|ness, soft′heart′ed|ness,** *n.*

**soft|ie** (sôf′tē, sof′-), *n. Informal.* a softy.

**soft|ish** (sôf′tish, sof′-), *adj.* somewhat soft; rather tender: *A bed of softish limestone* (Thomas H. Huxley).

**soft-land** (sôft′land′, soft′-), *v., n.* **—*v.t.*** to land (a spacecraft or instruments) slowly so as to avoid serious damage: *The four "feet" of the vehicle scheduled to soft-land two U.S. astronauts on the moon ... received a patent from the U.S. Patent Office* (Science News Letter).
**—*v.i.*** to make a soft landing: *The National Aeronautics and Space Administration (NASA) launched the Surveyor I spacecraft on a mission to soft-land on the moon and photograph its surface* (Mitchell R. Sharpe).
**—*n.*** a soft landing: *Soft-lands in bright areas— the lowlands— are ... easier from an engineering point of view* (London Times).
[back formation < *soft landing*]

**soft-land|er** (sôft′lan′dər, soft′-), *n.* a spacecraft designed to make a soft landing.

**soft landing,** the landing of a spacecraft or instruments, on a body in outer space at such slow speed as to avoid serious damage to the landing object: *The Soviet Union launched another unmanned spacecraft toward the moon ... in an apparent attempt to achieve a soft landing of an instrument package* (New York Times).

**soft lens,** a contact lens made of a porous plastic that becomes soft when it absorbs the moisture of the eyes and causes less discomfort or irritation than the harder type of lens.

**soft line,** a moderate, flexible attitude or policy, especially in politics: *Canada, Norway, Denmark and Italy prefer a "soft" line and want to leave the Council where it is to minimise the rupture with France* (Sunday Times).

**soft-lin|er** (sôft′lī′nər, soft′-), *n.* a person who adopts or follows a soft line.

**soft loan,** *U.S.* a loan at a very low rate of interest and a long period in which to repay it, as in foreign aid.

**soft money,** = paper money.

**soft|ness** (sôft′nis, soft′-), *n.* **1** the condition or quality of being soft. **2** *Figurative.* mildness; gentleness. **3** *Figurative.* weakness of character or disposition. **4** ease; comfort; luxury.

**soft palate,** the fleshy back part of the roof of the mouth. See picture under **mouth.**

**soft-paste porcelain** (sôft′pāst′, soft′-), a creamy white, translucent porcelain made from a white firing clay combined with a fusible silicate or mass of glass, sand, broken china, or the like.

**soft pedal,** a pedal for softening the tone of a piano.

**soft-ped|al** (sôft′ped′əl, soft′-), *v.*, **-aled, -al|ing** or (*especially British*) **-alled, -al|ling.** **—*v.t.*** **1** to soften the sound of by means of the soft pedal. **2** *Figurative.* to tone down; play down: *State Department officials soft-pedal any speculation that dramatic new accords may emerge from the talks* (Wall Street Journal).
**—*v.i.*** **1** to use a pedal on a piano, or organ to soften musical tones. **2** *Figurative.* to tone down: *Both parties are at present "soft-pedalling" on the world-revolution thesis* (London Daily Express).

**soft rays,** radiation of low penetrating power, such as is obtained from tubes of low vacuum.

**soft rock,** a low-keyed, rhythmically free, sophisticated form of rock'n'roll: *His songs delve ingeniously into hard and soft rock, blues, gospel, even country rock* (Time).

**soft rot,** a plant disease caused by bacteria or fungi that dissolve the substance cementing the cell walls together. The result is a general decay, or rot, of fleshy tissues.

**soft science,** any of the social or behavioral sciences, such as political science, economics, sociology, and psychology: *One may define technology to mean political technique as well as nuts and bolts; that is, the soft sciences along with the hard* (Ward Just).

**soft sculpture,** a sculpture made out of cloth, plastic, foam rubber, or other soft, pliable material.

**soft sell,** *Informal.* a relaxed way of selling, by suggestion and persuasion rather than by pressure or aggressiveness.

**soft-shell** (sôft′shel′, soft′-), *adj., n.* **—*adj.*** = soft-shelled.
**—*n.*** a person or animal that is soft-shelled.

**soft-shell** or **soft-shelled clam,** = soft clam.

**soft-shell** or **soft-shelled crab,** the common blue crab when it has shed its hard shell and not yet grown another.

**soft-shelled** (sôft′sheld′, soft′-), *adj.* **1** having a soft shell: *a soft-shelled lobster.* **2** *Informal.* **a** that adopts or is in favor of a moderate policy or temperate course. **b** that is soft-hearted.

**soft-shelled turtle,** any freshwater turtle of a family with flexible, leatherlike shells.

**soft-shoe** (sôft′shü′, soft′-), *v.*, **-shoed, -shoe|ing,** *adj.* **—*v.i.*** to dance or move as if dancing the soft shoe: *We soft-shoed out and, in a corridor adjoining the gym, were introduced to a lady* (New Yorker). **—*adj.*** of or having to do with the soft shoe: *soft-shoe dancing.*

**soft shoe, 1** a form of tap dancing in which the dancers wear shoes that have no metal taps. **2** the type of shoe used for this.

**soft soap, 1** a liquid or semiliquid soap. **2** *Informal.* flattery: *He and I are great chums, and a little soft soap will go a long way with him* (Thomas Hughes).

**soft-soap** (sôft′sōp′, soft′-), *v.t.* **1** *Informal.* to flatter; cajole. **2** to treat or coat with soft soap. **—soft′-soap′er,** *n.*

**soft-spo|ken** (sôft′spō′kən, soft′-), *adj.* **1** speaking with a soft voice. **2** *Figurative.* persuasive: *a bland, soft-spoken scoundrel.* **3** spoken softly: *a soft-spoken reproof.* **—soft′-spo′ken|ness,** *n.*

**soft spot, 1** a weak part; condition open to attack; sensitive weakness: *[His] soft spot as a social critic is that, sharp though his critical faculties are, he is of rather too amiable a disposition* (Atlantic). **2** an area in the atmosphere where the winds are of lesser force than those around it: *a type of radar that can spot rainfall and locate areas of rough air, enabling the pilot to avoid them or to find a "soft spot" through which he could fly safely* (Wall Street Journal). **3** = fontanel (def. 1).

**soft steel,** steel containing only a small percentage of carbon (less than 0.35 per cent); mild steel.

**soft technology,** = appropriate technology: *Soft technology ... is gentle on its surroundings, responds to it, incorporates it, feeds it. A nuclear power-generating station doesn't qualify. A wooden windmill with cloth sails grinding local grain does* (Harper's).

**soft top,** the folding canvas top of a convertible automobile.

**soft touch,** *U.S. Informal.* a person from whom money can easily be obtained for a loan, contribution, or the like: *His neighbors knew him as a soft touch for every charity drive* (Atlantic).

**soft|ware** (sôft′wãr′, soft′-), *n.* **1** the designs, instructions, routines, and other printed matter, required for the operation of a computer or other automatic machine: *Software is the general term used to describe various levels of the language of computer instructions; it includes compilers and assemblers, as well as application programs in high-level languages such as FORTRAN* (Max Tochner). **2** the plans, fuel, and other related material, of a rocket, missile, or other space vehicle: *The US government ... procures goods and services with sophisticated technological components (e.g. weapons, rocket boosters and analytical "software")* (New Scientist). **3** anything thought of as not directly related to some operation, principal function, or objective, such as the non-mechanized elements of a system: *Generally speaking standardization means persuading the several services to buy identical "software"— that is, the thousand and one everyday housekeeping items ranging from paint brushes to belt buckles that aren't directly related to combat efficiency* (Wall Street Journal).

**soft wheat,** wheat having a soft kernel, used especially for making cakes, crackers, and breakfast foods.

**soft|wood** (sôft′wu̇d′, soft′-), *n., adj.* **—*n.*** **1** any wood that is easily cut. **2** any tree that has needles or does not have broad leaves. Pines and firs are softwoods; oaks and maples are hardwoods. **3** the wood of such trees.
**—*adj.*** **1** having such wood. **2** made of such wood: *a softwood cabinet.*

**soft X ray,** a weakly penetrating X ray, produced by low voltage.

**soft|y** (sôf′tē, sof′-), *n., pl.* **soft|ies.** *Informal.* **1** a soft, silly, or weak person: *Our youth seldom walk if they can drive ... Are we becoming a nation of "softies?"* (Newsweek). **2** a person who is easily imposed upon: *I'm a sentimental old softy* (Sunday Times).

**sog** (sog), *v.*, **sogged, sog|ging,** *n. Especially British Dialect.* **—*v.i., v.t.*** to make or become soggy. **—*n.*** a bog.

**Sog|di|an** (sog′dē ən), *n.* **1** a member of an Iranian group that formerly lived in Sogdiana, now Bokhara, a region in the Soviet Union north of Afghanistan. **2** the Iranian language of this group.

**sog|gy** (sog′ē), *adj.*, **-gi|er, -gi|est.** **1** thoroughly wet; soaked: *The wash on the line was soggy from the rain.* **2** damp and heavy: *soggy bread, a soggy day.* [< *sog* + *-y*[1]] **—sog′gi|ly,** *adv.* **—sog′gi|ness,** *n.*

**soh** (sō), *interj.* = so.

**so|ho** (sō hō′), *interj.* ho there! hello! (a shout of hailing, encouragement, or discovery, originally used by huntsmen).

**soi-di|sant** (swȧ′dē zäN′), *adj. French.* **1** calling oneself thus; self-styled: *a soi-disant aristocrat.* **2** so-called: *a soi-disant literary classic.*

**soi|gné** (swȧ nyā′), *adj. French.* **1** very neat and well-dressed: *Diaghilev had left nothing to chance, including the soigné audience* (Newsweek). **2** finished or cared for to the smallest detail: *a soigné party. She has a lot of soigné clothes* (New Yorker).

**soi|gnée** (swȧ nyā′), *adj. French.* the feminine form of **soigné.**

**soil**[1] (soil), *n.* **1** the ground or earth; the top layer of the earth's surface, composed of rock and mineral particles mixed with animal and vegetable matter; dirt: *A farmer tills the soil. Roses grow best in rich soil. Soil is a well-organized and highly complicated layer of debris covering most of the earth's land surface* (White and Renner). **2** *Figurative.* something thought of as a place for growth or development: *A rich moral soil ... for aesthetic growth* (G. K. Chesterton). **3** a land; country; region: *This is my native soil.* [< Anglo-French *soil* (literally) one's piece (of ground) < Latin *solium* seat, influenced by Latin *solum* soil]

**soil**[2] (soil), *v., n.* **—*v.t.*** **1** to make dirty: *He soiled his clean clothes.* SYN: daub, begrime, besmirch. **2** to spot; stain: *The splashing paint soiled the wall.* **3** *Figurative.* to disgrace; dishonor: *False rumors have soiled the family name.* **4** *Figurative.* to corrupt morally.
**—*v.i.*** to become dirty: *White shirts soil easily.*
**—*n.*** **1** a spot; stain: (*Figurative.*) *The only soil of his fair virtue's gloss ... Is a sharp wit matched with too blunt a will* (Shakespeare). **2a** the act of soiling. **b** the condition of being soiled. **3** dirty or foul matter; filth; sewage; ordure. **4** manure or compost.

---

**Pronunciation Key:** hat, āge, cãre, fär; let, ēqual, tėrm; it, īce; hot, ōpen, ôrder; **oi**l, **ou**t; cup, pu̇t, rüle; **ch**ild; lo**ng**; **th**in; ᴛʜen; **zh**, measure; ə represents **a** in about, **e** in taken, **i** in pencil, **o** in lemon, **u** in circus.

[< Old French *soillier,* ultimately < Latin *suile* pigsty < *sus* pig]
**soil**[3] (soil), *n., v.* —*n.* a pool or marshy place in which deer or other animals take refuge.
—*v.i.* to take refuge in water or marshy ground. [Middle English *soyle* < Old French *soil* < *soillier;* see etym. under **soil**[2]]
**soil**[4] (soil), *v.t.* **1** to stall-feed with green fodder to fatten. **2** to feed green fodder to purge. [origin uncertain, perhaps < *soil*[2] in sense of "manure"]
**soil|age** (soi′lij), *n.* **1** green fodder fed to livestock in a barn or feed lot. **2** = zero pasture.
**soil bank,** *U.S.* a program adopted by the Federal government in 1956 through which farmers were paid to stop cultivating certain crops to reduce surpluses. The soil bank was replaced by other programs in the early 1960's.
**soil binder,** a plant which serves to protect a clayey or loamy soil from washing.
**soil|borne** (soil′bôrn′, -bōrn′), *adj.* carried in or transmitted by the soil: *soilborne viruses.*
**soil cap,** *Geology.* a layer of soil and detritus covering bedrock.
**soil-ce|ment** (soil′sə ment′), *n.* a low-cost material, used especially for paving roads, consisting of compacted soil, portland cement, and water.
**soil conditioner,** any synthetic chemical or natural substance that improves the soil's structure.
**soil creep,** the slow movement or settling of surface soil down a slope.
**-soiled,** *combining form.* having ___ soil or earth: *Black-soiled = having black soil.*
**soil|less** (soil′lis), *adj.* without soil: *soilless cultivation of plants.*
**soilless growth** or **gardening,** the growing of plants without soil, nutrition being supplied by a water solution; hydroponics.
**soil map,** a map which shows the distribution of different kinds of soils.
**soil mechanics,** the study of the physical characteristics of soil and other loose materials on which buildings, highways, and other structures may be erected.
**soil pipe,** a drain pipe for a sink, tub, toilet, or other plumbing fixture, or from a house to the sewer line.
**soil science,** the study of soils; pedology.
**soil scientist,** an expert in soil science; pedologist.
**soil|ure** (soil′yər), *n. Archaic.* **1** a soiling. **2** a being soiled. **3** a stain; spot. [< Old French *soilleure* < *soillier;* see etym. under **soil**[2]]
**soi|ree** or **soi|rée** (swä rā′), *n.* an evening party or social gathering: *Pierre is startling the guests at Anna Pavlovna's soiree by defending Napoleon* (Harper's). [< French *soirée* < *soir* evening < Old French *seir,* ultimately < Latin *sērō* late]
**so|ja** (sō′jə, -yə), *n.,* or **soja bean,** = soybean. [< New Latin *soja,* perhaps < Dutch < Japanese *shōyu;* see etym. under **soy**]
**so|journ** (*v.* sō jėrn′, sō′jėrn; *n.* sō′jėrn), *v., n.* —*v.i.* to dwell for a time: *The Israelites sojourned in the land of Egypt. And that is why I sojourn here, Alone and palely loitering* (Keats).
—*n.* a brief stay; stay that is not permanent: *During his sojourn in Africa he learned much about native customs. The entire family enjoyed a sojourn in Europe last month.*
[Middle English *sojornen* < Old French *sojorner,* ultimately < Latin *sub-* under + *diurnus* of the day < *diū* by day < *diēs* day] —**so|journ′er,** *n.*
**soke** (sōk), *n.* in early English law: **1** a right to local jurisdiction, as to hold court or collect fines, over a certain district. **2** a district over which such a right was exercised; a minor local division. [Middle English *sok* < Medieval Latin *soca* < Old English *sōcn;* see etym. under **socage**]
**soke|man** (sōk′mən), *n., pl.* **-men.** a tenant holding land in socage; socman.
**So|kol** (sō′kôl), *n.* a member of a Slavic gymnastic organization in eastern Europe and the United States, stressing the physical and moral development of young people. [< Czech *sokol* falcon]
**sol**[1] (sōl), *n. Music.* the fifth tone of the scale; G. Also, **so.** [Middle English *sol;* see etym. under **gamut**]
**sol**[2] (sōl), *n., pl.* **sols** (sōlz), **so|les** (sō′lās). **1** a unit of money of Peru, equal to 100 centavos. **2** a sliver coin or note having this value. [< Spanish *sol* sun < Latin *sōl, sōlis*]
**sol**[3] (sol), *n.* a former French silver or copper coin and money of account worth 1/20 of a livre. [< Old French *sol* < Latin *solidus* gold (coin). See etym. of doublets **sou, soldo, solid.**]

**Pronunciation Key:** hat, āge, cãre, fär; let, ēqual, tėrm; it, īce; hot, ōpen, ôrder; oil, out; cup, pu̇t, rüle; child; long; thin; ᴛʜen; zh, measure; ə represents **a** in about, **e** in taken, **i** in pencil, **o** in lemon, **u** in circus.

**sol**[4] (sol, sōl), *n.* a colloidal solution: *A sol is usually a solid dispersed in a liquid; but it may also be a gas or a liquid in a liquid* (A. B. Garrett). [< *sol*(ution)]
**Sol** (sol), *n.* **1** the Roman god of the sun. The Greeks called him Helios. **2** the sun, personified. **3** *Obsolete.* (in alchemy) gold. [< Latin *sōl, sōlis* (literally) the sun]
**sol.,** 1 soluble. **2** solution.
**Sol.,** 1 Solicitor. **2** Solomon.
**so|la**[1] (sō′lə), *adj. Latin.* the feminine form of **solus.**
**so|la**[2] (sō′lə), *n.* plural of **solum.**
**so|la**[3] (sō′lə), *n.* **1** a tall East Indian plant of the pea family. **2** its robust stem, the dried pith of which is used in making sun hats; spongewood. [< Urdu and Bengali *solā*]
**sol|ace** (sol′is), *n., v.,* **-aced, -ac|ing.** —*n.* **1** comfort or relief: *She found solace from her troubles in listening to music.* SYN: consolation. **2** something that gives comfort or consolation: *Though sight be lost, Life yet hath many solaces* (Milton).
—*v.t.* **1** to comfort; cheer; relieve; soothe: *She solaced herself with a book. ... fevered with ivy poison and solacing his woes with tobacco and Shakespeare* (Francis Parkman). **2** *Archaic.* to make (a place) cheerful or pleasant. **3** *Obsolete.* to entertain.
—*v.i. Obsolete.* to give comfort or relief.
[Middle English *solas* < Old French < Latin *sōlācium* < *sōlārī* to console, soothe. See etym. of doublet **solatium.**] —**sol′ace|ment,** *n.* —**sol′acer,** *n.*
**so|lan** (sō′lən), *n.,* or **solan goose,** = gannet. [variant of Middle English *soland,* perhaps < Scandinavian (compare Old Icelandic *súla* gannet, *and-, ond* duck)]
**sol|a|na|ceous** (sol′ə nā′shəs), *adj.* belonging to the nightshade family: *Tobacco, potatoes, tomatoes, and petunias are solanaceous plants.* [< New Latin *Solanaceae* the family (< *Solanum* the typical genus < Latin *sōlānum* nightshade) + English *-ous*]
**sol|a|nin** (sol′ə nin, sō′lə-), *n.* = solanine.
**sol|a|nine** (sol′ə nēn, -nin; sō′lə-), *n.* a poisonous alkaloid obtained from the black nightshade and other kinds of solanum. *Formula:* $C_{45}H_{73}NO_{15}$ [< *solan*(um) + *-ine*[2]]
**so|la|no** (sō lä′nō), *n.* a dry, very warm easterly wind that blows in the southeastern coastal region of Spain in the summer. [< Spanish *solano* < Latin *Sōlānus* the east wind; properly, adjective, of the sun < *sōl, sōlis* sun]
**so|la|num** (sō lā′nəm), *n.* any one of a large genus of erect or climbing herbs, shrubs, or small trees of the nightshade family, such as the nightshade, eggplant, and common white potato. [< New Latin *Solanum* the genus name < Latin *sōlānum* nightshade]
**so|lar** (sō′lər), *adj.* **1** of the sun: *a solar eclipse.* **2** having to do with the sun: *solar research.* **3** coming from the sun: *Solar heat is less in winter than in the summer. Solar energy is given off by atomic reactions taking place inside the sun.* **4** measured or determined by the earth's motion in relation to the sun: *solar time.* **5** working by means of the sun's light or heat. A solar telegraph uses mirrors to reflect flashes of sunlight. [< Latin *sōlāris* < *sōl, sōlis* sun]
**solar apex,** the point in space, situated in the constellation Hercules, toward which the sun is moving.
**solar battery,** a device that uses silicon crystals to trap sunlight and convert it into electrical energy: *The tiny solar batteries can get all the power they need to run the radio for as long as a year* (Science News Letter).
**solar cell,** a device that converts solar radiation into electrical energy: *Solar cells ... are widely employed for supplying electricity from sunlight in space vehicles* (Scientific American).
**solar constant,** the amount of heat from the sun that would reach one square centimeter of the earth's surface in one minute if no heat were lost in the atmosphere and the earth's surface were perpendicular to the sun's rays.
**solar day,** = mean solar day.
**solar disk,** (in ancient Egyptian art) a disk that stood for the sun, put upright on the head of an idol of a sun god.
**solar flare,** a sudden eruption of hydrogen gas on the surface of the sun, usually associated with sunspots, accompanied by a burst of ultraviolet radiation that travels toward the earth. Solar flares cause ionization in the upper atmosphere and are responsible for the fading of high-frequency radio reception. ... *the solar flare, the most violent activity on the face of the sun* (Scientific American).
***solar furnace,** a furnace heated by energy from the sun. It is used especially in research because the usual accompanying impurities of burning fuel are absent. *Solar furnaces, reaching temperatures of 3,000 degrees centigrade, focus the sun's heat by one or more mirrors* (Science News Letter).

***solar furnace**

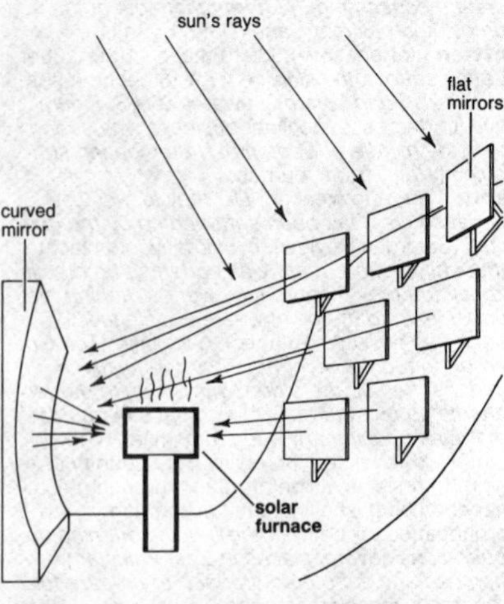


**so|lar|ism** (sō′lə riz əm), *n.* the interpretation of a myth by reference to the sun, especially such interpretation carried to an extreme.
**so|lar|i|um** (sə lãr′ē əm), *n., pl.* **-i|a** (-ē ə). a room or porch where people can lie or sit in the sun.
**so|lar|i|za|tion** (sō′lər ə zā′shən), *n.* **1** exposure to sunlight. **2** *Photography.* **a** overexposure to light. **b** the effects of this on a print.
**so|lar|ize** (sō′lə rīz), *v.,* **-ized, -iz|ing.** —*v.t.* **1** to affect by sunlight. **2** *Photography.* to overexpose to light.
—*v.i.* **1** to be affected by sunlight. **2** *Photography.* to be overexposed to light.
**solar month,** one twelfth of a solar year.
**solar panel,** a panel of solar cells: *Electrical energy was derived from sunlight by two solar panels unfolded by the astronauts from either side of the device* (Walter Sullivan).
**solar physics,** the astrophysical study of the sun.
**solar plexus, 1** a large network of sympathetic nerves connected with the abdominal organs, situated at the upper part of the abdomen, behind the stomach and in front of the aorta. **2** *Informal.* the pit of the stomach. [< New Latin *solar plexus* (because of its radial shape)]
**solar radiation,** radiant energy of the sun.
**solar salt,** a coarse salt derived from solar evaporation of salt water.
**solar still,** a device that uses the sun's energy to desalinate water: *The roof-type solar still consists of a blackened tray and a glass roof with condensation troughs along each side* (New Scientist).
***solar system,** the sun and all the planets, satellites, comets, and other heavenly bodies, that revolve around it. See picture below on next page.
**solar time,** = apparent solar time.
**solar wind,** a continuous stream of charged particles, mainly protons and electrons, ejected by the sun and extending in all directions through interplanetary space: *The speed of the solar wind as it passes the earth has been measured at several hundred kilometers per second* (Hugh Odishaw). See picture under **magnetosphere.**
**solar year,** the period of time required for the earth to make one complete revolution around the sun, from one vernal equinox to the next; tropical year; astronomical year. The solar year lasts 365 days, 5 hours, 48 minutes, 45.51 seconds.
**so|la|ti|um** (sō lā′shē əm), *n., pl.* **-ti|a** (-shē ə). a compensation, as for suffering, loss, or hurt feelings. [< Latin *sōlātium* < *sōlārī* to console, soothe. See etym. of doublet **solace.**]
**sola topee,** = pith helmet.
**sold** (sōld), *v.* the past tense and past participle of **sell:** *He sold his car a week ago. He has sold his car.*
**sol|dan** (sol′dən), *n.* the supreme ruler in the Middle Ages of a Moslem country, especially Egypt. [< Old French *soldan* < Arabic *sulṭān.* Compare etym. under **sultan.**]
**sol|der** (sod′ər; *British* sol′dər, sod′ər), *n., v.* —*n.* **1** any metal or alloy that can be melted and used for joining or mending metal surfaces or parts. **2** *Figurative.* anything that unites firmly or joins closely: *the very solder of Nature* (John Tyndall).
—*v.t.* **1** to fasten, mend, or join with solder: *He soldered the broken wires together. He soldered a hole in the pan. There have been instances in which two fragments [of old bronze] not belonging to each other have been soldered together to form a complete and spurious object of art*

(George Savage). 2 *Figurative.* to unite firmly; join closely: *unite and solder up their several schemes to join against the Church* (Jonathan Swift). 3 *Figurative.* to mend; repair; patch: *to solder ... the flaws and imperfections of nature* (Jonathan Swift).
– *v.i.* 1 to become soldered. 2 to become united by soldering: (*Figurative.*) *Their* [*children's*] *little brittle bones quickly solder* (W. H. Hudson).
[< Old French *soldure* < *solder* solidify < Latin *solidāre* < *solidus* solid] – **sol′der\|a\|ble**, *adj.* – **sol′der\|er**, *n.*

**sol\|der\|ing gun** (sod′ər ing; *British* sol′dər-, sod′ər-), a fast-heating soldering iron with a wire tip for the point and a pistol-shaped handle.

**soldering iron**, 1 an electric tool consisting of a long rod in a handle and a pointed copper tip that heats to melt solder. 2 a tool like this heated in a flame.

**sol\|dier** (sōl′jər), *n., v.* – *n.* 1 a person who serves in an army: *The trade of the soldier is war* (E. A. Parkes). 2 an enlisted man in the army, not a commissioned officer: *The common soldiers were in tents while their officers slept in cabins.* 3 a man having skill or experience in war. 4 *Figurative.* a person who serves in any cause: *soldiers of science, Christian soldiers.* 5 *U.S. Slang.* = button man. 6 *Zoology.* **a** one of a type of workers with a large head and powerful jaws in a colony of certain kinds of ants. **b** one of a kind of large-headed individuals in a colony of termites.
– *v.i.* 1 to act or serve as a soldier: *Caesar went off to soldier in Asia, at 18, and won both honor and disgrace* (Time). 2 *Informal.* **a** to pretend to work but do very little. **b** to pretend to be ill.
**soldier on**, *British.* to carry on under adverse conditions, as a soldier would: *The report suggests that some means be found of rewarding specially those who soldier on in the more difficult schools* (London Times).
[Middle English *soudeour* < Old French *soldier* < *solde, soulde* pay, coin < Latin *solidus* a Roman gold coin; see etym. under **solid**]

**soldier beetle**, any one of a group of beetles resembling the firefly, whose larva destroys other insects.

**soldier bug**, any one of various hemipterous insects which prey upon cutworms and other destructive larvae, such as the stinkbug.

**soldier crab**, = hermit crab.

**sol\|dier\|ing** (sol′jər ing), *n.* 1 the act or condition of being a soldier; military service or duty. 2 *Informal.* the act or practice of pretending to work; malingering.

**sol\|dier\|like** (sōl′jər līk′), *adj., adv.* – *adj.* 1 having the character or bearing of a soldier: *neat, clean, and soldierlike.* 2 befitting a soldier.
– *adv.* in a manner befitting a soldier: *to march soldierlike.*

**sol\|dier\|ly** (sōl′jər lē), *adj.* like a soldier; like that of a soldier; suitable for a soldier: *a soldierly manner.* – **sol′dier\|li\|ness**, *n.*

**soldier of fortune**, a man serving or ready to serve as a soldier under any government for money, adventure, or pleasure.

**soldiers' cap**, 1 = Dutchman's-breeches. 2 = monkshood.

**sol\|dier\|ship** (sōl′jər ship), *n.* 1 the condition or profession of a soldier. 2 soldierly qualities or skill.

**soldiers' home**, a government institution that provides shelter and care for disabled or homeless veterans: *After the Civil War the Congress established a number of soldiers' homes.*

**Soldier's Medal**, a military decoration given to a member of the United States armed forces for bravery involving the risk of life on noncombat duty.

**sol\|dier\|y** (sōl′jər ē), *n., pl.* **-dier\|ies.** 1a soldiers as a group: *the soldiery of the Allies.* **b** all military personnel as a group. 2 a body of soldiers: *The mercenaries were ... a fierce and rapacious soldiery* (Scott). 3 military training or knowledge.

**sol\|do** (sol′dō), *n., pl.* **-di** (-dē). an Italian copper coin, 1/20 of a lira. [< Italian *soldo* < Latin *solidus.* See etym. of doublets **sol**[3], **solid, sou.**]

**sold-out** (sōld′out′), *adj.* being a sellout; having no unsold seats or standing room left: *This spring they played a Beethoven sonata series in Vienna to sold-out houses* (New York Times).

**sole**[1] (sōl), *adj.* 1a one and only; single: *He was the sole heir to the fortune when his aunt died. Is that your sole objection?* SYN: See syn. under **single. b** of matchless quality; unique; singular: *The evil time's sole patriot* (Emerson). 2 only: *We three were the sole survivors from the wreck.* SYN: See syn. under **single**. 3 of or for only one person or group and not others; exclusive: *the sole right of use.* 4 without help; alone: *a sole undertaking.* 5 *Law.* unmarried: *a feme sole.* [< Old French *soul* < Latin *sōlus* alone] – **sole′ness**, *n.*

**sole**[2] (sōl), *n., v.,* **soled, sol\|ing.** – *n.* 1 the bottom or undersurface of the foot. 2a the bottom of a shoe, slipper, or boot. **b** a piece of leather or rubber cut in the same shape. 3 the undersurface; underpart; bottom: *the sole of an iron. The sole of a golf club is the part of the head that comes closest to the ground.*
– *v.t.* 1 to put a sole on: *I must have my shoes soled.* 2 *Golf.* to place the sole of (a club) on the ground behind the ball.
[< Old French *sole,* ultimately < Latin *solea* sandal, shoe < *solum* bottom, ground]

**sole**[3] (sōl), *n., pl.* **soles** or (*collectively*) **sole.** 1 a kind of flatfish much used for food. Soles have small mouths and small, close-set eyes. They comprise a family of fishes. 2 any one of certain related fishes, such as some of the flounders. [< Old French *sole* < Vulgar Latin *sola* < Latin *solea;* see etym. under **sole**[2]]

**sol\|e\|cism** (sol′ə siz əm), *n.* 1 a mistake in using words; violation of the grammatical or other accepted usages of a language: *"I done it" is a solecism.* 2 a mistake in social behavior; breach of good manners or etiquette: *unused to society and ... afraid of making herself ... conspicuous by some solecism or blunder* (Charlotte Brontë). [< Latin *soloecismos* < Greek *soloikismós,* reputedly < *Sóloi,* an Athenian colony in Cilicia, whose form of Attic dialect the Athenians considered barbarous]

**sol\|e\|cist** (sol′ə sist), *n.* a person who commits a solecism.

**sol\|e\|cis\|tic** (sol′ə sis′tik), *adj.* of the nature of a solecism; characterized by solecisms. – **sol′e\|cis′ti\|cal\|ly**, *adv.*

**sol\|e\|cize** (sol′ə sīz), *v.i.,* **-cized, -ciz\|ing.** to commit solecisms.

**-soled**, *combining form.* having ___ soles: *Thick-soled = having thick soles.*

**so\|le\|i\|form** (sə lē′ə fôrm), *adj.* having the form of a slipper. [< Latin *solea* slipper + English *-form*]

**so\|leil** (sō lā′), *n.* felt, wool, rayon, or other cloth with a silky texture. [< French *soleil* sun]

**sole leather**, strong, thick hide or leather.

**sole\|ly** (sōl′lē), *adv.* 1 as the only one or ones; alone: *You will be solely responsible for providing lunch.* 2 only: *Bananas grow outdoors solely in warm climates. He uses a car solely for convenience.*

**sol\|emn** (sol′əm), *adj.* 1a serious, grave, or earnest: *a solemn face, to speak in a solemn voice, solemn meditations. Why do you bend such solemn brows on me?* (Shakespeare). **b** formal: *to enter into a solemn agreement. He gave his solemn promise to do better.* 2 causing serious or grave thoughts: *The organ played solemn music. There reigned a solemn silence over all* (Edmund Spenser). SYN: impressive. 3 done with form and ceremony: *a solemn procession.* 4 connected with religion; observing certain religious rites; sacred: *a solemn Requiem.* 5 gloomy; dark; somber in color: *These heroes sleep in the land they made free ... under the solemn pines* (Robert G. Ingersoll). 6 legally correct. [Middle English *solempne* < Latin *sollempnis,* variant of *sollemnis* established, festal, religious] – **sol′emn\|ly**, *adv.* – **sol′emn\|ness**, *n.*

**Solemn High Mass** or **Solemn Mass**, = High Mass.

**so\|lem\|ni\|fy** (sə lem′nə fī), *v.t.,* **-fied, -fy\|ing.** to make solemn.

**sol\|em\|nise** (sol′əm nīz), *v.,* **-nised, -nis\|ing.** *Especially British.* solemnize.

**so\|lem\|ni\|ty** (sə lem′nə tē), *n., pl.* **-ties.** 1 solemn feeling; seriousness; impressiveness: *The solemnity of the church service was felt even by the children.* 2 Often, **solemnities.** a solemn, formal ceremony: *Passover and Easter are observed with solemnity. The solemnities were concluded with a prayer by the chaplain.* 3 *Law.* a formality necessary to make an act or document valid.

**sol\|em\|ni\|za\|tion** (sol′əm nə zā′shən), *n.* 1 the act of solemnizing. 2 the condition of being solemnized.

**sol\|em\|nize** (sol′əm nīz), *v.,* **-nized, -niz\|ing.** – *v.t.* 1 to observe with ceremonies: *Christian churches solemnize the resurrection of Christ at Easter.* 2 to hold or perform (a ceremony or service): *The marriage was solemnized in the cathedral.* 3 to make serious or grave.
– *v.i.* to speak or meditate solemnly.

**sol\|em\|niz\|er** (sol′əm nī′zər), *n.* 1 a person who solemnizes. 2 a person who performs a solemn rite.

**solemn vow**, a public vow taken by a Roman Catholic religious under which ownership of property is forbidden and marriage becomes invalid. Solemn vows are perpetual and irrevocable.

**so\|le\|no\|don** (sə lē′nə don), *n.* either of two related animals about the size of a squirrel, the almiqui of Cuba and a related variety of Haiti; opossum shrew. They look like the opossum and feed on insects. [< New Latin *Solenodon* the genus name < Greek *sōlên* channel + *odoús, odóntos* tooth]

**so\|le\|no\|dont** (sə lē′nə dont), *adj., n.* – *adj.* 1 of or having to do with the solenodons. 2 like the solenodon. – *n.* = solenodon.

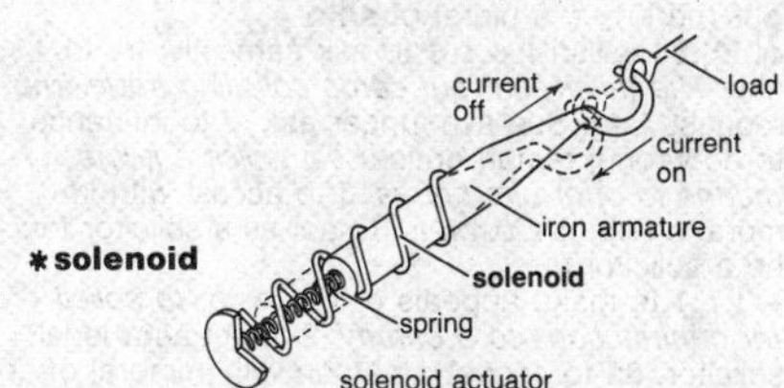

***solenoid**

***so\|le\|noid** (sō′lə noid), *n.* a spiral or cylindrical coil of wire that acts like a magnet when an elec-

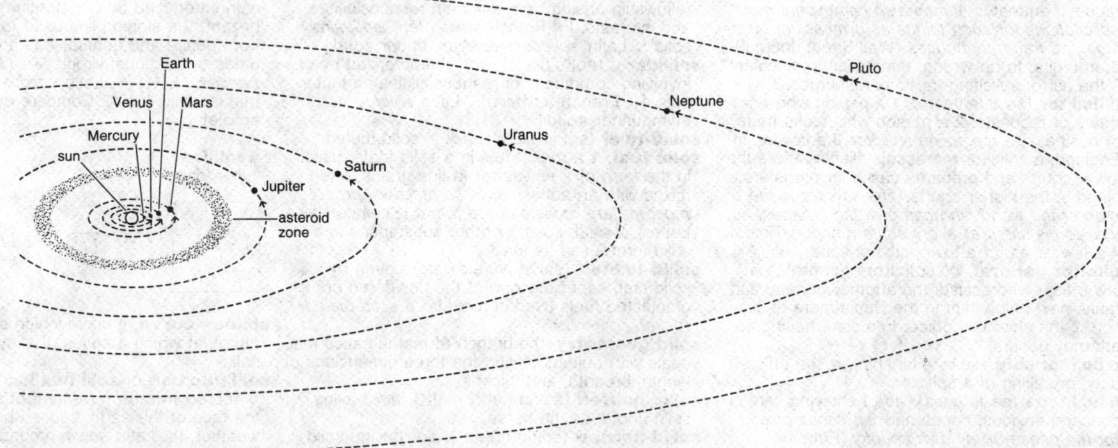

***solar system**

tric current passes through it. Solenoids are used in circuit breakers, automobile directional flashers, and mechanical sorting devices. [< French *solénoïde* < Greek *sōlēn, -ēnos* channel + *eîdos* form]

**so|le|noi|dal** (sō′lə noi′dəl), *adj.* **1** of or having to do with a solenoid. **2** of the nature of or resembling a solenoid. – **so′le|noi′dal|ly**, *adv.*

**sole|plate** (sōl′plāt′), *n.* **1** the base of a flatiron. **2** = bedplate. **3** the back part of a bucket in a water wheel. **4** the casting underneath a large bearing for a shaft. **5** protoplasm located at the end of several motor nerve fibers, containing their nuclei.

**sole|print** (sōl′print′), *n.* an impression of the sole of a foot for purposes of identification. Some hospitals take the soleprints of newborn babies.

**so|le|ra** (sō lā′rä), *adj., n.* – *adj.* of or having to do with a method of producing sherry, by blending various grades through a system of graded casks to achieve a uniform blend.
– *n.* **1** one of the graded casks used in this process. **2** the wine produced by these means.
[< Spanish *solera*]

**sole source**, *U.S.* a single firm contracted by a government agency to manufacture or supply a product: *When a sole source is awarded a contract, no competitive bids are requested by the government.*

**so|le|us** (sō′lē us), *n., pl.* **so|le|i** (sō′lē ī). a broad, flat muscle of the calf of the leg, situated immediately in front of and deeper than the gastrocnemius. See diagram under **leg**. [< New Latin *soleus* < Latin *solea*; see etym. under **sole**[2]]

**sol-fa** (sōl′fä′), *n., adj., v.,* **-faed, -fa|ing.** – *n.* the system of singing the syllables, *do, re, mi, fa, sol, la, ti, do* to tones of the scale; solmization.
– *adj.* of or having to do with this system of singing: *sol-fa notation, a sol-fa scale.*
– *v.i.* to use the sol-fa syllables in singing.
– *v.t.* to sing to the sol-fa scale.
[< Italian *solfa* < *sol* + *fa*; see etym. under **gamut**]

**sol-fa|ist** (sōl′fä′ist), *n.* a person who uses or believes in using the sol-fa syllables in singing.

**sol-fa syllables**, the sol-fa system of singing; sol-fa.

**sol|fa|ta|ra** (sōl′fä tä′rä), *n.* a volcanic vent or area that gives off only sulfurous gases, steam, and the like. [< Italian *Solfatara*, a volcano near Naples < *solfo* sulfur < Latin *sulfur, sulphur*]

**sol|fège** (sol fezh′), *n.* = solfeggio. [< French *solfège* < Italian *solfeggio*]

**sol|feg|gio** (sol fej′ō, -ē ō), *n., pl.* **-feg|gios** (-fej′ōz, -ē ōz), **-feg|gi** (-fej′ē). *Music.* **1a** an exercise for the voice in which the sol-fa syllables are used. **b** any exercise for voice. **2** the use of the sol-fa syllables. [< Italian *solfeggio* < *solfa*; see etym. under **sol-fa**]

**so|li** (sō′lē), *n.* a plural of **solo**.

**so|lic|it** (sə lis′it), *v.t.* **1** to ask earnestly; try to get: *The tailor sent out cards soliciting trade.* SYN: request, beg. See syn. under **ask**. **2** to influence to do wrong; tempt; entice: *To solicit a judge means to offer him bribes.* **3** to accost with immoral offers. **4** *Obsolete.* to act as a solicitor for; be a solicitor in.
– *v.i.* **1** to make appeals or requests: *to solicit for contributions to a charity.* **2** to act as a legal solicitor. **3a** to accost a person with immoral offers. **b** to try to get orders.
[earlier, manage affairs, disturb < Latin *sollicitāre*; see etym. under **solicitous**]

**so|lic|i|tant** (sə lis′ə tənt), *adj., n.* – *adj.* soliciting.
– *n.* a person who solicits.

**so|lic|i|ta|tion** (sə lis′ə tā′shən), *n.* **1** an earnest request; entreaty: *Alumni also can expect more solicitations for such things as gymnasium buildings and fraternity houses* (Wall Street Journal). **2** an urging to do wrong; temptation; enticement. **3** the act of soliciting for immoral purposes.

**so|lic|i|tor** (sə lis′ə tər), *n.* **1** a person who entreats or requests. **2** a person who seeks trade or business: *a magazine solicitor.* **3** a lawyer. In England, a solicitor represents clients before the lower courts and prepares cases for barristers to plead in the higher courts. *The solicitor is the man of the world who can give the broadest advice to his client at every stage* (London Times). **4** a lawyer as for a town, city, or state.

**solicitor general**, *pl.* **solicitors general**. **1** a law officer who assists the attorney general and ranks next below him in the Department of Justice. **2** the chief law officer in a state having no attorney general.

**so|lic|i|tor|ship** (sə lis′ə tər ship), *n.* the office, duty, or calling of a solicitor.

**so|lic|i|tous** (sə lis′ə təs), *adj.* **1** showing care or concern; anxious; concerned: *solicitous chiefly for the peace of my own country* (Edmund Burke). *Parents are solicitous for their children's progress in school.* **2** desirous; eager: *solicitous to please.* **3** very careful or attentive; particular: *solicitous in the meeting of an obligation.* [< Latin *sollicitus* (with English *-ous*) < *sollicitāre* to disturb < Old Latin *sollus* whole, all + Latin *ciēre* arouse] – **so|lic′i|tous|ly**, *adv.* – **so|lic′i|tous|ness**, *n.*

**so|lic|i|tude** (sə lis′ə tüd, -tyüd), *n.* anxious care; anxiety; concern: *... the tender solicitude of a parent* (Lytton Strachey). SYN: See syn. under **care**.
**solicitudes**, cares; troubles; causes of anxiety: *To her the destinies of mankind ... made the solicitudes of feminine fashion appear an occupation for bedlam* (George Eliot).

**so|lic|i|tu|di|nous** (sə lis′ə tü′də nəs, -tyü′-), *adj.* full of solicitude.

**sol|id** (sol′id), *adj., adv., n.* – *adj.* **1** not a liquid or a gas: *Water becomes solid when it freezes. A block of stone is solid material ... no matter where you put it, it keeps its shape* (Beauchamp, Mayfield, and West). **2** not hollow: *A bar of iron is solid; a pipe is hollow.* **3** strongly put together; hard; firm: *They were glad to leave the boat and put their feet on solid ground.* SYN: compact, stable. See syn. under **firm**. **4** alike throughout: *solid gold. The cloth is a solid blue. There wasn't a light on; the house was in solid darkness.* **5a** firmly united: *The country was solid for peace.* **b** *U.S. Informal.* regular in attendance; steady in support: *I'm solid for Mr. Peck every time* (William Dean Howells). **6** serious; not superficial or trifling: *a background of solid study. Chemistry and physics are solid subjects.* **7** genuine; real: *solid comfort; ... a debt of solid gratitude* (Edward A. Freeman). **8** that can be depended on: *He is a solid citizen.* **9** having or based on good judgment; sound; sensible; intelligent: *a solid book by a solid thinker, a solid argument. These men ... have some of the solidest information available* (Newsweek). **10** financially sound or strong: *a solid business. "The gasoline market is the solidest in two years," says one Oklahoma refiner* (Wall Street Journal). **11** whole; entire; complete: *He spent a solid hour on his arithmetic.* **12** undivided; continuous: *a solid wall, a solid row of houses.* **13** having length, breadth, and thickness. A sphere is a solid figure. **14** written without a hyphen or space: *"Earthworm" is a solid word.* **15** *Printing.* having the lines of type not separated by leads; having few open spaces. **16** *U.S. Informal.* on a friendly, favorable, or advantageous footing: *to get in solid with one's employer.* **17** thorough; downright; vigorous; substantial: *a good solid dose of medicine, a good solid blow.* **18** *U.S. Slang.* good; excellent; first-rate: *"It sounds good!" he shouted. "Solid!"* (New Yorker).
– *adv. Informal.* full; completely: *The train was packed solid with tourists. 86th Street, which had been parked solid the night before, was denuded of cars* (New York Times).
– *n.* **1** a substance that is not a liquid or a gas such as iron, wood, or ice: *In a solid, the molecules resist any force that tends to change their relative positions or distances* (John C. Duncan). **2** a body that has length, breadth, and thickness. A cube is a solid.
[< Latin *solidus*. See etym. of doublets **sol**[3], **soldo, sou.**] – **sol′id|ly**, *adv.* – **sol′id|ness**, *n.*

**sol|i|da|go** (sol′ə dā′gō), *n., pl.* **-gos.** = goldenrod. [< New Latin *Solidago* the genus name, ultimately < Latin *solidāre* strengthen < *solidus* solid (because of its supposed healing power)]

**solid angle**, an angle formed by three or more planes intersecting at a common point.

**sol|i|dar|ic** (sol′ə dar′ik), *adj.* characterized by solidarity.

**sol|i|dar|i|ty** (sol′ə dar′ə tē), *n., pl.* **-ties.** unity or fellowship arising from common responsibilities and interests. [< French *solidarité* < *solidaire* solid < Latin *solidus*; see etym. under **solid**]

**sol|i|dar|y** (sol′ə der′ē), *adj.* characterized by or involving community of responsibilities and interests. [< French *solidaire* < Latin *solidus*; see etym. under **solid**]

**sol|id-fu|el** (sol′id fyü′əl), *adj.* = solid-fueled.

**solid fuel**, **1** a rocket fuel in a solid state, usually in the form of a powder or in fine grains, often mixed with an adhesive: *Solid fuels will propel most military rockets in the future* (Science News Letter). **2** coal, coke, or other substances in a solid form, used as fuel.

**sol|id-fu|eled** (sol′id fyü′əld), *adj.* driven by a solid fuel, especially one of the powdered or granulated fuels used in rockets: *a solid-fueled rocket.*

**solid geometry**, the branch of mathematics that deals with objects having the three dimensions of length, breadth, and thickness.

**sol|id-hoofed** (sol′id hůft′, -hüft′), *adj.* having solid hoofs, as the horse.

**sol|id-horned** (sol′id hôrnd′), *adj.* having solid horns, as deer.

**sol|i|di** (sol′ə dī), *n.* plural of **solidus**.

**so|lid|i|fi|a|ble** (sə lid′ə fī′ə bəl), *adj.* that can be solidified.

**so|lid|i|fi|ca|tion** (sə lid′ə fə kā′shən), *n.* **1** the act or process of solidifying: *The origin of present practices and beliefs is lost in centuries of sociological solidification* (Atlantic). **2** the state of being solidified. **3** *Physics.* the passage of a body from a liquid or gaseous to a solid state, accompanied by loss of heat and a change in volume.

**so|lid|i|fy** (sə lid′ə fī), *v.,* **-fied, -fy|ing.** – *v.t.* **1** to make solid; harden: *Extreme cold will solidify water into ice.* **2** *Figurative.* to unite firmly. **3** to crystallize.
– *v.i.* **1** to become solid; be converted from a liquid to a solid: *Jelly solidifies as it gets cold.* **2** *Figurative.* to become firmly united: *The opposition in Congress to the President's proposal solidified over the next two weeks.* **3** to become crystallized.
[< *solid* + *-fy*]

**so|lid|i|ty** (sə lid′ə tē), *n., pl.* **-ties.** **1** the condition or quality of being solid; firmness or hardness; density: *the solidity of marble or steel. Transparency is one goal of the architect, says Breuer, "but transparency needs also solidity"* (Newsweek). **2** substantial quality, as of a person's learning, judgment, or character: *the solidity of George Washington's character.* **3** *Geometry.* volume; cubic content.

**solid mechanics**, mechanics that deals with bodies at rest or in motion, as distinguished from fluid mechanics.

**solid propellant**, = solid fuel.

**solid rocket**, a rocket using solid fuel. See picture under **rocket**[1].

**Solid South**, *U.S.* the Southern states that have usually supported the Democratic Party as a unit since the Reconstruction period: *The old eleven-state structure of the Solid South, which has stood with Bourbon pride and purpose and faded gallantry for a century or more* (Harper's).

**sol|id-state** (sol′id stāt′), *adj.* **1** of or having to do with solid-state physics and electronics: *solid-state phenomena.* **2** made with transistors, printed circuits, and other devices, using the conductive or other properties of solid materials: *The availability of solid-state devices has resulted in the introduction of a new line of equipment which supersedes older vacuum-tube versions to provide improved performance, increased reliability, smaller size, and in some cases lower cost* (U.S. Berger).

**solid-state electronics**, the branch of electronics that deals with semiconductors, masers, and similar electronic devices developed from studies in solid-state physics.

**solid-state maser**, a maser that amplifies radio signals by means of a solid material, such as synthetic ruby, surrounded by a magnetic field: *Known as the solid-state maser, the device would amplify the very faint signals received from space* (Science News Letter).

**solid-state physicist**, a person who studies solid-state physics.

**solid-state physics**, the branch of physics that deals with the physical properties of solid materials, such as mechanical strength, the movement of electrons, and the nature of crystals. Research in solid-state physics has produced the transistor and other semiconductor devices. *In one sense, solid-state physics can be described as a combination of chemistry and electronics* (Wall Street Journal).

**sol|id|un|gu|late** (sol′ə dung′gyə lit, -lāt), *adj., n.* – *adj.* belonging to the group of mammals with solid hoofs, such as the horse.
– *n.* a solidungulate animal.

* **sol|i|dus** (sol′ə dəs), *n., pl.* **-di.** **1** a Roman gold coin introduced by Constantine, later called a bezant. **2** a sloping line used to separate shillings from pence and generally as a dividing line, as in dates or fractions; virgule: 2/6 (*2 shillings, 6 pence*); 1/2, 1/3. [< Latin *solidus* (*nummus*) gold, that is, solid (coin). Compare etym. under **sou, soldier.**]

* **solidus**
definition 2

**solidus curve**, a curve which shows the temperatures at which a series of alloys are completely solid.

**sol|i|fluc|tion** or **sol|i|flux|ion** (sol′ə fluk′shən), *n.* the downward movement of soil and rock on the face of the earth, caused by the action of the weather. [< Latin *solum* ground, earth + English *fluxion*]

**so|lil|o|quist** (sə lil′ə kwist), *n.* **1** a person who soliloquizes. **2** a person who writes soliloquies.

**so|lil|o|quize** (sə lil′ə kwīz), *v.i.*, **-quized, -quiz|ing. 1** to talk to oneself: *Soliloquizing with the lucidity of genius* (Harper's). **2** to speak a soliloquy. **– so|lil′o|quiz′er,** *n.* **– so|lil′o|quiz′ing|ly,** *adv.*

**so|lil|o|quy** (sə lil′ə kwē), *n., pl.* **-quies. 1** a talking to oneself. **2** a speech made by an actor to himself, especially when alone on the stage. It reveals his thoughts and feelings to the audience, but not to the other characters in the play. **3** a similar speech by a character in a book, poem, or other literary work. [< Late Latin *sōliloquium* (introduced by Saint Augustine) < Latin *sōlus* alone + *loquī* speak]

**sol|i|on** (sol′ī′ən), *n.* a small electronic device containing ions in solution, that can detect and amplify minute changes, as in current, pressure, or temperature.

**sol|i|ped** (sol′ə ped), *adj., n.* = solidungulate. [< New Latin *solipes, -pedis* < Latin *solidus* solid + *pēs, pedis* foot]

**sol|ip|sism** (sol′ip siz əm), *n. Philosophy.* the theory that self is the only object of real knowledge or that nothing but self exists: *In him, personality was more than egotism, more even than egomania; it reached the level of solipsism* (New Yorker). [< Latin *sōlus* alone + *ipse* self]

**sol|ip|sist** (sol′ip sist), *n.* a person who believes in solipsism.

**sol|ip|sis|tic** (sol′ip sis′tik), *adj.* of or characterized by solipsism: *His solipsistic view of the world neatly prevents ... purposive behaviour because he refuses to admit the initial premise of the existence of anything beyond his own ego* (Manchester Guardian). **– sol′ip|sis′ti|cal|ly,** *adv.*

**sol|i|taire** (sol′ə tãr), *n.* **1** a card game played by one person, usually an attempt to put cards in a given order. **2** a diamond or other gem set by itself. **3** either one of two species of birds related to and resembling the dodo that lived on two islands in the Indian Ocean and became extinct in the 1700's. **4** a solitary; recluse. [< French *solitaire,* Old French, learned borrowing from Latin *sōlitārius.* See etym. of doublet **solitary.**]

**sol|i|tar|y** (sol′ə ter′ē), *adj., n., pl.* **-tar|ies.** **– *adj.*** **1a** alone or single; only: *A solitary rider was seen in the distance.* **SYN:** lone, sole. **b** being the only one; standing by itself; unparalleled: *not a single, solitary exception to the rule. The result, not of solitary conjecture, but of practice and experience* (Samuel Johnson). **2a** without companions; lonely: *The trapper leads a solitary life in the mountains. Secret, and self-contained, and solitary as an oyster* (Dickens). **SYN:** unattended. **b** away from people; remote; secluded: *The house is in a solitary spot miles from town.* **3a** *Zoology.* living alone, rather than in colonies: *a solitary bee.* **b** *Botany.* growing separately; not forming clusters: *a solitary stipule.*
**– *n.*** **1** a person living alone, away from people. **2** a person who is left alone: *An orphan and a solitary whose mother's death ... had amounted to a tragedy* (Arnold Bennett). **3** = solitary confinement.
[< Latin *sōlitārius,* ultimately < *sōlus* alone. See etym. of doublet **solitaire.**] **– sol′i|tar′i|ly,** *adv.* **– sol′i|tar′i|ness,** *n.*

**solitary confinement,** the separate confinement of a prisoner in complete isolation as a penalty for misbehavior.

**solitary greenlet,** = solitary vireo.

**solitary sandpiper,** a sandpiper with dark wings and back and a white breast, that nests in northern North America and migrates in winter to tropical America.

**solitary vireo,** the blue-headed vireo of the United States.

**solitary wasp,** any one of various wasps that do not live in communities, but build separate nests.

**sol|i|tude** (sol′ə tüd, -tyüd), *n.* **1** a being alone: *He likes company and hates solitude.* **2** a lonely place: *This forest is a solitude.* **3** loneliness: *to travel through regions of solitude.* [perhaps < Old French *solitude,* learned borrowing from Latin *sōlitūdō* < *sōlus* alone]
**– *Syn.*** **1 Solitude, isolation** mean a state of being alone. **Solitude,** applying to a state of being either where there are no other people for company or cut off voluntarily or involuntarily from those around, emphasizes aloneness, the fact or feeling of being entirely by oneself, without companions: *Both the prospector in the desert and the shy person in the city live in solitude.* **Isolation** emphasizes being separated from others or standing apart from the rest of the world: *A single mountain peak rose in splendid isolation.*

**sol|lar** or **sol|ler** (sol′ər), *n.* **1** a loft in a church, especially in a steeple. **2** *Archaic.* a garret or attic in a house. [Middle English *solar, soler* upper room (exposed to the sun) < Old French *solier* < Latin *sōlārium* solarium < *sōl* sun]

**sol|ler|et** (sol′ə ret, sol′ə ret′), *n.* a flexible shoe made of steel plates that formed a part of medieval armor. See picture under **armor.** [< Old French *solleret* (diminutive) < *soller* shoe]

**sol|mi|zate** (sol′mə zāt), *v.,* **-zat|ed, -zat|ing.** *Music.* **– *v.t.*** to express by solmization.
**– *v.i.*** to use solmization syllables.

**sol|mi|za|tion** (sol′mə zā′shən), *n.* **1** a system of singing the syllables *do, re, mi, fa, sol, la, ti, do* to the tones of the scale; sol-fa. **2** a medieval system of singing plain-song melodies on six syllables, *ut, re, mi, fa, sol, la.* [< French *solmisation* < *sol* + *mi;* see etym. under **gamut**]

**so|lo** (sō′lō), *n., pl.* **-los** or **-li,** *adj., v.,* **-loed, -lo|ing,** *adv.* **– *n.*** **1** a piece of music for one voice or instrument: *She sang three solos.* **2** anything done without a partner, companion, teacher, or aid, such as a flight made alone in an airplane. **3a** any one of certain card games in which one person plays alone against others. **b** a bid to play without discarding.
**– *adj.*** **1** arranged for and performed by one voice or instrument: *a solo part.* **2** playing the solo part: *a solo violin.* **3** without a partner, companion, teacher, or aid; alone: *a solo flight across the ocean, a solo dance. Back of the bar, in a solo game, sat Dangerous Dan McGrew* (Robert W. Service).
**– *v.i.*** **1** to make a solo flight in an airplane. **2** to sing or play a solo.
**– *adv.*** by oneself; alone: *She flew solo for the first time yesterday.*
[< Italian *solo* alone < Latin *sōlus*]

**so|lo|ist** (sō′lō ist), *n.* a person who performs a solo or solos.

**so|lo|is|tic** (sō′lō is′tik), *adj.* of or for a soloist or soloists: *thin, transparent soloistic instrumentation* (Harper's).

**Solo man,** a type of prehistoric man, found near the Solo River in Java, and regarded as more advanced than Pithecanthropus.

**Sol|o|mon** (sol′ə mən), *n.* **1** a king of Israel who lived in the 900's B.C. Solomon was a son of David and was famous for his wisdom, and for the great temple which he had built in Jerusalem (in the Bible, I Kings 3:5-28). **2** a man of great wisdom. **3** a self-proclaimed wise man; wiseacre: *Solomon of saloons And philosophic diner-out* (Robert Browning).

**Sol|o|mo|ni|an** (sol′ə mō′nē ən), *adj.* **1** of or having to do with Solomon, king of Israel. **2** like that of Solomon; suggesting his wisdom.

**Sol|o|mon|ic** (sol′ə mon′ik), *adj.* = Solomonian.

**Sol|o|mon's-seal** (sol′ə mənz sēl′), *n.* any one of a genus of perennial herbs of the lily family, with small, greenish flowers hanging from the bases of the leaves and a rootstock with scars resembling Solomon's seals. [translation of Medieval Latin *sigillum Solomonis* (because of scars on its rootstock)]

**Solomon's seal,** a mystic star-shaped figure formed of two equilateral triangles, one interlaced with or placed upon the other.

**So|lon** (sō′lən, -lon), *n.* **1** a wise man; sage. **2** *U.S. Informal.* a member of a legislature. [< *Solon,* about 638 B.C. to about 558 B.C., a wise Athenian lawgiver]

**so long,** *Informal.* good-by; farewell.

**So|lo|ni|an** (sə lō′nē ən), *adj.* of or having to do with Solon, an Athenian lawgiver who lived from about 638 B.C. to about 558 B.C.

**So|lon|ic** (sə lon′ik), *adj.* Solonian.

**solo organ,** a section of an organ, containing stops especially suited for solo use against an accompaniment by another section or manual.

**solr.,** solicitor.

***solstice**
definition 1

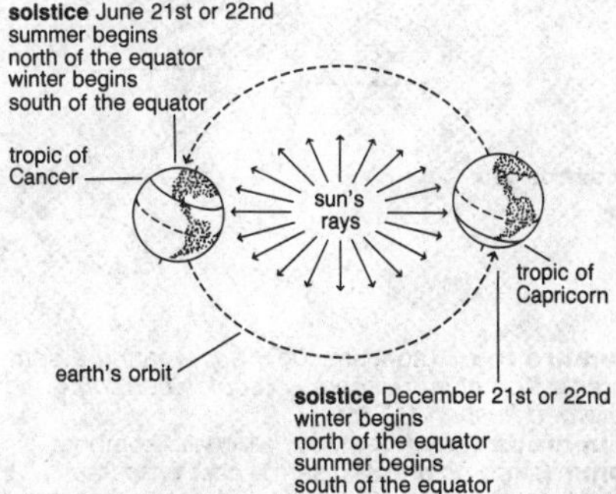


***sol|stice** (sol′stis), *n.* **1** either of the two times in the year when the sun is at its greatest distance from the celestial equator. In the Northern Hemisphere the summer solstice, about June 21, is the longest day of the year, and the winter solstice, about December 21 or 22, is the shortest. In the Southern Hemisphere the solstices are reversed. **2** either of the two points reached by the sun at these times. **3** *Figurative.* a turning or culminating point; furthest limit; crisis. [< Old French *solstice,* learned borrowing from Latin *sōlstitium* < *sōl, sōlis* sun + *sistere* stand still, related to *stāre* to stand]

**sol|sti|tial** (sol stish′əl), *adj.* **1** of or having to do with a solstice: *the solstitial heat being over now* (W. H. Hudson). **2** happening at or near a solstice: *solstitial rains.* **3** that is like the climate of the summer solstice. [< Latin *sōlstitiālis* < *sōlstitium;* see etym. under **solstice**]

**sol|u|bil|i|ty** (sol′yə bil′ə tē), *n., pl.* **-ties. 1** the quality that substances have of dissolving or being dissolved easily: *Anyone can see the solubility of sugar in water. Solubility is another property which varies with temperature* (William N. Jones). **2** the quality that problems, difficulties, questions, or other hurdles, have of being solved or explained.

**sol|u|bil|i|za|tion** (sol′yə bə lə zā′shən), *n.* the act or process of solubilizing.

**sol|u|bil|ize** (sol′yə bə līz), *v.t.,* **-ized, -iz|ing.** to make soluble; dissolve: *These dirt-collecting films, which tend to build up on linoleum, tile and other floor surfaces, are solubilized and prevented from re-forming* (Scientific American). **– sol′u|bil|iz′er,** *n.*

**sol|u|ble** (sol′yə bəl), *adj.* **1** that can be dissolved or made into liquid: *Salt is soluble in water.* **2** that can be solved; solvable: *soluble puzzles. This problem is hard but soluble.* [< Late Latin *solūbilis* < *solvere* dissolve] **– sol′u|ble|ness,** *n.*

**soluble glass,** = water glass.

**soluble RNA,** = transfer RNA. *Abbr:* sRNA (no periods).

**soluble starch,** a product of the hydrolysis of starch, soluble in hot water, obtained as by treating with weak acids or heating with glycerol.

**sol|u|bly** (sol′yə blē), *adv.* in a soluble manner.

**so|lum** (sō′ləm), *n., pl.* **-la.** *Law.* ground; a piece of ground. [< Latin *solum*]

**so|lus** (sō′ləs), *adj. Latin.* by himself; alone (used chiefly as a stage direction). The feminine form is *sola.*

**sol|ute** (sol′yüt, sō′lüt), *n., adj.* **– *n.*** a solid, gas, or liquid that is dissolved in a liquid to make a solution: *Salt is a solute in seawater. Stems ... act as channels through which water and solutes reach the leaves* (Fred W. Emerson).
**– *adj.*** **1** dissolved; in solution. **2** *Botany.* not adhering; free.
[< Latin *solūtus,* past participle of *solvere* dissolve, loosen]

**so|lu|tion** (sə lü′shən), *n.* **1** the act or process of solving a problem: *That problem was hard; its solution required many hours.* **2** an explanation or answer: *The police are seeking a solution of the crime.* **3** the process of dissolving: **a** the changing of a solid or gas to a liquid by mixing with a liquid: *The solution of gases in liquids is usually accompanied by heat.* **b** the uniform mixing of a solid, liquid, or gas with another solid, liquid, or gas. **4** a liquid or homogeneous mixture formed by dissolving: *Every time you put sugar in lemonade you are making a solution. The components of a solution cannot be distinguished with the aid of a microscope* (Parks and Steinbach). **5** the condition of being dissolved: *Sugar and salt can be held in solution in water.* **6** a separating into parts; dissolving. **7** *Mathematics.* any number which makes an open sentence a true statement. *Example:* The number 4 is a solution of $3y + 2 = 14$ because $3 \times 4 + 2 = 14$. **8** *Medicine.* **a** the termination of a disease. **b** the crisis of a disease. **9** *Obsolete, Law.* a payment; discharge (of a contract or obligation).
[< Latin *solūtiō, -ōnis* a loosing < *solvere* loosen, dissolve]

**so|lu|tion|al** (sə lü′shə nəl), *adj.* of, having to do with, or forming a solution.

**so|lu|tion|ist** (sə lü′shə nist), *n.* **1** a person who solves problems; problemist. **2** an expert in solving crossword puzzles.

**solution set,** *Mathematics.* the set which contains all the solutions of an open sentence.

**So|lu|tre|an** or **So|lu|tri|an** (sə lü′trē ən), *adj., n.* **– *adj.*** of or belonging to the period of the late Pleistocene.
**– *n.*** the late Pleistocene.
[< *Solutré,* France, where a cave was discovered containing flint implements of the late Pleistocene + *-an*]

**solv|a|bil|i|ty** (sol′və bil′ə tē), *n., pl.* **-ties. 1** the quality or condition of being solvable; solubility:

**Pronunciation Key:** hat, āge, cãre, fär; let, ēqual, tėrm; it, īce; hot, ōpen, ôrder; oil, out; cup, pu̇t, rüle; child; long; thin; ᴛʜen; zh, measure; ə represents a in about, e in taken, i in pencil, o in lemon, u in circus.

*the solvability of an equation.* **2** *Obsolete.* solvency.

**solv|a|ble** (sol′və bəl), *adj.* **1** capable of being solved. **2** capable of being dissolved; soluble.

**sol|vate** (sol′vāt), *n., v.,* **-vat|ed, -vat|ing.** *—n.* a chemical substance produced by the combination of the ions or molecules of a solvent and a solute. *—v.i., v.t.* to become or cause to become a solvate.

**sol|va|tion** (sol vā′shən), *n.* **1** the combination of a solute with its solvent. **2** the degree to which this takes place.

**Sol|vay process** (sol′vā), a process for deriving sodium carbonate from ordinary salt by dissolving carbon dioxide in a solution of salt and ammonia to produce sodium bicarbonate which is converted into sodium carbonate. [< Ernest *Solvay,* 1838-1922, a Belgian chemist, who invented it]

**solve** (solv), *v.t.,* **solved, solv|ing. 1** to find the answer to; clear up; explain: *The detective solved the mystery. He has solved all the problems in the lesson. She solved the puzzle.* **2** to pay. **3** to melt. [< Latin *solvere* to loosen, dissolve] —**solv′er,** *n.*

**sol|ven|cy** (sol′vən sē), *n., pl.* **-cies.** the ability to pay all one owes.

**sol|vent** (sol′vənt), *adj., n.* —*adj.* **1** able to pay all one owes: *A bankrupt firm is not solvent.*
**2** able to dissolve: *Gasoline is a solvent liquid that removes grease spots.*
*—n.* **1** a substance, usually a liquid, that can dissolve other substances: *Water is a solvent of sugar and salt.* **2** a thing that solves, explains, or settles.
[< Latin *solvēns, -entis,* present participle of *solvere* loosen (used in *rem solvere* to free one's property and person from debt)] —**sol′vent|ly,** *adv.*

**sol|vent|less** (sol′vənt lis), *adj.* not containing a solvent: *solventless paints.*

**solvent molding,** = shell molding.

**sol|vol|y|sis** (sol vol′ə sis), *n.* a chemical reaction in which a solvent reacts with the solute to form a new, usually intermediate, compound. [< *solv*(ent) + *-olysis,* as in *hydrolysis, thermolysis*]

**sol|vo|lyt|ic** (sol′və lit′ik), *adj.* having to do with or producing solvolysis.

**so|ma**[1] (sō′mə), *n., pl.* **-ma|ta** (-mə tə). all the tissues and organs of an animal or plant except the germ cells: *We need to know more about the interrelationships of the psyche and the soma, the mind and the body* (William C. Menninger).
[< New Latin *soma* < Greek *sôma, -atos* body; earlier, corpse]

**so|ma**[2] (sō′mə), *n.* **1** an East Indian twining plant of the milkweed family that yields a mildly acid, milky juice. **2** an intoxicating drink of ancient India used in religious rites, made from the juice of this or related plants. [< Sanskrit *soma*]

**So|ma|li** (sə mä′lē), *n., pl.* **-li** or **-lis. 1** a member of a people living in eastern Africa, of Negro, Arab, and other descent. **2** their Cushitic language.

**So|ma|li|an** (sə mä′lē ən), *adj., n.* —*adj.* of or having to do with Somalia, or the Somali Republic, in East Africa, or its people.
*—n.* a native or inhabitant of Somalia.

**so|ma|lo** (sō mä′lō), *n., pl.* **-li** (-lē). a former unit of money of Italian Somaliland (now a part of Somalia). [< Italian *somalo*]

**so|ma|plasm** (sō′mə plaz əm), *n.* = somatoplasm.

**so|ma|scope** (sō′mə skōp), *n.* a device used to detect diseases difficult to locate by means of X ray or fluoroscope. It aims very high-frequency sound waves at the body and converts the echoes into visual signals that may be photographed. [< Greek *sôma* body + English *-scope*]

**so|mat|ic** (sō mat′ik), *adj.* **1** of or having to do with the body. **2** having to do with the cavity of the body, or its walls. **3** having to do with the soma, especially as contrasted with the mind or nervous system. [< Greek *sōmatikós* < *sôma, -atos* body] —**so|mat′i|cal|ly,** *adv.*

**somatic cell,** any cell of an animal or plant, except a germ cell.

**so|mat|ics** (sō mat′iks), *n.* = somatology.

**so|ma|to|chrome** (sō′mə tə krōm), *n.* a nerve cell which possesses a well-marked cell body surrounding the nucleus on all sides and staining deeply in basic aniline dyes. [< Greek *sôma, -atos* body + *chrôma* color]

**so|ma|to|gen|ic** (sō′mə tə jen′ik), *adj.* of somatic origin; developing from the somatic cells.

**so|ma|to|log|ic** (sō′mə tə loj′ik), *adj.* = somatological.

**so|ma|to|log|i|cal** (sō′mə tə loj′ə kəl), *adj.* **1** of or having to do with somatology. **2** physical; material.

**so|ma|tol|o|gist** (sō′mə tol′ə jist), *n.* a person skilled in somatology.

**so|ma|tol|o|gy** (sō′mə tol′ə jē), *n.* **1** the science of the human body, especially as a branch of anthropology. **2** the science of material bodies or substances; physics. [< New Latin *somatologia* < Greek *sôma, -atos* body + *-logiā* -logy]

**so|ma|to|plasm** (sō′mə tə plaz′əm), *n.* the protoplasm of the somatic cells; all the living substance in the cells of the body, except the germ plasm. [< Greek *sôma, -atos* body + *plásma* something molded]

**so|ma|to|plas|tic** (sō′mə tə plas′tik), *adj.* of or having to do with the somatoplasm.

**so|ma|to|pleu|ral** (sō′mə tə plůr′əl), *adj.* **1** of or having to do with the somatopleure. **2** forming somatopleure.

**so|ma|to|pleure** (sō′mə tə plůr), *n. Embryology.* the outer of the two layers into which the mesoderm of craniate vertebrates splits, and which forms the body wall. [< Greek *sôma, -atos* body + *pleurā* side]

**so|ma|to|pleu|ric** (sō′mə tə plůr′ik), *adj.* = somatopleural.

**so|ma|to|psy|chic** (sō′mə tə sī′kik), *adj.* **1** having to do with or consisting of mind and body. **2** having to do with a somatic disease which causes secondary psychological symptoms.

**so|ma|to|sen|so|ry** (sō′mə tə sen′sər ē), *adj.* of or having to do with sensations involving the parts of the body that are not associated with the eyes, tongue, ears, and other primary sense organs: *somatosensory cortex.* [< Greek *sôma, -atos* body + English *sensory*]

**so|ma|to|stat|in** (sō′mə tə stat′in, -stā′tin), *n.* a hormone produced by the hypothalamus that inhibits the secretion of various other hormones, especially the growth hormone somatotropin: *Somatostatin consists of a long peptide chain of 14 amino acids and can now be synthesized in the laboratory* (Earl A. Evans, Jr.). *Somatostatin might have application in diabetes, because ... researchers have found evidence that an excess of growth hormone was implicated in the eye problems common among diabetics* (Newsweek). [< *somato*(tropin) + *-stat* + *-in*[2]]

**so|ma|to|troph|in** (sō′mə tə trof′in), *n.* = somatotropin.

**so|ma|to|tro|pic hormone** (sō′mə tə trō′pik), = somatotropin. *Abbr:* STH (no periods).

**so|ma|to|tro|pin** (sō′mə tə trō′pin), *n.* the pituitary hormone that regulates the growth of the body. [< Greek *sôma, -atos* body + *tropē* a turning + English *-in*]

**so|ma|to|type** (sō′mə tə tīp), *n., v.,* **-typed, -typ|ing.** *—n.* a general classification of human body types within which certain distinct types are arranged. In one classification somatotypes are described as ectomorphic, mesomorphic, and endomorphic: *fraternal somatotypes.*
*—v.t.* to classify according to body type.
[< Greek *sôma, -atos* body + English *type*]

**som|ber** (som′bər), *adj.* **1** dark; gloomy; having deep shadows: *to dress in somber browns and grays. A cloudy winter day is somber. It was a somber room with dark furniture and heavy black hangings.* SYN: murky. **2** melancholy; dismal: *a somber expression. His losses made him very somber. He does not understand his more somber-minded colleagues and their preoccupation with the tragic and grotesque* (Time). SYN: depressing. [< French *sombre;* origin uncertain] —**som′ber|ly,** *adv.* —**som′ber|ness,** *n.*

**som|bre** (som′bər), *adj. Especially British.* somber. —**som′bre|ly,** *adv.* —**som′bre|ness,** *n.*

***som|bre|ro** (som brãr′ō), *n., pl.* **-ros.** a broad-brimmed hat, worn in the southwest United States, Mexico, and Spain. [< Spanish *sombrero,* ultimately < Latin *sub-* under + *umbra* shade]

***sombrero**

**som|bre|roed** (som brãr′ōd), *adj.* wearing a sombrero: *The plump señora ... scolds her sombreroed husband* (Time).

**som|brous** (som′brəs), *adj. Archaic.* somber.

**some** (sum; *unstressed* səm), *adj., pron., adv.,* —*adj.* **1** certain or particular, but not known or named: *Some dogs are large; some dogs are small. Some people sleep more than others. Every nation is fitted ... for some particular employments or manufactures* (John Ruskin). **2** a number of: *Ask some boys to help you. He left the city some years ago.* **3** a quantity of: *to wait for some time, some degree of confidence. Drink some milk.* **4** a; any: *Ask some salesclerk to wait on us. Can't you find some kind person who will help you? Some mute inglorious Milton here may rest* (Thomas Gray). **5** about: *a place some seventy miles distant. Some twenty men asked for work.* **6** *U.S. Informal.* uncommonly big, good, bad, etc.; remarkable: *That was some storm!*
*—pron.* **1** certain unnamed persons or things: *Some think so.* **2** a certain number or quantity: *I ate some and threw the rest away.*
*—adv.* **1** *Informal.* to some degree or extent; somewhat: *He is some better today.* **2** *U.S. Informal.* to a great degree or extent: *That's going some!*
**and then some,** *U.S. Slang.* and a good deal or a great many in addition: ... *a Western film which is a Western and then some* (Wall Street Journal).
[Old English *sum*]

**-some**[1], *suffix forming adjectives.* **1** (*added to verbs*) tending to ___: *Meddlesome = tending to meddle.*
**2** (*added to nouns*) causing ___: *Troublesome = causing trouble.*
**3** (*added to adjectives*) ___ to a considerable degree: *Lonesome = lone to a considerable degree.*
[Middle English *-some,* Old English *-sum*]

**-some**[2], *suffix added to numbers.* a group of ___: *Twosome = a group of two. Foursome = a group of four.* [Old English *sum* some (used after numerals)]

**-some**[3], *combining form.* ___ body: *Chromosome = color body. Ribosome = ribose body. Monosome = single body.* [< Greek *sôma*]

**some|bod|y** (sum′bod′ē, -bə dē), *pron., n., pl.* **-bod|ies.** *—pron.* a person not known or named; some person; someone: *Somebody has taken my pen.*
*—n.* a person of importance: *She acts as if she were a somebody since she won the prize.*

**some|day** (sum′dā′), *adv.* at some future time.

**some|deal** (sum′dēl′), *n., adv. Archaic.* somewhat.

**some|how** (sum′hou), *adv.* in a way not known or not stated; in one way or another: *I'll finish this work somehow.*
**somehow or other,** in one way or another: *His father ... maintained that every pfennig of tax collected was somehow or other returned to the people* (New Yorker).

**some|one** (sum′wun, -wən), *pron., n.* —*pron.* some person; somebody: *Someone has to lock up the house.* —*n.* = somebody.

**some|place** (sum′plās), *adv. Informal.* in or to some place; somewhere: *Let's go someplace for dinner.*

**som|er|sault** (sum′ər sôlt), *n., v.* —*n.* a roll or jump, turning the heels over the head: *I jerked out of the forward somersault into a backward one* (New Yorker).
*—v.i.* to roll or jump, turning the heels over the head.
**turn a somersault,** to somersault: *I turned a somersault on the lawn.*
Also, **summersault.**
[< Middle French *sombresault* < Old Provençal *sobresaut,* ultimately < Latin *suprā* over + *saltus, -ūs* a leaping, jump < *salīre* to leap]

**som|er|set** (sum′ər set), *n., v.i.,* **-set|ted, -set|ting.** = somersault.

**so|mes|thet|ic** (sō′mes thet′ik), *adj.* of or having to do with bodily sensation. [< Greek *sôma* body; patterned on *anesthetic*]

**some|thing** (sum′thing), *n., adv.* —*n.* **1** some thing; particular thing not named or known: *I'm sure I've forgotten something. He has something on his mind. Something there is that doesn't love a wall* (Robert Frost). **2** a certain amount or quantity; a part; a little: *There is something of his father in his smile. Something yet of doubt remains.* **3** a thing or person of some value or importance: *He thinks he's something. For if a man think himself to be something, when he is nothing, he deceiveth himself* (Galatians 6:3). **4** a thing or person that is to a certain extent an example of what is named: *There is something of the saint in her. Albert Einstein was something of a violinist.*
*—adv.* somewhat; to some extent or degree; rather: *He is something like his father.*
**something else,** *U.S. Slang.* something special: *"The sound effects are going to be something else." ... "Wait 'til you hear that thing," Buterakos said. "It'll make the golfers jump into the next county"* (George Plimpton).
**something for nothing,** that which is sought or obtained without giving something in return: ... *not the fly-by-night variety, looking for something for nothing* (Newsweek).

**some|time** (sum′tīm), *adv., adj.* —*adv.* **1** at one time or another: *Come to see us sometime.* **2** at an indefinite time: *It came sometime in March.* **3** *Archaic.* sometimes. **4** *Archaic.* formerly.

—***adj.*** **1** former: *Alice Brown, a sometime pupil of our school, is now a teacher there.* **2** *Informal.* irregular; occasional: *In . . . areas where disasters are unknown or rare, civil defense is a sometime thing* (New York Times).

**some|times** (sum′tīmz), *adv.* now and then; at times: *She comes to visit sometimes.*

**some|way** (sum′wā), *adv.* in some way: *She was someway clever enough to get the job.*

**some|ways** (sum′wāz), *adv.* = someway.

**some|what** (sum′hwot), *adv., n.* —***adv.*** to some extent or degree; slightly: *somewhat embarrassed. My hat is somewhat like yours.*
—***n.*** **1** some part; some amount: *somewhat of a musician. A joke loses somewhat of its fun when you hear it the second time.* **2** a little. **3** a thing or person of value or importance.

**some|when** (sum′hwen), *adv.* at some indefinite time: *. . . a single tongue, spoken somewhere and somewhen in the past* (William Dwight Whitney).

**some|where** (sum′hwãr), *adv., n.* —***adv.*** **1** in or to some place; in or to one place or another: *They live somewhere in the neighborhood. He is somewhere about the house. He said he had to go somewhere to see someone about something* (W. H. Hudson). **2** at some time: *It happened somewhere in the past.* **3** approximately: *The total was somewhere around forty dollars.*
—***n.*** some place.
**get somewhere,** to accomplish something; be successful: *Such a clever and ambitious young woman will surely get somewhere in life.*

**some|wheres** (sum′hwãrz), *adv., n. Dialect or Informal.* somewhere: *"Hey, don't I know you from somewheres?"* (New Yorker).

**some|while** (sum′hwīl), *adv.* **1** at times. **2** for some time. **3** = sometime. **4** = formerly.

**some|whith|er** (sum′hwiᴛʜ ər), *adv.* to some place: *Somewhither would she have thee go with her* (Shakespeare).

**some|why** (sum′hwī), *adv.* for some reason.

**some|wise** (sum′wīz), *adv. Obsolete.* someway.

**so|mi|tal** (sō′mə təl), *adj.* = somitic.

**so|mite** (sō′mīt), *n. Zoology.* any one of a longitudinal series of more or less similar parts or segments composing the body of certain animals, such as the earthworm; metamere. [< Greek *sôma, -atos* body + English *-ite*[1]]

**so|mit|ic** (sō mit′ik), *adj.* **1** like a somite: *the somitic divisions of the body.* **2** of or having to do with somites: *a somitic ring or joint.*

**som|me|lier** (sô mə lyā′), *n. French.* a wine steward in a restaurant: *The sommelier then proffered the wine selected for us* (Maclean's).

**som|nam|bu|lance** (som nam′byə ləns), *n.* = somnambulism.

**som|nam|bu|lant** (som nam′byə lənt), *adj., n.* —***adj.*** walking in sleep. —***n.*** = sleepwalker.

**som|nam|bu|lar** (som nam′byə lər), *adj.* having to do with a somnambulist or somnambulism.

**som|nam|bu|late** (som nam′byə lāt), *v.i., v.t.,* **-lat|ed, -lat|ing.** to walk during sleep. —**som|nam′bu|la′tion,** *n.*

**som|nam|bu|la|tor** (som nam′byə lā′tər), *n.* = sleepwalker.

**som|nam|bule** (som nam′byül), *n.* = sleepwalker. [< French *somnambule*]

**som|nam|bu|lic** (som nam′byə lik), *adj.* = somnambular.

**som|nam|bu|lism** (som nam′byə liz əm), *n.* = sleepwalking. [< Latin *somnus* sleep + *ambulāre* walk + English *-ism*]

**som|nam|bu|list** (som nam′byə list), *n.* = sleepwalker.

**som|nam|bu|lis|tic** (som nam′byə lis′tik), *adj.* having to do with sleepwalking or sleepwalkers. —**som|nam′bu|lis′ti|cal|ly,** *adv.*

**som|ni|al** (som′nē əl), *adj.* having to do with or involving dreams. [< Latin *somniālis* < *somnium* a dream < *somnus* sleep]

**som|ni|fa|cient** (som′nə fā′shənt), *n., adj.* —***n.*** a drug that causes sleep. —***adj.*** causing sleep, as some drugs. [< Latin *somnus* sleep + *faciens, -entis,* present participle of *facere* do]

**som|nif|er|ous** (som nif′ər əs), *adj.* **1** causing sleep. **2** = sleepy. [< Latin *somnifer* (< *somnus* sleep + *ferre* to bring) + English *-ous*] —**som|nif′er|ous|ly,** *adv.*

**som|nif|ic** (som nif′ik), *adj.* causing sleep. [< Latin *somnificus* < *somnus* sleep + *facere* do, make]

**som|nil|o|quism** (som nil′ə kwiz əm), *n.* = somniloquy.

**som|nil|o|quist** (som nil′ə kwist), *n.* a person who talks in his sleep.

**som|nil|o|quy** (som nil′ə kwē), *n., pl.* **-quies.** the act or habit of talking in one's sleep. [< Latin *somnus* sleep + *loquī* speak]

**som|niv|o|len|cy** (som niv′ə lən sē), *n., pl.* **-cies.** something that induces sleep; soporific. [< Latin *somnus* sleep + *volentia* will < *velle* to wish]

**som|no|lence** (som′nə ləns), *n.* sleepiness; drowsiness.

**som|no|len|cy** (som′nə lən sē), *n.* = somnolence.

**som|no|lent** (som′nə lənt), *adj.* **1** sleepy; drowsy: *a somnolent expression.* **2** tending to produce sleep: *The sound of the babbling brook had a pleasant and somnolent effect.* [< Latin *somnolentus* < *somnus* sleep] —**som′no|lent|ly,** *adv.*

**Som|nus** (som′nəs), *n.* the Roman god of sleep. [< Latin *Somnus* (originally) sleep]

**SOMPA** (som′pə), *n.* System of Multicultural Pluralistic Assessment (an intelligence test that compares individual scores with the scores of others from similar cultural backgrounds to compensate for the cultural bias of standard IQ tests): *The SOMPA technique would remove the "retarded" stigma from many children but leaves them in a position where they still need special educational attention* (Edward B. Fiske).

**son** (sun), *n.* **1a** a male child. A boy is the son of his father and mother. *Abbr:* s. **b** = son-in-law. **c** a kindly term of address to a boy, as from an older person, priest, or the like. **2a** a male descendant: *Adam's sons are my brethren* (Shakespeare). **b** *Figurative.* a boy or man attached to a country, cause, organization, project, or other undertaking, as a child is to its parents: *Sam Rayburn was a son of Texas. Many Boston citizens were Sons of Liberty. Affliction's sons are brothers in distress* (Robert Burns). **c** anything thought of as a son in relation to its origin: *Man, who is a worm, and the son of a worm* (John Morley). [Old English *sunu*]

**Son** (sun), *n.* Jesus Christ.

**so|nance** (sō′nəns), *n.* **1** sonant quality or condition. **2** *Obsolete.* **a** a sound. **b** a melody; tune.

**so|nan|cy** (sō′nən sē), *n.* = sonance.

**so|nant** (sō′nənt), *adj., n.* —***adj.*** **1** of sound; having sound; sounding. **2** pronounced with the vocal cords vibrating; voiced.
—***n.*** a sound pronounced with the vocal cords vibrating; voiced sound. *Z* and *v* are sonants; *s* and *f* are not.
[< Latin *sonāns, -antis,* present participle of *sonāre* to sound < *sonus* a sound]

***so|nar** (sō′när), *n.* **1** a device for detecting and locating objects under water by the reflection of sound waves: *Sonar revealed details of lake and ocean coastline bottoms in a new, quick and less costly method of sounding* (Science News Letter). **2** any device or system using the reflection of sound waves: *In our studies of bats . . . we use an apparatus which translates the bats' high-pitched, inaudible sonar signals into audible clicks* (Scientific American). [< *so*(und) *na*(vigation) *r*(anging)]

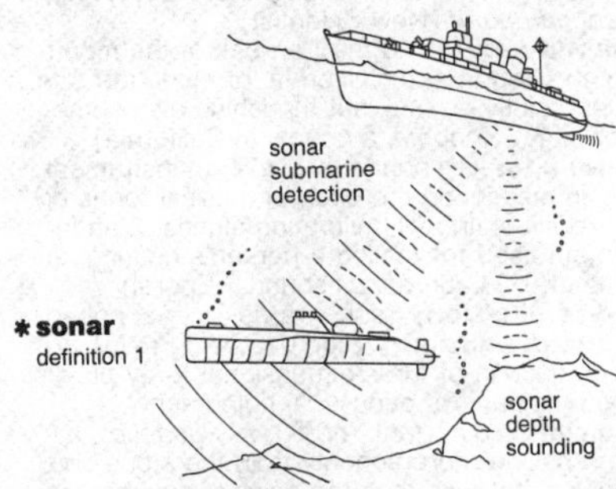


***sonar**
definition 1

**so|nar|man** (sō′när man′), *n., pl.* **-men.** a person who operates sonar: *Sonarmen hunched over their listening posts, monitoring the traffic in the North Atlantic shipping lane overhead* (Newsweek).

**so|na|ta** (sə nä′tə), *n.* **1** a piece of music, for one or two instruments, having three or four movements in contrasted rhythms and keys. **2** (originally) any instrumental composition, as contrasted with a vocal composition or cantata. [< Italian *sonata* (literally) sounded (played on an instrument, contrasted with singing) < Latin *sonāre* to sound]

**so|na|ta da ca|me|ra** (sə nä′tə dä kä′me rä), an Italian instrumental composition of the 1600's in four movements, performed by two or more stringed instruments with keyboard accompaniment. [< Italian *sonata da camera* (literally) chamber sonata]

**so|na|ta da chie|sa** (sə nä′tə dä kyā′zä), a composition similar to the sonata da camera but in a more serious, contrapuntal style suitable for performing in a church. [< Italian *sonata da chiesa* (literally) church sonata]

**sonata form,** a complicated form for a movement, usually the first movement, of a sonata, symphony, or concerto, consisting of the exposition, the development, and the recapitulation, often followed by a coda.

**son|a|ti|na** (son′ə tē′nə), *n., pl.* **-nas -ne** (-nā). a short or simplified sonata. [< Italian *sonatina* (diminutive) < *sonata;* see etym. under **sonata**]

**so|na|tion** (sō nā′shən), *n.* the giving forth of a sound; sounding. [< Medieval Latin *sonatio, -onis* < Latin *sonāre* to sound]

**sonde** (sond), *n.* = radiosonde.

**sone** (sōn), *n.* a unit of loudness. One sone is equivalent to a simple tone having a frequency of 1,000 cycles per second, 40 decibels above the listener's threshold. [< Latin *sonus* sound]

**son et lu|mière** (sôɴ′ ā ly myãr′), *French.* **1** a theatrical spectacle or pageant using subtle light effects and recorded music and narrative instead of actors and conventional stage settings: *We turned into Central Park south of the Metropolitan Museum, whose façade was floodlit as if for a performance of son et lumière* (New Yorker). **2** (literally) sound and light.

**song** (sông, song), *n.* **1** something to sing; short poem set to music: *Songs are thoughts, sung out with the breath when people are moved by great forces and ordinary speech no longer suffices* (Beals and Hoijer). **2** poetry that has a musical sound: *The mightiest chiefs of British song, Scorn'd not such legend, to prolong* (Scott). **3** music to fit a poem that is to be sung. **4** the act or practice of singing: *The canary burst into song.* **5** *Figurative.* any sound like singing: *the cricket's song, the song of the teakettle, the song of the brook.* **6** a mere trifle; low price: *a house offered at a song.*
**for a song,** very cheap: *Two men bought them [dogs], harness and all, for a song* (Jack London).
[Old English *sang*]

**song and dance,** *Informal.* an explanation or account, not necessarily true, and often intended to impress or deceive: *If the Soviet leaders did not make such a song and dance about international trade . . .* (Manchester Guardian).

**song-and-dance** (sông′ən dans′, -däns′; song′-), *adj.* of or having to do with singing and dancing, especially in a vaudeville act or a musical comedy: *a song-and-dance team.*

**song|bird** (sông′bėrd′, song′-), *n.* **1** a bird that sings. **2** a woman singer.

**song|book** (sông′bu̇k′, song′-), *n.* **1** a book containing a collection of songs: *Songbooks were passed around, and the hundred or so men on hand began singing to the accompaniment of a piano* (New Yorker). **2** = hymnbook. **3** the breviary used in the Anglo-Saxon church. [Old English *sangbōc* < *sang* song + *bōc* book]

**song|craft** (sông′kraft′, song′-; -kräft′), *n.* the art of composing songs; skill in versification.

**song cycle,** a group of art songs related in style or subject, usually written by one composer, and intended to be performed in a series: *Schubert's "Winterreise" is one of the earliest song cycles, and the greatest of them all* (London Times).

**Son|ge** (sông′gā, song′-), *n., pl.* **-ge** or **-ges.** a member of a Bantu-speaking people of the eastern Congo (now Zaire) in central Africa, noted for their use of fetish figures.

**song|fest** (sông′fest, song′-), *n. U.S.* an informal gathering or concert at which folk songs, popular songs, or the like, are sung, often with members of the audience joining the performers.

**song|ful** (sông′fəl, song′-), *adj.* full of song; musical; melodious: *. . . smoothly songful in passages where such sound is indispensable* (Saturday Review). —**song′ful|ly,** *adv.* —**song′ful|ness,** *n.*

**Song|hai** (sông hī′, song-; -gī′), *n., pl.* **-hai** or **-hais,** *adj.* —***n.*** **1** a member of a Negro Moslem people of western Africa, now living chiefly in Mali and Niger. **2** their Sudanic language.
—***adj.*** of or having to do with this people or their language: *the Songhai empire.*

**song|less** (sông′lis, song′-), *adj.* not able to sing; not singing; without song: *a songless bird.*

**song|like** (sông′līk′, song′-), *adj.* of the nature of song or singing: *(Figurative.) The songlike tenderness of her cantabile* (London Times).

**song|man** (sông′mən, song′-), *n., pl.* **-men.** a singer, especially a singer of songs.

**song of degrees** or **song of ascents,** any one of the fifteen Psalms from 120 to 134, inclusive. [because they were sung by pilgrims as they ascended steps or high places of worship]

**Song of Solomon,** a book of the Old Testament, attributed to Solomon; Canticles. *Abbr:* S. of Sol.

**Song of Songs,** = Song of Solomon.

**Song of the Three Children,** a book of the Old Testament Apocrypha, included in the canon of the Greek and Roman Catholic Bibles as part of Daniel.

---

**Pronunciation Key:** hat, āge, cãre, fär; let, ēqual, tėrm; it, īce; hot, ōpen, ôrder; oil, out; cup, pu̇t, rüle; child; long; thin; ᴛʜen; zh, measure; ə represents **a** in about, **e** in taken, **i** in pencil, **o** in lemon, **u** in circus.

**song|smith** (sông′smith, song′-), *n.* a composer of songs: *The book is realistic in appraising the professional songsmith versus the one-shot wonders* (Saturday Review).

**song sparrow**, a small, brown North American sparrow having a streaked breast with a dark central spot.

**song|ster** (sông′stər, song′-), *n.* **1** = singer. **2** a writer of songs or poems. **3** = songbird. [Old English *sangestre* < *sang* song + *-estre* -ster]

**song|stress** (sông′stris, song′-), *n.* **1** a woman singer. **2** a woman writer of songs or poems; poetess. **3** a female songbird.

**song thrush**, **1** = wood thrush (def. 1). **2** a common European thrush with a yellowish-brown back, spotted breast, and white belly, noted for its song; mavis.

**song|writ|er** (sông′rī′tər, song′-), *n.* a composer of popular songs or tunes.

**son|hood** (sun′hůd), *n.* the condition or relation of being a son.

***son|ic** (son′ik), *adj.* **1** of, having to do with, or using sound waves: *sonic impact.* **2** having to do with the rate at which sound travels in air. Sonic speed in air at sea level is about 1,100 feet per second (335 meters). [< Latin *sonus* sound + English *-ic;* perhaps patterned on *phonic*]

***sonic**
definition 2

**sonic: 740 mph (1,190 kph) speed of sound**

hypersonic:
5 or more times 740 mph (1,190 kph)

supersonic:
more than 740 mph (1,190 kph)

subsonic:
less than 740 mph (1,190 kph)

speeds at sea level

**son|i|cal|ly** (son′ə klē), *adv.* with regard to sound or its qualities: *A vigorous, passionate work whose rich coloration took on a special sheen in the sonically clean, echoless hall* (Time).

**son|i|ca|tion** (son′ə kā′shən), *n.* the use of high-frequency sound waves to break up matter: *Amoebae were washed once with cold ... buffer (pH 7.5) suspended in the same buffer, and broken by sonication* (Science).

**sonic bang**, *British.* sonic boom.

**sonic barrier** or **wall**, = sound barrier.

**sonic boom**, a loud noise made by shock waves which are produced by an aircraft traveling at a rate greater than the speed of sound.

**sonic depth finder**, a device for determining depth of water by sending sound waves through the water and timing their return from the bottom; fathometer.

**sonic mine**, a container holding an explosive charge that is put under water and exploded by propeller vibrations; acoustic mine.

**son|ics** (son′iks), *n.* **1** = acoustics. **2** the use of acoustic science in solving technical problems of sound; practical or applied acoustics.

**sonic speed**, the speed of sound.

**so|nif|er|ous** (sō nif′ər əs), *adj.* carrying or producing sound. [< Latin *sonus* sound + English *-ferous*]

**So|nin|ke** (sō ning′kā), *n., pl.* **-kes** or **-ke.** a member of a native Negro people of western Africa.

**son-in-law** (sun′in lô′), *n., pl.* **sons-in-law.** the husband of one's daughter.

**son|less** (sun′lis), *adj.* having no son; without a son.

**son|like** (sun′līk′), *adj.* like that of a son; filial: *He has a sonlike respect for his teacher.*

**son|ly** (sun′lē), *adj.* = sonlike.

**son|net** (son′it), *n., v.,* **-et|ed, -et|ing** or (*especially British*) **-et|ted, -et|ting.** —*n.* a poem having 14 lines, usually in iambic pentameter, and a formal arrangement of rhymes. Elizabethan and Italian sonnets differ in the arrangement of the rhymes.
—*v.i.* to compose sonnets.
—*v.t.* to celebrate in a sonnet or sonnets.
[< Middle French *sonnet,* or Italian *sonetto* < Old Provençal *sonet* (diminutive) < *son* sound < Latin *sonus*]

**son|net|eer** (son′ə tir′), *n., v.* —*n.* **1** a writer of sonnets. **2** an inferior poet: *Our little sonnetters ... have too narrow souls to judge of Poetry* (John Dryden).
—*v.i.* to write sonnets.

**son|net|ist** (son′ə tist), *n.* = sonneteer.

**son|net|ize** (son′ə tīz), *v.,* **-ized, -iz|ing.** —*v.i.* to compose sonnets.
—*v.t.* to make the subject of a sonnet; celebrate in a sonnet: *Now could I sonnetize thy piteous plight* (Robert Southey).

**sonnet sequence**, a series of sonnets by one poet, usually having a single theme.

**son|ny** (sun′ē), *n., pl.* **-nies.** little son (used as a pet name or as a way of speaking to a little boy or a man younger than the speaker).

**son|o|buoy** (son′ə boi′, -bü′ē), *n.* a radio device floated in a buoy or dropped from an airplane to receive and transmit underwater sounds, used especially in submarine detection. [< Latin *sonus* sound + English *buoy*]

**son|o|chem|i|cal** (son′ə kem′ə kəl), *adj.* of, having to do with, or produced by phenomena of sonochemistry.

**son|o|chem|is|try** (son′ə kem′ə strē), *n.* the use of high-frequency sound waves to produce chemical reaction: *Research ... has shown that organic fluids can be broken down by "sonochemical" means ... The suggestion has been made that sonochemistry may be a route to novel syntheses for rocket propellants* (New Scientist). [< Latin *sonus* sound + English *chemistry*]

**son of a gun**, *Slang.* **1** a wicked or mischievous person; scoundrel; rascal: *"Why, you son of a gun, you snuck out 11 cabs today"* (New York Times). **2** a wretched person; unfortunate. *"Them poor son of a guns live the same way ..., eat the same as the kids—slop"* (San Francisco Chronicle). **3** an exclamation used to greet a friend, express surprise, joy, etc.: *"Mac, old boy!" he shouted heartily. "Beddoes, you ... you son of a gun!"* (New Yorker).

**Son of God**, Jesus Christ (in the Bible, Matthew 26:63).

**Son of Man**, Jesus Christ, especially as the Messiah.

**son|o|gram** (son′ə gram), *n.* **1** = sound spectrogram. **2** = sonograph.

**son|o|graph** (son′ə graf, -gräf), *n.* **1a** a device for producing a graphic representation of sounds. **b** the representation, usually in the form of phonetic characters, produced by this device. **2** a three-dimensional picture produced by acoustical holography; an acoustical hologram. [< Latin *sonus* sound + English *-graph*]

**so|nog|ra|phy** (sə nog′rə fē), *n.* = acoustical holography.

**son|o|lu|mi|nes|cence** (son′ə lü′mə nes′əns), *n.* light given off when liquid containing dissolved gas is permeated by high-frequency sounds. [< Latin *sonus* sound + English *luminescence*]

**son|o|lu|mi|nes|cent** (son′ə lü′mə nes′ənt), *adj.* of or having to do with sonoluminescence: *On a sonoluminescent viewing screen, ... each part of the image will fluctuate in brightness according to its sound output* (New Scientist).

**So|no|ma oak** (sə nō′mə), an oak of the mountains of Oregon and California, of moderate size, valued chiefly as fuel, but furnishing also some tanbark. [< *Sonoma,* a county in California]

**so|nom|e|ter** (sə nom′ə tər), *n.* **1** an instrument used in measuring the pitch of musical tones or for experimenting with vibrating strings. **2** an instrument used for testing a person's hearing; audiometer. [< Latin *sonus* sound + English *-meter*]

**son|o-ra|di|o buoy** (son′ə rā′dē ō), = sonobuoy.

**son|o|ra|di|og|ra|phy** (son′ə rā′dē og′rə fē), *n.* the production of three-dimensional X-ray pictures by means of acoustical holography.

**so|no|rant** (sə nôr′ənt, -nōr′-), *n. Phonetics.* a sound having more sonority than the stops and fricatives, but less than the vowels, occurring in both syllabic and nonsyllabic position, as *l, m, n, ng,* and *r;* sonant. [< *sonor*(ous) + *-ant*]

**so|no|rif|ic** (sō′nə rif′ik, son′ə-), *adj.* producing sound or noise, as the organs that a cricket rubs together to make its chirping sound. [< Latin *sonor, -ōris* a sound + *facere* to make]

**so|nor|i|ty** (sə nôr′ə tē, -nor′-), *n., pl.* **-ties.** sonorous quality or condition: *He has a richer melodic gift than most, ... the ability to invent new sonorities without striving for far-fetched effects* (New York Times).

**so|no|rous** (sə nôr′əs, -nōr′-), *adj.* **1** giving out or having a deep, loud sound: *a big, sonorous church bell.* **2** full and rich in sound: *a round, deep, sonorous voice* (Dickens). **3** having an impressive sound; high-sounding: *sonorous phrases, a sonorous style.* [< Latin *sonōrus* (with English *-ous*) < *sonor, -ōris* a sound < *sonāre* to sound < *sonus* sound] —**so|no′rous|ly,** *adv.* —**so|no′rous|ness,** *n.*

**sonorous figures**, figures which are formed by vibration of a sounding body, as in a layer of fine sand strewn on a disk of glass or metal, which is caused to vibrate by the bow of a violin drawn across its edge.

**son|ship** (sun′ship), *n.* the condition or relation of being a son.

**son|sy** or **son|sie** (son′sē), *adj.,* **-si|er, -si|est.** *Scottish and Irish.* **1** bringing good fortune; lucky. **2** plump. **3** comely. **4** cheerful; jolly. **5** comfortable-looking. [Middle English *sonse* prosperity < Scottish Gaelic *sonas* < *sona* fortunate]

**son|tag** (son′tag), *n.* a woman's knitted cape with long ends crossed over the breast and fastened together at the back. [< Henriette *Sontag,* 1806-1854, a German singer]

**sook**[1] (sük), *n.* = suq.

**sook**[2] (sůk), *n. Australian Slang.* a cowardly person, especially a child.

**sool** (sül), *v.t. Australian.* **1** to incite (usually, a dog) to attack someone. **2** to attack or snap at.

**soom** (süm), *n., v.,* **soomed, soom|ming.** *Scottish.* swim.

**soon** (sün), *adv.* **1** in a short time; before long: *I will see you again soon.* SYN: shortly, presently. **2** before the usual or expected time; early: *Why have you come so soon?* **3** promptly; quickly: *As soon as I hear, I will let you know.* **4** readily; willingly: *The brave soldier would as soon die as yield to such an enemy.* **5** *Obsolete.* forthwith; straightaway.
**had** (or **would**) **sooner**, would more readily; prefer to: *Why, I'd sooner stay in prison all my life!* (T. A. Guthrie).
**sooner or later**, at some future time; in the end; inevitably: *sooner or later ... I felt sure that you'd want something out of me* (Graham Greene).
[Old English *sōna* at once, quickly]
▶ **sooner than.** After *no sooner* the connective used is *than,* not *when: The fly had no sooner hit the water than* [not *when*] *a huge trout snapped at it.*

**soon|er** (sü′nər), *n.* **1** *U.S. Slang.* a person who settles on government land before it is legally opened to settlers in order to gain the choice of location. **2** *U.S. Slang.* a person who gains an unfair advantage by getting ahead of others. **3** a person who acts prematurely.

**Soon|er** (sü′nər), *n.* a nickname for a native or inhabitant of Oklahoma.

**Sooner State**, a nickname for Oklahoma.

**soot** (sůt, süt), *n., v.* —*n.* a black substance in the smoke from burning coal, wood, oil, or other fuel. Soot is caused chiefly by incomplete burning and makes smoke dark. It collects on the inside of chimneys.
—*v.t.* to cover or blacken with soot.
[Old English *sōt*]

**soot|fall** (sůt′fôl′, süt′-), *n.* **1** the fall of soot left in the air especially by smokestacks in an industrial area. **2** the amount of soot falling within a certain time and area.

**sooth** (süth), *n., adj. Archaic.* —*n.* truth: *He speaks sooth.*
—*adj.* **1** true. **2** soothing; soft. **3** smooth.
**in sooth**, in truth; truly; really: *Are you in sooth Lancelot?*
[Old English *sōth*]

**soothe** (süᴛʜ), *v.,* **soothed, sooth|ing.** —*v.t.* **1** to quiet; calm; comfort: *The mother soothed the crying child. Music hath charms to soothe a savage breast* (William Congreve). **2** to make less painful; ease; relieve: *Heat soothes some aches; cold soothes others.* **3** *Obsolete.* to cajole by consenting.
—*v.i.* to have or exercise a soothing influence: *Ah, thought which saddens while it soothes* (Robert Browning). [Old English *sōthian* to verify < *sōth* sooth] —**sooth′er,** *n.*

**sooth|fast** (süth′fast′, -fäst′), *adj. Archaic.* **1** true. **2** truthful. **3** loyal. [Old English *sōthfæst* < *sōth* sooth + *fæst* fast, firm] —**sooth′fast′ly,** *adv.* —**sooth′fast′ness,** *n.*

**sooth|ful** (süth′fəl), *adj. Archaic.* **1** true. **2** truthful; trustworthy.

**sooth|ing** (sü′ᴛʜing), *adj.* **1** that soothes: *soothing words.* **2** that relieves pain or tension or brings sleep, especially in children: *soothing cough syrup.* —**sooth′ing|ly,** *adv.* —**sooth′ing-ness,** *n.*

**sooth|ly** (süth′lē), *adv. Archaic.* truly; in truth: *Soothly, other shores I fain would see* (William Morris).

**sooth|say** (süth′sā′), *v.,* **-said, -say|ing,** *n.* —*v.i.* = prophesy.
—*n.* **1** = prophecy. **2** = omen.
[back formation < *soothsayer*]

**sooth|say|er** (süth′sā′ər), *n.* a person who claims to tell what will happen; person who makes prophecies or predictions: *A soothsayer bids you beware the ides of March* (Shakespeare). [< *sooth* + *sayer*]

**sooth|say|ing** (süth′sā′ing), *n.* **1** the foretelling of future events: *Divinations, and soothsayings, and dreams, are vain* (Ecclesiasticus 34:5). **2** a prediction or prophecy.

**soot|less** (sůt′lis, süt′-), *adj.* free from soot.

**soot|y** (sůt′ē, sü′tē), *adj.,* **soot|i|er, soot|i|est,** *v.,* **soot|ied, soot|y|ing.** —*adj.* **1** covered or blackened with soot: *a sooty chimney, sooty hands.* **2** dark-brown or black; dark-colored.
—*v.t.* to black or foul with soot. —**soot′i|ly,** *adv.* —**soot′i|ness,** *n.*

**sooty albatross**, a wide-ranging species of albatross in southern and south temperate seas, of a sooty brown color, with black feet and bill, the latter having a yellow stripe on the side of the under mandible.

**sooty mold**, 1 a black, fungous growth on plants, produced by fungi growing on the honeydew secreted by insects. 2 the fungus producing such a growth.

**sooty shearwater**, a shearwater common on the Atlantic coast of North America, of medium size and entirely sooty brown plumage.

**sooty tern**, a partly white and partly glossy black tern whose eggs are used for food, found in abundance along the coasts of most warm and temperate seas; wide-awake.

**sop** (sop), *n., v.*, **sopped, sop|ping.** — ***n.*** 1 a piece of food dipped or soaked in milk, broth, or the like. 2 *Figurative.* something given to soothe or quiet; bribe: *Concessions are a sop to the malcontents in the organization.* 3 a person or thing that is thoroughly soaked. 4 an accumulation of some liquid: *a great pool and sop of blood* (Hawthorne).
— ***v.t.*** 1 to dip or soak: *to sop bread in milk.* 2 to take up (water or other liquid); wipe; mop: *Please sop up that water with a cloth.* 3 to soak thoroughly; drench.
— ***v.i.*** 1 to be drenched. 2 to soak in or through.
**sopping wet.** See under **sopping.**
[Old English *sopp,* noun]

**sop.**, soprano.

**SOP** (no periods) or **S.O.P.**, standing (or standard) operating procedure: *Presumably this was S.O.P.—standard operating procedure—by which they made themselves difficult targets from the ground* (Ralph Ingersoll). *I've been going around for years reminding people SOP is an abbreviation of the Army phrase "standing operating procedure," but everyone still says "standard"* (Jerome Beatty, Jr.).

**soph** (sof), *n. U.S. Informal.* sophomore.

**Soph.**, 1 Sophocles. 2 sophomore.

**So|pher** (sō′fər), *n., pl.* **-pher|im.** a scribe; one of the ancient teachers or expounders of the Jewish oral law. [< Hebrew *sopher*]

**So|pher|ic** (sō′fər ik), *adj.* pertaining to the Sopherim, or to their teachings or labors.

**So|pher|im** (sō′fər im), *n.* plural of **Sopher.**

**soph|ic** (sof′ik), *adj.* of, having to do with, or teaching wisdom. [< Greek *sophikós* < *sophós* wise, clever]

**soph|ism** (sof′iz əm), *n.* a clever but misleading argument; argument based on false or unsound reasoning: *But no sophism is too gross to delude minds distempered by party spirit* (Macaulay). [< Latin *sophisma* < Greek *sóphisma, -atos* < *sophízesthai* become wise < *sophós* clever]

**soph|ist** (sof′ist), *n., adj.* — ***n.*** 1 a person who makes use of a sophism or sophisms, especially intentionally or habitually; a clever but misleading reasoner: *The self-torturing sophist, wild Rousseau* (Byron). *Be neither saint nor sophist led, but be a man* (Matthew Arnold). 2 Often, **Sophist.** one of a class of teachers especially of rhetoric, philosophy, or ethics, in ancient Greece. 3 a man of learning.
— ***adj.*** Also, **Sophist.** of or having to do with sophists or sophism.
[< Latin *sophista* < Greek *sophistês* < *sophízesthai* become wise < *sophós* wise, clever]

**soph|ist|er** (sof′ə stər), *n.* 1 a student in his second or third year at Cambridge or Oxford universities. 2 an unsound reasoner; sophist. [< Old French *sophistre,* and *soffistre,* learned borrowing from Latin *sophista;* see etym. under **sophist**]

**so|phis|tic** (sə fis′tik), *adj.* = sophistical.

**so|phis|ti|cal** (sə fis′tə kəl), *adj.* 1 clever but misleading; based on false or unsound reasoning: *a sophistical proof. It is a reasoning weak, rotten and sophistical* (Edmund Burke). 2 using clever but misleading arguments; reasoning falsely or unsoundly: *a sophistical rhetorician, inebriated with the exuberance of his own verbosity* (Benjamin Disraeli). 3 of or having to do with sophists or sophistry. — **so|phis′ti|cal|ly,** *adv.* — **so|phis′ti|cal|ness,** *n.*

**so|phis|ti|cate** (*v., adj.* sə fis′tə kāt; *n.* sə fis′tə kāt, -kit), *v.*, **-cat|ed, -cat|ing,** *n., adj.* — ***v.t.*** 1 to make experienced in worldly ways; cause to lose one's natural simplicity and frankness; make worldly-wise: *They spoke out their thoughts with a rude freedom which ... proved that they had not been sophisticated into prigs* (Lisle Carr). 2 to make more advanced; make complex: *Modifications in the exuberance of the design of the station were made partly as a result of ... the sophisticating of the equipment* (London Times). 3 to mislead: *Books of casuistry, which sophisticate the understanding and defile the heart* (Robert Southey). 4 to involve in sophistry; misstate: *I have ... Sophisticated no truth, Nursed no delusion* (Matthew Arnold). 5 to adulterate; debase: *to sophisticate a commodity.*
— ***v.i.*** *Archaic.* to use sophistry; quibble.
— ***n.*** a sophisticated person.
— ***adj.*** = sophisticated.
[< Medieval Latin *sophisticare* (with English *-ate*[1]) to cheat, quibble < Latin *sophisticus* sophistical < Greek *sophistikós* < *sophistês;* see etym. under **sophist**]

**so|phis|ti|cat|ed** (sə fis′tə kā′tid), *adj.* 1 experienced in worldly ways; changed from natural simplicity or frankness; worldly-wise; knowledgeable: *a charming, witty, and thoroughly sophisticated young lady.* 2 appealing to the tastes of sophisticated people: *sophisticated humor.* 3 very complex and advanced in design: *a sophisticated missile. India is heavily armed with modern, sophisticated equipment* (New York Times). 4 = misleading. — **so|phis′ti|cat′ed|ly,** *adv.*

**so|phis|ti|ca|tion** (sə fis′tə kā′shən), *n.* 1 a lessening or loss of naturalness, simplicity, or frankness; worldly experience or ideas; urbanity: *The sophistication of the human intellect formed what we now call language* (Hawthorne). *Among your 40,000-plus teachers are a good many whose intellectual sophistication is scarcely matched in any other big city* (Harper's). 2 advanced refinement or complexity: *The development of semiconductor devices ... has permitted a new level of sophistication in physics experiments* (John Woolston). *Here is an area where continuing sophistication of the equipment and techniques is required* (Canada Month). 3 = sophistry. 4 adulteration; debasement.

**so|phis|ti|ca|tor** (sə fis′tə kā tər), *n.* a person who sophisticates, especially one who adulterates.

**soph|ist|ry** (sof′ə strē), *n., pl.* **-ries.** 1 unsound reasoning. 2 a clever but misleading argument: *The parson's cant, the lawyer's sophistry* (Alexander Pope). 3 the art, practice, or learning of the ancient Greek sophists, especially of their type of argument.

**Soph|o|cle|an** (sof′ə klē′ən), *adj.* of, having to do with, or characteristic of the ancient Greek tragic poet Sophocles, his works, or his style: *a Sophoclean tragedy.*

**soph|o|more** (sof′ə môr, -mōr; sof′môr, -mōr), *n., adj.* — ***n.*** a student in the second year of a four-year high school or college.
— ***adj.*** 1 of or having to do with the second-year students: *the sophomore year.* 2 of or for sophomores.
[earlier *sophumer* (originally) (one) taking part in dialectic exercises < *sophom, -um,* variant of *sophisme* sophism]

**soph|o|mor|ic** (sof′ə môr′ik, -mor′-), *adj.* 1 of, having to do with, or like a sophomore or sophomores. 2 *U.S.* conceited and pretentious, but crude and ignorant.

**Soph|o|ni|as** (sof′ə nī′əs), *n.* (in the Douay Bible) Zephaniah.

**so|pho|ra** (sə fôr′ə, -fōr′-), *n.* any one of a group of temperate or semitropical trees and shrubs of the pea family, with odd-pinnate leaves and spikes of white, yellow, or violet flowers. [< New Latin *Sophora* the genus name < Arabic *sofāra* a yellow plant < *asfar* yellow]

**So|phy** or **so|phy** (sō′fē, sof′ē), *n.* a former title of the ruler of Persia. [< Persian *ṣafī* < Arabic *ṣafī-d-dīn* purity of religion]

**so|pite** (sə pīt′), *v.t.*, **-pit|ed, -pit|ing.** 1 to put to sleep; dull. 2 to put an end to; settle. [< Latin *sōpītus,* past participle of *sōpīre* put to sleep]

**so|por** (sō′pər, -pôr), *n.* a deep, unnatural sleep. [< Latin *sopor, -ōris* deep sleep]

**so|po|rif|er|ous** (sō′pə rif′ər əs, sop′ə-), *adj.* bringing sleep; causing sleep. [< Latin *sopōrifer* (< *sopor, -ōris* deep sleep + *ferre* to bring) + English *-ous*] — **so′po|rif′er|ous|ly,** *adv.* — **so′po|rif′er|ous|ness,** *n.*

**so|po|rif|ic** (sō′pə rif′ik, sop′ə-), *adj., n.* — ***adj.*** 1 causing or tending to cause sleep: *a soporific sermon.* 2 sleep; drowsy.
— ***n.*** a drug that causes sleep.
[< Latin *sopor, -ōris* deep sleep + *facere* to make]

**so|po|rose** (sō′pə rōs, sop′ə-), *adj.* characterized by a deep, unnatural sleep.

**sopped** (sopt), *adj.* soaked; drenched.

**sop|ping** (sop′ing), *adj.* soaked; drenched.
**sopping wet,** soaked; drenched: *He came in out of the rain sopping wet.*
— **sop′ping|ly,** *adv.*

**sop|py** (sop′ē), *adj.*, **-pi|er, -pi|est.** 1 soaked; very wet: *soppy ground, soppy weather.* 2 *Informal, Figurative.* full of insincere sentiment. — **sop′pi|ness,** *n.*

**so|pra|ni|no** (sōp rə nē′nō), *adj., n., pl.* **-nos.**
— ***adj.*** (of a musical instrument) having a higher pitch than the soprano of the same family of instruments: *a sopranino cornet or saxophone.*
— ***n.*** a sopranino instrument.
[< Italian *sopranino* little soprano]

**so|pran|ist** (sə pran′ist, -prä′nist), *n.* = soprano.

**so|pran|o** (sə pran′ō, -prä′nō), *n., pl.* **-pran|os,** *adj.* — ***n.*** 1 the highest singing voice in women and boys. 2 a singer with such a voice. 3 a part in music for such a voice or for a corresponding instrument. 4 an instrument playing such a part.
— ***adj.*** of, for, or having to do with a soprano.
[< Italian *soprano,* adjective to *sopra* above < Latin *suprā*]

*****soprano clef**, *Music.* a C clef when placed on the bottom line of a staff.

*****soprano clef**

middle C

**so|ra** (sôr′ə, sōr′-), *n.*, or **sora rail,** a small, brown and gray, short-billed North American rail; Carolina rail; ortolan. [American English; origin uncertain]

**sorb**[1] (sôrb), *v.t.* to absorb or adsorb: *At 78°C (the temperature of solid carbon dioxide) both oxygen and nitrogen are sorbed readily* (New Scientist).

**sorb**[2] (sôrb), *n.* 1 either of the two European service trees. 2 the European mountain ash. 3 the fruit of any one of these trees. [< Middle French *sorbe* the serviceberry, learned borrowing from Latin *sorbum*]

**Sorb** (sôrb), *n.* 1 one of a Slavic people living in central Germany; Wend. 2 their language; Sorbian. [< German *Sorbe,* variant (influenced by Medieval Latin *Sorabi* Sorbs) of *Serbe* < Sorbian *Serb*]

**sorb apple,** 1 the fruit of the service tree. 2 the tree.

**sor|bate** (sôr′bāt), *n.* a salt of sorbic acid.

**sor|be|fa|cient** (sôr′bə fā′shənt), *adj., n.* — ***adj.*** promoting absorption.
— ***n.*** a sorbefacient agent.
[< Latin *sorbēre* absorb + *faciens, -entis,* present participle of *facere* to do]

**sorb|ent** (sôr′bənt), *n.* anything that absorbs or adsorbs: *A mixture of chemical compounds is applied to a stationary sorbent (blotting paper demonstrates the effect) and is then made to migrate along the sorbent* (L. J. Morris).

**sor|bet** (sôr′bit), *n.* = sherbet.

**Sor|bi|an** (sôr′bē ən), *adj., n.* — ***adj.*** of or having to do with the Sorbs or their language.
— ***n.*** 1 the West Slavic language of the Sorbs; Wendish. 2 = Sorb.

**sor|bic acid** (sôr′bik), an acid found in the berries of the mountain ash and produced synthetically, used to prevent mold in yeast, cheese, and other foods, often put into food wrappers. *Formula:* $C_6H_8O_2$

**sor|bite** (sôr′bīt), *n. Metallurgy.* a granular constituent of steel related to pearlite, formed during the tempering process. [< Henry C. *Sorby,* 1826-1908, an English geologist + *-ite*[1]]

**sor|bit|ic** (sôr bit′ik), *adj.* 1 having to do with sorbite. 2 containing sorbite.

**sor|bi|tol** (sôr′bə tōl, -tol), *n.* a sweet crystalline substance derived from the berries of the mountain ash, certain other berries and fruits, and corn sugar, used as a softner in candy, as a sugar substitute for diabetics, in making ascorbic acid, and as a moisture conditioner in leather and tobacco. *Formula:* $C_6H_{14}O_6$

**Sor|bon|ist** (sôr′bə nist), *n.* a student or doctor of the Sorbonne.

**Sor|bonne** (sôr bon′; *French* sôr bôn′), *n.* 1 the seat of the faculties of letters and science of the University of Paris. 2 (formerly) the theological college of the University of Paris. [< Old French *Sorbonne* < Robert de *Sorbon,* 1201-1274, who founded the original college]

**sorb|ose** (sôr′bōs), *n.* a monosaccharide sugar produced from sorbitol, used in synthesizing vitamin C. *Formula:* $C_6H_{12}O_6$ [< Latin *sorbum* the serviceberry + English *-ose*[2]]

**sor|cer|er** (sôr′sər ər), *n.* a person who practices magic with the supposed aid of evil spirits; wizard; magician: *Sorcerer and witch doctor ... are still an integral part of the African pattern* (Atlantic).

**sor|cer|ess** (sôr′sər is), *n.* a woman who practices magic with the supposed aid of evil spirits; witch: *Again she [Medea] grew to be the sorceress, Worker of fearful things* (William Morris).

**sor|cer|ize** (sôr′sə rīz), *v.t.*, **-ized, -iz|ing.** to transform by sorcery: *A Lombard was sorcerized into a goose* (Frederick James Furnivall).

**sor|cer|ous** (sôr′sər əs), *adj.* using, involving, or resembling sorcery: *sorcerous* spells. — **sor′cer|ous|ly,** *adv.*

**sor|cer|y** (sôr′sər ē), *n., pl.* **-cer|ies.** magic per-

**Pronunciation Key:** hat, āge, cãre, fär; let, ēqual, tėrm; it, īce; hot, ōpen, ôrder; oil, out; cup, pu̇t, rüle; child; long; thin; ᴛʜen; zh, measure; ə represents **a** in about, **e** in taken, **i** in pencil, **o** in lemon, **u** in circus.

formed with the supposed aid of evil spirits; witchcraft: *The prince had been changed into a toad by sorcery.* **SYN**: necromancy. [< Old French *sorcerie,* ultimately < Latin *sors, sortis* lot, fate]

**sor|da|men|te** (sôr′dä men′tā), *adv. Music.* in a muted or muffled manner; softly. [< Italian *sordamente* < *sordo* deaf, dull]

**sor|del|li|na** (sôr′də lē′nä), *n.* a small bagpipe. [< Italian *sordellina* < *sordo* mute]

**sor|des** (sôr′dēz), *n.* **1a** dirt; filth. **b** foul matter such as that gathering on the teeth or in the stomach. **2** *Medicine.* scabs from fever blisters. [< Latin *sordēs*]

**sor|did** (sôr′did), *adj.* **1** dirty; filthy: *The poor family lived in a sordid hut.* **SYN**: foul, squalid. **2a** caring too much for money; meanly selfish: *His ambitions are a little sordid ... he is too intent upon growing rich* (Winston Churchill). **SYN**: greedy. **b** mean; low; base: *It is through Art ... that we shield ourselves from the sordid perils of actual existence* (Oscar Wilde). **SYN**: contemptible, ignoble, degraded. **3** of a dull or dirty color, as some birds and fishes. [< Latin *sordidus* dirty < *sordēre* be dirty, related to *sordēs, -is* dirt] —**sor′did|ly,** *adv.* —**sor′did|ness,** *n.*

**sor|dine** (sôr′dēn), *n. Music.* **1** a mute, as for a trumpet; sourdine. **2** a trumpet fitted with this. [< Italian *sordina:* see etym. under **sourdine**]

**sor|di|no** (sôr dē′nō), *n., pl.* **-ni** (-nē). *Music.* a mute. [< Italian *sordino* (diminutive) < *sordo* < Latin *surdus* deaf, mute]

**sor|dor** (sôr′dər), *n.* sordid character: *the sordor of civilisation* (Byron). [< Latin *sordēre* be dirty, related to *sordēs* dirt + English *-or,* as in *squalor*]

**sore** (sôr, sōr), *adj.,* **sor|er, sor|est,** *n., adv.* —*adj.* **1** causing sharp or continuous pain; painful; aching; smarting; tender: *a sore finger.* **2** sad; sorrowful or grieving; distressed: *The suffering of the poor makes her heart sore. Why speak I vain words to a heart still sore With sudden death of happiness?* (William Morris). **3** *Figurative.* easily angered or offended; irritable; touchy. **SYN**: sensitive. **4** *Informal, Figurative.* offended; angered; vexed: *He is sore at missing the game.* **5** *Figurative.* causing pain, misery, anger, or offense; vexing: *Their defeat is a sore subject with the members of the team.* **6** severe; distressing: *Your going away is a sore grief to us. For want of money the poor family was in sore need.*
—*n.* **1** a painful place on the body where the skin or flesh is infected, broken, or bruised. **2** *Figurative.* a cause of pain, sorrow, sadness, anger, or offense. **SYN**: affliction.
—*adv. Archaic.* in a sore manner.
[Old English *sār*] —**sore′ly,** *adv.* —**sore′ness,** *n.*

**so|re|di|al** (sə rē′dē əl), *adj. Botany.* having the appearance of a soredium.

**so|re|di|um** (sə rē′dē əm), *n., pl.* **-di|a** (-dē ə). *Botany.* a gonidium of a lichen that is able to develop into a new thallus when detached from the surface of the thallus. [< New Latin *soredium* < Greek *sōrós* heap]

**sore|fal|con** (sôr′fôl′kən, -fal′-, -fô′-; sōr′-), *n.* a falcon in the reddish-brown plumage of the first year. [< Anglo-French *sore,* Old French *sor* reddish-brown + English *falcon;* origin uncertain]

**sore|head** (sôr′hed′, sōr′-), *n., adj. U.S. Informal.* —*n.* **1** a person who is easily angered or offended. **2** a disappointed politician.
—*adj.* soreheaded; irritable: *In a special issue in 1956, it offered a sorehead view of Harvard and a garish mix of ideas* (Harper's).
[American English < *sore* + *head*]

**sore|head|ed** (sôr′hed′id, sōr′-), *adj. U.S. Informal.* feeling angered or offended: *You were soreheaded about something* (Sinclair Lewis).

**sore|hon** (sôr′hən), *n.* = sorren.

**sore spot,** something that angers or offends easily: *Everybody has a few sore spots, such as an embarrassing occurrence he would rather not discuss.*

**sore throat,** inflammation of the throat, causing pain especially when one is swallowing.

***sor|ghum** (sôr′gəm), *n.* **1** a tall cereal grass resembling corn. One kind of sorghum has a sweet juice used for making molasses or syrup. Some kinds provide food for livestock either by their grain or as hay, and other furnish material for brushes or brooms. See picture below. **2** molasses or syrup made from a sweet sorghum plant. [< New Latin *Sorghum* the genus name < Italian *sorgo;* see etym. under **sorgo**]

**sor|go** (sôr′gō), *n., pl.* **-gos.** any one of the sweet sorghums. [< Italian *sorgo* < Medieval Latin *surgum,* variant of Latin *syricum,* neuter adjective, Syrian]

**so|ri** (sôr′ē, sōr′-), *n.* plural of **sorus.**

**sor|i|cine** (sôr′ə sīn, -sin; sor′-), *adj.* **1** of or belonging to the family comprising the shrews. **2** shrewlike. [< Latin *sōricīnus* < *sōrex, -icis* shrew]

**so|ri|tes** (sō rī′tēz), *n., pl.* **-tes.** a form of argument having several premises and one conclusion. A sorites can be resolved into a number of syllogisms, the conclusion of each being the premise of the next. [< Latin *sōrītēs* < Greek *sōreítes* < *sōrós* a heap]

**so|rit|i|cal** (sō rit′ə kəl), *adj.* **1** having to do with a sorites. **2** resembling a sorites.

**sorn** (sôrn), *v.i. Scottish.* to sponge for food or lodging. [< *sorren*]

**sor|o|ban** (sôr′ə ban, -bän), *n.* the type of abacus used in Japan: *The Japanese start using the abacus or soroban in the fourth grade and develop a concrete familiarity with numbers* (Scientific American). Compare **suan pan.** [< Japanese *soroban*]

**so|ro|che** (sō rō′chē), *n.* (in the Andes Mountains) mountain sickness; puna. [< Quechua *sorochi*]

**So|rop|ti|mist** or **so|rop|ti|mist** (sə rop′tə mist), *n.* a member of an international organization of service clubs for professional and executive businesswomen. [< *sor*(ority) + *optimist*]

**so|ro|ral** (sə rôr′əl, -rōr′-), *adj.* **1** having to do with a sister. **2** = sisterly. [< Latin *soror* sister]

**so|ror|ate** (sôr′ə rāt, sōr′-), *n.* the custom among some primitive peoples that allows or requires a man to marry his deceased wife's younger sister. [< Latin *soror* sister + English *-ate*[2]]

**so|ror|i|cid|al** (sə rôr′ə sī′dəl, -rōr′-), *adj.* **1** of or having to do with sorricide. **2** tending towards sororicide.

**so|ror|i|cide**[1] (sə rôr′ə sīd, -rōr′-), *n.* the act of killing one's sister. [< Latin *sorōricīdium* < *soror, -ōris* sister + *-cīdium* act of killing]

**so|ror|i|cide**[2] (sə rôr′ə sīd, -rōr′-), *n.* a person who kills one's sister. [< Latin *sorōricīda* < *soror, -ōris* sister + *-cīda* killer]

**so|ror|i|ty** (sə rôr′ə tē, -rōr′-), *n., pl.* **-ties.** **1** a club or society of women or girls, especially at a college. **2** a sisterhood. [probably < Medieval Latin *sororitas* < Latin *soror, -ōris* sister]

**so|ro|sis** (sə rō′sis), *n., pl.* **-ses** (-sēz). **1** *Botany.* a fleshy multiple fruit composed of the ovaries, receptacles, and associated parts of an entire cluster of flowers, as in the pineapple and mulberry. **2** *U.S.* a society, especially a women's society or club. [< New Latin *sorosis* < Greek *sōrós* a heap]

**sorp|tion** (sôrp′shən), *n.* **1** = absorption. **2** = adsorption.

**sorp|tive** (sôrp′tiv), *adj.* = absorptive.

**sor|rel**[1] (sôr′əl, sor′-), *adj., n.* —*adj.* reddish-brown. —*n.* **1** a reddish brown. **2** a horse of this color. **3** a three-year-old buck (deer).
[< Old French *sorel* < *sor* yellowish-brown, *sor,* or *sore* hawk with red plumage]

**sor|rel**[2] (sôr′əl, sor′-), *n.* **1** a plant with sour leaves. It is a small perennial herb that belongs to the buckwheat family. **2** any one of various plants resembling this. **3** = oxalis. [< Old French *surele* < *sur* sour < Germanic (compare Old High German *sūr*)]

**sorrel tree,** = sourwood.

**sor|ren** (sôr′ən, sor′-), *n.* **1** hospitality formerly due to the lord or his men in Ireland and Scotland. **2** a tax imposed instead of this. [< obsolete Irish *sorthan*]

**sor|row** (sor′ō, sôr′-), *n., v.* —*n.* **1** grief, sadness, or regret: *She felt sorrow at the loss of her kitten. Sorrow comes with years* (Elizabeth Barrett Browning). **2** a cause of grief, sadness, or regret; trouble; suffering; misfortune: *Her sorrows, have aged her. Call ignorance my sorrow, not my sin* (Robert Browning). **SYN**: affliction, woe.
—*v.i.* to feel or show grief, sadness, or regret; be sad; feel sorry; grieve: *She sorrowed over the lost kitten.* **SYN**: mourn.
[Old English *sorg*] —**sor′row|er,** *n.*
—*Syn. n.* **1 Sorrow, grief, distress** mean sadness or mental suffering caused by loss or trouble. **Sorrow** suggests deep and usually prolonged sadness or anguish: *Not knowing what had happened to her son brought great sorrow to the woman.* **Grief** suggests acute but usually not prolonged sorrow: *Her grief when he died was almost unbearable.* **Distress** suggests the strain or pressure of pain (physical or mental), grief, fear, anxiety, or the like: *War causes widespread distress.*

**sor|row|ful** (sor′ə fəl, sôr′-), *adj.* **1** full of sorrow; feeling sorrow; sad: *a sorrowful person.* **SYN**: unhappy, mournful. **2** showing sorrow: *a sorrowful smile.* **SYN**: unhappy, mournful. **3** causing sorrow: *A death in the family is a sorrowful occurrence.* —**sor′row|ful|ly,** *adv.* —**sor′row|ful|ness,** *n.*

**sor|row|less** (sor′ō lis, sôr′-), *adj.* feeling no sorrow; free from sorrow.

**sor|ry** (sor′ē, sôr′-), *adj.,* **-ri|er, -ri|est.** **1** feeling pity, regret, or sympathy; sad: *I am sorry that you are sick. We are sorry that we cannot come to the party. Everyone is sorry for a blind animal.* **SYN**: distressed, sorrowful. **2** wretched; poor; pitiful: *The baron ... grew fat and wanton, and a sorry brute* (Emerson). *Slipshod handling once the packages reach the grocery can reduce even the finest brand to a sorry and sometimes dangerous mess* (Wall Street Journal). **3** painful; distressing: *The blind beggar in his ragged clothes was a sorry sight. Nothing dear goes cheap except for a sorry reason* (New Yorker). **4** worthless: *a sorry excuse.* [Old English *sārig* < *sār* sore] —**sor′ri|ly,** *adv.* —**sor′ri|ness,** *n.*

**sort**[1] (sôrt), *n., v.* —*n.* **1a** a group of things having common or similar characteristics; kind or class: *I like that sort of candy best. This sort of fish is abundant along our coast.* **SYN**: type. See syn. under **kind**[2]. **b** a certain class, order, or rank of people: *the meaner sort, the better sort.* **c** a person or thing of a certain kind or quality: *He is a good sort, generous and kind.* **2** character; quality; nature: *materials of an inferior sort. What sort of work do you do? I hate to ... take the risk of breaking up a friendship of the sort that ours has gotten to be* (Ernest Hemingway). **3** manner; method; fashion; way: *She was named after, or in some sort related to, the Abbey at Westminster* (Dickens).
—*v.t.* **1** to arrange by kinds or classes; arrange in order: *to sort mail. Sort these cards according to their colors.* **SYN**: assort, classify, select. **2** to separate from others; put: *Sort out the best apples for eating and cook the rest. They will sort out the good from the evil* (Edmund Burke). **3** to rank; class: *I will not sort you with the rest of my servants* (Shakespeare). **4** *Scottish.* to arrange or put in order; put to rights.
—*v.i.* **1** *Archaic.* to be in harmony; agree; accord (with): *Different styles with different subjects sort* (Alexander Pope). **2** *Scottish.* to associate; consort: *to sort with queer people.*
**a sort of,** something like; a kind of: *They use a sort of jabber* (Jonathan Swift).
**of sorts, a** of one kind or another: *The Alcalde ... was ... police officer, petty magistrate of sorts* (W. H. Hudson). **b** of a poor or mediocre quality: *We've a fountain of sorts; we're very vain of our shabby fountain!* (Leonard Merrick).
**out of sorts,** slightly ill, cross, or uncomfortable: *We've had a hot day and are all are tired and out of sorts* (Robert L. Stevenson).
**sort of,** *Informal.* somewhat; rather: *sort of foolish. In spite of her faults I sort of like her.*
**sorts,** *Printing.* a letter or piece in a font of type: *The expense ... in casting a fount of letter with such a number of heavy sorts will be considerable* (Charles Stower).
[< Old French *sorte* < Vulgar Latin *sorta* < Late Latin *sors, sortis* rank, class < Latin, lot] —**sort′a|ble,** *adj.* —**sort′er,** *n.*
► See **kind**[2] for usage note.

**sort**[2] (sôrt), *n. Obsolete.* **1** destiny; fate; fortune. **2** lot: *Make a lottery, Any by device let blockish Ajax draw the sort to fight with Hector* (Shakespeare). [< Old French *sort,* learned borrowing from Latin *sors, sortis* lot, fortune. Compare etym. under **sort**[1].]

**sor|tie** (sôr′tē), *n.* **1a** a sudden rushing forth of troops from a besieged fort, town, castle, or other structure or specifically-held area, to attack the besiegers; sally: *The troops ... were ... annoyed by the frequent and vigorous sorties of the besieged* (John F. Kirk). **b** the group that makes

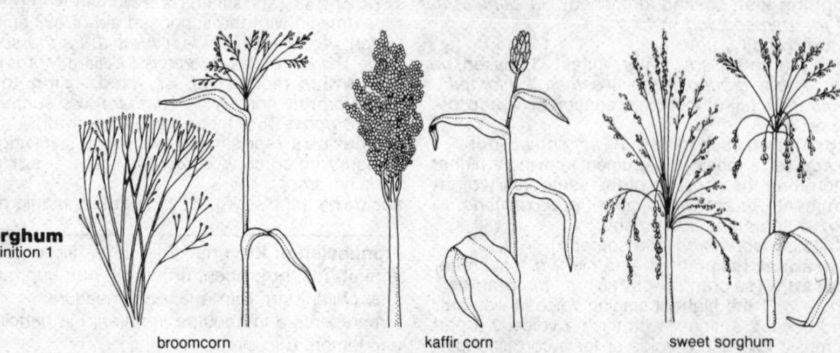

***sorghum** definition 1

a sortie: *They were a sortie of the besieged* (G. K. Chesterton). **2** a single round trip of an aircraft against the enemy; combat mission. [< French *sortie* < *sortir* go out < Old French, able, obtain by lot < Latin *sortīrī* cast lots < *sors, sortis* lot]

**sor|ti|lege** (sôr′tə lij), *n.* divination by the casting or drawing of lots: *They endeavoured by sortilege ... to find as it were a byroad to the secrets of futurity* (Scott). [< Medieval Latin *sortilegium* < Latin *sortilegus* diviner < *sors, sortis* lot, sort[2] + *legere* choose]

**sor|ti|le|gious** (sôr′tə lē′jəs), *adj.* of, having to do with, or characteristic of sortilege.

**sort|ing yard** (sôr′ting), = switchyard.

**sor|ti|tion** (sôr tish′ən), *n.* **1** the casting or drawing of lots; determination or selection by lot. **2** an instance of determining by lot. [< Latin *sortītiō, -ōnis* < *sortīrī*; see etym. under **sortie**]

**so|rus** (sôr′əs, sōr′-), *n., pl.* **-ri**. any one of the dotlike clusters of spore cases on the underside of the frond of a fern. [< New Latin *sorus* < Greek *sōrós* heap]

**sor|va** (sôr′və), *n.* **1** the milky juice of a Brazilian tree related to the cow tree, which is coagulated and boiled for use as a gum base in making chewing gum. **2** the tree itself. [< Portuguese *sorva*]

***S O S** (es′ō′es′), **1** a signal of distress consisting of the letters *s o s* of the international Morse code used in wireless telegraphy especially by ships, and by others calling for help. **2** *Informal.* any urgent call for help.

···———···

***S O S** definition 1

**so-so** (sō′sō′), *adj., adv.* — ***adj.*** neither very good nor very bad, but inclining toward bad; fairly good; mediocre: *The sermon was only so-so, but we enjoyed the singing.*
— ***adv.*** in a passable or indifferent manner or degree; tolerably: *"How is he doing his work?" "So-so."* **SYN**: passably, indifferently.

**sos|te|nu|to** (sos′tə nü′tō), *adj., adv., n., pl.* **-tos, -ti** (-tē). *Music.* — ***adj., adv.*** **1** sustained, as a note held for or over its full time value or a passage whose notes are thus held. **2** prolonged, as a passage played at a uniformly decreasing rate of speed.
— ***n.*** a movement or passage performed in this manner.
[< Italian *sostenuto,* past participle of *sostenere* sustain < Latin *sustinēre*]

**sot** (sot), *n.* a person made stupid and foolish by drinking too much alcoholic liquor; one who habitually drinks too much; drunkard. [Old English *sot* < Medieval Latin *sottus* stupid; a fool]

**so|te|ri|o|log|i|cal** (sō tir′ē ə loj′ə kəl), *adj.* of or having to do with soteriology.

**so|te|ri|ol|o|gy** (sō tir′ē ol′ə jē), *n.* the branch of theology dealing with salvation through Jesus Christ. [< Greek *sōtēríā* salvation (< *sōtḗr, -êros* savior < *sṓzein* save)]

**So|thic** (sō′thik, soth′ik), *adj.* of or having to do with Sothis or Sirius, the Dog Star. [< Greek *Sô-this* Sothis + English *-ic*]

**Sothic cycle** or **period**, a cycle or period of 1,460 Sothic years.

**Sothic year**, the fixed year of the ancient Egyptians, comprising 365 days, determined by the annual heliacal ring of Sirius.

**So|this** (sō′this), *n.* = Sirius. [< Greek *Sôthis*]

**So|tho** (sō′thō), *n., pl.* **-tho** or **-thos**. **1** = Basuto. **2** the Bantu language of the Basuto; Sesotho.

**so|tol** (sō′tōl, sō tōl′), *n.* any one of a group of plants of the lily family, resembling the yucca, and growing in the southwestern United States and in Mexico. [American English < Mexican Spanish *sotol,* also *zotol* < Nahuatl *tzotolli*]

**sot|ted** (sot′id), *adj.* = besotted.

**sot|tish** (sot′ish), *adj.* **1** stupid and foolish from drinking too much alcoholic liquor; drunken. **2** of or like a sot; stupid and coarse. — **sot′tish|ly,** *adv.* — **sot′tish|ness,** *n.*

**sot|to vo|ce** (sot′ō vō′chē), **1** in a low tone. **2** *Figurative.* aside; privately: *"She makes herself too cheap," Mrs. Van Buren said sotto voce* (Leonard Merrick). [< Italian *sotto voce* (literally) below (normal) voice < Latin *subter,* and *vōx, vōcis*]

**sot-weed** (sot′wēd′), *n. Informal.* tobacco.

**sou** (sü), *n., pl.* **sous** (süz; *French* sü). **1a** a former French coin, worth 5 centimes or 1/20 of a franc. **b** any one of various earlier French bronze, copper, silver, or gold coins, varying in value. **2** anything of little value. [< French *sou* < Old French *sol.* See etym. of doublets **sol**[3], **soldo, solid.**]

**sou|a|ri nut** (sü ä′rē), the large, edible nut of a tall, tropical American tree; butternut. [< Galibi (Guiana) *sawarra*]

**sou|bise** (sü bēz′), *n.,* or **soubise sauce**, a sauce flavored with a purée of onions. [< French *sauce soubise* < Prince Charles de Rohan *Soubise,* 1715-87, a French general]

**sou|bre|saut** (sü′brə sō′), *n.* a ballet jump with the body erect and the legs clinging together. [< French *soubresaut* < Middle French *sombresault;* see etym. under **somersault**]

**sou|brette** (sü bret′), *n.* **1** a maidservant or lady's maid in a play or opera, especially one of a coquettish, pert, and intriguing character; a lively or pert young woman character. **2** an actress or singer taking such a part. [< French *soubrette* < Provençal *soubreto* coy < *soubrar* to set aside < Latin *superāre* rise above < *super* over]

**sou|bret|tish** (sü bret′ish), *adj.* of or like a soubrette; coquettish; pert.

**sou|bri|quet** (sü′brə kā), *n.* = sobriquet.

**sou|car** (sou′kär), *n.* (in India) a Hindu banker or moneylender. Also, **sowcar**. [< Hindustani *sāhūkār* < Sanskrit *sādhu*]

**sou|chong** or **Sou|chong** (sü′shong′, -shông′), *n.* a fine variety of black tea, originally from China. [< Cantonese *siu chung* small, or fine, sort]

**Sou|da|nese** (sü′də nēz′, -nēs′), *adj., n.* = Sudanese.

**souf|fle** (sü′fəl), *n.* a murmuring or blowing sound, as heard when listening to the heart with a stethoscope. [< French *souffle* < Old French *souffler;* see etym. under **soufflé**]

**souf|flé** (sü flā′, sü′flā), *n., adj.* — ***n.*** a frothy baked dish usually made light by folding in beaten egg whites with the other ingredients and cooking very quickly in a hot oven: *a cheese soufflé, a chocolate soufflé.*
— ***adj.*** made very light in texture, especially by being puffed up in cooking: *potatoes soufflé.*
[< French *soufflé,* past participle of *souffler* puff up]

**souf|fléed** (sü flād′, sü′flād), *adj.* = soufflé.

**sou|gan** (sü′gən, sug′ən), *n.* = sugan.

**sough** (suf, sou), *v., n.* — ***v.i.*** **1** to make a rustling, rushing, or murmuring sound: ... *branches soughing with the four winds* (William O. Douglas). **2** *Scottish.* **a** to sigh deeply. **b** to die.
— ***v.t.*** **1** to express by a soughing sound. **2** *Scottish.* to utter in a sighing tone. **3** *Scottish.* to hum (a tune).
— ***n.*** **1** a rustling or murmuring sound, such as one made by wind or water: *It is the sough of the wind among the bracken* (Scott). **2** a deep sigh or breath. **3** *Scottish.* a canting or whining way of speaking, especially in preaching or praying: *I ken the sough o' her texts* (Scott). **4** *Scottish.* a rumor; vague report.
[Middle English *swoghen,* Old English *swōgan*]

**sought** (sôt), *v.* the past tense and past participle of **seek**: *For days she sought a safe hiding place. He was sought and found.*

**sought-af|ter** (sôt′af′tər, -äf′-), *adj.* wanted; in demand; popular.

**souk** (sük), *n.* = suq.

**soul** (sōl), *n., adj.* — ***n.*** **1** the part of the human being that thinks, feels, and makes the body act; the spiritual part of a person as distinct from the physical. Many religions believe that in death the soul and the body are separated and that the soul lives forever. *For what shall it profit a man, if he shall gain the whole world, and lose his own soul?* (Mark 8:36). *The soul selects her own society, Then shuts the door* (Emily Dickinson). *Breathes there the man, with soul so dead, Who never to himself hath said, This is my own, my native land!* (Scott). **2** energy or power of mind or feelings; spirit; fervor: *She puts her whole soul into her work.* **SYN**: heart. **3** *Figurative.* the cause of inspiration and energy; leading spirit; prime mover: *Florence Nightingale was the soul of the movement to reform nursing.* **4** *Figurative.* the essential part: *Brevity is the soul of wit* (Shakespeare). **SYN**: essence, substance. **5** a person; individual: *Don't tell a soul.* **SYN**: mortal, man. **6** *Figurative.* the embodiment of some quality; personification: *He is the soul of honor.* **7** the spirit of a dead person: *John Brown's body lies a-mouldering in the grave, His soul goes marching on* (Thomas B. Bishop). **SYN**: ghost. **8 Soul,** God (in the belief of Christian Scientists). **9a** the quality that stirs emotion or sentiment, especially in a distinctive spirit of Negro culture: *Ray Charles ... is the quintessence of soul: it's not what he sings but the way he sings it* (Time). **b** = soul music. **10** *U.S. Informal.* **a** a soul brother or soul sister. **b** = soul food.
— ***adj.*** **1** stirring the emotion or sentiment, especially in a distinctive spirit of Negro culture: *Sonny Charles, the organist, took over, singing with a soul appeal that caught up even this predominantly white audience* (New York Times). **2** belonging to or owned by Negroes; black: *Long before "black capitalism" became a politically popular catch phrase, Negro-owned "soul banks" started sprouting in ghetto areas* (Time).
**upon my soul!** as I hope to be saved! indeed! well!: *Upon my soul, a lie; a wicked lie* (Shakespeare).
[Old English *sāwol*]

**soul brother**, **1** *U.S.* a male Negro or, sometimes, one closely identified with Negro interests, especially in civil rights: *The session was a gathering of "soul brothers"—Negro military men and civilians, including a correspondent* (New York Times). **2** a man who belongs to the same or a similar group as another: *Even Vancouver's soul brothers, the Toronto Maple Leafs and Montreal Canadiens, turned thumbs down* (Maclean's).

**-souled,** *combining form.* having a ___ soul: *Great-souled = having a great soul.*

**soul food**, food typically popular among black Americans especially in the Southern United States, such as chitterlings, corn bread, pig's feet, turnip greens, and fried catfish: *Soul food may be said to embrace all the food created or developed over the centuries by the Negro cooks of the South ... It embraces such obvious dishes as fried chicken, spareribs, black-eyed peas, candied yams, mustard, turnip and collard greens cooked for hours with salt pork or fat back* (Craig Claiborne).

**soul|ful** (sōl′fəl), *adj.* **1** full of feeling; deeply emotional: *soulful music.* **2** expressing or suggesting deep feeling: *a soulful sigh.* — **soul′ful|ly,** *adv.* — **soul′ful|ness,** *n.*

**soul kiss,** = French kiss.

**soul|less** (sōl′lis), *adj.* **1** having no life or soul. **2** without spirit, courage, or noble feelings: *Do you think, because I am poor ... I am soulless and heartless?* (Charlotte Brontë). **3** without vivacity, animation, or the like; dull; insipid. — **soul′less|ly,** *adv.* — **soul′less|ness,** *n.*

**soul mate**, **1** an intimate associate or companion: ... *a need for an intellectual soul mate* (Newsweek). **2** = lover.

**soul music**, **1** a blend of music based on elements of jazz, rhythm and blues, and gospel music, developed and popularized by Negro singers: *As the greatest living exponent of gospel music, one of the main sources of the currently fashionable soul music, she should be assured of a sell-out* (Punch). **2** a composition of such music.

**soul rock**, rock'n'roll music influenced by soul music.

**soul-search|ing** (sōl′sėr′ching), *n., adj.* — ***n.*** a close, vigorous, and serious examination of one's motives, beliefs, or the like, especially at a critical time: *"There will be a great deal of soul-searching," predicted a retired judge ... "because there is no retreat from whatever choice we make"* (Newsweek).
— ***adj.*** of, engaged in, or requiring such examination.

**soul session**, a discussion, usually on civil rights or Negro culture: *The soul session, which has become a tradition of the movement in the South, is a kind of marathon group therapy, with a dash of mysticism* (New Yorker).

**soul-sick** (sōl′sik′), *adj.* spiritually depressed; sick at heart; deeply dejected: ... *the masses made blind and soul-sick by materialism and agnosticism* (Dublin Review).

**soul sister**, *U.S.* a Negro woman or girl: *Negro-owned establishments ... displayed the words, "Soul Brother" or "Soul Sister"* (New York Times).

**sou mar|kee** or **mar|quee** (sü′ mär kē′), *U.S.* **1** sou marqué. **2** a trifling sum or amount; little or nothing: ... *he didn't have a sou markee* (George Ade). [American English < French *sou marqué*]

**sou mar|qué** (sü′ mȧr kā′), *French.* a coin of base metal and low value, used in the 1700's.

**sound**[1] (sound), *n., v.* — ***n.*** **1** that which is or can be heard; sensation perceived in the organs of hearing by vibrations transmitted through the air or some other medium: *The birds fill the woods with tuneful sound.* **2** the energy in the form of vibrations causing this sensation. Sound travels through air in waves about 1,100 feet (335 meters) per second under normal conditions of pressure and temperature. **3** a noise, note, or tone, whose quality indicates its source or nature: *the sound of music, the sound of thunder, the sound of a baby.* **4** the distance within which a noise can be heard; earshot: ... *in sound of the swallowing sea* (Matthew Arnold). **5** one of the simple elements that make up speech, pro-

**Pronunciation Key:** hat, āge, cãre, fär; let, ēqual, tėrm; it, īce; hot, ōpen, ôrder; oil, out; cup, pu̇t, rüle; child; long; thin; ᴛʜen; zh, measure; ə represents **a** in about, **e** in taken, **i** in pencil, **o** in lemon, **u** in circus.

duced by a single position, movement, or set of movements of the vocal organs of the speaker: *a vowel sound.* **6** *Figurative.* the effect produced on the mind by what is heard: *a warning sound, a queer sound. Your predictions have a hopeful sound.* **7** mere noise, without meaning or importance: *A tale told by an idiot, full of sound and fury, signifying nothing* (Shakespeare). **8** *Archaic.* a report or rumor; news; tidings.

— ***v.i.*** **1** to make a sound or noise: *The wind sounds like an animal howling. The alarm began to sound. The whistle of the locomotive ... sounding like the scream of a hawk sailing over some farmer's yard* (Thoreau). **2** to be pronounced: *"Rough" and "ruff" sound just alike.* **3a** to be heard, as a sound: *Her voice sounds shrill. As if the words of an oracle sounded in his ears* (Scott). **b** to issue or pass as sound: *From you sounded out the word of the Lord* (I Thessalonians 1:8). **c** to be mentioned: *Wherever I went my name sounded* (Benjamin Disraeli). **4** to be filled with sound; resound: *The street sounds to the soldiers' tread* (A. E. Housman). **5** to summon: *The trumpet sounds for battle.* **6** *Figurative.* to give an impression or idea; seem; appear: *That excuse sounds peculiar. Your story sounds improbable.* **7** to make a sound, as on an instrument: *The singers sang, and the trumpeters sounded* (II Chronicles 29:28). **8** *Law.* to be capable of measurement in money for damages: *The action sounds in damages.*

— ***v.t.*** **1** to cause to make a sound: *Sound the trumpets; beat the drums* (Thomas Morell). **2** to give forth (a sound): *When winter's roar Sounded o'er earth and sea its blast of war* (Shelley). **3** to announce, order, or direct by a sound: *Sound the retreat. I sound my barbaric yawp over the roofs of the world* (Walt Whitman). **4** to pronounce or express; say so one can hear: *to sound each syllable.* **5** to make known; announce; utter: *The trumpets sounded the call to battle. Everyone sounded his praises.* **6** to celebrate; honor: *Nations unborn your mighty names shall sound* (Alexander Pope). **7** to test by noting sounds: *to sound a person's lungs.*

**sound off,** *U.S. Informal.* **a** to talk frankly or complain loudly: *He would sound off on domestic and international issues as he sees fit* (Wall Street Journal). **b** to give one's name, serial number, or other response, especially in military formations: *The soldiers sounded off smartly during the inspection.*

**within sound,** near enough to hear: *The incoming train was within sound when we reached the railroad station.*

[Middle English *soun* < Old French *son* < Latin *sonus;* the *-d* is a later addition]

**sound[2]** (sound), *adj., adv.* — ***adj.*** **1** free from disease; healthy: *a sound body, a sound mind.* **SYN:** robust. **2** free from injury, decay, or defect; in good condition: *sound walls, a sound ship, sound fruit.* **SYN:** uninjured, intact, flawless. **3** financially strong; safe; secure: *sound investments, sound credit, a sound business firm.* **4a** solid; massive; compact: *sound rock, a sound foundation.* **b** substantial, ample, or thorough: *a sound recovery, a sound investigation.* **5a** in accord with or based on fact, reason, or good sense; correct; right; reasonable; good: *sound advice, sound religious teaching, a sound objection, sound judgment. Remarks as sound as they are acute and ingenious* (Edmund Burke). **SYN:** just. **b** well-grounded in principles or knowledge; well-informed; reliable: *a sound teacher, a sound critic of music.* **6a** morally good; honest; upright: *No sounder piece of ... manhood was put together in that eighteenth century of time* (Thomas Carlyle). **SYN:** honorable, straightforward. **b** loyal; true; trusty: *... the requisites that form a friend, a real and sound one* (William Cowper). *Old soldiers ... are surest, and old lovers are soundest* (John Webster). **7** free from error or logical defect: *sound reasoning, a sound argument.* **SYN:** See syn. under **valid.** **8** without any legal defects: *a sound title.* **9a** having conventional or orthodox ideas or views: *politically sound, a sound conservative.* **b** theologically correct; orthodox: *He ordinarily preached sound doctrine* (John Evelyn). **10** deep; heavy; profound: *a sound sleep.* **11** vigorous; thorough; hearty: *a sound beating.*

— ***adv.*** deeply; profoundly: *The tired boy slept long and sound.* **SYN:** thoroughly.

[short for Middle English *isund,* Old English *gesund*]

**sound[3]** (sound), *v., n.* — ***v.t.*** **1a** to measure the depth of (water) by letting down a weight fastened on the end of a line, or by some other means; fathom: *to sound the channel in order to keep a boat in deep water.* **b** to measure (depth) in this way. **2** to examine or test (the bottom of the sea or other body of water) especially with a line arranged to bring up a sample: *to sound the bay for specimens of marine life.* **3a** to try to find out the views or feelings of; test; examine; investigate: *We sounded Mother on the subject of a picnic.* **SYN:** probe. **b** to seek to find out (as a person's views or opinions): *Cardinal Granvelle was instructed to sound the disposition of Francis* (James A. Froude). **SYN:** probe. **4** *Medicine.* to examine with a sound (instrument): *to sound the bladder.*

— ***v.i.*** **1** to use a sounding device, such as a line and weight, to determine depth or the nature of the bottom of the sea: *Men went overboard with pails ... sounding for deeper water* (Daniel Defoe). **2** to sink and reach bottom, as the weight on a line does. **3** to go toward the bottom; dive: *Some ... whales sound to great depths in their search for food* (Raymond M. Gilmore). **4** to make inquiry or investigation: *His thoughts ... had sounded into the depths of his own nature* (Thomas Carlyle).

— ***n.*** *Medicine.* a long, slender instrument used in examining body cavities.

[< Old French *sonder,* perhaps < the Germanic source of *sound[4]*]

**sound[4]** (sound), *n.* **1** long, narrow strip of water joining two larger bodies of water, or between the mainland and an island: *Long Island Sound.* See picture under **bay[1]**. **2** an inlet or arm of the sea: *Puget Sound.* **SYN:** firth. See picture under **bay[1]**. [partly Old English *sund* water, sea; partly < Scandinavian (compare Old Icelandic *sund* a strait)]

**sound[5]** (sound), *n.* a sac in fishes, containing air or gas, that helps them in floating; air bladder. [< Scandinavian (compare Old Icelandic *sundmagi,* Norwegian *sund*)]

**sound|a|ble** (soun′də bəl), *adj.* that can be sounded.

**sound-and-light** (sound′ən līt′), *adj.* **1** having to do with the combined use of light effects and recorded sound: *a sound-and-light discothèque.* **2** having to do with son et lumière: *a sound-and-light performance.* [translation of French *son et lumière*]

**sound and light,** = son et lumière.

**sound barrier,** a point near the speed of sound (about 1,100 feet or 335 meters per second in air at sea level) at which an aircraft or projectile meets a sudden increase in air resistance and creates a shock wave; sonic barrier. This point is viewed as a barrier separating subsonic from supersonic speed. *Jet aircraft ... have already penetrated what was thought ... to be an insuperable obstacle—the sound barrier* (Bulletin of Atomic Scientists).

***sound|board** (sound′bôrd′, -bōrd′), *n.* **1** a thin, resonant piece of wood forming part of a musical instrument such as a violin or piano, to increase the fullness of its tone. **2** = sounding board (def. 1).

***soundboard**
definition 1

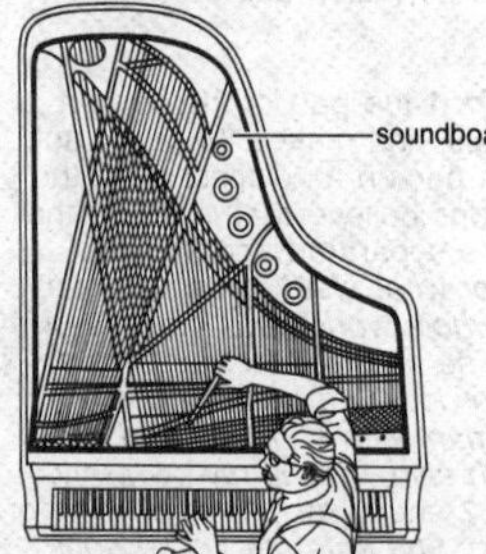


**sound bow** (bō), the thickest part of a bell, against which the clapper strikes.

**sound|box** (sound′boks′), *n.,* or **sound box,** **1** a hollow part of a musical instrument, as of a violin or harp, for strengthening the sonority of its tone; sounding box. **2** the part of a phonograph holding the sound-reproducing apparatus.

**sound effects,** sounds, as of thunder, blows, animals, or traffic, imitated by various devices or reproduced by recordings as part of the background of a play, motion picture, radio or television production, or the like.

**sound|er[1]** (soun′dər), *n.* **1** a person or thing that makes a sound or causes something to sound. **2** an electromagnetic receiving instrument that converts a telegraphic message into sound.

**sound|er[2]** (soun′dər), *n.* a person or thing that measures the depth of water.

**sound film,** **1** a motion-picture film with a sound track. **2** = sound motion picture.

**sound|head** (sound′hed′), *n.* a device in a motion-picture projector that converts the sound track of a film into electrical signals which are then amplified and reproduced.

**sound-hole** (sound′hōl′), *n.* a curvilinear opening, usually in pairs, in the soundboard of stringed instruments; f-hole.

**sound|ing[1]** (soun′ding), *adj.* **1** that sounds; causing, emitting, or producing a sound or sounds. **2** making loud sounds; resounding; resonant. **3** sounding fine, but meaning little; pompous; bombastic: *She used to repeat sounding phrases from books* (Charlotte Brontë). — **sound′ing|ly,** *adv.*

**sound|ing[2]** (soun′ding), *n.* **1** the act or process of measuring the depth of water with a sounding line, fathometer, sonar, or other means. **2** the depth of water found by this means. **3** an investigation. **4** an examining with a sound or probe.

**soundings,** **a** depths of water found by a sounding: *Up to the very brink of the coral rampart there are no soundings* (Herman Melville). **b** water not more than 100 fathoms (600 feet) deep, which can be measured by an ordinary sounding line: *We were soon out of soundings, and well into the Bay of Biscay* (Frederick Marryat).

**take soundings,** to try to find out quietly how matters stand: *Old Dan bears you no malice, I'd lay fifty pounds on it! But, if you like, I'll just step in and take soundings* (Charles J. Lever).

**sounding balloon,** a small, free balloon containing meteorological equipment, sent up to investigate and record atmospheric conditions.

**sounding board,** **1** a structure used to direct sound toward an audience. **2** *Figurative.* a means of bringing opinions, or ideas, out into the open: *In view of the prolonged and still unsettled wage negotiations in the industry, the convention is expected to be the sounding board for bitter recriminations* (New York Times). **3** = soundboard (def. 1).

**sounding box,** = soundbox.

**sounding lead,** the lead or plummet at the end of a sounding line.

**sounding line,** a line having a weight fastened to the end and marked in fathoms by various colors or materials, used to measure the depth of water; lead line.

**sounding machine,** any one of various machines for taking deep-sea or other soundings.

**sounding rocket,** a rocket containing scientific instruments for investigating conditions at high altitudes: *to send up sounding rockets to find out more about the nature of the space which satellite and space vehicles will traverse* (Wall Street Journal).

**sound|ings** (soun′dingz), *n.pl.* See under **sounding[2]**.

**sound|less[1]** (sound′lis), *adj.* without sound; making no sound; quiet or silent; noiseless or still: *soundless steps, a soundless night: ... a soundless waste, a trackless vacancy* (Wordsworth). — **sound′less|ly,** *adv.*

**sound|less[2]** (sound′lis), *adj.* so deep that the bottom cannot be reached with a sounding line; unfathomable. *the soundless depths of the ocean.* **SYN:** fathomless.

**sound|ly** (sound′lē), *adv.* **1** in a sound manner; deeply; heavily; profoundly: *The tired child slept soundly.* **2** vigorously; strongly; severely: *Father scolded us soundly.* **3** thoroughly; completely; properly. **4** with good judgment or common sense: *He decided soundly to keep out of trouble.*

**sound man,** = sound mixer.

**sound mixer,** a person who regulates the quality of the sound recorded as on films or tapes.

**sound motion picture,** a motion picture in which the actors can be heard to speak, sing, and move, the speech, music, and other sounds being recorded on a sound track.

**sound|ness** (sound′nis), *n.* **1** good health: *soundness of body and mind.* **SYN:** vigor. **2** freedom from weakness or defect. **SYN:** perfection. **3** good judgment; correctness and reliability: *We have confidence in the doctor's soundness.* **SYN:** discernment.

**sound pollution,** = noise pollution.

**sound post,** a thin rod inside a violin or similar instrument, underneath the bridge, that conducts the sound from the front to the back of the instrument and serves as a support against the pressure of the strings.

**sound|proof** (sound′prüf′), *adj., v.* — ***adj.*** not letting sound pass through; that absorbs or deadens sound: *a soundproof room or ceiling.*

— ***v.t.*** to make soundproof: *The halls at school are soundproofed.*

**sound radio,** *British.* the medium of broadcasting by radio; radiobroadcast.

**sound ranging,** echo ranging; echolocation.

**sound|scape** (sound′skāp), *n.* a range of sounds; musical panorama. [< *sound[1]* + *-scape*]

**sound spectrogram,** a graphic representation made by a sound spectrograph; sonogram.

**sound spectrograph,** an electronic instrument which produces a graphic representation of sound, with vertical marks representing frequency and horizontal marks representing time.

**sound stage**, the set on which a sound motion picture is filmed.

**sound track**, a recording of the sounds of words, music, and action, made along one edge of a motion-picture film. It is synchronized with the pictures of the action and reconverted into sound by the projector.

**sound truck**, *U.S.* a truck with one or more loudspeakers, used in making public announcements.

**sound wave**, any of the longitudinal progressive vibrations of a material medium by which sounds are transmitted.

**soup** (süp), *n., v.* —***n.*** **1** a liquid food made by boiling meat, fish, or vegetables in water, milk, or the like. Broth is thin soup. *He ate a bowl of hot chicken soup.* **2** anything resembling this, such as a mixture of chemical elements: *Life probably arose from "a soup of amino-acid-like molecules" some 3,000,000,000 years ago* (John G. Lepp). **3** *Slang.* a heavy, wet fog or cloud formation: *to fly on instruments through soup.* **4** *Slang.* power; horsepower. **5** *Surfing Slang.* the foam or froth formed by a wave breaking on the beach.
—***v.t.*** **soup up**, *Slang.* **a** to increase the horsepower of (an engine) by adjusting the mechanism, enriching the fuel mixture, adding special parts, or the like: *to soup up an engine.* **b** to make (an automobile or motorcycle) able to accelerate more quickly or attain a higher speed by doing this to its engine or engines: *to soup up a car.* **c** *Figurative: to soup up a story or song.*
**from soup to nuts**, from beginning to end: *The ideal organisation, it is suggested, is integration of production from raw material to the point of sale, doing the whole job from soup to nuts* (Sunday Times).
**in the soup**, *Informal.* in difficulty: *Hog producers are going to be in the soup by fall .... There'll be overproduction there just as sure as God made little apples* (Maclean's).
[< French *soupe* < a Germanic word]

**soup-and-fish** (süp′ən fish′), *n. Informal.* a man's formal evening suit. [because soup and fish are served at formal dinners]

**soup|bone** (süp′bōn′), *n.* a bone (with some meat on it) used for making soup stock, usually the shank of beef.

**soup|çon** or **soup|con** (süp sôɴ′, süp′sôɴ), *n.* a slight trace or flavor; very small amount; suspicion; suggestion: *to add a soupçon of salt to a salad. A soupçon of financial stability came* [*to the Paris Review*] *in 1956* (New York Herald Tribune Books). **SYN:** whit, dash. [< French *soupçon* < Old French *sospeçon* < Vulgar Latin *suspectiō, -ōnis,* for Latin *suspīciō;* see etym. under **suspicion**]

**soup|fin** (süp′fin′), *n.,* or **soupfin shark**, a shark whose fin is used by the Chinese for making soup, especially common on the coast of California.

**soup kitchen**, a place where food is served free or at a very low charge to poor or unemployed people or to victims of a flood, fire, or other disaster: *The nation was in the full grip of the depression, and on the sidewalks of New York was heard the shuffling of feet at the bread lines and the soup kitchens* (Newsweek).

**soup meat**, meat used for soup, especially to make the stock of soup.

**soup plate**, a rather large, deep plate used for serving soup.

**soup spoon**, a medium-sized, round spoon used for eating soup. See picture under **silverware**.

**soup|y** (sü′pē), *adj.,* **soup|i|er, soup|i|est.** like soup in consistency or appearance: *The weather was soupy and visibility was reduced* (New Yorker).

**sour** (sour), *adj., v., n., adv.* —***adj.*** **1** having a taste like that of vinegar or lemon juice; sharp and biting: *Most green fruit is sour.* **SYN:** acid, acidulous, tart. **2** fermented; acid as a result of fermentation; spoiled. Sour milk is healthful, but most foods are not good to eat when they have become sour. *During their absence the food in the cupboard turned sour.* **SYN:** rancid, curdled. **3** having a foul or rank smell: *sour breath, a sour medicine.* **4** *Figurative.* **a** disagreeable, bad-tempered, or peevish: *a sour face, a sour remark. Sour to them that loved him not; but to those men that sought him, sweet as summer* (Shakespeare). **b** dull; flat; stale: *The TV joke that may turn sour* (Observer). *Many a marriage or career has gone sour when it need not have* (Good Housekeeping). **5** unusually acid: *sour soil.* **6** cold and wet; damp: *sour weather.* **7** possessing contaminating amounts of sulfur: *sour gasoline.*
—***v.i., v.t.*** to become or make sour; turn sour: *The milk soured while it stood in the hot sun.* (*Figurative.*) *Such suffering would probably have soured the kindest temper* (William Godwin). (*Figurative.*) *After they had a 31-25 lead at halftime, the Wildcats' shooting soured* (New York Times). (*Figurative.*) *The low profits have held down dividends and ... soured investors on their industry* (Wall Street Journal).
—***n.*** **1** something sour, distasteful, or disagreeable: *the sweets we wish for, turn to loathed sours* (Shakespeare). **2** *U.S.* a sour alcoholic drink, such as whiskey and lemon juice: *a whiskey sour.* **3** a mildly acid bath or steep, used in bleaching, and dyeing.
—***adv.*** in a sour manner: (*Figurative.*) *to look sour.* **SYN:** disagreeably, crossly.
[Old English *sūr*] —**sour′ly**, *adv.* —**sour′ness**, *n.*
—***Syn.*** *adj.* **4 Sour, tart, acid**, used figuratively to describe a person, or his looks, disposition, words, manner of expression, or the like, mean having a quality of harshness or sharpness. **Sour** suggests bad temper, surly rudeness, grouchiness, or sullenness: *a sour disposition.* **Tart** suggests sharp and stinging qualities: *Her tart answer showed her slight irritation.* **Acid** suggests biting, sarcastic, severly critical qualities: *I read an acid comment on the acting in our school play.*

**sour|ball** (sour′bôl′), *n.* a hard, round piece of candy with a sour taste.

**source** (sôrs, sōrs), *n.* **1** the place from which anything comes or is obtained; origin: *Mines are the chief source of diamonds. One great original source of revenue ... the wages of labour* (Adam Smith). **2** a person, book, document, statement, or any other thing, that supplies information or evidence: *A newspaper gets news from many sources. What is the source of your belief?* **3** the beginning of a brook or river; spring; fountain: *Lake Tear-of-the-Clouds is the source of the Hudson River.* **4** a person, company, or other enterprise, that pays interest, dividends, or other return on investment. [< Old French *sourse* < *sourdre* to rise, spring up < Latin *surgere* rise; see etym. under **surge**]

**source|book** (sôrs′bůk′, sōrs′-), *n.* a book of fundamental documents, records, testimony, or evidence, which serve as firsthand or primary sources of information for the study of a subject.

**source language**, **1** *Linguistics.* the language from which something is translated. In a translation from German into English, German is the source language and English the target language. **2** *Education.* the language in which a foreign language is taught; native language. In teaching Russian to Americans, English is the source language and Russian is the object language.

**sour cherry**, a cherry with tart, edible fruit much used in cooking and baking. The amarelles and morellos are sour cherries.

**sour clover**, a kind of sweet clover used almost entirely as a cover crop, especially in the western United States.

**sour cream**, a thick cream made sour by a culturing process, used as a dressing for salads and certain other dishes.

**sour|dine** (sůr dēn′), *n. Music.* **1** a mute, as for a trumpet. **2** a small violin, used formerly by dance teachers. [< French *sourdine* < Italian *sordina* sordino (diminutive) < *sordo, sorda* deaf, muted]

**sour dock**, = sheep sorrel.

**sour|dough** (sour′dō′), *n., adj. Informal.* —***n.*** **1a** a prospector or pioneer in Alaska or Canada, especially in the Yukon. **b** any old resident, experienced hand, or the like; person who is not a tenderfoot. **2** Also, **sour dough.** fermented dough saved from one baking to start fermentation in the next, such as was used by the original prospectors in the Yukon.
—***adj.*** having sourdough as the leavening agent: *sourdough pancakes.*
[American English < the practice of saving sour dough (def. 2) < earlier British, leaven]

**sour gourd**, **1** the acid fruit of an Australian tree of the bombax family. **2** the tree itself; bottle tree. **3** = baobab.

**sour grapes**, a thing that a person pretends to dislike because he cannot have it: *Pearson is also aware ... that too vigorous an attack on the ... administration might sound like sour grapes* (Maclean's).

**sour gum**, **1** any one of various large North American trees of the same family as the tupelo, especially the black gum. **2** the wood of one of these trees.

**sour|ish** (sour′ish), *adj.* somewhat sour.

**sour mash**, *U.S.* **1** a fermenting grain mash. **2** a whiskey made from this.

**sour orange**, **1** a bitter-tasting orange used especially in making Eau de Cologne and preserves. **2** the tree on which it grows, widely cultivated for its rootstock, on which sweet oranges and other citrus fruits are grafted.

**sour|puss** (sour′půs′), *n. U.S. Informal.* a sullen or surly person; grouch: *One sourpuss ... grumbled ... that the company was probably infiltrated with spies* (Saturday Review).

**sour salt**, crystals of citric acid, used as a flavoring.

**sour|sop** (sour′sop′), *n.* **1** the large, edible fruit of a tropical American tree of the custard-apple family, having a white, somewhat acid pulp. **2** the small evergreen tree that bears this fruit.

**sour|wood** (sour′wůd′), *n.* **1** a tree of the heath family, native to the eastern United States, having a hard, close-grained wood, dark, glossy leaves that turn bright scarlet in the fall, and spikes of small, white, egg-shaped flowers; sorrel tree. **2** its wood, used especially to make handles for tools and the like.

**sou|sa|phone** (sü′zə fōn), *n.* a spiral bass tuba with a wide, flaring bell facing forward, used in brass bands. [American English < John Philip *Sousa,* 1854-1932, an American musical conductor and composer]

**souse**[1] (sous), *v.,* **soused, sous|ing,** *n.* —***v.t.*** **1** to plunge into liquid: *He soused me head and ears into a pail of water* (Sir Richard Steele). **2** to throw liquid over; soak in a liquid; drench with water or other liquid: *Then the engines arrived and soused the burning houses* (George Meredith). **3** to dash or pour (a quantity of water or other liquid). **4** to soak, as in vinegar or brine; pickle. **5** *Slang.* to make drunk.
—***v.i.*** **1** to be or become soaked or drenched; plunge into water or other liquid; soak: *Down I soused into the water* (Thackeray). **2** *Slang.* to become drunk.
[probably < noun]
—***n.*** **1** the act of plunging into a liquid; drenching: *Keeping her hand on his collar, she gave him two or three good souses in the watery fluid* (Scott). **2** a liquid used for pickling. **3** something soaked or kept in pickle, especially the head, ears, and feet of a pig. **4** *Slang.* a drunkard.
[< Old French *sous, soult* pickled pork < Germanic (compare Old High German *sulza* brine)]

**souse**[2] (sous), *n., v.,* **soused, sous|ing,** *adv. Archaic.* —***n.*** *Falconry.* **1** the rise of a bird from the ground, that gives the hawk an opportunity to strike. **2** the swooping down of a hawk upon a bird.
—***v.i., v.t.*** to swoop or pounce (on or upon), as an attacking hawk.
—***adv.*** suddenly; without warning.
[apparently alteration of *source,* in obsolete sense "the rise, spring (of a bird)"]

**sous-sous** (sü′sü′), *n.* a soubresaut performed by springing forward on the toes and bringing the legs tightly together. [< French *sous-sus* < (*des*)*sous*-(*des*)*sus* under-over]

**sou|tache** (sü′tash, sü tash′), *n.* a narrow ornamental braid, such as of wool or silk, used for trimming. [< French *soutache* < Hungarian *sujtás* soutache, braid, gold lace]

**sou|tane** (sü tän′), *n.* a cassock, such as that worn by priests of the Roman Catholic Church. [< French *soutane* < Italian *sottana,* adjective to *sotto* under < Latin *subtus,* adverb < *sub,* preposition]

**sou|ter** (sü′tər), *n. Scottish.* a shoemaker; cobbler. [Old English *sūtere* < Latin *sūtor, -ōris* cobbler < *suere* to sew, stitch]

**sou|ter|rain** (sü′tə rān′), *n.* an underground chamber, storeroom, passage, or the like. [< French *souterrain* < *sous* under + *terre* earth]

**south** (*n., adj., adv.* south; *v.* souтн, south), *n., adj., adv., v.* —***n.*** **1** the direction to the right as one faces the rising sun; direction just opposite north. South is one of the four cardinal points of the compass. *Abbr:* S (no period). **2** Also, **South.** the part of any country or region toward or at the south.
—***adj.*** **1** toward the south; farther toward the south: *He lives on the south side of town.* **2** from the south: *a south wind.* **3** in the south; facing the south: *A south window of a house catches the noonday sunshine.* **4** in the southern part; southern.
—***adv.*** toward the south; southward: *a flock of geese flying south. Drive south forty miles.*
—***v.i.*** to move or turn toward the south; blow more from the south: *About sundown the wind southed a point or two* (John M. Falkner).
**south of**, further south than: *New York is south of Boston.*
[Old English *sūth*]
▶ A *south* or *southerly* wind carries a ship sailing before it *north* or on a *northerly* course.

**South** (south), *n., adj.* —***n.*** **1** the southern part of the United States; the states south of Pennsylvania, the Ohio River, and Missouri, making up most of the states that formed the Confederate side in the Civil War. **2** = Confederacy. **3** the bridge player sitting opposite and in partnership

---

**Pronunciation Key:** hat, āge, cãre, fär; let, ēqual, tėrm; it, īce; hot, ōpen, ôrder; oil, out; cup, půt, rüle; child; long; thin; ᴛʜen; zh, measure; ə represents **a** in about, **e** in taken, **i** in pencil, **o** in lemon, **u** in circus.

with North. In most written illustrations of bridge hands, South is the declarer. **4** the developing countries of the world: *Today, any regional struggle over who is to become managing director of I.M.F. is far less likely to be one between the United States and Western Europe as between the "North" and "South"* (New York Times).
—***adj.*** of or having to do with the southern part, as of a country, region, or people.

**South African**, **1** of or having to do with southern Africa, especially the Republic of South Africa, or its people. **2** a person born or living in southern Africa or in the Republic of South Africa, especially an Afrikaner.

**South African Dutch**, **1** = Afrikaans. **2** the Afrikaners; Boers.

**South American**, **1** of or having to do with South America or its people: *a South American nation.* **2** a person born or living in South America.

**south|bound** (south′bound′), *adj.* going south; bound southward.

**south by east**, the point of the compass or the direction one point or 11 degrees 15 minutes to the east of south.

**south by west**, the point of the compass or the direction one point or 11 degrees 15 minutes to the west of south.

**South Carolinian**, **1** of or having to do with South Carolina. **2** a native or inhabitant of South Carolina.

**south celestial pole**, the zenith of the southern end of the earth's axis from which every direction is north; South Pole.

**South Dakotan**, **1** of or having to do with South Dakota. **2** a native or inhabitant of South Dakota.

**South|down** (south′doun′), *n.* any one of an English breed of small, hornless sheep raised for mutton. [< *South Downs,* an area in Sussex and Hampshire, England, where the breed originated]

**south|east** (south′ēst′; *Nautical* sou′ēst′), *adj., n., adv.* —***adj.*** **1** halfway between south and east. **2** coming from the southeast: *a southeast wind.* **3** lying toward or situated in the southeast: *a southeast district.* **4** facing the southeast: *A southeast window catches the mid-morning sun.*
—***n.*** **1** a southeast direction; the point of the compass or the direction midway between south and east. *Abbr:* SE (no periods). **2** a place that is in the southeast part or direction.
—***adv.*** **1** toward the southeast. **2** from the southeast. **3** in the southeast.
**the Southeast**, the southeastern part of the U.S.

**southeast by east**, the point of the compass or the direction one point or 11 degrees 15 minutes to the east of southeast.

**southeast by south**, the point of the compass or the direction one point or 11 degrees 15 minutes to the south of southeast.

**south|east|er** (south′ēs′tər; *Nautical* sou′ēs′tər), *n.* a wind or storm coming from the southeast.

**south|east|er|ly** (south′ēs′tər lē; *Nautical* sou′ēs′tər lē), *adj., adv.* **1** toward the southeast. **2** from the southeast.

**south|east|ern** (south′ēs′tərn; *Nautical* sou′ēs′tərn), *adj.* **1** toward the southeast. **2** coming from the southeast: *a southeastern wind.* **3** of or in the southeast.

**South|east|ern** (south′ēs′tərn), *adj.* of, having to do with, or in the Southeast.

**south|east|ern|er** (south′ēs′tər nər), *n.* a person born or living in the southeast.

**South|east|ern|er** (south′ēs′tər nər), *n.* a person born or living in the Southeast.

**south|east|ern|most** (south′ēs′tərn mōst; *Nautical* sou′ēs′tərn mōst), *adj.* lying furthest to the southeast.

**south|east|ward** (south′ēst′wərd; *Nautical* sou′ēst′wərd), *adv., adj., n.* —***adv.***, ***adj.*** toward the southeast. —***n.*** = southeast.

**south|east|ward|ly** (south′ēst′wərd lē; *Nautical* sou′ēst′wərd lē), *adj., adv.* **1** toward the southeast. **2** from the southeast: *southeastwardly winds.*

**south|east|wards** (south′ēst′wərdz; *Nautical* sou′ēst′wərdz), *adv.* = southeastward.

**south|er** (sou′ᴛʜər), *n.* a wind or storm coming from the south. [< *south* + *-er*[1]]

**south|er|li|ness** (sᴜᴛʜ′ər lē nis), *n.* the state of being southerly.

**south|er|ly** (sᴜᴛʜ′ər lē), *adj., adv., n., pl.* **-lies.** —***adj.*** **1** toward the south: *a southerly exposure.* **2** coming from the south: *a southerly wind.* **3** of the south. —***adv.*** **1** toward the south; southward: *The windows face southerly.* **2** from the south.

**Pronunciation Key:** hat, āge, cãre, fär; let, ēqual, tėrm; it, īce; hot, ōpen, ôrder; oil, out; cup, pu̇t, rüle; child; long; thin; ᴛʜen; zh, measure; ə represents **a** in about, **e** in taken, **i** in pencil, **o** in lemon, **u** in circus.

—***n.*** a southerly wind: *Finally, the fleet got under way with the aid of a light and fluky southerly* (New York Times).
► See **south** for a usage note.

**south|ern** (sᴜᴛʜ′ərn), *adj., n.* —***adj.*** **1** toward the south: *the southern side of a building.* **2** coming from the south: *a southern breeze.* **3** of or in the south: *He has traveled in southern countries.* **4** *Astronomy.* of or in the southern half of the celestial sphere: *Sirius and Canopus are southern stars.*
—***n.*** **1** Often, **Southern.** a person living in a southern region; southerner or Southerner: *Both Southern fierce and hardy Scot* (*Scott*). **2** a south wind; souther.
[Old English *sūtherne*]

**South|ern** (sᴜᴛʜ′ərn), *adj., n.* —***adj.*** of or in the southern part of the United States: *Atlanta, Georgia, is a Southern city.*
—***n.*** **1** a person living in a southern region. **2** the dialect of American English spoken in the South of the United States.

**Southern Baptist**, a member of a church belonging to the Southern Baptist Convention, a group of Baptist churches founded in Georgia in 1845.

**southern circle**, = tropic of Capricorn.

**Southern Cross**, a group of four bright stars in the form of a cross, visible in the Southern Hemisphere and often used in finding the direction south; Crux: *The Southern Cross appears too far south to be seen in the United States, except for a few places* (J. M. Levitt).

**Southern Crown**, a southern constellation near Sagittarius.

**south|ern|er** (sᴜᴛʜ′ər nər), *n.* a person born or living in the south.

**South|ern|er** (sᴜᴛʜ′ər nər), *n.* a person born or living in the southern part of the United States.

**Southern Fish**, a southern constellation near Aquarius, containing the bright star Fomalhaut.

**South|ern-fried chicken** (sᴜᴛʜ′ərn frīd′), *U.S.* chicken fried with a coating of flour and breadcrumbs.

**Southern Hemisphere**, the half of the earth that is south of the equator.

**South|ern|ism** (sᴜᴛʜ′ər niz′əm), *n.* **1** devotion or attachment to the South, especially to its customs, traditions, or other institutions. **2** a word, phrase, or meaning originating or much used in the South. **3** a custom or trait peculiar to the South.

**southern lights**, = aurora australis.

**south|ern|ly** (sᴜᴛʜ′ərn lē), *adj., adv.* = southerly.

**southern magnolia**, the evergreen magnolia of the southern United States, popular for its large, fragrant, whitish flowers; bull bay.

**south|ern|most** (sᴜᴛʜ′ərn mōst), *adj.* farthest south.

**South|ern|ness** (sᴜᴛʜ′ər nis), *n.* the state or quality of being Southern.

**southern prickly ash**, a species of prickly ash with large flowers and a warty trunk, growing on the sand coast of Virginia and southward.

**southern red lily**, a lily with erect, bright, red and yellow flowers spotted with purple, found along the southeastern coast of the United States.

**Southern Triangle**, a small constellation in the south polar zone near the Milky Way, containing three bright stars.

**south|ern|wood** (sᴜᴛʜ′ərn wu̇d′), *n.* a shrubby wormwood of Europe, grown in gardens for its finely divided, aromatic leaves.

**south geographic pole**, = South Pole.

**south|ing** (sou′ᴛʜing), *n.* **1** the distance of latitude reckoned southward from the last point of reckoning: *The latest southing was 1 degree 15 minutes from our position at sunrise.* **2** the distance southward covered by a ship on any southerly course: *On the first day of the voyage the southing was 200 knots.* **3** *Astronomy.* **a** a declination measured southward. **b** a crossing or approaching of the meridian by a heavenly body: *the southing of the moon.*

**South Jersey glass**, = Wistarberg glass.

**South Korean**, **1** of or having to do with South Korea or its people. **2** a native or inhabitant of South Korea.

**south|land** (south′lənd, -land′), *n.* the land in the south; southern part of a country.

**south|land|er** (south′lən dər, -lan′-), *n.* a native or inhabitant of the southland.

**south magnetic pole**, the point on the earth's surface toward which one end of a magnetic needle points. Its location varies but is approximately 1,600 miles from the South Pole, in Wilkes Land.

**south|most** (south′mōst), *adj.* farthest south; southernmost.

**south|paw** (south′pô′), *n., adj. Slang.* —***n.*** **1** a person who throws with the left hand, especially a left-handed baseball pitcher. **2** any left-handed person.
—***adj.*** left-handed, especially in pitching.
[American English < *south* "left" as an individual faces west + *paw*]

**south pole**, the pole of a magnet that points south.

**South Pole**, **1** the southern end of the earth's axis; point on the earth's surface from which every direction is north. It was first reached in 1911 by Roald Amundsen (1872-1928), a Norwegian explorer. See picture under **Antarctic Circle**. **2** = south magnetic pole. **3** = south celestial pole.

**south|ron** (sᴜᴛʜ′rən), *adj., n., pl.* **-rons** or **-ron.** —***adj.*** = southern.
—***n.*** Also, **Southron.** **1** *U.S.* a Southerner. **2** a native of the south of Great Britain; Englishman.
**the southron**, Englishmen: *In Ireland the Scotch and the southron were strongly bound together by their common Saxon origin* (Macaulay).
[Scottish alteration of *southern*]

**South Sea arrowroot**, = pia[2].

**South Sea Islander**, a native or inhabitant of the South Sea Islands.

**south-south|east** (south′south ēst′; *Nautical* sou′ sou ēst′), *n., adj., adv.* —***n.*** the point of the compass or the direction midway between south and southeast, two points or 22 degrees 30 minutes to the east of south.
—***adj., adv.*** of, from, or toward the south-southeast.

**south-south|west** (south′south west′; *Nautical* sou′sou west′), *n., adj., adv.* —***n.*** the point of the compass or the direction midway between south and southwest, two points or 22 degrees 30 minutes to the west of south.
—***adj., adv.*** of, from, or toward the south-southwest.

**South Vietnamese**, **1** of or having to do with South Vietnam or its people. **2** a native or inhabitant of South Vietnam.

**south|ward** (south′wərd), *adv., adj., n.* —***adv.*** toward the south; in a southerly direction: *He walked southward.*
—***adj.*** toward, facing, or at the south; southerly; south: *The orchard is on the southward slope of the hill.*
—***n.*** the direction or part that lies to the south; south.

**south|ward|ly** (south′wərd lē), *adj., adv.* **1** toward the south. **2** coming from the south: *southwardly winds.*

**south|wards** (south′wərdz), *adv.* = southward.

**south|west** (south′west′; *Nautical* sou′west′), *adj., n., adv.* —***adj.*** **1** halfway between south and west. **2** coming from the southwest: *a southwest wind.* **3** lying toward or situated in the southwest. **4** facing the southwest.
—***n.*** **1** the point of the compass or the direction midway between south and west. *Abbr:* SW (no periods). **2** a place that is in the southwest part or direction.
—***adv.*** **1** toward the southwest. **2** from the southwest. **3** in the southwest.
**the Southwest**, the southwestern part of the United States.

**southwest by south**, the point of the compass or the direction one point or 11 degrees 15 minutes to the south of southwest.

**southwest by west**, the point of the compass or the direction one point or 11 degrees 15 minutes to the west of southwest.

***south|west|er** (south′wes′tər *or Nautical* sou′wes′tər *for 1;* sou′wes′tər *for 2*), *n.* **1** a wind or storm coming from the southwest. **2** a waterproof hat having a broad brim behind to protect the neck. Southwesters are worn especially by seamen. Also, **sou′wester.**

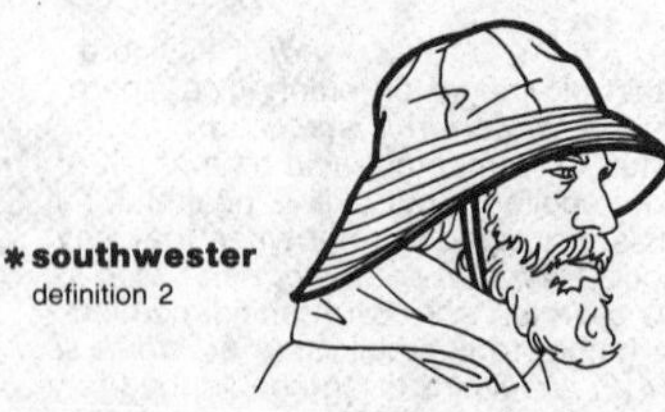
***southwester** definition 2

**south|west|er|ly** (south′wes′tər lē; *Nautical* sou′wes′tər lē), *adj., adv.* **1** toward the southwest. **2** from the southwest.

**south|west|ern** (south′wes′tərn; *Nautical* sou′wes′tərn), *adj.* **1** toward the southwest. **2** coming from the southwest: *a southwestern wind.* **3** of or in the southwest.

**South|west|ern** (south′wes′tərn), *adj.* of, having to do with, or in the southwestern part of the United States.

**south|west|ern|er** (south′wes′tər nər), *n.* a person born or living in the southwest.

**South|west|ern|er** (south′wes′tər nər), *n.* a person born or living in the Southwest.

**south|west|ern|most** (south′wes′tərn mōst;

*Nautical* sou'wes'tərn mōst), *adj.* lying farthest to the southwest.

**south|west|ward** (south'west'wərd; *Nautical* sou'west'wərd), *adv., adj., n.* —**adv., adj.** toward the southwest.
—*n.* = southwest.

**south|west|ward|ly** (south'west'wərd lē; *Nautical* sou'west'wərd lē), *adj., adv.* **1** toward the southwest. **2** from the southwest.

**south|west|wards** (south'west'wərdz; *Nautical* sou'west'wərdz), *adv.* = southwestward.

**sou|ve|nir** (sü'və nir', sü'və nir), *n.* something given or kept to remind one of a place, person, or occasion; token of remembrance; keepsake. **SYN**: memento, remembrance, reminder, token.
[< French *souvenir* (originally, infinitive) to remember < Latin *subvenīre* come to mind < *sub-* up + *venīre* come]

**sou'west|er** (sou'wes'tər), *n.* = southwester.

**SOV.**, sovereign.

**sov|er|eign** (sov'rən, suv'-), *n., adj.* —*n.* **1** the supreme ruler; king or queen; monarch. Queen Victoria was the sovereign of Great Britain from 1837 to 1901. *It was not for me to bandy civilities with my sovereign* (Samuel Johnson). **2** a person, group, or nation having supreme control or dominion; ruler; governor; lord; master: *sovereign of the seas.* **3** a British gold coin, worth one pound or formerly 20 shillings.
—*adj.* **1** having the rank or power of a sovereign: *a sovereign prince. Here lies our sovereign lord the king* (John Wilmot). **2** greatest in rank, authority, or power: *a sovereign court, sovereign jurisdiction.* **3** independent of the control of another government or governments: *a sovereign state. When the thirteen colonies won the Revolutionary War, America became a sovereign nation.* **4a** above all others; supreme; greatest: *Character is of sovereign importance. The knowledge of Truth ... is the sovereign good of human nature* (Francis Bacon). **SYN**: chief, paramount. **b** greatest in degree; utmost; extreme: *... a sovereign contempt for everyone* (Henry James). **5** excellent or powerful: *There is no sovereign cure for colds.* **6** of, belonging to, or characteristic of a sovereign or sovereignty: *sovereign power, a sovereign proclamation.*
[< Old French *soverain* < Vulgar Latin *superānus* < Latin *super* over] —**sov'er|eign|ly**, *adv.*

**sov|er|eign|ty** (sov'rən tē, suv'-), *n., pl.* **-ties.** **1** supreme power or authority; supremacy: *the sovereignty of the sea. The United States of America is a sovereign nation, but the 50 states which compose it do not have full sovereignty* (Payson S. Wild). **2** freedom from outside control; independence in exercising power or authority: *Countries that are satellites lack full sovereignty. Our* [*national*] *sovereignty is not something to be hoarded, but something to be used* (Wendell Willkie). **3** a state, territory, community, or other political area, that is independent or sovereign. **4** the rank, power, or jurisdiction of a sovereign; royal authority or dominion.

**so|vi|et** (sō'vē et, -it; sov'ē-; sō'vē et'), *n., adj.* —*n.* **1** Often, **Soviet.** in the Soviet Union: **a** either of two governing councils or assemblies concerned with local government (village soviets, town soviets). Each is composed of elected representatives of the people. **b** any one of the larger assemblies elected by local assemblies, culminating in the Supreme Soviet or Council, the national legislative body. **2** a council; assembly.
—**adj.** of or having to do with a soviet or soviets.
[< Russian *sovet* council < Old Russian *sŭvětŭ* < Old Church Slavonic < *sŭ-* together + *větŭ* counsel, agreement, translation of Greek *symboúlion*]

**So|vi|et** (sō'vē et, -it; sov'ē-; sō'vē et'), *adj., n.* —**adj.** of or having to do with the Soviet Union.
—*n.* **Soviets, a** Russians. **b** = Kremlin.
[< *soviet*]

**so|vi|et|ize** (sō'vē ə tīz, sov'ē-; sō'vē et'īz, sov'ē-), *v.t.,* **-ized, -iz|ing.** to change to a government by soviets, or to communism. —**so'vi|et|i|za'tion**, *n.* —**so'vi|et|iz'er**, *n.*

**So|vi|et|ize** (sō'vē ə tīz, sov'ē-; sō'vē et'īz, sov'ē-), *v.t.,* **-ized, -iz|ing.** to put under the control or influence of the Soviet Union or its system of government: *The satellite armies vary considerably in strength and capabilities but all of them have been more or less Sovietized* (New York Times). —**So'vi|et|i|za'tion**, *n.*

**So|vi|et|ol|o|gist** (sō'vē ə tol'ə jist, sov'ē-), *n.* = Kremlinologist.

**So|vi|et|ol|o|gy** (sō'vē ə tol'ə jē, sov'ē-), *n.* = Kremlinology.

**sov|khoz** (sov koz'; *Russian* sof hôs'), *n., pl.* **-khoz|es, -khoz|y** (-hô'zē). a farm in the Soviet Union that is owned by the state, as distinguished from a kolkhoz or collective farm. [< Russian *sovkhoz,* abbreviation of *sovetskoe khozjajstvo* soviet management]

**sov|nar|khoz** (sov'när koz'; *Russian* sof'närhôs'), *n., pl.* **-khoz|es, -khoz|y** (-hô'zē). a regional economic council in the Soviet Union that is responsible for the planning and production of all industrial enterprises. [< Russian *sovnarkhoz,* abbreviation of *sovnarkom khozjajstvo* council of people's commissars management]

**sov|ran** (sov'rən, suv'-), *n., adj. Poetic.* sovereign. [introduced by Milton < Italian *sovrano*]

**sov|ran|ty** (sov'rən tē, suv'-), *n., pl.* **-ties.** *Poetic.* sovereignty.

**sow**[1] (sō), *v.,* **sowed, sown** or **sowed, sow|ing.** —*v.t.* **1** to scatter (seed) on the ground; plant (a crop) in this way: *He sows more wheat than oats.* **2** to plant seed in: *The farmer sowed the field with oats.* **3** *Figurative.* to scatter (anything); spread abroad; disseminate: *to sow distrust, to sow the gospel among all nations. The enemy tried to sow discontent in our men.* **4** *Figurative.* to implant: *to sow the germ of dissension.*
—*v.i.* to scatter seed: *to sow once a year.*
[Old English *sāwan*] —**sow'er**, *n.*

**sow**[2] (sou), *n.* **1** a fully grown female pig. **2a** a large mass of solidified iron or other metal formed in the channel through which the molten metal passes from the smelting furnace to the series of parallel channels in which the pigs form. **b** the channel in which it is formed. [Old English *sugu*]

**so|war** (sə wär', -wôr'), *n.* (formerly) a native soldier in India in the British service, either as a member of a cavalry unit or as a mounted orderly. [< Hindustani, Persian *sawār* horseman]

**sow|bel|ly** (sou'bel'ē), *n. U.S. Informal.* salt pork consisting mostly of fat.

**sow bug** (sou), = wood louse.

**sow|car** (sou'kär), *n.* = soucar.

**sow|ens** (sō'ənz, sü'-), *n.pl. Scottish and Irish.* a kind of coarse porridge made from steeped oat husks. [earlier *sowannis* < Gaelic *súghan* broth used in preparing sowens < *súgh* juice, sap]

**sown** (sōn), *v.* a past participle of **sow**[1]: *The field had been sown with oats.*

**sow thistle** (sou), any coarse weed of a group of the composite family, with thistlelike leaves, yellow flowers, and milky juice.

**sox** (soks), *n.pl. Informal.* socks (stockings).

**soy** (soi), *n.* **1** Also, **soy sauce.** a salty, brown sauce made from fermented soybeans, used especially in Chinese and Japanese cooking to give flavor and color, as to meat and fish. **2** = soybean. [< Japanese *shōyu* < Chinese (Peking) *chiang -yu*]

**soy|a** (soi'ə), *n. British.* soy.

**soy|bean** (soi'bēn'), *n.* **1** a bean native to Asia, now grown in other parts of the world. Soybeans are used in making flour and oil and as a food. **2** the plant that it grows on, used as fodder for cattle. It belongs to the pea family. See picture under **pea family.** Also, **soja, soja bean.**

**soybean oil**, the pale yellow oil extracted from soybeans, used in the manufacture of margarine, shortenings, and salad and cooking oil. It is also an ingredient in paints, lacquers, soap, and ink.

**so|zin** (sō'zin), *n.* any protein normally present in the animal body and protecting it against disease. [< Greek *sôzein* save + English *-in*]

**soz|zled** (soz'əld), *adj. Slang.* intoxicated; drunk.

**sp.**, an abbreviation for the following:
**1** special.
**2** species.
**3** specific.
**4** specimen.
**5** spelling.
**6** spirit.

**s.p.**, **1** *Printing.* small pica. **2** *Banking.* supra protest. **3** *Law.* without issue (Latin, *sine prole*).

**Sp.**, **1** Spain. **2** Spaniard. **3** Spanish.

**SP** (no periods), **1** shore patrol. **2** specialist (def. 4).

**S.P.**, shore patrol.

**spa** (spä), *n.* **1** a mineral spring. **2** a town, locality, or resort where there is a mineral spring or springs. [< *Spa,* a Belgian resort]

***space** (spās), *n., adj., v.,* **spaced, spac|ing.** —*n.* **1** the unlimited room or place extending in all directions and in which all things exist: *The earth moves through space.* **2a** a part of this in a given instance; area; room: *The larger a house, the more space it occupies. Children need a lot of space to play in.* **b** a limited place or area: *to find a parking space. Is there space in the car for another person? This brick will fill a space 2½ by 4 by 8 inches.* **3** an extent or area, as of ground, surface, or sky; expanse: *The trees covered acres of space.* **4** = outer space: *the conquest and exploration of space, a rocket launched into space.* See picture below. **5** a distance between two or more points or objects: *The road is bad for a space of two miles. The trees are set at equal spaces apart.* **6** length of time; duration: *The flowers died in the space of a day. He had not seen his brother for the space of ten years. Many changes occur within the space of a man's life.* **7** *Archaic.* an interval of time; a while: *After a space, he continued his story.* **8** a blank between words or lines in written or printed matter: *Fill in the spaces as directed.* **9** *Printing.* one of the small pieces of blank type used to separate words, or other matter, or to justify a line. **10a** extent or room in a periodical, book, letter, or other printed or written matter, available for, or occupied by, written or printed matter. **b** *Advertising.* the part of a page or the number of lines in a periodical, newspaper, or other printed matter, available or used for advertising. **11** *Music.* one of the open places between the lines of a staff. **12** accommodations such as on a train, airplane,

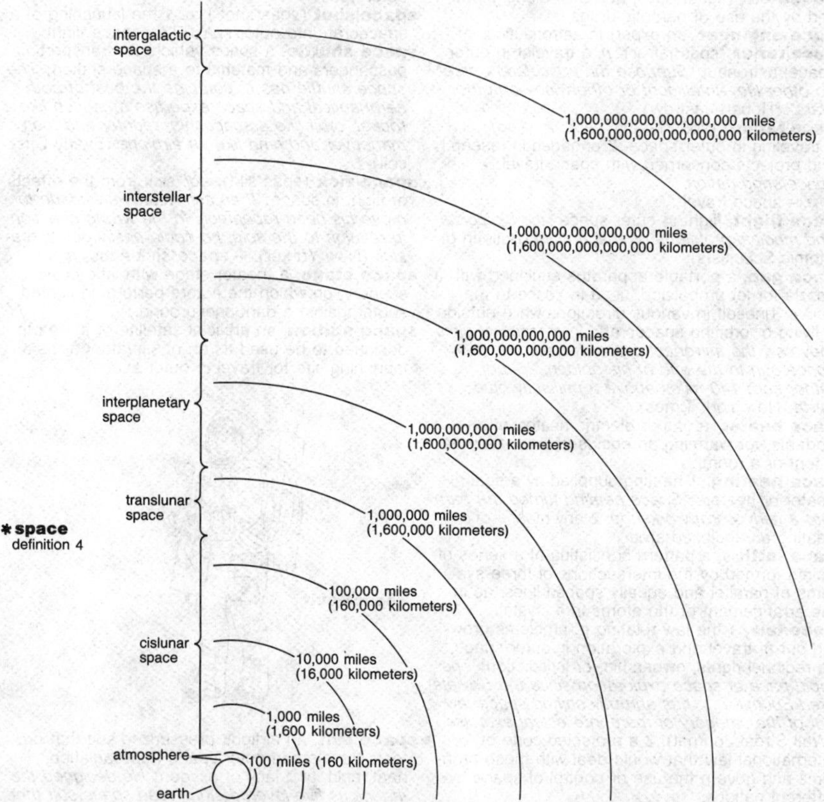

***space** definition 4

or ship. **13** *Telegraphy.* an interval in the transmission of a message in Morse code or a similar system when the key is not in contact and no signal is transmitted. **14** *Mathematics.* a set of points or elements that usually fulfills certain necessary conditions.

—***adj.*** **1** of or having to do with outer space: *space exploration, space dust.* **2** of or for space travel: *a space vehicle, the space industry, space technology.*

—***v.t.*** **1** to fix the space or spaces of; divide into spaces: *to space a chart.* **2** to separate by spaces: *Space your words evenly when you write.* **3** *Printing.* to extend to a required length by inserting additional space between the words or lines: *to space out a word or a line.*

[< Old French *espace,* learned borrowing from Latin *spatium*]

**space age** or **Space Age**, the current period in history, as marked by the advances made in the exploration and conquest of outer space through the launching and orbiting of artificial satellites and other space vehicles: *The conquest of space has moved ahead with breath-taking speed since the Space Age began on Oct. 4, 1957. On that day, Russian scientists launched the first true space traveler, an artificial satellite called Sputnik I* (Harold L. Goodwin). —**space′-age′, Space′-Age′,** *adj.*

**space bar**, the horizontal bar on a typewriter keyboard that is pressed down to move the carriage one or more spaces to the left.

**space|borne** (spās′bôrn′, -bōrn′), *adj.* **1** carried into outer space: *He also suggests applying continuous flight acceleration to the craft once it is spaceborne* (Science News Letter). **2** carried by spacecraft: [*The*] *Department of Defense plans to double its spaceborne network of radio relay stations* (Science News).

**space capsule**, a spacecraft consisting of a closed receptacle or chamber, designed to contain one or more persons, animals, or special equipment for carrying out an experiment or operation in space: *A space capsule containing both a monkey and a rat would be rocket-launched high above the earth ... to provide clues to human intellectual reaction caused by weightlessness in space travel* (Wall Street Journal).

**space charge**, the electric charge distributed through the area between the filament and the plate in a vacuum tube.

**space|craft** (spās′kraft′, -kräft′), *n., pl.* **-craft.** any vehicle used for flight in outer space; spaceship: *The whole spacecraft would rotate slowly about its long axis to provide artificial gravity, through centrifugal force, for the crew* (Science News Letter).

**spaced-out** (spāst′out′), *adj. U.S. Slang.* stupefied by the use of narcotic drugs.

**space engineer**, an expert in astronautics.

**space|far|er** (spās′fãr′ər), *n.* a traveler in outer space; astronaut: *Suppose the spacefarers meet no other life—intelligent or otherwise—on other stars?* (Robert Jastrow).

**space|far|ing** (spās′fãr′ing), *adj., n.* —***adj.*** **1** traveling in outer space. **2** engaged in research and projects concerned with space travel: *a spacefaring nation.*

—***n.*** = space travel.

**space flight**, flight in outer space: *the biological and medical problems of space flight* (Bulletin of Atomic Scientists).

**space gun**, a portable apparatus equipped with a nozzle for jet propulsion, used in space to maneuver oneself in various directions while outside a flying or orbiting spacecraft: *In a series of films they saw the astronaut propel himself with his space gun to the end of his golden, 25-foot tether cord 140 miles above a brilliantly blue earth* (New York Times).

**space heater**, a gas or electric heater, often portable, for warming an enclosed area, such as a tent or a room.

**space heating**, **1** heating supplied by a space heater or heaters: *Space heating turned the barn into a fairly warm workshop.* **2** any means of heating an enclosed area.

**space lattice**, a pattern consisting of a series of points formed by the intersections of three systems of parallel and equally spaced lines, as in the arrangement of the atoms in a crystal.

**space law**, **1** the law relating to problems growing out of travel and exploration in outer space, as regional rights, ownership, or jurisdiction: *The rapid pace of space exploration since the Soviets fired Sputnik I ... has abruptly shifted space law out of the category of mere intellectual exercise* (Wall Street Journal). **2** a projected code of international law that would deal with these problems and govern the use or control of space by different nations.

**space|less** (spās′lis), *adj.* **1** independent of space; not limited by space; infinite; boundless: *the spaceless reaches of the universe.* **2** occupying no space. —**space′less|ness,** *n.*

**space|man** (spās′man′), *n., pl.* **-men.** **1** a person skilled in or trained for space navigation; astronaut. **2** a person, especially a scientist, engaged in research or other projects concerned with space travel: *U.S. spacemen ... fired a satellite farther into space than any other man-made object* (Time).

**space|mark** (spās′märk′), *n.* an object in outer space used as a guide in space flight: *Interstellar navigation, however, will be tougher, because the spacemarks will constantly shift* (Science News). [patterned after *landmark*]

**space mark**, the symbol used to show that space is to be left, usually between two words.

**space medicine**, the branch of medicine dealing with the effects of space travel on the body, including the body's capacity to endure space travel and the prevention, cure, or alleviation of illnesses or diseases that may be expected to result from space travel; aerospace medicine.

**space platform**, = space station.

**space|port** (spās′pôrt′, -pōrt′), *n.* a place where spacecraft can take off or land.

**space probe**, a rocket with scientific instruments, shot into space to record certain phenomena and carry on research; probe.

**spac|er** (spā′sər), *n.* **1** a device for spacing words or letters, as in a typesetting machine, or typewriter. **2** an instrument that reverses a telegraphic current to increase the speed of transmission.

**space race**, the competition between the Soviet Union and the United States for first place in the exploration of outer space.

**space rate**, the rate of payment for space writing: *Our local newspaper pays free-lance writers at space rates.*

**space rocket**, = spaceship.

**space satellite**, = artificial satellite.

**space-sav|ing** (spās′sā′ving), *adj.* that saves or tends to save available space; that helps to use space more efficiently: *When stationary, on the other hand, the machines are sensationally space-saving; since they have flat tops, they can be set one on top of the other* (New Yorker).

**space science**, **1** any science or branch of science dealing with outer space, such as astronautics or space medicine. **2** the group of studies concerned with problems related to the exploration of outer space, including those branches of physics, biology, chemistry, and geology, that deal with extraterrestrial phenomena.

**space scientist**, an expert in or student of space science or any of the space sciences.

**space|ship** (spās′ship′), *n.* a spacecraft by which it is possible to travel between the planets or in outer space.

**space|shot** (spās′shot′), *n.* **1** the launching of a spacecraft into outer space. **2** = space flight.

**space shuttle**, a space vehicle for transporting passengers and material to a space station: *The space shuttle has to combine the best of both aeronautical and space expertise to launch like a rocket, orbit like a spaceship, reenter and then maneuver and land like an airplane* (Everly Driscoll).

**space|sick** (spās′sik′), *adj.* sick from the effects of flight in space: *If an astronaut were made to move his head repeatedly in the wrong direction in relation to the spin, he could easily get spacesick* (New Yorker). —**space′sick′ness,** *n.*

**space stage**, a theater stage with little or no scenery, on which the actors perform in lighted spots against a dark background.

**space station**, an artificial satellite of the earth designed to be used as an observatory or as a launching site for travel in outer space.

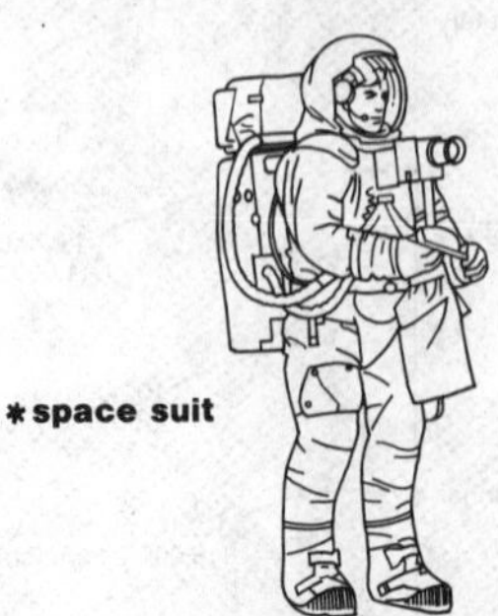

***space suit**

***space suit**, an airtight, pressurized suit that protects travelers in outer space from radiation, heat, cold, and lack of oxygen: *He designed the ingenious five-layered aluminized space suit that will meet the human needs of space flight* (Newsweek).

**space thunder**, thunder that follows the arcs of the earth's magnetic field out into space, and that is inaudible except as a whistle on a radio.

**space time**, **1** the frame of reference within which, according to the theory of relativity, any physical event has particularity of existence, consisting of the three traditional dimensions of physical being (length, breadth, thickness) and the fourth dimension (time). **2** = space-time continuum.

**space-time continuum** (spās′tīm′), *Physics.* space conceived as a continuum of four dimensions (length, width, height, and time), within which physical events can be located exactly.

**space travel**, travel through outer space, especially in spacecraft: *Satellites and moon rockets promise that space travel will one day be possible* (New Scientist).

**space tug**, a space vehicle for servicing and linking orbiting spacecraft and space stations: *The so-called "space tug" ... like the shuttle, would be manned but served for transport between the space station and other objects in space, rather than between Earth and the station* (New Scientist).

**space|walk** (spās′wôk′), *n., v.* —***n.*** the act of moving or floating in space while outside a spacecraft; extravehicular motion or activity.

—***v.i.*** to move or float in space while outside a spacecraft. —**space′walk′er,** *n.*

**space|ward** (spās′wərd), *adv.* upward or outward into outer space: *The world hopes desperately that Russia and the United States will continue to launch their giant rockets spaceward instead of at each other* (Atlantic).

**space|wom|an** (spās′wu̇m′ən), *n., pl.* **-wom|en.** a woman astronaut: *Valentina* [*Tereshkova*], *history's first spacewoman, is inspiring proof of the distances women have advanced in the secular world of the last hundred years* (Maclean's).

**space|wor|thy** (spās′wėr′ᴛʜē), *adj.* capable of being used in space flight: *to launch a really spaceworthy ship* (New Yorker).

**space writer**, a writer in newspaper and other literary work who is paid on the basis of the amount of space his accepted writing fills when it is set in type.

**space writing**, in newspaper work: **1** the system of payment to reporters or other writers in proportion to the space allowed to their articles in print. **2** writing or work done under this system.

**spa|cial** (spā′shəl), *adj.* = spatial.

**spac|ing** (spā′sing), *n.* **1** the fixing or arranging of spaces. **2** the manner in which spaces are arranged: *even, close, or open spacing in printed matter.* **3** a space or spaces in printing or other work.

**spa|cious** (spā′shəs), *adj.* **1** containing much space; with plenty of room; large; roomy: *The rooms of the palace were spacious.* SYN: capacious, commodious. **2** of great extent or area; extensive; vast: *the spacious plains of Kansas and Iowa.* SYN: wide, broad. **3** *Figurative.* broad in scope or range; not limited or narrow; expansive: *a spacious mind; ... the spacious times of great Elizabeth* (Tennyson). [< Latin *spatiōsus* < *spatium* space] —**spa′cious|ly,** *adv.* —**spa′cious-ness,** *n.*

**Spack|le** (spak′əl), *n., v.,* **-led, -ling.** —***n.*** *Trademark.* a powder which when mixed with water to form a paste is used to fill cracks and holes in walls and ceilings before painting or papering.

—***v.t.*** to apply Spackle paste to (a surface); repair with Spackle.

***spade¹**
definition 1

***spade¹** (spād), *n., v.,* **spad|ed, spad|ing.** —***n.*** **1** a tool for digging, having an iron blade, which can be pressed into the ground with the foot, and a long handle with a grip or crosspiece at the top. It is a kind of shovel. **2** any one of various spadelike knives used by whalers, especially in flensing a whale. **3** the sharp end of a gun trail sunk into the ground to hold the carriage in place during recoil.

—***v.i., v.t.*** to dig, cut, or remove with a spade: *to spade up worms and rocks. Spade up the garden.*

**call a spade a spade,** to call a thing by its real name; speak plainly and frankly, without mincing words: *If it is absolutely necessary to call a spade a spade then it must be done in a whisper* (Punch).
[Old English *spadu*] —**spad′er,** *n.* —**spade′like′,** *adj.*

**∗spade[2]** (spād), *n.* **1** a black figure shaped somewhat like the blade of a leaf, used on playing cards. **2** a card bearing such figures: *The spade took the trick.* **3** *U.S. Slang.* a male Negro (used in an unfriendly way).
**in spades,** *U.S. Informal.* **a** to the utmost degree; plentifully: *"Bob Taft did not have political ... appeal," says a conservative strategist. "But Barry has it—in spades"* (Newsweek). **b** without holding back; with a vengeance: [*He*] *hopes to reply to his competition not only in kind but in spades* (Time).
**spades,** the suit of playing cards bearing black spade figures, usually the highest-ranking suit: *"Let spades be trumps!" she said, and trumps they were* (Alexander Pope).
[< Italian *spade,* feminine plural of *spada* sword < Latin *spatha* < Greek *spáthē* sword. See etym. of doublets **épée, spathe.**]

**∗spade[2]**
definition 1

**spade beard,** a beard cut or trimmed to the shape of a pointed or broad spade blade.

**spade|fish** (spād′fish′), *n., pl.* **-fish|es** or (*collectively*) **-fish.** **1** any one of a group of deep-bodied, spiny-finned food fish, as a variety found along the eastern coast of the United States. **2** = paddlefish.

**spade foot,** a kind of tapered enlargement of the leg of a piece of furniture, common especially in Hepplewhite.

**spade|foot** (spād′fu̇t′), *n., pl.* **-foots.** Also, **spadefoot toad.** any one of a large group of toads of Europe, northern Africa, southern Asia, and North America that can burrow or dig deep holes quickly by means of a spadelike projection on the side of the foot.

**spade|ful** (spād′fu̇l), *n., pl.* **-fuls.** as much as a spade can hold.

**spade|work** (spād′wėrk′), *n.* **1** a digging, cutting, or removing with a spade. **2** *Figurative.* preparatory work, such as intensive research, investigation, or discussion, serving as a basis for further work or activity.

**spa|di|ceous** (spā dish′əs), *adj.* **1** *Botany.* **a** in the form or of like a spadix. **b** bearing a spadix. **2** reddish or brownish; chestnut. [< New Latin *spadiceus* (with English *-ous*) < Latin *spādīx, -īcis* date, date-colored, nut-brown; see etym. under **spadix**]

**spa|dix** (spā′diks), *n., pl.* **spa|dix|es, spa|di|ces** (spā dī′sēz). a spike composed of minute flowers set closely on a thick, fleshy stem. A spadix is usually enclosed in a petallike leaf called a spathe, as in the jack-in-the-pulpit and the calla lily. [< Latin *spādīx, -īcis* < Greek *spádīx, -īkos* any branch (especially a palm) torn off a tree < *spân* pluck off, out]

**spae** (spā), *v.t., v.i.,* **spaed, spae|ing.** *Scottish.* to foretell; prophesy. [< Scandinavian (compare Old Icelandic *spā*)]

**spaetz|le** (shpets′lə, spets′-), *n., pl.* **-le** or **-les.** = spätzle.

**spa|ghet|ti** (spə get′ē), *n.* **1** a dried mixture of wheat flour and water made up into long sticks and cooked by boiling in water. Spaghetti is thinner than macaroni and not hollow. See picture under **pasta. 2** *Electricity.* an insulating cloth or plastic tubing used for protecting bare wire. [< Italian *spaghetti,* plural of *spaghetto* cord, twine (diminutive) < *spago* cord < Late Latin *spacus*]

**spa|ghet|ti|ni** (spa gə tē′nē), *n.* a thin kind of spaghetti. [< Italian *spaghettini* (diminutive) < *spaghetti*]

**spaghetti western,** *U.S. Slang.* a cowboy motion picture or western produced by the Italian movie industry.

**Spa|gnuo|lo** (spä nyō′lō), *n., pl.* **-gnuo|li** (-nyō′lē). a Sephardic Jew of Turkey or the Balkan States. [< Italian *Spagnuolo* (literally) Spaniard]

**spa|gyr|ic** or **spa|gir|ic** (spə jir′ik), *adj., n. Obsolete.* —*adj.* having to do with alchemy; alchemical.
—*n.* an alchemist.
[< New Latin *spagiricus,* perhaps < Greek *spân* draw, separate, pluck + *ageírein* assemble]

**spa|hi** or **spa|hee** (spä′hē), *n.* **1** a member of a former special corps of Algerian cavalry in the French army. **2** a member of an élite body of cavalry in the Turkish army from about 1500 to about 1800. [< Turkish *sipahi* < Persian *sipāhī* < *sipāh* army. Compare etym. under **sepoy.**]

**spake** (spāk), *v. Archaic.* a past tense of **speak:** *Thus spake the Lord.*

**spale** or **spail** (spāl), *n. Scottish.* a chip, splinter, or thin strip of wood.

**spall** (spôl), *n., v.* —*n.* a chip, splinter, or small piece of stone or ore.
—*v.t.* to chip or break up roughly, as ore, preparatory to sorting.
—*v.i.* to chip off.
[Middle English *spalle;* origin uncertain]

**spal|la|tion** (spə lā′shən), *n.* the ejection from a nucleus of protons and neutrons as the result of intense bombardment or excitation by foreign particles. [< *spall* + *-ation*]

**spal|peen** (spal pēn′, spal′pēn), *n. Irish.* a scamp; rascal. [Anglo-Irish < Irish *spailpīn* bully; (originally) migratory laborer]

**∗span[1]** (span), *n., v.,* **spanned, span|ning.** —*n.* **1a** the part between two supports: *The bridge crossed the river in three spans.* **b** the distance between two supports: *The arch had a fifty-foot span.* **2** *Figurative.* a space of time: *This pupil has a short attention span. His life's span is nearly over. Did many talents gild thy span?* (Robert Burns). **3** the distance between the tip of a man's thumb and the tip of his little finger when the hand is spread out; about 9 inches. **4** something of the length of a span; very small extent: *There was not a span free from cultivation* (Mountstuart Elphinstone). **5** the full extent or reach of anything: (*Figurative.*) *the span of memory.* **6** the lateral distance of an airplane, or of a wing, from wing tip to wing tip.
—*v.t.* **1** to extend over or across: *A bridge spanned the river.* **2** to measure by the hand spread out: *This post can be spanned by one's two hands.* **3** to encircle or encompass (as the waist or wrist) with the hand or hands. **4** to provide with something that stretches over or across: *to span a river with a bridge.* **5** *Figurative.* to reach or extend over: *Memory spans the past.*
[Old English *spann*]

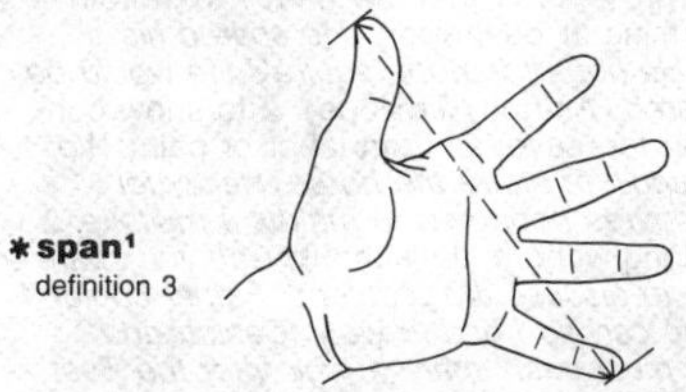
**∗span[1]**
definition 3

**span[2]** (span), *n., v.,* **spanned, span|ning.** —*n.* a pair of horses, mules, or other draft animals harnessed and driven together: ... *comfortable carry-alls drawn by steady spans* (Booth Tarkington).
—*v.t.* to harness (horses or other draft animals) to a vehicle.
[American English, probably < Dutch *span* < *spannen* to stretch, yoke]

**span[3]** (span), *v. Archaic.* a past tense of **spin:** *When Adam delved, and Eve span, who was then a gentleman?* (John Ball).

**Span.,** Spanish.

**span|dex** (span′deks), *n.* a synthetic fiber made from a polymer containing at least 85 per cent polyurethane, used as an elastic. [anagram of *expands*]

**∗span|drel** (span′drəl), *n.* **1** the triangular space between the outer curve of an arch and the rectangular molding or framework enclosing the arch. **2** the space between the outer curves of two adjacent arches and the molding above them. [perhaps < Anglo-French *spaundre,* short for Old French *espandre* expand < Latin *expandere.* Compare etym. under **expand.**]

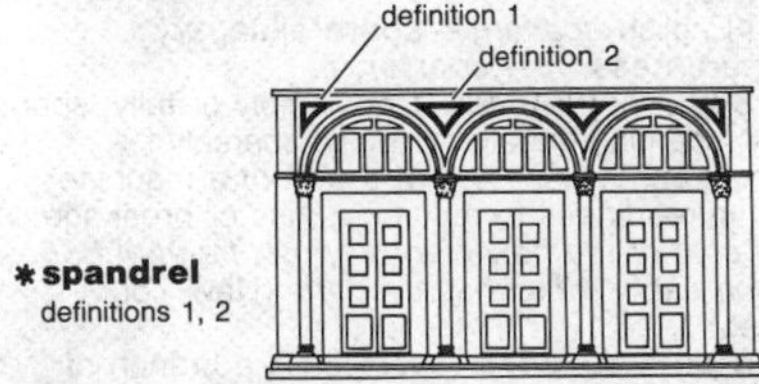

**∗spandrel**
definitions 1, 2

**span|dy** (span′dē), *adj., adv.* —*adj. Especially U.S. Informal.* very good or fine; smart: *My silk stockings and two pairs of spandy gloves are my comfort* (Louisa May Alcott).
—*adv.* wholly; perfectly: *a spandy new suit.*
[probably variant of dialectal *spander*(-new) < *span-new;* see etym. under **span-new**]

**spa|ne|mi|a** or **spa|nae|mi|a** (spə nē′mē ə), *n.* = anemia. [< New Latin *spanaemia* < Greek *spanós* scarce + *haîma* blood]

**spang** (spang), *adv. U.S. Informal.* with a sudden spring or impetus; slap; smack.
**right spang, a** entirely; quite: *He was good at making up stories right spang out of his own head.* **b** exactly: *The bullet landed right spang in the middle of the target.*
[American English, perhaps < dialectal *spang* a jerk, sharp rap, smack]

**span|gle** (spang′gəl), *n., v.,* **-gled, -gling.** —*n.* **1** a small piece of glittering metal used for decoration: *The dress was covered with spangles.* **2** any small, bright bit: *This rock shows spangles of gold.*
—*v.t.* **1** to decorate with spangles: *The dress was spangled with gold.* **2** to sprinkle with small, bright bits: (*Figurative.*) *The sky is spangled with stars.*
—*v.i.* to sparkle with or as if with spangles; glitter.
[perhaps diminutive form of Old English *spang* clasp, buckle]

**Span|glish** (span′glish), *n., adj.* —*n.* a blend of Spanish and English spoken in parts of the western United States and Latin America: *a historical pageant known as a "Texas Fandangle"—border-country Spanglish for fandango, the frenetic Mexican dance* (Time).
—*adj.* of or in Spanglish.
[blend of *Spanish* and *English*]

**span|gly** (spang′glē), *adj.,* **-gli|er, -gli|est.** covered with spangles; glittering with or as if with spangles: *a spangly starfish, a spangly flag.* (*Figurative.*) *Rockefeller Plaza is as spangly and tinkly as ever* (Manchester Guardian).

**Span|iard** (span′yərd), *n.* a person born or living in Spain.

**∗span|iel** (span′yəl), *n.* **1** any one of various breeds of dogs, usually of small or medium size, with long, silky hair and drooping ears. Spaniels are very gentle and affectionate. **2** *Figurative.* a person who yields too easily to others: *Perish shall all which makes a spaniel of the man* (John Greenleaf Whittier). [< Old French *espagneul* (literally) Spanish < Latin *Hispāniolus* < *Hispānia* Spain]

**∗spaniel**
definition 1
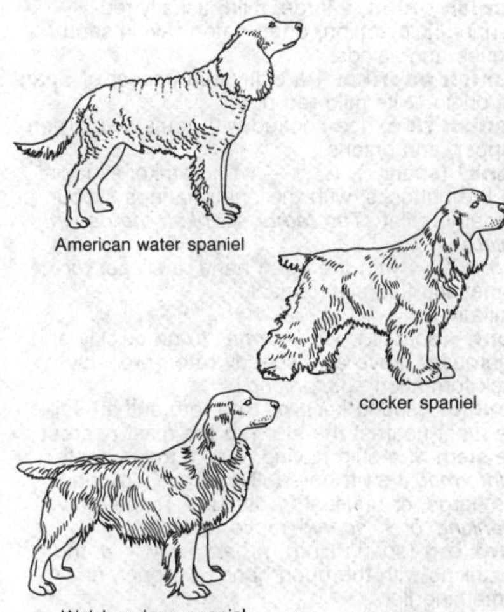
American water spaniel
cocker spaniel
Welsh springer spaniel

**Span|ish** (span′ish), *adj., n.* —*adj.* of or having something to do with Spain, a country in southwestern Europe, its people, or their language: *Spanish custom normally puts the father's family name first and the mother's last* (Newsweek).
—*n.* **1** *pl. in use.* the people of Spain. **2** the Romance language of Spain. It is also the language of most Latin American countries. *Abbr:* Sp.

**Span|ish-A|mer|i|can** (span′ish ə mer′ə kən), *adj.* **1** of or having to do with Spain and America, or with Spain and the United States: *Spanish-American relations.* **2a** of or having to do with the parts of America where Spanish is the principal language. **b** of or having to do with Americans whose origin or descent is from such parts.

**Spanish American, 1** a person born or living in a Spanish-American country, especially a person of Spanish descent. **2** *Southwestern U.S.* a person born in the United States whose parents or

---

**Pronunciation Key:** hat, āge, cãre, fär; let, ēqual, tėrm; it, īce; hot, ōpen, ôrder; oil, out; cup, pu̇t, rüle; child; long; thin; ᴛʜen; zh, measure; ə represents **a** in about, **e** in taken, **i** in pencil, **o** in lemon, **u** in circus.

forebears were from a part of America where Spanish is the principal language.

**Spanish bayonet**, any one of several desert plants or yuccas of the agave family, having narrow, rigid, evergreen leaves with spines at the tips.

**Spanish beard**, = Spanish moss.

**Spanish black**, a black paint used by artists, made from burnt cork shavings; cork black.

**Spanish broom**, a plant common to the Mediterranean region, with rushlike branches or twigs used in basketwork and in the manufacture of cords, and coarse cloths.

**Spanish chestnut**, a European chestnut tree that bears large, sweet, edible nuts called marrons.

**Spanish cream**, a dessert made with gelatin and a mixture of milk, egg yolk, sugar, and vanilla, often flavored with sherry.

**Spanish fly**, a bright-green European blister beetle whose dried and powdered body is a source of cantharides, used in medicine for raising blisters on the skin; cantharis.

**Spanish grippe** or **influenza**, influenza, especially in the virulent form that was pandemic in the United States and elsewhere in 1918-1919.

**Spanish heel**, a curved high heel for a woman's dress shoe, similar to the French heel but with a straight heel breast and broader base.

**Spanish jasmine** or **jessamine**, a jasmine of India, having large, fragrant, white flowers.

**Spanish mackerel**, any one of a group of marine food fishes related to the tuna and mackerel, such as the cero.

**Spanish moss**, a mosslike, epiphytic plant of the pineapple family, growing on the branches of certain trees, from which it hangs in gray streamers, found in the southern United States and tropical America; Florida moss. See picture under **pineapple family**.

**Spanish needles**, **1** an annual weed of the composite family, having barbed fruits. **2** its barbed fruits.

**Span|ish|ness** (span′ish nis), *n.* the quality or state of being Spanish or of Spanish descent.

**Spanish omelet**, an omelet served with a spiced tomato sauce usually containing green pepper, onion, and often chopped celery or peas.

**Spanish onion**, a large, mild, usually red-skinned, juicy onion, often eaten raw in sandwiches and salads.

**Spanish paprika**, **1** a cultivated pepper of Spanish origin. **2** its mild red pod.

**Spanish rice**, rice cooked with tomatoes, green pepper, and onions.

**spank**[1] (spangk), *v., n.* – ***v.t.*** to strike, especially on the buttocks, with the open hand, a slipper, or something flat: *The father spanked the naughty child.*
– ***n.*** a blow with the open hand, a slipper, or something flat; slap; smack.
[imitative]

**spank**[2] (spangk), *v.i. Informal.* to go quickly and vigorously; move at a speedy rate. [probably back formation < *spanking*]

**spank|er** (spang′kər), *n.* **1a** a fore-and-aft sail on the mast nearest the stern. **b** the mast nearest the stern of a ship having four or more masts. **2** *Informal.* a swift horse. **3** *Informal.* anything fine, large, or unusual for its kind. [apparently < *spanking*, or < *spank*[2] move fast]

**spank|ing** (spang′king), *n., adj., adv.* – ***n.*** the act of striking with the open hand, a slipper, or something flat.
– ***adj.*** **1** blowing briskly: *a spanking breeze.* **2** moving with a quick, lively pace: *a spanking team of horses.* **3** quick and vigorous: *a spanking pace.*
– ***adv.*** *Informal.* unusually fine, great, large, or otherwise remarkable: *a spanking good time, a spanking new building.*
[< earlier, fast-moving (of horses). Compare Danish *spanke* to strut.] – **spank′ing|ly**, *adv.*

**span|less** (span′lis), *adj.* that cannot be spanned.

**span loading**, the gross weight of an aircraft divided by the span of its wings.

**span|ner** (span′ər), *n.* **1** a person or thing that spans: *the spanners of a bridge.* **2** a wrench of fixed size, especially for a special purpose. **3** *Especially British.* any wrench other than a monkey wrench. [< German *Spanner* < *spannen* fasten, draw tight]

**span-new** (span′nü′, -nyü′), *adj.* entirely new; brand-new: *The men were exuberant, sprawling over their tanks, all span-new Shermans* (New Yorker). [< Scandinavian (compare Old Icelandic *spān-nȳr* < *spānn* chip + *nȳr* new)]

**span|sule** (span′səl, -syül), *n.* **1** a capsule containing tiny grains of medicine that dissolve at different times to maintain a constant infusion of medicine into the body over the dosage period; time-release capsule: *He swallowed a fifteen-milligram dextro-amphetamine-sulphate spansule with his coffee, looked briefly at his watch, and calculated the time span of his awareness* (Jesse Hill Ford). **2 Spansule**, a trademark for such a capsule. [< *span* + (cap)*sule*]

**span|worm** (span′wėrm′), *n.* = measuring worm.

**spar**[1] (spär), *n., v.,* **sparred, spar|ring.** – ***n.*** **1** a stout pole used to support or extend one of the sails of a ship; mast, yard, gaff, or boom. **2** the main horizontal support of an airplane wing, to which the ribs are attached.
– ***v.t.*** to equip (a ship) with spars; put a spar or spars on.
[Middle English *sparre* a rafter. Compare Old English *gespearrian* to shut, bar (as a door).]

**spar**[2] (spär), *v.,* **sparred, spar|ring,** *n.* – ***v.i.*** **1** to make motions of attack and defense with the arms and fists; box. **2** *Figurative.* to dispute or argue cautiously, as if to test one's opponent; bandy words: *The two old men were sparring about who would win the election.* **3** to fight, as roosters do, with the feet or spurs.
– ***n.*** **1** a boxing match. **2** a sparring motion. **3** *Figurative.* a dispute.
[< Middle French *esparer* to kick < Italian *sparare* to fling < *s-*, intensive (< Latin *ex-*) + *parare* to parry, ward off, protect]

**spar**[3] (spär), *n.* any one of various crystalline, shiny minerals that split into flakes easily, such as calcspar and fluorspar. [< Middle Low German *spar,* related to Old English *spær* in *spærstān* gypsum, *spæren* of plaster]

**SPAR** or **Spar** (spär), *n.* a member of the Women's Reserve of the United States Coast Guard Reserve. [< *s*(*emper*) *par*(*atus*) always ready (the motto of the Coast Guard)]

**spar|a|ble** (spar′ə bəl), *n.* a small, headless, wedge-shaped iron nail used in shoemaking. [alteration of earlier *sparrow-bill*]

**spar buoy**, a buoy shaped like a short, thick pole. See picture under **buoy**.

**spar deck**, the upper deck of a ship, extending from one end to the other.

**spare** (spãr), *v.,* **spared, spar|ing,** *adj.,* **spar|er, spar|est,** *n.* – ***v.t.*** **1** to show mercy to; refrain from harming or destroying: *He spared his enemy. He hoped that the squire's life would be long spared* (Anthony Trollope). **2** to show consideration for; save, as from labor or pain: *We walked uphill to spare the horse. Her cruel tongue spares nobody who makes a mistake.* **3** to get along without; do without: *Can you spare a moment to discuss the problem? Father couldn't spare the car; so I had to walk. Caesar and Pompey must each spare a legion for the East* (James A. Froude). **4** to make (a person) free from (something); relieve or exempt (a person) from (something): *She did the dishes to spare Mother. I did the work to spare you the trouble. Spare me the gory details.* **5** to refrain from using; forego, omit; forbear: *"Spare the rod and spoil the child."* **6** to use in small quantities or not at all; be saving of; stint: *to spare no expense.* **7** to set aside; keep in reserve for a particular use or purpose; have free: *to spare some time for reading, to have an hour to spare, to spare some pasture for a crop.*
– ***v.i.*** **1** to show mercy; refrain from doing harm: *spare not for spoiling of thy steed* (Scott). **2** to be saving, economical, or frugal: *I, who at some times spend, at others spare* (Alexander Pope).
– ***adj.*** **1** free for other use; surplus: *spare time.* **2** not in actual or regular use; in reserve; extra: *a spare tire, a spare room.* **3** not fat or plump; thin; lean: *Lincoln was a tall, spare man.* SYN: lank, gaunt. **4** small in quantity; meager; scanty: *a spare meal.* **5** frugal or economical, especially in regard to food: *To get thin, one should live on a spare diet.*
– ***n.*** **1** a spare thing, such as a part, tire, or room. **2** *Bowling.* **a** the knocking down of all the pins with two rolls of the ball. **b** the score for doing this.
[Old English *sparian*] – **spare′a|ble**, *adj.* – **spare′ness**, *n.* – **spar′er**, *n.*

**spare|ly** (spãr′lē), *adv.* **1** not amply or fully; sparingly; scantily; frugally. **2** thinly; sparsely.

**spare part**, a duplicate of a part of a machine kept in readiness to replace a loss or breakage: *The cost of the new planes ... will be about $8 million each, without spare parts* (New York Times).

**spare-part surgery** (spãr′pärt′), a branch of surgery dealing with the replacement of damaged organs, such as the heart, lungs, kidneys, and liver, either by transplantation or by the grafting of manufactured devices: *What surgeons in all fields of spare-part surgery needed was some way of switching off the immune reaction against their grafts without at the same time lowering the body's defences against genuinely harmful foreigners* (John Newell).

**spare|rib** (spãr′rib′), *n.* a rib of pork having less meat than the ribs near the loin. [probably alteration of earlier *ribspare* < Middle Low German *ribbespēr* rib cut]

**sparge** (spärj), *v.,* **sparged, sparg|ing,** *n.* – ***v.t., v.i.*** **1** to dash, splash, or sprinkle about. **2** to bespatter; besprinkle.
– ***n.*** **1** a sprinkling or splashing. **2** a sprinkle; dash (as of liquor).
[earlier, to plaster over, apparently < Old French *espargier* < Latin *spargere* to sprinkle] – **sparg′er**, *n.*

**Spar|ine** (spãr′ēn), *n. Trademark.* promazine.

**spar|ing** (spãr′ing), *adj.* **1** that spares. **2** avoiding waste; economical; frugal: *a sparing use of sugar.* SYN: parsimonious, stingy. – **spar′ing|ly**, *adv.*

**spark**[1] (spärk), *n., v.* – ***n.*** **1** a small bit of fire: *The burning wood threw off sparks.* **2a** the flash given off when electricity jumps across an open space. An electric spark ignites the gas in the engine of an automobile. **b** the discharge itself. **c** the discharge in a spark plug. **d** the mechanism generating and controlling this discharge. **e** = spark transmitter. **f** = spark transmission. **3** a bright flash; gleam; sparkle: *We saw a spark of light through the trees.* **4** *Figurative.* a small amount; trace; indication: *I haven't a spark of interest in the plan. They still kept alive the sparks of future friendship* (Washington Irving). **5** *Figurative.* a trace (of life or vitality): *O speak, if any spark of life remain* (Thomas Kyd). **6** a glittering bit: *The moving sparks we saw were fireflies.*
– ***v.i.*** **1** to send out small bits of fire; produce sparks: *This wood burns steadily with no sparking* (William O. Douglas). **2** to flash; gleam; sparkle: (*Figurative.*) *Her eyes did spark, at every glance, like diamonds in the dark* (Francis Quarles). **3** to issue or fall as or like sparks. **4** to operate properly in forming sparks, as the ignition in an internal-combustion engine.
– ***v.t.*** **1** to stir to activity; stimulate: *to spark a revolt, to spark sales.* SYN: animate, excite. **2** to make (one's friends, teammates, or associates) enthusiastic or determined.
[Old English *spearca*] – **spark′less**, *adj.*

**spark**[2] (spärk), *n., v.* – ***n.*** **1** a gay and showy young man: *A fop came ... a fine spark, and gave them fine words* (Stanley J. Weyman). SYN: dandy. **2** a beau; lover: *A ... woman ... daring death just for the sake of thee, her handsome spark!* (Robert Browning).
– ***v.t., v.i.*** *Informal.* to court; woo: *His master was courting, or, as it is termed, 'sparking' within* (Washington Irving).
[earlier, a beauty, a wit, perhaps special use of *spark*[1]] – **spark′er**, *n.*

**spark arrester**, **1** anything that keeps sparks from flying, such as a piece of mesh on the top of a chimney. **2** *Electricity.* a device for preventing or minimizing injurious sparking at points where frequent interruptions of the circuit occur, such as in telegraph keys or relays.

**spark chamber**, a gas-filled chamber containing metal plates connected to a source of electricity. Subatomic particles passing through leave a trail of bright sparks which may be photographed.

**spark coil**, an induction coil for producing electric sparks, used especially in an internal-combustion engine and wireless telegraphy equipment.

**spark|er** (spär′kər), *n.* **1** a person or thing that produces sparks. **2** *Electricity.* a spark arrester.

**spark gap**, an open space between two electrodes across which a discharge of electricity travels.

**spark generator**, an alternating-current generator that uses the electric discharge of a condenser across a spark gap as the power source.

**spark|ing plug** (spär′king), *British.* a spark plug.

**spark|ish** (spär′kish), *adj.* of or like a spark; gay and showy.

**spark killer**, *Electricity.* a spark arrester.

**spar|kle** (spär′kəl), *v.,* **-kled, -kling,** *n.* – ***v.i.*** **1** to shine as if giving out sparks; shine; glitter; flash; gleam: *The diamonds sparkled.* (*Figurative.*) *Disdain and scorn ride sparkling in her eyes* (Shakespeare). **2** *Figurative.* to be brilliant; be lively: *His wit sparkles.* **3** to send out little sparks: *The children's fireworks sparkled.* **4** to bubble, as champagne and ginger ale do.
– ***v.t.*** to cause to sparkle: *The ... sun ... sparkling the landscape with a thousand dewy gems* (Washington Irving).
– ***n.*** **1** a little spark: *to count the sparkles which flew from the horses' hoofs* (Scott). **2** a shine; glitter; flash; gleam: (*Figurative.*) *People always mention the sparkle of her eyes.* SYN: See syn. under **flash**. **3** *Figurative.* brilliance; liveliness.
[< *spark,* noun + *-le* (frequentative)]

**spar|kler** (spär′klər), *n.* **1** a person or thing that sparkles. **2** a firework that sends out little sparks. **3** a sparkling gem, especially a diamond.

**spar|kling** (spär′kling), *adj.* **1** that sparkles: *a sparkling fire.* **2** shining; glittering; flashing: *sparkling stars, a sparkling gem.* **3** *Figurative.* brilliant;

lively: *He has a sparkling wit.* **4** effervescent; bubbling: *Ginger ale and champagne are sparkling drinks.* — **spar′kling|ly**, *adv.*

***spark plug**, **1** a device in the cylinder of an internal-combustion engine by which the mixture of gasoline and air is exploded by an electric spark. **2** *Informal, Figurative.* a person who gives energy or enthusiasm to others: *The shortstop is the spark plug of our baseball team.*

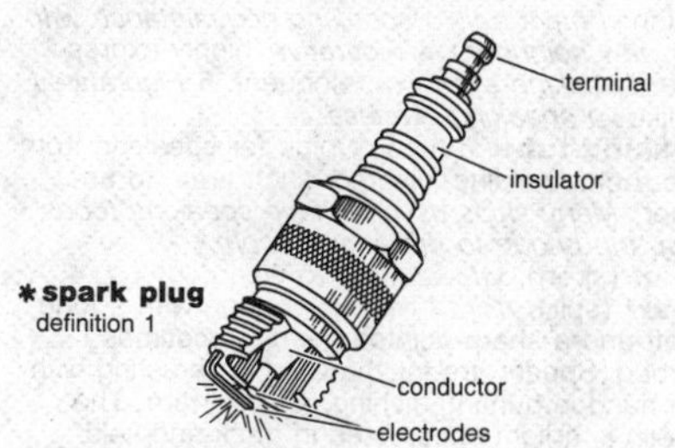


***spark plug**
definition 1

**spark-plug** or **spark|plug** (spärk′plug′), *v.t.*, **-plugged, -plug|ging.** *Informal.* **1** to be the spark plug of (a group, organization or cause). **2** to be the originator of; lead in bringing about: *He spark-plugged the investigation of corruption in the town.*

**sparks** (spärks), *n. Slang.* a telegraph or radio operator, as on a ship.

**spark spectrum**, the spectrum a metal or other conduction substance produces when an electric spark is passed between electrodes made of the metal or other substance.

**spark transmission**, radio transmission by means of a spark transmitter.

**spark transmitter**, a radio transmitter that uses the electric discharge of a condenser across a spark gap to provide its alternating-current power.

**spark|y** (spär′kē), *adj.*, **spark|i|er, spark|i|est.** **1** emitting sparks. **2** *Figurative.* lively; vivacious: *a never adjourned discussion brightened by the sparky friction of ideas on ideas* (New Yorker). — **spark′i|ly**, *adv.*

**spar|ling** (spär′ling), *n.* the smelt of Europe. Also, **sperling.** [Middle English *sperlinge* < Old French *esperlinge* < Germanic (compare Low German *spierling,* Middle Dutch *spirlinc*)]

**spar|mate** (spär′māt′), *n.* = sparring partner.

**spar|oid** (spãr′oid, spar′-), *adj., n.* — *adj.* **1** of or belonging to a group of marine fishes related to the grunts and snappers, having spiny fins and deep bodies, including the sea bream, scup, and porgy. **2** like a porgy.
— *n.* a sparoid fish.
[< Latin *sparus* gilthead (< Greek *spáros* sea bream) + English *-oid*]

**spar|rer** (spär′ər), *n.* a person who spars or boxes.

**spar|ring partner** (spär′ing), a boxer hired to keep another in practice while training for a fight.

**spar|row** (spar′ō), *n.* **1** any one of various small, usually brownish birds common in North and South America, such as the chipping sparrow, song sparrow, field sparrow, sage sparrow, swamp sparrow, and vesper sparrow. **2** any one of various related birds native to Europe, Asia, and Africa. English sparrows and some other kinds live near houses; others live in woods and fields. **3** any one of several similar birds, such as the hedge sparrow or dunnock of Europe (a warbler). [Old English *spearwa*] — **spar′row|like′**, *adj.*

**spar|row|grass** (spar′ō gras′), *n. Dialect.* asparagus. [alteration by folk etymology of obsolete *sparagus* < Medieval Latin, short for *asparagus* < Latin]

**sparrow hawk**, **1** a small North American falcon that feeds on large insects and small animals. **2** a hawk of Europe and Asia that feeds on small birds.

**spar|ry** (spär′ē), *adj.* full of spar; like spar (the mineral).

**sparse** (spärs), *adj.*, **spars|er, spars|est.** **1** thinly scattered; occurring here and there: *The sparse population of the country, sparse hair; ... an unorganised mob—thick in one place, sparse in another* (Walter Besant). SYN: See syn. under **scanty. 2** scanty; meager: *a sparse diet.* [< Latin *sparsus,* past participle of *spargere* to scatter] — **sparse′ly**, *adv.* — **sparse′ness**, *n.*

**spar|si|ty** (spär′sə tē), *n.* sparse or scattered condition; sparseness.

**Spar|ta|cist** (spär′tə sist), *n.* a member of a party of German socialist extremists formed in 1918, led by Karl Liebknecht, who had adopted the pseudonym *Spartakus* in his political tracts. [< German *Spartakist*]

**Spar|tan** (spär′tən), *adj., n.* — *adj.* **1** of or having to do with Sparta, a city of ancient Greece famous for its soldiers, or its people. **2** *Figurative.* like the Spartans; simple; frugal; severe, sternly disciplined, brave, and concise: *Spartan fortitude, Spartan taste.*
— *n.* **1** a person who was born or lived in Sparta. The Spartans were noted for living simply, saying little, being brave, and enduring pain without complaining. **2** *Figurative.* a person who is like the Spartans. **3** a style of sans-serif printing type. — **Spar′tan|ly**, *adv.*

**Spar|tan|ism** (spär′tə niz əm), *n.* **1** the beliefs and methods of ancient Sparta. **2** any discipline, method, etc., like that of the ancient Spartans.

**spar|te|ine** (spär′tē ēn, -in), *n.* a bitter, poisonous liquid alkaloid obtained from certain species of broom and lupine, used in medicine as a heart stimulant. *Formula:* $C_{15}H_{26}N_2$ [< New Latin *Spartium* the broom genus (< Greek *spártos* Spanish broom) + English *-ine*[2]]

**spar tree**, a tall tree used to support the cable for carrying other trees in high-lead logging.

**spar varnish**, an oleoresinous, weather-resistant varnish used for exterior surfaces, especially on ships.

**spasm** (spaz′əm), *n.* **1** a sudden, abnormal, involuntary contraction of a muscle or muscles. A clonic spasm is characterized by alternate contraction and relaxation of the muscles, and a tonic spasm by prolonged contraction without relaxation for some time. *The child in a spasm kept twitching his arms and legs.* SYN: convulsion. **2** *Figurative.* any sudden brief fit or spell of unusual energy or activity: *a spasm of temper, a spasm of enthusiasm. He caused her a spasm of anguish* (George Meredith). *Between the spasms of violence there were long quiet intervals when the ordinary occupations of men went on as usual* (James A. Froude). [< Latin *spasmus* < Greek *spasmós* < *spân* draw (up), tear away]

**spas|mod|ic** (spaz mod′ik), *adj.* **1** having to do with spasms; resembling a spasm: *a spasmodic cough.* **2** *Figurative.* **a** sudden and violent, but brief: *spasmodic rage.* **b** occurring very irregularly; intermittent: *a spasmodic interest in reading.* SYN: fitful. **3** *Figurative.* having or showing bursts of excitement: *Miss Tox immediately became spasmodic* (Dickens). **4** *Figurative.* disjointed; choppy: *a spasmodic style, spasmodic writing.* SYN: jerky. [< Medieval Latin *spasmodicus* < Greek *spasmṓdēs* < *spasmós;* see etym. under **spasm**]

**spas|mod|i|cal** (spaz mod′ə kəl), *adj.* = spasmodic. — **spas|mod′i|cal|ly**, *adv.*

**spas|mo|lyt|ic** (spaz′mə lit′ik), *adj., n.* — *adj.* of or for the relief of muscular spasms.
— *n.* a spasmolytic substance.

**spas|tic** (spas′tik), *adj., n.* — *adj.* **1** of, having to do with, or characterized by spasms, especially tonic spasms: *a spastic disease.* **2** caused by a spasm or spasms: *spastic pain.* **3** having spastic paralysis.
— *n.* a person suffering from a form of paralysis marked by prolonged contraction of a muscle or muscles.
[< Latin *spasticus* < Greek *spastikós* < *spân* draw (up)] — **spas′ti|cal|ly**, *adv.*

**spas|tic|i|ty** (spas tis′ə tē), *n.* **1** the tendency to go into spasms. **2** the state of being spastic: *Elaborate animal experiments have been attempted to try to relate how damage to the brain causes spasticity* (New Scientist).

**spastic paralysis**, paralysis characterized by prolonged contraction of a muscle or muscles with exaggerated reflexes, caused by brain damage.

**SPASUR** (spā′sər), *n.* a radar system that detects artificial satellites such as those used for surveillance that broadcast only on command from the ground. [< *Spa*(ce) *Sur*(veillance)]

**spat**[1] (spat), *n., v.,* **spat|ted, spat|ting.** — *n.* **1** a slight quarrel; tiff: *They got into kind of a spat about which one'd make the best actress* (Booth Tarkington). **2** a light blow; slap.
— *v.i.* **1** *Informal.* to quarrel slightly or briefly: *The dog and cat spatted before the dog chased the cat up the tree.* **2** to give a slap or slaps.
— *v.t.* to slap lightly.
[American English; perhaps imitative]

**spat**[2] (spat), *v.* a past tense and a past participle of **spit**[1]: *The cat spat at the dog.*

**spat**[3] (spat), *n.* See under **spats.**

**spat**[4] (spat), *n., v.,* **spat|ted, spat|ting.** — *n.* **1** the spawn of oysters or certain other shellfish. **2** a young oyster.
— *v.i.* (of oysters or certain other shellfish) to spawn.
[origin uncertain. Perhaps related to **spit**[1].]

**spa|tan|gus** (spə tang′gəs), *n., pl.* **-gi** (-gē). any one of a group of sea urchins, some of which are heart-shaped. [< New Latin *Spatangus* the genus name < Greek *spatángēs* a kind of sea urchin]

**spatch|cock** (spach′kok′), *n., v.* — *n.* a freshly killed fowl, split and broiled.
— *v.t.* **1** to cook as or in the manner of a spatchcock. **2** *Especially British Informal, Figurative.* to insert or interpolate; sandwich in: *The new matter consists of long quotations from secondary sources ... and of over-written descriptive paragraphs, spatchcocked into the old text* (Manchester Guardian).
[earlier, to cook hastily < phrase *dispatch cock* (originally) a chicken prepared with dispatch]

**spate** (spāt), *n.* **1** a sudden outburst; violent outpouring: *a spate of words or of anger.* **2** a large number; great quantity: *a spate of new books on astronomy.* **3** *British.* **a** a sudden flood; freshet: *Is the torrent in spate? He must ford it or swim* (Rudyard Kipling). **b** a sudden, heavy downpour of rain. [origin uncertain]

**spa|tha|ceous** (spə thā′shəs), *adj.* **1** furnished with or enclosed by a spathe. **2** of or like a spathe.

**spa|thal** (spā′thəl), *adj.* = spathaceous.

**spathe** (spāᴛʜ), *n.* a large bract or pair of bracts, often colored, that encloses a flower cluster. The calla lily has a white spathe around a yellow flower cluster. [< Latin *spatha* < Greek *spáthē* broad, flat blade. See etym. of doublets **épée, spade**[2].]

**spathed** (spāᴛʜd), *adj.* having or surrounded by a spathe.

**spath|ic** (spath′ik), *adj.* = spathose[1]. [earlier *spath, spat* spar[3] (< German *Spath*) + *-ic*]

**spath|i|form** (spath′ə fôrm), *adj.* resembling spar in form: *a spathiform variety of uranite.*

**spath|ose**[1] (spath′ōs), *adj.* like or consisting of spar; foliated; sparry.

**spa|those**[2] (spā′thōs, spath′ōs), *adj. Botany.* like or formed like a spathe.

**spath|u|late** (spath′yə lit, -lāt), *adj. Botany.* spatulate.

**spa|tial** (spā′shəl), *adj.* **1** of or having to do with space. **2** existing in space. **3** occupying or taking up space. Also, **spacial.** [< Latin *spatium* space + English *-al*[1]] — **spa′tial|ly**, *adv.*

**spa|ti|al|i|ty** (spā′shē al′ə tē), *n.* spatial quality or character.

**spa|ti|o-tem|po|ral** (spā′shē ō tem′pər əl), *adj.* belonging to both space and time: *linked in a manner transcending the spatio-temporal order, and hence wholly outside the ambit of "the laws of mechanics"* (New Scientist). [< Latin *spatium* space + English *temporal*] — **spa′ti|o-tem′po|ral|ly**, *adv.*

**Spät|le|se** (shpāt′lā′zə), *n., pl.* **-le|sen** (-lā′zən). a naturally sweet wine made from grapes picked after the harvest. [< German *Spätlese* (literally) late gathering]

***spats** (spats), *n.pl.* short gaiters worn over the instep and reaching just above the ankle, usually fastened by straps under the feet and buttons on one side. [short for *spatterdash*]

***spats**
***spatterdash**

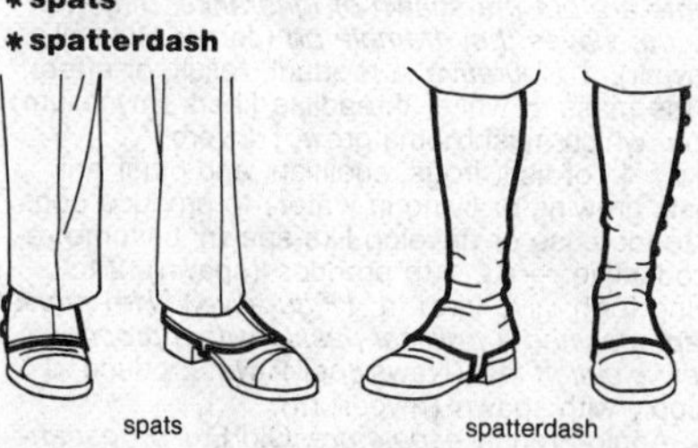

spats spatterdash

**spat|ter** (spat′ər), *v., n.* — *v.t.* **1** to scatter or dash in drops or particles; splatter: *to spatter paint, to spatter mud.* **2** to strike in a shower; strike in a number of places: *Bullets spattered the wall.* **3a** to sprinkle or spot with something that soils or stains; bespatter: *to spatter a white dress with mud.* **b** *Figurative.* to stain with something that harms: *to spatter a person with disgrace.* SYN: smear.
— *v.i.* **1** to send out or throw off drops or particles. **2** to fall in drops or particles: *Rain spatters on the sidewalk.*
— *n.* **1** a spattering: *a spatter of bullets.* **2** the sound of spattering: *the spatter of rain on a roof.* **3** a spot caused by something splashed; splatter. [apparently a frequentative form. Compare Dutch or Low German *spatten* to spout.] — **spat′ter|ing|ly**, *adv.*

**spatter cone**, a clot or hardened mass of lava in the form of a steep-sloped cone.

***spat|ter|dash** (spat′ər dash′), *n.* Often, **spatter-**

**Pronunciation Key:** hat, āge, cãre, fär; let, ēqual, tėrm; it, īce; hot, ōpen, ôrder; oil, out; cup, pu̇t, rüle; child; long; thin; ᴛʜen; zh, measure; ə represents **a** in about, **e** in taken, **i** in pencil, **o** in lemon, **u** in circus.

**dashes**. a long gaiter or legging of leather or cloth worn to keep the trousers or stockings from being splashed with mud, as in riding. [< *spatter* + *dash*]

**spat|ter|dock** (spat′ər dok′), *n.* **1** an aquatic plant of the water-lily family, with large erect leaves and rounded yellow flowers, common in stagnant waters of the eastern United States. **2** any one of various related water plants. [American English, earlier *splatterdock* < *splatter* + *dock*[4]]

**spat|ter|ware** (spat′ər wãr′), *n.* earthenware with a design produced by spatterwork.

**spat|ter|work** (spat′ər wėrk′), *n.* decorative work in which a design is produced on a surface by spattering ink or the like over exposed parts.

**spat|u|la** (spach′ə lə), *n.* a tool with a broad, flat, flexible blade, used for mixing, spreading, scrapping, or stirring soft substances, such as plaster or frosting, and for mixing powders. [< Late Latin *spatula* spoon (diminutive) < Latin *spatha* broad, flat blade < Greek *spáthē*]

**spat|u|lar** (spach′ə lər), *adj.* of or like a spatula.

**spat|u|late** (spach′ə lit, -lāt), *adj.* **1** shaped somewhat like a spatula: *a spatulate blade.* **2** *Botany.* having a broad, rounded end and a long, narrow base: *a spatulate leaf.* **3** wide at the tips: *spatulate fingers.*

**spat|ule** (spach′ůl), *n.* **1** = spatula. **2** *Zoology.* a spatulate formation or part, as at the end of the tail feathers of a bird. [< French *spatule* < Late Latin *spatula*]

**spätz|le** (shpets′lə, spets′-), *n., pl.* **-le** or **-les**. a kind of small dumpling made with flour, eggs, salt, and water. Also, **spaetzle**. [< German dialect (Swabia) *Spätzle*]

**spav|in** (spav′ən), *n.* **1** a disease of horses in which a bony swelling forms at the hock, causing lameness. **2** a less serious disease of horses in which the capsule of tissue at the hock fills with fluid. [< Old French *espavain,* probably < a Germanic word]

**spav|ined** (spav′ənd), *adj.* **1** having spavin. **2** *Figurative.* lame; crippled: *Even by its own spavined standards the native product is poor* (London Times).

**spawl**[1] (spôl), *v.i. Archaic.* to spit; expectorate. [origin unknown]

**spawl**[2] (spôl), *n., v.* = spall.

**spawn** (spôn), *n., v.* —*n.* **1a** the eggs of fish, frogs, shellfish, and other animals growing or living in water: *The boys dug up some little pockets of spawn at the water's edge.* **SYN**: roe. **b** the young that are newly hatched from such eggs: *The water was full of wriggling spawn.* **2** offspring, especially a large number of offspring; swarming brood. **SYN**: progeny. **3** *Figurative.* a person regarded as the offspring of some stock, or as imbued with some quality or principle: *Tyrants are but the spawn of Ignorance, Begotten by the slaves they trample on* (James Russell Lowell). **4** *Figurative.* a product, result, or effect. **5** the mass of white, threadlike fibers (mycelium) from which mushrooms grow. [< verb]
—*v.i.* **1** (of fish, frogs, shellfish, and other animals growing or living in water) to produce eggs. **2** to increase or develop like spawn; become reproductive. —*v.t.* **1** to produce (spawn). **2** to bring forth; give birth to: (*Figurative.*) [*He*] *himself had spawned a political hassle with a proposed new election law* (Newsweek). **SYN**: produce. **3** to supply with spawn (mycelium).
[< Anglo-French *espaundre,* Old French *espandre* < Latin *expandere* spread out. See etym. of doublet **expand**.] —**spawn′er**, *n.*

**spawn|ing bed** (spô′ning), a bed or nest made by salmon, trout, and other fish, in the bottom of a stream to deposit their spawn and milt.

**spawning ground**, **1** the place where fish spawn or to which they return to spawn. **2** *Figurative.* a place in which something commonly originates; breeding place: *Boxing's spawning grounds, the neighborhood clubs, are ... unable to compete with the fights on TV* (Newsweek).

**spawning screen**, a frame or screen on which the spawn of fish is collected.

**spay**[1] (spā), *v.t.* to remove the ovaries of (a female animal). [< Anglo-French *espeier* cut with a sword, ultimately < Old French *espee* sword, épée < Latin *spatha;* see etym. under **spathe**]

**spay**[2] (spā), *n. Archaic.* a male red deer in its third year. [origin unknown]

**SPC** (no periods), South Pacific Commission.

**S.P.C.A.** or **SPCA** (no periods), Society for the Prevention of Cruelty to Animals.

**S.P.C.C.**, Society for the Prevention of Cruelty to Children.

**speak** (spēk), *v.,* **spoke** or (*Archaic*) **spake, spoken** or (*Archaic*) **spoke, speak|ing.** —*v.i.* **1** to say words; talk; converse: *to speak with a stranger, to speak about something. A person with a cold often has trouble speaking distinctly. We speak a hundred times for every once we write* (George Herbert Palmer). **2a** to make a speech: *Who is going to speak at the meeting? Some lecturers speak without notes.* **b** to deliver, as an argument or plea: *to speak against a bill before Congress. Speak softly and carry a big stick* (Theodore Roosevelt). **3** *Figurative.* to express an idea, feeling, or the like; communicate: *Actions speak louder than words. For the heart must speak when the lips are dumb* (Kate P. Osgood). **4** to tell; express: (*Figurative.*) *Her eyes speak of suffering.* **5** to communicate in written or printed words: *The daily press speaks to millions of people.* **6** to make sounds: *The violins spoke at the nod of the conductor. The cannons spoke.* **7** (of dogs) to bark when told: *Speak for the candy, Fido.*
—*v.t.* **1** to say or utter (a word or words): *No one spoke a word to him.* **2** to tell or express in words or speech: *to speak nonsense. Speak the truth. On an occasion of this kind it becomes more than a moral duty to speak one's mind.* **3** to use (a language): *Do you speak French?* **4** *Figurative.* **a** to indicate by expression: *His face spoke hope.* **SYN**: manifest. **b** to reveal; indicate; make known: *The loud laugh that spoke the vacant mind* (Oliver Goldsmith). **SYN**: betoken, denote. **5** to speak to or with; converse with; address: *Lancelot ever spake him pleasantly* (Tennyson). *The great master ... can't be spoke by you* (Daniel Defoe). **6** to communicate with (a passing vessel) at sea; hail. **7** *Archaic.* to show to be; characterize: *His conduct speaks him honorable.*

**so to speak**, to speak in such a manner; to use that expression: *He has a chance to win the election; he is, so to speak, still in the running. Pearl ... was the leading spirit of the pair, and led Maud by the nose, so to speak* (J. S. Winter).

**speak for**, **a** to speak in the interest of; represent: *He spoke for the group that wanted a picnic. Why don't you speak for yourself, John?* (Longfellow). *They are slaves who fear to speak For the fallen and the weak* (James Russell Lowell). **b** to ask or apply for: *We ought to speak for reserved seats ahead of time.*

**speak of**, to mention; refer to: *He spoke of this matter to me. I shall have occasion to speak again of these books at the next session. Speaking of school, how do you like the new gym?*

**speak out** (or **up**), to speak loudly, clearly, or freely: *Bullies count on the fact that no one dares speak out against them. Speak out: what is it thou hast heard, or seen?* (Tennyson).

**speak up** (or **out**) **for**, to speak strongly on behalf or in defense of: *It's all very well for you to speak up for him ... You'll get a fortune by him* (Dickens). *Two thirds said in next November's election they would vote for candidates who spoke out for peace* (Maclean's).

**speak well for**, to give a favorable idea of; be evidence in favor of: *Her behavior speaks well for her.*

**to speak of**, worth mentioning: *I have no complaints to speak of.*

[Old English *specan*]
—*Syn. v.i.* **1 Speak, talk** mean to say or use words. **Speak** suggests more formality than **talk** or, when applied to children, more fluency: *He spoke at the banquet. She talks readily on almost any subject. My little daughter is learning to talk, but she cannot really speak yet.*

**speak|a|ble** (spē′kə bəl), *adj.* that can be spoken.

**speak|eas|y** or **speak-eas|y** (spēk′ē′zē), *n., pl.* **-eas|ies.** *U.S. Slang.* a place where alcoholic liquors are sold contrary to law, especially one that sold such liquor by the drink during the period of national prohibition. [American English < *speak* + *easy* (perhaps because of the quiet nature of the conversation therein)]

**speak|er** (spē′kər), *n.* **1** a person who speaks, especially one who speaks formally or skillfully before an audience; orator. **2** Usually, **Speaker.** a person who presides over a legislative assembly, especially the United States House of Representatives or a house of the British parliament: *The Lord Chancellor need not be a member of the House of Lords of which he is the Speaker* (Law Times). **3** any one of various devices for reproducing sound, as in a radio, phonograph, or television set; loudspeaker. **4** a book containing pieces for recitation or reading aloud.

**Speaker of the House**, the presiding officer of the United States House of Representatives.

**speak|er|phone** (spē′kər fōn′), *n.* a telephone incorporating a loudspeaker and a microphone: *Speakerphones ... permit an executive to conduct a phone conversation while standing several feet away from his desk* (Time).

**speak|er|ship** (spē′kər ship), *n.* the office or position of speaker in a legislative assembly.

**speak|ing** (spē′king), *n., adj.* —*n.* **1a** the act of a person who speaks; talking: *Within an hour from the time of my speaking* (Scott). **b** speech; talk; discourse: *So sweet his speaking sounded* (William Morris). **2** the making of speeches: *public speaking, after-dinner speaking.*
—*adj.* **1** used in, suited to, or involving speech: *a person's speaking voice, to be within speaking distance, a speaking part in a play.* **2** that speaks; giving information as if by speech: *a speaking example of a thing.* **3** permitting conversation: *I have only a speaking acquaintance with our new neighbors.* **4** *Figurative.* highly expressive: *speaking eyes.* **SYN**: eloquent. **5** *Figurative.* lifelike: *a speaking likeness.*

**speaking tube**, a tube or pipe for speaking from one room, building, or other such area, to another: *Many ships used to have speaking tubes from the bridge to the engine room.*

**spean** (spēn), *v.t. Scottish.* to wean.

***spear**[1] (spir), *n., v.* —*n.* **1** a weapon with a long shaft and a sharp-pointed head, sometimes barbed. Spears are for throwing or thrusting with the hand in hunting, fishing, and warfare. The javelin is a light spear used in track-and-field sports. **2** *Archaic.* a spearman.
—*v.t.* **1** to pierce with a spear: *The Indian speared a fish. I think it a gain to be speared by a foe rather than to be stabbed by a friend* (Cardinal Newman). **2** to pierce or stab with anything sharp: *to spear string beans with a fork.*
—*v.i. Figurative: His reproachful gaze speared into my heart. Long shafts of light ... spearing right down into the ... night below* (Margaret Kennedy). **SYN**: penetrate.
[Old English *spere*] —**spear′er**, *n.*

***spear** [1]
definition 1

***spearfish**

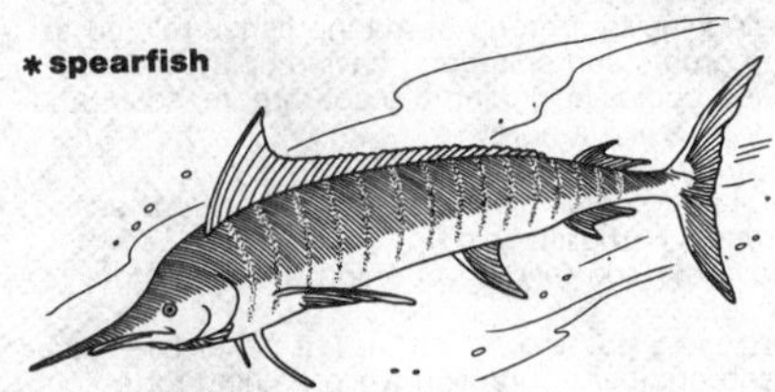

**spear**[2] (spir), *n., v.* —*n.* a sprout or shoot of a plant: *a spear of grass.*
—*v.i.* to sprout or shoot into a long stem; germinate: *The first blades of grass speared out of the earth.*
[earlier, a church spire, variant of *spire*[1]; perhaps influenced by *spear*[1]]

**spear beak**, a long, sharp beak, like that of a heron, that can be used to catch fish.

**spear crowfoot**, a yellow-flowered spearwort introduced into Newfoundland and Nova Scotia from Europe.

***spear|fish** (spir′fish′), *n., pl.* **-fish|es** or (*collectively*) **-fish**, *v.* —*n.* any one of various large, powerful, ocean fishes having a long, pointed beak or spear, related to the swordfishes and sailfishes; marlin: *He said the spearfish weighed up to 1,000 lbs. and could travel through the water at 68 miles an hour* (London Times).
—*v.i.* to engage in spearfishing; fish with a spear or speargun.

**spear|fish|er|man** (spir′fish′ər mən), *n., pl.* **-men.** person skilled or engaged in spearfishing.

**spear|fish|ing** (spir′fish′ing), *n.* the sport of fishing with a spear or speargun.

**spear grass**, any one of various grasses with a spearlike leaf, flower cluster, or other part, such as the couch grass.

**spear|gun** (spir′gun′), *n.* an underwater weapon used to shoot steel darts at fish. It operates by spring action like a crossbow or by the expansion of compressed carbon dioxide gas. Spearguns are often used by scuba divers.

**spear|head** (spir′hed′), *n., v.* —*n.* **1** the sharp-pointed striking end of a spear. **2** *Figurative.* the driving force in an attack or undertaking: *A spearhead of tanks and fighter planes led the infantry attack.*

—*v.t.* to lead or clear the way for; head: *He commanded the 505th Parachute Infantry Regiment, which spearheaded the allied assault in Sicily* (Newsweek).

**spear|man** (spir′mən), *n., pl.* **-men.** a soldier or hunter armed with a spear.

**spear|mint** (spir′mint′), *n.* a common garden mint, a fragrant herb much used for flavoring. It yields a fragrant oil. See picture under **mint family.** [< *spear*[1] (perhaps because of the shape of the flowers) + *mint*[1]]

**spear|point** (spir′point′), *n., v.* —*n.* **1** the point of a spear; spearhead. **2** *Figurative.* a person or thing that acts as a spearhead: *He was the spearpoint of the new power growing up in the rural areas* (London Times). —*v.t.* = spearhead.

**spear side,** the male line of descent: *Such and such qualities he got from a grandfather on the spear side* (James Russell Lowell).

**spear thistle,** the common thistle with lance-shaped leaves.

**spear|wort** (spir′wėrt′), *n.* any one of several crowfoots with lance-shaped leaves, such as the spear crowfoot.

**spear|y** (spir′ē), *adj.* spearlike; sharp-pointed.

**spec** (spek), *n. Informal.* speculation (def. 3).

**spec., 1a** special. **b** specially. **2** specification. **3** specimen. **4** spectrum.

**spe|cial** (spesh′əl), *adj., n.* —*adj.* **1** of a particular kind; distinct from others; not general; certain: *money set aside for a special purpose, a special edition of a book, special prices for the clearance sale. A safe has a special lock. A play may be violent, full of motion; yet it has that special kind of repose which allows contemplation* (Tennessee Williams). **2** more than ordinary; unusual; exceptional: *special care, a matter of special importance. Lions and tigers are a topic of special interest.* **3** having a particular purpose, function, or use: *special permission to leave school early, a special correspondent from the Congo, a special application of a theory. The railroad ran special trains on holidays. Send the letter by special messenger.* **4** belonging exclusively as to a person or thing: *a scholar's special field of knowledge, the special merits of a plan. Every country has its special attractions.* **5** held in high regard; great; chief: *a special friend, a special favorite.* **6** specific: *special instructions.*

—*n.* **1** a special train, car, bus, or the like. **2** any special person or thing. **3a** a special edition of a newspaper. **b** a special article in or communication to a newspaper: *a Washington special.* **4** *U.S.* a specially featured product or service; sale: *This week's special is ham and eggs.* **5** a television show, produced especially for a single broadcast, usually out of the pattern of regular daily or weekly programs: *In news and public affairs, specials were planned covering such subjects as air pollution, organized crime, air safety, drugs* (S. Taishoff and R. W. Crater).

[< Latin *speciālis* < *speciēs, -ēī* appearance; see etym. under **species.** See etym. of doublet **especial.**] —**spe′cial|ness,** *n.*

—*Syn. adj.* **1 Special, particular** mean belonging or relating to one person, thing, or group, as distinguished from others. **Special** implies being different from others of its kind: *Babies need special food.* **Particular** implies being or treated as being unique: *the particular meaning of a word. This particular brand of milk is sold only in one store.*

**special checking account,** a checking account with no minimum balance required.

**special delivery,** the delivery of a letter or package by a special messenger rather than by the regular mailman. Special delivery mail has much higher rates, but it is handled faster and delivered sooner than regular mail.

**Special Drawing Rights** or **special drawing rights,** a monetary reserve of the International Monetary Fund from which member nations may draw credit in proportion to their contribution to the Fund; paper gold. *Abbr:* S.D.R. or S.D.R.s

**special effects,** illusory effects created by various techniques in a motion picture.

**Special Forces,** a unit of the U.S. Army whose members are trained in unconventional warfare, especially guerrilla and antiguerrilla fighting. Special Forces men wear green berets.

**special handling,** the handling and sending of fourth-class postal matter (parcel post) at a faster than normal rate, for an additional fee. It is not sent by special delivery.

**spe|cial-in|ter|est group** (spesh′əl in′tər ist, -trist), a group of people seeking to protect their interests, especially by means of a lobby: *I deplore nothing more than this fragmentation of our democratic society into special-interest groups—labor, farmers, business* (Adlai E. Stevenson).

**spe|cial|ise** (spesh′ə līz), *v.i., v.t.,* **-ised, -is|ing.** *Especially British.* specialize.

**spe|cial|ism** (spesh′ə liz əm), *n.* **1** devotion or restriction to one particular branch, as of study, research, or business. **2** a special field of study; specialty.

**spe|cial|ist** (spesh′ə list), *n., adj.* —*n.* **1** a person who devotes or restricts himself to one particular branch of study, research, business, or organization: *a specialist in colonial American history.* **2** a physician or surgeon who limits his practice to the study or treatment of particular diseases or a part of the body: *an eye specialist. Dr. White is a specialist in diseases of the nose and throat.* **3** a broker on the floor of a stock exchange who is in charge of regulating the supply and demand of a particular security or securities and who executes special orders to buy or sell shares of that security. **4** an enlisted man in the U.S. Army with administrative or technical duties, ranking above a private first class, and ranging from specialist four to specialist seven who has the same pay as a sergeant first class.

—*adj.* = specialistic.

**spe|cial|is|tic** (spesh′ə lis′tik), *adj.* of or having to do with specialism or specialists.

**spé|cia|li|té de la mai|son** (spe′syä lē tā′ də lȧ me zôN′), *French.* specialty of the house: *There is also Le Drug Store on the Champs Elysées, where the spécialités de la maison are hamburgers* (Time).

**spe|ci|al|i|ty** (spesh′ē al′ə tē), *n., pl.* **-ties. 1** a special, limited, or particular character: *In the general ordinances . . . it would have been out of place because of its speciality* (James G. Murphy). **2** a special quality or characteristic; distinctive property or feature of a thing; peculiarity: *Weather is a literary speciality, and no untrained hand can turn out a good article on it* (Mark Twain). **3** a special point; particular; detail. **4** *British.* any special thing, such as a pursuit, branch of study, or product; specialty. [< Latin *speciālitās* < *speciālis;* see etym. under **special**]

**spe|cial|i|za|tion** (spesh′ə lə zā′shən), *n.* **1** the act of specializing. **2** the condition of being specialized.

**spe|cial|ize** (spesh′ə līz), *v.,* **-ized, -iz|ing.** —*v.i.* **1** to pursue some special branch of study, research, or work: *to specialize in early American history. Many students specialize in engineering. Some doctors specialize in taking care of children.* **2** *Biology.* to develop in a special way; take on a special form or use; become specialized. **3** to go into particulars or details.

—*v.t.* **1** to make special or specific; give as a special character or function to: *All the Allied infantrymen tend to become specialized, as machine gun men, and so on* (H. G. Wells). **2** to adapt to a special function or condition: *a specialized organ. Lungs and gills are specialized for breathing.* **3** to develop in a special way: *Animals and plants are specialized to fit their surroundings.* **4** to mention specially; specify. SYN: particularize. **5** to endorse (a bill, note, draft, or other security) so that only one payee may receive payment.

**spe|cial|iz|er** (spesh′ə lī′zər), *n.* a person who specializes; specialist.

**special jury,** *Law.* a jury specially selected for a purpose instead of being chosen at random. A blue-ribbon jury and a struck jury are special juries.

**spe|cial|ly** (spesh′ə lē), *adv.* in a special manner or degree; particularly; unusually: . . . *Writing it almost as though they were creating a new language specially invented for the purposes of their poetry* (Manchester Guardian Weekly). SYN: expressly.

**special partner,** a partner who invests a certain amount in a business and whose liability is no greater than the amount of his investment.

**special plea,** *Law.* a plea which does not answer the charge, but alleges some new fact on the basis of which the suit should be delayed or dismissed.

**special pleading, 1** *Law.* a pleading that does not deny what is alleged by the opposition but claims that other or additional points deriving from the case will offset it. **2** any pleading or arguing that ignores or sets aside points or features that are unfavorable to one's own side.

**special sessions,** a sitting or meeting of a court, council, legislature, or other body, for an extraordinary purpose and outside of the usually appointed time.

**special theory of relativity,** = relativity (def. 4a).

**spe|cial|ty** (spesh′əl tē), *n., pl.* **-ties. 1a** a special line of work, profession, or trade: *Straightening teeth is that dentist's specialty. Steel manufacturing is a specialty of that region.* **b** a special field or subject of study or research: *American history is the specialty of my social studies teacher.* **2** a product or article to which special attention is given, or for which a particular person or place is noted: *This store makes a specialty of children's clothes. Fine linen is a specialty of Ireland.* **3** special character or quality: *The specialty of Lincoln's wisdom made him one of the great leaders of history.* **4** a special or particular characteristic; peculiarity: *A specialty of the tribe was its belief in one supreme god.* **5** a special point or item; particular; detail. **6** *Law.* a special contract, bond, obligation, or the like, expressed in an instrument under seal. [earlier, special attachments; a mark of favor < Old French *especialte* < Latin *speciālitās;* see etym. under **speciality**]

**specialty fiber,** fiber from the hair of animals other than sheep and goats; fiber from the hair of the camel, alpaca, llama, and vicuña, provided it has never been reclaimed from any woven or felted wool product.

**specialty shop** or **store,** a store, usually small, selling an assortment of one kind of thing, such as hats, or a limited number of closely related things, such as books and stationery.

**spe|ci|ate** (spē′shē āt), *v.i.,* **-at|ed, -at|ing.** to form new species by evolutionary process: *Hybridization prevents plants from speciating.* —**spe′ci|a′tion,** *n.*

**spe|cie** (spē′shē), *n.* money in the form of coins; metal money. Silver dollars are specie.

**in specie, a** in kind: *The power of the advocate, though . . . less in degree is in specie the same with the power of the judge* (Jeremy Bentham). **b** in actual coin: *Our coin . . . whether we send it in specie . . . or . . . melt it down here to send it in bullion* (John Locke).

[earlier, coin < *in specie* in the real or actual form; in kind < Latin *in speciē* in kind, ablative of *speciēs* kind, form]

**spe|cies** (spē′shēz), *n., pl.* **-cies** (-shēz). **1** a group of animals or plants that have certain permanent characteristics in common and are able to interbreed. A species ranks next below a genus and may be divided into several varieties, races, or breeds. All species of apples belong to the same genus. Wheat is a species of grass. The domestic cat is one species of cat. **2** a distinct kind or sort; kind; sort: *There are many species of advertisements. That species of writing which is called the marvellous* (Henry Fielding). *He fought for the species of freedom which is the most valuable* (Macaulay). **3** *Logic.* **a** a number of individuals having certain common characteristics or essential qualities and a common name. **b** the individuals belonging to one species. **4a** the consecrated bread and wine used in the Mass. **b** either of these elements.

**the species,** the human race: *The female of the species is more deadly than the male* (Rudyard Kipling).

[earlier, common properties marking a class < Latin *speciēs* kind, sort; (originally) appearance. See etym. of doublet **spice.**]

**spe|cies|ism** (spē′shēz iz əm), *n.* discrimination in favor of one species of animal over another, especially in regard to the misuse or exploitation of various animals by human beings.

**spe|cies|ist** (spē′shēz ist), *adj.* practicing or supporting speciesism: *The public tends to be "speciesist" in its reaction to animal experimentation: For many people, a test is permissible when it inflicts pain on a "lower" animal like a hamster, but not when the victim is a dog* (Patricia Curtis).

**spe|cies-spe|cif|ic** (spē′shēz spi sif′ik), *adj.* limited in reaction or effect to one species: *It has become apparent that viruses, which had been thought to be species-specific, can cross from one species to another and thus spread disease* (New Scientist).

**specif.,** specifically.

**spec|i|fi|a|ble** (spes′ə fī′ə bəl), *adj.* that can be specified: *He cannot even claim that specifiable laws of physics are violated* (Science).

**spe|cif|ic** (spi sif′ik), *adj., n.* —*adj.* **1** definite; precise; particular: *a specific command or request, a specific sum of money. There was no specific reason for the quarrel. When you describe something, be specific.* SYN: explicit. **2** specially belonging to a thing or group of things; characteristic (of); peculiar (to): *A scaly skin is a specific feature of snakes. Feathers are a feature specific to birds.* SYN: distinctive. **3a** preventing or curing a particular disease: *a specific remedy.* **b** produced by a special cause or infection: *a specific disease.* **4** of, having to do with, or characteristic of a species: *the specific name of a plant.*

—*n.* **1** any specific statement, quality, or subject: *He still doesn't know specifics on all issues, but his general knowledge is sharpening and his instincts are surer* (Birmingham Post-Herald). **2** a

---

**Pronunciation Key:** hat, āge, cãre, fär; let, ēqual, tėrm; it, īce; hot, ōpen, ôrder; **oil, out;** cup, pu̇t, rüle; **child;** long; **thin; ŧʜen; zh,** measure; **ə** represents **a** in about, **e** in taken, **i** in pencil, **o** in lemon, **u** in circus.

cure for some particular disease; specific remedy: *Quinine is a specific for malaria. Vitamin $B_{12}$ is a specific for pernicious anemia.*
[< Late Latin *specificus* making up a species < Latin *speciēs* sort, kind + *facere* to make] —**spe·cif'ic|ness**, *n.*

**spe|cif|i|cal|ly** (spi sif'ə klē), *adv.* in a specific manner; definitely; particularly: *The doctor told her specifically not to eat eggs.*

**spec|i|fi|ca|tion** (spes'ə fə kā'shən), *n.* **1** the act of specifying; definite mention; detailed statement of particulars: *She made careful specification as to the kinds of cake and candy needed for her party.* **2** Often, **specifications. a** a detailed description of the dimensions, materials, or quantities, for a building, road, dam, boat, or like thing to be made or constructed. **b** the document containing this. **3** something specified; particular article, item, or the like: *statements unsupported by specifications.* **4** a description or definition according to specific or particular characters.

**specific duty**, a duty or tariff on a certain kind of article or on a given quantity of an article, without reference to its value or market price.

**specific gravity**, the ratio of the weight or mass of a given volume of any substance to that of an equal volume of some other substance taken as a standard, usually water at 4 degrees centigrade for solids and liquids, and hydrogen or air for gases. The specific gravity of gold is 19 because any volume of gold weighs 19 times as much as the same volume of water. A hydrometer is often used to find the specific gravity of a liquid. *Abbr:* sp.gr.

**specific heat**, *Physics.* **1** the number of calories of heat needed to raise the temperature of one gram of a given substance one degree centigrade. **2** the ratio of the amount of heat required to raise a unit mass of a substance one degree in temperature to that required to raise the same mass of some other substance, taken as a standard, one degree.

**specific impulse**, the thrust in pounds of a rocket motor or engine produced by burning one pound of a specified fuel with its oxidizer in one second.

**spec|i|fic|i|ty** (spes'ə fis'ə tē), *n.* specific quality: **a** the quality of having specific character or relation: *There has always been a certain lack of specificity about these fears; people have been bothered ... without being able to say precisely why* (New Yorker). **b** the quality of being specific in operation or effect: *It is also known that the protein coat determines the specificity of the virus, i.e., whether or not it will attack a certain bacterium* (Scientific American).

**spec|i|fi|er** (spes'ə fī'ər), *n.* a person who specifies.

**spec|i|fy** (spes'ə fī), *v.t.*, **-fied, -fy|ing. 1** to mention or name definitely; state or describe in detail: *Did you specify any particular time for us to call? He delivered the paper as specified.* **2** to include in the specifications: *The contractor couldn't use shingles for the roof because slate was specified.* **3** to give as a condition or requisite: *Punctuality was specified as the first requisite for the situation.* [< Old French *specifier,* learned borrowing from Late Latin *specificāre* < *specificus;* see etym. under **specific**]

**spec|i|men** (spes'ə mən), *n., adj.* —*n.* **1** one of a group or class taken to show what the others are like; single part or thing regarded as an example of its kind; sample: *He collects specimens of all kinds of rocks and minerals. The statue is a fine specimen of Greek sculpture. Abbr:* sp. **SYN:** instance. **2** *Informal.* a human being; person: *The tramp was a shabby specimen.*
—*adj.* taken or regarded as a specimen; typical: *a strong desire to see something more of Christendom than a specimen whaler or two* (Herman Melville). **SYN:** representative.
[< Latin *specimen, -inis* < *specere* to view]

**specimen plant**, a plant set out by itself and cultivated for its ornamental effect.

**spe|ci|os|i|ty** (spē'shē os'ə tē), *n., pl.* **-ties. 1** the quality of being specious; speciousness: *Speciosity ... usurps the place of reality ... ; instead of performance, there is appearance of performance* (Thomas Carlyle). **2** a specious act, appearance, remark, etc.

**spe|cious** (spē'shəs), *adj.* **1** seeming desirable, reasonable, or probable, but not really so; apparently good or right, but without real merit: *a specious appearance of fair play. The teacher saw through that specious excuse. This specious reasoning is nevertheless false* (Thomas Hobbes). **2** making a good outward appearance in order to deceive: *a specious friendship, a specious flatterer.* **3** *Archaic.* showy; beautiful; lovely. [< Latin *speciōsus* < *speciēs, -ēī* appearance] —**spe'cious|ly**, *adv.* —**spe'cious|ness**, *n.*

**speck** (spek), *n., v.* —*n.* **1** a small spot or mark; stain: *Can you clean the specks off this wallpaper? In beauty faults conspicuous grow, The smallest speck is seen on snow* (John Gay). **SYN:** speckle. **2** a tiny bit; particle: *a speck of dust, to have a speck in one's eye.* (*Figurative.*) *He has not a speck of humor or of sense.* **SYN:** mite.
—*v.t.* to mark with or as if with specks: *This fruit is badly specked.*
[Old English *specca*] —**speck'less**, *adj.*

**speck|le** (spek'əl), *n., v.*, **-led, -ling.** —*n.* a small spot or mark; speck: *This hen is gray with white speckles.*
—*v.t.* to mark with or as if with speckles: *The dog is speckled with paint. That boy is speckled with freckles.*
[probably < *speck* + *-le* (frequentative)]

**speck|led alder** (spek'əld), the common North American species of alder, growing from Hudson Bay south to Maryland and west to the Dakotas.

**speckled trout**, = brook trout.

**speckled wood**, wood having speckled or mottled markings, as: **a** = letterwood. **b** palmyra wood when cut transversely into veneers.

**specs** (speks), *n.pl. Informal.* spectacles.

**spec|ta|cle** (spek'tə kəl), *n.* **1** a thing to look at; sight; something presented to the view as noteworthy or striking: *the spectacle of a storm at sea. The children at play among the flowers made a charming spectacle. A quarrel is an unpleasant spectacle.* **2** a public show or display: *The parade was the crowning spectacle of the day.* **SYN:** exhibition, parade, pageant. **3** a person or thing set before the public view as an object of curiosity, contempt, wonder, or admiration.
**make a spectacle of oneself**, to behave in public view in such a manner as to become an object of curiosity, contempt, or wonder: *She was greatly embarrassed when her partner made a spectacle of himself on the dance floor.*
**spectacles, a** a pair of glasses to help a person's sight or protect his eyes; eyeglasses: *Spectacles and reading glasses are among the simplest and most useful of optical instruments* (David Brewster). **b** *Figurative.* a means or medium through which anything is viewed or regarded; point of view: *Subjects are to look upon the faults of princes with the spectacles of obedience and reverence* (John Donne). **c** anything like spectacles, such as the device attached to a railway semaphore for displaying lights of different colors by means of colored glass, or the pattern of contrasting scales on the hood of a cobra: *... two varieties of cobra, one with the spectacles and the other without them* (E. M. Gordon).
[< Latin *spectāculum* < *spectāre* to watch (frequentative) < *specere* to view]

**spec|ta|cled** (spek'tə kəld), *adj.* **1** provided with or wearing spectacles: *a scholar spectacled and slippered* (Edward G. Bulwer-Lytton). **2** having markings resembling spectacles: *the spectacled cobra.*

**spectacled bear**, a small black bear of the Andes, having white markings around the eyes that look like spectacles.

**spectacled snake**, the cobra of India that commonly has a black and white marking like spectacles on the back of the hood; Indian cobra.

**spectacled warbler**, a small European warbler resembling the whitethroat, with straw-colored legs and white markings around the eyes.

**spec|tac|u|lar** (spek tak'yə lər), *adj., n.* —*adj.* **1** making a great display or show; very striking or imposing to the eye: *a spectacular storm; ... a spectacular display of wrath* (Arnold Bennett). *Motion pictures present spectacular scenes like battles, processions, storms, or races.* **SYN:** showy. **2** having to do with a spectacle or show. **SYN:** theatrical.
—*n.* **1** a spectacular display: *Our scientific studies of outer space ... have easily matched those of the Soviet Union, notwithstanding the greater publicity given to the Soviet technological spectaculars* (Bulletin of Atomic Scientists). **2** a lengthy motion picture or television show, usually produced on an extravagant scale; special: *Its big feature ... will be a series of costly and lavish ninety-minute "spectaculars"—opera, drama, musical comedy, circuses, ice shows, etc.* (New York Times). —**spec|tac'u|lar|ly**, *adv.*

**spec|tac|u|lar|i|ty** (spek tak'yə lar'ə tē), *n.* spectacular quality or character.

**spec|tate** (spek'tāt), *v.i.*, **-tat|ed, -tat|ing.** to be a spectator: *Hearing that a big match was under way here, ... we repaired to the arena, and asked leave to spectate* (New Yorker). [back formation < *spectator*]

**spec|ta|tion** (spek tā'shən), *n.* spectatorship: *President Kennedy called upon Americans to spend less time in athletic spectation and more time in athletic participation* (George McNickle).
[< Latin *spectātiō, -ōnis* < *spectāre;* see etym. under **spectacle**]

**spec|ta|tor** (spek'tā tər, spek tā'-), *n.* **1** a person who looks on without taking part: *There were many spectators at the game. The Puritan hated bear-baiting, not because it gave pain to the bear, but because it gave pleasure to the spectators* (Macaulay). **SYN:** observer, witness, onlooker, bystander. **2** = spectator pump. [< Latin *spectātor* < *spectāre;* see etym. under **spectacle**]

**spec|ta|to|ri|al** (spek'tə tôr'ē əl, -tōr'-), *adj.* having to do with or characteristic of a spectator.

**spec|ta|tor|ism** (spek tā'tə riz'əm), *n.* the practice of being a spectator or onlooker at sports or games; spectatorship: *... a still-to-be-assessed turn from cool spectatorism to active involvement* (Harper's).

**spec|ta|tor|i|tis** (spek tā'tə rī'tis), *n.* excessive or undue spectatorism: *"Spectatoritis is the nation's No. 1 fitness problem," said* [*the*] *executive director of the President's Council on Youth Fitness* (Time).

**spectator pump**, a woman's sports pump with a medium or high heel, usually white but having a dark-colored heel and toe.

**spec|ta|tor|ship** (spek tā'tər ship), *n.* **1** the act of watching as a spectator. **2** the state or occupation of being a spectator.

**spectator sport**, a sport which usually attracts a large number of spectators, as distinguished from a sport, such as boating or hunting, in which more people participate than watch: *Baseball, football, and basketball rank high among the most popular spectator sports in the United States* (Elmer D. Mitchell).

**spec|ta|tress** (spek'tā tris, spek tā'-), *n.* a woman spectator: *To be spectatress at interminable and frequently incomprehensible sports is part of the lot of women* (Prudence Glynn).

**spec|ter** (spek'tər), *n.* **1** a phantom or ghost, especially one of a terrifying nature or appearance. **SYN:** See syn. under **ghost. 2** *Figurative.* a thing that causes terror or dread: *the grim specter of war.* [< Latin *spectrum* appearance; see etym. under **spectrum**]

**specter of the Brocken**, = Brocken specter.

**spec|tra** (spek'trə), *n.* a plural of **spectrum**.

**spec|tral** (spek'trəl), *adj.* **1** of or like a specter; ghostly: *the spectral form of a ship surrounded by fog. He saw the spectral form of the headless horseman.* **2a** of or produced by the spectrum: *spectral colors.* **b** carried out or performed by means of the spectrum: *spectral analysis.*
—**spec'tral|ly**, *adv.* —**spec'tral|ness**, *n.*

**spectral class**, any one of the classes into which stars are divided on the basis of their spectra. Spectral classes range from very hot blue stars to very cool red stars.

**spec|tral|i|ty** (spek tral'ə tē), *n.* the quality or state of being spectral.

**spectral line**, any of the dark or bright lines in stellar spectra caused by the transition of atoms from one energy level to another and indicating the presence of a particular chemical element; absorption line or emission line: *Because spectral lines are very narrow, it is unlikely that two molecules will have a line at the very same wave length. In fact, a molecule can often be identified on the basis of a single spectral line* (Patrick Thaddeus).

**spectral series**, a series of spectral lines.

**spec|tre** (spek'tər), *n.* = specter.

**spectro-**, *combining form.* having to do with the spectrum or with spectrum analysis: *Spectroscope = an instrument for spectrum analysis. Spectrogram = a photograph of a spectrum.* [< *spectrum*]

**spec|tro|bo|lom|e|ter** (spek'trō bō lom'ə tər), *n.* an instrument consisting of a combined spectroscope and bolometer, used in determining the distribution of radiant heat or energy in a spectrum.

**spec|tro|chem|i|cal** (spek'trō kem'ə kəl), *adj.* of or having to do with spectrochemistry.

**spec|tro|chem|is|try** (spek'trō kem'ə strē), *n.* the branch of chemistry that deals with the techniques and findings of spectrum analysis.

**spec|tro|flu|o|rom|e|ter** (spek'trō flü'ə rom'ə-tər), *n.* an instrument which measures the spectra of fluorescence.

**spec|tro|flu|o|ro|met|ric** (spek'trō flü'ər ə met'-rik), *adj.* of, having to do with, or using a spectrofluorometer.

**spec|tro|gram** (spek'trə gram), *n.* **1** a photograph or picture of a spectrum: *If the spectroscope is arranged for photographic observation, so the spectral lines can be photographed side by side on a film or plate, the instrument is called a spectrograph, and the picture a spectrogram* (Shortley and Williams). **2** = sound spectrogram.

**spec|tro|graph** (spek'trə graf, -gräf), *n.* **1** an instrument for photographing a spectrum. **2** = sound spectrograph.

**spec|tro|graph|ic** (spek'trə graf'ik), *adj.* of or by means of a spectrograph. —**spec'tro|graph'i|cal|ly**, *adv.*

**spec|trog|ra|phy** (spek trog'rə fē), *n.* the art of

using the spectrograph.

**spec|tro|he|li|o|gram** (spek′trō hē′lē ə gram), *n.* a photograph of the sun taken with a spectroheliograph.

**spec|tro|he|li|o|graph** (spek′trō hē′lē ə graf, -gräf), *n.* an apparatus for photographing the sun with light of a single wave length, in order to show the details of various solar phenomena, such as sun spots, as they would appear if only one kind of light were emitted.

**spec|tro|he|li|o|scope** (spek′trō hē′lē ə skōp), *n.* **1** an instrument like the spectroheliograph but used for visual rather than photographic observations of the sun. **2** = spectroheliograph.

**spec|tro|log|i|cal** (spek′trə loj′ə kəl), *adj.* of, having to do with, or determined by spectrology: *spectrological analysis.*

**spec|trol|o|gy** (spek trol′ə jē), *n.* the scientific study of spectra.

**spec|trom|e|ter** (spek trom′ə tər), *n.* a spectroscope equipped with a scale for measuring wave lengths of spectra.

**spec|tro|met|ric** (spek′trə met′rik), *adj.* of or having to do with a spectrometer or spectrometry. — **spec′tro|met′ri|cal|ly,** *adv.*

**spec|trom|e|try** (spek trom′ə trē), *n.* **1** the science that deals with the use of the spectrometer and the analysis of spectra. **2** the use of the spectrometer.

**spec|tro|pho|tom|e|ter** (spek′trō fō tom′ə tər), *n.* an instrument used to compare the intensities of two spectra, or the intensity of a given color with that of the corresponding color in a standard spectrum.

**spec|tro|pho|to|met|ric** (spek′trō fō′tə met′rik), *adj.* of or by means of the spectrophotometer. — **spec′tro|pho′to|met′ri|cal|ly,** *adv.*

**spec|tro|pho|tom|e|try** (spek′trō fō tom′ə trē), *n.* **1** the science that deals with the use of the spectrophotometer. **2** the use of the spectrophotometer.

***spec|tro|scope** (spek′trə skōp), *n.* an instrument for producing and examining the spectrum of a ray from any source. The spectrum produced by passing a light ray through a prism can be examined to determine the composition of the source of the ray. *With the possible exception of the telescope itself, no astronomical instrument has excelled the simple spectroscope in importance for our knowledge of the material universe* (Harlow Shapley).

***spectroscope**

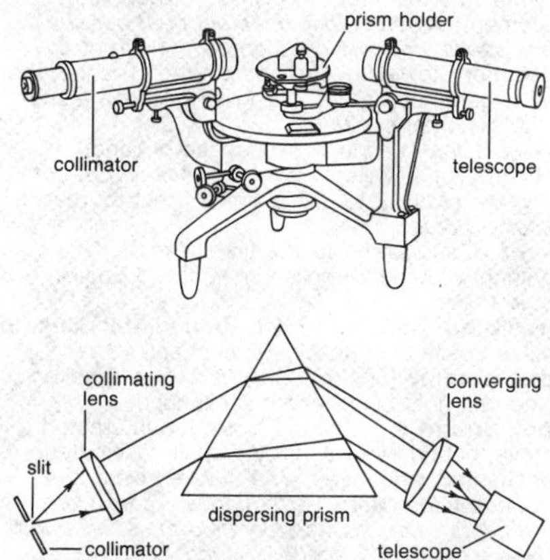


**spec|tro|scop|ic** (spek′trə skop′ik), *adj.* of or having to do with the spectroscope or spectroscopy: *a spectroscopic prism.* — **spec′tro|scop′i|cal|ly,** *adv.*

**spec|tro|scop|i|cal** (spek′trə skop′ə kəl), *adj.* = spectroscopic.

**spectroscopic binary,** *Astronomy.* a binary star whose two components are so close that they cannot be separated with a telescope and are known to exist only through spectrum analysis.

**spec|tros|co|pist** (spek tros′kə pist, spek′trə skō′-), *n.* a person skilled in spectroscopy.

**spec|tros|co|py** (spek tros′kə pē, spek′trə skō′-), *n.* **1** the science having to do with the examination and analysis of spectra. **2** the use of the spectroscope.

**spec|trum** (spek′trəm), *n., pl.* **-tra** or **-trums.** **1** the band of colors formed when a beam of white light is broken up by being passed through a prism or by some other means. A rainbow has all the colors of the spectrum: red, orange, yellow, green, blue, indigo, and violet. **2** the band of colors formed when any other form of radiant energy is broken up. The ends of such a band are not visible to the eye, but are studied by photography and heat effects. *Unfortunately, the spectra of galaxies provide information only with regard to motion along our line of sight, not at right angles to it* (Sky and Telescope). **3** the wavelength range between 30,000 meters and 3 centimeters; radio spectrum. **4** *Figurative.* range; scope; compass: *a broad spectrum of electronic knowledge. Hear ... the full spectrum of sound the next time you visit your music dealer* (Atlantic). [< New Latin *spectrum* < Latin; see etym. under **specter**]

**spectrum analysis,** the examination and study of bodies and substances by means of the spectra they form.

**spec|u|la** (spek′yə lə), *n.* a plural of **speculum.**

**spec|u|lar** (spek′yə lər), *adj.* **1** of or like a mirror; reflecting. **2** of, having to do with, or like a speculum. **3** *Medicine.* by means of a speculum: *specular examination.* [< Latin *speculāris* < *speculum* mirror; see etym. under **speculum**] — **spec′u|lar|ly,** *adv.*

**specular iron,** hematite, especially in its brilliant crystalline form.

**spec|u|lar|i|ty** (spek′yə lar′ə tē), *n.* the quality or state of being specular; reflectivity.

**specular schist,** a rock made up chiefly of quartz, specular iron ore, and mica.

**spec|u|late** (spek′yə lāt), *v.,* **-lat|ed, -lat|ing.** — *v.i.* **1** to think carefully; reflect; meditate; consider: *The philosopher speculated about time and space. She ... speculated without reserve on the coming of many grandsons* (Rudyard Kipling). **SYN:** pore, ponder. **2** to guess; conjecture: *She refused to speculate about the possible winner.* **3** to buy or sell when there is a large risk, with the hope of making a profit from future price changes: *He became poor after speculating in what turned out to be worthless oil wells.* **4** to take part or invest in a risky business enterprise or transaction in the hope of making large profits: *Would he be what he is if he hadn't speculated?* (Dickens).
— *v.t.* **1** to invest (money) in a risky enterprise. **2** *Obsolete.* to consider; contemplate: *If we do but speculate the folly ... of avarice* (Thomas Browne).
[< Latin *speculārī* (with English *-ate*[1]) < *specula* watchtower < *specere* to look]

**spec|u|la|tion** (spek′yə lā′shən), *n.* **1** careful thought; reflection: *Former speculations about electricity were often mere guesses. If the world were good for nothing else, it is a fine subject for speculation* (William Hazlitt). *Science carries us into zones of speculation where there is no habitable city for the mind of man* (Robert Louis Stevenson). **2** the action or process of guessing; conjecture: *His estimates of the cost were based on speculation.* **3** the act or practice of buying or selling when there is a large risk, with the hope of making a profit from future price changes: *His speculations in unsound stocks made him poor.* **4** the act or fact of taking part in any risky enterprise or transaction.

**spec|u|la|tive** (spek′yə lā′tiv, -lə-), *adj.* **1** carefully thoughtful; reflective: *a speculative turn of mind.* **2** theoretical rather than practical: *speculative knowledge.* **SYN:** academic. **3** = risky. **4** of or involving buying or selling land, stocks, or commodities at a large risk: *speculative ventures in real estate, speculative buying of cotton futures.* — **spec′u|la′tive|ly,** *adv.* — **spec′u|la′tive|ness,** *n.*

**spec|u|la|tor** (spek′yə lā′tər), *n.* **1** a person who speculates, usually in business or financial enterprises. **2** a person who buys tickets, as for shows or games, in advance, hoping to sell them later at a higher price. **SYN:** scalper. [< Latin *speculātor* explorer, spy < *speculārī;* see etym. under **speculate**]

**spec|u|la|to|ry** (spek′yə lə tôr′ē, -tōr′-), *adj.* **1** = speculative. **2** serving for observation; giving an outlook or view.

**spec|u|lum** (spek′yə ləm), *n., pl.* **-la** or **-lums.** **1** a mirror or reflector of polished metal. A reflecting telescope contains a speculum. **2** a surgical instrument for enlarging an opening in order to examine a cavity. **3** a patch of color on the wing of many ducks and certain other birds. In ducks it is often an iridescent green or blue. [< Latin *speculum* mirror < *specere* to view, look]

**sped** (sped), *v.* a past tense and a past participle of **speed**: *The police car sped down the road.*

**speech** (spēch), *n.* **1** the act of speaking; uttering of words or sentences; talk: *Men ... express their thoughts by speech* (George Berkeley). **SYN:** discourse. **2** the power of speaking: *Animals lack speech. Pity the man who has no gift of speech* (A. W. H. Eaton). **3** manner of speaking; dialect, language, or tongue: *His speech showed that he was from the South. The native speech of most Americans is English.* **4** what is said; the words spoken: *We made the usual farewell speeches.* **SYN:** utterance, remark, declaration. **5** a public, usually formal, talk or address: *The President gave an excellent speech.* **6** a number of lines spoken by an actor in a single sequence. **7** the study and practice of the spoken language: *to take a course in speech.* **8** *Archaic.* rumor; mention; report: *Dr. Clement, what's he? I have heard much speech of him* (Ben Jonson). [Old English *spǣc*]
— *Syn.* **5 Speech, address, oration** mean a talk made to an audience. **Speech** is the general word applying to any kind of talk made for some purpose: *Many after-dinner speeches are dull.* **Address** means a prepared formal speech, usually of some importance or given on an important occasion: *Who gave your commencement address?* **Oration** means a formal address on a special occasion, and suggests artistic style, dignity, and eloquence: *Daniel Webster's speech defending the Compromise of 1850 is a famous oration.*

**speech area,** the area in which a particular language or dialect is spoken.

**speech clinic,** a clinic where speech disorders, such as lisping and stuttering, are treated.

**speech clinician,** = speech therapist.

**speech community,** a group of people who speak the same language or dialect: *A group of people who use the same system of speech signals is a speech community* (Leonard Bloomfield).

**speech day,** the periodical examination day of an English public school.

**speech form,** = linguistic form.

**speech from the throne** or **Speech from the Throne, 1** a statement of foreign and domestic affairs and of the chief measures to be considered by the British Parliament or any legislative body in the Commonwealth, read by the sovereign at the opening of parliamentary sessions; King's (or Queen's) speech. **2** such a parliamentary statement by any sovereign or his representative.

**speech|ful** (spēch′fəl), *adj.* **1** full of speech; loquacious. **2** speaking or expressive. — **speech′ful|ness,** *n.*

**speech|i|fy** (spē′chə fī), *v.i.,* **-fied, -fy|ing.** *Informal.* to make a speech or speeches; orate: *A man always makes a fool of himself speechifying* (George Eliot). **SYN:** harangue. — **speech′i|fi′er,** *n.*

**speech island,** an area in which the people speak a different language from that spoken in the surrounding area.

**speech|less** (spēch′lis), *adj.* **1** not able to speak for a time: *He was speechless with anger.* **SYN:** See syn. under **dumb.** **2** not able to speak; mute or dumb: *Animals are speechless. Today as a result of electronic developments ... thousands of persons throughout the world who were once speechless can communicate again* (New York Times). **SYN:** See syn. under **dumb.** **3** not expressed in speech or words; silent: *... speechless pride and rapture* (Eugene Field). — **speech′less|ly,** *adv.* — **speech′less|ness,** *n.*

**speech|mak|er** (spēch′mā′kər), *n.* a person who makes a speech or speeches, especially in public; orator: *If the speechmakers confined themselves to statements of true fact ... maybe the oridinary citizen would not become so terribly confused on election day* (Wall Street Journal).

**speech|mak|ing** (spēch′mā′king), *n.* the act or fact of making or delivering a speech or speeches.

**speech reading,** = lip reading.

**speech-song** (spēch′sông′, -song′), *n.* a vocal style or part in music similar to but less sustained than recitative; Sprechgesang: *Schoenberg would probably have criticized her for not making a sharp enough distinction between song and speech-song* (Joan Chissel).

**speech sound,** a sound produced by the organs of speech, especially such a sound viewed as a minimal unit of speech; phone.

**speech therapist** or **pathologist,** a specialist in speech therapy.

**speech therapy** or **pathology,** the treatment of speech problems and disorders, such as stuttering, lisping, slow language development, and aphasia: *Experts in the profession of speech therapy work with children and adults whose speech interferes with communication* (Hugo H. Gregory).

**speech|way** (spēch′wā′), *n.* a habit or way of speech peculiar to a certain people or region: *For it is a fact that Americans differ from one another in their speechways, as they differ in their modes of life and in their occupations* (Donald J. Lloyd).

**speech|writ|er** (spēch′rī′tər), *n.* a person who

**Pronunciation Key:** hat, āge, cãre, fär; let, ēqual, tėrm; it, īce; hot, ōpen, ôrder; **oi**l, **ou**t; cup, pu̇t, rüle; **ch**ild; lo**ng**; **th**in; ᴛʜen; **zh**, measure; ə represents **a** in about, **e** in taken, **i** in pencil, **o** in lemon, **u** in circus.

writes speeches for another: *a presidential speechwriter.*

**speed** (spēd), *n., v.,* **sped** or **speed|ed, speed·ing.** —*n.* **1** swift or rapid movement; quickness in moving from one place to another or in doing something: *to work with speed, the amazing speed with which a cat jumps on a mouse. He could run with the speed of a deer.* **SYN:** rapidity, celerity, swiftness. See syn. under **hurry. 2** rate of movement: *to regulate the speed of machines. The boys ran at full speed.* **3** an arrangement of gears to give a certain rate of movement. An automobile usually has three speeds forward and one backward. **4** *Baseball.* the ability of a pitcher to throw balls hard: *So many men are like the pitcher. Plenty of speed but poor control* (H. W. Raper). **5** *Archaic.* luck; success; prosperity: *The king wished us good speed* (Daniel Defoe). **6** *Slang.* methamphetamine: *The user tends to be nervous ... because the "speed" dries up the membranes of the nose and mouth, leaving an uncomfortable, itchy feeling* (Maclean's).

—*v.t.* **1** to make go fast; hasten: *to speed a horse. Let's all help speed the work.* **2** to send fast; hurry: *to speed reinforcements to the front.* **3** to help forward for further; promote: *to speed a bill through Congress, to speed an undertaking.* **4** to further the going or progress of: *Welcome the coming, speed the parting guest* (Alexander Pope). **5** to give a certain speed to (a machine or other mechanism). **6** *Archaic.* to give success or prosperity to: *God speed you.*

—*v.i.* **1** to go fast: *The boat sped over the water.* **2** to go faster than is safe or lawful: *The car sped by the school bus. The car was caught speeding near the school zone.* **3** *Archaic.* to succeed; prosper; thrive: *The affair speeds well.* **4** *Slang.* to use methamphetamine: *Heavy speeding invariably produces two psychic nightmares: hallucinations and paranoia* (New York Times Magazine).

**speed up,** to go or cause to go faster; increase in speed; accelerate: *The United States has agreed to speed up delivery of 36 F-104 Starfighters to Jordan* (Manchester Guardian Weekly).

[Old English *spēd* luck, success, advancement]

**speed|ball** (spēd′bôl′), *n. U.S.* **1** a game resembling soccer except that a ball caught in the air can be passed or thrown with the hands. **2** a fast ball pitched in baseball. **3** *Informal, Figurative.* a person who moves quickly: *When it comes to work around the house, she isn't exactly a speedball.* **4** *Slang.* a mixture of cocaine and another drug, especially heroin, morphine, or amphetamine.

**speed|ball|er** (spēd′bôl′ər), *n. U.S.* a fast baller.

**speed|boat** (spēd′bōt′), *n.* a motorboat built to go fast, especially for use on lakes and rivers.

**speed|boat|er** (spēd′bō′tər), *n.* a person who engages in speedboating.

**speed|boat|ing** (spēd′bō′ting), *n.* the act or sport of riding in a speedboat.

**speed brake,** any flap designed for slowing down an airplane in flight.

**speed counter** or **indicator,** any one of various devices for indicating the speed of an engine, such as a tachometer or speedometer.

**speed|cup** (spēd′kup′), *n.* a cuplike device to which the dial and pointer of a speedometer are attached.

**speed demon,** *Informal.* a speedster; one who enjoys moving at high speeds.

**speed|er** (spē′dər), *n.* a person or thing that speeds, especially a person who drives an automobile at a higher speed than is safe or lawful: *the judge's crackdown on speeders.*

**speed freak,** *U.S. Slang.* a person addicted to the use of amphetamines, especially methamphetamine.

**speed|i|ly** (spē′də lē), *adv.* with speed; quickly; soon; rapidly.

**speed|i|ness** (spē′dē nis), *n.* speedy quality; quickness; rapidity.

**speed limit,** the speed that a vehicle is forbidden by law or other regulation to exceed on a street, road, or highway, or part of it.

**speed midget,** a small flashbulb that produces an extremely bright light for a short time (about 1/200 of a second).

**speed|om|e|ter** (spē dom′ə tər), *n.* **1** an instrument to indicate the speed of an automobile or other vehicle. **2** a similar instrument for indicating distance traveled; odometer. **3** = tachometer. [< *speed* + *-meter*]

**speed-read** (spēd′rēd′), *v.t.,* **-read** (-red′), **-read·ing.** to read rapidly by taking in several words, phrases, or sentences at a glance: *I speed-read a detective novel and fall asleep by midnight* (New Yorker). [back formation < *speed reading*] —**speed′-read′er,** *n.*

**speed reading,** a method of reading rapidly by taking in several words, phrases, or sentences at a glance: *Speed reading has been adopted by many harried business executives and government officials as a cure-all for paperwork pile-ups* (New York Times).

**speed skating,** skating in competition, such as in a race against others or as a race against a set time limit.

**speed|ster** (spēd′stər), *n.* **1** a person who drives, flies, or otherwise goes at high or reckless speed; speeder: *The speedsters, who pass each other on the autobahns at seventy-five and eighty miles an hour, were responsible ... for a tragic 21.7 per cent increase in accidents* (New York Times). **2** a speedboat, racing car, or the like: *The new ... pleasure line will include a 14-foot outboard, a 17-foot sports speedster ... and a 25-foot deluxe cabin cruiser* (Wall Street Journal). **3** a very fast runner: *He watched speedsters ... place one-two in the 100-meter dash* (Newsweek).

**speed trap,** a section of a highway under surveillance by concealed patrolmen, electronic devices for measuring speed, or by aircraft, along which even slight infraction of the speed limit may be penalized.

**speed-up** or **speed|up** (spēd′up′), *n.* an increase in speed, as in some process or work: *Among the urgent areas for study, the report included ... speed-up of boarding and deplaning procedures* (Science News Letter).

**speed|walk** (spēd′wôk′), *n.* a conveyor belt on a level or slight incline used to transport passengers a short distance; moving platform or sidewalk: *The Merrion centre also has a speedwalk 66 feet long for carrying shoppers up to first floor level* (Manchester Guardian).

**speed|way** (spēd′wā′), *n.* **1** a highway for fast driving. **2** a track for motor racing: *Here is how they finished ... in the thirteenth annual 500-mile motor classic on the Indianapolis speedway yesterday* (Kansas City Star). [American English]

**speed|well** (spēd′wel), *n.* any one of various low plants with leafy stems and small blue, purple, pink, or white flowers; veronica. The speedwells comprise a genus of plants of the figwort family.

**Speed|writ|ing** (spēd′rī′ting), *n. Trademark.* a shorthand system using letters of the alphabet instead of symbols, in which words are written as they sound. *Examples: You* is written as *u, are* is written as *r,* and *eye* is written as *i.*

**speed|y** (spē′dē), *adj.,* **speed|i|er, speed|i|est. 1** moving, going, or acting with speed; swift: *speedy workers. Most of them* [*ponies*] *are small, wiry beasts, not very speedy* (Theodore Roosevelt). **2** done with or characterized by speed; rapid; fast: *a speedy flight, speedy progress.* **3** rapidly coming or brought to pass: *a speedy change.* **4** coming, given, or arrived at quickly or soon; prompt: *a speedy reply, a speedy decision.*

**speel** (spēl), *Scottish.* —*v.i.* to climb; clamber. —*v.t.* to climb (as a hill or tree): *Sma' heart hae I to speel the steep Parnassus* (Robert Burns). [origin uncertain]

**speer** or **speir** (spir), *Scottish.* —*v.i.* to make inquiries; ask: *Speer as little about him as he does about you* (Scott).

—*v.t.* **1a** to make inquiries about. **b** to ask for (advice). **c** to beg (leave). **2** to seek (out) by inquiry: *Oh that people would speer out Christ!* (Samuel Rutherford). Also, **spier.**

[Old English *spyrian* ask about; (originally) seek, follow (or make) a track]

**speiss** (spīs), *n.* an impure metallic compound of arsenic or antimony, often containing nickel, cobalt, or iron, produced in the smelting of certain ores. [< German *Speise* speiss; (originally) food < Vulgar Latin *spēsa* < Latin *expēnsa,* feminine past participle of *expendere* weigh out; expend]

**spe|le|an** or **spe|lae|an** (spi lē′ən), *adj.* **1** having to do with or like a cave: *spelean darkness.* **2** living in or frequenting caves. [< Latin *spēlaeum* cave (< Greek *spēlaion*) + English *-an*]

**spe|le|o|log|i|cal** or **spe|lae|o|log|i|cal** (spē′lē ə loj′ə kəl), *adj.* of or having to do with speleology.

**spe|le|ol|o|gist** or **spe|lae|ol|o|gist** (spē′lē ol′ə jist), *n.* an expert in speleology.

**spe|le|ol|o|gy** or **spe|lae|ol|o|gy** (spē′lē ol′ə jē), *n.* the scientific study of caves. [< French *spéléologie* < Greek *spēlaion* cave + French *-logie* -logy]

**spell**[1] (spel), *v.,* **spelled** or **spelt, spell|ing.** —*v.t.* **1** to say, write, or signal the letters of (a word or syllable) in order: *"Cat" is easy to spell; "phthisis" is difficult.* **2** (of letters) to make up or form (a word or syllable): *"K" "e" double "n" "e" "d" "y" spells Kennedy.* **3** *Figurative.* to amount to; mean: *Delay spells danger. Those clouds spell a storm. I'd like to talk about five important lessons ... which I feel have made me a better catcher. Any one of them can spell the vital difference in a game* (Del Crandall). **SYN:** signify, imply, involve. **4a** Often, **spell out.** to read very slowly or with difficulty; read letter by letter: *to spell out a message. You spell out the words when you read the newspaper still* (Thackeray). **b** to make (one's way) letter by letter in reading: *to spell one's way through a message.* **5** *Figurative.* to discover or make out by close study or observation: *to spell out the truth of a matter.* **SYN:** discern.

—*v.i.* to write or say the letters of a word or syllable in order: *We learn to spell in school. She cannot spell well. A foolish opinion ... that we ought to spell exactly as we speak* (Jonathan Swift).

**spell down,** *U.S.* to outdo in spelling; surpass in a spelling bee: *"I could beat the world spelling! I could spell everybody in this reunion down right now," she offered. "Give me a word"* (Eudora Welty).

**spell out,** to explain carefully, step by step, and in detail: *The Defense Department proposed a new set of rules that would spell out in greater detail the costs a manufacturer may pass along to the Government* (Wall Street Journal).

[< Old French *espeller* < Germanic (compare Old High German *spellōn* to tell). Compare etym. under **gospel.**]

**spell**[2] (spel), *n., v.,* **spelled, spell|ing.** —*n.* **1** a word or set of words supposed to have magical powers; charm; incantation: *I'm a dealer in magic and spells* (William S. Gilbert). **2** *Figurative.* a magic influence; power of charming or attracting; fascination: *A spell of mystery seemed to hang over the old castle. We were under the spell of the beautiful music.*

—*v.t.* to charm; bewitch.

**cast a spell on** (or **over**), **a** to put under the influence of a spell; hex: *The witch cast an evil spell on Sleeping Beauty.* **b** *Figurative.* to influence or have an effect on someone as if he were put under a spell; fascinate: *The magic of the beautiful ballet cast a spell over the audience.*

**under a spell, a** controlled by a spell. **b** *Figurative.* fascinated; spellbound: *The explorer's story held the children under a spell.*

[Old English *spell* story, discourse]

**spell**[3] (spel), *n., v.,* **spelled, spell|ing.** —*n.* **1** a period of work or duty: *The sailor's spell at the wheel was four hours.* **2** a period or time of anything; turn; bout: *a spell of crying. The child has spells of coughing. There was a long spell of rainy weather in April.* **3** *Informal.* a brief period: *to rest for a spell. You hold on ... for a spell, and I'll be back* (Bret Harte). **4** the relief of one person by another in doing something. **5** *U.S. Informal.* an attack or fit of illness or nervous excitement: *When Hepsy does get beat out she has spells, and she goes on awful* (Harriet Beecher Stowe). **6** *Australian.* a rest. [earlier, the relief gang, perhaps Old English *gespelia* a substitute; perhaps < verb]

—*v.t.* **1** *Informal.* to work in place of (another person) for a while; relieve: *I'll spell you at cutting the grass.* **2** to give a time of rest to; rest: *to spell a horse.*

—*v.i. Australian.* to take a time of rest.

[variant of Middle English *spelen,* Old English *spelian*]

**spell|bind** (spel′bīnd′), *v.t.,* **-bound, -bind|ing.** to make spellbound; fascinate; enchant.

**spell|bind|er** (spel′bīn′dər), *n. U.S.* a speaker who can hold his listeners spellbound.

**spell|bound** (spel′bound′), *adj.* too interested to move; bound by or as if by a spell; fascinated; enchanted; entranced: *The children were spellbound by the circus performance. There were moments when his wizardry held me spellbound* (New Yorker). [< *spell*[2] + *bound*[1]]

**spell|down** (spel′down′), *n. U.S.* a spelling bee.

**spell|er** (spel′ər), *n.* **1** a person who spells words: *a poor speller.* **2** a book for teaching spelling; spelling book.

**spell|ing** (spel′ing), *n.* **1** the writing or saying of the letters of a word in order: *He is poor at spelling.* **2** the way that a word is spelled: *"Ax" has two spellings, "ax" and "axe."* **3** manner of writing or expressing words with letters; orthography: *An instance of futile classicism ... is the conventional spelling of the English language* (Thorstein Veblen).

**spelling bee,** a contest in spelling. The winner is the person or side that spells the most words correctly.

**spelling book,** a book containing exercises or instructions in spelling; speller.

**spelling pronunciation,** a pronunciation influenced by the written form of a word. *Example: often* pronounced as (ôf′tin) because of the *t* in the spelling.

**spelling reform,** regulation of the spelling of the words of a language according to systematic principles, to secure greater uniformity or simplicity or a more satisfactory representation of the sound of the spoken words.

**spelt**[1] (spelt), *v.* spelled; a past tense and a past participle of **spell**[1].

**spelt**[2] (spelt), *n.* a species of wheat grown chiefly in Europe. It is now used mainly to develop new varieties of wheat. [Old English *spelt* < Late Latin *spelta*]

**spel|ter** (spel′tər), *n.* zinc, usually in the form of small bars. [origin uncertain. Compare Low German *spialter.*]

**spe|lunk|er** (spi lung′kər), *n.* a person who explores and maps caves as a hobby: *No spelunker with any respect for his own skill will venture into a perilous cave without ... a climbing rope* (New Yorker). [< Latin *spelunca* cave (< Greek *spêlaion*)]

**spe|lunk|ing** (spi lung′king), *n.* the act or hobby of exploring and mapping caves.

**spence** (spens), *n. Archaic or Dialect.* **1** a pantry. **2** a cupboard. Also, **spense.** [short for Old French *despense*]

**spen|cer**[1] (spen′sər), *n.* a short coat or jacket for men or women, usually knitted. [< George John *Spencer,* second Earl Spencer, 1758-1834]

**spen|cer**[2] (spen′sər), *n.* = trysail. [origin uncertain]

**Spen|ce|ri|an**[1] (spen sir′ē ən), *adj., n.* —*adj.* of or having to do with the English philosopher Herbert Spencer (1820-1903) or with Spencerianism. —*n.* a follower or adherent of Herbert Spencer or Spencerianism.

**Spen|ce|ri|an**[2] (spen sir′ē ən), *adj.* of or having to do with a style of handwriting characterized by rounded letters that slant to the right. [< Platt R. *Spencer,* 1800-1864, an American penmanship expert, who originated it + *-ian*]

**Spen|ce|ri|an|ism** (spen sir′ē ə niz′əm), *n.* the philosophical views of Herbert Spencer or his followers. The basic idea is that the universe and all its phenomena can be explained in terms of an evolutionary process that operates mechanistically according to the laws of science.

**spend** (spend), *v.,* **spent, spend|ing.** —*v.t.* **1** to pay out: *She spent ten dollars shopping for food today.* **2** to use (labor, material, thought, or some other resource) to some purpose; use: *Spend more time on that lesson. Why do you spend many words and speak in many ways on this subject?* (Benjamin Jowett). **3** to pass (as time or one's life) in a particular manner, occupation, or place: *to spend one's spare time reading. We spent last summer at the seashore. All his life had been spent confronting others with the truth about themselves* (Morris L. West). **4** to use up; exhaust or consume by use; wear out: *The storm has spent its force. He spends himself in foolish activities.* **5** to waste; squander: *He spent his fortune on horse racing.* **6** to lose, as for a cause: *To royalize his blood, I spent mine own* (Shakespeare).

—*v.i.* **1** to pay out money: *Earn before you spend.* **2** *Obsolete.* to be exhausted, consumed, or used up: *The sound spendeth, and is dissipated in the open air* (Francis Bacon).

[Middle English *spenden,* Old English *-spendan,* as in *forspendan* use up < Latin *expendere.* See etym. of doublet **expend.**] —**spend′er,** *n.*

—***Syn.*** *v.t.* **1 Spend, expend, disburse** mean to pay out money: *She spends all she earns.* **Expend** is used chiefly of paying out large amounts for definite and serious purposes: *The United States has expended vast sums to strengthen her allies.* **Disburse** implies the payment from a fund for definite purposes in authorized amounts: *The treasurer reports what he disburses.*

**spend|a|ble** (spen′də bəl), *adj.* capable of being spent: *Traveler's checks are safe and spendable anywhere* (New Yorker).

**spendable earnings** or **income,** the amount left to a worker after taxes, social security, and other payroll deductions have been taken from his pay; net earnings.

**spend|ing** (spen′ding), *n.* expenditure: *Federal spending has become the main issue on which the tax-cut vote in the House will turn next week* (Wall Street Journal).

**spending money,** money used or available for small, miscellaneous expenses; pocket money.

**spend|thrift** (spend′thrift′), *n., adj.* —*n.* a person who spends wastefully or extravagantly; prodigal: *Fie, what a spendthrift is he of his tongue* (Shakespeare).

—*adj.* wastefully extravagant; wasteful: *spendthrift ways.* **SYN:** improvident, thriftless.

**Speng|ler|i|an** (speng glir′ē ən), *adj., n.* —*adj.* of or having to do with the philosophy of Oswald Spengler (1880-1936) who interpreted the history of mankind as a series of cultures completing identical cycles, the last of eight cultures being Western civilization.

—*n.* a student or follower of Spengler's philosophy.

**spense** (spens), *n. Archaic or Dialect.* spence.

**Spen|se|ri|an** (spen sir′ē ən), *adj., n.* —*adj.* of, having to do with, or characteristic of the English poet Edmund Spenser (1552?-1599) or his work. —*n.* **1** a poet of the school of Spenser. **2** = Spenserian stanza. **3** a poem in the meter of the Spenserian stanza.

**Spenserian sonnet,** a sonnet in which the fourteen lines follow this special rhyme pattern: *ababbcbccdcdee.*

**Spenserian stanza,** the stanza used by Spenser in *The Faerie Queene,* consisting of eight iambic pentameter lines and a final alexandrine, with three rhymes arranged thus: *ababbcbcc.*

**spent** (spent), *v., adj.* —*v.* the past tense and past participle of **spend:** *Saturday was spent in playing. How have you spent your time today?* —***adj.*** **1** used up. **2** worn out; tired: *a spent swimmer, a spent horse.*

**spe|os** (spē′os), *n. Archaeology.* a temple or tomb excavated in solid rock. [< Greek *speos* cave]

**sper|ling** (spėr′ling), *n.* = sparling.

**sperm**[1] (spėrm), *n., pl.* **sperm** or **sperms. 1** the fluid of a male that fertilizes the eggs of the female; semen. **2** one of the sperm cells in the semen; spermatozoon. [< Late Latin *sperma* < Greek *spérma, -atos* seed < *speirein* to sow[1]]

**sperm**[2] (spėrm), *n.* **1** = spermaceti. **2** = sperm whale. **3** = sperm oil. [short for *spermaceti*]

**sper|ma|cet|i** (spėr′mə set′ē, -sē′tē), *n.* a pale or whitish, waxy substance obtained from the oil in the head of the sperm whale and used in making fine candles, ointments, and cosmetics. [< Medieval Latin *sperma ceti* sperm of a whale < Late Latin *sperma* sperm[1], seed, and Latin *cētus* large sea animal < Greek *kêtos*]

**sper|ma|duct** (spėr′mə dukt), *n.* an organ conveying sperm; a spermatic duct. [< New Latin *spermaductus* < Late Latin *sperma* sperm[1] + Latin *ductus* duct]

**sper|ma|go|ni|um** (spėr′mə gō′nē əm), *n., pl.* **-ni|a** (-nē ə). = spermogonium.

**sper|ma|ry** (spėr′mər ē), *n., pl.* **-ries.** the organ or gland in which spermatozoa are generated in male animals; testis. [< New Latin *spermarium* < Late Latin *sperma;* see etym. under **sperm**[1]]

**sper|ma|the|ca** (spėr′mə thē′kə), *n., pl.* **-cae** (-sē). a receptacle in the oviduct of many female invertebrates, for receiving and holding spermatozoa. [< Late Latin *sperma* (see etym. under **sperm**[1]) + Greek *thēkē* receptacle]

**sper|ma|the|cal** (spėr′mə thē′kəl), *adj.* of or having to do with a spermatheca.

**sper|mat|ic** (spėr mat′ik), *adj.* **1** of or having to do with sperm; seminal; generative. **2** containing, conveying, or producing sperm or seed; seminiferous. **3** of or having to do with a sperm-producing gland.

**spermatic cord,** the cord by which the testicle is suspended within the scrotum, enclosing the vas deferens, the blood vessels and nerves of the testicle, and extending to the groin.

**spermatic fluid,** = semen.

**sper|ma|tid** (spėr′mə tid), *n.* a cell that develops into a spermatozoon. It results from the meiotic division of a secondary spermatocyte.

**sper|ma|ti|um** (spėr mā′shē əm), *n., pl.* **-ti|a** (-shē ə). **1** the nonmotile male gamete that fuses with the carpogonium of the red algae. **2** one of the tiny, cylindrical or rod-shaped bodies in certain lichens and fungi that are produced like spores in spermogonia. The spermatia are conjectured to be the male fertilizing organs. [< New Latin *spermatium* < Greek *spermátion* (diminutive) < *spérma* sperm[1], seed]

**spermato-,** *combining form.* seed; sperm: *Spermatocyte = a germ cell that produces spermatozoa. Spermatophyte = a plant that produces seeds.* [< Greek *spérma, -atos* sperm[1]]

**sper|mat|o|cid|al** (spėr mat′ə sī′dəl, spėr′mə tə-), *adj.* of or having to do with spermatocides.

**sper|mat|o|cide** (spėr mat′ə sīd, spėr′mə tə-), *n.* a substance that kills spermatozoa.

**sper|mat|o|cyte** (spėr mat′ə sīt, spėr′mə tə-), *n.* a germ cell that gives rise to spermatozoids or to spermatozoa. A primary spermatocyte divides by meiosis to form two secondary spermatocytes which, in turn, undergo meiosis to form spermatids which are converted into spermatozoa.

**sper|mat|o|gen|e|sis** (spėr mat′ə jen′ə sis, spėr′mə tə-), *n.* the formation and development of spermatozoa.

**sper|mat|o|ge|net|ic** (spėr mat′ō jə net′ik, spėr′mə tō-), *adj.* of or having to do with spermatogenesis.

**sper|mat|o|gen|ic** (spėr mat′ə jen′ik, spėr′mə tə-), *adj.* = spermatogenetic.

**sper|ma|tog|e|nous** (spėr′mə toj′ə nəs), *adj.* producing spermatozoa.

**sper|mat|o|go|ni|al** (spėr mat′ə gō′nē əl; spėr′mə tə-), *adj.* of or having to do with a spermatogonium or spermatogonia.

**sper|mat|o|go|ni|um** (spėr mat′ə gō′nē əm, spėr′mə tə-), *n., pl.* **-ni|a** (-nē ə). **1** a primitive germ cell that divides and gives rise to spermatocytes. **2** = spermogonium. [< New Latin *spermatogonium* < Greek *spérma, -atos* seed + a root *gen-* to bear]

**sper|ma|toid** (spėr′mə toid), *adj.* like sperm.

**sper|ma|toph|o|ral** (spėr′mə tof′ər əl), *adj.* of or having to do with a spermatophore.

**sper|mat|o|phore** (spėr mat′ə fôr, spėr′mə tə-; -fōr), *n.* a capsule or case containing many spermatozoa, produced by the male of many insects, mollusks, annelids, and some vertebrate animals.

**sper|ma|toph|o|rous** (spėr′mə tof′ə rəs), *adj.* = spermatophoral.

**sper|mat|o|phyte** (spėr mat′ə fīt, spėr′mə tə-), *n.* any one of a large group of plants that produce seeds. The spermatophytes are the most highly developed plants and form the largest division of the plant kingdom. They are divided into two groups, the angiosperms and the gymnosperms. Also, **spermophyte.**

**sper|mat|o|phyt|ic** (spėr mat′ə fit′ik, spėr′mə tə-), *adj.* of or having to do with a spermatophyte.

**sper|ma|tor|rhe|a** or **sper|ma|tor|rhoe|a** (spėr′mə tə rē′ə), *n.* an involuntary and frequent discharge of semen without orgasm. [< *spermato-* + Greek *rheîn* flow]

**sper|ma|to|zo|al** (spėr′mə tə zō′əl), *adj.* **1** of or having to do with spermatozoa. **2** like a spermatozoon.

**sper|ma|to|zo|an** (spėr′mə tə zō′ən), *adj.* = spermatozoal.

**sper|ma|to|zo|ic** (spėr′mə tə zō′ik), *adj.* = spermatozoal.

**sper|ma|to|zo|id** (spėr′mə tə zō′id), *n. Botany.* one of the tiny motile male gametes produced in an antheridium by which the female organs are fertilized; antherozoid. [< *spermatozo*(on) + New Latin *-id,* a suffix meaning "belonging to"]

**sper|ma|to|zo|oid** (spėr′mə tə zō′oid), *n.* = spermatozoid.

***sper|ma|to|zo|on** or **sper|ma|to|zo|ön** (spėr′mə tə zō′ən), *n., pl.* **-zo|a** (-zō′ə). a male reproductive cell; sperm cell. A typical spermatozoon has a head, neck, and long, threadlike tail. [< *spermato-* + Greek *zôion* animal]

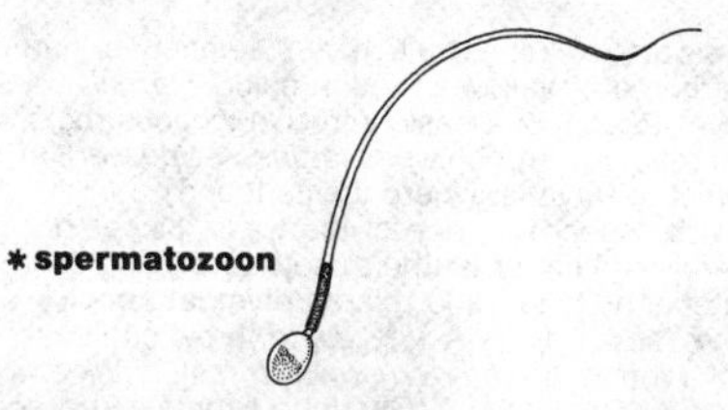

***spermatozoon**

**sperm cell, 1** the reproductive cell produced by a male animal; male germ cell. A sperm cell unites with an egg cell to fertilize it. **2** = spermatozoid.

**sper|mic** (spėr′mik), *adj.* of or having to do with sperm or seed.

**sper|mi|cid|al** (spėr′mə sī′dəl), *adj.* = spermatocidal.

**sper|mi|cide** (spėr′mə sīd), *n.* = spermatocide.

**sper|mi|dine** (spėr′mə dēn, -din), *n.* a crystalline basic substance found in semen and in some animal tissues: *Substances in sperm which have been reported to kill bacteria are spermine and spermidine, both of which are nitrogenous bases* (London Times). *Formula:* $C_7H_{19}N_3$

**sper|mine** (spėr′mēn, -min), *n.* a crystalline basic substance found in semen, sputum, yeast, and other substances. *Formula:* $C_{10}H_{26}N_4$

**sper|mi|o|gen|e|sis** (spėr′mē ō jen′ə sis), *n.* the production of sperm or spermatozoa.

**sper|mo|go|ni|um** (spėr′mə gō′nē əm), *n., pl.* **-ni|a** (-nē ə). one of the cup-shaped cavities or receptacles in which the spermatia of certain lichens and fungi are produced; spermatogonium. Also, **spermagonium.** [< New Latin *spermogonium* < Greek *spérma* seed + a root *gen-* to bear]

**sperm oil,** a light-yellow oil from the head of the sperm whale, used for lubricating delicate mechanisms.

**sper|mo|phile** (spėr′mə fīl, -fil), *n.* any one of various squirrellike burrowing rodents, including the ground squirrels and certain related forms that do much damage to crops. [< New Latin *spermophilus* < Greek *spérma* seed + *philos* loving]

**sper|mo|phyte** (spėr′mə fīt), *n.* = spermatophyte.

**sper|mous** (spėr′məs), *adj.* of or like sperm; spermatic.

**sperm whale,** a large, toothed whale with a

**Pronunciation Key:** hat, āge, cãre, fär; let, ēqual, tėrm; it, īce; hot, ōpen, ôrder; oil, out; cup, pu̇t, rüle; child; long; thin; ᴛʜen; zh, measure; ə represents **a** in about, **e** in taken, **i** in pencil, **o** in lemon, **u** in circus.

square head; cachalot. The sperm whale has a large cavity in its head filled with sperm oil and spermaceti. It sometimes forms ambergris in its alimentary canal.

**sper|ry|lite** (sper′ē līt), *n.* a mineral, an arsenide of platinum, occurring in minute, silvery white, isometric crystals. It is the only compound of platinum known to occur in nature. *Formula:* $PtAs_2$ [< Francis L. *Sperry,* a Canadian scientist of the 1800's, who discovered it near Sudbury, Ontario + *-lite*]

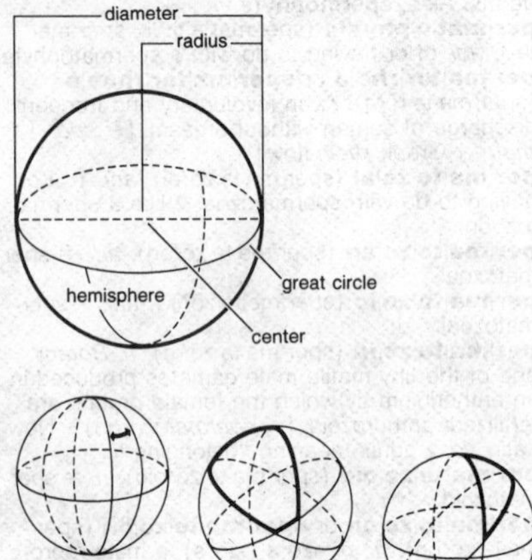


***sphere**
definition 1a

**spes|sart|ite** (spes′ər tīt), *n.* **1** a variety of garnet that is red or yellowish-red in color. *Formula:* $Mn_3Al_2(SiO_4)_3$ **2** a basic intrusive igneous rock. [alteration of French *spessartine* < *Spessart,* a district in Bavaria, where it was found]

**spetch** (spech), *n.* one of the waste pieces or parings of hide or leather, used for making such material as glue. [see related etym. at **speck**]

**spew** (spyü), *v., n.* —*v.t., v.i.* to throw out; cast forth; vomit: *A crater-crust which may crack and spew fire any day ...* (Charlotte Brontë). *The encampment began to spew out men* (H. G. Wells). —*n.* something that is spewed; vomit. Also, **spue.** [Old English *spīwan*] —**spew′er,** *n.*

**spew|y** (spyü′ē), *adj.,* **spew|i|er, spew|i|est.** exuding moisture; wet or moist: *spewy ground.*

**sp. gr.,** specific gravity.

**sphac|e|late** (sfas′ə lāt), *v.t., v.i.,* **-lat|ed, -lat|ing.** to affect or be affected with gangrene; mortify. [< New Latin *sphacelare* (with English *-ate*[1]) < *sphacelus;* see etym. under **sphacelus**] —**sphac′e|la′tion,** *n.*

**sphac|e|lus** (sfas′ə ləs), *n.* **1** a gangrenous or mortified tissue or part; slough. **2** gangrene; mortification. [< New Latin *sphacelus* < Greek *sphákelos*]

**sphag|nous** (sfag′nəs), *adj.* **1** consisting of or like sphagnum. **2** producing sphagnum; full of sphagnum.

**sphag|num** (sfag′nəm), *n.* **1** any one of a genus of soft mosses, found chiefly in boggy or swampy places, which, when decomposed and compacted, form peat. Sphagnum is one kind of peat moss. **2** a mass or quantity of this moss used by florists in potting and packing plants and in surgery for making dressings for wounds. [< New Latin *sphagnum* < Latin, a kind of moss < Greek *sphágnos* a spiny shrub]

**sphal|er|ite** (sfal′ə rīt, sfā′lə-), *n.* the main ore of zinc, a native zinc sulfide, occurring both crystalline and massive; blende; zinc blende; blackjack. *Formula:* ZnS [< Greek *sphalerós* deceptive, slippery (< *sphállein* overthrow, baffle)]

**sphene** (sfēn), *n.* the mineral titanite, especially in its yellowish or greenish variety. [< French *sphène* < Greek *sphēn, sphēnós* a wedge (because of its crystalline shape)]

**sphe|nic** (sfē′nik), *adj.* = wedge-shaped.

**sphe|no|don** (sfē′nə don), *n.* a lizardlike reptile native to New Zealand; tuatara. It is the only remaining rhynchocephalian and has much in common with the forerunners of present-day reptiles. [< New Latin *Sphenodon* the genus name < Greek *sphēn* wedge + *odoús, odóntos* tooth]

**sphe|no|graph|ic** (sfē′nə graf′ik), *adj.* of or having to do with sphenography.

**sphe|nog|ra|phy** (sfē nog′rə fē), *n.* the study and description of cuneiform writings. [< Greek *sphēn* a wedge + English *-graphy*]

**sphe|noid** (sfē′noid), *adj., n.* —*adj.* **1** wedge-shaped: *a sphenoid crystal.* **2** of or having to do with a compound bone of the base of the skull. —*n.* this bone. [< New Latin *sphenoides* < Greek *sphēnoeidês* < *sphên* wedge + *eîdos* form]

**sphe|noi|dal** (sfi noi′dəl), *adj.* = sphenoid.

**spher|al** (sfir′əl), *adj.* **1** = spherical. **2** symmetrically rounded, or perfect: *The poet, whose verses are to be spheral and complete ...* (Emerson).

**sphe|ral|i|ty** (sfi ral′ə tē), *n.* spheral or spherical quality or state; sphericality.

**spher|a|tor** (sfir′ā tər), *n.* a device in which highly ionized gas is confined by a magnetic field produced by a current in a superconducting ring: *A sperator ... has a single ring inside a current-carrying elliptical chamber* (Ernest P. Gray). [< *sphere* + *-ator,* as in *stellarator*]

***sphere** (sfir), *n., v.,* **sphered, spher|ing.** —*n.* **1a** a round body whose surface is at all points equally distant from the center. See diagram opposite. **b** any rounded body approximately of this form; ball; globe. A baseball is a sphere. **2** one of the stars or planets. The earth, sun, and moon are spheres. **3** the place or surroundings in which a person or thing exists, acts, or works: *A teacher's sphere is the classroom. People used to say that woman's sphere was the home.* **4** extent; region: *a sphere of interest. Extending principles which belong altogether to building, into the sphere of architecture proper* (John Ruskin). **5** a place, position, or rank in society: *the sphere of the aristocracy.* **6** a supposed hollow globe, with the earth at its center, enclosing the stars, sun, and planets; celestial sphere. **7a** any one of a series of such globes, one inside another, in which the stars and planets were supposed by ancient astronomers to be set. Movement of the spheres was believed to cause the stars and planets to revolve around the earth and produce a harmonious sound known as the music of the spheres. **b** the particular sphere occupied by each of the fixed stars and planets. **8** the heavens; the sky.
—*v.t.* **1** to enclose in or as if in a sphere; encircle; surround: *Mourners, sphered by their dark garb in a sacred and touching solitude ...* (William R. Alger). **2** to make into a sphere. **3** to place among the heavenly spheres; set aloft: *But thou art as a planet sphered above* (Shelley).
[< Late Latin *sphēra,* in Latin *sphaera* < Greek *sphaîra*] —**sphere′less,** *adj.* —**sphere′like′,** *adj.*

**sphere of influence, 1** a small and usually underdeveloped nation or geographical area over which a powerful nation exercises economic or political control or influence: *Southeast Asia is conceded to be Peking's natural sphere of influence* (New York Times). **2** such economic or political control or influence: *[Several nations] are thought here to be ... opposing Washington's effort to retain a sphere of influence in Southeast Asia* (New York Times).

**spher|ic** (sfer′ik), *adj.* spherical: **a** = globular. **b** formed in or on a sphere. **c** of or having to do with a sphere or spheres.

**spher|i|cal** (sfer′ə kəl), *adj.* **1** shaped like a sphere; globular. **2** formed in or on a sphere: *spherical lines or figures.* **3** of or having to do with a sphere or spheres; dealing with the properties of the sphere or spherical figures. **4** of or having to do with the heavenly spheres. **5** *Astrology.* planetary. —**spher′i|cal|ly,** *adv.*

**spherical aberration,** *Optics.* aberration of rays of light resulting in a blurred or indistinct image, and arising from the spherical shape of the lens or mirror: *Spherical aberration is found in all lenses bounded by spherical surfaces. The marginal portions of the lens bring rays of light to a shorter focus than the central region* (Scientific American).

***spherical angle,** *Geometry.* an angle formed by two intersecting arcs of great circles of a sphere.

**spherical geometry,** the branch of geometry that deals with figures formed on the surface of a sphere.

**spher|i|cal|i|ty** (sfer′ə kal′ə tē), *n.* spherical state or form.

***spherical polygon,** *Geometry.* a polygon formed on the surface of a sphere by arcs of great circles.

**spherical sailing,** the plotting of a ship's course in which allowance is made for the arc of the earth's curvature.

***spherical triangle,** *Geometry.* a triangle formed on the surface of a sphere by intersecting arcs of three great circles.

**spherical trigonometry,** the trigonometry of spherical triangles.

**sphe|ric|i|ty** (sfi ris′ə tē), *n., pl.* **-ties.** spherical form or quality; roundness.

**spher|ics**[1] (sfer′iks), *n.* the study of figures, such as circles and triangles, formed on the surface of a sphere, comprising spherical geometry and trigonometry.

**spher|ics**[2] (sfer′iks), *n.* the study and detection of distant atmospheric disturbances by electronic instruments. Also, **sferics.** [< (atmo)*spheric* + *-s*[1]]

**spher|i|form** (sfir′ə fôrm), *adj.* formed or existing as a sphere; spherical.

**sphe|roid** (sfir′oid), *n., adj.* —*n.* a body shaped somewhat like a sphere, but not perfectly round, especially one formed by the revolution of an ellipse about one of its axes.
—*adj.* = spheroidal.

**sphe|roi|dal** (sfi roi′dəl), *adj.* **1** shaped somewhat like a sphere: *a spheroidal galaxy.* **2** having to do with a spheroid or spheroids. —**sphe|roi′dal|ly,** *adv.*

**sphe|roi|dic|i|ty** (sfir′oi dis′ə tē), *n.* the quality or state of being spheroidal.

**sphe|rom|e|ter** (sfi rom′ə tər), *n.* an instrument for measuring the curvature of spheres and curved surfaces. [< French *sphéromètre* < Greek *sphaîra* sphere + French *-mètre* -meter]

**spher|o|plast** (sfer′ə plast), *n.* a bacterial cell that has lost most or all of its cell wall.

**spher|u|lar** (sfer′ů lər), *adj.* **1** having the form of a spherule; resembling a spherule. **2** of or having to do with spherulites; spherulitic.

**spher|ule** (sfer′ül), *n.* a small sphere or spherical body.
[< Late Latin *sphērula* (diminutive) < *sphēra* sphere]

**spher|u|lite** (sfer′ů līt), *n.* a small, spherical, concretionary mass formed in certain igneous rocks. [< Late Latin *sphērula* (see etym. under **spherule**) + English *-ite*[1]]

**spher|u|lit|ic** (sfer′ů lit′ik), *adj.* **1** of or containing spherulites. **2** like a spherulite.

**spher|u|li|tize** (sfer′ə lə tīz), *v.t.,* **-tized, -tiz|ing.** to change into spherulites; cause to assume a spherulitic form.

**spher|y** (sfir′ē), *adj.,* **spher|i|er, spher|i|est. 1** = spherical. **2** like a heavenly body; starlike.

**sphex** (sfeks), *n.* any one of a group of large digging or burrowing wasps. [< New Latin *Sphex* the genus name < Greek *sphêx* wasp]

**sphinc|ter** (sfingk′tər), *n.* a ringlike muscle that surrounds an opening or passage of the body, and can contract to close it. [< Late Latin *sphincter* < Greek *sphinktēr* < *sphíngein* to squeeze, bind]

**sphinc|ter|al** (sfingk′tər əl), *adj.* of or like a sphincter.

**sphin|gid** (sfin′jid), *n., adj.* —*n.* any moth of a group including the sphinx, sphinx moth, or hawk moth.
—*adj.* of or belonging to this group.
[< New Latin *Sphingidae* the family name < Latin *sphinx;* see etym. under **Sphinx**]

**sphin|go|lip|id** (sfing′gō lip′id, -lī′pid), *n.* any one of a class of lipids that yield sphingosine upon hydrolysis. [< *shingo*(sine) + *lipid*]

**sphin|go|my|e|lin** (sfing′gō mī′ə lin), *n.* any one of a class of phosphatides found in the brain, kidney, liver, and some other organs, consisting of choline, sphingosine, phosphoric acid, and a fatty acid. [< Greek *sphíngein* squeeze, bind + English *myelin*]

**sphin|go|sine** (sfing′gə sēn, -sin), *n.* a basic amino alcohol found in sphingomyelin and cerebroside. [< *sphingo*(myelin) + (cerebro)*si*(de) + *-ine*[2]]

***Sphinx** (sfingks), *n.* **1** a huge stone statue with a man's head and a lion's body, near Cairo, Egypt. **2** *Greek Mythology.* a monster with the head of a woman, the body of a lion, and wings. The Sphinx proposed a riddle to every passer-by and killed those unable to guess it. [< Latin *Sphinx* < Greek *Sphínx, Sphingós sphíngein* squeeze, bind]

***Sphinx**
definitions 1, 2

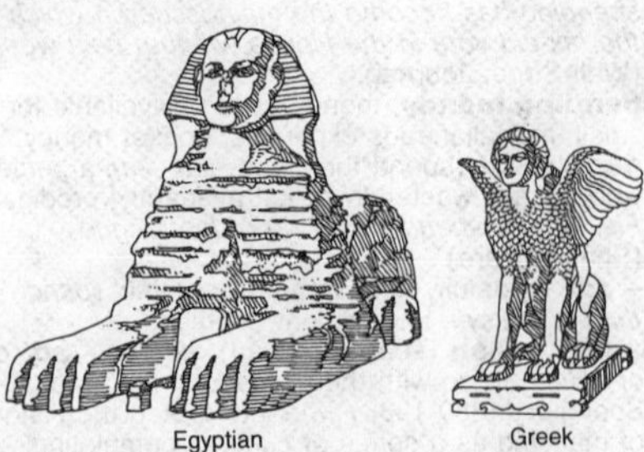


**sphinx** (sfingks), *n., pl.* **sphinx|es, sphin|ges** (sfin′jēz). **1** a statue of a lion's body with the head of a man, ram, or hawk. Egyptian sphinxes usually have male heads and wingless bodies; in the Greek type the head is female and the body winged. **2** *Figurative.* a puzzling, mysterious person. SYN: enigma. **3** = hawk moth. [< *Sphinx*] —**sphinx′like′,** *adj.*

**sphinx moth**, = hawk moth.
**sphrag|ide** (sfraj′id), *n.* = Lemnian earth. [< Greek *sphrāgís, -îdos* seal, Lemnian earth bearing the seal of the priestess of Lemnos]
**sphra|gis|tic** (sfrə jis′tik), *adj.* of or having to do with engraved seals or signet rings. [< Greek *sphrāgistós* stamped with the public seal (< *sphrāgís, -îdos* seal, signet) + English *-ic*]
**sp. ht.**, specific heat.
**sphyg|mic** (sfig′mik), *adj.* of or having to do with the pulse. [< New Latin *sphygmicus* < Greek *sphygmikós* < *sphygmós* pulse[1]; see etym. under **sphygmus**]
**sphygmo-**, *combining form.* the pulse; pulsation: *Sphygmograph = an instrument that records pulse beats.* [< Greek *sphygmós* throbbing, heartbeat; see etym. under **sphygmus**]
**sphyg|mo|gram** (sfig′mə gram), *n.* a diagram of the pulse beats recorded by a sphygmograph.
**sphyg|mo|graph** (sfig′mə graf, -gräf), *n.* an instrument that records characteristics of a pulse, such as the rate and strength, by means of tracings; pulsimeter.
**sphyg|mo|graph|ic** (sfig′mə graf′ik), *adj.* of or by a sphygmograph.
**sphyg|moid** (sfig′moid), *adj.* resembling the pulse; pulselike.
***sphyg|mo|ma|nom|e|ter** (sfig′mō mə nom′ə tər), *n.* an instrument for measuring blood pressure, especially in an artery. [< *sphygmo-* + Greek *manós* at intervals + English *-meter*]

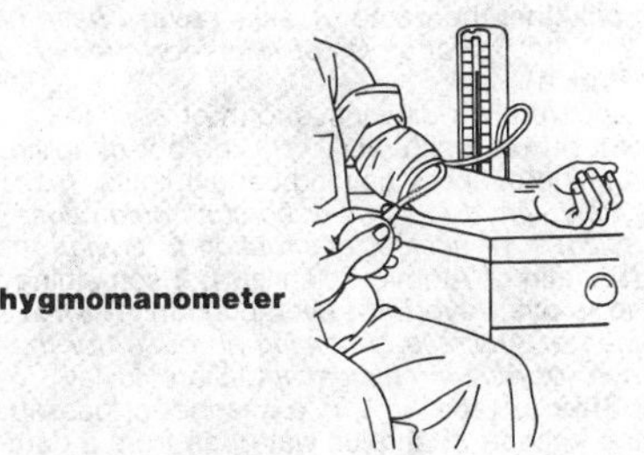
***sphygmomanometer**

**sphyg|mom|e|ter** (sfig mom′ə tər), *n.* = sphygmomanometer.
**sphyg|mo|phone** (sfig′mə fōn), *n.* an instrument that makes pulse beats audible.
**sphyg|mo|scope** (sfig′mə skōp), *n.* an instrument that makes pulse beats visible.
**sphyg|mus** (sfig′məs), *n.* = pulse[1] (def. 1). [< New Latin *sphygmus* < Greek *sphygmós* pulse[1]; a throbbing < *sphýzein* to beat, throb]
**spi|ca** (spī′kə), *n., pl.* **-cae** (-sē). **1** *Botany.* a spike. **2** *Surgery.* a spiral bandage with reversed turns. [< Latin *spīca* spike[2]. See etym. of doublet **spike**[2].]
**Spi|ca** (spī′kə), *n.* a very bright star in the constellation Virgo: *Follow the curve of the Dipper's handle through Arcturus to Spica* (Zim and Baker). [< Latin *Spīca* (originally) spike[2]]
**spic-and-span** (spik′ən span′), *adj.* = spick-and-span: ... *handsome men and beautiful women, with their spic-and-span, smiling children* (Edmund Wilson).
**spi|cate** (spī′kāt), *adj.* **1** *Botany.* **a** having spikes: *a spicate plant.* **b** arranged in spikes: *a spicate flower.* **2** *Zoology.* having the form of a spike; pointed: *a spicate appendage.* [< Latin *spīcātus,* past participle of *spīcāre* furnish with spikes < *spīca* spike[2]; see etym. under **spica**]
**spic|ca|to** (spi kä′tō), *adj., n., pl.* **-tos**. *Music.* —*adj.* separate; distinct; played with short, springing movements of the bow, achieving a staccato effect (a direction for violins, and other stringed instruments played with a bow, marked with dots or little wedges above or below notes): *The scherzo ... allowed Mr. Campoli to unfold long stretches of the most prodigious spiccato bowing* (London Times).
—*n.* a spiccato movement or passage: *a bow technique that encompasses remarkable pianissimos, cascading spiccatos* (New Yorker).
[< Italian *spiccato,* (literally) past participle of *spiccare* to detach < *picco* peak]
**spice** (spīs), *n., v.,* **spiced, spic|ing.** —*n.* **1a** any one of various seasonings obtained from plants, used to flavor or preserve food. Pepper, cinnamon, cloves, ginger, and nutmeg are common spices. **b** such substances considered collectively or as a material: *The dead ... with precious gums and spice fragrant, and incorruptibly preserved* (Robert Southey). **2** a spicy, fragrant odor. **3** *Figurative.* something that adds flavor or interest: *"Variety is the spice of life."* **4** *Figurative.* a slight touch or trace: *The world loves a spice of wickedness* (Longfellow).
—*v.t.* **1** to put a spice or spices in; season: *to spice peach jam.* **2** *Figurative.* to add flavor or interest to: *The principal spiced his speech with stories and jokes. ... days of adventure, all the pleasanter for being spiced with danger* (W. H. Hudson).
[< Old French *espice, espece,* learned borrowings from Latin *speciēs* kind, sort; produce, especially spices. See etym. of doublet **species**.]
—**spice′less**, *adj.*
**spice|ber|ry** (spīs′ber′ē, -bər-), *n., pl.* **-ries**. **1** the North American wintergreen; checkerberry. **2** a small tree of the myrtle family, grown in Florida and the West Indies for its edible, blackish or orange fruit.
**spice box**, a box for holding spices, especially a box enclosing several smaller boxes for holding the various spices used in cooking.
**spice|bush** (spīs′bu̇sh′), *n.* a North American shrub of the laurel family, with small yellow flowers that bloom in early spring and spicy-smelling bark and leaves.
**spicebush swallowtail**, = troilus butterfly.
**spice cake**, a cake flavored with a mixture of spices.
**spiced** (spīst), *adj.* **1** seasoned or flavored with spice: *spiced apples, spiced ham.* **2** *Figurative.* fragrant as if with spice; spicy: *spiced groves of ceaseless verdure* (Herman Melville).
**spic|er|y** (spī′sər ē), *n., pl.* **-er|ies**. **1** spices. **2** spicy flavor or fragrance: *The pine forest exhaled the fresher spicery* (Bret Harte). **3** *Obsolete.* a room or part of a house for keeping spices. [< Old French *espicerie* < *espice;* see etym. under **spice**]
**spice tree**, an evergreen tree of the laurel family, growing in Oregon and California, with aromatic leaves and a hard brown wood used in furniture and building.
**spice|wood** (spīs′wu̇d′), *n.* = spicebush.
**spi|ci|form** (spī′sə fôrm), *adj.* having the form of a spike. [< Latin *spīca* (see etym. under **spica**) + English *-form*]
**spic|i|ly** (spī′sə lē), *adv.* in a spicy manner; piquantly.
**spic|i|ness** (spī′sē nis), *n.* spicy flavor or smell.
**spick-and-span** (spik′ən span′), *adj.* **1** neat and clean; spruce or smart; trim: *a spick-and-span room, apron, or uniform.* **2** fresh or new; brand-new. [short for earlier *spick-and-span-new* new as a recently made spike and chip; *spick,* variant of *spike*[1]; *span-new* < Scandinavian (compare Old Icelandic *spān-nȳr* < *spānn* chip + *nȳr* new)]
**spi|cose** (spī′kōs), *adj.* = spicous.
**spi|cos|i|ty** (spī kos′ə tē), *n.* the state of being spicous.
**spi|cous** (spī′kəs), *adj. Botany.* having spikes or ears like corn. [< New Latin *spicosus* < Latin *spīca* spike, ear]
**spic|u|la**[1] (spik′yə lə) *n., pl.* **-lae** (-lē). **1** = spicule. **2** a sharp-pointed crystal, especially of frost or ice. [< New Latin *spicula,* variant of Latin *spīculum* (diminutive) < *spīca;* see etym. under **spica**]
**spic|u|la**[2] (spik′yə lə), *n.* plural of **spiculum**.
**spic|u|lar** (spik′yə lər), *adj.* = spiculate.
**spic|u|late** (spik′yə lāt, -lit), *adj.* **1** having, consisting of, or covered with spicules. **2** like a spicule; slender and sharp-pointed. [< New Latin *spiculatus,* past participle of *spiculare* provide with a spicula; see etym. under **spicula**[1]]
**spic|u|la|tion** (spik′yə lā′shən), *n.* formation into a spicule or spicules.
**spic|ule** (spik′yül), *n.* **1** a small, slender, sharp-pointed piece, usually bony or crystalline. **2** one of such pieces that form the skeleton of a sponge. **3** a small spike of flowers; spikelet. **4** a small solar prominence. [< Latin *spīculum;* see etym. under **spiculum**]
**spic|u|lif|er|ous** (spik′yə lif′ər əs), *adj.* bearing spicules or spicula. [< Latin *spīculum* + English *-ferous*]
**spic|u|li|form** (spik′yə lə fôrm), *adj.* formed like a spicule; sharp-pointed.
**spic|u|lum** (spik′yə ləm), *n., pl.* **-la**. *Zoology.* **1** a sharp-pointed process or formation, as a spine of an echinoderm. **2** = spicule. [< Latin *spīculum* sharp point, dart (diminutive) < *spīca* spica]
**spic|y** (spī′sē), *adj.,* **spic|i|er, spic|i|est**. **1** flavored with spice: *The cookies were rich and spicy.* **2** like spice; sharp and fragrant: *Those apples have a spicy smell and taste.* **SYN:** aromatic. **3** *Figurative.* lively and keen; spirited: *spicy conversation full of gossip.* **4** *Figurative.* somewhat improper or indelicate: *a spicy joke.* **SYN:** salacious. **5** producing spices; rich in spices: *on India's spicy shores* (William Cowper).
**spi|der** (spī′dər), *n.* **1a** a small animal with eight legs and no wings. Spiders belong to the class of arachnids. Most kinds produce a silky thread for spinning webs to catch insects for food, and for making cocoons and nests. **b** any one of various similar arachnids, such as a harvestman (daddy longlegs). **2** *Figurative: He was one of the kind sports call a spider, All wiry arms and legs* (Robert Frost). **3** a kind of frying pan, originally one with short legs. **4** *U.S.* a frame with three legs to support a pot or pan over a fire. **5** a device for pulverizing the soil, to be attached to a cultivator. **6** a highly flexible fiber ring which centers the voice coil of a loudspeaker. [Middle English *spither,* unrecorded Old English *spīthra* < *spinnan* to spin] —**spi′der|like′**, *adj.*
**spider bug**, a heteropterous insect of the United States having a very slender body with threadlike middle and hind legs, and spinous forelegs adapted for seizing; stick bug.
***spider crab**, any one of a group of crabs having long legs and retractable eyes, as a common variety found along the Atlantic coast of the United States, and the giant crab of Japan. See picture below.
**spider hole**, *U.S. Military Slang.* a hole in the ground concealing a sniper.
**spi|der|let** (spī′dər lit), *n.* = spiderling.
**spider line**, one of the threads of a spider's web used in forming the cross hairs of a telescope or the like.
**spi|der|ling** (spī′dər ling), *n.* a little or young spider.
**spi|der|man** (spī′dər man′, -mən), *n., pl.* **-men**. *Especially British.* a construction worker who erects the steel framework of a tall building: *The four wings, assembled by competing teams of French and Belgian spidermen, are suspended from giant steel girders* (Sunday Times).
**spider mite**, any one of various mites parasitic on insects, birds, and other animals, and on plants.
**spider monkey**, any one of a genus of monkeys of South and Central America, having a long, slim body and limbs, a long, prehensile tail, and rudimentary thumbs or none at all.
***spider orchid**, a European orchid with small brown flowers resembling a spider in shape.
**spider phaeton**, a lightweight, high carriage with a rear seat for a footman and a closed seat in front.
**spider plant**, = spiderwort.
**spider wasp**, any wasp which stores its nest with spiders for its young.
**spider web**, or **spi|der|web** (spī′dər web′), *n.* **1** the web spun by a spider; cobweb. **2** *Figurative.* any design or construction of interwoven lines or parts similar to a spider web: *Driving a rented car from Tempelhof Airport ... I soon became lost in a spiderweb of new freeways* (New Yorker).
**spi|der-web** (spī′dər web′), *v.t.,* **-webbed, -webbing.** to cover with a network resembling a spider web: *The Communists have spider-webbed*

***spider crab**
***spider orchid**

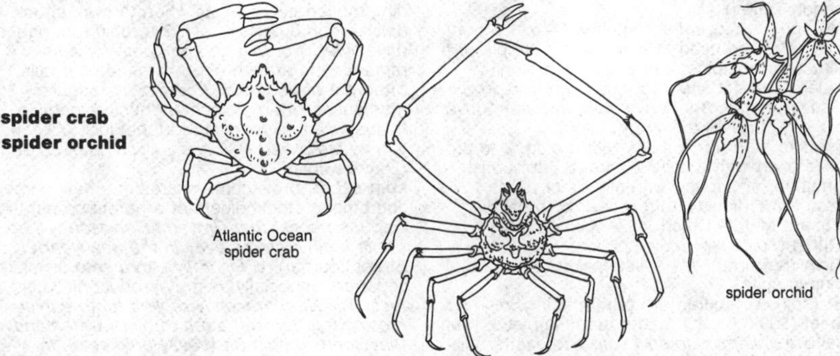
Atlantic Ocean spider crab
Japanese spider crab
spider orchid

**Pronunciation Key:** hat, āge, cãre, fär; let, ēqual, tėrm; it, īce; hot, ōpen, ôrder; oil, out; cup, pu̇t, rüle; child; long; thin; ᴛʜen; zh, measure; ə represents a in about, e in taken, i in pencil, o in lemon, u in circus.

*southern China and Laos with roads leading to the Thai and Burmese borders* (Time).

**spi|der|wort** (spī′dər wėrt′), *n.* any one of a genus of erect or trailing plants that bear clusters of blue, purple, or white flowers. One trailing species takes root at the knots of its stems.

**spiderwort family**, a group of dicotyledonous herbs growing mostly in tropical or subtropical regions. The family includes the dayflower, wandering Jew, and spiderwort.

**spi|der|y** (spī′dər ē), *adj.* **1** like the legs of a spider; long and thin: *a person with spidery arms.* **2** suggesting a spider web or cobweb. **3** full of, or infested with, spiders: *a spidery attic.*

**spied** (spīd), *v.* the past tense and past participle of **spy**: *The hunter spied the stag in the distance. Who spied on us?*

**spie|gel** (spē′gəl), *n.* = spiegeleisen.

**spie|gel|ei|sen** (spē′gəl ī′zən), *n.* a crystalline and lustrous variety of pig iron containing 15 to 30 per cent of manganese, used in making steel. [< German *Spiegeleisen* < *Spiegel* mirror + *Eisen* iron]

**spiegel iron**, = spiegeleisen.

**spiel**[1] (spēl, shpēl), *n., v. U.S. Slang.* —*n.* **1** a talk; speech; harangue, especially one of a cheap, noisy nature. **2** any glib or wordy talk or speech; line: *a salesman's spiel.* [< the verb]
—*v.i., v.t.* to talk; speak; say in or as a spiel: *He's always spieling about the "value of languages"* (Sinclair Lewis).
[American English < German *spielen* to play]

**spiel**[2] or **'spiel** (spēl), *n. British, Canadian.* a curling match; bonspiel: *This year's 'spiel has produced the usual number of close contests* (Winnipeg Free Press). [short for *bonspiel*]

**spiel|er**[1] (spē′lər), *n. Slang.* **1** *U.S.* a person who spiels. **2** *Australian.* a cardsharper or professional swindler.

**spiel|er**[2] or **'spiel|er** (spē′lər), *n. British, Canadian.* a player in a spiel or curling match; curler.

**spi|er**[1] (spī′ər), *n.* = spy.

**spier**[2] (spir), *v.i., v.t. Scottish.* speer.

**spiff** (spif), *v.i. Slang.* to make neat, spruce, or fine; dress neatly or smartly: *We flatter ourselves that we are spiffed out; at all events we've got our best dresses on* (William S. Gilbert). [origin unknown]

**spiff|ing** (spif′ing), *adj. Slang.* excellent; first-rate; very good: *We like to say that if he shaved his [head] he would make a spiffing monk* (Punch).

**spif|fli|cate** (spif′lə kāt), *v.t.,* **-cat|ed, -cat|ing.** *Informal.* spiflicate.

**spiff|y** (spif′ē), *adj.,* **spiff|i|er, spiff|i|est.** *Slang.* **1** smart; neat; trim: *a spiffy appearance.* **2** very enjoyable: *a spiffy time.*

**spif|li|cate** (spif′lə kāt), *v.t.,* **-cat|ed, -cat|ing.** *Informal.* **1** to confound or dismay. **2** to overcome; destroy; kill. [a coined word]

**spif|li|ca|tion** (spif′lə kā′shən), *n. Informal.* a spiflicating.

**Spi|ge|li|an** (spī jē′lē ən), *adj.* of or having to do with Spigelius, (1578-1625), a Belgian anatomist and botanist at Padua.

**Spigelian lobe**, a small lobe on the upper, posterior side of the right lobe of the liver.

**spig|ot** (spig′ət), *n.* **1** a valve for controlling the flow of water or other liquid, as from a pipe, tank, or barrel: *By opening the spigot in the barrel she let out all the wine.* **2** *U.S.* a faucet. **3** a peg or plug used to stop the small hole of a cask, barrel, or keg; bung; spile. [Middle English *spigote;* origin uncertain]

**spike**[1] (spīk), *n., v.,* **spiked, spik|ing.** —*n.* **1** a large, strong nail or pin usually of iron, used for fastening rails to the ties or heavy timbers in place: *Many spikes stuck out of the rotting timbers on the fishing boat.* **2** a sharp-pointed piece or part of metal or wood fastened in something with the point outward, as at the top of a wall, gate, or the like, for defense or to hinder passage: *He caught his pants on a spike while climbing over the iron fence.* **3** one of the metal points or sharp cleats, or a plate of them, attached to the sole of a shoe to prevent slipping. **4** anything like a spike, such as a bony projection of certain fishes, for example the marlin or the sailfish. **5a** the antler of a young deer, when straight and without snag or tine. **b** a young mackerel six or seven inches long. **6** *Aerospace.* a projection in front of a ramjet engine, used to control shock waves. **7** *Physics.* a sudden, sharp uprise or peak, as in a motion, voltage, or current: *An infinitely sharp spike would have an energy uncertainty of zero* (Scientific American). **8** any tip or high point on a linear graph: *... brain-wave patterns characterized by six- and 14-per-second spikes in the brain-wave tracing* (Science News Letter). **9** a sharp downward striking of a volleyball over the net into the opponents' court.
—*v.t.* **1** to fasten with spikes: *The men spiked the rails to the ties when laying the tracks.* **2** to provide or fit with or as if with spikes: *Runners wear spiked shoes to keep from slipping.* **3** to pierce with or as if with a spike. **4** to injure (an opponent or other player) with the spikes of one's shoes. **5** to make (a cannon) useless by driving a spike into the opening where the powder is set off. **6** *Figurative.* to put an end or stop to; make useless; block; thwart: *The extra guard spiked the prisoner's attempt to escape.* **7** to hit (a volleyball) sharply downward over the net into the opponents' court. **8** *Informal.* to add alcoholic liquor to (a drink or punch).
—*v.i.* to project up or out like a spike.
**spikes**, a pair of shoes fitted with spikes, used in baseball, track, and other sports to prevent slipping: *Wearing spikes is forbidden in football, since in this game spikes can cause serious injuries.*
[< Scandinavian (compare Old Icelandic *spīkr*)] —**spike′like′**, *adj.*

✱**spike**[2] (spīk), *n.* **1** an ear of grain. **2** a long, pointed cluster of flowers. [< Latin *spīca.* See etym. of doublet **spica.**]

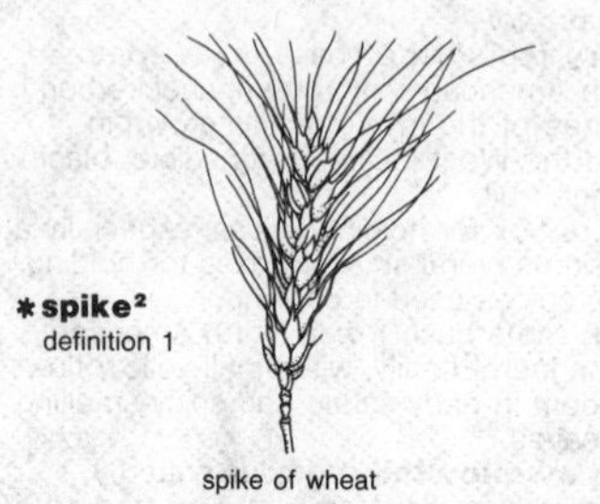

✱**spike**[2] definition 1

spike of wheat

**spike buck**, *U.S.* a male deer in its first or second year, when its antlers are in the form of straight spikes.

**spiked heel** (spīkt), = spike heel.

**spike heel**, a high, usually narrow and tapered heel on a woman's dress shoe; stiletto heel.

**spike horn**, **1** a deer's horn in the form of a spike. **2** = spike buck.

**spike lavender**, a lavender native to the Mediterranean region, having spikes of pale-purple flowers and yielding an oil used in painting.

**spike|let** (spīk′lit), *n.* a small spike or flower cluster, especially a small spike in the compound inflorescence of grasses or sedges.

**spike|nard** (spīk′nərd, -närd), *n.* **1** a sweet-smelling ointment used by the ancients. **2** the fragrant East Indian plant from which it was probably obtained; nard. It belongs to the same family as the valerian. **3** a tall American herb of the ginseng family, having greenish flowers and a fragrant root. [< Medieval Latin *spica nardi* ear of nard < Latin *spīca* spica, and *nardus* nard]

**spik|er** (spī′kər), *n.* **1** a person or thing that spikes. **2** a workman who drives the spikes in the ties in laying railroad tracks.

**spike rush**, any plant of a group of the sedge family, having simple stems with a solitary terminal spike and closely overlapping scales.

**spikes** (spīks), *n.pl.* See under **spike**[1].

**spike team**, *U.S.* a team of three draft animals, one leading the other two, that are harnessed abreast.

**spik|i|ly** (spī′kə lē), *adv.* in a spiky manner; like spikes.

**spik|y** (spī′kē), *adj.,* **spik|i|er, spik|i|est.** **1** having spikes; set with sharp, projecting points: *Being tough and spiky, cacti are relatively poor fodder* (Science News). **2** having the shape of a spike. **3** *Figurative.* **a** sharp; cutting: *"There's this chapel," she said, feeling a spiky nostalgia* (New Yorker). *She makes spiky statements about, say, original sin* (Manchester Guardian Weekly). **b** sharp-tongued; irritable; cross: *He is a controversial, occasionally spiky, man of steely intellect* (London Times).

**spile** (spīl), *n., v.,* **spiled, spil|ing.** —*n.* **1** a peg or plug of wood used to stop the small hole of a cask or barrel; spigot; bung. **2** *U.S.* a small wooden or metal spout for drawing off sap from the sugar maple. **3** a heavy stake or beam driven into the ground as a support; pile.
—*v.t.* **1** to stop up (a hole) with a plug. **2** to provide (a tree) with a spile or spout. **3** to furnish, strengthen, or support with stakes or piles. **4** *Dialect.* to draw (liquid) from a cask by broaching. [compare Middle Dutch *spīle* splinter, peg]

**spil|i|kin** (spil′ə kin), *n.* = spillikin.

**spil|ing** (spī′ling), *n.* **1** spiles; piling. **2** the act of driving in spiles.

**spill**[1] (spil), *v.,* **spilled** or **spilt, spill|ing,** *n.* —*v.t.* **1** to let (liquid or any matter in loose pieces) run or fall: *to spill milk, to spill salt.* **2** to scatter; disperse. **3** to shed (blood), as in killing or wounding: *blood spilled on the battlefield.* **4** *Informal.* to cause to fall from a horse, cart, boat, or the like: *The boat upset and spilled the boys into the water.* **5** to let wind out of (a sail). **6** *Slang, Figurative.* to make known; tell: *to spill a secret.* SYN: divulge, disclose.
—*v.i.* **1** to fall or flow out: *Water spilled from the pail.* **2** to become empty of wind: *The ship turned slowly to the wind, pitching and chopping as the sails were spilling* (Frederick Marryat).
—*n.* **1** the act of spilling. **2** the quantity spilled. **3** *Informal.* a fall: *He got a bad spill trying to ride that horse.* **4** *Informal.* a downpour (of rain). **5** = spillway.
[Old English *spillan* destroy, kill] —**spill′a|ble**, *adj.* —**spill′er**, *n.*

**spill**[2] (spil), *n.* **1** a thin piece of wood, or a folded or twisted piece of paper, used to light a candle, pipe, or fire, as from a fire or another candle: *candle-lighters, or "spills" ... of coloured paper* (Elizabeth Gaskell). **2** a splinter; sliver. **3** a pin or slender rod upon which anything turns; spindle. **4** a spile; bung. [Middle English *spille.* Perhaps related to **spile.**]

**spill|age** (spil′ij), *n.* **1** the act of spilling: *The food dishes should be about two inches high and have steep sides to prevent spillage* (Scientific American). **2** what is spilled; amount spilled: *... eating the spillage of grain and fruit manhandled through the port by our laborers* (Harper's).

**spil|li|kin** (spil′ə kin), *n.* = jackstraw. Also, **spilikin.**
**spillikins**, the game of jackstraws: *I have heard that the Bishops play spillikins for cups of tea* (Punch).
[apparently a diminutive form of *spill*[2]]

**spill|o|ver** (spil′ō′vər), *n.* **1** the act of spilling or running over, as beyond certain limits: *Inaccurately aimed low-power bombs could cause a spillover of nuclear destruction to civilian areas* (Bulletin of Atomic Scientists). **2** something that spills over; overflow; overabundance: *Thus the idea of Australia becoming an outlet for the spill-over of Asia is chimerical* (Julian Huxley).

**spill|way** (spil′wā′), *n.* a channel or passage for the escape of surplus water, as from a dam or river.

**spi|lo|site** (spī′lə sīt), *n.* a greenish schistose rock resulting from metamorphism of slate. [< Greek *spílos* spot, speck + English *-ite*[1]]

**spilt** (spilt), *v.* spilled; a past tense and a past participle of **spill**[1]: *Don't cry over spilt milk. For we ... are as water spilt on the ground, which cannot be gathered up again* (II Samuel 14:14).

**spilth** (spilth), *n. Archaic.* **1** the act of spilling. **2** something spilled.

**spin** (spin), *v.,* **spun** or (*Archaic*) **span, spun, spin|ning,** *n.* —*v.t.* **1** to make turn around or revolve rapidly: *The boy spins his top.* SYN: twirl, whirl, rotate. **2** to draw out and twist (cotton, flax, or wool) into thread, either by hand or by machinery. **3** to make (thread or yarn) by drawing out and twisting cotton, flax, or wool. **4** to make (a thread, web, or cocoon) by giving out from the body sticky material that hardens into thread. A spider spins a web. **5** to make (glass, gold, or other solid material) into thread. **6** *Figurative.* to produce, draw out, or tell in a manner suggestive of spinning: *The old sailor used to spin yarns about adventures at sea. ... spinning their dark intrigues* (Benjamin Disraeli). **7** to shape on a lathe or wheel.
—*v.i.* **1** to turn around rapidly: *the wheels spun on the ice. Let the great world spin forever down the ringing grooves of change* (Tennyson). SYN: twirl, whirl, rotate. **2** to feel as if one were whirling around; feel dizzy or giddy: *My head is spinning.* **3** to run, ride, or drive rapidly: *The automobile spun over the smooth expressway.* **4** to fish or troll with a spinner or spinning reel. **5** to draw out and twist the fibers of cotton, flax, or wool into thread. **6** to produce, as a thread, web, or cocoon, from a sticky material, as spiders do.
—*n.* **1** the act of spinning. **2** a twisting or spinning motion, as of a ball when thrown, struck, or delivered in a certain way. **3** a rapid run, ride, or drive: *Get your bicycle and come for a spin.* **4** a rapid turning around of an airplane as it falls, often out of control. **5** *Physics.* the angular momentum of an elementary nuclear particle. **6** *Australian.* experience; fortune; luck: *I know you've 'ad a bad spin and ... you're all on edge* (Ray Lawlor).
**spin off**, **a** to distribute shares in a new corporation among stockholders of a parent corporation: *Reports persist that Grayson-Robinson will spin off its Klein's stores early in the new year* (Wall Street Journal). **b** *Figurative.* to create or make separate, especially as a by-product or copy: *In fact, Willi Stoph recently replied to an earlier Kiesinger letter with a return missive demanding that Bonn ... spin off West Berlin as an independent "free city"* (Time).

**spin out**, to make long and slow; draw out; prolong: *to spin out negotiations. The old fisherman always spun out the tales of his adventures at sea.*
[Old English *spinnan*] —**spin′less**, *adj.*

**spi|na bi|fi|da** (spī′nə bī′fə də), a congenital gap or cleft in the posterior wall of the spinal canal. [< New Latin *spina bifida* a bifid or cleft spine]

**spi|na|ceous** (spi nā′shəs), *adj.* **1** of or like spinach. **2** belonging to the family of plants that includes spinach. [< New Latin *Spinacia* the spinach family (< Medieval Latin *spinachia;* see etym. under **spinach**) + English *-ous*]

**spin|ach** (spin′ich, -ij), *n.* **1** a plant whose green leaves are cooked and eaten as a vegetable, or used uncooked in a salad. It belongs to the goosefoot family. See picture under **goosefoot family**. **2** its leaves. [< Old French *espinache,* or *espinage* < Medieval Latin *spinachia* < Spanish *espinaca,* probably ultimately < Arabic *isbānakh*]

**spi|nal** (spī′nəl), *adj., n.* —*adj.* **1** of or having to do with the spine or backbone: *a spinal nerve, a spinal anesthetic.* **2** in the region of the spine. **3** resembling a spine in form or function: *a spinal ridge or hill.* **4** of or having to do with spines or sharp-pointed parts or bodies.
—*n. Informal.* a spinal anesthetic: *to administer a spinal.*
[< Late Latin *spīnālis* < Latin *spīna;* see etym. under **spine**] —**spi′nal|ly**, *adv.*

**spinal anesthesia**, anesthesia by injection into the spinal canal, affecting the lower part of the body and the legs.

**spinal block**, an obstructing of the flow of cerebrospinal fluid by the injection of an anesthetic into the nerves of the spinal canal.

**spinal canal**, the duct formed by the openings of the articulated vertebrae, containing the spinal cord.

**spinal column**, = backbone.

**spinal cord**, the thick, whitish cord of nerve tissue which extends from the brain down through most of the backbone and from which nerves to various parts of the body branch off. The spinal cord begins at its upper end in the medulla oblongata. See diagram under **brain**.

**spinal marrow**, the tissue of the spinal cord, found in the cavity running through the chain of vertebrae.

**spinal tap**, the removal of some cerebrospinal fluid from the base of the spine to analyze it for symptoms of brain or spinal disease or to replace it with an anesthetic.

**spin|ar** (spin′är), *n.* a rapidly spinning galactic body. [< *spin* + *-ar,* as in *pulsar, quasar*]

**spi|nate** (spī′nāt), *adj.* bearing spines.

**spi|na|tion** (spī nā′shən), *n.* **1** the condition of having spines. **2** the arrangement of spines.

**spin-cast|ing** (spin′kas′ting, -käs′-), *n.* = spinning (def. 2).

**spin|dle** (spin′dəl), *n., adj., v.,* **-dled, -dling.** —*n.* **1** a rod or pin used in spinning to twist, wind, and hold thread. In hand spinning, the spindle is a round, usually wooden rod, tapering toward each end, that revolves and twists into thread the fibers drawn out from the bunch of wool, flax, or other material, on the distaff. In machine spinning, a spindle is one of the many steel rods on which a bobbin is placed to hold the thread as it is spun. **2** a certain quantity or measure of yarn, such as 15,120 yards for cotton and 14,400 yards for linen. **3** any rod or pin that turns around or on which something turns. Axles and shafts are spindles. The two shaftlike parts of a lathe that hold the work are spindles. The small shaft passing through a lock, upon which the knobs or handles are fitted, is also a spindle. **4** something shaped like a spindle. **5** *Biology.* the group of achromatic fibers along which the chromosomes are arranged during mitosis and meiosis. The spindle joins the two newly formed nuclei and forms a rounded figure which tapers from the middle toward each end. See diagram under **meiosis**[1]. **6** one of the turned or circular, supporting parts of a baluster or stair rail. **7** an iron rod or post fixed to a rock, reef, or the like, to warn navigators. **8** = hydrometer.
—*v.i.* **1** to grow long and thin. **2** (of a plant) to shoot up or grow into a long, slender stalk or stem.
—*v.t.* to form into the shape of a spindle.
[Middle English *spindel,* alteration of Old English *spinel,* related to *spinnan* to spin]

**spindle cell**, a spindle-shaped or fusiform cell: *Spindle cells found in the gill covers, chest and throat regions of the minnow Phoxinus laevis ... were in fact closely associated with what seemed to be nerve fibers* (New Scientist).

**spin|dle|ful** (spin′dəl fu̇l), *n., pl.* **-fuls.** as much thread or yarn as a spindle can hold.

**spin|dle-leg|ged** (spin′dəl leg′id, -legd′), *adj.* having long, thin legs.

**spin|dle|legs** (spin′dəl legz′), *n. Informal.* a person with long, thin legs.

**spin|dle-shanked** (spin′dəl shangkt′), *adj.* = spindle-legged.

**spindle side**, the female side, or line of descent, of a family; distaff side.

**spindle tree**, any one of a group of trees and shrubs of the staff-tree family, whose hard, fine-grained, yellowish wood was formerly much used for spindles.

**spin|dling** (spin′dling), *adj., n.* —*adj.* very long and slender; too tall and thin: *a weak, spindling plant.*
—*n.* **1** a spindling plant or animal. **2** the action of twisting something.

**spin|dly** (spin′dlē), *adj.,* **-dli|er, -dli|est.** = spindling.

**spin|drift** (spin′drift′), *n.* spray blown or dashed up from the waves: *It ... began to blow with furious gusts which angrily tore the small waves of the inland sea into spindrift* (Norman Macleod). **SYN:** scud. Also, **spoondrift.** [originally Scottish variant of *spoondrift,* probably < Scottish pronunciation of *spoon*]

***spine** (spīn), *n.* **1** the series of small bones down the middle of the back in man and other vertebrates; backbone; spinal column. **2a** anything like a backbone; long, narrow ridge or support: *the spine of a mountain.* **b** *Figurative.* courage or determination, such as that by which a person is supported in the face of danger or adversity: *Threats merely stiffened his spine.* **3** *Botany.* a stiff, sharp-pointed growth of woody tissue: *The cactus and hawthorn have spines.* **4** *Zoology.* **a** a stiff, pointed, thornlike part or projection: *A procupine's spines are called quills.* **b** a sharp, rigid fin ray of a fish. **c** = spicule. **5** a slender, pointed process, as of a bone. **6** the supporting back portion of a book cover. [< Latin *spīna* (originally) thorn] —**spine′like′**, *adj.*

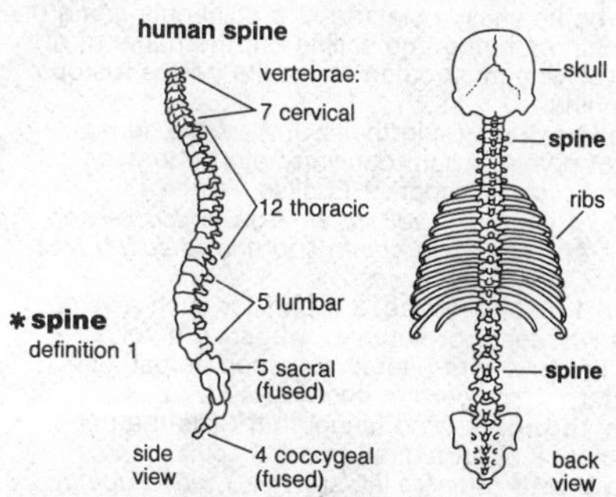

***spine** definition 1

**spine-chill|ing** (spīn′chil′ing), *adj.* that causes the spine to tingle with chilling fright; terrifying; exciting: *Edgar Allan Poe wrote many spine-chilling short stories.*

**spined** (spīnd), *adj.* having a spine or spines.

**spi|nel** (spi nel′, spin′əl), *n.* a crystalline mineral, consisting chiefly of oxides of magnesium and aluminum, that occurs in various colors. Transparent spinel is used for jewelry. [< Middle French *spinelle* < Italian *spinella* < *spina* thorn < Latin *spīna;* see etym. under **spine**]

**spine|less** (spīn′lis), *adj.* **1** having no spine or backbone; invertebrate: *A jellyfish is a spineless animal.* **2** having a weak or diseased spine; limp. **3** *Figurative.* without courage, determination, or moral force; weak-willed; feeble: *a spineless coward.* **SYN:** irresolute. **4** having no spines or sharp-pointed processes: *a spineless cactus.* —**spine′less|ly**, *adv.* —**spine′less|ness**, *n.*

**spi|nelle** (spi nel′, spin′əl), *n.* = spinel.

**spinel ruby**, a deep-red variety of the gem spinel; ruby spinel.

**spi|nes|cence** (spī nes′ens), *n.* the condition of being spinescent.

**spi|nes|cent** (spī nes′ənt), *adj.* **1** *Botany.* **a** developing into, or ending in, a spine or thorn. **b** bearing or covered with spines. **2** *Zoology.* coarse and spinelike, as feathers or hair. [< Late Latin *spīnēscēns, -entis,* present participle of *spīnēscere* grow thorny < Latin *spīna;* see etym. under **spine**]

**spin|et** (spin′it, spi net′), *n.* **1** an old-fashioned musical instrument like a small harpsichord. **2** a compact upright piano. [< French *espinette* < Middle French < Italian *spinetta,* perhaps < Giovanni *Spinetti,* around 1500, an Italian inventor; perhaps < Latin *spīna;* see etym. under **spine** (because the strings were plucked with quills)]

**spine|tail** (spīn′tāl′), *n.* any one of various swifts (birds) having tail feathers with stiff, spinelike points.

**spine-tailed** (spīn′tāld′), *adj.* having stiff, spine-like points on the tail feathers.

**spine-tin|gling** (spīn′ting′gling), *adj.* = spine-chilling: *This mission itself, its spine-tingling dangers [and] hairbreadth escapes, is worthy of an entire book* (Wall Street Journal).

**spin fisherman**, a person who engages in spin fishing.

**spin fishing**, = spinning (def. 2).

**spi|nif|er|ous** (spī nif′ər əs), *adj.* having or covered with spines; spiny. [< Latin *spīnifer* (< *spīna;* see etym. under **spine**; + *ferre* to bear) + English *-ous*]

**spin|i|fex** (spin′ə feks), *n.* any one of a group of Australian grasses with seeds that have elastic spines. [< New Latin *Spinifex* the genus name < Latin *spīna* thorn, spine + *facere* make]

**spi|ni|form** (spī′nə fôrm), *adj.* having the form of a spine; spinelike.

**spi|nig|er|ous** (spī nij′ər əs), *adj.* bearing spines; spiniferous.

**spi|ni|grade** (spī′nə grād), *adj.* moving by means of spines or spinous parts, as a starfish and sea urchin. [< Latin *spīna* (see etym. under **spine**) + *gradī* to walk]

**spin|i|ness** (spī′nē nis), *n.* spiny quality or state.

**spink** (spingk), *n. Dialect.* the chaffinch. [imitative]

**spin|na|ble** (spin′ə bəl), *adj.* that can spin or be spun: *a spinnable fiber.*

***spin|na|ker** (spin′ə kər), *n.* a large, triangular sail carried especially by yachts and sloops, on the side opposite the mainsail when running before the wind. [origin uncertain]

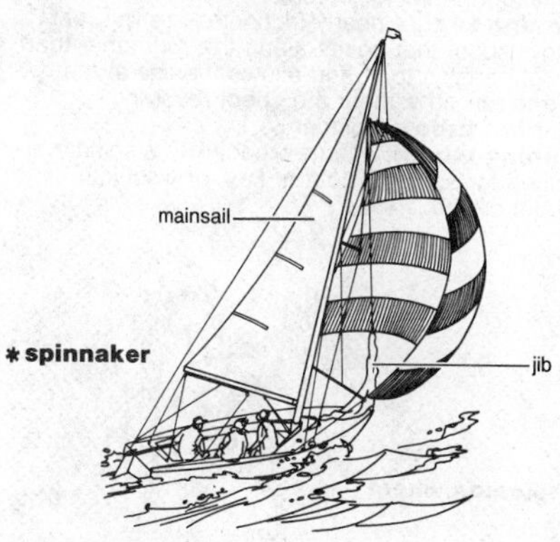

***spinnaker**

**spinnaker boom**, a long, light spar to which the foot of a spinnaker is attached.

**spin|ner** (spin′ər), *n.* **1** a person, animal, or thing that spins: (*Figurative.*) *I am a spinner of long yarns* (Hawthorne). **2** a revolving hook or lure, especially a spoon, used in trolling or casting. **3** a football maneuver or play in which the player receiving the ball from the center turns with his back to the line to fake or hand the ball to a teammate. **4** *Aeronautics.* the conical or parabolic sheet of metal attached to and revolving with the propeller hub to reduce drag or air resistance. **5** a cricket ball bowled with a spin: *Greensmith ... pitched his spinners to the right spot* (London Times).

**spin|ner|et** (spin′ə ret), *n.* **1** the organ by which spiders, and certain insect larvae such as silkworms, spin their threads for webs and cocoons. **2** Also, **spinnerette.** a small, metal device with tiny holes through which the viscous chemical solution is pressed out to form filaments or threads in the production of synthetic fibers. [< *spinner* + *-et*]

**spin|ner|u|lar** (spi ner′ů lər), *adj.* of or having to do with spinnerules.

**spin|ner|ule** (spin′ər ül), *n.* any one of a number of tubules on the spinneret of a spider. Silk in liquid form flows through the spinnerules from silk glands in the spider's abdomen to the outside of the body. The silk then hardens into a thread.

**spin|ner|y** (spin′ər ē), *n., pl.* **-ner|ies.** a mill or factory for spinning thread or yarn; spinning mill.

**spin|ney** (spin′ē), *n., pl.* **-neys.** *British.* a small wood with undergrowth, especially one preserved for sheltering game birds; small group of trees; thicket; copse. Also, **spinny.** [< Old French *espinee,* ultimately < Latin *spīna;* see etym. under **spine**]

**spin|ning** (spin′ing), *adj., n.* —*adj.* that spins: *a spinning top, a spinning mill or machine, a spinning lure.*
—*n.* **1** the act of a person or thing that spins. **2** the sport or technique of casting with a very light line and a spinning reel.

**spinning field**, the tip of a spinneret, the surface of which is covered with spinnerules.

**Pronunciation Key:** hat, āge, cãre, fär; let, ēqual, tėrm; it, īce; hot, ōpen, ôrder; **oil**, **out**; cup, pu̇t, rüle; **ch**ild; lo**ng**; **th**in; **ᴛʜ**en; **zh**, measure; ə represents **a** in about, **e** in taken, **i** in pencil, **o** in lemon, **u** in circus.

**spinning frame**, a machine for spinning and winding yarn.

*** spinning jenny**, an early type of spinning machine having several spindles, on which one person could spin a number of threads at the same time; jenny.

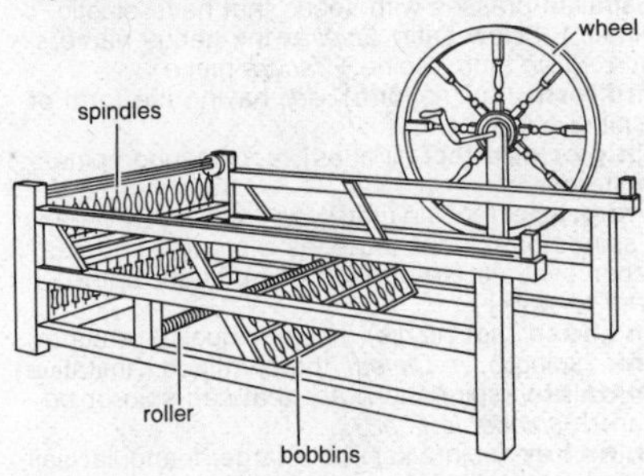


*** spinning jenny**

**spinning mule**, a machine for drawing and spinning cotton, wool, or other fibers into yarn and winding it on spindles; mule.

**spinning reel**, a nearly frictionless fishing reel with a spool that points along the rod rather than at right angles to it, and allows the line at the end to run off without the spool revolving.

**spinning tube** = spinnerule.

*** spinning wheel**, a large wheel with a spindle arranged for spinning cotton, flax, or wool into thread or yarn.

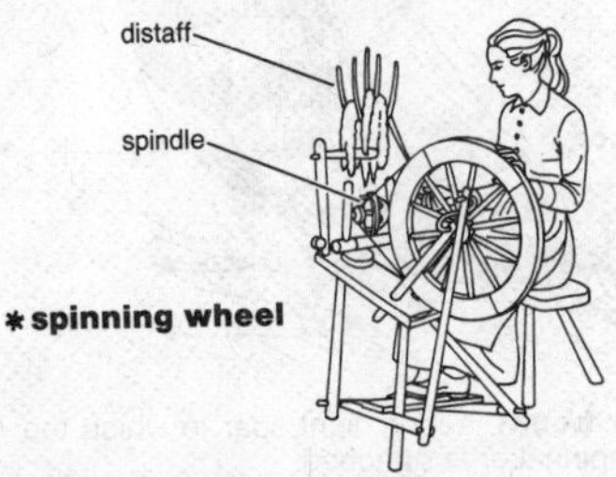


*** spinning wheel**

**spin|ny** (spin′ē), *n., pl.* **-nies**. *British.* a spinney.

**spi|node** (spī′nōd), *n.* that point on a curve where a point generating the curve has its motion precisely reversed; cusp.
[< Latin *spīna* (see etym. under **spine**) + English *node*]

**spin-off** (spin′ôf′, -of′), *n.* **1** the distribution of the stocks of a new or subsidiary company among the stockholders of the controlling company: *On May 31, 1957, all the capital stock of Republic Industrial Corp. … was distributed by Barium Steel Corp. to its shareholders in a tax-free spin-off* (Wall Street Journal). **2** *Figurative.* a by-product of research or similar activity, usually unexpected; fallout: *The vaccine is the result of a new type of ultrahigh-speed centrifuge that is a spin-off from atomic weapons work* (New York Times). *Water pollution is among the most undesirable spin-offs of heavy industrialization and technological progress* (Science News).

**spin|or** (spin′ôr, -ər), *n. Physics.* a vector used in quantum mechanics to describe particle spin. [< *spin* + *-or,* as in *vector, tensor*]

**spi|nose** (spī′nōs), *adj.* having or full of spines; thorny; spinous. [< Latin *spīnōsus* < *spīna* thorn] —**spi′nose|ly**, *adv.*

**spi|nos|i|ty** (spī nos′ə tē), *n., pl.* **-ties**. **1** the fact or condition of being spinous or spinose; thorniness; sharpness. **2** *Figurative.* a rude or disagreeable remark. **3** *Figurative.* a difficult argument or theory.

**spi|nous** (spī′nəs), *adj.* **1** *Botany.* covered with spines; having or full of spines or thorns; thorny. **2** *Zoology.* armed with or bearing spines or sharp-pointed processes: *The porcupine has a spinous back.* **3** slender and sharp-pointed; spinelike; sharp. —**spi′nous|ness**, *n.*

**spinous process**, a process, especially of a vertebra, shaped like a spine or thorn.

**spin|out** (spin′out′), *n.* a spin causing an automobile to run off the road, especially when rounding a corner at high speed: *Also popular: decorative features such as racing stripes … and "spoilers" —vertical flaps that put pressure on the rear wheels to prevent spinouts* (Time).

**Spi|no|zism** (spi nō′ziz əm), *n.* the philosophy of Spinoza, essentially an expression of pantheism in which all reality consists of God (the Substance) in one or the other of two aspects (thought and extension, or mind and matter).

**Spi|no|zist** (spi nō′zist), *n.* an adherent of Spinozism.

**Spin|o|zis|tic** (spin′ō zis′tik), *adj.* of, having to do with, or characteristic of Spinoza or his followers: *Spinozistic pantheism.*

**spin|ster** (spin′stər), *n.* **1** an elderly woman who has not married; old maid: *a middle-aged spinster. He was a beau of all the elder ladies and superannuated spinsters* (Washington Irving). **2** an unmarried woman. **3** *British.* any girl or woman of marriageable age who has yet to marry (used since the 1600's as a legal description): *I, Anthony Lumpkin, Esquire … refuse you, Constantia Neville, spinster* (Oliver Goldsmith). **4** a woman who spins flax, wool, or the like, into thread: *the spinsters and the knitters in the sun* (Shakespeare). **5** *Archaic.* any unmarried gentlewoman.

**spin|ster|hood** (spin′stər hu̇d), *n.* the condition of being a spinster.

**spin|ster|ish** (spin′stər ish), *adj.* like or befitting a spinster: *a spinsterish high-necked dress* (Sinclair Lewis).

**spin|ster|ly** (spin′stər lē), *adj.* = spinsterish.

**spin|ster|ship** (spin′stər ship), *n.* = spinsterhood.

**spin|stress** (spin′stris), *n.* **1** a woman spinner. **2** = spinster.

**spin|stry** (spin′strē), *n.* the work or occupation of spinning.

**spin|thar|i|scope** (spin thar′ə skōp), *n.* an instrument in which the alpha particles emitted by radioactive substances are evidenced by the production of tiny sparks when the particles strike a fluorescent screen; scintilloscope. [< Greek *spintharis* a spark + English *-scope*]

**spin|thar|i|scop|ic** (spin thar′ə skop′ik), *adj.* of or by means of a spinthariscope.

**spin the bottle**, **1** a game of spinning a bottle and kissing the partner of the opposite sex that the bottle finally points to. **2** a children's game of spinning a bottle and calling out the name of a player who must catch the bottle before it stops spinning.

**spin|ther|ism** (spin′thə riz əm), *n.* the sensation as of points of light dancing before the eyes. [< Greek *spinthḗr* spark + English *-ism*]

**spin|to** (spin′tō), *adj., n., pl.* **-tos**. *Music.* —*adj.* high and strong: *a spinto soprano, a spinto lyric tenor, spinto passages.*
—*n.* **1** a spinto voice. **2** a part for such a voice. **3** a lyric tenor or soprano with such a voice.
[< Italian *spinto* (literally) pushed, thrust, ultimately < *spingere* to push]

**spin tunnel**, a wind tunnel that tests the performance of an aircraft in a tail spin.

**spin|u|late** (spin′yə lāt, spīn′yə-), *adj. Zoology.* covered with little spines: *spinulate hairs.*

**spin|u|lat|ed** (spin′yə lā′tid, spīn′yə-), *adj.* = spinulate.

**spin|ule** (spīn′yül, spin′yül), *n.* a small, sharp-pointed spine. [< Latin *spīnula* (diminutive) < *spīna* thorn, spine] —**spi′nule|like′**, *adj.*

**spin|u|les|cent** (spin′yə les′ənt, spīn′yə-), *adj. Botany.* producing small spines; somewhat spiny. [< *spinul*(e) + *-escent*]

**spin|u|lose** (spin′yə lōs, spīn′yə-), *adj.* **1** provided with spinules. **2** spinulelike. —**spin′u|lose|ly**, *adv.*

**spin wave**, *Nuclear Physics.* a wave propagated by the deviation of a nuclear spin; magnon.

**spin|y** (spī′nē), *adj.,* **spin|i|er, spin|i|est**. **1** covered with spines; having spines; thorny: *a spiny cactus, a spiny porcupine.* **2** stiff and sharp-pointed; spinelike: *the spiny quills of a porcupine.* **3** *Figurative.* difficult; troublesome; thorny: *His spiny disposition made it difficult to approach him.*

**spiny anteater**, = echidna.

**spiny dogfish**, any one of a family of small sharks with a spine in front of each dorsal fin.

**spin|y-finned** (spī′nē find′), *adj.* having fins with sharp, rigid, unsegmented rays: *The bass and perch are spiny-finned.*

**spin|y-head|ed worm** (spī′nē hed′id), = acanthocephalan.

**spiny lobster**, any one of various lobsters much like the usual kind but lacking the enlarged pair of claws; sea crayfish.

**spin|y-rayed** (spī′nē rād′), *adj.* = spiny-finned.

**spin|y-skinned** (spī′nē skind′), *adj.* having or covered with skin consisting of spinelike projections; echinodermatous: *Like the familiar starfish, sea urchins, and sand dollars, they are in the general category of spiny-skinned animals known as echinoderms* (Science News Letter).

**spi|ra|cle** (spī′rə kəl, spir′ə-), *n.* **1** a small opening for breathing. Insects take in air through tiny spiracles. A whale breathes through a spiracle in the top of its head. A shark or ray gives off water through a spiracle. **2** an opening in the ground by which underground vapors are given off; air hole. [< Latin *spīrāculum* < *spīrāre* to breathe]

**spi|rac|u|lar** (spī rak′yə lər), *adj.* **1** of or having to do with spiracles. **2** serving as a spiracle.

**spi|rae|a** (spī rē′ə), *n.* a shrub that has clusters of small white, pink, or red flowers with five petals. The spiraeas comprise a genus of plants of the rose family. The bridal wreath and meadowsweet are two kinds. Also, **spirea**. [< Latin *spīraea* meadowsweet < Greek *speiraiā* privet < *speîra* coil]

**spi|ral** (spī′rəl), *n., adj., v.,* **-raled, -ral|ing** or (*especially British*) **-ralled, -ral|ling**. —*n.* **1** a winding and gradually widening curve or coil. A watch spring is a spiral. The thread of a screw is a spiral. **2** one of the separate circles or coils of a spiral object. **3** *Figurative.* a continuous and expanding increase or decrease, as in prices, wages, or employment: *an inflationary spiral, a deflationary spiral.* **4** the descent of an aircraft in a spiral path. **5** *Football.* a kick or pass in which the ball spins through the air on its longer axis. **6** = helix.
—*adj.* **1** winding or coiling around a fixed center while moving away or toward it; coiled; helical: *a spiral staircase. A snail's shell has a spiral shape.* **2** having to do with or like a spiral or coil.
—*v.i.* **1** to move or wind in a spiral: (*Figurative.*) *There is no security for anyone in a spiraling arms race* (Saturday Review). **2** (of an airplane) to descend in a spiral course.
—*v.t.* to form into a spiral; approach in a spiral: *The plane spiraled the airport before landing.*
[< Medieval Latin *spiralis* < Latin *spīra* a coil < Greek *speîra*] —**spi′ral|ly**, *adv.*

**spiral binding**, a binding for a notebook, booklet, or the like in which a spiral coil of wire or plastic passes through holes on the edge of each page to hold the pages together.

**spi|ral-bound** (spī′rəl bound′), *adj.* bound with a spiral coil of wire or plastic looping the pages together: *a spiral-bound notebook.*

**spiral galaxy** or **nebula**, a galaxy or nebula appearing as one or more spiraling streams issuing from a center: *Our Milky Way system seems to be a spiral galaxy, presumably very much resembling in outline and appearance the Great Spiral in Andromeda* (Bart J. Bok).

**spiral gear**, = helical gear.

**spi|ral|i|form** (spī ral′ə fôrm), *adj.* **1** having the form of a spiral. **2** having to do with a type of decoration based on the spiral, common in primitive art, especially the Mycenaean in Greece and Crete.

**spi|ral|i|ty** (spī ral′ə tē), *n.* spiral quality; degree of being spiral.

**spi|rant** (spī′rənt), *n., adj. Phonetics.* = fricative. [< Latin *spīrāns, -antis,* present participle of *spīrāre* to breathe]

**spire¹** (spīr), *n., v.,* **spired, spir|ing**. —*n.* **1a** the top part of a tower or steeple that narrows to a point: *The steeple, which has a spire to it, is placed in the middle of the church* (Laurence Sterne). **b** a tall structure rising from a tower, roof, or other structure, and ending in a slender point; steeple: *that sweet city with her dreaming spires* (Matthew Arnold). **2** *Figurative.* anything tapering or pointed: *the spire of an icicle, a spire of flame, the spire of a sword.* **3** *Figurative.* the highest point of something; peak; summit: *The sunset shone on the rocky spires of the mountains.* **4a** a young or tender shoot or sprout. **b** a blade or shoot of grass, etc.; spear.
—*v.i.* to shoot up; rise into a spire: (*Figurative.*) *The crowded firs spire from thy shores* (Samuel Taylor Coleridge).
—*v.t.* to furnish with a spire or spires.
[Old English *spīr* spike, blade] —**spire′like′**, *adj.*

**spire²** (spīr), *n., v.,* **spired, spir|ing**. —*n.* **1** a coil; spiral. **2** a single twist of a coil or spiral. **3** the upper part of a spiral shell, excluding the body whorl.
—*v.i.* to wind spirally; move with a coiling or spiral movement: *The worms … spired about his bones* (William Butler Yeats). (*Figurative.*) *The smoke spired upwards.*
[< Latin *spīra* < Greek *speîra* coil]

**spi|re|a** (spī rē′ə), *n.* = spiraea.

**spired¹** (spīrd), *adj.* **1** having a tapering, sharp-pointed top; peaked: *the spired roof of a silo.* **2** having or carrying a spire: *a spired tower.*

**spired²** (spīrd), *adj.* having a spire or coil: *a spired shell.*

**spi|reme** (spī′rēm), *n.* the threadlike coils appearing in the nucleus of a cell at the beginning of the prophase of mitosis, which give rise to the chromosomes. [< German *Spirem* < Greek *speirēma, -atos,* variant of *speirāma* a coiling < *speirâsthai* be coiled < *speîra* a coil]

**spi|ri|cle** (spī′rə kəl), *n. Botany.* one of the delicate coiled threads on the surface of certain seeds and fruits, which uncoil when wet. [< New Latin *spiricula,* diminutive of Latin *spīra* spire; see etym. under **spire²**]

**spi|rif|er|ous** (spī rif′ər əs), *adj.* **1** having a spire, as a univalve shell. **2** having spiral appendages, as a brachiopod. [< Latin *spīra* (see etym. under **spire²**) + English *-ferous*]

**spi|ril|lum** (spī ril′əm), *n., pl.* **-ril|la** (-ril′ə). **1** any bacteria of a group having long, rigid, spirally twisted forms and bearing a tuft of flagella. They comprise a genus of bacteria. See picture under **bacteria**. **2** any one of various spirally twisted microorganisms. [< New Latin *spirillum* < Latin *spīra;* see etym. under **spire²**]

**spir|it** (spir′it), *n., v., adj.* —*n.* **1** the immaterial part of man; soul: *He is present in spirit, though absent in body. Many religions teach that at death the spirit leaves the body. And the spirit shall return unto God who gave it* (Ecclesiastes 12:7). **2** man's moral, religious, or emotional nature: *Create in me a clean heart, O God; and renew a right spirit within me* (Psalms 51:10). **3** a supernatural being. God is a spirit. Ghosts and fairies are spirits. *... the Spirit of Christmas Past* (Dickens). SYN: phantom, specter, apparition. **4** a person; personality: *Hers is a brave spirit. He was one of the leading spirits of the revolution. Robert E. Lee was a noble spirit.* **5** an influence that stirs up and rouses: *a spirit of reform, the spirit of independence. A spirit of progress is good for people.* **6** courage; vigor; liveliness: *a man of spirit. A race horse must have spirit.* SYN: animation, mettle, vivacity. **7** enthusiasm and loyalty: *school spirit.* SYN: ardor, zeal. **8a** what is really meant as opposed to what is said or written: *The spirit of a law is more important than its words.* **b** the prevailing character, quality, or tendency: *the spirit of our institutions.* **9** any one of various mordant solutions used in dyeing, usually prepared from tin salts. **10** *Chemistry, Obsolete.* a liquid essence or extract of a substance, especially one obtained by distillation. **11** *Alchemy.* one of four substances: sulfur, sal ammoniac, mercury, or orpiment. **12 Spirit,** God (in the belief of Christian Scientists).

—*v.t.* **1** to carry (away or off) secretly: *The child has been spirited away.* **2** to stir or cheer up; encourage; cheer. **3** to produce as if by magic; conjure (up).

—*adj.* **1** of or having to do with spirits or spiritualism: *the spirit world.* **2** of or having to do with alcoholic spirits.

**out of spirits,** sad or gloomy: *Who can be out of spirits in such weather?* (Edward G. Bulwer-Lytton).

**spirits, a** a state of mind; disposition; temper; humor; mood: *He is in good spirits.* **b** vigor; liveliness; cheerfulness: *The horse would roll when he was bringing him up from the stable; he's so full of spirits* (Harriet Beecher Stowe). **c** a solution of a volatile substance in alcohol: *spirits of camphor.* **d** a strong alcoholic liquor. Whiskey and brandy are spirits. *He drinks beer and wine but no spirits.*

**the Spirit, a** God: *The apostolic power with which the Spirit Has filled its elect vessels* (Shelley). **b** the Holy Ghost: *... if ye through the Spirit do mortify the deeds of the body, ye shall live* (Romans 8:13).

[< Latin *spīritus, -ūs* (originally) breath, related to *spīrāre* to breathe. See etym. of doublets **esprit, sprite.**]

**spir|it-child** (spir′it chīld′), *n., pl.* **-chil|dren.** the form in which every individual was created by God before the earth was made, according to the teachings of the Mormon Church.

**spirit duplicator,** a duplicator that uses a master sheet on which the image to be copied is impregnated with a dye, a portion of which is dissolved by an alcohol-base fluid and transferred to the copy paper.

**spir|it|ed** (spir′ə tid), *adj.* **1** full of energy and spirit; lively; dashing; bold: *a spirited race horse. He entered into a spirited discussion concerning the relative merits of the imperishable Master of Baker Street* (Anthony Boucher). SYN: animated, mettlesome. **2** having a spirit or spirits: *good-spirited, mean-spirited, low-spirited.* —**spir′it|ed|ly,** *adv.* —**spir′it|ed|ness,** *n.*

**spirit gum,** a quick-drying preparation of gum used by actors and others to glue false hair to the head or face.

**spir|it|ism** (spir′ə tiz əm), *n.* = spiritualism.

**spir|it|ist** (spir′ə tist), *n.* = spiritualist.

**spir|it|is|tic** (spir′ə tis′tik), *adj.* = spiritualistic.

**spirit lamp,** a lamp in which alcohol is burned.

**spir|it|less** (spir′it lis), *adj.* **1** without spirit or courage; without vigor; depressed; dejected: *tired, spiritless soldiers.* **2** without liveliness; not spirited; tame: *The evening was passed in spiritless conversation* (Fanny Burney). —**spir′it|less|ly,** *adv.* —**spir′it|less|ness,** *n.*

**spirit level,** an instrument used to find out whether a surface is level, using an air bubble in an alcohol-filled glass tube. When the air bubble is exactly in the middle of the tube, the surface is level. See picture under **level.**

**spir|i|to|so** (spir′ə tō′sō), *adj. Music.* spirited; lively. [< Italian *spiritoso* < Vulgar Latin *spīritōsus* < Latin *spīritus;* see etym. under **spirit**]

**spir|it|ous** (spir′ə təs), *adj.* **1** *Archaic.* like an essence or distilled product; pure. **2** alcoholic; spirituous.

**spirit rapping,** rapping or knocking, believed to be a form of communication from or with spirits.

**spir|its** (spir′its), *n.pl.* See under **spirit.**

**spirits** or **spirit of hartshorn,** a water solution of ammonia.

**spirits** or **spirit of turpentine,** = oil of turpentine.

**spirits** or **spirit of wine,** = alcohol.

**spir|i|tu|al** (spir′ə chů əl), *adj., n.* —*adj.* **1** of or having something to do with the spirit or soul: *an outward and visible sign of an inward and spiritual grace given unto us* (Book of Common Prayer). **2** caring much for things of the spirit or soul: *Great men are they who see that spiritual is stronger than any material force* (Emerson). **3** of or having to do with spirits; supernatural: *Millions of spiritual creatures walk the earth unseen* (Milton). **4** of or having to do with the church: *spiritual lords.* **5** sacred; religious: *spiritual writings, a spiritual order. A minister is a spiritual leader.*

—*n.* a religious song which originated among the Negroes of the southern United States: *While the Negro was being assimilated, however, America was adding such Negro contributions as jazz music and spirituals to its cultural store* (Ogburn and Nimkoff).

**spirituals, a** matters primarily concerning religion or the church: *The civil power does best absolutely and unreservedly to ignore spirituals* (John Morley). **b** spiritual matters, affairs, or ideas: *He [Dante] assigns supremacy to the pope in spirituals, and to the emperor in temporals* (James Russell Lowell).

[< Latin *spīrituālis* < *spīritus;* see etym. under **spirit**] —**spir′i|tu|al|ly,** *adv.* —**spir′i|tu|al|ness,** *n.*

**spiritual bouquet,** a card listing prayers, Masses, or good works done in behalf of a living or dead person, sent by Roman Catholics on special occasions.

**spiritual idealism,** *Philosophy.* spiritualism.

**spir|i|tu|al|ism** (spir′ə chů ə liz′əm), *n.* **1** the belief that the spirits of the dead can communicate with the living, especially through persons called mediums; spiritism. **2** *Philosophy.* the doctrine or belief that spirit alone is real. **3** spiritual quality; emphasis or insistence on the spiritual: *He often checked Seth's argumentative spiritualism by saying "Eh, it's a big mystery"* (George Eliot).

**spir|i|tu|al|ist** (spir′ə chů ə list), *n., adj.* —*n.* **1** a person who believes that the dead communicate with the living. **2** a believer in or adherent of spiritualism as a philosophical doctrine. **3** a person who sees or interprets things from a spiritual point of view.

—*adj.* = spiritualistic.

**spir|i|tu|al|is|tic** (spir′ə chů ə lis′tik), *adj.* of or having to do with spiritualism or spiritualists.

**spir|i|tu|al|i|ty** (spir′ə chů al′ə tē), *n., pl.* **-ties. 1** devotion to spiritual things instead of worldly things: *Prayer is, undoubtedly, the life and soul of spirituality* (John Jebb). **2** the fact or quality of being spiritual; being neither corporeal nor material: *That He is invisible is accounted for by His spirituality* (James Tait). **3** *Archaic.* the clergy: *He blamed both spirituality and laity* (John Strype).

**spiritualities, a** spiritual things: *So these pretended successors of Peter ... have notoriously imitated that example of Simon in buying and selling spiritualities* (Henry More). **b** properties or revenues of the church or of a clergyman in his official capacity: *Their spiritualities, the tithes and oblations, were not to be taxed* (William Stubbs).

**spir|i|tu|al|ize** (spir′ə chů ə līz), *v.t.,* **-ized, -iz|ing. 1** to make spiritual. **2** to give a spiritual sense or meaning to: *The works of Richardson ... are romances as they would be spiritualized by a Methodist preacher* (Horace Walpole). —**spir′i|tu|al|i|za′tion,** *n.* —**spir′i|tu|al|iz′er,** *n.*

**spir|i|tu|als** (spir′ə chů əlz), *n.pl.* See under **spiritual.**

**spir|i|tu|al|ty** (spir′ə chů əl tē), *n., pl.* **-ties. 1** Often, **spiritualties.** the property or revenue of the church or of a clergyman. **2** the clergy.

**spir|i|tu|el** (spir′ə chů el′; *French* spē rē tʏ el′), *adj.* showing a refined mind or wit. [< French *spirituel* < Old French, learned borrowing from Latin *spīrituālis;* see etym. under **spiritual**]

**spir|i|tu|elle** (spir′ə chů el′; *French* spē rē tʏ el′), *adj.* **1** = spirituel. **2** delicate; graceful. [< French *spirituelle,* feminine of *spirituel;* see etym. under **spirituel**]

**spir|i|tu|ous** (spir′ə chů əs), *adj.* **1** having to do with, containing, or like alcohol; alcoholic: *spirituous liquors.* **2** distilled, not fermented. —**spir′i|tu|ous|ness,** *n.*

**spir|i|tus as|per** (spir′ə təs as′pər), *Greek Grammar.* rough breathing.

**spir|i|tus fru|men|ti** (spir′ə təs frü men′tī), *Latin.* whiskey. [< New Latin *spiritus frumenti* < Latin *spīritus* (see etym. under **spirit**), *frūmentī,* genitive of *frūmentum* grain]

**spir|i|tus le|nis** (spir′ə təs lē′nis), *Greek Grammar.* smooth breathing.

**spirit varnish,** a varnish made of resins that are dissolved in a quickly-evaporating solvent such as alcohol.

**spirit wrestlers,** = Doukhobors. [translation of Russian *dukhoborstsy*]

**spir|it|y** (spir′ə tē), *adj.* full of spirit, animation, energy, or vivacity; spirited: *He is a most active, spirity man, and by his great mental exercises keeps himself from anything like a lethargy* (Lord Malmesbury).

**spir|ket** (spėr′kit), *n.* a space forward or aft between the floor timbers of a ship [origin unknown]

**spir|ket|ing** or **spir|ket|ting** (spėr′kə ting), *n.* the inside planking between the waterways and the ports of a ship.

**spi|ro|che|tal** or **spi|ro|chae|tal** (spī′rə kē′təl), *adj.* of or having to do with spirochetes.

*****spi|ro|chete** or **spi|ro|chaete** (spī′rə kēt), *n.* any one of a large group of active bacteria. They are slender, spiral, very flexible, and able to expand and contract. One kind causes syphilis, and another causes relapsing fever. The spirochetes comprise an order of bacteria. [< New Latin *Spirochaetales* the order name < Greek *speîra* a coil + *chaítē* hair]

*** spirochete**

**spi|ro|che|ti|cide** or **spi|ro|chae|ti|cide** (spī′rəkē′tə sīd), *n.* an agent for destroying spirochetes. [< *spirochete* + *-cide¹*]

**spi|ro|che|to|sis** or **spi|ro|chae|to|sis** (spī′rəkē tō′sis), *n.* an infectious, often fatal, blood disease of poultry and other birds, caused by a spirochete.

**spi|ro|gram** (spī′rə gram), *n.* a graphic record of a person's lung capacity made by a spirometer. [< Latin *spīrāre* breathe + English *-gram*]

**spi|ro|graph** (spī′rə graf, -gräf), *n.* an instrument for recording respiratory movements. [< Latin *spīrāre* breathe + English *-graph*]

**spi|ro|graph|ic** (spī′rə graf′ik), *adj.* of or having to do with a spirograph.

**spi|ro|gy|ra** (spī′rə jī′rə), *n.* any one of a large group of green algae that grow in masses like scum in freshwater ponds or tanks. The cells have one or more bands of chlorophyll winding spirally to the right. The spirogyras comprise a genus of plants. See diagram under **conjugation.** [< New Latin *Spirogyra* the genus name < Greek *speîra* a coil + *gŷros* circle]

**spi|roid** (spī′roid), *adj.* tending to be spiral in form; like a spiral: *a spiroid curve, a spiroid shell.* [< New Latin *spiroides* < Greek *speiroeidḗs* coiled < *speîra* a coil + *eîdos* form]

**spi|rom|e|ter** (spī rom′ə tər), *n.* an instrument for measuring the capacity of the lungs, by the amount of air that can be breathed out after the lungs have been filled as full as possible. [< Latin *spīrāre* breathe + English *-meter*]

**spi|ro|met|ric** (spī′rə met′rik), *adj.* of or having to do with the spirometer or spirometry.

**spi|rom|e|try** (spī rom′ə trē), *n.* **1** the measurement of breathing power or lung capacity. **2** the use of the spirometer.

**spirt** (spėrt), *v.i., v.t., n.* = spurt.

**spir|u|la** (spir′yə lə, spir′ə-), *n., pl.* **-lae** (-lē). any of a group of small cephalopods having an internal, chambered, spiral shell and ten tentacles. [< New Latin *spirula* (diminutive) < Latin *spīra;* see etym. under **spire²**]

**spir|y¹** (spīr′ē), *adj.* **1** having the form of a spire; tapering: *a spiry turret or steeple, spiry grass or rocks.* **2** having many spires: *The spiry habitable city* (Robert Louis Stevenson).

**spir|y²** (spī′rē), *adj.* spiral; coiled; curving.

**spis|sat|ed** (spis′ā tid), *adj.* made thick, dense, or compact; inspissated. [< Latin *spissātus,* past participle of *spissāre* thicken (< *spissus* thick) + English *-ed²*]

**spis|si|tude** (spis′ə tüd, -tyüd), *n.* thickness; density; compactness. [< Latin *spissitūdo, -inis* < *spissus* thick]

**spit¹** (spit), *v.,* **spat** or **spit, spit|ting,** *n.* —*v.i.* **1** to throw out something from the mouth: *It is illegal to spit on the floor of buses, trains, and*

---

**Pronunciation Key:** hat, āge, cãre, fär; let, ēqual, tėrm; it, īce; hot, ōpen, ôrder; **oil, out;** cup, pu̇t, rüle; **ch**ild; lo**ng**; **th**in; **ᴛʜ**en; **zh,** measure; **ə** represents **a** in about, **e** in taken, **i** in pencil, **o** in lemon, **u** in circus.

*other public conveyances.* **2** to spit (at or on) a person or thing to express hatred or contempt: *You call me misbeliever ... And spit upon my Jewish gabardine* (Shakespeare). (*Figurative.*) *The wit of fools that slovenly will spit on all things fair* (George Chapman). **3** to make a spitting or hissing sound: *The cat spits when angry.* **4** to sputter: *The sausage began to spit in the pan.* **5** to rain or snow suddenly or lightly, as in a brief flurry.
**—*v.t.*** **1** to throw out (something) from the mouth; expectorate: *Spit your gum out before you come into the classroom.* **2** *Figurative.* to throw out as if by spitting: *The gun spits fire. He spat curses.* **3** to light (a fuse).
**—*n.*** **1** the liquid produced in the mouth; saliva. **2** the sound or act of spitting. **3a** the frothy secretion given off by some insects. **b** any one of these insects; spittle insect. **4** a light rain or snow.
**spit and image,** *Informal.* the exact image; spitting image: *My mother was the spit and image of Queen Wilhelmina* (New Yorker).
**spit up,** to throw up; regurgitate: *It is common for infants to spit up a little milk after being fed* (Sidonie M. Gruenberg).
**the spit of,** *Informal.* just like: *He is the very spit of his father.*
[< Old English *spittan*] **—spit′like′,** *adj.*
▶ See **expectorate** for usage note.

**spit**[2] (spit), *n., v.,* **spit|ted, spit|ting.** **—*n.*** **1** a sharp-pointed, slender rod or bar on which meat is roasted or broiled. **2** a narrow point of land running into the water. **3** a long, narrow reef, shoal, or sandbank extending from the shore. See picture under **peninsula.**
**—*v.t.*** **1** to run a spit through; put on a spit: *He lighted a fire, spitted a leg of mutton* (Tobias Smollett). **2** to pierce or stab with a sharp-pointed weapon; impale on something sharp: *The hunters spitted two rabbits.*
[Old English *spitu*]

**spit|al** (spit′əl), *n.* **1** a shelter or other place of refuge, as for travelers, paupers, etc. **2** a hospital for the poor or diseased, especially for lepers; lazaretto. [alteration (influenced by *hospital*) of earlier *spittle,* Middle English *spitell,* ultimately < Medieval Latin *hospitale.* See etym. of doublets **hospital, hostel, hotel.**]

**spit and polish,** *Informal.* great or too much attention to neatness, orderliness, and smart appearance, especially as part of the discipline of a sailor or soldier: *The army concentrated on spit and polish, retreat formations, and parades* (Dwight D. Eisenhower). *They looked weather-beaten, there was little spit and polish to them* (New Yorker).

**spit|ball** (spit′bôl′), *n., v. U.S.* **—*n.*** **1** a small ball of chewed-up paper, used as a missile. **2** *Baseball.* an illegal curve pitched after wetting one side of the ball with saliva.
**—*v.i.*** **1** to throw a spitball: *Birdie Tebetts, the Cincinnati manager, accused Burdette of spitballing* (Newsweek). **2** *Slang, Figurative.* to express one's immediate ideas without thought or preparation; brainstorm: *We're just spitballing, of course, but here are a few* [*ideas*] *we'll hand along* (New Yorker).
**—*v.t.*** *Slang, Figurative: "Never mind—spitball some dialogue to give the general idea," said Gallwise* (S. J. Perelman).
[American English < *spit*[1] + *ball*[1]]

**spit|ball|er** (spit′bô′lər), *n. U.S.* a baseball player who throws spitballs.

**spitch|cock** (spich′kok′), *n., v.* **—*n.*** an eel split, cut up into pieces, and broiled or fried.
**—*v.t.*** to split, cut up, and broil or fry (an eel).
[origin uncertain]

**spit curl,** *U.S. Informal.* a small lock of hair dampened, originally with saliva, and curled flat on the cheek or forehead: *Her face was firm and strong, but heavily rouged and framed with spit curls* (New Yorker).

**spite** (spīt), *n., v.,* **spit|ed, spit|ing.** **—*n.*** **1** desire to annoy or harm another; ill will or malice, or an instance of it; grudge: *They trampled his flowers out of spite.* **2** *Obsolete.* misfortune; insult; injury: *The time is out of joint: O cursed spite, That ever I was born to set it right!* (Shakespeare).
**—*v.t.*** to show ill will toward; annoy; irritate: *They left their yard dirty to spite the people who lived next door.*
**in spite of,** not prevented by; notwithstanding: *The children went to school in spite of the storm.*
[short for Middle English *despit* despite]
**—*Syn.*** ***n.*** **1 Spite, malice, grudge** mean ill will against another. **Spite** suggests envy or mean disposition, and applies to active ill will shown by doing mean, petty things to hurt or annoy: *He ruined her drawing out of spite.* **Malice** emphasizes actual wish or intention to injure, and suggests hatred or, especially, a disposition delighting in doing harm or seeing others hurt: *Many gossips are motivated by malice.* **Grudge** suggests wishing to get even for real or imagined injury, and applies to ill will nursed for a long time: *She bears grudges.*

**spite|ful** (spīt′fəl), *adj.* full of spite; eager to annoy; behaving with ill will and malice: *a spiteful remark. The spiteful little girl tore up her older sister's papers.* **SYN:** malicious, malevolent.
**—spite′ful|ly,** *adv.* **—spite′ful|ness,** *n.*

**spite|less** (spīt′lis), *adj.* free from spite.

**spit|fire** (spit′fīr′), *n.* **1** a person, especially a woman or girl, who has a quick and fiery temper. **2** something that sends forth fire, such as a cannon or certain fireworks.

**spit|rack** (spit′rak′), *n.* an iron rack formerly used to support a spit before a fire.

**spit|ter** (spit′ər), *n.* **1** a person who spits. **2** *Baseball.* a spitball: *"I gotta laugh at the players which favor the return of the spitter," said the cynical Stengel* (New York Times).

**spit|ting cobra** (spit′ing), any one of various Asian and African cobras that spit their venom at the face and eyes of their victims, especially the ringhals.

**spitting image,** *Informal.* the exact likeness; spit and image: *She is the spitting image of her mother.*

**spit|tle** (spit′əl), *n.* **1** saliva; spit. **2** the secretion produced by a spittle insect. [alteration of obsolete *spattle* (influenced by *spit*[1]), Old English *spātl* saliva < *spittan* spit]

**spit|tle|bug** (spit′əl bug′), *n.* a spittle insect; froghopper.

**spittle insect,** any one of various homopterous insects whose larvae cover themselves with a protective foamy secretion.

**spit|toon** (spi tün′), *n.* a container to spit into; cuspidor. [American English < *spit*[1] + *-oon,* as in *saloon*]

**spitz** (spits), *n.,* or **spitz dog,** any one of various sturdy, small dogs with long hair, pointed nose and ears, and a tail curled up over the back, especially a white variety of Pomeranian. [< German *Spitz* < *spitz* pointed]

**spitz|en|berg** or **Spitz|en|berg** (spit′sən bėrg), *n.* = spitzenburg.

**spitz|en|burg** or **Spitz|en|burg** (spit′sən bėrg), *n.* any one of several varieties of fine-flavored winter apple. They are red, sometimes streaked with yellow. [American English; origin uncertain; perhaps < Dutch *spits* pointed + *berg* mountain (because of its shape)]

**spitz|flute** (spits′flüt′), *n.* an organ stop having conical pipes of metal, which give a thin, somewhat reedy tone. [half-translation of German *Spitzflöte* < *spitz* pointed + *Flöte* flute]

**spiv** (spiv), *n. British Slang.* a person who makes a living as by petty thievery, blackmail, or pimping. [probably < *SPIV,* abbreviation of *Suspected Person Itinerant Vagabond* (a police charge)]

**spiv|ver|y** (spiv′ər ē), *n. British Slang.* the activities or practices of spivs.

**SPIW** (no periods) or **S.P.I.W.,** Special Purpose Individual Weapon (a gun equipped with separate barrels for firing fléchettes and grenades).

**splake** (splāk), *n., pl.* **splakes** or (*collectively*) **splake.** a Canadian trout developed in 1946 from a cross between the brook or speckled trout and the lake trout. [blend of *speckled* trout and *lake* trout]

**splanch|nic** (splangk′nik), *adj.* of, having to do with, or in the region of the viscera; visceral. [< New Latin *splanchnicus* < Greek *splanchnikós* < *splánchnon,* singular of *splánchna* the inward parts, viscera < *splēn, splēnós;* see etym. under **spleen**]

**splanch|nol|o|gy** (splangk nol′ə jē), *n.* the scientific study of the viscera. [< Greek *splánchnon* (see etym. under **splanchnic**) + English *-logy*]

**splanch|no|pleure** (splangk′nə plůr), *n. Embryology.* the inner layer of the mesoderm combined with the endoderm. It gives rise to the connective and muscle tissue of most of the intestinal tracts. [< Greek *splánchnon* (see etym. under **splanchnic**) + *pleurā* side]

**splanch|not|o|my** (splangk not′ə mē), *n., pl.* **-mies.** the dissection or anatomy of the viscera. [< Greek *splánchnon* (see etym. under **splanchnic**) + *-tomiā* a cutting]

**splash** (splash), *v., n.* **—*v.t.*** **1** to cause (water, mud, or the like) to fly about so as to wet or soil: *The baby likes to splash the water in his tub.* **2** to cause to scatter a liquid about: *He splashed the oars as he rowed.* **3** to wet, spatter, or soil: *Our car is all splashed with mud.* **4** to make (one's way) with splashing: *The boat splashed its way up the river.* **5** to mark with spots or patches: *The careless painter splashed the furniture.* **6** to move (logs) by opening a dam and releasing a flood of water.
**—*v.i.*** **1** to dash water, mud, or the like, about: *The baby likes to splash in his tub.* **2** to dash in scattered masses or drops: *Muddy water splashed on our windshield. The waves splashed on the beach.* **3** to fall, move, or go with a splash or splashes: *The dog splashed across the brook.*
**—*n.*** **1** the act, result, or sound of splashing: *The splash of the wave knocked him over. The boat upset with a loud splash.* **2** a spot of liquid splashed upon a thing: *She has splashes of grease on her dress.* **3** a large or uneven patch or spot: *The dog is white with brown splashes.* **4a** the moving of logs by splashing. **b** the water released from a dam in order to splash logs.
**make a splash,** *Informal.* to attract attention; cause excitement: *He is free from the desire to make a splash, or the impulse of some academics to bite their former mentors in the leg* (Marcus Cunliffe).
**splash down,** to land in the ocean after a space flight: *The mission will be over, however, when the ... spacecraft plunges back through the atmosphere to splash down in the Pacific Ocean northwest of Hawaii* (New York Times).
[probably alteration of *plash*[1]]

**splash|back** (splash′bak′), *n.* a guard in the back of a cookstove or on a wall to protect against splashes.

**splash|board** (splash′bôrd′, -bōrd′), *n.* **1** a guard in front of the driver's seat, or one over or beside a wheel, to prevent mud or water, from splashing into the vehicle; dashboard; mudguard. **2** a screen rising from the deck of a boat to block off water or spray. **3** a plank for closing the sluice or spillway of a dam.

**splash dam,** a dam built to store a head of water for driving logs.

**splash|down** (splash′doun′), *n.* the landing of a capsule or other spacecraft in the ocean after reentry: *Just after splashdown, frogmen reaching the space capsule plugged a floating telephone into a socket on the craft's exterior and immediately established communications with* [*the*] *astronauts* (Science News Letter).

**splash|er** (splash′ər), *n.* **1** a person or thing that splashes. **2** something that protects from splashes; splashboard.

**splash guard,** = mudguard.

**splash lubrication,** a lubricating system for an internal-combustion engine in which oil is splashed by the moving parts onto all parts of the engine.

**splash|y** (splash′ē), *adj.,* **splash|i|er, splash|i|est.** **1** making a splash. **2** full of irregular spots or streaks; done in splashes. **3** *Informal.* attracting attention; causing excitement or comment; showy: *The star of the show made a splashy entrance. Around the World in 80 Days—a big, splashy, funny review of the Jules Verne fantasy* (New Yorker). **—splash′i|ly,** *adv.* **—splash′i|ness,** *n.*

**splat**[1] (splat), *n.* a broad, flat piece of wood, especially one forming the central upright part of the back of a chair. [origin uncertain, apparently < Middle English *splat* to split open, cut up]

**splat**[2] (splat), *v.,* **splat|ted, splat|ting,** *n., interj.*
**—*v.t.*** to cause to spatter or splash against a hard surface; splatter: *He splats lemons against a wall* (Harper's).
**—*v.i.*** to make a dull, flat sound, as of splattering or splashing: *A full wallet splatted to the sand* (Barnaby Conrad).
**—*n., interj.*** a spattering, splashing, or slapping sound: *The splat occurs when a stream of fine droplets of molten metals lands on a solid surface* (New Scientist). *The grapefruit went "splat!" and came down in a shower of juice* (New York Times). [back formation < *splatter*]

**splatch** (splach), *n., v.t.* = splotch.

**splat|ter** (splat′ər), *v., n.* **—*v.t., v.i.*** to splash or spatter: *The cotton is ... white, splattered with stylized red and black snowflakes* (New Yorker).
**—*n.*** a splash or splatter.
[perhaps blend of *spatter* and *splash*]

**splay** (splā), *v., adj., n.* **—*v.t.*** **1** to spread out; expand; extend. **2** to make slanting, as the jambs or sides of a window; bevel. **3** to dislocate, as a horse's shoulder.
**—*v.i.*** **1** to have or lie in a slanting direction; slope. **2** to spread out; flare.
**—*adj.*** **1** spread out; wide and flat; turned outward: *splay feet.* **2** awkward; clumsy; ungainly. **3** oblique; awry.
**—*n.*** **1** a spread; flare. **2** a surface that makes an oblique angle with another, such as the beveled jamb of a window or door; slanting surface.
[Middle English *splayen,* short for *displayen* display]

**splay|foot** (splā′fůt′), *n., pl.* **-feet,** *adj.* **—*n.*** a broad, flat foot, especially one turned outward.
**—*adj.*** = splay-footed.

**splay-foot|ed** or **splay|foot|ed** (splā′fůt′id), *adj.* **1** having splayfeet. **2** awkward; clumsy.

**splay-kneed** (splā′nēd′), *adj.* having the knees turned outward.

**splay-leg|ged** (splā′leg′id, -legd′), *adj.* = bowlegged.

**splay-toed** (splā′tōd′), *adj.* having the toes spread out.

✱**spleen** (splēn), *n.* **1** a ductless, glandlike organ at the left of the stomach in man, and near the stomach or intestine in other vertebrates. It stores blood and helps filter foreign substances from the blood. The spleen was once believed to cause low spirits, bad temper, and spite. **2** bad temper; spite; anger: *This is the land where hate should die, No feuds of faith, no spleen of race* (Denis A. McCarthy). **3** low spirits; moroseness; melancholy. **4** *Obsolete.* a whim; caprice: *A thousand spleens bear her a thousand ways* (Shakespeare). [Middle English *splen,* and *splene* < Latin *splēn* < Greek *splēn, splēnós*] —**spleen′-like′**, *adj.*

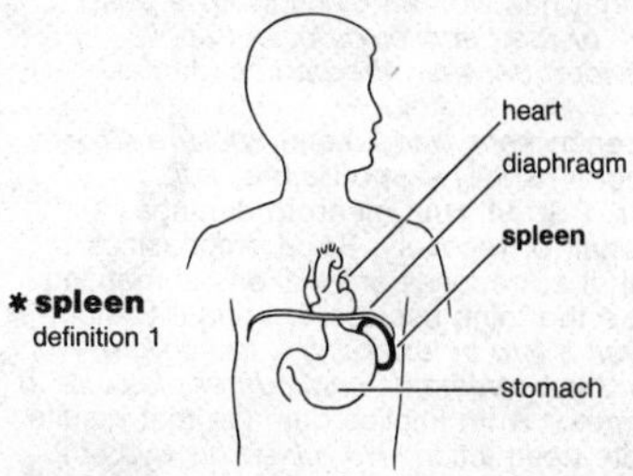


✱**spleen** definition 1

**spleen|ful** (splēn′fəl), *adj.* irritable or peevish; spiteful. —**spleen′ful|ly**, *adv.*

**spleen|less** (splēn′lis), *adj.* having no spleen.

**spleen|wort** (splēn′wėrt′), *n.* any one of a group of ferns having oblong spore cases situated obliquely on the upper surface of small veins. [< *spleen* + *wort* (because it was believed to be medically helpful)]

**spleen|y** (splē′nē), *adj.* full of or characterized by spleen; spleenful.

**splen|da|cious** (splen dā′shəs), *adj.* very splendid; gorgeous; magnificent: *The room is papered with some splendacious pattern in blue and gold* (Blackwood's Magazine). [< *splend*(id) + (viv)*acious*]

**splen|dent** (splen′dənt), *adj. Archaic.* **1** shining brightly; brilliant: *... splendent planets* (Sir Thomas Browne). **2** gleaming; lustrous: *... splendent Parian marble* (Thackeray). **3** *Figurative.* splendid; gorgeous: *splendent in gold lace* (Thomas Carlyle). [< Latin *splendēns, -entis,* present participle of *splendēre* be bright]

**splen|did** (splen′did), *adj.* **1** brilliant; glorious; magnificent; grand: *a splendid sunset, splendid jewels, a splendid palace, a splendid victory. Give me the splendid silent sun with all his beams full-dazzling* (Walt Whitman). SYN: See syn. under **magnificent**. **2** very good; fine; excellent: *a splendid chance, a splendid time.* [< Latin *splendidus* < *splendēre* be bright] —**splen′did|ly**, *adv.* —**splen′did|ness**, *n.*

**splen|dif|er|ous** (splen dif′ər əs), *adj. Informal.* splendid; magnificent: *The splendiferous hotel was surely the set where the Marx brothers had gambolled through "A Night in Casablanca"* (Sunday Express). [< Late Latin *splendifer,* for Latin *splendōrifer* (< *splendor, -ōris* splendor + *ferre* to bear) + English *-ous*] —**splen|dif′er|ous|ly**, *adv.* —**splen|dif′er-ous|ness**, *n.*

**splen|dor** (splen′dər), *n.* **1** great brightness; brilliant light or luster: *The sun set in a golden splendor. ... splendor of coral seas* (William O. Douglas). **2** great display of riches or costly things; magnificent show; pomp: *the splendor of a royal wedding.* **3** brilliant glory: *How the grand band-wagon shone with a splendor all its own* (James Whitcomb Riley). [< Latin *splendor, -ōris* < *splendēre* be bright]

**splen|dor|ous** (splen′dər əs), *adj.* full of splendor: *A light that spreads a finer joy, Than cloudless noon-tide splendorous o'er the world* (George MacDonald).

**splen|dour** (splen′dər), *n. Especially British.* splendor.

**splen|dour|ous** (splen′dər əs), *adj. Especially British.* splendorous.

**splen|drous** (splen′drəs), *adj. Especially British.* splendorous.

**sple|nec|to|mize** (spli nek′tə mīz), *v.t.,* **-mized, -miz|ing.** to subject to splenectomy; remove the spleen of.

**sple|nec|to|my** (spli nek′tə mē), *n., pl.* **-mies.** the surgical removal of the spleen. [< Greek *splēn, splēnós* spleen + *ektomē* a cutting out]

**sple|net|ic** (spli net′ik), *adj., n.* —*adj.* **1** of or having to do with the spleen. **2** bad-tempered; irritable; peevish; irascible: *a splenetic woman, who must have someone to find fault with* (Samuel Richardson).
—*n.* a person who is splenetic in disposition. [< Late Latin *splēnēticus* < Latin *splēn;* see etym. under **spleen**] —**sple|net′i|cal|ly**, *adv.*

**sple|net|i|cal** (spli net′ə kəl), *adj.* = splenetic.

**sple|ni|al** (splē′nē əl), *adj.* of or having to do with the splenius.

**splen|ic** (splen′ik, splē′nik), *adj.* of, having to do with, or in the region of the spleen. [< Latin *splēnicus* < Greek *splēnikós* < *splēn, splēnós* spleen]

**sple|ni|tis** (spli nī′tis), *n.* inflammation of the spleen. [< Greek *splēnîtis* < *splēn, splēnós* spleen]

**splen|i|tive** (splen′ə tiv), *adj.* **1** splenetic; ill-humored; irritable. **2** spleenful; impetuous; passionate: *I am not splenitive and rash* (Shakespeare).

**sple|ni|us** (splē′nē əs), *n.* a broad, flat muscle extending from the upper vertebrae to the neck and base of the skull. It serves to move the head and neck. [< New Latin *splenius* < Greek *splēnion* bandage, compress (especially, one used for the spleen) < *splēn, splēnós* spleen (because of its shape)]

**sple|ni|za|tion** (splē′nə zā′shən), *n. Medicine.* a change produced in the lungs by inflammation, in which they resemble the form of the spleen.

**sple|noid** (splē′noid), *adj.* spleenlike.

**sple|no|meg|a|ly** (splē′nō meg′ə lē, splen′ō-), *n.* enlargement of the spleen. [< Greek *splēn, splēnós* spleen + *mégas, megálou* big + English *-y*[3]]

**sple|not|o|my** (spli not′ə mē), *n., pl.* **-mies.** a surgical incision into the spleen. [< Greek *splēn, splēnós* spleen + *-tomiā* a cutting]

**spleu|chan** (splü′ʜən), *n. Scottish and Irish.* a pouch for holding tobacco, sometimes used as a purse. [< Gaelic *spliùchan*]

✱**splice** (splīs), *v.,* **spliced, splic|ing,** *n.* —*v.t.* **1** to join together (ropes or cables) by weaving together ends that have been pulled out into separate strands. **2a** to join together (two pieces of timber) by overlapping. **b** *Figurative:* *to write a speech by splicing parts of several old talks.* **3** to join together (film, tape, wire, or the like) by gluing or cementing the ends. **4** *Informal.* to marry: *We never meant to be spliced in the humdrum way of other people* (Charlotte Brontë).
—*n.* **1a** the act or process of joining ropes, timbers, film, or the like, by splicing: *How neat a splice can you make?* **b** the joint so formed. **2** *Slang.* a marriage; wedding. [perhaps < Middle Dutch *splissen*]

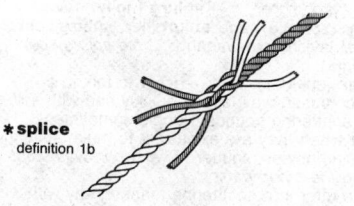

✱**splice** definition 1b

**splice graft,** *Horticulture.* a graft made by cutting the scion and stock diagonally, fitting them together, and tying them with waxed string.

**splice grafting,** the act or method of making a splice graft.

**splic|er** (splī′sər), *n.* **1** a person who splices. **2** a device for splicing film, tape, or the like: *One of the basic tools of film editing is the splicer, on which the shots chosen by the editor are pieced together* (Samuel Allen).

**spline** (splīn), *n., v.,* **splined, splin|ing.** —*n.* **1** a long, narrow, relatively thin strip of wood or metal; slat. **2** a long, flexible strip of wood or the like, used as a guide in drawing curves. **3** *Machinery.* **a** a flat, rectangular key fitting into a groove or slot between parts, as in a shaft or wheel. **b** the groove for such a key.
—*v.t.* **1** to fit with a spline or key. **2** to provide with a groove for a spline or key. [origin uncertain]

**splint** (splint), *n., v.* —*n.* **1** an arrangement of wood, metal, or plaster to hold a broken or dislocated bone in place: *The man's broken arm was set in splints to hold it in position.* **2** a thin, flexible strip of wood, such as is used in making baskets: *My basket is woven from splints.* **3** a thin metal strip or plate. Old armor often had overlapping splints to protect the elbow, knee, or other part of the body, and allow easy movement. **4** a hard, bony growth on the splint bone of a horse, mule, or the like. **5** *Dialect.* a splinter of wood or stone; chip.
—*v.t.* **1** to secure, hold in position, or support by means of a splint or splints. **2** *Figurative.* to support as if with splints. [probably < Middle Low German *splinte*]

**splint|age** (splin′tij), *n.* the application or use of splints.

**splint armor,** armor made of overlapping plates or strips of metal.

**splint bone,** either one of the two smaller bones on either side of the large bone between the hock and the fetlock of a horse, mule, or the like.

**splint-bot|tomed** (splint′bot′əmd), *adj.* having the bottom or seat made of splints, usually interwoven: *a splint-bottomed chair.*

**splint coal,** a hard, bituminous coal with a dull, grayish-black color and a splintery structure, producing a hot fire.

**splin|ter** (splin′tər), *n., adj., v.* —*n.* **1** a thin, sharp piece of wood, bone, stone, glass, or the like; sliver: *He got a splinter in his hand. The mirror broke into splinters.* **2** a dissenting group that breaks away from the main group.
—*adj.* of or having to do with dissenting groups that break away from regular political groups, religious organizations, or other associations: *a splinter party. A few other splinter Socialist groups exist* (Harper's).
—*v.t.* to split or break into splinters: *The fireman splintered the locked door with an ax.*
—*v.i.* to be split or broken into splinters; break off in splinters: *The mirror splintered. There were few men in the room who did not remember 1931, when the Labor Party ... splintered hopelessly* (Time).
[< Middle Dutch *splinter*]

**splinter bar,** **1** a crossbar between the shafts, as of a carriage, to which the traces are attached. **2** = singletree.

**splin|ter|proof** (splin′tər prüf′), *adj.* proof against splinters, as of bursting shells.

**splin|ter|y** (splin′tər ē), *adj.* **1** apt to splinter: *splintery wood.* **2** of or like a splinter. **3** *Figurative.* rough and jagged, as if from splintering: *The ridgy precipices ... showed their splintery and rugged edges* (Scott). **4** full of splinters. **5** characterized by the production of small splinters.

**split** (split), *v.,* **split, split|ting,** *n., adj.* —*v.t.* **1a** to break or cut from end to end, or in layers; cleave: *a tree split by lightning. The man is splitting the logs into firewood. She split the cake and filled it with jelly.* **b** to rip violently; tear: *sails split by a hurricane.* **2** to separate into parts; divide: *The two men split the cost of the dinner between them. The old farm has been split up into house lots.* **3** to divide into different groups, parties, or factions: *Disagreements split the club into rival factions.* **4** to cast (a vote or a ballot) for candidates of different political parties in the same election: *He split his vote by voting for a Democratic mayor and a Republican sheriff.* **5a** to divide (a molecule) into two or more individual atoms or atomic groups. **b** to remove by such a process. **c** to divide (an atomic nucleus) into two portions of approximately equal mass by forcing the absorption of a neutron. **6** to issue a certain number of new shares of (stock) for each share currently held: *American Tobacco Co. directors voted to split its common stock two-for-one* (Wall Street Journal).
—*v.i.* **1a** to come apart or break open by or as if by being split: *The huge tree split when it was struck by lightning. The rock split into two.* (*Figurative.*) *She complains that her head is splitting from the noise.* (*Figurative.*) *I laughed till I thought I should split* (Jonathan Swift). **b** to be capable of being split: *Birch splits easily.* **2** to separate into parts; divide: *There are two peaks where the mountain splits into two parallel ranges.* **3** to divide into different groups, parties, or factions: *After the party, the company split up. The membership of the club was at the point of splitting.* **4** *U.S. Slang, Figurative.* **a** to leave a place; go away: *The door was open, and Howard split. As soon as I realized he was gone, I went out looking for him* (New Yorker). **b** to run away; desert: *They [draftees] 'split' for different reasons—anything from personal problems to political resistance* (Listener). **5** *Informal.* to become separated or divorced; break up: *After years of quarreling, she and her husband finally split up.* **6** *British Slang.* to turn informer; peach: *I might have got clear off, if I'd split upon her* (Dickens).
—*n.* **1** an act or instance of splitting; break; crack; fissure: *a split in the door. Frost caused the split in the rock.* **2** a division in a group, party, or faction: *There was a split in the club for a time, but harmony was soon restored.* **3** *Slang.* a share; portion: *to get a split of the profits.* **4** the act or process of issuing a certain number of new shares of stock for each currently held. **5** *Informal.* a bottle of a drink half the usual size; about seven fluid ounces. **6** a sweet dish made of ice cream, sliced fruit, syrup, and nuts: *a ba-*

**Pronunciation Key:** hat, āge, cãre, fär; let, ēqual, tėrm; it, īce; hot, ōpen, ôrder; **oi**l, **ou**t; cup, pu̇t, rüle; **ch**ild; lo**ng**; **th**in; ᴛʜen; **zh**, measure; ə represents **a** in about, **e** in taken, **i** in pencil, **o** in lemon, **u** in circus.

*nana split.* **7** Often, **splits.** an acrobatic trick of sinking to the floor with the legs spread far apart in opposite directions. **8** the wide separation of two or more standing pins after the first roll in bowling, making a spare very difficult. **9** one of the thin sheets of leather into which a skin is sometimes sliced before or during tanning. **10** one of the strips into which osiers are cut in basketmaking.
—*adj.* **1** broken or cut from end to end; divided; cleft: *a split log, a split door.* **2** (of a stock market quotation) given in sixteenths rather than eighths (the usual way of quoting stock).
**split hairs.** See under **hair.**
[apparently < Middle Dutch *splitten*]

**split-bot|tomed** (split′bot′əmd), *adj.* = splint-bottomed.

**split decision,** a decision that is not unanimous, as in a boxing match: *Ezzard Charles ... got off the canvas after a second-round knockdown to gain a ten-round split decision over Paul Andrews in the Chicago Stadium* (New York Times).

**split end,** *Football.* an end separated a few yards from the line of scrimmage to enable him to get quickly downfield to catch passes.

**split-hair** (split′hãr′), *adj.* extremely narrow or close; very precise; hairline.

**split infinitive,** an infinitive having one or more words between *to* and the verb. *Example:* He wants to never work, but to always play.
▶ **split infinitive.** Awkward split infinitives should be avoided. Awkward: *After a while I was able to, although not very accurately, distinguish the good customers from the sulky ones.* Improved: *After a while I was able to distinguish—though not very accurately—the good customers from the sulky ones.*

**split jump,** a jump in the air made in dancing with the legs spread far apart in opposite directions.

**split-lev|el** (split′lev′əl), *n., adj.* —*n.* a house with two or more floor levels, each level about half a story above or below the adjacent level: *that youthful American dream, a split-level in the suburbs* (Harper's).
—*adj.* having an upper level about half a floor above the lower or main level: *a split-level house, a split-level church, a split-level parking lot. The tallest block contains six floors, including a split-level basement-ground floor* (London Times).

**split-off** (split′ôf′, -of′), *n.* **1** something that is split or divided from something else: *Split-offs from the parent clumps are best planted four inches apart* (Punch). **2** the distribution of stock in a new corporation to stockholders of the parent corporation in partial exchange for old stock: *Company officials declined to explain the split-off other than to say "it is for good business reasons"* (Wall Street Journal).

**split page,** the front page of the second section of a newspaper.

**split pattern,** a pattern for a casting that consists of two halves that can be fitted and held together with pins.

**split peas,** husked peas split for making pea soup.

**split personality,** **1** *Informal.* schizophrenia: *Split personality, or schizophrenia, is a psychosis characterized by a personality which is split, or separated, from reality* (Atlantic). **2** a personality that shows markedly inconsistent or contradictory patterns of behavior.

**split-phase** (split′fāz′), *adj.* of or having to do with an alternating single-phase current in a divided circuit where there is a difference of phase between the currents in the two branches.

**split-rail fence** (split′rāl′), *U.S.* a fence made up of rails split from a log: *an expanse of lawn bordered by a split-rail fence* (New Yorker).

**splits** (splits), *n.pl.* See under **split** (*n.* def. 7).

**split|saw** (split′sô′), *n.* a kind of ripsaw.

**split screen,** **1** the showing of two or more images simultaneously on separate sections of a motion-picture or television screen. **2** the images shown this way: *Among them was a split screen —live action on one half, tape rerun on the other— of two skiers apparently racing each other down the same slope, although they actually competed at different times* (New York Times). —**split′-screen′,** *adj.*

**split second,** a very brief moment of time; instant: *It disappears in a split second* (Science News Letter).

**split-sec|ond** (split′sek′ənd), *adj.* instantaneous; very quick: *split-second timing.*

**split shift,** a working shift divided into two or more periods: *"With a lot of us working a split shift, it used to be hard to find something to do with the couple of free hours in the afternoon"* (Wall Street Journal).

**split stroke** or **shot,** *Croquet.* a stroke or shot made in such a way that two balls placed in contact are driven in different directions.

**split|tail** (split′tāl′), *n.* a cyprinoid fish of California rivers. The upper lobe of its caudal fin is much more developed than the lower.

**split|ter** (split′ər), *n.* **1** a person or thing that splits. **2** *Figurative.* a person who splits hairs.

**split ticket,** **1** a ballot marked or cast by a voter for some candidates of one party and some candidates of another party. **2** a ballot that lists candidates of more than one party.

**split|ting** (split′ing), *adj.* **1** that splits. **2** *Figurative.* **a** very severe; extreme; violent: *a splitting headache.* **b** aching severely: *a splitting head.*

**split|tism** (split′iz əm), *n.* = fractionalism.

**split-up** (split′up′), *n.* **1** division; separation; breakup: *a family split-up.* **2** an issuing of a number of new shares of stock for each currently held; split: *a stock split-up.* **3** the exchange of all the stocks of a parent corporation for the stocks of one or more newly formed or subsidiary corporations, resulting in the dissolution of the parent corporation.

**splodge** (sploj), *n.* a thick, heavy, or clumsy splotch. [compare etym. under **splotch**]

**splodg|y** (sploj′ē), *adj.,* **splodg|i|er, splodg|i|est.** full of splodges; showing coarse splotches of color.

**splore** (splôr, splōr), *n. Scottish.* **1** a frolic; merrymaking; revel. **2** an embroilment; scrape. [origin unknown]

**splosh** (splosh), *n., v.* —*n.* **1** = splash. **2** *Slang.* money. —*v.t., v.i.* splash.

**splotch** (sploch), *n., v.* —*n.* a large, irregular spot; splash: ... *instead of wiping away the tomato splotch he ... put out a tasting finger* (Frederic Morton).
—*v.t.* to make a splotch or splotches on; splash. [origin uncertain. Compare Middle English *splotty* spotty.]

**splotch|y** (sploch′ē), *adj.,* **splotch|i|er, splotch|i|est.** marked with splotches.

**splurge** (splėrj), *v.,* **splurged, splurg|ing,** *n. Informal.* —*v.i.* **1** to spend lavishly; be extravagant: *to splurge on a new coat.* **2** to show off.
—*v.t.* to spend lavishly: *We ... splurged the threadbare housekeeping kitty far into the red* (Punch).
—*n.* **1** the action of showing off; ostentatious display: *a splurge of wealth.* **2** an outburst: *a sudden splurge of energy.*
[American English; perhaps blend of *splash* and *surge*] —**splurg′er,** *n.* —**splurg′ing|ly,** *adv.*

**splurg|y** (splėr′jē), *adj.,* **splurg|i|er, splurg|i|est.** *Informal.* lavish; extravagant: ... *big splurgy parties* (Time).

**splut|ter** (splut′ər), *v., n.* —*v.i.* **1** to talk in a hasty, confused way; speak quickly and with spitting or sputtering sounds. People sometimes splutter when they are excited. **2** to make spitting or popping noises; sputter: *The bacon was spluttering in the frying pan.*
—*v.t.* to utter in a spluttering manner; say with spluttering: *to splutter out an apology.*
—*n.* a spluttering.
[perhaps variant of *sputter*] —**splut′ter|er,** *n.*

**splut|ter|y** (splut′ər ē), *adj.* that splutters; spluttering.

**Spock|i|an** (spok′ē ən), *adj.* of or having to do with Benjamin M. Spock (born 1903), an American physician noted for his books on child care.

**Spode** or **spode** (spōd), *n., adj.* —*n.* fine china or porcelain, commonly in Oriental style, of the type perfected by Josiah Spode (1754-1827), one of the first great potters of Staffordshire, England: *to buy a set of Spode.*
—*adj.* of such china or porcelain: *a Spode platter.*

**spod|u|mene** (spoj′ů mēn), *n.* a mineral, a silicate of aluminum and lithium, usually occurring in flat prismatic crystals. It is hard, transparent to translucent, and varies in color from grayish-, yellowish-, or greenish-white to emerald-green and purple. Some varieties are used as gems. *Formula:* $LiAlSi_2O_6$ [< French *spodumène* < German *Spodumen* < Greek *spodoúmenos,* past participle of *spodoûsthai* be burned to ashes < *spodós* ashes, powder (because it powders under the blowtorch)]

**spof|fish** (spof′ish), *adj. British Slang.* bustling; fussy; officious. [origin unknown]

**spoil** (spoil), *v.,* **spoiled** or **spoilt, spoil|ing,** *n.* —*v.t.* **1** to damage or injure (something) so as to make it unfit or useless; destroy: *Rain spoiled the picnic. He spoils a dozen pieces of paper before he writes a letter.* **2** to injure the character or disposition of, especially by being too kind, generous, or lenient: *That child is being spoiled by too much attention.* **3** *Archaic.* **a** to strip (as a person, country, or house) of goods, possessions, or valuables by force; plunder; despoil; sack: *to spoil a poor widow of her savings.* SYN: pillage. **b** to seize (goods) by force; carry off as plunder; rob; steal.
—*v.i.* **1** to be damaged or injured; become bad or unfit for use; deteriorate; decay: *The fruit spoiled because I kept it too long.* SYN: rot. **2** *Archaic.* to plunder; ravage; rob.
—*n.* **1** Often, **spoils.** things taken by force; things won; booty; loot: *The soldiers carried the spoils back to their own land.* **2** objects of art, books, or the like, which have been acquired by special effort. **3** an object of plundering; prey. **4** the act or practice of plundering; spoliation. **5** earth or refuse matter from excavating, mining, or dredging.
**be spoiling for,** *Informal.* to be longing for (a fight or argument); desire: *He is spoiling for a fight.*
**spoils,** government offices and positions, together with their advantages, filled by the political party that has won an election: *The post ... is "spoils" of the humbler order but spoils equally divided between the parties* (James Bryce).
[< Old French *espoillier* < Latin *spoliāre* < *spolium* booty, spoil] —**spoil′a|ble,** *adj.*
—*Syn. v.t.* **1 Spoil, ruin** mean to damage beyond repair or recovery. **Spoil** emphasizes damage that so reduces or weakens something as to make the thing useless or bring it to nothing: *to spoil a film by exposing it to sunlight. Her friend's unkind comments spoiled her pleasure in her new dress.* **Ruin** implies damage that results in complete destruction: *He ruined his eyes by reading in a poor light.*

**spoil|age** (spoi′lij), *n.* **1** the act of spoiling. **2** the fact of being spoiled: *Lower grades of rubber will be purchased to replace material in the stockpile that has been damaged by spoilage* (Wall Street Journal). **3** something spoiled.

**spoil|a|tion** (spoi lā′shən), *n.* the act of spoiling or damaging something: *the destruction and spoilation of a parkland property.*

**spoil|bank** (spoil′bangk′), *n.* a bank or mound of refuse earth, stone, or other waste material: *Owners of colliery spoilbanks are required to take all practicable steps to minimize the emission of smoke and fumes* (London Times). [< *spoil,* noun + *bank*[1]]

**spoil|er** (spoi′lər), *n.* **1** a person or thing that spoils. **2** a person who takes spoils. **3** a movable flap on the upper surface of the wing of an airplane, to help in slowing down or in decreasing lift, as in descending or landing. See picture under **aileron.** **4** an airflow deflector on an automobile that helps reduce the danger of spinouts by keeping the rear wheels on the track. **5** *U.S.* a political candidate who cannot win but who takes away enough votes to spoil another candidate's chances of winning.

**spoiler party,** *U.S.* a third political party formed especially to split one of the two regular parties so as to spoil its chances of winning in an election: *Mr. Javits ... described the six-year-old Conservative party as "a faction" that had been set up as "a spoiler party"* (New York Times).

**spoil|five** (spoil′fīv′), *n.* a card game for from three to ten players having five cards each. The game is said to be "spoiled" if no player can take three tricks.

**spoils** (spoilz), *n.pl.* See under **spoil.**

**spoils|man** (spoilz′mən), *n., pl.* **-men.** **1** a person who gets or tries to get a government office or job as a reward for his service to the successful political party. **2** a person who supports the spoils system.
[American English < *spoils* + *man*]

**spoil|sport** (spoil′spôrt′, -spōrt′), *n.* a person who acts so as to spoil or hinder the enjoyment or plans of others: *It is unusual for a candidate to win first time around, and if one does, he arouses a certain amount of resentment as a spoilsport* (New Yorker).

**spoils system,** *U.S.* the system or practice in which public offices with their advantages are awarded to supporters of the winning political party for its own (rather than the public) interest: *Adams was a remarkable President in many ways* (*such as his iron refusal to adopt the spoils system*) *but he failed in his chief aims* (Newsweek).

**spoilt** (spoilt), *v.* spoiled; a past tense and a past participle of **spoil.**

**spoke**[1] (spōk), *v.* **1** a past tense of **speak:** *She spoke about that yesterday.* **2** *Archaic.* spoken; a past participle of **speak.**

✱**spoke**[2] (spōk), *n., v.,* **spoked, spok|ing.** —*n.* **1** one of the set of bars from the center of a wheel to the rim. The spokes support the rim. **2** one of the set of handles projecting radially from the wheel by which the rudder of a ship or other vessel is controlled. **3** any one of various sets of radially projecting pieces similar to either of these in appearance or function. **4** a rung of a ladder. **5** *Figurative.* a thing that prevents or hinders; hindrance; obstruction: *I did hope the policy would have put a spoke in our tour, but, unluck-*

*ily, it gives me latitude to travel* (Thomas Hood).
**— *v.t.*** to furnish or provide with spokes.
**put a spoke in one's wheel**, to stop or hinder one: *Capitalists ... were trying to put a spoke in the wheel of Socialism* (Manchester Examiner). [Old English *spāca*] — **spoke'like'**, *adj.*

***spoke²**
definition 1

**spo|ken** (spō'kən), *v., adj.* — ***v.*** a past participle of **speak**: *They have spoken about having a picnic.*
— ***adj.*** **1** expressed with the mouth; uttered; oral: *the spoken word. A child understands a spoken direction better than a written one.* **2** made known by any utterance; expressed; told: *a spoken opinion.*
**-spoken**, *combining form.* speaking in a ______ way: *Soft-spoken = speaking in a soft way.*
**spoke|shave** (spōk'shāv'), *n.* a cutting tool having a blade with a handle at each end, used for smoothing and shaping curved surfaces or for making shingles or beams; drawknife.
**spokes|man** (spōks'mən), *n., pl.* **-men.** a person who speaks for another or others: *He was the spokesman for the workers in the strike against the factory owners.*
**spokes|man|ship** (spōks'mən ship), *n.* the office or position of a spokesman: *He felt there was some fitness in his spokesmanship that evening, for he was the representative of an institution* (London Daily News).
**spokes|per|son** (spōks'pėr'sən), *n.* = spokesman: *The role of colleges and universities in ... reducing unemployment is seldom discussed by spokespersons for higher education* (Science).
**spokes|wom|an** (spōks'wům'ən), *n., pl.* **-women.** a woman who speaks for another or others; a female advocate or representative: *The frosty comment of a spokeswoman for Brighton's Roedean School: "We have absolutely no intention of modifying our uniform"* (Time).
**spoke|wise** (spōk'wīz), *adv.* in the manner of, or like the movements of spokes of, a wheel.
**spo|li|ate** (spō'lē āt), *v.t.,* **-at|ed, -at|ing.** to spoil, plunder, or despoil. [< Latin *spoliāre* (with English *-ate*¹) < *spolium* booty]
**spo|li|a|tion** (spō'lē ā'shən), *n.* **1** the act of plundering or pillaging; robbery; despoliation. **SYN**: brigandage. **2** the authorized plundering of neutrals at sea in time of war. **3** *Law.* **a** the act of destroying a document, or of tampering with it so as to destroy its value as evidence. **b** the destruction of a ship's papers, as to conceal an illegal act.
**spo|li|a|tive** (spō'lē ā'tiv), *adj.* (of a disease) diminishing the quantity of blood.
**spo|li|a|to|ry** (spō'lē ə tôr'ē, -tōr'-), *adj.* of the nature of or characterized by spoliation.
**spon|da|ic** (spon dā'ik), *adj.* **1** of a spondee. **2** consisting of spondees. **3** having a spondee where a different foot is normal, especially in the fifth foot of a hexameter line. [< Latin *spondaicus,* variant of *spondīacus* < Greek *spondeiakós* < *spondeîos;* see etym. under **spondee**]
**spon|dee** (spon'dē), *n.* **1** a foot in English verse consisting of two accented syllables. *Example* (in the first three metrical feet): Rocks', caves', /lakes', fens',/bogs', dens',/and shades'/of death' (Milton). **2** a foot in Greek and Latin verse consisting of two long syllables. *Example: hērōs.* [< Latin *spondēus* < Greek *spondeîos* the meter originally used in chants accompanying libations < *spondḗ* libation < *spéndein* offer a drink]
**spon|du|licks** or **spon|du|lix** (spon dü'liks), *n. Slang.* money; cash. [American English; origin unknown]
**spon|dy|li|tis** (spon'də lī'tis), *n.* inflammation of the vertebrae. [< New Latin *spondylitis* < Latin *spondylus* (< Greek *spóndylos* vertebra) + New Latin *-itis* -itis]
**sponge** (spunj), *n., v.,* **sponged, spong|ing.** — ***n.*** **1** any one of a group of water animals having a tough, elastic skeleton or framework of interlaced fibers; poriferan. Sponges are free-swimming as larvae but soon become attached, as to stones or plants where they exist in large, complex colonies, usually on the bottom of the ocean. The sponges comprise a phylum of animals. *Sponges ... for a long time were thought to be plants because they spend most of their life attached in one place and are not active in the sense that most animals are* (A. M. Winchester). **2** the soft, light, porous framework of any one of these animals after the living matter has been removed. Sponges readily soak up liquids and yield them on pressure, and are much used in bathing and cleansing surfaces. **3** a similar article made artificially of rubber or plastic: *cellulose sponges.* **4a** the act of sponging. **b** the act of bathing with a sponge, especially in a small amount of water. **5** *Figurative.* **a** a person or thing that absorbs, drains, or sucks up in the manner of a sponge: *His active mind was a sponge, soaking up impressions and information.* **b** a person who drinks heavily: *I will do any thing, Nerissa, ere I will be married to a sponge* (Shakespeare). **6** *Informal, Figurative.* a person who continually lives at the expense of others; parasite. **7** something like a sponge. **8** a sterile pad, usually of cotton gauze, used to absorb blood or other fluid during surgical operations. **9** in cookery: **a** the soft, fermenting dough of which bread is made. **b** a fluffy pudding made with gelatin, egg whites, and flavoring. **c** = sponge cake. **10** metal, such as platinum or iron, in a porous or spongelike form, usually obtained by reduction without fusion: [*The Corporation*] *expects to be in full production this fall at the rate of 3,600 tons of sponge a year* (Wall Street Journal). **11** a mop for cleaning the bore of a cannon.
— ***v.t.*** **1** to wipe or rub with a wet sponge; make clean or damp in this way: [*She*] *sponged herself, dressed, and had a quiet breakfast* (New Yorker). **2** to remove or wipe (away or off) with a sponge: *Sponge the mud spots off the car.* **3** to absorb or take (up) with a sponge: *Sponge up the spilled water.* **4** Often **sponge out**, to rub or wipe out as if with a sponge; blot out; remove all traces of; obliterate; efface: *Time ... That sponges out all trace of truth* (Eliza Cook). **5** *Informal, Figurative.* to get from another or at another's expense in a mean or parasitic way; cadge: *He sponges all his lunches.* **6** to preshrink (cloth) before making it into clothing.
— ***v.i.*** **1** to absorb or take up, as a sponge does. **2** to gather sponges. **3** *Informal, Figurative.* to live or profit at the expense of another in a mean way: *That lazy man won't work, but sponges on his family.*
**throw in** (or **up**) **the sponge**, to abandon a contest or struggle; admit defeat; give up (from the practice of a boxer's seconds' tossing a sponge into the ring in acknowledgment of defeat): *The tax-reform program was so badly battered that the administration threw in the sponge* (Harper's). [Old English *spynge* < Latin *spongia* < Greek *spongiā,* variant of *sphóngos*] — **sponge'a|ble**, *adj.* — **sponge'like'**, *adj.*
**sponge|bag** (spunj'bag'), *n. British.* a waterproof bag used to carry a bath sponge and other toilet articles.
**sponge cake**, or **sponge|cake** (spunj'kāk'), *n.* a light, spongy cake made with eggs, sugar, and flour, but no shortening.
**sponge cloth**, a cotton fabric of loose texture, used for women's clothing.
**sponge gourd**, **1** the fruit of the loofah. **2** the plant itself.
**sponge iron**, iron ore rendered light and porous by the removal of foreign matter.
**sponge mop**, a mop consisting of a sponge fastened at the end of a stick, usually with a wringing device.
**spong|er** (spun'jər), *n.* **1** a person who sponges. **2a** a machine for sponging cloth. **b** a person who sponges cloth. **3** a person or vessel engaged in gathering sponges. **4** *Informal.* a person who gets on at the expense of others.
**sponge rubber**, rubber similar to foam rubber, used especially for cushions and insulators. It is made from dried natural rubber or latex by adding chemicals that release air bubbles, inflating the rubber into a spongy mass.
**sponge|ware** (spunj'wãr'), *n.* **1** an Early American glazed earthenware having a mottled surface produced by applying glaze with sponges. **2** any imitation of this type of earthenware.
**sponge|wood** (spunj'wůd'), *n.* **1** the stem of the sola, a plant of the East Indies. **2** its dried pith, used in making sun hats. **3** the plant itself; sola.
**spon|gin** (spun'jin), *n.* a horny protein substance secreted by sponges. In many sponges it forms a fibrous skeleton without spicules; in others it serves to unite or cement spicules.
**spong|ing house** (spun'jing), a building formerly maintained by a sheriff's officer in England for the temporary confinement of debtors, from which a person could obtain release through the satisfaction of his creditor or creditors, or be committed to prison.
**spon|gi|ose** (spun'jē ōs), *adj.* spongy; porous.
**spon|goid** (spong'goid), *adj.* spongelike; spongy. [< Greek *spongoeidēs* < *spongiā* sponge + *-oeidēs* -oid]
**spon|gy** (spun'jē), *adj.,* **-gi|er, -gi|est.** **1** like a sponge; soft, light, elastic, and full of holes: *spongy moss, a spongy dough, spongy soil.* **2** having an open, porous structure; full of small holes: *spongy ice, a spongy rock.* **3** *Obsolete.* having much rain; wet: *I saw ... the Roman eagle wing'd From the spongy South* (Shakespeare). — **spon'gi|ness**, *n.*
**spongy cell**, any one of the loosely-packed, irregularly shaped cells lying below the palisade cells in a leaf. Spongy cells use light energy to split water molecules into the hydrogen and oxygen necessary for photosynthesis.
**spongy parenchyma**, the tissue formed by a layer of spongy cells.
**spon|sion** (spon'shən), *n.* a solemn or formal engagement, promise, or pledge, often one entered into or made on behalf of another person. [< Latin *spōnsiō, -ōnis* < *spondēre* promise solemnly]
**spon|son** (spon'sən), *n.* **1** a structure built out from the side of a vessel for support or protection, especially a platform for handling gear or an armored structure containing a turret and gun, such as was common on large naval vessels built in the late 1800's: *The new tugs will have a length of 145 ft. between perpendiculars and a beam of 58 ft. across the paddle sponsons* (London Times). **2** a projecting structure to increase stability: **a** an air-filled compartment on either side of the hull of a canoe. **b** a short, winglike protuberance on either side of the hull of a seaplane. **c** a float on each side of the hull of a hydroplane (motorboat). [origin uncertain]
**spon|sor** (spon'sər), *n., v.* — ***n.*** **1** a person or group of persons responsible for a person or thing: *the sponsor of a law, the sponsor of a student applying for a scholarship.* **2** a person who makes a formal promise or pledge on behalf of another; surety. **3** a person who stands with the parents at an infant's baptism, agreeing to assist in the child's religious upbringing if necessary; godfather or godmother. **4** a company, store, or other business firm that pays the costs of a radio or television program during which its products or services are advertised: *A television sponsor is shopping for a replacement for "My Favorite Husband"* (New York Times). **5** a person or group that arranges or promotes an organization, meeting, or the like. **6** a person who pledges or gives a certain amount of financial assistance to an organization: *A contribution of $25 entitles you to be a sponsor; $15 to be a sustaining member.*
— ***v.t.*** to act as sponsor for; be the sponsor of: *The local churches sponsor our scout troop.* [< Latin *spōnsor* < *spondēre* give assurance, promise solemnly]
**spon|so|ri|al** (spon sôr'ē əl, -sōr'-), *adj.* of or having to do with a sponsor.
**spon|sor|ship** (spon'sər ship), *n.* the position and duties of a sponsor.
**spon|ta|ne|i|ty** (spon'tə nē'ə tē), *n., pl.* **-ties.** **1** the quality, condition, or fact of being spontaneous: [*The*] *quartet was ... possessed more of expert workmanship than any great feeling of spontaneity* (New York Times). **2** a spontaneous action or movement on the part of a living organism, especially activity of physical organs in the absence of any external stimulus.
**spon|ta|ne|ous** (spon tā'nē əs), *adj., adv.* — ***adj.*** **1** caused by natural impulse or desire; of one's own choice; not forced or compelled; not planned beforehand: *Both sides burst into spontaneous cheers at the skillful play.* **SYN**: See syn. under **voluntary**. **2** taking place without external cause or help; caused entirely by inner forces; of itself: *A pile of oily rags will sometimes break into a spontaneous flame. The eruption of a volcano is spontaneous.* **3** growing or produced naturally without cultivation or labor; not planted or cultivated.
— ***adv.*** in a spontaneous manner.
[< Late Latin *spontāneus* (with English *-ous*) < Latin *sponte* of one's own accord] — **spon|ta'ne|ous|ly**, *adv.* — **spon|ta'ne|ous|ness**, *n.*
**spontaneous combustion**, the act of a substance bursting into flame without anyone's setting it on fire. In spontaneous combustion, the heat produced by chemical action within the substance itself causes it to catch fire.
**spontaneous emission**, *Physics.* the release of excess energy in the form of light by an excited atom: *Light produced by the sun and by ordinary electric lights is the result of spontaneous emission caused by heat* (James P. Gordon).
**spontaneous generation**, the supposed pro-

**Pronunciation Key:** hat, āge, cãre, fär; let, ēqual, tėrm; it, īce; hot, ōpen, ôrder; oil, out; cup, pu̇t, rüle; child; long; thin; ᴛʜen; zh, measure; ə represents **a** in about, **e** in taken, **i** in pencil, **o** in lemon, **u** in circus.

duction of living organisms from nonliving matter; abiogenesis; autogenesis: *worms from mud, maggots from decaying meat. ... This is the view that came to be called spontaneous generation* (Scientific American).

**spon|toon** (spon tün′), *n.* a type of pike, having a short shaft, carried by officers, especially officers up to the rank of captain, in the British infantry from about 1740 until the early 1800's. [< French *esponton* < Italian *spontone,* and *spuntone,* variant of *puntone* < *punto* a point < Latin *pungere* to pierce]

**spoof** (spüf), *n., v. Informal.* —*n.* **1** a trick, joke, or hoax. **2** a light satirical parody; take-off: ... *to the Imperial Theatre to see "Silk Stockings," a musical spoof of a Soviet woman commissar's trip to Paris* (New York Times).
—*v.t., v.i.* **1** to treat or offer as a spoof; make fun of; ridicule; joke; fool. **2** to make a light satirical parody on: *The most successful part of the show is his spoofing of TV programs and commercials* (Newsweek).
[earlier, a game involving hoaxing (invented and named by Arthur Roberts, 1852-1913, a British comedian)] —**spoof′er,** *n.*

**spoof|er|y** (spü′fər ē), *n. Informal.* **1** cheating; deceit. **2** the act of making fun (of); mockery; parody.

**spook** (spük), *n., v.* —*n.* **1** *Informal.* a ghost; specter: *There did I see a spook, sure enough —milk-white and moving round* (E. G. Paige). **SYN:** wraith, apparition. **2** *U.S. Slang.* **a** a spy. **b** a Negro (used in an unfriendly way).
—*v.t. Informal.* **1** to scare; frighten: *Lights on the water during night fishing are apt to spook the fish away* (Wall Street Journal). **2** to haunt (a person or place).
—*v.i. Informal.* to become frightened: *He spooks at the slightest noise.*
[American English < Dutch *spook*]

**spook|er|y** (spü′kər ē), *n., pl.* **-er|ies.** that which is spooky or characteristic of spooks.

**spook|i|ly** (spü′kə lē), *adv.* in a spooky manner: *The owl hooted spookily from the dark woods.*

**spook|i|ness** (spü′kē nis), *n.* the quality or condition of being spooky: *"All the spookiness began on the afternoon of Feb. 3," [she] said with a frown* (Newsweek).

**spook|ish** (spü′kish), *adj. Informal.* **1** like a spook or ghost; ghostly. **2** given over to spooks; haunted: *a spookish house.* **3** affected by a sense or fear of ghosts; suggestive of the presence or agency of spooks: *a spookish sensation.* —**spook′ish|ly,** *adv.* —**spook′ish|ness,** *n.*

**spook|y** (spü′kē), *adj.,* **spook|i|er, spook|i|est.** *Informal.* like a spook; suited to spooks; suggesting spooks: ... *the view from the North Church belfry of the spooky and moonlit harbor* (New Yorker).

**spool** (spül), *n., v.* —*n.* **1** a small cylinder of wood or metal on which thread, wire, cord, tape, or yarn is wound; bobbin; quill; reel. **2** something like a spool in shape or use.
—*v.t.* to wind on a spool.
—*v.i.* to wind spools.
[< Middle Dutch *spoele*] —**spool′er,** *n.*

**spool furniture,** an American style of machine-made furniture especially popular during the 1800's, characterized by posts and supports carved in a series of knobs or spools.

**spoon** (spün), *n., v.* —*n.* **1** a utensil consisting of a small, shallow bowl at the end of a handle. Spoons are used to take up or stir food or drink: *The captain loudly slurped hot soup from his spoon.* **2** something shaped like a spoon or the bowl of a spoon. **3** a golf club with a wooden head, having a slightly shorter and more rigid shaft and a face with greater slope than a driver or brassie. **4** = spoon bait. **5** a curved projection at the top of a torpedo tube to keep the torpedo going in a horizontal path.
—*v.t.* **1** to take up with or as if with a spoon: *She negligently spooned her soup, and then, after much parade, sent it away untouched* (Benjamin Disraeli). **2** to hollow out or form in the shape of the bowl of a spoon. **3** *Informal.* to make love to by hugging and kissing: *He's spooning our schoolmarm* (Owen Wister). **4** to push (a croquet ball) with the mallet instead of hitting it. **5** to hit (a golf ball) feebly with a lifting motion, as in a sand trap. **6** *Cricket.* to hit (the ball) into the air weakly. **7** to troll for or catch (fish) with a spoon bait.
—*v.i.* **1** to spoon a croquet, golf, or cricket ball. **2** to fish or troll with a spoon bait. **3** *Informal.* to make love by hugging and kissing.
**born with a silver spoon in one's mouth,** born lucky or rich: *There never was a child so plainly born with the traditional silver spoon in his mouth as Waller* (Edmund W. Gosse).
[Old English *spōn* chip, shaving; meaning probably influenced by Scandinavian (compare Old Icelandic *spōnn, spānn* chip; wooden spoon)] —**spoon′like′,** *adj.*

**spoon back,** the back of a chair slightly curved to fit the sitter's form.

**spoon bait,** a bright, spoon-shaped piece of metal swiveled just in front of the hook or hooks, used as a lure in casting or trolling for fish.

**spoon beak,** a spoonlike beak, such as that of a spoonbill, used to gather shellfish and water insects from shallow waters.

**spoon|bill** (spün′bil′), *n.* **1** a long-legged pink wading bird that has a long, flat bill with a spoon-shaped tip. Spoonbills belong to the same family as the ibises. **2** any one of certain other birds having such a bill. **3** = paddlefish.

**spoon|billed** (spün′bild′), *adj.* **1** having a spoon-like or spatulate bill, dilated at the end: *a spoonbilled bird.* **2** having a spatulate snout, as a sturgeon; shovel-nosed.

**spoonbilled catfish,** = paddlefish.

**spoon bread,** a mixture of corn meal, and sometimes rice, with milk, eggs, and shortening, cooked by baking but always soft enough to be served with a spoon.

**spoon|drift** (spün′drift′), *n.* = spindrift. [< obsolete *spoon* to sail before the wind (origin unknown) + *drift,* noun]

**spoon|er|ism** (spü′nə riz əm), *n.* an accidental transposition of sounds, usually the initial sounds, of two or more words, such as "well-boiled icicle" for "well-oiled bicycle." [< Reverend William A. *Spooner,* 1844-1930, of New College, Oxford, who was famous for such mistakes + *-ism*]

**spoon|ey** (spü′nē), *adj.,* **spoon|i|er, spoon|i|est,** *n., pl.* **spoon|eys.** = spoony.

**spoon-fash|ion** (spün′fash′ən), *adv.* like spoons put close together; with the face of one to the back of the other and with the knees bent.

**spoon-fed** (spün′fed′), *adj.* **1** protected and coddled, like a child who must be fed with a spoon; pampered: *a spoon-fed industry.* **2** discouraging or minimizing independence of thought and action, especially by avoiding what is difficult, controversial, or otherwise unpleasant: *spoon-fed education.*

**spoon-feed** (spün′fēd′), *v.t., v.i.,* **-fed, -feed|ing.** to feed with or as if with a spoon; coddle; pamper: *Nobody has yet come up with a solution of how to spoon-feed an industry without stifling it* (Time).

**spoon|ful** (spün′fül), *n., pl.* **-fuls.** as much as a spoon can hold: *I take only one spoonful of sugar with my coffee.*

**spoon hook,** a hook with a spinning lure (spoon) attached.

**spoon oar,** an oar which is slightly curved lengthwise at the end of its broad blade.

**spoon|y** (spü′nē), *adj.,* **spoon|i|er, spoon|i|est,** *n., pl.* **spoon|ies.** *Informal.* —*adj.* foolish or silly in lovemaking; demonstratively fond: *I was never in love myself, but I've seen many others spoony* (Frederick Marryat).
—*n.* **1** a sentimental or overfond lover. **2** = simpleton. —**spoon′i|ly,** *adv.* —**spoon′i|ness,** *n.*

**spoor** (spůr), *n., v.* —*n.* the trail of a wild animal or a person; track: *The spoor of every species of game could be found* (V. Pohl). *Only ... Bushmen ... could have made that spoor* (London Times).
—*v.t.* to track by a spoor.
—*v.i.* to follow a spoor.
[< Afrikaans *spoor* < Middle Dutch] —**spoor′er,** *n.*

**spor-,** *combining form.* the form of **sporo-** before vowels, as in *sporulate.*

**spo|rad|ic** (spə rad′ik), *adj.* **1** appearing now and then or at intervals in time; occasional: *sporadic outbreaks.* **2** being or occurring apart from others; isolated: *The sporadic meteors, which appear to be independent travelers, seem to be divided between stony and metallic* (Robert H. Baker). **3** occurring in scattered instances; not epidemic: *sporadic cases of scarlet fever.* **4** occurring singly or widely apart in locality; scattered; dispersed: *sporadic genera of plants.* [< Medieval Latin *sporadicus* < Greek *sporadikós* scattered < *sporás, -ados* scattered < *sporá;* see etym. under **spore**] —**spo|rad′i|cal|ly,** *adv.*

**sporadic E,** an area of high ionization in the E layer of the ionosphere which interferes with the normal reflection of short-wave radio: *Sporadic E is ... sometimes only a few hundred feet thick and occurs at times now unpredictable* (Science News).

**spo|ra|dic|i|ty** (spôr′ə dis′ə tē, spōr′-), *n.* sporadic quality.

**spo|ra|do|sid|er|ite** (spôr′ə dō sid′ə rīt, spōr′-), *n.* a stony meteorite containing grains of iron. [< Greek *sporás, -ados* scattered + English *siderite*]

**spo|ral** (spôr′əl, spōr′-), *adj.* of or having to do with spores.

**spo|ran|gi|a** (spə ran′jē ə), *n.* plural of **sporangium.**

**spo|ran|gi|al** (spə ran′jē əl), *adj.* **1** of or having to do with the sporangium: *the sporangial layer.* **2** containing spores. **3** having the character of a sporangium.

**spo|ran|gi|o|phore** (spə ran′jē ə fôr, -fōr), *n.* the structure or receptacle which bears sporangia.

**spo|ran|gi|um** (spə ran′jē əm), *n., pl.* **-gi|a.** a receptacle or case in which asexual spores are produced; spore case. The little brown spots sometimes seen on the underside of ferns are groups of sporangia. The sporangium receives different names according to the kind of spores produced, such as *macrosporangium, microsporangium.* In mosses *sporangium* is usually the same as *capsule.* See diagram under **alternation of generations.** [< New Latin *sporangium* < Greek *sporá* seed (see etym. under **spore**) + *angeîon* vessel]

**spore** (spôr, spōr), *n., v.,* **spored, spor|ing.** —*n.* **1** a single cell which becomes free and is capable of developing into a new plant or animal. Ferns and other flowerless plants produce spores; mold grows from spores. Some protozoans produce spores. The spores of flowerless plants are analogous to the seeds of flowering plants. Spores are produced asexually (asexual spores) or sexually (sexual spores) by the fusion of gametes. *These organisms not only flourish without oxygen, but also form resistant spores which survive pasteurization* (J. A. Barnett). **2** a germ; seed.
—*v.i.* to form or produce spores.
[< New Latin *spora* < Greek *sporá* seed; a sowing < *speírein* to sow]

**spore case,** a receptacle containing spores; sporangium. The little brown spots on the underside of ferns are spore cases.

**spore fruit,** any part of a plant that produces spores, such as an ascocarp.

**spore|ling** (spôr′ling, spōr′-), *n. Botany.* a young plant, such as a fern, developed from a spore.

**spo|ri|cid|al** (spôr′ə sī′dəl, spōr′-), *adj.* destructive of spores. [< *spore* + *-icidal,* as in *fungicidal*]

**spo|rif|er|ous** (spə rif′ər əs), *adj.* bearing or producing spores. [< New Latin *spora* (see etym. under **spore**) + English *-ferous*]

**spork** (spôrk), *n. U.S.* a plastic spoon having blunt tines at the tip of the bowl for use as a fork: *They [schoolchildren] try to cut meat, scoop up soup or wind up spaghetti with a spork* (New York Times). [blend of *spoon* and *fork*]

**sporo-,** *combining form.* spore or spores: *Sporogenesis = the formation of spores.* Also, **spor-** before vowels. [< Greek *sporá,* or *spóros* seed; a sowing < *speírein* to sow]

**spo|ro|carp** (spôr′ə kärp, spōr′-), *n. Botany.* **1** a multicellular body serving essentially for the formation of spores, as in red algae and ascomycetous fungi. **2** (in mosses) = sporogonium. **3** a sorus in certain aquatic ferns. [< *sporo-* + Greek *karpós* fruit]

**spo|ro|cyst** (spôr′ə sist, spōr′-), *n.* **1** a cyst formed by sporozoans during reproduction, in which sporozoites develop. **2** an encysted sporozoan. **3** a capsule or sac containing germ cells, that develops from the embryo of trematode worms, usually within the body of a snail. **4** *Botany.* a resting cell which produces asexual spores, as in algae.

**spo|ro|cys|tic** (spôr′ə sis′tik, spōr′-), *adj.* of or having to do with a sporocyst.

**spo|ro|cyte** (spôr′ə sīt, spōr′-), *n. Botany.* a cell from which a spore is derived.

**spo|ro|duct** (spôr′ə dukt, spōr′-), *n.* a duct in which spores are lodged or through which they pass.

**spo|ro|gen|e|sis** (spôr′ə jen′ə sis, spōr′-), *n. Biology.* **1** the formation of spores. **2** reproduction by means of spores.

**spo|ro|gen|ic** (spôr′ə jen′ik, spōr′-), *adj.* = sporogenous.

**spo|rog|e|nous** (spə roj′ə nəs), *adj.* **1** reproducing or reproduced by means of spores. **2** bearing or producing spores: *There is an operculum, as usual, but the sporogenous cells form a dome-shaped mass* (Fred W. Emerson).

**spo|ro|go|ni|um** (spôr′ə gō′nē əm, spōr′-), *n., pl.* **-ni|a** (-nē ə). the spore case of mosses and liverworts; sporocarp. [< New Latin *sporogonium* < Greek *sporá* (see etym. under **spore**) + a root *gen-* to bear]

**spo|rog|o|ny** (spə rog′ə nē), *n.* reproduction by means of spores, especially in certain protozoans.

**spo|ront** (spôr′ont, spōr′-), *n.* = gamont.

**spo|ro|phore** (spôr′ə fôr, spōr′ə fōr), *n. Botany.* **1** the branch or portion of a sporophyte which bears spores. In fungi, it is a single hypha or branch of a hypha. **2** = sporophyte (in ferns and mosses).

**spo|roph|o|rous** (spə rof′ə rəs), *adj.* **1** bearing spores. **2** of or having to do with the sporophore.

**spo|ro|phyll** or **spo|ro|phyl** (spôr′ə fil, spōr′-), *n. Botany.* any leaf or leaflike organ, usually more or less modified, which bears spores or spore cases. [< *sporo-* + Greek *phýllon* leaf]

**spo|ro|phyte** (spôr′ə fīt, spōr′-), *n. Botany.* the individual plant or the generation of a plant which produces asexual spores, in a plant which reproduces both sexually and asexually: *In other words, the moss sporophyte acts as a parasite on the gametophyte* (Fred W. Emerson). See diagram under **alternation of generations.** [< *sporo-* + *-phyte*]

**spo|ro|phyt|ic** (spôr′ə fit′ik, spōr′-), *adj.* having to do with, resembling, or characteristic of a sporophyte.

**spo|ro|pol|len|in** (spôr′ə pol′ə nin, spōr′-), *n.* a highly resistant and durable substance that forms the outer wall of all pollen grains except those of aquatic plants. [< *sporo-* + *pollen* + *-in*]

**spo|ro|tri|cho|sis** (spôr′ō tri kō′sis, spōr′-), *n.* a fungous disease of horses, dogs, cats, and man, characterized by cutaneous lesions along the lymph vessels. [< New Latin *Sporotrichum* the genus name (< Greek *sporá* spore + *thríx, trichós* hair)]

**spo|ro|zo|an** (spôr′ə zō′ən, spōr′-), *n., adj.* **—*n.*** any one of a class of minute parasitic protozoans which absorb food through the body wall and reproduce sexually and asexually in alternate generations. Certain sporozoans cause diseases of man and animals, such as malaria. Plasmodia belong to this class.
**—*adj.*** of or belonging to the sporozoans.
[< New Latin *Sporozoa* the class name (< Greek *sporá* spore + *zôion* animal)]

**spo|ro|zo|ite** (spôr′ə zō′īt, spōr′-), *n.* any of the minute, immature bodies, often infective, produced by the division of the spore of certain sporozoans, each of which develops into an adult sporozoan.

**spo|ro|zo|on** (spôr′ə zō′on, spōr′-), *n., pl.* **-zo|a** (-zō′ə). = sporozoan. [< *sporo-* + Greek *zôion* animal]

***spor|ran** (spôr′ən, spor′-), *n.* a large purse or pouch, usually covered with fur and ornamental tassels, worn hanging from the belt in front of the kilt by Scottish Highlanders. [< Scottish Gaelic *sporan*]

*** sporran**

**sport** (spôrt, spōrt), *n., v., adj.* **—*n.* 1** a game, contest, or other pastime requiring some skill and usually a certain amount of physical exercise. Football, baseball, tennis, hunting, golf, and fishing are outdoor sports. Basketball and bowling are indoor sports. *Of all sports, only mountain-climbing, bullfighting, and automobile racing really tried a man … the rest were recreations* (Atlantic). **SYN:** See syn. under **play. 2** any pastime or amusement; diversion: *He spends all his time in sport and play. After love, book collecting is the most exhilarating sport of all* (A. S. W. Rosenbach). **3** playful joking; fun: *That was great sport. There is no sport in hate* (Shelley). **4** ridicule: *His awkward pitching motion was a source of sport to his classmates.* **5** an object of joking or ridicule; laughingstock: *A very fat boy is sometimes the sport of other boys.* **6** something driven or whirled about, especially by the wind or waves, as in sport; plaything: *the sport of chance. His hat blew off and became the sport of the wind.* **7** a person who follows or participates in sports or a particular sport; sportsman. **8** *Informal.* a young man; fellow. **9** a good fellow; one who behaves in a sportsmanlike manner: *to be a sport, to be a good sport.* **10** *Informal.* a betting man; gambler. **11** *Informal.* a flashy person; one who wears showy clothes, lives a fast life, or the like. **12** an animal, plant, or part of a plant that varies suddenly or in a marked manner from the normal type or stock. A white blackbird would be a sport. *These differences were not the slight variations emphasized by Darwin but were wide differences, known among plant and animal breeders of today as sports* (Harbaugh and Goodrich). **13** *Obsolete.* amorous dalliance.
**—*v.i.* 1** to amuse or entertain oneself; frolic; gambol; play: *Lambs sport in the fields. The kitten sports with its tail. If all the year were playing holidays, to sport would be as tedious as to work* (Shakespeare). **2** to participate in or follow a sport or sports, especially an open-air sport. **3** to deal (with) in a light or trifling way; jest; dally: *To sport with Amaryllis in the shade* (Milton). *It was selfishness which made him sport with your affections* (Jane Austen). **4** *Biology.* to vary markedly from the normal type; exhibit spontaneous mutation. **5** *Botany.* to show bud variation.
**—*v.t.* 1** *Informal.* to wear, display, or use: *to sport a new hat. If a man … sports loose views on morals at a decent dinner party, he is not asked again* (James A. Froude). **2** *Obsolete.* to amuse or entertain (oneself).
**—*adj.* 1** of sports; suitable for sports: *sport equipment.* **2** designed for informal, outdoor, or athletic wear: *sport clothes.*
**for** (or **in**) **sport**, for fun; in jest or as a joke; not seriously: *to say a thing for sport. The man teased the child in sport.*
**make sport of**, to make fun of; laugh at; ridicule: *Don't make sport of someone who doesn't understand something.*
**turn to sport**, to turn into or take as a matter for jesting or mirth: *Thrice I deluded her, and turn'd to sport Her importunity* (Milton).
[ultimately short for *disport*] **—sport′er**, *n.*

**sport car**, = sports car.

**sport|cast** (spôrt′kast′, -käst′; spōrt′-), *n. Informal.* a sportscast.

**sport|cast|er** (spôrt′kas′tər, -käs′-; spōrt′-), *n. Informal.* a sportscaster.

**sport fish**, a fish caught for sport, such as a game fish.

**sport|fish|er|man** (spôrt′fish′ər mən, spōrt′-), *n., pl.* **-men. 1** a person who engages in sportfishing. **2** a motorboat used in sportfishing.

**sport|fish|ing** (spôrt′fish′ing, spōrt′-), *n., adj.* **—*n.*** fishing for sport, especially from a motorboat: *to go sportfishing in the Caribbean.*
**—*adj.*** of or engaged in sportfishing: *a sportfishing team, a sportfishing boat.*

**sport|ful** (spôrt′fəl, spōrt′-), *adj.* **1** playful; sportive. **2** diverting; entertaining; recreational.
**—sport′ful|ly**, *adv.* **—sport′ful|ness**, *n.*

**spor|tif** (spôr tēf′), *adj. French.* sportive.

**sport|ing** (spôr′ting, spōr′-), *adj.* **1** of, interested in, or engaging in sports. **2** used or suitable for hunting, especially by scent: *Pointers, setters, retrievers, and spaniels are sporting dogs. The sporting group includes 24 breeds* (Josephine Z. Rine). **3** playing fair: *Letting the little boy throw the ball first was a sporting gesture.* **4** willing to take a chance. **5** *Informal.* involving risk; uncertain: *He took a sporting chance in crossing the stream by jumping from rock to rock.* **—sport′ing|ly**, *adv.*

**sporting goods**, clothing and equipment used in sports.

**spor|tive** (spôr′tiv, spōr′-), *adj.* **1** playful; frolicsome; merry; gay: *The old dog seemed as sportive as the puppy.* **2** not earnest or serious; jesting: *a sportive remark.* **3** smart or flashy in dress; sporty: *Another contrast was offered by the sportive, male-inspired look … The sportive look thrived by day* (Oleg Cassini). **4** sporting: *It was now not a sportive combat, but a war to the death* (Macaulay). **5** *Archaic.* amorous; wanton: *Where sportive ladies leave their doors ajar* (Robert Browning). **—spor′tive|ly**, *adv.* **—spor′tive|ness**, *n.*

**sport of kings**, horse racing: *It is often called the sport of kings because at one time only kings and noblemen took part in it* (Joe Agrella).

**sports** (spôrts, spōrts), *adj.* **1** of or having to do with athletic sports: *the sports column or page, the sports editor of a paper.* **2** designed or suitable for outdoor, athletic, or casual wear: *a sports shirt, a sports coat. Everyone wore leather patches on the elbows of perfectly new Harris tweed sports jackets* (Punch).

**sports car**, a small, low, fast car, usually with two seats and an open top: *The Mille Miglia is a race for sports cars, not racing cars, but in recent years the distinction between the two has narrowed almost to the vanishing point* (Atlantic).

**sports|cast** (spôrts′kast′, -käst′; spōrts′-), *n. Informal.* a broadcast or telecast of a sporting event.

**sports|cast|er** (spôrts′kas′tər, -käs′-; spōrts′-), *n. Informal.* a person who does the spoken part of a sportscast.

**sports|cast|ing** (spôrts′kas′ting, -käs′-; spōrts′-), *n. Informal.* **1** the occupation or work of a sportscaster. **2** the making of a sportscast: *It amounts to the most spectacularly accurate piece of reportage in the history of sportscasting* (Newsweek).

**sports|drome** (spôrts′drōm, spōrts′-), *n.* a sports stadium; hippodrome.

**sport shirt**, a comfortable shirt designed for informal wear, usually without a tie: *He was barefoot and barelegged, wearing only floppy khaki shorts and a checked sport shirt, its tail tumbling outside* (Atlantic).

**sport-shirt|ed** (spôrt′shėr′tid, spōrt′-), *adj.* wearing a sport shirt.

**sports|man** (spôrts′mən, spōrts′-), *n., pl.* **-men. 1** a person who takes part in sports, especially hunting, fishing, riding, or racing. **2** a person who likes sports: *Martin, a more sedentary sportsman occasionally goes on a boat ride … but mostly to be affable* (New Yorker). **3** *Figurative.* a person who plays fair. **4** a person who is willing to take a chance.

**sports|man|like** (spôrts′mən līk′, spōrts′-), *adj.* like or suitable for a sportsman: (*Figurative.*) *That was a sportsmanlike gesture from a great pilot* (Atlantic). **SYN:** fair, honorable.

**sports|man|ly** (spôrts′mən lē, spōrts′-), *adj.* like a good sportsman; sportsmanlike.

**sports|man|ship** (spôrts′mən ship, spōrts′-), *n.* **1** the qualities or conduct of a good sportsman; fair play: *She would have been raised by solid people … and would respect all the … virtues: courage, good sportsmanship … and honor* (New Yorker). **2** ability in sports.

**sports-rac|ing car** (spôrts′rā′sing, spōrts′-), a sports car with a sleek body, very powerful engine, and often specially designed parts, used for road races such as the Grand Prix.

**sport|ster** (spôrt′stər, spōrt′-), *n.* a sports car: *A sportster, it looks like a miniature Alfa Romeo, carries two tall adults in comfort* (London Times). [< *sport* + *-ster*, as in *roadster*]

**sports|wear** (spôrts′wãr′, spōrts′-), *n.* clothes designed for informal, outdoor, or athletic wear, originally designed to be worn for active participation in sports.

**sports|wom|an** (spôrts′wu̇m′ən, spōrts′-), *n., pl.* **-wom|en.** a woman who engages in or is interested in sports.

**sports|writ|er** (spôrts′rī′tər, spōrts′-), *n.* a journalist who writes about sports.

**sports|writ|ing** (spôrts′rī′ting, spōrts′-), *n.* the occupation or work of writing about sports: *He dissects the drama … with a racy enthusiasm that is nowadays more likely to be found in sportswriting* (New Yorker).

**sport|y** (spôr′tē, spōr′-), *adj.,* **sport|i|er, sport|i|est.** *Informal.* **1** dashing or fast; flashy: *She knew he was associating with … "a sporty crowd"* (Sinclair Lewis). **SYN:** showy. **2** smart in dress, appearance, manners, etc.: *She looked very sporty in tweeds and boots.* **SYN:** natty. **3** sportsmanlike; sporting. **—sport′i|ly**, *adv.* **—sport′i|ness**, *n.*

**spor|u|late** (spôr′yə lāt, spōr′-), *v.,* **-lat|ed, -lat|ing.** *Biology.* **—*v.i.*** to form spores or sporules.
**—*v.t.*** to convert into spores.

**spor|u|la|tion** (spôr′yə lā′shən, spōr′-), *n. Biology.* the formation of or conversion into spores or sporules: *Propagation by sporulation is characteristic of a class of the Protozoa known as the Sporozoa* (Harbaugh and Goodrich).

**spor|ule** (spôr′yül, spōr′-), *n. Biology.* **1** a small spore. **2** any spore. [< French *sporule* < New Latin *sporula* (diminutive) < *spora;* see etym. under **spore**]

**sposh** (sposh), *n. U.S.* slush; watery matter; mud. [probably imitative]

**spot** (spot), *n., v.,* **spot|ted, spot|ting,** *adj.* **—*n.* 1** a small mark or stain that discolors or disfigures; stain; speck: *a spot of ink on the paper. You have grease spots on your suit. That spot on her cheek is a bruise.* **SYN:** fleck, blotch, blot. **2** *Figurative.* a blemish or flaw in character or reputation; moral defect; fault: *His record is without a spot. Sublimely mild, a spirit without spot* (Shelley). **3** a small part unlike the rest in color, material, or finish; dot: *a leopard's spots. His tie is blue with white spots.* **4** a small extent of space; place; site; locality: *From this spot you can see the ocean. A lonely spot by a woodside* (George Glissing); *the most pleasant spot in Italy* (John Evelyn). **5** *Especially British Informal, Figurative.* a small amount or quantity; little bit: *a spot of lunch, a spot of brandy.* **6** *Informal.* a position or place with reference to employment, radio or television scheduling, or the like: *Its time spot … put it in head-on competition with the season's most popular show* (Newsweek). **7** *Informal.* a spotlight. **8** a figure or dot on a playing card, domino, or die to show its kind or value. **9** a small sciaenoid food fish of the Atlantic coast of North America, having a dark marking on each side. **10** a variety of domestic pigeon, having white plumage with a spot of another color above the beak. **11** = sunspot. **12** *Botany.* leaf spot. **13** *U.S. Slang.* a piece of paper money; bill: *a five spot, a ten spot.* **14** = spot announcement.
**—*v.t.* 1** to make spots on; stain: *He has spotted the tablecloth.* **2** *Figurative.* to stain, sully, or tarnish (as character or reputation): *He spotted his*

**Pronunciation Key:** hat, āge, cãre, fär; let, ēqual, tėrm; it, īce; hot, ōpen, ôrder; **oi**l, **ou**t; cup, pu̇t, rüle; **ch**ild; lo**ng**; **th**in; **ᴛʜ**en; **zh**, measure; ə represents **a** in about, **e** in taken, **i** in pencil, **o** in lemon, **u** in circus.

*reputation by lying repeatedly.* **3** to mark, cover, or decorate with spots. **4** *Informal.* to pick out; find out; recognize or detect: *I spotted my sister in the crowd. The teacher spotted every mistake in my paper.* **5** to place in a certain spot or area; scatter in various spots: *to spot a billiard ball. Lookouts were spotted all along the coast.* **6** to locate (as an enemy position or weapon) exactly on the ground or a map. **7** *Informal.* to give or allow a lead or handicap to: *Wisconsin spotted Illinois a first-period touchdown, then turned loose a sharp ground attack to down the nation's third ranking football team, 34-7, today* (New York Times).

—***v.i.*** **1** to make a spot or stain. **2** to become spotted; have spots: *This silk will spot with rain.*

—***adj.*** **1** on hand; ready: *a spot answer.* **2a** for immediate cash payment and delivery: *a spot sale.* **b** having to do with or specializing in cash transactions: *A leading spot firm said there was a decided improvement in mill buying* (Wall Street Journal). **3** done or reported on the spot: *spot news coverage.* **4a** inserted between or in regular radio or television programs: *There are many variations of this procedure, allowing for the placing of national and local "spot" commercials* (London Times). **b** produced by and broadcast from a local station.

**hit the spot**, *Informal.* to be just right; be satisfactory: *A cool drink on a hot day is certain to hit the spot.*

**in a spot**, in trouble or difficulty: *I was in a spot when my car ran out of gas on that lonely road.*

**in spots, a** in one spot, part, place, or point and another: *an argument weak in spots.* **b** at times; by snatches: *Mammy has a kind of obstinacy about her, in spots, that everybody don't see as I do* (Harriet Beecher Stowe).

**on** (or **upon**) **the spot, a** at that very place: *You know in business there's nothing like being on the spot* (Lord Dunsany). **b** *Figurative.* at once; immediately; straightway: *He expected his orders to be carried out on the spot.* **c** *Informal, Figurative.* in trouble or difficulty; in an awkward or embarrassing position: *He put the speaker on the spot by asking a question he could not answer.*

**put on the spot**, *Slang.* to mark (someone) for death by assassination: *You get rid of inconvenient subordinates ... by putting them on the spot—that is, deliberately sending them to their death* (Punch).

**spot on**, *British Informal.* exactly right; perfectly correct: [*He*] *is a man whose forecasts are usually spot on* (Sunday Times). *Like the words, the setting must be spot on* (Manchester Guardian Weekly).

[compare Middle Dutch *spot* speck] —**spot′table**, *adj.*

**spot announcement**, a short advertisement or other announcement inserted by a local radio or television station before or during a regular network program.

**spot bowling**, a method of bowling in which the player chooses a spot on the alley over which the ball must pass in order to hit the pins correctly.

**spot card**, any playing card identified by the number of pips on it; any card from ace to ten.

**spot cash**, money paid just as soon as goods are delivered or work is done.

**spot check**, **1** a brief, rough sampling: *The number of people waiting in line to make withdrawals or deposits was normal in most banks around the city, a spot check and talks with bankers showed* (Wall Street Journal). **2** a checkup made without warning: *Russian negotiators at Geneva have made a special point of trying to limit ... the numbers of spot checks* (Manchester Guardian).

**spot-check** (spot′chek′), *v.t.* to make a spot check of: *Tons of gold—and silver too—are being spot-checked for purity and weight* (New York Times).

**spot|face** (spot′fās′), *v.t.,* **-faced, -fac|ing.** to face (a spot) around a hole drilled for a bolt or screw: *The heads ... drill and countersink holes, spotface them ... and face the outer surfaces* (Newsweek).

**spot lamp**, *Especially British.* spotlight.

**spot|less** (spot′lis), *adj.* **1** without a spot; absolutely clean; immaculate: *a spotless kitchen. She wore a spotless white apron.* **2** *Figurative.* without a stain or blot; unblemished: *a spotless reputation.* —**spot′less|ly**, *adv.* —**spot′less|ness**, *n.*

**spot|light** (spot′līt′), *n., v.,* **-light|ed** or **-lit, -light|ing.** —***n.*** **1a** a spot or circle of bright light thrown upon a particular person or object, leaving the rest of the stage more or less unilluminated. **b** a lamp that gives such a light: *a spotlight in a theater.* **2** any one of various somewhat similar lamps, such as an electric lamp of the type mounted on certain police cars, having a powerful, narrowly focused beam that can be pointed in any desired direction. **3** *Figurative.* public notice; anything that directs attention on a person or thing: *Movie stars are often in the spotlight.* **SYN**: publicity.

—***v.t.*** **1** to light up with a spotlight or spotlights: *At night, the baseball field is spotlighted.* **2** *Figurative.* to call attention to; give public notice to; highlight: *The newspaper will spotlight an industry that few Americans know about.*

**spot market**, any place where a commodity, such as cotton, is bought and sold for immediate delivery.

**spot news**, news reported at once from where it happens: *The newspapers, wire services, and networks sent their best men, top-seasoned hands to handle the fast-breaking spot news* (Harper's).

**spot pass**, *Football.* a pass timed to meet a receiver at a certain spot on the field.

**spot|ted** (spot′id), *adj.* **1** marked with spots: *a spotted dog.* **SYN**: speckled, dappled. **2** *Figurative.* stained with or as if with spots, especially morally stained; blemished: *a spotted reputation.* —**spot′ted|ness**, *n.*

**spotted adder**, = milk snake.

**spotted alder**, = witch hazel.

**spotted aphid** or **spotted alfalfa aphid**, a tiny yellow aphid that is very destructive to alfalfa, found in the warmer parts of North America.

**spotted bass**, a variety of bass smaller than largemouth bass.

**spotted cavy**, = paca.

**spotted cowbane**, a North American water hemlock with mottled stems and poisonous roots.

**spotted crake**, a small European rail related to the American sora; water crake.

**spotted crane's-bill**, common wild geranium of North America, with purplish or white flowers.

**spotted deer**, the axis deer of Southeast Asia.

**spotted eagle ray**, an eagle ray of tropical Atlantic waters, with white or yellowish spots on the upper side.

**spotted fever**, any one of various fevers characterized by the appearance of spots on the skin, especially cerebrospinal meningitis, typhus, or Rocky Mountain spotted fever: *Spotted fever is a serious disease that infects cattle, and expensive dipping of cattle for tick eradication is a necessity in many of the cattle-raising regions of the country* (A. M. Winchester).

**spot|ted-fe|ver tick** (spot′id fē′vər), the tick that transmits Rocky Mountain spotted fever.

**spotted hemlock**, = spotted cowbane.

**spotted hyena**, a grayish hyena with dark spots, found throughout most of Africa.

**spotted jewfish**, a large edible grouper of warm American seas.

**spotted moray**, a kind of moray common in West Indian waters.

**spotted salamander**, a bluish-black salamander with two rows of yellow spots along the back and tail, common in the eastern United States and Canada.

**spotted sandpiper**, a North American sandpiper with large spots on a white breast.

**spotted skunk**, a small North American skunk with black and white stripes on the body and a white-tipped tail.

**Spotted Swine**, any swine of an American breed similar to the Poland China hog breed.

**spotted wilt**, a variety of wilt disease characterized by the inward and downward curling of the youngest leaves and reddish spotting or metallic bronzing of the foliage.

**spot|ter** (spot′ər), *n.* **1** a person who makes or removes spots: *After drying, the garment goes to a highly-skilled worker called a spotter ... to remove any stains* (George P. Fulton). **2** a device for making or removing spots. **3** a person who watches for and reports the presence of unidentified aircraft. **4** a person who observes a wide area of enemy terrain, as from an aircraft or high point on the ground, in order to locate, and direct artillery fire against, any of various targets, such as enemy gun emplacements or troop concentrations. **5** a person employed to watch employees or customers for evidence of dishonesty or other misconduct, usually one who watches from a hidden place or whose identity is concealed. **6** a person or airplane whose job is to watch for or spot any situation which may require attention: *Crevasse spotters at the MacMurdo Sound base tragically missed a perfect score* (Newsweek). **7** a machine that automatically sets up the pins in a bowling alley; pinspotter.

**spot test**, **1** = spot check. **2** a chemical analysis in which a drop of the sample to be analyzed is mixed with a reagent, as on a filter paper or glass plate, used to identify the presence of metals, alkaloids, or other substances.

**spot|ting scope** (spot′ing), a small, portable telescope used especially in hunting and target shooting.

**spot|ty** (spot′ē), *adj.,* **-ti|er, -ti|est. 1** having spots; spotted: *dirty, spotty clothes.* **2** *Figurative.* not of uniform quality; irregularly good and bad: *His work was spotty.* —**spot′ti|ly**, *adv.* —**spot′ti|ness**, *n.*

**spot-weld** (spot′weld′), *v.t.* to weld by passing electric current through the contacting spots and applying pressure: *It has also proved possible to spot-weld electrically studs and stiffener brackets to the steel back of the laminate without damaging the film on the surface* (New Scientist).

**spot weld**, a weld made by spot-welding.

**spous|al** (spou′zəl), *n., adj. Archaic.* —***n.*** Often, **spousals.** the ceremony of marriage; nuptials.

—***adj.*** of or having to do with marriage; nuptial. [short for Old French *espousaille* espousal]

**spouse** (spous, spouz), *n., v.,* **spoused, spous|ing.** —***n.*** a husband or wife; married person: *Mr. Smith is Mrs. Smith's spouse, and she is his spouse. The family plan allows the purchaser of a full-fare, first-class ticket to take his spouse and children ... along at half the one-way fare* (Wall Street Journal).

—***v.t.*** *Archaic.* to marry; wed.

[< Old French *espous, espouse* < Latin *spōnsus* bridegroom, *spōnsa* bride (in Medieval Latin, spouse) < *spondēre* bind oneself, promise solemnly] —**spouse′less**, *adj.*

**spout** (spout), *v., n.* —***v.t.*** **1** to throw out (a liquid, vapor, or the like) in a stream or spray: *The fountain spouts water. A whale spouts hot, moist air when it breathes.* **2** to pour forth in quantity: *Machines now in operation spout quotations at a 500-character clip* (Wall Street Journal). **3** *Informal, Figurative.* to speak, especially in loud and emotional tones; declaim: *The old-fashioned actor used to spout his lines.* [*He*] *is spouting clichés in the same fashion as he accuses Dr. Roberts* (Science News). **4** *Slang.* to pawn.

—***v.i.*** **1** to throw out a liquid, vapor, or the like, in a jet or stream: *The fountain spouted up high.* **2** to flow out with force: *Water spouted from a break in the pipe.* **SYN**: gush, jet, squirt, spurt. **3** *Informal, Figurative.* to spout or declaim as words or lines in a play: *There he took his stand in a vacant lot ... and spouted to the rustic crowd* (Newsweek).

—***n.*** **1** a discharge of water or other fluid, in some quantity and with some force; jet; stream: *A spout of water shot up from the hole in the pipe.* **2** a pipe, tube, or trough for carrying off water or other liquid: *Rain runs down a spout from our roof to the ground.* **3** a tube or lip by which liquid is poured. A teakettle and a coffeepot have spouts. **4** a chute, as for grain, coal, or flour. **5** = waterspout. **6** a column of spray thrown into the air by a whale in breathing: *When the whale surfaces after a dive and empties its lungs, the foam expelled is the visible spout* (Time). **7** a lift or shaft formerly used by pawnbrokers to take up pawned articles for storage. **8** *Slang.* a pawnshop. [apparently < verb]

**go up the spout**, *Slang.* to be hopelessly lost; ruined: *Everything I owned has gone up the spout.*

**put up the spout**, *Slang.* to put in pawn: *I put my watch up the spout last week.*

[Middle English *spouten* < Middle Dutch *spouten*] —**spout′er**, *n.* —**spout′less**, *adj.*

**spout hole**, a blowhole or spiracle of a whale or other cetacean.

**spout shell**, **1** the shell of any one of a group of snaillike marine gastropods. **2** the animal itself, so called from the spoutlike aperture.

**spp.**, species (plural of *specie*).

**S.P.Q.R.**, the Roman Senate and People (Latin, *Senatus Populusque Romanus*).

**Sprach|ge|fühl** (shpraʜ′gə fyl′), *n. German.* feeling for language; sensitivity to what is right or proper in speech: *It doesn't take much Sprachgefühl to recognize that Mr. Wilder is ... being a mite folksy* (New Yorker).

**sprack** (sprak), *adj. Especially British Dialect.* active; lively; brisk; smart. [origin unknown]

**sprad|dle** (sprad′əl), *v.,* **-dled, -dling.** —***v.i.*** = sprawl.

—***v.t.*** **1** to spread or stretch (one's legs) wide apart: *He stood with legs spraddled over a large grass basket* (Jack London). **2** to stretch over or across; straddle: *Overnight, refineries spraddled the shore of the Persian Gulf* (Time).

**sprad|dle-foot|ed** (sprad′əl fu̇t′id), *adj.* with feet spread wide apart.

**sprad|dle-leg|ged** (sprad′əl leg′id, -legd′), *adj.* with legs spread wide apart: *He runs spraddle-legged, his trainer says, throwing his legs every which way* (New Yorker).

**sprag**[1] (sprag), *n., v.,* **spragged, sprag|ging.** —***n.*** a device to keep a carriage, wagon, or the like, from rolling backwards on a hill, especially: **a** a piece of wood placed under the wheel or between the spokes. **b** a rod or bar attached to the rear axle and lowered against the ground as needed.

— ***v.t.*** to check or stop (a wheel) by using a sprag.
[origin unknown]

**sprag²** (sprag), *n.* a young cod. [earlier, a lively fellow; origin unknown]

**Sprague's pipit** (sprāgz), a buff-colored pipit of the North American plains, with a streaked back and white-edged tail. [< Isaac *Sprague,* 1811-1895, an American botanical illustrator]

**sprain** (sprān), *v., n.* — ***v.t.*** to injure (the ligaments or muscles of a joint) by a sudden twist or wrench: *He sprained his ankle.*
— ***n.*** an injury caused by such a sudden twist or wrench: *He got a bad sprain in his ankle when he missed the lower step. What with climbing and falling, running and throwing, and general zestful physical activity, almost all children suffer a sprain sometime or other* (Sidonie M. Gruenberg).
[perhaps < Old French *espreindre* force out < Vulgar Latin *expremere,* for Latin *exprimere.* Compare etym. under **express.**]

**sprang** (sprang), *v.* a past tense of **spring**: *The wounded tiger sprang at the man.*

**sprat** (sprat), *n., pl.* **sprats** or (*collectively*) **sprat.** **1** a small herring of the Atlantic and Mediterranean coasts of Europe. **2** any one of certain similar herrings. [variant of earlier *sprot,* Old English *sprott*]

**sprat|tle** (sprat′əl), *n., v.,* **-tled, -tling.** *Scottish.* struggle or scramble. [origin uncertain]

**sprawl** (sprôl), *v., n.* — ***v.i.*** **1** to toss or spread the limbs about, like an infant or an animal lying on its back: *reading contentedly with his legs sprawled over the arm of the couch.* **2** to lie or sit with the limbs spread out, especially ungracefully: *The people sprawled on the beach in their bathing suits.* **3** to spread out in an irregular or awkward manner; straggle: *His large handwriting sprawled across the page. Vines sprawl over the old wall.* **4** to crawl in a struggling or ungraceful manner; move awkwardly; scramble.
— ***v.t.*** to spread or stretch out (the limbs), especially ungracefully: *to sprawl out one's legs.*
— ***n.*** **1** the act or position of sprawling: *Any kind of sprawl is ungraceful.* **2** a straggling array or display (of something): (*Figurative.*) *London's great sprawl ...* (London Times).
[Old English *sprēawlian*] — **sprawl′er,** *n.*

**sprawl|ing** (sprô′ling), *adj.* spread out in an irregular or rambling fashion: (*Figurative.*) *New York's sprawling apparel industry* (New York Times).

**sprawl|y** (sprô′lē), *adj.,* **sprawl|i|er, sprawl|i|est.** of a sprawling character; straggly.

**spray¹** (sprā), *n., v.* — ***n.*** **1a** liquid going through the air in small drops: *We were wet with the sea spray.* **b** small drops, as of medicine, insecticide, disinfectant, cosmetic, paint, or starch, blown on something by compressed air or gas: *Big advantage of the internal poison is that it protects the whole young plant, while sprays ... may leave some parts unprotected* (Time). **2** *Figurative.* something like this: *A spray of bullets hit the target.* **3a** an instrument that sends a liquid out as spray. **b** = spray can.
— ***v.t.*** **1** to throw in the form of spray; scatter in small drops: *Spray this paint on the cupboard.* **2** to sprinkle with spray; wet with small drops or particles: *to spray paint, to spray a lawn with water. Spray the apple tree to kill the worms.* **3** *Figurative.* **a** to direct numerous small missiles upon: *to spray the enemy with bullets.* **b** to distribute or scatter here and there; sprinkle: *Then he sprays questions* (New Yorker). *These pages are sprayed with identifying footnotes* (Orville Prescott).
— ***v.i.*** **1** to throw up or scatter spray. **2** to issue or rise as spray.
[apparently < Middle Dutch *sprayen, spraeien* to sprinkle] — **spray′a|ble,** *adj.* — **spray′er,** *n.*

**spray²** (sprā), *n.* **1** a small branch or piece of some plant with its leaves, flowers, or fruit, especially when used for decoration or ornament: *a spray of lilacs, a spray of berries.* **2** any ornament, pattern, or design resembling this: *a spray of diamonds.* **3** small or slender twigs of trees or shrubs collectively, either still growing or cut off. [Middle English *sprai, spray;* compare Danish *sprag*]

**spray can,** a can containing an insecticide, cosmetic, paint, cleaning fluid, starch, or other product under pressure, that may be released as a spray or mist; aerosol bomb or container. See diagram under **aerosol bomb.**

**spray drain,** a drain formed, as in grassland, by burying brush or the spray of trees in the earth to keep open a channel.

**spray|dry** (sprā′drī′), *v.t.,* **-dried, -dry|ing.** to dehydrate (food) by spraying and drying in powdery particles.

**spray|ey¹** (sprā′ē), *adj.* forming or scattering spray; in the form of spray.

**spray|ey²** (sprā′ē), *adj.* **1** consisting of sprays, as of a plant. **2** resembling sprays.

**spray gun,** a device to spray paints, insecticides, or other liquids over a surface: *The nylon, 8-ounce spray gun handles all types of paints and can easily be cleaned for spraying insecticides* (Newsweek).

**spray nozzle,** an attachment to the nozzle of a hose for spreading liquid insecticides and fungicides in the form of a fine spray.

**spray-on** (sprā′on′), *adj.* applied in the form of a spray: *a spray-on paint.*

**spray-paint** (sprā′pānt′), *v.t., v.i.* to paint with a spray gun or spray can.

**spray plane,** = crop duster.

**spray steel,** steel made by pouring molten iron directly from the blast furnace through a ring of oxygen jets that oxidize impurities much faster than the means by which conventional steel is made.

**spread** (spred), *v.,* **spread, spread|ing,** *n., adj.*
— ***v.t.*** **1** to cause to cover a large or larger area; stretch out (anything folded, piled, or rolled up) to a greater or its greatest extent; open out; lay out; unfold: *to spread rugs on a floor, to spread a blanket over a child, to spread papers on a table.* **SYN**: unroll. **2** to unfurl: *to spread all possible sail.* **3** to move outward or farther apart; extend outward: *to spread wings, to spread one's arms. Spread out your fingers.* **4** to move the sides of outward by force, especially: **a** to extend the circumference of: *He spread the head of the rivet with a hammer.* **b** to displace and push outward from the line of vertical thrust: *walls spread by too much weight.* **5** to cause to be protracted in time; break down the total of into parts distributed (over a period of time): *to spread a shipment over two months, to spread the repayment of a debt over a year.* **6** to scatter; distribute: *to spread seed, to spread fertilizer.* **7** to make widely or generally known; diffuse; disseminate: *to spread the rumor of victory. He spread the news.* **SYN**: circulate. **8** to make widely or generally prevalent; propagate: *to spread a religion.* **9** to cover with a layer; coat or overlay (with): *to spread a slice of bread with butter.* **10** to put as a layer; smear (on): *to spread jam on bread. Spread the paint evenly.* **11** to prepare (a table) for a meal or other purpose; set; lay. **12** to put food on (a table). **13** to make a written record of; enter in or as if in minutes.
— ***v.i.*** **1** to cover a large or larger area; expand; unfold; open out: *a fan that spreads when shaken.* **2** to move outward or further apart: *The rails of the track have spread.* **3** to extend or grow outward from a trunk or center: *The roots of the tree spread.* **4** to lie; extend: *Fields of corn spread out before us.* **5** to become widely or generally known or prevalent; be distributed: *The disease spread rapidly.* **6** to be or to be able to be put on as a layer: *This paint spreads evenly.*
— ***n.*** **1** the act or process of spreading: *to fight the spread of an infection, to encourage the spread of knowledge.* **2** the amount of or capacity for spreading; limit of expanding or ability to expand outward; width; extent: *the great spread of an eagle's wings, the spread of elastic.* **3** the wingspan of an aircraft. **4** a stretch; expanse: *a great spread of green fields.* **5** a cloth covering for a bed or table; tablecloth or blanket. **6** *Informal.* food for a meal put on the table, especially in abundance; feast; banquet: *Cousin Anna ... had pancakes and coffee going and a big spread on the table* (Saul Bellow). **7** an article of food to be spread on bread, crackers, or the like. Butter and jam are spreads. *Our beefsteaks are homogenized into hamburger, and Roquefort cheese is now a "spread"* (Atlantic). **8** a piece of advertising, a news story, or the like, occupying a number of adjoining columns or pages in a magazine or newspaper: *The advertisement was a three-column spread.* **9** two facing pages of a newspaper, magazine, or, sometimes, a book, viewed as a single unit in makeup. **10a** the difference between what something is bought for and what it is sold to another for: *a 30-cent spread in the buying and selling prices of wheat.* **b** any difference, as between two prices or rates: *a serious spread between actual and scheduled production.* **11** *Commerce.* a contractual privilege, usually purchased, of both a put and a call, similar to a straddle except that the price of the put is different from the price of the call. **12** *U.S. Informal.* **a** a ranch or farm: *He owned the 2,560-acre spread west of the Pecos River* (Time). **b** a large house or dwelling: *"What gives with that spread of yours while you're away? You renting it?"* (New Yorker).
— ***adj.*** stretched out; expanded; extended: *Front and low vowels are more easily pronounced with lips unrounded, that is, spread or neutral* (Simeon Potter).

**spread oneself,** *Informal.* **a** to try hard to make a good impression; exert oneself: *He had promised ... to spread himself in the preparation of this meal* (S. H. Hammond). **b** to display one's abilities fully: *The gentleman who had just spread himself was very angry at having the effect of his speech thus spoiled* (Edward Kinglake).
[Middle English *spreden,* Old English *-sprǣdan* (compare *sprǣdung* spreading)]

**spread|a|bil|i|ty** (spred′ə bil′ə tē), *n.* the quality or condition of being spreadable: *In spreadability ... margarine wins hands down* (New Scientist).

**spread|a|ble** (spred′ə bəl), *adj.* that spreads or can be spread: *spreadable illness or cheese.*

**spread city,** *U.S.* a sprawling extension of a city into and beyond the suburbs.

✱**spread eagle, 1** a representation of an eagle with outspread wings, used as an emblem of the United States and certain other countries. **2** a boastful, self-assertive person, especially an American with an excess of national or regional pride. **3** a figure executed in skating, consisting of a sideways glide with the arms outstretched and the legs widely opened.

✱**spread eagle**
definition 1

**spread-ea|gle** (spred′ē′gəl), *adj., v.,* **-gled, -gling.** — ***adj.*** **1** having or suggestive of the form or appearance of a spread eagle. **2** *U.S.* boastful or high-sounding, especially in praise of the United States: *spread-eagle oratory. It wasn't a spread-eagle speech, but he* [*Daniel Webster*] *made you see it* (Stephen Vincent Benét). **SYN**: grandiloquent, bombastic.
— ***v.t.*** **1** to stretch out flat and sprawling as if in a spread eagle: *The man ... fell and lay spread-eagled on the snow* (New Yorker). **2** to tie (a person) with the arms and legs spread widely to the sides as a form of punishment or torture. **3** to beat thoroughly, as by lapping one's opponents: [*He*] *virtually spread-eagled the field with a perfect start and lengthy strides* (New York Times).
— ***v.i.*** **1** to do a spread eagle or spread eagles in skating. **2** to stretch out flat; sprawl: *The horse pulled up* [*to the fence*] *and spread-eagled among the poles* (Manchester Guardian Weekly).

**spread|er** (spred′ər), *n.* a person or thing that spreads: *After the fabrics dry, spreaders pile them on a large table* (Betsy Talbot Blackwell). *More expensive than all of these tools put together is a spreader for lawn seed, fertilizer and weedkiller* (New York Times).

**spread F,** a patchy or diffuse pattern of reflected radio signals from the F layer of the ionosphere: *A natural phenomenon known as spread F ... occurs at night under certain natural conditions and suggests instabilities in the ionospheric plasma* (Science News).

**spread formation,** *Football.* an offensive formation in which the ends and some of the backs spread out laterally at a relatively great distance from the center.

**spread|ing adder** (spred′ing), = hognose snake.

**spreading decline,** a disease affecting citrus trees, caused by a nematoid worm.

**spreading dogbane,** a perennial herb of North America, having light-green leaves, clusters of pale pink flowers, and a bitter root sometimes used to induce vomiting.

**spreading factor,** a substance able to disperse colloids, especially the enzyme hyaluronidase.

**Sprech|ge|sang** (shpreн′gə zäng′), *n. German.* **1** a vocal style or part in music, halfway between speaking and singing, similar to recitative, but less sustained; speech-song: [*The*] *drama is considerably enhanced by Meller's use of Sprechgesang ... and ordinary speech as well as song* (London Times). **2** (literally) speaking song.

**spree** (sprē), *n.* **1** a lively frolic; gay time: *To celebrate victory the whole team went on a spree in town, including dinner and a movie.* **2** a long spell of drinking intoxicating liquor; drunken carousal: *He described both ... as excessive drinkers who would leave the children alone while they went on sprees* (New York Times).
[origin uncertain]

---

**Pronunciation Key:** hat, āge, cãre, fär; let, ēqual, tėrm; it, īce; hot, ōpen, ôrder; oil, out; cup, pu̇t, rüle; child; long; thin; ᴛʜen; zh, measure;
ə represents **a** in about, **e** in taken, **i** in pencil, **o** in lemon, **u** in circus.

**sprent** (sprent), *adj. Archaic.* sprinkled: *the brown hair sprent with grey* (Matthew Arnold). [past participle of obsolete *spreng,* Old English *sprengan* to sprinkle]

**sprew** (sprü), *n.* = sprue[1].

**spri|er** (sprī′ər), *adj.* spryer; a comparative of **spry.**

**spri|est** (sprī′ist), *adj.* spryest; a superlative of **spry.**

**sprig** (sprig), *n., v.,* **sprigged, sprig|ging.** —*n.* **1** a shoot, twig, or small branch: *a sprig of holly. He wore a sprig of lilac in his buttonhole.* **2** an ornament or design shaped like a sprig or spray: *glasses covered with little gold sprigs* (Henry James). **3** *Figurative.* a scion or offspring as of some person, class, or institution. **4** *Figurative.* a young fellow; youth; stripling: *a sprig whom I remember with a whey face and a satchel not so very many years ago* (Scott). **5** a small wedge of tin or zinc, used to hold glass in a sash until the putty dries. **6** a small, headless nail or brad. **7** *U.S.* a sprigtail.
—*v.t.* **1** to decorate (pottery, fabrics, or wallpaper) with designs representing sprigs. **2** to strip a sprig or sprigs from (a plant or tree). **3** to fasten with sprigs or brads.
[Middle English *sprigge;* origin uncertain] —**sprig′ger,** *n.*

**sprigged** (sprigd), *adj.* adorned or ornamented with sprigs (used especially of fabrics or wallpaper): *some friendly flounces of sprigged muslin ...* (Lytton Strachey).

**sprig|ging** (sprig′ing), *n.* the planting or repair of a lawn by means of grass sprigs rather than seed: *Sprigging is ... used where the grass being planted is a poor-seeding or non-seeding species* (Roy Wiggans).

**spright** (sprīt), *n. Obsolete.* sprite.

**spright|ful** (sprīt′fəl), *adj.* sprightly; spirited: *Spoke like a sprightful noble gentleman* (Shakespeare). —**spright′ful|ly,** *adv.* —**spright′fulness,** *n.*

**spright|ly** (sprīt′lē), *adj.,* **-li|er, -li|est,** *adv.* —*adj.* lively; gay: *a sprightly kitten, a sprightly bounce to one's walk. This brought a sprightly note into the conversation* (Atlantic). SYN: spirited, animated, vivacious.
—*adv.* in a sprightly manner; vivaciously.
—**spright′li|ness,** *n.*

**sprig|tail** (sprig′tāl′), *n. U.S.* **1** the pintail duck. **2** the ruddy duck.

**sprig-tailed** (sprig′tāld′), *adj.* having a sprigged or sharp-pointed tail.

***spring** (spring), *v.,* **sprang** or **sprung, sprung, spring|ing,** *n., adj.* —*v.i.* **1** to rise or move suddenly and lightly; leap or jump: *to spring to attention. I sprang to my feet. The dog sprang at the thief. He sprang to his sleigh, to his team gave a whistle* (Clement C. Moore). SYN: bound, vault. **2** to fly back or away as if by elastic force: *The door sprang to. The branch sprang up when I dropped from it.* SYN: rebound, recoil. **3** to be flexible, resilient, or elastic; be able to spring: *This branch springs enough to use as a snare.* **4** to come from some source; arise; grow: *A wind has sprung up. Plants spring from seeds. (Figurative.) The alliance sprang from their mutual peril.* SYN: emerge, emanate. **5** to derive by birth or parentage; be descended; be the issue of: *He springs from New England stock.* **6** to begin to move, act, or grow suddenly; burst forth: *Towns sprang up where oil was discovered. Sparks sprang from the fire.* **7** to crack, split, warp, bend, strain, or break: *Cracks all along the concrete wall showed where it had sprung.* **8** to extend upward; rise; tower: *a cliff springing sheer to a height of 2,000 feet.* **9** to take a curving or slanting upward course from some point of support. Arches, vaults, and rafters are said to spring. **10** to rise from cover, as partridges do. **11** of a mine: **a** to explode. **b** to be exploded.
—*v.t.* **1** to cause to spring; cause to act by a spring: *to spring a trap.* **2** *Figurative.* to bring out, produce, or make suddenly: *to spring a surprise on someone.* **3** *Figurative.* to announce or reveal suddenly and usually unexpectedly: *to spring the news of an engagement.* **4** to force open, apart, or out of position; crack, split, warp, bend, or break: *Cracks all along the surface showed where frost had sprung the rock wall. Miles of travel along rocky roads had sprung the wagon shaft. The burglar was able to spring the lock quite easily.* **5** to jump over: *to spring a distance of 12 feet, to spring a wall.* **6** to cause (partridges or other birds or game) to rise from cover: *I would throw her off, wait until she was up, and spring the birds* (T. H. White). **7** to provide or fit with a spring or springs: *to spring a watch or a carriage.* **8** *Slang.* to secure the release of (a person) from prison by bail or otherwise: *After a stretch in a Parma jail, [he] was sprung conditionally, time off for good behavior* (Time).
—*n.* **1** a leap or jump; bound: *The boy made a spring over the fence.* SYN: vault. **2** the distance covered or that can be covered by a spring. **3** an elastic device that returns to its original shape after being pulled or held out of shape. A spring consists of one or more strips or plates, usually of metal, bent, coiled, or otherwise shaped or adjusted. Springs are variously used to communicate or regulate motion and lessen concussion. *Beds have wire springs. The springs in a watch make it go.* **4** elastic quality or capacity; elasticity: *There is no spring left in these old rubber bands. (Figurative.) The old man's knees have lost their spring.* SYN: resiliency, buoyancy. **5a** a flying back or recoil from a forced position: *the bow well bent, and smart the spring* (William Cowper). **b** *Figurative.* something that produces action; moving force or motive: *the springs of progress.* **6** the season of the year after winter, when plants begin to grow in the temperate and colder regions of the earth (in North America, the months of March, April, and May; in Great Britain, February, March, and April): *O, Wind, If Winter comes, can Spring be far behind?* (Shelley). **7** *Astronomy.* the three months between the vernal equinox and the summer solstice. **8** *Figurative.* the first and freshest or most vigorous stage of anything, especially of life; period of youth: *Young people are in the spring of life.* **9** a stream of water flowing naturally from the earth: *The largest springs ... where the water flows underground in cavelike channels* (Eldred D. Wilson). **10** *Figurative.* a source of anything; origin; cause; wellspring: *the springs of emotion.* **11** a crack, split, warp, bend, strain, or break, especially a vertical split or transverse crack as in a mast or spar of a ship or other vessel. **12** the point at which an arch or vault springs or rises from its abutment or impost; rise of an arch: *It was just under five feet above the floor at the spring of the vaulting, a little over seven feet down the middle* (Oliver La Farge). **13** *Scottish.* a quick or lively tune: *Robin took the pipes, and played a little spring* (Robert Louis Stevenson).
—*adj.* **1** fitted with a spring or springs; operating by means of springs: *a spring balance.* **2** hung or suspended on springs: *a spring cart.* **3** of or having to do with the season of spring: *Probably the most welcome of all flowers are the spring flowers.* **4** characteristic of or suitable for the season of spring: *spring weather, new spring hats.* **5** from a spring: *spring salts.*
**spring a leak.** See under **leak.**
**spring a mine.** See under **mine**[2].
[Old English *springan* to move suddenly; come to sight; grow up] —**spring′a|ble,** *adj.* —**spring′less,** *adj.*

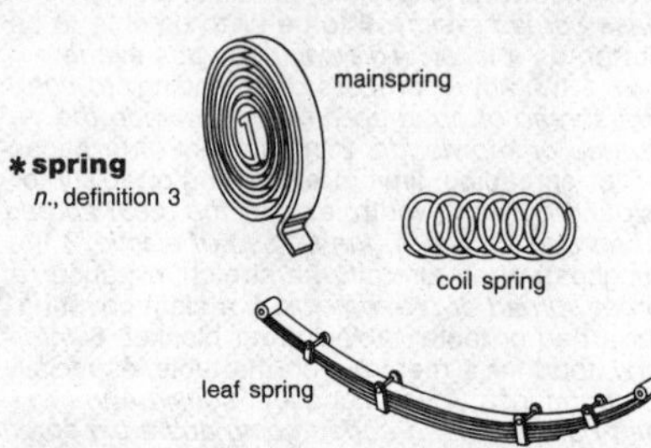

***spring** *n.,* definition 3

**spring|al**[1] (spring′əl), *n. Archaic.* a youth; springald.

**spring|al**[2] (spring′əl), *n. Archaic.* a kind of catapult; springald.

**spring|ald**[1] (spring′əld), *n. Archaic.* a young man; youth; stripling. [Middle English *sprynhold;* origin uncertain]

**spring|ald**[2] (spring′əld), *n.* a machine of war used in the Middle Ages for throwing heavy stones or other missiles; a kind of catapult. [apparently < Anglo-French *springalde,* Old French *espringalle* < *espringuer* to spring < Germanic (compare Old English *springan* to spring)]

**spring azure,** a small butterfly with a sky-blue color.

**spring balance,** a balance hanging or resting on a spring attached to a pointer which indicates the weight on a dial.

**spring beauty, 1** any one of a group of North American herbs of the purslane family producing small pink or white flowers in early spring; good-morning-spring. **2** the small pink or white flowers of any one of these plants.

**spring-blade** (spring′blād′), *n.,* or **spring-blade knife,** = switch blade.

**spring|board** (spring′bôrd′, -bōrd′), *n., v.* —*n.* **1** a flexible board used to give added spring in diving, jumping, or vaulting. It is mounted at one or both ends. **2** *Figurative.* anything that serves as a way to get to something else: *Hard work was his springboard to success. This will give us among other things entry into the British market and a springboard to the Continent* (Wall Street Journal).
—*v.i., v.t.* to make a great leap or departure, as if by using a springboard: *Robert H. Goddard and other 20th-century experimenters springboarded from the heritage of the 19th-century rocket motor design* (Science). *Matisse springboarded his way into the mid-twentieth century already in 1899, when he painted the "Still Life with Oranges"* (Sunday Times).

**spring|bok** (spring′bok′), *n., pl.* **-boks** or (*collectively*) **-bok.** a small antelope of southern Africa. It leaps almost directly upward when excited or disturbed. *If you are lucky you will see a springbok standing still and graceful before he leaps away* (Allan Gordon). [< Afrikaans *springbok* < *springen* to leap (< Dutch) + *bok* antelope (< Dutch)]

**spring|buck** (spring′buk′), *n., pl.* **-bucks** or (*collectively*) **-buck.** = springbok.

**spring cankerworm,** the caterpillar of a geometrid moth.

**spring chicken, 1** a young chicken, especially one only a few months old, used for frying or broiling because of its tenderness. **2** *Slang, Figurative.* a young person: *"She's no spring chicken," she would say of another woman* (New Yorker). *He's no spring chicken, 30 years old, but ... the envy of his younger rivals* (Sunday Times).

**spring-clean** (spring′klēn′), *v.t.* to clean thoroughly when mild weather sets in: *It's time to spring-clean the office and open up a few more windows* (Punch).

**spring-clean|ing** (spring′klē′ning), *n.* **1** the general cleaning of a house, or other building or office, when mild weather sets in. **2** *Figurative: [He] has called for "a good spring-cleaning" within the N.A.T.O. alliance* (Manchester Guardian Weekly). SYN: cleanup.

**spring clip,** a clip fitted with a spring: *the spring clip of a clipboard.*

**spring-clip pan** (spring′klip′), *Especially British.* = spring-form pan.

**springe** (sprinj), *n., v.,* **springed, spring|ing.** —*n.* a snare for catching small game, especially a noose attached to a twig bent over and released by a trigger.
—*v.t.* to catch in a springe; snare.
—*v.i.* to set a springe or springes.
[apparently < Old English *sprengan* burst, crack; (in unrecorded sense "cause to spring")]

**spring|er** (spring′ər), *n.* **1** a person or thing that springs. **2** the support or impost from which an arch springs. **3** the stone at each end of an arch next to this. **4** = springer spaniel. **5** = springbok. **6** = grampus. **7** = spring chicken. **8** = spring lamb. **9** a tin can containing spoiled food that has forced the ends of the can to bulge; swell.

**springer spaniel,** any one of certain of the larger breeds of field spaniels used to spring or flush game, such as the English springer spaniel and the Welsh springer spaniel.

**spring fever,** a listless, lazy, or restless feeling felt by some people during the first sudden warm weather of spring: *It's spring fever ... when you've got it you want—oh, you don't quite know what it is you do want, but it just fairly makes your heart ache, you want it so* (Mark Twain).

**Spring|field rifle** (spring′fēld), **1** a type of breechloading rifle, .30 caliber, with bolt action, adopted by the U.S. Army in 1903. **2** a muzzleloading, single-shot rifle, .58 caliber, used by the U.S. Army in the Civil War. [< *Springfield,* a city in Massachusetts, where a United States Army arsenal is located]

**spring-form pan** (spring′fôrm′), a baking pan with a round, high rim that can be loosened and removed by opening a clamp or clip on the side. Spring-form pans are used for baking cheese cakes and other cakes of delicate texture that are hard to remove from the pan after baking.

**spring frog, 1** = green frog. **2** = leopard frog.

**spring garden,** *Especially British.* a public pleasure garden, as formerly in Hyde Park and at Vauxhall, London.

**spring gun, 1** a gun fixed in place as a booby trap to fire at the person or animal who touches a trip wire attached to the trigger: *So it went on, a gripping chronicle of folly and ill-fortune ... gamekeepers tripping over their own spring guns* (Punch). **2** a gun in which the missile is discharged by the release of a spring: *They wore rubber flippers, underwater goggles, and carried spring guns with which to slaughter anything submarine* (Manchester Guardian).

**spring|haas** (spring′häs′), *n.* = jumping hare. [< Afrikaans *springhaas* < *spring* jump + *haas* hare]

**spring|halt** (spring′hôlt′), *n.* a diseased condition of the hind legs of a horse; stringhalt.

**spring hare,** = jumping hare.

**spring|head** (spring′hed′), *n.* a fountainhead; wellspring.

**spring-heeled** (spring′hēld′), *adj. Especially Brit-*

*ish.* **1** having a spring in one's step; light-footed: *Kath is forty-one but gallivants about the sitting room ... like a spring-heeled eurhythmics teacher* (Punch). **2** *Figurative.* sprightly; jaunty: *The orchestra sounded both suave and spring-heeled* (Charles Reid).

**spring house**, or **spring|house** (spring′hous′), *n. U.S.* a small outbuilding constructed over a spring or brook, used as a dairy or a place to keep milk, meat, or other perishables, cool.

**spring|ing** (spring′ing), *n.* **1** the spring of an arch. **2** an arrangement of springs; fitting of a spring or springs: *Many auto men consider independent front springing ... as the last major advance in softening auto riding* (Wall Street Journal).

**springing line**, = springing (def. 1).

**spring lamb**, a young and tender lamb, originally one born after January 1st and brought to market in April.

**spring|let** (spring′lit), *n.* a little spring (of water): *Out from the little hill Oozes the slender springlet still* (Scott).

**spring|like** (spring′līk′), *adj.* of or characteristic of the spring; vernal: *a drowsy springlike sultriness, mild springlike days.*

**spring lizard**, *U.S. Dialect.* a salamander (def. 1).

**spring-load|ed** (spring′lō′did), *adj.* held in place or operated by a spring.

**spring lock**, a lock that fastens automatically by a spring.

**spring peeper**, a small, brown tree frog with a dark patch across the face, whose peeping call is heard early in the spring: *The first faint, hesitant announcement by the spring peeper that the earth's sleep is not the sleep of death* (Atlantic).

**spring salmon**, the Chinook salmon, a large salmon of the Pacific coast.

**spring|tail** (spring′tāl′), *n.* any one of an order of small, wingless insects that have forked, taillike appendages at the end of the abdomen under the body which act as a spring, giving them great jumping ability; collembola.

**spring|tide** (spring′tīd′), *n.* = springtime.

**spring tide**, **1** the exceptionally high and low tides which come at the time of the new moon or the full moon, especially the highest level of high tide: *Approximately twice monthly the sun, moon, and earth are nearly in line and at these times the sun and moon combine their tide-raising forces to produce the greatest tides, called spring tides* (Wasley S. Krogdahl). See picture under **tide**[1]. **2** *Figurative.* any great flood, swell, or rush; copious flow: *With Kleist we are on the spring tide of German romanticism* (London Times).

**spring|time** (spring′tīm′), *n.* **1** the season of spring: *Flowers bloom in the springtime.* **2** *Figurative.* the first or earliest period: *the springtime of life.*

**spring-tooth harrow** (spring′tüth′), a harrow with hooklike teeth made of springs that tear into the soil when the harrow moves.

**spring water**, water issuing or obtained from a spring: *Spring water usually reaches the surface through either hydrostatic pressure or gravity flow* (White and Renner).

**spring wheat**, a variety of wheat sown in the spring.

**spring|wood** (spring′wu̇d′), *n.* **1** a light ring or layer of wood formed around a tree each spring. It has large open spaces and thin cell walls to allow for the rapid passage of water to the growing parts. **2** a wood or thicket of young trees: *the wide expanse of country beyond the cypress groves and springwoods* (Sir Osbert Sitwell).

**spring|y** (spring′ē), *adj.*, **spring|i|er, spring|i|est.** **1** that springs; elastic; resilient: *Her step was springy. Curves in the backbone give it a springy quality.* **2** having many springs of water. **3** spongy with moisture, such as soil in the area of a subterranean spring or springs. —**spring′i|ly**, *adv.* —**spring′i|ness**, *n.*

**sprin|kle** (spring′kəl), *v.*, **-kled, -kling**, *n.* —*v.t.* **1** to scatter in drops or tiny bits; strew: *He sprinkled sand on the icy sidewalk.* **SYN:** spatter, besprinkle. **2** to spray or cover with small drops or particles: *She sprinkled the flowers with water.* **3** *Figurative.* **a** to dot or vary with something scattered here and there: *a countryside sprinkled with farmhouses.* **b** to distribute here and there; disperse.
—*v.i.* **1** to scatter something in drops or small particles. **2** to rain a little.
—*n.* **1** the act of sprinkling: *Baptizing the Christian infant with a solemn sprinkle* (Milton). **2** a sprinkling; small number or quantity: *a sprinkle of salt. The cook put a sprinkle of nuts on the cake.* **3** a light rain.
[compare Dutch *sprenkelen*]

**sprin|kler** (spring′klər), *n.* **1** a person who sprinkles. **2** a device or apparatus for sprinkling water.

**sprin|klered** (spring′klərd), *adj.* equipped with a sprinkler system: *a modern, 6 story building, 100 per cent sprinklered.*

**sprinkler head**, the nozzle of a water sprinkler.

**sprinkler system**, a system of pipes with nozzles spaced regularly to carry water, especially as used to spray lawns and orchards or to help control fire by releasing water as the temperature rises: *Fire departments encourage the use of automatic sprinkler systems* (Robert C. Byrns).

**sprin|kling** (spring′kling), *n.* **1** the act of a person or thing that sprinkles: *regular sprinkling of a lawn.* **2** a small quantity sprinkled: *a sprinkling of rain.* **3** *Figurative.* **a** a small quantity or number scattered here and there: *a sprinkling of gray hairs.* **b** a small or slight quantity or amount: *a sprinkling of knowledge.* **SYN:** dash.

**sprint** (sprint), *v., n.* —*v.i.* to run at full speed, especially for a short distance: *The runners sprinted to the finish line.*
—*n.* **1** a short race at full speed: *The first of the added-money runs was the $22,725 Autumn Day Handicap, a sprint for fillies and mares* (New York Times). **2** any short spell of running, rowing, or other exercise, at full speed. **3** *Figurative: to finish the job with a sprint of very hard work.*
[Middle English *sprenten*, probably < Scandinavian (compare Old Icelandic *spretta*)]
—**sprint′er**, *n.*

**sprint car**, a very fast, medium-sized racing car used for races over short distances.

**sprit** (sprit), *n.* a small pole running diagonally from the foot of a mast up to the top corner of a fore-and-aft sail, to support and stretch it. [Old English *sprēot* pole]

**sprite** (sprīt), *n.* **1** an elf; fairy; goblin. **SYN:** pixie. **2** = sand crab. **3** *Obsolete.* a ghost; spirit. [< Old French *esprit* spirit < Latin *spīritus.* See etym. of doublets **esprit, spirit.**]

**sprite|ly** (sprīt′lē), *adj.*, **-li|er, -li|est**, *adv. Especially British.* sprightly. —**sprite′li|ness**, *n.*

**sprit|sail** (sprit′sāl′; *Nautical* sprit′səl), *n.* any fore-and-aft sail supported and stretched by a sprit: *It is beamy, with a rounded bow, and it carries a broad mainsail—spritsail rigged* (Listener).

**spritz|er** (sprit′sər), *n.* a cold drink made with syrup or wine and carbonated water. [< German *Spritzer* < *spritzen* to squirt, splash]

**sprock|et** (sprok′it), *n.* **1** one of a set of parts sticking out from the rim of a wheel, arranged to fit into the links of a chain. The sprockets keep the chain from slipping. **2** = sprocket wheel. [origin uncertain]

**sprock|et|less** (sprok′it lis), *adj.* without a sprocket or sprockets: *New projectors had sprocketless film transport and ... projection, permitting a wide range of projection speeds* (Walter Clark).

**sprocket wheel**, a wheel made with sprockets that are arranged to fit into the links of a chain.

**sprog** (sprog), *n. British Slang.* **1** a green or raw recruit: *I was twenty-two then—a sprog, as they called the green ones in the air force—and this was to be my first operational mission* (James N. Kirk). **2** a small child; youngster: *The guilt feelings of the father intensify when the sprog arrives* (Punch). [origin unknown]

**sprout** (sprout), *v., n.* —*v.i.* **1** to begin to grow; shoot forth; bud; germinate: *Buds sprout in the spring. Weeds have sprouted in the garden.* **2** to bring forth or produce shoots or shootlike growths: *After a shower a meadow sprouts with the yellow buds of the dandelion* (Theodore Winthrop). **3** *Figurative.* to shoot forth or develop rapidly or naturally: *A straggling black moustache sprouted on his upper lip* (Robert S. Hichens). *Community theatres have sprouted in several cities* (Manchester Guardian). *Doubts sprout among Federal analysts about summer business prospects* (Wall Street Journal).
—*v.t.* **1** to cause to sprout; produce by sprouting; grow: *to sprout wings. The rain sprouted the corn.* **2** *Informal.* to remove sprouts from: *He sprouted the potatoes twice every winter.*
—*n.* **1** a shoot from a branch, root, or stump of a tree, shrub, or other plant. **2** the young shoot, such as from a germinating seed or from a rhizome or tuber: *bean sprouts. The gardener was setting out sprouts.* **3** *Figurative.* something like a sprout in appearance, formation, or growth.
**a course of sprouts.** See under **course.**
**sprouts**, Brussels sprouts: *sprouts served in cream sauce.*
[Old English *-sprūtan*, as in *āsprūtan*]

**sprout|ing broccoli** (sprou′ting), = Italian broccoli.

**sprout|ling** (sprout′ling), *n.* a little or young sprout.

**sprouts** (sprouts), *n.pl.* See under **sprout.**

**spruce**[1] (sprüs), *n.* **1** any one of a group of evergreen trees with cones and with needle-shaped leaves arranged spirally around the branches. The spruce belongs to the pine family. It is often used as a Christmas tree in America. **2** any one of various other coniferous trees, such as the Douglas fir or Douglas spruce, the hemlock spruce, or the balsam spruce. **3** the wood of any of these trees. [earlier, adjective < Middle English *Spruce*, variant of *Pruce* Prussia (perhaps because the trees first came from there)]

**spruce**[2] (sprüs), *adj.*, **spruc|er, spruc|est**, *v.*, **spruced, spruc|ing.** —*adj.* smart in appearance; neat; trim: *He looked very spruce in his new suit. A good-looking man; spruce and dapper and very tidy* (Anthony Trollope). **SYN:** dapper, jaunty.
—*v.t.* to make spruce: *He spruced himself up for dinner. Border posts are to be spruced up with paint and flowers* (New York Times).
—*v.i.* to become spruce.
[perhaps special use of Middle English *Spruce* Prussia. Compare *spruce leather* (*jerkin*), a popular style in the 1500's (made in Prussia and considered smart-looking)] —**spruce′ly**, *adv.*
—**spruce′ness**, *n.*

**spruce beer**, a fermented beverage made from an extract of spruce needles and twigs boiled with molasses or sugar, formerly used especially as a diuretic and antiscorbutic.

**spruce budworm**, the larva of a small, thick-bodied moth that feeds on the bud tips of spruce, fir, and related trees.

**spruce fir**, a spruce, especially the Norway spruce.

**spruce grouse**, a grouse of the coniferous forests of northern North America; Canada grouse.

**spruce gum**, a resinous exudation from various spruces and firs, used as a chewing gum, or as an ingredient of chewing gum.

**spruce partridge**, = spruce grouse.

**spruce pine**, any one of various American pines or hemlocks with light, soft wood, such as the black spruce.

**sprue**[1] (sprü), *n. Metallurgy.* **1** an opening or passage through which molten metal is run into the gate and then into the mold. **2** the waste piece of metal cast in this passage. [origin uncertain]

**sprue**[2] (sprü), *n.* **1** a chronic disease characterized by emaciation, anemia, inflammation of the mouth, and digestive upsets, occurring especially in tropical countries: *Many sufferers of sprue and celiac disease, a digestive illness, cannot digest ordinary bread* (Science News Letter). **2** = thrush[2] (def. 1). [probably < Dutch *spruw*]

**sprui|ker** (sprü′kər), *n. Australian.* a fluent speaker who urges people to buy a product, see an exhibit, or the like; barker; spieler.

**spruit** (sprīt, sproit, sprœ′it), *n.* a small stream or watercourse in South Africa, usually dry except after rain. [< Afrikaans *spruit*]

**sprung** (sprung), *v., adj.* —*v.* a past tense and the past participle of **spring:** *The trap was sprung.*
—*adj.* **1** that has worked loose from a fastening, as a part of a tool. **2** split or cracked, as a mast. **3** bent or warped, as a board. **4** *Slang.* tipsy or drunk.

**sprung rhythm**, *Prosody.* rhythm which has feet that vary greatly in the number of syllables, usually having between one and four, but that always have equal time length, the stress being on the first syllable. It was much used by both Gerard Manley Hopkins and Dylan Thomas.

**spry** (sprī), *adj.*, **spry|er** or **spri|er, spry|est** or **spri|est.** full of health and spirits; lively; nimble; active; brisk: *The spry old lady traveled all over the country.* **SYN:** sprightly. [origin uncertain]
—**spry′ly**, *adv.* —**spry′ness**, *n.*

**SPS** (no periods), Service Propulsion System (the main rocket system of a service module).

**spt.**, seaport.

**spud** (spud), *n., v.*, **spud|ded, spud|ding.** —*n.* **1** a spadelike tool with a narrow blade for digging up weeds or cutting their roots. **2** a tool something like a wide chisel, used for removing bark. **3** *Informal.* a potato: *Spuds and yams show some price recovery* (Wall Street Journal). **4** a leg or support for a dredging or oil-drilling platform. **5** a spadelike surgical instrument for removing foreign bodies especially from the eye and ear.
—*v.t.* **1** to remove or dig up by means of a spud. **2** to drill (a hole) as part of the preliminary stages of sinking an oil well: *The third well was down 4,000 feet at last report and the fourth had just been spudded in* (Wall Street Journal).
—*v.i.* to dig with a spud: *He spudded among the vines for weeds.*
[Middle English *spudde* a short knife; origin uncertain]

**spud|der** (spud′ər), *n.* **1** = spud (def. 2). **2** a ma-

**Pronunciation Key:** hat, āge, cãre, fär; let, ēqual, tėrm; it, īce; hot, ōpen, ôrder; **oi**l, **ou**t; cup, pu̇t, rüle; **ch**ild; lo**ng**; **th**in; **ᴛʜ**en; **zh**, measure; ə represents **a** in about, **e** in taken, **i** in pencil, **o** in lemon, **u** in circus.

chine for spudding oil wells.
**spud|dy** (spud′ē), *adj.,* **-di|er, -di|est.** short and fat or thick: *spuddy hands.*
**spue** (spyü), *v.t., v.i.,* **spued, spu|ing,** *n.* = spew.
**spume** (spyüm), *n., v.,* **spumed, spum|ing.** *—n.* frothy matter, such as that on the crest of a wave; foam; froth.
*—v.i.* to foam or froth: *No longer do all the raging rivers spume untamed down to the fiords* (Newsweek).
[< Latin *spūma*]
**spu|mo|ne** or **spu|mo|ni** (spə mō′nē), *n.* an Italian ice cream made with layers of different colors and flavors, usually containing candied fruit and nuts. [< Italian *spumone,* singular, *spumoni,* plural < *spuma* foam < Latin *spūma*]
**spu|mous** (spyü′məs), *adj.* consisting of froth or scum; foamy: *The boat made a spumous track upon the water.*
**spum|y** (spyü′mē), *adj.,* **spum|i|er, spum|i|est.** covered with foam; foamy; frothy.
**spun¹** (spun), *v.* a past tense and the past participle of **spin**: *The car skidded and spun on the ice. She spun all day yesterday. The thread was spun from silk.*
**spun²** (spun), *n.* a fabric made of spun rayon. [apparently short for *spun rayon*]
**spun-dyed** (spun′dīd′), *adj.* dyed before being spun or pulled out into filaments: *Spun-dyed rayon and acetate yarn hold colors fast.*
**spun glass,** glass drawn into fine threads while in a liquid state. Fiberglass is one kind of spun glass.
**spunk** (spungk), *n., v.* *—n.* **1** *Informal.* courage; pluck; spirit; mettle: *a little puppy full of spunk.* **SYN**: nerve. **2** *Scottish.* **a** a spark. **b** a friction match. **3** touchwood; punk.
*—v.i.* **1** *U.S.* to show spunk or spirit: *Just spunk up to the old codger—let him know you are not afraid of him* (Elbridge G. Paige). **2** *Scottish.* to flare up with anger: *He spunked up like tinder. "Do you call me a liar?" he said* (Neil Munro).
**get one's spunk up,** *Informal.* **a** to show courage, pluck, or spirit: *How a woman got her spunk up and left the country* (M. Thompson). **b** to become angry: *My spunk is getting up a little about it* (Jamestown Journal).
**spunk of fire,** a small fire; bit of flame: *Ye might light a spunk of fire in the red room* (Scott).
**spunk up.** See verb above.
[< Scottish Gaelic *spong* tinder, pith; (churlish) spirit, perhaps ultimately < Latin *spongia;* see etym. under **sponge**]
**spunk|ie** (spung′kē), *n. Scottish.* **1** a will-o'-the-wisp. **2** whiskey or other strong drink. [< *spunk* + *-ie*]
**spunk|y** (spung′kē), *adj.,* **spunk|i|er, spunk|i|est.** *Informal.* courageous; plucky; spirited: *He is a spunky fellow.* **SYN**: mettlesome. — **spunk′i|ly,** *adv.* — **spunk′i|ness,** *n.*
**spun rayon, 1** any one of various rayon fabrics made to resemble linen, wool, cotton, or silk. **2** the yarn, made from rayon, used for these.
**spun silk,** silk waste spun into yarn: *Short fibers spun from the silk from pierced cocoons is called spun silk* (Bernice G. Chambers).
**spun sugar,** sugar drawn out or worked up into a threadlike form, used in making cotton candy, and as an ornament and frosting for desserts.
**spun yarn,** a line composed of two or more rope yarns loosely twisted together.
***spur** (spėr), *n., v.,* **spurred, spur|ring.** *—n.* **1** a pricking instrument consisting of a small spike or spiked wheel, worn on a horseman's heel for urging a horse on. **2** *Figurative.* anything that urges on: *Ambition was the spur that made him work.* **SYN**: stimulus, incentive, incitement. **3** something like a spur; point sticking out. **4** a protuberance on the inner side of the leg of a fowl, either knotlike or pointed, according to the age and sex of the fowl. **5** a piercing or cutting device fastened to each of a gamecock's legs; gaff. **6** a sharp-pointed, bony growth on some part of the body, especially on the heel or in the nose: *Because there is no swelling, pain or tenderness to show the spur, team mates and coaches may think the player is shirking* (Science News Letter). **7** a short or stunted branch or shoot of a tree. **8** = spur track. **9** a slender, generally hollow, projection from a flower part, as from the calyx of columbine; calcar. **10** a fungous disease of cereal plants; ergot. **11** a climbing iron used in mounting telephone poles or the like. **12** a range, ridge, mountain, hill, or a part of one of these, projecting from the main mass: *A spur of rock stuck out from the mountain.* **13** *Architecture.* **a** a brace, especially one set diagonally to support a post; shore; prop. **b** a sloping buttress. **c** an ornament at the base of a column; griffe. **14** a buttress or platform of masonry strengthening an outwork of a fortification.
*—v.t.* **1** to prick (a horse) with spurs; urge on with spurs: *The rider spurred his horse on.* **2** *Figurative: Pride spurred the boy to fight. He had spurred his party till he could no longer curb it* (Thackeray). **SYN**: stimulate, incite. **3** to provide with a spur or spurs. **4** to strike or wound with a spur or gaff.
*—v.i.* **1** to ride quickly by urging on one's horse with spurs. **2** = hasten.
**on the spur of the moment,** on a sudden impulse or without previous thought or preparation: *He went in on the spur of the moment and was taken on as an English translator* (Manchester Guardian Weekly).
**set** (or **put**) **spurs to,** to start or impel by or as if by applying spurs: *Hawker ... set spurs to his noble chestnut horse* (Henry Kingsley).
**win one's spurs,** to make a reputation for oneself or attain distinction: *The painter ... executed his task with a patience ... worthy of one who had to win his spurs* (George Walter Thornbury).
[Old English *spura*] — **spur′less,** *adj.* — **spur′like′,** *adj.* — **spur′rer,** *n.*

***spur**
definition 1

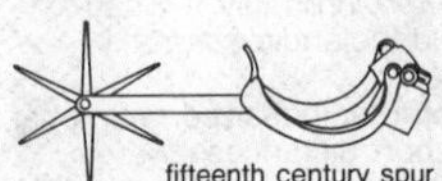
fifteenth century spur

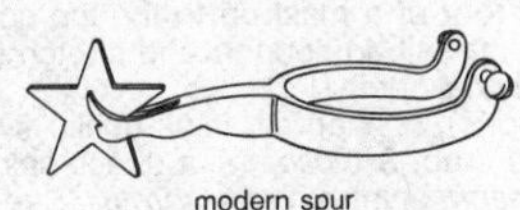
modern spur

**spur|dog** (spėr′dôg, -dog), *n., pl.* **-dogs** or (*collectively*) **-dog.** = spur dogfish.
**spur dogfish,** a variety of the common dogfish with two pectinated spurs on its upper side; spiny dogfish.
**spurge** (spėrj), *n.* any one of a genus of plants, many of which have an acrid, milky juice possessing purgative or medicinal properties, such as the poinsettia; euphorbia. [< Old French *espurge* < *espurgier* to purge < Latin *expūrgāre* < *ex-* out + *pūrgāre* to purge, cleanse]
**spur gear, 1** a simple gearwheel, having teeth on its rim set radially and with faces parallel to the axle: *Spur gears have the teeth parallel to the shaft, while helical gear teeth are at an angle* (Purvis and Toboldt). See picture under **gear**. **2** Also, **spur gearing.** gearing using such gearwheels.
**spurge family,** a group of dicotyledonous herbs, shrubs, and trees, some of which are fleshy and have a milky juice. The family includes the spurge, croton, cassava, castor-oil plant, and candlenut.
**spurge laurel,** an Old World laurellike evergreen shrub of the mezereum family with yellow flowers.
**spu|ri|ous** (spyůr′ē əs), *adj.* **1** not genuine or authentic, especially: **a** not having the source, origin, or author claimed for it; forged; counterfeit: *a spurious painting, a spurious document.* **b** false; sham: *spurious anger.* **2** *Botany.* superficially resembling but differing in form and structure. **3** = illegitimate. [< Latin *spurius* (with English *-ous*) illegitimate child] — **spu′ri|ous|ly,** *adv.* — **spu′ri|ous|ness,** *n.*
**spurious fruit,** *Botany.* a pseudocarp.
**spurious wing,** = bastard wing.
**spur line,** = spur track.
**spurn** (spėrn), *v., n.* *—v.t.* **1** to refuse with scorn; reject contemptuously; scorn: *to spurn an offer of friendship. The judge spurned the bribe.* **SYN**: despise, contemn. **2** to strike with the foot or feet; kick away; trample: *With flying foot the heath he spurned* (Scott). *—v.i.* **1** to oppose with scorn; protest strongly or rebel: *to spurn at restraint.* **2** *Obsolete.* to kick (at something).
*—n.* **1** disdainful rejection; contemptuous treatment. **2** = kick.
[Old English *spurnan* strike (the foot) on something; reject] — **spurn′er,** *n.*
**spur-of-the-mo|ment** (spėr′əv ᴛʜə mō′mənt), *adj.* made or occurring suddenly, without deliberation: *to deal with a crisis in a spur-of-the-moment decision. Most women say they do only spur-of-the-moment buying* (New York Times).
**spurred** (spėrd), *adj.* **1** having spurs or a spur: *a spurred boot, spurred feet.* **2** having sharp spines, such as those on the legs of a gamecock. **3** *Botany.* calcarate.
**spur|rey** (spėr′ē), *n., pl.* **-reys.** = spurry.
**spur|ri|er** (spėr′ē ər), *n.* a person who makes spurs.
**spur royal,** an English gold coin of the time of James I, worth fifteen shillings, named from a figure on the reverse suggesting the rowel of a spur.
**spur|ry** (spėr′ē), *n., pl.* **-ries. 1** a small European herbaceous weed of the pink family, having white flowers and very narrow, whorled leaves. **2** any one of several related or similar herbs. [< Dutch *spurrie,* earlier Flemish *speurie,* perhaps related to Medieval Latin *spergula*]
**spurt** (spėrt), *v., n.* *—v.i.* **1** to flow suddenly in a stream or jet; gush out; squirt: *Blood spurted from the wound.* **2** to come forth as if by spurting; spring: *Dust spurted out from the wall when the bullets struck.* **3** to put forth great effort for a short time; show great activity for a short time: *The runners spurted near the end of the race.*
*—v.t.* to cause to gush out; squirt: *to spurt blood.*
*—n.* **1** a sudden rushing forth; jet: *Spurts of flame broke out all over the building.* **2** a great increase of effort or activity for a short time: *To win the race he put on a spurt of speed at the end.* **3** a sudden outburst as of feeling: *He had ceased to be aggressive except in momentary spurts* (H. G. Wells). **4** a sudden rise in prices, improvement in business, or the like. **5** the period of this. Also, **spirt.**
[earlier *spirt,* variant of *sprit,* Old English *spryttan*] — **spurt′er,** *n.*
**spur|tle** (spėr′təl), *n. Scottish.* a wooden stick for stirring porridge, and the like.
**spur track,** a branch railroad track or line connected with the main track or line at one end only.
**spur wheel,** = spur gear.
**spur-winged** (spėr′wingd′), *adj.* having one or more horny spurs projecting from the bend of the wing.
**sput|nik** (sput′nik, spůt′-), *n.* an artificial earth satellite, especially one of a series launched by the Soviet Union. The first Russian sputnik was put into orbit on October 4, 1957. [< Russian (*Iskusstvennyj*) *Sputnik* (*Zemli*) (Artificial) Satellite (of the Earth) < *sputnik* (literally) companion]
**sput|ter** (sput′ər), *v., n.* *—v.i.* **1** to make spitting or popping noises: *fat sputtering in the frying pan. The firecrackers sputtered.* **2** to throw out drops of saliva, bits of food, etc., in excitement or in talking too fast. **3** to speak so rapidly and vehemently as to seem to spit out the words; speak confusedly and indistinctly.
*—v.t.* **1** to throw out (drops of spit, bits of food, etc.) in excitement or in talking too fast. **2** to say (words or sounds) in haste and confusion: *He would sputter uneasy protest* (Sinclair Lewis). **3** to emit in small amounts with slight explosions: *A burning green stick sputters out smoke.* **4** to coat (a surface) with a thin film of metal by bombarding with particles of the metal moving at high speed.
*—n.* **1** confused talk; splutter. **2** the act of sputtering; sputtering noise: *When he began working with the torch ... a few window-watchers seemed annoyed at the glare and sputter* (Newsweek). **3** matter ejected in or by sputtering.
[probably related to **spout**] — **sput′ter|er,** *n.*
**spu|tum** (spyü′təm), *n., pl.* **-ta** (-tə). **1** saliva; spittle; spit. **2** a mixture of saliva and mucus coughed up from the lungs and throat and spat out. [< Latin *spūtum,* neuter past participle of *spuere* to spit]
**spy** (spī), *n., pl.* **spies,** *v.,* **spied, spy|ing.** *—n.* **1** a person who keeps secret watch upon the actions of others: *She used her little sister as a spy against her brother and his friends. The informer had been a spy for the police. The secret police had spies everywhere. Soupert was a commercial spy [who] procured information regarding industrial processes* (London Times). **2** a person who tries to get secret information, especially about the enemy in time of war, usually by entering the enemy's territory in disguise: *One feels again a chilled amazement at the achievements of this shrewd, fearless, and determined spy* (New Yorker). **3** the act of spying; secret observation or watching. [< Old French *espie* < *espier;* see the verb]
*—v.i.* **1** to keep secret watch: *He saw two men spying on him from behind a tree.* **2** to act as a spy; be a spy. The punishment for spying in wartime is death. *The Russians think inspection is spying ... And so we watch each other spy and arm on the brink of disaster* (R. S. Emrich). **3** to be on the lookout; keep watch, especially with a telescope. **4** to examine or inspect something carefully.
*—v.t.* **1** to catch sight of; descry; discover; see: *She was the first to spy the rescue party in the distance.* **2** to watch (someone) in a secret or stealthy manner; keep under constant observation. **3** to look at or examine closely or carefully, as with a telescope.
**spy out, a** to watch or examine secretly or carefully: *Peder Pederson and a lieutenant ... slipped out Sunday to spy out the situation* (Harper's). **b** to find out by watching secretly or carefully: *She spies out everything that goes on in the neighborhood.*

[< Old French *espier* < Germanic (compare Old High German *spehōn*)]

**spy|glass** (spī′glas′, -gläs′), *n.* a small telescope, especially one not requiring a tripod or other mount in order to be used: *This type of instrument was very common before the invention of the prism binocular and is well known to everyone as the spyglass of the old-time sea captain* (Hardy and Perrin).

**spy|hole** (spī′hōl′), *n.* a hole for spying; peephole: *a spyhole in a door.*

**spy|mas|ter** (spī′mas′tər, -mäs′-), *n.* a person who directs the activities of, and acts as a clearing agent for, an organized group of spies (spy ring).

**spy|plane** (spī′plān′), *n.* a high-altitude aircraft for secret reconnaissance of foreign defense installations by means of aerial photographs and tape recordings of radio and radar emissions.

**spy ship**, a ship operating under false pretenses in foreign waters for the purpose of making secret reconnaissance by means of electronic equipment: *Two Soviet spy ships, posing as trawlers,* [*were*] *operating off Australia* (Sunday Times).

**sq.**, 1 sequence. 2 square. 3 the following (Latin, *sequens*, singular, or *sequentia*, plural).

**Sq.**, 1 squadron. 2 square (street).

**sq. ch.**, square chain or square chains.

**sq. ft.**, square foot or square feet.

**sq. in.**, square inch or square inches.

**sq. km.**, square kilometer or square kilometers.

**sq. mi.**, square mile or square miles.

**squab** (skwob), *n., adj.* —*n.* **1** a very young pigeon, such as is preferred for eating. **2** any very young bird; fledgling. **3** a short, stout person. **4** a thick or soft cushion: *Deeper, softer seats and squabs on both models give extra comfort* (Economist). **5** a sofa or couch.
—*adj.* **1** newly hatched; still unfledged: *a squab turkey.* **2** (of persons) short and stout.
[origin uncertain. Compare Swedish dialectal *sqvabb* loose or fat flesh, Norwegian dialectal *skvabb* soft, wet mass.]

**squab|ble** (skwob′əl), *n., v.,* **-bled, -bling.** —*n.* a petty, noisy quarrel: *Children's squabbles annoy their parents.*
—*v.i.* to take part in a petty, noisy quarrel; wrangle or argue disagreeably: *I won't squabble over a nickel.*
—*v.t. Printing.* to throw (type) out of line; disarrange or mix (lines of type).
[perhaps imitative. Compare German *schwabbeln* babble, prate.] —**squab′bler**, *n.*

**squab|by** (skwob′ē), *adj.,* **-bi|er, -bi|est.** short and stout; squat; thick-set.

**squac|co** (skwak′ō), *n.* a small, crested heron of Africa, southern Europe, and parts of Asia. [< Italian dialectal *sguacco;* probably imitative]

**squad** (skwod), *n., v.,* **squad|ded, squad|ding.** —*n.* **1** a military unit usually made up of eleven men and a squad leader, and composing the basic unit for drill, inspection, or work. A squad is the smallest unit in an army and is usually commanded by a sergeant or a corporal. There are usually four squads in a platoon. **2** any small group of persons working, training, or acting together: *a squad of police. He hired a squad of boys to clean up the yard.* SYN: corps.
—*v.t.* to form into a squad or squads.
[< earlier French *esquade,* variant of *escadre* < Italian *squadra* battalion; (literally) square, ultimately < Latin *ex-* out + *quadrāre* to quarter. Compare etym. under **cadre, square.**]

**squad car**, an automobile used by police, which is equipped with a special radio to keep in communication with headquarters; prowl car: *They got us out of there with billy clubs swinging, bundled us into squad cars and hustled us to the police station* (Maclean's).

**squad|die** or **squad|dy** (skwod′ē), *n., pl.* **-dies.** *British Informal.* a member of a military squad.

**squad|ron** (skwod′rən), *n., v.* —*n.* **1a** a tactical unit of the U.S. Air Force, consisting of a formation of eight or more airplanes, usually two or three flights, that fly or fight together. **b** the basic tactical unit of any air force. **2** a part of a naval fleet used for special service or duty, consisting of two or more divisions, usually of the same type of ship: *a destroyer squadron.* **3** a military unit made up of two or more troops of cavalry or armored cavalry, usually having from 120 to 200 men and commanded by a major or a lieutenant colonel. It corresponds to a battalion in other branches of the army. **4** any group or formation: *A stately squadron of snowy geese were riding in an adjoining pond* (Washington Irving).
—*v.t.* to form into a squadron or squadrons.
[< Italian *squadrone* < *squadra* squad; see etym. under **squad**]

**squadron leader**, a commissioned officer in the Australian, British, or Canadian Air Force, corresponding in rank to a major in the United States Air Force.

**squad room**, **1** the sleeping quarters of a group of soldiers in a barracks. **2** *U.S.* a room used in a police station for assembly, inspection, and the like.

**squads|man** (skwodz′mən), *n., pl.* **-men.** a member of a squad.

**squal|ene** (skwol′ēn, skwā′lēn), *n.* a colorless oil occurring in vegetable and animal fats including human sebum: *Recent researches suggest a material called squalene has an ameliorating effect on the ability of particular materials* (*called carcinogens*) *to cause cancer* (New York Times). *Formula:* $C_{30}H_{50}$
[< New Latin *Squalus* the shark genus (because it was first found in shark liver)]

**squal|id** (skwol′id), *adj.* **1** very dirty; filthy: *squalid tenements. It is futile to expect a hungry and squalid population to be anything but violent and gross* (T. H. Huxley). **2** *Figurative.* morally repulsive or wretched; degraded: *His life had been squalid and mean. The squalid belief in witchcraft* (James Harvey Robinson). [< Latin *squālidus* < *squālēre* be filthy] —**squal′id|ly**, *adv.* —**squal′id|ness**, *n.*

**squall**[1] (skwôl), *n., v.* —*n.* **1** a sudden, violent gust of wind, often with rain, snow, or hail. Squalls may be accompanied by thunder and lightning. SYN: blast. **2** *Informal, Figurative.* a disturbance or commotion; trouble: *The squall of criticism which has blown around the Administration's ten-year $101 billion roadbuilding program ...* (Newsweek).
—*v.i.* to undergo or give rise to a squall or squalls.
[compare Swedish *skval* impetuous rush of water < *skvala* to stream, gush]

**squall**[2] (skwôl), *v., n.* —*v.i.* to cry out loudly; scream violently: *The baby squalled.*
—*v.t.* to cry (out) in a loud, discordant tone.
—*n.* a loud, harsh cry: *The parrot's squall was heard all over the house.*
[perhaps imitative. Compare Old Icelandic *skvala* cry out, Swedish *skvaller* idle talk.] —**squall′er**, *n.*

**squall cloud**, a small cloud that forms below the front edge of a thundercloud.

**squall line**, a line of thunderstorms preceding a cold front, characterized by severe thunder, strong wind squalls, and heavy rains and lightning, and very often producing tornadoes.

**squall|y** (skwô′lē), *adj.,* **squall|i|er, squall|i|est.** **1** having many sudden and violent gusts of wind: *squally weather.* **2** blowing in squalls; gusty: *It was raining again with a squally wind* (Arnold Bennett). **3** *Informal, Figurative.* threatening; troublous.

**squa|loid** (skwā′loid), *adj.* **1** sharklike. **2** having to do with sharks. [< New Latin *Squalus* (see etym. under **squalus**) + English *-oid*]

**squal|or** (skwol′ər), *n.* **1** misery and dirt; filth: *By modern standards people in medieval Europe lived in indescribable squalor. Hovel piled upon hovel—squalor immortalized in undecaying stone* (Hawthorne). **2** *Figurative.* the quality or condition of being morally squalid.
[< Latin *squālor* < *squālēre* be filthy; see etym. under **squalid**]

**squa|lus** (skwā′ləs), *n., pl.* **-li** (-lī). any shark of a group comprising many of the spiny dogfishes.
[< New Latin *Squalus* the genus name < Latin *squalus* a sea fish]

**squam** (skwom), *n. U.S.* a waterproof, oilskin hat with a broad brim in the back; southwester. [< *Annisquam,* Massachusetts]

**squa|ma** (skwā′mə), *n., pl.* **-mae** (-mē). a scale or scalelike part, especially the thin vertical portion of the temporal bone in man and other vertebrates: *a squama of bone.* [< Latin *squāma*]

**squa|mate** (skwā′māt), *adj.* having or covered with squamae or scales. [< Latin *squāmātus* < *squāma* squama]

**squa|ma|tion** (skwə mā′shən), *n.* **1** the condition of being covered with scales. **2** the arrangement or pattern of the scales covering an animal. **3** the scales covering an animal.

**squa|mi|form** (skwā′mə fôrm), *adj.* having the shape of a scale; squamous.

**squa|mo|sal** (skwə mō′səl), *adj., n.* —*adj.* **1** of or having to do with the squama of the temporal bone. **2** = scaly.
—*n.* the squama of the temporal bone.

**squa|mose** (skwā′mōs), *adj.* = squamous. —**squa′mose|ly**, *adv.* —**squa′mose|ness**, *n.*

**squa|mous** (skwā′məs), *adj.* **1** furnished with, covered with, or formed of scales. **2** characterized by the development of scales; scalelike: *An epithelium is designated cubical, columnar, or squamous, according to the shape of its component cells* (A. Franklin Shull). (*Figurative.*) *Immense, of fishy form and mind, Squamous ...* (Rupert Brooke). **3** having to do with the squama of the temporal bone. [< Latin *squāmōsus* < *squāma* scale, squama] —**squa′mous|ly**, *adv.* —**squa′mous|ness**, *n.*

**squam|u|lose** (skwam′yə lōs, skwā′myə-), *adj. Botany.* provided or covered with small scales. [< Latin *squāmula* (diminutive) < *squāma* scale + English *-ose*[1]]

**squan|der** (skwon′dər), *v., n.* —*v.t.* **1** to spend or use foolishly; waste: *He squandered his fortune in gambling. Do not squander time* (Benjamin Franklin). SYN: dissipate. **2** to cause to scatter; disperse. —*v.i.* to be squandered: *Youth was made to squander.*
—*n.* **1** the act of squandering. **2** an instance of squandering.
[origin uncertain] —**squan′der|er**, *n.* —**squan′der|ing|ly**, *adv.*

**square** (skwãr), *n., adj.,* **squar|er, squar|est,** *v.,* **squared, squar|ing,** *adv.* —*n.* **1** a plane figure with four sides and four right angles: *Use a ruler to draw a square.* **2** anything having this shape or nearly this shape: *a square of light, a square of chocolate.* **3** a space in a city or town bounded by streets on four sides; block: *The automobile factories fill several squares.* **4** the distance along one side of such a space: *We live three squares from the school.* **5** an open space in a city or town bounded by streets on all sides, often planted with grass or trees: *Times Square, Berkeley Square. The soldiers' monument is in the square opposite the city hall. Abbr:* Sq. **6** any similar open space, such as at the meeting of streets. **7** the buildings surrounding such a space: *one of the houses of Washington Square.* **8** a body of troops drawn up in a square formation, such as was common before the development of automatic weapons. **9** an instrument like a T or an L, used for drawing right angles and testing the squareness of anything, especially in carpentry and drawing. **10** the product obtained when a number is multiplied by itself; the second power of a number or quantity: *16 is the square of 4.* **11** the bracts subtending a cotton blossom: *White flowers blossom from the squares, or buds* (Burt Johnson). **12** *Slang.* a person who is too conventional or old-fashioned; person who is not familiar with the latest fashions in popular entertainment and culture: *Junior, of course, is a square* (Wall Street Journal). **13** *Informal.* a square meal: *The animals are seen performing their customary tasks, which mostly consist of making certain that they obtain three squares daily* (New Yorker). [Middle English *squyr* (originally) a carpenter's square < Old French *esquire,* ultimately < Latin *ex-* out of + *quadrāre;* see the verb]
—*adj.* **1** having four equal sides and four right angles. **2** that is square or rectangular in cross section: *a square file.* **3** that is square or rectangular in both vertical and lateral section; having six sides, each one of which is at a right angle to the four that adjoin it: *a square box. A block of stone is usually square.* **4** equal to a square having a specified length on each side: *a room ten feet square.* **5** having breadth more nearly equal to length or height than is usual: *a square jaw.* **6** forming a right angle; turning at 90 degrees: *This table has four square corners.* **7** (of a yard) at right angles to the mast and keel. **8** plumb and level in its vertical and horizontal surfaces, respectively; straight and proper; even. **9** correctly built or finished. **10** *Figurative.* having no unbalanced amount on either side; settled; balanced: *Five dollars more and our accounts will be square.* **11** just; fair; honorable; honest: *to be absolutely square in one's business dealings.* SYN: equitable. **12** straightforward; plain; direct: *a square refusal. His ideas being square, solid and tangible* (Hawthorne). **13** satisfying and solid; substantial; plentiful: *At our house we have three square meals each day.* **14** designating an area each of whose dimensions is that unit of length; squared: *a square yard.* **15** based on such units; in square measure: *square measurement.* **16** multiplied by itself; squared: *3 square equals 9.* **17** solid and strong; sturdy. **18** *Slang.* not up to date; too conventional or old-fashioned: *He thought we had flipped our beanies. He was real square* (Time). **19** having the same number of warp ends and picks of filling yarn in each inch of cloth: *The price of 80-square print cloth ... has remained steady* (Wall Street Journal).
—*v.t.* **1** to make square, rectangular, or cubical in shape: *to square a block of granite.* **2** to mark out in squares: *The children squared off the sidewalk to play hopscotch.* **3** to bring to the form of a right angle: *to square the corners of a board.* **4** to make straight, level, or even; place accu-

---

**Pronunciation Key:** hat, āge, cãre, fär; let, ēqual, tėrm; it, īce; hot, ōpen, ôrder; **oi**l, **ou**t; cup, pu̇t, rüle; **ch**ild; lo**ng**; **th**in; **ᴛʜ**en; **zh**, measure; **ə** represents **a** in about, **e** in taken, **i** in pencil, **o** in lemon, **u** in circus.

rately in position: *to square a picture on a wall, to square up a gun mount.* **5** to test with a square or other instrument for deviation from a right (or the desired) angle or line. **6** *Figurative.* to adjust; settle; balance: *Let us square our accounts.* **7** *Figurative.* to settle (a debt); pay up: *At present the Italian balance of payments is squared only because of the offshore orders and other dollar expenditures in Italy of the United States Government* (New York Times). **8** *Figurative.* to guide or regulate: *I cannot square my conduct to time, place, or circumstance* (Keats). **9** in mathematics: **a** to find or describe a square equivalent in area to: *to square a circle.* **b** to calculate the number of square units of measure in. **c** to multiply (a number or quantity) by itself: *25 squared makes 625.* **10** *Sports.* to bring (the score of a game or contest) to equality; tie: *to square the score with a touchdown in the third quarter.* **11** *Slang.* to win over, conciliate, or secure the silence or consent of, especially by bribery; bribe: *Is there a word of truth in the suggestion that you paid Stevenson £200 to "square" him?* (London Times).

—*v.i.* **1** *Figurative.* to agree, accord, or fit; conform: *His acts do not square with his promises.* **2** *Sports.* to equalize the scores; become equal in score.

—*adv.* **1** *Informal.* fairly or honestly: *to speak fair and square.* **2** so as to be square; in a square or rectangular form. **3** at right angles; perpendicularly. **4** directly; precisely: *to hit someone square between the eyes.* **5** firmly; solidly.

**all square,** *U.S. Informal.* **a** having paid what is owing or done what is needed: *Am I all square now, or do I still owe you something?* **b** even; tied: *The two teams were all square at the end of the second quarter.*

**back at** (or **to**) **square one,** *Informal.* back where or to where one began; at an impasse: *The argument over the rise in mortgage rates seems to be back to square one* (Sunday Times).

**on** (or **upon**) **the square, a** at right angles: *That crooked picture is not hanging on the square.* **b** *Figurative.* face to face; directly: *He is awkward, and out of place ... He cannot meet you on the square* (Charles Lamb). **c** *Figurative.* justly; fairly; honestly: *He had played on the square with them* (Tobias Smollett).

**out of square, a** not at right angles: *The sagging windows are out of square in the old house.* **b** *Figurative.* out of order or proportion: *Something must be wrong in the inner man of the world, since its outer man is so terribly out of square!* (Thomas Carlyle).

**square away, a** to set the sails so that the ship will stay before the wind: *We squared away to a spanking breeze* (Frank T. Bullen). **b** *Figurative.* to make a new start: *He said if I didn't get squared away I'd get into combat some day and come back in a wooden coffin* (New York Times).

**square off,** *Informal.* to put oneself in a position of defense or attack; prepare to fight, especially with the fists: *As usual, the extremists square off and argue about everything but the root cause of the trouble* (Wall Street Journal).

**square oneself,** *Informal.* **a** to make up for something one has said or done: *She decided to square herself with her mother after their quarrel* **b** to get even: *He departed angrily, vowing to square himself before long.*

**square up,** to pay what one owes; settle an account: *Square up everything whatsoever that it has been necessary to buy* (Dickens).

[< Old French *esquarer,* ultimately < Latin *ex-* out + *quadrāre* make square < *quadrus* a square < *quattuor* four] —**squar′a|ble,** *adj.* —**square′ly,** *adv.* —**square′ness,** *n.*

**square|bash** (skwãr′bash′), *v.i. British Slang.* to do military foot drill: *When he wasn't square-bashing, young Private Lowery was swotting* (London Times). —**square′bash′er,** *n.*

***square bracket,** an opening or closing bracket used in printed matter, not a parenthesis.

***square bracket**

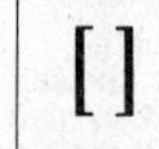

"The reason for this [the amendment]...

**square chain,** a unit of square measure used in surveying, equal to an area 1 chain by 1 chain: *Ten square chains equal one acre.*

**square dance,** a dance performed by a set of couples arranged about a square or in some set form, such as the quadrille and Virginia reel: *The square dances are socially stimulating, and recently have been recovering some of their lost popularity* (Emory S. Bogardus).

**square-dance** (skwãr′dans′, -däns′), *v.i.,* **-danced, -danc|ing.** to do a square dance. —**square′-danc′er,** *n.*

**squared circle** or **ring** (skwãrd), *Informal.* a ring for boxing bouts; prize ring.

**square deal, 1** *Informal.* fair and honest treatment. **2** an honest deal of cards.

**square division,** a division of the United States Army before World War II, made up of two infantry brigades and one field artillery brigade.

**square|dom** (skwãr′dəm), *n. Slang.* **1** the condition of being a square: *There has to be another choice than monolithic squaredom or disheveled bohemianism* (David Boroff). **2** all those who are squares.

**square|flip|per** (skwãr′flip′ər), *n.* a large gray and yellowish seal of arctic regions with a bristly beard and weighing up to 1,000 pounds.

**square foot,** a unit of square measure, equal to an area 1 foot by 1 foot or 0.0929 square meter. *Abbr:* sq. ft.

**square|head** (skwãr′hed′), *n. U.S. Slang.* **1** a slow-witted person; dolt. **2** a Scandinavian or a German (used in an unfriendly way).

**square inch,** a unit of square measure, equal to an area 1 inch by 1 inch or 6.4516 square centimeters: *A jet plane traveling 1,500 mph hits the rain drops with a force of 70,000 pounds per square inch* (Newsweek). *Abbr:* sq. in.

**square-jawed** (skwãr′jôd′), *adj.* having a square jaw.

**square kilometer,** a unit of square measure, equal to an area 1 kilometer by 1 kilometer. *Abbr:* sq. km.

**square knot,** a knot firmly joining two loose ends of rope or cord. It is tied with two overhand knots so the free ends come out alongside of the standing parts. A square knot will not slip and is easily untied. See picture under **knot**[1].

**square leg, 1** the position in the cricket field to the left of the batsman and nearly on a line with the wicket. **2** the fielder stationed at this point.

**square matrix,** *Mathematics.* a matrix having an equal number of rows and columns.

**square meal,** *U.S.* a substantial or satisfying meal.

**square measure,** a system for measuring area:

| | |
|---|---|
| 144 square inches | = 1 square foot or 0.0929 square meter |
| 9 square feet | = 1 square yard or 0.8361 square meter |
| 30¼ square yards | = 1 square rod or 25.293 square meters |
| 160 square rods | = 1 acre or 0.4047 hectare |
| 640 acres | = 1 square mile or 1 section or 258.9998 hectares |
| 36 sections | = 1 township |

**square mile,** a unit of square measure, equal to an area 1 mile by 1 mile or 258.9998 hectares. *Abbr:* sq. mi.

**square number,** the product of a number multiplied by itself, as 25 (5 × 5), or 36 (6 × 6).

**square peg,** person or thing unfit or unsuitable: *You can't put a square peg in a round hole.*

**square piano,** a rectangular piano having horizontal strings parallel to the keyboard.

**squar|er** (skwãr′ər), *n.* a person who reduces wood, stone, or other material to a square form.

**square-rigged** (skwãr′rigd′), *adj.* having the principal sails set at right angles across the masts.

***square-rigger**

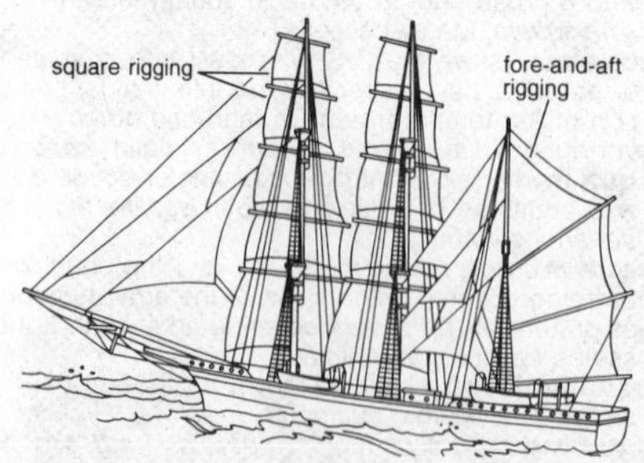


***square-rig|ger** (skwãr′rig′ər), *n.* a square-rigged ship: *In Boston ... you could look over the harbor at the big square-riggers anchored in the stream* (Atlantic).

**square rod,** a unit of square measure, equal to an area 1 rod by 1 rod or 25.293 square meters.

***square root**

$\sqrt{16} = 4$ (4 × 4 = 16) square root

$\sqrt[3]{125} = 5$ (5 × 5 × 5 = 125) cube root

***square root,** a number that produces a given number when multiplied by itself: *The square root of 16 is 4. The genius of William Hamilton sought the square root of minus one* (Walter de la Mare).

**square sail,** any four-sided sail carried on a yard across the mast.

**square set,** a set of four couples forming a square in square-dancing.

**square shake,** = square deal.

**square shooter,** *Informal.* a fair and honest person: *I trust businessmen and their wives, who buy annually, as square shooters* (Wall Street Journal).

**square shooting,** *Informal.* the behavior or activities of a square shooter.

**square-shoul|dered** (skwãr′shōl′dərd), *adj.* having shoulders that are high, not sloping, and well braced back: *She was ... tall, square-shouldered, and erect* (Harper's).

**squares|ville** (skwãrz′vil), *n., adj. Slang.* —*n.* the world or society of squares: *The book is intended to be the apotheosis of squaresville* (Sunday Times).

—*adj.* not up to date; unfashionable; square: *On campus ... it was squaresville to flip for the rock scene* (Time).

**square|tail** (skwãr′tāl′), *n.* **1** = brook trout. **2** = prairie chicken.

**square-toed** (skwãr′tōd′), *adj.* **1** having a broad, square toe: *square-toed shoes.* **2** *Figurative.* old-fashioned and homely, as in habits or ideas: *We old people must retain some square-toed predilection for the fashions of our youth* (Edmund Burke). —**square′-toed′ness,** *n.*

**square-toes** (skwãr′tōz′), *n.* a precise, formal, old-fashioned person, having strict or narrow ideas of conduct.

**square wave,** *Electronics.* a wave with a rectangular shape, which alternately takes on two fixed values for equal periods of time.

**square yard,** a unit of square measure, equal to an area 1 yard by 1 yard or 0.8361 square meter.

**squar|ish** (skwãr′ish), *adj.* nearly square; having breadth more nearly equal to length or height than is usual. —**squar′ish|ly,** *adv.* —**squar′ish-ness,** *n.*

**squar|rose** (skwar′ōs, skwo rōs′), *adj.* **1** *Botany.* **a** composed of or covered with scales, bracts, or other processes standing out at right angles or more widely, as a calyx or involucre. **b** standing out at right angles or more widely, as scales or bracts. **2** rough with spreading scales or other processes. [< Latin *squarrōsus* scurfy, scabby]

**squash**[1] (skwosh), *v., n., adv.* —*v.t.* **1** to squeeze or press into a flat mass or pulp; crush: *The boy squashed the bug. The package was squashed in the mail.* **2** to put an end to; stop by force; suppress; quash: *The principal moved quickly to squash any rumors of a holiday.* **3** *Informal, Figurative.* to silence or disconcert (a person) with a crushing argument, reply, or sarcastic remark. —*v.i.* **1** to be pressed into a flat mass; flatten out on impact or under pressure: *Carry the cream puffs carefully, for they squash easily.* **2** to make a splashing sound; move or walk with a splash: *We heard him squash through the mud and slush.* **3** to crowd; squeeze.

—*n.* **1** something squashed; crushed mass: *The grapes are just a squash and not fit to eat.* **2** the act, fact, or sound of squashing or crushing. **3** the impact of a soft, heavy body falling on a surface. **4** the sound produced by this. **5** = squash tennis. **6** = squash rackets. **7** *British.* a beverage made with fruit juice and (usually) carbonated water: *I'll have a lemon squash if you don't mind* (Graham Greene).

—*adv.* with a squash; squashily: *He came down, in less than no time, squash on his nose, and broke it* (F. E. Paget).

[< Old French *esquasser,* ultimately < Latin *ex-* out + *quassāre* < *quatere* to shake. Compare etym. under **quash**[1].] —**squash′er,** *n.*

**squash**[2] (skwosh), *n., pl.* **squash** or **squash|es.** **1** the fruit of any one of various vinelike plants, often eaten as a vegetable or made into a pie. **2** any one of these plants. Squash are annual plants that belong to the gourd family. [American English, short for earlier *squantersquash* < Algonkian (compare Narraganset *askútasquash* the green things that may be eaten raw)]

**squash bug,** a large, foul-smelling, dark-colored hemipterous insect of North America, injurious to squash vines and certain other plants.

**squash racquets** or **squash rackets,** a game similar to rackets but played on a smaller court with a shorter racket.

**squash tennis,** a game somewhat like handball and tennis, played with rackets and a hollow rubber ball in a walled court.

**squash|y** (skwosh′ē), *adj.,* **squash|i|er, squash|i-est. 1** having a soft or pulpy consistency; easily squashed: *squashy cream puffs.* **2** soft and wet: *squashy ground.* **3** having a squashed or flattened look: *a squashy nose.* —**squash′i|ly,** *adv.* —**squash′i|ness,** *n.*

**squat** (skwot), *v.*, **squat|ted** or **squat**, **squat|ting**, *adj., n.* —*v.i.* **1** to sit on the heels; crouch: *He found it difficult to squat on his heels for more than a few minutes.* **2** to sit on the ground or floor, with the legs closely drawn up beneath or in front of the body: *The Indians squatted around the fire. The two of them were squatting on this dirt road, talking the way farmers do* (Newsweek). **3** to crouch close to the ground to avoid observation or capture, as a hare does: *Some tenth-rate poeticule ... now squats in his hole like the tailless fox* (Algernon Charles Swinburne). **4** to settle on land without title or right: *He was a Kentucky man, of the Ohio, where he had "squatted"* (Frederick Marryat). **5** to settle on public land to acquire ownership of it under government regulation.
—*v.t.* to cause to squat; seat (oneself) with the legs drawn up.
—*adj.* **1** seated in a squatting position, crouching: *A squat figure could be seen in front of the fire.* **2** short and thick, like the figure of an animal squatting; low and broad; flattened: *a squat building. The Indian was a squat, dark man. That is a squat teapot.* SYN: dumpy.
—*n.* **1** the act of squatting or sitting close to the ground; crouching. **2** a squatting posture.
[< Old French *esquatir* to crush, ultimately < Latin *ex-* out + *coactāre* constrain < *cogere* drive together < *co-* together + *agere* drive] —**squat'ly**, *adv.* —**squat'ness**, *n.*

**squat|ter¹** (skwot'ər), *n.* **1** a person who settles on land without title or right: *Judging from the treatment of squatters on similar lands in Manitoba, there need be no fear of settling on lands within the reserves* (Saskatoon Herald). **2** a person who settles on public land to acquire ownership of it under government regulation. **3** a person or animal that crouches or squats. **4** a person who operates a sheep ranch or farm in Australia. [< *squat* + *-er¹*]

**squat|ter²** (skwot'ər), *v.i.* to plunge into or through water; move in water with much splashing or flapping. [origin uncertain]

**squatter's** or **squatter right**, *U.S.* the right or claim of a squatter to the land on which he has settled: *Gramp ... took up the land, by squatter's right, about 1892* (Atlantic).

**squatter sovereignty**, *U.S.* the right claimed by the settlers of new territories to make their own laws, especially in regard to slavery; popular sovereignty: *the doctrine of "squatter sovereignty" (local determination of the status of slavery)* (R. B. Morris).

**squat|toc|ra|cy** (skwo tok'rə sē), *n. Australian.* squatters, especially the socially and politically important sheep ranchers: *For England's "county" aristocracy, Australia substituted its own "squattocracy"—men who had carved out for themselves sheep or cattle stations the size of Maryland and sent their sons to Cambridge or Oxford* (Time).

**squat|ty** (skwot'ē), *adj.*, **-ti|er**, **-ti|est**. short and thick; low and broad; squat: *a squatty little shack behind the garage.*

**squaw** (skwô), *n.* **1** a North American Indian woman or wife. **2** *Slang.* any girl or woman. **3** *Slang.* a female spouse; wife. [American English, earlier, an Indian woman or wife < Algonkian (compare Massachusetts *squa*)]

**squaw|ber|ry** (skwô'ber'ē, -bər-) *n., pl.* **-ries**. a low-growing shrub of the eastern United States bearing tart, inedible berries; deerberry.

**squaw|fish** (skwô'fish'), *n., pl.* **-fish|es** or (*collectively*) **-fish**. any one of several large, slender carps, common in rivers of the Pacific coast of North America.

**squawk** (skwôk), *v., n.* —*v.i.* **1** to make a loud, harsh sound; squall or screech hoarsely: *Hens and ducks squawk when frightened.* **2** to give out a discordant sound; creak or squeak harshly. **3** *Slang, Figurative.* to complain loudly; give vent to vigorous protests: *Machine tool builders squawk as the Air Force buys $500,000 worth of tools abroad* (Wall Street Journal).
—*v.t.* to utter harshly and loudly, with or as if with a squawk.
—*n.* **1** a squawking; loud, harsh sound. **2** *Slang, Figurative.* a loud complaint; vigorous protest. **3** = black-crowned night heron.
[probably imitative]

**squawk|box** (skwôk'boks'), *n.*, or **squawk box**, *U.S. Slang.* a loudspeaker in a public-address system or intercom.

**squawk|er** (skwô'kər), *n.* **1** a person or thing that squawks. **2** a speaker of intermediate size, as in a phonograph or tape recorder, designed to reproduce frequencies in the middle range.

**squawl** (skwôl), *v.i., v.t.* to cry out loudly: *Hardly was the White House meeting over than the Soviet Union started squawling about how the U.S. was "playing with fire"* (Time). [variant of *squall²*]

**squaw man**, a white man living with an Indian squaw, especially one who has more or less abandoned white customs (used in an unfriendly way).

**squaw|root** (skwô'rüt', -rut'), *n.* a fleshy, leafless plant related to the beechdrops, with yellowish flowers, growing as a parasite usually on oak roots. It is found in eastern North America.

**squaw winter**, a brief period of prematurely cold weather early in autumn.

**squdge** (skwuj), *v.t., v.i.*, **squdged**, **squdg|ing**. to squish; squash. [imitative]

**squdg|y** (skwuj'ē), *adj.*, **squdg|i|er**, **squdg|i|est**. **1** squishy; squashy: *A pretty squdgy mass you have underfoot at that* (Punch). **2** *Figurative: He made haste to shake Joseph Bluett's squdgy hand and escape* (G. Warwick Deeping).

**squeak** (skwēk), *v., n.* —*v.i.* **1** to make a short, sharp, shrill sound: *A mouse squeaks.* **2** *Informal.* to get or pass (by or through) with difficulty: *The Senate will block it even if it squeaks through the House* (Wall Street Journal). **3** *Slang.* **a** to turn informer; squeal. **b** to confess.
—*v.t.* **1** to cause to squeak. **2** to utter in a squeaking manner or with a squeaky voice: *to squeak out an apology.*
—*n.* **1** a short, sharp, shrill sound: *We heard the squeak of the stairs.* **2** *Informal.* a chance to get by or through; chance of escape: *a close squeak. The bill passed by a narrow squeak.*
[probably imitative. Compare Swedish *sqväka* to croak.] —**squeak'ing|ly**, *adv.*

**squeak|er** (skwē'kər), *n.* **1** a person or thing that squeaks. **2** *Informal.* a contest whose outcome is uncertain until the final moment or period: *The game was a squeaker until the Yankees exploded for three runs in the eighth* (New York Times).

**squeak|y** (skwē'kē), *adj.*, **squeak|i|er**, **squeak|i|est**. **1** characterized by squeaking sounds; tending to squeak: *a squeaky window.* **2** squeaking; thin and shrill: *a squeaky voice.* —**squeak'i|ly**, *adv.* —**squeak'i|ness**, *n.*

**squeal** (skwēl), *v., n.* —*v.i.* **1** to make a long, sharp, shrill cry: *A pig squeals when it is hurt.* **2** *Slang.* to inform on another. **3** *Informal, Figurative.* to complain loudly; squawk.
—*v.t.* to utter sharply and shirlly: *to squeal out a command.*
—*n.* **1** a long, sharp cry; shrill scream or sound: *the squeal of a pig.* **2** *Informal.* an act of informing against another. **3** *Figurative.* an act of complaining loudly.
[probably imitative]

**squeal|er** (skwē'lər), *n.* **1** a person or thing that squeals. **2** the young of the grouse, partridge, quail, or pigeon. **3** a young pig. **4** *Slang.* an informer.

**squeam|ish** (skwē'mish), *adj.* **1** too proper, modest, or decent; easily shocked; prudish: *a squeamish old maid.* **2** excessively fastidious or punctilious; too particular; too scrupulous: *Trifles magnified into importance by a squeamish conscience* (Macaulay). SYN: fussy. **3** slightly sick at one's stomach; nauseated; sickish: *He turned squeamish at the sight of blood.* **4** readily affected with nausea; easily turned sick or faint; queasy. [Middle English *squaymish*, variant of *scoymous* < Anglo-French *escoymous* disdainful, shy; origin uncertain] —**squeam'ish|ly**, *adv.* —**squeam'ish|ness**, *n.*

**squee|gee** (skwē'jē), *n., v.*, **-geed**, **-gee|ing**. —*n.* **1** a tool consisting of a blade of rubber or sponge and a handle, used for sweeping water from wet decks, removing water from windows after washing, or cleaning a sink: *A small squeegee or an automatic automobile windshield wiper will help in the cleaning job* (Scientific American). **2** any one of various similar devices. **3** a device with a roller, as for pressing water from photographic prints.
—*v.t.* to sweep, scrape, or press with a squeegee.
[perhaps < earlier *squeege*, variant of *squeeze*]

**squeez|a|bil|i|ty** (skwē'zə bil'ə tē), *n.* the quality or condition of being squeezable.

**squeez|a|ble** (skwē'zə bəl), *adj.* that can be squeezed: *squeezable bottles.* —**squeez'a|bly**, *adv.*

**squeeze** (skwēz), *v.*, **squeezed**, **squeez|ing**, *n.* —*v.t.* **1** to press hard; compress: *to squeeze a sponge or a lemon. Don't squeeze the kitten, or you will hurt it.* **2a** to hug; embrace: *She squeezed her child.* SYN: clasp. **b** to press (the hand) in friendship or affection. SYN: clasp. **3** to force by pressing; thrust or cause to pass forcibly: *to squeeze oneself through a narrow opening. I can't squeeze another thing into my trunk.* **4** to force out or extract by pressure; cause to ooze or flow out by or as if by pressing: *to squeeze juice from a lemon. Lady Kew could ... squeeze out a tear over a good novel too* (Thackeray). **5** to get by force, pressure, or effort; extort: *The dictator squeezed money from the people. When it comes to squeezing a profit out of you ...* (Dickens). **6** *Informal, Figurative.* to put pressure on or try to influence (a person or persons) to do something, especially to pay money: *The blackmailer squeezed his victim for more money.* **7** *Figurative.* to burden or oppress: *Heavy taxes squeezed the people.* **8** to make a facsimile impression of. **9** *Bridge.* to compel (an opponent) to discard or unguard a winning card.
—*v.i.* **1** to yield to pressure: *Sponges squeeze easily.* **2** to force a way: *He squeezed through the crowd.* **3** to press hard; exert pressure, especially with the hand: *to squeeze on the tube until some toothpaste comes out.*
—*n.* **1** the act of squeezing; tight pressure: *She gave her sister's arm a squeeze.* **2** the state of being squeezed: *Her squeeze was severe enough to make her get a loan.* **3** a friendly or affectionate pressing: *a squeeze of the hand.* **4** a hug; close embrace. **5** a crush; crowd: *It's a tight squeeze to get five people in that little car.* **6** a small quantity or amount squeezed out. **7** an impression of an inscription, design, or the like, made by pressing a plastic substance around or over it. **8** *Informal, Figurative.* a situation from which escape is difficult, as when a retailer is caught between low prices and high costs: *a cost-price squeeze.* **9** *Informal, Figurative.* pressure used to extort a favor, influence, or money. **10** a squeeze play in baseball or bridge. **11** a shortage or the intense competition resulting from this: *Top manufacturers in all categories are warning that there will be a squeeze on desirable merchandise ... this fall and winter* (New York Times). **12** the act or state of forcing a short seller to pay a high price, as for securities.
[apparently variant of dialectal *squize*, *squiss*, and *quease*; all perhaps ultimately Old English *cwȳsan*] —**squeez'er**, *n.*

**squeeze bottle**, a plastic bottle squeezed to force out its contents in a spray or small quantity through a nozzle: *Some cosmetics and lotions are sold in squeeze bottles.*

**squeeze|box** (skwēz'boks'), *n. Informal.* an accordion: *A German in lederhosen broke out the squeezebox and played "Lili Marlene" for hours* (Listener).

**squeeze cage**, a cage having one or more walls that can be moved by a crank from the outside, used to squeeze a wild, injured, or sick animal into a narrow space where it can be controlled and treated.

**squeeze play**, **1** *Baseball.* a play in which a runner on third base starts for home as soon as the pitcher is legally committed to pitch and the batter bunts the ball away from the catcher, giving the runner a good chance to score. It is usually attempted with not more than one man out. **2** *Bridge.* a play or series of plays in which the holder of a card that may win a trick is compelled to discard it or to unguard another possible winner. **3** *Figurative.* any pressure applied to force a result: *The great Soviet squeeze play for Germany was developing according to plan* (Newsweek).

**squeg|ger** (skweg'ər), *n. Electronics.* an oscillator in which squegging occurs. [probably < *s*(elf)-*que*(nching)*g* (oscillator) + *-er¹*]

**squeg|ging** (skweg'ing), *n. Electronics.* a form of oscillation that builds up periodically to a certain point and then suddenly stops, usually due to blocking or resistance in the grid circuit.

**squelch** (skwelch), *v., n.* —*v.t.* **1** to cause to be silent; crush: *to squelch an annoying child. She squelched him with a look of contempt.* **2** to strike or press on with crushing force; put down; squash; suppress: *to squelch a student demonstration or an evil rumor.* SYN: quell.
—*v.i.* **1** to walk or tread heavily in mud, water, or wet ground, or with water in the shoes, so as to make a splashing sound: *... drillers squelching through the mud back to their barges* (London Times). SYN: slosh. **2** to make the sound of one doing so.
—*n.* **1** *Informal.* something that serves to squelch, such as a crushing retort or sharp command. **2** a splashing sound made by walking in mud, water, or wet shoes.
[apparently imitative] —**squelch'er**, *n.*

**squelch|y** (skwel'chē), *adj.* **1** soft and wet; marshy: *Down there in that squelchy river basin Edward the Confessor was born* (Manchester Guardian). **2** causing or characterized by squelching sounds: *At each stamp his shoes had made a squelchy squeak* (Westminster Gazette).

**sque|teague** (skwē tēg'), *n., pl.* **-teague**. **1** the

---

**Pronunciation Key:** hat, āge, cãre, fär; let, ēqual, tėrm; it, īce; hot, ōpen, ôrder; **oi**l, **ou**t; cup, pu̇t, rüle; **ch**ild; lo**ng**; **th**in; **ᴛʜ**en; **zh**, measure; **ə** represents **a** in about, **e** in taken, **i** in pencil, **o** in lemon, **u** in circus.

weakfish of the Atlantic coast. **2** any one of certain other related fishes. [American English < the Algonkian (Narraganset) name]

**sque|tee** (skwē tē′), *n., pl.* **-tee.** = squeteague.

**squib** (skwib), *n., v.,* **squibbed, squib|bing.** —*n.* **1** a short, witty or satirical attack in speech or writing; sharp sarcasm; lampoon: *The play was a virulent one-act squib lasting just over an hour* (Kenneth Tynan). **2** a brief item in a newspaper used mainly to fill space. **3** a broken firecracker. **4** a small firework that burns with a hissing noise and finally explodes: *It's only ... that people amuse themselves by lighting squibs and throwing rockets* (Atlantic). **5** = squib kick. **6** *Especially British.* a mean, paltry, or cowardly person.
—*v.i.* **1** to say, write, or publish a squib or squibs. **2** to let off or fire a squib. **3** to move (about) restlessly or swiftly. **4** to make a slight, sharp report like that of a squib.
—*v.t.* **1** to assail or attack with squibs; lampoon. **2** to cast, throw, or use like a squib. **3** *Australian.* to evade (as an action or issue) in a cowardly way.
**damp squib,** *Especially British Slang.* something that has no effect or that fails completely; anything ineffective: *There is little danger of this meeting turning out a damp squib* (London Times).
[origin uncertain; perhaps imitative]

**squib kick,** *Football.* a short kick, usually made in midfield to cause a fumble or to make the ball stop near the goal line.

***squid** (skwid), *n., pl.* **squids** or (*collectively*) **squid,** *v.,* **squid|ded, squid|ding.** —*n.* a sea animal like an octopus but having ten arms instead of eight around its mouth, and a pair of tail fins. Squids are cephalopod mollusks and are related to the cuttlefish. Small squids are much used as bait.
—*v.i.* to fish with a squid as bait.
[origin uncertain]

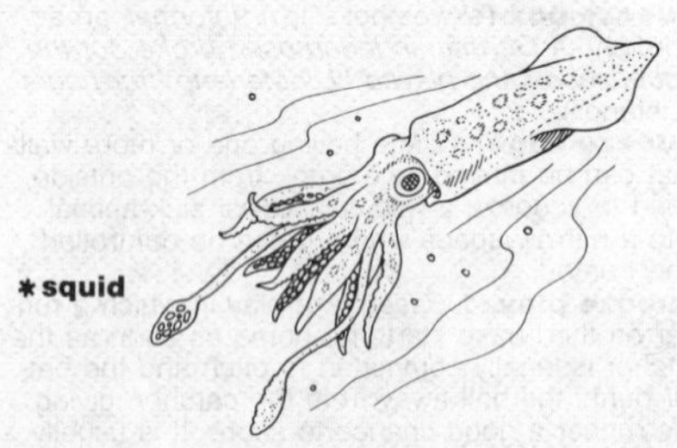
***squid**

**squidge** (skwij), *n.* a large disk used to flick the smaller disks into the cup in the game of tiddlywinks. [origin unknown]

**squid-jig|ger** (skwid′jig′ər), *n.* a device for catching squids, consisting of a number of hooks soldered together by the shanks so that the points radiate in all directions. It is dragged or jerked through the water.

**squiffed** (skwift), *adj. Slang.* squiffy.

**squif|fy** (skwif′ē), *adj. Slang.* intoxicated; drunk. [origin unknown]

**squig|gle** (skwig′əl), *n., v.,* **-gled, -gling.** —*n.* a wriggly twist or curve: *He may, for example, point to a squiggle in one corner of the card and say, "That looks like a caterpillar"* (Science News Letter).
—*v.t.* to make with twisting or curving lines: *The automatic pens squiggling recordings on numerous graphs traced eminently satisfactory data* (New York Times).
—*v.i.* to twist and turn about; writhe; squirm; wriggle: *Then a squiggling, squirming mass of eels made an exodus into the sea* (Science News Letter).
[origin unknown]

**squig|gly** (skwig′lē), *adj.* full of twists and turns: *Students pored over the squiggly lines that are man's first clues to the geography of outer space* (Time).

**squil|gee** (skwil′jē, skwil jē′), *n., v.,* **-geed, -gee|ing.** —*n.* **1** = squeegee. **2** a line bearing toggles with which a studding sail is set.
—*v.t.* = squeegee.

**squill** (skwil), *n.* **1** a plant of the lily family, whose onionlike bulb is sliced and dried for medicinal use, especially as an expectorant; sea onion. **2** Often, **squills.** its bulb. **3** any one of a group of Old World plants of the lily family, bearing small flowers on a leafless stalk, such as the bluebell or wood hyacinth. **4** the bulb of any one of these plants. [< Latin *squilla,* variant of *scilla* sea onion; prawn < Greek *skilla*]

**squil|la** (skwil′ə), *n., pl.* **squil|las, squil|lae** (skwil′ē), any one of a group of stomatopod crustaceans, somewhat like the mantis, which burrow into the shallow ocean bottom along the shore; mantis crab. [< Latin *squilla;* see etym. under **squill**]

**squinch¹** (skwinch), *n.* a straight or arched support constructed across an interior angle between walls in order to carry some superstructure, such as the side of an octagonal spire superimposed on a square tower. [short for Middle English *scuncheon* < Old French *escoinson,* apparently < *es-* out (< Latin *ex-*) + *coin* angle < Latin *cuneus* wedge]

**squinch²** (skwinch), *v.t.* to screw or distort (as the face or eyes): *How it will make her squinch her face, won't it?* (Thomas Haliburton). —*v.i.* to squeeze up so as to take up less space: *The bench was crowded so we all squinched together to make more room.* [origin uncertain]

**squin|ny** (skwin′ē), *v.,* **-nied, -ny|ing,** *n., pl.* **-nies.** *Dialect.* —*v.i.* to squint.
—*v.t.* to cause (the eyes) to squint.
—*n.* a squint.

**squint** (skwint), *v., n., adj.* —*v.i.* **1** to look or gaze with the eyes partly closed: *The bright sun made him squint at the sky to see the airplane.* **2** to look sideways; glance obliquely or in other than the direct line of vision. **3** to glance hastily; peep. **4** to be cross-eyed or affected with strabismus. **5** *Figurative.* to have an indirect bearing, reference, or implication; incline; tend: *The general's remark squinted toward treason.* **6** *Grammar.* to modify either a preceding or a following word or phrase. *Example:* In "A man who runs swiftly tires," the modifier *swiftly* squints. **7** to move, run, or go obliquely.
—*v.t.* **1** to hold (the eyes) partly closed, as in a bright light. **2** to cause to look sideways or obliquely.
—*n.* **1** the act or fact of looking with partly closed eyes: *The fisherman's squint made his eyes hard to see.* **2** a sidelong look: *She gave a squint to the handsome young man as he passed by.* **3** a hasty or casual glance; peep. **4** a tendency to look sideways: *She would be very pretty except for her squint.* **5** an inclination or tendency; drift; leaning. **6** an oblique or perverse tendency or bent. **7** a cross-eyed or walleyed condition; strabismus. **8** *Architecture.* a small opening in a chancel arch or wall; hagioscope.
—*adj.* **1** looking sideways or obliquely; looking askance: *A squint look at the answer.*
**2** cross-eyed or affected with strabismus: *His squint look improved when he wore his glasses.*
[short for *asquint*] —**squint′er,** *n.* —**squint′ing|ly,** *adv.*

**squint-eyed** (skwint′īd′), *adj.* **1** affected with strabismus; cross-eyed. **2** *Figurative.* narrowly and selfishly vindictive; malicious; spiteful: *squint-eyed jealousy. ... False and squint-eyed praise, which, seeming to look upwards on his glories, looks down upon my fears* (John Denham).

**squint|ing modifier** (skwin′ting), *Grammar.* a modifier placed in such a way that it may be taken to modify either a preceding or a following word or phrase; ambiguous modifier. See the example under **squint,** *v.i.,* def. 6.

**squint|y** (skwin′tē), *adj.,* **squint|i|er, squint|i|est.** having or characterized by a squint: *squinty eyes.*

**squir|arch** (skwīr′ärk), *n.* = squirearch.

**squir|ar|chy** (skwīr′är′kē), *n., pl.* **-chies.** = squirearchy.

**squire** (skwīr), *n., v.,* **squired, squir|ing.** —*n.* **1** a country gentleman in Great Britain, especially the chief landowner in a village or district (now often only a title of courtesy, but formerly the formal designation of such a person as the chief personage of his community, having specific legal responsibilities within it, and having the highest status of a gentleman, just below a knight). **2** *U.S.* a justice of the peace, magistrate, or local judge, especially in a rural community (used as a title of courtesy, especially in the 1700's and 1800's, when such persons were often comparable in community status to the squires of Great Britain). **3** a young man of noble family who attended a knight until he himself was made a knight. **4** a male personal attendant, especially of a sovereign or noble personage. **5** a woman's escort; gallant; lover.
—*v.t.* **1** to attend as squire. **2** to accompany as a squire; escort: *to squire a pretty girl about town.*
**squire it,** to act as a squire; play the squire: *Survey the Great, in City, Town, or Court, Who squire or lord it o'er the meaner sort* (Roger Bull).
[< Old French *esquier* < Latin *scūtārius* shield-bearer. Compare etym. under **esquire.**] —**squire′like′,** *adj.*

**squire|arch** (skwīr′ärk′), *n.* a member of the squirearchy: *Even the proudest of the neighbouring squirearchs always spoke of us as a very ancient family* (Edward G. Bulwer-Lytton).

**squire|ar|chal** (skwīr′är kəl), *adj.* = squirearchical.

**squire|ar|chi|cal** (skwīr′är′kə kəl), *adj.* of or having to do with a squirearchy: *A large-built, well-dressed man of military bearing and most squirearchical proportions* (Grant Allen).

**squire|ar|chy** (skwīr′är kē), *n., pl.* **-chies. 1** the collective body of squires, or landed proprietors; country gentry as a class, regarded especially in respect to political or social influence. **2a** government dominated by the country gentry, such as generally existed in England from the early 1700's until 1832. **b** a country, state, or community having such a government: *We should never have left home, home being something like an eighteenth-century English squirearchy* (Harper's). [< *squir(e)* + *-archy,* as in *hierarchy*]

**squir|een** (skwī rēn′), *n. Especially Irish.* a petty squire; a small landed proprietor. [< *squire* + Irish *-īn*]

**squire|hood** (skwīr′hu̇d), *n.* the state of being a squire; the rank or position of a squire.

**squire|ling** (skwīr′ling), *n.* **1** a petty squire. **2** a young squire.

**squire|ly** (skwīr′lē), *adj.* **1** of or having to do with a squire. **2** befitting a squire: *In recent years [he] led a squirely life in the Santa Barbara hills* (Time).

**squire of dames,** a man very attentive to women and much in their company: *"I'm not a squire of dames," Harris said with a poor attempt at pride* (Graham Greene).

**squir|ish** (skwīr′ish), *adj.* **1** characteristic of or befitting a squire: *Sancho Panza, in whom I think are united all the squirish graces* (Tobias Smollet). **2** having the appearance or character of a country squire: *He's settled down ... and has grown burly and squirish* (R. G. White).

**squirm** (skwėrm), *v., n.* —*v.i., v.t.* **1** to turn and twist; wriggle; writhe: *The restless boy squirmed in his chair. A rusting, war-built oil tanker squirmed its way into a dry dock* (Wall Street Journal). **2** *Figurative.* to show great embarrassment, annoyance, or confusion.
—*n.* a wriggle; writhe; twist.
[perhaps imitative]

**squirm|y** (skwėr′mē), *adj.,* **squirm|i|er, squirm|i|est.** squirming; wriggling: *To win the attention of squirmy teen-age audiences, Anita told the story of how she and Fawn were wakened by the sound of screams one night* (Time).

***squirrel**
definitions 1, 2

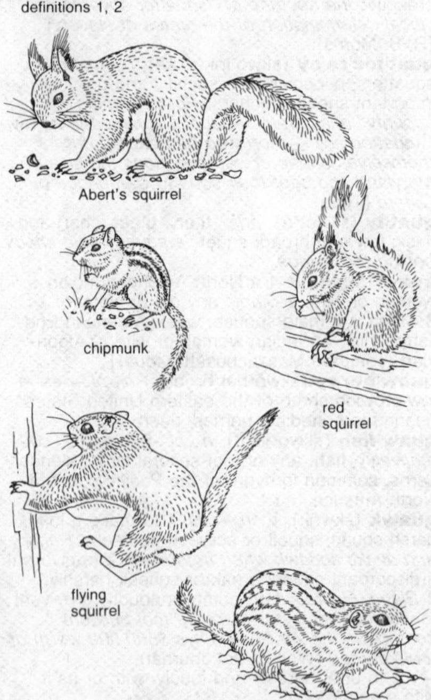


***squir|rel** (skwėr′əl), *n., v.,* **-reled, -rel|ing** or (*especially British*) **-relled, -rel|ling.** —*n.* **1** a small, slender, agile rodent with a long, bushy tail, that usually lives in trees and eats nuts, shoots, and bark. The fox squirrel and red squirrel are two kinds. **2** any one of numerous related rodents, such as the ground squirrels, chipmunks, woodchucks or marmots, and flying squirrels. **3** the gray, reddish, or dark-brown fur of any squirrel. **4** any one of various flying phalangers of Australia. **5** *Slang.* a reckless driver of a hot rod: *There was not a squirrel among them—no juvenile delinquent with wheels to zoom through traffic and terrorize the workaday motorist* (Time).
—*v.t.* to hide (away); bury or store (away): *She is*

*squirreling the stuff away, deep in one of the closets, and I stumbled on her cache this morning* (H. Allen Smith).
[< Anglo-French *esquirel,* Old French *escurel* < Vulgar Latin *sciūriolus* (diminutive) < Latin *sciūrus* < Greek *skíouros* < *skiâ* shadow + *ourâ* tail]
— **squir′rel|like′**, *adj.*
**squirrel cage**, **1** a cylindrical cage for squirrels, that revolves as they move. **2** any structure or situation similar to this.
**squirrel corn**, an American herb of the fumitory family, having finely divided leaves, cream-colored, heart-shaped flowers, and small tubers which resemble kernels of corn.
**squir|rel|fish** (skwėr′əl fish′), *n., pl.* **-fish|es** or (*collectively*) **-fish**. any one of a family of nocturnal, usually reddish, tropical fishes with large eyes and sharp spines and scales.
**squirrel frog**, a small green tree frog found in the southern United States.
**squirrel glider**, a flying phalanger (marsupial) found in isolated areas of eastern Australia, Papua, and Tasmania. It has a squirrellike face and a full parachute.
**squirrel grass**, = squirreltail.
**squirrel hake**, a species of hake found on the ocean bottom from Cape Hatteras to Labrador.
**squirrel hawk**, a large hawk of western North America with reddish-brown back and white underparts, so called because it preys extensively on ground squirrels.
**squir|rel|ly** (skwėr′ə lē), *adj. Slang.* very odd or peculiar; eccentric; crazy.
**squirrel monkey**, **1** any one of certain small South and Central American monkeys with a bushy, nonprehensile tail: *Although the squirrel monkey possesses a brain that is proportionately larger than man's, the animal is not particularly intelligent* (Science News Letter). **2** = marmoset.
**squir|rel|tail** (skwėr′əl tāl′), *n.* any one of various wild grasses related to the common barley.
**squir|rel|y** (skwėr′ə lē), *adj.* = squirrelly.
**squirt** (skwėrt), *v., n.* — ***v.t.*** **1** to force out (liquid) through a narrow opening: *to squirt water through a tube.* **2** to wet or soak (something) by shooting liquid in a jet or stream: *The elephant squirted me with his trunk.*
— ***v.i.*** to come out in a jet or stream; spurt: *Water squirted from the hose.*
— ***n.*** **1** the act of squirting. **2** a jet of liquid, or something like a liquid: *He soaked her with little squirts of water from the hose.* **3** a small pump, syringe, or other device that squirts. **4** *Informal.* **a** a small person. **b** an insignificant person who is impudent or conceited; whipper-snapper: *a little squirt of a man.*
[origin uncertain] — **squirt′er**, *n.*
**squirt gun**, = water pistol.
**squirt|ing cucumber** (skwėr′ting), a trailing Mediterranean plant of the gourd family whose ripened fruit separates from the stalk and expels the seeds and pulp with considerable force.
**squish** (skwish), *v., n.* — ***v.i.*** (of water, soft mud, or other watery mixture) to make a soft, splashing sound when walked in or on: *the caress of soft mud squishing up between the toes* (Rudyard Kipling).
— ***v.t.*** **1** to cause to make a soft, splashing sound. **2** *Dialect.* to squeeze or squash.
— ***n.*** a squishing sound: *Much of the pleasure appears purely sensuous—the squish and splatter of paints, the squash of clay* (New York Times).
[imitative]
**squish|y** (skwish′ē), *adj.* making or characterized by soft, splashing sounds; wet and soft.
— **squish′i|ly**, *adv.* — **squish′i|ness**, *n.*
**squush** (skwůsh, skwush), *v.i., v.t., n.* = squish.
**sq. yd.**, square yard or square yards.
**Sr** (no period), strontium (chemical element).
**Sr.**, an abbreviation for the following:
1 *Portuguese.* senhor.
2 senior.
3 *Spanish.* señor.
4 sir.
5 Sister.
**S.R.**, Sons of the Revolution.
**Sra.**, **1** *Portuguese.* senhora. **2** *Spanish.* señora.
**sra|dha** (srä′də), *n.* a Hindu funeral ceremony in honor of a deceased ancestor, at which food is offered, and gifts are made to Brahmans. Also, **shraddha**. [< Sanskrit *śrāddha*]
**SRAM** (no periods), short-range attack missile.
**Sra|nan-ton|go** (srä′nən tän′gō), *n.* a pidgin dialect of English spoken in Surinam; Taki-Taki.
**SRC** (no periods), Science Research Council (of Great Britain).
**S. Rept.**, Senate Report (used with a number).
**S. Res.**, Senate Resolution (used with a number).
**Sri** (shrē), *n.* **1** a Hindu form of address for a deity, holy person, or sacred book: ... *India's Holy Mother, Sri Sarada Devi* (New York Times). **2** this form of address used as a title of respect and equivalent to Mr. [< Sanskrit *śrī* (literally) exalted]
**S.R.I.**, Holy Roman Empire (Latin, *Sacrum Romanum Imperium*).
**Sri Lan|kan** (srē′ läng′kən), **1** a native or inhabitant of the Republic of Sri Lanka (formerly Ceylon); Ceylonese; Singhalese: *Thousands of Sri Lankans applauded May Day speakers* (New York Times). **2** of or having to do with the Republic of Sri Lanka or its people. [< *Sri Lanka* the Singhalese name of Ceylon + English *-an*]
**S.R.N.**, State Registered Nurse.
**sRNA** (no periods), soluble RNA.
**S.R.O.**, or **SRO** (no periods), **1** single-room occupancy. **2** standing room only: *The Carnegie Hall box office dusted off its S.R.O. sign* (Harper's).
**S.R.S.**, Fellow of the Royal Society (Latin, *Societatis Regiae Socius*).
**Srta.**, **1** *Portuguese.* senhorita. **2** *Spanish.* señorita.
**ss** (no period) or **ss.**, **1** *Law.* scilicet. **2** sections. **3** *Baseball.* shortstop.
**SS** (no periods), **1** Schutzstaffel. See **SS Troops. 2** steamship.
**S/S**, steamship.
**SS.**, **1** most holy (Latin, *sanctissimus*). **2** saints. **3** scilicet. **4** steamship.
**S.S.**, an abbreviation for the following:
1 Secretary of State.
2 Silver Star.
3 steamship.
4 Straits Settlements.
5 Sunday school.
**SSA** (no periods), Social Security Administration.
**SSB** (no periods), **1** single sideband. **2** Social Security Board.
**SSE** (no periods) or **S.S.E.**, south-southeast.
**S.Sgt.** or **S/Sgt.**, staff sergeant.
**S.S.J.**, Society of St. Joseph (the official name of the Josephites of the United States): *Father Philip Berrigan, S.S.J.*
**SSM** (no periods), surface-to-surface missile.
**SSR** (no periods) or **S.S.R.**, Soviet Socialist Republic.
**SSS** (no periods), Selective Service System.
**SST** (no periods), supersonic transport: *Boeing's SST could take off and land at the same speeds as supersonic jets* (Time).
**SS Troops**, a select military unit of fanatical Nazis who served as a bodyguard to Hitler, in special units, as a policing unit of the German army, and as the force in charge of concentration camps and deportation; Schutzstaffel.
**SSU** (no periods), semiconductor storage unit.
**SSW** (no periods) or **S.S.W.**, south-southwest.
**-st**, a suffix added to the numeral 1 or any numeral ending with 1 (except 11) to indicate the ordinal number: *1st Avenue, 181st Street, the 31st of May.*
**st.**, an abbreviation for the following:
1 stanza.
2 statute or statutes.
3 stere.
4 stet.
5 stitch or stitches.
6 stone (weight).
7 street.
8 strophe.
**s.t.**, short ton.
**St** (no period), stratus.
**St.**, **1** Saint. **2** statute or statutes. **3** strait. **4** Street.
**sta.**, **1** stationary. **2** stator.
**Sta.**, **1** Santa (*Spanish or Italian,* saint; holy). **2** station.
**stab** (stab), *v.,* **stabbed, stab|bing,** *n.* — ***v.t.*** **1** to pierce or wound with a pointed weapon, chiefly with a short weapon, such as a dagger. **2** to thrust (a weapon) into a person. **3** *Figurative.* to wound sharply or deeply in the feelings: *The mother was stabbed to the heart by her son's lack of gratitude. Lord, thy most pointed pleasure take And stab my spirit broad awake* (Robert Louis Stevenson).
— ***v.i.*** **1** to thrust with a pointed weapon; aim a blow. **SYN**: jab. **2** to penetrate suddenly and sharply; pierce: (*Figurative.*) *She speaks poniards, and every word stabs* (Shakespeare).
— ***n.*** **1** an act of stabbing; thrust or blow made with a pointed weapon: *Oh! deathful stabs were dealt apace* (Tennyson). **2** any thrust or sudden, sharp blow. **3** a wound made by stabbing: *A hasty bandage covered the stab of a bayonet.* **4** *Figurative.* an injury to the feelings. **5** *Informal, Figurative.* an attempt at something; try: *The conference was primarily an initial, amiable stab at getting acquainted* (Time).
**have** (or **make**) **a stab at**, to try; attempt: *Even if you've never done it before, make a stab at it.*
**stab in the back**, **a** an act of unexpected treachery: *He absorbed this political stab in the back with the best grace he could muster* (Harper's). **b** to attempt to injure in a sly, treacherous manner: *When Mussolini entered World War II on the side of Hitler, people said he had stabbed France in the back.*
[originally Scottish; apparently variant of *stob,* noun variant of *stub.* Compare Swedish *stabbe* stump, stub.] — **stab′ber**, *n.*
**Sta|bat Ma|ter** (stä′bät mä′ter; stā′bat mā′tər), **1** a celebrated Latin hymn of the 1200's, beginning "Stabat mater dolorosa," about the sorrows of the Virgin Mary at the Crucifixion. **2** the musical setting of this. **3** one of several other hymns beginning with the same words. **4** a musical setting of any one of these hymns. [< Medieval Latin *Stabat Mater* the Mother was standing (the first two words of the hymn)]
**stab|bing** (stab′ing), *adj.* **1** that stabs: *stabbing spears.* **2** sharp and sudden: *stabbing pain.* **3** *Figurative.* piercing; penetrating; incisive: *This stabbing satire of a playgirl's progress from obscurity to celebrity owes much to [her] stunning presence* (Time). — **stab′bing|ly**, *adv.*
**sta|bile** (stā′bəl, stab′əl), *adj., n.* — ***adj.*** **1** having stability; stable. **2** *Medicine.* **a** designating or having to do with treatment by electricity in which an electrode is kept stationary over the part treated. **b** not affected by an ordinary amount of heat.
— ***n.*** a stationary sculpture made of colored spheres, disks, and wires, or of large cut and bent sheets of metal.
[< Latin *stabilis;* see etym. under **stable**[2]]
**sta|bil|i|fy** (stə bil′ə fī), *v.t.,* **-fied, -fy|ing.** to render stable, fixed, or firm; establish or stabilize.
[< Latin *stabilis* (see etym. under **stable**[2])]
**sta|bi|lise** (stā′bə līz), *v.t., v.i.,* **-lised, -lis|ing.** *Especially British.* stabilize.
**sta|bil|i|tate** (stə bil′ə tāt), *v.t.,* **-tat|ed, -tat|ing.** to give stability to; make stable; stabilize. [< Latin *stabilitāre* (with English *-ate*[1]) < *stabilis;* see etym. under **stable**[2]]
**sta|bil|i|ty** (stə bil′ə tē), *n., pl.* **-ties. 1** the capacity to remain in position; ability to resist being dislodged, overturned, or otherwise unsettled or upset: *A concrete wall has more stability than a light wooden fence.* **SYN**: steadiness, equilibrium. **2** the state of being fixed in position; firmness of position: *the stability of the sun and the motion of the earth.* **3** the capacity to resist destruction or essential change; enduring quality; permanence: *A party of order or stability, and a party of progress or reform, are both necessary elements of a healthy state of political life* (John Stuart Mill). *Every quotation contributes something to the stability or enlargement of the language* (Samuel Johnson). **4** firmness of character, purpose, or resolution; steadfastness: *the stability of George Washington's character and devotion.* **5** the ability of an object to return to its original or normal position, especially the ability of an aircraft or ship to regain a position of equilibrium when forced from it by the wind or sea. **6** a fourth vow, made by a Roman Catholic Benedictine, binding him to continuance in his profession and residence for life in the same monastery. **7** *Obsolete.* solidity.
**sta|bi|li|za|tion** (stā′bə lə zā′shən), *n.* the act of making stable or the condition of being made stable.
**stabilization fund**, a fund established by a country to keep stable the foreign exchange rates of its currency and to influence the domestic currency market.
**sta|bi|lize** (stā′bə līz), *v.,* **-lized, -liz|ing.** — ***v.t.*** **1** to make stable or firm; confer stability on: *to stabilize a government.* **2** to prevent changes in, especially further changes; hold steady: *to stabilize prices.* **3** to keep well-balanced: *to stabilize an aircraft in level flight after hitting an air pocket.* **4** to give stability to (an aircraft or ship) by the manner of its design or loading or by special devices such as gyroscopic controls.
— ***v.i.*** to become stable: *This situation has fairly stabilized and we do not expect such an outbreak next year* (New York Times).
[< French *stabiliser* < Latin *stabilis;* see etym. under **stable**[2]]
**sta|bi|liz|er** (stā′bə lī′zər), *n.* **1** a person or thing that stabilizes. **2** a device for keeping an aircraft or ship steady: *a gyroscopic stabilizer. The stabilizers can be rotated on a horizontal axis to fit varying conditions at sea* (New York Times). **3** *Aeronautics.* the horizontal airfoil in the tail of an aircraft; horizontal stabilizer. **4** a substance added to an explosive to make it less liable to spontaneous decomposition. **5** a substance such as gelatin, agar, or gum, added to commercial foods to produce or retain smoothness or softness or preserve an emulsion.

---

**Pronunciation Key:** hat, āge, cãre, fär; let, ēqual, tėrm; it, īce; hot, ōpen, ôrder; **oi**l, **ou**t; cup, pu̇t, rüle; **ch**ild; lo**ng**; **th**in; **ᴛʜ**en; **zh**, measure; **ə** represents **a** in about, **e** in taken, **i** in pencil, **o** in lemon, **u** in circus.

**sta|ble**[1] (stā′bəl), *n., v.,* **-bled, -bling.** —*n.* **1** a building fitted with stalls and rack and manger, in which horses are kept: *The horses were led into the stable and each put in a stall.* **2** a barn, shed, or other building in which any domestic animals, such as cattle or goats, are kept. **3** a group of animals housed in such a building. **4** a group of race horses belonging to one owner: *The black horse is one of Mr. King's stable.* **5** the grooms, trainers, and helpers, who work for a racing stable. **6** *Figurative.* a group of people joined for a common purpose or interest or who work for a particular business: *It was found that the gamble of financing a Broadway production required the assembly of a whole stable of backers* (Times Literary Supplement).
—*v.t.* to put or keep in a stable: *to stable a horse for the night.*
—*v.i.* to be lodged in a stable.
**stables,** the buildings and grounds where race horses are quartered and trained: *to work at the stables.*
[< Old French *estable* < Latin *stabulum* (literally) a standing place < *stāre* to stand]

**sta|ble**[2] (stā′bəl), *adj.* **1** not likely to fall or be overturned: *a stable government.* **2** not likely to give way; steady; firm: *a stable support. Concrete reinforced with steel is stable.* **3** not likely to change in nature or purpose; steadfast: *a calm, stable person, a stable resolve. The world needs a stable peace.* **SYN:** constant, unwavering. **4** not liable to destruction or essential change; permanent: *a stable design.* **5** able to maintain or return to its original or normal position: *a stable ship.* **6** *Chemistry.* not easily decomposed: *a stable compound.* **7** not capable of decay; not radioactive: *a stable nuclear particle.* [< Old French *estable* < Latin *stabilis* (literally) able to stand < *stāre* to stand] —**sta′ble|ness,** *n.*

**sta|ble|boy** (stā′bəl boi′), *n.* a boy or man who works in a stable.

**stable fly,** a common fly of Europe and North America that resembles the housefly but has a severe bite.

**sta|ble|man** (stā′bəl man′), *n., pl.* **-men.** a man who is employed in a stable to groom, feed, and otherwise look after the horses.

**sta|ble|mate** (stā′bəl māt′), *n.* **1** a horse which shares the same stable as another; horse which belongs to the same stable as another. **2** *Figurative.* any person, group, or thing sharing the same ownership, purpose, or interest.

**sta|bler** (stā′blər), *n.* a person who provides stabling for horses.

**sta|bles** (stā′bəlz), *n.pl.* See under **stable**[1].

**sta|bling** (stā′bling), *n.* **1** the act of placing or accommodating horses in a stable. **2** stable accommodation: *There's stabling in this place for a dozen horses* (Dickens). **3** a building, or buildings, comprising a stable.

**stab|lish** (stab′lish), *v.t. Archaic.* establish.

**stab|lish|ment** (stab′lish mənt), *n. Archaic.* establishment.

**sta|bly** (stā′blē), *adv.* in a stable manner; firmly; fixedly; securely.

**stacc.,** staccato.

**∗staccato**
definition 1

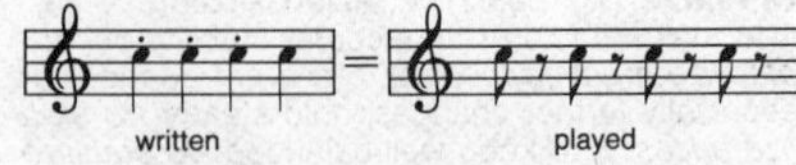


**∗stac|ca|to** (stə kä′tō), *adj., adv., n., pl.* **-tos** or **-ti** (-tē). —*adj.* **1** *Music.* with breaks between the successive tones; detached; disconnected: *His piano Bach is in the approved lighter, percussive, and staccato style* (Harper's). **2** *Figurative.* abrupt: *Her manner to her husband was ... a little staccato; she was nervous* (Margaret Kennedy).
—*adv. Music.* in a staccato manner.
—*n.* **1** *Music.* a succession of disconnected or staccato notes; passage played in a staccato manner. **2** *Figurative.* anything of an abrupt or disconnected nature, as speech: *His characters converse with curt clinical efficiency. This staccato creates a delicious undercurrent of venom* (Punch).
[< Italian *staccato* (literally) detached, short for *distaccato,* past participle of *distaccare* to detach]

**staccato mark,** *Music.* a dot or pointed stroke added over or under a note to indicate a staccato rendering.

**Pronunciation Key:** hat, āge, cãre, fär; let, ēqual, tėrm; it, īce; hot, ōpen, ôrder; oil, out; cup, pu̇t, rüle; child; long; thin; ᴛʜen; zh, measure; ə represents **a** in about, **e** in taken, **i** in pencil, **o** in lemon, **u** in circus.

**stack** (stak), *n., v.* —*n.* **1** a large pile of hay, straw, or grain in the sheaf. Haystacks are often round and arranged so as to shed water. **2** an orderly pile, heap, or group of anything: *a stack of wood, a stack of boxes.* **3** a number of chimneys, flues, or pipes standing together in one group: *a stack of chimneys.* **4** a chimney or funnel as of a factory, locomotive, or steamship. **5** a number of rifles arranged to support each other on the ground in a cone or pyramid with their muzzles together. **6** a rack with shelves for books. **7** a pile of poker chips, usually 20, sold by the banker to a player. **8** an English unit of measure for cut wood or coal, equal to 108 cubic feet. **9** a tall pillar of rock, detached from the main part of a cliff, and rising out of the sea. See picture under **peninsula**. **10** an arrangement of airplanes at different altitudes above an airport, awaiting landing instructions. **11** *Informal, Figurative.* a large number or quantity: *a stack of compliments. Sometimes a stack of people would come there* (Mark Twain).
—*v.t.* **1** to pile, arrange, or build in a stack: *to stack hay, to stack firewood, to stack rifles.* **2** to fill or load with stacks of something: *The left hand half of every step of the stairs was stacked with books* (Arnold Bennett). **3** to arrange (playing cards) unfairly. **4** *Figurative.* to arrange in such a way as to force or urge a predisposed result; load: *This committee is one of two or three in the House whose memberships are stacked to give the majority party substantial control* (New York Times).
**blow one's stack,** *Slang.* to lose one's temper: *It takes ... three times the normal self-control necessary to keep from blowing your stack over trifles* (Saturday Evening Post).
**stacks,** in libraries: **a** the part of a library in which the main collection of books is shelved: *He is up in the library stacks of our Investment Research department* (New Yorker). **b** a large bookcase, usually accessible from both sides: *the top shelf of the stacks.* **c** a number of bookcases arranged so as to save space: *to return borrowed books to the stacks.*
**stack up, a** to pile materials on to make (a fire): *We stacked up the fire* (H. Rider Haggard). **b** to pile up one's chips at poker: *to stack up before dealing.* **c** *Informal, Figurative.* to measure up; compare (against): *Stacked up against what's happening in the industry, these actions point to far-reaching changes* (Wall Street Journal). **d** to arrange (aircraft) at different altitudes above an airport: *Jet planes cannot be stacked up at the landing site while awaiting landing instructions* (Science News Letter).
[< Scandinavian (compare Old Icelandic *stakkr*)] —**stack′er,** *n.*

**stack|a|bil|i|ty** (stak′ə bil′ə tē), *n.* the condition of being stackable.

**stack|a|ble** (stak′ə bəl), *adj.* that can be stacked: *stackable tableware.*

**stacked** (stakt), *adj. Slang.* well-built; voluptuous: *Can I help it if this Mexican spitfire is fantastically stacked and wears a flimsy blouse?* (S. J. Perelman).

**stack|er** (stak′ər, stäk′-), *v.i. British Dialect.* to totter or reel; stagger. Also, **stacher.** [< Scandinavian (compare Old Icelandic *stakra* stagger < *staka* push)]

**stack|ing** (stak′ing), *n.* the circling of an airport by aircraft in a controlled pattern while awaiting landing instructions.

**stack room,** a room in a library in which books are stacked.

**stacks** (staks), *n.pl.* See under **stack**.

**stac|te** (stak′tē), *n.* a fragrant, sweet spice used by the Hebrews in the holy incense (in the Bible, Exodus 30:34). [< Latin *stactē* < Greek *staktḗ* sweet spice; oil of myrrh, ultimately < *stázein* to drop]

**stac|tom|e|ter** (stak tom′ə tər), *n.* an instrument for measuring a liquid in drops. [< Greek *staktós* distilling in drops (< *stázein* to drop) + English *-meter*]

**stad|dle** (stad′əl), *n.* **1** the lower part of a stack of hay, straw, or the like. **2** the platform on which this stands. **3** a supporting framework. Also, **stadle**. [Old English *stathol* foundation, support, base]

**stade**[1] (stād), *n.* an ancient unit of linear measure; stadium. [shortened form of *stadium*]

**stade**[2] (stād), *n. Geology.* a subdivision of a glacial stage; the period of time represented by a glacial substratum. [< French *stade* stage < Latin *stadium;* see etym. under **stadium**]

**stad|hold|er** (stad′hōl′dər), *n.* **1** the chief executive of the former republic of the United Provinces of the Netherlands. **2** (originally) the viceroy or governor of a province in the Netherlands. Also, **stadtholder**.
[< Dutch *stadhouder, stadthouder* < *stad, stadt* town, city + *houder* holder]

**stad|hold|er|ate** (stad′hōl′dər it), *n.* **1** the office of stadholder. **2** the rule or government of a stadholder. **3** a province or state governed by a stadholder. Also, **stadtholderate**.

**stad|hold|er|ship** (stad′hōl′dər ship), *n.* the office of stadholder. Also, **stadtholdership**.

**sta|di|a**[1] (stā′dē ə), *n., adj.* —*n.* **1** an instrument for measuring distances or heights by means of angles. A surveyor's transit is one kind of stadia. **2** a method of measuring distances by using such an instrument. **3** = stadia rod. **4** a surveying station. **5** a crude type of range finder consisting of a graduated rod held vertically at arm's length to indicate the distance of the target.
—*adj.* of or having to do with surveying by means of a stadia.
[apparently < Italian *stadia* lengths < Latin *stadia,* plural of *stadium* stadium]

**sta|di|a**[2] (stā′dē ə), *n.* a plural of **stadium**.

**sta|di|al** (stā′dē əl), *n., adj. Geology.* —*n.* a subdivision of a glacial stage; stade.
—*adj.* of or having to do with such a subdivision.

**stadia rod,** a staff or graduated rod placed at one end of the distance to be measured by a stadia.

**sta|dim|e|ter** (stə dim′ə tər), *n.* an optical instrument for measuring distances of objects, especially ships, of which the heights are known.

**sta|di|om|e|ter** (stā′dē om′ə tər), *n.* **1** an instrument consisting of a rolling wheel with spaced teeth, used for measuring the length of a line or curve. **2** a modified theodolite in which the directions are not read off but marked upon a small sheet, which is changed at each station. [< Greek *stádion* + English *-meter*]

**sta|di|um** (stā′dē əm), *n., pl.* **-di|ums** or **-di|a.** **1** a place shaped like an oval or a U, consisting of tiers of seats around an open field: *The stadium was filled for the final baseball game.* **SYN:** amphitheater. **2** an ancient Greek running track for footraces, with tiers of seats along each side and at one end. The stadium at Athens was about 607 feet long. **3** a unit of linear measure used in various parts of the ancient world, varying according to time and place, but most commonly equal to slightly over 600 feet or 1/8 of a Roman mile. **4a** *Biology.* a stage of a process. **b** a stage of a disease. [< Latin *stadium* < Greek *stádion* 607 feet (see def. 2)]
► In the sense of def. 1, the plural is usually *stadiums.* In the senses of defs. 2, 3, and 4, the plural is regularly *stadia.*

**stad|le** (stad′əl), *n.* = staddle.

**stadt|hold|er** (stat′hōl′dər), *n.* = stadholder.

**stadt|hold|er|ate** (stat′hōl′dər it), *n.* = stadholderate.

**stadt|hold|er|ship** (stat′hōl′dər ship), *n.* = stadholdership.

**staff**[1] (staf, stäf), *n., pl.* **staves** or **staffs** *for 1, 2, 7,* **staffs** *for 3-6, adj., v.* —*n.* **1** a stick, pole, or rod: **a** a stick carried in the hand as a support in walking or climbing: *The old man leaned on his staff.* **b** a stick or club used as a weapon; cudgel: *Robin Hood fell under Little John's staff.* **c** a pole from which a flag is flown: *The flag was flown at half-staff.* **d** a rod or wand as an emblem of office, such as the crosier of episcopal authority. **e** a rod used in surveying for measuring distances and heights. **2** *Figurative.* something or someone that supports or sustains. Bread is called the staff of life because it will support life. *They had one son, who had grown up to be the staff and pride of their age* (Washington Irving). **3** a group of people assisting a chief; group of employees: *the editorial staff of a paper, a hospital staff. Our school has a staff of twenty teachers.* **4** *Military.* a group of officers that assists a commanding officer with administration and planning but does no fighting. **5** a similar group assisting or attending a governor, president, or other executive. **6** the set of five horizontal lines and four spaces between them, on which music is written; stave. **7** *Archaic.* the long handle of a spear, lance, poleax, or halberd.
—*adj.* having to do with or belonging to a military or administrative staff: *staff duties. The gate was partly blocked by a staff car* (Harper's).
—*v.t.* to provide with a staff of officers, teachers, or employees: *Staffing the administrative services of the new republic has also been difficult* (Manchester Guardian).
[Old English *stæf*]

**staff**[2] (staf, stäf), *n.* a building material consisting of plaster of Paris, cement, and fibrous material, used for temporary ornamental work. [apparently < German *staffieren* to trim]

**staff angle,** a square strip of wood, standing flush with the wall on each of its sides, at the external angles of plastering, to protect them from injury.

**staf|fel|ite** (staf′ə līt), *n.* a greenish mineral, a phosphate and carbonate of calcium, occurring in botryoidal forms of a fibrous structure. [< German *Staffelit* < *Staffel,* Prussia, where it was found + *-it* -ite[1]]

**staff|er** (staf′ər, stäf′-), *n. Informal.* a member of a staff.

**staff|man** (staf′man′, stäf′-), *n., pl.* **-men.** a member of a staff: *Public relations men, whether as corporate staffmen or as hired counsel, are acquiring power and acceptance in America's executive suites* (Vance Packard).

**staff officer,** 1 a commissioned officer in the armed forces who belongs to the staff of a commanding officer. A staff officer is charged with executive and administrative duties, but has no command over a combat force. 2 a commissioned officer in the U.S. Navy, such as a surgeon or chaplain, who is not eligible to assume military command.

**staff of life,** 1 bread: *The staff of life is frequently of such spongy substance that it is incapable of giving much support* (New York Times). 2 any basic or staple food: *Water [for geese] is their staff of life* (Punch). *Broad beans form one of the staves of life in Sicily* (D. Sladen).

**Staf|ford|shire terrier** (staf′ərd shir, -shər), any dog of a sturdy breed having a short stiff coat, weighing 35 to 50 pounds, and developed from the bulldog and a terrier. [< *Staffordshire,* a county in England, where the breed originated]

**staff ride,** a course of instruction in the field for officers of a general staff.

**staff|room** (staf′rüm′, stäf′-), *n. Especially British.* a room for the use of the staff only, as in a school.

**staff sergeant,** 1 a noncommissioned officer in the U.S. Army, Air Force, or Marine Corps ranking next above a sergeant. 2 a noncommissioned officer in the Australian, British, or Canadian armed forces, usually ranking with or next above a sergeant. *Abbr:* S. Sgt.

**staff tree,** any one of a group of twining shrubs, especially the bittersweet.

**staff-tree family** (staf′trē′, stäf′-), a group of dicotyledonous, climbing, shrubs or trees including the American bittersweet, strawberry bush, wahoo, and kat.

**staff|work** (staf′wėrk′, stäf′-), *n.* work by a staff; administrative work.

**stag** (stag), *n., adj., adv., v.,* **stagged, stag|ging.** —*n.* 1 a full-grown male deer, especially the European red deer; hart. 2 the male of many other large animals of the group including deer. 3 the male of various other animals. 4 an animal, especially a hog, castrated when full-grown. 5 *Informal.* a person, especially a man, who goes to a dance, party, or other social function unaccompanied by a person of the opposite sex. 6 *Informal.* a dinner or party attended by men only: *In summer, the men from the mill hold a stag every Wednesday night at the golf club* (Maclean's). 7 *Scottish.* a young horse, especially one that is unbroken. 8 *British.* a person who seeks to buy stocks in a corporation to sell them immediately at a profit: *The stock is obviously a useful investment and expectations are for a higher premium when the stags have finished selling* (Economist). —***adj.*** *Informal.* 1 attended by, or for, men only: *a stag dinner, a stag party.* 2 intended for stag parties; pornographic: *He continued with a profitable avalanche of skin flicks and stag movies, all totally explicit* (London Times).
—***adv.*** *Informal.* without the company of a person of the opposite sex: *to go stag to a party.*
—***v.i.*** *Informal.* to go to a dance or party unaccompanied by a person of the opposite sex.
—***v.t.*** 1 *British.* to purchase or deal in (stock) as a stag. 2 *British Slang.* to observe; watch. 3 *Obsolete, Slang.* to detect.
[Old English *stagga* stag]

**stag beetle,** any one of various large lamellicorn beetles, some of the males of which have mandibles resembling antlers; giant stag. See picture under **beetle**[1].

**stag|bush** (stag′bu̇sh′), *n.* = black haw.

***stage** (stāj), *n., adj., v.,* **staged, stag|ing.** —*n.* 1 one step or degree in a process; period of development. An insect passes through several stages before it is full-grown. Frogs pass through a tadpole stage. Childhood, adolescence, and adulthood are stages in a person's life. *The communicable diseases are most contagious in this early stage* (Time). 2 the raised platform in a theater on which actors perform: *Like a lone actor on a gloomy stage* (Thomas Hardy). *All the world's a stage And all the men and women merely players* (Shakespeare). *Thirty feet above its stage floor was the grid—a set of rafters from which hung scenery, lights, and drapes* (New Yorker). See picture below. 3 *Figurative.* the scene of action: *Bunker Hill was the stage of a famous battle.* SYN: arena. 4 a section of a rocket or missile having its own engine and fuel and other component parts. A three-stage rocket has three engines, one in each stage, which separate one after another from the rocket or missile after the fuel is burned up. *Russia said the next to last stage of the vehicle burned up in the atmosphere about 50 miles up* (Wall Street Journal). 5 a stagecoach or bus. SYN: diligence. 6 a place of rest on a journey, especially a regular stopping place, as for stagecoaches, where horses were changed. SYN: station. 7 the distance between two places on a journey; distance between stops. 8a a platform; flooring. **b** the small platform on which an object is placed to be viewed through a microscope: *The doctor looked through the microscope at the slide on the stage.* 9 a scaffold for workmen and their tools; staging. 10 *Geology.* two or more related beds of stratified rocks. It is the division of rocks ranking below a series. 11 *Electronics.* one element in some complex apparatus, such as one tube and its accessory equipment in an amplifier consisting of several tubes; stop. 12 a single set each of stationary blades or nozzles and of moving blades or rotor buckets in a turbine. 13 *U.S.* a level (of water): *During last year's flood, the river rose to record stages at four different locations.*
—***adj.*** of or having to do with the stage or theater; theatrical: *a stage production, a stage designer, stage business, the stage critics.*
—***v.t.*** 1 to arrange; put on a stage or in an exhibit: *to stage an art exhibit. The play was very well staged.* 2 *Figurative.* **a** to arrange to have an effect; plan and carry out: *Mother had staged a surprise for the children's party by hiring a magician. The angry people staged a riot.* **b** to present or display; exhibit: *During the week the stock market staged a mild recovery* (New York Times). 3 to burn out and detach from a rocket or missile: *to stage a motor or a fuel tank.* 4 to carry out or do by stages: *The West called for staged reduction of both atomic and conventional weapons* (New York Times). —***v.i.*** 1 to be suited to the theater: *That scene will not stage well.* 2 to travel by stagecoach.

**by easy stages,** a little at a time; often stopping; slowly: *We climbed the mountain by easy stages.*

**hold the stage,** to be the center of attention: *He held the stage all the time. He went on to say that he had killed three of four people* (London Times).

**on stage,** on a stage; before the audience or public: *Yet we are on stage, whether we like it or not ... the curtain is about to go up ... and the world is watching* (Harper's).

**on the stage,** being an actor or actress; in the acting profession: *If he had gone on the stage*

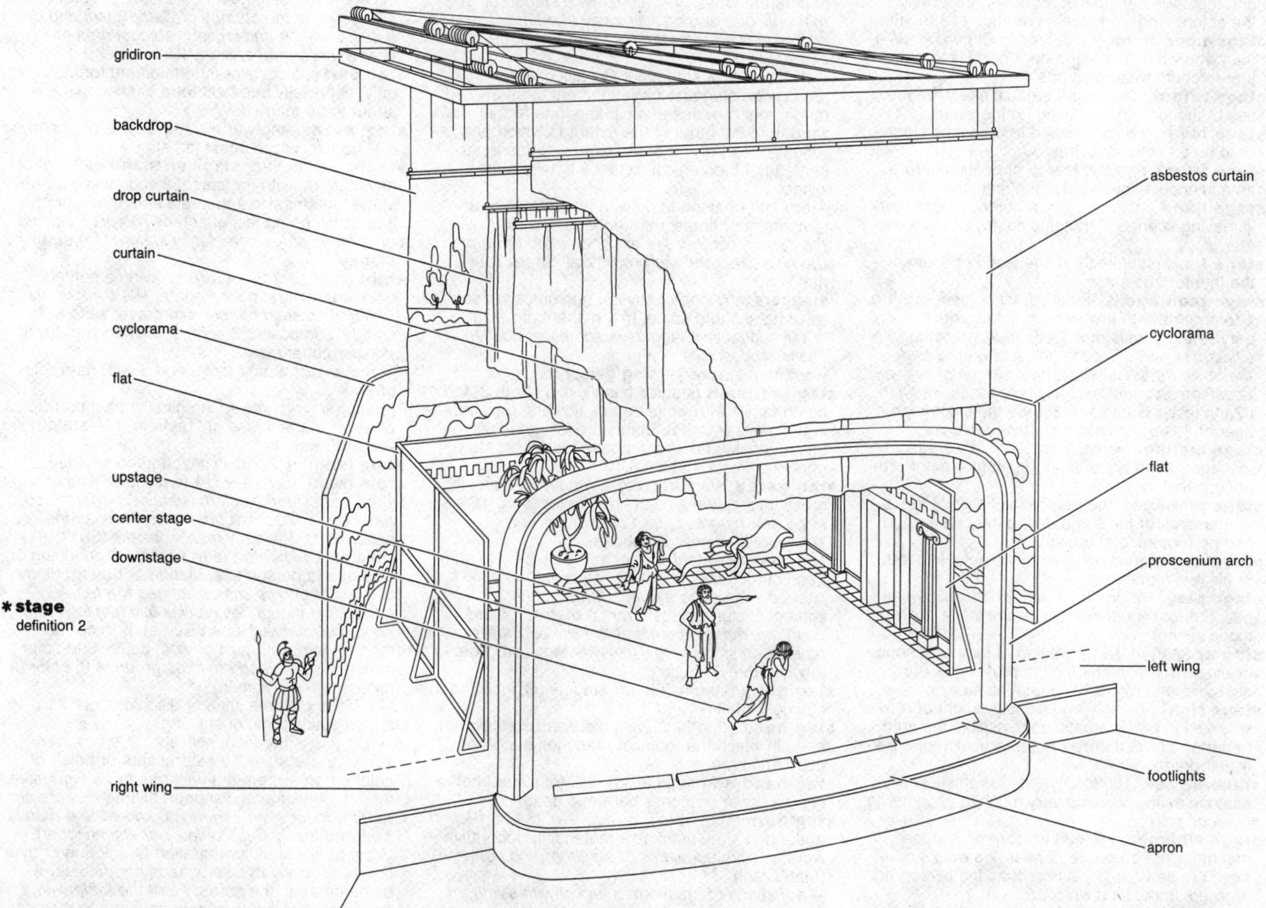


***stage**
definition 2

*he'would have made a good actor* (E. F. Adeline Sergeant).
**set the stage**, to prepare the way; set up the necessary conditions: *The House set the stage for possible widespread grass roots protest* (New York Times). *It's hoped the venture will set the stage for later U.S.-Soviet efforts* (Wall Street Journal).
**the stage**, the theater; the drama; the actor's profession: *Shakespeare wrote for the stage.*
[< Old French *estage* < Late Latin *staticum* < Latin *stāre* to stand] —**stage'like'**, *adj.*

**stage|a|ble** (stāj'ə bəl), *adj.* that can be staged or put on stage.

**stage box**, a box in a theater, in or close to the proscenium arch, seating several spectators.

**stage carriage**, *British.* stagecoach.

***stage|coach** (stāj'kōch'), *n.* a horse-drawn coach carrying passengers and parcels over a regular route: *Stagecoaches made the coaching inn, railroads the terminal hotel* (Saturday Review).

***stagecoach**

**stage|craft** (stāj'kraft', -kräft'), *n.* skill in, or the art of, writing, adapting, or presenting plays: *The theater badly needs workmen who are wise in stagecraft and anxious to use their talents* (Newsweek).

**stage designer**, a person who designs the stage setting for plays, operas, motion pictures, or television programs.

**stage direction**, a direction in a written or printed play to indicate the appropriate action or arrangement of the stage.

**stage director**, *Theater.* **1** *Especially U.S.* a director. **2** *Especially British.* a stage manager.

**stage door**, the door giving access to the stage and the parts behind it in a theater, especially the actors' and workmen's entrance to a theater.

**stage-door Johnny** (stāj'dôr', -dōr'), *Informal.* a man who waits at a stage door or goes to a theater to court an actress or showgirl.

**stage effect**, a striking theatrical effect, as the use of thunder and lightning on the stage.

**stage fever**, a strong desire to go on the stage, or to be an actor or actress.

**stage fright**, nervous fear of appearing before an audience, especially for the first time.

**stage|hand** (stāj'hand'), *n.* a person whose work is moving scenery, arranging lights, etc., in a theater.

**stage|land** (stāj'land'), *n.* the world or realm of the theater; the stage.

**stage-man|age** (stāj'man'ij), *v.t.*, **-aged, -ag|ing.** **1** to arrange with a view to dramatic effect; supervise the details of closely: *to stage-manage a Christmas party. But the hours of waiting had their own theatrical shape, a prologue of high expectation splendidly stage-managed by tradition* (Manchester Guardian). **2** to be the stage manager of. [back formation < *stage manager*]

**stage management**, **1** the work of a stage manager. **2** the act of stage-managing a performance, event, or the like.

**stage manager**, the person in charge of the arrangements of the stage during the preparation and performance of a play.

**stage name**, a name used by an actor instead of his real name.

**stage play**, **1** a dramatic performance. **2** a play adapted for representation on the stage. **3** dramatic acting.

**stag|er** (stā'jər), *n.* **1** a person of long experience or employment in an office, a profession, etc.; old hand; veteran. **2** = coach horse.

**stage right**, the sole and exclusive right of representation of a dramatic composition; the right to perform or authorize the performance of a particular drama.

**stage-struck** (stāj'struk'), *adj.* extremely interested in acting; wanting very much to become an actor or actress.

**stage whisper**, **1** a loud whisper on a stage, meant for the audience to hear. **2** a whisper meant to be heard by others than the person addressed. **3** any loud whisper.

**stage-whis|per** (stāj'hwis'pər), *v.i., v.t.* to speak or say in a stage whisper: *"Why don't you fellows call this whole thing off," he stage-whispered to the nearby press table* (Time).

**stage|wor|thy** (stāj'wėr'ᴛʜē), *adj.* worthy of representation on the stage: [*The* ]*new play is a skillfully stageworthy adaptation of his novel* (London Times). —**stage'wor'thi|ness**, *n.*

**stage|y** (stā'jē), *adj.*, **stag|i|er, stag|i|est.** = stagy.

**stag|fla|tion** (stag flā'shən), *n.* a condition of continuous inflation combined with a stagnant rate of business and industrial expansion: *A lack of high competitiveness leads to stagflation, which tends to become a permanent feature of the economic system* (Manchester Guardian Weekly). [blend of *stagnation* and *inflation*]

**stag|fla|tion|ar|y** (stag flā'shə ner'ē), *adj.* of or characterized by stagflation: *This was discussion of ways in which the antitrust movement could play a part in curing the stagflationary disease—the combination of rising prices and rising unemployment* (Sunday Times).

**stag|gard** (stag'ərd), *n.* a four-year-old male red deer. [Middle English *stagard* < *stag* stag]

**stag|gart** (stag'ərt), *n.* = staggard.

**stag|ger** (stag'ər), *v., n., adj.* —*v.i.* **1** to sway or reel from side to side when trying to stand or walk, as from weakness, a heavy load, or being drunk; move unsteadily; totter: *The boy staggered and fell under the heavy load of books. I saw him staggering up the street in a state of intoxication* (George Borrow). SYN: See syn. under **reel**². **2** to become unsteady; give way; waver: *The troops staggered under the severe gunfire. A prince's banner wavered, then staggered backward, hemmed by foes* (E. R. Sill). **3** *Figurative.* to begin to doubt or waver; become less confident or determined; hesitate: *He staggered at the idea of corruption in such high offices of government.*
—*v.t.* **1** to make sway or reel: *The blow staggered me for a moment.* **2** to cause to doubt, waver, or falter; cause to hesitate: *a fire from the militia which ... staggered the regulars* (James Fenimore Cooper). **3** *Figurative.* to confuse or astonish greatly; shock; nonplus; overwhelm; bewilder: *The difficulty of the examination staggered me. The size of the debt staggered us. He was staggered by the news of his friend's death.* **4** to make helpless. **5** to arrange in a zigzag order or way, as spokes in a wheel hub. **6** to arrange (the wings of a biplane) so that the leading edge of one is set farther forward on the fuselage than the leading edge of the other. **7** to arrange to be at different times: *Vacations were staggered so that only one person was away at a time. The school was so crowded they had to stagger the classes.*
—*n.* **1** an act of staggering; swaying, tottering, or reeling. **2** a staggered arrangement. **3** an arrangement of wings of a biplane, one farther forward than the other. **4** the extent to which one wing is ahead of the other, expressed as a percentage of the vertical distance between the wings.
—*adj.* of or having to do with an alternating arrangement of times, work, jobs, or the like: *... the current stagger system of electing three of the nine directors each year* (Wall Street Journal).
**staggers**, any one of several nervous diseases, as of horses and cattle, that make them stagger or fall suddenly: *Staggers is sometimes called "blind staggers."*
[variant of *stacker*] —**stag'ger|er**, *n.*

**stag|ger|bush** (stag'ər bůsh'), *n.* a shrub of the heath family with white or pink flowers, growing in the eastern United States. Its foliage is poisonous to stock, and was supposed to cause staggers in animals that ate it.

**stag|gered** (stag'ərd), *adj.* arranged in a progressing sequence as of time, or location: *12 large new plants ... built on a staggered schedule* (Scientific American).

**stag|ger|ing** (stag'ər ing), *adj.* **1** causing to stagger; confounding; shocking: *a staggering surprise, a staggering thought.* **2** enormous; immense; stupendous: *From a material standpoint, the achievements of the United States ... have been staggering* (Newsweek). —**stag'ger|ing|ly**, *adv.*

**stag|ger|y** (stag'ər ē), *adj.* staggering; inclining to stagger or fall.

**stag|head** (stag'hed'), *n.* a diseased condition of trees in which the topmost branches become dead and bare.

**stag-head|ed** (stag'hed'id), *adj.* (of a tree) having the upper branches bare and dead.

**stag|horn** (stag'hôrn'), *n., adj.* —*n.* the horn or antler of a stag, used as a material in decorative work: *... carved pieces of staghorn and bone* (Matt Clark).
—*adj.* made of staghorn: *a jacket with staghorn buttons.*

**staghorn coral**, any one of various madreporic corals having a branched skeleton that resembles the antlers of a stag.

**staghorn sumac**, a tall species of sumac of eastern North America, with branchlets covered with velvety hairs.

**stag|hound** (stag'hound'), *n.* any large hound of a breed resembling the foxhound but larger, formerly used for hunting deer and wolves.

**stag|ing** (stā'jing), *n.* **1** a temporary flooring with posts and boards for support, used as a platform by workmen or builders; scaffolding. **2** the act, process, or art of putting a play on the stage. **3** the act of releasing a stage in a rocket or spacecraft. **4** the act of assembling personnel or equipment before a military movement or expedition. **5** a traveling by stages or by stagecoach. **6** the business of running or managing stagecoaches.

**staging area**, **1** an area where troops, equipment, or the like are prepared before a military movement. **2** *Figurative.* any place or area of preparation: *Downs Park is a prep school—a staging area from which little boys can go on to the public schools* (Time).

**staging post**, *British.* staging area. *France is the principal staging post between the Orient and the United States in the opium chain* (Manchester Guardian Weekly).

**Stag|i|rite** (staj'ə rīt), *n.* a native or inhabitant of ancient Stagira, a city in ancient Macedonia, especially Aristotle, who was born there.

**stag line**, *U.S. Informal.* the men, or place for men, who have no dancing partners.

**stag|nan|cy** (stag'nən sē), *n.* stagnant condition.

**stag|nant** (stag'nənt), *adj.* **1** not running or flowing; lacking motion or current: *stagnant air, stagnant water.* SYN: stationary. **2** foul from standing still: *a stagnant pool of water.* **3** *Figurative.* not active; sluggish; dull: *During the summer, business is often stagnant. There is always a chance that the perfect society might be a stagnant society* (Harper's). SYN: inactive, quiescent. [< Latin *stāgnāns, -antis,* present participle of *stāgnāre;* see etym. under **stagnate**] —**stag'nant|ly**, *adv.*

**stagnant anoxia**, a decrease in oxygen in the blood caused by a slowdown in the circulation.

**stag|nate** (stag'nāt), *v.*, **-nat|ed, -nat|ing.** —*v.i.* to be or become stagnant.
—*v.t.* to make stagnant.
[< Latin *stāgnāre* (with English *-ate*¹) < *stāgnum* standing water]

**stag|na|tion** (stag nā'shən), *n.* **1** the condition of becoming stagnant. **2** the act or process of making stagnant. **3** stagnant condition: (*Figurative.*) *France ... is the country of Catholicism and disbelief, tradition and impiety, stagnation and drama, order and anarchy* (Newsweek).

**stag party**, a party or entertainment for men only, especially one held for a bachelor who is about to be married.

**stag|worm** (stag'wėrm'), *n.* the larva of one of several botflies which infest the stag.

**stag|y** (stā'jē), *adj.*, **stag|i|er, stag|i|est.** **1** of or having to do with the stage. **2** suggestive of the stage; theatrical in appearance, manner, or style. **3** artificial; pompous; affected: *The play, closing on a lame, stagy note, lacks stature* (Time). Also, **stagey**.

**staid** (stād), *adj., v.* —*adj.* **1** having a settled, quiet character; sober; sedate: *We think of the Puritans as staid people.* SYN: grave, serious, steady, composed. **2** settled; unchanging; fixed. SYN: permanent, set.
—*v. Archaic.* a past tense and a past participle of **stay**¹.
[earlier *steyed, stayed,* (originally) past participles of *stay*¹ in the sense of "restrain"] —**staid'ly**, *adv.* —**staid'ness**, *n.*

**staig** (stāg), *n. Scottish.* a young horse; stag.

**stain** (stān), *v., n.* —*v.t.* **1** to discolor (something); spot; soil: *The tablecloth is stained where food has been spilled. Let not women's weapons, waterdrops, Stain my man's cheeks* (Shakespeare). **2** *Figurative.* **a** to spot by wrongdoing or disgrace (a person's reputation or honor); blemish; dishonor: *His crimes stained the family honor. But thoughtless follies laid him low, And stain'd his name* (Robert Burns). **b** to corrupt morally; taint with guilt or vice; defile. **3** to color or dye: *She stained the chair green.* **4** to color (a microscopic specimen).
—*v.i.* **1** to cause a stain or discoloration. **2** to take a stain; admit of staining.
—*n.* **1** a discoloration; soil; spot: *He has ink stains on his shirt.* **2** a natural spot or patch of color different from the background. **3** *Figurative.* a mark of disgrace; dishonor; stigma: *His character is without stain. When you know the dream is true And lovely with no flaw nor stain* (Robert Graves). **4** a liquid preparation of coloring or dye used especially to color woods and fabrics, by penetrating the pores: *Paint the table with a brown stain.* **5** a dye or pigment used to make

visible transparent or very small structures, or to differentiate tissue elements by coloring, for microscopic study: ... *many of the various stains used in microscopic work have a selective effect on bacteria, coloring some species and leaving others more or less unaffected* (Fred W. Emerson).
[probably fusion of short form of Middle English *distainen* (< Old French *desteign-*, stem of *desteindre* take out the color, ultimately < Latin *dis-* off + *tingere* to dye), and a Scandinavian borrowing (compare Old Icelandic *steina* to paint)]
— **stain′a|ble**, *adj.* — **stain′er**, *n.* — **stain′like′**, *adj.*

**stain|a|bil|i|ty** (stā′nə bil′ə tē), *n.* the ability of a cell or a part of a cell to take up a stain.

**stained** (stānd), *adj.* discolored; colored by staining: *a stained white uniform.*

**stained glass**, **1** colored glass used in sheets or fitted pieces in church windows to form a picture, or in mosaic or composite designs. **2** any enameled or painted glass.

**stain|less** (stān′lis), *adj., n.* — *adj.* without stain; spotless.
— *n.* = stainless steel. — **stain′less|ly**, *adv.* — **stain′less|ness**, *n.*

**stainless steel**, steel containing a high percentage of chromium (from 10 to 25 per cent), making it very resistant to rust and corrosion.

**stair** (stãr), *n.* **1** one of a series of steps for going from one level or floor to another. **2** a set of such steps; staircase; stairway: *We climbed the winding stair to the tower.* **3** *Figurative: He passed one after another of his associates on the stair to success.*
**stairs**, the series of steps for going from one level or floor to another: *the top of the stairs.*
[Old English *stǣger* stair, related to *stīgan* to climb] — **stair′less**, *adj.*

***stair|case** (stãr′kās′), *n.* a flight, or a series of flights, of stairs with their supporting framework, and balusters; stairs.

***staircase**

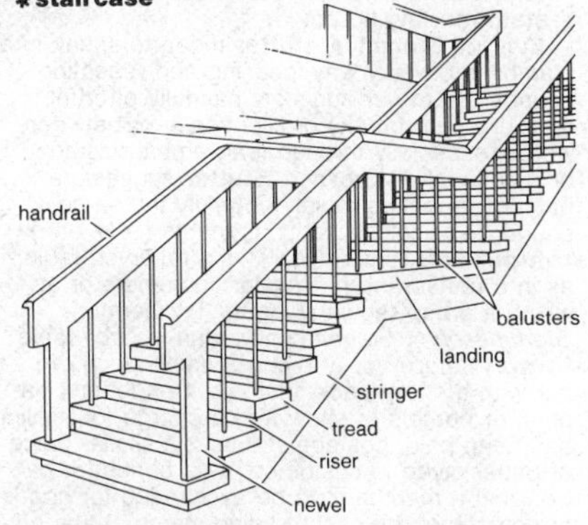


**staircase shell**, **1** the shell of any one of a group of gastropods of tropical seas, that suggests in its appearance a spiral staircase. **2** the animal itself; wentletrap.

**stair|head** (stãr′hed′), *n.* the top of a staircase or flight of stairs.

**stair|step** (stãr′step′), *n., adj.* — *n.* **1** one of the steps in a flight of stairs; stair. **2** *Informal.* one of a number of siblings differing in age and height by regular intervals.
— *adj.* **1** arranged like steps in a flight of stairs: *Stairstep terraces are used in soil conservation.* **2** *Figurative.* rising or falling in a series of steps: *a stairstep tax reduction.*

**stair|way** (stãr′wā′), *n.* a way up or down a flight of stairs; flight or flights of stairs; stairs; staircase: *the back stairway.*

**stair|well** (stãr′wel′), *n.,* or **stair well**, the vertical passage or open space containing the stairs of a building.

**stake**[1] (stāk), *n., v.,* **staked, stak|ing.** — *n.* **1** a stout stick or post pointed at one end for driving into the ground. Stakes are used to form part of a fence, mark a boundary, support a plant, or the like: *He built a fence of stakes with rope tied between to keep people out of his flower garden.* **2** each of the posts which fit into sockets on the edge of a wagon, truck, flatcar, or boat, to prevent the load from slipping off. **3a** a district within the authority of the Mormon Church made up of a number of wards; diocese. **b** the see or jurisdiction of a Mormon president.
— *v.t.* **1** to fasten with a stake or stakes: *to stake down a tent.* **2** to tether (an animal) to a stake. **3** to support (a plant, tree, or vine) with a stake or stakes. **4** to mark (out or off) with stakes; mark the boundaries of: *The miner staked out his claim. The surveyor staked off the district boundaries.* **5** to close (up or in), keep (out), or shut (off) with a barrier of stakes.
**drive stakes**, *Informal.* **a** to pitch one's tent or camp: *We stopped near the river and drove stakes for the night.* **b** to stake off a claim: *In the gold rush of '49, he succeeded in driving stakes in the San Fernando valley.* **c** to establish oneself; settle: *After drifting about several years I finally drove stakes on the Spokane River* (Outing).
**pull up stakes**, *Informal:* to move away; change the place where one lives: *Constant flooding of their land led the farmers to pull up stakes and leave the valley for the highlands. Many of the South's best educated citizens ... are among those pulling up stakes* (Wall Street Journal).
**stake out**, **a** to maintain surveillance over (an area, building, person, or group): *The police staked out his home, hoping he would return to get the money.* **b** to assign (someone) to maintain surveillance: *Department stores staked out a cameraman in a room across from the store to photograph unloading trucks* (Time). **c** to set aside for a special purpose; reserve: [*He*] *is demanding that the office of Borough President of Manhattan be permanently staked out as the inheritance of "a black man or a black woman"* (New York Times).
**the stake**, **a** a post to which a person was tied and then burned to death: *Joan of Arc was burned at the stake.* **b** death by being burned at a stake: *I know that I would go to the stake for you* (Thackeray).
[Old English *staca,* noun] — **stak′er**, *n.*

**stake**[2] (stāk), *v.,* **staked, stak|ing,** *n.* — *v.t.* **1** to risk (money or something valuable) on the result of a game, race, or cast of dice, or on any chance: *He staked all his money on the black horse.* **SYN**: bet, wager. **2** *Figurative.* to risk the loss of; hazard. **3** *U.S. Informal.* to grubstake: *For the last time he staked the old prospector.* **4** *Informal, Figurative.* to assist (a person) with money or other resources (to something): *I'll stake you to a dinner if you'll come.*
— *n.* **1** money risked; what is staked: *The men played for high stakes.* **2** the sum of money with which a gambler operates. **3** *Figurative.* something to gain or lose; share, such as in a property or business; interest: *Each of us has a stake in the future of our country.* **4** *U.S. Informal.* a grubstake.
**at stake**, to be won or lost; in jeopardy; risked: *His honor is at stake.*
**stakes**, **a** the prize in a contest or race: *The stakes were divided up among the winners. ... whose game was empires, and whose stakes were thrones* (Byron). **b** a race for a prize, usually a sum of money: *He made a two-dollar bet at the stakes.*
— **stak′er**, *n.*

**stake|boat** (stāk′bōt′), *n.* a boat moored or otherwise fixed to serve as a starting point or mark for racing boats.

**stake body**, the body or platform of a stake truck.

**stake driver**, *U.S.* the bittern, a small heron whose cry suggests the sound of a stake being driven into mud.

**stake|hold|er** (stāk′hōl′dər), *n.* the person who takes care of what is bet and gives it to the winner.

**stake|out** (stāk′out′), *n.* surveillance of an area where criminal activity is expected: *Detectives ... got her picture identified, discovered her modus operandi, and put a stakeout on her neighborhood* (Time).

**stake race** or **stakes race**, a horse race in which part or all of the stake is put up by the owners of the horses running in the race.

**stakes** (stāks), *n.pl.* See under **stake**[2].

**stake truck**, a flat-bed truck having brackets or sockets around the edge of the platform so that stakes can be inserted to help hold a load.

**Sta|kha|nov|ism** (stə hä′nə viz əm), *n.* (in the Soviet Union) a system of rewarding individual enterprise (especially in factories) and thereby increasing output. Stakhanovism is based on voluntary cooperation among workers divided into units or teams, in which each man does a part of the job at which he is most skilled and is paid for the work on a piecework basis. [< Aleksey G. *Stakhanov,* a coal miner whose record output in two shifts in 1935 was taken as a model for the system + *-ism*]

**Sta|kha|nov|ite** (stə hä′nə vīt), *n., adj.* — *n.* (in the Soviet Union) a worker who regularly increases his output and is rewarded for it under Stakhanovism.
— *adj.* of, having to do with, or characteristic of Stakhanovites or Stakhanovism: *One young biochemist ... regularly works Stakhanovite hours in his Midwestern laboratory* (Harper's).

**sta|lac|tic** (stə lak′tik), *adj.* having to do with or like stalactites or a stalactite; stalactitic.

***sta|lac|tite** (stə lak′tīt, stal′ək-), *n.* **1** a formation of lime, shaped like an icicle, hanging from the roof or sides of a cave. It is formed by dripping water that contains lime. *Perfect stalactites, as thin as straws and untouched by man, have been found in a cave on North Island, New Zealand* (Science News Letter). **2** any formation shaped like this. [< New Latin *stalactites* < Greek *stalaktós* dripping < *stalássein* to trickle]

***stalactite** definition 1
***stalagmite** definition 1

**stal|ac|tit|ic** (stal′ək tit′ik), *adj.* **1** of the nature of or like a stalactite or stalactites. **2** characteristic or suggestive of stalactites: *the stalactitic structure of some minerals.* **3** having stalactites: *a stalactitic cave.* — **stal′ac|tit′i|cal|ly**, *adv.*

**sta|lag** (stä′läg; *German* shtä′läk′), *n.* a German camp for noncommissioned prisoners of war: [*He*] *spent two years in various ... stalags in Germany before he broke free* (New Yorker). [< German *Stalag* < *Sta*(*mm*)*lag*(*er*) base camp]

***sta|lag|mite** (stə lag′mīt, stal′əg-), *n.* **1** a formation of lime, shaped like a cone, built up on the floor of a cave. It is formed by water dripping from the roof of a cave. *A fluffy stalagmite shaped like a knife blade shot skyward* (Newsweek). **2** any formation shaped like this. [< New Latin *stalagmites* < Greek *stalagmós* a dropping, or *stálagma, -atos* a drop, drip < *stalássein* to trickle]

**stal|ag|mit|ic** (stal′əg mit′ik), *adj.* **1** of the nature of or like a stalagmite or stalagmites. **2** characteristic of a stalagmite or stalagmites. — **stal′ag-mit′i|cal|ly**, *adv.*

**stale**[1] (stāl), *adj.,* **stal|er, stal|est,** *v.,* **staled, stal-ing.** — *adj.* **1** that has lost some or all of its softness, flavor, or consistency through age; not fresh: *stale bread.* **2** flat; having lost its effervescence: *stale ginger ale.* **3** *Figurative.* no longer new or interesting; worn-out; hackneyed: *a stale joke. How weary, stale, flat and unprofitable Seems to me all the uses of this world* (Shakespeare). **SYN**: trite, banal. **4** out of condition through overtraining or too long continued exertion, as an athlete or race horse: *The horse has gone stale from too much running. The team has gone stale from too much practice.* **5** *Figurative.* temporarily lacking, as in vigor or nimbleness, especially through unremitting application to one kind of thing: *a stale mind.* **6** *Law.* (of a claim or demand in a court of equity) having been allowed to lie dormant for so long that it has lost validity.
— *v.t.* **1** to make stale: *These are things which cannot be staled by repetition* (George Gissing). **2** *Obsolete.* to lower in value or estimation; cheapen.
— *v.i.* to become stale: (*Figurative.*) *To see her was a delight that never staled* (Somerset Maugham).
[Middle English *stale.* Compare etym. under **stalemate, stall**[1].] — **stale′ly**, *adv.* — **stale′ness**, *n.*

**stale**[2] (stāl), *v.,* **staled, stal|ing,** *n.* — *v.i.* (of horses and cattle) to urinate.
— *n.* the urine of horses and cattle.
[origin uncertain. Compare Old French *estaler,* Dutch and Middle High German *stallen.*]

**stale|mate** (stāl′māt′), *n., v.,* **-mat|ed, -mat|ing.** — *n.* **1** *Chess.* a draw which results when a player whose turn it is to move cannot move any of his pieces without putting his own king in check. **2** *Figurative: The prolonged stalemate outside Richmond* [*in 1864*] *made a sinister impression upon the North* (Sir Winston Churchill). *The military and diplomatic stalemate in Europe had freed Soviet hands for evil work elsewhere* (Newsweek). **SYN**: deadlock, standstill.

**Pronunciation Key:** hat, āge, cãre, fär; let, ēqual, tėrm; it, īce; hot, ōpen, ôrder; oil, out; cup, pu̇t, rüle; child; long; thin; ᴛʜen; zh, measure; ə represents a in about, e in taken, i in pencil, o in lemon, u in circus.

— *v.t.* **1** *Chess.* to subject to a stalemate. **2** *Figurative: House and Senate Republicans have stalemated each other* (Time). SYN: deadlock.
[Middle English *stale* stalemate (perhaps < Anglo-French *estale* a standstill < a Germanic word; compare etym. under **stale**[1]) + *mate*[2]]

**Sta|lin|ism** (stä′lə niz əm), *n.* the theory or system of Communism associated with Joseph Stalin, especially as characterized by coercion and severe oppression of opposition: *There was widespread hope of relief from the excesses of Stalinism* (Atlantic). [< Joseph *Stalin,* 1879-1953, a Soviet political leader, and premier of the Soviet Union 1941-1953 + *-ism*]

**Sta|lin|ist** (stä′lə nist), *n., adj.* — *n.* a follower of Stalin or Stalinism.
— *adj.* of, having to do with, or characteristic of Stalinism.

**Sta|lin|i|za|tion** (stä′lə nə zā′shən), *n.* the act or process of Stalinizing.

**Sta|lin|ize** (stä′lə nīz), *v.t.,* **-ized, -iz|ing.** to make Stalinist; cause to adopt the principles and practices of Stalinism: *The Stalinized parties ... lost sight of the interests and aspirations of the working classes* (Listener).

**stalk**[1] (stôk), *n.* **1** the stem or main axis of a plant, which rises directly from the root, and which usually supports the leaves, flowers, and fruit: *It is a long green reed, like the stalk of the maize* (Fanny Kemble). **2** any slender, supporting, or connecting part of a plant. A flower or a leaf blade may have a stalk. **3** any similar slender connecting or supporting part of an animal. The eyes of a crayfish are on stalks. **4** a slender, upright support: *a wineglass with a tall stalk.* **5** *Obsolete.* a quill. [Middle English *stalke;* origin uncertain; perhaps diminutive form of Old English *stela* stalk] — **stalk′like′,** *adj.*

**stalk**[2] (stôk), *v., n.* — *v.t.* to approach or pursue without being seen or heard: *The hunter stalked the lion. The detective stalked the suspect only to lose him in a crowd. He stalked his quarry without avail.*
— *v.i.* **1** to walk with slow, stiff, or haughty strides: *Offended, she stalked out of the room.* **2** to hunt or come up to something or someone stealthily: *He stalked with camera instead of gun.* **3** *Figurative.* to spread silently and steadily: *Disease stalked through the land.* **4** *Obsolete.* to walk softly, cautiously, or stealthily.
— *n.* **1** a stiff or haughty gait. **2** the act of stalking, especially a stealthy approach to game.
[Old English *-stealcian,* as in *bestealcian* steal along] — **stalk′er,** *n.*

**stalked** (stôkt), *adj.* having a stalk or stem: *a stalked barnacle or crinoid.*

**-stalked,** *combining form.* having a ___ stalk or stalks: *Tall-stalked = having tall stalks.*

**stalk-eyed** (stôk′īd′), *adj.* having the eyes set upon stalks, as certain crustaceans.

**stalk|ing-horse** (stô′king hôrs′), *n.* **1** a horse, or figure of a horse or some other animal, behind which a hunter conceals himself in stalking game. **2** *Figurative.* anything used to hide plans or acts; something put forward to conceal one's real intentions, desires, or motives; pretext. **3** *U.S.* a candidate used as a blind to conceal the identity of a more important candidate or to divide the opposition.

**stalk|less** (stôk′lis), *adj.* having no stalk.

**stalk|let** (stôk′lit), *n.* a diminutive stalk, especially a secondary stalk; pedicel.

**stalk|y** (stô′kē), *adj.,* **stalk|i|er, stalk|i|est. 1** consisting of stalks. **2** abounding in stalks. **3** of the nature of a stalk or stalks; long and slender like a stalk.

**stall**[1] (stôl), *n., v.* — *n.* **1** a place in a stable for one animal: *Each horse was put in a separate stall.* **2** a stable or shed for horses or cattle. **3** *Especially British.* a small place for selling things or in which some business is conducted: *At the public market different things were sold in different stalls under one big roof.* **4** a seat for the use of the clergy in the choir of a church. A stall is partly or entirely enclosed at the back and sides. **5** a pew in a church. **6** *British.* a seat in the front part of a theater; orchestra seat. **7** one of the sheaths for the fingers in a glove. **8** any one of various other sheaths or receptacles. **9** a parking space for a vehicle. **10** the condition resulting from stalling; failure to remain in operation.
— *v.t.* **1** to put, keep, or confine (an animal) in a stall: *The horses were safely stalled in the barn.* **2** to stop or bring to a standstill, usually against one's wish: *to stall an engine.* **3** to cause to become stuck, as in mud or snow: *We were stalled in the mud.*
— *v.i.* **1** to live in a stall, stable or kennel. **2** to come to a stop or standstill, usually against one's wish: *The car always stalls on this hill.* **3** to become stuck, as in mud or snow. **4** (of an airplane or airfoil) to lose speed or lift so that controlled flight cannot be maintained: *An airplane tends to drop when it stalls.*
**stalls,** *British.* **a** the orchestra section of an auditorium: *From our places in the stalls we could see our four friends ... in the loge* (Thackeray). **b** those who occupy it: *Why should the stalls stand to oblige the pit?* (Sunday Express).
[Old English *steall,* probably related to *stæl* a place] — **stall′-like′,** *adj.*

**stall**[2] (stôl), *n., v. Informal.* — *n.* a pretense to avoid doing something; pretext to prevent or delay action or the accomplishment of a purpose: *His excuse was just a stall.*
— *v.i.* **1** to act or speak evasively, deceptively, or hesitantly so as to prevent action; delay: *You have been stalling long enough. Every time I ask her to set the date she stalls.* **2** *Sports.* to play worse or more slowly than one is capable of, especially to use up the remaining time.
— *v.t.* Usually, **stall off,** to put off or prevent by evasive tactics, a plausible tale, or the like; delay; evade: *[He] did his best ... to ... stall off the awful truth with discreet shrugs and simpers* (George A. Sala).
[perhaps < Anglo-French *estale* decoy < a Germanic word]

**stall bars,** a series of wooden bars, like the rungs of a ladder, held against a wall and used for exercises in gymnastics.

**stall end,** the end of a stall or seat, as in the choir of a church, often richly carved.

**stall-feed** (stôl′fēd′), *v.t.,* **-fed, -feed|ing.** to feed (an animal) in a stall, especially to fatten for eating, selling, or showing.

**stall gate,** the gate in front of the row of stalls in which horses stand at the start of a race: *The fourteen three-year-olds put on a thriller from the moment the stall gates flew open* (New Yorker).

**stall|hold|er** (stôl′hōl′dər), *n. Especially British.* a person who owns, rents, or runs a stall in a market: *I bought ... an old Italian colored print from one of the artistic little stallholders who set up shop there every day* (Maclean's).

**stall-in** (stôl′in′), *n.* the act of deliberately stalling automobiles on a thoroughfare as a form of protest or demonstration: *Demonstrators have ... staged stall-ins on busy bridges, and refused to leave public buildings, all claiming in court (unsuccessfully) that their acts were constitutionally protected "speech"* (Fred P. Graham).

**stall|ing speed** (stôl′ing), the lowest speed an aircraft can travel in level flight without losing altitude: *If a plane's angle of attack is too great, the plane will stall even when flying at twice its normal stalling speed* (Martin Caidin).

**stal|lion** (stal′yən), *n.* a male horse that can be used for breeding purposes. [Middle English *stalyone,* alteration of *staloun* < Old French *estalon* < Germanic (because it was kept in a stall) (compare Old High German *stal* stable, stall)]

**stalls** (stôlz), *n.pl.* See under **stall**[1].

**stall shower,** a small enclosure for taking a shower bath.

**stal|wart** (stôl′wərt, stol′-), *adj., n.* — *adj.* **1** strongly and stoutly built; sturdy; robust: *She was proud of her stalwart, good-looking son* (Booth Tarkington). SYN: stout, muscular, powerful. **2** strong and brave; valiant: *a stalwart knight.* SYN: bold. **3** firm; steadfast; resolute; determined: *a stalwart refusal.*
— *n.* **1** a stalwart person. **2** a loyal supporter of a political party.
[(originally) Scottish variant of Middle English *stalworth,* Old English *stælwierthe* serviceable < *stæl* place, position + *wierthe* worthy. See related etym. at **stall**[1].] — **stal′wart|ly,** *adv.* — **stal′wartness,** *n.*

**stal|worth** (stôl′wərth, stol′-), *adj. Archaic.* stalwart.

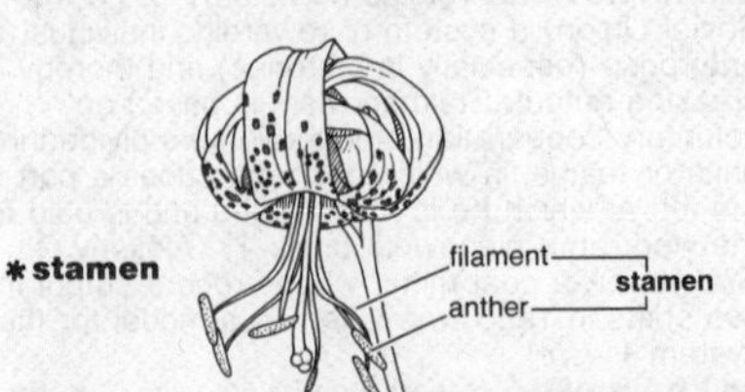

**✱stamen**

**✱sta|men** (stā′mən), *n., pl.* **sta|mens** or **stam|i|na.** the part of a flower that contains the pollen. The stamens are surrounded by the petals. A stamen consists of a slender stem or filament like a thread, which supports the anther. *When the flower is fully open numerous stamens are revealed, forming a circle just inside the ring of petals* (Fred W. Emerson). [< New Latin *stamen* < Latin *stāmen, -inis* warp, thread]

**stam|i|na**[1] (stam′ə nə), *n.* power to resist, sustain, or recover from that which weakens, such as fatigue or illness; strength; endurance: *moral stamina, a man of great physical stamina. Reading aloud requires stamina in the reader as well as in those read to* (London Times). [< Latin *stāmina* threads (of life, spun by the Fates), plural of *stāmen;* see etym. under **stamen**]

**stam|i|na**[2] (stam′ə nə), *n.* stamens; a plural of **stamen.**

**stam|i|nal** (stam′ə nəl), *adj.* **1** having to do with stamens. **2** consisting of stamens.

**stam|i|nate** (stam′ə nit, -nāt), *adj.* **1** having stamens but no pistils. **2** having a stamen or stamens; producing stamens. [< New Latin *staminatus* < Latin *stāminātus* < *stāmen, -inis* stamen]

**stam|i|nif|er|ous** (stam′ə nif′ər əs), *adj. Botany.* bearing or having stamens. [< Latin *stamēn, -inis* (see etym. under **stamen**) + English *-ferous*]

**stam|i|no|di|um** (stam′ə nō′dē əm), *n., pl.* **-di|a** (-dē ə). *Botany.* **1** a sterile or abortive stamen. **2** an organ resembling an abortive stamen. [< New Latin *staminodium* < *stamen* (see etym. under **stamen**) + *-odium,* a suffix meaning "resembling"]

**stam|i|no|dy** (stam′ə nō′dē), *n. Botany.* the metamorphosis of various organs of a flower, as a sepal, petal, pistil, or bract, into a stamen. [< Latin *stāmen, -inis* + English *-ody,* as in *phyllody*]

**stam|mel** (stam′əl), *n.* a coarse woolen fabric or linsey-woolsey, usually dyed red, formerly used for garments. [perhaps < obsolete French *estamel*]

**stam|mer** (stam′ər), *v., n.* — *v.i.* to repeat the same sound in an effort to speak; hesitate in speaking; speak haltingly, as from nervousness or embarrassment. *Example:* I s-s-see a d-d-dog. *Stammering was relieved when the stammerer was prevented from monitoring his own speech* (Science News Letter). — *v.t.* to utter in this way: *to stammer an excuse.*
— *n.* a stammering; stuttering: *He has a nervous stammer.*
[Old English *stamerian*] — **stam′mer|er,** *n.* — **stam′mer|ing|ly,** *adv.*
— *Syn. v.i.* **Stammer, stutter** mean to speak in a stumbling or jerky way, pausing and repeating sounds. **Stammer** suggests painfully effortful speaking with breaks or silences in or between words, especially through fear, embarrassment, or emotional disturbance. **Stutter** suggests a habit of repeating rapidly or jerkily the same sound, especially initial consonants (*s, p,* etc.).

**stamm|tisch** (shtäm′tish′), *n.* a reserved table, as in a restaurant, for regular customers or at which a group regularly meets. [< German *Stammtisch* < *Stamm* family, clan + *Tisch* table]

**stamp** (stamp), *n., v.* — *n.* **1** a small piece of paper with a sticky back, that is put on letters, papers, or parcels to show that a charge for mailing has been paid; postage stamp. **2** a similar piece of paper given to customers as a bonus for patronizing a merchant, to be exchanged for goods or sometimes for cash; trading stamp. **3** any official mark or label required by law to be affixed to a paper or other item to show that a fee, duty, or tax has been paid. **4** an official mark certifying quality, genuineness, validity, or other condition: (*Figurative.*) *The South wants the stamp of national approval upon slavery* (John Drinkwater). **5** the act of bringing down (the foot) with force: *The horse gave a stamp of his foot.* **6** an instrument that cuts, shapes, or impresses a design, characters, or words on paper, wax, or metal; thing that puts a mark on: *The stamp had her name on it.* **7** the mark, impression, or imprint made with such an instrument. **8** *Figurative.* a distinguishing or distinctive mark; impression; imprint: *Her face bore the stamp of suffering. Man, with all his noble qualities ... still bears in his bodily frame the indelible stamp of his lowly origin* (Charles Darwin). **9** *Figurative.* character; kind; type; make; cast: *Men of his stamp are rare.* **10a** a mill or machine that crushes rock, or the like. **b** a heavy metal pestle for crushing ores; one of the pestles of a stamp mill.
— *v.t.* **1** to put postage on: *to stamp a letter.* **2** to make a mark on; impress with an official stamp or mark: *to stamp a deed. He stamped the papers with the date.* **3** to bring down (one's foot) with force on the ground, a floor, or the like: *He stamped his foot in anger.* **4** to strike or beat (something) by bringing down one's foot forcibly: *to stamp the floor in fury.* **5** to pound, crush, trample, drive, or otherwise affect by stamping: *to stamp the snow from one's boots.* **6** *Figurative.* to fix firmly or deeply; imprint; impress: *an event stamped on one's memory. Her words were stamped on my mind.* **7** to mark (paper, fabric, leather, wax, metal, or other material) with an instrument that cuts, shapes, or impresses a design, characters, or words. **8** to impress, mark, or cut out (a design, characters, or words) on something, as to indicate genuineness, quality,

inspection, ownership, or the like. **9** *Figurative.* to show to be of a certain quality or character; indicate; characterize: *His speech stamps him as an educated man.*

**—*v.i.*** **1** to bring down the foot forcibly, as in crushing or beating down something, for emphasis, or to express anger: *He stamped on the spider.* **2** to walk with a heavy, pounding tread: *The children stamped up the stairs.*

**stamp out, a** to put out or extinguish by trampling or stamping: *Stamp out the fire.* **b** to put an end to or suppress by force or vigorous measures: *to stamp out a rebellion.*

[Middle English *stampen* stamp with the foot, pound in a mortar, partly unrecorded Old English *stampian,* partly < Old French *estamper* < Germanic (compare Old Frisian *stâmpa* club, cudgel)] **—stamp′less,** *adj.*

**stamp|age** (stam′pij), *n.* **1** the act of stamping. **2** an impression made by stamping. **3** the amount charged or paid for stamps; postage.

**stamp album,** a blank book or album used by collectors for the classification and display of postage stamps.

**stamp book,** a book in which to collect stamps, such as trading stamps: *The 60-year-old ... concern has ... 450 stores where housewives can trade their stamp books for premiums* (Wall Street Journal).

**stamp collecting,** = philately.

**stamp collector,** = philatelist.

**stamp duty,** *Especially British.* stamp tax.

**stamped** (stampt), *adj.* **1** crushed by stamping. **2** beaten down with the feet. **3** impressed with a design, characters, or words. **4** ornamented with an embossed device or design; cut out or shaped by stamping. **5** impressed with an official mark or device showing that a duty or charge has been paid. **6** bearing an adhesive paper stamp, such as a revenue stamp or a postage stamp. **7** impressed on something by means of a stamp, as a device.

**stam|pede** (stam pēd′), *n., v.,* **-ped|ed, -ped|ing.** **—*n.*** **1** a sudden scattering, confused rush, or headlong flight of a frightened herd, as of cattle or horses: *The cowboys could not control the stampede.* **2** *Figurative.* any headlong flight of a large group: *the panic-stricken stampede of the audience from a burning theater.* **3** *Figurative.* a general rush: *a stampede to newly discovered gold fields. Steel demand is assuming the proportions of a mild stampede* (Wall Street Journal). **4** *U.S.* a sudden, apparently unconcerted rush of the delegates at a political convention to support a particular candidate. **5** a rodeo; rodeo-like entertainment: *How did you like the Calgary Stampede?* (Maclean's).

**—*v.i.*** **1** to scatter or flee in a stampede: *Cattle sometimes stampede in a thunderstorm.* **2** *Figurative.* to make a general rush.

**—*v.t.*** to cause to stampede: *Thunder stampeded the cattle.* (*Figurative.*) *We should not allow ourselves to be stampeded by undue fears into exaggerated positions* (Atlantic).

[American English < Mexican Spanish *estampida* (in Spanish, an uproar) < Spanish *estampar* to stamp, press, ultimately < a Germanic word. Compare etym. under **stamp.**] **—stam|ped′er,** *n.*

**stamp|er** (stam′pər), *n.* **1** a person who uses a stamp or operates a stamping machine: *a metal stamper, a die stamper.* **2** a person who applies the postmark and cancels the postage stamps in a post office. **3** an instrument or machine used in stamping. **4** the final hard metal copy used to make a finished phonograph record. **5** pestle. **stampers,** the pestle or each of several pestles in a crushing apparatus, especially in a stamping mill: *It is beat by iron-headed stampers upon an iron bed* (John Smeaton).

**stamp|ing** (stam′ping), *n.* a part or thing made with a stamper or stamping machine.

**stamping ground,** *U.S.* a person's or animal's habitual place of resort: *He is back on his old stamping ground doing the thing he loves best* (Time).

**stamping mill,** an apparatus used to crush ores by means of a pestle (stamp) or series of pestles operated by machinery.

**stamp machine,** a machine from which to obtain postage stamps by dropping in a coin.

**stamp mill,** = stamping mill.

**stamp tax,** *U.S.* any tax or duty paid to the government through the purchase of the official stamps that must be affixed to certain products and documents; stamp duty.

**stamp weed,** = Indian mallow (formerly used to stamp designs on butter).

**stance** (stans), *n.* **1** the position of the feet of a player when making a swing or a stroke in golf or other games: *He has changed his stance a bit and I think it has helped* (New York Times). **2** manner of standing; posture: *an erect stance.* **3** *Figurative: to adopt the stance of the Tammany politician to whom nothing matters but victory* (Saturday Review). **SYN:** attitude, point of view. **4** *Scottish.* **a** a standing place, station, or position. **b** a site. [< Old French *estance,* ultimately < Latin *stāre* to stand. See etym. of doublet **stanza.**]

**stanch**[1] (stônch, stänch, stanch), *v.t.* **1** to stop or check the flow of (blood or other fluid). **2** to stop or check the flow of blood from (a wound). **3** *Obsolete.* to satisfy (thirst or hunger). **4** *Obsolete.* to put an end to (strife, rebellion, or other commotion); quell. **—*v.i.*** to cease flowing. Also, **staunch.** [< Old French *estanchier* stop, hinder, perhaps ultimately < Vulgar Latin *tancare* to fix, hold < unrecorded Celtic *tanko* I join] **—stanch′er,** *n.* **—stanch′less,** *adj.*

**stanch**[2] (stônch, stänch, stanch), *adj.* = staunch[2]. **—stanch′ly,** *adv.* **—stanch′ness,** *n.*

**stan|chion** (stan′shən), *n., v.* **—*n.*** **1** an upright bar, post, or pillar used as a support, as for a window, a roof, or the deck of a ship. **2** a framework of two vertical bars which fasten loosely around the neck of a cow to hold her in place while in a stall.

**—*v.t.*** **1** to fasten (cattle) by stanchions. **2** to strengthen or support with stanchions.

[< Old North French *estanchon* < *estance;* see etym. under **stance**]

**stand** (stand), *v.,* **stood, stand|ing,** *n.* **—*v.i.*** **1** to be upright on one's feet: *Don't stand if you are tired, but sit down.* **2** to have a certain height when upright: *She stands five feet tall.* **3** to rise to one's feet: *He stood when she entered the room. The children stood to salute the flag.* **4** to be set upright: *a chair standing in a corner. The box stands over there. Pillars stand on each side of the door.* **5** to be set, placed, or fixed; rest; lie: *Some food stood on the table.* **6** to be situated in a specified position; be located: *The house stood in a forest.* **7** to be at a particular degree: *The thermometer stands at 32°.* **8** *Figurative.* to be in a certain place, rank, position, or scale: *He stands first in his class for service to the school. There are men and classes of men that stand above the common herd* (Robert Louis Stevenson). **9** to take or hold the office, position, or responsibility indicated: *to stand godfather.* **10** to take or keep a certain position or condition: *to stand aside. "Stand back!" called the policeman to the crowd.* **11** to become or remain motionless; stop moving; halt; stop: *The cars stood and waited for the light to change. "Stand!" cried the sentry.* **12** *Figurative.* to remain steadfast, firm, or secure; take a way of thinking or acting: *to stand with those who seek justice.* **13** *Figurative.* to be or remain in a specified condition: *He stands innocent of any wrong. The poor man stood in need of food and clothing. The door stood ajar.* **14** to stay in place; resist destruction or decay; last: *The old house has stood for a hundred years.* **15** to collect and remain: *Tears stood in her eyes. Flood water stands in low-lying fields.* **16** *Figurative.* to be unchanged; hold good; remain the same: *The rule against being late will stand.* **17** to grow erect: *corn standing in the fields.* **18** *Figurative.* to show a (specified) position of the parties concerned: *The score stands in his favor. The account stands square.* **19** to take or remain in a certain course or direction: *The ship stood due north.* **20** *Hunting.* (of a dog) to point. **21** *Obsolete.* (in a negative clause) to hesitate; scruple: *He would not stand at stealing.*

**—*v.t.*** **1** to cause to stand; place or leave standing; set upright or in an indicated position or condition: *to stand a ladder against a wall. Stand the box over there.* **2** to be submitted to (a trial, test, or ordeal); undergo: *to stand a rigid examination.* **3** to bear the brunt of without flinching or retreating; withstand; confront; face: *to stand enemy fire.* **4** *Figurative.* to endure, especially without hurt or damage, or without succumbing or giving way: *This cloth will not stand washing. Those plants cannot stand cold.* **SYN:** See syn. under **bear**[2]. **5** to act as: *to stand guard, stand sentinel.* **6** *Informal, Figurative.* to bear the expense of; pay for: *I'll stand you a dinner.*

**—*n.*** **1** the act of standing: *All we have to ask is whether a man's a Tory, and will make a stand for the good of the country?* (George Eliot). **2** the act of coming to a position of rest; pause; halt; stop: *The hikers made a stand and pitched their tents.* **SYN:** stay. **3** a stop, as of moving troops, for defense or resistance: *We made a last stand against the enemy.* (*Figurative.*) *to make a stand against oppression.* **4** a halt made on a theatrical tour to give a performance or performances: *a one-night stand.* **5** a town where such a halt is made. **6** *Figurative.* a state of arrested progress (as of affairs or natural processes); standstill: *Business was at a stand.* **7** a place where a person stands; position; station: *to take one's stand on the stage. The school crossing guard took her stand at the street corner.* **SYN:** post. **8** *Figurative.* a position or attitude, such as on a moral question, a policy, or a person: *to take a new political stand. The town clergymen took a strong stand against gambling.* **9** Also, **stands.** a raised place where people can sit or stand, especially a structure for spectators, as at a race course, football field, or gymnasium, or for a band or other group of performers: *The mayor sat on the reviewing stand at the parade. The crowd in the stands cheered the winning team.* **10** the place where a witness stands or sits to testify in court. **11** a stall, booth, or table for the display of goods for sale or for business: *a vegetable stand, a newspaper stand.* **12** a position, site, or building for a business. **13** a station for a row of vehicles available for hire: *a stand for taxis.* **14** the row of vehicles occupying such a station. **15** a framework, table, or other thing to put things on or in: *a stand for a microscope. Leave your wet umbrella in the stand in the hall.* **16** a small, light table. **17** a group of growing trees or plants, especially those of a particular species on a given area: *a stand of timber, a stand of cotton. We have a fair stand of oaks that covers the path leading up to the top of our ridge* (Atlantic). **18** *Archaic.* a complete set: *a stand of armor.*

**stand a chance.** See under **chance.**

**stand by, a** to be near; be present: *His son and daughter stood by him at the bar* (Macaulay). **b** *Figurative.* to be faithful or loyal to; side with; help; support; defend: *to stand by a friend.* **c** *Figurative.* to adhere to or abide by (as a statement or agreement); keep; maintain: *to stand by one's promise.* **d** to be or make ready for use or action; be prepared to perform some act (used chiefly in the imperative, as a word of command): *The starboard watch ... left the ship to us for a couple of hours, yet with orders to stand by for a call* (Richard Henry Dana). **e** *Radio.* (1) to be prepared to transmit signals, or messages, but not actually do so: *The radio operator was ordered to stand by.* (2) to remain tuned in to a station until it starts sending messages or for the continuance of a program: *The station asked its listeners to stand by for an announcement.* **f** to be laid aside with disregard: *And now everything stands by for the discussion of Home Rule* (Sketch).

**stand down, a** to step down and leave the witness stand after giving evidence: *I will not trouble the court by asking him any more questions. Stand down, Sir* (Dickens). **b** to withdraw from a contest or competition: *The coach forced the new runner to stand down in favor of the more experienced senior classman.*

**stand easy,** *British Military.* to stand completely at ease: *Soldiers standing easy are permitted to talk.*

**stand for, a** to represent; be in the place of; mean: *What does the abbreviation "St." stand for? The olive branch stands for peace.* **b** *Figurative.* to be on the side of; take the part of; uphold: *to stand for liberty. Our school stands for fair play.* **c** to be a candidate for: *to stand for mayor.* **d** *Informal, Figurative.* to put up with; tolerate: *The teacher said she would not stand for talking during class.* **e** to sail or set the course toward: *They hoisted sail and stood for the nearest island.*

**stand in, a** *Informal.* to be on good terms; have a friendly or profitable understanding: *to stand in well with the police.* **b** to act as a stand-in; take the place of another: *The understudy stood in for the star in one scene.* **c** to cost: *Dinner stood me in a lot of money.*

**stand off, a** *Informal.* to keep off; keep away; evade: *to stand off an angry crowd, to stand off a questioner.* **b** *Figurative.* to hold oneself aloof, as from an offer or appeal or friendship: *He stood off from her plea.* **c** *Nautical.* to sail away from the shore: *We tacked about again and stood off to sea* (John Glanville).

**stand on,** *Nautical.* to keep one's course; remain on the same tack: *The Admiral continued, with a press of sail, standing on close to the wind* (Robert Beatson).

**stand on** (or **upon**), **a** to depend on; be based on: *to stand on the facts. Your future stands on your decision. He does not stand upon ceremony.* **b** *Figurative.* to demand; assert; claim: *to stand on one's rights.*

**stand one's ground.** See under **ground**[1].

**stand on one's own feet.** See under **feet.**

**stand out, a** to project or protrude: *His ears stood out.* **b** to be noticeable or prominent: *Certain facts stand out.* **c** *Figurative.* to refuse to yield; oppose; resist: *to stand out against popular*

---

**Pronunciation Key:** hat, āge, cãre, fär; let, ēqual, tėrm; it, īce; hot, ōpen, ôrder; oil, out; cup, pu̇t, rüle; child; long; thin; ᴛʜen; zh, measure; **ə** represents **a** in about, **e** in taken, **i** in pencil, **o** in lemon, **u** in circus.

*opinion.* **d** to refuse to come in or join others: *The ladies proposed a dance .... The captain himself stood out* (National Observer). **e** *Figurative.* to endure to the end: *to stand out the war.*
**stand over,** to be left or reserved for later treatment, consideration, or settlement: *His accounts are balanced at the close of each season, and no bad debts are allowed to stand over* (Saturday Review).
**stand to, a** to support or uphold, as a cause or interest: *We stood to our fellow student right loyally* (Tait's Magazine). **b** *Figurative.* to apply oneself manfully to (a fight, contest, or task): *The peasants stood to it like men* (Sir Arthur Conan Doyle). **c** to be or make ready; stand by: *The platoon stood to for battle.*
**stand up, a** to get to one's feet; rise: *He stood up and began to speak.* **b** *Figurative.* to endure; last: *The smaller boy, ... though still standing up pluckily, was getting decidedly the worst of it* (A. E. Houghton). **c** *Informal.* to break a date with; fail to meet: *To keep the date, Sheridan has to stand up Shelley, the pretty librarian* (Newsweek).
**stand up and be counted,** to take a public stand (on a controversial issue) as an individual; state one's own position openly and fearlessly: *One can understand the desire of Americans who oppose their government's Vietnam policy to stand up and be counted* (K. H. Hecht).
**stand up for,** to take the part of; support; defend: *to stand up for a friend.*
**stand up to,** to meet or face boldly: *to stand up to an enemy.*
**stand up with,** *Informal.* to act as best man, bridesmaid, or other sponsor or assistant, to: *I want to tell you ... about the wedding. ... We had no one to stand up with us, as we wished to have a simple service* (Chicago Sunday Tribune).
**take the stand,** to go on the witness stand and give evidence: *The judge called on the witness to take the stand for the cross-examination.*
[Old English *standan*] —**stand′er,** *n.*

**stand|ard** (stan′dərd), *n., adj.* —*n.* **a** anything taken as a basis of comparison; level or degree of excellence considered as a goal or as adequate; model: *Your work is not up to the class standard. They have no general standard of taste, or scale of opinion* (William Hazlitt). **2** a rule, test, or requirement; criterion: *applying his English standards to the examination of the American system* (James Bryce). **3** anything established, familiar, or common: *That book is a standard among campers. Average-sized cars are often called standards. Most of the royalties ... come from the handful of well-known songs such as "Star Dust," known in music circles as "standards"* (New York Times). **4** an authorized weight or measure by which the accuracy of all others is determined. **5** a commodity that is given a fixed value in order to serve in a monetary system as a measure of value for all other commodities, such as a metal (monometallic standard), usually gold (gold standard) or silver (silver standard), or gold and silver, in a fixed relationship (bimetallic standard). **6** the legally prescribed proportion of metal and alloy to be used in coins. **7** the prescribed degree of fineness for gold or silver. **8** *Commerce.* in commercial use) the lowest level or grade of excellence. **9** a grade or class in British elementary schools. **10** a flag, emblem, or symbol: *The dragon was the standard of China.* **11** a military or naval flag of a particular kind, usually longer and more tapering than a banner and broader than a pennon.
**12** the flag of a cavalry unit in the United States and Great Britain. **13** an upright support: *The floor lamp has a long standard.* **14** *Horticulture.* a tree, shrub, or other plant growing on an erect stem of full height, not dwarfed or trained on a wall, trellis, or espalier: *There are bush roses, standards and climbing roses on arches and towers* (New York Times). **15a** *Botany.* a vexillum. **b** one of the three upper petallike segments of an iris. **16** a unit of measure for lumber, equal to 16⅔ cubic feet or 1,980 board feet.
—*adj.* **1a** serving as or conforming to the prescribed weight, measure, or value: *a standard pint or gallon, the standard unit of heat.* **b** of the accepted or normal size, amount, power, or quality: *the standard rate of pay, a standard fit.*
**2** serving as or fitted to serve as a standard of comparison or judgment: *standard pitch, a standard text.* **3** having recognized excellence or authority: *a standard reference book. Dickens and Mark Twain are standard authors.* **4** usual, regular, or established: *an orchestra's standard repertoire, standard equipment for campers, the standard practice or procedure, a standard pronunciation.* **5** characteristic of the speech of cultivated persons and of the language used in writing and in the conduct of public affairs, schools, courts, and churches; socially acceptable: *standard usage, standard spelling.* **6** *Printing.* of the usual height, width, or weight: *standard type.* **7a** of the lowest grade or quality: *Canners use brand names that correspond to their best, or fancy, products; their medium, or extra-standard, grades; and their lowest, or standard, products* (John T. R. Nickerson). **b** being a grade of meat not good, choice, or prime but superior to various commercial meats and cut from cattle not over four years old, with little fat and a mild flavor, but usually lacking juiciness. *Abbr:* std.
[< Old French *estandart* < a Germanic word]
—*Syn. n.* **1 Standard, criterion** mean something used as a means of measuring or judging a person or thing. **Standard** applies to any rule or model generally accepted as a basis of comparison in quality, value, quantity, or social, moral, or intellectual level: *to set high standards for admission to college.* **Criterion** applies to a test or rule by which one may determine the value, excellence, or the like of something already in existence: *Popularity by itself is not a criterion of a good motion picture.*

**Stand|ard** (stan′dərd), *n.* a widely used style of sans-serif printing type.

**standard atmosphere,** a hypothetical atmosphere having an arbitrarily selected set of atmospheric conditions, used as a standard for purposes of comparing the performance of aircraft, resolving problems in ballistics, or designing pressure altimeters.

**stand|ard|bear|er** or **stand|ard-bear|er** (stan′dərd bãr′ər), *n.* **1** an officer or soldier who carries a flag or standard; colorbearer. **2** a person who carries a banner in a procession. **3** *Figurative.* a conspicuous leader, as of a movement, political party, or any cause.

**standard book number,** a group of nine numbers identifying an edition of a book and its publisher, used to facilitate ordering of books.

**stand|ard|bred** (stan′dərd bred′), *adj., n.* —*adj.* **1** (of a horse) bred and trained primarily for harness racing, as a trotter or pacer. **2** bred to the standard of excellence prescribed by some authority.
—*n.* Often, **Standardbred.** a standardbred horse.

**standard candle,** = candle (def. 3c).

**standard cell,** a voltaic cell that is used as a standard of measurement for voltage.

***standard deviation,** *Statistics.* the square root of the mean of the deviations from the arithmetic mean in a frequency distribution; root-mean-square deviation. A distance of one standard deviation on each side of the mean of a normal curve includes 68.27 per cent of the cases in the frequency distribution.

***standard deviation**

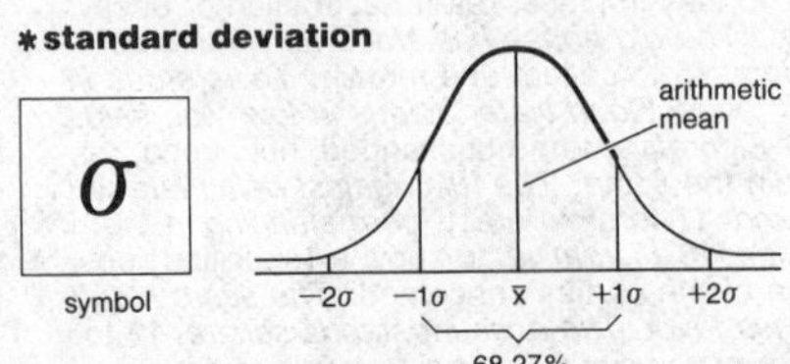


**standard dollar,** the value of a U.S. dollar in gold.

**Standard English,** the English language, both formal and informal, as it is currently spoken and written by educated people: *I do not suppose that there are now any linguists who hold that ... Standard English must fit some logical ... scheme apart from the test of usage* (Paul Roberts).

**standard error,** *Statistics.* the standard deviation of the sample in a frequency distribution.

**standard gauge,** the distance between railroad rails or between the right and left wheels, as of an automobile or wagon. The standard gauge between rails is 56½ inches. See picture at **gauge.**

**stand|ard|ise** (stan′dər dīz), *v.t., v.i.,* **-ised, -is|ing.** *Especially British.* standardize.

**stand|ard|i|za|tion** (stan′dər də zā′shən), *n.* **1** the act or process of standardizing. **2** the fact or state of being standardized.

**stand|ard|ize** (stan′dər dīz), *v.,* **-ized, -iz|ing.** —*v.t.* **1** to make standard in size, shape, weight, quality, or strength: *The parts of an automobile are standardized.* **2** to regulate by a standard. **3** to test by a standard.
—*v.i.* to establish a standard or standards; adopt something as the standard: *The no-pay interval can be 13, 14, or 15 hours depending on the region of the country. "Where do you standardize?" asks an industry official* (Wall Street Journal). —**stand′ard|iz′er,** *n.*

**standard of living,** the way of living that a person or community considers necessary to provide enough material things for comfort, happiness, and well-being: *Even those Americans who can't afford to buy all the gadgets that have become synonymous with the American standard of living still are better off than people anywhere else in the world* (Newsweek).

**standard operating procedure,** = standing operating procedure.

**standard schnauzer,** the breed of schnauzer intermediate between the giant and miniature breeds, being from 18 to 20 inches high.

**standard score,** the score of an individual in a psychological, educational, or other test that shows a deviation from the average score of the group, expressed in units of the standard deviation of the distribution.

**standard star,** a star whose position and proper motion are particularly well known, used in determining the positions of other stars, instrumental constants, time, and latitude.

**standard time,** the time officially adopted as the standard for a region or country. Each meridian 15 degrees east or west of Greenwich, England, marks a time difference of one hour. Noon is usually reckoned in a given region as the time the sun apparently passes the meridian closest to that region.

**stand|a|way** (stand′ə wā′), *adj.* made to stand up straight, curled, or in folds away from the rest of the garment or from the body: *A favorite coat has a broad standaway collar, dropped shoulders, and three-quarter sleeves* (New Yorker).

**stand-by** or **stand|by** (stand′bī′), *n., pl.* **-bys,** *adj.* —*n.* **1** a person or thing that can be relied upon; chief support; ready resource: *Verdi's music for this old stand-by never fails* (Wall Street Journal). **2a** a ship, boat, or other vessel kept in readiness for emergencies. **b** an order or signal for a vessel to stand by. **3** a person or thing that stands by to serve as a substitute or replacement: **a** a person waiting to replace an airplane passenger who fails to show up or cancels his trip: *Flight No. 55 out of New York ... was filled. Disappointed stand-bys were left behind* (Atlanta Constitution). **b** a motion-picture stand-in: *He ... was Phil Silver's stand-by in "Do Re Mi"* (New York Times).
—*adj.* in a position of readiness or reserve: *a stand-by loan, stand-by passengers.*
**on stand-by,** waiting in readiness or reserve: *During the emergency, nurses and doctors were on stand-by twenty-four hours a day.*

**stand|ee** (stan dē′), *n. U.S. Informal.* a person who has to stand, as in a theater or on a bus, because he cannot obtain a seat. [American English < *stand* + *-ee*]

**stand|er-by** (stan′dər bī′), *n.* a person who stands near or looks on but does not take part; bystander.

**stand|fast** (stand′fast′, -fäst′), *adj., n.* —*adj.* that holds stubbornly to an opinion, attitude, etc.; stubborn.
—*n.* a fixed or stable position.

**stand-in** (stand′in′), *n.* **1** a person whose work is standing in the place of a motion-picture actor or actress while the lights, camera, or costumes, are being arranged, or during scenes in which dangerous action occurs. **2** *Figurative: Certainly, the New Dealing Advisory Council of the National Democratic Committee has been an inadequate stand-in for a national party leader* (Wall Street Journal). SYN: substitute. **3** *Informal.* a favorable position; good standing. **4** *U.S.* the presence of Negroes in a line of persons waiting to enter a theater or other public accommodation or entertainment, as a protest against racial segregation in a public place.

**stand|ing** (stan′ding), *n., adj.* —*n.* **1a** rank or position in society, a profession or business, religion, or the like; social, professional, or commercial reputation; status: *a person of good standing. What people say behind your back is your standing in the community* (E. W. Howe). **b** *Law.* the right or qualification to institute a lawsuit because of a personal interest or stake in its outcome: *Federal District Judge William B. Jones ruled in Washington that neither group had standing to sue* (New York Times). **2** good or high rank or reputation. **3** length of service, experience, residence, or the like, especially as determining position, wages, or privileges. **4** *Figurative.* length of existence; duration: *a feud of long standing between two families.* **5** the act of one who stands, in any sense. **6** the time at, in, or during which one stands. **7** a place in which to stand; post; station.
—*adj.* **1** straight up; erect; upright: *standing timber.* SYN: perpendicular. **2** done from or in an erect position: *a standing jump. The audience's greeting ... was in the form of a standing ovation* (New York Times). **3** that stands up, upright, or on end: *a standing lamp or collar.* **4** established; permanent: *a standing invitation, a standing joke.* SYN: lasting, enduring. **5** remaining at rest or in a fixed position: **a** not flowing; stagnant: *standing water.* **b** not in operation; at a standstill: *a stand-*

*ing machine.* **c** remaining stationary, especially while another part moves.

**standing army**, **1** the regular army, as a permanently organized military force. **2** an army, or that part of it, which is under arms and ready for immediate action, especially in time of peace, and usually including reservists and conscripts as well as members of the regular army.

**standing broad jump**, a broad jump made from a standing position, without a running start.

**standing committee**, a permanent committee, as of a legislative body or club, selected or elected to deal with all matters in a particular sphere.

**standing high jump**, a high jump made from a standing position without a running start.

**standing operating procedure**, any fixed procedure such as standardized instructions for carrying out a particular task. *Abbr:* SOP (no periods) or S.O.P. Also, **standard operating procedure**.

**standing order**, *Military.* a regulation for operation or procedure mandatory for an entire command, or for specified members of it, and not subject to change by subordinate or temporary commanders.

**standing orders**, the regular rules for procedure in parliamentary bodies, in force from session to session unless specifically rescinded or repealed: *Both houses have agreed, at various times, to standing orders, for the permanent guidance and order of their proceedings* (Thomas Erskine May).

**standing rigging**, the ropes, stays, and other lines supporting the masts and fixed spars.

**standing room**, **1** space to stand in after all the seats are taken; accommodation for a standee or standees: *standing room at the back of a theater.* **2** space to stand in, especially space having sufficient headroom for a person to stand erect in.

**standing wave**, *Physics.* a wave characterized by lack of vibration at certain points, between which areas of maximum vibration occur periodically; stationary wave. Standing waves are produced by the interference of two similar waves traveling at the same time in opposite directions, as in the vibration of a violin string. See diagram under **node**.

**stand|ish** (stan′dish), *n.* a stand containing ink, pens, and other writing materials and accessories; inkstand. [taken by folk etymology to be < *stand,* verb + *dish,* noun]

**stand-off** or **stand|off** (stand′ôf′, -of′), *n., adj.* —*n.* **1** a tie or draw in a game. **2** *Figurative: It is far easier to maintain a stand-off between two superpowers than between three or four* (Bulletin of Atomic Scientists). **3** a standing off or apart; reserve; aloofness.
—*adj.* = stand-offish.
[American English < *stand* + *off*]

**stand-off bomb**, a guided missile fired from an airplane at a ground target several hundred miles away.

**stand-off halfback** or **half**, *Rugby Football.* the halfback who takes a position between the scrum-half and the three-quarter back; outside half.

**stand-off|ish** or **stand|off|ish** (stand′ôf′ish, -of′-), *adj.* reserved; aloof. **SYN**: distant, unapproachable. —**stand′-off′ish|ly, stand′off′ish|ly,** *adv.* —**stand′-off′ish|ness, stand′off′ish|ness,** *n.*

**stand oil**, linseed oil or tung oil made heavy and thick by heating under pressure, used as a medium in paint and varnish.

**stand-out** or **stand|out** (stand′out′), *n., adj. U.S.* —*n.* **1** a person or thing that is outstanding of its kind, especially in excellence: *Kudos ... to the hostess who is ever on the lookout for goodies to make the cookout a stand-out* (New Yorker). **2** *Informal.* a person who refuses to act with the others of a group or accept the desires of the majority.
—*adj. Informal.* outstanding: *He has written a lot of stand-out stories in his time* (Newsweek).

**stand|pat** (stand′pat′), *adj. Informal.* standing firm for things as they are; opposing any change.

**stand|pat|ter** (stand′pat′ər), *n. Informal.* a person who stands firm for things as they are and opposes any change, especially in politics. **SYN**: do-nothing.

**stand|pat|tism** (stand′pat′iz əm), *n. Informal.* the principles or conduct of standpatters; condition of being a standpatter.

**stand|pipe** (stand′pīp′), *n.* a large, upright pipe or tower to hold water at a height great enough to provide pressure for a water system, especially one used as a reservoir or auxiliary to a reservoir.

**stand|point** (stand′point′), *n.* the point at which one stands to view something; point of view; mental attitude: *From his standpoint, combing one's hair is a waste of time. To judge of the total scientific achievement of any age, the standpoint of a succeeding age is desirable* (William Tyndall).

**St. An|drew's cross** (an′drüz), = Saint Andrew's cross.

**stand|still** (stand′stil′), *n., adj.* —*n.* **1** a complete stop; halt; pause: *All activity about the place had come to a standstill at noontime.* **SYN**: cessation, deadlock. **2** a state of being unable to proceed, owing to exhaustion: *[Robert E.] Lee could not extricate himself and his supply trains without fighting Meade's army to a standstill* (Sir Winston Churchill).
—*adj.* **1** that is at a standstill: *The old standstill Mexico of mañana and the travel posters is scrambling toward prosperity* (Time). **2** of the nature of a standstill. **3** causing a standstill: *The standstill strike forced industry to negotiate a work contract.*

**stand-up** (stand′up′), *adj.* **1** that stands erect; upright: *a stand-up collar.* **2** performed or taken while standing: *a stand-up dinner.* **3** designed and built for standing upright: *a stand-up lunch counter. The new plane is designed for full comfort, with a roomy stand-up cabin.* **4** performing alone before an audience: *a stand-up comedian.* **5** standing up fairly to each other without flinching or evasion: *They wouldn't let us make a stand-up fight of it* (George Bernard Shaw). *A gray fox, casting vulpine caution to the winds, fought a stand-up battle with a dog its own size* (New York Times).

**stane** (stān), *n., adj., v.t.,* **staned, stan|ing.** *Scottish.* stone.

**Stan|ford-Bi|net test** (stan′fərd bə nā′), an adaptation of the Binet-Simon intelligence test to American problems and situations. [< *Stanford* University, in California, where the revisions were made]

**stang**[1] (stang), *v. Archaic.* a past tense of **sting.**

**stang**[2] (stang), *n. British and Scottish Dialect.* a pole, bar, or rail.

**ride the stang**, to be carried about in public mounted astride on a pole, in an old popular mode of punishment, as for wife beating, the culprit being sometimes represented by an effigy or a proxy: *In some Scottish and northern English villages, one who is found working on New Year's Day has to ride the stang or pay a forfeit.* [< Scandinavian (compare Old Icelandic *stöng*). Compare Old English *steng* pole.]

**stang**[3] (stang), *v.t., v.i., n. Especially Scottish.* sting. [< Scandinavian (compare Old Icelandic *stanga* to jab, goad)]

**stan|hope** (stan′hōp, -əp), *n.* a light, open carriage having one seat and two or four wheels. [< Fitzroy *Stanhope,* 1787-1864, a British clergyman, for whom it was first made]

**stan|iel** (stan′yəl), *n.* = kestrel. [Old English *stāngella* < *stān* stone + *gellan* yell]

**Stan|i|slav|sky** or **Stan|i|slav|ski method** (stan′i släf′skē), a system of acting developed and taught by Konstantin Stanislavsky (or Stanislavski, 1863-1938), a Russian actor and director, that stresses the importance of realism in acting and feeling and living the part one is playing; the Method.

**stank**[1] (stangk), *v.* a past tense of **stink**: *The dead fish stank.*

**stank**[2] (stangk), *n. British Dialect and Scottish.* **1** a pond or pool. **2** a ditch of slowly moving water; moat. **3** a dam or weir. [< Old French *estanc,* ultimately < Latin *stāgnum* standing water]

**Stan|ley** (stan′lē), *n., pl.* **-leys.** = Stanley Steamer.

**Stanley Cup**, the trophy awarded annually to the champion of the National Hockey League in the United States and Canada. [< Sir Frederick A. *Stanley,* 1841-1908, a British statesman, governor general of Canada from 1888 to 1893]

* **Stanley Steamer**, an early make and type of automobile that ran on steam power, built by Francis and Freelan Stanley, American inventors of the 1800's.

***Stanley Steamer**

**stan|na|ry** (stan′ər ē), *n., pl.* **-ries. 1** a region or district where tin is mined. **2** *British.* a tin mine. [< Medieval Latin *stannaria* < Late Latin *stannum* tin; see etym. under **stannum**]

**stan|nate** (stan′āt), *n.* a salt of stannic acid. [< *stann*(ic) + *-ate*[2]]

**stan|nic** (stan′ik), *adj.* **1** of or having to do with tin. **2** containing tin, especially with a valence of four. [< Late Latin *stannum* tin + English *-ic*]

**stannic acid**, any one of several white or colorless acids of tin, used in making stannates.

**stannic chloride**, a colorless, caustic liquid made from tin and chlorine, used as a dye and color brightener, for coating objects, and as a bleaching agent. *Formula:* $SnCl_4$

**stannic oxide**, a white powder found in nature as cassiterite and produced synthetically, used to glaze and color ceramics and glass, to polish glass and metal, and in making cosmetics. *Formula:* $SnO_2$

**stannic sulfide**, = mosaic gold.

**stan|nite** (stan′īt), *n.* a mineral, a sulfide of tin, copper, and iron; tin pyrites. It is a brittle, steel-gray or iron-black mineral with a metallic luster. *Formula:* $Cu_2FeSnS_4$ [< Late Latin *stannum* tin + English *-ite*[1]]

**stan|nous** (stan′əs), *adj.* **1** of or having to do with tin. **2** containing tin, especially with a valence of two.

**stannous chloride**, a crystalline compound made by dissolving tin with hydrochloric acid, used to galvanize tin, remove ink stains, silver mirrors, and as a reducing agent for various chemicals. *Formula:* $SnCl_2$

**stannous fluoride**, a fluoride of tin, added to toothpaste or applied topically to prevent tooth decay. *Formula:* $SnF_2$

**stan|num** (stan′əm), *n.* tin. *Symbol:* Sn (no period). [< New Latin *stannum* < Late Latin, tin; earlier, an alloy of silver and lead, variant of Latin *stagnum*]

**St. An|tho|ny's fire** (an′thə nēz, -tə-), **1** any one of various inflammations of the skin, such as erysipelas. **2** = ergotism (def. 2). Also, **Saint Anthony's fire.**

**stan|za** (stan′zə), *n.* **1** a group of lines of poetry, usually four or more, arranged according to a fixed plan; verse of a poem. This plan may regulate the number of lines, the meter, the pattern of rhymes, or the words or thoughts: *They sang the first and last stanzas of "America." Abbr:* st. **2** *Sports.* any period of time in, or division of, a game, such as an inning in baseball or a quarter in football. [< Italian *stanza* (originally) a stopping place, ultimately < Latin *stāre* to stand. See etym. of doublet **stance.**]

**-stanzaed**, *combining form.* having ____ stanzas: *Two-stanzaed = having two stanzas.*

**stan|za|ic** (stan zā′ik), *adj.* **1** of or having to do with a stanza. **2** forming a stanza. **3** composed of stanzas. —**stan|za′i|cal|ly,** *adv.*

**sta|pe|dec|to|my** (stā′pə dek′tə mē), *n., pl.* **-mies.** the surgical repair or replacement of the stapes. [< New Latin *stapes, -edis* stapes + English *-ectomy*]

**sta|pe|di|al** (stə pē′dē əl), *adj.* of or having to do with the stapes.

**sta|pe|li|a** (stə pē′lē ə), *n.* any one of a group of African plants of the milkweed family, with fleshy, leafless stems and oddly mottled flowers with a fetid odor. [< New Latin *Stapelia* the genus name < Jan Bode van *Stapel,* died 1636, a Dutch botanist]

**sta|pes** (stā′pēz), *n., pl.* **sta|pes, sta|pe|des** (stā′pə dēz). the innermost of the three small bones of the tympanum or middle ear of mammals (the other two being the incus and the malleus); stirrup bone. See picture under **ear**[1]. [< New Latin *stapes* < Medieval Latin, stirrup]

**staph** (staf), *n. Informal.* staphylococcus or staphylococci: *Staph are among the most common germs ever to bother man* (Wall Street Journal).

**staph|y|lin|id** (staf′ə lin′id), *adj., n.* —*adj.* of or belonging to the family of insects comprising the rove beetles: *Certain staphylinid beetles secrete "appeasement substances" to ward off attacking worker ants* (New Scientist).
—*n.* a staphylinid beetle; rove beetle.
[< New Latin *Staphylinidae* the family name < Greek *staphylē* bunch of grapes]

**staph|y|lo|coc|cal** (staf′ə lə kok′əl), *adj.* **1** having to do with staphylococcus. **2** produced by staphylococcus: *staphylococcal infections.*

**staph|y|lo|coc|cic** (staf′ə lə kok′sik), *adj.* = staphylococcal.

**staph|y|lo|coc|cus** (staf′ə lə kok′əs), *n., pl.* **-coc|ci** (-kok′sī). any one of a group of spherical parasitic bacteria that usually bunch together in irregular masses, such as the micrococcus which causes the formation of pus. Several species are

**Pronunciation Key:** hat, āge, cãre, fär; let, ēqual, tėrm; it, īce; hot, ōpen, ôrder; oil, out; cup, půt, rüle; child; long; thin; ᴛʜen; zh, measure; ə represents **a** in about, **e** in taken, **i** in pencil, **o** in lemon, **u** in circus.

capable of causing serious infections in human beings and other organisms. *The penicillin-resistant staphylococci protect themselves by producing an enzyme, penicillinase, which destroys penicillin* (New Scientist). [< New Latin *Staphylococcus* the genus name < Greek *staphylê* bunch of grapes + New Latin *coccus* coccus (because of the shape they assume)]

**sta|ple[1]** (stā′pəl), *n., v.,* **-pled, -pling.** —*n.* **1** a piece of metal with pointed ends bent into a U shape. Staples are driven into wood to hold a hook, pin, or bolt. **2** a bent piece of wire used to hold together papers or parts of a book.
—*v.t.* to fasten or secure with a staple or staples: *to staple together the pages of a report.*
[Old English *stapol* post]

**sta|ple[2]** (stā′pəl), *n., adj., v.,* **-pled, -pling.** —*n.* **1** the most important or principal article regularly grown or manufactured in a place: *Cotton is the staple in many southern states.* **2** any major article of commerce or trade; something of recognized quality or in constant demand. **3** *Figurative.* the chief element, ingredient, material, or constituent of anything; chief item: *Politics is often a staple of conversation.* **4** the material of which anything is made; raw material. **5** a fiber of cotton or wool considered with regard to its length and fineness. **6** a particular length and degree of fineness in fiber, as of cotton or wool. **7** = staple fiber. **8** (formerly) a town or place in which a body of merchants was granted by royal authority the exclusive right to buy certain goods for export: *He had borrowed a great sum of money of the merchants of the staple* (Holinshed's "Chronicles"). **9** *Archaic.* the principal market of a place; chief center of trade.
—*adj.* **1** most important; chief; principal: *Bread is a staple food. The weather was their staple topic of conversation.* **2** established and important in commerce; leading: *a staple trade or industry.* **3** regularly produced in large quantities for the market; foremost among the exports of a country or place: *Corn is a staple commodity of Iowa.*
—*v.t.* to sort according to fiber: *to staple wool.*
[< Anglo-French, Old French *estaple* mart < Germanic (compare Dutch *stapel* pile, heap)]

**-stapled,** *combining form.* having a ____ staple: *Long-stapled wool = wool that has a long staple.*

**staple fiber,** the short fiber lengths of rayon, acetate, or the like that are spun into yarn: *Staple fibers are those used to spin yarns, as distinguished from filament, or continuous, yarns already suitable for weaving into cloth* (Wall Street Journal).

**sta|ple|punc|ture** (stā′pəl pungk′chər), *n.* the insertion of tiny wire staples into the external ear as a form of acupuncture supposed to reduce the appetite or eliminate drug-withdrawal symptoms: *Staplepuncture ... is based on the theory —so far unconfirmed—that there are "obesity nerve endings" in the ear* (Time). [< *staple*[1] + (acu)*puncture*]

**sta|pler[1]** (stā′plər), *n.* a machine for fastening things together with wire staples, such as several sheets of paper, parts of a book, screening or upholstery to a frame, or sheets of insulation to rafters.

**sta|pler[2]** (stā′plər), *n.* a person who sorts and grades fibers, as of wool or cotton.

**stapp** (stap), *n.* a unit of measure used in aviation medicine, equal to the force exerted by one G acting on the body for one second. [< John P. *Stapp,* born 1911, a U.S. Air Force medical officer, who did research on rocket sled acceleration and deceleration]

**star** (stär), *n., v.,* **starred, star|ring,** *adj.* —*n.* **1** any one of the heavenly bodies appearing as bright points in the sky at night: *There were so many clouds we could not see many stars last night.* **2** any heavenly body that is not a planet, moon, comet, meteor, or nebula. Stars are hot, luminous, gaseous bodies varying in size from those slightly larger than the earth to those several million times as large as the sun. The majority of stars, including the sun, fall into one pattern (the main sequence) when plotted on a graph according to luminosity and type of spectrum. **3** any heavenly body. **4** *Astrology.* a planet or constellation of the zodiac, considered as influencing people and events. **5** one's fortune, rank, destiny, or temperament, viewed as determined by the stars; fate: *The fault, dear Brutus, is not in our stars, But in ourselves, that we are underlings* (Shakespeare). **6** a figure having usually five points, sometimes six, taken to represent a star of the sky. **7** something having or suggesting this shape. **8** = asterisk. **9** *U.S.* a representation of a star symbolizing one of the states in the Union. **10** *U.S.* any one of the military medals or awards having a star-shaped design. **11** *Figurative.* **a** a person having brilliant qualities or talents in some art, science, or other field: *an athletic star.* **b** an actor, singer, or other entertainer who is exceptionally well known or prominently advertised, or who has the leading part in a particular production; lead: *an opera star, the star of the new musical. All stars have one characteristic in common ... some magnetic quality which sets them apart on the screen from all other actors* (New York Times). **12** *Physics.* a star-shaped pattern of lines radiating outward from the nucleus of an atom that is exploded by high-energy particles, as seen in a photograph of this effect produced in a cloud chamber. **13** any one of a class of racing sailboats that are about 23 feet in length and have large sails, Marconi rigs, and fin keels.
—*v.t.* **1** to set, adorn, or ornament with stars; bespangle: *Her cards were starred for perfect attendance.* **2** to mark with an asterisk. **3** to single out for special notice or recommendation. **4** to give a leading part to (an actor or actress); present to the public as a star. —*v.i.* **1** to be a leading performer; perform the leading part: *She has starred in many motion pictures.* **2** to shine above others; be brilliant or outstanding; excel.
—*adj.* brilliant or outstanding; chief; excellent; best; leading: *the star player on a football team.*
**see stars,** to see flashes of light as a result of a hard blow on one's head: *Quicker than thought, in comes his right, and if you only see stars you are pretty lucky* (John D. Astley).
**thank one's (lucky) stars,** to be thankful for one's good luck: *You may thank your stars, my lad, that I followed Master Barns tonight* (Joseph Hatton).
**with stars in one's eyes,** full of idealism or optimism; starry-eyed: *The depressing thing to one whose entire ancestry, immediate and remote, is British, and who came to England with stars in his eyes, is the bleakness of the future* (Atlantic).
[Old English *steorra*]

**star anise,** **1** a shrub or small tree of the magnolia family, native to Asia, having purplish-red flowers and fruits of anise scent. **2** a spice obtained from the fruit.

**star apple,** **1** the apple-shaped, edible fruit of a tropical American evergreen tree of the sapodilla family, whose carpels present a star-shaped figure when cut across. **2** the tree itself.

**star|board** (stär′bərd, -bôrd, -bōrd), *n., adj., adv., v.* —*n.* the right side of a boat or ship when facing forward.
—*adj.* on, at, or of the right side of a boat or ship.
—*adv.* to or toward the right side of a boat or ship.
—*v.t., v.i.* to turn or move (the helm) to or in the direction of the right side of a boat or ship.
[Old English *stēorbord* side on which a vessel was steered. Compare etym. under **steer**[1], **board.**]

**star|burst** (stär′bėrst′), *n., adj.* —*n.* **1** something shaped like the bursting forth of a star's rays; a star-shaped figure or design: *... a flamboyant 55-ft. neon trademark with a starburst on top* (Sunday Times). **2** = star shell.
—*adj.* having the shape or appearance of a starburst: *starburst chandeliers, a starburst clock.*

**starch** (stärch), *n., v.* —*n.* **1** a white, odorless, tasteless food substance. It is chemically a complex carbohydrate, found in all parts of a plant which store plant food. It is an important ingredient in the diet, reacting with certain enzymes to form dextrose, maltose, and other sugars, and is widely used commercially. Potatoes, wheat, rice, and corn contain much starch. *Formula:* $(C_6H_{10}O_5)_n$ **2** a preparation of this substance used to stiffen clothes, curtains, and other cloth, to give a finish to certain textiles, and to size paper. **3** *Figurative.* a stiff, formal manner; stiffness. **4** *Informal.* vigor; energy; zest.
—*v.t.* to stiffen with starch; apply starch to: *Starch the curtains.*
**starches,** foods containing much starch: *to lose weight by avoiding starches.*
**starch up,** *Obsolete.* to make formal or rigid: *She starched up her behaviour with a double portion of reserve* (Tobias Smollett).
**take the starch out of,** *Informal.* to cause to lose courage, confidence, or determination: *This apparently took the starch out of the fast-crumpling opposition* (New York Times).
[Old English unrecorded *stercan* (in *stercedferhth* stouthearted) < *stearc* stiff, strong. Compare etym. under **stark.**] —**starch′like′,** *adj.*

**Star Chamber,** a court that existed in England from 1487 until 1641, enabled to proceed and act without regard for the common law, in secret session, without a jury, and in which confessions were often obtained by torture. [Middle English *sterred chambre,* translation of Medieval Latin (England) *camera stellata* a room in Westminster Palace where the king's council first met (probably so called from a decoration of stars on its ceiling).]

**star chamber,** any court, committee, or group like the Star Chamber in its procedures.

**star-cham|ber** (stär′chām′bər), *adj.* **1** of or having to do with a star chamber. **2** characteristic of a star chamber, especially in holding secret sessions: *His constitutional rights were violated by "star-chamber" proceedings in which he was not allowed to confront or cross-examine his accusers* (New York Times).

**star chart,** a chart which shows the stars in a certain portion of the sky.

**starched** (stärcht), *adj.* **1** stiffened with starch: *a starched collar.* **2** *Figurative.* stiff; rigidly formal: *throwing aside all the starched reserve of her ordinary manner* (Hawthorne).

**starch|er** (stär′chər), *n.* **1** a person who starches. **2** a machine for starching.

**starch|ness** (stärch′nis), *n.* stiffness of manner; preciseness.

**starch syrup,** = glucose (def. 2).

**starch|y** (stär′chē), *adj.,* **starch|i|er, starch|i|est.** **1** like starch. **2** composed of starch. **3** containing starch. **4** stiffened with starch. **5** *Figurative.* stiff in manner; formal: *Sir William Haley, the starchy editor of The Times, has donned his black cap and passed his savage sentence* (Newsweek). SYN: prim. —**starch′i|ly,** *adv.* —**starch′i|ness,** *n.*

**star cloud,** a group of stars that look like a bright, hazy area when seen without a telescope.

**star cluster,** a group of stars that are relatively close together, classified as either galactic or globular clusters.

**star-con|nect|ed** (stär′kə nek′tid), *adj.* having a star connection.

**star connection,** an arrangement in a polyphase system, as in a transformer, by which the coils or circuits have a common junction while the free ends are connected with the terminals of the line wires.

**star coral,** any one of various stony corals with radiating septa that give the cuplike depression of the skeleton a starlike appearance.

**star|craft** (stär′kraft′, -kräft′), *n.* knowledge of the stars; astrology.

**star-crossed** (stär′krôst′, -krost′), *adj.* born under an evil star; ill-fated: *So the star-crossed lovers and the perplexed older people moved step by step into tragedy* (New York Times).

**star|dom** (stär′dəm), *n.* **1** the fact of being a star actor or performer. **2** star actors or performers as a group.

**star drift,** *Astronomy.* a gradual movement of groups of stars in one direction; motion common to a group of stars.

**star dust,** or **star|dust** (stär′dust′), *n.* **1** masses of stars that look so small as to suggest particles of dust. **2** particles from meteors falling from space to earth. **3** *Informal, Figurative.* glamour; happy enchantment.

**stare** (stãr), *v.,* **stared, star|ing,** *n.* —*v.i.* **1** to look long and directly with the eyes wide open; gaze fixedly. A person stares in wonder, surprise, stupidity, curiosity, or from mere rudeness. *The little girl stared in wonder at the doll in the window.* SYN: gape. See syn. under **gaze.** **2** to be very striking or glaring: *His eyes stared with anger.* **3** to stand on end (now chiefly of hair, feathers, or fibers). —*v.t.* to bring to a (specified) condition by staring: *to stare a person into silence.*
—*n.* a long and direct look with the eyes wide open: *The doll's eyes were set in an unchanging stare. A stony British stare* (Tennyson).
**stare down,** to confuse or embarrass by staring; abash: *The Colombian government and foreign groups complete formalities for the resumption of aid after almost a year of trying to stare each other down* (New York Times).
**stare up and down,** to gaze at or survey from head to foot: *They are staring me up and down like a wild animal* (Henry Seton Merriman).
[Old English *starian*]

**sta|re de|ci|sis** (stãr′ē di sī′sis), *Latin.* **1** to abide by things decided. **2** the legal principle that precedents are, or define law.

**star|er** (stãr′ər), *n.* a person who stares.

**sta|rets** or **sta|retz** (stä′rets), *n.* a saintly religious teacher or holy man in Russia: *Unbounded faith in the powers of his staretz may well have helped to halt the Tsarevitsch's haemophilia* (Sunday Times). [< Russian *starets*]

**star facet,** one of the eight small triangular facets sloping down from the flat top of a gem cut as a brilliant.

**star field,** the stars in a portion of the sky seen through a telescope.

**star finder,** a map or chart of the stars used in celestial navigation.

* **star|fish** (stär′fish′), *n., pl.* **-fish|es** or (*collectively*) **-fish.** any one of a group of star-shaped sea animals with flattened bodies; asteroid. Starfish consist of five or more arms or rays radiating from a central disk, with a mouth under this disk and rows of tubular walking feet. The rays are sometimes very short or altogether absent. Star-

fish are not fish. They belong to a group of animals called echinoderms. Starfish feed on organic matter; some are carnivorous and do great damage to oyster beds.

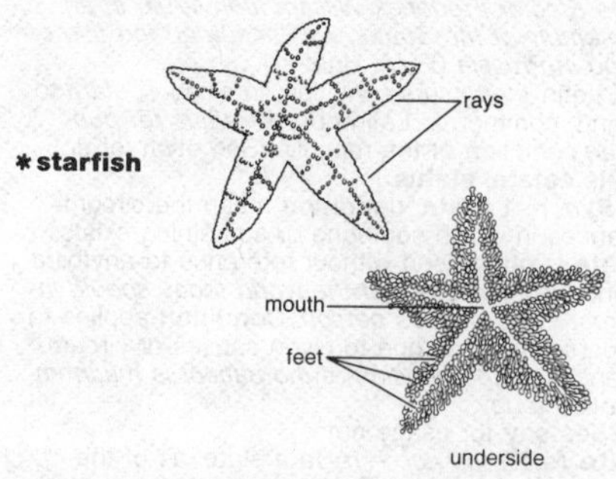


***starfish**

**star|flow|er** (stär′flou′ər), *n.* any one of various star-shaped flowers or the plants bearing them, especially: **a** = star-of-Bethlehem. **b** any one of a group of low, white-flowered plants of the primrose family.

**star|gaze** (stär′gāz′), *v.i.,* **-gazed, -gaz|ing. 1** to gaze at the stars; study the heavens. **2** *Figurative.* to be absent-minded; daydream.

**star|gaz|er** (stär′gā′zər), *n.* **1** a person who studies the heavens, such as an astronomer or astrologer. **2** *Figurative.* a person given to daydreaming. **3** any one of a family of spiny-finned marine fishes having both eyes on the top of the head.

**star|gaz|ing** (stär′gā′zing), *n., adj.* — *n.* **1** attentive observation and study of the stars; astronomy or astrology. **2** *Figurative.* daydreaming.
— *adj.* **1** given to the observation and study of the stars. **2** *Figurative.* given to daydreaming; absent-minded.

**star grass,** any one of several grasslike plants with star-shaped flowers or a starlike arrangement of leaves, especially: **a** any one of a group of herbs of the amaryllis family. **b** = colicroot.

**star|ing** (stãr′ing), *adj.* **1** very conspicuous; too bright; that cannot be overlooked; glaring: *a staring blunder. ... printed in great black letters on a staring broad sheet* (Dickens). **2** gazing with a stare; wide-open. — **star′ing|ly,** *adv.*

**stark** (stärk), *adj., adv.* — *adj.* **1** downright; complete; sheer; absolute: *That fool is talking stark nonsense. She moved with the stark simplicity of a Martha Graham dancer* (Newsweek). **SYN:** utter. **2** stiff, especially from rigor mortis; rigid: *The dog lay stark in death.* **3** bare; barren; desolate: *a stark landscape.* **4** *Dialect.* (of climate or weather) harsh; inclement. **5** *Archaic.* (of persons) stern; severe: *He is ... stark as death To those that cross him* (Tennyson). **6** *Archaic.* strong; sturdy.
— *adv.* **1** to the fullest extent or degree; entirely; completely; absolutely; utterly: *stark, raving mad. The boys went swimming stark naked.* **SYN:** wholly. **2** in a stark manner.
[Old English *stearc* stiff, strong] — **stark′ly,** *adv.* — **stark′ness,** *n.*

**Stark effect** (stärk), *Physics.* the splitting of spectral lines when an emitting atom is under the influence of a strong electric field: *The Stark effect ... was detected in simple atomic gases in 1913 by Johannes Stark, awarded the Nobel Prize for this work in 1919* (Science News). [< Johannes *Stark,* 1874-1957, a German physicist, who discovered it]

**stark|ers** (stär′kərz), *adj. British Slang.* stark naked. [< *stark* + *-ers,* as in *bonkers*]

**star|less** (stär′lis), *adj.* without stars or starlight; having no stars visible: *a cloudy, starless night.*

**star|let** (stär′lit), *n.* **1** a young actress or singer who is being trained and publicized for leading roles in motion pictures: *Some remote Hollywood starlet's marriage was on the rocks* (J. D. Salinger). **2** a little star.

**star|light** (stär′līt′), *n., adj.* — *n.* light from the stars: *By starlight and by candlelight ... She comes to me* (Herbert Trench).
— *adj.* **1** lighted by the stars; starlit. **2** done by starlight.

**star|light|ed** or **star-light|ed** (stär′lī′tid), *adj.* = starlit.

**starlight scope,** a device for spotting rifle targets at night, similar to the sniperscope, but using nocturnal light from the sky to light up targets by means of a network of glass fibers, sensitized film, and electrons: *Unlike the older infrared sniperscope, the compact starlight scope sends out no radiation of its own and hence cannot be detected by the enemy* (New York Times).

**star|like** (stär′līk′), *adj.* **1** shaped like a star: *a pattern of starlike snowflakes.* **SYN:** stellate. **2** shining like a star. **SYN:** sparkling.

**star lily,** = sand lily.

**star|ling¹** (stär′ling), *n.* **1** a common European and American perching bird with a short tail and glossy greenish-black or brownish-black feathers that are speckled with buff in the winter. Starlings often nest about buildings and fly in large flocks. **2** any one of certain North American blackbirds, such as the redwing. [Old English *stærling* < *stær* starling]

**star|ling²** (stär′ling), *n.* a projecting outwork of piles to protect a pier of a bridge.

**star|lit** (stär′lit′), *adj.* lighted by the stars: *a starlit night. There, by the starlit fences, The wanderer halts* (A. E. Housman).

**star|lite** (stär′līt′), *n.* a variety of zircon which, on special treatment with heat, becomes a brilliant blue gem.

**star map,** a map or chart of part or all of the heavens, showing the fixed stars as they appear from the earth and usually indicating their magnitudes.

**star|nose** (stär′nōz′), *n.* = star-nosed mole.

**star-nosed mole** (stär′nōzd′), a mole of eastern North America that has a star-shaped circle of small, fleshy processes at the end of its nose.

**star-of-Beth|le|hem** (stär′əv beth′lē əm, -lə hem), *n.* an Old World plant of the lily family, naturalized in eastern North America, that grows from a bulb and has a tall cluster of green-and-white, star-shaped flowers. [because of the shape of its flowers]

**Star of Bethlehem,** the star described in Matthew 2:2, 9-10, that heralded Christ's birth and was followed by the Three Wise Men to the manger where the Christ child lay.

***Star of David,** a Jewish emblem, consisting of a six-pointed star formed of two triangles, one interlaced with or placed upon the other; magen David.

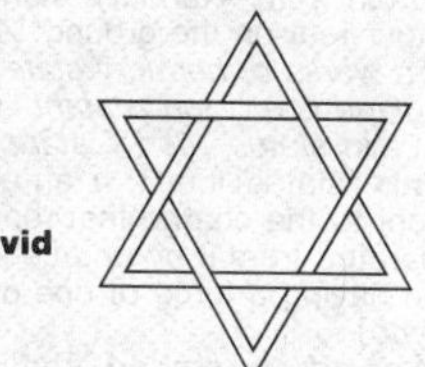

***Star of David**

**star|quake** (stär′kwāk′), *n.* a series of rapid changes in the shape of a star or in the distribution of its matter, detected from sudden acceleration of the star's pulse rate: *Starquakes may change a pulsar's pulse* (New Scientist).

**star quartz,** asteriated quartz.

**starred** (stärd), *adj.* **1** full of stars; starry. **2** decorated with stars: *Gartered peers and starred ambassadors* ... (Benjamin Disraeli). **3** marked with a star or asterisk. **4** presented as a star actor or performer. **5** influenced by the stars or by fate.

**star route,** (in the U.S. Postal Service) a route, other than the ordinary routes, over which mail is carried by special contract with private individuals, rather than by the usual carriers (so called from asterisks used to mark such routes in official papers).

**star ruby,** a ruby exhibiting asterism, like the more common star sapphire or asteria.

**star|ry** (stär′ē), *adj.,* **-ri|er, -ri|est. 1** containing many stars: *a starry sky.* **2** lighted by stars; starlit: *a starry night.* **3** shining like a star or like stars; very bright: *starry eyes.* **4** like a star in shape. **SYN:** stellate. **5** of or having to do with the stars. **SYN:** astral. **6** consisting of stars. — **star′ri|ly,** *adv.* — **star′ri|ness,** *n.*

**star|ry-eyed** (stär′ē īd′), *adj.* tending to view too favorably or idealistically; unrealistic; dreamy: *He's no starry-eyed optimist* (Margery Allingham). — **star′ry-eyed′ness,** *n.*

**Stars and Bars,** the first flag of the Confederacy. It had two horizontal red stripes with a white stripe between and a blue square containing a circle of seven white stars.

**Stars and Stripes,** the flag of the United States. When first adopted by the Continental Congress on June 14, 1777, it contained 13 stripes and 13 stars. It now contains 13 stripes and 50 stars.

**star sapphire,** a sapphire which exhibits by reflected light a star of bright rays, resulting from its crystalline structure.

**star saxifrage,** a small saxifrage found northward in both hemispheres having white starry flowers.

**star-shaped** (stär′shāpt′), *adj.* shaped like a star; having rays proceeding from, or angular points disposed in a regular outline about, a central point.

**star shell,** a flare which bursts into bright starlike clusters or a single light, suspended by a parachute, used in war to illuminate enemy positions or, in various colors, as a signal or firework.

**star|shine** (stär′shīn′), *n.* = starlight.

**star shower,** = meteor shower.

**star-span|gled** (stär′spang′gəld), *adj.* sprinkled with stars.

**Star-Spangled Banner, 1** the national anthem of the United States. The words were composed by Francis Scott Key in 1814. **2** the flag of the United States; Stars and Stripes.

**star-stud|ded** (stär′stud′id), *adj.* **1** star-spangled: *a star-studded canopy.* **2** having or featuring many stars or celebrities: *a star-studded show.*

**star system, 1** the system or practice of developing star performers and exploiting their popularity to attract large audiences: *the Hollywood star system. The Kirstein-Balanchine troupe would not ... adopt a star system for its dancers* (New York Times). **2** *Figurative: America's U.N. ambassadors—Henry Cabot Lodge, Stevenson, Arthur Goldberg—usually have been appointed under "the star system"* (Harper's).

**start¹** (stärt), *v., n.* — *v.i.* **1** to begin to move, go, or act: *to start in business, to start from the beginning, to start to school. The train started on time.* **SYN:** go. **2** to begin or commence, as a process, performance, or the like: *The play started at nine.* **3** to give a sudden, involuntary jerk or twitch; move suddenly: *to start backward, to start from one's seat, to start to one's feet.* (*Figurative.*) *He started in surprise.* (*Figurative.*) *To start at shadows* (Scott). **4** to come, rise, or spring suddenly: *Tears started from her eyes.* **5** to burst out: *eyes seeming to start from their sockets.* **6** to be displaced, as by pressure or shrinkage; become loose.
— *v.t.* **1** to begin; commence: *to start reading a book, start work, start a song, start an argument.* **SYN:** See syn. under **begin. 2** to cause to begin moving, going, acting, operating, or otherwise functioning; set going; put into action: *to start a car, to start a fire, to start a business, to start a rumor.* **3** to cause or enable (a person) to begin some course of action or career: *He started his son in business.* **4** to induce (a person) to begin to talk on some subject. **5** to introduce (as a subject or topic); broach. **6** to rouse suddenly into action, motion, or flight, as an animal from its lair: *to start a rabbit.* **7** to displace, as by pressure; make loose; cause to loosen or lose hold: *to start a plank, to start an anchor. The huge waves had started some of the ship's bolts.* **8** to begin the flow of (a liquid) from a container; empty (a vessel); tap. **9** to enter in a race, especially a horse race. **10** to cause (a race or contestants in a race) to begin. **11** *Obsolete.* to startle.
— *n.* **1** an act of setting in motion: *He pushed the car to give the motor a start.* **2** the act or fact of beginning to move, go, or act; starting or setting out: *to see a race from start to finish.* **3** a sudden, involuntary movement of the body, as from surprise or terror; jerk: *to give someone a start. On seeing the snake, the man sprang up with a start. I awoke with a start.* **4** the act or fact of beginning ahead of others; advantage: *He got the start of his rivals.* **5** a chance or assistance given for entering on a career or course of action: *to get a start in life. His father gave him a start in business.* **6** a spurt of energy or activity: *to work by fits and starts.* **7** *Archaic.* an outburst, sally, or flight, as of wit, humor, passion, or grief: *some starts of his former ... vivacity break out* (Fanny Burney). **8** the place or line at which a race begins. **9** a part that has started; displaced or loosened part. **10** a break, opening, or other condition resulting from this.

**start in** (or **out**), to begin to do something: *The duckling started in swimming as soon as he was set in the water.*

**start up, a** to rise suddenly; spring up: *Chaerephon ... started up and ran to me, seizing my hand* (Benjamin Jowett). **b** to come suddenly into being or notice: *I am surrounded by difficulties, and as fast as I get the better of one, another starts up* (Earl Carlisle). **c** to begin to do something: *He started up fishing as soon as spring came.* **d** to cause (an engine) to begin operating: *Before starting up the engine make sure that the gear lever is in the central or neutral position* (Morris Owner's Manual).
[variant of Old English *styrtan* leap up]

**start²** (stärt), *n.* the tail of an animal (now used only in compounds). [Old English *steort* tail]

**start|er** (stär′tər), *n.* **1** a person or thing that starts. **2** an official who gives the signal to begin a race. **3** an official who is responsible for main-

**Pronunciation Key:** hat, āge, cãre, fär; let, ēqual, tėrm; it, īce; hot, ōpen, ôrder; oil, out; cup, pu̇t, rüle; child; long; thin; ᴛʜen; zh, measure; ə represents **a** in about, **e** in taken, **i** in pencil, **o** in lemon, **u** in circus.

taining the schedule and sequence of departures from a station, and who signals buses, subways, trains, elevators, and other conveyances, to start out. **4** any contestant who sets out in a race. **5** the first in a series of things: *This request was only a starter.* **6** an apparatus for starting a machine, especially an automobile; self-starter. **7** a chemical agent or bacterial culture used to start a reaction, as in the formation of acid in making cheese, sour cream, or vinegar. **8** *Cribbage.* turnup.

**as** (or **for**) **a starter,** *Informal.* as a beginning; to begin with; for a start: *For a starter we'll have soup and then eat the main course later. As a starter the diners ordered various appetizers.*

**for starters,** *Informal.* to begin with; as a starter: *For starters, there is a countess who wants to keep him, but ... he will have none of it* (Eliot Fremont-Smith).

**starter sheet,** a thin sheet of pure copper which serves as a cathode in the electrolytic refining of copper.

**star thistle, 1** a low, spreading, European composite weed having small heads of purple flowers surrounded by radiating spines; caltrop. **2** a related weed of more erect habit and having yellow flowers.

**star|throat** (stär′thrōt′), *n.* a hummingbird having the throat spangled with the scales of the gorget.

**start|ing blocks** (stär′ting), a pair of triangular blocks against which a runner braces his feet at the start of a race to get a fast start.

**starting gate,** a device by which race horses are aligned at the start of a race; barrier.

**starting point,** a point from which a person or thing starts; place of starting; beginning: *Inspection is the starting point for any realistic system of disarmament* (Time).

**star|tle** (stär′təl), *v.,* **-tled, -tling,** *n.* —*v.t.* to frighten suddenly; surprise: *The dog jumped at the girl and startled her.* SYN: scare, alarm, shock, stun.

—*v.i.* to move suddenly in fear or surprise.

—*n.* an experience of being startled; a sudden start or shock of surprise or fright.

[probably Old English *steartlian* to kick, stumble]

**star|tler** (stär′tlər), *n. Informal.* **1** a startling thing. **2** a person who does startling things.

**star|tling** (stär′tling), *adj.* that causes a shock of surprise; surprising; frightening: *startling tales.* —**star′tling|ly,** *adv.*

**start-up** (stärt′up′), *n., adj.* —*n.* the beginning of an operation or production: *The system is completely automatic after the initial start-up* (Edward H. Owen).

—*adj.* of or having to do with the process of beginning an operation or production: *start-up costs.*

**star turn,** the principal person or item in a show; starred performer or feature: *The return of Ann Corio, as M.C., star turn, and director of an old-time burlesque show* (New Yorker).

**star|va|tion** (stär vā′shən), *n., adj.* —*n.* **1** the action or process of starving: *Starvation of prisoners is barbarous.* **2** the condition of being starved; suffering from extreme hunger: *Starvation caused his death.*

—*adj.* that causes or is bound to cause starvation: *a starvation diet, starvation wages. Kept ... on starvation rations through lack of supplies, the men sickened, and many died of yellow fever and dysentery* (Time).

**starve** (stärv), *v.,* **starved, starv|ing.** —*v.i.* **1** to die because of hunger; perish from lack or insufficiency of food. **2** to suffer because of hunger; famish: *Let not poor Nellie* [*Nell Gwyn*] *starve* (Charles II of England). **3** *Informal.* to feel very hungry. **4** to suffer extreme proverty and need: *She ended up starving in a New York tenement* (Time). **5** *Dialect.* to die or suffer from exposure to extreme cold. **6** *Obsolete.* to die.

—*v.t.* **1** to weaken or kill with hunger: *That cruel man half starves his horses.* **2** to force or subdue by lack of food: *The enemy starved the men in the fort into surrendering.* **3** *Figurative.* to weaken or destroy through lack of something needed: *The powers of their minds are starved by disuse* (John Locke). **4** *Dialect.* to cause to die or suffer from cold.

**starve down** (or **out**), to force or subdue from lack of food: *After a siege of many weeks the garrison of the castle was starved out.*

**starve for,** to suffer from the lack of (something); have a strong desire or craving for (a thing): *to starve for news. The lonely child is starved for affection.*

[Old English *steorfan* to die] —**starv′er,** *n.*

**starve|ling** (stärv′ling), *adj., n.* —*adj.* **1** starving; hungry: *Women nursed their starveling infants* (Katherine Anne Porter). **2** = poverty-stricken.

—*n.* a person or animal that is suffering from lack of food.

**star|ward** (stär′wərd), *adv., adj.* toward the stars.

**star|wort** (stär′wėrt′), *n.* **1** any one of various chickweeds with white star-shaped flowers. **2** any plant of the group including the asters. **3** = water starwort.

**stase** (stās), *n.* a fossil plant deposit that has remained in its original position. [< Greek *stásis;* see etym. under **stasis**]

**stash¹** (stash), *v., n.* —*v.t.* **1** *Slang.* to hide or put away for safekeeping or future use: *Better stash some cash in the bank* (Wall Street Journal). *Banks stash away part of their profits in hidden reserves* (Maclean's). SYN: cache. **2** *British or Archaic.* **a** to bring to an end; stop. **b** to quit (a place).

—*n. Slang.* **1** a hiding place: *The husband breaks-and-enters and the wife's skirts are the stash* (Harper's). **2** something to be hidden: *Cisco loads the stash into his guitar case* (Time). [origin uncertain]

**stash²** (stash), *n. U.S. Slang.* mustache.

**sta|sis** (stā′sis, stas′is), *n., pl.* **-ses** (-sēz). **1** a stoppage or stagnation of the flow of any fluid of the body, as in the blood vessels or the intestines. **2** *Figurative.* a static or stagnant condition: *Listeners have been driven off by the increasing stasis of jazz's establishment performers* (New Yorker). [< New Latin *stasis* < Greek *stásis* a standing < *sta-,* a root of *histánai* to stand]

**-stat,** *combining form.* **1** a mechanical device or instrument that causes something to be or become stable, as in *rheostat,* and *thermostat.* **2** any regulating, stablizing, or controlling center, agent, or device, as in *appestat.*

[probably < Greek *-státēs,* a noun agent suffix < *sta-,* a root of *histánai* cause to stand, or stop]

**stat.,** **1a** statuary. **b** statue. **2a** statute (miles). **b** statute or statutes.

**stat|a|ble** (stā′tə bəl), *adj.* that can be stated: *statable relationships.* Also, **stateable.**

**sta|tant** (stā′tənt), *adj. Heraldry.* standing in profile with all four feet on the ground: *All the current standard works of heraldry state that the Crest of England is a "Lion Statant"* (Sunday Times). [< Latin *status, -ūs* (< *stāre* to stand)]

**stat|cou|lomb** (stat′kü lom′), *n.* an electrostatic unit equivalent to the charge that repels a like charge, separated from it by one centimeter in a vacuum, and having a force of one dyne. [< *stat-*(ic) + *coulomb*]

**state** (stāt), *n., adj., v.,* **stat|ed, stat|ing.** —*n.* **1** the condition of a person or thing at a certain time; situation: *the state of the weather, a state of war, a person's state of mind, the state of our present knowledge of the solar system. He is in a state of poor health. The house is in a bad state of repair. Let us pray for the whole state of Christ's Church* (Book of Common Prayer). **2** a particular condition of mind or feeling: *a state of uncertainty, a state of excitement.* **3** physical condition with regard to composition, form, structure, phase or stage of existence, or the like. A substance may exist in a solid, liquid, or gaseous state. Ice is water in a solid state. **4** spiritual existence; the mode of existence of a spiritual being: *the state of grace, our mortal state.* **5a** a group of people occupying a given area under a government; commonwealth; nation. **b** Often, **State.** one of several organized political groups which together form a nation: *Hawaii is the fiftieth state of the United States.* **c** the territory, government, or authority of a state. **d** the civil government; highest civil authority: *affairs of state.* **6a** a person's position in life; rank: *He is a man of humble state.* SYN: standing, status. **b** high rank; greatness; eminence. **c** *Archaic.* a person of high status; noble. **7** high style of living; dignity; pomp: *a coach of state. Kings lived in great state.*

—*adj.* **1a** of or having to do with a state of the United States: *a state road, state police, a state flag.* **b** of, having to do with, or belonging to the civil government or highest civil power or authority: *state control.* **2** of ceremony; used on or reserved for very formal and special occasions; ceremonious; formal: *state robes.* **3** with or involving ceremony and pomp: *state occasions, a state banquet.*

—*v.t.* **1** to tell in speech or writing; express; say: *to state one's reasons. State your opinion of the new school rules.* SYN: declare. See syn. under **say. 2** to set forth formally or in proper form: *to state a question, to state a case. Every argument was stated with logical precision* (Edward Bulwer-Lytton). **3** to specify; fix; settle: *to state a price.*

**be in a state,** *Informal.* **a** to be in a bad or disordered condition: *He leaves things lying around, and look what a state his room is in!* **b** to be in an agitated or excited condition of mind or feeling: *Don't you remember when she went away, what a state you were in and how you raged?* (Violet Jacob).

**lie in state,** to lie in a coffin to be seen formally and publicly before being buried: *The dead king lay in state one day in the main hall of the royal palace.*

**states** or **States,** the bodies from which a national legislature, such as the States-General, was formed; estates (chiefly in historical use): *The Elector Frederick William III in 1701, in an assembly of the States, was accorded the title of King in Prussia* (F. M. Hueffer).

[< Latin *status, -ūs* condition, position < *stāre* to stand; common in Latin phrase *status rēī publicae* condition of the republic. See etym. of doublets **estate, status.**]

—***Syn.*** *n.* **1 State, condition** mean the circumstances in which someone or something exists. **State** is often used without reference to anything concrete: *The state of the world today should interest every serious person.* **Condition** applies to a particular state due to given causes or circumstances: *The condition of the patient is much improved today.*

▶ See **say** for usage note.

**State** (stāt), *n., adj.* —*n.* **1a** a state, as of the United States (used especially in its official name): *The State of Texas is one of the United States.* **b** a nation. **2** the territory, government, or authority of a state: *Never any State was ... so open to receive strangers into their body, as were the Romans* (Francis Bacon). **3** the civil government; highest civil authority: *The State is properly ... the nation in its collective and corporate capacity* (Matthew Arnold).

—*adj.* of or having to do with a nation or a state, especially a state of the United States: *a State road, State police.*

**the States,** the United States (used especially abroad): [*The trend*] *apparently started in the States, where women are now said to own more capital than men* (Punch).

[< *state*]

▶ **State, state.** The capitalized form is now used chiefly to emphasize the authority, sovereignty, or official character of a nation or other political entity or its government.

**state|a|ble** (stā′tə bəl), *adj.* = statable.

**state aid,** *U.S.* financial or other assistance given by a Federal or state government, especially to a local or private enterprise. —**state′-aid′,** *adj.*

**state bank, 1** a bank owned or controlled by a government, especially an institution through the agency of which currency is issued or controlled. **2** *U.S.* a bank that has a charter from a state government.

**state bird,** a bird chosen as the emblem of a state of the United States.

**state capitalism,** a form of capitalism in which the government controls the direction and overall operation of a nation's economy.

**state church,** = established church.

**state college,** a college maintained by a state of the United States, often as part of a state university. Some state colleges are agricultural or junior colleges.

**state|craft** (stāt′kraft′, -kräft′), *n.* **1** skill in the management of public or national affairs; statesmanship. **2** crafty statesmanship.

**stat|ed** (stā′tid), *adj.* **1** put into words; said; told: *the stated facts of a case.* **2** fixed; settled; specified: *for a stated fee. School begins daily at a stated time.* **3** explicitly set forth; formulated: *a stated rule or penalty.* —**stat′ed|ly,** *adv.*

**State Department,** an executive division of the United States government charged with the conduct of foreign affairs. It is presided over by the Secretary of State.

**state flower,** a flower chosen as the emblem of a state of the United States. The forget-me-not is the state flower of Alaska.

**state|hood** (stāt′hu̇d), *n.* the condition or status of being a state, especially a state of the United States.

**State|house** or **state|house** (stāt′hous′), *n.,* or **state house,** *U.S.* the building in which the legislature of a state meets; capitol of a state.

**state|less** (stāt′lis), *adj.* **1** not belonging to any country; having no citizenship or nationality: *a stateless refugee.* **2** in which national sovereignty does not exist: *a stateless world.* —**state′lessness,** *n.*

**state|let** (stāt′lit), *n.* a small state.

**state|li|ly** (stāt′lə lē), *adv.* in a stately manner.

**state line,** any boundary line between states of the United States.

**state|li|ness** (stāt′lē nis), *n.* stately quality or character.

**state|ly** (stāt′lē), *adj.,* **-li|er, -li|est,** *adv.* —*adj.* **1** having dignity; deliberate: *to speak and move in a slow, stately manner.* SYN: dignified. **2** imposing; grand; majestic: *the stately music of Handel, a region of stately homes. The Capitol at Washington is a stately building.* SYN: See syn. under **grand.**

—*adv.* in a stately manner; with stately or dignified bearing, movement, or expression.

**state medicine,** a system under which medical

care and hospital services are provided by the government for all in the state, the costs being borne by some form of taxation.

**state|ment** (stāt′mənt), *n.* **1** something stated; account; report: *His statement was correct.* **2** the act of stating or manner of stating something: *The statement of an idea helps me to remember it.* **3** a summary of an account, showing the amount owed, due, or on hand: *a bank statement.* **4** a song, painting, design, or the like, that expresses a point of view, concept, or theme: *Jesse Taylor's albums have always been very personal statements about the artist's changing life* (New York Times). *The medium for his [Andrew Wyeth's] most sustained ... statements is egg tempera* (Atlantic). *Mrs. Barton's costume was "a simple statement"—a sleeveless satin dress with a tulle veil* (Marylin Bender). **5** *Mathematics.* an idea expressed by a closed sentence. *Example:* 5 = 2 + 3 is a statement expressing the true idea that 5 is the sum of 2 and 3.

**state of the art**, the level of development in a field or industry: *These brief reports of current research are presumably intended to give an accurate idea of the 'state of the art', or of important 'break-throughs' in particular fields* (Science Journal).

**state-of-the-art** (stāt′əv ᴛʜi ärt′), *adj.* involving facilities or techniques already known or developed; not experimental or at the research-and-development stage.

**State of the Union message**, an address by the President of the United States to Congress in which he reviews the nation's development of the past year and outlines his program for the coming year.

**state prison**, *U.S.* a prison maintained by and operated under the penal code of the state in which it is situated.

**stat|er¹** (stā′tər), *n.* **1** a person who states: *the stater of a case.* **2** a person who favors, belongs to, or has to do with a certain kind of state: *a welfare stater.*

**sta|ter²** (stā′tər), *n.* any one of various gold, silver, or electrum coins of the ancient Greek states or cities, varying in value. [< Latin *statēr* < Greek *statḗr* (originally) a weight < *sta-*, a stem of *histánai* cause to stand; place in the balance]

**state religion**, the official religion of a nation, such as Anglicanism in England and Roman Catholicism in Italy.

**state rights** or **State rights**, = states' rights.

**state|room** (stāt′rüm′, -rům′), *n.* **1** a private room on a ship with sleeping and (now usually) toilet facilities for a single person or small group of persons; cabin. **2** a private room on certain American railroad cars of the late 1800's resembling the drawing room or bedroom of today.

**states** (stāts), *n.pl.* See under **state.**

**States** (stāts), *n.pl.* **the**. See under **State**.

**state's attorney**, *U.S.* the law officer responsible for preparation and presentation of the case of the state in a court action.

**state's evidence**, **1** *U.S.* testimony given in court by an accused person against one or more of his alleged associates in a crime. **2** evidence brought forward by the government in a criminal case.

**turn state's evidence**, *U.S.* to testify in court against one's alleged associates in a crime: *Hoping to get a lighter sentence, the man accused of being part of a smugglers' ring agreed to turn state's evidence.*

**States-Gen|er|al** (stāts′jen′ər əl, -jen′rəl), *n.* **1** the legislative body of France from 1302 to 1789, consisting of representatives of the three estates, the clergy, the nobility, and the common people; Estates-General. **2** the lawmaking body of the Netherlands.

**State Shinto**, (formerly) Shinto stressing patriotism and divinity of the Japanese emperor. It was abolished after World War II.

**state|side** (stāt′sīd′), *adj., adv. Informal.* —***adj.*** from or in the United States, especially the continental United States: *American soldiers abroad are happy to have stateside magazines.*
—***adv.*** to or in the United States, especially the continental United States: *to fly stateside.*

**state|sid|er** (stāt′sī′dər), *n. U.S. Informal.* a person born or living in the continental United States; mainlander.

**states|man** (stāts′mən), *n., pl.* **-men**. a person skilled in the management of public or national affairs: *Abraham Lincoln was a famous American statesman. Wise statesmen ... foresee what time is thus bringing, and endeavor to shape institutions and to mold men's thought and purpose in accordance with the change* (Viscount Morley). **SYN**: See syn. under **politician**.

**states|man|like** (stāts′mən līk′), *adj.* having the qualities of a statesman.

**states|man|ly** (stāts′mən lē), *adj.* like, worthy of, or befitting a statesman.

**states|man|ship** (stāts′mən ship), *n.* the qualities of a statesman; skill in the management of public or national affairs.

**state socialism**, a form of socialism involving government control, management, or ownership of all or certain enterprises, especially in the industrial, commercial, and financial realms, with the purpose of improving social conditions.

**state socialist**, an adherent of state socialism.

**state song**, a song chosen as the anthem of a state of the United States.

**state's prison**, = state prison.

**states' righter** or **States' righter**, *U.S. Informal.* an advocate or supporter of states' rights.

**states' rights** or **States' rights**, the rights and powers considered as belonging to the individual states of the United States under the Constitution. The doctrine of states' rights holds that all powers which the Constitution does not specifically delegate to the Federal government, and does not specifically deny to the individual states, belong to the states. Some states have interpreted this doctrine further so as to exclude activity on the part of the Federal government of the United States in any area, such as education or voting laws, that is normally under the control of the individual states.

**states|wom|an** (stāts′wům′ən), *n., pl.* **-wom|en**. a woman skilled in the management of public or national affairs.

**state tree**, a tree chosen as the emblem of a state of the United States.

**state trooper**, *U.S.* a member of the police force of a state.

**state university**, a university maintained by a state of the United States as a unit of or adjunct to its system of public education.

**state-wide** or **state|wide** (stāt′wīd′), *adj., adv.* —***adj.*** covering an entire state; over all of a state: *a state-wide election campaign.*
—***adv.*** in an entire state; over a whole state: *[He] supported Mr. Kennedy in 1960, but now he'll go Republican locally, statewide, and nationally* (Wall Street Journal).

**stat|ic** (stat′ik), *adj., n.* —***adj.*** **1** in a fixed or stable condition; not in a state of progress or change; at rest; standing still: *a static character in a novel. Life does not remain static, but changes constantly.* **SYN**: passive, immobile. **2a** having to do with bodies at rest or with forces that balance each other. **b** acting by weight without producing motion: *static pressure.* **3a** of or having to do with stationary electrical charges that balance each other. Static electricity can be produced by rubbing a glass rod with a silk cloth. **b** producing such electricity. **4** of, having to do with, or caused by atmospheric electricity that interferes with radio and television reception. **5** *Economics.* having to do with the conditions and problems occurring in a relatively stable society.
—***n.*** **1** electrical disturbances in the air; atmospherics. Static interferes with radio and television broadcasting by causing crackling sounds in the receiver. Some static is caused by electrical storms. **2** noises and other interference with radio and television reception caused by such electrical disturbances; strays: *Thin squeaks of radio static* (Hart Crane).
[< Greek *statikós* causing to stand < *sta-*, a stem of *histánai* cause to stand or stop] —**stat′i|cal|ly**, *adv.*

**stat|i|cal** (stat′ə kəl), *adj.* = static.

**stat|i|ce** (stat′ə sē), *n.* **1** any one of a group of small herblike plants related to the leadwort, with rosettes of narrow evergreen leaves on the ground and globular heads of pink, purplish, or white flowers; thrift. **2** any one of a group of related herbs or shrubs growing especially in sandy areas of the Old World; sea lavender. [< New Latin *Statice* the genus name < Latin *staticē* an astringent herb < Greek *statikḗ*, feminine of *statikós*; see etym. under **static**]

**static line**, a line attached at one end to a closed parachute and at the other end to a cord suspended from a cable inside the aircraft, serving as a rip cord to open the parachute.

**stat|ics** (stat′iks), *n.* the branch of mechanics that deals with bodies at rest or forces that balance each other.

**static testing**, the testing of a rocket, missile, or engine, on the ground.

**static tube**, a small tube for measuring the static pressure of the air or other fluids, used especially on aircraft.

**sta|tion** (stā′shən), *n., v.* —***n.*** **1a** a place to stand in; place or spot that a person is appointed to occupy in the performance of some duty; assigned post: *The policeman took his station at the corner.* **SYN**: position, location. **b** a locality or post assigned for military duty to a person or unit. **c** a place or region to which a naval vessel or fleet is assigned for duty. **d** a place at which naval vessels or aircraft are regularly located: *a naval air station.* **e** (formerly, in India) the place of residence of the British officials of a district or officers of a garrison. **2a** a place to which people are assigned and where equipment is set up for some particular kind of work, research, or the like: *a postal station, a biological station, a weather station.* **b** the police headquarters of a district. **c** the place or equipment for sending out or receiving programs or messages by radio or television. **3a** a regular stopping place: *a bus station.* **b** the building or buildings erected at such a place; depot: *Father met me at the coffee shop in the railroad station.* **4** a cattle or sheep farm in Australia or New Zealand: *Stations either for sheep or cattle were spotted about ... over the whole country* (Samuel Butler). **5** social position; rank: *A serf was a man of humble station in life.* **6** *Figurative.* situation or position, as in a class, scale of estimation, or the like: *The masters told his parents he was dull and advised them to take him out; they were only wasting their money trying to educate him beyond his station* (Edmund Wilson). **7** *Surveying.* **a** each of the selected points at which observations are taken. **b** a fixed uniform distance into which a survey line is divided. **8** *Biology.* the condition or position of an animal or plant in its habitat, or its relation to its environment. **9** the act or posture of standing on the feet. **10** the condition or fact of standing still: *Her motion and her station are as one; She shows a body rather than a life* (Shakespeare).
—***v.t.*** to assign a station to; place: *The faithful dog stationed himself at the door behind which his master lay sick in bed. The soldier was stationed at Fort Hays.*
[< Latin *statiō, -ōnis* < *stāre* to stand]

**station agent**, = stationmaster.

**sta|tion|al** (stā′shən əl), *adj.* of or having to do with a station.

**sta|tion|ar|y** (stā′shə ner′ē), *adj.* **1a** having a fixed station or place; not movable: *A factory engine is stationary.* **SYN**: immovable. **b** residing or established in one place; not itinerant or migratory: *I deemed it advisable to ... change my late wandering life for a stationary one* (William Godwin). **2** standing still; not moving: *A parked car is stationary.* **SYN**: motionless. **3** without change, as in size, number, or activity: *The population of this town has been stationary for ten years at about 5,000 people.* **SYN**: invariable. [< Latin *statiōnārius* (*mīlitēs*) (soldier) belonging to a military station < *statiō*; see etym. under **station**] —**sta′tion|ar′i|ly**, *adv.* —**sta′tion|ar′i|ness**, *n.*
▶ **Stationary** and **stationery** are usually pronounced identically and as a consequence sometimes carelessly confused in writing.

**stationary front**, *Meteorology.* a surface between two dissimilar air masses neither of which is displacing the other and usually resulting in mild temperatures and cloudy weather. See picture under **front**.

**stationary wave**, = standing wave.

**station bill**, a list posted in a ship containing the appointed station of each member of the ship's company in any emergency.

**station break**, a pause in a radio or television program, or between programs, to identify the broadcasting station or network by its call letters or number and location. Station breaks usually occur on the hour or half hour. *After the Topsawyer commercial came a station break* (Russell Baker).

**sta|tion|er** (stā′shə nər), *n.* **1** a person who sells paper, pens, pencils, and other writing materials, and now, often, newspapers, magazines, some books, tobacco, and trinkets. **2a** a bookseller, especially one dealing primarily in books published by himself, such as was common in England in the early days of publishing. **b** *Obsolete.* a publisher. [< Medieval Latin *stationarius* shopkeeper, especially, a bookseller; (originally) a stationary seller, as distinct from a roving peddler < Late Latin, a postmaster at a military post-station]

**sta|tion|er|y** (stā′shə ner′ē), *n., adj.* —***n.*** writing materials, such as paper, cards, and envelopes.
—***adj.*** of or having to do with stationery.
▶ See **stationary** for usage note.

**station house**, a building used as a station, especially as a police station.

**sta|tion|mas|ter** (stā′shən mas′tər, -mäs′-), *n.* the person in charge of a railroad station, usually an employee of a particular railroad by which the station is owned, but sometimes an employee of a separate corporation, such as one owning a

**Pronunciation Key:** hat, āge, cãre, fär; let, ēqual, tėrm; it, īce; hot, ōpen, ôrder; **oi**l, **ou**t; cup, pu̇t, rüle; **ch**ild; lo**ng**; **th**in; ᴛʜen; **zh**, measure; ə represents **a** in about, **e** in taken, **i** in pencil, **o** in lemon, **u** in circus.

station used by two or more railroads.

**sta|tions of the cross** or **Sta|tions of the Cross** (stā′shənz), **1** a series of scenes (usually fourteen) of successive incidents of Christ's Passion, usually painted or sculptured and placed around the walls of a church or along a road leading to a shrine, to be visited for meditation and prayer. **2** the prayers used at these stations.

**sta|tion-to-sta|tion** (stā′shən tə stā′shən), *adj.* designating a long-distance telephone call in which the person calling will speak to anyone who answers at the number called.

**station wagon**, a closed automobile with a rear door for loading and unloading the back part, and seats in the rear that can be folded down or removed, for use as a light truck.

▶ **station wagon, beach wagon**. The latter term, relatively common especially in the eastern United States in the 1920's and early 1930's, now survives for all practical purposes only in the fiction of that period.

**stat|ism** (stā′tiz əm), *n.* **1** highly centralized governmental control, as of the economy and information media of a state or nation. **2** advocacy of the sovereignty of a state, especially of a state of a republic.

**stat|ist** (stā′tist), *n., adj.* **—*n.*** **1** a person who advocates statism. **2** = statistician.
**—*adj.*** having to do with or advocating statism.

**sta|tis|tic** (stə tis′tik), *adj., n.* **—*adj.*** = statistical. **—*n.*** **1** any value, item, or fact used in statistics: *an important statistic.* **2** = statistics.

**sta|tis|ti|cal** (stə tis′tə kəl), *adj.* of or having to do with statistics; consisting of or based on statistics.

**statistical independence**, *Statistics.* the absence of correlation between two or more ways of classifying a group.

**sta|tis|ti|cal|ly** (stə tis′tə klē), *adv.* in a statistical manner; according to statistics.

**stat|is|ti|cian** (stat′ə stish′ən), *n.* an expert in statistics; person who prepares statistics.

**sta|tis|tics** (stə tis′tiks), *n.* **1** numerical facts, such as those about people, the weather, or business conditions. Statistics are collected and classified systematically. *Wherever statistics are kept, the numbers of births and of deaths rise and fall in nearly parallel lines* (William R. Inge). **2** the science of collecting and using such facts: *The process by which numerical data are collected and eventually presented in a usable and understandable form is an important part of the mathematical science of statistics* (F. J. Crosswhite). [< German *Statistik,* apparently < New Latin *statisticum collegium* lecture course on state affairs < *statista* one skilled in statecraft < Latin *status;* see etym. under **state**]

▶ **Statistics** is plural in form and in the sense of def. 1 is plural in use: *Statistics are classified systematically;* but in the sense of def. 2 it is singular in use: *Statistics is taught in many colleges.*

**sta|tive** (stā′tiv), *adj.* (of certain Hebrew verbs) expressing a state or condition.

**Stat. L.**, Statutes at Large.

**stat|o|blast** (stat′ə blast), *n.* any one of the horny buds developed within certain freshwater bryozoans that are set free when the parent colony dies, remain inactive throughout the winter, and give rise to new individuals in the spring. [< Greek *statós* standing, static + *blastós* sprout, germ]

**stat|o|cyst** (stat′ə sist), *n. Zoology.* an organ of balance found in various crustaceans, flatworms, and other invertebrates, consisting of a sac containing particles (statoliths), as of sand or lime, suspended in fluid. [< Greek *statós* standing, static + English *cyst*]

**stat|o|lith** (stat′ə lith), *n.* a particle, as of sand or lime, suspended in fluid, contained in a statocyst. [< Greek *statós* standing, static + *lithos* stone]

**sta|tor** (stā′tər), *n.* a stationary portion enclosing rotating parts in a steam turbine, an electric generator or motor, or other machine. See picture at **motor**. [< New Latin *stator* < Latin *stātor* sustainer < *sistere* cause to stand < *stāre* to stand]

**stat|o|scope** (stat′ə skōp), *n.* **1** a form of aneroid barometer for measuring very small variations of atmospheric pressure. **2** an instrument for detecting a small rise or fall in the altitude of an aircraft. [< Greek *statós* standing + English *-scope*]

**stat|u|ar|y** (stach′ů er′ē), *n., pl.* **-ar|ies**, *adj.* **—*n.*** **1** statues collectively. **2** the art of making statues; sculpture. **3** a sculptor: *He* [*Byron*] *had a head which statuaries loved to copy* (Macaulay).
**—*adj.*** of or having to do with the making of statues; suitable for statues: *statuary marble.*

**stat|ue** (stach′ü), *n.* an image of a person or animal carved in stone or wood, cast in metal, or molded in clay, wax, or other material: *Nearly every city has a statue of some famous man. He sat rigid, immovable, like a statue* (F. Marion Crawford). SYN: sculpture.

**statues**, a game in which the players become suddenly motionless at a signal after having spun around and are judged on the awkwardness and ridiculousness of their poses.

[< Old French *statue,* learned borrowing from Latin *statua* < *status, -ūs* a standing still, condition < *stāre* to stand] **—stat′ue|like′**, *adj.*

**Statue of Liberty** or **statue of liberty**, a play in football in which a back holds the ball up as if to pass and another back comes around behind him and takes it. [< *Statue of Liberty,* a huge statue of the goddess of liberty holding aloft a lighted torch, given to the United States by France, and standing in New York harbor]

**stat|ues** (stach′üz), *n.pl.* See under **statue**.

**stat|u|esque** (stach′ů esk′), *adj.* like a statue in dignity, formal grace, or classic beauty. **—stat′u-esque′ly**, *adv.* **—stat′u|esque′ness**, *n.*

**stat|u|ette** (stach′ů et′), *n.* a small statue; figurine. [< French *statuette* (diminutive) < Old French *statue;* see etym. under **statue**]

**stat|ure** (stach′ər), *n.* **1** the height of a person or thing; tallness: *A man six feet tall is above average stature.* **2** *Figurative.* mental or moral growth; distinguished development or achievement: *Thomas Jefferson was a man of great stature among his countrymen. His diligent espousal of the cause of world peace as a practical ideal gave great stature to a long ... life* (New York Times). *Two Catholic theologians of stature ... attempt to sort out the theological issues* (John Cogley). *If we are true to plan, Our statures touch the skies* (Emily Dickinson). [< Old French *stature,* learned borrowing from Latin *statūra* < *stāre* to stand]

**stat|ured** (stach′ərd), *adj.* **1** having stature; tall. **2** having a certain kind of stature: *fair-statured.*

**sta|tus** (stā′təs, stat′əs), *n.* **1a** social or professional standing; position; rank: *the status of a doctor. What is her status in the government? Making way for no one under the status of a priest* (Rudyard Kipling). *Mr. Polly's status was that of a guest pure and simple* (H. G. Wells). SYN: footing, station. **b** standing, position, or rank considered to be desirable: *to seek status, to lose status.* **2** condition; state: *Diplomats are interested in the status of world affairs. The status of the world in 1970 was discouraging to lovers of peace.* **3** legal position of a person as determined by his membership in some class of persons with certain rights or limitations: *the status of the foreign-born in America.* SYN: classification. [< Latin *status, -ūs* < *stāre* to stand. See etym. of doublets **estate, state**.]

**sta|tus in quo** (stā′təs in kwō′, stat′əs), *Latin.* status quo.

**status quo** (kwō), **1** the way things are; the existing state of affairs: [*He*] *represents a new breed of Soviet university officials—with more of an eye on innovation than on the preservation of the status quo* (Fred. M. Hechinger). **2** the way things were previously: *to restore the status quo.* [< Latin *status quō* the state in which; see etym. under **status**]

**status quo an|te** (an′tē), *Latin.* the way things were previously.

**status symbol**, something that is supposed to indicate or represent a desirable status in society.

**stat|u|ta|ble** (stach′ů tə bəl), *adj.* = statutory.

**stat|ute** (stach′üt), *n.* **1a** a law enacted by a legislative body of a state or nation and recorded in a formal document: *The statutes for the United States are made by Congress.* SYN: See syn. under **law**. **b** the document recording such a law. *Abbr:* stat. **2** a formally established rule; law; decree: *the statutes of a university.* **3** *International Law.* an instrument annexed or subsidiary to an international agreement such as a treaty. [< Old French *statut,* learned borrowing from Late Latin *statūtum* < Latin *statuere* establish < *stāre* to stand]

**statute book**, a collection or record of statutes.

**statute law**, law expressed or stated by statutes; written law.

**statute mile**, 5,280 feet or 1.6093 kilometers; mile (the standard mile for land measurement throughout the English-speaking world).

**statute of limitations**, a statute limiting the time during which rights or claims can be enforced by legal action, or crimes (except murder or other serious crimes) can be prosecuted.

**statute staple**, *Obsolete.* a bond of record acknowledged before the mayor of a staple, giving a creditor power to seize the property of a debtor who fails to pay his financial obligation at the appointed time.

**stat|u|to|ri|ly** (stach′ů tôr′ə lē, -tōr′-), *adv.* in a statutory manner; by statutory enactment; in accordance with the provisions of the statutes.

**stat|u|to|ry** (stach′ů tôr′ē, -tōr′-), *adj.* **1** having to do with or consisting of statutes: *a statutory part of the law, a statutory code.* **2** fixed by statute: a statutory copyright. **3** punishable by statute: *a statutory crime or offense.* **4** conforming to the provisions of a statute: *statutory regulations.*

**statutory law**, = statute law.

**statutory rape**, *U.S.* sexual intercourse with a girl who has not yet attained the age of consent, with or without the exercise of force by the male.

**stat|volt** (stat′vōlt′), *n.* an electrostatic unit of charge with a potential of one erg per statcoulomb, equal to about 300 volts.

**St. Au|gus|tine grass** (ô′gəs tēn), a type of lawn grass used in warm, humid regions. It is propagated by stolons or sprigs. Also, **Saint Augustine grass**. [< *St. Augustine,* a city in Florida]

**staum|rel** (stôm′rəl), *adj., n. Scottish.* **—*adj.*** very stupid; half-witted.
**—*n.*** a very stupid person; half-wit.
[< dialectal *staumer,* variant of *stammer*]

**staunch**[1] (stônch, stänch), *v.t., v.i.* = stanch[1].
**—*staunch′less*,** *adj.*

**staunch**[2] (stônch, stänch), *adj.* **1** able to resist or repel attack; firm; strong: *staunch walls, a staunch defense.* **2** not to be turned aside; unwavering; loyal; steadfast: *a staunch friend, a staunch supporter of the law.* SYN: constant, true, faithful, steady, unswerving. **3** soundly built and calked; watertight: *a staunch boat.* Also, **stanch**. [< Old French *estanche,* feminine of *estanc* < *estanchier;* see etym. under **stanch**[1]] **—staunch′ly**, *adv.* **—staunch′ness**, *n.*

**stau|ro|lite** (stôr′ə līt), *n.* a mineral, a silicate of aluminum and iron, yellowish-brown to dark-brown in color, found frequently twinned in the form of a cross. *Formula:* $FeAl_4Si_2O_{10}(OH)_2$ [< French *staurolite* < Greek *staurós* a cross; (originally) stake + French *-lite* -lite]

**stau|ro|lit|ic** (stôr′ə lit′ik), *adj.* having to do with, resembling, or characterized by the presence of staurolite.

**stau|ro|scope** (stôr′ə skōp), *n.* an instrument used in the microscopic examination of crystals, to find the position of planes of light vibration. [< Greek *staurós* cross + English *-scope*]

**stau|ro|scop|ic** (stô′rə skop′ik), *adj.* of, having to do with, or made by means of the stauroscope: *stauroscopic examination.* **—stau′ro|scop′i|cal|ly**, *adv.*

**stave** (stāv), *n., v.,* **staved** or **stove, stav|ing**.
**—*n.*** **1** one of the thin, narrow, curved pieces of wood which form the sides of a barrel, cask, tub, or the like. **2** a stick, staff, rod, bar, or pole. **3** a rung of a ladder or a crossbar between the legs of a chair. **4** a verse or stanza of a poem or song. **5** *Music.* staff[1].
**—*v.t.*** **1** to break a hole in (a barrel, cask, or other such container): *having staved a cask of port ...* (Tobias Smollett). **2** to smash (a hole), as in a boat or door. **3** to break up (as a barrel, cask, or boat). **4** to furnish with staves. **5** to drive off or beat with a staff or stave.
**—*v.i.*** **1** to become smashed or broken in: *Like a vessel of glass she stove and sank* (Longfellow). **2** *Dialect.* to go with a rush or dash.
**stave off**, to put off; keep back; delay or prevent: *The lost campers ate birds' eggs to stave off starvation.*
[back formation < *staves,* plural of *staff*]

▶ The variant past tense and past participle form **stove** is used chiefly with reference to the breaking of boats and the like: *The waves stove* (or *staved*) *the boat in,* but *He staved off his creditors.*

**staves** (stāvz), *n.* **1** a plural of **staff**[1]. **2** plural of **stave**.

**staves|a|cre** (stāvz′ā kər), *n.* **1** an Old World larkspur whose seeds are violently emetic and cathartic. **2** its seeds. [alteration of Middle English *staphisagre* < Medieval Latin *staphisagria* < Greek *staphìs agría* (literally) wild raisin < *staphís* raisin, and *ágrios* wild]

**stav|ing** (stā′ving), *n.* staves collectively.

**stay**[1] (stā), *v.,* **stayed** or (*Obsolete*) **staid, stay|ing**, *n.* **—*v.i.*** **1a** to continue to be; remain: *Stay here till I tell you to move. The cat stayed out all night. Shall I go or stay?* **b** to continue to be as indicated; keep: *to stay clean, stay thin. Stay still.* **2** to live for a while, especially as a guest; dwell: *to stay at a hotel. She is staying with her aunt while her mother is ill.* SYN: lodge, sojourn, abide, reside. **3** to come to a stop; halt (often used as a command to pause or to cease doing something): *We have no time to stay. Stay, stay, until the hasting day, Hath run but to the evensong* (George Herrick). **4** to pause; wait; tarry; delay: *Time and tide stay for no man.* **5a** to last, hold out, or endure: *I was unable to stay to the end of the race.* **b** to keep up (with a competitor in a race). **6** to make a stand; stand firm: *Give them leave to fly that will not stay* (Shakespeare). **7** *Poker.* to call or see a bet; continue playing a hand. **8** *Archaic.* to cease or desist: *The little girl was unable to stay from crying.*
**—*v.t.*** **1** to put off; hold back; delay: *The teacher stayed judgment till she could hear both sides. If*

*I could stay this letter an hour* (John Donne). SYN: detain. **2** to prevent (a person or thing) from doing something; check; restrain: *Stay, stay thy hands, thou art an Amazon* (Shakespeare). **3** to put an end to for a while; satisfy (as hunger or appetite): *He ate some bread and butter to stay his hunger until dinner.* **4** to bring under control or suppress (as strife or rebellion). **5** to remain for, during, or throughout: *We stayed the night in the spare room.* **6** *Informal.* to last for (a certain distance or time): *He cannot stay a mile.* **7** *Archaic.* to wait for; await: *My father stays my coming* (Shakespeare).

*—n.* **1** the act or fact of staying; stop; time spent: *a pleasant stay in the country, a week's stay at the seashore.* **2** the act or fact of stopping; check; restraint: *a stay on someone's activity.* **3** the act or fact of coming to a standstill; halt; pause: *without stop or stay* (Matthew Prior). **4** *Law.* a delay in carrying out the order of a court: *The judge granted the condemned man a stay for an appeal.* **5** *Informal.* staying power; endurance. **6** *Obsolete.* **a** a cause of stoppage; obstacle; hindrance. **b** control; restraint.

**stay out**, to remain to the end of or beyond the limit of: *It seemed as if we had stayed our English welcome out* (Hawthorne).

**stay put**, *Informal.* to remain where or as placed; remain fixed: *[a shirt] with big oversized French cuffs and generous shirttails that really stay put* (New Yorker).

[probably < unrecorded Anglo-French *estaier*, variant of Old French *ester* stand < Latin *stāre*]

*—Syn. v.i.* **1a Stay, remain** mean to continue in a stated place or condition. **Stay** emphasizes keeping on in the present or specified place or condition without leaving or stopping: *I decided to stay in college another year.* **Remain**, often used interchangeably with *stay*, may emphasize staying after the departure of others: *Of all the charter members of the club, he alone remains.*

**stay**[2] (stā), *n., v.,* **stayed, stay|ing.** *—n.* **1** a support; prop; brace. **2** *Figurative:* *The oldest son was the family's stay.* [probably < verb]

*—v.t.* **1** to support; prop; hold up. SYN: brace. **2** *Figurative.* to strengthen mentally or spiritually; fix or rest in dependence or reliance. SYN: sustain.

**stays**, a corset, especially a stiffened one: *Susan ... had suddenly become so very upright that she seemed to have put an additional bone in her stays* (Dickens).

[probably < Old French *estayer* < a Germanic word]

***stay**[3] (stā), *n., v.,* **stayed, stay|ing.** *—n.* **1** one of the strong ropes, often of wire, that support the mast of a ship. **2** any rope or chain attached to something to steady it; guy. A broadcasting antenna or a flagpole may have stays.

*—v.t.* **1** to support, secure, or attach (as a mast) by means of a stay or stays. **2** to incline (a mast) forward or aft by stays.

*—v.i.* (of a ship) to change to the other tack.

**in stays**, in the act of changing from one tack to another: *"Christabel" was sailed ... and was remarkably quick in stays* (London Times).

[Old English *stæg*]

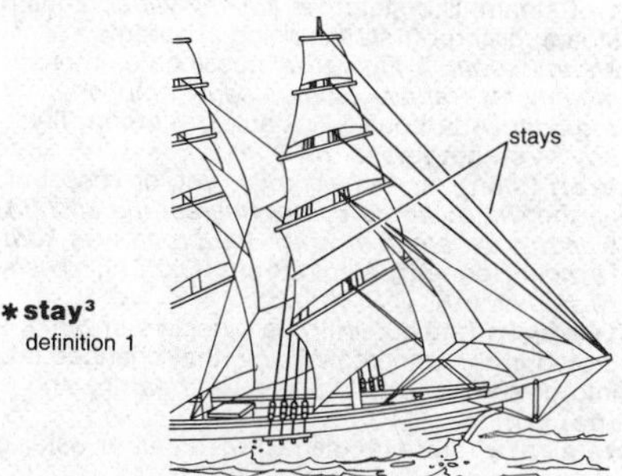


***stay**[3]
definition 1

**stay-at-home** (stā′ət hōm′), *n., adj.* *—n.* a person who would much rather remain at home than travel, go out, or engage in public activity: *This stay-at-home was delighted to sit by the fire and watch the Hibiscus Stakes ... on television* (New Yorker).

*—adj.* that is a stay-at-home; characteristic of or befitting a stay-at-home; choosing to remain at home in preference to going out, traveling, or engaging in public activity: *Then a person traveling at close to light's speed would not age as fast as his stay-at-home twin* (Science News Letter).

**stay bar**, *Architecture.* a horizontal iron bar extending in one piece from jamb to jamb along the top of the mullions of a traceried window.

**stay bolt**, a bolt or rod binding together opposite plates, as in a boiler, to enable them to sustain each other against internal pressure.

**stay|er**[1] (stā′ər), *n.* **1** a person who stays or remains: *a stayer at home.* **2** a person or animal having great staying power, especially a race horse. **3** a person or thing that stops or restrains.

**stay|er**[2] (stā′ər), *n.* a person who stays or supports.

**stay|ing power** (stā′ing), the power to hold out and not give in even though weakened or tired; power or will to endure: *The old fellow's staying powers were really extraordinary* (W. H. Hudson).

**stay-in strike**, or **stay-in** (stā′in′), *n. British.* a sit-down strike.

**Stay|man** (stā′mən), *n.* a popular variety of apple developed from the Winesap.

**stay of execution**, a delay in carrying out a sentence, granted to a prisoner by the court that sentenced him.

**stays** (stāz), *n.pl.* See under **stay**[2].

**stay|sail** (stā′sāl′; *Nautical* stā′səl), *n.* any fore-and-aft sail fastened on a stay.

**S.T.B.**, Bachelor of Sacred Theology (Latin, *Sacrae Theologiae Baccalaureus*).

**St. Bernard**, = Saint Bernard.

**std.**, standard.

**STD** (no periods), Subscriber Trunk Dialing (the British system of direct long-distance dialing).

**S.T.D.**, Doctor of Sacred Theology (Latin, *Sacrae Theologiae Doctor*).

**Ste.** or **Ste** (no period), Sainte.

**stead** (sted), *n., v.* *—n.* **1** the place or function (of a person or thing) as held by a substitute or a successor: *Our regular baby sitter could not come, but sent her sister in her stead.* SYN: lieu. **2** *Obsolete or Dialect.* **a** a tract or property in land. **b** a farm; homestead.

*—v.t. Archaic.* to avail, profit, or be of use to (a person): *There's none but truth can stead you* (Walt Whitman).

**stand in good stead**, to be of advantage or service to: *His ability to swim stood him in good stead when the boat upset.*

[Old English *stede*]

**stead|fast** (sted′fast, -fäst, -fəst), *adj.* **1** loyal; unwavering; not changing; firm of purpose: *Benjamin Franklin was a steadfast servant of his country.* SYN: unswerving. **2** firmly fixed; not moving: *a steadfast gaze. ... this tall pile ... By its own weight made steadfast and immovable* (William Congreve). **3** (of a law or condition of things) firmly settled; unchangeable; established. Also, **stedfast.** [Old English *stedefæst* < *stede* a place + *fæst* fast[1], firm] **—stead′fast|ly**, *adv.* **—stead′fast|ness**, *n.*

**stead|i|er** (sted′ē ər), *n.* a person or thing that steadies: *She uses her cane for a steadier.*

**stead|i|ly** (sted′ə lē), *adv.* in a steady manner; with regularity in habits; firmly; evenly; uniformly; unwaveringly; steadfastly: *[He] saw life steadily and saw it whole* (Matthew Arnold).

**stead|i|ness** (sted′ē nis), *n.* steady character, quality, or condition; firmness: *It will be your duty ... to set an example of discipline and perfect steadiness under fire* (Horatio H. Kitchener).

**stead|ing** (sted′ing), *n. Scottish.* a farmhouse and outbuildings. [< *stead* a farm + *-ing*[1]]

**stead|y** (sted′ē), *adj.,* **stead|i|er, stead|i|est,** *v.,* **stead|ied, stead|y|ing,** *interj., n., pl.* **stead|ies,** *adv.* **—adj. 1a** changing little; uniform; regular: *a steady breeze, a steady price, a steady barometer. He is making steady progress at school.* **b** regularly doing a particular thing; constant: *a steady worker, a steady playgoer.* **2a** firmly fixed; not swaying or shaking; firm: *a steady hand. The post is steady as a rock. Hold the ladder steady.* **b** assured in movement or action; not faltering or tremulous: *a steady aim.* **3** not easily excited; calm: *a steady mind or head, steady nerves.* **4** resolute; steadfast: *a steady belief, a steady purpose, steady friendship.* SYN: unwavering. **5** having good habits; reliable: *He is a steady young man.* SYN: trustworthy, dependable. **6** (of a ship) keeping nearly upright and on course, especially in a heavy sea. **7** *Informal.* being one's regular sweetheart: *Mary was his steady girl.*

*—v.t.* **1** to make or keep steady; keep from shaking or swaying: *Steady the ladder while I climb to the roof.* **2** to make regular in character and conduct: *Don't be nervous; steady yourself. She was too confused to steady her thoughts. His experiences abroad steadied his character.* *—v.i.* **1** to become steady; regain or maintain an upright or stable position or condition: *Our sails filled as the wind steadied from the east. The horses' pace steadied. The market steadied after a week's fluctuation.* **2** to become regular in conduct or stable in character: *After the playboy married, he steadied down.*

*—interj.* **1** be calm! don't get excited! **2** *Nautical.* hold the helm as it is! keep on course!

*—n. U.S. Informal.* one's regular sweetheart: *I heard this Russell was ... your ... friend Mildred's steady* (Booth Tarkington).

*—adv.* in a steady manner; steadily: *to steer steady.*

**go steady**, *Informal.* to be a boy's steady girlfriend or a girl's steady boyfriend: *"Going steady" ... undoubtedly is a factor in building toward early marriage* (Paul H. Landis).

[< *stead* + *-y*[1]]

*—Syn. adj.* **1a, b Steady, regular** mean constant or uniform in acting, doing, moving, or happening. **Steady** emphasizes the absence of interruption or change: *He has been unable to find steady work.* **Regular** emphasizes a fixed, usual, or uniform procedure, practice, program, or pattern: *He is a regular subscriber to several magazines.*

**stead|y-go|ing** (sted′ē gō′ing), *adj.* steady in action, habits, or purpose.

**steady motion**, motion of a fluid maintained at a velocity constant in magnitude and direction at any point.

**steady state**, *Physics.* the condition in which all or most changes or disturbances have been eliminated from a system: *We see examples of the steady state in the equilibrium phase of chemical reactions ... and in the "balance of nature"* (Emilio Q. Daddario).

**stead|y-state** (sted′ē stāt′), *adj.* **1** *Physics.* unchanging, or changing very little, in quality or behavior: *a steady-state current.* **2** *Astronomy.* having to do with the steady-state theory: *a steady-state universe, the steady-state hypothesis.*

**stead|y-stat|er** (sted′ē stā′tər), *n.* a supporter of the steady-state theory.

**steady-state theory**, the theory that the universe is in appreciably the same state as it has always been, for, although matter has been and is being lost or dispersed, other matter is continuously created to take its place.

**steak** (stāk), *n.* **1** a slice of beef, especially one cut from the hindquarter, for broiling or frying; beefsteak. **2** a slice of any meat or fish for broiling or frying: *a salmon steak.* **3** finely ground meat, especially beef but sometimes beef mixed with pork, veal, or other ingredients, shaped and cooked somewhat like a steak: *hamburger steak, a Salisbury steak.* [probably < Scandinavian (compare Norwegian *steik* < Old Icelandic *steikja* to roast)]

**steak house**, or **steak|house** (stāk′hous′), *n.* a restaurant that serves broiled steaks as its specialty; grill.

**steak knife**, a table knife with a sharp blade for cutting beefsteak.

**steal** (stēl), *v.,* **stole, sto|len, steal|ing,** *n.* **—v.t. 1** to take (something) that does not belong to one; take dishonestly: *Robbers stole the money. Who steals my purse, steals trash* (Shakespeare). **2** to take or appropriate (another's work, words, or ideas) without permission or acknowledgment; pass off as one's own: *No man like you for stealing other men's inventions* (Scott). **3** to take, get, or do secretly: *to steal a kiss, to steal a look at someone. She stole time from her lessons to read a story.* **4** to take, get, or win by art, charm, or gradual means: *The baby stole our hearts. At the circus, the trained bears stole the act from the clowns.* **5** to place, move, or pass slowly, gently, or imperceptibly: *She stole her hand into his.* **6** *Baseball.* to run to (second base, third base, or home plate) as the pitcher delivers the ball to the batter. A player steals a base when he reaches it without the help of a hit, base on balls, error, passed ball, wild pitch, or balk. **7** to make (as a play or point) unexpectedly.

*—v.i.* **1** to commit or practice theft: *From childhood she had stolen whenever she had a chance.* **2** to move, come, or leave secretly or quietly: *She had stolen softly out of the house. A mink steals out of the marsh ... and seizes a frog* (Thoreau). SYN: sneak, skulk, slink. **3** to move, pass, come, or go slowly, gently, or imperceptibly: *The years steal by. A feeling of drowsiness stole over me. Her hand stole timidly into his.* **4** *Baseball.* to steal a base.

*—n.* **1** *Informal.* **a** the act of stealing. **b** the thing stolen. **2** *Informal.* something obtained at a very low cost or with very little effort: *This table is such a bargain it's a steal.* **3** *Informal.* a dishonest or unethical transaction at a great profit: *Of all the swindles and steals that have ever been proposed or carried out in our State, this is the largest and boldest* (Daily Gazette [Little Rock, Arkansas]). **4** *Baseball.* a safe advance from one base to another by stealing: *Davis overthrew second in an attempt to nail Hale on a steal* (Oregonian).

---

**Pronunciation Key:** hat, āge, cãre, fär; let, ēqual, tėrm; it, īce; hot, ōpen, ôrder; oil, out; cup, pu̇t, rüle; child; long; thin; ᴛʜen; zh, measure; ə represents **a** in about, **e** in taken, **i** in pencil, **o** in lemon, **u** in circus.

**steal a march**. See under **march**[1].
**steal one's** (or **the**) **thunder**. See under **thunder**.
**steal the show**. See under **show**.
[Old English *stelan*] —**steal′er**, *n.*
—*Syn. v.t.* **1 Steal, pilfer, filch** mean to take dishonestly or wrongfully and secretly something belonging to someone else. **Steal** is the general and common word: *Thieves stole the silver.* **Pilfer** means to steal and carry away in small amounts: *In many department stores hidden guards watch for people who pilfer merchandise.* **Filch** implies stealthy or furtive pilfering, usually of objects of little value: *The children filched some candy from the counter.*

**steal|ing** (stē′ling), *n., adj.* —*n.* the act of one who steals: *Stealing is a crime.*
—*adj.* that steals or moves stealthily.
**stealings**, what is stolen: *I asked how much his office was worth, and his answer was six hundred dollars, besides stealings* (Frederick Marryat).

**stealth** (stelth), *n.* **1** secret or sly action: *She obtained the letter by stealth, taking it while nobody was in the room. The greatest pleasure I know is to do a good action by stealth, and to have it found out by accident* (Charles Lamb). **2** *Obsolete.* the act of stealing or going furtively into or out of a place: *I told him of your stealth into this wood* (Shakespeare). [Middle English *stelthe*, apparently unrecorded Old English *stælth* (compare *stælthing* theft), related to *stelan* steal]

**stealth|ful** (stelth′fəl), *adj.* = stealthy.

**stealth|y** (stel′thē), *adj.*, **stealth|i|er, stealth|i|est.** done in a secret manner; secret; sly: *The cat crept with stealthy movements toward the bird.* SYN: furtive, sneaking, underhand, surreptitious. —**stealth′i|ly**, *adv.* —**stealth′i|ness**, *n.*

**steam** (stēm), *n., v., adj.* —*n.* **1a** water in the form of vapor or gas. Boiling water gives off steam. **b** the white cloud or mist formed by the condensation, when cooled, of the invisible vapor from boiling water. **2a** the vapor of boiling water used, especially by confinement in special apparatus, to generate mechanical power and for heating and cooking. **b** the power thus generated. **3** *Informal, Figurative.* power; energy; force: *That old man still has a lot of steam left in him.* **4** a vapor or fume; exhalation.
—*v.i.* **1** to give off steam or vapor: *The cup of coffee is steaming.* **2** to become covered with condensed vapor: *The windshield had completely steamed up inside the heated car.* **3** to rise or issue in the form of steam: *Several damp gentlemen, whose clothes … began to steam* (Dickens). **4** (of an engine, boiler, or other device) to generate or produce steam. **5** to move by steam: *The ship with its cargo steamed off.* **6** *Informal, Figurative.* **a** to run or go quickly, as if powered by steam; move with speed and vigor: *The runner steamed into second base for a double.* **b** to show anger or irritation; fume: *The boss rushes in, steaming about figures in the Randall account* (St. Louis Post-Dispatch). *We see this guy, a book critic, … really steamed* (Life).
—*v.t.* **1** to cook, remove, soften, freshen, or disinfect by steam: *to steam vegetables, to steam a plum pudding, to steam stamps off an envelope, to steam surgical instruments.* **2** to give off or emit (steam or vapor); send out in the form of vapor. **3** to transport or cause to move by steam. **4** *Informal, Figurative.* to make angry or agitated: *The mayor got further steamed up when the press lambasted him, … and his volatile temper boiled over* (New Yorker).
—*adj.* **1** of, having to do with, or consisting of steam. **2** cooking, softening, washing, heating, or treating by steam: *a steam laundry, a steam kettle.* **3** propelled by or with a steam engine: *a steam train.* **4** operated by steam or a steam engine. **5** containing, conveying, or regulating steam: *a steam valve.* **6** *British Informal, Figurative.* ordinary; conventional: *I suspect the steam telephone is actually a better means of communication than look-as-you-talk television* (Tom Dalyell).
**get up steam**, *Informal.* to work up the necessary energy: [*He*] *tried to work, but could not get up steam* (Sunday Times).
**let** (or **blow**) **off steam**, *Informal.* **a** to get rid of excess energy: *The children ran around the playground at recess, letting off steam.* **b** to relieve one's feelings: *He let off steam by yelling at a clerk.*
[Old English *stēam* vapor, fume] —**steam′like′**, *adj.*

**steam bath**, **1** a bath taken in a steam room: *He keeps fit by daily visits to the gymnasium for steam baths* (New York Times). **2** a Turkish bath or a sauna. **3** a bath of steam, used in a laboratory. **4** laboratory apparatus containing such a bath.

**steam|boat** (stēm′bōt′), *n.* a boat moved by steam.

**steam boiler**, a boiler in which water is heated to make steam, as for working a steam engine or a steam turbine.

**steam|car** (stēm′kär′), *n.* **1** an automobile driven by steam; steamer. **2** *U.S., Archaic.* a railroad car.

**steam chest** or **box**, the chamber through which the steam of an engine passes from the boiler to the cylinder.

**steam cylinder**, the cylinder of a steam engine.

**steamed-up** (stēmd′up′), *adj. Informal.* excited; agitated; angry.

***steam engine**, an engine operated by steam. A steam engine is usually one in which a sliding piston in a cylinder is moved by the expansive action of steam generated in a boiler. Locomotives, ships, and large machines may be driven by steam engines. —**steam′-en′gine**, *adj.*

***steam engine**

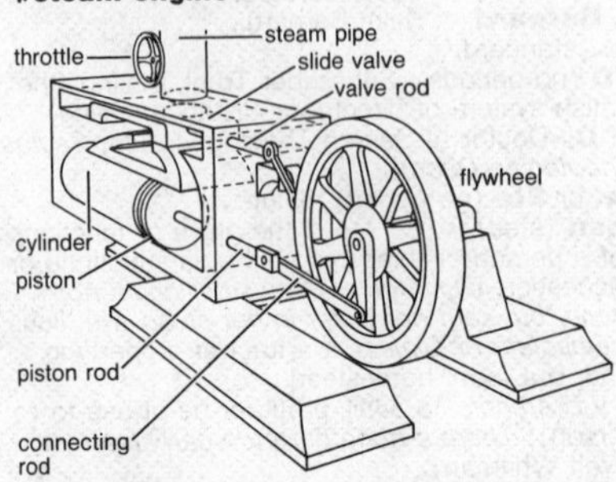


**steam|er** (stē′mər), *n.* **1** a steamboat; steamship. **2** an engine run by steam. **3** a container in which something is steamed or kept warm, as for sterilization or cooking. **4** a boiler or other vessel for generating steam. **5** = steamcar.

***steamer chair**, a kind of reclining chair used by passengers on the deck of a ship.

***steamer chair**
***steamer trunk**

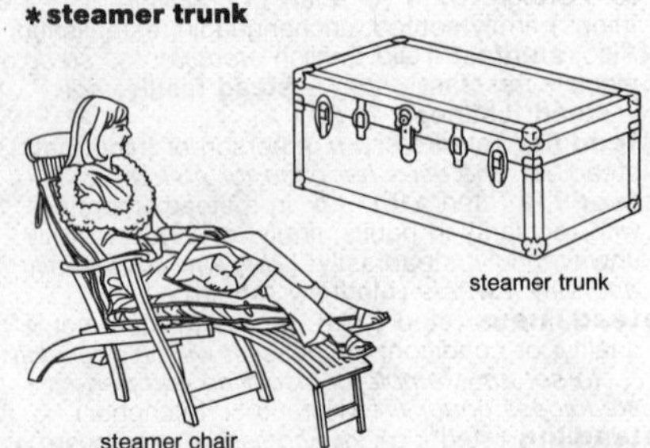


**steamer clam**, = soft clam.

**steamer duck**, a duck of Patagonia and nearby islands whose movement in water suggests a steamboat.

**steamer rug**, a heavy blanket, especially one used to keep a person warm in a chair on the deck of a ship.

***steamer trunk**, a small trunk suitable for use in a ship's stateroom.

**steam fitter**, a person who installs and repairs steam pipes, radiators, boilers, air-conditioning systems, and the like.

**steam fitting**, the work of a steam fitter.

**steam fog**, fog that appears when cold air picks up moisture as it passes over warmer water.

**steam gauge**, an attachment to a boiler to indicate the pressure of steam.

**steam generator**, a unit for producing high-pressure steam, consisting of a combined boiler and superheater.

**steam hammer**, a powerful hammer for forging steel and for other heavy jobs, operated by steam power.

**steam heat**, heat given off by steam in radiators and pipes.

**steam|ing** (stē′ming), *adj., n.* —*adj.* emitting steam or vapor: *a steaming glass of tea. He … pulled up his steaming horse by the station* (Joseph S. Le Fanu).
—*n.* travel by steamboat or steamship.
**steaming hot**, piping hot; very hot: *a cup of steaming hot coffee.*

**steam iron**, an electric iron in which water is heated to produce steam, which is released through holes in or near its undersurface to dampen cloth while pressing it.

**steam jacket**, an enclosure or jacket into which steam passes, built round a tank, kettle, or the like, in order to heat it.

**steam locomotive**, a locomotive that moves by means of steam generated in its own boiler.

**steam pipe**, a pipe through which steam is conveyed.

**steam point**, a standard of measurement for temperature, equal to the temperature at which water boils under normal atmospheric pressure; 100 degrees centigrade (Celsius).

**steam power**, the power of steam applied to move machinery or produce any other result.

**steam radio**, *British Informal.* sound radio.

**steam-roll** or **steam|roll** (stēm′rōl′), *v.t., v.i.* = steam-roller.

***steam roller**, or **steam|roll|er**[1] (stēm′rō′lər), *n.* **1** a heavy roller, formerly run by steam but now usually by an internal-combustion engine, used to crush and level materials in making and repairing roads. **2** *Informal, Figurative.* a means of crushing opposition.

***steam roller**
definition 1

**steam-roll|er** or **steam|roll|er**[2] (stēm′rō′lər), *v., adj.* —*v.t.* **1** *Informal.* **a** to override by crushing power or force; crush: *to steam-roller all opposition.* **b** to force (into or through) by this means. **2** to make level or smooth with a steam roller.
—*v.i. Informal.* to override or crush a person or thing that is in opposition.
—*adj. Informal.* crushing as if with a steam roller; overriding: *steam-roller methods.*

**steam room**, a room filled with dry or wet steam for sweating, as in a Turkish bath.

**steam|ship** (stēm′ship′), *n.* a ship moved by steam. *Abbr:* SS (no periods).

**steam shovel**, a machine for digging, formerly always operated by steam, but now often by an internal-combustion engine; power shovel.

**steam table**, a fixture resembling a shallow tank in which water is heated or into which steam is piped, with holes in its upper surface into which containers are fitted. It is used especially by restaurants and institutional kitchens to keep food warm.

**steam-tight** (stēm′tīt′), *adj.* impervious to the passage of steam under pressure.

**steam trap**, a device permitting the passage of condensed water out of pipes and radiators while preventing the escape of steam.

**steam turbine**, a rotary engine operated by steam.

**steam|y** (stē′mē), *adj.*, **steam|i|er, steam|i|est.** **1** of steam; like steam: *a steamy vapor.* **2** full of steam; giving off steam; rising in steam: *a steamy room.* **3** *Figurative.* passionate; intense: *a steamy love affair. … the steamy emotionalism of the fight* (Ada Louise Huxtable). —**steam′i|ly**, *adv.* —**steam′i|ness**, *n.*

**stean** (stēn), *n. Archaic.* a jar, pot, or vessel of earthenware: *In the corner nearest the kitchen was a great stean in which the bread was kept* (Arnold Bennett). Also, **steen.** [Old English *stǣne* < *stān* stone]

**ste|ap|sin** (stē ap′sin), *n.* a digestive enzyme, secreted in the pancreatic juice, that changes fat into glycerol and fatty acids. [< *stea*(rin) and (pe)*psin*]

**ste|a|rate** (stē′ə rāt, stir′āt), *n.* a salt or ester of stearic acid. [< *stear*(ic) + *-ate*[2]]

**ste|ar|ic** (stē ar′ik, stir′-), *adj.* of, having to do with, or obtained from stearin, suet, or fat. [< *stearic* (acid)]

**stearic acid**, a white, odorless, tasteless, saturated fatty acid, obtained chiefly from tallow and other hard fats by saponification. Stearic acid exists in combination with glycerol as stearin, in beef and mutton fat, and in several vegetable fats. *Formula:* $C_{18}H_{36}O_2$ [< French *acide stéarique* < *stéarine* stearin]

**ste|a|rin** (stē′ər in, stir′in), *n.* **1** a white, odorless, crystalline solid substance, an ester of stearic acid and glycerol, that is the chief constituent of many animal and vegetable fats. *Formula:* $C_{57}H_{110}O_6$ **2** a mixture of fatty acids used especially for making candles and solid alcohol. **3** the solid or higher melting parts of any fat. [< French *stéarine* < Greek *stéār, stéātos* fat + French *-ine* -ine[2]]

**ste|a|rine** (stē′ər in, -ə rēn; stir′in, -ēn), *n.* = stearin.

**ste|a|rop|tene** (stē′ə rop′tēn), *n.* the solid part of an essential oil. [< Greek *stéār* fat + *ptēnós* winged < *pétesthai* to fly (because of its volatility)]

**ste|ar|rhe|a** or **ste|ar|rhoe|a** (stē′ə rē′ə), *n.* = seborrhea. [< Greek *stéār, stéātos* fat, tallow + *rheîn* to flow]

**ste|a|ryl alcohol** (stē′ə rəl, stir′əl), a solid alcohol produced from stearic acid, occurring as white flakes or granules, used in pharmaceuticals and cosmetics, and as a lubricant and detergent. *Formula:* $C_{18}H_{38}O$

**ste|a|tite** (stē′ə tīt), *n.* a rock composed of impure talc, with a smooth, greasy feel; soapstone. [< Latin *steatītis* soapstone < Greek *stéār, stéātos* fat, tallow]

**ste|a|tit|ic** (stē′ə tit′ik), *adj.* of, having to do with, like, or made of steatite.

**ste|a|to|py|gi|a** (stē′ə tə pī′jē ə, -pij′ē-), *n.* an excessive deposit of fat on the buttocks and thighs, prevalent especially among the women of the Hottentots and certain other native African peoples.
[< New Latin *steatopygia* < *steatopyga* a protuberance of the buttocks < Greek *stéār, stéātos* fat, suet + *pȳgē* rump, buttocks]

**ste|a|to|pyg|ic** (stē′ə tə pij′ik), *adj.* having to do with, characterized by, or exhibiting steatopygia.

**ste|a|to|py|gous** (stē′ə tə pī′gəs), *adj.* = steatopygic.

**ste|a|tor|rhe|a** or **ste|a|tor|rhoe|a** (stē′ə tə-rē′ə), *n.* **1** = seborrhea. **2** an abnormally great proportion of fat in the bowel movements, caused by poor absorption of fat in the small intestine.
[< Greek *stéār, stéātos* tallow, fat + *rheîn* to flow]

**ste|a|to|sis** (stē ə tō′sis), *n.* **1** fatty degeneration. **2** any disease of the sebaceous glands. [< New Latin *steatosis* < Greek *stéār, stéātos* fat + New Latin *-osis* -osis]

**sted|fast** (sted′fast, -fäst, -fəst), *adj.* = steadfast. — **sted′fast|ly**, *adv.* — **sted′fast|ness**, *n.*

**steed** (stēd), *n.* **1** a horse, especially a riding horse: *I set her on my pacing steed* (Keats). **2** a high-spirited horse. **3** a war horse. **4** *Figurative.* anything, such as a person or vehicle, likened to either of these. [Old English *stēda* stallion]

**steed|less** (stēd′lis), *adj.* without a steed.

**steek** (stēk), *v., n. Scottish.* — ***v.t.*** **1** to shut. **2** to stitch.
— ***v.i.*** **1** to close a place; lock a door. **2** to sew.
— ***n.*** (in needlework or knitting) a stitch.
[Middle English *steken,* probably unrecorded Old English *stecan*]

**steel** (stēl), *n., adj., v.* — ***n.*** **1** an alloy of iron and carbon. Steel is produced by separating a given amount of carbon from molten pig iron. Steel contains less than 1.7 per cent of carbon, and less than the amount contained in cast iron, but more than that in wrought iron. It has greater hardness and flexibility than cast iron and hence is much used for tools, machinery, and girders. See also **hard steel, medium steel, soft steel.** **2** something made from steel: **a** a sword or knife of steel. **b** a piece of steel for striking sparks from flint. **c** a rod of steel for sharpening knives. **d** a narrow strip of steel used for stiffening and support, as in a corset or dress. **3** *Figurative.* steellike hardness or strength: *true as steel. The brave soldier had nerves of steel.* **4** the market quotation for stock in a steel company.
— ***adj.*** **1** made or consisting of steel. **2** like steel, as in color or hardness. **3** of, having to do with, or used for the production of steel.
— ***v.t.*** **1** to point, edge, or cover with steel. **2** *Figurative.* to make hard or strong like steel: *The miser steeled his heart against the sufferings of the poor. The soldiers steeled themselves to withstand the attack.* **SYN:** harden, indurate, inure.
**steels,** shares of stock, bonds, or other securities issued by steel companies: *Steels ... registered substantial gains yesterday* (Wall Street Journal).
[Old English *stēle*] — **steel′like′**, *adj.*

***steel band**

***steel band**, a West Indian musical band that performs on various percussion instruments usually made from the heads of oil drums.

**steel blue**, a lustrous dark blue, like the color of tempered steel. — **steel′-blue′**, *adj.*

**steel engraving**, *Graphic Arts.* **1** the art or process of engraving upon a steel plate. **2** a print or impression from such a plate.

**steel gray**, a dull, dark gray color, having a tinge of blue. — **steel′-gray′**, *adj.*

**steel guitar**, = Hawaiian guitar.

**steel|head** (stēl′hed′), *n.* a rainbow trout that enters the sea before it returns to freshwater streams to spawn.

**steel|ie** (stē′lē), *n.* **1** a steel marble: *McGurk took all his marbles, including a good steelie* (Harper's). **2** = steelhead.

**steel|i|ness** (stē′lē nis), *n.* steely nature or quality.

**steel|less** (stēl′lis), *adj.* containing no steel.

**steel|mak|er** (stēl′mā′kər), *n.* a manufacturer of steel.

**steel|mak|ing** (stēl′mā′king), *n., adj.* — ***n.*** the manufacture of steel.
— ***adj.*** of or having to do with steelmaking: *a steelmaking furnace.*

**steel|man** (stēl′man′), *n., pl.* **-men.** *U.S.* **1** = steelmaker. **2** a seller of steel.

**steel|mas|ter** (stēl′mas′tər, -mäs′-), *n. Especially British.* steelmaker.

**steel mill**, a place where steel is made.

**steels** (stēlz), *n.pl.* See under **steel**.

**steel trap**, a trap with jaws and spring of steel.

**steel-trap** (stēl′trap′), *adj.* resembling or suggesting a steel trap; sharp and powerful: *steel-trap cunning.*

**steel wool**, a mass of long, fine steel shavings, used for cleaning or polishing surfaces.

**steel|work** (stēl′wėrk′), *n.* tools, parts, framing, or other objects, made of steel.

**steel|work|er** (stēl′wėr′kər), *n.* a person who works in a place where steel is made.

**steel|works** (stēl′wėrks′), *n.pl. or sing.* a place where steel is made.

**steel|y** (stē′lē), *adj.,* **steel|i|er, steel|i|est.** **1** made of steel. **2** like steel in color, strength, or hardness.

***steel|yard¹** (stēl′yärd′, stil′yərd), *n.* a type of scale for weighing, having arms of unequal length. The longer one has a movable weight and is marked in units of weight; the shorter one has a hook for holding the object to be weighed. [apparently < *steel* + *yard²* rod, beam; probably influenced by *Steelyard*]

***steelyard¹**

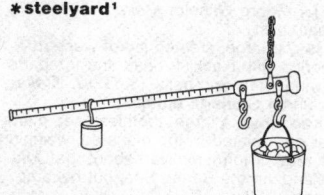

**Steel|yard** or **steel|yard²** (stēl′yärd′), *n.* in English history: **1** a place in London where the Hanseatic merchants formerly had an establishment. **2** the merchants themselves. **3** a similar establishment elsewhere. [mistranslation of Middle Low German *stâlhof* < *stâl* (pronounced "steel") pattern + *hof* courtyard]

**steel|y-eyed** (stē′lē īd′), *adj.* having hard eyes; cold-eyed; emotionless; impassive: *a group of steely-eyed Secret Service men* (New Yorker).

**steen** (stēn), *n.* = stean.

**steen|bok** (stēn′bok′, stān′-), *n.* any one of various small African antelopes with straight, slender horns, frequenting rocky places. Also, **steinbock, steinbok, steinbuck.** [< Afrikaans *steenbok* < *steen* stone + *bok* buck¹]

**steep¹** (stēp), *adj., n.* — ***adj.*** **1a** having a sharp slope: *a very steep hill, a steep grade.* **b** almost straight up and down: *a steep cliff.* **2** *Figurative.* **a** unreasonably high; exorbitant: *a steep price.* **b** sharply rising or falling: *a steep gain in exports, a steep decline in the rate of employment.* **3** *Informal.* exaggerated; incredible: *a steep story.* **4** *Obsolete.* headlong: *from that steep ruin to which he had nigh brought them* (Milton). **5** *Obsolete.* elevated; lofty.
— ***n.*** a steep slope; precipitous place.
[Old English *stēap*] — **steep′ly**, *adv.* — **steep′ness**, *n.*
— ***Syn.*** *adj.* **1a, b Steep, abrupt, precipitous** mean having a sharp slope. **Steep** suggests having a slope sharp enough to be hard to go up or down: *I do not like to drive up a steep hill. Steep Hill—Use Low Gear.* **Abrupt** suggests a very steep slope suddenly broken off from the level: *From the rim they made their way down the abrupt sides of the canyon.* **Precipitous** suggests a nearly vertical slope, like that of a cliff: *The climbers will attempt to scale the precipitous eastern slope of the peak.*

**steep²** (stēp), *v., n.* — ***v.i.*** to undergo soaking; soak: *Let the tea leaves steep in boiling water for five minutes.*
— ***v.t.*** **1** to permit to steep; soak, especially in order to soften, cleanse, or extract an essence: *She steeped the tea in boiling water.* **2** to make thoroughly or frequently wet (with); saturate (in): *His shirt was steeped with sweat. She steeped her handkerchief in tears as she cried.* **3** *Figurative.* to involve deeply in something; immerse; imbue: *to steep oneself in knowledge of the Middle Ages. The professor steeps himself in Latin.*
— ***n.*** **1** the process of soaking. **2** the liquid in which something is soaked. **3** *Obsolete.* a steeping vessel.
**steeped in**, filled with; permeated by: *ruins steeped in gloom, a mind steeped in hatred. The whole of modern thought is steeped in science* (Thomas H. Huxley).
[Middle English *stepen,* perhaps unrecorded Old English *stēpan* (compare *stēap* bowl)]

**steep|en** (stē′pən), *v.i.* to become steep or steeper.
— ***v.t.*** to make steep or steeper.

**steep|er** (stē′pər), *n.* **1** a person or thing that steeps or soaks. **2** a vessel used in steeping.

**steep|grass** (stēp′gras′, -gräs′), *n.* = butterwort.

**steep|ish** (stē′pish), *adj.* rather steep.

**stee|ple** (stē′pəl), *n.* **1** a high tower on a church, temple, or other public building. Steeples usually have spires and often contain bells. ... *spire steeples ... point as with silent finger to the sky* (Samuel Taylor Coleridge). **2** a spire on the top of the tower or roof of a church or similar building. [Old English *stēpel,* related to *stēap* steep¹] — **stee′ple|like′**, *adj.*

**stee|ple|bush** (stē′pəl bu̇sh′), *n. U.S.* a hardhack.

**stee|ple|chase** (stē′pəl chās′), *n., v.,* **-chased, -chas|ing.** — ***n.*** **1a** a horse race over a course having ditches, hedges, and other obstacles. **b** a cross-country horse race in which the contestants hurdle such obstacles as fences and brooks. **2** a cross-country footrace in which the runners jump over hurdles and a ditch filled with water.
— ***v.i.*** to ride or run in a steeplechase.
[because formerly it was a race with a church steeple in view as goal] — **stee′ple|chas′er**, *n.*

**stee|ple-crowned** (stē′pəl kround′), *adj.* having a tall, pointed crown, as a hat.

**stee|pled** (stē′pəld), *adj.* having a steeple or steeples or abounding in steeples: *many a steepled town* (John Greenleaf Whittier).

**steeple hat**, a steeple-crowned hat.

**stee|ple|jack** (stē′pəl jak′), *n., v.* — ***n.*** a person who climbs steeples, towers, tall chimneys, or the like to make repairs or do other work.
— ***v.i.*** to do the work of a steeplejack: *[He] steeplejacked, punched cows in Texas, got married at 21* (Time).

**steeple top**, **1** the top of a steeple. **2** = Greenland whale (because its spout holes end in a sort of cone).

**steep-to** (stēp′tü′), *adj.* descending almost perpendicularly into water, as a shore or shoal bordering navigable water; abruptly steep.

**steep|wa|ter** (stēp′wôt′ər, -wot′-), *n.* the water in which a thing is soaked or macerated.

**steep|y** (stē′pē), *adj. Archaic.* steep.

**steer¹** (stir), *v., n.* — ***v.t.*** **1** to guide the course of: *to steer a car, steer one's plans toward success. And all I ask is a tall ship and a star to steer her by* (John Masefield). **2** to guide; lead; conduct; pilot: *to steer a person through a crowd, steer a horse to victory.* **3** *Figurative.* to set and follow (a certain course): *That country steers a middle course between war and peace with its neighbors. He was bravely steering his way across the continent* (Washington Irving).
— ***v.i.*** **1** to guide the course of a ship, automobile, bicycle, horse, or other conveyance or animal: *The sail collapsed, and the captain steered for the harbor.* **2** to admit of being steered; be guided: *This car steers easily.* **3** *Figurative.* to direct one's way or course: *Steer away from trouble. He steered along the street by her side* (Elizabeth Gaskell).
— ***n.*** *U.S. Slang.* an idea or a suggested course of action; tip: *Of the selling jobs advertised ... maybe there might be a real steer in one* (James T. Farrell). *[The] navigator gave Mosbacher a bum steer—laying a course to the wrong buoy* (Time).

**Pronunciation Key:** hat, āge, cãre, fär; let, ēqual, tėrm; it, īce; hot, ōpen, ôrder; oil, out; cup, pu̇t, rüle; child; long; thin; ᴛʜen; zh, measure; ə represents **a** in about, **e** in taken, **i** in pencil, **o** in lemon, **u** in circus.

**steer clear of**, to keep away from; avoid: *Steer clear of him until he calms down. We would have steered clear of them, and cared not to have them see us, if we could help it* (Daniel Defoe). [Old English *stēran*] —**steer′er**, *n.*

**steer²** (stir), *n.* **1** a young male of cattle that has been castrated; young ox, usually two to four years old, especially one being raised for beef. **2** any male of beef cattle. [Old English *stēor*]

**steer³** (stir), *v.t., v.i., n. Dialect.* stir.

**steer|a|bil|i|ty** (stir′ə bil′ə tē), *n.* the quality of being steerable: *the steerability of a sled.*

**steer|a|ble** (stir′ə bəl), *adj.* that can be steered.

**steer|age** (stir′ij), *n.* **1** the part of a passenger ship occupied by passengers traveling at the cheapest rate. Steerage was replaced on most lines originally by third class and now by tourist class. **2a** the act or process of steering a boat or ship. **b** the manner in which a ship is affected by the helm. **3** *Figurative.* direction; guidance: *the steerage of a country through war.*

**steer|age|way** (stir′ij wā′), *n.* the amount of forward motion a ship must have before it can be steered; speed below which a vessel will not answer the helm.

**steer|hide** (stir′hīd′), *n.* **1** the hide of a steer. **2** leather made from it.

**steer|ing column** (stir′ing), the cylindrical shaft connecting the steering gear of an automobile with the steering wheel.

**steering committee**, *U.S.* a committee, in a lawmaking or other body, that is responsible for deciding which items shall be considered and in what order.

**steering gear**, **1a** the mechanism by which the front wheels of an automobile are turned to right or left. See diagram under **power steering**. **b** the mechanism by which the rudder of a ship is turned to port or starboard. **2** any apparatus for steering: *the steering gear of a bicycle.*

**steering wheel**, the wheel that is turned to steer an automobile, ship, or other conveyance.

**steer|less** (stir′lis), *adj.* having no rudder. [Old English *steōrleās* < *steōr* rudder + *-leās* -less]

**steers|man** (stirz′mən), *n., pl.* **-men.** a person who steers a boat or ship: *By and by ... nearly every pilot on the river had a steersman* (Mark Twain). **SYN:** helmsman.

**steers|man|ship** (stirz′mən ship), *n.* the office or art of a steersman; skill in steering.

**steeve¹** (stēv), *n., v.,* **steeved, steev|ing.** —*n.* a long derrick or spar with a block at one end, used in stowing cargo.
—*v.t.* to stow (cargo) in the hold or on the deck of a ship: *Each morning we ... brought off as many hides as we could steeve in the course of the day* (Richard H. Dana).
[< Old French *estiver* or Italian *stivare* < Latin *stīpāre* to press, crowd; pack in. Compare etym. under **stevedore.**]

**steeve²** (stēv), *v.,* **steeved, steev|ing,** *n.* —*v.i.* (of a bowsprit) to extend upward at an angle rather than horizontally with the keel.
—*v.t.* to set (a bowsprit or spar) at an angle upward.
—*n.* the angle upward of a bowsprit.
[origin uncertain]

**steev|ing** (stē′ving), *n.* = steeve².

**Stef|an-Boltz|mann law** (stef′ən bōlts′mən), the law stating that the total energy radiated per second by each unit area of a perfect black body is proportional to the fourth power of its absolute temperature. [< Josef *Stefan*, 1835-1893, and Ludwig *Boltzmann*, 1844-1906, Austrian physicists]

**steg|o|ce|pha|li|an** (steg′ə sə fā′lē ən), *adj.* of or having to do with a group of extinct tailless amphibians whose skulls were protected by bony plates. [< New Latin *Stegocephalia* the name of the order (< Greek *stégos* roof + *kephalē* head)]

**steg|o|don** (steg′ə don), *n., pl.* **-dons** or (*collectively*) **-don.** any one of a group of very large extinct mammals with ridged teeth, related to the elephants and mastodons. [< New Latin *Stegodon* the genus name < Greek *stégos* roof + *odoús, odóntos* tooth (because their teeth are ridged)]

**steg|o|saur** (steg′ə sôr), *n.* = stegosaurus.

***steg|o|sau|rus** (steg′ə sôr′əs), *n., pl.* **-sau|ri** (-sôr′ī). a large, extinct, plant-eating reptile (about 18 feet long) with heavy, bony armor. The stegosauri comprised a genus of ornithischian dinosaurs. [< New Latin *Stegosaurus* the genus name < Greek *stégos* house, roof + *saûros* lizard]

**stein** (stīn), *n.* **1** a mug for beer. A stein is usually of earthenware or glass and holds from twelve to sixteen ounces. **2** the amount of beer that a stein holds. [< German *Stein* stone, short for *Steinkrug* stone jug]

**stein|bock** or **stein|bok** (stīn′bok′), *n.* **1** = steenbok. **2** = ibex. [< German *Steinbock* < *Stein* stone + *Bock* buck¹]

**stein|buck** (stīn′buk′), = steenbok.

**Stein|heim man** (stīn′hīm′), an early type of pre-Neanderthal man similar to Homo sapiens, identified from the skull fragments found at Steinheim, a town in West Germany.

**ste|la** (stē′lə), *n., pl.* **-lae** (-lē), **-las.** = stele (defs. 1, 2, and 3). [< Latin *stela* < Greek *stēlē*]

**ste|lar** (stē′lər), *adj. Botany.* of or having to do with a stele.

**ste|le** (stē′lē), *n., pl.* **-lae** (-lē), **-les. 1** an upright slab or pillar of stone bearing an inscription, sculptured design, or the like. **2** a prepared surface on the face, as of a building or a rock, bearing an inscription or the like. **3** an upright slab or pillar of stone used in ancient Greece and Rome to mark a grave. **4** *Botany.* the central cylinder of conducting tissue formed by the network of vascular bundles in the stems and roots of plants. It includes, typically, those tissues within the endodermis, such as the pericycle, xylem, phloem, and pith. [< Greek *stēlē* slab, pillar]

**stel|la** (stel′ə), *n.* a gold coin with a star on its reverse, minted with a value of $4 in the United States in 1879 and 1880. [< Latin *stēlla* star]

**stel|lar** (stel′ər), *adj.* **1** of or having to do with the stars or a star; like a star: *stellar magnitudes.* **SYN:** astral, sidereal. **2** *Figurative.* chief; principal: *to play the stellar role in a government.* **3** of or having to do with a star performer: *a stellar part in a play.* [< Latin *stellāris* < *stēlla* star]

**stel|la|ra|tor** (stel′ə rā′tər), *n.* a device in which highly ionized gas is confined in an endless tube by means of an externally applied magnetic field, used to produce controlled thermonuclear power: *Medium-density plasma containers ... include the stellarators, originally developed at the Princeton Plasma Physics Laboratory, and the tokamaks, originally developed at the I.V. Kurchatov Institute of Atomic Energy near Moscow* (Scientific American). [< *stellar* (gener)*ator;* so called from the expectation that stellar temperatures may be generated by such a device]

**stellar wind**, a stream of charged particles ejected from the corona of a star into space.

**stel|late** (stel′āt, -it), *adj.* spreading out like the points of a star; star-shaped. [< Latin *stellātus,* past participle of *stellāre* to set or cover with stars < *stēlla* star] —**stel′late|ly,** *adv.*

**stel|lat|ed** (stel′ā tid), *adj.* = stellate.

**Stel|ler's eider** (stel′ərz), an eider duck of the northern polar regions, the male of which has a white head, black collar, and black rings around the eyes. [< Georg Wilhelm *Steller*, 1709-1745, a German naturalist]

**Steller's jay**, a large, crested jay of western North America with blackish head and foreparts and blue wings, tail, and belly. [< G. W. *Steller;* see etym. under **Steller's eider**]

**Steller's sea cow**, a large, toothless sea mammal similar and related to the manatee, weighing up to four tons. It formerly lived about the Commander Islands in the Bering Sea, but became extinct in the 1760's.

**Steller's sea eagle**, a large gray sea eagle of the northern Pacific coast of Asia, with white tail and shoulders.

**Steller's sea lion**, a large sea lion of the Pacific coast of North America; northern sea lion.

**stel|lif|er|ous** (ste lif′ər əs), *adj.* abounding with stars. [< Latin *stēllifer* (< *stēlla* star + *ferre* to bear) + English *-ous*]

**stel|li|form** (stel′ə fôrm), *adj.* = star-shaped. [< New Latin *stelliformis* < Latin *stēlla* star + *-formis* -form]

**stel|li|fy** (stel′ə fī), *v.t.,* **-fied, -fy|ing.** to turn into or cause to resemble a star; convert into a constellation; make glorious.

**stel|lion** (stel′yən), *n.* any one of a group of Old World lizards with the scales of the tail arranged in whorls. [< Latin *stēlliō, -ōnis* < *stēlla* star]

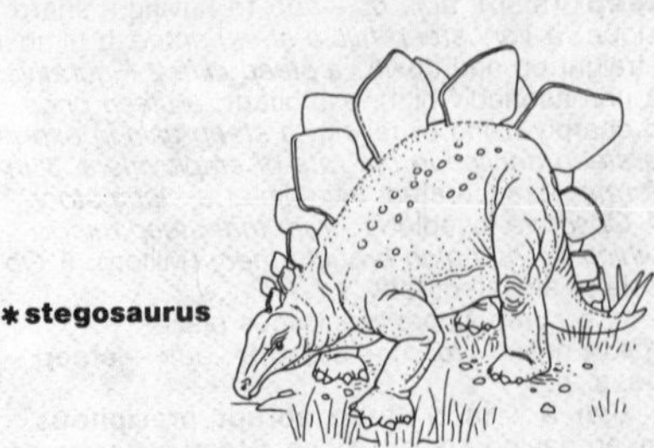

***stegosaurus**

**stel|lion|ate** (stel′yə nāt, -nit), *n.* (in civil or Scottish law) any fraud not distinguished by a special name and not defined by any written law, especially the sale of the same property to two or more different buyers. [< Late Latin *stēlliōnātus* trickery < *stēlliō, -ōnis* knave; (literally) newt, lizard]

**stel|lu|lar** (stel′yə lər), *adj.* having the form of a small star or small stars. [< Late Latin *stellula* (diminutive) < Latin *stēlla* star + English *-ar*]

**St. El|mo's fire** or **light** (el′mōz), a ball of light, due to a discharge of atmospheric electricity, often seen on masts of ships, towers, and the like; corposant. Also, **Saint Elmo's fire** or **light.** [< *St. Elmo*, a Syrian martyr who was considered the patron saint of sailors, died 303]

**stem¹** (stem), *n., v.,* **stemmed, stem|ming.** —*n.* **1a** the main part of a tree, shrub, or other plant, usually above the ground. The stem supports the branches. The trunk of a tree and the stalks of corn are stems. Most stems are more or less cylindrical. **b** the ascending axis (whether above or below ground) of a plant, bearing the remaining aerial parts of the plant (distinguished from the root or descending axis). **2** the part of a flower, leaf, or fruit that joins it to the plant or tree: **a** the peduncle of the fructification. **b** the pedicel of a flower. **c** the petiole or stalk of a leaf. **3** a bunch of bananas. **4** anything like the stem of a plant, such as: **a** the tube of a tobacco pipe. **b** the upright, cylindrical support of a goblet or wineglass. **c** the shaft connecting the mechanism of a watch to the knob by which the watch is wound. **d** the cylindrical rod in certain locks, about which the key fits and turns. **e** *Printing.* the upright stroke of a letter. **f** *Music.* the vertical line forming part of any note smaller than a whole note. **5a** the line of descent of a family. **b** ancestry; pedigree. **6** the part of a word to which endings are added and in which changes occur. *Run* is the stem of *running, runner,* and *ran.* **7** the upright at the bow of a ship between the keel and the bowsprit, to which the side planking or plates are joined. **8** the bow or front end of a boat or ship; prow.
—*v.t.* **1** to remove the stem from (a leaf or fruit). **2** to provide with a stem.
**from stem to stern**, **a** from one end of a ship to the other: *The sea ran high, and swept the little craft from stem to stern* (Charles J. Lever). **b** *Figurative: They searched the train from stem to stern, looking for the missing suitcase.*
**stem from**, to come from; have as a source or cause; originate or develop from; spring from: *The difficulty stems from their failure to plan properly. Newspapers stemmed from the invention of the printing press.*
[Old English *stefn, stemn*] —**stem′like′**, *adj.*

**stem²** (stem), *v.,* **stemmed, stem|ming,** *n.* —*v.t.* **1a** to dam up (as a stream). **b** *Figurative: It was the Spanish power indisputably which stemmed the Reformation* (James A. Froude). **SYN:** stop, check, hinder, restrain. **2** to plug or tamp (a hole for blasting); make tight (a joint). **3** *Scottish.* to stop or stanch (bleeding). **4** (in skiing) to turn (one or both skis) so that the tips converge.
—*v.i.* (in skiing) to slow down or stop by turning the back of one or both skis outward so that the tips converge.
—*n.* (in skiing) a maneuver involving stemming with one ski (single stem) or both skis (double stem).
[perhaps < Scandinavian (compare Old Icelandic *stemma*)]

**stem³** (stem), *v.t.,* **stemmed, stem|ming. 1** to make progress against: *When you swim upstream you have to stem the current.* **2** *Figurative.* to make progress against (opposition of any kind); go counter to. **SYN:** breast. [Middle English *stemmen* to head, or urge, the stem (of a ship or boat) toward < *stem*¹]

**stem borer**, an insect whose larva bores in the stems of plants.

**stem cell**, an embryonic or primitive cell that gives rise to specialized cells.

**stem christie**, = stem turn.

**stem cup**, a cup or bowl on a stem.

**stem eelworm**, a minute nematoid which causes stem sickness in clover.

**stem-end rot** (stem′end′), **1** a fungous disease infecting the end of the stem of watermelons and other fruit after harvesting. **2** the fungus causing this disease.

**stem leaf**, a leaf growing from the stem; a cauline leaf.

**stem|less** (stem′lis), *adj.* having no stem, or having no visible stem.

**stem|let** (stem′lit), *n.* a little stem.

**stem|ma** (stem′ə), *n., pl.* **stem|ma|ta** (stem′ə tə). **1** the recorded genealogy of an ancient Roman family. **2a** a geneological tree. **b** any chart or diagram showing genetic relationships. **3** *Zoology.* a simple eye, or a single facet of the compound eye, in invertebrates. [< Latin *stemma* garland placed on an ancestral image; ancestry; pedigree < Greek *stémma* garland]

**stemmed** (stemd), *adj.* **1** having or bearing a stem or stems (used chiefly in combination). **2** having the stem removed: *stemmed blueberries, stemmed tobacco leaves.*

**stem|mer** (stem′ər), *n.* a person or thing that

removes stems, as from tobacco leaves or grapes.
**stem|mer|y** (stem′ər ē), *n., pl.* **-mer|ies.** a factory where tobacco is stripped from the stem.
**stem mother,** a female plant louse which, being hatched in the spring from a winter egg, is the foundress of a summer colony of aphids.
**stem|my** (stem′ē), *adj.,* **-mi|er, -mi|est. 1** having or bearing many stems: *stemmy bluegrasses.* **2** like a stem; long and slender.
**stem|ple** (stem′pəl), *n.* a small timber driven into the wall or placed crosswise in a mine, to prevent caving, to serve as a support for a platform or as a step, or for other purposes. [compare Dutch *stempel* mark, stamp]
**stem rot, 1** a fungous disease attacking the stem of the tomato, banana, sweet potato, and other plants, causing it to wilt. **2** the fungus causing this disease.
**stem rust, 1** a fungous disease attacking the head and stem of wheat, barley, and other grains, robbing the plant of its nutriments and water, and leaving small rust-colored spots on the stem. **2** the fungus causing this disease.
**stem sickness,** a disease of clover caused by the stem eelworm, that brings about first a stunted condition and finally the death of the plant.
**stem|son** (stem′sən), *n.* a curved timber in the bow of a ship extending from the keelson to the stem. [< *stem*[1]; patterned on *keelson*]
**stem stitch,** a stitch used in embroidery and in making bobbin lace to form a thick, braidlike stripe for the stems of flowers, tendrils, and the like.
**stem turn,** (in skiing) a method of turning in which a skier stems the ski opposite the direction of turn and applies his weight to it.
**stem|ware** (stem′wãr′), *n.* glasses or goblets with stems, used for wine, alcoholic liquor, liqueur, and water.
**stem-wind|er** (stem′wīn′dər), *n.* **1** a watch with a stem and knob for winding. **2** *U.S. Informal.* a first-rate person or thing.
**stem-wind|ing** (stem′wīn′ding), *adj.* **1** wound by turning a knob on the stem: *a stem-winding watch.* **2** *U.S. Informal, Figurative.* winding up the emotions; rousing; impassioned: *a stem-winding orator. His sermons are a far cry from the stem-winding exercises in dour purple prose that 19th century congregations loved* (Time).
**Sten** (sten), *n.* = Sten gun.
**stench** (stench), *n.* a very bad smell; foul odor; stink: *the stench of burning rubber, the stench of a barnyard. A narrow winding street, full of offence and stench* (Dickens). **SYN:** fetor. [Middle English *stenche,* Old English *stenc* odor (pleasant or not), related to *stincan* to smell]
**stench bomb,** = stink bomb.
**stench|ful** (stench′fəl), *adj.* full of bad smells; stinking.
**stench|y** (sten′chē), *adj.* having a stench or offensive smell.
**sten|cil** (sten′səl), *n., v.,* **-ciled, -cil|ing** or (*especially British*) **-cilled, -cil|ling.** —*n.* **1** a thin sheet of metal, paper, cardboard, or other material, having letters or designs cut through it. When it is laid on a surface and ink or color is spread on, these letters or designs appear on the surface. *I put my name on packages with a stencil.* **2** the letters or designs so made.
—*v.t.* **1** to mark or paint (a surface) with a stencil: *The curtains have a stenciled border.* **2** to produce (letters or designs) by means of a stencil.
[earlier *stanesile* < Old French *estenceler,* ultimately < Latin *scintilla* spark. See etym. of doublets **scintilla, tinsel.**] —**sten′cil|er,** *especially British,* **sten′cil|ler,** *n.*
**sten|cil|i|za|tion** (sten′sə lə zā′shən), *n.* the act of stenciling or state of being stenciled.
**sten|cil|ize** (sten′sə līz), *v.t.,* **-ized, -iz|ing.** = stencil.
**Sten gun,** a light machine gun of simple design, the standard weapon of British forces in World War II. [< *S*(heppard) and *T*(urner), English inventors of the 1900's + *En*(gland)]
**sten|o** (sten′ō), *n., pl.* **sten|os.** *U.S. Informal.* a stenographer: *My girl friend who got me in there was steno to the boss* (Saturday Evening Post). [< *steno*(grapher)]
**steno-,** *combining form.* narrow; small: *Stenocephalic = narrow-headed. Stenopetalous = having narrow petals.* [< Greek *stenós*]
**sten|o|bath|ic** (sten′ə bath′ik), *adj.* having a narrow range of depth, said of animals living in the water between definite limits of depth. [< *steno-* + Greek *báthos* depth + English *-ic*]
**sten|o|ce|phal|ic** (sten′ə sə fal′ik), *adj.* narrow-headed. [< *steno-* + Greek *kephalê* head + English *-ic*]
**sten|o|chro|mat|ic** (sten′ə krə mat′ik), *adj.* of or having to do with stenochromy.
**sten|o|chro|my** (sten′ə krō′mē), *n.* the art or process of printing in several colors at one impression. [< *steno-* + Greek *chrôma* color + English *-y*[3]]
**ste|nog** (stə nog′), *n. Informal.* a stenographer.
**sten|o|graph** (sten′ə graf, -gräf), *n., v.* —*n.* **1** a writing in shorthand. **2** any one of various keyboard machines, somewhat resembling a typewriter, used for writing in shorthand.
—*v.t., v.i.* to write in shorthand.
[back formation < *stenographer*]
**ste|nog|ra|pher** (stə nog′rə fər), *n.* a person whose work is making a record in shorthand of words as they are spoken and reproducing it, especially with a typewriter; one whose work is stenography.
**sten|o|graph|ic** (sten′ə graf′ik), *adj.* **1** of or having to do with stenography. **2** made by stenography. **3** using stenography. **4** concise: *a stenographic style.* —**sten′o|graph′i|cal|ly,** *adv.*
**sten|o|graph|i|cal** (sten′ə graf′ə kəl), *adj.* = stenographic.
**ste|nog|ra|phist** (stə nog′rə fist), *n.* = stenographer.
**ste|nog|ra|phy** (stə nog′rə fē), *n.* **1** shorthand and typing, as the primary skills of the modern stenographer: *to study stenography.* **2** a method of rapid writing that uses symbols and abbreviations; shorthand: *I bought an approved scheme of the noble art and mystery of stenography ... and plunged into a sea of perplexity* (Dickens). **3** the act of writing in shorthand. [< *steno-* + *-graphy*]
**sten|o|ha|line** (sten′ə hā′lin, -līn; -hal′in, -īn), *adj. Biology.* capable of living only in water whose degree of saltiness is within a narrow range: *a stenohaline animal or plant.* [< *steno-* + Greek *háls* brine + English *-ine*[1]]
**sten|o|morph** (sten′ə môrf), *n.* a plant that is unusually small due to a cramped habitat, as from crowding by other plants. [< *steno-* + Greek *morphê* form]
**sten|o|pa|ic** (sten′ə pā′ik), *adj. Optics.* having to do with, characterized by, or of the nature of a small or narrow opening. [< *steno-* + Greek *opê* an opening + English *-ic*]
**stenopaic spectacles,** spectacles in which each lens is covered by an opaque plate with a small central aperture.
**sten|o|pet|al|ous** (sten′ə pet′ə ləs), *adj.* having narrow petals.
**ste|noph|a|gous** (stə nof′ə gəs), *adj. Zoology.* living on a small variety of foods. [< *steno-* + Greek *phageîn* eat + English *-ous*]
**sten|o|phyl|lous** (sten′ə fil′əs), *adj.* having narrow leaves. [< *steno-* + Greek *phýllon* leaf + English *-ous*]
**sten|o|rhyn|chous** (sten′ə ring′kəs), *adj.* having a narrow beak or bill. [< *steno-* + Greek *rhýnchos* snout + English *-ous*]
**ste|nosed** (sti nōst′, sten′ōzd), *adj.* affected with stenosis; abnormally narrowed or constricted. [< *stenos*(is) + *-ed*[2]]
**ste|no|sis** (sti nō′sis), *n. Medicine.* the contraction or stricture of a passage, duct, or canal. [< New Latin *stenosis* < Greek *sténōsis* a narrowing < *stenoûn* to narrow < *stenós* narrow]
**sten|o|therm** (sten′ə thėrm′), *n. Biology.* a stenothermal organism.
**sten|o|ther|mal** (sten′ə thėr′məl), *adj. Biology.* incapable of enduring a great range of temperature; not found in places having a broad range of temperatures.
**sten|o|ther|mic** (sten′ə thėr′mik), *adj.* = stenothermal.
**ste|not|ic** (sti not′ik), *adj.* having to do with or characterized by stenosis: *a stenotic condition, valve, or duct.*
**sten|o|top|ic** (sten′ə top′ik), *adj. Biology.* able to tolerate only a narrow range of variations in environmental conditions. [< *steno-* + Greek *tópos* place + English *-ic*]
**sten|o|trop|ic** (sten′ə trop′ik), *n. Biology.* having narrow limits of adaptation to changes in environment. [< *steno-* + Greek *tropê* a turning + English *-ic*]
**sten|o|type** (sten′ə tīp), *n., v.,* **-typed, -typ|ing.** —*n.* **1** a letter or group of letters used for a sound, word, or phrase in stenotypy. **2a** a keyboard machine, like a small typewriter, used to print such letters; shorthand machine. **b** Also, **Stenotype.** a trademark for this kind of machine.
—*v.t., v.i.* to write or record with a stenotype.
**sten|o|typ|ist** (sten′ə tī′pist), *n.* a person who is skilled in stenotypy, especially one whose work is to write in stenotypy or on a stenotype.
**sten|o|typ|y** (sten′ə tī′pē, stə not′ə-), *n.* **1** a form of shorthand that uses ordinary letters. **2** the use of a stenotype machine to record speeches, court testimony, or the like.
**stent** (stent), *v.t., v.i., n.* = stint[1].
**sten|ter** (sten′tər), *n., v.t., v.i., British.* = tenter[1]. [ultimately < Latin *extentus,* past participle of *extendere* to stretch out]
**Sten|tor** (sten′tôr), *n. Greek Legend.* a Greek herald in the Trojan War, whose voice (as described in the *Iliad*) was as loud as the voices of fifty men.
**sten|tor**[1] (sten′tôr), *n.* a man of powerful voice. [< *Stentor*]
**sten|tor**[2] (sten′tôr), *n.* any one of a genus of trumpet-shaped protozoans that are among the largest of all single-celled animals. [< New Latin *Stentor* the genus name < Greek *Sténtōr* Stentor (because it is shaped like a speaking trumpet)]
**sten|to|ri|an** (sten tôr′ē ən, -tōr′-), *adj.* very loud or powerful in sound: *The stentorian voice ... rang through the valley* (James Fenimore Cooper). **SYN:** sonorous, thundering. —**sten|to′ri|an|ly,** *adv.*
**sten|to|ri|ous** (sten tôr′ē əs, -tōr′-), *adj.* = stentorian. —**sten|to′ri|ous|ly,** *adv.*
**step** (step), *n., v.,* **stepped** or (*Archaic*) **stept, step|ping.** —*n.* **1** a movement made by lifting the foot and putting it down again in a new position; one motion of the leg in walking, running, or dancing: *to make a long step to the side, walk with short steps, a polka step, a gliding step, a dance with fancy steps.* **2** the distance covered by one such movement: *She was three steps away when he called her back.* **3** a short distance; little way: *The school is only a step from our house.* **4** a way of walking, dancing, or running; gait; stride: *a brisk step. Light of step and heart was she* (Walter de la Mare). **5a** a pace uniform with that of another or others or in time with music: *to keep step.* **b** a particular marching pace: *a quick step.* **6** a place for the foot in going up or coming down. A stair or a rung of a ladder is a step. **7** the sound made by putting the foot down; footstep: *I hear steps on the stairs.* **8** a footprint: *to see steps in the mud.* **9** *Figurative.* an action: *the first step toward peace.* **SYN:** measure, proceeding. **10** a degree in a scale; a grade in rank; stage: *A colonel is three steps above a captain.* (*Figurative.*) *College is often a step to higher advancement.* **11** *Music.* **a** a degree of the staff or scale. **b** the interval between two adjoining degrees of the scale, called a *half step* (semitone) or a *whole step* (two semitones). **c** (popularly) a whole step. **12** an offset, or part of a machine, fitting, or the like, resembling a step in outline. **13** a frame or support in which the lower end or heel of a mast is set to hold it upright: *the step of a mast.* [Old English *steppa*]
—*v.i.* **1** to move the legs as in walking, running, or dancing: *to step to the side. Step lively!* **2** to walk a short distance: *to step across the road. Step this way.* **3** to put the foot down; tread (on, upon): *He stepped on a bug. I stepped on the accelerator.* **4** *Informal, Figurative.* to go fast; move quickly.
—*v.t.* **1a** to measure (off) by taking steps; pace (off): *Step off the distance from the door to the window.* **b** to mark (off) as with dividers or compasses. **2** to make or arrange like a flight of steps. **3a** to set (a mast) in place; fix or place in a support. **b** to fit (as a deck or rail) in position on a ship. **4** to move (the foot) forward as in walking: *to step foot into a room.* **5** to go through the steps of (a dance); perform: *He stepped a minuet gravely and gracefully.*
**break step, 1** to stop marching in step: *The troops had to break step in order to cross the narrow bridge.* **2** *Figurative.* to disagree or be out of harmony with one's associates or regulations: *He broke step with his party and supported a rival candidate.*
**change step,** to fall into marching step more correctly: *One of the marchers quickly changed step to keep in time with the music.*
**in step, a** making one's steps fit those of another person or persons; at a uniform pace with others or in time with music: *She had difficulty keeping in step with the rest of the marchers.* **b** *Figurative.* making one's actions or ideas agree with those of another person or persons; in harmony or agreement: *The new price increase is in step with the rising costs of production.*
**out of step, a** not keeping pace with others or in time with music: *That boy was out of step during most of the parade.* **b** *Figurative.* not in harmony or accord: *People who live solitary lives are often out of step with the times.*
**pick one's steps,** to move with great care and caution over treacherous ground, a difficult situation, or the like: (*Figurative.*) *The dashing stream stays not to pick his steps among the rocks* (Arthur H. Clough).
**step aside, a** to move away a small distance;

retire a few steps: *Please step aside to make room for the luggage.* **b** *Figurative.* to withdraw: *Recently he stepped aside from his diplomatic role to speak to a New York audience out of his own Buddhist faith* (Maclean's).
**step back, a** to move a little distance to the rear; go backward: *The favorite of the Princess, looking into the cavity, stepped back and trembled* (Samuel Johnson). **b** *Figurative.* to withdraw; retire: *Bobby* [*Kennedy*] *stepped back before the overriding claims of Jack's fight for the White House* (Maclean's).
**step by step,** little by little; slowly: *the revolution which human nature desires to effect step by step in many ages* (Benjamin Jowett). *Step by step Wykeham rose to the highest dignities* (George W. Thornbury).
**step down, a** to come down: *In robe and crown the king stept down* (Tennyson). **b** *Figurative.* to surrender or resign from an office or position of precedence: *Last week Editor Hutchinson, 65, announced that he was stepping down to devote all his time to writing* (Time). **c** *Figurative.* to lower by steps or degrees; decrease: *Congress voted to step down government spending.*
**step in,** to come in; intervene; take part: *But where the Federal government must step in, it will* (Newsweek).
**step into,** to come into, acquire, or receive, especially without particular effort or by chance: *to step into a fortune.*
**step on it,** *Informal.* to go faster; hurry up: *If you want to catch the train, you'd better step on it.*
**step out,** *U.S. Informal.* **a** to leave a place, usually for a short time: *Mother's stepped out, and I'm alone up here* (R. O'Reilly). **b** *Informal.* to go out for entertainment: *We're celebrating by stepping out tonight.* **c** *Figurative.* to withdraw; retire: *He intended to remain as president of the World's Fair. "There is no possibility at all of getting me to step out"* [*he said*] (New York Times). **d** to walk or march with longer or more vigorous steps: *At the command, "Step out!" the marching soldiers lengthened their pace.*
**steps, a** a stepladder: *Steps, nails, and hammer were quickly at the disposal of the stranger* (F. W. Robinson). **b** a path traversed; course or way: *to retrace one's steps.*
**step up, a** to go up; ascend: *The instructor stepped up onto the stage to deliver his lecture.* **b** *Figurative.* to increase: *My salary was stepped up last week.* **c** *Figurative.* to raise by steps or degrees; make go faster or higher: *to step up production of automobiles, to step up the pressure in a boiler.* **d** *Informal.* to come forward (used by a carnival barker): *Step right up, ladies and gentlemen!*
**take steps,** to adopt, put into effect, or carry out measures considered to be necessary or desirable: *Steps have already been taken to deal with the emergency.*
**watch one's step,** to be careful: *Watch your step when you ride down that steep hill on the bicycle. The ... chairman warned that "Congress should watch its step" in trying to regulate economic pressures* (Wall Street Journal).
[Old English *steppan*]

**step-,** *prefix.* related by the remarriage of a parent, not by blood, as in *stepmother, stepsister, stepaunt.* [Old English *stēop-*, probably meaning "bereaved, orphaned"]

**step|broth|er** (step′bruᴛʜ′ər), *n.* a stepfather's or stepmother's son by a former marriage: *If her father marries a widow with a little boy, this boy will be her stepbrother.*

**step-by-step** (step′bī step′), *adj.* taking one step at a time; doing something gradually or by degrees: *This book is a step-by-step manual* (New York Times). *The war ... can be ended only by step-by-step concessions* (Manchester Guardian).

**step|child** (step′chīld′), *n., pl.* **-chil|dren. 1** a child of one's husband or wife by a former marriage; stepson or stepdaughter. **2** *Figurative.* something or someone not treated as one's own; one that is neglected or ignored: *The Commerce Department has for many years been a stepchild of city government* (New York Times).

**step cut,** an ornamental design in gem cutting with long, steplike facets cut into the top and back of the stone; trap cut.

**step|dame** (step′dām′), *n. Archaic.* a stepmother.

**step dance,** a dance marked by originality, variety, or difficulty in the steps; dance in which the steps are more important than the figure.

**step|daugh|ter** (step′dô′tər), *n.* a daughter of one's husband or wife by a former marriage.

**step deal, 1** a contract offered to an independent producer by a motion-picture studio, giving the studio the right to withdraw financing at any point up to the time filming is ready to begin. **2** a similar contract offered to anyone in motion pictures.

**step-down** (step′doun′), *adj., n.* —*adj.* **1** that decreases gradually. **2** *Electricity.* lowering the voltage of a current, especially by means of a transformer.
—*n.* a decrease or reduction: *a clear, tangible military step-down* (Time).

**step|fa|ther** (step′fä′ᴛʜər), *n.* a man who has married one's mother after the death or divorce of one's real father.

**step fault, 1** one of a series of small, nearly parallel faults by which strata have been dislocated so as to occupy a position resembling a series of steps or stairs. **2** the compound fault comprising such a series.

**steph|a|ne** (stef′ə nē), *n. Greek Antiquity.* a bandlike headdress or coronal widest at the front and narrowing toward the sides, often seen on representations of the goddess Hera. [< Greek *stephánē* < *stéphein* put round]

**steph|an|ite** (stef′ə nīt), *n. Mineralogy.* a soft, brittle, black mineral with a metallic luster, an ore of silver; brittle silver ore. *Formula:* $Ag_5SbS_4$ [< German *Stephanit*]

**steph|a|nos** (stef′ə nos), *n., pl.* **-noi** (-noi). *Greek Antiquity.* **1** a wreath or crown serving as a prize or a mark of honor. **2** a coronal like the stephane but of the same width all around. [< Greek *stéphanos* crown]

**steph|a|no|tis** (stef′ə nō′tis), *n.* any one of a group of tropical twining shrubs of the milkweed family, as a variety often grown in greenhouses for its fragrant, waxy, white or cream-colored flowers. [< New Latin *Stephanotis* the genus name < Greek *stephanōtis* fit for a crown < *stéphanos* crown]

**Ste|phen** (stē′vən), *n.* **Saint,** the first Christian martyr (in the Bible, Acts 7:59).

**step-in** (step′in′), *adj., n.* —*adj.* put on by being stepped into: *step-in shoes or slippers.*
—*n.* a step-in garment, shoe, or the like.

**step-ins** (step′inz′), *n.pl.* a garment, especially a woman's undergarment with short legs, that one may put on by stepping into it and pulling it up over the body.

**step|lad|der** (step′lad′ər), *n.* a ladder with flat steps instead of rungs. Stepladders are usually four-legged and often hinged at the top.

**step|less** (step′lis), *adj.* having no step or steps: *a stepless entrance.*

**step|like** (step′līke′), *adj.* resembling a step or series of steps.

**step|moth|er** (step′muᴛʜ′ər), *n.* a woman who has married one's father after the death or divorce of one's real mother.

**step|moth|er|ly** (step′muᴛʜ′ər lē), *adj.* **1** having to do with or suitable to a stepmother. **2** *Figurative.* harsh or neglectful.

**step-out** (step′out′), *n.* **1** the act of stepping or getting outside: *In preparation for his step-out into space, White spent sixty hours in vacuum chambers* (Time). **2** = step-out well.

**step-out well,** a well dug near another that has been proven to yield oil or gas, as for confirmation of the area's productivity.

**step|par|ent** (step′pãr′ənt), *n.* a stepfather or stepmother.

**steppe** (step), *n.* **1** one of the vast, level, treeless plains in southeastern Europe and in Asia, especially as found in the Soviet Union north of the Caspian and Aral seas. **2** any vast, treeless plain. **SYN:** savanna, prairie. [< Russian *step′*]

**stepped** (stept), *adj.* having a step or steps; formed in a series of steps: *a stepped pyramid.*

**stepped-up** (stept′up′), *adj.* increased in size, speed, or extent.

**steppe eagle,** an eagle of central Asia, living in treeless plains and often nesting on the ground. Steppe eagles migrate to Africa in the winter.

**step|per** (step′ər), *n.* a person or animal that steps, especially in a certain way: *a high stepper, a fast stepper.*

**step|ping-off place** (step′ing ôf′, -of′), a point of departure; jumping-off place.

**step|ping stone** (step′ing), **1** a stone or one of a line of stones in shallow water, a marshy place, or the like, used in crossing. **2** a stone for use in mounting or ascending. **3** *Figurative.* anything serving as a means of advancing or rising: *Students from various minority groups* [*are*] *intent on using education as a stepping stone to a better life* (Fred M. Hechinger). **SYN:** springboard.

**step rocket,** a multistage rocket.

**step-roof** (step′rüf′, -ru̇f′), *n.* a roof shaped like stairsteps, found on many Dutch colonial houses in the northeastern United States.

**steps** (steps), *n.pl.* See under **step.**

**step|sis|ter** (step′sis′tər), *n.* one's stepfather's or stepmother's daughter by a former marriage.

**step|son** (step′sun′), *n.* a son of one's husband or wife by a former marriage.

**step|stool** (step′stül′), *n.* a stool with several steps that often may be folded and hidden under the seat, used both as a stool and as a small stepladder.

**stept** (stept), *v. Archaic.* a past tense and a past participle of **step.**

**step|toe** (step′tō′), *n. Northwestern U.S.* a hill or mountain surrounded and isolated by a large flow or plain of lava.

**step turn,** a method of turning in which a skier lifts and turns first the inner ski and then the outer one until the turn is complete.

**step-up** (step′up′), *adj., n.* —*adj.* **1** that increases gradually. **2** *Electricity.* increasing the voltage of a current, especially by means of a transformer.
—*n.* an increase: *a gradual step-up in the production.*

**step|way** (step′wā′), *n.* a way or passage formed by steps.

**step|wise** (step′wīz′), *adv., adj.* —*adv.* in the manner of steps; by steps: *Another suggestion, adopted immediately, was to proceed stepwise* (Bulletin of Atomic Scientists).
—*adj.* occurring step by step; gradual: *... the stepwise activation of particular components of the genetic code* (New Scientist).

**-ster,** *suffix.* **1** a person who ____s: *Trickster = a person who tricks.*
**2** a person who makes or handles ____: *Rhymester = a person who makes rhymes.*
**3** a person who is ____: *Youngster = a person who is young.*
**4** special meanings, as in *gangster, roadster, teamster.*
[Middle English *-estre*, a feminine agent suffix, Old English *-istre, -estre* a feminine suffix]

**ster.,** sterling.

**sterad** (no period), steradian.

**ste|ra|di|an** (sti rā′dē ən), *n. Geometry.* a unit of measurement of solid angles. It is the solid angle subtended at the center of a sphere by the area of the surface of the sphere equal to the square of its radius. [< Greek *stereós* solid + English *radian*]

**ster|co|ra|ceous** (stėr′kə rā′shəs), *adj.* **1** of, like, or having to do with dung or feces. **2** frequenting or feeding on dung, as certain beetles, flies, or other animals do. [< Latin *stercorāceus* (with English *-ous*) < *stercus, -oris* dung]

**Ster|co|ra|nism** (stėr′kər ə niz′əm), *n.* the doctrine or belief of the Stercoranists.

**Ster|co|ra|nist** (stėr′kər ə nist), *n.* a person who believes that consecrated elements of the Eucharist are digested just as ordinary food is. [< Medieval Latin *Stercoranistae*, plural < Latin *stercus, -oris* dung]

**ster|co|rar|y** (stėr′kə rer′ē), *adj., n., pl.* **-rar|ies.**
—*adj.* = stercoraceous.
—*n.* a place for putting or storing dung or manure.
[< Latin *stercorārius* < *stercus, -oris* dung]

**ster|co|ric|o|lous** (stėr′kə rik′ə ləs), *adj.* living in dung or feces. [< Latin *stercus, -oris* dung + *colere* inhabit + English *-ous*]

**ster|co|rous** (stėr′kər əs), *adj.* = stercoraceous.

**ster|cu|li|a|ceous** (stər kyü′lē ā′shəs), *adj.* belonging to the sterculia family of plants. [< New Latin *Sterculiaceae* the order name]

**ster|cu|li|a family** (stər kyü′lē ə), a group of dicotyledonous, chiefly tropical, trees, shrubs and herbs, including the bottle tree, cacao, kola, and flame-tree. [< New Latin *Sterculia* the typical genus < Latin *stercus, -oris* dung (from the fetid odor of some species)]

**stere** (stir), *n.* a unit of measure, used especially for wood, equal to one cubic meter. [< French *stère* < Greek *stereós* solid]

**ster|e|o¹** (ster′ē ō, stir′-), *n., adj.* —*n.* **1** a system or equipment reproducing stereophonic sound: *And so, each Friday night, I flip on Swan Lake and Bolero on the stereo* (Harper's). **2** stereophonic sound reproduction.
—*adj.* = stereophonic.

**ster|e|o²** (ster′ē ō, stir′-), *n., adj.* —*n.* **1** a stereo camera or a print made with it. **2** = stereophotography.
—*adj.* = stereoscopic: *a stereo image, picture, or viewer.*

**stereo-,** *combining form.* **1** hard, firm, or solid: *Stereobate = a solid mass of masonry.*
**2** three-dimensional: *Stereoscopic = seen as three-dimensional. Stereomicroscope = a three-dimensional microscope.*
[< Greek *stereós* solid]

**stereo.,** stereotype.

**ster|e|o|bate** (ster′ē ə bāt, stir′-), *n.* **1** a solid mass of masonry serving as a base for a wall or other structure; foundation. **2** the substructure of a row of columns, including the stylobate. See picture under **Ionic.** [< Latin *stereobata* a foundation wall or substructure for a colonnade < Greek *stereós* solid + *bátēs* step(ping); obstructed < *bainein* step]

**ster|e|o|bat|ic** (ster′ē ə bat′ik, stir′-), *adj.* of, having to do with, or like a stereobate.

**stereo camera,** a camera with twin lenses that take simultaneous photographs, the resulting pairs of prints or slides giving an effect of three dimensions when seen in a stereoscope.

**ster|e|o|chem|i|cal** (ster′ē ō kem′ə kəl, stir′-), *adj.* having to do with stereochemistry. —**ster′e|o-chem′i|cal|ly,** *adv.*

**ster|e|o|chem|is|try** (ster′ē ō kem′ə strē, stir′-), *n.* **1** the branch of chemistry dealing with the relative position in space of atoms in relation to differences in the optical and chemical properties of the substances. Stereochemistry is used in making certain plastics by building molecules with definite arrangements of atoms. **2** the arrangement or position of atoms or molecules in a substance.

**ster|e|o|chrome** (ster′ē ə krōm, stir′-), *n.* **1** a process of mural painting in which water glass is used as a vehicle or as a preservative coating. **2** a picture produced by this process. [< German *Stereochrom* < Greek *stereós* solid + *chrôma* color]

**ster|e|o|chro|mic** (ster′ē ə krō′mik, stir′-), *adj.* of, having to do with, or produced by stereochrome.

**ster|e|o|com|pa|ra|tor** (ster′ē ō kom′pə rā′tər, -kəm par′ə-; stir′-), *n.* an instrument on the stereoscopic principle, used to superpose a pair of astronomical photographs taken at an interval of time, and detect any movement of a star or other object which has taken place in that interval.

**ster|e|o|gram** (ster′ē ə gram, stir′-), *n.* **1** a diagram representing a solid object on a plane, especially a drawing in which the inequalities or curvature of a surface is indicated by contour lines or shading. **2** = stereograph. [< *stereo-* + *-gram*]

**ster|e|o|graph** (ster′ē ə graf, -gräf; stir′-), *n., v.* —*n.* a pair of nearly identical pictures, giving a three-dimensional effect when viewed in a stereoscope.
—*v.t., v.i.* to take a stereograph or stereoscopic photograph (of).
[< *stereo-* + *-graph*]

**ster|e|o|graph|ic** (ster′ē ə graf′ik, stir′-), *adj.* showing the whole of a sphere on the whole of an infinite plane, while preserving the angles. —**ster′e|o|graph′i|cal|ly,** *adv.*

**ster|e|o|graph|i|cal** (ster′ē ə graf′ə kəl, stir′-), *adj.* = stereographic.

**ster|e|og|ra|phy** (ster′ē og′rə fē, stir′-), *n.* the art of representing the forms of solid bodies on a plane; a branch of solid geometry that deals with the construction of all regularly defined solids.

**ster|e|o|i|so|mer** (ster′ē ō ī′sə mər, stir′-), *n. Chemistry.* one of two or more isomeric compounds that are held to differ by virtue of a difference in the spatial arrangement (not in the order of connection) of the atoms in the molecule. [< *stereo-* + *isomer*]

**ster|e|o|i|so|mer|ic** (ster′ē ō ī′sə mer′ik, stir′-), *adj. Chemistry.* characterized by stereoisomerism.

**ster|e|o|i|som|er|ism** (ster′ē ō ī som′ə riz əm, stir′-), *n. Chemistry.* isomerism in which the atoms are joined in the molecule in the same way but differ in their spatial arrangement.

**ster|e|ol|o|gy** (ster′ē ol′ə jē, stir′-), *n.* the scientific study of the three-dimensional characteristics of objects that are normally viewed only two-dimensionally: *Up to now it has not been easy to measure brain area but the rather new science of stereology, employing statistico-geometrical methods, now makes it possible to draw conclusions concerning three-dimensional structures from flat images, such as cut sections* (Science Journal). [< *stereo-* + *-logy*]

**ster|e|om** (ster′ē om, stir′-), *n.* = stereome.

**ster|e|ome** (ster′ē ōm, stir′-), *n.* **1** the elements which give strength to a fibrovascular bundle in plants. **2** the hard tissue of the body of invertebrates. Also, **stereom.** [< Greek *sterëōma* a solid body < *stereós* solid]

**ster|e|o|met|ric** (ster′ē ə met′rik, stir′-), *adj.* having to do with or performed by stereometry. —**ster′e|o|met′ri|cal|ly,** *adv.*

**ster|e|o|met|ri|cal** (ster′ē ə met′rə kəl, stir′-), *adj.* = stereometric.

**ster|e|om|e|try** (ster′ē om′ə trē, stir′-), *n.* the measurement of solid figures; solid geometry.

**ster|e|o|mi|cro|scope** (ster′ē ə mī′krə skōp, stir′-), *n.* a microscope with two eyepieces, used to obtain a three-dimensional image of the object viewed; stereoscopic microscope.

**ster|e|o|phon|ic** (ster′ē ə fon′ik, stir′-), *adj.* **1** of or giving the effect of lifelike sound by using two or more microphones, placed apart, and an equal number of loudspeakers, also placed apart. Stereophonic sound has the same effects of depth and direction as the original sound. **2** of or having to do with the sound thus reproduced. [< *stereo-* + *phonic*] —**ster′e|o|phon′i|cal|ly,** *adv.*

**ster|e|oph|o|ny** (ster′ē of′ə nē, stir′-), *n.* stereophonic sound reproduction: *The differentiation between the directions of the direct sounds from the musical instruments ... can be simulated by means of stereophony* (New York Herald Tribune).

**ster|e|o|pho|to|graph|ic** (ster′ē ō fō′tə graf′ik, stir′-), *adj.* of or having to do with stereophotography.

**ster|e|o|pho|tog|ra|phy** (ster′ē ō fə tog′rə fē, stir′-), *n.* the making of stereoscopic pictures, as with a stereo camera.

**ster|e|o|pho|to|mi|crog|ra|phy** (ster′ē ō fō′tō mī-krog′rə fē, stir′-), *n.* the art of making stereoscopic or three-dimensional photomicrographs.

**ster|e|o|pla|ni|graph** (ster′ē ō plā′nə graf, -gräf; stir′-), *n.* a machine that draws contour maps from aerial photographs. [< *stereo-* + Latin *plānus* level + English *-graph*]

**ster|e|o|plot|ter** (ster′ē ō plot′ər, stir′-), *n.* a stereoscopic device that automatically records coordinates in three dimensions.

**ster|e|o|plot|ting** (ster′ē ō plot′ing, stir′-), *n.* the plotting of maps or charts from aerial photographs by means of a stereoplotter.

**ster|e|op|sis** (ster′ē op′sis, stir′-), *n.* stereoscopic vision. [< New Latin *stereopsis* < Greek *stereós* solid + *-ópsis* vision]

**ster|e|op|ti|can** (ster′ē op′tə kən, stir′-), *adj.* of, resembling, or having to do with a stereopticon: *stereoptican vision.*

**ster|e|op|ti|cian** (ster′ē op tish′ən, stir′-), *n.* a person trained in the use of a stereopticon.

**ster|e|op|ti|con** (ster′ē op′tə kən, stir′-), *n.* a projector arranged to combine two images of the same object or scene upon a screen, so that one passes gradually into the other with three-dimensional effect. [American English < *stereo-* + Greek *optikón,* neuter of *optikós* relating to vision]

**ster|e|o|ra|di|o|graph** (ster′ē ō rā′dē ō graf, -gräf; stir′-), *n.* a stereoscopic X-ray photograph.

**ster|e|o|reg|u|lar** (ster′ē ō reg′yə lər, stir′-), *adj.* of or having to do with a polymer that has a definite and regular spatial arrangement of the atoms in its repeating units: *stereoregular rubber.*

**ster|e|o|reg|u|lar|i|ty** (ster′ē ō reg′yə lar′ə tē, stir′-), *n.* the quality or state of being stereoregular.

***ster|e|o|scope** (ster′ē ə skōp, stir′-), *n.* an instrument through which two pictures (usually photographs) of the same object or scene, taken from slightly different angles, are viewed, one by each eye. The object or scene thus viewed appears to have three dimensions.

***stereoscope**

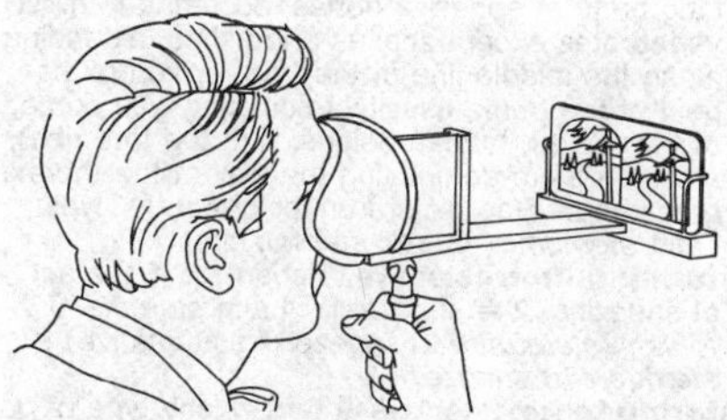

**ster|e|o|scop|ic** (ster′ē ə skop′ik, stir′-), *adj.* **1** seeming to have depth as well as height and breadth; three-dimensional. **2** having to do with stereoscopes.

**ster|e|o|scop|i|cal** (ster′ē ə skop′ə kəl, stir′-), *adj.* = stereoscopic.

**ster|e|o|scop|i|cal|ly** (ster′ē ə skop′ə klē, stir′-), *adv.* by means of a stereoscope.

**ster|e|os|co|pist** (ster′ē os′kə pist, stir′-), *n.* a person skilled in the use or construction of stereoscopes.

**ster|e|os|co|py** (ster′ē os′kə pē, stir′-), *n.* **1** the use or construction of stereoscopes. **2** the study of stereoscopic systems or effects. **3** the viewing of an object or scene in three dimensions.

**ster|e|o|ski|ag|ra|phy** (ster′ē ō skī ag′rə fē, stir′-), *n.* the taking of several X-ray pictures at different angles in order to produce a stereoscopic effect. [< *stereo-* + *skiagraphy*]

**ster|e|o|son|ic** (ster′ē ə son′ik, stir′-), *adj. Especially British.* stereophonic.

**ster|e|o|spe|cif|ic** (ster′ē ō spi sif′ik, stir′-), *adj.* of or having to do with a chemical process in which a steroid, alkaloid, or other product is used to form a specific stereoisomer of related structure, usually with the aid of a catalyst.

**ster|e|o|spe|cif|i|cal|ly** (ster′ē ō spi sif′ə klē, stir′-), *adv.* in a stereospecific manner.

**ster|e|o|spec|i|fic|i|ty** (ster′ē ō spes′ə fis′ə tē, stir′-), *n.* the quality or state of being stereospecific: *stereospecificity of enzymic reactions.*

**ster|e|o|tac|tic** (ster′ē ə tak′tik, stir′-), *adj.* **1** *Biology.* of, having to do with, or exhibiting stereotaxis; thigmotactic. **2** = stereotaxic.

**ster|e|o|tape** (ster′ē ō tāp′, stir′-), *n.* a magnetic tape reproducing stereophonic sound.

**ster|e|o|tax|ic** (ster′ē ə tak′sik, stir′-), *adj.* involving or based upon three-dimensional surveys of the brain that allow operation or research on otherwise inaccessible parts of the brain: *Utilizing three-dimensional anatomical maps of the brain* (*stereotaxic atlases*) *and stereotaxic instruments which hold the head of an anesthetized animal in a predetermined plane, it is possible to insert electrodes through small holes in the skull into almost any brain structure* (Elliot S. Valenstein and Verne C. Cox). —**ster′e|o|tax′i|cal|ly,** *adv.*

**ster|e|o|tax|is** (ster′ē ə tak′sis, stir′-), *n.* **1** *Biology.* a movement of an organism as a result of contact with a solid body; thigmotaxis. **2** the use of stereotaxic methods and equipment to locate areas deep in the brain. [< *stereo-* + Greek *táxis* arrangement]

**ster|e|o|trope** (ster′ē ə trōp, stir′-), *n.* an optical device based on the same principle as a zoetrope but fitted with a stereoscope, giving solidity to the figures in motion. [< *stereo-* + Greek *-tropos* turned]

**ster|e|o|trop|ic** (ster′ē ə trop′ik, stir′-), *adj. Biology.* bending or turning under the stimulus of contact with a solid body.

**ster|e|ot|ro|pism** (ster′ē ot′rə piz əm, stir′-), *n. Biology.* a tendency to bend or turn in response to contact with a solid body or rigid surface. [< *stereo-* + *tropism*]

**ster|e|o|type** (ster′ē ə tīp, stir′-), *n., v.,* **-typed, -typ|ing.** —*n.* **1** a method or process of printing in which a solid plate, usually of type metal, is cast from a mold of composed type; stereotypy. The mold, of papier-mâché, plastic, or rubber, is taken from the surface of a form of type, and the printing is done from the plate instead of the form. **2** a printing plate cast from a mold. **3** *Figurative.* a fixed form, expression, character, or image; something stereotyped; conventional type. Long John Silver, in Stevenson's *Treasure Island,* is the stereotype of a pirate. *Its* [*a play's*] *villains are often more stereotypes than people* (Wall Street Journal). *Today we know that each immigrant's worth is best judged by personal qualities and skills, not by group stereotypes* (New York Times).
—*v.t.* **1** to make a stereotype of. **2** to print from stereotypes. **3** *Figurative.* to give a fixed or settled form to.
[< French *stéréotype* < Greek *stereós* solid + *týpos* type] —**ster′e|o|typ′er,** *n.*

**ster|e|o|typed** (ster′ē ə tīpt, stir′-), *adj.* **1** cast in the form of, or printed from, a stereotype. **2** *Figurative.* fixed or settled in form; conventional: *stereotyped characters in a novel. "It gives me great pleasure to be with you tonight" is a stereotyped opening for a speech.*

**ster|e|o|typ|ic** (ster′ē ə tip′ik, stir′-), *adj.* of or relating to stereotype.

**ster|e|o|typ|i|cal** (ster′ē ə tip′ə kəl, stir′-), *adj.* = stereotypic: (*Figurative.*) *In her passionate rejection of all stereotypical thinking she has, in fact, become something of a stereotype herself* (Mary Lowrey Ross). —**ster′e|o|typ′i|cal|ly,** *adv.*

**ster|e|o|typ|i|cal|i|ty** (ster′ē ə tip′ə kal′ə tē, stir′-), *n.* the quality or state of being stereotypic: (*Figurative.*) *These magazines are boring in their inevitable stereotypicality of regimented subject matter* (London Times).

**ster|e|o|typ|y** (ster′ē ə tī′pē, stir′-), *n.* **1** the process of making stereotype plates. **2** the process of printing from stereotype plates. **3** *Figurative.* persistence as of a fixed or stereotyped idea or mode of action, as in certain types of insanity.

**ster|ic** (ster′ik, stir′-), *adj. Chemistry.* of or having to do with the arrangement in space of the atoms in a molecule. [< Greek *stereós* solid + English *-ic*] —**ster′i|cal|ly,** *adv.*

**ster|i|cal** (ster′ə kəl, stir′-), *adj.* = steric.

**ste|rig|ma** (stə rig′mə), *n., pl.* **-ma|ta** (-mə tə). **1** a ridge extending down a stem below the point of attachment of a decurrent leaf. **2** a stalk or filament bearing a spore in a fungus. **3** a branch or outgrowth of a basidium. [< Greek *stērigma* a support < *sterízein* to support]

**ster|ig|mat|ic** (ster′ig mat′ik), *adj.* having to do with or like a sterigma.

**ster|i|lant** (ster′ə lənt), *n.* a chemical or other agent that sterilizes, such as a chemical that destroys an insect's ability to reproduce.

**ster|ile** (ster′əl), *adj.* **1** free from living germs or microorganisms: *The nurse kept the surgeon's instruments sterile.* **2** not producing seed, offspring, or crops; not fertile; barren; unproductive: *a sterile cow. Desert soil is usually sterile.* **SYN:** infertile. **3a** not bearing fruit or spores: *a sterile plant.* **b** producing only stamens, or producing neither stamens nor pistils: *a sterile flower.*

**Pronunciation Key:** hat, āge, cãre, fär; let, ēqual, tėrm; it, īce; hot, ōpen, ôrder; oil, out; cup, pu̇t, rüle; child; long; thin; ᴛʜen; zh, measure; ə represents **a** in about, **e** in taken, **i** in pencil, **o** in lemon, **u** in circus.

4 *Figurative.* **a** not producing results: *sterile hopes.* **b** mentally or spiritually barren: *verbal logic drawing sterile conclusions from untested authority* (John Morley). [< Latin *sterilis*] — **ster′ile|ly,** *adv.*

**ster|i|lise** (ster′ə līz), *v.t.,* **-lised, -lis|ing.** *Especially British.* sterilize.

**ste|ril|i|ty** (stə ril′ə tē), *n., pl.* **-ties.** sterile condition or character; barrenness.

**ster|i|liz|a|ble** (ster′ə lī′zə bəl), *adj.* capable of being sterilized.

**ster|i|li|za|tion** (ster′ə lə zā′shən), *n.* **1** the act or operation of sterilizing: *the sterilization of dishes by boiling them.* **2** condition of being sterilized.

**ster|i|lize** (ster′ə līz), *v.t.,* **-lized, -liz|ing.** **1** to make free from living germs or microorganisms, as by heating or otherwise: *By boiling the water we sterilized it, making it fit to drink.* **SYN**: disinfect, purify. **2** to deprive of fertility; make incapable of producing offspring by removing the organs of reproduction or by the inhibition of their function. **3** *Figurative.* to make unproductive, unprofitable, or useless.

**ster|i|liz|er** (ster′ə lī′zər), *n.* any device for killing germs or microorganisms, such as a vessel containing boiling water, with or without disinfecting liquids, through which live steam may be passed to kill the germs.

**ster|let** (stėr′lit), *n.* a small sturgeon especially of the Black Sea and Caspian Sea, highly esteemed for its flavor and for the superior caviar from its roe. [< Russian *sterljad′* < German *Störling* (diminutive) < *Stör* sturgeon]

**ster|ling** (stėr′ling), *adj., n.* — ***adj.*** **1** containing 92.5 per cent pure silver; of standard quality for silver. *Sterling* is stamped on solid silver knives, forks, and the like. **2** made of sterling silver. **3** *Figurative.* genuine; reliable; excellent; dependable: *Everyone admires our doctor's sterling character.* **SYN**: sound. **4** of British money; payable in British money.
— ***n.*** **1** sterling silver or things made of it. **2a** British money, especially the pound as the standard British monetary unit in international trade: *to pay in sterling.* **b** the standard of fineness for silver or gold coin in Great Britain, that of silver being .500 at present, and that for gold .9166. Since 1946 British coins are made of a cupronickel alloy. *Abbr:* stg. **3** (in Australia) persons born in Great Britain or Ireland.
[Middle English *sterling* silver penny, Old English *steorra* star (which was on certain early Norman coins) + *-ling*] — **ster′ling|ly,** *adv.* — **ster′ling|ness,** *n.*

**sterling area,** a group of countries in the Commonwealth of Nations, certain dependent territories, and other countries that use the British pound sterling as the unit of currency in foreign trade: *Canada, being in the dollar area, is outside the sterling area.*

**sterling bloc,** a group of countries that have adjusted their currencies and foreign exchange in accordance with the value of the British pound sterling.

**sterling silver,** solid silver; silver that is 92.5 per cent pure (the original British standard of fineness for silver coin).

**stern**[1] (stėrn), *adj.* **1** severe; strict; harsh: *a stern master, a stern religion. His stern frown frightened the children.* **SYN**: See syn. under **severe.** **2** not yielding; hard; firm: *stern necessity, stern reality. ... ambition should be made of sterner stuff* (Shakespeare). **3** *Figurative.* forbidding in nature or aspect; grim: *a stern climate, stern mountains. ... a stern and rock-bound coast* (Felicia D. Hemans). [Old English *styrne*] — **stern′ly,** *adv.* — **stern′ness,** *n.*

**stern**[2] (stėrn), *n., adj.* — ***n.*** **1** the rear part of a ship or boat, beginning where the sides curve inward. See picture under **ship.** **2** the rear part of an aircraft. **3a** the buttocks. **b** the hinder part of any creature.
— ***adj.*** of, at, or having to do with the stern.
[Compare Old Frisian *stiārne* stern, rudder, Old Icelandic *stjōrn* a steering]

**ster|nal** (stėr′nəl), *adj.* **1** of or having to do with the breastbone or sternum. **2** in the region of the sternum.

**stern board,** *Nautical.* a backward motion of a vessel.

**stern|cas|tle** (stėrn′kas′əl, -käs′-), *n.* a high structure at the stern of a caravel, cog, or similar vessel.

**stern chase,** a chase in which the pursuing ship is directly following in the wake of another.

**stern chaser,** a gun in the stern of a ship for protection against an enemy ship following in its wake.

**stern drive,** = inboard-outboard.

**-sterned,** *combining form.* having a ____ stern: *A high-sterned vessel = a vessel having a high stern.*

**stern|er sex** (stėr′nər), the male sex; men as a group: *There are some very skilled embroiderers among members of the sterner sex who are not in the least effeminate* (London Times).

**stern|fore|most** (stėrn′ fôr′mōst, -məst; -fōr′-), *adv.* **1** with the stern first; backwards. **2** *Figurative.* clumsily; awkwardly.

**ster|nine** (stėr′nīn), *adj.* of or like a tern; belonging to a subfamily of birds including the terns. [< New Latin *sterninus* < *Sterna* the tern genus. Compare Old English *stearn* a sea bird.]

**ster|nite** (stėr′nīt), *n. Zoology.* the ventral part of each segment of the body of an insect or other arthropod. [< Greek *stérnon* chest + English *-ite*[1]]

**stern knee,** = sternson.

**stern|most** (stėrn′mōst, -məst), *adj.* **1** nearest the stern. **2** farthest in the rear.

**ster|no|cla|vic|u|lar** (stėr′nō klə vik′yə lər), *adj.* of, having to do with, or connecting the breastbone (sternum) and clavicle.

**ster|no|clei|do|mas|toid** (ster′nō klī′dō mas′toid), *adj.* connecting the breastbone (sternum), the clavicle, and the mastoid process of the temporal bone (applied to each of two muscles of the neck that serve to turn and nod the head). [< New Latin *sternum* breastbone + Greek *kleís, kleidós* clavicle + English *mastoid*]

**ster|no|cos|tal** (stėr′nō kos′təl), *adj.* of, having to do with, or connecting the sternum and the ribs. [< New Latin *sternum* breastbone + English *costal*]

**ster|no|mas|toid** (stėr′nō mas′toid), *adj.* = sternocleidomastoid.

**ster|no|scap|u|lar** (stėr′nō skap′yə lər), *adj.* of or having to do with the sternum and the scapula: *a sternoscapular muscle.*

**stern|post** (stėrn′pōst′), *n.* the upright timber or metal bar at the stern of a ship. It extends from the keel to the deck, and it usually supports the rudder.

**stern|sheets** (stėrn′shēts′), *n.pl.* the space at the stern of an open boat.

**stern|son** (stėrn′sən), *n.,* or **sternson knee,** a timber or metal bar set in the angle between the keelson and the sternpost to strengthen the joint; stern knee. [< *stern*[2]; patterned on *keelson, stemson*]

**stern-steer|er** (stėrn′stir′ər), *n.* an iceboat steered by the runner at the rear.

**ster|num** (stėr′nəm), *n., pl.* **-na** (-nə), **-nums.** a long bone or series of bones, occurring in most vertebrates except snakes and fishes, extending along the middle line of the front or ventral aspect of the trunk, usually articulating with some of the ribs (in human beings, with the true ribs), and with them completing the wall of the thorax; breastbone. See picture under **chest.** [< New Latin *sternum* < Greek *stérnon* chest]

**ster|nu|ta|tion** (stėr′nyə tā′shən), *n.* **1** the act of sneezing. **2** = sneeze. [< Latin *sternūtātiō, -ōnis* < *sternūtāre* to sneeze (frequentative) < *sternuere* to sneeze]

**ster|nu|ta|tor** (stėr′nyə tā′tər), *n.* any type of gas designed to cause irritation of the nose, coughing, and tears.

**ster|nu|ta|to|ry** (stər nyü′tə tôr′ē, -tōr′-), *adj., n., pl.* **-ries.** — ***adj.*** having to do with or causing sneezing.
— ***n.*** a substance that causes sneezing, such as snuff.
[< Medieval Latin *sternutatorius* < Latin *sternūtāre;* see etym. under **sternutation**]

**stern|ward** (stėrn′wərd), *adv., adj.* toward the stern; astern.

**stern|wards** (stėrn′wərdz), *adv.* = sternward.

**stern|way** (stėrn′wā′), *n.* the movement of a ship in reverse, with the stern preceding the bow.

**stern-wheel** (stėrn′hwēl′), *adj.* that is a sternwheeler.

**stern-wheel|er** (stėrn′hwē′lər), *n.* a steamboat driven by a paddle wheel at the stern. See picture under **paddlewheeler.**

**ster|oid** (ster′oid), *n., adj.* — ***n.*** *Biochemistry.* any one of a large class of structurally related compounds containing the carbon ring of the sterols, and including the sterols, various hormones, saponins, and acids found in bile.
— ***adj.*** = steroidal.
[< *ster*(ol) + *-oid*]

**ste|roi|dal** (stə roi′dəl), *adj.* **1** of, resembling, or having to do with a steroid. **2** of, resembling, or having to do with a sterol: *a steroidal ketone.*

**ster|ol** (ster′ōl, -ol), *n.* any one of a group of solid, chiefly unsaturated alcohols, such as ergosterol or cholesterol, present in animal and plant tissues. [< (chole)*sterol,* (ergo)*sterol*]

**Ster|o|pe** (stėr′ō pē), *n. Greek Mythology.* one of the Pleiades.

**ster|tor** (stėr′tər), *n.* a heavy snoring sound caused especially by the passage of air through mucus in the trachea. [< New Latin *stertor* < Latin *stertere* to snore]

**ster|to|rous** (stėr′tər əs), *adj.* making a heavy snoring sound: *stertorous breathing.* [< New Latin *stertor* snoring + English *-ous*] — **ster′to|rous|ly,** *adv.* — **ster′to|rous|ness,** *n.*

**stet** (stet), *n., v.,* **stet|ted, stet|ting.** *Printing.* — ***n.*** "let it stand" (do not delete), a direction on printer's proof, a manuscript, or the like, to retain matter that had been marked for deletion. The passage to be retained is usually underlined with a series of dots. *Abbr:* st.
— ***v.t.*** to mark with such a direction.
[< Latin *stet* let it stand]

**steth|o|graph** (steth′ə graf, -gräf), *n.* an instrument for recording the respiratory movements of the chest. [< Greek *stêthos* breast, chest + English *-graph*]

**steth|o|graph|ic** (steth′ə graf′ik), *adj.* of, having to do with, or obtained by means of the stethograph.

**ste|thom|e|ter** (ste thom′ə tər), *n.* an instrument for measuring the expansion of the chest in respiration. [< Greek *stêthos* breast, chest + English *-meter*]

**steth|o|met|ric** (steth′ə met′rik), *adj.* having to do with or obtained by means of a stethometer.

**steth|o|phone** (steth′ə fōn), *n.* a kind of stethoscope. [< Greek *stêthos* breast, chest + English *-phone*]

***steth|o|scope** (steth′ə skōp), *n., v.,* **-scoped, -scop|ing.** — ***n.*** an instrument used by doctors when listening to sounds in the heart, lungs, or other parts of the body.
— ***v.t.*** to examine with a stethoscope.
[< Greek *stêthos* breast, chest + English *-scope*]

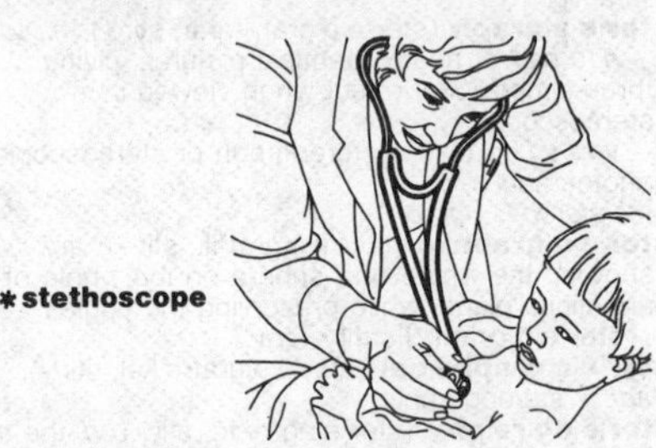
***stethoscope**

**steth|o|scop|ic** (steth′ə skop′ik), *adj.* **1** having to do with the stethoscope or its use. **2** made or obtained by the stethoscope. — **steth′o|scop′i|cal|ly,** *adv.*

**steth|o|scop|i|cal** (steth′ə skop′ə kəl), *adj.* = stethoscopic.

**ste|thos|co|pist** (ste thos′kə pist), *n.* a person skilled in the use of the stethoscope.

**ste|thos|co|py** (ste thos′kə pē), *n.* the art or process of using the stethoscope.

***Stet|son** or **stet|son** (stet′sən), *n.* **1** a soft felt hat with a broad brim and high crown, worn especially in the western United States. **2** any similar broad-brimmed hat: *In a corner of the plaza there are two cowboys wearing straw stetsons, plaid shirts, and string ties* (Maclean's). [< *Stetson,* trademark of a company that manufactures hats]

***Stetson**
definition 1

**Steu|ben glass** or **glassware** (stü′bən, styü′-; stü ben′, styü-), a handmade American glass or glassware made of heavy lead crystal. [< *Steuben* Glass, Incorporated, a company in Corning, New York]

**ste|ve|dore** (stē′və dôr, -dōr), *n., v.,* **-dored, -dor|ing.** — ***n.*** a person employed at a port to load and unload ships.
— ***v.t.*** to load or unload (a vessel or cargo).
— ***v.i.*** to work as a stevedore.
[American English < Spanish *estibador* < *estibar* to stow cargo < Latin *stīpāre* pack down; press. Compare etym. under **steeve**[1].]

**stevedore's knot,** a type of knot forming a bulge to keep a rope from going through a hole or block.

**Ste|ven|graph** (stē′vən graf, -gräf), *n.* a picture woven in silk. [< Thomas *Stevens,* died 1888, an English weaver]

**Ste|ven|so|ni|an** (stē′vən sō′nē ən), *adj., n.* — ***adj.*** having to do with, characteristic of, or like the Scottish author Robert Louis Stevenson (1850-1894) or his writings: *Mr. Muller's dramatization carefully preserved the bright Steven-*

*sonian colours* (London Times).
— *n.* an admirer of Stevenson or his writings.

**ste|vi|o|side** (stē′vē ə sīd), *n.* a glucoside obtained from the leaves of a South American composite plant, that is 300 times as sweet as ordinary cane sugar. *Formula:* $C_{38}H_{60}O_{18}$ [< New Latin *Stevia* the genus name + English *-ose*² + *-ide*]

**stew** (stü, styü), *v., n.* — *v.t.* to cook by slow boiling in a closed vessel: *Mother stewed the chicken for a long time.*
— *v.i.* **1** to be or be able to be stewed. **2** *Informal, Figurative.* to worry; fret: *to stew about an imagined insult. Retailers still stew about the taxability of a number of items* (Wall Street Journal).
— *n.* **1** food cooked by slow boiling, especially pieces of meat such as beef, veal, lamb, or mutton, and one or more of various vegetables. Stews are served with the sauce produced in cooking. **2** *Informal, Figurative.* a state of worry; fret: *to be in a perpetual stew. She is all in a stew over her lost suitcase. You'll be worried and fretted and kept in a stew* (Samuel Dodge). **SYN:** dither, agitation.
[< Old French *estuver* < Vulgar Latin *extūfāre* < Latin *ex-* out + Greek *tŷphos* vapor; fever. Compare etym. under **typhus.**]

**stew|ard** (stü′ərd, styü′-), *n., v.* — *n.* **1** a man who has charge of the food and table service for a club, ship, railroad train, or airplane. **2** a servant on a ship: *a deck steward. A cabin steward waits on passengers in their staterooms.* **3** a man who manages another's property: *He is the steward of that great estate.* **SYN:** manager. **4** *British.* a person appointed to manage a dinner, ball, race meeting, or other public event. **SYN:** chairman. **5** = shop steward.
— *v.i.* to be a steward; serve as steward: *We have with us two boys to cook and steward for us* (J. Chalmers).
— *v.t.* to be a steward for; manage as a steward: *to steward a property or a concert. The Athenian Commander ... ill stewarded the Treasury of the Commonwealth* (J. Yates).
[Middle English *stuard,* and *styward,* Old English *stīgweard* house guardian < *stig* hall, building + *weard* keeper, ward]

**stew|ard|ess** (stü′ər dis, styü′-), *n.* **1** a woman employed on a ship or airplane to wait on passengers. **2** a woman steward.

**stew|ard|ship** (stü′ərd ship, styü′-), *n.* **1** the position or work of a steward. **2** management for others.

**stewed** (stüd, styüd), *adj.* **1a** cooked by stewing: *stewed meat.* **b** cooked by boiling until very soft: *stewed fruit.* **2** *Slang.* drunk: *stewed to the gills.*

**stew|pan** (stü′pan′, styü′-), *n.* a pot, or a heavy saucepan, used for stewing.

**stew|pond** (stü′pond′, styü′-), *n. Especially British.* a pond or tank in which fish are kept until needed for the table.

**stew|pot** (stü′pot′, styü′-), *n.* a covered pot for making soups and stews: *Italian cooking ... to be at its best, requires a wood or charcoal fire ... and earthenware stewpots* (Atlantic).

**St. Ex.,** stock exchange.

**stey** (stā), *adj. Scottish.* (of a mountain, cliff, and other geological formations) steep.

**stg.,** sterling.

**stge.,** storage.

**St. George's cross,** = Saint George's cross.

**St. George's Day,** April 23, observed by the English in honor of Saint George, the patron saint of England.

**STH** (no periods), somatotropic hormone.

**sthe|ni|a** (sthi nī′ə, sthē′nē-), *n. Medicine.* abnormal or excessive bodily strength or action. [< New Latin *sthenia* < Greek *sthénos* strength; patterned on *asthenia*]

**sthen|ic** (sthen′ik), *adj.* **1** having to do with vigor or nervous energy. **2** (of diseases or symptoms) characterized by abnormal or excessive action of the vital processes. [< New Latin *sthenicus* < Greek *sthénos* strength]

**Sthe|no** (sthē′nō, sthen′ō), *n. Greek Legend.* one of the Gorgons.

**stiac|cia|to** (styät chä′tō), *adj., n.* — *adj.* (of a relief) very flat or shallow, as on a coin.
— *n.* a carving or modeling in very low relief.
[< Italian *stiacciato* flattened, past participle of *stiacciare* to crush, variant of *schiacciare* crack a nut, perhaps < a Germanic word]

**stib|i|al** (stib′ē əl), *adj.* like or having the qualities of antimony; antimonial.

**stib|ine** (stib′ēn, -in), *n.* a colorless, poisonous, gaseous compound; a hydride of antimony. *Formula:* $SbH_3$ [< *stib*(ium) + *-ine*²]

**stib|i|um** (stib′ē əm), *n.* = antimony. *Symbol:* Sb [Middle English *stibium* stibnite; kohl < Latin < Greek *stíbi,* variant of *stímmi*]

**stib|nite** (stib′nīt), *n.* a lead-gray mineral occurring in orthorhombic crystals and also massive. It is the most important ore of antimony. *Formula:* $Sb_2S_3$ [< *stibine* + *-ite*¹]

**stich** (stik), *n.* a line, especially of verse; verse. [< Greek *stíchos* row, line, verse < *steíchein* to walk, march (in a line)]

**sti|che|ron** (sti kir′on), *n., pl.* **-ra** (-rə). = troparion. [< Medieval Greek *sticheron,* neuter of *sticheros* < Greek *stíchos* verse]

**stich|ic** (stik′ik), *adj.* having to do with a verse or line; consisting of verses or lines; linear.

**stich|o|met|ric** (stik′ə met′rik), *adj.* of or having to do with stichometry.

**stich|o|met|ri|cal** (stik′ə met′rə kəl), *adj.* = stichometric.

**sti|chom|e|try** (sti kom′ə trē), *n.* the writing of a prose text in lines each one of which is a unit of sense or cadence. This was felt to be sometimes necessary before the development of punctuation permitted the separation of phrases, clauses, and other units, within the same line. [< Late Greek *stichometriā* < Greek *stíchos* line + *-metriā* a measuring < *métron* measure]

**stich|o|myth|i|a** (stik′ə mith′ē ə), *n.* dialogue in alternating single lines, as in Greek drama. [< New Latin *stichomythia* < Greek *stíchos* row, line + *mŷthos* word, speech]

**sti|chom|y|thy** (sti kom′ə thē), *n., pl.* **-thies.** = stichomythia.

**stich|wort** (stich′wėrt′), *n.* = stitchwort.

**stick**¹ (stik), *n., v.,* **sticked, stick|ing.** — *n.* **1a** a long, thin piece of wood: *Put some sticks on the fire.* **SYN:** rod, staff. **b** such a piece of wood shaped for a special use: *a walking stick, a hockey stick.* **c** such a piece used as a weapon; club; cudgel. **2** a slender branch or twig of a tree or shrub, especially when cut or broken off. **3** something like a stick in shape: *a stick of candy, a stick of cinnamon.* **4** a stalk of celery, rhubarb, or the like. **5** *Informal, Figurative.* a stiff, awkward, or stupid person: *a prig, a stick, a petrified poser* (George Meredith). **6** the device by which the ailerons, elevator, and rudder of an airplane are manipulated, originally a simple sticklike lever projecting upward between the pilot's knees as he sat in the cockpit. **7a** a mast or a section of a mast. **b** = yard². **8** *Informal.* a portion of alcoholic liquor added to a drink, especially of tea or coffee. **9** *Printing.* **a** a small metal tray in which type is set by hand; composing stick. **b** the amount of type so set; stickful of type. **10** a number of bombs capable of being released from an aircraft so as to strike the target in a line. **11a** = hockey stick. **b** = crosse. **c** a drumstick or baton. **d** = hurdle (def. 1). **12** *Slang.* a group of paratroopers jumping in succession in a single pass over an area: *Two "sticks" of parachutists made drops in which they delayed opening their canopies until they were no more than 1,000 feet from the ground* (London Times). **13** *U.S. Slang.* a marijuana cigarette.
— *v.t.* **1** to furnish with a stick or sticks to support or prop. **2** *Printing.* to arrange (type) in a composing stick.

**in a cleft stick,** *Especially British.* in a position from which it is impossible either to advance or retreat; in a dilemma: *The other side are in a cleft stick; they cannot go on long as they are, and they cannot stir into any new path without demolishing the ... Laws* (P. Thompson).

**shake a stick at,** *U.S. Informal.* to take notice of: *There were just a few flakes, not enough snow to shake a stick at.*

**sticks, a** pieces of cut or broken branches or pieces of cut and chopped wood, used as fuel: *Mr. Phillips has laid the paper, the sticks, and the coals neatly in the grate* (Arthur Symons). **b** wooden pieces of anything: *... the simple house with its few sticks of furniture* (Listener). **c** a breach of rule involving improper handling of a hockey stick: *to be penalized for sticks.*

**the sticks,** *U.S. Informal.* the outlying or undeveloped districts; backwoods: *The past theatrical season may have been the worst in living memory, but it was a series of flops in Manhattan, not in the sticks* (Saturday Review).
[Old English *sticca* rod, twig, spoon] — **stick′like′,** *adj.*

**stick**² (stik), *v.,* **stuck, stick|ing,** *n.* — *v.t.* **1a** to pierce with a pointed instrument: *to stick a potato with a fork.* **b** to thrust (a point) into; stab: *He stuck his fork into the potato.* **2** to kill by stabbing or piercing: *stick him like a calf* (Tennyson). **3** to fasten by thrusting the point or end into or through something: *He stuck a flower in his buttonhole.* **4a** to fix on a pointed implement; impale: *Their heads were stuck upon spears* (Edmund Burke). **b** to mount by transfixing with pins: *I have not stuck an insect this term* (Charles Darwin). **5** to put into a position; place: *to stick a finger in the pie. Don't stick your head out of the window.* **6** to fasten; attach: *to stick a notice on the bulletin board. Stick a stamp on the letter.* **7** to set into or adorn the surface of: *to stick a ham with cloves.* **8** to bring to a stop: *Our work was stuck by the breakdown of the machinery.* **9** *Informal, Figurative.* to puzzle: *That problem in arithmetic still sticks me.* **10** *Informal.* to smear (with an adhesive, plaster, or other gluey substance). **11** *Slang, Figurative.* **a** to impose upon by or as if by fraud; cheat; swindle: *to stick the public with shoddy goods.* **b** to leave (a person) with, as something to pay: *How much did they stick you for this lot?* (Arnold Bennett). **12** *Informal, Figurative.* to stand or put up with; tolerate: *I won't stick his insults much longer.*
— *v.i.* **1** to be thrust; extend: *His arms stick out of his coat sleeves.* **2** to keep close: *The little boy stuck to his mother's heels. He sticks here instead of getting out into the world and enjoying the fight* (Sinclair Lewis). **3** to be or become fastened; become fixed: *an arrow stuck in a tree. Two pages of the book stuck together.* **4** to come to or be at a standstill: *Our car stuck in the mud.* **5** to hold one's position; keep on; hold fast; cling: *to stick on a horse's back. He sticks to a task until he finishes it.* (*Figurative.*) *Being very stubborn he had a tendency to stick to his opinions.* **6** *Informal, Figurative.* to remain; stand; last: *He cannot make his charges stick. The scenes of his childhood stuck in his memory for years. It would be just a matter of guessing whether the rise will stick* (Wall Street Journal). **7** *Figurative.* to hesitate; be puzzled: *He always stuck in the middle, everybody recollecting the latter part except himself* (Washington Irving).
— *n.* **1** a thrust; stab. **2** sticky condition or quality; adhesiveness. **3** a standstill; stop. **4** a cause of delay; obstacle; impediment: *That should be no stick to you* (Stevenson). *When we came to the Hill Difficulty he made no stick at that* (John Bunyan).

**stick around,** *Informal.* **a** to stay or wait nearby: *I'll stick around for a while, but then I must go.* **b** to remain in a place; stay on: *The members of the office staff who stick around long enough to get to know him swear by Adams* (Time).

**stick at,** to hesitate or stop for: *He sticks at nothing in order to get his own way. She's not a woman to stick at trifles* (George Meredith).

**stick by** (or **to**), to remain resolutely faithful or attached to; refuse to desert: *He sticks by his friends when they are in trouble.*

**stick it out,** *Informal.* to put up with unpleasant conditions or circumstances; endure: *Try to stick it out for a few more days.*

**stick out, a** *Informal.* to put up with until the end: *By this method, companies, and sometimes whole battalions, which had stuck out the shellfire, were overwhelmed and annihilated* (E. W. Hamilton). **b** to stand out; be plain: *His inefficiency sticks out like a sore thumb.*

**stick together,** to keep or cling together; stay united; support each other or one another: *While we live we will stick together; one fate shall belong to us all* (Elisha K. Kane).

**stick up,** *Slang.* to hold up; rob: *The [hotel's] long-suffering night clerk ... has been stuck up three times in the last two months* (Time).

**stick up for,** *Informal.* to stand up for; support; defend: *I shall always like him [Whittier] the better for sticking up for old New England* (James Russell Lowell).
[Middle English *stikien,* Old English *stician*]
— ***Syn.*** *v.i.* 3, 4, 5 **Stick, adhere** mean to be firmly or closely attached to something. **Stick,** the common and general word, suggests being fastened as if by gluing: *Flies stick to flypaper. He stuck to his work.* **Adhere,** a more formal word sometimes used as a dignified substitute for *stick,* suggests clinging fast or being firmly attached by itself or of one's own accord: *This adhesive tape will adhere evenly to very smooth surfaces. Churchill firmly adhered to his announced aim of winning the war.*

**stick|a|bil|i|ty** (stik′ə bil′ə tē), *n.* **1** capacity for sticking or remaining stuck. **2** *Informal.* endurance; perseverance: *To be able to take rebuffs happily and still go on requires ... stickability* (British Weekly).

**stick|a|ble** (stik′ə bəl), *adj.* **1** capable of sticking or remaining stuck: *an absolutely stickable glue.* **2** *Informal.* capable of enduring or persevering.

**stick|ball** (stik′bôl′), *n.* a form of baseball played in small areas such as streets and vacant back lots, and played with a rubber ball and a stick or broom handle for a bat.

**stick bug, 1** = walking stick. **2** = spider bug.

**stick-but|ton** (stik′but′ən), *n.* = burdock.

**stick dance,** a folk or ritual dance marked by the symbolic use or beating of sticks, found throughout the world in many forms.

**Pronunciation Key:** hat, āge, cãre, fär; let, ēqual, tėrm; it, īce; hot, ōpen, ôrder; oil, out; cup, pu̇t, rüle; child; long; thin; ᴛʜen; zh, measure; ə represents **a** in about, **e** in taken, **i** in pencil, **o** in lemon, **u** in circus.

**stick|er** (stik′ər), *n.* **1** a person or thing that sticks. **2** *U.S.* a gummed label. **3** a bur; thorn. **4** *Informal.* a puzzle.

**stick figure**, the figure of a person or animal drawn with straight lines except for a circle to represent the head.

**stick|ful** (stik′fu̇l), *n., pl.* **-fuls.** *Printing.* as much type as a composing stick will hold.

**stick|han|dle** (stik′han′dəl), *v.i.,* **-dled, -dling.** to keep control of the hockey puck by skillful handling of the stick: *The Canuck veteran ... neatly stickhandled through the defense and scored from close in* (Grand Prairie Herald-Tribune).

**stick|han|dler** (stik′han′dlər), *n.* **1** a hockey player who stickhandles. **2** any hockey player: *New York stickhandlers took an astounding 65 shots at [the] goalie* (Time).

**stick|ing plaster** (stik′ing), a cloth coated with a sticky substance, used to cover and close slight cuts and wounds; adhesive tape.

**sticking point, 1** the place in which a thing stops and holds fast: *The nut has been screwed on the bolt to the sticking point. He screwed up his courage to the sticking point.* **2** *Figurative: The shippers and the union are apart on every issue, with the ... coastwide contract demand the key sticking point* (Wall Street Journal).

**stick insect**, = walking stick.

**stick-in-the-mud** (stik′in ᴛʜə mud′), *n., adj. Informal.* — *n.* **1** a person who prefers old methods or ideas to new; very dull or conservative person; old fogy. **2** a person who lacks initiative; backward, unresourceful person.
— *adj.* narrow in outlook; backward; provincial: *You have used the standards of some stay-at-home, stick-in-the-mud place to judge those progressive attitudes that have become part of the universally approved heritage of all Americans* (Harper's).

**stick|it** (stik′it), *adj. Scottish.* **1** imperfect or bungled; unfinished. **2** having failed, as in a calling or profession. [alteration of *sticked,* adjective < obsolete past participle of *stick*[2], verb]

**stick|lac** (stik′lak′), *n.,* or **stick lac**, a natural, dark-red, transparent resin deposited on the twigs of trees in India and southern Asia by certain insects; shellac (in its natural state); lac.

**stick|le** (stik′əl), *v.,* **-led, -ling,** *n.* — *v.i.* **1** to make objections about trifles; contend or insist stubbornly: *Flying for life, one does not stickle about his vehicle* (Thomas Carlyle). **2** to feel difficulties about trifles; have objections; scruple. **SYN:** demur.
— *n. Dialect or Informal.* **1** fuss; ado; disturbance: *Sometimes the victims may feel that the letter-writer's main purpose in ... reading has been to find cause for a good stickle* (London Times). **2** an agitated or bewildered state of mind; consternation.
[apparently variant of Middle English *stightlen* to regulate (a contest), mediate, arrange (frequentative) < Old English *stihtan* arrange]

***stick|le|back** (stik′əl bak′), *n., pl.* **-backs** or (*collectively*) **-back.** a small, scaleless fish with a row of sharp spines on its back. The male builds an elaborate nest for the eggs. The sticklebacks comprise a family of fishes. [Middle English *stykylbak* < Old English *sticel* a prick, sting + *bæc* back[1]]

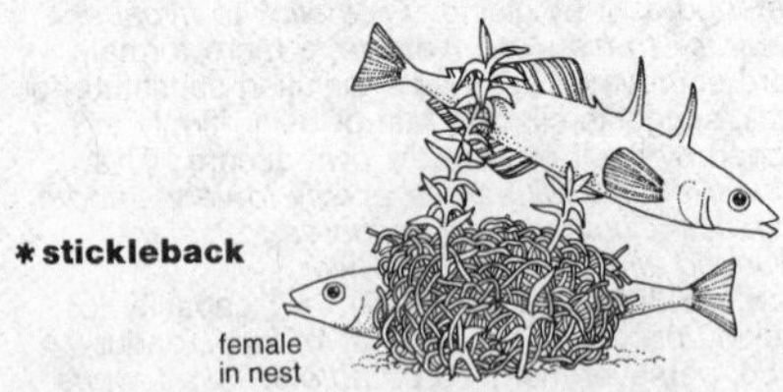

***stickleback**

**stick|ler** (stik′lər), *n.* a person who contends or insists stubbornly, sometimes over trifles: *a stickler for punctuality.*

**stick|man** (stik′man′), *n., pl.* **-men.** *U.S. Slang.* **1** a gambling house employee; croupier. **2** a person who handles a stick or bat in sports, such as a batter in baseball. **3** = drummer (def. 1).

**stick-out** (stik′out′), *n., adj. Informal.* — *n.* a person or thing that stands out: *He was clearly a stick-out in an otherwise lackluster, fifteen horse field* (Time).
— *adj.* that sticks out; prominent or conspicuous: *a stick-out athlete.*

**stick|pin** (stik′pin′), *n.* a long, slender pin having a decorated head, worn in a necktie or scarf for ornament; tiepin. [American English < *stick*[2] + *pin*]

**sticks** (stiks), *n.pl.* See under **stick**[1].

**stick|seed** (stik′sēd′), *n.* any one of a group of herbs of the borage family with flowers whose prickly seeds stick to clothing, such as the burseed.

**stick|shift** (stik′shift′), *n.* a lever projecting from the floor of an automobile, used to shift or change the speed of gears.

**stick|tight** (stik′tīt′), *n.* any one of a group of weedy herbs of the composite family, having flat, barbed seedlike fruits that stick to clothing; bur marigold; beggar's-lice.

**stick-to-it|ive** (stik′tü′ə tiv), *adj. U.S. Informal.* persistent; persevering.

**stick-to-it|ive|ness** (stik′tü′ə tiv nis), *n. U.S. Informal.* persistence; perseverance.

**stick|um** (stik′əm), *n. Slang.* any sticky substance; gum; adhesive: *postage stamp stickum.*

**stick-up** or **stick|up** (stik′up′), *n. Informal.* a holdup; robbery. [American English < *stick up,* idiom]

**stick|wa|ter** (stik′wôt′ər, -wot′-), *n.* a sticky solution obtained from the steam processing of fish for industrial use.

**stick|weed** (stik′wēd′), *n.* = ragweed.

**stick|work** (stik′wėrk′), *n.* **1** the way a player manipulates his stick in such sports as hockey and lacrosse. **2** *U.S. Informal.* skill in baseball batting. **3** a drummer's use of drumsticks. **4** a conductor's use of the baton.

**stick|y** (stik′ē), *adj.,* **stick|i|er, stick|i|est. 1** that sticks: *sticky glue.* **SYN:** adhesive, viscous, mucilaginous. **2** that makes things stick; covered with adhesive matter: *sticky paper to catch flies.* **3** *Informal.* hot and damp: *sticky weather.* **SYN:** humid. **4** *Informal, Figurative.* difficult: *a sticky problem. A night carrier landing can be a very sticky thing* (Saturday Evening Post). **5** *Informal, Figurative.* selling with difficulty: *Used car stocks ... are somewhat improved, although currently sticky* (Wall Street Journal). **6** *Slang, Figurative.* unpleasant; extremely disagreeable: *A few years ago this old peasant would have certainly joined up with wreckers and saboteurs and have reached a sticky end* (London Times). — **stick′i|ly,** *adv.* — **stick′i|ness,** *n.*

**stick|y|beak** (stik′ē bēk′), *n. Australian.* a prying, inquisitive person.

**stick|y-fin|gered** (stik′ē fing′gərd), *adj. Slang.* inclined to steal; thievish.

**sticky wicket, 1** *Cricket.* the condition when the ground around the wicket is wet and sticky, so that the ball bounces low. **2** *Especially British, Figurative.* a bad arrangement; difficult situation; unfavorable condition; rough deal: *Could the Commonwealth survive if the British Government decreed a sticky wicket for the West Indies?* (London Times).

**Stie|gel glass** (stē′gəl), a type of fine American glassware to which patterns were applied by molding, enameling, and engraving, made in Manheim, Pennsylvania between 1763 and 1774 by Henry William Stiegel.

**stiff** (stif), *adj., adv., n., v.* — *adj.* **1** not easily bent; fixed; rigid: *a stiff brush. He wore a stiff collar.* **2** hard to move: *a stiff gear. The old hinges on the barn door are stiff.* **3** not able to move easily: *a stiff neck. The old man's joints were stiff and sore.* **4** drawn tight; tense; taut: *a stiff cord, to keep a stiff rein.* **5** not fluid; firm: *a stiff cake batter. That jelly is stiff enough to stand alone.* **6** dense; compact: *stiff soil.* **7** *Figurative.* not easy or natural in manner; formal: *He made a stiff bow to his partner. He writes in a stiff style.* **SYN:** stilted, affected, constrained, ceremonious. **8** lacking grace of line, form, or arrangement: *stiff geometrical designs.* **9** *Figurative.* resolute; steadfast; unyielding: *a stiff resistance. He ... was as stiff about urging his point as ever you could be* (Charlotte Brontë). **10** strong and steady in motion: *a stiff breeze.* **11** harsh or severe: *a stiff penalty.* **12** *Informal, Figurative.* **a** more than seems suitable: *He asks a stiff price for his house.* **SYN:** immoderate, excessive. **b** firm, as prices, a commodity, or a market. **13a** *Informal.* very strong; potent: *Bobby poured everybody a stiff drink of bourbon* (James Dickey). **b** *U.S. Slang.* drunk: *Both laughed some more, which proves beyond doubt that both ... were stiff* (Atlantic). **14** *Figurative.* hard to deal with; hard; laborious: *a stiff fight, stiff opposition. The teacher gave us a stiff test.* **SYN:** rigorous. **15** (of a ship) carrying a press of canvas in the wind without heeling or veering excessively. **16** *Scottish.* strongly built; stalwart; sturdy.
— *adv.* **1** in a stiff manner or condition; rigidly: *to be frozen stiff.* **2** *Informal.* very much; extremely; completely: *The movie bored me stiff. I'm scared stiff of that dog.* **3** hard by; close: *He ... lays long iron shots stiff to the pin* (Tuscaloosa News).
— *n. Slang.* **1** a dead body; corpse: *They piled the stiffs outside the door* (John Hay). **2** *Figurative.* a stiff, formal, or priggish person: *These old stiffs of teachers just give you a lot of junk about literature and economics* (Sinclair Lewis). **3** any worker; fellow; person: *... a directory that appears to contain the name and assignment of every working news stiff in the capital* (New York Times). **4** a person who fails to tip for service. **5** a hopeless or incorrigible fellow. **6** *U.S.* a hobo; tramp: *stiffs riding the rods of Western freight cars* (Time). **7** an unskilled dockworker. **8** a drunken person.
— *v.t. Slang.* to leave without tipping or paying: *to stiff a waiter or bellhop. He stiffed the landlady for the month's rent he owed her.*
[Old English *stīf*] — **stiff′ly,** *adv.* — **stiff′ness,** *n.*
— *Syn. adj.* **1 Stiff, rigid** mean not easily bent. **Stiff** implies a hard firmness that resists bending: *a book with a stiff cover.* **Rigid** often implies so stiff that it will not bend without breaking: *rigid icicles. The gate has a rigid iron frame.*

**stiff-arm** (stif′ärm′), *v.t., n.* = straight-arm.

**stiff-backed** (stif′bakt′), *adj.* **1** erect or rigid of posture, as a soldier at attention. **2** *Figurative.* stiffly precise; rigid; formal: *There is nothing stiff-backed about the furnishings of her mind* (New Yorker).

**stiff|en** (stif′ən), *v.t.* to make stiff or stiffer: *She stiffened the shirt with starch.* — *v.i.* to become stiff or stiffer: *The jelly will stiffen as it cools. The wind was stiffening as the storm approached.* (*Figurative.*) *He stiffened with anger.* — **stiff′en|er,** *n.*

**stiff|en|ing** (stif′ə ning, stif′ning), *n.* **1** a making or becoming stiff or stiffer. **2** something used to stiffen a thing.

**stiff-heart|ed** (stif′här′tid), *adj. Archaic.* stubborn; contumacious.

**stiff|ish** (stif′ish), *adj.* rather stiff: *Most of Balmain's best coats have this stiffish skirt* (New York Times). (*Figurative.*) *The climb up from the beach is a stiffish one* (Sunday Times).

**stiff-lamb disease** (stif′lam′), = white muscle disease.

**stiff-lipped** (stif′lipt′), *adj.* showing no emotion; reserved; stoical: *This [ceremony] was conducted in a drenching rain in the presence of 1,100 stiff-lipped British soliders standing wetly to attention* (Time).

**stiff-necked** (stif′nekt′), *adj.* **1** having a stiff neck. **2** *Figurative.* stubborn; obstinate: *The stiff-necked old aristocrat ...* (George Gissing). **SYN:** mulish, intractable, refractory. — **stiff′-neck′ed|ness,** *n.*

**stiff upper lip**, bravery or endurance in facing trouble; stoicism: *Hemingway preaches the stiff upper lip* (Atlantic). *He manages to combine hysteria with a stiff upper lip* (Time).

**sti|fle**[1] (stī′fəl), *v.,* **-fled, -fling.** — *v.t.* **1a** to stop the breath of; smother; suffocate: *The smoke stifled the firemen.* **SYN:** strangle. **b** to choke to death. **SYN:** strangle. **2** to keep back or down; stop; suppress: *to stifle a cry, stifle a yawn,* (*Figurative.*) *stifle business activity,* (*Figurative.*) *to stifle a rebellion.* **SYN:** repress. **3** to smother or extinguish: *to stifle a flame. The fog ... stifled the roar of the traffic of London* (Rudyard Kipling).
— *v.i.* **1** to be unable to breathe freely: *I am stifling in this hot room.* (*Figurative.*) *Brother, the creed would stifle me That shelters you* (Karle Wilson). **SYN:** choke, strangle. **2** to die or become unconscious by being unable to breathe.
[Middle English *stuflen* or *stifflen* < *stuffen* to stuff, stifle; perhaps influenced by Scandinavian. Compare Old Icelandic *stīfla* dam up (water).] — **sti′fler,** *n.*

**sti|fle**[2] (stī′fəl), *n.,* or **stifle joint**, the joint of the upper hind leg of various animals, such as horses or dogs, corresponding to the knee of a human being. See picture at **horse**. [origin unknown]

**sti|fling** (stī′fling), *adj.* that stifles; suffocating; oppressively close: *stifling heat.* — **sti′fling|ly,** *adv.*

**stig|ma** (stig′mə), *n., pl.* **-mas** or **-ma|ta. 1** a mark of disgrace or shame; stain or reproach on one's reputation: *But, in the lapse of ... years ... the scarlet letter ceased to be a stigma which attracted the world's scorn* (Hawthorne). *They were suffering from the stigma of a crushing defeat* (John L. Motley). **2** a distinguishing mark or sign. **3a** an abnormal spot or mark in the skin, especially one that bleeds or turns red during hysteria. **b** an indication of a particular condition, such as hysteria. **4** the part of the pistil in flowering plants that receives the pollen. It is situated either directly on the ovary or at the top (more rarely the side) of the style. See picture under **flower**. **5** *Zoology.* **a** the pigmented eyespot of a protozoan. **b** a spiracle of an insect. **6** *Archaic.* a special mark burned on a slave or criminal; brand. [< Latin *stigma* < Greek *stígma, -atos* mark, puncture < *stig-,* root of *stízein* to mark, tattoo]

**stig|mal** (stig′məl), *adj.* of or having to do with a stigma; stigmatic.

**stig|mas|ter|ol** (stig mas′tə rōl, -rol), *n.* a crystalline alcohol, a sterol, occurring in the oil of the Calabar bean and in soybean and other vegetable oils, used in the preparation of some sex hormones. *Formula:* $C_{29}H_{48}O$ [< New Latin (*Physio*)-*stigma* the Calabar bean genus + English *sterol*]

**stig|ma|ta** (stig′mə tə), *n.* **1** a plural of **stigma**. **2** marks or wounds like the five wounds on the crucified body of Christ, in the hands, feet, and side, said to appear supernaturally on the bodies of certain persons. [< Greek *stígmata,* plural of *stígma;* see etym. under **stigma**]

**stig|mat|ic** (stig mat′ik), *adj., n.* —*adj.* **1** of or having to do with a stigma; like that of a stigma; marked by a stigma. **2** having to do with or accompanying the stigmata. **3** *Optics.* anastigmatic (applied especially to rays that converge to a single point).
—*n.* a person bearing marks suggestive of the wounds of Christ.

**stig|mat|i|cal|ly** (stig mat′ə klē), *adv.* **1** with stigma. **2** with a mark of infamy or deformity.

**stig|ma|tise** (stig′mə tīz), *v.t.,* **-tised, -tis|ing.** *Especially British.* stigmatize.

**stig|ma|tism** (stig′mə tiz əm), *n.* **1** a condition characterized by the presence of stigmata. **2** the absence of astigmatism.

**stig|ma|tist** (stig′mə tist), *n.* a person on whom the stigmata appear.

**stig|ma|ti|za|tion** (stig′mə tə zā′shən), *n.* **1** the act of stigmatizing. **2** the condition of being stigmatized.

**stig|ma|tize** (stig′mə tīz), *v.t.,* **-tized, -tiz|ing.** **1** to set some mark of disgrace on; reproach: *He always felt that his father's prison record stigmatized both of them.* **SYN**: villify, defame. **2** to brand: *As to their white wines, he stigmatizes them as mere substitutes for cider* (Washington Irving). **3** to produce stigmas or stigmata on. —**stig′ma|tiz′er,** *n.*

**stilb** (stilb), *n.* a unit of brightness or luminance equal to one candle per square centimeter of a surface. [< Greek *stílbein* to glitter]

**stil|bene** (stil′bēn), *n.* a crystalline hydrocarbon, used in the manufacture of dyes. *Formula:* $C_{14}H_{12}$ [< Greek *stílbein* to glitter + English *-ene*]

**stil|bes|trol** or **stil|boes|trol** (sil bes′trōl, -trol), *n.* = diethylstilbestrol. *Formula:* $C_{18}H_{20}O_2$ [< *stilb*-(ene) + (o)*estr*(us) + *-ol*[1]]

**stil|bite** (stil′bīt), *n.* a mineral, a hydrous silicate of aluminum, calcium, and sodium, usually occurring in radiated or sheaflike tufts of crystals with a pearly luster. It varies in color from white to brown or red. [< French *stilbite* < Greek *stílbein* to glitter + French *-ite* -ite[1]]

**stile[1]** (stīl), *n.* **1** a step or steps for getting over a fence or wall, while forming a barrier to the passage of sheep or cattle: *past the village, and down over the stile, into a field path* (John Galsworthy). **2** = turnstile. [Old English *stigel,* related to *stīgan* climb]

**stile[2]** (stīl), *n.* a vertical piece in a paneled wall, the side of a door, or the like. [perhaps < Dutch *stijl* doorpost, pillar]

**sti|let|to** (stə let′ō), *n., pl.* **-tos** or **-toes,** *v.,* **-toed, -to|ing.** —*n.* **1** a type of dagger with a narrow, pointed blade: *a sharp, double-edged stiletto* (Frederick Marryat). **2** a small, sharp-pointed instrument for making eyelet holes in embroidery.
—*v.t.* to stab with a stiletto: *They* [*robbers*] *stiletto all the men* (Washington Irving).
[< Italian *stiletto* (diminutive) < *stilo* dagger < Latin *stilus* pointed instrument]

**stiletto heel,** = spike heel.

**still[1]** (stil), *adj., n., v., adv., conj.,* —*adj.* **1** staying in the same position or at rest; without motion; stationary: *Sit still.* **SYN**: motionless. **2a** without noise; quiet; tranquil: *a still night. The room was so still that you could have heard a pin drop.* **b** unruffled or undisturbed; free from waves, violent current, winds, or the like: *a pool of still water. The lake is still today.* **3** making no sound; silent: *to keep still. Peace, and be still* (Shakespeare). **4** not loud; soft; low; subdued: *a still, small voice.* **5** not sparkling or bubbling: *a still wine.* **6a** having to do with or designating a single photograph or an individual frame of a motion picture: *still pictures, a still print.* **b** taking or showing single photographs as distinguished from a motion picture: *a still camera, a still projector, a still photographer.*
—*n.* **1** a single photograph, as distinguished from a motion picture; photograph of a person or object at rest. **2** an individual picture or frame of a motion picture, or a photograph of an actor or a scene, used especially in advertising or publicity. **3** *Informal.* **a** a still-life picture. **b** = still alarm. **4** stillness; silence; hush; calm.
—*v.t.* **1** to make calm or quiet: *The mother stilled the crying baby. The people prayed that the storm might be stilled.* **SYN**: silence, hush, tranquilize, pacify. **2** to stop the movement or activity of.
—*v.i.* to become calm or quiet: *After an hour, the storm stilled.*
—*adv.* **1** even; yet: *still more, still worse. You can read still better if you will try.* **2** in spite of some event, circumstance, or statement; nevertheless: *Though she has new dolls, she still loves her old ones best. Proof was given, but they still doubted.* **3** at this time; at that time: *They came yesterday and they are still here.* **4** even to this time; even to that time: *Was the store still open? The teacher's question is still unanswered.* **5** in the future as in the past: *It will still be here.* **6** without moving; quietly. **7** *Archaic.* steadily; constantly; always; ever: *still achieving, still pursuing* (Longfellow).
—*conj.* and yet; but yet; nevertheless; notwithstanding: *He was hungry; still he would not eat. She has many friends; still she likes to stay home.*

**still and all,** *U.S. Informal.* after all; nevertheless: *Still and all, he's a good man and knows the law* (New Yorker).
[Old English *stille*]
—*Syn. adj.* **1, 2a Still, quiet** mean without noise or activity. **Still** suggests being silent and at rest: *Her hands are never still.* **Quiet** suggests being calm and peaceful: *They live in a quiet little town.*

***still[2]** (stil), *n., v.* —*n.* **1** an apparatus for distilling liquids, especially alcoholic liquors, consisting essentially of a vessel in which the liquid to be distilled is heated and a device to condense the vapor thus produced. **2** a place where alcoholic liquors are distilled; distillery. **3** *U.S. Slang.* a heat exchanger.
—*v.t. Obsolete.* **1** to distill. **2** to give forth in drops.
—*v.i. Obsolete.* **1** to drip. **2** to issue from something that is being distilled.
[short for *distill*]

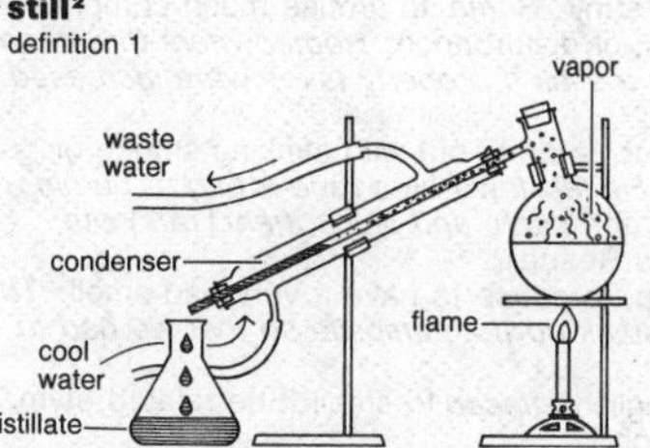

***still[2]**
definition 1

**stil|lage** (stil′ij), *n.* a low stool or bench, such as in a factory, used to keep manufactured products from coming in contact with the floor. Some stillages can be tilted to allow articles placed on them to slide into packing boxes. [probably < Dutch *stellage* platform, stand]

**still alarm,** a fire alarm communicated to the fire department by telephone or by any means other than a signal box or other apparatus activating the alarm bell in the firehouse.

**still|birth** (stil′bėrth′), *n.* **1** the birth of a dead child. **2** a child dead at birth.

**still|born** (stil′bôrn′), *adj.* **1** dead when born. **2** *Figurative.* **a** destined never to be realized: *stillborn hopes.* **b** that fails utterly to attract an audience: *a stillborn book or play.* **SYN**: abortive.

**still-burn** (stil′bėrn′), *v.t.,* **-burned** or **-burnt, -burn|ing.** to burn in the process of distillation: *to still-burn brandy.*

**still hunt,** quiet or secret pursuit, especially a pursuit of game stealthily or under cover; stalking.

**still-hunt** (stil′hunt′), *v.t., v.i.* = stalk.

**stil|li|form** (stil′ə fôrm), *adj.* drop-shaped. [< Latin *stilla* a drop + English *-form*]

**still life, 1** *no pl.* fruit, flowers, furniture, pottery, dead game, or the like, shown in a picture: *He painted still life, oranges and lemons ...* (Horace Walpole). **2** *pl.* **still lifes** or **still lives.** a picture of such things: *His fine still lives date from the last decades of the nineteenth century* (London Times). —**still′-life′,** *adj.*

**still|man** (stil′mən), *n., pl.* **-men.** a workman employed to attend to a still.

**still|ness** (stil′nis), *n.* **1** absence of noise; quiet; silence: *the stillness of the grave, to listen in sullen stillness.* **SYN**: hush. **2** absence of motion; calm: *the stillness of a mill pond.* **SYN**: immobility.

**still-room** (stil′rüm′, -rům′), *n. British.* **1** (originally) a room in a house in which cordials and other alcoholic liquors were distilled: *A hundred years ago every lady in the country had her still-room* (Thackeray). **2** (later) a room where cordials, preserves, or the like, are kept, and tea and coffee are prepared. [< *still*[2] + *room*]

**Still's disease** (stilz), a chronic disease of children, in which the spleen and lymphatic glands become enlarged and many of the joints inflamed. It is a kind of rheumatoid arthritis. [< George F. *Still,* 1868-1941, an English pediatrician]

**Still|son wrench** (stil′sən), *Trademark.* a wrench with an adjustable L-shaped jaw that tightens as pressure on the handle is increased, used for turning pipes and other round objects.

**stil|ly** (*adj.* stil′ē; *adv.* stil′lē), *adj.,* **-li|er, -li|est,** *adv.* —*adj.* quiet; still; calm.
—*adv.* calmly; quietly.

***stilt** (stilt), *n., pl.* **stilts** or (*for 3, collectively*) **stilt,** *v.* —*n.* **1** one of a pair of poles, each with a support for the foot at some distance above the ground. Stilts are used for walking in shallow water, or by children for amusement. **2** a long post or pole used to support a house, shed, or other building, above water or swampland. **3** a wading bird with very long, slender legs and a slender, sharp bill, that lives in marshes.
—*v.t.* to raise on or as if on stilts.
[Middle English *stilte* a crutch] —**stilt′like′,** *adj.*

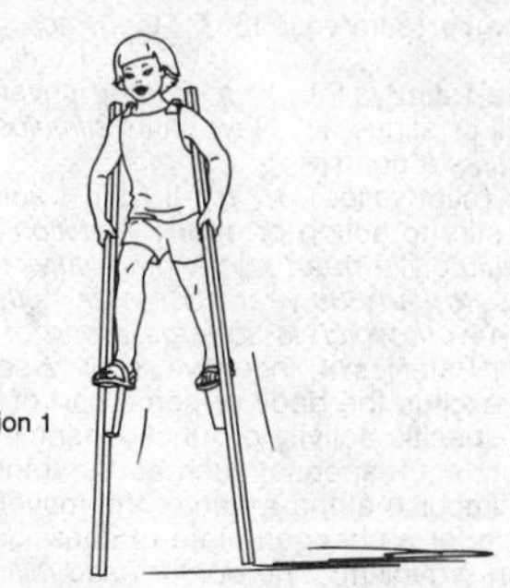
***stilt**
definition 1

**stilt|bird** (stilt′bėrd′), *n.* = stilt (def. 3).

**stilt|ed** (stil′tid), *adj.* **1** stiffly dignified or formal: *stilted conversation. He has a stilted manner of speaking. There were letters of stilted penitence to his father, for some wrong-doing* (Elizabeth Gaskell). **SYN**: pompous. **2** supported on props or posts so as to be raised above the ground. **3** raised as if on stilts. **4** raised above the general level by a course of masonry. A vault that does not spring immediately from the top of a pier or other apparent point of impost is a stilted vault. —**stilt′ed|ly,** *adv.* —**stilt′ed|ness,** *n.*

**stilt|er** (stil′tər), *n.* a person who walks on or as if on stilts.

**Stil|ton cheese,** or **Stil|ton** (stil′tən), *n.* a rich white cheese veined with mold when well ripened. Stilton cheese is much like Roquefort cheese and is classed as one of the great cheeses of England. [< *Stilton,* a village in Huntingdonshire, England, where it was sold at a coaching inn]

**stilt root,** = prop root.

**stilt sandpiper,** a long-legged American sandpiper with a gray back and white rump.

**stilt|y** (stil′tē), *adj.* inflated; pompous; stilted.

**sti|lya|ga** (sti lyä′gä), *n., pl.* **sti|lya|gi** (sti lyä′gē), a young person in the Soviet Union, who seeks to cultivate the style of dress, uninhibited manners, and tastes associated with the younger generation in Western countries: *There have, of course, been unofficial movements of dress reform in recent years among young Russians —such as the bright shirts and drainpipe trousers worn by the stilyagi* (Manchester Guardian). [< Russian *stil′yaga* (literally) style chaser < *stil′* style + (slang) *yaga* chaser < German *Jäger* hunter]

**stime** (stīm), *n. Scottish and Irish.* a glimmer or glimpse.

**stim|u|la|bil|i|ty** (stim′yə lə bil′ə tē), *n.* the state or quality of being stimulable.

**stim|u|la|ble** (stim′yə lə bəl), *adj.* that can be stimulated.

**stim|u|lant** (stim′yə lənt), *n., adj.* —*n.* **1** a food, drug, or medicine, that temporarily increases the activity of the body or some part of the body. Tea and coffee are stimulants: *Some stimulants ... make a drowsy person more wakeful* (Edward F. Domino). **2** something that excites, stirs, or stimulates; motive or influence that rouses one to action: *Hope is a stimulant.* **SYN**: stimulus. **3** *Informal.* an alcoholic drink.
—*adj.* = stimulating.
[< Latin *stimulāns, -antis,* present participle of *stimulāre;* see etym. under **stimulate**]

**stim|u|late** (stim′yə lāt), *v.,* **-lat|ed, -lat|ing.** —*v.t.* **1** to spur on; stir up; rouse to action: *Praise stimulated her to work hard.* **SYN**: prick, goad, incite, encourage, impel, urge. **2** to increase temporarily the functional activity of (the body or some part of the body, especially a nerve). **3** to

**Pronunciation Key:** hat, āge, cãre, fär; let, ēqual, tėrm; it, īce; hot, ōpen, ôrder; **oi**l, **ou**t; cup, pu̇t, rüle; **ch**ild; lo**ng**; **th**in; ᴛʜen; **zh**, measure; ə represents **a** in about, **e** in taken, **i** in pencil, **o** in lemon, **u** in circus.

excite with alcoholic liquor; intoxicate. —***v.i.*** to act as a stimulant or a stimulus. [< Latin *stimulāre* (with English *-ate*[1]) < *stimulus* (originally) a goad]

**stim|u|lat|er** (stim′yə lā′tər), *n.* = stimulator.

**stim|u|lat|ing** (stim′yə lā′ting), *adj.* rousing to (mental or physical) action; stirring; inspiring: *a stimulating speech, article.* —**stim′u|lat′ing|ly,** *adv.*

**stim|u|la|tion** (stim′yə lā′shən), *n.* the act of stimulating or condition of being stimulated: *Lazy people need stimulation to make them work.*

**stim|u|la|tive** (stim′yə lā′tiv), *adj., n.* —***adj.*** tending to stimulate; stimulating. —***n.*** a stimulating thing; stimulus. —**stim′u|la′tive|ly,** *adv.*

**stim|u|la|tor** (stim′yə lā′tər), *n.* a person or thing that stimulates.

**stim|u|la|to|ry** (stim′yə lə tôr′ē, -tō′-), *adj.* = stimulative.

**stim|u|lose** (stim′yə lōs), *adj. Botany.* covered with stimuli or stings. [< New Latin *stimulosus* < Latin *stimulus* a goad]

**stim|u|lus** (stim′yə ləs), *n., pl.* **-li** (-lī). **1** something that stirs to action or effort: *Ambition is a great stimulus. We need some imaginative stimulus ... to carry us year after year ... through the routine work which is so large a part of our life* (Walter Pater). **SYN:** incentive, spur. **2** something that excites the body or some part of the body to a specific activity or function; something that produces a response, such as the transmitting of an impulse along a nerve, the movement of a muscle, or a changed state of consciousness, in an organism: *The doctor used mild electric shocks as a stimulus to keep the patient's heart beating. The stimulus of a loud sound, carried by nerves to the brain, made the baby cry.* **3** *Botany.* a sting, such as a stinging hair on a nettle. [< Latin *stimulus* (originally) a goad]

**stimulus threshold,** *Psychology.* the minimum stimulus to produce a conscious effect.

**sti|my** (stī′mē), *n., pl.* **-mies,** *v.,* **-mied, -my|ing.** = stymie.

**sting** (sting), *v.,* **stung** or (*Archaic*) **stang, sting-ing,** *n.* —***v.t.*** **1** to pierce or wound with a sharp-pointed organ (often) bearing a poisonous fluid: *If a honeybee stings you, remove the stinger.* **2** (of certain plants or substances) to produce irritation, rash, or inflammation in (a person's skin) by contact. **3** to affect with a tingling pain, burning sensation, sharp hurt, or the like: *Mustard stings the tongue. The electric spark stung his arm.* **4** *Figurative.* to affect with a sudden, sharp mental pain; cause to suffer mentally: *He was stung by the jeers of the other children.* **5** *Figurative.* to drive or stir up as if by a sting: *Their ridicule stung him into making a sharp reply.* **6** *Slang, Figurative.* to impose upon; charge too much; cheat: *Guess I'll have to get down to the office now and sting a few clients* (Sinclair Lewis).
—***v.i.*** **1** to use a sting: *Bees, wasps, and hornets sting.* **2** to cause a feeling like that of a sting: *Mustard stings.* **3** *Figurative.* to feel sharp mental or physical pain or distress; smart: *The groans of a person stinging under defeat* (Thackeray).
—***n.*** **1** the act of stinging. **2a** a wound caused by stinging; prick; wound: *Put mud on the sting to take away the pain.* **b** the pain or smart of such a wound. **3** the sharp-pointed part of an insect, animal, or plant that pricks or wounds and often poisons: *A wasp's sting is not left in the wound.* **4** *Botany.* a stiff, sharp-pointed, glandular hair that emits an irritating fluid when touched, as on the nettle; stinging hair. **5** *Figurative.* a sharp pain or wound: *the stings of remorse. The ball team felt the sting of defeat. O death, where is thy sting? O grave, where is thy victory?* (I Corinthians 15:55). **6** something that causes a sharp pain. **7** *Figurative.* something that drives or urges sharply; stimulus; incitement. **8** stinging quality; capacity to sting or hurt: (*Figurative.*) *This passage ... has been deprived of half its sting* (Sir George Trevelyan). **9** *U.S. Slang.* an illegal scheme, such as a swindle, theft, or confidence game: *Cosby, a safecracker, and Poitier, a con man, pull off separate, spectacular stings at the film's outset* (Time).
[Old English *stingan*] —**sting′ing|ly,** *adv.*

**sting|a|ree** (sting′ə rē, sting′ə rē′), *n.* = sting ray. [American English, alteration of *sting ray*]

**stinged** (stingd), *adj.* having a sting, as an insect.

**sting|er**[1] (sting′ər), *n.* **1** the part of an insect or animal that stings. **2** anything that stings: *Keep away from yellow jackets; they are stingers.* **3** *Informal, Figurative.* a stinging blow, remark, or the like.

**sting|er**[2] (sting′ər), *n.* **1** *U.S.* a cocktail consisting of brandy and white crème de menthe. **2** *British Informal.* Scotch whisky and soda. [alteration of *stengah* < a Malay word meaning "half"]

**sting|ing hair** (sting′ing), *Botany.* a sting.

**stinging nettle, 1** a variety of Eurasian nettle now naturalized in eastern North America, having bristles on the stems and leaves that irritate the skin when touched; great nettle. **2** any nettle that bears stings.

**sting|less** (sting′lis), *adj.* having no sting.

**stin|go** (sting′gō), *n. British Slang.* **1** strong ale or beer. **2** *Figurative.* vigor; energy; zip. [< *sting,* verb (from its sharp taste)]

**sting ray,** or **sting|ray** (sting′rā′), *n.* a broad, flat fish that can inflict severe wounds with the sharp spine on its long tail.

**stin|gy**[1] (stin′jē), *adj.,* **-gi|er, -gi|est. 1** mean about spending or giving money; not generous: *She tried to save money without being stingy.* **SYN:** miserly, parsimonious, niggardly, penurious. **2** poor in quantity or amount; scanty; meager: *a stingy helping of dessert.* [see related etym. at **sting**] —**stin′gi|ly,** *adv.* —**stin′gi|ness,** *n.*

**sting|y**[2] (sting′ē), *adj.,* **sting|i|er, sting|i|est.** having a sting; stinging. [< *sting* + *-y*[1]]

**stink** (stingk), *n., v.,* **stank** or **stunk, stunk, stink|ing.** —***n.*** **1** a very bad smell: *... the deep-sea stink of the hot shore* (Saul Bellow). **SYN:** stench. **2** *Informal, Figurative.* loud complaint or criticism; public clamor: *There's been such a stink about stag hunting on Exmoor* (Joanna Ostrow). *"Say, remember the time we shoved bonehead Vinc Curley ... and there was a big stink"* (James T. Farrell).
—***v.i.*** **1** to have a very bad smell: *Decaying fish stink.* **2** *Figurative.* **a** to have a very bad reputation; be in great disfavor. **b** to savor offensively (of): *His remark stinks of treason.* **c** *Informal.* to be poor in quality; be inferior: *"Anyway, you're too slow and your math stinks"* (New Yorker). [*At*] *any game without a ball we tend, unfortunately, to stink* (J. D. Salinger).

**raise a stink,** *Slang.* to arouse much complaint, criticism, or disturbance: *Homeowners threatened to raise a stink if property taxes were increased again.*

**stink out,** to drive out with stinking smoke or fumes: *He let down by a rope a bag of burning sulphur and pitch, and stunk them* [*rats*] *out* (Charles Reade).

**stink up,** to cause to have a very bad smell: *The skunk stank up the campsite so that we had to move.*

[Old English *stincan* to smell. See related etym. at **stench.**]

▶ **Stunk** as the past tense form was once common, but is now rare in Standard English.

**stin|kard** (sting′kərd), *n.* **1** any one of various ill-smelling animals: **a** = polecat. **b** = badger. **2** a person who stinks (formerly often used as a term of abuse).

**stink|ball** (stingk′bôl′), *n.* a ball or missile containing explosives, or other chemicals, for generating offensive and suffocating vapors, used in warfare for throwing among the enemy.

**stink|bird** (stingk′bėrd′), *n. Informal.* the hoatzin. [supposedly because of its strong musky odor]

**stink bomb,** a can, jar, or other container filled with certain chemicals that gives off a disagreeable smell when exploded or burst.

**stink|bug** (stingk′bug′), *n.* any bad-smelling bug, especially one of a family of large, flat bugs with a disagreeable odor. [American English < *stink* + *bug*[1]]

**stink|er** (sting′kər), *n.* **1** a thing that stinks, especially: **a** any one of several large ill-smelling petrels. **b** = stinkpot. **2** a person who stinks. **3** *Informal, Figurative.* a low, mean, contemptible person. **4** *Slang, Figurative.* something very difficult: *It is also a very dreary sort of a place and whoever has the job of redeveloping it has his job cut out. It is a real stinker ...* [*but*] *just the place to tackle* (Manchester Guardian).

**stink fly,** any one of a family of green-colored lacewings that are commonly attached to lights at night, and give off a strong odor when handled.

**stink grass,** an ill-smelling grass native to Europe and Asia and widely naturalized in the United States.

**stink|horn** (stingk′hôrn′), *n.* a very unpleasant smelling fungus that often grows in backyards and under open stairways; fetid wood witch.

**stink|ing** (sting′king), *adj., adv.* —***adj.*** **1** that stinks; having an offensive smell: *a stinking pigpen.* **2** *Informal, Figurative.* very bad; terrible. *It's a stinking shame.* **3** *Slang.* very drunk.
—***adv.*** *Slang.* very; extremely: *If I was willing to leave all you lovely people ... I'd be a stinking rich talent scout living in Beverly Hills* (John Updike). —**stink′ing|ly,** *adv.*

**stinking nightshade,** = henbane.

**stinking smut,** = bunt[3].

**stink|o** (sting′kō), *adj. Slang.* **1** drunk. **2** unpleasant; offensive.

**stink|pot** (stingk′pot′), *n.* **1** a potlike metal vessel filled with combustibles that produce a suffocating, bad-smelling smoke, formerly flung at an enemy, especially in naval warfare, to drive him into the open or overcome his capacity to resist assault. **2** *Informal.* a person who stinks; stinker. **3** *Slang.* a motorboat: *Most of the time sailors regard our "stinkpots" as a lower order, reserving their rivalry for racing boats of their own class* (Maclean's).

**stink|stone** (stingk′stōn′), *n.* any stone the gives out a fetid odor on being scratched or struck, because of rotten organic matter.

**stink|weed** (stingk′wēd′), *n.* any one of several ill-smelling plants, especially the jimson weed.

**stink|wood** (stingk′wu̇d′), *n.* **1** any of various trees whose wood has an unpleasant odor. **2** the wood.

**stink|y** (sting′kē), *adj.,* **stink|i|er, stink|i|est.** that stinks; stinking: *A dirty, stinky, uncared-for closet-size section of a great city* (Claude Brown).

**stint**[1] (stint), *v., n.* —***v.t.*** **1** to keep on short allowance; be saving or careful in using or spending; limit: *The parents stinted themselves of food to give it to their children.* **2** *Archaic.* to stop; cease.
—***v.i.*** **1** to be saving; get along on very little. **2** *Archaic.* to cease action; desist.
—***n.*** **1** limit; limitation: *The generous man gives without stint.* **2** an amount or share set aside. **3** an allotted portion of work; task assigned: *Washing the breakfast dishes was her daily stint. My cousin has just completed a three-year stint in the army.* **4** *Archaic.* a stop. Also, **stent.** [Middle English *stinten,* Old English *styntan* to blunt, make dull] —**stint′er,** *n.* —**stint′ing|ly,** *adv.* —**stint′less,** *adj.*

**stint**[2] (stint), *n.* any one of various small sandpipers, especially the dunlin or the least sandpiper. [Midddle English *stynte*]

**stip.,** stipend.

**stipe** (stīp), *n.* **1** *Botany.* a stalk or stem, especially of a mushroom, fern, or seaweed, or of a small organ such as a pistil: **a** the stalk in flowering plants formed by the receptacle or some part of it, or by a carpel. **b** the stalk or petiole of a frond, especially of a fern or seaweed. **c** the stalk or stem in certain fungi which supports the pileus or cap: *the stipe of a mushroom.* **2** *Zoology.* a stalklike part or organ. [< French *stipe* < New Latin *stipes;* see etym. under **stipes**]

**sti|pel** (stī′pəl), *n. Botany.* a secondary stipule situated at the base of the leaflets of a compound leaf. [< New Latin *stipella* (diminutive) < Latin *stipula;* see etym. under **stipule**]

**sti|pel|late** (stī pel′āt, -it; stī′pə lāt, -lit), *adj.* having stipels.

**sti|pend** (stī′pend), *n.* **1** fixed or regular pay; salary: *A postman receives a stipend.* **2** a fixed, periodic allowance, as to a student holding a scholarship. [< Latin *stipendium* < *stips, stipis* gift (in small coin), soldier's pay; (originally) coin + *pendere* weigh out]

▶ **Stipend** is the usual word in England for the pay of a curate or other clergyman remunerated at a fixed rate, of a professor, of a judge, and of certain other professional persons. The official income of a minister of state, on the other hand, or that of a civil servant, is more commonly called *salary.*

**sti|pen|di|ar|y** (stī pen′dē er′ē), *adj., n., pl.* **-ar|ies.** —***adj.*** **1** receiving a stipend. **2** paid for by a stipend. **3** of or having to do with a stipend. **4** performing services for regular pay: *the insidious spy, the stipendiary informer* (Henry Hallam). **5** that renders or is obligated to render services, tribute, or the like especially under feudal or ancient Roman law.
—***n.*** **1** a person who receives a stipend; salaried clergyman, official, or the like. **2** a stipendiary person or piece of property in ancient Rome. [< Latin *stīpendiārius* < *stipendium;* see etym. under **stipend**]

**stipendiary magistrate,** a salaried official in Great Britain, Canada, and Australia, having judicial functions similar to those of the unpaid justices of the peace.

**sti|pes** (stī′pēz), *n., pl.* **stip|i|tes** (stip′ə tēz). **1** *Zoology.* a part or organ resembling a stalk, especially the second section of one of the maxillae of a crustacean or insect. **2** *Botany.* a stipe. [< New Latin *stipes* < Latin *stīpes, -itis* tree trunk, post, stalk]

**sti|pi|form** (stī′pə fôrm), *adj. Botany, Zoology.* having the form or character of a stipe.

**stip|ple** (stip′əl), *v.,* **-pled, -pling,** *n.* —***v.t.*** **1** to paint, draw, or engrave by using dots or small, light strokes. **2** to produce a stippled effect on.
—***n.*** **1** the method of painting, drawing, or engraving by stippling. **2** an effect produced by or as if by this method: *rose-moles all in stipple upon trout that swim* (Gerard Manley Hopkins). **3** stippled work.
[< Dutch *stippelen* (frequentative) < *stippel* prick, speckle < *stip* a point] —**stip′pler,** *n.*

**stip|pling** (stip′ling), *n.* **1a** the act, method, or work of a person or thing that stipples. **b** the design or shading so produced; dotted work. **2** any natural appearance resembling stippled painting or engraving.

**stip|u|lar** (stip′yə lər), *adj. Botany.* **1** of or having to do with stipules. **2** resembling stipules. **3** having stipules. **4** situated on, near, or in the place of a stipule.

**stip|u|late**[1] (stip′yə lāt), *v.*, **-lat|ed, -lat|ing.** —*v.t.* to arrange definitely; demand as a condition of agreement: *He stipulated that he should receive a month's vacation every year if he took the job.* —*v.i.* **1** to make an express demand or arrangement (for): *In accepting the job she stipulated for a raise every six months.* **2** *Obsolete.* to make a bargain or contract; covenant.
[< Latin *stipulārī* (with English *-ate*[1]) stipulate, perhaps related to *stips;* see etym. under **stipend**]

**stip|u|late**[2] (stip′yə lit, -lāt), *adj. Botany.* having stipules.

**stip|u|lat|ed**[1] (stip′yə lā′tid), *adj.* stated; agreed upon: *a stipulated amount, the stipulated conditions in a contract.*

**stip|u|lat|ed**[2] (stip′yə lā′tid), *adj. Botany.* having stipules; stipulate.

**stip|u|la|tion** (stip′yə lā′shən), *n.* **1** a definite arrangement; agreement; bargain. **SYN:** contract. **2** a condition in an agreement or bargain: *We rented the house with the stipulation that certain rooms should be papered and painted by the owner.* **SYN:** proviso. **3** the act of stipulating.

**stip|u|la|tor** (stip′yə lā′tər), *n.* a person who stipulates.

**stip|u|la|to|ry** (stip′yə lə tôr′ē, -tōr′-), *adj.* having to do with or characterized by stipulation.

***stip|ule** (stip′yül), *n.* one of a pair of little leaflike parts at the base of a leaf stem. [earlier *stipula* < New Latin use of Latin *stipula* stem, stalk (of hay). See etym. of doublet **stubble.**]

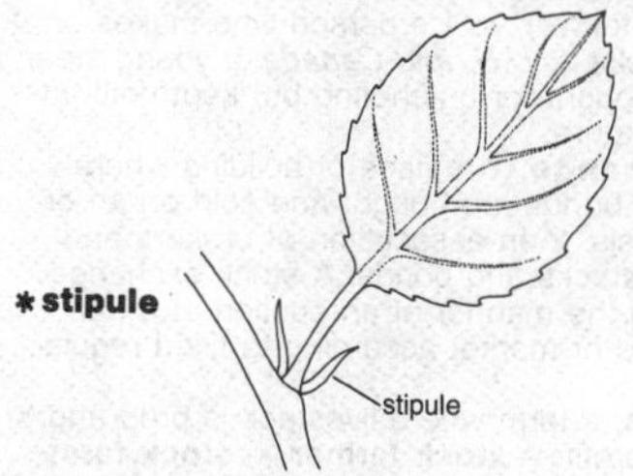

***stipule**

**stir**[1] (stėr), *v.*, **stirred, stir|ring,** *n.* —*v.t.* **1** to set in motion; move; shake: *The wind stirs the leaves.* **2** to change the position or situation of; move, especially slightly: *Thy companion had been slain by thy side ... without thy stirring a finger to his aid* (Scott). **3** to mix by moving around with a spoon, fork, stick, or some other implement or device; or with the hand: *to stir the fire with a poker. He stirs the sugar in his tea with his spoon. She stirred her soup to quicken its cooling.* **4** to excite to feeling, emotion, or passion; affect strongly; move: *Words ... that really stir the soul* (Anthony Trollope). *Abraham Lincoln was stirred to the depths of his being by the passing of the Kansas-Nebraska Act* (Sir Winston Churchill). **5** to move to action; incite; instigate: *The untruth of the stories by which they had been stirred to rebellion* (James A. Froude). **SYN:** rouse, animate, agitate. **6** to bring into notice or debate.
—*v.i.* **1** to move about; be active: *No one was stirring in the house.* **2** to pass from rest or inaction to motion or action; begin to move, especially slightly; budge: *They dare not stir.* **3** to become active, much affected, or excited: *The countryside was stirring with new life.* **4** to be in circulation; be current: *There is no news stirring here now* (William Dean Howells). **5** to be mixed with a spoon, fork, or some other implement, or with the hand: *This dough stirs hard.*
—*n.* **1** movement; action: *There was a stir in the bushes where the boys were hiding.* **SYN:** motion, activity. **2** a state of motion, activity, briskness, or bustle. **3** excitement: *The coming of the queen caused a great stir.* **4** emotion; impulse; feeling. **5** the act of stirring: *She gave the mixture a hard stir.* **6** a jog; thrust; poke. **7** *Archaic.* a public disturbance, tumult, or revolt.
**stir oneself,** to move briskly; bestir: *The French ambassador ... stirred himself not only to keep this project alive, but to bring it to a practical conclusion* (John H. Burton).
**stir up, a** to set going; incite; stimulate: *He stirs up the other children to mischief.* **b** to excite; provoke; induce: *to stir up a mutiny.*
[Old English *styrian*] —**stir′rer,** *n.*
—*Syn. n.* **2, 3 Stir, bustle, ado** mean excitement or excited activity. **Stir** suggests disturbance or excitement where there has been quiet: *There was a stir in the courtroom.* **Bustle** suggests a great deal of noisy, excited, energetic activity: *All week before the class picnic, studying gave way to the bustle of preparations.* **Ado** suggests much busyness and fuss over something not worth it: *They made much ado about a comfortable bed for the kitten.*

**stir**[2] (stėr), *n. Slang.* prison: *He's just out of stir.* [origin uncertain]

**stir|a|bout** (stėr′ə bout′), *n. British.* a porridge made with corn meal or oatmeal.

**stir-cra|zy** (stėr′krā′zē), *adj. U.S. Slang.* mentally disturbed because of long confinement or subjection to dull, restrictive routine: *They go through little rituals, crouching in a corner and rubbing a hand ceremoniously or sitting motionless for hours in apparent catatonia—"just stir-crazy," as one staff man phrased it* (Scientific American).

**stir-fry** (stėr′frī′), *v.t., v.i.,* **-fried, -fry|ing.** to stir very fast while frying in a little oil or fat: *Stir-frying is the technique most often used in Chinese food preparation* (Jean Hewitt).

**stirk** (stėrk), *n.* a bullock or heifer between one and two years old. [Old English *stirc*]

**stir|less** (stėr′lis), *adj.* without stir or movement; not stirring; motionless.

**Stir|ling cycle** (stėr′ling), *Thermodynamics.* a modified form of the Carnot cycle in which all the heat is added and rejected at the highest and lowest temperatures reached. [< Robert *Stirling,* a Scottish engineer of the 1800's, who first proposed it]

**Stirling engine,** an external-combustion heat engine using the Stirling cycle: *The Stirling engine burns its fuel in a continuous low pressure combustion system outside the cylinders* (Science Journal).

**Stir|ling's formula** (stėr′lingz), *Mathematics.* a formula for approximating the value of higher factorials, using transcendental numbers pi and *e.* [< James *Stirling,* 1692-1770, a Scottish mathematician]

**stirp** (stėrp), *n.* **1** a stock or family. **2** lineage: *Some maid Of royal stirp* (James Russell Lowell). [< Latin *stirps, stirpis* stem, stock]

**stirps** (stėrps), *n., pl.* **stir|pes** (stėr′pēz). **1** stock; family. **2** *Law.* the person from whom a family is descended. **3** *Biology.* the organic units present in a newly fertilized ovum.

**stir|ring** (stėr′ing), *adj.* **1** moving, active, or lively: *stirring times.* **SYN:** bustling, brisk. **2** rousing; exciting: *a stirring appeal.* **SYN:** stimulating, inspiring. —**stir′ring|ly,** *adv.*

**stir|rup** (stėr′əp, stir′-), *n.* **1** a support for a rider's foot, that hangs from the side of a saddle. A stirrup is usually a loop of metal or wood with the bottom part flattened and often broadened. *The rider stood up in his stirrups to get a better view.* **2** something shaped like a stirrup, especially a U-shaped clamp or support. **3** *Nautical.* one of the short ropes hanging from a yard, with an eye at the lower end through which a footrope is passed and thus supported. **4** = stapes. [Old English *stigrāp,* ultimately < *stige* a climbing, ascent < *rāp* rope] —**stir′rup|like′,** *adj.*

**stirrup bone,** the innermost of the three bones in the middle ear, resembling a stirrup; stapes.

**stirrup cup, 1** a cup of wine or other liquor handed to a rider when already on horseback setting out for a journey, or to mounted huntsmen at the beginning of a fox hunt. **2** a drink, especially an alcoholic drink, taken or offered just before leaving or at parting.

**stirrup leather** or **strap,** the leather strap by which a stirrup hangs from the saddle.

**stirrup pump,** a hand pump held by the foot in a stirruplike bracket, used to put out fires with water pulled from a bucket, tank, or pond.

**stir-up** (stėr′up′), *n.* the action of stirring up or condition of being stirred up; agitation; commotion: *How it gives the heart and soul a stir-up* (Robert Browning).

**stitch**[1] (stich), *n., v.* —*n.* **1** one complete movement of a threaded needle through cloth in sewing or embroidery, or through skin, or flesh, in surgery: *Take long stitches when you baste your skirt hem.* **2** one complete movement of the needle or other implement, as in knitting, crocheting, tatting, or lacemaking. **3** a particular method of taking stitches, or the kind of work thus produced: *blanket stitch, buttonhole stitch.* **4** a loop or portion, as of thread or yarn, made by a stitch: *Rip out these long stitches. The doctor will take the stitches out of the wound tomorrow.* **5** a piece of cloth or clothing: *He hadn't a dry stitch on.* **6** *Informal, Figurative.* a small bit: *The lazy girl wouldn't do a stitch of work.* **7** a sudden, sharp, stabbing pain, especially a spasmodic one in the intercostal muscles: *After running all the way home, he had a stitch in his side. Laugh yourself into stitches* (Shakespeare).
—*v.t.* **1** to make stitches in; fasten or ornament with stitches: *She stitched a pocket on the new apron. The doctor stitched the cut to close it.* **2** to fasten (cartons or the like) by stapling.
—*v.i.* to work with a needle and thread; make stitches; sew.
**in stitches,** laughing uncontrollably: *With this Latin outburst* [*he*] *had Oxford masters and deans in stitches today* (New York Times).
[Old English *stice* a puncture. See related etym. at **stick**[1].] —**stitch′er,** *n.* —**stitch′like′,** *adj.*

**stitch**[2] (stich), *n. Dialect.* a linear or temporal span, viewed as a fragment or part of a whole.
**a good stitch,** a considerable distance or period: *You have gone a good stitch; you may well be weary; sit down* (John Bunyan).
[Old English *stycce* fragment, piece]

**stitch|er|y** (stich′ər ē), *n.* the process or the product of stitching or sewing; needlework: *yards of fine stitchery.*

**stitch|ing** (stich′ing), *n.* **1** the act or work of a person who stitches: *She continued her stitching.* **2** stitches collectively.

**stitch|work** (stich′wėrk), *n.* stitchery; needlework.

**stitch|wort** (stich′wėrt′), *n.* any one of certain plants of the pink family, especially a white-flowered species supposed to cure a stitch in the side. Also, **stichwort.** [< *stitch*[1] a sharp pain + *wort* plant (because of its reputed medicinal value)]

**stith|y** (stiᴛʜ′ē, stith′-), *n., pl.* **stith|ies,** *v.,* **stith|ied, stith|y|ing.** —*n.* **1** = anvil. **2** a forge; smithy. —*v.t. Obsolete.* to forge.
[Middle English *stithi* < Scandinavian (compare Old Icelandic *stethi*)]

**sti|ver** (stī′vər), *n.* **1** a Dutch coin or unit of money. **2** *Figurative.* anything having small value.
**not a stiver,** not at all; nothing: *They did not care a stiver if my head was blown off* (Blackwood's Magazine).
[< Duch *stuiver,* or Middle Flemish *stuver*]

**St.-John's-bread** (sānt jonz′bred′), *n.* the edible bean of the carob. [< the account of *Saint John* the Baptist's diet while in the wilderness. See Matthew 3:4, where "locusts" refers to the *locust bean* or *carob.*]

**St. John's Day,** June 24, Midsummer Day, named for Saint John the Baptist.

**St. John's Eve,** the night before St. John's Day, long celebrated with bonfires and other festivities in various countries of Europe, apparently in continuation of an ancient heathen festival of the summer solstice.

**St. John's evil,** = epilepsy.

**St.-John's-wort** (sānt jonz′wėrt′), *n.* any one of a large genus of herbs or shrubs that have clusters of showy, mostly yellow flowers and translucent dots in the leaves; hypericum.

**stk.,** stock.

**S.T.L.,** Licentiate of Sacred Theology (Latin, *Sacrae Theologiae Licenciatus*).

**St. Law|rence skiff** (lôr′əns, lor′-), a type of small, light boat with a single sail and a centerboard. [< *St. Lawrence* River]

**St. Lou|is encephalitis** (lü′is), a form of viral encephalitis that first occurred epidemically around St. Louis, Missouri, and is now endemic in America.

**St. Luke's Day** (lüks), the feast day of St. Luke, October 18.

**St. Luke's summer,** a period of mild weather occurring about St. Luke's Day.

**S.T.M.,** Master of Sacred Theology (Latin, *Sacrae Theologiae Magister*).

**St. Mar|tin's Day** (mär′tənz), = Martinmas.

**St. Martin's summer,** a period of mild weather occurring about St. Martin's Day.

**St. Nich|o|las's clerk** (nik′ə lə siz), *Obsolete.* a highwayman; thief.

***stoa**

***sto|a** (stō′ə), *n., pl.* **sto|ae** (stō′ē), **sto|as.** a portico or roofed colonnade, usually detached and of considerable length, often walled on one side and open on the other, used as a promenade or meeting place in ancient Greece. [< Greek *stoā̂*]

**Pronunciation Key:** hat, āge, cãre, fär; let, ēqual, tėrm; it, īce; hot, ōpen, ôrder; oil, out; cup, pu̇t, rüle; child; long; thin; ᴛʜen; zh, measure; ə represents a in about, e in taken, i in pencil, o in lemon, u in circus.

**Sto·a** (stō′ə), *n.* **the,** a public walk at Athens, where the Stoic philosopher Zeno taught; the Porch. He founded the philosophy of Stoicism. [< Greek *stoâ*]

**stoat** (stōt), *n.* **1** an ermine in its summer coat of brown. **2** any weasel. [Middle English *stote;* origin uncertain]

**stob** (stob), *n. Dialect.* **1** a stake or post. **2** a gibbet. [variant of *stub*]

**stoc·ca·do** (sto kä′dō, -kā′-), *n., pl.* **-dos** or **-does.** *Archaic.* a thrust or stab with a sword or the like. [< Italian *stoccata*]

**sto·chas·tic** (stō kas′tik), *adj.* having to do with a random variable or variables; involving chance or probability: *Stochastic processes arise in physics, astronomy, economics, genetics, ecology, and many other fields of science. The simplest and most celebrated example of a stochastic process is the Brownian motion of a particle* (Scientific American). — **sto·chas′ti·cal·ly,** *adv.* [< Greek *stochastikós* conjectural, ultimately < *stóchos* aim, guess]

***stock** (stok), *n., adj., v.* — *n.* **1a** things for use or for sale; supply used as it is needed: *a stock of words, a stock of canned goods. This store keeps a large stock of toys.* **SYN:** fund, store, goods, merchandise, wares. **b** the undistributed remainder of a pack of cards, set of dominoes, or other pieces, after the players have taken their allotted number, placed on the table to be drawn from according to the rules. **2** cattle or other farm or ranch animals; livestock: *The farm was sold with all its stock.* **3a** the capital of a company or corporation, divided into portions or shares of uniform amount which are represented by transferable certificates. The holder of one of these is considered a part owner, rather than a creditor, of the company. **b** the shares or portions of one such company or corporation. The profits of a company are divided among the owners of stock. *Father owns some stock in that railroad.* **4** a debt owed, especially by a nation, city, or other government, to individuals who receive a fixed rate of interest. **5** *Figurative.* the estimation in which a person or thing is held: *to set great stock by a remedy.* **6** *Figurative.* **a** the descendants of a common ancestor or ethnic group; family or race; lineage: *She is of New England stock. The people who built this house were of Dutch stock with whom thrift was second nature* (Wall Street Journal). **b** an original ancestor of a family, tribe, or race: *Their stock was King Alfred.* **7** *Figurative.* a race or other group of closely related animals or plants in a breed or species. **8** *Figurative.* an ancestral type from which various races, species, or kinds have diverged. **9** *Figurative.* a group of related languages. **10** the main upright part of anything; vertical beam. **11** a part used as a support or handle; part in which other parts are inserted or to which they are attached, especially: **a** the wooden or metal piece to which the barrel and firing mechanism of a rifle or other firearm are attached: *the wooden stock of a rifle.* **b** a similar part on certain automatic weapons. **c** the trail on the carriage of a field gun. **d** the handle of a whip, fishing rod, or the like. **e** an adjustable wrench for holding screw-cutting dies. **f** the basic part of a plow, to which all the other parts are fastened. **12a** a carpenter's boring tool; brace. **b** the body of a carpenter's plane, consisting of the frame or block which holds the blade. **13** the part of an anchor across the top of the shank. **14** the raw material from which anything is made: *soap stock. Rags are used as a stock for making paper.* **15** water in which meat, fish, or vegetables have been cooked, used as a base for soups, sauces, and gravies. **16a** the various plays produced by a stock company. **b** a stock company, or such companies and their activities as a category or type of theatrical production (used without article): *She is playing in summer stock.* **17** the lower part of a tree trunk left standing; stump. **18a** the main stem of a plant or tree, as distinguished from the root and branches. **b** an underground stem like a root; rhizome. **19a** a stem, tree, or plant that furnishes slips or cuttings for grafting. **b** a stem in which a graft is inserted and which is its support. See picture under **graft**[1]. **20a** a block of wood; log. **b** something lifeless, motionless, or void of sensation: *"You stocks and stones!"* **c** a person who is senseless and lifeless like a block or log; stupid person. **21** an old-fashioned stiff neckcloth, used in place of the modern collar and tie: *Around his throat he had negligently fastened a stock of black silk* (James Fenimore Cooper). **22a** any one of a genus of garden plants of the mustard family, that have large flowers of various colors, such as the gillyflower. **b** cabbage or colewort. **23** *Zoology.* a compound organism consisting of a colony of zooids. **24** *Archaic.* **a** the part of a tally that a creditor received as evidence of a debt. **b** the money represented by this tally. **25** *Obsolete or Dialect.* a stocking.

— *adj.* **1** kept on hand regularly: *stock sizes of dresses.* **2** having as one's employment the care or handling of stock: *a stock clerk.* **3** *Figurative.* in common use; commonplace; everyday: *The weather is a stock subject of conversation. He merely got the stock answer that the matter was under consideration* (Time). **4** of, having to do with, or devoted to the raising of livestock: *a stock farm.* **5** of or having to do with stock or stocks: *a stock certificate.* **6a** having to do with, presenting, or acting in a stock company or repertory company: *a stock play, a stock actor.* **b** appearing or recurring in various productions because of convention, custom, or unfailing appeal: *a stock character in pantomime, a stock situation in melodrama.*

— *v.t.* **1** to lay in a supply of; supply: *Our camp is well stocked with food for a short stay.* **SYN:** furnish, store. **2** to keep regularly for use or sale: *A toy store stocks toys.* **3** to furnish with horses, cattle, or other livestock: *to stock a farm.* **4** to furnish with wildlife: *to stock a lake with fish.* **5** to fasten to or fit with a stock: *to stock a plow, bell, anchor, or rifle.* **6** to sow (land) with grass, clover, or the like. **7** *Obsolete.* to put in the stocks, as an offender.

— *v.i.* **1** to lay in a stock or supply: *a store that stocks up yearly, to stock up for the winter.* **2** (of corn, grass, or some other plants) to send out shoots.

**in stock,** ready for use or sale; on hand: *I intend to dispose of the whole of goods in stock* (W. J. Greenwood).

**on the stocks, a** being built: *In addition to the Britannia, at least one other long-range turboprop airliner was on the stocks* (Edwin C. Shepherd). **b** being planned; in preparation: *I have had a long letter on the stocks for you for the last fortnight* (Cardinal Newman).

**out of stock,** no longer on hand; lacking: *The supplies he needs are out of stock, but they should be arriving soon.*

**take stock, a** to find out how much stock one has on hand: *The business of the servant of the company was ... to take stock* (Macaulay). **b** *Figurative.* to make an estimate or examination: *The end of fifty years is a convenient moment to take stock* (London Times).

**take stock in, a** *Informal.* to take an interest in; consider important; trust: *He took little stock in the story.* **b** to take shares in (a company): *He made money by taking stock in two new airlines.*

**take stock of, a** to reckon up; evaluate: *to take stock of one's holdings.* **b** *Informal.* to look at with suspicion or interest: *to take stock of a stranger.*

**the stocks, a** a heavy wooden frame with holes to put a person's feet and sometimes his hands through, formerly used as a punishment. **b** the framework on which a ship or boat is supported while being built: *One of the galleys* [*is*] *planked and completely rigged on the stocks* (New York Mercury). **c** a frame in which an animal, such as a horse, is confined for shoeing: *The frisky horse was put into the stocks when the blacksmith arrived.*

[Old English *stocc* stump, post]

**the stocks** definition a

***stock**

**stock account,** an account in a ledger showing on one side the amount of the original stock with accumulations, and on the other the amount used up.

**stock·ade** (sto kād′), *n., v.,* **-ad·ed, -ad·ing.** — *n.* **1** a defensive wall or fence of large, strong posts fixed upright in the ground: *A heavy stockade around the cabins protected the pioneers from attack.* **2a** a pen or other place of confinement for human beings or animals, now especially one enclosed by a wire fence. **b** *U.S.* a place of confinement on a military post for soldiers awaiting court-martial or sentenced to relatively short terms of incarceration.

— *v.t.* to protect, fortify, or surround with a stockade. [< French *estocade,* alteration of *estacade,* ultimately < Provençal *estaca* stake < Germanic (compare Dutch *staake*)]

**stock·age** (stok′ij), *n.* **1** the act of stocking up. **2** stock; store: *stockages of supplies.*

**stock·a·teer** (stok′ə tir′), *n. Slang.* a person dealing in fraudulent stocks. [< *stock* + (racke)*teer*]

**stock·book** (stok′bu̇k′), *n. Australian.* a book in which a rancher keeps records of his cattle.

**stock·boy** (stok′boi′), *n.* a boy who unpacks and puts merchandise in its place in a store.

**stock breeder,** a person who raises or breeds livestock; stock farmer; stock raiser.

**stock breeding,** the breeding of livestock; stock farming; stock raising.

**stock·bro·ker** (stok′brō′kər), *n.* a person who buys and sells stocks and bonds for others for a commission.

**stock·bro·ker·age** (stok′brō′kər ij), *n.* the business of a stockbroker.

**stock·bro·king** (stok′brō′king), *n.* = stockbrokerage.

**stock car, 1** a standard passenger car modified for racing: *A stock car racer can be almost anything from a Cadillac convertible to a jig-saw puzzle on wheels* (Newsweek). **2** (originally) a car kept in stock; any standard automobile. **3** a railroad freight car for livestock.

**stock certificate,** a transferable certificate evidencing ownership of one or more shares of a corporation's capital stock.

**stock company, 1** a theatrical company employed more or less permanently under the same management, usually at one theater but sometimes on tour, to perform many different plays. **2** a company whose capital is divided into shares; joint-stock company or corporation.

**stock dividend, 1** a dividend payable in additional shares of the company. **2** any dividend payable in cash to a stockholder.

**stock dove,** a wild pigeon of Europe.

**stock·er** (stok′ər), *n.* **1** a person who makes or fits gunstocks. **2** *U.S. and Canada.* a young steer or heifer, bought for butchering but kept until fattened or mature.

**stock exchange, 1** a place or building where stocks and bonds are bought and sold on an organized basis. **2** an association of brokers and dealers in stocks and bonds. A stock exchange operates in the manner of an auction at a particular place or market according to fixed regulations.

**stock farm,** a farm where livestock is bred and raised for profit. — **stock farmer.** — **stock farming.**

**stock·fish** (stok′fish′), *n., pl.* **-fish·es** or (*collectively*) **-fish.** fish, such as cod, haddock, or hake, preserved by splitting and drying in the air without salt.

**stock·hold·er** (stok′hōl′dər), *n.* a person who owns stock; holder of a share or shares in a company; shareholder.

**stock·hold·ing** (stok′hōl′ding), *adj., n.* — *adj.* that owns stock.

— *n.* the owning of a share or shares in a company.

**stock·horse** (stok′hôrs′), *n. Australian.* a horse used in herding cattle.

**stock·i·net** or **stock·i·nette** (stok′ə net′), *n.* an elastic, machine-knitted fabric used especially for making underwear. [apparently short for earlier *stocking-net*]

**stockinette stitch,** a stitch used in knitting, where one row is knit and the next row is purled.

**stock·ing** (stok′ing), *n.* **1** a close-fitting, usually knitted covering of wool, cotton, nylon, silk, or other fabric, for the foot and leg. **2** anything suggesting a stocking, such as a patch of color on an animal's leg: *a chestnut horse with four white stockings.* [< *stock* stocking] — **stock′ing·less,** *adj.*

**stocking cap,** a close-fitting, knitted cap somewhat resembling a long, tapering stocking, with a long, pointed end that falls over the back or shoulder, worn for skiing, sledding, or skating or by children in the winter.

**stocking doll,** a doll made of stockings stuffed with cotton, rags, newspaper, or the like.

**stock·inged** (stok′ingd), *adj.* wearing stockings: *stockinged legs.*

**stocking feet,** the feet covered only with stockings: *he ... being at least six feet three inches in his stocking feet* (Weir Mitchell).

**stocking mask,** a nylon stocking pulled over the head or wrapped around the face to conceal identity: *Three men in stocking masks raided Martins Bank in South Audley Street* (London Times).

**stock-in-trade** (stok′in trād′), *n.,* or **stock in trade, 1** the stock of a dealer or company: *Half its stock-in-trade is glossy paperbacks* (Punch). **2** a workman's tools or materials. **3** *Figurative.* resources or skills: *She could and did stage emotional outbursts at will and ... it was part of her stock-in-trade to do so* (London Times).

**stock·ish** (stok′ish), *adj.* stupid; dull. — **stock′ish·ly,** *adv.* — **stock′ish·ness,** *n.*

**stock|ist** (stok′ist), *n. British.* a person who keeps a stock of certain goods for sale at retail; merchant; dealer.

**stock|job|ber** (stok′job′ər), *n.* **1** *U.S.* a stockbroker. **2** *British.* a member of the stock exchange who deals with other members, as in wholesale amounts, but does not deal with the public.

**stock|job|ber|y** (stok′job′ər ē), *n.* the business or practice of a stockjobber.

**stock|job|bing** (stok′job′ing), *n., adj.* —***n.*** = stockjobbery.
—***adj.*** that deals in stocks and shares; concerned with stockjobbery.

**stock|keep|er** (stok′kē′pər), *n.* **1** a person in charge of the stock of a warehouse. **2** a person who raises or looks after livestock.

**stock|less** (stok′lis), *adj.* without a stock: *a stockless gun, a stockless anchor.*

**stock list**, a list published daily or periodically in connection with a stock exchange, enumerating stocks dealt in, current prices, actual transactions, and the like.

**stock|mak|er** (stok′mā′kər), *n.* a person who makes gunstocks.

**stock|man** (stok′mən), *n., pl.* **-men.** **1a** a man who raises livestock, especially cattle or sheep. **b** a man employed to look after livestock, especially cattle or sheep. **2** a man in charge of a stock of materials or goods.

**stock|man|ship** (stok′mən ship), *n.* the work or skill of breeding and raising livestock.

**stock market**, **1** a place where stocks and bonds are bought and sold; stock exchange: *the New York stock market.* **SYN:** bourse. **2** the buying and selling in such a place. **3** the trend of prices of stocks and bonds.

**stock option**, an option giving a person, especially an employee or executive, the right to purchase stock from a corporation at a given price and within a given time.

**stock|pile** (stok′pīl′), *n., v.,* **-piled, -pil|ing.** —***n.*** **1** a supply of raw materials or essential items, built up and held in reserve for use during time of emergency or shortage: *the national stockpiles of strategic materials and farm commodities* (Arthur Krock). **2** such a reserve of weapons for warfare, especially atomic weapons. **3** *Figurative.* a supply or reserve of anything: *The Soviets ... drew upon their vast stockpile of superb performers and came up with four men* (Herman Weiskopf).
—***v.t., v.i.*** to collect or bring together as a stockpile: *Food and drinking water were stockpiled, but the supplies ran out* (Abigail L. Kuflik).
—**stock′pil′er,** *n.*

**stock|pot** (stok′pot′), *n.* **1** a large pot in which meat, bones, and vegetables are simmered with water to make stock for soup, sauces, or gravies. **2** any vessel in which a mixture of things is prepared for use by long, slow cooking.

**stock|proof** (stok′prüf′), *adj.* that will not let livestock through: *a stockproof fence.*

**stock raiser**, a person who raises livestock.

**stock raising**, the business of raising livestock.

**stock-rid|er** (stok′rī′dər), *n.* (in Australia) a mounted stockman.

**stock|room** (stok′rüm′, -rům′), *n.,* or **stock room**, **1** a room where stock is kept, especially one in which reserve stock is kept. **2** a room, especially in a hotel, where salesmen can show their samples and receive orders from retailers and wholesalers.

**stocks** (stoks), *n.pl.* See under **stock**.

**stock saddle**, = Western saddle.

**stock-share** (stok′shãr′), *adj.* of or having to do with a form of agriculture in which the owner and tenant each get an agreed-on share of the livestock sold.

**stock split**, the division of the shares of stock of a corporation into a larger number of shares, in which the value of the total shares remains the same but each individual share is less. A 3-for-1 stock split of 100 shares worth $12.00 each, would give the stockholder 300 shares worth $4.00 each.

**stock-still** (stok′stil′), *adj.* as still as a post or log; motionless. **SYN:** stationary, immobile.

**stock|tak|ing** (stok′tā′king), *n.* **1** a periodical examination and inventorying of the stock of goods in a shop, warehouse, or the like. **2** *Figurative.* an accounting or reckoning up of resources, weaknesses, achievements, and failures; appraisal; evaluation: *a spiritual stocktaking.*

***stock ticker**, a telegraphic instrument that prints stock quotations and other market news automatically; ticker.

**stock|whip** (stok′hwip′), *n. British.* a herder's whip, having a short handle and long thong.

**stock|y** (stok′ē), *adj.,* **stock|i|er, stock|i|est.** having a solid or sturdy form or build; thick for its height: *a stocky building. He is a stocky, round-faced man.* —**stock′i|ly,** *adv.* —**stock′i|ness,** *n.*

**stock|yard** (stok′yärd′), *n.* a place with pens and sheds for cattle, sheep, hogs, or horses. A stockyard is often connected with a slaughterhouse, railroad, or market. [American English]

**stodge** (stoj), *v.,* **stodged, stodg|ing,** *n.* —***v.t., v.i.*** to gorge; stuff; cram: *He grabs the Leader and leaves me to stodge myself with his Times* (George Bernard Shaw).
—***n.*** **1** a thick, heavy, usually starchy food. **2** *Figurative.* dull, stodgy subjects, articles, or composition: *This symposium devoted to the arts ... was never planned as a solemn magazine of esoteric stodge* (Punch).

**stodg|er** (stoj′ər), *n. Informal.* a person who is lacking in spirit and liveliness; stodgy person.

**stodg|y** (stoj′ē), *adj.,* **stodg|i|er, stodg|i|est.** **1** dull or uninteresting; tediously commonplace: *a stodgy book, a stodgy mind or character.* **2** thick and heavy in consistency; very filling: *stodgy food.* **3** heavily built: *a stodgy person.* **4** stuffed full: *a stodgy bag.* [< *stodge* to stuff + *-y*[1]]
—**stodg′i|ly,** *adv.* —**stodg′i|ness,** *n.*

**stoe|chi|ol|o|gy** (stē′kē ol′ə jē), *n.* = stoichiology.

**stoep** (stüp), *n.* (in South Africa) a raised porch around the front and often the sides of a house: *Tante Let was still sitting on the stoep when Gijs returned from the veld* (L. H. Brinkman). [< Afrikaans *stoep* < Dutch, doorstep]

**sto|gie** or **sto|gy** (stō′gē), *n., pl.* **-gies.** **1** a long, slender, cheap cigar, usually rather strong in flavor: *Mr. Born listened politely, tilting his stogie this way and that* (New Yorker). **2** a rough, heavy kind of boot or shoe. [American English, earlier *stoga,* short for *Conestoga,* Pennsylvania (reputedly because drivers of Conestoga wagons favored them)]

**Sto|ic** (stō′ik), *n., adj.* —***n.*** a member of the ancient school of philosophy founded at Athens by Zeno (335?-265? B.C.). This school taught that virtue is the highest good and that men should be free from passion and unmoved by life's happenings.
—***adj.*** having to do with or belonging to the school of the Stoics or its system of philosophy.
[< Latin *stōicus* < Greek *stōïkós* pertaining to a *stoâ* portico (especially the one in Athens where Zeno taught)]

**sto|ic** (stō′ik), *n., adj.* —***n.*** a person who remains calm, represses his feelings, and is indifferent to pleasure and pain: *A stoic of the woods—a man without a tear* (Thomas Campbell). *The sternest seeming stoic is human after all* (Charlotte Brontë).
—***adj.*** = stoical.
[< *Stoic*]

**Sto|i|cal** (stō′ə kəl), *adj.* = Stoic.

**sto|i|cal** (stō′ə kəl), *adj.* **1** like a stoic; indifferent to pleasure and pain; self-controlled: *a stoical person.* **2** of or like that of a stoic: *stoical courage.* —**sto′i|cal|ly,** *adv.* —**sto′i|cal|ness,** *n.*

**stoi|chei|ol|o|gy** (stoi′kī ol′ə jē), *n.* = stoichiology.

**stoi|chi|ol|o|gy** (stoi′kē ol′ə jē), *n.* the study of the elements comprising animal tissues. Also, **stoechiology, stoicheiology.** [< German *Stöchiologie* < Greek *stoicheîon* element (< *steichein* to step, walk) + German *-logie* -logy]

**stoi|chi|o|met|ric** (stoi′kē ə met′rik), *adj.* having to do with stoichiometry. —**stoi′chi|o|met′ri|cal|ly,** *adv.*

**stoi|chi|om|e|try** (stoi′kē om′ə trē), *n.* **1** the process or art of calculating the equivalent and atomic weights of the elements participating in any chemical reaction. **2** the branch of science that deals with the relationships between the elements making up substances and the properties of the substances. [< German *Stöchiometrie* < Greek *stoicheîon* element (< *steichein* to step, walk) + German *-metrie* -metry]

**Sto|i|cism** (stō′ə siz əm), *n.* the philosophy of the Stoics.

**sto|i|cism** (stō′ə siz əm), *n.* patient endurance; indifference to pleasure and pain: *William so far forgot his wonted stoicism as to utter a passionate exclamation at the way in which the English regiments had been sacrificed* (Macaulay).

***stock ticker**

**stoit** (stoit), *v., n. Scottish.* —***v.i.*** to move unsteadily; stumble or lurch.
—***n.*** a lurch; stumble. [perhaps < Dutch *stuiten* rebound, bounce]

**stoke**[1] (stōk), *v.,* **stoked, stok|ing.** —***v.t.*** **1** to stir up and feed (a fire). **2** to tend the fire in (a furnace) or under (a boiler).
—***v.i.*** to tend a fire; stoke or stoke up anything.
**stoke up, a** to get or supply with fuel: *Stoke up the furnace. The ship is stoking up.* **b** *Figurative.* to stir up: *Neither the British nor the German soldier has been able to stoke up that virulent hate* (Blackwood's Magazine). **c** *Figurative.* to gird or be girded; prepare: *Now she is stoking up for a personal-appearance tour to promote her biggest and best part yet* (Time).
[back formation < *stoker*]

**stoke**[2] (stōk), *n.* in the centimeter-gram-second system, a unit for measuring the kinematic viscosity of a fluid (the viscosity of a fluid divided by its density). [< Sir George *Stokes,* 1819-1903, a British mathematician and physicist]

**stoke|hold** (stōk′hōld′), *n.* **1** the place in a steamship where the furnaces and boilers are. It adjoins or includes the engine room and is usually below the water line. **2** = stokehole.

**stoke|hole** (stōk′hōl′), *n.* **1** the hole through which fuel is put into a furnace, especially into a coal-burning furnace. **2** the space in front of a furnace where stokers shovel in coal and take out ashes.

**stok|er** (stō′kər), *n.* **1** a worker who tends the fires of a furnace or boiler. **2** a mechanical device for putting coal in a furnace automatically. [< Dutch *stoker* < *stoken* stoke, feed (a fire)]

**Stokes-Ad|ams disease** (stōks′ad′əmz), a slow, progressive degeneration of the heart muscle, accompanied by fainting and dizzy spells, convulsions, dropsy, slow pulse, and shortness of breath. [< William *Stokes,* 1804-1878, and Robert *Adams,* 1791-1875, Irish physicians]

**Stokes' aster** (stōks), = stokesia.

**sto|ke|si|a** (stō kē′zhē ə, -sē-), *n.* a composite perennial herb of the southern United States, that has large terminal heads of blue, purplish, or white flowers. [< New Latin *Stokesia* the genus name < Jonathan *Stokes,* 1755-1831, an English botanist]

**Stokes' law** (stōks), *Physics.* the law that the frequency of luminescence excited by radiation is usually not higher than the frequency of the exciting radiation. [< Sir George *Stokes,* 1819-1903, a British mathematician and physicist]

**STOL** (stôl), *n.* short take-off and landing (a type of aircraft with a greatly reduced take-off and landing distance): *The STOL plane tends to be slower than a conventional plane and much slower than a jet airliner but it is faster than a helicopter. It is able to use a field much smaller than the strip that a jetliner needs. But it needs more room than a helicopter* (New York Times).

**sto|la** (stō′lə), *n., pl.* **-lae** (-lē). a long, ample robe worn by matrons in ancient Rome. [< Latin *stola;* see etym. under **stole**[2]]

**stole**[1] (stōl), *v.* the past tense of **steal**: *Who stole my money?*

***stole**[2]
definitions 1, 2

definition 1

definition 2

***stole**[2] (stōl), *n.* **1** a narrow strip of silk or other material worn over the shoulders by a clergyman during certain church functions. **2** a woman's scarf or similar garment of fur or cloth, worn usually with the ends hanging down in front: *She wore a cloth coat, preferring it to a mink stole she won in a raffle a year ago* (Newsweek). **3** *Archaic.* a long robe. [Old English *stole* < Latin *stola* < Greek *stolḗ* garment; equipment, related to *stéllein* to place, array]

**stoled** (stōld), *adj.* wearing a stole.

**stole fee**, a fee paid to a Roman Catholic priest

**Pronunciation Key:** hat, āge, cãre, fär; let, ēqual, tėrm; it, īce; hot, ōpen, ôrder; oil, out; cup, pu̇t, rüle; child; long; thin; ᴛʜen; zh, measure; ə represents **a** in about, **e** in taken, **i** in pencil, **o** in lemon, **u** in circus.

for a religious service, such as a marriage, christening, or funeral.

**sto|len** (stō′lən), *v.* the past participle of **steal**: *The money was stolen by a thief.*

**stol|id** (stol′id), *adj.* hard to arouse; not easily excited; showing no emotion; seeming dull: *a stolid person, a stolid face, a stolid refusal. The Prime Minister is immensely popular among the stolid and dour northerners* (New York Times). **SYN**: impassive. [< Latin *stolidus*] — **stol′id|ly**, *adv.* — **stol′id|ness**, *n.*

**sto|lid|i|ty** (stə lid′ə tē), *n., pl.* **-ties**. stolid quality or condition.

**Stol|len** (shtô′lən), *n. German.* a rich, fancy bread, often containing nuts, fruits, and spices.

***sto|lon** (stō′lon), *n.* **1** *Botany.* **a** a slender branch along the ground that takes root at the tip and grows into a new plant. A very slender, naked stolon with a bud at the end is a runner. **b** a rhizome or rootstock of certain grasses, used for propagation. **2** *Zoology.* a rootlike growth in a compound organism. It is a process of the soft tissue joining a bud or zooid to the main part. [< Latin *stolō, -ōnis* a shoot, sucker of a plant]

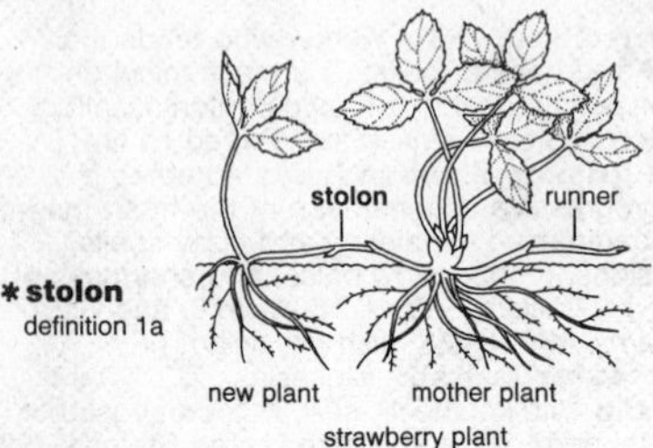


***stolon** definition 1a

**sto|lo|nif|er|ous** (stō′lə nif′ər əs, stol′ə-), *adj.* producing stolons. — **sto′lo|nif′er|ous|ly**, *adv.*

**sto|lo|ni|za|tion** (stō′lə nə zā′shən), *n.* the producing of stolons.

**STOL|port** or **stol|port** (stôl′pôrt′, -pōrt′), *n.* an airport for STOL planes.

**sto|ma** (stō′mə), *n., pl.* **-ma|ta** or **-mas**. **1** an opening or pore in a plant; breathing pore. A leaf contains many stomata which let water and gases in and out of the plant. **2** a mouthlike opening in an animal body, especially a small or simple aperture in a lower animal. [< New Latin *stoma* < Greek *stóma, -atos* mouth]

**stom|ach** (stum′ək), *n., v.* — *n.* **1a** the large muscular bag in the body which first receives the food and digests some of it before passing it on to the intestines. In human beings, it is a saclike dilation of the alimentary canal, occupying the upper part of the left side of the abdomen. See diagram under **digestion**. **b** any portion of the body of an invertebrate capable of digesting food. **2** the part of the body containing the stomach; abdomen; belly: *He poked the other boy in the stomach.* **3** appetite for food. **4** *Figurative.* desire; liking: *I have no stomach for killing harmless creatures.* **5** *Figurative.* disposition: *a bold stomach.* **6** *Obsolete.* **a** spirit; temper; heart. **b** pride; haughtiness: *He was a man of unbounded stomach, ever ranking himself with princes* (Shakespeare). **c** anger; irritation.
— *v.t.* **1** to be able to eat or keep in one's stomach. **2** *Figurative.* to put up with; bear; endure: *He could not stomach such an insult. They could stomach even the fugitive slave law if—and only if—they could be sure that some day no such laws would be necessary* (Bruce Catton).
— *v.i. Obsolete.* to be offended (at): *What one ... doth not stomach at such contradiction?* (Richard Hooker).
**turn one's stomach**, to nauseate; disgust extremely: *This filthy smile ... Quite turns my stomach* (Alexander Pope).
[< Old French *estomac*, learned borrowing from Latin *stomachus* < Greek *stómachos* (originally) the throat < *stóma* mouth]

**stom|ach|a|ble** (stum′ə kə bəl), *adj.* that can be stomached.

**stom|ach|ache** (stum′ək āk′), *n.* a pain in the stomach or abdomen.

**stom|ach|al** (stum′ə kəl), *adj.* **1** having to do with the stomach; gastric. **2** good for the stomach, as a remedy. **3** of the nature of a stomach.

**-stomached**, *combining form.* having a ___ stomach: *Large-stomached = having a large stomach.*

***stom|ach|er** (stum′ə kər; *formerly* stum′ə chər), *n.* an ornamental covering for the stomach and chest, formerly worn by women under the lacing of the bodice.

**stom|ach|ful** (stum′ək fu̇l), *n., pl.* **-fuls**. as much as one can stomach; sufficiency and more besides.

**sto|mach|ic** (stō mak′ik), *adj., n.* — *adj.* **1** of or having to do with the stomach; gastric: *stomachic disturbances.* **2** beneficial to the stomach, digestion, or appetite.
— *n.* a medicine for the stomach. — **sto|mach′i|cal|ly**, *adv.*

**stomach poison**, an insecticide that kills when the insect eats it.

**stomach pump**, a pump or syringe used for emptying the stomach.

**stomach sweetbread**, the pancreas of a young animal, especially a calf, used for food; sweetbread.

**stomach tooth**, a canine milk tooth of the lower jaw (because gastric disturbance frequently accompanies its appearance).

**stomach worm**, a nematode worm that infests the stomach of sheep; wireworm.

**stom|ach|y** (stum′ə kē), *adj. British Dialect.* **1a** high-spirited. **b** irritable. **2** big-bellied; portly.

**sto|ma|ta** (stō′mə tə, stom′ə-), *n.* a plural of **stoma**.

**stom|a|tal** (stom′ə təl, stō′mə-), *adj. Biology.* **1** having to do with or connected with a stoma or stomata; of the nature of a stoma. **2** having stomata; stomatous.

**sto|mate** (stō′māt), *adj., n.* — *adj.* having stomata or a stoma. — *n.* = stoma.

**sto|mat|ic** (stō mat′ik), *adj.* **1a** of or having to do with the mouth. **b** curing diseases of the mouth. **2** *Biology.* stomatal. [< Greek *stóma, -atos* mouth + English *-ic*]

**sto|ma|ti|tis** (stō′mə tī′tis, stom′ə-), *n.* inflammation of the mouth. [< New Latin *stomatitis* < Greek *stóma, -atos* mouth + New Latin *-itis* inflammation, -itis]

**sto|ma|to|log|i|cal** (stō′mə tə loj′ə kəl, stom′ə-), *adj.* having to do with stomatology.

**sto|ma|tol|o|gy** (stō′mə tol′ə jē, stom′ə-), *n.* the branch of medicine dealing with the mouth and the diagnosis and treatment of its diseases.

**stom|a|to|pod** (stom′ə tə pod, stō′mə-), *adj., n.* — *adj.* of or belonging to an order of marine crustaceans having the gills on abdominal appendages.
— *n.* a stomatopod crustacean, such as the squilla.
[< New Latin *Stomatopoda* the order name < Greek *stóma, -atos* mouth + *poús, podós* foot]

**stom|a|tous** (stom′ə təs, stō′mə-), *adj.* having or furnished with stomata; stomatal.

**-stome**, *combining form.* mouth; mouthlike part; opening: *Pneumostome = an opening for the passage of air.* [< Greek *stóma* mouth]

**sto|mi|a|toid** (stō′mē ə toid), *adj., n.* — *adj.* of or belonging to a group of deep-sea fishes having a large, deep mouth and a long, narrow body with delicate scales, found in Atlantic waters.
— *n.* a stomiatoid fish.
[< New Latin *Stomiatidae* the family name (ultimately < Greek *stóma, -atos* mouth) + English *-oid*]

**sto|mo|dae|al** (stō′mə dē′əl, stom′ə-), *adj.* = stomodeal.

**sto|mo|dae|um** (stō′mə dē′əm, stom′ə-), *n., pl.* **-dae|a** (-dē′ə). = stomodeum.

**sto|mo|de|al** (stō′mə dē′əl, stom′ə-), *adj.* having to do with or having the character of a stomodeum.

**sto|mo|de|um** (stō′mə dē′əm, stom′ə-), *n., pl.* **-de|a** (-dē′ə). the anterior or oral portion of the alimentary canal of the embryo, beginning as an invagination of the ectoderm. [< New Latin *stomodeum* < Greek *stóma, -atos* mouth + *hodaîos* (something) on the way (to) < *hodós* way, road]

**stomp** (stomp), *v., n.* — *v.t.*, *v.i.* to stamp with the foot: *In Luxembourg we first met the custom of hearing the audience stomp their feet in addition to applauding for numbers they really liked* (Musical America).
— *n.* **1** the act of stomping. **2** *U.S.* a form of jazz music and accompanying dance especially popular before and during the 1930's, marked by a spirited rhythm and the stamping of feet.
[variant of *stamp*] — **stomp′er**, *n.*

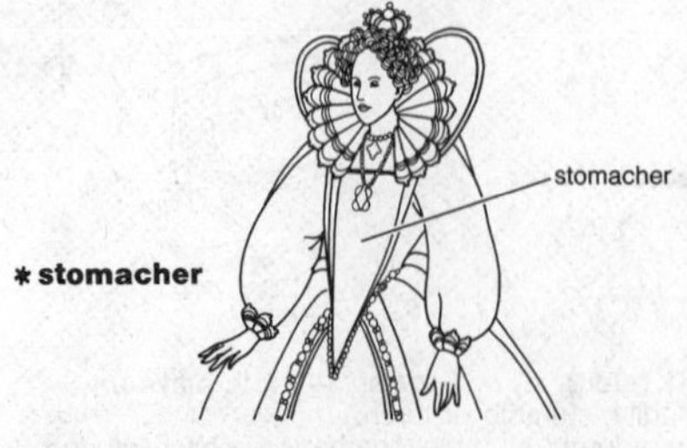


***stomacher**

**stomp|down** (stomp′doun′), *n. U.S. Dialect.* a square dance or a party with square dancing.

**stone** (stōn), *n., pl.* **stones** (*but for def. 11* **stone**), *adj., v.,* **stoned, ston|ing.** — *n.* **1** the hard, compact mineral material of which rocks are made up; hard matter that is not metal. Stone, such as granite and marble, is much used in building. **2** a particular kind of rock or hard mineral matter. **3** a piece of rock, especially one of a small or moderate size: *The boys threw stones into the pond.* **SYN**: pebble. **4a** a piece of rock of definite size or shape, used for a particular purpose, such as building or paving: *foundation stones.* **b** a block, slab, or pillar set up as a monument, boundary mark, or the like: *His grave is marked by a fine stone.* **c** a shaped piece of rock for grinding or sharpening something; grindstone, millstone, or whetstone. **5** a precious stone; gem; jewel: *The queen's diamonds were very fine stones.* **6** a small, hard, rounded object resembling a stone or pebble, such as a hailstone. **7** any impure material, such as sand particles, embedded in glass. **8** the hard covering of a seed, especially that of a soft, pulpy fruit: *peach stones, plum stones.* **9** *Medicine.* **a** something hard and rounded like a stone, that sometimes forms in the kidney, urinary bladder, or gall bladder, causing sickness and pain; calculus. **b** a disease characterized by the presence of such a formation. **10** a British measure of weight, equal to 14 pounds or 6.35 kilograms for man and large animals, and of varying weight for various commodities: *He has the best part of a stone in weight to lose before he reaches his fastest and his best* (London Times). **11** *Printing.* a flat table with a top of stone or (now usually) metal on which type is imposed; imposing stone or table. **12** the block of fine-grained limestone used in lithography, especially the smooth printing surface of it. **13** one of the pieces used in playing certain games, such as backgammon or dominoes.
— *adj.* **1** made or built of stone; consisting of stone: *a stone wall, a stone house.* **2** having to do with stone: *a stone quarry.* **3** *Figurative.* resembling stone: *The stone strength of the past* (Robinson Jeffers). **4** made of coarse, hard pottery.
— *v.t.* **1** to put stones on; pave, build, line, or support with stone. **2a** to throw stones at; drive by throwing stones: *The cruel boys stoned the dog. They stoned her out of Thrums* (James Barrie). **b** to kill by throwing stones: *The martyr was stoned by the heathens.* **3** to rub or polish with a stone; sharpen on a stone. **4** to take the stones or seeds out of: *to stone cherries or plums for canning.*
**cast the first stone**, to be the first to criticize, attack, or condemn (in allusion to John 8:7): *Let the juror who is without sin cast the first stone against the accused in this trial.*
**leave no stone unturned**, to do everything that can be done to bring about a desired result: *We'll leave no stone unturned to develop workable disarmament* (Wall Street Journal).
**throw** (or **cast**) **stones** (**at**), to make an attack (on); bring an accusation (against): *In view of the British record so far, no one in this country is in any position to throw stones at the attitudes of American voters to racial discrimination and civil rights* (Manchester Guardian Weekly).
[Old English *stān*] — **stone′like′**, *adj.*

**Stone Age**, the earliest known period of human culture, in which people used tools and weapons made from stone. It was followed by the Bronze Age. The Stone Age is divided into the paleolithic, mesolithic, and neolithic periods.

**stone-blind** (stōn′blīnd′), *adj.* totally blind. — **stone′-blind′ness**, *n.*

**stone|boat** (stōn′bōt′), *n. U.S. and Canada.* **1** a flat-bottomed sled without runners for hauling stones or other heavy objects over short distances. **2** a platform hung below the axles of a wagon, used for similar purposes.

**stone-broke** (stōn′brōk′), *adj. Slang.* totally without funds; penniless; ruined; stony. Also, **stony-broke**.

**stone bruise**, a bruise caused by a stone or other hard object, especially one on the sole of the foot or the side of a tire.

**stone canal**, a duct in the water-vascular system of an echinoderm, usually with calcareous walls, leading from the madreporite to a vessel around the mouth.

**stone|cat** (stōn′kat′), *n.* a yellowish-brown, freshwater catfish of North America that reaches a length of about one foot.

**stone cell**, *Botany.* a short, hardened cell that serves to support other tissues, found especially in seeds and fruit; sclereid.

**stone|chat** (stōn′chat′), *n.* a small European songbird, related to the thrushes, whose alarm note sounds like pebbles striking together. [< stone + *chat* (reputedly from its note of alarm resembling pebbles striking together)]

**stone china**, = ironstone china.

**stone coal**, **1** mineral coal, or coal dug up from

the earth, as distinguished from charcoal. **2** a hard variety of such coal; anthracite.

**stone-cold** (stōn′kōld′), *adj., adv.* —*adj.* cold as stone; quite cold: *a meal of stone-cold leftovers.* —*adv.* completely; thoroughly; quite: *stone-cold dead. No passion can last forever at boiling point, and ... men wake up one morning stone-cold middleaged* (New Yorker).

**stone color**, **1** a dark, dull bluish gray. **2** a brownish gray.

**stone-col|ored** (stōn′kul′ərd), *adj.* **1** dark, dull bluish-gray. **2** brownish-gray.

**stone crab**, an edible crab of the Atlantic coast of the southern United States. See picture under **crab**[1].

**stone|cress** (stōn′kres′), *n.* any one of a group of woody herbs of the mustard family native to the Mediterranean region, with racemes of usually white or pinkish flowers.

**stone|crop** (stōn′krop′), *n.* **1** any one of a group of low plants of the orpine family, especially a creeping, mosslike herb with small, fleshy leaves and clusters of small, yellow flowers, that grows in masses on rocks, old walls, and the like; sedum. **2** any one of various allied plants. [Old English *stāncrop* (supposedly from its growing on rocks or old walls)]

**stone curlew**, any brown or grayish bird of a group similar to the plover and curlew, with thick knees and large yellow eyes. It is found in the Old World and tropical America, especially on dry, stony ground.

**stone|cut|ter** (stōn′kut′ər), *n.* **1** a person who cuts or carves stone. **2** a machine for cutting, shaping, or dressing stone.

**stone|cut|ting** (stōn′kut′ing), *n.* the business of cutting, shaping, or dressing stone.

**stoned** (stōnd), *adj.* **1** having a stone or stones. **2** having the stones removed: *stoned cherries.* **3** *Slang.* intoxicated by alcohol or drugs.

**stone-dead** (stōn′ded′), *adj.* dead as stone; lifeless: *This collection finally kills an old legend stone-dead* (Manchester Guardian).

**stone-deaf** (stōn′def′), *adj.* totally deaf.

**stone|face** (stōn′fās′), *n.* any one of a group of stemless, succulent, South African plants of the carpetweed family, with the leaves forming a stonelike body from the top of which a single yellow or white flower grows.

**stone-faced** (stōn′fāst′), *adj.* = stony-faced.

**stone|fish** (stōn′fish′), *n., pl.* **-fish|es** or (*collectively*) **-fish.** a very poisonous fish, found in shallow water in the tropics of the Indian and Pacific Ocean. It is a scorpionfish that resembles a rock as it lies partly buried in sand on the ocean floor.

**stone fly**, any one of an order of insects, the nymphs of which are aquatic and frequently found under stones. The adults are much used as fish bait.

**stone fruit**, a fruit having the seed covered with a hard shell (stone) that is surrounded by a layer of pulp; drupe: *Peaches are stone fruit.*

**stone hammer**, a large hammer used for breaking stone. See picture under **hammer**.

**stone|hand** (stōn′hand′), *n.* a typesetter who imposes pages of type on a stone and secures them in the chase for electrotyping or printing.

**Stone|henge** (stōn′henj′), *n.* a prehistoric ruin in southern England, near Salisbury, consisting of huge slabs or megaliths of roughly shaped stone in a circular arrangement. It may have been a kind of observatory used by astronomers.

**stone|less** (stōn′lis), *adj.* having no stone or stones.

**stone lily**, a fossil flower-shaped sea animal or crinoid.

**stone|man** (stōn′mən), *n., pl.* **-men.** **1** = stonemason. **2** = stonehand.

**stone marten**, **1** a marten of Europe and Asia that has a patch of white fur on the throat and breast. **2** the fur of this animal.

**stone|ma|son** (stōn′mā′sən), *n.,* or **stone mason**, a person who cuts stone or builds walls or other structures of stone.

**stone|ma|son|ry** (stōn′mā′sən rē), *n., pl.* **-ries.** the art of, or work done by, a stonemason.

**stone oak**, an oak found in Java and other islands, having a thick, bony, ridged acorn.

**stone oil**, = petroleum.

**stone parsley**, an Old World herb of the parsley family, with aromatic seeds which are used as a seasoning; honewort.

**stone pine**, a pine native to southern Europe, related to the piñon and producing pine nuts.

**ston|er** (stō′nər), *n.* a person who stones or pelts with stones.

**stone roller**, **1** a fish of the eastern United States and Mexico, related to the carps. **2** an American sucker.

**stone sheep**, a wild sheep of British Columbia, a brownish-black variety of the Dall sheep; bighorn.

**stone's throw**, a short distance: *The parson lives only a stone's throw from the church.*

**stone-still** (stōn′stil′), *adj.* still as a stone; absolutely motionless: *She lay stone-still in a trance of terror* (George Meredith).

**stone|wall** (stōn′wôl′), *v.i.* **1** (in cricket) to bat solely to protect the wicket. **2a** *Especially British.* to obstruct business, especially parliamentary business, by long speeches or other delaying tactics. **b** to obstruct or prevent any action by evasive or delaying tactics: *He and his aides schemed to "stonewall," to make empty claims of "national security," ... to maneuver prosecutors—all in order to keep the facts from coming out* (Anthony Lewis).
—*v.t.* **a** *Especially British.* to obstruct (parliamentary business) by long speeches or other delaying tactics. **b** to obstruct or prevent (any action) by evasive or delaying tactics: *Let the courts clamor for documents, the Judiciary Committee subpena tapes, the President ... will "stonewall it" to the bitter end* (New York Post). —**stone′-wall′er**, *n.*

**stone wall**, **1** a wall built of stones. **2a** *Especially British.* an obstruction of business, especially parliamentary business, by long speeches or other delaying tactics. **b** any insurmountable obstruction or obstacle.

**stone|ware** (stōn′wãr′), *n.* a coarse, hard pottery. Stoneware is made from very siliceous clay, or a mixture of clay with a considerable amount of flint, sand, prefired clay, or the like, to give it greater strength, fired higher (about 2,300 degrees Fahrenheit) than earthenware, and often glazed with salt.

**stone|work** (stōn′wėrk′), *n.* **1** work done in or with stone. **2a** a wall or other structure made of stone. **b** the part of a building made of stone. **3** artistic work of any kind executed in stone.

**stone|work|er** (stōn′wėr′kər), *n.* a person who shapes or cuts stone for use in buildings or other structures or sculpture.

**stone|works** (stōn′wėrks′), *n.pl.* **1** a factory or shop where stone is cut and shaped for building, or ornamental work; stonecutter's establishment. **2** a place where stoneware is made.

**stone|wort** (stōn′wėrt′), *n.* any green algae of a group whose jointed stems are frequently encrusted with deposits of lime, commonly growing submerged in fresh water.

**ston|ey** (stō′nē), *adj.,* **ston|i|er, ston|i|est.** = stony.

**stone|yard** (stōn′yärd′), *n.* a yard in which stonecutting is carried on.

**ston|i|ly** (stō′nə lē), *adv.* in a stony manner; stiffly; harshly; coldly.

**ston|i|ness** (stō′nē nis), *n.* the quality of being stony.

**ston|ker** (stong′kər), *v.t. Australian.* **1** to strike heavily; beat. **2** to catch off guard; outwit.

**ston|y** (stō′nē), *adj.,* **ston|i|er, ston|i|est.** **1** having many stones or outcroppings of rock: *The beach is stony.* **2** hard like stone; very hard: *concrete hardened to a stony consistency.* **3** *Figurative.* **a** cold and unfeeling: *The cruel man has a stony heart.* **b** without expression or feeling: *a stony stare.* **c** petrifying; stupefying: *stony fear, stony grief.* **4** *Slang.* stone-broke. **5** *Obsolete.* made of stones or stone. **6** *Obsolete.* (of a fruit) having a stone.

**ston|y-broke** (stō′nē brōk′), *adj. British Slang.* stone-broke.

**stony coral**, any coral of an order that secrete a hard calcareous skeleton.

**ston|y-faced** (stō′nē fāst′), *adj.* having or showing a cold, unfeeling expression; expressionless: [*The senator*] *listened, stony-faced, tight-lipped, and angry* (Atlantic).

**ston|y-heart|ed** (stō′nē här′tid), *adj.* cruel; unfeeling; merciless.

**stood** (stůd), *v.* the past tense and past participle of **stand**: *He stood in the corner for five minutes. I had stood in line all morning to buy tickets to the game.*

**stooge** (stüj), *n., v.,* **stooged, stoog|ing.** *Informal.* —*n.* **1a** a person on the stage who asks questions of a comedian and is the butt of the comedian's jokes. **b** (in vaudeville) an actor in the audience who heckles a comedian. **2** a person who follows and flatters another; hanger-on.
—*v.i.* to be or act as a stooge (for): *to stooge for a comedian.*
[American English; origin uncertain]

**stook** (stük, stůk), *n., v.* —*n.* a shock (of grain).
—*v.t.* to set up in shocks: *the grain was cut and stooked* (Atlantic).
[Middle English *stouk;* origin uncertain]

**stool** (stül), *n., v.* —*n.* **1** a seat for one person without arms and, usually, without a back. **2** a similar article used to rest the feet on, or to kneel on; footstool. **3** a stump or root of a plant from which shoots grow: **a** the stump of a felled tree, or a group of stumps. **b** the stump or base of a tree felled or headed to produce saplings or young timber, or of a plant cut down to produce branches for layering. **c** the base of plants producing new stems or foliage annually. **4** a cluster of shoots, or a shoot or layer from a plant. **5** *Hunting.* **a** a decoy. **b** a movable pole to which a bird is fastened as a decoy. **6a** a movement of the bowels; waste matter from the bowels. **b** an article or place to be used as a toilet. **7** = window sill.
—*v.i.* **1** to send out shoots or stems; form a stool. **2** to evacuate the bowels.
**fall between two stools**, to make a complete failure by hesitating between two opportunities or trying to use both: *Asked to develop two patterns of thought he may well fall between two stools and develop neither* (Technology).
[Old English *stōl*] —**stool′like′**, *adj.*

**stool end**, a part of rock left unworked in a mine to support the rest.

**stool pigeon**, **1** *Slang.* a spy for the police; informer: *Everybody in the plant was regarding everybody else as a possible stool pigeon* (Maclean's). **2a** a pigeon fastened to a stool and used to lead other pigeons into a net or other trap. **b** *Slang.* a person employed as a decoy, as by gamblers.

**stool|y** or **stool|ie** (stü′lē), *n., pl.* **stool|ies.** *U.S. Slang.* a stool pigeon.

**stoop**[1] (stüp), *v., n.* —*v.i.* **1** to bend forward: *He stooped to pick up the money. She stoops over her work.* **2** to carry the head and shoulders bent forward: *The old man stoops.* **3** (of trees, precipices, or other natural outgrowths) to bend forward and downward; slope. SYN: incline. **4** *Figurative.* to lower oneself; descend: *He stooped to cheating. When lovely woman stoops to folly* (Oliver Goldsmith). SYN: condescend, deign. **5** *Figurative.* to swoop like a hawk or other bird of prey: *the comic muse, who should be taught to stoop only at the ... blacker crimes of humanity* (Richard Brinsley Sheridan). **6** *Archaic, Figurative.* to submit; yield. **7** *Obsolete.* to descend from a height.
—*v.t.* **1** to lower by bending forward; bow: *A superb-looking warrior stooped the towering plumes of his head-dress ... and entered the house* (Herman Melville). SYN: incline. **2** *Archaic, Figurative.* to humble; subdue; subject.
—*n.* **1** an act of stooping; bending forward. **2** a forward bend. **3** a forward bend of the head and shoulders: *My uncle walks with a stoop.* **4** *Figurative.* condescension. **5** the swoop of a bird of prey on its quarry: *The peregrine in its "stoop" attains 175 an hour, the highest speed ever recorded for a bird* (Scientific American).
[Old English *stūpian*] —**stoop′er**, *n.*

**stoop**[2] (stüp), *n. U.S.* a porch or platform at the entrance of a house. [American English < Dutch *stoep*]

**stoop**[3] (stüp), *n.* = stoup.

**stoop**[4] (stüp), *n. Dialect.* a post or pillar. [< Scandinavian (compare Old Icelandic *stolpe*)]

**stoop|ball** (stüp′bôl′), *n. U.S.* a variation of baseball, usually played in city streets, in which a rubber ball is thrown against the stoop of a house or building and players on the opposing team try to catch the ball before it bounces.

**stoop labor**, *U.S.* labor requiring much stooping or bending over, as picking, weeding, or other such farm labor in the fields.

**stoop-shoul|dered** (stüp′shōl′dərd), *adj.* having a habitual stoop in the shoulders and back.

**stop** (stop), *v.,* **stopped** or (*Archaic*) **stopt, stop|ping,** *n.* —*v.t.* **1a** to keep from moving, acting, doing, being, or working: *to stop work, stop a speaker, stop a car. The men stopped the boys from teasing the cat. I stopped the clock.* **b** to hold back; restrain; prevent: *If anyone wants to go, I shan't stop him.* SYN: hinder, deter, impede. **2** to cut off; withhold: *to stop supplies, stop a person's pay.* SYN: discontinue, intermit, suspend. **3** to put an end to; interrupt; check: *to stop a noise.* **4** to close (a hole or opening) by filling (it); fill holes in; close: *to stop a crack, stop a leak, stop a wound. Father stopped up the rats' holes.* **5** to close (a vessel) with a cork, plug, or the like; shut up (something) in a closed vessel or place: *to stop a bottle.* **6** to block (a way); obstruct: *A fallen tree stopped traffic. A big box stops up the doorway.* **7** to check, counter, or parry (a stroke, blow, weapon, attack or maneuver); ward off. **8** to defeat by a knockout in boxing: *He was stopped in the second round.* **9** to defeat (in various games). **10** to bring down or kill by the action of a weapon. **11** = punctuate. **12** *Music.* **a** to close (a finger hole) in order to produce a particular tone from a wind instrument. **b** to press down (a string as of a violin or guitar)

**Pronunciation Key:** hat, āge, cãre, fär; let, ēqual, tėrm; it, īce; hot, ōpen, ôrder; oil, out; cup, půt, rüle; child; long; thin; ᴛʜen; zh, measure; ə represents a in about, e in taken, i in pencil, o in lemon, u in circus.

in order to alter the pitch of tone produced. Stopping a string shortens its vibrating length and thus produces a higher tone than that of the unstopped (open) string. **c** to produce (a tone or sound) by this means. **13** to instruct a bank not to honor (a check, bill, or other negotiable form) when presented. **14** to issue a stop order on (a particular security). **15** to have (a suit in bridge) guarded or blocked by holding a high card and cards to protect it and thus to prevent an opponent from running all the tricks in the suit.
—***v.i.*** **1** to cease to move; stay; halt: *Stop, look, and listen.* **2** to halt and remain; stay on: *to stop for the night at a hotel. She stopped at the bank for a few minutes. Because I could not stop for Death—He kindly stopped for me* (Emily Dickinson). **3** to leave off acting, doing, or being; come to an end; discontinue; cease: *All work stopped. The rain is stopping.* **4** to be or become plugged or clogged: *The drain stopped.*
—***n.*** **1a** the act of coming to a halt; cessation of onward movement: *Her sudden stop startled us.* **b** a cessation of an activity or process; end: *The singing came to a stop.* **c** a stay or halt in the course of a journey: *a short stop for lunch.* **d** a blocking, hindering, checking, or obstructing: *to be the cause of a complete stop of traffic.* **2** the fact or condition of being stopped. **3** a place where a stop is made: *a bus stop.* **4** a thing that stops; obstacle: *The old brick was set against the open door as a stop to keep it from blowing shut.* **5** a plug or cork; stopper. **6** any piece or device that serves to check or control movement or action in a mechanism. **7a** a punctuation mark that normally indicates some kind of pause, such as a comma, semicolon, colon, question mark, exclamation point, and dash. **b** a full stop; period. **8** a word used in telegrams and cables, instead of a period. **9** *Music.* **a** the closing of a finger hole or aperture in the tube of a wind instrument, or the act of pressing with the finger on a string of a violin or similar instrument, so as to alter the pitch of its tone. **b** a key or other device that controls the pitch of an instrument. **c** a graduated set of organ pipes of the same kind, producing tones of the same quality: *One music from a thousand stops and strings* (Henry Augustin Beers). **d** the handle or knob that controls them; stop knob. See picture under **organ**. **e** a similar set of reeds in a reed organ. **10** *Photography.* the aperture of a lens, or the f/number indicating this: *The next stop smaller than f/3.5 is f/2.* **11** *Phonetics.* **a** a sudden, complete stopping of the breath stream either in the glottis, at some point in the mouth, or at the lips, followed by its sudden release. **b** a consonant that involves such a stopping; explosive. *P, b, t, d, k,* and *g* (as in *go*) are stops. **c** (in some classifications) a speech sound articulated, with the nasal passage either open or closed, by completely stopping the breath stream at some point, thus including also the nasals, such as English *m, n,* and *ng.* **12a** an instruction to a bank or banker not to honor a check, bill, or other negotiable form. **b** = stop order. **13** *Nautical.* any piece of small rope, cloth, etc., used to hold or tie something, especially a furled sail. **14** a high card or group of cards in a suit that protects the holder against an opponent's run in that suit.
**pull out all (the) stops,** to do something in the biggest way possible; exert maximum effort: *But perhaps the best scene in the show is Art Smith's shrewd lawyer pulling out all stops to get Volpone acquitted* (Saturday Review).
**put a stop to,** to stop; end: *Henry ... put a stop to this* (M. J. Guest). *The coal trade at Newcastle was for some time put a stop to by a mutiny* (John Brand).
**stop by** (or **in**), to stop for a short visit: *He stopped in, not at all sure that on this first occasion he would be able to broach the dangerous subject* (Theodore Dreiser).
**stop down,** *Photography.* to reduce the aperture of a lens and thus the amount of light reaching the film or plate: *The sharpness of the picture can ... be greatly improved by the simple expedient of "stopping down"* (J. A. Hodges).
**stop off,** *Informal.* to stop for a short stay: *Yet would I counsel the traveler whose way lies by Avignon to stop off, if only for an hour, in order to ascend the Rocher des Doms* (Outing).
**stop out, a** *U.S.* to interrupt one's education to pursue some other activity for a brief period: *The trend of stopping out is growing, however, partly because the draft law now gives young men with high lottery numbers a new freedom* (Time).
**b** *Etching.* to stop (certain parts of a plate) from being further exposed to the acid: *Before the second and successive acid bath, he [the artist] uses either ground or varnish to stop out ... areas of the plate having the desired depth* (Andrew J. Stasik, Jr.).
**stop over, a** to make a short stay: *By stopping over at Dalhousie [in Canada] ... the following localities may be visited* (J. W. Dawson). **b** *Informal.* to stop in the course of a trip: *You renewed your ticket after stopping over in Baltimore* (Mark Twain).
[Old English *-stoppian* (in *for-stoppian*), ultimately < Latin *stuppa* tow[2], oakum < Greek *stýppē.* See etym. of doublet **estop.**]
—*Syn. v.t.* **1a Stop, arrest, check** mean to put an end to action, movement, or progress. **Stop,** the general word, means to bring any kind of advance or movement to an end: *He stopped the car.* **Arrest** suggests halting by forceful and usually deliberate action: *He grabbed the child to arrest its fall.* **Check** means to stop or arrest suddenly, sharply, or with force, sometimes only temporarily: *An awning over the sidewalk checked his fall and saved his life.* *-v.i.* **2 Stop, cease, pause** mean to leave off. **Stop,** the general word, means to leave off doing, acting, moving, or going ahead: *The train stopped.* **Cease,** a more formal word, means to come to an end, and therefore is used of things that are existing or lasting, or to emphasize that action or movement has stopped permanently: *All life has ceased.* **Pause** means to stop for a time, but suggests going on again: *He paused to tie his shoe.*

**stop-ac|tion** (stop′ak′shən), *adj., n.* —***adj.*** of or having to do with a method of photography in which a quick action or movement is broken down into a series of still pictures somewhat like stop-motion or time-lapse photography, but without omitting any action: *a stop-action photo of a high jump.*
—***n.*** stop-action photography: *Through "stop-action," the electron shells could be shown interacting* (Isaac Asimov).

**stop bath,** an acid solution used to halt the developing process in photography; shortstop.

**stop|cock** (stop′kok′), *n.* a device for turning the flow of a liquid or gas on or off; faucet; valve.

**stope** (stōp), *n., v.,* **stoped, stop|ing.** —***n.*** a steplike excavation in a mine to take out the ore after shafts have been sunk.
—***v.t., v.i.*** to mine in stopes.
**stope out,** to stope: *to stope out salt.*
[probably related to **step,** noun]

**stop|gap** (stop′gap′), *n., adj.* —***n.*** **1** a thing or person that fills the place of something lacking; temporary substitute: *We ought to send them our surplus food and clothing as a stopgap, until we can do something more permanent for them* (Atlantic). **2** an utterance intended to fill up a gap or an awkward pause in conversation or discourse: *a mere conversational stopgap, to be dropped now that the real business could be commenced* (H. G. Wells).
—***adj.*** serving as a stopgap: *U.S. economists consider stabilization plans only short-term, stopgap methods of straightening out world markets* (Time).

**stop-go** (stop′gō′), *n., adj. British.* —***n.*** a period or condition of alternating inflation and deflation; go-stop: *The victims of stop-go and unemployment are union members* (Manchester Guardian Weekly).
—***adj.*** of or characterized by stop-go: *a stop-go economy.*

**stop knob,** a handle used to turn an organ stop on or off; stop.

**stop|light** (stop′līt′), *n.* **1** a red light on the rear end of a vehicle that turns on automatically when the brakes are applied. **2** = traffic light.

**stop-loss** (stop′lôs′, -los′), *adj.* of the nature of or having to do with a stop order: *Stop-loss orders have not been much of a factor in the price decline* (Wall Street Journal).

**stop motion,** a method of taking motion pictures at extended intervals so that a slow movement or process, such as the opening of a flower, will appear much accelerated; time-lapse photography. —**stop′-mo′tion,** *adj.*

**stop|off** (stop′ôf′, -of′), *n. U.S. Informal.* a stopover.

**stop order,** an order given to a broker to buy or sell a stock whenever the market reaches a set price, especially to prevent a loss from a further change in the market price.

**stop-out** (stop′out′), *n. U.S.* a college student who interrupts his education to pursue some other activity for a year. [patterned on *drop-out*]

**stop|o|ver** (stop′ō′vər), *n.* **1** the act of stopping over in the course of a journey, especially with the privilege of proceeding later on the ticket originally issued for the journey. **2** a place where a journey is broken: *We'd have to keep driving steadily if we were to reach our first stopover point in time for a decent night's rest* (New Yorker). [American English < *stop* + *over*]

**stop|pa|ble** (stop′ə bəl), *adj.* capable of being stopped.

**stop|page** (stop′ij), *n.* **1** the act of stopping: *The foreman called for a stoppage of operations to oil the machinery.* **2** the condition of being stopped: *During the work stoppage many workers looked for other jobs.* **3** a block; an obstruction.

**stop payment,** an instruction to a bank or banker by the maker of a check not to pay that check.

**stopped** (stopt), *adj.* **1a** obstructed; blocked. **b** (of a hole or crevice) filled up. **2** (of a vessel or tube) closed with a plug or stopper. **3** brought to a standstill. **4a** (of an organ pipe) having the upper end closed, thereby being about an octave lower in pitch than an open pipe of equal length. **b** (of the string of a violin or other stringed instrument) pressed down with the finger. **c** (of a tone or note) produced by stopping a string or finger hole of an instrument. **d** (of a French horn) having the sound muffled by the placing of the player's hand in the bell. **5** *Phonetics.* articulated as a stop.

**stop|per** (stop′ər), *n., v.* —***n.*** **1** a plug or cork for closing the opening of a bottle, tube, or other container. **2** a person or thing that stops. **3** *Cards.* a card or cards which prevents the running of a suit by the opponents. **4** a picture, slogan, or other advertising device, designed to catch the attention and arouse interest. **5** *Baseball Slang.* a very skillful pitcher, especially a relief pitcher.
—***v.t.*** **1** Also, **stopper down.** to close or secure (a bottle, tube, or other container) with a stopper. **2** to fit with a stopper.

**stop|ple** (stop′əl), *n., v.,* **-pled, -pling.** —***n.*** a stopper as for a bottle; plug.
—***v.t.*** to close or fit with a stopper.
[partly < *stop;* partly short for *estoppel*]

**stop-press** (stop′pres′), *n., adj. British.* —***n.*** a newspaper column containing late news inserted after printing has begun: *Look at ... the racing news in the stop-press* (London Times).
—***adj.*** containing late or the latest news: *a stop-press newspaper.*

**stop sign,** a traffic sign posted at an intersection to signal motorists going toward it to come to a full stop: *Police believed that the farm workers' truck had run through a stop sign at the intersection and directly into the path of the tractor-trailer* (Newsweek).

**stop street,** a street with a stop sign at the intersection.

**stopt** (stopt), *v. Archaic.* stopped; a past tense and a past participle of **stop.**

**stop watch,** or **stop|watch** (stop′woch′, -wôch′), *n.* a watch having a hand or hands that can be stopped or started at any instant. A stop watch indicates fractions of a second and is used for timing races and other contests.

**stop|work** (stop′wėrk′), *n.* a device attached to a watch, clock, music box, or other clockwork, to prevent overwinding.

**stor|a|bil|i|ty** (stôr′ə bil′ə tē, stōr′-), *n.* the quality of being storable.

**stor|a|ble** (stôr′ə bəl, stōr′-), *adj.* that can be stored: *storable commodities.*

**stor|age** (stôr′ij, stōr′-), *n.* **1a** the act or fact of storing goods: *room for storage, the storage of furs in summertime.* **b** the condition of being stored. Cold storage is used to keep eggs and meat from spoiling. *She removed her winter clothes from storage.* **2** a place for storing: *She has put her furniture in storage.* **3** the price for storing, especially rent paid for warehousing: *She paid $30 storage on her furniture.* **4** the production by electric energy of chemical reactions that can be reversed to produce electricity, especially that occurring in and exemplified by the charging of a storage battery. **5a** a device for storing information in a computer; memory. **b** the storing of such information: *long-term storage of data.* **c** the amount of information stored: *an 800,000-bit storage.*

**storage battery,** a battery that stores, but does not produce, electrical energy. A storage battery converts chemical energy into direct-current electrical energy. When the cells of the battery have been discharged, they may be charged again by passing a current through them in a direction opposite to that of the current flow when discharging.

**storage cell,** = storage battery.

**storage ring,** *Nuclear Physics.* a device for storing a beam of accelerated particles in a circular track and causing it to collide with an opposing beam to produce the necessary energy for the creation of new particles.

**storage tank,** a tank for storing water, oil, liquid gas, or other liquids.

**sto|rax** (stôr′aks, stōr′-), *n.* **1** a solid resin resembling benzoin, with an odor like that of vanilla, obtained from a small styracaceous tree of Asia Minor and Syria, formerly used in medicine and perfume. **2** the tree itself. **3** any other tree or shrub of the same group, found chiefly in warm regions of Asia and America, such as the species from which benzoin is obtained. **4** a fragrant gum resin or balsam obtained from various species of liquidambar, especially the inner bark, used in medicine and perfumery. [< Latin *storax,* variant of *styrax* < Greek *stýrax, -akos*]

**store** (stôr, stōr), *n., adj., v.,* **stored, stor|ing.** —*n.* **1** a place where goods are kept for sale; shop: *a clothing store.* **2** a thing or things put away for future use; supply; stock: *a squirrel's store of nuts. Mother has a store of vegetables in the freezer.* **3** a place where supplies are kept for future use; storehouse; warehouse. **4** storage; reserve; keeping: *Half of our stock is for use, the other half for store.* **5** stock; supply: *My desk usually contained a store of ... miscellaneous volumes* (Scott). (*Figurative.*) *They're forever provoking their families to add to their store of guilt* (New Yorker). **6** *Especially British.* storage (def. 5). **7** *Archaic.* quantity; abundance: *We wish them a store of happy days* (Tennyson). [short for Middle English *astore* < Old French *estor,* noun < *estorer;* see the verb]
—*adj. U.S.* that has been or can be bought in a store: *store clothes, store goods.*
—*v.t.* **1** to supply or stock: *These studies ... store a man's mind with valuable facts* (Washington Irving). **2** to put away for use later; lay up; accumulate: *He stores old coins in a metal box.* **3** to put in a warehouse or other place for preserving or safekeeping: *We stored our furs during the summer.*
**in store, a** saved for future use; on hand; in reserve: *It was determined ... that a hundred and seventy thousand barrels of gunpowder should constantly be kept in store* (Macaulay). **b** to be expected; awaiting (a person, group, or enterprise): *Eight of the nation's leading economic seers ... let the world know just what was in store ... for business in the year ahead* (Newsweek).
**set store by,** to value; esteem: *She sets great store by her father's opinions.*
**store away** (or **up**), to put away for future use; lay up; accumulate: *The squirrel stores away nuts.*
**stores, a** the things needed, such as food, clothing, and arms, to equip and maintain an army, ship, household, hospital, or other institution; supplies: *naval stores.* **b** a thing or things laid up for future use: *She puts up stores of preserves and jellies every year.*
[short for Middle English *astoren* < Old French *estorer* construct, erect, furnish, store, restore < Latin *instaurāre* restore < *in-* in + unrecorded *staurus* pillar]

**store-bought** (stôr′bôt′, stōr′-), *adj. U.S. Informal.* bought in a store; not homemade: *a store-bought suit, store-bought bread.*

**store cheese,** *U.S.* American cheese.

**store|front** (stôr′frunt′, stōr′-), *n., adj. U.S.* —*n.* the front or front room of a store: *The façade of the office is a storefront* (New Yorker).
—*adj.* **1** situated in a storefront: *a storefront church or chapel.* **2** of or belonging to a church situated in a storefront: *a storefront preacher, a storefront congregation.* **3** taking place in a storefront: *a storefront meeting, to conduct a storefront campaign.*

**storefront school,** *U.S.* free school.

**store|house** (stôr′hous′, stōr′-), *n.* **1** a place where things are stored; warehouse: *This factory has many storehouses for its product.* **2** *Figurative: A library is a storehouse of information.*

**store|keep|er** (stôr′kē′pər, stōr′-), *n.* **1** a person who owns or manages a retail store or stores. **2** *Especially British.* a person who has charge of receiving and issuing supplies, especially military or naval supplies.

**store|keep|ing** (stôr′kē′ping, stōr′-), *n.* the keeping of a store; business of a storekeeper.

**store|man** (stôr′man′, stōr′-), *n., pl.* **-men. 1** *U.S.* an owner or manager of a store, especially a department store. **2** a man in charge of stores or supplies, as on a ship or in a store.

**stor|er** (stôr′ər, stōr′-), *n.* a person who lays up or accumulates a store.

**store|room** (stôr′rüm′, -rům′; stōr′-), *n.* a room where things are stored.

**stores** (stôrz, stōrz), *n.pl.* See under **store.**

**store|ship** (stôr′ship′, stōr′-), *n.* a government ship detailed to carry naval or military stores.

**store|wide** (stôr′wīd′, stōr′-), *adj. U.S.* applying to an entire store, especially a department store: *an official storewide policy. A storewide sale includes all the merchandise in a store.*

**sto|rey** (stôr′ē, stōr′-), *n., pl.* **-reys.** = story².

**sto|reyed** (stôr′ēd, stōr′-), *adj.* = storied².

**sto|ri|at|ed** (stôr′ē ā′tid, stōr′-), *adj.* = historiated.

**sto|ried¹** (stôr′ēd, stōr′-), *adj.* **1** celebrated in story or history: *the storied Wild West.* **2** ornamented with designs representing happenings in history or legend: *storied tapestry.* [< *story*¹ + *-ed*²]

**sto|ried²** (stôr′ēd, stōr′-), *adj.* having stories or floors: *a storied tower, a two-storied house.* [< *story*² + *-ed*²]

**sto|ri|ette** (stôr′ē et′, stōr′-), *n.* a very short story. [American English]

**sto|ri|ol|o|gy** (stôr′ē ol′ə jē, stōr′-), *n.* the study of popular tales and legends, their origin and distribution. [< *story*¹ + *-logy*]

**stork** (stôrk), *n.* a large wading bird with long legs, a long neck, and a long, stout bill. Storks comprise a family of birds, related to the ibises and herons. They are found in most warm parts of the world. [Old English *storc*] —**stork′like′,** *adj.*

**stork's-bill** (stôrks′bil′), *n.* any one of a group of plants that includes most of the cultivated varieties of geraniums; pelargonium. [< the beaklike prolongation of the seed pod]

**storm** (stôrm), *n., v.* —*n.* **1a** a strong wind with rain, snow, hail, or thunder and lightning: *One of the worst storms of the winter suddenly swept down on the Northeast* (Newsweek). **b** = sandstorm. **2** a heavy fall of rain, hail, or snow, or a violent outbreak of thunder and lightning, without strong wind. **3** *Meteorology.* a wind having a velocity of 64-73 miles per hour (on the Beaufort scale, force 11). **4** anything like a storm: *a storm of arrows.* **5** *Figurative.* a violent attack: *The castle was taken by storm.* **6** *Figurative.* a violent outburst or disturbance: *a storm of tears, a storm of angry words, a storm of applause.*
—*v.i.* **1** to blow hard; rain, snow, or hail: *It stormed last night.* **2** *Figurative.* to be violent; rage: *She curses and storms at me like a trooper* (Samuel Richardson). *Why look you, how you storm, I would be friends with you* (Shakespeare). **3** to rush to an assault or attack: *troops storming up the hill.* **4** *Figurative.* to rush violently: *He stormed out of the room.*
—*v.t.* **1** to attack violently: *The enemy stormed the castle. Troops stormed the city.* **2** *Figurative.* to attack or trouble violently, as if with a storm: *He laid siege to her affections and stormed her heart. A fickle maid ... Storming her world with sorrow's wind and rain* (Shakespeare). **3** *Figurative.* **a** to address loudly and angrily. **b** to affect as if with a storm: *His curses stormed the air.*
**storm in a teacup,** *Especially British.* a great commotion about a small matter: *[He] described the mystery of his whereabouts at the weekend as "a storm in a teacup"* (London Times).
**take by storm,** to win over completely: *The musical ... took the audience by storm* (New York Times).
**up a storm,** *Informal.* to the utmost; aplenty; copiously: *to sweat up a storm, to curse up a storm. You can ... shop up a storm in the Avenida Madero* (New Yorker).
[Old English *storm*]

**Storm|a|long** (stôr′mə lông, -long), *n.* **Alfred Bulltop,** a gigantic hero of American sailors' folklore.

**storm and stress,** = Sturm und Drang.

**storm belt,** a belt or zone in which storms occur in a regular pattern of frequency.

**storm|bird** (stôrm′bėrd′), *n.* **1** = stormy petrel. **2** any bird that seems to foretell bad weather by its cries or other actions.

**storm|bound** (stôrm′bound′), *adj.* confined or detained by a storm.

**storm cellar,** *U.S.* a cellar for shelter during cyclones and tornadoes.

**storm center, 1** the center of a cyclone, where there is very low air pressure and comparative calm. **2** *Figurative.* any center of trouble, or tumult: *She was a troublemaker, a constant storm center at school.*

**storm cloud, 1** a cloud that brings or threatens storm. **2** *Figurative: He ran out of capital ... as the storm clouds of the second world war began to gather* (Harper's).

**storm|coat** (stôrm′kōt′), *n.* a thick, usually lined and waterproof coat.

**storm|cock** (stôrm′kok′), *n.* **1** = fieldfare. **2** = green woodpecker. [from the belief that they are stormbirds]

**storm cone,** *British.* a cone-shaped device used as a storm signal.

**storm door,** *U.S.* an extra door outside of an ordinary door, to keep out snow, cold winds, and rain.

**storm drain,** = storm sewer.

**storm|er** (stôr′mər), *n.* **1** a person who takes by storm; member of a storming party. **2** *Figurative.* a person who rages.

**storm|ful** (stôrm′fůl), *adj.* having or troubled by many storms. —**storm′ful|ness,** *n.*

**storm jib,** a small jib made of heavy canvas for use in bad weather.

**storm|less** (stôrm′lis), *adj.* without storms.

**storm petrel,** = stormy petrel.

**storm|proof** (stôrm′prüf′), *adj.* resistant to storms; that can withstand a storm.

**storm sewer,** a sewer for carrying off rain from paved streets.

**storm signal, 1** a signal displayed along a seacoast or lakeshore to give warning of the approach of high winds and storms. It usually consists of a square red flag with a black center during the day or two vertical red lights at night. **2** *Figurative: Recession storm signals are going up in Europe even while inflation remains a chronic threat* (Wall Street Journal).

**storm surge,** a sudden onrush of tidal waves caused by strong gales.

**storm trooper, 1** a member of the Sturmabteilung of Nazi Germany, the private army formed by Adolf Hitler in 1923; brown shirt. **2** an extremely brutal or vicious individual.

**storm troops,** = Sturmabteilung.

**storm|ward** (stôrm′wərd), *adv., adj.* toward the storm.

**storm warning, 1** a display of storm signals or a broadcast predicting a storm and its probable intensity: *The storm warnings that flew Lake Michigan's length changed that night into "whole gale" warnings* (Time). **2** *Figurative.* a sign of trouble to come.

**storm window,** an extra window outside of an ordinary window, to keep out snow, cold winds, and rain.

**storm|y** (stôr′mē), *adj.,* **storm|i|er, storm|i|est. 1** having a storm or storms; likely to have storms; troubled by storms: *a stormy sea, a stormy night, stormy weather.* SYN: tempestuous, blustery, windy. **2** *Figurative.* rough and disturbed; violent: *They had stormy quarrels.* SYN: wild. —**storm′i|ly,** *adv.* —**storm′i|ness,** *n.*

**stormy petrel, 1** any one of several small, black-and-white sea birds whose presence is supposed to give warning of a storm. **2** *Figurative.* anyone believed likely to cause trouble or to indicate trouble: *He [Sinclair Lewis] was a stormy petrel in his life as in his books* (Basil Davenport). Also, **storm petrel.**

**Stor|ting** or **Stor|thing** (stôr′ting′, stōr′-), *n.* the national legislature of Norway. [< Norwegian *Storting, Storthing* < *stor* great + *ting, thing* assembly]

**sto|ry¹** (stôr′ē, stōr′-), *n., pl.* **-ries,** *v.,* **-ried, -ry|ing.** —*n.* **1** an account of some happening or group of happenings: *the story of the boy's disappearance, the story of the gold rush. The man told the story of his life.* SYN: relation, narrative, recital, record, chronicle. **2** such an account, either true or made-up, intended to interest the reader or hearer; tale: *fairy stories, ghost stories, stories of adventure, a speech abounding in good stories, the short stories of Poe.* **3** *Informal.* a falsehood: *That boy is a liar; he tells stories.* SYN: fib, lie. **4** stories as a branch of literature: *famous in song and story.* **5** the plot or succession of incidents as of a play or novel: *If you were to read [Samuel] Richardson for the story, your impatience would be so much fretted that you would hang yourself* (Samuel Johnson). **6** *U.S.* **a** a newspaper article. **b** the subject or material for this. **7** *Archaic.* history: *well-read in story.*
—*v.t.* **1** to ornament with sculptured or painted scenes from history or legend. **2** *Archaic.* to tell the history or story of; relate.
[< Anglo-French *estorie,* learned borrowing from Latin *historia* < Greek *historiā.* See etym. of doublet **history.**]
—*Syn. n.* **2 Story, anecdote, tale** mean a spoken or written account of some happening or happenings. **Story** applies to any such account, true or made-up, long or short, in prose or verse, intended to interest another: *the story of King Arthur.* **Anecdote** applies to a brief story about a single incident, usually funny or with an interesting point, often in the life of a famous person: *He knows many anecdotes about Mark Twain.* **Tale** usually applies to a longer story: *an ancient Persian tale. She reads tales of frontier days.*

**sto|ry²** (stôr′ē, stōr′-), *n., pl.* **-ries. 1** one of the structural divisions in the height of a building; floor or the space between two floors: *a house of two stories. There are four rooms on the third story.* **2** a room or set of rooms on the same level or floor of a building: *The third story is for rent.* **3** each of a number of tiers or rows (of columns, windows, or other building parts) placed horizontally one above another. Also, **storey.** [perhaps ultimately a special use of *story*¹]

***sto|ry|board** (stôr′ē bôrd′, -bōrd′; stōr′-), *n.* a series of drawings to show the sequence of a planned motion picture, television program, commercial, or the like, each drawing representing a

---

**Pronunciation Key:** hat, āge, cãre, fär; let, ēqual, tėrm; it, īce; hot, ōpen, ôrder; oil, out; cup, pu̇t, rüle; child; long; thin; ᴛʜen; zh, measure; ə represents **a** in about, **e** in taken, **i** in pencil, **o** in lemon, **u** in circus.

major change of scene or action and usually including script and directions for sound effects.

***storyboard**

Little Red Riding Hood leaving home . . . waving

. . . in woods . . . sees wolf . . .

. . . wolf runs ahead . . .

wolf in bed . . . Little Red Riding Hood enters . . .

**sto|ry|book** (stôr′ē bu̇k′, stōr′-), *n., adj.* —***n.*** a book containing one or more stories or tales, especially for children.
—***adj.*** of or like that of a storybook; romantic; fictional: *a storybook hero, a storybook ending.*

**sto|ry|less** (stôr′ē lis, stōr′-), *adj.* without a story or stories.

**story line**, the line or plan of development of a story, novel, play, or the like: *The screen writers may have trouble developing a story line and picking a hero* (Harper's).

**sto|ry|tell|er** (stôr′ē tel′ər, stōr′-), *n.* **1** a person who tells stories. **2** *Informal.* a person who tells falsehoods; liar.

**sto|ry|tell|ing** (stôr′ē tel′ing, stōr′-), *n., adj.* —***n.*** **1** the act or art of telling stories, either true or made-up. **2** *Informal.* the telling of falsehoods.
—***adj.*** **1** that tells stories: *the storytelling power of the camera's eye* (Newsweek). **2** *Informal.* lying.

**stoss** (stos; *German* shtōs), *adj.* turned toward a former oncoming glacier: *the stoss side of a hill, the stoss end of a rock.* [< German *Stoss* a thrust, push]

**sto|tin|ka** (stō ting′kə), *n., pl.* **-ki** (-kē). a Bulgarian coin, worth 1/100 of a lev. [< Bulgarian *stotinka* < *stotna* one hundredth]

**stound** (stound, stünd, stün), *n., v.* —***n.*** **1** *Especially Scottish.* **a** a sharp pain; a pang. **b** a fierce attack; a shock. **c** a thrill of delight. **2** *Obsolete except Dialect.* **a** a time; while. **b** a short time; moment.
—***v.i.*** *Scottish.* to start; throb.
[Old English *stund* a time, moment; time of trouble]

**stoup** (stüp), *n.* **1a** a cup, flagon, tankard, or other drinking vessel: *a stoup of wine.* **b** the amount it holds. **2** a basin for holy water, usually set in or against the wall at a church entrance. Also, **stoop**. [Middle English *stowpe* < Scandinavian (compare Old Icelandic *staup*)]

**stour**¹ (stůr), *n. Scottish.* **1** tumult; uproar. **2** a storm. **3a** flying dust or spray. **b** a deposit of dust. **4** a fight. [< Anglo-French *estur,* Old French *estour, estorn* conflict, tumult < Germanic (compare Old High German *sturm*)]

**stour**² (stůr), *adj. Scottish.* **1** coarse in texture; harsh; rough. **2** stern; surly. **3** strong; sturdy. [Old English *stōr* great, big, strong]

**stoush** (stoush), *n. Australian Informal.* a battering; beating; brawl.

**stout** (stout), *adj., n.* —***adj.*** **1** fat and large: *a stout body. That boy could run faster if he weren't so stout.* SYN: stocky, plump, portly. See syn. under **fat**. **2** strongly built; firm; strong: *a stout dam, a stout fighting ship. The fort has stout walls.* SYN: durable, tough, sturdy, hardy. **3** brave; bold: *a stout heart. Robin Hood was a stout fellow.* SYN: valiant. **4** not yielding; stubborn; resolute; uncompromising: *stout resistance, a stout advocate or enemy.* SYN: determined. **5** characterized by endurance or staying power: *a stout horse, a stout engine.*
—***n.*** **1** a strong, heavy, dark-brown beer. **2a** a stout person. **b** a garment designed for such a person. **c** the size of this garment.
[< Old French *estout,* earlier *estolt* strong < Germanic (compare Middle Dutch *stout*)] —**stout′ly,** *adv.* —**stout′ness,** *n.*

**stout|en** (stou′tən), *v.t.* to make stout. —*v.i.* to grow stout.

**stout-heart|ed** or **stout|heart|ed** (stout′här′tid), *adj.* having courage; brave; bold: *a stout-hearted person, stout-hearted defense.* SYN: courageous. —**stout′-heart′ed|ly, stout′heart′ed|ly,** *adv.* —**stout′-heart′ed|ness, stout′heart′ed|ness,** *n.*

**stout|ish** (stou′tish), *adj.* somewhat stout.

**Stov|ar|sol** (stov′ər sol), *n. Trademark.* acetarsone.

**stove**¹ (stōv), *n., v.,* **stoved, stov|ing.** —***n.*** **1** an apparatus for cooking food and heating. There are wood, coal, gas, oil, and electric stoves. **2** a heated room or box for some special purpose, such as a hothouse or kiln.
—***v.t.*** to heat in a stove: *Layers were glued, one by one, over moulds in the shapes of boxes and lids, and then stoved at about 100 degrees Fahrenheit* (London Times).
[< perhaps Middle Dutch *stove* a hot room < Germanic (compare Old High German *stuba*)]

**stove**² (stōv), *v.* a past tense and a past participle of **stave**: *The barrel was stove in when it dropped off the truck.*
▶ See **stave** for usage note.

**stove bolt**, a bolt with a slotted head and coarse thread. See picture under **bolt**¹.

**stove|mak|er** (stōv′mā′kər), *n.* a manufacturer of stoves.

**stove|pipe** (stōv′pīp′), *n.* **1** a metal pipe that carries smoke and gases from a stove to a chimney, or to the outside of a building. **2** *Informal.* a tall silk hat.

**stovepipe trousers** or **pants**, narrow, tight trousers: *The low-slung stovepipe pants are pinstriped* (New Yorker).

**stove plant**, a plant cultivated in a hothouse.

**sto|ver** (stō′vər), *n.* **1** stalks of grain without the ears, used as fodder. **2** winter food for cattle. **3** *British Dialect.* any fodder. [short for Middle English *estovers* in sense of "necessary provisions"]

**stow**¹ (stō), *v.t.* **1** to put away to be stored; pack: *to stow books in a trunk. The cargo was stowed in the ship's hold.* **2** to pack things closely in; fill by packing: *The boys stowed the little cabin with supplies for the trip.* SYN: cram. **3** *Slang.* to stop. **4** to have room for; hold.
**stow away, a** to hide on a ship, airplane, train, or bus to get a free ride or to make an escape: *They escaped and reached Gibraltar on a steamer on which they had stowed away* (London Daily Chronicle). **b** to put away in a safe place or to be out of the way: *The bales of merchandise ... could not be stowed away before dark* (Harriet Martineau).
[Middle English *stowen* to put in a certain place or position, ultimately < Old English *stōw* a place] —**stow′a|ble,** *adj.* —**stow′er,** *n.*

**stow**² (stō), *v.t. Scottish.* to cut or trim close; crop. [apparently < unrecorded Middle English *stuven,* ultimately < Scandinavian (compare Old Icelandic *stūfr* stump)]

**stow|age** (stō′ij), *n.* **1** the act of stowing. **2** the state or manner of being stowed. **3** a room or place for stowing. **4** what is stowed. **5** a charge for stowing something.

**stow|a|way** (stō′ə wā′), *n.* a person who hides on a ship, airplane, train, or bus to get a free passage or to make an escape.

**STP** (no periods), **1** standard (conditions of) temperature and pressure. **2** a hallucinogenic drug chemically related to mescaline and amphetamine (for *Scientifically Treated Petroleum,* a trademark for a gasoline additive): *STP is a drug with similar effects to LSD* (London Times).

**str.**, an abbreviation for the following:
**1** steamer.
**2** strait.
**3** *Music.* string or strings.
**4** *Mechanics.* stroke.

**stra|bis|mic** (strə biz′mik), *adj.* **1** = cross-eyed. **2** of or having to do with strabismus. **3** *Figurative.* distorted: *The six sprightly clowns who people this excellent revue seem to have no difficulty in adjusting to the author's hopelessly strabismic view of the world* (New Yorker).

**stra|bis|mom|e|ter** (strā′biz mom′ə tər), *n.* an instrument for measuring strabismus.

**stra|bis|mus** (strə biz′məs), *n.* a disorder of vision due to the turning of one eye or both eyes from the normal position so that both cannot be directed at the same point or object at the same time; cross-eye or walleye; cast; squint. [< New Latin *strabismus* < Greek *strabismós* < *strabízein* to squint < *strabós* squint-eyed, related to *stréphein* to turn]

**stra|bot|o|my** (strə bot′ə mē), *n., pl.* **-mies.** the surgical incision of one or more of the muscles of the eye to cure strabismus. [< New Latin *strabotomia* < Greek *strabós* squint-eyed + *-tomiā* a cutting]

**STRAC** (no periods), *U.S.* Strategic Army Corps (an emergency force kept ready for duty anywhere on short notice): *STRAC includes 36,000 combat troops poised for quick movement abroad on short notice* (Wall Street Journal).

**Strad** (strad), *n. Informal.* a Stradivarius.

**strad|dle** (strad′əl), *v.,* **-dled, -dling,** *n.* —***v.i.*** **1** to walk, stand, or sit with the legs wide apart: *to straddle over a fence watching cars go by.* **2** (of the legs) to stand wide apart. **3** *Informal, Figurative.* to avoid taking sides; attempt to favor both sides: *All three political candidates straddled on the tariff issue.* **4** *Commerce.* to buy and sell stocks, or other securities, so as to balance a long holding against a short holding.
—***v.t.*** **1** to spread (the legs) wide apart. **2** to have a leg on each side of (a horse, bicycle, chair, ditch, or the like); bestride. **3** to stand or lie across; be on both sides of: *A pair of field glasses straddled his nose.* SYN: span. **4** *Informal, Figurative.* to attempt to favor both sides of (a question).
—***n.*** **1** the act of straddling. **2** the distance straddled. **3** an attempt to favor both sides of a question, especially in politics. **4** a contractual privilege, usually purchased, covering both a put and a call, allowing the holder either to demand certain securities or commodities, of its issuer, or to deliver certain securities or commodities, to its issuer within a given period, and at the same specified price: *A straddle is the purchase of a commodity for delivery in one month and the simultaneous sale of a commodity (generally the same one) for delivery in another month* (New York Times). **5** a high jump with the legs straddling the bar.
[a frequentative form of a variant of *stride*]
—**strad′dler,** *n.* —**strad′dling|ly,** *adv.*

**straddle carrier** or **truck**, a vehicle with motor and driver located on a raised frame, so that a load of lumber, pipe, or other material can be straddled and carried beneath it.

**strad|dle-legged** (strad′əl legd′), *adj., adv.*
—***adj.*** having the legs set wide apart: *The monstrous straddle-legged figure of that legitimate monarch, Henry VIII* (William Hazlitt).
—***adv.*** with the legs astride: *The wives ... who sit straddle-legged on the tiniest of donkeys* (William Howard Russell).

**Strad|i|var|i** (strad′ə vär′ē), *n.* = Stradivarius.

**Strad|i|var|i|us** (strad′ə vär′ē əs), *n.* a violin, viola, or cello made by the Italian violin maker Antonio Stradivari (1644?-1737). [< Latinized form of *Stradivari*]

**strafe** (strāf, sträf), *v.,* **strafed, straf|ing,** *n.* —***v.t.*** **1** to fly low over enemy positions and attack with machine-gun fire: *to strafe a line of soldiers. The planes strafed the deck of the ship.* **2** to shell or bomb heavily.
—***n.*** the act of strafing.
[originally, to punish < the German World War I slogan *Gott strafe England* God punish England]
—**straf′er,** *n.*

**strag|gle** (strag′əl), *v.,* **-gled, -gling,** *n.* —***v.i.*** **1** to wander in a scattered fashion: *Cows straggled along the lane.* SYN: roam, range, rove. **2** to stray from the rest; wander: *to straggle from a herd.* (*Figurative.*) *Children ... cannot keep their minds from straggling* (John Locke). **3** to spread in an irregular, rambling manner: *Vines straggled over the yard.*
—***n.*** **1** a group or body of scattered persons or objects: *A straggle of late Victorian tourists totter over a glacier, umbrellas up against the glare* (Manchester Guardian Weekly). **2** an irregular or fitful emergence (of something): *Here are some private utterances of his, throwing a straggle of light on those points* (Thomas Carlyle).
[perhaps < unrecorded Middle English *strakelen* (frequentative) < *straken* to move, go, extend. Probably related to **stretch**.] —**strag′gler,** *n.*

**strag|gling** (strag′ling), *adj.* **1** that straggles; wandering or straying: *any such casual accidental landing of straggling people from the main* (Daniel Defoe). **2** wandering apart from a line of march or a main body: *straggling soldiers.* **3** spreading irregularly in growth; rambling; spindling; *straggling plants.* **4** extending or scattered irregularly over an area: *It was a straggling little town.* **5** winding irregularly: *a straggling road.*
—**strag′gling|ly,** *adv.*

**strag|gly** (strag′lē), *adj.* spread out in an irregular, rambling way; straggling: *straggly rhododendrons.*

**strag|u|lum** (strag′yə ləm), *n.* the back and folded wings of a bird taken together as a distinguishing feature; mantle; pallium. [< Latin *strāgulum* spread, covering]

**straight** (strāt), *adj., adv., n.* —***adj.*** **1a** without a bend or curve: *a straight edge, a straight line, a straight path.* SYN: undeviating, unswerving. **b** evenly formed or set; not crooked: *a straight back, a straight nose. Keep your shoulders straight.* **c** not curly or wavy: *straight hair.* **2** going in a line; direct: *a straight course, straight aim, a straight throw.* **3** *Figurative.* **a** frank; honest; upright: *a straight answer, straight talking, a man straight in all his dealings.* SYN: honorable. **b** right; correct: *straight thinking, a straight clear thinker.* **4** in proper order or condition: *Our ac-*

*counts are straight. Set the room straight.* **5a** without interruption or break; continuous: *in straight succession.* **b** in an unbroken series: *straight sets, to lose 15 straight games.* **6** *U.S.* **a** supporting the candidates of one party only: *to vote the straight Democratic ticket.* **b** without reservations or exceptions; thorough-going or unreserved: *a straight Republican.* **7** *U.S.* **a** unmixed; undiluted: *straight gin.* **b** without qualification; unmodified: *a straight comedy, straight poker or whist.* **8** showing no emotion or humor: *He kept a straight expression, though he wanted to laugh.* **9** serious rather than comic; natural rather than eccentric: *a straight part in a play, a straight performance.* **10** *Informal, Figurative.* reliable; sure; authoritative: *a straight tip, straight information.* **11** *Slang.* **a** behaving in a conventional manner; holding orthodox views; square: *Elvin had once been into drugs, but now he was straight* (Atlantic). *There are ... groups to advise "straight" family members who are trying to understand a homophile relative* (Time). **b** conventional; standard; normal: *Now rock has its own problems, which may well prove to be more basic than those of straight music* (Listener). **12** made up of a sequence of five cards: *a straight flush in poker.* **13** (of an internal-combustion engine) having its cylinders in one straight line rather than radially or in a V-shaped pattern: *a straight eight.*
—***adv.*** **1a** in a line; directly: *to go straight home, to walk straight ahead, to look someone straight in the eye, to shoot straight at a target.* **b** not crookedly: *to write or walk straight, to hang a picture straight.* **c** in an erect position; upright: *Stand up straight. Sit straight.* **2** *Figurative.* honorably; uprightly; honestly: *Live straight.* **3** continuously to the end; all the way: *a hole straight through a wall, to drive straight on.* **4** without delay; immediately; straightway: *The bridge must straight go down* (Macaulay). **5** *Figurative.* without qualification or reservation; frankly; outspokenly: *straight from the shoulder. Tell me straight out what you think.* **6** *Informal.* selling at a fixed price regardless of quantity: *cigars selling at 10 cents straight.*
—***n.*** **1** straight condition; straight form, position, or line: *to be out of the straight.* **2** a straight part, as of a race track. **3** *Slang.* a person who is straight; conventional person, especially one who holds orthodox views; a square: *The Silent Majority ... that includes blue and white collars, small businessmen, professionals, and assorted "straights"* (Time). **4a** a sequence of five cards in poker, ranking above three of a kind and below a flush. **b** a hand containing such a sequence: *to deal a player a straight.* **5** *Sports.* a series of shots or plays producing a perfect score. **6** = straight whiskey.
**straight away** (or **off**), at once: *Your ma went straight off to see what was needed* (Louisa May Alcott).
**the straight**, the home stretch of a race track: *There was no important change in the order of running until after the turn into the straight* (London Times).
[Middle English *streit,* Old English *streht,* past participle of *streccan* to stretch]
—**straight′ly**, *adv.* —**straight′ness**, *n.*

**straight-A** (strāt′ā′), *adj. U.S.* having or showing the highest grade in all courses at school: *The chance for scholarships is much better for straight-A students* (New York Times).

**straight and narrow**, conventional standards or requirements of proper behavior: *These flirtations almost prove disastrous but Tung and Chen finally return to the straight and narrow* (Sunday Times).

**straight angle**, an angle of 180 degrees.

**straight-arm** (strāt′ärm′), *v., n.* —*v.t.* **1** to prevent (an opponent) from making a tackle in football by holding one's free arm stiffly extended. **2** to keep (a person) away by holding one's arm straight out; fend off: (*Figurative.*) *"We're not going to be straight-arming the customers any more," he declared. "We're going to inform everyone what their entitlements are"* (New York Times).
—***n.*** the act of straight-arming.

**straight arrow**, *U.S. Informal.* a very proper, upright, straightforward person: *Smith, a wonderfully old-fashioned straight arrow, was right in character when ... he said, "I don't call that gamesmanship. I call that rudeness"* (New Yorker).

**straight-arrow** (strāt′ar′ō), *adj. U.S. Informal.* very proper, upright, or straightforward: *The new eco-activists include groups as straight-arrow as the Girl Scouts* (Time).

**straight\|a\|way** (strāt′ə wā′), *n., adj., adv.* —***n.*** a straight course.
—***adj.*** in a straight course.
—***adv.*** as quickly as possible; at once; immediately; straightway.

**straight chain**, *Chemistry.* an arrangement of atoms in an organic molecule represented in a structural formula by a straight line with no forks or branches.

**straight\|edge** (strāt′ej′), *n.* **1** a strip of plastic, wood, or metal having one edge accurately straight, used in obtaining or testing straight lines and level surfaces. **2** = straight razor.

**straight\|en** (strā′tən), *v.t.* **1** to make straight: *Straighten your shoulders. He straightened the bent pin.* **2** to put in the proper order or condition: *to straighten out an account. Please straighten up your room.*
—***v.i.*** **1** to become straight: *Suddenly resolved, he straightened and marched out of the room.* **2** *U.S. Informal.* to mend one's ways; reform.
—**straight′en\|er**, *n.*

**straight face**, a face or expression that shows no emotion, humor, or thought: *He kept a straight face while telling the joke.*

**straight-faced** (strāt′fāst′), *adj.* showing no emotion, humor, or thought; with a straight face: *a straight-faced comedian, a straight-faced joke. He is not a debunker; he achieves his effects not by wisecracks but by straight-faced deadly irony* (Atlantic). —**straight′-faced′ly**, *adv.* —**straight′-faced′ness**, *n.*

**straight flush**, (in poker) a sequence of five cards in the same suit, ranking higher than four of a kind.

**straight\|for\|ward** (strāt′fôr′wərd), *adj., adv.*
—***adj.*** **1** honest; frank: *a straightforward answer. He has a reputation for being straightforward. He has written for the most part a straightforward and unvarnished drama* (Wall Street Journal). **SYN**: forthright, downright, aboveboard. **2** going straight ahead; direct.
—***adv.*** directly. —**straight′for′ward\|ly**, *adv.*
—**straight′for′ward\|ness**, *n.*

**straight\|for\|wards** (strāt′fôr′wərdz), *adv.* = straightforward.

**straight-from-the-shoul\|der** (strāt′frəm ᴛʜə shōl′dər), *adj.* straightforward; frank; direct.

**straight-grained** (strāt′grānd′), *adj.* (of timber) having the grain running straight, or parallel to the length, instead of at cross directions.

**straight\|ish** (strā′tish), *adj.* somewhat straight.

**straight\|jack\|et** (strāt′jak′it), *n., v.t.* = straitjacket.

**straight-laced** (strāt′lāst′), *adj.* = strait-laced.

**straight life insurance**, a plan of life insurance in which premiums are paid as long as the insured lives.

**straight-line** (strāt′līn′), *adj.* **1** having the main parts placed in a straight line, as a machine. **2** acting or exerted in a straight line: *straight-line movement, a straight-line force.* **3** producing or transferring motion in a straight line, as a system of rods so linked as to change rotating or oscillating movement into movement that acts in a straight line.

**straight-line depreciation**, a method of depreciation in which the original cost of machinery, equipment, or other investment, less the estimated resale value, is divided evenly over the number of years of expected use, and the percentage thus fixed is periodically charged off.

**straight man**, a person who serves as a foil for a comedian: *A BBC comedian asked his straight man to read the day's news* (Time).

**straight-out** (strāt′out′), *adj. U.S. Informal.* out-and-out; complete; thorough: *It was a case of straight-out dishonesty.*

**straight razor**, a heavy blade fixed to a handle, used chiefly by barbers for shaving.

**straight-run gasoline** (strāt′run′), gasoline of low octane rating distilled and condensed from crude petroleum.

**straight shooter**, *Informal.* a person who is honest and free from deceit or fraud.

**straight-time** (strāt′tīm′), *adj., adv.* —***adj.*** for or based on regular working hours: *The straight-time base pay in logging camps and sawmills is now $1.80 an hour* (Wall Street Journal).
—***adv.*** at regular hours: *On this job everyone works straight-time.*

**straight\|way** (strāt′wā′), *adv.* at once; immediately; straightaway: *He read the letter and burned it straightway.*

**straight whiskey**, whiskey distilled and aged without blending either with neutral spirits or with other whiskeys: *He predicted that straight whiskies would gain in favor at the expense of blends* (New York Times).

**straight-wing** (strāt′wing′), *adj.* having the wing's leading edge and the fuselage form a right angle: *an airplane with a straight-wing design.*

**strain¹** (strān), *v., n.* —*v.t.* **1** to draw tight; stretch: *His weight strained the rope.* **2** to stretch as much as possible or beyond the proper or reasonable limit: (*Figurative.*) *She strained the truth in telling that story.* (*Figurative.*) *The political system* [*in 1860*] *was being strained beyond its limit* (Bruce Catton). **3** to use to the utmost: *He strained every muscle to lift the rock. She strained her eyes to see.* **4a** to injure by too much effort or by stretching: *The runner strained his leg. She strained her back in scrubbing the floor.* **SYN**: wrench, sprain. **b** to damage or weaken by too much tension, pressure, or force: *The heavy cargo strained the ship's hold.* **5a** to press or pour through a strainer: *Strain the soup before serving it. Babies eat strained foods.* **b** to remove or keep back (dense or solid parts) in this way: *to strain lumps from a sauce.* **6** *Figurative.* to make excessive demands upon; tax severely: *to strain one's credit.* **7** to press closely; squeeze; hug: *She strained her child to her breast.* **8** *Physics.* to cause alteration of form, shape, or volume in (a solid). **9** *Obsolete.* to force; constrain as by extortion: *The quality of mercy is not strain'd* (Shakespeare).
—***v.i.*** **1** to pull hard: *The dog strained at his leash.* **SYN**: tug. **2a** to make a very great effort: *Both sides were straining to reconcile the most repulsive difficulties* (Benjamin Disraeli). **b** to exert oneself to the utmost; strive: *a rower straining against the current.* **3a** to be injured or damaged by too much effort, tension, or pressure. **b** to undergo too much tension or pressure. **4** to drip through. **SYN**: filter, trickle, percolate.
—***n.*** **1** any force or weight that stretches, pulls apart, or drags from a position: *The strain on the rope made it break.* **2a** a great muscular or physical effort. **b** too much effort. **c** an injury caused by too much effort or by stretching; sprain: *The injury to his back was only a slight strain.* **3** *Figurative.* **a** any severe, trying, or wearing pressure: *the strain of worry, the strain of debts. The strain of sleepless nights made her ill.* **b** the effect of such pressure on the body or mind. **4** Often, **strains.** a part of a piece of music complete in itself; melody; song; tune: *In sweet Italian strains our shepherds sing* (William Congreve). **5** *Figurative.* **a** a manner or style of doing or speaking: *a playful strain, a poem in a melancholy strain.* **b** mood; tone: *a moralizing or thoughtful strain.* **6** a passage of poetry. **7** a flow or burst of language, or eloquence. **8** *Physics.* **a** alteration of form, shape, or volume caused by external forces; deformation. **b** stress.
**strain a point**. See under **point**.
**strain at**, to have difficulty accepting: *Even his best friend strained at such an obvious lie.*
[< Old French *estreind-,* stem of *estreindre* bind tightly < Latin *stringere* draw tight]

**strain²** (strān), *n.* **1a** a line of descent; race; stock: *Charlemagne, And the long heroes of the Gallic strain* (Matthew Prior). **b** ancestry; descent; lineage: *He is of a noble strain* (Shakespeare). **2** any one of various lines of ancestry united in an individual or a family: *His Irish strain gives him a sense of humor.* **3a** a group of animals or plants that form part of a race, breed, or variety, and are distinguished from related organisms by some feature: *Certain strains of hybrid corn yield more hardy seed than others.* **b** an artificial variety of a domestic animal. **4** *Figurative.* **a** an inherited tendency, quality, or character: *a strain of madness. There is a strain of musical talent in that family.* **b** a trace or streak: *a scientist with a strain of superstition. That horse has a mean strain.* **5** a kind, class, or sort: *His ambition was of a noble and generous strain* (Edmund Burke). **6** *Archaic.* offspring; progeny. **7** *Obsolete.* a begetting; generation; procreation. [variant of Middle English *strene,* Old English *strēon* a gain, begetting, short form of *gestrēon*]

**strained** (strānd), *adj.* not natural; forced: *Her greeting was cold and strained.*

**strain\|er** (strā′nər), *n.* **1** a thing that strains. A filter, a sieve, and a colander are strainers. **2** a device for stretching or tightening.

**strain gauge**, any one of various gauges for measuring strains or pressures, such as stresses exerted on steel. One type consists of a small, flattened coil of fine wire which varies in electrical resistance according to the degree of deformation.

**strain hardening**, *Physics.* the hardening of metals or alloys by a change in structure due to strain or deformation: *Strain hardening results from the breakdown of the metal's microscopic grains* (Scientific American).

**strain\|ing** (strā′ning), *n.* the act of a person or thing that strains.

**straining arch**, *Architecture.* an archlike structure, such as a flying buttress, designed to resist pressure like a strut.

**straining beam** or **piece**, the horizontal timber

---

**Pronunciation Key:** hat, āge, cãre, fär; let, ēqual, tėrm; it, īce; hot, ōpen, ôrder; oil, out; cup, pu̇t, rüle; child; long; thin; ᴛʜen; zh, measure; ə represents **a** in about, **e** in taken, **i** in pencil, **o** in lemon, **u** in circus.

or beam in a roof truss between the tops of two queen posts, which holds them in place.

**strain|me|ter** (strān′mē′tər), *n.* an instrument used by seismologists to detect and measure strain in the earth's surface. [< *strain*[1] + *-meter*]

**strains** (strānz), *n.pl.* See under **strain**[1] (*n.* def. 4).

**strait** (strāt), *n., adj., adv.* — ***n.*** **1** Often, **straits.** a narrow channel or passage connecting two larger bodies of water: *The Strait of Gibraltar connects the Mediterranean Sea and the Atlantic Ocean.* *Abbr:* str. See picture under **bay**[1]. **2** *Archaic.* an isthmus. **3** *Obsolete.* a narrow, confined place or space.
— ***adj.*** *Archaic.* **1** narrow; limited; confining: *It matters not how strait the gate* (W. E. Henley). **2** strict; rigorous: *The nun took strait vows.*
— ***adv.*** *Obsolete except Dialect.* in a narrow manner; tightly; closely.
**straits,** difficulty; need; distress; plight: *He was in desperate straits for money. Low prices for fish products ... left Iceland's economy in dire straits* (Raymond E. Lindgren). **SYN:** crisis, emergency.
[< Old French *estreit* < Latin *strictus* drawn tight, bound, past participle of *stringere.* See etym. of doublets **strict, stretto.**] — **strait′ly,** *adv.* — **strait′ness,** *n.*

**strait|en** (strā′tən), *v.t.* **1** to limit by the lack of something; restrict. **SYN:** hamper, impede. **2** to make narrow; contract. **3** *Archaic.* to confine within narrow limits; confine.

**strait|ened** (strā′tənd), *adj.* **1** limited or reduced, especially to insufficiency: *straitened means or income.* **2** needing money badly; hampered by insufficiency of means: *The day before payday found him in straitened circumstances.* **3** *Archaic.* narrowed or contracted; narrowly confined. **4** *Obsolete.* drawn tight.

***strait|jack|et** or **strait-jack|et** (strāt′jak′it), *n., v.* — ***n.*** **1** a strong coat with long sleeves that can be tied to hold the arms close to the sides. It keeps a violent person from harming himself or others. **2** *Figurative: The programs of the community colleges are not tied to the straitjacket of a statewide, uniform curriculum* (Fred M. Hechinger). **SYN:** restriction, restraint.
— ***v.t.*** to restrain or confine in a straitjacket: (*Figurative.*) *The campaign is strait-jacketed by lack of funds* (Newsweek). (*Figuative.*) *Scientists suddenly found themselves strait-jacketed by security regulations which limited severely their contacts with fellow scientists* (Scientific American). Also, **straightjacket.**

***straitjacket**
definition 1

**strait-laced** (strāt′lāst′), *adj.* **1** very strict in matters of conduct; prudish: *I'm not strait-laced, but I tell you we got to have decent women in our schools* (Sinclair Lewis). **SYN:** stiff, formal. **2** *Archaic.* **a** tightly laced. **b** wearing tightly laced garments. Also, **straight-laced.** — **strait′-laced′ly,** *adv.* — **strait′-laced′ness,** *n.*

**straits** (strāts), *n.pl.* See under **strait.**

**Straits dollar,** a silver coin of the Straits Settlements, a former British colony in southeastern Asia.

**strait waistcoat,** *Especially British.* straitjacket.

**strake** (strāk), *n.* a single breadth of planks or metal plates along the side of a ship from the bow to the stern. [Middle English *strake* iron rim of a wheel. Apparently related to **stretch.**]

**stram** (stram), *v.,* **strammed, stram|ming,** *n. U.S. Dialect.* — ***v.i.*** to walk with ungraceful strides; tramp: *Don't go stramming off another afternoon* (Harriet Beecher Stowe).
— ***n.*** a long, hard walk; tramp.

**stra|mash** (strə mash′, stram′ish), *n. Scottish.* a disturbance; uproar; row. [apparently imitative]

**stra|min|e|ous** (strə min′ē əs), *adj.* **1a** of or like straw. **b** *Figurative.* valueless. **2** *Botany.* straw-colored. [< Latin *strāmineus* (with English *-ous*) < *strāmen, -inis* straw, related to *sternere* to spread, scatter]

**stra|mo|ni|um** (strə mō′nē əm), *n.* **1** = jimson weed. **2** a drug made from its dried leaves, used as an antispasmodic and as a sedative, in the treatment of asthma. [< New Latin *stramonium;* origin uncertain]

**stram|o|ny** (stram′ə nē), *n.* = stramonium.

**strand**[1] (strand), *v., n.* — ***v.t., v.i.*** **1** to run aground; drive on the shore: *The ship was stranded on the rocks.* **2** *Figurative.* to bring or come into a helpless position: *He was stranded a thousand miles from home with no money.* [< noun]
— ***n.*** shore; land bordering a sea, lake, or river: *wandering on a foreign strand* (Scott). **SYN:** beach, coast.
[Old English *strand*]

**strand**[2] (strand), *n., v.* — ***n.*** **1** one of the threads, strings, or wires that are twisted together to form a rope, cord, line, cable, or electric conductor: *This is a rope of three strands.* **2** one of the threads or strips of a woven or braided material. **3** a string, thread, or tress: *a strand of beads or pearls, a strand of hair.* **4** a fiber in animal or plant tissue.
— ***v.t.*** **1** to form (a rope) by the twisting of strands. **2** to break one or more of the strands of (a rope).
[perhaps < Old French *estran* < Germanic (compare Old High German *streno*)]

**strand**[3] (strand), *n.* **1** *Scottish.* a channel or gutter. **2** *Scottish and English Dialect.* a stream, brook, or rivulet. [Middle English; origin uncertain]

**strand|ed**[1] (stran′did), *adj.* aground; helpless: *a stranded vessel,* (*Figurative.*) *stranded travelers searching for shelter.*

**strand|ed**[2] (stran′did), *adj.* made of strands; having a certain number of strands: *a three-stranded rope.* — **strand′ed|ness,** *n.*

**strand|ing** (stran′ding), *n.* the act or process of being stranded.

**strand line,** *Geology.* the line of contact between a lake or ocean and the land.

**strand|loop|er** (strand′lü′pər), *n.* a Bushman living on the coast in South Africa and working largely along the shore. [< Afrikaans *strandlooper* < Dutch *strand* shore + *looper* runner]

**strange** (strānj), *adj.,* **strang|er, strang|est,** *adv.* — ***adj.*** **1** unusual; odd; queer; peculiar: *a strange accident. What a strange experience! She wears strange, old-fashioned clothing. 'Tis strange—but true; for truth is always strange; Stranger than fiction* (Byron). **2** not known, seen, or heard of before; not familiar: *strange faces, a strange language. She is moving to a strange place. A strange cat is on our steps. The custom was strange to them.* **SYN:** unfamiliar, new, novel. **3** not used (to); unaccustomed (to); inexperienced (at): *He is strange to the work but will soon learn.* **4** out of place; not at home: *a strange dog walking down a street. The poor child felt strange in the palace.* **5** distant or cold; reserved. **6** *Archaic.* foreign; alien.
— ***adv.*** in a strange manner.
[< Old French *estrange* < Latin *extrāneus* foreign. See etym. of doublet **extraneous.** See related etym. at **estrange.**] — **strange′ly,** *adv.*
— ***Syn.*** *adj.* **1 Strange, odd, peculiar,** mean unusual or out of the ordinary. **Strange** applies to what is unfamiliar, unknown, or unaccustomed: *A strange quiet pervaded the city.* **Odd** applies to what is irregular or puzzling: *That house has been painted with an odd combination of colors.* **Peculiar** applies to what is unique or different from others: *Raising frogs is a peculiar way to make a living.*

**strange|ness** (strānj′nis), *n.* **1** the quality or condition of being strange. **2** *Nuclear Physics.* a property of certain elementary particles, used in explaining their relatively slow rate of decay. *Abbr:* S (no period).

**strange particle,** *Nuclear Physics.* any of the heavier, unstable elementary particles, comprising the heavy mesons and the hyperons, so called because their relatively long life appeared to be inconsistent with existing atomic theories.

**stran|ger** (strān′jər), *n., adj., v.* — ***n.*** **1** a person not known, seen, or heard of before: *She is a stranger to us.* **2** a person or thing new to a place; newcomer: *He is a stranger in New York.* **3** a person who is out of place or not at home in something: *He is no stranger to hard work.* **4** visitor; guest: ... *thy stranger that is within thy gates* (Exodus 20:10). **5** a person from another country; foreigner; alien: *The king received the strangers with kindness.* **6** *Law.* a person who has no legal interest or standing in an action or transaction.
— ***adj.*** **1** that is a stranger: *a stranger prince or knight, a stranger gentleman.* **2** foreign; alien: *stranger troops, a stranger nation.*
— ***v.t.*** *Obsolete.* to make a stranger of; alienate: *Dow'rd with our curse, and stranger'd with our oath, Take her or leave her* (Shakespeare).

**stran|gle** (strang′gəl), *v.,* **-gled, -gling,** *n.* — ***v.t.*** **1** to kill by squeezing the throat to stop the breath: *Hercules strangled a snake with each hand.* **2** to choke; suffocate: *His high collar seemed to be strangling him.* **SYN:** throttle, stifle. **3** *Figurative.* to choke down; suppress; keep back: *to strangle a yawn, to strangle a nation's economy by too many taxes. He strangled an impulse to cough.*
— ***v.i.*** to be strangled; choke: *She almost strangled on a piece of meat that caught in her throat.*
— ***n.*** **strangles,** an acute, infectious disease as of horses and mules caused by a bacterium, and characterized by fever and inflammation of the mucous membranes.
[< Old French *estrangler* < Latin *strangulāre.* Compare etym. under **strangulate.**] — **stran′gler,** *n.*

**stran|gle|hold** (strang′gəl hōld′), *n.* **1** a wrestling hold for stopping an opponent's breath. **2** *Figurative: The processes of maturity had me in a grim stranglehold ... and the joys of the intellectual life were beginning to overwhelm me* (Punch).

**strangler fig,** a fig tree of Florida and the Bahama Islands that begins its growth as a parasite on another tree, reaches its top, and then gradually strangles the existing tree in a mass of roots, finally standing in place of the original tree.

**strangler tree,** = clusia.

**stran|gles** (strang′gəlz), *n.* See under **strangle.**

**stran|gu|late** (strang′gyə lāt), *v.,* **-lat|ed, -lat|ing.** — ***v.t.*** **1** *Medicine.* to constrict or compress so as to stop the circulation in, or hinder the action of: *The danger of abdominal hernia is that the abdominal muscles may contract, strangulating ... the part of the bowel that protrudes* (Hyman S. Rubinstein). **2** to strangle; choke.
— ***v.i.*** *Medicine.* to become strangulated.
[< Latin *strangulāre* (with English *-ate*[1])]

**stran|gu|lat|ed** (strang′gyə lā′tid), *adj.* **1** *Medicine.* compressed or constricted so as to prevent circulation or suppress function: *In a strangulated hernia, the circulation in the protruded part is arrested.* **2** *Botany.* irregularly contracted and expanded: *a strangulated stem.* **3** strangled; choked: *He sings in such a fiercely strangulated manner as to torment the music* (Atlantic).

**stran|gu|la|tion** (strang′gyə lā′shən), *n.* **1** the act of strangling or condition of being strangled: *death by strangulation.* (*Figurative.*) *Today vast urban areas ... suffer from traffic strangulation* (Wall Street Journal). **2** *Medicine.* constriction of a bodily organ, duct, or the like so as to stop circulation or the passage of fluids.

**stran|gu|ry** (strang′gyər ē), *n.* a slow, painful emission of urine, drop by drop. [< Latin *strangūria* < Greek *strangouriā* < *stránx, strangós* a drop squeezed out + *oûron* urine]

**strap** (strap), *n., v.,* **strapped, strap|ping.** — ***n.*** **1** a narrow strip of leather or other material that bends easily: *the straps of a wheel or pulley, to beat someone with a strap.* **SYN:** thong. **2** a narrow, flat band or strip of cloth: *The general wore straps on the shoulders of his uniform.* See also **shoulder strap. 3** a narrow strip for fastening things together or in position, or for holding together timbers, parts of machinery, or the like: *Put a strap around the trunk. He had a strap around his books. The box was strengthened by straps of steel.* **4** a narrow strip of leather to sharpen razors on; strop. **5** a looped band suspended from a bar, as in a bus, train, or car, for passengers to hold on to, to steady themselves. **6** a looped band attached to a boot to help pull it on.
— ***v.t.*** **1** to fasten, bind, or secure with a strap or straps: *We strapped the trunk.* **2** to beat with a strap. **3** to sharpen (a razor or knife) on a strap or strop. **4** to dress and bandage.
[dialectal variant of *strop,* partly Old English < Latin *stroppus;* partly < Old French *estrop* < Latin *stroppus* < Greek *stróphos* < *stréphein* to turn] — **strap′like′,** *adj.*

**strap|hang** (strap′hang′), *v.i.,* **-hung, -hang|ing.** *Informal.* to be a straphanger: *You cannot straphang in an airliner as you can on a London bus* (New Scientist).

**strap|hang|er** (strap′hang′ər), *n. Informal.* a passenger in a bus, subway, or train, who cannot get a seat and stands holding on to a strap, rod, or other support.

**strap hinge,** a hinge with a long band of metal, usually on each side, by which it is secured to a door and a post. See picture at **hinge.**

**strap|less** (strap′lis), *adj., n.* — ***adj.*** having no strap or straps; not fitted with straps: *a strapless gown.*
— ***n.*** a strapless garment or undergarment.

**strap-on** (strap′on′, -ôn′), *adj., n.* — ***adj.*** attached to a space vehicle or engine for additional thrust: *The vehicle seen on television appeared to have a two-stage core with four strap-on boosters* (New Scientist).
— ***n.*** a strap-on booster or engine.

**stra|pon|tin** (strə pon′tin), *n.* **1** a folding seat as used in automobiles. **2** a similar type of seat used in theaters: *I spotted her once on a backless strapontin, lost to the world, her shining face uplifted to the stage* (New Yorker). [< French *strapontin*]

**strap|pa|do** (strə pā′dō, -pä′-), *n., pl.* **-does.** **1** a form of human torture in which the victim was raised by a rope and suddenly let fall the length of the rope. **2** the mechanism for doing this. [alteration of Middle French *estrapade* < Italian *strappata* < *strappare* to drag, snatch < Vulgar Latin *extirpāre* extirpate, fused with Latin *trahere* to drag]

**strapped** (strapt), *adj.* **1** fastened or provided with straps. **2** finished with bands of cloth, as seams or garments. **3** *Informal.* short of money: *Over the country, banks were more strapped for funds than they have been in the last 10 months* (Wall Street Journal).

**strap|per** (strap′ər), *n.* **1** a person or thing that straps. **2** *Informal.* a tall, robust person.

**strap|ping** (strap′ing), *adj., n.* —*adj. Informal.* **1** tall, strong, and healthy; robust: *a fine, strapping boy. There is a strong gleam of didacticism under his rather strapping prose* (Manchester Guardian). **SYN:** sturdy, husky. **2** very big; great; whopping: *a strapping lie.*
—*n.* thin, narrow steel straps or bands used to reinforce crates, cartons, packages, etc., for shipping.

**strap|work** (strap′wėrk′), *n.* architectural design consisting of folded, crossed, and interlaced fillets or bands.

**strap|wort** (strap′wėrt′), *n.* a coastal herb native to the Mediterranean region and western Europe, with many slender trailing stems and small white flowers in little heads or cymes, the sepals petallike on the margin.

**Stras|bourg goose** (stras′bėrg), a goose that is specially fattened to enlarge its liver for use in making pâté de foie gras. [< *Strasbourg,* a city in northeastern France where these geese are raised]

**strass**[1] (stras), *n.* a brilliant glass containing oxide of lead, used in making artificial gems; paste. [< German *Strass,* reputedly < Joseph *Strasser,* who invented it]

**strass**[2] (stras), *n.* silk waste that remains after working up skeins. [< French *strasse,* earlier *estrasse* or *estrace* < Italian *straccio*]

**stra|ta** (strā′tə, strat′ə), *n.* a plural of **stratum.**

**strat|a|gem** (strat′ə jəm), *n.* **1** a scheme or trick for deceiving an enemy: *The spy got into the castle by the stratagem of dressing as a beggar.* **2** a trick; trickery. [< Middle French *stratagème,* learned borrowing from Latin *stratēgēma* < Greek *stratēgēma, -atos* < *stratēgeîn* be a general < *stratēgós* general; see etym. under **strategy**]
—*Syn.* **1, 2 Stratagem, ruse, artifice** mean a scheme to trick or mislead others. **Stratagem** applies to a careful and sometimes complicated scheme for gaining advantage against an enemy or opponent: *a clever political stratagem. The general planned a stratagem to trap the enemy.* **Ruse** is applied to any trick used to hide one's real purpose or present a false impression, often as a means of cheating another: *Her headache was a ruse to leave early. The shoplifter knew many ruses to distract attention from his stealing.* **Artifice** emphasizes the ingenuity involved and is sometimes applied to a device built primarily to mislead: *The Trojan horse was the artifice used by the Greeks to gain entry into Troy.*

**stra|tal** (strā′təl), *adj.* having to do with a stratum or strata.

**stra|te|gic** (strə tē′jik), *adj.* **1** of or having to do with strategy; based on strategy; useful in strategy: *a strategic retreat.* **2** important in strategy: *The Panama Canal was once a strategic link in our national defense.* **3** having to do with raw material necessary for warfare which must be obtained, at least partially, from an outside country: *The government plans to continue limited direct purchases of ... lead and zinc for the strategic stockpile* (Wall Street Journal). **4** specially made or trained for destroying key enemy bases, industry, or communications behind the lines of battle, rather than for supporting combat units on land or sea: *a strategic bomber.*

**Strategic Air Command,** *U.S.* a branch of the Air Force carrying out strategic air operations.

**stra|te|gi|cal** (strə tē′jə kəl), *adj.* = strategic.

**stra|te|gi|cal|ly** (strə tē′jə klē), *adv.* in a strategic manner; by strategy: *a strategically important area.*

**strategic hamlet,** a village fortified militarily against incursions by guerrillas.

**stra|te|gics** (strə tē′jiks), *n.* = strategy.

**strat|e|gist** (strat′ə jist), *n.* a person trained or skilled in strategy: *a brilliant military strategist, a chess strategist, a football strategist.*

**strat|e|gy** (strat′ə jē), *n., pl.* **-gies. 1** the planning and directing of military movements and operations; science or art of war: *Tactics are used to win an engagement, strategy to win a campaign or a war* (Bulletin of Atomic Scientists). **SYN:** strategics. **2** the skillful planning and management of anything: ... *the faulty strategy of idealists who have too many illusions when they face realists who have too little conscience* (Reinhold Niebuhr). **3** a plan based on or involving strategy: *Strategy is needed to keep the boys at work.* **SYN:** maneuver. [< Greek *stratēgíā* < *stratēgós* general < *stratós* army + *ágein* to lead]
▶ **Strategy** differs from **tactics.** *Strategy* refers to the overall plans of a nation at war. *Tactics* refers to the disposition of armed forces in combat.

**strath** (strath), *n. Scottish.* a wide valley. [< Scottish Gaelic *srath*]

**strath|spey** (strath′spā′, strath′spā′), *n.* **1** a vigorous Scottish dance, usually in 4/4 time, somewhat like a reel. **2** the music for this dance. [supposedly < *Strathspey,* a place name in Scotland]

**stra|tic|u|late** (strə tik′yə lit, -lāt), *adj. Geology.* arranged in thin layers of strata. [< a diminutive form of *stratum* + *-ate*[1]]

**stra|tic|u|la|tion** (strə tik′yə lā′shən), *n.* arrangement in thin layers.

**strat|i|fi|ca|tion** (strat′ə fə kā′shən), *n.* **1** the act or fact of stratifying or being stratified; arrangement in layers or strata: *the stratification of society.* **2** *Geology.* **a** the formation of strata; deposition or occurrence in strata. **b** a stratum.

**strat|i|fi|ca|tion|al** (strat′ə fə kā′shə nəl), *adj. Linguistics.* having to do with a method of analyzing language by arranging its components into a series of interrelated strata, each stratum consisting of units such as phonemes, morphemes, lexemes, and sememes: *stratificational grammar.*

**strat|i|fi|ca|tion|al|ist** (strat′ə fə kā′shə nə list), *n.* a student or follower of stratificational linguistics.

**stra|ti|fied-charge engine** (strat′ə fīd chärj′), an internal-combustion engine whose cylinders are divided into two chambers containing different mixtures of fuel and air: *In the stratified-charge engine ... there are zones that are fuel-rich or fuel-poor* (H. Martin Malin, Jr.). *Fuel economy and reduced exhaust emissions can both be obtained in so-called stratified-charge engines* (London Times).

**strat|i|form** (strat′ə fôrm), *adj.* **1** *Geology.* arranged in strata; forming a stratum or layer. **2** *Anatomy.* occurring in thin layers in bones: *stratiform cartilage.* **3** having the form of stratus clouds. [< French *stratiforme* < Latin *strātum* (see etym. under **stratum**) + *-formis* -form]

**strat|i|fy** (strat′ə fī), *v.,* **-fied, -fy|ing.** —*v.t.* **1** to arrange in layers or strata; form into layers or strata: ... *a sample selected from a population which has been stratified, part of the sample coming from each stratum* (Kendall and Buckland). **2** *Geology.* to deposit (sediment) in strata; form strata in. **3** to preserve (seeds) by putting them between alternate layers of earth or sand.
—*v.i.* to form strata: *Already a few of the new settlers are starting to rise in the world, to stratify and to disperse* (Punch).
[< Medieval Latin *strātificāre* < Latin *strātum* (see etym. under **stratum**) + *facere* to make]

**stra|tig|ra|pher** (strə tig′rə fər), *n.* a person skilled in stratigraphy.

**strat|i|graph|ic** (strat′ə graf′ik), *adj.* of or having to do with stratigraphy. —**strat′i|graph′i|cal|ly,** *adv.*

**stra|tig|ra|phy** (strə tig′rə fē), *n.* **1** the branch of geology that deals with the order and position of strata. **2** the order and position of the strata (of a country or region): *The stratigraphy of river deposits can pose obdurate problems* (G. H. Dury).

**strato-,** *combining form.* **1** horizontal layers: *Stratosphere = area of the atmosphere where the winds are mainly horizontal.*
**2** of the stratosphere; having to do with high altitudes: *Stratotanker = a tanker that refuels at high altitudes.* [< *stratus*]

**stra|to-cir|rus** or **stra|to|cir|rus** (strā′tō sir′əs), *n.* a cloud closely resembling a cirro-stratus, but more compact, and formed at a lower altitude.

**stra|toc|ra|cy** (strə tok′rə sē), *n., pl.* **-cies.** government by the army; military government. [< Greek *stratós* army + *-kratíā* rule]

**strat|o|crat|ic** (strat′ə krat′ik), *adj.* of or having to do with stratocracy.

**stra|to-cu|mu|lus** or **stra|to|cu|mu|lus** (strā′tō-kyü′myə ləs), *n., pl.* **-li** (-lī). a cloud formation made up of large, dark, rounded masses above a flat, horizontal base, usually seen in winter and occurring at heights under 6,000 feet.

**strat|o|lab** (strat′ə lab), *n.* a manned gondola equipped with scientific instruments, suspended from a balloon at high altitudes for meteorological or other investigation.

**strat|o|pause** (strat′ə pôz′, strā′tə-), *n.* the area of atmospheric demarcation between the stratosphere and the mesosphere.

**strat|o|scope** (strat′ə skōp), *n.* a balloon carrying a telescope with a camera for photographing the sun from heights of over 80,000 feet.

**stra|tose** (strā′tōs), *adj. Botany.* arranged in strata or layers.

**strat|o|sphere** (strat′ə sfir, strā′tə-), *n.* **1** the region of the atmosphere between the troposphere and mesosphere. It extends from 10 to 20 miles above the earth. In the stratosphere temperature varies little with changes in altitude, and the winds are chiefly horizontal. See diagram under **atmosphere. 2** (formerly) the stratosphere and ionosphere together. **3** *Figurative.* a high or rarefied region: *On one point he seemed to take off into a stratosphere of fancy* (Wall Street Journal). [< French *stratosphère* < Latin *strātus, -ūs* a spreading out (see etym. under **stratus**) + French *-sphère,* as in *atmosphère* atmosphere]

**strat|o|spher|ic** (strat′ə sfer′ik, strā′tə-), *adj.* of or having to do with the stratosphere: (*Figurative.*) *But that would mean tax rates would stay at their present stratospheric height* (Wall Street Journal). —**strat′o|spher′i|cal|ly,** *adv.*

**strat|o|tank|er** (strat′ə tang′kər), *n.* a tanker plane that can refuel bombers at high altitudes.

**stra|tum** (strā′təm, strat′əm), *n., pl.* **-ta** or **-tums. 1** a layer of material, especially one of several parallel layers placed one upon another: *to lay several strata of gravel on a road. In digging the well, the men struck a stratum of sand, then one of clay and finally a stratum of rock.* **2** *Geology.* a bed or formation of sedimentary rock consisting throughout of approximately the same kind of material. **3** *Figurative.* a social level; group having about the same education, culture, development, or taste: *Tramps are in a low stratum of society.* **SYN:** caste. **4** *Biology.* a layer of tissue; lamella. **5** a region of the atmosphere or of the sea assumed as bounded by horizontal planes for purposes of calculation. **6** *Linguistics.* any one of several levels in which language can be analyzed. A word may be analyzed at the phonemic, morphemic, or semantic stratum. [< New Latin *stratum* < Latin *strātum* something spread out; coverlet; pavement; neuter past participle of *sternere* to spread out]

**stratum cor|ne|um** (kôr′nē əm), the horny outer layer of the skin, consisting of broad, thin cells. [< New Latin *stratum corneum* horny layer]

**stra|tus** (strā′təs), *n., pl.* **-ti** (-tī). a low, uniform, horizontal layer of gray cloud that spreads over a large area, occurring at heights under 6,500 feet. See picture under **cloud.** [< Latin *strātus, -ūs* a spreading out < *sternere* to spread out]

**Strauss|i|an** (strou′sē ən), *adj., n.* —*adj.* of or having to do with the German musical composer and conductor Richard Strauss (1864-1949) or his musical style, theories, or compositions.
—*n.* a follower of Richard Strauss or his works.

**stra|vage** (strə vāg′), *v.i.,* **-vaged, -vag|ing.** = stravaig.

**stra|vaig** (strə vāg′), *v.i. Scottish and Northern English.* to wander about aimlessly; roam: *The squadron leader said ... "I don't want you lot stravaiging around the town"* (Listener). [< probably alteration of Medieval Latin *extravagari* wander outside limits; see etym. under **extravagant**]

**Stra|vin|ski|an** (strə vin′skē ən), *adj., n.* —*adj.* of or having to do with the Russian-born American composer Igor Stravinsky (1882-1971) or his musical style and works: ... *Stravinskian cacophony* (New Yorker).
—*n.* a follower of Igor Stravinsky or his works.

**straw** (strô), *n., adj.* —*n.* **1** the stalks or stems of grain after drying and threshing. Straw is used for bedding for horses and cows, for making hats, and for many other purposes. **2** one such stem or stalk. Straws are hollow. **3** a tube. Straws made of waxed paper, plastic, or glass are used for sucking up drinks. **4** *Figurative.* **a** a bit; trifle: *He doesn't care a straw.* **b** a minor thing that indicates how something else may turn out: *Already there are a few straws which the Republican National Committee is eying hopefully* (Harper's). **5** *Informal.* a straw hat: *I've already talked about her glorious flower-laden straws* (New Yorker).
—*adj.* **1** made of straw: *a straw hat.* **2** of the color of straw; pale-yellow; straw-colored: *a straw coat.* **3** *Figurative.* of little value or consequence; worthless: *a straw bid.* **4** of or having to do with an unofficial or informal collecting of votes: *If the straw ballots are accurate, the Conservative candidate may draw as many as 400,000 votes* (New York Times).
**grasp** (or **clutch,** or **catch**) **at straws** (or **at a straw**), to try anything in desperation: *Girls desperate for friendship and kindness ... tend to clutch at straws* (Manchester Guardian Weekly). *A drowning man will catch at a straw, the prov-*

**Pronunciation Key:** hat, āge, cãre, fär; let, ēqual, tėrm; it, īce; hot, ōpen, ôrder; **oil, out;** cup, pu̇t, rüle; **ch**ild; lo**ng**; **th**in; **ᴛʜ**en; **zh,** measure; ə represents **a** in about, **e** in taken, **i** in pencil, **o** in lemon, **u** in circus.

*erb says* (Samuel Richardson).
**straw in the wind**, something taken as an indication of a trend: *A more specific election straw in the wind can be found in yesterday's heavy buying of steel shares* (Wall Street Journal).
[Old English *strēaw*. Probably related to **strew**.] —**straw′like′**, *adj.*

**straw bail**, bail furnished by a person not possessing the property he pretends to have.

**straw bass**, = largemouth bass.

**straw|ber|ry** (strô′ber′ē, -bər-), *n., pl.* **-ries**. **1** a small, juicy, red fruit that is good to eat. It has many tiny, yellow seeds on the skin. **2** the low plant that it grows on. The varieties of strawberry comprise a genus of the rose family.

**strawberry bass**, = calico bass.

**strawberry blite**, a low, weedy plant of the goosefoot family with globular clusters of flowers and bright-red fruit.

**strawberry blonde** or **blond**, a person, especially a girl or woman, with reddish blonde hair.

**strawberry bush**, **1** a low, upright or straggling North American shrub of the staff-tree family with crimson fruit and seeds with scarlet coverings. **2** = wahoo[1].

**strawberry finch**, = amadavat.

**strawberry guava**, **1** a species of guava growing in Brazil and yielding a dark-red fruit. **2** the fruit.

**strawberry leaf**, the trifoliate leaflike ornament on the coronet of a duke, marquis, or earl, commonly taken as the symbol of the rank involved.

**strawberry mark**, a soft, reddish birthmark slightly raised above the skin.

**strawberry shrub**, *U.S.* any one of various shrubs having brownish or purplish-red flowers with a fragrance like that of strawberries.

**strawberry tomato**, **1** the small, edible, yellowish or greenish fruit of a ground cherry that looks like a tomato. **2** the plant it grows on.

**strawberry tree**, a low evergreen tree of the heath family having a bright-scarlet fruit resembling a strawberry, cultivated for ornament.

**straw|board** (strô′bôrd′, -bōrd′), *n.* a coarse, yellowish cardboard made of straw pulp, used for boxes and packing.

**straw boss**, *U.S. Informal.* an assistant foreman.

**straw cloth**, cloth of natural or synthetic straw, used especially for hats and handbags.

**straw color**, the color of straw; pale yellow.

**straw-col|ored** (strô′kul′ərd), *adj.* of a straw color; pale-yellow: *straw-colored hair.*

**straw|flow|er** (strô′flou′ər), *n.* any one of various flowers that keep their shape and color when dry, especially a tall annual herb of the composite family, having yellow, orange, red, or white flowers.

**straw-hat** (strô′hat′), *adj. U.S.* of or having to do with plays, concerts, or the like, performed during the summer in suburban or country areas: *a straw-hat theater. The show tried out with some success on the straw-hat circuits this summer* (Time). [< *straw hat* (because they are worn in the summer)]

**straw man**, **1** an imaginary opponent or opposing argument, put up in order to be defeated or refuted; man of straw. **2** a person put up as a surety in a fraudulent action: *The usual procedure ... is for straw men to set up the Corporation and then resign to turn it over to its directors* (Wall Street Journal). **3** = puppet (def. 1b).

**straw poll**, an unofficial poll taken to estimate the amount of support for or strength of opposing candidates or opinions on various issues: *A straw poll shows him leading other contenders for the nomination* (Time).

**straw ride**, *U.S.* a hayride.

**straw|stack** (strô′stak′), *n.* a large, outdoor pile of straw.

**straw vote**, an unofficial vote taken to find out general opinion or to estimate the strength of opposing candidates: *The continued strength of the Labor party is suggested by straw votes* (New York Times).

**straw wine**, wine made from grapes dried or partly dried in the sun on straw, usually sweet and rich.

**straw|worm** (strô′wėrm′), *n.* **1** the larva of certain chalcid flies, that attacks grain stalks. **2** = caddis worm.

**straw|y** (strô′ē), *adj.* **1** of, containing, or like straw. **2** strewn or thatched with straw.

**straw|yard** (strô′yärd′), *n.* **1** a yard littered with straw, in which horses and cattle are wintered. **2** *Informal.* a man's straw hat.

**stray** (strā), *v., adj., n.* —*v.i.* **1** to lose one's way; wander; roam: *straying about in a strange city. Our dog has strayed off somewhere.* **SYN**: rove, straggle. See syn. under **wander**. **2** *Figurative.* to turn from the right course; go wrong: *We have erred and strayed from thy ways like lost sheep* (Book of Common Prayer). *Most of us have ... a readiness to stray far, ever so far, on the wrong road* (Joseph Conrad). **SYN**: deviate, err. **3** *Figurative.* to wander, as in mind or purpose; digress: *I am straying from the question* (Oliver Goldsmith).
—*adj.* **1** wandering; lost: *A stray cat is crying at the door.* **2** here and there; scattered: *a stray customer or two, stray thoughts. There were a few stray fishermen's huts along the beach.* **3** separated from the rest; isolated: *a stray copy of a book.*
—*n.* **1** an animal that has wandered away from its flock, home, or owner; lost animal; wanderer: *That cat is a stray that we took in.* **2** any homeless or friendless person or animal. **3** something that has wandered from its usual or proper place.
**strays**, *Electronics.* static: *Thomas Edison ... says, "Marvellous! marvellous! but let us not forget that there are such things as electric strays"* (Westminster Gazette).
[short for Old French *estraier*, (originally) adjective < Vulgar Latin *strātārius* roaming the streets < Late Latin *strāta*, for Latin (*via*) *strāta* paved (street). Compare etym. under **estray**.] —**stray′er**, *n.*

**streak** (strēk), *n., v.* —*n.* **1** a long, thin mark or line: *He has a streak of dirt on his face. We saw streaks of lightning. She gets up at the first streak of daylight. A window, through which the first streaks of light could be seen* (Time). **2a** a layer: *Bacon has streaks of fat and streaks of lean.* **b** a stratum or vein of ore. **3** *Figurative.* a vein; strain; element: *He has a streak of humor though he looks very serious.* **SYN**: trace, touch. **4** *Informal, Figurative.* a brief period; spell: *a streak of luck.* **5** *Mineralogy.* the line of colored powder produced by scratching a mineral or rubbing it on a harder surface, forming an important distinguishing character. Hematite has a red streak, magnetite a black streak. **6** *Bacteriology.* the distribution of material to be inoculated over the surface of a medium in a line or stripe. **7** a flash of lightning: *A dazzling streak lit up the sky.* **8** an act or instance of streaking.
—*v.t.* to put long, thin marks or lines on: *The Indians used to streak their faces with paint. She usually streaks her brown hair with a blond color.*
—*v.i.* **1** to become streaked or streaky. **2** *Informal.* to move very fast; go at full speed: *Our man streaked past the others and over the finishing line.* **3** to dash naked through a public area, especially as a fad.
**like a streak**, *Informal.* very fast; at full speed: *The dog ran like a streak across the lawn.*
[Middle English *streke*, Old English *strica*]

**streak camera**, a high-speed camera for photographing rapidly moving objects, such as a bird or a bullet in flight: *The best streak cameras ... attained time resolutions of around 40 picoseconds* (New Scientist).

**streak color**, the typical color of a mineral's streak. The streak color of pyrite, a yellow mineral, is black.

**streaked** (strēkt), *adj.* **1** marked or diversified with streaks; streaky. **SYN**: striated. **2** *U.S. Dialect.* perturbed; uneasy; alarmed.

**streak|er** (strē′kər), *n.* a person who engages in streaking.

**streak|ing** (strē′king), *n.* the practice of running or riding naked through a public area, especially as a fad.

**streak photography**, the photographing of rapidly moving objects; photography by means of a streak camera.

**streak plate**, a piece of unglazed porcelain on which to rub or scratch a mineral in testing the streak.

**streak|y** (strē′kē), *adj.,* **streak|i|er**, **streak|i|est**. **1** marked with streaks; streaked: *an old man with a streaky gray chin-beard* (Booth Tarkington). **2** occurring in streaks. **3** *Figurative.* varying; uneven: *The dress has faded so much that the color is streaky.* —**streak′i|ly**, *adv.* —**streak′i|ness**, *n.*

**stream** (strēm), *n., v.* —*n.* **1** a flow of water in a channel or bed. Small rivers and large brooks are both called streams. **2** a steady current of water, as in a river or in the ocean. **3a** any current or flow: *a stream of blood pouring from a wound, a stream of tears, a stream of air, gas, or electricity.* **b** a ray or beam: *a stream of light.* **4** *Figurative.* a steady or continuous flow: *a stream of shoppers, a stream of cars, a stream of words.* **5** *Figurative.* trend; drift; course: *the prevailing stream of opinion.* **6** *British.* any of several classes of a secondary school into which students of the same grade are divided on the basis of ability or aptitude; track: *Opponents of streaming have for a long time said that middle-class children get put in the top streams because they have learnt at home to use words precisely* (Manchester Guardian Weekly).
—*v.i.* **1** to flow: *Tears streamed from her eyes.* **SYN**: See syn. under **flow**. **2** *Figurative.* **a** to move steadily in large numbers: *People streamed out of the theater.* **b** to move swiftly; streak: *A meteor streamed across the sky.* **3** to be so wet as to drip in a stream; run; drip; overflow: *a streaming umbrella, eyes streaming with tears, a face streaming with perspiration.* **4** to float or wave: *Flags streamed in the wind.* **5** to hang loosely and waving: *streaming hair.* **6** to extend in straight lines: *The sunshine streamed across the room.* **7** to be carried or given off in a stream or trail: *dust streaming out behind the car.*
—*v.t.* **1** to cause to flow; pour out: *to stream water on a fire. The gash in his arm streamed blood.* **2** to cause to stream. **3** *British.* to divide (students) into separate classes according to level of ability or aptitude: *Most of the schools streamed pupils into A, B, C, or D classes* (London Times).
**on stream**, in full production: *Part of the new plant is now in operation ... and the remainder will be on stream later this month* (Wall Street Journal).
[Old English *strēam*] —**stream′like′**, *adj.*
—*Syn. n.* **1, 2 Stream, current** mean a flow of water. **Stream** emphasizes a continuous flow, as of water in a river or from a spring or faucet: *Because of the lack of rain many streams dried up.* **Current** emphasizes a strong or rapid, onward movement in a certain direction, and applies particularly to the more swiftly moving part of a stream, ocean, or body of air: *We let the boat drift with the current.*

**stream|er** (strē′mər), *n.* **1** any long, narrow, flowing thing: *Streamers of ribbon hung from her hat. We saw streamers of snow blowing around the hilltop.* **2** a long, narrow, pointed flag or pennon. **SYN**: pennant. **3** a newspaper headline that runs all the way across a page. **4** a ribbonlike column of light shooting across the heavens in the aurora borealis.

**streamer chamber**, a large type of bubble chamber in which the tracks of the charged particles appear as streams of sparks.

**streamer fly**, any of various large artificial fishing flies with long wings extending past the hook, made to imitate a minnow.

**stream|flow** (strēm′flō′), *n.* the volume of water flowing in a stream at a given time.

**stream|ing** (strē′ming), *n.* **1** *Biology.* the flowing motion or rotation of protoplasm in a cell. **2** *British.* the division of students of a school into separate classes according to level of ability or aptitude, as determined by examinations; tracking: *There is far too little research evidence on the effects of streaming and other forms of in-school organization* (New Scientist).

**stream|let** (strēm′lit), *n.* a small stream; rivulet. **SYN**: creek, brook.

**stream|line** (strēm′līn′), *adj., v.,* **-lined, -lin|ing**, *n.* —*adj.* **1** = streamlined. **2** of or having to do with a motion or flow that is free from disturbance, as of a particle in a steadily flowing mass of fluid.
—*v.t.* **1** to give a streamlined shape to: *to streamline a racing car.* **2** *Figurative.* to bring up to date; make more efficient: *to streamline train service between Chicago and New York, to streamline an office.*
—*n.* **1** a streamlined shape. **2** *Physics.* the path of a particle in a steadily flowing mass of fluid.

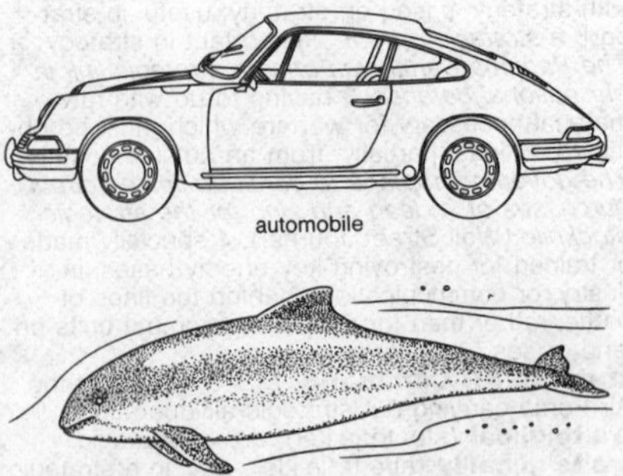

*** streamlined**
definition 1

*** stream|lined** (strēm′līnd′), *adj.* **1** having a shape or body that offers the least possible resistance to air or water. The fastest automobiles, airplanes, and trains have streamlined bodies. **2** *Figurative.* brought up to date; made more efficient: *streamlined methods of production, a streamlined organization.*

**streamline flow**, a steady flow of a fluid past a body, in which the fluid remains smooth and relatively unchanged.

**stream|lin|er** (strēm′lī′nər), *n.* a streamlined railroad train or other vehicle: *Light-weight, low-slung streamliners whisk you from city to city in* record time (Wall Street Journal).

**stream of consciousness**, the freely flowing thoughts and associations of any one of the characters in a story.

**stream-of-con|scious|ness** (strēm′əv kon′shəs nis), *adj.* of or having to do with a method of storytelling in which the author tells the story through the freely flowing thoughts and associations of one of the characters.

**stream|side** (strēm′sīd′), *n., adj.* —*n.* the margin or bank of a stream.
—*adj.* beside a stream; on the bank of a stream: *streamside trees.*

**stream table**, a tray for sand, earth, and water, used to study streamflow and other geological processes.

**stream|way** (strēm′wā′), *n.* **1** the shallow bed of a stream; watercourse. **2** the main current of a river.

**stream|y** (strē′mē), *adj.*, **stream|i|er, stream|i|est.** **1** full of streams or watercourses. **2** flowing in a stream; streaming.

**streek** (strēk), *v., n. Scottish.* —*v.t.* **1** to stretch. **2** to lay out (a corpse).
—*v.i.* to stretch.
—*n.* extent.
[variant of Middle English *strecchen,* Old English *streccan* stretch]

**street** (strēt), *n., adj.* —*n.* **1** a public road in a city or town, usually with buildings on both sides, and including the sidewalks or paths as well as the roadway. A street is maintained by the city or town, a highway by the county or state. *Abbr:* St. **2** a place or way for automobiles, wagons, or other vehicles to go: *Be careful in crossing the street.* **3** the people who live in the buildings on a street: *The whole street welcomed him home.*
—*adj.* **1** of a street: *a street corner, a street cleaner.* **2** in a street or streets: *a street scene, a street gang, street fighting, street games.* **3** level with the street: *the department store's street floor.* **4** for use on the street: *to change into street clothes.* **5** showing the location of streets: *a street guide, a street map.* **6** = streetwalking: *street women.*

**be streets ahead**, *Especially British.* to be far ahead in a contest; be far superior: *When it came to pure boxing ability, Winstone was streets ahead* (London Times).

**by a street**, *British.* by a large margin: *to win by a street. Instead of beating Chelsea by a street, they went home ... only with a draw* (Sunday Times).

**on easy street**, *Informal.* in comfortable circumstances; financially secure or independent: *He tried one scheme after another, looking for the quickest way to get on easy street.*

**out on the street**, without a home or a job: *They worked hard ... and now they have maybe a wife and a child, and they are out on the street and naturally they feel cheated* (Harper's).

**take to the streets**, to make a public demonstration: *The small shopkeeper ... finds the bill intolerably heavy and is now taking to the streets to protest against it* (London Times).

**the Street**, *Informal.* Wall Street: *"They still know me in the Street," he added* (New Yorker).

**up one's street**, *Especially British Informal.* suited to one's interests or abilities; pleasing for one; up one's alley: *I have never found his films very much up my street* (Punch).

[Old English *strēt, strǣt* < Late Latin *strāta,* for Latin (*via*) *strāta* paved (road), feminine past participle of *sternere* lay out] —**street′like′**, *adj.*

**street Arab**, a homeless child who wanders about the streets and lives by his wits, as by begging or stealing. **SYN:** waif.

**street|car** (strēt′kär′), *n.* a car that runs on rails in the streets and carries passengers; trolley car.

**street Christian**, *U.S.* one of the Jesus People: *Street Christians ... are the latest incarnation of that oldest of Christian phenomena: footloose, passionate bearers of the Word* (Time).

**street club**, *U.S.* a juvenile gang in a city block or district, especially one assigned to a street-worker. —**street′-club′**, *adj.*

**street|ed** (strē′tid), *adj.* having streets.

**street|ful** (strēt′fu̇l), *n., pl.* **-fuls.** as much or as many as a street will hold.

**street furniture**, the fixtures of streets: *The Department of Transportation commissioned a study for coordinating "street furniture"—lampposts, trash bins, street signs, telephone booths—in U.S. cities* (Philip M. Hauser).

**street lamp**, a lamp that lights a street.

**street-length** (strēt′lengkth′, -length′), *adj.* of a length suitable for everyday wear on the street; not full-length: *street-length dresses.*

**street light**, = street lamp.

**street name**, *U.S.* the name of a broker or brokerage firm. A person usually buys stocks in a street name for convenience in the safekeeping, handling, and transfer of the stocks.

**street people**, people who have rejected traditional social values including homes, so that they are usually found congregating on streets, in parks, and other public places: *Then came the street people, ... the alienated societal dropouts of today* (New York Times). *Tens of thousands of the street people, or those seeking an alternative society, are expected* (London Times).

**street piano**, a small mechanical piano set on wheels and operated by turning a crank, formerly played in the streets for gratuities; hurdy-gurdy.

**street railway**, **1** a route or routes served by streetcars in a city or town. **2** a company owning or operating such a route or routes.

**street|scape** (strēt′skāp), *n.* **1** a view or appearance of a street: *Closer inspection reveals a streetscape of despair: low, glum buildings, boarded-up store fronts, infrequent parks, broken curbs* (Time). **2** a picture of a street.

**street|side** (strēt′sīd′), *n., adj.* —*n.* the side of a street: *Along the streetside were the remains of a narrow building* (John Ward).
—*adj.* beside a street: *Carpenters hammered together streetside reviewing stands for his big show* (Time).

**street theater**, **1** a theater performance on the street. **2** = guerrilla theater.

**street value**, the cost of a product in illegal trafficking or on the black market: *the street value of heroin, the street value of bootleg cigarettes.*

**street virus**, a virus directly isolated from a rabid animal: *Street virus is not entirely restricted to nervous tissues and is found particularly in the salivary glands of rabid animals* (Science Journal). [translation of French *virus des rues;* so called to distinguish it from the laboratory strains of virus, the two strains showing different incubative and other characteristics]

**street|walk|er** (strēt′wô′kər), *n.* a prostitute who frequents the streets or other public places in search of customers.

**street|walk|ing** (strēt′wô′king), *n., adj.* —*n.* the work or activities of a streetwalker.
—*adj.* of or like a streetwalker.

**street|ward** (strēt′wərd), *adv., adj.* near or toward the street; looking out on the street.

**street|wear** (strēt′wãr′), *n.* clothes designed for everyday wear on the street.

**street|wise** (strēt′wīz′), *adj. U.S.* familiar with local people and their problems; wise to the ways and needs of people on the street: *No mayor can function effectively unless he has around him competent and streetwise people who can assume much of his responsibility* (New York Times Magazine).

**street|work|er** (strēt′wėr′kər), *n. U.S. and Canada.* a social worker who befriends and tries to help troubled or delinquent youngsters of a neighborhood: *The streetworker has become so friendly with them that he can sometimes return stolen goods before the police are even aware of the theft* (Maclean's).

**stre|ga** (strā′gä), *n.* a yellow Italian liqueur with a sweet, perfumed taste. [< *Strega,* the trademark of the product]

**streng|ite** (streng′īt), *n.* a purplish or deep pink mineral, a hydrous phosphate of iron, occurring mainly in botryoidal form. *Formula:* $FePO_4 \cdot 2H_2O$ [< German *Strengit*]

**strength** (strengkth, strength), *n.* **1** the quality or condition of being strong; power; force; vigor: *Because of his strength he could lift heavy weights. The strength of a dog's love for his master is well known. A nation's strength does not lie in material things alone; a rich nation can also be a decaying one* (Newsweek). **SYN:** See syn. under **power.** **2** mental or moral power: *strength of memory or of judgment. The queen had great strength of character. He did not have enough strength of mind to refuse.* **3** power to resist or endure; toughness: *the strength of a fort, the strength of a rope.* **4** military force measured in numbers, as of soldiers or warships: *an army or fleet at full strength.* **5** power derived from authority, the law, influence, the possession of resources, or the like: *the strength of public opinion, the strength of a leader.* **6** power or capacity for producing effects; cogency or potency; weight: *the strength of words, arguments, or evidence.* **7** degree of strength; intensity: *the strength of a wind, stream, or current of electricity, the strength of a color, sound or light. Take this cough medicine at full strength. Some flavorings lose their strength in cooking.* **8** something that makes strong; support: *God is our refuge and strength* (Psalms 46:1). **9** the existence of a firm or rising level of stock or commodity prices on an exchange: *Strength in the railroads highlighted last week's stock market* (Wall Street Journal). **10** energy or vigor of literary or artistic conception or treatment.

**by main strength**, by using full strength: *It was only by main strength that he was able to raise the cart and save the man trapped beneath its wheels.*

**go from strength to strength**, to have increasing or continued success: *She has gone from strength to strength, pushing through two notable reforms* (Sunday Times).

**on the strength of**, relying or depending on; with the support or help of: *Father bought the dog on the strength of my promise to take care of it. He read the book on the strength of his teacher's recommendation.*

[Old English *strengthu* < *strang* strong]

**strength|en** (strengk′thən, streng′-), *v.t.* to make stronger: *The soldiers strengthened their defenses.* **SYN:** reinforce, fortify. —*v.i.* to grow stronger: *Steel prices strengthen as demand continues moving up* (Wall Street Journal).
—**strength′en|er**, *n.*

**strength|less** (strengkth′lis, strength′-), *adj.* lacking strength.

**stren|u|os|i|ty** (stren′yu̇ os′ə tē), *n., pl.* **-ties.** **1** the quality or condition of being strenuous. **2** a strained effect or a straining for effect.

**stren|u|ous** (stren′yu̇ əs), *adj.* **1** very active: *We had a strenuous day moving into our new house. I wish to preach, not the doctrine of ignoble ease, but the doctrine of the strenuous life* (Theodore Roosevelt). **SYN:** See syn. under **vigorous.** **2** full of energy: *Beavers are strenuous workers. The gym teacher is a strenuous man.* **SYN:** See syn. under **vigorous.** **3** requiring much energy: *Running is strenuous exercise.* [< Latin *strēnuus* (with English *-ous*)] —**stren′u|ous|ly**, *adv.* —**stren′u|ous|ness**, *n.*

**strep** (strep), *n. Informal.* streptococcus: *Special attention to "strep" infections is necessary to guard children against rheumatic fever* (Newsweek). [short for *streptococcus*]

**streph|o|sym|bo|li|a** (stref′ō sim bō′lē ə), *n.* **1** a reading difficulty in certain children characterized by confusion between similar letters, such as *b* and *d,* or *n* and *u.* **2** a visual disorder in which objects appear reversed, as in a mirror. [< New Latin *strephosymbolia* < Greek *stréphein* twist + *sýmbolon* symbol]

**strep|i|tant** (strep′ə tənt), *adj.* = strepitous.

**strep|i|to|so** (strep′ə tō′sō), *adv., adj. Music.*
—*adv.* in a noisy manner; accompanied with much noise.
—*adj.* noisy.
[< Italian *strepitoso* < *strepito* noise < Latin *strepitus, -ūs*]

**strep|i|tous** (strep′ə təs), *adj.* noisy: *a strepitous movement in a symphony.* [< Latin *strepitus, -ūs* noise, clatter (< *strepere* make a noise) + English *-ous*]

**strep|o|gen|in** (strep′ə jen′in), *n.* a peptide found in insulin and other proteins that is essential to the growth of mice and certain microorganisms. [< *strep* + *-gen* + *-in*]

**strep|sic|e|ros** (strep sis′ə rəs), *n.* any antelope of a group with twisted or spiral horns, including the kudu and the nyala. [< New Latin *Strepsiceros,* the genus name < Greek *strepsikerōs,* an animal with twisted horns]

**strep|sip|ter|an** (strep sip′tər ən), *adj., n.,* —*adj.* of or belonging to an order of tiny insects that are parasitic on bees, wasps, and crickets, and are characterized (in the male) by front wings reduced to twisted filaments and large, fan-shaped hind wings. The females are wingless.
—*n.* a strepsipteran insect, such as the stylops.
[< New Latin *Strepsiptera* the order name < Greek *strepsi-* (*stréphein* to twist) + *pterón* wing]

**strep throat**, septic sore throat.

**strepto-**, *combining form.* **1** twisted or linked; resembling chains: *Streptococcus = a group of bacteria that occur in chains.*
**2** streptococcus: *Streptokinase = an enzyme derived from streptococci.*
[< Greek *streptós* twisted; a chain or linked collar < *stréphein* to twist, turn]

**strep|to|ba|cil|lus** (strep′tə bə sil′əs), *n., pl.* **-cil|li** (-sil′ī). a bacillus that occurs as part of a chain of bacilli. One kind of streptobacillus causes an infection transmitted by the bite of a rat. [< *strepto-* + *bacillus*]

**strep|to|coc|cal** (strep′tə kok′əl), *adj.* having to do with or caused by streptococci.

**strep|to|coc|cic** (strep′tə kok′sik), *adj.* = streptococcal.

**strep|to|coc|cus** (strep′tə kok′əs), *n., pl.* **-coc|ci** (-kok′sī). any one of a group of spherical bacteria that multiply by dividing in only one direction, usually forming chains; strep. The streptococcus is a Gram-positive bacterium. The various kinds comprise a genus of bacteria. Many serious infections and diseases, such as scarlet fever, erysipelas, and septicemia, are caused by streptococci. [< New Latin *Streptococcus* the genus name < Greek *streptós* (see etym. under **strepto-**) + *kókkos* a grain, kernel; berry]

**strep|to|dor|nase** (strep′tō dôr′nās), *n.* an enzyme produced by certain bacteria, used in combination with, and having effects similar to, streptokinase. [< *streptod*(e)*o*(cy)*r*(ibo)*n*(ucle)*ase*]

**strep|to|ki|nase** (strep′tō kī nās′), *n.* a protein enzyme that loosens or dissolves blood clots, pus, and other waste matter associated with infections. It is derived from streptococcal bacteria.

**strep|to|ly|sin** (strep′tə lī′sin), *n.* any one of various hemolysins derived from streptococcal bacteria.

**strep|to|my|ces** (strep′tə mī′sēz), *n., pl.* **-ces.** any soil microbe of a group sometimes considered fungi, sometimes bacteria, which is the source of streptomycin and other antibiotics. [< New Latin *Streptomyces* the genus name < Greek *streptós* twisted + *mýkēs* fungus]

**strep|to|my|cin** (strep′tə mī′sin), *n.* a powerful antibiotic similar to penicillin, obtained from a kind of streptomyces. It is effective against tuberculosis, typhoid fever, tularemia, and certain other bacterial infections. *Formula:* $C_{21}H_{39}N_7O_{12}$

**strep|to|nig|rin** (strep′tō nig′rin), *n.* a very toxic, dark brown, crystalline antibiotic produced by a variety of streptomyces, and active against various forms of tumors. *Formula:* $C_{24}H_{20}N_4O_8$ [< *strepto-* + Latin *niger* black + English *-in*]

**strep|to|thri|cin** or **strep|to|thry|sin** (strep′tə-thrī′sin), *n.* an antibiotic obtained from a soil microorganism. It is similar to streptomycin in its action. [< New Latin *Streptothrix* the genus name of the fungus (< Greek *streptós;* see etym. under **strepto-**; + *thríx, trichós* a hair) + English *-in*]

**strep|to|va|ri|cin** (strep′tō və rī′sin), *n.* an antibiotic obtained from a kind of streptomyces, used against tuberculosis.

**stress** (stres), *n., v.* **—*n.*** **1** great pressure or force; strain: *the stress of poverty, war, or weather. Under the stress of hunger the man stole some food. Other animals have like tensions ... know the deadly effects of stress* (William O. Douglas). *My purpose was to teach students how to think under stress* (Time). **2** great effort. **3** *Figurative.* emphasis; importance: *More high schools today lay stress upon science and mathematics.* SYN: significance, weight. **4** *Physics.* **a** the internal forces interacting between contiguous parts of a body, caused by the external forces, such as tension or shear, which produce the strain. **b** the intensity of these forces, generally measured in pounds per square inch. **c** a force or system of forces causing strain. **5a** the greater or lesser force given to certain syllables or words; accent. In *hero,* the stress is on the first syllable. **b** a stressed syllable. **6** *Prosody.* **a** the relative loudness or prominence given a syllable or word in a metrical pattern. **b** any accented syllable in a foot. **7** *Music.* an accent.
**—*v.t.*** **1** to put pressure upon. **2** *Figurative.* to treat as important; emphasize: *Stress the important words of the sentence. The English curriculum should stress both composition and reading.* **3** to pronounce with stress: *"Accept" is stressed on the second syllable.*
[partly short for Middle English *destresse* distress, partly < Old French *estrece* narrowness, oppression, ultimately < Latin *strictus,* past participle of *stringere* draw tight]

**stressed-skin construction** (strest′skin′), a type of aircraft construction, such as monocoque, in which the skin bears all or part of the stresses arising in the aircraft.

**stress|ful** (stres′fəl), *adj.* full of stress; subject to strain: *to keep on doing one's job under stressful conditions.* — **stress′ful|ly,** *adv.* — **stress′ful-ness,** *n.*

**stress|less** (stres′lis), *adj.* **1** not under stress or strain: *a stressless life.* **2** unstressed: *Some languages—Hindi, Marathi, and Japanese—may be described as stressless* (Simeon Potter). — **stress′less|ness,** *n.*

**stress|or** (stres′ər), *n. Psychology.* any stimulus that produces stress or strain: *Experimental stressors, for obvious reasons, are very mild, the most usual being distracting or painful noises, electric shocks, the stress of examinations* (New Scientist).

**stress syndrome,** *Medicine.* a group of symptoms caused by overactivity of the pituitary and adrenal glands in response to psychological stress: *Hypertension, atherosclerosis, and adrenal deterioration are typical of the ... stress syndrome* (Scientific American).

**stretch** (strech), *v., n., adj.* **—*v.t.*** **1** to draw out; extend (oneself, body, limbs, wings, or the like) to full length: *The bird stretched its wings. He stretched himself out on the grass to rest.* **2** to extend so as to reach from one place to another or across a space: *Father stretched a clothesline from a tree to a pole.* **3** to reach (out); hold (out): *I stretched out my hand for the money.* **4** to draw out to greater size; lengthen or widen: *Please stretch this shoe a little until it fits.* **5** to draw tight; strain: *to stretch a muscle. He stretched the violin string until it broke.* **6** *Figurative.* to extend beyond proper or natural limits: *to stretch one's credit. They stretched the law to suit their own purpose.* **7** *Informal, Figurative.* to exaggerate: *to stretch the truth. There was things which he stretched, but mainly he told the truth* (Mark Twain). **8** *Dialect.* to straighten the limbs of (a dead person). **9** *Informal.* to hang (a person).
**—*v.i.*** **1** to extend one's body, or limbs at full length, as in lying down, yawning, or reaching: *She stretched out on the couch.* **2** to continue over a distance; fill space; spread: *The forest stretches for miles. The hours stretched by like years* (Alfred Noyes). **3** to extend one's hand; reach for something: *to stretch out to get a book.* **4** *Figurative.* to make great effort. **5** to become longer or wider without breaking: *Rubber stretches.* **6** *Informal, Figurative.* to go beyond the strict truth. **7** *Informal.* to be hanged.
**—*n.*** **1a** an unbroken length or extent: *A stretch of sand hills lay between the road and the ocean.* **b** an uninterrupted period: *to work for a stretch of five hours.* **2** *Slang.* **a** a term of imprisonment. **b** *British.* a year's term in prison. **3** *Figurative.* the act or fact of stretching or straining something beyond its proper limits: *a stretch of authority or of the law, no great stretch of the imagination.* **4a** the act of stretching or the condition of being stretched: *With a sudden stretch he took the cap off the tall boy's head.* **b** the act of stretching the legs; walk for exercise. **5** capacity for being stretched; extent to which something can be stretched: *The stretch of that bird's wings is two feet. She shouted the insult at the stretch of her voice.* **6** one of the two straight sides of a race course. The part between the first and second turns is called the backstretch; the part between the last turn and the finish line is called the home stretch. *Down the back stretch, Needles was still lost in the pack* (Time). **7** *Mining, Geology.* the course or direction of a seam or stratum. **8** the ability of an aircraft to be modified and improved in design, performance, or capacity after its original construction: *[It] is capable of considerable further stretch in power and efficiency, already claimed to equal or exceed that of other engines* (Wall Street Journal).
**—*adj.*** of a material that stretches easily to fit all sizes: *stretch gloves, stretch socks, stretch pants.*
**stretch a point.** See under **point.**
**stretch one's legs.** See under **leg.**
**the stretch,** = home stretch.
[spelling variant of Middle English *strecchen,* Old English *streccan.* Compare etym. under **streek.**]
— **stretch′a|ble,** *adj.*

**stretch|a|bil|i|ty** (strech′ə bil′ə tē), *n.* the ability to stretch or be stretched.

**stretched-out** (strecht′out′), *adj.* drawn out beyond the original size; extended; prolonged.

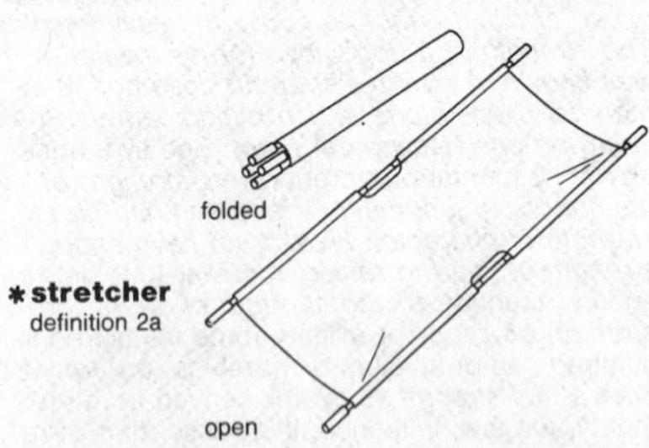

**∗stretcher**
definition 2a

**∗stretch|er** (strech′ər), *n.* **1** a person or thing that stretches: *A glove stretcher makes gloves larger.* **2a** canvas stretched on a frame for carrying the sick, wounded, or dead. SYN: litter. **b** a high bed or cot on wheels, that can be raised or lowered by means of collapsible legs, used for transporting patients to and from ambulances and in hospitals. **3a** a bar, beam, or rod used as a tie or brace, as between the legs of a chair. **b** a brick or stone laid with its length in the direction of the face of the wall. **4** a wooden frame on which an artist's canvas is spread and drawn tight, usually by means of tacks along the sides and small wedges in the angles. **5** *Informal.* an exaggerated tale; yarn: *... mostly a true book, with some stretchers* (Mark Twain).

**stretch|er-bear|er** (strech′ər bãr′ər), *n.* one of the persons who carry a stretcher, as in moving a sick, injured, or dead person.

**stretcher bond,** = running bond.

**stretch marks,** glistening white lines on the abdomen and thighs caused by stretching of the skin during pregnancy; striae gravidarum.

**stretch|out** (strech′out′), *n., adj.* **—*n.*** *Informal.* **1** a postponement, especially of the date for filling defense orders: *Such cuts might take the form of a stretchout of defense goals so that their cost might be distributed over a longer period* (New York Times). **2** a system in which factory or other workers are required to do additional work without overtime pay.
**—*adj.*** of or having to do with a stretchout.

**stretch receptor,** a sense organ that is sensitive to any stretching of the tissue in which it is found. The muscle spindle is a stretch receptor.

**stretch|y** (strech′ē), *adj.,* **stretch|i|er, stretch|i-est.** *Informal.* **1** elastic; stretchable. **2** liable to stretch too much.

**stretch yarn,** any synthetic yarn treated to give it elasticity.

**stret|ta** (stret′tä), *n., pl.* **-te** (-tā), **-tas.** *Music.* **1** a passage, especially a final passage, performed in quicker or accelerated time for climactic effect, a device often used in oratorio and opera. **2** stretto in a fugue or canon. [< Italian *stretta,* feminine of *stretto;* see etym. under **stretto**]

**stret|to** (stret′tō), *n., pl.* **-ti** (-tē), **-tos.** *Music.* **1a** (in a fugue or canon) an overlapping of subject and answer so as to produce a rapidly cumulative effect. **b** the third section of the fugue, after exposition and development, in which this device is often used. **c** a canon in which this device is used. **2** a final passage; stretta. [< Italian *stretto* close, narrow < Latin *strictus.* See etym. of doublets **strait, strict.**]

**streu|sel** (stroi′zəl, strü′-; *German* shtroi′zəl), *n.* a crumb topping for cake, usually made of flour, sugar, and nuts. [< German *Streusel* (literally) sprinkling]

**strew** (strü), *v.t.,* **strewed, strewed** or **strewn** (strün), **strew|ing. 1** to scatter or sprinkle: *She strewed seeds in her garden. The boy strewed his clothes all over the floor.* **2** to cover with something scattered or sprinkled: *In the fall the ground was strewn with leaves. Wild tornadoes strewing yonder sea with wrecks* (William Cowper). **3** to be scattered or sprinkled over: *Photographs strewed the low tables* (Edith Wharton). **4** *Figurative.* to spread about; disseminate: *All heaven bursts her starry floors, And strews her lights below* (Tennyson). *For so I have strewed it in the common ear* (Shakespeare). [Old English *strēowian.* Probably related to **straw.**]

**strew|ment** (strü′mənt), *n. Archaic.* something strewed, as flowers: *She is allow'd ... Her maiden strewments* (Shakespeare).

**strewn** (strün), *v.* strewed; a past participle of **strew.**

**stri|a** (strī′ə), *n., pl.* **stri|ae** (strī′ē). **1** a slight furrow or ridge; small groove or channel, as produced on a rock by moving ice, or on the surface of a crystal or mineral by its structure. **2** a linear marking; narrow stripe or streak, as of color or texture, especially one of a number in parallel arrangement. **3** *Architecture.* a fillet between the flutes of columns. [< Latin *stria* a facet or flute (of a column)]

**striae grav|i|da|rum** (grav′ə dãr′əm), *Medicine.* stretch marks. [< New Latin *striae gravidarum* (literally) stripes of pregnancy]

**stri|ate** (strī′āt), *v.,* **-at|ed, -at|ing,** *adj.* **—*v.t.*** to mark or score with striae; furrow; stripe; streak.
**—*adj.*** = striated.
[< Latin *striāre* (with English *-ate*[1]) to furrow, channel < *stria;* see etym. under **stria**]

**stri|at|ed** (strī′ā tid), *adj.* marked with striae; striped; streaked; furrowed: *striated rock.*

**∗striated muscle**

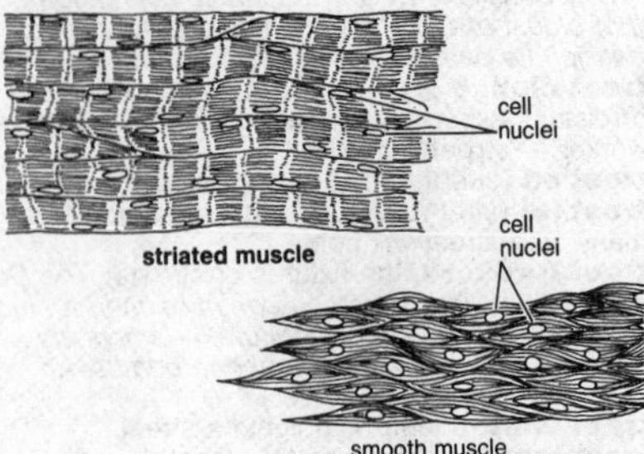


**∗striated muscle,** a type of muscle with fibers of cross bands usually contracted by voluntary action, such as the muscles that move the arms, legs, and neck; voluntary muscle.

**stri|a|tion** (strī ā′shən), *n.* **1** striated condition or appearance. **2** one of a number of parallel striae; stria.

**stri|a|ture** (strī′ə chər), *n.* **1** disposition of striae; striation. **2** = stria. [< Latin *striātūra* < *stria;* see etym. under **stria**]

**strick** (strik), *n.* **1** a bundle of broken hemp, flax, or jute, for hackling. **2** a bunch of silk fiber for the second combing. [apparently variant of *strike*]

**strick|en** (strik′ən), *adj., v.* — *adj.* **1** hit, wounded, or affected (by a weapon, disease, trouble, sorrow, disaster, or the like): *a stricken deer, a city stricken by fire, a sorrow-stricken face, a poverty-stricken family. The stricken man was taken immediately to a hospital.* **SYN**: afflicted. **2** filled level to the top or brim; full but not heaped up: *a stricken measure or container of grain.*
— *v.* struck; a past participle of **strike**.
**stricken in years,** old: *He was stricken in years long before his time.*

**strick|le** (strik′əl), *n., v.,* **-led, -ling.** — *n.* **1** a straight piece of wood used to level a measure of grain in a container. **2** a piece of wood covered with emery, used for whetting or sharpening scythes; rifle. **3** *Metallurgy.* **a** a straightedge used to level off sand in a flask. **b** a specially shaped piece used in sweeping patterns in sand or loam.
— *v.t.* to sweep off or level (as grain) with a strickle.
[Old English *stricel* wheel, pulley, related to *strīcan* to pass over a surface; strike]

**strict** (strikt), *adj.* **1** very careful in following a rule or in making others follow it: *Our teacher is strict but fair.* **2** harsh; severe; stern: *strict discipline, strict justice. Cinderella's stepmother was very strict with her.* **3** *Figurative.* exact; precise; accurate: *the strict meaning of a word. He told the strict truth. A strict construction of the Constitution is a literal interpretation of its words.*
**4** *Figurative.* complete; perfect; absolute: *strict neutrality. The secret was told in strict confidence.* **5** *Figurative.* careful or minute: *a strict method, a strict inquiry.* **6** *Botany.* close or narrow and upright: *a strict stem or inflorescence.*
**7** *Archaic.* tight; close. [< Latin *strictus,* past participle of *stringere* bind tight. See etym. of doublets **strait, stretto.**] — **strict′ly,** *adv.* — **strict′ness,** *n.*
— *Syn.* **1, 2 Strict, rigid, rigorous** mean severe and unyielding or harsh and stern. **Strict** emphasizes showing or demanding a very careful and close following of a rule, standard, or requirement: *Our teacher is strict and insists that we follow instructions to the letter.* **Rigid** emphasizes being firm and unyielding, not changing or relaxing for anyone or under any conditions: *He maintains a rigid working schedule.* **Rigorous** emphasizes the severity, harshness, or sternness of the demands made, conditions imposed, or the like: *We believe in rigorous enforcement of the laws.*

**stric|tion** (strik′shən), *n.* a drawing tight; constriction. [< Latin *strictiō, -ōnis* < *strictus;* see etym. under **strict**]

**stric|ture** (strik′chər), *n.* **1** an unfavorable criticism; critical remark: *We may now and then add a few strictures of reproof* (Samuel Johnson).
**2** an unhealthy narrowing of some canal, duct, or tube of the body, as of the urethra, esophagus, or intestine. **3** a binding or tightening; binding restriction; constriction: *A windless stricture of frost had bound the air* (Robert Louis Stevenson). *They are heterodox Moslems, accepting the Prophet's precepts but rejecting some of his strictures, e.g., their women go unveiled* (Time).
**4** *Obsolete.* strictness: *A man of stricture and firm abstinence* (Shakespeare). [< Latin *strictūra* < *strictus;* see etym. under **strict**]

**stride** (strīd), *v.,* **strode** or (*Obsolete*) **strid** (strid), **strid|den** (strid′ən) or (*Obsolete*) **strid, strid|ing,** *n.* — *v.i.* **1** to walk with long steps: *The tall man strides rapidly down the street.* **SYN**: See syn. under **walk**. **2** to take a long step; pass (over or across) with a long step: *He strode over the brook.*
— *v.t.* **1** to walk with long steps: *to stride the streets. He strode the halls of the building, looking for the exit.* **2** to go over or across with one long step: *to stride a brook.* **3** to sit or stand with one leg on each side of; straddle; bestride: *to stride a fence.*
— *n.* **1** a striding; long step: *The child could not keep up with his father's stride.* **2** the progressive movement of a horse or certain other animals, completed when all the feet are returned to the same position as at the beginning. **3** the distance covered by a stride.
**hit one's stride,** to reach one's regular speed or normal activity: *At first the comedian's monologue fell flat, but after a few minutes he hit his stride.*
**make great** (or **rapid**) **strides,** to make great progress; advance rapidly: *The Corporation ... is making great strides in bringing ample power, irrigation, and agricultural extension services to the land-rich Cauca Valley* (Atlantic).
**take in** (**one's**) **stride,** to deal with in one's normal activity; do or take without difficulty, hesitation, or special effort: *I'd want something that would look more easy and natural, more as if I took it in stride* (Edith Wharton).
[Old English *strīdan*] — **strid′er,** *n.*

**stri|dence** (strī′dəns), *n.* the quality of being strident.

**stri|den|cy** (strī′dən sē), *n.* = stridence.

**stri|dent** (strī′dənt), *adj.* **1** making or having a harsh sound; creaking; grating; shrill: *The strident voice sounded harsher than ever* (Mrs. Humphry Ward). *The details make pretty strident reading* (Atlantic). **SYN**: piercing. **2** having a harsh voice; rasping; shrill: *a strident person.* [< Latin *strīdēns, -entis,* present participle of *strīdere* sound harshly, screech] — **stri′dent|ly,** *adv.*

**stride piano,** *Jazz Slang.* ragtime piano playing consisting of single notes on the first and third beats of the bar and chords on the second and fourth beats. — **stride pianist.**

**stri|dor** (strī′dər), *n.* **1** a harsh, shrill sound; strident noise. **2** *Medicine.* a harsh respiratory sound, caused by obstruction of the air passages.
[< Latin *strīdor, -ōris* < *strīdere* to creak, screech, sound harshly]

**strid|u|lant** (strij′ə lənt), *adj.* stridulating.

**strid|u|late** (strij′ə lāt), *v.i.,* **-lat|ed, -lat|ing.** **1** to make a shrill, grating sound, as a cricket or katydid does, by rubbing together certain parts of the body. **2** to shrill; chirr. [< New Latin *stridulare* (with English *-ate*[1]) < Latin *strīdulus;* see etym. under **stridulous**]

**strid|u|la|tion** (strij′ə lā′shən), *n.* the act or sound of stridulating.

**strid|u|la|to|ry** (strij′ə lə tôr′ē, -tōr′-), *adj.* having to do with stridulation; stridulating.

**strid|u|lous** (strij′ə ləs), *adj.* **1** making a harsh or grating sound; strident: *She ... closed her eyes in halcyon tranquillity, enjoying everything—even the stridulous cries of the gulls, even the windless heat* (New Yorker). **2** *Medicine.* of, having to do with, or characterized by stridor. [< Latin *strīdulus* (with English *-ous*) < *strīdere* creak, sound harshly] — **strid′u|lous|ly,** *adv.* — **strid′u|lous|ness,** *n.*

**stri|é** (strē ā′), *adj. French.* striated: *strié silks, strié velvets.*

**strife** (strīf), *n.* **1** the act of quarreling; fighting: *bitter strife between rivals.* **SYN**: conflict, contention. **2** a quarrel; fight: *to find out the cause of a strife.* **SYN**: struggle, dispute. **3** *Archaic.* rivalry; competition; emulation: *I strove with none, for none was worth my strife* (Walter S. Landor).
**4** *Archaic.* a strong effort; endeavor. [< Old French *estrif* < a Germanic word, related to *estriver* strive] — **strife′less,** *adj.*

**strig|il** (strij′əl), *n.* **1** a scraper for the skin, used after a bath or gymnastic exercise by the ancient Greeks and Romans. **2** one of a set of curved flutings or reedings, used in Roman architecture. **3** a brushlike part on the legs or abdomen of certain insects, such as the bee. [< Latin *strigilis,* related to *stringere* strip off, scrape; draw tight, bind]

**strig|i|la|tion** (strij′ə lā′shən), *n.* vigorous friction with a strigil or the like.

**stri|gose** (strī′gōs, stri gōs′), *adj.* **1** *Botany.* covered with stiff and straight bristles or hairs; hispid. **2** *Zoology.* marked with fine, closely set ridges, grooves, or points. [< New Latin *strigosus* < *striga* stiff bristle < Latin, row of grain cut down, swath, stubble, related to *stringere;* see etym. under **strigil**]

**strike** (strīk), *v.,* **struck, struck** or **strick|en,** or (*Obsolete*) **strook** or **struck|en, strik|ing,** *n.*
— *v.t.* **1** to deal a blow to; hit: *He struck his enemy in anger. The ship struck a rock. The car struck a fence. Lightning struck the barn.* **SYN**: smite, beat, buffet, slap. **2** to wound with fangs or sting: *The snake struck the man's hand.* **3** to deal out or forth; give: *He struck a blow in self-defense.* **4** to cause to hit; dash; knock: *The child struck her head against the crib. He struck his fist against the table and called for order.*
**5** to make as by stamping or printing: *They will strike a medal in memory of the great victory.*
**6** to set on fire by hitting or rubbing: *to strike a spark, to strike a light, to strike a match.* **7** *Figurative.* to have a strong effect on the mind or feelings of; impress: *The plan strikes me as silly. That play strikes my fancy.* **8** to sound: *This clock strikes the hour and the half hour.* **9a** to overcome by death, disease, or suffering: *The town was struck with a flu epidemic.* **b** to attack: *The enemy struck the town at dawn.* **c** *Figurative: They were struck with terror.* **10** *Figurative.* to occur to: *An amusing thought struck her.* **11** to come upon, sometimes suddenly; find: *to strike water, to strike oil. After years of prospecting the old man finally struck gold. We shall strike the main road soon.* **12** to cross; rub; cancel; expunge: *Strike his name from the list.* **13** to take away by a blow: *Strike the weapon from his hand.* **14** *Figurative.* to assume: *He struck an attitude of friendliness.* **15** to send (a root) down or out: *The cuttings have struck roots.* **16a** to get by figuring: *to strike an average.* **b** to balance: *to strike a ledger.* **17** *Figurative.* to enter upon; make; decide: *to strike a bargain, to strike a compromise. The employer and the workmen have struck an agreement.* **18a** to lower (as a flag or sail) in a salute or sign of surrender: *The ship struck her flag.* **b** to lower (an object) into a ship's hold with a rope and tackle. **19** to remove the tents of; break (camp): *to strike camp in the morning.* **20a** to remove (a scene) from the stage: *Strike the set.* **b** to remove the scenery of (a play). **21a** to make level with the top edge of a measure: *to strike grain.* **b** to level with a strickle: *to strike up sand.* **22** to cause to enter; penetrate: *The wind struck a chill into her bones.* **23** *Figurative.* to fall on; touch; reach; catch: *The sun struck her eyes. A whistle struck his ear. The waving palm trees struck my view.* **24** to go on strike against (an employer): *The pilots struck the country's major international airline* (New York Times). **25a** to harpoon (a whale). **b** to hook (a fish) by pulling or jerking the line. **26** to alter one's pace into (a faster movement): *The horses struck a canter.* **27** to leave off (work) at the close of the day or at meal times. **28** *Dialect.* to stroke; smooth: *to strike one's beard.* **29** *Informal.* to make a sudden and pressing demand upon: *to strike a friend for a loan.* **30** *Obsolete.* to fight (a battle).
— *v.i.* **1** to deal or aim a blow: *to strike at a person with a whip.* **2** to tap, rap, or knock: *He struck upon the window.* **3** to wound, or try to wound, prey with the fangs or sting: *The snake struck at my hand.* **4** to attack: *The enemy will strike at dawn.* **5** to use one's weapons; fight: *to strike for freedom.* **6** to be set on fire by hitting or rubbing: *The match wouldn't strike.* **7** to sound with blows; sound: *The clock struck twelve times at noon.* **8** to stop work to get better pay or shorter hours, or to force an employer to meet some other demand: *The coal miners struck when the company refused to improve safety conditions in the mine.* **9** to go; advance: *to strike into a gallop. We walked along the road a mile, then struck across the fields.* **SYN**: proceed. **10** to make a stroke with one's arms or legs in swimming or with one's oar in rowing. **11** to send roots or take root: *The roots of oats strike deep.* **12** to seize the bait and the hook: *The fish are striking well today.* **13** to collide: *The car struck against a wall. The ship struck against a reef.* **14** to fall; catch: *The sunlight struck on his face. A sound struck on his ear.* **15** *Figurative.* to make an impression on the mind or senses. **16** to move quickly; dart; shoot. **17** to come; light: *to strike upon a new book.* **18a** to lower a flag, or colors, as a signal of surrender or to honor or salute a dignitary. **b** to raise a white flag in surrendering.
— *n.* **1a** the act or fact of finding rich ore in mining or oil in boring: *He made a rich strike in the Yukon. Drilling crews recently have hit at least ... seven strikes in the same vicinity* (Wall Street Journal). **b** *Figurative.* a sudden success: *He made a strike with his first play.* **2a** the act of stopping work in order to get better pay or shorter hours, or to force an employer to meet some other demand: *The workers were home for six weeks during the strike last year.* **b** any stoppage of normal activity to protest some action or condition: *a rent strike, a student's strike.* **3** the action of striking. **4** *Baseball.* the failure of a batter to swing at a pitched ball in the strike zone, to hit a pitched ball at which he swings, or to hit a pitched ball into fair territory under the rules of the game. After two strikes, a batter may hit any number of foul balls, provided they are not caught by any fielder. After three strikes, the batter is out. **5** in bowling: **a** an upsetting of all the pins with the first ball bowled: *Some proprietors offer baby sitters while mother seeks a strike or a spare on the alley* (Wall Street Journal). **b** the score so made. **6** the action of a taking hold of the bait and the hook: *He got a strike at his first cast in the lake.* **7** *Mining, Geology.* the linear course or direction of a stratum, vein, or other feature or structure of rock; direction with regard to the points of the compass. The strike of a vein is perpendicular to the direction of the dip. **8** an attack upon a target: *The bombardiers reported clearing weather and "good to excellent" results in both strikes* (New York Times). **9** the number of coins minted at one time. **10** a metal piece in

**Pronunciation Key:** hat, āge, cãre, fär; let, ēqual, tėrm; it, īce; hot, ōpen, ôrder; **oi**l, **ou**t; cup, pu̇t, rüle; **ch**ild; lo**ng**; **th**in; **ᴛʜ**en; **zh**, measure; **ə** represents **a** in about, **e** in taken, **i** in pencil, **o** in lemon, **u** in circus.

a doorjamb, into which the latch of a lock fits when the door closes. **11** a strickle for leveling a measure, as of grain or salt. **12** *Obsolete.* **a** the degree of strength of ale or beer. **b** the unit proportion of malt in ale or beer.
**on strike**, stopping work to get better pay or shorter hours, or to force an employer to agree to meet some other demand: *Most of the workers voted to go on strike.*
**strike an attitude**. See under **attitude**.
**strike down**, **a** to knock down; overcome; defeat: *Then is sin struck down like an ox* (Shakespeare). **b** *Figurative: As early as 1936, the* [*Supreme*] *Court had begun striking down state criminal convictions based on confessions coerced from defendants* (New Yorker).
**strike off**, **a** to take off; cancel; remove: *The first person who flouts her shall be struck off my visiting list* (Matilda Betham-Edwards). **b** to print: *to strike off a hundred copies.*
**strike out**, **a** to cross out; rub out: *His name was struck out of the list of privy councillors* (Macaulay). **b** to fail to hit three pitches in baseball; be called out on strikes: *The batter struck out.* **c** to cause to fail to hit three pitches: *The pitcher struck out six men.* **d** *Informal, Figurative.* to fail: *He tried to borrow money from several banks but struck out each time.* **e** to use arms and legs to move forward: *The swimmer struck out across the lake.* **f** to hit violently: *Striking out at the tall reeds by the river with his stick* ... (D. Russell). **g** *Figurative.* to go or proceed energetically: *He ... struck out in the direction in which it* [*the pitfall*] *lay* (Frederick Marryat). *Gluck's music ... strikes out on a revolutionary path, the way of free emotion* (Saturday Review). **h** *Figurative.* to open up; make for oneself (a path, course, or line): *The men who act must strike out practical lines of action* (Woodrow Wilson).
**strike up**, **a** to begin: *to strike up a conversation. The two boys struck up a friendship.* **b** to begin or cause to begin to play, sing, or sound: *to strike up a song. Strike up the band.* **c** to raise, as by hammering: *to strike up a dent in the metal of a fender.*
[Old English *strīcan* to pass lightly (over a surface); to rub, stroke; to beat, hit] — **strike′less**, *adj.*

**strike-a-light** (strīk′ə līt′), *n.* a piece of trimmed flint used with pyrites or steel for producing fire from the sparks: *Strike-a-lights have often appeared among prehistoric findings.*

**strike|bound** (strīk′bound′), *adj.* having its operations stopped by a labor strike: *The company has been strikebound since August* (Wall Street Journal).

**strike|break|er** (strīk′brā′kər), *n.* a person who helps to break up a strike of workers by taking a striker's job or by furnishing persons who will do so. SYN: scab.

**strike|break|ing** (strīk′brā′king), *n.* forceful measures taken to halt a strike.

**strike fault**, *Geology.* a fault whose trend is roughly parallel to the strike of the rocks in which it occurs.

**strike force**, an armed force, equipped for attack; striking force: *In December 1960, the U.S. first proposed to help NATO develop its own nuclear strike force* (Time).

**strike|out** (strīk′out′), *n.* **1** *Baseball.* **a** an out earned by a pitcher throwing three strikes against a batter. **b** the act of striking out: *"Casey at the Bat," which builds up to one of the biggest letdowns in all literature—Casey's strikeout with two men on and two out* (Time). **2** *U.S.* an ex-convict forbidden to work as a longshoreman because of his undesirable associations.

**strike|o|ver** (strīk′ō′vər), *n.* the act of striking a typewriter key over a character to replace it, make it sharper, or cross it out.

**strik|er** (strī′kər), *n.* **1** a person or thing that strikes. **2** a worker who is on strike: *The union won't accept any settlement that does not greatly improve the working conditions of the strikers.* **3** the hammer that rings the alarm or strikes the hour in certain clocks. **4** an assistant worker who wields the heavy hammer in working metal. **5a** *U.S. Army.* an orderly. **b** *U.S. Navy.* an enlisted man serving an apprenticeship for a petty officer's rating. **6a** a person who strikes fish with a spear or harpoon. **b** = harpoon. **7** *Cricket.* a batsman.

**strike zone**, the area over home plate through which a baseball must be pitched for it to be called a strike, if the batter does not swing: *The size of the strike zone was reduced, making it from the armpits* [*of the batter*] *to the top of the knees instead of from the shoulders to the knees* (James O. Dunaway).

**strik|ing** (strī′king), *adj.* **1** that strikes. **2** attracting attention; very noticeable: *a striking woman, a striking change, a striking performance by an actor.* SYN: remarkable, impressive. — **strik′ing|ly**, *adv.* — **strik′ing|ness**, *n.*

**striking distance**, the distance within which it is possible to strike effectively.

**striking force**, **1** the means to attack an enemy: *The Strategic Air Command's striking force consists of medium bombers ...* (Newsweek). **2** = strike force.

**Strine** (strīn), *n., adj. Slang.* — ***n.*** the form of English spoken in Australia: *Anyone who goes to Australia thinking he speaks the Queen's English is in for a shock called "Strine," meaning Australian—the cockney-like vernacular that most Aussies spout* (Time).
— ***adj.*** Australian: *Strine English.*
[< the supposed Australian pronunciation of *Australian*]

**string** (string), *n., v.,* **strung, strung** or **stringed**, **string|ing**, *adj.* — ***n.*** **1** a thick thread; small cord or very thin rope: *The package is tied with red string.* SYN: twine. **2** a thread, cord, or chain with things on it: *She wore a string of beads around her neck.* **3** a special cord of gut, silk, fine wire, or nylon, as for musical instruments, bows, or tennis rackets. **4** anything used for tying: *apron strings.* **5** a cordlike part of plants. String beans have little strings connecting the two halves of a pod. **6a** a number of people, animals, or things in a line or row; file: *A string of cars came down the street.* SYN: series, chain. **b** a continuous series or succession: *a string of questions or stories.* SYN: series, chain. **7** *Informal, Figurative.* a condition; proviso: *an offer with strings attached to it. Our aid programs to non-Communist nations must be free of political strings* (Atlantic). **8** a group of players forming one of the teams of a squad, ranked according to relative skill: *The first string will practice against the second string.* **9a** the race horses belonging to a particular stable or owner. **b** a group of persons or things under the same ownership or management: *He owns a string of newspapers.* **10** *Architecture.* **a** a stringcourse. **b** a sloping board supporting the ends of the treads and risers in a staircase; stringer. **11a** a stroke in billiards made to determine the order of play, in which each player attempts to place his ball closest to the head cushion or the string line after bouncing it off the opposite cushion. **b** = string line. **12** *Journalism.* a strip of paper used to paste up the printed stories of a part-time correspondent who is paid by the line. **13** = string bikini. **14** *Obsolete.* a tendon, nerve, or muscle fiber.
— ***v.t.*** **1** to put on a string: *The child is stringing beads.* **2** to furnish with a string or strings: *to string a tennis racket.* **3** to tie with a string or rope. **4a** to hang with a string or rope: *We dry herbs by stringing them from rafters in the barn. Lights were strung on the Christmas tree.* **b** to furnish or ornament with something hanging: *a street strung with Christmas lights.* **5** to extend or stretch from one point to another: *to string a cable.* (*Figurative.*) *to string together a wordy speech.* **6** to extend in a line, row, or series: *Cars were strung for miles bumper to bumper.* **7** to adjust or tighten the strings of; tune: *to string a violin or guitar.* **8** to make tight; brace; strengthen. **9** *Figurative.* to make tense or excited: *I suppose it was despair that strung my nerves* (Edgar Allan Poe). **10** to remove the strings from: *to string beans.*
— ***v.i.*** **1** to move in a line or series. **2** to form into a string or strings; become stringy. **3** to make a stroke in billiards to determine the order of play.
— ***adj.*** made up of stringed instruments: *a string band, a string trio. The ovation given the string ensemble was stirring.*
**have two strings to one's bow**, to have more than one possible course of action: *As he that has two strings to his bow, And burns for love and money too* (Samuel Butler).
**on a string**, under someone's control: *Mr. H. said he was not a candidate on a string; he had his own convictions* (Westminster Gazette).
**pull strings**, to use secret influence: *I pulled strings and got myself into school, but I had to pay a lot of money to do it* (Atlantic).
**pull the strings**, to control the course of affairs; direct the actions of others secretly: *Persons ... who pull the strings of the Catholic world in the city of Rome* (John Bright).
**string along**, *Informal.* **a** to fool; hoax: *That boy is so easy to string along that you can convince him of just about anything.* **b** to go along (with); agree (with): *"I'll string along with your chairman about this being the greatest country," he began* (New Yorker). **c** to believe in; trust completely. **d** to keep (a person) waiting; stall off: *He has been stringing us along for too long, and now we want a decision.*
**string out**, *Informal.* to prolong; stretch; extend: *The program was strung out too long.*
**strings**, **a** violins, cellos, and other stringed instruments: *Praise him upon the strings and the pipe* (Book of Common Prayer). **b** the players of stringed instruments in an orchestra: *With the orchestra little fault could be found beyond the weakness of the strings* (London Daily Telegram).
**string up**, *Informal.* to hang: *to string up a criminal.*
[Old English *streng* harp string, rope, sinew] — **string′less**, *adj.* — **string′like′**, *adj.*

**string bass** (bās), = double bass.

**string bean**, **1** any one of various bushes or vines bearing long, green or yellow pods; snap bean. String beans belong to the pea family. **2** the pod of any of these plants. String beans contain smooth, somewhat flat seeds and are eaten as vegetables while still unripened. **3** *Informal.* a tall, thin, gangling person: *Phil took one look at the happy-go-lucky string bean with the outsize hands, and saw just what he was looking for* (Time).

**string bikini**, a bikini held up by a string or cord.

**string|board** (string′bôrd′, -bōrd′), *n.* a board or facing that covers the ends of steps in a stair.

**string-col|ored** (string′kul′ərd), *adj.* of a light grayish-brown color, as lace; ficelle.

**string correspondent**, *U.S.* **1** a part-time or local correspondent for a newspaper or magazine. **2** a newspaper correspondent paid on the basis of linage.

**string|course** (string′kôrs′, -kōrs′), *n.* a decorative horizontal band around a building, often at floor level; cordon.

**stringed** (stringd), *adj., v.* — ***adj.*** **1** having a string or strings. **2** produced by a stringed instrument or instruments: *stringed music.* **3** held together or caused to close by a string or strings.
— ***v.*** a past participle of **string**.

**stringed instrument**, a musical instrument having strings, usually played either with a bow or by plucking. A harp, a violin, and a guitar are stringed instruments.

**strin|gen|cy** (strin′jən sē), *n., pl.* **-cies**. **1** strictness; severity; rigorousness. SYN: harshness. **2** lack of ready money; tightness. SYN: scarcity. **3** convincing force; cogency: *the stringency of a debater's argument.*

**strin|gen|do** (strin jen′dō), *adj., adv. Music.* accelerating the tempo (a direction, used sometimes on a passage approaching a climax). [< Italian *stringendo,* present participle of *stringere* < Latin, draw tight]

**strin|gent** (strin′jənt), *adj.* **1** strict; severe: *stringent laws against speeding.* SYN: rigid, rigorous, exacting, binding. **2** lacking ready money; tight: *a stringent market for mortgage loans.* **3** convincing; forcible; cogent: *stringent arguments.* [< Latin *stringēns, -entis,* present participle of *stringere* bind, draw tight] — **strin′gent|ly**, *adv.*

***string|er** (string′ər), *n.* **1** a person or thing that strings: *a stringer of pearls.* **2a** a horizontal timber or girder connecting uprights, as in a framework or supporting a floor. **b** a tie beam: *There were oak beams connecting the pillars and supporting a crisscrossed network of stringers, made of peeled saplings* (New Yorker). **c** *Architecture.* string (def. 10b). **3** a heavy, horizontal timber or girder supporting the ties of a railroad trestle or bridge or the flooring of a wooden bridge. **4** *U.S.* a string correspondent. **5** *Geology.* a narrow vein of a mineral. **6** a member of a team or other person ranked according to ability: *a first-stringer.*

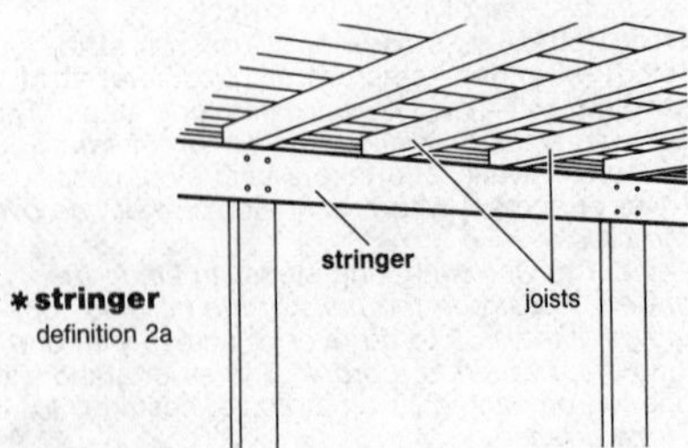

***stringer**
definition 2a

**string figure**, **1** a figure or design made with a string passed over the fingers of both hands. **2** a game in which such figures are made; cat's cradle.

**string|halt** (string′hôlt′), *n.* a diseased condition of horses that causes jerking of the hind legs in walking; springhalt. [apparently < *string* tendon + *halt*[2], adjective and noun]

**string|halt|ed** (string′hôl′tid), *adj.* suffering from stringhalt.

**string line**, a line in billiards and pool from behind which the cue ball is played after being out of play.

**string|piece** (string′pēs′), *n.* a long, heavy, horizontal beam in a framework, used to strengthen or connect other parts.

**string player**, a person who plays a stringed instrument or instruments, especially in an orchestra.
**string puppet**, = marionette.
**string quartet**, **1** a quartet of stringed instruments, usually consisting of two violins, a viola, and a cello. **2** a composition for such a quartet.
**strings** (stringz), *n.pl.* See under **string**.
**string tie**, a short, narrow necktie, usually knotted into a bow, sometimes worn with ends dangling.
**string|y** (string′ē), *adj.*, **string|i|er, string|i|est.** **1** like a string or strings. **2** forming strings: *a stringy syrup.* **3** having tough fibers: *a piece of tough, stringy meat, a dry, stringy radish.* **4** lean and sinewy: *a tall and stringy boy.* —**string′i-ness**, *n.*
**stringy bark**, **1** any one of a group of Australasian gum trees having a strong, fibrous bark. **2** the bark of such a tree.
**strip[1]** (strip), *v.*, **stripped** or (*Rare*) **stript, stripping,** *adj.* —*v.t.* **1** to make bare or naked; undress (as a person or thing): *The boys had stripped themselves to go swimming when the sheriff showed up.* **2** to take off the covering of: *to strip a tree of its bark. The monkey stripped the banana by taking off the skin.* SYN: skin, peel. **3** to remove; tear off; pull off: *to strip paper from a wall, to strip fruit from a tree, to strip off one's gloves.* **4** to make bare; clear out; empty: *to strip a house of its furniture, to strip a forest of its timber.* **5** to take away the equipment of; dismantle; disassemble: *to strip a car in a junkyard, to strip a ship of its guns.* **6** to rob; plunder: *Thieves stripped the house of everything valuable.* SYN: despoil. **7** *Figurative.* to take away the titles, rights, office, reputation, or self-respect of (a person or thing). **8a** to tear off the teeth of (a gear). **b** to break the thread of (a bolt, nut, or pipe). **9a** to separate the leaves from the stalks of (tobacco) after curing. **b** to remove the midrib and large veins from (tobacco leaves) after curing. **10** to milk (a cow) thoroughly; draw the last milk from (a cow). **11** to mine (a mineral) from the surface by removing overlying layers of earth; lay bare (a mineral deposit). **12** to pluck a dog, removing the long hair.
—*v.i.* **1** to take off the clothes or covering; undress; uncover; become undressed or uncovered: *Other lads than I Strip to bathe on Severn shore* (A. E. Housman). **2** to perform a striptease. **3** to be stripped; peel.
—*adj.* that features stripteasers: *a strip club, strip bar, strip joint, strip show.*
[Old English *-strīepan,* as in unrecorded *bestrīepan* to plunder] —**strip′pa|ble**, *adj.*
**strip[2]** (strip), *n., v.,* **stripped, strip|ping.** —*n.* **1a** a long, narrow, flat piece (of cloth, paper, bark, metal, wood, or the like). **b** a flat piece of rolled steel less than 24 inches wide: *Galvanized steel sheets are being slit into strips, which in turn will be formed into moulding channels* (Newsweek). **2** a long, narrow tract, as of land, territory, or forest. **3a** a long, narrow runway for aircraft to take off from and land on; landing strip; airstrip. **b** = flight strip. **4** a long stretch of commercial development along a highway, especially outside a city or town. **5** a horizontal or vertical row of three or more stamps. **6** a continuous series of pictures in a newspaper or magazine: *a comic strip, a cartoon strip.* **7** = strip chart. **8** a local, minor civil division in Maine. **9** *U.S.* a special area or course set aside for drag racing: *The strips are scattered through 37 states, according to the National Hot Rod Association* (Wall Street Journal).
—*v.t.* **1** to cut into strips. **2** Sometimes, **strip in.** to arrange and fix film or printed or drawn material to photograph for making a printing plate. **3** to affix cloth to the gathered pages of a book before they are put in the case.
**tear a strip** (or **strips**) **off,** *Slang.* to reprimand: *A quiet English girl gave a surprising display of bilingualism herself by tearing strips off Jacques-Robert Rivart in some French no nice English girl should know* (Maclean's).
[apparently variant of *stripe[1]*]
**strip cartoon**, *British.* comic strip.
**strip chart**, a graphic representation of data in the form of a long strip of paper on which the course of something, such as a patient's fever, is charted.
**strip city**, *U.S.* a long, narrow stretch of urban development between two or more relatively distant cities: *By 1980 or so, 80 per cent of us will live in cities, and the strip city—Boston to Washington, Los Angeles to San Diego, and Milwaukee to Cleveland—will have made its appearance* (Saturday Review).
**strip cropping** or **planting**, = strip farming.
**stripe[1]** (strīp), *n., v.,* **striped, strip|ing.** —*n.* **1** a long, narrow band, as of a different color, material, or weave from the rest of a surface or thing: *A tiger has stripes. The American flag has thirteen stripes.* SYN: stria. **2** a striped material or cloth. **3** a strip or narrow piece. **4** *Figurative.* sort; type; class: *a man of quite a different stripe. Of a democratic, liberal stripe* (Edmund C. Stedman). SYN: kind, stamp. **5** a narrow line painted or marked as a line of demarcation: *Temple [football team], which gained most of its yardage in its own territory, was unable to get past the midfield stripe in the last quarter* (New York Times).
—*v.t.* to mark or ornament with a stripe or stripes: *The stick of candy was striped with red.*
**stripes, a** a number or combination of strips of braid on the sleeve of a uniform to show rank, length of service, or function: *to earn one's stripes.* **b** *Slang.* chevrons: *sergeant's stripes.*
[< Middle Dutch *strīpe*]
**stripe[2]** (strīp), *n.* **1** a stroke or lash, as with a whip, scourge, or rod. **2** *Archaic.* the mark made by a stroke or lash; weal; welt. [probably special use of *stripe[1]*]
**striped** (strīpt, strī′pid), *adj.* having stripes; marked with a stripe or stripes: *Zebras are striped.*
**striped bass**, a sea bass with blackish stripes along the sides, found in North American coastal waters.
**striped gopher**, = striped spermophile.
**striped maple**, = moosewood.
**striped marlin**, a small marlin of the Pacific with vertical bars across the back and sides.
**striped-pants** (strīpt′pants′), *adj. Informal.* **1** of or having to do with the diplomatic corps: *Pakistan's ... Mohammed Ali, 45, ambassador to the U.S. ... was reappointed to his old striped-pants post in the capital* (Time). **2** of diplomacy; characteristic of diplomacy: *striped-pants formality or protocol.*
**striped skunk**, the common black skunk or the black-and-white skunk, found throughout the United States and spreading into northern Mexico and southern Canada.
**striped snake**, = garter snake.
**striped spermophile**, a common striped ground squirrel of the western plains of North America; striped gopher.
**striped squirrel**, = chipmunk.
**striped tabby**, = tiger cat (def. 2).
**strip|er** (strī′pər), *n.* **1** *Slang.* a naval officer whose rank is indicated by the stripes on his sleeve: *A three-striper is a commander.* **2** *Slang.* any serviceman whose rank or length of service is indicated by a stripe or stripes on the sleeve. **3** = striped bass.
**stripes** (strīps), *n.pl.* See under **stripe[1]**.
**strip farming**, the growing of rows of crops with strong root systems between rows of crops having weak root systems, along the contour of a slope, in order to prevent excessive erosion of topsoil.
**strip|film** (strip′film′), *n.* a reel of film with still frames; filmstrip.
**strip|ing** (strī′ping), *n.* **1** the act of forming stripes or ornamenting with stripes. **2** a series or pattern of stripes: *sport slacks with blue and white stripings.*
**strip|light** (strip′līt′), *n.* a row of lamps set in a narrow, rectangular trough and placed on the floor or elsewhere to light a stage, set, scene, and the like.
**strip|ling** (strip′ling), *n.* a boy just coming into manhood; youth; lad.
**strip method**, a conservative method of lumbering in which trees are reproduced on cleared strips by self-sown seeds from an adjoining forest.
**strip mill**, a rolling mill producing strips of steel.
***strip mine**, a mine which is operated from the surface by removing the overlying layers of earth.

***strip mine**

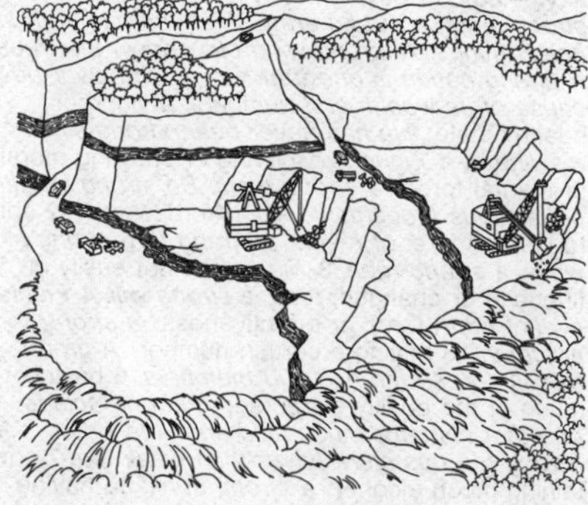

**strip-mine** (strip′mīn′), *v.t.,* **-mined, -min|ing.** to take (a mineral or ore) from a strip mine: *The ore is near hydro-electric power and can be strip-mined after removal of a small amount of overburden* (Wall Street Journal).
**strip mining**, the work or business of operating a strip mine.
**stripped** (stript), *adj.* = stripped-down.
**stripped-down** (stript′doun′), *adj.* reduced to the bare essentials: *Detroit has found that the stripped-down car is not what most people want* (Newsweek).
**strip|per** (strip′ər), *n.* **1** a person or thing that strips, such as a varnish or paint remover. **2** an oil well that can produce oil only a few hours a day, requiring several hours to rebuild enough pressure for the oil to flow freely through the sand. **3** *Informal.* a stripteaser.
**strip|ping** (strip′ing), *n.* **1** the act of a person or thing that strips. **2** something removed by this act. **3** = strip mining.
**strippings,** the last milk drawn from a cow.
**strip poker**, a form of poker in which the players take off a piece of clothing each time they lose a hand.
**strip|tease** (strip′tēz′), *n., v.,* **-teased, -teas|ing.** —*n.* a dance in which a woman slowly and coyly removes her clothing piece by piece to music, as in a burlesque show or night club.
—*v.i.* to do a striptease.
**strip|teas|er** (strip′tē′zər), *n.* a performer of the striptease.
**strip|teuse** (strip tœz′), *n., pl.* **-teuses** (-tœz′). = stripteaser. [< *stript*(ease) + (dans)*euse*]
**strip|y** (strī′pē), *adj.* **1** having stripes; striped. **2** occurring in or suggestive of stripes.
**stri|sci|an|do** (strē′shē än′dō), *adj., adv. Music.* —*adj.* creeping or gliding.
—*adv.* in a creeping or gliding manner.
[< Italian *strisciando,* present participle of *strisciare* to creep, glide]
**strive** (strīv), *v.i.,* **strove** or **strived, striv|en, striv|ing.** **1** to try hard; work hard: *to strive for self-control. Strive to succeed.* SYN: endeavor. **2** to struggle (with); fight (against): *The swimmer strove against the tide.* SYN: contend, battle. **3** *Obsolete.* to compete. [short for Old French *estriver* < a Germanic word] —**striv′er**, *n.* —**striv′ing|ly**, *adv.*
► Verbs borrowed from Old French normally have been conjugated in English with *-ed* in the past tense and past participle. **Strive**, an exception, was early attracted into the class of *ride, drive,* and the like. Alongside of *strove, striven,* however, the form *strived* is also recorded from the fourteenth century and is still in use. At present it occurs more often as past participle than as past tense.
**striv|en** (striv′ən), *v.* a past participle of **strive**: *She has striven hard to make the party a success.*
**strob** (strob), *n. Physics.* a unit of velocity for bodies moving in a circular path, equal to one radian per second. [< Greek *stróbos;* see etym. under **stroboscope**]
**strobe** (strōb), *n., v.,* **strobed, strob|ing.** —*n.* **1** = strobe light. **2** = stroboscope.
—*v.i.* to produce flashes from, or as if from, a strobe light.
[< *stroboscope*]
**strobe light**, an electronic flash gun for action photography. Its neon- or xenon-filled tube can be used over and over in contrast to the flashbulb, which must be replaced after each picture.
**strob|ic** (strob′ik), *adj.* spinning or whirling; appearing to spin or whirl. [< Greek *stróbos* (see etym. under **stroboscope**) + English *-ic*]
**strobic circles**, a group of concentric circles that appear to spin round or revolve when the paper or object they are drawn on is moved about.
**strobic disk**, a disk containing strobic circles or the like.
**strob|il** (strob′əl), *n.* = strobile.
**stro|bi|la** (strə bī′lə), *n., pl.* **-lae** (-lē). **1** the body of a tapeworm, as distinct from the head, consisting of a chain of segments. **2** a stage in the development of certain jellyfish in which a series of disk-shaped bodies split off to form new individuals. [< New Latin *strobila* < Greek *strobī́lē* cone-shaped plug of lint < *stróbīlos* pine cone; (originally) any twisting thing < *streblós* twisted, related to *stréphein* to turn, twist]
**strob|i|la|ceous** (strob′ə lā′shəs), *adj.* **1** of or like a strobile. **2** bearing strobiles. [< New Latin *strobilaceus* (with English *-ous*) < Late Latin *strobīlus;* see etym. under **strobile**]
**strob|i|la|tion** (strob′ə lā′shən), *n.* an asexual form of reproduction in which segments of the

**Pronunciation Key:** hat, āge, cãre, fär; let, ēqual, tėrm; it, īce; hot, ōpen, ôrder; oil, out; cup, pu̇t, rüle; child; long; thin; ᴛʜen; zh, measure; ə represents **a** in about, **e** in taken, **i** in pencil, **o** in lemon, **u** in circus.

body separate to form new individuals, as in tapeworms and scyphozoans. [< *strobil*(a) + *-ation*]

**strob|ile** (strob′əl), *n. Botany.* any seed-producing cone, such as a pine cone, or a compact mass of scalelike leaves that produce spores, such as the cone of the club moss; strobil. [< Late Latin *strobīlus* < Greek *stróbīlos* pine cone; see etym. under **strobila**]

**strob|i|li|za|tion** (strob′ə lə zā′shən), *n.* = strobilation.

**strob|i|lus** (strob′ə ləs), *n., pl.* **-li** (-lī). = strobile.

**strob|o|graph** (strob′ə graf, -gräf), *n.* a device that makes a record of the phenomena observed with a stroboscope or similar instrument.

**strob|o|graph|ic** (strob′ə graf′ik), *adj.* of or having to do with a strobograph.

**strob|o|scope** (strob′ə skōp), *n.* an instrument for studying the successive phases of the periodic motion of a body by means of periodically interrupted light. [< German *Stroboskop* < Greek *stróbos* a twisting, related to *stréphein* to twist, turn + German *-skop* < Greek *skopeîn* look at]

**strob|o|scop|ic** (strob′ə skop′ik), *adj.* of or having to do with a stroboscope. — **strob′o|scop′i|cal|ly**, *adv.*

**stroboscopic light**, = strobe light.

**strob|o|tron** (strob′ə tron), *n.* an electron tube containing a rare gas, or mixture of such gases, used as a source of light in a stroboscope.

**strode** (strōd), *v.* a past tense of **stride**: *He strode over the ditch.*

**stroke**[1] (strōk), *n., v.,* **stroked, strok|ing.** — *n.* **1** the act of striking; blow: *a stroke of the fist or of an ax, a backhand stroke. He drove in the nail with one stroke of the hammer. The house was hit by a stroke of lightning.* **SYN**: See syn. under **blow. 2** the sound made by striking, as of a bell or clock: *We arrived at the stroke of three o'clock.* **3** *Figurative.* a piece of luck or fortune, or other unexpected happening: *a stroke of bad luck.* **4a** a single complete movement to be made again and again, especially of a moving part or parts of a machine, in one direction: *the stroke of a piston.* **b** the distance traveled by this part. **5** a throb or pulsing, as of the heart; pulsation. **6** a movement or mark made by a pen, pencil, or brush: *He writes with a heavy downstroke.* **7** *Figurative.* **a** a vigorous attempt to attain some object: *a bold stroke for freedom.* **b** a measure or expedient adopted for some purpose: *a great stroke of politics.* **8** *Figurative.* **a** a very successful effort or achievement: *a stroke of wit or genius.* **b** an effective, clever, or characteristic touch in literary composition. **9** a single effort; act, piece, or amount of work: *a good stroke of business. That lazy boy has not done a stroke of work all day.* **10a** a sudden attack (of illness). **b** an attack of paralysis caused by injury to the brain when a blood vessel breaks or becomes obstructed; apoplexy: *With newer therapeutic methods and modern rehabilitation, strokes need no longer be considered a hopeless and helpless condition* (New York Times). **11** *Figurative.* a sudden action like a blow in its effect, as in causing pain, injury, or death: *a stroke of fate, the stroke of death.* **12a** one of a series of propelling movements in swimming, involving the pull of one arm (or both together) with one or more kicks. **b** a style or method of swimming: *She swims a fast stroke.* **13** in rowing and canoeing: **a** a single pull of the oar or paddle. **b** the style or rate of pulling the oars or a paddle: *He rows with a strong stroke.* **c** the rower or paddler who sets the time for the other oarsmen or paddlers. **d** the position of this rower or paddler. In rowing, the stroke is at the stern; in canoes and kayaks, at the bow.
— *v.t.* **1** to be the stroke of; set the stroke for: *Who stroked the Yale crew?* **2** to mark with a stroke or strokes; cancel by drawing a line or lines across. **3** to hit. **4** (of a clock) to sound (the time) by striking. **5** to make a specified number of strokes per minute in rowing or paddling: *The winner stroked an average of 28 to Gunther's 30* (London Times). — *v.i.* to execute a stroke; make the motions of stroking.
**keep stroke**, to make strokes at the same time, as in rowing: *I, being unable to keep stroke with the rest, was well beaten* (James Wadsworth).
[unrecorded Old English *strāc*. Compare etym. under **stroke**[2].]

**stroke**[2] (strōk), *v.,* **stroked, strok|ing,** *n.* — *v.t.* **1** to move the hand gently over: *to stroke a child's hair. She likes to stroke her kitten.* **2** *Figurative.* **a** to manipulate by cajoling; persuade by soothing words or flattery: *The White House counsel received a "happy Easter" phone call from the President, but he recognized it ... as a 'stroking' call* (Newsweek). **b** to boost the ego of: *It's Show Biz, man—a bunch a' egomaniacal people using a captive audience to stroke themselves* (Atlantic).
— *n.* **1** a stroking movement: *She brushed away the crumbs with a quick stroke.* **2** an act or means of stroking someone: (*Figurative.*) *It is the function of the Parent to enforce an Injunction ... along with reinforcing "strokes"* (New York Times Magazine).
[Middle English *stroken*, Old English *strācian*. See related etym. at **strike**.]

**stroke oar**, **1** the oar nearest the stern of a boat. **2** the rower that pulls the stroke oar. The stroke oar sets the time for the other oarsmen.

**stroke play**, **1** (in golf) medal play. **2** the quality or style of one's stroke or stroking movement.

**strok|er** (strō′kər), *n.* **1** a person who strokes. **2** *Archaic.* a person who claims to cure diseases by stroking. **3** *British.* a kind of wood or bone paper folder that brings forward separate sheets of paper to a printing machine.

**strokes|man** (strōks′mən), *n., pl.* **-men.** the oarsman nearest to the stern of a boat, who sets the stroke for the other oarsmen.

**stroke stitch**, a running stitch in embroidery made twice to form a continuous line on both sides of the fabric.

**stroll** (strōl), *v., n.* — *v.i.* **1** to take a quiet walk for pleasure; walk: *We were strolling about under the trees.* **SYN**: saunter, ramble, roam. **2** to go from place to place: *strolling Gypsies.* **SYN**: rove.
— *v.t.* to stroll along or through: *He noticed three people strolling the muddy street* (Sinclair Lewis).
— *n.* a leisurely walk: *We went for a stroll in the park. My life is like a stroll upon the beach* (Thoreau). **SYN**: saunter. [origin uncertain]

**stroll|er** (strō′lər), *n.* **1** a person who strolls or rambles; wanderer: *holiday strollers in the park.* **2** a strolling player or actor. **3** a wandering vagrant; tramp. **4** a kind of light baby carriage in which an older baby or small child sits erect: *Children were everywhere: in strollers, in mothers' arms, and perched on curbs* (Newsweek).

**stro|ma** (strō′mə), *n., pl.* **-ma|ta** (-mə tə). *Anatomy.* **1** the connective tissue, nerves, and vessels that form the framelike support of an organ or part. **2** the spongy, colorless framework of a red blood corpuscle or other cell. [< Latin *strōma, -ātis* bed cover < Greek *strôma, -atos* a spread to lie or sit on]

**stro|mal** (strō′məl), *adj.* of or having to do with the stroma or with stromata.

**stro|mat|ic** (strō mat′ik), *adj.* of or like stroma.

**stro|mat|o|lite** (strō mat′ə līt), *n.* a calcareous rock formation containing fossil deposits of blue-green algae. [< Greek *strôma, -atos* a spread + English *-lite*]

**stro|mat|o|lit|ic** (strō mat′ə lit′ik), *adj.* of or having to do with stromatolites.

**stromb** (strom), *n.* **1** a large marine gastropod of the West Indies whose delicate-pink shell is used for ornament and cameo cutting. **2** the shell of such a gastropod. [< New Latin *Strombus* the genus name < Latin *strombus* spiral shell < Greek *strómbos*, related to *stréphein* to twist]

**strom|boid** (strom′boid), *adj., n.* — *adj.* having to do with or resembling a stromb. — *n.* = stromb.

**Strom|bo|li|an volcano** (strom bō′lē ən), a volcano having thick lava with many incandescent rock fragments and somewhat violent eruptions. [< *Stromboli*, a volcano in the Lipari Islands, Italy]

**strom|bu|li|form** (strom′byə lə fôrm), *adj. Botany.* twisted or coiled into the form of a screw, helix, or spiral. [< New Latin *strombuliformis* < Latin *strombus* (see etym. under **stromb**) + *forma* form]

**stro|meyer|ite** (strō′mī′ə rīt), *n.* a steel-gray mineral, a sulfide of silver and copper, with a metallic luster, occurring massive and in crystals. [< Friedrich *Stromeyer*, died 1835, a German chemist + *-ite*[1]]

**strong** (strông, strong), *adj.,* **strong|er** (strông′gər, strong′-), **strong|est** (strông′gəst, strong′-), *adv.* — *adj.* **1a** having much force or power: *strong arms, a strong army. A strong man can lift heavy things. A strong wind blew down the trees. A strong nation is one that has much power because of its wealth and numbers.* **b** vigorous; healthy; hale: *He has never been strong since his illness.* **c** *Figurative.* having or showing moral or mental force: *a strong mind. Be strong in faith, bid anxious thoughts lie still* (Wordsworth). **2** able to last, endure, or resist: *a strong fort, strong walls, a strong rope.* **3** *Figurative.* not easily influenced or changed; firm: *a strong will.* **4** *Figurative.* of great force or effectiveness: *a strong argument.* **5** having a certain number: *A group that is 100 strong has 100 members.* **6** having much of the quality expected: *A strong acid is one that contains much acid and little water. Strong tea has more flavor than weak tea.* **7** containing much alcohol: *a strong drink.* **8a** having much flavor or odor: *strong seasoning, strong perfume, a strong cigar.* **b** having an unpleasant taste or smell: *strong butter.* **9a** loud and firm; powerful: *a strong voice.* **b** vivid or intense: *a strong light, a strong color.* **c** *Figurative.* marked; definite: *a strong resemblance, a strong impression.* **d** powerful in working effect: *a strong poison, strong glasses.* **10** *Figurative.* vigorous; forceful; emphatic: *a strong speech, a protest in strong terms.* **11** hearty; zealous; ardent: *a strong dislike, a strong Republican, a strong sense of duty.* **12** well-skilled; well-versed; proficient: *I am not very strong in spelling* (Thackeray). **13** *Commerce.* steadily good or advancing; firm; active: *a strong market, strong prices.* **14** *Grammar.* **a** inflected for tense by a vowel change within the stem rather than by adding endings; irregular. *Examples:* find, found; give, gave, given. **b** belonging to the vocalic declensions; having a stem originally ending with a vowel. Certain Germanic nouns and adjectives are called strong. **15** *Phonetics.* stressed.
— *adv.* **1** with force; powerfully. **2** in a strong manner; vigorously: *When we left, the party was still going strong.*
[Old English *strang*] — **strong′ly**, *adv.* — **strong′ness**, *n.*
— *Syn. adj.* **1a, b Strong, sturdy, robust** mean having or showing much power, force, or vigor. **Strong**, the general word, suggests great power or force in acting, resisting, or enduring: *a strong grip, strong walls. Lumberjacks need strong backs and arms.* **Sturdy** suggests power coming from solid construction: *Children need sturdy clothes.* **Robust** suggests healthy vigor of mind or body: *Team sports make children robust.*

**strong-arm** (strông′ärm′, strong′-), *adj., v. Informal.* — *adj.* using force or violence: *strong-arm methods.* — *v.t.* to use force or violence on: *to strong-arm an opponent.* [American English]

**strong|back** (strông′bak′, strong′-), *n.* **1** *Nautical.* a spar across boat davits, to which the boat is secured at sea. **2** a piece of wood or iron over the windlass, to haul up and secure the chain when the windlass is ready to be used.

**strong|bark** (strông′bärk′, strong′-), *n.* any small tree or shrub of a group of the borage family growing in the West Indies and southern Florida, having a strong, hard, brown wood streaked with orange.

**strong|box** (strông′boks′, strong′-), *n.* a strongly made box to hold valuable things.

**strong breeze**, a wind between 25 and 31 miles per hour.

**strong drink**, **1** a drink containing much alcohol: *Whiskey, brandy, and rum are strong drinks compared with wine or beer.* **2** such drinks as a class.

**strong|er sex** (strông′gər, strong′-), the male sex; men as a group.

**strong force**, = strong interaction.

**strong gale**, a wind between 47 and 54 miles per hour.

**strong-head|ed** (strông′hed′id, strong′-), *adj.* **1** = headstrong. **2** having a strong intellect. — **strong′-head′ed|ness**, *n.*

**strong|hold** (strông′hōld′, strong′-), *n.* **1** a strong place; fort; fortress. **SYN**: bulwark. **2** *Figurative: The robbers have a stronghold in the mountains.*

**strong interaction**, an interaction between elementary particles that is stronger than any other known force. The strong interaction causes neutrons and protons to bind in the nuclei of atoms.

**strong|ish** (strông′ish, strong′-), *adj.* somewhat or rather strong: *a simple-minded man, with a strongish will* (Alexander W. Kinglake).

**strong|man** (strông′man′, strong′-), *n., pl.* **-men.** **1** a strong man, especially one who performs feats of strength, as in a circus or carnival. **2** *Figurative.* a leader who uses force to obtain and hold power; despot; dictator: *Strongman Porfirio Díaz took over after Juárez in 1876, ruled* [*Mexico*] *with an iron hand* (Time).

**strong mayor**, *U.S.* a mayor in a mayor-council type of government who has large executive authority. A strong mayor appoints the heads of municipal departments and directs city administration.

**strong-mind|ed** (strông′mīn′did, strong′-), *adj.* **1a** having a strong mind; mentally vigorous. **b** determined to the point of being stubborn. **2** having or affecting masculine mentality or rights: *a strong-minded woman.* — **strong′-mind′ed|ly**, *adv.* — **strong′-mind′ed|ness**, *n.*

**strong|point** (strông′point′, strong′-), *n.* = stronghold.

**strong room**, or **strong|room** (strông′rüm′, -rům′; strong′-), *n.* a room like a vault for keeping or storing valuable things.

**strong side**, the side of a football formation to which the greater number of players have shifted.

**strong suit**, **1** = long suit (def. 1). **2** *Figurative.* a strong point: *Ireland's strong suit that afternoon was desperate defence, since they were seldom allowed to suggest attack* (London Times).

**strong-willed** (strông′wild′, strong′-), *adj.* strong-minded; stubborn; obstinate.

**stron|gyle** or **stron|gyl** (stron′jəl), *n.* any one of a group of roundworms, many of which are disease-producing parasites, as in men or horses. [< New Latin *Strongylus* the genus name < Greek *strongýlos* round < *stránx, strangós* drop (of liquid)]

**stron|gy|lo|sis** (stron′jə lō′sis), *n.* a disease due to the presence of strongyles in the organs and tissues.

**stron|ti|a** (stron′shē ə), *n.* **1** a grayish-white, amorphous powder resembling lime; strontium oxide: *Formula:* SrO **2** a colorless powder formed by treating strontium oxide with water; strontium hydroxide. *Formula:* $Sr(OH)_2$ [< *strontian*]

**stron|ti|an** (stron′shē ən, -shən), *n.* **1** = strontianite. **2** = strontia. **3** = strontium. [< *Strontian,* a parish in Argyllshire, Scotland, location of the lead mines where strontium was first found]

**stron|ti|an|ite** (stron′shē ə nīt), *n.* a mineral consisting of strontium carbonate, occurring in massive, fibrous forms and varying color from white to yellow and pale green. *Formula:* $SrCO_3$ [< *strontian* + *-ite*[1]]

**stron|tic** (stron′tik), *adj.* having to do with strontium.

***stron|ti|um** (stron′shē əm, -tē-), *n.* a soft, silver-white metallic chemical element which occurs only in combination with other elements, as in strontianite and celestite. It is one of the alkaline-earth metals and resembles calcium. Strontium is used in making alloys and in fireworks and signal flares. *Fall-out contains strontium made radioactive* (New York Times). [< New Latin *strontium* < *Strontian;* see etym. under **strontian**]

***strontium**

| symbol | atomic number | atomic weight | oxidation state |
|---|---|---|---|
| Sr | 38 | 87.62 | 2 |

**strontium 90**, a radioactive isotope of strontium which occurs in the fallout from a hydrogen-bomb explosion; radiostrontium. It is extremely dangerous because it is easily absorbed by the bones and tissues and may eventually replace the calcium in the body.

**strontium carbonate**, a white, odorless powder, in its natural state the constituent of strontianite, used in sugar refining and in the making of iridescent glass, fireworks, and salts of strontium. *Formula:* $SrCO_3$

**strontium hydroxide**, = strontia.

**strontium nitrate**, a white powder that burns with a crimson flame, used in flares and fireworks. *Formula:* $Sr(NO_3)_2$

**strontium oxide**, = strontia.

**strontium titanate**, a crystalline substance almost as brilliant and clear as diamond, made by fusing strontium, titanium, and oxygen, used for lenses and in jewelry. *Formula:* $SrTiO_3$

**strook** (strůk), *v. Obsolete.* struck; a past participle of **strike**.

**strop** (strop), *n., v.,* **stropped, strop|ping.** **—*n.*** **1** a leather strap used for sharpening razors: *Men who shave with straight-edged razors are always on the lookout for a good strop* (New Yorker). **2** any band, strip, or thong of leather; strap.
**—*v.t.*** to sharpen on a strop.
[Old English *strop* < Latin *stroppus;* see etym. under **strap**]

**stro|phan|thin** (strō fan′thin), *n.* a bitter, poisonous glucoside obtained from the seeds of various tropical African shrubs or small trees of the dogbane family. It is used as a heart stimulant. [< *strophanth(us)* + *-in*]

**stro|phan|thus** (strō fan′thəs), *n.* **1** any one of a group of tropical African shrubs or small trees of the dogbane family, the seeds of which are used in making strophanthin. **2** the seeds. [< New Latin *Strophanthus* the genus name < Greek *stróphos* twisted cord (< *stréphein* to turn) + *ánthos* flower (from the twisted sections of the corolla)]

**stro|phe** (strō′fē), *n.* **1a** the part of an ancient Greek choric ode sung by the chorus while moving from right to left. **b** the movement itself. **2a** one of two or more groups of lines of a lyric poem; stanza. The groups are related metrically. **b** a series of lines forming a division of a poem and having metrical structure which is repeated in a second group of lines (the antistrophe), especially in ancient Greek choral and lyric poetry. [< Greek *strophḗ* (originally) a turning; section sung by the chorus while turning and moving in one direction < *stréphein* to turn]

**stroph|ic** (strof′ik, strō′fik), *adj.* of or having to do with a strophe.

**stroph|i|cal** (strof′ə kəl, strō′fə-), *adj.* = strophic.

**strophic song,** *Music.* a song having the same melody or music for every stanza.

**stroph|i|o|late** (strof′ē ə lāt, strō′fē-), *adj.* bearing a strophiole.

**stroph|i|ole** (strof′ē ōl, strō′fē-), *n. Botany.* a cellular outgrowth near the hilum in certain seeds; caruncle. [< Latin *strophiolum* (diminutive) < *strophium* band of cloth < Greek *stróphion* (diminutive) < *stróphos* twisted band < *stréphein* twist]

**stro|phi|um** (strō′fē əm), *n.* a tight band of cloth like a corset, worn with the stola by women in ancient Rome. [< Latin *strophium* < Greek *stróphion* (diminutive); see etym. under **strophiole**]

**stroph|oid** (strof′oid, strō′foid), *n. Geometry.* a curve that is the locus of intersections of two lines rotating uniformly about two fixed points in a plane. [< French *strophoïde* < Greek *stróphos* twisted band + French *-oïde* -oid]

**stroph|u|lus** (strof′yə ləs), *n.* a pimply eruption of the skin of infants; red gum. [< New Latin *strophulus,* apparently alteration of Medieval Latin *scrofulus* red gum, alteration of Latin *scrōfulae* scrofula]

**strop|per** (strop′ər), *n.* **1** a person who strops. **2** a device for stropping.

**stroud** (stroud), *n.* a large, coarse blanket formerly used in bartering with North American Indians. [origin uncertain]

**strove** (strōv), *v.* a past tense of **strive**: *They strove hard, but did not win the game.*

**strow** (strō), *v.t.,* **strowed, strown** (strōn) or **strowed, strow|ing.** *Archaic.* to strew.

**stroy** (stroi), *v.t. Archaic.* to destroy. [short for *destroy*]

**struck** (struk), *v., adj.* **—*v.*** a past tense and past participle of **strike**: *The clock struck four. The barn was struck by lightning.*
**—*adj.*** closed or affected in some way by a strike of workers: *a struck factory.*

**struck|en** (struk′ən), *v. Obsolete.* struck; a past participle of **strike**.

**struck jury,** a special jury selected from a list (usually of 48 persons) by having the lawyers on both sides strike out the same number of names.

**struck measure,** a stricken or leveled measure, as of grain.

**struc|tur|al** (struk′chər əl), *adj.* **1** of, having to do with, or used in building; constructional: *structural materials. Blue-gray structural glass and stainless steel will be used on the outside of the first three floors* (New York Times). **2** of or having to do with structure or structures: (*Figurative.*) *the structural unity of a novel.* **3** *Biology.* of or having to do with the organic structure of an animal or plant; morphological. **4** *Geology.* having to do with the structure of rock, the earth's crust, or the structure of some heavenly body; tectonic: *The geologist showed the structural difference in rocks of different ages.* **5** *Chemistry.* of or showing the placement or manner of attachment of the atoms that make up a particular molecule. **6** *Economics.* caused by the economic structure: *the structural fluctuation of prices.*

**structural formula,** a chemical formula that differs from a molecular formula in that it shows how the atoms in a molecule are arranged.

**structural gene,** the part of an operon that determines the sequence of amino acids and the structure of the proteins: *The first known class consists of structural genes, which determine the amino acid sequence and three-dimensional shape of proteins; the second is regulatory genes, which specify whether structural genes will function, and therefore control the rate of enzyme synthesis* (Science News).

**structural geology,** a branch of geology dealing with the positions, shapes, and compositions of rocks.

**structural iron** or **steel, 1** iron or steel in shapes or lengths for use in building, such as I-beams or girders. **2** the type or composition of iron or steel so used.

**struc|tur|al|ism** (struk′chər ə liz′əm), *n.* **1** *Psychology.* the study of the structure of consciousness, or what it consists of, as opposed to its function, or what it does. **2** = structural linguistics. **3** any study or theory which regards structure as more important than function.

**struc|tur|al|ist** (struk′chər ə list), *n., adj.* **—*n.*** a follower of or believer in structuralism.
**—*adj.*** = structuralistic.

**struc|tur|al|is|tic** (struk′chər ə lis′tik), *adj.* of, having to do with, or characteristic of structuralism.

**structural linguistics,** the study of linguistic structure to determine and describe patterns and their interrelationships of language.

**struc|tur|al|ly** (struk′chər ə lē), *adv.* with regard to structure: *The new church is structurally perfect, but it is not beautiful.*

**struc|tur|als** (struk′chər əlz), *n.pl.* heavy steel members, beams, or other supports used in construction.

**struc|ture** (struk′chər), *n., v.,* **-tured, -tur|ing.** **—*n.*** **1** something built; building or construction: *The city hall is a large stone structure. Dams, bridges, tunnels, and office buildings are great and useful structures.* **SYN:** See syn. under **building. 2** anything composed of parts arranged together: *The human body is a wonderful and complex structure.* **3** the way parts are made or put together; manner of building; construction: *The structure of the new school is excellent.* **4** the relation of the parts or elements of a thing, especially as it determines its peculiar nature or character: *the structure of society, sentence structure, the structure of a language, the structure of a story.* **5** *Biology.* the arrangement of tissues, parts, or organs of a whole organism: *the structure of a flower. The cytoplasm of plant cells usually exhibits a considerable amount of structure as seen with the microscope* (Fred W. Emerson). **6** *Geology.* **a** the character of rocks as determined by stratification and faults. **b** the features of rocks that are due to fracture or to the arrangement of heterogeneous components. **7** *Chemistry.* the manner in which the atoms making up a particular molecule are attached to one another.
**—*v.t.*** to make into a structure; build; construct; fabricate: *to structure a building, to structure a sentence. Language is not only dependent on its culture, but in turn structures reality for this culture* (Herbert Hackett).
[< Latin *structūra* < *struere* build, arrange]

**struc|tured** (struk′chərd), *adj.* having a definite structure: *Linguists have often been favoured with the most obviously structured material with which to work* (Henry A. Gleason, Jr.).

**struc|ture|less** (struk′chər lis), *adj.* having no definite structure; amorphous. *To interpret the scattering of neutrons one idealizes the nucleus as a structureless sphere* (New Scientist).
**—struc′ture|less|ness,** *n.*

**struc|tur|ism** (struk′chə riz əm), *n.* art that emphasizes basic geometric forms or structures: *Biederman himself, having grandly declared that both painting and sculpture were obsolete, arrived at ... "structurism"—reliefs that have the dimension of sculpture and the color of painting* (Time).

**struc|tur|ist** (struk′chər ist), *n., adj.* **—*n.*** an artist whose work emphasizes basic geometric forms or structures.
**—*adj.*** of or characterized by structurism.

**struc|tur|i|za|tion** (struk′chə rə zā′shən), *n.* the process of arranging any complex matter into an organized structure.

**struc|tur|ize** (struk′chə rīz), *v.t.,* **-ized, -iz|ing.** to arrange in the form of an organized structure: *Research capacities are being structurized to the optimum in every single economic branch in order to meet the country's requirements of the scientific and technological revolution* (London Times).

**stru|del** (strü′dəl; *German* shtrü′dəl), *n.* a pastry, usually consisting of fruit or cheese covered by a very thin dough: *apple strudel.* [< German *Strudel* (literally) whirlpool]

**strug|gle** (strug′əl), *v.,* **-gled, -gling,** *n.* **—*v.i.*** **1** to make great efforts with the body; work hard against difficulties; try hard: *The poor have to struggle for a living. The swimmer struggled against the tide. She struggled to keep back the tears.* **SYN:** strive, labor, toil, contend. **2** to fight: *The dog struggled fiercely with the wildcat.* **3** to get, move, or make one's way with great effort: *to struggle through, to struggle along, to struggle to one's feet.*
**—*v.t.*** **1** to bring, put, do, or otherwise achieve by struggling. **2** *Obsolete.* to contest (a point) persistently.
**—*n.*** **1** great effort; hard work: *It is a struggle for the widow to send her six children to college. Making the baby eat his spinach is a struggle.* **SYN:** exertion, labor, endeavor. **2** the act of fighting; conflict. **SYN:** strife, contest.
[Middle English *struglen;* origin uncertain]
**—strug′gler,** *n.*

**struggle for existence** or **life,** *Biology.* the competition between living animals or plants for survival; natural selection. Often, the circumstances helping one form survive cause another to die out.

**strug|gling** (strug′ling), *adj.* **1** that struggles. **2** having a struggle to make a living: *a struggling professional man, a struggling periodical.* **—strug′gling|ly,** *adv.*

**strum** (strum), *v.,* **strummed, strum|ming,** *n.* **—*v.t., v.i.*** **1a** to play by running the fingers

**Pronunciation Key:** hat, āge, cãre, fär; let, ēqual, tėrm; it, īce; hot, ōpen, ôrder; **oi**l, **ou**t; cup, pu̇t, rüle; **ch**ild; lo**ng**; **th**in; **ᴛʜ**en; **zh**, measure; ə represents **a** in about, **e** in taken, **i** in pencil, **o** in lemon, **u** in circus.

across the strings or keys, often carelessly and with a light touch: *to strum a guitar, to strum on the piano.* **b** to play by strumming: *to strum a melody, to strum out a few chords.* **2** to tap against or strike as if strumming: *to strum one's fingers impatiently on a table, to strum on a table with one's fingers.*
—*n.* **1** the act of strumming. **2** the sound of strumming.
[perhaps imitative] —**strum′mer,** *n.*

**stru|ma** (strü′mə), *n., pl.* **-mae** (-mē). **1** *Medicine.* **a** scrofula. **b** goiter. **2** *Botany.* a cushionlike swelling or dilatation of or on an organ, as at one side of the base of the capsule in many mosses, or at the tip of the petiole in many leaves. [< New Latin *struma* < Latin *strūma* scrofulous tumor]

**stru|mose** (strü′mōs), *adj.* **1** *Medicine.* strumous. **2** *Botany.* having a struma or strumae.

**stru|mous** (strü′məs), *adj. Medicine.* affected with or characteristic of struma.

**strum|pet** (strum′pit), *n.* = prostitute. [origin uncertain]

**strung** (strung), *v.* the past tense and a past participle of **string**: *The children strung along after the teacher. The vines were strung on poles.*
**strung out,** *Slang.* to be or become addicted to a drug: *He is strung out on heroin.*

**strung-out** (strung′out′), *adj.* sick, weak, or disturbed, especially from drug addiction: *"These are very strung-out kids with individual hangups," said Jim Fouratt ... describing the modern runaway* (New York Times).

**strunt** (strunt), *n., v. Scottish.* —*n.* **1** a fit of ill humor; the sulks. **2** alcoholic liquor.
—*v.i.* **1** to sulk. **2** to strut.
[origin uncertain]

**strun|zite** (strun′zīt), *n.* a yellowish mineral consisting chiefly of iron, manganese, and phosphorus, with small amounts of magnesium and zinc. [< Hugo *Strunz,* a German mineralogist of the 1900's + *-ite*[1]]

**strut**[1] (strut), *v.,* **strut|ted, strut|ting,** *n.* —*v.i.* to walk in a vain, important, or affected manner: *The rooster struts about the barnyard.*
—*v.t.* to walk upon or over with a vain, self-important, or affected manner: *to strut the stage.*
—*n.* a strutting walk: *after our little hour of strut and rave* (James Russell Lowell).
[Old English *strūtian* stand out stiffly] —**strut′ter,** *n.*
—*Syn. v.i.* **Strut, swagger** mean to walk or hold oneself with an air of importance. **Strut** suggests sticking the chest out and holding the head and body stiffly and proudly to show how important one is: *The little boy put on his father's medals and strutted around the room.* **Swagger** suggests showing off how much better one is than others by strutting boldly, rudely, or insultingly: *After being put on probation again, the boys swaggered out of the principal's office.*

*** strut**[2] (strut), *n., v.,* **strut|ted, strut|ting.** —*n.* a supporting piece that resists pressure in a framework, such as a diagonal brace that acts as a support for a beam of a bridge or the rafter of a roof; brace.
—*v.t.* to brace or support by a strut or struts.
[ultimately related to **strut**[1]]

*** strut**[2]

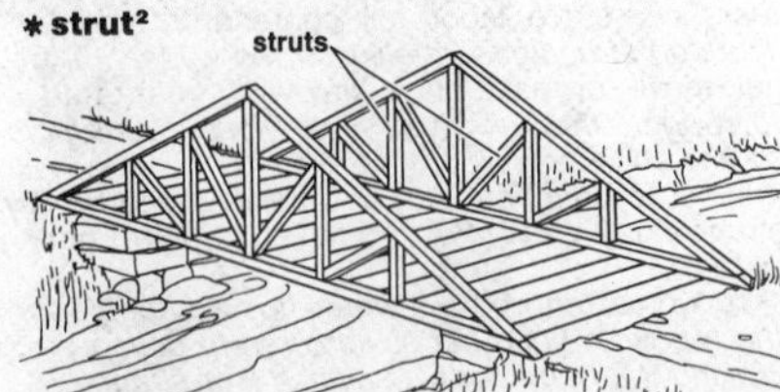


**stru|thi|oid** (strü′thē oid), *adj.* = struthious.

**stru|thi|ous** (strü′thē əs), *adj.* **1** of or belonging to a large group of flightless birds including the ostriches and, sometimes, other birds with unkeeled sternums, such as the emus and cassowaries. **2** of or like the ostrich: *struthious tactics.* [< Late Latin *strūthio* ostrich, short for Latin *strūthiocamēlus* (< Greek *strouthokámēlos* < *strouthós* sparrow + *kámēlos* camel) + English *-ous;* because of the bird's long neck]

**strut|ting** (strut′ing), *adj.* that struts or is like a strut: *a strutting rooster, a strutting drum major.* —**strut′ting|ly,** *adv.*

**strut|ty** (strut′ē), *adj.,* **-ti|er, -ti|est.** walking with an affected air of dignity; strutting: *A tough, strutty little man said, "I believe in capital punishment"* (Truman Capote).

**strych|nin** (strik′nin), *n.* = strychnine.

**strych|nine** (strik′nin, -nēn, -nīn), *n.* a highly poisonous drug consisting of colorless crystals. It is an alkaloid obtained from the nux vomica and related plants. Strychnine is used in medicine in small doses as a tonic, and as a stimulant to the central nervous system. *Formula:* $C_{21}H_{22}N_2O_2$ [< French *strychnine* < New Latin *Strychnos* the genus name of the nux vomica plant < Greek *strýchnos* a kind of nightshade; various emetic plants]

**strych|nin|ism** (strik′nə niz əm), *n.* a disordered condition produced by too great a use of strychnine.

**strych|nos** (strik′nos), *n.* any tropical tree or shrub of a group with usually poisonous bark, roots, or seeds, such as the nux vomica. [< New Latin *Strychnos;* see etym. under **strychnine**]

**sts.,** **1** stanzas. **2** stitches.

**STS** (no periods), Serologic Test for Syphilis.

**Stu|art** (stü′ərt, styü′-), *n.* a member of the royal family that ruled Scotland from 1371 to 1603, and England and Scotland from 1603 to 1714. James I, Charles I, Charles II, James II, Mary II, and Queen Anne were the Stuarts who reigned after 1603.

**stub** (stub), *n., v.,* **stubbed, stub|bing,** *adj.* —*n.* **1** a short piece that is left: *the stub of a pencil, the stub of a cigar.* **2a** the short piece of each leaf, as in a checkbook, kept as a record. **b** a similar part of a motion-picture or theater ticket. **3** something short and blunt; short, thick, piece or part. **4** a pen having a short, blunt point. **5** the stump of a tree, a broken tooth, or lost limb. **6** = stub nail.
—*v.t.* **1** to strike (one's toe) against something: *He stubbed his toe against the doorsill.* **2** to clear (land) of tree stumps. **3** to dig up by the roots; grub up (roots). **4** to put out (a cigarette) by pressing the lighted end of the stub against a hard object: *He hesitated, took it, smoked it only half way before stubbing it out* (Cape Times).
—*adj.* squat; stubby.
[Old English *stybb* stump]

**stub|bed** (stub′id, stubd), *adj.* **1** reduced or worn down to a stub. **2** cut close to the skin, stubbly: *stubbed hair.* **3** having many stubs. **4** sturdy; hardy. —**stub′bed|ness,** *n.*

**stub|ble** (stub′əl), *n.* **1** the lower ends of stalks of grain left in the ground after the grain is cut: *The stubble hurt the boy's bare feet. The long-lasting stubbles, with their spilled grain, were also the partridge's winter granaries* (London Times). **2** any short, rough growth: *He had a three days' stubble on his unshaven face.* SYN: bristle. [< Old French *estuble,* ultimately < Late Latin *stupula,* variant of Latin *stipula* stem. See etym. of doublet **stipule.**]

**stub|bled** (stub′əld), *adj.* covered with stubble.

**stubble field,** a field from which grain has been cut; stubbled piece of ground.

**stub|bly** (stub′lē), *adj.,* **-bli|er, -bli|est.** **1** covered with stubble: *stubbly waste land* (Sinclair Lewis). **2** like stubble; bristly: *a stubbly moustache.*

**stub|born** (stub′ərn), *adj.* **1** fixed in purpose or opinion; not giving in to argument or requests; unyielding: *The stubborn boy refused to listen to reasons for not going out in the rain.* SYN: dogged, resolute. See syn. under **obstinate.** **2** characterized by obstinacy: *a stubborn refusal to listen to reason, a stubborn defense of a belief.* SYN: dogged, resolute. See syn. under **obstinate.** **3** hard to deal with or manage: *a stubborn cough, a stubborn metal. Facts are stubborn things. Not a plough had ever disturbed a grain of that stubborn soil* (Thomas Hardy). SYN: unruly, ungovernable, refractory. [probably ultimately < *stub*] —**stub′born|ly,** *adv.* —**stub′born|ness,** *n.*

**stub|by** (stub′ē), *adj.,* **-bi|er, -bi|est.** **1a** short and thick or broad: *stubby fingers, a stubby figure. His stubby-fingered, thick-veined hands and his short, corded arms were like steel and leather* (Atlantic). **b** short and blunt as the result of wear: *a stubby pencil.* **2** short, thick, and stiff: *a stubby beard.* **3** having many stubs or stumps. —**stub′bi|ness,** *n.*

**stu|be** or **Stu|be** (shtü′bə, stü′-), *n., pl.* **-bes, -ben** (-bən). = bierstube. [< German *Stube* (literally) room]

**stub nail,** **1** a short, thick nail. **2** a worn or broken nail, especially an old horseshoe nail.

**stub pen,** = stub (def. 4).

**stub wing,** or **stub|wing** (stub′wing′), *n.* **1** that part of a wing on certain aircraft that lies next to the fuselage, to which the rest of the wing, separately built, is attached. **2** a short wing, especially as used on certain autogiros.

**stuc|co** (stuk′ō), *n., pl.* **-coes** or **-cos,** *v.,* **-coed, -co|ing.** —*n.* **1** plaster used for covering walls, which sets with a hard, stonelike coat. One kind, made of portland cement, sand, and lime, is used for covering the outer walls of buildings. Another kind, made of lime and crushed marble, is used for cornices, moldings, and other interior decorations. *The white stucco buildings were trim and gay in the sunlight* (Harper's). **2** = stuccowork.
—*v.t.* to cover, coat, or decorate with stucco: *We had out house stuccoed last year.*
[< Italian *stucco* < Germanic (compare Middle High German *stucke* piece)] —**stuc′co|er,** *n.*

**stuc|co|work** (stuk′ō wėrk′), *n.* work or decoration done in stucco.

**stuck** (stuk), *v.* past tense and past participle of **stick**[2]: *She stuck out her tongue. We were stuck in the mud.*

**stuck-up** (stuk′up′), *adj. Informal.* too proud; conceited; vain; haughty. SYN: egotistical. —**stuck′up′-ness,** *n.*

*** stud**[1] (stud), *n., v.,* **stud|ded, stud|ding.** —*n.* **1** a head of a nail, or a knob, or boss sticking out from a surface, used for ornament or protection: *The belt was ornamented with silver studs. Some snow tires have metal studs to provide more traction.* **2** a kind of small button that fits through eyelets or buttonholes, used as a collar fastener on men's shirts or as an ornament. **3** an upright post to which boards, laths, or panels are nailed in making walls in houses. **4** a projecting pin or socket on a machine, such as one in which the end of an axle or pin fits or one that serves as a support, axis, or stop. **5** a crosspiece put in each link of a chain cable to strengthen it. **6** = stud poker.
—*v.t.* **1** to set or ornament with studs or something like studs: *a sword hilt studded with jewels.* **2** to be set or scattered over: *a city studded with factories. Little islands stud the harbor.* **3** to set like studs; scatter at intervals: *Shocks of corn were studded over the field.* **4** to provide, frame, or support (a wall, ceiling, or floor) with studs.
[Old English *studu* pillar, post]

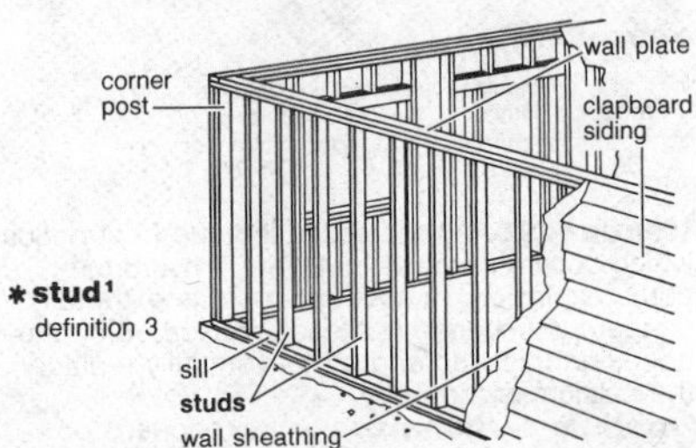


*** stud**[1]
definition 3

**stud**[2] (stud), *n., adj.* —*n.* **1** a collection of horses kept for breeding, hunting, or racing. **2** a place where such a collection is kept; studfarm. **3** *U.S.* a male horse kept for breeding; stallion. **4** any male animal kept for breeding.
—*adj.* **1** of or having to do with a studhorse. **2** kept for breeding purposes.
**at stud,** ready for use in breeding: *a stallion at stud.*
[Old English *stōd.* Compare etym. under **steed.**]

**stud.,** student.

**stud|book** (stud′bu̇k′), *n.,* or **stud book,** a book giving the pedigrees and performance records of thoroughbred horses and dogs.

**stud|ded** (stud′id), *adj.* provided with studs: *studded tires, a high-studded parlor.*

**stud|ding** (stud′ing), *n.* **1** the studs of a wall, house, or other structure. **2** lumber for making studs.

**stud|ding|sail** (stud′ing sāl′; *Nautical* stun′səl), *n.,* or **studding sail,** a light sail set at the side of a square sail, as on a square-rigged ship; stunsail; stuns'le. [origin unknown]

**stu|dent** (stü′dənt, styü′-), *n.* **1** a person who studies: *a student of human nature. She is a student of birds.* **2** a person who is studying at a school, college, or university: *That high school has 3,000 students. A student is a person who is learning to fulfill his powers and to find ways of using them in the service of mankind* (Harold Taylor). [< Latin *studēns, -entis,* present participle of *studēre* apply oneself to learning; (originally) be eager]
—*Syn.* **1, 2 Student, pupil, scholar** mean a person who is studying or being taught. **Student,** emphasizing the idea of studying, applies to anyone who loves to study, but especially to someone attending a higher school, college, or university: *Several high-school students were there.* **Pupil,** emphasizing personal supervision by a teacher, applies to a child in school or someone studying privately with a teacher: *He is a pupil in the third grade. My aunt is a pupil of an opera singer.* **Scholar** now applies chiefly to a learned person who is an authority in some field or to a student who has a scholarship: *He is a distinguished classical scholar.*

**student body,** the collective community of students studying at a school, college, or university.

**student council,** a group of students elected by their classmates to represent them in the management of school or college activities.

**student government,** the participation of students in the government of a school, college, or university, usually through a student council or similar organization that represents the students' interests.

**student lamp**, an adjustable lamp for reading at a table or desk. The old-fashioned kind burned kerosene.

**student power**, the control of a school, college, or university by members of the student body: *The place is no longer under the direction of its professors ... but is operating under what is called "student power"* (New Yorker). [patterned on *Black Power*]

**Student's distribution** or **Student's t-distribution**, *Statistics.* a distribution used to estimate the standard deviation of a population on the basis of the standard deviation of a small sample; t-distribution. As the size of the sample increases, the distribution approaches normal distribution. [< *Student,* the pseudonym of William Sealy Gosset, 1876-1947, a British statistician]

**stu|dent|ship** (stü′dənt ship, styü′-), *n.* **1** the fact or condition of being a student. **2** a scholarship or fellowship granted to a student in a college or university.

**student teacher**, a college or university student who teaches in a school for a certain period to qualify for a teacher's certificate or diploma; practice teacher.

**student teaching**, the practice of a student teacher.

**student union**, a building set aside at a college or university for student activities, usually with dining facilities and lounges.

**stud|farm** (stud′färm′), *n.* = stud$^2$ (*n.* def. 2).

**stud fee**, the fee charged for the use of a male animal for breeding: *When the horse retires ... his stud fee will be $15,000* (Newsweek).

**stud|fish** (stud′fish′), *n., pl.* **-fish|es** or (*collectively*) **-fish**. any one of several bluish or greenish killifish found in rivers of the central and southern United States.

**stud|horse** (stud′hôrs′), *n.* a male horse kept for breeding; stallion.

**stud|ied** (stud′ēd), *adj.* **1** resulting from or characterized by deliberate effort; carefully planned; done on purpose: *a studied air of simplicity, a studied laugh. What she said to me was a studied insult. While its performances of popular songs and jazz tunes are dexterous, they are a bit too studied for my taste* (New Yorker). **SYN**: premeditated, intentional. See syn. under **elaborate**. **2** = learned. — **stud′ied|ly**, *adv.* — **stud′iedness**, *n.*

**stud|i|er** (stud′ē ər), *n. Rare.* a person who studies; student: *a studier of nature.*

**stud|ies** (stud′ēz), *n.pl.* See under **study**.

**stu|di|o** (stü′dē ō, styü′-), *n., pl.* **-di|os**, *adj.* — *n.* **1a** the workroom of a painter, sculptor, photographer, or other artist. **SYN**: atelier, workshop. **b** a room in which a music teacher, dramatic coach, or other artist gives lessons. **2** a place where motion pictures are made. **3** a place where a radio or television program originates.
— *adj.* of or having to do with a studio.
[< Italian *studio* a study; study < Latin *studium* study, enthusiasm, related to *studēre;* see etym. under **student**. See etym. of doublets **étude**, **study**.]

**studio apartment**, a one-room apartment with a bathroom and sometimes a small kitchen or kitchenette.

**studio couch**, an upholstered couch, without a back or arms, that can be used as a bed.

**stu|di|ous** (stü′dē əs, styü′-), *adj.* **1** fond of study: *That studious boy likes school.* **2** showing careful attention or consideration; careful; thoughtful: *She is always studious of her mother's comfort. The clerk made a studious effort to please customers.* **SYN**: earnest, painstaking, solicitous, zealous, assiduous. **3** studied; deliberate: *The study was furnished with studious simplicity* (John Galsworthy). **4** *Archaic.* used for or suited to study: *To walk the studious cloisters ...* (Milton). [< Latin *studiōsus* < *studium;* see etym. under **study**] — **stu′di|ous|ly**, *adv.* — **stu′di|ous|ness**, *n.*

**stud poker**, a form of poker in which each player is dealt one card face down and another face up. At each round of betting, another card is dealt face up to each remaining player, until five cards are distributed.

**stud|work** (stud′wėrk′), *n.* **1** building or structures built with or supported by studs. **2** fabrics or leather set with knobs or studs.

**stud|y** (stud′ē), *n., pl.* **stud|ies**, *v.,* **stud|ied**, **stud|y|ing**. — *n.* **1** the effort to learn by reading or thinking: *After an hour's hard study he knew his lesson. Study to him was pleasure and delight* (George Crabbe). **2** a careful examination; investigation: *to make a study of a case at law, a man's life or character, or the causes of a depression. Such a study, brought down to date, would show the same expansion going on in the last six years* (Newsweek). **3** a subject that is studied; branch of learning; thing investigated or to be investigated. Arithmetic, spelling, and geography are three school studies. *The proper study of mankind is Man* (Alexander Pope). **4** a room for study, reading, or writing: *The minister was reading in his study.* **5** a piece of writing or a work of art that deals in careful detail with one particular subject: *a study of art in Germany. The face of Nature* [*was*] *a study in old gold* (Kenneth Grahame). **6** a sketch, as for a picture or story. **7** a piece of music for practice or testing; étude. **8** earnest effort, or the object of endeavor or effort: *Her constant study is to please her parents.* **9** deep thought; reverie: *to be in a brown study. The judge was absorbed in study about the case.* **10** a person, usually an actor, with respect to his ability to memorize: *a quick or slow study.*
— *v.t.* **1** to try to learn by oneself or in school: *to study the rules of a game or contest, to study philosophy, to study law. She studied her spelling lesson for half an hour.* **2** to examine carefully or in detail; investigate: *to study the customs of society, to study a man's character, to study a poem. We studied the map to find the shortest road home.* **SYN**: scrutinize. **3** to read carefully to learn or understand: *to study the Bible.* **4** to memorize or try to memorize: *to study one's part in a play.* **5** to consider with care; thing out; plan; devise: *to study a suitable answer, to study out a new procedure. The prisoner studied ways to escape.* **SYN**: ponder. See syn. under **consider**. **6** to give care and thought to; try hard for; aim at: *The three villians studied nothing but revenge* (Daniel Defoe).
— *v.i.* **1** to try to learn or gain knowledge by means of books, observation, or experiment: *He is studying to be a doctor.* **2** to be a student: *to study for a master's degree, to study under a famous musician.* **3** to think intently; meditate; ponder. **4** to try hard; endeavor: *The grocer studies to please his customers. I studied to appear calm* (W. H. Hudson).
**studies**, a person's work as a student: *to return to one's studies after a vacation.*
[< Latin *studium* study; (originally) eagerness, related to *studēre;* see etym. under **student**. See etym. of doublets **étude**, **studio**.]

**study group**, a group of people who come together or are appointed to study a particular subject or problem.

**study hall**, a large room in a school or college for studying, reading, and preparing assignments.

**stu|fa** (stü′fä), *n., pl.* **-fas**, **-fe** (-fā). a jet of steam issuing from a fissure in the earth in a volcanic region. [< Italian *stufa.* Compare etym. under **stove**$^1$.]

**stuff** (stuf), *n., v.* — *n.* **1** what a thing is made of; material: *Clay is the stuff of which pottery is made. There are even greater difficulties in "managing" the stuff of history than in understanding it* (Bulletin of Atomic Scientists). *We are such stuff as dreams are made on* (Shakespeare). **2** any woven fabric, especially a woolen or worsted one: *She bought some white stuff for curtains.* **3** a thing or things; substance: *The doctor rubbed some kind of stuff on the burn.* **4** goods; belongings; possessions: *I was told to move my stuff out of the room.* **5** worthless material; useless objects; refuse: *The attic is full of old stuff.* **SYN**: rubbish, trash. **6** silly words and thoughts: *a lot of stuff and nonsense.* **7** *Figurative.* inward qualities; character; capabilities: *... places where a man has got to show the stuff that's in him* (Joseph Conrad). *He was not naturally of the stuff of which martyrs are made* (Hawthorne). **8** *Baseball, Slang.* the ability to throw a variety of pitches with deception: *Pitch for pitch, many of his contemporaries have what the trade calls "more stuff"* (Time). **9** *U.S. Slang.* **a** marijuana. **b** heroin.
— *v.t.* **1** to pack full; fill: *She stuffed the pillow with feathers.* **SYN**: cram. **2** to stop (up); block; choke (up): *to stuff one's ears with cotton, to stuff a hole with rags, a stuffed nose. My head is stuffed up by a cold.* **3** to fill the skin of (a dead animal) to make it look as it did when alive: *We saw many stuffed birds in the museum.* **4** to fill (a chicken, turkey, fish, or piece of another animal, such as lamb or pork) with breadcrumbs, meat, chestnuts, and seasoning, before cooking. **5** to force; push; thrust: *He stuffed his clothes into the drawer. He stuffed his hands into his pockets.* **6** *U.S.* to put more votes in (a ballot box) than there are rightful voters. **7** to fill with food, information, or rubbish: *After he stuffed himself with candy, he felt sick.* (*Figurative.*) *Don't stuff up your mind with useless facts.* (*Figurative.*) *We are the hollow men We are the stuffed men ... Headpiece filled with straw* (T. S. Eliot). **8** to fill or pack together tightly: *a box stuffed with old letters, to stuff tobacco in a pipe, people stuffed in an elevator.* **SYN**: cram. **9** *Basketball.* to jam (a basketball) into the basket from above. **10** to treat (a hide) with a compound of tallow and other substances to soften, waterproof, and preserve it.
— *v.i.* **1** to eat too much; gorge oneself with food. **2** *Basketball.* to make a stuff shot.
**do one's stuff**, *Informal.* to perform, especially with skill: *Quite a few people come to our fair city to see the King* [*a dancer*] *do his stuff* (New Yorker).
**know one's stuff**, *Informal.* to be competent or well-informed, especially in a particular field; be knowledgeable: *For all the clarity and originality of his presentation, this is very much a book for those who know their stuff* (Scientific American).
**strut one's stuff**, *Slang.* to show off one's looks, clothing, abilities, or accomplishments: *A "dandy look" struts its stuff this spring* (New York Times).
[< Old French *estoffe,* perhaps ultimately < Latin *stuppa* tow$^2$, oakum < Greek *stýppē.* Compare etym. under **stop**.]

**stuffed shirt** (stuft), *Slang.* a person who tries to seem more important than he really is: *His deliberately offensive behavior to academic stuffed shirts* (David Daiches).

**stuff|er** (stuf′ər), *n.* **1** a person or thing that stuffs. **2** material used to stuff something.

**stuff|ing** (stuf′ing), *n.* **1** material used to fill or pack something. **2** a seasoned mixture of breadcrumbs with sausage or oysters, chestnuts, or some other food, used to stuff a chicken, turkey, or other animal, before cooking. **3** the act of a person or thing that stuffs.
**knock the stuffing out of**, *Informal.* to overcome; defeat; beat: *He was at the time going as well as any, but this error knocked the stuffing out of him* (London Times).

**stuffing box**, a chamber through which a piston rod or shaft passes and which is packed with an elastic material impermeable by a particular liquid or gas, in order to prevent leakage of the liquid or gas at the orifice through which the shaft passes: *Their metal bearings are kept lubricated by oil-soaked waste in a stuffing box* (Scientific American).

**stuffing nut**, a nut which when tightened reduced the cubic capacity of a stuffing box, so as to compress the elastic material contained in it and thus seal its orifice against leakage of a particular liquid or gas.

**stuff shot**, *Basketball.* a shot in which the ball is jammed into the basket from above; dunk shot.

**stuff|y** (stuf′ē), *adj.,* **stuff|i|er**, **stuff|i|est**. **1** lacking fresh air: *a stuffy room.* **2** lacking freshness or interest; dull; stodgy: *a stuffy speech. Lewis Cass of Michigan, very old and very dignified and very stuffy, was Secretary of State* (Bruce Catton). **3** stopped up: *A cold makes my head feel stuffy.* **4** *Informal.* easily shocked or offended: prim; strait-laced: *a stuffy chaperone.* **5** *Informal.* angry or sulky: *They never growl at us or get stuffy* (Rudyard Kipling). — **stuff′i|ly**, *adv.* — **stuff′i|ness**, *n.*

**Stu|ka** (stü′kə), *n.* a powerful German dive bomber used in World War II. [< German *Stuka* < *Stu*(*rz*)*ka*(*mpfflieger*) < *Sturz* a plunge + *Kampf* battle + *Flieger* flyer]

**stull** (stul), *n. Mining.* **1** a heavy timber secured in an excavation to provide support for a mine working. **2** a platform or framework of timber to support workmen or protect miners from falling stones. [perhaps < German *Stollen* a prop]

**stul|ti|fi|ca|tion** (stul′tə fə kā′shən), *n.* **1** the action of stultifying. **2** the state of being stultified: *Our simple survival is not worth so much that it is to be purchased at the cost of intellectual stultification* (Bulletin of Atomic Scientists).

**stul|ti|fi|er** (stul′tə fī′ər), *n.* a person or thing that stultifies.

**stul|ti|fy** (stul′tə fī), *v.t.,* **-fied**, **-fy|ing**. **1** to make worthless, useless, weak, or futile; frustrate: *to stultify a person's efforts or incentive, a program of reform stultified by public indifference, the stultifying atmosphere of a prison or dictatorship. It was infinitely dreary, stultifying, and meaningless* (Harper's). **2** to cause to appear foolish or absurd; reduce to foolishness or absurdity: *Many oldline companies ... clinging to their past practices, their stale traditions and stultifying smugness* (Christian Science Monitor). **3** *Law.* to allege (a person or oneself) to be of unsound mind. [< Late Latin *stultificāre* < Latin *stultus* foolish + *facere* to make] — **stul′ti|fy′ing|ly**, *adv.*

**stul|til|o|quence** (stul til′ə kwəns), *n.* foolish or silly talk; senseless babble. [< Latin *stultiloquentia* < *stultiloquus* speaking foolishly, ultimately < *stultus* foolish + *loquī* speak]

**Pronunciation Key:** hat, āge, cãre, fär; let, ēqual, tėrm; it, īce; hot, ōpen, ôrder; **oi**l, **ou**t; cup, pu̇t, rüle; **ch**ild; lo**ng**; **th**in; **ŦH**en; **zh**, measure; **ə** represents **a** in about, **e** in taken, **i** in pencil, **o** in lemon, **u** in circus.

**stul|til|o|quent** (stul til′ə kwənt), *adj.* given to stultiloquence.

**stum** (stum), *n., v.,* **stummed, stum|ming.** *—n.* **1** unfermented or partly fermented grape juice, often used for toning up flat wines. **2** wine toned up with must.
*—v.t.* **1** to tone up (wine) with unfermented or partly fermented grape juice. **2** to stop the fermentation of (new wine).
[perhaps < Dutch *stom,* noun use of adjective, stupid, insipid]

**stum|ble** (stum′bəl), *v.,* **-bled, -bling,** *n. —v.i.* **1** to trip by striking the foot against something: *He stumbled over the stool in the dark kitchen.* **2** to walk or move in an unsteady way: *The tired old man stumbled along.* **3** *Figurative.* to speak, act, or proceed in a clumsy or hesitating way: *The boy made many blunders as he stumbled through his recitation.* **4** *Figurative.* to make a mistake; do wrong; err: *The officials stumbled repeatedly in carrying out the new program.* **5** *Figurative.* to come by accident or chance: *While in the country, she stumbled upon some fine old pieces of furniture.* **6** to take offense; find an obstacle to belief; falter (at).
*—v.t.* **1** to cause to stumble; trip. **2** *Figurative.* to puzzle; perplex; nonplus.
*—n.* **1** a wrong act; mistake; blunder. **2** the act of stumbling.
[origin uncertain. Compare Swedish dialectal *stambla.*] **—stum′bler,** *n.* **—stum′bling|ly,** *adv.*

**stum|ble|bum** (stum′bəl bum′), *n. Slang.* **1** a person who moves about awkwardly or unsteadily as if in a daze or drunk. **2** a person of little ability; unskilled or inept person.

**stum|bling block** (stum′bling), **1** an obstacle; hindrance; impediment: *A big stumbling block preventing settlement was the union's demand for a cost-of-living escalator clause* (Wall Street Journal). **2** something that makes a person stumble.

**stum|bly** (stum′blē), *adj.* **1** apt to stumble. **2** apt to cause stumbling.

**stu|mer** (stü′mər, styü′-), *n. British Slang.* a forged or worthless check; counterfeit bank note or coin; sham. [origin unknown]

**stump** (stump), *n., v. —n.* **1a** the lower end of a tree or plant, left after the main part is broken or cut off: *We sat on top of a stump in the middle of a clearing.* **b** a standing tree trunk from which the upper part and the branches have been removed. **2** anything left after the main or important part has been removed or used up; stub; butt: *the stump of a pencil, the stump of a candle, the stump of a cigar, the stump of a tooth. The dog wagged his stump of a tail.* **3a** a place where a political speech is made. It was formerly the stump of a large felled tree. **b** public speaking around the country as a candidate or in support of a cause: *The senator is on the stump.* **4** a person with a short, thick build. **5a** a heavy step or gait, as of a lame or wooden-legged person. **b** a sound made by stiff walking or heavy steps; clump. **6a** a wooden leg. **b** *Slang.* a leg: *to stir one's stumps.* **7** *U.S. Informal.* a dare; challenge. **8** a tight roll of paper, soft leather, rubber, or other soft material, pointed at the ends and used to soften or blend pencil, charcoal, or crayon marks in drawing. **9** *Cricket.* one of the three upright sticks on the tops of which the bails are laid to form a wicket.
*—v.t.* **1** *U.S.* to remove stumps from (land). **2** to reduce to a stump; cut off; lop. **3** *U.S.* to make political speeches in: *The candidates for governor will stump the state.* **4** *Informal, Figurative.* to make unable to do or answer; cause to be at a loss; nonplus; baffle: *The unexpected question stumped him. Nobody could think of anything to do—everybody was stumped* (Mark Twain). **5** *U.S. Informal.* to dare or challenge (a person) to do something. **6** *U.S. Informal.* to stub (one's toe). **7** to tone or treat (lines or drawings) with a stump. **8** *Cricket.* (of the wicketkeeper) to put (a batsman) out by dislodging a bail, or knocking down a stump, with the ball held in the hand, when the batsman is out of the area within which he may bat.
*—v.i.* **1** to walk in a stiff, clumsy, or noisy way, as if one had a wooden leg: *The lame man stumped along.* **2** *U.S.* to make political speeches: *The candidate for senator stumped through every county of the state. Stumping it through England for seven years made* [*him*] *a consummate debater* (Emerson).
**go on** (or **take**) **the stump,** to go on a political campaign tour: [*They*] *said they would take the political stump to offset any Texas rebellion on the offshore oil issue* (New York Times).
**up a stump,** *U.S. Informal.* unable to act or answer; impotent; baffled: *We've got the map … but we ain't no nearer to finding the valley. … We're up a stump, and no mistake* (K. Munroe).
[compare Middle Low German *stump*] **—stump′-like′,** *adj.*

**stump|age** (stum′pij), *n.* **1a** standing timber with reference to its value or quantity. **b** the monetary value of such timber. **2** the right to cut such timber. **3** the price or tax paid for this.

**stump|er** (stum′pər), *n. U.S. Informal.* **1** a person or thing that stumps. **2** *Figurative.* a puzzling or baffling question or problem: *This was a stumper; I had been asked it dozens of times since I had arrived in Britain* (New Yorker). **3** = stump speaker.

**stump|jump plough** or **plow** (stump′jump′), *Australian.* a machine by which land can be plowed without clearing it of stumps.

**stump|knock|er** (stump′nok′ər), *n.* a sunfish of the southeastern United States with red or bronze spots on the body.

**stump|land** (stump′lənd, -land′), *n.* land covered with tree stumps.

**stump speaker,** a person who makes political speeches.

**stump speech,** a political speech: [*He*] *is no mean speaker himself, but all the editors got was a stump speech that ticked off the glories of the Democratic Party* (Vermont Royster).

**stump tracery,** a form of tracery in medieval German architecture, in which the molded bar passes through itself and is cut off short to form a stump.

**stump|wood** (stump′wu̇d′), *n.* wood from the stump of a tree, often valued in cabinetmaking.

**stump work,** a kind of embroidery made in England in the 1600's, in which lace, brocade, satin, corals, feathers, and other materials were stitched together and raised on pieces of wood or wool pads in fantastic shapes.

**stump|y** (stum′pē), *adj.,* **stump|i|er, stump|i|est.** **1** short and thick; squat and broad: *a stumpy person, a stumpy figure.* **2** having many stumps: *stumpy ground.* **—stump′i|ly,** *adv.* **—stump′i|ness,** *n.*

**stun** (stun), *v.,* **stunned, stun|ning,** *n. —v.t.* **1** to make senseless; knock unconscious: *He was stunned by the fall.* **2** to daze; bewilder; shock; overwhelm: *She was stunned by the news of a friend's death.* **SYN:** stupefy, dumfound, astound, amaze.
*—n.* **1a** the act of stunning or dazing. **b** the condition of being stunned. **2** a thing that stuns; stunner.
[Old English *stunian* to crash, resound; influenced by Old French *estoner* to resound, stun, ultimately < Latin *ex-* out, from + *tonāre* to thunder]

**stung** (stung), *v.* a past tense and past participle of **sting:** *A wasp stung him. He was stung on the neck.*

**stun gas,** an incapacitating gas; incapacitant: *Police across the country have … adopted Mace, a chemical stun gas in a pressurized can, as a means of coping with rioters and unruly suspects* (Time).

**stun gun,** a long-barreled gun that shoots a compressed bag filled with sand, bird shoot, or the like, used especially in riot control.

**stunk** (stungk), *v.* a past tense and past participle of **stink:** *The garbage dump stunk. The rotten eggs had stunk up the kitchen.*
▶ See **stink** for usage note.

**stun|ner** (stun′ər), *n.* **1** a person, thing, or blow that stuns. **2** *Informal.* a very striking or attractive person or thing. **3** *Informal.* an expert: *The cook … was really a stunner for tarts* (Thackeray).

**stun|ning** (stun′ing), *adj.* **1a** very attractive or good-looking; strikingly pretty: *a stunning girl, a stunning new hat.* **b** excellent or delightful; first-rate; splendid: *a stunning performance.* **2** that stuns or dazes; bewildering: *a stunning blow, a stunning piece of news.* **—stun′ning|ly,** *adv.*

**stun|sail** or **stun|s'le** (stun′səl), *n.* = studding-sail.

**stunt¹** (stunt), *v., n. —v.t.* **1** to check in growth or development: *Lack of proper food often stunts a child.* **2** to decrease the rate of; retard: *to stunt the growth of a plant.*
*—n.* **1** a stunting. **2** a stunted animal or plant.
[earlier to bring to a stand, nonplus < Middle English *stunt* foolish, Old English]

**stunt²** (stunt), *n., v. Informal. —n.* a feat to attract attention; act showing boldness or skill: *to do stunts in the water or with an airplane. Circus riders perform stunts on horseback.*
*—v.i.* to perform a stunt or stunts.
*—v.t.* to perform a stunt or stunts with: *to stunt an airplane.*
[perhaps variant of *stint* a task]

**stunt|ed** (stun′tid), *adj.* **1** checked in growth or development; undeveloped; dwarfed: *a knot of stunted hollies* (Thomas Hardy). **2** disproportionately or abnormally short or small. **3** (of growth or development) checked or arrested. **—stunt′ed|ly,** *adv.* **—stunt′ed|ness,** *n.*

**stunt|i|ness** (stun′tē nis), *n.* a being stunted or stunty; stuntedness.

**stunt|man** (stunt′man′), *n. pl.* **-men.** a man who performs dangerous or difficult feats as a profession, especially in motion pictures where he often acts as a double for an actor.

**stunt|y¹** (stun′tē), *adj.* = stunted.

**stunt|y²** (stun′tē), *adj.* done for display; showy: *Writing should be literate but not fine, amusing but not facetious, attractive but not stunty* (Observer).

∗**stu|pa** (stü′pə), *n.* (in the Buddhist countries) a dome-shaped monumental structure erected to commemorate some event or to mark a sacred spot. [< Sanskrit *stūpa*]

∗ **stupa**
Great Stupa at Sanchi, India

**stupe¹** (stüp, styüp), *n.* **1** a piece of flannel or other cloth soaked in hot, usually medicated, water and wrung out, applied as a counterirritant to an inflamed area. **2** a small compress of soft material, used in dressing a wound. [< Medieval Latin *stupa* < Latin *stūpa,* variant of *stuppa* coarse flax < Greek *stýppē*]

**stupe²** (stüp, styüp), *n. Slang.* a stupid person. [< *stupid*]

**stu|pe|fa|cient** (stü′pə fā′shənt, styü′-), *adj., n. —adj.* stupefying.
*—n.* a drug or agent that produces stupor.
[< Latin *stupefaciēns, -entis,* present participle of *stupefacere;* see etym. under **stupefy**]

**stu|pe|fac|tion** (stü′pə fak′shən, styü′-), *n.* **1** dazed or senseless condition; stupor. **SYN:** torpor. **2** overwhelming amazement, shock, or consternation. **SYN:** petrifaction. **3** the action of stupefying or state of being stupefied.

**stu|pe|fac|tive** (stü′pə fak′tiv, styü′-; stü′pə fak′-, styü′-), *adj.* stupefying; stupefacient.

**stu|pe|fi|er** (stü′pə fī′ər, styü′-), *n.* a person or thing that stupefies.

**stu|pe|fy** (stü′pə fī, styü′-), *v.t.,* **-fied, -fy|ing.** **1** to make stupid, dull, or senseless: *to be stupefied by a drug.* **SYN:** deaden. **2** to overwhelm with shock or amazement; astound: *They were stupefied by the calamity.* **SYN:** stun. [< Latin *stupefacere* < *stupēre* be amazed + *facere* to make]

**stu|pe|fy|ing|ly** (stü′pə fī′ing lē, styü′-), *adv.* in a manner that is stupefying: *This stupefying tedious excursion into the past loses itself in a yawn* (Observer).

**stu|pend** (stü pend′, styü-), *adj. Archaic.* stupendous.

**stu|pen|dous** (stü pen′dəs, styü-), *adj.* amazing; marvelous; immense: *Niagara Falls is a stupendous sight.* **SYN:** astounding, prodigious. [< Latin *stupendus* to be wondered at, gerundive of *stupēre* be amazed] **—stu|pen′dous|ly,** *adv.* **—stu|pen′dous|ness,** *n.*

**stu|pe|ous** (stü′pē əs, styü′-), *adj.* **1** *Entomology.* covered with long, loose scales, like tow. **2** *Botany.* woolly. [< Latin *stūpeus* (with English *-ous*) made of tow < *stūpa;* see etym. under **stupe¹**]

**stu|pid** (stü′pid, styü′-), *adj., n. —adj.* **1** not intelligent; dull: *a stupid person, a stupid remark.* **2** not interesting; tiresome; boring: *a stupid book, to have a stupid time.* **SYN:** vapid. **3** dazed; stunned: *to be stupid with grief.* **SYN:** senseless.
*—n. Informal.* a stupid person or persons: *The wrath of the stupid has laid waste the world quite as often as has the craft of the bright* (Time).
[< Latin *stupidus* < *stupēre* be dazed, amazed] **—stu′pid|ly,** *adv.* **—stu′pid|ness,** *n.*
*—Syn. adj.* **1 Stupid, dull** mean having or showing little intelligence. **Stupid,** describing people or what they say or do, suggests a natural lack of good sense or ordinary intelligence: *Running away from an accident is stupid.* **Dull** suggests a slowness of understanding and a lack of alertness either by nature or because or overwork, poor health, or other such oppressive condition: *The mind becomes dull if the body gets no exercise.*

**stu|pid|i|ty** (stü pid′ə tē, styü-), *n., pl.* **-ties.** **1** lack of intelligence; dullness. **SYN:** obtuseness. **2** a foolish act or idea. **SYN:** folly.

**stu|por** (stü′pər, styü′-), *n.* **1** a dazed condition; loss or lessening of the power to feel: *The injured man lay in a stupor, unable to tell what had* *happened to him.* **SYN**: lethargy, torpor. **2** intellectual or moral numbness: *a joyless stupor* (John Woolman). **SYN**: apathy. [< Latin *stupor, -ōris* < *stupēre* be dazed, amazed]

**stu|por|ous** (stü′pər əs, styü′-), *adj.* characterized by or in a stupor; dazed.

**stu|pose** (stü′pōs, styü′-), *adj. Biology.* bearing tufts or mats of long hairs; composed of matted filaments like tow. [< Medieval Latin *stuposus* < Latin *stūpa;* see etym. under **stupe**[1]]

**stur|died** (stėr′dēd), *adj.* (of sheep) afflicted with sturdy or gid.

**stur|dy**[1] (stėr′dē), *adj., -***di|er**, **-di|est. 1** strong; stout: *a sturdy child, a sturdy chair, a sturdy plant, sturdy legs.* **SYN**: hardy, robust, muscular. See syn. under **strong. 2** not yielding; firm: *sturdy resistance, sturdy defenders.* **SYN**: resolute, indomitable. **3** simple and vigorous in character; downright; uncompromising: *sturdy courage, honesty, or common sense.* [Middle English *stourdy* reckless, violent, strong < Old French *esturdi* violent; (originally) dazed, past participle of *estourder* to stun, daze] —**stur′di|ly**, *adv.* —**stur′di|ness**, *n.*

**stur|dy**[2] (stėr′dē), *n.* a kind of staggers in sheep; gid. [< Old French *estordie* giddiness < *estourder;* see etym. under **sturdy**[1]]

**stur|geon** (stėr′jən), *n., pl.* **-geons** or (*collectively*) **-geon.** a large food fish whose long body has a tough skin with rows of bony plates. The various kinds comprise a family of fishes. Caviar and isinglass are obtained from sturgeons. [< Anglo-French *esturgeon,* ultimately < Germanic (compare Old High German *sturion,* accusative)]

**stur|ine** (stėr′ēn, -in), *n.* a protamine obtained from sturgeon's sperm.

**Sturm|ab|tei|lung** (shtůrm′äp′tī lůng), *n. German.* **1** a paramilitary Nazi Party organization, known as the brown shirts and noted for its terroristic activities. After 1934 it was replaced by the Schutzstaffel (SS). **2** (*literally*) storm division.

**Sturm und Drang** (shtůrm′ ůnt dräng′), *German.* **1** storm and stress; upheaval; turmoil: *The Metropolitan was not the only opera company beset by Sturm und Drang this week* (Newsweek). **2** a phrase applied to a period of rebellion against convention in German literature during the latter half of the 1700's and typified by a play of the same name, written by F. Klinger in 1776.

**sturt** (stėrt), *n. Scottish.* contention; quarreling. [alteration of *strut*[1]]

**stuss** (stus), *n.* a gambling game with cards, resembling faro. [< German *Stoss* push, hit, stroke]

**stut** (stut), *v.i., v.t.,* **stut|ted, stut|ting.** *British and Scottish Dialect.* to stutter. [Middle English *stutten;* see etym. under **stutter**]

**stut|ter** (stut′ər), *v., n.* —*v.i., v.t.* **1** to repeat (the same sound) in an effort to speak, as a result of nervous spasms or of a speech impediment. *Example:* C-c-c-c-can't th-th-th-they c-c-c-come? **SYN**: See syn. under **stammer. 2** to make any sound resembling this: (*Figurative.*) *the stuttering rifles' rapid rattle* (Wilfred Owen).
—*n.* the act, habit, or sound of stuttering.
[frequentative form of Middle English *stutten* stutter. Compare Dutch *stotteren.*] —**stut′ter|er**, *n.* —**stut′ter|ing|ly**, *adv.*

**Stutt|gart pitch** (stut′gärt; *German* shtůt′gärt), = international pitch. [< *Stuttgart,* a city in Germany]

**STV** (no periods), subscription television.

**St. Vi|tus dance** (sānt vī′təs), = St. Vitus's dance.

**St. Vitus's dance**, a nervous disorder, which affects children more often than adults, characterized by involuntary twitching of the muscles; chorea. [< *St. Vitus,* legendary martyr during the reign of Diocletian, venerated for his gift of healing, especially by dancing before his image at his festival]

**sty**[1] (stī), *n., pl.* **sties**, *v.,* **stied** or **styed, sty|ing.** —*n.* **1** a pen for pigs. **2** *Figurative.* any filthy or disgusting place: *I see ... human beings living in sties* (Thoreau).
—*v.t.* to keep or lodge in or as if in a sty: *The most beggarly, vile place that ever pigs were styed in* (Robert Louis Stevenson).
—*v.i.* to live in or as if in a sty.
[Old English *stig* building]

**sty**[2] (stī), *n., pl.* **sties.** a small, painful swelling on the edge of the eyelid. A sty is like a small boil. [probably < misdivision of Middle English *styanye* (taken as "sty on eye"), ultimately Old English *stīgend* a rising, riser, sty + *ēage* eye]

**stye** (stī), *n.* = sty[2].

**Styg|i|an** (stij′ē ən), *adj.* **1** of or having to do with the river Styx or the lower world. **2** Also, **stygian.** *Figurative.* black as the river Styx; dark; gloomy: *a Stygian sky. Its Stygian blackness prohibits plant life, which depends on sunlight* (Scientific American). **3** infernal; hellish. **4** completely binding; inviolable like the oath by the Styx, which the gods themselves feared to break: *a Stygian oath.* [< Latin *Stygius* (< Greek *Stýgios* < *Stýx, Stygós* the river Styx) + English *-an*]

**sty|lar** (stī′lər), *adj.* of, having to do with, or like a style for writing on wax.

**sty|late** (stī′lāt, -lit), *adj.* **1** *Zoology.* **a** having a style or stylet. **b** styloid; styliform. **2** *Botany.* having a persistent style.

**style** (stīl), *n., v.,* **styled, styl|ing.** —*n.* **1** fashion; manner or custom that prevails: *Paris, London, Rome, and New York set the style of dress for the world. Her dress is out of style.* **SYN**: See syn. under **fashion. 2** manner; method; way: *a lecturer with a free and easy style, the Gothic style of architecture, an opera in the Wagnerian style, styles of acting, to entertain in a lavish style. She learned several styles of swimming.* **3** a way of writing or speaking: *Books for children should have a clear, easy style.* **4** good style; fashionable appearance: *She dresses in style. That otherwise impalpable quality which women call style* (William Dean Howells). **5** excellence of form or expression, as in literature, speech, or art: *a model of style, a master of literary style. Get your facts right first: that is the foundation of all style* (Time). *Style is the dress of thoughts* (Lord Chesterfield). *Proper words in proper places, make the true definition of a style* (Jonathan Swift). **6** an official name; title: *Salute him with the style of King.* **7** a kind, sort, or type: *There was something in her style of beauty* (Jane Austen). **8** a pointed instrument for writing on wax; stylus. **9** something like this in shape or use, such as an etching needle, a graver, a pen, or a phonograph needle. **10** the pointer on a dial or chart, especially the gnomon of a sundial. **11** the stemlike part of the pistil of a flower, having the stigma at its top. Pollen is passed along the style to the ovules. See picture under **flower. 12** *Zoology.* a small, slender, pointed process or part; stylet. **13** the rules of spelling, punctuation, typography, and other matters of writing and setting in type, used by printers or followed by a particular editorial department or publication. **14** a method of reckoning time and dates, such as Old Style (Julian calendar) and New Style (Gregorian calendar). **15** a surgical probe with a blunt point; stylet.
—*v.t.* **1** to make in or conform to a given or accepted style; stylize: *Her poem is styled with care.* **2** to design according to a style or fashion: *His suits are styled by a famous designer.* **3** to name; call: *Joan of Arc was styled "the Maid of Orléans."*
**cramp one's style**, *Informal.* to keep one from showing his skill or ability: *The presence of curious onlookers watching him paint cramped his style.*
[< Old French *estile* < Latin *stilus* (originally) pointed writing instrument; influenced in modern spelling by Greek *stŷlos* column. See etym. of doublet **stylus.**] —**styl′er**, *n.*

**style|book** (stīl′bůk′), *n.* **1** a book containing the rules of punctuation, capitalization, and other matters of style followed by a printing or editorial office, school or college, or other institution that publishes. **2** a book showing fashions, usually in dress.

**style|less** (stīl′lis), *adj.* without style; of no particular style: *Her art deserved a better epitaph than this styleless, half-baked concoction* (Saturday Review). —**style′less|ness**, *n.*

**style|set|ter** (stīl′set′ər), *n.* a person or thing that sets a style for others to follow.

**sty|let** (stī′lit), *n.* **1a** a slender surgical probe. **b** a wire inserted in a catheter or cannula to stiffen it. **2** *Zoology.* a style. **3** a stiletto or dagger. [< French *stylet* < Italian *stiletto* stiletto]

**sty|li** (stī′lī), *n.* a plural of **stylus.**

**sty|li|form** (stī′lə fôrm), *adj.* shaped like a stylus or style: *a styliform bone, a styliform projection of rock.* [< New Latin *styliformis* < *stylus* style + *-formis* -form]

**styl|ing** (stī′ling), *n.* the way in which something is styled: *simplicity of styling.*

**styl|ise** (stī′līz), *v.,* **-ised, -is|ing.** *Especially British.* stylize.

**styl|ish** (stī′lish), *adj.* **1** having style; in the current fashion; fashionable: *a stylish woman. She wears stylish clothes.* **SYN**: modish, chic. **2** graceful and polished; skillful and smooth: *a stylish performance.* —**styl′ish|ly**, *adv.* —**styl′ish|ness**, *n.*

**styl|ism** (stī′liz əm), *n.* (in art and literature) excessive concern for style, with little consideration of content.

**styl|ist** (stī′list), *n.* **1** a writer, speaker, artist, musician, or the like, considered to be an expert or a master of style; person who takes much pains with his style: *an excellent stylist. He did turn out to have qualities as a musician and stylist that shone to advantage in this particular concerto* (New Yorker). **2** a person who designs, arranges, or advises concerning things such as interior decorations, clothes, or hairstyles.

**sty|lis|tic** (stī lis′tik), *adj.* of or having to do with style, especially in literature, music, or art: *I should like to hear music ... that is free of self-conscious formulas and tricks of stylistic sleight of hand* (New Yorker).

**sty|lis|ti|cal|ly** (stī lis′tə klē), *adv.* with regard to style; in matters of style: *The text itself is loaded with clichés, grossly repetitive and stylistically dull* (Scientific American).

**sty|lis|ti|cian** (stī′lə stish′ən), *n.* an expert in stylistics: *Some stylisticians say that literary style is defined by its deviance from speech* (Listener).

**sty|lis|tics** (stī lis′tiks), *n.* **1** the study of literary style. **2** the stylistic features of a written work: *the stylistics of the New Testament.*

**sty|lite** (stī′līt), *n.* any one of various Christian ascetics of the early Middle Ages who lived on the tops of pillars or columns. [< Late Greek *stȳlītēs* < Greek *stŷlos* a pillar]

**sty|lit|ic** (stī lit′ik), *adj.* of or like the stylites.

**styl|i|za|tion** (stī′lə zā′shən), *n.* **1** the act or process of stylizing: *The stage was empty except for fragmentary décors of a roof or a fence as stylizations of a wrecked home and loneliness* (New Yorker). **2** the fact or condition of being stylized.

**styl|ize** (stī′līz), *v.t., v.i.,* **-ized, -iz|ing.** to make or design according to a particular or conventional style: *We prefer to stylize and indicate—we do our best to avoid ambiguity* (New Yorker). **SYN**: regularize, conventionalize. —**styl′iz|er**, *n.*

**sty|lo** (stī′lō), *n., pl.* **-los.** = stylograph.

**sty|lo|bate** (stī′lə bāt), *n. Architecture.* a continuous base under a row of columns; the top part or surface of a stereobate. See picture under **Ionic.** [< Latin *stȳlobata* < Greek *stȳlobátēs* < *stŷlos* pillar + *baínein* to walk, step]

**sty|lo|graph** (stī′lə graf, -gräf), *n.* an old fountain pen similar to a modern ballpoint pen, in which the writing point consists of a fine metal tube instead of a nib. [< New Latin *stylus* style (< Latin *stilus*) + English *-graph*]

**sty|lo|graph|ic** (stī′lə graf′ik), *adj.* of or having to do with a stylograph or stylography. —**sty′lo-graph′i|cal|ly**, *adv.*

**sty|lo|graph|i|cal** (stī′lə graf′ə kəl), *adj.* = stylographic.

**stylographic pen**, = stylograph.

**sty|log|ra|phy** (stī log′rə fē), *n.* writing, drawing, or engraving with a stylus.

**sty|lo|hy|oid** (stī′lō hī′oid), *adj.* of or having to do with the styloid process of the temporal bone and the hyoid bone.

**sty|loid** (stī′loid), *adj.* **1** like a style; slender and pointed. **2** of or having to do with a styloid process. [< New Latin *styloides* < Greek *stȳloeidēs* < *stŷlos* pillar (sense influenced by Latin *stilus* style) + *eîdos* form]

**styloid process**, **1** a sharp spine pointing down at the base of the temporal bone in man. **2** the pointed projection at the lower extremity of the ulna, on the inner and posterior side.

**sty|lo|lite** (stī′lə līt), *n.* a columnar structure in limestones and certain other rocks, consisting of vertical layers at right angles to the stratification. [< Greek *stŷlos* pillar + English *-lite*]

**sty|lo|man|dib|u|lar** (stī′lō man dib′yə lər), *adj.* connecting the styloid process of the temporal bone and the lower jawbone: *a stylomandibular ligament.*

**sty|lo|mas|toid** (stī′lō mas′toid), *adj.* common to the styloid and mastoid processes of the temporal bone.

**sty|lo|max|il|lar|y** (stī′lō mak′sə ler′ē), *adj.* = stylomandibular.

**Sty|lo|my|cin** (stī′lə mī′sin), *n. Trademark.* puromycin.

**sty|lo|po|di|um** (stī′lə pō′dē əm), *n., pl.* **-di|a** (-dē ə). *Botany.* one of the double, fleshy disks surmounting the ovary and supporting the styles in plants of the parsley family. [< New Latin *stylopodium* < *stylus* (< Greek *stŷlos* pillar) + *-podium* little foot < Greek *poús, podós* foot]

**sty|lops** (stī′lops), *n.* a tiny insect that lives as a parasite in the bodies of bees, wasps, and other insects. The stylops is a typical strepsipteran insect. [< New Latin *Stylops* the genus name < Greek *stŷlos* pillar + *ōps* eye]

**sty|lo|sta|tis|tics** (stī′lō stə tis′tiks), *n.* the use of statistical methods to analyze the style of a writer or group of writers: *There are two essays in stylostatistics ... and both show that frequency of items or classes of items can be shown to correlate with time and type of writing* (Archibald A. Hill).

---

**Pronunciation Key:** hat, āge, cãre, fär; let, ēqual, tėrm; it, īce; hot, ōpen, ôrder; **oi**l, **ou**t; cup, půt, rüle; **ch**ild; lo**ng**; **th**in; **ŧħ**en; **zh**, measure; **ə** represents **a** in about, **e** in taken, **i** in pencil, **o** in lemon, **u** in circus.

*** sty|lus** (stī′ləs), *n., pl.* **-lus|es** or **-li. 1** a pointed instrument for writing on wax or a waxlike surface, as a mimeograph stencil; style. **2a** a phonograph needle: *If the turntable is shaken by extraneous vibration ... this will be picked up by the stylus and reproduced in mixture with the music* (Atlantic). **b** a needlelike device for cutting the sound grooves in a phonograph record. The record then can either by played back by itself or used as a mold to make other records. **3** the lightweight pen that records lines on a moving drum or chart on an oscillograph, galvanometer, or the like. **4** a V-shaped tool used in electronic engraving to cut or burn lines or dots into a metal or plastic. **5** *Botany, Zoology.* a style. [< New Latin *stylus* < Latin *stilus,* also *stylus;* spelling influenced by Greek *stŷlos* pillar. See etym. of doublet **style.**]

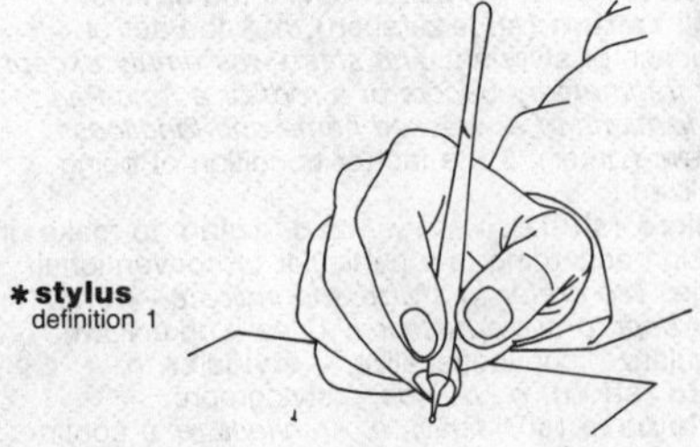
*** stylus**
definition 1

**sty|mie** (stī′mē), *n., pl.* **-mies,** *v.,* **-mied, -mieing.** —*n. Golf.* **1** the position or occurrence of a ball on a putting green directly between the player's ball and the hole for which he is playing. **2** (formerly) the position or occurrence of an opponent's ball on a putting green when it is directly between the player's ball and the hole for which he is playing, and when the distance between the balls is more than six inches.
—*v.t.* **1** *Golf.* to hinder or block with a stymie. **2** to stop or halt the progress of; block completely; hinder; thwart: *to be stymied by a problem or by lack of money. A brilliant talent, but he, too, stymied himself working in a distasteful environment* (S. J. Perelman). Also, **stimy.**
[origin uncertain]

**sty|my** (stī′mē), *n., pl.* **-mies,** *v.,* **-mied, -my|ing.** = stymie.

**styph|nic acid** (stif′nik), a yellow crystalline compound obtained from resorcinol or the wood of certain trees, used in making explosives. *Formula:* $C_6H_3N_3O_8$

**styp|tic** (stip′tik), *adj., n.* —*adj.* able to stop or check bleeding; astringent.
—*n.* something that stops or checks bleeding by contracting the tissue. Alum is a common styptic. [< Latin *stypticus* < Greek *stŷptikós* < *stýphein* to constrict]

**styp|ti|cal** (stip′tə kəl), *adj.* = styptic.

**styp|tic|i|ty** (stip tis′ə tē), *n.* the property of being styptic; astringency.

**styptic pencil,** a small stick of alum or other styptic substance, used on slight wounds to stop bleeding.

**sty|ra|ca|ceous** (stī′rə kā′shəs), *adj.* belonging to the family of dicotyledonous shrubs and small trees that includes the storax and silver bell. [< Latin *styrax, -acis* storax + English *-aceous*]

**sty|rax** (stī′raks), *n.* = storax. [< Latin *styrax* < Greek *stýrax, -akos*]

**sty|rene** (stī′rēn, stir′ēn), *n.* **1** an aromatic unsaturated liquid hydrocarbon, produced by distilling storax and by other methods and used in making synthetic rubber and plastics. *Formula:* $C_8H_8$ **2** = polystyrene: *chrome with rich chip-slip proof styrene handle* (Wall Street Journal). [< Latin *styrax, -acis* storax + English *-ene*]

**sty|rene-bu|ta|di|ene** (stī′rēn byü′tə dī′ēn, -dīēn′; stir′ēn-), *n.* a common type of synthetic rubber derived from petroleum, capable of withstanding very high temperature and pressure, used especially in automobile tires and footwear: *Dow probably will build a plant within the common market area to make a line of styrene-butadiene latexes* (Wall Street Journal).

**styrene resin,** = polystyrene.

**Sty|ro|foam** (stī′rə fōm′), *n. Trademark.* a polystyrene foam.

**sty|rol** (stī′rol), *n.* = styrene.

**sty|ro|lene** (stī′rə lēn), *n.* = styrene.

**Sty|ron** (stī′ron), *n. Trademark.* a colorless polystyrene material resistant to the effects of weather, sun, and acids.

**stythe** (stīth), *n. Dialect.* chokedamp. [origin uncertain]

**Styx** (stiks), *n. Greek Mythology.* a river in the lower world. The souls of the dead were ferried across it into Hades by Charon. [< Latin *Styx* < Greek *Stýx, Stygós,* related to *stygeîn* to hate]

**su-,** *prefix.* the form of **sub-** before *sp,* as in *suspect.*

**Su.,** Sunday.

**su|a|bil|i|ty** (sü′ə bil′ə tē), *n.* the state of being suable; liability to be sued.

**su|a|ble** (sü′ə bəl), *adj.* that can be sued; liable to be sued.

**su|a|bly** (sü′ə blē), *adv.* in a suable manner.

**suan pan** (swän′ pän′), the type of abacus used in China: *The Chinese suan pan, also used in Korea, has beads shaped like tiny doughnuts that move almost frictionlessly along bamboo rods* (Scientific American). [< Chinese (Peking) *suan p'an* counting board]

**sua|sion** (swā′zhən), *n.* an advising or urging; persuasion: *Moral suasion is persuasion exerted through or acting upon the moral nature or sense. The effectiveness of rules must never be based on paper promises or moral suasion* (Bulletin of Atomic Scientists). [< Latin *suāsiō, -ōnis* < *suādēre* to persuade]

**sua|sive** (swā′siv), *adj., n.* —*adj.* advising or urging; persuasive.
—*n.* a suasive speech, influence, or the like.
—**sua′sive|ly,** *adv.* —**sua′sive|ness,** *n.*

**sua|so|ry** (swā′sər ē), *adj.* = suasive.

**suave** (swäv), *adj.* smoothly agreeable or polite: *a suave and slippery scoundrel, a suave manner.* SYN: urbane, bland. [< Middle French *suave,* learned borrowing from Latin *suāvis* agreeable]
—**suave′ly,** *adv.* —**suave′ness,** *n.*

**sua|vi|ter in mo|do, for|ti|ter in re** (swav′ə tər in mō′dō, fôr′tə tər in rē′), *Latin.* gently in manner, vigorously in deed.

**sua|vi|ty** (swä′və tē, swav′ə-), *n., pl.* **-ties.** smoothly agreeable quality or behavior; smooth politeness; blandness: *These words, delivered with a cutting suavity* (Dickens). *The suavity and elegance of his prose is ... a little benumbing* (Scientific American).

**sub**[1] (sub), *n., adj., v.,* **subbed, sub|bing.** *Informal.* —*n., adj.* **1** = substitute. **2** = submarine. **3** = subordinate. **4** = subaltern. **5** *Photography.* substratum; subbing. **6** = subway.
—*v.i.* to act as a substitute; substitute (for).
—*v.t.* = subedit.

**sub**[2] (sub), *n., v.,* **subbed, sub|bing.** *British.* —*n.* an advance of money, especially on account of wages due at the end of a certain period.
—*v.t., v.i.* to pay or receive an advance of money: *A workman who was erroneously given a full pay packet when he had already subbed most of his week's wages, did not commit theft when he failed to return the money* (Sunday Times).
[< *sub*(sistence) money]

**sub-,** *prefix.* **1** under; below: *Subnormal = below normal.*
**2** down; further; again: *Subdivide = divide again.*
**3** near; nearly: *Subtropical = nearly tropical.*
**4** lower; subordinate; assistant: *Subcommittee = a lower or subordinate committee. Subhead = a subordinate head.*
**5** resulting from further division: *Subsection = a section resulting from further division of something.*
**6** slightly; somewhat: *Subacid = slightly acid.*
Also, **su-,** before *sp;* **suc-,** before *c;* **suf-,** before *f;* **sug-,** before *g;* **sum-,** in some cases before *m;* **sup-,** before *p;* **sur-,** before *r;* **sus-,** in some cases before *c, p, t.*
[< Latin *sub* underneath, under, beneath]

**sub.,** an abbreviation for the following:
1 subaltern.
2 subject.
3 submarine.
4 subscription.
5 substitute.
6 suburb.
7 suburban.

**S.U.B.** or **SUB** (no periods), supplemental unemployment benefits (money paid by a company to unemployed workers, in addition to their unemployment compensation).

**sub|ac|e|tate** (sub as′ə tāt), *n.* an acetate in which there is an excess of the base or metallic oxide beyond the amount that reacts with the acid to form a normal salt; basic acetate: *Verdigris is a subacetate of copper.*

**sub|ac|id** (sub as′id), *adj.* slightly acid: *An orange is a subacid fruit.* —**sub|ac′id|ly,** *adv.* —**sub|ac′id|ness,** *n.*

**sub|a|cid|i|ty** (sub′ə sid′ə tē), *n.* subacid quality or state.

**sub|a|cute** (sub′ə kyüt′), *adj.* **1** somewhat or moderately acute. **2** *Medicine.* between acute and chronic: *Antibiotics have made possible a recovery rate of better than 75 per cent in subacute bacterial endocarditis, an infection of the lining of the heart that was once invariably fatal* (New York Times). —**sub′a|cute′ly,** *adv.*

**su|ba|dar** (sü′bə där′), *n.* = subahdar.

**sub|a|dult** (sub′ə dult′, sub ad′ult), *adj., n.* —*adj.* nearly full grown; approaching adulthood.
—*n.* = subimago.

**sub|aer|i|al** (sub ãr′ē əl), *adj.* taking place, existing, operating, or formed in the open air or on the earth's surface. —**sub|aer′i|al|ly,** *adv.*

**sub|a|gent** (sub ā′jənt), *n.* a person employed as the agent of an agent.

**su|bah|dar** (sü′bə där′), *n.* **1** (formerly) the chief native officer of a company of native troops in the British Indian service: *an old loyal pensioned subahdar of our former Indian Army* (London Times). **2** any one of various former high administrative officials under the Mogul emperors in India, especially one appointed as his viceroy by the emperor in a particular province. [Anglo-Indian < Hindustani *ṣūbahdār* < *ṣūbah* province (< Arabic) + *dār* master]

**sub|a|late** (sub ā′lāt), *adj.* somewhat like a wing; thin and triangular.

**sub|al|ka|line** (sub al′kə līn, -lin), *adj.* slightly alkaline.

**sub|al|pine** (sub al′pīn), *adj.* **1** of, having to do with, or characteristic of mountain regions next in elevation below those called alpine, usually between 4,000 and 5,500 feet in most parts of the North or South Temperate Zones: *a subalpine climate, a subalpine tree or plant.* **2** of or having to do with regions at the foot of the Alps.

**sub|al|tern** (sə bôl′tərn, sub′əl-), *n., adj.* —*n.* **1** any commissioned officer in the British Army ranking below a captain: *His Majesty presented the Colours to two subalterns* (London Times). **2** = subordinate. **3** *Logic.* a subaltern proposition. [< adjective]
—*adj.* **1** *British.* ranking below a captain. **2** having lower rank; subordinate: *Todd's mode is distinctly romantic; but he is one of those subaltern figures of romanticism who can smile at the main current even while it carries them along* (Hayden Carruth). **3** *Logic.* (of a proposition) particular, in relation to a universal of the same quality. *Example:* "Some men are mortal" is a subaltern proposition inferred from the universal proposition "All men are mortal."
[< Late Latin *subalternus* < Latin *sub-* under + *alternus* alternate < *alter* other]

**sub|al|ter|nate** (sub ôl′tər nit), *adj., n.* —*adj.* **1** having lower rank; subordinate. **2** *Botany.* alternate, but with a tendency to become opposite.
—*n. Logic.* a subaltern proposition. —**sub|al′ternate|ly,** *adv.*

**sub|al|ter|na|tion** (sub′ôl tər nā′shən), *n. Logic.* the relation between a universal and a particular of the same quality.

**sub|ant|arc|tic** (sub′ant ärk′tik, -är′tik), *adj.* near or just above the antarctic region; having to do with or occurring in a region just north of the Antarctic Circle: *subantarctic islands.*

**sub|ap|i|cal** (sub ap′ə kəl, -ā′pə-), *adj.* beneath or near an apex; nearly apical.

**sub|ap|os|tol|ic** (sub′ap ə stol′ik), *adj.* of, having to do with, or being the period succeeding that of the apostles: *subapostolic literature.*

**sub|a|quat|ic** (sub′ə kwat′ik, -kwot′-), *adj.* **1** = subaqueous. **2** partly aquatic, as plants or animals.

**sub|a|que|ous** (sub ā′kwē əs, -ak′wē-), *adj.* **1** under water; suitable for use under water: *At the skin-diving stall, a movie was being shown on a TV-size screen of flipper-footed people snaking their way through coral formations as a male voice intoned subaqueous aphorisms* (New Yorker). **2** *Geology.* existing, formed, or occurring under water. **3** *Biology.* living or growing under water.

**sub|a|rach|noid** (sub′ə rak′noid), *adj., n.* —*adj.* situated or taking place beneath the arachnoid membrane: *subarachnoid hemorrhage.*
—*n.* the space between the arachnoid membrane and the pia mater.

**sub|arc|tic** (sub ärk′tik, -är′-), *adj.* near or just below the arctic region; having to do with or occurring in regions just south of the Arctic Circle: *a subarctic climate, a subarctic exploration.*

**sub|ar|e|a** (sub ãr′ē ə), *n.* a part or division of an area; subsection.

**sub|ar|id** (sub ar′id), *adj.* moderately arid.

**sub|as|sem|bly** (sub′ə sem′blē), *n., pl.* **-blies.** **1** a putting together of parts or components to be used in forming the main or final assembly of a finished product. **2** a single such part or component: *A new production technique divides television circuits into 20 subassemblies, each having an electron tube and associated components* (Science News Letter).

**sub|as|tral** (sub as′trəl), *adj.* situated under the stars or heavens; terrestrial.

**sub|as|trin|gent** (sub′ə strin′jənt), *adj.* slightly astringent.

**sub|at|om** (sub at′əm), *n.* a constituent of an atom: *Protons and electrons are subatoms.*

**sub|a|tom|ic** (sub′ə tom′ik), *adj.* **1** of or having to do with the constituents of an atom or atoms or phenomena connected with them: *Like all other subatomic bits of matter, electrons have wave-like as well as particle-like properties* (Scientific American). **2** of or having to do with the interior of an atom or any phenomenon occurring there.

**sub|au|di|ble** (sub ô′də bəl), *adj.* slightly or barely audible.

**sub|au|di|tion** (sub′ô dish′ən), *n.* **1** the act of implying something that is not expressed. **2** something that is inferred or understood. [< Late Latin *subaudītiō, -ōnis* < *subaudīre* to supply an ellipsis, understand < Latin *sub-* under, slightly + *audīre* hear]

**sub|au|ric|u|lar** (sub′ô rik′yə lər), *adj.* below an auricle, especially of the ear.

**sub|ax|il|lar|y** (sub ak′sə ler′ē), *adj.* **1** *Botany.* situated or placed beneath an axil. **2** *Anatomy.* situated beneath the axilla.

**sub|base** (sub′bās′), *n.* **1** the lowest part of a base that is divided horizontally. **2** a base placed under the bottom of a machine or other apparatus to raise it higher from the ground. **3** = subbass. **4** a secondary base of supplies.

**sub|base|ment** (sub′bās′mənt), *n.* any basement below the first or main basement of a building: (*Figurative.*) *Beneath the level of obvious fraud ... was a subbasement of chicanery where we were all fooling one another* (Harper's).

**sub|bass** (sub′bās′), *n.* a pedal stop producing the lowest tones of an organ; bourdon.

**sub|bing** (sub′ing), *n.* a thin layer of gelatinous material between the emulsion and the supporting layer of a photographic film or plate; substratum.

**sub|bi|tu|mi|nous coal** (sub′bə tü′mə nəs, -tyü′-), a black coal with a dull to glossy luster, lower in quality and value than bituminous coal, but higher than peat and lignite.

**sub|bot|nik** or **Sub|bot|nik** (sə bôt′nik, -bot′-), *n.* in the Soviet Union: **1** a day of unpaid voluntary work for the state, usually a Saturday. **2** a person who volunteers for such work. **3** (originally) a non-Jew who observed Saturday as a day of rest; Sabbatarian. [< Russian *subbotnik* < *subbota* Saturday + *-nik*]

**sub|branch** (sub′branch′, -bränch′), *n.* **1** a subdivision of a branch. **2** = subphylum.

**sub|breed** (sub′brēd′), *n.* a recognizable strain or subdivision of a breed.

**sub|cab|i|net** (sub kab′ə nit, -kab′nit), *n.* a subordinate cabinet, chosen by the leader of a government, and acting under the principal cabinet.

**sub|cal|i|ber** or **sub|cal|i|bre** (sub kal′ə bər), *adj.* **1** (of a shell, bullet, or other projectile) having a diameter less than that of the bore of the gun from which it is fired. Subcaliber projectiles are fitted with a disk the size of the bore or fired from a tube attached to the inside or the outside of the gun, and are used in practice firing as a substitute for more costly full-sized projectiles. **2** using or involving the use of such ammunition: *a subcaliber gun, subcaliber practice.*

**Sub|car|bon|if|er|ous** (sub′kär bə nif′ər əs), *adj., n. Geology.* —*adj.* of or having to do with a geological period or a system of rocks of the earlier or lower portion of the Carboniferous period or system; Mississippian.
—*n.* the Subcarboniferous period or system.

**sub|car|ri|er** (sub kar′ē ər), *n.* a carrier wave that is used to modulate another carrier wave.

**sub|car|ti|lag|i|nous** (sub′kär tə laj′ə nəs), *adj.* **1** partially or incompletely cartilaginous. **2** below or beneath cartilage.

**sub|caste** (sub′kast′, -käst′), *n.* a subdivision of a caste: *The whole situation is made far more intricate by the fact that each caste is divided into subcastes with special distinctions and privileges* (Santha Rama Rau).

**sub|cat|e|go|ry** (sub kat′ə gôr′ē, -gōr′-), *n., pl.* **-ries.** a subordinate category; subdivision of a category: *Under the agreement, quotas apply to subcategories in each of the major classifications* (New York Times).

**sub|ce|les|tial** (sub′sə les′chəl), *adj., n.* —*adj.* **1a** situated or existing below the heavens. **b** *Figurative.* terrestrial; mundane. **2** *Astronomy.* directly under the zenith.
—*n.* a subcelestial being.

**sub|cel|lar** (sub′sel′ər), *n.* a cellar beneath another cellar.

**sub|cel|lu|lar** (sub sel′yə lər), *adj.* smaller in size than ordinary cells: *subcellular particles.*

**sub|cen|ter** (sub′sen′tər), *n.* a subordinate or secondary center: *The system is highly centered on San Francisco, with Oakland as a subcenter* (Scientific American).

**sub|cen|tral** (sub sen′trəl), *adj.* **1** being under the center. **2** nearly central; a little off center. —**sub-cen′tral|ly**, *adv.*

**subch.**, subchapter.

**sub|chas|er** (sub′chā′sər), *n.* = submarine chaser.

**sub|chief** (sub′chēf′), *n.* an official next in rank to the chief, as of a tribe or clan: *Below the chief, subchiefs were appointed for certain districts* (New Yorker).

**sub|chlo|ride** (sub klôr′īd, -id; -klōr′-), *n.* a chloride that contains a relatively small proportion of chlorine.

**sub|class** (sub′klas′, -kläs′), *n. Biology.* a group of animals or plants ranking above an order and below a class; superorder.

**sub|cla|vi|an** (sub klā′vē ən), *adj., n. Anatomy.* —*adj.* **1** beneath the clavicle or collarbone. **2** of or having to do with the subclavian artery, vein, groove, or muscle.
—*n.* a subclavian artery, vein, groove, or muscle. [< New Latin *subclavius* < *sub-* under (< Latin) + *clavis* clavicle (< Latin *clāvis* key) + English *-an*]

**subclavian artery**, the large artery forming the trunk of the arterial system of the arm or forelimb. See picture under **circulation**.

**subclavian groove**, either of two shallow depressions on the first rib for the subclavian artery and vein.

**subclavian muscle**, a small muscle extending from the first rib to the clavicle.

**subclavian vein**, the part of the main vein of the arm lying under the clavicle. See picture under **circulation**.

**sub|cli|max** (sub klī′maks), *n. Biology.* a climax whose normal development has been arrested by some factor.

**sub|clin|i|cal** (sub klin′ə kəl), *adj.* having mild symptoms that are not readily apparent in clinical tests: *a subclinical infection.* —**sub|clin′i|cal|ly**, *adv.*

**sub|col|lege** (sub kol′ij), *adj. U.S.* below college level: ... *two-year community colleges, technical institutes, and other subcollege institutions* (New York Times).

**sub|com|mis|sion** (sub′kə mish′ən), *n.* a subordinate commission chosen from and acting under a larger commission for some special duty: *The bank is being sponsored by ECAFE, a U.N. subcommission* (New York Times).

**sub|com|mit|tee** (sub′kə mit′ē), *n.* a small committee chosen from a larger general committee for some special duty.

**sub|com|mu|ni|ty** (sub′kə myü′nə tē), *n., pl.* **-ties.** *U.S.* a suburban community: *I went to an Iowa reunion picnic in the L.A. subcommunity of Long Beach* (Christopher Rand).

**sub|com|pact** (sub kom′pakt), *n.* a passenger car similar to a sports car and smaller than a compact car.

**sub|con|scious** (sub kon′shəs), *adj., n.* —*adj.* **1** not wholly conscious; on the border of consciousness. **2** beneath or beyond consciousness; existing in the mind but not fully perceived or recognized: *a subconscious fear, subconscious desires, a subconscious suggestion. Her poor grades caused a subconscious irritation that made her cross.*
—*n.* Often, **the subconscious. 1** thoughts or feelings present in the mind but not fully perceived or recognized; subconscious mental activity. **2** (loosely) the unconscious. —**sub|con′scious|ly**, *adv.*

**sub|con|scious|ness** (sub kon′shəs nis), *n.* **1** the quality of being subconscious. **2** = subconscious.

**sub|con|ti|nent** (sub kon′tə nənt), *n.* **1** a land mass that is very large, but smaller than a continent; very large island: *the subcontinent of New Guinea.* **2** a large section of a continent having a certain geographical or political independence: *the subcontinent of India.*

**sub|con|ti|nen|tal** (sub′kon tə nen′təl), *adj.* of, having to do with, or characteristic of a subcontinent: *Arabia, a block of subcontinental size, ... was formerly a part of Africa* (New Scientist).

**sub|con|tract** (sub kon′trakt; *also for v.* sub′kən-trakt′), *n., v.* —*n.* a contract under a previous contract; contract for carrying out a previous contract or a part of it: *The contractor for the new school building gave out subcontracts to a plumber, an electrician, and a steam fitter.*
—*v.i.* to make a subcontract.
—*v.t.* to make a subcontract for.

**sub|con|trac|tor** (sub kon′trak tər, sub′kən-trak′-), *n.* a person who contracts to carry out a previous contract or part of it.

**sub|con|tra|oc|tave** (sub′kon trə ok′tiv), *n. Music.* the octave below the contraoctave, as on an organ; fourth octave below middle C.

**sub|con|tra|ri|e|ty** (sub kon′trə rī′ə tē), *n. Logic.* the relation existing between subcontrary propositions.

**sub|con|tra|ry** (sub kon′trer ē), *adj., n., pl.* **-ries.** *Logic.* —*adj.* (of a pair of propositions) so related that both may be true but only one may be false. *Example:* "Some birds are blue" and "Some birds are not blue" are subcontrary propositions.
—*n.* a subcontrary proposition.

**sub|cor|tex** (sub kôr′teks), *n., pl.* **-ti|ces** (-tə sēz). the white matter beneath the cortex of the brain.

**sub|cor|ti|cal** (sub kôr′tə kəl), *adj.* **1** of or having to do with the subcortex: *the subcortical regions of the brain.* **2** situated beneath the cortex of a sponge or the cortex or bark of a tree.

**sub|crit|i|cal** (sub krit′ə kəl), *adj.* having or using less than the amount of fissionable material necessary to sustain a chain reaction: *a subcritical reactor.*

**sub|crust** (sub′krust′), *n.* the under portion of the crust of the earth, from about 15 to about 40 miles below the surface.

**sub|crus|tal** (sub krus′təl), *adj.* happening or located below the earth's crust: *Earth's subcrustal mantle must have a much larger mechanical strength than previously believed in order to support the pear-like shape* (Science News Letter).

**sub|cul|tur|al** (sub kul′chər əl), *adj.* of or having to do with a subculture.

**sub|cul|ture** (sub kul′chər), *n., v.,* **-tured, -tur-ing.** —*n.* **1** a group of people with distinct cultural traits within a culture or society: *Most of his work has been with ... a youth subculture dominated by gang-joining potentially explosive teenagers* (Newsweek). **2** a bacteriological culture derived from a previous culture.
—*v.t.* to cultivate (a bacteriological culture) from a previous culture: *I subculture the water into a nutrient medium as soon as possible—preferably as soon as we bring the specimens out of the cave* (New Scientist).

**sub|cur|rent** (sub′kėr′ənt), *n.* a secondary or subordinate current: (*Figurative.*) *One of the historical subcurrents he believes to be a constant inhuman development is a tendency to equate the traditional with art* (Harper's).

**sub|cu|ta|ne|ous** (sub′kyü tā′nē əs), *adj.* **1** under the skin: *subcutaneous tissue.* **2** living under the skin: *a subcutaneous parasite.* **3** placed or performed under the skin: *a subcutaneous injection.* —**sub′cu|ta′ne|ous|ly**, *adv.*

**sub|cu|tis** (sub′kyü′tis, sub kyü′-), *n.* the deeper part of the cutis.

**sub|dea|con** (sub dē′kən), *n.* a member of the clergy next below a deacon in rank.

**sub|dea|con|ate** (sub dē′kə nit), *n.* the office or order of subdeacon.

**sub|dean** (sub′dēn′), *n.* an official next below a dean in rank, and acting as his deputy.

**sub|deb** (sub′deb′), *n. Informal.* a subdebutante.

**sub|deb|u|tante** (sub deb′yə tänt, -tant; sub deb′-yə tänt′), *n.* a young girl soon to make her debut in society. [American English < *sub-* + *debutante*]

**sub|del|e|gate** (sub del′ə git, -gāt), *n., v.,* **-gat-ed, -gat|ing.** —*n.* a subordinate delegate.
—*v.t.* to delegate (powers or responsibilities) to a subordinate delegate.

**sub|del|e|ga|tion** (sub′del ə gā′shən), *n.* the act of subdelegating.

**sub|den|tate** (sub den′tāt), *adj.* imperfectly dentate; having indistinct notches.

**sub|de|pot** (sub dep′ō), *n.* a branch military depot, nearer the regiment than a depot.

**sub|di|ac|o|nate** (sub′dī ak′ə nit), *n.* = subdeaconate.

**sub|di|a|lect** (sub dī′ə lekt), *n.* a division or variety of a dialect.

**sub|dis|ci|pline** (sub dis′ə plin), *n.* a subdivision of a discipline: *Anthropologists have long shown an interest in native or folk medical systems, and medical anthropology is emerging as a specialized subdiscipline* (Raymond D. Fogelson).

**sub|dis|trict** (sub′dis′trikt), *n.* a division or subdivision of a district.

**sub|di|vide** (sub′də vīd′, sub′də vīd), *v.t., v.i.,* **-vid|ed, -vid|ing. 1** to divide again; divide into smaller parts. **2** to divide (land) into lots for houses, buildings, or other development: *A builder bought the farm, subdivided it into lots, and built homes on them.* —**sub′di|vid′er**, *n.*

**sub|di|vis|i|ble** (sub′də viz′ə bəl, sub′də viz′-), *adj.* that can be subdivided.

**sub|di|vi|sion** (sub′də vizh′ən, sub′də vizh′-), *n.* **1** a division into smaller parts. **2** a part of a part. **3** *Botany.* a group of related plants ranking below a division; subphylum. **4** a tract of land divided into building lots.

**sub|di|vi|sion|al** (sub′də vizh′ə nəl, sub′də-vizh′-), *adj.* of or having to do with subdivision.

**sub|dom|i|nant** (sub dom′ə nənt), *n., adj. Music.* —*n.* the tone or note next below the dominant; fourth tone or note from the tonic in the ascending scale, and the fifth in the descending scale. See picture under **dominant**.
—*adj.* of or having to do with this tone: *a subdominant chord.*

**sub|drain|age** (sub drān′ij), *n.* an underground

---

**Pronunciation Key:** hat, āge, cãre, fär; let, ēqual, tėrm; it, īce; hot, ōpen, ôrder; oil, out; cup, pu̇t, rüle; child; long; thin; ᴛʜen; zh, measure; ə represents **a** in about, **e** in taken, **i** in pencil, **o** in lemon, **u** in circus.

drainage system.

**sub|du|a|ble** (səb dü′ə bəl, -dyü′-), *adj.* that can be subdued.

**sub|du|al** (səb dü′əl, -dyü′-), *n.* **1** the act of subduing. **2** the state of being subdued.

**sub|duct** (səb dukt′), *v.t., v.i.* **1** to draw down or downward. **2** to take away; subtract; deduct. [< Latin *subductus,* past participle of *subdūcere* to lead away < *sub-* away + *dūcere* to lead]

**sub|duc|tion** (səb duk′shən), *n.* the act or process of taking away or withdrawing; subtraction.

**sub|due** (səb dü′, -dyü′), *v.t.,* **-dued, -du|ing. 1** to overcome by superior force; conquer: *Our army subdued the enemy. The Spaniards subdued the Indian tribes in Mexico. He who ... subdues mankind Must look down on the hate of those below* (Byron). SYN: vanquish, subjugate, enslave. **2** to get the better of; prevail over: *Swords conquer some, but Words subdue all men* (Matthew Prior). **3** to gain control over; keep down; hold back; suppress: *We subdued a desire to laugh.* **4** to tone down; soften: *Pulling down the window shades subdued the light in the room.* **5** to reduce or allay: *to subdue a fever or a boil.* **6** to bring (land) under cultivation. [ultimately < Latin *subdūcere* draw, lead away < *sub-* from under + *dūcere* lead; meaning influenced by Latin *subdere* subdue < *sub-* under + *dare* put] — **sub|du′er,** *n.*

**sub|dued** (səb düd′, -dyüd′), *adj.* **1** reduced to subjection; made submissive. **2** reduced in intensity or force; toned down: *a sort of boudoir, pervaded by a subdued, rose-coloured light* (Henry James). — **sub|dued′ly,** *adv.* — **sub|dued′ness,** *n.*

**sub|due|ment** (səb dü′mənt, -dyü′-), *n.* = subdual.

**sub|du|ple** (sub′dü pəl, -dyü-), *adj.* being half of a quantity or number; having a proportion of one to two. [< Late Latin *subduplus* < Latin *sub-* under + *duplus* double]

**sub|du|pli|cate** (sub dü′plə kit, -dyü′-), *adj.* being that of the square roots of the quantities. *Example:* 2 : 3 is the subduplicate ratio of 4 : 9.

**sub|du|ral** (sub dúr′əl, -dyúr′-), *adj.* situated or existing below the dura mater: *a subdural hemorrhage.*

**sub|dwarf** (sub′dwôrf′), *n.,* or **subdwarf star,** any star of a group lying just below the main sequence in the Russell diagram, being relatively small and dim when compared to a main-sequence star of the same spectral class.

**sub|e|co|nom|ic** (sub′ē kə nom′ik, -ek ə-), *adj.* below what is economically proper or desirable; not up to economic standards: *We still suffer from subeconomic rates of freight* (London Times).

**sub|ed|it** (sub ed′it), *v.t.* **1** to edit under the direction of a chief editor. **2** *British.* to read and edit (manuscript); copyread.

**sub|ed|i|tor** (sub ed′ə tər), *n.* **1** a subordinate or assistant editor. **2** *British.* a copyreader.

**sub|ed|i|to|ri|al** (sub′ed ə tôr′ē əl, -tōr′-), *adj.* of or having to do with a subeditor.

**sub|ed|i|tor|ship** (sub ed′ə tər ship), *n.* the position or responsibility of a subeditor.

**sub|em|ployed** (sub′em ploid′), *adj.* unemployed or underemployed. — **sub′em|ploy′ment,** *n.*

**sub|en|try** (sub′en′trē), *n., pl.* **-tries.** a subordinate entry, as in a list.

**sub|e|qual** (sub ē′kwəl), *adj.* nearly equal.

**sub|e|qua|to|ri|al** (sub′ē kwə tôr′ē əl, -tōr′-), *adj.* near or adjoining the equatorial region.

**su|ber|ate** (sü′bə rāt), *n.* a salt of suberic acid.

**su|be|re|ous** (sü bir′ē əs), *adj.* of or like cork; corky. [< Latin *sūbereus* (with English *-ous*) < *sūber, -eris* cork, cork oak, probably < Greek *sŷphar* anything wrinkled]

**su|ber|ic** (sü ber′ik), *adj.* of or having to do with cork. [< French *subérique* < Latin *sūber, -eris* cork, cork oak]

**suberic acid,** a crystalline dicarboxylic acid prepared by the action of nitric acid on cork, paper, fatty acids, and various other substances, used in making plastics and dyes. *Formula:* $C_8H_{14}O_4$

**su|ber|in** (sü′bər in), *n.* a substance in cork tissue that gives cork its waterproof quality. [< Latin *sūber* (see etym. under **subereous**) + English *-in*]

**su|ber|i|za|tion** (sü′bər ə zā′shən), *n. Botany.* the making of cell walls into cork by the formation of suberin.

**su|ber|ize** (sü′bə rīz), *v.t.,* **-ized, -iz|ing.** *Botany.* to change (a cell wall) into cork tissue by the formation of suberin. [< Latin *sūber, -eris* (see etym. under **subereous**) + English *-ize*]

**su|ber|ose** (sü′bə rōs), *adj.* of or like cork; corky; subereous.

**su|ber|ous** (sü′bər əs), *adj.* = suberose.

**sub|fam|i|ly** (sub fam′ə lē, sub′fam′-), *n., pl.* **-lies.** *Biology.* a group of related plants or animals ranking above a genus and below a family.

**sub|fer|tile** (sub fėr′təl), *adj.* not wholly fertile: *In three to five months the centre is usually able to list a couple as fertile, subfertile (requiring surgery or other special treatment), or sterile* (Maclean's).

**sub|field** (sub′fēld′), *n.* **1** a subdivision of a field of study; subdiscipline: *In almost every case a technological invention preceded much of the explosive growth in many subfields of physics* (Science). **2** *Mathematics.* a field that is a subset of another field.

**sub|floor** (sub′flôr′, -flōr′), *n.* an underlying floor used as a base for the finished floor.

**sub|floor|ing** (sub flôr′ing, -flōr′-), *n.* a flooring of wood, concrete, stone, or other material forming the base of the floor of a room.

**sub|fos|sil** (sub fos′əl), *adj., n.* — *adj.* partly fossilized.
— *n.* a subfossil animal or plant.

**sub|freez|ing** (sub frē′zing), *adj.* below freezing.

**sub|fusc** or **sub|fusk** (sub fusk′), *adj.* somewhat dark or dusky; brownish: *a subfusc hue like that of old furniture* (John Galsworthy). [< Latin *subfuscus* < *sub-* under, away + *fuscus* dark]

**sub|fus|cous** (sub fus′kəs), *adj.* = subfusc.

**sub|ge|ner|ic** (sub′jə ner′ik), *adj.* of, having to do with, or being a subgenus. — **sub′ge|ner′i|cal|ly,** *adv.*

**sub|ge|nus** (sub jē′nəs, sub′jē′-), *n., pl.* **sub|gen|er|a** (sub jen′ər ə, sub′jen′-), **sub|ge|nus|es.** *Biology.* a group of related plants or animals ranking above a species and below a genus.

**sub|gi|ant** (sub′jī′ənt), *n.,* or **subgiant star,** any star of a group lying just above the main sequence in the Russell diagram, being relatively large and bright when compared to a main-sequence star of the same spectral class.

**sub|gla|cial** (sub glā′shəl), *adj.* existing or formed beneath a glacier: *a subglacial stream.* — **sub|gla′cial|ly,** *adv.*

**sub|grade** (sub′grād′), *n.* a layer of earth or rock below the surface, leveled off as a foundation for a road or structure.

**sub|grav|i|ty** (sub grav′ə tē), *n.* a gravitational effect or state characterized by less than the normal force of gravity (usually less than one G).

**sub|group** (sub′grüp′), *n.* **1** a subordinate group; subdivision of a group, especially in botany and zoology: *Two subordinate types of this subgroup can be distinguished as far as the English elms are concerned* (R. H. Richens). **2** *Chemistry.* a division of a group in the periodic table; family.

**sub|gum** (sub′gum′), *adj.* (of Chinese food) served with mixed vegetables: *subgum fried noodles, subgum chicken chow mein.* [< Chinese pidgin English *subgum*]

**sub|head** (sub′hed′), *n.* **1** a subordinate head or title, as in a book, chapter, or article. **2a** a subordinate division of a head or title. **b** a short heading used to break up the paragraphs of a long news story. **3** an official next in rank to the head, as of a college.

**sub|head|ing** (sub′hed′ing), *n.* = subhead.

**sub|hu|man** (sub hyü′mən), *adj., n.* — *adj.* **1** below the human race or type; less than human. **2** almost human.
— *n.* a subhuman creature.

**sub|hu|man|i|ty** (sub′hyü man′ə tē), *n.* **1** subhumans taken as a group. **2** the fact of being subhuman; subhuman character or quality: *What the rescuers of the Nottingham's crew take off Boon Island after nearly a month is ten scarecrows who are close to subhumanity* (Time).

**sub|hu|mid** (sub hyü′mid), *adj.* having sufficient rainfall to support the growth of tall grass or similar vegetation: *The prairies of the United States and the pampas of South America have subhumid climates.*

**sub|i|ma|go** (sub′i mā′gō), *n., pl.* **-i|ma|gos, -i|mag|i|nes** (-i maj′ə nēz). a May fly just after it emerges from the nymph stage. The subimago sheds its skin to become an imago.

**sub|in|dex** (sub in′deks), *n., pl.* **-di|ces** (-də sēz). a figure or letter following and slightly below a symbol; subscript. *Example:* 2 is the subindex in $H_2O$ and $b_2$.

**sub|in|feud** (sub′in fyüd′), *v.t., v.i.* = subinfeudate.

**sub|in|feu|date** (sub′in fyü′dāt), *v.t., v.i.,* **-dat|ed, -dat|ing.** to grant by subinfeudation.

**sub|in|feu|da|tion** (sub′in fyü dā′shən), *n.* in feudal law: **1** the granting of lands by a feudal tenant to a subtenant, who held them on terms similar to those of the grant to the tenant. **2** the tenure so established. **3** an estate or fief so created.

**sub|in|feu|da|to|ry** (sub′in fyü′də tôr′ē, -tōr′-), *n., pl.* **-ries.** a person who holds by subinfeudation.

**sub|ir|ri|gate** (sub ir′ə gāt), *v.t.,* **-gat|ed, -gat|ing.** to irrigate beneath the surface of the ground, as by underground pipes.

**sub|ir|ri|ga|tion** (sub′ir ə gā′shən), *n.* the act of subirrigating: *These pipes provide subirrigation from flowing wells* (New York Times).

**su|bi|ta|ne|ous** (sü′bə tā′nē əs), *adj. Obsolete.* sudden; unexpected; hasty. [< Latin *subitāneus* (with English *-ous*); see etym. under **sudden**]

**su|bi|to** (sü′bi tō), *adv. Music.* quickly; suddenly (a direction): *piano subito.* [< Italian *subito* < Latin *subitō,* ablative of *subitus;* see etym. under **sudden**]

**subj.,** an abbreviation for the following:
**1** subject.
**2** subjective.
**3** subjectively.
**4** subjunctive.

**sub|ja|cen|cy** (sub jā′sən sē), *n.* the state of being subjacent.

**sub|ja|cent** (sub jā′sənt), *adj.* **1** situated underneath or below; underlying. **2** forming the basis or substratum. **3** being in a lower situation, though not directly beneath; at or near the base, as of a mountain. [< Latin *subjacēns, -entis,* present participle of *subjacēre* < *sub-* below + *jacēre* to lie] — **sub|ja′cent|ly,** *adv.*

**sub|ject** (*n., adj.* sub′jikt, -jekt; *v.* səb jekt′), *n., adj., v.* — *n.* **1** something thought about, discussed, or studied: *a subject of discussion or negotiation, the subject of a sermon. The subject for our composition was "An Exciting Moment."* **2** something learned or taught; course of study in some branch of knowledge: *English, history, arithmetic, and science are some of the subjects we take up in school.* SYN: discipline. **3a** a person under the rule of a state, government, sovereign, or other individual or system: *the subjects of a king. The kings of our own day very much resemble their subjects in education and breeding* (Benjamin Jowett). **b** a person who is under the power, control, or influence of another: *The slaves refused to remain the master's subjects and made plans to break free.* **4** a person or thing that undergoes or experiences something: *Rabbits and mice are often subjects for medical experiments. The patient of a doctor or psychologist is his subject. Medical students dissect dead bodies which they call subjects.* **5** *Grammar.* the word or group of words about which something is said in a sentence. The subject is usually the performer of the action of an active verb or the receiver of the action of a passive verb. *I* is the subject of the following sentences: I see the cat. I am seen by the cat. I can see. *Abbr:* subj. **6a** the theme of a book, poem, or other literary work. **b** a figure, scene, object, or incident, chosen by an artist for representation. **c** *Music.* the theme or melody on which a work or movement is based. **7** *Philosophy.* **a** the substance of anything, as contrasted with its qualities or attributes. **b** the mind or self, as contrasted with everything outside the mind. **c** substance or reality, as contrasted with appearance. **8** *Logic.* **a** the term of a proposition of which the other term (predicate) is affirmed or denied. **b** the thing about which such affirmation or denial is made. **9** a ground, motive, or cause: *Lateness and carelessness are subjects for complaint.*
— *adj.* **1** under the power or influence of; bound by loyalty or allegiance (to): *We are subject to our country's laws.* **2** under some power or influence: *the subject nations of an empire.* **3** likely to have; liable to suffer from; prone (to): *subject to decay. I am subject to colds. Japan is a country subject to earthquakes. Human affairs are all subject to changes and disasters* (Daniel Defoe). **4** likely to receive; exposed or open (to): *This play is subject to criticism.* **5** depending on; on the condition of: *I bought the car subject to your approval.*
— *v.t.* **1** to bring under some power or influence: *Ancient Rome subjected all Italy to her rule.* **2** to make subordinate or submissive: *to subject the minds of a people.* **3** to cause to undergo or experience something: *The savages subjected their captives to torture. The lawyer subjected the witness to grueling cross-examination.* **4** to make liable (to have or receive); lay open (to); expose: *The location of the island in the middle of the ocean subjects it to frequent hurricanes. Credulity subjects one to impositions.* **5** *Obsolete.* to put, lay, or spread under.
[< Latin *subjectus,* past participle of *subicere* place under < *sub-* under + *jacere* throw]
— *Syn. n.* **1 Subject, topic** mean the main thing or idea thought, talked, or written about, as in a conversation, lecture, essay, or book. **Subject** is the general word: *She tried to change the subject. Juvenile delinquency is a broad subject.* **Topic** particularly applies to a limited and definitely stated subject often having to do with a current event or problem that is, or is to be, discussed in a lecture, essay, or the like, or some part of it: *"The need for a recreation center here" is today's topic.*

**subject catalog,** a card catalog, or part of one, in which books are entered by subject.

**sub|jec|ti|fy** (səb jek′tə fī), *v.t.,* **-fied, -fy|ing.** to make subjective; identify with the subject. — **sub-jec′ti|fi|ca′tion,** *n.*

**sub|jec|tion** (səb jek′shən), *n.* **1** the act or process of bringing under some power or influence; conquering; subjugating: *The subjection of the rebels took years.* **2** the condition of being under some power or influence; subjugation: *Women used to live in subjection to men.*

**sub|jec|tion|al** (səb jek′shə nəl), *adj.* **1** having to do with subjection. **2** based upon subjection.

**sub|jec|tive** (səb jek′tiv), *adj.* **1** existing in the mind; belonging to the person thinking rather than to the object thought of. Ideas and opinions are subjective; facts are objective. **2** about the thoughts and feelings, as of the speaker, writer, or painter; personal. Lyric poetry is subjective, expressing the feelings of the poet; narrative poetry is generally objective, telling a story. **3** *Grammar.* being or serving as the subject of a sentence; nominative. **4** *Psychology.* **a** originating within or dependent on the mind of the individual rather than an external object. **b** = introspective. **5** *Philosophy.* **a** of or relating to reality as perceived by the mind, as distinct from reality as independent of the mind. **b** influenced by an individual's state of mind: *a subjective perception or apprehension.* **c** having to do with the substance of anything, as opposed to its qualities and attributes. **6** *Medicine.* (of symptoms) discoverable by the patient only. **7** *Obsolete.* of or having to do with someone who is subject to rule or control. —**sub|jec′tive|ly**, *adv.* —**sub|jec′tive|ness**, *n.*

**sub|jec|tiv|ism** (səb jek′tə viz əm), *n.* **1** the theory that all knowledge is subjective. **2** any theory that emphasizes the subjective elements in experience or learning. **3a** the ethical theory that conceives the aim of morality to be the attainment of states of feeling. **b** the ethical theory that an individual's feelings are a criterion of values.

**sub|jec|tiv|ist** (səb jek′tə vist), *n., adj.* —***n.*** a person who believes in or advocates a theory of subjectivism.
—***adj.*** = subjectivistic.

**sub|jec|ti|vis|tic** (səb jek′tə vis′tik), *adj.* having to do with or characterized by subjectivism.

**sub|jec|tiv|i|ty** (sub′jek tiv′ə tē), *n.* **1** subjective quality or condition; existence in the mind only; absorption in one's own mental states or processes; tendency to view things through the medium of one's own individuality. **2** = subjectivism.

**sub|jec|tiv|ize** (səb jek′tə vīz), *v.t.*, **-ized, -iz|ing.** to make subjective: *The picture seems to me sentimentalized and subjectivized out of all proportion* (Harper's).

**sub|ject|less** (sub′jikt lis, -jekt-), *adj.* without a subject or subjects: *subjectless art.*

**subject matter**, **1** something thought about, discussed, studied, written about, or otherwise considered: *While an ingenious questionnaire might be devised to meet these contingencies, it is usually better, where the subject matter is complex, to use the unguided interview* (Anthony H. Richmond). **2** what a talk, book, play, motion picture, or other presented material is about, as distinguished from its form or style: *The lecturer's subject matter was better than his presentation.*

**sub|join** (sub join′), *v.t.* **1** to add at the end of something spoken or written; append. **2** to place in immediate sequence or juxtaposition to something else. [< Middle French *subjoindre* < Latin *subjungere* < *sub-* under + *jungere* to join]

**sub ju|di|ce** (sub jü′də sē), *Latin.* **1** still before the court; under consideration; not decided: *The Kastner-Gruenwald case is sub judice, but it will now be ... an election issue* (London Times). **2** (literally) under judgment.

**sub|ju|gate** (sub′jə gāt), *v.t.*, **-gat|ed, -gat|ing.** **1** to subdue; conquer. **2** to bring under complete control; make subservient or submissive: *His love and his hatred were of that passionate fervour which subjugates all the rest of the being* (George Eliot). [< Latin *subjugāre* (with English *-ate*[1]) < *sub-* under + *jugum* yoke]

**sub|ju|ga|tion** (sub′jə gā′shən), *n.* conquest; subjection: *the subjugation of Greece by the Ottomans.*

**sub|ju|ga|tor** (sub′jə gā′tər), *n.* a person who subjugates.

**sub|junc|tion** (səb jungk′shən), *n.* **1** the act of subjoining. **2** the state of being subjoined. **3** something subjoined. [< Late Latin *subjunctiō, -ōnis* < Latin *subjungere;* see etym. under **subjoin**]

**sub|junc|tive** (səb jungk′tiv), *adj., n. Grammar.* —***adj.*** having to do with a verb form which expresses a state, act, or event as possible, conditional, or dependent, rather than as actual.
—***n.*** **1** the mood of a verb which expresses this. *Abbr:* subj. **2** the form of a verb in this mood. *Examples:* I insist that he *go,* if this *be* treason, if I *were* you.
[< Late Latin *subjunctīvus* < Latin *subjungere;* see etym. under **subjoin**]

**sub|king|dom** (sub king′dəm, sub′king′-), *n. Biology.* a primary division of the animal or plant kingdom, often omitted from classifications.

**sub|lan|guage** (sub lang′gwij), *n.* a secondary or minor language differing from a standard language; the special language or speech of a group or class of people within a culture: *Jargon, the sublanguage peculiar to any trade, contributes to euphemism when its terms seep into general use. The stock market, for example, rarely "falls" in the words of Wall Street analysts. Instead it is discovered to be "easing" or found to have made a "technical correction" or "adjustment"* (Time).

**sub|lap|sar|i|an** (sub′lap sãr′ē ən), *adj., n.* —***adj.*** of or having to do with sublapsarianism or its adherents.
—***n.*** an adherent of the doctrine of sublapsarianism.
[< New Latin *sublapsarius* (< Latin *sub-* under, after + *lapsus, -ūs* a lapse, fall + *-ārius* -ary) + English *-an*]

**sub|lap|sar|i|an|ism** (sub′lap sãr′ē ə niz′əm), *n.* the Calvinist doctrine that the fall of man, while foreseen by God, was not decreed as part of the plan of creation and that election and damnation are therefore correctives that came after the Fall; infralapsarianism.

**sub|late** (sub lāt′), *v.t.*, **-lat|ed, -lat|ing.** **1** to cancel or negate. **2** (in Hegelian dialectics) to preserve (a negated element) as part of the synthesis. **3** to remove or detach. [< Latin *sublatus* < *sub-* up + *-latus,* suppletive past participle of *ferre* carry] —**sub|la′tion**, *n.*

**sub|lease** (*n.* sub′lēs′; *v.* sub lēs′, sub′lēs′), *n., v.*, **-leased, -leas|ing.** —***n.*** a lease granted by a person on property which has been leased to him.
—***v.t.*** to grant or take a sublease of.

**sub|les|see** (sub′le sē′), *n.* the receiver or holder of a sublease.

**sub|les|sor** (sub les′ər), *n.* the grantor of a sublease.

**sub|let** (sub let′, sub′let′), *v.*, **-let, -let|ting,** *n.* —***v.t.*** **1** to rent to another (something that has been rented to oneself); give a sublease of: *We sublet our house for the summer.* **2** to take a sublease of: *I have sublet an apartment whose tenants went away for the summer.* **3** to give part of (a contract) to another: *The contractor for the whole building sublet the contract for the plumbing.*
—***n.*** a building, apartment, or other space, structure, or right, that has been sublet: *... the hapless couple's horrid little furnished sublet in the city* (New Yorker).

**sub|le|thal** (sub lē′thəl), *adj.* not causing death; short of being fatal: *In experimental animals ... sublethal doses of radiation appreciably reduce the life span* (Scientific American). —**sub|le′thal|ly**, *adv.*

**sub|lev|el** (sub′lev′əl), *n.* a lower level; substratum.

**sub|lieu|ten|an|cy** (sub′lü ten′ən sē; *in general British usage, except in the navy* sub′lef ten′ənsē), *n.* the position or rank of a sublieutenant.

**sub|lieu|ten|ant** (sub′lü ten′ənt; *in general British usage, except in the navy* sub′lef ten′ənt), *n.* **1** a subordinate lieutenant. **2** (in the British Army and Navy) a commissioned officer ranking next below a lieutenant.

**sub|lim|a|ble** (sə blī′mə bəl), *adj.* that can be sublimed.

**sub|li|mate** (*v.* sub′lə māt; *adj., n.* sub′lə mit, -māt), *v.*, **-mat|ed, -mat|ing,** *adj., n.* —***v.t.*** **1** to purify; refine: *The heat of Milton's mind may be said to sublimate his learning* (Samuel Johnson). **2** to change (an undesirable impulse or trait) into a more desirable or acceptable activity. **3** to sublime (a solid substance).
—***v.i.*** to become sublimated.
—***adj.*** sublimated.
—***n.*** a material obtained when a substance is sublimed. Bichloride of mercury is a very poisonous sublimate.
[< Latin *sublīmāre* (with English *-ate*[1]) to raise < *sublīmis* lofty; see etym. under **sublime**]

**sub|li|ma|tion** (sub′lə mā′shən), *n.* **1** the act or process of sublimating or subliming; purification: *This direct transition from solid to vapor is called sublimation* (Sears and Zemansky). **2** the resulting product or state, especially, mental elevation or exaltation: *that enthusiastic sublimation which is the source of greatness and energy* (Thomas L. Peacock). **3** the highest stage or purest form of a thing. **4** a chemical sublimate.

**sub|lime** (sə blīm′), *adj., n., v.*, **-limed, -lim|ing.** —***adj.*** **1** noble; grand; majestic; lofty: *Mountain scenery is often sublime.* **2** exalted; excellent; eminent; supreme: *sublime devotion. How sublime a thing it is To suffer and be strong* (Longfellow). **3** expressing lofty ideas in a grand manner: *sublime poetry.* **4a** of lofty bearing or appearance: *In his simplicity sublime* (Tennyson). **b** *Obsolete.* haughty; proud. **5** *Archaic.* set or raised aloft. **6** *Obsolete.* elated.
—***n.*** **1** something that is lofty, noble, exalted, or majestic: *the sublime in literature and art. No, never need an American look beyond his own country for the sublime and beautiful of natural scenery* (Washington Irving). **2** the highest degree or example (of): *Your upward gaze at me now is the very sublime of faith, truth, and devotion* (Charlotte Brontë).
—***v.t.*** **1** to make higher or nobler; make sublime: *A judicious use of metaphors wonderfully raises, sublimes and adorns oratory* (Oliver Goldsmith). **2a** to heat (a solid substance) and condense the vapor given off; purify; refine. **b** to cause to be given off by this or a similar process. —***v.i.*** **1** to pass off as a vapor and condense as a solid without going through the liquid state; become purified or refined. **2** to be changed into a gas directly from the solid state.

**from the sublime to the ridiculous**, from one extreme to the other: *His writing is very uneven, running the gamut from the sublime to the ridiculous.*
[< Latin *sublīmis* (originally) sloping up (to the lintel) < *sub-* up + *līmen, -inis* threshold] —**sub|lime′ly**, *adv.* —**sub|lime′ness**, *n.* —**sub|lim′er**, *n.*

**Sublime Porte**, = Porte.

**sub|lim|i|nal** (sub lim′ə nəl, -lī′mə-), *adj., n. Psychology.* —***adj.*** **1** below the threshold of consciousness; subconscious: *the subliminal self. For years psychologists have been experimenting with subliminal stimulation—exposing subjects to stimuli which are too faint or too fleeting to be noticed consciously but which nevertheless evoke a response* (Scientific American). **2** too weak or small to be felt or noticed: *a subliminal stimulus.*
—***n.*** = subconscious.
[< *sub-* + Latin *līmen, -inis* threshold + English *-al*[1]] —**sub|lim′i|nal|ly**, *adv.*

**subliminal advertising**, advertising by flashing messages before a viewer so fast he does not see them consciously but absorbs them through the subconscious mind.

**sub|lim|i|ty** (sə blim′ə tē), *n., pl.* **-ties.** **1** lofty excellence; grandeur; majesty; exalted state: *There was an awful sublimity in the hoarse murmuring of the thunder* (Francis Parkman). **2** something sublime; sublime person or thing: *The soul ... retains an obscure sense Of possible sublimity* (Wordsworth).

**sub|li|mize** (sub′lə mīz), *v.t.*, **-mized, -miz|ing.** to make sublime; elevate; exalt.

**sub|lin|e|ar** (sub lin′ē ər), *adj.* **1** nearly linear. **2** placed below a written or printed line: *Hebrew has sublinear vowel signs.*

**sub|lin|e|ate** (sub lin′ē āt), *v.t.*, **-at|ed, -at|ing.** to underline; underscore. [< *sub-* + *lineate*]

**sub|lin|e|a|tion** (sub′lin ē ā′shən), *n.* the act of sublineating.

**sub|lin|gual** (sub ling′gwəl), *adj., n. Anatomy.* —***adj.*** situated under or on the under side of the tongue: *a sublingual gland, artery, cyst, etc.*
—***n.*** a sublingual gland, artery, or the like.
[< *sub-* + *lingual*]

**sub|lit|er|ar|y** (sub′lit′ə rer′ē), *adj.* of, having to do with, or characteristic of subliterature: *Even aficionados of murder fiction will concede, in a moment of honesty, that except in the hands of a few writers it has been a subliterary product* (Charles J. Rolo).

**sub|lit|er|ate** (sub lit′ər it), *adj., n.* —***adj.*** below the accepted standard of literacy; semi-educated: *Subliterate, they were not in any sense skilled and therefore could not earn good wages* (New Scientist).
—***n.*** a subliterate person.

**sub|lit|er|a|ture** (sub′lit′ər ə chùr, -chər; -lit′rə-), *n.* **1** writings with little or no literary merit; substandard literature: *The Tarzan books ... from a lofty view ... are subliterature* (Edmund Fuller). **2** written accounts, such as laboratory reports and discussions, mimeographed or printed in impermanent form for use within the organization that prints them.

**sub|lit|to|ral** (sub lit′ər əl), *adj., n.* —***adj.*** **1** near the seacoast: *a sublittoral plant.* **2** of or having to do with the area of an ocean from low tide to the edge of the continental shelf.
—***n.*** a sublittoral area or region.

**sub|lu|nar** (sub lü′nər), *adj.* = sublunary.

**sub|lu|nar|y** (sub′lü ner′ē, sub lü′nər-), *adj.* beneath the moon; earthly: *the vanity of all sub-*

---

**Pronunciation Key:** hat, āge, cãre, fär; let, ēqual, tėrm; it, īce; hot, ōpen, ôrder; oil, out; cup, pùt, rüle; child; long; thin; ᴛʜen; zh, measure; ə represents a in about, e in taken, i in pencil, o in lemon, u in circus.

*lunary things* (Benjamin Disraeli). *The Van Allen radiation belt is the chief feature of sublunary space* (New Scientist). [< New Latin *sublunaris,* ultimately < Latin *sub-* under + *lūna* moon]

**sub|lu|nate** (sub lü′nāt), *adj.* almost crescent-shaped: *a sublunate mark.*

**sub|lux|ate** (sub luk′sāt), *v.t.,* **-at|ed, -at|ing.** to dislocate partially: *The patient is told ... that his troubles are due to just one thing: a subluxated vertebra* (Maclean's).

**sub|lux|a|tion** (sub′luk sā′shən), *n.* a partial dislocation; sprain: *Do you shrug off shooting pains in the wrist, ascribing them to a mere passing subluxation of the radial head?* (Punch). [< New Latin *subluxatio, -onis* < Latin *sub-* under, away + *luxāre* dislocate]

**sub|ma|chine gun** (sub′mə shēn′), a small, lightweight automatic or semiautomatic gun, designed to be fired from the shoulder or hip.

**sub|man|dib|u|lar** (sub′man dib′yə lər), *adj.* situated under the jaw, especially the lower jaw: *a submandibular gland.*

**sub|mar|gin|al** (sub mär′jə nəl), *adj.* **1** below the margin; not up to the minimum standard: *submarginal housing, submarginal intelligence.* **2** not productive enough to be worth cultivating or developing: *submarginal farmland. Lots of Soviet land is submarginal by U.S. standards* (Wall Street Journal). **3** *Biology.* near the margin or edge of a body or organ. — **sub|mar′gin|al|ly,** *adv.*

**sub|ma|rine** (*n., v.* sub′mə rēn; *adj.* sub′mə rēn′), *n., v.,* **-rined, -rin|ing,** *adj.* — *n.* **1** a boat that can go under water. Submarines are used in warfare for attacking enemy ships with torpedoes and for launching guided missiles. *Nuclear-powered submarines have broken all earlier records for speed, endurance, and time submerged* (Raymond V. B. Blackman). **2a** an organism that lives under water. **b** anything designed to be used under water, such as a mine or other explosive device. **3** *U.S. Slang.* a hero sandwich.
— *v.t.* to attack, damage, or sink by a submarine.
— *v.i. Football.* to charge very low against and upset a lineman.
— *adj.* **1** happening, growing, done, or used below the surface of the sea; underwater: *submarine plants, a submarine mine. The continental terrace is one of the main subjects of investigation in submarine geology today* (Scientific American). **2** of or carried out by a submarine or submarines: *submarine tactics, submarine warfare, a submarine attack.*

**submarine chaser,** a small, fast warship for pursuing and destroying submarines. It is usually smaller than a destroyer.

**submarine pen,** an underground shelter along the shore for docking and refueling submarines. Many partly exposed submarine pens are reinforced with concrete.

**sub|ma|rin|er** (sub′mə rē′nər; -mar′ə nər), *n.* a member of the crew of a submarine.

**sub|ma|ri|no** (sub′mə rē′nō), *n., pl.* **-nos.** an undersea oceanographic vessel; submersible. [< Spanish *submarino* submarine (adopted to distinguish this type of vessel from armed submarines)]

**sub|max|il|la** (sub′mak sil′ə), *n., pl.* **-max|il|lae** (-mak sil′ē). the lower jaw or lower jawbone in man and other vertebrates. [< Latin *sub-* under + *maxilla* maxilla]

**sub|max|il|lar|y** (sub mak′sə ler′ē), *n., pl.* **-lar|ies,** *adj.* — *n.* **1** the lower jawbone. **2** a salivary gland situated beneath the lower jaw on either side.
— *adj.* **1** of, having to do with, or beneath the lower jaw or lower jawbone: *a submaxillary fracture.* **2** having to do with the submaxillary glands.

**submaxillary gland,** either of a pair of salivary glands beneath the lower jaw.

**sub|me|di|an** (sub mē′dē ən), *adj.* situated near but not at the middle.

**sub|me|di|ant** (sub mē′dē ənt), *n. Music.* **1** the tone next above the dominant in the scale. **2** a key in which the submediant is the tonic: *The slow movement was in the submediant.*

**sub|men|tum** (sub men′təm), *n.* the lower part of the labium in insects. [< New Latin *submentum* < Latin *sub-* under + *mentum* chin]

**sub|merge** (səb mėrj′), *v.,* **-merged, -merg|ing.**
— *v.t.* **1** to put under water; cover with water: *A big wave submerged us. At high tide this path is submerged. The flooded river submerged most of the farmland in the valley.* **SYN:** plunge, immerse, submerse. **2** *Figurative.* to cover; bury: *His talent was submerged by his shyness.*
— *v.i.* **1** to go below the surface of a body of water; sink under water: *The submarine submerged to escape enemy attack.* **2** *Figurative.* to sink out of sight; be lost to view.
[< Latin *submergere* < *sub-* under + *mergere* to plunge]

**sub|merged** (səb mėrjd′), *adj.* **1** sunk under water or beneath the surface of something. **2** *Figurative.* living in extreme poverty and misery: *the submerged classes of society.* **3** *Botany.* growing under water.

**sub|mer|gence** (səb mėr′jəns), *n.* **1** the act of submerging. **2** the condition of being submerged.

**sub|mer|gi|bil|i|ty** (səb mėr′jə bil′ə tē), *n.* = submersibility.

**sub|mer|gi|ble** (səb mėr′jə bəl), *adj., n.* = submersible.

**sub|merse** (səb mėrs′), *v.t., v.i.,* **-mersed, -mers|ing.** = submerge. [< Latin *submersus,* past participle of *submergere;* see etym. under **submerge**]

**sub|mersed** (səb mėrst′), *adj.* **1** = submerged. **2** *Botany.* growing under water, as the leaves of aquatic plants.

**sub|mers|i|bil|i|ty** (səb mėr′sə bil′ə tē), *n.* the quality or state of being submersible.

**sub|mers|i|ble** (səb mėr′sə bəl), *adj., n.* — *adj.* that can be submerged: *To preserve future catches, Millot is designing a large submersible cage* (Scientific American).
— *n.* **1** an undersea vessel used for oceanographic research and exploration, such as a bathyscaph or mesoscaph: *A true submersible ... supports itself by the buoyancy of its very strong and relatively light hull* (New Scientist). *... an overview of Sealab II and other deep submersibles, and the human performance aboard* (Science News). **2** = submarine.

**sub|mer|sion** (səb mėr′zhən, -shən), *n.* **1** the action of submerging. **2** the condition of being submerged.

**sub|me|tal|lic** (sub′mə tal′ik), *adj.* imperfectly or partially metallic.

**sub|mi|cron** (sub mī′kron), *adj.* having to do with or consisting of particles that are each smaller than a micron, or 10,000 to 20,000 times smaller than a millimeter: *Finest glass fibers ever made may serve to screen out submicron dust and particles such as would result from atomic explosions* (Science News Letter).

**sub|mi|cro|scop|ic** (sub′mī krə skop′ik), *adj.* so tiny or minute as to be invisible through the normal microscope: *It is composed of submicroscopic cigar-shaped particles of iron* (Scientific American). — **sub′mi|cro|scop′i|cal|ly,** *adv.*

**sub|mil|li|me|ter** (sub mil′ə mē′tər), *adj.* smaller than a millimeter.

**sub|min|i|a|ture** (sub min′ē ə chər, -min′ə-), *adj.* smaller than the standard small size; microminiature: *A subminiature radio receiver, small enough to be plugged into an ear* (Science News Letter).

**sub|min|i|a|tur|ize** (sub min′ē ə chə rīz, -min′ə-chə-), *v.t.,* **-ized, -iz|ing.** to reduce to subminiature size; microminiaturize: *The proliferation of transistorized and "subminiaturized" tape recording devices—many of them easily concealed or disguised ...* (Saturday Review). — **sub|min′i|a|tur|i|za′tion,** *n.*

**sub|min|i|mal** (sub min′ə məl), *adj.* below the minimum; not up to the minimum standard: *... a subminimal public education program* (New York Times).

**sub|min|i|mum** (sub min′ə məm), *adj.* = subminimal.

**sub|miss** (səb mis′), *adj. Archaic.* submissive; humble: *In adoration at his feet I fell submiss* (Milton). [< Latin *submissus,* past participle of *submittere;* see etym. under **submit**]

**sub|mis|sion** (səb mish′ən), *n.* **1a** the act of yielding to the power, control, or authority of another; submitting: *The defeated general showed his submission by giving up his sword.* **SYN:** compliance, acquiescence, surrender. **b** the condition or an instance of having submitted. **2** humble obedience: *They bowed in submission to the queen's order.* **SYN:** humbleness. **3a** the act or process of referring or the fact of being referred to the consideration or judgment of some person or group. **b** something submitted to another for decision or consideration: *The Government Departments have contributed letters, reports and submissions to the Queen* (Sunday Times). *They spitefully submitted a sonnet by Keats. This was returned as speedily as the other submissions* (Maclean's). [< Latin *submissiō, -ōnis* a lowering < *submittere;* see etym. under **submit**]

**sub|mis|sion|ist** (səb mish′ə nist), *n.* a person who believes in or advocates submission.

**sub|mis|sive** (səb mis′iv), *adj.* yielding to the power, control, or authority of another; inclined to submit; obedient; humble: *He was proud, when I praised, he was submissive when I reproved him; but he did never love me* (Charles Lamb). *Between the overstrict and the easygoing fathers, Dr. Block found striking personality differences. The restrictive men were submissive, indecisive, ... and unconfident* (Newsweek). — **sub|mis′sive|ly,** *adv.* — **sub|mis′sive|ness,** *n.*

**sub|mit** (səb mit′), *v.,* **-mit|ted, -mit|ting.** — *v.i.* to yield to the power, control, or authority of some person or group; surrender: *The thief submitted to arrest by the police. He submitted to the decision of fate with ... humility* (G. K. Chesterton). **SYN:** comply, succumb, bow. See syn. under **yield.**
— *v.t.* **1** to refer to the consideration or judgment of another or others: *The secretary submitted a report of the last meeting.* **2** to suggest or urge in a respectful manner: *I submit that more proof is needed to support the case.* **3a** to yield (oneself) to the power, control, or authority of a person or agency. **b** to cause (a thing) to be subordinated to another.
[< Latin *submittere* < *sub-* under + *mittere* let go, send] — **sub|mit′ter,** *n.*

**sub|mit|tal** (səb mit′əl), *n.* the act of submitting.

**sub|mol|e|cule** (sub mol′ə kyül), *n.* a particle smaller than a molecule: *DNA molecules are made up of two very long strands connected to each other by hundreds of thousands of short submolecules, which are set in place like the rungs of a ladder* (Time).

**sub|mon|tane** (sub mon′tān), *adj.* under or beneath a mountain or mountains; of or at the foothills or lower slopes. [< *sub-* + *montane*]
— **sub|mon′tane|ly,** *adv.*

**sub|mu|co|sa** (sub′myü kō′sə), *n., pl.* **-sae** (-sē). the connective tissue lying beneath the mucous membrane.

**sub|mu|co|sal** (sub′myü kō′səl), *adj.* = submucous.

**sub|mu|cous** (sub myü′kəs), *adj.* of or having to do with the submucosa; beneath the mucosa.

**sub|mul|ti|ple** (sub mul′tə pəl), *n., adj.* — *n.* a number or quantity that divides another without a remainder; factor.
— *adj.* being or having to do with such a number or quantity.

**sub|mun|dane** (sub mun′dān), *adj.* existing under the world; underground; subterranean.

**sub|mus|cu|lar** (sub mus′kyə lər), *adj.* situated beneath a muscle.

**sub|nar|cot|ic** (sub′när kot′ik), *adj.* (of a drug) moderately narcotic.

**sub|nor|mal** (sub nôr′məl), *adj., n.* — *adj.* **1** below normal; less than normal: *a subnormal temperature, subnormal sales.* **2** inferior to the normal, as in mental capacity: *a subnormal person.*
— *n.* a subnormal individual: *Most subnormals require schooling to the age of sixteen because of mental and social immaturity* (Sunday Times).

**sub|nor|mal|i|ty** (sub′nôr mal′ə tē), *n.* the quality or condition of being subnormal.

**sub|nu|cle|ar** (sub nü′klē ər, -nyü′-), *adj.* **1** of or belonging within an atomic nucleus; being smaller than a nucleus: *The restless genius of man, standing midway between the boundless fields of interstellar space and the tiny, teeming jungles of subnuclear particles* (Newsweek). **2** of or having to do with the study of subnuclear particles: *Consider the vast sums ... happily sunk in the most far-out varieties of subnuclear physics because subnuclear research once delivered the military goods* (New Scientist).

**sub|nu|cle|on** (sub nü′klē on, -nyü′-), *n.* a hypothetical constituent of the known nuclear particles: *Dr. Yock postulates that all known particles are composed of six subnucleons* (Science News). [< *subnuclear* + *-on*]

**sub|ob|so|lete** (sub ob′sə lēt), *adj. Zoology.* nearly obsolete; almost disappearing.

**sub|o|ce|an|ic** (sub′ō shē an′ik), *adj.* existing, formed, or occurring beneath the ocean.

**sub|oc|tave** (sub′ok′tiv, -tāv), *n. Music.* the octave below a given note.

**sub|of|fice** (sub′ôf′is, -of′-), *n.* a branch office.

**sub|of|fi|cer** (sub′ôf′ə sər, -of′-), *n.* a subordinate officer.

**sub|of|fi|cial** (sub′ə fish′əl), *adj., n.* — *adj.* not fully official: *a subofficial program.*
— *n.* a subordinate official.

**sub|op|ti|mal** (sub op′tə məl), *adj.* not up to the optimal standard; inferior: *Many workers live in much older and suboptimal quarters* (Arthur W. Galston).

**sub|op|ti|mi|za|tion** (sub op′tə mə zā′shən), *n.* a failure to make the most of anything: *The suboptimization of existing weapons is not a competent alternative* (Scientific American).

**sub|op|ti|mize** (sub op′tə mīz), *v.t., v.i.,* **-mized, -miz|ing.** to fail to make the most of (a system, process, plan, or the like): *It is more difficult for them to sense needs beyond those institutions ... In the language of the systems analyst, they have a strong tendency to suboptimize* (Atlantic).

**sub|op|ti|mum** (sum op′tə məm), *adj.* = suboptimal.

**sub|or|bit|al** (sub ôr′bə təl), *adj., n.* — *adj.* **1** *Anatomy.* situated below the orbit of the eye, or on the floor of the orbit, as a cartilage or nerve. **2** of less than a full orbit: *a suborbital space flight.*
— *n.* a suborbital cartilage or nerve.

**sub|or|der** (sub′ôr′dər, sub ôr′-), *n. Biology.* a group of related plants or animals ranking above a family and below an order.

**sub|or|di|na|cy** (sə bôr′də nə sē), *n.* a subordinate position or state; subordination.

**sub|or|di|nal** (sə bôr′də nəl), *adj.* of, having to do with, or ranked as a suborder.

**sub|or|di|nar|y** (sub ôr′də ner′ē), *n., pl.* **-nar|ies.** *Heraldry.* any one of various simple charges or bearings regarded as less important than the ordinaries.

**sub|or|di|nate** (*adj., n.* sə bôr′də nit; *v.* sə bôr′də-nāt), *adj., n., v.,* **-nat|ed, -nat|ing.** —*adj.* **1** lower in rank: *In the army, lieutenants are subordinate to captains.* **2** having less importance; secondary; minor: *An errand boy has a subordinate position.* **3** under the control or influence of something else; dependent. **SYN:** subject, subservient. **4** *Grammar.* **a** dependent. **b** subordinating. *Because, since, if, as,* and *whether* are subordinate conjunctions. **5** *Obsolete.* submissive.
—*n.* a subordinate person or thing: *Platoons of subordinates jump when he twitches* (Time).
—*v.t.* to place in a lower order or rank; make subordinate or dependent: *A polite host subordinates his wishes to those of his guests. He to whose will our wills are to be subordinated* (Thomas Carlyle).
[< Medieval Latin *subordinatus,* past participle of *subordinare* < Latin *sub-* under + *ordināre* arrange, put in order < *ōrdō, -inis* order] —**sub|or′di|nate|ly,** *adv.* —**sub|or′di|nate|ness,** *n.*

**subordinate clause,** a clause in a complex sentence that cannot act alone as a sentence; dependent clause. In "If I go home, my dog will follow me," *If I go home* is a subordinate clause.

**sub|or|di|nat|ing** (sə bôr′də nā′ting), *adj.* joining a subordinate clause to a main clause: *a subordinating conjunction.*

**sub|or|di|na|tion** (sə bôr′də nā′shən), *n.* **1** the act of subordinating. **2** the condition of being subordinated. **3** subordinate position or importance. **SYN:** subjection. **4** submission to authority; willingness to obey; obedience. **SYN:** subservience, dependence.

**sub|or|di|na|tion|ism** (sə bôr′də nā′shə niz əm), *n. Theology.* the doctrine that the second and third persons of the Trinity are inferior to the first.

**sub|or|di|na|tion|ist** (sə bôr′də nā′shə nist), *n., adj.* —*n.* a believer in the doctrine of subordinationism.
—*adj.* of or having to do with this doctrine.

**sub|or|di|na|tive** (sə bôr′də nā′tiv), *adj.* tending to subordinate; involving or expressing subordination or dependence.

**sub|orn** (sə bôrn′), *v.t.* **1a** to persuade (a person) to do an illegal or evil deed. **b** to make disloyal; corrupt. **2** to persuade or cause (a witness) to give false testimony in court: *He had no case without suborning witnesses* (George Meredith). **3a** to get by bribery or other unlawful means. **b** to obtain (evidence) by such means. [< Latin *subornāre* suborn; (originally) equip < *sub-* under + *ornāre* equip] —**sub′or|na′tion,** *n.* —**sub-orn′er,** *n.*

**subornation of perjury,** *Law.* the crime of persuading or causing a witness to give false testimony in court.

**sub|or|na|tive** (sə bôr′nə tiv), *adj.* having to do with subornation.

**sub|ox|id** (sub ok′sid), *n.* = suboxide.

**sub|ox|ide** (sub ok′sīd, -sid), *n.* a compound of oxygen and another element or radical, containing a small proportion of oxygen.

**sub-par** (sub′pär′), *adj.* **1** below average: *A New York importer claims a Turkish trader sent him a shipment of sub-par sunflower seeds; he wants ... damages* (Newsweek). **2** (in golf) under par: *Continuing his sub-par play ... the British open champion had a point total of 22* (New York Times).

**subpar.,** subparagraph.

**sub|par|a|graph** (sub par′ə graf, -gräf), *n.* a secondary or supplementary paragraph.

**sub|par|ti|cle** (sub pär′tə kəl), *n.* a constituent of a particle: *All ribosomes are constructed from two unequal subparticles* (Science Journal). *The question now is whether "elementary" particles such as protons have ... subparticles of some kind* (Gary Mitchell).

**sub|pe|na** (sə pē′nə), *n., v.,* **-naed, -na|ing.** = subpoena.

**sub|phy|lum** (sub′fī′ləm, sub fī′-), *n., pl.* **-la** (-lə). *Biology.* **1** a group of related animals ranking above a superclass and below a phylum. **2** = subdivision (def. 3).

**sub|plot** (sub′plot′), *n.* a minor or subordinate plot, as in a play or novel; underplot: *When several of the subplots must somehow be tied together, the work shows strain and becomes contrived* (New Yorker).

**sub|poe|na** (sə pē′nə), *n., v.,* **-naed, -na|ing.** —*n.* an official written order commanding a person to appear in court or before another legal body, such as a committee of the U.S. Congress. A subpoena is delivered by an officer of the court or other legal body to the person specified in it, who becomes liable to penalty for failure to comply with it. *Mr. Bell has said that if necessary he will call the corporation officers on subpoena* (London Times).
—*v.t.* to summon with such an order; serve a subpoena on: *They were cited for refusing to turn over to the committee ... documents subpoenaed from them* (New York Times). Also, **subpena.**
[< Medieval Latin *sub poena,* the first words of the writ < Latin *sub* under + *poenā,* ablative of *poena* penalty]

**subpoena ad tes|ti|fi|can|dum** (ad tes′tə fə-kan′dəm), *Law.* a subpoena requiring a person to appear in court as a witness. [< New Latin *subpoena ad testificandum* (literally) under penalty to testify]

**subpoena du|ces te|cum** (dü′kās tā′kəm), *Law.* a subpoena requiring a person to bring into court with him certain specified things, such as papers, books, financial records, or other documents. [< New Latin *subpoena duces tecum* (literally) under penalty bring with you]

**sub|point** (sub′point′), *n.* = substellar point.

**sub|po|lar** (sub pō′lər), *adj.* **1** below or adjoining the poles or polar seas of the earth in latitude. **2** beneath the pole of the heavens: *the subpolar passage of a star.*

**sub|pop|u|la|tion** (sub pop′yə lā′shən), *n.* a part or subdivision of a population.

**sub-post office** (sub′pōst′), *British.* a branch of a post office.

**sub|po|ten|cy** (sub pō′tən sē), *n. Biology.* a lessening in the power to transmit inherited characteristics.

**sub|po|tent** (sub pō′tənt), *adj.* having or exhibiting subpotency.

**sub|pre|fect** (sub prē′fekt), *n.* an assistant or deputy prefect.

**sub|pre|fec|ture** (sub prē′fek chər), *n.* **1** the office or position of a subprefect. **2** a division of a prefecture.

**sub|prin|ci|pal** (sub prin′sə pəl), *n.* **1** an assistant or deputy principal, as of a school or university. **2** an auxiliary rafter in the framework of a roof. **3** *Music.* a subbass of the open diapason class in an organ.

**sub|pri|or** (sub′prī′ər), *n.* the deputy or assistant of a prior. [< Medieval Latin *subprior* < *sub-* sub- + Latin *prior* prior]

**sub|prob|lem** (sub′prob′ləm), *n.* a problem that is part of a larger problem: *The computer would be programmed to split the problem into subproblems* (Scientific American).

**sub|pro|fes|sion|al** (sub′prə fesh′ə nəl, -fesh′-nəl), *adj., n.* —*adj.* **1** below what is professional; not up to the professional level: *subprofessional assistants, subprofessional talent.* **2** = paraprofessional.
—*n.* a paraprofessional: *Dr. Gardner is training workers from the community, many of whom lack even high school diplomas, to act as therapists. The bulk of the therapeutic work is done by these subprofessionals* (Science News).

**sub|pro|gram** (sub′prō′gram, -grəm), *n.* **1** a part of a computer program. **2** = subroutine (def. 2).

**sub|pul|sa|tion** (sub′pul sā′shən), *n.* a part or constituent of a pulsation.

**sub|pulse** (sub′puls′), *n.* a part or constituent of a pulse; a pulse that forms a part of a main pulse: *Subpulses have been observed in the pulsar* (New Scientist).

**sub|ra|mose** (sub rā′mōs, sub′rə mōs′), *adj. Botany.* branching only slightly.

**sub|re|gion** (sub′rē′jən), *n.* a division or subdivision of a geographical region, especially with reference to animal distribution.

**sub|re|gion|al** (sub rē′jə nəl), *adj.* of or having to do with a subregion.

**sub|rep|tion** (sub rep′shən), *n.* **1** the suppression of facts in order to obtain something, as ecclesiastical dispensation or preferment. **2** a fallacious or deceptive representation or an inference derived from it. [< Latin *subreptiō, -ōnis* < *subripere* remove secretly, steal < *sub-* under + *rapere* snatch. Compare etym. under **surreptitious.**]

**sub|rep|ti|tious** (sub′rep tish′əs), *adj.* **1** obtained by subreption. **2** clandestine or surreptitious. —**sub′rep|ti′tious|ly,** *adv.*

**sub|res|in** (sub rez′ən), *n.* the part of a resin which dissolves in boiling alcohol, and is deposited as the alcohol cools.

**sub|ro|gate** (sub′rə gāt), *v.t.,* **-gat|ed, -gat|ing.** **1** to put (a person) into the place of another in respect to a legal right or claim. **2** to substitute (a thing) for another. Also, **surrogate.** [< Latin *subrogāre* (with English *-ate*[1]) < *sub-* under, away + *rogāre* to pray] —**sub′ro|ga′tion,** *n.*

**sub ro|sa** (sub rō′zə), **1** in strict confidence; privately; secretly: *In Israel one can eat pork only sub rosa* (Listener). **2** confidential; private; secret: *A few ... had purchased in a sub rosa sort of way neckties which remained to be exhibited in public* (Harper's). [< Latin *sub* under, *rosā,* ablative of *rosa* rose (because it was apparently an ancient symbol of secrecy)]

**sub|rou|tine** (sub′rü tēn′), *n.* **1** a part of a routine. **2** a sequence of instructions directing an electronic computer to carry out a well-defined mathematical or logical operation.

**sub|sa|line** (sub sā′līn), *adj.* moderately saline or salty.

**sub|salt** (sub′sôlt′), *n.* a basic salt.

**sub|sam|ple** (sub′sam′pəl, -säm′-), *n., v.,* **-pled, -pling.** —*n.* a sample taken from a group of samples; part of a large sampling.
—*v.t.* to take a subsample of.

**sub|sat|el|lite** (sub sat′ə līt), *n.* an object carried into orbit inside an artificial earth satellite and then ejected: *... a subsatellite carrying particle detectors and a magnetometer* (New Scientist).

**sub|sat|u|rat|ed** (sub sach′ə rā′tid), *adj.* partly or incompletely saturated.

**sub|sat|u|ra|tion** (sub sach′ə rā′shən), *n.* partial or incomplete saturation.

**sub|scap|u|lar** (sub skap′yə lər), *adj., n.* —*adj.* beneath, or on the anterior surface of, the scapula: *a subscapular gland or artery.*
—*n.* a subscapular muscle, artery, etc.

**sub|sci|ence** (sub sī′əns), *n.* a branch or subdivision of a science: *She was ... one of the first to develop the subscience of semiotics* (Time).

**sub|scrib|a|ble** (səb skrī′bə bəl), *adj.* that can be subscribed to: *The new bond is subscribable only by holders of 2⅞ per cent bonds* (New York Times).

**sub|scribe** (səb skrīb′), *v.,* **-scribed, -scrib|ing.** —*v.t.* **1a** to promise to give or pay (a sum of money): *He subscribed $5 to the hospital fund.* **b** to give or pay (money) in fulfillment of such a promise. **2** to write (one's name) at the end of a document or the like; sign (one's name): *The old man subscribed his mark at the end of the will.* **3a** to sign one's name to (a document, petition, or the like); show one's consent or approval by signing: *Thousands of citizens subscribed the petition.* **b** to attest (as a statement or will) by signing. **4** *Obsolete.* to give one's consent, approval, or support to; sanction: *Orestes ... chose rather to encounter the rage of an armed multitude, than to subscribe the ruin of an innocent people* (Edward Gibbon).
—*v.i.* **1a** to promise to give or pay money: *to subscribe to several charities.* **b** to give or pay money in fulfillment of such a promise; contribute. **2** to promise to taken and pay for a number of copies of a newspaper, magazine, or other form of publication: *We subscribe to a few magazines. I am subscribing for some of the books of a book club.* **3** to give one's consent, approval, or support; agree: *She will not subscribe to anything unfair. I do not expect you to subscribe to my opinion.* **4** to sign one's name to something, as to show agreement or approval, or as a witness: *John Hancock was the first man to subscribe to the Declaration of Independence.* [< Latin *subscrībere* < *sub-* under + *scrībere* write]

**sub|scrib|er** (səb skrī′bər), *n.* a person who subscribes: *The magazines make a special offer to new subscribers.*

**sub|script** (sub′skript), *n., adj.* —*n.* a number, letter, or other symbol written underneath and usually to one side of the number, letter, or symbol to which it applies. In $H_2SO_4$ the *2* and *4* are subscripts.
—*adj.* **1** written underneath or low on the line. **2** *Mathematics.* of or having to do with a subindex.
[< Latin *subscrīptus,* past participle of *subscrībere;* see etym. under **subscribe**]

**sub|scrip|tion** (səb skrip′shən), *n.* **1** the act or process of subscribing. **2a** the money subscribed; contribution: *His subscription to the Fresh Air Fund was $5.* **b** *British.* dues for a society, club, or other organization. **3** the right to receive a magazine, newspaper, or other form of publication, obtained by paying a certain sum: *Your subscription to the newspaper expires next week.* **4** a sum of money raised by a number of persons; fund: *We are raising a subscription for the new hospital.* **5** something written at the end of a document, petition, or the like; signature. **6** a signed declaration, statement, or other document. **7** consent, agreement, or support given by signing one's name. **8a** assent to a set of articles of faith, principles, or doctrines which are intended to further uniformity. **b** (in the Church of England) assent to the Thirty-nine Articles of 1563 and the Book of Common Prayer.

**subscription book,** **1** a book containing the

names of subscribers, along with the amounts of their subscription: *Less than 48 hours after brokers opened subscription books on the largest financial dealing in history, the entire issue had been snapped up* (Newsweek). **2** a book sold by subscription. **3** a book of tickets for a series of events: *Shops will sell subscription books for the ... series of Stadium Concerts* (New York Times).

**subscription television**, television broadcasting paid for by the viewers and transmitted over cable or scrambled and decoded by a device on a subscriber's set.

**sub|scrip|tive** (səb skrip′tiv), *adj.* **1** of or having to do with a subscription or signature. **2** having to do with the subscribing of money. — **sub|scrip′tive|ly**, *adv.*

**sub|sea** (sub sē′), *adj.* undersea; submarine: *subsea oil deposits.*

**subsec.**, subsection.

**sub|sec|tion** (sub′sek′shən), *n.* a part of a section.

**sub|sen|si|ble** (sub sen′sə bəl), *adj.* deeper than the range of the senses; too deep or subtle for the senses to grasp.

**sub|sep|tate** (sub sep′tāt), *adj.* not perfectly septate; having an incomplete septum.

**sub|se|quence¹** (sub′sə kwəns), *n.* **1** the fact or condition of being subsequent. **2** a subsequent event or circumstance; sequel.

**sub|se|quence²** (sub sē′kwəns), *n.* a subordinate or secondary sequence: *a subsequence of numbers.*

**sub|se|quen|cy** (sub′sə kwən sē), *n., pl.* **-cies.** = subsequence¹.

**sub|se|quent** (sub′sə kwənt), *adj.* coming after; following; later: *Subsequent events proved that he was right. The story will be continued in subsequent issues of the magazine.*

**subsequent to**, after; following; later than: *on the day subsequent to your visit.*

[< Latin *subsequēns, -entis,* present participle of *subsequī* < *sub-* from under + *sequī* follow] — **sub′se|quent|ness**, *n.*

**sub|se|quen|tial** (sub′sə kwen′shəl), *adj.* = subsequent.

**sub|se|quent|ly** (sub′sə kwənt lē), *adv.* afterward; later: *At first we thought we would go; subsequently we learned we were needed at home.*

**subsequently to**, after; following; later than: *In North America ... the large quadrupeds lived subsequently to that period* (Erasmus Darwin).

**sub|sere** (sub′sir′), *n. Ecology.* a subordinate or secondary succession of plant communities: ... *the species composition of early stages of the subsere* (New Scientist). [< *sub-* + *sere²*]

**sub|serve** (səb sėrv′), *v.t.,* **-served, -serv|ing.** to help or assist (as a purpose, action, or function): *Chewing food well subserves digestion. Liberty is to be subserved whatever occurs* (Walt Whitman). *When words no longer subserve thought but are granted a value of their own equal to that of thought itself, the mediocre mind is sorely tempted to use them, to the detriment of constructive thinking* (Atlantic). [< Latin *subservīre* < *sub-* under + *servīre* serve]

**sub|ser|vi|ence** (səb sėr′vē əns), *n.* **1** slavish politeness and obedience; tame submission; servility. **2** the condition or quality of being of use or service.

**sub|ser|vi|en|cy** (səb sėr′vē ən sē), *n.* = subservience.

**sub|ser|vi|ent** (səb sėr′vē ənt), *adj.* **1** slavishly polite and obedient; tamely submissive; servile: *The lawyers had been subservient beyond all other classes to the Crown* (John R. Green). **SYN**: obsequious, truckling. **2** useful as a means to help a purpose or end; serviceable (to): *A street of small shops subservient to the needs of poor people* (W. Somerset Maugham). **3** subordinate or subject (to). [< Latin *subserviēns, -entis,* present participle of *subservīre;* see etym. under **subserve**] — **sub|ser′vi|ent|ly**, *adv.*

***sub|set** (sub′set′), *n. Mathematics.* a set, each of whose members is a member of another set or series of terms. The set of numbers from 2 to 5 is a subset of the set of numbers 0 to 10.

***subset**

**set of numbers**

{0, 1, **2, 3, 4, 5**, 6, 7, 8, 9, 10}

subset

**sub|shell** (sub′shel′), *n.* any part or segment of the space occupied by the orbit of an electron: *The relation arises from the disposition of electrons around a nucleus in a series of shells and subshells, which are really a simplified physical representation of quantum-mechanical energy levels* (Scientific American).

**sub|shrub** (sub′shrub′), *n.* a plant with a somewhat woody base; small shrub; undershrub.

**sub|shrub|by** (sub′shrub′ē), *adj.* like a subshrub; suffruticose.

**sub|side** (səb sīd′), *v.i.,* **-sid|ed, -sid|ing. 1** to grow less; become less active; die down: *The waves subsided when the wind stopped. Her fever subsided after she took the medicine. Her anger now subsiding into grief* (Frances Burney). **SYN**: abate, decrease, ebb, wane. **2** to sink to a lower level: *Several days after the rain stopped, the flood waters subsided.* **3** to sink or fall to the bottom; settle. **4** to sink down, as into a chair. [< Latin *subsīdere* < *sub-* down + *sīdere* to settle]

**sub|sid|ence** (səb sī′dəns, sub′sə-), *n.* the act or process of subsiding: *the subsidence of a flood or a fever.*

**sub|sid|i|ar|y** (səb sid′ē er′ē), *adj., n., pl.* **-ar|ies.** — *adj.* **1** useful to assist or supplement; auxiliary; supplementary: *The teacher sold books as a subsidiary occupation.* **2** subordinate; secondary: *a subsidiary issue. Only as a subsidiary reason does the message advocate more trade to help assure our own economic growth* (Wall Street Journal). **3** maintained by a subsidy or subsidies. — *n.* **1** a person or thing that assists or supplements. **2** a company having over half of its stock owned or controlled by another company: *The bus line was a subsidiary of the railroad.* **3** *Music.* a secondary theme or subject.

[< Latin *subsidiārius* < *subsidium* reserve troops; see etym. under **subsidy**] — **sub|sid′i|ar′i|ly**, *adv.*

**sub|si|dise** (sub′sə dīz), *v.t.,* **-dised, -dis|ing.** *Especially British.* subsidize.

**sub|si|dize** (sub′sə dīz), *v.t.,* **-dized, -diz|ing. 1** to aid or assist with a grant of money or by guaranteeing a market: *The government subsidizes airlines that carry mail. Many universities subsidize research and publications.* **2** to buy the aid or assistance of with a grant of money. **3** = bribe. [< *subsid*(y) + *-ize*] — **sub′si|di|za′tion**, *n.*

**subsidized adoption**, *U.S.* a government program that provides financial assistance to persons who adopt children: *Subsidized adoption is a way to increase the number of available adoptive homes* (Frances A. Mullen).

**sub|si|diz|er** (sub′sə dī′zər), *n.* a person or group that subsidizes.

**sub|si|dy** (sub′sə dē), *n., pl.* **-dies. 1** a grant or contribution of money, especially one made by a government in support of an undertaking or the upkeep of a thing: *a subsidy for education. Under the price-support program, the farmer is given a subsidy to encourage him to produce surpluses* (Newsweek). **2** money formerly granted to the sovereign by the British Parliament to meet special needs. [< Anglo-French *subsidie,* learned borrowing from Latin *subsidium* aid, reserve troops < *sub-* under + *sedēre* to sit]

**sub si|len|ti|o** (sub sī len′tē ō), *Latin.* in silence; without a remark being made; without notice being taken: *Sometimes passing a thing sub silentio is evidence of consent* (John Bouvier).

**sub|sist** (səb sist′), *v.i.* **1** to keep alive; live: *People in the far north subsist chiefly on fish and meat.* **2** to continue to be; exist: *Many superstitions still subsist. A club cannot subsist without members.* **3** *Philosophy.* **a** to stand as fact or truth; hold true. **b** to be logically necessary, probable, or conceivable. **4** *Obsolete.* to continue in a condition or position; remain as such. — ***v.t.*** to provide for; feed; support. [< Latin *subsistere* stand firm; support < *sub-* up to + *sistere* to stand < *stāre* to stand]

**sub|sist|ence** (səb sis′təns), *n.* **1** the condition or fact of keeping alive; living: *Selling papers was the poor old man's only means of subsistence.* **2** a means of keeping alive; livelihood: *The sea provides a subsistence for fishermen.* **3** continued existence; continuance. **4** *Philosophy.* **a** the individualizing of substance, especially as a particular rational (human) being standing apart from all others but possessing certain rights, powers, and functions in common with all others of the same type. **b** the condition of subsisting. **5** *Obsolete.* the condition or quality of inhering or residing (in something). [< Late Latin *subsistentia* < Latin *subsistēns, -entis,* present participle of *subsistere;* see etym. under **subsist**]

**subsistence farming**, farming that produces only the minimum amount of food necessary to sustain the farmer and his family, with little or no surplus or profit: *A settled community now enjoys a cash crop instead of the insecurity of crude subsistence farming* (Manchester Guardian Weekly).

**sub|sist|ent** (səb sis′tənt), *adj.* existing of or by itself; existing; subsisting.

**sub|soil** (sub′soil′), *n., v.* — *n.* the layer of earth that lies just under the surface soil: *Below this layer is a gradual transition to a yellowish stratum of clay ... called subsoil* (Fred W. Emerson). — ***v.t.*** to plow, till, or dig so as to cut into the subsoil. — **sub′soil′er**, *n.*

**sub|so|lar** (sub sō′lər), *adj.* **1** directly underneath the sun; having the sun in the zenith. **2** *Figurative.* terrestrial; mundane. **3** between the tropics.

**sub|son|ic** (sub son′ik), *adj.* **1** having to do with or designed for use at a speed less than the speed of sound (about 1,100 feet or 335 meters per second in air). **2** that moves at a speed slower than the speed of sound: *a subsonic airplane.* — **sub|son′i|cal|ly**, *adv.*

**sub|space** (sub′spās′), *n. Mathematics.* a subset of a space.

**sub|spe|cial|ize** (sub spesh′ə līz), *v.i.,* **-ized, -iz|ing.** to pursue a subspecialty: *to subspecialize in transplant surgery or child psychology.* — **sub|spe′cial|ist**, *n.* — **sub|spe′cial|i|za′tion**, *n.*

**sub|spe|cial|ty** (sub spesh′əl tē), *n., pl.* **-ties.** a subdivision of a branch of science or research; specialty within a specialty: *There is no subspecialty of social or community psychiatry* [*in Russia*] *because every psychiatrist works in an overall social effort as public health officer* (Science News).

**sub spe|ci|e ae|ter|ni|ta|tis** (sub spē′shē ē ē-tėr′nə tā′tis), *Latin.* under the form of eternity; in its essential form or character.

**sub|spe|cies** (sub′spē′shēz, sub spē′-), *n., pl.* **-cies. 1** *Biology.* a group of related plants or animals ranking below a species. **2** a subdivision of a species: *We include within the Mongoloid subspecies three major races; the Asiatic Mongoloid, the Indonesian-Malay, and the American Indian* (Beals and Hoijer).

**sub|spe|cif|ic** (sub′spi sif′ik), *adj.* of, having to do with, or like a subspecies. — **sub′spe|cif′i|cal|ly**, *adv.*

**sub|spher|i|cal** (sub sfer′ə kəl), *adj.* not completely spherical; spheroidal: ... *subspherical curvatures* (Scientific American).

**subst.**, **1** substantive. **2** substitute.

**sub|stage** (sub′stāj′), *n.* **1** a subdivision of a stage: *The specimens come from different substages of the same* [*geological*] *formation* (Charles Darwin). **2** a device beneath the ordinary stage of a compound microscope to support mirrors and other accessories.

**sub|stance** (sub′stəns), *n.* **1** what a thing consists of; matter; material: *Ice and water consist of the same substance in different forms. The wool-gray air is all about him like a living substance* (Thomas Wolfe). **2** the real, main, or important part of anything; essence: *The substance of an education is its effect on your life, not just learning lessons.* **3** the real meaning; gist: *Give the substance of the speech in your own words.* **SYN**: purport. **4** solid quality; body: *Pea soup has more substance than water.* **5** wealth; property; possessions: *a man of substance. He spent his substance in bookstores.* **6** a particular kind of matter; stuff: *a chemical substance. The little pond is covered with a green substance. This variety of substances, which compose the internal parts of our globe* (Oliver Goldsmith). **7** *Philosophy.* **a** something that underlies all phenomena, and in which accidents or attributes inhere; something that receives modifications and is not itself a mode. **b** something that subsists by itself; separate or distinct thing.

**in substance**, **a** essentially; substantially; mainly: *In substance, obviously, this is a moving story* (New Yorker). **b** really; actually: *We know that the monarchy did not survive the hierarchy, no, not even in appearance, for many months; in substance, not for a single hour* (Edmund Burke).

[< Old French *substance,* learned borrowing from Latin *substantia* < *substāre* stand firm; be present < *sub-* up to + *stāre* stand]

— ***Syn.*** **1, 2 Substance, matter, material** mean what a thing consists or is made of. **Substance** applies both to things existing in the physical world and to those given form only in the mind: *The substance of the plan is good.* **Matter** applies to any substance that occupies space and that physical objects consist of: *Matter may be gaseous, liquid, or solid.* **Material** applies to any matter from which something is made: *Oil is an important raw material.*

**sub|stance|less** (sub′stəns lis), *adj.* without substance; unsubstantial.

**sub|stand|ard** (sub stan′dərd, sub′stan′-), *adj.* **1** below standard: *Basically furnished quarters* (*may for a time be substandard but adequate*) *at low rentals* (London Times). **2** not conforming to the accepted standards of speech or writing. **3** *Law, U.S.* below the standard required by law and not so labeled.

**sub|stan|tial** (səb stan′shəl), *adj., n.* — *adj.* **1** having substance; real; actual: *People and things are substantial; dreams and ghosts are not.* **SYN**: material. **2** strong; firm; solid: *That house is substantial enough to last a hundred years.* **3** large; important; ample: *a substantial profit. By hard study he made a substantial improvement in arithmetic.* **4** providing ample or abundant nourishment: *Eat a substantial break-*

*fast.* **5** in the main; for the most part; in essentials: *The stories told by the two boys were in substantial agreement.* **6** well-to-do; wealthy; influential: *He ... introduced us to a number of substantial-looking middle-aged civilians* (New Yorker). **7** of real or solid worth or value; weighty; sound: *substantial criticism, substantial evidence. The substantial comforts of a good coal fire* (Mary R. Mitford). **8a** being a substance; being real. **b** essential; material: *the substantial truth of the story* (John Hay). **9** *Philosophy.* of, having to do with, or inherent in substance, rather than accident.
—*n.* **substantials**, something substantial: *His judgment in substantials, like that of Johnson, is always worth having* (James Russell Lowell).
[< Latin *substantiālis* < *substantia;* see etym. under **substance**] — **sub|stan′tial|ness**, *n.*

**sub|stan|tial|ism** (səb stan′shə liz əm), *n. Philosophy.* **1** the doctrine that substantial realities or real substances underlie all phenomena. **2** the doctrine that matter is a tangible substance and is definable in terms of weight and volume, rather than energy and interacting fields of force, even in its smallest particles.

**sub|stan|tial|ist** (səb stan′shə list), *n.* an adherent of a doctrine of substantialism.

**sub|stan|ti|al|i|ty** (səb stan′shē al′ə tē), *n., pl.* **-ties**. **1** real existence. **2** solidity; firmness. **3** real worth or value. **4** something substantial; substantial article of food.

**sub|stan|tial|ize** (səb stan′shə līz), *v.t.,* **-ized, -iz|ing.** to make substantial; give reality to.

**sub|stan|tial|ly** (səb stan′shə lē), *adv.* **1** essentially; mainly: *This report is substantially correct.* **2** really; actually. **3** strongly; solidly: *a substantially built house.*

**sub|stan|tials** (səb stan′shəlz), *n.pl.* See under **substantial.**

**sub|stan|ti|ate** (səb stan′shē āt), *v.t.,* **-at|ed, -at|ing.** **1** to establish by evidence; prove; verify: *to substantiate a rumor, to substantiate a claim, to substantiate a theory. Many of these theories could be disproved or substantiated* (Saturday Review). **SYN**: See syn. under **confirm.** **2** to give concrete or substantial form to; embody. **3** to give substantial existence to; make physically real. — **sub|stan′ti|a′tion**, *n.* — **sub|stan′ti|a′tor**, *n.*

**sub|stan|ti|a|tive** (səb stan′shē ā′tiv), *adj.* serving to substantiate.

**sub|stan|ti|fy** (sub′stən tə fī), *v.t.,* **-fied, -fy|ing.** = substantivize.

**sub|stan|ti|val** (sub′stən tī′vəl), *adj.* of, having to do with, or consisting of a substantive or substantives. — **sub′stan|ti′val|ly**, *adv.*

**sub|stan|tive** (sub′stən tiv), *adj., n. Grammar.*
—*adj.* **1a** real; actual; essential: *The substantive issue of what constitutes forbidden political activity has rarely been faced* (Bulletin of Atomic Scientists). **b** = substantial. **2** *Grammar.* **a** used as a noun. **b** (of verbs) showing or expressing existence. The verb *to be* is a substantive verb. **3** standing of or by itself; independent; self-sufficient. **4** having a firm or solid basis. **5** not requiring a mordant, but adhering directly to the material: *a substantive dye.* **6** *Law.* dealing with rights rather than the procedures of obtaining them.
—*n.* **1** a noun or pronoun. *Abbr:* subst. **2** any word or group of words used as a noun.
[< Latin *substantīvus* < *substantia;* see etym. under **substance**] — **sub′stan|tive|ly**, *adv.* — **sub′stan|tive|ness**, *n.*

**sub|stan|tiv|ize** (sub′stən tə vīz), *v.t.,* **-ized, -iz|ing.** to make a substantive of; use as a substantive.

**sub|sta|tion** (sub′stā′shən), *n.* a branch station; subordinate station: *Besides the main post office in our city, there are six substations.*

**sub|stel|lar point** (sub stel′ər), the point on the earth's surface directly below any particular star.

**sub|stit|u|ent** (səb stich′ů ənt), *n., adj. Chemistry.*
—*n.* an atom or group of atoms taking the place of another atom or group in a compound.
—*adj.* having to do with such an atom or group of atoms.
[< Latin *substituēns, -entis,* present participle of *substituere;* see etym. under **substitute**]

**sub|sti|tut|a|bil|i|ty** (sub′stə tü′tə bil′ə tē, -tyü′-), *n.* the quality or condition of being substitutable: *There is a high degree of substitutability among types of loans and lending institutions* (New York Times).

**sub|sti|tut|a|ble** (sub′stə tü′tə bəl, -tyü′-), *adj.* that can be substituted: *substitutable food.*

**sub|sti|tute** (sub′stə tüt, -tyüt), *n., v.,* **-tut|ed, -tut|ing,** *adj.* —*n.* **1** a thing used instead of another; person taking the place of another: *Margarine is a common substitute for butter. A substitute taught us at school today.* **SYN**: expedient, alternate. **2** a person who took the place of a draftee in the army or navy, usually for pay, as in the American Civil War. **3** *Grammar.* a word or other linguistic form which under certain circumstances replaces any one of a class of other words or linguistic forms. **4** a small flag used in the flag signaling system of a ship to repeat the flag or penant flying above it; repeater. Substitutes make it unnecessary to carry extra sets of flags and pennants to show the same signal several times.
—*v.t.* **1** to put in place of another: *We substituted brown sugar for molasses in these cookies.* **2** to cause to take the place of: *For real wit he is obliged to substitute vivacity* (Oliver Goldsmith). **SYN**: replace.
—*v.i.* **1** to take the place of another; be a substitute: *The retired teacher substituted for our regular teacher, who was sick.* **2** *Chemistry.* to replace one or more equivalents of an element or radical by a like number of equivalents of another.
—*adj.* put in for or taking the place of another: *a substitute teacher.*
[< Latin *substitūtus,* past participle of *substituere* < *sub-* under + *statuere* establish < *stāre* stand]

**sub|sti|tu|tion** (sub′stə tü′shən, -tyü′-), *n.* **1** the use of one thing for another; putting (one person or thing) in place of another; taking the place of another: *substitution of a kind word for a cross one.* **2** *Chemistry.* the replacing of one or more elements or radicals in a compound by other elements or radicals.

**sub|sti|tu|tion|al** (sub′stə tü′shə nəl, -tyü′-), *adj.* **1** having to do with or characterized by substitution. **2** acting or serving as a substitute. — **sub′sti|tu′tion|al|ly**, *adv.*

**sub|sti|tu|tion|ar|y** (sub′stə tü′shə ner′ē, -tyü′-), *adj.* = substitutional.

**substitution system**, a cryptographic system in which the letters of the plaintext retain their original positions but are replaced by other letters.

**sub|sti|tu|tive** (sub′stə tü′tiv, -tyü′-), *adj.* **1** having to do with or involving substitution. **2** serving as, or capable of serving as, a substitute. — **sub′sti|tu′tive|ly**, *adv.*

**sub|stra|ta** (sub strā′tə, -strat′ə), *n.* a plural of **substratum.**

**sub|stra|tal** (sub strā′təl), *adj.* underlying; fundamental.

**sub|strate** (sub′strāt), *n.* **1** = substratum. **2** *Biochemistry.* the material that an enzyme or ferment acts upon.

**sub|stra|tive** (sub strā′tiv), *adj.* forming a substratum; underlying.

**sub|strat|o|sphere** (sub strat′ə sfir, -strā′tə-), *n.* the region of the earth's atmosphere just below the stratosphere, an altitude high enough to require special aids for flying, such as oxygen masks, pressurized aircraft cabins, and superchargers.

**sub|stra|tum** (sub strā′təm, -strat′əm), *n., pl.* **-ta** or **-tums.** **1** a layer lying under another: *Beneath the sandy soil there was a substratum of clay ten feet thick.* **2** a layer of earth lying just under the surface soil; subsoil. **3** *Figurative.* basis; foundation: *The story has a substratum of truth.* **4** *Biology.* the medium or matter on which an organism grows. **5** *Photography.* a thin layer of gelatinous material placed on a film or plate to help hold the emulsion; subbing. **6** *Metaphysics.* something that is regarded as supporting attributes or accidents; substance in which qualities inhere or from which phenomena derive: *Substances (in the phenomenon) are the substrata of all determinations of time* (Immanuel Kant). [< New Latin *substratum,* neuter of Latin *substrātus,* past participle of *substernere* < *sub-* under + *sternere* to spread]

**sub|struc|tion** (sub struk′shən), *n.* an understructure, as of a building; foundation; substructure. [< Latin *substrūctiō, -ōnis* < *substruere* construct beneath < *sub-* under + *struere* build]

**sub|struc|tur|al** (sub struk′chər əl), *adj.* of, having to do with, or like a substructure.

**sub|struc|ture** (sub′struk′chər, sub struk′-), *n.* **1** the underlying and supporting structure of a building; foundation. **2** the base of earth, concrete, stone, or other material, upon which the ballast of a railroad is laid or the superstructure of a bridge is built. **3** *Figurative: a substructure for religious belief.* **SYN**: groundwork, basis.

**sub|sul|tive** (səb sul′tiv), *adj.* characterized by sudden leaps or starts; jerky; convulsive: *subsultive earthquake shocks.* [< Latin *subsultus,* past participle of *subsilīre* leap up (< *sub-* under + *salīre* leap) + English *-ive*]

**sub|sul|to|ry** (səb sul′tər ē), *adj.* = subsultive.

**sub|sume** (səb süm′), *v.t.,* **-sumed, -sum|ing.** **1** to bring (an idea, term, principle, proposition, or the like) under another; bring (a case or instance) under a rule. **2** to take up into, or include in, a larger or higher class or the like. [< New Latin *subsumere* < Latin *sub-* under + *sūmere* assume, take]

**sub|sump|tion** (səb sump′shən), *n.* **1a** the act or process of subsuming. **b** the state of being subsumed. **2a** *Logic.* a proposition subsumed under another; minor premise. **b** an assumption. [< New Latin *subsumptio, -onis* < *subsumere;* see etym. under **subsume**]

**sub|sump|tive** (səb sump′tiv), *adj.* of or involving subsumption.

**sub|sur|face** (sub sėr′fis), *adj., n.* —*adj.* under the surface; underlying; underground: *subsurface nuclear tests, subsurface rock, water, or oil.*
—*n.* the space or matter immediately below the surface.

**sub|sys|tem** (sub′sis′təm, sub sis′-), *n.* **1** a part or subdivision of a system. **2** *Aerospace.* a component system within a major system of a missile or rocket: *Flight tests demonstrate the compatibility of airframe, engine, and autopilot subsystems* (Air Force Report on the Ballistic Missile).

**sub|tan|gent** (sub tan′jənt), *n. Geometry.* the part of the axis of a curve cut off between the tangent and the ordinate of a given point in the curve.

**sub|teen** (sub′tēn), *n., adj. Informal.* —*n.* = subteen-ager.
—*adj.* of or for subteen-agers: *a subteen dance or party.*

**sub|teen-ag|er** (sub tēn′ā′jər), *n. Informal.* a boy or girl nearly thirteen years old.

**sub|tem|per|ate** (sub tem′pər it), *adj.* of, having to do with, or found in the colder regions of the Temperate Zone.

**sub|ten|an|cy** (sub ten′ən sē, sub′ten′-), *n., pl.* **-cies.** the status, right, or holding of a subtenant.

**sub|ten|ant** (sub ten′ənt, sub′ten′-), *n.* a tenant of a tenant; person who rents land, a house, or other building, or a right, from a tenant.

**sub|tend** (səb tend′), *v.t.* **1** to extend under; stretch across; be opposite to: *The chord of an arc subtends the arc.* **2** *Botany.* to enclose in the angle between a leaf or bract and its stem. [< Latin *subtendere* < *sub-* under + *tendere* to stretch]

**sub|tense** (səb tens′), *n. Geometry.* the chord of an arc or any other subtending line.

**subter-**, *prefix.* underneath; beneath; below; less than, as in *subterconscious, subterposition.* [< Latin *subter,* related to *sub* under, beneath]

**sub|ter|con|scious** (sub′tər kon′shəs), *adj.* = subconscious. [< *subter-* + *conscious*]

**sub|ter|fuge** (sub′tər fyüj), *n.* a trick, excuse, or expedient used to escape something unpleasant: *The girl's headache was only a subterfuge to avoid going to school.* **SYN**: artifice, ruse. [< Late Latin *subterfugium* < Latin *subterfugere* to escape < Latin *subter* beneath + *fugere* flee]

**sub|ter|nat|u|ral** (sub′tər nach′ər əl), *adj.* below what is natural; less than natural. [< *subter-* + *natural*]

**sub|ter|po|si|tion** (sub′tər pə zish′ən), *n.* the state of being placed or of lying underneath something else; position underneath.

**sub|ter|rane** (sub′tə rān), *n.* **1** *Geology.* the bedrock under a deposit. **2** an underground cave, chamber, or dwelling. [< Latin *subterrāneus* < *sub-* under + *terra* earth]

**sub|ter|ra|ne|an** (sub′tə rā′nē ən), *adj., n.* —*adj.* **1** beneath the earth's surface; underground: *A subterranean passage led from the castle to the cave. Mammoth Cave, the biggest of the subterranean caverns in the limestone deposits of central Kentucky* (Newsweek). **2** *Figurative.* carried on secretly; hidden: *subterranean plotting.* **SYN**: clandestine, surreptitious.
—*n.* a person who lives or works underground: *The strange, sad subterraneans who lived and died in the city beneath the sea* (Punch).
[< Latin *subterrāneus* (< *sub-* under + *terra* earth) + English *-an*] — **sub′ter|ra′ne|an|ly**, *adv.*

**sub|ter|ra|ne|ous** (sub′tə rā′nē əs), *adj.* = subterranean. — **sub′ter|ra′ne|ous|ly**, *adv.* — **sub′ter|ra′ne|ous|ness**, *n.*

**sub|ter|res|tri|al** (sub′tə res′trē əl), *adj.* underground; subterranean.

**sub|ter|sur|face** (sub′tər sėr′fis), *adj.* lying below the surface; subsurface. [< *subter-* + *surface*]

**sub|ter|tian malaria** (sub tėr′shən), = falciparum malaria. [< *sub-* + *tertian*]

**sub|test** (sub′test′), *n.* a test that is part of a series of tests: *In the reasoning subtest a typical item consists of drawings of five abstractions* (Scientific American).

**sub|text** (sub′tekst′), *n.* the underlying meaning of a literary or dramatic text: *"The Lodger" demonstrates a beautiful sense of subtext—of the gap between what people say and what is on their minds—which is rather an astonishing achievement in a silent picture* (Penelope Gilliatt).

---

**Pronunciation Key:** hat, āge, cãre, fär; let, ēqual, tėrm; it, īce; hot, ōpen, ôrder; **oi**l, **ou**t; cup, pu̇t, rüle; **ch**ild; lo**ng**; **th**in; **ᴛʜ**en; **zh**, measure; **ə** represents **a** in about, **e** in taken, **i** in pencil, **o** in lemon, **u** in circus.

**sub|theme** (sub′thēm′), *n.* a subordinate or secondary theme; subtopic: *"Man and His World" has been divided into ten subthemes, such as "Man and Work," "Man the Visionary," and "Man and the Infinite"* (Time).

**sub|thresh|old** (sub thresh′ōld, -hōld), *adj.* below the point where a given stimulus is perceptible or two stimuli can be differentiated: *The Subliminal Projection process is a method of conveying an advertising message to the subthreshold area of the human mind* (Bulletin of Atomic Scientists).

**sub|tile** (sut′əl, sub′təl), *adj.* **1** not dense or heavy; thin; delicate; rare: *a subtile liquid, a subtile fabric, a subtile powder.* (*Figurative.*) *after living ... within the subtile influence of an intellect like Emerson's* (Hawthorne). **2** *Archaic.* subtle: *And with such subtile toils enveloped him* (Robert Southey). [< Middle French *subtil,* learned borrowing from Latin *subtīlis.* Compare etym. under **subtle.**] —**sub′tile|ly,** *adv.* —**sub′tile|ness,** *n.*

**sub|til|i|sin** (sub til′ə sin), *n.* a proteolytic enzyme produced by a common species of soil bacteria, used in tanning and experimentally in chemical synthesis. [< New Latin (*Bacillus*) *subtilis* the species of soil bacteria (< Latin *subtīlis* subtle) + English *-in*]

**sub|til|i|ty** (sub til′ə tē), *n., pl.* **-ties.** *Archaic.* subtlety.

**sub|til|ize** (sut′ə līz, sub′tə-), *v.,* **-ized, -iz|ing.** —*v.t.* to make subtle; introduce subtleties into. —*v.i.* to make subtle distinctions; argue or reason in a subtle manner; split hairs: *Men ... who subtilize upon the commonest duties until they no longer appear binding* (Oliver Goldsmith). —**sub′til|i|za′tion,** *n.*

**sub|til|ty** (sut′əl tē, sub′təl-), *n., pl.* **-ties.** = subtlety.

**sub|ti|tle** (sub′tī′təl), *n., v.,* **-tled, -tling.** —*n.* **1** an additional or subordinate title of a book or article. **2a** a repetition of the chief words of the full title of a book at the top of the first page of text. **b** = half title. **3** a word or words shown on a motion-picture screen, especially as the translation of the words spoken in a foreign-language film; caption.
—*v.t.* to give a subtitle or subtitles to: *This delightful, cheerful collection might easily be subtitled grim fairy tales for adults* (Harper's).

**sub|tle** (sut′əl), *adj.,* **-tler, -tlest. 1** very fine; thin; delicate: *Some subtle odors are hard to recognize.* **SYN:** tenuous, rare. **2** so fine or delicate as to elude observation or analysis: *subtle distinctions. Subtle jokes are often hard to understand.* **3** faint; mysterious: *a subtle smile or wink.* **4** having a keen, quick mind; discerning; acute: *She is a subtle observer of slight differences in things.* **SYN:** discriminating. **5** sly; crafty; tricky: *a subtle scheme to get some money.* **SYN:** artful, cunning, wily. **6** skillful; clever; expert: *a subtle worker in gold and silver, a subtle design.* **7** working unnoticeably or secretly; insidious: *a subtle poison or drug.*
[< Old French *soutil* < Latin *subtīlis*] —**sub′tle|ness,** *n.*

**sub|tle|ty** (sut′əl tē), *n., pl.* **-ties. 1** subtle quality: *Guides cannot master the subtleties of the American joke* (Mark Twain). *His style is artfully simple and flowing, his portraiture full of subtlety and charm* (Atlantic). **2** something subtle; cunning; craft: *The laws were violated by power, or perverted by subtlety* (Edward Gibbon).

**sub|tly** (sut′lē), *adv.* in a subtle manner; with subtlety.

**sub|ton|ic** (sub ton′ik), *n. Music.* the seventh tone of a scale; tone next below the upper tonic; leading tone.

**sub|to|pi|a** (sub tō′pē ə), *n. British.* countryside that has developed into an industrial urban area: *Harrow-on-the-Hill is ... a linear ridge-top town above green fields on either side, a simultaneous oasis of both town and country in a sea of subtopia* (Observer). [< *sub-* + (u)*topia*]

**sub|to|pi|an** (sub tō′pē ən), *adj. British.* of or characteristic of a subtopia: *... subtopian wastes of semidetached houses and bungaloid growths left by the industrialists of the nineteenth century, and the 'spec' builders of the twentieth* (Manchester Guardian).

**sub|to|pi|an|ize** (sub tō′pē ə nīz), *v.t.,* **-ized, -iz|ing.** *British.* to change into a subtopia.

**sub|top|ic** (sub′top′ik), *n.* a subordinate or secondary topic, included under a major topic.

**sub|tor|rid** (sub tôr′id, -tor′-), *adj.* = subtropical.

**sub|to|tal** (sub′tō′təl), *adj., n., v.,* **-taled, -tal|ing** or (*especially British*) **-talled, -tal|ling.** —*adj.* not quite total; less than complete: *Subtotal counts will be handed to the press every 30 minutes* (New York Times).
—*n.* something less than the total; partial sum: *The figure you see is a subtotal and not the final amount.*
—*v.t.* **1** to find the subtotal of: *Subtotal the third column of figures.* **2** to amount to the subtotal of: *This column of figures subtotals 107,963.*

**sub|tract** (səb trakt′), *v.t., v.i.* **1** to take away: *Subtract 2 from 10 and you have 8.* **2** to take away (something) from a whole. [< Latin *subtractus,* past participle of *subtrahere* < *sub-* from under + *trahere* draw] —**sub|tract′er,** *n.*
—*Syn.* **1 Subtract, deduct** mean to take away. **Subtract** is chiefly used in its mathematical sense, meaning to take away one number from another: *She subtracted 89 from 200.* **Deduct** means to take away a quantity or amount from a total or whole: *The butcher deducted 89 cents in tax from the delivery boy's wage of $10.*

***sub|trac|tion** (səb trak′shən), *n.* **1** the act or process of taking one number or quantity from another; finding the difference between two numbers or quantities: *10 − 2 = 8 is a simple subtraction.* **2a** the act or process of taking away. **b** the fact or state of being taken away.

| ***subtraction** definition 1 | 25 minuend<br>− 9 subtrahend<br>16 remainder | minuend, subtrahend: 25–9 = 16 :remainder |
|---|---|---|

**sub|trac|tive** (səb trak′tiv), *adj.* **1** of or having to do with subtraction. **2** tending to subtract; having power to subtract. **3** to be subtracted; having the minus sign.

**subtractive process,** a process in color photography, in which two or more colorants are used to absorb, in varying degree, their complementary colors from white light.

**sub|tra|hend** (sub′trə hend), *n.* a number or quantity to be subtracted from another number or quantity: *In 10 − 2 = 8, the subtrahend is 2.* [< Latin *subtrahendus* to be subtracted, gerundive of *subtrahere;* see etym. under **subtract**]

**sub|treas|ur|y** (sub′trezh′ər ē, -trā′zhər-; sub-trezh′-, -trā′zhər-), *n., pl.* **-ur|ies. 1** a branch treasury. **2** any branch of the United States treasury.

**sub|tribe** (sub′trīb′), *n.* a division of a tribe, especially of animals or plants.

**sub|trip|li|cate** (sub trip′lə kit), *adj.* being that of the cube roots of the quantities. *Example:* 2 : 3 is the subtriplicate ratio of 8 : 27.

**sub|trop|ic** (sub trop′ik), *adj.* = subtropical.

**sub|trop|i|cal** (sub trop′ə kəl), *adj.* **1** bordering on the tropics. **2** characteristic of subtropical regions; nearly tropical: *to swim in warm, subtropical waters.*

**sub|trop|ics** (sub′trop′iks, sub trop′-), *n.pl.* a region or regions bordering on the tropics.

**sub|type** (sub′tīp′), *n.* a subordinate type; type included in a general type.

**sub|typ|i|cal** (sub tip′ə kəl), *adj.* **1** of or having to do with a subtype. **2** not quite typical, or true to the type.

**su|bu|late** (sü′byə lit), *adj. Biology.* slender, more or less cylindrical, and tapering to a point; awl-shaped: *a subulate leaf.* [< New Latin *subulatus* < Latin *sūbula* awl]

**sub|u|nit** (sub yü′nit), *n.* a lower or secondary unit; unit of a unit.

**sub|urb** (sub′ərb), *n.* **1** a town, village, or other community near a city or larger town. **2** any district just outside the boundary of a city or town: *He was aware that the U.S. with its ... growing suburbs ... could well afford to buy more new cars than it ever had before* (Time).
**the suburbs,** a residential section or sections near the boundary of a city or town; outlying parts; outskirts: *Many people who work in the city live in the suburbs.*
[< Old French *suburbe,* learned borrowing from Latin *suburbium* < *sub-* below + *urbs, urbis* city]

**sub|ur|ban** (sə bėr′bən), *adj., n.* —*adj.* **1** of, having to do with, or in a suburb: *a suburban school, a suburban shopping center. We have excellent suburban train service.* **2** characteristic of a suburb or its inhabitants: *suburban life.*
—*n.* = suburbanite.

**sub|ur|ban|ite** (sə bėr′bə nīt), *n.* a person who lives in a suburb: *Suburbanites who get carried away by "do-it-yourself" projects often get carried away, period!* (Newsweek).

**sub|ur|ban|i|za|tion** (sə bėr′bə nə zā′shən), *n.* the act or process of suburbanizing or being suburbanized: *The suburbanization of American life and growth of the middle class* (Harper's).

**sub|ur|ban|ize** (sə bėr′bə nīz), *v.t.,* **-ized, -iz|ing.** to make suburban: *to suburbanize a district, suburbanize a rural village.*

**sub|ur|bi|a** (sə bėr′bē ə), *n.* **1a** the suburbs of a particular city or town. **b** suburbs in general: *In our part of suburbia, there's a get-together somewhere almost every week* (Maclean's). **2** people who live in the suburbs; suburbanites.

**sub|ur|bi|car|i|an** (sə bėr′bə kãr′ē ən), *adj.* of or having to do with the dioceses (now six in number) around Rome of which the pope is metropolitan and whose bishops are cardinals. [< Late Latin *suburbicārius* (< Latin *suburbium;* see etym. under **suburb**) + English *-an*]

**sub|va|ri|e|ty** (sub′və rī′ə tē), *n., pl.* **-ties.** a subordinate or minor variety, especially of a domestic animal or cultivated plant.

**sub|vene** (səb vēn′), *v.i.,* **-vened, -ven|ing.** to come as a relief or remedy or in support. [< Latin *subvenīre;* see etym. under **subvention**]

**sub|ven|tion** (səb ven′shən), *n.* **1** money granted to aid or support some cause, institution, or undertaking; subsidy: *A subvention will insure the publication of his doctoral thesis.* **2a** the providing of help, support, or relief. **b** an instance of this. [< Late Latin *subventiō, -ōnis* < Latin *subvenīre* come to one's aid < *sub-* under + *venīre* come]

**sub|ven|tion|ar|y** (səb ven′shə ner′ē), *adj.* of or like a subvention.

**sub ver|bo** (sub vėr′bō), *Latin.* under the word; under the heading (directing the reader to a reference). *Abbr:* s.v.

**sub|ver|sal** (səb vėr′səl), *n.* = subversion.

**sub|ver|sion** (səb vėr′zhən, -shən), *n.* **1** the act or process of subverting or condition of being subverted; overthrow; destruction; ruin: *They steer clear of harsher reprisals and keep the road open for victory by the more classic means of subversion* (Newsweek). **2** anything that tends to overthrow or destroy; cause of ruin: *... protecting from subversion either from within or without* (E. H. Litchfield). [< Late Latin *subversiō, -ōnis* < Latin *subvertere;* see etym. under **subvert**]

**sub|ver|sive** (səb vėr′siv), *adj., n.* —*adj.* tending to overthrow; causing ruin; destructive: *He was rearrested on an old indictment charging him with being a member of a subversive organization advocating the forceful overthrow of the Government* (New York Times).
—*n.* a person who seeks to overthrow or undermine a government or other existing institution.
—**sub|ver′sive|ly,** *adv.* —**sub|ver′sive|ness,** *n.*

**sub|vert** (səb vėrt′), *v.t.* **1** to overthrow (something established or existing); cause the downfall or destruction of; ruin; destroy: *Dictators subvert democracy.* **2** to undermine the principles of; corrupt: *A Red plan to subvert all Africa came to light* (Newsweek). [< Latin *subvertere* < *sub-* under + *vertere* to turn] —**sub|vert′er,** *n.*

**sub|vert|i|ble** (səb vėr′tə bəl), *adj.* that can be subverted.

**sub|ver|ti|cal** (sub vėr′tə kəl), *adj.* almost vertical.

**sub|vi|ral** (sub vī′rəl), *adj.* having to do with or caused by a subvirus: *subviral carcinogenesis.*

**sub|vi|rus** (sub vī′rəs), *n.* a viral protein or other basic constituent of a virus that has some of the properties of a virus: *Research in the United States and England linked several human diseases, including multiple sclerosis, with a tiny subvirus that causes the sheep disease, scrapie* (Science News).

**sub|vo|cal** (sub vō′kəl), *adj.* **1** having to do with the formulation of words in the mind, with little or no vocal articulation. **2** = subaudible. —**sub|vo′cal|ly,** *adv.*

**sub|way** (sub′wā′), *n.* **1** *U.S.* an electric railroad running beneath the surface of the streets in a city. **2** an underground passage, tunnel, or way, as for conveying water and gas pipes, telegraph, telephone, or electrical wires, or for pedestrians to pass from one area to another, as beneath a busy street or railroad station.
► **subway** (def. 1). In England it is called an *underground;* in France and certain other European countries, it is called a *Métro.*

**sub|ze|ro** (sub′zir′ō, sub zir′ō), *adj.* **1** below zero on the scale of a thermometer: *subzero temperatures.* **2** characterized by or used in subzero temperatures: *subzero weather, subzero lubricants.*

**sub|zone** (sub′zōn′), *n.* a subdivision of a zone.

**suc-,** *prefix.* the form of **sub-** before *c,* as in *succeed.*

**Su|car|yl** (sü′kər əl), *n. Trademark.* a sweet-tasting, white, crystalline calcium or sodium salt, used as a substitute for sugar; cyclamate calcium or sodium.

**suc|cah** (sůk′ə, sů kä′), *n.* = sukkah.

**suc|ce|da|ne|ous** (suk′sə dā′nē əs), *adj.* acting or serving as a substitute.

**suc|ce|da|ne|um** (suk′sə dā′nē əm), *n., pl.* **-ne|a** (-nē ə), **-ne|ums.** = substitute. [< New Latin *succedaneum,* neuter of Latin *succēdāneus* substituted, succeeding < *succēdere* go near to; see etym. under **succeed**]

**suc|ceed** (sək sēd′), *v.i.* **1** to turn out well; do well; have success: *His plans succeeded.* **SYN:** prosper, thrive, flourish. **2** to accomplish what is attempted or intended: *to succeed in finding an empty seat. The attack succeeded beyond all expectations.* **3** to come next after; follow another; take the place of another: *When George VI died, Elizabeth II succeeded to the throne.* **4** to have (good or ill) success: *I have succeeded very badly* (George Macdonald). **5** *Obsolete.* (of an estate) to devolve.

— ***v.t.*** to come next after; take the place of; follow: *John Adams succeeded Washington as President. Week succeeds week.* **SYN**: See syn. under **follow**.

[< Latin *succēdere* go after, go near to < *sub-* up or near + *cēdere* go] — **suc|ceed′er,** *n.*

**suc|cen|tor** (sək sen′tər), *n. Ecclesiastical.* a precentor's deputy. [< Late Latin *succentor, -ōris* < Latin *succinere* sing so as to accompany < *sub-* under + *canere* sing]

**suc|cès de scan|dale** (syk se′ də skäɴ dål′). *French.* **1** a success due to scandal or notoriety; anything that wins popularity or profit by scandalizing the public or because of its connection with a scandal. **2** (literally) success of scandal.

**suc|cès d'es|time** (syk se′ des tēm′), *French.* **1** a play, novel, or other piece of writing that is praised by the critics but largely ignored by the public. **2** critical acclaim accompanied by popular indifference: *The public's indifference ... prevented it from having more than a succès d'estime, in spite of the extraordinary music* (Listener). **3** (literally) success of esteem.

**suc|cès fou** (syk se′ fü′), *French.* **1** a success marked by wild enthusiasm: *In France, where the antinovel is in, it has been a succès fou* (Punch). **2** (literally) mad success.

**suc|cess** (sək ses′), *n.* **1** a favorable result; wished-for ending; good fortune: *Success in school comes from intelligence and hard work. Success in one field does not assure success in another* (Newsweek). **2** the gaining of wealth, position, or other advantage: *He has had little success in life.* **3** a person or thing that succeeds: *The girl from the small village became a social success in the city. The party was a great success.* **4** result; outcome; fortune: *What success did you have in finding a new apartment?* [< Latin *successus,* past participle of *succēdere;* see etym. under **succeed**]

**suc|cess|ful** (sək ses′fəl), *adj.* **1** having success; accomplishing what is desired or intended; ending in success: *a successful campaign. The books of a successful writer are liked by the public. Many of these seeds are imperfect, but occasional ones give rise to successful plants* (Fred W. Emerson). **2** having succeeded in gaining wealth, position, or other advantage; prosperous; fortunate: *a successful businessman, a successful match or marriage.* — **suc|cess′ful|ly,** *adv.* — **suc|cess′ful|ness,** *n.*

**suc|ces|sion** (sək sesh′ən), *n.* **1** a group of persons or things coming one after another; series: *a rapid succession of victories. A succession of accidents spoiled our automobile trip. Succession thus is the process of migration of one type of people after another into a given area, or the migration of one type of land usage after another into a particular area* (Emory S. Bogardus). **SYN**: See syn. under **series**. **2** the coming of one person or thing after another. **3** the act, right, or process of succeeding to an office, property, or rank: *There was a dispute between the brothers about the rightful succession to the throne.* **4** the order or arrangement of persons having such a right of succeeding: *The king's oldest son is first in succession to the throne. The Speaker is ... second in succession to the Presidency, following only the Vice-President* (New York Times). **5** *Law.* the legal change involved when a person succeeds to the rights and liabilities of a predecessor.

**in succession,** one after another: *We visited our sick friend several days in succession.*

[< Latin *successiō, -ōnis* < *succēdere;* see etym. under **succeed**]

**suc|ces|sion|al** (sək sesh′ə nəl), *adj.* **1** of or having to do with succession. **2** following or occurring in succession. **3** passing by succession or descent. — **suc|ces′sion|al|ly,** *adv.*

**succession duty** or **tax,** *Especially British.* a tax on inherited property; inheritance tax.

**suc|ces|sive** (sək ses′iv), *adj.* **1** coming one after another; following in order; consecutive: *It has rained for three successive days.* **2** characterized by or involving succession. — **suc|ces′sive|ly,** *adv.* — **suc|ces′sive|ness,** *n.*

— ***Syn.* 1 Successive, consecutive** mean following one after another. **Successive** implies coming one after another in regular order: *I have worked on three successive Saturdays.* **Consecutive** implies coming one after another without interruption or a break: *I worked three consecutive days last week.*

**suc|cess|less** (sək ses′lis), *adj.* without success; unsuccessful. — **suc|cess′less|ly,** *adv.* — **success′less|ness,** *n.*

**suc|ces|sor** (sək ses′ər), *n.* **1** a person who follows or succeeds another in office, position, or ownership of property: *John Adams was George Washington's successor as President.* **2** a person or thing that comes next after another in a series. [< Latin *successor, -ōris* < *succēdere;* see etym. under **succeed**]

**suc|ces|sor|ship** (sək ses′ər ship), *n.* the position or condition of a successor.

**success story, 1** a real or fictitious narrative recounting the rise of someone, usually poor or unknown, to fame and fortune: *The Horatio Alger myth is the American archetype of the success story.* **2** a person, thing, or event that achieves outstanding, and usually unexpected, success: *Among the major Protestant denominations in Canada, the United Church is the great success story of our times* (Maclean's).

**suc|ci|nate** (suk′sə nāt), *n.* a salt of succinic acid.

**suc|cinct** (sək singkt′), *adj.* **1** expressed briefly and clearly; expressing much in few words; concise: *His letter was succinct, with all the major points on one page. A tale should be judicious, clear, succinct* (William Cowper). **SYN**: compressed, condensed. See syn. under **concise**. **2** characterized by brevity or conciseness: *a succinct writer, speaker, or style.* **SYN**: terse, curt. **3** *Archaic.* (of garments) not full; close-fitting; short; scant. [< Latin *succinctus,* past participle of *succingere* tuck up clothes for action; to gird from below < *sub-* under + *cingere* gird] — **succinct′ly,** *adv.* — **suc|cinct′ness,** *n.*

**suc|cinc|to|ri|um** (suk′singk tôr′ē əm, -tōr′-), *n., pl.* **-to|ri|a** (-tôr′ē ə, -tōr′-). a vestment worn on solemn occasions by the pope, similar in shape to a maniple, and hanging on his left side from the girdle or cincture. [< Late Latin *succinctorium* < Latin *sub-* under + *cinctorium* girdle < *cingere* gird]

**suc|cinc|to|ry** (suk singk′tər ē), *n., pl.* **-ries.** = succinctorium.

**suc|cin|ic** (suk sin′ik), *adj.* of, having to do with, or derived from amber. [< French *succinique* < Latin *succinum* amber, variant of *sūcinum*]

**succinic acid,** a colorless, crystalline dicarboxylic acid present in amber, but usually produced synthetically from tartaric acid, used in making dyes and perfumes and in photography. *Formula:* $C_4H_6O_4$

**suc|cin|yl|cho|line** (suk′sə nəl kol′ēn, -kō′lēn), a white, odorless crystalline powder, used to relax the muscles in surgery; scoline: *Anesthetists commonly infuse succinylcholine by vein* (Sumner M. Kalman). *Formula:* $C_{14}H_{30}Cl_2N_2O_4{\cdot}2H_2O$

**suc|cin|yl|sul|fa|thi|a|zole** (suk′sə nəl sul′fə thī′ə zōl), *n.* a derivative of sulfathiazole, less toxic than sulfaguanidine, and used orally for the prevention and treatment of bacterial infections of the gastrointestinal tract. *Formula:* $C_{13}H_{13}N_3O_5S_2{\cdot}H_2O$

**suc|cise** (sək sīs′), *adj. Botany.* appearing as if cut or broken off at the lower end. [< Latin *succīsus,* past participle of *succīdere* cut below < *sub-* under + *caedere* cut]

**suc|cor** (suk′ər), *n., v.* — ***n.*** a person or thing that helps, relieves, or assists; help; aid; assistance.

— ***v.t.*** to help, aid, or assist (a person) in time of need, distress, or danger; support; relieve: *Mr. Harding thought ... of the worn-out, aged men whom he had succored* (Anthony Trollope). Also, *especially British,* **succour.**

[< Anglo-French *succor,* Old French *succurre* < Medieval Latin *succursus, -us* < Latin *succurrere* run to help < *sub-* up (to) + *currere* run] — **suc′cor|er,** *n.*

**suc|cor|a|ble** (suk′ər ə bəl), *adj.* **1** capable of being succored or relieved. **2** *Archaic.* affording succor or relief.

**suc|cor|less** (suk′ər lis), *adj.* without succor, help, or relief.

**suc|co|ry** (suk′ər ē), *n.* = chicory. [alteration of earlier *sycory* chicory]

**Suc|cos** (sůk′əs), *n.* = Sukkoth.

**suc|cose** (suk′ōs), *adj.* juicy; succulent. [< Latin *succōsus* < *succus,* or *sūcus* juice]

**suc|co|tash** (suk′ə tash), *n.* kernels of sweet corn and beans, usually Lima beans, cooked together: *Since corn was their principal product, the Indians devised numerous ways of preparing it ... They made succotash, a mixture of corn and beans boiled* (Science News Letter). [American English < Algonkian (Narraganset) *m'sickquatash* green corn boiled whole]

**Suc|coth** (sü kōth′), *n.* = Sukkoth.

**suc|cour** (suk′ər), *n., v.t. Especially British.* succor.

**suc|cu|ba** (suk′yə bə), *n., pl.* **-bae** (-bē). = succubus. [< Late Latin *succuba* strumpet < Latin, supplanter, rival; (literally) one lying under < *sub-* under + *cubāre* lie]

**suc|cu|bus** (suk′yə bəs), *n., pl.* **-bi** (-bī), **-bus|es. 1** a demon in female form supposed to have carnal intercourse with men in their sleep. **2** any evil spirit; demon. [< Medieval Latin *succubus* < Late Latin *succuba;* see etym. under **succuba**; patterned on *incubus*]

**suc|cu|lence** (suk′yə ləns), *n.* = juiciness.

**suc|cu|len|cy** (suk′yə lən sē), *n.* = succulence.

**suc|cu|lent** (suk′yə lənt), *adj., n.* — ***adj.* 1** full of juice; juicy: *a succulent peach.* **2** *Figurative.* interesting; not dull. **3** *Botany.* having thick or fleshy and juicy leaves or stems: *The houseleek and the cactuses are succulent plants.*

— ***n.*** a succulent plant: *Most desert surfaces carry a scattered grass growth, dotted with thorny shrubs and succulents* (White and Renner).

[< Latin *succulentus* < *succus,* or *sūcus* juice] — **suc′cu|lent|ly,** *adv.*

**suc|cumb** (sə kum′), *v.i.* **1** to give way; yield: *He succumbed to the temptation and stole the money.* **2** to die: *He succumbed of old age.*

**succumb to,** to die of: *Mr. Picken has since succumbed to his injuries* (Pall Mall Gazette).

[< Latin *succumbere* < *sub-* down + *-cumbere* lie, related to *cubāre*]

**suc|cur|sal** (sə kėr′səl), *adj.* that is or is like a subsidiary or auxiliary: *A succursal church is dependent on the main church.* [< French *succursale* < Latin *succursus,* past participle of *succurrere;* see etym. under **succor**]

**suc|cus** (suk′əs), *n., pl.* **suc|ci** (suk′sī). **1** the juice in the body. **2** the extracted juice of a plant for use in medicine. [< Latin *succus* juice]

**suc|cuss** (sə kus′), *v.t.* **1** to shake up. **2** *Medicine.* to subject (a patient) to succussion. [< Latin *succussus,* past participle of *succutere* < *sub-* under + *quatere* shake]

**suc|cus|sa|tion** (suk′ə sā′shən), *n.* = succussion.

**suc|cus|sa|to|ry** (sə kus′ə tôr′ē, -tōr′-), *adj.* = succussive.

**suc|cus|sion** (sə kush′ən), *n.* **1** the action of shaking or condition of being shaken with violence. **2** *Medicine.* a shaking of the body to detect the presence of fluid in the thorax or other cavity. [< Latin *succusiō, -ōnis* < *succutere;* see etym. under **succuss**]

**suc|cus|sive** (sə kus′iv), *adj.* characterized by a shaking motion, especially an up-and-down movement.

**such** (such), *adj., adv., pron.* — ***adj.* 1** of that kind; of the same kind or degree: *Such men as Washington and Lincoln are rare. I have never seen such a sight.* **2** of the kind that; of a particular kind: *The child had such a fever that he nearly died. She wore such thin clothes it is no wonder she caught cold.* **3** of the kind already spoken of or suggested: *flour, sugar, salt, and other such staples. The ladies took only tea and coffee and such drinks.* **4** to the extent described; so great, so bad, or so good: *He is such a liar! Such weather!*

— ***adv.* 1** so very: *Our neighbors are such nice, friendly people. We had such good times together.* **2** in such a manner; so: *The speakers are chosen such that each one has a turn.*

— ***pron.* 1** such a person or thing; such persons or things: *Take from the blankets such as you need. Such as sit in darkness and in the shadow of death* (Psalms 107:10). **2** such a person or thing, or such persons or things, now or before mentioned or described: *Such was the outcome of the debate.*

**as such, a** as being what is indicated or implied; in that capacity: *A leader, as such, deserves obedience.* **b** in or by itself; intrinsically considered: *Mere good looks, as such, will not take you far.*

**such and such,** some; certain: *We were told that such and such a bank was offering such and such gifts if we opened an account there.*

**such as, a** of the kind or degree that; of a particular kind: *Her behavior was such as might be expected of a young child. The food, such as it was, was plentiful.* **b** of the same character or quality as; like: *There are few writers such as Dickens.* **c** for example: *members of the dog family, such as the wolf, fox, and jackal.*

[Old English *swylc, swelc,* originally a compound of *swā* so + *līc* like. Compare etym. under **which.**]

**such-and-such** (such′ən such′), *adj., pron.*

— ***adj.*** some; certain; such and such: *We sense that this isn't how such-and-such a thing really happened* (New Yorker).

— ***pron.*** some (unnamed) person or thing: *It informed me ... that my board would be number such-and-such* (Manchester Guardian Weekly).

**such|like** (such′līk′), *adj., pron.* — ***adj.*** of such kind; of a like kind; of the before-mentioned sort or character: *dreams, signs, and suchlike fanciful superstitions.*

— ***pron.*** things of such kind: *She showed me some old clothes, household articles, pictures, and suchlike.*

---

**Pronunciation Key:** hat, āge, cãre, fär; let, ēqual, tėrm; it, īce; hot, ōpen, ôrder; **oi**l, **ou**t; cup, půt, rüle; **ch**ild; lo**ng**; **th**in; **ᴛʜ**en; **zh**, measure; **ə** represents **a** in about, **e** in taken, **i** in pencil, **o** in lemon, **u** in circus.

—*pron.* things of such kind; the like: *deceptions, disguises, and suchlike* (Joseph Conrad).

**such|ness** (such′nis), *n.* **1** the state or quality of being such; a particular or characteristic quality. **2** *Buddhism.* the state or quality of nature which transcends reality and is absolute and eternal: ... *the essential Suchness of the world, which is at once immanent and transcendent* (Aldous Huxley).

**suck** (suk), *v., n.* —*v.t.* **1** to draw into the mouth by using the lips, cheeks, and tongue: *to suck juice from an orange. Lemonade can be sucked through a straw.* **2** to draw juice or other liquid from with the mouth: *to suck an orange.* **3** to drink, take, or absorb: *A sponge sucks in water. Plants suck up moisture from the earth.* **4** to hold in the mouth and lick: *a baby sucking his thumb. The child sucked a lollipop.* **5** to draw in; swallow: *The whirlpool sucked down the boat.* **6** to render (as specified) by sucking.

—*v.i.* **1** to draw liquid, especially milk from the breast or a bottle, into the mouth. **2** to draw or be drawn by sucking: *He sucked at his pipe. The crimson cheeks of the trumpeters sucked in and out* (Arnold Bennett). **3** to draw air instead of water, as from low water or a defective valve: *The pump sucked nosily.*

—*n.* **1** the act of sucking; suction by the mouth or other means: *The baby took one suck at the bottle and pushed it away.* **2** a sucking force or sound. **3** milk or other substance drawn into the mouth by sucking. **4** *Informal.* a small draft of liquid; sip.

**suck in, a** *Informal.* to pull in; flatten out: *to suck in the stomach.* **b** *Slang.* to cheat; trick; take in: *He got sucked in by a swindler.*

**suck up to,** to curry favor with; toady to: *That [his strength], and his less enviable gifts for sucking up to the general foreman, got him made a ganger after a month* (Manchester Guardian).

[Old English *sūcan.* Ultimately related to **soak.**]

**suck|er** (suk′ər), *n., v.* —*n.* **1** an animal or thing that sucks. **2** a young mammal before it is weaned, especially a suckling pig. **3** any one of various freshwater fishes that suck in food or have toothless, fleshy mouths that suggest sucking. **4** an organ adapted for sucking or absorbing nourishment by suction, such as the proboscis of an insect. **5** a part or organ for holding fast to an object by a sucking force, such as that of a leech or snail: *the animal [tapeworm] clings to the inner wall of the alimentary canal by means of hooks and suckers* (Hegner and Stiles). See picture under **remora. 6a** a shoot growing from an underground stem or root. **b** an adventitious shoot from the trunk or a branch of a tree or plant. **c** one of the small roots of a parasitic plant; haustorium. **7** the piston of a suction pump. **8** the valve of such a piston. **9** a pipe or tube through which anything is drawn by suction. **10** a lump of hard candy, especially a lollipop: *She was greeted by two little boys with suckers in their jaws* (New Yorker). **11** *Slang, Figurative.* **a** a person easily deceived; simpleton; greenhorn: *Most people saw the urgency of the economic situation but nobody wanted "to be played for a sucker"* (London Times). **b** a sponger; parasite.

—*v.t.* **1** to strip off suckers or shoots from; remove superfluous young shoots from (as tobacco or corn). **2** *U.S. Slang.* to treat as a fool or simpleton; deceive; dupe: *Let's face it, the real reason why we got suckered into this ... business was plain fright* (Harper's).

—*v.i.* to form or throw up suckers.

**sucker bait,** *U.S. Slang.* an enticement to attract a person in order to mislead or take advantage of him, especially in monetary matters: *They alluded constantly to bets on long shots and absurd propositions that even yokels recognize as sucker bait* (Saturday Evening Post).

**suck|er|el** (suk′ər əl), *n.* a long, slender sucker living in large streams and impounded lakes of the Mississippi Valley, with a small head and bluish body. [diminutive of *sucker*]

**suck|er|fish** (suk′ər fish′), *n., pl.* **-fish|es** or (*collectively*) **-fish.** a fish of the western coast of the United States, having a sucker on the ventral side with which it clings to objects.

**sucker list,** *U.S. Slang.* a list of persons who can readily be misled or taken advantage of, especially in monetary matters.

**Sucker State,** a nickname of Illinois.

**suck|fish** (suk′fish′), *n., pl.* **-fish|es** or (*collectively*) **-fish. 1** = suckerfish. **2** = remora.

**suck|ing** (suk′ing), *adj.* **1** that sucks; not yet weaned. **2** very young; immature; unfledged.

**sucking louse,** any one of an order of wingless, bloodsucking lice that are parasitic on mammals and transmit many diseases, such as typhus fever.

**suck|le** (suk′əl), *v.,* **-led, -ling.** —*v.t.* **1** to feed with milk from the breast or udder; give suck to; nurse: *The cat suckles her kittens.* **2** *Figurative.* to bring up; nourish: *suckled on the literature of Spain* (W. H. Hudson). *A Pagan suckled in a creed outworn* (Wordsworth). —*v.i.* to suck at the breast or udder. [Middle English *sukle,* perhaps back formation < *suckling;* perhaps (frequentative) < Middle English *suken* suck]

**suck|ler** (suk′lər), *n.* **1** a young animal not yet weaned; suckling. **2** an animal that suckles its young; mammal.

**sucklers,** *British.* the flowering heads of clover: *a pasture of white sucklers.*

**suck|ling** (suk′ling), *n., adj.* —*n.* a very young animal or child, especially one not yet weaned: ... *babes and sucklings* (Psalms 8:2). SYN: nursling.

—*adj.* **1** very young. **2** not yet weaned; sucking: *a suckling pig.*

**su|crase** (sü′krās), *n.* = invertase. [< French *sucre* sugar + English *-ase*]

**su|crate** (sü′krāt), *n. Chemistry.* a compound of a metallic oxide with a sugar: *calcium sucrate.* [< French *sucrate* < *sucre* sugar + *-ate* -ate²]

**su|cre** (sü′krā), *n.* **1** the basic Ecuadorian monetary unit, equal to 100 centavos. **2** a silver coin or bank note worth this amount. [< Antonio José de *Sucre,* 1795-1830, a South American general and liberator]

**su|cri|er** (sʏ krē ā′), *n. French.* sugar bowl.

**su|crose** (sü′krōs), *n.* ordinary sugar obtained as from sugar cane or sugar beets; cane sugar; beet sugar; saccharose. Sucrose is a crystalline disaccharide sugar. Hydrolysis changes sucrose to fructose and glucose. *Formula:* $C_{12}H_{22}O_{11}$ [< French *sucre* sugar + English *-ose*²]

**suc|tion** (suk′shən), *n., adj.* —*n.* **1** the process of drawing liquids or gases into a space or of causing surfaces to stick together by producing a vacuum. Lemonade is drawn through a straw by suction. **2** the force caused by suction. **3** the act or process of sucking. **4** any part or device, such as a pipe, which effects, or operates by, suction, or by pressures less that that of the atmosphere.

—*adj.* **1** causing a suction; working by suction: *a suction valve.* **2** in which suction occurs; into or through which something is forced or drawn by suction: *a suction line.*

[< Late Latin *sūctiō, -ōnis* < Latin *sūgere* to suck]

**suction cup,** a cup-shaped piece of rubber, plastic, or glass, that can stick to a surface by suction: *Mixing bowls ... have been provided with a removable suction cup designed to hold them firmly to a table or counter* (Science News Letter).

**suction pump,** any pump of various types in which liquid is drawn into the line to the pump by suction, especially the common hand-operated water pump, in which downward and upward strokes of a piston create a partial vacuum in the line, into which water is forced by atmospheric pressure with each upward stroke.

**suction stop,** *Phonetics.* a stop which is released by inward suction, rather than the more usual outward explosion of the checked breath stream. The most familiar suction stops are clicks.

**suc|to|ri|al** (suk tôr′ē əl, -tōr′-), *adj.* **1** adapted for sucking or adhering by suction. **2** having organs adapted for feeding by sucking or adhering by suction. [< New Latin *suctorius* (< Latin *sūgere* to suck) + English *-al*¹]

**suc|to|ri|an** (suk tôr′ē ən, -tōr′-), *n.* an animal with a mouth or other organ adapted for sucking or adhering by suction: *The lamprey, leech, and flea are examples of suctorians.*

**suc|to|ri|ous** (suk tôr′ē əs, -tōr′-), *adj.* = suctorial.

**sud** (sud), *n.* singular of **suds.**

**su|dam|i|na** (sü dam′ə nə), *n.pl. Medicine.* minute, whitish vesicles appearing on the skin in various fevers from the accumulation of sweat in the upper layers of the skin. [< New Latin *sudamina* < Latin *sūdāre* to sweat; see etym. under **sudatory**]

**su|dam|i|nal** (sü dam′ə nəl), *adj.* of or having to do with sudamina.

**Su|dan** (sü dan′), *n. Trademark.* any one of a group of yellow, brown, and red dyes used to stain biological specimens and color oils and fats.

**Su|dan durra** (sü dan′), a grain sorghum used for fodder; feterita.

**Su|da|nese** (sü′də nēz′), *adj., n., pl.* **-nese.** —*adj.* of or having to do with the Sudan, a country in Africa south of Egypt, or its people.

—*n.* a person born or living in the Sudan. Also, **Soudanese.**

**Sudan grass,** a variety of sorghum from the Sudan, grown in the United States for hay and forage.

**Su|dan|ic** (sü dan′ik, -dä′nik), *adj., n.* —*adj.* of or belonging to a group of languages of northern Africa that are not related to the Bantu or Hamitic languages. The Sudanic languages include Tshi, Mandingo, and Yoruba.

—*n.* the Sudanic language group.

**Su|dan|i|za|tion** (sü′də nə zā′shən), *n.* the act or process of Sudanizing.

**Su|dan|ize** (sü′də nīz), *v.t.,* **-ized, -iz|ing.** to make Sudanese.

**su|dar|i|um** (sü dãr′ē əm), *n., pl.* **-i|a** (-ē ə). **1** the handkerchief of Saint Veronica miraculously impressed, according to legend, with the features of Christ when He wiped His face with it on the way to Calvary. **2** a portrait of Christ on a cloth; veronica. **3** any handkerchief (a humorous use): *The most intrepid veteran ... dares no more than wipe his face with his cambric sudarium* (Sydney Smith). [< Latin *sūdārium* < *sūdor, -ōris* sweat]

**su|da|ry** (sü′dər ē), *n., pl.* **-ries.** = sudarium. [Middle English *sudary* < Latin *sūdārium* sudarium]

**su|da|tion** (sü dā′shən), *n.* the process of sweating.

**su|da|to|ri|um** (sü′də tôr′ē əm, -tōr′-), *n., pl.* **-to|ri|a** (-tôr′ē ə, -tōr′-). a heated room in a bathing establishment, used to induce sweating. [< Latin *sūdātōrium,* noun use of neuter of *sūdātōrius;* see etym. under **sudatory**]

**su|da|to|ry** (sü′də tôr′ē, -tōr′-), *adj., n., pl.* **-ries.**

—*adj.* **1** of or having to do with a sudatorium. **2** producing sweating.

—*n.* = sudatorium.

[< Latin *sūdātōrius* < *sūdāre* to sweat, related to *sūdor* sweat]

**sudd** (sud), *n.* a mass of floating vegetable matter on the White Nile which occasionally obstructs navigation. [< Arabic *sudd* < *sadda* he closed, obstructed]

**sud|den** (sud′ən), *adj., adv., n.* —*adj.* **1** happening or coming without notice, warning, or premonition; not expected: *a sudden stop, a sudden rise to power. Our troops made a sudden attack on the enemy. The snake ... His notice sudden is* (Emily Dickinson). SYN: See syn. under **unexpected. 2** found or hit upon unexpectedly; abrupt: *a sudden shift in foreign policy. There was a sudden turn in the road.* **3** speedy; immediate; quick; rapid: *The cat made a sudden jump at the mouse. The sudden hush as he took his place at the desk on the dais ...* (James Hilton). **4** *Archaic.* done or acting without forethought; rash; unpremeditated; hasty: *Jealous in honour, sudden and quick in quarrel* (Shakespeare).

—*adv.* suddenly.

—*n. Obsolete.* a sudden need, danger, or other emergency.

**(all) of a sudden,** in a sudden manner; without warning or preparation; suddenly; unexpectedly or quickly: *As he gazed, he saw of a sudden a man steal forth from the wood* (Arthur Conan Doyle). *Then all of a sudden appears Caligula, and demands that Claudius should be ... his slave* (Frederic W. Farrar).

**on** (or **upon**) **a sudden,** *Archaic.* suddenly; unexpectedly: *My crop promis'd very well, when on a sudden I found I was in danger of losing it all again* (Daniel Defoe).

[< Anglo-French *sodein,* or *sudein,* Old French *subdain* < Latin *subitāneus* < *subitus* sudden; (originally) past participle of *subīre* < *sub-* under + *īre* come, go] —**sud′den|ness,** *n.*

**sudden death, 1** instant death occurring without warning: *If I were worthy I would pray God for a sudden death* (Scott). **2** *Sports.* the immediate ending of a game as soon as one team scores in an overtime period to resolve a tie: *He won the sudden death playoff on the first extra hole.*

**sudden infant death syndrome,** = crib death.

**sud|den|ly** (sud′ən lē), *adv.* in a sudden manner; without warning or preparation; all at once: *Suddenly he turned from the window and rushed out into the night* (Ernest Hemingway). SYN: abruptly, unexpectedly.

**Su|de|ten** (sü dā′tən), *n.* a native or inhabitant of the Sudetenland, a region in northern Czechoslovakia.

**su|dor** (sü′dôr), *n.* = sweat. [< Latin *sūdor, -ōris* sweat]

**su|dor|al** (sü′dər əl), *adj.* of or having to do with sweat.

**su|dor|if|er|ous** (sü′də rif′ər əs), *adj.* secreting or causing sweat. [< Late Latin *sūdōrifer* (< Latin *sūdor, -ōris* sweat + *ferre* to bear) + English *-ous*] —**su′dor|if′er|ous|ness,** *n.*

**su|dor|if|ic** (sü′də rif′ik), *adj., n.* —*adj.* **1** causing or promoting sweat. **2** secreting sweat.

—*n.* a sudorific agent or remedy.

[< New Latin *sudorificus* < Latin *sūdor, -ōris* sweat + *facere* to make]

**su|dor|ip|a|rous** (sü′də rip′ər əs), *adj.* secreting sweat. [< New Latin *sudoriparus* (with English *-ous*) < Latin *sūdor, -ōris* sweat + *parere* to bear]

**Su|dra** (sü′drə), *n.* a member of the lowest of the four major Hindu castes. [< Sanskrit *śūdra*]

**suds** (sudz), *n., v.* —*n.pl.* **1** soapy water: *She rested in a bath of warm suds.* **2** bubbles and

foam on soapy water; soapsuds: *The children blew the suds off the top of the water.* **3** any froth or foam. **4** *U.S. Slang.* beer.
—*v.t.* to wash with soapy water: *We noticed four New Yorkers carefully sudsing and hosing their cars* (New Yorker).
—*v.i.* to make suds; form foam on soapy water: *Some detergents suds too much.*
[perhaps < Middle Dutch *sudse* bog]

**suds|er** (sud′zər), *n.* something that produces suds: *The washer has a built-in sudser* (Science News Letter).

**suds|less** (sudz′lis), *adj.* without suds; forming no suds: *a sudsless soap.*

**suds|y** (sud′zē), *adj.,* **suds|i|er, suds|i|est.** *Especially U.S.* **1** full of soapsuds. **2** full of foam: *sudsy beer.* **3** *Slang.* characteristic of soap operas; soap-operatic: *cloying sentimentality and the pseudodramatic froth typical of sudsy afternoon television dilemmas* (New York Times).

**sue** (sü), *v.,* **sued, su|ing.** —*v.t.* **1** to start a lawsuit against (a person, company, or other group); prosecute in court; bring a civil action against: *He sued the railroad because his cow was killed by the engine.* **2** to appeal to (a court) for legal redress. **3** to appeal to; petition: *Then will I sue thee to forgive* (Byron). **4** *Archaic.* to be a suitor to; court; woo: *They would sue me and woo me and flatter me* (Tennyson). —*v.i.* **1** to take civil action in law; bring suit: *to sue for damages.* **2** to beg or ask (for); petition; plead: *Messengers came suing for peace.* **3** *Archaic.* to be a suitor; woo.
**sue out, a** to apply before a court for the granting of (a writ or other legal process): *A party detained without any warrant must sue out his habeas corpus at common law* (Henry Hallam). **b** to proceed with (a legal action) to a decision; gain judicially: *After a man's body was taken in execution, no other process could be sued out against his lands or his goods* (Edward Poste).
[Middle English *suwen* follow, proceed < Anglo-French *suer,* or *siwer,* Old French *sivre,* later *suivre* < Late Latin *sequere,* for Latin *sequī* follow]

**suede** or **suède** (swād), *n., adj.* —*n.* **1** a soft leather that has a velvety nap on one or both sides. **2** a kind of cloth that has a similar appearance; suede cloth.
—*adj.* made of suede: *suede shoes, a suede jacket.*
[< French *Suède* Sweden; (originally) in phrase *gants de Suède* Swedish gloves]

**suede cloth** or **suède cloth,** a fabric with a napped finish resembling suede.

**sued|ed** or **suèd|ed** (swā′did), *adj.* having a napped finish: *sueded calf, a sueded cotton pullover.*

**suede|head** (swād′hed′), *n.* a young British working-class tough, distinguished from a skinhead by a slightly longer growth of hair.

**sue|dette** (swā det′), *n.* a suede imitation or substitute: *Swimming in suede is the new thing; swimming in cotton suedette the next best* (Sunday Times). [< *suede* + *-ette,* as in *leatherette*]

**su|er** (sü′ər), *n.* a person who sues or petitions.

**su|et** (sü′it), *n.* the hard fat about the kidneys and lions of certain animals, especially cattle and sheep. Suet is used in cooking and for making tallow. [probably < unrecorded Anglo-French *suet* (diminutive) < *sue,* variant of Old French *sieu* tallow < Latin *sēbum*]

**suet pudding,** a pudding made of flour, chopped suet, breadcrumbs, and raisins, and usually served with a sauce.

**su|et|y** (sü′ə tē), *adj.* **1** of or like suet; fat: *his suety face and alderman's stomach* (Time). **2** containing or made with suet.

**suf-,** *prefix.* the form of **sub-** before *f,* as in *suffer, suffice.*

**suf.** or **suff.,** suffix.

**suff** (suf), *n. Informal.* a suffragist.

**Suff.,** **1** Suffolk. **2** suffragan.

**suf|fer** (suf′ər), *v.i.* **1** to have pain, grief, or injury: *to suffer in silence, to suffer from malaria. She suffers from a headache. Very sick people may suffer. He suffered from the constant heckling of his guards.* **2** to experience harm or loss: *His business suffered greatly during the war. Neither plane nor passengers suffered much from the forced landing.* **3** to undergo punishment or be executed. **4** *Obsolete.* to endure patiently: *Charity suffereth long and is kind* (I Corinthians 13:4).
—*v.t.* **1** to have or feel (pain, grief, or injury): *to suffer great strain. He suffered harm from being out in the storm.* **2** to be subjected to; experience; undergo: *The party suffered a serious defeat in the last election.* **3** to allow; permit: *Suffer the little children to come unto me* (Mark 10:14). **4** to bear (something) with patience; endure; tolerate: *I will not suffer such insults. For ye suffer fools gladly, seeing ye yourselves are wise* (II Corinthians 11:19).
[< Anglo-French *suffrir,* Old French *sufrir,* < Latin *sufferre* < *sub-* up + *ferre* to bear] —**suf′fer|er,** *n.*

**suf|fer|a|ble** (suf′ər ə bəl, suf′rə-), *adj.* that can be endured; tolerable; bearable. —**suf′fer|a|ble-ness,** *n.*

**suf|fer|a|bly** (suf′ər ə blē, suf′rə-), *adv.* in a sufferable manner; tolerably.

**suf|fer|ance** (suf′ər əns, suf′rəns), *n.* **1** permission or consent given only by a failure to object or prevent. **2** power to bear or endure; patient endurance. **3** *Archaic.* suffering.
**on sufferance,** allowed or tolerated, but not really wanted; under conditions of passive acquiescence or bare tolerance: *They were a Ministry on sufferance when they appealed to the country* (Justin McCarthy).

**suf|fer|ing** (suf′ər ing, suf′ring), *n., adj.* —*n.* **1** the condition of being in pain; pain: *Hunger causes suffering. Motherhood will give the mother much suffering to bear* (Newsweek). *Those little anodynes that deaden suffering* (Emily Dickinson). **SYN:** distress, agony, misery. **2** the enduring of pain, trouble, or distress: *the suffering of a poor family.* **SYN:** distress, agony, misery.
—*adj.* that suffers or is characterized by the suffering of pain, grief, or injury: *The suffering human race* (Matthew Arnold). —**suf′fer|ing|ly,** *adv.*

**suf|fice** (sə fīs′), *v.,* **-ficed, -fic|ing.** —*v.i.* **1** to be enough; be sufficient: *Fifty dollars will suffice to buy that coat.* **2** to have the necessary ability, capacity, or resources (for doing something); be competent or able (to do something).
—*v.t.* to meet the desires, needs, or requirements of (a person); make content; satisfy: *A small amount of cake sufficed the baby.*
**suffice it,** let it suffice or be sufficient: *Suffice it to say that the party was a success.*
[< Old French *suffis-,* stem of *suffire* < Latin *sufficere* < *sub-* up (next to) + *facere* to make]
—**suf|fic′er,** *n.* —**suf|fic′ing|ly,** *adv.* —**suf|fic′ing|ness,** *n.*

**suf|fi|cien|cy** (sə fish′ən sē), *n., pl.* **-cies. 1** a sufficient amount; large enough supply: *The ship had a sufficiency of provisions for the voyage.* **SYN:** plenty. **2** the condition or fact of being sufficient; adequacy; ability. **SYN:** competence, capacity. **3** = self-confidence. **4** an income or means adequate for living in a (specified) manner: *a modest sufficiency.*

**suf|fi|cient** (sə fish′ənt), *adj.* **1** as much as is needed; enough: *sufficient proof. The poor child did not have sufficient clothing for the winter.* **SYN:** adequate, ample. See syn. under **enough. 2** *Archaic.* competent; capable; able. [< Latin *sufficiēns, -entis,* present participle of *sufficere;* see etym. under **suffice**] —**suf|fi′cient|ly,** *adv.*

**sufficient condition,** *Logic.* an antecedent from which the consequent must inevitably follow.

*** suf|fix** (*n.* suf′iks; *v.* sə fiks′, suf′iks), *n., v.* —*n.* **1a** a syllable or syllables put at the end of a word to change its meaning or to make another word, such as *-ly* in bad*ly,* *-ness* in good*ness,* *-ful* in spoon*ful,* and *-ment* in amaze*ment.* **b** an inflectional ending, which adapts a word to indicate person, number, or tense, or to show its grammatical relationship to other words, such as *-s* in believe*s* (third-person singular), *-s* in cat*s* (plural), or *-ed* in jump*ed* (past tense). **2** *Mathematics.* a subindex.
—*v.t.* **1** to add at the end; put after. **2** to attach as a suffix. **3** to fix or place under; subjoin.
[< New Latin *suffixum,* noun use of Latin, neuter past participle of *suffīgere* < *sub-* upon + *fīgere* fasten]

*** suffix**
definition 1a
con - figur - ation
prefix root suffix

**suf|fix|al** (suf′ik səl), *adj.* **1** having to do with a suffix. **2** of the nature of a suffix.

**suf|fix|a|tion** (suf′ik sā′shən), *n.* the forming of suffixes.

**suf|fix|ion** (sə fik′shən), *n.* **1** the act of suffixing, especially the attaching of a suffix at the end of a word. **2** the state of being suffixed.

**suf|flate** (sə flāt′), *v.t.,* **-flat|ed, -flat|ing.** *Obsolete.* to inflate. [< Latin *sufflāre* (with English *-ate*[1]) < *sub-* up + *flāre* to blow]

**suf|fla|tion** (sə flā′shən), *n. Obsolete.* inflation.

**suf|fo|cate** (suf′ə kāt), *v.,* **-cat|ed, -cat|ing.** —*v.t.* **1** to kill by stopping the breath; choke to death: *The prison may catch fire and he may be suffocated not with a rope, but with common ordinary smoke* (Samuel Butler). **2** to keep from breathing; hinder in breathing; stifle; choke. **3** *Figurative.* to smother; suppress.
—*v.i.* **1** to gasp for breath; choke. **2** to die for lack of air; be suffocated: *The dog suffocated in the small box.*
[< Latin *suffōcāre* (with English *-ate*[1]) (originally) to narrow up < *sub-* up + *faucēs,* plural, throat, narrow entrance] —**suf′fo|cat′ing|ly,** *adv.*

**suf|fo|ca|tion** (suf′ə kā′shən), *n.* **1** the act of suffocating: (*Figurative.*) *aisles crammed almost to suffocation* (Bruce Catton). **2** the condition of being suffocated: *The body must always be able to take in good air and get rid of bad air; when the body cannot do this, we have suffocation* (Beauchamp, Mayfield, and West).

**suf|fo|ca|tive** (suf′ə kā′tiv), *adj.* = stifling.

**Suf|folk** (suf′ək), *n.* **1** any one of an English breed of hornless sheep raised especially for meat. **2** any one of an English breed of heavy-bodied, chestnut-colored work horses. **3** any one of an English breed of small black swine. [< *Suffolk,* a former county in southeastern England]

**Suffolk Punch,** = Suffolk (def. 2).

**Suffr.,** suffragan.

**suf|fra|gan** (suf′rə gən), *n., adj.* —*n.* **1** a bishop consecrated to assist another bishop. **2** any bishop considered in relation to his archbishop or metropolitan.
—*adj.* assisting.
[< Anglo-French *suffragan,* learned borrowing from Medieval Latin *suffraganeus* one owing suffrage < Latin *suffrāgium;* see etym. under **suffrage**]

**suffragan bishop,** = suffragan.

**suf|fra|gan|ship** (suf′rə gən ship), *n.* the position of suffragan.

**suf|frage** (suf′rij), *n.* **1** the right to vote, especially the right to vote as a citizen in national or local elections, referendums, and the like; franchise: *The United States granted suffrage to women in 1920.* **2** the exercise of this right; casting of votes; voting. **3** a vote, usually in support of a proposal or candidate; ballot cast in an election, referendum, or the like: *The election of a new emperor was referred to the suffrage of the military order* (Edward Gibbon). **4** a short prayer or supplication. **5** *Archaic.* approval; assent; sanction; consent. [< Latin *suffrāgium* supporting vote < *sub-* nearby + *fragor* din, crash (as an outbreak of shouts of approval from the crowd), related to *frangere* to break]

**suf|fra|gette** (suf′rə jet′), *n.* a woman supporter of the cause of suffrage for women.

**suf|fra|get|tism** (suf′rə jet′iz əm), *n.* the support of suffrage for women.

**suf|fra|gism** (suf′rə jiz əm), *n.* the advocacy of the grant or extension of political suffrage, especially to women.

**suf|fra|gist** (suf′rə jist), *n., adj.* —*n.* a person who favors or actively supports giving suffrage to more people, especially to women.
—*adj.* of or having to do with a suffragist or suffragists: *suffragist literature.*

**suf|fru|tes|cent** (suf′rü tes′ənt), *adj. Botany.* somewhat woody or shrubby at the base. [< New Latin *suffrutescens, -entis* < *sub-* somewhat + Late Latin *frutēscēns, -entis* frutescent]

**suf|fru|tex** (suf′rü teks), *n., pl.* **suf|fru|ti|ces** (sə-frü′tə sēz). *Botany.* **1** an undershrub, or very small shrub; a low plant with decidedly woody stems, as the trailing arbutus. **2** a plant having a woody base but a herbaceous annual growth above. [< New Latin *suffrutex* < *sub-* under + *frutex* frutex]

**suf|fru|ti|cose** (sə frü′tə kōs), *adj. Botany.* **1** having the character of a suffrutex; small with woody stems. **2** woody at the base but herbaceous above. [< New Latin *suffruticosus* < *suffrutex, -icis* suffrutex]

**suf|fu|mi|gate** (sə fyü′mə gāt), *v.t.,* **-gat|ed, -gat|ing.** to fumigate from below. [< Latin *suffumigāre* (with English *-ate*[1]) < *sub-* from under + *fumigāre* fumigate]

**suf|fu|mi|ga|tion** (sə fyü′mə gā′shən), *n.* fumigation from below.

**suf|fuse** (sə fyüz′), *v.t.,* **-fused, -fus|ing.** to overspread (as with a color, liquid, or dye): *At twilight the sky was suffused with color. Her eyes were suffused with tears.* (*Figurative.*) *A broad smile suffused his face.* **SYN:** cover. [< Latin *suffūsus,* past participle of *suffundere* < *sub-* under + *fundere* to pour]

**suf|fu|sion** (sə fyü′zhən), *n.* **1** the action of suffusing. **2** the condition of being suffused. **3** that with which anything is overspread. **4** a flush of color: *There was a healthful suffusion on their cheeks* (Hawthorne). **SYN:** blush, glow.

**suf|fu|sive** (sə fyü′siv), *adj.* tending to suffuse.

**Su|fi** (sü′fē), *n.* **1** a sect of Moslem mystics and ascetics, especially in Persia, that originated early in the history of Islam. The monastic and ascetic

**Pronunciation Key:** hat, āge, cãre, fär; let, ēqual, tėrm; it, īce; hot, ōpen, ôrder; oil, out; cup, pu̇t, rüle; child; long; thin; ᴛʜen; zh, measure; ə represents **a** in about, **e** in taken, **i** in pencil, **o** in lemon, **u** in circus.

dervishes and fakirs derive from this sect. **2** an adherent of this sect. [< Arabic *ṣūfī* (literally) man of wool < *ṣūf* wool (probably because of their ascetic garments)]

**Su|fic** (sü′fik), *adj.* of or having to do with the Sufi or their mystical system.

**Su|fism** (sü′fiz əm), *n.* the mystical system of the Sufi, using a symbolism popular with Moslem poets.

**Su|fis|tic** (sü fis′tik), *adj.* = Sufic.

**sug-**, *prefix.* the form of **sub-** before *g*, as in *suggest.*

**su|gan** (sü′gən, sug′ən), *n.* **1** *Especially Irish.* **a** a straw rope. **b** a saddle of straw or rushes. **2** *Irish, Western U.S.* a heavy coverlet, as for a bed. Also, **sougan.** [< Irish *sūgān*]

**sug|ar** (shu̇g′ər), *n., v.* —*n.* **1a** a sweet, white or brown, usually crystalline substance, obtained chiefly from sugar cane or sugar beets and used commonly in food products; sucrose; saccharose. *Formula:* $C_{12}H_{22}O_{11}$ **b** *Especially British.* a lump or piece of this substance: *"I just know how many sugars each ... needs in his tea"* (Sunday Times). **2** *Chemistry.* any one of the class of carbohydrates to which this substance belongs. Glucose, lactose, and maltose are sugars. Most plants manufacture sugar. Sugars are soluble in water, sweet to the taste, and either directly or indirectly fermentable. According to their chemical structure, sugars are classified as monosaccharides, disaccharides, and trisaccharides. **3** something resembling sugar in form or taste. **4** *Figurative.* sweet or honeyed words; flattery. **5** *U.S. Informal.* darling; dear: *"I could use a drink, sugar," I said* (James Dickey). **6** *Slang, Figurative.* money.

—*v.t.* **1** to put sugar in; sweeten with sugar: *She sugared her tea.* **2** to cover with sugar; sprinkle with sugar: *to sugar doughnuts.* **3** *Figurative.* to cause to seem pleasant or agreeable; sugarcoat: *He sugared his criticism of the play with some praise for the performers. The ... sugared ... cajoleries that the two women directed upon him* (Arnold Bennett).

—*v.i.* to form crystals of sugar; granulate: *Honey sugars if kept too long.*

**sugar off**, to make maple sugar by boiling down the maple sap: *Families that you find up in the hills ... sugaring off in the spring* (William D. Howells).

**sugar up**, *Informal.* to flatter; butter up: *He never sugars up these guys on the committees, although he knows it might make life easier* (Atlantic).

[Middle English *sucere,* and *sugure* < Old French *sucre,* and *sukere* < Medieval Latin *succarum* < Arabic *sukkar* < Persian *shakar* < Sanskrit *śarkarā* candied sugar; (originally) grit. See related etym. at **saccharine.**] —**sug′ar|like′**, *adj.*

**sugar apple**, = sweetsop.

**sugar beet**, a large beet with a white root used in making sugar. See picture under **beet**[1].

**sug|ar|ber|ry** (shu̇g′ər ber′ē), *n., pl.* **-ries.** = hackberry.

**sug|ar|bird** (shu̇g′ər bėrd′), *n.* **1** any one of various small birds that feed on the nectar of flowers, such as the honey eater and certain South African sunbirds. **2** *U.S.* the evening grosbeak (believed by the Indians to like maple sugar).

**sugar bowl**, a small, bowl-shaped dish, usually with a cover and often with handles, used for sugar at the table.

**sug|ar|bush** (shu̇g′ər bu̇sh′), *n.* **1** a grove or plantation of sugar maples; sugar orchard. **2** the sugar maples on a particular tract or in a particular area, as distinguished from other kinds of trees.

**sugar candy**, **1** candy made by boiling pure sugar and allowing it to crystallize. **2** *Figurative.* anything like sugar candy; something sweet, pleasant, or delicious: *Lord John Russell, to whom a rap at the University was always sugar candy* (Frederic E. Gretton).

**sug|ar-can|dy** (shu̇g′ər kan′dē), *adj.* sugared; honeyed; excessively sweet: (*Figurative.*) *sugar-candy hymns,* (*Figurative.*) *sugar-candy words of flattery.*

**sugar cane**, a very tall grass, with a strong, jointed stem and long, flat leaves, growing in warm regions. Sugar cane is one of the chief sources of manufactured sugar. See picture under **grass family.**

**sug|ar-coat** (shu̇g′ər kōt′), *v.t.* **1** to cover with sugar; put a coating of sugar on: *to sugar-coat pills.* **2** *Figurative.* to cause to seem more pleasant or agreeable: *to sugar-coat discipline with humor. Through front organizations and membership on semiofficial committees, they will propagate sugar-coated versions of their main ideas* (New York Times).

**sug|ar-coat|ing** (shu̇g′ər kō′ting), *n.* **1** a covering with sugar. **2** *Figurative.* a thing that makes something seem more pleasant or agreeable.

**sugar corn**, = sweet corn.

**sugar daddy**, *U.S. Slang.* an older man generous with gifts to younger women.

**sugar diabetes**, = diabetes mellitus.

**sug|ared** (shu̇g′ərd), *adj.* **1** containing, impregnated, or coated with sugar; sweetened with sugar. **2** *Figurative.* honeyed: *sugared words of flattery.*

**sug|ar|house** (shu̇g′ər hous′), *n.* **1** *U.S.* a building near or in a sugar orchard, in which the sap from the sugar maples is reduced, by boiling, into maple syrup or maple sugar. **2** a sugar factory; sugarworks.

**sug|ar|i|ness** (shu̇g′ər ē nis), *n.* sugary quality.

**sug|ar|ing off** (shu̇g′ər ing), *U.S.* **1** the act or process of making maple sugar, by boiling off the free liquid from maple sap. **2** a gathering of neighbors at a sugarhouse to help in the making of maple sugar, marked traditionally by much jollity and humor. **3** a social gathering patterned on this, now often for the entertainment of tourists or visitors.

**sug|ar|less** (shu̇g′ər lis), *adj.* without sugar: *sugarless soda pop or chewing gum.*

**sugar loaf**, **1** a solid, cone-shaped mass of hard, refined sugar. It is the form in which sugar was generally sold during most of the period from the late Middle Ages to the middle of the 1800's. **2** something shaped like a sugar loaf, especially: **a** a high, cone-shaped hill: *here and there the outline of a wooded sugar loaf in black* (Robert L. Stevenson). **b** a tall, cone-shaped hat.

**sug|ar-loaf** (shu̇g′ər lōf′), *adj.* shaped like a sugar loaf.

**sugar maple**, a maple tree of eastern North America, highly valued for its heavy, hard, tough wood and for its sweet sap, from which maple sugar and maple syrup are made.

**sugar mill**, a machine or factory for making sugar, as by pressing the juice out of sugar cane.

**sugar nucleotide**, *Biochemistry.* any one of a group of sugars which are bound to the phosphate group of nucleotides, are intermediates in the conversion of one sugar to another, and serve as a source of sugar units in forming polysaccharides: *Research all over the world ... has produced more than 100 different sugar nucleotides—essential components in biochemical reactions* (Science Journal).

**sugar of lead**, = lead acetate.

**sugar of milk**, = lactose.

**sugar orchard**, = sugarbush (def. 1).

**sugar pine**, a tall pine of California, Oregon, Nevada, and Mexico, which gives off a sugarlike resin when cut deep into the wood. It bears very large cones.

**sug|ar|plum** (shu̇g′ər plum′), *n.* a small piece of candy; bonbon: *The children were nestled all snug in their beds While visions of sugarplums danced in their heads* (Clement C. Moore). **SYN:** confection, comfit.

**sugar soap**, an alkaline substance that resembles sugar, used for cleansing a surface before painting.

**Sugar State**, a nickname for Louisiana.

**sugar tongs**, small tongs for lifting cubes of sugar from a bowl.

**sugar tree**, **1** = sugar maple. **2** any tree from which sugar syrup or sugary sap can be obtained.

**sugar vinegar**, vinegar made of the waste juice of sugar cane.

**sug|ar|works** (shu̇g′ər wėrks′), *n.pl.* (*sing. in use*). a place where sugar is made.

**sug|ar|y** (shu̇g′ər ē), *adj.* **1** consisting of or containing much sugar. **2** like sugar; sweet. **3** *Figurative.* outwardly, but not sincerely, pleasant or agreeable; deceitfully or flatteringly pleasant: *a sugary greeting.* **4** *Figurative.* excessively or offensively sweet: *The pudding was too sugary for my taste.*

**sug|gest** (səg jest′, sə-), *v.t.* **1** to bring to mind; call up the thought of: *The thought of summer suggests swimming, tennis, and hot weather. Democratic Athens, oligarchic Rome, suggest to us Pericles and Brutus* (James Bryce). **2** to put forward; propose: *He suggested a swim, and we all agreed. I suggest that you follow me immediately.* **3** to provide the motive for; prompt: *Prudence suggested the necessity of a temporary retreat* (Edward Gibbon). **4** to show in an indirect way; hint; intimate: *His yawns suggested that he would like to go to bed. Bad manners suggest a lack of proper home training. The first* [*report*] *sounded as though the administration was about ready to throw Negro troops into the war, while the later one suggested that the administration was still hesitating* (Carl Sandburg). **SYN:** insinuate. [< Latin *suggestus,* past participle of *suggere* suggest, supply, put under < *sub-* under, next to + *gerere* bring] —**sug|gest′er**, *n.*

**sug|gest|i|bil|i|ty** (səg jes′tə bil′ə tē, sə-), *n.* the quality or condition of being suggestible: *Crowd emotionality is perhaps best interpreted in terms of heightened suggestibility, that is the tendency of an individual in a crowd to respond uncritically to the stimuli provided by the other members* (Ogburn and Nimkoff).

**sug|gest|i|ble** (səg jes′tə bəl, sə-), *adj.* **1** capable of being influenced by suggestion; readily swayed or influenced: *We are tremendously suggestible. Our mechanism is much better adapted to credulity than questioning* (James Harvey Robinson). **2** capable of being influenced by hypnotic suggestion. **3** that can be suggested; capable of suggestion: *a suggestible solution.*

**sug|ges|ti|o fal|si** (səg jes′tē ō fôl′sī), *Latin.* suggestion of the false; indirect lie; conscious misrepresentation, whether by words, conduct, or artifice: *Despite ... unqualified denials from Washington which reached London long before the evening papers went to press, the process of suggestio falsi continued, and for obvious political reasons* (Harold Hutchinson).

**sug|ges|tion** (səg jes′chən, sə-), *n.* **1** the act of suggesting; the putting into the mind of an idea, course of action, or the like: *The trip was made at her suggestion.* **2** a thing suggested; proposal: *The picnic was an excellent suggestion.* **3** the action of calling up one idea by another because they are connected or associated in some way. **4** a very small amount; slight trace; hint; inkling: *There was a suggestion of anger in Father's voice when he called us in from play for the third time. The foreigner spoke English with just a suggestion of his native accent.* **SYN:** soupçon, touch. **5** *Psychology.* **a** the insinuation of an idea, belief, or impulse into the mind, especially a hypnotized person's mind, with avoidance of normal critical thought or contrary ideas. **b** the idea, belief, or impulse so insinuated.

**suggestion box**, a box in which written suggestions for improvement are put, as by employees in a factory or business or patrons in a theater or restaurant: *The majority of employers utilizing suggestion boxes award cash for accepted ideas* (New York Times).

**sug|ges|tive** (səg jes′tiv, sə-), *adj.* **1** tending to suggest ideas, acts, or feelings: *The teacher gave an interesting and suggestive list of composition subjects.* **SYN:** See syn. under **expressive.** **2** conveying a suggestion or hint (of something): *a tone suggestive of anger.* **3** tending to suggest something improper or indecent: *Bribery is a suggestive incentive to many weak politicians.* —**sug|ges′tive|ly**, *adv.* —**sug|ges′tive|ness**, *n.*

**su|gi** (sü′gē), *n.* a tall Japanese tree of the pine family, whose wood is compact, very white, soft, and much used in construction. [< Japanese *sugi*]

**su|i|cid|al** (sü′ə sī′dəl), *adj.* **1** of or having to do with suicide: *a suicidal individual, a suicidal weapon.* **2** leading to or causing suicide: *suicidal behavior, the suicidal impulse. War has become so obviously self-defeating and suicidal* (Atlantic). **3** *Figurative.* ruinous to one's own interests; disastrous to oneself: *It would be suicidal for a store to sell many things below cost. We still await the arrival of a time of political maturity among candidates ... when courageous discussion of taxation is not considered suicidal in a bid for public office* (New York Times). —**su′i|cid′al|ly**, *adv.*

**su|i|cide**[1] (sü′ə sīd), *n., adj., v.,* **-cid|ed, -cid|ing.** —*n.* **1** the act of killing oneself on purpose: *The police think the death was suicide.* **2** *Figurative.* the destruction of one's own interests or prospects.

—*adj.* **1** designating a military action or operation that is certain, or almost certain, to result in the death of the person or persons involved; suicidal: *a suicide attack, suicide missions.* **2** undertaking such actions or operations: *a suicide pilot, suicide squads.* **3** used in such actions or operations: *a suicide airplane, suicide bombs.*

—*v.i., v.t.* to commit suicide; kill (oneself).

**commit suicide**, to kill oneself on purpose: *to commit suicide in a moment of wild despair.*

[< New Latin *suicidium* < Latin *suī* of oneself + *-cīdium* -cide[2]]

**su|i|cide**[2] (sü′ə sīd), *n.* a person who kills himself on purpose: *Christian burial has usually been denied suicides* (Newsweek). [< New Latin *suicida* < Latin *suī* of oneself + *cīda* -cide[2]]

**suicide seat**, *Informal.* the seat next to the driver in an automobile: *Those who drive with dogs in their laps, or with young children bouncing about on the "suicide seat" next to them ... are equally irresponsible* (Scotsman).

**suicide squad**, **1** a group of soldiers or guerrillas who undertake suicide missions in enemy territory. **2** *Football Slang.* a group of players specially selected for kickoffs and punting.

**su|i|cid|ol|o|gist** (sü′ə sī dol′ə jist), *n.* a person engaged in the study of suicide and in its prevention: *... suicidologists working in the 300 suicide-prevention centers operating round the country* (Time).

**su|i|cid|ol|o|gy** (sü′ə sī dol′ə jē), *n.* the study of suicide and suicidal behavior.

**su|i ge|ne|ris** (sü′ī jen′ər is), *Latin.* of his, her, its, or their peculiar kind; unique: *Indeed, society itself is ... an entity sui generis, something real in itself and unlike a mere sum of the individuals of which it is composed* (Hinkle and Hinkle). **SYN**: unmatchable.

**su|i ju|ris** (sü′ī jůr′is), *Law.* that is of age and presumably sane, and therefore legally competent to act and legally responsible for actions: *I made it a rule never to take for treatment anyone who was not sui juris, independent of others in all the essential relations of life* (Sigmund Freud). [< Latin *suī jūris* (literally) of one's own right; *suus, suī* one's own, *jūs, jūris* (legal) right]

**su|il|line** (sü′ə līn, -lin), *adj.* of or having to do with swine. [< Latin *suillus* (< *sūs* swine) + English *-ine*[1]]

**su|i|mate** (sü′ə māt′, sü′ī-), *n.* = self-mate. [< Latin *suī* of oneself + English *mate*[2]]

**su|ine** (sü′in), *n.* a mixture of oleomargarine with lard or other fatty substances, used as a substitute for butter. [< Latin *sūs* swine + English *-ine*[2] (because it was made from pig lard)]

**su|int** (sü′int, swint), *n.* dried perspiration found in the natural grease of sheep's wool, containing potash. [< French *suint* < Middle French *suin* < *suer* to sweat < Latin *sūdāre*]

**suit** (süt), *n., v.* —*n.* **1** a set of clothes to be worn together. A man's suit consists of a coat, trousers, and sometimes a vest. A woman's suit consists of a coat and either a skirt or trousers. *The knight wore a suit of armor. His suit of ancient black* (Vachel Lindsay). **2** a civil action brought before a law court; application to a court for justice: *He started a suit to collect damages for his injuries in the automobile accident. The Plaintiff in the suit ... was adjudged to have not proved his charge* (George Meredith). **3** a request; asking; wooing: *The prince's suit was successful and Cinderella married him.* **4a** one of the four sets of cards (spades, hearts, diamonds, and clubs) making up a deck. **b** all the cards of any one of these sets held in a player's hand at one time: *He had a good heart suit.* **5** = suite. **6** (originally) attendance by a tenant at the court of a feudal lord.

—*v.t.* **1** to make suitable or appropriate; make fit: *The teacher suited the punishment to the offense by making the student sweep up the bits of paper he had thrown.* **SYN**: adjust. **2** to be good for; agree with: *A cold climate suits apples and wheat, but not oranges and tea.* **3** to be agreeable, convenient, or acceptable to; please; satisfy: *Which time suits you best? It is hard to suit everybody.* **SYN**: gratify, content. **4** to be becoming to: *Her blue hat suits her fair skin. A small ring suits a small hand.* **5** to provide with a suit of clothes; clothe; attire: [*She*] *made her reputation with frivolous promotions like ... suiting up the stewardesses in Pucci pajamas. I'll disrobe me Of these Italian weeds and suit myself As does a Briton peasant* (Shakespeare).

—*v.i.* **1** to be suitable; be convenient; be fitting. **2** *Archaic.* to agree or harmonize.

**bring suit,** to start a lawsuit: *The landlord brought suit to collect the money which the tenant owed him.*

**follow suit, a** to play a card of the same suit as that first played: *Having but two or three small trumps, he should never force his partner to trump, if he finds he cannot follow suit* (J. Beaufort). **b** *Figurative.* to follow the example of another: *Kenya and Sierra Leone ... too must consider the possibility of following suit if Zambia quits the Commonwealth* (Manchester Guardian Weekly).

**suit oneself,** to do as one pleases: *If you will not take my advice, suit yourself.*

**suit up,** to put on a special suit or uniform: *Two husky football players suited up in the University of Colorado's field house at Boulder* (Time). *He could be suited up and sent off to war* (Russell Baker).

[Middle English *sywte* attendance at a court; the company attending; then, their livery < Anglo-French *siwte,* or *suite* < Vulgar Latin *sequita,* ultimately < Latin *sequī* follow. See etym. of doublet **suite.**]

**suit|a|bil|i|ty** (sü′tə bil′ə tē), *n.* a being suitable; fitness; appropriateness.

**suit|a|ble** (sü′tə bəl), *adj.* right for the occasion; fitting; proper; appropriate: *A simple dress is suitable for school wear. The park gives the children a suitable playground.* **SYN**: See syn. under **fit**[1].
—**suit′a|ble|ness,** *n.*

**suit|a|bly** (sü′tə blē), *adv.* in a suitable manner; fitly; appropriately; agreeably.

**suit|case** (süt′kās′), *n.* a flat, rectangular traveling bag. **SYN**: valise, grip.

**suitcase farmer,** *U.S.* a farmer, especially a dry-land farmer, who lives away from the farm most of the year.

**suit-dress** (süt′dres′), *n.* a woman's outfit consisting of a skirt or dress and matching jacket or coat.

**suite** (swēt; *also* süt *for 2*), *n.* **1** a set of connected rooms to be used by one person, family, or other group of associated persons: *She has a suite of rooms at the hotel—a living room, bedroom, and bath.* **SYN**: apartment. **2** a set of furniture that matches: *a dining room suite.* **3** any set or series of like things. **4** *Music.* **a** a series of connected instrumental movements varying in number and character, sometimes concert arrangements of ballet or stage music: *a suite for strings.* **b** a series of dances in the same or related keys, arranged for one or more instruments; partita. The typical movements are allemande, courante, saraband, and gigue; between saraband and gigue, intermezzos are inserted, the most important being the minuet. **5** a group of followers, attendants, or servants; retinue: *The queen traveled with a suite of twelve.* **SYN**: cortège. [< French, Old French *suite* < Vulgar Latin *sequita.* See etym. of doublet **suit.**]

**-suited,** *combining form.* wearing a ___ suit or suits: *Gray-suited = wearing a gray suit.*

**suit|ing** (sü′ting), *n.* fabric for making suits.

**suit|or** (sü′tər), *n.* **1** a man who is courting a woman, especially with a view to marriage: *The princess had many suitors. You think that you are Ann's suitor* [*but*] *... it is you who are the pursued ... the destined prey* (George Bernard Shaw). **SYN**: beau. **2** a person bringing suit in a law court. **SYN**: litigant. **3** anyone who sues or petitions; petitioner; suppliant. **SYN**: supplicant.

**suit|or|ship** (sü′tər ship), *n.* the state or condition of being a suitor.

**suit|ress** (sü′tris), *n. Archaic.* a woman suitor.

**suk**[1] (sük), *n., pl.* **suk.** a Korean unit of measure for grain, vegetables, and other dry commodities, equal to about five bushels. [< Korean *suk*]

**suk**[2] (sůk), *n.* = suq.

**Suk** (sük), *n., pl.* **Suk** or **Suks.** a member of a Nilotic people of Kenya.

**su|ki|ya|ki** (sü′kē yä′kē, skē yä′-), *n.* a Japanese dish consisting of thin strips of meat, sliced onions, bamboo shoots, shredded spinach, and other vegetables cooked for a very short time in a mixture of soy sauce, stock, sugar, and sweet sake. [< Japanese *sukiyaki,* perhaps < *suki* slicing + *-yaki* cooking, roasting]

**suk|kah** (sůk′ə, sů kä′), *n.* a temporary bower or hut covered with branches, built on the premises of a house or synagogue as a place to eat in and sometimes sleep in during Sukkoth: *Midday meal in the sukkah, the festival tent set up in the quadrangle* (Harper's). Also, **succah.** [< Hebrew *sukkå* a booth]

**Suk|kos** (sůk′əs), *n.* = Sukkoth.

**Suk|koth** or **Suk|kot** (sů kōth′), *n.* a Jewish festival of eight or nine days celebrated in Tishri (September–October) by building temporary bowers or huts in remembrance of those the Israelites used during their wanderings in the desert; Feast of Booths. Leviticus 23:33-44. Also, **Succos, Succoth.** [< Hebrew *Sukkoth,* plural of *sukkå* a booth]

**sul|cate** (sul′kāt), *adj.* marked with parallel furrows or grooves, as a stem. [< Latin *sulcātus,* past participle of *sulcāre* to plow, furrow < *sulcus* furrow]

**sul|cat|ed** (sul′kā tid), *adj.* = sulcate.

**sul|ca|tion** (sul kā′shən), *n.* **1** a furrow, channel, or sulcus. **2** a set of sulci collectively. **3** the state of being sulcated. **4** the act, manner, or mode of grooving.

**sul|cus** (sul′kəs), *n., pl.* **-ci** (-sī). *Anatomy.* **1** a groove or furrow in a body, organ, or tissue. **2** a shallow groove between two convolutions of the surface of the brain. [< Latin *sulcus* a furrow, trench, wrinkle]

**sul|fa** (sul′fə), *adj., n.* —*adj.* of or having to do with a family of drugs containing sulfurous anhydride ($SO_2$), derived from sulfanilamide, and used in treating various bacterial infections.
—*n.* a sulfa drug. Also, **sulpha.**
[abstracted < *sulfanilamide*]

**sul|fa|di|a|zine** (sul′fə dī′ə zēn, -zin), *n.* a sulfa drug of the sulfonamide group, a white or yellowish powder, less toxic than sulfanilamide, sulfapyridine, or sulfathiazole, and used in treating various bacterial infections. *Formula:* $C_{10}H_{10}N_4O_2S$ [< *sulfa* + *diazine*]

**sul|fa|di|meth|ox|ine** (sul′fə dī′mə thok′sēn), *n.* a sulfonamide used against general body infections. *Formula:* $C_{12}H_{14}N_4O_4S$ [< *sulfa* + *di-*[1] + *meth*(yl) + *ox*(ygen) + *-ine*[2]]

**sulfa drugs,** a family of drugs containing sulfur dioxide ($SO_2$), especially those derived from sulfanilamide, that are generally powerful in checking the growth of certain bacteria. Members of the group are used (sometimes with antibiotics) chiefly to combat streptococcic, pneumococcic, meningococcic, and staphylococcic infections, but all are more or less toxic and are restricted in use. *Sulfa drugs became available just before World War II and played an important role in preventing deaths from wound infection on the battlefield* (Sidonie M. Gruenberg).

**sul|fa|guan|i|dine** (sul′fə gwan′ə dēn, -din; -gwä′nə-), *n.* a sulfa drug of the sulfonamide group, a white, crystalline powder, comparatively nontoxic, and used chiefly against bacillary dysentery. *Formula:* $C_7H_{10}N_4O_2S{\cdot}H_2O$

**sul|fa|mer|a|zine** (sul′fə mer′ə zēn, -zin), *n.* a sulfa drug of the sulfonamide group, a white or yellowish, crystalline powder similar to sulfadiazine, but more readily absorbed. *Formula:* $C_{11}H_{12}N_4O_2S$ [< *sulfa* + Greek *méros* part, taken as "member of a similar group" + English *azine*]

**sul|fa|meth|a|zine** (sul′fə meth′ə zēn, -zin), *n.* a sulfa drug used for the treatment of various bacterial infections. *Formula:* $C_{12}H_{14}N_4O_2S$ [< *sulfa* + (di)*meth*(yl) + *azine*]

**sul|fam|ic acid** (sul fam′ik), a white, crystalline solid obtained by heating urea with sulfuric acid, used for cleaning and electroplating metal, as a fire retardant, and in organic synthesis. *Formula:* $HSO_3NH_2$

**sul|fa|nil|a|mide** (sul′fə nil′ə mīd, -mid), *n.* a white, crystalline substance derived from coal tar. It was the first sulfa drug to be widely used in treating various infections. Sulfanilamide is the amide of sulfanilic acid and is the basis for most of the sulfa drugs. *Formula:* $C_6H_8N_2O_2S$ [< *sulfanil*(ic acid) + *amide*]

**sul|fa|nil|ic acid** (sul′fə nil′ik), a grayish-white, crystalline acid produced by heating aniline with sulfuric acid, used especially in the manufacture of dyes. *Formula:* $C_6H_7NSO_3{\cdot}H_2O$ [< *sulf*(uric acid) + *anil*(ine) + *-ic*]

**sul|fa|nil|yl|guan|i|dine monohydrate** (sul′fə-nil′əl gwan′ə dēn, -din; -gwä′nə-), = sulfaguanidine. [< (acetyl)*sulfanilyl* (chloride), a chemical compound + *guanidine*]

**sul|fa|pyr|a|zine** (sul′fə pir′ə zēn, -zin), *n.* a sulfa drug with uses similar to sulfadiazine. *Formula:* $C_{10}H_{10}N_4O_2S$

**sul|fa|pyr|i|dine** (sul′fə pir′ə dēn, -din), *n.* a sulfa drug, of the sulfonamide group, used against certain skin infections and pneumonia, but now superseded for general use by less toxic derivatives. *Formula:* $C_{11}H_{11}N_3O_2S$

**sul|fa|qui|nox|a|line** (sul′fə kwi nok′sə lēn, -lin), *n.* a synthetic drug used in the treatment of coccidiosis, fowl cholera, dysentery, and other diseases of cattle, sheep, swine, rabbits, and domestic fowl. *Formula:* $C_{14}H_{12}N_4O_2S$

**sulf|ar|se|nid** (sulf är′sə nid), *n.* = sulfarsenide.

**sulf|ar|se|nide** (sulf är′sə nīd, -nid), *n. Chemistry.* a compound which is a double salt of sulfur and arsenic. [< *sulf*(ide) + *arsenide*]

**sulf|ars|phen|a|mine** (sulf′ärs fen′ə mēn, -min; -fen am′in), *n.* a sulfa drug containing arsenic, used in the treatment of syphilis. *Formula:* $C_{14}H_{14}As_2N_2Na_2O_8S_2$

**Sul|fa|sux|i|dine** (sul′fə suk′sə dēn, -din), *n. Trademark.* a preparation of succinylsulfathiazole.

**sul|fa|tase** (sul′fə tās), *n.* an enzyme that catalyzes the hydrolysis of esters of sulfuric acid. One kind is commonly found in animal and plant tissues; another is present in bacteria.

**sul|fate** (sul′fāt), *n., v.,* **-fat|ed, -fat|ing.** —*n.* any salt or ester of sulfuric acid: *Most sulfates are soluble in water, but such sulfates as barium, strontium, and lead sulfates do not dissolve in water.*
—*v.t.* **1** to combine or treat with sulfuric acid or a sulfate. **2** to change into a sulfate. **3** *Electricity.* to form a scaly deposit of a compound containing lead sulfate on (the plates of a storage battery).
—*v.i.* to become sulfated.
[< French *sulphate* < New Latin *sulphatum* (*acidum*) (literally) acid of sulfate < Latin *sulfur,* and *sulphur*]

**sulfate paper,** any paper of various grades and types made from pulp produced by the sulfate process, as kraft and other stocks intended for commercial use and certain types of inexpensive typewriter paper.

**sulfate process,** a papermaking process in which wood chips are converted into pulp by cooking under pressure in a solution of sodium sulfide, sodium hydroxide, and water.

**sul|fa|thi|a|zole** (sul′fə thī′ə zōl, -zol), *n.* a sulfa drug of the sulfonamide group, used especially in treating gonorrhea and pneumonia, but superseded for general use by sulfadiazine. *Formula:* $C_9H_9N_3O_2S_2$

---

**Pronunciation Key:** hat, āge, cãre, fär; let, ēqual, tėrm; it, īce; hot, ōpen, ôrder; oil, out; cup, pu̇t, rüle; child; long; thin; ᴛʜen; zh, measure; ə represents **a** in about, **e** in taken, **i** in pencil, **o** in lemon, **u** in circus.

**sul|fa|tion** (sul fā′shən), *n.* **1** the act or process of sulfating: *The additive would … ward off the harmful effects … of sulfation in lead-acid storage batteries which causes efficiency to drop off* (Wall Street Journal). **2** the scaly deposit formed on the plates of a storage battery by this process.

**sul|fat|i|za|tion** (sul′fə tə zā′shən), *n.* the act or process of sulfatizing.

**sul|fat|ize** (sul′fə tīz), *v.t.,* **-ized, -iz|ing.** to change (as sulfide ores) into sulfates, especially by roasting.

**sul|fe|trone** (sul′fə trōn), *n.* a drug, one of the sulfone compounds, used in the treatment of leprosy. *Formula:* $C_{30}H_{28}N_2O_{14}S_5Na_4$ [< *sulf*(one) + (t)*etr*(a)- fourth (because this is the position of one of the radicals on the chain) + *-one*]

**sulf|hy|drate** (sulf hī′drāt), *n.* = hydrosulfide.

**sulf|hy|dric acid** (sulf hī′drik), = hydrogen sulfide. Also, **sulphydric acid.**

**sulf|hy|dryl** (sulf hī′drəl), *n.* the univalent radical -SH; thiol. [< *sulf*(ur) + *hydr*(ogen) + *-yl*]

**sul|fid** (sul′fid), *n.* = sulfide.

**sul|fide** (sul′fīd), *n.* any compound of sulfur with another element or radical; salt of hydrogen sulfide; sulfuret. [< *sulf*(ur) + *-ide*]

**sul|fi|nyl** (sul′fə nəl), *n. Chemistry.* a bivalent organic radical, -SO; thionyl. [< *sulf*(ur) + *-in* + *-yl*]

**sul|fi|sox|a|zole** (sul′fə sok′sə zōl, -zol), *n.* a white or yellowish sulfa drug used to treat various bacterial infections, especially infections of the urinary tract. *Formula:* $C_{11}H_{13}N_3O_3S$

**sul|fite** (sul′fīt), *n.* a salt or ester of sulfurous acid. [< French *sulfite,* arbitrary alteration of *sulphate;* see etym. under **sulfate.** Compare etym. under **-ite**[2].]

**sulfite process,** a method of producing wood pulp by cooking wood chips in a solution of bisulfite of calcium, magnesium, sodium, or ammonium. It is used mainly with softwoods, such as fir and hemlock.

**sul|fit|ic** (sul fit′ik), *adj.* of or having to do with a sulfite or sulfites.

**Sul|fo|nal** (sul′fə nal, sul′fə nal′), *n. Trademark.* sulfonmethane.

**sul|fon|a|mide** (sul fon′ə mīd; sul′fə nam′īd, -id), *n.* **1** any one of a group of sulfa drugs, derivatives of sulfanilamide, which check bacterial infections, chiefly by preventing the synthesis in the body of certain substances necessary to the growth of disease-producing bacteria. Their use is governed by factors such as rate of absorption and resistance of the bacteria. Other drugs, such as sodium bicarbonate, are often administered with them to reduce their toxic effects. **2** *Chemistry.* **a** an organic compound which contains the univalent radical $-SO_2NH_2$. **b** the radical itself. [< *sulfon*(yl) + *amide*]

**sul|fo|nate** (sul′fə nāt), *n., v.,* **-nat|ed, -nat|ing.** *Chemistry.* **—*n.*** a salt or ester of a sulfonic acid. **—*v.t.*** to convert into a sulfonic acid.

**sul|fo|na|tion** (sul′fə nā′shən), *n. Chemistry.* the introduction of one or more sulfonic acid radicals $-SO_2OH$ into an organic compound.

**sul|fone** (sul′fōn), *n. Chemistry.* any one of a group of compounds containing the radical $-SO_2$ united to two hydrocarbon radicals: *Widespread use of sulfone drugs has made recovery* [*from leprosy*] *increasingly common* (Time). [< German *Sulfon* < *Sulfur* sulfur + *-on* -one]

**sul|fon|ic** (sul fon′ik), *adj. Chemistry.* **1** of or denoting the univalent acid radical $-SO_2OH$ (or $-SO_3H$). **2** of or having to do with an acid containing this radical. [< *sulfon*(e) + *-ic*]

**sulfonic acid,** any one of a group of organic acids containing the univalent radical $-SO_2OH$, considered as sulfuric acid derivatives by the replacement of a hydroxyl radical (-OH). They are used especially in making phenols, dyes, and drugs.

**sul|fo|ni|um** (sul fō′nē əm), *n. Chemistry.* a univalent radical formed by the addition of a proton to hydrogen sulfide. *Formula:* $-H_3S$ [< *sulf*(ur), + *-onium,* on the analogy of *ammonium*]

**sul|fon|meth|ane** (sul′fōn meth′ān, -fon-), *n.* a soluble, white, crystalline substance used as a hypnotic; Sulfonal. *Formula:* $C_7H_{14}O_4S_2$ [< *sulfon*(e) + *methane*]

**sul|fo|nyl** (sul′fə nəl, -nēl), *n. Chemistry.* a bivalent radical, $-SO_2$; sulfuryl.

**sulfonyl chloride,** = sulfuryl chloride.

**sul|fo|nyl|u|re|a** (sul′fə nəl yů rē′ə), *n.* any one of a group of drugs, compounds of sulfonyl and urea, related to the sulfa drugs and used as a substitute for insulin in the treatment of diabetes.

**sulf|ox|ide** (sulf ok′sīd), *n. Chemistry.* an organic compound containing an -SO group linked to two carbon atoms.

***sul|fur** (sul′fər), *n., adj., v.* **—*n.*** **1** a light-yellow, nonmetallic chemical element that burns in the air with a blue flame and a stifling odor; brimstone. Sulfur is found abundantly in volcanic regions, occurring free in nature as a brittle, crystalline solid or in combination with metals and other substances, and is also a constituent of proteins. It is used in making matches, gunpowder, paper pulp, fertilizers, medicines, and insecticides, and for vulcanizing rubber and in bleaching. **2** a greenish yellow; sulphur.
**—*adj.*** greenish-yellow; sulphur.
**—*v.t.*** to combine or treat with sulfur; sulfurate. Also, **sulphur.**
[Middle English *soufre,* and *sulfre* < Anglo-French *sulfere,* Old French *soufre* < Latin *sulfur,* or *sulphur*]

***sulfur**
definition 1

| symbol | atomic number | atomic weight | oxidation state |
|---|---|---|---|
| S | 16 | 32.064 | -2,+4,+6 |

**sul|fu|rate** (sul′fə rāt, -fyə-), *v.,* **-rat|ed, -rat|ing,** *adj.* **—*v.t.*** to combine, impregnate with, or subject to the action of sulfur or a sulfur compound; sulfurize.
**—*adj.*** **1** made of or consisting of sulfur. **2** resembling sulfur.
[< Late Latin *sulphurātus* < Latin *sulphur* sulfur]

**sul|fu|ra|tion** (sul′fə rā′shən, -fyə-), *n.* **1** the act or process of treating with sulfur. **2** the state of being treated or impregnated with sulfur.

**sul|fu|ra|tor** (sul′fə rā′tər, -fyə-), *n.* **1** an apparatus for treating, impregnating, or sprinkling with sulfur. **2** an apparatus for fumigating or bleaching with the fumes of burning sulfur.

**sul|fur-bot|tom** (sul′fər bot′əm), *n.* = sulphur-bottom.

**sulfur dioxide,** a heavy, colorless, poisonous gas or liquid with a sharp odor, used as a bleach, disinfectant, preservative, and refrigerant, and in making sulfuric acid. *Formula:* $SO_2$

**sul|fu|re|ous** (sul fyůr′ē əs), *adj.* **1** consisting of or containing sulfur. **2** having to do with sulfur. **3** like sulfur. **4** = sulphureous (def. 2). [< Latin *sulphureus* (with English *-ous*) < *sulphur* sulfur] **—sul|fu′re|ous|ly,** *adv.* **—sul|fu′re|ous|ness,** *n.*

**sul|fu|ret** (sul′fyə ret), *v.,* **-ret|ed, -ret|ing** or (*especially British*) **-ret|ted, -ret|ting,** *n.* **—*v.t.*** to combine or treat with sulfur. [< noun]
**—*n.*** (formerly) a sulfide.
[< New Latin *sulphuretum*]

**sul|fu|ret|ed** or **sul|fu|ret|ted** (sul′fyə ret′id), *adj.* **1** combined or treated with sulfur. **2** containing sulfur or a sulfur compound.

**sul|fu|ric** (sul fyůr′ik), *adj.* **1** of or having to do with sulfur. **2** containing sulfur, especially with a valence of six.

**sulfuric acid,** a heavy, oily, colorless, and very corrosive acid derived from sulfur; oil of vitriol; vitriol. Sulfuric acid is used in making explosives and fertilizers, in refining petroleum, and in many other industrial processes. *Formula:* $H_2SO_4$

**sul|fu|ri|za|tion** (sul′fyər ə zā′shən, -fər-), *n.* the act or process of sulfurizing.

**sul|fu|rize** (sul′fyə rīz, -fə-), *v.t.,* **-rized, -riz|ing.** **1** to cause to combine with, or to be impregnated by, sulfur or a sulfur compound; sulfurate. **2** to fumigate with burning sulfur.

**sul|fur|ous** (sul′fər əs, -fyər-; *in Chemistry, also* sul fyůr′əs), *adj.* **1a** of or having to do with sulfur. **b** containing sulfur, especially with a valence of four. **2** like burning sulfur; fiery. **3** like sulfur in color; sulphurous: *The city, unreal as a mirage in the desert, lay bathed in a sulfurous yellow light* (Edgar Maass). **4** *Figurative.* of or like the fires of hell; hellish. **5** *Figurative.* angry, blasphemous, or profane: *sulfurous language.* **—sul′fur|ous|ly,** *adv.* **—sul′fur|ous|ness,** *n.*

**sulfurous acid,** a colorless acid, consisting of a solution of sulfur dioxide in water, used especially as a bleach and reducing agent. It is known chiefly in the form of its salts, the sulfites. *Formula:* $H_2SO_3$

**sulfur trioxide,** a chemical compound used chiefly as an intermediate in the production of sulfuric acid. *Formula:* $SO_3$

**sul|fur|y** (sul′fər ē), *adj.* of or like sulfur; sulfurous.

**sul|fur|yl** (sul′fər əl, -fə rēl; -fyər əl, -fyə rēl), *n. Chemistry.* a bivalent radical, $-SO_2$, occurring in sulfuric acid; sulfonyl.

**sulfuryl chloride,** a colorless, pungent liquid compound, used as a chlorinating agent, as a solvent, and in plastics. *Formula:* $SO_2Cl_2$

**sulk** (sulk), *v., n.* **—*v.i.*** to keep aloof from others in moody silence; indulge in sullen ill humor; be sulky: *The bride sat crying in one corner of the carriage and the bridegroom sulked in the other* (Samuel Butler). **SYN:** mope.
**—*n.*** a sulking; fit of sulking. **SYN:** sullenness.
**the sulks,** ill humor shown by sulking: *That little girl seems to have a fit of the sulks.*
[perhaps back formation < *sulky*[1]] **—sulk′er,** *n.*

**sulk|i|ly** (sul′kə lē), *adv.* in a sulky manner.

**sulk|i|ness** (sul′kē nis), *n.* sulky behavior; sullenness; moroseness.

**sulk|y**[1] (sul′kē), *adj.,* **sulk|i|er, sulk|i|est.** **1** silent because of bad humor; sullen: *She gets sulky and won't play if she can't be leader.* **SYN:** See syn. under **sullen.** **2** showing bad humor: *a sulky silence.* [origin uncertain. Compare Old English *āsolcen* lazy, past participle of *āseolcan* become relaxed, languid.]

***sulk|y**[2] (sul′kē), *n., pl.* **sulk|ies,** *adj.* **—*n.*** a very light carriage with two wheels, sometimes without a body, for one person. A sulky is pulled by one horse, and is now commonly used in trotting races.
**—*adj.*** (of farming equipment) having a seat for the driver: *a sulky plow.*
[probably related to *sulky*[1] (because the rider is alone)]

***sulky**[2]

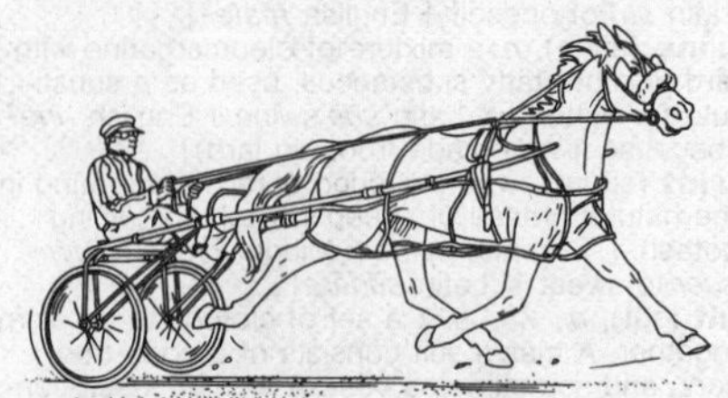

**sulky racing,** = harness racing.

**sul|la** (sul′ə), *n.* a plant of the pea family, with flowers resembling those of the red clover, cultivated for forage in Mediterranean countries. [< Spanish *sulla*]

**sul|lage** (sul′ij), *n.* **1** sewage: *The people themselves feel the misery of having no channels to remove sullage away clear from every habitation* (Florence Nightingale). **2** the silt washed down and deposited by a stream or flood. **3** (in founding) the scoria which rises to the surface of the molten metal in the ladle. **4** *Obsolete.* filth. [earlier *sollage,* perhaps < unrecorded Anglo-French *souillage* < Old French *souiller;* see etym. under **soil**[2]. Compare etym. under **soilage.**]

**sul|len** (sul′ən), *adj.* **1** silent because of bad humor or anger: *a sullen disposition. That boy becomes sullen if he is punished. The sullen child refused to answer my questions.* **2** showing bad humor or anger: *a sullen silence.* **SYN:** surly. **3** gloomy or dismal: *a gray and sullen sea. The sullen skies threatened rain.* **4** of a deep, dull, or mournful tone: *sullen thunder.* **5** *Obsolete.* baleful; malignant. [earlier, also *sollen,* Middle English *soleine* < unrecorded Anglo-French *solain,* and *solein* < Vulgar Latin *sōlānus* < Latin *sōlus* alone] **—sul′len|ly,** *adv.* **—sul′len|ness,** *n.*
**—*Syn.*** **1 Sullen, sulky, glum** mean silent and bad-humored or gloomy. **Sullen** suggests an ill-natured refusal to talk or be cooperative because of anger or bad humor or disposition: *It is disagreeable to have to sit at the breakfast table with a sullen person.* **Sulky** suggests moody or childish sullenness because of resentment or discontent: *Dogs sometimes become sulky because they are jealous.* **Glum** emphasizes silence and low spirits because of some depressing condition or happening: *He is glum about the results of the election.*

**sul|lens** (sul′ənz), *n.pl.* sullen humor: *a fit of sullens.*

**sul|ly** (sul′ē), *v.,* **-lied, -ly|ing,** *n., pl.* **-lies.** **—*v.t.*** to soil, stain, or tarnish: *False rumors sullied the lawyer's reputation. Smog sullied the usually attractive skyline of the city. When he had washed his face, which was a little sullied by his fall …* (Richard Graves). **—*v.i.*** *Obsolete.* to become sullied: *Look you Francis, your white … doublet will sully* (Shakespeare).
**—*n.*** *Obsolete.* a stain or blemish: *Without the least sully in their virtue …* (Henry Fielding).
[probably < Old French *souiller;* see etym. under **soil**[2]]

**sul|pha** (sul′fə), *adj., n.* = sulfa.

**sul|pha|nil|a|mide** (sul′fə nil′ə mīd, -mid), *n.* = sulfanilamide.

**sul|phate** (sul′fāt), *n., v.t., v.i.,* **-phat|ed, -phat|ing.** = sulfate.

**sul|phide** (sul′fīd), *n.* = sulfide.

**sul|phite** (sul′fīt), *n.* = sulfite.

**sul|phur** (sul′fər), *n., adj., v.* **—*n.*** **1** = sulfur. **2** any one of a family of yellow or orange butterflies, such as the common sulphur of the eastern and Midwestern United States. **3** a pale yellow with a tinge of green; lemon; sulfur.
**—*adj.*** pale-yellow with a tinge of green; lemon; sulfur.
**—*v.t.*** = sulfur.

**sul|phu|rate** (sul′fə rāt, -fyə-), *v.t.,* **-rat|ed, -rat|ing,** *adj.* = sulfurate.

**sul|phur-bot|tom** (sul′fər bot′əm), *n.* a whalebone whale, sometimes growing to over 100 feet in length, the largest of all known living creatures, blue-gray with yellowish underparts; blue whale. It lives in the Antarctic and northern Atlantic and Pacific oceans. Also, **sulfur-bottom.**

**sul|phu|re|ous** (sul fyu̇r′ē əs), *adj.* **1** = sulfureous (def. 1-3). **2** of the color of sulphur. —**sul|phu′re|ous|ly**, *adv.* —**sul|phu′re|ous|ness**, *n.*

**sul|phu|ric** (sul fyu̇r′ik), *adj.* = sulfuric.

**sul|phur|ous** (sul′fər əs, -fyər-; *in Chemistry, also* sul fyu̇r′əs), *adj.* = sulfurous (def. 1-3, 5). —**sul′phur|ous|ly**, *adv.*

**sulphur whale**, = sulphur-bottom.

**Sul|pi|cian** (sul pish′ən), *n.* a priest of a Roman Catholic order established about 1645 to train young men for holy orders. [< French *sulpicien* < St. *Sulpice,* the parish of the founder + *-en* -an]

**sul|tan** (sul′tən), *n.* **1** the ruler of any one of certain Mohammedan countries. Turkey was ruled by a sultain until 1922. **2** an absolute ruler. **3** = sultana (def. 4). [< Arabic *sulṭān* ruler; power]

**Sul|tan** (sul′tən), *n.* a breed of chicken having white plumage and characterized especially by stiff quill feathers extending backward from the thighs.

**sul|tan|a** (sul tan′ə, -tä′nə), *n.* **1** the wife or concubine of a sultan. **2** the mother, sister, or daughter of a sultan. **3** a small, seedless raisin produced in the neighborhood of Smyrna (Izmir). **4** any one of various gallinules having brilliant plumage, especially the purple gallinule. [< Italian *sultana,* feminine of *sultano* sultan < Arabic *sulṭān*]

**sultana bird**, = sultana (def. 4).

**sul|tan|ate** (sul′tə nāt), *n.* **1** the position, authority, or period of rule of a sultan. **2** the territory ruled over by a sultan: *Egypt was now a Turkish sultanate* (H. G. Wells).

**sul|tan|ess** (sul′tə nis), *n.* = sultana (def. 1, 2).

**sul|tan|ic** (sul tan′ik), *adj.* **1** of or having to do with a sultan. **2** suggestive of a sultan: *sultanic luxury.*

**sul|tan|ship** (sul′tən ship), *n.* the office or dignity of a sultan.

**sul|tri|ly** (sul′trə lē), *adv.* in a sultry manner; oppressively.

**sul|tri|ness** (sul′trē nis), *n.* sultry condition or quality; heat with moist or close air.

**sul|try** (sul′trē), *adj.,* **-tri|er, -tri|est. 1** hot, close, and moist: *We expect some sultry weather during July.* **SYN**: muggy. **2** hot or fiery; glowing with heat: *beneath the burning sky, And sultry sun ...* (John Dryden). **SYN**: sweltering. **3** *Figurative.* characterized by the heat of passion, lust, or anger: *a sultry glance.*
[< obsolete *sulter* swelter + *-y*[1]. See related etym. at **swelt.**]

**su|lu** (sü′lü), *n.* a sarong worn by men of the Fiji Islands: *Sulus for men are often handsome woolen wrap-arounds, and the police wear white ones with saw-tooth edges* (Saturday Review). [< Fijian *sulu*]

**Su|lu** (sü′lü), *n.* **1** a member of a native Moslem tribe inhabiting the Sulu Archipelago, a group of islands in the southwestern part of the Philippine Islands. **2** the Malayan language of these people. [< Malay *Sulu′*]

**Su|lu|an** (sü′lü ən), *adj., n.* —*adj.* of or having to do with the natives, inhabitants, or language of the Sulu Archipelago.
—*n.* = Sulu.

**sum** (sum), *n., v.,* **summed, sum|ming.** —*n.* **1** an amount of money: *He paid the sum of $7 for a new hat.* **2** the number or quantity obtained by adding two or more numbers or quantities together; total: *The sum of 2 and 3 and 4 is 9.* **SYN**: See syn. under **number. 3** a series of two or more numbers or quantities to be added. **4** a problem in arithmetic: *He can do easy sums in his head, but he has to use pencil and paper for hard ones.* **5** the whole amount; total amount; aggregate; totality: *an immense sum of misery* (Macaulay). *To win the prize seemed to her the sum of happiness.* **6** *Figurative.* the essence or gist of anything; pith: *That the Sermon on the Mount contains the sum and substance of Christianity ...* (Frederick W. Robertson). **7** *Mathematics.* union (def. 9). **8** *Archaic.* a summary; epitome.
—*v.t.* **1** to find the total number or amount of: *Nature's true-born child, who sums his years* (*like me*) *with no arithmetic but tears* (Henry King). **2** to summarize; sum up: *The phase ... may be summed in a word—Penitence* (Charles Reade).
—*v.i.* to amount (to): *How can the nine digits be placed in a square array to form eight intersecting sets of three digits ..., each summming to the same number?* (Scientific American).
**in sum, a** in a few words; briefly: *My meaning, in sum, is, that whereas ...* (F. Hall). **b** to conclude in a few words; in short: *In sum, I seriously protest, that no man ever had ... a greater veneration for Chaucer than myself* (John Dryden).
**sum up, a** to reckon, count, or total: *to sum up the advantages of the offer.* **b** to express or tell briefly; summarize; epitomize: *to sum up the week's work. Sum up the main points of the lesson in three sentences.* **c** to review the chief points of: *The judge summed up the evidence for the jury.* **d** *Figurative.* to form an estimate of the qualities or character of; size up: *They were not obviously staring, but he knew that they were rapidly summing him up* (Hugh Walpole). **e** to bring or collect into a whole or in a small compass: *to sum up strength to deal a final blow.*
[Middle English *summe,* and *somme* < Anglo-French *summe* < Latin *summa,* noun use of adjective, feminine of *summus* highest]

**sum-**, *prefix.* the form of **sub-** before *m,* as in *summon.*

**su|mac** or **su|mach** (sü′mak, shü′-), *n.* **1** a shrub or small tree having divided leaves that turn scarlet in the autumn and long clusters of small, red or white, one-seeded fruit. In some species, such as the poison sumac and poison ivy, the foliage is poisonous to the touch. See picture under **cashew family. 2** the dried and powdered leaves and shoots of certain species, used in tanning and dyeing. **3** the wood of any of these plants. [< Old French *sumac,* or Medieval Latin *sumach* < Arabic *summāq*]
▶ The (sh) of the second pronunciation arose during the Early Modern period, as in *sure* and *sugar.* Today the more common educated pronunciation appears to be the first, where the (s) has been restored, as in *assume, ensue, suit,* and the like, which were also at one time often pronounced with (sh).

**sumac family**, = cashew family.

**Su|ma|tran** (su̇ mä′trən), *adj., n.* —*adj.* of or having to do with the island of Sumatra, in western Indonesia, its people, or its language.
—*n.* **1** a native or inhabitant of Sumatra. **2** the Indonesian language of the Sumatrans.

**sum|bul** (sum′bəl, su̇m′bu̇l), *n.* **1** any one of several aromatic or medicinal plants, such as the East Indian spikenard. **2** the root of such a plant. **3** a root, used as a nerve tonic and antispasmodic. [< French *sumbul* < Arabic *sunbul*]

**Su|me|ri|an** or **Su|mi|ri|an** (sü mir′ē ən), *adj., n.* —*adj.* of or having to do with the people of Sumer, an ancient region in the lower part of Mesopotamia (now Iraq), or their language.
—*n.* **1** a person who was born or lived in Sumer: *In Dr. Gelb's view the Sumerians, that fabled people of Mesopotamia who for at least 1,500 years dominated the culture of the Near East, took the first step toward a "fully developed writing"* (Scientific American). **2** a non-Semitic language of Sumer, recorded in cuneiform inscriptions.

**su|mi** (sü′mē), *n.* a black stick made of carbon and glue, dipped in water for writing and drawing by Japanese artists. [< Japanese *sumi*]

**sum|less** (sum′lis), *adj. Archaic.* that cannot be summed or reckoned up; incalculable: *sumless treasures.*

**sum|ma** (su̇m′ə, sum′-), *n., pl.* **-mas, -mae** (-mē). a summary treatise dealing with a particular field or subject, or with the whole of human knowledge: *Although they acknowledged that God was ultimately unknowable, the medieval scholastics devoted page after learned page of their summas to discussions of the divine attributes* (Time). [< Latin *summa;* see etym. under **sum**]

**sum|ma|bil|i|ty** (sum′ə bil′ə tē), *n.* the condition of being mathematically summable.

**sum|ma|ble** (sum′ə bəl), *adj.* that can be summed.

**sum|ma cum lau|de** (su̇m′ə ku̇m lou′də; sum′ə kum lô′dē), with the highest distinction. These words are added to the diploma of a student who has done unusually good academic work. [< New Latin *summa cum laude* < Latin *summā,* feminine, ablative of *summus* highest, *cum* with, *laude,* ablative of *laus* praise]

**sum|mand** (sum′and, sum and′), *n.* one of two or more numbers or quantities to be added together. [< Medieval Latin *summandus,* gerundive of *summare* to sum]

**sum|ma|ri|ly** (sum′ər ə lē, sə mer′-), *adv.* in a summary manner; without delay; briefly.

**sum|ma|ri|ness** (sum′ər ē nis), *n.* the character of being summary.

**sum|ma|rise** (sum′ə rīz), *v.t., v.i.,* **-rised, -ris|ing.** *Especially British.* summarize.

**sum|ma|rist** (sum′ər ist), *n.* the maker of a summary.

**sum|ma|ri|za|tion** (sum′ər ə zā′shən), *n.* **1** the act or process of summarizing. **2** an instance of summarizing.

**sum|ma|rize** (sum′ə rīz), *v.t., v.i.,* **-rized, -riz|ing.** to make a summary of; give only the main points of; express briefly; sum up: *to summarize the story of a book. It may be too early as yet to summarize any results* (London Times).

**sum|ma|riz|er** (sum′ə rī′zər), *n.* = summarist.

**sum|ma|ry** (sum′ər ē), *n., pl.* **-ries,** *adj.* —*n.* a brief statement giving the main points or substance of a matter; epitome; abstract; abridgment: *This history book has a summary at the end of each chapter.* [< Latin *summārium* < *summa* sum (in genitive, main points)]
—*adj.* **1** containing or comprising the chief points; concise and comprehensive; brief; short: *a summary account.* **SYN**: terse, succinct. **2** direct and prompt; without delay: *The soldier took summary vengeance by killing both his enemies. He cleared the table by the summary process of tilting everything upon it into the fireplace* (Dickens). **3** carried out or determined rapidly, with the omission of certain formalities usually required by law: *summary proceedings. The governor took summary action to aid the flood victims.*
[< Medieval Latin *summarius* < Latin *summa* sum]
—*Syn. n.* **Summary, digest** mean a brief presentation of facts or subject matter. **Summary** applies to a brief statement, often in different words, giving only the main points of an article, chapter, book, speech, subject, proposed plan, or the like: *Give a summary of today's lesson.* **Digest** applies to a shortened form, as of a book or article, leaving out less important details but keeping the original order, emphasis, and words: *Some magazines contain digests of books.*

**sum|mate** (sum′āt), *v.t., v.i.,* **-mat|ed, -mat|ing.** to add; sum; find the total of.

**sum|ma|tion** (su mā′shən), *n.* **1** the process of finding the sum or total; addition: *the ... summation of a grotesque assembly of faults* (H. G. Wells). **2** the total. **SYN**: aggregate. **3** *Law.* the final presentation of facts and arguments by the counsel for each side.

**sum|ma|tion|al** (su mā′shə nəl), *adj.* produced or expressed by summation or addition.

**summation sign**, *Mathematics.* the Greek capital letter sigma, used to denote the sum of a series of quantities.

**sum|ma|tive** (sum′ə tiv), *adj.* involving summation or addition; additive.

**sum|mer**[1] (sum′ər), *n., adj., v.* —*n.* **1** the warmest season of the year; season of the year between spring and autumn: *Shall I compare thee to a summer's day? Thou art more lovely and more temperate* (Shakespeare). **2** *Figurative.* anything considered like summer in its warmth, full beauty, healthy maturity, or the like: *a young man in the summer of his life. But thy eternal summer shall not fade* (Shakespeare). *I only know that summer sang in me A little while, that in me sings no more* (Edna St. Vincent Millay).
—*adj.* **1** of summer; in summer: *a summer night, summer flowers, summer heat.* (*Figurative.*) *Some happy summer isle* (William Morris). **2** used in summer; for summer: *summer clothes, a summer cottage.* **3** held in or during the summer: *a summer job, summer sessions, a summer program, summer theater.*
—*v.i.* to spend the summer: *to summer at the seashore.*
—*v.t.* to keep or feed during the summer; arrange or manage during the summer: *to summer the stock, to summer cattle in the mountains.*
[Old English *sumor*]

**sum|mer**[2] (sum′ər), *n.* **1** a horizontal bearing beam in a building, especially the main beam supporting the girders or joists of a floor (or occasionally the rafters of a roof). **2** a large stone laid over a column in beginning a cross vault. **3** = lintel. [< Anglo-French *sumer,* and *somer,* variant of Old French *somier* (originally) beast of burden < Late Latin *saumārius,* for Latin *sagmārius* pack horse < *sagma* pack saddle < Greek *ságma, -atos* < *sáttein* to pack, stuff]

**summer avalanche**, = ice avalanche.

**summer camp**, a camp for health and recreation, especially for children, open during the summer.

**summer cypress**, an erect, many-branched bushy annual plant of the goosefoot family, grown for its colorful foliage, which turns purplish red in the fall.

**summer fallowing**, the practice in dry regions of plowing land in the summer and planting the next spring.

**summer flounder**, a greenish flounder of the Atlantic coast of North America with white spots on the body and both eyes on the left side of the head.

---

**Pronunciation Key:** hat, āge, cãre, fär; let, ēqual, tėrm; it, īce; hot, ōpen, ôrder; oil, out; cup, pu̇t, rüle; child; long; thin; ᴛʜen; zh, measure; ə represents **a** in about, **e** in taken, **i** in pencil, **o** in lemon, **u** in circus.

**sum|mer|house** (sum′ər hous′), *n.* a building in a park or flower garden to afford shade and shelter from showers in the summer. Summerhouses often have a railing but no walls.

**summer house**, a home for the summer.

**sum|mer|i|ness** (sum′ər ē nis), *n.* summery character.

**sum|mer|less** (sum′ər lis), *adj.* having no summer; without summer weather: *In the high latitudes, in the vicinity of the poles, are the summerless polar regions* (Finch and Trewartha).

**sum|mer|like** (sum′ər līk′), *adj.* resembling summer; summery.

**summer lilac**, = buddleia.

**sum|mer|li|ness** (sum′ər lē nis), *n.* = summeriness.

**sum|mer|ly** (sum′ər lē), *adj.* = summerlike.

**summer oil**, a thick oil for use in automobile engines during hot weather.

**summer resort**, a place in the mountains, on a lake, at the seashore, or other place of recreation, where people go in the summer: *The islands have become summer resorts, and for the most part cottages and metal beach chairs stand where the vineyards once flourished* (New Yorker).

**sum|mer|sault** (sum′ər sôlt), *n., v.i.* = somersault.

**summer sausage**, uncooked sausage that is smoked or dried by air.

**summer savory**, an annual European herb of the mint family much used as a flavoring ingredient in cooking.

**summer school**, a school conducted in the summer to help students make up credits or accelerate their studies toward a degree: *I will have to get some credits in summer school if I wish to teach in September.*

**sum|mer|set** (sum′ər set), *n., v.i.* = somersault.

**summer solstice**, **1** the solstice that occurs about June 21. It is the time in the Northern Hemisphere when the sun is farthest north from the equator. In the Southern Hemisphere this is the winter solstice. **2** the northernmost point of the ecliptic, which the sun reaches at this time. It is now in the constellation Gemini.

**summer squash**, any one of various squashes that ripen quickly and are intended to be eaten while the skins are still tender, such as the crookneck squash or the zucchini.

**summer stock**, **1** a theatrical stock company that performs during the summer: *Many famous actors began their careers as stagehands in summer stock.* **2** the repertory or theater of such a company.

**summer sweet**, a shrub of the eastern United States with alternate, serrate leaves and racemes of fragrant, white or pink flowers.

**summer tanager**, a tanager of the southern United States, the male of which has rosy-red feathers.

**sum|mer|tide** (sum′ər tīd′), *n.* = summertime.

**sum|mer|time** (sum′ər tīm′), *n.* **1** the season of summer; summer. **2** *Figurative.* any period in which energy is greatest or talent most productive: *in the summertime of life.*

**summer time**, *Especially British.* daylight-saving time.

**summer triangle**, a group of three bright stars, Vega, Deneb, and Altair, especially prominent in summer.

**summer wheat**, any wheat of a variety that is planted in the spring, and ripens in the same summer; spring wheat.

**summer White House**, a residence occupied in summer by the President of the United States.

**sum|mer|wood** (sum′ər wu̇d′), *n.* a dark ring or layer of wood formed around a tree each summer, composed of relatively small, compact cells with thick walls; latewood.

**sum|mer|y** (sum′ər ē), *adj.*, **-mer|i|er, -mer|i|est. 1** of summer. **SYN**: estival. **2** for summer: *a summery dress.* **3** like summer: *a summery day.*

**sum|ming-up** (sum′ing up′), *n., pl.* **sum|mings-up. 1** the act or process of summarizing: *... an opportunity for philosophical reflection or summing-up* (Scientific American). **2** a summary: *It is read in the Netherlands as a summing-up of the experiences of so many Hollanders* (London Times). **3** a recapitulation of the chief points of the evidence to a jury before it retires to consider a verdict: *The Judge, resuming his summing-up yesterday, said ...* (Sunday Times). **4** *Figurative.* an estimate of the qualities or character of a person or thing; size-up: *The profile of President Lowell is the fairest, saltiest summing-up I have ever read* (Atlantic).

**sum|mist** (sum′ist), *n.* a medieval writer of a summary or compendium, especially of theology, such as Saint Thomas Aquinas. [< Medieval Latin *summista* < Latin *summa* sum; see etym. under **sum**]

**sum|mit** (sum′it), *n., adj.* —*n.* **1** the highest point, as of a mountain or hill; topmost peak or ridge; top: *We could see the summit of a mountain twenty miles away.* **SYN**: pinnacle, zenith. See syn. under **top**. **2** *Figurative.* **a** the topmost part of anything; apex: *The summits of emotion can only be reached at rare intervals* (W. Somerset Maugham). *It is sometimes necessary at the summit of authority ... to remain calm when others panic* (Sir Winston Churchill). **SYN**: pinnacle, zenith. See syn. under **top**. **b** the highest point of ambition, hope, skill, energy, or other accomplishment; acme: *The summit of her ambition was to be an actress.* **SYN**: pinnacle, zenith. See syn. under **top**. **3** the highest level of authority, especially the leaders of individual governments, as dealing in international affairs. **4** *Informal.* a conference at the highest level; summit meeting: *A Foreign Ministers' Conference ... might be allowed as much as two months to prepare for a "summit"* (Sunday Times).

—*adj.* of or having to do with a summit meeting: *summit talks, summit decisions.*

**at the summit**, at the level of diplomacy involving heads of government; at the highest level: *Fruitful negotiations on East-West tension can be achieved only at the summit* (London Times).

[Middle English *somette* < Old French *somete,* feminine, or *somet,* masculine (diminutive) < *som,* or *sum* summit < Latin *summum,* noun use of adjective, neuter of *summus* highest. Compare etym. under **sum**.]

**sum|mit|al** (sum′ə təl), *adj.* of or having to do with a summit.

**sum|mit|eer** (sum′ə tir′), *n. Informal.* a participant in a summit meeting: *The summiteers signed a series of accords on cooperation in medicine, pollution control, science, and space flights* (Pittsburgh Press).

**sum|mit|less** (sum′it lis), *adj.* having no summit.

**summit meeting** or **conference**, a meeting between heads of governments, especially for the purpose of settling disagreements and lessening international tensions: *All the big European questions were taken up by the "summit" conference at Geneva* (London Times).

**sum|mit|ry** (sum′ə trē), *n. Informal.* **1** the conducting of summit meetings: *He is one of the old hands at Commonwealth summitry, having attended the 1953 conference shortly after succeeding his late father as Prime Minister* (Manchester Guardian). **2** summit meetings.

**sum|mon** (sum′ən), *v.t.* **1** to call with authority; order to come; send for: *to summon men to defend their country. Summon the children to dinner. A telegram summoned him home.* (*Figurative.*) *It is a knell That summons thee to heaven or to hell* (Shakespeare). **SYN**: See syn. under **call**. **2** to call together by authority for action or deliberation; convoke: *to summon a legislative body.* **3** to order or notify formally to appear before a court or judge, especially to answer a charge. **4** to call upon to do something: *The church bells summon people to worship.* **5** to call upon (a fort, army, or other group or installation) to surrender. **6** *Figurative.* to stir to action or effort; call up; arouse: *He summoned his courage and entered the deserted house.* [Middle English *sumunen,* or *somenen* < Anglo-French, Old French *sumun-,* stem of *somondre* < Vulgar Latin *summonere* to call, cite, for Latin *summonēre* hint to < *sub-* underneath + *monēre* warn] —**sum′mon|a|ble**, *adj.*

**sum|mon|er** (sum′ə nər), *n.* **1** a person who summons. **2** (formerly) a petty officer whose duty was to warn persons to appear in court.

**sum|mons** (sum′ənz), *n., pl.* **-mons|es**, *v.* —*n.* **1a** a formal order or notice to appear before a law court or judge, especially to answer a charge. **b** the writ (writ of summons) by which such an order is made: *He received a summons for fast driving.* **2** an urgent call for the presence or attendance of a person; a summoning command, knock, message, or signal: *I hurried in response to my friend's summons for help. Death is a common friend or foe ... And at his summons each must go* (M. J. Barry). **3** an authoritative call to appear at a place named, or to attend to some public duty. **4** a call to do something, especially to surrender.

—*v.t. Informal.* to take out a summons against; summon to court: *Say another word and I'll summons you* (Dickens).

[< Anglo-French *somonse* < *somondre;* see etym. under **summon**]

**sum|mum bo|num** (sum′əm bō′nəm), *Latin.* the highest or ultimate good: *Bentham, the founder of Utilitarianism, ... held as the summum bonum the greatest good for the greatest number and believed that there was no limit to the benefits a good education could confer* (Scientific American).

**sum|mum ge|nus** (sum′əm jē′nəs), *Latin.* the highest genus or class.

**sum|mum jus** (sum′əm jus′), *Latin.* the strictest law or legal right.

✱**su|mo** (sü′mō), *n.* a Japanese form of wrestling with fewer throws than in jujitsu. [< Japanese *sumō* wrestling]

✱**sumo**

**su|mo|ist** (sü′mō ist), *n.* a person who practices sumo: *Kirinji, if you follow the theory, was not lucky to win, he was the superior sumoist* (Manchester Guardian Weekly).

**sump** (sump), *n.* **1** a pit or reservoir for collecting water, sewage, factory wastes, or other liquid, such as a cesspool or septic tank: *We have instituted a conservation program of over 400 sumps which are turning back millions of gallons of rain water into the ground, instead of letting it run off into the Atlantic Ocean or Long Island Sound* (New York Times). **2** a reservoir for oil or other lubricating fluid at the lowest point in a lubricating system, especially that beneath the crankcase of an internal-combustion engine. **3** the bottom of a mine shaft, where water collects and from which it is pumped. **4** a shaft or tunnel excavated in front of the main shaft or tunnel of a mine or boring. [< Middle Low German *sump,* or Middle Dutch *somp.* Compare etym. under **swamp**.]

**sum|pi|tan** (sum′pə tən), *n.* a kind of blowgun used by the Dyaks and Malays of Borneo for shooting darts, which are often poisoned. [< Malay *sumpītan* < *sumpit* blowpipe; (originally) narrow]

**sump pump**, a pump used to remove liquid, especially water that collects in a cellar sump.

**sump|si|mus** (sump′sə məs), *n.* a correct expression for replacing an incorrect but popular one. [< Latin *sumpsimus* (literally) we have taken. Compare etym. under **mumpsimus**.]

**sump|ter** (sump′tər), *n., adj.* —*n.* a horse or mule for carrying baggage; pack animal.

—*adj.* for carrying baggage: *Camels, mules, and horses are sumpter animals.*

[Middle English *sumter* < Old French *sommetier* < Vulgar Latin *sagmatārius* < Latin *sagma.* See related etym. at **summer²**.]

**sump|tu|ar|y** (sump′chu̇ er′ē), *adj.* having to do with the spending of money; regulating expenses, especially to control extravagance or waste. A law prohibiting any family from owning more than one car would be a sumptuary law. [< Latin *sūmptuārius* < *sūmptus, -ūs* expense < *sūmere* spend, buy; (originally) take]

**sump|tu|os|i|ty** (sump′chu̇ os′ə tē), *n.* expensiveness; costliness.

**sump|tu|ous** (sump′chu̇ əs), *adj.* **1** costly; magnificent; rich: *sumptuous clothes. The king gave a sumptuous banquet.* **SYN**: luxurious, lavish. **2** splendid or magnificent in appearance: *She spoke and turn'd her sumptuous head* (Tennyson).

[< Middle French, Old French *somptueux* (with English *-ous*), learned borrowing from Latin *sūmptuōsus* < *sūmptus, -ūs* expense; see etym. under **sumptuary**] —**sump′tu|ous|ly**, *adv.* —**sump′tu|ous|ness**, *n.*

**sump|weed** (sump′wēd′), *n.* = marshelder.

**sum total**, the total amount; aggregate; totality; sum: *The sum total of our expenses on the trip came to $55.30.*

**sum-up** (sum′up′), *n.* a summary; estimate; summing-up: *The sum-up: You can expect a different, more positive U.S. program for dealing with Russia* (Newsweek).

✱**sun** (sun), *n., v.,* **sunned, sun|ning.** —*n.* **1** the brightest heavenly body in the sky; star around which the earth and other planets revolve and which supplies them with light and heat. The sun is a glowing ball of hot gases, chiefly hydrogen and helium. Its mean distance from the earth is slightly less than 93,000,000 miles (150,000,000 km.). Its mean diameter is about 865,000 miles (1,392,000 km), its volume about 1,300,000 times that of the earth, and its mass about 333,000 times that of the earth. *... the high temperature of the sun, which is more than sufficient to vaporize all known substances* (George Hale). See picture on opposite page. **2** the sun, as with reference to its position in the sky, its aspect, visibility, heat, or other attribute: *a tropical sun. The* *clouds that gather round the setting sun ...* (Wordsworth). **3** the light and warmth of the sun; sunshine; sunlight: *The cat likes to sit in the sun.* **4** any heavenly body like the sun. Many stars are suns and have their worlds that travel around them. **5** *Figurative: Knowledge ... is the great sun in the firmament* (Daniel Webster). *Sun of my soul, thou Saviour dear* (John Keble). *But, soft! what light through yonder window breaks? It is the east, and Juliet is the sun* (Shakespeare). **6** a figure, image, or ornament made to resemble the sun, such as a heraldic bearing, usually charged with human features, or a kind of circular firework. **7** *Archaic.* a day, as being determined by the rising of the sun. **8** *Archaic.* a year; revolution of the earth around the sun: *Vile it were For some three suns to store and hoard myself* (Tennyson). *The thoughts of men are widen'd with the process of the suns* (Tennyson).

*—v.t.* **1** to expose to the sun's rays to warm, dry, or air; put in the light and warmth of the sun: *The swimmers sunned themselves on the beach.* **2** to bring or get into a specified condition by exposure to the sun.

*—v.i.* to expose oneself to the sun's rays; bask in the sun: *We were sunning on the pier* (Arthur S. M. Hutchinson).

**against the sun**, in the direction contrary to the apparent movement of the sun: *When the wind shifts against the sun, trust it not, for back it will run* (Frederick Bedford).

**from sun to sun**, from sunrise to sunset: *Man's work's from sun to sun, Woman's work's never done* (old rhyme).

**under the sun**, on earth; in the world: *There is no new thing under the sun* (Ecclesiastes 1:9). *... Speakers' Corner in Hyde Park, where anyone gets up on a soapbox and delivers opinions on anything under the sun* (Maclean's).

**with the sun**, in the direction of the apparent movement of the sun: *The starborad cable should be bitted with the sun, and the port cable against the sun* (H. Stuart).

[Old English *sunne*] —**sun′like′**, *adj.*

**Sun.**, Sunday.

**Sun|a|pee trout** (sun′ə pē), a trout related to the arctic char and the European char, found especially in Sunapee Lake, New Hampshire, and Flood Pond, Maine, and noted for its brilliant coloring.

**sun|back** (sun′bak′), *adj.* (of a garment) cut low in the back; allowing exposure of the back to the sun: *Printed voiles and dotted Swiss cotton sleeveless and sunback dresses are particularly strong sellers* (New York Times).

**sun-baked** (sun′bākt′), *adj.* **1** baked by exposure to the sun, as bricks or pottery. **2** excessively heated by the sun; dried up, parched, or hardened by heat of the sun: *the sun-baked earth.*

**sun bath**, **1** the exposure of the body to the direct rays of the sun; basking in the sun. **2** the exposure of the body to a sun lamp.

**sun|bathe** (sun′bāᴛʜ′), *v.i.*, **-bathed**, **-bath|ing.** to expose oneself to the sun's ray or to a sun lamp: *You will sunbathe on golden sands beside coral seas* (New Yorker). —**sun′bath′er**, *n.*

**sun|beam** (sun′bēm′), *n.* a ray of sunlight: *A sunbeam brightened the child's hair to gold.*

**sun bear**, a small bear of southern Asia, black with white or yellowish markings on the chest; Malayan bear. See picture under **bear**[1].

**Sun|belt** or **sun|belt** (sun′belt′), *n. U.S.* the southern rim of the United States, extending from Virginia to southern California: *Every city in the Sunbelt, from Richmond to Los Angeles, has some transplanted Yankees* (Roy Reed). *... the nation's fastest-growing region, the Sunbelt* (New York Times).

**sun|ber|ry** (sun′ber′ē, -bər-), *n., pl.* **-ries. 1** the edible berry of a cultivated variety of the black nightshade. **2** the plant bearing this fruit.

**sun|bird** (sun′bėrd′), *n.* **1** any one of a family of small birds with brilliant and variegated plumage, resembling hummingbirds, found in tropical and subtopical regions of Africa, Asia, and Australia. **2** = sun bittern.

**sun bittern**, a long-legged, long-necked, tropical American bird, related to the cranes and rails.

**sun block**, a chemical substance that prevents sunburn and most suntanning, used especially on sensitive parts of the body such as the eyelids and nose: *Then there is ... a sunscreen, less protective than a sun block, for the body* (Angela Taylor).

**sun|bon|net** (sun′bon′it), *n.* a large bonnet that shades the face and neck from the sun.

**sun|bon|net|ed** (sun′bon′ə tid), *adj.* wearing a sunbonnet: *a sunbonneted frontierswoman.*

**sun|bow** (sun′bō′), *n. Archaic.* an arch of prismatic colors like a rainbow, formed by refraction of sunlight in spray or vapor: *The sunbow's rays still arch The torrent with the many hues of heaven* (Bryon).

**sun|break** (sun′brāk′), *n.* **1** a burst of sunshine; sunburst. **2** = sunrise.

**sun|break|er** (sun′brā′kər), *n.* a louvered structure of wood or other material over a window or other opening to keep out direct sunlight, especially during the summer.

**sun|burn** (sun′bėrn′), *n., v.,* **-burned** or **-burnt**, **-burn|ing.** *—n.* **1** a burning condition of the skin caused by the sun's rays or by a sun lamp. A sunburn is often red and painful. *Bad sunburns often cause freckles.* **2** the color of red or tan resulting from sunburn.

*—v.i.* **1** to burn the skin by the sun's rays. **2** to become burned by the sun: *Her skin sunburns very quickly.* *—v.t.* **1** to affect with sunburn: *He is sunburned from a day on the beach.* **2** to burn (the skin) by exposure to the sun.

**sun|burned** (sun′bėrnd′), *adj., v.* *—adj.* burned, scorched, or browned by the sun; tanned: *sunburned grass.* *—v.* a past tense and a past participle of **sunburn**.

**sun|burnt** (sun′bėrnt′), *v.* sunburned; a past tense and a past participle of **sunburn**.

**sun|burst** (sun′bėrst′), *n.* **1** a sudden shining of the sun through a break in clouds: *a dazzling sunburst.* **2** a brooch or other piece of jewelry with jewels arranged to resemble the sun with its rays. **3** *Figurative.* anything resembling or suggesting a bursting forth of the sun: *The villas ... support cornices that are sunbursts of frilly lattice* (Russell Lynes). *The orchestra opens into a sunburst of orchestral sound* (Harper's).

**sun clock**, **1** = sundial. **2** a clock which shows solar time.

**sun compass**, a compass that uses the sun to indicate true north, formerly used in air navigation.

**sun-cured** (sun′kyůrd′), *adj.* dried and prepared by direct exposure to sunlight: *Farms producing both fire-cured Virginia tobacco and sun-cured Virginia tobacco* (Wall Street Journal).

**Sund.**, Sunday.

**sun|dae** (sun′dē), *n.* a dish of ice cream served with syrup, and, often, crushed fruits, nuts, and whipped cream over it. [American English; origin uncertain; probably < *Sunday* (because it was originally sold on this day only)]

**sun dance**, a religious ceremony in honor of the sun, performed by North American Plains Indians at the summer solstice.

**Sun|da|nese** (sun′də nēz′, -nēs′), *adj., n., pl.* **-nese.** *—adj.* of western Java, its people, or their language.

*—n.* **1** a native of western Java. **2** the Malayo-Polynesian language spoken in western Java.

**Sun|day** (sun′dē, -dā), *n., adj.* *—n.* **1** the first day of the week. *Abbr:* Sun. **2** the day of rest and worship for most Christians; the Christian Sabbath.

*—adj.* **1** of, taking place on, or characteristic of Sunday: *a Sunday concert, a Sunday picnic.* **2** not everyday or regular; off-and-on; occasional: *a Sunday driver, Sunday painters.*

[Old English *sunnandæg,* ultimately translation of Latin *diēs sōlis* day of the sun, translation of Late Greek *hēméra hēlíou*]

► **Sunday, Sabbath** are not true synonyms. **Sunday** is the name of the first day of the week, which is generally observed among Christians as a day of worship and rest from ordinary business. **Sabbath**, literally meaning a time of rest from work, applies to the seventh day of the week (Saturday) among the Jews and some Christians. But it is commonly applied to Sunday in the religious sense of a day for abstaining from work or activity of any kind except religious: *Some keep the Sabbath going to church—I keep it staying at home* (Emily Dickinson).

**Sunday best**, *Informal.* best clothes: *O, he was in his Sunday best!* (Robert Southey).

**Sun|day-go-to-meet|ing** (sun′dē gō′tə mē′ting), *adj. Informal or Dialect.* suitable for use in attending church; best and most presentable: *Sunday-go-to-meeting clothes.*

**Sun|day|ish** (sun′dē ish, -dā-), *adj.* characteristic of or like Sunday: *a Sundayish leisureliness.*

**Sunday punch**, *Slang.* **1** a boxer's most powerful blow: *The champion floored his opponent in the second round with a Sunday punch.* **2** *Figurative: Some feel that if air power and our nuclear weapons are to be the main threat, we are not spending enough on aircraft to give us the "Sunday punch" needed* (New York Times). [probably < *Sunday,* in the informal sense of "best," as in *Sunday best*]

**Sunday school**, **1** a school held on Sunday for teaching religion. **2** its students and teachers. Also, **Sabbath school**.

► The word *school* in **Sunday school** is capitalized only when it is part of a proper name, as in *St. Mark's Sunday School.*

**sun|deck** (sun′dek′), *n.* **1** the upper deck of a passenger ship: *Around the spacious sundeck, 24 aluminum life boats ... glisten in the sun* (Time). **2** a level, terrace, porch, or the like, such as one on, alongside, or above a building or swimming pool for sunbathing and lounging: *Many of the proposed suites will have sundecks with a view over a wide sweep of the East River* (New York Times).

**sun|der** (sun′dər), *v., n.* *—v.t., v.i.* to put asunder; separate; part; sever; split: *Time and distance often sunder friends.* SYN: divide, disjoin, disconnect.

*—n.* **in sunder**, apart; asunder: *Lightning tore the tree in sunder.*

[Old English *syndrian, sundrian* < *sundor* apart. Compare etym. under **asunder.**]

**sun|der|ance** (sun′dər əns), *n.* severance; separation.

**sun|dew** (sun′dü′, -dyü′), *n.* a small herb that grows in bogs and has hairy, sticky leaves with which it captures and absorbs insects; drosera. It belongs to the same family as the Venus's-flytrap. See picture under **carnivorous**.

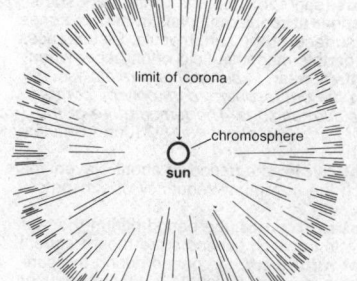

***sun** definition 1

symbol

sun's atmosphere:

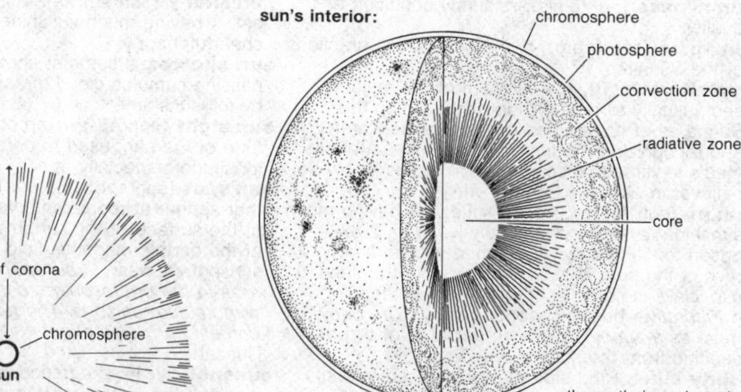


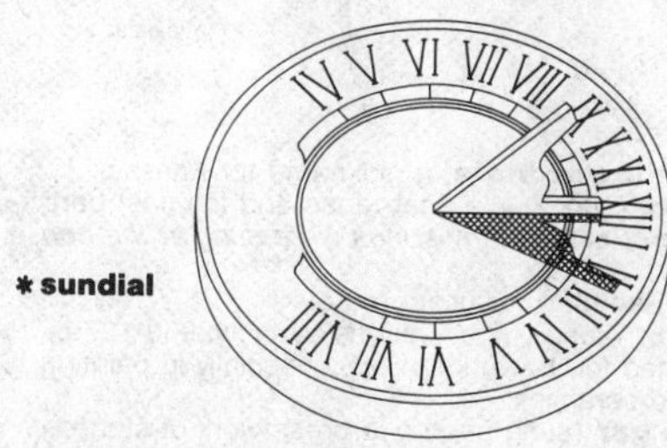


***sundial**

***sun|di|al** (sun′dī′əl), *n.* an instrument for telling the time of day by the position of a shadow cast by the sun; dial.

**Pronunciation Key:** hat, āge, cãre, fär; let, ēqual, tėrm; it, īce; hot, ōpen, ôrder; **oi**l, **ou**t; cup, pu̇t, rüle; **ch**ild; lo**ng**; **th**in; ᴛʜen; **zh**, measure; ə represents **a** in about, **e** in taken, **i** in pencil, **o** in lemon, **u** in circus.

**sun disk**, **1** the disk of the sun. **2** a figure of the sun, used in religious symbolism, especially as an attribute of the Egyptian sun god Ra.
**sun|dog** (sun′dôg′, -dog′), *n.* **1** = parhelion. **2** a small or incomplete rainbow. [origin uncertain]
**sun|down** (sun′doun′), *n.* = sunset (def. 2).
**sun|down|er** (sun′dou′nər), *n.* **1** *Australian Slang.* a tramp who makes a practice of arriving at a farm, ranch, or other establishment, about sunset under the pretense of seeking work, so as to obtain food and a night's lodging. **2** a drink of alcoholic liquor taken at sunset (especially in South Africa): *White settlers of the Salisbury area were comfortably settled on the veranda ... sipping their customary sundowners* (Time). **3** *Western U.S.* a person who lives toward the sundown or west.
**sun|down|ing** (sun′dou′ning), *n.* the practice of a sundowner.
**sun-drenched** (sun′drencht′), *adj.* overspread with sunlight: *the sun-drenched cane fields of Cuba* (Newsweek).
**sun dress**, a sleeveless dress with a low-cut neckline in the front and back.
**sun-dried** (sun′drīd′), *adj.* dried by exposure to the sun: *sun-dried raisins. The Pueblo Indians built with sun-dried bricks.*
**sun|dries** (sun′drēz), *n.pl.* sundry things; items not named; odds and ends: *My expenses included $36.00 for room and board, $9.50 for shirts, $3.25 for books, and $1.60 for sundries.*
**sun|dries|man** (sun′drēz mən), *n., pl.* **-men.** *Especially British.* a dealer in sundries.
**sun|drops** (sun′drops′), *n., pl.* **-drops.** any one of various evening primroses having yellow flowers that bloom by day.
**sun|dry** (sun′drē), *adj.* **1** a number of; several; various: *From sundry hints, I guessed I was to be given a bicycle for my birthday.* **2** composed of diverse elements or items; miscellaneous: *a box of sundry trinkets.*
**all and sundry**. See under **all.**
[Old English *syndrig* separate, special, ultimately related to *sundor* separately, apart]
**sun|fast** (sun′fast′, -fäst′), *adj.* that sunlight will not fade: *sunfast material for a dress.* SYN: sunproof. [< *sun* + *fast*[1] fixed]
**sun|fish** (sun′fish′), *n., pl.* **-fish|es** or (*collectively*) **-fish.** **1** a large fish having tough flesh and a short, deep, compressed body, sometimes growing as large as 11 feet long. Sunfish live in tropical or temperate seas. **2** a small freshwater fish of North America, found especially in lakes and ponds, and often used for food. Sunfish are related to perch. **3** any other related fish.
***sun|flow|er** (sun′flou′ər), *n.* **1** a tall plant having yellow or reddish flowers with yellow, purplish, or brown centers. Sunflowers produce seeds which are used as food for stock and which yield an edible oil. The common yellow-and-brown sunflower is the state flower of Kansas. **2** any one of a genus of plants of the composite family to which the sunflower belongs.

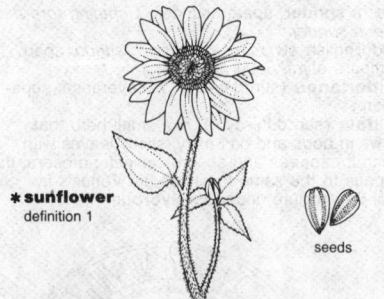

***sunflower**
definition 1

seeds

**Sunflower State**, a nickname for Kansas.
**sung** (sung), *v.* a past tense and the past participle of **sing:** *Many songs were sung at the concert.*
▶ See **sing** for usage note.
**Sung** (sùng), *n.* a Chinese dynasty, 960-1279, noted for its works of art, especially in painting and ceramics.
**sun|gar** (sung′gər), *n.* a breastwork of stone. Also, **sangar.** [< Hindustani *sángar*]
**sun gear**, the central gear around which the planetary gears revolve: *For reverse ... the front clutch is released and the rear clutch engaged so that the large sun gear is now connected to the turbine* (Jud Purvis). See picture under **planetary.**
**sun|glass** (sun′glas′, -gläs′), *n.* a lens for concentrating the rays of the sun; burning glass.
**sun|glass|es** (sun′glas′iz, -gläs′-), *n.pl.* eyeglasses to protect the eyes from the glare of the sun. They are usually made with colored lenses.
**sun|glow** (sun′glō′), *n.* **1** the glow of the sun. **2** a diffused, hazy light sometimes visible before sunrise or after sunset, due to fine, solid particles in the atmosphere.
**Sung Mass**, = missa cantata.
**sun god**, or **sun-god** (sun′god′), *n.* a god representing the sun. Many different peoples have worshiped sun gods. Helios, Apollo, Sol, and Ra were sun gods.
**sun|graz|er** (sun′grā′zər), *n.* a comet that comes very near to the sun: *During the past 100 or 150 years, about seven of these sungrazers have been spotted, some of which broke into pieces as they whirled back into space* (Science News Letter).
**sun-grebe** (sun′grēb′), *n.* a finfoot of Africa or South America, having feet like a grebe's.
**sun hat**, a broad-brimmed hat worn to protect the head from the sun.
**sun helmet**, a helmet worn to protect the head from the sun; pith helmet; topi.
**sun hemp**, = sunn.
**sunk** (sungk), *v.* a past tense and a past participle of **sink:** *The ship had sunk to the bottom.*
**sunk|en** (sung′kən), *adj., v.* —*adj.* **1** that has sunk in water: *a sunken ship.* **2** submerged; under water: *a sunken rock.* **3** situated below the general level: *a sunken living room, a sunken garden.* **4** fallen in; hollow: *sunken eyes, sunken cheeks.*
—*v.* a past participle of **sink.**
▶ **Sunken** is now used chiefly as an adjective.
**sun|ket** (sung′kit, sùng′-), *n. Scottish.* **1** a dainty; tidbit. **2** something, especially something to eat. [probably < Scottish *sumquhat* somewhat]
**sunk fence**, = ha-ha.
**sun|kissed** (sun′kist′), *adj.* **1** that has been exposed to sunshine: *Harvesters take the sun-kissed grapes into the lagares or wine presses to extract the juice* (New Yorker). **2** sunshiny: (*Figurative.*) *a sunkissed production of "The Boys from Syracuse"* (New York Times).
**sun lamp**, or **sun|lamp** (sun′lamp′), *n.* **1** a lamp for producing ultraviolet rays similar to those in sunlight, used for therapeutic treatments, as for some skin diseases. **2** a large lamp used in motion-picture studios which reflects its light by means of parabolic mirrors.
**sun|less** (sun′lis), *adj.* without sun; without sunlight: *Most flowers will not grow in a sunless place.* SYN: dark, shady.
**sun|let** (sun′lit), *n.* a little sun.
**sun|light** (sun′līt′), *n.* the light of the sun: *Outdoor sunlight is very good for the health.* SYN: sunshine.
**sun|lit** (sun′lit′), *adj.* lighted by the sun.
**sun lounge**, a sunroom; sun parlor.
**sunn** (sun), *n.,* or **sunn hemp**, **1** an East Indian shrub of the pea family, with long, narrow leaves, slender branches, and bright-yellow flowers. **2** its inner bark, from which a hemplike fiber is obtained. **3** the fiber, used for rope, cordage, and bags. [< Hindi *san* < Sanskrit *śaṇa* hemp]
**Sun|na** or **Sun|nah** (sùn′ə), *n.* the traditional part of Moslem law, not directly attributed to Mohammed, but believed to derive from his sayings and actions as recorded by his disciples. As a guide, the Sunna is accepted as being as authoritative as the Koran by the Sunnite or orthodox Moslems but is rejected by the Shiites. [< Arabic *sunna* (literally) form, course, rule]
**Sun|ni** (sùn′ē), *n., pl.* **-ni** or **-nis.** **1** an orthodox Moslem; a Sunnite. **2** the Sunnites as a group: *The Sunni ... compose about 90 per cent of present-day Islam* (Newsweek).
**sun|ni|ly** (sun′ə lē), *adv.* in a sunny manner.
**sun|ni|ness** (sun′ē nis), *n.* sunny condition or quality.
**Sun|nism** (sùn′iz əm), *n.* the beliefs and practices of the Sunnites.
**Sun|nite** (sùn′īt), *n.* a Moslem of the majority sect, usually termed orthodox, accepting the Sunna as of equal importance with the Koran and recognizing the first four caliphs as Mohammed's legitimate successors. [< Arabic *sunnī* a believer in *Sunna* + English *-ite*[1]]
**sun|ny** (sun′ē), *adj.,* **-ni|er, -ni|est.** **1** having much sunshine: *a sunny day, sunny weather.* **2** exposed to, lighted by, or warmed by the direct rays of the sun: *a sunny room.* **3** like the sun, especially in color; bright yellow or golden. **4** *Figurative.* bright; cheerful; happy: *The baby gave us a sunny smile.* SYN: genial. **5** of or proceeding from the sun: *sunny beams.*
**sunny side**, **1** the side that is exposed to sunlight: *the sunny side of the street.* **2** *Figurative.* the pleasant side or aspect of anything: *Then, only looking at the sunny side of things, all was bright* (Edward J. Trelawny).
**on the sunny side of**, younger than; under the age of: *Still on the sunny side of 50 himself,* [*he*] *wants to lower his Cabinet's average age* (London Times).
**sun|ny-side up** (sun′ē sīd′), fried only on one side, so that the egg yolk is on top.
**sun parlor**, a room with many windows to let in sunlight.
**sun porch**, a porch enclosed largely by glass.
**sun-pow|ered** (sun′pou′ərd), *adj.* powered by sunlight or by energy from sunlight.
**sun|proof** (sun′prüf′), *adj.* impervious to or unaffected by the rays of the sun: *These are sunproof curtains; they will not fade.*
**sun|ray** (sun′rā′), *n.* a ray of the sun; sunbeam.
**sun|rise** (sun′rīz′), *n.* **1** the coming up of the sun; first appearance of the sun in the morning. **2** the time when the sun comes up; beginning of day. SYN: daybreak, dawn. **3** the display of light or color in the sky at this time: *The scarlet shafts of sunrise* (Tennyson).
**sun roof**, a section of an automobile roof that can slide open.
**sun|room** (sun′rüm′, -rům′), *n.* a room with many windows to let in sunlight; sun parlor.
**sun|rose** (sun′rōz′), *n.* **1** a plant often grown in rock gardens, having flowers which expand in sunlight; rockrose. **2** the flower of this plant.
**sun|scald** (sun′skôld′), *n.* injury to a plant, such as permanent wilting of the leaves, due to excessive exposure to very bright sunlight.
**sun|screen** (sun′skrēn′), *n.* a chemical substance that screens ultraviolet rays, used in suntan lotions.
**sun|seek|er** (sun′sē′kər), *n.* **1** a person who seeks out places of sunshine and warmth to vacation in: *Sunseekers are beginning to look farther afield than the popular Spanish mainland* (London Times). **2** a photoelectric device in an artificial satellite or manned spacecraft which causes instruments to be oriented toward the sun at all times.
**sun|set** (sun′set′), *n.* **1** the going down of the sun; last appearance of the sun in the evening: *After sunset, the horizon burned and glowed with rich crimson and orange lustre* (Hawthorne). **2** the time when the sun goes down; close of day. SYN: sundown. **3** the display of light and color in the sky at this time: *Then in the sunset's flush they went aloft* (John Masefield). **4** *Figurative.* decline or close, especially of a period of prosperity or the like: *the sunset of life* (Thomas Campbell).
**sunset law**, *U.S.* **1** a law requiring a government regulatory agency to undergo periodic review for its continued usefulness. **2** a law providing that state agencies created by a governor or a legislature be terminated after a specified period.
**sun|shade** (sun′shād′), *n.* **1** = parasol. **2** protection against the sun. **3** an awning, especially one over the outside of a window.
**sunshades**, *Slang.* sunglasses; shades.
**sun|shine** (sun′shīn′), *n.* **1** the shining of the sun; light of the sun: *Occasionally, when the wind opened seams in the roof of cloud, there were brief splashes of ... sunshine* (Hugh MacLennan). **2** the warmth, light, and beneficial effects deriving from the rays of the sun. **3** a place or area exposed to sunshine. **4** *Figurative.* **a** brightness; cheerfulness; happiness. **b** a source of this.
**sunshine law**, *U.S.* a law that requires government records and procedural bodies to be open to the public: *The Federal Government and several state governments have ... sunshine laws aimed at reopening decision-making processes that have become cloaked in secrecy* (Iver Peterson).
**Sunshine State**, a nickname for Florida and for South Dakota.
**sunshine vitamin**, = vitamin $D_3$.
**sun|shin|y** (sun′shī′nē), *adj.,* **-shin|i|er, -shin|i|est.** **1** having much sunshine. **2** *Figurative.* bright; cheerful; happy.
**sun shower**, a summer shower of rain from a passing cumulus cloud, preceded and followed by full sunshine.
**sun|sight** (sun′sīt′), *n.* an observation of the altitude of the sun, used to determine latitude and longitude, especially at sea.
**sun|spot** (sun′spot′), *n.* one of the dark spots that appear at regular intervals in certain zones of the surface of the sun; macula. Disturbances of the earth's magnetic field often occur when sunspots appear. *A sunspot is a relatively cool area in the photosphere, dark only by contrast with its surroundings. The temperature of the darkest part ... is about 4000°C* (John Charles Duncan).
**sunspot cycle**, the period of about eleven years in which the maximum frequency of sunspots recurs.
**sunspot maximum**, the period during the sunspot cycle in which sunspots are most frequent.
**sunspot minimum**, the period during the sunspot cycle in which sunspots are least frequent.
**sun star**, any one of various starfishes having many rays.

**sun|stone** (sun′stōn′), *n.* any one of several varieties of feldspar showing red or golden-yellow reflections.

**sun|stroke** (sun′strōk′), *n.* a sudden illness caused by too long exposure to the sun's rays or by too much heat. Sunstroke results in extreme exhaustion and, often, loss of consciousness.

**sun|struck** (sun′struk′), *adj.* overcome by the heat of the sun; affected with sunstroke.

**sun|suit** (sun′süt′), *n.* short pants held up by shoulder straps often attached to a bib and worn without a shirt by children for playing in the sun.

**sun|swept** (sun′swept′), *adj.* swept by the sun; exposed to steady sunlight: *sunswept port towns* (New Yorker).

**sun|tan** (sun′tan′), *n., adj.* **—*n.*** **1** the reddish-brown color of a person's skin tanned by the sun: *He had collected a walnut suntan from the top of his bald head to practically his toes* (Punch). **2** a light, yellowish brown; khaki: *Sizes 8 to 18 in suntan, white, aqua ... and black* (New Yorker).
**—*adj.*** light yellowish-brown; khaki.
**suntans,** a tan military uniform for summer wear; khaki shirt and trousers: *Tough ... soldiers in suntans deployed briskly* (Time).

**suntan lotion,** a lotion containing a chemical substance that screens the sun's ultraviolet rays and prevents sunburn.

**sun-tanned** or **sun|tanned** (sun′tand′), *adj.* having a suntan: *His blue eyes were startlingly clear, and, like most sun-tanned people, he looked very healthy* (New Yorker).

**sun|tans** (sun′tanz′), *n.pl.* See under **suntan.**

**sun time,** = apparent solar time.

**sun trap,** a place or device for catching sunshine: *As it is protected by the cliffs, this beach is a real sun trap* (Observer).

**sun|up** (sun′up′), *n.* = sunrise (def. 2).

**sun visor, 1** a flap above the windshield of a car, truck, bus, locomotive, or airplane, that can be lowered to shield the eyes from the sun: *Their automobile has sun visors that can swing from the front to the side.* **2** a fixed sheet of metal or tinted plastic on the outside of a car, truck, bus, or locomotive, to shield the eyes from the sun.

**sun|ward** (sun′wərd), *adv., adj.* toward the sun: *He glanced briefly sunward as the cloud cast its shadow* (adv.). *Apples grow larger on the sunward side of the tree* (adj.).

**sun|wards** (sun′wərdz), *adv.* = sunward.

**sun|wise** (sun′wīz′), *adv.* from left to right; clockwise.

**sun worship,** the worship of the sun, especially as the symbol of the deity or as a source of light and heat.

**SUNY** (no periods) or **S.U.N.Y.,** State University of New York.

**su|o ju|re** (sü′ō jür′ē), *Latin.* in one's own right.

**su|o lo|co** (sü′ō lō′kō), *Latin.* in its own or proper place.

**sup**[1] (sup), *v.,* **supped, sup|ping.** **—*v.i.*** to eat the evening meal; take supper: *He supped alone on bread and milk.*
**—*v.t.*** to give a supper to or for.
[< Old French *souper* < *soupe;* see etym. under **soup**]

**sup**[2] (sup), *v.t., v.i.,* **supped, sup|ping,** *n.* = sip. [Old English *sūpan*]

**sup-,** *prefix.* the form of **sub-** before *p,* as in *suppress.*

**sup.,** an abbreviation for the following:
**1** superior.
**2** superlative.
**3** supine.
**4a** supplement. **b** supplementary.
**5** supply.
**6** supra (above).
**7** supreme.

**Sup. Ct., 1** Superior Court. **2** Supreme Court.

**supe** (süp), *n. Slang.* super.

**su|per** (sü′pər), *n., adj., v.* **—*n.*** **1** *Informal.* a superintendent, especially of an apartment house or office building. **2** *Informal.* an extra person or thing; supernumerary. **3** *Informal.* a supernumerary actor; extra: *to use 300 supers for a mob scene.* **4** *Commerce.* goods of extremely fine quality, superior grade, or very large size. **5** a thin, starched cotton of open weave used in reinforcing books: *On most sewed books, the machine glues a strip of reinforcing mesh fabric, called super, to the rounded backbone. This super is about two inches wider than the thickness of the book* (Frank B. Myrick). **6** = superhive.
**—*adj. Slang.*** **1** of superlative quality; excellent: *super-deluxe accommodations.* **2** superior; extraordinary: *a super gentleman, super elegance.*
**—*v.t.*** to reinforce (books) with super.
[< *super-*]

**super-,** *prefix.* **1** over; above: *Superimpose = to impose over or above.*
**2** besides; further: *Superadd = to add besides or further.*
**3** in high proportion; to excess; exceedingly: *Superabundant = abundant to excess.*
**4** surpassing: *Supernatural = surpassing the natural.*
[< Latin *super,* adverb, preposition]

**super., 1** superfine. **2** superior.

**su|per|a|bil|i|ty** (sü′pər ə bil′ə tē), *n.* the quality of being superable.

**su|per|a|ble** (sü′pər ə bəl), *adj.* that can be overcome or vanquished; surmountable. **SYN:** conquerable, vincible. [< Latin *superābilis* < *superāre* to overcome < *super* over] **—su′per|a|ble|ness,** *n.*

**su|per|a|bly** (sü′pər ə blē), *adv.* so as to be superable: *a superably built obstacle.*

**su|per|a|bound** (sü′pər ə bound′), *v.i.* **1** to be very abundant; occur in great quantity or numbers. **2** to be too abundant; occur in excessive quantity or numbers.

**su|per|a|bun|dance** (sü′pər ə bun′dəns), *n.* **1** a very great abundance: *a superabundance of rain.* **SYN:** profusion. **2** a greater amount than is needed: *a superabundance of evidence* (William Dwight Whitney). **SYN:** superfluity.

**su|per|a|bun|dant** (sü′pər ə bun′dənt), *adj.* **1** very abundant; ample. **2** too abundant; more than enough; excessive. **—su′per|a|bun′dant|ly,** *adv.*

**su|per|ac|id** (sü′pər as′id), *adj.* excessively acid.

**su|per|ac|ti|nide series** (sü′pər ak′tə nīd), a predicted series of superheavy chemical elements which is to follow the transactinide series in the periodic table.

**su|per|a|cute** (sü′pər ə kyüt′), *adj.* excessively acute.

**su|per|add** (sü′pər ad′), *v.t.* **1** to add besides; add further (to what already exists): *A toothache was superadded to her other troubles. Jealousy was now superadded to a deeply-rooted enmity* (John F. Kirk). **2** to add over and above; add to what has been added: *A French war is added to the American; and there is ... reason ... to expect a Spanish war to be superadded to the French* (Edmund Burke). [< Latin *superaddere* < *super-* besides, over + *addere* add]

**su|per|ad|di|tion** (sü′pər ə dish′ən), *n.* **1** the act of superadding. **2** the state of being superadded. **3** something that is superadded.

**su|per|aer|o|dy|nam|ics** (sü′pər ãr′ō dī nam′iks, -di-), *n.* the branch of aerodynamics that deals with bodies in motion at very high altitudes and speeds, and with the motion of air that contains only a few molecules.

**su|per|a|gen|cy** (sü′pər ā′jən sē), *n., pl.* **-cies.** a large agency, especially of the government, which is in charge of a group of smaller agencies: ... *proposed the creation of a superagency that eventually would coordinate all transportation in the tri-state metropolitan area* (New York Times).

**su|per|al|loy** (sü′pər al′oi), *n.* an alloy developed to resist high temperatures, stresses, and oxidation: *Superalloys such as nickel and cobalt-base alloys, even though some of them can withstand temperatures as high as 1,800 degrees F., will not hold up under the high-temperature requirements of upcoming jets, reactors, and rockets* (Science News).

**su|per|al|tar** (sü′pər ôl′tər), *n. Ecclesiastical.* **1** a portable stone slab consecrated for use upon an unconsecrated altar, a table, or the like. **2** a structure above and at the back of an altar, such as a reredos or a gradin. [< Medieval Latin *superaltare* < Latin *super-* over + *altāre* altar]

**su|per|an|nu|a|ble** (sü′pər an′yů ə bəl), *adj. Especially British.* qualifying one for a pension: *Posts are superannuable and an allowance of £50 per child is paid* (Economist).

**su|per|an|nu|ate** (sü′pər an′yů āt), *v.t., v.i.,* **-at|ed, -at|ing. 1** to retire or be retired on a pension because of age or infirmity. **2** to make or become old-fashioned or out of date: *Each year the new car models superannuate the old.* [back formation < *superannuated*] **—su′per|an′nu|a′tion,** *n.*

**su|per|an|nu|at|ed** (sü′pər an′yů ā′tid), *adj.* **1** retired on a pension; pensioned off. **2** too old for work or service; old and infirm. **SYN:** timeworn, decrepit. **3** old-fashioned; out-of-date: *Nothing is more tiresome than a superannuated pedagogue* (Henry Adams). **SYN:** passé. [< Medieval Latin *superannuatus* cattle more than a year old < Latin *super annum* beyond a year]

**su|per|a|tom|ic bomb** (sü′pər ə tom′ik), = hydrogen bomb.

**su|perb** (sů pėrb′), *adj.* **1** grand and stately; majestic; magnificent; splendid: *Mountain scenery is superb. The queen's jewels are superb.* **SYN:** imposing. See syn. under **magnificent. 2** grandly and sumptuously equipped, arrayed, or decorated; rich; elegant: *a superb dinner.* **3** very fine; excellent; first-rate: *The actor gave a superb performance.* [< Latin *superbus* < *super* above] **—su|perb′ly,** *adv.* **—su|perb′ness,** *n.*

**su|per|bi|ty** (sů pėr′bə tē), *n.* pride; arrogance: *the superbity of youth.*

**su|per|block** (sü′pər blok′), *n. U.S.* a large, landscaped city block closed to automobile traffic: *Cambridge is full of mid-nineteenth-century superblocks, with economical cul-de-sacs ... and spacious gardens that have proved a happy barrier to overcrowding* (New Yorker).

**su|per|bomb** (sü′pər bom′), *n.* = hydrogen bomb.

**su|per|bomb|er** (sü′pər bom′ər), *n.* a large, long-range bomber capable of delivering superbombs.

**su|per|brain** (sü′pər brān′), *n.* = electronic brain.

**su|per|bridge** (sü′pər brij′), *n.* a very high bridge, especially especially one built over a mountain barrier.

**su|per|cal|en|der** (sü′pər kal′ən dər), *v., n.* **—*v.t.*** to subject (paper) to additional calendering, so as to produce a highly glazed surface.
**—*n.*** a roller or machine used in making supercalendered paper.

**su|per|cal|en|dered paper** (sü′pər kal′ən dərd), paper with a highly glazed surface produced by additional calendering.

**su|per|car|go** (sü′pər kär′gō), *n., pl.* **-goes** or **-gos.** an officer on a merchant ship who acts for the owner and has charge of the cargo and the business affairs of the voyage. [alteration of earlier *supracargo* < Spanish *sobrecargo* < *sobre* over (< Latin *suprā*) + *cargo*]

**su|per|car|go|ship** (sü′pər kär′gō ship), *n.* the position or business of a supercargo.

**su|per|car|ri|er** (sü′pər kar′ē ər), *n.* a very large aircraft carrier.

**su|per|cav|i|tat|ing propeller** (sü′pər kav′ə tā-ting), a type of propeller with square-ended blades that overcome loss of speed due to cavitation, designed especially for ships operating at high speeds.

**su|per|cen|ter** (sü′pər sen′tər), *n.* a very large shopping center, especially in a suburb.

**su|per|charge** (sü′pər chärj′), *v.t.,* **-charged, -charg|ing. 1** to increase the power of (an internal-combustion engine) by fitting with a supercharger. **2** to fit the engine or engines of (a vehicle or aircraft) with a supercharger or superchargers. **3** *Figurative.* to charge to excess with excitement, emotion, force, or vigor: *The atmosphere at the trial was supercharged with tension.*

**su|per|charg|er** (sü′pər chär′jər), *n.* a blower, pump, or similar device fitted on an internal-combustion engine, by means of which a greater amount of air is forced into the cylinders than the action of the pistons would draw. Superchargers are used especially on the engines of racing cars and of aircraft designed to fly at high altitudes.

**su|per|church** (sü′pər chėrch′), *n.* a large church formed by the unification of a group of separate churches.

**su|per|cil|i|ar|y** (sü′pər sil′ē er′ē), *adj.* **1** of or having to do with the eyebrow. **2** in the region of the eyebrow. **3** designating or having to do with a prominence (superciliary arch) of the frontal bone over the eye. **4** *Zoology.* **a** situated over the eye: *a superciliary line or patch of color.* **b** having a marking above the eye, as various birds do. [< New Latin *superciliaris* < Latin *supercilium* eyebrow; see etym. under **supercilious**]

**su|per|cil|i|ous** (sü′pər sil′ē əs), *adj.* showing scorn or indifference because of a feeling of superiority; haughty, proud, and contemptuous; disdainful: *The duchess looked down at the workman with a supercilious stare.* **SYN:** See syn. under **proud.** [< Latin *superciliōsus* < *supercilium* pride; (originally) brow, eyebrow < *super* above + unrecorded *celium* a cover < *cēlāre* to cover, conceal] **—su′per|cil′i|ous|ly,** *adv.* **—su′per|cil′i|ous|ness,** *n.*

**su|per|cit|y** (sü′pər sit′ē), *n., pl.* **-cit|ies. 1** a large urban area formed by the expansion and gradual coalescence of two or more relatively distant cities: *I have the recurrent nightmare of the supercities that threaten us today, the titanic conurbations—already growing before our eyes—single vast towns from Boston to Baltimore, Pittsburgh to Chicago, London to Birmingham* (James Cameron). **2** a very large city; megalopolis: *He planned arcologies, gigantic supercities high in the air or floating on water, as a means of preventing man from destroying himself and his environment* (John Fowler).

**su|per|civ|i|li|za|tion** (sü′pər siv′ə lə zā′shən), *n.* a civilization above or beyond the civilization of the earth: *If the radio transmissions from CTA-21 and CTA-102 are actually attempts to communicate, they must come from supercivilizations with incredibly vast amounts of energy at their disposal* (Time).

**su|per|class** (sü′pər klas′, -kläs′), *n. Biology.* **1** a

---

**Pronunciation Key:** hat, āge, cãre, fär; let, ēqual, tėrm; it, īce; hot, ōpen, ôrder; oil, out; cup, pu̇t, rüle; child; long; thin; ᴛʜen; zh, measure; ə represents a in about, e in taken, i in pencil, o in lemon, u in circus.

group of related plants or animals ranking below a subphylum and above a class. **2** = subphylum.

**su|per|clus|ter** (sü′pər klus′tər), *n.* a very large cluster of galaxies: *Most astronomers believe that superclusters are the largest groups that can be told apart in the universe* (A. G. W. Cameron).

**su|per|cold** (sü′pər kōld′), *adj.* **1** extremely cold: *supercold temperatures.* **2** using extremely low temperatures; cryogenic: *Supercold surgery is known as cryosurgery.*

**su|per|co|los|sal** (sü′pər kə los′əl), *adj.* extremely large; huge; gigantic; vast: *supercolossal wealth, a supercolossal movie.* —**su′per|co|los′sal|ly,** *adv.*

**su|per|co|lum|nar** (sü′pər kə lum′nər), *adj. Architecture.* **1** above a column or columns. **2** having to do with supercolumniation.

**su|per|co|lum|ni|a|tion** (sü′pər kə lum′nē ā′shən), *n. Architecture.* the setting of one order of columns upon another.

**su|per|con|duct** (sü′pər kən dukt′), *v.i.* to act as a superconductor; conduct electric current with no resistance at temperatures near absolute zero: *Metals and alloys stop superconducting when exposed to a magnetic field.*

**su|per|con|duc|tion** (sü′pər kən duk′shən), *n.* **1** the conducting of electric current by means of a superconductor. **2** = superconductivity.

**su|per|con|duc|tive** (sü′pər kən duk′tiv), *adj.* capable of or having superconductivity: *Strangely, the best electrical conductors, copper and silver, do not become superconductive* (Scientific American).

**su|per|con|duc|tiv|i|ty** (sü′pər kon′duk tiv′ə tē), *n.* the ability of some metals, such as lead and tin, to conduct electric current with no resistance at temperatures near absolute zero: *Physicists today are still hunting for an explanation of ... superconductivity, which seems to contradict some of our basic ideas about nature* (Scientific American).

**su|per|con|duc|tor** (sü′pər kən duk′tər), *n.* a metal, such as lead or tin, that can conduct electric current with no resistance at temperatures near absolute zero.

**su|per|con|ti|nent** (sü′pər kon′tə nənt), *n.* any one of several great land masses, or a single great land mass, that is thought to have originally comprised the present continents and that later split up into smaller masses which drifted to form the present continents; protocontinent: *Dietz discounts an alternative hypothesis that all continents once were a single land mass called Pangaea. Rather he favours the notion of two supercontinents, eloquently advocated a half century ago by Wegener. Wegener's other supercontinent, called Laurasia, combined North America, Europe, and Asia* (New Scientist).

**su|per|cool** (sü′pər kül′), *v.t.* to cool (a liquid) below the normal freezing point without causing it to solidify. —*v.i.* to undergo supercooling.

**su|per|cooled** (sü′pər küld′), *adj.* (of a liquid, especially water) cooled below its usual freezing point without solidifying.

**su|per|coun|try** (sü′pər kun′trē), *n., pl.* **-tries.** an extremely powerful country; superpower.

**su|per|crit|i|cal** (sü′pər krit′ə kəl), *adj.* **1** *Nuclear Physics.* having more than the amount of fissionable material necessary for sustaining a chain reaction: *a supercritical mass, a supercritical reactor.* **2** *Aeronautics.* able to maintain a supersonic flow of air from the leading edge to the trailing edge without any drag: *The supercritical wing ... has a shape differing greatly from conventional wings, which have a pronounced curvature from front to back so that the airflow across the wing reaches the speed of sound before the aircraft itself does* (London Times). —**su′per|crit′i|cal|ly,** *adv.*

**su|per|cur|rent** (sü′pər kėr′ənt), *n.* the electric current of a superconductor; current that flows through a metal conductor chilled to temperatures near absolute zero without meeting resistance or requiring voltage to drive it on.

**su|per|dense** (sü′pər dens′), *adj.* extremely dense or compact: *The idea that superdense bodies could be formed as end products of supernova explosions is not new. Hypothetical superdense stars composed almost entirely of neutrons were conceived ... by the Russian physicist L. D. Landau and independently by J. Robert Oppenheimer* (Scientific American).

**su|per|dom|i|nant** (sü′pər dom′ə nənt), *n. Music.* submediant.

**su|per|dread|nought** (sü′pər dred′nôt), *n.* any very large, heavily armored warship of the battleship class built between about 1910 and the end of World War II, usually having a main armament of eight or more guns of a single caliber in the range from 12 inches upward.

**su|per-du|per** (sü′pər dü′pər), *adj., n. U.S. Slang.* —*adj.* very great; most excellent; stupendous; colossal: *Your mileage is calculated for you by roadside signs screaming—"Only ten miles to tupelo honey," ... or "Twelve miles to Sandy's super-duper jumbo hamburgers"* (Alistair Cooke). —*n.* the greatest or most excellent of its kind.

**su|per|e|go** (sü′pər ē′gō, -eg′ō), *n. Psychoanalysis.* that part of a person's psyche that determines right or wrong conduct; conscience. The superego, comprising rules, as of conduct, morality, and ethics, assimilated from parents and others in the environment, governs the repression or expression by the ego of the drives of the id.

**su|per|el|e|va|tion** (sü′pər el′ə vā′shən), *n.* the amount of elevation of the outer rail above the inner rail at a curve on a railway, or of one side of a road above another.

**su|per|em|i|nence** (sü′pər em′ə nəns), *n.* the state of being supereminent; eminence superior to what is common; distinguished eminence: *the supereminence of Demosthenes as an orator* (Milton).

**su|per|em|i|nent** (sü′pər em′ə nənt), *adj.* of superior eminence, rank, or dignity; standing out or rising above others. **SYN:** preeminent, distingué. [< Latin *superēminēns, -entis,* present participle of *superēminēre* rise above < *super-* above, over + *ēminēre* be prominent, stand out. Compare etym. under **eminent.**] —**su′per|em′i|nent|ly,** *adv.*

**su|per|en|ci|pher** (sü′pər en sī′fər), *v.t.* to encipher (a message already in code or cipher): *Codes are often superenciphered: The code words or code numbers are enciphered by some cipher system just as if they were ordinary plain text* (Scientific American). —**su′per|en|ci′pher|ment,** *n.*

**su|per|er|o|gate** (sü′pər er′ə gāt), *v.i.,* **-gat|ed, -gat|ing. 1** to do more than is commanded or required. **2** to make up (for) by excess: *The fervency of one man in prayer cannot supererogate for the coldness of another* (Milton). [< Late Latin *superērogāre* (with English *-ate*[1]); see etym. under **supererogation**]

**su|per|er|o|ga|tion** (sü′pər er′ə gā′shən), *n.* the action of doing more than duty or circumstances require. [< Late Latin *superērogātiō, -ōnis* < *superērogāre* pay or do additionally < *super-* above, over + *ērogāre* pay out < *ex-* out + *rogāre* ask (consent)]

**su|per|e|rog|a|to|ry** (sü′pər ə rog′ə tôr′ē, -tōr′-), *adj.* **1** doing more than duty requires; of the nature of supererogation. **2** unnecessary; superfluous. **SYN:** needless.

**su|per|ette** (sü′pə ret′), *n. U.S.* a small supermarket.

**su|per|ex|cel|lence** (sü′pər ek′sə ləns), *n.* superior excellence.

**su|per|ex|cel|lent** (sü′pər ek′sə lənt), *adj.* of superior or surpassing excellence: *Tobacco, divine, rare, superexcellent tobacco* (Robert Burton). —**su′per|ex′cel|lent|ly,** *adv.*

**su|per|fam|i|ly** (sü′pər fam′ə lē), *n., pl.* **-lies. 1** *Biology.* a group of animals or plants ranking above a family and below an order or, according to some, below a suborder: *A common superfamily, Hominoidae, ... sets apes and man off from monkeys* (William Howells). **2** *Nuclear Physics.* supermultiplet.

**su|per|fec|ta** (sü′pər fek′tə), *n. U.S.* a form of betting on a horse race in which the bettor must pick in their exact order the first four horses to finish the race: *The superfecta is a betting gimmick popular at the trots* (New Yorker). [American English, blend of *super-* and *perfecta*]

**su|per|fe|cun|da|tion** (sü′pər fē′kən dā′shən, -fek′ən-), *n. Physiology.* the fertilization of two or more ova at the same period of ovulation by two or more acts of coition.

**su|per|fe|tate** (sü′pər fē′tāt), *v.i.,* **-tat|ed, -tat|ing.** *Physiology.* to conceive during pregnancy. [< Latin *superfētāre* (with English *-ate*[1]) < *super* over, above + *fētāre* to produce, bear < *fētus, -ūs* offspring, fruit]

**su|per|fe|ta|tion** (sü′pər fi tā′shən), *n.* **1** *Physiology.* a second conception before the birth of the offspring of the first conception. This occurs normally in some animals. **2** *Botany.* the fertilization of the same ovule by two different kinds of pollen. **3** *Figurative.* **a** additional production; growth or accretion (of one upon another). **b** an instance of this.

**su|per|fice** (sü′pər fis), *n.* = superficies. [< Latin *superficiēs;* see etym. under **superficial**]

**su|per|fi|cial** (sü′pər fish′əl), *adj.* **1** of the surface: *a superficial measurement.* **2** on the surface; at the surface: *His burns were superficial and soon healed.* **3a** concerned with or understanding only what is on the surface; not thorough; shallow: *superficial knowledge. Girls used to receive only a superficial education. Men of superficial understanding and ludicrous fancy* (James Boswell). **SYN:** cursory. **b** not real or genuine: *a superficial friendship.* [< Latin *superficiālis* < *superficiēs* surface < *super-* above + *faciēs* (external) form. Compare etym. under **face.**] —**su′per|fi′cial|ness,** *n.*

**su|per|fi|cial|ist** (sü′pər fish′ə list), *n.* **1** a person who deals with things superficially. **2** a person of superficial knowledge or attitudes.

**su|per|fi|ci|al|i|ty** (sü′pər fish′ē al′ə tē), *n., pl.* **-ties. 1** superficial quality or condition; shallowness. **2** something superficial.

**su|per|fi|cial|ize** (sü′pər fish′ə līz), *v.t.,* **-ized, -iz|ing.** to make superficial; treat superficially.

**su|per|fi|cial|ly** (sü′pər fish′ə lē), *adv.* in a superficial manner; on the surface; not thoroughly: *superficially attractive.*

**su|per|fi|ci|es** (sü′pər fish′ē ēz), *n., pl.* **-es. 1** a surface. **2** the surface area. **3** *Figurative.* the outward appearance as distinct from the inner or real nature or condition. [< Latin *superficiēs;* see etym. under **superficial**]

**su|per|fine** (sü′pər fīn′), *adj.* **1** that is the very best of its kind; very fine; extra fine: *superfine goods.* **2** too refined; too nice, fastidious, or elegant. —**su′per|fine′ly,** *adv.* —**su′per|fine′ness,** *n.*

**su|per|fix** (sü′pər fiks), *n. Linguistics.* a suprasegmental feature, such as the stress pattern of a word, phrase, or sentence. [< *super-* + *-fix,* as in *prefix, suffix*]

**su|per|flu|id** (sü′pər flü′id), *n., adj.* —*n.* a fluid, especially liquid helium, characterized by the complete disappearance of viscosity at temperatures near absolute zero.
—*adj.* extremely fluid; completely lacking viscosity: *The bottom layer, rich in helium-4, is superfluid and can pass through extremely fine cracks that can not be penetrated by other gases and liquids* (Science News Letter).

**su|per|flu|id|i|ty** (sü′pər flü id′ə tē), *n.* extreme fluidity; lack of viscosity: ... *the superfluidity of liquid helium, the frictionless flow of entire atoms, demonstrated in the liquid's ability to flow through the tiniest tubes or narrowest slits* (Scientific American).

**su|per|flu|i|ty** (sü′pər flü′ə tē), *n., pl.* **-ties. 1** a greater amount than is needed; excess: *Our orchard gives us a superfluity of apples.* **SYN:** superabundance. **2** something not needed: *Luxuries are superfluities.*

**su|per|flu|ous** (sù pėr′flü əs), *adj.* **1** more than is needed or desired; excessive; surplus: *In writing telegrams it pays to omit superfluous words. Divinely superfluous beauty ... The incredible beauty of joy* (Robinson Jeffers). **2** needless; unnecessary: *A raincoat is superfluous on a clear day. Many a poem is marred by superfluous verse* (Longfellow). [< Latin *superfluus* (with English *-ous*) < *super-* over + *fluere* to flow] —**su|per′flu|ous|ly,** *adv.* —**su|per′flu|ous|ness,** *n.*

**su|per|flux** (sü′pər fluks), *n.* **1** an overflowing, or an excessive flow, as of water. **2** a superabundant amount. **3** a superfluous amount, or surplus. [< Medieval Latin *superfluxus,* noun use of past participle of Latin *superfluere;* see etym. under **superfluous**]

**su|per|foe|ta|tion** (sü′pər fi tā′shən), *n.* = superfetation.

**Su|per|fort** (sü′pər fôrt′, -fōrt′), *n.* **1** a large, heavily armored, American bombing plane used especially against Japan in the latter part of World War II, officially designated as a B-29. **2** a similar bombing plane officially designated as a B-50. [< *super-* + *fort*(ress), as in *flying fortress*]

**Su|per|for|tress** (sü′pər fôr′tris, -fōr′-), *n.* = Superfort.

**su|per|fu|el** (sü′pər fyü′əl), *n.* a fuel that surpasses all others in energy and performance: *This giant booster probably burned the usual kerosene fuel and liquid-oxygen oxidizer rather than some new superfuel* (Newsweek).

**su|per|fuse** (sü′pər fyüz′), *v.t., v.i.,* **-fused, -fus|ing. 1** to pour on something. **2** to be poured on something. **3** = supercool. [< Latin *superfūsus,* past participle of *superfundere* to flow over or on < *super-* over + *fundere* to pour]

**su|per|fu|sion** (sü′pər fyü′zhən), *n.* **1** the act or process of superfusing or pouring liquid over something. **2** the cooling of a liquid below its freezing point without solidification taking place.

**su|per|ga|lac|tic** (sü′pər gə lak′tik), *adj.* of a supergalaxy.

**su|per|gal|ax|y** (sü′pər gal′ək sē), *n., pl.* **-ax|ies.** a cluster of galaxies: *the supergalaxy of which the Milky Way is a part* (Scientific American).

**su|per|gene** (sü′pər jēn′), *n.* a group of genes that function as a single gene in genetic transmission, usually as a result of an inversion in the normal arrangement of genes in the chromosomes: *These supergenes are visible in the giant chromosomes of Drosophila larvae* (Scientific American).

**su|per|gi|ant** (sü′pər jī′ənt), *n.,* or **supergiant star,** any one of various extremely large and brilliant stars, ranging in luminosity from 100 to 10,000 or more times that of the sun. They are most common in the spiral galaxies and many can be seen in the Large (Magellanic) Cloud. *Supergiant stars are extraordinarily large and luminous giants. Examples are Rigel and Betelgeuse* (Robert H. Baker).

**su|per|gla|cial** (sü′pər glā′shəl), *adj.* situated or occurring upon a surface of ice, especially of a glacier. —**su′per|gla′cial|ly**, *adv.*

**su|per|gov|ern|ment** (sü′pər guv′ərn mənt, -ər-), *n.* **1** a central organization formed by a group of governments to regulate relations among members and on matters of common interest: *The UN represents not a supergovernment, not a separate institutional personality, but one of a number of forums on which governments communicate with one another* (Atlantic). **2** a government which has very extensive powers. **3** rule by a supergovernment: *As long as we expect supergovernment from the UN, we'll remain disillusioned over its "failure"* (Maclean's).

**su|per|group** (sü′pər grüp′), *n.* a rock'n'roll group made up of members or former members of other rock groups.

**su|per|hawk** (sü′pər hôk′), *n. U.S.* a person who favors total war, including the use of atomic weapons, as a solution in a conflict; an extreme militant.

**su|per|heat** (*v.* sü′pər hēt′; *n.* sü′pər hēt′), *v., n.* —*v.t.* **1** to heat to a very high temperature; heat too hot; heat hotter than usual: *It's hard to manage vapor that's been superheated ... to five or more times the boiling point of water* (Wall Street Journal). **2** to heat (a liquid) above its normal boiling point without causing vaporization: *The tracks of particles reveal themselves as lines of bubbles in superheated liquid* (New Scientist). **3** to heat (steam) apart from water until it contains no suspended water droplets. The steam then resembles and will remain a dry or perfect gas at the specified pressure.
—*n.* **1** the excess heat which a vapor acquires when it is superheated from a dry and saturated condition. **2** the temperature range through which the vapor passes.

**su|per|heat|er** (sü′pər hē′tər), *n.* a device for superheating steam: *Only 151,000 kilowatts will come from nuclear heat and the remainder from an oil-fired superheater* (Wall Street Journal).

**su|per|heav|y** (sü′pər hev′ē), *adj., n., pl.* **-heav·ies**. —*adj.* **1** having a higher atomic number or greater atomic mass than those of the heaviest elements known: *Nuclear theorists have speculated ... about the possible existence of stable superheavy elements ... Superheavy elements are generally created by accelerating heavy ions, such as argon, for interactions with heavier elements, such as uranium* (New Scientist). **2** of or belonging to superheavy elements: *superheavy nuclei.*
—*n.* a superheavy element: *The superheavies are particularly interesting because some of them may be relatively stable, lasting millions of years instead of fractions of a second* (Science News).

**su|per|het** (sü′pər het′), *adj., n. Informal.* superheterodyne: *The real heart of a superhet set is the first detector* (Glasgow Herald).

**su|per|het|er|o|dyne** (sü′pər het′ər ə dīn), *adj., n.* —*adj.* of or having to do with a kind of radio reception which reduces modulated waves (above audibility) to a lower frequency and in later stages rectifies the signals to audio-frequency amplification: *Almost all modern radio sets make use of the superheterodyne principle* (Sears and Zemansky).
—*n.* a superheterodyne radio receiving set.

**su|per|high frequency** (sü′pər hī′), any radio frequency between 3,000 and 30,000 megahertz. *Abbr:* SHF (no periods).

**su|per|high|way** (sü′pər hī′wā′), *n.* a highway for fast driving. Superhighways are often very long and divided in the middle, with two or more lanes for traffic in each direction. *Thruways and superhighways make industrial parks feasible on the edge of a city rather than in congested downtown areas* (Wall Street Journal).

**su|per|hive** (sü′pər hīv′), *n.* a removable upper compartment of a beehive.

**su|per|hu|man** (sü′pər hyü′mən), *adj.* **1** above or beyond what is human: *Angels are superhuman beings.* **2** above or beyond ordinary human power, experience, or ability: *By a superhuman effort the hunter choked the leopard to death. With a superhuman effort, the high-jumper soared to a new Olympic record. He has not raised himself to that superhuman level of reason which should correspond to the possession of superhuman strength* (Wall Street Journal). —**su′per|hu′man|ly**, *adv.* —**su′per|hu′man|ness**, *n.*

**su|per|hu|man|i|ty** (sü′pər hyü man′ə tē), *n.* the character of being superhuman.

**su|per|hu|man|ize** (sü′pər hyü′mə nīz), *v.t.,* **-ized, -iz|ing.** to make superhuman.

**su|per|im|pos|a|ble** (sü′pər im pō′zə bəl), *adj.* that can be superimposed: *Any compound will theoretically do this if one form is not superimposable on its mirror image* (Ralph C. Dougherty).

**su|per|im|pose** (sü′pər im pōz′), *v.t.,* **-posed, -pos|ing.** **1** to put (one object on top of something else); lay above or on the top. **2** to put or join as an addition.

**su|per|im|po|si|tion** (sü′pər im′pə zish′ən), *n.* **1** the act of superimposing. **2** the state of being superimposed: *Here we have the sudden, more or less complete superimposition of one culture upon an alien one* (Ogburn and Nimkoff).

**su|per|in|cum|bence** (sü′pər in kum′bəns), *n.* the state or condition of lying upon something.

**su|per|in|cum|ben|cy** (sü′pər in kum′bən sē), *n.* = superincumbence.

**su|per|in|cum|bent** (sü′pər in kum′bənt), *adj.* **1** lying or resting on something else; overlying (chiefly in scientific use). **2** situated or suspended above; overhanging: *It can scarce uplift The weight of the superincumbent hour* (Shelley). **3** exerted from above: *a superincumbent pressure.* [< Latin *superincumbēns, -entis,* present participle of *superincumbere* rest on < *super-* on, above + *incumbere.* Compare etym. under **incumbent**.]

**su|per|in|duce** (sü′pər in düs′, -dyüs′), *v.t.,* **-duced, -duc|ing.** to bring in or develop as an addition; introduce in addition: *Their improvement cannot come from themselves, but must be superinduced from without* (John Stuart Mill). [< Late Latin *superindūcere* add, cover over < Latin *super-* over, above + *indūcere.* Compare etym. under **induce**.] —**su′per|in|duc′tion**, *n.*

**su|per|in|fec|tion** (sü′pər in fek′shən), *n.* infection caused a second time or more often by the same kind of germ: *Continual superinfection, year in, year out, wet season and dry season ... kills or renders immune long before childhood has ended* (New Scientist).

**su|per|in|tend** (sü′prin tend′, -pər in-), *v.t.* to oversee and direct (work or workers); manage (a place or institution); supervise. **SYN**: administer. [< Late Latin *superintendere* < Latin *super-* above + *intendere* to direct. Compare etym. under **intend**.]

**su|per|in|tend|ence** (sü′prin ten′dəns, -pər in-), *n.* guidance and direction; supervision; management. **SYN**: administration, surveillance.

**su|per|in|tend|en|cy** (sü′prin ten′dən sē, -pər in-), *n., pl.* **-cies.** the position, authority, or work of a superintendent.

**su|per|in|tend|ent** (sü′prin ten′dənt, -pər in-), *n., adj.* —*n.* a person who oversees, directs, or manages; supervisor: *a superintendent of schools, a superintendent of a factory or apartment house. Abbr:* Supt. **SYN**: controller.
—*adj.* superintending.

**su|per|in|tend|ent|ship** (sü′prin ten′dənt ship, -pər in-), *n.* the position of superintendent.

**su|pe|ri|or** (sə pir′ē ər, sü-), *adj., n.* —*adj.* **1** above the average; very good; excellent: *to do superior work in school, a superior intellect. Schools were selected because of their educational provisions for the superior pupil* (Science). **2** higher in degree, amount, or quality; better; greater: *a superior blend of coffee, a superior legal claim, to win by superior play. Our army had to fight off a superior force.* **3** higher in position, rank, or importance; more exalted in official or social status: *a superior judge, superior officers. The mystic feels ... sometimes as if he were grasped and held by a superior power* (William James). **4** showing a feeling of being above others; proud, supercilious, or dictatorial: *superior airs. The other girls disliked her superior manner.* **5** more elevated in place; higher; upper. **6** *Botany.* growing above some other part or organ, as: **a** the ovary when situated above or free from the (inferior) calyx. **b** the calyx when adherent to the sides of the (inferior) ovary and thus seeming to rise from its top. **7** *Printing.* set above the main line of type, and often smaller than the body type, as symbols for footnotes, numerals or letters in chemical formulas, or other characters: *In $x^2y^3$, the 2 and 3 are superior.* **8** *Astronomy.* **a** designating those planets whose orbits lie outside that of the earth (originally, according to the Ptolemaic astronomy, as having their spheres above that of the sun). **b** on the far side of the sun from the earth: *a superior conjunction of Mercury with the sun.* **c** above the horizon: *the superior passage of a star.*
—*n.* **1** a person who is higher or greater than another in position, rank, dignity, ability, or the like: *A captain is a lieutenant's superior. As a violin player he has no superior. We return to face our superiors ... those whom we obey* (Joseph Conrad). *Not the least of the marks of a military genius is his capacity to bend both subordinates and superiors to his plans of action* (Newsweek). **2** the head of a monastery, convent or abbey. **3** *Printing.* a superior letter or figure.

**superior to, a** higher in quality or position than; above: *Man considers himself superior to the beasts.* **b** greater, better, or more inclusive than: *to be superior to an enemy in weapons.* **c** not giving in to; above yielding to; indifferent to: *A wise man is superior to flattery or revenge.*
[< Latin *superior, -ōris,* comparative of *superus,* adjective, above < *super,* preposition, above]
—**su|pe′ri|or|ly**, *adv.*

**superior court**, *U.S.* **1** the ordinary court of general jurisdiction in many states. **2** a court above the courts of limited or special jurisdiction, and below the court or courts of appeal in some states.

**su|pe|ri|or|ess** (sə pir′ē ər is, sü-), *n.* **1** a woman superior. **2** a woman who is the head of a convent or order of nuns.

**superior general**, *pl.* **superiors general**. the head of a religious order or congregation; superior: *It was the first time a Superior General of the Society of Jesus had addressed an audience in the United States* (New York Times).

**su|pe|ri|or|i|ty** (sə pir′ē ôr′ə tē, -or′-; sü-), *n., pl.* **-ties**. superior condition or quality: *No one doubts the superiority of modern ways of traveling over those of olden times. All nobility in its beginnings was somebody's natural superiority* (Emerson). **SYN**: preeminence.

**superiority complex**, an exaggerated feeling of superiority to others, sometimes the result of overcompensation for an inferiority complex.

**superior vocal cords**, the upper of the two pairs of vocal cords, which do not directly aid in producing voice; false vocal cords.

**su|per|ja|cent** (sü′pər jā′sənt), *adj.* overlying (now chiefly in technical use). [< Latin *superjacēns, -entis,* present participle of *superjacēre* < *super-* over + *jacēre* to lie, rest]

**su|per|jet** (sü′pər jet′), *n.* a large jet aircraft; jumbo jet: *a 747 superjet.*

**superl.**, superlative.

**su|per|la|tive** (sə pėr′lə tiv, sü-), *adj., n.* —*adj.* **1** of the highest kind; above all others; supreme; supereminent: *King Solomon was a man of superlative wisdom.* **2** exaggerated; excessive; hyperbolic: *Such superlative praise could not be sincere.* **3** showing the highest degree of comparison of an adjective or adverb. *Fairest, best,* and *most slowly* are the superlative forms of *fair, good,* and *slowly.*
—*n.* **1** a person or thing above all others; supreme example. **2** the highest or utmost degree of something; height; acme. **3a** the highest degree of comparison of an adjective or adverb. **b** a form or phrase in this degree. *Fairest, fastest,* and *best* are the superlatives of *fair, fast,* and *good.*
**in superlatives**, in an exaggerated way: *She overflowed with enthusiasm, describing the school play in superlatives, calling it stupendous and terrific.*
[< Late Latin *superlātīvus* < *superferre* carry over or beyond, or to extremes < *super-* beyond + *ferre* carry] —**su|per′la|tive|ness**, *n.*

**su|per|la|tive|ly** (sə pėr′lə tiv lē, sü-), *adv.* to the highest degree; above all others; supremely.

**su|per|lin|e|ar** (sü′pər lin′ē ər), *adj.* placed above a written or printed line: *superlinear punctuation.*

**su|per|lin|er** (sü′pər lī′nər), *n.* an ocean liner, able to travel several thousand miles without refueling and carrying many more passengers and crewmen than the ordinary liner.

**su|per|long** (sü′pər lông′, -long′), *adj.* exceedingly long: *The greatest aid to superlong casting is ultra-light line* (Observer).

**su|per|lu|nar** (sü′pər lü′nər), *adj.* = superlunary.

**su|per|lu|na|ry** (sü′pər lü′nər ē), *adj.* **1** of or having to do with the heavens beyond the orbit of the moon; situated beyond the moon. **2** belonging to a higher world; celestial. [< *super-* + Latin *lūna* moon + English *-ary*]

**su|per|male** (sü′pər māl′), *n.* an overaggressive male, especially one born with the extra male sex chromosome characteristic of the XYY syndrome.

**su|per|man** (sü′pər man′), *n., pl.* **-men**. **1** a man having more than human powers: *The folk-tale superman really is a superman, a creature of the elements* (New York Times). **2** a man imagined by Friedrich Nietzsche, the German philosopher, as the ideal human being, achieved by evolution through selection and the elimination of inferior members: *The idea of attaining a race of "supermen" by eugenical selection of mutations in man depends upon the rate of occurrence of mutations in man* (Ogburn and Nimkoff). [translation of German *Übermensch* (coined by Friedrich W. Nietzsche, 1844-1900) literally, above man]

**Pronunciation Key:** hat, āge, cãre, fär; let, ēqual, tėrm; it, īce; hot, ōpen, ôrder; oil, out; cup, pu̇t, rüle; child; long; thin; ᴛʜen; zh, measure; ə represents **a** in about, **e** in taken, **i** in pencil, **o** in lemon, **u** in circus.

**su|per|mar|ket** (sü′pər mär′kit), *n.* a large store for groceries and household articles in which customers select items from open shelves and pay for them just before leaving: *The function of the supermarket is to provide the housewife with all the necessities—for her table, her home, her family* (Time).

**su|per|mart** (sü′pər märt′), *n.* = supermarket.

**su|per|mol|e|cule** (sü′pər mol′ə kyül), *n.* a molecule consisting of several smaller molecules.

**su|per|mul|ti|plet** (sü′pər mul′tə plit), *n. Nuclear Physics.* a group of multiplets: *The omega minus particle was required by the eightfold way to complete a supermultiplet, or superfamily, of 10 particles that share certain basic characteristics* (Scientific American).

**su|per|mun|dane** (sü′pər mun′dān), *adj.* being above the world; belonging to a region above the world: *A practical rocket man has worried that his fellow astronauts might someday create serious supermundane traffic problems* (Newsweek). [< Medieval Latin *supermundanus* < Latin *super-* above + *mundus* world]

**su|per|nac|u|lum** (sü′pər nak′yə ləm), *adv., n., pl.* **-la** (-lə). —*adv.* until no more liquor remains than will rest on the thumbnail; to the last drop. —*n.* **1** wine or other liquor good enough to be drunk to the last drop; fine liquor. **2** a draft that empties the cup or glass to the last drop. **3** a full cup or glass; a bumper. [< New Latin *super naculum,* translation of German *auf den Nagel* (*trinken*) (drink off) liquor to the last drop; literally, (drink) on the nail]

**su|per|nal** (sů pėr′nəl), *adj.* **1** existing in or deriving from the realm above or beyond life on earth; heavenly; divine: *a supernal being.* **2** = supernatural. **3** of lofty status; very high in rank or dignity; elevated; exalted. **4** supremely great or excellent: *supernal wisdom, supernal beauty.* **5** situated in or belonging to the sky; celestial: *the supernal stars.* [probably < Middle French, Old French *supernal* < Latin *supernus* < *super* above] —**su|per′nal|ly,** *adv.*

**su|per|na|tant** (sü′pər nā′tənt), *adj., n.* —*adj.* floating above or on the surface: *oil supernatant on water.* —*n.* a supernatant substance: *Cells from the culture were found 100% effective against the disease while the fluid or supernatant that rises on the culture offered far less protection* (Science News Letter). [< Latin *supernatāns, -antis,* present participle of *supernatāre* float or swim on the surface < *super-* above + *natāre* to swim, float]

**su|per|na|tion|al** (sü′pər nash′ə nəl, -nash′nəl), *adj.* above and beyond or independent of national limitations; supranational: *Europe is gradually uniting in extra-governmental and supernational organizations: the Iron and Steel Community, the European Economic Commission, Euratom* (*for atomic energy*), *the Common Market* (Harper's).

**su|per|na|tion|al|ism** (sü′pər nash′ə nə liz′əm, -nash′nə liz-), *n.* extreme nationalism: *India ... doesn't want supernationalism to scare away the Western capital Asia so badly needs* (Newsweek).

**su|per|na|tion|al|ist** (sü′pər nash′ə nə list, -nash′nə-), *n., adj.* —*n.* an extreme nationalist. —*adj.* favoring supernationalism; extremely nationalistic: *a supernationalist patriotic organization; ... such uneasy partners as a Buddhist party, a Trotskyite group and the supernationalist Ceylon Freedom Party* (Time). —**su′per|na′tion|al|is′tic,** *adj.*

**su|per|nat|u|ral** (sü′pər nach′ər əl, -nach′rəl), *adj., n.* —*adj.* above or beyond what is natural: *supernatural powers. Angels and devils are supernatural beings.* —*n.* **the supernatural,** supernatural agencies, influences, or phenomena: *With the development of the present-day exact scientific methods, beliefs in the "supernatural" gradually faded away and came to be considered superstition* (Bulletin of Atomic Scientists). [< Medieval Latin *supernaturalis* < Latin *super-* above + *nātūra* nature] —**su′per|nat′u|ral|ly,** *adv.* —**su′per|nat′u|ral|ness,** *n.*

**su|per|nat|u|ral|ism** (sü′pər nach′ər ə liz′əm, -nach′rə liz-), *n.* **1** supernatural character or quality. **2** a system or collection of supernatural agencies or events. **3** the belief in the supernatural: *Man must first emancipate himself from supernaturalism before he can see himself as a natural being* (George Simpson). **4** a theory or doctrine that supernatural forces are at work in the universe. —**su′per|nat′u|ral|ist,** *n., adj.*

**su|per|nat|u|ral|is|tic** (sü′pər nach′ər ə lis′tik, -nach′rə-), *adj.* **1** of or having to do with supernaturalism. **2** of the nature of supernaturalism.

**su|per|nat|u|ral|ize** (sü′pər nach′ər ə līz, -nach′rə-), *v.t.,* **-ized, -iz|ing.** to make supernatural; impart or attribute a supernatural character to.

**su|per|nor|mal** (sü′pər nôr′məl), *adj.* **1** exceeding that which is normal: *Hybrid vigour is not anything supernormal: it is rather the degenerate parents which are subnormal* (Eric Ashby). **2** of or designating phenomena of an extraordinary but not necessarily supernatural kind. —**su′per|nor′mal|ly,** *adv.*

**su|per|nor|mal|i|ty** (sü′pər nôr mal′ə tē), *n.* the quality or condition of being supernormal.

**su|per|no|va** (sü′pər nō′və), *n., pl.* **-vae** (-vē), **-vas.** *Astronomy.* a nova far brighter than an ordinary nova, being from 10 to 100 million times as luminous as the sun. A supernova appeared in 1885 in the Andromeda galaxy and in a few days radiated more light than the sun does in a million years. *Astronomers observe as a "supernova" the sudden spectacular brightening of a star* (Arthur Beer).

**su|per|nu|mer|ar|y** (sü′pər nü′mə rer′ē, -nyü′-), *adj., n., pl.* **-ar|ies.** —*adj.* **1** beyond the usual or necessary number; additional; extra. **2** beyond the number needed or desired; superfluous. —*n.* **1** an extra person or thing; one beyond the usual, regular, or prescribed number. **2** a person who appears on the stage but usually has no lines to speak, as in scenes requiring crowds; extra: *In addition to the regular actors, there were 20 supernumeraries for the mob scene.* [< Late Latin *supernumerārius* excessive in number (of soldiers added to a full legion) < Latin *super numerum* beyond the number]

**su|per|or|der** (sü′pər ôr′dər), *n. Biology.* a group of animals or plants ranking above an order and below a class.

**su|per|or|di|nal** (sü′pər ôr′də nəl), *adj.* of or having to do with a superorder.

**su|per|or|di|nar|y** (sü′pər ôr′də ner′ē), *adj.* above or beyond the ordinary.

**su|per|or|di|nate** (sü′pər ôr′də nit), *adj., n.* —*adj.* superior in rank or importance; not subordinate: *a superordinate position, a superordinate requirement.* —*n.* a superordinate person or thing: *Getting along for many of us these days more and more involves the ability to manipulate, to sell, perhaps to con our ... subordinates and superordinates, and perhaps—most of all—ourselves* (New York Times).

**su|per|or|gan|ic** (sü′pər ôr gan′ik), *adj.* above or outside of the organic realm.

**su|per|or|gan|ism** (sü′pər ôr′gə niz əm), *n.* a group of organisms that function as a social unit. A colony of social insects is a superorganism.

**su|per|os|cu|late** (sü′pər os′kyə lāt), *v.t.,* **-lat|ed, -lat|ing.** *Geometry.* to osculate at more consecutive points than usually suffice to determine the locus.

**su|per|os|cu|la|tion** (sü′pər os′kyə lā′shən), *n. Geometry.* the act or process of superosculating.

**su|per|o|vu|late** (sü′pər ō′vyə lāt), *v.,* **-lat|ed, -lat|ing.** —*v.i.* to produce more than the normal number of eggs at one time, especially through hormonal treatment: *Farm animals could be induced to superovulate* (New Scientist). —*v.t.* to cause to superovulate: *It is planned to superovulate the infertile patients with a dose of gonadotrophin hormones* (London Times).

**su|per|o|vu|la|tion** (sü′pər ō′vyə lā′shən), *n.* **1** the process of inducing the ovaries of animals to greater than normal activity, as by the injection of a hormone serum: *The scientists here claim that superovulation doesn't affect the fertility of the donor animal* (Wall Street Journal). **2** the greater production of eggs resulting from this treatment: *The agent that is capable of producing this superovulation ... is the pituitary's gonad-stimulating hormone* (Scientific American).

**su|per|par|a|sit|ic** (sü′pər par′ə sit′ik), *adj.* having to do with superparasitism.

**su|per|par|a|sit|ism** (sü′pər par′ə sī tiz′əm), *n.* the infestation of parasites by other parasites.

**su|per|pa|tri|ot** (sü′pər pā′trē ət; *British* -pat′rē ət), *n.* an extremely or excessively patriotic person.

**su|per|pa|tri|ot|ic** (sü′pər pā′trē ot′ik; *British* -pat′rē ot′ik), *adj.* extremely or excessively patriotic: *New York City's Society of Tammany adopted its own constitution as a superpatriotic club for 100%-pure Americans* (Time).

**su|per|pa|tri|ot|ism** (sü′pər pā′trē ə tiz′əm; *British* -pat′rē ə tiz′əm), *n.* extreme or excessive patriotism.

**su|per|phos|phate** (sü′pər fos′fāt), *n. Chemistry.* **1** any one of various phosphates, such as bone or boneblack, which have been treated with sulfuric acid to increase their solubility for use as fertilizers. **2** a phosphate containing an excess of phosphoric acid; acid phosphate.

**su|per|phys|i|cal** (sü′pər fiz′ə kəl), *adj.* above or outside of the physical realm; hyperphysical.

**su|per|plas|tic** (sü′pər plas′tik), *adj.* **1** capable of plastic deformation under very small stress at high temperature: *Superplastic materials ... are characterized by a very small grain size ... and an immense capacity for plastic deformation at elevated temperatures, without fracture occurring* (New Scientist). **2** made out of a superplastic material: *Superplastic cars should be quieter, and their scrap value far higher than that of steel cars* (Geoffrey Charles). **3** having to do with or characteristic of superplastic materials: *Some alloys, when deformed at certain rates and in certain temperature ranges, can stretch out like chewing gum and be tremendously deformed without breaking. This superplastic behavior is being studied ... to put it to industrial use* (O. Cutler Shepard). —**su′per|plas′ti|cal|ly,** *adv.*

**su|per|plas|tic|i|ty** (sü′pər plas tis′ə tē), *n.* the property or quality of being superplastic: *Key to achieving superplasticity is in the compounding of proper metals, neither of which can have crystals more than a few millionths of an inch in diameter* (Science News).

**su|per|pol|y|mer** (sü′pər pol′ē mər), *n.* a polymer having very large molecules.

**su|per|pos|a|ble** (sü′pər pō′zə bəl), *adj.* that can be superposed; not interfering with one another, or not rendering one another impossible, as two displacements or strains.

**su|per|pose** (sü′pər pōz′), *v.t.,* **-posed, -pos|ing.** **1** to place above or on something else; superimpose: *Ordinarily, the antennas are vertically superposed a specific distance apart* (L. F. B. Carini). **2** to add onto something else, by or as if by superimposing. **3** *Geometry.* to place (a figure) upon another so that the two coincide. **4** to arrange (the wings of a biplane) one directly over the other. [< French *superposer* < *super-* above (< Latin) + *poser* to place. Compare etym. under **pose**[1].]

**su|per|posed** (sü′pər pōzd′), *adj. Botany.* situated directly over some other part (used especially of a whorl of organs arranged opposite or over another instead of alternately).

**su|per|po|si|tion** (sü′pər pə zish′ən), *n.* **1** the act of placing one thing above or on something else; superposing: *The lattice may be considered as resulting from the superposition of two lattices* [*of atoms*], *say A and B* (P. E. Hodgson). **2** the condition of being so placed: *Such clues as the superposition of later carvings on earlier ones ... helped to determine the sequence of execution* (Scientific American). **3** the thing so placed: *a superposition of gravel on bedrock.* **4** *Geometry.* the transferring of one figure into the position occupied by another, so as to show that they are coincident.

**su|per|pow|er** (sü′pər pou′ər), *n.* **1** power on an extraordinary or extensive scale. **2** a nation so great or strong as a power that its actions and policies greatly affect those of smaller, less powerful nations. The United States and the Soviet Union are superpowers. *It marked the beginning of new forms of competition between the superpowers* (New Yorker). **3** a supernational political entity having authority in the international realm that transcends that of all or most world powers, existing as a concept in political science and reflected to a limited extent in the formal structure of such bodies as the League of Nations and the United Nations. **4** electric power on an extraordinary scale developed by linking together all available power sources in a given area, for providing more efficient and economical power production and distribution.

**su|per|pow|ered** (sü′pər pou′ərd), *adj.* having or provided with extremely high power: *a superpowered rocket fuel, gunboats superpowered by jet engines.*

**su|per|pure** (sü′pər pyůr′), *adj.* extremely pure: *Demand for "superpure" aluminum* (*99.99%*) *has steadily increased* (Harris and Mitchell).

**su|per|race** (sü′pər rās′), *n.* a race regarded as superior to another or others.

**su|per|ra|tion|al** (sü′pər rash′ə nəl, -rash′nəl), *adj.* above or beyond what is rational; transcending reason. —**su′per|ra′tion|al|ly,** *adv.*

**su|per|re|gen|er|a|tion** (sü′pər ri jen′ə rā′shən), *n.* (in wireless telegraphy and telephony) a method of effecting an abnormally great regeneration.

**su|per|re|gen|er|a|tive** (sü′pər ri jen′ə rā′tiv), *adj.* (in wireless telegraphy and telephony) effecting an abnormally great regeneration.

**su|per|sales|man** (sü′pər sālz′mən), *n., pl.* **-men.** a very successful salesman; person who is very skillful and effective in persuading others: *The indomitable Churchill ... put at the head of the party organization no political routineer but a supersalesman, Lord Woolton* (Newsweek).

**su|per|sales|man|ship** (sü′pər sālz′mən ship), *n.* very skillful or effective salesmanship: *Though trained as an architect,* [*he*] *was a slick businessman with a flair for supersalesmanship* (Time).

**su|per|salt** (sü′pər sôlt′), *n. Chemistry.* an acid salt.

**su|per|sat|u|rate** (sü′pər sach′ə rāt), *v.t.,* **-rat|ed,**

**-rat|ing.** **1** to saturate to excess: *Cholesterol gallstones form when excess cholesterol precipitates from bile supersaturated with cholesterol* (Joseph B. Kirsner). **2** to dissolve more of a solute in (a solvent) than is sufficient to saturate it. A supersaturated solution is one in which more of a substance is dissolved than the solvent will hold under normal conditions.

**su|per|sat|u|ra|tion** (sü′pər sach′ə rā′shən), *n.* **1** the act or process of saturating to excess, or of adding to beyond saturation: *supersaturation bombing with nuclear and atomic weapons* (Bulletin of Atomic Scientists). **2** the state or condition of being supersaturated.

**su|per|scribe** (sü′pər skrīb′), *v.t.,* **-scribed, -scrib|ing.** **1** to write (words, letters, or one's name) above, on, or outside of something. **2** *Archaic.* to address (a letter or parcel). [< Late Latin *superscrībere* write over or above (in Latin, to do this as a correction) < *super-* above + *scrībere* write]

**su|per|script** (sü′pər skript), *adj., n.* —*adj.* written above a letter, or above the line of writing. —*n.* a number, letter, or other symbol written above and to one side of another symbol. *Example:* In $a^3 = b^n$, the *3* and *n* are superscripts. *The superscript . . . is the total number of particles in the nucleus, and is the nearest integer to the atomic weight* (Sears and Zemansky). [< Late Latin *superscriptus,* past participle of *superscrībere;* see etym. under **superscribe**]

**su|per|scrip|tion** (sü′pər skrip′shən), *n.* **1** a writing above, on, or outside of something. **2** something written above or on the outside, such as the address on a letter or parcel. **3** the symbol ℞ (for Latin *recipe,* "take") at the head of a prescription.

**su|per|se|cret** (sü′pər sē′krit), *adj.* = top-secret.

**su|per|sede** (sü′pər sēd′), *v.t.,* **-sed|ed, -sed|ing.** **1** to take the place of; cause to be set aside; displace: *Electric lights have superseded gaslights in most American homes. Atomic reactors have superseded coal furnaces in many power plants.* **SYN:** See syn. under **replace.** **2** to fill the place of (someone removed from an office); succeed and supplant; replace: *A new governor superseded the old one.* **SYN:** See syn. under **replace.** **3** to set aside or ignore in promotion; promote another over the head of. [< Middle French, Old French *superceder,* learned borrowing from Latin *supersedēre* be superior to, refrain from (in Medieval Latin, succeed to an estate) < *super-* above + *sedēre* sit]

**su|per|se|de|as** (sü′pər sē′dē as), *n., pl.* **-de|as.** *Law.* a writ ordering a delay in legal proceedings or suspending the powers of an officer, especially from a court of appeal to a lower court: *The judge also ruled that . . . the defendants could file a supersedeas bond* (Wall Street Journal). [< Medieval Latin *supersedeas* you shall stay, present subjunctive of Latin *supersedēre*]

**su|per|sed|ence** (sü′pər sē′dəns), *n.* = supersession.

**su|per|sed|er** (sü′pər sē′dər), *n.* a person or thing that supersedes.

**su|per|se|dure** (sü′pər sē′jər), *n.* = supersession.

**su|per|sen|ior|i|ty** (sü′pər sēn yôr′ə tē, -yor′-), *n., pl.* **-ties.** seniority not based upon age or length of service: *The Board's five members unanimously found that the award of "superseniority" to replacements for strikers is a form of discrimination against employees engaged in economic walkouts* (Wall Street Journal).

**su|per|sen|si|ble** (sü′pər sen′sə bəl), *adj.* outside or above the sensory realm; supersensory.

**su|per|sen|si|bly** (sü′pər sen′sə blē), *adv.* in a supersensible manner.

**su|per|sen|si|tive** (sü′pər sen′sə tiv), *adj.* extremely or abnormally sensitive; hypersensitive: *Sound was supplied by a supersensitive miniature microphone pinned to Philip's lapel* (Newsweek). —**su′per|sen′si|tive|ly,** *adv.* —**su′per|sen′si|tive|ness,** *n.*

**su|per|sen|si|tiv|i|ty** (sü′pər sen′sə tiv′ə tē), *n.* extreme sensitivity; hypersensitivity.

**su|per|sen|so|ry** (sü′pər sen′sər ē), *adj.* outside or above the sensory realm; independent of the organs of sense; extrasensory.

**su|per|sen|su|al** (sü′pər sen′shü əl), *adj.* **1** = supersensory. **2** = spiritual.

**su|per|serv|ice|a|ble** (sü′pər sėr′və sə bəl), *adj.* **1** extremely serviceable. **2** doing or offering service beyond what is desired; officious.

**su|per|ses|sion** (sü′pər sesh′ən), *n.* **1** the act of superseding: *The progressive subordination of such [military] alliances to, and their ultimate supersession by, the collective security system of the United Nations, should be an integral part of the process of general and complete disarmament by stages* (Bulletin of Atomic Scientists). **2** the condition of being superseded. [< Medieval Latin *supersessio, -onis* < Latin *supersedēre;* see etym. under **supersede**]

**su|per|ses|sive** (sü′pər ses′iv), *adj.* superseding.

**su|per|size** (sü′pər sīz′), *adj.* = supersized.

**su|per|sized** (sü′pər sīzd′), *adj.* of very great size; oversized.

**super slurper,** a material that absorbs several thousand times its weight in water or some solution of water. Super slurpers are made by combining starch molecules with synthetic polymers. *The U.S. Department of Agriculture (USDA) increased the absorbability of its super slurper almost threefold. The newest modified version of this substance soaks up 5,000 times its weight of water* (Frederick C. Price).

**su|per|son|ic** (sü′pər son′ik), *adj., n.* —*adj.* **1** of or having to do with sound waves beyond the limit of human audibility (above frequencies of 20,000 cycles per second); ultrasonic: *When mutations are induced in fruit flies by . . . supersonic vibrations or some other artificial means, most of them are lethal* (Scientific American). **2** greater than the speed of sound in air at normal pressure and temperature (about 1,100 feet or 335 meters per second): *The difference in air flow between subsonic and supersonic speeds in turn has created a wholly new branch of aerodynamics* (Scientific American). **3** capable of moving at a speed greater than the speed of sound: *supersonic aircraft.* —*n.* a supersonic wave. —**su′per|son′i|cal|ly,** *adv.*

**su|per|son|ics** (sü′pər son′iks), *n.* the science dealing with the nature and uses of supersonic waves and the phenomena associated with them; ultrasonics.

**supersonic transport,** a large jet aircraft that flies 1200 to 1800 miles per hour: *Supersonic transports might modify the stratosphere, globally . . . and their climatic consequences, must . . . be removed* (New Scientist). *Abbr:* SST (no periods).

**su|per|space** (sü′pər spās′), *n. Physics.* a theoretical expanse in which all three-dimensional spaces are points: *Superspace is a mathematical construction that allows physicists to order all the possible three-dimensional spaces in such a way that they can be compared with one another in the way physical theories apply to them* (Science News). *In superspace there is no time* (New Scientist).

**su|per|spe|cies** (sü′pər spē′shēz, sü′pər spē′-), *n., pl.* **-cies** (-shēz). a group of species which are related, especially on a geographical or ecological basis.

**su|per|spec|ta|cle** (sü′pər spek′tə kəl), *n.* a very spectacular show or production: *"Spartacus" is a new kind of Hollywood movie: a superspectacle with spiritual vitality and moral force* (Time).

**su|per|speed** (sü′pər spēd′), *n.* extremely high speed, especially sonic or supersonic speed: *Planes at superspeeds encounter stresses not ordinarily met* (Science News Letter).

**su|per|star** (sü′pər stär′), *n.* **1** an exceptionally successful star, as in sports or motion pictures: *Why don't they wait until he's been in the league for six, seven or eight years before they begin comparing him with the great stars, let alone superstars like Musial* (Birmingham News). **2a** an exceptionally large star or other heavenly body: *If it stemmed from the explosion of a star, it must have been a truly gigantic explosion— the disintegration of a superstar at least 100,000 times more massive than our sun!* (Scientific American). **b** a heavenly body that is a powerful source of electromagnetic waves.

**su|per|state** (sü′pər stāt′), *n.* a very large or powerful state.

**su|per|sti|tion** (sü′pər stish′ən), *n.* **1** an unreasoning fear of what is unknown, mysterious, or imaginary, especially in connection with religion; worship based on fear or ignorance; unreasoning expectation: *Superstition is the religion of feeble minds* (Edmund Burke). **2** a belief or practice founded on ignorant fear or mistaken reverence: *A common superstition considers 13 an unlucky number. New truths . . . begin as heresies and . . . end as superstitions* (Thomas H. Huxley). [< Latin *superstitiō, -ōnis* excessive fear of the gods < *superstāre* stand on, or over < *super-* above + *stāre* stand]

**su|per|sti|tious** (sü′pər stish′əs), *adj.* full of superstition; likely to believe superstitions; caused by superstition: *a superstitious habit, a superstitious belief. Gamblers and adventurers are generally superstitious* (Bret Harte). —**su′per|sti′tious|ly,** *adv.* —**su′per|sti′tious|ness,** *n.*

**su|per|stra|tum** (sü′pər strā′təm), *n., pl.* **-ta** (-tə), **-tums.** a stratum or layer deposited over or upon something. [< New Latin *superstratum,* noun use of neuter past participle of Latin *supersternere* to spread over < *super-* over + *sternere* lay down]

**su|per|struct** (sü′pər strukt′), *v.t.* to build upon something else; erect as a superstructure: (*Figurative.*) *Those . . . on whose approbation his esteem of himself was superstructed* (Samuel Johnson). [< Latin *superstructus,* past participle of *superstruere* < *super-* over + *struere* to build]

**su|per|struc|tur|al** (sü′pər struk′chər əl), *adj.* of or having to do with a superstructure.

**su|per|struc|ture** (sü′pər struk′chər), *n.* **1** a structure built on something else as a foundation. **2** all of a building above the foundation. **3** the parts of a ship, especially a naval vessel, above the main deck: *The lifeboats, the great funnels, and the bulk of her superstructure are of aluminum* (Newsweek). **4** the part of a bridge supported by the piers and abutments. **5** the ties and rails of a railroad line, supported by the ballast.

**su|per|sub|ma|rine** (sü′pər sub′mə rēn), *n.* a large and powerful type of submarine.

**su|per|sub|tle** (sü′pər sut′əl), *adj.* extremely or excessively subtle.

**su|per|sub|tle|ty** (sü′pər sut′əl tē), *n., pl.* **-ties.** excessive subtlety; overnicety of discrimination.

**su|per|sys|tem** (sü′pər sis′təm), *n.* a very large or extensive system: *a galactic supersystem. An example of the supersystem of the future is . . . an ultrasophisticated computer communications system* (M. W. Martin).

**su|per|tank|er** (sü′pər tang′kər), *n.* a huge tanker, ranging above 70,000 tons: *Existing supertankers sometimes must transfer their cargo to smaller tankers because harbor facilities are inadequate to handle the giant ships* (Wall Street Journal).

**su|per|task** (sü′pər task′, -täsk′), *n.* any one of various logical paradoxes involving the challenge to complete an infinite sequence of tasks.

**su|per|tax** (sü′pər taks′), *n.* a tax in addition to a normal tax; surtax.

**su|per|ter|ra|ne|an** (sü′pər tə rā′nē ən), *adj.* that is above the earth's surface; not subterranean.

**su|per|ter|res|tri|al** (sü′pər tə res′trē əl), *adj.* = superterranean.

**su|per|ton|ic** (sü′pər ton′ik), *n. Music.* the second tone or note of a scale; tone or note next above the tonic. See picture under **dominant.**

**su|per|trans|u|ran|ic** (sü′pər trans′yü ran′ik), *adj., n.* —*adj.* surpassing in mass the transuranic elements (those with atomic numbers higher than uranium); superheavy. —*n.* a supertransuranic element.

**su|per|vene** (sü′pər vēn′), *v.i.,* **-vened, -ven|ing.** to come as something additional or interrupting; come directly or shortly after something else, either as a consequence of it or in contrast with it: *Those further away are likely to suffer from "radiation sickness," followed by changes in the blood; these changes may continue for up to a month, after which death may supervene* (London Times). [< Latin *supervenīre* to follow closely < *super-* upon + *venīre* to come]

**su|per|ven|ience** (sü′pər vēn′yəns), *n.* **1** the fact of being supervenient. **2** the act of supervening; supervention.

**su|per|ven|ient** (sü′pər vēn′yənt), *adj.* supervening.

**su|per|ven|tion** (sü′pər ven′shən), *n.* a supervening.

**su|per|vis|al** (sü′pər vī′zəl), *n., adj.* —*n.* = supervision. —*adj.* = supervisory.

**su|per|vise** (sü′pər vīz), *v.t.,* **-vised, -vis|ing.** to look after and direct (work, workers, or a process); oversee; manage; superintend: *Study halls are supervised by teachers.* [< Medieval Latin *supervisus,* past participle of *supervidēre* < Latin *super-* over + *vidēre* to see]

**su|per|vi|sion** (sü′pər vizh′ən), *n.* **1** the act or function of supervising or overseeing; management; direction; oversight: *The house was built under the careful supervision of an architect.* **SYN:** superintendence. **2** *U.S.* **a** the management and evaluation of instruction, especially in a public school or school system. **b** the authority for this.

**su|per|vi|sor** (sü′pər vī′zər), *n.* **1** a person who supervises: *The music supervisor had charge of the school band, chorus, and orchestra.* **SYN:** administrator, director. **2** *U.S.* an official whose duties are to supervise and assist the teachers of a particular subject, especially in a public school or school system. **3** *U.S.* (in certain states) an official who is the elected administrative head of a town or other division of a county and who is a member of the governing board of the county.

**su|per|vi|sor|ship** (sü′pər vī′zər ship), *n.* the position or authority of a supervisor.

**su|per|vi|so|ry** (sü′pər vī′zər ē), *adj.* **1** of a supervisor; having to do with supervision. **2** supervising.

**su|per|volt|age** (sü′pər vōl′tij), *n.* any very high

**Pronunciation Key:** **h**a**t**, **ā**ge, c**ã**re, f**ä**r; l**e**t, **ē**qual, t**ė**rm; **i**t, **ī**ce; h**o**t, **ō**pen, **ô**rder; **oi**l, **ou**t; c**u**p, p**ů**t, r**ü**le; **ch**ild; lo**ng**; **th**in; **ᵺ**en; **zh**, measure; **ə** represents **a** in about, **e** in taken, **i** in pencil, **o** in lemon, **u** in circus.

voltage, especially radiation voltage ranging above 500,000 volts: *Only a few of the nation's largest hospitals have these big, supervoltage X-ray machines* (Science News Letter).

**su|per|wa|ter** (sü′pər wôt′ər, -wot′-), = polywater.

**su|per|weap|on** (sü′pər wep′ən), *n.* any military weapon greatly superior to other existing or conventional weapons: *They warn the solid-fuel Minuteman won't be a superweapon, it can't carry as big a warhead as the liquid-fuel jobs* (Wall Street Journal).

**su|per|wom|an** (sü′pər wu̇m′ən), *n., pl.* **-wom|en.** a woman of extraordinary or superhuman powers: *The novel's heroine, a toothsome superwoman who runs a railroad* (Atlantic).

**su|pi|nate** (sü′pə nāt), *v.,* **-nat|ed, -nat|ing.** — ***v.t.*** to hold or turn (the hand or forelimb) so that the palm faces up or forward.
— ***v.i.*** to be supinated; undergo supination.
[< Latin *supīnāre* (with English *-ate*[1]) < *supīnus;* see etym. under **supine**, adjective]

**su|pi|na|tion** (sü′pə nā′shən), *n.* **1** a rotation of the hand or forelimb so that the palm faces up or forward. **2** a similar movement of the foot, hindlimb, shoulder, or the like. **3** the position which results from this rotation.

**su|pi|na|tor** (sü′pə nā′tər), *n.* a muscle, especially of the forearm, that effects or assists in supination. [< New Latin *supinator* < Latin *supīnāre* supinate]

**su|pine** (*adj.* sü pīn′; *n.* sü′pīn), *adj., n.* — ***adj.*** **1** lying flat on the back: *a supine person.* **2** recumbent with the face or front upward: *a supine position.* **3** *Figurative.* lazily inactive; listless, especially morally or mentally. **SYN**: languid, indolent, inert. **4** not active; passive. **5** sloping or inclining backwards: *like the young moon supine* (Shelley). **6** supinated. [< Latin *supīnus,* related to *super* above]
— ***n.*** **1** either of two Latin verbal nouns formed from the stem of the past participle, one ending in *-tum* or *-sum* and the other ending in *-tū* or *-sū.* **2** a verbal form of similar function in another language.
[< Late Latin *supīnum* (*verbum*) supine (word), noun use of *supīnum,* neuter of *supīnus;* see the adjective] — **su|pine′ly,** *adv.* — **su|pine′ness,** *n.*

**supp.,** supplement.

**sup|per** (sup′ər), *n.* **1** the evening meal; meal eaten early in the evening if dinner is near noon, or late in the evening if dinner is at six or later. **2** the hour at which this is eaten; suppertime. **3** such a meal made the occasion of a social or festive gathering: *a church supper.* [Middle English *super,* or *soper* < Old French *soper,* noun use of infinitive, to sup, dine]

**supper club,** = night club.

**sup|per|less** (sup′ər lis), *adj.* having no supper; going without supper: *The disobedient boy was sent to bed supperless.*

**sup|per|time** (sup′ər tīm′), *n.* the time at which supper is served: *Then I went back to the hotel and sat around until it got close to suppertime* (New Yorker).

**suppl.,** supplement.

**sup|plant** (sə plant′, -plänt′), *v.t.* **1** to take the place of; displace or set aside; supersede: *Machinery has largely supplanted hand labor in making shoes.* **SYN**: See syn. under **replace. 2** to take the place of by unfair methods: *The general plotted to supplant the king with the help of the army.* **SYN**: See syn. under **replace. 3** to remove from its position; get rid of; oust. [< Latin *supplantāre* trip up < *sub-* under + *planta* sole of the foot] — **sup|plant′er,** *n.*

**sup|plan|ta|tion** (sup′lən tā′shən), *n.* **1** the act of supplanting. **2** the condition of being supplanted.

**sup|plant|ment** (sə plant′mənt, -plänt′-), *n.* = supplantation.

**sup|ple** (sup′əl), *adj.,* **-pler, -plest,** *v.,* **-pled, -pling.** — ***adj.*** **1** bending or folding easily, without breaking or cracking; pliant: *a supple birch tree, supple leather.* **SYN**: pliable. **2** capable of bending easily; moving easily or nimbly: *a supple dancer. "In my youth," said the sage ... "I kept all my limbs very supple By the use of this ointment"* (Lewis Carroll). **3** *Figurative.* readily adaptable to different ideas, circumstances, or people: **a** flexible; elastic: *a keen and supple mind.* **SYN**: plastic. **b** yielding readily to persuasion or influence; compliant: *She gets along well with people because of her supple nature.* **4** artfully or servilely complaisant or obsequious.
— ***v.t.*** to make supple: *To set free, to supple and to train the faculties* (James Russell Lowell).
— ***v.i.*** to grow supple.
[Middle English *souple* < Old French *souple,* and *supple* < Latin *supplex, -icis* submissive; (literally) bending, related to *supplicāre;* see etym. under **supplicate**] — **sup′ple|ly,** *adv.* — **sup′ple|ness,** *n.*

**sup|ple|jack** (sup′əl jak′), *n.* any one of various climbing and twining shrubs with tough, pliable stems, found in tropical and subtropical forests.

**sup|ple|ment** (*n.* sup′lə mənt; *v.* sup′lə ment), *n., v.* — ***n.*** **1** something added to complete a thing, or to make it larger or better. Newspapers have supplements that are usually of a special character and issued as an additional feature. *There is a travel supplement in the Sunday newspaper. That history book has a supplement containing an account of what has happened since 1970.* **2** something added to supply a deficiency: *a diet supplement.* **3** the amount needed to make an angle or arc equal to 180 degrees. *Abr:* supp.
— ***v.t.*** to supply what is lacking in; add to; complete: *He supplements his diet with vitamin pills.* **SYN**: See syn. under **complement.**
[< Latin *supplēmentum* < *supplēre;* see etym. under **supply**[1]] — **sup′ple|ment|er,** *n.*
— ***Syn.*** *n.* **1 Supplement, appendix** mean something added to a book or paper to complete or improve it. **Supplement** applies to a section added later or printed separately to bring the information up to date, correct mistakes, or present special features: *This encyclopedia has a supplement covering recent events.* **Appendix** applies to a section added at the end of a book or document to give extra information: *The appendix contains a list of dates.*

**sup|ple|men|tal** (sup′lə men′təl), *adj., n.* = supplementary.

**sup|ple|men|ta|ri|ly** (sup′lə men′tər ə lē, -trə lē), *adv.* in a supplementary manner.

**sup|ple|men|ta|ry** (sup′lə men′tər ē, -trē), *adj., n., pl.* **-ries.** — ***adj.*** **1** additional: *a volume supplementary to the original encyclopedia.* **SYN**: extra, auxiliary. **2** added to supply what is lacking: *The new members of the class received supplementary instruction.*
— ***n.*** something which is supplementary; supplement: *Mr. Callaghan added a string of supplementaries to Mr. Wilson's simple challenge* (Manchester Guardian Weekly). **SYN**: addition, appendage.

**supplementary angle,** either of two angles which together form an angle of 180 degrees (a straight line): *A 60-degree angle is the supplementary angle of a 120-degree angle.* See diagram under **angle**[1].

**sup|ple|men|ta|tion** (sup′lə men tā′shən), *n.* **1** the act of supplementing: *Supplementation of the diet with egg-yolk ... resulted in a fall in recurrences of rheumatic fever* (New Scientist). **2** a supplementary addition.

**sup|plete** (sə plēt′), *v.t.,* **-plet|ed, -plet|ing.** *Obsolete.* to supplement. [< Latin *supplētus,* past participle of *supplēre;* see etym. under **supply**[1]]

**sup|ple|tion** (sə plē′shən), *n. Grammar.* the occurrence or use of suppletive forms.

**sup|ple|tive** (sə plē′tiv, sup′lə-), *adj. Grammar.* **1** (of a word or form) used as the inflected form in a paradigm that lacks one or more inflected forms, as *went* in "go, went, gone," and *better, best* in "good, better, best." **2** (of a paradigm) containing one or more such words or forms. [< Medieval Latin *suppletivus* < Latin *supplēre;* see etym. under **supply**[1]]

**sup|ple|to|ry** (sup′lə tôr′ē, -tōr′-), *adj.* = supplementary. [< Late Latin *supplētōrium* a supplement]

**sup|pli|ance** (sup′lē əns), *n.* = supplication.

**sup|pli|ant** (sup′lē ənt), *adj., n.* — ***adj.*** asking or praying humbly and earnestly; supplicating: *lifting suppliant hands in a prayer for mercy. He sent a suppliant message for help.* **SYN**: beseeching.
— ***n.*** a person who asks humbly and earnestly: *She knelt as a suppliant at the altar.* **SYN**: supplicant.
[< Middle French, Old French *suppliant* (originally) present participle of *supplier* to pray < Latin *supplicāre;* see etym. under **supplicate**. See etym. of doublet **supplicant.**] — **sup′pli|ant|ly,** *adv.*

**sup|pli|cant** (sup′lə kənt), *adj., n.* = suppliant. [< Latin *supplicāns, -antis,* present participle of *supplicāre;* see etym. under **supplicate**. See etym. of doublet **suppliant.**] — **sup′pli|cant|ly,** *adv.*

**sup|pli|cat** (sup′lə kat), *n.* a formal petition for a degree or its equivalent at an English university. [< Latin *supplicat* he supplicates < *supplicāre* to beg, supplicate]

**sup|pli|cate** (sup′lə kāt), *v.,* **-cat|ed, -cat|ing.**
— ***v.t.*** **1** to beg (a person) humbly and earnestly; address an entreaty to: *The mother supplicated the judge to pardon her son.* **SYN**: entreat, beseech, petition. **2** to beg humbly for (something); seek by entreaty.
— ***v.i.*** to pray humbly; present a humble petition.
[< Latin *supplicāre* (with English *-ate*[1]) beg, beseech < *sub-* under, down + *plicāre* to bend, kneel] — **sup′pli|cat′ing|ly,** *adv.*

**sup|pli|ca|tion** (sup′lə kā′shən), *n.* **1** the action of supplicating: *He knelt in supplication. Their grave, white faces lifted in a single supplication to the ship* (Thomas Wolfe). **2** Usually, **supplications.** a humble and earnest request or prayer: *Supplications to God arose from all the churches of the besieged town.*

**sup|pli|ca|tor** (sup′lə kā′tər), *n.* a person or thing that supplicates; suppliant.

**sup|pli|ca|to|ry** (sup′lə kə tôr′ē, -tōr′-), *adj.* supplicating.

**sup|pli|er** (sə plī′ər), *n.* a person or thing that supplies; provider; purveyor: *Ask your supplier to show you how expressive your letterhead looks* (Time).

**sup|plies** (sə plīz′), *n.pl.* See under **supply**[1].

**sup|ply**[1] (sə plī′), *v.,* **-plied, -ply|ing,** *n., pl.* **-plies.**
— ***v.t.*** **1** to provide (what is wanted or needed); furnish: *to supply power to a factory. The school supplies books for the children. The records did not supply a description of him* (Thomas B. Costain). **SYN**: afford. **2** to furnish or provide (a person or persons) with what is wanted or needed: *He is supplying us with milk. Brazil supplies us with much of our coffee.* **3** to furnish (a thing) with something needed: *to supply plants with water and sunlight.* **4** to make up for (a loss, lack, or absence); compensate for: *to supply a deficiency.* **5** to satisfy (a need or want): *There was just enough to supply the demand.* **6** to fill (a place, vacancy, pulpit, or other position) as a substitute. **7** to fill: *Rocks and stumps supplied the place of chairs at the picnic.* — ***v.i.*** to fill another's place, pulpit, or other position temporarily; be a substitute.
— ***n.*** **1** a quantity ready for use; stock; store: *The school gets its supplies of books, papers, pencils, and chalk from the city. The United States has very large supplies of coal. The amount of the blood supply is therefore all-important to the heart* (Scientific American). **2** the act of supplying a need, desire, want, loss, lack, or vacancy. **3** a quantity or amount supplied or provided: *a new supply of paper.* **4** *Economics.* the quantity of any commodity in the market ready for purchase, especially at a given price: *a supply of coffee.* **5** a sum of money appropriated by a national legislature to meet the expenses of government. **6** a person who fills a place, vacancy, pulpit, or other position as a substitute for another. **7** *Obsolete.* reinforcements. **8** *Obsolete.* assistance; aid.
**supplies,** the food and equipment necessary for an army, expedition, or the like: *The invaders remained until their supplies were exhausted* (Benjamin Jowett).
[< Old French *supplier* < Latin *supplēre* < *sub-* from under + *-plēre* to fill]

**sup|ply**[2] (sup′lē), *adv.* in a supple manner. [reduction of *supple* + *-ly*[1]]

**supply and demand,** the interplay of the quantity of goods offered for sale at specified prices and the quantity of goods purchased at those prices in a free market: *The meeting would decide whether ... export quotas should be changed in the light of supply and demand* (New York Times).

**supply pastor,** a preacher who fills a pulpit during the temporary absence of the pastor: *He was licensed as a lay preacher, and during his college years he spent his weekends as a supply pastor* (Time).

**supply reel,** the reel of a tape recorder or motion-picture camera or projector that holds the tape or film to be wound up by the take-up reel.

**sup|port** (sə pôrt′, -pōrt′), *v., n.* — ***v.t.*** **1** to keep from falling or sinking; bear the weight of; hold up; sustain: *Walls support the roof. Crutches supported the injured man.* **2** to give strength, courage, or confidence to; keep up; help: *Hope supports us in time of trouble.* **3** to supply with the necessities of life; provide for: *Parents usually support their children.* **SYN**: keep. **4** to supply funds or means for: *to support the expenses of government.* **5** to maintain, keep up, or keep going: *a town which is able to support two orchestras.* **6** to be in favor of (a person, party, cause, or course of action); back; second: *to support a motion, to support the foreign-aid bill. The members of his cabinet supported the President's view.* **7** to help prove; bear out: *The facts support their claim. The primary assumption made in the theory was supported by evidence* (A. W. Haslett). **SYN**: verify, confirm, substantiate. **8** to put up with; bear; endure; tolerate: *She couldn't support life without friends.* **SYN**: suffer. **9** to provide a military unit with supplies, transportation, reserves, or protection: *Naval fire supported the marine landings.* **10** *Theater.* **a** to act with (a leading actor); play a subordinate, though often important, part to; assist. **b** to act or play (a part) with success.
— ***n.*** **1a** the act of supporting: *Columns serve for support. He spoke in support of the proposal.* **b** the condition of being supported: *A building must have support. This argument lacks support.* **2** help or assistance; aid: *He needs the support of a scholarship. Inability to enlist informed and*

*enthusiastic public participation and support ...* (New York Times). SYN: backing. **3** maintenance; means of livelihood: *That family lacks support.* SYN: See syn. under **living**. **4** a person or thing that supports; prop; stay: *The neck is the support of the head. Wheat supports are due to fall faster than those on other crops* (Wall Street Journal). **5** *Military.* **a** the assistance or protection given to one unit or element by another. **b** a unit or a part of a unit which provides supplies, transportation, reserves, or protection to another unit or to the rest of the unit: *Aviation may be used as a support for infantry.* **c** the part of any unit held in reserve during the initial phase of an attack. **6** the material used as a foundation for a painting, such as a canvas, a wooden panel, or a sheet of paper.

[< Old French *supporter,* learned borrowing from Latin *supportāre* convey, bring up < *sub-* (up from) under + *portāre* carry] —**sup|port′ing|ly,** *adv.*

—***Syn.*** *v.t.* **1, 2 Support, maintain, uphold** mean to hold up or keep up, literally or figuratively. **Support** suggests bearing the weight or giving needed strength to prevent something or someone from falling or sinking: *Teammates supported the injured player.* **Maintain** suggests keeping up in a certain condition by providing what is needed to prevent loss of strength, value, or some other desirable quality: *The state maintains the highways.* **Uphold** chiefly suggests giving aid or moral support to a person, cause, belief, or institution: *He upheld his brother's honor.*

**sup|port|a|bil|i|ty** (sə pôr′tə bil′ə tē, -pōr′-), *n.* the quality or condition of being supportable.

**sup|port|a|ble** (sə pôr′tə bəl, -pōr′-), *adj.* that can be supported; bearable or endurable: *Future wars must have limited objectives, attainable by limited means and making defeat a painful, but supportable blow to the loser* (Bulletin of Atomic Scientists). —**sup|port′a|ble|ness,** *n.*

**sup|port|a|bly** (sə pôr′tə blē, -pōr′-), *adv.* in a supportable manner; so as to be supportable or endurable.

**sup|port|er** (sə pôr′tər, -pōr′-), *n.* **1** a person who supports, especially one who sides with, backs up, or assists a person or cause; adherent; partisan. **2** a thing that supports, especially something worn to hold up a garment, such as a garter, or some part of the body, such as a jockstrap. **3** *Heraldry.* either of two figures, as of animals or human beings, standing one on each side of an escutcheon, and often depicted as holding it.

**sup|port|ing** (sə pôr′ting, -pōr′-), *adj.* **1** keeping from falling: *The veins and veinlets combine supporting and conductive tissues* (Fred W. Emerson). **2** keeping from giving way; sustaining; giving assistance or relief: *a strong supporting cast, a topnotch director* (Time). **3** confirmatory; corroborative.

**sup|por|tive** (sə pôr′tiv, -pōr′-), *adj.* providing support; supporting; sustaining: *supportive evidence, a supportive arch. Mr. Jones has always played a supportive role at board meetings* (Harper's). —**sup|por′tive|ly,** *adv.*

**supportive therapy** or **treatment, 1** a moderate form of psychotherapy to arrive at a practical solution to a patient's problems by direct and sympathetic discussion with him: *In supportive therapy ... the doctor merely makes an effort to understand sympathetically the problem, sorting out reactions, and advising the patient about his course of conduct* (Newsweek). **2** medical therapy to relieve the symptoms of a disease or disturbance without direct treatment, such as the use of blood transfusions in the treatment of shock.

**sup|port|less** (sə pôrt′lis, -pōrt′-), *adj.* having no support.

**support price,** *U.S.* the price, set in relation to the parity ratio, at which the government is ready to purchase commodities as a part of price support: *High support prices have encouraged farmers to overproduce* (Wall Street Journal). *Lower support prices will have an offsetting effect on net income for wheat farmers* (Mark V. Keeler).

**sup|por|tress** (sə pôr′tris, -pōr′-), *n.* a woman supporter.

**sup|pos|a|ble** (sə pō′zə bəl), *adj.* that can be supposed.

**sup|pos|a|bly** (sə pō′zə blē), *adv.* in a supposable degree or way; as may be supposed or presumed.

**sup|pos|al** (sə pō′zəl), *n.* supposition; assumption; conjecture. [< Old French *supposaille* < *supposer* suppose + *-aille* -al[2]]

**sup|pose** (sə pōz′), *v.,* **-posed, -pos|ing.** —*v.t.* **1** to consider as possible; take for granted; assume: *Suppose we leave early in the morning. Suppose we are late, what will the teacher say? Suppose that the sum of the angles equals 90 degrees.* **2** to consider as true or probably true; incline to think or believe: *Where do you suppose I left my purse? This furniture is supposed to have been in the family for 150 years.* **3** to believe, think, or imagine; presume: *I suppose that she will come as usual. Did you suppose that all snakes were poisonous? Happiness depends ... less on exterior things than most suppose* (William Cowper). **4** to presume the existence or presence of: *We have no reason to suppose ... any radical difference of language* (William Ewart Gladstone). **5** to require as a condition; involve as necessary; imply; presuppose: *An invention supposes an inventor.* **6** to expect (used in the passive): *I'm supposed to be there early.*

—*v.i.* to conjecture; think; imagine.

[< Old French *supposer* < *sub-* under + *poser.* Compare etym. under **pose**[1].]

**sup|posed** (sə pōzd′), *adj.* **1** accepted as true, but without actual or final proof; assumed: *a supposed fact. The supposed beggar was really a prince.* **2** considered as possible or probable; hypothetical: *a supposed limit to human development.* **3** imaginary: *a supposed insult.*

**sup|pos|ed|ly** (sə pō′zid lē), *adv.* according to what is supposed or was supposed. SYN: presumably, probably.

**sup|pos|ing** (sə pō′zing), *conj.* in the event that; if: *Supposing it rains, shall we still go to the zoo?*

**sup|po|si|tion** (sup′ə zish′ən), *n.* **1** the act of supposing: *a policy based on the supposition of continued peace.* **2** a thing supposed; belief; opinion: *to abandon a basic supposition. The speaker planned his talk on the supposition that his hearers would be schoolchildren.* SYN: assumption, conjecture. [< Old French *supposition,* learned borrowing from Latin *suppositiō, -ōnis* a placing under, substitution (in Medieval Latin, a translation of Greek *hypóthesis* hypothesis) < *suppōnere* to substitute < *sub-* under + *ponere* to place]

**sup|po|si|tion|al** (sup′ə zish′ə nəl), *adj.* of or based on supposition; hypothetical; supposed. —**sup′po|si′tion|al|ly,** *adv.*

**sup|po|si|tious** (sup′ə zish′əs), *adj.* **1** of or based on supposition; hypothetical; supposed: *suppositious enemies, a suppositious relationship.* **2** not genuine; spurious; false: *a suppositious testimony.*

**sup|pos|i|ti|tious** (sə poz′ə tish′əs), *adj.* **1** put by fraud in the place of the genuine or original thing or person: *a supposititious copy in place of the original.* **2** not genuine; pretended; false: *a supposititious science.* SYN: spurious, counterfeit. **3** involving or based on supposition; hypothetical; supposed: *a supposititious case.* **4** illegitimate: *a supposititious son.* [< Latin *suppositīcius* (with English *-ous*) < *suppōnere;* see etym. under **supposition**] —**sup|pos′i|ti′tious|ly,** *adv.* —**sup|pos′i|ti′tious|ness,** *n.*

**sup|pos|i|tive** (sə poz′ə tiv), *adj., n.* —*adj.* **1** of the nature of, implying, or grounded on supposition; supposed. **2** *Grammar.* expressing a supposition; conditional.

—*n. Grammar.* a suppositive word. —**sup|pos′i|tive|ly,** *adv.*

**sup|pos|i|to|ry** (sə poz′ə tôr′ē, -tōr′-), *n., pl.* **-ries.** a medicine in the form of a cone or cylinder to be put into a body cavity, such as the rectum, vagina, or urethra, for any of various purposes; bougie. [< Medieval Latin *suppositorium,* noun use of adjective, neuter of *suppositorius* < Latin *suppōnere;* see etym. under **supposition**]

**sup|press** (sə pres′), *v.t.* **1** to put an end to; stop by force; put down: *The police suppressed a riot by firing over the heads of the mob.* SYN: subdue, quell, crush. **2** to keep in; hold back; keep from appearing: *to suppress a smile. She suppressed a yawn. Each nation suppressed news that was not favorable to it. Newspapers had easily gotten copies of the Cameron report and published the suppressed paragraph alongside the final official one* (Carl Sandburg). SYN: restrain, repress. **3** to subdue (as a feeling, thought, or habit): *suppressed desires. Gradually the child's unconscious fills more or less deliberately with things forgotten (suppressed) because they are unpleasant* (Time). **4** to check the flow of: *to suppress bleeding.* **5** to keep secret; refrain from disclosing or divulging: *to suppress the truth.* [< Latin *suppressus,* past participle of *supprimere* < *sub-* down, under + *premere* to press]

**sup|pres|sant** (sə pres′ənt), *adj., n.* —*adj.* that suppresses an attack, symptom, reaction, or the like; suppressive: *a suppressant drug or medicine.*

—*n.* **1** a suppressant medicine: *cough suppressants.* **2** a substance that suppresses an effect or reaction: *a fire suppressant.*

**sup|pres|sed|ly** (sə pres′id lē), *adv.* in a suppressed or restrained manner: *to laugh suppressedly.*

**sup|press|er** (sə pres′ər), *n.* = suppressor.

**sup|press|i|ble** (sə pres′ə bəl), *adj.* that can be suppressed.

**sup|pres|sion** (sə presh′ən), *n.* **1** the act of putting down by force or authority; putting an end to: *Soldiers were used in the suppression of the revolt.* **2** the act of keeping in; holding back: *the suppression of a childish, silly fear. The suppression of facts may be as dishonest as the telling of lies.* **3** *Psychoanalysis.* **a** the conscious controlling or inhibiting of a desire or impulse. **b** = repression.

**sup|pres|si|o ver|i** (sə pres′ē ō ver′ī), *Latin.* suppression of the true; misrepresentation of the truth by concealing facts which ought to be made known: *The English Church Union could hardly subscribe ex animo to an interpretation containing an important suppressio veri* (Spectator).

**sup|pres|sive** (sə pres′iv), *adj.* tending to suppress; causing suppression: *The drug, which is synthesized from readily available raw materials, is of the suppressive type, which means it would not provide a cure but would be used to control the disease* (Science News Letter). —**sup|pres′sive|ness,** *n.*

**sup|pres|sor** (sə pres′ər), *n.* **1** a person or thing that suppresses, crushes, or quells. **2** a person or thing that represses, checks, or stifles: *Sound suppressors put the finger squarely on the solution of the jet noise problem* (Wall Street Journal). **3** a person who conceals.

**Supp. Rev. Stat.,** Supplement to the Revised Statutes.

**sup|pur|ant** (sup′yər ənt), *adj., n.* = suppurative.

**sup|pu|rate** (sup′yə rāt), *v.i.,* **-rat|ed, -rat|ing.** to form or discharge pus; fester; maturate: *The infected wound suppurated badly.* [< Latin *suppūrāre* (with English *-ate*[1]) < *sub-* under + *pūs, pūris* pus]

**sup|pu|ra|tion** (sup′yə rā′shən), *n.* **1** the formation or discharge of pus; festering; maturation. **2** = pus.

**sup|pu|ra|tive** (sup′yə rā′tiv), *adj., n.* —***adj.*** **1** promoting suppuration. **2** attended or characterized by suppuration. **3** suppurating.

—*n.* an agent or remedy that promotes suppuration.

**supr.,** supreme.

**su|pra** (sü′prə), *adv.* **1** above. **2** before, in a book or writing. [< Latin *suprā,* related to *super* over]

**supra-,** *prefix.* on; above; beyond, as in *supraliminal, supranational, suprarenal.* [< Latin *suprā,* adverb, preposition, related to *super* over]

**su|pra|e|so|phag|e|al** (sü′prə ē′sə faj′ē əl), *adj.* situated above or on the dorsal side of the esophagus: *supraesophageal ganglia.*

**su|pra|hu|man** (sü′prə hyü′mən), *adj.* = superhuman.

**su|pra|lap|sar|i|an** (sü′prə lap sãr′ē ən), *n., adj.* —*n.* an adherent of the doctrine of supralapsarianism.

—*adj.* of or having to do with supralapsarianism or its adherents.

**su|pra|lap|sar|i|an|ism** (sü′prə lap sãr′ē ə niz′-əm), *n.* the Calvinist doctrine that the division of mankind into the elect and the damned is God's basic purpose and that the fall of man was an instrumentality to achieve this end, consequent on that original purpose, and formed part of the divinely decreed plan of the creation of the world. [< New Latin *supralapsarius* (< Latin *supra-* + *lapsus, -ūs* a fall + *-ārius* having to do with) + English *-ian* + *-ism*]

**su|pra|lim|i|nal** (sü′prə lim′ə nəl), *adj.* above the margin or threshold of consciousness; conscious.

**su|pra|max|il|la** (sü′prə mak sil′ə), *n., pl.* **-max|il|lae** (-mak sil′ē). *Anatomy, Zoology.* **1** the upper jaw. **2** the upper jawbone.

**su|pra|max|il|lar|y** (sü′prə mak′sə ler′ē), *adj., n., pl.* **-lar|ies.** *Anatomy.* —***adj.*** of or having to do with the upper jaw or upper jawbone.

—*n.* the upper jawbone.

**su|pra|mo|lec|u|lar** (sü′prə mə lek′yə lər), *adj.* **1** above, or having more complexity than, a molecule. **2** made up of more than one molecule.

**su|pra|mun|dane** (sü′prə mun′dān), *adj.* = supermundane.

**su|pra|na|tion|al** (sü′prə nash′ə nəl, -nash′nəl), *adj.* above or beyond a nation or state, as in authority; supernational: *The conception of a supranational organization solving the world's quarrels ... is an attractive one* (Punch). —**su′pra|na′tion|al|ly,** *adv.*

**su|pra|na|tion|al|ism** (sü′prə nash′ə nə liz′əm, -nash′nə liz-), *n.* the principle or practice of international cooperation above and beyond national limitations: *In the Council of Ministers, composed of cabinet ministers of all six nations, supranationalism meets nationalism* (Time).

**Pronunciation Key:** hat, āge, cãre, fär; let, ēqual, tėrm; it, īce; hot, ōpen, ôrder; oil, out; cup, pu̇t, rüle; child; long; thin; ᴛʜen; zh, measure; ə represents **a** in about, **e** in taken, **i** in pencil, **o** in lemon, **u** in circus.

**su|pra|na|tion|al|i|ty** (sü′prə nash′ə nal′ə tē), *n.* the state of being supranational: *The [European Economic] Community was bound to develop supranationality as the six countries agreed to common policies* (New York Times).

**su|pra|nat|u|ral** (sü′prə nach′ər əl, -nach′rəl), *adj., n.* = supernatural. — **su′pra|nat′u|ral|ly**, *adv.*

**su|pra|or|bit|al** (sü′prə ôr′bə təl), *adj.* above the orbit of the eye: *Most apes posses a marked bulge of bone, called a supraorbital ridge, which extends unbroken across the region of the skull just over the eyes* (Beals and Hoijer).

**su|pra|per|son|al** (sü′prə pėr′sə nəl, -pėrs′nəl), *adj.* above or beyond the personal: *I refer to the needs of adventure, of risk, and hardship in the search for personal significance by way of suprapersonal goals* (Bulletin of Atomic Scientists).

**su|pra|pro|test** (sü′prə prō′test), *n.* an acceptance or a payment of a bill by a third person to save the reputation of the drawer after protest (official notice) that the drawee has refused to accept or pay it. [Latinization of Italian *sopra protesto* upon protest; *sopra* upon (< Latin *suprā*), *protesto* < *protestare* to protest < Latin *prōtestārī*]

**su|pra|ra|tion|al** (sü′prə rash′ə nəl, -rash′nəl), *adj.* above or beyond the rational; not comprehensible by reason alone: *Revealed theology, by contrast, is suprarational, and although consonant with reason ... reason alone could not have attained to it* (Listener).

**su|pra|re|nal** (sü′prə rē′nəl), *adj., n.* — *adj.* **1** situated above or on the kidney; adrenal. **2** of or from the suprarenal glands.
— *n.* = suprarenal gland, body, or capsule.
[< New Latin (*capsulae*) *suprarenales,* (literally) suprarenal (capsules) < Latin *suprā* above + *renēs* kidneys]

**suprarenal extract**, a solution of the hormone secreted by the suprarenal glands, from which commerical adrenalin is made.

**suprarenal gland, body,** or **capsule**, one of the two ductless glands on or near the upper part of the kidneys, which secrete important hormones, such as adrenalin and cortin; adrenal gland; renal gland.

**su|pra|seg|men|tal** (sü′prə seg men′təl), *adj., n.* — *adj.* **1** above or beyond the segmental: *... the functional organization of the central nervous system as a series of interconnected segmental and suprasegmental pathways* (Science). **2** *Linguistics.* **a** extending over or representing more than one speech sound: *a suprasegmental phoneme. Stress, pitch, juncture, and intonation are the suprasegmental features of an utterance.* **b** of or having to do with suprasegmental features: *suprasegmental phonology.*
— *n. Linguistics.* a suprasegmental feature; superfix.

**su|pra|ther|mal ion detector** (sü′prə thėr′məl), an instrument for recording the flux, quantity, density, velocity, and energy per unit of positive ions near the lunar surface: *the suprathermal ion detector that was designed to record the presence of any gases on the moon* (Time).

**su|prem|a|cist** (sə prem′ə sist, sù-), *n.* a person who believes in the supremacy of one group or person over another: *a male supremacist, a white supremacist.*

**su|prem|a|cy** (sə prem′ə sē, sù-), *n.* **1** the condition or quality of being supreme: *Nature is loth To yield to art her fair supremacy* (Robert Bridges). **2** supreme authority or power. SYN: domination, predominance, mastery. **3** supreme position in achievement, character, or estimation.

**su|prem|a|tism** (sə prem′ə tiz əm, sù-), *n.* a style in modern art originated in Russia by Kasimir Malevich (1878-1935), characterized by simple geometric shapes painted with a limited selection of colors: *Malevich's suprematism began with a black square on a white ground but soon dealt with very original color effects* (London Times). [< French *suprématie* supremacy + English *-ism*]

**su|prem|a|tist** (sə prem′ə tist, sù-), *n.* an artist who follows the style of suprematism: *He never joined either of the violent opposing factions in Russian revolutionary art, the suprematists and the constructivists* (London Times).

**su|preme** (sə prēm′, sù-), *adj., n.* — *adj.* **1** highest in rank or authority: *a supreme ruler, a supreme commander.* SYN: chief, paramount. **2** of or belonging to a person or thing that is supreme: *supreme authority. German reunification constituted an obligation on the part of the four Powers who assumed supreme power in Germany* (London Times). **3** highest in degree; greatest; utmost; extreme: *supreme disgust.* **4** highest in quality: *With supreme courage she snatched the baby from in front of the car.* **5** highest or greatest in character or achievement: *a supreme optimist, a supreme pianist.* **6** last; final: *Soldiers who die for their country make the supreme sacrifice.*
— *n.* = suprême (defs. 3 and 4).
[< Latin *suprēmus,* superlative of *superus* a thing above < *super* above] — **su|preme′ly**, *adv.* — **su|preme′ness**, *n.*

**su|prême** (sə prēm′, -prām′; sü-), *n.* **1** a white sauce or velouté made from chicken stock; sauce suprême. **2** a dish made or served with this sauce. **3** Also, **supreme**. a shallow bowl or glass on a pedestal. **4** Also, **supreme**. an appetizer or dessert served in such a bowl or glass: *It was Mrs. Whitney who selected [the] suprême of fresh fruit* (New York Times). [< French *suprême* < Latin *suprēmus;* see etym. under **supreme**]

**Supreme Being**, = God.

**Supreme Court**, **1a** the highest court in the United States, consisting of the Chief Justice and eight associate justices. It meets at Washington, D.C. *The Supreme Court decision is the law of the land* (Estes Kefauver). **b** the highest court in most states of the United States. **2** a similar court in certain other countries.

**Supreme Soviet**, **1** the bicameral legislature of the Soviet Union: *The plan was presented by [the] finance minister ... before a special session of the Supreme Soviet* (Wall Street Journal). **2** any of certain legislatures, such as those of the constituent republics of the Soviet Union.

**su|pre|mo** (sə prē′mō), *n., pl.* **-mos**. *British.* a person who is highest in command or authority; the overall head or chief of one or of several organizations: *The creation of a national police Supremo, with greater power over Britain's police than anyone has had before, is under consideration by the Home Secretary* (Sunday Times). [< Spanish *supremo* commander in chief, generalissimo < *supremo,* adjective, supreme]

**Supt.** or **supt.**, superintendent.

**suq** (sük), *n.* an Arab market place, especially in the Middle East: *the Jerusalem suq.* Also, **souk, suk, sook**. [< Arabic *sūq*]

**sur-**[1], *prefix.* over; above; beyond, as in *surcoat, surname, surpass, surtax.* [< Middle French *sur-* < Old French *sour-, sor-* < Latin *super-* super-]

**sur-**[2], *prefix.* the form of **sub-** before *r,* as in *surreptitious.*

**sur.**, surplus.

**su|ra** (sùr′ə), *n.* a chapter of the Koran. The 114 suras are arranged, without regard to chronology or subject, according to length, beginning with the longest (after the opening prayer). [< Arabic *sūra* (literally) row or layer of stones]

**su|rah** (sùr′ə), *n.* a soft, twilled fabric of silk, or silk and rayon. [earlier *surat* an uncolored cotton fabric < *Surat,* a city in India, where it was produced; pronunciation and form influenced by French *surah*]

**su|ral** (sùr′əl), *adj.* of or having to do with the calf of the leg: *spasm of the sural muscles.* [< New Latin *suralis* < Latin *sūra* calf of the leg]

**sur|ba|har** (sür′bə här′), *n.* a guitarlike instrument of India similar to the sitar but having a lower pitch. It has 7 main strings and 7 sympathetic strings. [< Hindi *sūrbahhār*]

**sur|ba|har|ist** (sür′bə här′ist), *n.* a player of the surbahar.

**sur|base** (sėr′bās′), *n. Architecture.* a border or molding above any base, such as at the top of wainscoting or a pedestal.

**sur|based** (sėr′bāst′), *adj. Architecture.* **1** having a surbase. **2** depressed; flattened. **3** designating an arch, vault, or dome whose rise is less than half the span. [(def. 1) < *surbase*(*e*) + *-ed*[2]; (def. 3) half-translation of French *surbaissé* < *sur-* exceedingly + *baissé* lowered, past participle of Old French *baisser,* or *baissier* to lower. Compare etym. under **abase**.]

**sur|base|ment** (sėr bās′mənt), *n. Architecture.* the condition of being surbased.

**sur|cease** (sėr sēs′), *n., v.,* **-ceased, -ceas|ing**. — *n.* end; cessation: *There is no surcease in the torrent of Princes ... who continue to pour into the capital* (Daily Telegraph). *Vainly I had sought to borrow from my books surcease of sorrow* (Edgar Allan Poe).
— *v.i.* to stop; cease: *The great Arch-Angel from his warlike toil surceas'd* (Milton). *Intrigues ... would of necessity surcease* (John L. Motley).
— *v.t.* to desist from (as a course of action): *The hobby horse surceased his capering* (Scott).
[< Anglo-French *sursise* omission, noun use of Old French, feminine past participle of *surseoir* to refrain < Latin *supersedēre* supersede; spelling influenced by English *cease*]

**sur|charge** (*n.* sėr′chärj′; *v.* sėr chärj′), *n., v.,* **-charged, -charg|ing**. — *n.* **1** an additional charge; extra charge: *The express company made a surcharge for delivering the trunk outside of the city limits.* **2** an additional mark printed on a postage stamp as to change its value or date. **3** a stamp bearing such a mark. **4** *Figurative.* an additional or excessive load, burden, or supply: *The surcharge of the learned, might in time be drawn off to recruit the laboring class of citizens* (Thomas Jefferson). **5** the act of showing an omission in an account. **6** a statement showing such an omission. [< French *surcharge* < Old French *surcharger;* see the verb]
— *v.t.* **1** to charge extra. **2** to overcharge. **3** *Figurative.* to overload; overburden; oppress; overwhelm: *The widow's heart was surcharged with grief.* **4** to put an additional and usually excessive physical burden or weight upon; weigh down. **5** to print a surcharge on (a postage stamp). **6** to show an omission in (an account) which the accounting party should have charged himself with.
[< Middle French, Old French *surcharger* < *sur-* over + *charger* to charge, load down < Late Latin *carricāre* to load < *carrus* load, wagon. Compare etym. under **car**.]

**sur|charg|er** (sėr chär′jər), *n.* a person who surcharges.

**sur|cin|gle** (sėr′sing gəl), *n.* **1** a heavy strap or belt around a horse's body to keep a saddle, blanket, or pack in place. **2** a girdle or belt for fastening a cassock. [< Old French *surcengle* < *sur-* over + *cengle* a girdle < Latin *cingula,* and *cingulum* < *cingere* to gird]

* **sur|coat** (sėr′kōt′), *n.* **1** an outer coat or garment of rich material, often worn by knights over their armor and depicting their heraldic arms. **2** a long sleeveless garment worn by women in the Middle Ages over long sleeved gowns. **3** an outer coat, slightly longer than a jacket, worn by men and boys. [< Old French *surcote* < *sur-* over + *cote* coat, tunic]

* **surcoat**
definition 1

**sur|cu|lose** (sėr′kyə lōs), *adj. Botany.* producing shoots or suckers. [< Latin *surculōsus* woody, twiglike < *surculus* young shoot, twig (diminutive) < *surus* branch]

**surd** (sėrd), *n., adj.* — *n.* **1** *Phonetics.* a sound uttered without vibration of the vocal cords; voiceless sound. The sounds of *f, k, p, s* (as in *sit*), and *t* are surds. **2** *Mathematics.* an irrational number, such as $\sqrt{2}$.
— *adj.* **1** *Phonetics.* uttered without vibration of the vocal cords; voiceless. **2** *Mathematics.* that cannot be expressed as a whole number or common fraction; irrational.
[< Latin *surdus* unhearing; unheard; silent, dull, related to *susurrus* a muttering, whispering]

**sure** (shùr), *adj.,* **sur|er, sur|est**, *adv., n.* — *adj.* **1** free from doubt; certain; having ample reason for belief; confident; positive: *Are you sure you locked the door? He is sure of success in the end. I am sure of his guilt.* **2** to be trusted; safe; reliable: *You can trust him, he is a sure messenger.* **3** never missing, slipping, or failing; unerring: *sure aim, a sure touch.* SYN: unfailing. **4** admitting of no doubt or question: *sure proof.* **5** firm: *to stand on sure ground.* **6** certain to come or happen; inevitable: *Misery is the sure result of war.* **7** destined; bound: *He is sure to return.* **8** *Archaic.* secure or safe.
— *adv. Informal.* **1** certainly; undoubtedly; of course: *This year a new 427-inch engine showed up at the track ... and it sure rocked the racing fraternity* (Ray Brock). **2** without fail; for certain: *I'll call you later this week, then, sure.*
— *n.* for certain; undoubtedly: *Who could know for sure how the public was going to respond to color television* (Vance Packard).

**be sure**, to be careful or certain (to do something specified); do not fail: *Be sure to leave plenty of time.*

**for sure**. See above **sure**, *n.*

**make sure, a** to act so as to make something certain: *Make sure you have the key.* **b** to get sure or certain knowledge; ascertain: *That fellow rode up to the house to make sure Tristram was away* (M. Notley).

**sure enough**, certainly; undoubtedly; of course; to be sure: *And you were so angry with me when you went off—I saw it, sure enough* (J. S. Winter). *Sure enough, just as they prophesied, most of these painters ... became enormously fashionable* (Harper's).

**to be sure**, of course; surely; certainly; undoubtedly: *For some, to be sure, openness of speech is more than an occasional matter* (Harper's). *Good circumstantial evidence, to be sure, but we had nothing concrete* (Saturday Review).

[< Old French *sur,* and *seür* < Latin *sēcūrus.* See etym. of doublets **secure, sicker.**] —**sure′ness,** *n.*

—*Syn. adj.* **1 Sure, certain, confident** mean having no doubt. **Sure** implies being free from doubt in one's own mind: *Police are sure he was kidnaped.* **Certain** implies having positive reasons or proof to eliminate all doubt: *They have been certain since they uncovered new evidence.* **Confident** implies having a strong belief that admits no doubt: *They are confident they will solve the case soon.*

► **Sure,** as an adverb, is considered inappropriate in standard written English. In informal English, it is widely used, particularly as a sentence modifier (*Sure, I'm coming*) and not infrequently as an intensifier (*I'm sure tired*).

**sure-e|nough** (shůr′i nuf′), *adj. U.S. Informal.* genuine; real: *It was at once agreed that he "wasn't the sure-enough bronco-buster he thought himself"* (Theodore Roosevelt).

**sure-fire** (shůr′fīr′), *adj. Informal.* definite; certain; unfailing: *a sure-fire success. In the repertoire of the nation's comedians, Hoboken, N.J., ranks almost on a par with Brooklyn, N.Y., and Kokomo, Ind., as a sure-fire laugh-getter* (Newsweek).

**sure-foot|ed** (shůr′fůt′id), *adj.* not liable to stumble, slip, or fall: *The elephant is a sure-footed animal* (*Figurative.*) *The new salesman proved to be sure-footed and reliable.* —**sure′-foot′ed|ly,** *adv.* —**sure′-foot′ed|ness,** *n.*

**sure-hand|ed** (shůr′han′did), *adj.* dexterous; skillful: *The conductor had a sure-handed mastery of the orchestra.* —**sure′-hand′ed|ness,** *n.*

**sure|ly** (shůr′lē), *adv.* **1** certainly; undoubtedly; assuredly; truly: *Half a loaf of bread is surely better than none at all.* **2** as may be confidently supposed; as must be the case: *Surely it will not rain all week.* **3** without mistake; without missing, slipping, or failing; firmly; unerringly: *The goat leaped surely from rock to rock. Surely he hath borne our griefs, and carried our sorrows* (Isaiah 53:4). **4** without fail: *slowly but surely.*

**Sû|re|té** (shůr′ə tā′; *French* syr tā′), *n.* the criminal department of a prefecture of police in France, lower Canada, and other countries where French is spoken: *Across the counter at the Montreal Sûreté the sergeant leaned on his elbow and waited to hear me out* (Maclean's). [< French *Sûreté* < Old French *surtey.* See related etym. at **surety.**]

**sure thing,** a certainty; safe thing; a bet that one cannot lose: *A host of horseplayers think he's a sure thing* (New Yorker).

**sur|e|ty** (shůr′ə tē, shůr′tē), *n., pl.* **-ties.** **1** security against loss, damage, or failure to do something: *An insurance company gives surety against loss by fire.* **SYN:** guaranty, pledge. **2** a ground of certainty or safety; guarantee. **3** a person who agrees to be legally responsible for the debt, default, or conduct of another: *He was surety for his brother's appearance in court on the day set.* **SYN:** bondsman, bail, sponsor. **4** *Archaic.* **a** a sure thing; certainty: *Of a surety he will come.* **b** the condition of being sure; certain knowledge; sureness. **5** *Obsolete.* a sponsor at baptism. [Middle English *sewrte* < Old French *surtey, seurte* < Latin *sēcūritās* < *sēcūrus* sure, secure]

**surety bond,** a bond guaranteeing the performance of an obligation or a contract within a given period.

**sur|e|ty|ship** (shůr′ə tē ship, shůr′tē-), *n.* the obligation of a person to answer for the debt, fault, or conduct of another.

**surf** (sėrf), *n., v.* —*n.* **1** the waves or swell of the sea breaking in a foaming mass on the shore, or over a shoal, reef, or the like. The surf is high just after a storm. *The shooting surf comes hissing in* (John Betjeman). **2** the deep pounding or thundering sound of this.
—*v.i.* **1** to travel on the crest of a wave, especially with a surfboard. **2** to wade or go swimming in the surf.
[alteration of earlier *suff;* origin uncertain]

**surf|a|ble** (sėr′fə bəl), *adj.* that can be surfed or used for surfing.

**sur|face** (sėr′fis), *n., adj., v.,* **-faced, -fac|ing.** —*n.* **1** the outside of anything: *the surface of a golf ball, the surface of a mountain. An egg has a smooth surface.* **2a** any face or side of a thing: *A cube has six surfaces. The upper surface of the plate has pictures on it.* **b** the top of the ground or soil, or of a body of water or other liquid: *The stone sank below the surface.* **3** *Figurative.* the outward appearance; what appears on a slight or casual view or without examination: *a meaning that lies below the surface* (Fred A. Paley). *Beneath his rough surface he is really a very kind person.* **4** *Geometry.* that which has length and breadth but no thickness: *a plane surface.* **5** *Aeronautics.* any level part which provides lift, support, or stability, such as an airfoil.
—*adj.* **1** of the surface; on the surface; having something to do with the surface: *surface mining, a surface current, the surface temperature of the sun.* **2** by land or water; not by air or underground: *surface transit.* **3** *Figurative.* superficial; external: *surface emotions, surface knowledge, surface comprehension, a surface relationship.*
—*v.t.* **1** to put a surface on; make smooth: *The town must surface this road.* **2** to direct or steer (a submarine) to the surface. **3** *Figurative.* to bring into the open; reveal; expose: *He surfaces the resentment of his scientific colleagues against the* [*Communist*] *Party's Central Committee overseer for science affairs* (Saturday Review).
—*v.i.* **1** to rise to the surface: *The nuclear-powered "Triton" was the first submarine to go around the world without surfacing* (Raymond V. B. Blackman). *Whales surface to breath.* **2** to mine near the surface. **3** *Figurative.* to come out into the open; emerge; appear: *He has plunged into the archives and surfaced with a long volume* (Andrew Sinclair).
**scratch the surface,** to do very little about something; touch upon something superficially: *What is said here only scratches the surface of a vast literature* (Scientific American).
[< French *surface* < *sur-* above + *face* face, patterned on Latin *superficiēs.* Compare etym. under **superficial.**]

**sur|face-ac|tive** (sėr′fis ak′tiv), *adj.* of or having to do with a group of chemical substances that have the property of reducing the surface tension of water or other liquid. Certain sulfates or sulfonates made from animal and vegetable fats are surface-active and are used in making household detergents.

**surface burst,** a bomb explosion on or near the ground or water.

**surface car,** *U.S.* a car moving on the surface of the ground, as distinguished from one moving on an elevated or underground railway.

**surface color,** an opaque color that is the hued counterpart of any neutral surface.

**-surfaced,** *combining form.* having a ___ surface: *Smooth-surfaced = having a smooth surface.*

**sur|face-ef|fect ship** (sėr′fis ə fekt′), *U.S.* an air cushion vehicle for use on water.

**surface mail,** **1** mail sent by railroad, ship, or truck, as distinguished from air mail. **2** the system of sending mail by surface transportation.

**sur|face|man** (sėr′fis mən), *n., pl.* **-men.** a person who works on the surface, as on the roadbed of a railway, or in a mining or military operation.

**surface mining,** mining carried on close to the surface of the earth; shallow mining.

**surface of revolution,** *Geometry.* a surface which is generated by the revolution of a curve around an axis.

**surface plate,** a metal plate for testing the accuracy of a flat surface.

**sur|fac|er** (sėr′fə sər), *n.* **1** that which produces a smooth or even surface. **2** a person who mines near the surface.

**surface ship,** any naval ship that is not a submarine.

**surface structure,** *Linguistics.* the formal structure or phonetic expression of a sentence, as distinguished from its deep structure: *"John loves Mary" is the surface structure of the sentence. It constitutes the sort of "physical signal," or phonetic articulation, to which we can perfectly well apply the traditional syntax we have learned in school: noun, verb, object, and so on. But this surface structure tells us little and obviously differs for every language* (George Steiner).

**surface tension,** the tension of the surface film of a liquid that makes it contract to a minimum area. It is caused by molecular forces and measured in terms of force per unit length.

**sur|face-to-air** (sėr′fis tů ãr′), *adj.* **1** launched from the ground or a ship to intercept and destroy flying aircraft or missiles: *surface-to-air missiles.* **2** between the ground or a ship and an aircraft: *surface-to-air rescue.*

**sur|face-to-sur|face** (sėr′fis tů sėr′fis), *adj.* **1** launched from the ground or a ship at a target on the sea or on the ground. **2** between two ships or two points on the ground: *surface-to-surface communication.*

**sur|face-to-un|der|wa|ter** (sėr′fis tů un′dər wôt′ər, -wot′-), *adj.* **1** launched from the ground or a ship at a target beneath the surface of the sea. **2** between a surface ship and a submarine, diver, or other object underwater.

**surface water,** **1** water that collects on the surface of the ground. **2** the surface layer of a body of water.

**surface wave,** a wave created by an earthquake and traveling along the surface of the earth.

**sur|fac|ing** (sėr′fi sing), *n.* **1** the action or process of giving a smooth or even surface to something. **2** the material with which a body is surfaced.

**sur|fact|ant** (sėr fak′tənt), *n.* a surface-active agent or solution. [< *surf*(ace-)*act*(ive) *a*(ge)*nt*]

**surf bird,** a shore bird related to the plover, that nests in Alaska and winters along the Pacific coast of North and South America.

***surf|board** (sėrf′bôrd′, -bōrd′), *n., v.* —*n.* a long, narrow board on which to be carried on the crest of a wave as it mounts and breaks as surf on a beach.
—*v.i.* to ride the waves on a surfboard; surf. —**surf′board′er,** *n.*

***surfboard**

***surfing**

**surf|board|ing** (sėrf′bôr′ding, -bōr′-), *n.* the act of riding a surfboard.

**surf|boat** (sėrf′bōt′), *n.* a strong boat designed especially for use in heavy surf.

**surf|cast** (sėrf′kast′, -käst′), *v.i.,* **-cast, -cast|ing.** to cast a fishing line from the shore into the surf: *Later I tried to teach my oldest son how to surfcast with a drail, but he kept fouling his line and getting sand in the reel, and we had a quarrel* (John Cheever).

**surf|cast|er** (sėrf′kas′tər, -käs′-), *n.* a fisherman who casts the line from the shore into the surf: *The holiday surfcasters found the striped bass cooperative along the Rhode Island beaches* (New York Times).

**surf|cast|ing** (sėrf′kas′ting, -käs′-), *n.* the act of fishing by casting the line from the shore into the surf.

**surf clam,** a large, edible clam that lives near the surf on the Atlantic coast of the United States.

**surf duck,** a scoter, especially the surf scoter.

**sur|feit** (sėr′fit), *n., v.* —*n.* **1** an excessive amount of something; too much; excess: *A surfeit of food makes one sick.* (*Figurative.*) *A surfeit of advice annoys me.* **2** disgust or nausea caused by this; painful satiety. **3** gluttonous indulgence, especially gluttonous eating or drinking. **4** an abnormal condition caused by gluttony; derangement of the digestive system arising from gluttony or intemperance: *He died of a surfeit caused by intemperance* (Oliver Goldsmith).
—*v.t.* to feed or supply to excess; force down or on (a person) in such quantity as to cause nausea or disgust: (*Figurative.*) *He is weary and surfeited of business* (Samuel Pepys).
—*v.i.* to eat, drink, or indulge in something to excess; take one's fill and more (of); feast gluttonously (upon): *They are as sick that surfeit with too much as they that starve with nothing* (Shakespeare). **SYN:** glut, gorge. See syn. under **satiate.**
[< Old French *surfet,* and *surfait* excess; (originally) past participle of *surfaire* overdo < *sur-* over + *faire* do < Latin *facere*] —**sur′feit|er,** *n.*

**surf|er** (sėr′fər), *n.* = surf rider.

**surf fish,** any one of a family of small to medium-sized viviparous fishes frequenting shallow water along the Pacific coast of North America; seaperch; surfperch.

**sur|fi|cial** (sėr fish′əl), *adj.* of the surface or outside of something; surface: *Erosion quickly erases the surficial expression of terrestrial craters* (New Scientist). [< *surf*(ace) + *-icial,* as in *superficial*]

***surf|ing** (sėr′fing), *n.* the act of riding waves on a surfboard; surfboarding. See picture above.

**surf|man** (sėrf′mən), *n., pl.* **-men.** **1** a man skilled in handling boats in surf. **2** = lifeguard.

**Pronunciation Key:** hat, āge, cãre, fär; let, ēqual, tėrm; it, īce; hot, ōpen, ôrder; oil, out; cup, půt, rüle; child; long; thin; ᴛʜen; zh, measure; ə represents a in about, e in taken, i in pencil, o in lemon, u in circus.

**surf|man|ship** (sėrf′mən ship), *n.* skill in managing a surfboat.

**surf|mat** (sėrf′mat′), *n.* a strong mat sometimes used by surfers in place of a surfboard.

**surf|perch** (sėrf′pėrch′), *n.* = surf fish.

**surf rider**, a person who rides the surf, especially on a surfboard: *A surf rider moves through the water because his board, perched on the front of a spilling wave, is perpetually sliding downhill* (Scientific American).

**surf scoter**, a North American sea duck, dark with white markings about the head.

**surf|y** (sėr′fē), *adj.* **1** having much surf or heavy surf: *a surfy beach.* **2** forming or resembling surf.

**surg.**, **1** surgeon. **2** surgery. **3** surgical.

**surge** (sėrj), *v.*, **surged, surg|ing**, *n.* —*v.i.* **1** to rise and fall, as a ship does on the waves; ride at anchor or over the waves: *The ship surged in the stormy seas, rolling and pitching with each wave.* **2** to rise or swell with great force: *A great wave surged over us.* **3** to sweep forward as waves do; move like waves: *The mob surged through the streets.* **4** *Figurative.* to rise (up) violently or excitedly, as feelings or thoughts. **5** *Physics.* to increase or oscillate suddenly or violently, as an electrical current. **6** *Nautical.* **a** (of a rope or cable) to slip back or slacken, especially when wound around a capstan or windlass. **b** (of a ship) to sweep, pull, or jerk in a certain direction.
—*v.t.* **1** to cause to move in, or as if in, swelling waves or billows. **2** *Nautical.* to cause (a rope or cable) to slip back or slacken.
—*n.* **1** a high, rolling swell of water; swelling wave; billow: *The sea was rolling in immense surges* (Richard Henry Dana). **2** a sweep or rush of waves; the swelling and rolling of the sea: *Laced with white foam from the eternal surge* (Charles Kingsley). **3** something like a wave; a swelling or sweeping forward like that of waves: *a sudden surge of smoke, the surge of the mob through the streets.* **4** *Figurative.* a violent or excited rising or swelling up as of feelings or thoughts: *a surge of anger, a surge of public opinion. The surge of encouragement ...* (Sir Winston Churchill); *... the surge and thunder of the Odyssey* (Andrew Lang). **5** *Physics.* **a** a sudden or violent rush or oscillation of electrical current in a circuit. **b** a wave of pressure in a liquid system caused by a sudden stoppage of flow. **6** *Nautical.* **a** a slipping back or slackening of a rope or cable. **b** the tapered part of a capstan or windlass, upon which the rope surges.
[probably < Middle French, Old French *sourgeon* a spring < Latin *surgere* to rise < *sub-* (up from) under + *regere* to reach; rule]

**surge chamber**, a chamber or tank which absorbs surges of flow in a liquid system: *At the outlet of the tunnel there is a surge chamber* (London Times).

**surge|less** (sėrj′lis), *adj.* free from surges; smooth; calm.

**sur|geon** (sėr′jən), *n.* a doctor who performs operations; medical practitioner whose specialty is surgery: *A surgeon removed the boy's tonsils.* *Abbr:* surg. [Middle English *surgeoun* < Anglo-French *surgien*, Old French *cirurgien* < *cirurgie;* see etym. under **surgery**. See etym. of doublet **chirurgeon.**]

**surgeon bird**, a jaçana of the East Indies, having a long tail like a pheasant's, and a white head and white wings.

**sur|geon|cy** (sėr′jən sē), *n., pl.* **-cies**. the position or duties of a surgeon.

**sur|geon|fish** (sėr′jən fish′), *n., pl.* **-fish|es** or (*collectively*) **-fish**. any one of a group of fishes having long, sharp spines growing near the tail, found especially in tropical seas and near coral reefs; doctorfish; tang.

**surgeon general**, *pl.* **surgeons general**. **1** the chief medical officer of a particular branch of the armed forces of the United States. **2** a member of the medical staff of the British army.

**Surgeon General**, *pl.* **Surgeons General**. the chief medical officer of the United States Public Health Service (formerly the Bureau of Public Health). *Abbr:* Surg. Gen.

**surgeon's knot**, any one of various knots used by surgeons in tying ligatures and bandages.

**sur|ger|y** (sėr′jər ē), *n., pl.* **-ger|ies**. **1** the art and science of treating diseases, injuries, or deformities by operations and instruments: *Malaria can be cured by medicine, but a ruptured appendix requires surgery.* **2** the operating room or other area where surgical operations are performed. **3** the work performed by a surgeon. **4** *Figurative:* *to save a tree by skillful surgery. Nonconformity had entered far too deeply into the nation's life to be eradicated by the severest surgery of law* (H. W. Clark). **5** *British.* the office of a doctor or dentist. [< Old French *surgerie*, or *cirurgerie*, earlier *cirurgie*, learned borrowing from Latin *chīrūrgia* < Greek *cheirourgíā* < *cheirourgós* surgeon < *cheír* hand + *érgon* work]

**Surg. Gen.**, Surgeon General.

**sur|gi|cal** (sėr′jə kəl), *adj.* **1** of surgery; having something to do with surgery: *a surgical patient, surgical experience.* **2** used in surgery: *surgical instruments. Surgical gloves, should, of course, present an impermeable barrier to bacteria on the skin* (New Scientist). **3** performed by a surgeon. **4** following or resulting from an operation or other treatment by a surgeon: *surgical fever.* —**sur′gi|cal|ly**, *adv.*

**surg|y** (sėr′jē), *adj.*, **surg|i|er, surg|i|est**. **1** surging; swelling; billowy. **2** produced by surges: *The surgy murmurs of the lonely sea* (Keats).

**su|ri|cat** (sůr′ə kat), *n.* = suricate.

**su|ri|cate** (sůr′ə kāt), *n.* a small, burrowing, carnivorous mammal of the civet family, found in South Africa. [< French *surikate;* origin uncertain; perhaps influenced by Dutch *surikat* the macaque]

**Su|ri|nam toad** (sůr′ə nam), an aquatic toad of northern South America, notable for the manner in which the eggs, distributed by the male over the back of the female, are retained there, in cells of the skin which form about them, until fully developed into young. [< *Surinam*, a Dutch territory in South America]

**sur|li|ly** (sėr′lə lē), *adv.* in a surly manner; crabbedly; morosely.

**sur|li|ness** (sėr′lē nis), *n.* surly condition or character; gloomy moroseness; crabbed ill-nature.

**sur|loin** (sėr′loin), *n.* = sirloin.

**sur|ly** (sėr′lē), *adj.*, **-li|er, -li|est**. **1** bad-tempered and unfriendly; rude; gruff: *The grouchy old man grumbled a surly reply.* **SYN**: sullen, churlish, cross. **2** *Obsolete.* haughty; arrogant: *Be opposite with a kinsman; surly with servants* (Shakespeare). [Middle English *sirly*, perhaps < *sir* lord + *-ly*²]

**sur|mise** (sər mīz′; *n. also* sėr′mīz), *v.*, **-mised, -mis|ing**, *n.* —*v.t., v.i.* to infer; guess: *We surmised that the traffic delay was caused by some accident on the highway.* **SYN**: suppose. See syn. under **guess**. [< Old French *surmise*, past participle of *surmettre* < *sur-* upon + *mettre* to put < Latin *mittere* send]
—*n.* **1** the formation of an idea with little or no evidence; guessing: *His guilt was a matter of surmise; there was no proof.* **2** a conjecture; guess: *a shrewd surmise. To trust the soul's invincible surmise* (George Santayana).
[< Old French *surmise* accusation, verbal noun of *surmettre;* see the verb] —**sur|mis′er**, *n.*

**sur|mount** (sər mount′), *v.t.* **1** to rise above; surpass in height; be higher than; overtop: *Mount Rainier surmounts all the peaks near it.* **2** to be situated above; rest on top of; top; crown: *a steeple surmounting a church. A statue surmounts the monument.* **3** to go up and across; get over: *to surmount a hill.* **4** to prevail over; get the better of; overcome: *Lincoln surmounted many difficulties before he rose to be President.* [< Old French *surmonter* < *sur-* over + *monter.* Compare etym. under **mount**¹.]

**sur|mount|a|ble** (sər moun′tə bəl), *adj.* that can be surmounted.

**sur|mul|let** (sėr mul′it), *n.* = red mullet. [< French *surmulet* < Old French *sormulet*, probably < *sor* reddish-brown + *mulet.* Compare etym. under **mullet**¹.]

**sur|name** (sėr′nām′), *n., v.*, **-named, -nam|ing**.
—*n.* **1** a last name; family name. A person shares his surname with all the other members of his immediate family, and he is identified by it as belonging to a particular family group. In the English-speaking world a surname usually derives from one's father and is one's last name. *Smith is the surname of John Smith.* **2** a name added to a person's real name or names, especially one derived from the place of his birth or from some outstanding quality, achievement, or other distinguishing feature; epithet; agnomen. *Examples:* Francis (*of Assisi*), Ivan (*the Terrible*), William (*the Conqueror*).
—*v.t.* to give a surname to; call or identify by a surname: *Simon was surnamed Peter.*
[Middle English alteration (influenced by *name*) of *surnoun* < Anglo-French *sournoun*, variant of Old French *surnom* < *sur-* over + *nom* name < Latin *nōmen, -inis*]

**sur|nom|i|nal** (sėr nom′ə nəl), *adj.* of or having to do with surnames.

**sur|pass** (sər pas′, -päs′), *v.t.* **1** to do more or better than; be greater than; excel: *She surpasses her sister in arithmetic. His work surpassed expectations. The sense of accomplishment I felt in actually aiding birth surpassed any feeling I'd had before* (Parents' Magazine). **SYN**: outdo, outstrip, outrun, eclipse. See syn. under **excel**. **2** to be too much or too great for; go beyond; transcend; exceed: *The horrors of the battlefield surpassed description.* [< Middle French *surpasser* < *sur-* beyond + *passer* to pass, go by]

**sur|pass|a|ble** (sər pas′ə bəl, -päs′-), *adj.* that can be surpassed.

**sur|pass|ing** (sər pas′ing, -päs′-), *adj., adv.* —*adj.* greatly exceeding or excelling others; of the highest degree or quality: *Helen of Troy was a surpassing beauty.*
—*adv. Poetic.* in a surpassing degree; exceedingly: *a gracious damsel and surpassing fair.*
—**sur|pass′ing|ly**, *adv.* —**sur|pass′ing|ness**, *n.*

***sur|plice** (sėr′plis), *n.* **1** a broad-sleeved, white gown worn by clergymen and choir singers over their other clothes. **2** an arrangement of folds on a blouse or the bodice of a dress that cross one another from the waist up to the opposite shoulder. [Middle English *surplis* < Anglo-French *surpliz*, contraction of Old French *surpelize* < *sur-* over + *pelice* fur garment < Medieval Latin *pellicia* < Latin *pellis* hide]

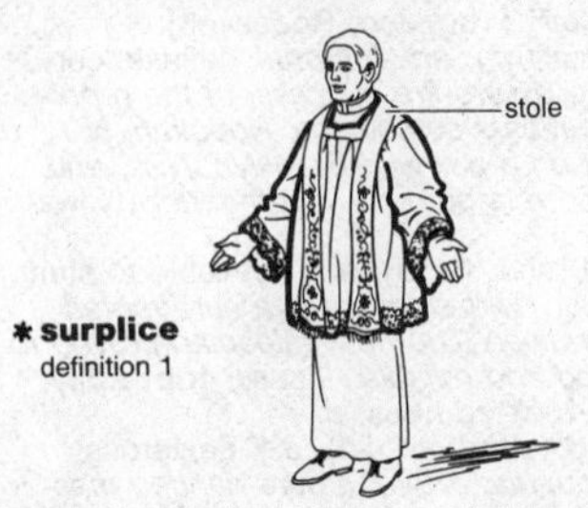


***surplice**
definition 1

**sur|pliced** (sėr′plist), *adj.* wearing a surplice: *Throughout the day, surpliced priests, accompanied by acolytes carrying pots of holy water, visited every business and residential section of Rome, blessing homes and offices* (New York Times).

**sur|plus** (sėr′pləs, -plus), *n., adj.* —*n.* **1** an amount over and above what is needed; extra quantity left over; excess: *The bank keeps a large surplus of money in reserve.* **SYN**: residue, remainder. **2** *Accounting.* **a** an excess of assets over liabilities. **b** an excess of assets over dividends, interest, and other fixed charges within some given period of time.
—*adj.* more than is needed; extra; excess: *Surplus wheat is put in storage and shipped abroad.* [< Old French *surplus* < *sur-* over + *plus* more < Latin]

**sur|plus|age** (sėr′plu sij), *n.* **1** a surplus; excess. **2** an excess of words; unnecessary words. **3** *Law.* nonessential or irrelevant material in a pleading or plea.

**surplus value**, *Economics.* the greater value or profit which, according to Marxian theory, an employer obtains from the services of a worker in relation to the amount he pays the worker for his services.

**sur|print** (sėr′print′), *v., n.* —*v.t.* **1** to print over (something already printed) with new matter. **2** to print (new matter) over something already printed.
—*n.* surprinted matter.

**sur|pris|al** (sər prī′zəl), *n.* the act of surprising or state of being surprised; surprise.

**sur|prise** (sər prīz′), *n., v.*, **-prised, -pris|ing**, *adj.*
—*n.* **1** the feeling caused by something happening suddenly or unexpectedly; astonishment; wonder; amazement: *His face showed surprise at the news.* **2** anything which causes this feeling; something unexpected: *Mother always has a surprise for the children on holidays. Life is a series of surprises* (Emerson). **3** the act of coming upon suddenly and without warning; catching unprepared: *The fort was captured by surprise.*
—*v.t.* **1** to cause to feel surprise; astonish: *The victory surprised us.* **2** to come upon suddenly; take unawares; take or catch in the act. **3** to attack suddenly and without warning; catch unprepared; make an unexpected assault upon (as an unprepared place, army, or person): *Our army surprised the enemy while they were sleeping.* **4** to betray (into doing something not intended); lead or bring (a person, etc.) unawares: *The news surprised her into tears.* **5** *Figurative.* to find or discover (something) by a sudden or unexpected question, attack, or other maneuver; detect or elicit: *to surprise the truth of the matter from him.* **6** *Obsolete.* to capture by an unexpected assault or attack.
—*adj.* that is not expected; coming as a surprise; surprising: *a surprise party, a surprise visit.*
**take by surprise**, **a** to come upon suddenly and unexpectedly; catch unprepared: *That he was taken by surprise is true. But he had twelve hours to make his arrangements* (Macaulay). **b** to astonish because unexpected; amaze: *This statement, I confess, took me by surprise* (John Tyndall).
[< Old French *surprise*, noun use of feminine

past participle of *surprendre* < *sur-* over + *prendre* to take < Latin *prehendere*]

—***Syn.*** *v.t.* **1 Surprise, astonish, amaze** mean to cause a feeling of wonder. **Surprise** emphasizes the sudden reaction produced by something unexpected: *Her frank answer surprised him.* **Astonish** emphasizes the wonder caused by something extraordinary or incredible: *The young prodigy astonished everyone with her phenomenal memory.* **Amaze** implies bewildered or admiring wonder: *The landing of astronauts on the moon amazed the whole world.*

**sur|pris|ed|ly** (sər prī′zid lē), *adv.* in a manner indicating surprise; with surprise.

**sur|pris|er** (sər prī′zər), a person or thing that surprises.

**sur|pris|ing** (sər prī′zing), *adj.* causing surprise: *a surprising recovery.* **SYN**: astonishing, amazing. —**sur|pris′ing|ly**, *adv.* —**sur|pris′ing|ness**, *n.*

**sur|ra** (sůr′ə), *n.* an acute, infectious blood disease, usually fatal, of horses and other domesticated animals, occurring chiefly in India, China, and the Philippines and caused by a protozoan. [< Marathi *sūra* a wheezing; air breathed through the nostrils]

**sur|re|al** (sə rē′əl, sėr rē′-), *adj.* **1** = surrealistic. **2** characterized by a dreamlike distortion of reality; eerie; bizarre. [back formation < *surrealism*]

**sur|re|al|ism** (sə rē′ə liz əm), *n.* a modern movement in painting, sculpture, literature, motion pictures, and other forms of art, that tries to show what takes place in dreams and in the subconscious mind. Surrealism is characterized by unexpected arrangements and distortions of images. *Dadaism, the school of determinedly impromptu expression, was giving way to the more rigidly formulated doctrines of surrealism* (New Yorker). [< French *surréalisme* < *sur-* beyond, sur-[1] + *réalisme* realism]

**sur|re|al|ist** (sə rē′ə list), *n., adj.* —***n.*** an artist or writer who uses surrealism: *The surrealists' intention [in painting] was to discover and explore ... the world of psychic experience as it had been revealed by psychoanalytical research* (Helen Gardner).
—***adj.*** of or having to do with surrealism or surrealists; surrealistic: *surrealist art, a surrealist painter.*

**sur|re|al|is|tic** (sə rē′ə lis′tik), *adj.* **1** of or having to do with surrealism or surrealists. **2** characterized by a dreamlike distortion of reality; surreal: *a surrealistic atmosphere, a motion picture's surrealistic imagery.* —**sur|re′al|is′ti|cal|ly**, *adv.*

**sur|re|al|i|ty** (sə rē al′ə tē, sėr′rē-), *n.* a dreamlike distortion of reality; surreal quality or condition. [blend of *surreal* and *reality*]

**sur|re|al|ly** (sə rē′ə lē, sėr rē′-), *adv.* in a surreal way.

**sur|re|but** (sėr′ri but′), *v.i.*, **-but|ted, -but|ting.** *Law.* (of a plaintiff) to reply to a defendant's rebutter.

**sur|re|but|tal** (sėr′ri but′əl), *n. Law.* a plaintiff's evidence or giving of evidence to refute the defendant's rebuttal.

**sur|re|but|ter** (sėr′ri but′ər), *n. Law.* a plaintiff's answer to the defendant's rebutter.

**sur|re|join** (sėr′ri join′), *v.i. Law.* to reply to a defendant's rejoinder.

**sur|re|join|der** (sėr′ri join′dər), *n. Law.* a plaintiff's answer to the defendant's rejoinder (the fifth step in ordinary pleadings).

**sur|ren|der** (sə ren′dər), *v., n.* —***v.t.*** **1** to give up (something) to the possession or power of another; yield (to): *to surrender a town to the enemy, to surrender an office or privilege.* **SYN**: relinquish. **2** *Figurative.* **a** to give up or abandon (as hope, joy, or comfort): *As the storm increased, the men on the raft surrendered all hope.* **b** to give (oneself or itself) up to a dominating thing or influence: *He surrendered himself to bitter grief.* **3** *Obsolete.* to give back or return (thanks, etc.). —***v.i.*** to yield to the power of another; submit: *The captain had to surrender to the enemy.*
—***n.*** **1** the act of surrendering; the giving up of something or of oneself into the possession or power of another: *The surrender of the soldiers saved them from being killed.* **2** *Insurance.* the abandonment of an insurance policy by the party insured, in return for a sum of money (surrender value), the amount payable depending upon the amount of the premiums paid. **3** *Law.* the deed by which an estate, lease, or other holding or right is legally surrendered.
[< Anglo-French *surrender*, Old French *surrendre* < *sur-* over, sur-[1] + *rendre.* Compare etym. under **render.**] —**sur|ren′der|er**, *n.*

**sur|rep|ti|tious** (sėr′əp tish′əs), *adj.* **1** acting by stealth or secretly; stealthy: *a surreptitious look.* **SYN**: secret. **2** taken, obtained, used, or done by stealth; secret and unauthorized; clandestine: *surreptitious meetings.* [< Latin *surreptīcius*, or *surreptītius* (with English *-ous*) < *surripere* seize secretly < *sub-* under + *rapere* to snatch] —**sur′rep|ti′tious|ly**, *adv.* —**sur′rep|ti′tious|ness**, *n.*

✱**sur|rey** (sėr′ē), *n., pl.* **-reys.** a light carriage with four wheels and two seats facing forward. A surrey sometimes has a top. [American English < earlier *surrey cart* < *Surrey*, a county in England]

**✱surrey**

**sur|ro|gate** (*n., adj.* sėr′ə gāt, -git; *v.* sėr′ə gāt), *n., adj., v.*, **-gat|ed, -gat|ing.** —***n.*** **1** a substitute; deputy. **2** the deputy of an ecclesiastical judge, usually of a bishop. **3** *U.S.* a judge or judicial officer in certain states who has charge of the probate of wills, the administration of estates, and the like.
—***adj.*** that takes the place of or stands for something else; representative; substitute: *To support this idea, by now stale, of Communism as a surrogate religion, [he] feels free to rewrite the early history of the Russian Revolution* (Time). [< Latin *surrogātus*, (originally) past participle of *surrogāre*; see the verb]
—***v.t.*** **1** *Law.* **a** to designate (another) to succeed oneself. **b** = subrogate. **2** to put instead of another; substitute. [< Latin *surrogāre* (with English *-ate*[1]) to substitute < *sub-* in the place of, under + *rogāre* ask for (by election)]

**sur|ro|gate|ship** (sėr′ə gāt ship, -git-), *n.* the office or authority of a surrogate.

**sur|ro|ga|tion** (sėr′ə gā′shən), *n.* the act of surrogating; substitution.

**sur|round** (sə round′), *v., n.* —***v.t.*** **1** to shut in on all sides; enclose; encompass: *A high fence surrounds the field.* **2** to be around; extend around; encircle: *inscriptions surrounding the base of a monument.* **3** *Figurative.* to make available to in abundance; provide unstintingly: *They surrounded the sick girl with every comfort.* **4** to encompass and beset on all sides with hostile military force, especially so as to cut off from supplies, reinforcements, or retreat: *to surround a city.*
—***n.*** a border or edging of a particular material, nearly or completely surrounding a central piece: *the plastic surround of the television screen.*
[< Anglo-French *surounder* surpass; (originally) overflow < Late Latin *superundāre* overflow < Latin *super-* over + *undāre* to flow (in waves) < *unda* wave; meaning influenced by *round*]

**sur|round|ings** (sə roun′dingz), *n.pl.* surrounding things or conditions; environment: *The poor child had never had cheerful surroundings.*

**sur|round-sound** (sə round′sound′), *n., adj. British.* —***n.*** any high-fidelity sound reproduction or transmission that creates a sense of sound coming from all parts of a room: *The record ... demolishes the pontifications that at least four audio channels are needed for surround-sound* (New Scientist).
—***adj.*** of or having to do with surround-sound: *The new surround-sound systems recognize that sound can come from literally any direction* (London Times).

**sur-roy|al** (sėr roi′əl), *n.* an upper or terminal branch of an antler, above the royal antler.

**sur|sum cor|da** (sėr′səm kôr′də), *Latin.* **1** lift up your hearts (words said before the Preface of the Mass). **2** words used to incite or encourage.

**sur|tax** (sėr′taks′), *n., v.* —***n.*** an additional or extra tax on something already taxed; supertax. The surtax on incomes usually increases in graded steps in proportion to the amounts by which incomes exceed a certain sum.
—***v.t.*** to subject to a surtax.
[< French *surtaxe* < *sur-* over, sur-[1] + *taxe* tax]

**sur|tax|a|ble** (sėr tak′sə bəl), *adj.* that can be surtaxed: *surtaxable income.*

**✱surtout**

✱**sur|tout** (sėr tüt′, -tü′), *n.* a kind of single-breasted frock coat with pockets cut diagonally in front, especially one of the type worn by men during the latter 1800's. [< French *surtout* < *sur-* over, sur-[1] + *tout* all < Latin *tōtus* everything]

**surv.**, **1** surveying. **2** surveyor. **3** surviving.

**SURV** (no periods), Standard Underwater Research Vessel (a type of research submersible made in Great Britain).

**sur|veil|lance** (sər vā′ləns, -vāl′yəns), *n.* **1** watch or guard kept over a person or thing, especially over a suspected person, a prisoner, or the like. **2** supervision: *The teachers promised they would ... supply exam-room surveillance to guard against cheating* (Newsweek).
**under surveillance**, subject to a watch or guard: *The police kept the criminal under surveillance.*
[< French *surveillance* < *surveiller;* see etym. under **surveillant**]

**sur|veil|lant** (sər vā′lənt, -vāl′yənt), *n.* a person who keeps watch over another or others. [< French *surveillant*, noun use of present participle of *surveiller* oversee < *sur-* over, sur-[1] + *veiller* to watch < Latin *vigilāre* < *vigil*, *-ilis* vigil]

**sur|veille** (sər vāl′), *v.t.*, **-veilled, -veil|ling.** to keep under surveillance; watch or guard closely: *From foregoing, [I] suspect we are surveilling wrong party* (Harper's). [back formation < *surveillance*]

**sur|vey** (*v.* sər vā′; *n.* sėr′vā, sər vā′), *v., n., pl.* **-veys.** —***v.t.*** **1** to look over; view, examine, consider, or contemplate as a whole: *to survey accounts. Grandma surveyed me with a stern look. The buyers surveyed the goods offered for sale.* (*Figurative.*) *The mayor surveyed the situation before recommending action.* **2** to measure for size, shape, position, or boundaries; use linear and angular measurements and apply geometric and trigonometric principles so as to construct a map, plan, or detailed description: *Men are surveying the land before it is divided into lots.*
—***v.i.*** to survey land.
—***n.*** **1** the act of viewing or considering something as a whole; general or comprehensive look; view; examination; inspection: *We were pleased with our first survey of the house. After a moment's survey of her face ...* (Dickens). **2** *Figurative.* a comprehensive literary examination, discussion, or description: *a survey of contemporary poetry.* **3** *Figurative.* a formal or official inspection, study, or poll: *a survey of public opinion, a research center for business surveys.* **4** *Figurative.* a statement or description embodying the result of such examination: *a published survey of population trends.* **5** the process of measuring for size, shape, position, or boundaries: *A survey of the property showed that the northern boundary was not correct.* **6** a plan or description of such a measurement: *He pointed out the railroad on the government survey.*
[< Anglo-French *surveier*, or Old French *sourveeir* < Medieval Latin *supervidere* < Latin *super-* over + *vidēre* to see]

**sur|vey|a|ble** (sər vā′ə bəl), *adj.* that can be surveyed.

**survey course**, *Education.* an introductory course giving a general view of a subject: *required freshmen survey courses in the four-year colleges* (Fred M. Hechinger).

**sur|vey|ing** (sər vā′ing), *n.* **1** the process, act, or business of making surveys of land. **2** mathematical instruction in the principles and art of making surveys.

**sur|vey|or** (sər vā′ər), *n.* **1** a person who surveys, especially one who surveys land: *The surveyor set up his transit and began to make a survey of the road.* **2** *U.S.* a customs official with the duty of determining the quantity or value of commodities brought into a port from another country. **3** *British.* **a** a quantity surveyor. **b** *Archaic.* an architect, especially one in charge of construction.

**surveyor general**, *pl.* **surveyors general**, **1** a principal or head surveyor. **2** an officer of the United States government who supervises the surveys of public lands.

**surveyor's chain**, a measuring instrument used by surveyors, consisting of 100 interlinked metal rods; Gunter's chain.

**surveyor's compass** or **dial**, an instrument for determining the horizontal direction of a line in reference to the direction of a magnetic needle.

**sur|vey|or|ship** (sər vā′ər ship), *n.* the position of a surveyor.

**surveyor's level**, an instrument used by a surveyor to determine whether a surface is level; dumpy level.

**surveyor's measure**, a system of measuring

used by surveyors. In the United States, the unit is usually a chain 66 ft., or 20.1168 meters, long with links 7.92 in., or 20.1168 centimeters, long.

1 square link = 62.73 square inches or 404.709 square centimeters
625 square links = 1 square pole or 25.2920 square meters
16 square poles = 1 square chain or 404.6724 square meters
10 square chains = 1 acre or 0.4047 hectare
640 acres = 1 section or 1 square mile or 2.5899 square kilometers
36 sections = 1 township or 93. 2364 square kilometers

**sur|view** (sėr′vyü′), *n. Archaic.* a view, especially a mental view, of something; survey. [< Old French *surveue* < *sourveeir;* see etym. under **survey**]

**sur|viv|a|bil|i|ty** (sər vī′və bil′ə tē), *n.* capability of surviving or lasting: *retaliatory missile systems of high survivability* (Bulletin of Atomic Scientists).

**sur|viv|a|ble** (sər vī′və bəl), *adj.* capable of surviving or lasting.

**sur|viv|al** (sər vī′vəl), *n.* **1** the act or fact of surviving; continuance of life; living or lasting longer than others: *No small number of what the English stigmatize as Americanisms are cases of survival from former good usage* (William D. Whitney). **2** something that continues to exist after the cessation of something else, or of other things of the kind. **3** a person, thing, custom, or belief that has lasted from an earlier time: *Belief in the evil eye is a survival of ancient magic. Thanksgiving Day is a survival from before the American Revolution.*

**survival kit**, food, water, medicine and other emergency supplies, in a kit given to the crew of an airplane for use in case of a crash or forced landing: *They wore long cotton underwear ... winter flying gloves, wool socks, A-13A oxygen masks, B-5 parachutes, and carried A-1 survival kits* (Newsweek).

**survival of the fittest**, *Biology.* the fact or the principle that those organisms which are best adapted to their environment continue to live and pass on their favorable features to their offspring, while those of the same or related species which are less adapted perish; the process or result of natural selection.

**survival value**, *Biology.* usefulness of any part, characteristic, or function of an organism in enabling the organism to survive: *Over many generations certain genetically controlled characteristics tend to grow scarce within a population as others gradually replace them, owing to a difference in their survival values* (Atlantic).

**sur|viv|ance** (sər vī′vəns), *n.* = survival.

**sur|vive** (sər vīv′), *v.*, **-vived, -viv|ing.** —*v.t.* **1** to live longer than; outlive: *He survived his wife by three years.* **2** to remain alive after; not die during: *Only ten of the crew survived the shipwreck. She survived a serious operation.* **3** to sustain the effects of and continue to live; outlast: *The crops survived the drought.*
—*v.i.* **1** to continue to live; remain alive; live on: *Yea, though I die, the scandal will survive* (Shakespeare). **2** to continue to exist; remain; last on: *Books have survived from the time of the ancient Egyptians.* [< Anglo-French *survivre,* Old French *sourvivre* < Latin *supervīvere* < *super-* above + *vīvere* to live]

**sur|viv|ing** (sər vī′ving), *adj.* that survives: **a** still living after another's death. **b** still remaining after the cessation of something else.

**sur|vi|vor** (sər vī′vər), *n.* **1** a person, animal, or plant that remains alive; thing that continues to exist: *He is the only survivor of a family of nine. There were two survivors from the plane crash.* **2** *Law.* the one of two or more joint tenants or other persons with a joint interest in property who outlives the other or others.

**sur|vi|vor|ship** (sər vī′vər ship), *n. Law.* **1** the condition of a survivor, or the fact of one person surviving another or others, considered in relation to some right or privilege depending on such survival or the period of it. **2** the right of the survivor or survivors of two or more joint tenants or other persons having a joint interest in property, to take the whole on the death of the other.

**sus-**, *prefix.* the form of **sub-** sometimes before *c, p,* or *t,* as in *susceptible, suspend, sustain.*

**Sus.**, Susanna (book of the Apocrypha).

**Su|san|na** (sü zan′ə), *n.* **1** a character in the Old Testament Apocrypha. Susanna was accused of adultery but was proved innocent by Daniel's cross-examination of her accusers. **2** the book of the Old Testament Apocrypha telling her story, included in the canon of the Greek and Roman Catholic Bibles as part of the Book of Daniel. *Abbr:* Sus.

**sus|cep|ti|bil|i|ty** (sə sep′tə bil′ə tē), *n., pl.* **-ties.** **1** the quality or condition of being susceptible; sensitiveness; sensibility. **2** *Physics.* the capacity of a substance to be magnetized, measured by the ratio of the magnetization to the magnetizing force. *Symbol:* k (no period).
**susceptibilities**, sensitive feelings: *Blunt susceptibilities are very consistent with strong propensities* (Charlotte Brontë).
**susceptibility to**, capability of receiving, being affected by, or undergoing: *a susceptibility to infection.*

**sus|cep|ti|ble** (sə sep′tə bəl), *adj.* **1** easily influenced by feelings or emotions; very sensitive; impressionable: *Poetry appealed to her susceptible nature.* **SYN**: See syn. under **sensitive**. **2** subject to some physical affection, such as infection.
**susceptible of**, **a** capable of receiving, undergoing, or being affected by: *Oak is susceptible of a high polish.* **b** sensitive to: *Her young heart was susceptible only of pleasure and curiosity* (Edward G. Bulwer-Lytton).
**susceptible to**, easily affected by; liable to; open to: *Young children are susceptible to many diseases. Vain people are susceptible to flattery. I ... am peculiarly susceptible to draughts* (Oscar Wilde).
[< Late Latin *susceptibilis* < Latin *suscipere* sustain, support, acknowledge; take on oneself < *sub-* (up from) under + *capere* take] —**sus|cep′ti|ble|ness**, *n.*

**sus|cep|ti|bly** (sə sep′tə blē), *adv.* in a susceptible manner.

**sus|cep|tion** (sə sep′shən), *n.* **1** merely passive mental reception. **2** *Obsolete.* the act of taking up, assuming, or receiving.

**sus|cep|tive** (sə sep′tiv), *adj.* **1** having the quality of taking or receiving; receptive. **2** susceptible; impressionable. —**sus|cep′tive|ness**, *n.*

**sus|cep|tiv|i|ty** (sus′ep tiv′ə tē), *n.* the capacity of admitting; susceptibility.

**su|shi** (sü′shē), *n.* a Japanese and Hawaiian dish of cold cooked rice, fish, and vegetables, rolled in pressed seaweed. [< Japanese *sushi*]

**Su|sie-Q** (sü′zē kyü′), *n.* a kind of shuffling, sideways dance step, especially popular in the 1930's: *... where happy feet first stomped out the Lindy Hop, Big Apple, and Susie-Q* (Time).

**sus|lik** (sus′lik), *n.* **1** a small grayish ground squirrel of Europe and Asia. **2** its fur. [< Russian]

**sus|pect** (*v.* sə spekt′; *n.* sus′pekt; *adj.* sus′pekt, sə spekt′) *v., n., adj.* —*v.t.* **1** to think (something) likely; imagine to be so; surmise: *The old fox suspected danger and did not touch the trap. I suspect that some accident has delayed him. I suspect his knowledge did not amount to much* (Charles Lamb). **SYN**: conjecture. **2** to believe (a person or thing) guilty, false, or bad without enough proof or knowledge: *The policeman suspected the thief of lying.* **3** to feel no confidence in; be very skeptical of; doubt: *The judge suspected the truth of the defendant's alibi.*
—*v.i.* to imagine something, especially some evil, to be possible or likely; be suspicious. [< adjective, and < French *suspecter* suspect, ultimately < Latin *suspectus;* see the adjective]
—*n.* a person suspected of some offense, evil intention, or the like: *The police have arrested two suspects in connection with the bank robbery.* [< adjective]
—*adj.* open to or viewed with suspicion; suspected: *As for the aims and ideals of Marxism, there is one feature of them that is now rightly suspect* (Edmund Wilson). [< Latin *suspectus,* past participle of *suspicere* esteem, look up to < *sub-* under + *specere* to look]

**sus|pect|a|ble** (sə spek′tə bəl), *adj.* that may be suspected; open to suspicion.

**sus|pect|ed** (sə spek′tid), *adj.* **1** that one suspects to be such; possible; likely: *The medical aid to expectant mothers is intended to avert premature births, a suspected cause of mental retardation* (Wall Street Journal). **2** regarded with suspicion; imagined guilty or faulty; suspect: *The hoodlum is the suspected thief.*

**sus|pect|ful** (sə spekt′fəl), *adj. Obsolete.* **1** inclined to suspect. **2** causing suspicion.

**sus|pend** (sə spend′), *v.t.* **1** to hang down by attaching to something above, especially so as to allow movement about the point of attachment: *The lamp was suspended from the ceiling.* **SYN**: dangle, swing. **2** to hold in place as if by hanging; cause to be held up by gravity, buoyancy, or other force: *We saw the smoke suspended in the still air.* **3** to hold or cause to be held in suspension. **4** to stop for a time: *to suspend work on a road until more funds are voted. We suspended building operations during the winter. The hurricane suspended all ferry service for three days.* **SYN**: interrupt, intermit. **5** to remove or exclude for a time from some office, privilege, or job; debar temporarily: *He was suspended from school for a week for bad conduct.* **6** to defer temporarily (sentence on a convicted person). **7** to cause (a law or rule) to be for a time no longer in force; abrogate or make inoperative temporarily: *The privilege of the writ of habeas corpus shall not be suspended* (Constitution of the United States). **8** to keep undecided or undetermined; put off: *Let us suspend judgment until we know all the facts. The court suspended judgment until next Monday.* **SYN**: defer. —*v.i.* **1** to come to a stop for a time. **2** to stop payment; be unable to pay debts or claims.
[< Latin *suspendere* < *sub-* down, under + *pendere* hang]

**sus|pend|ed animation** (sə spen′did), a temporary suspension of breathing, pulse, and other vital functions, especially that due to asphyxia.

**sus|pend|er** (sə spen′dər), *n.* **1** *British.* a garter. **2** a person or thing that suspends. **3** that by which something is suspended.
**suspenders**, straps worn over the shoulders and attached to the trousers to hold them up. In British English the term is *braces.*

**sus|pense** (sə spens′), *n., adj.* —*n.* **1** the condition of being mentally uncertain, especially: **a** such a condition induced by art or craft in order to hold the attention of a reader or audience: *The detective story kept me in suspense until the last chapter.* **b** anxious uncertainty; anxiety: *Mothers feel suspense when their children are very sick.* **2** the condition of being undecided or undetermined; suspending of judgment. **3** *Obsolete.* suspending of action; suspension.
—*adj.* of suspense; suspenseful: *He will do a remake of one of his successful suspense stories* (New York Times).
[< Anglo-French *suspens,* in phrase (*en*) *suspens* (in) abeyance, or < Old French *suspense,* delay < Medieval Latin *suspensus* a checking or withholding, and Vulgar Latin *suspēnsa* < Latin *suspendere;* see etym. under **suspend**]

**suspense account**, an account in which sums received or spent are temporarily entered until their proper place in the books is determined.

**sus|pense|ful** (sə spens′fəl), *adj.* characterized by or full of suspense: *superbly acted suspenseful entertainment* (Saturday Review). *This time there was an even longer and more suspenseful silence before the answer came* (New Yorker).
—**sus|pense′ful|ly**, *adv.*

**sus|pen|si|bil|i|ty** (sə spen′sə bil′ə tē), *n.* the capability of being suspended.

**sus|pen|si|ble** (sə spen′sə bəl), *adj.* that can be suspended.

**sus|pen|sion** (sə spen′shən), *n.* **1a** the act of suspending: *the suspension of a boy from school for bad conduct, suspension of judgment or opinion, the suspension of a driver's license for speeding.* **SYN**: interruption, intermission, stop, postponement, respite. **b** the condition of being suspended: *a suspension from office.* **SYN**: interruption, intermission, stop, postponement, respite. **2** a support on which something is suspended. **3** the arrangement of springs, shock absorbers, or similar devices above the axles, for supporting the body of an automobile, railroad car, or the like. **4a** a mixture in which very small particles of a solid remain suspended without dissolving: *Muddy water is a suspension of tiny dirt particles in water* (John P. Fackler, Jr.). **b** the condition of the solid in such a mixture. **c** a solid in such condition. **5** inability to pay one's debts; failure: *the suspension of a bank.* **6** the temporary deprivation of a clergyman of his right to perform his sacred duties or to receive his ecclesiastical dues. **7** *Electricity.* a wire or filament for supporting the moving part of various instruments. **8** the method or mechanism by which the pendulum or balance wheel is suspended in a clock or watch. **9** *Music.* **a** a prolonging of one or more tones of a chord into the following chord, usually producing a temporary discord until the part or parts prolonged are allowed to proceed. **b** the tone or tones so prolonged. **10a** the act of keeping in suspense. **b** the state of being kept in suspense.

***suspension bridge**

***suspension bridge**, a bridge that has its roadway hung on cables and chains between towers.

**suspension point**, one of a series of dots showing an omission or a longer than usual pause in written or printed matter.

***suspension system**, the shock absorbers, springs, torsion bars, or similar devices, suspended between the wheels and the frame of an automobile to protect the body and mechanical parts from road shock.

***suspension system**

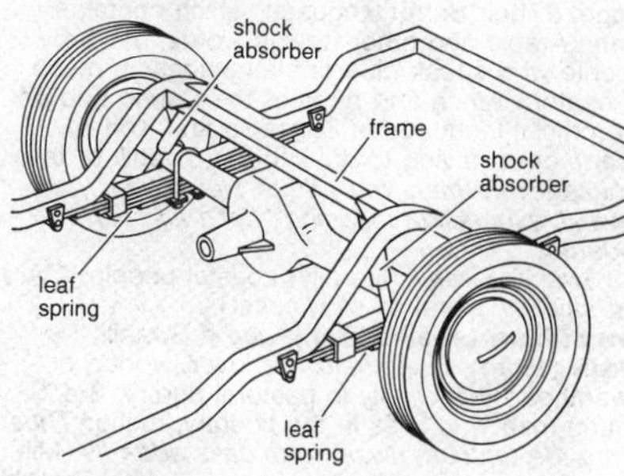


**suspension vase**, a vase with a handle or handles by which it may be suspended without spilling the contents.

**sus|pen|sive** (sə spen′siv), *adj.* **1** inclined to suspend judgment; undecided in mind. **2** having to do with or characterized by suspense, uncertainty, or apprehension: *a suspensive hush.* **3** having the power or effect of suspending, deferring, or temporarily stopping the operation of something: *a suspensive veto.* **4** involving such suspension (applied in law to a condition or obligation of which the operation is suspended until some event takes place). —**sus|pen′sive|ly**, *adv.*

**sus|pen|soid** (sə spen′soid), *n. Chemistry.* a colloidal system in which solid particles are dispersed in a liquid medium.

**sus|pen|sor** (sə spen′sər), *n.* **1** a suspensory muscle, ligament, bandage, or other part or device. **2** *Botany.* a group of cells at the extremity of the embryo that help position the embryo in relation to its food supply. [< Medieval Latin *suspensor* < Latin *suspendere;* see etym. under **suspend**]

**sus|pen|so|ry** (sə spen′sər ē), *adj., n., pl.* **-ries.** —*adj.* **1** serving or fitted to hold up or support: *a suspensory bandage.* **2** stopping for a while; leaving undecided.
—*n.* a muscle, ligament, bandage, or other part or device that holds up or supports a part of the body.

**suspensory ligament**, a supporting ligament, especially the membrane that holds the lens of the eye in place.

**sus. per coll.**, hanged by the neck (Latin, *suspendatur per collum*): *that lamentable note of sus. per coll. at the name of the last male of her line* (Thackeray).

**sus|pi|cion** (sə spish′ən), *n., v.* —*n.* **1** the state of mind of one who suspects; act of suspecting: *The real thief tried to turn suspicion toward others.* **2** an instance of this: *Her suspicions were aroused.* **3** the condition of being suspected. **4** a very small amount; slight trace; suggestion: *She spoke with a suspicion of spite.* **5** a slight belief or idea; faint notion; inkling: *not a suspicion of danger.*
—*v.t. U.S. Dialect.* to suspect: *She naturally suspicioned most things she read* (Dayton Rommel).
**above suspicion**, not to be suspected: *Our old servants are above suspicion. The wife of Caesar must be above suspicion* (Charles Merivale). *The rare red-brown sixpenny Barbados* [*stamp*], *unperforated, ... is not altogether above suspicion* (Philatelist).
**on suspicion**, because of being suspected: *He was arrested on suspicion of robbery. As the result of a student demonstration in which he had played no important part, he* [*Lenin*] *was dismissed from the University of Kazan on suspicion as the brother of the terrorist* (Edmund Wilson).
**under suspicion**, suspected: *He was under suspicion as an accomplice in the theft.*
[< Latin *suspīciō, -ōnis* < Latin *suspicer* to suspect]
—*Syn. n.* **1 Suspicion, distrust, doubt** mean lack of trust or confidence in someone. **Suspicion** suggests fearing, or believing without enough or any proof, that someone or something is guilty, wrong, or false: *Suspicion points to him, but the evidence is circumstantial.* **Distrust** suggests lack of confidence or trust, and may suggest certainty of guilt or falseness: *I could not explain my distrust of the stranger.* **Doubt** suggests merely lack of certainty: *He had no doubt about his son's honesty.*
► **suspicion**. As a verb *suspicion* is substandard: *Nobody suspicioned who it was. Suspect* is the formal and informal verb.

**sus|pi|cion|al** (sə spish′ə nəl), *adj.* **1** of or having to do with suspicion. **2** having to do with or characterized by morbid or insane suspicions.

**sus|pi|cious** (sə spish′əs), *adj.* **1** causing one to suspect; deserving of or exciting suspicion: *A man was hanging about the house in a suspicious manner.* SYN: questionable, doubtful. **2** feeling suspicion; suspecting; mistrustful: *Our dog is suspicious of strangers.* **3** showing or characterized by suspicion: *The dog gave a suspicious sniff at my leg.* —**sus|pi′cious|ly**, *adv.* —**sus|pi′cious|ness**, *n.*

**sus|pi|ra|tion** (sus′pə rā′shən), *n.* a sigh: *windy suspirations of forced breath* (Shakespeare).

**sus|pire** (sə spīr′), *v.*, **-pired, -pir|ing.** *Poetic.* —*v.i.* **1** to sigh or long; yearn. **2** to breathe.
—*v.t.* to breathe forth: *a bolt from heaven ... suspiring flame* (Robert Browning).
[< Latin *suspīrāre* draw a deep breath < *sub-* (from) under + *spīrāre* breathe]

**Sus|que|han|na** (sus′kwə han′ə), *n., pl.* **-na** or **-nas.** a member of an Iroquoian tribe living along the Susquehanna River.

**suss** (sus), *v.t. British Slang.* Usually, **suss out.** to figure out: *Do not, please, tell me ... that youth susses things out for itself* (Anthony Burgess). *Then there are those people who reckon they have got you all sussed out* (Listener). [perhaps originally short for *suspect*]

**Suss.**, Sussex.

**Sus|sex** (sus′iks), *n.* **1** any one of an English breed of chicken raised for meat and eggs. It has white skin and light, speckled, or red plumage, and lays eggs with brown shells. **2** any one of an English breed of beef cattle. [< *Sussex,* a county in England where they were first developed]

**Sussex spaniel**, any one of an English breed of spaniel developed in the 1800's, having a bright liver color, short neck and legs, and reaching a height of about 16 inches and weight of about 45 pounds.

**sus|tain** (sə stān′), *v.t.* **1** to keep up; keep going; maintain; prolong: *Hope sustains him in his misery. The arts by which he sustains the reader's interest* (Benjamin Jowett). ... *Sympathy's sustaining bread* (Louisa May Alcott). SYN: aid, assist, comfort. **2** to supply as with food or provisions: *to sustain a family. She eats barely enough to sustain life.* **3** to hold up; support: *Columns and arches sustain the weight of the roof.* **4** to bear; endure: *The sea wall sustains the shock of the waves.* SYN: withstand, stand. **5** to suffer; experience: *to sustain a broken leg. She sustained a great loss in the death of her husband.* SYN: undergo. **6** to allow; admit; favor: *The court sustained his claim.* **7** to agree with; confirm: *The facts sustain her theory.* SYN: corroborate, sanction. [< Anglo-French *sustein-,* stem of *sustenir* < Latin *sustinēre* < *sub-* (from) under + *tenēre* to hold] —**sus|tain′er**, *n.*

**sus|tain|a|ble** (sə stā′nə bəl), *adj.* that can be sustained.

**sus|tained** (sə stānd′), *adj.* **1** kept up without intermission or flagging: *a sustained attack, sustained illness. Her sustained chatter was unbearable.* **2** maintained uniformly, especially at a high pitch or level: *the best sustained performance.* **3** *Music.* of a tone or note: **a** held to its full time value. **b** maintained for several beats or measures in one part while the other parts progress.

**sus|tain|ed|ly** (sə stā′nid lē), *adv.* in a sustained manner.

**sustained yield**, the continuing yield of a biological resource, such as a forestry or fishery crop, by special, controlled harvesting, usually aimed at a steady optimum yield.

**sus|tain|er engine** (sə stā′nər), a rocket engine that maintains the speed reached by a booster engine.

**sus|tain|ing program** (sə stā′ning), a radio or television program having no commercial sponsor but maintained at the expense of a station or network.

**sus|tain|ment** (sə stān′mənt), *n.* **1** the act of sustaining. **2** the state of being sustained. **3** a person or thing that sustains; means of support; sustenance.

**sus|te|nance** (sus′tə nəns), *n.* **1** means of sustaining life; food or provisions; nourishment: *The lost campers went without sustenance for two days.* **2** means of living or subsistence; support: *He gave money for the sustenance of his aged relatives.* **3** the act or process of sustaining. **4** the condition of being sustained. [< Anglo-French *sustenaunce* < *sustenir;* see etym. under **sustain**]

**sus|ten|tac|u|lar** (sus′ten tak′yə lər), *adj. Anatomy.* supporting: *sustentacular muscle fibers.* [< New Latin *sustentaculum* sustaining (in Latin, a prop, stay, support; in Late Latin, sustenance or nourishment) < Latin *sustentāre* (frequentative) < *sustinēre* (see etym. under **sustain**) + *-ar*]

**sus|ten|ta|tion** (sus′ten tā′shən), *n.* **1** the act of keeping up an establishment, building, or institution; upkeep; maintenance. **2** preservation of a condition or state, especially human life. **3** the act of maintaining a person or concrete thing in being or activity (used especially in the 1600's of divine support).. **4** support; sustenance. [< Latin *sustentātiō, -ōnis* < *sustentāre* (frequentative) < *sustinēre;* see etym. under **sustain**]

**sus|ten|ta|tive** (sus′ten tā′tiv, sə sten′tə-), *adj.* having the quality of sustaining.

**sus|ten|tion** (sə sten′shən), *n.* **1** the act of sustaining or keeping up something, such as a condition or feeling. **2** the holding on of a musical tone. **3** the quality of being sustained in argument or style. [< *sustain;* patterned on *retention*]

**sus|ten|tive** (sə sten′tiv), *adj.* having the quality or property of sustaining.

**su|su¹** (sü′sü), *n.* a blind freshwater mammal related to and resembling the dolphin, found in the Indus, Ganges, and other large rivers of India. [< Bengali *susu*]

**su|su²** (sü′sü), *n. Anthropology.* a kinship group, such as found among the Dobus, consisting of a woman, her brother, and children of the woman. [< Dobu *susu* (literally) mother's milk]

**Su|su** (sü′sü), *n., pl.* **-su** or **-sus**, *adj.* —*n.* **1** a member of a cattle-herding people of Guinea and Sierra Leone. **2** their Mandingo language.
—*adj.* of this people or their language.

**su|sur|rant** (sü sėr′ənt), *adj.* softly rustling or murmuring; whispering. [< Latin *susurrāns, -antis,* present participle of *susurrāre* to whisper, hum < *susurrus* susurrus]

**su|sur|rate** (sü sėr′āt), *v.i.*, **-rat|ed, -rat|ing.** *Obsolete.* to whisper. [< Latin *susurrāre* (with English *-ate*¹) < *susurrus* susurrus]

**su|sur|ra|tion** (sü′sə rā′shən), *n.* **1** a whispering. **2** a rustling murmur. [< Late Latin *susurrātiō, -ōnis* < Latin *susurrāre* to whisper, hum < *susurrus* susurrus]

**su|sur|rous** (sü sėr′əs), *adj.* = susurrant.

**su|sur|rus** (sü sėr′əs), *n.* a low, soft, whispering sound; whisper: *the soft susurrus and sighs of the branches* (Longfellow). [< Latin *susurrus* a whispering. Compare etym. under **surd.**]

**Su|sy-Q** (sü′zē kyü′), *n.* = Susie-Q.

**SU(3) symmetry**, *Nuclear Physics.* eightfold way. [< *S*(pecial) *U*(nitary) (group in *3* dimensions) *symmetry*]

**sut|ler** (sut′lər), *n.* a merchant who follows or camps near an army and sells provisions to the soldiers. [< early Dutch *soeteler* small tradesman < *soetelen* ply a low trade; do mean duties]

**sut|ler|ship** (sut′lər ship), *n.* the office or occupation of a sutler.

**su|tra** (sü′trə), *n.* **1** any one of certain aphoristic rules, consisting typically of one line and dealing with such various realms as grammar, philosophy, and law, that form part of the link between Vedic and later Sanskrit literature. **2** any one of various collections of such rules, from some of which in varying degree both Hinduism and Buddhism derive certain rules, as of social ceremony and family life. **3** a division of (Pali) Buddhist sacred literature containing general expositions of doctrine, the sermons of Buddha, and other writings. [< Sanskrit *sūtra* rule; (originally) thread]

**sut|ta** (sůt′ə), *n.* = sutra.

**sut|tee** (su tē′, sut′ē), *n.* **1** the Hindu custom, now forbidden by law but still occasionally practiced, of burning a widow alive with the body of her husband: *He was cremated yesterday in a secret place to prevent demonstrations and perhaps suttee* (London Times). **2** a woman who dies by suttee; widow who throws herself, or is thrown, on the funeral pyre of her husband and is burned alive. Also, **sati.** [< Hindustani *sattī* < Sanskrit *satī* faithful wife; feminine of *sat* good, wise; (literally) present participle of *as* to be]

**sut|tee|ism** (su tē′iz əm), *n.* the practice of suttee.

**su|tur|al** (sü′chər əl), *adj., n.* —*adj.* **1** of or having to do with a suture. **2** *Botany.* taking place at, or otherwise relating to, a suture.
—*n.* any one of various small, irregular bones sometimes found in the sutures of the skull.
—**su′tur|al|ly**, *adv.*

**su|ture** (sü′chər), *n., v.*, **-tured, -tur|ing.** —*n.* **1** the sewing together or joining of two surfaces, especially the edges of a cut or wound. **2** a seam formed in sewing up a wound, the ends of a severed tendon or nerve, or the like. **3** one of the stitches or fastenings used. **4** the material used, such as catgut, linen, or silk. **5** the act of

sewing together or joining as if by sewing. **6** a stitch or seam. **7** *Anatomy.* **a** the line or seam where two bones, especially of the skull, join in an immovable joint. **b** the immovable joint itself: *All of these* [*bones*] *are firmly united by immovable joints called sutures* (Beals and Hoijer). **8** *Zoology.* the line between adjoining parts, such as that along which clamshells join: *The sutures, the lines of junction of the septa with the wall of the shell, were nearly straight or only slightly curved* (A. Franklin Shull). **9** *Botany.* the seam or line of junction between two edges, such as that along which pea pods split.
*—v.t.* to unite by suture or in a similar manner.
[< Latin *sūtūra* < *suere* sew]

**su|um cui|que** (sü′əm kī′kwē, kwī′kwē), *Latin.* his own to each; (render) to each his due: [*He*] *had invested in it, but I suggested that Irwin invest somewhere else. Suum cuique, as it were* (New Yorker).

**su|ze|rain** (sü′zər in, -zə rān), *n., adj.* *—n.* **1** a feudal lord. **2** a ruler, state, or government exercising political control over a dependent state.
*—adj.* of or like a suzerain; sovereign: *a suzerain power.*
[< French *suzerain,* earlier *suserain* < *sus* above < Latin *sūrsum* upward < *sub* (from) under + *versus* turned; patterned on Old French *souverain* sovereign]

**su|ze|rain|ty** (sü′zər in tē, -zə rān′-), *n., pl.* **-ties.** the position, rank, or authority of a suzerain.

**Su|zu|ki method** (sə zü′kē), a method of teaching music, especially on the violin, to very young children, based on the elements of imitation and repetition used in learning how to talk; talent education method: *... the Suzuki method of introducing tiny violins to tiny, sticky fingers practically from birth* (Sunday Times). [< Shinichi *Suzuki,* a Japanese music teacher, who devised the method in 1945]

**s.v.,** sub verbo or sub voce (under the word or heading).

**S.V.,** Sons of Veterans.

**svan|berg|ite** (svän′bər gīt), *n.* a mineral occurring in rhombohedral crystals of a yellow, red, or brown color. It consists of sulfate and phosphate of aluminum and calcium. [< Lars F. *Svanberg,* a Swedish chemist of the 1800's + *-ite*[1]]

**Sved|berg unit** (sved′bėrg, svā′ber ē), a measure of the rate of sedimentation of a protein or other large molecule in a centrifugal field, equal to $10^{-13}$ centimeter per second: *In the tadpole we find a single protein peak with a sedimentation constant of 4.3 Svedberg units* (Scientific American). *Abbr.:* S (no period). [< Theodor *Svedberg,* 1884-1971, a Swedish chemist]

**svelte** (svelt), *adj.* slender; lithe; slim; willowy: *The countess was tall, svelte, and very pale. This dazzling, svelte charmer ... wheedles her way into our hearts with stunning brilliance* (London Times). [< French *svelte* < Italian *svelto* (literally) past participle of *svellere* to tear up; probably < Latin *ex-* out + *vellere* to pluck, or < Vulgar Latin *solvitus* free, released < Latin *solvere* loosen] **—svelte′ly,** *adv.*

**Sven|ga|li** (sven gä′lē), *n.* **1** a musician who hypnotizes and gains control over the heroine of the novel *Trilby* (1894), by George du Maurier (1834-1896), an English novelist. **2** a person with irresistible hypnotic powers.

**Sw.,** **1** Sweden. **2** Swedish.

**SW** (no periods), **1** short wave. **2** Southwest. **3** Southwestern.

**s.w.,** **1** southwest. **2** southwestern.

**S.W.,** an abbreviation for the following:
**1** South Wales.
**2** Southwest.
**3** Southwestern.
**4** (South-Western (postal district of London).

**S.W. (2d),** Southwestern Reporter, second (series).

**SWA** (no periods), South West Africa.

**swab** (swob), *n., v.,* **swabbed, swab|bing.** *—n.* **1** a long-handled mop for cleaning decks, floors, and the like. **2** a bit of sponge, cloth, or cotton for cleansing some part of the body or for applying medicine to it: *There are swabs which can be left in the body after an operation to dissolve harmlessly in the blood* (London Times). **3** a specimen taken with such a bit of sponge, cloth, or cotton. **4** a patch of cloth for cleaning the bore of a firearm. **5** *Slang.* an awkward, clumsy person. **6** *U.S. Slang.* swabby.
*—v.t.* to clean with a swab; apply a swab to: *to swab the deck, to swab a person's throat. Main decks of battleships, which receive rough treatment and constant swabbing, are usually surfaced with teak* (New Yorker). Also, **swob.**
[back formation < *swabber*]

**Swab.,** **1** Swabia. **2** Swabian.

**swab|ber** (swob′ər), *n.* **1** a person who uses a swab. **2** a mop; swab. **3** a kind of mop for cleaning ovens. **4** *Slang.* a swab. [< earlier Dutch *zwabber* < *zwabben* swab]

**swab|by** or **swab|bie** (swob′ē), *n., pl.* **-bies.** *U.S. Slang.* a sailor of enlisted rank; gob: *He was, after all, the luckiest swabby in Uncle Sam's Navy* (Time).

**Swa|bi|an** (swā′bē ən), *adj., n.* *—adj.* of or having to do with Swabia, a former duchy in southwest Germany, or its people.
*—n.* a native or inhabitant of Swabia.

**swad|dle** (swod′əl), *v.,* **-dled, -dling,** *n.* *—v.t.* **1** to wrap (a baby) with long, narrow strips of cloth. **2** to bind (anything) tightly with clothes, bandages, or other wrapping; envelop; swathe. **3** *Figurative.* to restrict the action of (any person or thing); halt or hinder the movement of by or as if by binding or enfolding: [*His thoughts*] *have been cramped and twisted and swaddled into lifelessness and deformity* (William Hazlitt).
*—n.* cloth used for swaddling; swaddling clothes.
[Middle English *swathelen* < *swethel* a swaddle, Old English *swethel.* See related etym. at **swathe**[1].]

***swad|dling clothes, bands,** or **clouts** (swod′ling), **1a** long, narrow strips of cloth used for wrapping a newborn infant so as to prevent its free movement: *And she brought forth her firstborn son, and wrapped him in swaddling clothes, and laid him in a manger* (Luke 2:7). **b** long clothes for an infant. **2** *Figurative.* **a** the earliest period of existence of a person or thing, when movement or action is restricted; infancy. **b** the restrictions so imposed.

***swaddling clothes**
definition 1a

**Swa|de|shi** (swə dā′shē), *n.* that part of the movement for Indian political autonomy (swaraj) that involved the boycott of foreign, especially British, commodities in favor of those made or processed in India. [< Bengali *Swadeshi* (literally) own-country things < Sanskrit *svadeśin* native < *svadeśa* native land]

**swag** (swag), *n., v.,* **swagged, swag|ging.** *—n.* **1** *Slang.* **a** things stolen; booty; plunder: *What'll we do with what little swag we've got left?* (Mark Twain). **b** dishonest gains, especially dishonest political gains. **2** *Australian.* a bundle of personal belongings, especially of a traveler in the bush, a tramp, or a miner. **3** an ornamental festoon of flowers, leaves, or ribbons: *He got out the stepladder ... and began to unfasten the crêpe-paper swags* (New Yorker). **4** a swaying or lurching movement. [< verb. Compare Middle English *swagge* bag.]
*—v.i.* **1** to move unsteadily or heavily from side to side or up and down; sway without control; lurch. **2** to hang loosely or heavily; sag.
**swag it,** *Australian.* to carry one's swag: *The solitary pedestrian, with the whole of his supplies ... strapped across his shoulders* [*was*] *"swagging it"* (T. M'Combie).
[probably < Scandinavian (compare dialectal Norwegian *svagga* to sway). See related etym. at **sway.**]

**swage** (swāj), *n., v.,* **swaged, swag|ing.** *—n.* **1** a tool for bending cold metal to the required shape. **2** a die or stamp for shaping metal, as on an anvil or in a press. **3** = swage block.
*—v.t.* to bend or shape by using a swage.
[earlier, a molding, mounting < Old French *souage,* perhaps < Late Latin *sōca* rope]

**swage block,** a heavy iron or steel block with holes and grooves of various sizes, for shaping bolts or other objects.

**swag|ger** (swag′ər), *v., n., adj.* *—v.i.* **1** to walk with a bold, rude, or superior air; strut about or show off in a vain or insolent way: *The bully swaggered into the schoolyard.* SYN: See syn. under **strut. 2** to boast or brag noisily: *By swaggering could I never thrive* (Shakespeare). **3** to bluster; bluff.
*—v.t.* to affect by bluster, especially to bring (into or out of a state) by blustering talk; bluster; bluff.
*—n.* the act of swaggering; swaggering way of walking, acting, or speaking: *The pirate captain moved among his prisoners with a swagger.*
*—adj. Informal.* showily or ostentatiously smart or fashionable.
[apparently < *swag,* verb + *-er*[6]] **—swag′ger|er,** *n.* **—swag′ger|ing|ly,** *adv.*

**swagger cane,** = swagger stick.

**swagger coat,** a woman's loosely fitting, beltless sportcoat.

**swagger stick,** a short, light stick or cane, sometimes carried by army officers or soldiers.

**swag|gie** (swag′ē), *n. Australian.* swagman.

**swag|man** (swag′mən), *n., pl.* **-men.** *Australian.* a man who travels with a swag.

**swags|man** (swagz′mən), *n., pl.* **-men.** = swagman.

**Swa|hi|li** (swä hē′lē), *n., pl.* **-li** or **-lis,** *adj.* *—n.* **1** a member of a Bantu people living along the east coast of Africa, from Somalia to Mozambique. **2** their Bantu language, which contains many Arabic and other foreign words, used, by people who speak different languages, in much of eastern Africa and parts of the Congo and as the official language of Tanzania and Kenya.
*—adj.* of or having to do with the Swahili or their language: *Farmers roared ... "Harambee!", a Swahili expression meaning "Let's all push together"* (Time).
[< Swahili *Swahili* (literally) coastal people < Arabic *sawāḥil,* plural of *sāḥil* coast]

**Swa|hi|li|an** (swä hē′lē ən), *adj.* = Swahili.

**swain** (swān), *n. Archaic.* **1** a lover, wooer, or sweetheart, especially in pastoral poetry. **2** a young man who lives in the country; rustic: *Thus sang the uncouth swain to th'oaks and rills* (Milton). **3** a country gallant or lover. [Middle English *swein* < Scandinavian (compare Old Icelandic *sveinn* boy)]

**swain|ish** (swā′nish), *adj.* **1** having to do with a swain. **2** resembling a swain; rustic; boorish. **—swain′ish|ness,** *n.*

**Swain|son's hawk** (swān′sənz), a brownish hawk, often with white throat and abdomen, found in South America and western North America. [< William *Swainson,* 1789-1855, an English naturalist]

**Swainson's thrush,** = olive-backed thrush.

**Swainson's warbler,** a warbler of the southeastern United States with olive back and dull whitish breast.

**Swa|kar|a** (swə kär′ə), *n.* **1** the fur of a lamb of South West Africa, similar to karakul. **2** the lamb, bred from a stock imported originally from Bukhara. [< *SWA* (abbreviation of South West Africa) + *kara*(kul)]

**swale** (swāl), *n.* **1** a low, wet piece of land; low place: *The bear we spotted in a grassy swale was already fattened after his winter sleep* (Paul Brooks). **2** *Dialect.* a shady place. [probably < Scottish *swaill* low, hollow place, or < dialectal *swale* or *swell* shady place. Compare Old Icelandic *svalr* cool.]

**swal|low**[1] (swol′ō), *v., n.* *—v.t.* **1** to take into the stomach through the throat: *We swallowed all our food and drink.* **2** *Figurative.* **a** to take in completely; absorb: *Big cities ... don't have the legal authority to easily swallow outlying areas* (Wall Street Journal). **b** to make away with; cause to disappear completely; engulf: *The scene was swallowed in a hush* (James T. Farrell). **3** *Informal, Figurative.* to believe too easily; accept without question or suspicion; drink in: *He will swallow any story.* **4** *Figurative.* to put up with; take meekly; accept without opposing or resisting; bear: *I had to swallow the insult. He doesn't give you more than you can swallow and he makes you feel you are part of the team* (Harper's). **5** *Figurative.* to keep from expressing; keep back; repress: *to swallow one's anger. She swallowed her displeasure and smiled.* **6** *Figurative.* to take back; retract; recant: *to swallow words said in anger.*
*—v.i.* to take food, drink, etc., into the stomach through the throat; perform the act of swallowing: *I cannot swallow because my throat is so sore.*
*—n.* **1** an act of swallowing; gulp: *He took the medicine at one swallow.* **2** an amount swallowed at one time; mouthful: *There are only about four swallows left in the bottle.* **3** the capacity for swallowing; appetite. **4** the throat; gullet. **5** *Nautical.* the space between the sheave and the shell in a pulley block, through which the rope is passed.
**swallow up, a** to take in as if by devouring or absorbing; consume; destroy; engulf: *The waves swallowed up the little boat. Must not all things at last be swallowed up in death?* (Benjamin Jowett). **b** to absorb or appropriate (a territory or other possession); take for oneself or into oneself: *The French King ... swallow'd up almost all Flanders* (John Evelyn). **c** to take up completely: *The first printing was swallowed up before publication* (New Yorker).
[Middle English *swalewen,* Old English *swelgan*] **—swal′low|er,** *n.*

**swal|low**[2] (swol′ō), *n.* **1** any one of a large group of small, swift-flying birds with long, pointed wings and weak feet used only for perching. Swallows are noted for their migrations, in large numbers and over long distances, to avoid cold or find food. Some kinds have deeply forked tails. The bank swallow or sand martin, the barn swallow, the cliff swallow, and the purple martin are some of the kinds in the swallow family. *Some listen for the first ... swallow, but at least one countryman awaits more eagerly the liquid call of the first quail* (London Times). **2** any one of certain swifts that resemble swallows, such as the chimney swift (also called the chimney swallow). [Old English *swealwe*] —**swal′low|like′**, *adj.*

**swal|low|a|ble** (swol′ō ə bəl), *adj.* **1** that can be swallowed. **2** *Figurative.* that can be believed; credible.

**swallow dive**, *Especially British.* a swan dive.

**swallow hole**, *Especially British.* an opening or cavity, common in limestone formations, through which a stream disappears underground; sinkhole.

***swal|low|tail** (swol′ō tāl′), *n.* **1** a large butterfly, having taillike extensions of the hind wings. The tiger swallowtail and the zebra swallowtail are two kinds. *Swallowtails ... include some of the most beautifully colored butterflies* (A. M. Winchester). **2** a thing shaped like or suggesting the deeply forked tail of certain swallows. **3** a tail like that of a swallow; forked tail. **4** = swallow-tailed coat.

***swallowtail**
definitions 1, 3, 4

butterfly

barn swallow

swallow-tailed coat

**swal|low-tailed** (swol′ō tāld′), *adj.* **1** having a tail like that of a swallow. **2** of the form of a swallow's tail.

**swallow-tailed coat**, a man's coat with tails, worn at formal evening parties.

**swallow-tailed kite**, a graceful black and white hawk with a long, black, forked tail, found in the southern United States and south to Argentina.

**swal|low|wort** (swol′ō wėrt′), *n.* **1** any one of several plants of the milkweed family, especially a European herb whose pods suggest a swallow with outspread wings. It has a root with emetic, cathartic, and diuretic properties. **2** = celandine (def. 1).

**swam** (swam), *v.* the past tense of **swim**: *When the boat sank, we swam to shore.*

**swa|mi** (swä′mē), *n., pl.* **-mis. 1** a Hindu religious teacher (often used as a title). **2** a person who is like a swami; an expert; pundit: *The former Liberal campaign chairman ... is presenting himself as the swami who can best draft a vote-getting platform* (Canadian Saturday Night). [< Hindi *svāmī* master (used as term of address) < Sanskrit *svāmin* lord, master]

**swamp** (swomp, swômp), *n., adj., v.* —*n.* **1** wet, soft land; mire; bog; marsh: *The farmer will drain the swamp so that he can plant crops there.* **SYN:** morass, fen, slough, quagmire. **2** (originally) a tract of rich soil having a growth of trees and other vegetation, but too moist for cultivation.
—*adj.* **1** having to do with a swamp or swamps. **2** living in a swamp or swamps: *a swamp bird.* **3** growing in a swamp or swamps: *swamp grass.*
—*v.t.* **1** to plunge or sink in or as if in a swamp: *The horses were swamped in the stream.* **2** to fill (a boat) with water and sink: *The wave swamped the boat.* **3** to flood, submerge, or soak, as with water. **4** *Figurative.* to overwhelm with difficulties or by superior numbers; make helpless: *to be swamped by debts, swamped with work. That factory is swamped with orders it cannot fill.* **5** to clear out underbrush or fell trees in, in order to make logging roads or to haul out logs on a skidway: *The clearing was swamped in three days.*
—*v.i.* **1** to sink by filling with water: *Their boat swamped.* **2** to sink or stick in or as if in a swamp or water. **3** *Figurative.* to become involved with difficulties or sink under superior numbers; become helpless: *Their small force soon swamped amid the onrushing horde of Tartars.*
[American English, apparently variant of *sump*]

**swamp azalea** or **honeysuckle**, a variety of azalea with white or pinkish flowers, growing in swampy areas of the eastern United States.

**swamp bay**, **1** = sweet bay (def. 1). **2** a tree or shrub of the Atlantic coast with tiny yellow flowers and pale green leaves. It belongs to the laurel family.

**swamp blackbird**, = redwing.

**swamp buggy**, *U.S.* **1** a motor vehicle with a high body and large, thick tires, used for traveling over swampland. **2** an airboat.

**swamp buttercup**, a North American buttercup commonly found in wet or damp places.

**swamp cabbage**, = skunk cabbage.

**swamp cypress**, = bald cypress.

**swamp deer**, = marsh deer.

**swamp|er** (swom′pər, swôm′-), *n. U.S.* **1** a person who lives in a swamp or swampy region: *Everybody thought we were just a state of hillbillies and swampers* (Time). **2a** a person who works clearing roads for lumberjacks or clearing fallen trees of limbs and knots for the men who cut the trunks into logs. **b** a person who hauls logs out of the woods on a skidway.

**swamp fever**, **1** = malaria. **2** = leptospirosis. **3** a usually fatal virus disease of horses and other animals, often characterized by anemia: *The regulatory action grew out of a mounting concern by state veterinary agencies throughout the country over the incidence of equine infectious anemia—swamp fever* (New York Times).

**swamp|fish** (swomp′fish′, swômp′-), *n., pl.* **-fishes** or (*collectively*) **-fish.** a small striped fish with a transparent skin covering its eyes, found in swamps and streams of the Atlantic coastal plain of the southern United States.

**swamp forest**, a forest of trees growing in a swamp. Swamp forests are found in Georgia and Florida.

**swamp gas**, = marsh gas.

**swamp hare**, = swamp rabbit.

**swamp hickory**, a species of hickory that grows in swamps and bears nuts with a bitter kernel; bitternut.

**swamp|i|ness** (swom′pē nis, swôm′-), *n.* swampy quality or condition: *... studies of tides, rainfall, and swampiness in that area* (New Yorker).

**swamp|ish** (swom′pish, swôm′-), *adj.* swampy, as land: *when all this flat central country was swampish and hadn't been drained off yet* (Booth Tarkington).

**swamp|land** (swomp′land′, swômp′-), *n.* a tract of land covered by swamps.

**swamp|less** (swomp′lis, swômp′-), *adj.* without a swamp or swamps: *Mountain regions are usually swampless.*

**swamp loosestrife**, a woody North American herb of the loosestrife family, having purplish-red flowers and commonly found in marshes; slinkweed.

**swamp magnolia**, = sweet bay (def. 1).

**swamp maple**, a common variety of maple of eastern North America often growing in swampy areas; red maple.

**swamp oak**, = pin oak.

**swamp ore**, = bog iron ore.

**swamp owl**, **1** = barred owl. **2** = short-eared owl.

**swamp partridge**, = spruce grouse.

**swamp rabbit**, a large, coarse-haired rabbit, a species of cottontail, most common in wet areas of the lower Mississippi Valley.

**swamp robin**, **1** = towhee. **2** any one of various American thrushes.

**swamp rose mallow**, a rose mallow with white or pink flowers that grows wild in marshes of the eastern United States, sometimes growing seven feet high.

**swamp sparrow**, a sparrow of the marshes of eastern North America, with a white throat and rusty crown.

**swamp spruce**, = black spruce.

**swamp white oak**, an oak having a flaky gray bark, found in swamps in eastern North America.

**swamp|y** (swom′pē, swôm′-), *adj.,* **swamp|i|er, swamp|i|est. 1** like a swamp; soft and wet: *swampy ground. The front yard is swampy from the heavy rain.* **SYN:** boggy, marshy. **2** containing swamps: *a swampy region.* **3** of swamps.

**swa|my** (swä′mē), *n., pl.* **-mies.** = swami.

***swan¹**
definition 1

mute swan

***swan¹** (swon, swôn), *n., v.,* **swanned, swan|ning.** —*n.* **1** a large, graceful water bird with a long, slender, curving neck. The grown male is usually pure white. Swans are closely related to geese and ducks. **2** *Figurative.* a person or thing that is considered faultless and has purity, great beauty, or other similar physical attribute thought of in relation to the swan. **3** *Figurative.* a sweet singer; poet; bard: *Sweet swan of Avon* (Ben Jonson).
—*v.i. Especially British.* to move like a swan; float; drift: *I shall swan about in my bachelor flat in Prince of Wales Drive* (Christopher Matthew).
**swan it**, *Informal.* to go by swanning; drift; roam: *He'll be all right for another year or two, swanning it around the islands* (Atlantic).
[Old English *swan*] —**swan′like′**, *adj.*

**swan²** (swon, swôn), *v.i. U.S. Dialect.*
**I swan**, I declare: *If you haven't observed it, I have, and a queer one it is, I swan* (Thomas C. Haliburton).
[American English, perhaps contraction of dialectal (New England) *I s'warn* I shall warrant; *warrant,* in the sense of "swear"]

**Swan** (swon, swôn), *n.* the northern constellation Cygnus. [translation of Latin *Cygnus* Cygnus]

**swan dive**, a graceful dive in which the legs are held straight, the back is arched, and the arms are spread like the wings of a gliding bird.

**swang** (swang), *v. Archaic and Dialect.* swung; a past tense of **swing¹**.

**swan grebe**, = western grebe.

**swan|herd** (swon′hėrd′, swôn′-), *n.* a person who looks after swans.

**swan-hop|per** (swon′hop′ər, swôn′-), *n.* = swan-upper.

**swan-hop|ping** (swon′hop′ing, swôn′-), *n.* = swan-upping.

**swank¹** (swangk), *adj., v., n.* —*adj.* **1** *Slang.* stylish; smart; dashing. **2** *Scottish.* agile; active; nimble.
—*v.i. Slang.* to show off; bluff; swagger.
—*n. Slang.* **1** ostentatious or pretentious behavior or talk; showing off: *I do not mind his money, but I do not like his swank* (G. K. Chesterton). **2** style; smartness; dash.
[origin uncertain; perhaps (originally) variant of *swing¹*, in sense of "swing the body," related to Scottish *swank* active, agile. Compare Old English *swancor* lithe.]

**swank²** (swangk), *v. Archaic.* a past tense of **swink.**

**swank|i|ly** (swang′kə lē), *adv. Slang.* in a swanky manner.

**swank|i|ness** (swang′kē nis), *n. Slang.* the state or quality of being swanky.

**swank|y** (swang′kē), *adj.,* **swank|i|er, swank|i|est,** *n., pl.* **swank|ies.** —*adj.* **1** *Slang.* **a** stylish; smart; dashing. **b** swaggering. **2** *Scottish.* swank.
—*n. Scottish.* a smart, active, strapping young fellow.

**swan maiden**, a fabulous creature able to appear in the guise of either a young maiden or swan by taking off or putting on a magic garment of swan's feathers, or by invoking the power of a magic ring or golden chain, versions of which are encountered in Teutonic and Asian folklore and myth.

**swan-mark** (swon′märk, swôn′-), *n. British.* the official mark cut on the beak of a swan in swan-upping.

**swan|neck** (swon′nek′, swôn′-), *n.* **1** a neck like that of a swan, as in length, slenderness, or whiteness. **2** something shaped like or suggesting the neck of a swan, as a curved section of a pipe.

**swan-necked** (swon′nekt′, swôn′-), *adj.* **1** having a neck like that of a swan, as in length, whiteness, or slenderness. **2** shaped or curved like the neck of a swan.

**swan|ner|y** (swon′ər ē, swôn′-), *n., pl.* **-ner|ies.** a place where swans are kept and reared.

**Swans|combe man** (swonz′kəm), an early type of pre-Neanderthal man similar to Homo sapiens, identified from skull bones found at Swanscombe, England.

**swan's-down** (swonz′doun′, swônz′-), *n.* **1** the soft down of a swan, used for dress trimmings, powder puffs, and the like. **2** Also, **swansdown. a** a fine, thick, soft cloth, usually made from wool, used especially for babies' coats and bathrobes. **b** = cotton flannel.

**swan shift**, a garment made of swan's feathers which the swan maiden put on to assume her guise as a swan.

**swan|skin** (swon′skin′, swôn′-), *n., adj.* —*n.* **1** the skin of a swan, with the feathers on. **2** any one of various soft fabrics, as cotton flannel.
—*adj.* made or consisting of swanskin.

**Pronunciation Key:** hat, āge, cãre, fär; let, ēqual, tėrm; it, īce; hot, ōpen, ôrder; oil, out; cup, pu̇t, rüle; child; long; thin; ᴛʜen; zh, measure; ə represents **a** in about, **e** in taken, **i** in pencil, **o** in lemon, **u** in circus.

**swan song**, **1** the song which, according to fable, a swan sings as it is about to die. It is melancholy but surpassingly beautiful. **2** *Figurative.* a person's last piece of work, farewell performance, or final statement, especially a last work of literature, music, or art.

**swan-up|per** (swon′up′ər, swôn′-), *n. British.* an official who takes up and marks swans.

**swan-up|ping** (swon′up′ing, swôn′-), *n. British.* **1** the act or practice of taking up swans and marking them with nicks on the beak in token of being owned by the Crown or somebody chartered by the Crown. **2** the annual expedition to do this on the Thames, carried out under the aegis of the sovereign. [< *swan*¹ + *upping,* gerund of *up,* verb]

**swap** (swop), *v.,* **swapped, swap|ping,** *n. Informal.* **—*v.t., v.i.*** to exchange, barter, or trade: *It is dangerous to swap horses in midstream. Since he liked my radio and I liked his camera, we decided to swap. The old friends often got together to swap stories.*
**—*n.*** **1** an exchange, barter, or trade: *Getting that new camera for my old radio was the best swap I've ever made.* **2** = swap fund. Also, **swop.**
[Middle English *swappen* strike, strike the hands together; probably imitative; the modern sense is from the practice of "striking hands" as a sign of agreement in bargaining. Compare the phrase "to strike a bargain."]

**swap fund**, a mutual fund that accepts blocks of common stock from investors in exchange for shares in the fund: *Swap funds differ from most mutual funds in that the amount of shares they issue is limited to the value of the securities accepted in establishing the fund* (Wall Street Journal).

**swap line**, a reciprocal credit arrangement between banks of different countries: *the Bank of England's swap line with the Federal Reserve Bank.*

**swap meet**, *U.S.* a bazaar or market where articles are bartered or traded.

**swap|per** (swop′ər), *n. Informal.* **1** a person who swaps. **2** *Especially British.* something very big; whopper.

**swa|raj** (swə räj′), *n., adj.* **—*n.*** political autonomy for India; establishment of India as a self-governing political unit.
**—*adj.*** of or having to do with swaraj.
[< Sanskrit *svarāja* self-ruling < *sva* one's own + *rāj* reign, rule]

**Swa|raj** (swə räj′), *n.* the party in India primarily devoted to swaraj during the latter period of British domination. [< *swaraj*]

**swa|raj|ism** (swə rä′jiz əm), *n.* the swaraj principle or movement.

**swa|raj|ist** (swə rä′jist), *n., adj.* **—*n.*** an advocate of swaraj; a member of the Swaraj party.
**—*adj.*** of or having to do with swaraj.

**sward** (swôrd), *n., v.* **—*n.*** a grassy surface; turf.
**—*v.i.*** to form a sward; become covered with grassy turf. **—*v.t.*** to cover with a sward (used chiefly in the passive). [Old English *sweard* skin, rind]

**sware** (swãr), *v. Archaic.* swore; a past tense of **swear.**

**swarf** (swôrf, swärf), *n.* **1** the greasy grit that collects on a knife as it is sharpened on a stone, or on an axle as it revolves in a bearing. **2** filings or shavings that come as from a drilled hole: *Every "do-it-yourself" driller knows that it is important when drilling a long small diameter hole to withdraw the drill every so often to clear the swarf and debris* (New Scientist). [Old English *geswearf* filings < *sweorfan* to file. See related etym. at **swerve.**]

**swarm**¹ (swôrm), *n., v.* **—*n.*** **1** a large group of honeybees, led by a queen, that leave a hive and fly off together to start a new colony. **2** a group of honeybees settled together in a hive. **3** a large group of insects flying or moving about together. **4** *Figurative.* a great number or multitude, especially one moving about together; crowd; throng: *Swarms of children were playing in the park.* **SYN:** See syn. under **crowd. 5** *Biology.* a cluster of free-swimming or free-floating cells or one-celled organisms, such as zoospores, moving in company.
**—*v.i.*** **1** to fly off together to start a new colony: *The bees swarmed on a sunny June day.* **2** to fly or move about in great numbers: *The flies swarmed about us.* **3** *Figurative.* to be in very great numbers; come together in a dense crowd; collect, assemble, or congregate thickly and confusedly; crowd; throng. **4** to be crowded (with); contain great numbers; abound; teem: *The swamp swarms with mosquitoes.* **5** *Biology.* to escape from the parent organism in a swarm, with characteristic movement.
**—*v.t.*** to fill or beset with, or as if with, a swarm; throng: *Mosquitoes swarmed the open tent.*

**swarm off**, to leave a hive or colony to start another or others: *The number of monks increased so rapidly that they were soon obliged to swarm off, like bees, into new monasteries of the same Order* (Joseph T. Fowler).
[Old English *swearm*]

**swarm**² (swôrm), *v.i., v.t.* to climb; shin: *to swarm up a tree.* [origin uncertain]

**swarm cell**, = swarm spore.

**swarm|er** (swôr′mər), *n.* **1** one of a number that swarm; one of a swarm, as of insects. **2** *Biology.* swarm spore.

**swarm spore**, *Biology.* any tiny motile spore produced in great abundance; zoospore.

**swart** (swôrt), *adj.* dark in color; dusky; swarthy. [Old English *sweart*] **—swart′ness,** *n.*

**swarth**¹ (swôrth), *adj. Archaic.* swarthy. [variant of *swart*]

**swarth**² (swôrth), *n. Dialect.* turf; sward. [Old English *swearth,* variant of *sweard* sward]

**swarth**³ (swôrth), *n. Dialect.* swath.

**swarth|i|ly** (swôr′ᴛʜə lē, -thə-), *adv.* with a swarthy hue.

**swarth|i|ness** (swôr′ᴛʜē nis, -thē-), *n.* the condition of being swarthy; dusky or dark complexion; tawniness: *The swarthiness of the fisherman's skin bespoke his days in the sun.*

**swarth|y** (swôr′ᴛʜē, -thē), *adj.,* **swarth|i|er, swarth|i|est.** having a dark skin; dark in color; dusky (used especially of the skin or complexion, or of persons in respect to these): *The sailor was swarthy from the sun of the tropics.* **SYN:** See syn. under **dusky.** [apparently < *swarth*¹ + *-y*¹. Compare obsolete *swarty* < *swart* + *-y*¹.]

**swash**¹ (swosh, swôsh), *v., n.* **—*v.t.*** **1** to dash (water or other liquid) about; splash. **2** to dash water or other liquid upon; souse.
**—*v.i.*** **1** to dash with a splashing sound; splash (about, against). **2** = swagger.
**—*n.*** **1** a swashing action or sound: *the swash of waves against a boat.* **2** a swagger; swashbuckling. **3** a channel of water through or behind a sandbank. **4** ground under water or over which water washes.
[probably imitative]

**swash**² (swosh, swôsh), *adj., n. Printing.* **—*adj.*** having or characterized by ornamental strokes or flourishes: *swash capitals, swash italics.* See also **swash letters.**
**—*n.*** an ornamental stroke or flourish on a letter or font.
[< obsolete *swash* slanting, abstracted from obsolete *aswash* aslant; origin uncertain]

**swash|buck|le** (swosh′buk′əl, swôsh′-), *v.,* **-led, -ling,** *n.* **—*v.i.*** to swagger in a noisy, blustering, or boasting manner: *[He] sings and swashbuckles in eighteenth-century costume* (Newsweek).
**—*v.t.*** to make by swashbuckling: *... dashing soldiers of fortune who swashbuckled their way to legend* (Wall Street Journal).
**—*n.*** the act of swashbuckling.
[back formation < *swashbuckler*]

**swash|buck|ler** (swosh′buk′lər, swôsh′-), *n.* a swaggering swordsman, bully, or boaster: *He had a garrison after his own heart ... guzzling, deep-drinking swashbucklers* (Washington Irving).

**swash|buck|ler|ing** (swosh′buk′lər ing, swôsh′-), *n., adj.* = swashbuckling.

**swash|buck|ling** (swosh′buk′ling, swôsh′-), *n., adj.* swaggering; bullying; boasting: *political swashbuckling* (n.), *a swashbuckling swordsman* (adj.).

**swash|er** (swosh′ər, swôsh′-), *n.* = swashbuckler.

**swash|ing** (swosh′ing, swôsh′-), *adj., n.* **—*adj.*** **1** (of water or other liquid) dashing and splashing. **2** swaggering; swashbuckling: *We'll have a swashing and a martial outside, As many other mannish cowards have* (Shakespeare).
**—*n.*** **1** a dashing or splashing action of water: *A rising tide creates ... swashings and swirlings and a continuous slapping against the rocky rim of the land* (New Yorker). **2** *Archaic.* swaggering; ostentatious behavior.

***swash letters**, letters, especially italic capital letters, of a style characterized by ornamental strokes or flourishes on the top or bottom.

***swash letters** *ABCDE*

**swash|plate** (swosh′plāt′, swôsh′-), *n.* a rotating circular plate inclined to the plane of its revolution, which gives and receives reciprocal motion to and from other parts of the mechanism: *A swashplate or like system links the pistons to a central shaft* (New Scientist).

**swash|y** (swosh′ē, swôsh′-), *adj.,* **swash|i|er, swash|i|est.** soft and watery; splashy: *Bulldozers cleared the course in fine style for the reopening last Friday, but ... the footing was still a little swashy* (New Yorker).

***swas|ti|ka** or **swas|ti|ca** (swos′tə kə), *n.* **1** an ancient symbol or ornament like a cross with each arm bent in the same way to form a right angle; fylfot. Swastikas were thought in early times to bring good luck. **2** such a figure with arms turning clockwise, used as the official emblem of the Nazi Party and Nazi Germany. [< Sanskrit *svastika* < *svasti* luck < *sū* well + *astī,* noun, being < *as* to be]

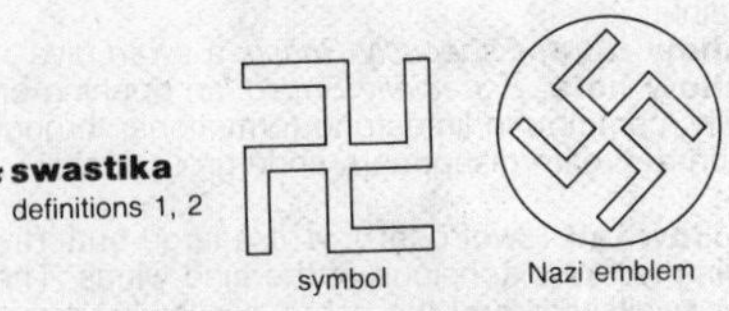


***swastika** definitions 1, 2

**swat**¹ (swot), *v.,* **swat|ted, swat|ting,** *n. Informal.* **—*v.t.*** to hit sharply or violently: *to swat a fly, to swat a home run.* **—*n.*** a sharp or violent blow. Also, **swot.** [apparently imitative]

**swat**² (swot), *v.i. v.t.,* **swat|ted, swat|ting,** *n. British Slang.* swot².

**swat**³ (swot), *v. Obsolete.* sweat; a past tense and past participle of **sweat.**

**SWAT** or **S.W.A.T.** (swot), *n. U.S.* a police unit trained in the use of special weapons and tactics. [< *S*(pecial) *W*(eapons) *a*(nd) *T*(actics) or *S*(pecial) *W*(eapons) *A*(ttack) *T*(eam)]

**swatch** (swoch), *n.* **1** a sample of cloth or other material: *a swatch of calico. After picking a model from samples and a fabric from an assortment of swatches ...* (New Yorker). **2** a specimen of anything: *Over cocktails and frequent swatches of non-dance music, one can take an eagle's-nest gander at New York* (New Yorker).
[earlier, a tally or its counterpart; origin uncertain]

**swath** (swoth, swôth), *n.* **1a** the space covered by a single cut of a scythe or by one cut of a mowing machine. **b** the grass, hay, or standing grain within such a space. **c** a row of grass, hay, or grain cut by a scythe or mowing machine. **d** something compared to grass, hay, or grain falling before the scythe or mowing machine. **2** *Figurative.* a strip, belt, or lengthwise extent (of something).

**cut a swath**, to make a showy display; attract attention: *You folks been cuttin' a pretty wide swath here in New York* (H. L. Wilson). *He wasn't a bad-looking guy, and ... he could cut a swath all togged up* (James T. Farrell).
[Old English *swæth* track, trace, footprint]

**swathe**¹ (swāᴛʜ), *v.,* **swathed, swath|ing,** *n.* **—*v.t.*** **1** to wrap up closely or fully: *swathed in a blanket.* **2** to bind, wrap, or bandage. **3** *Figurative.* to envelop or surround like a wrapping; enwrap; enfold: *White clouds swathed the mountain.* **—*n.*** a wrapping; bandage.
[Old English *swathian* < *swath-* a band of cloth. See related etym. at **swaddle.**]

**swathe**² (swāᴛʜ), *n.* = swath. [Middle English *swathe,* Old English *swæth* swath]

**swath|er**¹ (swā′ᴛʜər), *n.* a device with curved arms extending diagonally backward, fixed to the end of the cutter bar of a reaper or mower to lift up uncut stalks, and throw those that are cut in such a way as to mark a line of separation between the uncut and the cut. [< *swath* + *-er*¹]

**swath|er**² (swā′ᴛʜər), *n.* a person who swathes.

**swath|ing** (swā′ᴛʜing), *n.* **1** the act of a person or thing that swathes. **2** that with which something is swathed: *Lady Frensham has arrived ... by automobile; she appeared in veils and swathings* (H. G. Wells).

**swats** (swots), *n.pl. Scottish.* new small beer or ale. [Old English *swātan* beer]

**swat|ter** (swot′ər), *n. Informal.* **1** a person or thing that swats. **2** something to swat with: *a fly swatter.*

**swave** (swāv), *adj. U.S. Slang.* fine; excellent; swell. [origin uncertain; possible satirical mispronunciation of *suave*]

**S wave**, = secondary wave.

**sway** (swā), *v., n.* **—*v.i.*** **1** to swing back and forth; swing from side to side or to one side: *She swayed and fell in a faint. Branches sway in the wind. The pail swayed in his hands as he ran.* **SYN:** wave, fluctuate, oscillate. See syn. under **swing. 2** to bend or move to one side or downward; turn aside; lean: *The horse swayed left at the crossroads.* **3** *Figurative.* to change in opinion, feeling, or the like; vacillate. **4** *Figurative.* to have control; rule; govern: *Where still doth sway the triple tyrant* (Milton).
**—*v.t.*** **1** to make move; cause to sway: *The wind sways the tall grass.* **2** to cause to incline or bend down on one side. **3** *Figurative.* to cause to change in opinion or feeling: *Nothing could sway her after she had made up her mind.* **4** *Figurative.* to cause to be inclined to one side, party, argument, opinion, or the like; influence: *to try to sway an election with bribery. The speaker's words swayed his audience. ... an enormously*

popular man with a quite remarkable ability to sway and lead the masses (Harper's). 5 *Figurative.* to have control of; direct; govern: *The will of man is by his reason sway'd* (Shakespeare). 6 *Archaic.* to rule, as a sovereign. 7 to wield as an emblem of sovereignty: *to sway the scepter.*
—*n.* 1 the action of swaying; swinging back and forth or from side to side: *The sway of the pail caused some milk to spill out. Regardless of the sweeping whirlwind's sway* (Thomas Gray). 2 *Figurative.* influence, control, or rule: *Few countries are now under the sway of kings. They bent before the sway of his vehement and impetuous will* (John F. Kirk).
**sway up**, *Nautical.* to raise or set aloft (a yard, topmast, or the like): *Forward there, Jacob, and sway up the mast* (Frederick Marryat).
[Middle English *sweye* to go, sink, probably < Scandinavian (compare Old Icelandic *sveigja*)]
—**sway'er**, *n.* —**sway'ing|ly**, *adv.*

**sway|back** or **sway-back** (swā'bak'), *adj., n.*
—*adj.* = sway-backed.
—*n.* an exaggerated sag or downward curvature of the spinal column of an animal, especially of a horse.

**sway-backed** or **sway|backed** (swā'bakt'), *adj.* 1a having the back sagged or hollowed to an unusual degree: *a sway-backed horse.* b strained in the back, as by overwork. 2 that sags in the middle, especially through age or lack of care: *a sway-backed old wagon or barn.*

**sway brace**, a diagonal brace used on a tower, bridge, or other structure, to resist side or swaying strains.

**swayed** (swād), *adj.* = sway-backed.

**sway|less** (swā'lis), *adj.* not swaying; without sway: *Front-wheel drive, combined with ... advanced suspension design, provides swayless directional stability for relaxed driving* (Scientific American).

**Swa|zi** (swä'zē), *n., pl.* **-zi** or **-zis**, *adj.* —*n.* 1 a native or inhabitant of Swaziland, a country in southeastern Africa, especially one of a Bantu people of Zulu origin: *The Swazis are a Zulu offshoot who settled in their present country just over a hundred years ago* (Napier Davitt). 2 the language of this people; siSwati.
—*adj.* of the Swazi or Swaziland.

**sweal** (swēl), *Dialect.* —*v.i.* 1 of a candle, tallow, or the like: a to melt (away). b to gutter. 2 *Figurative.* to waste away. —*v.t.* to cause to waste away like a guttering candle: ... *the time not spent in study, for the most part swealed away* (C. Mather). [fusion of Old English *swǣlan* to burn (something), and of *swelan* to burn. See related etym. at **swelter**.]

**swear** (swãr), *v.,* **swore** or (*Archaic*) **sware**, **sworn**, **swear|ing**. —*v.i.* 1 to make a solemn statement, appealing to God or some other sacred being or object; take an oath. 2 to promise solemnly; vow: *The knights swear to be true to their king.* 3 to testify under oath; make a declaration under oath (to or against): *Will you swear to the truth of what you said?* 4 to use profane language; curse: *The pirate raged and swore. It's 'most enough to make a deacon swear* (James Russell Lowell). **SYN:** See syn. under **curse**.
—*v.t.* 1 to declare, calling God to witness; declare on oath: *A witness at a trial is asked, "Do you swear to tell the truth, the whole truth, and nothing but the truth, so help you God?"* 2 to bind by an oath; require to promise: *Members of the club were sworn to secrecy.* 3 to admit to office or service by administering an oath: *to swear a witness.* 4 to promise on oath or solemnly (to observe or do something); pledge; vow: *to swear allegiance, swear revenge.* 5 to declare or affirm emphatically or confidently: *I swear I'll never go near the place again. Major Scobie, when I lent you money, I swear it was for friendship, just friendship* (Graham Greene). 6 to take or utter (an oath), either solemnly or profanely. 7 to bring, set, take, or otherwise act by swearing: *to swear a person's life away.* 8 to take an oath as to the fact or truth of; testify under oath: *He swore treason against his friend* (Samuel Johnson).
**swear by**, a to name (God or a sacred being or object) as one's witness in taking an oath: *They had sworn by the sacred head of the emperor himself* (Edward Gibbon). b to have great confidence in: *The members of the office staff who stick around long enough to get to know him swear by Adams* (Time).
**swear in**, to admit to an office or service by giving an oath: *to swear in a jury. Immediately after this election the new Cabinet will be sworn in* (Manchester Guardian Weekly).
**swear off**, *Informal.* to promise to give up: *to swear off smoking.*
**swear out**, to get by swearing that a certain charge is true: *He swore out a warrant for the arrest of the man who had hit him.*
[Old English *swerian.* Compare etym. under **answer**.] —**swear'er**, *n.*

**swear|word** (swãr'wėrd'), *n.* a word used in cursing; profane word; oath: *The poor man's supply of swearwords was evidently not enough for the situation and it quickly ran out after his extravagant expenditure* (Atlantic).

**sweat** (swet), *n., v.,* **sweat** or **sweat|ed**, **sweat-ing**. —*n.* 1 moisture coming through the pores of the skin, usually as a result of heat, exertion, or emotion; perspiration: *After mowing the lawn he wiped the sweat from his face. His brow is wet with honest sweat* (Longfellow). 2 a fit or condition of giving out moisture through the pores of the skin: *I was in a cold sweat from fear.* 3 such a condition induced for a purpose, especially a therapeutic purpose. 4 *Informal, Figurative.* a condition of anxiety, impatience, or anything that might make a person sweat: *We were all in a sweat over the big test we would get on Monday. He was in quite a sweat that his father would find out about the damaged car.* 5 moisture given out by something or gathered on its surface: *the sweat on a pitcher of ice water.* 6 the act of exuding moisture from something, or the process of producing an exudation, as part of certain industrial processes such as tanning. 7 a run given to a horse as part of his training for a race. 8 *Figurative.* anything that causes sweat; hard work or strenuous exertion; labor: *I have nothing to offer but blood, toil, tears, and sweat* (Sir Winston Churchill). 9 *Obsolete.* the sweating sickness. [Middle English *swete* < *sweten;* see the verb]
—*v.i.* 1 to give out moisture through the pores of the skin; perspire: *We sweated because it was very hot.* 2 to gather moisture from the air by condensation, so that it appears in drops on the surface: *A pitcher of ice water sweats on a hot day.* 3a to give out moisture, as before storage or preparation for use. b (of tobacco) to ferment. 4 to come out in drops; ooze. 5 *Informal, Figurative.* to work very hard: *He sweated over his written reports. Some, lucky, find a flowery spot, for which they never toiled nor sweat* (Robert Burns). 6 *Figurative.* to be annoyed or vexed; fume: *to sweat over a delay.* 7 to suffer severely, especially as a penalty: *They will sweat for the wrong they have done.*
—*v.t.* 1 to give out through the pores of the skin: *He's always cold, and never seems to sweat even a drop of water.* (*Figurative.*) *Some people sweat blood when they have to memorize something.* 2 to cause (a person or animal) to sweat: *He sweated his horse by riding him too hard.* 3 to get rid of by or as if by sweating (off, out): *to sweat off excess weight.* 4 to send out (moisture) in drops or small particles like sweat. 5 to wet, soak, or stain with sweat: *to sweat one's collar.* 6a to cause to give out moisture; force the moisture out of: *to sweat hides in preparing them for use.* b to ferment (tobacco) by removing moisture. 7 *Figurative.* to cause to work hard and under bad conditions: *That employer sweats his workers.* 8 *Figurative.* to wait out or work out as by sweating: *to sweat out a prison sentence, to sweat out a divorce, to sweat out a difficult exam.* 9a to heat (solder) until it melts; fasten or join by applying heat after soldering, so as to produce partial fusion. b to heat (metal) in order to remove an easily fusible constituent. 10 *Informal.* to be anxious or worry about (something): ... *told him to lay it on, that he was all ears, and not to sweat a thing because he was on their side* (New Yorker). 11 to remove bits of metal from (a coin, especially of gold), as by shaking it with others in a bag. 12 *Informal.* to extract or try to extract information from (a person, especially a prisoner) by long, hard questioning. 13 *Slang.* to deprive of or cause to give up something, especially money; rob; fleece.
**no sweat**, *Slang.* no trouble at all; no effort: *For most of those involved in this Strategic Air Command operation it was routine. As Capt. Smith or one of his crew would say, "It's no sweat"* (Birmingham News).
**sweat it out**, *Informal, Figurative.* to wait anxiously or nervously for something to happen: *And they were continuing to tilt it* [*a rocket*] *at X minus ten seconds. In the blockhouse, at the control board, Fred Marmo sweated it out* (Saturday Review).
[Middle English *sweten,* Old English *swǣtan* < *swāt* sweat] —**sweat'less**, *adj.*
—*Syn. n.* 1 **Sweat, perspiration** mean moisture coming through the pores of the skin. **Sweat** is the direct native English word, used when speaking of animals or things and often of people: *Sweat streamed down the horse's flanks, and the rider's shirt was stained with sweat.* **Perspiration**, seldom used except when speaking of human beings, is preferred by some people for that reason: *Tiny drops of perspiration formed at her temples.*

**sweat|band** (swet'band'), *n.* 1 a band of leather or cloth on the inside of a hat or cap, protecting it from perspiration. 2 a band worn around the head to absorb perspiration from the forehead: *The sweatband, which keeps spectacles and goggles clear, is feather-light* (Science News Letter). [American English < *sweat,* noun + *band*[2]]

**sweat bee**, any small blackish bee of a family that nests in tunnels in the ground, so called from its habit of alighting on the skin of a perspiring person.

**sweat|box** (swet'boks'), *n.* 1 any one of various boxlike enclosures within which certain commodities, such as hides and figs, are caused to give out or lose moisture preparatory to use or sale. 2 *Slang.* a very small, narrow cell in which a prisoner is confined as a means of punishment or torture: *Just let me out of this third-degree sweatbox and I'll sign anything you like* (Punch).

**sweat|ed** (swet'id), *adj.* 1a employed in a sweatshop; overworked and underpaid: *We had all benefited in the past from the cheap food and raw materials produced by ... sweated labour* (London Times). b utilizing or produced by sweated workers. 2 = sweaty.

**sweat|er** (swet'ər), *n.* 1 a knitted jacket or pullover, usually of wool or nylon, worn for warmth: *She also finds time for social engagements and such normal pastimes as knitting a sweater* (Newsweek). 2 an agent or remedy that causes sweating; sudorific. 3 a person or company that grossly overworks and underpays employees; operator of a sweatshop. 4 a person who perspires, especially one who does so to lose weight or as part of the process of a Turkish bath.

**sweat|ered** (swet'ərd), *adj.* wearing a sweater: *Sweatered young men sat on stools and jibed at the jaded values of a commercial society* (New York Times).

**sweater girl**, *Informal.* a young woman, especially an actress or model, having shapely or prominent bosom.

**sweat|ful** (swet'fəl), *adj.* abounding in, attended with, or inducing sweat; toilsome.

**sweat gland**, one of the many small, coiled glands that secrete sweat. Human sweat glands are found in the deeper layer of the skin of most of the body, connecting with the surface through a tube or duct that ends in a pore. *Excretion in the skin is done by the sweat glands, of which there are about two million in man* (A. Franklin Shull). See picture under **skin**.

**sweat|ing sickness** (swet'ing), a febrile disease characterized by profuse sweating, that was epidemic in England at various times during the 1400's and 1500's; miliary fever.

**sweating system**, a system of employment involving abuse of workers, as by employing them at low wages, during overlong hours, under unsanitary or otherwise unfavorable conditions, or letting work out by contract to middlemen, to be done in inadequate workshops or at the homes of the workers.

**sweat pants**, a pair of baggy pants gathered in at the ankles, worn especially by athletes to keep warm before and after exercise.

**sweat room**, a room in which tobacco or other agricultural produce is sweated.

**sweat shirt**, a heavy, pullover jersey with long sleeves, sometimes with a fleece lining, worn especially by athletes to keep warm before and after exercise.

**sweat|shop** (swet'shop'), *n.* a place where workers are employed for long hours under bad conditions of work and at very low wages: *A ... minimum wage will help to eliminate unfair competition based on sweatshop wages in the clothing industry* (Wall Street Journal). [American English < *sweat,* noun + *shop,* noun]

**sweat socks**, woolen ankle-length socks, usually white, worn with casual shoes or sneakers, especially for sports.

**sweat suit**, a suit consisting of a sweat shirt and sweat pants, used by athletes and by people trying to lose weight by sweating: *A lank-haired boy in a blue sweat suit was wielding dumbbells on the third-floor landing* (New Yorker).

**sweat|y** (swet'ē), *adj.,* **sweat|i|er**, **sweat|i|est**. 1 covered or wet with sweat; sweating. 2 causing sweat: *the sweaty forge* (Matthew Prior). 3 laborious; toilsome. —**sweat'i|ly**, *adv.* —**sweat'i|ness**, *n.*

**Swed.**, 1 Sweden. 2 Swedish.

**Swede** (swēd), *n.* 1 a person born or living in Sweden. 2 Also, **swede**. = rutabaga. [< Middle Low German, or Middle Dutch *Swede*]

**Swe|den|bor|gi|an** (swē'dən bôr'jē ən), *n., adj.*

---

**Pronunciation Key:** hat, āge, cãre, fär; let, ēqual, tėrm; it, īce; hot, ōpen, ôrder; oil, out; cup, pu̇t, rüle; child; long; thin; ᴛʜen; zh, measure; ə represents a in about, e in taken, i in pencil, o in lemon, u in circus.

—*n.* a believer in the theology and religious doctrines of Emanuel Swedenborg (1688-1772), a Swedish philosopher, scientist, and mystic.
—*adj.* having to do with Swedenborg, his doctrines, of his followers. —**Swe'den|bor'gi|an|ism, Swe'den|borg|ism,** *n.*

**Swed|ish** (swē'dish), *adj., n.* —*adj.* of or having to do with Sweden, a country in northern Europe, its people, or their language.
—*n.* **1** *pl. in use.* the people of Sweden. **2** the Scandinavian language of Sweden.

**Swedish clover,** = alsike clover.

**Swedish cress,** = winter cress.

**Swedish massage,** a massage in which Swedish movements are used.

**Swedish movements,** a series of exercises designed to tone up the different muscles and joints.

**Swedish turnip,** = rutabaga.

**swee|ny** (swē'nē), *n.* atrophy of the shoulder muscles of a horse, due to damage to a nerve or disuse of the limb. [probably < dialectal German *Schweine* atrophy (< *schweinen* become emaciated) + English *-y*³]

**sweep** (swēp), *v.,* **swept, sweep|ing,** *n.* —*v.t.* **1a** to clean or clear (a floor, deck, or the like) with a broom or brush; use a broom or something like one to remove dirt; brush: *The campers swept the floor of their cabin every morning. Sweep the steps.* **b** to make safe or passable by sweeping; clear of what impedes or endangers: *to sweep the sidewalk after a snowfall, to sweep a passage through a minefield.* **2** to move, drive, or take away with a broom or brush: *They swept the dust into a pan.* (*Figurative.*) *The wind sweeps the snow into drifts.* (*Figurative.*) *She swept the change off the table into her purse.* **3** to remove with a sweeping motion; carrying along: *cargo swept off the deck of a ship by waves. A flood swept away the bridge.* (*Figurative.*) *He kept abreast of the times and was not just swept along with them as his work ... proved* (London Times). **4** to trail upon: *Her dress sweeps the ground.* **5** *Figurative.* to pass over with a steady movement: *Her fingers swept the strings of the harp. His eyes swept the sky, searching for signs of rain.* **6** *Figurative.* to range over; scour: *Enthusiasm for the candidate swept the country.* **7** to win a complete victory in: *to sweep a baseball series.*
—*v.i.* **1** to use a broom or something like one to remove dirt; clean a room or surface by sweeping. **2** *Figurative.* to move swiftly; pass swiftly: *Pirates swept down on the town. The wind sweeps over the valley. When the deer sweeps by, and the hounds are in cry* (Scott). **3** to move with dignity: *The lady swept out of the room.* **4** *Figurative.* to move or extend in a long course or curve; stretch: *The shore sweeps to the south for miles.*
—*n.* **1** an act of sweeping; clearing away; removing: *to give a room a good sweep.* (*Figurative.*) *He made a clean sweep of all his debts.* **2** a steady, driving motion or swift onward course of something: *The sweep of the wind kept the trees from growing tall.* (*Figurative.*) *The sheer sweep of dramatic events carried many men along* (Bruce Catton). **3** a smooth, flowing motion or line; dignified motion: *the regular sweep of an oar,* (*Figurative.*) *the stately sweep of heroic verse.* **4** a curve; bend: *the sweep of a road.* **5** a swinging or curving motion: *He cut the grass with strong sweeps of his scythe.* **6** *Figurative.* a continuous extent; stretch; expanse: *The house looks upon a wide sweep of farming country. The full length of civilization, as we know it, seemed hardly a second in the sweep of geological history unfolded in this painted canyon* (William O. Douglas). **7** *Figurative.* reach; range; extent: *The mountain is beyond the sweep of your eye. The Western plan had sweep and imagination* (Time). **8** a winning of all the games in a series, match, or contest; complete victory. **9** a person who sweeps, especially chimneys, streets, and floors: *The sweep will dump his soot there* (Manchester Guardian). **10** a long oar used in rowing and sometimes in steering: *Their sweeps were shorter, the oarsmen pulled in shorter arcs* (Time). **11a** a long pole which pivots on a high post and is used to lower and raise a bucket in a well. **b** a pump handle. **12** anything collected by or as if by sweeping; refuse. **13** = sweepstakes. **14a** a slam in whist. **b** a pairing or combining of all the cards on the board, and so taking them, in cassino. **15** *Physics.* a process of settling, or tending to settle, into thermal equilibrium. **16** *Football.* end run.
**sweep off one's feet.** See under **feet.**
**sweeps,** gold and silver waste salvaged from the work of goldsmiths and silversmiths; sweepings: *The inhabitants of Africa ... dress their gold dust in small bowls, after the manner that goldsmiths wash their sweeps* (William Pryce).
**sweep the board.** See under **board.**
[Middle English *swepen* < Old English *geswǣpa* sweepings, related to *swāpan* to sweep]

**sweep|back** (swēp'bak'), *n.* the acute angle at which the wing of an aircraft slopes or slants backwards from the fuselage to the wing tip: *The wings pivot in such a way that they can be ranged with almost no sweepback for take-off and landing* (Observer).

**sweep|er** (swē'pər), *n.* **1** a person or thing that sweeps: *a carpet sweeper, a street sweeper.* **2** = minesweeper.

**sweep hand,** a second hand of a clock or watch that is mounted together with the minute and hour hands and sweeps across the entire dial once every minute; sweep-second hand: *the silent inevitability of the sweep hand of a watch* (Punch).

**sweep|ing** (swē'ping), *adj., n.* —*adj.* **1** passing over a wide space: *Her sweeping glance took in the whole room.* **2** having a wide range: *a sweeping victory, a sweeping statement. New York's Senate unanimously voted a sweeping investigation of illegal wire tapping* (Wall Street Journal). *Uncle Billy included the whole party in one sweeping anathema* (Bret Harte).
—*n.* the act of a person or thing that sweeps.
**sweepings, a** dust, scraps, or rubbish swept out or up: *She just shoved the sweepings into the closet.* **b** *Figurative.* the most worthless people: *the sweepings of the city.* **c** the metal-yielding scraps of an establishment where precious metals are worked: *Goldsmiths and refiners are wont ... carefully to save the very sweepings of their shops* (Robert Boyle).
—**sweep'ing|ly,** *adv.* —**sweep'ing|ness,** *n.*

**sweep net, 1** a large net enclosing a wide space, used in fishing. **2** a net used for catching insects, as by sweeping it over herbage.

**sweep oar,** = sweep (def. 10).

**sweeps** (swēps), *n.pl.* See under **sweep.**

**sweep-sec|ond hand** (swēp'sek'ənd), = sweep hand.

**sweep|stake** (swēp'stāk'), *n.* **1** = sweepstakes. **2** *Obsolete.* **a** a person who wins all the stakes in a game. **b** a person who takes all or everything. **3** *Obsolete.* **a** a sweeping in or winning of all the stakes in a game. **b** any total removal or clearance.

**sweep|stakes** (swēp'stāks'), *n., pl.* **-stakes. 1** a system of gambling on horses, races, or other contests. People buy tickets, and from the money they pay prizes are awarded to the holder or holders of winning tickets. **2a** a race or contest by which the winner or winners are determined under such a system of gambling. **b** a race or contest in which the prize or prizes derive from a pooling of the stakes of the contestants, with or without additional contributions by the sponsor or sponsors of the contest. **3** a prize in such a race or contest.
[< *sweep,* in obsolete sense of "to win all the stakes in a game" + *stake*² + *-s*¹]

**sweep|swing|er** (swēp'swing'ər), *n.* an oarsman in a racing crew: *Right from the start, Navy's powerful sweepswingers made it clear they intended to get in front and stay there* (Time). [< *sweep,* (*n.* def. 10) + *swinger*¹]

**sweep ticket,** a ticket giving a chance in a sweepstakes.

**sweep|y** (swē'pē), *adj.* characterized by sweeping movement or form; sweeping.

**sweer** (swir), *adj. Scottish.* **1** inactive; indolent; slothful. **2** reluctant; unwilling. [Old English *swǣr* heavy, oppressive]

**sweet** (swēt), *adj., adv., n.* —*adj.* **1** having a taste like sugar or honey: *Pears are much sweeter than lemons.* **SYN:** saccharine. **2** having a pleasant taste or smell: *a sweet flower. Perfume is sweet.* **SYN:** fragrant, perfumed. **3** *Figurative.* pleasing to the ear; having or giving a pleasant sound; musical; melodious; harmonious: *a sweet singer, a sweet song. Like sweet bells, jangled out of tune* (Shakespeare). *Jonah Jones, who heads a quartet, keeps his cornet sweet* (New Yorker). **4** *Figurative.* pleasing to the eye; of charming appearance; lovely: *a sweet face, a sweet smile.* **5** *Figurative.* pleasant; agreeable: *a sweet child, sweet sleep, sweet words of praise. What a sweet hat!* **SYN:** pleasing, winning. **6** free from disagreeable taste or smell; not sour or spoiled; fresh: *He drinks sweet milk.* **7** not salted or salty: *I like sweet butter better than salted butter.* **8** having a sweet taste; not bitter: *sweet wine.* **9** fertile, not acid or sour; good for farming: *sweet soil.* **10** *Figurative.* dearly loved or prized; dear; darling: *sweet sir.* **11** *Figurative.* excessively or offensively pleasant or agreeable; saccharine. **12** easily managed, handled, or dealt with: *a sweet ship. The clutch is exceptionally sweet in operation* (London Times). **13a** *Metallurgy.* free from corrosive salt, sulfur, and acid. **b** *Chemistry.* lacking any sulfur compounds, as gasoline. **14** blandly melodious: *sweet jazz.*
—*adv.* in a sweet manner; so as to be sweet; sweetly.
—*n.* **1** something sweet: *Becky Sharp was probably rolling a sweet on her prettily pointed tongue* (Carlos Baker). **2** *British.* a sweet dessert. **3** *Informal.* a sweet potato. **4** *Figurative.* a dear; darling. **5** sweetness of taste or smell.
**be sweet on** (or **upon**), *Informal.* to be in love with: *I think he is sweet upon your daughter* (Dickens).
**sweets, a** candy or other sweet things: *She was carrying a bag of sweets* (London Times). **b** *Figurative.* pleasant or agreeable things: *The Gods have envy'd me the sweets of life* (John Dryden).
[Old English *swēte*] —**sweet'ly,** *adv.*

**sweet alyssum,** a common, low-growing garden plant of the mustard family, with clusters of small, fragrant, white or purple flowers.

**sweet-and-sour** (swēt'ən sour'), *adj.* **1** made with sugar and vinegar or lemon juice: *a sweet-and-sour sauce.* **2** flavored with a sweet-and-sour sauce: *sweet-and-sour chicken, beef, or pork.*

**sweet|bag** (swēt'bag'), *n.* a small bag filled with a scented or aromatic substance, used especially for perfuming the air and clothes; sachet: *Hast thou no perfumes and sweetbags* (Scott).

**sweet basil,** = basil.

**sweet bay, 1** an American magnolia, a shrub or small tree with round, fragrant, white flowers, common in swamps along the Atlantic coast from Massachusetts southward; bay. **2** the bay or European laurel.

**sweet|bells** (swēt'belz'), *n.pl.* a shrub of the heath family growing in the eastern United States, having racemes of white or pink flowers.

**sweet birch,** a birch tree of the eastern United States, having a hard, dark-colored, and close-grained wood used especially for furniture, and an aromatic bark yielding a volatile oil similar to oil of wintergreen; cherry birch; black birch.

**sweet|bread** (swēt'bred'), *n.* the pancreas or thymus especially of a calf or lamb, used as meat. [probably < *sweet* + Middle English *brede,* Old English *brǣd* roasted or grilled meat]

**sweet|bri|er** or **sweet|bri|ar** (swēt'brī'ər), *n.* a wild rose with strong, hooked prickles on a tall stem, pink, single flowers, and small, aromatic leaves; eglantine; wild brier.

**sweet cassava,** a variety of cassava of Brazil with starchy, edible roots.

**sweet cherry,** a kind of cherry with sweet, edible, yellow or red fruit; mazzard. The bigarreaus and geans are sweet cherries.

**sweet chervil,** = sweet cicely.

**sweet chestnut, 1** a chestnut of Spain and Italy that is larger, and less sweet, than the American variety. **2** the tree it grows on: *The Romans are thought to have introduced the sweet or Spanish chestnut to Britain* (London Times).

**sweet cicely,** a European plant of the parsley family, with white flowers, fernlike leaves, and aromatic roots.

**sweet cider,** unfermented cider.

**sweet clover,** any one of a genus of herbs of the pea family, grown for hay and pasture and to improve the soil.

**sweet corn, 1** a kind of corn eaten by people when it is young and tender; corn; sugar corn. The kernels of sweet corn are rich in sugar. Sweet corn is eaten either directly from the ear or after being cut from the ear. *It is better to plant sweet corn in blocks rather than in single rows* (Sunday Times). See picture under **corn**¹. **2** an ear or ears of such corn, at the milky stage; green corn.

**sweet|en** (swē'tən), *v.t.* **1** to make sweet or sweeter: *to sweeten the air of a room. He sweetened his coffee with two lumps of sugar. All the perfumes of Arabia will not sweeten this little hand* (Shakespeare). **2** *Informal.* **a** to increase the collateral of (a loan) by adding further securities of a high grade. **b** to improve the terms of (an offer, bid, or contract): *The companies ... have indicated recently that they are ready to "sweeten" their offer somewhat* (Wall Street Journal). **3** to increase the value of (a pot) in poker, especially by an ante of money or chips additional to that required as a preliminary to play: (*Figurative.*) *To sweeten the pot, county associations now offer additional rewards of up to $1,000* (Time). —*v.i.* to become sweet or sweeter: *Those pears will sweeten as they ripen.* [< *sweet* + *-en*¹] —**sweet'en|er,** *n.*

**sweet|en|ing** (swē'tə ning, swēt'ning), *n.* **1** something that sweetens; sweetener. Sugar is the most common sweetening. **2** the act of a person or thing that sweetens.

**sweet fern, 1** a small shrub of North America of the same family as the wax myrtle, with fragrant, fernlike leaves. **2** any one of various ferns.

**sweet flag, 1** a water plant with long, swordshaped leaves and a thick, creeping rootstock; calamus; sweetroot. It belongs to the arum family. **2** its fragrant root, used in perfumes and medicines and sometimes preserved with sugar and eaten as candy.

**sweet gale**, a low, aromatic shrub of Europe, Asia, and North America with yellowish fruit; gale.

**sweet gas**, natural gas containing little or no hydrogen sulfide, used for fuel.

**sweet goldenrod**, a goldenrod of the eastern United States having fragrant leaves from which a medicinal tea is brewed.

**sweet grass**, any grass that has a sweet taste and is used for fodder: *It is found throughout the Ethiopian region wherever there is water, sweet grass and shelter from the midday heat* (New Scientist).

**sweet gum**, **1** a large North American tree, of the same family as the witch hazel, with shining, star-shaped leaves that turn scarlet in the fall; bilsted; red gum. In warm regions it exudes a balsam, used in the preparation of chewing gum and in medicine. **2** the balsam from this tree; liquidambar. **3** the reddish-brown wood of this tree.

**sweet|heart** (swēt′härt′), *n.* **1** a loved one; lover. **SYN**: suitor, beau, swain. **2** a girl or woman loved: —*that old sweetheart of mine* (James Whitcomb Riley). **3** *Informal.* darling; dear: *He ... listened to the voice of his old math teacher, "Criss" Cross, that sweetheart, droning through the open window of 104* (Philip Roth).

**sweetheart agreement**, = sweetheart contract.

**sweetheart contract**, *U.S.* a secret contract between an employer and an unscrupulous union leader by which workers are made to join a union but receive substandard wages: *Management and union officials who conspire to the detriment of working people, as in "sweetheart contracts," could be punished equally* (Wall Street Journal).

**sweetheart neckline**, a low-cut neckline whose lower edge is heart-shaped.

**sweet|ie** (swē′tē), *n. Informal.* a sweetheart; darling: *The club is noisy with theatrical patter—"Yes, he's a sweetie—and quite a good actor too"* (Harper's).

**sweeties**, *British Informal.* candy; sweets: *Burnt almonds, chocolate, and sweeties of every flavour* (Christina Rossetti).

**sweet|ie-pie** (swē′tē pī′), *n. Informal.* a sweetheart; darling: *"I've got a quarter of an hour to catch the London train. Be a sweetie-pie and run me over there"* (V. S. Pritchett).

**sweet|ing** (swē′ting), *n.* **1** a sweet apple. **2** *Archaic.* sweetheart; darling. [Middle English *sweting* < *swete* sweet + *-ing,* a noun suffix that meant "one having the designated quality"]

**sweet|ish** (swē′tish), *adj.* **1** somewhat sweet. **2** too sweet; cloying. —**sweet′ish|ly,** *adv.* —**sweet′ish|ness,** *n.*

**sweet|leaf** (swēt′lēf′), *n.* any one of a group of shrubs or trees of tropical and subtropical regions sometimes grown for ornament, as the sapphireberry.

**sweet|lips** (swēt′lips′), *n., pl.* **-lips.** any one of various small, marine, percoid fishes of the Indian and Pacific Oceans.

**sweet marjoram**, a marjoram commonly used as a flavoring for meats, vegetables, and salads.

**sweet|meats** (swēt′mēts′), *n.pl.* **1** candied fruits, sugar-covered nuts, or the like; candy; bonbons. **SYN**: confectionery. **2** preserves.

**sweet|ness** (swēt′nis), *n.* a sweet quality: *He likes candy because of its sweetness.* (*Figurative.*) *The sweetness of her manners made everyone like her.*

**sweetness and light**, **1** a person or thing exhibiting unusual tolerance, understanding, or sympathy (often used ironically when such a display is entirely out of character): *Now that they need us they are suddenly all sweetness and light. Politics is neither "sweetness and light" nor "too dirty to get into," [she] said* (New York Times). **2** a union of moral, intellectual, and aesthetic qualities, regarded as the highest cultural ideal of mankind: *Their ideal of beauty and sweetness and light, and a human nature complete on all its sides* (Matthew Arnold). *Instead of dirt and poison, we have rather chosen to fill our lives with honey and with wax thus furnishing mankind with the two noblest things, which are sweetness and light* (Jonathan Swift).

**sweet nothings**, *Informal.* words of endearment between lovers: *And whispered sweet nothings in her ear* (Frank Sullivan). *The sweet nothings that men whisper into my ear don't mean a thing to me* (Wall Street Journal).

**sweet oil**, any mild or pleasant, edible oil, especially olive oil.

**sweet orange**, the common orange, an evergreen tree of the rue family with fragrant white blossoms and oval leaves.

**sweet pea**, **1** an annual climbing plant with delicate, fragrant flowers of various colors. It belongs to the pea family. **2** the flower.

**sweet pepper**, **1** any one of various mild-flavored pepper plants. See picture under **pepper**. **2** the fruit of any one of various mild-flavored pepper plants, used especially as a vegetable and for stuffing; green pepper.

**sweet potato**, **1** the sweet, thick, yellow or reddish root of a creeping vine, used as a vegetable. **2** the vine that it grows on, much cultivated in warm regions. It belongs to the morning-glory family. *The sweet potato, a New World plant, was found by the first white explorers all over Polynesia* (Harper's). See picture under **morning-glory family**. **3** *Music, Informal.* an ocarina.

**sweet potato weevil**, a weevil whose larva feeds in the stems or roots of sweet potatoes and related plants.

**sweet rocket**, a perennial garden plant of Europe and Asia with showy white, pinkish, and purplish flowers.

**sweet|root** (swēt′rüt′, -rút′), *n.* **1** = licorice. **2** = sweet flag.

**sweets** (swēts), *n.pl.* See under **sweet**.

**sweet scabious**, a plant with long, tough stems and dense flower heads, a kind of scabious much cultivated in flower gardens.

**sweet-scent|ed** (swēt′sen′tid), *adj.* having a sweet scent; sweet-smelling; fragrant.

**sweet|shop** (swēt′shop′), *n. British.* a candy store.

**sweet|sop** (swēt′sop′), *n.* **1** the sweet, edible, pulpy fruit of a tropical American tree of the custard-apple family; sugar apple. It has a thick, green, scaly rind and black seeds. **2** the tree itself.

**sweet sorghum**, any one of a group of cultivated varieties of sorghum used for making molasses or syrup and as food for livestock; sorgo.

**sweet spirit of niter**, an alcoholic solution of ethyl nitrite, used as a diuretic and as a means of increasing sweating.

**sweet talk**, *Informal.* pleasant, agreeable, usually insincere talk to convince, befriend, or set at ease; cajolery: *As a man of good will he had to ... give them a chance to back up their sweet talk with action* (Newsweek).

**sweet-talk** (swēt′tôk′), *Informal.* —*v.t.* to try to convince, befriend, or set at ease by pleasant, agreeable talk; charm; cajole: *But he argues that the most effective tactics of gaining peace don't always consist of sweet-talking our enemies* (Wall Street Journal). **SYN**: mollify.
—*v.i.* to use sweet talk; be charming or flattering.

**sweet-tem|pered** (swēt′tem′pərd), *adj.* having a gentle or pleasant nature. **SYN**: amiable, affable.

**sweet tooth**, a fondness for sweets.

**sweet wil|liam** or **sweet Wil|liam** (wil′yəm), a plant with dense, rounded clusters of small flowers of various shades of white, purple, and red, usually variegated or parti-colored; bunch pink. It is a kind of pink.

**sweet|wood** (swēt′wúd′), *n.* **1** any one of various trees and shrubs, chiefly of the laurel family, of the West Indies and tropical America. **2** the wood of such a tree or shrub.

**sweet woodruff**, a species of woodruff with a sweet fragrance when dried. It has been used as a flavoring and in perfumes.

***swell** (swel), *v.,* **swelled, swelled** or **swol|len, swell|ing,** *n., adj.* —*v.i.* **1** to grow bigger: *Bread dough swells as it rises.* **SYN**: inflate, distend, dilate. See syn. under **expand**. **2** to be larger or thicker in a particular place; stick out: *A barrel swells in the middle.* **SYN**: bulge. **3** to increase in amount, degree, or force: *Savings may swell into a fortune. The ranks swelled with volunteers.* **4a** to rise above the usual or general level, as a river: *Rounded hills swell gradually from the village plain.* **b** to rise in waves, as the sea does during and after a storm. **c** to rise to the brim, as a spring; well up, as tears. **5** to grow louder or more intense, as sound or music: *Once again the organ swells* (John Greenleaf Whittier). *The murmur gradually swelled into a fierce and terrible clamor* (Macaulay). **6** *Figurative.* to become filled with emotion: *to swell with pride or indignation.* **7** *Figurative.* to behave proudly, arrogantly, or pompously: *He would come home and swell around his town in his blackest and greasiest clothes* (Mark Twain).
—*v.t.* **1** to make bigger; increase in size: *The bee sting had swelled his finger.* **SYN**: dilate, distend. **2** to cause to bulge out or protrude. **3** to make greater in amount, degree, or force: *Volunteers were swelling the ranks. The government brought four army regiments ... to swell ... military strength* (Newsweek). **4** to cause to rise above the usual level: *Rain swelled the river.* **5** to make louder: *All joined in to swell the chorus.* **6** *Figurative.* to fill with emotion. **7** *Figurative.* to make proud or conceited: *swollen with pride, swollen with his own importance.*
—*n.* **1** the act of swelling; increase in amount, degree, or force: (*Figurative.*) *The swell of insolence* (Samuel Johnson). **2** the condition of being swollen or increased in size. **3** a part that rises or swells out. **4** a piece of higher ground; rounded hill. **5** a long; unbroken wave, or waves, as after a storm: *riding out a gale which was accompanied by as big a swell as we have ever seen* (London Times). *The boat rocked in the swell.* **6** a swelling tone or sound. **7** *Music.* **a** a gradual increase in sound followed by a decrease; crescendo followed by diminuendo. **b** the sign for this. **c** a device, as in an organ or harpsichord, to control the volume of sound. **8** *Informal.* a fashionable, stylishly dressed, or distinguished person: *I never was a gentleman—only a swell* (Frederick Marryat). **9** a tin can with swelled or bulging ends; springer.
—*adj.* **1** *Informal.* stylish; grand. **2** *Slang.* excellent; very satisfactory: *a swell time, a swell worker. The woman is a lot better. That was swell medicine you gave her* (Sinclair Lewis).
[Old English *swellan*]
► Both **swelled** and **swollen** are in common use as past participles (*had swelled* or *swollen*); as an attributive adjective *swelled* is occasionally employed, as in the informal, figurative phrase *a swelled head,* but *swollen* is usual.

***swell**
*n.,* definitions 7a, b

**swell box**, = swell organ.

**swell|dom** (swel′dəm), *n. Informal.* swells collectively; the fashionable world.

**swelled** (sweld), *adj.* **1** = swollen. **2** *Informal, Figurative.* having an overdeveloped sense of one's own importance or merits: *a swelled ego. He has a bad case of swelled head.*

**swelled-head|ed|ness** (sweld′hed′id nis), *n. Informal.* conceit; arrogance.

**swell|fish** (swel′fish′), *n., pl.* **-fish|es** or (*collectively*) **-fish.** a fish that can inflate the body by swallowing air; puffer.

**swell front**, any horizontally convex projection in furniture or architecture, such as a bow window.

**swell-head** (swel′hed′), *n. Informal.* a swell-headed person.

**swell-head|ed** or **swell|head|ed** (swel′hed′id), *adj. Informal.* conceited; arrogant. —**swell′head′ed|ness, swell′head′ed|ness,** *n.*

**swell|ing** (swel′ing), *n., adj.* —*n.* **1** an increase in size. **2** a swollen part: *There is a swelling on his head where he bumped it. Inoculation of the virus resulted in the development of a localized swelling of the skin* (Fenner and Day). **SYN**: protuberance.
—*adj.* that swells.

**swell|ish** (swel′ish), *adj. Informal.* characteristic of a swell; fashionable; stylish.

**swell mob**, *British Slang.* a class of criminals who go about fashionably dressed to avoid suspicion.

**swell-mobs|man** (swel′mobz′mən), *n., pl.* **-men.** *British Slang.* a fashionably dressed criminal.

**swell organ**, the chief enclosed section of an organ, containing a set of pipes or reeds, and having shutters somewhat resembling Venetian blinds, that are opened and closed as by a pedal, to vary the volume of sound.

**swelt** (swelt), *Scottish.* —*v.i.* **1** to die. **2** to faint or swoon. **3** to languish or swelter with oppressive heat.
—*v.t.* to oppress or overcome with heat; cause to swelter.
[Old English *sweltan* to die. See related etym. at **sultry, swelter.**]

**swel|ter** (swel′tər), *v., n.* —*v.i.* **1** to suffer from heat: *We sweltered ... in the stagnant superheated air* (Joseph Conrad). **2** to perspire freely; sweat.
—*v.t.* **1** to oppress with heat. **2** to exude (venom, poison, or the like) like sweat: *A reptile contemporary has recently sweltered forth his black venom* (Dickens).
—*n.* a sweltering condition.
[< *swelt* be faint with heat + *-er*[6]. See related etym. at **sweal.**]

**swel|ter|ing** (swel′tər ing, -tring), *adj.* **1** (of heat, weather, or a season) oppressively hot: *The heat was sweltering, and he became very tired* (John Galsworthy). **2** suffering from or overpowered by oppressive heat. —**swel′ter|ing|ly,** *adv.*

**swel|try** (swel′trē), *adj.* oppressively hot; swelter-

**Pronunciation Key:** hat, āge, cãre, fär; let, ēqual, tėrm; it, īce; hot, ōpen, ôrder; oil, out; cup, pút, rüle; child; long; thin; ᴛʜen; zh, measure; ə represents **a** in about, **e** in taken, **i** in pencil, **o** in lemon, **u** in circus.

ing; sultry: *The fierce heat of the sun had rendered the atmosphere sweltry and oppressive* (Blackwood's Magazine). [< *swelter* + *-y*[1]. See related etym. at **sultry**.]

**swept** (swept), *v., adj.* —*v.* the past tense and past participle of **sweep**: *She swept the room. It was swept clean.*
—*adj.* = swept-back.

**swept-back** (swept′bak′), *adj.* extending outward and sharply backward from the fuselage: *It has swept-back wings to permit high speed, and is equipped with six ... turbo-jet engines* (Science News Letter).

**swept-for|ward** (swept′fôr′wərd), *adj.* extending outward and forward from the fuselage: *Swept-forward wings are used in high-speed jets.*

**swept|wing** (swept′wing′), *n., adj.* —*n.* a swept-back wing.
—*adj.* having swept-back wings.

**swerp|ing** (swėr′ping), *n. U.S.* a sound distortion on a magnetic tape, supposedly produced by an automatic tape recorder as it accelerates to full recording speed after being actuated by a sound: *Swerping ... normally obscures the first few syllables spoken after the interruption of speech* (J. Fred Buzhardt). [imitative]

**swerve** (swėrv), *v.,* **swerved, swerv|ing,** *n.* —*v.i., v.t.* to turn aside: *to swerve off the road. The car swerved and hit a tree.* (*Figurative.*) *Nothing could swerve him from doing his duty.* (*Figurative.*) *The world has swerved from truth and right* (William Morris). **SYN**: deviate, diverge, stray.
—*n.* a turning aside: *The swerve of the ball made it hard to hit.*
[Middle English *swerven* go off, turn aside, Old English *sweorfan* to rub, file]

**swerve|less** (swėrv′lis), *adj.* unswerving: *His gaze at the preacher had become swerveless* (Owen Wister).

**swerv|er** (swėr′vər), *n.* a person or thing that swerves.

**swev|en** (swev′ən), *n.* **1** *Archaic.* a dream or vision. **2** *Obsolete.* sleep. [Middle English *sweven,* Old English *swefen* a dream; sleep]

**S.W.G.,** standard wire gauge.

**swift** (swift), *adj., adv., n.* —*adj.* **1** moving very fast; able to move very fast: *a swift horse, a swift automobile.* **SYN**: fleet, speedy, rapid. **2** made or done at high speed; quick: *a swift pace, the swift clicking of the knitting needles.* **3** coming, happening, or performed quickly; prompt: *a swift answer.* **4** quick, rapid, or prompt to act; ready; alert (to): *swift to suspect. He is swift to repay a kindness.* **5** passing quickly; that is soon over; brief: *Swift Summer into the Autumn flowed* (Shelley).
—*adv.* in a swift manner; swiftly.
—*n.* **1** a small bird with long, strong wings, noted for its rapidity of flight. It is related to the hummingbird and goatsucker but looks somewhat like a swallow. The chimney swift of North America often builds its nest in an unused chimney. *The swift ... has a wingspread of some 16 inches, which makes it an incomparable little flying machine* (Scientific American). **2** any one of certain small lizards that run quickly. **3** any one of a family of large moths distinguished by their rapid flight; ghost moth. **4** a kind of reel, usually adjustable in diameter, used for winding skeins of yarn, silk, and thread. **5** a cylinder in a carding machine.
[Old English *swift*] —**swift′ly,** *adv.* —**swift′ness,** *n.*

**swift|en** (swif′tən), *v.t., v.i.* to make or become swift or swifter; hasten. [< *swift* + *-en*[1]]

**swift|er** (swif′tər), *n., v. Nautical.* —*n.* **1** a rope passed through holes or notches in the outer ends of capstan bars and drawn taut to keep the bars in their sockets while the capstan is being turned. **2** the forward shroud of a lower mast, extending to either side of the mast. **3** a rope encircling a boat or ship lengthwise to strengthen and protect its sides.
—*v.t.* to hold tight or draw together with a swifter.
[apparently < Middle English *swift* to make fast + *-er*[1]]

**swift-foot|ed** (swift′fůt′id), *adj.* able to run swiftly.

**swift fox,** = kit fox.

**swift|let** (swift′lit), *n.* a little or young swift, especially a small species of swift that constructs the edible bird's-nest of southeastern Asia.

**swift|walk|er** (swift′wô′kər), *n.* a bicycle of the early 1800's, such as the draisine.

**swift|y** (swif′tē), *n., pl.* **swift|ies.** *U.S.* a type of adverbial pun. *Examples:* "Hands up," said Jesse James disarmingly. "I have a puncture in my tire," the driver said flatly. [American English < Tom *Swift,* the hero of a popular series of boys' books by Edward L. Stratemeyer, 1862-1930, + *-y*[2]; so called because of the author's habit of having Tom always say something "slowly," "soberly," "excitedly," or in some other manner expressed by an adverb]

**swig** (swig), *n., v.,* **swigged, swig|ging.** *Informal.* —*n.* a big or hearty drink.
—*v.t., v.i.* to drink heartily or greedily: *I am ... drinking as much tea ... as I can swig* (John Ruskin).
[origin uncertain]

**swig|ger** (swig′ər), *n.* a person who swigs.

**swill** (swil), *n., v.* —*n.* **1a** kitchen refuse, especially when partly liquid; garbage; slops; hogwash. Swill is sometimes fed to pigs. **b** any one of various other foods for animals resembling this in consistency, such as a mixture of water and used distillery mash, sometimes with added grain or dried waste from slaughterhouses. **2** very unappetizing food. **3** a deep drink; swig. **4** the act of eating or drinking greedily; gluttonous ingestion. [< verb]
—*v.t.* **1** to drink (down) greedily or too much; guzzle: *a number of well-dressed people ... devouring sliced beef and swilling port* (Tobias Smollett). *She had seen them swilling down champagne with a couple of unknown Americans* (Atlantic). **2** to fill with drink: *to swill my belly with wine* (Robert Louis Stevenson). **3** to wash or rinse out by flooding with water. —*v.i.* **1** to drink greedily; drink too much; tipple: *Ye eat, and swill, and sleep, and gourmandise* (Richard Brinsley Sheridan). **2** to move or dash about, as liquid shaken in a vessel does; flow freely or forcibly. **3** to let water wash over soil, gravel, or the like, especially as a way of panning gold: *There was a certain glamour about the old gold-rush boys, swilling hopefully away with their little tin pannikins* (Punch).
[Old English *swilian, swillan* to wash] —**swill′er,** *n.*

**swim** (swim), *v.,* **swam** or (*Dialect*) **swum, swum, swim|ming,** *n.* —*v.i.* **1** to move on or in the water by using arms, legs, or fins: *Fish and dogs swim; cats will swim if they must. Most girls and boys like to swim.* **2** to float or seem to float: *a leaf swimming on a pond. The roast lamb was swimming in gravy.* **3** *Figurative.* to be overflowed or flooded (with or in): *Her eyes were swimming with tears.* **4** *Figurative.* to go smoothly; glide, as if on water: *The white clouds swam across the sky. She ... swam across the floor as though she scorned the drudgery of walking* (Robert Louis Stevenson). **5** *Figurative.* to be dizzy or feel giddy; whirl or seem to whirl: *Whirling around makes my head swim.* —*v.t.* **1** to go or do by swimming: *to swim a mile, unable to swim a stroke.* **2** to move in, on, or over by swimming; swim across: *We swam the river.* **3** to make swim or float: *He swam his horse across the stream.* **4** to provide with enough water for (something) to swim in or float on.
—*n.* **1** an act, time, motion, or distance of swimming: *Her swim had tired her. She had had an hour's swim.* **2** *Figurative.* a smooth gliding motion or movement, especially of the body. **3** = swim bladder.
**the swim,** *Informal, Figurative.* the popular current of affairs; what is going on; activities: *An active and sociable person likes to be in the swim.*
[Old English *swimman* to move in or on the water, to float]

**swim bladder,** a sac in fishes containing air or gas and serving as an organ of flotation; structure homologous with the lungs of air-breathing animals: *Certain fishes have a swim bladder, which aids in diffusion of gases* (Harbaugh and Goodrich). See also **air bladder**. See picture under **air bladder**.

**swim fin,** a rubber, paddlelike attachment worn on the foot to increase kicking power in swimming; fin: *The next day I bought a pair of swim fins and I have been skin diving ever since* (Scientific American). See picture under **aquagun**.

**swim|ma|ble** (swim′ə bəl), *adj.* that can be swum.

**swim meet,** a swimming and diving contest, usually consisting of several events.

**swim|mer** (swim′ər), *n.* a person or animal that swims.

**swim|mer|et** (swim′ə ret), *n.* an abdominal limb or appendage in many crustaceans, used in respiration and for carrying eggs (in females), and usually adapted for swimming; pleopod. [< *swimmer* + *-et*]

**swimmer's itch,** an inflammation of the skin caused by burrowing schistosomes.

**swim|ming** (swim′ing), *n., adj.* —*n.* **1** the practice or sport of moving along or in water by using arms, legs, or fins: *My brother is an expert at both swimming and diving.* **2** the act of moving this way: *Can you reach the island by swimming?* **3** *Figurative.* a state of dizziness or giddiness; vertigo.
—*adj.* **1a** of or for swimming or swimmers: *a swimming teacher, a swimming pool.* **b** that swims habitually: *a swimming bird or insect.* **2** *Figurative.* filled with tears; watery: *swimming eyes.* **3** *Figurative.* faint; dizzy: *a swimming sensation.* **SYN**: giddy, vertiginous.

**swimming bath,** *British.* a swimming pool: *There is a pleasant garden round the house and a beautiful swimming bath* (Cape Times).

**swimming crab,** any crab of a family that includes the blue crab and the lady crab.

**swimming hole,** a pool, as in a small stream, with sufficient depth of water to swim in: *The boy's love for the water, his affection for the old swimming hole* (J. H. Moore).

**swim|ming|ly** (swim′ing lē), *adv.* with great ease or success: *Everything went swimmingly at our party. The ... light opera program moves along swimmingly with the current revival* (Wall Street Journal). *I found the association went on swimmingly* (Benjamin Franklin). **SYN**: easily, smoothly.

**swimming meet,** = swim meet.

**swimming pool,** a large tank, usually of concrete, metal, or plastic, used for swimming and diving: *to build an outdoor swimming pool.*

**swimming pool reactor,** a nuclear reactor partly immersed in a tank of water that absorbs heat, slows down nuclear fission, and is a radiation shield.

**swim|my** (swim′ē), *adj.,* **-mi|er, -mi|est. 1** slightly dizzy or giddy; light-headed: *The blow on the head left him feeling swimmy.* **2** not seeing clearly; blurred: *Through the smoke his swimmy eyes made out a vague shape.*

**swim pool,** = swimming pool.

**swim|suit** (swim′süt′), *n.* = bathing suit.

**swim|wear** (swim′wãr′), *n.* clothes worn for swimming: *The most exciting collection of coordinated swimwear* (New Yorker).

**swin|dle** (swin′dəl), *v.,* **-dled, -dling,** *n.* —*v.t.* **1** to cheat; defraud: *Honest merchants do not swindle their customers.* **SYN**: rook. **2** to get (something) by fraud. —*v.i.* to be guilty of swindling another or others; practice fraud.
—*n.* an act of swindling: *to suspect a swindle.*
[back formation < *swindler*] —**swin′dle|a|ble,** *adj.*

**swin|dler** (swin′dlər), *n.* a person who cheats or defrauds. [< German *Schwindler* < *schwindeln* to befog, confuse; cheat]

**swindle sheet,** *U.S. Slang.* an expense account: *To catch a few suspected swindle sheet artists, the Internal Revenue Service has now decided to crack down on all ... who get so much as a penny of their expenses paid by their employers* (Wall Street Journal).

**swin|dling** (swin′dling), *n.* the act of a person who swindles or defrauds.

**swine** (swīn), *n., pl.* **swine. 1a** hogs or pigs: *... and he sent him into his fields to feed swine* (Luke 15:15). **b** a hog or pig. **2** *Figurative.* a coarse or beastly person. [Old English *swīn.* See related etym. at **sow**[2].]

**swine fever,** = hog cholera.

**swine flu,** a virulent form of influenza caused by a filterable virus originally isolated in swine: *The very possibility that the swine flu virus had once again become infectious to humans was enough to trigger a series of triphammer decisions* (New York Sunday News).

**swine|herd** (swīn′hėrd′), *n.* a person who tends pigs or hogs, especially for hire.

**swine plague,** an infectious disease of swine, caused by a specific bacterium, and marked by internal hemorrhage, fever, and often pneumonia and pleurisy.

**swine pox, 1** an infectious disease of hogs, caused by a virus and characterized by itching skin lesions, especially on the underparts. **2** *Obsolete.* chicken pox.

**swing**[1] (swing), *v.,* **swung** or (*Dialect*) **swang, swung, swing|ing,** *n., adj.* —*v.t.* **1** to move (something) back and forth, especially with a regular motion: *He swings his arms as he walks.* **2** to hang or suspend so as to turn freely: *We swung the hammock between two trees.* **3** to cause to turn in alternate directions or in either direction, on or as if on an axle or pivot: *to swing a door open.* **4** to cause to move in a curve: *to swing a lasso. He swings the club twice around his head. She swung the automobile around a corner.* **5** *Informal, Figurative.* to manage or influence successfully: *to swing a business deal. Princeton's financial-aid officer tells how to swing the high cost of higher education* (Saturday Evening Post).
—*v.i.* **1** to move freely or regularly back and forth, as an object suspended from above; oscillate, as a pendulum does: *The hammock swings.* **2** to move back and forth through the air on a suspended rope or ropes as a sport. **3** to hang: *They all lovingly swung together at Execution-Dock* (Daniel Defoe). **4** to turn in alternate directions, or in either direction, on or as if on an axle or pivot; wheel: *A gate swings on its hinges. He swung around to see who was speaking. The*

*ship, swinging to her anchor with the flood tide* (Herman Melville). **5** to move in a curve; sweep. **6** to move with a free, swaying motion: *The camels, swinging at a steady trot* (J. A. Stewart). **7** to hit with a swinging motion: *I swung at the ball.* **8** *Slang.* to be up to date, lively, and exciting: *"This magazine has got to swing, like other magazines swing," Ackerman had once said, and he had not meant simply that it should be fashionable but that it should be aware of the way society moved* (Harper's). **9** *Slang.* to exchange partners for sexual purposes.

—*n.* **1** the act or manner of swinging: *He brought the hammer down with a mighty swing.* **2** the amount of swinging. **3** something that swings or is swung, especially a seat hung from ropes, chains, or rods, on which one may sit and swing. **4** a swinging movement or gait: *An easy swing in my walk* (Washington Irving). **5a** the act of swinging or flourishing, as a weapon. **b** a curving movement, such as that made in flourishing a weapon. **6** a steady, marked swinging rhythm: *The song "Dixie" has a swing. His poetry lacked the swing of ... Kipling* (Sinclair Lewis). **7** *Figurative.* freedom of action; free scope: *The giving free swing to one's temper and instincts* (Matthew Arnold). **8** *Figurative.* movement; activity, especially vigorous activity: *to get into the swing of working after a vacation.* **9** a trip around a country or region; tour: *a swing through the United States.* **10** *Archaic.* forcible motion of something; impetus.

—*adj.* **1** capable of turning to and fro; swinging: *a swing lamp, a swing gate.* **2** *Figurative.* that can influence the outcome of an election or other issue: *swing voters, a swing district.*

**in full swing,** going on actively and completely; without restraint: *By five o'clock the party was in full swing. The Victorian Age was in full swing* (Lytton Strachey).

**swing around the circle,** *U.S.* a political swing or tour: *Will the appropriated money be available for campaigning swings around the circle?* (Springfield Republican).

[Old English *swingan* to beat, strike; move violently. See related etym. at **swinge, swingle.**]

—*Syn. v.i.* **1 Swing, rock, sway** mean to move back and forth or from side to side. **Swing** applies to the movement of something hanging free or loose, and usually suggests a regular or rhythmical movement: *The lantern hanging overhead swung in the wind.* **Rock** applies to movement back and forth upon a base, either gentle (*I rocked quietly until the baby fell asleep*) or violent (*The house rocked in the storm*). **Sway** suggests an unsteady motion: *The unexpected blow caused him to sway and lose his balance. The branches sway in the breeze.*

**swing[2]** (swing), *n., v.,* **swung, swing|ing,** *adj.* —*n.* Also, **swing music.** jazz, especially jazz for dancing, of the type popular between about 1935 and 1944, in which the players improvise freely on the original melody: *The sextet's style is swing, and it swings in the most dexterous manner imaginable* (New Yorker).

—*v.t.* to play (music) as swing.

—*v.i.* **1** to play or sing with a lively, swinging rhythm: *There is little that is new or startlingly original in the arrangements themselves, but how they swing!* (Saturday Review). **2** *Slang.* to be satisfying, pleasing, exciting, or lively: *"The first old-fashioned specialty store around here ... had gotten slightly old ladyish. Now it swings"* (New York Times).

—*adj.* of or having to do with swing or its style: *Tatum ... created "swing" piano and anticipated nearly all the rhythmic and harmonic idioms of the modern period* (John Mehegan).

[special use of *swing*[1]]

**swing|back** (swing′bak′), *n.* **1** a reversion, as of opinion; turning back to formerly held beliefs or ideas. **2** a backward swing, as of the body or a weapon.

**∗swing bridge**

**∗swing bridge,** a bridge that pivots on its center to open and let ships pass.

**swing|by** (swing′bī′), *n.* the passing of a spacecraft through the gravitational field of a planet in order to achieve the orbit necessary to change course, usually for a more distant planet: *Venus swing-bys to Mercury can be accomplished* (Science Journal). *It* [*a mission*] *is planned as a swing-by past Jupiter or Saturn and is of relatively long duration* (New Scientist).

**swing door,** = swinging door.

**swinge[1]** (swinj), *v.t.,* **swinged, swinge|ing.** **1** *Archaic.* to beat; flog; whip: *Saint George, that swinged the Dragon* (Shakespeare). **2** *Obsolete.* to chastise or castigate. [variant of Old English *swengan* (causative) < *swingan;* see etym. under **swing**[1]]

**swinge[2]** (swinj), *v.t.,* **swinged, swinge|ing.** *Dialect.* to singe or scorch. [perhaps alteration of *singe*]

**swinge|ing** (swin′jing), *adj. Informal.* very forcible, strong, or large of its kind: *He and his editor are swiftly haled before the bench and swingeing penalties ... are demanded* (Punch). —**swinge′ing|ly,** *adv.*

**swing|er[1]** (swing′ər), *n.* **1** a person or thing that swings: *a lasso swinger, a good swinger.* **2** *Slang.* a person who is up-to-date and lively, especially in an unrestrained way: *The go-go spirit of today's glamorized young swingers is hardly conducive to interest in exact and abstract reasoning* (New York Times). **3** *Slang.* a person who exchanges partners for sexual purposes.

**swing|er[2]** (swin′jər), *n.* **1** *Informal.* anything very forcible, great, or large, such as a blow, or a lie; whopper. **2** a person or thing that swinges.

**swing|ing** (swing′ing), *adj.* **1** moving freely in either direction upon a fixed center or axis, as a stool or a door. **2** moving or proceeding with a swing, as a pace or gait, or a rhythm in verse or music. **3** *Slang.* up-to-date and lively, especially in an unrestrained way: [*She*] *and a troop of other notable models played host at a champagne luncheon at noon and a swinging party at night* (London Times). —**swing′ing|ly,** *adv.* —**swing′ing|ness,** *n.*

**swinging door,** a door that swings shut by itself and opens from either direction: *the swinging door into the butler's pantry gave its old swish and slap* (New Yorker).

**swin|gle** (swing′gəl), *n., v.,* **-gled, -gling.** —*n.* **1** a wooden instrument shaped like a large knife, used for beating flax or hemp and scraping from it the woody or coarse portions. **2** the striking part of a flail; swiple.

—*v.t.* to clean, beat, and scrape (flax or hemp). [Middle English *swingle,* Old English *swingel* a stroke, whip < *swingan* beat]

**swin|gle|bar** (swing′gəl bär′), *n.* = whiffletree.

**swin|gle|tree** (swing′gəl trē′), *n.* = whiffletree.

**swing|man** (swing′man′, -mən), *n., pl.* **-men.** **1** *U.S.* one of the outriders who keeps a moving herd of cattle in order. **2** a musician who plays swing: *Swingman Benny Goodman* [*was*] *named ... for his contributions to world culture and American music* (Time). **3** *Slang, Figurative.* a person who casts the decisive vote: *The swingman, Justice Harlan, voted to reverse Estes' conviction* (New York Times).

**swing music,** = swing[2].

**swing-over** (swing′ō′vər), *n.* **1** a change to an opposite side, position, or opinion: *An odd phenomenon in American postwar life is the swing-over of young women from ambitious career girls to full-time housewives* (London Times). **2** an acrobatic movement of hanging from one arm and swinging the body in a complete vertical circle: [*She*] *is shown doing the rhythmic swing-overs that entitle her to center ring position as a star* (New York Times).

**swing shift,** the hours between the day and night shifts, usually from 4 p.m. to midnight, designated as a working day in factories and other operations that are on a 24-hour basis: *In addition to his swing shift job at Douglas,* [*he*] *works days as an airplane mechanic* (Wall Street Journal). [American English, perhaps < *swing*[1] (because the shift is the middle one)]

**swing shifter,** a person who works on the swing shift.

**swing tail,** an airplane tail that swings open on hinges to facilitate loading and unloading, especially of large and heavy pieces of freight. —**swing′-tail′,** *adj.*

**swing|tree** (swing′trē′), *n.* = whiffletree.

**swing-wing** (swing′wing′), *n., adj.* —*n.* **1** a wing that can be swung in flight to vary the motion of an aircraft for slow, intermediate, or supersonic speeds; variable-sweep wing. **2** an aircraft having such a wing: *a squadron of swing-wings.*

—*adj.* of or having to do with a swing-wing: *a swing-wing jet fighter.*

**swing|y** (swing′ē), *adj.,* **swing|i|er, swing|i|est.** of or in the style of swing music; lively; jazzy: *... an impressive collection of 12 swingy ballads* (Saturday Review).

**swin|ish** (swī′nish), *adj.* **1** very selfish; greedy. **2** dirty; filthy; beastly. **3** having to do with or fit for swine: *in swinish sleep* (Shakespeare). —**swin′ish|ly,** *adv.* —**swin′ish|ness,** *n.*

**swink** (swingk), *n., v.,* **swank** or **swonk, swonken, swink|ing.** *Archaic.* —*n.* labor; toil. [Old English *swinc*]

—*v.i.* to labor; toil. —*v.t.* to weary with toil; overwork. [Old English *swincan.* Ultimately related to **swing**[1].] —**swink′er,** *n.*

**swinked** (swingkt), *adj. Archaic.* wearied with toil: *the swink'd hedger at his supper sat* (Milton).

**swipe** (swīp), *n., v.,* **swiped, swip|ing.** —*n.* **1** *Informal.* a sweeping stroke; hard, driving blow: *I made two swipes at the golf ball without hitting it.* (*Figurative.*) [*He*] *managed to get in a few casually phrased but tough swipes at the fair for presenting a largely unreal, euphemistic view of the world* (New Yorker). **2** a kind of lever for raising a weight, especially for raising water. **3** harmony, in barbershop quartet singing, that changes several times on a single note of the melody. **4** *U.S. Slang.* a person who rubs down horses at a racing stable.

—*v.t.* **1** *Informal.* to strike with a sweeping blow. **2** *Slang.* to steal. SYN: snatch.

—*v.i.* to make a sweeping blow or stroke.

**take a swipe at,** *Informal.* to seek to hit; deliver a blow at: *A pampered but kindly king ... takes a good-natured swipe at conformity and some unsuccessful attempts to resist it* (New York Times).

[partly variant of *sweep;* partly variant of obsolete *swip* to strike, move hastily, Middle English *swippen,* perhaps Old English *swippan,* variant of *swipian.* Compare Old English *swipu* a stick, scourge.]

**swipes** (swīps), *n.pl. British Slang.* **1** poor, weak beer; small beer. **2** alcoholic malt beverages in general; beer. [< *swipe,* in obsolete sense of "to drink hastily" + *-s*[1]]

**swi|ple** or **swip|ple** (swip′əl), *n.* the part of a flail that strikes the grain in threshing; swingle. [Middle English *swepell* a besom, and *swipyll* a swipple. Probably related to **sweep, swipe.**]

**swirl** (swėrl), *v., n.* —*v.i.* **1** to move or drive along with a twisting motion; whirl: *dust swirling in the air, a stream swirling over rocks.* (*Figurative.*) *The heat and noise made my head swirl.* **2** to twist or curl: *a lock of hair swirled against the neck.*

—*v.t.* **1** to give a whirling motion to: *Add the firm butter to the sauce in little curls, swirling the pan* (New York Times). **2a** to give a twisted or curled form to: *Gold is used as an accent to emphasize the swirled pattern on a round table* (New York Times). **b** to wrap around (with something).

—*n.* **1** a swirling movement; whirl; eddy: (*Figurative.*) *the swirl of city life.* **2** a twist or curl: *a swirl of whipped cream on top of a sundae. Her hat had a swirl of lace around it.*

[Middle English *swirle* eddy, probably < dialectal Norwegian *svirla.* Compare Dutch *zwirrelen* to whirl.] —**swirl′ing|ly,** *adv.*

**swirl|y** (swėr′lē), *adj.* **1** twisted. **2** knotty; gnarled.

**swish[1]** (swish), *v., n.* —*v.i.* **1** to move with a thin, light, hissing or brushing sound: *The whip swished through the air.* **2** to make such a sound: *The long gown swished as she danced across the floor.*

—*v.t.* to cause to swish: *The cow swished her tail. She swished the stick.*

—*n.* a swishing movement or sound: *the swish of little waves on the shore; the swish of paddles in dark water* (William O. Douglas). *A few shots and swishes of scimitars and it was all over* (Newsweek). —**swish′er,** *n.* —**swish′ing|ly,** *adv.*

**swish[2]** (swish), *adj., n. Slang.* —*adj.* **1** elegant; classy; posh: *Her new premises in Bruton Street are swish* (Sunday Times). **2** effeminate; homosexual.

—*n.* a homosexual.

[special use of *swish*[1]]

**swish|y** (swish′ē), *adj.,* **swish|i|er, swish|i|est.** **1** characterized by a swishing sound or motion. **2** *Slang.* effeminate; homosexual.

**swiss** (swis), *n.* = Swiss muslin.

**Swiss** (swis), *adj., n., pl.* **Swiss.** —*adj.* **1** of or having to do with Switzerland, a small country in central Europe, or its people. **2** characteristic of Switzerland or its people.

—*n.* **1** a person born or living in Switzerland. **2** *pl. in use.* the people of Switzerland. **3** = Swiss muslin.

[< French *suisse* < Middle High German *Swiz*]

**Swiss chard,** any one of several varieties of

---

**Pronunciation Key:** hat, āge, cãre, fär; let, ēqual, tėrm; it, īce; hot, ōpen, ôrder; **oi**l, **ou**t; cup, pu̇t, rüle; **ch**ild; lo**ng**; **th**in; **ᴛʜ**en; **zh**, measure; **ə** represents **a** in about, **e** in taken, **i** in pencil, **o** in lemon, **u** in circus.

beets whose leaves are often eaten as a vegetable; chard: *For brilliant foliage no other vegetable quite equals the ... Swiss chard* (New York Times).

**Swiss cheese**, a firm, pale-yellow or whitish cheese with many large holes.

**Swiss franc**, the unit of money of Switzerland, equal to 100 centimes.

**Swiss Guards**, a body of Swiss soldiers that acts as a bodyguard to the pope in the Vatican.

**Swiss muslin**, a kind of thin muslin often with raised dots or figures in various patterns, used especially for curtains; Swiss.

**Swiss roll**, a sponge cake rolled up with a layer of jam or jelly; jellyroll.

**Swiss steak**, a slice of beef, veal, or lamb, kneaded with flour, browned, and cooked with gravy and tomato sauce: *To stimulate more beef-eating, the Agriculture Department is putting out recipes for ... ragout of beef and Swiss steak* (Wall Street Journal).

**Swiss system**, a system used in chess tournaments, in which players with like or nearly like scores are paired with each other in successive rounds. The highest scorer at the end of the final round is declared the winner or champion.

**Swit.**, Switzerland.

**switch** (swich), *n., v.* —*n.* **1** a slender stick used in whipping or beating, especially a riding whip. **2** a thin, flexible shoot cut from a tree: *Not so long ago, exasperated mothers snatched off a switch from the lilac bush while ushering junior to the shed.* **3** a blow with or as if with a switch; stroke; lash: *The big dog knocked a vase off the table with a switch of his tail.* **4** a bunch or coil of long hair, often of false hair, worn by a woman in addition to her own hair. **5** any one of various devices for changing the direction of something, for making or breaking a connection, or for other purposes: **a** a lever, plug, or other device for making or breaking a connection in an electric circuit or for altering the connections in a circuit. **b** a pair of movable rails, pivoted at one end, by which a train can shift from one track to another. **6** the act of operating any of these devices. **7** *Figurative.* a change; turn; shift: *a last-minute switch of plans. He lost the election when his supporters made a switch of their votes to the other candidate. In Peking, the Red Chinese Government pulled another switch* (Newsweek). **8** a turning to another suit in bidding or play at bridge: *Don't double if there is a probability of a switch into some other call which you cannot possibly double* (A. M. Foster). **9** a hold that enables a wrestler to change from defense to offense through arm leverage.
—*v.t.* **1** to whip with or as if with a switch; strike: *He switched the boys with a birch switch.* **2** to swing or flourish like a switch; jerk suddenly; whisk: *The horse switched his tail to drive off the flies.* **3a** to connect or disconnect with an electric current by using a switch; turn (an electric light, current, or the like, on or off): *Switch off the lights before you go to bed.* **b** to shift to another circuit. **4a** to shift (a train or railroad car) from one track to another by a swtich; shunt. **b** to form (a train) by joining or removing cars; join or remove (cars). **5** *Figurative.* to turn, shift, or divert; change: *to switch the subject, to switch places. The girls switched hats. The Middle East's awakening nations ... could switch the balance of world power* (Newsweek). **6** to shift (suits) in bidding or play at bridge.
—*v.i.* **1** to strike a blow or blows with or as if with a switch. **2** to shift from or as if from one railroad track to another. **3** to change or shift, as in direction or suits in cards: *At contract he has the additional and highly important duty of raising the opener's bid as far towards a game or slam contract as his hand permits, and if he switches, of deciding whether to make a pre-emptive bid or not* (London Daily Telegraph).
[probably < variant of Low German *swutsche*]
—**switch′a|ble**, *adj.* —**switch′like′**, *adj.*

**switch|back** (swich′bak′), *n., v.* —*n.* **1** a section of a railroad or highway built in a zigzag course up a steep grade, as on the side of a mountain, by means of which the rate of climb of the roadbed is held within a tolerable range: *The trail began suddenly to rise in sharp switchbacks from the valley floor* (Paul Brooks). **2** *Especially British.* a roller coaster.
—*v.i.* to take a zigzag course: *For three miles, without either village or cottage, this narrow ... byroad switchbacked up and down across the high ground* (Geoffrey Household).

**switch|blade** (swich′blād′), *n.,* or **switch blade knife**, a pocketknife with a blade that springs out at the push of a button or knob on the handle: *A large quantity of guns and switchblade knives were scooped up by police* (Birmingham News).

**switch|board** (swich′bôrd′, -bōrd′), *n.* a panel or group of panels with electric switches and plugs for opening, closing, combining, controlling, measuring, and protecting a number of electric circuits. Some telephone switchboards have plugs for connecting one line to another.

**switch box**, a box containing the parts of one or more electric switches.

**switch cane**, a short-stemmed grass of the southern United States, found in wet areas and used as fodder.

**switched-on** (swicht′on′), *adj. Slang.* smart; up-to-date; stylish: *The women were in short, swtiched-on dresses* (New Yorker). ... *the new, switched-on world of "swinging" London* (Maclean's).

**switch engine**, an engine used in railroad yards for moving and switching trains and railroad cars; switcher.

**switch|er** (swich′ər), *n.* **1** a person or thing that switches. **2** *U.S.* a railroad engine used for switching cars and making up trains in a railroad yard: *The Atchison, Topeka and Santa Fe Railway ordered 25 ... road switchers* (Wall Street Journal). **3** a piece of television equipment used to change scenes or combine scenes from two or more cameras or other video sources.

**switch|er|oo** (swich′ə rü′), *n. U.S. Slang.* a sudden, startling change, as in character, appearance, or action; sudden reversal: *As things seem to be moving toward a sordid triangle case,* [*she*] *pulls her switcheroo* (Newsweek).

**switch|gear** (swich′gir′), *n.* the device operating switches in electric circuits.

**switch|grass** (swich′gras′, -gräs′), *n.* a tall panic grass found from the Atlantic coast to the Rocky Mountains, used especially for hay.

**switch-hit** (swich′hit′), *v.i.,* **-hit, -hit|ting.** to bat either right-handed or left-handed; be a switch-hitter.

**switch-hit|ter** (swich′hit′ər), *n.* a baseball player who bats either right- or left-handed: *For a while Lloyd talked of baseball ... how he'd practiced batting left-handed so he could be a switch-hitter like Mickey Mantle* (New York Times).

**switch-hit|ting** (swich′hit′ing), *n., adj.* hitting right-handed or left-handed; being a switch-hitter.

**switch|man** (swich′mən), *n., pl.* **-men. 1** a man in charge of one or more railroad switches, as at a junction or siding. **2** a man who helps with the shifting of cars and makeup of trains, as at a sorting yard or freight terminal.

**switch|o|ver** (swich′ō′vər), *n.* the act of switching or changing over (to); conversion: *Now that the campaign is over, the big problem is the switchover to a new administration* (Newsweek).

**switch plant**, *Botany.* a plant that bears slender green shoots or rodlike branches with small leaves or without leaves: *Leaves may be omitted altogether and the green food-making surface confined to modified stems, as in ... such switch plants* (Science News Letter).

**switch plate**, a plate for covering a switch box so that the lever, plug, or other switch protrudes.

**switch selling**, the selling of a more expensive item to customers than the one advertised at a much lower price: *All its salesmen are, and always have been, expressly forbidden to attempt 'switch selling'* (Sunday Times).

**switch|yard** (swich′yärd′), *n.* a railroad yard where cars are switched from one track to another and put together to make trains; sorting yard.

**swith** (swith), *adv., interj. Archaic.* —**adv. 1** at a rapid rate; very quickly. **2** instantly; immediately.
—***interj.*** quick! hence! away!
[Old English *swīthe*]

**swith|er** (swiᴛʜ′ər), *v., n.* —*v.i. Scottish.* to falter; hesitate.
—*n.* **1** a state of agitation or excitement; flurry or fluster: *The novelty of having women appear in pants suits has headwaiters across the country in a swither* (Time). **2** *Scottish.* a state of perplexity or hesitation; doubt or uncertainty: [*He*] *stands some time in jumbled swither, to ride in this road, or that ither* (Allan Ramsay).
[origin uncertain. Compare Old English *geswithrian* weaken.]

**Switz.**, Switzerland.

**Switz|er** (swit′sər), *n.* a Swiss. [ultimately < Middle High German *Switzer,* or < Middle Dutch *Switser,* and *Swytzer* < *Switzen* Switzerland; (literally) the canton of Schwyz]

**swive** (swīv), *v.t., v.i.,* **swived, swiv|ing.** *Informal.* to have sexual intercourse. [Middle English *swiven,* Old English *swīfan* to move in a course, sweep] —**swiv′er**, *n.*

**swiv|el** (swiv′əl), *n., v.,* **-eled, -el|ing** or (*especially British*) **-elled, -el|ling.** —*n.* **1a** a simple fastening or coupling device that allows the thing fastened to turn around freely upon it. **b** a chain link having two parts, one of which turns freely in the other. **2** a support on which a chair can turn around. **3a** the flexible support of a swivel gun, by which the weapon is permitted to be elevated or depressed, or to range to right or left. **b** a gun that turns on such a support; swivel gun: *Mounted high up in the rigging, however, the ships had a few smaller guns, called swivels* (New Yorker).
—*v.i.* **1** to turn (anything) on a swivel. **2** to swing around; rotate; turn.
—*v.t.* **1** to turn on a swivel. **2** to furnish with a swivel; fasten or support by means of a swivel: *Leitzel, as every circus familiar knows, performed on Roman rings and on a swivelled rope in the tent top* (New Yorker). **3** to swing around; rotate; turn.
[Middle English *swivell,* related to Old English *swīfan* to move in a course, sweep]

**swivel chair**, a chair having a seat that turns on a swivel.

**swivel gun**, a gun, especially any of various relatively light pieces of artillery formerly used on land and at sea, having a barrel mounted on a swivel so that it can be turned in any direction.

**swiv|el-hip** (swiv′əl hip′), *v.i.,* **-hipped, -hip|ping.** to walk or move with a swinging motion of the hips: *"Garçon!" he cried, as a waiter swivel-hipped ... down one of the aisles, holding his tray high overhead* (New Yorker).

**swivel knife**, a knife used in leathercraft to carve designs into leather.

**swiv|et** (swiv′it), *n. U.S. Slang.* great excitement; frenzy; stir; dither: [*He*] *flew into a swivet over the fact that two Texas pelicans died recently in the London zoo* (Time). [origin uncertain]

**swizz** (swiz), *n. Slang.* a swindle; fraud: *Amanda said, in tones of desperation. "It's a swizz. Michael is never going to die"* (New Yorker). [origin uncertain]

**swiz|zle** (swiz′əl), *n., v.,* **-zled, -zling.** —*n.* **1** a drink consisting of rum or other alcoholic liquor, crushed ice, bitters, sugar, and lemon or lime juice. **2** any other mixed alcoholic drink.
—*v.t. Informal.* to drink habitually and to excess; swill.
[apparently variant of earlier *switchel*]

**swizzle stick**, a stick used for stirring swizzles and other drinks: *Swizzle sticks coated with rock candy are a unique gadget for sweetening old fashioneds, collins drinks, tea or coffee* (New York Times).

**swob** (swob), *n., v.t.,* **swobbed, swob|bing.** = swab. —**swob′ber**, *n.*

**swol|len** (swō′lən), *adj., v.* —***adj.*** swelled; enlarged; bulging: *a swollen ankle.* (*Figurative.*) *His swollen heart almost bursting* (Dickens). *Swollen mountain streams burst out of the woods like furious brown snakes, swallowing topsoil and drowning animals* (Time). **SYN:** puffy, tumid.
—*v.* a past participle of **swell**: *Her ankle has swollen considerably since she fell. The controversy about bomb tests has swollen in the last three years into a torrent of words* (Eugene Rabinowitch).

**swollen shoot**, a disease of cacao trees caused by a virus carried by mealy bugs feeding on tree sap: *The swollen shoot virus ... has cut cocoa bean production by as much as three-fourths in some Gold Coast areas* (Science News Letter).

**swoln** (swōln), *adj. Archaic.* swollen.

**swonk** (swungk), *v. Archaic.* a past tense of **swink**.

**swonk|en** (swung′kən), *v. Archaic.* the past participle of **swink**.

**swoon** (swün), *v., n.* —*v.i.* **1** to faint: *She swoons at the sight of blood.* **2** to fade or die away gradually. **3** to go into a state of great joy; become thrilled with overwhelming delight; become enraptured: [*He*] *is a wonderful man: the ladies have been swooning all over him and keeping the dregs from his tea in cologne bottles* (Edmund Wilson).
—*n.* **1** a faint; syncope: *Cold water will bring her out of the swoon.* **2** *Obsolete.* a deep or sound sleep.
[Middle English *swonen,* ultimately < Old English *geswōgen* in a swoon] —**swoon′ing|ly**, *adv.*

**swoop** (swüp), *v., n.* —*v.i.* **1** to come down with a rush; sweep rapidly down (upon) in a sudden attack: *The pirates swooped down on the towns. One night the Indians swooped down on an unsuspecting village and burned it.* **2** to make a rapid sweeping descent through the air, as a bird of prey does, in order to seize, kill, or destroy: *The flying death that swoops and stuns* (Dorothy Sayers).
—*v.t.* **1** to snatch: *She rushed after the child and swooped him up in her arms.* **2** *Obsolete.* to sweep (up, away, or off).
—*n.* a rapid downward sweep; sudden, swift descent or attack: *With one swoop the hawk seized the chicken and flew away. Influenza came down upon me with a swoop* (Thomas H. Huxley).
**in** (or **at**) **one fell swoop**, in a single blow or stroke; in one sweeping act: *No longer are the governments, East or West, under any illusion*

*that they can settle all the problems of the world in one fell swoop* (Wall Street Journal). [apparently dialectal variant of obsolete *swope,* Old English *swāpan* to sweep] — **swoop′er**, *n.*

**swoop|stake** (swüp′stāk′), *adv. Obsolete.* by or as if by sweeping all the stakes at once; indiscriminately: *... is't writ in your revenge, That, swoopstake, you will draw both friend and foe, Winner and loser?* (Shakespeare). [alteration of *sweepstake*]

**swoosh** (swüsh), *v., n. Informal.* — ***v.i.*** to move very swiftly with a whirling, brushing sound: *Jet planes swooshed overhead* (New York Times).
— ***v.t.*** to cause to swoosh: *to swoosh air through a tunnel. The propellers of the plane swooshed a gale.*
— ***n.*** a swooshing movement or sound: *the swoosh of jets flying past.* [imitative]

**swop** (swop), *v.t., v.i.,* **swopped, swop|ping,** *n.* = swap. — **swop′per,** *n.*

***sword** (sôrd, sōrd), *n.* **1** a weapon, usually metal, with a long, sharp blade fixed in a handle or hilt. **SYN**: rapier, saber, blade, cutlass, scimitar. **2** *Figurative.* something that wounds or kills; destroying agency: *He hath loosed the fateful lightning of His terrible swift sword* (Julia Ward Howe). *This avarice ... hath been the sword of our slain kings* (Shakespeare). **3** a symbol of power or authority, especially to judge and impose sentence. **4** the swordlike projection of the upper jaw of a swordfish.
**be at swords' points,** to be very unfriendly; be avowed enemies: *They were at swords' points as a result of the election.*
**cross swords, a** to fight: *Few men ventured to cross swords with him* (Scott). **b** *Figurative: They rarely met without crossing swords on one matter if not another* (Lynn Linton).
**draw the sword,** to begin a war: *He would not draw the sword against his king.*
**measure swords, a** to fight with swords: *You ... wanted to measure swords with Mohun, did you?* (Thackeray). **b** *Figurative: The senator has often measured swords with his colleagues on the issue of foreign relations.*
**put to the sword,** to kill with a sword; slaughter at war: *De Thermes ... took the fortress of Broughty, and put the garrison to the sword* (David Hume).
**sheathe the sword,** to end a war: *The sword should not be sheathed till he had been brought to condign punishment as a traitor* (Macaulay).
**the sword, a** war: *If I were young again the sword should end it* (Shakespeare). **b** fighting or military power: *Those that live by the sword shall perish by the sword. The pen is mightier than the sword* (Edward G. Bulwer-Lytton). **c** the army: *This influential portion was formed by ... the sword, the ... clergy, and the members of the parliaments* (John Austin).
[Old English *sweord*] — **sword′like′,** *adj.*

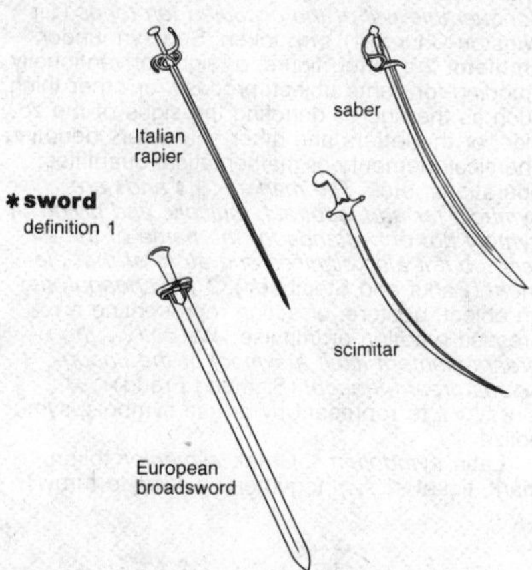


***sword**
definition 1

**sword arm,** the arm, usually the right arm, with which the sword is wielded.

**sword bayonet,** a bayonet with a long, narrow blade able to be used as a sword in close combat, especially one of, or patterned on, those originally used in the French army.

**sword|bear|er** (sôrd′bãr′ər, sōrd′-), *n.* the person by whom the sword of a great or noble warrior was cared for and carried when not in use.

**sword|bill** (sôrd′bil′, sōrd′-), *n.* a South American hummingbird with a slender bill longer than its body.

**sword-billed hummingbird** (sôrd′bild′, sōrd′-), = swordbill.

**sword cane,** a weapon resembling a light cane or walking stick, but having a hollow core within which is a steel blade that may be drawn out or snapped out by a spring.

**sword|craft** (sôrd′kraft′, -kräft′; sōrd′-), *n.* **1** the art of or skill in using the sword; swordsmanship. **2** military power.

**sword dance,** any one of various dances with swords, especially naked swords laid on the ground: *In Syria's Damascus the celebration was wilder. Bedouins whirled through the Arab sword dance* (Time).

**sword dancer,** a person who performs a sword dance.

**sword dollar,** a Scottish silver coin of the reign of James VI, with a sword on its reverse.

**sword|ed** (sôr′did, sōr′-), *adj.* armed with a sword.

**sword fern,** a tropical or subtropical fern with long, pinnate fronds.

**sword|fight** (sôrd′fīt′, sōrd′-), *n.* a combat or fight with swords: *where with single swordfight they ended their quarrel, by dying both* (James Hayward).

**sword|fish** (sôrd′fish′, sōrd′-), *n., pl.* **-fish|es** or (*collectively*) **-fish.** a very large saltwater food fish with a long, swordlike bone sticking out from its upper jaw.

**sword|fish|ing** (sôrd′fish′ing, sōrd′-), *n.* fishing for swordfish: *Swordfishing is the most popular way of spending the day* [*at Block Island*] (The Congregationalist).

**sword grass,** any one of various plants with sword-shaped leaves, such as the gladiolus and various grasses and sedges, and, sometimes, the iris.

**sword knot,** a looped strap, ribbon, or the like attached to the hilt of a sword, serving as a means of supporting it from the wrist or as an ornament.

**sword|less** (sôrd′lis, sōrd′-), *adj.* without a sword: *His hand fell upon his swordless belt* (William Morris).

**sword lily,** = gladiolus.

**sword|man** (sôrd′mən, sōrd′-), *n., pl.* **-men.** *Archaic.* a swordsman.

**sword** or **Sword of Damocles,** disaster that may occur at any moment (with allusion to the sword suspended by a single hair over the head of Damocles): *In old age we live under the shadow of Death, which, like a sword of Damocles may descend at any moment* (Samuel Butler).

**sword|play** (sôrd′plā′, sōrd′-), *n.* the action, practice, or art of wielding a sword; fencing: *The large Stratford company ... manage swordplay and panoplied pageantry with great facility* (Newsweek).

**sword|play|er** (sôrd′plā′ər, sōrd′-), *n.* a person skilled in swordplay; fencer.

**swords|man** (sôrdz′mən, sōrdz′-), *n., pl.* **-men.** **1** a person skilled in using a sword. **2** a person using a sword in sport; fencer. **3** a warrior; soldier.

**swords|man|ship** (sôrdz′mən ship, sōrdz′-), *n.* the act of a swordsman; skill in using a sword.

**sword|stick** (sôrd′stik′, sōrd′-), *n.* = sword cane.

**sword swallower,** a person who entertains by swallowing or pretending to swallow a sword: *He was traveling through the Balkans with a small circus, doubling as sword swallower and magician* (Time).

**sword|tail** (sôrd′tāl′, sōrd′-), *n.* any one of a group of small tropical American freshwater fishes, the male of which has a long sword-shaped tail, frequently kept in aquariums.

**sword-tailed** (sôrd′tāld′, sōrd′-), *adj.* having a long and sharp tail or tail fin, as the horseshoe crab and other sea animals.

**swore** (swôr, swōr), *v.* past tense of **swear**: *He swore to be a loyal American when he became a citizen.*

**sworn** (swôrn, swōrn), *v., adj.* — ***v.*** the past participle of **swear**: *A solemn oath of loyalty was sworn by all the knights.*
— ***adj.*** **1** having taken an oath; bound by an oath: *There were ten sworn witnesses.* **2** declared or promised with an oath: *We have his sworn statement.*

**swot**[1] (swot), *v.t.,* **swot|ted, swot|ting,** *n.* = swat[1].

**swot**[2] (swot), *v.,* **swot|ted, swot|ting,** *n. British Slang.* — ***v.i.*** to work hard at one's studies: *He has swotted at his books since the age of eleven* (New Yorker).
— ***v.t.*** Usually, **swot up.** to work hard at; study hard: *He really should swot up his history* (London Times).
— ***n.*** **1a** hard study at school or college: *For three years of sweat and swot I had imagined that my graduation day would be a solemn occasion* (Punch). **b** labor; toil. **2** a person who studies hard: *He mischievously incites ... the innocent swot* (Observer). Also, **swat.**
[apparently Scottish variant of *sweat*]

**swound** (swound), *v.i., n. Archaic.* swoon; faint. [Middle English *swoune* swoon; the *-d* is a later addition]

**'swounds** (zwoundz, zoundz), *interj. Archaic.* a shortened form of *God's wounds,* used as an oath.

**Swtz.,** Switzerland.

**swum** (swum), *v.* **1** a past participle of **swim**: *He had never swum before.* **2** *Archaic.* swam; a past tense of **swim.**

**swung** (swung), *v.* a past tense and past participle of **swing**[1]: *He swung his arms as he walked. The door had swung open.*

**swy** (swī), *n. Australian.* two-up. [alteration of German *zwei* two]

**sy-,** *prefix.* the form of **syn-** before *z* or before *s* plus a consonant, as in *syzygy, system.*

**S.Y.,** steam yacht.

**Syb|a|rite** (sib′ə rīt), *n.* an inhabitant of Sybaris, an ancient Greek city of southern Italy, proverbial for its luxury. [< Latin *Sybarīta* < Greek *Sybarītēs*]

**syb|a|rite** (sib′ə rīt), *n.* a person who cares very much for luxury and pleasure; voluptuary: *Once the luxurious guest house ... was a Mecca for starved sybarites from Baghdad* (London Times). [< *Sybarite*]

**syb|a|rit|ic** (sib′ə rit′ik), *adj.* characterized by or caring very much for luxury; luxurious; voluptuous: *Meanwhile, the Egyptians mercilessly attack Saudi Arabia's rulers as corrupt and sybaritic* (Time). — **syb′a|rit′i|cal|ly,** *adv.*

**Syb|a|rit|ic** (sib′ə rit′ik), *adj.* of or having to do with Sybaris or its inhabitants. — **Syb′a|rit′i|cal|ly,** *adv.*

**syb|a|rit|i|cal** or **Syb|a|rit|i|cal** (sib′ə rit′ə kəl), *adj.* = sybaritic or Sybaritic.

**syb|a|rit|ism** (sib′ə rī tiz′əm), *n.* sybaritic life, practices, or luxury.

**syc|a|mine** (sik′ə min, -mīn), *n. Archaic.* a kind of mulberry tree. [< Latin *sycamīnus* mulberry tree < Greek *sȳkámīnos* < Aramaic *shiqmin,* plural]

**syc|a|more** (sik′ə môr, -mōr), *n.* **1** a tall, North American shade tree with large leaves, small, round fruit, and bark that peels off in thin scales; buttonwood; plane tree. **2** Also, **sycamore maple.** a large maple tree of Europe and Asia, grown as a shady ornamental tree and for its wood. **3** a fig tree of Egypt and Syria with leaves somewhat resembling those of the mulberry. The sycamore is grown as a shade tree and bears a sweetish fruit that is good to eat. [Middle English *sycomour* a fig tree < Old French *sichamor* < Latin *sȳcomorus* < Greek *sȳkómoros* < *sȳkon* fig + *móron* mulberry]

**sycamore fig,** a fig tree of Egypt, Syria, and surrounding areas.

**sycamore maple,** a variety of maple of Europe and western Asia with leaves similar to those of a sycamore, and fine hard wood used especially in making furniture, violins, and carvings.

**syce** (sīs), *n. Anglo-Indian.* **1** a servant who attends to horses; groom. **2** an attendant who follows on foot a mounted horseman or a carriage. Also, **sais, sice.** [< Hindustani and Arabic *sā'is* servant; administrator < Arabic *sāsa* he managed]

**sy|cee** (sī sē′), *n.* fine uncoined silver in lumps of various sizes, usually stamped with a banker's or assayer's seal, formerly used in China as a medium of exchange. [< Cantonese *sai-si* fine silk (because, if pure, it may be drawn out into fine threads)]

**sycee silver,** = sycee.

**sych|no|car|pous** (sik′nə kär′pəs), *adj. Botany.* capable of bearing fruit many times without perishing, as a tree.
[< Greek *sychnós* many + *karpós* fruit + English *-ous*]

**sy|co|ni|um** (sī kō′nē əm), *n., pl.* **-ni|a** (-nē ə). *Botany.* a multiple fruit developed from numerous flowers embedded in a hollow fleshy receptacle, as in the fig. [< New Latin *syconium* < Greek *sȳkon* fig]

**syc|o|phan|cy** (sik′ə fən sē), *n., pl.* **-cies.** servile flattery; self-seeking flattery: *The people, like the despot, is pursued with adulation and sycophancy* (John Stuart Mill).

**syc|o|phant** (sik′ə fənt), *n., adj.* — ***n.*** a servile or self-seeking flatterer; parasite; toady; lickspittle. Great men are likely to be surrounded by sycophants who want favors. **SYN**: fawner.
— ***adj.*** = sycophantic.
[< Latin *sȳcophanta* < Greek *sȳkophántēs* informer, slanderer; probably (originally) one who makes the insulting gesture of the "fig," that is, sticking the thumb between index and middle finger < *sȳkon* fig + *phaínein* to show]

**Pronunciation Key:** hat, **ā**ge, c**ã**re, f**ä**r; let, **ē**qual, t**ė**rm; it, **ī**ce; hot, **ō**pen, **ô**rder; **oi**l, **ou**t; cup, p**u̇**t, r**ü**le; **ch**ild; lo**ng**; **th**in; **ᴛʜ**en; **zh**, measure; **ə** represents **a** in about, **e** in taken, **i** in pencil, **o** in lemon, **u** in circus.

**syc|o|phan|tic** (sik′ə fan′tik), *adj.* having to do with, characteristic of, or acting as a sycophant: *one man, surrounded by the constant incense of sycophantic adulation* (Wall Street Journal). **SYN**: parasitic. —**syc′o|phan′ti|cal|ly**, *adv.*

**syc|o|phan|ti|cal** (sik′ə fan′tə kəl), *adj.* = sycophantic.

**syc|o|phan|tish** (sik′ə fan′tish), *adj.* like a sycophant; sycophantic. —**syc′o|phan′tish|ly**, *adv.*

**syc|o|phant|ism** (sik′ə fən tiz′əm), *n.* = sycophancy.

**sy|co|sis** (sī kō′sis), *n.* an inflammatory disease of the hair follicles, especially of the beard, characterized by the eruption of crust-forming pimples; barber's itch. [earlier, an ulcer < New Latin *sycosis* < Greek *sýkōsis* < *sýkon* fig (because of its similar shape) + *-ōsis* -osis]

**Syd|en|ham's chorea** (sid′ən əmz, -hamz), the ordinary, mild form of chorea; St. Vitus's dance. [< Thomas *Sydenham,* 1624-1689, an English physician]

**Syd|ney|sid|er** (sid′nē sī′dər), *n.* a person born or living in Sydney, Australia.

**sy|e|nite** (sī′ə nīt), *n.* a crystalline, igneous rock composed of feldspar with certain other minerals, such as hornblende. Also, **sienite**. [< Latin *Syēnitēs* (*lapis*) (stone) from *Syēnē* (modern Aswan), a city in Egypt]

**sy|e|nit|ic** (sī′ə nit′ik), *adj.* **1** containing syenite. **2** like syenite, or possessing some of its properties.

**syke** (sīk), *n. Scottish.* sike.

**syl-**, *prefix.* form of **syn-** before *l,* as in *syllogism.*

**syl.** or **syll.**, syllable.

**syl|i** (sil′ē), *n., pl.* **syl|i** or **syl|is**. the unit of money of Guinea. Also, **sily**. [< a native name]

**syl|la|bar|i|um** (sil′ə bãr′ē əm), *n., pl.* **-i|a** (-ē ə). = syllabary.

**syl|la|bar|y** (sil′ə ber′ē), *n., pl.* **-bar|ies**. **1** a collection, set, system, list, or table of syllables, especially a list of symbols or characters each of which represents a syllable, used in writing certain languages. **2** a language using a syllabary. [< New Latin *syllabarium* < Latin *syllaba* syllable]

**syl|lab|ic** (sə lab′ik), *adj., n.* —*adj.* **1** of, having to do with, or made up of syllables. **2** forming a separate syllable by itself. The second *l* in *little* is syllabic. **3** pronounced syllable by syllable; uttered with distinct separation of syllables. **4** representing a syllable; consisting of signs representing syllables. **5** *Prosody.* denoting versification based on the number of syllables in a line rather than on the arrangement of accents or quantities: *English metre, according to many theorists, is neither syllabic nor quantitative, but simply accentual* (Times Literary Supplement).
—*n.* a syllabic speech sound. —**syl|lab′i|cal|ly**, *adv.*

**syl|lab|i|cate** (sə lab′ə kāt), *v.t.,* **-cat|ed, -cat|ing**. to form or divide into syllables; syllabify. [back formation < *syllabication*]

**syl|lab|i|ca|tion** (sə lab′ə kā′shən), *n.* division into syllables. [< Medieval Latin *syllabicatio, -onis,* ultimately < Latin *syllaba* syllable]

**syl|lab|i|fi|ca|tion** (sə lab′ə fə kā′shən), *n.* division into syllables.

**syl|lab|i|fy** (sə lab′ə fī), *v.t.,* **-fied, -fy|ing**. to divide into syllables.

**syl|la|bism** (sil′ə biz əm), *n.* **1** the use of syllabic characters. **2** a division into syllables. **3** syllabic verse.

**syl|la|bize** (sil′ə bīz), *v.t.,* **-bized, -biz|ing**. **1** to form or divide into syllables. **2** to utter with careful distinction of syllables.

**syl|la|ble** (sil′ə bəl), *n., v.,* **-bled, -bling**. —*n.* **1** a word or part of a word pronounced as a unit, usually consisting of a vowel alone or a vowel with one or more consonants. *A mer i can and Al a bam a* are words of four syllables. *Do, this,* and *stretch* are words of one syllable. Certain consonant sounds may be used as a vowel sound in syllables, such as the (l) in *bottle* (bot′l) or the (n) in *hidden* (hid′n). **2** one or more letters in a printed or written word that may be separated from other syllables of the word by a space, hyphen, or other mark to show where the word may be divided at the end of a line. *Strength* has only one syllable; *ap prox i mate* has four. **3** the slightest bit; word: *He promised not to breathe a syllable of the secret to anyone.*
—*v.t.* **1** to pronounce in syllables; utter distinctly; articulate: *Airy tongues, that syllable men's names On sands and shores and desert wildernesses* (Milton). **2** to represent by syllables.
—*v.i.* to utter syllables; speak.
[< Anglo-French *sillable,* variant of Old French *sillabe* < Latin *syllaba* < Greek *syllabḗ* (originally) a taking together < *syn-* together + *lab-,* stem of *lambánein* to take]

**-syllabled**, *combining form.* having _____ syllable or syllables: *One-syllabled = having one syllable.*

**syl|la|bub** (sil′ə bub), *n.* = sillabub.

**syl|la|bus** (sil′ə bəs), *n., pl.* **-bus|es, -bi** (-bī). **1** a brief statement of the main point, as of a speech, a book, or a course of study. **SYN**: abstract, synopsis. **2** *Law.* a brief summary, at the beginning of the report of a case, of the rulings of a court on the legal points involved. [< New Latin *syllabus* < Late Latin, misreading of Greek *sillybos* parchment label]

**syl|lep|sis** (sə lep′sis), *n., pl.* **-ses** (-sēz). *Grammar.* formal grammatical agreement with one word but not with another. *Example:* Neither he nor we are willing. [< Latin Latin *syllēpsis* < Greek *sýllēpsis* < *syn-* together + *lēpsis* a taking < *lambánein* to take]

**syl|lep|tic** (sə lep′tik), *adj.* of, having to do with, or containing syllepsis. —**syl|lep′ti|cal|ly**, *adv.*

**syl|lep|ti|cal** (sə lep′tə kəl), *adj.* = sylleptic.

**syl|lo|gism** (sil′ə jiz əm), *n.* **1** a form of argument or reasoning, consisting of two statements (the major premise and the minor premise) and a third statement (the conclusion) drawn necessarily from them. *Example:* All tree have roots; an oak is a tree; therefore, an oak has roots. **2** reasoning or argumentations in this form; deduction. **3** *Figurative.* a specious or very subtle argument; deviously crafty piece of reasoning. [< Latin *syllogismus* < Greek *syllogismós* (originally) inference, conclusion < *syllogízesthai* reckon up < *syn-* together + *logízesthai* to reckon, count < *lógos* a reckoning]

**syl|lo|gist** (sil′ə jist), *n.* a person who reasons by or is skilled in using syllogisms.

**syl|lo|gis|tic** (sil′ə jis′tik), *adj., n.* —*adj.* of, having to do with, of the nature of, or consisting of a syllogism or syllogisms; using syllogisms: *Dottie follows a logical, syllogistic construction; she is more of a technician and a scientist* (Time).
—*n.* syllogistic reasoning; branch of logic dealing with syllogisms. —**syl′lo|gis′ti|cal|ly**, *adv.*

**syl|lo|gis|ti|cal** (sil′ə jis′tə kəl), *adj.* = syllogistic.

**syl|lo|gis|tics** (sil′ə jis′tiks), *n.* = syllogistic.

**syl|lo|gi|za|tion** (sil′ə jə zā′shən), *n.* a reasoning by syllogisms.

**syl|lo|gize** (sil′ə jīz), *v.i., v.t.,* **-gized, -giz|ing**. **1** to argue or reason by syllogisms. **2** to deduce by syllogism: *those who, as Dante says, syllogize hateful truths* (James Russell Lowell). —**syl′lo|giz′er**, *n.*

**sylph** (silf), *n.* **1** a slender, graceful girl or woman. **2** an imaginary spirit of the air, typically slender and graceful. Sylphs were supposed by Paracelsus to exist as the inhabitants of the air, having mortality but lacking souls. [< New Latin *sylphes,* plural (coined by Paracelsus)] —**sylph′like′**, *adj.*

**sylph|id** (sil′fid), *n.* a little or young sylph. [< French *sylphide* < *sylphe* sylph < New Latin *sylphes* sylphs]

**sylph|id|ine** (sil′fə din, -dīn), *adj.* like a sylphid. [< *sylphid* + *-ine*[1]]

**syl|va** (sil′və), *n., pl.* **-vas, -vae** (-vē). = silva.

**syl|van** (sil′vən), *adj., n.* —*adj.* **1** of or in the woods; consisting of woods; having woods: *a sylvan scene, a sylvan glade, a sylvan region. They lived in a sylvan retreat.* **SYN**: woodsy. **2** rural; rustic.
—*n.* **1** a denizen of the woods; sylvan being. **2** a person living or working in a woodland region; forester. **3** = rustic. Also, **silvan**.
[< Latin *sylvānus,* variant of *silvānus* < *silva* forest, grove]

**Syl|van|er** (sil vä′nər), *n.* **1** an aromatic white wine made in the Rhine region and in California. **2** the grape from which this wine is made. [< German *Sylvaner* < Latin *sylvānus* sylvan]

**syl|van|ite** (sil′və nīt), *n.* a telluride of gold and silver, occurring in crystals or masses of gray, white, or yellow, with metallic luster. [< (*Tran*)*sylvania,* a region in Romania, where it is found + *-ite*[1]]

**syl|vat|ic** (sil vat′ik), *adj.* **1** of, belonging to, or found in woods; sylvan: *sylvatic animals, sylvatic trees.* **2** of, carried by, or transmitted by woodland or jungle animals or insects, such as rodents, monkeys, or mosquitoes: *Sylvatic plague is comparable to typhus,* [*and*] *relapsing fever ... which smolder silently and often unnoticed in their reservoir hosts, only flaring into epidemics when they come in contact with vectors that habitually or frequently bite human beings* (Asa C. Chandler). [< Latin *silvāticus* < *silva* forest]

**syl|ves|tral** (sil ves′trəl), *adj.* belonging to or growing in woods. [< Latin *sylvestris,* or *silvestris* + English *-al*[1]]

**syl|vics** (sil′viks), *n.* = silvics.

**syl|vi|cul|tur|al** (sil′və kul′chər əl), *adj.* = silvicultural.

**syl|vi|cul|ture** (sil′və kul′chər), *n.* = silviculture.

**syl|vi|cul|tur|ist** (sil′və kul′chər ist), *n.* = silviculturist.

**syl|vin** or **syl|vine** (sil′vin), *n.* = sylvite. [< French *sylvine* < New Latin *sal digestivus sylvii;* see etym. under **sylvite**]

**syl|vi|nite** (sil′və nīt), *n.* = sylvite.

**syl|vite** (sil′vīt), *n.* a mineral, potassium chloride, occurring in white or colorless cubes or octahedrons. It is an important source of potassium. *Formula:* KCl [abstracted < New Latin *sal digestivus sylvii* (literally) digestive salt of *Sylvius* (probably François de la Boe *Sylvius,* 1614-1672, a Flemish anatomist) + English *-ite*[1]]

**sym-**, *prefix.* the form of **syn-** before *b, m,* or *p,* as in *symbol, symmetry, sympathy.*

**sym.**, **1** symbol. **2** *Chemistry.* symmetrical. **3** symphony.

**Sym|bi|o|nese** (sim′bē ə nēz′, -nēs′), *adj. U.S.* of or belonging to a secret paramilitary group of terrorists formed in 1974: *the Symbionese Liberation Army.* [< Greek *symbiôn* living together (see etym. under **symbiont**) + English *-ese*]

**sym|bi|ont** (sim′bī ont, -bē-), *n. Biology.* an organism that lives in a state of symbiosis: *Instead of depending on its symbiont only for support, it also takes water and practically all of its food from it* (Fred W. Emerson). [< Greek *symbiôn, -ountos,* present participle of *symbioûn* live together; see etym. under **symbiosis**]

**sym|bi|on|tic** (sim′bī on′tik, -bē-), *adj.* of or having to do with a symbiont or symbionts.

**sym|bi|o|sis** (sim′bī ō′sis, -bē-), *n., pl.* **-ses** (-sēz). **1** *Biology.* **a** the association or living together of two unlike organisms for the benefit of each other. Symbiosis is the opposite of *parasitism,* in which one organism feeds on the body of the other. Most lichens, which are composed of an alga and a fungus, are examples of symbiosis; the alga provides the food, and the fungus provides water and protection. *Symbiosis covers those associations where neither is harmed, and one or both benefit* (David Park). **b** any association or living together of two unlike organisms, as in commensalism or parasitism. **2** *Figurative.* a mutually beneficial relationship: *Newsmen support the committees because the committees feed the newsmen: they live together in happy symbiosis* (Daniel J. Boorstin). [< New Latin *symbiosis* < Greek *symbíōsis* < *symbioûn* live together < *sýmbios* (one) living together (with another); partner < *syn-* together + *bios* life]

**sym|bi|ot|ic** (sim′bī ot′ik, -bē-), *adj.* having to do with symbiosis; living in symbiosis. —**sym′bi|ot′i|cal|ly**, *adv.*

**sym|bi|ot|i|cal** (sim′bī ot′ə kəl, -bē-), *adj.* = symbiotic.

***sym|bol** (sim′bəl), *n., v.,* **-boled, -bol|ing** or (*especially British*) **-bolled, -bol|ling**. —*n.* **1** something that stands for or represents something else, especially an idea, quality, or condition: *The lion is the symbol of courage; the lamb, of meekness; the olive branch, of peace; the cross, of Christianity ... Metaphysical myths ... the symbols of vital beliefs* (Jacques Maritain). *We are symbols and inhabit symbols* (Emerson). *All civilizations have been generated, and are perpetuated, only by the use of symbols* (Beals and Hoijer). *The V sign is the symbol of the unconquerable will of the occupied territories* (Sir Winston Churchill). **SYN**: token. See syn. under **emblem**. **2** a letter, figure, or sign conventionally standing for some object, process, or other thing, such as the figures denoting the signs of the zodiac, or the letters and other characters denoting chemical elements or mathematical quantities, operations, etc.: *The marks* +, ‖, ∎ *and* ∎ *are symbols for add, subtract, multiply, and divide. A symbol not only stands for the name of the element, but it also signifies one atom of that element* (Parks and Steinbach). **3** *Psychoanalysis.* an object, gesture, or action representing a repressed emotion or impulse: *We call ... the dream-element itself a symbol of the unconscious dream-thought* (Sigmund Freud).
—*v.t., v.i.* to represent by or use symbols; symbolize.
[< Latin *symbolum* < Greek *sýmbolon* token, mark, ticket < *syn-* together + *bállein* to throw]

***symbol** definition 1

peace symbol

peace emblem

**sym|bol|a|try** (sim bol′ə trē), *n., pl.* **-tries**. = symbololatry.

**sym|bo|le|og|ra|phy** or **sym|bo|lae|og|ra|phy** (sim′bə lē og′rə fē), *n.* the art of drawing up legal documents. [< Greek *symbolaiographíā* < *symbolaiográphos* notary < *symbólaion* a contract (< *syn-* together + *bállein* to throw) + *-graphíā* -graphy]

**sym|bol|ic** (sim bol′ik), *adj.* **1** used as a symbol: *A lily is symbolic of purity.* **SYN**: emblematic, representative. **2** of a symbol; expressed by a symbol or set of symbols; using symbols: *Writing is a* *symbolic form of expression. As far as we know, man is the only animal capable of symbolic behavior* (Beals and Hoijer). **3** consisting of, denoted by, or involving the use of written symbols: *Shorthand is a symbolic method of writing.* **4** (in art and literature) having the characteristics of symbolism. **5** *Semantics.* expressing a mere relation. — **sym|bol′i|cal|ly**, *adv.* — **sym|bol′i|cal-ness**, *n.*

**sym|bol|i|cal** (sim bol′ə kəl), *adj.* = symbolic.

**symbolical books**, those books containing the fundamental doctrines, creeds, and the like, of the several churches, such as the Augsburg Confession of the Lutherans.

**symbolic logic**, the most recently developed branch of formal logic, deriving from advanced mathematics, and utilizing the methods and symbols of mathematics as its principal tools of inquiry and definition; mathematical logic: *It is possible to translate this problem into the notation of symbolic logic and solve it by appropriate techniques* (Martin Gardner).

**sym|bol|ics** (sim bol′iks), *n.* the branch of theology that treats of the history and matter of Christian creeds and confessions of faith.

**sym|bol|ise** (sim′bə līz), *v.,* **-ised, -is|ing.** *Especially British.* symbolize.

**sym|bol|ism** (sim′bə liz əm), *n.* **1** the use of symbols; representation by symbols. **2** a system of symbols; organized set or pattern of symbols: *The cross, the crown, the lamb, and the lily are parts of Christian symbolism. Symbolisms developed in the church to add impressiveness to the setting and liturgy* (Matthew Luckiesh). **3** symbolic meaning or character: *Symbolism, then, is a second and independent factor in dream-distortion, existing side by side with the censorship* (Sigmund Freud). **4** (in literature or art) the principles or practice of a symbolist or the symbolists: *Their sculpture and architecture glow with color ... and full-dimensional symbolism* (Time).

**sym|bol|ist** (sim′bə list), *n., adj.* —*n.* **1** a person who uses symbols or symbolism. **2** any one of a school of French and Belgian poets (including Verlaine, Mallarmé, and Maeterlinck) of the late 1800's, who sought to represent ideas and emotions by indirect suggestion, attaching a symbolic meaning as to particular objects and words, in a reaction against realism: *The symbols of the symbolist school are usually chosen arbitrarily by the poet to stand for special ideas of his own* (Edmund Wilson). **3** a painter who aims at symbolizing ideas rather than representing the form or aspect of actual objects, especially one of a recent school of painters who use representations of objects and schemes of color to suggest ideas or states of mind. **4** a person who has experience in the study or interpretation of symbols or symbolism. **5a** a person who uses or advocates the use of symbolism in religious ceremonies. **b** a person who holds that the elements of the Eucharist are not transubstantiated but are mere symbols.
—*adj.* = symbolistic.

**Sym|bol|ist** (sim′bə list), *n.* **1** a symbolist poet or artist: *The outstanding characteristic of the Symbolist movement lay in the fact that it evoked, rather than described; reflected, rather than stated* (Atlantic). **2** a person who holds that the elements of the Eucharist are symbols.

**sym|bol|is|tic** (sim′bə lis′tik), *adj.* of or having to do with symbolism or symbolists. — **sym′bol|is′ti-cal|ly**, *adv.*

**sym|bol|i|za|tion** (sim′bə lə zā′shən), *n.* a representation by symbols; symbolizing: *The more intricate and variable is the situation we wish to describe the more dependent we become upon mathematical systems of symbolization* (George Simpson).

**sym|bol|ize** (sim′bə līz), *v.,* **-ized, -iz|ing.** —*v.t.* **1** to be a symbol of; stand for; represent: *A dove symbolizes peace.* **2** to represent by a symbol or symbols: *to symbolize a nation by its flag. The Indians and the settlers symbolized their friendship by smoking the peace pipe.* **3** to make into or treat as a symbol; regard as symbolic or emblematic.
—*v.i.* to use symbols: *Men symbolize, that is, bestow meanings upon physical phenomena, in almost every aspect of their daily lives* (Beals and Hoijer). — **sym′bol|iz′er**, *n.*

**sym|bo|log|i|cal** (sim bə loj′ə kəl), *adj.* of or having to do with symbology.

**sym|bol|o|gist** (sim bol′ə jist), *n.* a person who is versed in symbology; symbolist.

**sym|bol|o|gy** (sim bol′ə jē), *n.* **1** the science or study of symbols. **2** the use of symbols; symbolism: *one not unfamiliar with cartoon symbology* (Carl Rose). [< New Latin *symbologia* < Greek *sýmbolon* (see etym. under **symbol**) + New Latin *-logia* -logy]

**sym|bol|ol|a|try** (sim′bə lol′ə trē), *n., pl.* **-tries.** worship of or excessive reverence for symbols. [< *symbol* + *-latry,* as in *idolatry*]

**sym|bo|lo|pho|bi|a** (sim′bə lō fō′bē ə), *n.* an abnormal fear of having one's actions interpreted symbolically.

**sym|me|tal|lic** (sim′mə tal′ik), *adj.* of or having to do with symmetallism.

**sym|met|al|lism** or **sym|met|al|ism** (sim met′ə liz əm), *n.* a proposed monetary system in which the standard metal is a combination of two or more precious metals in a fixed proportion, usually a gold-silver alloy: *The arrangement that there should be a joint demand for gold and silver money might, perhaps be called symmetallism, to distinguish it from the arrangement that there should be a composite supply which is called bimetallism* (F. Y. Edgeworth).

**sym|met|ric** (si met′rik), *adj.* = symmetrical.

***sym|met|ri|cal** (si met′rə kəl), *adj.* **1** having symmetry; regular in form; well-proportioned: *symmetrical figures ... Symmetrical as an endless row of lead soldiers* (Newsweek). SYN: balanced. **2** *Botany.* **a** (of a flower) having the same number of parts (sepals, petals, stamens, and carpels) in each whorl; isomerous. **b** (of a flower). divisible vertically into similar halves either by one plane only (bilaterally symmetrical or zygomorphic) or by two or more planes (radially symmetrical or actinomorphic). **3** *Chemistry.* **a** having a structural formula characterized by symmetry. **b** denoting a derivative of benzene in which hydrogen atoms occupying positions one, three, and five have been replaced. **4** *Logic, Mathematics.* (of propositions, equations, and the like) so constituted that the value or truth is not changed by interchanging the terms. **5** *Medicine.* (of a disease) affecting corresponding organs or parts at the same time, as both arms or both lungs or both ears equally: *a symmetrical infection.* — **sym-met′ri|cal|ly**, *adv.* — **sym|met′ri|cal|ness**, *n.*

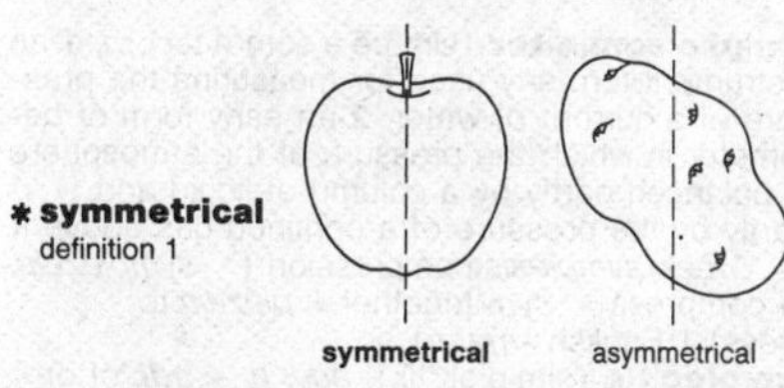


***symmetrical**
definition 1

**sym|me|trist** (sim′ə trist), *n.* a person who studies or favors symmetry.

**sym|me|trize** (sim′ə trīz), *v.t.,* **-trized, -triz|ing.** to make symmetrical; reduce to symmetry.
— **sym′me|tri|za′tion**, *n.*

**sym|me|try** (sim′ə trē), *n., pl.* **-tries.** **1** a regular, balanced form, or arrangement on opposite sides of a line or plane, or around a center or axis: *Its asymmetry was deliberate, for the Japanese believe that symmetry stunts the imagination* (Atlantic). **2** pleasing proportions between the parts of a whole; well-balanced arrangement of parts; harmony: *A swollen cheek spoiled the symmetry of his handsome face. In a scale passage ... you have symmetry of timing—whether the notes follow each other at even intervals or not* (Time). **3** *Botany.* agreement in number of parts among the cycles of organs that compose a flower. [< Latin *symmetria* < Greek *symmetriā* < *sýmmetros* symmetrical < *syn-* together + *métron* a measure]

**sym|pa|thec|to|my** (sim′pə thek′tə mē), *n., pl.* **-mies.** the surgical removal of a section of a sympathetic nerve: *A nerve-cutting operation called sympathectomy helps many with early cases of severe high blood pressure* (Science News Letter). [< *sympathe*(tic) + Greek *ektomḗ* a cutting out]

**sym|pa|thet|ic** (sim′pə thet′ik), *adj., n.* —*adj.* **1** having or showing kind feelings toward others; sympathizing: *She is an unselfish and sympathetic friend. ... an unusually tender and sympathetic audience* (Dickens); *a look of sympathetic concern* (Fanny Burney). SYN: compassionate, commiserating, tender. **2** approving; agreeing: *The teacher was sympathetic to the class's plan for a trip to the museum. When the third volume of Das Kapital came out, even economists sympathetic to Marx expressed disillusion and disappointment* (Edmund Wilson). **3** enjoying the same things and getting along well together. **4** harmonious; agreeable: *a sympathetic environment.* SYN: congenial. **5a** of or having to do with the sympathetic nervous system. **b** of or having to do with the entire autonomic nervous system. **6** *Physics.* **a** produced in one body by transmission of vibrations of the same frequency from another body: *sympathetic vibrations.* **b** produced by responsive vibrations induced in one body by transmission of vibrations of the same frequency through the air or other medium from another: *The phenomena of resonance are examples of sympathetic sound.*
—*n.* **1** a nerve of the sympathetic nervous system. **2** = sympathetic nervous system.

**sym|pa|thet|i|cal|ly** (sim′pə thet′ə klē), *adv.* in sympathetic manner; with kindness: *The doctor spoke sympathetically while he bandaged my leg. If one cannot be sure one knows enough to advise, it still is possible to listen ... sympathetically* (Harper's).

**sympathetic ink**, any one of certain colorless liquid compositions used as ink. The writing done remains invisible until the color is developed by the application of heat or some chemical reagent.

**sympathetic magic**, **1** = contagious magic. **2** magic based on the belief that similarity between actions and things makes them identical. An example of such magic is sticking pins into the image of an enemy to cause him pain or death.

**sympathetic nervous system**, the part of the autonomic nervous system that produces involuntary responses opposite to those produced by the parasympathetic nervous system, such as increasing the rate of the heartbeat and slowing down the activity of glands and digestive and reproductive organs. It consists of two groups of ganglia connected by nerve cords, one on either side of the spinal column.

**sympathetic ophthalmia**, inflammation in one eye due to lesion or other injury to the other eye: *Eye wounds are particularly dangerous because of "sympathetic ophthalmia," a complication in the good eye that usually results in complete blindness, unless the injured eye is removed at once* (New York Times).

**sympathetic strike**, = sympathy strike.

**sympathetic string**, any one of the strings of certain musical instruments, such as the sitar and the baryton, that are not played upon but reinforce the sound by sympathetic vibrations.

**sym|pa|thin** (sim′pə thin), *n.* a substance released at the endings of the sympathetic nerves that has an effect on the body similar to that produced by epinephrine.

**sym|pa|thique** (saN pȧ tēk′), *adj. French.* likable and pleasant; agreeable; congenial: *He looked smaller somehow than he had been on my last visit, and for that reason, perhaps, more sympathique* (Atlantic).

**sym|pa|thise** (sim′pə thīz), *v.i.,* **-thised, -this|ing.** *Especially British.* sympathize.

**sym|pa|thize** (sim′pə thīz), *v.i.,* **-thized, -thiz|ing.** **1** to feel or show sympathy: *The girl sympathized with her little brother who had hurt himself.* SYN: condole, commiserate. **2** to share in or agree with a feeling or opinion: *My mother sympathizes with my plan to be a doctor.* **3** to enjoy the same things and get along well together. **4** to respond sympathetically to some influence or to some disorder of the body. [< French *sympathiser* < *sympathie* sympathy, learned borrowing from Latin *sympathīa;* see etym. under **sympathy**] — **sym′-pa|thiz′ing|ly**, *adv.*

**sym|pa|thiz|er** (sim′pə thī′zər), *n.* a person who sympathizes with another; person who is favorably inclined toward a particular belief or person; person who feels sympathy: *The issue of whether he was a "sympathizer," a "promoter" or a "follower" of communism involved forbidden inquiry into a man's beliefs* (New York Times).

**sym|pa|tho|lyt|ic** (sim′pə thō lit′ik), *adj., n.* —*adj.* that opposes the effects of stimulation of the sympathetic nervous system.
—*n.* a sympatholytic drug or chemical.

**sym|pa|tho|mi|met|ic** (sim′pə thō′mi met′ik, -mī-), *adj., n.* —*adj.* that imitates or mimics the action of the sympathetic nervous system: *The medical profession is using drugs called "sympathomimetic amines" to treat depression* (Wall Street Journal).
—*n.* a sympathomimetic drug or chemical.

**sym|pa|thy** (sim′pə thē), *n., pl.* **-thies.** **1** a sharing of another's sorrow or trouble: *We feel sympathy for a person who is ill. Sympathy ... enables one to put himself in the place of his fellows and to understand them* (Emory S. Bogardus). *The dedicated doctor knows that sympathy and understanding are just as important as scientific knowledge* (New York Times). SYN: compassion, commiseration. See syn. under **pity**. **2** the condition or fact of having the same feeling; agreement in feeling: *The sympathy between the twins was so great that they smiled or cried at the same things.* SYN: harmony, affinity. **3** agreement; favor; approval: *He is in sympathy with my plan.* **4a** an affinity between certain things, whereby

**Pronunciation Key:** hat, āge, cãre, fär; let, ēqual, tėrm; it, īce; hot, ōpen, ôrder; oil, out; cup, pu̇t, rüle; child; long; thin; ᴛʜen; zh, measure; ə represents **a** in about, **e** in taken, **i** in pencil, **o** in lemon, **u** in circus.

they are similar or correspondingly affected by the same influence. **b** an action or response induced by such a relationship.
**c** *Physiology.* a relation between parts or organs such that a disorder or any condition in one produces an effect, often a similar one, on the other. **d** *Physics.* a relation between two vibratile bodies such that when one is thrown into vibration it transmits its vibration to the other through air or some other medium. [< Latin *sympathīa* < Greek *sympátheia,* or *sympathês* having a fellow feeling < *syn-* together + *páthos* a feeling]

**sympathy strike,** a strike by workers, not to enforce demands on their own employer, but to help or give moral support to workers on strike against another employer or other employers.

**sym|pat|ric** (sim pat′rik), *adj.* of or having to do with sympatry; existing in the same region without interbreeding: *sympatric species.* —**sym|pat′ri|cal|ly,** *adv.*

**sym|pa|try** (sim′pə trē), *n.* the existence of plant or animal species in the same area without hybridization through interbreeding. [< Greek *syn-* together + *pátrā* fatherland, native country + English *-y*[3]]

**sym|pel|mous** (sim pel′məs), *adj.* (of birds) having the two deep flexor tendons of the toes blended into one before dividing to proceed to the digits. Also, **synpelmous.** [< *sym-* + Greek *pélma* sole of the foot + English *-ous*]

**sym|pet|al|ous** (sim pet′ə ləs), *adj. Botany.* gamopetalous. Also, **synpetalous.**

**sym|phi|lism** (sim′fə liz əm), *n.* = symphily.

**sym|phi|lous** (sim′fə ləs), *adj.* of or having to do with symphily.

**sym|phi|ly** (sim′fə lē), *n.* the occurrence in ant or termite colonies of guest insects which establish a mutually beneficial relation with their hosts; friendly commensalism. [< Greek *symphilía* mutual friendship < *syn-* + *philía* friendship]

**sym|pho|nette** (sim′fə net′), *n.* **1** an orchestra similar to a symphony orchestra but having fewer members and playing less elaborate compositions. **2** a musical composition similar to a symphony but shorter and usually less elaborate: *Morton Gould's Latin-American symphonette is in keeping with the festive mood of the rest of the record* (Atlantic).

**sym|phon|ic** (sim fon′ik), *adj.* **1** of, having to do with, or like a symphony: *symphonic music. Massine, using it frankly as theatre music, made it into a setting for a "symphonic" ballet* (Winthrop Sargeant). **2** of or having to do with symphony or harmony of sounds; similar in sound: *Nature's symphonic world drowned by man's industrial cacophony.* —**sym|phon′i|cal|ly,** *adv.*

**symphonic poem,** an orchestral composition similar in character and dimensions to a symphony but freer in form and usually consisting of only one movement; tone poem. It is a musical description of some story, series of images, or program, poetic in nature, upon which its form depends, often employing leitmotifs to represent each character or sentiment.

**sym|pho|ni|ous** (sim fō′nē əs), *adj.* = harmonious. —**sym|pho′ni|ous|ly,** *adv.*

**sym|pho|nist** (sim′fə nist), *n.* a composer of symphonies: *The European symphonists have their American counterparts in Harris, Piston and William Schuman* (New York Times).

**sym|pho|nize** (sim′fə nīz), *v.i.,* **-nized, -niz|ing.** to agree; harmonize.

**sym|pho|ny** (sim′fə nē), *n., pl.* **-nies. 1a** an elaborate musical composition for an orchestra. It usually has four movements in different rhythms but related keys. **b** an instrumental passage in a vocal composition or between movements in an oratorio. **c** = (formerly) sinfonia (def. 2). **2** = symphony orchestra: *the Chicago Symphony.* **3** harmony of sounds. **SYN:** concord, consonance. **4** *Figurative.* harmony of colors: *In autumn the woods are a symphony in red, brown, and yellow.* **5** *Figurative.* anything having a harmonious combination of elements: *What I had experienced was a symphony of the wilderness* (William O. Douglas). [Middle English *symphanye* any of various instruments; harmony < Latin *symphōnia* < Greek *symphōníā* harmony; a concert; orchestra < *sýmphōnos* harmonious < *syn-* together + *phōnê* voice, sound]

**symphony orchestra,** a large orchestra for playing symphonic works, made up of brass, woodwind, percussion, and stringed instruments: *These selections are all thrilling brand-new performances played by world-famous symphony orchestras* (Time).

**sym|phy|lid** (sim′fə lid), *n.* any one of a group of very small centipedes with 12 pairs of legs and a pair of long antennae, that includes the garden centipede. [< New Latin *Symphyla* the class name < Greek *syn-* together + *phȳlê* tribe, clan]

**sym|phys|i|al** or **sym|phys|e|al** (sim fiz′ē əl), *adj.* of, having to do with, situated at, or forming a symphysis.

***sym|phy|sis** (sim′fə sis), *n., pl.* **-ses** (-sēz). **1** *Anatomy.* **a** the union of two bones originally separate, either by the fusion of the bony substance or by intervening cartilage, especially of two similar bones on opposite sides of the body in the median line, as that of the pubic bones or of the two halves of the lower jawbone. **b** the part or line of junction thus formed. **c** an articulation in which bones are united by cartilage without a synovial membrane. **d** a union or line of junction or other parts either originally or normally separate. **2** *Botany.* a fusion or coalescence of parts of a plant normally distinct. [< Greek *sýmphysis* a natural growing together or articulation (especially, of bones) < *symphýein* to unite < *syn-* together + *phýein* grow]

***symphysis**
definition 1b

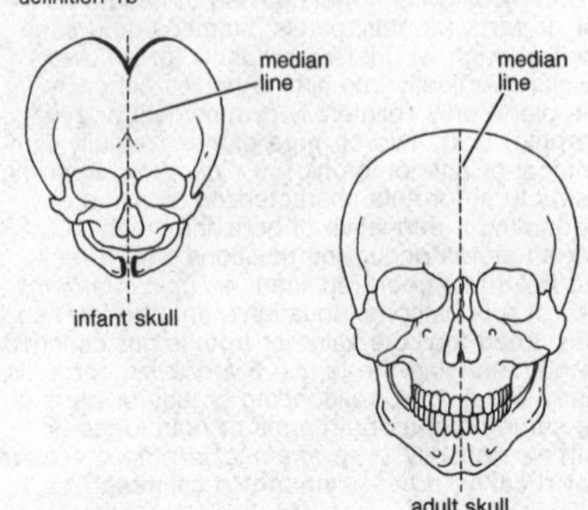


**sym|pi|e|som|e|ter** (sim′pē ə som′ə tər), *n.* **1** an instrument formerly used for measuring the pressure of a current of water. **2** an early form of barometer in which the pressure of the atmosphere is balanced partly by a column of liquid and partly by the pressure of a confined gas above it. [< Greek *sympíesis* compression (< *sympiézein* to compress < *syn-* together + *piézein* to press) + English *-meter*]

**sym|plec|tic** (sim plek′tik), *adj., n.* —*adj.* of or having to do with a bone of the lower jaw of fishes that unites certain other bones. —*n.* the symplectic bone. [< Greek *symplektikós* twining together < *symplékein* to twine together < *syn-* together + *plékein* to twine, weave]

**sym|po|di|al** (sim pō′dē əl), *adj.* having to do with, of the nature of, or producing a sympodium. See picture under **branch.** —**sym|po′di|al|ly,** *adv.*

**sym|po|di|um** (sim pō′dē əm), *n., pl.* **-di|a** (-dē ə). *Botany.* an axis or stem that imitates a simple stem, but is made up of the bases of a number of axes that arise successively as branches one from another, as in the grapevine. [< New Latin *sympodium* < *syn-* syn- + Greek *poús, podós* foot]

**sym|po|si|ac** (sim pō′zē ak), *adj., n.* —*adj.* of, suitable for, or like a symposium.
—*n.* **1** a symposiac meeting, or the conversation at it. **2** an account of such a meeting or conversation.
[< Late Latin *symposiacus* < Greek *symposiakós* < *sympósion;* see etym. under **symposium**]

**sym|po|si|al** (sim pō′zē əl), *adj.* **1** of or having to do with a symposium. **2** *Music.* having to do with or consisting of a group of variations on a given theme, each written by a different composer: *a symposial quartet.*

**sym|po|si|arch** (sim pō′zē ärk), *n.* **1** the master or director of an ancient symposium. **2** = toastmaster. [< Greek *symposiarchos* < *sympósion* (see etym. under **symposium**) + *árchein* to rule]

**sym|po|si|ast** (sim pō′zē ast), *n.* a person who takes part in a symposium or social affair. [< *symposi*(um) + *-ast,* as in *enthusiast*]

**sym|po|si|as|tic** (sim pō′zē as′tik), *adj.* = symposiac.

**sym|po|si|um** (sim pō′zē əm), *n., pl.* **-si|ums, -si|a** (-zē ə). **1** a meeting or conference for the discussion of some subject: *Our school will hold a symposium on science during Science Week. Our next problem ... is setting up seminars and symposia to digest all the data* (Newsweek). **2** a collection of the opinions of several persons on some subject: *This magazine contains a symposium on sports.* **3a** a convivial meeting for drinking, conversation, and intellectual entertainment among the ancient Greeks. **b** any convivial meeting, dinner, or other gathering, considered as resembling this. [< Latin *symposium* < Greek *sympósion* < *syn-* together + *pósis* a drinking < *pīnein* to drink]

**symp|tom** (simp′təm), *n.* **1** a sign or indication: *Quaking knees and paleness are symptoms of fear.* **SYN:** token, mark. **2** a noticeable change in the normal working of the body that indicates or accompanies disease, sickness, or other malfunction: *Fever is a symptom of illness. The doctor made his diagnosis after studying the patient's symptoms.* [< Late Latin *symptōma, -atis* < Greek *sýmptōma, -atos* a happening, accident, disease < *sympíptein* to befall < *syn-* together + *píptein* to fall]

**symp|to|mat|ic** (simp′tə mat′ik), *adj.* **1** being a sign; signifying; indicative: *Headaches may be symptomatic of eyestrain. Riots are symptomatic of political or social unrest. The present tendency of scientists to emphasize uncertainty is symptomatic of the times* (Bulletin of Atomic Scientists). **2a** indicating or accompanying a disease or other malfunction: *The infection caused a symptomatic fever. Headaches are sometimes symptomatic.* **b** of or having to do with symptoms of disease or other malfunction: *symptomatic treatment.* —**symp′to|mat′i|cal|ly,** *adv.*

**symp|to|mat|i|cal** (simp′tə mat′ə kəl), *adj. Obsolete.* symptomatic.

**symp|to|mat|o|log|i|cal** (simp′tə mat′ə loj′ə kəl), *adj.* of or having to do with symptomatology. —**symp′to|mat′o|log′i|cal|ly,** *adv.*

**symp|tom|a|tol|o|gy** (simp′tə mə tol′ə jē), *n.* the branch of medicine dealing with symptoms; semeiology. [< New Latin *symptomatologia* < Greek *sýmptōma, -atos* (see etym. under **symptom**) + *-logīā* -logy]

**symptom complex,** = symptom group.

**symptom group,** a group of symptoms frequently occurring together, and constituting a syndrome.

**symp|tom|ize** (simp′tə mīz), *v.t.,* **-ized, -iz|ing. 1** to be a symptom of: *The condition ... could also symptomize other ailments, such as kidney block* (New York Times). **2** to characterize or indicate as a symptom: *Demoniacal possession ... was symptomized by superhuman manifestations* (James Tait).

**symp|tom|less** (simp′təm lis), *adj.* **1** without symptoms. **2** not attended with the usual symptoms, as a disease: *A symptomless attack* [*of polio*] *early in life confers lifetime immunity* (New York Times).

**symp|tom|ol|o|gy** (simp′tə mol′ə jē), *n.* = symptomatology.

**syn-,** *prefix.* with; together; jointly; at the same time; alike, as in *synagogue, synchronous, syndrome, synonym, synthesis, synecology.* Also: **sy-** before *z* and before *s* plus a consonant; **syl-** before *l;* **sym-** before *b, m,* or *p.* [< Greek *sýn* together, with]

**syn.,** **1** synonym. **2** synonymous. **3** synonymy.

**syn|ac|tic** (si nak′tik), *adj.* working together; cooperating; synergetic. [< Greek *synaktikós* able to bring together < *synágein;* see etym. under **synagogue**]

**syn|aer|e|sis** (si ner′ə sis), *n.* **1** contraction, especially of two vowels, into a diphthong or simple vowel. **2** *Chemistry.* the loss of liquid and resulting contraction of a gel or clot. **3** *Grammar, Prosody.* synizesis (def. 1). Also, **syneresis.** [< Greek *synaíresis* (literally) contraction, drawing together < *synaireîn* to contract, take as one < *syn-* together + *haireîn* to take]

**syn|aes|the|sia** (sin′es thē′zhə), *n.* = synesthesia.

**syn|aes|thet|ic** (sin′es thet′ik), *adj.* = synesthetic. —**syn′aes|thet′i|cal|ly,** *adv.*

**syn|a|gog** (sin′ə gôg, -gog), *n.* = synagogue.

**syn|a|gog|al** (sin′ə gôg′əl, -gog′-), *adj.* = synagogical.

**syn|a|gog|i|cal** (sin′ə goj′ə kəl), *adj.* of or having to do with a synagogue.

**syn|a|gogue** (sin′ə gôg, -gog), *n.* **1** a building or place used by Jews for worship and religious instruction; temple. **2** an assembly of Jews for religious instruction and worship constituting, since the destruction of the Temple (A.D. 70), the sole form of Jewish public worship; Jewish congregation. **3** the Jewish religion. [< Latin *synagōga* < Greek *synagōgê* (literally) assembly < *synágein* to assemble < *syn-* together + *ágein* bring]

**syn|a|loe|pha** or **syn|a|le|pha** (sin′ə lē′fə), *n.* the contraction or coalescence of two syllables into one, especially of two vowels at the end of one word and the beginning of the next. [< Latin *synaloepha* < Greek *synaloiphḗ,* variant of *synaliphḗ* a coalescing < *synaleíphein* coalesce, gloss over; (literally) smear or melt together < *syn-* together + *aleíphein* anoint]

**syn|a|loe|phe** or **syn|a|le|phe** (sin′ə lē′fē), *n.* = synaloepha.

**Syn|a|non** (sin′ə non), *n.* a private association of former drug addicts organized for mutual help and rehabilitation. [< *syn-* together + *anon*(ymous)]

**syn|an|ther|ous** (si nan′thər əs), *adj. Botany.* characterized by stamens that are coalescent by means of their anthers, as a composite plant. [< *syn-* + *anther* + *-ous*]

**syn|an|thous** (si nan′thəs), *adj. Botany.* **1** characterized by the abnormal union of two or more flowers. **2** having flowers and leaves that appear at the same time. [< *syn-* + Greek *ánthos* flower + English *-ous*]

**syn|an|thy** (si nan′thē), *n. Botany.* the abnormal union of two or more flowers. [< *syn-* + Greek *ánthos* flower + English *-y*³]

**syn|apse** (si naps′, sin′aps), *n., v.,* **-apsed, -aps·ing.** —*n.* the place where a nerve impulse passes from one nerve cell to another. A synapse is between the axon of one nerve cell and the dendrite of the other. *Changes at the synapse are thought to be involved in the learning process* (S. A. Barnett). See diagram at **neuron.** —*v.i.* to form a synapse: *An inhibitory neuron acts to inhibit all cells with which any of its terminals synapse* (Scientific American).
[< Greek *sýnapsis* conjunction < *synáptein* to clasp < *syn-* together + *háptein* to fasten]

**syn|ap|sis** (si nap′sis), *n., pl.* **-ses** (-sēz). **1** *Biology.* the union of paternal and maternal paired chromosomes, the first step in meiosis; syndesis. **2** *Physiology.* synapse. [< New Latin *synapsis* < Greek *sýnapsis;* see etym. under **synapse**]

**syn|ap|te** (si nap′tē), *n., pl.* **-tai** (-tī). a litany in the Greek Orthodox Church. [< Greek *synaptḗ,* feminine of *synaptós* joined together < *synáptein* to clasp, join together; see etym. under **synapse**]

**syn|ap|tic** (si nap′tik), *adj.* having to do with a synapsis or a synapse: *Any one neuron may have as many as a thousand synaptic connexions* (Science News). —**syn|ap′ti|cal|ly,** *adv.*

**syn|ap|tol|o|gy** (sin′ap tol′ə jē), *n.* the study of synapses.

**syn|ar|chy** (sin′är kē), *n., pl.* **-chies.** joint rule or sovereignty. [< Greek *synarchíā* < *synárchein* to rule jointly with < *syn-* together + *árchein* to rule]

**syn|ar|thro|di|a** (sin′är thrō′dē ə), *n., pl.* **-di|ae** (-dē ē). = synarthrosis. [< New Latin *synarthrodia* < Greek *syn-* together + *arthrōdíā* kind of jointing with slightly concave or convex surfaces < *árthron* a joint]

**syn|ar|thro|di|al** (sin′är thrō′dē əl), *adj. Anatomy.* having to do with or of the nature of a synarthrosis. —**syn′ar|thro′di|al|ly,** *adv.*

**syn|ar|thro|sis** (sin′är thrō′sis), *n., pl.* **-ses** (-sēz). *Anatomy.* a kind of articulation admitting of no movement, as in the sockets of the teeth. [< New Latin *synarthrosis* < Greek *synárthrōsis* immovable articulation < *syn-* together, completely + *árthrōsis* a jointing < *árthron* joint]

**syn|ax|is** (si nak′sis), *n., pl.* **syn|ax|es** (si nak′sēz). in the early Church, an assembly for public worship, especially for the Eucharist. [< Late Latin *synaxis* < Late Greek *sýnaxis* a gathering < *synágein* to bring together < *syn-* together + *ágein* to drive, lead]

**sync** (singk), *n., v. Informal.* —*n.* synchronization of sound and action or of speech and lip movement, as in a television or motion picture.
—*v.i., v.t.* to synchronize. Also, **synch.**
**in sync,** synchronized: *When you line up the three ... then you're in sync* (Harper's).
**out of sync,** not synchronized: *You're coming in weak and out of sync* (Charles Fowler).

**syn|carp** (sin′kärp), *n. Botany.* **1** an aggregate fruit. **2** a multiple fruit. [< New Latin *syncarpium* < Greek *syn-* together + *karpós* fruit]

**syn|car|pous** (sin kär′pəs), *adj. Botany.* **1** of or having the character of a syncarp. **2** consisting of united or coherent carpels.

**syn|car|py** (sin′kär pē), *n. Botany.* **1** the state of having united carpels. **2** the abnormal union or fusion of two or more fruits.

**syn|cat|e|gor|e|mat|ic** (sin kat′ə gôr′ə mat′ik, -gōr′-), *adj. Logic.* (of a word) that cannot be used by itself as a term, but must be connected with another word or words, as *all, some,* or *it.*

**syn|cer|e|bral** (sin ser′ə brəl, -sə rē′brəl), *adj.* of, having to do with, or constituting a syncerebrum.

**syn|cer|e|brum** (sin ser′ə brəm), *n., pl.* **-brums, -bra** (-brə). the compound brain of an insect. [< New Latin *syncerebrum* < *syn-* + Latin *cerebrum* brain]

**synch** (singk), *n.* = sync.

**syn|chon|dro|si|al** (sing′kon drō′sē əl), *adj.* of or having to do with synchondrosis.

**syn|chon|dro|sis** (sing′kon drō′sis), *n., pl.* **-ses** (-sēz). *Anatomy.* **1** an articulation in which the bones are so fused by intervening cartilage that the joint has little or no motion. **2** symphysis. [< New Latin *synchondrosis* < *syn-* together + Greek *chóndros* lump, cartilage + New Latin *-osis* -osis]

**syn|chro** (sing′krō), *n., pl.* **-chros,** *adj.* —*n.* **1** = synchro unit. **2** flash synchronization.
—*adj.* working by or using synchronization: *a synchro mechanism, generator, or motor.*
[short for *synchronization*]

**syn|chro-cy|clo|tron** or **syn|chro|cy|clo|tron** (sing′krō sī′klə tron, -sik′lə-), *n.* a cyclotron that accelerates charged particles by changing the frequency of the alternating electric field so that it synchronizes with the particles: *A ... synchrocyclotron discovered that high-energy proton beams are strongly polarized after being scattered from a hydrogen target* (Scientific American).

**syn|chro|flash** (sing′krə flash′), *adj. Photography.* that synchronizes the flashbulb circuit with the shutter of a camera.

**syn|chro|mesh** (sing′krə mesh), *n., adj.* —*n.* a system of gears in an automobile transmission synchronized to mesh without shock or grinding when the driver shifts from one gear to another: *There is no synchromesh on first gear, but it is hardly ever necessary to change to that gear* (London Times).
—*adj.* **1** having synchromesh: *a synchromesh transmission.* **2** of, having to do with, or utilizing synchromesh transmission: *synchromesh action or shifting.*

**syn|chro|nal** (sing′krə nəl), *adj.* = synchronous.

**syn|chro|ne|i|ty** (sing′krə nē′ə tē), *n.* = synchronism.

**syn|chron|ic** (sin kron′ik, sing-), *adj.* **1** dealing with a subject or event only as it occurs at a given stage, without reference to anything but its own characteristics: *A man may surely make a rational and satisfying synchronic or descriptive study of a language now or for any time in the past, but, if that study is to remain one hundred per cent synchronic, he must at no point ask or state the reason why, for that will ineluctably bring in diachronic or historical factors* (Simeon Potter). **2** = synchronous. —**syn|chron′i|cal|ly,** *adv.*

**syn|chron|i|cal** (sin kron′ə kəl, sing-), *adj.* = synchronic.

**syn|chro|nic|i|ty** (sing′krə nis′ə tē), *n., pl.* **-ties.** = synchronism.

**syn|chro|nise** (sing′krə nīz), *v.,* **-nised, -nis|ing.** *Especially British.* synchronize.

**syn|chro|nism** (sing′krə niz əm), *n.* **1** occurrence at the same time; agreement in time: *Human thought ... is a complex of relationships that must come out of the knowledge of certain specific facts and synchronisms* (Atlantic). **2** the arrangement of historical events or persons according to their dates, as in a history: *The laws of synchronism ... bring strange partners together, and we may pass at once from Luther to Ariosto* (Henry Hallam). **3** *Physics.* the condition of being synchronous.

**syn|chro|nis|tic** (sing′krə nis′tik), *adj.* having to do with or exhibiting synchronism; synchronous; simultaneous.

**syn|chro|nis|ti|cal** (sing′krə nis′tə kəl), *adj.* = synchronistic.

**syn|chro|ni|za|tion** (sing′krə nə zā′shən), *n.* **1** the act or process of synchronizing (used especially of clocks). **2** the occurrence of events at the same time.

**syn|chro|nize** (sing′krə nīz), *v.,* **-nized, -niz|ing.** —*v.i.* **1** to occur at the same time; agree in time. SYN: coincide. **2** to move or take place at the same rate and exactly together.
—*v.t.* **1** to make agree in time; cause to go at the same rate: *to synchronize all the clocks in a building.* **2** to assign to the same time or period. **3a** to make (dialogue and other sounds) coincide with the action in the preparation of a motion picture. **b** to make sound and action coincide in (a sound motion picture): *A synchronized picture differs from a true talkie in that the scenes are first taken silent and then accompaniment is added* (B. Brown).
[< Greek *synchronízein* < *sýnchronos;* see etym. under **synchronous**] —**syn′chro|niz′er,** *n.*

**syn|chro|nized shifting** (sing′krə nīzd), a shifting of gears in a motor vehicle that includes a device that brings both of any pair of gears to the same speed just before meshing; synchromesh shifting.

**synchronized swimming,** = water ballet.

**syn|chron|o|scope** (sin kron′ə skōp), *n. Electricity.* an instrument for determining the synchronism between two alternating-current machines.

**syn|chro|nous** (sing′krə nəs), *adj.* **1** occurring at the same time; simultaneous. SYN: coincident, contemporaneous. **2** going on at the same rate and exactly together: *the synchronous movements of the two ballet dancers.* **3** *Physics.* having coincident frequency, as an alternating electric current: *a synchronous compensator for an open-air hydrogen-cooling installation in Italy* (New Yorker). **4** operating at a speed exactly proportional to the frequency of the applied current: *a synchronous motor.* **5** *Aerospace.* **a** orbiting at the same rate as the earth rotates; geostationary: *a synchronous communications satellite.* **b** synchronized with the speed of the earth's rotation: *a synchronous orbit.* **c** of or having to do with a synchronous satellite or orbit: *a synchronous altitude of 36,000 kilometers, a synchronous course.*
[< Late Latin *synchronus* (with English *-ous*) < Greek *sýnchronos* < *syn-* together + *chrónos* time] —**syn′chro|nous|ly,** *adv.* —**syn′chro|nous·ness,** *n.*

**synchronous converter,** *Electricity.* a synchronous machine for changing alternating current into direct current, or direct current into alternating current; rotary.

**synchronous machine,** *Electricity.* a dynamo-electric machine, either a generator, motor, or converter, that operates at a speed exactly proportional to the frequency of the current.

**synchronous satellite,** an artificial satellite whose orbit is synchronous with the rotation of the earth on its axis. It orbits the earth once every 24 hours at a fixed altitude above the equator, and thus appears to be stationary; geostationary satellite.

**synchronous speed,** *Electricity.* a speed, proportional to the frequency of the supply current, at which an alternating-current machine must operate to produce an electromotive force at a specified frequency.

**syn|chro|ny** (sing′krə nē), *n.* coincidence in time; synchronism.

**syn|chrop|ter** (sing′krop tər), *n.* a helicopter having twin synchronized rotors with intermeshing blades. [< *synchro*(nized rotor) + (helico)*pter*]

**syn|chro|scope** (sing′krə skōp), *n. Electricity.* an electromagnetic device for indicating the synchronism between two alternating-current machines, or two or more engines, as in aircraft. [< *synchro*(nism) + *-scope*]

**syn|chro|tron** (sing′krə tron), *n.* a particle accelerator that accelerates atomic particles to extremely high speed by increasing the magnetic field and changing the frequency of the electric field: *Synchrotrons accelerate particles by spinning them around a circular path* (Science News Letter). [< *synchro*(nous) + *-tron*]

**synchrotron radiation,** a form of electromagnetic radiation produced by the spiraling motion of high-speed electrons around a magnetic field, as in a synchrotron or in some galactic nebulae.

**synchro unit,** *Electricity.* an alternating-current motor for maintaining the rotational angle possessed by the electrically connected rotating element of a similar motor.

**syn|clas|tic** (sin klas′tik), *adj. Mathematics, Physics.* of or having to do with a surface, as that of a ball or egg, which is curved similarly (either convexly or concavely) in all directions. [< *syn-* alike + Greek *klastós* broken, taken as "bent" (< *klân* to break) + English *-ic*]

**syn|cli|nal** (sin klī′nəl, sing′klə-), *adj., n. Geology.* —*adj.* **1a** sloping downward from opposite directions so as to form a trough or inverted arch. **b** of or having to do with a syncline. **2** inclined or sloping toward each other, or characterized by such inclination. —*n.* = syncline.
[< Greek *synklīnḗs* inclining together (< *synklī́nein* to lean, incline < *syn-* together + *klī́nein* to lean) + English *-al*¹]

**synclinal axis,** *Geology.* the axis toward which the slopes of a syncline converge.

**synclinal line,** *Geology.* the line from which a syncline slopes.

**syn|cline** (sing′klīn), *n. Geology.* a fold or folds of rock strata sloping downward from opposite directions so as to form a trough or inverted arch. See picture under **fold**¹.

**syn|cli|no|ri|um** (sing′klī nôr′ē əm, -nōr′-), *n., pl.* **-no|ri|a** (-nôr′ē ə, -nōr′-), **-no|ri|ums.** *Geology.* a compound syncline, consisting of a series of subordinate synclines and anticlines, the whole formation having the general contour of an inverted arch. [< New Latin *synclinorium* < Greek *synklī́nein* (see etym. under **synclinal**) + *óros* mountain]

**Syn|com** (sing′kəm), *n.* any one of a series of United States synchronous communications satellites: *The 150-pound Syncom was designed to relay radio and telephone conversations between North America and South Africa from a synchronous or 24-hour orbit* (Science News Letter). [< *syn*(chronous) + *com*(munications satellite)]

**syn|co|pal** (sing′kə pəl), *adj. Medicine.* having to do with or marked by syncope.

**syn|co|pate** (sing′kə pāt), *v.t.,* **-pat|ed, -pat|ing.** **1** *Music.* **a** to begin (a tone) on an unaccented beat and hold it into an accented one. **b** to shift (accents) to regularly unaccented beats. **c** to introduce syncopation into (a passage). **2** *Grammar.* to shorten (a word) by omitting sounds or letters from the middle: *Gloucester is usually syncopated to Gloster.* **3** *Figurative.* to cut short: *to*

---

*syncopate a long report.* [< Late Latin *syncopē* (see etym. under **syncope**) + English *-ate*[1]. Compare Late Latin *syncopāre* to faint, swoon.]

**syn|co|pat|ed** (sing′kə pā′tid), *adj.* **1** *Music.* characterized by syncopation: *a syncopated style, syncopated rhythm.* **2** *Grammar.* contracted by omission of one or more syllables or sounds in the middle. **3** *Figurative.* cut short; abbreviated.

**syn|co|pa|tion** (sing′kə pā′shən), *n.* **1a** the act of syncopating or quality of being syncopated; a shifting or anticipating of the accent to a normally unaccented beat, produced for example by beginning a note on a normally unaccented beat and holding it into a normally accented beat, by beginning a note between any two beats and holding it into the following beat, or by using accents (sforzandos) on normally unaccented beats. **b** music marked by syncopation, such as jazz or ragtime. **c** a rhythm, dance step, or passage based upon syncopation. **2** *Grammar.* syncope: *The syncopation of words ending in "ary" and "ory" ... is an Anglicism which never fails to delight the American ear* (Scientific American).

**syn|co|pa|tor** (sing′kə pā′tər), *n.* a member of a jazz band; person devoted to jazz.

**syn|co|pe** (sing′kə pē), *n.* **1** *Grammar.* contraction of a word by omitting sounds or letters from the middle, as in *ne'er* for *never: Syncope is common in proper names: Bennett* (*Benedict*), *Dennis* (*Dionysus*), *Jerome* (*Hieronymus*) (Scientific American). **2** *Medicine.* a temporary loss of consciousness caused by a lessening of the flow of blood to the brain; faint. [< Late Latin *syncopē* < Greek *synkopê* (originally) a cutting off, ultimately < *syn-* together, thoroughly + *kóptein* to cut]

**syn|cop|ic** (sin kop′ik), *adj.* = syncopal.

**syn|cop|tic** (sin kop′tik), *adj.* = syncopal.

**syn|cret|ic** (sin kret′ik), *adj.* of or having to do with syncretism; characterized by syncretism: *Toynbee's prophetic vision is essentially syncretic—a kind of spiritual Noah's ark carrying a specimen of every "higher religion"* (Time). — **syn|cret′i|cal|ly**, *adv.*

**syn|cre|tism** (sing′krə tiz əm), *n.* **1** attempted union or reconciliation of diverse or opposite tenets or practices, especially in philosophy or religion. **2** *Grammar.* the merging or union of originally different inflectional categories, usually the result of phonetic change. **3** a process in the growth of religions in which the religious doctrines, rituals, deities, and the like, of one creed or belief are adopted, adapted, or identified with its own by another, which thus gains adherents from the first. **4** the doctrines of the Lutheran, George Calixtus (1586-1656), and his followers, who aimed at harmonizing the Protestant sects and ultimately effecting the union of all Christian denominations. [< New Latin *syncretismus* < Greek *synkrētismós* (< *synkrētízein* to combine, ally, apparently originally a union or federation of Cretan communities < *Krês, Krētôs* Crete) + *-ismos* -ism]

**syn|cre|tist** (sing′krə tist), *n., adj.* — *n.* a person who practices or favors syncretism.
— *adj.* = syncretistic.

**syn|cre|tis|tic** (sing′krə tis′tik), *adj.* of, having to do with, or characterized by syncretism: *syncretistic sects which combine elements of several religions, including Confucianism and Taoism* (Atlantic).

**syn|cre|tis|ti|cal** (sing′krə tis′tə kəl), *adj.* = syncretistic.

**syn|cre|tize** (sing′krə tīz), *v.*, **-tized, -tiz|ing.**
— *v.i.* to practice syncretism; attempt to combine different or opposing tenets or systems.
— *v.t.* to treat in the way of syncretism; combine, as different systems.
[< New Latin *syncretizare* < Greek *synkrētízein*; see etym. under **syncretism**]

**syn|cri|sis** (sing′krə sis), *n.* *Obsolete.* a figure by which opposite things are compared. [< Late Latin *syncrisis* < Greek *sýnkrisis* < *synkrínein* to compound, compare < *syn-* syn- + *krínein* to separate]

**syn|cy|tial** (sin sish′əl, -sit′ē əl), *adj.* of or having to do with a syncytium.

**syn|cy|ti|um** (sin sish′ē əm, -sit′-), *n., pl.* **-cy|ti|a** (-sish′ē ə, -sit′-), *Biology.* **1** a single cell containing several nuclei, formed either by fusion of a number of cells without fusion of the nuclei, or by division of the nucleus without division of the cell substance. **2** a structure composed of such cells, as one forming the outermost fetal layer of the placenta. [< New Latin *syncytium* < Greek *syn-* syn- + *kýtos* anything hollow, cell]

**syn|dac|tyl** or **syn|dac|tyle** (sin dak′təl), *adj., n.*
— *adj.* having some or all of the digits wholly or partly fused, as the hind feet of the kangaroo or the feet of certain birds.
— *n.* a syndactyl animal.
[< French *syndactyle* < Greek *syn-* together + *dáktylos* finger, toe]

**syn|dac|tyl|ism** (sin dak′tə liz əm), *n.* the condition of being syndactyl: *inherited syndactylism.*

**syn|dac|ty|lous** (sin dak′tə ləs), *adj.* = syndactyl.

**syn|dac|ty|ly** (sin dak′tə lē), *n.* the condition of having fused or webbed digits.

**syn|de|sis** (sin′də sis), *n., pl.* **-sis** (-sēz). *Biology.* a synapsis. [< New Latin *syndesis* < Greek, a binding together < *syndeîn* to bind together, connect; see etym. under **syndetic**]

**syn|des|mo|sis** (sin′des mō′sis), *n., pl.* **-ses** (-sēz). an articulation in which the bones are connected by ligaments, membranes, or other structures, other than those which enter into the composition of the joint. [< New Latin *syndesmosis* < Greek *sýndesmos* a fastening, bond, binding together (as of sinews) < *syndeîn;* see etym. under **syndetic**]

**syn|des|mot|ic** (sin′des mot′ik), *adj.* bound together by a fascia, as two bones; of or having to do with syndesmosis.

**syn|det** (sin′det), *n.* a synthetic detergent. [< *syn*(thetic) *det*(ergent)]

**syn|det|ic** (sin det′ik), *adj.* serving to unite or connect; connective; copulative. [< Greek *syndetikós* < *syndeîn* connect, unite < *syn-* together + *deîn* bind. Compare etym. under **diadem.**] — **syn|det′i|cal|ly**, *adv.*

**syn|det|i|cal** (sin det′ə kəl), *adj.* = syndetic.

**syn|dic** (sin′dik), *n.* **1** a person who manages the business affairs of a university or other corporation, especially of any one of various British or European universities designated by charter as corporate bodies. **2** a government official, such as the chief official of certain cities or other communities, especially in Europe; magistrate. [< Middle French *syndic* chief representative or delegate, learned borrowing from Late Latin *syndicus* < Greek *sýndikos* public advocate < *syn-* together + *díkē* defendant's justice; judgment, right < *deiknýnai* bring to light, prove]

**syn|di|cal** (sin′də kəl), *adj.* **1** of or having to do with syndicalism; syndicalist: [*He*] *said that the syndical organization of the people fought for ideals and interests* (London Times). **2** of or having to do with a syndic. **3** of or having to do with a craft union. [< French *syndical* < Middle French *syndic;* see etym. under **syndic**]

**syn|di|cal|ism** (sin′də kə liz′əm), *n.* **1** a movement to put industry and government under the control of labor unions by means of the general strike, sabotage, and any one of various other kinds of violence: *Syndicalism is an extreme form of socialism, which aims at a complete overthrow of society by violent means* (Emory S. Bogardus). **2** the body of theory and doctrine underlying this movement, certain formal elements of which influenced Mussolini in his structural reorganization of Italian industry and government. [< French *syndicalisme,* ultimately < Middle French *syndic;* see etym. under **syndic**]

**syn|di|cal|ist** (sin′də kə list), *n., adj.* — *n.* a person who favors and supports syndicalism: *The syndicalist would have his syndicate, or unions, assume general control in society* (Emory S. Bogardus).
— *adj.* = syndical.

**syn|di|cal|is|tic** (sin′də kə lis′tik), *adj.* = syndical.

**syn|di|cate** (*n.* sin′də kit; *v.* sin′də kāt), *n., v.,* **-cat|ed, -cat|ing.** — *n.* **1a** a combination of persons or companies formed to carry out some commercial undertaking, especially one requiring a large capital investment, such as the underwriting of an issue of securities. **b** a combination of persons formed for the promotion or continuation of any enterprise: *a labor union syndicate.* **2** an agency that sells special articles, photographs, comic strips, and news stories to a large number of newspapers or magazines for publication at the same time: *This syndicate supplies stories to a hundred newspapers.* **3** a council or body of syndics. **4** *U.S.* a group of criminals that organizes and controls criminal activities, such as gambling, prostitution, or traffic in narcotics: *Crime reporters in America have* [*been*] *referring to organized crime simply as "the mob" or "the syndicate"* (Canadian Saturday Night).
— *v.t.* **1** to combine into a syndicate. **2** to control or manage by a syndicate. **3** to publish through a syndicate: *a syndicated newspaper columnist.*
— *v.i.* to unite in a syndicate.
[< French *syndicat* < Middle French *syndic* (see etym. under **syndic**) + *-at* -ate[3]]

**syn|di|ca|tion** (sin′də kā′shən), *n.* the action of syndicating or state of being syndicated: *Red Smith became, statistically in terms of syndication, the number one sports writer in the country* (Harper's).

**syn|di|ca|tor** (sin′də kā′tər), *n.* a person who forms or is part of a syndicate: *Syndicators must also file annual reports, including profit and loss statements, with the office and all investors* (Wall Street Journal).

**syn|drome** (sin′drōm), *n.* **1** a group of signs and symptoms considered together as characteristic of a particular disease: *In many cases of the rheumatoid syndrome the joint structures may be little or not at all involved* (Ralph Pemberton). **2** any group of signs characteristic of a type of behavior: *What I guess about you is that you have a nobility syndrome* (Saul Bellow). *His only syndrome was the cookery syndrome* (Geoffrey T. Hellman). *The contest syndrome is no less acute in packaging than in any other industry* (Sales Management). [< New Latin *syndrome* < Greek *syndromḗ* concurrence of symptoms; concourse < *sýndromos* (literally) running together < *syn-* with + *drómos* course, related to *drameîn* to run]

**syn|drom|ic** (sin drom′ik), *adj.* of or having to do with a syndrome or syndromes.

**syne** (sīn), *adv., prep., conj. Scottish.* since. [contraction of *sithen*]

**syn|ec|do|che** (si nek′də kē), *n.* *Rhetoric.* a figure of speech by which a part is put for the whole, or the whole for a part, the special for the general, or the general for the special, or the like. *Examples:* a factory employing 500 *hands* (persons); to eat of the *tree* (its fruit); a *Solomon* (wise man); a *marble* (a statue) on its pedestal. [< Late Latin *synecdoche* < Greek *synekdochḗ* < *synekdéchesthai* supply a thought or word; take with (something else) < *syn-* with + *ex-* out + *déchesthai* to receive]

**syn|ec|doch|ic** (sin′ek dok′ik), *adj.* of the nature of or expressed by synecdoche. — **syn′ec|doch′i|cal|ly**, *adv.*

**syn|ec|doch|i|cal** (sin′ek dok′ə kəl), *adj.* = synecdochic.

**syn|ec|do|chism** (si nek′də kiz′əm), *n.* **1** synecdochic style; the use of synecdoche. **2** the use in contagious magic of a part of an object or person as an equivalent of the whole object or person, so that anything done with the part is held to take effect upon the whole: *One or more pieces of the skull* (*for in synecdochism the piece carries the virtue of the whole*) *of the slain were used as amulets* (Report of the Bureau of American Ethnology).

**syn|e|cious** (si nē′shəs), *adj.* = synoecious.

**syn|e|co|log|i|cal** (sin′ek ə loj′ə kəl), *adj.* of or having to do with synecology. — **syn′e|co|log′i|cal|ly**, *adv.*

**syn|e|col|o|gist** (sin′ə kol′ə jist), *n.* an expert in synecology.

**syn|e|col|o|gy** (sin′ə kol′ə jē), *n.* the branch of ecology dealing with communities as distinguished from individual species: *Synecology deals with plant communities, as related to soil, light, climate, and other environmental factors* (Heber W. Youngken). [< *syn-* together + *ecology*]

**syn|ec|thry** (sin′ek thrē), *n.* the occurrence in ant or termite colonies of insects to which the hosts are unfriendly but which remain in the colony as unwelcome guests; hostile commensalism. [< *syn-* + Greek *échthros* hostile + English *-y*[3]]

**syn|ec|tic** (si nek′tik), *adj.* of or having to do with synectics: *There appears to be a problem-solving mechanism at work in the "mind" which can be stimulated to resolve problems adversely affecting survival, and which stimulates in a synectic fashion solutions to problems of a creative nature which enhance survival* (New Scientist). — **synec′ti|cal|ly**, *adv.*

**syn|ec|tics** (si nek′tiks), *n.* the free and unrestrained exchange of ideas among a group of people, used as a method of developing new ideas, solving problems, and making discoveries: *A new philosophy, "synectics," which is said to liberate the creative instinct and so stimulate inventiveness, is gaining a following among big corporations* (London Times). [probably < *syn-* together + (dial)*ectics*]

**syn|ed|ri|al** (si ned′rē əl), *adj.* of or having to do with the Sanhedrin.

**syn|ed|ri|on** (si ned′rē ən), *n., pl.* **-ri|a** (-rē ə). = Sanhedrin. [< Greek *synédrion;* see etym. under **Sanhedrin**]

**syn|er|e|sis** (si ner′ə sis), *n.* = synaeresis.

**syn|er|ga|my** (si nėr′gə mē), *n.* a form of marriage in which three or more people live together as husbands and wives to each other. [< Greek *synergós* working together + English *-gamy*]

**syn|er|get|ic** (sin′ər jet′ik), *adj.* working together, as a group of muscles for the production of some movement; cooperating; synergistic. [< Greek *synergētikós* < *synergeîn* cooperate; see etym. under **synergy**] — **syn′er|get′i|cal|ly**, *adv.*

**syn|er|gic** (si nėr′jik), *adj.* = synergetic. — **syn|er′gi|cal|ly**, *adv.*

**syn|er|gism** (sin′ər jiz əm, si nėr′-), *n.* **1** the combined action of different agents or organs, producing a greater effect than the sum of the various individual actions, as in a medicine composed of several drugs; synergy: *Synergism ... has also been demonstrated in other phases of plant development* (New Scientist). **2** *Theology.* the doctrine that the human will cooperates with divine grace in the work of regeneration. [< New Latin *synergismus* < Greek *synergeîn;* see etym. under **synergy**]

**syn|er|gist** (sin′ər jist), *n.* **1** a bodily organ or a medicine that cooperates with another or others. **2** *Theology.* a person who holds the doctrine of synergism.

**syn|er|gis|tic** (sin′ər jis′tik), *adj.* **1** of, having to do with, or producing synergism. **2** cooperating with another; acting as a synergist; synergetic: *a synergistic organ. The drugs have what is called a synergistic effect, which means they increase each other's effectiveness* (Wall Street Journal). **3** interacting or interdependent; mutually stimulating or responsive: *The synergistic action of these basic facets of our national economy—public information, public approval, public action—can be the difference between success and failure, survival and disintegration for the modern corporation* (Saturday Review). **—syn′er|gis′ti|cal|ly,** *adv.*

**syn|er|gis|ti|cal** (sin′ər jis′tə kəl), *adj.* = synergistic.

**syn|er|gize** (sin′ər jīz), *v.,* **-gized, -giz|ing.** **—*v.i.*** to act as a synergist. **—*v.t.*** to cooperate with and enforce the activity of: *The catalyst synergizes chemical reaction. Stress-corrosion cracking . . . is initiated by localized corrosion synergized by sustained tensile stress at the surface* (Scientific American).

**syn|er|gy** (sin′ər jē), *n., pl.* **-gies. 1** a combined or correlated action of a group of organs of the body, such as nerve centers or muscles, or of two or more drugs or remedies. **2** the action or behavior of any system in a way that cannot be predicted by the action or behavior of its individual parts; combined action whose total effect is greater than the sum of the individual actions: *A continuous interchange of knowledge and experience gives customers the benefit of synergy at work* (Scientific American). [< New Latin *synergia* < Greek *synergíā* < *synergós* working together < *synergeîn* work together, help in work < *syn-* together + *érgon* work]

**syn|e|sis** (sin′ə sis), *n. Grammar.* a construction according to sense, not strictly grammatical. [< Greek *sýnesis* sagacity; comprehension; (originally) quickness at putting together < *syn-* together + *hīénai* to send]

**syn|es|the|sia** (sin′es thē′zhə, -zhē ə), *n.* **1** *Physiology.* a sensation in one part of the body produced by a stimulus applied to another part. **2** *Psychology.* a phenomenon in which the stimulation of one sense produces a mental impression associated with a different sense, as when hearing certain sounds causes a person to see certain colors: *As I tasted it, a tune came into my head* (*this association of two sensory memories is, I believe, called synesthesia*) (New Yorker). Also, **synaesthesia.**

**syn|es|thet|ic** (sin′es thet′ik), *adj.* of or having to do with synesthesia: *synesthetic impressions.* Also, **synaesthetic.** **—syn′es|thet′i|cal|ly,** *adv.*

**syn|gam|ic** (sin gam′ik), *adj.* having to do with syngamy.

**syn|ga|mous** (sing′gə məs), *adj.* = syngamic.

**syn|ga|my** (sing′gə mē), *n. Biology.* the union of two cells, as of gametes in fertilization.

**syn|gas** (sin′gas′), *n.* synthetic gas made especially from low-grade coal: *Becoming a feedstock for "syngas" would open a major new potential for coal, especially the now stymied high-sulfur varieties* (Time). [< *syn*(thetic) + *gas*[1]]

**syn|ge|ne|ic** (sin′jə nē′ik), *adj. Genetics.* having an identity of genotype. [< Greek *syngéneia* kinship, relationship + English *-ic*]

**syn|ge|ne|sious** (sin′jə nē′shəs), *adj. Botany.* (of stamens) united by the anthers so as to form a ring or tube.

**syn|gen|e|sis** (sin jen′ə sis), *n. Biology.* the formation of the germ by fusion of the male and female elements, so that the substance of the embryo is derived from both parents; sexual reproduction. [< *syn-* + *genesis*]

**syn|ge|net|ic** (sin′jə net′ik), *adj. Biology.* reproduced by means of both parents; of or having to do with syngenesis. **—syn′ge|net′i|cal|ly,** *adv.*

**syn|i|ze|sis** (sin′ə zē′sis), *n.* **1** *Linguistics.* the fusion of two syllables into one by the coalescence of two adjacent vowels (or of a vowel and a diphthong) without the formation of a recognized diphthong. **2** *Biology.* the clustering of the nuclear chromatin before the maturation division. **3** *Medicine.* closure of the pupil of the eye. [< Latin *synīzēsis* < Greek *synízēsis* (literally) collapsing < *synizánein* sink down < *syn-* together, completely + *hizánein* to seat oneself, settle down (causative) < *hízein* to sit]

**syn|kar|y|on** (sin kar′ē on), *n. Biology.* a nucleus produced by the fusion of two nuclei, as in fertilization. [< *syn-* + Greek *káryon* nut, taken as "nucleus"]

**syn|ki|ne|sis** (sin ki nē′sis), *n.* a reflex or involuntary synergetic movement, especially of muscles. [< New Latin *synkinesis* < *syn-* together + *kinesis* kinesis < Greek *kī́nesis* motion]

**syn|ki|net|ic** (sin ki net′ik), *adj.* of or having to do with synkinesis.

**syn|od** (sin′əd), *n.* **1** an assembly called together to discuss and decide church affairs; church council. **2** a governing body or council of the Presbyterian Church ranking next above the presbytery. **3** an assembly, convention, or council of any kind. SYN: convocation, meeting. [< Late Latin *synodus* < Greek *sýnodos* assembly, meeting, conjunction (of planets) < *syn-* together + *hodós* a going, a way]

**syn|od|al** (sin′ə dəl), *adj.* having to do with a synod.

**syn|od|ic** (si nod′ik), *adj.* = synodical.

**syn|od|i|cal** (si nod′ə kəl), *adj.* **1** having to do with the conjunction of two heavenly bodies, especially with respect to the sun. The synodical period of the moon is the time between one new moon and the next. **2** of, having to do with, or transacted in a synod; synodal. [(def. 1) < Late Greek *synodikós* < *sýnodos;* see etym. under **synod**; (def. 2) < Late Latin *synodicus* < Late Greek; + English *-al*[1]] **—syn|od′i|cal|ly,** *adv.*

**synodical** or **synodic month,** the interval between one new moon and the next, about 29½ days; lunar month: *The synodic month is the interval between successive conjunctions of the moon and sun, from new moon to new moon again* (Robert H. Baker).

**syn|oe|cious** (si nē′shəs), *adj. Botany.* **1** having male and female flowers in one head, as some composite plants. **2** having male and female organs in the same receptacle, as some mosses. Also, **synecious.** [< *syn-* + *-ecious,* as in *diecious.* Compare Greek *synoikíā* community of persons living together.]

**syn|oe|cism** (si nē′siz əm), *n.* the uniting of several towns or villages into one city or community. [< Greek *synoikismós* < *synoikízein* to synoecize < *syn-* together + *oikízein* to found as a community < *oîkos* house]

**syn|oe|cize** (si nē′sīz), *v.t.,* **-cized, -ciz|ing.** to unite into a city or community. [< Greek *synoikízein,* see etym. under **synoecism**]

**syn|oi|cous** (si noi′kəs), *adj.* = synoecious.

**syn|o|nym** (sin′ə nim), *n.* **1** a word that means the same or nearly the same as another word in the same language. *Keen* is a synonym of *sharp. He needs all his wits about him as well, in quickly finding synonyms for words he can't pronounce* (London Times). *Abbr:* syn. **2** a word or expression generally accepted as another name for something; metonym: *Albert Einstein's name has become a synonym for scientific genius. Many people are apt to think that public interest is a synonym for consumer interest* (London Times). SYN: equivalent. **3** *Biology.* a scientific name discarded as being incorrect or out of date. [< Latin *synōnymum* < Greek *synṓnymon,* (originally) noun use of neuter of *synṓnymos;* see etym. under **synonymous**]

**syn|o|nym|ic** (sin′ə nim′ik), *adj.* = synonymous.

**syn|o|nym|i|cal** (sin′ə nim′ə kəl), *adj.* = synonymous.

**syn|o|nym|ics** (sin ə nim′iks), *n.* the study of synonyms; synonymy.

**syn|on|y|mist** (si non′ə mist), *n.* a person who makes a study or prepares lists of synonyms.

**syn|o|nym|i|ty** (sin′ə nim′ə tē), *n.* the quality of being synonymous; synonymy.

**syn|on|y|mize** (si non′ə mīz), *v.t.,* **-mized, -miz|ing. 1** to give the synonyms of. **2** to furnish with lists of synonyms. **3** to make synonymous.

**syn|on|y|mous** (si non′ə məs), *adj.* having the same or nearly the same meaning; having the character of a synonym. *Little* and *small* are synonymous. *Being good was . . . represented to me as synonymous with keeping silence* (Harriet Beecher Stowe). (*Figurative.*) *Americans who can't afford to buy all the gadgets that have become synonymous with the American standard of living still are better off than people anywhere else in the world* (Newsweek). [< Medieval Latin *synonymus* (with English *-ous*) < Greek *synṓnymos* < *syn-* together + dialectal *ónyma* name] **—syn|on′y|mous|ly,** *adv.*

**syn|on|y|my** (si non′ə mē), *n., pl.* **-mies. 1** the quality of being synonymous; equivalence in meaning. **2** the study of synonyms. **3** *Rhetoric.* the use or coupling of synonyms in discourse for emphasis or amplification. **4** a set, list, or system of synonyms. **5** *Biology.* **a** a list of the several different scientific names that have been applied to a species or other group by various describers or classifiers. **b** such names collectively.

**synop.,** synopsis.

**syn|op|sis** (si nop′sis), *n., pl.* **-ses** (-sēz). a brief statement giving a general view, as of some subject, book, or play; summary: *Write a synopsis of "Treasure Island" in 200 words or less.* SYN: digest. [< Late Latin *synopsis* < Greek *sýnopsis* a general view < *synorân* to see altogether, all at once < *syn-* together + *horân* to see, view]

**syn|op|size** (si nop′sīz), *v.t.,* **-sized, -siz|ing.** to make a synopsis of: *The opera was called "Vaiva," and before we went to hear it, we asked an Intourist woman to synopsize the action for us* (New Yorker).

**syn|op|tic** (si nop′tik), *adj., n.* **—*adj.* 1** furnishing a general view of some subject: *Nearly 20 agencies . . . combined their facilities to make a great synoptic oceanographic survey* (Science). **2** having to do with, involving, or taking a comprehensive view of something. **3** Often, **Synoptic. a** having an approximately parallel point of view. *Matthew, Mark,* and *Luke* are called the *Synoptic Gospels* because they are much alike in content, order, and statement. **b** of or having to do with the Synoptic Gospels. **4** *Meteorology.* **a** of or having to do with a chart showing meteorological data from simultaneous observations at many points: *Marks were allotted on a system based on synoptic data, height of cloud-top in relation to freezing level* (A. W. Haslett). **b** of or having to do with the branch of meteorology that deals with the compilation or analysis of such data. **—*n.*** one of the Synoptic Gospels or their authors; Matthew, Mark, or Luke. [< New Latin *synopticus* < Greek *synoptikós* < *sýnopsis;* see etym. under **synopsis**] **—syn|op′ti|cal|ly,** *adv.*

**syn|op|ti|cal** (si nop′tə kəl), *adj.* = synoptic.

**Synoptic Gospels,** the Gospels of Matthew, Mark, and Luke.

**syn|op|tist** (si nop′tist), *n.* any one of the writers of the Synoptic Gospels; Matthew, Mark, or Luke.

**syn|os|te|o|sis** (si nos′tē ō′sis), *n.* = synostosis.

**syn|os|to|sis** (sin′os tō′sis), *n., pl.* **-ses** (-sēz). *Anatomy.* union by means of ossified cartilage or bone; ankylosis. [< New Latin *synostosis* < Greek *syn-* together + *ostéon* bone + New Latin *-osis* - osis]

**syn|ou|si|acs** (si nü′sē aks), *n.* the branch of knowledge that deals with societies. [< Greek *synousíā* society (< *synoûsa,* feminine, present participle of *synéinai* be with < *syn-* with + *eînai* be) + English *-(i)cs*]

**syn|o|vec|to|my** (sin′ə vek′tə mē), *n., pl.* **-mies.** the surgical removal of a synovium. [< *synov*(ium) + *-ectomy*]

**syn|o|vi|a** (si nō′vē ə), *n.* a viscid, clear, lubricating liquid secreted by certain membranes, such as those lining the joints. [< New Latin *synovia* (coined by Paracelsus) various body fluids; gout]

**syn|o|vi|al** (si nō′vē əl), *adj.* consisting of, containing, or secreting synovia: *a synovial membrane or capsule. The ends of the bones are padded with cartilage at the joints and there is a lubricating liquid, the synovial fluid, that further reduces friction* (A. M. Winchester).

**syn|o|vi|tis** (sin′ə vī′tis), *n.* inflammation of a synovial membrane. [< *synov*(ia) + *-itis*]

**syn|o|vi|um** (si nō′vē əm), *n.* the membrane lining a joint of the body; a synovial membrane: *Among the causes of pain in rheumatoid arthritis are inflammation of the synovium . . .* (Time). [< New Latin *synovium* < *synovia*]

**syn|pel|mous** (sin pel′məs), *adj.* = sympelmous.

**syn|pet|al|ous** (sin pet′ə ləs), *adj.* = gamopetalous.

**syn|sep|al|ous** (sin sep′ə ləs), *adj.* = gamosepalous.

**syn|sper|mous** (sin spėr′məs), *adj.* characterized by synspermy.

**syn|sper|my** (sin spėr′mē), *n.* union or coalescence of two or more seeds.

**syn|tac|tic** (sin tak′tik), *adj.* of or having to do with syntax; in accordance with the rules of syntax: *The parts of speech, for example, in any new language under examination, should be determined either by their inflexions or, if completely uninflected, by their syntactic function* (Simeon Potter). **—syn|tac′ti|cal|ly,** *adv.*

**syn|tac|ti|cal** (sin tak′tə kəl), *adj.* = syntactic.

**syn|tac|tics** (sin tak′tiks), *n.* **1** the formal syntactic system or structure of a language without reference to meaning. **2** the study of such a system or structure.

**syn|tag|ma** (sin tag′mə), *n., pl.* **-ma|ta** (-mə tə), **-mas. 1** *Linguistics.* a syntactic unit or construction; group of words forming a sentence, clause, or phrase. **2** a systematically arranged treatise. [< Greek *sýntagma* < *syntássein* to arrange together; see etym. under **syntax**]

**syn|tag|mat|ic** (sin′tag mat′ik), *adj. Linguistics.* of or having to do with a syntagma or syntagmata.

**syn|tax** (sin′taks), *n.* **1a** the way in which the

**Pronunciation Key:** hat, āge, cãre, fär; let, ēqual, tėrm; it, īce; hot, ōpen, ôrder; oil, out; cup, pu̇t, rüle; child; long; thin; ᴛʜen; zh, measure; ə represents a in about, e in taken, i in pencil, o in lemon, u in circus.

words and phrases of a sentence are arranged to show how they relate to each other; sentence structure: *In syntax and vocabulary the message of the written record is unmistakable, and it exerts a tremendous effect upon the standard language* (Leonard Bloomfield). **b** the patterns of such arrangement in a given language: *The team wants to analyze the syntax of one pair of languages (German and English) in terms of mathematical symbolism* (Newsweek). **c** the use or function of a word, phrase, or clause in a sentence. **d** the part of grammar dealing with the construction and function of phrases, clauses, and sentences: *The object in syntax is still to discover the relations between the parts of the expression* (Joshua Whatmough). **2** *Obsolete.* an orderly or systematic arrangement of parts or elements; connected order or system of things: *Concerning the syntax and disposition of studies, that men may know in what order ... to read* (Francis Bacon). [< Late Latin *syntaxis* < Greek *sýntaxis* < *syntássein* < *syn-* together + *tássein* arrange]

**syn|tech|nic** (sin tek′nik), *adj.* of or having to do with unrelated animals that resemble each other due to the influence of a similar environment.

**syn|tex|is** (sin tek′sis), *n. Geology.* the process by which magma is formed by the melting of different types of rocks. [< Greek *sýntēxis* a melting away < *syntḗkein* to melt together < *syn-* together + *tḗkein* to thaw]

**syn|the|sis** (sin′thə sis), *n., pl.* **-ses** (-sēz). **1a** the combination of parts or elements into a whole: *in the opinion of several competent critics the best synthesis of Baudelaire that had appeared in English* (London Times). *I cannot believe that we can achieve a synthesis between Thomas Aquinas and Marx* (Gyorgy Lukas). **b** a body of things put together thus. An idea or concept may be a synthesis of several other ideas. *The happiest synthesis of the divine, the scholar and the gentleman* (Samuel Taylor Coleridge). **2** the formation of a compound or a complex substance by the chemical union of various elements or by the combination of simpler compounds. Alcohol, ammonia, and rubber can be artificially produced by synthesis. *A total synthesis implies that in theory a substance has been elaborated from its elements, in this case carbon, hydrogen and oxygen* (A. J. Birch). **3** *Philosophy, Logic.* **a** the combination or unification of particular phenomena, observed or hypothesized, into a general body or abstract whole. **b** according to Immanuel Kant, the action of the understanding in combining and unifying the isolated data of sensation into a cognizable whole. **c** according to Thomas Hobbes, Isaac Newton, and others, deductive reasoning.
[< Latin *synthesis* a collection, set; the composition (of a medication) < Greek *sýnthesis* composition (logical, mathematical) < *syntithénai* to combine < *syn-* together + *tithénai* put, place. Compare etym. under **thesis.**]

**syn|the|sise** (sin′thə sīz), *v.t., v.i.,* **-sised, -sis|ing.** *Especially British.* synthesize.

**syn|the|sist** (sin′thə sist), *n.* a person who uses synthesis or a synthetic method.

**syn|the|si|za|tion** (sin′thə sə zā′shən), *n.* the act or process of synthesizing: *The ... basic ingredients are human beings, which no doubt will always defy synthesization* (Wall Street Journal).

**syn|the|size** (sin′thə sīz), *v.,* **-sized, -siz|ing.**
—*v.t.* **1** to put together or combine into a complex whole. **2** to make by combining parts or elements: *Gottlieb's ... effort to synthesize antitoxin* (Sinclair Lewis). **3** to produce or manufacture by chemical synthesis; treat or form synthetically: *to synthesize rubber. Every natural drug from quinine to penicillin has been synthesized* (Philip Wylie).
—*v.i.* to come together or combine into a complex whole: *The other chain took eight days to synthesize and showed a final yield of 37 percent* (Scientific American).

**syn|the|siz|er** (sin′thə sī′zər), *n.* **1** a person or thing that synthesizes: *Sir Winston Churchill [was] the great synthesizer of foreign affairs, a man of global vision and striking phrase* (New York Times). **2** an electronic device that simulates and blends conventional and ultrasonic sounds: *The synthesizer ... generates its own sound electronically and, at least in theory, can synthesize from five basic sound-elements any musical effect ever conceived, or imaginable in the future* (Harper's).

**syn|the|tase** (sin′thə tās), *n.* = ligase. [< *synthet*(ize) + *-ase*]

**syn|thet|ic** (sin thet′ik), *adj., n.* —*adj.* **1** of, having to do with, or involving synthesis: *synthetic chemistry.* **2** made artificially by chemical synthesis. Many kinds of fabrics, furs, dyes, resins, and drugs are synthetic products. *Synthetic vanillin is chemically indistinguishable from vanillin obtained from the bean* (New York Times). SYN: See syn. under **artificial. 3** *Figurative.* not real or genuine; artificial: *synthetic laughter.* **4** *Linguistics.* characterized by the use of affixes and inflectional endings rather than by the use of separate words, such as auxiliary verbs and prepositions, to express the same idea. Latin is a synthetic language, while English is analytic. For example, the Latin *amabitur* expresses in one word the English *he will be loved.*
—*n.* a product made by chemical synthesis: *Goodyear used a synthetic called "Natsyn," the molecular duplicate of tree-grown latex* (Charles C. Cain).
[< New Latin *syntheticus* < Greek *synthetikós,* ultimately < *syntithénai;* see etym. under **synthesis**] —**syn|thet′i|cal|ly,** *adv.*

**syn|thet|i|cal** (sin thet′ə kəl), *adj.* = synthetic.

**synthetic cubism,** a form of cubism in which different views of an object are shown in the same picture, often superimposed on each other; simultaneism.

**synthetic fiber,** any fiber developed by chemical processes from natural substances such as cellulose, petroleum, and coal: *Rayon, fiberglass, and nylon are well-known synthetic fibers. Some imaginative chemists began to experiment with synthetic fibers, and the non-wovens started to take on a new character* (Science News Letter).

**synthetic geometry,** geometry treated without algebra or coordinates, as distinguished from analytic geometry; ordinary Euclidean geometry.

**syn|thet|i|cism** (sin thet′ə siz əm), *n.* synthetic methods or procedure.

**synthetic philosophy,** the philosophy of Herbert Spencer, an English philosopher, so called by himself as bringing the various sciences into a systematic whole.

**synthetic rubber,** any rubberlike substance or elastomer developed by chemical processes chiefly from butadiene as a substitute for natural rubber, usually having special properties, such as resistance to heat, cold, age, and harmful chemicals: *... On the basis of usefulness, synthetic rubber is nearing the limits where it can seize a big new piece of the market* (Wall Street Journal).

**syn|thet|ics** (sin thet′iks), *n.* **1** man-made substances formed by chemical synthesis. Plastics are synthetics. *Today's synthetics are by and large either better than their natural counterparts or have no counterparts at all* (Newsweek). **2** the field of science or industry dealing with the making of synthetic products: *Only recently did it [a firm] make a halfhearted attempt to get into synthetics* (Time).

**syn|the|tism** (sin′thə tiz əm), *n.* **1** a synthetic system or doctrine. **2** *Medicine.* the complete treatment of a fracture from its reduction to the removal of the splints and restoration of the function of the limb. **3** (in art) symbolism.

**syn|the|tist** (sin′thə tist), *n.* = synthesist.

**syn|the|tize** (sin′thə tīz), *v.t.,* **-tized, -tiz|ing.** = synthesize.

**syn|thet|o|graph** (sin thet′ə graf, -gräf), *n.* a composite drawing, as from two or more specimens of a new species.

**syn|ton|ic** (sin ton′ik), *adj.* **1** of or having to do with the tuning of a transmitter and receiver, so that the receiver responds only to the vibrations of the transmitter. **2** of or having to do with resonance, especially of radio frequency. **3** of or having to do with a personality responding emotionally to the environment readily and appropriately. [< *syn-* + Greek *tónos* tone + English *-ic*] —**syn|ton′i|cal|ly,** *adv.*

**syn|ton|i|cal** (sin ton′ə kəl), *adj.* = syntonic.

**syn|to|nism** (sin′tə niz əm), *n.* = syntony.

**syn|to|ni|za|tion** (sin′tə nə zā′shən), *n.* the act of making syntonic.

**syn|to|nize** (sin′tə nīz), *v.t.,* **-nized, -niz|ing.** to make syntonic. —**syn′to|niz′er,** *n.*

**syn|to|ny** (sin′tə nē), *n.* the condition of being syntonic. [< *synton*(ic) + *-y*[3]]

**syn|u|ra** (si nu̇r′ə, -nyu̇r′-), *n., pl.* **syn|u|rae** (si nu̇r′ē, -nyu̇r′-), **syn|u|ras.** a flagellate, freshwater protozoan (sometimes classed as an alga), occurring in radially arranged, globose clusters in pools, swamp waters, and sometimes in reservoirs; oilbug. The synura gives off an oily matter of cucumberlike or fishy flavor, which, though harmless, may make the water unpleasant for drinking. [< New Latin *Synura* the genus name < Greek *syn-* together + *ourá* tail (because of its shape)]

**syph** (sif), *n. Slang.* syphilis.

**sy|pher** (sī′fər), *v.t.* to fit together the chamfered edges of (boards) in a joint so as to form one continuous surface. [variant of *cipher,* verb, in obsolete meaning of "to bevel"]

**sypher joint,** a joint in which the edges of the boards overlap so as to leave a plane surface.

**syph|i|lide** (sif′ə lid), *n.* a syphilitic skin eruption.

**syph|i|lis** (sif′ə lis), *n.* a contagious venereal disease that attacks the skin, internal organs, and finally the bones, brain, and spinal cord; lues; pox. Syphilis is caused by a spirochete. [< New Latin *syphilis,* apparently < *Syphilis, sive Morbus Gallicus,* the title of a poem by Girolamo Fracastoro, 1483-1553, an Italian physician and poet < *Syphilus,* the hero of the poem who is described as the first sufferer of the disease]

**syph|i|lit|ic** (sif′ə lit′ik), *adj., n.* —*adj.* **1** of, having to do with, or caused by syphilis: *syphilitic lesions.* **2** affected with syphilis.
—*n.* a person who has syphilis.

**syph|i|loid** (sif′ə loid), *adj.* characteristic of syphilis.

**syph|i|lol|o|gist** (sif′ə lol′ə jist), *n.* a specialist in syphilology.

**syph|i|lol|o|gy** (sif′ə lol′ə jē), *n.* the branch of medicine that deals with the diagnosis and treatment of syphilis.

**syph|i|lous** (sif′ə ləs), *adj.* = syphilitic.

**sy|phon** (sī′fən), *n., v.t., v.i.* = siphon.

**syr.,** *Pharmacy.* syrup.

**Syr.,** **1** Syria. **2** Syriac. **3** Syrian.

**Syr|a|cu|san** (sir′ə kyü′sən, -zən), *adj., n.* —*adj.* **1** of or belonging to Syracuse, a city in Sicily: *The Syracusan expedition was the deathblow of the Athenian Empire* (John Buchan). **2** of or belonging to Syracuse, a city in central New York State.
—*n.* **1** a native or inhabitant of Syracuse, Sicily: *Dionysius ... obliged the Syracusans to accept his tokens in place of silver coins* (William Stanley Jevons). **2** a native or inhabitant of Syracuse, New York.

**sy|ren** (sī′rən), *n., adj.* = siren.

**Syr|i|ac** (sir′ē ak), *adj., n.* —*adj.* of or having to do with Syria or its language.
—*n.* the ancient Semitic language of Syria, a dialect of Aramaic. *Abbr:* Syr.
[< Latin *Syriacus* < *Syriā* Syria]

**Syr|i|an** (sir′ē ən), *adj., n.* —*adj.* of or having to do with Syria, a country in southwestern Asia, or its people.
—*n.* **1** a native or inhabitant of Syria. **2** = Zyrian.

**Syrian hamster,** = golden hamster.

**sy|rin|ga** (sə ring′gə), *n.* **1** a shrub with fragrant white flowers blooming in early summer; mock orange; philadelphus. Syringa belongs to the saxifrage family. The blossom of one kind is the state flower of Idaho. **2** any lilac. [< New Latin *Syringa* the mock orange (because of its use for pipe stems); later, the lilac genus < Greek *sŷrinx, -ingos* shepherd's pipe]

**sy|ringe** (sə rinj′, sir′inj), *n., v.,* **-ringed, -ring|ing.**
—*n.* **1** a narrow tube fitted with a piston or rubber bulb for drawing in a quantity of fluid and then forcing it out in a stream. Syringes are used for cleaning wounds and injecting fluids into the body. **2** = hypodermic syringe. **3** a similar instrument used for various purposes, such as exhausting or compressing air or squirting water over plants.
—*v.t.* to clean, wash, or inject by means of a syringe.
[Middle English *siryng,* and *searing* < Medieval Latin *sirynga* < Greek *sŷrinx, -ingos* shepherd's pipe; spelling and pronunciation influenced by Greek plural *sŷringes*]

**sy|rin|ge|al** (sə rin′jē əl), *adj.* of, having to do with, or connected with the syrinx in a bird or birds.

**sy|rin|go|my|e|li|a** (sə ring′gō mī ē′lē ə), *n.* a chronic disease characterized by the formation of abnormal tubular cavities in the central canal of the spinal cord. [< New Latin *syringomyelia* < Greek *sŷrinx, -ingos* shepherd's pipe + *myelós* marrow, taken as "spinal cord"]

**sy|rin|go|my|el|ic** (sə ring′gō mī el′ik), *adj.* of or having to do with syringomyelia.

**syr|inx** (sir′ingks), *n., pl.* **sy|rin|ges** (sə rin′jēz), **syr|inx|es. 1** = Panpipe. **2** the vocal organ of birds, situated at or near the division of the trachea into the right and left bronchi. **3** = Eustachian tube. [< Latin *sŷrinx, -ingis* < Greek *sŷrinx, -ingos* shepherd's pipe. See related etym. at **syringa, syringe.**]

**syr|phi|an** (sėr′fē ən), *n., adj.* = syrphid.

**syr|phid** (sėr′fid), *n., adj.* —*n.* = syrphus fly.
—*adj.* of or having to do with syrphus flies. [< New Latin *Syrphidae* the family name < *Syrphus;* see etym. under **syrphus fly**]

**syr|phus fly** (sėr′fəs), any fly of a family that feed on the nectar of flowers and often resemble bees or wasps, whose larvae live on decaying matter or plant lice. [< New Latin *Syrphus* the genus name < Greek *sŷrphos* gnat, some small insect]

**syr|tic** (sėr′tik), *adj.* having to do with or resembling a syrtis or quicksand.

**syr|tis** (sėr′tis), *n., pl.* **-tes** (-tēz). *Archaic.* a quicksand: *Quencht in a boggy Syrtis, neither sea, Nor good dry land* (Milton). [< Latin *syrtis* < Greek *Sýrtis* (originally) either of two quicksands (Syrtis Major and Syrtis Minor) off the northern coast of Africa < *sýrein* to drag]

**syr|up** (sir′əp, sėr′-), *n.* **1** sugar boiled in water or fruit juice: *cherries canned in syrup.* **2** a solution of sugar in a medicated liquid: *cough syrup.* **3** a sweet, thick liquid obtained especially in the manufacture of sugar, glucose, cornstarch, and sorghum, such as molasses, corn syrup, and maple syrup. **4** *Figurative.* excessive sweetness or sentimentality: *Spiritual life is not all syrup, and* [*these*] *poems are almost all of them syrup* (Spectator). Also, **sirup**. [Middle English *sirop* < Old French < Arabic *sharāb* a drink. Compare etym. under **sherbet**, **shrub**[2].] —**syr′up|like′**, *adj.*

**syr|up|y** (sir′ə pē, sėr′-), *adj.* **1** like syrup in consistency or sweetness: *The solution of the acid ... is a colorless syrupy liquid* (William H. Jones). **2** having to do with syrup. **3** *Figurative.* like syrup; overly sweet or sentimental: *a syrupy voice. An amusing, if slightly syrupy, display of paintings and drawings ...* (New Yorker). Also, **sirupy**.

**sys|sar|co|sis** (sis′är kō′sis), *n. Obsolete.* the union of bones by means of intervening muscle. [< New Latin *syssarcosis* < Greek *syssárkōsis* < *syssarkóesthai* unite with flesh (< *syn-* + *sárx, sarkós* flesh) + New Latin *-osis* -osis]

**syst.**, system.

**sys|tal|tic** (sis tal′tik), *adj.* **1** of the nature of contraction; contracting. **2** of or having to do with movement in which there is alternate contraction (systole) and dilatation (diastole): *the systaltic action of the heart.*
[< Late Latin *systalticus* < Greek *systaltikós* depressing < *syn-* together + *staltikós* astringent < *stéllein* to send; place. Compare etym. under **systole**.]

**sys|tem** (sis′təm), *n.* **1** a set of things or parts forming a whole: *a mountain system, a railroad system. Title to most of the nation's gold is held by the Federal Reserve System* (Wall Street Journal). *Not every system is treated in cybernetics. Cybernetics is only concerned with controlled systems* (V. G. Drozin). **2** an ordered group of facts, principles, or beliefs: *a system of government, a system of education. "Uncle Tom's Cabin" ... presented ... a succession of simple, poignant incidents inseparable from a system of slavery* (Sir Winston Churchill). **3** a theory or hypothesis, especially of the arrangement and relationship of the heavenly bodies by which their observed movements and phenomena are explained: *the Copernican system.* **4** a plan, scheme, or method: *a system of classification, a system for betting. The little boy has a system for always getting a ride home from school.* SYN: arrangement. **5** an orderly way of getting things done: *to read without system. She works by system, not by chance.* SYN: organization. **6a** a set of organs or parts in the body having the same or similar structure, or serving to perform some function: *the digestive system, the respiratory system. In all the more complex animals the systems are everywhere made up of unlike parts, each contributing a different portion of the general process* (A. Franklin Shull). See also **nervous system**. **b** the animal body as a whole; the organism in relation to its vital processes or functions: *to take food into the system. His sickness weakened his entire system. The living system is essentially an "open" thermodynamic system in which the cells are capable of exchanging energy with outside sources* (Atlantic). **c** each of the primary groups of tissues or parts in the higher plants. **7** a group of heavenly bodies forming a whole that follows certain natural laws: *the solar system.* **8** the world; universe. **9** *Geology.* a major division of rocks including two or more series and formed during a geological period: *Heterogeneous systems are made up of matter in different states of aggregation* (Parks and Steinbach). *Major segments of the geologic column, which are deemed to have worldwide application, are known as systems* (Raymond C. Moore).
**10** *Chemistry.* **a** a portion of matter made up of an assemblage of substances which are in, or tend to approach, equilibrium. A system is binary when it is made up of two substances, ternary if made up of three, and so on. **b** a substance, or an assemblage of substances, considered as a separate entity, isolated, at least in mind, for the purpose of restricted study: *Any system, such as a normal atom, containing equal numbers of protons and electrons, exhibits no net charge* (Sears and Zemansky).
**the system**, the network of established political, social, and economic institutions that control a country; the establishment; power structure: *Their ideologies differ, but in general their rationale is that "the system" is incapable of real change* (Time).
[< Late Latin *systēma, -atis* musical interval (in Medieval Latin, the universe) < Greek *sýstēma, -atos* < *synistánai* bring together < *syn-* together + *histánai* stand, place]

**sys|tem|at|ic** (sis′tə mat′ik), *adj.* **1** according to a system; having a system, method, or plan: *systematic work, a systematic investigation. The subject matter of all science is essentially the same: systematic observation and systematic presentation of the observations in communicable form* (F. H. George). *During the time when systematic classification was beginning to develop there was on foot a movement to give precise names to plants* (Fred W. Emerson). SYN: See syn. under **orderly**. **2** orderly in arranging things or in getting things done: *a very systematic person.* SYN: See syn. under **orderly**.
**3** regularly organized, done, or carried on, especially for an evil purpose: *a systematic attack on another person's character.* **4a** of, following, or arranged according to a system of classification. **b** = taxonomic. **5** *Statistics.* affecting all of a set of measurements; not random or chance: *a systematic error, systematic bias.*

**sys|tem|at|i|cal** (sis′tə mat′ə kəl), *adj.* = systematic.

**sys|tem|at|i|cal|ly** (sis′tə mat′ə klē), *adv.* with system; according to some plan or method.

**sys|tem|at|ic|ness** (sis′tə mat′ik nis), *n.* the quality of being systematic.

**sys|tem|at|ics** (sis′tə mat′iks), *n.* the subject or study of systems, especially of classification: *There are a number of works on the morphology and systematics of many of these animals* (Science).

**sys|tem|a|tise** (sis′tə mə tīz), *v.t.*, **-tised**, **-tis|ing**. *Especially British.* systematize. —**sys′tem|a|tis′er**, *n.*

**sys|tem|a|tism** (sis′tə mə tiz′əm), *n.* systematizing.

**sys|tem|a|tist** (sis′tə mə tist), *n.* **1** a person who constructs, or adheres to a system. **2** a naturalist who constructs or is expert in systems of classification; taxonomist: *It has been said that John Ray ... an Englishman, was the first true systematist* (A. Franklin Shull).

**sys|tem|a|tize** (sis′tə mə tīz), *v.t.*, **-tized**, **-tiz|ing**. to arrange according to a system; make into a system; make more systematic. SYN: organize, order. —**sys′tem|a|ti|za′tion**, *n.* —**sys′tem|a|tiz′er**, *n.*

**sys|tem|a|tol|o|gy** (sis′tə mə tol′ə jē), *n.* the science of systems or their formation.

**sys|temed** (sis′təmd), *adj.* made into a system; systematized: *Ere systemed suns were globed and lit The slaughters of the race were writ* (Thomas Hardy).

**sys|tem|ic** (sis tem′ik), *adj., n.* —*adj.* **1** having to do with, supplying, or affecting the body as a whole: *systemic sensations, systemic circulation. A systemic poison is absorbed into the plant itself, not merely sprayed on the outside* (Harper's). **2** having to do with or affecting a particular system of parts or organs of the body, especially the nervous system: *systemic lesion.* **3** of or having to do with a system: *Systemic patterns are blocks or pieces of culture or language sharing a content that is of common origin and is arranged in a common pattern* (Alfred L. Kroeber).
—*n.* a systemic insecticide or other poison: *These ... systemics spread as the plant grows and do not wash off in rain* (Science News Letter).

**sys|tem|i|cal|ly** (sis tem′ə klē), *adv.* in a systemic manner; in or on the body as a whole.

**systemic circulation**, the part of the circulatory system that carries the blood from the heart to the other parts of the body.

**systemic insecticide**, an insecticide that a plant is able to absorb throughout its circulatory system without harm to itself: *These systemic insecticides are all compounds of phosphorus, and by preparing them from radioactive phosphorus the scientists are able to trace their course after they are sprayed onto plants* (Science News Letter).

**sys|tem|ic|i|ty** (sis′tə mis′ə tē), *n.* the quality or condition of being systemic.

**systemic lupus erythematosus**, the acute, fatal form of lupus erythematosus, attacking both the skin and viscera of the body.

**systemic painting**, **1** painting in the style of minimal art. **2** a painting done in this style.

**sys|tem|ist** (sis′tə mist), *n.* = systematist.

**sys|tem|ize** (sis′tə mīz), *v.t.*, **-ized**, **-iz|ing**. = systematize. —**sys′tem|i|za′tion**, *n.* —**sys′tem|iz′er**, *n.*

**sys|tem|less** (sis′təm lis), *adj.* without system.

**sys|tems analysis** (sis′təmz), the scientific and mathematical analysis of systems to improve their efficiency, accuracy, or general performance, especially through the optimal use of electronic computer or data-processing machines; operations research: *Systems analysis has gotten its biggest boost from the space industry, which could scarcely hope that huge rockets and space vehicles, made in pieces by 40 or 50 subcontractors, would work when put together without some overall way of keeping track of all the loose ends* (Science News).

**systems analyst**, an expert in systems analysis: *A systems analyst in an industrial plant might analyze time studies, inventory records, marketing forecasts, and equipment downtime to develop a computer-based, integrated production system* (Steven Norwood).

**systems engineer**, an expert in systems engineering.

**systems engineering**, that branch of engineering that specializes in the technical and economic aspects of production systems.

**sys|tem|wide** (sis′təm wīd′), *adj.* covering the entire system; over and throughout all of a system: *The central board's plan provides for a systemwide school curriculum that would meet city as well as state standards* (New York Times).

**sys|to|le** (sis′tə lē), *n.* **1** the normal, rhythmical contraction of the heart, especially that of the ventricles, when blood is pumped from the heart into the arteries. Systole alternates with diastole, the two together constituting the cardiac cycle. **2** the shortening of a long syllable in Greek or Latin verse. [< New Latin *systole* < Greek *systolḗ* contraction < *syn-* together + *stéllein* to put]

**sys|tol|ic** (sis tol′ik), *adj.* of, having to do with, or characterized by a contraction of the heart.

**Sys|tox** (sis′toks), *n. Trademark.* = demeton.

**syz|y|get|ic** (siz′ə jet′ik), *adj.* having to do with a syzygy or syzygies.

**syz|y|get|i|cal|ly** (siz′ə jet′ə klē), *adv.* with reference to a syzygy or syzygies.

**sy|zyg|i|al** (si zij′ē əl), *adj.* having to do with or of the nature of a syzygy.

**syz|y|gy** (siz′ə jē), *n., pl.* **-gies**. **1** *Astronomy.* the conjunction or opposition of two heavenly bodies, or either of the points at which these occur, especially with respect to the sun and the moon: *Cognate problems are the determination of the syzygies, last visibilities of the moon, and eclipses* (I. Bernard Cohen). **2** (in Greek and Latin prosody) a dipody, or combination of two like feet (or sometimes of two unlike feet). [< Latin *sȳzygia* < Greek *sȳzygíā* yoke (pair); any union (of two) < *syzygeîn* to yoke (in pairs) < *syn-* together + *zygón* yoke]

# T t

***T¹**, **t** (tē), *n., pl.* **T's** or **Ts**, **t's** or **ts**. **1** the 20th letter of the English alphabet. There are two *t*'s in *tablet.* **2** any sound represented by this letter.
**3** (used as a symbol for) the 20th, or more usually 19th, of an actual or possible series (either *I* or *J* being omitted).
**cross one's** (or **the**) **t's**, to be minutely exact; emphasize even small points: *Cross his t's and polish up his manuscript* (Manchester Examiner).
**to a T**, exactly; perfectly: *That suits me to a T.*

**T²** (tē), *n., pl.* **T's**, *adj.* —*n.* anything shaped like the letter T.
—*adj.* shaped like the letter T.

**'t**, *Poetic and Dialect.* contraction of *it* with a verb, as in *'twas, see't.*

**-t**, *suffix.* a variant of the ending **-ed** in certain verbs, as in *slept, meant, built.* See **-ed¹** and **-ed²**.

**t** (no period), *Statistics.* distribution.

**t.**, an abbreviation for the following:
**1** in the time of (Latin, *tempore*).
**2** metric ton (French, *tonneau*).
**3** tare.
**4** teaspoon or teaspoons.
**5** temperature.
**6** tempo.
**7** tenor.
**8** time.
**9** ton or tons.
**10** town.
**11** volume (French, *tome* or Latin, *tomus*).

**T** (no period), an abbreviation or symbol for:
**1** temperature (absolute).
**2** (surface) tension.
**3** tera-.
**4** tesla.
**5** thymine.
**6** *Physics.* time.
**7** *Astronomy.* time of passing perihelion.
**8** firing time or launch time, as of a rocket: *At T minus 139 minutes, wispy white plumes of supercold liquid oxygen will stream out of the Thor's side vents* (Newsweek).
**9** time reversal.
**10** *Chemistry.* tritium.

**T.**, an abbreviation for the following:
**1** tablespoon or tablespoons.
**2** tenor.
**3** ton or tons.
**4** Tuesday.
**5** Turkish.
**6** Turkish (pounds).

**ta** (tä), *interj., n. Especially British Informal.* thank you; thanks: *Not that he said so much as a ta but it isn't the thanks you look for* (Punch). [a child's word]

**Ta** (no period), tantalum (chemical element).

**TA** (no periods), an abbreviation for the following:
**1** teaching assistant.
**2** technology assessment.
**3** therapeutic abortion.
**4** toxin-antitoxin.
**5** transactional analysis.
**6** Transit Authority.

**T-A** (no periods), toxin-antitoxin.

**T.A.**, an abbreviation for the following:
**1** teaching assistant.
**2** *British.* Territorial Army.
**3** toxin-antitoxin.
**4** Transit Authority.

**TAA** (no periods), Technical Assistance Administration (for projects in economic development, social welfare, and public administration in various countries).

**Taal** (täl), *n.* a dialect of Dutch spoken in South Africa; Afrikaans; Cape Dutch: *He speaks the Taal better than a Hollander can, and can understand the Boers better* (Westminster Gazette). [< Afrikaans *Taal,* Dutch, language, speech < Middle Dutch *tāle* speech]

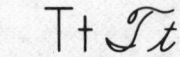

**Ta|a|nith Es|ther** (tä'ä nit' es ter', tä'nəs es'tər), *Hebrew.* Fast of Esther.

**tab¹** (tab), *n., v.,* **tabbed, tab|bing.** —*n.* **1** a small flap, strap, loop, or piece of some material: *He wore a fur cap with tabs over the ears.* **2** a small extension of or attachment to a card, usually used for labeling, numbering, coding, or otherwise marking in filing. **3** = label (def. 1). **4** *Aeronautics.* an auxiliary control surface set into or attached to a larger one such as a rudder.
**5** *British.* **a** a colored strap or strip worn by a staff officer: *The officer ... who cannot stand the glory of his tabs* (Newsweek). **b** a staff officer.
**6** a small, narrow drop curtain in a theater: *will perform a thrilling twenty-minute excerpt from next week's play, in front of the tabs* (Punch). **7** a piece of leather worn by an archer on the fingers to protect them from the bowstring.
—*v.t.* **1** to put a tab on (something). **2** to name, mark, or identify.
[origin uncertain]

**tab²** (tab), *n., adj., v.,* **tabbed, tab|bing.** *Informal.* —*n.* **1** a bill or check; expense: *The company picked up the tab for the annual picnic.* **2** = tabulator. —*adj.* tabulating. —*v.t.* = tabulate.
**keep tab** (or **tabs, a tab**) **on** (or **upon**), *Informal.* to keep track of; keep watch on; check: *A mother keeps tabs on her children. The foreman kept tab on the workmen.*
[short for *table* and *tabulation*]

**tab³** (tab), *n. Informal.* a tabloid: *a lively, well-edited tab.* [short for *tabloid*]

**tab⁴** (tab), *n. U.S. Informal.* a tablet: *an amphetamine tab.* [short for *tablet*]

**tab.**, table or tables.

**tab|a|nid** (tab'ə nid, tə ban'id), *adj., n.* —*adj.* of or belonging to the family of dipterous insects comprising the horseflies.
—*n.* a tabanid insect; horsefly.
[< New Latin *Tabanidae* the family name < Latin *tabanus* horsefly]

***tab|ard** (tab'ərd), *n.* **1** a short, loose coat worn by heralds, emblazoned with the arms of their sovereign. **2** a mantle worn by knights over their armor, generally embroidered with the arms of the wearer. **3** coarse outer garment worn by the poor during the Middle Ages. [< Old French *tabart,* later *tabar* < Latin *tapēte* figured cloth, tapestry]

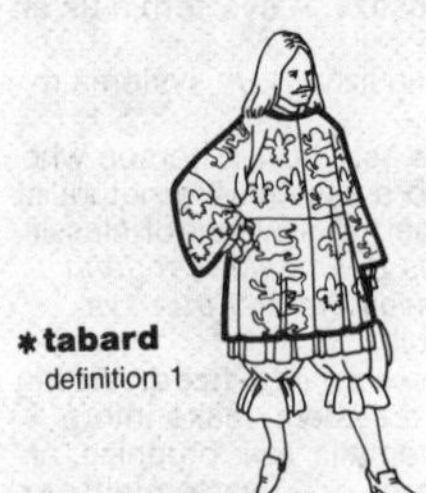

***tabard**
definition 1

**tab|ard|ed** (tab'ər did), *adj.* wearing a tabard: *The Queen ... marched ... past lines of tabarded heralds* (Time).

**tab|a|ret** (tab'ər it), *n.* an upholstery material with alternate satin and watered stripes. [compare etym. under **taboret**]

**Ta|bas|co** (tə bas'kō), *n. Trademark.* a kind of peppery sauce, used on fish or meat, prepared from the fruit of a variety of capsicum. [American English < *Tabasco,* a state in Mexico]

**tab|a|sheer** or **tab|a|shir** (tab'ə shir'), *n.* a siliceous concretion formed in the joints of the bamboo, used in the East as a medicine. [< Arabic, Persian, Hindustani *tabāshīr*]

**ta|ba|tière** (tȧ bȧ tyer'), *n. French.* a snuffbox.

**tab|by¹** (tab'ē), *n., pl.* **-bies,** *adj.* —*n.* **1** a brown, gray, or tawny cat with darker streaks and spots. **2** a female cat. **3** an old maid; spinster. **4** *Figurative.* a spiteful female gossip: *a lot of old tabbies always busy criticising* (Sinclair Lewis). **5** *Australian Slang.* a woman or girl.
—*adj.* brown, gray, or tawny with darker streaks and spots; brindled: *a tabby cat.*
[probably alteration (influenced by the proper name *Tabby* < *Tabitha*) of earlier *tibby,* type name for a female (paired with *Tom* for a male). Compare *Tibbert,* a typical cat name in medieval Reynard stories.]

**tab|by²** (tab'ē), *n., pl.* **-bies,** *adj., v.,* **-bied, -by|ing.** —*n.* any silk cloth with a striped, wavy, or watered pattern or marking, such as silk taffeta.
—*adj.* **1** like tabby. **2** made of the fabric tabby.
—*v.t.* to give a wavy appearance to (silk or other material) by calendering.
[< French *tabis* < Middle French *atabis* < Arabic *'Attābiy* a section of Bagdad where such cloth was first made]

**tab card**, a punch card for an electronic tabulator.

**tab|e|fac|tion** (tab'ə fak'shən), *n.* the fact or process of wasting away or consumption of the body by disease; emaciation; tabes. [< Late Latin *tābefactus,* past participle of *tābefacere* cause to waste away (< Latin *tābēre* waste away + *facere* make) + English *-ion*]

**ta|ber** (tā'bər), *n., v.i., v.t.* = tabor.

**Tab|er|nac|le** (tab'ər nak'əl), *n.* the covered wooden framework carried by the Jews for use as a place of worship during their journey from Egypt to Palestine; Tent of Meeting (in the Bible, Exodus 25-27). [< Latin *tabernāculum* tent, shed, place for religious rites (diminutive) < *taberna* cabin, booth]

**tab|er|nac|le** (tab'ər nak'əl), *n., v.,* **-led, -ling.** —*n.* **1** a temporary dwelling; tent. **2** *Figurative.* the human body thought of as the temporary dwelling of the soul. **3** a place of worship for a large congregation, such as a meeting house used chiefly by Baptists and Methodists in England, or a Congregationalist or Independent place of worship in Scotland. **4** a Jewish temple; synagogue. **5** a recess covered with a canopy and used as a shrine. **6** a container for something holy or precious; container for the consecrated bread used in the Mass.
—*v.i.* to dwell for a time; sojourn.
—*v.t.* to enshrine: *In thee the light, Creation's eldest born, was tabernacled* (Henry H. Milman).
[< *Tabernacle*]

**Tab|er|nac|les** (tab'ər nak'əls), *n.pl.* the Jewish festival of Sukkoth. It is marked by the building of temporary dwellings symbolizing the tabernacles used by the Jews in their journey to Palestine. *More than any other of the Jewish festivals, Tabernacles claims to be a holy day distinctly commemorative of the harvest* (Westminster Gazette).

**tabernacle work**, *Architecture.* **1** ornamental work of tracery used in tabernacles or canopies over tombs and stalls, and in the carved screens of churches. **2** work in which tabernacles form the characteristic feature.

**tab|er|nac|u|lar** (tab'ər nak'yə lər), *adj.* **1** having to do with a tabernacle. **2** like or characteristic of a tabernacle.

**ta|bes** (tā'bēz), *n.* **1** = tabes dorsalis. **2** *Obsolete.* a gradually progressive emaciation; consumption. [< Latin *tābēs, -is* a wasting disease; (literally) a melting away]

**ta|bes|cence** (tə bes'əns), *n.* = tabefaction.

**ta|bes|cent** (tə bes'ənt), *adj.* wasting away. [< Latin *tābēscēns, -entis,* present participle of *tābēscere* < *tābēre* waste away < *tābēs;* see etym. under **tabes**]

**ta|bes dor|sa|lis** (tā'bēz dôr sā'lis), a disease of the spinal cord marked by loss of control over walking and other movements; locomotor ataxia. [< New Latin *tabes dorsalis* consumption of the back]

**ta|bet|ic** (tə bet'ik), *adj., n.* —*adj.* **1** having to do with tabes dorsalis. **2** suffering from tabes dorsalis.
—*n.* a person who has tabes dorsalis.
[< Latin *tābēs* (see etym. under **tabes**); patterned on *diabetic*]

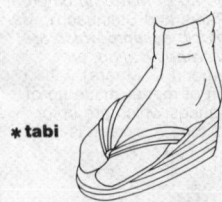

***tabi**

***ta|bi** (tä'bē), *n., pl.* **-bi.** *Japanese.* a low, white or blue cotton, silk, or nylon sock, with a thick sole and a separate part for the big toe, worn with a

***T¹**
definition 1

Script letters look like examples of fine penmanship. They appear in many formal uses, such as invitations to social functions.

Handwritten letters, both manuscript or printed (left) and cursive (right), are easy for children to read and to write.

Roman letters have *serifs* (finishing strokes) adapted from the way Roman stonecutters carved their letters. This is *Times Roman* type.

Sans-serif letters are often called *gothic.* They have lines of even width and no serifs. This type face is called *Helvetica.*

Between roman and gothic, some letters have thick and thin lines with slight flares that suggest serifs. This type face is *Optima.*

Computer letters can be sensed by machines either from their shapes or from the magnetic ink with which they are printed.

sandal or wooden clog: *A Japanese in rubber-soled tabi and a workman's short black jacket finished a bottle* (New Yorker).

**tab|id** (tab′id), *adj.* = tabetic.

**tab|la** (tä′blä), *n.* a small drum of India played with the hand and tuned to various notes. [< Hindustani *tabla* < Arabic *tabl* drum]

**tab|la|ture** (tab′lə chər), *n.* **1** an old name for musical notation in general, especially for systems differing from ordinary staff notation by using letters, numbers, or other symbols to indicate the strings and frets to be played: *Organ tablature was a system of writing the notes without the stave by means of letters* (Stainer and Barrett). **2** *Obsolete.* a tabular formation or structure having an inscription or design. **3** *Obsolete.* a painting; picture: *He prefers the Saracen's head upon a signpost before the best tablature of Raphael* (Henry H. Kames). [< Middle French *tablature* < Old French *table,* learned borrowing from Latin *tabula* slab for writing or painting]

**ta|ble** (tā′bəl), *n., adj., v.,* **-bled, -bling.** *—n.* **1** a piece of furniture having a smooth, flat top on legs: *a dining table, a surgeon's operating table.* **2** a table upon which food is served: *to set the silverware on a table.* **3** food put on a table to be eaten; fare: *Your mother sets a good table.* **4** the entertainment of a family or guests at a table; eating; feasting. **5** the persons seated at a table, especially at a dinner or for discussion: *The whole table joined in the conversation.* **6** an arrangement of numbers, words, or other items in columns and lines to show some relation distinctly; tabulated form: *the multiplication table, tables of weights or measure, insurance tables.* **7** information in a very brief form; list: *the table of contents in the front of a book.* **SYN**: schedule, synopsis. **8** a flat or plane surface like that of a table; level area. **9** = tableland. **10** *Architecture.* **a** a horizontal molding, especially a cornice. **b** a panel (of a wall). **11** the flat surface at the top of a jewel. **12** *Anatomy.* either of the two large bones of the skull separated by the diploë. **13** a thin, flat piece of wood, stone, metal, or other material; tablet: *The Ten Commandments were written on tables of stone.* **14** matter inscribed or written on tables. **15** either of the two leaves of a backgammon board.

*—adj.* **1** of or for a table: *a cloth for table use, a table-model television, a table lamp.* **2** suitable for or used at meals: *a table glass, table manners.*

*—v.t.* **1** to make a list or statement in tabulated form; tabulate; catalog. **2** to put (a card, money, or token) on a table. **3** *U.S.* **a** to put off discussing (a bill or motion) until a future time by voting to leave it on the table of the presiding officer. **b** = shelve. **4** *British.* to submit (a bill or motion) for discussion or consideration; bring forward. **5** to provide with meals.

**lay** (or **set**) **the table,** to put dishes and silver, but not food, on the table for a meal: *You may as well set the table for two* (J. T. Trowbridge).

**on** (or **upon**) **the table,** (of a report, motion, bill, or the like) on the table of the presiding officer so that the discussion is postponed: *that for the present this report be received and laid on the table* (Transactions of the Philological Society).

**tables,** the multiplication table: *She has already memorized her tables.*

**the tables,** certain collections of ancient Greek and Roman laws cut or carved on thin, flat pieces of stone: *In the comparison of the tables of Solon with those of the Decemvirs, some casual resemblance may be found* (Edward Gibbon).

**turn the tables (on),** to reverse conditions or circumstances completely: *They had won the first game, but we turned the tables on them and won the second.*

**under the table,** not in the open; secretly; stealthily: *Some money changed hands under the table.*

[Old English *tabule, tabele,* ultimately < Latin *tabula* slab for writing or painting]

**tab|leau** (tab′lō, tab lō′), *n., pl.* **tab|leaux** (tab′lōz, tab lōz′), *less frequently,* **tab|leaus** (tab′lōz, tab-lōz′). **1** a striking scene; picture. **2** a representation of a person, statue, picture, scene, or incident, by a person or group posing in appropriate costume. Tableaux are silent and motionless. *Our school is going to present several tableaux from American history. Those who stumbled through the blackened halls and who could still keep their eyes open were rewarded with wax tableaus on which certain figures suddenly came alive only to freeze again* (Saturday Review). **3** *Figurative.* a picturesque or graphic description: *The book starts out with a tableau which in its intellectual irrelevance and mawkish sentimentality is the kind of journalism one has come to expect* (Hans J. Morgenthau). [< French *tableau* (diminutive) < Old French *table;* see etym. under **tablature**]

**ta|bleau vi|vant** (tȧ blō′ vē väɴ′), *pl.* **ta|bleaux vi|vants** (tȧ blō′ vē väɴ′). = tableau. [< French *tableau vivant* (literally) living picture]

**table chair,** a piece of furniture used either as a table or chair, the top turning back to a vertical position on the hinge.

**ta|ble|cloth** (tā′bəl klôth′, -kloth′), *n.* a cloth covering for a table: *Spread the tablecloth and set the table for dinner.*

**table cut,** a form of ornamentation in diamond cutting in which a usually flat stone is cut with long facets and bordered by beveled edges or smaller facets.

**ta|ble d'hôte** (tab′əl dōt′, tä′bəl), a meal served at a fixed time and price. In meals table d'hôte, there is one price for the whole meal; but in meals à la carte, a person chooses what he wants and pays for each article. [< French *table d'hôte* (literally) host's table]

**ta|ble|ful** (tā′bəl fu̇l), *n., pl.* **-fuls. 1** as many persons as can be seated at a table. **2** as many things as a table will hold.

**ta|ble-hop** (tā′bəl hop′), *v.i.,* **-hopped, -hop|ping.** *Informal.* to move from one table to another making brief visits, as in a restaurant or a night club: *An urbane raconteur,* [*he*] *spends much of his time happily table-hopping at fashionable restaurants* (Newsweek).

**table knife,** a knife used while eating, especially to cut meat.

**table lamp,** a lamp to light the surface of a table, usually placed on the table.

**ta|ble|land** (tā′bəl land′), *n.* a large, high plain; plateau: *These lofty plats of tableland seem to form a peculiar feature in the American continents* (Washington Irving). **SYN**: mesa, table. See picture under **plain**¹.

**ta|ble|less** (tā′bəl lis), *adj.* without a table; not furnished with a table.

**table lifting,** = table rapping.

**table linen,** tablecloths, napkins, doilies, and place mats.

**table mat,** a table covering, made of fabric, plastic, or wood, for an individual place setting; place mat.

**table|mate** (tā′bəl māt′), *n.* a person sitting next to one at a table or sharing at table with one.

**table money,** *British.* an extra allowance to higher officers of the British Army and Navy for expenses of official hospitality.

**table napkin,** a napkin used at meals.

**table of organization,** a table or publication that prescribes the organizational structure and personnel for a military unit.

**table rapping,** the production of raps or knocking sounds on a table without apparent physical means, used by spiritualists as a supposed means of communicating with departed spirits.

**table rock,** a flat-topped rock.

**ta|bles** (tā′bəlz), *n.pl.* See under **table.**

**table salt,** ordinary salt for use at the table; sodium chloride.

**tables of the law, 1** the stone slabs on which the Ten Commandments were inscribed. **2** = decalogue.

**ta|ble|spoon** (tā′bəl spün′, -spu̇n′), *n.* **1a** a spoon larger than a teaspoon or dessert spoon, used to serve food at the table and to eat soup and cereal from. **b** any large spoon used to serve vegetables and other food at the table; serving spoon. **2** a spoon used as a unit of measure in cooking. It holds the same amount as three teaspoons or ½ fluid ounce or 1.4786 centiliters. **3** = tablespoonful. *Abbr:* tbs., tbsp.

**ta|ble|spoon|ful** (tā′bəl spün fu̇l′, -spu̇n-), *n., pl.* **-fuls. 1** a standard unit of liquid measure used in cooking, equal to ½ fluid ounce; ¹⁄₁₆ cup; 3 teaspoonfuls or 1.4786 centiliters. **2** as much as a tablespoon holds.

**tab|let** (tab′lit), *n., v.,* **-let|ed, -let|ing** or **-let|ted, -let|ting.** *—n.* **1** a number of sheets of writing paper fastened together at one edge, often with a stiff back and a cover; pad: *A tablet of scratch paper was kept near the telephone.* **2a** a small, flat piece of medicine or candy; pill; lozenge: *That box contains twelve aspirin tablets.* **b** *British.* a cake of soap. **3** a small, flat surface with an inscription or bas-relief: *The Hall of Fame is a building that has many tablets in memory of famous people. Idealism ... is not static, not something writ on tablets, but a constantly developing attitude of heart and mind capable of embracing and giving new meaning to twentieth century society* (Listener). **4** a small, smooth place of stone, wood, ivory, or other material, used in ancient times to write or draw on; sheet or slab. A tablet was covered with wax or clay and often hinged with another. The ancient Romans used tablets as we use pads of paper.

*—v.t.* **1** to make into a tablet or tablets: *Their figures did not include the cost of tableting and distributing the bulk powder* (New Yorker). **2** to furnish with a tablet or tablets: [*The*] *chapel* [*is*] *tableted with the names of some who have died in their country's service* (Westminster Gazette).

[< Old French *tablete,* later *tablette* < *table;* see etym. under **tablature**]

**table talk, 1** conversation at meals: *The role of family table talk has not been generally appreciated* (Emory S. Bogardus). **2** the social conversation of famous men or intellectual circles, especially as reproduced in literary form. **3** a subject for table talk: *To be the table talk of clubs upstairs* (William Cowper).

**table tennis,** a game played on a large table marked somewhat like a tennis court, using small wooden rackets and a light, hollow plastic ball; ping-pong.

**ta|ble|top** (tā′bəl top′), *n., adj.* *—n.* **1** the upper surface of a table. **2** the flat top of a hill, rock, or other like surface.

*—adj.* designed to be used on a tabletop: *a tabletop radio.*

**ta|ble|ware** (tā′bəl wãr′), *n.* the dishes, knives, forks, spoons, and linen used at meals.

**table wine,** a wine that is generally served with meals.

**ta|ble-work** (tā′bəl wėrk′), *n. Printing.* the setting of columns of figures, tables, or other copy in very narrow measure.

**ta|bli|er** (tȧ bli ā′), *n. French.* **1** an apron. **2** an apronlike piece in a woman's dress: *The bride ... wore a dress of striped white satin with pearl tablier in front and net veil* (Pall Mall Gazette).

**tab|loid** (tab′loid), *n., adj.* *—n.* **1** a newspaper, usually having half the ordinary size newspaper page, that has many pictures and gives the news in short articles and large, often sensational, headlines: *He launches another tabloid, "Municipal News," for mayors and civic officials* (Canada Month). **2** a tablet of medicine or a chemical; pill; pellet: *Burroughs Wellcome registered the word Tabloid years ago, and rise up in reproof whenever they see it spelt with a small T* (Punch).

*—adj.* in the form of a summary, capsule, or digest; condensed: *tabloid writing.*

[originally *Tabloid,* a trademark for compressed or concentrated chemicals < *tabl*(et) + *-oid*]

**ta|boo** (tə bü′, ta-), *adj., v.,* **-booed, -boo|ing,** *n., pl.* **-boos.** *—adj.* **1** forbidden by custom or tradition; banned; prohibited: *Eating human flesh is taboo in civilized countries. The mention of her neighbours is evidently taboo, since ... she is in a state of affront with nine-tenths of them* (Mary R. Mitford). **2** set apart as sacred or cursed. Among the Polynesians certain things, places, and persons are taboo.

*—v.t.* **1** to make taboo; forbid; ban; prohibit: *The Scandinavians, the Dutch and the Swiss all taboo masculine tears* (David Gunston). **SYN**: proscribe. **2** to forbid social contact with; ostracize; boycott: *You cannot taboo a man who has got a vote* (Lord Bryce).

*—n.* **1** any ban on a practice or on the use of something: prohibition. **SYN**: interdiction. **2** a ban on association with someone; exclusion from social relations; ostracism. **3a** the system or act of setting things apart as forbidden. The Polynesians have many taboos under which certain things, places, and persons are set apart or prohibited as sacred, unclean, or cursed. *The sacred protection of an express edict of the taboo, declaring his person inviolable for ever* (Herman Melville). **b** the fact or condition of being so placed: *whoever violates the taboo will presumably be stricken to death by unseen beings* (Emory S. Bogardus). **c** the prohibition or interdict itself: *Taboos were enforced by invoking fear* (Emory S. Bogardus). Also, **tabu.**

[< Tongan *tabu*]

▶ **taboo, tabu.** *Taboo* is more generally used than *tabu,* except in anthropology.

**ta|bor** or **ta|bour** (tā′bər), *n., v.* *—n.* a small drum, used especially by a person playing a pipe or fife to accompany himself: *The whole neighbourhood came out to meet their minister ... preceded by a pipe and tabor* (Oliver Goldsmith).

*—v.i.* to beat or play on a tabor.

*—v.t. Obsolete.* to beat (anything); thrash. Also, **taber.**

[< Old French *tabour, tabur* < Persian *tabīrah* drum] —**ta′bor|er, ta′bour|er,** *n.*

**tab|o|ret** or **tab|ou|ret** (tab′ər it, tab′ə ret′), *n.* **1** a stool: *He had bought a new easel and two rush-bottomed tabourets* (W. C. Morrow). **2** a small, low table; stand. **3** = embroidery frame. **4** *Archaic.* a small tabor; timbrel. [< French *tabouret* < Middle French (diminutive) < Old French *tabour;* see etym. under **tabor**]

**tab|o|rin, tab|o|rine,** or **tab|ou|rine** (tab′ər in),

*n.* a drum narrower and longer than the tabor. [< Middle French *tabourin* (diminutive) < Old French *tabour*]

**tab|ret** (tab′rit), *n. Archaic.* a small tabor.

**Ta|briz** (tə brēz′), *n.* a Persian rug of cotton and wool with a medallion design, originally woven in Tabriz, a city in northwestern Iran.

**ta|bu** (tə bü′, ta-), *adj., v.,* **-bued, -bu|ing,** *n., pl.* **-bus.** = taboo.
➤ See **taboo** for usage note.

**tab|u|la** (tab′yə lə), *n., pl.* **-lae** (-lē). **1** in ancient Rome: **a** a table or tablet, especially a writing tablet. **b** a writing or document. **c** a legal instrument or record. **2** *Ecclesiastical.* a wooden or metal frontal. [< Latin *tabula;* see etym. under **table**]

**tab|u|lar** (tab′yə lər), *adj.* **1** of tables or lists. **2** entered in a table or arranged in lists; written or printed in columns: *tabular data.* **3** (of a quantity) read from or calculated by means of tables. **4** flat like a table: *a tabular rock.* **5** having the form of a tablet, slab, or tablature; flat and usually thin. **6** tending to split into flat, thin pieces, as a rock. [< Latin *tabulāris* having to do with a slab or plate < *tabula* slab; see etym. under **table**] —**tab′u|lar|ly,** *adv.*

**ta|bu|la ra|sa** (tab′yə lə rā′sə, rā′sə), *pl.* **ta|bu|lae ra|sae** (tab′yə lē rā′sē, rā′sē). *Latin.* **1** the mind before it is developed and changed by experience: *The mind for* [*Locke*] *is entirely passive, a clean blackboard, tabula rasa, on which the experiences of the individual write their own impressions* (Norbert Wiener). *No scientist starts with a tabula rasa, a clean slate* (George Simpson). **2** (literally) an erased (wax) tablet.

**tab|u|lar|ize** (tab′yə lə rīz), *v.t.,* **-ized, -iz|ing.** to make tabular; put into tabular form; tabulate. —**tab′u|lar|i|za′tion,** *n.*

**tab|u|late** (*v.* tab′yə lāt; *adj.* tab′yə lit, -lāt), *v.,* **-lat|ed, -lat|ing,** *adj.* —*v.t., v.i.* to arrange (facts or figures) in tables or lists.
—*adj.* **1** shaped like a table or a tablet; tabular. **2** having horizontal partitions: *tabulate corals.* [< Latin *tabula* (see etym. under **table**) + *-ate*[1]]

**tab|u|lat|ing machine** (tab′yə lā′ting), = tabulator.

**tab|u|la|tion** (tab′yə lā′shən), *n.* **1** the process of arranging in tables or lists: *In 1950, it took 1,400 people a year to prepare the census takers' findings for tabulation* (Newsweek). **2** the fact or condition of being arranged in tables or lists.

**tab|u|la|tor** (tab′yə lā′tər), *n.* **1** a person or thing that tabulates. **2** a typewriter attachment for spacing figures in neat columns. **3** a computing machine that takes in punch cards and instructions and produces lists, totals, and tabulations of the information on separate forms or on continuous paper.

**ta|bun** (tä bün′), *n.* a toxic nerve gas for military use, first synthesized in Germany. *Formula:* $C_5H_{11}N_2O_2P$ [< German *Tabun*]

**TAC** (no periods), Tactical Air Command (a branch of the United States Air Force which provides air support for land and sea forces, ready for use in any part of the world).

**tac|a|ma|hac** (tak′ə mə hak), *n.* **1** an aromatic gum resin, used in incense, in ointments, and formerly in medicines: **a** (originally) a resin from a Mexican tree. **b** (later) any similar resin from various trees of tropical America, Madagascar, or the East Indies. **c** resin from the buds of the North American balsam poplar. **2** any one of these trees, especially the balsam poplar. Also, **tacmahac, tacmahack.** [< Spanish *tacamahaca* < Nahuatl *tecamaca*]

**tac|a|ma|hac|a** (tak′ə mə hak′ə), *n.* = tacamahac.

**TACAN** (no periods), or **Tac|an** (tak′an), *n.* Tactical Air Navigation (an electronic unit in an aircraft that supplies a pilot with continuous readings of his distance and bearing from a fixed station, by an emitted pulse and automatic reply).

**ta|ces** (tā′sēz), *n.pl. Obsolete.* tasses.

**ta|cet** (tā′sit), *v.i. Music.* to be silent (used as an indication that an instrument or voice is to be silent for a time). [< Latin *tacet,* third person singular, present indicative of *tacēre* to be silent]

**tache** or **tach** (tach), *n. Archaic.* **1** any device for fastening, such as a clasp, buckle, hook and eye, or hook: *Taches of gold ... connecting together the curtains of the tabernacle* (Hugh Macmillan). **2** *Figurative: Finally, the word became ... a tach between the external object and the internal impression* (Frederic W. Farrar). **SYN:** link, bond. [< Old French *tache* a pin, brooch, nail < the same root as in *attach, attack, tack*]

**tach|e|om|e|ter** (tak′ē om′ə tər), *n.* = tachymeter.

**tach|i|na fly** (tak′ə nə), any one of a group of dipterous insects resembling the housefly whose larvae are parasitic in caterpillars and other insects. [< New Latin *Tachina* the genus name < Greek *tachinē* swift]

**Ta Ch'ing** (dä′ ching′), the Manchu dynasty, 1644-1912; Ch'ing.

**tach|i|nid** (tak′ə nid), *adj., n.* —*adj.* of or belonging to a family of thick-set, quick-moving dipterous insects including the tachina fly.
—*n.* a tachinid insect.
[< New Latin *Tachinidae* the family name < *Tachina* the tachina fly genus]

**tach|i|ol** (tak′ē ōl, -ol), *n.* a yellowish, crystalline compound, used as an antiseptic; silver fluoride. *Formula:* $AgF \cdot H_2O$ [< *tachy-* + *-ol*[2]]

**tach|isme** or **tach|ism** (tash′iz əm; *French* tà shēz′mə), *n.* a style of painting in which colors are splashed or daubed on the canvas, allowing impulse rather than conscious effort to control the form and content of the picture; action painting. [< French *tachisme* < *tache* blot, stain + *-isme, -ism*]

**tach|ist** (tash′ist), *n., adj.* = tachiste.

**tach|iste** (tash′ist; *French* tà shēst′), *n., adj.*
—*n.* a painter who uses the style or technique of tachisme.
—*adj.* of or having to do with tachisme or tachistes: *The eucalyptus trees with their stringy bark like dribbled tachiste paintings drooped* (Manchester Guardian).
[< French *tachiste*]

**ta|chis|to|scope** (tə kis′tə skōp), *n.* an apparatus which exposes to view, for a selected brief period of time, an object or group of objects such as letters or words. The tachistoscope is used especially in experimental psychology. [< Greek *táchistos* swiftest, superlative of *tachýs* swift + English *-scope*]

**ta|chis|to|scop|ic** (tə kis′tə skop′ik), *adj.* of or having to do with a tachistoscope: ... *tachistoscopic flashes on a screen* (Bulletin of Atomic Scientists).

**tach|o|gram** (tak′ə gram), *n.* a record made by a tachograph.

**tach|o|graph** (tak′ə graf, -gräf), *n.* **1** a tachometer which makes a record of its readings over a period of time. **2** = tachogram.

**ta|chom|e|ter** (tə kom′ə tər), *n.* **1** an instrument for measuring the speed of rotation, as of a shaft or wheel. **2** any one of various instruments for measuring or indicating speed, as of a river or the blood. [< Greek *táchos* speed + English *-meter*]

**ta|chom|e|try** (tə kom′ə trē), *n.* the measurement of velocity.

**tachy-,** *combining form.* swift; rapid: *Tachycardia = excessively fast heartbeat. Tachygraphy = the art of rapid writing.* [< Greek *tachýs*]

**tach|y|car|di|a** (tak′ə kär′dē ə), *n. Medicine.* excessively fast heartbeat. [< *tachy-* + Greek *kardíā* heart]

**tach|y|car|di|ac** (tak′ə kär′dē ak), *adj., n. Medicine.* —*adj.* of or having to do with tachycardia.
—*n.* a person with tachycardia: *One of my tachycardiacs began to ride a bicycle two years ago, and with much advantage* (Thomas C. Allbutt).

**tach|y|graph** (tak′ə graf, -gräf), *n.* **1** a tachygraphic writing or manuscript. **2** a writer of shorthand: *The other tachygraph, Phocas, had also reported this sermon* (Frederic W. Farrar). **3** a device for measuring the rate of flow of arterial blood.

**ta|chyg|ra|pher** (tə kig′rə fər), *n.* a writer of shorthand.

**tach|y|graph|ic** (tak′ə graf′ik), *adj.* **1** of tachygraphy. **2** written in shorthand. —**tach′y|graph′i|cal|ly,** *adv.*

**tach|y|graph|i|cal** (tak′ə graf′ə kəl), *adj.* = tachygraphic.

**ta|chyg|ra|phist** (tə kig′rə fist), *n.* = tachygrapher.

**ta|chyg|ra|phy** (tə kig′rə fē), *n.* **1** the art or practice of writing quickly. **2** shorthand, especially the ancient Greek and Roman form. **3** the art of writing in abbreviations, as in some Greek and Latin written in the Middle Ages. **4** cursive as letters.

**tach|y|lyte** or **tach|y|lite** (tak′ə līt), *n.* a black, glassy basalt of volcanic origin that is readily fusible: *Tachylites commonly occur as bombs and cinders, or scoria, thrown out by volcanoes* (Fenton and Fenton). [< German *Tachylit* < Greek *tachýs* swift + *lytós* soluble < *lýein* to loosen (because it is easily fusible)]

**tach|y|lyt|ic** (tak′ə lit′ik), *adj.* **1** composed of tachylyte. **2** resembling tachylyte. **3** containing tachylyte.

**ta|chym|e|ter** (tə kim′ə tər), *n.* **1** an instrument used especially to determine distances rapidly in a survey. **2** = tachometer.

**tach|y|met|ric** (tak′ə met′rik), *adj.* of or having to do with a tachymeter or tachymetry.

**ta|chym|e|try** (tə kim′ə trē), *n.* the use of the tachymeter.

**tach|y|on** (tak′ē on), *n.* a hypothetical elementary particle with a speed greater than that of light, whose existence has been inferred mathematically from Einstein's special theory of relativity: *At the velocity of light a tachyon would possess infinite energy and momentum; as the particle lost energy, it would speed up, until at zero energy its velocity would be infinite!* (New Scientist). [(coined by Gerald Feinberg, born 1933, an American physicist) < Greek *tachýs* swift + English *-on*]

**tach|yp|noe|a** (tak′ip nē′ə), *n. Medicine.* excessively rapid respiration. [< New Latin *tachypnoea* < Greek *tachýs* swift + *pneîn* breathe]

**ta|chys|ter|ol** (tə kis′tə rol), *n. Biochemistry.* a substance formed by irradiating ergosterol, becoming calciferol when further irradiated. *Formula:* $C_{28}H_{44}O$

**tac|it** (tas′it), *adj.* **1** implied or understood without being openly expressed: *His eating the food was a tacit admission that he liked it.* **SYN:** implicit. **2** saying nothing; still; silent: *Edward Strachey was ... a man rather tacit than discursive* (Thomas Carlyle). **3** unspoken; silent: *a tacit prayer.* **SYN:** unuttered, unexpressed. **4** *Law.* existing out of custom or from silent consent but not expressly stated. [< Latin *tacitus,* past participle of *tacēre* be silent] —**tac′it|ly,** *adv.* —**tac′it|ness,** *n.*

**Tac|i|te|an** (tas′ə tē′ən), *adj.* **1** of or having to do with Tacitus. **2** having a graphic, incisive style of writing: *His style is uneven, but redeemed by the occasional Tacitean touch* (Economist). [< *Tacitus,* A.D. 55?-about 120, a Roman historian, known for this style of writing + *-an*]

**tac|i|turn** (tas′ə tėrn), *adj.* saying very little; not fond of talking; inclined to silence: *At the Council board he was taciturn and ... never opened his lips* (Thackeray). **SYN:** reserved. See syn. under **silent.** [< Latin *taciturnus* < *tacitus;* see etym. under **tacit**] —**tac′i|turn|ly,** *adv.*

**tac|i|tur|ni|ty** (tas′ə tėr′nə tē), *n.* the habit of keeping silent; disinclination to talk much: *The secrets of nature Have not more gift in taciturnity* (Shakespeare). **SYN:** reserve, reticence.

***tack¹**
definition 6b

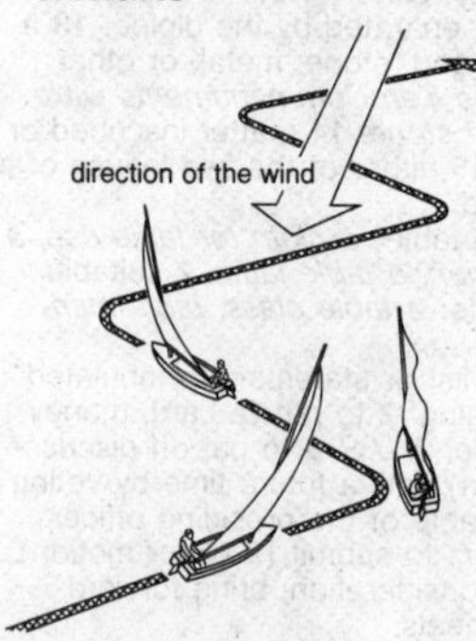


***tack¹** (tak), *n., v.* —*n.* **1** a short, sharp-pointed nail or pin with a flat, broad head: *We bought some carpet tacks.* **2** a long, loose stitch used as a temporary fastening before final sewing. **3** any very slight, loose fastening: *hanging by a tack.* **4a** the act of fastening lightly or temporarily. **b** the condition of being fastened this way. **5** adhesiveness; tackiness. **6** *Nautical.* **a** the direction in which a ship moves in regard to the direction of the wind and the position of her sails. When on port tack, a ship has the wind on her left. **b** a slanting or zigzag course against the wind. See picture above. **c** one of the straight runs in a zigzag course. **d** the act of zigzagging; turn from one straight run to the next. **7** *Figurative.* any zigzag movement. **8** *Figurative.* a course of action or conduct: *To demand what he wanted was the wrong tack to take with his father. They think the House will take a tougher tack on dollar-a-year men* (Wall Street Journal). **9** *Nautical.* the rope to hold in place the outer lower corner of some sails. The rope securing a course on a square-rigged ship and the rope securing a studding-sail to the end of the boom are both tacks. **b** the corner held by any such rope, such as the forward lower corner of a fore-and-aft sail. **10** saddles, harnesses, and other equipment for horses. **11** a bar or strip to hold up shoots or stems, in gardening. **12** a brace to hold a pipe to a wall.
—*v.t.* **1** to fasten with tacks (short nails): *to tack up a notice. She tacked mosquito netting over the windows.* **2** to sew with temporary stitches. **3** *Figurative.* to join together, often artificially or clumsily: *Traditional tales, tacked together without regard to place or chronology* (John Lingard). **4** *Figurative.* to attach (something separate); add (a supplement); append; annex: *She tacked a postscript to the end of her letter.* **5** *Nautical.* **a** to sail (a ship) in a zigzag course against the wind. **b** to turn (a ship) to sail at the same angle to the wind on the other side; change from one leg of a zigzag course to the next: *to tack ship.*

—*v.i.* 1 *Nautical.* of sailors or ships: **a** to sail in a zigzag course into the wind: *The ship was tacking, trying to make the harbor. The craft could tack … an art unknown to Europeans at the time of Columbus* (Beals and Hoijer). **b** to turn and sail at the same angle to the wind on the other side. **2** *Figurative.* to move along any zigzag route. **3** *Figurative.* to change one's attitude, conduct, or course of action. **4** *Figurative.* to use indirect methods.
[< Anglo-French *taque* nail, clasp, Old French *tache* < Germanic root] —**tack′er,** *n.*

**tack**[2] (tak), *n.* **1** things; stuff. **2** *Slang.* food: *I thought the canteen tack the nastiest stuff I had ever tasted* (D. C. Murray). [origin uncertain]

**tack**[3] (tak), *n. Scottish.* **1** tenancy of land, especially leasehold tenure. **2** the tenure of a benefice. **3** the period of tenure. [< Scottish *tac, tak* take]

**tack-driv|er** (tak′drī′vər), *n.* **1** a machine which automatically places and drives a series of tacks. **2** = tack-hammer.

**tack-ham|mer** (tak′ham′ər), *n.* a light hammer for driving tacks.

**tack|i|ly** (tak′ə lē), *adv.* = stickily.

**tack|i|ness** (tak′ē nis), *n.* = stickiness.

**tack|le** (tak′əl), *n., v.,* **-led, -ling.** —*n.* **1** any equipment; apparatus; gear. Fishing tackle means the rod, line, hooks, or other equipment used in catching fish. **2** a device consisting of a set of ropes and pulleys for lifting, lowering, or moving heavy things. It is usually designated as single or double tackle by the number of sheaves in a block, or by the object it moves; block and tackle. See picture under **block**. **3** *Nautical.* the rigging of a ship, especially the ropes and blocks by which the sails are raised and lowered. **4** a purchase consisting of a rope passed over sheaves or pulleys in two or more blocks. **5** any arrangement of rope passed through or over several blocks on sheaves. **6** *Football.* **a** the act of throwing the ball carrier to the ground. **b** an offensive or defensive player between the guard and the end on either side of the line. **c** any act of tackling.
—*v.t.* **1** to try to deal with, solve, or master (a task, difficulty, or problem); grapple with: *Everyone has his own problems to tackle. My brother usually tackles his homework before supper.* **2** to grip (a person or animal) physically; lay hold of; fasten upon; seize or attack: *The policeman tackled the thief and threw him.* **3** (in football and Rugby) to seize and stop or throw to the ground (an opponent who has the ball). **4** (in soccer) to obstruct (an opponent) in order to get the ball away from him. **5** to begin to eat (food). **6** to harness (a horse): *Go out and tackle the old mare, and have our wagon round to the house* (Harriet Beecher Stowe).
—*v.i.* **1** *Football.* to bring down and stop an opponent who has the ball: *That big fullback tackles hard.* **2** *Especially British Informal.* to set to; grapple: *We'll tackle to* (Anthony Trollope).
**tackle up,** to harness a horse: *I shall just tackle up and go over and bring them children home agin* (Harriet Beecher Stowe).
[Middle English *takel* gear, especially of a ship; hoisting apparatus, probably < Middle Low German] —**tack′ler,** *n.*

**tackle box,** a covered box to carry fishing tackle.

**tack|ling** (tak′ling), *n.* gear; tackle; equipment.

**tack room,** a room for storing gear and supplies, especially for riding.

**tacks|man** (taks′mən), *n., pl.* **-men.** *Scottish.* a person who holds a tack or lease of land from another; a tenant or lessee: *His grandfather, Malcolm, was "tacksman" of a farm … at the extreme north of the island* (Sunday Times). [< *tack's* (possessive of *tack*[3]) + *man*]

**tack|y**[1] (tak′ē), *adj.,* **tack|i|er, tack|i|est.** very sticky or gummy; adhesive: *A tacky disk surface permits changing the abrasives* (Science News Letter). [< *tack*[1] + *-y*[1]]

**tack|y**[2] (tak′ē), *adj.,* **tack|i|er, tack|i|est. 1** *Informal.* shabby; dowdy; tatty: [*They*] *have the knack of looking tacky even when they are wealthy and titled* (Kansas City Star). **2** *Slang, Figurative.* unpleasant; disagreeable: *They are quite tacky about drum beating, horn tooting and other such commercialistic clamor* (New Yorker). [American English; origin uncertain]

**tac|ma|hac** or **tac|ma|hack** (tak′mə hak), *n.* = tacamahac.

**ta|co** (tä′kō), *n., pl.* **-cos.** a rolled-up tortilla filled with chopped meat, chicken, cheese, onion, beans, and seasoning, and served hot. [< Mexican Spanish *taco*]

**tac|o|nite** (tak′ə nīt), *n.* a variety of chert which is about a third iron ore, occurring especially in the Mesabi Range: *At taconite plants, miners blast the rock from the ground, crush it to talcum fineness and separate a rich, black ore* (Wall Street Journal). [< the *Taconic* range, mountains on the western edge of New England + *-ite*[1]]

**tact** (takt), *n.* **1** the ability to say and do the right things; skill in dealing with people or handling difficult situations without giving offense; delicacy; diplomacy: *Mother's tact kept her from talking about things likely to be unpleasant to the guests. Tact consists in knowing how far we may go too far* (Jean Cocteau). SYN: finesse, tactfulness. **2** the practice of not giving offense. **3** the sense of touch; touch. **4** good judgment; sense. [< Latin *tāctus, -ūs* < *tangere* to touch]

**tact|ful** (takt′fəl), *adj.* **1** having tact: *Mother is a tactful person.* SYN: diplomatic. **2** showing tact: *A tactful reply does not hurt a person's feelings.* —**tact′ful|ly,** *adv.* —**tact′ful|ness,** *n.*

**tac|tic** (tak′tik), *n., adj.* —*n.* **1** a detail of military tactics; maneuver. **2** *Figurative.* any skillful move; tack; gambit. **3** a system of tactics; tactics. **4** *Mathematics.* (formerly) the study dealing with order and arrangement.
—*adj.* **1** *Biology.* **a** having to do with taxis. **b** characteristic of taxis. **2** having to do with arrangement or order.
[< Late Latin *tacticus* expert in arms < Greek *taktikós*; see etym. under **tactics**]

**tac|ti|cal** (tak′tə kəl), *adj.* **1** of tactics; concerning tactics. **2** having to do with the direction of military or naval forces in battle: *a tactical advantage.* **3** organized for or used in action against enemy troops, rather than against enemy bases or industry behind the lines of battle: *tactical air force, a tactical bomber. The distinction between tactical nuclear weapons and strategic nuclear weapons is almost entirely one of use* (Manchester Guardian). **4** *Figurative.* **a** characterized by skillful procedure, methods, or expedients; adroit; clever. **b** having to do with ways and means. —**tac′ti|cal|ly,** *adv.*

**Tactical Air Command,** = TAC.

**Tactical Air Navigation,** = TACAN.

**tactical dispersal,** (in civil defense) the movement of people outward from the center of a target area.

**tactical unit,** a unit of an army activated or organized to fight the enemy.

**tac|ti|cian** (tak tish′ən), *n.* an expert in tactics: (*Figurative.*) *He accumulated the experience that made him a political tactician who was useful to his party and to his country* (Wall Street Journal).

**tac|tics** (tak′tiks), *n.* **1** the art or science of directing military or naval forces in battle; science of disposition and maneuver. **2** a method or process of doing this. **3** the operations themselves: *The tactics of pretending to cross the river and of making a retreat fooled the enemy. Tactics are used to win an engagement, strategy to win a campaign or a war* (Bulletin of Atomic Scientists). **4** *Figurative.* procedures to gain advantages or success; methods: *When coaxing failed, she changed her tactics and began to cry. To some the obvious answer was to fight fire with fire, to reply in kind if* [*they*] *resorted to bully-boy tactics* (Newsweek). [plural of *tactic* < New Latin *tactica* < Greek *taktikḗ* (*téchnē*) (art of) arrangement, ultimately < *tássein* arrange]
▶ **Tactics,** meaning the science, is plural in form and singular in use: *Tactics differs from strategy, which refers to the overall plans of a nation at war.* Otherwise, it is plural in form and use: *The general's tactics were successful. His tactics in winning the class election were hardly ethical.* See **strategy** for another usage note.

**tac|tile** (tak′təl), *adj., n.* —*adj.* **1** of or having to do with the sense of touch: *a tactile stimulus.* SYN: tactual. **2** having the sense of touch. **3** that can be felt by touch; tangible. SYN: palpable.
—*n.* **1** *Psychology.* a person in whose mind tactile images are predominant or especially distinct. **2** a work of art designed to appeal to or stimulate the tactile sense: *"The image in my art transcends the visible," he* [*Yaakov Agam*] *said, brushing his hand over one of his "tactiles," a field of silver buttons mounted in springs* (New York Times).
[< Latin *tāctilis* tangible < *tangere* to touch]

**tactile bud** or **corpuscle,** any one of numerous minute, oval bodies which occur in sensitive parts of the skin and are involved with the sense of touch.

**tac|til|i|ty** (tak til′ə tē), *n.* the quality or condition of being tactile.

**tac|tion** (tak′shən), *n.* the act of touching, or a state of contact: *They neither can speak nor attend to the discourses of others, without being roused by some external taction upon the organs of speech and hearing* (Jonathan Swift).

**tact|less** (takt′lis), *adj.* **1** without tact; blunt; gauche: *a tactless person.* **2** showing no tact; undiplomatic: *a tactless reply.* —**tact′less|ly,** *adv.* —**tact′less|ness,** *n.*

**tac|tom|e|ter** (tak tom′ə tər), *n.* an instrument for determining the acuteness of the sense of touch. [< Latin *tāctus, -ūs* touch + English *-meter*]

**tac|tu|al** (tak′chů əl), *adj.* **1** of or having to do with touch; tactile: *Despite repeated experience of the tactual solidity of the glass, the animals never learned to function without optical support* (Scientific American). **2** caused by or due to touch. **3** causing touch; giving sensations of touch. [< Latin *tāctus, -ūs* (< *tangere* to touch) + English *-al*[1]]

**tac|tu|al|i|ty** (tak′chů al′ə tē), *n.* tactual quality.

**tac|tu|al|ly** (tak′chů ə lē), *adv.* **1** by means of touch. **2** as regards touch.

**tad** (tad), *n. U.S. Informal.* **1** a very small boy; chap: *One of the bellboys at the hotel, cute little tad, knew the town like a book* (Sinclair Lewis). **2** a very small amount. [probably short for *tadpole*]

**Ta|djik** (tä′jik), *n., pl.* **-djik.** = Tadzhik.

**Ta|dji|ki** (tä′ji kē, tä jē′-), *n.* = Tadzhiki.

***tad|pole** (tad′pōl′), *n.* a very young frog or toad in the larval stage when it lives in water and has gills and a long tail; polliwog. Tadpoles gradually adapt to life out of water by developing lungs and limbs, losing gills, and changing internally. [Middle English *taddepol* < *tadde* toad + *pol* (perhaps) poll, head]

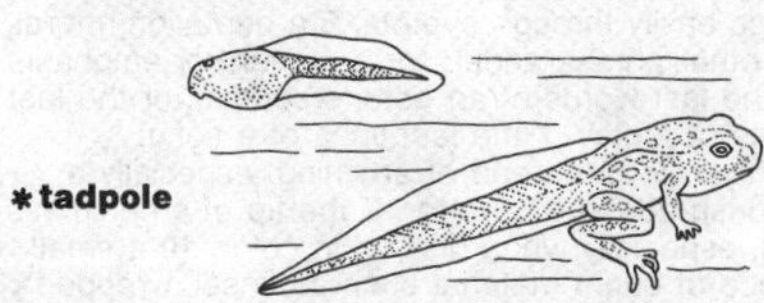

***tadpole**

**Ta|dzhik** (tä′jik), *n., pl.* **-dzhik.** one of an Iranian people living in Tadzhikistan and Afghanistan. Also, **Tadjik, Tajik.**

**Ta|dzhi|ki** (tä′ji kē, tä jē′-), *n.* the Iranian language of the Tadzhik. Also, **Tadjiki, Tajiki.**

**tae** (tā), *prep. Scottish.* to.

**tae|di|um vi|tae** (tē′dē əm vī′tē), *Latin.* weariness of life; a feeling of unbearable weariness and dissatisfaction with life: *A cloud of vague depression rests on the man, who shuns society, falls off in fat, becomes restless … and feels strongly the taedium vitae* (T. S. Clouston).

**tae kwon do** (tī′ kwon dō′), the Korean form of karate. [< Korean *tae kwon do*]

**tael** (tāl), *n.* **1** any one of several east Asian units of weight, varying according to locality, especially one equal to 1⅓ ounces avoirdupois. **2** a former Chinese unit of money, originally a tael, in weight, of silver. [< Portuguese *tael* < Malay *tahil*]

**ta'en** (tān), *v. Archaic.* taken: *The Prince hath ta'en it hence* (Shakespeare).

**tae|ni|a** (tē′nē ə), *n., pl.* **-ni|ae** (-nē ē), **-ni|as. 1** *Archaeology.* a headband; fillet; hair ribbon. **2** *Architecture.* a band separating the Doric architrave from the frieze. **3** *Anatomy.* a ribbonlike structure, as the longitudinal muscles of the colon. **4** *Zoology.* a tapeworm. Also, **tenia.** [< Latin *taenia* < Greek *tainíā* band, fillet, tapeworm, related to *teínein* to stretch]

**tae|ni|a|cid|al** (tē′nē ə sī′dəl), *adj.* of or having to do with a taeniacide.

**tae|ni|a|cide** (tē′nē ə sīd), *n.* an agent or remedy that destroys tapeworms.

**tae|ni|a|fuge** (tē′nē ə fyüj), *adj., n.* —*adj.* expelling tapeworms.
—*n.* an agent or remedy that expels tapeworms.
[< *taenia* tapeworm + Latin *fugere* flee]

**tae|ni|a|sis** (tē nī′ə sis), *n. Medicine.* the condition of being infested with taeniae or tapeworms.

**tae|ni|cid|al** (tē′nə sī′dəl), *adj.* = taeniacidal.

**tae|ni|cide** (tē′nə sīd), *n.* = taeniacide.

**tae|ni|oid** (tē′nē oid), *adj.* **1** of a ribbonlike shape; like a tapeworm. **2** related to the tapeworms.

**taff** (taf), *n.* = teff.

**Taff** (taf), *n.* = Taffy.

**taf|fe|ta** (taf′ə tə), *n., adj.* —*n.* **1** a light, stiff silk cloth with a smooth, glossy surface. **2** a similar cloth, as of linen or rayon. **3** (originally) a plain, woven, glossy silk.
—*adj.* **1** of taffeta. **2** *Figurative.* like taffeta: *taffeta phrases, silken terms* (Shakespeare). **3** having to do with taffeta.
[< Middle French *taffeta* < Old French *taffetas* < Persian *tāftah* silk, or linen cloth]

**taf|fi|a** (taf′ē ə), *n.* = tafia.

**taff|rail** (taf′rāl′), *n.* **1** the rail around the stern of a ship. **2** the upper part of the stern of a ship. [alteration of earlier *tafferel* (carved) panel < Dutch *tafereel* panel (for painting or carving), ultimately < *tafel* table]

**taffrail log,** a log to measure the distance traveled by a ship.

---

**Pronunciation Key:** hat, āge, cãre, fär; let, ēqual, tėrm; it, īce; hot, ōpen, ôrder; oil, out; cup, pu̇t, rüle; child; long; thin; ᴛʜen; zh, measure; ə represents **a** in about, **e** in taken, **i** in pencil, **o** in lemon, **u** in circus.

**taf|fy** (taf′ē), *n., pl.* **-fies.** **1** a kind of chewy candy made of brown sugar or molasses boiled down, often with butter: *saltwater taffy.* **2** *Informal, Figurative.* flattery: *There will be a reaction, and the whole party will unite in an offering of taffy* (New York Tribune). **SYN:** blarney, blandishment. Also, **toffee, toffy.** [originally Scottish, an earlier form of *toffee*]

**Taf|fy** (taf′ē), *n., pl.* **-fies.** a nickname for a Welshman; Taff. [< Welsh pronunciation of *Davy* or *David* (in Welsh *Dafydd*)]

**taf|i|a** (taf′ē ə), *n.* a liquor similar to rum, made in Haiti from low-grade molasses, refuse brown sugar, or the like. [American English; origin uncertain]

**tag¹** (tag), *n., v.,* **tagged, tag|ging.** —*n.* **1** a card or small piece of paper, leather, or other material, to be tied or fastened to something, especially as a label: *Each coat in the store has a tag with the price on it.* **2** a small hanging piece; loosely attached piece; loose end; tatter: *Mother cut all the tags off the old frayed rug.* **3** a tab or loop by which a coat is hung up. **4** a metal point on the end of a shoelace or string, to make it pass easily through eyelets. **5** a quotation, moral, or other phrase added for ornament or emphasis. **6** the last words of an actor's speech, or the last lines of a play. **7** the last lines of a song. **8** *Figurative.* the end of anything, especially a flourish added to a letter. **9** the tip of an animal's tail, especially when distinct in color. **10** a small piece of bright material such as tinsel, wrapped around the shank of a fishhook near the tail of an artificial fly. **11** a matted lock of wool on a sheep; tag-lock. **12** a radioactive tracer: *Carbon 14 is used as a "tracer" or "tag" in research or industrial processes* (Wall Street Journal). **13** a unit of information used in computer programming to identify or label other information: *Along with the bits making up each word would be stored "tag" bits giving some information about the word* (New Scientist). **14** *Obsolete.* the mob.

—*v.t.* **1** to add for ornament or emphasis. **2** to furnish (a speech or composition) with tags, such as quotations. **3** to add on as an afterthought; fasten or tack on: *to tag a moral to a story.* **4** to mark, label, or identify with a tag or tags: *All his suitcases and trunks are tagged with his name and address. A carbon atom can be tagged ... by substituting the deuterium isotope for one or more of the associated hydrogen atoms* (Harold C. Urey). **5** *Informal.* to follow closely: *The dog tagged them all the way home.* **6** to cut off tags from (a sheep).

—*v.i.* to trail along; follow: *The younger children tagged after the older ones. We didn't invite him to go with us but he tagged along anyway.*

[origin uncertain] —**tag′ger,** *n.*

**tag²** (tag), *n., v.,* **tagged, tag|ging.** —*n.* **1** a children's game in which one child who is "it" chases the others until he touches one. The one touched is then "it" and must chase the others. **2** *Baseball.* the act of touching a base runner with the ball, or a base with the foot while holding the ball, to make a putout.

—*v.t.* **1** to touch or tap with the hand. **2** *Baseball.* **a** to touch (a base runner) with the ball to make a putout: *The runner was caught off base and tagged out.* **b** to touch (a base) with the foot while holding the ball to make a putout.

—*v.i.* **tag up,** *Baseball.* to stay on, or return to stay on, the base occupied until after a fly ball is caught, before advancing to the next base: *Edwin had no little trouble understanding why a base runner must tag up before running if a fly ball is caught* (New Yorker).

[origin uncertain]

**Ta|gal** (tä gäl′), *n.* = Tagalog.

**Ta|ga|la** (tä gä′lä, tə gal′ə), *adj., n.* —*adj.* **1** having to do with Tagalog, the branch of the Austronesian linguistic family that includes the languages of the Philippines. **2** having to do with Tagalog, the chief language of the Philippines.

—*n.* = Tagalog.

**Ta|ga|log** (tä gä′log, tag′ə-), *n., pl.* **-logs** or **-log.** **1** a member of the chief Malay people in the Philippines. **2** their Indonesian language on which the official language of the Philippines is based. **3** the Austronesian linguistic family that includes the languages of the Philippines.

**tag|a|long** (tag′ə lông′, -long′), *n., adj. Informal.* —*n.* a person who follows along: *"And me, I can say something too," said the little tagalong who was never to be outdone by her sisters or brother* (Harper's).

—*adj.* that is a tagalong: *For the first time in recent history, the No. 2 man on each ticket will not be a tagalong candidate* (Newsweek).

**tag|board** (tag′bôrd′, -bōrd′), *n.* a kind of strong cardboard used for making tags, posters, and book covers.

**tag day,** *U.S.* a day when contributions to a certain charity are solicited and contributors are each given a tag to wear.

**tag end,** **1** the very end; last part: *They had been together all season and seemed to resent our coming in on the tag end of it* (Harper's). **2** a remaining scrap or fragment: *... work pieced together from tag ends of everything* (New York Times).

**tagged** (tagd), *adj.* having a tag or tags.

**tag|gers** (tag′ərz), *n.pl.* iron in very thin sheets, usually coated with tin.

**ta|glia|ri|ni** (tal′yə rē′nē), *n.* a kind of pasta in the form of flat, ribbonlike strips: *The Bolognese sauce that accompanies the tagliarini is pedestrian* (New York Times). [< Italian *tagliarini* < *tagliare* to cut]

**ta|glia|tel|le** (tal′yə tel′ā), *n.* a kind of pasta similar to but broader than tagliarini. [< Italian *tagliatelle* (diminutive) < *tagliare* to cut]

**tag line,** **1** the last part of an actor's speech or of a play; tag. **2** = punch line. **3** a catch phrase, as in advertising: *The author of the article picks out a few pat tag lines: "Unbelievable—but absolutely true! Nothing like it on any screen! A picture you will never forget"* (New York Times).

**tag-lock** (tag′lok′), *n.* a tag of wool.

**tag|meme** (tag′mēm), *n. Linguistics.* the smallest meaningful unit of grammatical form. [(coined by Leonard Bloomfield, 1887-1949, an American linguist) < Greek *tágma* order, arrangement (< *tássein* to arrange) + English *-eme,* as in *phoneme*]

**tag|me|mic** (tag mē′mik), *adj.* of or having to do with tagmemes or tagmemics.

**tag|me|mi|cist** (tag mē′mə sist), *n.* a linguist who specializes in tagmemics.

**tag|me|mics** (tag mē′miks), *n. Linguistics.* a method of analyzing language by the ordering of grammatical units into various levels, with the tagmeme as the basic unit.

**tag|rag** (tag′rag′), *n.* **1** the riffraff; rabble. **2** a shred; tatter.

**tagrag and bobtail,** the riffraff; rabble.

**tag sale,** *U.S.* a private sale of used furniture, appliances, and other household items, each item carrying a price tag.

**tag team,** a team of wrestlers who take turns wrestling with members of another team.

**ta|ha** (tä′hä), *n.* **1** a South African weaverbird, the male of which has yellow and black feathers. **2** any one of various related birds. [< a native name]

**tah|bun** (tä bün′), *n.* a wraparound cotton cloth worn by men in Pakistan. [< Urdu *tahbūn*]

**Ta|hi|tian** (tə hē′shən, -hē′tē ən), *adj., n.* —*adj.* of or having to do with the island of Tahiti, its people, their language, or their way of life.

—*n.* **1** a person born or living in Tahiti. **2** the Polynesian language of Tahiti.

**tahr** (tär), *n.* any one of several beardless wild goats with short curved horns of the Himalayan mountains and southeastern Arabia. Also, **tehr.** [< the native name in the Himalayas]

**tah|sil|dar** or **tah|seel|dar** (tə sēl′där′), *n.* (in India) a revenue officer. [< Hindustani *tauṣīldār* < Persian < Arabic *taḥṣīl* collection + Persian *dār* holder]

**Tai** (tī), *n., adj.* = Thai.

**tai|a|ha** (tī′ä hä), *n.* a kind of club or staff about six feet long, carved at one end and frequently ornamented with feathers, used by Maori chiefs as a badge of office, and sometimes for fighting. [< Maori]

**Ta|ic** (tä′ik, tī′-), *adj., n.* = Thai.

**tai chi** (tī′ jē′), a Chinese method of exercise and self-defense that excludes extreme movements and emphasizes balance, coordination, and effortlessness: *Tai chi ... depends less on strength and speed than do other martial arts* (Herman Kauz). [short for *tai chi chuan* < Chinese (Peking) *t'ai chi ch'üan* great art of boxing]

**tai chi chuan** (tī′ jē′ chwän′), = tai chi.

**tai|ga** (tī′gə), *n.* **1** the swampy, coniferous evergreen forest land of subarctic Siberia between the tundra and the steppes. **2** the similar forest land in North America. [< Russian *tajga*]

**tail¹** (tāl), *n., v., adj.* —*n.* **1** the part of an animal's body that sticks out beyond the back of the main part. Rabbits have very short tails. Mice have long tails. *My dog wags his tail.* **2** some thing, part, or appendage like an animal's tail: *to write a "g" with a long tail. Rags tied together made the tail of my kite.* **3** the part of an airplane at the rear of the fuselage, which includes the stabilizers and fins to which the elevators and rudders are hinged. **4a** the hind part of anything; back; rear: *the tail of a cart. A crowd of small boys formed the tail of the procession.* **b** *Slang.* buttocks. **5** *Astronomy.* a luminous trail of small particles from the head of a comet, extending away from the sun: *The tail is by far the most spectacular of the comet's features* (Bernhard, Bennett, and Rice). **6** a long braid or tress of hair. **7** *Figurative.* a part at the end of anything; conclusion: *towards the tail of his letter.* **8** *Printing.* the end of a page, chapter, or book. **9** *Prosody.* the lines at the end of certain types of poems, such as the sonnet; coda. **10** the part of a millrace below the wheel; lower end of a pool or stream; tailrace. **11** the open end of a rivet. **12** *Figurative.* the least valuable part of anything, especially tin scraps; refuse. **13** any group of followers, such as a retinue. **14** *Slang.* a person who follows another to watch and report on his movements.

—*v.t.* **1** to form the tail of; follow close behind. **2** to furnish with any kind of tail. **3** *Slang.* to follow closely and secretly, especially in order to watch or prevent escaping. **4** to fasten (timber) by an end in, into, or on a wall or other structure. **5** to join (one thing) to the end of another. **6** to dock the tail of (an animal).

—*v.i.* **1** to form a tail, especially to move in a file: *Some of the children tailed after the parade.* **2a** to occur less and less; gradually stop; diminish; subside; die away: *The protests tailed off into only an occasional mutter. ... a good many numbers, often built round a good idea, that tail away without making an effective point* (Punch). **b** to fall behind; lag; straggle. **3** (of a timber) to be held by an end in, into, or on a wall or other structure. **4** (of a boat or other floating object) to swing its stern or free end away from a wind or current: *tailing upstream in the wind.*

—*adj.* **1** at the tail, back, or rear. **2** coming from behind: *a tail wind.*

**at the tail of,** following: *She ... had ... come to Morocco at the tail of a Spanish embassy* (Hall Caine).

**on one's tail,** *Informal.* following closely; on one's heels: *One motorist ... said: "Lorries were travelling right on my tail, flashing their lights and blaring their horns to try to make me go faster ..."* (London Times).

**tail off,** *Informal.* **a** to run away: *He ducked his head; made a slouching bow; tailed off to his pigs* (Francis E. Paget). **b** to come gradually to an end; peter out: *South Africa's gold and mineral bonanza is beginning to tail off* (Manchester Guardian Weekly).

**tail of one's eye,** the outside corner of one's eye: *Mrs. Westropp watched him with the tail of her eye as she talked to Lady Trevor* (James Payn).

**tails,** *Informal.* **a** the reverse side of a coin: *heads or tails.* **b** Also, **tail coat.** a coat with long tails, worn on formal occasions: *The groom wore tails and a top hat.* **c** full dress: *The party called for tails and gowns.*

**turn tail,** to run away, as from danger or trouble; retreat or flee: *The wolves turned tail* (Daniel Defoe). *You are going to turn tail on your former principles* (E. S. Barrett).

**twist the lion's tail.** See under **lion.**

**with one's tail between one's legs,** afraid, humiliated, or dejected: *We shall have you back here very soon ... with your tail between your legs* (William E. Norris).

[Old English *tægel*] —**tail′like′,** *adj.*

**tail²** (tāl), *n., adj. Law.* —*n.* the limitation of an inheritance or title to one's lineal descendants or to a specified line of heirs; entail: *an estate in tail male.*

—*adj.* limited as to tenure by an entail.

[< Anglo-French *taile,* variant of Old French *taillie,* past participle of *taillier* allot, cut to shape < Late Latin *tāliāre*]

**tail assembly,** the stabilizers and control surfaces at the rear of an aircraft; empennage.

**tail|back** (tāl′bak′), *n. Football.* the offensive halfback in the single wing formation whose position is farthest back from the line of scrimmage.

**tail bandage,** a bandage divided into strips at the end.

**tail bay,** **1** the space between a girder and the wall. **2** the narrow water space just below a canal lock, opening out into the lower pond.

**tail beam,** a tailpiece in building.

**tail|board** (tāl′bôrd′, -bōrd′), *n.* the tailgate of a truck or wagon.

**tail|bone** (tāl′bōn′), *n.* **1** any one of the caudal vertebrae of an animal. **2** = coccyx.

**tail boom,** a projecting spar or frame on certain aircraft, connecting the stabilizers and control surfaces of the tail with a main supporting member.

**tail coat,** = swallow-tailed coat.

**tail|coat|ed** (tāl′kō′tid), *adj.* wearing a tail coat.

**tail cone,** the cone-shaped assembly behind a turbojet engine through which the exhaust gases are discharged.

**tail coverts,** the feathers concealing the bases of a bird's tail feathers.

**-tailed,** *combining form.* having a ___ tail: *Short-tailed = having a short tail.*

**tail end,** **1** the hindmost, lowest, or concluding part of anything: *Our plane landed at the new airfield on the tail end of a sandstorm that had swept against us for some hours* (New Yorker).

2 the end or tip of a tail.
**tail-end|er** (tāl′en′dər), *n.* a person or thing at the tail end.
**tail|er** (tā′lər), *n.* **1** *British.* a device for securing a fish by the tail, consisting of a movable loop on a handle. **2** a fish whose tail breaks the surface of the water.
**tail feather**, a feather in the tail of a bird.
**tail fin**, **1** a fin at the tail end of the body of a fish, whale, or the like: *It has two powerful pectoral fins at the front and a tail fin which acts as a skid at the rear* (New Scientist). **2** any object like this, as that which sticks out on the tail of an airplane or on the rear fenders of an automobile.
**tail|first** (tāl′fėrst′), *adv.* with the tail leading; backwards: *Ordinarily virus particles attach themselves tailfirst to the cell wall* (Scientific American).
**tail|fore|most** (tāl′fôr′mōst, -fōr′-), *adv.* = tailfirst.
**tail|gate** (tāl′gāt′), *n., v.,* **-gat|ed, -gat|ing,** *adj.* **—n. 1** a board at the back of a wagon, truck, or station wagon that can be let down or removed when loading or unloading: *They have a leisurely barbecue, using the tailgate of a station wagon as the buffet table* (Sunset). **2** *Especially British.* the lower gate or pair of gates of a canal lock.
**—*v.i., v.t.*** **1** to drive a truck or car too close to the one ahead of it. **2** *U.S.* to serve or eat a meal or refreshments on the tailgate of a station wagon: *Tailgating started ... at Ivy League games, where alumni would serve genteel picnics from the backs of their station wagons* (Time).
**—*adj.*** of or designating a style of jazz used in playing the trombone, characterized by extensive use of slides (so called from the place of trombone players on a truck during parades): *tailgate blues, a tailgate trombone.*
**tail|gat|er** (tāl′gā′tər), *n.* **1** *Slang.* a musician who plays tailgate jazz. **2** a driver who tailgates. **3** *U.S.* a picnicker who tailgates.
**tail gun**, a gun at the rear of an airplane.
**tail|gun|ner** (tal′gun′ər), *n.* a person who operates a tail gun.
**tail|gun|ning** (tāl′gun′ing), *adj., n.* **—*adj.*** having to do with a tail gun.
**—*n.*** the operating of a tail gun.
**tail-heav|y** (tāl′hev′ē), *adj.* (of an airplane) with the tail tending to pitch down in flight. **—tail′-heav′i|ly,** *adv.* **—tail′-heav′i|ness,** *n.*
**tail|ing** (tā′ling), *n.* that end of a projecting stone or brick that is built into a wall.
**tailings**, any residue or rejects; leavings; scraps: *Tailings are a familiar part of any mine landscape; after all, one has to put the stuff somewhere* (New Yorker).
**tail lamp**, = tail light.
**taille** (tāl; tä′yə), *n.* a tax levied by former French kings or lords: *The great fiscal grievance of old France was the taille, a tax raised ... only on the property and income of the unprivileged classes* (John Morley). [< Old French *taille* assessment < *taillier;* see etym. under **tail**[2]]
**tail|less**[1] (tāl′lis), *adj.* having no tail, in any sense; acaudal; anurous: *An ape is a kind of tailless monkey.*
**—tail′less|ly,** *adv.* **—tail′less|ness,** *n.*
**tail|less**[2] (tāl′lis), *adj. Law.* without a tail.
**tailless airplane**, any type of powered aircraft without a tail, such as a flying wing.
**tail|leur** (tä yœr′), *n.* a woman's tailor-made suit or dress. [< French *tailleur* tailor, Old French *tailor;* see etym. under **tailor**]
**tail light**, or **tail|light** (tāl′līt′), *n.* a warning light, usually red, at the rear of a car, truck, train, or other vehicle.
**tai|lor** (tā′lər), *n., v.* **—*n.*** a person whose business is making, altering, or mending clothes.
**—*v.t.*** **1** to make or fashion by tailor's work: *The suit was well tailored.* **2** to fit or furnish (a person) with clothes made by a tailor; outfit. **3** *Figurative.* to make specially to fit; adjust; adapt: *The clinic tailors its treatment to individual needs* (Scientific American).
**—*v.i.*** to make or mend clothes.
[< Anglo-French *taillour,* Old French *tailleor* < Late Latin *tāliāre* to cut < *tallia,* for Latin *tālea* rod, cutting] **—tai′lor|less,** *adj.*
**tai|lor|a|ble** (tā′lər ə bəl), *adj.* that can be made into something to wear: *This highly tailorable stuff has been molded into classic clothes* (New Yorker).
**tailor bee**, any one of various bees that cut leaves and line their nests with the pieces.
**tai|lor|bird** (tā′lər bėrd′), *n.* any one of several small passerine songbirds of Asia and Africa that stitch leaves together to form and hide their nests.
**tai|lored** (tā′lərd), *adj.* **1** cut and sewn: *Paleolithic peoples living at the borders of the great glaciers made tailored skin clothing at least as early as the Solutrean* (Beals and Hoijer). **2** *Figurative.* simple and functional to suit a special purpose: *He sits down with the dealer and a designer and they plan a tailored office* (Wall Street Journal). **3** of superior fabric, having simple, straight lines and a minimum of ornament: *a tailored suit.*
**tai|lor|ess** (tā′lər is), *n.* a woman tailor.
**tai|lor|ing** (tā′lər ing), *n.* **1** the business or work of a tailor. **2** the clothes or workmanship of a tailor: *British tailoring.*
**tai|lor-made** (tā′lər mād′), *adj., n.* **—*adj.*** **1** made by or as if by a tailor; simple and fitting well. **2** *Figurative.* made to fit a certain person, object, or purpose: *Not too many years ago a car would run on most any kind of gasoline, but now engines require fuels that are virtually tailor-made* (Wall Street Journal). **3** *Informal.* manufactured, rather than rolled by hand: *a tailor-made cigarette.*
**—*n.*** a tailor-made article: *She wore English tailor-mades and pale billowy scarves* (New Yorker).
**tai|lor-make** (tā′lər māk′), *v.t.,* **-made, -mak|ing.** to make especially to fit a person, object, or situation: *they'll tailor-make an itinerary to suit you* (Sunset).
**tail|piece** (tāl′pēs′), *n.* **1** a piece forming the end; endpiece. **2** a piece added on; appendage; addition. **3** *Printing.* a small decorative engraving, usually at the end of a chapter. **4** *Music.* a triangular block, usually of ebony, near the lower end of a violin, viola, or other stringed instrument, to which the strings are fastened. **5** a short beam, rafter, or joist built into a wall and supported by a header; tail beam.
**tail pin**, a slender pin or peg projecting from the lower end of a cello, used to support it on the floor while it is being played.
**tail pipe**, **1** the intake pipe of a suction pump. **2** the pipe that discharges the spent gases of an automobile, bus, truck, or airplane engine. See picture under **exhaust pipe**.
**tail plane**, = horizontal stabilizer.
**tail|race** (tāl′rās′), *n.* **1** the part of a millrace, flume, or channel below the water wheel that leads the water away. **2** *Mining.* a channel for carrying away refuse (tailings) in water.
**tail|rope** (tāl′rōp′), *n.* a rope fastened to the back of anything.
**tails** (tālz), *n.pl.* See under **tail**[1].
**tail|sit|ter** (tāl′sit′ər), *n.* an airplane that can take off from or land on its tail.
**tail skid**, a runner at the back of certain aircraft, used instead of a wheel as a support in landing or on the ground.
**tail|slide** (tāl′slīd′), *n.* a rearward motion which an airplane may be made to take after having been brought into a stalling position.
**tail spin**, or **tail|spin** (tāl′spin′), *n.* **1** the downward spiraling movement of an airplane with the nose first and the tail spinning above it; spin. **2** *Informal, Figurative.* mental confusion or agitation; panic.
**tail|stock** (tāl′stok′), *n.* the adjustable rear frame of a lathe or grinder, carrying the nonrevolving pin.
**tail|wag|ging** (tāl′wag′ing), *n.* a wide turn at high speed, made with the skis parallel.
**tail|walk** (tāl′wôk′), *v.i.* (of a fish) to leap repeatedly from the water, as if walking or hopping supported by the tail: *The great fish roars out of the water, sometimes jumping 12 ft. or more, as he goes raging and tailwalking across the ocean* (Time).
**tail water**, the water running downstream from a millrace, canal, or dam.
**tail wind**, a wind blowing toward the direction in which a ship or aircraft is moving and helping to move it: *The North Star had picked up a high tail wind and was climbing between the cloud layers at a speed estimated at 240 miles an hour* (Maclean's).
**tain** (tān), *n.* **1** a thin tin plate. **2** tinfoil for silvering mirrors. [< French *tain* tinfoil < Old French *étain* tin < Latin *stagnum* stannum]
**Tai|no** (tī′nō), *n., pl.* **-nos** or **-no. 1** one of the extinct Indian aborigines of the Bahamas and Greater Antilles. **2** their Arawakan language.
**taint** (tānt), *n., v.* **—*n.*** **1** a trace of any harmful or undesirable quality, often: **a** a condition of contamination, infection, or decay. **b** a trace of discredit, dishonor, or disgrace; slur: *a taint of bribery. No taint of dishonor ever touched George Washington.* **c** a touch, shade, or tinge of discoloration; spot or stain; blemish. **2** a cause of any such condition, especially a contaminating or corrupting influence; cause of decay. **3** *Obsolete.* a color, hue, or dye.
**—*v.t.*** **1** to give a taint to; spoil, corrupt, or contaminate: *Flies sometimes taint what they touch. His character was tainted from following the ways of bad companions.* SYN: sully. **2** *Obsolete.* to color; dye. **—*v.i.*** to become tainted; decay: *Meat will taint if it is left too long in a warm place.* [partly short for *attaint;* partly < Old French *teint,* past participle of *teindre* to dye < Latin *tingere.* See etym. of doublets **tint, tinct.**] **—taint′less,** *adj.*
**taint|ed** (tān′tid), *adj.* **1** affected with any taint; stained, tinged, contaminated, infected, corrupted, or depraved: *The death toll from tainted liquor in Spain rose to 22 ... and officials feared that it would go higher* (New York Times). **2** *Archaic.* smelling of an animal's scent. **—taint′ed|ly,** *adv.* **—taint′ed|ness,** *n.*
**tain|ter gate** (tān′tər), a vertically curved dam gate with a horizontal pivotal axis. [< Burnham *Tainter,* an American inventor of the 1800's]
**tain|ture** (tān′chər), *n.* any taint.
**tai|pan**[1] (tī′pan), *n.* a large poisonous snake of Australia and New Guinea, related to the cobra. [< a native Australian name]
**tai|pan**[2] (tī′pan), *n.* a wealthy Chinese tradesman. [< Chinese *tai pan*]
**Tai|ping** (tī′ping′), *n.* a person who took part in a large and unsuccessful rebellion in southern China against the Manchu dynasty between 1850 and 1864. [< Chinese (Peking) *t'ai p'ing* great peace (the name of the native dynasty proclaimed by the rebels)]
**Tai|wa|nese** (tī′wä nēz′, -nēs′), *n., pl.* **-nese,** *adj.* **—*n.*** **1** a native or inhabitant of Taiwan: *Excepting 105,000 Malay aborigines, the Taiwanese are of Chinese stock and have kept their Chinese culture* (Newsweek). **2** the form of Chinese spoken by many Taiwanese, including many borrowings from English.
**—*adj.*** of Taiwan or its people.
**taj** (täj), *n.* **1** a crown or diadem: *He also gave him a taj ... which kings only were accustomed to wear* (John C. Atkinson). **2** the conical cap of a Moslem dervish. [< Arabic *taj*]
**Ta|jik** (tä′jik), *n., pl.* **-jik.** = Tadzhik.
**Ta|ji|ki** (tä′ji kē, tä jē′-), *n.* = Tadzhiki.
**ta|ka** (tä′kə), *n., pl.* **-ka.** the unit of money of Bangladesh, worth 100 paise, established in 1972. [< Bengali *taka*]
**tak|a|ble** (tā′kə bəl), *adj.* = takeable.
**ta|ka|he** (tə kä′hē), *n.* = notornis. [< Maori]
**tak|a|mak|a** (tak′ə mak′ə), *n.* = tacamahac.
**take** (tāk), *v.,* **took, tak|en, tak|ing,** *n.* **—*v.t.*** **1** to lay hold of; grasp: *A little child takes its mother's hand in walking.* **2a** to seize; capture: *to take a fortress, to take someone prisoner.* **b** to catch; snare: *Wild animals are taken in traps.* **c** to come upon suddenly: *to be taken by surprise.* **3a** to accept; accept and act upon; be guided by; comply with: *to take a hint. Take my advice. The man won't take a cent less for the car.* **b** to charge; collect; solicit: *to take money for admission, to take contributions to the Red Cross.* **c** to accept (a bet). **4a** to get; receive; assume the ownership or possession of: *to take a bribe. She took the gifts with a smile of thanks and opened them. She takes lodgers.* **b** to obtain in marriage: *He took a wife.* **c** to bring or receive (a person into some relation): *Take him into your confidence.* **5a** to win: *The visiting team took the game 8 to 1. He took first prize.* **b** to receive (something bestowed, conferred, or administered: *to take a degree in science, to take a sacrament.* **6** to receive in an indicated manner: *to take it all in good fun. She took the news calmly. He was really good-humoured and kind-hearted if you took him the right way* (Lytton Strachey). **7** to receive into the body; swallow, inhale, drink: *to take food, to take a drink, to take snuff.* **8** to absorb: *Wool takes a dye well. Marble takes a high polish.* **9a** to get; have: *to take cover. Take a seat. Now, in his old age, he takes refuge from his loneliness ... in returning to a vein of childhood memories* (Edmund Wilson). **b** to obtain from a source; derive: *Washington, D.C., takes its name from George Washington.* **c** to extract; quote: *a passage taken from Keats.* **10a** to make use of; use: *to take an opportunity of leaving, to take the Lord's name in vain. He hates to take medicine. "Take a stick to him!"* (Lewis Carroll). **b** to use to travel: *to take a bus. We took a train to go to Boston.* **11** to indulge in: *to take a nap, to take a vacation.* **12a** to submit to; put up with: *to take a beating, to take hard punishment, taking things as I found them.* SYN: endure, undergo, bear. **b** to study: *to take history.* **13** *Slang, Figurative.* to swindle; cheat. **14** to need; require: *It takes time and patience to learn how to drive an automobile. The trip takes five hours. He takes a seven in shoes.* **15** to pick out; choose; select: *to take sides. Take the shortest way home.* **16** to carry away; remove: *Please take the wastebasket away and empty it.* **17** to remove by death: *Pneumonia took him. The devil take him.* **18** to subtract; deduct: *If you take 2 from 7, you*

**Pronunciation Key:** hat, āge, cãre, fär; let, ēqual, tėrm; it, īce; hot, ōpen, ôrder; **oi**l, **ou**t; cup, pu̇t, rüle; **ch**ild; lo**ng**; **th**in; **ŦH**en; **zh**, measure; **ə** represents **a** in about, **e** in taken, **i** in pencil, **o** in lemon, **u** in circus.

have 5. **19** to lead: *Where will this road take me?* **20** to go with; escort: *Take her home. He likes to take his dog out for a walk.* **21** to carry; convey: *Take your lunch along. We took flowers to our sick friend.* **22** to do; make; obtain by some special method: *Take a walk. Please take my photograph.* **23** to form and hold in mind; feel: *to take it under consideration, to take a dislike to him. She takes pride in her schoolwork.* **24** to find out: *The doctor took my temperature.* **25** *Figurative.* to act upon; have effect with. **26a** to understand: *I take the meaning.* **b** to understand the acts or words of; interpret: *How did you take his remark?* **27** to suppose: *I take it you won't go to school since you feel sick.* **28** to regard; consider; view: *Let us take an example.* **29a** to assume; undertake (a function, responsibility, right, or oath): *to take all the blame, to take a vow, to take the trouble. She took charge of the household.* **b** to assume (as a form or nature); develop as: *The cloud took the form of a face.* **30** to engage; hire; lease: *to take furnished lodgings. We have taken a cottage for the summer.* **31** to write down; record: *to take dictation, to take minutes at a meeting.* **32** to receive and pay for regularly; receive regularly; subscribe for: *to take a magazine.* **33** *Grammar.* to be used with: *A plural noun takes a plural verb.* **34** to photograph: *to take a scene of a movie.* **35** to become affected by: *to take cold.* **36** *Figurative.* to please; attract; charm: *The new song took our fancy.* **37** *Figurative.* to cause to go: *What takes you into the city today?* **38** to attempt to get over, through, around, or under: *My horse took the fence easily.* **39** (of a batter in baseball) to let (a pitched ball) pass without swinging at it. **40** *Cricket.* **a** to catch and to put out: *A minute later Walker was smartly taken at the wicket* (Daily Telegraph). **b** to capture (a wicket), especially by striking it with the ball. **41** *Archaic.* to hear and receive (something said to one): *Take our defiance loud and high* (Scott).

—*v.i.* **1** to catch hold; lay hold: *The fire has taken.* **2** *Informal.* to become: *He took sick.* **3** to lessen; remove something; detract: *The billboards take away from the scenery. Her paleness takes from her beauty.* **4** to act; have effect: *The medicine seems to be taking; the fever is better. The inoculation took. Skin grafts from donors do not "take" permanently* (Science News Letter). **5** to make one's way; go: *to take across the fields.* **6** *Informal.* to appear in one's photographs: *He takes badly.* **7** to stick to a surface; stick; adhere: *This ink doesn't take on glossy paper. The snow was not taking on the wet street* (New Yorker). **8** to win favor: *Do you think the new play will take with the public?* **9a** to be readily taken (out, off, up, down, or under). **b** to be adapted for this: *That machine takes apart.* **10** (of a plant, seed, or graft) to begin to grow; strike root. **11** (of fish) to seize the bait; bite. **12** *Law.* to acquire ownership; inherit: *Since he left no will, his eldest son will take.* **13** *Archaic.* to accept what is offered: *And when he had given thanks, he brake it, and said, Take, eat: this is my body, which is broken for you: this do in remembrance of me* (I Corinthians 11:24). **14** *Dialect.* (of a road, a river, or other way or course) to run in some direction.

—*n.* **1** the act of taking. **2** the fact of being taken: *Sometimes there is no "take" on the first vaccination, and it is assumed that the child is immune* (Sidonie M. Gruenberg). **3** that which is taken. **4** *Slang.* receipts; profits: *the box-office take.* **5** the act of transplanting or grafting: *Research has demonstrated that permanently successful takes of cross-grafted skin are possible in chicks less than four days old* (Science News Letter). **6a** a scene or sequence photographed or televised at one time. **b** the act of making a photograph or a scene in a motion picture or television program. **7a** the act or process of making a recording for a record, tape, or the like. **b** a record or tape of this: *The performance that you buy ... is as often as not compounded of bits and pieces chosen from a number of takes and edited by a skilled technician* (Punch). **8** the amount taken: *a great take of fish.* **9** *Journalism.* any one of the portions into which a long story or article is divided to allow the printer to begin preparing it for the press.

**on the take**, looking for personal gain, usually by illegal means: *When you have a police force of more than 26,000 men there are sure to be some who are on the take* (New York Times).

**take about**, to conduct, especially on a round of sightseeing; escort: *He seems to have taken the ... ladies about a good deal* (Annie W. Patterson).

**take after**, **a** to follow (someone's) example: *His followers all take after him in this particular* (Peter Heylin). **b** *Figurative.* to be like; resemble in nature, character, habits, or appearance: *She takes after her mother.* **c** to follow, especially to chase: *The dog took after the rabbit.*

**take against**, to take sides against; oppose: *The barons took against King John and supported the people in their cause.*

**take (it) amiss**, to be offended at (something not intended to be offensive): *You ... therefore cannot take it amiss that I have never written* (Samuel Johnson).

**take and**, *U.S. Dialect.* to proceed to: *I'll take and bounce a rock off'n your head* (Mark Twain).

**take apart**, **a** to dismantle; remove the parts from: *He spent the afternoon taking apart his old Model T Ford.* **b** *Figurative: The reviewer mercilessly took apart the young writer's first novel.*

**take back**, **a** to withdraw; retract: *He refused and so took back his offer to go. I had ... made some complaints of you, but I will take them all back again* (Abigail Adams). **b** *Figurative.* to remind of the past: *The letter took her back ten years.*

**take down**, **a** to write down (what is said): *to take down a speech.* **b** to pull down; dismantle: *The circus men took down the tent after the last show.* **c** *Figurative.* to lower the pride of; humble: *to take him down a peg.*

**take for**, to suppose to be: *to be taken for a fool, to be taken for one's sister.*

**take in**, **a** to receive; admit; accept: *to take in boarders.* **b** to do (work) at home for pay: *to take in laundry.* **c** to understand: *He took in the situation at a glance. Many tragedies on ships and in the air have been due to the failure of a telephone or radio listener to hear or "take in" the message given them* (Science News Letter). **d** to visit or attend: *It's too late to take in her party now.* **e** to make smaller; tighten: *Mother took in the waist of her skirt. Sure every one of me frocks must be taken in—it's such a skeleton I'm growing* (Thackeray). **f** *Informal, Figurative.* to deceive; cheat; trick: *Some feel he has been taken in by the Administration* (Newsweek). **g** to include; comprise: *His jurisdiction now takes in this village.* **h** *Especially British.* to subscribe to (a newspaper, magazine, or other publication): *Many of them take in the French paper just as they buy Punch* (Blackwood's Magazine).

**take it**, **a** to suppose: *I take it your own business calls on you* (Shakespeare). **b** to accept as true or correct; believe (something told one): *Take it from me that he means what he says.* **c** *Slang.* to endure abuse or punishment: *He can dish it out but he can't take it.*

**take it or leave it**, to accept or reject without modification: *Too many firms adopt a take it or leave it attitude towards overseas customers* (Economist).

**take it out of**, **a** *Informal.* to exhaust; fatigue: *The sort of day that takes it out of a man* (May Laffan). **b** to take (something) from a person in compensation; exact satisfaction from: *If any one steals from me, ... and I catch him, I take it out of him on the spot. I give him a jolly good hiding* (Henry Mayhew).

**take it out on**, *Informal.* to relieve one's anger or annoyance by scolding or hurting: *The nice old lady from Missoula, Montana, who gets hot consommé spilled on her ... shoes, doesn't take it out on the waitress* (Maclean's).

**take kindly to**, to look favorably upon; be friendly toward: *Freud took kindly to Rank, ... encouraged him to finish Gymnasium ... and get a Ph.D.* (Time).

**take lying down**, *Informal.* to take without a protest: *He's not going to take this insult lying down.*

**take off**, **a** to make a take-off; leave the ground or water: *Three airplanes took off at the same time. Well over a hundred flights a day wing in from or take off for some foreign port* (New York Times). **b** *Informal.* to give an amusing imitation of; mimic: *to take off a classic.* **c** *Informal.* to rush away: *He took off at the first sign of trouble.* **d** *Informal.* to attack: *Committee Democrats ... immediately took off on the Secretary, demanding to know how the loophole got into the ... program* (Wall Street Journal).

**take on**, **a** to engage; hire: *The large manufacturers are ... taking on a considerable number of hands* (Examiner). **b** to undertake to deal with: *to take on an opponent.* **c** to acquire: *to take on the appearance of health. The neighborhood has taken on a fresh look since the new park was built.* **d** *Informal.* to show great excitement, grief, or other emotion: *She took on so about the tiny spot on her dress that we thought she must be extremely vain.*

**take one out of oneself**, to distract from inner worries; divert: *A drive in the country will take her out of herself.*

**take one tardy**, *Obsolete.* to surprise in a crime, fault, error, or the like; detect; catch: *He took her tardy with a plain lie* (Nicolas Udall).

**take one up on**, *Informal.* to accept: *He invited me to dinner and I took him up on it.*

**take out**, **a** to remove: *to take a book out, to take out a stain.* **b** to apply for and obtain (a license, patent, or other privilege): *The Bishops were obliged to take out new commissions from the King ... for holding their Bishoprics* (Gilbert Burnet). **c** to escort: *It was awfully good of you to take the children out, Charlie* (J. Ashby Sterry). **d** to set out: *They took out on a boat to explore the lake.* **e** to destroy: *Our initial response might be to take out a couple of Communist airfields by conventional bombing* (Newsweek). **f** to make a different and usually higher bid in bridge than that bid by one's partner.

**take over**, **a** to take the ownership or control of: *The company was formed ... for the purpose of taking over the business ... carried on by the plaintiff* (Law Reports). **b** to adopt; take up: *He had taken over from his father the gift of meeting all sorts of people and dealing with them on their own terms* (Edmund Wilson).

**take to**, **a** to form a liking for; become fond of: *Good students take to books. That "instant" coffee so many hurried housewives are taking to lately is exerting a heavy impact* (Wall Street Journal). **b** to adopt; take up: *If the changes are presented well and explained, then people take to them quite easily* (Maclean's). **c** to adapt: *A tree which is late transplanted seldom takes well to the soil* (Examiner). **d** make one's way to; go to: *The cat took to the woods and became wild.*

**take up**, **a** to soak up; absorb: *A sponge takes up liquid.* **b** to begin; undertake: *to take up the conversation, to take up residence, to take up law. He took up piano lessons in the summer.* **c** to tighten, especially to shorten: *Mother took up the hem of the red dress.* **d** to pay off: *I am disposed to try and find the money to take up these mortgages* (H. Rider Haggard). **e** to lift; pry up: *to take up a stone.* **f** to purchase: *The whole of the limited edition ... was taken up by the booksellers on the day of publication* (Picture World). **g** to collect: *They take up a collection and bury him* (Mark Twain). **h** *Figurative.* to adopt (as an idea or purpose): *There has, as yet, been no indication whether their resignations will be taken up* (London Times). **i** to secure the loose end of (a stitch): *This operation of taking up a stitch ... is one of the slowest* (Maria Edgeworth). **j** *Figurative.* to reprove; rebuke: *to take someone up short.* **k** to reduce or remove (lost motion, etc.); tighten: *to take up the slack.*

**take upon oneself**, to assume as one's duty or obligation: *This militia must take upon itself to distribute such food as there was* (Edmund Wilson).

**take up with**, *Informal.* to begin to associate or be friendly with: *He takes up with younger folks, Who for his wine will bear his jokes* (Jonathan Swift).

[Old English *tacan* < Scandinavian (compare Old Icelandic *taka* take, lay hold)]

► See **bring** for a usage note.

**take|a|ble** (tā′kə bəl), *adj.* that can be taken: *We took everything that was takeable.*

**take-all** (tāk′ôl′), *n.* a fungous disease which attacks wheat and certain other grains, especially in soils which do not have proper nutritional balance.

**take|a|way** (tāk′ə wā′), *adj. British.* take-out: *a Liverpool chain of take-away chicken houses* (Sunday Times).

**take|down** (tāk′doun′), *n., adj.* —*n.* **1** the act of taking down. **2** the fact of being taken down. **3** a rifle or similar firearm that can be taken apart and reassembled readily. **4** the nut, bolt, joint, or other piece, between its parts. **5** *Wrestling.* the act or process of forcing an opponent to the mat. **6** *Informal.* the act of humiliating or condition of being humiliated.

—*adj.* easy to take apart and put back together; collapsible.

**take-home pay** (tāk′hōm′), the wages or salary left after deductions, such as taxes and health insurance, have been made: *Based on their current take-home pay, some of the workers probably could spend a good deal more than they do* (Wall Street Journal).

**take-home sale**, *British.* the sale of alcoholic liquor for consumption off the premises; off-sale.

**take-in** (tāk′in′), *n. Informal.* **1** any deception, especially a cheat or swindle. **2** any deceiving thing or person; fraud.

**take-leave** (tāk lēv′), *n.* the act of saying good-by.

**tak|en** (tā′kən), *v.* past participle of **take**: *I have taken his toy from the shelf.*

**take-off** or **take|off** (tāk′ôf′, -of′), *n., adj.* —*n.* **1** the leaving of the ground in leaping or in beginning a flight in an aircraft; taking off: *Vertical take-offs and landings long have been a goal of aircraft engineers and builders* (Wall Street Journal). **2** the place from which one takes off. **3** a leap into the air. **4** *Informal.* an amusing imitation;

mimicking; caricature; burlesque: *This piece, a take-off on the school and its faculty, is done in typical sophomoric style* (Maclean's). **5** a disadvantage. **6** *Figurative.* **a** the act of starting out: *We could try to postpone China's economic take-off* (Manchester Guardian Weekly). **b** a beginning; starting point: *Britain's long-awaited take-off in exports may have arrived at last* (Wall Street Journal).
—*adj.* of or for a take-off: *in take-off position.*

**take|out** (tāk′out′), *n.* **1** that which is taken out or removed: *The city promised the takeout from the take-home pay will decline to normal* (New York Times). **2** a magazine article printed on full and successive pages and easily removable as a unit: *There is no doubt that Mailer's journalistic pieces, especially the long takeouts in Esquire, are charged with the energy of art* (Atlantic).

**take-out** (tāk′out′), *adj. U.S.* designating or dealing with food prepared to be eaten away from the premises; carry-out: *take-out pizza pies.*

**takeout double,** (in bridge) an informatory double.

**take-o|ver** or **take|o|ver** (tāk′ō′vər), *n.* the act of taking over; seizure of ownership or control: *a take-over of a country by the military. In industry there is a continuing healthy ferment of amalgamations and take-overs* (Punch).

**take-over bid,** *British.* an offer to buy out another company.

**tak|er** (tā′kər), *n.* **1** a person or thing that takes. **2** a person who accepts a bet.

**tak|est** (tā′kist), *v. Archaic.* take (used only with *thou*). "Thou takest" means "you take."

**tak|eth** (tā′kith), *v. Archaic.* takes.

**take-up** (tāk′up′), *n.* **1** any taking up, especially forming pleats, engaging a clutch, or reeling in slack. **2** a gather in a dress. **3** a machine or device for tightening such things as slack ropes or cables, or absorbing waste motion, especially: **a** = take-up reel. **b** a device in a sewing machine for tightening the thread in the stitch.

**take-up reel,** the reel onto which tape or film is wound in a tape recorder or motion-picture camera or projector.

**ta|kin** (tä′kin), *n.* a goatlike horned antelope found at high altitudes in the eastern Himalayas. [< the native name]

**tak|ing** (tā′king), *adj., n.* —*adj.* **1** attractive or pleasing; winning; fetching: *a taking smile.* **SYN:** captivating, fascinating. **2** *Informal.* easy to catch; infectious; contagious. **3** injurious; harmful: *taking airs* (Shakespeare).
—*n.* **1** the act of one who takes. **2** capture; seizure: *the taking of game.* **3** apprehension by the police; arrest. **4** anything that is taken, especially the fish or animals caught on one trip; bag or catch.
**in a taking, a** in an agitated state of mind: *Lord! what a taking poor Mr. Edward will be in when he hears of it* (Jane Austen). **b** in unhappy circumstances; in trouble: *The poor boy was in a pitiful taking* (Samuel Pepys).
**takings,** any money taken in; receipts, winnings, or profits: *The takings from the Spencer show will go to the church* (Manchester Guardian Weekly).

**Ta|ki-Ta|ki** (tä′kē tä′kē), *n.* a pidgin dialect of English somewhat mixed with Dutch, spoken in Surinam (Dutch Guiana). [a reduplicative variant of *talk*]

**tak|y** (tā′kē), *adj. Informal.* pleasing; attractive; taking.

**ta|la**[1] (tä′lə), *n., pl.* **-las.** a set rhythmic pattern used in traditional Hindu music: *triple, quintuple, and septuple rhythmic patterns inside a tala of eight fundamental beats* (London Times). [< Sanskrit *tāla*]

**ta|la**[2] (tä′lä), *n., pl.* **-la** or **-las.** the basic unit of money of Western Samoa. [< Samoan *tala* < English *dollar*]

**tal|a|poin** (tal′ə poin), *n.* **1** a Buddhist monk of southeast Asia. **2** a small West African monkey. [< Portuguese *talapão* < Talaing (a Burmese language) *tala pôi* (literally) my lord as a title]

**talapoin monkey,** = talapoin.

**tal|a|ri** (tal′ər ē), *n.* an Ethiopian silver coin. [< Arabic *talari* (originally) the Maria Theresa dollar < German *Thaler* dollar]

**ta|lar|i|a** (tə lãr′ē ə), *n.pl. Roman Mythology.* the winged sandals or small wings on the ankles of some gods, especially Mercury (Hermes). [< Latin *tālāria,* neuter plural of *tālāris* relating to the heel or ankle < *tālus* ankle, heel]

**Ta|la|ve|ra** (tä′lä vā′rä), *n.* **1** a variety of spring wheat. **2** a kind of Spanish majolica of the 1500's. [< *Talavera* (*de la Reina*), a town in Spain]

**tal|bot** (tôl′bət), *n.* a former variety of English hunting hound, with hanging ears and heavy jaws, from which the bloodhound and other hounds were developed. [earlier, the name of a dog, perhaps < *Talbot,* a family whose coat of arms had a dog]

**tal|bo|type** (tôl′bə tīp), *n.* = calotype. [< W. H. F. *Talbot,* 1800-1877, who invented it]

**talc** (talk), *n., v.,* **talced** (talkt), **talc|ing** (tal′king) or **talcked, talck|ing.** —*n.* a soft, smooth mineral, a hydrated silicate of magnesium. It usually consists of slippery, translucent, white, apple-green, or gray sheets, and is used in making face powder and chalk, as filler in paper, and as a lubricant. Soapstone or steatite is a kind of talc. *Talc is the softest mineral known* (Frederick H. Pough). *Formula:* $Mg_3Si_4O_{10}(OH)_2$
—*v.t.* to apply talc to, especially to coat (a photographic plate) with talc.
[< Medieval Latin *talcum* any of various shiny minerals < Arabic *ṭalq*]

**talc|ose** (tal′kōs), *adj.* abounding in or consisting largely of talc.

**tal|cum** (tal′kəm), *n.* **1** = talcum powder. **2** = talc.

**talcum powder,** a powder made of purified white talc, for use on the face and body.

**tale** (tāl), *n.* **1** a story of an event or incident, especially a made-up story: *a tale about ghosts. The old sea captain told the children tales of his adventures. Tales, which are customarily distinguished from myths because of their secular character, are often regarded as an unwritten record of tribal history* (Melville J. Herskovits). **SYN:** See syn. under **story. 2** a falsehood; lie; fabrication. **3** an improper disclosure of a secret. **4** a piece of gossip or scandal; rumor. **5** a number; count: *His tale of sheep amounted to over three hundred. By measures of forty bushels each, the tale is kept* (Anthony Trollope). **6** *Obsolete.* conversation; talk.
**tell tales, a** to spread gossip or scandal: *Dead men tell no tales* (George P. R. James). **b** to tell lies: *He was punished for telling too many tales.*
**tell tales out of school,** to reveal confidential matters: *A very handsome ... supper, at which, to tell tales out of school ... the guests used to behave abominably* (Thomas A. Trollope).
**tell the tale,** to tell a tale of woe to evoke pity or sympathy: *We all tell the tale when we want money* (London Daily Express).
[Old English *talu.* See related etym. at **tell.**]

**tale|bear|er** (tāl′bãr′ər), *n.* a person who spreads gossip or scandal: *These words were spoken in private, but some talebearer repeated them to the Commons* (Macaulay). **SYN:** gossip, scandalmonger, telltale.

**tale|bear|ing** (tāl′bãr′ing), *n., adj.* —*n.* the spreading of gossip or scandal.
—*adj.* spreading gossip or scandal.

**tal|ent** (tal′ənt), *n.* **1** a special natural ability; aptitude: *She has a talent for music. Genius does what it must, and Talent does what it can* (Owen Meredith). *If a man has a talent and cannot use it, he has failed* (Thomas Wolfe). *Women with the talent for raising the tantrum to an art form and the conniption fit to a way of life* (Time). **SYN:** faculty, capacity, gift. See syn. under **ability. 2** a person or persons with talent: *to introduce new talent on stage. That young singer is a real talent.* **3a** an ancient unit of weight or money, varying with time and place. **b** the value of a talent weight as a money of account. **4** *Slang.* bookmakers' customers collectively; gamblers. **5** *Obsolete.* what one prefers; one's liking. [(def. 3) Old English *talente* unit of weight, money < Latin *talentum* < Greek *tálanton;* the obsolete sense < Medieval Latin *talentum* inclination, desire; the other meanings < a figurative sense of money or value. See Matthew 25:14-30.] —**tal′ent|less,** *adj.*

**tal|ent|ed** (tal′ən tid), *adj.* having natural ability; gifted: *a talented musician.* **SYN:** endowed.

**talent education method,** = Suzuki method.

**talent money,** a bonus given, especially to a professional athlete, for an outstanding performance.

**talent scout,** a person whose work is discovering talented people, as for motion pictures, professional athletics, or business.

**ta|ler** (tä′lər), *n., pl.* **-ler.** = thaler.

**ta|les** (tā′lēz), *n.* **1** *pl. in use:* **a** persons chosen to fill out a jury when the original panel has been depleted because of challenges. **b** *British.* common jurors summoned to serve on a special jury. **2** *sing. in use:* **a** one or more people so provided. **b** the writ ordering them to serve. [< Anglo-French *tales* < Latin *tālēs dē circumstantibus* similar persons from those standing around]

**ta|les-book** (tā′lēz bu̇k′), *n.* a book recording the names of persons summoned on a tales.

**tales|man** (tālz′mən, tā′lēz-), *n., pl.* **-men.** a person chosen from among the bystanders or those present in court to serve on a jury when too few of those originally summoned are qualified to be on a jury: *With the consent of the Court, the People will excuse the talesman* (Theodore Dreiser).

**tale|tell|er** (tāl′tel′ər), *n.* **1** = talebearer. **2** a teller of tales or stories; narrator: *You are reminded of those oriental taletellers of the marketplace, whose hands are as eloquent as their voices* (Harper's). **3** a person who tells a tale or lie with the object of deceiving or misleading.

**tale|tell|ing** (tāl′tel′ing), *n., adj.* = talebearing.

**Tal|go** (tal′gō), *n.* a lightweight railroad train with a very low center of gravity that enables it to travel at high speed around curves. [< Spanish *t*(ren) *a*(rticulado) /(igero) (literally) a light jointed train + *G*(oicoechea), who invented it + *O*(riol), who backed the project in Spain]

**ta|li**[1] (tā′lī), *n.* plural of **talus**[1].

**ta|li**[2] (tä′lē), *n.* a Hindu ornament of gold, engraved with the likeness of the goddess Lakshmi, and suspended by a consecrated string of many fine yellow threads. It is worn by married women in India. [< Hindi]

**tal|i|grade** (tal′ə grād), *adj.* walking with the weight on the outer side of the foot. [< Latin *tālus* ankle + *gradī* to walk]

**tal|i|on** (tal′ē ən), *n.* the principle of making the punishment just like the injury; an eye for an eye, a tooth for a tooth; retaliation. [< Middle French *talion* < Latin *tāliō, -ōnis* < *tālis,* such, the like]

**tal|i|ped** (tal′ə ped), *adj., n.* —*adj.* **1** having to do with or affected with talipes; clubfooted. **2** (of a foot) deformed; misshapen.
—*n.* a person who has talipes, especially a clubfoot.
[< New Latin *talipes, talipedis;* see etym. under **talipes**]

**tal|i|pes** (tal′ə pēz), *n.* **1** any one of various foot defects, especially congenital ones, such as clubfoot, characterized by a twisting of the foot to the outside or the inside. **2** a clubfooted condition. [< New Latin *talipes, talipedis* < Latin *tālus* ankle + *pēs, pedis* foot]

**tal|i|pot** (tal′ə pot), *n.* a tall fan palm of Sri Lanka, India, Malaya, and the Philippines, with large leaves that are used as fans, umbrellas, wallpaper, and material to write on. [< Singhalese *talapata* < Sanskrit *tālapattra* < *tālas* the fan palm + *pattra* leaf. Compare etym. under **toddy.**]

**tal|is|man** (tal′is mən, -iz-), *n., pl.* **-mans. 1** a stone, ring, or other object engraved with figures supposed to have magic power; charm. A talisman is usually worn as an amulet to avert evil. *He had stolen from Henry ... a Talisman, which rendered its wearer invulnerable* (Bishop William Stubbs). **SYN:** phylactery. **2** *Figurative.* **a** anything that acts as a magic token or charm. **b** anything that seems to produce extraordinary results. [< French *talisman* < Arabic *ṭilsam* < Late Greek *télesma, -atos* talisman, religious rite, payment < Greek, consecration ceremony; payment; completion < *teleîn* perform (religious rites) < *télos* services due; completion; tax]

**tal|is|man|ic** (tal′is man′ik, -iz-), *adj.* **1** having to do with a talisman. **2** serving as a talisman: *The name has acquired a talismanic significance* (Harper's). —**tal′is|man′i|cal|ly,** *adv.*

**talk** (tôk), *v., n.* —*v.i.* **1** to use words; speak: *Baby is learning to talk.* See syns. under **speak** and **say. 2** to exchange words; converse. **3** to consult; confer: *to talk with one's doctor.* **4** to spread rumors; gossip; blab: *She talked behind their backs.* **5** to spread ideas by other means than speech; communicate: *to talk by signs.* **6** to speak idly; chatter away; prate. **7** to communicate with voices; make sounds that resemble speech: *The birds were talking loudly.* **8** to give an informal speech. **9** *Informal.* to reveal secret information; inform: *The prisoner talked to the police.*
—*v.t.* **1** to use in speaking; speak (a kind of speech or language): *to talk sense. Can you talk French?* **2** to bring, put, drive, or influence, by talk; persuade: *We talked him into joining the club.* **3** to speak about; discuss: *to talk politics, to talk business.*
—*n.* **1** the act or process of speaking; use of words; spoken words; speech: *We had talk enough, but no conversation; there was nothing discussed* (Samuel Johnson). **2** conversation, especially when familiar, empty, or idle: *mere talk. The old friends met for a good talk.* **3** rumor, gossip, or speculation: *There is talk of a gasoline shortage.* **4** an informal speech: *The coach gave the team a talk about the need for more team spirit.* **5** a way of speaking; style; manner: *baby talk.* **6** a language, dialect, or lingo: *thieves' talk.* **7** a conference; council: *summit talks, peace talks, a top-level talk.* **8** a subject for talk or gossip: *She is the talk of the town.*
**talk about, a** to speak in reference to; mention: *Talk about English people being fond of eating,*

**Pronunciation Key:** hat, āge, cãre, fär; let, ēqual, tėrm; it, īce; hot, ōpen, ôrder; **oil, out;** cup, pu̇t, rüle; **ch**ild; lo**ng**; **th**in; **ᴛʜ**en; **zh,** measure;
**ə** represents **a** in about, **e** in taken, **i** in pencil, **o** in lemon, **u** in circus.

*that Canadian party beat all I had ever seen* (E. Roper). **b** to consider with a view of doing: *He talks about retiring soon from business.*

**talk around**, to discuss at length without coming to the point or to a conclusion: *The Cabinet members talked around the proposal for several hours before adjourning.*

**talk away**, to spend (time) in talking; pass by talking: *I am very well content to talk away an evening with you on the subject* (Joseph Addison).

**talk back**, *Informal.* to answer rudely or disrespectfully: *The boy was punished for talking back to the teacher.*

**talk big**, *Slang.* to talk boastfully; brag: *We are able to talk big about light and freedom* (Connop Thirlwall).

**talk down, a** to make silent by talking louder or longer; outtalk: *Her that talk'd down the fifty wisest men* (Tennyson). **b** to belittle; disparage: *He talks down his competitor's products.* **c** to give radio instructions for landing an airplane because of instrument failure or poor visibility: *The pilot must rely upon the maintenance staff ... when it is necessary for him to be talked down by Ground Controlled Approach* (Punch).

**talk down to**, to speak to in a superior tone: *College students resent teachers that talk down to them.*

**talk of, a** to speak in reference to; mention: *Talking of Switzerland—have you ever been there in winter?* **b** to consider with a view to doing: *He talks of moving to a warmer climate.*

**talk off** (or **out of**) **the top of one's head**. See under **top**[1].

**talk out, a** to discuss thoroughly: *Let's talk this out before we do anything.* **b** (in the British Parliament) to discuss (a bill) until the time for adjournment and so prevent its being put to a vote: *... a form of filibustering to keep all rival records off the air as a politician talks out his opponent* (Punch).

**talk over, a** to consider together; discuss: *We will talk over the matter as we go* (Frederick Marryat). **b** to persuade or convince by arguing: *He talked over Trevittick, who sulkily acquiesced* (Henry Kingsley).

**talk up**, to talk earnestly in favor of; campaign for: *Two years ago he went to the federal-provincial conference in Ottawa and talked up the idea of a centennial project in Charlottetown* (Maclean's).

[Middle English *talken.* See related etym. at **tell.**]

▶ See **say** for usage note.

**talk|a|thon** (tô′kə thon), *n.* **1** *Informal.* a lengthy period of speaking or debating, similar to a filibuster. **2** a way of political campaigning, by answering questions for an unlimited amount of time before a radio or television audience.

**talk|a|tive** (tô′kə tiv), *adj.* having the habit of talking a great deal; fond of talking: *He became very talkative over his second bottle of port* (George Eliot). —**talk′a|tive|ly**, *adv.* —**talk′a|tive|ness**, *n.*

—*Syn.* **Talkative, loquacious** mean talking much. **Talkative**, the common word, emphasizes a fondness for talking and having the habit of talking a great deal: *He is a merry, talkative old man, who knows everybody on our street.* **Loquacious**, a formal word, adds the idea of talking smoothly and easily and suggests a steady stream of words: *The president of the club is a loquacious woman.*

**talk-down** (tôk′doun′), *n.* the act of talking down an airplane: *Poor talk-down on the part of the controller, the man in the control tower, contributed to the crash of the plane* (British Broadcasting Company).

**talked-a|bout** (tôkt′ə bout′), *adj.* discussed: *Certainly she is one of the century's most talked-about authors* (Wall Street Journal).

**talked-of** (tôkt′uv′, -ov′), *adj.* familiarly or vaguely spoken about.

**talk|er** (tô′kər), *n.* **1** any person who talks: *The most fluent talkers ... are not always the justest thinkers* (William Hazlitt). **SYN**: speaker, lecturer. **2** a talkative person. **SYN**: gossip. **3** *Informal.* a barker for a side show.

**talk|fest** (tôk′fest′), *n. Informal.* **1** a long or drawn-out talk, discussion, or debate: *They saw no reason ... to propose resumption of the truce conference if it was to be just another futile talkfest* (Newsweek). **2** a period of light, often aimless discussion: *There must be discipline, because without it classes degenerate into mere talkfests, with the conversation wandering far from the main theme* (Wall Street Journal).

**talk|ie** (tô′kē), *n. Informal.* a motion picture with a synchronized sound track; talking picture: *It was not until the talkies came that the cinema divorced itself from reading* (London Times).

**talk|ie-talk|ie** (tô′kē tô′kē), *n. British.* talky talk.

**talk-in** (tôk′in′), *n.* **1** a protest demonstration in which the participants take turns to speak up on the issues. **2** *Informal.* a lecture or talk. **3** *Informal.* a conference or discussion.

**talk|ing book** (tô′king), a phonograph record or tape recording of a book, article, or other publication, especially for blind persons.

**talking head**, a person being interviewed or discussing some issue on television or a person shown narrating a program or documentary motion picture: *... the audience is more likely to be engrossed by visual excitement than by "talking heads"* (New Yorker). *Television often achieves its best effects by moving in close. 'Talking heads' can be superb television* (Listener).

**talking machine**, *Archaic.* a phonograph.

**talking myna**, = hill myna.

**talking picture**, a motion picture with a synchronized sound track: *The "talking picture" ... sent well-known stars to the scrap heap* (Emory S. Bogardus).

**talk|ing-point** (tô′king point′), *n.*, or **talking point**, a subject for talk, especially something to use as an argument: *Many of these tax-free groups can solicit contributions with the powerful talking-point that the gifts are tax-deductible* (Wall Street Journal).

**talking stage**, a stage or period when some plan has not yet been settled but is still only a matter of discussion.

**talk|ing-to** (tô′king tü′), *n., pl.* **talk|ing-tos** or **talk|ings-to**. *Informal.* a scolding; reprimand.

**talk jockey**, *U.S. Informal.* a radio announcer on a program consisting mainly of light talk or conversation, especially with listeners who call in on the telephone: *Some of the new talk jockeys ... still play music, but it is always subordinate to their dialogue with listeners* (Time). [patterned after *disk jockey*]

**talk show**, *Especially U.S.* a television or radio show in which guests are interviewed: *Promoting her book in the United States, the ... scholar rapidly became a familiar figure on television's talk shows, equally at ease in the role of host or guest* (Lawrence R. Van Gelder).

**talk|y** (tô′kē), *adj.*, **talk|i|er, talk|i|est**. **1** = talkative. **2** too full of talk.

**talky talk**, *Informal.* trivial conversation; small talk: *Probably she'd be called the typical New York girl, if you wanted to talk talky talk* (H. L. Wilson).

**tall** (tôl), *adj., adv.* —*adj.* **1a** higher than the average; having great height; high: *New York has many tall buildings.* **SYN**: lofty, towering. See syn. under **high**. **b** high or lofty, especially in proportion to width: *tall chimneys, a tall mast.* **2** standing as high as specified, having the height of; in height: *The man is 5 feet 8 inches tall. The tree is one hundred feet tall.* **3** *Informal, Figurative.* high or large in amount; extravagant: *a tall price.* **4** *Informal, Figurative.* hard to believe; exaggerated: *That is a tall tale.* **5** *Obsolete.* praiseworthy in various senses; good: **a** strong in combat; brave. **b** good-looking; handsome. **c** proper; fitting; decent. **d** skillful; dexterous; handy.

—*adv.* **1** *Slang.* in an exaggerated manner: *to talk tall.* **2** *Informal.* with the head high; proudly: *to walk tall.*

[Middle English *tall;* Old English *getæl* prompt, active] —**tall′ness**, *n.*

**tal|lage** (tal′ij), *n., v.*, **-laged, -lag|ing**. —*n.* **1** any tax, toll, or levy. **2** in English history: **a** a tax levied by kings on the royal boroughs and crown lands. **b** a tax levied on feudal dependents by their lords.

—*v.t.* to tax.

[Middle English *taillage* < Old French < *taillier* determine the form; (literally) cut to shape; see etym. under **tail**[2]]

**tall|boy** (tôl′boi′), *n.* **1** *British.* a highboy. **2** a kind of tall chimney pot. **3** *Dialect.* a long-stemmed glass; goblet.

**tall buttercup**, a common, tall, weedy buttercup native to Europe, sometimes grown for its double yellow flowers.

**tall fescue**, a variety of meadow fescue.

**tal|li|a|ble** (tal′ē ə bəl), *adj. Archaic.* that can be tallaged; subject to tallage.

**tal|li|ate** (tal′ē āt), *v.t.*, **-at|ed, -at|ing**. to tax; tallage. [< Medieval Latin *talliare* (with English *-ate*[1]) impose a tax. Compare etym. under **tail**[2].]

**tal|lied** (tal′ēd), *adj.* corresponding; matched; suited.

**tal|li|er** (tal′ē ər), *n.* **1a** a person or thing that tallies. **b** a person who keeps a tally. **2** the banker in certain card games.

**tal|lis** (tä′lis), *n., pl.* **tal|lei|sim** (tä lā′sim). a prayer shawl; tallith. [< Yiddish *tallis* < Hebrew *tallith;* see etym. under **tallith**]

**tall|ish** (tô′lish), *adj.* **1** inclining toward tallness; rather tall: *a tallish, vigorous man.* **2** somewhat exaggerated: *a tallish tale.*

**tal|lit** (tä′lit), *n., pl.* **tal|li|tim** (tal′ə tim′). a prayer shawl; tallith.

**✱tal|lith** (tal′ith, -it; tä′lis), *n., pl.* **tal|liths, tal|li|thim** (tal′ə thim′, tä lä′sim). a fringed mantle or shawl of wool, silk, or linen, worn by Orthodox Jewish men at morning prayer. [< Hebrew *tallith* < Aramaic *ṭlal* cover, shelter]

**✱tallith**

**tall oil** (täl), a resinous liquid by-product of the manufacture of pine wood pulp, used especially in making soap, varnish, and turpentine. [American English, half-translation of German *Tallöl*, a half-translation of Swedish *tallolja* (literally) pine oil]

**tall|ol** (tä′lôl, -lol), *n.* = tall oil. [< German *Tallöl;* see etym. under **tall oil**]

**tall order**, a large requirement, demand, request, or proposal.

**tal|low** (tal′ō), *n., v.* —*n.* **1** the hard, white fat from around the kidneys of sheep, cows, oxen, or other animals, used for making candles and soap and in dressing leather. **2** the fat or adipose tissue of an animal; suet. **3** any one of various kinds of grease or greasy substances, especially those obtained from plants.

—*v.t.* to grease with tallow: *I ... tallowed my nose, and went to bed* (J. K. Jerome).

[Middle English *talowe*, oblique case of *talgh*]

**tal|low|ber|ry** (tal′ō ber′ē), *n., pl.* **-ries**. **1** a small malpighiaceous tree of the West Indies and Florida Keys. **2** the edible fruit of this tree.

**tallow bush**, *U.S.* the wax myrtle.

**tallow chandler**, a person whose business is making and selling tallow candles.

**tallow chandlery, chan|dler|ing** (chan′dlər-ing), or **chan|dling** (chan′dling), **1** the business or work of a tallow chandler. **2** his place of work.

**tallow dip**, a tallow candle.

**tal|low-faced** (tal′ō fāst′), *adj.* (of a person) having a pale, yellowish-white face; pallid (used in an unfriendly way).

**tallow gourd**, **1** an East Indian climbing plant of the gourd family, that exudes a waxy substance from its fruit when ripe; wax gourd; white gourd. **2** its edible fruit.

**tal|low|ish** (tal′ō ish), *adj.* resembling tallow: *The cheeks, formerly tallowish ..., became ruddy* (Augustus B. Granville).

**tallow nut**, a thorny tree of tropical America, bearing a plumlike fruit containing a white seed or nut.

**tallow nutmeg**, a South American nutmeg tree, whose seed yields oil of nutmeg.

**tallow shrub**, = bayberry.

**tal|low-top** (tal′ō top′), *n.* a gem cut as a cabochon; carbuncle.

**tal|low-topped** (tal′ō topt′), *adj.* **1** having a slightly rounded or convex surface. **2** (of a gem) cut as a cabochon.

**tallow tree**, any one of several trees yielding waxy or fatty substances: **a** an Asian tree of the spurge family, introduced into North America, whose seeds are used to make soap and candles. **b** a tree of tropical Africa whose seeds yield a fat used in cooking and for making soap; butter tree. **c** = tallowwood (def. 1).

**tal|low|wood** (tal′ō wu̇d′), *n.* **1** a large Australian eucalyptus tree which yields a very hard, greasy, durable wood. **2** the tallow nut.

**tal|low|y** (tal′ō ē), *adj.* **1** like tallow; fat; greasy; sebaceous. **2** yellowish-white; pallid; pale. **3** (of an animal) fat.

**tall ship**, a high-masted sailing ship, especially a square-rigger. *... 16 of the world's largest windjammers, or tall ships* (Time). [< the line "And all I ask is a *tall ship* and a star to steer her by" in John Masefield's poem "Sea-Fever"]

▶The modern usage almost certainly derives from Masefield's poem, although in the days when sailing ships were prevalent the term was known from the 1500's for any large sailing vessel.

**tall thistle**, a branching species of thistle with light-purple flowers.

**tal|ly** (tal′ē), *n., pl.* **-lies**, *v.*, **-lied, -ly|ing**. —*n.* **1** a stick in which notches are cut to represent numbers. Tallies were formerly used to show the amount of a debt or payment. **2** a number or group used in tallying; lot: *The dishes were counted in tallies of 20.* **3** a notch, stroke, or mark made on a tally; mark made for a certain number of objects in keeping account. **4** any

board or other thing on which a score or account is kept. **5** the account or score kept; reckoning: *a tally of a game.* **6** a thing that matches another: **a** a part that fits; counterpart. **b** one like it; duplicate. **7** *Figurative.* correspondence; agreement. **8** any symbol of an amount, such as a token or ticket. **9** a distinguishing mark; label; tag. **10** (formerly in Britain) the charge-account system. **11** *Sports.* a scoring point; run, goal, or other score.
— ***v.t.*** **1** to mark on a tally; enter; register: *to tally a score.* **SYN**: record, number, score. **2** to count up; inventory. **3** to mark with an identifying label; tag. **4** *Figurative.* to cause to fit, suit, or correspond. **5** *Sports.* to score: *The hockey team tallied seven goals in their last game.*
— ***v.i.*** **1** to correspond, match, or agree; fit: *Your account tallies with mine. It is hard that a man's exterior should tally so little sometimes with his soul* (W. Somerset Maugham). **SYN**: conform, accord. **2** = duplicate. **3** *Sports.* to make scoring points: *The best scorer failed to tally in only one game all season. Larry Jeffrey and Alex Delvecchio tallied in a 49-second span to put Detroit ahead, 4-2* (New York Times).
[probably < Anglo-French *tallie* < Medieval Latin *tallia* < Late Latin *tālea* a cutting, rod. See related etym. at **tail²**.]

**tally board**, a board on which a tally or score is kept, as by notches or chalk marks; scoreboard.

**tally clerk**, **1** a clerk who checks merchandise against a loading list. **2** *U.S.* a clerk who helps count votes; teller.

***tal|ly|ho** (*interj., v.* tal'ē hō'; *n.* tal'ē hō'), *interj., n., pl.* **-hos**, *v.,* **-hoed** or **-ho'd**, **-ho|ing**. *Especially British.* — ***interj.*** a hunter's cry on catching sight of the fox; view halloo.
— ***n.*** **1** a large private or mail coach pulled by four horses. **2** a sounding of "tallyho" by a hunter.
— ***v.t.*** **1** to urge (hounds) by this call. **2** to cry this upon sighting (a fox). — ***v.i.*** to call "tallyho."
[earlier *tallio,* apparently alteration of French *taïaut* < Old French *taho* or *tielau*]

***tallyho**
definition 1

**tal|ly|man** (tal'ē mən), *n., pl.* **-men**. **1** a man who keeps a tally. **2** a person who makes entries on a tally.

**tally sheet**, a sheet on which a record or score is kept: *The TV tally sheet already lists 62 shows ... devoted to some variation of Cops and Robbers* (Time).

**tally shop**, (formerly) a shop selling cheap goods on credit.

**tal|ma** (tal'mə), *n.* a kind of cape or cloak formerly worn by men or women: *He wore a wide hat and a talma—a cloak with full, dashing lines* (New Yorker). [< François *Talma,* 1763-1826, a French tragedian]

**Tal|mud** (tal'məd), *n.* **1** a collection of 63 books containing the body of Jewish civil and canonical law derived by interpretation and expansion of the teachings of the Old Testament; the Mishnah together with the Gemara. **2** the Gemara, a commentary on the Mishnah, in Palestinian and Babylonian versions, both completed about 500 A.D. [< Hebrew *talmūd* instruction < *lāmad* he taught]

**Tal|mud|ic** (tal müd'ik), *adj.* of or having to do with the Talmud: *a Talmudic scholar, Talmudic studies, Talmudic tradition.* — **Tal|mud'i|cal|ly**, *adv.*

**Tal|mud|i|cal** (tal müd'ə kəl), *adj.* = Talmudic.

**Tal|mud|ist** (tal'mə dist), *n.* **1** a person learned in the Talmud and literature about it. **2** one of the authors or editors of the Talmud. **3** a person who accepts the doctrines of the Talmud.

**Tal|mud|is|tic** (tal'mə dis'tik), *adj.* = Talmudic.

**Tal|mud To|rah** (täl'müd tôr'ə, tōr'-), *pl.* **Talmud To|rahs**, **Tal|mu|dei To|rah** (täl mü'dā tôr'ə, tōr'-), a Hebrew School. [< Hebrew *talmūd tōrāh* (literally) study of the Torah]

**tal|on** (tal'ən), *n.* **1** the claw of an animal, especially a bird of prey: *The eagle seized a chicken with it talons.* **2** a clawlike, grasping finger. **3** cards not dealt; stock; pile. **4** the projection on the bolt that the key engages in a lock; shoulder. **5** *Architecture.* an ogee molding. **6** the heel of a sword blade. **7** *Commerce.* a certificate after the last coupon on a bond, to be sent in for more coupons.
**talons,** clawlike fingers; grasping hands: (*Figurative.*) *the talons of despotism* (Edmund Burke).
[< Old French *talon* heel < Medieval Latin *talo, -onis* < Latin *tālus* ankle]

**tal|oned** (tal'ənd), *adj.* having talons.

**tal|pa|ta|te** (täl'pä tä'tā), *n.* **1** a cementlike rock composed chiefly of sand and volcanic ash. **2** a poor soil composed chiefly of volcanic ash. [< American Spanish *talpatate* < a Nahuatl word]

**tal|pe|ta|te** (täl'pə tä'tā), *n.* = talpatate.

**tal|pine** (tal'pin), *adj.* **1** having to do with the mole. **2** allied to the mole; molelike. [< Late Latin *talpīnus* < Latin *talpa* mole]

**ta|luk** (tə lük'), *n.* in India: **1** a subdivision of a tax district, covering several villages, under a collector. **2** (formerly) the ancestral estate of an Indian family. [Anglo-Indian < Hindustani *tāluk* estate, proprietary tract < Arabic *ta'alluq* attachment, dependence]

**ta|luk|dar** (tə lük'där), *n.* in India: **1** the holder of a hereditary taluk. **2** the collector in charge of a taluk. [< Hindustani *tālukdār* < *tāluk* taluk + *-dār* holding]

**ta|lus¹** (tā'ləs), *n., pl.* **-li**. **1** the human anklebone; astragalus. See picture under **ankle**. **2** the human ankle. [< Latin *tālus* ankle]

**ta|lus²** (tā'ləs), *n., pl.* **-lus|es**. **1** *Geology.* a sloping mass of rocky fragments that has fallen from a cliff: *Piles of talus (earth and rocks dislodged from above by the processes of weathering, which the forces of erosion are unable to remove as fast as they accumulate) lie in abundance against the bases of dry-land escarpments* (Finch and Trewartha). **2** a sloping side of a wall, rampart, trench, or the like. **3** any slope. [< Old French *talu* < Latin *talūtium* a sign of gold near the surface]

**tam** (tam), *n.* = tam-o'-shanter.

**tam|a|ble** (tā'mə bəl), *adj.* = tameable.

**tam|a|bly** (tā'mə blē), *adv.* = tameably.

**ta|main** (tə mīn'), *n.* = tamein.

**ta|ma|le** (tə mä'lē), *n.* a Mexican food made of corn meal and ground meat, seasoned with red peppers, wrapped in cornhusks, and roasted or steamed. [American English < Mexican Spanish *tamales,* plural of *tamal* < Nahuatl *tamal*]

**tam|an|du** (tam'ən dü), *n.* = tamandua.

**ta|man|dua** (tä'mən dwä'), *n.* a small arboreal anteater of tropical America, with four toes on the front feet, a prehensile tail, and no teeth. [< Portuguese *tamanduá* < Tupi (Brazil) *tamanduá*]

**tam|a|noir** (tam'ə nwär), *n.* = ant bear (def. 1). [< French *tamanoir,* alteration of *tamanduá* tamandua]

**tam|a|rack** (tam'ə rak), *n.* **1** a larch of northern North America with reddish-brown bark, which yields strong, heavy timber; hackmatack. **2** any one of certain similar larches. **3** the wood of any larch tree. [American English, apparently < an Algonkian word]

**ta|ma|rau** (tä'mə rou'), *n.* a small, shaggy, black buffalo of Mindoro Island, in the Philippines, with very thick, short horns.

**tam|a|rin** (tam'ər in), *n.* any of various small South American monkeys allied to the marmosets, having a long, nonprehensile tail and hooked claws. [< French *tamarin,* probably < the Carib name in French Guiana]

**tam|a|rind** (tam'ər ind), *n.* **1** a tropical fruit, a brown pod with juicy, acid pulp, used in foods, drinks, and medicine. **2** the evergreen tree bearing this fruit. It belongs to the pea family. Tamarind is also widely grown for its fragrant yellow flowers, streaked with red, and its hard, heavy, yellowish wood. [< Old French *tamarindes,* plural < Arabic *tamr hindī* (literally) date of India]

**tam|a|risk** (tam'ər isk), *n.* **1** an ornamental shrub or small tree with fine, feathery branches and minute, scalelike leaves. It is an evergreen tree of the Mediterranean region. **2** any related Old World tree or shrub. [< Late Latin *tamariscus,* variant of Latin *tamarīx, -īcis*]

**ta|ma|sha** (tə mä'shə), *n.* (in India) a public entertainment, display, or ceremony; function or show. [< Hindustani, Arabic *tamāshā* strolling for fun < Arabic *tamashshā* he walked]

**tam|bac** (tam'bak), *n.* = tombac.

**tam|ba|la** (tam bä'lə), *n., pl.* **-la** or **-las**. a unit of money in Malawi, equal to 1/100 of a kwacha. [< the native name, meaning "cockerel"]

**tam|bo** (tam'bō), *n., pl.* **-bos**. an end man in a minstrel troupe who plays on the tambourine. [short for *tambourine*]

**tam|bo|ri|to** (täm'bō rē'tō), *n., pl.* **-tos**. a Panamanian folk dance in which a man and a woman dance together in the center of a circle. [< Spanish *tamborito* little drum < *tambor* drum]

**tam|bour** (tam'bůr), *n., v., adj.* — ***n.*** **1** a drum, especially a bass drum. **2** a drummer: *Twice a day, the tambour ... would read aloud the latest dispatches in the village square* (New Yorker). **3** a pair of hoops, one fitting within the other, for holding cloth stretched for embroidering; pair of embroidery hoops. **4** embroidery done on this. **5** one of the three hazards in court tennis, projecting from the back wall on the hazard side, to make the ball rebound erratically. **6** a palisade protecting a gate, road, or entrance. **7** *Especially British.* a circular vestibule. **8** *Architecture.* one of the cylindrical stones in a column; drum. **9** the cylinder on a recording instrument.
— ***v.t., v.i.*** to embroider on a tambour.
— ***adj.*** made of strips or slats of wood with half-rounded upper surfaces for sliding easily across rounded surfaces: *... a compartment of pigeonholes, which is concealed by a small tambour door* (New Yorker).
[< Middle French *tambour,* variant of Old French *tabour;* see etym. under **tabor**]

**tam|bou|ra** (täm bůr'ə), *n.* an Oriental musical instrument of the lute family consisting of four strings and producing a droning sound, used as accompaniment to the sitar or sarod. Also, **tambura**. [< Persian *ṭanbūr*]

**tam|bou|rin** (tam'bůr in; *French* täɴ bü ʀaɴ'), *n.* **1** a long, narrow drum or tabor used in Provence. **2** a Provençal dance, originally accompanied by the tambourin or tabor. **3** the music for it. [< French *tambourin* (diminutive) < Middle French *tambour;* see etym. under **tambour**]

***tam|bou|rine** (tam'bə rēn'), *n.* **1** a small, shallow drum with only one head, and metal disks around the sides, played by shaking it or by striking it with the knuckles; timbrel: *The banjos rattled, and the tambourines Jing-jing-jingled in the hands of Queens* (Vachel Lindsay). **2** an African pigeon with a resonant call. [apparently < French *tambourin;* see etym. under **tambourin**]

***tambourine**
definition 1

**tam|bour-lace** (tam'bůr lās'), *n.* a modern lace of needlework designs on machine-made net, resembling tambour embroidery.

**tambour stitch**, **1** the loop-stitch used in tambour embroidery. **2** a stitch used in crochet to make ridges that intersect at right angles.

**tam|bu|ra** (täm bůr'ə), *n.* = tamboura.

**tam|bu|rit|za** (tam bə rit'sə), *n.* a long-necked stringed instrument of Yugoslavia resembling a large mandolin. [< Serbo-Croatian *tamburica,* ultimately < Persian *ṭanbūr* tamboura]

**tame** (tām), *adj.,* **tam|er**, **tam|est**, *v.,* **tamed**, **tam|ing**. — ***adj.*** **1** not wild or savage; domestic: *Cows are tame animals.* **2a** taken from the wild state and made obedient: *The man has a tame bear.* **SYN**: domesticated. **b** without fear or shyness; gentle: *The birds are so tame they will eat out of our hands.* **SYN**: docile. **3** *Figurative.* fawning; servile. **4** *Figurative.* without spirit; colorless; insipid; dull: *a tame story. The party was tame because we were sleepy.* **5** *Figurative.* not dangerous or harmful: *The reactor was built for tame atomic energy use* (Science News Letter). **6a** (of plants or land) cultivated. **b** (of a fruit) improved by artificial breeding or other methods. **7** not inclined to criticize.
— ***v.t.*** **1** to make tame; break in: *The lion was tamed for the circus.* **2** *Figurative.* to take spirit, courage, or interest from; make dull: *Harsh punishment in childhood had tamed him and broken his will.* **SYN**: curb, repress. **3** *Figurative.* to reduce in strength; tone down; subdue; soften; mellow: *The pill will contain living polio virus "tamed" by growing through many generations* (Science News Letter).
— ***v.i.*** to become tame: *She tamed down considerably. White rats tame easily.*
[Old English *tam*] — **tame'ly**, *adv.* — **tame'ness**, *n.*

**tame|a|ble** (tā'mə bəl), *adj.* **1** that can be tamed or subdued. **2** that can be reclaimed from a wild or savage state. Also, **tamable**.

**tame|a|bly** (tā'mə blē), *adv.* in a tameable manner; so as to tame. Also, **tamably**.

**tame cat**, *Informal.* a person who is easy to impose upon; tractable person.

---

**Pronunciation Key:** hat, āge, cãre, fär; let, ēqual, tėrm; it, īce; hot, ōpen, ôrder; **oi**l, **ou**t; cup, půt, rüle; **ch**ild; lo**ng**; **th**in; **ᴛʜ**en; **zh**, measure; **ə** represents **a** in about, **e** in taken, **i** in pencil, **o** in lemon, **u** in circus.

***ta|mein** or **ta|mehn** (tə mīnʹ), *n.* a brightly colored silk or cotton garment worn by Burmese women. Also, **tamain, te-mine.** [< a Burmese word]

***tamein**

**tame|less** (tāmʹlis), *adj.* **1** that has never been tamed. **2** that cannot be tamed: *The leopardess is tameless* (Charlotte Brontë). —**tameʹless|ly,** *adv.* —**tameʹless|ness,** *n.*

**tame-poi|son** (tāmʹpoiʹzən), *n.* an herb of the milkweed family native to Europe whose root was formerly used as an antidote to poisons.

**tam|er** (tāʹmər), *n.* a person who tames: *a lion tamer.*

**Tam|il** (tamʹəl), *n., adj.* —*n.* **1** a Dravidian language spoken in southern India, Ceylon (Sri Lanka), Singapore, and Malaysia. **2** one of the people who speak this language.
—*adj.* of or having to do with the Tamils or their language.

**tam|is** (tamʹis), *n.* **1** a cloth strainer; sieve; tammy. **2** the fabric used in it. [< French *tamis* sieve of wire, silk, hair]

**tam|is-cloth** (tamʹis klôthʹ, -klothʹ), *n.* = tamis (def. 2).

**Tam|ma|ny** (tamʹə nē), *n., adj.* —*n.* an influential organization of Democratic politicians of New York City, founded as a fraternal and benevolent organization in 1789, notorious for corruption in the 1800's.
—*adj.* of or having to do with this organization or its politics, methods, or members: *An old Tammany sachem once remarked that he would rather have the "New York Times" against him than for him* (Time).
[American English < *Tamanen* or *Tamanend,* a Delaware Indian chief of the 1600's; (literally) the affable one]

**Tammany Hall,** = Tammany.

**Tam|ma|ny|ism** (tamʹə nē izʹəm), *n.* the system or principles of Tammany.

**Tam|ma|ny|ite** (tamʹə nē īt), *n.* an adherent of Tammany; follower of Tammanyism.

**Tam|muz** (tämʹmüz; *Biblical* tamʹuz), *n.* **1** the tenth month of the Jewish civil year and the fourth month of the ecclesiastical year, occurring in June and often part of July. **2** *Babylonian Mythology.* a god of the springtime and plant growth, who annually returned to earth from the lower world, symbolizing the rebirth of vegetation in spring. Also, **Thammuz.** [< Hebrew *tammūz* < Babylonian *dumuzi*]

**tam|my**[1] (tamʹē), *n., pl.* **-mies. 1** *Especially British.* a tam-o'-shanter; tam. **2** *British Informal.* a Scotsman.

**tam|my**[2] (tamʹē), *n.* a fine worsted cloth, often with a glazed finish, used in the 1600's and 1700's.
[perhaps alteration of obsolete *tamin,* short for French *étamine*]

**tam|my**[3] (tamʹē), *n., pl.* **-mies.** a strainer; tamis. [apparently < French *tamis;* see etym. under **tamis**]

***tam-o'-shan|ter** (tamʹə shanʹtər), *n.* a soft woolen cap, originally of Scotland, with a flat, round crown and often with a tassel; tam. [< *Tam o' Shanter,* the hero of a poem by Robert Burns]

***tam-o'-shanter**

**tamp** (tamp), *v., n.* —*v.t.* **1** to pack down or in by a series of light blows: *to tamp tobacco into a pipe, to tamp the earth about a newly planted tree.* **2** (in blasting) to fill (the hole containing the explosive) with dirt or other nonexplosive material.
—*n.* **1** the act or an instance of tamping. **2** something used for tamping.
[perhaps < *tampin,* variant of *tampion,* taken as *tamping,* present participle; influenced by *stamp*]

**tam|per**[1] (tamʹpər), *v.i.* **1** to meddle (with); meddle in an improper way (with): *Do not tamper with the lock.* SYN: See syn. under **meddle. 2** to work secretly; scheme; plot.
**tamper with, a** to influence improperly; bribe; corrupt: *Crooked politicians had tampered with the jury.* **b** to change so as to damage or falsify: *to tamper with the accounts of a company. They might not consent to such drastic tampering with the basic structure of the play* (New Yorker).
[earlier, to work clay, apparently variant of *temper,* verb] —**tamʹper|er,** *n.*

**tamp|er**[2] (tamʹpər), *n.* **1** a tool used for tamping concrete. **2** a person or thing that tamps. **3** a heavy sheath of lead or tungsten around the explosive elements of a nuclear bomb to prevent the escape of neutrons and to keep the bomb from flying apart too soon.

**tam|per|proof** (tamʹpər prüfʹ), *adj.* that resists being tampered with: *A tamperproof, nonresettable meter keeps count of checks signed* (Newsweek).

**tam|pi|on** (tamʹpē ən), *n.* **1** a wooden plug in the muzzle of a gun that is not being used, to keep out dampness and dust. **2** a plug for the top of a stopped organ pipe. Also, **tompion.** [< Middle French *tampon,* variant of Old French *tapon* < *tape* < *taper* to plug < a Germanic word]

**tam|pon** (tamʹpon), *n., v.* —*n.* **1** a plug of cotton or other absorbent material inserted in a body cavity or wound to stop bleeding or absorb secretions. **2** a two-headed drumstick used to produce a roll. —*v.t.* to fill or plug with a tampon. [< French, Middle French *tampon;* see etym. under **tampion**]

**tam-tam** (tumʹtumʹ), *n.* **1** a large gong, especially one used in a symphony orchestra: *Mahler's Sixth is ... colored by such exotic instruments as cowbells, chimes, tam-tam, and a special musical hammer devised by Mahler himself* (Atlantic). **2** = tom-tom. [variant of *tom-tom;* ultimately imitative]

**ta|mu|re** (tä müʹrā), *n.* = schnapper. [< a Maori word]

**Tam|worth** (tamʹwėrthʹ), *n.* an English breed of pigs of a reddish color, raised chiefly for bacon. [< *Tamworth,* a town in Staffordshire where this breed was developed]

**tan** (tan), *adj., n., v.,* **tanned, tan|ning.**
—*adj.* **1** light yellowish-brown in color: *He wore tan shoes.* **2** having to do with tanning. **3** used in tanning.
—*n.* **1** a yellowish brown; light brown or darkish buff. **2** the brown color of a person's skin caused by being in the sun and air. An artificial tan can be obtained by exposure to a sun lamp or by applying a tanning substance. *His arms and legs had a dark tan.* **3** the liquid used in tanning hides, usually containing tannin, extracted from the bark of oaks, hemlocks, and similar trees. **4** the bark used in tanning hides and also for covering riding tracks and circus rings; tanbark. **5** the astringent acid in it; tannin.
—*v.t.* **1** to make brown by exposure to sun and air, or to a sun lamp, or by applying a tanning substance: *Sun and wind had tanned the sailor's face.* **2** to make (a hide) into leather by soaking in a special liquid, especially one containing tannin, extracted from the bark of oak or hemlock trees. **3** *Informal.* to thrash or beat in punishment.
—*v.i.* to become tanned: *If you lie on the beach in the sun you will tan.*
[Old English *tannian* < Medieval Latin *tannare* < *tannum* oak bark, probably < Celtic (compare Breton *tann* oak tree)]

**tan** (no period) or **tan.,** tangent.

**ta|na**[1] (täʹnə), *n.* in India: **1** a police station. **2** (formerly) a military station or fortified post. Also, **thana.** [< Hindi *thāna*]

**ta|na**[2] (täʹnä), *n., pl.* **ta|na|im.** = tanna.

**ta|na|dar** (täʹnə därʹ), *n.* the head officer of a tana. Also, **tannadar, thanadar.** [< Hindi *thānadār* < *thāna* tana[1] + *-dar* agent]

**tan|a|ger** (tanʹə jər), *n.* any one of various small American songbirds related to the finches. Tanagers usually have brilliant plumage. The scarlet tanager, the summer tanager, the hepatic tanager, and the western or Louisiana tanager of North America are four of the kinds that comprise the tanager family. [< New Latin *tanagra,* alteration of Portuguese *tángara* < Tupi (Brazil) *tangara*]

**Tan|a|gra figurine** (tanʹə grə), a terra-cotta figurine found in the ruins of the ancient Greek city of Tanagra.

**tan|a|grine** (tanʹə grin), *adj.* of or having to do with the tanagers.

**ta|na|im** (tä näʹim), *n.* plural of **tana**[2].

**tan|bark** (tanʹbärkʹ), *n.* **1** the crushed bark, as of oak and hemlock, containing tannin and used in tanning hides; tan. Riding tracks and circus rings are often covered with used tanbark. **2** a riding track or circus ring so covered: *Out on the tanbark the show will go on much as usual, with the frivolous fun of cavorting clowns* (Wall Street Journal).

**tan|bay** (tanʹbāʹ), *n.* = loblolly bay.

***tan|dem** (tanʹdəm), *adv., adj., n., v.* —*adv.* one behind the other; in single file: *to drive horses tandem, to paddle a canoe tandem instead of by oneself.*
—*adj.* having animals, seats, or parts arranged one behind the other: *A tandem helicopter has one overhead rotor in the front of the long narrow fuselage and another in the back* (New York Times).
—*n.* **1** two horses harnessed one behind the other. **2** a high, two-wheeled open carriage, pulled by two horses harnessed tandem. **3** Also, **tandem bicycle.** a bicycle built with two or more seats, one behind the other. **4** a truck or other vehicle with two attached units, such as a cab for pulling and a trailer to carry the load.
—*v.i., v.t.* to harness or drive in tandem.
**in tandem, a** one behind the other; in tandem formation: *mounted in tandem.* **b** *Figurative.* closely together; in cooperation: *She and her husband were a writing team working in tandem on the book.*
[< a pun on Latin *tandem* at length < *tam* so]
—**tanʹdem|ly,** *adv.*

***tandem**
definitions 2, 3

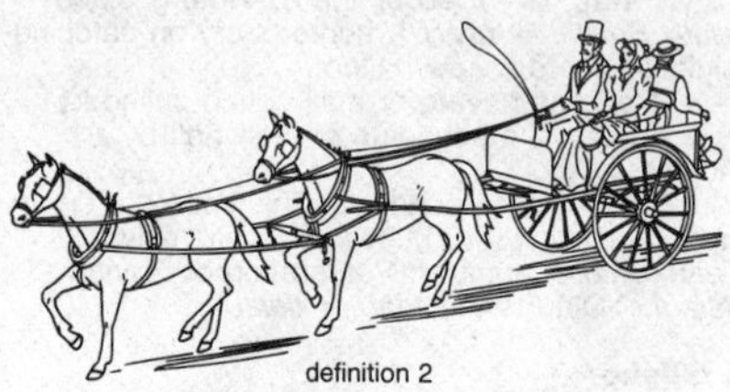
definition 2

definition 3

**tandem accelerator,** *Informal.* Van de Graaff generator.

**tandem play,** a football play in which one player runs close behind another to try to break through the opponent's line.

**tan|dem-ro|tor** (tanʹdəm rōʹtər), *n.* a helicopter with two main rotors, one at each end of the body, powered by the same engine.

**tan|dem-ro|tored** (tanʹdəm rōʹtərd), *adj.* having tandem rotors.

**tan|dour** (tanʹdůr), *n.* (in the Middle East) a heater consisting of a square table with a brazier under it, to warm those who sit around it. [< French *tandour* < Turkish *tandir* < Arabic *tannūr* < Hebrew < Assyrian *tinūru* furnace, oven]

**ta|ne|ka|ha** (täʹne käʹhä), *n.* an evergreen tree of New Zealand with strong wood and a bark containing tannic acid and a red dye. [< a Maori word]

**tang**[1] (tang), *n., v.* —*n.* **1** a strong taste or flavor, often an aftertaste: *the tang of mustard.* SYN: pungency. **2** a disagreeable taste absorbed from something else: *a strong tang of onion in the butter.* **3** the distinctive quality of a thing; flavor; nature; characteristic: *The substance of it was pure Russian but the flavor of it had an international tang* (Wall Street Journal). **4** *Figurative.* a slight touch or suggestion; trace: *The language has a tang of Shakespeare* (Thomas Gray). **5** a characteristic odor: *the salt tang of sea air.* **6** a penetrating smell. **7** the long, slender projecting point, strip, or prong on a chisel, file, or the like, that fits into the handle. **8** = surgeonfish.
—*v.t.* **1** to provide with a spike, flange, or other tang. **2** to give a distinct taste or flavor to: *tanged with orange* (New Yorker).
[< Scandinavian (compare Old Icelandic *tangi* point)] —**tangʹer,** *n.*

**tang**[2] (täng), *n., v.* —*n.* a sharp, ringing sound.
—*v.i., v.t.* to make a sharp, ringing sound; ring; clang.
[imitative]

**tang**[3] (täng), *n. Dialect.* any one of several large, coarse seaweeds; sea wrack; tangle. [< Scandinavian (compare Danish *tang*)]

**Tang** or **T'ang** (täng), *n.* a Chinese dynasty, 618-907, under which China expanded toward central Asia, Buddhism gained its political influence, printing was invented, and poetry reached its finest development.

**tan|ga** (tang′gə), *n.* any one of various coins formerly used in south and central Asia. [perhaps < Portuguese *tanga,* ultimately < Sanskrit *ṭaṅka* a weight, and a coin]

**tan|ga|lung** (tang′gə lung), *n.* a civet of Sumatra and Java. [< Malay *tanggālung*]

**Tan|gan|yi|kan** (tan′gən yē′kən, tang′-), *n., adj.* —*n.* a native or inhabitant of the former country of Tanganyika.
—*adj.* of or having to do with the former country of Tanganyika or its people.

**Tan|ga|ro|a** (tan′gə rō′ə), *n.* the supreme god of Polynesia.

**tan|ge|lo** (tan′jə lō), *n., pl.* **-los.** **1** a hybrid tree of the tangerine and the grapefruit. **2** its fruit. [< *tang*(erine) + (pom)*elo*]

**tan|gen|cy** (tan′jən sē), *n.* the quality or condition of being tangent.

***tan|gent** (tan′jənt), *adj., n.* —*adj.* **1** *Geometry.* touching a curve or surface at one point only and not intersecting. These circles are tangent: ○○. **2** *Figurative.* in contact; touching; contiguous. **3** having the spokes tangent to the hub: *a tangent wheel on a bicycle or tricycle.*
—*n.* **1** a tangent line, curve, or surface. **2** *Trigonometry.* the ratio of the length of the side opposite an acute angle in a right triangle to the length of the side adjacent to the acute angle. The tangent, sine, and secant are the three fundamental trigonometric functions. **3** *Geometry.* the part of a line tangent to a curve from the point of tangency to the horizontal axis. **4** *Music.* the upright metal pin or wedge at the back of a clavichord key, which presses up against the string to produce its sound. **5** the straight part of a survey line between curves, as on a railroad or highway curve. *Abbr:* tan (no period).
**fly** (or **go**) **off at** (or **on**) **a tangent,** to change suddenly from one course of action or thought to another: *Then his mind went off at a tangent in another direction* (H. G. Wells).
[< New Latin *linea tangens* tangent line < Latin *tangens, -entis,* present participle of *tangere* to touch]

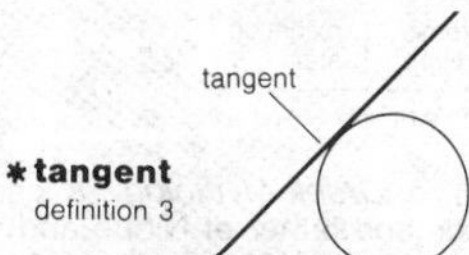


***tangent**
definition 3

**tan|gen|tal** (tan jen′təl), *adj.* = tangential.

**tangent balance,** a balance in which the weight is shown on a graduated arc by a pointer attached to the beam.

**tan|gen|tial** (tan jen′shəl), *adj.* **1** of or having to do with a tangent or tangency. **2** having the nature of a tangent; being a tangent: *The two halves of the chamber are connected by a tangential throat* (New Scientist). **3** acting in the direction of a tangent: *a tangential motion or force.* **4** *Figurative.* wandering off the subject; diverging. **SYN:** digressive, erratic. **5** slightly connected with a subject; marginal. —**tan|gen′tial|ly,** *adv.*

**tan|ge|rine** (tan′jə rēn′), *n.* **1** a small, deep-colored citrus fruit with a very loose peel and segments that separate easily. A tangerine has a sweet, spicy pulp. It is a variety of mandarin which is much grown in the United States. **2** a deep, slightly reddish-orange color. [< French *Tanger* Tangier, a seaport in North Africa (where these fruits were first obtained) + English *-ine*[1]]

**Tan|ge|rine** (tan′jə rēn′), *n., adj.* —*n.* a native of Tangier.
—*adj.* of or having to do with Tangier or its people.

**tang|ey** (tang′ē), *adj.,* **tang|i|er, tang|i|est.** = tangy.

**tan|ghan** (täng′gən, tang′-), *n.* = tangun.

**tan|ghin** (tang′gin), *n.* **1** an evergreen shrub of Madagascar. **2** its fruit. **3** a poison made from its kernels. [< French *tanghin* < Malagasy *tangena*]

**tang|i**[1] (tang′ē), *n. New Zealand.* a formal ceremony, poem, or song of lamentation, as a dirge or coronach. [< Maori *tangi* lament]

**tan|gi**[2] (tang′gē), *n.* (in Pakistan) a sharp, narrow gorge or defile. [< Pushtu *tangi,* plural of *tangai* < Persian *tang* narrow]

**tan|gi|bil|i|ty** (tan′jə bil′ə tē), *n., pl.* **-ties.** **1** the quality or condition of being tangible. **2** a tangible object or matter; reality.

**tan|gi|ble** (tan′jə bəl), *adj., n.* —*adj.* **1** that can be touched or felt by touch; physical; material: *A chair is a tangible object.* **2** that can be detected by touching: *a tangible roughness.* **3** *Figurative.* **a** of some importance, moment, or effect; not imaginary; actual: *There has been a tangible improvement in his work.* **b** specific enough to be understood and dealt with; not vague; real; actual; definite: *tangible evidence.* **4** whose value can be accurately appraised: *Real estate is tangible property. The good will of a business is not as tangible as its buildings and stock.*
—*n.* **1** something tangible: *Fighting hunger* [*and*] *disease is a tangible that everybody can understand* (Atlantic). **2** a tangible property, asset, or other thing: *National income comprises both tangibles and intangibles* (Wall Street Journal).
[< Late Latin *tangibilis* < Latin *tangere* touch]
—**tan′gi|ble|ness,** *n.*

**tan|gi|bly** (tan′jə blē), *adv.* in a tangible manner; so as to be tangible.

**tan|gle**[1] (tang′gəl), *v.,* **-gled, -gling,** *n.* —*v.t.* **1** to twist and twine together in a confused mass; jumble (threads); mat; knot; snarl: *The kitten had tangled the ball of twine.* **SYN:** entangle, interweave. **2** to hinder, hamper, or obstruct; involve or catch and hold: (*Figurative.*) *tangl'd in the fold Of dire necessity* (Milton). **3** *Figurative.* to mix up; bewilder; confuse: *He had cut the knot which the Congress had only twisted and tangled* (Macaulay).
—*v.i.* to be or become tangled: *Long hair tangles easily.*
—*n.* **1** a confused or tangled mass; knot or jumble: *The climbing vines are all in a tangle and need to be pruned and tied up.* **2** *Figurative.* **a** anything complicated and confused; muddle; puzzle: *a tangle of words. Her quick temper gets her into one tangle after another.* **b** perplexed state of mind; bewilderment: *in a tangle of contradictory statements.* **3** the condition of being tangled; twistedness; obstructedness; confusion; trapping.
[apparently variant of Middle English *tagilen* entangle < Scandinavian (compare Swedish dialectal *taggla* to disorder)] —**tan′gler,** *n.*

**tan|gle**[2] (tang′gəl), *n.* any one of various large seaweeds. [< Scandinavian (compare Old Icelandic *thangulr,* probably < *thang* tang[3])]

**tan|gle|ber|ry** (tang′gəl ber′ē), *n., pl.* **-ries.** a huckleberry of the northeastern United States. Also, **dangleberry.**

**tan|gled** (tang′gəld), *adj.* **1** thoroughly intertwined; matted; tangly: *the fishermen's tangled nets.* **2** *Figurative.* **a** mixed up; confused; jumbled; complicated: *His affairs were hopelessly tangled.* **b** bewildered.

**tan|gle|foot** (tang′gəl fu̇t′), *adj., n.* —*adj.* complicated; confusing; perplexing.
—*n.* **1** anything tangling or confusing. **2** *U.S. Slang.* an intoxicating beverage, especially whiskey.

**tan|gle|foot|ed** (tang′gəl fu̇t′id), *adj.* having tangled feet; stumbling.

**tan|gle-legs** (tang′gəl legz′), *n. U.S.* **1** a popular name of the hobblebush. **2** *Slang.* strong beer or liquor.

**tan|gle|ment** (tang′gəl mənt), *n.* **1** the state of being tangled: *When he declared bankruptcy his business affairs were in an awful tanglement.* **2** = tangle.

**tangle net,** = gill net.

**tangle picker,** *British Dialect.* the turnstone.

**tan|gle|toad** (tang′gəl tōd′), *n. British Dialect.* a variety of buttercup with double yellow flowers, that sends out long runners which root themselves.

**tan|gly** (tang′glē), *adj.* **1** in a tangle. **2** full of tangles.

**tan|go** (tang′gō), *n., pl.* **-gos,** *v.,* **-goed, -go|ing.** —*n.* **1** a Spanish-American dance in rather slow duple time, with long, gliding steps and many figures and poses. **2** music for it.
—*v.i.* to dance the tango.
[< Cuban Spanish *tango*]

**Tan|go** (tang′gō), *n. U.S.* a code name for the letter *t,* used in transmitting radio messages.

**tan|go|ist** (tan′gō ist), *n.* a person who dances the tango.

**tan|gor** (tan′jôr, -jor), *n.* a hybrid between a tangerine and an orange: *They are natural hybrids, almost certainly tangors ... and they are so sweet that people on diets sometimes eat them before dinner in order to throttle their appetites* (New Yorker). [< *tang*(erine) + *or*(ange)]

***tan|gram** (tang′grəm), *n.* a Chinese puzzle of five triangles, a square, and a parallelogram to arrange into a large square, then into many other figures: *The Chinese puzzle game called tangram* [*is*] *believed to be thousands of years old* (Scientific American). [origin uncertain; *-gram,* probably as in *anagram, cryptogram*]

**tan|gun** (tang′gən, tang′-), *n.* a strong and surefooted little Tibetan pony. [< Hindi *ṭāṅghan* < Tibetan *Tāṇāṇ* < *Ta* horse]

**tang|y** (tang′ē), *adj.,* **tang|i|er, tang|i|est.** **1** having a tang; piquant: *Scandal is always a tangy bit of news.* **2** having a disagreeable taste: *The water from the old well has a tangy bitter taste. Also,* **tangey.**

**tan|house** (tan′hous′), *n.* a building in which tanning is carried on.

**tan|ia** (tan′yə), *n.* a potatolike plant of the arum family related to the taro, cultivated in tropical America and Africa for its edible tubers and leaves. [< Tupi (Brazil) *taña, taya,* Carib *taya*]

**tan|ist** (tan′ist, thô′nist), *n.* (in Irish history) a Celtic chief's heir apparent, elected by the tribe during his lifetime, usually his most vigorous adult kinsman. [< Irish, Scottish Gaelic *tánaiste*]

**tan|ist|ry** (tan′ə strē, thô′nə-), *n.* the practice of electing tanists, usually during the chief's lifetime: *Despite tanistry ... Scotland managed to have real monarchs when Ireland had none* (Times Literary Supplement).

**tank**[1] (tangk), *n., v.* —*n.* **1** a large container for a liquid or gas, usually rectangular or cylindrical: *He always kept plenty of gasoline in the car's tank.* **SYN:** cistern, reservoir. **2** a pool or lake, often an artificial earthen pool, especially for irrigation or watering livestock.
—*v.t.* to put or store in a tank.
**tank up, a** *Informal.* to fill up the fuel tank of an automobile, or other vehicle, with gasoline: *We tanked up at the service station before getting onto the turnpike.* **b** *Slang.* to drink heavily: *Both of 'em are tankin' up next door, and layin' for you and the whole bunch* (Clinton H. Stagg).
[apparently < Portuguese *tanque* < Latin *stagnum* pool; (def. 2) perhaps < Hindustani *ṭāṅkh* cistern]

***tank**[2] (tangk), *n.* a heavily armored combat vehicle carrying machine guns and usually a cannon, moving on an endless track of linked steel treads on each side. Tanks can travel over rough ground, fallen trees, and other obstacles. [special use of *tank*[1], a label to disguise the content of crates which housed the vehicles during transport in the first World War] —**tank′like′,** *adj.*

***tank**[2]

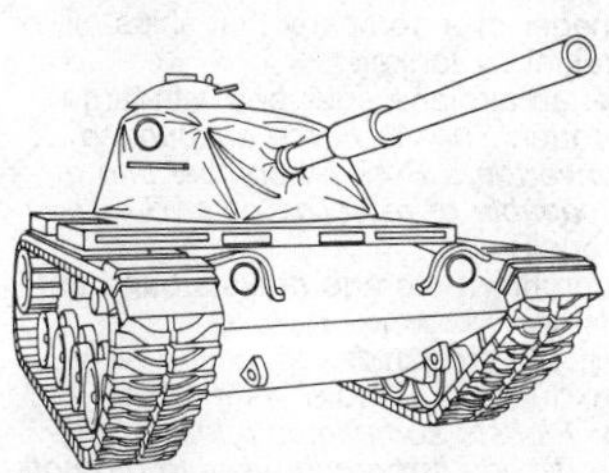

**tan|ka**[1] (täng′kə), *n., pl.* **-ka** or **-kas.** a Japanese poem or verse form of 31 syllables arranged in five lines of 5, 7, 5, 7, and 7 syllables. [< Japanese *tanka*]

**tan|ka**[2] (tang′kə), *n.* a descendant of an aboriginal people of Canton, China, who live entirely in the boats by which they make a living. [< Chinese (Cantonese) *tan* egg + *ka* family, people]

**tan|ka**[3] (täng′kə), *n.* a Tibetan religious scroll painting carried as a banner. [< Tibetan *thaṅka*]

**tank|age** (tang′kij), *n.* **1** the capacity of a tank or tanks. **2** storage in tanks. **3** the cost of such storage. **4** fertilizer and coarse feed made in slaughterhouses of carcasses after their fat has been rendered.

***tangram**

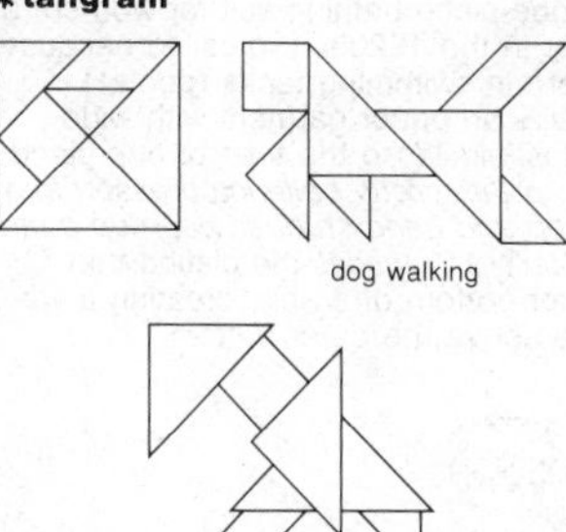


**tank|ard** (tang′kərd), *n.* a large drinking mug, usually with a handle and a hinged cover; flagon. [compare Middle Dutch *tanckaert*]

**tank|bust|er** (tangk′bus′tər), *n. Slang.* an airplane equipped with antitank cannon.

**Pronunciation Key:** hat, āge, cãre, fär; let, ēqual, tėrm; it, īce; hot, ōpen, ôrder; **oi**l, **ou**t; cup, pu̇t, rüle; **ch**ild; lo**ng**; **th**in; **ᴛʜ**en; **zh**, measure; ə represents **a** in about, **e** in taken, **i** in pencil, **o** in lemon, **u** in circus.

***tank car**, a railroad car with a tank for carrying liquids or gases: *New Orleans is becoming one huge chemical plant, linked by webs of pipelines, strings of tank cars, fleets of barges* (Newsweek).

***tank car**

**tank destroyer**, a fast, lightly armored vehicle carrying a heavy gun for destroying tanks.
**tank drama**, *Slang.* **1** a sensational play including adventures in a tank of water, especially a drowning rescue. **2** any sensational melodrama.
**tanked** (tangkt), *adj. Slang.* drunk.
**tank|er** (tang′kər), *n., v.* **—*n.*** **1** a ship for carrying liquid freight, especially oil: *The tanker Salem Maritime had just finished taking on 130,000 barrels of gasoline, kerosene, and oil at Lake Charles* (Newsweek). **2** any vehicle carrying liquid freight, such as a tank truck or tanker plane. **3** a soldier who fights in a tank: *The Army's tankers are hoping, however, that these tanks ... will be supplemented eventually* (New York Times).
**—*v.t.*** to transport in a tanker: *Most of Saudi Arabia's oil is tankered to market* (Wall Street Journal).
**tank|er|ing** (tang′kər ing), *n.* the loading and unloading of tankers.
**tank|er|man** (tang′kər mən), *n., pl.* **-men.** the owner or manager of a company that ships oil, or other liquid freight by tanker.
**tanker plane**, an airplane equipped with large tanks to carry fuel: *The Air Force announced ... that it had converted a B-47 jet bomber into a tanker plane capable of refueling other B-47's in flight* (New York Times).
**tank farm**, a group of storage tanks around an oil field or refinery.
**tank farming**, = hydroponics.
**tank|ful** (tangk′fu̇l), *n., pl.* **-fuls.** as much as a tank will hold: *Florists sometimes release tankfuls of carbon dioxide in greenhouses to promote plant growth* (Scientific American).
**tank|ie** (tang′kē), *n. British Naval Slang.* an officer or sailor in charge of the freshwater tanks; captain of the hold.
**tank|less** (tangk′lis), *adj.* without a tank: *a tankless toilet.*
**tank locomotive**, *U.S.* a railway engine carrying fuel and water itself, not in a separate tender.
**tank|man** (tangk′mən), *n., pl.* **-men. 1** a member of a tank crew. **2** = tankie.
**tank runner**, a jaçana of Indonesia, Ceylon (Sri Lanka), and surrounding areas with a tail like a pheasant's that lives near watering places and marshes.
**tank|ship** (tangk′ship′), *n.* = tanker (def. 1).
**tank station**, a place with tanks, especially to supply water to railroad engines.
**tank suit**, a one-piece bathing suit for women, of a type popular in the 1920's. [so called because they were worn in swimming tanks (pools)]
***tank top**, **1** *U.S.* an upper garment with wide shoulder straps, similar to the tops of one-piece bathing suits: *a tall, pretty ballerina dressed in a purple tank top and baggy rubber warm-up pants* ... (New Yorker). **2** *Nautical.* the plating that forms the inner bottom of a ship, creating a watertight space above the outer bottom.

***tank top**
definition 1

**tank town**, *U.S.* **1** a small town where trains stop mainly to get water. **2** *Informal.* any small town; hick town. **—tank′-town′**, *adj.*
**tank trailer**, a trailer for transporting liquid cargoes, such as oil, milk, or chemicals.
**tank trap**, any one of a number of obstacles, such as concrete blocks, ditches, and mines, put up to stop tanks.
**tank truck**, a truck for carrying liquids: *an oil tank truck, a milk tank truck.*
**tank|wag|on** (tangk′wag′ən), *n.* a tank truck for transporting liquid cargoes.
**tank waste**, the insoluble sediment from the dissolving tanks in alkali works.
**tank|worm** (tangk′wėrm′), *n.* a parasitic nematode worm found in the mud in India, probably the young of the Guinea worm.
**tan|na** (tä′nä), *n., pl.* **tan|na|im.** any one of the Jewish scholars whose teachings are found in the Mishnah. The tannaim lived about 10-200 A.D. Also, **tana.** [< Hebrew *tannā* teacher]
**tan|na|ble** (tan′ə bəl), *adj.* that can be tanned.
**tan|na|dar** (tä′nə där′), *n.* = tanadar.
**tan|nage** (tan′ij), *n.* **1** the act or process of tanning hides. **2** the result of tanning; material which has been tanned. **3** a browning of the skin; tan: *They should have got his cheek fresh tannage* (Robert Browning). **4** *Scottish.* a tannery.
**tan|na|im** (tä nä′im), *n.* plural of **tanna.**
**tan|na|ite** (tä′nə īt), *n.* one of the tannaim; tanna.
**tan|na|it|ic** (tä′nə it′ik), *adj.* **1** of or having to do with the tannaim. **2** like the tannaim.
**tan|nate** (tan′āt), *n.* a salt or ester of tannic acid.
**tanned** (tand), *adj.* **1** (of a hide) made into leather. **2** made brown by the sun or wind. **3** reddish-brown; tawny color.
**tan|ner**[1] (tan′ər), *n.* **1** a person whose work is making hides into leather by tanning them. **2** a chemical substance applied to the skin to produce a tan.
**tan|ner**[2] (tan′ər), *n. British Slang.* a sixpence. [origin uncertain]
**tanner's** or **tanners' bark**, = tanbark.
**tanners' sumac**, a European sumac whose leaves and shoots are dried and chopped for tanning. Also, **tanning sumac.**
**tanners' tree**, **1** a low deciduous shrub of southern Europe used in tanning. **2** = tanners' sumac.
**tan|ner|y** (tan′ər ē), *n., pl.* **-ner|ies.** a place where hides are tanned; tanyard.
**Tann|häu|ser** (tän′hoi′zər, tan′-), *n. German Legend.* a knight and poet who, after a time of wicked pleasure, was refused pardon by the pope.
**tan|nic** (tan′ik), *adj.* **1** of or like tannin. **2** derived from tanbark.
**tannic acid**, **1** the white, amorphous, strongly astringent principle derived from nutgalls. *Formula:* $C_{14}H_{10}O_9$ **2** any one of various other astringent organic substances, especially the principle derived from oak bark.
**tan|nier** (tan′yər), *n.* = tania.
**tan|nif|er|ous** (ta nif′ər əs), *adj.* containing or yielding tannin.
**tan|nin** (tan′ən), *n.* a vegetable acid, especially common tannin, the whitish tannic acid obtained from the bark or galls of oaks and from certain other plants. Tannis is used in tanning, dyeing, and making ink, and in medicine. [< French *tanin* < *tan* (< Medieval Latin *tannum;* see etym. under **tan**)] **—tan′nin|like′**, *adj.*
**tan|ning** (tan′ing), *n.* **1** the work, process, or art of converting hides or skins into leather: *True tanning, as opposed to curing with animal fats, is limited to the Old World and to the technologically more advanced cultures* (Beals and Hoijer). **2** the action of making or an instance of becoming brown by exposure to the sun. **3** *Informal.* a beating; thrashing; whipping; flogging.
**tannin glycerol**, glycerin of tannic acid.
**tanning sumac**, = tanners' sumac.
**tan|noy** (tan′oi), *n. British.* a public-address system: *It was just one of the hundreds of routine messages broadcast daily over the tannoy of any international airport* (Manchester Guardian Weekly). [< *Tannoy,* a trademark for such a system]
**tan oak**, an oak that yields tanbark.
**Ta|no|an** (tä′nō ən), *n., adj.* **—*n.*** a family of American Indian languages spoken in northern New Mexico.
**—*adj.*** of or having to do with this family of languages.
**tan|rec** (tan′rek), *n.* = tenrec.
**tan|sy** (tan′zē), *n., pl.* **-sies. 1** a coarse, strong-smelling, bitter-tasting plant with notched, divided leaves and clusters of small, yellow flowers. Tansy belongs to the composite family. It was formerly much used as a seasoning and in medicine as a stomachic. *Equally vivid along the road and in winter bouquets is the pungent herb called tansy* (New York Times). **2** any other plant of the same genus. **3** any one of various other plants, such as the silverweed. **4** = tansy ragwort. **5** a cake or pudding flavored with tansy.
**like a tansy**, *Archaic.* perfectly: *I would work ... like a horse, and make fortifications for you ... like a tansy* (Laurence Sterne).
[< Old French *tanesie,* short for *athanasie* < Late Latin *athanasia* < Greek *athanasiā* elixir; (originally) immortality < *a-* without + *thánatos* death]
**tansy ragwort**, a toxic weed of the composite family native to Europe and naturalized in North America, poisonous to cattle; felonweed.
**tan|ta|late** (tan′tə lāt), *n.* a salt of tantalic acid.
**tan|ta|le|an** or **tan|ta|li|an** (tan tā′lē ən), *adj.* **1** of or having to do with Tantalus. **2** like that of Tantalus; tantalizing.
**tan|tal|ic** (tan tal′ik), *adj.* **1** of or having to do with tantalum. **2** containing tantalum, especially with a valence of five.
**tantalic acid**, a colorless, crystalline acid, known mainly in the form of its salts, the tantalates. *Formula:* $HTaO_3$
**tan|ta|lise** (tan′tə līz), *v.t.,* **-lised, -lis|ing.** *Especially British.* tantalize.
**tan|ta|lis|ing** (tan′tə lī′zing), *adj. Especially British.* tantalizing. **—tan′ta|lis′ing|ly**, *adv.*
**tan|ta|lite** (tan′tə līt), *n.* a rare, heavy, black crystalline mineral with a submetallic luster, iron tantalate, rarely found without manganese or niobium. It is the chief ore of tantalum. [< German *Tantalit*]
**tan|ta|li|za|tion** (tan′tə lə zā′shən), *n.* **1** a tantalizing. **2** a being tantalized.
**tan|ta|lize** (tan′tə līz), *v.t.,* **-lized, -liz|ing. 1** to torment by keeping some desired thing in sight but out of reach. **SYN:** plague, vex. **2** *Figurative.* to tease by holding out hopes that are repeatedly disappointed: *He tantalized the hungry dog by pretending to feed him.* **SYN:** plague, vex. [< *Tantalus*] **—tan′ta|liz′er**, *n.*
**tan|ta|liz|ing** (tan′tə lī′zing), *adj.* exciting desire, curiosity, or appetite; enticing; tempting; provocative: *a tantalizing concept. He lives with the tantalizing knowledge that his late father's millions lie just beyond his reach in a Swiss bank* (Maclean's). **—tan′ta|liz′ing|ly**, *adv.*
**tan|ta|lous** (tan′tə ləs), *adj.* **1** of or having to do with tantalum. **2** derived from tantalum. **3** containing tantalum, especially with a valence of three.
***tan|ta|lum** (tan′tə ləm), *n.* a hard, shiny, grayish-white metallic chemical element occurring with niobium in tantalite, columbite, and other rare minerals. It is very resistant to corrosion and is used as an alloy in nuclear reactors and in surgical and dental equipment. [< Swedish *Tantalum* < Latin *Tantalus* Tantalus (because it cannot absorb acid though immersed in it)]

***tantalum**

| symbol | atomic number | atomic weight | oxidation state |
|---|---|---|---|
| Ta | 73 | 180.948 | 5 |

**Tan|ta|lus** (tan′tə ləs), *n. Greek Mythology.* a king of Phrygia, son of Zeus and father of Niobe and Pelops, whose punishment in the lower world, for betraying the gods' secrets, was to stand in the river Tartarus up to his chin, under branches of fruit. Whenever he tried to drink or eat, the water or fruit withdrew from his reach, and a rock continually threatened to fall on him.
**tan|ta|lus** (tan′tə ləs), *n.* **1** *British.* a rack of decanters which seem free but must be unlocked to be used. **2a** a genus of storks. **b** a species of these; wood ibis. [< *Tantalus*] **—tan′ta|lus|like′**, *adj.*
**tan|ta|mount** (tan′tə mount), *adj., v.* **—*adj.*** as much as; equivalent: *The withdrawal of his statement is tantamount to an apology.* **SYN:** See syn. under **equal.** [< verb]
**—*v.i.*** *Obsolete.* to be or become equivalent; amount.
[< Anglo-French *tant amunter* amount to as much < *tant* as much (< Latin *tantum*) + *amunter* amount to]
**tan|tar|a** (tan tar′ə, -tär′-; tan′tər ə), *n.* **1** a flourish or blast of a trumpet or horn; fanfare. **2** any similar sound. [(originally) interjection used as a poetic refrain; imitative (especially of a trumpet)]
**tante** (täɴt), *n. French.* aunt.
**Tan|te** (tän′tə), *n. German.* aunt.
**tan|tiv|y** (tan tiv′ē), *interj., n., pl.* **-tiv|ies,** *adv., adj., v.,* **-tiv|ied, -tiv|y|ing.** **—*interj.*** full gallop! (a cry in hunting).
**—*n.*** **1** a ride at full gallop; rush. **2** a hunting cry when in full gallop. **3** a High Churchman or Tory.
**—*adv., adj.*** at full gallop; headlong.
**—*v.i.*** to ride at full gallop; rush: *Midnight roundabout riders tantivying under the fairylights* (Atlantic).
**—*v.t.*** to call "tantivy."
[perhaps imitative of hoofbeats]
**tant mieux** (täɴ myœ′), *French.* all the better.
**tan|to** (tän′tō), *adv. Music.* so; so much; too much (used in a direction). [< Italian *tanto* < Latin *tantum* so much]
**tan|to|ny bell** (tan′tə nē), **1** = handbell. **2** a small church bell. [short for *Saint Anthony,* whose emblem was a bell]
**tantony pig**, **1** the smallest pig of a litter.
**2** *Figurative.* a person who follows another slavishly: *To see you dangling after me everywhere,*

*like a tantony pig* (Isaac Bickerstaffe).

**tant pis** (täN pē′), *French.* all the worse.

**tan|tra** or **Tan|tra** (tan′trə), *n.* **1** one of a class of Hindu religious works in Sanskrit, of comparatively late date, related to the puranas, in which mysticism and magic play a great part. **2** one of a class of Buddhist works of a somewhat similar character. [< Sanskrit *tantra* loom, warp; principle, doctrine < *tan* to stretch]

**tan|tric** or **Tan|tric** (tan′trik), *adj.* of or having to do with the tantras.

**tan|trism** or **Tan|trism** (tan′triz əm), *n.* the doctrines or teachings of the tantras: *What is marginal in Indian tradition—mantra, mandala, pilgrimage and circumambulation—is focal in Tantrism* (Listener).

**tan|trist** or **Tan|trist** (tan′trist), *n.* an adherent or follower of tantrism.

**tan|trum** (tan′trəm), *n.* a fit of bad temper or ill humor intended to get what one wants: *The spoiled child had a tantrum whenever she did not get her own way.* [origin uncertain]

**tan|trum|y** (tan′trə mē), *adj.* given to tantrums; characterized by fits of bad temper: *tantrumy behavior, a tantrumy child.*

**Tan|tum Er|go** (tan′təm ėr′gō), **1** the hymn of Saint Thomas Aquinas, "Pange lingua gloriosi Corporis mysterium." **2** the last two stanzas, sung at Benediction. **3** a setting of these. [< Latin *tantum* (*sacramentum*) so great (a sacrament); *ergo* therefore (words from the hymn)]

**tan|yard** (tan′yärd′), *n.* = tannery.

**Tan|za|ni|an** (tan zə nē′ən), *adj., n.* —*adj.* of or having to do with the republic of Tanzania (formed in 1964 by the union of Tanganyika and Zanzibar) or its people.
—*n.* a native or inhabitant of Tanzania.

**tan|za|nite** (tan′zə nīt), *n.* a semiprecious gemstone, a blue variety of zoisite, found in northern Tanzania. [< *Tanzania* + *-ite*[1]]

**Tao** (tou, dou), *n.* **1** (in Taoism) the moving force of the universe. **2** (in Confucianism) the path of virtue or righteousness; the ideal way of life. [< Chinese *tao;* see etym. under **Taoism**]

**taoi|seach** (tē′shok), *n.* a prime minister of Ireland. [< Irish *taoiseach*]

**Tao|ism** (tou′iz əm, dou′-), *n.* **1** one of the main religions of China, founded on the principles of the ancient philosopher Lao Tzu. Taoism teaches natural simplicity and humility as a way to peace and harmony in life. **2** the system of philosophy on which this religion was based. [< Chinese *tao* the right way, or path, in the title *Tao te Ching* (*The Way and Its Power*) by Lao Tzu, 604?-531 B.C., a philosopher]

**Tao|ist** (tou′ist, dou′-), *n., adj.* —*n.* a believer in Taoism.
—*adj.* of or having to do with Taoists or Taoism.

**Tao|is|tic** (tou is′tik, dou-), *adj.* = Taoist.

**Ta|os** (tä′ōs, tous), *n., pl.* **-os.** **1** a member of an American Indian tribe living in New Mexico. **2** the Tanoan language of this tribe.

**tap**[1] (tap), *v.,* **tapped, tap|ping,** *n.* —*v.t.* **1** to strike lightly, often so that one can hear: *Tap him on the shoulder.* **2** to use (one's hand, foot, or a hammer or other object) in knocking; cause to strike lightly: *She tapped her foot on the floor.* **3** to make, put, or move by light blows: *to tap a rhythm, to tap out a message, to tap the ashes out of a pipe.* **4** to put a repair (the heel or sole of a shoe) with leather. **5** to select; choose.
—*v.i.* to strike a light blow or series of blows: **a** to hit slightly; tamp. **b** to signal by knocking; rap: *He tapped on the window.*
—*n.* **1** a light blow, often one that can be heard: *There was a tap at the door.* **2** the sound of a light blow. **3** a piece of leather used to repair the bottom of a shoe. **4** a small steel plate on a shoe to reduce wear or to make a louder tap in tap-dancing. **5** = tap-dancing. **6** *Bowling.* the appearance of having knocked over all the pins when actually one is still standing.
**taps.** See under **taps.**
[< Old French *taper,* probably < a Germanic word]

**✱tap**[2] (tap), *n., v.,* **tapped, tap|ping.** —*n.* **1** a simple wooden faucet for a barrel or the like, consisting of a short pipe with a peg stopper inserted crosswise like a setscrew or cotter pin to stop the flow. See picture above. **2** any faucet; spigot; cock: *He left the tap open to fill the kitchen sink with water.* **3** a hole in a barrel made for a spigot. **4** any opening cut into a supply of liquid, especially for a branch pipe. **5** liquor taken from a certain tap. **6** a certain variety or quality of liquor; brew. **7** *Informal.* a room where liquor is sold and drunk; bar. **8a** an electric connection on a coil somewhere other than at an end. **b** any place where an electric connection can be made; outlet. **9** any long, tapering cylinder, especially a taproot: *The tap of the oak will make its way downward* (Charles Marshall). **10** a tool for cutting screw threads on the inner surface of a cylinder or opening. **11** = wiretap. **12** *Especially British.* an issue of notes or securities, usually by a government, that are put on continuous sale and may be purchased in unrestricted quantity.
—*v.t.* **1** to make a hole in to let out liquid: *They tapped the sugar maples when the sap began to flow.* **2** to remove the plug from (a cask); pierce: *to tap a cask.* **3** to let out (liquid) by piercing or by drawing a plug. **4** to provide (a barrel) with a tap. **5** to let out liquid from by surgery. **6** *Figurative.* to make (resources or reserves) accessible; make (any potential) available; penetrate; open up: *Chicago is the only inland port in America which can* (*and does*) *tap the two great inland water routes* (Newsweek). *Many here believed that his full potential had not been tapped* (New York Times). **7** to attach a listening device to (a telephone line) in order to eavesdrop; wiretap. **8** to make an internal screw thread in (a pipe). **9** *Informal, Figurative.* to ask (a person) for money, help, or the like: *[He] was tapped by NBC-TV to appear on "Today"* (Saturday Review).
**on tap, a** ready to be let out of a keg, cask, or barrel and be served: *There is good beer on tap down at the Red Lion.* **b** *Figurative.* ready for use; on hand; available: *Mother keeps a box of stationery on tap so that she won't run out of it unexpectedly. Much of [television's] appeal comes from its being on tap* (Manchester Guardian). **c** with a spigot inserted for drawing off; broached: *The tavernkeeper had three barrels on tap for the evening's celebration.* **d** *Figurative.* obtainable when required at a fixed rate; on call: *It is some time since additional Treasury Bills have been on tap at so low a rate as 1⅞ per cent* (Westminster Gazette).
[Old English *tæppa.* See related etym. at **tip**[1].]

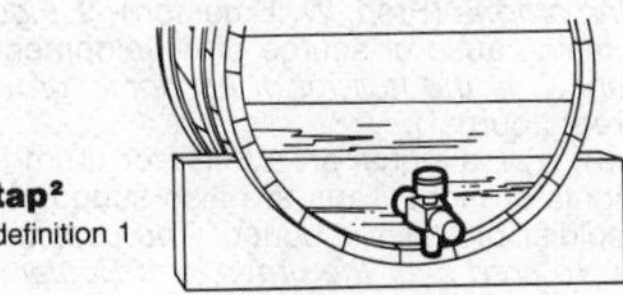

**✱tap**[2]
definition 1

**tap**[3] (tap), *n.* (in India) malaria. [< Persian *tap* fever, heat < Sanskrit *tāpa* heat, pain]

**ta|pa**[1] (tä′pə), *n.* **1** an unwoven cloth of the Pacific islands, made by soaking and pounding the soft inner bark of the paper mulberry tree. **2** this bark. [< Polynesian *tapa*]

**ta|pa**[2] (tä′pə), *n.* an hors d'oeuvre served with a drink: *All the south of Spain drinks sherry, generally ... accompanied by tapas in the form of olives, anchovies, or strips of raw Serrano ham* (London Times). [< Spanish *tapa* (literally) lid (because tapas were once served on lids placed over the glass)]

**tap|a|de|ra** (tap′ə dãr′ə), *n., pl.* **-ras.** a heavy leather housing for the front of a stirrup of a Mexican saddle, to keep the foot from slipping forward and to protect it against thorny underbrush. [< Spanish *tapadera* < *tapar* to cover]

**tap bar,** a bar placed in a cementation furnace and withdrawn for testing during the process.

**tap bond** or **issue,** a United States government bond on sale in unlimited amount for an indefinite period of weeks, intended to attract as capital idle funds from outside the usual sources.

**tap dance,** a dance in which the steps are accented by sharp taps of the foot, toe, or heel.

**tap-dance** (tap′dans′, -däns′), *v.i.,* **-danced, -danc|ing.** to do a tap dance.

**tap-danc|er** (tap′dan′sər, -dän′-), *n.* a person who tap-dances.

**tap-danc|ing** (tap′dan′sing, -dän′-), *n., adj.* —*n.* the act or art of a person who tap-dances.
—*adj.* **1** of or having to do with a tap dance. **2** like a tap dance.

**tape** (tāp), *n., v.,* **taped, tap|ing.** —*n.* **1** a long, narrow, woven strip or ribbon of durable cotton, linen, or other fabric, used to bind seams, to make loops, etc.: *fancy tape to tie packages.* **2** any thin, flexible strip, such as a cloth or steel tape measure: *Surveyors measure with a steel tape.* **3** a strip, string, or ribbon stretched across a finish line, especially of a footrace, to be broken by the winner. **4** a ribbon across the entrance of a new building, bridge, road, or other facility, cut during the official opening ceremony. **5** the strip of paper on which a teletypewriter prints messages; ticker tape: *Stock quotations are printed on paper tape.* **6a** a thin, narrow strip of paper or plastic coated with magnetized iron oxide to record sound, as for a tape recorder; magnetic tape. **b** a recording thus made; tape recording. **7** = videotape. **8** = adhesive tape. **9** = red tape.
—*v.t.* **1** to fasten with tape; wrap with tape; tie: *The doctor taped up the wound.* **2** to join the sections of (a book) with tape. **3** to attach a tape or tapes to. **4** to measure with a tape measure. **5** to get the range of (a position); hit and silence. **6** to record on tape; tape-record or videotape: *to tape a telephone conversation. The President's arrival was taped to show on a television news program in the evening.*
**breast the tape,** *Sports.* (of a runner) to break the ribbon stretched across the finish line and win the race: *Masters was able to sprint ahead and breast the tape.*
**have** or **get one taped,** *Especially British Slang.* to understand one: *But I guess I had you all pretty well taped* (Mellen Cole).
[Middle English *tape,* variant of *tappe,* Old English *tæppe*] —**tape′less,** *adj.* —**tape′like′,** *adj.*

**tape-car|ri|er** (tāp′kar′ē ər), *n.* a frame in which a tape sprinkled with powdered corundum acts as a cutting or filing instrument.

**tape-con|trolled** (tāp′kən trōld′), *adj.* controlled by instructions recorded on a tape.

**tape deck, 1** the mechanical component of a tape recorder, used in high-fidelity systems, computers, and the like: *The simplest playback machine is the tape deck, which has to be plugged into one's own hi-fi equipment* (Harper's). **2** = tape player.

**tape|fish** (tāp′fish′), *n., pl.* **-fish|es** or (*collectively*) **-fish.** a fish with a long, flat body like an eel; ribbonfish.

**tape grass,** an underwater herb of the frogbit family with narrow, grasslike leaves.

**tape line,** = tape measure.

**tape machine,** any machine that uses tape, especially: **a** = tape recorder. **b** = teletypewriter. **c** a ticker-tape machine. **d** (in weaving) a machine for sizing the cotton warp threads.

**tape|man** (tāp′mən), *n., pl.* **-men.** (in surveying) one of the two men who measure with the tape measure.

**tape measure,** a strip of cloth or steel marked in inches, feet, meters, etc., for measuring, often compactly rolled on a spring when not in use.

**tape player,** a machine for playing back sound recorded on magnetic tapes or in cassettes: *Incar entertainment covers radios and tape players* (London Times).

**tap|er**[1] (tā′pər), *n.* person who tapes something.

**ta|per**[2] (tā′pər), *v., n., adj.* —*v.i.* **1** to become gradually smaller toward one end: *The church spire tapers to a point.* **2** *Figurative.* to grow steadily less in amount, force, activity, or quality; diminish: *His business tapered to nothing as people moved away.* **SYN:** subside, shrink, decrease.
—*v.t.* **1** to make gradually smaller toward one end: *The carpenter tapered the end of the fence post with an axe.* **2** to shape like an awl or wedge. [< noun]
—*n.* **1** a becoming smaller toward one end: *Iron plugs ... upon a very gentle taper* (John Smeaton). **2** *Figurative.* a gradual lessening of activity, force, capacity, or quality. **3** a figure that tapers to a point; slender cone or pyramid; spire. **4** a very slender candle. **5** a long wick coated with wax, for lighting a candle, cigarette, cigar, or the like, from an open fire.
—*adj.* becoming smaller toward one end.
**taper off,** to make gradually less in amount, force, activity, or quality; reduce steadily: *to taper off smoking.*
[Old English *tapor*] —**ta′per|ing|ly,** *adv.* —**ta′perness,** *n.*

**tape-re|cord** (tāp′ri kôrd′), *v.t., v.i.* to record on a tape recorder: *Unlike many interviews between politicians and reporters it was not off the record; it was tape-recorded, and the transcript is now before me* (Harper's).

**tape recorder,** a machine that records sounds or other electrical signals, magnetically on plastic tape and plays them back after they are recorded: *In space missiles, tape recorders provide a record of the speed, stresses, temperatures, and other scientific data encountered during flight* (H. W. McMahan).

**tape recording, 1** the recording of sound on a tape. **2** a tape on which sounds or other electrical signals have been recorded: *A tape recording, after all, is basically nothing more than an organized magnetic pattern arranged in the iron particles which coat a plastic base* (David Sarser). **3** the sounds or other electrical signals recorded: *Tape recordings were played of his conversations with two Seattle gamblers* (Wall Street Journal).

**ta|per|er** (tā′pər ər), *n.* a person who carries a taper or slender candle in a religious ceremony.

**tape-stretch|er** (tāp′strech′ər), *n.* a device to

---

**Pronunciation Key:** hat, āge, cãre, fär; let, ēqual, tėrm; it, īce; hot, ōpen, ôrder; **oi**l, **ou**t; cup, pu̇t, rüle; **ch**ild; lo**ng**; **th**in; **ᴛʜ**en; **zh,** measure; **ə** represents **a** in about, **e** in taken, **i** in pencil, **o** in lemon, **u** in circus.

keep a uniform tension on the measuring line when surveying.
**tap|es|tried** (tap′ə strēd), *adj.* **1** adorned with or as if with tapestry: *tapestried walls.* **2** woven in the manner of tapestry: *elaborately tapestried quilts.*
**tap|es|try** (tap′ə strē), *n., pl.* **-tries**, *v.*, **-tried**, **try-ing**. —*n.* **1** a fabric with pictures or designs woven in it, used to hang on walls or to cover furniture: *Tapestry and velvet hangings decorated walls in Europe during the 1500's* (Effa Brown). **2** a similar machine-woven fabric. **3** a picture in tapestry: (*Figurative.*) *Bushes are now entering a season in which their foliage acquires its most persuasive tints, a planting of any size presenting a delightful tapestry of softly interwoven colors* (London Times).
—*v.t.* **1** to picture in tapestry. **2** to cover or hang with tapestry. **3** *Figurative.* to cover with a pattern like that of tapestry.
[variant of Middle English *tapesery* < Old French *tapisserie* < *tapisser* cover with a carpet < *tapis;* see etym. under **tapis**] —**tap′es|try|like′**, *adj.*
**tapestry beetle**, a dermestid beetle whose larva eats tapestry, woolens, and the like.
**tapestry brick**, a type of face brick having a rough surface.
**tapestry carpet**, a carpet in which the warp yarn is colored in advance, to produce a pattern when woven.
**ta|pe|tal** (tə pē′təl), *adj.* of or having to do with a tapetum.
**tap|e|ti** (tap′ə tē), *n.* a small South American rabbit. [< Tupi (Brazil) *tapetí*]
**ta|pe|tum** (tə pē′təm), *n., pl.* **-ta** (-tə). **1** *Botany.* a cell or sheath of cells in a spore case, serving to supply nourishment to the maturing spores: *The tapetum cells disorganize, supplying the nourishment that is used in the development of the pollen mother-cells* (Fred. W. Emerson). **2** any one of certain layers of membrane in the eye, such as those that make cats' eyes shine at night. [< New Latin *tapetum,* alteration of Latin *tapēta,* or *tapēte, -is* carpet < Greek *tápēs, -ētos*]
**tape unit**, the tape deck of a computer, used to record information.
**tape|worm** (tāp′wėrm′), *n.* a long, flat worm that lives as a parasite in the intestines of man and other vertebrates; cestode. Tapeworms consist of many separable parts and have no digestive tract. *Man gets his commonest tapeworms from insufficiently cooked pork* (A. Franklin Shull).
**tap|hole** (tap′hōl′), *n.* **1** a hole in a steelmaking furnace, ladle, or pot through which molten metal or slag may be tapped. **2** a hole made in a maple or other tree to collect the sap.
**tap|house** (tap′hous′), *n. Especially British.* **1** a place where liquor is sold and drunk; bar. **2** one of the rooms in a tavern; taproom; barroom; bar.
**tap-in** (tap′in′), *n.* a scoring shot in basketball in which a player leaps up to deflect the ball through the hoop with his fingers.
**tap|ing** (tā′ping), *n.* **1** = tape recording. **2** data on punched or magnetic tape that regulates an electronic computing machine: *The orders given the machine may be fed into it by a taping which is completely predetermined* (Norbert Wiener).
**tap|i|o|ca** (tap′i ō′kə), *n.* a starchy, granular food obtained from the root of the cassava plant. It is used especially in puddings, for thickening soups, and as a postage-stamp adhesive. [ultimately < Tupi (Brazil) *tipioca*]
**ta|pir** (tā′pər), *n., pl.* **-pirs** or **-pir**. a large piglike mammal with a flexible snout. The tapir has hoofs, is herbivorous, and is related to the horse and rhinoceros. It lives in tropical America and southern Asia. [ultimately < Tupi (Brazil) *tapira*]
**tap|is** (tap′ē, tap′is, ta pē′), *n., pl.* **-is**. *Obsolete.* any rug, tablecloth, hanging, or other tapestry.
**on the tapis**, being given attention; under discussion: *This view was held by Mr. Stansfield when his successor's bill was on the tapis* (Manchester Guardian).
[< Middle French *tapis* < Old French, ultimately < Greek *tápēs, -ētos* rug]
**ta|pis|se|rie** (tȧ pē′se rē′), *n. French.* tapestry.
**ta|pis|sier** (tȧ pē syā′), *n. French.* a maker or weaver of tapestries.
**tap-off** (tap′ôf′, -of′), *n.* = jump ball.
**tap|pa|ble** (tap′ə bəl), *adj.* capable of being tapped; fit for tapping: *tappable bark. Every member of the Communist Party* (*or alleged member*) *was* [*considered*] *a potential if not probable enemy agent whose phone was tappable* (Atlantic).
**tap|per¹** (tap′ər), *n.* **1** a telegraph key that makes a contact and breaks another in one motion. **2** a bell clapper. **3** a person who taps, as at a door. **4** a person who taps train wheels to test their soundness. **5** = cobbler.
**tap|per²** (tap′ər), *n.* **1** a person who taps trees for the sap. **2** = milking machine. **3** = wiretapper. [Old English *tæppere* a tapster < *tæppian* to tap² < *taeppe* tap²]
**✱tap|pet** (tap′it), *n.* a projecting arm, cam, or other part in a machine that strikes another part of the machine at intervals to transmit an irregular motion.

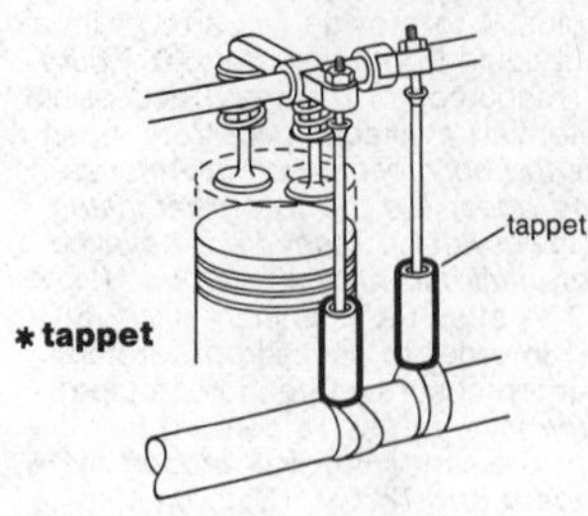

**✱tappet**

**tap|ping¹** (tap′ing), *n.* **1** the act of striking gently. **2** a sound made in this way.
**tap|ping²** (tap′ing), *n.* **1** the act of a person who taps pipes, electricity, resources, or anything else. **2** something that runs from a tap.
**tap|pit hen** (tap′it), **1** *Scottish.* a hen having a crest or topknot. **2** *British Dialect.* a woodpecker. [variant of *topped*]
**tap plate**, a tool for cutting an outside pipe thread.
**tap|room** (tap′rüm′, -rům′), *n.* = barroom.
**tap|root** (tap′rüt′, -rům′), *n.* **1** a main root growing deep downward from the stem. A taproot is thick at the top, tapers to a point, and sprouts subsidiary lateral roots. *Trees that have well-developed taproots are especially well equipped to withstand wind storms* (Fred. W. Emerson). **2** *Figurative.* the main cause or source of development: *Investment ... is the taproot of economic growth* (Wall Street Journal).
**taps** (taps), *n.pl.* a signal on a bugle or drum to put out lights at night. Taps are also sounded when a soldier or sailor is buried. *The customary volleys were fired over the grave, and Bugler Fitzgerald sounded taps, the soldier's last sad farewell* (Cambridge Tribune).
► **Taps** is plural in construction but may be singular or plural in use.
**tap|sal|tee|rie** (tap′səl tē′rē), *adv. Scottish.* topsy-turvy.
**tap|ster** (tap′stər), *n.* a person who draws beer, wine, or other alcoholic liquor from barrels, kegs, casks, or the like, to serve in a tavern or barroom. [Old English *tæppestre;* (originally) feminine of *tæppere;* see etym. under **tapper²**]
**tap|stress** (tap′stris), *n. Archaic.* a barmaid.
**tap-tap** (tap′tap′), *n., v.,* **-tapped**, **-tap|ping**. —*n.* a repeated tap; series of taps: *Mr. Tressle's man ... ceased his tap-tap upon the coffin* (Thackeray).
—*v.i.* to make a series of tapping sounds or movements.
**Ta|pu|ya** (tä pü′yə), *n., pl.* **-ya**. **1** a member of a primitive group of tribes, once numerous throughout Central South America but now found only in the remote regions of Brazil. **2** any speaker of Tapuyan. [< Portuguese *Tapuya* < Tupi (Brazil) *tapuya* enemy, savage]
**Ta|pu|yan** (tä pü′yən), *n., adj.* —*n.* **1** a family of American Indian languages formerly widely spoken in central Brazil, now restricted to remote areas. **2** = Tapuya.
—*adj.* of or having to do with the Tapuya or with the Tapuyan family of languages.
**tap water**, water from a pipe.
**tar¹** (tär), *n., v.,* **tarred**, **tar|ring**, *adj.* —*n.* **1** a dark-brown or black, sticky substance obtained by distillation, especially of wood or coal. Tar is used to cover and patch roads and to keep telephone poles and other timber from rotting. **2** a brownish-black substance produced by the burning of tobacco: *cigarette tar.* **3** a pitch distilled from coal tar.
—*v.t.* **1** to cover or smear with tar; soak in tar. Tarred paper is used on sheds to keep out water. *The street in front of our house is tarred.* **2** *Figurative.* to dirty as with tar; soil; smear: *to tar a person's character or reputation. If it* [*the policy*] *goes badly, people who now approve of the policy will be tarred as warmongers* (New York Times).
—*adj.* of, like, or covered with tar.
**beat** (or **knock**, **whip**, or **whale**) **the tar out of**, *Informal.* to beat unmercifully: *If he was sore at me for something, he'd save up ..., then beat the tar out of me* (New Yorker).
**tar and feather**, to pour heated tar on and cover with feathers as a punishment: *If I escape from town without being tarred and feathered, I shall consider it good luck* (Hawthorne).
**tarred with the same brush** (or **stick**), having similar faults or defects: *They are all tarred with the same stick—rank Jacobites and Papists* (Scott).
**tar with** (a specified) **brush**, to disgrace in some way; stigmatize: [*He*] *intends to tar his opponent with the Tory brush* (London Times).
[Old English *teoru, teru*] —**tar′like′**, *adj.* —**tar′rer**, *n.*
**tar²** (tär), *n.* a sailor or seaman; Jack tar. [probably short for *tarpaulin* (in early meaning) sailor]
**tar³** (tär), *v.t.*, **tarred**, **tar|ring**. to incite; provoke; hound (on): *The cries, the squealings of children, ... tarring them on, as the rabble does when dogs fight* (Thomas Carlyle). [Middle English *terren*]
**tar|a|did|dle** (tar′ə did′əl), *n. Especially British Informal.* **1** a trifling falsehood; petty lie; fib: *Everybody told us it would be very cold, and as usual, everybody told taradiddles* (Thomas H. Huxley). **2** something of little importance or consequence. Also, **tarradiddle**. [origin uncertain]
**Ta|ra|hu|ma|ra** (tä′rə hü mä′rə), *n., pl.* **-ras** or **-ra**. **1** a member of an American Indian people living in Chihuahua and adjacent parts of northern Mexico. **2** the Uto-Aztecan language of this people.
**ta|ra|ma|sa|la|ta** (tä′rä mä sä lä′tä), *n.* a Greek appetizer consisting of a creamy paste of salted fish roe mixed with bread or potato and seasoned with lemon juice. [< New Greek *taramasalata* < Turkish, roe salad]
**ta|ran|ta|ra** (tə ran′tər ə), *n.* = tantara.
**ta|ran|tass** or **ta|ran|tas** (tä′rän täs′), *n.* a large, four-wheeled carriage on long, flexible wooden bars with no springs, used in Russia in the 1800's. [< Russian *tarantas*]
**tar|an|tel|la** (tar′ən tel′ə), *n.* **1** a rapid whirling, southern Italian folk dance in very quick rhythm, usually performed by a single couple. It was once a supposed cure for tarantism. *Williams' screenplay, like his drama, revolves with the frantic formlessness of a tarantella* (Newsweek). **2** a ballroom dance based on it. **3** music for either of these dances. **4** any music in this rhythm. [< Italian *tarantella* < *Taranto* Taranto, a city in Italy < Latin *Tarentum;* popularly associated with *tarantula,* and supposedly a cure for *tarantism*]
**tar|ant|ism** (tar′ən tiz′əm), *n.* a nervous disorder characterized by an extreme impulse to dance, epidemic in southern Italy from the 1400's to the 1600's and popularly attributed to the bite of the tarantula; dancing mania: *Tarantism ... occurred at the height of the summer heat, in July and August* (Scientific American). [< New Latin *tarantismus* < Italian *tarantismo* < *Taranto* Taranto. Compare etym. under **tarantula**.]
**✱ta|ran|tu|la** (tə ran′chə lə), *n., pl.* **-las**, **-lae** (-lē). **1** a large, hairy spider of southern Europe, whose slightly poisonous bite was once imagined to cause an insane desire to dance: *The tarantula's powerful body is covered with long hairs that transmit a delicate sense of touch* (Science News Letter). **2** any one of a family of large, hairy spiders with a painful but not serious bite, found in the southwestern United States and South and Central America: *A typical southwestern U.S. tarantula has a body about two inches long and a leg span of about six inches* (Science News Letter). [< Medieval Latin *tarantula* < Italian *tarantola* < *Taranto* Taranto, a city in Italy, near which the spider is found]

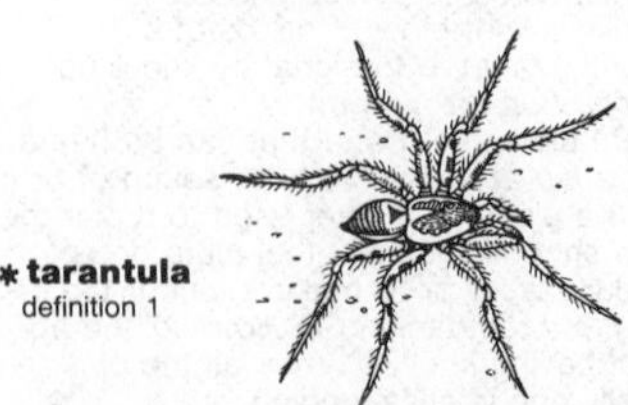
**✱tarantula**
definition 1

**Ta|ras|can** (tə ras′kən), *n., adj.* —*n.* **1** a member of a tribe of Indians living in Mexico. **2** their language.
—*adj.* of or having to do with the Tarascans or their language.
**ta|ra|ta** (tə rä′tə), *n.* an evergreen tree of New Zealand with fragrant yellow flowers; lemonwood. [< Maori *tarata*]
**ta|rax|a|cum** (tə rak′sə kəm), *n.* **1** any one of a group of composite herbs, such as the dandelion. **2** dried dandelion roots, used as a tonic, laxative, and diuretic. [< New Latin *Taraxacum* the genus name < Medieval Latin *tarasacon,* probably misreading of Arabic *ṭarakhshaqōq* < Persian *talkh chakūk* bitter herb]
**ta|rax|ein** (tə rak′sēn, -sē in), *n.* a protein substance extracted from the blood serum of schizophrenic persons: *Taraxein ... causes symptoms similar to schizophrenia when injected into normal volunteers* (Time). [< Greek *taraxē* confusion (< *taràssein* to trouble, confuse) + English *-in*]

**tar|board** (tär′bôrd′, -bōrd′), *n., adj.* —*n.* a strong millboard made especially of tarred rope.
—*adj.* made of this.

***tar|boosh** (tär büsh′), *n.* a cloth or felt brimless cap, usually red and with a tassel on top, worn by Moslem men, sometimes inside a turban. Also, **tarbush.** [< Arabic *ṭarbūsh*]

***tarboosh**

**tar|boy** (tär′boi′), *n. Australian.* a boy who dabs tar on sheep cut during shearing.

**tar|bush¹** (tär′bu̇sh′), *n. U.S.* any of a group of California shrubs of the waterleaf family.

**tar|bush²** (tär büsh′), *n.* = tarboosh.

**Tar|de|nois|i|an** (tär′də noi′zi ən), *adj.* of or having to do with a mesolithic culture, remains of which were first discovered in Tardenois, France.

**tar|di|grade** (tär′də grād), *adj., n.* —*adj.* **1** moving or walking slowly. **2** of or having to do with a class or subclass of very small arthropods with little-developed circulatory and respiratory systems and four pairs of short legs, either marine or inhabiting damp places, often found as slime on ponds.
—*n.* any tardigrade animal.
[< French *tardigrade* < Latin *tardigradus* slow-paced < *tardus* slow + *gradī* to walk]

**tar|di|ly** (tär′də lē), *adv.* slowly; late; with delay: *The night rolled tardily away* (William Cowper).

**tar|di|ness** (tär′dē nis), *n.* the quality of being tardy; slowness of action; lateness: *A tardiness in nature, Which often leaves the history unspoke That it intends to do* (Shakespeare).

**tar|do** (tär′dō), *adj. Music.* slow (used as a direction). [< Italian *tardo* < Latin *tardus* slow]

**tar|dy** (tär′dē), *adj.,* **-di|er, -di|est,** *adv.* —*adj.* **1** behind time; late. **SYN:** behindhand. **2** late for a meeting, school, or appointment; unpunctual. **3** taking rather long to make little progress; slow in motion or action; sluggish: *The old bus was tardier than ever.* **SYN:** dilatory. See syn. under **late.** **4** delaying; reluctant.
—*adv.* **come tardy off.** See under **come.**
[Middle English *tardyve* < Middle French *tardif, -ive,* ultimately < Latin *tardus* slow]

**tare¹** (tãr), *n.* **1** any one of various fodder plants, especially a common species with light-purplish flowers; vetch. **2** a vetch seed, often a symbol of smallness. **3** an injurious weed, possibly the darnel (in the Bible, Matthew 13:24-30): *Tares killed the wheat.* [compare Middle Dutch *tarwe* wheat]

**tare²** (tãr), *n., v.,* **tared, tar|ing.** —*n.* **1** a deduction made from the gross weight of goods to allow for the weight of the wrapper, box, container, or vehicle they are in. **2** the weight deducted. **3** the weight of any empty motor vehicle, without passengers, load, or fuel. **4** *Chemistry.* **a** the weight of a vessel, subtracted from its weight with a substance in it, to determine the weight of the substance. **b** a counterweight to the vessel.
—*v.t.* to mark or allow for the tare of.
[< Old French *tare* < Medieval Latin *tara* deduction < Arabic *ṭarḥah* thing rejected]

**tare-fitch** (tãr′fich′) or **tar|fitch** (tär′fich′), *n.* = tarevetch.

**tare|vetch** (tãr′vech′), *n. British Dialect.* any of various vetches or tares. Also, **tarvetch.**

**targe** (tärj), *n. Archaic.* a light, circular shield or buckler. [< Old French *targe* < Germanic (compare Old Icelandic *targe*)]

**targe|man** (tärj′mən), *n., pl.* **-men.** *Archaic.* a man who carries a targe or shield.

***tar|get** (tär′git), *n., v.* —*n.* **1a** a mark for shooting at, especially a design of a circle or concentric circles to be shot at in practice or competition. **b** any object shot at or thrown at. **2** *Figurative.* an object of abuse, scorn, or criticism: *His crazy ideas made him the target of jokes by everyone.* **SYN:** butt. **3** *Figurative.* any aim one tries to achieve; goal; objective: *The lower farm production targets in the new plan appeared to be more realistic* (Wall Street Journal). **4** a small shield or buckler, especially a round medieval shield fastened to the arm. **5** *Physics.* **a** a plate, often of platinum or tungsten, opposite the cathode in an X-ray tube, upon which the cathode rays impinge and produce X rays. **b** any substance subjected to bombardment by atomic particles. **6** a plate in a television camera tube that receives the image from the screen plate in the form of electrons, the image being picked up for transmission by a scanning beam. **7** *Surveying.* **a** the movable sight on a leveling staff; vane. **b** any marker for leveling a sight on. **8** a disk to show whether a railway switch is open or closed. **9** *Obsolete.* a cymbal.
—*v.t.* **1** to make or put up as a target: *In a statement released with the figures,* [*he*] *stated the company has targeted a profit for the year* (Wall Street Journal). **2** to guide to a target.
[Middle English *targat* light shield < Middle French *targuete,* variant of *targete* (diminutive) < Old French *targe;* see eytm. under **targe**] —**tar′get|less,** *adj.*

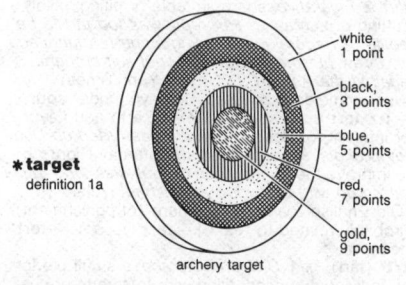

white, 1 point
black, 3 points
blue, 5 points
red, 7 points
gold, 9 points
archery target

***target**
definition 1a

**tar|get|a|ble** (tär′gə tə bəl), *adj.* that can be aimed at a target: *The United States will in the next few years add to its arsenal missiles capable of putting into space a number of individually targetable warheads* (New York Times).

**tar|get-card** (tär′git kärd′), *n.* a card used for scoring the shooters' respective hits.

**target date,** a date set for the beginning or completion of a project: *The idea would be to bring everything into readiness by a target date* (Science News Letter).

**tar|get|eer** (tär′gə tir′), *n.* **1** a person who tests the sights for accuracy on small arms. **2** = peltast.

**tar|get-fir|ing** (tär′git fīr′ing), *n. Especially British.* target practice.

**target language,** the language into which something is translated; object language.

**target pistol,** a pistol with a long barrel for accuracy, used for target practice.

**target practice,** practice at shooting to improve one's aim.

**target ship,** a condemned ship used as a practice target.

**tar|get-shoot|ing** (tär′git shü′ting), *n.* = target practice.

**Tar|ghee** (tär′gē), *n.* any one of an American breed of sheep, a cross between the Rambouillet and the Lincoln.

**Tar|gum** (tär′gum; *Hebrew* tär güm′), *n., pl.* **Targums, Tar|gu|mim** (tär′gü mēm′). any one of various Aramaic translations or paraphrases of almost all sections of the Old Testament. [< Hebrew *Targūm* < Aramaic, interpretation < *targem* to interpret]

**Tar|gum|ist** (tär′gə mist), *n.* a compiler of any of the Targums.

**Tar|gum|is|tic** (tär′gə mis′tik), *adj.* of or having to do with a Targumist or the Targumists.

**Tar|heel** (tär′hēl′), *n.* a nickname for a native or inhabitant of North Carolina. [American English < *tar*¹ + *heel*]

**Tarheel State,** a nickname for North Carolina.

**tar|iff** (tar′if), *n., v.* —*n.* **1** a list of duties or taxes that a government charges on imports or exports. **2** the system of duties or taxes on imports and exports. **3** any duty or tax in such a list or system: *There is a very high tariff on imported jewelry. Heavy revenue duties ... have the same effect as protective tariffs in obstructing free trade* (Time). **4** the table of prices in a hotel, restaurant, or similar establishment: *The tariff at the Grant Hotel ranges from $10 to $25 a day for a single room.* **5** any scale of prices; book of rates; schedule: *a revised tariff for passenger travel.* **6** *Obsolete.* an arithmetical table, especially one used to save calculating discounts; ready reckoner.
—*v.t.* **1** to put a tariff on. **2** to set a value or price for, according to a tariff. **3** to list the tariff or tariffs on.
[< Italian *tariffa* schedule of customs rates < Arabic *ta'rīf* information, notification]

**tariff reform,** *U.S.* a reduction of most import duties.

**Tariff Reform,** *British.* an increase or extension of most import duties.

**tariff wall,** = trade barrier.

**tar|iff-walled** (tar′if wôld′), *adj.* **1** of or having to do with a tariff wall. **2** like a tariff wall.

**tar|la|tan** (tär′lə tən), *n.* a thin, stiff muslin, transparent and unwashable, formerly glazed and used as for ballet skirts and bags for Christmas candy. [< French *tarlatane;* origin uncertain]

**tar|mac** (tar′mak′), *n. British.* any surface made of tarmacadam, especially a road, runway, or other part of an airfield.

**Tar|mac** (tär′mak′), *n. Trademark.* tarmacadam.

**tar|mac|ad|am** (tär′mə kad′əm), *n.* a paving material consisting of crushed rock in a tar and creosote binder; blacktop. [< *tar*¹ + *macadam*]

**tarn** (tärn), *n.* a small lake or pool in the mountains, especially one formed by glaciers. See picture under **mountain.** [Middle English *terne* < Scandinavian (compare Old Icelandic *tjörn,* Swedish *tjärn* pool, standing water)]

**tar|nal** or **'tar|nal** (tär′nəl), *adj., adv. Dialect.* tarnation. [alteration of *eternal*]

**tar|na|tion** (tär nā′shən), *n., adj., adv. U.S. Dialect.* —*n.* damnation.
—*adj.* confounded; damned: *a tarnation fool.*
—*adv.* awfully; inordinately: *Travelling is tarnation bad* (Harriet E. Comstock).
[probably < *tarn*(al) + (dam)*nation*]

**tar|nish** (tär′nish), *v., n.* —*v.t.* **1** to dull the luster or brightness of: *Salt will tarnish silver.* **SYN:** blacken. **2** *Figurative.* to bring disgrace upon (a reputation, one's honor, or the like); sully; taint: *The expedition's triumph was somewhat tarnished by dissension and subsequent recrimination* (Atlantic).
—*v.i.* **1** to lose luster or brightness; grow dull or dim; discolor: *The brass doorknob tarnished.* **SYN:** blacken. **2** *Figurative.* to grow less appealing; become uninviting; pall; fade.
—*n.* **1** the fact or condition of being tarnished; loss of luster or brightness. **2** a discolored coating, especially on silver. **3** *Figurative.* any unattractiveness or blemish; blot: *The Savoy operas are still a joy, no tarnish on them* (Punch).
[< Middle French *terniss-,* stem of *ternir* < *terne* dark, dull, perhaps < Germanic (compare Middle High German *tarnen, ternen* darken)] —**tar′nish|a|ble,** *adj.*

**ta|ro** (tä′rō, tar′ō), *n., pl.* **-ros. 1** a tropical plant grown in the Pacific islands and other regions for its starchy rootlike stem or corm, which is used as food. Taro belongs to the arum family. Its leaves, sprouts, and stems are acrid when raw, but not when cooked. See picture under **arum family. 2** its rootlike stem or corm, resembling a potato tuber. [< Polynesian *taro*]

**tar|oc, tar|ock,** or **tar|ok** (tar′ək), *n.* = tarot. [< Italian *tarocchi,* plural; origin unknown]

**tar|ot** (tar′ət), *n.* one of a set of Italian playing cards of the 1300's, consisting of 22 figured trumps added to a deck of 56 in four suits, also used in fortunetelling.
**tarots,** the game played with such cards: *to win at tarots.*
[< French *tarot,* alteration of Italian *tarocchi;* see etym. under **taroc**]

**tarp** (tärp), *n. U.S. Informal.* a tarpaulin: *There were tents by the creek, and tarps stretched from cars and wagons to make lean-to shelters* (Dan Cushman).

**tar|pan** (tär′pan), *n.* **1** a grayish-brown wild horse of central Asia, about the size of a mule. **2** a wild European horse that became extinct in the 1800's: *Tarpans are extinct; the last herds vanished in the 19th century, after ranging eastward to the steppes of the Ukraine* (Time). [< Tartar *tarpan*]

**tar paper,** heavy paper covered or impregnated with tar, used especially for waterproofing and windproofing buildings: *a tar paper shack.*

**tar|pau|lin** (tär pô′lən, tär′pə-), *n., v.* —*n.* **1** canvas or other coarse cloth made waterproof, as by painting, tarring, or rubberizing. **2** a sheet of this, used especially as a protection against rain. **3** a hat made of or covered with it, especially a sailor's hat. **4** a coat or other garment made of this. **5** a sailor; seaman; tar: *bandy-legged tarpaulins* (Robert Louis Stevenson).
—*v.t.* to cover with a tarpaulin: *On the dot of the announced time, a green-tarpaulined, mysterious-looking truck arrives* (Newsweek).
—*v.i.* to take shelter under a tarpaulin.
[probably < *tar*¹ + *pall*¹ covering + *-ing*¹]

**Tar|pe|ian** (tär pē′ən), *adj.* of or having to do with a rock on the Capitoline Hill in Rome, from which persons convicted of treason to the state were hurled. [< Latin *Tarpeianus* < *Tarpeia* Tarpeia, a legendary Roman maiden who committed treason by aiding the Sabines]

**tar|pon** (tär′pon), *n., pl.* **-pons** or (*collectively*) **-pon. 1** a large, silver-colored fish found in the warmer parts of the Atlantic Ocean; jewfish. The tarpon has large scales, weighs over 100 pounds, and is much sought as a game fish. **2** a similar East Indian species. [origin unknown]

**Pronunciation Key:** hat, āge, cãre, fär; let, ēqual, tėrm; it, īce; hot, ōpen, ôrder; **oi**l, **ou**t; cup, pu̇t, rüle; **ch**ild; lo**ng**; **th**in; **ŧh**en; **zh,** measure; ə represents **a** in about, **e** in taken, **i** in pencil, **o** in lemon, **u** in circus.

**tar|ra|did|dle** (tar′ə did′əl), *n.* = taradiddle.
**tar|ra|gon** (tar′ə gon), *n.* **1** a wormwood, native to eastern Europe and temperate Asia. **2** its leaves, used to flavor vinegar, salads, soups, chicken, and other food. [probably < Old Spanish *taragoncía,* or Middle French *targon* tarragon < Medieval Greek *tarchon* < Arabic *ṭarkhon,* apparently < Greek *drákōn* dragon]
**Tar|ra|go|na** (tar′ə gō′nə), *n.* a Spanish red wine of the port type. [< *Tarragona,* a province in Spain]
**tar|ras** (tar′əs), *n., v. Obsolete.* —*n.* trass.
—*v.t.* to cement with trass.
[probably < French *terrasser* to terrace]
**tarre** (tär), *v.t.,* **tarred, tar|ring.** *Obsolete.* to tar (on); incite; hound: *And, like a dog that is compell'd to fight, Snatch at his master that doth tarre him on* (Shakespeare). [earlier form of *tar*³, Middle English *terren*]
**tarred** (tärd), *adj.* smeared or covered with tar: *a tarred road.*
**tar|ri|ance** (tar′ē əns), *n. Archaic.* **1** delay: *I am impatient of my tarriance* (Shakespeare). **2** a brief stay; sojourn.
**tar|ri|er¹** (tar′ē ər), *n. Archaic.* a person who tarries; lingerer.
**tar|ri|er²** (tar′ē ər), *n.* a borer, especially one used to pull a bung. [< Old French *tarere* < Late Latin *taratrum.* Compare Greek *téretron* borer.]
**tar|ri|er³** (tär′ē ər), *adj.* the comparative of **tarry².**
**tar|rock** (tar′ək), *n. British Dialect.* any one of various sea birds, such as the arctic tern, kittiwake, gull, or guillemot.
**tar|row** (tar′ō), *v.i. Scottish.* to delay; hesitate; tarry. [apparently variant of *tarry*¹]
**tar|ry¹** (tar′ē), *v.,* **-ried, -ry|ing,** *n.* —*v.i.* **1** to delay leaving; remain; stay: *He tarried at the inn until he felt strong enough to travel. Time and tide tarry for no man* (Scott). **SYN:** linger, loiter. **2** to delay starting any action; be tardy; hesitate: *Why do you tarry so long?*
—*v.t. Archaic.* to wait for (a person or event).
—*n. Obsolete.* a tarrying.
[Middle English *tarien;* origin uncertain]
**tar|ry²** (tär′ē), *adj.,* **-ri|er, -ri|est. 1** of tar: *a tarry smell.* **2** like tar; sticky. **3** covered with tar; tarred: *a tarry road.* **4** = black. [< *tar*¹ + *-y*¹]
**tar|sal** (tär′səl), *adj., n.* —*adj.* **1** of or having to do with the tarsus: *The first ants to settle in a new place catch onto a rough or soft surface using these tarsal hooks* (Science News Letter). **2** of or having to do with the edges (tarsi) of the eyelids. —*n.* one of the bones or cartilages in the ankle. See diagram under **skeleton.**
**tarsal joint,** a joint of the tarsus: **a** (in man) the joint between the tibia and fibula and the astragalus or tarsus. **b** a corresponding joint in other vertebrates. **c** (in birds) the joint between the tibia and the metatarsus, or, strictly, between the tarsal elements of the tibia and the tarsal elements of the metatarsus.
**tar sand,** a Canadian sand containing tarry substances: *In addition to coal, oil, and natural gas, the earth's crust contains vast potential resources of oil shale and oil-bearing tar sands* (Scientific American).
**tar|sec|to|my** (tär sek′tə mē), *n., pl.* **-mies.** the removal of one or more tarsal bones.
**tar sheet,** = tarpaulin.
**Tar|shish** (tär′shish), *n.* a region mentioned in the Bible (II Chronicles 9:21). It was probably in southern Spain.
**tar|si** (tär′sī), *n.* plural of **tarsus.**
**tar|si|a** (tär′sē ə), *n.* a kind of inlay in wood of various colors. [< Italian *tarsia* inlay of bone, horn, wood, or ivory]
**tar|si|er** (tär′sē ər), *n.* any one of a genus of small, nocturnal primates of Indonesia and the Philippines, with large eyes and long, bare tails. They are related to the lemurs. [< French *tarsier* < *tarse* ankle < Medieval Latin *tarsus* (because of its long anklebones)]
**tar|si|ped** (tär′sə ped), *n., adj.* —*n.* a small marsupial mammal of West Australia with a prehensile tail, that feeds on nectar, pollen, and insects. —*adj.* of or belonging to the tarsiped family.
[< New Latin *Tarsipes, -pedis* the genus name < *tarsus* tarsus + Latin *pēs, pedis* foot]
**tar|so|met|a|tar|sal** (tär′sō met′ə tär′səl), *adj., n.* —*adj.* **1** having to do with the tarsus and the metatarsus. **2** resulting from a combination of tarsal and metatarsal bones, as a single compound bone. **3** having parts of the tarsus combined with itself, as a metatarsus. **4** of the tarsometatarsus.
—*n.* the tarsometatarsal bone.
**tar|so|met|a|tar|sus** (tär′sō met′ə tär′səs), *n., pl.* **-si** (-sī). **1** the leg bone or shank in birds and early reptilian types, consisting of united tarsal and metatarsal bones. **2** the third joint of the limb of a bird.
**tar|sus** (tär′səs), *n., pl.* **-si. 1a** the human ankle. **b** the group of small bones composing it; collective name for the seven small bones between the tibia and the metatarsus, part of the ankle joint and of the instep. **2** the corresponding part in most mammals, in some reptiles, and in amphibians. **3** the shank of a bird's leg; tarsometatarsus. **4** the last segment of the leg of an arthropod. **5** the thin plate of condensed connective tissue that gives form to the edge of the eyelid. [< New Latin *tarsus* < Greek *tarsós* sole of the foot; rim of the eyelid; (originally) flat basket]
**tart¹** (tärt), *adj., v.* —*adj.* **1** having a sharp taste; biting, acid, or sour: *tart plums. Some apples are tart.* **2** *Figurative.* sharp; irritable or biting; mildly cutting or sarcastic: *Her reply was too tart to be polite. A Federal judge, using some tart language, ... threw out the $1,000,000 libel suit brought against the A.F.L.-C.I.O.* (New York Times).
**SYN:** acrimonious, caustic. See syn. under **sour.**
—*v.t.* **tart up,** *Especially British.* **a** to add flavor or interest to: *Joseph Landon has tarted up Dudley Nichols' script* (Canadian Saturday Night). **b** to improve the appearance of: *galleries and pubs tarted up with driftwood and fishnet* (Atlantic).
[Old English *teart* painful, sharp (of punishment). Probably related to **tear**¹.] —**tart′ly,** *adv.* —**tart′ness,** *n.*
**tart²** (tärt), *n.* **1** *U.S. and Canada.* a small pie for an individual serving, filled with fruit, jam, or custard, and without a top crust. **2** *British.* any fruit pie. [< Old French *tarte;* origin uncertain]
**tart³** (tärt), *n. Informal.* a prostitute. [special use of *tart*²; originally, a girl or woman of loose morals]
**tar|tan¹** (tär′tən), *n., adj.* —*n.* **1** a plaid woolen cloth. Each Scottish Highland clan has its own pattern, usually both a hunting tartan and a dress tartan, that differ mainly in the background color. **2** the pattern or design itself. **3** any similar plaid design or fabric, as of silk or cotton.
—*adj.* **1** made of tartan. **2** of or like tartan. **3** having to do with tartan.
[< Old French *tiretanie* linsey-woolsey; influenced by Old French *tartarin* (cloth) of Tartary]
**tar|tan²** (tär′tən), *n.* a Mediterranean type of boat, having one mast rigged with a lateen sail and a jib. [< French *tartan* < Italian *tartana,* perhaps < Arabic *tarīdah* kind of ship]
**Tar|tan** (tär′tən), *n. Trademark.* a nylon material resembling a grassy surface, used for artificial playing fields and lawns.
**tar|taned** (tär′tənd), *adj.* **1** wearing a tartan. **2** (of cloth) having a tartan pattern.
**tar|tar¹** (tär′tər), *n.* **1a** an acid solid, potassium bitartrate, present in grape juice and deposited as a reddish crust in wine casks; argol. *Formula:* $KH_5C_4O_6$ **b** this substance partly purified. When pure as cream of tartar, it is mixed with baking soda to make baking powder. **2** a hard, yellowish substance formed on the teeth by the action of saliva on food particles. [< Old French *tartre* < Medieval Latin *tartarum* < Late Greek *tártaron,* perhaps < a Semitic word]
**tar|tar²** (tär′tər), *n.* **1** a person who has a bad temper; virago: *The old man was an awful tartar* (Dickens). **2** *Slang.* a person hard to beat or surpass in skill; champion. [< *Tartar*]
**Tar|tar** (tär′tər), *n., adj.* —*n.* **1** a member of a mixed horde of Mongols, Turks, and other tribes who overran Asia and eastern Europe in the 1200's and 1300's. **2** any descendant of these peoples living in parts of the Soviet Union and central and western Asia, especially one who speaks a Ural-Altaic language of the Turkic branch. **3** any such language, chiefly in west central Asia, such as Turkish or Kirghiz.
—*adj.* of or having to do with any of these peoples or their languages. Also, **Tatar.**
**catch a Tartar,** to attack someone who is too strong; get the worst of it: *You must give up flirting, my boy, or if I mistake not, you'll find you've caught a Tartar* (Florence Marryat).
[< Medieval Latin *Tartarus,* probably < Persian *Tātār* < Turkic; influenced by Latin *Tartarus* Tartarus]
**tar|tar|at|ed** (tär′tə rā′tid), *adj. Chemistry.* made into a tartrate; containing or obtained from tartar.
**Tar|tar|e|an** or **tar|tar|e|an** (tär tãr′ē ən), *adj.* of or having to do with Tartarus: *Drives the dead to dark, Tartarean coasts* (Alexander Pope).
**tartar emetic,** a poisonous, white, crystalline, granular salt with a sweetish, metallic taste, used in medicine as an expectorant and as a mordant in dyeing. It is a tartrate of potassium and antimony. *Formula:* $K(SbO)C_4H_4O_6 \cdot ½H_2O$
**tar|tar|e|ous** (tär tãr′ē əs), *adj.* **1** of the nature of tartar; tartarlike. **2** *Botany.* having a rough, crumbling surface.
**tar|tar|et** (tär′tə ret), *n.,* or **tartaret falcon,** a small falcon of Africa and Asia. [< Old French *tartaret* < Old French *Tartaire* Tartary (because they were thought to come from there)]
**Tar|tar|i|an** (tär tãr′ē ən), *adj.* **1** of or having to do with the Tartars. **2** *Figurative.* savage.
**tartarian bread,** a vegetable eaten in Hungary with oil, vinegar, and salt. It is the root of an East European perennial herb of the mustard family. [translation of Hungarian *tatár kenyér*]
**tartarian lamb,** an Asian fern with shaggy rhizomes suggesting a small lamb.
**tar|tar|ic** (tär tar′ik, -tär′-), *adj.* **1** of or having to do with tartar; containing tartar. **2** obtained from tartar.
**tartaric acid,** an acid used especially in dyeing, medicine, foods, and photography, occurring in four isomers. The common colorless, crystalline form is found in unripe grapes and prepared from argol. *Formula:* $C_4H_6O_6$
**tar|tar|i|za|tion** (tär′tər ə zā′shən), *n.* the act of tartarizing, or of forming tartar.
**tar|tar|ize** (tär′tə rīz), *v.t.,* **-ized, -iz|ing.** *Chemistry.* to combine or treat with tartar.
**tartar sauce,** a sauce, usually for fish, consisting of mayonnaise with chopped pickles, onions, olives, capers, and herbs. [< French *sauce tartare*]
**tartar steak,** a dish of minced raw beef, highly seasoned, and served or blended with uncooked egg yolk.
**Tar|ta|rus** (tär′tər əs), *n. Greek Mythology.* **1** a place of darkness where Zeus punished the Titans, as far below Hades as earth is from heaven. **2** (later) a place of eternal punishment for the spirits of the worst sinners. **3** the underworld; Hades; hell.
**tar|tine** (tär tēn′), *n.* a slice of bread and butter, jam, honey, or the like: *She placidly handed out this decoction, which we took with cakes and tartines* (Thackeray). [< French *tartine* < Old French *tarte* tart²]
**tart|ish** (tär′tish), *adj.* somewhat tart; slightly pungent or acid. —**tart′ish|ly,** *adv.*
**tart|let** (tärt′lit), *n.* a small tart, two or three inches across. [< Old French *tartelette* (diminutive) < *tarte* tart²]
**tar|tram|ide** (tär′tram′īd, -id), *n.* the amide of tartaric acid. *Formula:* $C_4H_4(NH_2)_2O_4$
**tar|trate** (tär′trāt), *n.* a salt or ester of tartaric acid. [< French *tartrate*]
**tar|trat|ed** (tär′trā tid), *adj.* formed into a tartrate; combined with tartaric acid.
**tar|tra|zine** (tär′trə zēn, -zin), *n.* a yellowish-orange powder used as a dye for cosmetics and wool. *Formula:* $C_{16}H_9N_4Na_3O_9S_2$
**tar|tron|ate** (tär′trə nāt), *n.* salt of tartronic acid.
**tar|tron|ic acid** (tär tron′ik), a dibasic acid occurring in large, colorless crystals. *Formula:* $C_3H_4O_5$
**tart-tongued** (tärt′tungd′), *adj.* biting or cutting in speech; caustic; sarcastic.
**Tar|tuffe** or **Tar|tufe** (tär tüf′; *French* tȧr tyf′), *n.* = hypocrite. [< *Tartuffe,* the central character of a French comedy by Molière, produced in 1667, famous for his hypocritical piety]
**Tar|tuff|er|y** (tär tü′fər ē), *n., pl.* **-er|ies.** the character or conduct of a Tartuffe; hypocrisy.
**Tar|tuff|i|an** or **Tar|tuf|i|an** (tär tü′fē ən), *adj.* hypocritical; pretentious.
**Tar|tuff|ism** or **Tar|tuf|ism** (tär tü′fiz əm), *n.* = Tartuffery.
**tart|y** (tär′tē), *adj. Informal.* of or like a tart; sharp; snippy.
**tar|vetch** (tär′vech), *n.* = tarevetch.
**tar|vi|a** (tär′vē ə), *n.* a road-surfacing material made chiefly of asphalt. [< *tar*¹ + Latin *via* way]
**tar-wa|ter** (tär′wôt′ər, -wot′-), *n.* an infusion of tar in cold water, formerly administered as a medicine.
**tar|weed** (tär′wēd′), *n. U.S.* **1** any one of a group of sticky plants of the composite family with a strong, tarry smell, found especially along the Pacific coast of America. **2** any one of various similar plants.
**Tar|zan** or **tar|zan** (tär′zan, -zən), *n.* a man endowed with great physical strength and skill: *Grinda, a tarzan of a Frenchman, with a thunderbolt of a service, was broken three times in all—twice in the opening set and once in the third* (London Times). [< *Tarzan,* the hero of a series of adventure stories by Edgar Rice Burroughs, 1875-1950, an American author]
**TAS** (no periods), true air speed (of an aircraft).
**Ta|sa|day** (tä′sä dī′), *n., pl.* **-day** or **days. 1** a member of a small tribe living like Stone Age people in caves on Mindanao, in the Philippines. The Tasaday were discovered in 1970-71. **2** the Malayo-Polynesian language of this tribe.
**ta|sa|jo** (tä sä′hō), *n.* strips of jerked beef. [< Spanish *tasajo*]
**Ta|ser** (tā′zər), *n., v.* —*n. Trademark.* a handheld weapon somewhat like a flashlight that fires a dart attached to long wires which transmit electric shock that immobilizes a person temporarily: *The Taser ... paralyzes you until the barbs are removed or the current is switched off* (New Scientist). —*v.t.* to attack or disable with a Taser. [< *T*(ele-)*A*(ctive) *S*(hock) *E*(lectronic) *R*(epulsion)]
**tash|lich** or **tash|lik** (täsh′liH), *n. Judaism.* **1** the custom of reciting a penitential prayer near a stream of water on the afternoon of Rosh Ha-

shanah, often symbolically casting away one's sins by throwing pieces of bread into the water. **2** the penitential prayer recited in this ritual. [< Hebrew *tashlīkh* thou shalt cast, future of *shālakh* to cast]

**TASI** (no periods), Time Assignment Speech Interpolation (a high-speed electronic switching system used in undersea telephone cables).

**ta|sim|e|ter** (tə sim′ə tər), *n.* an instrument for measuring differences of temperature and other factors, by changes in conductivity and pressure. [< Greek *tásis* tension + English *-meter*]

**tas|i|met|ric** (tas′ə met′rik), *adj.* of or having to do with the measurement of pressures, or with the tasimeter.

**ta|sim|e|try** (tə sim′ə trē), *n.* the measurement of pressures.

**task** (task, täsk), *n., v.* —*n.* **1** work to be done; work assigned or found necessary; duty: *Her task is to set the table. The silk-worm, after having spun her task, lays her eggs and dies (Joseph Addison).* **SYN**: assignment, undertaking, responsibility. **2** any piece of work; stint; job. **3** difficult or heavy work; chore. **4** *Obsolete.* tax.
—*v.t.* **1** to put work on; force to work: *The master tasked his slaves beyond their strength.* **2** to burden or strain: *Lifting the heavy box tasked him beyond his strength.* **3** *Obsolete.* to levy a tax on.
**take to task**, to blame, scold, or reprove: *The teacher took him to task for not studying. The Sultan of Johore ... took his people to task for their apathy toward political murder by terrorists* (London Times).
[< Old North French *tasque* job, tax, Old French *tasche* < Vulgar Latin *tasca,* variant of *taxa* < Latin *taxāre* appraise, evaluate] —**task′er**, *n.*

**task force**, **1** a temporary group of military units, especially naval units, assigned to one commander for carrying out a specific operation. **2** any group temporarily organized for a task: *[He] said that a "task force" representing his group had started a "crash program" in Newark* (New York Times).

**task|mas|ter** (task′mas′tər, täsk′mäs′-), *n.* **1** a very exacting boss or teacher. **2** a person who sets tasks for others to do. **SYN**: supervisor, overseer.

**task|mis|tress** (task′mis′tris, täsk′-), *n.* a woman who assigns tasks, especially in a household.

**task|work** (task′wėrk′, täsk′-), *n.* **1** = piecework. **2** any task, especially a burden: *I feel a dislike to order and to taskwork of all kinds* (Scott).

**Tas|ma|ni|an** (taz mā′nē ən, -mān′yən), *adj., n.* —*adj.* of or having to do with Tasmania, an island south of Australia, or its people.
—*n.* a native or inhabitant of Tasmania.

***Tasmanian devil**, a ferocious-looking, burrowing, carnivorous, black-and-white marsupial mammal of Tasmania, which resembles a very small bear and attacks sheep.

***Tasmanian devil**

**Tasmanian myrtle**, an evergreen tree of Tasmania and Victoria, Australia. It is related to the beech.

**Tasmanian wolf** or **tiger**, = thylacine.

**tass** (tas, täs), *n. Especially Scottish.* **1** a small drinking cup, especially of silver; goblet. **2** the drink in it; a small draft, especially of spirits. [< Old French *tasse* goblet, apparently < Arabic *ṭass* basin, probably < Persian *tast* cup, goblet]

**Tass** (tas, täs), *n.* a government agency of the Soviet Union which collects, censors, and distributes news. [< Russian *T(elegrafnoe) A(genstvo) S(ovetskovo) S(oyuza)* Telegraph Agency of the Soviet Union]

**tas|sel[1]** (tas′əl), *n., v.,* **-seled, -sel|ing** or (*especially British*) **-selled, -sel|ling.** —*n.* **1** a hanging bunch of threads, small cords, beads, or the like, fastened together at one end; pendant. **2** any bunch of hairs, threads, or the like, hanging like this. **3** the cluster of long stems bearing small flowers that hangs from the top of a cornstalk. **4** a hanging catkin, blossom, flower, or bud in any tree or plant.
—*v.t.* **1** to put tassels on, especially as decoration. **2** to gather into a tassel or tassels. **3** to take tassels from. —*v.i.* to grow tassels: *Corn tassels just before the ears form.*
[< Old French *tassel* mantle fastener, probably < Vulgar Latin *tassellus* stick for drawing lots, a die, alteration of Latin *taxillus* a small die]

**tas|sel[2]** (tas′əl), *n. Archaic.* a short board under the end of a beam where it rests on brickwork or stonework. Also, **torsel, tossel.** [< Old French *tassel* a plug < Latin *taxillus* a small die. Compare etym. under **tassel**[1].]

**tas|sel[3]** (tas′əl), *n. Obsolete.* tercel.

**tas|sel-bush** (tas′əl bu̇sh′), *n. Especially U.S.* an evergreen shrub with elegant, long, drooping catkins, native to California, Mexico, Cuba, and Jamaica.

**tas|sel-eared squirrel** (tas′əl ird′), a large squirrel of the southwestern United States and Mexico, with long ear tufts, a reddish-brown back, and a whitish tail.

**tas|seled** (tas′əld), *adj.* **1** decorated with a tassel or tassels: *a tasseled cap.* **2** (of a person) wearing a tassel or tassels. **3** gathered into tassels. **4** (of a fern) having divisions like tassels at the apex of each frond.

**tas|ses** (tas′iz), *n.pl.* armor thigh guards made of narrow, overlapping plates strapped below the waist plates, and forming a sort of kilt. See picture under **armor**. [< Old French *tasse* purse, holster]

**tas|sets** (tas′its), *n.pl.* = tasses.

**tast|a|ble** (tās′tə bəl), *adj.* **1** that can be tasted. **2** pleasant to the taste; savory; relishing: *We had a very tastable meal, even for leftovers.* —**tast′a|ble|ness**, *n.* —**tast′a|bly**, *adv.*

**taste** (tāst), *n., v.,* **tast|ed, tast|ing.** —*n.* **1** what is special about something when it touches the taste buds in the mouth and on the tongue; flavor; savor. Sweet, sour, salt, and bitter are four important tastes. *I think this milk is sour; it has a funny taste.* **2** the sense by which the flavor of things is perceived: *Her taste is unusually keen.* **3** a little bit; sample: *Give me just a taste of pudding.* (*Figurative.*) *The snowstorm will give you a taste of northern winter.* **4** a liking or enthusiasm for something; zest; yen: *a taste for sailing. Suit your own taste.* **SYN**: inclination, predilection, fondness. **5** the ability to recognize and enjoy what is beautiful and excellent: *Good books and pictures appeal to people of taste.* **6** a manner or style that shows this ability or lack of it; aesthetic quality or standards: *Her house is furnished in excellent taste.* **7** the prevailing, typical style in an age, class, or country: *in the Moorish taste.* **8** the act of tasting. **9** the fact of being tasted. **10** *Obsolete.* a trying; testing; trial. **11** *Obsolete.* feeling: **a** the sense of touch. **b** a touching.
—*v.t.* **1** to test the quality of (something) by taking a little into the mouth; try the flavor of: *The cook tastes everything to see that it is right.* **2** to get the flavor of by the sense of taste: *I taste almond in this cake. When I have a cold I can taste nothing.* **3** *Figurative.* to experience slightly; have or feel; sample: *Having tasted freedom, the bird would not return to its cage.* **4** to eat or drink a little bit of: *The children barely tasted their breakfast the day they went to the circus.* **5** to eat. **6** to perceive by any sense, especially smell. **7** *Archaic.* **a** to enjoy or like; relish. **b** to appreciate. **8** *Obsolete.* to put to the proof; try out; test. **9** *Obsolete.* to touch: **a** to feel; handle. **b** to come into contact with; strike.
—*v.i.* **1** to have or use the sense of taste; tell or distinguish flavors. **2** to have a certain flavor: *The butter tastes rancid.* **3** to test flavors, as of wines; act as taster.
**a bad** (or **nasty**) **taste in the mouth**, an unpleasant feeling or memory left by a distasteful experience; bad aftertaste: *They [Balzac's novels] leave such a bad taste in my mouth* (Charlotte Brontë).
**taste of, a** to have the flavor of; smack or savor of: *The soup tastes of onion.* **b** *Figurative.* to experience; feel; encounter; perceive: *to taste of fame.* **c** to eat or drink a little of: *I crave ... that we may taste of your wine* (Shakespeare). **d** *Figurative.* to suggest; smack of: *a sharp word that tastes of envy.*
**to one's taste**, in harmony with one's preferences; to one's liking; pleasing: *The other girl is more amusing, more to my taste* (Edward G. Bulwer-Lytton).
[Middle English *tasten* to examine by touch, feel < Old French *taster* to feel; taste, probably < Vulgar Latin *tastāre* < *taxitāre* (frequentative) < Latin *taxāre* evaluate. Compare etym. under **tax**, verb, **task**.]
—*Syn. n.* **1 Taste, flavor** mean the quality of a thing that affects the sense organs of the mouth. **Taste** is the general word: *Mineral oil has no taste.* **Flavor** means a characteristic taste, especially of a pleasant kind: *The flavor I like best is chocolate.*
► **Taste of** is used in certain dialects for *taste* (verb def. 1). Dialect: *He tasted of the lamb stew and made a face.* General: *He tasted the lamb stew and made a face.*

**taste bud**, one of the groups of cells, chiefly in the lining of the tongue or mouth, that are organs of taste: *In the tongue, taste buds located in different regions conduct specific taste sensations* (Martin E. Spencer).

**taste|ful** (tāst′fəl), *adj.* **1** having good taste. **SYN**: refined. **2** showing or done in good taste: *The room had tasteful furnishings of rugs, curtains, and furniture in soft colors that went well together.* **SYN**: tasty, pleasing. —**taste′ful|ly**, *adv.* —**taste′ful|ness**, *n.*

**taste|less** (tāst′lis), *adj.* **1** without taste; flavorless; insipid: *Hot food is tasteless and unpleasant when it is allowed to get cold.* **SYN**: flat, vapid. **2** *Figurative.* uninspiring; dull. **3** having poor taste. **4** showing or done in poor taste. **5** without the sense of taste; unable to taste. —**taste′less|ly**, *adv.* —**taste′less|ness**, *n.*

**taste|mak|er** (tāst′mā′kər), *n.* a person or thing that sets a style or acts as an indicator to mold popular opinion: *For they are the tastemakers and opinion formers—the one per cent of the population, roughly, who are imitated by the others* (Harper's).

**tast|er** (tās′tər), *n.* **1** any person who tastes, especially one whose work is judging the quality of wine, tea, coffee, cheese, or other foods or drinks, by the taste. **2** (formerly) a person who tasted food to safeguard his master against poison. **3** a shallow cup, usually metal, to taste wine in. **4** a utensil like a corer for sampling food, especially cheese. **5** a small sample, especially of food; taste. **6** *British Informal.* a portion of ice cream served in a shallow glass.

**taste-test** (tāst′test′), *v.t.* to test the quality of by tasting: *The commission taste-tested six samples of orange juice concentrate made from freeze damaged fruit last year* (Wall Street Journal).

**tast|ing** (tās′ting), *n.* **1** the action of a person or thing that tastes. **2** a small portion taken to try the taste; sampling.

**tast|y** (tās′tē), *adj.,* **tast|i|er, tast|i|est.** **1** tasting good; pleasing to the taste; delicious; piquant; appetizing: *a tasty morsel. The meal was very tasty.* **SYN**: palatable, savory. **2** *Informal.* having or showing good taste; tasteful; elegant: *tasty furnishings.* **3** *Informal, Figurative.* pleasant; agreeable; attractive: *a tasty personality.* —**tast′i|ly**, *adv.* —**tast′i|ness**, *n.*

**tat[1]** (tat), *v.t., v.i.,* **tat|ted, tat|ting.** to make a kind of lace by looping and knotting (threads) with a hand shuttle. [probably back formation < *tatting*]

**tat[2]** (tat), *n. British Slang.* **1** ragged things, especially shabby furnishings. **2** a rag. [perhaps < *tatter*[1]]

**tat[3]** (tat), *n.* **1** very thick hemp canvas used especially for mats, sacking, and screens. **2** a strip of it about 10 inches wide, for sewing into mats or screens. **3** such a mat. Also, **tatty, taut.** [< Hindi *ṭāṭ*]

**tat[4]** (tat), *n.* a native pony of India; tattoo. Also, **tatt.** [see etym. under **tattoo**[3]]

**TAT** (no periods), thematic apperception test.

**ta-ta** (tä′tä′), *interj.* = good-by.

**ta|ta|mi** (tä tä′mē), *n., pl.* **-mi** or **-mis.** a mat made of rice straw, used as a floor covering in a Japanese house: *In Japan they describe the size of a room as a twelve tatami room or a twenty-four tatami room according to the number of tatami it takes to cover the floor* (Atlantic). [< Japanese *tatami*]

**Ta|tar** (tä′tər), *n., adj.* = Tartar.

**Ta|tar|i|an** (tä tãr′ē ən), *adj.* = Tartarian.

**ta|ter** (tā′tər), *n. Dialect.* a potato.

**ta|tou** (tä tü′), *n.* a large armadillo of South America. Also, **tatu.** [ultimately < Tupi (Brazil) *tatu, tatuaí*]

**tatt** (tat), *n.* = tat[4].

**tat|ter[1]** (tat′ər), *n., v.* —*n.* **1** a torn or ragged piece dangling from any cloth or garment; rag: *After the storm the flag hung in tatters upon the mast.* **2** a piece of cloth, paper, or other material torn off; shred; scrap.
—*v.t.* to tear or wear to pieces; make ragged; fray.
—*v.i.* to be or become tattered.
**tatters, a** torn or ragged clothing: ... *a suit of rags and tatters on my back* (Samuel Rowlands). **b** *Figurative.* useless fragments of anything; pieces; bits: *After the explosion only tatters of the old barn were left.*
[ultimately < Scandinavian (compare Old Icelandic *tötturr* rag)]

**tat|ter[2]** (tat′ər), *n.* a person who tats.

**tat|ter[3]** (tat′ər), *n. Especially British Slang.* a rag-

**Pronunciation Key:** hat, āge, cãre, fär; let, ēqual, tėrm; it, īce; hot, ōpen, ôrder; oil, out; cup, pu̇t, rüle; child; long; thin; ŦHen; zh, measure; ə represents **a** in about, **e** in taken, **i** in pencil, **o** in lemon, **u** in circus.

and-bone man; junkman.

**tat|ter|de|mal|ion** (tat′ər di māl′yən, -mal′-; -ē-ən), *n., adj.* — ***n.*** a person in ragged clothes; ragamuffin.
— ***adj.*** tattered; ragged.

**tat|tered** (tat′ərd), *adj.* **1** full of tatters; torn; ragged: *a tattered dress.* **2** wearing torn or ragged clothes: *This is the man, all tattered and torn* (Nursery Rhyme).

**tat|ter|er** (tat′ər ər), *n. Especially British Slang.* a tatter[3].

**tat|ters** (tat′ərz), *n. pl.* See under **tatter[1]**.

**Tat|ter|sall** or **tat|ter|sall** (tat′ər sôl), *n., adj.* — ***n.*** a woven pattern of thin lines of bright or dark colors forming checks on a white or light background.
— ***adj.*** of such a pattern: *a Tattersall vest.*
[< *Tattersall's,* a sporting establishment and horse auction market in London, opened by Richard *Tattersall,* 1724-1795]

**tat|ter|y** (tat′ər ē), *adj.* = tattered.

**tat|tie** (tat′ē), *n. Scottish Dialect.* a potato.

**tat|ti|ly** (tat′ə lē), *adv. Especially British.* in a tatty manner; shabbily.

**tat|ti|ness** (tat′ē nis), *n. Especially British.* the quality or condition of being tatty; shabbiness.

***tat|ting** (tat′ing), *n.* **1** the process or work of making a kind of lace by looping and knotting strong cotton or linen thread with a hand shuttle. **2** lace made in this way. [perhaps < Scottish *tat* to tangle, *tatty* tangled + *-ing[1]*]

***tatting** definition 2

**tat|tle** (tat′əl), *v.,* **-tled, -tling,** *n.* — ***v.i.*** **1** to tell tales or secrets; blab: *Though his brother used to tease him, the little boy never tattled.* **2** to talk idly or foolishly; chatter; gossip: *The two old ladies tattled for hours about neighbors.*
— ***v.t.*** **1** to reveal by tattling; blurt out. **2** to say idly or foolishly.
— ***n.*** **1** idle or foolish talk; gossip: *the tattle of the day.* **2** the act of telling tales or secrets.
[earlier, stammer, prattle. Compare Middle Dutch *tatelen* to stutter; perhaps imitative.]

**tat|tler** (tat′lər), *n.* **1** = telltale (def. 1). **2** any one of a group of shore birds resembling sandpipers, with a noisy cry.

**tat|tle|tale** (tat′əl tāl′), *n., adj. Informal.* — ***n.*** a telltale.
— ***adj.*** revealing faults; telltale: *tattletale stains.*
[American English < *tattle;* patterned on *telltale*]

**tat|too[1]** (ta tü′), *n., pl.* **-toos,** *v.,* **-tooed, -too|ing.** — ***n.*** **1a** a signal on a bugle or drum calling soldiers or sailors to their quarters at night. **b** a drumbeat raising an alarm. **2** a series of raps, taps, or thumps: *The hail beat a loud tattoo on the windowpane.* **3** *Especially British.* a military display, especially music and parading by show units, usually outdoors in the evening and floodlit.
— ***v.i., v.t.*** to tap continuously; drum: *Don't tattoo with your fingers. He tattooed the table impatiently.*
[variant of *tap-too* < Dutch *taptoe* < *tap* tap of a barrel + *toe* pull to, shut]

**tat|too[2]** (ta tü′), *v.,* **-tooed, -too|ing,** *n., pl.* **-toos.** — ***v.t.*** **1** to mark (the skin) with designs or patterns by pricking a line of holes and putting in colors. **2** to put (such a design) on the skin in this way: *The sailor had a ship tattooed on his arm.*
— ***n.*** **1** a picture, design, or motto tattooed on the skin. **2** the act or practice of tattooing the skin.
[< Polynesian (Marquesan) *tatu*] — **tat|too′er,** *n.*

**tat|too[3]** (tat′ü), *n., pl.* **-toos.** = tat[4]. [< Hindi *ṭaṭṭū*]

**tat|too|ing** (ta tü′ing), *n.* **1** the practice or art of marking the skin with tattoos. **2** the marks or pattern so produced.

**tat|too|ist** (ta tü′ist), *n.* a tattooer.

**tat|ty[1]** (tat′ē), *adj.,* **-ti|er, -ti|est.** **1** *Especially British.* ragged or shabby: *The jobber scribbles something in a tatty notebook* (Manchester Guardian Weekly). **2** *Scottish.* (of hair, an animal, or its coat) tangled; matted; shaggy.

**Pronunciation Key:** hat, āge, cãre, fär; let, ēqual, tėrm; it, īce; hot, ōpen, ôrder; oil, out; cup, pu̇t, rüle; child; long; thin; ᴛʜen; zh, measure; ə represents **a** in about, **e** in taken, **i** in pencil, **o** in lemon, **u** in circus.

**tat|ty[2]** (tat′ē), *n., pl.* **-ties.** **1** a wet grass mat hung up to freshen the room. **2** = tat[3]. [< Hindi *ṭaṭṭī*]

**ta|tu** (tä tü′), *n.* = tatou.

***tau** (tô, tou), *n.* **1a** the 19th letter of the Greek alphabet, corresponding to English *T, t.* **b** tav, the last letter of the Hebrew alphabet. **2** a T-shaped cross, used especially as a sacred symbol, and in heraldry; Saint Anthony's cross. **3** (as a numeral) 300. **4** the last letter, as in Hebrew; Z.

| T | τ |
|---|---|
| capital letter | lower-case letter |

***tau** definition 1

**tau cross,** = Saint Anthony's cross.

**taught** (tôt), *v., n.* — ***v.*** the past tense and past participle of **teach**: *That teacher taught my mother. She has taught arithmetic for years.*
— ***n.*** a person who has been taught: *the teacher and the taught.*

**taun|gya** (tông′gyə), *n.* a Burmese system of cultivation, consisting of clearing a part of the jungle by burning, cultivating a year or two, then leaving it to the jungle again. Also, **toungya.** [< Burmese *taungya* < *taung* hill + *ya* garden]

**taunt[1]** (tônt, tänt), *v., n.* — ***v.t.*** **1** to jeer at; mock; reproach; ridicule: *Some mean girls taunted her because she was poor.* **SYN:** deride, gibe, flout. **2** to get or drive by taunts; provoke: *They taunted him into taking the dare.*
— ***v.i.*** to make mocking or insulting remarks; jeer.
— ***n.*** **1** a bitter or insulting remark; sarcasm; mocking; jeering. **2** an object of taunts: *So it shall be a reproach and a taunt … unto the nations* (Ezekiel 5:15). **3** *Obsolete.* a quip.
[compare French *tant pour tant* tit for tat < Latin *tantus prō tantus* so much for that] — **taunt′er,** *n.* — **taunt′ing|ly,** *adv.*

**taunt[2]** (tônt, tänt), *adj. Nautical.* unusually high or tall, as a mast. [apparently for *a-taunt* all sails set, perhaps < Middle French *autant* as much < Old French *al* again + *tant* so much < Latin *tantus*]

**taupe** (tōp), *n., adj.* — ***n.*** a dark, brownish gray; gray like a moleskin, often with yellow flecks.
— ***adj.*** of this color.
[< French *taupe* mole < Latin *talpa*]

**tau|pie** (tô′pē), *n. Scottish.* tawpie.

**Tau|ri** (tôr′ī), *n.* genitive of **Taurus.**

**tau|ri|form** (tôr′ə fôrm), *adj.* **1** having the form of a bull. **2** shaped like the horns of a bull.

**tau|rin** (tôr′in), *n.* = taurine[2].

**tau|rine[1]** (tôr′in, -īn), *adj.* **1** of or having to do with a bull; bovine. **2** like a bull. **3** of or having to do with the zodiacal sign Taurus. [< Latin *taurīnus* of a bull < *taurus* bull]

**tau|rine[2]** (tôr′ēn, -īn, -in), *n.* a neutral, crystallizable substance, found in the fluids of many animals' muscles, lungs, and other organs, also resulting from the hydrolysis of taurocholic acid. *Formula:* $C_2H_7NO_3S$

**tau|ro|cho|lic acid** (tôr′ə kō′lik, -kol′ik), a crystalline acid, present as a sodium salt in the bile of man, oxen, and most other animals, and hydrolyzing into taurine and cholic acid. *Formula:* $C_{26}H_{45}NSO_7$

**tau|ro|dont** (tôr′ə dont), *adj.* (of teeth) having the roots or ridges fused. [< Latin *taurus* bull + Greek *odoús, odóntos* tooth]

**tau|ro|ma|chi|an** (tôr′ə mā′kē ən), *adj.* of or having to do with tauromachy.

**tau|rom|a|chy** (tô rom′ə kē), *n., pl.* **-chies.** **1** = bullfighting. **2** = bullfight. [< Greek *tauromachiā* < *taûros* bull + *máchesthai* to fight]

**Tau|rus** (tôr′əs), *n., genitive* (def. 1) **Tau|ri.** **1** a northern constellation that was thought of as arranged in the shape of a bull; the Bull. It is between Aries and Gemini. **2** the second sign of the zodiac, which the sun enters about April 20; the Bull. **3** a person born under this sign. [< Latin *Taurus* bull, adaptation of Greek *Taûros* (literally) bull]

**taut[1]** (tôt), *adj.* **1** pulled tight; tense: *a taut rope.* **SYN:** See syn. under **tight.** **2** in neat condition; tidy; orderly: *The captain insists on a taut ship.* **3** *Figurative.* strict. [earlier *taught,* Middle English *toght*] — **taut′ly,** *adv.* — **taut′ness,** *n.*

**taut[2]** (tat), *n.* tat, a strip of heavy canvas.

**taut|en** (tô′tən), *v.t.* to make taut; tighten.
— ***v.i.*** to become taut.

**tauto-,** *combining form.* the same; identical: *Tautology = repetition of the same word or idea.* [< Greek *tautó* < *tò autó* the same]

**taut|o|chrone** (tô′tə krōn), *n. Mathematics.* the curve joining all points from which gravity takes the same length of time to draw a particle to some fixed point; cycloid. [< *tauto-* + Greek *chrónos* time]

**tau|tog** (tô tog′, -tôg′), *n.* a dark-colored food fish, a variety of wrasse, common on the Atlantic coast of the United States; blackfish. [American English < Algonkian (Narragansett) *tautauog* sheepsheads, apparently related to *taut* or *tautau* fish]

**tau|to|log|i|cal** (tô′tə loj′ə kəl), *adj.* **1** having to do with tautology. **2** characterized by or using tautology. — **tau′to|log′i|cal|ly,** *adv.*

**tau|tol|o|gise** (tô tol′ə jīz), *v.i.,* **-gised, -gis|ing.** *Especially British.* tautologize.

**tau|tol|o|gism** (tô tol′ə jiz əm), *n.* **1** useless repetition. **2** something so repeated.

**tau|tol|o|gist** (tô tol′ə jist), *n.* a person who uses repetition or tautology.

**tau|tol|o|gize** (tô tol′ə jīz), *v.i.,* **-gized, -giz|ing.** to use tautology.

**tau|tol|o|gous** (tô tol′ə gəs), *adj.* characterized by or using tautology; tautological; redundant: *Thus mathematical statements are tautologous: they assert nothing more than what is asserted in a statement of the type "All spinsters are unmarried"* (Saturday Review). — **tau|tol′o|gous|ly,** *adv.*

**tau|tol|o|gy** (tô tol′ə jē), *n., pl.* **-gies.** **1** a saying a thing over again in other words without adding clearness or force; useless repetition. *Example:* the *modern* college student of *today.* **SYN:** redundancy. **2** *Logic.* a statement, classification, or accounting that overlooks and excludes no possibility. *Example:* She is either married or not. **3** the stating or believing of a fact to be its own reason; confusion of cause and effect. *Examples:* It's wet because it has water on it. I know because I know. [< Late Latin *tautologia* < Greek *tautologiā* < *tautologeîn* repeat (what has been said) < *tautó* same + *lógos* saying < *légein* speak]

**tau|to|mer** (tô′tə mər), *n.* one of the isomeric forms exhibited in tautomerism.

**tau|to|mer|ic** (tô′tə mer′ik), *adj.* **1** of or having to do with tautomerism. **2** exhibiting tautomerism.

**tau|tom|er|ism** (tô tom′ə riz′əm), *n. Chemistry.* the existence of certain organic compounds in equilibrium in two or more structures (isomers or tautomers) that differ in the placement of a hydrogen atom and its double bond, able to react in either structure. [< German *Tautomerie* (< Greek *tautó* the same + *méros* a share + German *-ie* < Greek *-íā* act of) + *-ism*]

**tau|tom|er|i|za|tion** (tô tom′ər ə zā′shən), *n.* an acquiring of tautomerism.

**tau|tom|er|y** (tô tom′ər ē), *n.* = tautomerism.

**tau|to|nym** (tô′tə nim), *n. Biology.* a scientific name with the genus and species names alike, now professionally forbidden in botany, though often found in zoology. *Example: Cygnus cygnus,* the whooper swan. [< Greek *tautṓnymos* the same name]

**tau|to|nym|ic** (tô′tə nim′ik), *adj. Biology.* (of a scientific name) having the genus and species names alike.

**tau|ton|y|mous** (tô ton′ə məs), *adj.* = tautonymic.

**tau|ton|y|my** (tô ton′ə mē), *n. Biology.* **1** the use of tautonyms. **2** a list of tautonyms.

**tau|toph|o|ny** (tô tof′ə nē), *n., pl.* **-nies.** repetition of the same sound, especially a vowel. [< Medieval Greek *tautophonia* < Greek *tautó* the same + *phōnḗ* voice]

**tav** (tôf, täv), *n.* the twenty-second and last letter of the Hebrew alphabet. Also, **tau, taw.** [< Hebrew *tāw*]

**ta|va|rish** (tə vär′ish), *n.* = tovarish.

**tav|ern** (tav′ərn), *n.* **1** a place where alcoholic drinks are sold and drunk; bar; saloon. **2** a small local hotel or public house; inn. Hotels have taken the place of the old taverns. **SYN:** hostelry. [< Old French *taverne* < Latin *taberna* (originally) hut, shed]

**tav|er|na** (tav′ər nə), *n.* (in Greece) a small, plain restaurant: *In Greece, for instance, many residents will tell you that you can find the best Greek cooking in the basement taverna of the Athens Hilton* (Harper's). [< New Greek *tavérna*]

**tav|ern|er** (tav′ər nər), *n.* **1** *Archaic.* a tavernkeeper. **2** *Obsolete.* a drunkard. [< Anglo-French *taverner,* Old French *tavernier* tavernkeeper < *taverne,* see etym. under **tavern**]

**tav|ern|keep|er** (tav′ərn kē′pər), *n.* the proprietor of a tavern.

**taw[1]** (tô), *n., v.* — ***n.*** **1** a specially fine marble used for shooting, often streaked or variegated; glassy; monny. **SYN:** agate. **2** the game of marbles. **3** the line from which the players shoot their marbles. — ***v.i.*** to shoot a taw.
[origin uncertain] — **taw′er,** *n.*

**taw[2]** (tô), *v.t.* **1** to prepare (raw material) for further use; dress. **2** to tan (skins) by soaking in minerals rather than vegetable tanbark. **3** *Obsolete, Dialect.* to whip; flog; thrash. [Old English *tawian* make ready; harass, insult] — **taw′er,** *n.*

**taw[3]** (tôf, täv, tou), *n.* = tav.

**ta|wa** (tä′wə, tou′ə), *n.* **1** a tall New Zealand tree of the laurel family with damsonlike fruit. **2** its light, soft wood, used for making butter kegs. [< Maori *tawa*]

**ta|wai** (tä′wī), *n.* = tawhai.

**taw|dri|ly** (tô′drə lē), *adv.* in a tawdry manner.

**taw|dry** (tô′drē), *adj.*, **-dri|er, -dri|est,** *n., pl.* *-dries.* —*adj.* **1** showy and cheap; gaudy; flashy. **SYN:** garish. **2** dressed in gaudy and cheap clothes.
—*n.* tawdry clothes or ornaments.
[short for *tawdry lace,* alteration of *Saint Audrey's lace*] —**taw′dri|ness,** *n.*

**ta|whai** (tä′hwī), *n.* any one of several tall trees of New Zealand, usually called birches. [< Maori *tawhai*]

**ta|whi|ri** (tä hwē′rē, tä′-), *n.* a small New Zealand tree with fragrant, white blossoms and a tough wood. [< Maori *tawhiri*]

**taw|ie** (tô′ē), *adj. Scottish.* easy to deal with; manageable. [perhaps < *taw*[2]]

**ta|wi|ri** (tä wē′rē, tä′-), *n.* = tawhiri.

**taw|ney** (tô′nē), *adj. Obsolete.* tawny.

**taw|ny** (tô′nē), *adj.*, **-ni|er, -ni|est,** *n., pl.* **-nies.**
—*adj.* of a rich tan color; brownish-yellow: *A lion has a tawny coat.*
—*n.* a brownish yellow.
[Middle English *tauny* < Anglo-French *tauné,* Old French *tane,* past participle of *taner* to tan] —**taw′ni|ly,** *adv.* —**taw′ni|ness,** *n.*

**tawny bunting,** = snow bunting.

**tawny eagle,** a brownish-yellow eagle of Africa and India.

**tawny emperor,** a large, tawny nymphalid butterfly.

**tawny owl,** a tawny-colored owl of Europe, Asia, and northern Africa.

**tawny thrush,** = veery.

**taw|pie** or **taw|py** (tô′pē), *n. Scottish.* a foolish or thoughtless girl or woman. [compare Danish *taabe* simpleton, Norwegian *taap* half-witted person]

**taws** or **tawse** (tôz), *n. sing.* or (*especially Scottish*) *pl.* a leather strap divided into narrow strips, formerly much used to punish schoolboys. [apparently plural of *taw*[2]]

**tax** (taks), *n., v.* —*n.* **1** money paid by people for the support of the government and the cost of public works and services; money or sometimes goods collected from citizens by their rulers; assessment; levy: *Our parents pay taxes to the city, state, and federal government.* **SYN:** impost, duty, excise. **2** *Figurative.* any burden, duty, or demand that oppresses; strain: *Climbing stairs is a tax on a weak heart.* **3** *U.S. Informal.* the price for any article or service; charge. **4** work or goods required from people by the government. [< verb]
—*v.t.* **1** to require (a person) to pay a tax. People who own property are taxed in order to provide clean streets, good roads, protection against crime, and free education. **2** to put a tax on: *to tax cigarettes, to tax incomes.* **3** *Figurative.* to put a heavy burden on; make demands on; be hard on; strain: *The work taxed her strength. Reading in a poor light taxes the eyes.* **SYN:** task. **4** to criticize (a person); call to account; reprove; accuse; censure: *The teacher taxed him with having neglected his work.* **5** *Law.* to determine the amount of (costs, as of a lawsuit). **6** *U.S. Informal.* in New England: **a** to price (a thing at so much). **b** to charge (a price for a thing).
[< Old French *taxer,* learned borrowing from Medieval Latin *taxare* impose a tax; censure, take to task < Latin *taxāre* evaluate, estimate, assess, perhaps < *tangere* to touch. Compare etym. under **task, taste.**] —**tax′er,** *n.*

**tax|a** (tak′sə), *n.* plural of **taxon.**

**tax|a|bil|i|ty** (tak′sə bil′ə tē), *n.* the quality or condition of being taxable.

**tax|a|ble** (tak′sə bəl), *adj.* liable to be taxed; subject to taxation: *Churches are not taxable. The basic definition of taxable income [is]gross income less deductions* (Wall Street Journal). **SYN:** assessable. —**tax′a|ble|ness,** *n.* —**tax′a|bly,** *adv.*

**tax|a|ceous** (tak sā′shəs), *adj.* belonging to the same family of trees and shrubs as the yew. [< New Latin *Taxaceae* the family name < Latin *taxus* yew tree]

**tax|a|tion** (tak sā′shən), *n.* **1** the act or system of taxing: *Taxation is necessary to provide roads, schools, and police.* **2** the amount people pay for the support of the government; money raised by taxes; tax revenue; taxes. **3** the fact of a taxpayer or commodity being taxed. **4** a tax on anything.

**tax bond,** *U.S.* a state bond that may be surrendered in place of taxes.

**tax book** or **roll,** a list of property subject to taxation and the amount of the taxes.

**tax certificate,** *U.S.* a provisional deed given to the buyer at a tax sale by the authorized official.

**tax collector,** a government official who collects taxes.

**tax cut,** a reduction in the rate of a tax: *In times of depression the government may give a tax cut.*

**tax-de|duc|ti|ble** (taks′di duk′tə bəl), *adj.* that is allowed as a deduction in figuring income tax.

**tax deed,** *U.S.* the permanent deed delivered to a purchaser of land at a tax sale.

**tax-dodg|er** (taks′doj′ər), *n.* a person who avoids paying taxes.

**tax-dodg|ing** (taks′doj′ing), *adj., n.* —*adj.* avoiding paying taxes.
—*n.* the act or practice of avoiding paying taxes.

**tax|eme** (tak′sēm), *n. Linguistics.* any device in a language that affects or alters grammatical relationship, such as a change of ending (play*ed* — play*ing*), difference in word order (Is he?— He is.), choice of auxiliary verbs (Could be!— Must be!), or change of internal vowel (m*a*n— m*e*n). [< Greek *táxis* arrangement + English *-eme*]

**tax evader,** = tax-dodger.

**tax evasion,** = tax-dodging.

**tax-ex|empt** (taks′ig zempt′), *adj., n.* —*adj.* free from taxes; not taxed; not taxable.
—*n.* a tax-exempt security.

**tax farmer,** (formerly) a person who bought from his government the privilege of being tax collector in a certain region.

**tax-free** (taks′frē′), *adj.* not taxable; tax-exempt.

**tax gallon,** a standard United States gallon of 231 cubic inches capacity which contains 50 per cent by volume of ethyl alcohol.

**tax gatherer,** *Archaic.* a tax collector.

**tax haven,** *U.S.* a foreign country in which a person or company buys property or establishes a subsidiary because of the country's low or nonexistent taxes.

**tax|i** (tak′sē), *n., pl.* **tax|is** or **tax|ies,** *v.,* **tax|ied, tax|i|ing** or **tax|y|ing.** —*n.* = taxicab.
—*v.i.* **1** to ride in a taxicab; go by taxi. **2** (of an aircraft or flier) to move slowly on the ground or water before gathering speed to take off or after landing: *The airplane taxied off the field.*
—*v.t.* **1** to make (an airplane) move this way. **2** to take in a taxicab. [short for *taxicab*]

**tax|i|cab** (tak′sē kab′), *n.* an automobile for hire, usually with a meter for recording the fare. [short for *taximeter cab*]

**taxi dancer,** a dance partner paid by the dance, usually a woman.

**tax|i|der|mal** (tak′sə dėr′məl), *adj.* of or having to do with taxidermy.

**tax|i|der|mic** (tak′sə dėr′mik), *adj.* = taxidermal.

**tax|i|der|mist** (tak′sə dėr′mist), *n.* an expert in taxidermy.

**tax|i|der|my** (tak′sə dėr′mē), *n.* the art of preparing the skin of animals and stuffing and mounting them so that they look alive. [< Greek *táxis* taxis + *-dermiā* < *dérma, -atos* skin]

**tax|i|man** (tak′sē man′), *n., pl.* **-men.** a taxicab driver; cabman.

**tax|i|me|ter** (tak′sē mē′tər, tak sim′ə-), *n.* **1** a meter in a taxicab for indicating the fare at any moment. **2** a taxi with this. [< French *taximètre* < *taxe* fare, tariff + *-mètre* -meter]

**tax|in** (tak′sin), *n.* = taxine.

**tax|ine** (tak′sēn, -sin), *n.* a light-yellow, resinous, alkaloid poison obtained from the needles and seed of the English yew. *Formula:* $C_{37}H_{51}NO_{10}$ [< New Latin *Taxus* the yew genus]

**tax|ing** (tak′sing), *adj.* trying; burdensome; difficult: *The taxing central role . . . involves delivering practically nonstop monologues* (New Yorker). —**tax′ing|ly,** *adv.*

**taxing district,** a subdivision, as of a town or county, for assessment.

**taxing master,** *Especially British.* an officer in a law court who taxes.

**taxi pattern,** the route that an airplane follows to reach a take-off point or parking area.

**tax|i|plane** (tak′sē plān′), *n.* an airplane for hire or charter for short trips.

**tax|is** (tak′sis), *n.* **1** *Biology.* movement in a particular direction by a free organism or a cell, such as a zoospore, in reaction to an external stimulus, such as light. *Taxis* is a change of place, whereas *tropism* is a turning toward a different direction. **2** *Medicine.* the use of a manipulation rather than surgery to replace a dislodged part, reduce a hernia, or correct some malfunction. **3** = taxonomy. **4** any one of various sections or units of ancient Greek troops. [< New Latin *taxis* < Greek *táxis* < *tássein* arrange. Compare etym. under **tactic.**]

**taxi squad,** *U.S. Football Slang.* a group of players on a football team who participate in practice sessions but do not play in the games.

**taxi stand,** = cabstand.

**tax|ite** (tak′sīt), *n. Geology.* any lava consolidated from fragments from the same flow having different colors and textures.

**tax|it|ic** (tak sit′ik), *adj.* **1** of or having to do with taxite. **2** like taxite.

**tax|i|way** (tak′sē wā′), *n.* a path or surface area on an airfield for taxiing to or from the runway, ramp, or hanger.

**tax|less** (taks′lis), *adj.* = untaxed.

**tax lien,** *U.S.* lien of a state on taxable property.

**tax|man** (taks′man′), *n., pl.* **-men.** = tax collector.

**tax|o|di|um family** (tak sō′dē əm), a small group of mostly evergreen, gymnospermous trees with scalelike or needlelike leaves, sometimes included in the pine family. The family includes the cryptomeria, bald cypress, redwood, and big tree.

**tax|on** (tak′sən), *n., pl.* **tax|a.** a taxonomic division, such as a family or order: *Assignment to the taxon is not on the basis of a single property but on the aggregate of properties* (Scientific American). [back formation < *taxonomy*]

**tax|o|nom|ic** (tak′sə nom′ik), *adj.* of or having to do with taxonomy. —**tax′o|nom′i|cal|ly,** *adv.*

**tax|o|nom|i|cal** (tak′sə nom′ə kəl), *adj.* = taxonomic.

**tax|on|o|mist** (tak son′ə mist), *n.* an expert in taxonomy.

***tax|on|o|my** (tak son′ə mē), *n.* **1** classification, especially of plant and animal species. See picture below. **2** the branch of science dealing with classification; study of the general laws and principles of classification. **3** that branch of any subject which consists in or relates to classification. [< French *taxonomie* < Greek *táxis* arrangement (see etym. under **taxis**) + *-nomiā,* related to *némein* to distribute]

**tax-paid** (taks′pād′), *adj.* **1** paid for by taxes; supported or provided by tax revenues: *tax-paid public officials.* **2** on which taxes are paid: *It is estimated that Atlanta sells as much "moonshine" as it does tax-paid liquor* (Atlanta Journal).

**tax|pay|er** (taks′pā′ər), *n.* a person who pays a tax or is required by law to do so.

**tax|pay|ing** (taks′pā′ing), *n., adj.* —*n.* the payment of taxes: *Two groups of demonstrators assailed taxpaying* (New York Times).
—*adj.* paying taxes: *the taxpaying public.*

**tax rate,** the rate of taxation especially on income, land, or other holdings, or on purchases.

**tax revolt,** a public protest or uprising against excessive taxes, especially against rapidly increasing property taxes: *After California's decisive vote on Proposition 13 [calling for a rollback of property taxes], the entire country became aware of the tax revolt. The idea spread rapidly . . . and by Election Day (November 7) 1978, proposals to limit spending or taxes were on the ballot in about one-third of the states* (Edward Cowan).

**tax sale,** *U.S.* a government sale of property to collect the taxes that are overdue on it.

**tax shelter,** an investment, depletion allowance, or other means used by a person or company to reduce or avoid liability to income tax: *Other Administration proposals chip away at . . . such tax shelters as farm losses and certain trust income* (Time).

**tax-shel|tered** (taks′shel′tərd), *adj.* being or serving as a tax shelter.

**tax stamp,** a stamp put on a taxable article to show that the required tax has been paid.

**tax title,** *U.S.* the title conveyed by a tax deed.

***taxonomy**
definition 1

greyhound

**of an animal:**
kingdom: Animalia
phylum: Chordata
class: Mammalia
order: Carnivora
family: Canidae
genus: Canis
species: Canis familiaris

buttercup

**of a plant:**
kingdom: Plantae
phylum: Tracheophyta
class: Angiospermae
order: Ranales
family: Ranunculaceae
genus: Ranunculus
species: Ranunculus acris

**tax|us** (tak′səs), *n.* = yew (def. 1). [< Latin *taxus*]

**Ta|yg|e|ta** (tā ij′ə tə), *n. Greek Mythology.* one of Atlas's seven daughters who became the Pleiades.

**Tay|lor|ism** (tā′lə riz əm), *n.* a detailed system for organizing factory work to make it more efficient, especially by the use of time and motion study. [< Frederick W. *Taylor,* 1856-1915, an American engineer and efficiency expert, who developed it]

**Tay|lor's series** (tā′lərz), *Mathematics.* a power series for the expansion of a function $f(x)$ in a neighborhood of the reference point $(a)$, based on a theorem (**Taylor's theorem**) which describes approximating polynomials for the general function $f(x)$. [< Brook *Taylor,* 1685-1731, an English mathematician]

**tay|ra** (tī′rə), *n.* a small South American carnivorous mammal related to the weasel; tree otter. It is about two feet long, and has a long tail and black body. [< Tupi *taira*]

**Tay-Sachs disease** (tā′saks′), = amaurotic idiocy. [< Warren *Tay,* 1843-1927, an English ophthalmologist, and Bernard *Sachs,* 1858-1944, an American neurologist]

**ta|zi|a** (tə zē′ə), *n.* a model of the tombs of Husain and Hassan carried in the Muharram procession. [< Arabic *ta'zīyat* condolence]

**taz|za** (tät′sə; *Italian* tät′tsä), *n., pl.* **-zas,** *Italian* **-ze** (-tsā). a shallow, saucer-shaped ornamental bowl or vase, especially one on a pedestal. [< Italian *tazza* cup < Arabic *ṭassah* basin]

**t.b.,** 1 trial balance. 2 tubercle bacillus. 3 *Informal.* tuberculosis of the lungs.

**Tb** (no period), terbium (chemical element).

**TB** (no periods) or **T.B.,** *Informal.* tuberculosis of the lungs.

**T-band|age** (tē′ban′dij), *n.* a T-shaped bandage.

**T-bar** (tē′bär′), *n.* 1 a T-shaped ski lift. 2 a T-shaped girder.

**T-beam** (tē′bēm′), *n.* = T-bar.

**T-bone steak,** or **T-bone** (tē′bōn′), *n. U.S.* a steak containing a T-shaped bone, cut from the middle portion of a loin of beef. See picture under **beef.**

**tbs.** or **tbsp.,** tablespoon or tablespoons.

**tc.,** tierce or tierces (fencing stance).

**Tc** (no period), technetium (chemical element).

**TC** (no periods), teachers college.

**T cart,** an open, four-wheeled carriage with two seats, whose body resembles the letter T.

**T cell,** or **T-cell** (tē′sel′), *n.* a type of lymphocyte that attacks foreign bodies directly, destroying them chemically, derived from the thymus gland and distinguished from a B cell by its relatively smooth surface: *Since T cells do not secrete antibodies and B cells do, it seems plausible that T cells might cause B cells to produce antibodies* (Science News). [< *T*(hymus-derived) *cell*]

**Tchai|kov|ski|an** (chī kôf′skē ən), *adj.* of, having to do with, or characteristic of the Russian composer Peter Ilich Tchaikovsky, (1840-1893), his music, or his musical style.

**Tche|ka** (che′kə), *n.* = Cheka.

**tchick** (chik), *n., v.* —*n.* a sound produced by pressing the tongue against the palate and suddenly withdrawing it with suction or sucking out the air at one side, especially as used to start or quicken the pace of a horse.
—*v.i.* to make the sound of *tchick.* [imitative]

**tchr.,** teacher.

**TCP** (no periods), tricresyl phosphate.

**TD** (no periods), *Football.* touchdown.

**t-dis|tri|bu|tion** (tē′dis′trə byü′shən), *n.* = Student's distribution.

**TDY** (no periods), temporary duty.

**Te** (no period), tellurium (chemical element).

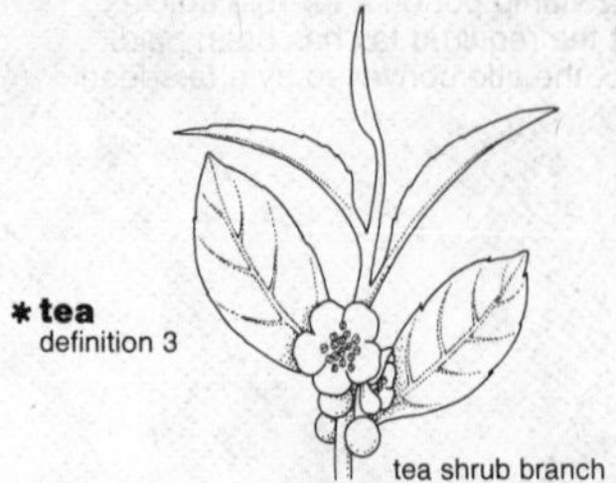

***tea** definition 3

***tea** (tē), *n.* 1 a common drink made by pouring boiling water over the dried and prepared leaves of a shrub grown chiefly in China, Japan, Ceylon (Sri Lanka), and India. Tea is slightly bitter, aromatic, and mildly stimulating. It is usually served with sugar and milk or lemon, either hot or iced. *Love and scandal are the best sweeteners of tea* (Henry Fielding). 2 the dried and prepared leaves from which this drink is made: *Mother buys tea at the grocery.* 3 the shrub these leaves grow on, bearing fragrant, white flowers and oval, evergreen, toothed leaves. 4 *British.* either of two late afternoon or early evening meals at which tea is served: **a** tea, bread and butter with jam, pastry, scones, crumpets, cake, and small sandwiches, but no meat or vegetables, at about 4 o'clock; afternoon tea. **b** supper, about 6:00, instead of afternoon tea and dinner; high tea. 5 a reception during which afternoon tea is served. 6 something to drink prepared from some other thing named: *sage tea, pepper tea, mint tea.* Beef tea is a strong broth made from beef. 7 the leaves, blossoms, or other parts of the plant, so used. 8 the plant they grow on. 9 *Slang.* marijuana.
**cup of tea.** See under **cup.**
[< Chinese (Amoy) *t'e*]

**tea bag,** tea leaves in a little bag of thin cloth or paper for easy removal from the cup or pot after use.

**tea ball,** *U.S.* 1 a perforated metal ball for tea leaves in brewing tea. 2 tea leaves in a little paper bag; tea bag.

**tea|ber|ry** (tē′ber′ē, -bər-), *n., pl.* **-ries.** 1 the spicy berry of the American wintergreen plant; checkerberry. 2 *U.S.* the plant, whose leaves are used to make tea.

**tea biscuit,** *British.* a shortbread or cooky, usually served with a cup of tea.

**tea|bowl** (tē′bōl′), *n.* a bowl from which tea is drunk: *an antique teabowl and saucer.*

**tea boy,** *Especially British.* a male servant.

**tea break,** *British.* the act or practice of stopping to have tea.

**tea caddy** or **canister,** a small can or tin-lined box for keeping tea fresh.

**tea cake** or **bread,** *British.* a kind of light bread or scone.

**tea|cart** (tē′kärt′), *n.* a small table on wheels, used in serving foods, as for tea; tea wagon; tea trolley.

**teach** (tēch), *v.,* **taught, teach|ing,** *n.* —*v.t.* 1 to help to learn; show how (to); make understand: *He is teaching his dog to shake hands.* SYN: train. 2 to give instruction to; instruct; inform: *He teaches his classes well. Teach me to ride.* 3 to give lessons in or instruction about (a subject): *She teaches music.* 4 (as a threat) to punish for (to). —*v.i.* to give lessons; act as teacher: *She teaches for a living.*
—*n. Slang.* teacher: *NBC will also begin a drama series ... with James Franciscus as the muscular teach* (Time).
[Old English *tǣcan* show, teach]
—*Syn. v.t.* 1, 2 **Teach, instruct** mean to convey knowledge or skill to someone. **Teach** implies giving individual guidance and training to the learner: *Some children learn to read by themselves, but most must be taught.* **Instruct** implies providing, in a systematic way, the necessary information or knowledge about a subject: *He instructs classes in chemistry.*
► See **learn** for usage note.

**teach|a|bil|i|ty** (tē′chə bil′ə tē), *n.* the fact or quality of being teachable.

**teach|a|ble** (tē′chə bəl), *adj.* capable of being taught: *Mr. Gatchell believes that anybody can train a teachable dog to learn the meaning of 2,000 words* (New Yorker). SYN: educable.
—**teach′a|ble|ness,** *n.*

**teach|a|bly** (tē′chə blē), *adv.* in a teachable manner; with docility.

**teach|er** (tē′chər), *n.* 1 a person who teaches, especially a person who teaches in a school; instructor: *The teacher trains individuals in developing skills, in doing things, in acquiring information* (Emory S. Bogardus). SYN: educator, pedagogue. 2 *Figurative:* *Experience is the best teacher.* —**teach′er|like′,** *adj.*

**teach|er|age** (tē′chər ij), *n.* a house provided as a residence for a schoolteacher, as in certain rural districts of the United States.

**teacher bird,** 1 the North American ovenbird. 2 = red-eyed vireo.

**teach|er|less** (tē′chər lis), *adj.* lacking a teacher or teachers: *teacherless classrooms.*

**teach|er|ly** (tē′chər lē), *adj.* of or like a teacher: *... the teacherly obsession to share all that they can learn* (Time).

**teachers college,** *U.S.* 1 a college or university for training teachers. 2 = normal school.

**teach|er|ship** (tē′chər ship), *n.* 1 the office or post of teacher. 2 an appointment as a teacher.

**tea chest,** *Especially British.* a box in which tea is shipped, often 2′ × 2′ × 2½′.

**teach-in** (tēch′in′), *n.* 1 a long meeting or session held by college or university teachers and students for the purpose of expressing dissenting or critical views on an important political or social issue: *Now shifting their targets to concern for the environment, students across the country are planning a massive ecological-environmental teach-in on university campuses* (Science News). 2 any forum or seminar patterned on the university teach-in: *A series of "teach-ins" on drug addiction are to be held soon, the National Association on Drug Addiction announced* (London Times).

**tea china,** a tea set of china.

**teach|ing** (tē′ching), *n.* 1 the work or profession of a teacher. 2 the act of a person who teaches. 3 what is taught: **a** instruction. **b** a precept or doctrine: *religious teachings.*

**teaching aid,** an audio-visual aid.

**teaching fellow,** a graduate student holding a fellowship that requires him to assume some teaching duties.

**teaching hospital,** a hospital connected with a medical school.

**teaching machine,** a device that gives information in a series of units, usually with a gradual increase in difficulty, and checks how well the information has been learned by a set of questions that the pupil must answer correctly before going on to new material.

**tea clam,** *U.S.* a very small clam.

**tea clipper,** a fast sailing ship carrying tea.

**tea cloth,** 1 *Especially British.* a small, ornamental tablecloth. 2 *British.* dishtowel.

**tea cooper,** *Especially British.* a docker who unloads tea and does necessary repairs to the packing.

**tea cozy** or **cosy,** a padded jacket to keep the teapot hot.

**tea|cup** (tē′kup′), *n.* 1 any cup for drinking tea. 2 = teacupful.

**tea|cup|ful** (tē′kup′fu̇l), *n., pl.* **-fuls.** as much as a teacup holds, usually four fluid ounces.

**tea dance,** an afternoon tea with dancing.

**tea drunkard,** a person who habitually drinks so much tea that it makes him ill.

**tea family,** a group of dicotyledonous, tropical and subtropical trees and shrubs, including the tea plant, camellia, loblolly bay, and Franklin tree.

**tea fight,** *British Slang.* noisy quarrel; tea party.

**tea garden,** *Especially British.* 1 an outdoor restaurant for tea and light refreshments, as in a park. 2 a tea plantation.

**tea gown,** a loose, long-sleeved, formal gown worn by women in the early part of the 1900's, resembling a modern housecoat, but more formal.

**tea-ho** (tē′hō′), *n. Australian.* a pause for tea during work, often of 10-20 minutes.

**tea|house** (tē′hous′), *n.* 1 a place where tea and other light refreshments are served. There are many teahouses in Japan and China. 2 (in Britain) any café. 3 *Especially British.* the offices of a firm that imports tea.

**teak** (tēk), *n.* 1 a hard, yellowish-brown, heavy, resinous wood of great strength and durability; teakwood. Teak is used in shipbuilding and in making fine furniture. 2 the large tree of the East Indies from which it comes. It belongs to the verbena family. 3 any one of various other trees producing strong or durable timber, such as a tropical African tree of the spurge family. [< Portuguese *teca* < Malayalam *tēkku*]

**tea|ket|tle** (tē′ket′əl), *n.* a kettle with a handle and spout for heating water.

**teak|wood** (tēk′wu̇d′), *n.* = teak (def. 1).

**teal** (tēl), *n., pl.* **teals** or (*collectively*) **teal.** a small, freshwater duck, such as the North American or European green-winged teal, and the North American blue-winged teal. Teals belong to the same genus as the mallard. [Middle English *tele*]

**tea-lead** (tē′led′), *n.* an alloy of lead with a little tin, used for lining tea chests.

**tea leaf,** any leaf of tea, especially after use.
**tea leaves,** such leaves used in telling fortunes.

**team** (tēm), *n., v., adj.* —*n.* 1 a number of people working or acting together, especially one of the sides in a game: *a football team, a debating team.* 2 two or more horses or other animals harnessed together to work. 3 one or more draft animals, their harness, and the vehicle they pull. 4 *British Dialect.* a brood or litter of animals. 5 *British Dialect.* any chain, as of sausage links. 6 *Obsolete.* a family line, either of descent or posterity; offspring, lineage, or descendants.
—*v.t.* 1 to join together in a team; combine; yoke. 2 to carry, haul, or otherwise work with a team. —*v.i.* 1 to join together in a team; combine: *Everybody teamed up to clean the room after the party.* 2 to drive a team; do teamster's work.
—*adj.* having to do with or performed by a team: *The Americans launched one of the most amazing team rallies on record* (New Yorker).
**a whole** (or **full**) **team,** *U.S.* a person who is very capable; expert or champion: [*He*] *was not only a whole team, but a team and a half* (James K. Paulding).
**in the team,** (of ships) in a line facing outward to watch an enemy: *Nothing can be more dull and monotonous than a blockading cruise in the team* (Frederick Marryat).
[Old English *tēam*]

**tea|mak|er** (tē′mā′kər), *n.* **1** a person who dries tea leaves and prepares the tea for commercial distribution. **2** a person or apparatus that makes or infuses tea.

**tea|man** (tē′man′), *n., pl.* **-men. 1** a merchant who deals in tea; tea dealer. **2** *British Slang.* a prisoner who is allowed one pint of tea every evening instead of gruel.

**team boat**, (formerly) a ferryboat with paddle wheels turned by horses.

**team|er** (tē′mər), *n.* = teamster (def. 1).

**team|less** (tēm′lis), *adj.* without a team.

**team|mate** (tēm′māt′), *n.* a fellow member of a team.

**team play**, joint action; cooperation.

**team spirit**, = esprit de corps.

**team|ster** (tēm′stər), *n.* **1** a person whose work is hauling things with a truck or driving a team of horses. **2** *U.S.* a member of the transportation workers' union.

**team teaching**, an educational program in which several teachers skilled in particular subjects alternately lecture, instruct, or otherwise meet with a group of students drawn from several regular classes.

**team|work** (tēm′wėrk′), *n.* **1** the acting together of a number of people to make the work of the group successful and effective: *Football requires teamwork even more than individual skill.* **SYN**: cooperation. **2** work done with horses. [American English < *team* + *work*]

**Te|an** (tē′ən), *adj.* = Teian.

**tea party**, **1** an afternoon party at which tea is drunk. **2** *Slang.* a noisy quarrel; brawl.

**tea pavilion**, *Cricket.* the pavilion, usually wooden, where players and spectators have tea halfway through the game.

**tea|plant|er** (tē′plan′tər, -plän′-), *n.* a person whose business is cultivating tea.

**tea|plant|ing** (tē′plan′ting, -plän′-), *n.* the occupation or business of cultivating tea.

**tea|pot** (tē′pot′), *n.* a container with a handle and a spout for making and serving tea.
**tempest in a teapot**. See under **tempest**.

**tea|pot|ful** (tē′pot′fu̇l), *n., pl.* **-fuls.** as much as a teapot contains.

**tea|poy** (tē′poi), *n.* a small, three-legged table for serving tea. [Anglo-Indian < Hindi *tīpāi* < *tīn-* (< *tir-* three-) + *pāya* foot]

**tear**[1] (tir), *n., v.* **—*n.* 1** a drop of salty water coming from the eye. Tears are secreted by the lacrimal glands to moisten the membrane covering the front of the eyeball and the lining of the eyelid. **2** something like or suggesting a tear, especially a pendant glass ornament or a kind of English candy. **3** a bead of liquid condensed on anything. **4** a small cavity or flaw, especially in glass. **5** a small, hardened drop of the fragrant gum or resin of frankincense or myrrh, used in making perfume or burned as incense.
**—*v.i.*** to shed tears; fill up with tears: *The smoke made his eyes tear.*
**dissolve in tears**, to shed many tears: *On hearing the news, she dissolved in tears.*
**in tears**, shedding tears or crying: *The baby is in tears because he is hungry. The people ... are all in tears and mourning* (John Daus).
[Old English *tēar*] **—tear′like′**, *adj.*

**tear**[2] (tãr), *v.,* **tore, torn, tear|ing,** *n.* **—*v.t.* 1** to pull apart by force; claw to pieces; rend; sunder: *to tear a box open. Don't tear up paper, but put it in the wastebasket. He tore the page in half.* **2** to make (a hole) by pulling apart: *She tore a hole in her dress.* **3** to make a hole or rent in by a pull; rip: *The nail tore her coat.* **4** to move by pulling hard or violently; wrench; wrest: *Tear out the page.* **5** to cut badly; wound: *The jagged stone tore his skin.* **SYN**: lacerate. **6** *Figurative.* to produce hostile, dissenting groups in; rend; divide; split: *The party was torn by two factions.* **7** *Figurative.* to plague, as with conflicts: *a person torn by doubts.* **8** *Figurative.* to make miserable; distress; harrow; distract: *His heart was torn by sorrow.*
**—*v.i.* 1** to be pulled apart; become torn: *Lace tears easily.* **2** to make jerking snatches; claw: *They ... kept tearin' at each other like a pack o' wolves* (W. E. Burton). **3** *Figurative.* to pull by force: *What, will you tear Impatient answers from my gentle tongue?* (Shakespeare). **4** *Informal, Figurative.* to move with great force or haste: *An automobile came tearing along the road. He would have nightmares, and ... get up and run screaming into the dining room, where he would tear around and around the table* (James T. Farrell).
**—*n.* 1** a torn place, especially in cloth; rent; hole: *She has a tear in her dress.* **2** the act of tearing. **3** the process of being torn. **4** *Informal, Figurative.* a hurry; rush. **5** *Slang, Figurative.* a spree. **6** *Figurative.* a fit of violent anger.
**be torn between**, to find it very hard to choose between (two opposite desires): *Agnes, torn between her interest in what was going on and her desire to get back to her mother, had at last hurriedly accepted this Mrs. Sherwood's offer* (Mrs. Humphry Ward).
**tear down, a** to pull down; raze; destroy: *The city tore down a whole block of apartment houses.* **b** *Figurative.* to bring about the wreck of; discredit; ruin: *She tried to tear down his reputation.*
**tear into, a** to set upon with great or destructive energy; attack violently: *Last summer's hurricanes killed 200 people ... as they tore into the coasts and back country* (New York Times). **b** *Figurative: A legion of critics stand ready to tear into him the moment they can prove him wrong* (Time).
**tear it**, *Especially British Slang.* to spoil one's chances; wreck one's hopes, plans, etc.: *"Good Lord, that's torn it," she panted. "I am ruined forever"* (Blackwood's Magazine).
**tear off**, *Informal.* to do or make quickly; toss off: *The reporter tore off a cable to the newspaper reporting the end of the strike.*
**tear oneself away** (or **from**), to leave with great reluctance; go very unwillingly: *He could not tear himself from that spot. They will watch the football [game] if they can bear to tear themselves away from delights elsewhere* (Manchester Guardian Weekly).
**tear up, a** to tear into ragged pieces; rip: *... engaged in tearing up old newspapers* (Thomas Hughes). **b** *Figurative.* to cancel by tearing; destroy: *to tear up a contract.*
[Old English *teran*] **—tear′a|ble,** *adj.* **—tear′a|bly,** *adv.*
**—*Syn.* *v.t.* 1 Tear, rip** mean to pull something apart by force. **Tear** means to pull apart or into pieces in such a way as to leave rough or ragged edges: *He tore the letter into tiny pieces.* **Rip** means to tear roughly or quickly, usually along a joining: *She ripped the hem in her skirt by catching her heel in it.*

**tear|a|way** (tãr′ə wā′), *n., adj.* **—*n.*** *British Informal.* a wild, uncontrollable person or animal.
**—*adj.*** impetuous; wild: *It is a very good budget. It avoids the danger of a tearaway boom* (Listener).

**tear bomb, shell,** or **grenade** (tir), a bomb, shell, or grenade filled with tear gas.

**tear bottle** (tir), a small bottle or phial, possibly used to hold the mourners' tears, found in an ancient tomb.

**tear-down** (tãr′doun′), *n.* the act or process of tearing down; destruction: *... a fast tear-down of all trade boundaries* (Maclean's).

**tear|drop** (tir′drop′), *n., adj.* **—*n.* 1** a tear. **2** something like or suggesting a tear: *crystal teardrops.* **3** an air bubble in glass, as in a tear glass.
**—*adj.*** of or like a teardrop.

**tear drop** (tir), = pig board.

**tear|duct** (tir′dukt′), *n.* any one of several ducts that carry tears from the lacrimal glands to the eyes or from the eyes to the nose.

**tear|er** (tãr′ər), *n.* **1** *U.S. Informal.* any violent person or thing, especially a storm. **2** = tearaway. **3** anyone who tears.

**tear-fall|ing** (tir′fô′ling), *adj. Archaic.* tearful.

**tear fault** (tãr), *Geology.* a big crevice left by a landslide.

**tear|ful** (tir′fəl), *adj.* **1** full of tears; weeping: *The tearful old man bid his son good-by.* **2** inclined to weep. **3** causing tears; very sad; pathetic: *Getting lost is a tearful experience for a young child.* **SYN**: mournful, melancholy. **—tear′ful|ly,** *adv.* **—tear′ful|ness,** *n.*

**tear gas** (tir), a gas that irritates the eyes and temporarily blinds them with tears. It is used in war and especially in dispersing rioters.

**tear-gas** (tir′gas′), *v.t.,* **-gassed, -gas|sing.** to attack with tear gas; force, subdue, or eject with tear gas.

**tear glass** (tir), a wineglass with a tear-shaped air bubble in the stem.

**tear|ing** (tãr′ing), *adj., adv.* **—*adj.* 1** that tears. **2** *Informal.* headstrong and boisterous; reckless. **3** *British Slang.* excellent; first-rate.
**—*adv.*** *British Slang.* extremely; very.

**tear-jerk|er** or **tear|jerk|er** (tir′jėr′kər), *n. Informal.* an overly sad or sentimental song, film, or story.

**tear-jerk|ing** (tir′jėr′king), *adj. Informal.* oversentimental.

**tear|less** (tir′lis), *adj.* **1** without tears; not crying. **2** dry, as the eyes. **3** *Figurative.* without emotion. **—tear′less|ly,** *adv.* **—tear′less|ness,** *n.*

**tear mask** (tir), a gas mask worn for protection against tear gas.

**tear-off** (tãr′ôf′, -of′), *adj.* that is removed by tearing, usually along a dotted, marked, or scored line; detachable: *a roll of tear-off plastic bags, a tear-off coupon.*

**tear|proof** (tãr′prüf′), *adj.* protected against tearing; resistant to tearing.

**tea|room** (tē′rüm′, -ru̇m′), *n.* a room or shop where tea, coffee, and light meals are served.

**tea rose**, any one of several varieties of cultivated rose, derived partly from the China rose, whose flowers have a delicate scent somewhat like that of tea.

**tear-shaped** (tir′shāpt′), *adj.* = pear-shaped.

**tear sheet** (tãr), *U.S.* a page torn out, as for filing, mounting, or marking.

**tear shell** (tir), a shell of tear gas.

**tear-stained** (tir′stānd′), *adj.* stained by tears.

**tear strip** (tãr), a scored strip of paper or tape, that is pulled or wound off to open a can, box top, or wrapper.

**tear-up** (tãr′up′), *n.* an uprooting.

**tear|y** (tir′ē), *adj.,* **tear|i|er, tear|i|est. 1** = tearful. **2** = salty.

**tea sage**, a species or variety of sage whose leaves are used for making sage tea.

**tea scrub**, *Australian.* a thicket of tea trees.

**tease** (tēz), *v.,* **teased, teas|ing,** *n.* **—*v.t.* 1** to vex or worry by jokes, questions, requests, or the like; annoy; plague: *The other boys teased him about his curly hair.* **2** to make a joke of without annoying; make affectionate, good-humored fun of; chaff: *teasing him about all the money he'd won.* **3** to separate the fibers of; comb out; shred or card (as wool or flax). **4** to backcomb (hair): *"We are all agreed that hair should be a medium length and only teased enough to be coaxed into place"* (Atlanta Constitution). **5** to raise nap on (cloth) by combing all the free fibers in one direction; teasel.
**—*v.i.*** to be annoying by making repeated requests; beg: *That child teases for everything he sees.*
**—*n.* 1** a person who teases, especially a nagging child: *Don't be a tease.* **2a** the act of teasing. **b** the condition of being teased.
[Old English *tǣsan* pluck, pull apart]
**—*Syn.* *v.t.* 1 Tease, plague, pester** mean to irritate by continous or persistent annoyance. **Tease** implies causing to lose patience and flare up in annoyance or anger, either by persistent begging or by unkind jokes or tricks: *Children teased the dog until he bit them.* **Plague** emphasizes that the irritation is severe: *The people were plagued with high taxes.* **Pester** emphasizes that the irritation is constantly repeated: *She is always pestering her mother for candy.*

***tea|sel** (tē′zəl), *n., v.,* **-seled, -sel|ing** or (*especially British*) **-selled, -sel|ling.** **—*n.* 1** any one of a genus of Eurasian and African herbs with prickly stems and flower heads, such as the fuller's teasel. **2** the dried flower head or burr of fuller's teasel, used for raising nap on cloth. **3** a brush with hooked prongs used for the same purpose.
**—*v.t.*** to raise a nap on (cloth) with teasels; dress with teasels. Also **teazel, teazle.**
[Old English *tǣsel,* apparently < *tǣsan* pluck, tease] **—tea′sel|er,** *especially British,* **tea′sel|ler,** *n.*

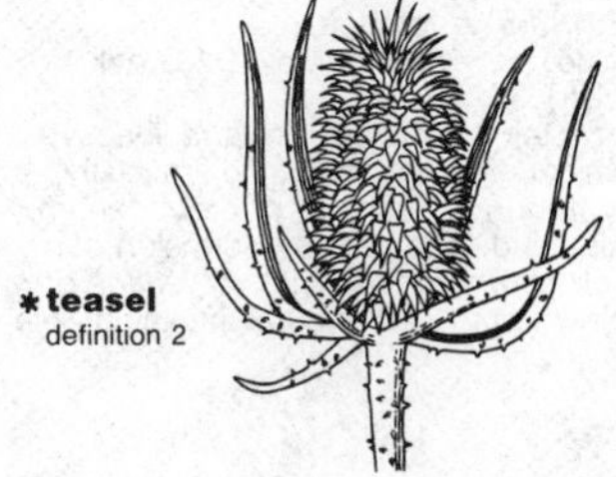

***teasel** definition 2

**teas|er** (tē′zər), *n.* **1** a person or thing that teases. **2** *Informal.* an annoying problem; puzzling task. **3** a short curtain hung from the top of the proscenium to mask overhead lights and to help frame the stage. **4** a person who regulates the furnace at a glassworks.

**tea service**, = tea set.

**tea set**, a set of china or silver, usually consisting of teapot, sugar bowl, creamer, teacups, and saucers, for use at tea.

**tea ship**, **1** a ship carrying tea. **2** a tea stand with two or more shelves.

**tea shop**, *Especially British.* a tearoom.

**teas|ing|ly** (tē′zing lē), *adv.* in a teasing way.

**tea|spoon** (tē′spün′, -spu̇n′), *n.* **1** a spoon, smaller than a tablespoon, commonly used to stir tea or coffee. It is larger in America than in Brit-

**Pronunciation Key:** hat, āge, cãre, fär; let, ēqual, tėrm; it, īce; hot, ōpen, ôrder; oil, out; cup, pu̇t, rüle; child; long; thin; ᴛʜen; zh, measure; ə represents **a** in about, **e** in taken, **i** in pencil, **o** in lemon, **u** in circus.

ain. **2** a spoon used as a unit of measure in cooking. It holds 1/3 as much as a tablespoon or 0.4928 centiliter. *Abbr:* t. **3** = teaspoonful.

**tea|spoon|ful** (tē′spün′fu̇l, -spu̇n′-), *n., pl.* **-fuls.** **1** a standard unit of liquid measure in cooking, equal to 1/3 tablespoonful or 1 1/3 fluid drams or 0.4928 centiliter. **2** as much as a teaspoon holds. *Abbr:* tsp.

**tea stick**, a stick cut from the Australian tea tree.

**tea stone**, a Chinese rose quartz resembling the cairngorm.

**teat** (tēt, tit), *n.* **1** the nipple of a female's breast or udder, from which the young suck milk. **2** a rubber or plastic nipple on a baby's feeding bottle. [< Old French *tete,* probably < a Germanic word (compare Old English *titt*)]

**tea|ta|ble** (tē′tā′bəl), *n., adj.* —*n.* **1** a table for tea. **2** the people who eat at it.
—*adj.* **1** of or having to do with the teatable. **2** frivolous; trivial: *teatable talk.*

**tea-tast|er** (tē′tās′tər), *n.* a person whose business is testing the quality of tea by tasting samples; a tea expert.

**tea-tast|ing** (tē′tās′ting), *n., adj.* —*n.* the occupation or business of a tea-taster.
—*adj.* of or having to do with tea-tasting.

**tea things**, *Especially British.* the teacups, teapot, and other parts of a tea set.

**tea time**, *Especially British.* the time in the afternoon at which tea is taken.

**tea|tow|el** (tē′tou′əl), *n.* = dishtowel.

**tea tray**, a tray on which tea is brought from the kitchen.

**tea tree**, **1** the shrub that yields tea. **2** any one of various trees or shrubs that belong to the myrtle family, having a heavy, durable wood, and leaves used as a substitute for tea. **3** an African shrub of the nightshade family, with violet flowers and spiny branches. **4** (in Great Britain) a flowering shrub related to the boxthorn, a native of China. **5** a native tree of Ceylon (Sri Lanka) and Coromandel with leaves like those of the tea shrub.

**tea trolley**, *Especially British.* a teacart.

**tea urn**, = samovar.

**tea wagon**, *Especially U.S.* a small table on wheels used in serving tea; teacart.

**tea|zel** (tē′zəl), *n., v.,* **-zeled, -zel|ing** or (*especially British*) **-zelled, -zel|ling.** = teasel. —**tea′zel|er,** *especially British,* **tea′zel|ler,** *n.*

**tea|zle** (tē′zəl), *n., v.,* **-zled, -zling.** = teasel. —**tea′zler,** *n.*

**te|bel|di** (tə bel′dē), *n.* = baobab.

**Te|bet** or **Te|beth** (tā vāth′, tā′ves), *n.* the fourth month of the Jewish civil year, or the tenth month of the ecclesiastical year, corresponding to December and sometimes part of January. [< Hebrew *ṭebeth* < Babylonian *ṭibitu*]

**tec** (tek), *n. British Slang.* a detective.

**tec|bir** (tek bir′), *n.* = tekbir.

**Tech** or **Tec** (tek), *n. Slang.* a technical institute: *Georgia Tech.*

**tech.**, **1a** technical. **b** technically. **2a** technological. **b** technologically. **c** technology.

**teched** (techt), *adj.* = tetched.

**tech|ne** (tek′nē), *n.* = technology. [< Greek *téchnē* art, skill]

***tech|ne|ti|um** (tek nē′shē əm), *n.* a radioactive metallic chemical element produced artificially, especially by fission of uranium or molybdenum. Technetium is used to inhibit the corrosion of iron. [< Greek *technētós* artificial (< *téchnē* an art, skill) + New Latin *-ium,* a suffix meaning "element"]

***technetium**

| symbol | atomic number | mass number | oxidation state |
|---|---|---|---|
| Tc | 43 | 97 | 4,6,7 |

**tech|ne|tron|ic** (tek′nə tron′ik), *adj.* having to do with or characterized by technological advances in electronics and communications: *Communications satellites ... mark the dawn of a technetronic era that will ultimately transform the Earth into a global village* (Saturday Review). [< Greek *téchnē* an art, skill + English (elec)*tronic*]

**tech|nic** (tek′nik), *n., adj.* —*n.* **1** any technique. **2** *Especially U.S.* a technical detail, point, term, etc.; technicality. **3** the science of technics.
—*adj.* = technical.
[< Latin *technicus* < Greek *technikós* of art < *téchnē* art, skill, craft]

**tech|ni|ca** (tek′nə kə), *n.pl.* technical details, methods, or skills; technics. [< Greek *techniká,* neuter plural of *technikós;* see etym. under **technic**]

**tech|ni|cal** (tek′nə kəl), *adj.* **1** of or having something to do with the special facts of a science or art: *"Electrolysis," "tarsus," and "protein" are technical words.* **2** of or having something to do with mechanical or industrial arts or with applied sciences; technological: *This technical school trains engineers, chemists, and architects.* **3** using technical terms; treating a subject technically: *a technical lecture.* **4** of or having to do with an art, science, discipline, or profession: *a word's technical sense.* **5** of or having to do with technique: *She has technical skill in singing, but her voice is weak.* **6** judged strictly by the rules, as of a certain science, art, or game; strictly interpreted. See also **technical knockout**. **7** (of a stock market, its prices, or trading) abnormally high or low because of heavy speculation. [< *technic* + *-al*[1]] —**tech′ni|cal|ness,** *n.*

**tech|ni|cal|ise** (tek′nə kə līz), *v.t.,* **-ised, -is|ing.** *Especially British.* technicalize.

**tech|ni|cal|ism** (tek′nə kə liz′əm), *n.* **1** technical style, method, or treatment. **2** overuse of technicalities.

**tech|ni|cal|ist** (tek′nə kə list), *n.* **1** an expert in technicalities. **2** a person addicted to technicalities.

**tech|ni|cal|i|ty** (tek′nə kal′ə tē), *n., pl.* **-ties.** **1** a technical matter, point, detail, term, or expression: *Books on engineering contain many technicalities which the ordinary reader does not understand.* **2** technical quality or character.

**tech|ni|cal|i|za|tion** (tek′nə kə lə zā′shən), *n.* **1** the act or process of technicalizing: *He said this cooperation was necessary as a balance against the growing "technicalization" of the Common Market* (London Times). **2** the state of being technicalized.

**tech|ni|cal|ize** (tek′nə kə līz), *v.t.,* **-ized, -iz|ing.** to make technical: *to technicalize one's language, technicalize a school.*

**technical knockout**, a knockout scored in a boxing match when the referee or physician decides that a fighter is too hurt or dazed to continue fighting, although he has not been knocked out.

**tech|ni|cal|ly** (tek′nə klē), *adv.* in a technical manner or respect; in technical terms; in a technical sense; in accordance with technical methods.

**technical officer**, *Especially British.* an industrial official engaged in investigation, research, and development work.

**technical sergeant**, a noncommissioned officer in the U.S. Air Force, ranking next above a staff sergeant and next below a master sergeant. *Abbr:* T.Sgt.

**tech|ni|cian** (tek nish′ən), *n.* **1** an expert in the details of a subject or skill, especially a mechanical one. **2** any artist, musician, or worker skilled in technique. **3** one of three former specialists' ratings (third, fourth, and fifth grades) in the United States Army, equivalent to staff sergeant, sergeant, and corporal respectively.

**Tech|ni|col|or** (tek′nə kul′ər), *n. Trademark.* a special process of making colored motion pictures by which three-color photographs are combined in one film. [American English < *techni*(cal) + *color*]

**tech|ni|col|or** (tek′nə kul′ər), *n., adj.* —*n.* bright, intense color: *The author has a fine visual imagination. She rolls it on in glorious technicolor* (Atlantic).
—*adj.* very colorful; vivid: *a technicolor sunset.* [< *Technicolor*]

**tech|nics** (tek′niks), *n.* **1** a study or science of the arts, especially the mechanical or industrial arts. **2** technic or technique.

**tech|ni|cum** or **tech|ni|kum** (tek′nə kəm), *n.* a secondary school in the Soviet Union that prepares students for jobs such as nursing. [< Russian *tekhnikum*]

**tech|nique** (tek nēk′), *n.* **1** the skill of a composing artist, such as a musician, painter, sculptor, or poet. **2** the method or way of performing the mechanical details of an art; technical skill: *The pianist's technique was excellent, though his interpretation of the music was poor.* **3** a special method or system used to accomplish something. [< French *technique* noun use of adjective < Greek *technikós;* see etym. under **technic**]

**techno-**, *combining form.* the arts and crafts, especially industrial arts; technics; technology: *Technocracy = government by technological principles.* [< Greek *téchnē* an art, method, system; skill]

**tech|noc|ra|cy** (tek nok′rə sē), *n., pl.* **-cies.** **1** governmental, social, and industrial management by technical experts: *The French Government is determined, however, to fight any attempt at uniting Europe under a "technocracy"* (New York Times). **2** the theory popular in the 1930's that such management would benefit everyone. **3** advocacy of this theory.

**tech|no|crat** (tek′nə krat), *n.* a supporter of technocracy: *In top positions there are too many technocrats—men of tremendous ability in their own sphere, but who lack the essential quality of being able to lead men* (London Times).

**tech|no|crat|ic** (tek′nə krat′ik), *adj.* of or having to do with technocracy or technocrats.

**tech|no|graph|ic** (tek′nə graf′ik), *adj.* of or having to do with technography.

**tech|nog|ra|phy** (tek nog′rə fē), *n. Anthropology.* the study of the geographical distribution of arts and crafts.

**technol.**, **1** technological. **2** technology.

**tech|no|lith|ic** (tek′nə lith′ik), *adj. Archaeology.* of or having to do with a group of stone implements made according to a particular design or pattern. [< *techno-* + Greek *líthos* stone + English *-ic*]

**tech|no|log|ic** (tek′nə loj′ik), *adj.* = technological.

**tech|no|log|i|cal** (tek′nə loj′ə kəl), *adj.* **1** of or having to do with technology. **2** used in technology. —**tech′no|log′i|cal|ly,** *adv.*

**technological gap**, the difference in technological advancement between two nations or groups of nations.

**technological unemployment**, unemployment caused by technical advances and inventions eliminating jobs or industries: *Automatic power looms in the textile industry and great improvements in making finished steel also contributed to technological unemployment in many countries* (Robert D. Patton).

**tech|nol|o|gist** (tek nol′ə jist), *n.* an expert in technology.

**tech|nol|o|gize** (tek nol′ə jīz), *v.t.,* **-gized, -giz|ing.** to make technological: *to technologize society or an industry.*

**tech|nol|o|gy** (tek nol′ə jē), *n., pl.* **-gies.** **1** the science of the mechanical and industrial arts; applied science: *He studied electronics at a school of technology.* **2** the body of tools, machines, materials, techniques, and processes used to produce goods and services and satisfy human needs: *Many people call the age we live in the age of technology. Science has contributed much to modern technology.* **3** a particular application of technology; any method, process, or system using special tools and techniques to achieve a goal: *medical technology, military technology, the technology of highway construction. To reach the ... conditions required for a net release of fusion power it is necessary to first develop many new technologies* (Scientific American). **4** technical words, terms, or expressions as used in an art or science; technical terminology or nomenclature. [< Greek *technologiā* < *téchnē* art, craft, or technique + *-logos* systematic treating of, -logy]

**technology assessment**, **1** the attempt to make advance assessments on the impact or effect of new technologies on society: *Technology assessment is a procedure designed to optimize the use of technology* (Scientific American). **2** a study or analysis of such a potential impact or effect: *The board would award contracts ... for specific technology assessments* (Science News).

**tech|no|pho|bi|a** (tek′nə fō′bē ə), *n.* fear of the adverse effect of technology on society or the environment.

**tech|nop|o|lis** (tek nop′ə lis), *n.* a society dominated by technology: *"Technopolis"—the society where our lives, thoughts and happiness are determined by the applications of a science and technology which often appears to be out of control ...* (New Scientist). [< *techno-* + Greek *pólis* city, polis]

**tech|no|pol|i|tan** (tek′nə pol′ə tən), *adj.* of or having to do with a technopolis.

**tech|no|struc|ture** (tek′nə struk′chər), *n.* any highly organized system operated by technical experts: ... *the technostructure of large-scale corporate enterprise today, where key decisions are made not by individual owners but by groups and committees of salaried scientists, technicians, engineers, and organization managers* (Eliot Fremont-Smith). [(coined by John Kenneth Galbraith, born 1908, an American economist) < *techno-* + *structure*]

**tech|y** (tech′ē), *adj.,* **tech|i|er, tech|i|est.** = tetchy. —**tech′i|ly,** *adv.* —**tech′i|ness,** *n.*

**tec|nol|o|gy** (tek nol′ə jē), *n.* the study of children. [< Greek *téknos* child + English *-logy*]

**tec|non|y|mous** (tek non′ə məs), *adj.* practicing tecnonymy.

**tec|non|y|my** (tek non′ə mē), *n. Anthropology.* the practice of identifying a person as the parent of his named child rather than by his personal name. [< Greek *téknos* child + *ónyma* name + English *-y*[3]]

**te|co|ma** (ti kō′mə), *n. Botany.* **1** any one of various plants of the bignonia family, consisting chiefly of erect, climbing, or twining shrubs with

**Pronunciation Key:** hat, āge, cãre, fär; let, ēqual, tėrm; it, īce; hot, ōpen, ôrder; oil, out; cup, pu̇t, rüle; child; long; thin; ᴛʜen; zh, measure; ə represents **a** in about, **e** in taken, **i** in pencil, **o** in lemon, **u** in circus.

showy, trumpet-shaped flowers, mostly red or yellow. **2** any one of several related tall trees with digitate leaves, used for timber and in medicine. [< New Latin *Tecoma* the genus name < Nahuatl *tecomaxochitl* < *tecomatl* calabash tree, earthen pot + *xochitl* rose, flower]

**tec|ta** (tek′tə), *n.* plural of **tectum.**

**tec|tal** (tek′təl), *adj.* of or having to do with a tectum; tectorial.

**tec|ti|branch** (tek′tə brangk), *adj., n. Zoology.* — ***adj.*** belonging to the marine gastropod mollusks, having the gills covered by the mantle, and small shells often concealed by the mantle.
— ***n.*** such a gastropod.
[< Latin *tectus, -ī* covered + *branchiae* gills]

**tec|ti|form** (tek′tə fôrm), *adj. Zoology.* **1** sloping down on each side from a ridge, as a wing. **2** serving as a covering or lid. [< Latin *tectus, -ī* covered + *forma* form]

**tec|to|log|i|cal** (tek′tə loj′ə kəl), *adj.* of or having to do with tectology.

**tec|tol|o|gy** (tek tol′ə jē), *n. Biology.* that branch of morphology which regards an organism as composed of morphons of different orders. [< German *Tektologie* < Greek *téktōn* builder + German *-logie* -logy]

***tec|ton|ic** (tek ton′ik), *adj.* **1** *Geology.* **a** belonging to the structure of the earth's crust and to general changes in it, such as folding or faulting. **b** resulting from these: *a tectonic ridge. Many geologists currently believe that the lithosphere is geographically divided into 6 major slablike sections, called tectonic plates, plus a number of smaller ones* (Edmund F. Grekulinski). See picture below. **2** of or having to do with the structure of buildings; constructional; architectural. [< Late Latin *tectonicus* < Greek *tektonikós* of building < *téktōn, -onos* builder] — **tec|ton′i|cal|ly,** *adv.*

**tec|ton|ics** (tek ton′iks), *n.* **1** the science or art of assembling, shaping, or ornamenting materials in construction; construction. **2** tectonic geology; structural geology (of the earth's crust). **3** the branch of zoology that deals with structure.

**tec|ton|ism** (tek′tə niz əm), *n. Geology.* tectonic activity; diastrophism.

**tec|to|no|phys|ics** (tek′tə nə fiz′iks), *n.* the application of the principles of physics to tectonic geology.

**tec|to|ri|al** (tek tôr′ē əl, -tōr′-), *adj.* covering like a roof; forming a protective structure over something: *the tectorial membrane of the ear.* [< Latin *tectōrium* a covering (< *tegere* to cover) + English *-al*[1]]

**tec|tri|cial** (tek trish′əl), *adj.* having to do with the tectrices.

**tec|trix** (tek′triks), *n., pl.* **tec|tri|ces** (tek trī′sēz, tek′trə-). a feather covering the base of wing and tail quills. [< New Latin *tectrix,* feminine of Latin *tector* one who covers < *tegere* to cover]

**tec|tum** (tek′təm), *n., pl.* **-ta.** any rooflike structure in the human or animal anatomy: *Anatomical studies had shown that not all the frog's optic nerve fibers pass to the tectum.* (Scientific American). [< Latin *tectum* roof < *tegere* to cover]

**ted** (ted), *v.t.,* **ted|ded, ted|ding.** to spread or scatter (new-mown grass) for drying. [compare Old Icelandic *tethja* spread manure]

**Ted** (ted), *n. British Slang.* a teddy-boy.

**ted|der** (ted′ər), *n.* a machine that spreads out hay for drying.

**ted|dy**[1] (ted′ē), *n., pl.* **-dies.** a combined chemise and drawers worn by women and girls as an undergarment, especially in the 1920's. [origin uncertain]

**ted|dy**[2] or **Ted|dy** (ted′ē), *n., pl.* **-dies.** *British Slang.* a teddy-boy.

**teddy bear,** a child's furry toy bear. [< *Teddy,* nickname of President Theodore Roosevelt, who was famous as a big-game hunter and was once shown in a cartoon sparing the life of a bear cub]

**ted|dy-boy** or **Ted|dy-boy** (ted′ē boi′), *n. British Slang.* an uncouth, rough, idle, usually low-class young tough (about 15 to 25 years old), often violent; juvenile delinquent. [< *Teddy,* a nickname of Edward; in allusion to their fancy suits, cut in the style of *Edward VII*]

**ted|dy-girl** or **Ted|dy-girl** (ted′ē gėrl′), *n. British Slang.* a teddy-boy's girl friend.

**Te De|um** (tē dē′əm), **1** an ancient hymn of praise and thanksgiving sung in the Roman Catholic and Anglican churches at morning prayers or on special occasions. **2** the music for this hymn. **3** a thanksgiving service in which this hymn is prominent. [< Late Latin *Te Deum* (*Laudamus*) Thee God (we praise), the first words of the hymn]

**te|di|ous** (tē′dē əs, tē′jəs), *adj.* **1** long and tiring; boring; irksome: *A long talk that you cannot understand is tedious. Life is as tedious as a twice-told tale* (Shakespeare). **SYN:** wearisome. **2** writing or talking on and on; wordy; wearying; long-winded. **SYN:** prolix. See syn. under **tiresome.**
[< Late Latin *taediōsus* < Latin *taedium* tedium]
— **te′di|ous|ly,** *adv.* — **te′di|ous|ness,** *n.*

**te|di|um** (tē′dē əm), *n.* **1** the condition of being wearisome; tiresomeness; tediousness. **SYN:** irksomeness. **2** ennui; boredom. [< Latin *taedium* < *taedet* it is wearisome]

**te|di|um vi|tae** (tē′dē əm vī′tē), = taedium vitae.

**tee**[1] (tē), *n., v.,* **teed, tee|ing.** — ***n.*** **1** a mark or place from which a player starts in playing each hole in golf, often slightly elevated. See picture under **golf course. 2** a little mound of sand or dirt or an inch-high stand of wood or plastic, on which a golf ball is set for the first drive. **3** a device for holding a football in position before it is kicked.
— ***v.t.*** to set (a golf ball) on a tee.
**tee off, a** to drive (a golf ball) from a tee: *A field of 134 will tee off tomorrow ... for the Professional Golfers Association championship* (New York Times). **b** *Figurative.* to begin any series of actions: *He will tee off this year's new ten-week course next Sunday with tips on "how to read a Shakespeare play"* (New York Times). **c** *Slang.* to make angry: *He was teed off when she failed to keep the date.*
**tee off on,** *Slang.* to denounce or criticize: ... *ample room to tee off slyly on hipsterism* (Oscar Cargill).
**tee up, a** to set (a golf ball) on a tee. **b** *Especially British.* to tee off.
[origin uncertain]

**tee**[2] (tē), *n.* the mark or peg aimed at in curling, quoits, and other games. [perhaps < *tee*[3]]

**tee**[3] (tē), *n., adj.* — ***n.*** **1** the letter *T, t.* **2** anything T-shaped, especially a pipe fitting with three openings, one at right angles to the other two. **3** = T-bar.
— ***adj.*** with a crosspiece on top; T-shaped.
**to a tee,** to a T; exactly: *Politicians ... are calculating to a tee how to extract the maximum advantage* (London Times).
[< Latin *tē* the letter T]

**tee**[4] (tē), *n.* an umbrella-shaped decoration, usually gilded and hung with bells on top of pagodas, especially in Burma. Also, **htee.** [< Burmese *h'ti* umbrella]

**tee-hee** (tē hē′), *interj., n., v.,* **-heed, -hee|ing.** = te-hee.

**teel** (tēl), *n.* = til[1].

**tee line,** a line running through the tee of a curling rink, perpendicular to the center line.

**teem**[1] (tēm), *v.i.* **1** to be full; abound; swarm: *The swamp teemed with mosquitoes.* **2** to be fertile, fruitful, or prolific: *His mind teemed with large schemes* (William E. H. Lecky). **3** *Obsolete.* to be or become pregnant; give birth. [Old English *tēman, tīeman* < *tēam* progeny] — **teem′er,** *n.*

**teem**[2] (tēm), *v.t.* **1** to empty (a vessel). **2** to pour off (the contents); decant. — ***v.i.*** to flow out. [< Scandinavian (compare Old Icelandic *tæma* to empty < *tōmr* empty)]

**teem|ful** (tēm′fəl), *adj.* **1** fruitful; teeming. **2** *British Dialect.* full to the top.

**teem|ing** (tē′ming), *adj.* **1** full (of); alive (with). **2** fruitful; prolific. — **teem′ing|ly,** *adv.* — **teem′ing-ness,** *n.*

**teem|less** (tēm′lis), *adj.* barren.

**teen**[1] (tēn), *n.* **1** *Archaic.* grief. **2** *Archaic.* pains; care. **3** *Obsolete.* revenge. [Old English *tēona* injury, damage, trouble]

**teen**[2] (tēn), *adj., n.* — ***adj.*** of or having to do with the teens or teen-agers; teen-age.
— ***n.*** = teen-ager.

**-teen,** *suffix added to numbers.* ten more than _____: *Seventeen = ten more than seven.* [Old English *-tēne* < *tēn* ten]

**teen-age** (tēn′āj′), *adj.* **1** of or for a teen-ager or teen-agers: *a teen-age club.* **2** in one's teens; being a teen-ager: *a teen-age girl.*

**teen-aged** (tēn′ājd), *adj.* being a teen-ager; in one's teens: *a teen-aged athlete.*

**teen-ag|er** (tēn′ā′jər), *n.* a person in his or her teens.

**teen|er** (tē′nər), *n.* a teen-ager; teen.

**teens** (tēnz), *n.pl.* the years of life from 13 to 19 inclusive; adolescence.

**teen|sy** (tēn′sē), *adj.,* **-si|er, -si|est.** *Informal.* very small; tiny: *Of course, Max was not, or only a teensy bit, to blame* (W. H. Auden).

**teen|sy-ween|sy** or **teen|sie-ween|sie** (tēn′sē wēn′sē), *adj. Informal.* teensy.

**teent|sy** (tēnt′sē), *adj.,* **-si|er, -si|est.** *Informal.* very small; tiny.

**tee|ny** (tē′nē), *adj.,* **-ni|er, -ni|est.** *Informal.* very small; tiny.

**tee|ny-bop|per** (tē′nē bop′ər), *n. Slang.* **1** a teen-ager, especially a girl, who shuns adult conventions and often adopts hippie ways: *Teeny-boppers ... flee to 4th Avenue in revolt against their parents* (Maclean's). **2** any teen-ager: *The Muscovite teeny-boppers in the auditorium appeared to be very square indeed* (London Times).

**tee|ny-wee|ny** or **tee|nie-wee|nie** (tē′nē wē′nē), *adj. Informal.* teeny.

**tee|pee** (tē′pē), *n.* = tepee.

**tee shirt,** = T-shirt.

**tee|soo** or **tee|so** (tē′sü), *n.* in India: **1** the brilliant orange-red flowers of the dhak or palas. **2** the yellow dye they yield. [< Hindi *tēsū*]

**tee|tee** (tē′tē), *n.* = titi[1]. [< Tupi *titi*]

**tee|ter** (tē′tər), *v., n.* — ***v.i., v.t.*** **1** to rock unsteadily; sway. **2** to balance on a seesaw.
— ***n.*** **1** a swaying movement; reeling. **2** = seesaw.

**tectonic plates:**

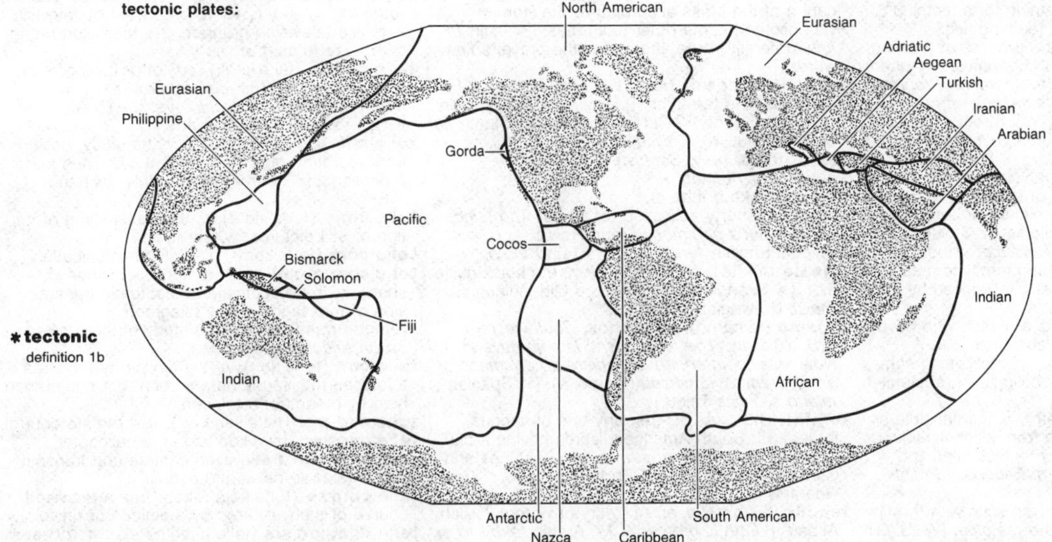


***tectonic**
definition 1b

3 hesitation between two alternatives; vacillation. [American English < Middle English *titeren* < Scandinavian (compare Old Icelandic *titra* shake, totter)]

**tee|ter-board** or **tee|ter|board** (tē′tər bôrd′, -bōrd′), *n. Especially U.S.* a seesaw.

**tee|ter|ing-board** (tē′tər ing bôrd′, -bōrd′), *n. Especially U.S.* a seesaw.

**tee|ter-tot|ter** (tē′tər tot′ər), *n.* = seesaw.

**tee|ter|y** (tē′tər ē), *adj. U.S.* unsteady; shaky.

**teeth** (tēth), *n.* plural of **tooth**: *You often show your teeth when you smile.*

**cut one's teeth, a** to have the teeth begin to grow through the gums; begin teething: *Their first child is just now cutting his teeth.* **b** *Figurative.* to get one's first training; have one's first experience: *The National Cinema School has been training a fine and aggressive group of young directors who are allowed to cut their teeth on short films and pictures made for TV* (Bosley Crowther).

**get** (or **sink**) **one's teeth into,** to become deeply involved with; take hold of; come to grips with: *When* [*he*] *gets his teeth into a good, meaty, high-calorie political issue, he does not let go easily* (New York Times). *Mr. Woodbridge is struggling valiantly to discover something that he can sink his teeth into* (London Times).

**in the** (or **one's**) **teeth, a** in direct opposition or conflict: *Others ... met the enemy in the teeth* (William Whiston). **b** *Figurative.* to one's face; openly: *Dost thou jeer and flout me in the teeth?* (Shakespeare).

**in the teeth of, a** straight against; in the face of: *They advanced in the teeth of the wind. They came on in the teeth of our men, fearless of danger* (Daniel Defoe). **b** *Figurative.* in defiance of; in spite of: *Why do you continue to live here in the teeth of these repeated warnings?* (Leigh Hunt).

**kick in the teeth,** *Informal.* to insult; betray; reject: *Is it not time to be more realistic, ... and, when a country kicks you in the teeth, withdraw aid?* (London Times).

**lie in one's teeth,** to lie brazenly and boldly: *He also accused* [*the*] *general secretary-treasurer of the union, of "lying in his teeth" in asserting the 30-day rule had been in practice 45 years* (Wall Street Journal).

**put teeth in** or **into,** to make effective or forceful: *to put teeth into a rule.* [*His*] *efforts help to put the strongest possible teeth into whatever the UN does* (Manchester Guardian Weekly).

**set one's teeth,** to prepare (for a struggle) with firmness: *"I think not!" replied Mr. Sawyer, setting his teeth for a catastrophe* (G. J. Whyte-Melville).

**set one's teeth on edge,** to be so unpleasant or annoying as to cause physical discomfort: *The screenplay is so arty that it constantly sets one's teeth on edge* (Brendan Gill).

**show one's teeth,** to show anger; threaten: *When the law shows her teeth, but dares not bite ...* (Edward Young).

**throw in one's teeth,** to blame or reproach for (especially something shameful): *This neglect of family devotions is often thrown in our teeth* (Francis Bragge).

**to the teeth,** completely: *armed to the teeth. I'm not trying to excuse the salesman, but I am fed up to the teeth with seeing him picked on all the time* (Colm Hogan).

**teethe** (tēᴛʜ), *v.i.,* **teethed, teeth|ing.** to grow teeth; cut teeth: *Baby is teething.*

**teeth|er** (tē′ᴛʜər), *n.* something for a teething baby to bite on, such as a teething ring.

**teeth|ing** (tē′ᴛʜing), *n.* **1** the process of growing or cutting teeth; dentition. **2** *Figurative.* any often painful or upsetting early development: *Progress thus far has exceeded expectations with unusually few teething troubles* (Wall Street Journal).

**teething ring,** a ring of plastic, bone, or ivory for a teething baby to bite on.

**teeth|ridge** (tēth′rij′), *n.* = alveoli.

**tee|to|tal** (tē tō′təl), *adj.* **1** of or having to do with total abstinence from alcoholic liquor. **2** urging total abstinence from alcoholic liquor. **3** pledged to drink no alcoholic liquor. **4** *Informal.* without exception; complete; entire. [apparently formed < *total,* with repetition of initial *t;* influenced by *teetotum*] — **tee|to′tal|ly,** *adv.*

**tee|to|tal|er** (tē tō′tə lər), *n.* a person who never takes alcoholic liquor. **SYN:** abstainer.

**tee|to|tal|ing** (tē tō′tə ling), *adj.* abstaining completely from the use of alcoholic liquor; abstemious.

**tee|to|tal|ism** (tē tō′tə liz əm), *n.* the principle or practice of total abstinence from alcoholic liquor.

**tee|to|tal|ist** (tē tō′tə list), *n.* = teetotaler.

**tee|to|tal|ler** (tē tō′tə lər), *n. Especially British.* teetotaler.

**tee|to|tum** (tē tō′təm), *n.* a top spun with the fingers: *She'll waltz away like a teetotum* (W. S. Gilbert). [for earlier *totum,* the original name (< Latin *tōtum* all), with *tee* = T, a letter stamped on one side of the toy]

**tee|vee** (tē′vē′), *n. Informal.* television: *I can see Calton sitting in there with his wife watching teevee* (Jesse Hill Ford). [pronunciation of *TV*]

**teff** or **tef** (tef), *n.* the principal cereal of Ethiopia, producing minute black or white grains from which bread is made, introduced elsewhere for fodder. Also, **taff.** [< Amharic *ṭêf*]

**te|fil|lin** (tə fil′ən), *n.pl.* phylacteries. Also, **tephillin.** [< Aramaic *təphillīn,* perhaps irregular plural of *təphillāh* prayer]

**TEFL** (tef′əl), *n. Education.* teaching English as a foreign language.

**Tef|lon** (tef′lon), *n. Trademark.* polytetrafluoroethylene.

**Tef|nut** (tef′nüt), *n.* the ancient Egyptian goddess of moisture.

**teg** or **tegg** (teg), *n. Especially British.* a sheep from its weaning till its first shearing in its second year. [perhaps < Scandinavian (compare Swedish *tacka* ewe)]

**teg|men** (teg′men), *n., pl.* **-mi|na** (-mə nə). **1** *Biology.* a cover, covering, or coating; integument. **2** *Botany.* the thin, soft, delicate inner coat of a seed, surrounding the embryo; integument. **3** *Entomology.* a forewing of an insect when modified to serve as a covering for the hind wings. [< Latin *tegmen, -minis* a covering < *tegere* to cover]

**teg|men|tal** (teg men′təl), *adj.* having to do with the tegmentum.

**teg|men|tum** (teg men′təm), *n., pl.* **-ta** (-tə). *Botany.* **1** the scaly coat which covers a leaf bud. **2** one of the scales of such a coat. [< Latin *tegmentum,* variant of *tegumentum* < *tegere* to cover]

**teg|mi|nal** (teg′mə nəl), *adj.* = tegumentary.

**te|gu** (tə gü′), *n., pl.* **-gus.** = teju.

**te|guex|in** (tə gwek′sin), *n.* a large South American lizard resembling a monitor. [< New Latin *teguexin* the species name < Nahuatl *tecoixin* lizard]

**teg|u|lar** (teg′yə lər), *adj.* **1** having to do with a tile. **2** like a tile. **3** consisting of or made of tiles. **4** arranged or fitted like tiles. [< Latin *tēgula* tile (< *tegere* to cover) + English *-ar*] — **teg′u|lar|ly,** *adv.*

**teg|u|ment** (teg′yə mənt), *n.* a natural covering; shell, capsule, or cocoon; integument. [< Latin *tegumentum* < *tegere* to cover]

**teg|u|men|tal** (teg′yə men′təl), *adj.* = tegumentary.

**teg|u|men|ta|ry** (teg′yə men′tər ē), *adj.* **1** of or having to do with integument. **2** composed or consisting of skin or other covering or investing part or structure.

**te-hee** (tē hē′), *interj., n., v.,* **-heed, -hee|ing.**
— ***interj.*** a word representing the sound of a tittering laugh.
— ***n.*** **1** the sound of a tittering laugh. **2** a titter; snicker; snigger; giggle.
— ***v.i.*** to titter; snicker; snigger; giggle. Also, **teehee.**
[Middle English *tihi, tehee;* imitative]

**tehr** (tãr), *n.* = tahr.

**Te|huel|che** (te wel′chā), *n., pl.* **-che** or **-ches.** **1** a member of a tribe of Araucanian Indians in Patagonia, renowned for their tallness. **2** the language of this tribe.

**Tei|an** (tē′ən), *adj.* **1** of Teos, in ancient Ionia, Greece. **2** of the poet Anacreon, who was a native of Teos. Also, **Tean.**

**te ig|i|tur** (tē ij′ə tər), the first prayer of the canon of the Mass according to the Roman Catholic and some other Latin rites. [< Latin *te igitur* (literally) thee, therefore (the prayer's first words)]

**teil** (tēl), *n.,* or **teil tree, 1** the linden tree. **2** (in the Bible) the terebinth. [partly < Medieval Latin *tilia* linden; partly < Old French *til, teil* < Latin *tiliolus* (diminutive) < *tilius* lime]

**teind** (tēnd), *n., v. Scottish.* — ***n.*** a tithe.
— ***v.i.*** to pay teinds.
— ***v.t.*** to take a tithe of.
**teinds,** property assessed for tithes: *The teinds are the kirk's patrimony* (John Row).
[Middle English *tende* tenth] — **teind′er,** *n.*

**teis|tie** (tēs′tē), *n. British Dialect.* the black guillemot. [< Scandinavian (compare Old Icelandic *theist,* Norwegian *teist*)]

**te|ja|no** (tā hä′nō), *n., pl.* **-nos.** *Southwestern U.S.* a Texan: *The term tejano is pejorative in New Mexico, intended to conjure up an image of an ignorant ... cowhand* (Harper's). [< Spanish *tejano* < *Tejas* Texas]

**te|ju** (tə zhü′), *n., pl.* **-jus.** any one of various large, swift South American lizards having a bluish-black back with crosswise yellow stripes and yellowish underparts. [< Portuguese *tejú* < Tupi-Guarani]

**tek|bir** (tek bir′), *n.* an Arab cry of victory, "Allah Akbar" ("God is greater"). [< Arabic *tekbīr* to exalt < *kabura* to be great]

**tek|ke** or **tek|keh** (tek′ke), *n.* = tekkieh.

**tek|ki|eh** (tek′kē ə), *n.* a Moslem monastery. [< Arabic *takīyah*]

**tek|tite** (tek′tīt), *n. Geology.* any one of various rounded, glassy objects of different shapes and weights, found in various parts of the world and thought to have come from outer space: *Tektites differ chemically from meteorites, but some of them contain small bits of meteoritic iron* (John A. O'Keefe). [< Greek *tēktós* molten (< *tēkein* to melt) + English *-ite*[1]]

**tek|tit|ic** (tek tit′ik), *adj. Geology.* of or having to do with tektites: *If the glass chemist were asked to formulate a material which would survive both hypersonic entry through the atmosphere and prolonged geological weathering, he could not improve upon the tektitic formula* (New Scientist).

**tel-,** *combining form.* a variant of **tele-,** as in *telelectric, teloptic.*

**tel.,** **1** telegram. **2** telegraph. **3** telephone.

**TEL** (no periods), tetraethyl lead (an antiknock additive for gasoline).

**Tel|a|mon** (tel′ə mon), *n. Greek Mythology.* the father of Ajax, king of the island of Salamis.

**tel|a|mon** (tel′ə mon), *n., pl.* **tel|a|mo|nes** (tel′ə-mō′nēz). *Architecture.* a figure of a man used as a column. [< *Telamon*]

**tel|an|gi|ec|ta|sia** (tə lan′jē ek tā′zhə, -zhē ə), *n.* = telangiectasis. [< New Latin *telangiectasia,* variant of *telangiectasis*]

**tel|an|gi|ec|ta|sis** (tə lan′jē ek′tə sis), *n., pl.* **-ses** (-sēz). *Medicine.* a disorder in which the capillaries are permanently dilated, as in red-faced alcoholics, or persons who spend much time out of doors. [< New Latin *telangiectasis* < Greek *télos* end + *angeîon* vessel + *éktasis* dilation < *ekout* + a root of *teínein* to stretch]

**tel|an|gi|ec|tat|ic** (tə lan′jē ek tat′ik), *adj.* **1** having to do with telangiectasis. **2** showing telangiectasis.

**Tel|an|thro|pus** (tel′an thrō′pəs), *n.* an extinct man, fragments of whom were discovered in 1952 near Johannesburg, South Africa. [< New Latin *Telanthropus* the genus name < Greek *télos* end + *ánthrōpos* man]

**tel|au|to|gram** (tel ô′tə gram), *n.* the record produced by a TelAutograph.

**Tel|Au|to|graph** (tel ô′tə graf, -gräf), *n. Trademark.* a telegraph for reproducing handwriting or pictures. The movements of a pen at one end are produced in facsimile by a pen at the other end.

**tel|au|to|graph|ic** (tel ô′tə graf′ik), *adj.* having to do with the TelAutograph.

**tel|au|tog|ra|phy** (tel′ô tog′rə fē), *n.* the use of the TelAutograph.

**tele-,** *combining form.* **1** having to go with operating over long distances: *Telegraph = an instrument to send messages over a long distance.* **2** having to do with television: *Telecast = to broadcast by television.* **3** telescopic: *Tele-camera = a telescopic camera.* Also, **tel-** before vowels.
[< Greek *tēle* far off]

**tel|e** (tel′ē), *n. British Slang.* television: *... people couldn't watch their favourite programmes on the "tele"* (Manchester Guardian Weekly). [< *tele*(vision)]

**Tel|e|bit** or **tel|e|bit** (tel′ə bit), *n.* a device in space satellites to store scientific data and transmit it to earth.

**tel|e-cam|er|a** (tel′ə kam′ər ə), *n.* a telescopic camera.

**tel|e|cast** (tel′ə kast′, -käst′), *v.,* **-cast** or **-cast|ed, -cast|ing,** *n.* — ***v.t., v.i.*** to broadcast by television.
— ***n.*** **1** a television program. **2** a television broadcast. — **tel′e|cast′er,** *n.*

**tel|e|chir|ic** (tel′ə kir′ik), *adj.* of or having to do with telechirics: *The job of patrolling ... would seem suited for a telechiric vehicle* (New Scientist). — **tel′e|chir′i|cal|ly,** *adv.*

**tel|e|chir|ics** (tel′ə kir′iks), *n.* the study, design, and operation of remote-control machines and processes. [< *tele-* + Greek *cheír, -os* hand + English *-ics*]

**tel|e|cin|e** (tel′ə sin′ē), *n.* the transmitting of motion or still pictures by television.

**tel|e|com** (tel′ə kom), *n.* = telecommunication.

**tel|e|com|mu|ni|ca|tion** (tel′ə kə myü′nə kā′shən), *n.* the electrical and electronic transmission of messages, as by telegraph.
**telecommunications,** the study of this: *to read up on telecommunications.*

**tel|e|con** (tel′ə kon), *n.* **1** a device that flashes teletyped messages on a screen. **2** a conference held by means of a telecon.

**tel|e|con|trol** (tel′ə kən trōl′), *n.* = remote control.

**tel|e|cop|ter** (tel′ə kop′tər), *n.* a helicopter equipped with a television camera and transmitter, to televise news and events.

**tel|e|course** (tel′ə kôrs′, -kōrs′), *n.* a televised course of study offered by a college or university.

**tel|e|di|ag|no|sis** (tel′ə dī əg nō′sis), *n., pl.* **-ses**

(-sēz). diagnosis of an illness performed by means of electronic equipment and closed-circuit television linking the physician to the patient.
[< *tele*(vision) *diagnosis*]

**tel|e|dra|ma** (tel′ə drä′mə, -dram′ə), *n.* a drama written or adapted for television; teleplay.

**tel|e|du** (tel′ə dü), *n.* a small carnivorous mammal of Indonesia, which is related to and resembles the skunk, except for a short tail, and can give off a very strong, unpleasant smell. [< Malay]

**tel|e|fac|sim|i|le** (tel′ə fak sim′ə lē), *n.* a method of transmitting printed materials over a telephone circuit, as by an acoustic coupler. [< *tele*(phone) *facsimile*]

**tel|e|fe|rique** (tel′ə fə rēk′), *n.* = ski lift. [< French *téléférique* < *téléphérage* transportation by telphers < English *telpherage*]

**tel|e|film** (tel′ə film′), *n.* a motion picture produced especially for television.

**teleg.,** 1 telegram. 2 telegraph. 3 telegraphy.

**te|le|ga** (te le′gə), *n.* a primitive, four-wheeled, springless Russian wagon. [< Russian *telega*]

**tel|e|gen|ic** (tel′ə jen′ik), *adj. Especially U.S.* appearing attractive on television; suitable for telecasting.

**tel|e|gon|ic** (tel′ə gon′ik), *adj.* of or having to do with telegony.

**te|leg|o|ny** (tə leg′ə nē), *n. Genetics.* the sire's supposed influence on the dam's offspring by later sires. [< *tele-* + Greek *-goniā* a begetting]

**tel|e|gram** (tel′ə gram), *n., v.,* **-grammed, -gram|ming.** —*n.* a message sent by telegraph: *Mother sent a telegram telling us what plane she was returning on.*
—*v.t.* to telegraph to.
—*v.i.* to send a telegram; telegraph.

**tel|e|gram|mat|ic** (tel′ə grə mat′ik), *adj.* = telegrammic.

**tel|e|gram|mic** (tel′ə gram′ik), *adj.* 1 of or having to do with a telegram. 2 *Figurative.* brief; concise; succinct.

**tel|e|graph** (tel′ə graf, -gräf), *n., v.* —*n.* an apparatus, system, or process for sending coded messages over wires by means of electricity.
—*v.t.* 1 to send (a message) by telegraph: *Mother telegraphed that she would arrive home by afternoon plane.* SYN: wire. 2 to send a message to (a person) by telegraph. SYN: wire. 3 *Figurative.* to signal (what one intends to do); show by a gesture, look, or other sign: *The boxer telegraphed his punches too often. Most dancers nowadays seem to telegraph to their audiences, "Watch for this one—it's tremendous"* (Clive Barnes).
—*v.i.* to signal or communicate by telegraph. SYN: wire.
[(originally) a semaphore < French *télégraphe* < Greek *têle* at a distance + *-graphos* writer < *gráphein* to write]

**telegraph boy,** *Especially British.* a boy who personally delivers telegrams.

**te|leg|ra|pher** (tə leg′rə fər), *n.* a person who sends and receives messages by telegraph.

**telegrapher's cramp,** painful cramps in the muscles of the arm and fingers, an occupational disorder of telegraphers.

**tel|e|graph|ese** (tel′ə gra fēz′, -fēs′), *n.* the concise and elliptical style in which telegrams are worded; cablese: *Another colleague rewrote the paper in telegraphese, leaving out most adjectives, inserting the word "stop" for periods* (Time).

**tel|e|graph|ic** (tel′ə graf′ik), *adj.* 1 of or having to do with a telegraph. 2 sent as a telegram. 3 *Figurative.* extremely concise; contracted: *a telegraphic style.* —**tel′e|graph′i|cal|ly,** *adv.*

**tel|e|graph|i|cal** (tel′ə graf′ə kəl), *adj.* = telegraphic.

**te|leg|ra|phist** (tə leg′rə fist), *n. Especially British.* a telegrapher.

**telegraph key,** a small lever to tap out messages by telegraph.

**te|leg|ra|phone** (tə leg′rə fōn), *n.* a form of telephone which receives and magnetically records the spoken message.

**tel|e|graph|o|scope** (tel′ə graf′ə skōp), *n.* a telegraphic device for transmitting and reproducing a still picture, such as a wirephoto.

**telegraph plant,** an East Indian tick trefoil plant, whose leaflets, spontaneously jerking up and down and rotating on their own axes, suggest a semaphore.

**telegraph pole,** *Especially British.* telephone pole.

**telegraph printer,** = ticker (def. 2).

**te|leg|ra|phy** (tə leg′rə fē), *n.* the act of making or operating of telegraphs.

**Tel|e|gu** (tel′ə gü), *n., pl.* **-gu** or **-gus,** *adj.* = Telugu.

**tel|e|guide** (tel′ə gīd′), *v.t.,* **-guid|ed, -guid|ing.** to guide by remote control: *The Russians were able to teleguide the last stage of their moon rocket* (New York Herald Tribune).

**tel|e|ki|ne|sis** (tel′ə ki nē′sis), *n.* = psychokinesis.

**tel|e|ki|net|ic** (tel′ə ki net′ik), *adj.* 1 like telekinesis. 2 having to do with telekinesis. —**tel′e|ki|net′i|cal|ly,** *adv.*

**tel|e|lec|tric** (tel′i lek′trik), *n., adj.* —*n.* transmission by electrical means.
—*adj.* having to do with transmission by electrical means.

**tel|e|lec|tro|scope** (tel′i lek′trə skōp), *n.* an electrical transmitter of motion pictures.

**tel|e|lec|ture** (tel′ə lek′chər), *n.* a lecture delivered by telephone to a classroom or other place for two-way communication: *Colleges today are ... piping the specialist's voice and face in by telelecture and televison* (Saturday Review).

**tel|e|lens** (tel′ə lenz′), *n.* = telephoto lens.

**Te|lem|a|chus** (tə lem′ə kəs), *n. Greek Legend.* the son of Penelope and Odysseus (Ulysses). When Odysseus returned from the Trojan War, Telemachus helped him slay Penelope's insolent suitors.

**tel|e|mark** (tel′ə märk, tā′lə-), *n.,* or **telemark turn,** a method of turning or stopping skis by advancing the outside ski. [< *Telemark,* a region in Norway, where it originated]

**tel|e|me|chan|ics** (tel′ə mə kan′iks), *n.* the science of transmitting electric power by radio, without wires.

**te|lem|e|ter** (tə lem′ə tər), *n., v.* —*n.* 1 a device for measuring heat, radiation, pressure, speed, or other quantity, and transmitting the information to a distant receiving station. 2 any one of various range finders used in surveying and gunnery. 3 *Physics.* a device to measure strains.
—*v.t., v.i.* to measure and transmit by telemeter.

**tel|e|met|ric** (tel′ə met′rik), *adj.* having to do with telemetry. —**tel′e|met′ri|cal|ly,** *adv.*

**tel|e|met|ri|cal** (tel′ə met′rə kəl), *adj.* = telemetric.

**te|lem|e|try** (tə lem′ə trē), *n.* the use of telemeters for measuring and transmitting information.

**tel|e|mo|tor** (tel′ə mō′tər), *n.* a hydraulic or electric system of remote control, especially of a ship's rudder.

**tel|en|ce|phal|ic** (tel′en sə fal′ik), *adj.* of or having to do with the telencephalon.

**tel|en|ceph|a|lon** (tel′en sef′ə lon), *n.* the anterior part of the forebrain in vertebrates, comprising mainly the cerebral hemispheres; endbrain.

**te|len|gi|scope** (tə len′jə skōp), *n.* an instrument which combines the functions of a telescope and a microscope. [< *tel-* + obsolete *engyscope* a microscope < Greek *engýs* near + English *-scope*]

**tel|e|o|log|i|cal** (tel′ē ə loj′ə kəl, tē′lē-), *adj.* 1 of or having to do with teleology. 2 having to do with a design or purpose. 3 of the nature of a design or purpose. —**tel′e|o|log′i|cal|ly,** *adv.*

**teleological argument,** the doctrine that teleology proves the existence of a Creator.

**tel|e|ol|o|gist** (tel′ē ol′ə jist, tē′lē-), *n.* a person who believes in or studies teleology.

**tel|e|ol|o|gy** (tel′ē ol′ə jē, tē′lē-), *n.* 1 the fact or quality of being purposeful. 2 purpose or design as shown in nature: *Either the world shows a teleology or it does not* (William R. Inge). 3 the doctrine that mechanisms alone cannot explain the facts of nature and that purposes have causal power. 4 the doctrine that all things in nature were made to fulfill a plan or design. [< New Latin *teleologia* < Greek *télos, -eos* end, goal + *-logíā* -logy]

**tel|e|on|o|my** (tel′ē on′ə mē, tē′lē-), *n.* a social system or group ruled by an overall purpose. [< *télos, -eos* end, goal + English *-nomy,* as in *autonomy*]

**tel|e|op|er|a|tor** (tel′ə op′ə rā′tər), *n.* a robot or similar mechanical device operated by remote control: *Remotely controlled devices with mobility, sensory and manipulative capabilities ... are often referred to as "teleoperators"* (New York Times). [< *tele-* + *operator*]

**tel|e|ost** (tel′ē ost, tē′lē-), *adj., n.* —*adj.* of or having to do with a large group of fishes with bony skeletons, including most common fishes, such as the perch or flounder, but not the sharks, rays, and lampreys.
—*n.* a teleost fish.
[< New Latin *Teleostei* the group name < Greek *téleios* finished, complete + *ostéon* bone]

**tel|e|os|te|an** (tel′ē os′tē ən, tē′lē-), *adj., n.* = teleost.

**tel|e|path** (tel′ə path′), *n.* = telepathist.

**tel|e|path|ic** (tel′ə path′ik), *adj.* 1 of or having to do with telepathy. 2 by telepathy. —**tel′e|path′i|cal|ly,** *adv.*

**te|lep|a|thist** (tə lep′ə thist), *n.* 1 a person who has telepathic power. 2 a student of or believer in telepathy.

**te|lep|a|thize** (tə lep′ə thīz), *v.,* **-thized, -thiz|ing.**
—*v.i.* to practice telepathy: *He guessed or telepathized to what I was imagining rather than what I was saying* (New Scientist).
—*v.t.* to communicate with or affect by telepathy.

**te|lep|a|thy** (tə lep′ə thē), *n.* the communication of one mind with another without using speech, hearing, sight, or any other sense used normally to communicate. [< *tele-* + *-pathy*]

**teleph.,** 1 telephone. 2 telephony.

**tel|e|phe|rique** (tel′ə fə rēk′), *n.* = teleferique.

* **tel|e|phone** (tel′ə fōn), *n., v.,* **-phoned, -phon|ing.**
—*n.* 1 an apparatus for sending sound or speech to a distant point over wires usually by means of electricity. 2 the process of, or system for, doing this. *Abbr:* tel.
—*v.t.* 1 to talk to or summon by telephone: *He decided ... to telephone her and free himself from the engagement* (Sinclair Lewis). 2 to send (a message) by telephone.
—*v.i.* to speak on the telephone: *We can telephone to your mother for a car* (John Galsworthy).
[American English < *tele-* + Greek *phōnḗ* sound, voice]
► As a noun, *telephone* occurs very often in an attributive position, as in *telephone call, telephone number, telephone exchange, telephone operator, telephone system,* and the like. Some of the less self-explanatory phrases in which it appears are given below as separate entries.

* **telephone**
definition 1

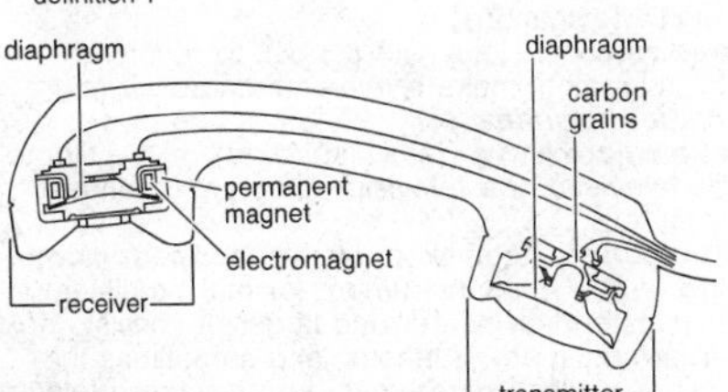


**telephone book,** = telephone directory.

**telephone booth,** a public booth with a telephone and coin box for making prepaid calls.

**telephone box,** *Especially British.* a telephone booth.

**telephone directory,** a list of the names, addresses, and telephone numbers of people or businesses with telephones in a certain area.

**telephone pole,** a pole to carry telephone wires, usually wooden and about 30 feet tall.

**tel|e|phon|er** (tel′ə fō′nər), *n.* a person who telephones.

**telephone receiver,** the earpiece of a telephone set, which changes electrical impulses into sound.

**tel|e|phon|ic** (tel′ə fon′ik), *adj.* 1 of or having to do with the telephone. 2 by the telephone. —**tel′e|phon′i|cal|ly,** *adv.*

**te|leph|o|nist** (tə lef′ə nist), *n. Especially British.* a telephone switchboard operator.

**tel|e|pho|ni|tis** (tel′ə fə nī′tis), *n.* an excessive or abnormal urge to make telephone calls (humorous use): *All the young ladies had telephonitis* (New York Times).

**tel|e|pho|no|graph** (tel′ə fō′nə graf, -gräf), *n.* a device to record and reproduce telephone messages.

**tel|e|pho|no|graph|ic** (tel′ə fō′nə graf′ik), *adj.* 1 having to do with a telephonograph. 2 by a telephonograph.

**te|leph|o|ny** (tə lef′ə nē), *n.* the making or operating of telephones.

**tel|e|pho|to** (tel′ə fō′tō), *adj., n., pl.* **-tos,** *v.*
—*adj.* 1 of or having to do with telephotography. 2 used in telephotography: *I climbed the barbed wire fence ... and made ready my eight-millimeter telephoto movie camera* (Harper's).
—*n.* 1 = telephotograph. 2 = wirephoto.
—*v.t., v.i.* = telephotograph.

**tel|e|pho|to|graph** (tel′ə fō′tə graf, -gräf), *n., v.*
—*n.* 1 a picture taken with a camera having a telephoto lens. 2 a picture sent by telegraphy.
—*v.i.* 1 to take a picture with a camera having a telephoto lens. 2 to send a picture by telegraphy or radio.
—*v.t.* 1 to photograph with a telephoto lens. 2 to send by telegraphy or radio.

**tel|e|pho|to|graph|ic** (tel′ə fō′tə graf′ik), *adj.* = telephoto.

**tel|e|pho|tog|ra|phy** (tel′ə fə tog′rə fē), *n.* 1 the method or process of photographing distant objects by using a camera with a telephoto lens. 2 the method or process of sending and reproducing pictures by radio or telegraph.

**Pronunciation Key:** hat, āge, cãre, fär; let, ēqual, tėrm; it, īce; hot, ōpen, ôrder; oil, out; cup, pu̇t, rüle; child; long; thin; ᴛʜen; zh, measure;
ə represents **a** in about, **e** in taken, **i** in pencil, **o** in lemon, **u** in circus.

**telephoto lens**, a lens used in a camera for producing an enlarged image of a distant object.

**tel|e|plasm** (tel′ə plaz əm), *n.* the ectoplasm of a medium in a trance. [< *tele-* + Greek *plásma* something formed]

**tel|e|plas|mic** (tel′ə plaz′mik), *adj.* of, having to do with, or like teleplasm.

**tel|e|play** (tel′ə plā′), *n.* a play produced especially for television: *The first was a well-written teleplay ... about the development of a Confederate submarine* (Time).

**tel|e|print|er** (tel′ə prin′tər), *n. Especially British.* a teletypewriter.

**tel|e|proc|ess|ing** (tel′ə pros′əs ing), *n.* the use of a computer that can process data which the computer collects from distant points by radio or telephone: *Earlier computer networks involving high-speed teleprocessing have been limited to such applications as the Mercury control system for space flight and defense and industrial installations* (Science News Letter).

**Tel|e|Promp|Ter** (tel′ə promp′tər), *n. Trademark.* a device consisting of a moving band that gives a prepared speech line for line, used by speakers who are being televised.

**tel|e|ran** (tel′ə ran), *n.* an aid to landing aircraft which sends radar maps of the sky, an airfield, or other area, by television. [< *Tele*(vision) *R*(adar) *A*(ir) *N*(avigation)]

**tel|e|re|cord** (tel′ə ri kôrd′), *v.t.* to record on film for televising; make a telerecording of: *a telerecorded performance.*

**tel|e|re|cord|ing** (tel′ə ri kôr′ding), *n.* **1** a film to be televised. **2** a television program broadcast from this.

***tel|e|scope** (tel′ə skōp), *n., v.,* **-scoped, -scoping.** *adj.* **—*n.*** an instrument for making distant objects appear nearer and larger. It consists of an arrangement of lenses, and sometimes mirrors, in one or more tubes. In a refracting telescope the image is produced by a lens and magnified by the eyepiece. In a reflecting telescope the image is produced by a concave mirror or speculum and magnified. The stars are studied by means of both kinds of telescopes. *After the invention of the telescope in 1609, observatories were established in many European cities* (Helmut Abt).
**—*v.t.*** **1** to force together one inside another, like the sliding tubes of some telescopes: *When the trains crashed into each other, the cars were telescoped.* **2** *Figurative.* to bring together and shorten; condense: *He telescoped the four-year course into three-years* (New York Times).
**—*v.i.*** **1** to fit or be forced together, one part inside another, like the parts of some telescopes. **2** *Figurative.* to be telescoped; come or run together: *The new theories telescope into the old ones in their common domain of application* (New Yorker).
**—*adj.*** = collapsible.
[< New Latin *telescopium* < Greek *tēleskópos* far-seeing < *têle* far + *skopeîn* to watch]

***telescope**

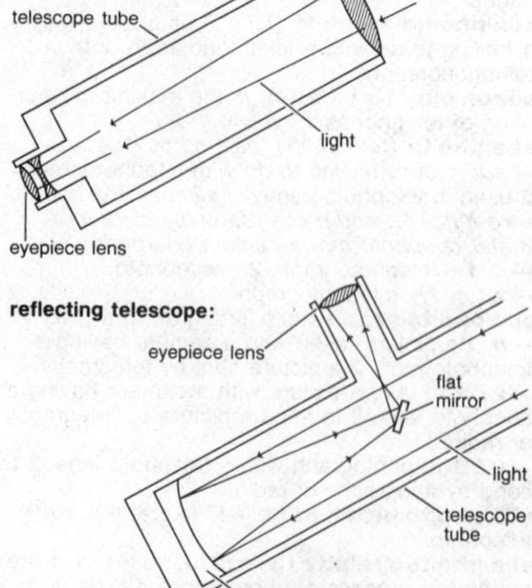


**telescope sight**, a small telescope used for aiming a gun.

**tel|e|scop|ic** (tel′ə skop′ik), *adj.* **1** of or having to do with a telescope. **2** obtained or seen by means of a telescope: *a telescopic view of the moon.* **3** visible only through a telescope. **4** *Figurative.* far-seeing. **5** making distant things look clear and close: *a telescopic lens.* **6** consisting of parts that slide one inside another like the tubes of some telescopes.

**tel|e|scop|i|cial** (tel′ə skop′ə kəl), *adj.* = telescopic.

**tel|e|scop|i|cal|ly** (tel′ə skop′ə klē), *adv.* **1** in a telescopic manner. **2** by means of a telescope; as seen through a telescope.

**telescopic rifle**, a rifle with a telescopic sight.

**Tel|e|sco|pi|i** (tel′ə skō′pē ī), *n.* genitive of **Telescopium.**

**te|les|co|pist** (tə les′kə pist), *n.* a person skilled in telescopy.

**Tel|e|sco|pi|um** (tel′ə skō′pē əm), *n. genitive* **Tel|e|sco|pi|i.** a southern constellation near Sagittarius. [< New Latin *telescopium*]

**te|les|co|py** (tə les′kə pē), *n.* **1** the science or practice of using telescopes. **2** the science or practice of making telescopes.

**tel|e|screen** (tel′ə skrēn′), *n.* a television screen.

**tel|e|seism** (tel′ə sī′zəm), *n.* an earth tremor remote from a place where it is recorded or indicated by a seismograph or the like. [< *tele-* + Greek *seismós* earthquake]

**tel|e|seis|mic** (tel′ə sīz′mik), *adj.* of or having to do with a teleseism: *a network of 20 to 30 teleseismic recording stations.*

**tel|e|sis** (tel′ə sis), *n.* the policy of using the forces of nature and society to accomplish a chosen end. [< New Latin *telesis* < Late Greek *télesis* event, fulfillment < Greek *teleîn* to finish, complete, related to *télos* end, goal]

**tel|e|spec|tro|scope** (tel′ə spek′trə skōp), *n.* an instrument consisting of a telescope with a spectroscope attached.

**tel|e|ster|e|o|scope** (tel′ə ster′ē ə skōp, -stir′-), *n.* **1** an instrument for viewing distant objects in three dimensions as in a stereoscope, consisting of two pairs of mirrors arranged to produce this effect; binoculars. **2** an optical range finder.

**tel|es|the|sia** (tel′əs thē′zhə; -zhē ə, -zē ə), *n.* = telepathy. Also, **telaesthesia.** [< New Latin *telesthesia* < Greek *têle* far off + *aisthēsis* perception]

**tel|es|thet|ic** (tel′əs thet′ik), *adj.* = telepathic. Also, **telaesthetic.**

**te|les|tich** (tə les′tik, tel′ə stik), *n.* a short poem in which the final letters of the lines, in order, spell a word or words. [< Greek *télos* end + *stíchos* line]

**tel|e|ther|a|py** (tel′ə ther′ə pē), *n.* radiotherapy of a high intensity, applied at a distance from the body or affected organ.

**tel|e|ther|mo|graph** (tel′ə thėr′mə graf, -gräf), *n.* **1** = telethermometer. **2** a record made by such a device.

**tel|e|ther|mom|e|ter** (tel′ə thər mom′ə tər), *n.* any one of various thermometers whose readings are automatically transmitted.

**tel|e|ther|mom|e|try** (tel′ə thər mom′ə trē), *n.* the use of a telethermometer.

**tel|e|thon** (tel′ə thon), *n.* a television program lasting many hours, especially one soliciting contributions, as for a charity.

**Tel|e|type** (tel′ə tīp), *n. Trademark.* teletypewriter.

**tel|e|type** (tel′ə tīp), *n., v.,* **-typed, -typ|ing.** *n.* a communication system of teletypewriters with their connecting circuits and other equipment.
**—*v.t.*** to send (a message) by teletypwriter.
[< *Teletype*] **—tel′e|typ′er,** *n.*

**Tel|e|type|set|ter** (tel′ə tīp′set′ər), *n.* **1** *Trademark.* a telegraphic device for sending signals by teletype. The signals cause holes to be punched in a tape that is put into a typesetting machine which sets printing type automatically. **2 teletypesetter.** any device or apparatus like this.

**tel|e|type|writ|er** (tel′ə tīp′rī′tər), *n.* a telegraphic device which resembles a typewriter, used in sending, receiving, and automatically printing out messages.

**tel|e|typ|ist** (tel′ə tī′pist), *n.* a person who operates a teletypewriter.

**te|leu|to|spore** (tel yü′tə spôr, -spōr), *n. Botany.* a teliospore. [< Greek *teleutḗ* end (< *teleîn* to complete) + English *spore*]

**te|leu|to|spor|ic** (tel yü′tə spôr′ik, -spōr′-), *adj. Botany.* teliosporic.

**tel|e|view** (tel′ə vyü′), *v.t., v.i.* to look at (a television program).

**tel|e|view|er** (tel′ə vyü′ər), *n.* a person who watches television.

**tel|e|vise** (tel′ə vīz), *v.,* **-vised, -vis|ing.**
**—*v.t.*** **1** to send by television: *to televise a baseball game.* **2** to receive or see by television.
**—*v.i.*** to broadcast television programs.

**tel|e|vi|sion** (tel′ə vizh′ən), *n.* **1** the process of sending pictures of an object, scene, or something happening through the air or over a wire by means of electricity so that people in many places can see them at once. In television, waves of light from an object are changed into electric waves which are sent to a receiving point, where they are changed back into waves of light that produce an image of the object on a screen. The sound which accompanies the image is sent by radio at the same time. **2** a view of scenes transmitted thus. **3** an apparatus on which these pictures may be seen; television set. **4** the business of broadcasting television programs; the television industry. *Abbr:* TV (no periods).
▶ **Television** is frequently used as an attributive, occurring in such phrases as *television show, television program, a television station, a television actor or announcer, television talk shows, a television stuido.* Such easily understood phrases are not separate entries in this dictionary.

**tel|e|vi|sion|al** (tel′ə vizh′ə nəl), *adj.* of or having to do with television. **—tel′e|vi′sion|al|ly,** *adv.*

**tel|e|vi|sion|ar|y** (tel′ə vizh′ə ner′ē), *adj.* = televisional.

**television set**, an apparatus for receiving and making visible television broadcasts.

**tel|e|vi|sor** (tel′ə vī′zər), *n.* **1** a television receiver or transmitter. **2** a person or studio that televises.

**tel|e|vis|u|al** (tel′ə vizh′ü əl), *adj. Especially British.* of or suitable for television: *a televisual subject.* **—tel′e|vis′u|al|ly,** *adv.*

**Tel|ex** (tel′eks), *n., v.* **—*n.*** **1** *Trademark.* a communications system of teletypewriters serving subscribers: *Telex, Western Union's direct-dial teleprinter service, had grown rapidly since its inauguration in 1958* (William H. Watts). **2 telex.** this or any similar system. **3** a machine in this system.
**—*v.t.*** Also, **telex.** **1** to send (messages) by Telex: *The instructions were telexed to Pretoria* (Cape Times). **2** to communicate with by Telex: *The departments for which each pallet is destined are telexed ahead of the train* (London Times).
[< *tel*(etype) *ex*(change)]

**tel|fer** (tel′fər), *n., v.t., adj.* = telpher.

**tel|fer|age** (tel′fər ij), *n.* = telpherage.

**tel|ford** (tel′fərd), *n., adj.* **—*n.*** a pavement consisting of layers of rolled stones.
**—*adj.*** **1** of or having to do with such a pavement. **2** made by layers of rolled stones.
[< Thomas *Telford,* 1757-1834, a Scottish engineer]

**tel|ford|ize** (tel′fər dīz), *v.t.,* **-ized, -iz|ing.** to pave with telford (pavement).

**tel|har|mo|ni|um** (tel′här mō′nē əm), *n.* an electrical keyboard instrument to produce music at a distance over an electrical circuit.

**tel|har|mo|ny** (tel här′mə nē), *n.* telharmonium music.

**te|li|al** (tē′lē əl, tel′ē-), *adj. Botany.* **1** of or having to do with a telium. **2** like a telium.

**telial stage**, *Botany.* the last phase in the life cycle of certain rust fungi, in which teliospores are produced.

**tel|ic** (tel′ik), *adj.* **1** *Grammar.* (of a conjunction or clause) expressing end or purpose. *Example:* He asked in order to find out. **2** done for a purpose; teleological. [< Greek *telikós* final < *télos* end, goal]

**tel|ics** (tel′iks), *n.* a branch of sociology dealing with planned and directed progress. [< Greek *télos* goal + English *-ics*]

**te|li|o|spore** (tē′lē ə spôr, -spōr; tel′ē-), *n. Botany.* a thick-walled spore produced by certain rust fungi generally in autumn, remaining in the tissues of the host during winter and germinating in the spring to produce basidia.

**te|li|o|spor|ic** (tē′lē ə spôr′ik, -spōr′-; tel′ē-), *adj. Botany.* having to do with or characterized by teliospores.

**te|li|o|stage** (tē′lē ə stāj′, tel′ē-), *n. Botany.* the telial stage.

**te|li|um** (tē′lē əm, tel′ē-), *n., pl.* **te|li|a** (tē′lē ə, tel′ē-). *Botany.* a sorus bearing teliospores, formed by certain rust fungi. [< New Latin *telium* < Greek *télos* end, goal]

**tell**[1] (tel), *v.,* **told, tell|ing.** **—*v.t.*** **1** to put in words; find a way of expressing; say; utter; express: *Tell the truth. I can't tell you how much I liked it.* **2** to give an account of; narrate; relate; report: *Tell us a story.* **3** to make known in words; communicate: *Tell him the news. He said much but told little.* SYN: mention. **4** to inform; let know: *They told us the way at the station.* **5** to disclose (private matters); reveal (a secret): *Promise not to tell this.* SYN: divulge. **6** to order (a person to do something); say to; direct; command: *Do as you are told. Tell him to wait.* **7** to say with assurance; be positive about: *I couldn't tell exactly when he came.* **8** to recognize well enough to identify; discern: *He couldn't tell which house it was.* **9** to understand the difference between; distinguish; discriminate: *He can't tell one twin from another.* **10** to count one by one; count off; count over: *The nun tells her beads.* **11** to count (votes or voters). **12** *Archaic.* to declare formally or state publicly; announce; proclaim; publish: *Tell it not in Gath* (II Samuel 1:20). **13** *Archaic.* to reckon up the number of; count up: *He could not tell twenty in English* (Daniel

Defoe). 14 *Obsolete.* to reveal.
—*v.i.* 1 to act as talebearer; report secrets; blab; tattle: *Promise not to tell.* 2 to be effective; count for something; have an effect or force: *Every blow told.* 3 *British Dialect.* to talk idly without acting.
**don't tell me**, an expression of incredulity or impatience: *Error of judgment! don't tell me. I know how these things happen quite well* (Cardinal Newman).
**I (can) tell you**, yes, indeed; I emphasize: *I tell you, it got on my nerves* (F. Young).
**let me tell you**, yes, indeed; I emphasize: *Let me tell you, I am not to be persuaded by metaphysical arguments* (Bishop Berkeley).
**tell good-by**, *U.S.* to say good-by to: *She told me to tell you good-by* (Booth Tarkington).
**tell it like it is**, *U.S. Slang.* to tell the truth, no matter how unpleasant: *The [TV] series' intention ... is "to tell it like it is for the young people while remaining palatable to older audiences"* (Time).
**tell me another**, an expression of incredulity or irony: *You lost your money. Indeed! Tell me another.*
**tell of**, to be an indication or sign of; show: *His hard hands and sinewy sunburnt limbs told of labour and endurance* (Charles Kingsley).
**tell off, a** to count off; count off and detach for some special duty: *Ten knights were then told off, and ten followers for every knight, to ride down to Doncaster* (James A. Froude). **b** to strike back sharply; reprimand; scold; reprove: *Monty came to see me and I had to tell him off for falling foul of both the King and the Secretary of State* (Maclean's).
**tell on, a** to inform on; tell tales about: *Promise not to tell on me.* **b** *Figurative.* to have a harmful effect on; break down: *The strain told on the man's heart.*
[Old English *tellan,* related to *talu* tale]

**tell²** (tel), *n.* an artificial hillock or mound, usually one covering the ruins of an ancient city: *Some Palestinian tells are 70 ft. thick and contain dozens of different layers of debris* (Time). [< Arabic *tall* hillock]

**Tell** (tel), *n.* **William**, a legendary hero in the Swiss struggle for independence against Austria.

**tell|a|ble** (tel′ə bəl), *adj.* that can be told; worth telling. —**tell′a|ble|ness**, *n.*

**tell|a|bly** (tel′ə blē), *adv.* in a manner that is tellable; so as to be tellable.

**tell|er** (tel′ər), *n.* 1 a person who tells, especially a story; narrator: *Our teacher is a good teller of stories.* 2 a person who counts, especially: **a** a bank cashier who takes in, gives out, and counts money. **b** an official who counts votes, especially in a legislature.

**tell|er|ship** (tel′ər ship), *n.* the office or post of teller; a position as teller.

**tell|ing** (tel′ing), *adj., n.* —*adj.* having effect or force; striking: *a telling blow. He is a master of a singularly lucid ... and telling style* (Times Literary Supplement). SYN: effective, potent, forceful.
—*n.* 1 the act of relating or making known: *something beautiful beyond all telling. The narrative loses nothing in the telling* (Athenaeum).
2 the act of counting: *This mixed telling did not mean mixed voting* (Scotsman). —**tell′ing|ly**, *adv.*

**tell|ing-off** (tel′ing ôf′, -of′), *n. Informal.* a scolding; rebuke.

**tell|tale** (tel′tāl′), *n., adj.* —*n.* 1 a person who tells tales on others; person who reveals private or secret matters from malice. SYN: talebearer, tattler. 2 *Figurative.* a warning sign; indication. 3 any one of various indicators or recording instruments, such as a time clock. 4 *Music.* an indicator of the pressure of the air supply to an organ. 5 a row of ribbons hung over a track before a tunnel, bridge, or other low structure, to warn trainmen off the roofs of cars. 6 *Nautical.* a device above deck to indicate the rudder's position. 7 (in squash and rackets) a metal strip across the front wall of the court that may not be hit with the ball. The squash telltale is 17 inches high, the rackets telltale 27.
—*adj.* 1 telling what is not supposed to be told; revealing: *a telltale fingerprint.* 2 showing, signaling, or warning of something.

**tel|lu|rate** (tel′yə rāt), *n. Chemistry.* a salt of telluric acid with a maximum of oxygen.

**tel|lu|ri|an¹** (te lůr′ē ən), *adj., n.* —*adj.* 1 having to do with the earth. 2 earthly; terrestrial.
—*n.* an inhabitant of the earth: *Our own case, the case of poor mediocre tellurians* (Thomas De Quincey).
[< Latin *tellūs, -ūris* earth + English *-an*]

**tel|lu|ri|an²** (te lůr′ē ən), *n.* = tellurion.

**tel|lu|ric¹** (te lůr′ik), *adj.* 1 of the earth; terrestrial. 2 arising from the soil; of earth. [< Latin *tellūs, -ūris* earth + *-ic*]

**tel|lu|ric²** (te lůr′ik), *adj. Chemistry.* 1 having to do with tellurium. 2 containing tellurium, especially with a valence of six.

**telluric acid**, an acid containing tellurium with a valence of six, obtained by oxidizing tellurium or its oxide. *Formula:* $H_6TeO_6$

**tel|lu|rid** (tel′yər id), *n.* = telluride.

**tel|lu|ride** (tel′yə rīd, -yər id), *n.* a compound of tellurium with an electropositive element or radical.

**tel|lu|rif|er|ous** (tel′yə rif′ər əs), *adj.* containing or yielding tellurium.

**tel|lu|ri|on** (tə lůr′ē ən), *n.* a model of the moving earth and the sun, showing how day and night and the changes in the seasons result from the earth's revolution about the sun. [< Latin *tellūs, -ūris* earth + Greek *-ion,* a neuter diminutive suffix]

**tel|lu|rite** (tel′yə rīt), *n.* 1 *Chemistry.* a salt of tellurous acid, containing less oxygen than a tellurate. 2 a mineral, a native dioxide of tellurium, usually found in clusters of minute, whitish or yellowish crystals. *Formula:* $TeO_2$

***tel|lu|ri|um** (te lůr′ē əm), *n.* silver-white, nonmetallic chemical element with some metallic properties. It is poisonous, brittle unless extremely pure, and similar to sulfur and selenium chemically. It usually occurs in nature combined with gold, silver, or various other metals. Tellurium is used as a coloring agent in ceramics. [< New Latin *Tellurium* < Latin *tellūs, -ūris* earth]

***tellurium**

| symbol | atomic number | atomic weight | oxidation state |
|---|---|---|---|
| Te | 52 | 127.60 | -2,+4,+6 |

**tel|lu|rize** (tel′yə rīz), *v.t.,* **-rized, -riz|ing.** to combine or treat with tellurium.

**tel|lu|rom|e|ter** (tel′yə rom′ə tər), *n.* an electronic device for measuring distances by the time it takes a radio microwave to travel from one point to another and back.

**tel|lu|rous** (tel′yər əs, te lůr′-), *adj.* 1 of tellurium. 2 containing tellurium, especially with a valence of four.

**tellurous acid**, an acid containing tellurium with a valence of four. It is a white, water-soluble powder. *Formula:* $H_2TeO_3$

**Tel|lus** (tel′əs), *n. Roman Mythology.* an ancient goddess who blessed crops and marriage.

**tel|ly** (tel′ē), *n. British Informal.* television. [alteration of *tele,* short for *television*]

**tel|ma|tol|o|gy** (tel′mə tol′ə jē), *n.* the science that deals with the formation and contents of peat bogs. [< Greek *télma, -atos* marsh + English *-logy*]

**tel|o|dy|nam|ic** (tel′ō dī nam′ik, -di-), *adj.* of or having to do with the transmission of power, especially by cables on pulleys. [< Greek *tēloû* far off + English *dynamic*]

**tel|o|lec|i|thal** (tel′ō les′ə thəl), *adj.* (of eggs) having the yolk in one end and the cytoplasm in the other end. [< Greek *télos* end + English *lecith*(in) + *-al*¹]

**tel|o|mer** (tel′ə mər), *n.* a reduced polymer formed by the reaction between a substance capable of being polymerized and an agent that arrests the growth of the chain of atoms: *Chemists found how to limit the number of atoms that link together to form a long-chain molecule, creating telomers in contrast to the long-chain polymers of earlier plastics* (Science News Letter). [< Greek *télos* end + English (poly)*mer*]

**tel|o|phase** (tel′ə fāz), *n. Biology.* the fourth and final stage of mitosis, when a membrane forms around each group of chromosomes in the cell and a nucleus is produced in each group, just before the cytoplasm of the cell constricts and the two new cells appear. See diagram at **mitosis**. [< Greek *télos* end + English *phase*]

**tel|o|phas|ic** (tel′ə fā′zik), *adj.* of or having to do with the telophase.

**te|los** (tē′los, tel′os), *n., pl.* **-loi** (-loi). end; purpose; ultimate object or aim: *a clash between the laws of the inorganic which has no telos, and the behavior of living creatures who have one* (New Yorker). [< Greek *télos* end]

**tel|pher** (tel′fər), *n., v., adj.* —*n.* 1 a car or other unit running from electric cables. 2 a system using these; telpherage.
—*v.t.* to carry or convey by a telpher.
—*adj.* 1 of or having to do with telpherage. 2 used in telpherage. Also, **telfer**.
[short for earlier *telephore* < *tele-* + Greek *phoreîn* to bear]

**tel|pher|age** (tel′fər ij), *n.* 1 a transportation system using telphers supplied with electric current by the cable. 2 a similar system in which cars are pulled by an endless cable worked by a motor. Also, **telferage**.

**tel|son** (tel′sən), *n.* the rearmost segment of the abdomen in certain crustaceans and arachnids, such as the middle flipper of a lobster's tail or the sting of a scorpion. [< Greek *télson* limit; headland]

**Tel|star** (tel′stär′), *n.* an active communications satellite launched by the United States to relay telephone calls, television programs, and other communications. [< *tel-* + *star*]

**Tel|u|gu** (tel′ə gü), *n., pl.* **-gu** or **-gus**, *adj.* —*n.* 1 a Dravidian language spoken in southeastern India. 2 one of the Dravidian people who speak this language.
—*adj.* of or having to do with this Dravidian people or their language. Also, **Telegu.**

**TEM** (no periods), triethylene melamine.

**tem|blor** (tem blôr′), *n., pl.* **-blors, -blo|res** (-blōr′ās). *U.S.* a tremor; earthquake. [American English < Spanish *temblor* a trembling < *temblar* to tremble < Vulgar Latin *tremulāre* < Latin *tremulus* trembling]

**Tem|bu** (tem′bü), *n., pl.* **-bu** or **-bus.** a member of a Kaffir tribe that lives in Tembuland, a region in Cape of Good Hope Province, South Africa.

**tem|er|ar|i|ous** (tem′ə rãr′ē əs), *adj.* characterized by temerity. [< Latin *temerārius* (with English *-ous*) rash; fortuitous < *temere* heedlessly]
—**tem′er|ar′i|ous|ly**, *adv.* —**tem′er|ar′i|ous|ness**, *n.*

**te|mer|i|ty** (tə mer′ə tē), *n.* reckless boldness; rashness: *What preposterous temerity—to analyze what happened in a half hour five billion years ago!* (Atlantic). SYN: foolhardiness, audacity. [< Latin *temeritās* < *temere* heedlessly]

**te-mine** (tə mīn′), *n.* = tamein.

**Tem|in enzyme** (tem′ən), an enzyme that causes the formation of DNA on a template or pattern of RNA in certain cancer-producing viruses; reverse transcriptase: *No form of cancer in humans has yet been shown to be caused by a virus but should this be the case, the Temin enzyme may offer an unprecedented chance of attacking the disease at its roots* (London Times). [< Howard M. *Temin,* an American biochemist, who discovered the enzyme]

**Tem|in|ism** (tem′ə niz′əm), *n.* a theory in molecular biology which maintains, in contravention to the central dogma, that RNA can act as a blueprint or template for the formation of DNA. [< Howard M. *Temin,* an American biochemist, who proposed this theory]

**Tem|ne** (tem′nā), *n.* 1 a tribe that inhabits part of Sierra Leone, a country on the western coast of Africa. 2 their Niger-Congo language.

**temp.**, 1 in the time of (Latin, *tempore*). 2 temperature. 3 temporary.

**tem|peh** (tem′pā), *n.* an Indonesian food made from fermented soybean curds. [< Indonesian *témpé*]

**tem|per** (tem′pər), *n., v.* —*n.* 1 state of mind; disposition; mood: *She has a sweet temper. She was in no temper to be kept waiting.* SYN: humor. See syn. under **disposition**. 2 an angry state of mind: *He flies into a temper at trifles. In her temper she broke a vase.* 3 a calm state of mind: *He became angry and lost his temper.* 4 the hardness, toughness, or flexibility of a substance, given by tempering: *The temper of the clay was right for shaping.* 5 a substance added to something to modify its properties or qualities. 6 *Archaic.* **a** a regulation; adjustment. **b** a middle course; mean. 7 *Obsolete.* the temperament. [< verb]
—*v.t.* 1 to moderate; soften: *Temper justice with mercy.* 2 to check; restrain; curb. 3 to bring to a proper or desired condition by mixing or preparing. A painter tempers his colors by mixing them with oil. *Clay is tempered by mixing or working it up with water.* 4 to harden (glass or metals, especially steel) by heating and then cooling in oil, water, or other liquid: *The structure of steel is changed by tempering it at various temperatures* (George S. Rose). 5 to tune or adjust the pitch of (a musical instrument, or voice, or a note). 6 *Obsolete.* to fit, adapt, or make suitable (to).
—*v.i.* to be or become tempered; be brought to a proper or desired condition by mixing or preparing.
[Middle English *tempren,* Old English *temprian* < Latin *temperāre* (originally) observe due measure < *tempus, -oris* time. Compare etym. under **tamper**¹.] —**tem′per|a|ble**, *adj.* —**tem′per|er**, *n.*

**tem|per|a** (tem′pər ə), *n.* 1 a method of painting in which colors are mixed with white or yolk of egg, the whole egg, or other substances instead of oil. 2 the paints used. [< Italian *tempera* < *temperare* to temper < Latin *temperāre.* Compare etym. under **distemper**².]

**tem|per|a|ment** (tem′pər ə mənt, -prə-), *n.* 1 a person's nature; make-up; disposition: *She has a nervous temperament. Her highly strung tempera-*

**Pronunciation Key:** hat, āge, cãre, fär; let, ēqual, tėrm; it, īce; hot, ōpen, ôrder; oil, out; cup, pu̇t, rüle; child; long; thin; ᴛʜen; zh, measure; ə represents **a** in about, **e** in taken, **i** in pencil, **o** in lemon, **u** in circus.

*ment made her uncertain ... capricious ... enchanting* (George Bernard Shaw). SYN: See syn. under **disposition**. **2** an easily irritated, sensitive nature, especially a nature or disposition that is not inclined to submit to ordinary rules or restraints. An artist, singer, or actress often has temperament. **3** *Music.* **a** the adjustment of the intervals of the natural scale by slightly varying the pitch. **b** a system according to which this is done. **4** *Archaic.* **a** moderation. **b** mitigation. **c** due regulation. **5** *Obsolete.* consistency; composition. **6** *Obsolete.* climate. **7** *Obsolete.* temperature. [< Latin *temperāmentum* mixture < *temperāre* to mix, temper]

**tem|per|a|men|tal** (tem′pər ə men′təl, -prə-), *adj.* **1** subject to moods and whims; easily irritated; sensitive. **2** showing a strongly marked individual temperament. **3** due to temperament; constitutional: *Cats have a temperamental dislike for water.* —**tem′per|a|men′tal|ly**, *adv.*

**tem|per|ance** (tem′pər əns, -prəns), *n.* **1** the state or quality of being moderate in action, speech, or habits; self-control: *Temperance should be applied not only to food and drink but also to work and play.* **2** the state or quality of being moderate in the use of alcoholic drinks: *Abstinence is as easy to me as temperance would be difficult* (Samuel Johnson). **3** the principle and practice of not using alcoholic drinks at all. SYN: abstinence. [< Anglo-French *temperaunce*, learned borrowing from Latin *temperantia* moderation < *temperāre* to temper]

**tem|per|ate** (tem′pər it, -prit), *adj.* **1** not very hot, and not very cold: *a temperate climate.* **2** moderate; self-restrained; using self-control: *She spoke in a temperate manner, not favoring either side especially.* SYN: calm, dispassionate. See syn. under **moderate**. **3a** moderate in using alcoholic drinks: *He is a temperate man, and never drinks too much.* **b** = abstemious. **4** *Music.* tempered. **5** of or having to do with the Temperate Zone: *New Zealand supported ... the orderly marketing ... of temperate agricultural products* (London Times). [< Latin *temperātus* restrained; duly regulated, past participle of *temperāre* (originally) observe due measure; see etym. under **temper**] —**tem′per|ate|ly**, *adv.* —**tem′per|ate|ness**, *n.*

**Temperate Zone** or **temperate zone**, either of the two regions of the earth between the tropics and the polar circles: *The United States is in the north Temperate Zone.*

**tem|per|a|ture** (tem′pər ə chər, -chůr; -prə-), *n.* **1** the degree of heat or cold. The temperature of freezing water is 32 degrees Fahrenheit. *The colour of a glowing opaque body depends only on its temperature and not on its composition* (Bondi and Bondi). *Abbr:* temp. **2** the degree of heat contained in a human or other living body, usually measured by a thermometer: *The temperature of a person who has a fever is over 98.6 degrees Fahrenheit.* **3** a body temperature higher than normal (98.6 degrees) F. or 37 degrees C.; fever: *A sick person may have a temperature.* **4** *Physics.* a measure of the kinetic energy of the molecules that make up a substance. **5** *Obsolete.* **a** moderation. **b** temperament. [< Latin *temperātūra* a tempering < *temperāre* to temper]

**temperature gradient**, the rate of change in temperature: *Though an intriguing possibility the use of temperature gradients in the oceans does not appear to be an important source of useful power* (J. J. William Brown).

**temperature-humidity index**, a combined measurement of temperature and humidity arrived at by adding degrees of temperature to percentage of relative humidity and dividing by two; discomfort index; humiture. It is issued during the summer months by the U.S. Weather Service. *Abbr:* THI (no periods).

**temperature inversion**, = thermal inversion.

**temper color**, any one of the colors formed on the surface of steel in the tempering process.

**tem|pered** (tem′pərd), *adj.* **1a** softened or moderated. **b** seasoned: (*Figurative.*) *tempered wisdom.* **2** having a (specified) state of mind: *a good-tempered person.* **3** treated so as to become hard but not too brittle: *The sword was made of tempered steel.* **4** *Music.* tuned or adjusted in pitch according to equal temperament.

**temper tantrum**, = tantrum.

**tem|pest** (tem′pist), *n., v.* —*n.* **1** a violent windstorm, usually accompanied by rain, hail, or snow: *The tempest drove the ship on the rocks.* SYN: gale. **2** *Figurative.* a violent disturbance: *a tempest of anger.* SYN: uproar, tumult.
—*v.t.* to affect by a tempest: (*Figurative.*) *The huge dolphin tempesting the main* (Alexander Pope).

**tempest in a teapot**, *Especially U.S.* a great disturbance over a small matter: *To Ferger the whole fracas was "a tempest in a teapot" and his major accuser "emotionally unstable"* (Time).
[< Old French *tempeste* < Vulgar Latin *tempestus*, or *tempesta*, variants of Latin *tempestās* storm; weather; season, related to *tempus, -oris* time, season]

**tem|pes|tu|ous** (tem pes′chů əs), *adj.* **1** stormy: *a tempestuous night.* **2** *Figurative.* violent: *a tempestuous argument. She burst into a tempestuous fit of anger.* —**tem|pes′tu|ous|ly**, *adv.* —**tem-pes′tu|ous|ness**, *n.*

**tem|pi** (tem′pē), *n.* tempos; a plural of **tempo**.

**Tem|plar** (tem′plər), *n.* **1** a member of a religious and military order called Knights Templars, founded among the Crusaders to protect the Holy Sepulcher and pilgrims to the Holy Land. **2** a member of an order of Masons, the Knights Templar. **3** Also, **templar**. *British.* a barrister or other person, who has chambers in the Inner or Middle Temple in London. [< Medieval Latin *templarius* < Latin *templum* temple (because the order occupied a building in Jerusalem near the site known as Solomon's Temple)]

**tem|plate** (tem′plit), *n.* **1** a pattern, gauge, or mold of a thin, flat piece of wood or metal, used in shaping a piece of work. **2** *Figurative.* any model on which something is formed or based; pattern: *There seems little doubt that ... only one strand of the DNA molecule serves as a template for RNA synthesis* (Scientific American). **3a** a horizontal piece under a girder, beam, or other long supporting piece to distribute downward thrust. **b** a piece for supporting joists or rafters, as over a doorway or window. **4** a wedge supporting the keel of a ship under construction. [variant of *templet;* probably influenced by *plate*]

**tem|ple[1]** (tem′pəl), *n.* **1** a building used for the service or worship of a god or gods: *Greek temples were beautifully built.* SYN: sanctuary, tabernacle. **2** Often, **Temple. a** any one of three buildings in ancient Jerusalem built at different times on the same spot by the Jews. **b** Also, **Temple of Solomon.** the first of these three buildings, built by Solomon and destroyed by the Babylonians (in the Bible, I Kings 6 and 7). **3** a building set apart for Christian worship; church. **4a** = synagogue. **b** the services conducted there. **5** a place in which God specially dwells. **6** a Mormon church. **7a** a building occupied by a local unit of a secret order. **b** a local unit of certain secret orders.
[Old English *tempel* < Latin *templum.* See etym. of doublets **temple[3]**, **templon.**]

**tem|ple[2]** (tem′pəl), *n.* **1** the flattened part on either side of the forehead. **2** *U.S.* the bow of eyeglasses. [< Old French *temple* < Vulgar Latin *tempula,* feminine < Latin *tempora,* neuter plural of *tempus, -oris* temple (of the head)]

**tem|ple[3]** (tem′pəl), *n.* an apparatus in a loom for keeping cloth stretched to its proper width. [< Middle French *temple* weaver's stretcher, learned borrowing from Latin *templum* small timber; temple. See etym. of doublets **temple[1]**, **templon.**]

**Tem|ple** (tem′pəl), *n.* either of two English legal societies (the Inner Temple and Middle Temple).

**temple block**, any one of various hollowed-out wooden vessels of different sizes and pitches, used with a stick as a percussion instrument in Korean and Chinese ritual music and sometimes in modern bands and orchestras.

**tem|pled** (tem′pəld), *adj.* furnished or adorned with a temple or temples.

**tem|plet** (tem′plit), *n.* = template.

**tem|plon** (tem′plon), *n.* (in the Greek Church) an iconostasis. [< Late Greek *témplon* < Latin *templum.* See etym. of doublets **temple[1]**, **temple[3]**.]

**tem|po** (tem′pō), *n., pl.* **-pos, -pi** (-pē). **1** *Music.* the time or rate of movement; proper or characteristic speed of movement: *the correct tempo for a dance tune. Hundreds of people identified themselves with the conductor, standing in front of their screens with rulers and pencils in their hands and giving the beat and tempo* (Time). **2** *Figurative: the fast tempo of modern life.* SYN: rhythm, pace. [< Italian *tempo* time < Latin *tempus.* See etym. of doublet **tense[2]**.]

**tem|po|ral[1]** (tem′pər əl, -prəl), *adj., n.* —*adj.* **1** of time. **2a** lasting for a time only. SYN: temporary, transient. **b** of this life only: *The things which are seen are temporal; but the things which are not seen are eternal* (II Corinthians 4:18). SYN: earthly, terrestrial. **3** not religious or sacred; worldly; secular. **4** *Grammar.* **a** expressing time, as an adverb or a clause. **b** of tense.
—*n.* Often, **temporals.** that which is temporal; a temporal thing or matter: *trying by some other way than through these homely temporals, to learn the spiritual life* (H. Drummond).
[< Latin *temporālis* < *tempus, -oris* time]

**tem|po|ral[2]** (tem′pər əl, -prəl), *adj., n.* —*adj.* of or situated in the temples or sides of the forehead: *a temporal artery, muscle, or vein.*
—*n.* **1** = temporal bone. **2** any temporal part.
[< Late Latin *temporālis* < Latin *tempora,* plural of *tempus, -oris* temple]

**temporal bone**, a compound bone that forms part of the side and base of the skull. See picture under **face**.

**temporal gland**, a gland situated in the temporal region of an elephant's brain that becomes active during the frenzied condition of the must period and secretes a dark, oily material with a strong smell.

**tem|po|ral|i|ty** (tem′pə ral′ə tē), *n., pl.* **-ties.** **1** temporal character or nature; temporariness. **2** something temporal; temporal power, jurisdiction, or authority. **3** the laity.
**temporalities**, the property or revenues of a church or clergyman: *The Pope ... gave to the said Nicholas the said Abbey, with all the said spiritualities and temporalities* (Roger Coke).

**tem|po|ral|ize** (tem′pər ə līz), *v.t.,* **-ized, -iz|ing.** **1** to make temporal; limit in time. **2** to make worldly; secularize.

**temporal lobe**, the lower lateral lobe of each cerebral hemisphere, in front of the occipital lobe. It is the center of hearing in the brain. See diagram under **brain**.

**tem|po|ral|ly** (tem′pər ə lē, -prə-), *adv.* in a temporal manner; as regards temporal matters.

**tem|po|rar|i|ly** (tem′pə rer′ə lē, tem′pə rãr′-), *adv.* for a short time; for the present: *They are living in a hotel temporarily. The work is postponed temporarily.*

**tem|po|rar|i|ness** (tem′pə rer′ē nis), *n.* the condition or character of being temporary.

**tem|po|rar|y** (tem′pə rer′ē), *adj., n., pl.* **-rar|ies.**
—*adj.* lasting for a short time only; used for the time being; not permanent: *temporary relief from pain. The hunter made a temporary shelter out of branches.*
—*n.* a person employed, enrolled, or otherwise accounted for temporarily; casual: *He entered the army as a temporary* (London Times).
[< Latin *temporārius* of seasonal character; lasting a moment of time < *tempus, -oris* time, season]
—*Syn. adj.* **Temporary, transient** mean lasting or staying only for a time. **Temporary** applies to something meant to last only for a time and liable to come to an end shortly: *He has a temporary job. Our school is housed in a temporary building.* **Transient** applies to something that is passing and hence will not stay long: *Her panic was transient, and ceased when she began to speak.*

**temporary duty**, limited military duty performed away from one's regular station or post.

**tem|po|rize** (tem′pə rīz), *v.i.,* **-rized, riz|ing.** **1** to evade immediate action or decision in order to gain time, avoid trouble, or otherwise put off something. SYN: hedge. **2** to fit one's acts to the time or occasion. SYN: trim. **3** to make or discuss terms; negotiate. SYN: parley. [< Middle French *temporiser,* learned borrowing from Medieval Latin *temporizare* pass time, perhaps < Vulgar Latin *temporāre* to delay < Latin *tempus, -oris* time] —**tem′po|ri|za′tion**, *n.* —**tem′po|riz′er**, *n.* —**tem′po|riz′ing|ly**, *adv.*

**temps per|du** (tän per dv′), *French.* **1** a former period of time; time past: *This nostalgic and gilded re-creation of temps perdu offers a banjo band, beer, and occasional old movies* (New Yorker). **2** (literally) time lost.

**tempt** (tempt), *v.t.* **1** to make or try to make (a person) do something: *The sight of the food tempted the hungry man to steal.* SYN: lure, inveigle, decoy. **2** to appeal strongly to; attract: *That candy tempts me.* SYN: allure, entice. **3** to dispose or incline: *to be tempted to disagree.* **4** to induce or persuade: *Nothing will tempt him to sell his business.* **5** to provoke: *It is tempting Providence to go in that old boat.* **6** *Archaic.* to test: *God tempted Abraham by asking him to sacrifice his son.* [< Anglo-French *tempter,* learned borrowing from Latin *temptāre,* later *tentāre* to try (intensive) < *tendere* to stretch (oneself), strive] —**tempt′a|ble**, *adj.* —**tempt′er**, *n.*

**temp|ta|tion** (temp tā′shən), *n.* **1** the act of tempting: *No temptation could make him false to a friend.* **2** the fact or condition of being tempted: *The Lord's Prayer says "Lead us not into temptation."* **3** a thing that tempts: *Money left carelessly about is a temptation. But in spite of all temptations he remains an Englishman* (W. S. Gilbert). SYN: attraction, lure, enticement, inducement.

**Tempt|er** (temp′tər), *n.* **the.** the Devil; Satan.

**tempt|ing** (temp′ting), *adj.* that tempts; alluring; inviting: *A nap is a tempting idea.* —**tempt′ing|ly**, *adv.* —**tempt′ing|ness**, *n.*

**tempt|ress** (temp′tris), *n.* a woman who tempts. SYN: siren.

**tem|pu|ra** (tem pür′ə; *Japanese* tem′pů rä), *n.* a dish of seafood or vegetables fried in batter. [< Japanese *tempura*]

**tem|pus e|dax re|rum** (tem′pəs ē′daks rir′əm), *Latin.* time the devourer of (all) things.

**tem|pus fu|git** (tem′pəs fyü′jit), *Latin.* time flies.

**ten** (ten), *n., adj.* —*n.* **1** one more than nine; 10.

2 a set of ten persons or things. **3** a playing card, throw of the dice, billiard ball, or other playing piece, with ten spots or a "10" on it. **4a** a ten-dollar bill. **b** a ten-pound note.
*—adj.* being one more than nine.
[Old English *tēn, tīen*]

**ten.,** **1** tenor. **2** *Music.* tenuto.

**ten|a|bil|i|ty** (ten'ə bil'ə tē), *n.* the fact or quality of being tenable.

**ten|a|ble** (ten'ə bəl), *adj.* that can be held or defended: *a tenable position,* (*Figurative.*) *a tenable theory.* **SYN:** defensible, unassailable. [< Middle French *tenable* < Old French *tenir* hold (< Latin *tenēre*)] **—ten'a|ble|ness,** *n.*

**ten|a|bly** (ten'ə blē), *adv.* in a tenable manner.

**ten|ace** (ten'ās), *n.* a combination of two cards lacking a third between them to form a sequence, such as ten and queen. [probably < Spanish *tenaza* (literally) pincers < Latin *forcipes tenāces* gripping forceps. Compare French *demeurer tenace* to have the tenace.]

**te|na|cious** (ti nā'shəs), *adj.* **1** holding fast: *the tenacious jaws of a bulldog, a person tenacious of his rights.* **2** *Figurative.* stubborn; persistent: *a tenacious salesman.* **SYN:** obstinate. **3** *Figurative.* able to remember: *a tenacious memory.* **SYN:** retentive. **4** holding fast together; not easily pulled apart. **5** sticky. [< Latin *tenax, -ācis* (with English *-ous*) < *tenēre* to hold] **—te|na'cious|ly,** *adv.* **—te|na'cious|ness,** *n.*

**te|nac|i|ty** (ti nas'ə tē), *n.* **1** firmness in holding fast. **SYN:** adhesion, grip. **2** *Figurative.* stubbornness; persistence. **SYN:** obstinacy. **3** *Figurative.* ability to remember. **SYN:** retentiveness. **4** firmness in holding together; toughness. **SYN:** cohesion. **5** sticky quality; sticky condition. **SYN:** viscosity. **6** *Physics.* tensile strength.

**te|nac|u|lum** (ti nak'yə ləm), *n., pl.* **-la** (-lə). a long-handled surgical instrument with a sharp hook, used especially to pick up parts and draw edges of wounds together. [< New Latin *tenaculum* (in Latin, a holder) < Latin *tenēre* to hold]

**te|naille** or **te|nail** (te nāl'), *n.* a low defensive structure built outside a main fortification between two bastions. [< Middle French *tenaille* < Old French, forceps, < unrecorded Latin *tenācula,* plural of *tenāculum;* see etym. under **tenaculum**]

**ten|an|cy** (ten'ən sē), *n., pl.* **-cies.** **1** the condition of being a tenant; occupying and paying rent for land or buildings: *Tenancy is the human condition in Manhattan* (New Yorker). **SYN:** occupancy. **2** the property so held. **SYN:** holding. **3** the length of time a tenant occupies a property. **SYN:** tenure.

**ten|ant** (ten'ənt), *n., v.* **—n. 1** a person paying rent for the temporary use of the land or buildings of another person: *That building has apartments for one hundred tenants.* **2** *Figurative: Birds are tenants of the trees.* **SYN:** inhabitant, occupant, dweller.
*—v.t.* to hold or occupy as a tenant; inhabit: *That old house has not been tenanted for many years.*
*—v.i.* to reside; dwell; live (in).
[< Old French *tenant,* (originally) present participle of *tenir* to hold < Latin *tenēre*] **—ten'ant|a|ble,** *adj.*

**tenant farmer,** a farmer who raises crops or livestock on land belonging to another, to whom he pays rent in cash or in a share of the crops or livestock: *The sharecropper and tenant farmers left the farm and turned to the rapidly growing opportunities in industry.*

**ten|ant|less** (ten'ənt lis), *adj.* without a tenant; vacant: *a dreary and tenantless mansion* (Longfellow).

**ten|ant|ry** (ten'ən trē), *n., pl.* **-ries.** **1** all the tenants on an estate: *The old Squire's visits to his tenantry were rare* (George Eliot). **2** = tenancy.

**ten|ant|ship** (ten'ənt ship), *n.* tenancy; occupancy.

**ten-cent store** (ten'sent'), *U.S. Informal.* dime store.

**tench** (tench), *n., pl.* **tench|es** or (*collectively*) **tench.** a freshwater fish of Europe, related to the carp, and noted for the length of time it can live out of water: *Tench are partial to foul and weedy waters* (William Bingley). [< Old French *tenche* < Late Latin *tinca*]

**Ten Commandments,** the ten rules for living and for worship that God revealed to Moses on Mount Sinai (in the Bible, Exodus 20:2-17; Deuteronomy 5:6-22); Decalogue.

**tend[1]** (tend), *v.i.* **1** to be apt; be likely; incline (to): *Fruit tends to decay. Modern industry tends toward consolidation. Farms tend to use more machinery now.* **2** to move (toward); be directed (toward): *The road tends to the south here.* [< Old French *tendre* < Latin *tendere* to aim, stretch out. See etym. of doublet **tender[2]**.]

**tend[2]** (tend), *v.t.* **1** to take care of; look after; attend to: *He tends shop for his father. A shepherd tends his flock. A nurse tends the sick.* **2** to serve; wait upon. **3** *Nautical.* to stand by and watch over (as a line or anchor cable). *—v.i.* **1** to serve (upon). **2** *Informal.* to pay attention. **3** *Obsolete.* to wait in expectation or readiness: *The time invites you, go, your servants tend* (Shakespeare). [short for *attend,* or *intend* apply oneself to. Compare etym. under **tent[3]**.]

**Ten|dai** (ten'dī), *n.* a Buddhist sect of Japan noted for its synthesis of all Buddhist doctrines: *Buddhism in Japan today has five major divisions: Tendai and Shingon, which came from China early in the ninth century, Zen, Jodo, and Nichiren* (Atlantic).

**tend|ance** (ten'dəns), *n.* attention; care.

**ten|den|cious** (ten den'shəs), *adj.* tendentious: *A false and tendencious account of what had taken place* (Contemporary Review). **—ten|den'cious|ly,** *adv.* **—ten|den'cious|ness,** *n.*

**tend|en|cy** (ten'dən sē), *n., pl.* **-cies.** **1** an inclination; leaning: *Boys have a stronger tendency to fight than girls.* **SYN:** bent, bias, proneness, propensity. **2** a natural disposition to move, proceed, or act in some direction or toward some point, end, or result: *Wood has a tendency to swell if it gets wet.* **SYN:** See syn. under **direction.** [< Medieval Latin *tendentia* < Latin *tendere* tend, incline]

**ten|den|tial** (ten den'shəl), *adj.* **1** marked by a tendency. **2** = tendentious.

**ten|den|tious** (ten den'shəs), *adj.* **1** having a tendency to take sides; one-sided: *a tendentious statement.* **2** troublemaking; rebellious: *a spoiled, tendentious child.* [< *tendency* + *-ous*] **—ten|den'tious|ly,** *adv.* **—ten|den'tious|ness,** *n.*

**ten|der[1]** (ten'dər), *adj., v., n.* **—adj. 1** not hard or tough; soft: *The meat is tender. Stones hurt the little child's tender feet.* **2a** not strong and hardy; delicate: *tender young grass. The leaves in spring are green and tender.* **SYN:** weak. **b** soft; subdued: *a tender blue.* **SYN:** delicate. **3** kind; affectionate; loving: *The mother spoke tender words to her baby. She sent tender messages to her friends.* **SYN:** compassionate, merciful. **4** not rough or crude; gentle: *He patted the dog with tender hands. The young plants need tender care.* **SYN:** mild, sympathetic. **5** young; immature: *Two years old is a tender age.* **6** sensitive; painful; sore: *a tender wound. The elbow joint is a tender spot.* **7a** feeling pain or grief easily: *She has a tender heart and would never hurt anyone.* **b** *Figurative.* sensitive to insult or injury; ready to take offense: *a man of tender pride.* **8** considerate or careful: *He handles people in a tender manner.* **9** *Figurative.* requiring careful or tactful handling: *a tender situation. Automobiles are a tender subject with Dad since he wrecked his.* **10** = crank[2].
*—v.t. Archaic.* **1** to make tender. **2** to weaken. **3** to feel or act tenderly toward.
*—v.i. Obsolete.* to become tender.
*—n. Obsolete.* care; regard; concern.
[Middle English *tendre* soft, delicate < Old French, earlier *tenre* < Latin *tener*] **—ten'der|a|ble,** *adj.* **—ten'der|ly,** *adv.*

**ten|der[2]** (ten'dər), *v., n.* **—v.t. 1** to offer formally: *to tender one's resignation. He tendered his thanks.* **SYN:** proffer, present. See syn. under **offer.** **2** *Law.* to offer (as money or goods) in payment of a debt or other obligation.
*—n.* **1** a formal offer: *She refused his tender of marriage.* **SYN:** proposal, proffer, overture. **2** the thing offered. Money that must be accepted as payment for a debt is called legal tender. **3** *Law.* an offer of, as of money or goods, to satisfy a debt or liability. **4** *Commerce.* a bid to supply or purchase: *All tenders must be enclosed in sealed envelopes* (Cape Times).
[< Middle French *tendre* to offer < Latin *tendere* extend. See etym. of doublet **tend[1]**.] **—ten'der|er,** *n.*

***tender[3]**
definition 3

***tend|er[3]** (ten'dər), *n.* **1** a person or thing that tends another: *a machine tender. He did not like his job as baby tender.* **2a** a boat or small ship used for carrying supplies and passengers to and from larger ships. **b** a small boat carried on or towed behind a larger boat or a ship for similar use. **3** the small car that carries wood, coal and water, or oil, attached behind a locomotive. See picture below. [probably < *tend[2]* + *-er[1]*]

**ten|der|foot** (ten'dər fůt'), *n., pl.* **-foots** or **-feet.** *Informal.* **1** a newcomer to the pioneer life of the western United States. **2** a person not used to rough living and hardships: *The tenderfoot, new to the sounds and solitude of the Canadian timber belt, wondered if indeed an occasional hot-dog stand or friendly filling station might not be desirable when the night closed in* (Wall Street Journal). **3** *Figurative.* an inexperienced person; beginner. **SYN:** tyro, novice. **4** Also, **Tenderfoot.** a beginning member of the Boy Scouts or Girl Scouts.

**ten|der-heart|ed** (ten'dər här'tid), *adj.* kindly; sympathetic; easily moved, as by pity or sorrow: *a tender-hearted smile.* **SYN:** compassionate. **—ten'der-heart'ed|ly,** *adv.* **—ten'der-heart'ed|ness,** *n.*

**ten|der|ize** (ten'də rīz), *v.t.,* **-ized, -iz|ing.** to make soft or tender: *to tenderize meat by pounding.* **—ten'der|i|za'tion,** *n.*

**ten|der|iz|er** (ten'də rī'zər), *n.* **1** any substance which tenderizes meat by breaking down the meat fibers. **2** a small, ridged mallet for pounding meat to make it tender before cooking.

**ten|der|loin** (ten'dər loin'), *n.* **1** a tender part of the loin of beef or pork. **2** a cut of beef or pork consisting of this part. See picture under **beef.**

**Ten|der|loin** (ten'dər loin'), *n. U.S. Slang.* **1** a city district or section that includes the great mass of theaters, hotels, and restaurants, and that is noted for the graft paid to the police for protection of vice. **2** (originally) a police district in New York City where the large amount of graft available was supposed to enable a corrupt policeman to live on a diet of tenderloin.

**tenderloin district** or **section,** = Tenderloin.

**ten|der-mind|ed** (ten'dər mīn'did), *adj.* **1** impractical: *He belongs in William James's well-known division of the human race, to the tender-minded* (Manchester Guardian). **2** tender-hearted: *To be tender-minded does not become a sword* (Shakespeare).

**ten|der|ness** (ten'dər nis), *n.* **1** the quality or condition of being tender. **2** a tender feeling: *She has a tenderness for cats.*

**tender offer,** a public offer to buy a company's stock at a price that usually exceeds the market price, for the purpose of gaining a controlling interest in the company: *The tender offer ... has clearly replaced the old-fashioned proxy fight as the favorite weapon for forcible corporate takeovers* (Time).

**ten|der|om|e|ter** (ten'də rom'ə tər), *n.* an instrument for measuring the tenderness of various types of foods: *The percentages of intramuscular fat were then related to tenderness, as measured both objectively, using a tenderometer, and subjectively, using a panel of tasters* (New Scientist).

**ten|di|ni|tis** (ten'də nī'tis), *n.* inflammation of a tendon; tenonitis: *Russ has bursitis in his elbow, tendinitis in his knee, and strained ligaments in his ankle* (Time). [< Medieval Latin *tēndo, -inis* tendon + English *-itis*]

**ten|di|nous** (ten'də nəs), *adj.* **1** of or like a tendon. **2** consisting of tendons.

**ten|don** (ten'dən), *n.* a tough, strong band or cord of tissue that joins a muscle to a bone or some other part and transmits the force of the muscle to that part; sinew: *They transplant tendons to enable the crippled to walk, and graft skin over tissue mutilated by fire, gunshot, and auto accident* (Arthur J. Snider). **SYN:** ligament. [< Medieval Latin *tendo, -inis,* alteration of Late Latin *tenōn, -ontis* < Greek *ténōn, -ontos* tendon; influenced by Latin *tendere* to stretch]

**tendon of Achilles,** = Achilles' tendon.

**ten|drac** (ten'drak), *n.* = tenrec.

**ten|dresse** (tän dres'), *n. French.* tender regard; tenderness.

**ten|dril** (ten'drəl), *n.* **1** a twisting, threadlike part of a climbing plant that attaches itself to something and helps support the plant. **2** something similar: *curly tendrils of hair.* [< Middle French *tendrillon* bud, shoot (diminutive) < *tendron* bud, tendril; (literally) clasper, < Old French *tendre;* see etym. under **tender[1]**; influenced by Middle French *tendre* to stretch]

**ten|dril|lar** (ten'drə lər), *adj.* **1** full of tendrils. **2** resembling a tendril.

**ten|dril|ous** (ten'drə ləs), *adj.* = tendrillar.

**Ten|e|brae** (ten'ə brē), *n.pl.* in the Roman Catholic Church: **1** the office of matins and lauds for

---

**Pronunciation Key:** hat, āge, cãre, fär; let, ēqual, tėrm; it, īce; hot, ōpen, ôrder; **oi**l, **ou**t; cup, pu̇t, rüle; **ch**ild; lo**ng**; **th**in; **ŦH**en; **zh**, measure; **ə** represents **a** in about, **e** in taken, **i** in pencil, **o** in lemon, **u** in circus.

the following day sung the afternoon or evening before each of the three days preceding Easter. **2** a public service at which this office is sung. [< Medieval Latin *Tenebrae* < Latin *tenebrae,* plural, darkness]

**ten|e|brif|ic** (ten′ə brif′ik), *adj.* causing or producing darkness; obscuring. [< Latin *tenebrae,* plural, darkness + English *-fic*]

**te|neb|ri|o|nid** (ten′ə brē ə nid), *adj., n.* —*adj.* of or having to do with a group of beetles living in arid places on decaying matter, and producing larvae that feed on grain and meal in storage. —*n.* a tenebrionid beetle. [< New Latin *Tenebrionidae* the family name < Latin *tenebrio, -onis* one who lurks in the dark < *tenebrae* darkness]

**te|neb|ri|ous** (tə neb′rē əs), *adj.* = tenebrous.

**ten|e|brism** or **Ten|e|brism** (ten′ə briz əm), *n.* a style of painting of the early 1600′s, inspired by the works of the Italian painter Caravaggio, in which extreme contrasts of light and shade were used, as by grouping figures against a plain, dark background and spotlighting them with an intense, revealing light. [< Latin *tenebrae* darkness + English *-ism*]

**ten|e|brist** or **Ten|e|brist** (ten′ə brist), *n., adj.* —*n.* any one of the group of painters who used tenebrism.
—*adj.* of the tenebrists or tenebrism.

**ten|e|brous** (ten′ə brəs), *adj.* full of darkness; dark; gloomy; dim. SYN: somber, murky, dusky. [< Latin *tenebrōsus* < *tenebrae,* plural, darkness] —**ten′e|brous|ness,** *n.*

**ten-eight|y** or **1080** (ten′ā′tē), *n.* a poisonous compound, used as a rat poison; sodium fluoroacetate. *Formula:* $C_2H_2FNaO_2$ [< the compound's laboratory serial number]

**ten|e|ment** (ten′ə mənt), *n.* **1** a building divided into sets of rooms occupied by separate families, especially such a building in a poor section of a city: *the shabby tenements along the railroad tracks.* **2** any house or building to live in; dwelling house: *The little cottage was a small tenement in the valley.* **3** the part of a house or building occupied by a tenant as a separate dwelling: *A two-family house has two tenements.* SYN: apartment, flat. **4** *Figurative.* an abode; habitation.
**tenements,** *Law.* anything permanent that one person may hold of another, such as land, buildings, franchises, or rents: *The Sheriffs of London* [*in*] *those days might lawfully enter into the ... tenements that the Abbot had within Middlesex* (Richard Grafton).
[earlier, tenure of immovable property < Anglo-French, Old French *tenement,* learned borrowing from Medieval Latin *tenementum* < Latin *tenēre* to hold]

**ten|e|men|tal** (ten′ə men′təl), *adj.* having to do with a tenement or tenements.

**ten|e|men|ta|ry** (ten′ə men′tər ē), *adj.* **1** that can be leased. **2** held by tenants.

**tenement house,** = tenement (def. 1).

**te|nes|mus** (ti nez′məs, -nes′-), *n. Medicine.* the continual inclination to void the contents of the bladder or bowels, with little or no discharge. [< Medieval Latin *tenesmus,* alteration of Latin *tēnesmos* < Greek *teinesmós* (literally) straining < *teínein* to strain, stretch]

**ten|et** (ten′it; *especially British* tē′nit), *n.* a doctrine, principle, belief, or opinion held as true by a school, sect, party, or person: *The practical consequences of any political tenet go a great way in deciding upon its value* (Edmund Burke). SYN: dogma, persuasion. [< Latin *tenet* he holds, third person singular of *tenēre* to hold]

**ten|fold** (ten′fōld′), *adj., adv., n.* —*adj.* **1** ten times as much or as many. **2** having ten parts.
—*adv., n.* ten times as much or as many.

**ten-gal|lon hat** (ten′gal′ən), *Western U.S.* a large, broad-brimmed hat, usually worn by cowboys.

**te|ni|a** (tē′nē ə), *n., pl.* **-ni|ae** (-nē ē), **-ni|as.** = taenia.

**te|ni|a|cide** (tē′nē ə sīd), *n.* = taeniacide.

**te|ni|a|fuge** (tē′nē ə fyüj), *adj., n.* = taeniafuge.

**te|ni|a|sis** (ti nī′ə sis), *n.* = taeniasis.

**Ten|ku** (teng′kü), *n.* = Tunku.

**Tenn.,** Tennessee.

**ten|nant|ite** (ten′ən tīt), *n.* a gray to black mineral, a sulfide of arsenic with copper and usually iron. It is an ore of copper. *Formula:* $Cu_3AsS_3$ [< Smithson *Tennant,* 1761-1815, an English chemist]

**ten|né** (ten′ē), *n. Heraldry.* the tawny color in coats of arms. [< Middle French *tenné,* variant of *tanné.* Compare etym. under **tawny.**]

**ten|ner** (ten′ər), *n. Informal.* **1** a ten-dollar bill or a ten-pound note. **2** anything that counts as ten.

**Ten|nes|se|an** (ten′ə sē′ən), *adj., n.* —*adj.* of or having to do with Tennessee.
—*n.* a native or inhabitant of Tennessee.

**Ten|nes|see Valley Authority** (ten′ə sē). = TVA.

**Tennessee walking horse,** an easy-gaited saddle horse originally bred from Morgan and standard bred stock by Southern plantation owners to obtain a horse with a comfortable mount.

**Tennessee warbler,** a warbler with an olive-green back and white breast, that nests in coniferous forests of northeastern North America.

***ten|nis** (ten′is), *n.* **1** a game played by two or four players on a special court, in which a ball is hit back and forth over a net with a racket; lawn tennis. **2** = court tennis. [Middle English *teneys,* apparently alteration of earlier *tenets* < Anglo-French *tenetz,* Old French *tenez* hold!, imperative of *tenir* < Latin *tenēre*]

***tennis**
definition 1

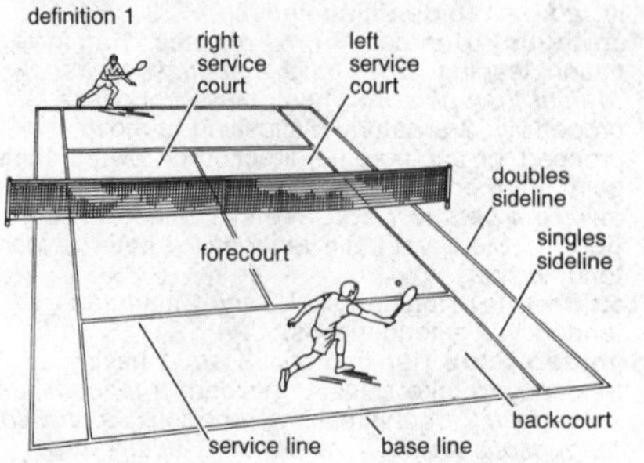

right service court
left service court
doubles sideline
singles sideline
forecourt
backcourt
service line
base line

**tennis ball,** a ball used in tennis, made of rubber with a cloth covering.

**tennis court,** a level, rectangular area divided by a low net stretched across its center, prepared and marked out for playing the game of tennis.

**tennis elbow,** inflammation or bursitis of the elbow, commonly associated with tennis and certain other sports.

**tennis racket,** the racket used in tennis.

**tennis shoes,** any pair of various shoes with rubber soles, worn for tennis; sneakers.

**ten|nist** (ten′ist), *n.* a tennis player. [< *tennis* + *-ist*]

**ten|no** or **Ten|no** (ten′ō), *n.* a title of the emperor of Japan. [< Japanese *tennō* (literally) heavenly ruler < *ten* heaven (< Chinese *tien*) + *nō* ruler (< Chinese *hwang*)]

**ten|ny** (ten′ē), *n.* = tenné.

**Ten|ny|so|ni|an** (ten′ə sō′nē ən), *adj.* of or having to do with the English Victorian poet, Alfred, Lord Tennyson (1809-1892), his style, or his works: *"Lohengrin" has a few strokes of magic and many pages of idyllic Tennysonian rapture* (Desmond Shawe-Taylor).

**ten|on** (ten′ən), *n., v.* —*n.* the end of a piece of wood cut so as to fit into the mortise in another piece and so form a joint.
—*v.t., v.i.* **1** to cut so as to form a tenon. **2** to fit together with tenon and mortise.
[< Middle French *tenon* < Old French *tenir* to hold < Latin *tenēre*]

**ten|o|ni|tis** (ten′ə nī′tis), *n.* = tendinitis. [< Late Latin *tenōn, -ontis* tendon + English *-itis*]

**ten|or** (ten′ər), *n., adj.* —*n.* **1** the general tendency; course: *The calm tenor of her life has never been disturbed by excitement or trouble.* SYN: direction. **2** the general meaning or drift: *I understand French well enough to get the tenor of his speech.* SYN: gist, purport. **3** *Music.* **a** the highest adult male voice. Bass and tenor are two parts of men's voices. **b** a singer with such a voice. **c** a part for such a voice or for an instrument of similar range. **d** an instrument that has the quality or range of this voice. **e** the largest bell of a peal, having the lowest tone. **4** *Law.* an exact copy of a document. **5** *Obsolete.* **a** nature. **b** condition.
—*adj. Music.* of or for a tenor; having the quality or range of a tenor: *a tenor voice, a tenor saxophone, a tenor drum.*
[< Latin *tenor* contents, course; (originally) a holding on < *tenēre* to hold; (def. 3) < Middle French, or Medieval Latin *tenor* holding (the melody)]

***tenor clef,** *Music.* the C clef when placed on the fourth line of the staff.

***tenor clef**
middle C

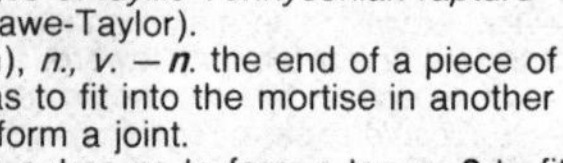

**te|no|re di gra|zi|a** (te nō′rā dē grät′sē ä), *n.* a tenor with a light, flexible, lyrical voice. [< Italian *tenore di grazia* (literally) tenor of grace]

**te|no|re ro|bus|to** (te nō′rā rō büs′tō), a tenor with a vigorous, powerful voice. [< Italian *tenore robusto* (literally) robust tenor]

**ten|or|ite** (ten′ə rīt), *n.* a black oxide of copper, found in thin, iron-black scales in lava. *Formula:* CuO

**ten|or|oon** (ten′ə rün), *n.* **1** an obsolete wooden reed instrument intermediate in pitch between the oboe and the bassoon: *The tenoroon ... has entirely gone out of use* (W. H. Stone). **2** a reed stop in an organ, resembling the oboe stop, but not extending below tenor C. **3** any stop not extending below tenor C. [< *tenor* + (bass)*oon*]

**te|nor|rha|phy** (tə nôr′ə fē, -nor′-), *n., pl.* **-phies.** the surgical suture of a tendon. [< Greek *ténōn* + *rhaphē* a seam or suture]

**te|not|o|my** (tə not′ə mē), *n., pl.* **-mies.** surgical incision into or through a tendon. [< Greek *ténōn* + *-tomiā* a cutting]

**ten|pence** (ten′pəns), *n.* **1** a sum of ten British pennies. **2a** a coin worth ten pennies (as one issued by the Bank of Ireland in the early 1800′s). **b** *Archaic.* any of various foreign coins worth about ten pennies.

**ten|pen|ny** (ten′pen′ē, -pə nē), *adj.* of the amount or value of tenpence: *a tenpenny piece, tenpenny lace. A tenpenny nail is 3 inches long, and it is so called because originally the nails cost tenpence per hundred.*

**ten-per|cent|er** (ten′pər sen′tər), *n. Slang.* **1** an agent, as of an actor or writer: *The ... ten-percenters retired to several of the town's toney hangouts* (Manchester Guardian Weekly). **2** any person whose commission is ten per cent of the profit or merchandise.

**ten|pin** (ten′pin′), *n.* one of the pins in tenpins.

**ten|pins** (ten′pinz′), *n. sing. or pl.* **1** a game played with ten wooden pins at which a ball is bowled to knock them down; bowling. **2** the pins used in this.
► **Tenpins,** the game (def. 1.), is plural in form and singular in use: *Tenpins is similar to ninepins. Tenpins,* the pins used in the game (def. 2), is plural in form and in use: *The tenpins were all knocked down.*

**ten-point** (ten′point′), *n.* a size of type.

**ten|pound|er** (ten′poun′dər), *n. Informal.* the ladyfish.

**ten|rec** (ten′rek), *n.* any one of certain insectivorous, quilled mammals of Madagascar, especially one that is tailless. Also, **tanrec, tendrac.** [< French *tanrec* < Malagasy *tàndraka,* variant of *tràndraka*]

**tense¹** (tens), *adj.,* **tens|er, tens|est,** *v.,* **tensed, tens|ing.** —*adj.* **1** stretched tight; strained to stiffness: *a tense rope, a face tense with pain.* SYN: taut, rigid. **2** *Figurative.* strained; keyed up: *tense nerves, a tense moment.* **3** *Phonetics.* pronounced with the muscles of the speech organs relatively tense.
—*v.t., v.i.* to stretch tight; stiffen; tighten: *I tensed my muscles for the leap.*
**tense up,** to make or become tense: *You're all tensed up* (Atlantic).
[< Latin *tēnsus,* past participle of *tendere* to stretch] —**tense′ly,** *adv.* —**tense′ness,** *n.*

***tense²** (tens), *n.* **1** the form of a verb that shows the time of the action or state expressed by the verb. *Examples: He obeys* is in the present tense. *He obeyed* is in the past tense. *He will obey* is in the future tense. **2** a set of such forms for the various persons. *Example:* The present tense of *obey* is: *I obey, thou obeyest, he obeys, we obey, you obey, they obey.* [< Old French *tens* time < Latin *tempus.* See etym. of doublet **tempo.**]

***tense²**
definition 1

she looks
present

she looked
past

she will look
future

she has looked
perfect

she had looked
past perfect

she will have looked
future perfect

**tense|less** (tens′lis), *adj.* having no tense: *a tenseless verb.*

**ten|si|ble** (ten′sə bəl), *adj.* that can be stretched. [< Late Latin *tēnsibilis* capable of tension < Latin *tendere* to stretch]

**ten|sile** (ten′səl), *adj.* **1** of or having to do with tension. **2** that can be stretched; ductile: *tensile metals.* [< New Latin *tensilis* < Latin *tendere* to stretch]

**tensile strength,** the maximum stress that a material can withstand before it breaks, expressed in pounds per square inch.

**ten|sil|i|ty** (ten sil′ə tē), *n.* tensile quality; ductility.

**ten|sim|e|ter** (ten sim′ə tər), *n.* an instrument for measuring the pressure or tension of vapor, as a manometer. [< Latin *tēnsus* past participle of *tendere* stretch + *-meter*]

**ten|si|om|e|ter** (ten′sē om′ə tər), *n.* **1** an instrument for measuring the tautness or tension of wire, fabric, and other material. **2** an instrument for measuring the surface tension of a liquid. Also, **tensometer**. [< Latin *tēnsiō, -ōnis* tension + English *-meter*]

**ten|si|o|met|ric** (ten′sē ə met′rik), *adj.* of or having to do with a tensiometer or with tensiometry.

**ten|si|om|e|try** (ten′sē om′ə trē), *n.* **1** the measurement of tension or tensile strength. **2** the study of tension or tensile strength.

**ten|sion** (ten′shən), *n., v.* —*n.* **1** the act of stretching: *His tension on the rope made it break.* **2** a stretched condition: *The tension of the bow gives its speed to the arrow.* **3** *Figurative.* mental or nervous strain: *A mother feels tension when her baby is sick.* **SYN**: anxiety, uneasiness. **4** *Figurative.* a strained condition: *political tension.* **5** stress caused by the action of a pulling force: *An elevator exerts tension on the cables supporting it.* **6** a device to control the pull or strain on something: *The tension in a sewing machine may be adjusted to hold the thread tight or loose.* **7** the pressure of a gas. **8** electromotive force or voltage: *high-tension wires.*
—*v.t.* to make tense; tighten; draw out: *tensioned steel rods.*
[< Latin *tēnsiō, -ōnis* < *tendere* to stretch]
—**ten′sion|less**, *adj.*

**ten|sion|al** (ten′shə nəl), *adj.* of or having to do with tension.

**ten|sion|er** (ten′shə nər), *n.* a device to control the pull or strain on something: *The overhead wire is strung with special tensioners to remain at a constant height above the track* (Bruce H. Frisch).

**ten|si|ty** (ten′sə tē), *n.* tense quality or condition: (*Figurative.*) *It braced him into such a tensity of spirit* (Thomas Carlyle).

**ten|sive** (ten′siv), *adj.* **1** causing tension. **2** denoting a sensation of tension in any part of the body.

**ten|son** (ten′sən), *n.* **1** a contest in verse between rival troubadours. **2** verse composed for or sung at such a contest. [< French *tenson* < Latin *tēnsiō, -ōnis*]

**ten|sor** (ten′sər, -sôr), *n.* **1** a muscle that stretches or tightens some part of the body. **2** *Mathematics.* a vector that can be defined only by reference to more than three components: *The gravitational equations of the general theory of relativity are written in a form of mathematics that deals with quantities called tensors* (Harper's). [< New Latin *tensor* < Latin *tendere* to stretch]

**ten spot**, *Informal.* a ten-dollar bill.

**ten-strike** (ten′strīk′), *n.* **1** a stroke that knocks down all ten pins in bowling; strike. **2** *Informal, Figurative.* any completely successful stroke or act.

***tent**[1] (tent), *n., v.* —*n.* **1** a movable shelter made of canvas or skins supported by a pole or poles. Modern tents often have fiberglass screen windows, sewed-in floors, and zippered openings. **2** a tentlike device to regulate the temperature and humidity of the air in treating certain respiratory diseases.
—*v.i.* to live in or as if in a tent: *We're tenting tonight on the old campground* (Walter Kittredge).
—*v.t.* **1** to cover with or as if with a tent. **2** to put up or lodge in a tent or tents.
[< Old French *tente* < Latin *tenta,* (originally) plural of *tentum,* variant past participle of *tendere* to stretch] —**tent′like′**, *adj.*

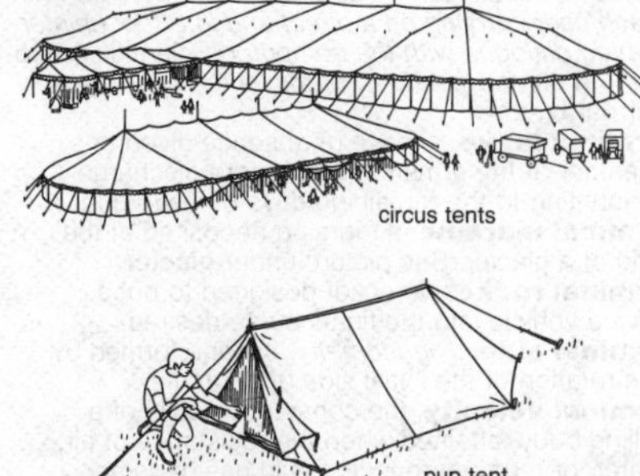
***tent**[1] definition 1

circus tents

pup tent

**tent**[2] (tent), *n., v. Medicine.* —*n.* **1** a roll of gauze that increases in size when wet, used to dilate an opening. **2** *Obsolete.* a probe.
—*v.t.* to keep open with a tent.
[< Old French *tente* < *tenter* to try, examine < Latin *temptāre;* see etym. under **tempt**]

**tent**[3] (tent), *n., v. Scottish.* —*n.* heed; care.
—*v.t.* **1** to take or have charge and care of. **2** to heed. **3** to hinder. **4** to teach.
[short for Middle English *attent* intent]

**ten|ta|cle** (ten′tə kəl), *n.* **1** one of the long, slender, flexible growths on the head or around the mouth of an animal, used to touch, hold, or move; feeler: *An octopus has eight tentacles.* See picture under **hydra**. **2** *Figurative.* any power or influence that has a far-reaching or strangling hold: *He began as the chairman of a Senate investigating committee to trace the tentacles of organised crime in the U.S.* (Alistair Cooke). **3** a sensitive, hairlike growth on a plant. [< New Latin *tentaculum* < Latin *tentāre,* earlier *temptāre;* see etym. under **tempt**]

**ten|ta|cled** (ten′tə kəld), *adj.* having a tentacle or tentacles: *The hydra has a wormlike trunk and a tentacled head.*

**ten|tac|u|lar** (ten tak′yə lər), *adj.* of, forming, or resembling tentacles: (*Figurative.*) *We checked in with Roger L. Stevens, the busiest producer of the era, as well as a real-estate man of tentacular scope* (New Yorker).

**tent|age** (ten′tij), *n.* equipment of tents.

**ten|ta|tion** (ten tā′shən), *n.* tentative operation.

**ten|ta|tive** (ten′tə tiv), *adj., n.* —*adj.* **1** done as a trial or experiment; experimental: *a tentative plan.* **2** hesitating: *a tentative laugh.*
—*n.* a trial; experiment: *I had even made some tentatives for ... a reconciliation* (H. G. Wells).
[< Medieval Latin *tentativus* < Latin *tentāre;* see etym. under **tempt**] —**ten′ta|tive|ly**, *adv.* —**ten′ta|tive|ness**, *n.*

**tent caterpillar**, a caterpillar that spins tentlike silken webs in which it lives. Tent caterpillars feed on leaves and do great damage to fruit and forest trees.

**tent coat**, a coat flaring to a wide skirt, resembling a tent.

**tent dress**, a loose-fitting dress having the shape of a tent.

**tent|ed** (ten′tid), *adj.* covered with tents: *A tented camp was set up, with facilities for journalists, photographers, and publicity agents* (Punch).

**ten|ter** (ten′tər), *n., v.* —*n.* a framework on which cloth is stretched so that it may set or dry evenly without shrinking.
—*v.t.* to stretch (cloth) on a tenter.
—*v.i. Obsolete.* to be able to be tentered, as cloth.
[ultimately < Latin *tentus,* variant past participle of *tendere* to stretch]

**ten|ter|hook** (ten′tər hu̇k′), *n.* one of the hooks or bent nails that hold cloth stretched on a tenter.
**on tenterhooks**, in painful suspense; anxious: *The parties here are on tenterhooks about the way the vote will go* (London Times).

**tenth** (tenth), *n., adj.* —*n.* **1** next after the ninth; last in a series of 10. **2** one of 10 equal parts: *A dime is a tenth of a dollar.* **3** *Music.* **a** a tone or note ten degrees from a given tone or note. **b** the interval between such tones or notes. **c** the combination of such tones or notes.
—*adj.* **1** next after the ninth; last in a series of 10. **2** being one of 10 equal parts.

**tenth|ly** (tenth′lē), *adv.* in the tenth place.

**tenth Muse**, **1** a goddess of some aspect of human effort not protected by the nine classical Muses. **2** *Figurative.* a woman of considerable literary talent.

**tent|mak|er** (tent′mā′kər), *n.* **1** a person who makes tents, as for a traveling circus. **2** any moth whose larvae spin large silken webs in trees.

**tent meeting**, *U.S.* a camp meeting held in a tent.

**Tent of Meeting**, = Tabernacle.

**tent peg** or **pin**, a stake driven into the ground, to fasten a tent rope.

**tent pole**, a pole used to hold up a tent.

**tent show**, a show performed in a tent, usually in rural areas where no theater is available: *Although it is described as a musical comedy it is really an old-fashioned tent show* (New Yorker).

**tent stitch**, the short, slanting, left-to-right stitch used in petit point.

**tent|y** (ten′tē), *adj.,* **tent|i|er**, **tent|i|est**. *Scottish.* watchful; observant.

**ten|u|is** (ten′yu̇ is), *n., pl.* **-u|es** (-yu̇ ēz). *Phonetics.* a voiceless stop, such as represented by English *p, t,* and *k.* [< Latin *tenuis* thin, fine; translation of Greek *psīlós* unaspirated, bare]

**ten|u|i|ty** (ten yü′ə tē, ti nü′-), *n.* rarefied condition; thinness; slightness.

**ten|u|ous** (ten′yu̇ əs), *adj.* **1** thin or slight; slender: *the tenuous thread of a spider's web.* **2** not dense; rare; rarefied: *The air ten miles above the earth is very tenuous.* **3** *Figurative.* having slight importance; not substantial: *a tenuous claim.* [< Latin *tenuis* thin] —**ten′u|ous|ly**, *adv.* —**ten′u|ous|ness**, *n.*

**ten|ure** (ten′yər), *n.* **1** the act or fact of holding or possessing. **2** the length of time of holding or possessing: *The tenure of office of the president of our club is one year.* **3** the manner of holding something, such as land or buildings, from a feudal lord or superior: *The military tenure of land had been originally created as a means of national defence* (Macaulay). **4** conditions or terms on which anything is held or occupied. **5** permanent status, granted after a period of trial, especially to a member of a faculty. [< Anglo-French, Old French *tenure* < Medieval Latin *tenitura* < Latin *tenēre* hold]

**ten|ured** ((ten′yərd), *adj.* having tenure: *The power of the central administration is offset by the counterweight of the tenured faculty who are safe from interference and dismissal* (New York Times).

**ten|u|ri|al** (te nyu̇r′ē əl), *adj.* of or having to do with a tenure. —**ten|u′ri|al|ly**, *adv.*

**te|nu|to** (te nü′tō), *adj., adv. Music.* (of a tone or chord) held or sustained to its full time value. [< Italian *tenuto,* past participle of *tenere* to hold < Latin *tenēre*]

**te|o|cal|li** (tē′ə kal′ē; *Spanish* tā′ō kä′yē), *n., pl.* **-lis**. an Aztec temple, constructed on top of a high pyramid, the remains of some of which survive in parts of Mexico and Central America. [< Spanish *teocalli* < Nahuatl, temple (literally) house of a god < *teotl* god + *calli* house]

**te|on|a|na|ca|tl** (tē on′ə nə ka′təl), *n.* **1** a drug that induces hallucination. **2** a mushroom from which the drug is derived. [< Nahuatl *teonanacatl*]

**te|o|sin|te** (tē′ə sin′tē), *n.* a tall, annual grass related to corn, native to Mexico and Central America, used for fodder and sometimes as a cereal: *Some botanists conjecture that the ancestor of the corn was the Mexican grass teosinte* (Science News Letter). [< Mexican Spanish *teosinte* < Nahuatl *teosintli,* the name of a wild grass]

**TEPA** (no periods), or **te|pa** (tē′pə), *n.* = triethylene phosphoramide.

**te|pal** (tē′pəl, tep′əl), *n. Botany.* a sepal or petal, especially when almost identical, as in many plants of the lily family. [anagram of *petal*]

**tep|a|ry** (tep′ər ē), *n., pl.* **-ries**. an annual, drought-resistant bean, native to the southwestern United States and Mexico. [< Mexican Spanish *tepari* < a Piman word]

***te|pee** (tē′pē), *n.* a tent of the North American Indians, especially of the Great Plains, formed of bark, mats, or animal skins stretched over poles arranged in the shape of a cone: *Tepee was the type of tent most commonly used by the Plains tribes* (Ruth M. Underhill). Also, **teepee, tipi.** [American English < Siouan (Dakota) *tipi* dwelling]

***tepee**

**tep|e|fac|tion** (tep′ə fak′shən), *n.* the act or process of making tepid.

**tep|e|fy** (tep′ə fī), *v.t., v.i.,* **-fied, -fy|ing**. to make or become tepid. [< Latin *tepefacere* < *tepēre* to be tepid + *facere* to make]

**Tep|ex|pan man** (tep′eks pän′), a very early form of man whose remains were discovered in Mexico, believed to have existed between 10,000 and 12,000 years ago. [< *Tepexpán,* a village in Mexico]

**te|phil|lin** (tə fil′ən), *n.pl.* = tefillin.

**teph|ra** (tef′rə), *n.* volcanic material, such as ash, dust, cinders, scoria, or pumice, given off in an eruption. [< Greek *téphra* ashes]

**teph|rite** (tef′rīt), *n.* any one of a group of volcanic rocks related to basalt. [< Greek *tephrós* ash-colored]

**teph|rit|ic** (tef rit′ik), *adj.* of the nature of tephrite; having to do with tephrite.

**tep|id** (tep′id), *adj.* moderately or slightly warm; lukewarm: *tepid soup, a tepid bath.* [< Latin *tep-*

**Pronunciation Key:** hat, āge, cãre, fär; let, ēqual, tėrm; it, īce; hot, ōpen, ôrder; oil, out; cup, pu̇t, rüle; child; long; thin; ᴛʜen; zh, measure; ə represents **a** in about, **e** in taken, **i** in pencil, **o** in lemon, **u** in circus.

*idus* < *tepēre* be warm] —**tep′id|ly**, *adv.* —**tep′id|ness**, *n.*
**te|pid|i|ty** (ti pid′ə tē), *n.* tepid condition.
**TEPP** (no periods), tetraethyl pyrophosphate.
**te|qui|la** (tə kē′lə, tā kē′lä), *n.* **1** a Mexican agave. The juices of its roasted stems are made into a distilled liquor. **2** this liquor. [American English < American Spanish *tequila* < *Tequila,* a town in Mexico]
**ter.**, **1** terrace. **2** territory.
**tera-**, *combining form.* one trillion___: *Teravolt = one trillion volts.* [< Greek *téras, -atos* monster; marvel]
**ter|a|bit** (ter′ə bit′), *n.* a unit of information equivalent to one trillion bits or binary digits: *The CG-100 computer is said to have a main memory capable of holding 10 million million bits* (*10 terabits*) *of information* (New Scientist and Science Journal). [< *tera-* + *bit*[4]]
**ter|a|cy|cle** (ter′ə sī′kəl), *n.* one trillion cycles per second.
**te|rai** (tə rī′), *n.*, or **terai hat**, a wide-brimmed felt hat, perforated at the sides for ventilation. [< Hindi *tarāī* moist land < *tar* moist]
**ter|a|phim** (ter′ə fim), *n.pl., sing.* **ter|aph** (ter′əf). images or idols of the household gods used as oracles by the ancient Hebrew and kindred peoples (in the Bible, Genesis 31:19). [< Late Latin *theraphim* < Hebrew *tərāfim* images]
**ter|a|to|gen** (ter′ə tə jən, -tō′-), *n.* a drug or other agent that causes teratogenesis: *Thalidomide's effect classified it as a teratogen, a substance which can alter a developing embryo and lead to malformations* (Malcolm A. Holliday).
**ter|a|to|gen|e|sis** (ter′ə tə jen′ə sis), *n. Biology.* the production of monstrous or misshapen organisms or growths. [< Greek *téras, -atos* monster; marvel + English *genesis*]
**ter|a|to|ge|net|ic** (ter′ə tə jə net′ik), *adj.* = teratogenic.
**ter|a|to|gen|ic** (ter′ə tə jen′ik), *adj.* having to do with teratogenesis; causing malformation of an embryo or fetus: *Recent reports from England indicate that preparations made from mandrake may be teratogenic, i.e., capable of deforming babies* (Maclean's). —**ter′a|to|gen′i|cal|ly**, *adv.*
**ter|a|to|ge|nic|i|ty** (ter′ə tə jə nis′ə tē), *n.* the quality of being teratogenic; tendency to cause malformations of the embryo or fetus: *The teratogenicity of thalidomide might have been missed had it not produced malformations rarely encountered* (New Yorker).
**ter|a|tog|e|ny** (ter′ə toj′ə nē), *n.* = teratogenesis.
**ter|a|toid** (ter′ə toid), *n.* like a monster. [< Greek *téras, -atos* monster + *-oid*]
**ter|a|to|log|i|cal** (ter′ə tə loj′ə kəl), *adj.* of or having to do with teratology.
**ter|a|tol|o|gist** (ter′ə tol′ə jist), *n.* an expert in teratology.
**ter|a|tol|o|gy** (ter′ə tol′ə jē), *n. Biology.* the study of monstrous or misshapen formations in animals or plants. [< Greek *téras, -atos* monster + *-logy*]
**ter|a|to|ma** (ter′ə tō′mə), *n., pl.* **-mas, -ma|ta** (-mə tə). a complex congenital tumor, often containing many different tissues, such as skin, hair, teeth, connective tissue, cartilage, bone, muscles, and glands. [< Greek *téras, -atos* monster + English *-oma*]
**ter|bic** (tėr′bik), *adj.* of or having to do with terbium.
***ter|bi|um** (tėr′bē əm), *n.* a silver-gray metallic chemical element found in gadolinite, monazite, and certain other minerals with yttrium and ytterbium. Terbium is a rare-earth element. [< New Latin *terbium* < (Yt)*terby,* a town in Sweden. Compare etym. under **erbium**, **yttrium**.]

***terbium**

| symbol | atomic number | atomic weight | oxidation state |
|---|---|---|---|
| Tb | 65 | 158.924 | 3 |

**terbium metals**, a group of closely related rare-earth elements, consisting of terbium, dysprosium, europium, and gadolinium.
**terbium oxide**, a brown powder, one of the rare earths. *Formula:* $Tb_4O_7$
**terce** (tėrs), *n.* = tierce.
**ter|cel** (tėr′səl), *n.* a male falcon or goshawk. [< Old French *tercel,* and *terçuel* < Vulgar Latin *tertiolus* (diminutive) < Latin *tertius* third]
**ter|cen|te|nar|y** (tėr sen′tə ner′ē, tėr′sen ten′ər-; *especially British* -sen tē′nər ē), *adj., n., pl.* **-naries.** —*adj.* of or having to do with a period of 300 years or a 300th anniversary: *a tercentenary anniversary.*
—*n.* **1** a 300th anniversary. **2** the celebration of this. **3** a period of 300 years.
[< Latin *ter* three times + English *centenary*]
**ter|cen|ten|ni|al** (tėr′sen ten′ē əl), *adj., n.* = tercentenary.

**ter|cet** (tėr′sit, tėr set′), *n.* **1** a group of three lines rhyming together, or connected by rhyme with the adjacent group or groups of three lines. **2** *Music.* a triplet. [< French *tercet,* Middle French *tiercet* < Italian *terzetto* (diminutive) < *terzo* third < Latin *tertius.* See etym. of doublet **terzetto.**]
**ter|e|bene** (ter′ə bēn), *n.* a liquid mixture of terpenes obtained from turpentine, used as an antiseptic and expectorant. [< French *térébène* < *térébinthe* terebinth + *-ène* - ene]
**te|reb|ic** (tə reb′ik, -rē′bik), *adj.* of or having to do with terebic acid.
**terebic acid**, a crystalline acid obtained from oil of turpentine. *Formula:* $C_7H_{10}O_4$
**ter|e|binth** (ter′ə binth), *n.* a tree of the cashew family, growing in the Mediterranean region, a source of crude turpentine. [< Latin *terebinthus* < Greek *terébinthos,* variant of earlier *térbinthos*]
**ter|e|bin|thine** (ter′ə bin′thin), *adj.* **1** of or having to do with turpentine. **2** of or having to do with the terebinth.
**ter|e|brate** (ter′ə brāt), *v.t., v.i.,* **-brat|ed, -brat|ing.** to bore or perforate. [< Latin *terebrāre* (with English *-ate*[1])] —**ter′e|bra′tion**, *n.*
**te|re|do** (tə rē′dō), *n., pl.* **-dos, -di|nes** (-də nēz). a small, wormlike marine clam that bores into and destroys the wood of ships, piers, and other wood surfaces exposed to salt water; shipworm. [< Latin *terēdo* < Greek *terēdōn* < *teirein* to rub away, weaken, bore]
**te|rel|la** (tə rel′ə), *n. Obsolete.* terrella.
**ter|eph|thal|ate** (ter′ef thal′āt), *n.* a salt or ester of terephthalic acid.
**ter|eph|thal|ic acid** (ter′ef thal′ik), a white, crystalline acid obtained from petroleum, used chiefly in making Dacron and other polyester fibers. *Formula:* $C_8H_6O_4$ [< *tere* (bene) + *phthalic acid*]
**te|rete** (tə rēt′, ter′ēt), *adj.* **1** having a cylindrical or slightly tapering form. **2** rounded and smooth. [< Latin *teres, -etis* rounded off < *terere* to rub, wear away]
**Te|reus** (tir′yüs, -ē əs), *n. Greek Mythology.* an evil king, the husband of Procne.
**ter|gal** (tėr′gəl), *adj. Zoology.* **1** of or on the back; dorsal. **2** of or having to do with a tergum or tergite.
**ter|gem|i|nate** (tėr jem′ə nit, -nāt), *adj.* (of a compound leaf) having at the base a pair of leaflets and then forking, with a pair on each branch. [< Latin *tergeminus,* variant of *trigeminus* triple + English *-ate*[1]]
**ter|gite** (tėr′jīt), *n.* the upper or dorsal plate of each segment or somite of an arthropod or other articulated animal. [< Latin *tergum* + *-ite*[1]]
**ter|gi|ver|sate** (tėr′jə vər sāt′), *v.i.,* **-sat|ed, -sat|ing.** **1** to change one's attitude or opinions with respect to a cause or subject; turn renegade. **2** to shift or shuffle; evade. [< Latin *tergiversārī* evade < *tergum* the back + *versāre* < *vertere* to turn]
**ter|gi|ver|sa|tion** (tėr′jə vər sā′shən), *n.* **1** change of attitude or opinions. **2** a backing out; evasion.
**ter|gi|ver|sa|tor** (tėr′jə vər sā′tər), *n.* a person who tergiversates.
**ter|gum** (tėr′gəm), *n., pl.* **-ga** (-gə). *Zoology.* the back or dorsal portion of an arthropod or other articulated animal. [< Latin *tergum* the back]
**ter|i|ya|ki** (ter′i yä′kē), *n.* a Japanese dish consisting of fish or meat with onions and green peppers, and soy sauce, often broiled and served on a skewer. [< Japanese *teriyaki.* Compare etym. under **sukiyaki.**]
**term** (tėrm), *n., v.* —*n.* **1** a word or group of words used in connection with some special subject, science, art, or business: *medical terms. "Acid," "base," and "salt" are terms commonly used in chemistry.* **2** any word or expression: *an abstract term, a term of reproach, a foreign term.* **3** a set period of time; length of time that a thing lasts: *the term of a lease. The President's term of office is four years.* SYN: duration. **4** one of the long periods into which the school year is divided: *Most schools have a fall term and a spring term.* SYN: semester. **6a** a set or appointed time or date, especially for the payment of rent, wages, or other money due. **b** the completion of the period of pregnancy; the normal time of childbirth: *A term baby is one born at or near term.* **7** *Mathematics.* **a** one of the members in a proportion or ratio; numerator or denominator in a fraction. **b** any part of an algebraic expression separated from the other parts by a plus or minus sign. In $13ax^2 - 2bxy + y$, $13ax^2$, $2bxy$, and $y$ are the terms. **c** a point, line, or surface that limits in geometry. **8** *Logic.* **a** the word or words that form the subject or predicate of a proposition. **b** one of the three parts of a syllogism. **9** a terminal or end figure. **10** *Archaic.* a boundary; end limit.
—*v.t.* to apply a term to; name; call: *He might be termed handsome.*
**bring to terms**, to compel to agree, assent, or submit; force to come to an agreement: *The company found out that the union could not be brought to terms without the promise of a new contract.*
**come to terms**, **a** to agree upon conditions; reach an understanding: *The two rivals cannot come to terms without someone going between them. The Chinese accuse the Soviets of planning to betray the cause of revolution by coming to terms with the United States* (Atlantic).
**b** *Figurative.* to accept a situation; become resigned: *Somehow the British public has never really come to terms with the phenomenon of women in politics* (Manchester Guardian Weekly).
**in terms of**, **a** in regard to: *The book* [*is*] *a big success in terms of the interest it aroused* (New Yorker). **b** in the phraseology or mode of thought belonging to: *Criticisms of M.I.T.'s warm embrace of business are often couched in terms of conflict of interest* (New York Times).
**terms**, **a** conditions; stipulations; provisions: *board and lodging on reasonable terms, the lowest terms offered. The terms of the peace treaty were very hard for the defeated nation.* **b** *Figurative.* a way of speaking: *He talked about you in very flattering terms.* **c** *Figurative.* personal relations: *on speaking terms. We are on good terms with all our neighbors.*
[< Old French *terme* limit < Latin *terminus* end, boundary line. See etym. of doublet **terminus.**]
**term.**, **1** terminal. **2** termination. **3** terminology.
**Ter|ma|gant** (tėr′mə gənt), *n.* a deity, supposed in medieval Europe to have been worshiped by the Moslems, appearing in morality plays as a violent, ranting, overbearing personage. [alteration of Middle English *Tervagant* < Old French *Tervagan,* origin uncertain]
**ter|ma|gant** (tėr′mə gənt), *n., adj.* —*n.* a violent, quarreling, scolding woman: *Tom's wife was a tall termagant, fierce of temper, loud of tongue, and strong of arm* (Washington Irving). SYN: shrew, virago. —*adj.* violent, quarreling, or scolding. SYN: shrewish. [< *Termagant*]
**term day**, **1** = quarter day. **2** each of a series of days appointed for taking systematic scientific observations, as of meteorological phenomena.
**term|er** (tėr′mər), *n.* a person who is serving a term as a public official: *a fourth-termer.*
**ter|mi|na|bil|i|ty** (tėr′mə nə bil′ə tē), *n.* the fact or quality of being terminable.
**ter|mi|na|ble** (tėr′mə nə bəl), *adj.* **1** that can be ended: *The contract was terminable by either party.* **2** coming to an end after a certain term: *a loan terminable in 10 years.* —**ter′mi|na|ble|ness**, *n.*
**ter|mi|na|bly** (tėr′mə nə blē), *adv.* in the way of being terminable.
**ter|mi|nal** (ter′mə nəl), *adj., n.* —*adj.* **1a** at the end; forming the end part: *a terminal appendage.* **b** *Botany.* growing at the end of a branch or stem: *a terminal bud or flower.* **2** coming at the end: *a terminal examination.* SYN: final, ultimate. **3** having to do with or completing a term: *a terminal payment.* **4a** at the end of a railroad line. **b** having to do with or for the handling of freight at a terminal. **5a** marking a boundary, limit, or end: *a terminal pillar.* **b** of or having to do with the end of life; approaching or resulting in death; fatal: *a terminal disease, terminal cancer.*
—*n.* **1** the end; end part. SYN: extremity. **2a** either end of a railroad line, airline, bus line, or shipping route, at which are located sheds, hangars, garages, offices, and stations to handle freight and passengers; terminus. **b** a city or station at the end of a railroad, bus route, or the like. **3** a device for making an electrical connection: *the terminals of a battery.* **4a** a teletype machine. **b** a typewriter keyboard or other device connected to a computer for remote input or output of data. Some terminals are connected to a video display unit that projects information on a cathode-ray tube. *As many as 30 terminals can be connected at one time, with each user carrying on a direct and in effect uninterrupted dialogue with the computer* (Scientific American). [Latin *terminālis* < *terminus* terminus] —**ter′mi|nal|ly**, *adv.*
**terminal leave**, a leave of absence given to a member of the armed forces before discharge, amounting to the remaining days of leave due.
**terminal moraine**, a moraine deposited at the end of a glacier. See picture under **glacier**.
**terminal rocket**, a rocket designed to put a space vehicle into the final course desired.
**terminal side**, *Trigonometry.* the line formed by the rotation of the initial side of an angle.
**terminal velocity**, the constant velocity of a falling body, attained when the resistance of air, water, or other surrounding fluid has become equal to the force of gravity acting upon the body: [*The*] *terminal velocity for a man is about 120 m.p.h.* (*e.g. for a parachutist delaying the opening of his chute*); *the corresponding velocity for a cat is probably 40 m.p.h. at the most* (New Scientist).

**ter|mi|nate** (tėr′mə nāt), *v.*, **-nat|ed, -nat|ing.** *— v.t.* **1** to bring to an end; put an end to; end: *to terminate a partnership. The policeman terminated the quarrel by sending the boys home.* **SYN:** conclude. **2** to occur at or form the end of; bound; limit: *land terminated by the sea.* **3** *U.S.* to dismiss from employment: *In the recession the company terminated a number of workers.* *— v.i.* **1** to come to an end; cease; close: *His contract terminates soon. The evening's entertainment will terminate in a dance.* **2** to form an end or limit; stop short: *The railroad line terminates in New York.* **3** to result: *The battle terminated in favor of the larger forces.* **4** *U.S.* to dismiss an employee or employees.
[< Latin *termināri* (with English *-ate*[1]) < *terminus* end, terminus]

**ter|mi|na|tion** (tėr′mə nā′shən), *n.* **1** the act of ending or the fact of being ended; end: *The termination of the agreement left the businessman free to do as he pleased. All human power has its termination sooner or later* (Cardinal Newman). **SYN:** conclusion. **2** an end part; limit: *The glacier was traced to its termination.* **SYN:** bound. **3** the ending of a word. *Example:* In *gladly,* the adverbial termination is *-ly.* **4** outcome; result: *He hopes for a successful termination of the court case.* **5** *U.S.* the abolition of the special relationship between American Indian tribes and the Federal government, especially the support and protection of reservations: *A number of tribes voted for termination ... But in most cases, termination took place too rapidly and with too little preparation for independence* (Merwyn S. Garbarino).

**ter|mi|na|tion|al** (tėr′mə nā′shə nəl), *adj.* **1** closing; final. **2** forming or formed by an inflected ending or suffix.

**ter|mi|na|tive** (tėr′mə nā′tiv), *adj.* tending or serving to terminate. — **ter′mi|na′tive|ly,** *adv.*

**ter|mi|na|tor** (tėr′mə nā′tər), *n.* **1** a person or thing that terminates. **2** *Astronomy.* the line separating the light and dark parts of the disk of the moon or a planet; circle of illumination.

**ter|mi|no|log|i|cal** (tėr′mə nə loj′ə kəl), *adj.* of or having to do with terminology: *terminological problems of science.* — **ter′mi|no|log′i|cal|ly,** *adv.*

**ter|mi|nol|o|gist** (tėr′mə nol′ə jist), *n.* a person skilled in terminology.

**ter|mi|nol|o|gy** (tėr′mə nol′ə jē), *n., pl.* **-gies.** **1** the special words or terms used in a science, art, business, or other endeavor: *medical terminology.* **2** *Obsolete.* the doctrine or scientific study of terms. [< German *Terminologie* < Medieval Latin *terminus* term (in Latin, end, terminus) + German *-logie* -logy]

**term insurance**, insurance expiring at the end of a period of time and payable only if loss occurs within that period.

**ter|mi|nus** (tėr′mə nəs), *n., pl.* **-ni** (-nī), **-nus|es.** **1** either end of a railroad line, bus line, airline, or shipping route; terminal. **2** a city or station at the end of a railroad, bus line, airline, or shipping route: *The Eastern Region termini in London ran 79 extra trains* (London Times). **3** an ending place; final point; goal; end. **SYN:** finale. **4** a stone, post, or the like, marking a boundary or limit; boundary marker. [< Latin *terminus.* See etym. of doublet **term.**]

**ter|mi|nus ad quem** (ter′mən əs ad kwem′), *Latin.* the end to which; finishing point.

**terminus a quo** (ā kwō′), *Latin.* the end from which; starting point.

**ter|mi|tar|i|um** (tėr′mə tãr′ē əm), *n., pl.* **-tar|i|a** (-tãr′ē ə). **1** = termitary (def. 1). **2** a cage or vessel for studying termites. [< New Latin *termitarium* < *termites* termite]

**ter|mi|tar|y** (tėr′mə tãr′ē), *n., pl.* **-tar|ies.** **1** nest of termites: *The formicary, the termitary, ... and the beehive send forth their thousands* (Kirby and Spence). **2** = termitarium (def. 2).

**✱termite**

**✱ter|mite** (tėr′mīt), *n.* an insect that has a soft, pale body and a dark head, and lives in colonies; isopteran. Termites look somewhat like white ants and eat the wood of buildings and furniture, provisions, paper, and other matter containing cellulose. Termite colonies consist of winged males and females and wingless, sterile soldiers. [< New Latin *termites,* plural of *termes, -mitis* < Late Latin, woodworm (in Latin, *tarmes, -itis*), related to *terere* to rub, wear]

**ter|mit|ic** (tėr mit′ik), *adj.* of, having to do with, or formed by termites.

**term|less** (tėrm′lis), *adj.* **1** not dependent on or limited by any terms or conditions; unconditional. **2** having no limit; boundless; endless: *infinite and termless complication of detail* (John Ruskin).

**term paper**, a required essay written for a course in a school term.

**term policy**, an insurance policy that provides term insurance.

**terms** (tėrmz), *n.pl.* See under **term**.

**terms of reference**, *Especially British.* the terms which define the scope of an inquiry.

**term time**, *Especially British.* **1** the period of study at a university or school. **2** the period during which the law courts are in session.

**tern**[1] (tėrn), *n.* any one of a group of sea birds, related to the gulls but with a more slender body and bill, long, pointed wings, and usually a long, forked tail. [< Scandinavian (compare Danish *terne*)]

**tern**[2] (tėrn), *n.* **1** a ternary; trio; triad. **2a** a combination of three winning numbers drawn in a lottery. **b** a prize won by the holder of such a combination. [< French *terne* < Old French *terne* or *ternes,* plural, double three in dice, ultimately < Latin *ternī* three each < *ter* thrice]

**ter|na|ry** (tėr′nər ē), *adj., n., pl.* **-ries.** *— adj.* **1** consisting of three; involving three; triple. **2** third in rank, order, or position. **3** *Mathematics.* **a** having three for the base: *a ternary scale.* **b** involving three variables. **4** *Metallurgy.* consisting of three elements or components: *a ternary alloy.* *— n.* **1** a set or group of three; trio; triad. **2** a number that is a multiple of three.
[< Latin *ternārius* < *ternī* three each < *ter* thrice]

**ter|nate** (tėr′nit, -nāt), *adj.* **1** consisting of three. **2** arranged in threes. **3** *Botany.* **a** having or consisting of three leaflets. **b** having leaves in whorls of three. — **ter′nate|ly,** *adv.*

**terne** (tėrn), *v.,* **terned, tern|ing,** *n.* *— v.t.* to plate with an alloy of tin and lead.
*— n.* terneplate.

**terne|plate** (tėrn′plāt′), *n.* a thin sheet of iron or steel coated with an alloy of lead and a small percentage of tin: *Terneplate ... is used in air cleaners and fuel tanks* (Wall Street Journal). [probably < obsolete *terne,* adjective, dull, dark + *plate*]

**ter|ni|on** (tėr′nē ən), *n.* **1** = ternary. **2** a section of paper for a book, containing twelve pages. [< Latin *terniō, -ōnis* a triad < *ternī* three each < *ter* thrice]

**ter|pene** (tėr′pēn), *n.* **1** any one of a group of isomeric hydrocarbons, such as pinene and limonene, many of which are produced by distilling the volatile oils of plants, especially conifers. *Formula:* $C_{10}H_{16}$ **2** any one of various alcohols derived from or related to terpene.

**ter|pe|nic** (tėr pē′nik), *adj.* of or derived from terpene.

**ter|pe|noid** (tėr′pə noid), *n., adj.* *— n.* any one of a group of compounds having a chemical structure similar to that of terpene.
*— adj.* of or having to do with a terpenoid.

**ter|phen|yl** (tėr fen′əl, -fē′nəl), *n.* a crystalline organic compound used as a moderator and coolant in certain nuclear reactors. *Formula:* $C_{18}H_{14}$ [< Latin *ter* three times (because it contains three benzene rings) + English *phenyl*]

**ter|pin** (tėr′pin), *n.* **1** a compound like alcohol, whose hydrate is prepared from oil of turpentine. *Formula:* $C_{10}H_{20}O_2$ **2** a compound isomeric with it. [< German *Terpin* < *Terpentin* turpentine]

**ter|pin|e|ol** (tėr pin′ē ōl, -ol), *n.* a tertiary colorless alcohol, found in essential oils, and also produced synthetically. It is used as a solvent and in making perfumes. *Formula:* $C_{10}H_{18}O(OH)$

**ter|pin|ol** (tėr′pə nōl, -nol), *n.* a mixture of the isomeric forms of terpineol.

**ter|pol|y|mer** (ter pol′i mer), *n. Chemistry.* a compound formed by the polymerization of three different compounds, each of which usually is able to polymerize alone. [< Latin *ter* thrice + English *polymer*]

**Terp|sich|o|re** (tėrp sik′ə rē), *n. Greek Mythology.* the Muse of dancing and choral singing.

**Terp|si|cho|re|an** (tėrp′sə kə rē′ən), *adj.* of or having to do with Terpsichore.

**terp|si|cho|re|an** (tėrp′sə kə rē′ən), *adj., n.* *— adj.* of or having to do with dancing: *terpsichorean art.* *— n.* a dancer (now in humorous use).

**terr** (ter), *n.* a black guerrilla in Rhodesia or South Africa (used in an unfriendly way by white Rhodesians and South Africans): *"The terrs move in groups of five to eight, one guy carries a light machine gun and another is trained to plant mines," a soldier here* [*in Rhodesia*] *said* (New York Times). [< *terr*(orist)]

**terr.**, **1** terrace. **2** territory.

**Terr.**, Territory.

**ter|ra** (ter′ə), *n., pl.* **ter|rae.** **1** the earth. **2** earth; soil. **3** any part of the lunar surface that is not one of the maria: *The terrae* [*consist*] *of a complex arrangement of level plains, gently rolling to rugged hills, and large craters* (N. J. Trask and H. E. Holt). [< Italian and Latin *terra* earth, land]

**Ter|ra** (ter′ə), *n. Roman Mythology.* a goddess of the earth. The Greeks called her Gaea.

**ter|ra al|ba** (ter′ə al′bə), = pipe clay. [< Latin *terra alba* (literally) white earth]

**✱ter|race** (ter′is), *n., v.,* **-raced, -rac|ing.** *— n.* **1** an outdoor space, usually paved or tiled, near a house, used for lounging or dining. **2** the flat roof of a house, especially of an Oriental or Spanish house. **3a** a street along the side or top of a slope. **b** a row of houses on such a street. **4a** a flat, raised piece of land, with a vertical or sloping front, or sides, faced as with masonry or turf, especially one of a series of such levels placed one above the other. **b** such a raised piece of land and the masonry, turf, or other material, together. **5** *U.S.* a parklike strip, as in the center of a road. *Abbr:* ter.
*— v.t.* to form into a terrace or terraces; furnish with terraces: *to terrace a hillside.*
[< Middle French *terrace* (originally) a heap of rubble (used to underlie a platform) < Vulgar Latin *terrācea* < Latin *terra* earth]

**✱terrace**
definition 1

**ter|raced** (ter′ist), *adj.* **1** furnished with a terrace or terraces: *a terraced garden, a terraced apartment.* **2** arranged or constructed in the form of a terrace.

**ter|rac|ing** (ter′ə sing), *n.* **1** the formation of terraces. **2** a terraced surface or formation. **3** a platform or stand with rows of seats rising in tiers behind each other.

**ter|ra cot|ta** (ter′ə kot′ə), **1** a kind of hard, often unglazed, and usually brownish-red or cream-colored earthenware, used for vases, statuettes, and decorations on buildings. **2** an object made of this substance. **3** a dull brownish red. [< Italian *terra cotta* < *terra* earth + *cotta* baked; (literally) cooked, feminine past participle of *cuocere* < Latin *coquere* to cook]

**ter|ra-cot|ta** (ter′ə kot′ə), *adj.* **1** having to do with or made of terra cotta: *The floor was made of terra-cotta tiles* (Atlantic). **2** of the color of terra cotta.

**ter|ra|dy|nam|ic** (ter′ə dī nam′ik, -di-), *adj.* having to do with or based on terradynamics.

**ter|ra|dy|nam|ics** (ter′ə dī nam′iks, -di-), *n.* **1** the study of the behavior and effect of objects penetrating the earth at high speeds. **2** the use of high-speed projectiles to penetrate the earth: *Terradynamics, a technique that uses a rocket for high-speed penetration of the earth, gives geologists a new method for studying the earth's crust* (James A. Pearre). [< Latin *terra* earth + English *dynamics;* patterned on *aerodynamics*]

**ter|rae** (ter′ē), *n.* plural of **terra**.

**ter|rae fi|li|us** (ter′ē fil′ē əs), *pl.* **ter|rae fi|li|i** (ter′ē fil′ē ī). **1** a student at Oxford University formerly appointed to make jesting satirical speeches. **2** *Archaic.* a person of obscure birth or low origin. [< Latin *terrae fīlius* a son of the earth, a man of unknown origin]

**ter|ra fir|ma** (ter′ə fėr′mə), solid earth; dry land. [< Latin *terra firma*]

**ter|rain** (te rān′, ter′ān), *n.* **1** any tract of land, especially considered with respect to its extent and natural features: *the hilly, rocky terrain of parts of New England.* **2** *Geology.* terrane. [< French *terrain* < Old French *terain* < Vulgar Latin *terrānum,* for Latin *terrēnum,* noun use of adjective, earthy < *terra* earth, land]

**ter|ra in|cog|ni|ta** (ter′ə in kog′nə tə), *pl.* **ter|rae in|cog|ni|tae** (ter′ē in kog′nə tē). an unknown or unexplored region: *Missionaries, entrepreneurs, a trickle of tourists, ... except for these, Asia remained terra incognita* (Arthur Goodfriend). (*Figurative.*) *Hungarian fiction since World War II is likely to constitute a sort of terra incognita for most English-speaking readers* (Saturday Re-

**Pronunciation Key:** hat, āge, cãre, fär; let, ēqual, tėrm; it, īce; hot, ōpen, ôrder; **oi**l, **ou**t; cup, pu̇t, rüle; **ch**ild; lo**ng**; **th**in; **ᴛʜ**en; **zh**, measure; **ə** represents **a** in about, **e** in taken, **i** in pencil, **o** in lemon, **u** in circus.

view). [< Latin *terra incognita* (literally) unknown land]

**ter|ra Ja|pon|i|ca** (ter′ə jə pon′ə kə), *pl.* **ter|rae Ja|pon|i|cae** (ter′ē jə pon′ə sē). **1** = gambier. **2** = catechu. [< New Latin *terra Japonica* (literally) Japanese land]

**Ter|ra|my|cin** (ter′ə mī′sin), *n. Trademark.* oxytetracycline.

**ter|rane** (tə rān′, ter′ān), *n. Geology.* a formation or a connected series of formations. [apparently alteration of *terrain*]

**ter|ra|pin** (ter′ə pin), *n.* **1** any one of certain North American turtles used for food. Terrapins live in fresh water or tidewater. The diamondback terrapin of the Atlantic and Gulf coasts is one kind. **2** any one of certain other turtles. [American English, alteration of Algonkian (Abnaki) *turepé* or (Delaware) *turpa*]

**ter|ra|que|ous** (te rā′kwē əs), *adj.* **1** consisting of land and water: *the terraqueous globe.* **2** living in land and water, as a plant. [< Latin *terra* land, earth + English *aqueous*]

***ter|rar|i|um** (tə rãr′ē əm), *n., pl.* **-i|ums, -i|a** (-ē ə). **1** a glass or plastic bowl or container in which small plants are grown in a soil mixture; a plant vivarium. **2** a similar enclosure in which small land animals are kept; an animal vivarium. [< New Latin *terrarium* < Latin *terra* land. Compare Late Latin *terrārius* earthly.]

***terrarium** definition 1

**ter|ra sig|il|la|ta** (ter′ə sij′ə lā′tə), = Lemnian earth. [< New Latin *terra sigillata* (literally) sealed earth]

**ter|rasse** (te räs′), *n. French.* terrace.

**ter|raz|zo** (te rät′sō), *n.* a flooring made of small pieces of marble set in a scattered pattern in cement. [< Italian *terrazzo* floor of broken stone and cement < Vulgar Latin *terrāceum* rubble, useless earth, noun use of neuter adjective < Latin *terra* earth. Compare etym. under **terrace.**]

**terre-à-terre** (ter′ə ter′), *adj.* **1** (of a kind of dance) performed close to the ground; performed with very little lifting of the feet. **2** *Figurative.* matter-of-fact; unimaginative: *He is content with such terre-à-terre foods as chicken salad and hamburger* (New Yorker). [< French *terre à terre* (literally) earth to earth]

**ter|rel|la** (te rel′ə), *n.* **1** a space capsule with an environment of the earth: *Sanitary engineers ... are figuring out how to dispose of wastes and insure the cleanliness of the terrella* (New Yorker). **2** a magnetic globe or other spherical object so placed that its poles, equator, and other points of orientation correspond exactly to those of the earth, and often marked with lines representing meridians and parallels, for illustrating magnetic phenomena of the earth. **3** *Obsolete.* a little earth; small planet. [< New Latin *terrella* (diminutive) < Latin *terra* earth, world]

**ter|rene** (te rēn′), *adj., n.* **—adj. 1** belonging to the earth; earthly; worldly. **2** of the nature of earth; earthy.
**—n. 1** the earth. **2a** a land. **b** = terrain.
[< Latin *terrēnus* earthly, worldly < *terra* earth, land. Compare etym. under **terrain.**]

**terre|plein** (ter′plān′), *n.* **1** the top of a rampart, on which cannon are placed. **2** the surface of a fortification in the field, especially for cannon. [< French *terreplein* < Italian *terrapieno,* ultimately < Latin *terra* earth + *plēna,* feminine of *plēnus* full]

**ter|res|tri|al** (tə res′trē əl), *adj., n.* **—adj. 1** of the earth, not of the heavens; having to do with the earth: *this terrestrial globe.* **2** of the land, not water: *Islands and continents make up the terrestrial parts of the earth.* **3** living on the ground, not in the air, water, or trees: *Cows, lions, and elephants are terrestrial animals. These animals are now able to crawl out on land and take their place as terrestrial vertebrates* (A. M. Winchester). **4** growing on land; growing in the soil: *terrestrial plants.* **5** worldly; earthly. **SYN**: mundane. See syn. under **earthly.**
**—n.** a terrestrial being, especially a human.
[< Late Latin *terrestria* earthly things (< Latin *terrestris* earthly, worldly < *terra* earth) + English *-al*[1]] **—ter|res′tri|al|ly,** *adv.*

**terrestrial globe, ball,** or **sphere, 1** the earth. **2** a sphere with a map of the earth on it.

**terrestrial magnetism,** = geomagnetism.

**terrestrial planet,** any one of the four planets nearest the sun and somewhat similar in size. They are the Earth, Mars, Venus, and Mercury.

**terrestrial space,** a zone from the earth's surface to about 4,000 miles into space, within which the earth's magnetic and electric influences are strongest.

**ter|ret** (ter′it), *n.* **1** one of the round loops or rings on the saddle of a harness, through which the driving reins pass. **2** a round loop or ring, especially one turning on a swivel, by which a string or chain is attached to anything. [Middle English *tyret,* variant of *toret,* probably < Old French *touret* (diminutive) < *tour* a circuit, tour]

**ter|ri|ble** (ter′ə bəl), *adj.* **1** causing great fear; dreadful; awful: *a terrible leopard, the terrible weapons of warfare. The terrible storm destroyed many lives.* **SYN**: frightful, appalling, horrible, shocking. **2** distressing; severe: *the terrible suffering caused by war.* **3** *Informal.* extremely bad or unpleasant: *a terrible student. She has a terrible temper.* [< Old French *terrible,* learned borrowing from Latin *terribilis* < *terrēre* to terrify] **—ter′ri|ble|ness,** *n.*

**ter|ri|bly** (ter′ə blē), *adv.* **1** in a terrible manner; dreadfully: *to be terribly afraid of lightning.* **2** *Informal.* extremely; very: *I'm terribly sorry I stepped on your toes.*

**ter|ric|o|lous** (te rik′ə ləs), *adj. Biology.* living on or in the ground. [< Latin *terricola* < *terra* earth + *colere* inhabit]

***ter|ri|er** (ter′ē ər), *n.* a kind of small, active, intelligent, and courageous dog, formerly used to pursue prey into its burrow. Some well-known breeds are fox terriers, Irish terriers, and Scottish terriers. The bull, Sealyham, Skye, Airedale, Dandie Dinmont, and schnauzer are also terriers. [Middle English *terrere* < Old French (*chien*) *terrier* terrier (dog) < Medieval Latin *terrārium,* noun use of adjective, neuter of Late Latin *terrārius* earthly < Latin *terra* earth] **—ter′ri|er|like′,** *adj.*

***terrier**[1]

**ter|rif|ic** (tə rif′ik), *adj.* **1** causing great fear or terror; terrifying: *a terrific storm. A terrific earthquake shook Japan.* **SYN**: awful. **2** *Informal.* very great or severe; remarkable; extraordinary: *terrific applause. A terrific hot spell ruined many of the crops.* **3** *Informal.* very good; wonderful: *He is a terrific football player. The party was terrific.* [< Latin *terrificus* < *terrēre* to terrify + *facere* to make]

**ter|rif|i|cal|ly** (tə rif′ə klē), *adv.* in a terrific manner; to a terrific degree: *Debussy ... believed that Beethoven had terrifically profound things to say* (Atlantic).

**ter|ri|fied** (ter′ə fīd), *adj.* filled with great fear; frightened: *Elizabeth ... hastened ... along the principal alley of the Pleasance, dragging with her the terrified Countess* (Scott). **SYN**: See syn. under **afraid.** **—ter′ri|fied|ly,** *adv.*

**ter|ri|fi|er** (ter′ə fī′ər), *n.* a person or thing that terrifies.

**ter|ri|fy** (ter′ə fī), *v.t.,* **-fied, -fy|ing.** to fill with great fear or terror; frighten very much: *Terrified by the sight of the bear, he ran into the cabin.* **SYN**: scare, alarm, horrify, appall. [< Latin *terrificāre* < *terrēre* terrify + *facere* to make]

**ter|ri|fy|ing|ly** (ter′ə fī′ing lē), *adv.* in a terrifying manner; to a terrifying degree: *Aunt Kate yelled terrifyingly from the back of the hall "I'm going to tell your mother"* (Time). *It includes some terrifyingly vivid writing* (Anthony West). *Much refuse from fission is low-level and short-lived but about one-third of it is terrifyingly radioactive* (Newsweek).

**ter|rig|e|nous** (tə rij′ə nəs), *adj.* **1** produced by the earth. **2** *Geology.* of or having to do with marine deposits from the neighboring land. [< Latin *terrigenus* (with English *-ous*) < *terra* earth + *gen-,* root of *gignere* beget]

**ter|rine** (te rēn′), *n.* **1** a bowllike earthenware vessel with a cover, and handles on either side: *As the waitress brought in a great terrine of potato soup, the boss asked me if I had eaten* (New Yorker). **2** the contents of such a vessel. [early form of *tureen*]

**ter|ri|to|ri|al** (ter′ə tôr′ē əl, -tōr′-), *adj., n.* **—adj. 1** of or having to do with territory or land: *The purchase of Louisiana was a valuable territorial addition to the United States.* **2** of a particular territory or district; restricted to a particular district: *a territorial governor. The gods ... were local and territorial divinities* (Joseph Priestley). **SYN**: local, sectional. **3** showing territoriality; defending an area possessively: *Unlike the lion and puma, the cheetah is not territorial, and several strangers tolerate each other within a certain hunting area* (George B. Schaller).
**—n.** a member of a territorial military force: *These territorials could also be used to suppress opposition groups ... during the crucial referendum on secession* (Maclean's). **—ter′ri|to′ri|al|ly,** *adv.*

**Ter|ri|to|ri|al** (ter′ə tôr′ē əl, -tōr′-), *adj., n.* **—adj. 1** of a United States Territory: *a Territorial legislature, Territorial laws.* **2** *British.* organized for home defense.
**—n.** *British.* a soldier of the Territorial Army.

**Territorial Army,** the portion of the British Army auxiliary to the regular army, especially for home defense; Home Guard.

**territorial imperative,** *Ethology.* the supposed innate character of certain animals to regard areas possessively and defend them from encroachment: *The "territorial imperative" does much to explain the causes of war, ... which I consider almost purely territorial* (Konrad Lorenz).

**ter|ri|to|ri|al|ism** (ter′ə tôr′ē ə liz′əm, -tōr′-), *n.* **1** the tendency among animals to defend their individual territories. **2** a theory that gives predominance in a state to the landed class; landlordism. **3** the theory of church government holding that ecclesiastical supremacy is inherently a prerogative of the civil power; territorial system.

**ter|ri|to|ri|al|ist** (ter′ə tôr′ē ə list, -tōr′-), *n.* an advocate of territorialism.

**ter|ri|to|ri|al|i|ty** (ter′ə tôr′ē al′ə tē, -tōr′-), *n.* **1** territorial quality, condition, position, or status. **2** a form of behavior in which an animal claims an area for itself and defends it from encroachment by others: *No room was left for doubting ... the territoriality of the owls* (Scientific American). *The cichlids' territoriality—defense of its territory—offers an interesting analogy to the institution of private property in the higher vertebrates* (New Yorker).

**ter|ri|to|ri|al|ize** (ter′ə tôr′ē ə līz, -tōr′-), *v.t.,* **-ized, -iz|ing. 1** to make territorial. **2** to associate with or allocate to a particular territory or district. **3** to make larger by increasing the territory of. **—ter′ri|to′ri|al|i|za′tion,** *n.*

**territorial system,** = territorialism.

**territorial waters,** the waters inland or off the coastline of a nation over which the nation exercises jurisdiction: *Canada proposed that the limit of territorial waters should be six miles, with an additional six miles of exclusive fishing rights for the coastal State* (Manchester Guardian Weekly).

**ter|ri|to|ry** (ter′ə tôr′ē, -tōr′-), *n., pl.* **-ries. 1** land; region: *to map an unexplored territory from the air. Much territory in the northern part of Africa is desert.* **SYN**: tract, area. **2a** land belonging to a government; land under the rule of a distant government: *Gibraltar is British territory.* **SYN**: dominion. **b** = Territory. **3** a region assigned to a salesman or agent. **4** *Figurative.* the facts investigated by some branch of science or learning: *the territory of biochemistry.* **SYN**: field. **5** an area within definite boundaries, such as a nesting ground, in which an animal lives and from which it keeps out others of its kind. [< Latin *territōrium,* apparently < *terra* land]

**Ter|ri|to|ry** (ter′ə tôr′ē, -tōr′-), *n., pl.* **-ries. 1** *U.S.* a district not admitted as a state but having its own lawmaking body: *Hawaii and Alaska were Territories before they became states.* **2** a district with a somewhat similar status elsewhere, as in Australia or Canada. *Abbr:* Terr. [< *territory*]

**ter|ror** (ter′ər), *n.* **1** great fear: *The child has a terror of thunder.* **SYN**: fright, alarm, dread, consternation. **2** a cause of great fear: *Pirates were once the terror of the sea. There is no terror, Cassius, in your threats* (Shakespeare). **3** deliberate violence against persons or groups by a government or another group. **4** *Informal.* a person or thing that causes much trouble and unpleasantness: *What an awful person! She must be a holy terror to live with* (Sinclair Lewis). [< Latin *terror* < *terrēre* to terrify]

**Ter|ror** (ter′ər), *n.* **1** a period when a community lives in fear of death or violence because of the methods used by a political party or group to win or keep power, such as the Reign of Terror in France. **2** a group or movement using such methods. [< *terror*]

**ter|ror|ise** (ter′ə rīz), *v.t.*, **-ised, -is|ing.** *Especially British.* terrorize.

**ter|ror|ism** (ter′ə riz əm), *n.* **1** the act of terrorizing; use of terror, especially the systematic use of terror by a government or other authority against particular persons or groups. **2** a condition of fear and submission produced by frightening people. **3** a method of opposing a government internally through the use of terror.

**ter|ror|ist** (ter′ər ist), *n., adj.* **—*n.*** a person who uses or favors terrorism: *Venezuelan terrorists attacked a prison in Caracas and about 600 prisoners were said to have escaped* (Wall Street Journal).
**—*adj.*** of or by terrorists; terroristic.

**ter|ror|is|tic** (ter′ə ris′tik), *adj.* using or favoring methods that inspire terror.

**ter|ror|ize** (ter′ə rīz), *v.t.*, **-ized, -iz|ing.** **1** to fill with terror: *The sight of the growling dog terrorized the little child.* **SYN:** terrify. **2** to rule or subdue by causing terror. **SYN:** browbeat, intimidate. **—ter′ror|i|za′tion,** *n.* **—ter′ror|iz′er,** *n.*

**ter|ror|less** (ter′ər lis), *adj.* **1** free from terror. **2** without terrors.

**ter|ror-strick|en** (ter′ər strik′ən), *adj.* = terrified.

**ter|ry** (ter′ē), *n., pl.* **-ries.** a rough cotton cloth made of uncut looped yarn. [perhaps < French *tiré* drawn]

**terry cloth,** = terry.

**terse** (tėrs), *adj.,* **ters|er, ters|est.** brief and to the point (said of writing and speaking, or writers and speakers): *"No" was Father's terse reply when I asked to play after bedtime.* **SYN:** See syn. under **concise.** [< Latin *tersus* clean-cut, burnished, past participle of *tergere* to rub, polish, wipe] **—terse′ly,** *adv.* **—terse′ness,** *n.*

**ter|tial** (tėr′shəl), *adj., n.* **—*adj.*** of or having to do with the flight feathers on the basal section of a bird's wing.
**—*n.*** a tertial feather.
[< Latin *tertius* third + English *-al*[1]]

**ter|tian** (tėr′shən), *n., adj.* **—*n.*** a fever, such as malaria, with a bad spell which recurs every other day.
**—*adj.*** recurring every other day.
[Middle English (*fever*) *tercian* < Latin *tertiāna* (*febris*) < *tertius* third]

**ter|ti|ar|y** (tėr′shē er′ē, -shər-), *adj., n., pl.* **-ar|ies.** **—*adj.*** **1** of the third order, rank, or formation; third. **2** *Chemistry.* **a** of or having to do with a carbon atom joined to three other carbon atoms in a chain or ring. **b** resulting from the replacement of three atoms or groups. **3** = tertial.
**—*n.*** **1** one of a bird's flight feathers; tertial feather. **2** a lay member of the third order of certain monastic fraternities of the Roman Catholic Church, not subject to the strict rule of the regulars.
[< Latin *tertiārius,* adjective, of or having to do with a (or the) third < *tertius* third]

**Ter|ti|ar|y** (tėr′shē er′ē, -shər-), *n., pl.* **-ar|ies,** *adj.* **—*n.*** **1** the earlier of the two periods making up the Cenozoic era, immediately following the Mesozoic. During this time the great mountain systems, such as the Alps, Himalayas, Rockies, and Andes, appeared, and rapid development of mammals occurred. **2** the rocks formed during this period.
**—*adj.*** of or having to do with this period or its rocks.

**tertiary color,** a color formed by mixing two binary colors.

**tertiary consumer,** *Ecology.* an animal that eats a secondary consumer in a food chain. In a food chain in which a grass-eating mouse (primary consumer) is devoured by a weasel (secondary consumer) and the weasel in turn is consumed by a hawk, the hawk is a tertiary consumer. See diagram under **food chain.**

**tertiary root,** a branch of a secondary root.

**tertiary syphilis,** the last stage of syphilis, with severe lesions of skin, bones, and brain.

**ter|ti|um quid** (tėr′shē əm kwid′), a third something; something related in some way to two things but distinct from both; something intermediate between two opposite things. [< Latin *tertium quid* some third thing; translation of Greek *tríton ti*]

**ter|ti|us** (tėr′shē əs), *adj.* **1** third (used in prescriptions). **2** (in some English schools) designating the youngest of three boys of the same surname: *Smith tertius hit the ball* (London Times). [< Latin *tertius* third]

**ter|va|lent** (tėr vā′lənt), *adj. Chemistry.* **1** trivalent. **2** having three valences. [< Latin *ter* thrice + English *-valent*]

**Ter|y|lene** (ter′ə lēn), *n. British Trademark.* Dacron.

**ter|za ri|ma** (ter′tsä rē′mä), an Italian form of iambic verse consisting of ten-syllable or eleven-syllable lines arranged in tercets, the middle line of each tercet rhyming with the first and third lines of the following tercet (*aba, bcb, cdc,* and so on). Dante's *Divine Comedy* and Shelley's *Ode to the West Wind* are in terza rima. [< Italian *terza rima* < *terza* third + *rima* rhyme]

**ter|zet** (tert′set), *n.* = terzetto.

**ter|zet|to** (ter tset′tō), *n., pl.* **-ti** (-tē). *Music.* a trio, especially a vocal trio. [< Italian *terzetto.* See etym. of doublet **tercet.**]

**TESL** (tes′əl), *n. Education.* teaching English as a second language: *A major curriculum emphasis is developing fluency in the English language using the linguistic approach of TESL* (Saturday Review).

**tes|la** (tes′lə), *n.* a unit for measuring magnetic flux density, equal to one weber per square meter. *Abbr:* T (no period). [< Nikola *Tesla,* 1856-1943, an American electrician and inventor, born in Croatia]

**Tesla coil,** an air-core transformer used to produce high-frequency alternating or oscillating currents. [< Nikola *Tesla,* who invented it]

**Tesla current,** a current generated by the Tesla coil.

**TESOL** (tes′ôl), *n. Education.* teachers of English to speakers of other languages: *TESOL texts and tapes.*

**tes|sel|la** (tes′ə lə), *n., pl.* **-lae** (-lē). a small tessera or block, as in mosaic. [< Latin *tessela,* variant of *tessera;* see etym. under **tessera**]

**tes|sel|late** (*v.* tes′ə lāt; *adj.* tes′ə lit, -lāt), *v.,* **-lat|ed, -lat|ing,** *adj.* **—*v.t.*** to make of small squares or blocks, or in a checkered pattern.
**—*adj.*** made in small squares or blocks or in a checkered pattern.
[< Medieval Latin *tessellare* (with English *-ate*[1]) < Latin *tessella,* variant of *tessera;* see etym. under **tessera**]

**tes|sel|la|tion** (tes′ə lā′shən), *n.* **1a** the act or art of tessellating. **b** tessellated condition. **2** a piece of tessellated work.

**tes|ser|a** (tes′ər ə), *n., pl.* **tes|ser|ae** (tes′ə rē). **1** a small piece of marble, glass, or the like, used in mosaic work. **2** a small square of bone, wood, or the like, used in ancient times as a token, tally, ticket, or die. [< Latin *tessera* (originally) a cube < Greek *téssera* four (because of the four corners)]

**tes|ser|act** (tes′ə rakt), *n. Mathematics.* a four-dimensional cube. [< Greek *téssera* four + *aktī́s* ray]

**tes|si|tur|a** (tes′ə tůr′ə), *n. Music.* the part of the total compass of a melody or voice part in which most of its tones lie; range. [< Italian *tessitura* texture]

**test**[1] (test), *n., adj., v.* **—*n.*** **1** an examination or trial: *The teacher gave us a test in arithmetic. People who want a license to drive an automobile must pass a test.* **SYN:** See syn. under **trial.** **2** a means of trial: *Trouble is a test of character.* **3** *Chemistry.* **a** the examination of a substance to see what it is or what it contains: *A test showed that the water was pure.* **b** the process or substance used in such an examination. **c** the result of such an examination. **4** a cupel used in assaying or refining precious metals. **b** examination by a test or cupel. **5** *British.* a Test match.
**—*adj.*** **1** of or having to do with a test: *There are other test issues* (New York Times). **2** taken, done, or made as a test: *a test specimen, test laws.*
**—*v.t.*** to put to a test of any kind; try out: *to hang on a rope testing it for strength. The doctor tested my eyes. He tested the boy's honesty by leaving money on the table. The teacher will test the class in spelling. The winter at Valley Forge tested the loyalty of the American troops* (Marshall Smelser).
**—*v.i.*** **1** to undergo a test; be tested: *Everybody wants to test for a part in the play.* **2** to show a certain result on a test: *The water tests pure. The car tested better on the highway than in city traffic.* **3** to give a test (for): *to test a child for comprehension, to test a patient for an allergy.*
[< Old French *test* small pot in which to treat ore to find out how much metal it has < Latin *testū* earthen container or pot, variant of *testa;* see etym. under **testa.**] **—test′a|ble,** *adj.*

**test**[2] (test), *n.* **1** *Zoology.* the hard covering of certain animals; shell. **2** *Botany.* testa. [< Latin *testa;* see etym. under **testa**]

**Test.,** Testament.

**tes|ta** (tes′tə), *n., pl.* **-tae** (-tē). **1** *Botany.* the hard outside coat of a seed. **SYN:** integument. **2** *Zoology.* test[2]. [< Latin *testa;* earthenware (pot)]

**test|a|bil|i|ty** (tes′tə bil′ə tē), *n.* the quality or state of being testable.

**tes|ta|cean** (tes tā′shən), *adj., n.* **—*adj.*** of or belonging to an order of shell-covered rhizopods.
**—*n.*** a testacean animal.
[< New Latin *Testacea* the order name (< Latin *testāceus* covered with a shell < *testa* testa) + English *-an*]

**tes|ta|ceous** (tes tā′shəs), *adj.* **1** of the nature or substance of a shell or shells. **2** having a hard shell. **3** *Biology.* of a dull brownish-red, brownish-yellow, or reddish-brown color. [< Latin *testāceus* (with English *-ous*); see etym. under **testacean**]

**tes|ta|cy** (tes′tə sē), *n.* the leaving of a will at death.

**Tes|ta|ment** (tes′tə mənt), *n.* **1** a main division of the Bible; the Old Testament or the New Testament. **2** *Informal.* the New Testament. **3** a copy of the New Testament. [< Latin *testāmentum* < *testārī;* see etym. under **testate**]

**tes|ta|ment** (tes′tə mənt), *n.* **1** written instructions telling what to do with a person's property after his death; will. **2** expression; manifestation: *There is here no ... reflection of his tender regard for Thomas Hardy, though there is many a testament of friendship* (Canadian Forum). **3** a statement of beliefs or principles: *[He] laid down his personal testament of what Canadian Conservation meant to him* (Maclean's). **4** (in the Bible) a covenant between God and man; dispensation. [< *Testament*]

**tes|ta|men|ta|ry** (tes′tə men′tər ē, -trē), *adj.* **1** of or having to do with a testament or will. **2** given, done, or appointed by a testament or will. **3** in a testament or will.

**tes|tate** (tes′tāt), *adj., n.* **—*adj.*** having made and left a valid will: *He clearly desired when he died to die testate and not intestate* (London Times).
**—*n.*** = testator (def. 2). [< Latin *testātus,* past participle of *testārī* make a will < *testis* witness]

**tes|ta|tor** (tes′tā tər, tes tā′-), *n.* **1** a person who makes a will. **2** a person who has died leaving a valid will.

**tes|ta|trix** (tes tā′triks), *n., pl.* **-tri|ces** (-trə sēz). a woman testator.

**test ban,** a ban on testing, especially of nuclear weapons.

**test bed,** **1** a base to hold equipment for testing: *the difficulties ... uncovered by operating experience with prototype reactors in ground test beds* (Scientific American). **2** an aircraft or rocket to test engines.

**test blank,** a form containing a test and blank spaces to fill in answers.

**test case,** a legal case whose outcome may set a precedent or test the constitutionality of a statute: *He had been one of the most active in pushing a test case that established the right of Negroes to vote in the Georgia primaries* (New Yorker).

**test drive,** a ride taken in an automobile to test its performance.

**test-drive** (test′drīv′), *v.t.,* **-drove, -driv|en, -driv|ing.** to drive (a motor vehicle) to test its performance.

**test|ee** (tes tē′), *n.* a person who takes a test.

**test|er**[1] (tes′tər), *n.* a person or thing that tests. **SYN:** examiner. [< *test*[1], verb + *-er*[1]]

**tes|ter**[2] (tes′tər), *n.* a canopy, especially one over a bed. [Middle English *testere,* probably < Old French *testre* headboard of a bed < *teste* head < Vulgar Latin *testa* head (in Latin, earthen pot)]

**tes|ter**[3] (tes′tər), *n.* **1** the teston of Henry VIII, especially as debased or depreciated. **2** *British Informal.* a sixpence. [earlier *testor* < *testorne,* alteration of *teston*]

**tes|tes** (tes′tēz), *n.* plural of **testis.**

**test-fire** (test′fīr′), *v.t.,* **-fired, -fir|ing.** to fire (a rocket or missile) as a test: *The Navy has been test-firing guided missiles from subs since 1955* (Newsweek).

**test flight,** a flight in which the performance of an aircraft or spacecraft is tested: *The experimental plane, the X-15, designed to carry man to the edge of outer space, began its series of power test flights* (Science News Letter).

**test-fly** (test′flī′), *v.t.,* **-flew, -flown, -fly|ing.** to subject to a test flight.

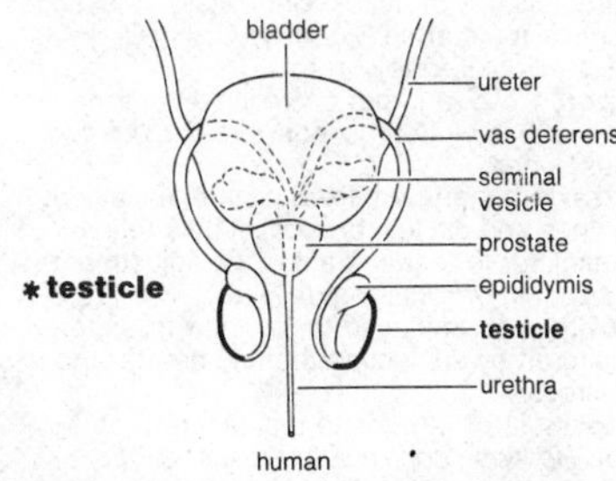

***testicle**

***tes|ti|cle** (tes′tə kəl), *n.* either one of the two reproductive glands of a male animal that secrete

**Pronunciation Key:** hat, āge, cãre, fär; let, ēqual, tėrm; it, īce; hot, ōpen, ôrder; oil, out; cup, pu̇t, rüle; child; long; thin; ᴛʜen; zh, measure; ə represents **a** in about, **e** in taken, **i** in pencil, **o** in lemon, **u** in circus.

sperm; testis. [< Latin *testiculus* (diminutive) < *testis* testis]

**tes|tic|u|lar** (tes tik′yə lər), *adj.* of or having to do with a testicle or testis.

**tes|tic|u|late** (tes tik′yə lit, -lāt), *adj.* formed like a testicle.

**tes|ti|fi|ca|tion** (tes′tə fə kā′shən), *n.* a testifying; testimony. [< Latin *testificātiō, -ōnis* < *testificārī;* see etym. under **testify**]

**tes|ti|fi|er** (tes′tə fī′ər), *n.* a person who gives testimony; witness.

**tes|ti|fy** (tes′tə fī), *v.,* **-fied, -fy|ing.** **—*v.i.*** **1** to give evidence; say as a witness: *The excellence of Shakespeare's plays testifies to his genius.* **2** to give evidence under oath in a law court: *He hated to testify against a friend.* **3** to bear testimony: *In vain thy creatures testify of thee* (William Cowper). **—*v.t.*** **1** to give evidence of; bear witness to: *The firm testified its appreciation of her work by raising her pay.* **2** to declare under oath in a law court: *The witness testified that the larger car had crowded the smaller one into the ditch.* **3** to declare solemnly; affirm.
[< Latin *testificārī* < *testis* witness + *facere* to make]

**tes|ti|mo|ni|al** (tes′tə mō′nē əl), *n., adj.* **—*n.*** **1** a certificate of character, conduct, qualifications, or value; recommendation: *The boy looking for a job has testimonials from his teachers and former employers.* **SYN:** credential, voucher. **2** something given or done to show esteem, admiration, gratitude, or worthiness: *The members of the church collected money for a testimonial to their retiring pastor.*
**—*adj.*** given or done as a testimonial: *a testimonial letter, a testimonial dinner.*

**tes|ti|mo|ni|al|ize** (tes′tə mō′nē ə līz), *v.t.,* **-ized, -iz|ing.** **1** to furnish with a recommendation. **2** to honor with a testimonial: *[He] was being testimonialized for 35 years of service to his state* (Time).

**tes|ti|mo|ny** (tes′tə mō′nē), *n., pl.* **-nies.** **1** a statement used for evidence or proof: *A witness gave testimony that the accused man was at home all day.* **SYN:** proof. See syn. under **evidence.** **2** evidence: *The pupils presented their teacher with a watch in testimony of their respect and affection.* **SYN:** proof. See syn. under **evidence.** **3** an open declaration or profession of one's faith. **4** *Archaic.* the Ten Commandments.
**testimonies,** the precepts of God; divine law: *to keep the Lord's testimonies and statutes.*
[< Latin *testimōnium* < *testis* witness]

**test|ing** (tes′ting), *n., adj.* **—*n.*** the act of subjecting to a test of any kind.
**—*adj.*** **1** having to do with or used for experimentation: *a testing station, testing mechanisms.* **2** that tests or puts to the test: *a testing crisis.*

**tes|tis** (tes′tis), *n., pl.* **-tes.** = testicle. [< Latin *testis* (originally) witness (because it bears witness to man's virility)]

**test-mar|ket** (test′mär′kit), *v.t.* to test by putting on sale or distributing in certain areas.

**Test** or **test match,** *British.* a contest or tournament for a cricket or Rugby championship.

**tes|ton** (tes′tən), *n.* **1** any one of various silver coins usually bearing a head, as one of certain early French silver coins or the English shilling of Henry VIII. **2** *Obsolete.* a sixpence. [< Middle French *teston* < Italian *testone* (augmentative) < *testa* head < Vulgar Latin, shell, (in Latin, testa, pot) (because the coin had a head or portrait on one face). Compare etym. under **tester**[3].]

**tes|toon** (tes tün′), *n.* = teston.

**tes|tos|ter|one** (tes tos′tə rōn), *n.* a hormone secreted by the testicles or produced synthetically. Testosterone is responsible for the secondary sex characteristics of males. Chemically, it is a white, crystalline steroid. *Formula:* $C_{19}H_{28}O_2$ [< *testis* + *ster*(ol) + *-one*]

**test paper,** **1** *U.S.* a paper on which a person taking a test has written his answers. **2** *Chemistry.* litmus paper.

**test pattern,** a standard, fixed picture, usually of straight lines and circles, broadcast by a television transmitter to test and aid in the adjustment of broadcasting or receiving devices.

**test pilot,** a pilot employed to test new or experimental aircraft by subjecting them to greater than normal stress.

**test-pi|lot** (test′pī′lət), *v.t.* to test (aircraft) as a test pilot: *He was soon recalled to test-pilot single-seater fighter planes* (New York Times).
**—*v.i.*** to be a test pilot; work as a test pilot: *Men risk and sometimes find death in many ways . . . mountain climbing, test-piloting, and war* (Wall Street Journal).

**test range,** **1** an area set aside for tests. **2** the extent of any test.

**test site,** a place where anything is tested.

**test stand,** a device to hold something that is being tested, such as a rocket engine.

**test track,** **1** a course for testing motor vehicles. **2** rails on which a vehicle moves at high speed to imitate flying conditions, such as rapid acceleration.

**test tube,** a thin glass tube closed at one end, used in making chemical or biological tests.

**test-tube** (test′tüb′, -tyüb′), *adj.* **1** of, having to do with, or contained in a test tube: *a test-tube experiment, test-tube cultures.* **2** *Figurative.* of or by chemical synthesis; synthetic: *a test-tube product.* **3** *Figurative.* born through artificial insemination: *test-tube cattle.*

**test-tube baby,** **1** (formerly) a baby that is conceived and develops outside the womb. **2** a baby conceived outside the womb that develops as a fetus after implantation in the womb: *The world's first test-tube baby, a girl, was born by Caesarean section to Lesley Brown just before midnight, on July 25 [1978], at Oldham and District General Hospital, Greater Manchester [England]. She weighed 5 pounds, 12 ounces* (T. J. O. Hickey). **3** a baby conceived through test-tube means.

**tes|tu|di|nal** (tes tü′də nəl, -tyü′-), *adj.* of, having to do with, or resembling a tortoise or tortoise shell.

**tes|tu|di|nate** (tes tü′də nit, -nāt; -tyü′-), *adj., n.* **—*adj.*** **1** arched; vaulted. **2** of or having to do with a tortoise or tortoises.
**—*n.*** a tortoise or turtle.
[< Latin *testūdinātus* arched < *testūdō, -inis* tortoise; see etym. under **testudo**]

**tes|tu|do** (tes tü′dō, -tyü′-), *n., pl.* **-di|nes** (-də nēz). **1a** a movable shelter with a strong and usually fireproof arched roof, used by the ancient Romans for protection in siege operations. **b** a shelter formed by a body of troops overlapping their shields above their heads. **2** any other shelter. [< Latin *testūdō, -inis* (literally) tortoise < *testa* shell, testa]

**test well,** a well made to test a site for oil.

**tes|ty** (tes′tē), *adj.,* **-ti|er, -ti|est.** easily irritated; impatient: *a very unpleasant and testy old man.* **SYN:** irascible, peevish, petulant, cross. [Middle English *testyf* headstrong < Anglo-French *testif* < *teste* head < Vulgar Latin *testa* pot] **—tes′ti|ly,** *adv.* **—tes′ti|ness,** *n.*

**Tet** (tet), *n.* the Vietnamese lunar New Year, celebrated in January or February for three or four days. [< Annamese *tet*]

**te|tan|ic** (ti tan′ik), *adj.* **1** having to do with tetanus. **2** having to do with tetany. **—te|tan′i|cal|ly,** *adv.*

**tet|a|nize** (tet′ə nīz), *v.t.,* **-nized, -niz|ing.** to cause (a muscle) to have tetanic spasms. **—tet′a|ni|za′tion,** *n.*

**tet|a|nus** (tet′ə nəs), *n.* **1a** a disease caused by certain bacilli usually entering the body through wounds, characterized by violent spasms, stiffness of many muscles, and even death. Tetanus of the jaw is called lockjaw. You can be protected against tetanus by inoculation. **b** the bacillus that causes this disease. **2** a condition of prolonged contraction of a muscle. [< Latin *tetanus* < Greek *tetanós* < *teínein* to stretch. See etym. of doublet **tetany.**]

**tet|a|ny** (tet′ə nē), *n.* a disease characterized by spasms of the muscles. [< French *tétanie,* or new Latin *tetania* < Latin *tetanus.* See etym. of doublet **tetanus.**]

**te|tar|to|he|dral** (ti tär′tō hē′drəl), *adj.* having one fourth of the number of faces required by the highest degree of symmetry belonging to its system: *a tetartohedral crystal.* [< Greek *tétartos* fourth (< *tetra-;* see etym. under **tetra-**) + *hédra* side, base + English *-al*[1]]

**tetched** (techt), *adj. U.S. Dialect.* slightly crazy; touched. Also, **teched.**

**tetch|y** (tech′ē), *adj.,* **tetch|i|er, tetch|i|est.** easily irritated or made angry; irritable; touchy. Also, **techy.** **—tetch′i|ly,** *adv.* **—tetch′i|ness,** *n.*

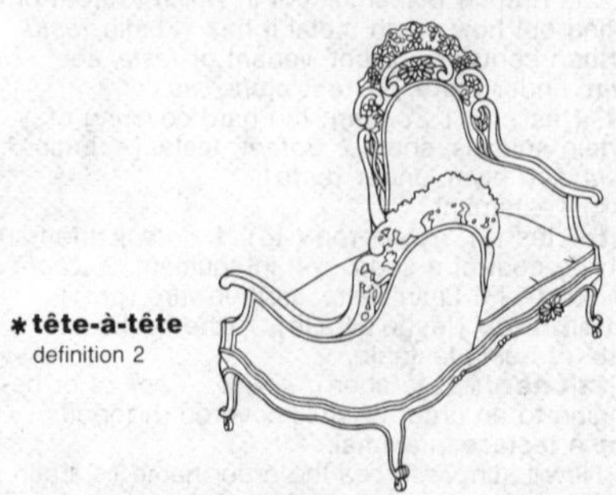

**✱tête-à-tête**
definition 2

**✱tête-à-tête** (tāt′ə tāt′, tet′ə tet′), *adv., adj., n.* **—*adv.*** two together in private: *They dined tête-à-tête.* **—*adj.*** of or for two people in private: *a tête-à-tête conversation.*
**—*n.*** **1** a private conversation between two people. **2** an S-shaped seat built so that two people can sit facing one another.
[< French *tête-à-tête* (literally) head to head; *tête* < Vulgar Latin *testa* (in Latin, pot)]

**tête-bêche** (tet′besh′), *adj.* (of two adjacent stamps) printed upside down or sideways in relation to each other. [< French *tête* head + *bêche,* reduction of *béchevet* double head of a bed < *bes-* twice (< Latin *bis*) + *chevet* head of a bed]

**tête-de-pont** (tet′də pôɴ′), *n., pl.* **têtes-de-pont** (tet′də pôɴ′). = bridgehead. [< French *tête de pont* (literally) bridge head]

**teth** (teth), *n.* the ninth letter of the Hebrew alphabet. [< Hebrew *ṭēth*]

**teth|er** (teᴛʜ′ər), *n., v.* **—*n.*** **1** a rope or chain for fastening an animal so that it can graze or move only within certain limits: *The cow had broken her tether and was in the garden.* **2** *Figurative.* something that acts as a chain or rope to limit, as ability, resources, or action: *We soon find the shortness of our tether* (Alexander Pope).
**—*v.t.*** to fasten with a tether: *The horse is tethered to the stake.* (*Figurative.*) *Need for money tethered the playboy to his job.*
**at the end of one's tether,** at the end of one's resources or endurance: *She is capable also of doing a little mothering of her son when he seems at the end of his tether* (London Times).
[< Scandinavian (compare Old Icelandic *tjóthr*)]

**teth|er|ball** (teᴛʜ′ər bôl′), *n.* **1** a game played by two persons with a ball fastened by a cord to the top of a tall post. The object of each person is to hit the ball so as to wind the cord around the post, in one direction or the other. **2** the ball used in this game.

**Te|thy|an** (tē′thē ən), *adj. Geology.* of or having to do with Tethys: *the Tethyan system of ocean trenches.*

**Te|thys** (tē′this), *n.* **1** *Greek Mythology.* the wife of Oceanus, daughter of Uranus and Gaea. **2** *Geology.* a large triangular sea that hypothetically separated Africa and Eurasia before the drifting of continents: *Long before the existence of the present Mediterranean, perhaps a quarter of a billion years ago, a giant waterway, the Tethys, extended across southern Europe, Iran and southern China to the Pacific Ocean. The Mediterranean is generally considered to be a remnant of the Tethys* (Science News). **3** a satellite of Saturn.

**Te|ton** (tē′ton), *n., pl.* **-ton** or **-tons.** **1** a member of the western division of the Sioux Indians. The best-known tribe of this division was the Oglala. **2** the language of this group, forming a dialect of Dakota.

**tetr-,** *combining form.* the form of **tetra-** sometimes before vowels, as in *tetrarch.*

**tet|ra** (tet′rə), *n.* any one of a group of small, brilliantly colored fishes of the upper Amazon region, such as the neon tetra and flame tetra. [< New Latin *Tetra* (*gonopterus*), genus name < Greek *tetrágōnon* tetragon + *pterón* wing]

**tetra-,** *combining form.* four, as in *tetrachloride, tetravalent.* Also, sometimes **tetr-** before vowels. [< Greek *tetra-,* for *téttares,* variant of *téssares*]

**tet|ra|ba|sic** (tet′rə bā′sik), *adj. Chemistry.* **1** (of an acid) having four hydrogen atoms that can be replaced by basic atoms or radicals. **2** having four atoms or radicals of a univalent metal. **3** containing four basic hydroxyl (-OH) radicals.

**tet|ra|bran|chi|ate** (tet′rə brang′kē it, -āt), *adj., n.* **—*adj.*** of or belonging to an order of cephalopods that have two pairs of gills and an external shell, as the pearly nautilus and certain fossil mollusks. **—*n.*** a tetrabranchiate cephalopod. [< New Latin *Tetrabranchiata* the order name (< Greek *tetra-* four + *bránchia* gills)]

**tet|ra|caine hydrochloride** (tet′rə kān), a drug used as a local anesthetic in the eye, nose, throat, and spinal canal; Pontocaine. *Formula:* $C_{15}H_{24}N_2O_2 \cdot HCl$ [< *tetra-* + (pro)*caine*]

**tet|ra|chlo|ride** (tet′rə klôr′īd, -id; -klōr′-), *n.* a compound containing four atoms of chlorine combined with another element or radical.

**tet|ra|chlo|ro|eth|yl|ene** (tet′rə klôr′ō eth′ə lēn, -klōr′-), *n.* = perchlorethylene.

**tet|ra|chord** (tet′rə kôrd), *n. Music.* **1** a diatonic scale series of four notes, the first and last being a perfect fourth apart (the most important unit of Greek melody and music theory); half an octave. **2** an ancient instrument with four strings. [< Latin *tetrachordon* < Greek *tetráchordon* < *tetrachordós* producing four tones < *tetra-* four + *chordē* string; (originally) gut]

**tet|ra|chor|dal** (tet′rə kôr′dəl), *adj.* having to do with a tetrachord; consisting of tetrachords.

**tet|ra|chot|o|mous** (tet′rə kot′ə məs), *adj.* **1** divided or dividing into four parts. **2** branching into four parts; giving off shoots by fours.

**tet|ra|chot|o|my** (tet′rə kot′ə mē), *n., pl.* **-mies.** division into four parts, classes, branches, or other divisions. [< Greek *tétracha* in four parts (< *tetra-* four) + *tomiā* a cutting, division]

**te|trac|id** (te tras′id), *adj., n. Chemistry.* —***adj.*** **1** (of a base or alcohol) having four hydroxyl (-OH) groups that may react with the hydrogen of an acid to form water, leaving a salt or ester. **2** having four acid atoms of hydrogen per molecule.
—***n.*** a base or an alcohol having four replaceable hydroxyl (-OH) groups.

**tet|ra|cy|clic** (tet′rə sī′klik, -sik′lik), *adj.* **1** passing through or having four cycles. **2** *Chemistry.* having four rings in the molecule. **3** *Botany.* having four whorls of floral organs.

**tet|ra|cy|cline** (tet′rə sī′klin), *n.* an antibiotic used in treating a wide variety of bacterial diseases, including pneumonia, tuberculosis, meningitis, and dysentery. *Formula:* $C_{22}H_{24}N_2O_8$ [< *tetra-* + *cycl-* + *-ine*[2] (because it contains four benzene rings)]

**tet|rad** (tet′rad), *n.* **1** a sum, group, or set of four. **2** *Chemistry.* an element, atom, or radical with a valence of four. **3** *Biology.* a group of four chromatids formed in various organisms when a pair of chromosomes splits longitudinally during meiosis. **4** *Botany.* a group of four cells, as of spores or pollen grains. See diagram under **alternation of generations**. [< Greek *tetrás, -ádos* (a group of) four < *tetra-* four]

**tet|ra|dac|tyl** (tet′rə dak′təl), *adj.* having four fingers, claws, toes, etc., on each limb. [< Greek *tetradáktylos* < *tetra-* four + *dáktylos* finger, toe]

**te|trad|ic** (te trad′ik), *adj.* of or having to do with a tetrad.

**tet|ra|drachm** (tet′rə dram′), *n.* a silver coin of ancient Greece, of the value of four drachmas.

**te|trad|y|mite** (te trad′ə mīt), *n. Mineralogy.* a telluride of bismuth, found in pale, steel-gray laminae with a bright, metallic luster. *Formula:* $Bi_2Te_3$ [< German *Tetradymit* < Greek *tetrádymos* fourfold + German *-it* -ite[1]]

**tet|ra|dy|na|mous** (tet′rə dī′nə məs, -din′ə-), *adj. Botany.* having six stamens, four longer, arranged in opposite pairs, and two shorter, inserted lower down (characteristic of flowers of the mustard family). [< New Latin *Tetradynamia* the former class name (< Greek *tetra-* four + *dýnamis* power, strength) + English *-ous*]

**tet|ra|eth|yl|am|mo|ni|um chloride** (tet′rə eth′ə lə mō′nē əm), a crystalline salt used as a drug to block the sympathetic nervous system during surgery, lower blood pressure in treating hypertensive conditions, etc. *Formula:* $C_8H_{20}ClN$

**tet|ra|eth|yl lead** (tet′rə eth′əl), a poisonous, colorless liquid, used in gasoline to reduce knocking. *Formula:* $Pb(C_2H_5)_4$ *Abbr:* TEL (no periods).

**tetraethyl pyrophosphate**, a crystalline compound, or a solution of it, used as an insecticide against mites and aphids, and in medicine as a stimulant in the treatment of certain diseases of the ocular, bulbar, and sacral nerves. *Formula:* $C_8H_{20}P_2O_7$ *Abbr:* TEPP (no periods).

**tet|ra|flu|o|ride** (tet′rə flü′ə rīd, -ər id), *n.* a fluoride with four atoms of fluorine.

**tet|ra|fluo|ro|eth|yl|ene** (tet′rə flôr′ō eth′ə lēn, -flü′ər ō-), *n.* a colorless, nonflammable gas used in making heat-resistant and acid-resistant plastics, such as Teflon. *Formula:* $F_2C{:}CF_2$

**tet|ra|gon** (tet′rə gon), *n.* a figure, especially a plane figure, having four angles and four sides, as a square or diamond. [< Greek *tetrágōnon* quadrangle < *tetra-* four + *gōniā* angle]

**te|trag|o|nal** (te trag′ə nəl), *adj.* **1** of or having to do with a tetragon; having four angles. **2** designating or having to do with a system of crystallization (**tetragonal system**) in which the three axes are at right angles, the two lateral axes being equal and the vertical of a different length; dimetric. See picture under **crystal**. —**te|trag′o|nal|ly**, *adv.*

**tet|ra|gram** (tet′rə gram), *n.* **1** a word of four letters, especially the Tetragrammaton. **2** *Geometry.* a figure formed by four straight lines in a plane and their six points of intersection; quadrilateral. [< Late Greek *tetrágrammon* < Greek *tetra-* four + *grámma* letter]

**Tet|ra|gram|ma|ton** (tet′rə gram′ə ton), *n.* the mysterious and sacred Hebrew word of four consonants, transliterated YHWH, YHVH, JHWH, or JHVH, standing for the Ineffable Name of God. The name is usually transcribed in English as *Yahweh* or *Jehovah.* [< Greek (*tó*) *tetragrámmaton* (literally) (the word) of four letters < *tetra-* four + *grámma, -atos* letter]

**tet|ra|gram|ma|ton** (tet′rə gram′ə ton), *n.* a word of four letters used as a symbol. [< *Tetragrammaton*]

**tet|ra|he|dral** (tet′rə hē′drəl), *adj.* **1** of or having to do with a tetrahedron; having four faces. **2** *Crystallography.* belonging to a division of the isometric system of which the regular tetrahedron is the characteristic form. —**tet′ra|he′dral|ly**, *adv.*

**tet|ra|he|drite** (tet′rə hē′drīt), *n. Mineralogy.* native sulfide of antimony and copper, with various elements sometimes replacing one or the other of these, often occurring in tetrahedral crystals. [< German *Tetraëdrit* < Greek *tetráedron* (see etym. under **tetrahedron**) + German *-it* -ite[1]]

***tet|ra|he|dron** (tet′rə hē′drən), *n., pl.* **-drons, -dra** (-drə). *Geometry.* a solid figure having four faces. The most common tetrahedron is a pyramid whose base and three sides are equilateral triangles. [< Greek *tetráedron* < *tetra-* four + *hédra* seat, base]

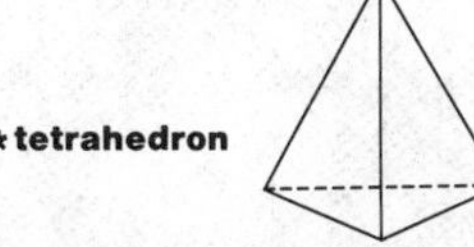

***tetrahedron**

**tet|ra|hy|dro|can|nab|i|nol** (tet′rə hī′drə kə nab′ə nôl, -nōl), *n.* the active principle in marijuana and hashish, obtained from the resin of the hemp plant or produced synthetically. *Abbr:* THC (no periods). [< *tetra-* + *cannabin* + *-ol*[2]]

**tet|ra|hy|dro|fu|ran** (tet′rə hī′drō fyu̇r′an), *n.* a flammable liquid ether, used as a chemical intermediate and as a solvent for vinyl resins. *Formula:* $C_4H_8O$ *Abbr:* THF (no periods).

**tet|ra|hy|drox|y** (tet′rə hī drok′sē), *adj. Chemistry.* having four hydroxyl (-OH) radicals.

**te|tral|o|gy** (te tral′ə jē), *n., pl.* **-gies**. **1** a series of four connected dramas, operas, or other dramatic or literary works. **2** (in ancient Greece) a series of four dramas, three tragic (the trilogy) and one satiric, exhibited at Athens at the festival of Dionysus. **3** any set of four things: *a tetralogy of speeches, a tetralogy of congenital defects.* [< Greek *tetralogiā* < *tetra-* four + *logiā* -logy]

**tetralogy of Fallot**, = Fallot's tetralogy.

**tet|ra|mer** (tet′rə mər), *n.* a chemical compound in which four molecules of the same substance are produced by polymerization.

**te|tram|er|al** (te tram′ər əl), *adj.* = tetramerous.

**te|tram|er|ous** (te tram′ər əs), *adj.* **1** having, consisting of, or characterized by four parts. **2** *Botany.* (of a flower) having four members in each whorl (generally written *4-merous*). **3** *Zoology.* having tarsi with four joints. [< New Latin *tetramerus* (with English *-ous*) < Greek *tetramerês* < *tetra-* four + *méros* part]

**te|tram|e|ter** (te tram′ə tər), *n., adj. Prosody.*
—***n.*** **1** a line of verse having four metrical feet. *Example:* "The stág / at éve / had drúnk / his fíll." **2** (in Greek and Latin verse) a line having four dipodies (eight feet), in trochaic, iambic, or anapestic meter.
—***adj.*** consisting of four measures or feet.
[< Latin *tetrametrus* < Greek *tetrámetron* < *tetra-* four + *métron* measure, -meter]

**tet|ra|meth|yl lead** (tet′rə meth′əl), a poisonous liquid, used in gasoline to reduce knocking. *Formula:* $Pb(CH_3)_4$

**tet|ra|mor|phic** (tet′rə môr′fik), *adj.* occurring in four distinct forms; exhibiting tetramorphism.

**tet|ra|mor|phism** (tet′rə môr′fiz əm), *n.* the occurrence in four different forms of a crystalline substance.

**te|tran|drous** (te tran′drəs), *adj. Botany.* having four stamens. [< *tetra-* + Greek *anḗr, andrós* male, man + English *-ous*]

**tet|ra|ni|tro|meth|ane** (tet′rə nī′trə meth′ān), *n.* a colorless, poisonous liquid insoluble in water, derived from the combination of fuming nitric acid with benzene, acetic anhydride, or acetylene, and used for rocket fuel and as an oxidant. *Formula:* $C(NO_2)_4$

**tet|ra|on|id** (tet′rə on′id), *adj., n.* —***adj.*** belonging to a family of gallinaceous birds including the grouse and allied forms. —***n.*** a tetraonid bird. [< New Latin *Tetraonidae* the family name < Latin *tetrāō, -ōnis* grouse < Greek *tetrā́ōn*]

**tet|ra|pet|al|ous** (tet′rə pet′ə ləs), *adj. Botany.* having four petals.

**tet|ra|phyl|lous** (tet′rə fil′əs), *adj. Botany.* having four leaves or leaflets. [< *tetra-* + Greek *phýllon* leaf + English *-ous*]

**tet|ra|ploid** (tet′rə ploid), *adj., n. Biology.* —***adj.*** having four times the number of chromosomes characteristic of the germ cells of the species: *Tetraploid snaps [snapdragons] are those that have been treated with colchicine to give them extremely large flowers, husky growth habit and good foliage* (New York Times).
—***n.*** a tetraploid organism or cell: *Tetraploids are the result of recent genetic research and practical flower breeding* (Gordon Morrison).
[< *tetra-* + *-ploid*, as in *haploid*]

**tet|ra|ploi|dy** (tet′rə ploi′dē), *n. Biology.* the state of having four times the chromosomes characteristic of the germ cells of the species.

**tet|ra|pod** (tet′rə pod), *n., adj.* —***n.*** **1a** an animal having four limbs; quadruped. **b** any one of a superclass of vertebrates including amphibians, reptiles, birds, and mammals but not fishes. **2** a very large concrete block with four legs that can be interlocked with another, used especially in building breakwaters and jetties.
—***adj.*** having four limbs; quadruped: *tetrapod mammals.*
[< Greek *tetrápous, -podos,* adjective, having four feet < *tetra-* four + *poús, podós* foot]

**tet|ra|pod|ic** (tet′rə pod′ik), *adj.* having four metrical feet.

**te|trap|o|dy** (te trap′ə dē), *n., pl.* **-dies**. *Prosody.* **1** a group of four metrical feet in a line of verse. **2** a line of verse having four metrical feet. [< Greek *tetrapodiā* < *tetrápous, -podos;* see etym. under **tetrapod**]

**te|trap|o|lis** (te trap′ə lis), *n.* a group of four cities or towns; political division consisting of four cities. [< Greek *tetrápolis* < *tetra-* four + *pólis* city]

**tet|ra|pol|i|tan** (tet′rə pol′ə tən), *adj.* of or having to do with a tetrapolis.

**te|trap|ter|ous** (te trap′tər əs), *adj.* **1** *Entomology.* having four wings. **2** *Botany.* having four winglike appendages, as certain fruits. [< New Latin *tetrapterus* (with English *-ous*) < Greek *tetrápteros* < *tetra-* four + *pterón* wing]

**tet|ra|py|lon** (tet′rə pī′lon), *n.* a pylon or arch with four gates, marking the intersection of two avenues, especially in ancient Rome.

**tet|rarch** (tet′rärk, tē′trärk), *n.* **1** the ruler of a part (originally a fourth part) of a subject country or province in the ancient Roman Empire. **2** any one of various subordinate rulers. **3a** a ruler of a fourth part. **b** one of four joint rulers, directors, or heads. [< Latin *tetrarchēs* < Greek *tetrárchēs* < *tetra-* four + *árchein* to rule]

**tet|rar|chate** (tet′rär kāt, tē′trär-), *n.* the office, jurisdiction, government, or territory of a tetrarch.

**te|trar|chic** (te trär′kik), *adj.* of, having to do with, or belonging to a tetrarch or tetrarchy.

**tet|rar|chy** (tet′rär kē, tē′trär-), *n., pl.* **-chies**. **1a** the government or jurisdiction of a tetrarch. **b** the territory governed by a tetrarch. **2** government by four persons. **3** a set of four rulers. **4** a country divided into four governments.

**tet|ra|sep|al|ous** (tet′rə sep′ə ləs), *adj. Botany.* having four sepals.

**tet|ra|sper|mous** (tet′rə spėr′məs), *adj. Botany.* four-seeded.

**tet|ra|spo|ran|gi|um** (tet′rə spô ran′jē əm, -spō-), *n., pl.* **-gi|a** (-jē ə). *Botany.* a sporangium producing or containing a group of four asexual spores, resulting from the division of a mother cell.

**tet|ra|spore** (tet′rə spôr, -spōr), *n. Botany.* one of a group of four asexual spores, resulting from the division of a mother cell, in certain algae.

**tet|ra|stich** (tet′rə stik, te tras′tik), *n.* a stanza or poem of four lines. [< Latin *tetrastichon* < Greek *tetrástichon,* neuter of *tetrástichos* having four rows < *tetra-* four + *stíchos* row, line of verse]

**tet|ra|stich|ic** (tet′rə stik′ik), *adj.* having to do with or constituting a tetrastich or tetrastichs.

**te|tras|ti|chous** (te tras′tə kəs), *adj. Botany.* **1** (of flowers) arranged in a spike having four vertical rows. **2** (of a spike) having the flowers arranged in four vertical rows. [< New Latin *tetrastichus* (with English *-ous*) < Greek *tetrásti-chos;* see etym. under **tetrastich**]

**tet|ra|style** (tet′rə stīl), *adj., n.* —***adj.*** having four columns in front, as a temple or a portico.
—***n.*** a tetrastyle structure.
[< Latin *tetrastȳlos* < Greek *tetrástȳlos* < *tetra-* four + *stȳlos* pillar, column]

**tet|ra|syl|lab|ic** (tet′rə sə lab′ik), *adj.* consisting of four syllables.

**tet|ra|syl|lab|i|cal** (tet′rə sə lab′ə kəl), *adj.* = tetrasyllabic.

**tet|ra|syl|la|ble** (tet′rə sil′ə bəl), *n.* a word of four syllables.

**tet|ra|tom|ic** (tet′rə tom′ik), *adj. Chemistry.* **1** containing four atoms; consisting of molecules containing four atoms each. **2** (incorrectly) quadrivalent. **3** having four atoms or groups that can be replaced. [< *tetr-* + *atomic*]

**tet|ra|va|lent** (tet′rə vā′lənt, te trav′ə-), *adj. Chemistry.* **1** having a valence of four; quadrivalent: *An element like carbon whose atom can hold four monovalent atoms in combination is called a tetravalent element* (Parks and Steinbach). **2** having four different valences; quadrivalent.

**te|trax|i|al** (te trak′sē əl), *adj.* having four axes. [< *tetra-* + *axial*]

**te|trax|ile** (te trak′səl, -sīl), *adj.* = tetraxial. [< *tetra-* + *axile*]

**tet|rode** (tet′rōd), *n.* a vacuum tube containing

**Pronunciation Key:** hat, āge, cãre, fär; let, ēqual, tėrm; it, īce; hot, ōpen, ôrder; oil, out; cup, pu̇t, rüle; child; long; thin; ᴛʜen; zh, measure; ə represents **a** in about, **e** in taken, **i** in pencil, **o** in lemon, **u** in circus.

four elements, commonly a cathode, anode, and two grids: *Tetrodes ... are able to operate at extremely high frequencies* (William C. Vergara). [< *tetr-* + (electr)*ode*]

**tet|ro|do|tox|in** (tet′rō də tok′sən), *n.* a potent nerve poison produced by certain globefishes and newts: *Tetrodotoxin ... is a remarkably potent and specific inhibitor of the membrane mechanisms responsible for changes in sodium permeability during the action potential in nerve and muscle* (Barry D. Lindley). *Formula:* $C_{11}H_{17}N_3O_8$ [< New Latin *Tetrodo*(n) the genus name of globefishes + English *toxin*]

**te|trox|id** (te trok′sid), *n.* = tetroxide.

**te|trox|ide** (te trok′sīd, -sid), *n. Chemistry.* an oxide containing four atoms of oxygen in each molecule with another element or radical.

**tet|ryl** (tet′rəl), *n.* **1** an explosive used especially to detonate the propelling or bursting charge of artillery shells. *Formula:* $C_7H_5N_5O_8$ **2** *Chemistry.* butyl.

**tet|ter** (tet′ər), *n.* any one of various itching skin diseases, such as eczema and psoriasis. [Old English *teter*]

**teugh** (tyüH), *adj. Scottish.* tough. **–teugh′ly,** *adv.* **–teugh′ness,** *n.*

**Teut., 1** Teuton. **2** Teutonic.

**Teu|ton** (tü′tən, tyü′-), *n., adj.* **–*n.* 1** = German. **2** a person belonging to the group of northern Europeans that speak Germanic languages, including the Germans, Dutch, and Scandinavians. **3** a member of the Teutones.
**–*adj.*** German; Teutonic; Germanic.
[< Latin *Teutonēs,* or *Teutonī,* plural, (originally) a tribe in northern Europe]

**Teu|to|nes** (tü′tə nēz, tyü′-), *n.pl.* an ancient Germanic tribe who in the 100's B.C. devastated Gaul and threatened the Roman republic. [< Latin *Teutonēs;* see etym. under **Teuton**]

**Teu|ton|ic** (tü ton′ik, tyü-), *adj., n.* **–*adj.* 1** of or having to do with the ancient Teutones or their language. **2** of or having to do with the Germanic languages; Germanic. **3** of or having to do with the Teutons; German. **4** of or having to do with the northern European peoples that speak Germanic languages. **5** = Nordic.
**–*n.*** = Germanic. **–Teu|ton′i|cal|ly,** *adv.*

**Teu|ton|i|cism** (tü ton′ə siz əm, tyü-), *n.* **1** a Teutonic or German character or practice. **2** a Teutonic or German idiom or expression; Germanism.

**Teutonic Knight,** a member of a military and religious order of German knights founded about 1190 to spread Christianity and help the needy.

**Teu|ton|ism** (tü′tə niz əm, tyü′-), *n.* **1** Teutonic or German feeling and action; spirit of Germany or the Germans. **2** = Teutonicism.

**Teu|ton|ist** (tü′tə nist, tyü′-), *n.* **1** a person versed in the history of the Teutonic races or languages. **2** a person whose writings have a Teutonic character or style.

**Teu|ton|ize** (tü′tə nīz, tyü′-), *v.t., v.i.,* **-ized, -iz|ing.** to make or become Teutonic or German.
**–Teu′ton|i|za′tion,** *n.*

**Teu|to|phobe** (tü′tə fōb, tyü′-), *n.* a person who fears or hates the Teutons or Germans. [< *Teuto*(n) + *-phobe*]

**tew** (tyü), *v., n. Obsolete.* **–*v.i.* 1** to work hard; toil. **2** to bustle (about).
**–*n.* 1** constant work and bustling. **2** a state of worry or excitement.
[Middle English *tewen* (originally) to taw leather, to prepare by beating or pounding, apparently variant of *taw*²]

**Tex., 1** Texan. **2** Texas.

**Tex|an** (tek′sən), *adj., n.* **–*adj.*** of or having to do with Texas or its people.
**–*n.*** a native or inhabitant of Texas.

**Tex|as** (tek′səs), *n., pl.* **-as** or **-as|es.** an American Indian belonging to a former confederation of Caddoan tribes, often allied against the Apache, that lived in the region of what is now the state of Texas. [< American Spanish *Texas* < a Caddoan word meaning "allies"]

**tex|as** (tek′səs), *n.* a structure on the hurricane deck of a river steamer where officers' cabins are situated. It has the pilot house in front or on top. [< *Texas,* one of the states of the United States]

**Texas armadillo,** = nine-banded armadillo.

**Texas fever,** an infectious disease of cattle that attacks the red blood cells, caused by a protozoan parasite and transmitted by cattle-infesting ticks.

**Texas fever tick,** the tick that transmits Texas fever; cattle tick.

**Texas leaguer,** *Baseball.* a fly falling between the infielders and outfielders. [< *Texas League,* one of the minor leagues]

**Texas longhorn,** = longhorn.

**Texas Rangers, 1** a group of mounted men in the state police of Texas. **2** a group of United States citizens who tried to maintain order during the early years of settling in Texas.

**Texas sparrow,** an olive-green finch of southern Texas and Mexico, with two brown stripes on the crown; greenfinch.

***Texas tower,** *U.S.* a platform built offshore on pilings sunk into the ocean floor and used as a radar station: *Radar-equipped ships, planes, blimps and Texas towers—offshore platforms modeled after oil drilling rigs—complete a warning fence that circles the continent* (Wall Street Journal). [< *Texas,* the state (because of its resemblance to the offshore oil derricks or rigs found there)]

***Texas tower**

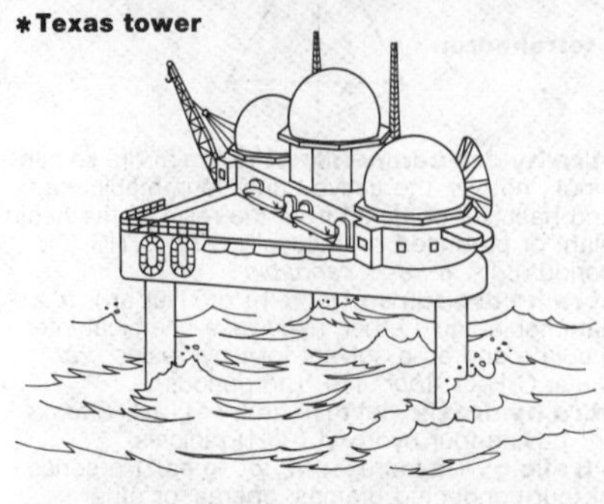

**text** (tekst), *n.* **1** the main body of reading matter in a book, as distinct from the notes, supplements, and indices: *This history book contains 300 pages of text and about 50 pages of maps, pictures, notes, explanations, and questions for study.* **2** the original words of a writer, especially a work in the original language, as distinct from a translation or rendering. A text is often changed here and there when it is copied. **3a** any one of the various wordings of a poem, play, or the like. **b** the wording adopted by an editor as (in his opinion) most nearly representing an author's original work. **c** a book or edition containing this. **4** a short passage from the Bible, used as the subject of a sermon or as proof of some belief: *The minister preached on the text "Blessed are the merciful."* **5** *Figurative.* a topic; subject: *Town improvement was the speaker's text.* **6** = textbook. **7a** the letter of Scripture. **b** the Scriptures themselves. **c** a reading of the Scriptures or a wording of a Scriptural passage taken as correct and authoritative. **8** = text hand. [< Middle French *texte* < Old French, learned borrowing from Medieval Latin *textus* the Scriptures; an authority; a treatise (in Late Latin, written account, content, characters) < Latin *textus, -ūs* style or texture of a work; (originally) a thing woven < *texere* to weave] **–text′less,** *adj.*

**text|book** (tekst′bu̇k′), *n., adj.* **–*n.*** a book for regular study by pupils, especially as an authority and standard in the study of a particular subject. Most books used in schools are textbooks. There are textbooks in arithmetic, geography, history, science, and most other subjects in school.
**–*adj.*** of or belonging in a textbook; accepted; standard; typical: *a textbook example. There are special conditions everywhere. The textbook answer can often be very wrong* (Ralph Allen).

**text|book|ish** (tekst′bu̇k′ish), *adj.* of the nature of a textbook: *He has put nearly everything into double columns, which I find textbookish and uninviting* (New Yorker).

**text edition,** the form of a book published for use as a textbook in schools and colleges, as distinguished from the trade edition of the same book.

**text hand, 1** a style of handwriting in which large, bold letters are formed. **2** (originally) one of the larger and more formal hands in which the text of a book was more often written, as distinct from the smaller or more cursive hand used for the gloss.

**tex|tile** (teks′təl, -tīl), *adj., n.* **–*adj.* 1** woven: *Cloth is a textile fabric.* **2** suitable for weaving: *Linen, cotton, silk, nylon, and wool are common textile materials.* **3** of or having something to do with weaving: *the textile arts.* **4** of or having to do with the making, selling, and designing of textiles: *His father was in the textile industry.*
**–*n.* 1** a woven fabric; cloth. **2** any material that can be woven.
[< Latin *textilis* woven < *texere* to weave]

**tex|tile|man** (teks′təl man′, -tīl-), *n., pl.* **-men.** a man engaged in the textile industry; a weaver or seller of cloth.

**textile mill,** place where textiles are made.

**tex|to|log|i|cal** (teks′tə loj′ə kəl), *adj.* of or having to do with the study of a text or texts: *textological comments.*

**tex|tu|al** (teks′chu̇ əl), *adj.* **1** of the text; having to do with the text: *A misprint is a textual error.* **2** based on, following, or conforming to the text, especially of the Scriptures. [alteration of Middle English *textuel,* probably < Anglo-French, Old French, learned borrowing from Medieval Latin *textualis* < Latin *textus, -ūs;* see etym. under **text**] **–tex′tu|al|ly,** *adv.*

**textual criticism,** = lower criticism.

**tex|tu|al|ism** (teks′chu̇ ə liz′əm), *n.* a strict adherence to the text, especially of the Scriptures.

**tex|tu|al|ist** (teks′chu̇ ə list), *n.* **1** a person who adheres strictly to, and bases his doctrine upon, the text of the Scriptures. **2** a person learned in the text of the Bible.

**tex|tu|ar|y** (teks′chu̇ er′ē), *adj., n., pl.* **-ar|ies.**
**–*adj.*** of or belonging to the text; textual.
**–*n.*** = textualist.

**tex|tur|al** (teks′chər əl), *adj.* of or having to do with texture: *They express, in varying degrees, the feeling for color, textural interest, and balanced design that marks a sensitive and imaginative artist* (New Yorker). **–tex′tur|al|ly,** *adv.*

**tex|ture** (teks′chər), *n., v.,* **-tured, -tur|ing.** **–*n.* 1** the arrangement of threads in a woven fabric: *Homespun is cloth that has a loose texture. A piece of burlap has a much coarser texture than a linen handkerchief.* **2a** *Figurative.* the arrangement of parts of anything; structure; constitution; makeup: *the granular texture of sandy soil. Her skin has a fine texture. The texture of marble makes it take a polish.* SYN: composition. **b** the structure or minute molding (of a surface). **3** *Fine Arts.* the representation of the structure and minute molding of a surface, especially of the skin, as distinct from its color. **4** the musical quality of combined voices, instruments, or parts: *the harsh texture of brass instruments.* **5** *Archaic.* a textile fabric.
**–*v.t.*** to provide with a particular texture; give a certain texture to: *... a smooth texturing of cotton and Arnel acetate* (New York Times). (*Figurative.*) *A bright faultless vision textured out of mere sunbeams* (Thomas Carlyle).
[earlier, the process of weaving < Latin *textūra* a web; texture; structure < *texere* to weave] **–tex′ture|less,** *adj.*

**tex|tured** (teks′chərd), *adj.* **1** having a particular texture: *thickly textured. Open-textured = having an open texture.* **2** given a bulky, soft texture by adding air to the filament strands to form kinks and loops: *textured yarn.*

**tex|tur|ize** (teks′chə rīz), *v.t.,* **-ized, -iz|ing.** to provide with texture: *Nylon makers work with yarn processors to give the fiber greater bulk and better feel by texturizing it* (Wall Street Journal).

**tex|tus re|cep|tus** (teks′təs ri sep′təs), the accepted text, especially the received text of the Greek New Testament. [< Latin *textus, -ūs* text, and *receptus,* past participle of *recipere* receive]

**Tez|cat|li|po|ca** (tes kot′lē pō′kə), *n.* a chief god of the Aztecs.

**T.F.,** Territorial Force.

**T-for|ma|tion** (tē′fôr mā′shən), *n. Football.* an offensive formation with the quarterback directly behind the center and the other three backs in a horizontal line a few yards behind him, in the general shape of a T.

**tfr.,** transfer.

**TFX** (no periods), tactical fighter, experimental (a jet warplane).

**t.g.,** type genus.

**T.G.I.F.,** thank God it's Friday: *We yield to no man in our appreciation of Friday as a day for rejoicing. T.G.I.F. is a sentiment we've often shared* (New Yorker).

**T-group** (tē′grüp′), *n.* **1** = encounter group. **2** a group of people undergoing sensitivity training. [< (Sensitivity) *T*(raining) *group*]

**TGWU** (no periods) or **T.G.W.U.,** Transport and General Workers' Union (of Great Britain).

**-th,** *suffix added to numbers* (*from fourth on*). number ___ in order or position in a series: *Sixth = number six in order or position in a series.* Also, **-eth.** [Old English *-tha,* or *-the*]

**Th** (no period), thorium (chemical element).

**Th., 1** Thomas. **2** Thursday.

**T.H.,** Territory of Hawaii (the official abbreviation before Hawaii became a State).

**tha** (ᴛʜə), *pron. British* (*Northern*) *Dialect.* **1** thee. **2** thou. **3** thy.

**thack** (thak), *n., v.t., v.i. Scottish.* **1** thatch. **2** roof. [Old English *thæc.* Compare etym. under **thatch.**]

**Thack|er|ay|an** (thak′ə rē ən), *adj.* of, having to do with, or characteristic of the English novelist William Makepeace Thackeray (1811-1863) or his works: *A certain cynical humor which is almost Thackerayan in quality* (Scottish Leader).

**Thad.,** Thaddaeus.

**Thad|dae|us** (tha dē′əs), *n.* Jude, or Saint Judas, one of the Apostles.

**thae** (ᴛʜā), *adj., pron. Scottish.* plural of **that.** [< Old English *thā.* Compare etym. under **those.**]

**Thai** (tī), *n., adj.* **–*n.* 1** the language of Thailand; Siamese. **2a** a family of languages spoken in Thailand and parts of Burma, Indochina, and

China, including Shan, Lao, and the language of Thailand. **b** any one of the people who speak these languages, especially a person born or living in Thailand: *Most Thais also still believe ... that the elephant is a "great and ample demonstration of the power and wisdom of almighty God"* (Time).
—***adj.*** **1** of or having to do with the Thai language family or the peoples that speak languages of this family. **2** of or having to do with Thailand (Siam); Siamese. Also, **Tai.**

**Thai|land|er** (tī′lən dər), *n.* = Thai (def. 2b).

**thal|a|men|ce|phal|ic** (thal′ə men sə fal′ik), *adj.* = diencephalic.

**thal|a|men|ceph|a|lon** (thal′ə men sef′ə lon), *n., pl.* **-la** (-lə). = diencephalon. [< *thalam*(us) + *encephalon*]

**tha|lam|ic** (thə lam′ik), *adj.* of or having to do with the thalamus. —**tha|lam′i|cal|ly,** *adv.*

**thal|a|mot|o|my** (thal′ə mot′ə mē), *n., pl.* **-mies.** a surgical incision into the thalamus, as in the treatment of severe emotional disturbance. [< *thalam*(us) + Greek *-tomiā* a cutting]

**thal|a|mus** (thal′ə məs), *n., pl.* **-mi** (-mī). **1** a large, oblong mass of gray matter in the posterior part of the forebrain, from which nerve fibers pass to the sensory parts of the cortex and which is connected with the optic nerve; optic thalamus: *Most physiologists believe that the site of salicylic acid's analgesic action is the thalamus, the chief sensory reception center, located in the forebrain* (New Yorker). **2** *Botany.* **a** the receptacle of a flower; torus. **b** thallus. [< New Latin *thalamus* (in Latin, inner room) < Greek *thálamos*]

**thal|as|se|mi|a** (thal′ə sē′mē ə), *n.* a hereditary blood disorder in which the red blood cells are misshapen and easily destroyed, leading to anemia; Mediterranean anemia. One form is often fatal in childhood. [< New Latin *thalassemia* < Greek *thálassa* sea; Mediterranean Sea + *haîma* blood (because it was originally thought that the disease was confined to those of Mediterranean origin)]

**tha|las|si|an** (thə las′ē ən), *adj., n.* —***adj.*** of or having to do with the sea; marine.
—***n.*** any sea turtle.
[< Greek *thalássios* marine (< *thálassa* sea) + English *-an*]

**tha|las|sic** (thə las′ik), *adj.* **1** of or having to do with the sea. **2** of or having to do with the smaller or inland seas, as distinct from the pelagic waters or oceans. **3** growing or living in, or formed in or by, the sea; marine.

**tha|las|so|chem|i|cal** (thə las′ō kem′ə kəl), *adj.* of or having to do with thalassochemistry.

**tha|las|so|chem|is|try** (thə las′ō kem′ə strē), *n.* the study of the chemistry of the sea. [< Greek *thálassa* sea + English *chemistry*]

**thal|as|soc|ra|cy** (thal′ə sok′rə sē), *n., pl.* **-cies.** **1** mastery at sea; sovereignty of the sea. **2** a kingdom having such mastery: *The Aegean was the nursery of thalassocracies, that is to say the sea kingdoms that grew fat and then split up through internal dissension or invasion, forming new colonies elsewhere* (New Scientist). [< Greek *thalassokratiā* < *thálassa* sea + *krátos* rule, power]

**tha|las|so|crat** (thə las′ə krat), *n.* a ruler or master of the sea.

**thal|as|sog|ra|phy** (thal′ə sog′rə fē), *n.* the science of the ocean; oceanography. [< Greek *thálassa* sea + English *-graphy*]

**tha|ler** (tä′lər), *n., pl.* **-ler.** **1** a large silver coin formerly used in Germany; taler. The thaler was replaced by the mark. **2** = Levant dollar. [< German *Thaler.* Compare etym. under **dollar.**]

**Tha|li|a** (thə lī′ə), *n. Greek Mythology.* **1** the Muse of comedy and idyllic poetry. **2** one of the three Graces. [< Latin *Thalia* < Greek *Tháleia* (literally) blooming, luxuriant < *thállein* to bloom]

**tha|lic|trum** (thə lik′trəm), *n.* any one of a group of plants of the crowfoot family; meadow rue. [< Latin *thalictrum* < Greek *tháliktron* meadow rue]

**tha|lid|o|mide** (thə lid′ə mīd′), *n.* a tranquilizing drug formerly used as a sedative and hypnotic, discontinued after its use during early pregnancy was found to cause malformation of the fetus, especially the failure of development of the limbs. *Formula:* $C_{13}H_{10}N_2O_4$

**thalidomide baby,** a malformed baby born to a woman who had taken thalidomide during pregnancy: *Because thalidomide babies have above average intelligence, Dr. Hauberg is theorizing about some mysterious process of natural compensation* (Time).

**thal|lic** (thal′ik), *adj. Chemistry.* **1** of thallium. **2** containing thallium, especially with a valence of three.

**thal|line** (thal′in, -ēn), *n.* a white, crystalline base yielding salts used as antipyretics. *Formula:* $C_{10}H_{13}NO$ [< Greek *thallós* a green shoot + English *-ine*[2] (because its spectrum is marked by a green band)]

***thal|li|um** (thal′ē əm), *n.* a soft, bluish-white, metallic chemical element. Thallium has a leaden luster, is extremely malleable, and is almost devoid of tenacity and elasticity. It occurs in small quantities in iron and zinc ores and in various minerals. Its compounds are extremely poisonous and are used to kill insects and rodents. Thallium is also used in making glass of high refractive power. [< New Latin *thallium* < Greek *thallós* green shoot < *thállein* to bloom (because its spectrum is marked by a green band)]

***thallium**

| symbol | atomic number | atomic weight | oxidation state |
|---|---|---|---|
| Tl | 81 | 204.37 | 1,3 |

**thallium sulfate,** a colorless, crystalline poison absorbed through the skin, used as a rodenticide and insecticide. *Formula:* $Tl_2SO_4$

**thal|loid** (thal′oid), *adj. Botany.* of, resembling, or consisting of a thallus. [< *thall*(us) + *-oid*]

**thal|lo|phyte** (thal′ə fīt), *n.* any one of a large group of plants in which the plant shows no differentiation into stem, leaf, and root. The simpler unicellular forms reproduce by cell division or by asexual spores; the higher forms reproduce both asexually and sexually. Bacteria, algae, fungi, and lichens are thallophytes. [< New Latin *Thallophyta* the division name < Greek *thallós* green shoot + *phytón* plant]

**thal|lo|phyt|ic** (thal′ə fit′ik), *adj.* of or having to do with the thallophytes.

**thal|lous** (thal′əs), *adj. Chemistry.* **1** of thallium. **2** containing thallium, especially with a valence of one.

**thal|lus** (thal′əs), *n., pl.* **thal|li** (thal′ī), **thal|lus|es.** a plant not divided into leaves, stem, and root; the plant body characteristic of thallophytes. Mushrooms, toadstools, and lichens are thalli. [< New Latin *thallus* < Greek *thallós* green shoot < *thállein* to bloom]

**Tham|muz** (täm′müz; *Biblical* tam′uz), *n.* = Tammuz.

**than** (ᴛʜan; *unstressed* ᴛʜən), *conj., prep.* —***conj.*** **1** in comparison with: *He is taller than his sister. This train is faster than that one.* **2** compared to that which: *She has more money than she needs.* **3** except; besides: *How else can we come than by airplane?*
—***prep.*** **than whom,** compared to whom: *Present also was Sheridan, than whom there was no abler speaker in the group.*
[Old English *thanne, thænne,* or *thonne;* (originally) the same word as *then*]
► **a** In clauses consisting of **than** plus a personal pronoun, the form of the latter is determined by its function as subject or object: *He is older than I* [am]. *I like his cousin better than* [I like] *him.* In sentences like the first of these, *than* is often treated as a preposition and the objective form of the pronoun is substituted: *He is older than me.* This construction, although very common in familiar speech, is regarded as nonstandard. **b** In comparison, the standard idiom is *other than* (not *different than*): *It was other than* (or *different from*) *what he expected.*
► See **then** for another usage note.

**tha|na** (tä′nə), *n.* = tana[1].

**tha|na|dar** (tä′nə där′), *n.* = tanadar.

**tha|nah** (tä′nə), *n.* = tana[1].

**than|a|tism** (than′ə tiz əm), *n.* the belief that at death the human soul ceases to exist.

**than|a|toid** (than′ə toid), *adj.* **1** resembling death; apparently dead: *We carted the old man into the restaurant and propped him up at a table. He looked exactly the same—thanatoid* (Truman Capote). **2** deadly, as a venomous snake. [< Greek *thánatos* death + English *-oid*]

**than|a|to|log|i|cal** (than′ə tə loj′ə kəl), *adj.* of or having to do with thanatology or thanatologists: *Undertakers from eleven European countries have organized the European Thanatological Association* (Time).

**than|a|tol|o|gist** (than′ə tol′ə jist), *n.* **1** a person who studies or is versed in thanatology. **2** an undertaker: *The embalmers of Quebec now prefer to be known as thanatologists* (American Speech).

**than|a|tol|o|gy** (than′ə tol′ə jē), *n.* the scientific study of death and its causes and phenomena. [< Greek *thánatos* death]

**than|a|top|sis** (than′ə top′sis), *n.* a contemplation of death; meditative viewing of the end of life. [< Greek *thánatos* death + *ópsis* a view of]

**Than|a|tos** (than′ə tos), *n. Greek Mythology.* death personified as a god, identified with the Roman Mors.

**thane** (thān), *n.* **1** (in early English history) a man who ranked between an earl and an ordinary freeman. Thanes held lands of the king or lord and gave military service in return. **2** (in Scottish history) a person, equal in rank to an earl's son, who held lands of the king; the chief of a clan, who became one of the king's barons; Scottish baron or lord: *All hail, Macbeth! hail to thee, thane of Glamis!* (Shakespeare). Also, **thegn.** [alteration of Middle English *thaine* king's baron, Old English *thegn* a military follower. Compare etym. under **thegn.**]

**thane|hood** (thān′hu̇d), *n.* **1** the condition or rank of a thane. **2** thanes collectively.

**thane|ship** (thān′ship), *n.* **1** the office, dignity, or character of a thane. **2** the land or tenure held by a thane.

**thank** (thangk), *v., n.* —***v.t.*** to say that one is pleased and grateful for something given or done; express gratitude to: *She thanked her teacher for helping her.* [Old English *thancian* < *thanc;* see the noun]
—***n.*** **1** *Archaic.* grateful thought; gratitude. **2** *Obsolete.* favorable thought or feeling; good will.
**have oneself to thank,** to be to blame: *You have yourself to thank if you eat too much.*
**thanks, a** I thank you: *Thanks for your good wishes.* **b** the act of thanking; expression of gratitude and pleasure for something given or done: *I return the book to you with my sincere thanks.* **c** a feeling of kindness received; gratitude: *You have our thanks for everything you have done.*
**thanks to, a** owing to or because of: *Thanks to his efforts, the garden is a great success. The passengers—thanks, I expect, to the bitter cold—behaved more quietly at night than in the morning* (Westminster Gazette). **b** thanks be given to, or are due to: *But (thanks to Homer) ... I live and thrive, Indebted to no prince or peer alive* (Alexander Pope).
[Old English *thanc* (originally) a thought; an expression of gratitude. See related etym. at **think**[1].]

**thank|ful** (thangk′fəl), *adj.* feeling or expressing thanks; grateful: *He is thankful for his good health.* **SYN:** See syn. under **grateful.** —**thank′ful|ly,** *adv.* —**thank′ful|ness,** *n.*

**thank|less** (thangk′lis), *adj.* **1** not feeling or expressing thanks; ungrateful: *The thankless boy did almost nothing for his mother. How sharper than a serpent's tooth it is To have a thankless child* (Shakespeare). **2** not likely to get thanks; not appreciated: *Giving advice is usually a thankless act.* **SYN:** unrewarded, unrequited. —**thank′less|ly,** *adv.* —**thank′less|ness,** *n.*

**thank offering,** **1** an offering made according to the Levitical law as an expression of gratitude to God. **2** any offering made by way of thanks or grateful acknowledgment.

**thanks** (thangks), *n.pl.* See under **thank.**

**thanks|giv|er** (thangks′giv′ər), *n.* a person who gives thanks.

**thanks|giv|ing** (thangks′giv′ing), *n.* **1** the giving of thanks, especially the act of giving thanks to God. **2** an expression of thanks: *They offered a thanksgiving to God for their escape.* **3a** a public celebration, often with religious services, held as a solemn acknowledgment of God's favor. **b** a day set apart for this purpose.

**Thanks|giv|ing** (thangks′giv′ing), *n.* = Thanksgiving Day.

**Thanksgiving Day,** a day set apart as a holiday on which to give thanks for God's kindness during the year. In the United States, Thanksgiving Day is the fourth Thursday in November and commemorates the harvest feast of the Pilgrims in 1621. In Canada, Thanksgiving Day is the second Monday in October.

**thank|wor|thy** (thangk′wėr′ᴛʜē), *adj.* worthy of thanks; deserving gratitude.

**thank-you** (thangk′yü′), *n.* a saying of "thank you"; an expression of thanks: *You wouldn't have got a thank-you for that service in the old days* (Punch).

**thank-you-ma'am** (thangk′yə mam′), *n. U.S. Informal.* **1** a ridge or hollow in a road causing persons riding over it in a vehicle to nod the head suddenly as if making a bow of acknowledgment. **2** such a ridge or hollow in a road on the face of a hill, designed to throw to one side descending rain water. [referring to the bob of the head, as if to say *"thank you, ma'am"*]

**than|na** or **than|nah** (tä′nə), *n.* = tana[1].

**thar** (ᴛʜär), *adv. British* (*Northern*) *Dialect.* there.

**tha|ros** (thär′os), *n.* a small North American butterfly with black, orange, and white coloration. [< New Latin *tharos* the species name]

**that** (ᴛʜat; *unstressed* ᴛʜət), *adj., pron., pl.* (*for defs. 1-3*) **those,** *conj., adv.* —***adj.*** **1** pointing out or indicating some one person, thing, or idea: *Shall we buy this book or that one? Who is that*

**Pronunciation Key:** hat, āge, cãre, fär; let, ēqual, tėrm; it, īce; hot, ōpen, ôrder; oil, out; cup, pu̇t, rüle; child; long; thin; ᴛʜen; zh, measure; ə represents **a** in about, **e** in taken, **i** in pencil, **o** in lemon, **u** in circus.

*lovely girl in the chair by the fire?* **2** indicating the farther of two or farthest of most things: *Shall I buy this dress or that one we saw yesterday? What is the name of that mountain beyond the others to the east?* **3** showing contrast: *This hat is prettier but that one costs less.*

—***pron.*** **1** some one person, thing, or idea: *That is the right way. That's a good boy!* **2** the farther of two or farthest of most things: *I like that better. I like that best.* **3** something contrasted: *Which hat do you want, this or that?* **4** who; whom: *Is he the man that sells dogs? She is the girl that you saw in the chair by the fire.* **5** which: *Bring the box that will hold most.* **6** at or in which; when: *It was the day that school began. 1960 was the year that we went to England.* **7** *Archaic.* the former.

—***conj.*** *That* is used: **1** to introduce a noun clause and connect it with a verb: *I know that 6 and 4 are 10.* **2** to show purpose, end, aim, or desire (often with *may, might,* or *should,* rarely *shall*): *Study that you may learn. He ran fast so that he would not be late.* **3** to show result: *I ran so fast that I was five minutes early.* **4** to show cause: *I wonder what happened, not that I care.* **5** to express a wish: *Oh, that she were here!* **6** to show anger, surprise, sorrow, indignation, or the like: *That one so fair should be so false!*

—***adv.*** to that extent; to such a degree; so: *The baby cannot stay up that late. I didn't know you cared that much.*

**at that,** *Informal.* **a** with no more talk, work, etc.: *If I'm invited to have a drink I just say "A fruit juice please" and leave it at that* (Manchester Guardian Weekly). **b** considering everything: [*He was*] *a shoemaker, and a poor one at that* (Francis Crawford).

**in that,** because: *I prefer her plan to yours, in that I think it is more practical.*

**that is,** that is to say; in other words: *Look at me, that is, look on me, and with all thine eyes* (Ben Jonson).

**that's that,** *Informal.* that is settled or decided: *"Well," he exclaimed, "that's that. At least I know where I'm going"* (P. Marks).

**with that,** when that occurred; whereupon: *The train reached the station, and, with that, our long trip ended.*

[Old English *thæt* (originally) neuter of *sē,* demonstrative pronoun and adjective. Compare etym. under **the**[1], **this.**]

▶ The relative pronouns **that, who,** and **which** are distinguished in present use as follows: (1) *That* may refer to persons, animals, or things, *who* only to persons (or personified abstractions of animals when thought of as having personality, as in children's stories), *which* to animals, things, or groups of people regarded impersonally: *the man that* (or *who*) *answered; the concert that* (or *which*) *was scheduled; the animals that* (or *which*) *are native to this region.* (2) *That* is used chiefly in restrictive clauses: *the man that answered. The book that she selected for her report was the longest on the list. Who* and *which* are used in both restrictive and nonrestrictive clauses. Restrictive: *the man who answered; the parcel which I received.* Nonrestrictive: *the parcel, which had been badly wrapped; my aunt, who is an accountant. The privilege of free speech, which we hold so dear, is now endangered.* (3) *That* is not used as the object of a preposition; it cannot be substituted in *the man to whom I spoke* or *the size for which he asked* (or *which he asked for*).

▶ See **this** for another usage note.

**that|a|way** (ᴛʜat′ə wā′), *adv. U.S. Dialect.* in that direction: *He went thataway.*

***thatch**
definition 2

***thatch** (thach), *n., v.* —***n.*** **1** straw, rushes, palm leaves, or the like, as a roof or covering. **2** a roof or covering made of thatch. **3** *Informal, Figurative.* the hair covering the head. **4** any one of various palms whose leaves are used to thatch.

—***v.t.*** to make or cover with thatch or as if with thatch.

[variant of *thack;* Old English *thæc*] —**thatch′er,** *n.*

**thatch|ing** (thach′ing), *n.* **1** = thatch. **2** the act or process of covering with thatch.

**thatch|less** (thach′lis), *adj.* having the thatch of the roof missing or destroyed.

**that'll** (ᴛʜat′əl), **1** that will. **2** that shall.

**that's** (ᴛʜats), **1** that is. **2** that has.

**thau|ma|tol|o|gy** (thô′mə tol′ə jē), *n.* the description or discussion of the miraculous; miracles, as a subject of study or systematic inquiry. [< Greek *thaûma, -atos* a marvel + English *-logy*]

**thau|ma|turge** (thô′mə tėrj), *n.* a worker of marvels or miracles; wonder-worker. [< Medieval Latin *thaumaturgus* < Greek *thaumatourgós;* see etym. under **thaumaturgy**]

**thau|ma|tur|gic** (thô′mə tėr′jik), *adj.* having to do with a thaumaturge or thaumaturgy; having the powers of a thaumaturge.

**thau|ma|tur|gist** (thô′mə tėr′jist), *n.* = thaumaturge.

**thau|ma|tur|gy** (thô′mə tėr′jē), *n.* the working of wonders or miracles; wonder-working; magic: *Romans put a good deal of faith in thaumaturgy; sophisticated and ignorant citizens alike* (New Yorker). [< Greek *thaumatourgíā* < *thaumatourgós* (one) conjuring < *thaûma, -atos* marvel + *érgon* work]

**thaw** (thô), *v., n.* —***v.t.*** **1** to melt (ice, snow, or anything frozen); free from frost: *The sun at noon thaws the ice on the roads very quickly.* **SYN:** See syn. under **melt.** **2** to make no longer frozen: *to thaw a frozen chicken, to thaw a package of frozen peas.* **3** *Figurative.* to make less stiff and formal in manner; soften.

—***v.i.*** **1** to become warm enough to melt ice and snow; rise above a temperature of 32 degrees Fahrenheit or 0 degrees centigrade (Celsius) (said of the weather, and used impersonally): *It thawed early last spring. If the sun stays out, it will probably thaw today.* **2** to become free, as of frost or ice: *Our sidewalk thawed yesterday. The pond freezes up in November and thaws out in April. Frozen peas thaw quickly in boiling water.* **3** *Figurative.* to become less cold, less formal, or less reserved in manner; soften: *His shyness thawed under her kindness.*

—***n.*** **1** the act or process of thawing. **2** weather above the freezing point (32 degrees Fahrenheit or 0 degrees centigrade, Celsius); time of melting: *In January we usually have a thaw.* **3** *Figurative.* the act of becoming less stiff and formal in manner; softening. **4** *Figurative.* a relaxation of authority or control; a lessening in rigidity or severity: *the exceptional freedoms granted to the Roman Catholic Church in Poland during the 1956 political "thaw"* (London Times).

[Old English *thawian*] —**thaw′er,** *n.*

**Th.B.,** Bachelor of Theology (Latin, *Theologiae Baccalaureus*).

**THC** (no periods), tetrahydrocannabinol.

**Th.D.,** Doctor of Theology (Latin, *Theologiae Doctor*).

**the**[1] (*unstressed before a consonant* ᴛʜə; *unstressed before a vowel* ᴛʜi; *stressed* ᴛʜē), *definite article.* The word *the* shows that a certain one (or ones) is meant: *The dog I saw had no tail. The boys on the horses are my brothers.* Various special uses are: **1** to mark a noun as indicating something well-known; the only: *the prodigal son, the Alps.* **2** denoting the time in question or under consideration, now or then present: *the hour of victory. Was that the moment to act?* **3** with or as part of a title: *the Duke of Wellington, the Right Honorable the Earl of Derby, the Reverend John Smith.* **4** to mark a noun as indicating the best or most important of its kind: *the place to dine.* **5** to mark a noun as being any one of its kind; any: *The dog is a quadruped.* **6** to indicate a part of the body or a personal belonging: *to hang the head in shame, to clutch at the sleeve of one's father.* **7** before adjectives used as nouns; that which is; those which are: *to visit the sick, a love of the beautiful.* **8** distributively, to denote any one separately: *candy at one dollar the pound, so much by the day.*

[Old English *thē, the,* reduction of oblique forms of *sē,* demonstrative pronoun and adjective. Compare etym. under **that, this.**]

**the**[2] (ᴛʜə, ᴛʜē), *adv.* The word *the* is used to modify an adjective or adverb in the comparative degree: **1** signifying "in or by that," "on that account," "in some or any degree": *If you start now, you will be back the sooner.* **2** used correlatively, in one instance with relative force and in the other with demonstrative force, and meaning "by how much ... by that much," "in what degree ... in that degree": *the more the merrier, the sooner the better. The longer you work, the more you get. The later I sit up, the sleepier I become.* [Old English *thē,* variant of *thȳ,* instrumental case of demonstrative *thæt* that]

**the-,** *combining form.* the form of **theo-** before vowels, as in *theanthropism.*

**The|a** (thē′ə), *n. Greek Mythology.* the wife of Hyperion and mother of Eos, Helios, and Selene.

**the|a|ceous** (thē ā′shəs), *adj.* belonging to the tea family. [< New Latin *Theaceae* the family name (< *Thea* the genus name < source of English *tea*)]

**T-head** (tē′hed′), *n., adj.* —***n.*** a bar, beam, or other support or part with a crosspiece at the end. —***adj.*** having the shape or form of a T: *a T-head bolt.*

**the|an|thro|pism** (thē an′thrə piz əm), *n.* **1** *Theology.* **a** the doctrine of the union of divine and human natures in Christ. **b** the manifestation of God as man in Christ. **2** the attribution of human character to the gods; anthropomorphism. [< Late Greek *theánthrōpos* (< Greek *theós* god + *ánthrōpos* man) + English *-ism*]

**the|ar|chic** (thē är′kik), *adj.* divinely sovereign or supreme.

**the|ar|chy** (thē′är kē), *n., pl.* **-chies.** **1** = theocracy. **2** an order or system of deities. [< Greek *thearchíā* < *theós* god + *árchein* to rule, lead]

**theat.,** theatrical.

**the|a|ter** (thē′ə tər), *n.* **1** a place where plays or motion pictures are shown. **2** the audience; house. **3** a place that looks like a theater in its arrangement of seats: *The surgeon performed an operation before the medical students in the operating theater.* **4** a natural formation or other place suggesting a theater, such as a bowllike indentation of the ground with naturally terraced sides. **5** *Figurative.* a place of action: *Europe was the theater of the First World War. Politicians are actors in the theater of public life.* **6a** plays; writing, acting in, or producing plays; drama; the stage: *He was interested in the theater and tried to write plays himself.* **b** a play, situation, dialogue, or part considered as to its effectiveness on the stage: *This scene is bad theater.* Also, **theatre.** [< Latin *theātrum* < Greek *théātron* < *theâsthai* to behold < *théā* a view]

▶ **Theater** is the preferred American spelling, but **theatre** is very commonly used in the names of theater houses.

**theater commander,** the commander in charge of a theater of operations.

**the|a|ter|go|er** or **the|a|tre|go|er** (thē′ə tər gō′ər), *n.* a person who attends the theater, especially one who goes often: *a devoted theatergoer.*

**the|a|ter|go|ing** or **the|a|tre|go|ing** (thē′ə tər gō′ing), *n., adj.* —***n.*** the practice or habit of attending the theater: *Ordinarily, my theatergoing ... does not extend ... far off Broadway* (New Yorker).

—***adj.*** attending the theater.

**the|a|ter-in-the-round** (thē′ə tər in ᴛʜə round′), *n. Especially U.S.* a theater in which the stage is surrounded by seats on all sides, whether in a permanent building, a tent, or out of doors; arena theater.

**Theater of Cruelty** or **theater of cruelty,** a form of theater based on the theories of the French actor and poet Antonin Artaud (1896-1948), in which dialogue, plot, and character are subordinated to a representation of harsh physical and sensual rituals in which the audience is often deliberately involved: *In the Theatre of Cruelty ... the boundaries between actor and audience are broken down; the spectator "is engulfed and physically affected" by the action* (Julius Novick).

**Theater of Fact** or **theater of fact,** a form of theater that draws its subjects from events of recent history, often utilizing excerpts from actual speeches, articles, and books to convey realism: *"Murderous Angels" is another example of The Theatre of Fact.* [*Conor*] *O'Brien has subtitled his play "A political tragedy and comedy in black and white," and the two main characters are Dag Hammarskjold and Patrice Lumumba* (Clive Barnes).

**theater of operations,** a military area in which air, land, or sea operations are conducted. It is usually divided into a combat zone and a communications zone.

**Theater of the Absurd** or **theater of the absurd,** a form of theater that uses fantasy and surrealism to dramatize the absurdity of the human condition in an irrational world: *Like the plays of the theater of the absurd, these new movies base their form on an absence of logic* (Atlantic).

**theater of war,** a military area or region that includes several theaters of operations.

**The|a|tine** (thē′ə tin), *n., adj.* —***n.*** a member of a Roman Catholic order of clerks regular, founded in 1524 to combat heresy and improve morals.

—***adj.*** of or having to do with this order.

[< New Latin *Theatinus* < *Theate,* Latin name of Chieti, a province of Italy; so called because one of its founders was Giovanni Caraffa, Bishop of Chieti, afterwards Pope Paul IV]

**the|at|ral** (thē at′rəl), *adj.* of or connected with the theater; theatrical; dramatic.

**the|a|tre** (thē′ə tər), *n.* = theater.
▶ See **theater** for usage note.
**theatre sister,** *British.* a nurse who works in an operating room.
**the|at|ric** (thē at′rik), *adj.* = theatrical.
**the|at|ri|cal** (thē at′rə kəl), *adj., n.* —*adj.* **1** of or having something to do with the theater, actors, or dramatic presentations: *theatrical performances, a theatrical company. Dark stools, placed on an unadorned stage, took on theatrical effectiveness* (Christian Science Monitor). **SYN**: histrionic. **2** suggesting a theater or acting; showy; spectacular: *a theatrical flourish.* **SYN**: See syn. under **dramatic. 3** *Figurative.* for display or effect; artificial; affected: *The new girl would have won more friends if she had not had such a theatrical manner.*
—*n.* **theatricals, a** dramatic performances, especially as given by amateurs: *private theatricals.* **b** matters having to do with the stage and acting: *He ... dedicated his mind to the study of theatricals* (W. H. Ireland). **c** *Figurative.* actions of a theatrical or artificial character: *It's only the usual theatricals, because he's ashamed to face us* (Ethel Voynich). —**the|at′ri|cal|ly,** *adv.* —**the|at′ri|cal|ness,** *n.*
**the|at|ri|cal|ism** (thē at′rə kə liz′əm), *n.* **1** the theory and methods of scenic representations. **2** theatrical practice, style, or character; staginess: *Director Victor Vicas has tilted the picture with such suave restraint that an air of deliberate theatricalism pervades most of it* (New York Times).
**the|at|ri|cal|ist** (thē at′rə kə list), *n.* a person who takes part in theatricals.
**the|at|ri|cal|i|ty** (thē at′rə kal′ə tē), *n.* the quality or condition of being theatrical: *He has a gift for the theatricality of nothing happening, for small sudden changes of key, for the humor of despair* (Time).
**the|at|ri|cal|ize** (thē at′rə kə līz), *v.t.,* **-ized, -izing.** to make theatrical; put in dramatic form; dramatize: *Folk-dance purists, therefore, may find his dances too ... theatricalized for their tastes* (Newsweek). —**the|at′ri|cal|i|za′tion,** *n.*
**the|at|rics** (thē at′riks), *n.* (*sing. or pl. in use*). **1** the art of producing plays. **2** *Figurative.* doings of a theatrical or artificial character; histrionics: *Pike's return to religion was quiet and without theatrics* (Saturday Evening Post).
**the|at|ro|ma|ni|a** (thē at′rə mā′nē ə), *n.* a mania or excessive fondness for theatergoing. [< *theatre* + *mania*]
**the|ba|in** (thē′bə in, thi bā′-), *n.* = thebaine.
**the|ba|ine** (thē′bə ēn; thi bā′-; -in), *n.* a highly poisonous alkaloid, obtained in colorless leaflets or prisms from opium. It produces spasms like those caused by strychnine. *Formula:* $C_{19}H_{21}NO_3$ [< Greek *Thêbai* Thebes, Egypt (because it was a chief source of opium) + English *-ine*[2]]
**The|ban** (thē′bən), *adj., n.* —*adj.* of or having to do with Thebes in ancient Greece or Thebes in ancient Egypt.
—*n.* a native or inhabitant of Thebes.
[< Latin *Thēbānus* < Greek *Thêbai;* see etym. under **Thebaic**]
**the|ca** (thē′kə), *n., pl.* **-cae** (-sē). **1** *Botany.* **a** a sac, cell, or capsule. **b** a vessel containing spores in various lower plants. **2** *Anatomy, Zoology.* a case or sheath enclosing an animal, such as an insect pupa, or some part of an animal, such as a tendon. [< Latin *thēca* < Greek *thêkē* case, cover < *tithénai* to place]
**the|cal** (thē′kəl), *adj.* having to do with or of the nature of a theca.
**the|cate** (thē′kit, -kāt), *adj.* having a theca; sheathed.
**the|co|dont** (thē′kə dont), *n.* any one of a group of extinct, carnivorous reptiles with long hind legs, teeth lodged in alveoli, and ribs hollowed on both ends. It is regarded as the ancestor of the dinosaurs. [< New Latin *Thecodontes* the family name < Greek *thêkē* case, cover + *odoús, odóntos* tooth]
**thé dan|sant** (tā′ dän sän′), *pl.* **thés dansants** (tā′ dän sän′). *French.* an afternoon tea with dancing; tea dance.
**thee** (ᴛʜē), *pron. Objective case of* **thou.** *Archaic.* you: *"The Lord bless thee and keep thee."* [Old English *thē,* dative of *thū* thou]
▶ **Thee** is generally used as the nominative by members of the Society of Friends (Quakers), and in some of the local dialects of England. In this use, especially by the Quakers, it always takes a verb in the third person: *Is thee going to Meeting?* Among Quakers, especially in the United States, the form is not now generally used in speaking to persons of other religious sects, except by some members of the older generation who use it very much as the French use *tu,* in speaking to close friends and young children.
▶ See **thou** for another usage note.
**thee|lin** (thē′lin), *n. Biochemistry.* the former name of estrone. [< Greek *thêlys* female (< *thêlê* nipple) + English *-in*]
**thee|lol** (thē′lōl, -lol), *n. Biochemistry.* the former name of estriol. [< *theel*(in) + *-ol*[1]]
**theft** (theft), *n.* **1** the act of stealing: *The man was put in prison for theft.* **SYN**: thievery, pilfering, larceny, robbery. **2** an instance of stealing: *The theft of the jewels caused much excitement.* **3** something stolen. [Middle English *thefte,* Old English *thēofth* < *thēof* thief]
**theft|proof** (theft′prüf′), *adj.* invulnerable to theft; safe from thievery: *The safe is theftproof.*
**thegn** (thān), *n.* = thane. [modern use of Old English *thegn.* Compare etym. under **thane.**]
**thegn|ly** (thān′lē), *adj., adv.* —*adj.* of or having to do with a thane.
—*adv.* in a manner suitable for a thane.
**the|ine** (thē′ēn, -in), *n.* a vegetable alkaloid, originally thought to be a principle peculiar to tea, but found to be identical with caffeine. [< New Latin *thea* tea (see etym. under **theaceous**) + English *-ine*[2]]
**their** (ᴛʜãr), *adj. Possessive form of* **they. 1** of them; belonging to them; having to do with them: *They like their school and do their lessons well.* **2** of or linked to a (particular or specified) group as something shared in the fact or capacity of doing or being done to: *Those fellows certainly know their physics. Such mistakes will lead to their defeat.* [< Scandinavian (compare Old Icelandic *theirra,* genitive plural)]
▶ **Their, theirs** are the possessive forms of *they. Their* is the adjectival form; *theirs* is the absolute (or substantive) form: *This is their farm. This farm is theirs.*
**theirs** (ᴛʜãrz), *pron. Possessive form of* **they. 1** of them; belonging to them: *Those books are theirs, not mine.* **2** the one or ones belonging to them: *Our house is white; theirs is brown.*
▶ See **their** for a usage note.
**the|ism** (thē′iz əm), *n.* **1** monotheism: **a** belief in one God (the Deity), the creator and ruler of the universe. **b** belief in (any) one god rather than many. **2** belief in a deity or deities; religious faith or conviction. [< Greek *theós* god + English *-ism.* Compare etym. under **deism.**]
**the|ist** (thē′ist), *n., adj.* —*n.* a believer in theism: *No one is to be called a theist who does not believe in a personal God* (Cardinal Newman).
—*adj.* = theistic.
**the|is|tic** (thē is′tik), *adj.* of or having to do with theism or a theist; according to the doctrine of theists. —**the|is′ti|cal|ly,** *adv.*
**the|is|ti|cal** (thē is′tə kəl), *adj.* = theistic.
**the|li|tis** (thi lī′tis), *n.* inflammation of the nipple. [< New Latin *thelitis* < Greek *thēlê* nipple + *-ītis* -itis]
**them** (ᴛʜem; *unstressed* ᴛʜəm), *pron. Objective case of* **they**: *The books are new; take care of them.* [< Scandinavian (compare Old Icelandic *theim*)]
▶ In many nonstandard dialects **them** is used as a demonstrative adjective, often strengthened by *there: them bales, them there bales.*
**Th-Em** (no periods), thorium emanation.
**the|mat|ic** (thē mat′ik), *adj.* **1** of or having to do with a theme or themes. **2** *Grammar.* of or having to do with the theme of a word. —**the|mat′i|cal|ly,** *adv.*
**thematic apperception test,** a psychological test to reveal traits of personality by a story written or told about a picture or the like. *Abbr:* TAT (no periods).
**thematic vowel,** a vowel occurring between the root and the inflectional ending of a verb or noun in some Indo-European languages.
**theme** (thēm), *n.* **1** a topic; subject: *Patriotism was the army captain's theme when he spoke at our school assembly.* **SYN**: text. **2** a short written composition: *Our school themes must be written in ink and on white paper.* **SYN**: essay. **3** *Music.* **a** the principal melody or subject in a piece of music. **b** a short melody or tune repeated in different forms or developed, as in an elaborate musical composition. **4** a melody used to identify a particular radio or television program; signature. **5** *Grammar.* the inflectional base or stem of a word, consisting of the root with modifications or additions, but without the inflectional endings. **6** *Obsolete.* **a** the text of a sermon. **b** a proposition to be discussed. [< Latin *thema* < Greek *théma, -atos* (literally) something set down < *tithénai* to put down, place] —**theme′less,** *adj.*
**theme park,** an amusement park in which all the attractions have to do with a single, or several themes, such as wildlife, marine life, fantasyland, or African and Asian culture.
**theme song, 1** a melody used to identify a particular radio or television program; theme. **2** a melody repeated so often in a stage play, musical comedy, motion picture, or operetta as to dominate it or establish its character.
**The|mis** (thē′mis), *n. Greek Mythology.* the goddess of law and justice, daughter of Uranus and Gaea and thus a Titaness.
**them|selves** (ᴛʜem selvz′, ᴛʜəm-), *pron.* **1** the intensifying or emphatic form of **they** or **them**: *They did it themselves. The teachers themselves said the test was too hard.* **2** the reflexive form of **them**: *The boys hurt themselves sliding downhill.* **3** their real selves: *The children are sick and are not themselves this morning.*
▶ **Theirselves,** composed of the possessive pronoun *their* plus *selves,* parallels *myself, yourself, ourselves, yourselves.* The form is old but in modern English is found only in the nonstandard dialects.
**then** (ᴛʜen), *adv., n., adj.* —*adv.* **1** at that time: *Father talked of his childhood, and recalled that prices were lower then. Will prices then be higher?* **2** soon afterward: *The noise stopped and then began again.* **3** next in time or place: *First comes spring, then summer.* **4** at another time: *First one boy was ahead in the race and then the other.* **5** also; besides: *The dress seems too good to throw away, and then it is very becoming.* **6** in that case; therefore: *If you broke the window, then you must pay for it.*
—*n.* that time: *By then we shall know the result of the election.*
—*adj.* being at that time; existing then: *the then President.*
**but then,** but at the same time; but on the other hand: *There was ... some difficulty in keeping things in order, but then Vivian Grey was such an excellent manager!* (Benjamin Disraeli).
**then and there,** at that precise time and place; at once and on the spot: *The Constable DeLacy ... was then and there to deliver to the Flemings a royal charter of their immunities* (Scott).
**what then?** See under **what.**
[Middle English *thenne,* variant of Old English *thanne, thonne;* (originally) the same word as *than*]
▶ **then, than.** These words are often carelessly confused in writing. *Then* is an adverb of time, *than* a conjunction in clauses of comparison: *Then the whole crowd went to the drugstore. I think that book was better than any other novel I read last year.*
**the|nar** (thē′när), *n., adj. Anatomy.* —*n.* **1** the palm of the hand. **2** the fleshy prominence at the base of the thumb. **3** the sole of the foot.
—*adj.* of or having to do with the palm or thenar. [< New Latin *thenar* < Greek *thénar, -aros* palm (of the hand), sole (of the foot)]
**thence** (ᴛʜens, thens), *adv.* **1** from that place; from there: *He went to Italy; thence he went to France. A few miles thence is a river. Homeward from thence by easy stages* (George Eliot). **2a** for that reason; therefore: *You didn't work, thence you will get no pay.* **b** (as an inference) from those premises or data; from that; therefrom: *He has given his decision and thence there is no appeal.* **3** from that time; after that; from then: *a few years thence.* [Middle English *thannes, thennes* < *thanne, thenne* (Old English *thanone*) + adverbial genitive *-s*]
**thence|forth** (ᴛʜens′fôrth′, -fōrth′; thens′-), *adv.* from then on; from that time forward: *Women were given the same rights as men; thenceforth they could vote.*
**thence|for|ward** (ᴛʜens′fôr′wərd, thens′-), *adv.* = thenceforth.
**thence|for|wards** (ᴛʜens′fôr′wərdz, thens′-), *adv.* = thenceforth.
**theo-,** *combining form.* a god or gods; God: *Theogony = the origin of the gods. Theocentric = centering in God. Theology = the study of God.* Also, **the-** before vowels. [< Greek *theós* god]
**Theo., 1** Theodore. **2** Theodosia.
**the|o|bro|mine** (thē′ə brō′mēn, -min), *n.* a bitter, volatile, poisonous alkaloid, resembling caffeine, contained in the seeds of the cacao, in kola nuts, and in tea. It is used medicinally (in the form of its salts) to stimulate the nerves and as a diuretic. *Formula:* $C_7H_8N_4O_2$ [< New Latin *theobroma* (*cacao*) the cacao tree; *theobroma* (literally) food of the gods (< Greek *theós* god + *brôma* food) + English *-ine*[2]]
**the|o|cen|tric** (thē′ə sen′trik), *adj.* centering or centered in God; having God as its center. —**the′o|cen′tri|cal|ly,** *adv.*
**the|o|cen|tric|i|ty** (thē′ə sen tris′ə tē), *n.* the quality or condition of being theocentric.
**the|o|cen|trism** (thē′ə sen′triz əm), *n.* adherence to theocentric views or doctrines.
**the|oc|ra|cy** (thē ok′rə sē), *n., pl.* **-cies. 1** a government in which God, or a god, is recognized as the supreme civil ruler and in which religious au-

**Pronunciation Key:** hat, āge, cãre, fär; let, ēqual, tėrm; it, īce; hot, ōpen, ôrder; oil, out; cup, pu̇t, rüle; child; long; thin; ᴛʜen; zh, measure; ə represents **a** in about, **e** in taken, **i** in pencil, **o** in lemon, **u** in circus.

thorities rule the state as God's, or a god's, representatives: *In the little theocracy which the Pilgrims established ... the ministry was the only order of nobility* (Harriet Beecher Stowe). **2** any government headed by religious authorities. **3** a country or state governed by a theocracy. [< Greek *theokratiā* < *theós* god + *krátos* a rule, regime]

**the|oc|ra|sy** (thē ok′rə sē), *n., pl.* **-sies. 1** a mixture of several gods in one deity or of the worship of different gods. **2** the intimate union of the soul with God in contemplation. [< Greek *theokrāsiā* a mingling with God < *theós* god + *krâsis* a mingling. Compare etym. under **crasis.**]

**the|o|crat** (thē′ə krat), *n.* **1** a person who rules in a theocracy, alone or as a member of a governing body. **2** a person who favors theocracy.

**the|o|crat|ic** (thē′ə krat′ik), *adj.* **1** of, having to do with, or of the nature of theocracy. **2** having a theocracy: *a theocratic state.* **—the′o|crat′i|cal|ly,** *adv.*

**the|o|crat|i|cal** (thē′ə krat′ə kəl), *adj.* = theocratic.

**The|oc|ri|te|an** (thē ok′rə tē′ən), *adj.* of, having to do with, or in the manner of Theocritus, the ancient Greek poet of country life and scenes; pastoral; idyllic.

**the|od|i|cy** (thē od′ə sē), *n., pl.* **-cies.** a vindication of the justice and holiness of God in establishing a world in which evil exists. [< French *Théodicée,* the title of a work of Leibnitz < Greek *theós* god + *díkē* justice]

**the|o|di|dact** (thē′ə di dakt′, -dī-), *adj., n.* **—*adj.*** taught by God: *Owing nothing to church or schools he [St. Francis] was truly theodidact* (Louise S. Houghton). **—*n.*** a person taught by God. [< Greek *theodidaktos* < *theós* god + *didáskein* teach]

***the|od|o|lite** (thē od′ə līt), *n.* a surveying instrument for measuring horizontal and vertical angles. [earlier *theodelitus,* probably coined by Leonard Digges, an English mathematician of the 1500's who reputedly invented it]

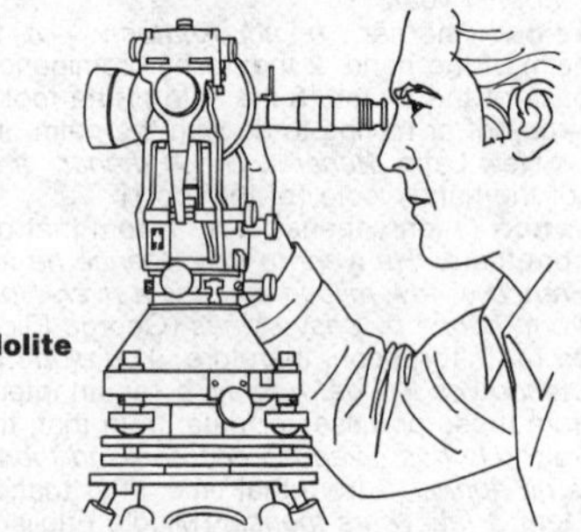

***theodolite**

**the|od|o|lit|ic** (thē od′ə lit′ik), *adj.* of or having to do with a theodolite; made by means of a theodolite.

**the|o|gon|ic** (thē′ə gon′ik), *adj.* of or relating to theogony.

**the|og|o|nist** (thē og′ə nist), *n.* a person skilled in theogony; person who writes about theogony.

**the|og|o|ny** (thē og′ə nē), *n., pl.* **-nies. 1** the origin of the gods. **2** an account of this; genealogical account of the gods. [< Greek *theogoniā* < *theós* god + *gónos* begetting, descent < *gignesthai* beget]

**theol., 1** theologian. **2** theological. **3** theology.

**the|o|log** (thē′ə lôg, -log), *n. U.S. Informal.* theologue.

**the|ol|o|gas|ter** (thē ol′ə gas′tər), *n.* a shallow theologian; pretender in theology. [< *theolog*(ian) + Latin *-aster,* a diminutive suffix]

**the|ol|o|gate** (thē ol′ə gāt), *n.* a theological college or seminary. [< New Latin *theologatus* < Latin *theológus* theologue + *-ātus* -ate[3]]

**the|o|lo|gian** (thē′ə lō′jən, -jē ən), *n.* an expert in theology, especially Christian theology; divine.

**the|o|log|ic** (thē′ə loj′ik), *adj.* = theological.

**the|o|log|i|cal** (thē′ə loj′ə kəl), *adj.* **1** of or having to do with theology. A theological school trains young people for the ministry. **2** of or having to do with the nature and will of God; scriptural.

**the|o|log|i|cal|ly** (thē′ə loj′ə klē), *adv.* according to theology: *It is clear then that the religions of Japan are, both theologically and institutionally, quite different from those of the Western world* (Atlantic).

**theological virtues,** faith, hope, and charity (I Corinthians 13:13).

**the|ol|o|gist** (thē ol′ə jist), *n.* = theologian.

**the|ol|o|gize** (thē ol′ə jīz), *v.,* **-gized, -giz|ing.** **—*v.i.*** to reason theologically; theorize or speculate on theological subjects.
**—*v.t.*** to make theological; treat theologically. **—the|ol′o|gi|za′tion,** *n.* **—the|ol′o|giz′er,** *n.*

**the|o|logue** (thē′ə lôg, -log), *n. U.S. Informal.* a theological student. Also, **theolog.** [< Latin *theológus* < Greek *theológos* < *theós* God + *-logos* treating of]

**the|ol|o|gy** (thē ol′ə jē), *n., pl.* **-gies. 1** the study of God and His relations with man and the universe. **2** the study of religion and religious beliefs. **3** a system of religious beliefs: *Calvinistic theology. Abbr:* theol. [< Late Latin *theologia* < Greek *theologiā* < *theológos* one discoursing on god; see etym. under **theologue**]

**the|o|mor|phic** (thē′ə môr′fik), *adj.* **1** having the form or likeness of God. **2** of or having to do with the doctrine that man is formed in God's image. [< Greek *theómorphos* (< *theós* god + *morphḗ* form) + English *-ic*]

**the|on|o|mous** (thē on′ə məs), *adj.* of or having to do with theonomy: *the outdated medieval concept of God as the "theonomous" controller of all forces in the universe* (Time). **—the|on′o|mous|ly,** *adv.*

**the|on|o|my** (thē on′ə mē), *n.* the condition of being ruled by God; government by God. [< German *Theonomie* < Greek *theós* god + *-nomiā* (< *nómos* law)]

**the|o|pa|thet|ic** (thē′ə pə thet′ik), *adj.* responsive to divine influence; emotionally sensitive to feelings inspired by contemplation of God. [< *theopathy;* patterned on *pathetic*]

**the|o|path|ic** (thē′ə path′ik), *adj.* = theopathetic.

**the|op|a|thy** (thē op′ə thē), *n., pl.* **-thies.** piety or a sense of piety. [< *theo-* + *-pathy.* Compare Greek *theopátheia* the divine suffering.]

**the|o|phan|ic** (thē′ə fan′ik), *adj.* of or having to do with theophany.

**the|oph|a|ny** (thē of′ə nē), *n., pl.* **-nies.** an appearance of God or a god to man. [< Late Latin *theophānia* < Greek *theophāniā* vision of God, apparently variant of *theopháneia* a festival at Delphi at which statues of Apollo and other gods were shown to the public < *theós* god + *phaínein* to show]

**the|o|pho|bi|a** (thē′ə fō′bē ə), *n.* the fear or dread of God.

**the|o|phyl|line** (thē′ə fil′ēn, -in), *n.* a poisonous, crystalline alkaloid, isomeric with theobromine, contained in tea leaves in very small amounts and used to treat hypertension and various heart conditions. *Formula:* $C_7H_8N_4O_2{\cdot}H_2O$ [< New Latin *thea* tea (see etym. under **theaceous**) + Greek *phýllon* leaf + English *-ine*[2]]

**theor.,** theorem.

***the|or|bo** (thē ôr′bō), *n., pl.* **-bos.** an obsolete kind of lute having two necks. [< French *théorbe* < Italian *tiorba,* probably < Turkish *torba*]

***theorbo**

**the|o|rem** (thē′ər əm, thir′əm), *n.* **1** *Mathematics.* **a** a statement that is to be proved or that has been proved. *Example:* In an isosceles triangle the angles opposite the equal sides are equal. **b** a rule or statement of relations that can be expressed by an equation or formula: *Geometrical theorems grew out of empirical methods* (Herbert Spencer). **2** any statement or rule that can be proved to be true. **3** a kind of picture produced by painting through one or more colored stencils, made especially in the 1800's. [< Latin *theōrēma* < Greek *theṓrēma, -atos* < *theōreîn* to consider; see etym. under **theory**]

**the|o|re|mat|ic** (thē′ər ə mat′ik, thir′ə-), *adj.* having to do with, by means of, or of the nature of a theorem: *theorematic truth.*

**the|o|ret|ic** (thē′ə ret′ik), *adj., n.* **—*adj.*** = theoretical.
**—*n.* theoretics,** theoretical matters; theory: *Morals come before contemplation, ethics before theoretics* (H. B. Wilson).
[< Late Latin *theōrēticus* < Greek *theōrētikós* < *theōrētós* perceivable < *theōreîn* to consider; see etym. under **theory**]

**the|o|ret|i|cal** (thē′ə ret′ə kəl), *adj.* **1** planned or worked out in the mind, not from experience; based on theory, not on fact; limited to theory. **SYN:** hypothetical. **2a** dealing with theory only; not practical: *City boys can get a theoretical knowledge of farming from textbooks.* **b** having the object of knowledge as its end; concerned with knowledge only, not with accomplishing anything or producing anything; purely scientific. **SYN:** speculative.

**theoretical arithmetic,** = theory of numbers.

**the|o|ret|i|cal|ly** (thē′ə ret′ə klē), *adv.* in theory; according to theory; in a theoretical manner.

**the|o|re|ti|cian** (thē′ər ə tish′ən), *n.* an expert in the theory of an art, science, etc.

**the|o|rist** (thē′ər ist, thir′ist), *n.* **1** a person who forms theories. **2** one who is adept in the theory (contrasted with practice) of a subject.

**the|o|rize** (thē′ə rīz), *v.i.,* **-rized, -riz|ing.** to form a theory or theories; speculate: *It is a capital mistake to theorize before one has data* (Sir Arthur Conan Doyle). **—the′o|ri|za′tion,** *n.* **—the′o|riz′er,** *n.*

**the|o|ry** (thē′ər ē, thir′ē), *n., pl.* **-ries. 1a** an explanation; explanation based on thought; explanation based on observation and reasoning, especially one that has been tested and confirmed as a general principle explaining a large number of related facts: *the theory of evolution. Einstein's theory of relativity explains the motion of moving objects. According to one scientific theory of life, the more complicated animals developed from the simpler ones.* **b** a hypothesis proposed as an explanation; conjecture: *Whether I am right in the theory or not ... the fact is as I state it* (Edmund Burke). **2** the principles or methods of a science or art rather than its practice: *the theory of music, the theory of modern warfare.* **3a** an idea or opinion about something: *I think the fire was started by a careless smoker. What is your theory?* **b** thought or fancy as opposed to fact or practice: *He is right only as to theory, because the facts contradict him.* **4** *Mathematics.* a set of theorems which constitute a connected, systematic view of some branch of mathematics: *the theory of probabilities.* **5** *Obsolete.* mental view; contemplation.
**in theory,** according to theory; theoretically: *In theory the plan should have worked.*
[< Late Latin *theōria* < Greek *theōriā* a looking at, thing looked at < *theōreîn* to consider, look at < *theōrós* spectator < *théā* a sight + *horán* to see]
**—*Syn.* 1a, b. Theory, hypothesis** as terms in science mean a generalization reached by inference from observed particulars and proposed as an explanation of their cause, relations, or the like. **Theory** implies a larger body of tested evidence and a greater degree of probability: *The red shift in the spectra of galaxies supports the theory that the universe is continuously expanding.* **Hypothesis** designates a merely tentative explanation of the data, advanced or adopted provisionally, often as the basis of a theory or as a guide to further observation or experiment: *Archeological discoveries strengthened the hypothesis that Troy existed.*

**theory of games,** a theory dealing with the strategies used by the competitors in games or other situations involving the interplay of chance and skill in determining action or choice, and the mathematical probabilities associated with these.

**theory of numbers,** the study of integers and their relationships; number theory.

**theos.** or **Theos., 1** theosophical. **2** theosophist. **3** theosophy.

**the|o|soph** (thē′ə sof), *n.* = theosophist.

**the|o|soph|ic** (thē′ə sof′ik), *adj.* of or having to do with theosophy. **—the′o|soph′i|cal|ly,** *adv.*

**the|o|soph|i|cal** (thē′ə sof′ə kəl), *adj.* = theosophic.

**the|os|o|phism** (thē os′ə fiz əm), *n.* = theosophy.

**the|os|o|phist** (thē os′ə fist), *n.* a person who believes in theosophy.

**the|os|o|phy** (thē os′ə fē), *n.* any system of philosophy or religion that claims to have a special insight into the divine nature through spiritual self-development. [< Medieval Latin *theosophia* < Late Greek *theosophiā* < Greek *theósophos* one wise about God < *theós* god + *sophós* wise]

**The|os|o|phy** (thē os′ə fē), *n.* the modern philosophical system of the Theosophical Society, founded in 1875 in the United States, which combines the teachings of various religions, especially Hinduism and Buddhism.

**the|o|tech|nic** (thē′ə tek′nik), *adj.* of or having to do with the action or intervention of the gods; operated or carried on by or as by the gods.

**therap., 1** therapeutic. **2** therapeutics.

**ther|a|peu|sis** (ther′ə pyü′sis), *n., pl.* **-ses** (-sēz). therapeutic treatment. [< New Latin *therapeusis* < Greek *therapeúein* to cure]

**ther|a|peu|tic** (ther′ə pyü′tik), *adj., n.* **—*adj.*** of or having to do with the treating or curing of disease; curative: *Heat has therapeutic value.* **SYN:** remedial, healing.
**—*n.* 1** a therapeutic agent; remedy: *The development of some therapeutic to neutralize or weaken ... antisocial rebellion* (A. Philip Randolph). **2** = therapeutist.
[< New Latin *therapeuticus* < Greek *therapeutikós* < *therapeutḗs* one ministering <

*therapeúein* to cure, treat < *théraps, -apos* attendant] — **ther′a|peu′ti|cal|ly**, *adv.*

**ther|a|peu|ti|cal** (ther′ə pyü′tə kəl), *adj.* = therapeutic.

**therapeutic community**, a residential mental-health clinic or institution in which various methods of psychotherapy are used, especially to rehabilitate drug addicts.

**therapeutic index**, a measure of the therapeutic value of a drug, based on the ratio of the drug's lethal dose to its effective dose: *The higher the therapeutic index, the better the drug, other factors being equal.*

**ther|a|peu|tics** (ther′ə pyü′tiks), *n.* the branch of medicine that deals with the treating or curing of disease.

**ther|a|peu|tist** (ther′ə pyü′tist), *n.* a person who specializes in therapeutics.

**ther|a|pist** (ther′ə pist), *n.* a person who specializes in some form of therapy, such as psychotherapy, electrotherapy, or speech therapy: *a physical therapist.*

**ther|ap|sid** (thə rap′sid), *n.* any one of a group of reptiles first appearing in the Permian period, that had differentiated teeth and skulls much like the mammals of which they are thought to be the ancestors; theriodont. [< New Latin *Therapsida* the order name < *théraps* attendant]

**ther|a|py** (ther′ə pē), *n., pl.* **-pies. 1** the treatment of diseases or disorders: *physical therapy, electrotherapy.* **2** curative power; healing quality. [< New Latin *therapia* < Greek *therapeíā* < *therapeúein;* see etym. under **therapeutic**]

**Ther|a|va|da** (ther′ə vä′də), *n.* the form of Buddhism predominant in southeastern Asia; Hinayana: *There are at present two main schools —Theravada or the Way of the Elders, a sect in Ceylon, Burma, Thailand, and Cambodia, stressing monastic salvation, and Mahayana or the Northern School, stressing every person's potential Buddhahood* (Virginia Carew). [< Pali *theravāda* (literally) way of the elders]

**ther|blig** (thėr′blig), *n.* a unit of physical movement or activity in time and motion study. [anagram formed from his own name by Frank B. *Gilbreth,* 1868-1924, an American engineer who developed time and motion study]

**there** (ᴛʜãr; *unstressed* ᴛʜər), *adv., n., interj.*
— ***adv.*** **1** in that place; at that place: *Sit there.* **2** to or into that place: *How did that get there? We are going there tomorrow.* **3** at that point or stage in action, proceeding, speech, or thought: *Finish reading the page and stop there. If you hadn't stopped there, you could have won in a few moves.* **4** in that matter: *You are mistaken there.* **5** *There* is also used in sentences in which the verb comes before its subject: *There are three new houses on our street. Is there a drugstore near here? There comes a time when ... There was heard a rumbling noise.* **6** *There* is used to call attention to some person or thing: *There goes the bell. There comes the mail.*
— ***n.*** that place; place yonder: *We go to New York first and from there to Boston.*
— ***interj.*** an expression of satisfaction, triumph, dismay, encouragement, comfort, or some other feeling: *There, there! Don't cry.*
**all there.** See under **all.**
[Old English *thǣr*]
▶ **there** (*adv.* def. 5). When *there* is used as a temporary substitute for the real subject, in careful speaking and writing the verb agrees in number with the real subject: *There was much work to be done. There are many answers in the back of the book.*

**there|a|bout** (ᴛʜãr′ə bout′), *adv.* = thereabouts.

**there|a|bouts** (ᴛʜãr′ə bouts′), *adv.* **1** near that place: *She lives in the main part of town, on Front Street or thereabouts.* **2** near that time: *He went home in the late afternoon, at 5 o'clock or thereabouts.* **3** near that number or amount: *to use 50 gallons of oil or thereabouts. It was very cold and the temperature fell to zero or thereabouts.*

**there|af|ter** (ᴛʜãr af′tər, -äf′-), *adv.* **1** after that; afterwards: *He was very ill as a child and was considered delicate thereafter.* **SYN:** subsequently. **2** accordingly.

**there|a|gainst** (ᴛʜãr′ə genst′), *adv. Archaic.* against or in opposition to that.

**there|a|mong** (ᴛʜãr′ə mung′), *adv.* among that, those, or them.

**there|at** (ᴛʜãr at′), *adv.* **1** when that happened; at that time. **2** because of that; because of it. **3** at that place; there.

**there|a|way** (ᴛʜãr′ə wā′), *adv.* **1** in that region; in those parts. **2** about that time, amount, or number: *for five or six months or thereaway* (Scott).

**there|by** (ᴛʜãr bī′, ᴛʜãr′bī), *adv.* **1** by means of that; in that way: *He wished to travel and thereby study the customs of other countries.* **2** in connection with that: *We won the game, and thereby hangs a tale.* **3** by or near that place; near there: *a farm lay thereby.* **4** *Scottish.* thereabouts (in number, quantity, or degree). **5** *Obsolete.* with reference thereto; apropos of that.

**there'd** (ᴛʜãrd), **1** there had. **2** there would.

**there|for** (ᴛʜãr fôr′), *adv.* for that; for this; for it: *He promised to give a building for a hospital and the land necessary therefor.*

**there|fore** (ᴛʜãr′fôr, -fōr), *adv.* for that reason; as a result of that; consequently: *She went to a party and therefore did not study her lessons.* [Middle English *therfore* < *ther,* Old English *thǣr* there + *fore,* variant of *for* for]
— ***Syn.*** **Therefore, consequently,** when used to connect two grammatically independent but logically related clauses, indicate that the second follows as a conclusion from the first. **Therefore** indicates formally and precisely that the second clause states the necessary conclusion to be drawn from the first: *He was the only candidate; therefore he was elected.* **Consequently,** also formal, indicates a reasonable or logical, though not necessary, conclusion: *She is the popular candidate; consequently, she will be elected. I overslept and, consequently, was late.*

**there|from** (ᴛʜãr from′, -frum′), *adv.* from that; from this; from it: *He opened his bag and took therefrom an apple.*

**there|in** (ᴛʜãr in′), *adv.* **1a** in that place, time, or thing: *God created the sea and all that is therein.* **b** into that place or thing. **2** in that matter; in that way: *The captain thought all danger was past; therein he made a mistake.*

**there|in|af|ter** (ᴛʜãr′in af′tər, -äf′-), *adv.* after in that document, statute, agreement, or the like; later in the same contract, deed, or other legal instrument.

**there|in|be|fore** (ᴛʜãr′in bi fôr′, -fōr′), *adv.* before in that document, statement, agreement, or the like.

**there|in|to** (ᴛʜãr in′tü, ᴛʜãr′in tü′), *adv.* **1** into that place; into it. **2** into that matter.

**there'll** (ᴛʜãrl), **1** there will. **2** there shall.

***ther|e|min** (ther′ə min), *n.* an electronic musical instrument whose sound is produced by two high-frequency electric circuits, the pitch of the tone and the volume depending upon the distance of the player's outstretched hands from two antennas, without touching them. [< Leo *Theremin,* born 1896, the Russian inventor]

***theremin**

**there|ness** (ᴛʜãr′nis), *n.* the quality of having location, situation, or existence in a particular point or place: *Giotto was ultimately responsible for the thereness of the figures in Sassetta's painting* (Listener).

**there|of** (ᴛʜãr ov′, -uv′), *adv.* **1** of that; of it. **2** from it; from that source.

**there|on** (ᴛʜãr on′, -ôn′), *adv.* **1** on that; on it: *Before the window was a table. A huge book lay thereon. A swan Swims on a lake, with her double thereon* (Thomas Hood). **2** immediately after that; thereupon: *Moses struck a rock with his staff. Thereon water flowed forth.*

**there|out** (ᴛʜãr out′), *adv. Archaic.* thence.

**there|o|ver** (ᴛʜãr ō′vər), *adv. Archaic.* over or above that.

**there's** (ᴛʜãrz), **1** there is. **2** there has.

**there|through** (ᴛʜãr thrü′), *adv.* **1** through that, it, or them. **2** by means of that; thereby.

**there|to** (ᴛʜãr tü′), *adv.* **1** to that; to it: *The castle stands on a hill, and the road thereto is steep and rough.* **2** in addition to that; besides; also; moreover: *The king gave his servant rich garments and added thereto a bag of gold.*

**there|to|fore** (ᴛʜãr′tə fôr′, -fōr′), *adv.* before that time; until then: *Its author was a man I had theretofore known only through references in the writings of others* (New Yorker). **SYN:** previously.

**there|un|der** (ᴛʜãr un′dər), *adv.* **1** under that; under it. **2** under the authority of that; according to that. **3** under or less than that (number, age, etc.).

**there|un|to** (ᴛʜãr un′tü, ᴛʜãr′un tü′), *adv.* **1** to that; to it. **2** *Obsolete.* in addition to that; thereto.

**there|up|on** (ᴛʜãr′ə pon′, -pôn′), *adv.* **1** immediately after that: *The President appeared. Thereupon the people clapped.* **2** because of that; therefore: *The stolen jewels were found in his room; thereupon he was put in jail.* **3** on that; on it: *The knight carried a shield with a cross painted thereupon.* **4** *Archaic.* on that subject or matter.

**there|with** (ᴛʜãr wiᴛʜ′, -with′), *adv.* **1** with that; with it: *The lady gave him a rose and a smile therewith.* **2** immediately after that; then: *"Avenge me!" said the ghost and therewith disappeared.* **3** besides; withal. **4** against that (or those).

**there|with|al** (ᴛʜãr′wiᴛʜ ôl′), *adv.* **1** with that; with this; with it. **2** in addition to that; also.

**the|ri|ac** (thir′ē ak), *n.* = theriaca.

**the|ri|a|ca** (thi rī′ə kə), *n.* **1** treacle or molasses. **2** *Obsolete.* an antidote for poisonous bites or for poisons, made up of many ingredients. [< Latin *thēriaca* < Greek *thēriakē* (*antídotos*), or *thēriakòn* (*phármakon*). See etym. of doublet **treacle.**]

**the|ri|a|cal** (thi rī′ə kəl), *adj.* having to do with theriaca; medicinal.

**the|ri|an|throp|ic** (thir′ē an throp′ik), *adj.* **1** part human and part animal, as a mermaid, sphinx, or centaur. **2** of or having to do with a deity or deities combining the form of a beast with that of a man. [< Greek *thēríon* (diminutive) < *thēr, thērós* wild beast + *ánthrōpos* man; + English *-ic*]

**the|ri|an|thro|pism** (thir′ē an′thrə piz əm), *n.* the worship of therianthropic deities.

**the|rid|i|id** (thə rid′ē id), *n., adj.* — ***n.*** one of a group of spiders, most of whom spin webs consisting of irregularly intersecting threads.
— ***adj.*** of or belonging to the theridiids.
[< New Latin *Theridium* the genus name < Greek *thēríon* (diminutive) < *thēr, thērós* wild beast]

**ther|i|o|dont** (thir′ē ə dont), *n.* = therapsid. [< Greek *thēr, thērós* wild beast + *odoús, odóntos* tooth]

**the|ri|o|mor|phic** (thir′ē ə môr′fik), *adj.* of or having to do with a deity worshiped in the form of a beast. [< Greek *thēriómorphos* < *thēríon* (diminutive) < *thēr* wild beast + *morphē* form]

**therm** (thėrm), *n. Physics.* any one of various units of heat: **a** the small calorie. **b** the large or great calorie. **c** a unit equivalent to 1,000 large calories. **d** a unit equivalent to 100,000 British thermal units, used as a basis of charge for gas supplied. Also, **therme.** [< Greek *thérmē* heat]

**therm-,** *combining form.* the form of **thermo-** before vowels, as in *thermal.*

**therm.,** **1** thermometer. **2** thermometric.

**ther|mae** (thėr′mē), *n.pl.* **1a** a public bathing establishment of the ancient Greeks or Romans, originally built over or near a natural hot spring or springs but later using water heated by artificial means. **b** the baths of such an establishment. **2** *Obsolete.* hot springs. [< Latin *thermae* < Greek *thérmai,* plural of *thérmē* heat]

**ther|mal** (thėr′məl), *adj., n.* — ***adj.*** **1** of or having to do with heat; determined, measured, or operated by heat; thermic: *The thermal balance of the earth is being upset by the carbon dioxide produced by burning coal and oil and already the concentration has been increased 10 per cent* (Science News Letter). **2a** naturally hot or warm: *a thermal spring.* **b** of, having to do with, or of the nature of thermae or hot springs. **c** having hot springs.
— ***n.*** a rising current of warm air: *Like gliding, ballooning depends for movement on luck with thermals* (New Yorker). — **ther′mal|ly,** *adv.*

**thermal barrier,** = heat barrier.

**thermal breeder,** a breeder reactor that uses slow neutrons to produce fissionable material.

**thermal cracking,** the application of steady heat and pressure in petroleum cracking.

**thermal equator,** = heat equator.

***thermal inversion,** an atmospheric condition in which a stationary layer of warm air settles over a layer of cool air near the ground, often causing a heavy concentration of pollutants in the air and mirages of light in the night sky. See diagram on the following page.

**ther|mal|ize** (thėr′mə līz), *v.t.,* **-ized, -iz|ing.** to lower the kinetic energy of (an atom or other particle) until it reaches the energy characteristic of the temperature of a particular medium. — **ther′mal|i|za′tion,** *n.*

**thermal noise,** noise generated in a radio receiver or amplifier by the agitation of electrons in a conductor as a result of heat.

**thermal pollution, 1** the discharge of artificially heated water into a natural body of water, causing a rise in natural water's temperature that is harmful to plant and animal life in it; heat pollution; hot water pollution. **2** the discharge of heated gases into the surrounding air, causing a rise in air temperature that sometimes affects local weather conditions; heat pollution; hot water pollution.

**thermal reactor**, = thermal breeder.
**thermal shock**, a drastic change in temperature that affects the composition or properties of some organic and inorganic matter.
**thermal spring**, = hot spring.
**thermal unit**, a unit adopted for measuring and comparing quantities of heat.
**therm|an|es|the|sia** or **therm|an|aes|the|sia** (thėrm′an əs thē′zhə, -zhē ə), *n.* = thermoanesthesia.
**therm|an|ti|dote** (thėrm an′tə dōt), *n.* a rotating wheellike apparatus, usually enclosed in wet tatties, fixed in a window, and used in India to cool the air.
**therme** (thėrm), *n. Physics.* therm.
**therm|es|the|sia** or **therm|aes|the|sia** (thėrm′es thē′zhə, -zhē ə), *n. Medicine.* sensitiveness to heat or cold; sensitivity to degree of heat. [< *thermo-* + *esthesia*]
**ther|mic** (thėr′mik), *adj.* of or having to do with heat; thermal. — **ther′mi|cal|ly**, *adv.*
**Ther|mi|dor** (thėr′mə dôr; *French* ter mē dôr′), *n.* the eleventh month of the French Revolutionary Calendar, beginning July 19. [< French *Thermidor* < Greek *thérmē* heat + *dōron* gift]
**therm|i|on** (thėrm′ī′ən, thėr′mē-), *n. Physics.* an electrically charged particle, either positive (an ion) or negative (an electron), given off by a heated body. [< *therm-* + *ion*]
**therm|i|on|ic** (thėrm′ī on′ik, thėr′mē-), *adj. Physics.* of or having to do with thermions: *thermionic emission. A thermionic generator is a vacuum or gas-filled device with two elements or electrodes insulated from one another* (J. J. William Brown). — **therm′i|on′i|cal|ly**, *adv.*
**thermionic converter**, an electronic device that changes heat directly into electricity. It consists of two metallic electrodes held in a tube at different temperatures and separated by a gas at low pressure. When the electrons on the surface of one electrode are heated, they pass to the other electrode and by their movement produce electric current.
**thermionic current**, **1** an electric current produced by movements of thermions. **2** a movement of thermions.
**thermionic emission**, the freeing of electrons by heat, as from a metal: *Thermionic emission was first disclosed in 1883 by Thomas A. Edison* (J. J. William Brown).
**therm|i|on|ics** (thėrm′ī on′iks, thėr′mē-), *n.* the science of thermionic phenomena.
**thermionic tube**, **1** a vacuum tube in which (usually) the cathode is heated to produce electron emission. **2** *Especially British.* vacuum tube.
**thermionic valve**, *Especially British.* vacuum tube.
**ther|mis|tor** or **ther|mist|er** (thėr mis′tər), *n.* a small electronic resistor whose conduction of electric current increases rapidly and predictably with a rise in temperature, used especially in heat measurement, and as a voltage regulator in communication circuits: *When the scanning mirror crosses the horizon of a planet, the increase or decrease registers on the thermister* (Science News Letter). [< *therm-* + (res)*istor*]
**ther|mite** (thėr′mīt), *n.* a mixture of powdered aluminum and the oxide of one or more chemically weak metals, usually iron, that produces an extremely high temperature when ignited, used in welding and in incendiary bombs. [< *therm-* + *-ite*[1]]
**thermo-**, *combining form.* **1** heat; temperature: *Thermoelectricity = electricity produced by heat.* **2** thermoelectric, as in *thermocurrent.* Also, **therm-** before vowels.
[< Greek *thermós* hot, and *thérmē* heat]
**ther|mo|an|es|the|sia** or **ther|mo|an|aes|the|sia** (thėr′mō an′əs thē′zhə, -zhē ə), *n. Medicine.* loss of thermesthesia; inability to feel heat or cold.
**ther|mo|bar|o|graph** (thėr′mō bar′ə graf, -gräf), *n.* an instrument that simultaneously records temperature and atmospheric pressure.
**ther|mo|ba|rom|e|ter** (thėr′mō bə rom′ə tər), *n.* **1** a thermometer that indicates the pressure of the atmosphere by the boiling point of water, used in the measurement of altitudes; hypsometer. **2** a siphon barometer that may be reversed for use as a thermometer.
**ther|mo|bat|ter|y** (thėr′mō bat′ər ē), *n., pl.* **-ter|ies**. a thermoelectric battery.
**ther|mo|cau|ter|y** (thėr′mō kô′tər ē), *n., pl.* **-ter|ies**. a cautery in which the metal end of the instrument is heated.
**ther|mo|chem|i|cal** (thėr′mō kem′ə kəl), *adj.* of or having to do with thermochemistry.
**ther|mo|chem|ist** (thėr′mō kem′ist), *n.* a person who is skilled in thermochemistry.
**ther|mo|chem|is|try** (thėr′mō kem′ə strē), *n.* the branch of chemistry dealing with the relations between chemical action and heat.
**ther|mo|chro|mic** (thėr′mə krō′mik), *adj.* of or having to do with thermochromy.
**ther|mo|chro|my** (thėr′mə krō′mē), *n.* a change of color occurring in a substance due to varying temperatures.
**ther|mo|cline** (thėr′mə klīn), *n.* a layer within a large body of water sharply separating parts of it that differ in temperature, so that the temperature gradient through the layer is very abrupt. [< *thermo-* + Greek *klīnein* to slope]
**ther|mo|cou|ple** (thėr′mō kup′əl), *n.* two dissimilar metallic conductors joined end to end, whose junction when heated, produces a thermoelectric current in the circuit of which they form a part; thermoelectric couple. Thermocouples are used as thermometers, to generate electricity, and to make refrigeration devices.
**ther|mo|cur|rent** (thėr′mō kėr′ənt), *n.* the electric current produced in a thermoelectric battery.
**ther|mo|dif|fu|sion** (thėr′mō di fyü′zhən), *n.* diffusion of heat.
**thermodyn.**, thermodynamics.
**ther|mo|dy|nam|ic** (thėr′mō dī nam′ik, -di-), *adj.* **1** of or having to do with thermodynamics. **2** using force due to heat or to the conversion of heat into mechanical or other forms of energy. — **ther′mo|dy|nam′i|cal|ly**, *adv.*
**ther|mo|dy|nam|i|cal** (thėr′mō dī nam′ə kəl, -di-), *adj.* = thermodynamic.
**ther|mo|dy|nam|i|cist** (thėr′mō dī nam′ə sist, -di-), *n.* a person skilled in thermodynamics.
**ther|mo|dy|nam|ics** (thėr′mō dī nam′iks, -di-), *n.* the branch of physics that deals with the relations between heat and other forms of energy or work, and the conversion of one into the other.

***thermal inversion**

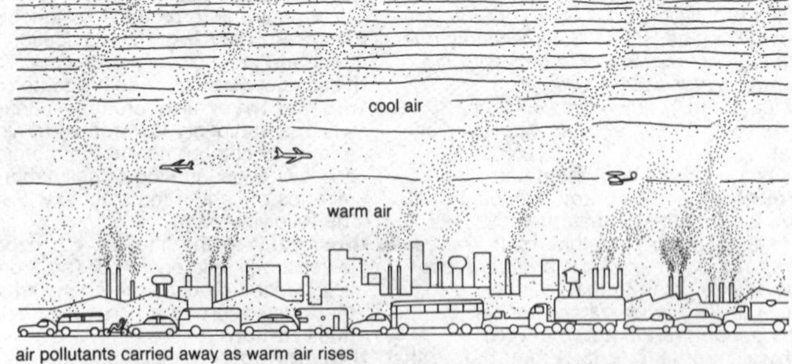

air pollutants carried away as warm air rises

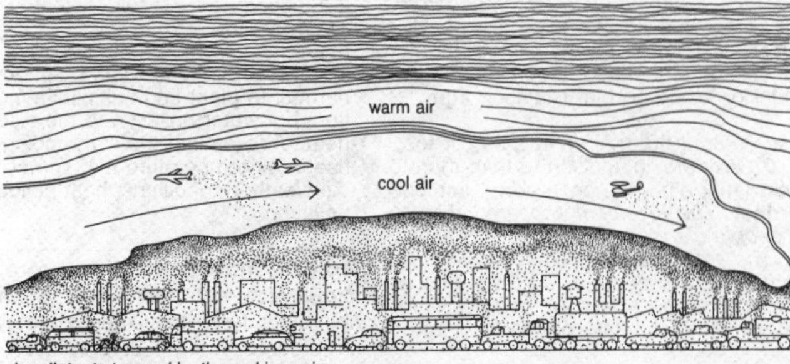

air pollutants trapped by thermal inversion

**ther|mo|e|lec|tric** (thėr′mō i lek′trik), *adj.* of or having to do with thermoelectricity: *A thermoelectric generator powered the scientific experiments left on the moon by the Apollo 12 astronauts in 1969* (Theodore Korneff). — **ther′mo|e|lec′tri|cal|ly**, *adv.*
**ther|mo|e|lec|tri|cal** (thėr′mō i lek′trə kəl), *adj.* = thermoelectric.
**thermoelectric couple** or **pair**, = thermocouple.
**ther|mo|e|lec|tric|i|ty** (thėr′mō i lek′tris′ə tē, -ē′lek-), *n.* **1** electricity produced directly by heat, especially that produced by a temperature difference between two different metals used as conductors in a circuit. **2** the branch of electrical science that deals with such electricity.
**thermoelectric thermometer**, an electric thermometer consisting essentially of a thermocouple and an indicator.
**ther|mo|e|lec|trom|e|ter** (thėr′mō i lek′trom′ə tər, -ē′lek-), *n.* an instrument for measuring the heating power of an electric current, or for determining the strength of a current by the heat produced.
**ther|mo|e|lec|tro|mo|tive** (thėr′mō i lek′trə mō′tiv), *adj.* of or having to do with electromotive force produced by heat.
**ther|mo|e|lec|tron** (thėr′mō i lek′tron), *n. Physics.* a negatively charged particle given off by a heated body.
**ther|mo|el|e|ment** (thėr′mō el′ə mənt), *n.* a thermocouple as an element of a battery: *A layer of silica on the silicongermanium alloy ... protects the thermoelements and renders them chemically inert* (New Scientist).
**ther|mo|form** (thėr′mə fôrm), *n., v.* — ***n.*** a process for shaping plastic by the application of heat: *A fairly new development ... is the thermoform process whereby thin plastic film ... is moulded into such objects as the subdivided holders in biscuit and chocolate boxes, and lightweight trays for serving meals in aircraft* (London Times).
— ***v.t., v.i.***, to shape (plastic substances) into desired forms by the application of heat.
**ther|mo|gal|va|nom|e|ter** (thėr′mō gal′və nom′ə tər), *n.* a thermoelectric instrument for measuring small electric currents.
**ther|mo|gen|e|sis** (thėr′mō jen′ə sis), *n.* the generation or production of heat, especially in an animal body.
**ther|mo|ge|net|ic** (thėr′mō jə net′ik), *adj.* of or having to do with thermogenesis.
**ther|mo|gen|ic** (thėr′mə jen′ik), *adj.* = thermogenetic.
**ther|mo|ge|og|ra|phy** (thėr′mō jē og′rə fē), *n.* the study of the geographical distribution and variation of temperature.
**ther|mo|gram** (thėr′mə gram), *n.* a measurement or record made by a thermograph: *In medicine, infrared is a supplement to X-ray diagnosis, providing doctors with a thermogram—a photograph that shows not what our eyes would see but what hundreds of thermometers would sense* (Science News Letter).
**ther|mo|graph** (thėr′mə graf, -gräf), *n.* **1** a thermometer that automatically records temperature. **2** the photographic or other apparatus used in thermography.
**ther|mo|graph|ic** (thėr′mə graf′ik), *adj.* of, having to do with, or obtained by a thermograph or thermography: *The thermographic method ... uses the heat of infrared rays, instead of light, for exposure* (R. F. Beckwith). — **ther′mo|graph′i|cal|ly**, *adv.*
**ther|mog|ra|phy** (thėr mog′rə fē), *n.* **1** the measurement of temperature by means of a thermograph. **2** a method of recording photographically or displaying visually infrared rays emitted by the body which show differences in temperature between healthy and unhealthy tissue: *In the treatment of burns ... thermography has been hailed as a tool as essential as the scalpel in healing large-area burns* (New Scientist). **3** a method of letterpress printing to produce a raised effect in the print by dusting the printed sheet with a special powder and then heating them until the printed letters appear to be engraved.
**ther|mo|hal|ine** (thėr′mō hal′īn, -hā′līn), *adj.* having to do with both the temperature and salt content of the ocean: *thermohaline circulation. In its thermohaline aspects, the ocean ... acts as a heat engine* (Scientific American). [< *thermo-* + Greek *háls, halós* salt + English *-ine*[1]]
**ther|mo|jet** (thėr′mō jet), *n.* a jet engine that forces gas out under great pressure. It is the commonest type of jet engine.
**ther|mo|junc|tion** (thėr′mō jungk′shən), *n.* the point of union of the two metallic conductors of a thermocouple.
**ther|mo|kin|e|mat|ics** (thėr′mō kin′ə mat′iks), *n.* the study of motion caused by heat.

**ther|mo|la|bile** (thėr′mō lā′bəl), *adj. Biochemistry.* liable to destruction or loss of characteristic properties at moderately high temperatures, as certain toxins.

**ther|mol|o|gy** (thėr′mol′ə jē), *n.* = thermotics.

**ther|mo|lu|mi|nes|cence** (thėr′mō lü′mə nes′əns), *n.* **1** the emission of light produced by heat or exposure to high temperature. **2** a method of determining the age of an archaeological specimen by heating it at a controlled rate and measuring the light it emits, the amount of such light being proportional to the age of the specimen: *Pottery and other heat-treated artifacts up to 500,000 years old can be accurately dated by means of thermoluminescence* (Scientific American).

**ther|mo|lu|mi|nes|cent** (thėr′mō lü′mə nes′ənt), *adj.* **1** having or showing thermoluminescence. **2** using thermoluminescence: *thermoluminescent dating of pottery. Another use of thermoluminescent testing is for the detection of faked artifacts* (Ralph M. Rowlett).

**ther|mol|y|sis** (thər mol′ə sis), *n.* **1** *Physiology.* the dispersion or dissipation of heat from the body. **2** *Chemistry.* decomposition or dissociation by heat. [< *thermo-* + Greek *lýsis* a loosening; patterned on German *Thermolyse*]

**ther|mo|lyt|ic** (thėr′mə lit′ik), *adj.* having to do with or producing thermolysis.

**thermom.**, **1** thermometer. **2** thermometric.

**ther|mo|mag|net|ic** (thėr′mō mag net′ik), *adj.* of or having to do with the effect of heat as modifying the magnetic properties of bodies.

**ther|mo|me|chan|i|cal** (thėr′mō mə kan′ə kəl), *adj.* having to do with the use of heat to do mechanical work.

***ther|mom|e|ter** (thər mom′ə tər), *n.* an instrument for measuring temperature. Most thermometers contain mercury or alcohol in a narrow tube. When the temperature outside it goes up, the liquid rises by expanding; when the temperature goes down, the liquid drops by contracting. [< French *thermomètre* < Greek *thérmē* heat + *métron* measure]

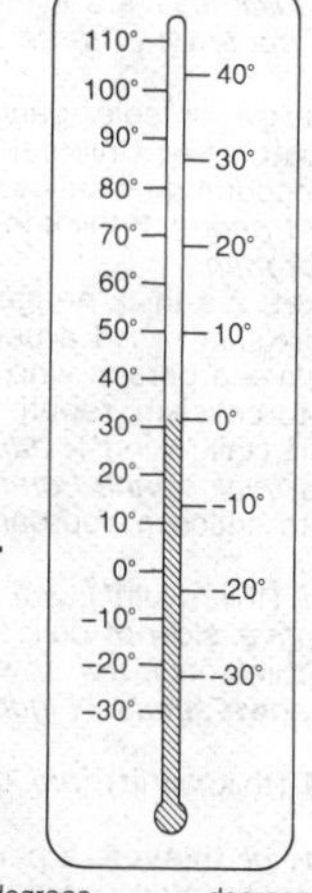


***thermometer**

**ther|mo|met|ric** (thėr′mə met′rik), *adj.* **1** of or having to do with a thermometer: *The thermometric scale.* **2** made by means of a thermometer: *thermometric observations.* — **ther′mo|met′ri|cal|ly**, *adv.*

**ther|mo|met|ri|cal** (thėr′mə met′rə kəl), *adj.* = thermometric.

**ther|mom|e|try** (thər mom′ə trē), *n.* **1** the measurement of temperature. **2** the science that deals with the construction of thermometers and their use.

**ther|mo|mo|tive** (thėr′mō mō′tiv), *adj.* **1** of, having to do with, or caused by heat applied to produce motion. **2** having to do with a thermomotor.

**ther|mo|mo|tor** (thėr′mō mō′tər), *n.* an engine driven by the expansive power of heated air or other gas.

**ther|mo|nu|cle|ar** (thėr′mō nü′klē ər, -nyü′-), *adj.* of or having to do with the fusion of atoms through very high temperature, as in the hydrogen bomb: *a thermonuclear reaction, a thermonuclear weapon.*

**ther|mo|nuke** (thėr′mə nük, -nyük), *n. U.S. Informal.* a thermonuclear weapon.

**Ther|mo|pane** (thėr′mə pān), *n. Trademark.* a double insulating glass for windows and doors.

**ther|mo|pause** (thėr′mə pôz′), *n.* the upper region of the thermosphere.

**ther|mo|pe|ri|od** (thėr′mō pir′ē əd), *n.* the length of time during which a plant is exposed to a particular temperature each day.

**ther|mo|pe|ri|od|ism** (thėr′mō pir′ē ə diz′əm), *n.* the response of a plant to daily changes in temperature.

**ther|mo|phile** (thėr′mə fīl, -fil), *n.* a bacterium, fungus, or other microorganism that requires a high temperature for its growth: *The thermophiles ... have a maximum temperature for growth at or above 50°C and a minimum greater than 20°C* (New Scientist).

**ther|mo|phil|ic** (thėr′mō fil′ik), *adj.* requiring high temperatures for development: *thermophilic bacteria.*

**ther|mo|phys|i|cal** (thėr′mō fiz′ə kəl), *adj.* of or having to do with the physical characteristics of substances under high temperature or increasing temperature.

**ther|mo|pile** (thėr′mō pīl), *n. Physics.* a device consisting of several thermocouples acting together for the production of a combined effect, as for generating currents or for ascertaining minute temperature differences. [< *thermo-* + *pile*[1]]

**ther|mo|plas|tic** (thėr′mō plas′tik), *adj., n.* — ***adj.*** becoming soft and capable of being molded when heated, as certain synthetic resins do.
— ***n.*** a thermoplastic material.

**ther|mo|plas|tic|i|ty** (thėr′mō plas tis′ə tē), *n.* thermoplastic property or condition.

**ther|mo|re|cep|tor** (thėr′mō ri sep′tər), *n.* a sense organ stimulated by a change in the temperature.

**ther|mo|reg|u|late** (thėr′mō reg′yə lāt), *v.i., v.t.,* **-lat|ed, -lat|ing.** to undergo or cause to undergo thermoregulation: *The next step is to ... see whether the monkeys will thermoregulate around the new set point* (New Scientist).

**ther|mo|reg|u|la|tion** (ther′mō reg′yə lā′shən), *n.* regulation of body temperature: *mammalian thermoregulation.*

**ther|mo|reg|u|la|tor** (thėr′mō reg′yə lā′tər), *n.* **1** an internal mechanism that regulates body temperature: *Our juncos, chickadees, and kinglets appear to use different thermoregulators than the ones ... in the Sudan* (New Scientist). **2** any device, such as a thermostat, that regulates temperature.

**ther|mo|reg|u|la|to|ry** (thėr′mō reg′yə lə tôr′ē, -tōr′-), *adj.* of or having to do with thermoregulation: *The thermoregulatory behaviour of mice was influenced by the intensity and duration of the heat they received* (New Scientist).

**ther|mo|rem|a|nence** (thėr′mō rem′ə nəns), *n.* **1** the magnetism remaining in a substance that was once molten and then cooled at the Curie point. **2** a method of determining the age of a rock or other substance by measuring its remanent or residual magnetism against the present-day magnetism of the earth.

**ther|mo|rem|a|nent** (thėr′mō rem′ə nənt), *adj.* of or having to do with thermoremanence.

**ther|mos** (thėr′məs), *n.* = thermos bottle.

**thermos bottle, flask,** or **jug**, a bottle, flask, or jug made with a vacuum between the inner and outer walls so that its contents remain at their original temperature for hours; vacuum bottle. [< *Thermos*, a trademark < Greek *thermós* hot]

**ther|mo|scope** (thėr′mə skōp), *n.* an instrument or device for indicating variations in temperature without measuring their amount.

**ther|mo|scop|ic** (thėr′mə skop′ik), *adj.* having to do with or made by means of the thermoscope.

**ther|mo|scop|i|cal** (thėr′mə skop′ə kəl), *adj.* = thermoscopic.

**ther|mo|set** (thėr′mə set), *adj., n.* = thermosetting.

**ther|mo|set|ting** (thėr′mō set′ing), *adj., n.* — ***adj.*** becoming hard and permanently shaped under the continued application of heat, as certain synthetic resins do.
— ***n.*** thermosetting action or quality.

**ther|mo|si|phon** (thėr′mō sī′fən), *n.* a siphon attachment by which the circulation in a system of hot-water pipes is increased or induced.

**ther|mo|sphere** (thėr′mə sfir), *n.* the region of the atmosphere above the mesopause, in which temperature increases with height: *The outermost part of the thermosphere is the fringe region where the earth's atmosphere merges with interplanetary gases* (Knudsen and McGuire). See diagram under **atmosphere**.

**ther|mo|sta|bil|i|ty** (thėr′mō stə bil′ə tē), *n.* the quality of being thermostable.

**ther|mo|sta|ble** (thėr′mō stā′bəl), *adj. Biochemistry.* able to undergo heat without loss to characteristic properties, as certain ferments or toxins.

**ther|mo|stat** (thėr′mə stat), *n.* **1** an automatic device for regulating temperature. In most thermostats, the expansion and contraction of a metal, liquid, or gas opens and closes an electric circuit, by which an appliance or device, such as an air conditioner, refrigerator, or oil burner, is made to work or to stop working. *Most furnaces and ovens are controlled by thermostats.* **2** any device that responds automatically to conditions of temperature, such as an automatic fire alarm or sprinkler system. [< *thermo-* + *-stat*]

**ther|mo|stat|ic** (thėr′mə stat′ik), *adj.* of, having to do with, or like a thermostat. — **ther′mo|stat′i|cal|ly**, *adv.*

**ther|mo|stat|ics** (thėr′mə stat′iks), *n.* the science dealing with the equilibrium of heat.

**ther|mo|tax|ic** (thėr′mō tak′sik), *adj.* of or having to do with thermotaxis.

**ther|mo|tax|is** (thėr′mō tak′sis), *n.* **1** *Biology.* the movement of an organism in response to changes in temperature. **2** *Physiology.* the regulation of body temperature.

**ther|mo|ten|sile** (thėr′mō ten′səl), *adj.* relating to tensile strength as affected by variations of temperature.

**ther|mo|ther|a|py** (thėr′mō ther′ə pē), *n.* therapy in which heat is used.

**ther|mot|ic** (thər mot′ik), *adj.* **1** of or having to do with heat. **2** of or having to do with thermotics.

**ther|mot|ics** (thər mot′iks), *n.* the science of heat. [< Greek *thermōtikós* warming (< *thermós* warm, hot) + English *-ics*]

**ther|mo|trop|ic** (thėr′mə trop′ik), *adj.* of, having to do with, or exhibiting thermotropism.

**ther|mot|ro|pism** (thər mot′rə piz əm), *n. Biology.* a tendency to bend or turn toward or away from the sun or other source of heat.

**the|roid** (thir′oid), *adj.* like or having the form of a brute; of a bestial nature or character. [< Greek *thḗr, thērós* wild beast + English *-oid.* Compare Greek *thēroeidḗs* having the forms of beasts.]

**the|rol|o|gy** (thi rol′ə jē), *n.* the science of mammals; mammalogy. [< Greek *thḗr, thērós* wild beast + English *-logy*]

**ther|o|pod** (thir′ə pod), *n., adj.* — ***n.*** any one of a suborder of carnivorous dinosaurs that walked on their hind legs.
— ***adj.*** of or belonging to this suborder.
[< New Latin *Theropoda* the suborder name < Greek *thḗr, thērós* wild beast + *poús, podós* foot]

**Ther|si|tes** (thər sī′tēz), *n. Greek Legend.* (in the *Iliad*) the most vindictive, ugly, and abusive of the Greeks at the siege of Troy, killed by Achilles (who was, with Odysseus (Ulysses), a chief target of his abuse).

**ther|sit|i|cal** (thər sit′ə kəl), *adj.* abusive; reviling; scurrilous: *thersitical satire.* [< Greek *Thersítēs* Thersites + English *-ic* + *-al*[1]]

**the|sau|ro|sis** (thi sə rō′sis), *n.* a disease in which the cells of the body store an excessive amount of exogenous or endogenous substances. [< Greek *thēsaurós* storehouse + English *-osis*]

**the|sau|rus** (thi sôr′əs), *n., pl.* **-sau|ri** (-sôr′ī). **1** a dictionary in which synonyms, antonyms, and other related words are classified under certain headings. **2** any dictionary, encyclopedia, or other book filled with information: *This work is one of five thesauri published under the auspices of Kang Hsi, the second Emperor of the present dynasty* (Westminster Gazette). **3** a treasury or storehouse. [< Latin *thēsaurus* < Greek *thēsaurós* storehouse, treasure. See etym. of doublet **treasure**.]

**these** (ᴛʜēz), *adj., pron.* plural of **this**: *These days are cold* (adj.). *These two problems are hard* (adj.). *These are my books* (pron.). [Old English *thēs* this, pronoun + *-e*, apparently patterned on the plural form of adjectives. Compare etym. under **those**.]
▶ For *these kind, these sort,* see **kind**.
▶ See **this** for another usage note.

**The|se|um** (thi sē′əm), *n.* **1** a temple or shrine dedicated to Theseus, the legendary hero and king of Athens. **2** a so-called temple of Theseus (now regarded as a temple of Hephaestus) at Athens, a beautiful Doric structure of Pentelic marble and the best-preserved of the Greek temples. [< Latin *Thēsēum* < Greek *Thēseîon* Thesion < *Thēseús* Theseus]

**The|se|us** (thē′sē əs, -süs), *n. Greek Legend.* the most important hero of Athens, son of Aegeus, King of Athens. He made his way through the Labyrinth at Crete (with Ariadne's help) and killed the Minotaur, killed Procrustes and other robbers, united the various states of Attica, fought the Amazons and married their princess, joined the Argonauts, and took part in the Calydonian boar hunt.

**the|sis** (thē′sis), *n., pl.* **-ses** (-sēz). **1a** a proposition or statement to be proved or to be maintained against objections. **b** a necessary

**Pronunciation Key:** hat, āge, cãre, fär; let, ēqual, tėrm; it, īce; hot, ōpen, ôrder; oil, out; cup, pu̇t, rüle; child; long; thin; ᴛʜen; zh, measure; ə represents **a** in about, **e** in taken, **i** in pencil, **o** in lemon, **u** in circus.

preliminary assumption, whether to be proved or taken for granted; postulate. **2a** an essay. **b** an essay or written report presented by a candidate for a diploma or degree: *a master's or doctoral thesis.* **3** *Music.* the strong or downward beat in a measure. **4** *Prosody.* **a** the accented (strong) part of a foot. **b** the unaccented (weak) syllable or syllables of a foot, the use originating in a misunderstanding of the Greek word. [< Latin *thesis* < Greek *thésis* a proposition, the downbeat (in music); (originally) any setting down or placing < *tithénai* to place]

**thes|mo|thete** (thez′mə thēt), *n.* **1** any one of the six lower judges or magistrates in ancient Athens. **2** any magistrate, judge, or legislator. [< Greek *thesmothetēs* < *thesmós* law + *-thetēs* one that sets down < *tithénai* to set down]

**Thes|pi|an** or **thes|pi|an** (thes′pē ən), *adj., n.* —*adj.* **1** of or having to do with the drama or tragedy; dramatic; tragic. **2** of or having to do with Thespis, a Greek tragic poet.
—*n.* an actor or actress: *Theatrical agents handle the affairs of all ... kinds of Thespians* (Punch).
[< Greek *Théspis* Thespis, a Greek poet of the 500's B.C., the traditional founder of Greek tragedy + English *-an*]

**Thess.**, Thessalonians.

**Thes|sa|li|an** (the sā′lē ən), *adj., n.* —*adj.* of or having to do with Thessaly, a district in east central Greece, or its people.
—*n.* a native or inhabitant of Thessaly.

**Thes|sa|lo|ni|an** (thes′ə lō′nē ən), *adj., n.* —*adj.* of or having to do with Thessalonica (Salonika), a seaport in northeastern Greece, or its people.
—*n.* a native or inhabitant of Thessalonica (Salonika).

**Thes|sa|lo|ni|ans** (thes′ə lō′nē ənz), *n.pl.* (*sing. in use*). either of two books of the New Testament, I Thessalonians and II Thessalonians, written by the Apostle Paul to the Christians of Thessalonica. *Abbr:* Thess.

***the|ta** (thā′tə, thē′-), *n.* the eighth letter of the Greek alphabet, corresponding to the English *th* in *thin.* [< Greek *thêta*]

***theta** — Θ capital letter; θ lower-case letter

**theta pinch**, *Nuclear Physics.* the rapid compression of a magnetic field surrounding highly ionized gas in order to produce a controlled fusion reaction.

**thet|ic** (thet′ik), *adj.* **1** characterized by laying down or setting forth; involving positive statement: *His* [*Mohammed's*] *genius was not thetic but synthetic, not creative but constructive* (A. M. Fairbairn). **2** *Prosody.* that bears the thesis; stressed. [< Greek *thetikós* positive; (literally) fit to be placed < *thetós* placed < *tithénai* to set down, place] —**thet′i|cal|ly**, *adv.*

**The|tis** (thē′tis), *n. Greek Mythology.* one of the Nereids, the mother of Achilles and wife of Peleus. She dipped Achilles in the river Styx and thus made him invulnerable except for the heel by which she held him.

**the|ur|gic** (thē ėr′jik), *adj.* of or having to do with theurgy. —**the|ur′gi|cal|ly**, *adv.*

**the|ur|gist** (thē′ėr jist), *n.* a person who believes in or practices theurgy.

**the|ur|gy** (thē′ėr jē), *n., pl.* **-gies.** **1** a system of magic, originally practiced by certain members of the Egyptian school of Neoplatonism, to procure communication with beneficent spirits, and by their aid produce miraculous effects. **2a** the operation of a divine or supernatural agency in human affairs, especially at the behest of a human being. **b** an instance of this; divine or supernatural act; miracle. [< Late Latin *theūrgia* < Greek *theourgiā* sorcery < *theós* god + *érgon* work]

**thewed** (thyüd, thüd), *adj.* having thews; muscled.

**thews** (thyüz, thüz), *n.pl.* **1** muscles. **2** sinews. **3** bodily force; might; strength; vigor. [Middle English *thewe* good qualities, virtues, Old English *thēaw* habit + *-s*[1]]

**they**[1] (ᵺā), *pron., pl. nom.; poss.,* **their, theirs**; *obj.,* **them.** **1** the nominative plural of **he, she,** or **it**: *I had three books yesterday. Do you know where they are? They are on the table.* **2** *Informal.* people in general; some people; any people; persons: *They say we should have a new school. In Scotland they wear kilts.* [< Scandinavian (compare Old Icelandic *their*)]
▶ Indefinite **they**, common in spoken English, is regularly avoided in standard written English: *There have been* (not *They have had*) *no serious accidents at that crossing for over two years. Germany was completely prostrate at the end of the war, but it has* (not *they have*) *made an amazing recovery.*

**they**[2] (ᵺā), *adv. Dialect.* there: *"They'll be work; they's got to be"* (Atlantic).

**they'd** (ᵺād), **1** they had. **2** they would.

**they'll** (ᵺāl), **1** they will. **2** they shall.

**they're** (ᵺãr), they are.

**they've** (ᵺāv), they have.

**THF** (no periods), tetrahydrofuran.

**THI** (no periods), temperature-humidity index (a combined measurement of temperature and humidity, used to indicate relative discomfort).

**thi-**, *combining form.* a variant of **thio-**, as in *thiamine.*

**thi|a|ben|da|zole** (thī′ə ben′də zōl), *n.* a drug used in the treatment of trichinosis and other parasitic diseases, especially of animals. [< *thia*(zolyl)*ben*(zimi)*dazole*]

**thi|al|dine** (thī al′dēn, -dīn), *n.* a white basic compound that has a powerful action on the heart. *Formula:* $C_6H_{13}NS_2$ [< *thi-* + *ald*(ehyde) + *-ine*[2]]

**thi|am|ide** (thī am′īd, -id), *n.* any of a class of compounds formed by replacing the oxygen of an amide by sulfur.

**thi|a|min** (thī′ə min), *n.* = thiamine.

**thi|a|mine** (thī′ə min, -mēn), *n.* a vitamin, a crystalline organic compound found in whole-grain cereals, yeast, meats, and certain vegetables, or prepared synthetically; vitamin $B_1$. It promotes growth and aids in preventing beriberi and neuritis. *Formula:* $C_{12}H_{17}ClN_4OS$ [< *thi-* + *amine*]

**Thian-shan sheep** (tyän′shän′), = Marco Polo sheep.

**thi|a|zin** (thī′ə zin), *n.* = thiazine.

**thi|a|zine** (thī′ə zin, -zēn), *n.* any compound of a group, each having a ring composed of four carbon atoms, one sulfur atom, and one nitrogen atom. The thiazines are the parent substances of certain dyes. [< *thi-* + *azine*]

**thi|a|zol** (thī′ə zōl, -zol), *n.* = thiazole.

**thi|a|zole** (thī′ə zōl), *n.* **1** a colorless basic liquid that has a pungent odor. It is the parent substance of certain dyes. *Formula:* $C_3H_3NS$ **2** any one of various compounds derived from this substance. [< *thi-* + *azole*]

**Thi|bet|an** (ti bet′ən), *adj., n.* = Tibetan.

**Thich** (tik), *n.* (in Vietnam) a Buddhist title of honor equivalent to reverend or venerable.

**thick** (thik), *adj., adv., n., v.* —*adj.* **1** with much space from one side to the opposite side; not thin: *a thick plank, a thick layer of paint. The castle has thick stone walls.* **2** measuring (so much) between two opposite sides: *This brick is 8 inches long, 4 inches wide, and 2½ inches thick.* **3** set close together; dense: *She has thick hair. It is a thick forest.* SYN: close, compact, crowded. **4** many and close together; abundant: *During its sale, the store was swarming with people thick as fleas.* SYN: plentiful, numerous. **5** filled; covered: *a room thick with flies.* **6** like glue or syrup, not like water; rather dense of its kind: *Thick liquids pour much more slowly than thin liquids.* **7** not clear; foggy: *The weather was thick and the airports were shut down.* SYN: misty, hazy. **8** difficult or impossible to see through: *the thick blackness of a moonless night.* **9** not clear in sound; hoarse: *She has a thick voice because of a cold.* SYN: indistinct, inarticulate, muffled. **10** *Figurative.* stupid; dull: *He has a thick head.* SYN: slow, obtuse. **11** *Informal, Figurative.* very friendly; intimate: *Those two boys are as thick as thieves.* **12** *Informal, Figurative.* too much to be endured: *That remark is a bit thick.*
—*adv.* in a thick manner; thickly.
—*n.* **1** the thickest part. **2** *Figurative.* the hardest part; place where there is the most danger or activity: *King Arthur was in the thick of the fight.*
—*v.t., v.i. Archaic.* to thicken: *The nightmare Life-in-Death was she, Who thicks men's blood with cold* (Samuel Taylor Coleridge).
**lay it on thick,** *Slang.* to praise or blame too much: *Isn't the bloke laying it on a bit thick, even for the American tourists?* (Maclean's).
**thick and fast,** in close or rapid succession; quickly: *The cars came thick and fast during the rush hour. Now things started to happen thick and fast* (Jonathan Eberhart).
**through thick and thin,** in good times and bad: *A true friend sticks through thick and thin. There's five hundred men here to back you up through thick and thin* (Hall Caine).
[Old English *thicce*]

**thick-and-thin** (thik′ən thin′), *adj.* **1** that is ready to follow in good times and bad; loyal; steadfast; unwavering: *a thick-and-thin supporter.* **2** (of a tackle-block) having one sheave larger than the other.

**thick|en** (thik′ən), *v.t.* to make thick or thicker: *to thicken a wall. Mother thickens the gravy with flour.* SYN: coagulate, congeal, condense.
—*v.i.* **1** to become thick or thicker: *The pudding will thicken as it cools. The weather has thickened over the Atlantic.* SYN: coagulate, congeal, condense. **2** *Figurative.* to become more involved or complicated: *In the second act of the play the plot thickens.* —**thick′en|er**, *n.*

**thick|en|ing** (thik′ə ning, thik′ning), *n.* **1** a material or ingredient used to thicken something: *to use cornstarch as thickening for a sauce.* **2** a thickened part or substance. **3** the act or process of making or becoming thick or thicker.

**thick|et** (thik′it), *n.* **1** a number of shrubs, bushes, or small trees growing close together: *We crawled into the thicket and hid.* SYN: shrubbery, copse, brake. **2** *Figurative.* a thick, dense mass; jumble: *a thicket of cables.* [Old English *thiccet* < *thicce* thick]

**thick|et|ed** (thik′ə tid), *adj.* covered with thick shrubs, bushes, or small trees.

**thick|et|y** (thik′ə tē), *adj.* = thicketed.

**thick film,** a thick layer of conductive material forming part of the electronic circuitry of an integrated circuit. —**thick′-film′**, *adj.*

**thick|head** (thik′hed′), *n.* a person who is dull of intellect; stupid fellow; blockhead.

**thick-head|ed** or **thick|head|ed** (thik′hed′id), *adj.* stupid; dull. SYN: doltish. —**thick′-head′ed-ness, thick′head′ed|ness**, *n.*

**thick|ish** (thik′ish), *adj.* somewhat thick: *a faded woman and thickish* (Sinclair Lewis).

**thick-knee** (thik′nē′), *n.* = stone curlew.

**thick|leaf** (thik′lēf′), *n., pl.* **-leaves.** any plant of a group of mostly South African herbs or shrubs of the orpine family, with thick, succulent leaves.

**thick|ly** (thik′lē), *adv.* **1** in a thick manner; closely; densely: *Most of New York City is thickly settled.* **2** in great numbers; in abundance: *Weeds grow thickly in rich soil.* **3** frequently: *The houses came more thickly as we got closer to the city.* **4** with thick consistency. **5** in tones that are hoarse or hard to understand; hoarsely.

**thick|ness** (thik′nis), *n.* **1** the quality or condition of being thick: *The thickness of the walls shuts out all sound.* **2** the distance between two opposite sides; the third measurement of a solid, not length or breadth: *The length of the board is 10 feet, the width 6 inches, the thickness 2 inches.* **3** the thick part: *Turn the board so you can walk across on its thickness.* **4** a layer or fold: *The bandage was made up of three thicknesses of gauze.*

**thickness gauge,** = feeler gauge.

**thick-set** or **thick|set** (thik′set′), *adj., n.* —*adj.* **1** growing or occurring closely together; thickly set: *a thick-set hedge.* **2** thick in form or build: *a short, thick-set man.*
—*n.* **1** = thicket. **2** a thick hedge.

**thick|skin** (thik′skin′), *n.* **1** a person with a thick skin. **2** *Figurative.* a person who is not sensitive in feeling, as to criticism, rebuff, or the like.

**thick-skinned** (thik′skind′), *adj.* **1** having a thick skin or rind: *a thick-skinned orange.* **2** *Figurative.* not sensitive to criticism, reproach, rebuff, or the like.

**thick-skulled** (thik′skuld′), *adj.* **1** having a thick skull. **2** *Figurative.* slow or dull; stupid.

**thick-sown** (thik′sōn′), *adj.* sown or scattered thickly: *thick-sown seeds,* (*Figurative.*) *thick-sown metaphors.*

**thick-wit|ted** (thik′wit′id), *adj.* dull of wit; stupid; thick-headed.

**thief** (thēf), *n., pl.* **thieves.** a person who steals, especially one who steals secretly and without using force; one who commits theft or larceny: *the story of Ali Baba and the Forty Thieves.* [Old English *thēof*]
—*Syn.* **Thief, robber** mean someone who steals. **Thief** applies to someone who steals in a secret or stealthy way: *A thief stole my bicycle from the yard.* **Robber** applies to someone who steals by force or threats of violence: *The robbers bound and gagged the night watchman.*

**thieve** (thēv), *v.i., v.t.,* **thieved, thiev|ing.** to steal: *He saw a boy thieving at school today.* [Old English *thēofian* < *thēof* thief]

**thiev|er|y** (thē′vər ē, thēv′rē), *n., pl.* **-er|ies.** **1** the act of stealing; theft. **2** something stolen.

**thieves** (thēvz), *n.* plural of **thief.**

**thieves' kitchen,** *British Slang.* an area where thieves congregate.

**thiev|ish** (thē′vish), *adj.* **1** having the habit of stealing; likely to steal. SYN: predatory. **2** like a thief; stealthy; sly: *That cat has a thievish look.* SYN: furtive. —**thiev′ish|ly**, *adv.* —**thiev′ish|ness**, *n.*

**thig** (thig), *v.t., v.i.,* **thigged, thig|ging.** *Scottish.* **1** to beg; cadge. **2** to borrow. [Middle English *thiggien* < Scandinavian (compare Old Icelandic *thiggja* receive, related to Old English *thicgean* accept; consume food)]

**thigh** (thī), *n.* **1** the part of the leg between the hip and the knee. **2** the similar but not corresponding part of a four-legged vertebrate animal, such as the horse; upper part of the hind leg. **3** the second segment of the leg of a bird, containing the tibia and the fibula. **4** the third seg-

ment of the leg of an insect. [Old English *thēoh, thēh*]
**thigh|bone** (thī′bōn′), *n.* the bone of the thigh between the hip and the knee; femur. See diagram under **leg**.
**thigh|boot** (thī′büt′), *n.* a boot with uppers reaching to the thigh: *The adjutant was pacing up and down in his dark thighboots* (Punch).
**thighed** (thīd), *adj.* having thighs.
**thig|mo|tac|tic** (thig′mə tak′tik), *adj.* of, having to do with, or exhibiting thigmotaxis.
**thig|mo|tax|is** (thig′mə tak′sis), *n. Biology.* stereotaxis. [< Greek *thígma, -atos* a touch + *táxis* arrangement]
**thig|mo|trop|ic** (thig′mə trop′ik), *adj. Biology.* bending or turning in response to a touch stimulus.
**thig|mot|ro|pism** (thig mot′rə piz əm), *n. Biology.* a tendency of some part of any organism to bend or turn in response to a touch stimulus. [< Greek *thígma, -atos* a touch + English *tropism*]
**thill** (thil), *n.* either of the shafts between which a single animal drawing a vehicle is placed. [Middle English *thille;* origin uncertain. Compare Old English *thille* board, boarding.]
**thim|ble** (thim′bəl), *n.* **1** a small cap of metal or plastic, worn on the finger to protect it when pushing the needle in sewing. Thimbles have many small indentations on the head to prevent the needle from slipping. **2** any one of various short metal tubes, rings, sleeves, bushings, or other fittings for machines. **3** a metal ring fitted as within a ring of rope, an open splice, or a perforation in a sail, to reduce wear or protect against chafing. [Middle English *thymbyl,* alteration (with intrusive *b*) of Old English *thȳmel* thumbstall < *thūma* thumb] —**thim′ble|like′**, *adj.*
**thim|ble|ber|ry** (thim′bəl ber′ē), *n., pl.* **-ries.** any one of various American raspberries with a thimble-shaped fruit, especially a thornless variety with large, white flowers.
**thim|bled** (thim′bəld), *adj.* wearing a thimble: *a thimbled finger* (Arnold Bennett).
**thim|ble|fish** (thim′bəl fish′), *n., pl.* **-fish|es** or (*collectively*) **-fish.** a jellyfish of tropical or warm seas, named from its shape.
**thim|ble|ful** (thim′bəl fu̇l), *n., pl.* **-fuls. 1** as much as a thimble will hold; very small quantity, especially of wine or alcoholic liquor; dram: *Could I trouble you for another thimbleful of brandy?* (H. G. Wells). **2** a very small amount of anything: (*Figurative.*) *a thimbleful of common sense.*
**thim|ble|rig** (thim′bəl rig′), *n., v.,* **-rigged, -rig|ging.** —*n.* **1** a swindling game in which the operator apparently covers a small ball or pea with one of three thimblelike cups, and then, moving the cups about, offers to bet that no one can tell under which cup the ball or pea lies. **2a** a person who cheats by this game. **b** *Figurative.* a deft swindler.
—*v.t.* **1** to cheat by the thimblerig. **2** *Figurative.* to swindle deftly.
[< *thimble* + *rig*[3]] —**thim′ble|rig′ger**, *n.*
**thim|ble|weed** (thim′bəl wēd′), *n.* any one of various plants whose fruiting heads have the form and markings of a thimble, such as an anemone and a rudbeckia.
**thi|mer|o|sal** (thī mer′ə sal, -mėr′-), *n.* a liquid preparation containing mercury, used as a germicide, fungicide, and antiseptic; Merthiolate. *Formula:* $C_9H_9HgNaO_2S$ [< *thi-* + *mer*(cury) + *sal*(icylate)]
**thin** (thin), *adj.,* **thin|ner, thin|nest,** *adv., v.,* **thinned, thin|ning,** *n.* —*adj.* **1** with little space from one side to the opposite side; not thick: *a thin book, thin paper, thin wire. The ice on the pond is too thin for skating.* SYN: narrow, slim, attenuated. **2** having little flesh; slender; lean: *a thin person.* **3** not set close together; scanty: *a thin stand of timber, thin foliage. He has thin hair.* **4** not dense; not rich in oxygen; rarefied: *The air on the top of those high mountains is thin.* **5** few and far apart; not abundant: *The actors played to a thin audience.* SYN: sparse. **6** like water; not like glue or syrup; not as thick as usual: *a thin soup, thin milk. The gravy is too thin.* **7** not deep or strong: *a shrill, thin voice.* **8** having little depth, fullness, or intensity: *a thin color, thin applause.* **9** *Figurative.* **a** without body; not strong of its kind; of low alcoholic strength; weak: *thin liquor.* **b** not full or rich; meager: *a thin diet.* **10** *Figurative.* easily seen through; flimsy: *It was a thin excuse that satisfied no one.* **11** *Photography.* relatively transparent, usually as a result of being underexposed or underdeveloped: *a thin negative.* **12** *Obsolete.* scarce; rare; few.
—*adv.* **1** in a thin manner; thinly. **2** *Obsolete.* in a poor or sparing manner.
—*v.t.* **1** to make thin or thinner: *Hunger had thinned her cheeks.* **2** to make less crowded or close by removing individuals: *to thin a row of beets.*
—*v.i.* **1** to become thin or thinner: *The smoke clouds were thinning away* (Rudyard Kipling). **2a** (of a place) to become less full or crowded. **b** (of a crowd) to become less numerous.
—*n.* **1** something which is thin: *The forms have tentatively been christened thins* (New Scientist). **2** the thinnest part: *in the thin of things.*
**wear thin.** See under **wear**[1].
[Old English *thynne*] —**thin′ly**, *adv.* —**thin′ness**, *n.*
—*Syn. adj.* **2 Thin, lean, gaunt** mean having little flesh. **Thin,** neither favorable nor unfavorable in connotation, suggests lack of the normal or usual amount of flesh: *She has a thin face.* **Lean,** favorable in connotation, suggests lack of fat: *The Olympic swimmer is lean and tanned.* **Gaunt,** unfavorable in connotation, suggests a bony, starved, or worn look: *Gaunt, bearded men stumbled into camp.*
**thine** (ᴛʜīn), *pron., adj. Archaic.* —**pron.** *Possessive case of* **thou.** the one or ones belonging to thee; yours: *My heart is thine.*
—*adj. Possessive form of* **thou.** thy; your (used only before a word beginning with a vowel or *h,* or after a noun): *thine enemies.*
[Old English *thīn,* genitive of *thū* thou. Compare etym. under **thy.**]
► See **thou** for a usage note.
**thin film,** a thin layer of conductive material forming part of the electronic circuitry of an integrated circuit. Thin films are deposited by evaporation in a high vacuum on the insulated base of a chip or wafer. —**thin′-film′**, *adj.*
**thing**[1] (thing), *n.* **1** any object or substance; what you see or hear or touch or taste or smell: *All the things in the house were burned. Put these things away. Food is a nourishing thing. Some drugs are dangerous things.* **2** whatever is done or to be done; act, deed, fact, event, or happening: *It was a good thing to do. A strange thing happened. The shipwreck was a tragic thing.* **3** whatever is spoken or thought of; idea; opinion: *a dangerous thing to repeat, a mind filled with the oddest things. That is a strange thing to think of.* **4** matter; affair; subject; business: *Let's settle this thing between us. How are things going?* **5** an attribute, quality, or property of an actual being or entity: *It is the small things about him that puzzle me.* **6** *Informal.* a person or animal: *I felt sorry for the poor thing. Galina Samtsova, a pretty young thing from the Ukrainian corn country ...* (Maclean's). **7a** an indefinable object or substance; something: *The poor fellow is seeing things that don't exist.* **b** an inanimate object or substance: *animals, plants, and things.* **8** *Philosophy.* that which has separate or individual existence (as distinct on the one hand from the totality of being, on the other hand from attributes or qualities). **9** *Law.* anything over which a person may exercise possession and control; property.
**a thing or two,** *Informal.* **a** things that one should know or find out about; wisdom; experience; knowledge: *Does anyone ... feel inclined to tell me that those old palm-oil chiefs have not learnt a thing or two during their lives?* (Mary Kingsley). **b** an example or experience serving as a warning; lesson: *The accident taught him a thing or two about carelessness.*
**do one's (own) thing,** *Informal.* to do what one likes best or does best: *Living on what they could scrounge from family ... they spent their aimless days "doing their thing," which chiefly involved introspection aided by drugs, meditation, exotic religion, and music* (New York Times). *A singer can do his own thing and still be commercially successful* (Time).
**for one thing,** as one point to be noted; in the first place: *For one thing, no one in these hospitals ever seems to do anything* (New Yorker).
**have a thing about,** *Informal.* to have a phobia or obsession about: *They have a thing about opening letters, and never do* (Punch).
**make a good thing of,** *Informal.* to profit from: *These dealers in ragged merchandise make a good thing of it* (St. Paul's Magazine).
**of all things,** *Informal.* what is least expected; very surprising: *For Christmas my brother gave me, of all things, a cowboy hat.*
**see things,** to have hallucinations: *Under the influence of the drug he began to see things.*
**(the) first thing,** at the earliest possible moment: *He is going first thing in the morning.*
**the thing, a** the fashion or style: *The silk is at once rich, tasty, and quite the thing* (Oliver Goldsmith). **b** the important fact or idea: *The thing about Michelangelo is this: he is not ... at the head of a class, he stands apart by himself* (John A. Symonds).
**things, a** personal belongings; possessions: *She packed up all her things and left him.* **b** clothes: *I know every part of their dress, and can name all their things by their names* (Sir Richard Steele). **c** outdoor clothes: *But having her things on, ... she thought it best to go* (Samuel Richardson). **d** implements or equipment for some specified use: *cooking things.*
[Old English *thing* entity, fact; action, a legal case before a court; (originally) a judicial or deliberative assembly. See related etym. at **thing**[2].]
**thing**[2] (thing, ting), *n.* (in Scandinavian countries) a legislative assembly, court of law, or other public meeting (used especially as the last element of a name): *Storthing, Landsthing.* Also, **ting.** [< Scandinavian (compare Icelandic *thing,* Swedish *ting*). See related etym. at **thing**[1].]
**thing|am|a|bob** (thing′ə mə bob), *n.* = thingumbob.
**thing|am|a|jig** (thing′ə mə jig), *n.* = thingumbob.
**thing-in-it|self** (thing′in it self′), *n. Philosophy.* a thing regarded apart from its attributes; noumenon. [translation of *Ding an sich,* a phrase used by Kant]
**thing|ish** (thing′ish), *adj.* characterized by thingism; concerned with physical objects and details: *... the "thingish" fiction of Sarraute and Robbe-Grillet* (New Yorker).
**thing|ism** (thing′iz əm), *n.* emphasis on or concern with physical objects and details in literature and art: *Godard is ... influenced, reportedly, by the poetry of Francis Ponge, which is concerned with "Thingism," the seeming life and effect of "things"* (New Republic). [translation of French *chosisme*]
**thing|ness** (thing′nis), *n.* the quality of a material thing; objectivity; actuality; reality.
**thing|um|a|bob** (thing′ə mə bob), *n.* = thingumbob.
**thing|um|a|jig** (thing′ə mə jig), *n.* = thingumbob.
**thing|um|bob** (thing′əm bob), *n. Informal.* something whose name one forgets or does not bother to mention. [< *thing*[1] + arbitrary suffix]
**thing|um|my** (thing′ə mē), *n., pl.* **-mies.** *Informal.* thingumbob: *There's no What's-his-name but Thingummy, and What-you-may-call-it is his prophet* (Dickens).
**think**[1] (thingk), *v.,* **thought, think|ing,** *n., adj.*
—*v.t.* **1** to have (a thought or idea) in the mind: *He thought that he would go. To think so base a thought* (Shakespeare). *O poor hapless nightingale thought I* (Milton). **2** to picture in one's mind; imagine: *You can't think how surprised I was. We think the ocean as a whole* (William James). **3** to have one's thoughts full of: *He thinks nothing but sports.* **4** to consider: *They think their teacher a fine man. I am afraid, to think what I have done* (Shakespeare). **5** to intend or plan (to do something); contemplate: *They think to escape punishment.* SYN: purpose, mean. **6** to believe possible or likely; expect: *I did not think to find you here. Do you think it will rain? We thought it might snow.* **7** to bring into or out of some specified condition by thinking: *to think one's way out of trouble.*
—*v.i.* **1** to have ideas; use the mind: *to learn to think clearly. I want to think about that question before I answer it.* **2** to have an idea: *He had thought of her as still a child.* SYN: conceive. **3** to consider the matter; reflect: *I must think before answering.* **4** to have an opinion; believe: *Do what you think fit.* **5** to have a (good, bad, etc.) opinion (of a person or thing): *to think well of a person's abilities.* **6** to have an expectation; look for.
—*n. Informal.* a thought: *Each country in the Six will have to have a long think about ... foreign trade* (Wall Street Journal).
—*adj. Informal.* devoted to thought; engaged in intellectual or theoretical work, study, or research: *The Institute of Defense Analysis is one of the think companies working for the Pentagon* (Jerry E. Bishop).
**think aloud** (or **out loud**), to say what one is thinking: *Often, he becomes a sounding board as the President walks about his desk, peers out the window, and "thinks out loud" on upcoming issues* (Newsweek).
**think better of.** See under **better**[1].
**think for,** to expect or suppose: *It will be better than you think for.*
**think little of.** See under **little.**
**think nothing of.** See under **nothing.**
**think of, a** to have in mind: *Nothing was thought of, but how to save ourselves* (Samuel Johnson). **b** to imagine: *He doesn't like apple pie. Think of that!* **c** to remember: *I can't think of his name.*
**think out, a** to plan or discover by thinking: *He meditated deeply on the philosophy of trade, and thought out by degrees a complete ... theory* (Macaulay). **b** to solve or understand by thinking: *to think out a puzzle, to think out a problem.* **c** to

think through to the end: *Oh, don't bother me ... I don't want to be uncivil, but I've got to think this out* (F. Anstey).
**think over**, to consider carefully: *He would think the matter over* (Frederick Marryat).
**think through**, to think about until one reaches an understanding or conclusion: *Had he been given time to think the question through, he would have come up with a better answer.*
**think twice**, to think again before acting; hesitate: *Scientists ought to think twice before venturing into the marts of trade* (New Yorker).
**think up**, to plan, discover, or compose by thinking: *The idea was a simple one, thought up* (*so the story goes*) *at a supper party* (Manchester Guardian Weekly).
[Middle English *thinken,* variant of *thenchen,* Old English *thencan.* See related etym. at **thank.**]
— **think'er**, *n.*
— ***Syn.*** *v.i.* **1 Think, reflect, meditate** mean to use the powers of the mind. **Think** is the general word meaning to use the mind to form ideas, reach conclusions, understand what is known, or make plans: *I must think about your offer before I accept it.* **Reflect** suggests quietly and seriously thinking or turning over a subject in one's mind: *They need time to reflect on their problems.* **Meditate** suggests focusing the thoughts on a subject from every point of view, to understand all its sides and relations: *He meditated on the nature of happiness.*

**think²** (thingk), *v.i.,* **thought, think|ing.** it seems (used impersonally, with an indirect object; now obsolete except in *methinks, methought*). [Middle English *thinken* variant of *thinchen,* Old English *thyncan*]

**think|a|ble** (thing'kə bəl), *adj.* capable of being thought; conceivable: *It is hardly thinkable that he could have behaved as he did.* **SYN**: imaginable. — **think'a|bly**, *adv.*

**think factory**, = think tank.

**think|ing** (thing'king), *adj., n.* — ***adj.*** **1** that thinks; reasoning: *Whatever withdraws us from the power of our senses ... advances us in the dignity of thinking beings* (Samuel Johnson). **2** given to thinking; thoughtful or reflective.
— ***n.*** mental action or activity; thought: *Thinking ... in its higher forms ... is a kind of poetry* (Havelock Ellis). **SYN**: contemplative, pensive, cogitative. — **think'ing|ly**, *adv.*

**thinking cap**,
**put on one's thinking cap**, to take time for thinking over something: *No expense has been spared; clearly everyone connected with the enterprise put on his thinking cap, and thought big* (New Yorker).

**thinking machine**, = electronic brain.

**think piece**, a magazine or newspaper article devoted to an extensive analysis or discussion of current news.

**think tank**, *Informal.* a center or institute for theoretical studies and research in solving problems of society, science, and technology; think factory: *The Urban Institute was set up by the Johnson Administration as a private, nonprofit corporation to serve as the Government's "think tank" for research into city problems* (New York Times).

**think-tank|er** (thingk'tang'kər), *n.* a member of a think tank.

**thin-lay|er chromatography** (thin'lā'ər), a method of analyzing the chemical substances of a mixture by passing it through a thin layer of filtering material.

**thin|ner** (thin'ər), *n.* **1** a liquid, especially turpentine, used to make paint more fluid. **2** a person or thing that thins.

**thin|ning** (thin'ing), *adj., n.* — ***adj.*** that thins: *thinning hair.*
— ***n.*** a decrease in thickness, closeness, density, or amount.
**thinnings**, slivers, particles, or shavings, removed in decreasing the thickness of wood or the like: *... a fir paling of the horizontal kind, made from the thinnings of trees of that kind* (R. W. Dickson).

**thin|nish** (thin'ish), *adj.* somewhat thin.

**thin-skinned** (thin'skind'), *adj.* **1** having a thin skin or rind: *a thin-skinned orange.* **2** *Figurative.* sensitive to criticism, reproach, rebuff, or the like; touchy: *When* [*the author*] *gets after the Americans the amusement turns sour and not, one thinks, because an American reader is necessarily thin-skinned* (Wall Street Journal).

**thio-**, *combining form.* sulfur (replacing oxygen atoms in the designated oxygen compound) as in *thioarsenate, thiocyanate.* Also, sometimes **thi-** before vowels. [< Greek *theîon* sulfur]

**thi|o|a|ce|tic acid** (thī'ō ə sē'tik, -set'ik), a liquid produced by heating glacial acetic acid with a sulfide of phosphorus, used as a reagent. *Formula:* $C_2H_4OS$

**thi|o|ac|id** (thī'ō as'id), *n.* an acid in which sulfur partly or wholly takes the place of oxygen.

**thi|o|al|de|hyde** (thī'ō al'də hīd), *n.* any compound of a group produced by treating aldehydes with hydrogen sulfides, and considered as aldehydes with sulfur substituted for the oxygen.

**thi|o|ar|se|nate** (thī'ō är'sə nāt), *n.* a salt of a thioarsenic acid.

**thi|o|ar|sen|ic acid**, (thī'ō är sen'ik), any one of a group of acids existing only in the form of their salts. *Formulas:* $H_3AsS_4$, $HAsS_3$, and $H_4As_2S_7$

**thi|o|ar|se|ni|ous acid** (thī'ō är sē'nē əs), any one of a group of hypothetical acids. *Formulas:* $H_3AsS_3$, $HAsS_2$, $H_4As_2S_5$, and $H_6As_4S_9$

**thi|o|ar|se|nite** (thī'ō är'sə nīt), *n.* a salt of a thioarsenious acid.

**thi|o|car|bam|id** (thī'ō kär bam'id), *n.* = thiocarbamide.

**thi|o|car|bam|ide** (thī'ō kär bam'id, -īd), *n.* = thiourea.

**thi|oc|tic acid** (thī ok'tik), one of the vitamins of the vitamin B complex, important in releasing sugar for conversion into energy, and in the proper functioning of the liver; lipoic acid. *Formula:* $C_8H_{14}O_2S_2$ [< *thi-* + *oct-* + *-ic* (because of the eight carbon atoms)]

**thi|o|cy|a|nate** (thī'ō sī'ə nāt), *n.* a salt or ester of thiocyanic acid, containing the radical -SCN. [< *thio-* + *cyanate*]

**thi|o|cy|an|ic acid** (thī'ō sī an'ik), a colorless, unstable liquid with a penetrating odor. *Formula:* HSCN

**thi|o|gua|nine** (thī'ō gwä'nēn, -nin), *n.* a drug that retards the growth of cells, used in the treatment of certain forms of cancer. *Formula:* $C_5H_5N_5S$

**Thi|o|kol** (thī'ə kol), *n. Trademark.* any of a group of synthetic rubbers produced from organic halides and metallic polysulfides, especially resistant to gasoline, oils, and typical organic solvents.

**thi|ol** (thī'ōl, -ol), *n.* **1** any organic compound of a series resembling the alcohols and phenols, but containing sulfur in place of oxygen; mercaptan. **2** the univalent radical -SH; sulfhydryl. [< *thio-* + *-ol¹*]

**thi|ol|a|ce|tic acid** (thī'ōl ə sē'tik, -ol; -set'ik), = thioacetic acid.

**thi|o|nate** (thī'ə nāt), *n.* a salt or ester of a thionic acid.

**thi|on|ic** (thī on'ik), *adj. Chemistry.* **1** of or containing sulfur. **2** having oxygen replaced by sulfur. [< Greek *theîon* sulfur + English *-ic*]

**thionic acid**, any unstable acid of a group represented by the formula $H_2S_nO_6$, where *n* equals two, three, four, five, and perhaps six.

**thi|o|nin** (thī'ə nin), *n.* = thionine.

**thi|o|nine** (thī'ə nēn, -nin), *n.* **1** a dark crystalline, basic compound derived from thiazine, used as a violet stain in microscopy. *Formula:* $C_{12}H_9N_3S$ **2** any of several allied dyes. [< Greek *theîon* sulfur + English *-ine²*]

**thi|o|nyl** (thī'ə nəl), *n.* a bivalent inorganic radical -SO; sulfinyl. [< Greek *theîon* sulfur + English *-yl*]

**thi|o|pen|tal sodium** (thī'ō pen'tal), a yellowish-white barbiturate similar to pentobarbital sodium, used as an anesthetic; Pentothal Sodium; sodium pentothal. *Formula:* $C_{11}H_{17}N_2O_2SNa$ [< *thio-* + *pent*(oth)*al*]

**thi|o|pen|tone** (thī'ō pen'tōn), *n.* = thiopental sodium.

**thi|o|phen** (thī'ə fən), *n.* = thiophene.

**thi|o|phene** (thī'ə fēn), *n.* a colorless liquid compound, present in coal tar, with an odor like that of benzene, and with properties similar to those of benzene. *Formula:* $C_4H_4S$

**thi|o|phe|nol** (thī'ə fē'nōl, -nol), *n.* a colorless mobile liquid with the odor of garlic, regarded as phenol with the oxygen replaced by sulfur. *Formula:* $C_6H_6S$ [< *thio-* + *phenol*]

**thi|o|phos|phate** (thī'ō fos'fāt), *n.* a salt or ester of thiophosphoric acid.

**thi|o|phos|phor|ic acid** (thī'ō fos fôr'ik, -for'-), an acid produced from phosphoric acid by replacing one or more oxygen atoms with an atom of sulfur.

**thi|o|rid|a|zine** (thī'ə rid'ə zēn), *n.* a drug used as a tranquilizer, especially in the treatment of schizophrenia and senility. *Formula:* $C_{21}H_{26}N_2S_2$ [< *thio-* + (pipe)*rid*(ine) + (thi)*azine*]

**thi|o|sem|i|car|ba|zone** (thī'ō sem'ē kär'bə zōn), *n.* a toxic, pale-yellow, crystalline compound, used in treating leprosy and pulmonary tuberculosis. *Formula:* $C_{10}H_{12}N_4OS$ [< *thio-* + *semi-* + *carb*(on) + *az*(o) + *-one*]

**thi|o|sin|am|ine** (thī'ə si nam'in, -sin'ə mēn'), *n.* a colorless crystalline compound having a garlicky odor, produced by heating mustard oil and alcohol with ammonia. It is used in medicine and in photography. *Formula:* $C_4H_8N_2S$ [< *thio-* + Latin *sināpis* mustard (< Greek *sínāpi*) + English *amine*]

**thi|o|sul|fate** (thī'ō sul'fāt), *n.* a salt or ester of thiosulfuric acid.

**thi|o|sul|fu|ric acid** (thī'ō sul fyůr'ik), an unstable acid, considered as sulfuric acid in which one atom of oxygen is replaced by sulfur. It occurs only in solution or in the form of its salts (thiosulfates). *Formula:* $H_2S_2O_3$

**thi|o|TE|PA** or **thi|o|te|pa** (thī'ō tē'pə), *n.* a crystalline drug derived from nitrogen mustard, used in arresting the growth of cancerous tissue by inhibiting cell division, as in the alleviation of leukemia. [< *thio-* + *TEPA*]

**thi|o|u|ra|cil** (thī'ō yůr'ə səl), *n.* a white crystalline powder used in treating hyperthyroidism. *Formula:* $C_4H_4N_2OS$ [< *thio-* + *ur*(ic) *ac*(id) + *-il,* a variant of *-yl*]

**thi|o|u|re|a** (thī'ō yů rē'ə, -yůr'ē-), *n.* a bitter, colorless crystalline substance, considered as urea with sulfur substituted for the oxygen; thiocarbamide. It is used especially in photography. *Formula:* $CH_4N_2S$

**thir** (ᴛʜir, ᴛʜėr), *pron., adj. Scottish.* these.

**thi|ram** (thī'ram), *n.* a white crystalline compound used as a fungicide, seed disinfectant, and bacteriostat. *Formula:* $C_6H_{12}N_2S_4$ [< (tetramethyl) *thi*(u)*ram* disulfide]

**third** (thėrd), *adj., n., v.* — ***adj.*** **1** next after the second; last in a series of three: *C is the third letter of the alphabet.* **2** being one of three equal parts. **3** *U.S.* of, having to do with, or designating the gear used for ordinary driving in an automobile with a standard transmission; high: *to shift into third gear.*
— ***n.*** **1** the next after the second; last in a series of three. **2** one of three equal parts into which a unit or total may be divided: *Mother divided the cake into thirds.* **3** the third of the subdivisions of any standard measure or dimension that is successively subdivided in a constant ratio; subdivision next below seconds. **4** *Music.* **a** a tone or note three diatonic degrees from a given tone or note. **b** the interval of two tones between such tones or notes. **c** the harmonic combination of such tones or notes. **d** the third tone or note of a scale, three diatonic degrees above the tonic; mediant. **5** *U.S.* third gear; high.
— ***v.t.*** **1** to divide (anything) into three equal parts; reduce to one third the number or bulk. **2** to speak in favor of (a motion, proposition, or the like) as third speaker; support the seconder: *A motion of the lord Wharton, seconded and thirded by the lords Somers and Halifax* (N. Luttrell).
**thirds**, **a** one third of the property of a deceased husband, to which the widow is entitled if there is a child or children. **b** a widow's dower.
[apparently Middle English alteration of Old English *thridda* < *thrēo* three]

**third base**, *Baseball.* **1** the base that must be touched third by a runner. **2** the position of the fielder covering the area near this base. — **third baseman.**

**third|bor|ough** (thėrd'bėr'ō), *n.* formerly in England: **1** the head of a frankpledge or tithing. **2** the peace officer of a tithing; petty constable of a township or manor.

**third class**, **1a** the lowest or next to the lowest class of accommodations on any one of various railroads in Europe, Great Britain, and elsewhere. **b** (formerly) the lowest class of accommodations on a passenger vessel; tourist class. **2** a class of mail consisting of printed matter other than newspapers or periodicals, usually not sealed and weighing less than 16 ounces. **3** *Especially British.* **a** the class next below the second in an examination list. **b** a place in this class.

**third-class** (thėrd'klas', -kläs'), *adj., adv.* — ***adj.*** **1** of or belonging to a class after the second. **2** of or having to do with third class. **3** of distinctly inferior quality; third-rate.
— ***adv.*** in or by a third-class conveyance or accommodations: *to travel third-class.*

**third-class matter**, (in the postal system of the United States) printed matter other than newspapers or periodicals, sent through the mails by the publishers at special rates.

**third degree**, **1** *Informal.* the use of severe treatment by the police to force a person to give information or make a confession. **2** the degree of master mason in Freemasonry.

**third-de|gree burn** (thėrd'də grē'), a deep burn, with charring and actual destruction of the skin and tissue.

**third dimension**, **1** the dimension of depth or thickness in a figure, object, or system. **2** *Figurative.* a quality that gives solidity or depth to anything; three-dimensional quality: *... music's third dimension—the expression of human drama by means of sound* (New Yorker).

**third-di|men|sion|al** (thėrd'də men'shə nəl), *adj.* having depth, as well as length and width; three-dimensional: *The mural is slightly curved, there is a balustrade and the lighting is so deftly placed that the effect is third-dimensional* (New York Times).

**third estate** or **Third Estate**, persons not in the nobility or clergy, especially in French history; common people.

**third eyelid,** = nictitating membrane.
**third force,** any person or group that tries to hold a middle course between extreme factions, especially a political group trying to hold such a position: *New York's Liberal Party—a powerful third force in New York politics* (Time).
**third-hand** (thėrd′hand′), *adj., adv.* —*adj.* **1** obtained, copied, or imitated from a second-hand source; further away from the original source, and so more stale, less authoritative, etc., than the second-hand source: *Second-hand and third-hand opinions and views ... are buzzing around this camp like flies* (J. D. Salinger). **2** dealing in third-hand goods.
—*adv.* from a source twice removed from the original: *Details from a Canadian reporter's first-hand description of a royal tour turn up third-hand in a biography* (Maclean's).
**Third House,** *U.S.* a body of lobbyists; group that tries to influence legislators: *And the power of the so-called "Third House"—the special interest lobbies that had long ruled Sacramento—was waning* (Harper's).
**Third International,** an organization formed by the Communist Party in Moscow in 1919 to promote communism outside Russia; Communist International; Comintern. It was officially dissolved in 1943.
**third|ly** (thėrd′lē), *adv.* in the third place.
**third market,** *U.S.* the market in listed stocks not traded on a stock exchange; over-the-counter trading in listed stocks, as distinguished from trading on a national exchange or in unlisted stocks: *the so-called third market, where brokers arrange private trades of listed stocks* (Time).
**third order** or **Third Order,** an order or rule of the Roman Catholic Church that is made up of lay associates of a monastic order, such as the Dominicans or Carmelites; any order of tertiaries.
**third party, 1** *U.S. and Canada.* a political party organized as an independent rival of the two major parties: *One of the major functions of third parties in Canada has always been to introduce imaginative ideas into our political life* (Canadian Forum). **2** a party or person besides the two primarily concerned, as in a law case.
**third person, 1** the person used when referring to someone or something spoken of. **2** the form of a pronoun or verb thus used. *He, she, it,* and *they* are pronouns of the third person. In *he walks* and *they walk,* the verbs are in the third person.
**third proportional,** *Mathematics.* the final term of a proportion having three variables, the second and third terms being the mean proportional. *Example:* In the proportion, 2 is to 4 as 4 is to 8, the third proportional is 8.
**third quarter, 1** the period between full moon and second half moon. **2** the phase of the moon represented by the second half moon, after full moon.
***third rail,** a rail paralleling the ordinary rails of a railroad. It carries a powerful electric current and is used on some railroads instead of an overhead wire. The power is picked up by a device (shoe) that extends out from the locomotive or car and fits over the rail. —**third′-rail′,** *adj.*

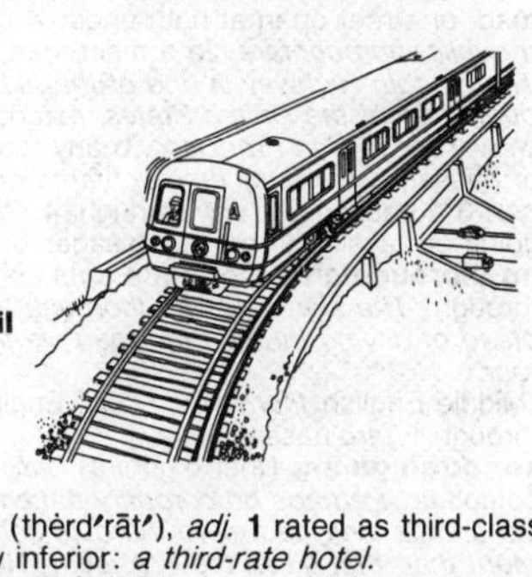

***third rail**

**third-rate** (thėrd′rāt′), *adj.* **1** rated as third-class. **2** distinctly inferior: *a third-rate hotel.*
**third-rat|er** (thėrd′rā′tər), *n.* a third-rate person or thing.
**Third Reich,** the totalitarian state in Germany (from 1933 to 1945) under Adolf Hitler.
**Third Republic,** the government of France from 1871 to 1946.
**third sex,** homosexuals.
**third stream,** a form of musical composition that attempts to combine the harmonic qualities of classical music with the rhythmic and improvisational elements of jazz. —**third′-stream′,** *adj.*
**Third World** or **third world, 1** the world of neutral or nonaligned nations; countries taking neither side in the cold war between Communist and Western nations: *China failed in its effort to isolate the Third World from both the United States and Russia* (New York Times). **2** the underdeveloped countries of the world: *Today's widespread poverty among the peoples of the Third World—of Asia, Africa, and Latin America—is as real a phenomenon as was that of late eighteenth century Britain as observed by Malthus* (New Scientist). **3** the minority groups of a country or society: *The Third World ... is composed of blacks, Mexican Americans, Chinese Americans and other racial minorities* (Time).
—**Third Worldism.**
**Third World|er** (wėrl′dər), a person belonging to the Third World, especially an African or Asian.
**thirl[1]** (thėrl), *v.t., v.i. British Dialect.* **1** to pierce; perforate. **2** to thrill. [Old English *thyrlian* < *thȳrel* hole, bore, ultimately < *thurh* through. Compare etym. under **nostril.**]
**thirl[2]** (thėrl), *n. Scottish.* thirlage. [alteration of obsolete *thrill* bondage, Old English *thrǣl.* Compare etym. under **thrall.**]
**thirl|age** (thėr′lij), *n.* in Scots and feudal law: **a** a requirement that tenants have their grain ground at a certain mill. **b** the charge for this grinding. [alteration of obsolete *thrillage* bondage < *thrill,* verb, to hold as thrall < *thrill,* noun; see etym. under **thirl[2]**]
**thirst** (thėrst), *n., v.* —*n.* **1** a dry, uncomfortable feeling in the mouth or throat caused by having had nothing to drink: *The traveler in the desert suffered from thirst.* **2** a desire for something to drink: *He satisfied his thirst at the spring.* **3** *Figurative.* a strong desire; craving: *Many young people have a thirst for adventure.*
—*v.i.* **1** to feel thirst; be thirsty. **2** *Figurative.* to have a strong desire or craving: *Some men thirst for power.*
[Old English *thurst*] —**thirst′er,** *n.*
**thirst|i|ly** (thėrs′tə lē), *adv.* in a thirsty manner.
**thirst|i|ness** (thėrs′tē nis), *n.* the condition of being thirsty; thirst.
**thirst|less** (thėrst′lis), *adj.* having no thirst.
**thirst|y** (thėrs′tē), *adj.,* **thirst|i|er, thirst|i|est.** **1** feeling thirst; having thirst: *The dog is thirsty; please give him some water.* **2** (of earth or plants) without water or moisture; dry, parched, or arid: *The land seemed thirstier than a desert.* **3** *Figurative.* having a strong desire or craving; eager: *The fellow was evidently thirsty for my blood* (W. H. Hudson). **4** *Informal.* that causes thirst.
**thir|teen** (thėr′tēn′), *n., adj.* three more than ten; 13: *She thinks thirteen is an unlucky number.* [Middle English *thirttene,* alteration of earlier *thrittene,* Old English *thrēotēne*]
**thir|teenth** (thėr′tēnth′), *adj., n.* **1** next after the 12th; last in a series of 13: *The thirteenth cookie made a baker's dozen.* **2** one, or being one, of 13 equal parts.
**thir|ti|eth** (thėr′tē ith), *adj., n.* **1** next after the 29th; last in a series of 30. **2** one, or being one, of 30 equal parts: *A day is about one thirtieth of a month.*
**thir|ty** (thėr′tē), *n., pl.* **-ties,** *adj.* —*n.* **1** three times ten; 30. **2** the figure "30" as a symbol placed at, and designating, the end of a news story or other piece of copy.
—*adj.* three times ten; 30.
[Middle English *thyrty,* alteration of *thrytty,* Old English *thrītig* < *thrī-* three + *-tig* -ty[1]]
**thir|ty-eight** or **.38** (thėr′tē āt′), *n.* a .38 caliber revolver or automatic pistol.
**thir|ty|fold** (thėr′tē fōld′), *adj., adv.* thirty times as great or as much; increased thirty times.
**thir|ty|ish** (thėr′tē ish), *adj.* about thirty years of age; looking thirty years old.
***thir|ty-sec|ond note** (thėr′tē sek′ənd), *Music.* a note played for one thirty-second as long as a whole note; demisemiquaver.

***thirty-second note**
***thirty-second rest**

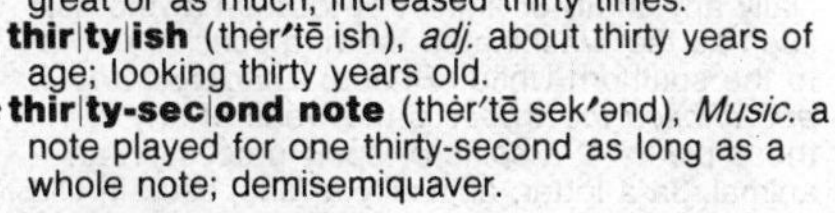

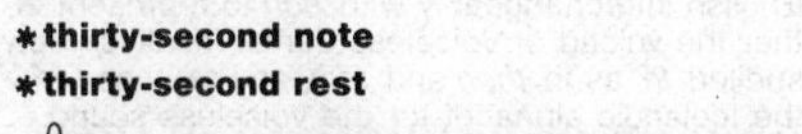

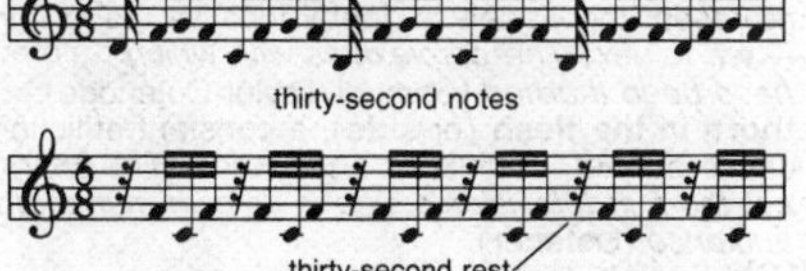


***thirty-second rest,** *Music.* a rest equivalent in time value to a thirty-second note.
**thir|ty-three** (thėr′tē thrē′), *n.* a phonograph record which revolves at 33⅓ revolutions per minute; long-playing record.
**thir|ty-two|mo** (thėr′tē tü′mō), *n., pl.* **-mos,** *adj.* —*n.* **1** a size of a book, or of its pages, made by folding a sheet of paper thirty-two times to form leaves about 3½ X 5½ inches. *Abbr:* 32mo or 32°. **2** a book having pages of this size.
—*adj.* of this size; having pages of this size.
[< *thirty-two* + *-mo,* as in *decimo*]
**this** (ᴛʜis), *adj., pron., pl.* **these,** *adv.* —*adj.* **1** present; near; spoken of; referred to: *this minute, this child, this idea.* **2a** indicating the nearer of two or nearest of several things in time or space: *Do you prefer this tie or that one in the closet?* **b** indicating one thing as distinct from another or others: *School begins at eight this year. You may have this one, this next one, or that one, but not all three.*
—*pron.* **1** the person, thing, event, quality, condition, or idea that is present, near, or referred to now: *This is my brother. After this you must go home.* **2** the one emphasized or contrasted with another called "that": *Take this, or this, but not that. Shall we buy this or that?*
—*adv.* to this degree or extent; so: *You can have this much.*
[Old English *this,* neuter demonstrative pronoun and adjective. Compare etym. under **these.**]
► **a This,** like *that,* is regularly used to refer to the idea of a preceding clause or sentence: *He had always had his own way at home, and this made him a poor roommate.* **b This, these, that, those** are called *demonstrative adjectives* when they modify substantives: *this company, that magazine.* When they stand alone, they are called *demonstrative pronouns: This is the one. That's what I want.*
**this-a-way** (ᴛʜis′ə wā′), *adv. U.S. Dialect.* in this fashion or direction: *It happened this-a-way* (New York Times).
**This|be** (thiz′bē), *n. Greek Legend.* a maiden loved by Pyramus. Pyramus killed himself thinking that Thisbe had been devoured by a lion, and she killed herself when she found him dead.
**this|ness** (ᴛʜis′nis), *n.* the state or quality of being this; the particular reality of a thing: *Each community has its particular identity, a thisness that makes it different from other places* (New Yorker).
***this|tle** (this′əl), *n.* **1** any one of various plants that have prickles on the stem and leaves and, usually, purple flowers. The blossom of one kind of purple thistle, the bull thistle, is the national flower of Scotland. **2** any one of several other prickly plants. [Old English *thistel*] —**this′tle|like′,** *adj.*

***thistle**
definition 1

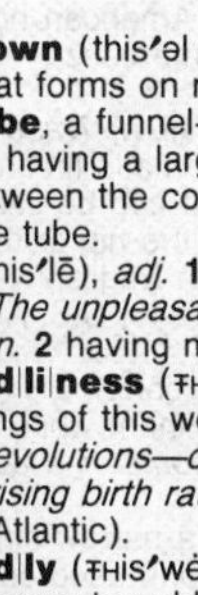

**this|tle|down** (this′əl doun′), *n.* the downy growth that forms on ripe thistle seeds.
**thistle tube,** a funnel-shaped glass tube used by chemists, having a large bulb like the head of a thistle between the conical flaring part and the rest of the tube.
**this|tly** (this′lē), *adj.* **1** like thistles; prickly: (*Figurative.*) *The unpleasant old man had a thistly disposition.* **2** having many thistles.
**this-world|li|ness** (ᴛʜis′wėrld′lē nis), *n.* devotion to the things of this world: *She speaks of four modern revolutions—of equality, of this-worldliness, of rising birth rates, and of driving scientific change* (Atlantic).
**this-world|ly** (ᴛʜis′wėrld′lē), *adj.* of or concerned with the present world or state of existence: *The guests were always this-worldly, and often profane* (Mark Twain).
**thith|er** (thiᴛʜ′ər, ᴛʜiᴛʜ′-), *adv., adj.* —*adv.* **1** to that place; toward that place; there. **2** *Obsolete.* to or toward that end, purpose, result, or action.
—*adj.* on that side; farther.
[variant of Middle English *thider, thedir,* Old English *thider,* variant of earlier *thæder;* influenced by Old English *hider* hither]
**thith|er|to** (thiᴛʜ′ər tü′, ᴛʜiᴛʜ′-; thiᴛʜ′ər tü′, ᴛʜiᴛʜ′-), *adv.* up to that time; until then.
**thith|er|ward** (thiᴛʜ′ər wərd, ᴛʜiᴛʜ′-), *adv.* toward that place; in that direction; thither: *Were thy vocation in truth thitherward!* (Scott).
**thith|er|wards** (thiᴛʜ′ər wərdz, ᴛʜiᴛʜ′-), *adv.* = thitherward.
**thix|o|trop|ic** (thik′sə trop′ik), *adj.* exhibiting or characterized by thixotropy.
**thix|ot|ro|py** (thik sot′rə pē), *n. Chemistry.* the

**Pronunciation Key:** hat, āge, cãre, fär; let, ēqual, tėrm; it, īce; hot, ōpen, ôrder; **oil, out;** cup, pu̇t, rüle; **child;** long; **th**in; **ᴛʜ**en; **zh,** measure;
ə represents **a** in about, **e** in taken, **i** in pencil, **o** in lemon, **u** in circus.

property of becoming fluid when stirred or agitated, as exhibited by gels. [< Greek *thíxis* a touching + *-tropos* a turning + English *-y*[3]]

**Th. M.**, Master of Theology.

**tho** or **tho'** (ᴛʜō), *conj., adv.* = though.

**thob** (tōb), *n.* = tobe. [< Arabic *thawb*]

**thole**[1] (thōl), *n.* a peg or pin, often one of a pair, on the gunwale of a boat to hold an oar in rowing. [Middle English *tholle,* probably Old English *thol*]

**thole**[2] (thōl), *v.,* **tholed, thol|ing.** *Archaic.* — ***v.t.*** to be subjected or exposed to (something evil); be afflicted with.
— ***v.i.*** to be patient; wait patiently.
[Old English *tholian* to bear (a burden)]

**tho|lei|ite** (thō′lē īt), *n.* a form of basalt, usually containing quartz and alkalic feldspar: *The tholeiites represent the primary magma generated in the upper mantle beneath the oceans* (Lawrence Ogden). [< German *Tholeiit* < *Tholei,* a village in Germany + *-it* -ite[1]]

**tho|lei|it|ic** (thō′lē it′ik), *adj.* of or containing tholeiite: *They concluded that the lunar rocks are most likely tholeiitic in composition* (George R. Tilton).

**thole|pin** (thōl′pin′), *n.* = thole.

**thol|o|bate** (thol′ə bāt), *n.* the circular substructure on which a dome or cupola rests. [< Greek *thólos* dome, cupola + *-batēs* one that goes < *baínein* to go]

**tho|los** (thō′los), *n., pl.* **-loi** (-loi), **-li** (-lī). **1** a circular domed building or structure; dome; cupola: *the painted tholos of Kazanlik in Bulgaria, whose colors were flaking off in layers* (Harold J. Plenderleith). **2** (in ancient Greece) a circular tomb of the Mycenaean age, domed and lined with masonry; beehive tomb. [< Greek *thólos*]

**Thom|as** (tom′əs), *n.* one of Christ's twelve apostles (in the Bible, John 11:16; 20:24-29). He at first doubted the Resurrection. In the Gospel of John he is surnamed Didymus.

**Tho|mism** (tō′miz əm, thō′-), *n.* the scholastic and theological doctrines of Saint Thomas Aquinas (1225?-1274), Italian philosopher and theologian of the Roman Catholic Church: *During the fifteenth century Thomism was reaching the position of ascendancy which it has held ever since in Catholic thinking* (Listener).

**Tho|mist** (tō′mist, thō′-), *n., adj.* — ***n.*** a follower of Saint Thomas Aquinas.
— ***adj.*** of or having to do with the Thomists or Thomism: *He belonged to the ... Thomist tradition in which he was formed as a philosopher but he was no uncritical disciple of Aquinas* (London Times).

**Tho|mis|tic** (tō mis′tik, thō-), *adj.* = Thomist.

**Thomp|son seedless** (tomp′sən), a variety of a light green or pale yellow grape much grown in California for use in the raisin industry. [< W. B. *Thompson,*1869-1930, an American horticulturist]

**Thomp|son's gazelle** (tomp′sənz), = Thomson's gazelle.

**Thompson submachine gun**, *Trademark.* a small, light, air-cooled, automatic firearm, using .45-caliber ammunition, that can be carried by one man, fired either from the hip or the shoulder; Tommy gun. [American English < General John T. *Thompson,* 1860-1940, U.S. Army, one of the inventors]

**Thom|son's gazelle** (tom′sənz), a small gazelle of East Africa, having prominent white markings on the face. [< Joseph *Thomson,* a Scottish explorer of the 1800's]

**thong** (thông, thong), *n.* **1** a narrow strip of leather or hide, especially one used as a fastening: *The ancient Greeks laced their sandals with thongs.* **2** the lash of a whip, especially one made of plaited strips of leather. [Middle English *thonge,* variant of *thwonge,* Old English *thwang.* See related etym. at **twinge, whang**[3].]

**Thor** (thôr), *n.* the ancient Scandinavian god of thunder and war, bringer of rain to the crops. He destroyed the giants, foes of the gods, with his magic hammer made by the dwarfs. [Old English *Thōr* < Scandinavian (compare Old Icelandic *thōrr*). Compare etym. under **Thursday**]

**tho|ra|cec|to|my** (thôr′ə sek′tə mē, thōr′-), *n., pl.* **-mies.** surgical removal of part of a rib. [< Latin *thōrāx, -ācis* thorax + Greek *ektomḗ* a cutting out]

**tho|rac|ic** (thô ras′ik, thō-), *adj.* of, having to do with, or in the region of the thorax. The thoracic cavity contains the heart and lungs.

**thoracic duct**, the main trunk of the lymphatic system, that passes through the thoracic cavity in front of the spinal column and empties lymph and chyle into the blood through the left subclavian vein.

**tho|rac|i|co|lum|bar** (thô ras′ə kō lum′bər, thō-), *adj.* of or having to do with the thoracic and lumbar regions.

**tho|ra|co|lum|bar** (thôr′ə kō lum′bər, thōr′-), *adj.* of or having to do with the thoracic and lumbar regions, especially of the spine or the sympathetic nervous system. [< Greek *thṓrāx, -ākos* thorax + English *lumbar*]

**tho|ra|co|plas|ty** (thôr′ə kō plas′tē, thōr′-), *n., pl.* **-ties.** plastic surgery on the thorax, especially removal of all or part of some of the ribs to collapse the chest wall, used in some cases of tuberculosis. [< Greek *thṓrāx, -ākos* thorax + *-plastós* something molded]

**tho|ra|cot|o|my** (thôr′ə kot′ə mē, thōr′-), *n., pl.* **-mies.** surgical incision into the thorax.

**tho|rax** (thôr′aks, thōr′-), *n., pl.* **tho|rax|es, tho|ra|ces** (thôr′ə sēz, thōr′-). **1** the part of the body between the neck and the abdomen. A man's chest is his thorax. The thorax contains the chief organs of circulation and respiration. **2** the second of the three main divisions of an insect's body, between the head and the abdomen. See picture under **abdomen.** [< Latin *thōrāx, -ācis* < Greek *thṓrāx, -ākos* chest]

**Tho|ra|zine** (thôr′ə zēn, -zin), *n. Trademark.* chlorpromazine.

**Tho|reau|vi|an** (thə rō′vē ən), *adj., n.* — ***adj.*** of or having to do with the American author and naturalist Henry David Thoreau (1817-1862) or his works: *The Garden City enthusiasts drank a bit too deeply at nature's bosom and intoxicated themselves with Thoreauvian ideals* (Harper's).
— ***n.*** a follower of Thoreau, his ideas, or practices: *The small-town Thoreauvian, the walker in the country* (Atlantic).

**tho|ri|a** (thôr′ē ə, thōr′-), *n.* a heavy white powder, an oxide of thorium, obtained from monazite, and used in making ceramics or as a catalyst. *Formula:* $ThO_2$ [< New Latin *thoria* < *thorium* thorium]

**tho|ri|a|nite** (thôr′ē ə nīt, thōr′-), *n.* a radioactive mineral consisting chiefly of the oxides of thorium, uranium, and other rare metals, found in small brownish-black crystals having a resinous luster.

**tho|ric** (thôr′ik, thōr′-), *adj.* of, having to do with, or derived from thorium.

**tho|rite** (thôr′īt, thōr′-), *n.* **1** a mineral, a silicate of thorium, occurring crystalline or massive, in color orange-yellow to brownish-black or black. *Formula:* $ThSiO_4$ **2** an explosive formerly used in artillery shells as a bursting charge. [< Swedish *thorit* < *Thor* Thor + *-it* -ite[1]]

***tho|ri|um** (thôr′ē əm, thōr′-), *n.* a dark-gray, radioactive, metallic chemical element present in thorite, monazite, and certain other rare minerals. When thorium is bombarded with neutrons, it changes into a form of uranium which is used as an atomic fuel. [< New Latin *thorium* < Swedish *Thor* Thor]

***thorium**

| symbol | atomic number | mass number | oxidation state |
|---|---|---|---|
| Th | 90 | 232 | 4 |

**thorium emanation**, = thoron.

***thorn** (thôrn), *n., v.* — ***n.*** **1a** a sharp point on a stem or branch of a tree or other plant. A thorn usually grows from a bud. *Blackberries, roses, hawthorns, and cacti have thorns.* **SYN:** spine, prickle. **b** a tree or other plant with thorns, especially any shrub or small tree of the hawthorns, such as the Washington thorn, a species native to the southern United States: *Thorns sprang up and choked the wheat.* **c** the wood of any of these plants. **2** a spine or spiny process in an animal. **3a** a letter, originally a rune, used in Old English interchangeably with *edh* to represent either the voiced or voiceless dental fricatives now spelled *th,* as in *then* and *thin,* and still used in the Icelandic alphabet for the voiceless sound. **b** the symbol used in phonetic transcriptions to represent the voiceless dental fricative, as in *thin.*
— ***v.t.*** to vex: *The perplexities with which ... I have been thorned* (Samuel Taylor Coleridge).
**thorn in the flesh** (or **side**), a constant affliction; cause of grief, trouble, or annoyance: *The sharpest thorn in television's side is its own mammoth audience* (Listener).
[Old English *thorn*] — **thorn′like′,** *adj.*

***thorn**
definition 3a

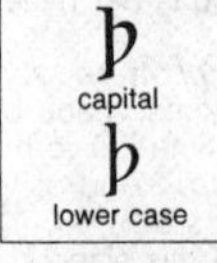

capital — Þacche=Thatch

lower case — þacche=thatch

**thorn apple**, **1a** the fruit of the hawthorn; haw. **b** = hawthorn. **2** the jimson weed or any other datura (so called from the prickly capsules).

**thorn|back** (thôrn′bak′), *n.* **1a** a spiny-backed European ray. **b** any one of certain similar American rays. **2** a large spider crab of Europe.

**thorn|bush** (thôrn′bu̇sh′), *n.* a shrub that produces thorns, such as the hawthorn or bramble: *one mud cabin fenced about with cactus and thornbush* (Manchester Guardian).

**thorned** (thôrnd), *adj.* having thorns.

**thorn forest**, a forest consisting mainly of scrubby and thorny trees, found in western Mexico, parts of India, northern Australia, and northeastern Brazil.

**thorn|less** (thôrn′lis), *adj.* without thorns.

**thorn letter**, = thorn (*n.* def. 3a).

**thorn|y** (thôr′nē), *adj.,* **thorn|i|er, thorn|i|est.** **1** full of thorns or spines; spiny; prickly: *He scratched his hands on the thorny bush.* **2** abounding in thorn-bearing or prickly plants; overgrown with brambles: *He tried to make his way through the thorny thicket.* **3** *Figurative.* troublesome; annoying: *The boys argued over the thorny points in the lesson. Life is thorny* (Samuel Taylor Coleridge). **SYN:** vexatious, difficult. — **thorn′i|ly,** *adv.* — **thorn′i|ness,** *n.*

**thor|o** (thėr′ō), *adj., adv., prep.* = thorough.

**tho|ron** (thôr′on, thōr′-), *n.* a radioactive, gaseous isotope of radon, formed by the disintegration of thorium; thorium emanation. [< *thor*(ium) + *-on*]

**thor|ough** (thėr′ō), *adj., adv., prep.* — ***adj.*** **1a** being all that is needed; complete: *Please make a thorough search for the lost money.* **b** that is fully what is expressed by the noun; thoroughgoing: *a thorough scoundrel.* **2** doing all that should be done; painstaking: *a thorough person. The doctor was very thorough in his examination of the sick child.* **3** going, passing, or extending through (now only in special applications, chiefly with nouns of action or position, being a kind of elliptical use of the adverb).
— ***adv., prep.*** *Archaic.* through. Also, **thoro.**
[Old English *thuruh,* variant of *thurh* through]
— **thor′ough|ly,** *adv.* — **thor′ough|ness,** *n.*

**thorough bass** (bās), *Music.* **1** a bass part extending throughout a piece, having written figures indicating the intended harmony; figured bass. **2** the system or method of so indicating harmonies. **3** the science of harmony in general.

**thorough brace**, or **thor|ough|brace** (thėr′ō brās′), *n.* either of a pair of two strong braces or bands of leather connecting the front and back springs and supporting the body of a coach, carriage, or the like.

**thor|ough|bred** (thėr′ō bred′), *adj., n.* — ***adj.*** **1** of pure breed or stock; bred from pure stock; purebred. **2** *Figurative.* well-bred; thoroughly trained. **3** *Figurative.* having those qualities that are traditionally associated with a thoroughbred horse; high-spirited; mettlesome.
— ***n.*** **1** a thoroughbred animal, especially a horse. **2** *Figurative.* a well-bred or thoroughly trained person.

**Thor|ough|bred** (thėr′ō bred′), *n., adj.* — ***n.*** any one of a breed of horses, used especially in racing, that were originally developed by crossing domestic English mares with Arabian stallions.
— ***adj.*** of, having to do with, or characteristic of Thoroughbreds.

**thor|ough|fare** (thėr′ō fãr′), *n.* **1** a passage, road, or street open at both ends: *A city street is a public thoroughfare.* **2a** a main road; highway: *The Lincoln Highway is one of the main thoroughfares of the United States, extending from New York to San Francisco.* **b** any road, street, or passage: *the busy thoroughfares of a great city.* **3** a passage or way through. **4** *Obsolete.* a going or passing through; passage.
**no thoroughfare**, people are forbidden to go through: *The sign said "no thoroughfare," so instead of driving through the road we took the detour.*
[Middle English *thurghfare* < Old English *thurh* through + *faru* passage, way]

**thor|ough|go|ing** (thėr′ō gō′ing), *adj.* thorough; complete: *Perhaps no coronary patient in medical annals ever had more thoroughgoing treatment than that given the President* (Newsweek).

**thor|ough|paced** (thėr′ō pāst′), *adj.* **1** (of a horse) trained in all paces. **2** *Figurative.* thoroughly trained or accomplished (in something): *A hearty thoroughpaced liar* (Charles Lamb).

**thor|ough|pin** (thėr′ō pin′), *n.* a swelling in the sheath of a tendon above a horse's hock, appearing on both sides of the leg as if a pin were passing through, sometimes causing lameness.

**thor|ough|wort** (thėr′ō wėrt′), *n.* **1** a North American composite herb that has opposite leaves, each pair united at the base so that the stem appears to grow through them, and large corymbs of numerous white flowers; boneset; agueweed; trumpetweed. It is valued for its tonic and diaphoretic properties. **2** any one of several other plants of the same group.

**thorp** or **thorpe** (thôrp), *n. Obsolete.* a hamlet, village, or small town. [Middle English *thorp,* alteration of Old English *throp;* perhaps influenced

by Scandinavian (compare Old Icelandic *thorp*)]
**thort|veit|ite** (thôrt vī′tīt, tôrt-), *n.* a grayish-green crystalline mineral, a silicate of scandium and yttrium. [< Olaus *Thortveit,* a Norwegian mineralogist of the 1900's + *-ite*[1]]
**Thos.,** Thomas.
**those** (ᴛʜōz), *adj., pron.* plural of **that:** *She owns that dog; the boys own those dogs* (adj.). *That is his book; those are my books* (pron.). [Middle English *thos* < *thō,* Old English *thā,* nominative plural of *sē*]
►For *those kind, those sort,* see **kind.**
►See **this** for another usage note.
**Thoth** (thōth, tōt), *n.* the ancient Egyptian god of speech, wisdom, and magic, and, as the scribe of the gods, inventor of letters and numbers, identified with the Greek god Hermes. He is represented with a human body and the head of an ibis or a baboon.
**thou**[1] (ᴛʜou), *pron., sing., nom.* **thou;** *poss.* **thy** or **thine;** *obj.* **thee;** *pl. nom.* **you** or **ye;** *poss.* **your** or **yours;** *obj.* **you** or **ye;** *v. Archaic.* **—*pron.*** the one spoken to; you: *Thou, God, seest me.*
**—*v.t., v.i.*** to use the pronoun *thou* to a person, especially familiarly, to an inferior, in contempt or insult, etc.
[Old English *thū.* Compare etym. under **thee, thy.**]
►**Thou, thy, thine, thee,** and **ye** are archaic pronouns for the second person, used now chiefly in the formal language of church services.
**thou**[2] (thou), *n., pl.* **thou** or **thous.** *Informal.* a thousand dollars, pounds, or other units of currency: *A player . . . went from twenty thou a year to thirty when he was drafted by Oakland* (Atlantic). [short for *thousand*]
**thou.,** thousand.
**though** (ᴛʜō), *conj., adv.* **—*conj.*** **1** in spite of the fact that; notwithstanding the fact that; although: *We take our medicine, though we do not like it. Though it was pouring, the girls went to school.* **2** yet; still; nevertheless; however: *He is better, though not yet cured.* **3** even if; even supposing that: *Though I fail, I shall try again.*
**—*adv.*** however; nevertheless: *I am sorry about our quarrel; you began it, though.* Also, **tho, tho'.**
**as though,** as if; as it would be if: *You look as though you were tired.*
[Middle English *thoh* < Scandinavian (compare Old Icelandic *thō*)]
**thought**[1] (thôt), *n.* **1** what a person thinks; idea; notion: *Her thought was to have a picnic.* **SYN:** See syn. under **idea. 2** the power or process of thinking; mental activity: *Thought helps us solve problems.* **SYN:** cogitation, deliberation, meditation. **3** reasoning: *He applied thought to the problem.* **4** care; attention; regard: *Show some thought for others than yourself. The old man was lost in thought and did not hear us come in.* **SYN:** consideration. **5** an intention; design; purpose: *He doesn't have a thought of leaving.* **6** conception, imagination, or fancy: *a pretty thought.* **7** *Figurative.* a very small amount; little bit; trifle: *Just a thought more sugar, please. Be a thought more polite.* **8** the characteristic thinking of a particular person, group, time, or place: *in modern scientific thought, 16th-century thought.* [Old English *thōht.* See related etym. at **think**[1].]
**thought**[2] (thôt), *v.* the past tense and past participle of **think:** *We thought it would snow yesterday.*
**thought control,** the strict limiting or regimentation of ideas, reasoning, education, research, and the like, in all persons so as to conform to that of a particular group or government.
**thought|ful** (thôt′fəl), *adj.* **1a** full of thought; thinking: *She was thoughtful for a while and then replied, "No."* **SYN:** reflective, meditative, contemplative. **b** indicating thought: *a thoughtful expression.* **2** careful; heedful: *Most speeders are not thoughtful of danger they pose to other drivers.* **3** careful of others; considerate: *She is always thoughtful of her mother.* **—thought′ful|ly,** *adv.* **—thought′ful|ness,** *n.*
**—*Syn.* 3 Thoughtful, considerate** mean giving careful attention to the comfort or feelings of others. **Thoughtful** emphasizes the performance of small services and acts of kindness which anticipate another's needs: *A thoughtful neighbor, knowing the girl was sick and alone, took her some food.* **Considerate** emphasizes concern with the feelings and rights of others and the desire to spare them from discomfort, pain, or unhappiness: *She is considerate enough to tell her parents where she goes.*
**thought|less** (thôt′lis), *adj.* **1** without thought; doing things without thinking; careless: *a thoughtless person, a thoughtless remark. He is a thoughtless boy and is always making blunders.* **SYN:** remiss, heedless. **2** not thinking; unmindful: *thoughtless of danger.* **3** showing little or no care or regard for others; not considerate: *It is thoughtless of her to keep us waiting so long.* **4** = stupid. **—thought′less|ly,** *adv.* **—thought′less|ness,** *n.*

**thought-out** (thôt′out′), *adj.* arrived at or developed by thinking; thoroughly considered: *It is heartening to see such a well-organized and thought-out project* (New York Times).
**thought reading,** = mind reading.
**thought transference,** = telepathy.
**thought|way** (thôt′wā′), *n.* a habit or manner of thinking: *. . . the dominance of technological thoughtways in which means float free of or determine ends* (John R. Seeley).
**thou|sand** (thou′zənd), *n., adj.* **—*n.*** **1** ten hundred; 1,000. *Abbr:* thou. **2** a large number: *thousands of people.*
**—*adj.*** being ten hundred; 1,000.
[Old English *thūsend*]
**thou|sand|fold** (thou′zənd fōld′), *adj., adv., n.* a thousand times as much or as many.
**Thousand Island dressing,** mayonnaise blended with catchup or chili sauce and various relishes. [< *Thousand Islands,* a group of islands in the St. Lawrence River]
**thou|sand-leg|ger** (thou′zənd leg′ər), *n.* a myriapod, especially a chilopod or centipede, as a species common in the southern United States, that infests houses and preys upon household insects: *The thousand-leggers or millipedes never have as many as a thousand legs* (Science News Letter).
**thou|sand-legs** (thou′zənd legz′), *n.* = thousand-legger.
**thou|sandth** (thou′zəndth), *adj., n.* **1** next after the 999th; last in a series of a thousand. **2** one, or being one, of a thousand equal parts.
**thow|less** (thou′lis), *adj. Scottish.* **1** inert; inactive. **2** spiritless; listless. [origin uncertain]
**THPC** (no periods), *Trademark.* a crystalline compound used in making cotton and rayon fabrics flame-resistant. *Formula:* $C_4H_{12}O_4PCl$
**Thra|cian** (thrā′shən), *adj., n.* **—*adj.*** of or having to do with ancient Thrace, a region in the eastern part of the Balkan Peninsula, or its people.
**—*n.*** **1** a person who was born or lived in ancient Thrace: *The Thracians were the most musical of the peoples of Greece* (Edith Hamilton). **2** the Indo-European language of the ancient Thracians, related to Illyrian.
**Thra|co-Il|lyr|i|an** (thrā′kō i lir′ē ən), *adj., n.* **—*adj.*** of or having to do with a branch of the Indo-European language family of which Albanian is the only surviving member.
**—*n.*** a Thraco-Illyrian language, especially Albanian.
**Thra|co-Phryg|i|an** (thrā′kō frij′ē ən, -frij′ən), *adj., n.* **—*adj.*** of or having to do with Thracian and Phrygian, two ancient Indo-European languages.
**—*n.*** either of those languages.
**thrall** (thrôl), *n., adj., v.* **—*n.*** **1** a person in bondage; slave; bondman: *The thralls did the work of the castle.* **SYN:** serf. **2** *Figurative.* a person who is a slave to something: *a thrall to alcohol. Slaves of drink and thralls of sleep* (Shakespeare). *I am . . . made up of likings and dislikings— the veriest thrall to sympathies, apathies, antipathies* (Charles Lamb). **3** bondage; slavery; thralldom: (*Figurative.*) *to be in thrall to drink.*
**—*adj.*** *Archaic.* that is a thrall; in thrall.
**—*v.t.*** *Archaic.* to put or hold in thralldom or bondage; enslave.
[Old English *thræl* < Scandinavian (compare Old Icelandic *thræll*)]
**thrall|dom** or **thral|dom** (thrôl′dəm), *n.* bondage; slavery; servitude: *A sorcerer had the knight in thralldom.*
**thrang** (thrang), *n., v., adj. Scottish.* throng.
**thrash** (thrash), *v., n.* **—*v.t.*** **1** to beat as punishment; flog: *The man thrashed the boy for stealing apples.* **SYN:** trounce. **2** to move, swing, or beat vigorously to and fro or up and down: *to thrash one's arms against one's body to keep warm, to thrash one's legs in the water.* **3** to thresh (wheat, rye, or other grain). **4** *Nautical.* to force (a ship) to move forward against a wind, sea, or tide.
**—*v.i.*** **1** to move violently; toss; lash: *children thrashing about in the water. Branches thrashed against the window. Unable to sleep, the patient thrashed about in his bed.* **2** to thresh grain. **3** *Nautical.* to make way against the wind, tide, or sea; beat.
**—*n.*** **1** the act of thrashing or threshing; beating. **2** *Nautical.* a making way against the wind, tide, or sea. **3** a swimming movement in which the legs are moved alternately and rapidly up and down; flutter kick.
**thrash out,** *Figurative.* to settle by thorough discussion: *. . . the problem has not always been fully and adequately thrashed out* (Manchester Guardian).
**thrash over,** *Figurative.* to go over again and again: *The jurors kept thrashing over the evidence without being able to reach a verdict.*
[variant of Middle English *threshen* to thresh]
**thrash|er**[1] (thrash′ər), *n.* **1** a person or thing that thrashes. **2** = thresher (def. 3). [< *thrash* + *-er*[1]]
**thrash|er**[2] (thrash′ər), *n.* any one of several long-tailed North American birds related to the mockingbird, such as the brown thrasher of eastern North America. A thrasher looks somewhat like a thrush. [American English, apparently variant (influenced by *thrasher*[1]) of English dialectal *thresher, thrusher,* probably < *thrush*[1]]
**thrasher shark,** = thresher (def. 3).
**thrash|ing** (thrash′ing), *n.* the act of beating or flogging.
**thra|son|ic** (thrə son′ik), *adj.* = thrasonical.
**thra|son|i|cal** (thrə son′ə kəl), *adj.* boasting; bragging. [< Latin *Thrasō, -ōnis,* a braggart soldier in Terence's *Eunuchus* (< Greek *Thrásōn* < *thrasýs* bold) + English *-ic* + *-al*[1]] **—thra|son′i|cal|ly,** *adv.*
**thraw**[1] (thrô, thrä), *n. Scottish.* **1** a turn or twist around, as to one side; wrench; crook; warp. **2** throe. [variant of *throe*]
**thraw**[2] (thrô, thrä), *v.t., v.i., n. Scottish.* throw.
**thrawn** (thrôn, thrän), *adj. Scottish.* **1a** twisted; crooked. **b** misshapen; distorted. **2a** perverse; contrary. **b** crabbed; peevish. [variant of *thrown*] **—thrawn′ly,** *adv.* **—thrawn′ness,** *n.*
**thread** (thred), *n., v., adj.* **—*n.*** **1a** cotton, silk, flax, or some similar material spun out into a fine cord. You sew with thread. **b** each of the lengths of yarn that form the warp and woof of a woven fabric. **c** an article of clothing; garment; stitch: *not a thread fit to wear.* **2** something long and slender or fine like a thread, such as a fine ligament, strand, stream, line, or streak: *a thread of sand pouring down an hourglass, a thread of light coming through the crack in the door. Threads of gold could be seen in the ore. The spider hung by a thread.* **3** *Figurative.* the main thought that connects the parts of a story, speech, or the like: *Something distracted him and he lost the thread of their conversation. I return to the thread of my story* (Edward G. Bulwer-Lytton). **4** the winding, sloping ridge of a bolt, screw, or pipe joint. The thread of a nut interlocks with the thread of a bolt. **5** *Figurative.* **a** a course; progression. **b** = thread of life.
**—*v.t.*** **1** to pass a thread through: *She threaded her needle.* **2** to string on a thread: *She threaded a hundred beads in a pattern to make a necklace.* **3** *Figurative.* to pass like a thread through; pervade. **4** *Figurative.* **a** to make (one's way) carefully or skillfully: *He threaded his way through the crowd.* **b** to find one's way through: *A labyrinth of narrow streets . . . rarely threaded by the stranger* (George Eliot). **5** to form a thread on (a bolt, screw, pipe joint, or nut): *Screws and nuts are threaded by special machines.* **6** *Electricity.* to cause the formation of lines of force around (a conductor).
**—*v.i.*** **1** to form into a thread: *Cook the syrup until it threads.* **2** *Figurative.* to make one's way; go in a winding course; weave in and out; wind: *The path threads through the forest. The speedy halfback threaded through the field for a touchdown.*
**—*adj.*** of, made of, or like thread or a thread.
**hang by** (or **on** or **upon**) **a thread,** to be in a precarious condition (often with reference to the legend of Damocles): *The old man's life hung by a thread.*
**threads,** *U.S. Slang.* clothes: *A down-to-earth club, whose youthful patrons seem more interested in music and dancing than in ogling other people's threads* (New Yorker).
[Old English *thrǣd* fine cord. See related etym. at **throw.**] **—thread′er,** *n.* **—thread′less,** *adj.* **—thread′like′,** *adj.*
**thread|bare** (thred′bãr′), *adj.* **1** having the nap worn off; worn so much that the threads show: *a threadbare coat. Nail to the mast her holy flag, Set every threadbare sail* (Oliver Wendell Holmes). **2** wearing clothes worn to the threads; shabby; seedy: *a threadbare beggar.* **3** *Figurative.* very poor; hard up. **4** *Figurative.* old and worn; stale: *a threadbare joke. Saying "I forgot" is a threadbare excuse.* **SYN:** hackneyed, trite. **—thread′bare′ness,** *n.*
**thread|fin** (thred′fin′), *n.* any one of a group of fishes having threadlike rays extending beyond the pectoral fins, such as the barbudo.
**thread glass,** glassware with threads of glass on the surface, usually on the necks of bottles, vases, and pitchers, and on the rims of plates.
**thread lace,** lace made of linen thread, as distinguished from cotton and silk laces.
**thread mark,** a thin, highly-colored thread put into paper money to make counterfeiting difficult.
**thread of life, the,** the imaginary thread spun

**Pronunciation Key:** hat, āge, cãre, fär; let, ēqual, tėrm; it, īce; hot, ōpen, ôrder; oil, out; cup, pu̇t, rüle; child; long; thin; ᴛʜen; zh, measure; ə represents **a** in about, **e** in taken, **i** in pencil, **o** in lemon, **u** in circus.

and cut by the Fates. It is supposed to symbolize the course and termination of one's existence.

**thread|worm** (thred′wėrm′), *n.* any one of various threadlike nematode worms, especially the pinworm or a filaria.

**thread|y** (thred′ē), *adj.*, **thread|i|er, thread|i|est.** **1** consisting of or resembling a thread; threadlike. **2a** composed of fine fibers; stringy; fibrous. **b** forming strings; viscid; ropy: *a thready liquid.* **3** thin and feeble: *The pulse becomes quick ... and so thready, it is not like a pulse at all, but like a string vibrating just underneath the skin* (Florence Nightingale). **4** lacking in fullness: *a thready voice.* —**thread′i|ness,** *n.*

**threap** (thrēp), *v.t. Scottish.* **1** to rebuke; chide; scold. **2** to assert or maintain obstinately. [Old English *thrēapian*]

**threat** (thret), *n., v.* —*n.* **1** a statement of what will be done to hurt or punish someone: *The boys stopped playing ball in the classroom because of the janitor's threats to report it to the principal.* **SYN:** commination, intimidation. **2** *Figurative.* a sign, cause, or source of possible evil or harm: *Those black clouds are a threat of rain. Poverty and disease are threats to society. Germany had been a threat, a menace* (H. G. Wells).
—*v.t., v.i. Archaic.* to threaten.
[Old English *thrēat* crowd, troop; oppression]

**threat|en** (thret′ən), *v.t.* **1** to make a threat against; say what will be done to hurt or punish: *to threaten a person with imprisonment. The farmer threatened to shoot any dog that killed one of his sheep.* **2** *Figurative.* to give warning of (coming trouble); be a sign of (possible evil or harm): *Black clouds threaten a storm.* **SYN:** portend, presage, forebode, augur. **3** *Figurative.* to be a cause or source of possible evil or harm to: *A flood threatened the city.* —*v.i.* **1** to be or pose a threat. **2** to say threats: *She threatens and scolds too much. Do you mean to threaten?* **3** to allow oneself to be threatened: *Say what you will, I don't threaten easily.* [Old English *thrēatnian* press; urge on; afflict < *thrēat*; see etym. under **threat**] —**threat′en|er,** *n.* —**threat′en|ing|ly,** *adv.*
—*Syn. v.t.* **1 Threaten, menace** mean to indicate the intention of harming someone. **Threaten** applies when one is trying to force someone to do (or not to do) something and warns him of the consequences if he does not obey: *The robber threatened to gag her if she screamed.* **Menace** applies when one tries to frighten someone by means of a look, movement, or weapon: *He menaced her with a gun.*

**three** (thrē), *n., adj.* —*n.* **1** one more than two; 3: *One yard is three feet.* **2** a set of three persons or things: *to arrive in threes.* **SYN:** trio, threesome, triplet. **3** a card domino, throw of dice, billiard ball, or other playing piece with three spots or a "3" on it; trey.
—*adj.* one more than two; 3. Three feet make one yard.
[Old English *thrēo,* feminine and neuter of *thrīe*]

**three-bag|ger** (thrē′bag′ər), *n. Slang.* a three-base hit in baseball; triple.

**three-ball** (thrē′bôl′), *adj.* played with three balls, as a golf match.

**three-base hit** (thrē′bās′), a safe hit for three bases in baseball; triple.

**three-card monte** (thrē′kärd′), a Mexican gambling game, in which three cards are thrown on the table face down, the opposing players betting on the position of one of the cards.

**three-col|or** (thrē′kul′ər), *adj.* of or having to do with a photomechanical process of printing in which a colored picture or letterpress is produced by the superposition of the three primary colors or their complementaries.

**three-cor|nered** (thrē′kôr′nərd), *adj.* **1** having three corners; tricornered: *a three-cornered hat.* **2** of, having to do with, or involving three persons or parties: *a three-cornered general election contest.*

**3-D** or **three-D** (thrē′dē′), *adj., n. Informal.* —*adj.* three-dimensional; stereoscopic: ... *a 3-D microscope which magnifies clearly and exactly the characteristics of blood cells* (Newsweek). ... *gift shops that sell 3-D tableaux of the Last Supper* (Time).
—*n.* **1** a three-dimensional form: *to see an image in 3-D.* **2** a photographic or optical system or process that produces three-dimensional images: *Anatomy has seized upon 3-D to give a new view for teaching and research purposes* (Science News Letter).

**three-day measles** (thrē′dā′), = German measles.

**three-deck|er** (thrē′dek′ər), *n.* **1a** a ship having three decks. **b** a warship that used to carry guns on three decks. **2** a thing having three stories, layers, or parts, such as a novel in three volumes or a sandwich made with three slices of bread.

**three-di|men|sion|al** (thrē′də men′shə nəl), *adj.* **1** having three dimensions: *The first quality to appreciate in sculpture is its volume or mass—the fact that it is three-dimensional* (Sir Herbert Read). **2** seeming to have depth as well as height and breadth; appearing to exist in three dimensions; stereoscopic: *a three-dimensional motion picture.* **3** *Figurative.* **a** real; substantial: *They [the characters] are less three-dimensional and more abstract in the ballet than in the play* (New York Times). **b** well-rounded; complete; solid: *a three-dimensional study of a problem.* Also, **third-dimensional, tridimensional.** —**three′-di|men′sion|al|ly,** *adv.*

**three-di|men|sion|al|i|ty** (thrē′də men′shə nal′ə tē), *n.* the condition or quality of being three-dimensional. Also, **tridimensionality.**

**three-dimensional sound,** sound by stereophonic reproduction.

**three|fold** (thrē′fōld′), *adj., adv., n.* —*adj.* **1** three times as much or as many. **SYN:** treble. **2** having three parts.
—*adv.* in a threefold manner; trebly; triply.
—*n.* three times as much or as many; three: *to increase by threefold.*

**three-four** (thrē′fôr′, -fōr′), *adj. Music.* with three quarter notes in a measure or bar: *a three-four time or rhythm.*

**three-is|land ship** (thrē′ī′lənd), a general cargo ship having a raised forecastle, bridge, and poop. [because the three structures stand out above the main deck like islands]

**three-leg|ged race** (thrē′leg′id, -legd′), a race run by couples, the right leg of one person being bound to the left leg of the other.

**three-line whip** (thrē′līn′), *British.* the strongest form of directive issued by a political party to its members to attend a parliamentary debate. It is underlined three times to emphasize its urgency.

**three-mast|er** (thrē′mas′tər, -mäs′-), *n.* a ship having three masts.

**three-mile limit** (thrē′mīl′), the distance from the shore that, according to international law, is included within the jurisdiction of the country possessing the coast.

**three of a kind,** three cards of the same rank, such as three aces.

**three-part time** (thrē′pärt′), *Music.* three beats, or a multiple of three beats, to the measure.

**three|pence** (thrip′əns, threp′-, thrup′-), *n.* **1** three British old pennies; three pence. **2** a British coin of this value, worth about 3 cents. It is no longer legal tender. Also, **thrippence.**

**three|pen|ny** (thrip′ə nē, thrip′nē; threp′-, thrup′-; thrē′pen′ē), *adj.* **1** worth, costing, or amounting to threepence. **2** *Figurative.* of little worth; cheap; paltry.

**threepenny bit** or **piece,** = threepence.

**three-phase** (thrē′fāz′), *adj.* **1** of or having to do with a combination of three electric currents caused by alternating electromotive forces differing in phase by one third of a cycle (120 degrees). **2** having three phases.

**three-piece** (thrē′pēs′), *adj.* having three pieces. A three-piece suit has trousers, jacket, and vest (for men), or skirt, jacket, and topcoat (for women).

**three-ply** (thrē′plī′), *adj.* having three thicknesses, layers, folds, or strands.

**three-point landing** (thrē′point′), a landing of an aircraft at an angle with the ground that is the same as that of the craft when at rest on the ground. Wheels of the main landing gear, and the skid under the tail, touch the ground at the same time.

**three-port** (thrē′pôrt′, -pōrt′), *adj.* of or having to do with a type of two-cycle internal-combustion engine having three ports for the intake, transfer, and exhaust.

**three-quar|ter** (thrē′kwôr′tər), *adj., n.* —*adj.* consisting of or involving three quarters of a whole. A three-quarter portrait usually shows three quarters of the figure.
—*n.* = three-quarter back.

**three-quarter back,** *Rugby.* one of the four backs whose normal position is in front of the fullback and behind the halfbacks.

**three-quarter binding,** a style of bookbinding in which the same material is used for the back, about one third of each cover, and sometimes the corners, the remainder of the covers having different material.

**three-quar|ter-bound** (thrē′kwôr′tər bound′), *adj.* (of a book) bound in three-quarter binding.

**three-ring circus** (thrē′ring′), **1** a very large circus that has three rings in which separate acts can be presented at the same time. **2** *Informal, Figurative.* any activity or undertaking having a great variety of things going on at the same time.

**three R's,** reading, writing, and arithmetic.

**three|score** (thrē′skôr′, -skōr′), *adj.* three times twenty; 60.

**three|some** (thrē′səm), *n., adj.* —*n.* **1** a group or set of three people. **2a** a game or match played by three people. **b** *Golf.* a match of three players using only two balls in which one player plays against the other two, each of whom takes alternate strokes at the second ball. **c** the players.
—*adj.* consisting or composed of three; performed by three together; threefold; triple.
[originally, Scottish adjective < Old English *thrēo* three + *-sum* -some[2]]

**three-square** (thrē′skwãr′), *adj.* having three equal sides; equilaterally triangular.

**three-toed sloth** (thrē′tōd′), a variety of sloth with three toes on each foot; ai.

**three-toed woodpecker,** either of two woodpeckers of northern North America that lack the inner hind toe and have a yellow crown.

**three-way** (thrē′wā′), *adj.* **1** going three ways; extending in three directions: *a three-way relationship.* **2** consisting of or involving three persons or groups: *a three-way race for Congress. A three-way partnership would be unusual* (New York Times). **3** used in three ways or for three purposes: *"Three-way grapes" ... are used as fresh table grapes, as wine grapes, and for raisins* (L. E. Davies). **4** providing three degrees of illumination: *a three-way electric bulb.* **5** having to do with or designating a valve or cock with one inlet and two alternative outlets.

**three-wheel|er** (thrē′hwē′lər), *n.* a tricycle or other vehicle running on three wheels.

**Three Wise Men,** three men who came from the East to honor the infant Jesus; the Magi. In medieval legend they became three kings, named Gaspar (or Kaspar), Melchior, and Balthasar.

**threm|ma|tol|o|gy** (threm′ə tol′ə jē), *n.* the science of breeding or propagating animals and plants under domestication. [< Greek *thrémma, -atos* nursling (< stem of *tréphein* nourish) + English *-logy*]

**thre|net|ic** (thri net′ik), *adj.* having to do with a threnody; mournful. [< Greek *thrēnētikós*]

**thre|net|i|cal** (thri net′ə kəl), *adj.* = threnetic.

**thre|node** (thrē′nōd, thren′ōd), *n.* = threnody.

**thre|no|di|al** (thri nō′dē əl), *adj.* having to do with or like a threnody.

**thre|nod|ic** (thri nod′ik), *adj.* = threnodial.

**thren|o|dist** (thren′ə dist), *n.* the composer of a threnody: *Peace, then, rhetoricians, false threnodists of false liberty!* (Thomas De Quincey).

**thren|o|dy** (thren′ə dē), *n., pl.* **-dies.** a song of lamentation, especially at a person's death; dirge: *Cyrus Sulzberger's "My Brother Death" is a profoundly moving threnody on man's fate* (New York Times). [< Greek *threnoidiā* < *thrênos* a lament (< *threîsthai* to shriek, cry aloud) + *ōidē* song, ode]

**thre|o|nine** (thrē′ə nēn, -nin), *n.* a crystalline amino acid considered essential to human nutrition. It is a product of the hydrolysis of proteins. *Formula:* $C_4H_9NO_3$

**thresh** (thresh), *v., n.* —*v.t.* **1** to separate the grain or seeds from (wheat, rye, or other grain); thrash: *Nowadays most farmers use a machine to thresh their wheat.* **SYN:** sift. **2** to toss about; move violently; thrash.
—*v.i.* **1** to thresh grain. **2** to toss about; move violently; thrash.
—*n.* the act of threshing.
**thresh out,** *Figurative.* to settle by thorough discussion; thrash out: *All this could have been threshed out in private, without a court of inquiry* (Maclean's).
**thresh over,** *Figurative.* to go over again and again; thrash over: *They threshed over the problem all night long.*
[Middle English *thresshen,* variant of Old English *therscan* to beat; thresh with a flail; (originally) to tread, tramp]

**thresh|er** (thresh′ər), *n.* **1** a person or thing that threshes. **2** a machine for threshing; threshing machine. **3** a large shark of the Atlantic, with a very long, curved tail; thrasher; thrasher shark. It supposedly beats the water with its tail to round up the small fish on which it feeds.

**thresher shark,** = thresher (def. 3).

**thresher whale,** = killer whale.

**threshing machine,** a machine used for separating the grain or seeds from the stalks and other parts of wheat, rye, or other grain; thresher.

**thresh|old** (thresh′ōld, -hōld), *n.* **1** a piece of wood or stone under a door; doorsill. **2** the entrance to a house or building; doorway. **3** *Figurative.* a point of entering; beginning point: *to be at the threshold of war. The scientist was on the threshold of an important discovery. I was on the threshold of a surprising adventure* (W. Somerset Maugham). **4** *Psychology, Physiology.* the point at which a given stimulus begins to be perceptible, or the point at which two stimuli can be differentiated; limen: *a person with a high threshold of pain.* [Old English *threscold.* Apparently related to **thresh** in the sense "to tread, tramp".]

**threw** (thrü), *v.* past tense of **throw:** *He threw a stone and ran away.*

**thrice** (thrīs), *adv.* **1** three times: *He knocked*

thrice. 2 in threefold quantity or degree: *The giant was thrice as strong as an ordinary man.* 3 *Figurative.* very; greatly; extremely. [Middle English *thriës,* Old English *thriwa* < *thrīe* three + adverbial genitive *-s*]

**thrid** (thrid), *v.,* **thrid|ded, thrid|ding.** *Archaic.* to thread.

**thrift** (thrift), *n.* **1** absence of waste; saving; economical management; habit of saving: *By thrift she managed to get along on her small salary. A bank account encourages thrift.* **SYN:** economy, frugality. **2** any one of a genus of low plants with pink, white, or lavender flowers that grow on mountains and along seashores; statice. **3** vigorous growth, as of a plant. **4** *Archaic or Dialect.* industry; labor; employment. **5** *Obsolete.* prosperity; success. [Middle English *thrift* < *thriven* to thrive; perhaps influenced by Scandinavian (compare Old Icelandic *thrift,* variant of *thrif* prosperity)]

**thrift|less**(thrift′lis), *adj.* without thrift; wasteful. **SYN:** improvident. —**thrift′less|ly,** *adv.* —**thrift′less|ness,** *n.*

**thrift shop,** *U.S.* a shop in which second-hand articles in good condition are sold at low prices and usually paid for by the shopkeeper after he has sold them: *The entire proceeds from the sale of donated articles at the thrift shop have gone to charity* (New York Times).

**thrift|y** (thrif′tē), *adj.,* **thrift|i|er, thrift|i|est.** **1** careful in spending; economical; saving: *a thrifty housewife.* **SYN:** provident, frugal, sparing. See syn. under **economical. 2** thriving; flourishing; vigorous: *a thrifty plant.* **3** prosperous; well-to-do; successful: *The countryside had many fine, thrifty farms.* —**thrift′i|ly,** *adv.* —**thrift′i|ness,** *n.*

**thrill** (thril), *n., v.* —*n.* **1** a shivering, exciting feeling: *a thrill of pleasure or fear, the thrill of adventure or discovery. She gets a thrill whenever she sees a parade.* **2** a vibration or quivering; throbbing; tremor. **3** an abnormal vibration or fine tremor that can be heard with a stethoscope when listening to the heart or lungs. [< verb]
—*v.t.* **1** to give a shivering, exciting feeling to: *Stories of adventure thrilled him.* **2** to cause to tremble or quiver; make vibrate: *to thrill the air with music.*
—*v.i.* **1** to have a shivering, exciting feeling: *The children thrilled with joy at the sight of the parade.* **2** to tremble; quiver: *Her voice thrilled with excitement.* **SYN:** vibrate, throb.
[variant of *thirl*[1]]

**thrill|er** (thril′ər), *n.* **1** a person or thing that thrills: *still smarting under the sting of losing last night's ten-inning thriller* (New York Times). *For 75 minutes the plane circled. The final landing was a thriller* (Time). **2** *Informal.* a play, story, or motion picture filled with excitement or suspense: *There has been no better thriller in London since the war than "Dial M for Murder," produced at the Westminster Theatre* (London Times).

**thrill|er-dill|er** (thril′ər dil′ər), *n. Slang.* a sensational story; thriller.

**thrill|ing** (thril′ing), *adj.* **1** affecting with a thrill of emotion: *wild thrilling sounds* (Herman Melville). **2** vibrating or quivering. **3** *Obsolete.* piercing or penetrating. —**thrill′ing|ly,** *adv.* —**thrill′ing|ness,** *n.*

**thrip|pence** (thrip′əns), *n.* = threepence.

**thrips** (thrips), *n.sing.* (*occasionally plural with singular* **thrip**). any one of an order of small, narrow, winged or wingless insects. The winged species usually have four narrow wings fringed with hairs. Most varieties are destructive to plants and grains. Some spread virus and fungus. [< Latin *thrips* < Greek *thrips, thripós* woodworm]

**thrive** (thrīv), *v.i.,* **throve** or **thrived, thrived** or **thriv|en** (thriv′ən), **thriv|ing. 1** to grow or develop well; grow vigorously: *Most flowers will not thrive without sunshine.* **SYN:** flourish. **2** to be successful; grow rich; turn out well; prosper: *He that would thrive Must rise at five He that hath thriven May lie till seven* (John Clarke). **SYN:** succeed. [Middle English *thrifen,* perhaps < Scandinavian (compare Old Icelandic *thrīfa*)] —**thriv′ing|ly,** *adv.*

**thriv|er** (thrī′vər), *n.* a person or thing that thrives.

**thro′** or **thro** (thrü), *prep., adv., adj.* = through.

∗**throat** (thrōt), *n., v.* —*n.* **1** the front of the neck, containing the passages from the mouth to the stomach and lungs: *She had a muffler wrapped around her throat.* **2** the passage from the mouth to the stomach or the lungs: *A bone stuck in his throat.* **3** any narrow passage: *The throat of the mine was blocked by fallen rocks.* **4** the narrow or narrowest part of anything, such as the shaft of a column, the handle of a racket, or the fluke of an anchor.
—*v.t.* **1** to utter from or in one's throat; speak or sing throatily. **2** to provide with a narrow part or passageway; groove, flute, or channel.
**at each other's throat** (or **throats**), fighting or quarrelling: *Nations that had formerly been at each other's throats had learned to live together via the trade route* (New York Times).
**cut one's throat,** to defeat or destroy one; put an end to someone: *Leaders who have been actively trying to cut each other's throats were suddenly enveloped in each other's arms* (Time).
**have** (or **hold**) **by the throat,** to have at one's mercy; hold in one's power: *They can expect no public sympathy for ... an attempt to inflate their salaries to vast levels by, as a body, holding a proud airline by the throat* (London Times).
**jump down one's throat,** *Informal.* to attack or criticize a person with sudden violence: *The fact that he has made a mistake is no excuse for jumping down his throat.*
**lie in one's throat,** to lie brazenly and boldly: *Whoever charged him with the plot lied in his throat* (Washington Irving).
**lump in one's throat.** See under **lump**[1].
**ram** (**force, shove,** or **cram**) **down one's throat,** to force (an opinion, situation, or circumstance) on one's acceptance: *The referendum proposal had to be rammed down the throats of De Gaulle's unhappy ministers* (Atlantic).
**stick in one's throat,** to be hard or unpleasant to say: *Amen stuck in my throat* (Shakespeare).
[Old English *throte.* See related etym. at **throttle.**]

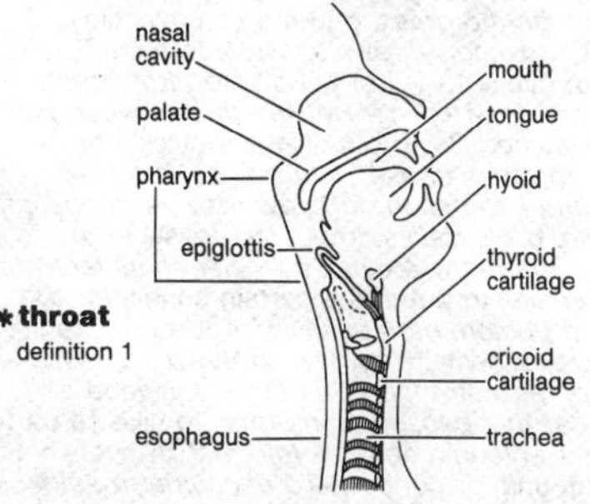


∗**throat**
definition 1

**throat-cut|ting** (thrōt′kut′ing), *n.,* or **throat cutting, 1** a cutting of the throat to maim or kill. **2** *Informal.* a deliberate attempt to harm or ruin another or others for personal advantage in a competitive situation.

**-throated,** *combining form.* having a ____ throat: *White-throated = having a white throat.*

**throat|latch** (thrōt′lach′), *n.* a strap that passes under a horse's throat and helps to hold the bridle in place. See picture at **harness.**

**throat sweetbread,** the thymus gland, especially of a calf, used as food.

**throat|y** (thrō′tē), *adj.,* **throat|i|er, throat|i|est. 1** produced or modified in the throat; guttural or velar: *The young girl had a throaty voice.* **2** low-pitched and resonant: *The engine started with a throaty roar.* —**throat′i|ly,** *adv.* —**throat′i|ness,** *n.*

**throb** (throb), *v.,* **throbbed, throb|bing,** *n.* —*v.i.* **1** to beat rapidly or strongly: *a heart throbbing with joy. The long climb up the hill made her heart throb. His wounded arm throbbed with pain.* **SYN:** pulsate, palpitate. **2** to beat steadily: *propellers or engines that throb.* **3** to quiver; tremble: *The leaves throbbed in the breeze.*
—*n.* **1** a rapid or strong beat: *A sudden throb of pain shot through his head.* **2** a steady beat: *the throb of a pulse.* **3** a quiver; tremble.
[probably imitative] —**throb′ber,** *n.* —**throb′bing|ly,** *adv.*

**throe** (thrō), *n.* a violent spasm or pang; great pain.
**throes, a** anguish; agony: *in the very throes of its fell despair* (Benjamin Disraeli). **b** *Figurative.* a desperate struggle; violent disturbance: *When a nation is in the throes of revolution, wild spirits are abroad in the storm* (James Froude). **c** labor pangs (in childbirth): *My womb ... Prodigious motion felt and rueful throes* (Milton).
[variant of Middle English *throwe;* origin uncertain]

**throm|bi** (throm′bī), *n.* plural of **thrombus.**

**throm|bin** (throm′bin), *n.* an enzyme in blood serum which reacts with fibrinogen to form fibrin, causing blood to clot.

**throm|bo|cyte** (throm′bə sīt), *n.* = blood platelet. [< Greek *thrómbos* a clot + English *-cyte*]

**throm|bo|cy|to|pe|ni|a** (throm′bə sī′tə pē′nē ə), *n.* an abnormal decrease of thrombocytes in the blood. [< *thrombocyte* + Greek *peniā* poverty]

**throm|bo|em|bol|ic** (throm′bō em bol′ik), *adj.* of, having to do with, or characterized by thromboembolism.

**throm|bo|em|bo|lism** (throm′bō em′bə liz əm), *n.* the obstruction of a blood vessel by a clot that has broken loose from its site of formation, a common and very serious complication of coronary thrombosis.

**throm|bo|gen** (throm′bə jen), *n.* = prothrombin.

**throm|bo|ki|nase** (throm′bō kī′nās, -kin′ās), *n.* an enzyme that promotes the conversion of prothrombin into thrombin and therefore is active in the clotting of blood. [< Greek *thrómbos* a clot + English *kinase*]

**throm|bo|phle|bi|tis** (throm′bō fli bī′tis), *n.* the formation of a thrombus in an injured or infected blood vessel, especially in one of the veins of an arm or leg. [< Greek *thrómbos* a clot + English *phlebitis*]

**throm|bo|plas|tic** (throm′bō plas′tik), *adj.* promoting or having to do with the clotting of blood. [< Greek *thrómbos* a clot + English *plastic*] —**throm′bo|plas′ti|cal|ly,** *adv.*

**throm|bo|plas|tin** (throm′bō plas′tin), *n.* **1** a protein substance found in the blood and in tissues, which promotes the conversion or prothrombin into thrombin. **2** = thrombokinase.

**throm|bosed** (throm bōzd′, throm′bōzd), *adj.* affected by thrombosis: *thrombosed arteries.*

**throm|bo|sis** (throm bō′sis), *n., pl.* **-ses** (-sēz). the formation of a thrombus or blood clot; coagulation of blood in a blood vessel or in the heart, causing an obstruction of the circulation. [< New Latin *thrombosis* < Greek *thrómbōsis,* ultimately < *thrómbos* a clot]

**throm|bot|ic** (throm bot′ik), *adj.* **1** of or like thrombosis. **2** caused by or having to do with thrombosis.

**throm|bus** (throm′bəs), *n., pl.* **-bi.** a fibrous clot which forms in a blood vessel or within the heart and obstructs the circulation: *Coronary thrombosis is the result of a ... thrombus, forming in a coronary artery and shutting off part of the blood supply of the heart muscles* (Nathan W. Shock). [< New Latin *thrombus* < Greek *thrómbos* a clot]

**throne** (thrōn), *n., v.,* **throned, thron|ing.** —*n.* **1** the chair on which a king, queen, pope, bishop, or other person of high rank sits during ceremonies: *Ye also shall sit upon twelve thrones, judging the twelve tribes of Israel* (Matthew 19:28). **2** the position, power, or authority of a king, queen, or other ruler: *a tottering throne, to gamble for a throne. The throne of England commands respect but does not command armies.* **SYN:** sovereignty, dominion. **3** a person who sits on a throne; sovereign: *to address oneself to the throne.*
—*v.t.* = enthrone.
—*v.i.* to be enthroned.
**ascend the throne,** to become king or queen: *Elizabeth II ascended the British throne in 1952.*
**take the throne,** to become king or reigning queen; succeed to the throne: *Upon the death of his father the young prince took the throne.*
**thrones,** the third order of angels, in the highest of the three hierarchies: *Thrones, who God's Judgments hear, and then proclaim* (Thomas Ken).
[< Latin *thronus* < Greek *thrónos* chair, seat, throne]

**throne room,** a palace room in which a sovereign formally receives visitors from the throne.

**throng** (thrông, throng), *n., v., adj.* —*n.* **1** a crowd; great number; multitude: *The streets were filled with throngs of people* (Dickens). *Not in the shouts and plaudits of the throng, But in ourselves are triumph and defeat* (Longfellow). **SYN:** host, mass, pack. See syn. under **crowd. 2** a pressing or crowding; crowded condition: *Went the summons forth Into all quarters, and the throng began* (William Cowper).
—*v.t.* **1** to crowd; fill with a crowd: *People thronged the theater to see the famous actress.* **SYN:** cram, stuff. **2** to crowd around and press upon; jostle.
—*v.i.* to come together in a crowd; go or press in large numbers: *The people thronged to see the king.* (*Figurative.*) *A thousand fantasies Begin to throng into my memory* (Milton).
—*adj. Especially Scottish.* crowded; thronged. Also, *Scottish,* **thrang.**
[Middle English *throng, thrang,* probably Old English *gethrang,* related to *thringan* to crowd] —**throng′er,** *n.*

**thros|tle** (thros′əl), *n. British.* **1** a thrush, especially the song thrush. **2** a kind of spinning machine that draws, twists, and winds cotton, wool, or other thread, in one continuous action. [Old English *throstle*]

**throt|tle** (throt′əl), *n., v.,* **-tled, -tling.** —*n.* **1** a valve regulating the flow of steam, gasoline va-

**Pronunciation Key:** hat, āge, cãre, fär; let, ēqual, tėrm; it, īce; hot, ōpen, ôrder; oil, out; cup, pu̇t, rüle; child; long; thin; ᴛʜen; zh, measure; ə represents **a** in about, **e** in taken, **i** in pencil, **o** in lemon, **u** in circus.

por, or other fuel or driving fluid or gas, to an engine: *He slowed down the motorcycle and closed the throttle.* See diagram under **carburetor**. **2** a lever, pedal, or other regulator working such a valve. The throttle of a car is connected to the accelerator. **3** *Informal* or *Dialect.* the throat or windpipe. **4** the fact or condition of being throttled: *excess throttle in the engine.* **5** *Figurative.* something that throttles: *a monetary throttle in the market. His left hand ... is on the throttle of policy* (Harper's).
—*v.t.* **1** to stop the breath of by pressure on the throat; strangle: *The thief throttled the dog to keep it from barking.* SYN: choke, suffocate, garrote. **2** *Figurative.* to check or stop the flow of; suppress: *High tariffs throttle trade between countries.* SYN: obstruct. **3** to silence or check as if choking. **4a** to check, stop, or regulate the flow of (fuel or other driving fluid or gas) to an engine. **b** to stop, check, or lessen the speed of (an engine) by closing a throttle: *to throttle a steam engine.* **c** to vary the thrust of (a rocket engine), especially by changing the pressure in the thrust chamber.
—*v.i.* to be choked; strangle; suffocate.
**go full throttle,** to go at full speed: *He starts at 8 a.m. and goes full throttle until after midnight* (Time). *Practically everything was going full throttle throughout the [musical] composition* (New Yorker).
[Middle English *throtel* < *throte* throat + frequentative suffix *-le*]

**throt|tle|a|ble** (throt′əl ə bəl), *adj.* that can be throttled: *a throttleable rocket engine.*

**Throt|tle|bot|tom** (throt′əl bot′əm), *n. U.S.* a harmlessly ineffective holder of public office. [< *Throttlebottom,* a character in the musical comedy *Of Thee I Sing* (1931) by George S. Kaufman and Morrie Ryskind]

**throt|tle|hold** (throt′əl hōld′), *n.* a strangling hold; suppressive or stifling control: (*Figurative.*) *a throttlehold on free speech.*

**throttle lever** or **pedal,** = throttle (*n.* def. 2).

**throt|tler** (throt′lər), *n.* a person or thing that throttles.

**throttle valve,** = throttle (*n.* def. 1).

**through** (thrü), *prep., adv., adj.* —*prep.* **1** from end to end of; from side to side of; between the parts of; from beginning to end of: *The soldiers marched through the town. The carpenter bored holes through a board. The men cut a tunnel through a mountain. Fish swim through the water.* **2** here and there in; over; around: *to stroll through the streets of a city. We traveled through New England and saw many old towns.* **3** because of; by reason of; on account of; owing to: *to fail through ignorance. The woman refused help through pride.* **4** by means of: *He became rich through hard work and ability.* See syn. under **with**. **5** having reached the end of; finished with; done with: *We are through school at three o'clock.* **6a** during the whole of; throughout: *to work from dawn through the day and into the night.* **b** during and until the finish of: *to help a person through hard times.*
—*adv.* **1** from end to end; from side to side; between the parts: *The bullet hit the wall and went through.* **2** completely; thoroughly: *He walked home in the rain and was wet through.* **3** from beginning to end: *She read the book all the way through.* **4** along the whole distance; all the way: *The train goes through to Boston.*
—*adj.* **1a** going all the way without change: *a through train from New York to Los Angeles.* **b** for the whole distance or journey: *a through ticket to Los Angeles.* **c** allowed or allowing movement or passage without stopping: *through traffic, a through highway.* **2** having reached the end; at an end; finished: *I will soon be through.* **3** passing or extending from one end, side, or surface to the other. Also, **thro, thro', thru.**
**get through.** See under **get.**
**go through.** See under **go**[1].
**see through.** See under **see**[1].
**through and through,** completely; thoroughly; wholly; entirely: *soaked through and through, a scoundrel through and through. "I shall write an opera only if I come across a subject capable of warming me through and through"* (Listener).
[Middle English *thurgh,* variant of Old English *thurh.* Compare etym. under **thorough.**]

**through-com|posed song** (thrü′kəm pōzd′), *Music.* a song having a different melody or music for each stanza.

**through|ly** (thrü′lē), *adv. Archaic.* fully; completely; thoroughly.

**through-oth|er** (thrü′uᴛʜ′ər), *adv. Scottish.* (mingled) through each other or one another; indiscriminately.

**through|out** (thrü out′), *prep., adv.* —*prep.* **1** in or to every part of: *The Fourth of July is celebrated throughout the United States.* **2** all the way through; through all: *He worked hard throughout his life.*
—*adv.* **1** in or to every part: *This house is well built throughout.* SYN: everywhere. **2** through the whole of a period or course of action.

**through|put** (thrü′pu̇t′), *n.* **1** the production and distribution of a product: *the throughput of crude oil, the throughput of canned meats.* **2** the quantity produced: *The average daily throughput was 1,370 short tons of ore* (Cape Times). **3** the amount of data put through a computer; a computer's input and output collectively: *Time-sharing (or multiprogramming) is already well established as a means of increasing the throughput and utilization of a computer* (New Scientist).

**through street, 1** a street that is not a dead end or extends through a town or other area. **2** a street on which motor vehicles can move without having to stop at intersections.

**through|way** (thrü′wā′), *n.* = thruway.

**throu|ther** (thrü′ᴛʜər), *adv. Scottish.* through-other.

**throve** (thrōv), *v.* a past tense of **thrive**: *She throve on hard work.*

**throw** (thrō), *v.,* **threw, thrown, throw|ing,** *n.*
—*v.t.* **1a** to send through the air with force; cast; toss; hurl; fling: *to throw a ball, to throw spray against a window,* (*Figurative.*) *to throw caution to the winds. The man threw water on the fire.* **b** to cause to go; project: *The tree throws a shadow on the grass.* **c** to fire (a projectile); shoot: *A cannon throws shells.* **2** to bring to the ground; cause to fall or fall off: *to throw one's opponent in wrestling. He was thrown when his horse bucked.* **3a** to put or move quickly or by force: *to throw oneself into a fight, to throw someone into prison, to throw reserve troops into a battle.* **b** *Figurative.* to put carelessly or in haste: *She threw a cloak over her shoulders.* **c** *Figurative.* to put into a certain condition: *to throw a person into confusion.* **4** to turn, direct, or move, especially quickly: *to throw a questioning look at a stranger. She threw a glance at each car that passed.* **5** *Informal.* to give (a party or other entertainment). **6** *Informal.* to overwhelm or confound; disconcert: *To encounter a setback ... was a bit daunting, but I wasn't going to let it throw me* (S. J. Perelman). **7a** to move (a lever or other device) that connects or disconnects parts of a switch, clutch, or other mechanism. **b** to connect or disconnect thus. **8** to project (one's voice) so that it seems to come from a different source, as a ventriloquist does. **9** to cast off: **a** to shed: *A snake throws its skin.* **b** to lose; drop: *The horse threw a shoe.* **10** (of some animals) to bring forth (young); bear: *The cow threw a healthy calf.* **11** *Informal.* to let an opponent win (a race, game, or other contest), often for money: *Ronald Howells, aged 29, pleaded Not Guilty to conspiring with Gould and others to defraud bookmakers by "throwing" the Scunthorpe v. Darby County match* (London Times). **12** to make (a specified cast) with dice. **13** to twist (silk) into threads. **14** to shape on a potter's wheel: *to throw a bowl from a ball of clay.* **15** *Especially Scottish.* **a** to twist; turn. **b** to strain; wrench.
—*v.i.* to cast, toss, or hurl something: *How far can you throw?*
—*n.* **1** a light scarf, wrap, blanket, or other covering: *a knitted throw.* **2** the distance a thing is or may be thrown: *a long throw.* **3** the act of throwing; cast, toss, or hurl: *That was a good throw from left field to the catcher.* **4** a cast at dice; venture: *a lucky throw.* **5** *U.S. Informal.* a single item or unit (of something): *Her book ... has sold more than 100,000 copies at $4.50 a throw* (Saturday Review). **6a** the reciprocating motion generated by a cam, eccentric, or the like. **b** the motion of a cam, eccentric, or the like. **c** the extent of this, measured on a straight line passing through the axis of motion. **d** any one of the cranks of the crankshaft of a gasoline engine. **7** *Geology.* **a** a fault. **b** the extent of vertical displacement produced by a fault. **8** *Obsolete.* a fall.
**throw away, a** to get rid of; discard: *Throw away those old shoes. They will ... throw away the blessings their hands are filled with because they are not big enough to grasp everything* (John Locke). **b** to waste: *Advice ... would be but thrown away upon them* (Spectator). **c** to fail to use: *Don't throw away your opportunities.*
**throw back, a** to give or send back; return; reflect: *The mirror threw back his image.* **b** to check, retard, or delay; set back: *The loss of a week threw him back in his work by nearly a month.* **c** to force to count or depend (on or upon): *The shortage of gas has thrown us back upon the use of bicycles.* **d** to revert to an ancestral type: (*Figurative.*) *He and his ideas throw back to the Middle Ages* (John Galsworthy).
**throw in, a** to put in as a supplement; add as a gift: *Our grocer often throws in an extra apple. [The] story turns ... on murder and revenge, with a little love thrown in* (Black & White). **b** to interpose or contribute (a remark or explanation); put in: *"Not a grain," threw in Julian, hotly* (Sabine Baring-Gould). **c** to share (one's lot, interests, or the like) with: *He willingly threw in his fortune with theirs* (England Illustrated Magazine).
**throw off, a** to get rid of; cast off: *to throw off a yoke.* **b** to give off; emit: *to throw off wastes with perspiration.* **c** to divest oneself of (a garment, a quality, a habit, or anything else); discard: *He throws off his gown and hypocrisy together* (E. Ward). **d** to cause to lose: *to throw a hound off the scent.* **e** *Informal.* to produce (a poem, sketch, song, or other artistic piece) in an offhand manner: *The new articles ... "thrown off at a heat," stood particularly in want of re-revision* (J. Badcock).
**throw oneself at,** to try very hard to get the love, friendship, or favor of: *As for the girls, Claire, they just throw themselves at a man* (Walter Besant).
**throw oneself on** (or **upon**), **a** to commit oneself entirely to (someone's generosity, will, or the like): *The criminal threw himself upon the mercy of the court.* **b** *Figurative.* to attack with violence or vigor; fall upon: *He threw himself upon the ragout, and the plate was presently [empty]* (Scott).
**throw open, a** to open suddenly or widely: *I had ordered the folding doors to be thrown open* (Joseph Addison). **b** *Figurative: labouring to throw open the gates of commerce* (Tait's Magazine).
**throw out, a** to get rid of; discard: *When the contract expires, this newspaper will throw out its linotype machines* (Indianapolis Typographical Journal). **b** to reject: *The Ballot Bill ... was thrown out by the Lords* (P. V. Smith). **c** to expel: *The servants threw out the intruder.* **d** to dismiss, as from a job: *He has been thrown out from his job.* **e** *Figurative.* to put or send forth (as a signal, question, or suggestion): *Athens unhesitatingly accepted the challenge thrown out* (A. W. Ward). *He began to throw out questions about our plans the following day* (George Woodcock). **f** *Figurative.* to send out; give off; emit: *The chimney threw out black smoke.* **g** *Baseball.* to put out (a base runner) by throwing the ball to a baseman.
**throw over, a** to give up; discard; abandon: *to throw over an old friend. Mr. Freeman ... throws over the latter part of Palgrave's theory* (William Stubbs). **b** to overthrow: *The government was thrown over by a rebel group.*
**throw together, a** to put together hastily or roughly: *She made supper from the leftovers she had thrown together.* **b** to bring into casual contact or association: *They had been thrown together at school, but had rarely met since.*
**throw up, a** *Informal.* to vomit: *It is easy to judge ... the cause by the substances which the patient throws up* (John Arbuthnot). **b** *Figurative.* to give up; abandon; quit: *He had felt tempted to throw up public life in disgust* (James A. Froude). **c** to build rapidly: *The Greeks threw up a great intrenchment to secure their navy* (Sir Richard Steele). **d** to raise (the hands) quickly and suddenly: *She threw up her hands in dismay.*
[Old English *thrāwan* to twist, turn; torture]
—**throw′er,** *n.*
—*Syn. v.t.* **1a Throw, toss, cast** mean to send something through the air by a sudden movement of the arm. **Throw** is the general word: *The children threw pillows at each other.* **Toss** means to throw lightly or carelessly with the palm up: *Please toss me the matches.* **Cast** is now often considered stiff and literary except figuratively or in special uses, as in games, voting, fishing, sailing: *They cast anchor. She cast dignity to the wind, and ran.*

**throw|a|way** (thrō′ə wā′), *n., adj.* —*n.* a handbill, pamphlet, or other short printed piece intended to be thrown away after reading.
—*adj.* **1** that can be thrown away or discarded; disposable: *a throwaway bottle. Throwaway umbrellas made of paper have just been marketed on an experimental basis by a Tokyo paper goods firm* (New Scientist). **2** *Figurative.* casual; offhand: *His songs give a better idea of the man than the few throwaway remarks he will volunteer about himself* (Manchester Guardian Weekly).

**throwaway line,** a casually or carelessly delivered line from a dialogue or script: *It takes a certain nerve for a comedian to try a throwaway line* (Time).

**throw|back** (thrō′bak′), *n.* **1** a throwing back. **2** a setback or check. **3a** a reversion to an ancestral type or character. **b** an example of this: *The boy seemed to be a throwback to his great-grandfather.*

**throw-in** (thrō′in′), *n.* the act of putting the ball in play by throwing it into fair territory, as in basketball, soccer, and Rugby.

**throw|ing** (thrō′ing), *n.* a step in the processing of textiles in which the yarn is twisted and doubled without drawing it out or stretching it to give it greater strength.

**thrown** (thrōn), *v.* the past participle of **throw**: *She has thrown her old toys away.*

**throw-out** (thrō′out′), *n.* **1** an act of throwing out; ejection: *The land areas ... must be controlled to avoid hazard from throw-out of material, dust, air blast, and ground shock* (Science News Letter). **2** a person or thing that is thrown out; discard: *Ursula is reminded of what she has lost by the sight of a heap of throw-outs* (Punch).

**throw pillow**, a light pillow, often embroidered, used on a chair, couch, or bed as a decoration or cushion.

**throw rug**, = scatter rug.

**throw|ster** (thrō′stər), *n.* a person who throws silk.

**throw weight**, the delivery power of a ballistic missile or rocket, expressed in megatons; size of a missile payload: *The SS-9 and the new SS-18 have throw weights capable of launching warheads packing 25 megatons* (Time).

**thru** (thrü), *prep., adv., adj.* = through.

**thrum**[1] (thrum), *v.,* **thrummed, thrum|ming,** *n.* **—*v.i.*** **1** to play on a stringed instrument by plucking the strings, especially in an idle, mechanical, or careless way; strum: *to thrum on a guitar.* **2** to sound when thrummed on, as a guitar or its strings. **3** to drum or tap idly with the fingers: *to thrum on a table.* **4** to speak or read monotonously; drone; mumble: *Boswell ... has thrummed upon this topic till it is threadbare* (Scott). **5** *Dialect.* (of a cat) to purr.
**—*v.t.*** **1** to play (a stringed instrument, or a tune on it) idly, mechanically, or carelessly: *to thrum a guitar.* **2a** to recite or tell in a monotonous way. **b** to hum over (a melody).
**—*n.*** the sound made by thrumming.
[apparently imitative] **—thrum′mer,** *n.*

**thrum**[2] (thrum), *n., v.,* **thrummed, thrum|ming.** **—*n.*** **1** an end of the warp thread left unwoven on the loom after the web is cut off. **2** any piece of loose thread or yarn. **3** a tuft, tassel, or fringe of threads at the edge of a piece of cloth. **4** *Scottish.* a tangle.
**—*v.t.*** **1** *Nautical.* to sew or fasten bunches of rope yarn over (a mat or sail) to produce a rough surface to prevent chafing or stop a leak. **2** *Obsolete or Dialect.* to furnish or adorn with thrums; cover with small tufts; make shaggy.
**thrums, a** the row or fringe of warp threads left unwoven on the loom when the web is cut off: *to cut off the thrums for use as frills.* **b** *Figurative.* odds and ends; scraps: *It is this, which ... makes life a whole instead of a parcel of thrums bound together by an accident* (John Morley). **c** *Nautical.* short pieces of coarse woolen or hempen yarn: *thrums used for mops in the cabins.*
[Old English *-thrum,* in *tungethrum* tongue ligament]

**thrush**[1] (thrush), *n.* **1** any one of a large group of migratory songbirds that includes the robin, the bluebird, the wood thrush, and the veery. Thrushes are usually medium-sized and have upper parts of a dull, solid color and a spotted or colored breast. **2** any one of various similar birds, such as the Louisiana water thrush. [Old English *thrysce*]

**thrush**[2] (thrush), *n.* **1** a contagious disease often attacking infants and associated with malnutrition, characterized by white specks on the inside of the mouth and throat and caused by a parasitic fungus; white mouth; infantile sore mouth. **2** a diseased condition of the horn of the central cleft of the frog in a horse's foot.
[perhaps < Scandinavian (compare Swedish *trosk*)]

force of bridge weight
thrust of arch
counterthrust of abutment

**∗thrust** definition 5

**∗thrust** (thrust), *v.,* **thrust, thrust|ing,** *n.* **—*v.t.*** **1** to push with force; shove; drive: *He thrust his hands into his pockets. He thrust a chair against the door.* (*Figurative.*) *A soldier thrusts himself into danger.* (*Figurative.*) *Some men are born great, some achieve greatness, and some have greatness thrust upon them* (Shakespeare). **2** to stab; pierce: *He thrust the knife into the apple. We thrust the tent pole deep into the ground.* **3** to put forth; extend: *The tree thrust its roots deep into the ground.*
**—*v.i.*** **1** to push with force; make a thrust. **2** to make a stab or lunge. **3** to push or force one's way, as through a crowd, between persons, or against obstacles: *The woman thrust past me into the room.*
**—*n.*** **1** a push with force; drive: *She hid the book behind the pillow with a quick thrust.* **SYN:** shove, punch. **2** a stab; lunge: *A thrust with the pin broke the balloon.* **3** a sudden, sharp attack; thrusting assault: (*Figurative.*) *a sarcastic thrust at a prevailing foible* (William Dean Howells). **4** *Mechanics.* the force of one thing pushing on another. **5** *Architecture.* the lateral force exerted, as by an arch, against an abutment or support. It must be counteracted to prevent the structure from collapsing. **6a** the push exerted by the rotation of a propeller, that causes an aircraft or ship to move. **b** the force driving a rocket or a jet plane forward as a reaction to the rearward escape of gases or burning fuels through a nozzle or exhaust: *Rocket engine thrust depends on the speed of the gases and particles shot out of the tail. The higher this speed, the greater the thrust provided by the exhaust gases which push the rocket in one direction while they rush away in the other* (Christian Science Monitor). **7** *Geology.* **a** a compressive strain in the earth's crust. **b** a thrust fault. **8** *Figurative.* an object, purpose, or goal: *Dr. Stanton said the practical thrust of the rules would be to create an incentive for the networks themselves* (New York Times).
**thrust out,** to expel; eject: *They were now, without any accusation, thrust out of their house* (Macaulay).
[Middle English *thrusten* < Scandinavian (compare Old Icelandic *thrȳsta*)]

**thrust chamber**, the chamber of a rocket in which the expansion of gases produces enough thrust for take-off.

**thrust|er** (thrus′tər), *n.* **1** a person or thing that thrusts or exerts thrust. **2** = thrustor.

**thrust fault**, *Geology.* a reversed fault, produced by horizontal compression.

**thrust|ful** (thrust′fəl), *adj.* full of thrust; forceful: *Now at last there is the prospect of some thrustful competition ... in one vitally important part of the work of the airlines* (New Scientist). **—thrust′ful|ly,** *adv.* **—thrust′ful|ness,** *n.*

**thrus|tor** (thrus′tər), *n.* an electrical engine or similar device for producing thrust, as in a rocket or spacecraft; reaction engine. Also, **thruster.**

**thrust stage**, a theatrical stage extending into the auditorium, with seats surrounding the stage on three sides.

**thru|way** (thrü′wā′), *n.* an express highway; throughway.

**Thu.**, Thursday.

**thud** (thud), *n., v.,* **thud|ded, thud|ding.** **—*n.*** **1** a dull, heavy sound: *The book hit the floor with a thud.* **2** a heavy blow; thump.
**—*v.i., v.t.*** to hit, move, or strike with a thud: *The heavy box fell and thudded on the floor. We didn't hear the five bullets that thudded into the wall a few feet from our heads until they arrived* (Maclean's).
[earlier, blast of wind; origin uncertain. Compare Old English *thyddan* to strike.]

**thug** (thug), *n.* **1** a ruffian or cutthroat: *One thug with a pistol struck the druggist on the head* (New York Times). **2** a member of a former religious organization of robbers and murderers in India, who strangled their victims. [< Hindi *thag* < Sanskrit *sthaga* rogue]

**thug|gee** (thug′ē), *n.* the system of robbery and murder practiced by the thugs of India. [< Hindi *thagī* < *thag;* see etym. under **thug**]

**thug|ger|y** (thug′ər ē), *n., pl.* **-ger|ies.** **1** the activities or practices of a thug or thugs. **2** = thuggee.

**thug|gish** (thug′ish), *adj.* of or like a thug or thugs; ruffianly; cutthroat.

**thu|ja** (thü′jə, thyü′-), *n.* any coniferous evergreen tree of a group of the cypress family; arbor vitae. A common American kind yields an aromatic oil (oil of thuja) that is used in medicine. Also, **thuya.** [< New Latin *Thuja* the genus name, ultimately < Greek *thyīā, thȳā* an African tree]

**Thu|le** (thü′lē), *n.* the part of the world that the ancient Greeks and Romans regarded as farthest north; some island or region north of Britain, sometimes identified as Iceland, a part of Denmark or Norway, or Mainland (largest of the Shetland Islands). [Old English *Tyle* < Latin *Thūlē,* or *Thȳlē* < Greek *Thoúlē*]

**thu|li|a** (thü′lē ə), *n.* a greenish-white, amorphous powder, an oxide of thulium. *Formula:* $Tm_2O_3$ [< *thulium*]

**∗thu|li|um** (thü′lē əm), *n.* a silver-white metallic chemical element of the yttrium group, found in gadolinite and various other minerals. It is a rare-earth element. An isotope of thulium is used as the radiating element in portable X-ray units. [< New Latin *thulium* < Latin *Thūlē* Thule]

**∗thulium**

| symbol | atomic number | atomic weight | oxidation state |
|---|---|---|---|
| Tm | 69 | 168.934 | 3 |

**thumb** (thum), *n., v.* **—*n.*** **1** the short, thick finger of the human hand, next to the forefinger. The thumb can be used in opposition to the other fingers. **2** the corresponding digit or part of the paw of an animal; pollex. **3** the part of a glove or mitten that covers the thumb: *There was a hole in the thumb of his mitten.* **4** *Architecture.* a convex molding; ovolo.
**—*v.t.*** **1** to soil or wear by handling with the thumbs: *Some of the books were badly thumbed.* **2** to turn pages of (a book or other sheets of paper) rapidly with a thumb, reading only portions. **SYN:** skim. **3** to handle awkwardly or clumsily. **SYN:** fumble. **4** *Informal.* to ask for or get (a free ride) by holding up one's thumb to motorists going in one's direction; hitchhike: *Some commuters abandoned the trains and thumbed rides* (New York Times). **—*v.i.*** **1** to turn pages rapidly with a thumb: *During the long patrol, crewmen ... thumb through books and magazines* (Time). **2** *Informal.* to travel by walking and getting free rides from motorists: *I went out on the road to start thumbing* (Saul Bellow).
**all thumbs,** very clumsy or awkward: *The team lost the game because two of the players were all thumbs and kept dropping the ball.*
**stick out like a sore thumb,** to appear unpleasantly conspicuous: *Wearing a sports coat at the formal dance, he stuck out like a sore thumb.*
**thumb down,** *Informal.* to reject: *Its power to thumb down first-rate political talent is often deplored* (Alistair Cooke).
**thumbs down,** a sign of disapproval or rejection: *There are expressions of surprise when many workers, as in the aerospace industry, turn thumbs down on a prime form of union security, the union shop* (Wall Street Journal).
**thumbs up,** a sign of approval or acceptance: *As the trial progressed, he would leave court each day to the smiles and thumbs up signs of the crowd* (New York Times).
**twiddle one's thumbs, a** to keep turning one's thumbs idly about each other: *The bishop was sitting in his easy chair, twiddling his thumbs* (Anthony Trollope). **b** to do nothing; have nothing to do; be idle: *You'd have all the world do nothing half its time but twiddle its thumbs* (D. Jerrold).
**under the thumb of** (or **one's thumb**), under the power or influence of: *The bully tried to keep us all under his thumb but we outwitted him. Her son-in-law was under the thumb of his women-folk* (Rudyard Kipling).
[Middle English *thoumbe,* Old English *thūma*]
**—thumb′like′,** *adj.*

**thumb index**, a series of grooves cut along the front edges of the pages of a book to show initial letters or titles, so that any division may be turned to by placing the thumb or finger on the proper initial or title.

**thumb-in|dex** (thum′in′deks), *v.t.* to furnish (a book) with a thumb index.

**thumb|kins** (thum′kinz), *n.pl. Scottish.* a thumbscrew, an instrument of torture.

**thumb knot**, = overhand knot.

**thumb|nail** (thum′nāl′), *n., adj.* **—*n.*** **1** the nail of the thumb. **2** *Figurative.* something very small or short.
**—*adj.*** *Figurative.* very small or short: *a thumbnail sketch.*

**thumb piano**, any one of various small African musical instruments played with the thumbs, such as the kalimba and mbira.

**thumb|piece** (thum′pēs′), *n.* **1** a part of a handle made to receive the thumb. **2** a lever, button, or other part of a mechanism operated by pressure of the thumb.

**thumb|print** (thum′print′), *n.* **1** an impression of the markings on the inner surface of the last joint of the thumb: *In the second century before Christ, the clever Chinese were already using thumbprints as a means of identification* (New Yorker). **2** *Figurative.* an impression; stamp: *He is tall, athletic and handsome, but his soul bears the thumbprint of his ruthless wife* (Time).

**thumb|ring** (thum′ring′), *n.,* or **thumb ring, 1** a ring, especially one with a seal, to be worn on

**Pronunciation Key:** hat, āge, cãre, fär; let, ēqual, tėrm; it, īce; hot, ōpen, ôrder; oil, out; cup, pu̇t, rüle; child; long; thin; ᴛʜen; zh, measure; ə represents **a** in about, **e** in taken, **i** in pencil, **o** in lemon, **u** in circus.

the thumb. **2** a ring for the thumb on the guard of a dagger or sword.

**thumb|screw** (thum′skrü′), *n.* **1** a screw with a flattened or winged head so that it can be turned with the thumb and a finger. **2** an old instrument of torture that squeezed the thumbs.

**thumb|stall** (thum′stôl′), *n.* **1** a kind of thimble worn over the thumb, especially by shoemakers, for pushing a needle. **2** a protective sheath, as of leather, worn over an injured thumb.

**thumb-suck|ing** (thum′suk′ing), *n.* the habit of sucking one's thumb.

**thumb|tack** (thum′tak′), *n., v.* —*n.* a tack with a broad, flat head, that can be pressed into a wall or board with the thumb.
—*v.t.* to fasten with a thumbtack: *Thumbtacked to another wall [was] a postcard mailed from Vienna* (New Yorker).
[American English < *thumb* + *tack*[1]]

**Thum|mim** (thum′im), *n.pl.* (in the Old Testament) certain objects worn in or upon the breastplate of the Jewish high priest. See **Urim.** [< Hebrew *thummīm*]

**thump** (thump), *v., n.* —*v.t.* **1** to strike with something thick and heavy; pound: *He thumped the table with his fist.* **2** to strike against (something) heavily and noisily: *The shutters thumped the wall in the wind.* **3** *Informal.* to beat or thrash severely.
—*v.i.* **1** to make a dull sound; pound heavily: *a fist thumping against the door. The hammer thumped against the wood. He thumped on the piano.* **2** to beat violently; throb heavily: *His heart thumped as he walked past the cemetery at night.* **3** to move heavily and noisily; bump or jolt along: *to thump across a room. The car thumped along on a flat tire.*
—*n.* **1** a blow with something thick and heavy; heavy knock: *He hit the thief a thump on the head.* **SYN:** whack, bang. **2** the dull sound made by a blow, knock, or fall: *We heard the thump as he fell.*
[imitative]

**thump|er** (thum′pər), *n.* **1** a person that thumps. **2** a device for producing a shallow seismic wave to test structural properties of the lunar surface.

**thump|ing** (thum′ping), *adj., adv. Informal.* —*adj.* very large; great; excellent.
—*adv.* very: *a thumping good time.*

**thun|der** (thun′dər), *n., v.* —*n.* **1** the loud noise that often follows a flash of lightning. It is caused by a disturbance of the air resulting from the discharge of electricity. **2** any noise like thunder; very loud or resounding noise: *the thunder of Niagara Falls.* **3** *Figurative.* a threat or denunciation. **4** = thunderbolt.
—*v.i.* **1** to give forth thunder: *It thundered a few times, but no rain fell.* **2a** to make a noise like thunder; roar: *The cannon thundered throughout the night.* **b** to rush or fall with great noise and commotion: *The waterfall thundered over the rocks.* **3** *Figurative.* to utter threats or denunciations: *From his pulpit he thundered against the ungodly.*
—*v.t.* **1** to utter very loudly; roar: *to thunder a reply.* **2** *Figurative.* to threaten or denounce.
**steal one's** (or **the**) **thunder, a** to take an effective or successful idea, method, or plan, originated by another person, and use as one's own so as to reduce or annul the effect of his words or actions: *"I'll be damned if he isn't stealing ... my thunder," thought Mason to himself at this point. "He's forestalling most of the things I intended to riddle him with"* (Theodore Dreiser). **b** to gain the success, applause, or other recognition that was meant for or belonged to another: *Although the result ... of England's final trial at Twickenham suggested [a draw], the junior team stole most of the thunder* (London Times).
[Middle English *thunder,* Old English *thunor*]

**thun|der|a|tion** (thun′də rā′shən), *n., interj. U.S. Dialect or Informal.* —*n.* the deuce; the devil: *Everybody wants to know who in thunderation Rache will marry* (Century Magazine).
—*interj.* an exclamation of surprise or annoyance: *"Thunderation!" he muttered indignantly* (Time).

***thunderbird**

Haida Indian carving

***thun|der|bird** (thun′dər bėrd′), *n.* a huge bird in the folklore of certain North American Indians, that produces thunder by flapping its wings and lightning by opening and closing its eyes.

**thun|der|bolt** (thun′dər bōlt′), *n., v.* —*n.* **1** a flash of lightning and the thunder that follows it. **2** *Figurative.* something sudden, startling, and terrible: *The news of his death came as a thunderbolt.* **3** *Figurative.* a person with great energy and drive. **4** a bolt or dart formerly believed to destroy when lightning strikes anything. **5** a fossil or stone formerly thought to have fallen from heaven with the lightning.
—*v.t.* to strike with a thunderbolt: (*Figurative.*) *It will not be long before he is thunderbolted to the quick by the physical similarities between East Anglia and China* (Punch). **SYN:** startle, terrify.

**thun|der|burst** (thun′dər bėrst′), *n.* = thunderclap.

**thun|der|clap** (thun′dər klap′), *n.* **1** a loud crash of thunder. **2** *Figurative.* something sudden or startling.

**thun|der|cloud** (thun′dər kloud′), *n.* a dark cloud that brings thunder and lightning.

**thunder egg,** a kind of round rock or stone formed from tuff or lava and containing chalcedony or some other mineral.

**thun|der|er** (thun′dər ər), *n.* a person or thing that thunders.

**Thun|der|er** (thun′dər ər), *n.* Jupiter; Zeus. [because Jupiter is frequently represented with a thunderbolt in his hand]

**thun|der|flash** (thun′dər flash′), *n.* **1** a loud explosion accompanied by a flash. **2** a tin can, blank artillery shell, or the like, filled with powder, that makes such an explosion.

**Thunder God vine,** a climbing perennial plant of the staff-tree family, imported into the United States from China for the insecticidal property of its roots.

**thun|der|head** (thun′dər hed′), *n.* one of the very tall, swelling masses of cumulus clouds often appearing before thunderstorms and frequently developing into thunderclouds.

**thun|der|ing** (thun′dər ing, -dring), *adj., adv.* —*adj.* **1** that thunders; very loud and deep: *a thundering herd of cattle,* (*Figurative.*) *a thundering voice.* **2** *Informal, Figurative.* very great or big; immense; too great: *a thundering lie.*
—*adv. Informal.* very: *a thundering high price.*
—**thun′der|ing|ly,** *adv.*

**thun|der|ous** (thun′dər əs, -drəs), *adj.* **1** producing thunder. **2** *Figurative: The famous actor received a thunderous burst of applause at the end of the play.* **SYN:** deafening. —**thun′der|ous|ly,** *adv.*

**thun|der|peal** (thun′dər pēl′), *n.* a clap of thunder; thunderclap.

**thun|der|pump** (thun′dər pump′), *n. U.S.* the bittern.

**thun|der|show|er** (thun′dər shou′ər), *n.* a shower with thunder and lightning.

**thun|der|squall** (thun′dər skwôl′), *n.* a squall with thunder and lightning.

**thunder stick, 1** = bull-roarer. **2** a musket, as supposedly called by the American Indians when they first saw firearms.

**thun|der|stone** (thun′dər stōn′), *n.* **1** any one of various stones or fossils formerly identified with thunderbolts, such as belemnites and meteorites. **2** *Archaic.* a thunderbolt.

**thun|der|storm** (thun′dər stôrm′), *n.* a storm with thunder and lightning and, usually, heavy rain.

**thun|der|strick|en** (thun′dər strik′ən), *adj.* = thunderstruck.

**thun|der|stroke** (thun′dər strōk′), *n.* a stroke of lightning.

**thun|der|struck** (thun′dər struk′), *adj.* **1** overcome, as if hit by a thunderbolt; astonished; amazed: *We were thunderstruck by the news of the war.* **SYN:** confounded, astounded. **2** *Obsolete.* struck by lightning.

**thun|der|y** (thun′dər ē), *adj.* = thunderous.

**thun|drous** (thun′drəs), *adj.* = thunderous.

**thunk** (thungk), *n., v.* —*n.* a flat metallic sound: *... the satisfying thunk of a metal pellet embedding itself in a hollow plastic object* (Punch).
—*v.i.* to make such a sound: *The [car] seats are soft and the doors thunk* (Time). [imitative]

**Thur.,** Thursday.

**thu|ri|ble** (thůr′ə bəl, thyůr′-), *n.* = censer. [< Latin *thūribulum* < *thūs, thūris* incense < Greek *thýos, thýeos* incense; (originally) burnt sacrifice < *thýein* to sacrifice]

**thu|ri|fer** (thůr′ə fər, thyůr′-), *n.* an altar boy or acolyte who carries the censer. [< New Latin *thurifer* < Latin *thūrifer* incense-bearing < *thūs, thūris* incense + *ferre* to bear, carry]

**thu|ri|fy** (thůr′ə fī, thyůr′-), *v.t.,* **-fied, -fy|ing.** to burn incense before or about; perfume with incense; cense. [< Old French *thurifier* < Late Latin *thūrificāre* < *thūs, thūris* incense + *facere* to make]

**Thu|rin|ger** (thůr′in jər, thyůr′-), *n.* a kind of mildly seasoned dry sausage. [German *Thüringer* (*Wurst*) Thuringian (sausage)]

**Thu|rin|gi|an** (thů rin′jē ən, thyů-), *adj., n.* —*adj.* **1** of or having to do with Thuringia, a region in southern East Germany, or its people. **2** *Geology.* of or having to do with the upper division of the Permian in Europe.
—*n.* **1** a native or inhabitant of Thuringia. **2** a member of a Germanic tribe that established a kingdom in central Germany that was conquered by the Franks in the 500's A.D.

**Thurs.,** Thursday.

**Thurs|day** (thėrz′dē, -dā), *n.* the fifth day of the week, following Wednesday: *In the United States, Thanksgiving Day is always the fourth Thursday in November. Abbr:* Thurs., Thur., Thu. [Old English *Thuresdæg, Thurresdæg,* perhaps variation of *Thunresdæg* (< *Thunor* god of thunder + *dæg* day), translation of Late Latin *diēs Jovis* day of Jupiter, or Jove]

**thus** (ᴛʜus), *adv.* **1** in this way; in the way just stated or indicated; in the following manner: *He spoke thus: "Friends, Romans, countrymen."* **2** accordingly; consequently; therefore: *He studied hard; thus he got high marks. Thus we decided that you were wrong.* **SYN:** hence. **3** to this extent; to this degree; so: *Yet you can speak thus calmly of unsaying All we have said* (Walter C. Smith).
**thus far, a** until now or then: *Thus far, we haven't heard from him.* **b** to this or that point: *Thus far you may go and no farther.*
[Old English *thus.* See related etym. at **this.**]

**thus-and-so** (ᴛʜus′ən sō′), *n.* any one of several things not named: *If the local authorities don't do thus-and-so, and at once, they will choke the streets with bigger mobs* (Wall Street Journal).

**thus|ly** (ᴛʜus′lē), *adv. Informal.* thus: *A Pisa pizza pie peddler we contacted commented thusly: "Balderdash!"* (Maclean's).

**thus|ness** (ᴛʜus′nis), *n. Informal.* the state of being thus: *What is the reason for this thusness?* (Artemus Ward).

**thus|wise** (ᴛʜus′wīz), *adv.* = thus.

**thu|ya** (thü′yə), *n.* = thuja.

**thwack** (thwak), *v., n.* —*v.t.* to strike vigorously with a stick or something flat; whack: *Take all my cushions down and thwack them soundly* (Thomas Middleton).
—*n.* a sharp blow with a stick or something flat; whack: *The man ... with his open palm gave the animal a resounding thwack* (Joseph Conrad).
[probably ultimately imitative] —**thwack′er,** *n.*

**thwart** (thwôrt), *v., n., adj., adv.* —*v.t.* **1** to oppose and defeat; keep from doing something: *The boy's lack of money thwarted his plans for college.* **SYN:** baffle, balk, foil. See syn. under **frustrate. 2** to go against; oppose; hinder. **3** *Obsolete.* to pass or extend across from side to side of; traverse; cross. [< adverb]
—*n.* **1** a seat across a boat, on which a rower sits. **2** a brace between the gunwales of a canoe. [< adjective or adverb]
—*adj.* **1** lying or passing across. **2** obstinate; stubborn. [< adverb]
—*adv.* across; crosswise; athwart.
[Middle English *thwert* < Scandinavian (compare Old Icelandic *thvert* across, neuter of *thverr* transverse)] —**thwart′er,** *n.*

**thy** (ᴛʜī), *adj. Possessive form of* **thou.** *Archaic.* your: *Thy kingdom come. Thy will be done* (Matthew 6:10). [Middle English *thi, thin,* Old English *thīn* thine]
► See **thou** for usage note.

**Thy|es|te|an** (thī es′tē ən), *adj.* of or having to do with Thyestes.

**Thyestean banquet** or **meal,** a repast at which human flesh is served; cannibal feast.

**Thy|es|tes** (thī es′tēz), *n. Greek Legend.* a son of Pelops, brother of Atreus, and father of Aegisthus. When Thyestes seduced Atreus' wife and plotted his murder, Atreus pretended reconciliation, but killed three sons of Thyestes and served them to him at a banquet.

**thy|la|cine** (thī′lə sīn, -sin), *n.* a doglike, carnivorous, marsupial mammal of Tasmania, now almost extinct; Tasmanian wolf. Thylacines are grayish or yellowish brown with dark brown stripes on their backs. [< French *thylacine* < Greek *thýlax, -akos* pouch, sack]

**thy|la|koid** (thī′lə koid), *n.* a saclike membrane that is the structural unit of the grana in the chloroplasts of plant cells and the site of chemical reactions essential in photosynthesis. [< Greek *thýlax, -akos* pouch, sack + English *-oid*]

**thyme** (tīm), *n.* any one of a group of herbs with fragrant, aromatic leaves that smell like mint. Thyme belongs to a genus of the mint family. The sweet-smelling leaves of the common garden thyme are used for seasoning. The common wild thyme is a creeping evergreen. [< Latin *thymum* < Greek *thýmon* < *thýein* burn as a sacrifice]

**thy|mec|to|mize** (thī mek′tə mīz), *v.t.,* **-mized, -miz|ing.** to subject to thymectomy.

**thy|mec|to|my** (thī mek′tə mē), *n., pl.* **-mies.** the

surgical removal of the thymus gland. [< *thymus* + *-ectomy*]

**thym|e|lae|a|ceous** (thim′ə lē ā′shəs), *adj.* belonging to the mezereum family of trees and shrubs. [< New Latin *Thymelaeaceae* the family name (< Greek *thymelaiā* < *thýmon* thyme + *elaiā* olive tree) + English *-ous*]

**thy|mic¹** (tī′mik), *adj.* having to do with or derived from thyme. [< *thym*(e) + *-ic*]

**thy|mic²** (thī′mik), *adj.* of or having to do with the thymus gland. [< *thym*(us) + *-ic*]

**thymic acid**, = thymol.

**thy|mi|dine** (thī′mə din, -dēn), *n.* a nucleoside of thymine occurring in DNA that stimulates growth in cells. *Formula:* $C_{10}H_{14}N_2O_5$

**thy|mine** (thī′min, -mēn), *n.* a substance present in nucleic acid in cells. It is one of the pyrimidine bases of DNA, corresponding to uracil in RNA. *Formula:* $C_5H_6N_2O_2$ *Abbr:* T (no period). [< *thym*(us) + *-ine²* (because it was originally extracted from the thymus gland)]

**thy|mo|cyte** (thī′mə sīt), *n.* a lymphocyte found in the thymus gland.

**thy|mol** (thī′mōl, -mol), *n.* an aromatic, white or colorless, crystalline phenol obtained from the volatile oil of thyme and various other plants or made synthetically, used chiefly as an antiseptic. *Formula:* $C_{10}H_{14}O$ [< *thym*(e) + *-ol¹*]

**thy|mo|sin** (thī′mə sin), *n.* a hormone of the thymus gland, associated with the production of lymphocytes that cause cellular immunity: *Thymosin treatment has raised the T-cell count in more than 75 per cent of the cancer patients* (Allan L. Goldstein).

**thy|mus** (thī′məs), *n., adj.* —*n.* = thymus gland. —*adj.* of or having to do with the thymus gland. [< New Latin *thymus* < Greek *thýmos* (originally) a warty excrescence]

**thymus gland**, a small, ductless gland near the base of the neck, found in young vertebrates. It disappears or becomes rudimentary in the adult. The thymus gland aids in the development of lymphocytes necessary to protect the young from disease. The thymus of lambs and calves is used for food and is called sweetbread. See picture under **endocrine gland**.

**thymus nucleic acid**, deoxyribonucleic acid, originally extracted from the thymus gland.

**thym|y** (tī′mē), *adj.* having to do with or like thyme; full of thyme: *thymy hills.*

**thy|ra|tron** (thī′rə tron), *n.* a gas-filled, three- or four-element vacuum tube containing a hot cathode, in which the grid initiates, but does not limit, the current. It is used mainly as an electronic switch. [< Greek *thýrā* door + English *-tron*]

**thy|ris|tor** (thī ris′tər), *n.* a transistor or semiconductor that forms an open circuit until signaled to switch to the conducting state by a controlling electrode: *If thyristors are used to control the motor of an electric car, the vehicle moves smoothly but with poor efficiency at low speeds* (New Scientist). [< *thyr*(atron) + (trans)*istor*]

**thy|ro|ac|tive** (thī′rō ak′tiv), *adj.* stimulating the activity of thyroxine and other secretions of the thyroid gland.

**thy|ro|ar|y|te|noid** (thī′rō ar′ə tē′noid), *adj.* having to do with or connecting the thyroid and arytenoid cartilages of the larynx. [< *thyro*(id) + *arytenoid*]

**thy|ro|cal|ci|to|nin** (thī′rō kal′sə tō′nən), *n.* = calcitonin.

**thy|ro|glob|u|lin** (thī′rō glob′yə lin), *n.* a protein of the thyroid gland that contains iodine, found in the colloid substance of the gland. [< *thyro*(id) + *globulin*]

**thy|roid** (thī′roid), *n., adj.* —*n.* **1** = thyroid gland. **2** a medicine made from the thyroid glands of certain domestic animals, used in the treatment of goiter, obesity, and other disorders caused by a deficiency in the thyroid gland. **3** = thyroid cartilage. **4** a part of the body, such as a vein, near the thyroid gland.
—*adj.* of or having to do with the thyroid gland or the thyroid cartilage: *thyroid extract.*
[< Greek *thyreoeidḗs* shield-shaped < *thyreós* oblong shield (< *thýrā* door) + *eîdos* form]

**thy|roi|dal** (thī roi′dəl), *adj.* = thyroid.

**thyroid body**, = thyroid gland.

**thyroid cartilage**, the principal cartilage of the larynx, which forms the lump called the Adam's apple in human beings.

**thy|roid|ec|to|mize** (thī′roi dek′tə mīz), *v.t.*, **-mized, -miz|ing.** to subject to thyroidectomy.

**thy|roid|ec|to|my** (thī′roi dek′tə mē), *n., pl.* **-mies.** the surgical removal of all or part of the thyroid gland. [< *thyroid* + *-ectomy*]

***thyroid gland**, an important ductless gland in the neck of vertebrates, near the larynx and upper windpipe, that affects growth and metabolism. An enlargement of the thyroid gland is called a goiter. Thyroxine is secreted by the thyroid gland.

**thy|roid|i|tis** (thī′roi dī′tis), *n.* inflammation of the thyroid gland.

**thy|ro|tox|i|co|sis** (thī′rō tok′sə kō′sis), *n. Medicine.* hyperthyroidism.

**thy|ro|tro|phic** (thī′rō trō′fik), *adj.* = thyrotropic.

**thy|ro|tro|phin** (thī′rō trō′fin), *n.* = thyrotropin.

**thy|ro|trop|ic** (thī′rō trop′ik, -trō′pik), *adj.* stimulating the thyroid gland; regulating thyroid activity: *thyrotropic hormone.*

**thy|ro|tro|pin** (thī′rō trō′pin), *n.* a hormone produced by the pituitary gland, that regulates the activity of the thyroid gland.

**thy|rox|in** (thī rok′sin), *n.* = thyroxine.

**thy|rox|ine** (thī rok′sēn, -sin), *n.* a white, crystalline amino acid, the principal secretion of the thyroid gland, which stimulates metabolism and, in children, affects growth. A synthetic form is used to treat goiter and other thyroid disorders. *Formula:* $C_{15}H_{11}I_4NO_4$

**thyrse** (thėrs), *n. Botany.* thyrsus.

**thyr|sus** (thėr′səs), *n., pl.* **-si** (-sī). **1** *Greek Mythology.* a staff or spear tipped with an ornament like a pine cone and sometimes wrapped around with ivy and vine branches. It was carried by Dionysus (Bacchus) and his followers. **2** *Botany.* a form of mixed inflorescence, a contracted panicle, in which the main ramification is indeterminate and the secondary or ultimate is determinate, as in the lilac and horse chestnut.
[< New Latin *thyrsus* < Latin < Greek *thýrsos* (literally) staff, stem]

**thy|sa|nu|ran** (thī′sə nůr′ən, -nyůr′-; this′ə-), *n., adj.* —*n.* any one of an order of wingless insects having long antennae, a scaly, flattened body that is silvery or gray in color, and two or three slender caudal appendages. Silverfishes and bristletails are thysanurans.
—*adj.* of or belonging to this order.
[< New Latin *Thysanura* the order name (< Greek *thýsanos* tassel, fringe + *ourā* tail) + *-an*]

**thy|self** (ᴛʜī self′), *pron. Archaic.* yourself.

**ti¹** (tē), *n. Music.* the seventh tone of the diatonic scale; si. [*ti* replaced earlier *si*, to avoid confusion with *sol;* see etym. under **gamut**]

**ti²** (tē), *n., pl.* **tis.** any one of various Polynesian and Asian palmlike shade trees and shrubs of the agave family; ti palm. The elongated leaves of one species are often used for food wrappers or hula skirts. [< Polynesian *ti*]

**Ti** (no period), titanium (chemical element).

**Tian-shan sheep** (tyän′shän′), = Marco Polo sheep. [< *Tian Shan*, mountain range in Asia]

***ti|ar|a** (tī ãr′ə, tē-; tē är′-), *n.* **1** a band of gold, jewels, or flowers worn by women around the head as an ornament. **SYN:** coronet. **2a** the triple crown worn by the pope as a symbol of his position. **b** *Figurative.* the position or authority of the pope. **3** an ancient Persian headdress worn by men. [< Latin *tiara* < Greek *tiārā*]

***tiara**
definitions 1, 2a

definition 1

definition 2a

**ti|ar|aed** (tī ãr′əd, tē-; tē är′-), *adj.* adorned with a tiara or tiaras.

**Tib|bu** (tib′bü), *n., pl.* **-bu** or **-bus.** a member of a Negro people of mixed ancestry living in the southeastern part of the Sahara.

**ti|bet** (ti bet′, tib′ət), *n.*, or **tibet cloth**, a soft, smooth, twilled woolen cloth. [< *Tibet*, a country (now part of China), where it was produced]

***thyroid gland**

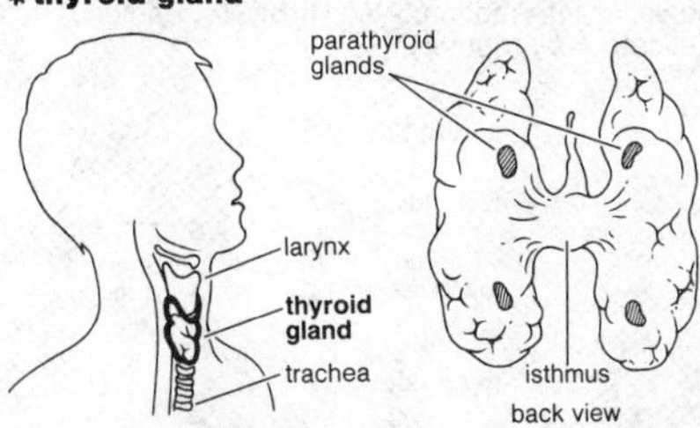

back view

**Ti|bet|an** (ti bet′ən), *adj., n.* —*adj.* of or having to do with Tibet, a region in southwestern China, its people, or their language.
—*n.* **1** a person born or living in Tibet. **2** the Sino-Tibetan language of Tibet. Tibetan is related to Burmese and Thai. Also, **Thibetan.**

**Tibetan terrier**, any one of a breed of dog that originated in Tibet. Tibetan terriers resemble Old English sheepdogs but are smaller, standing from 14 to 16 inches high, and have a fluffy tail that curls over the dog's back.

**Ti|bet|o-Bur|man** (ti bet′ō bėr′mən), *n.* a subdivision of the Sino-Tibetan language family, including Tibetan and Burmese.

**tib|i|a** (tib′ē ə), *n., pl.* **-i|ae** (-ē ē), **-i|as.** **1** the inner and thicker of the two bones of the leg, from the knee to the ankle; shinbone. See diagram under **leg**. **2** a corresponding bone in amphibians, birds, reptiles, and mammals. **3** the fourth section (from the body) of the leg of an insect. **4** an ancient Roman flute. **5** one of several organ stops, mostly of the flute family; flageolet. [< Latin *tībia* shinbone, pipe, or flute]

**tib|i|al** (tib′ē əl), *adj.* of or having to do with the tibia.

**tib|i|o|fib|u|lar** (tib′ē ō fib′yə lər), *adj.* of or having to do with both the tibia and the fibula: *the posterior tibiofibular ligament.*

**tic** (tik), *n.* **1** a habitual, involuntary twitching of the muscles, especially those of the face. **2** = tic douloureux. [< French *tic,* ultimately < a Germanic word]

**ti|cal** (ti käl′, -kôl′; tē′kəl), *n., pl.* **-cals** or **-cal.** **1** a former Siamese (Thai) monetary unit and silver coin, worth 100 satang, now replaced by the baht. **2** a former Siamese (Thai) unit of weight, equal to 231.5 grains, or about half an ounce troy. [< Thai *tical* < Malay *tikal*]

**tic dou|lou|reux** (tik′ dü′lü rü′; *French* tēk dü lü-rœ′), a severe facial neuralgia, especially of the trigeminal nerve, accompanied by twitching. [< French *tic douloureux* (literally) painful tic]

**tick¹** (tik), *n., v.* —*n.* **1** the quick, light sound made by a watch or clock. **2** a sound like it: *the tick of a moth against the windowpane.* **3** *Informal, Figurative.* a moment or second; instant: *I'll be with you in a tick.* **SYN:** jiffy. **4** a small mark, such as a check mark, made to indicate something: *He put a tick opposite each job that was done on his list.*
—*v.i.* **1** to make a tick or ticks: *The clock ticks louder and louder in a quiet room.* **2** *Informal.* to function, work, or go: *What makes the gadget tick?* —*v.t.* **1** to mark off: *The clock ticked away the minutes.* **2** to mark with a tick or ticks; check: *He ticked the items delivered one by one.*
**tick off, a** to mark or check off: *to tick off the items on a list.* **b** *Figurative.* to say quickly; rattle off: *She now has so many clothes ... and she can tick off the labels as readily as if they were the names of the songs she has recorded* (New York Times). **c** *Informal.* to reprove severely: *[He] tried to tick me off, once; and I lost my temper* (M. Cole). **d** *Informal.* to make angry: *And then Durward showed up for lunch an hour and 20 minutes late. Daddy was really ticked off* (Maclean's).
**tick over,** *British.* **a** to run slowly without transmitting power; idle. A motor ticks over when it is out of gear and running slowly. *The engines were started and allowed to tick over for about 10 minutes or so, to warm up gradually* (C. F. S. Gamble). **b** *Slang.* to work; function; operate: *Students ... would keep the place ticking over in the evening* (London Daily Telegraph).
[Middle English *tek* (originally) a light touch or tap; probably ultimately imitative]

***tick²**
definition 1

wood tick

***tick²** (tik), *n.* **1** a tiny eight-legged animal, related to the spider, that attaches itself to the skin of mammals, birds, and reptiles and sucks their blood. Ticks carry various infectious diseases which attack people or animals. *Meanwhile certain wise old Western cattle growers ... had a notion that Texas fever was caused by an insect living on the cattle and sucking blood ... called a tick* (Paul de Kruif). **2** a dipterous or wingless insect, such as the sheep tick, that sucks the blood of certain animals, including sheep, cattle, or deer.
[Middle English *tyke*, perhaps unrecorded Old English *tīca*]

**Pronunciation Key:** hat, āge, cãre, fär; let, ēqual, tėrm; it, īce; hot, ōpen, ôrder; **oi**l, **ou**t; cup, pů̇t, rüle; **ch**ild; lo**ng**; **th**in; ᴛʜen; **zh**, measure; ə represents **a** in about, **e** in taken, **i** in pencil, **o** in lemon, **u** in circus.

**tick**[3] (tik), *n.* **1** the cloth covering of a mattress or pillow. **2** *Informal.* ticking. [Middle English *tyke, teke,* or *tikke,* probably ultimately < Latin *thēca* case < Greek *thḗkē* < a root of *tithénai* to put, place]

**tick**[4] (tik), *n. Informal.* credit; trust: *to buy something on tick. This villainous habit of living upon tick* (Robert L. Stevenson). [apparently short for *on* (*the*) *tick*(et)]

**tick|bird** (tik′bėrd′), *n.* **1** the ani, a kind of cuckoo. It often feeds on ticks that infest cattle and other animals. **2** = oxpecker.

**tick|er** (tik′ər), *n.* **1** a person or thing that ticks. **2** a telegraphic instrument that prints market reports or news on a paper tape; stock ticker. **3** *Slang.* a watch or clock. **4** *Slang, Figurative.* the heart.

**ticker tape**, a cellophane or paper tape on which a ticker prints stock-market reports or news.

**tick|er-tape parade** (tik′ər tāp′), a parade through the streets of a city in honor of a visiting celebrity or dignitary, accompanied by showers of ticker tape or the like thrown from buildings.

**tick|et** (tik′it), *n., v.* —*n.* **1** a card or piece of paper that gives its holder a right or privilege: *a ticket to the theater, a railroad ticket, a lottery ticket, a laundry ticket.* **SYN**: voucher, coupon. **2** *Informal.* a summons given by a policeman to a person who has broken a law to pay a fine or appear in court, usually with reference to traffic violations: *a ticket for speeding, a parking ticket.* **3** a card or piece of paper attached to something to show its price, what it is or consists of, or some similar information. **4** the list of candidates to be voted on that belong to one political party: *to vote the Republican ticket.* **SYN**: slate. **5** *Banking.* a temporary record, as of transactions before their recording in a more permanent form. **6** *Slang.* a certificate: *a chief engineer's ticket.* **7** *Obsolete.* a notice posted in a public place; placard.
—*v.t.* **1** to put a ticket on; mark with a ticket: *All articles in the store are ticketed with the price.* **2** *Figurative.* to describe or mark as if by a ticket; label; designate; characterize. **3** to furnish with a ticket, especially an airplane or a railroad ticket: *We were 'ticketed through to the depot'* (Longfellow). **4** *Informal.* to serve with a summons: *ticketed for careless driving* (Time).
**the ticket**, *Informal.* the correct or proper thing: *A small, flat trailer ... would be just the ticket for an overnight stop in a throughway service area* (New Yorker).
[short for Middle French *etiquet* ticket < *estiquette* < *estiquer* to affix, stick < Dutch *stikken.* Compare etym. under **etiquette**.]

**tick|et|hold|er** (tik′it hōl′dər), *n.* a person who has a ticket of admission.

**tick|et|less** (tik′it lis), *adj.* having no ticket.

**ticket of leave**, *British.* a permit formerly given in Great Britain and Australia, granting a convict his liberty before his sentence has expired, provided he obeys certain conditions. —**tick′et-of-leave′**, *adj.*

**tick|et-of-leave man** (tik′it əv lēv′), *British.* a convict released on parole.

**tick|et|y-boo** (tik′ə tē bü′), *adj. Especially British.* all right; fine; OK.

**tick|ey** (tik′ē), *n., pl.* **-eys.** (in South Africa) a threepenny piece; threepence. Also, **ticky**.

**tick fever**, **1** a fever attacking people or cattle, transmitted by ticks, especially Rocky Mountain spotted fever. **2** an infectious blood disease of cattle, often fatal when acute, caused by an animal parasite that is carried by certain ticks, and characterized by fever, destruction of red blood corpuscles, and emaciation; Texas fever.

**tick|ing** (tik′ing), *n.* a strong cotton or linen cloth, used to cover mattresses and pillows and to make tents and awnings.

**tick|le** (tik′əl), *v.,* **-led, -ling,** *n., adj.* —*v.t.* **1a** to touch lightly, causing little thrills, shivers, or wriggles: *He tickled the baby's feet and made her laugh.* **b** to cause to have such a feeling: *Don't tickle me.* **2** *Figurative.* to excite pleasurably; amuse; please: *The child was tickled with his new toys. This joke will really tickle you.* **SYN**: divert. **3** to play, stir, get, or move with light touches or strokes: *to tickle a piano or guitar, to tickle a fire.* **4** to stir up or refresh (the memory).
—*v.i.* to have a tickling feeling: *My nose tickles from the dust and I want to scratch it.*
—*n.* **1** a tingling or itching feeling. **2** the act of tickling.
—*adj. Dialect.* easily upset or overthrown; insecure; tottering.
**be tickled pink**, *Informal.* to be very pleased; be delighted: *We were tickled pink to see our friends on television.*
[Middle English *tikelen;* origin uncertain]

**tick|ler** (tik′lər), *n.* **1** a person or thing that tickles, especially a small feather brush used to tickle the faces of others, as at a carnival or party. **2** *U.S.* a memorandum book, card index, or other device kept to remind, as of engagements or payments due. **3** *Informal.* a difficult or puzzling problem; teaser; puzzler. **4** *Electronics.* tickler coil.

**tickler coil**, *Electronics.* a small coil in a vacuum tube that couples inductively the plate circuit with the grid circuit, so that a portion of the amplified signal is returned for additional amplification.

**tick|lish** (tik′lish), *adj.* **1** sensitive to tickling: *The bottoms of the feet are ticklish.* **2** requiring careful handling; delicate; risky: *a ticklish assignment. Telling a person his faults is a ticklish job.* **SYN**: precarious. **3a** easily upset; unstable: *A canoe is a ticklish craft.* **SYN**: unsteady, shaky. **b** *Figurative: a very proud and ticklish fellow.* **SYN**: touchy. —**tick′lish|ly**, *adv.* —**tick′lish|ness**, *n.*

**tick|seed** (tik′sēd′), *n.* **1** any one of various plants with seeds that look like ticks, such as a coreopsis or a bugseed. **2** = tick trefoil.

**tickseed sunflower**, any one of various bur marigolds having conspicuous yellow flowers.

**tick-tack** (tik′tak′), *n.* **1** a device for making a ticking or tapping sound, as against a window or door in playing a practical joke. **2** = tick-tock. Also, **tic-tac**. [apparently imitative]

**tick-tack-toe** (tik′tak tō′), *n.* **1** a game in which two players alternately put circles or crosses in a figure of nine squares, each player trying to be the first to fill three spaces in a row with his mark. **2** a children's game in which the players, without looking, bring a pencil down on a slate or sheet of paper with a set of numbers drawn on it, the number hit being scored. **3** the practical joke of using a tick-tack. Also, **tic-tac-toe, tit-tat-toe.** [apparently extension of earlier *tick-tack* backgammon]

**tick-tock** (tik′tok′), *n., v.* —*n.* the sound made by a clock or watch.
—*v.i.* to make this sound; tick: *A tall clock tick-tocked on the stair.*

**tick trefoil**, any one of a group of plants of the pea family, having leaves consisting of three leaflets and jointed pods that stick like ticks to the fur of animals.

**tick|y**[1] (tik′ē), *n., pl.* **tick|ies.** = tickey.

**tick|y**[2] (tik′ē), *adj.* full of or infested by ticks.

**tick|y-tack|y** (tik′ē tak′ē), *adj., n. Informal.* —*adj.* uniformly cheap, tasteless, or inferior: *... row on row of ticky-tacky houses appear* (New York Times).
—*n.* ticky-tacky material.
[coined in 1964 by Malvina Reynolds, an American songwriter, apparently by reduplication of *tacky*[2]]

**tic|po|lon|ga** (tik′pə long′gə), *n.* = Russell's viper. [< Singhalese *tik* spot + *polongā* viper]

**tic-tac** (tik′tak′), *n.* = tick-tack.

**tic-tac-toe** (tik′tak tō′), *n.* = tick-tack-toe.

**tid|al** (tī′dəl), *adj.* **1** of tides; having tides; caused by tides. A tidal river is affected by the ocean's tide. **2** dependent on the state of the tide as to time of arrival and departure: *a tidal steamer.* —**tid′al|ly**, *adv.*

**tidal air**, the air that a person ordinarily inhales and exhales at each breath. Tidal air amounts to about a pint in adults.

**tidal current**, the movement of water toward and away from the coast as the tide rises and falls.

**tidal wave**, **1** a large wave or sudden increase in the level of water along a shore, caused by unusually strong winds. **2** a large, destructive ocean wave caused by an underwater earthquake or volcanic eruption. **3** either of two great swellings of the ocean surface (caused by the attraction of the moon and sun) that move around the globe on opposite sides and cause the tides. **4** *Figurative.* any great movement or manifestation of feeling, opinion, or the like; overwhelming outburst: *a tidal wave of popular indignation.*

**tid|bit** (tid′bit′), *n.* a very pleasing bit of food, news, or information. Also, **titbit**. [< earlier *tid* delicate + *bit* morsel]

**tid|dle|dy|winks** (tid′əl dē wingks′), *n.* = tiddlywinks.

**tid|dler** (tid′lər), *n.* **1** *Informal.* something or somebody small: **a** a fish of small size, especially a stickleback: *I could see that such a tiddler did not count for very much with the two Turkana fishermen who were with me* (New Yorker). **b** a small submarine, rocket, or other device: *But these would have a payload of only 150 lb.; ... scientists are apt to look contemptuously at tiddlers like this* (New Scientist). **c** a little child; tot. **2** a person who plays tiddlywinks.

**tid|dley** or **tid|dly** (tid′lē), *adj. Especially British. Slang.* intoxicated. [origin uncertain]

**tid|dly|winks** (tid′lē wingks′), *n.* a game in which the players try to make small colored disks jump from a flat surface into a cup by pressing on their edges with larger disks. [origin uncertain]

✱**tide**[1] (tīd), *n., v.,* **tid|ed, tid|ing,** *adj.* —*n.* **1a** the rise and fall of the ocean about every twelve hours, caused by the attraction of the moon and the sun: *We go swimming at high tide; at low tide we dig for clams.* See picture below. **b** the inward or outward flow or current resulting from this on a coast or in a river or bay. **2** = flood tide. **3** *Figurative.* anything that rises and falls like the tide: *the tide of popular opinion. There is a tide in the affairs of men, Which, taken at the flood, leads on to fortune* (Shakespeare). **4** a stream, current, or flood: *Feel this arm of mine —the tide within* (Tennyson). *Faith ... Stands a sea-mark in the tides of time* (Algernon Charles Swinburne). **5** a season; time; a church festival or anniversary (especially in compounds such as *Christmastide, springtide*). **6** *Archaic.* the right moment or occasion; opportune time.
—*v.t.* to carry as the tide does.
—*v.i.* **1** to float or drift with the tide. **2** to flow or surge as the tide does. **3** *Nautical.* to navigate a ship by taking advantage of favoring tides, and anchoring when the tide turns.
—*adj.* = tidal.
**swim against the tide**, to oppose the prevailing trends or conditions; favor or defend an unpopular cause: *We have not had to swim against the tide for our freedom* (Listener).
**tide over**, **a** to help along for a time: *His savings will tide him over his illness.* **b** to overcome (as a difficulty or problem): *We ... believe that for the moment the difficulty is tided over* (Manchester Examiner).
**turn the tide**, to change from one condition to the opposite: *A touchdown in the final minute of play turned the tide against us. The appearance of Joan of Arc turned the tide of war* (Henry Hallam).
[Old English *tīd* (originally) a point or portion of time]

**tide**[2] (tīd), *v.i.,* **tid|ed, tid|ing.** *Archaic.* to betide; happen; befall. [Old English *getīdan* < *tīd* tide[1]]

**tide|gate** (tīd′gāt′), *n.* **1** a gate through which water flows when the tide is in one direction but which closes when the tide is in the other direction. **2** a channel in which a tidal current runs.

**tide|land** (tīd′land′), *n.* **1** land flooded at high tide. **2** submerged coastal land within the historical boundaries of a state and belonging to that state (according to an act passed by the Congress of the United States in May, 1953).

**tide|less** (tīd′lis), *adj.* having no tide; without ebb and flow.

**tide|line** (tīd′līn′), *n.* = tidemark.

**tide|mark** (tīd′märk′), *n.* **1** a mark left or reached by the tide at high or low water; high-water mark or low-water mark. **2** a post or the like set up to mark the point reached by the tide.

**tide mill**, a mill driven by the flow of the tide against a water wheel: *It is natural that man should look for means of harnessing some of the power of the tides for his own benefit, and small tide mills have been operated in a few suitable localities for centuries* (New Scientist).

**tide|race** (tīd′rās′), *n.* a strong tidal current, especially one that flows in a tideway.

**tide rip**, a heavy wave or rough current caused by opposing tides or currents.

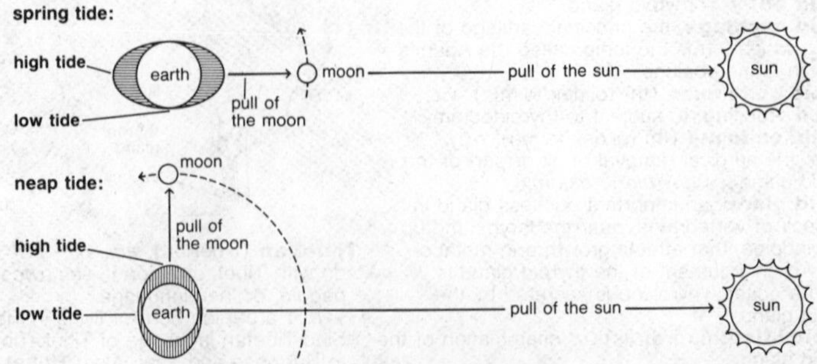

✱**tide**[1] definition 1a

**tide table**, a table that lists the time of high water at a place or places on each day during a particular period.

**tide|wait|er** (tīd′wā′tər), *n.* a customs officer who formerly waited for and boarded ships to prevent the evasion of the customs regulations.

**tide|wa|ter** (tīd′wôt′ər, -wot′-), *n., adj.* —*n.* **1** water in rivers and streams affected by the rise and fall of the tides. **2** water that is brought by the flood tide and overflows land. **3** low-lying land along a seacoast through which tides flow. **4** the seacoast or a region along a seacoast.
—***adj.*** of or along tidewater. Tidewater country is land along the seacoast.

**tide|way** (tīd′wā′), *n.* **1** a channel in which a tidal current runs. **2** a strong current running in such a channel.

**ti|di|er** (tī′dē ər), *n.* a person who tidies: *a most serviceable cleaner and tidier of things* (H. G. Wells).

**ti|ding** (tī′ding), *n. Obsolete.* a piece of news.

**ti|dings** (tī′dingz), *n.pl.* news; information: *joyful tidings. The messenger brought tidings from the battlefield.* **SYN**: word, message. [Old English *tīdung* < *getīdan* to happen, tide[2]]

**ti|dy** (tī′dē), *adj.*, **-di|er, -di|est,** *v.*, **-died, -dy|ing,** *n., pl.* **-dies.** —***adj.*** **1** neat and in order; orderly; trim: *a tidy room.* **SYN**: See syn. under **neat. 2** inclined to keep things neat and in order: *a tidy person.* **3** *Informal.* fairly large; considerable: *$500 is a tidy sum of money.* **4** *Informal.* fairly good.
—***v.t., v.i.*** to make neat; put in order: *She tidied the room. Be sure to tidy up before going out.*
—***n.*** a small cover to keep the back of a chair, etc., from becoming dirty or worn.
[Middle English *tidy* < *tide* time] —**ti′di|ly,** *adv.* —**ti′di|ness,** *n.*

**ti|dy|tips** (tī′dē tips), *n. sing. and pl.* any one of a group of California annual composite herbs with flower heads that have yellow rays tipped with white.

**tie** (tī), *v.*, **tied, ty|ing,** *n.* —***v.t.*** **1** to fasten with string, cord, rope, or the like; bind: *to tie a dog to a tree. Please tie this package.* **SYN**: secure. **2** to arrange to form a bow or knot: *to tie a ribbon in the hair. Mother tied the strings of her apron behind her back.* **3** to tighten and fasten the string or strings of: *to tie one's shoes, to tie an apron.* **4a** to fasten, join, or connect in any way; link: *to be tied to the mainland by an isthmus.* **b** to connect and make fast by a rod or beam; place a tie beam between. **5** *Figurative.* to restrain; restrict; limit; confine: *He did not want to be tied to a steady job.* **6** to make the same score as: *Harvard tied Yale in football.* **7** *Music.* to connect (notes) by a tie or ligature. **8** *Informal, Figurative.* to unite in marriage. **9** *Slang.* to offer or think of (something) to equal or surpass: *He eats my food, borrows my car, and thinks he's done me a favor. Can you tie that?*
—***v.i.*** **1** to fasten by tying; form a bow or knot: *a rope too heavy to tie. That ribbon doesn't tie well.* **2** to join or fasten together; make a bond or connection: *Where does this beam tie with the roof?* **3** to make the same score; be equal in points: *The two teams tied.*
—***n.*** **1** anything connecting or holding together two or more things or parts; fastening; connection; link. **2** a cord, chain, or the like, used for tying. **3** an ornamental knot, bow of ribbon, or the like; knot. **4** = necktie: *He always wears a shirt and tie.* **5** *Figurative.* a thing that unites; bond; obligation: *Family ties have kept him at home.* **SYN**: See syn. under **bond. 6** a heavy piece of timber or iron placed crosswise to form a foundation or support; crosstie: *The rails of a railroad track are fastened to ties.* **7** a connecting beam, rod, or the like; tie beam. **8a** equality in points, votes, etc.: *The game ended in a tie, 3 to 3.* **b** a match or contest in which this occurs; draw. **9** *Music.* a curved line set above or below two notes of the same pitch. A tie indicates that the tones are to be played or sung continuously.
**tie down, a** to limit; confine; restrict: *a hard man to tie down. She is tied down by her home and five children.* **b** to fasten or hold down by tying: *The dogs were accustomed to be tied down separately every night* (Daniel Johnson).
**tie in, a** to connect or be connected: *Where does this line tie in with the main circuit?* **b** *Figurative.* to make or have a connection; relate: *How does that statement tie in with what you said yesterday?* **c** to make subject to a tie-in sale: *Their advertised bargains are usually tied in with some product that's not on sale.*
**tie into,** *Slang.* to attack; lace into: *They girded up their loins, an' tied into him* (R. A. Wason).
**tie one on,** *Slang.* to drink heavily; go on a binge: *I'll tell you how you can tell ... any morning, whether I went and tied one on the night before* (John McNulty).
**ties,** *Informal.* low, laced shoes: *to wear Oxford ties.*
**tie up, a** to tie firmly or tightly: *They had tied up the luggage* (Dickens). **b** to wrap up: *You tie up the present while I make out the card.* **c** *Figurative.* to hinder; stop; delay: *The stalled truck tied up traffic for half an hour. They've tied us up for these two weeks* (S. Merwin). *Death that hath taken her hence ... ties up my tongue, and will not let me speak* (Shakespeare). **d** *Figurative.* to invest (money) or place (property) in such a way as to make it unavailable for other use: *Since his money was tied up in other investments, he was unable to buy the stocks and bonds.* **e** *Figurative.* to have one's program full; be very busy: *I can't go tomorrow; I'm all tied up.* **f** to connect; relate: *I tried to tie up all that had happened with the inexplicable quietness in Lena's eyes* (P. Perera). **g** *Figurative.* to associate: *There are ... well over one hundred booksellers who are tying up with the national advertising campaign* (Publishers' Weekly). **h** to moor; anchor: *Dale ... eased us into a dock, where we tied up* (Anthony Bailey). **i** *Figurative.* to complete (as a sale); conclude an agreement with: *to tie up a deal.*
[Old English *tīgan* < *tēag* a tie, rope] —**tie′less,** *adj.*

**tie-and-dye** (tī′ən dī′), *adj.* tie-dyed.

**tie|back** (tī′bak′), *n.* **1** a strip of material used to tie a curtain back from a window: *Draperies were trimmed with fringe, elaborate tiebacks, and swags* (G. McStay Jackson). **2** a curtain having such a strip of material.

**tie beam,** a timber or piece serving as a tie, especially, a horizontal beam connecting the lower ends of two opposite principal rafters, thus forming the base of a roof truss.

**tie-break** (tī′brāk′), *n. British.* a system for breaking a tie in tennis in which the player winning five points out of nine takes the set.

**tie-break|er** (tī′brā′kər), *n.* **1** a game played to break a tie between contestants in a match or matches. **2** anything used to break a tie and choose a winner, such as a lottery.

**tie clasp** or **clip,** a clasp or clip for holding a necktie in place by fastening it to the shirt front.

**tied house** (tīd), *British.* an inn or public house owned by or under contract to a brewery and from which all its liquor is purchased.

**tie-dye** (tī′dī′), *v.*, **-dyed, -dye|ing,** *n.* —***v.t., v.i.*** to dye (cloth) to produce a design or pattern, by tying parts of the material in tight knots so that the cloth inside the knot will not absorb the dye: *Simple bias-cut skirts are made of panne velvet tie-dyed by hand to rare shades* (New Yorker).
—***n.*** **1** the process or method of tie-dyeing. **2** a tie-dyed garment or fabric: *The stars fussed with their see-through dresses, tie-dyes, and black ties and then paraded up a red-carpeted walkway* (Time).

**tie-in** (tī′in′), *n., adj.* —*n.* **1** a connection; link; relationship: *Police suspected a tie-in between the murder and the international narcotics ring. Work is proceeding on ... installations of equipment and tie-ins with the main boiler plant* (New York Times). **2a** = tie-in sale. **b** advertising promotion associated with tie-in sales.
—***adj.*** having to do with or characteristic of a tie-in or tie-in sale.

**tie-in sale** (tī′in′), *U.S.* the sale of something desired or scarce on the condition that the buyer buy something else, often unneeded or of lesser value.

**tie|man|nite** (tē′mə nīt), *n.* a mineral, a selenide of mercury, occurring in dark-gray masses or granules with a metallic luster. *Formula:* HgSe [< W. *Tiemann,* a German mineralogist of the 1800's + *-ite*[1]]

**Tien-shan sheep** (tyen′shän′), = Marco Polo sheep. [variant of *Tian-shan sheep*]

**tie|on** (tī′on′, -ôn′), *adj.* that is fastened on by tying: *tie-on labels, a tie-on headband.*

**tie|pin** (tī′pin′), *n.*, or **tie pin,** = stickpin.

**tier**[1] (tir), *n., v.* —***n.*** one of several rows one above another: *tiers of seats in a football stadium.*
—***v.t., v.i.*** to arrange, or be arranged, in tiers.
[< Middle French *tire,* Old French, rank, sequence, order < *tirer* to draw.]

**ti|er**[2] (tī′ər), *n.* a person or thing that ties.

**tierce** (tirs), *n.* **1a** an old unit of liquid measure, equal to 42 United States gallons; one third of a pipe. **b** a cask holding this amount. **2** a sequence of three playing cards in the same suit. **3** *Fencing.* the third of the traditional series of eight defensive positions. The wrist of the hand holding the foil is faced inward with the fingernails downward, so that the foil is pointed upward and slightly to the right. **4a** the third of the seven canonical hours. **b** the service for this hour, following prime. Tierce is usually said about 9 A.M. **5** *Obsolete.* a third; third part. Also, **terce.** [< Old French *tierce,* noun use of feminine of *tiers* third < Latin *tertius* third, related to *trēs* three]

**tierce de Pic|ar|die** (tirs′ də pik′ər dē), *Music.* Picardy third. [< French *tierce de Picardie*]

**tier|cel** (tir′səl), *n.* = tercel. [< Old French *tercel, tiercel;* see etym. under **tercel**]

**-tiered,** *combining form.* having ______ tiers: *Three-tiered = having three tiers.*

**tie rod, 1** one of the rods connecting the front wheels of an automobile, moved by the steering mechanism when turning the wheels to the left or right. **2** = tie beam.

**tier|ra ca|lien|te** (tyer′ə ka lyen′tə), a very warm region or climatic zone, especially in high plateaus of tropical South America, extending from sea level to about 3,000 feet. [< Spanish *tierra caliente* hot land]

**tier|ra fri|a** (tyer′ə frē′ə), a cold region or climatic zone lying between 6,000 and 10,000 feet above sea level. In the mountains of tropical South America, it lies above the tierra templada. [< Spanish *tierra fría* cold land]

**tier|ra tem|pla|da** (tyer′ə tem plä′də), a temperate region or climatic zone lying between 3,000 and 6,000 feet above sea level, or midway between the tierra caliente and tierra fría of tropical South America. [< Spanish *tierra templada* temperate land]

**tiers é|tat** (tyer zā tä′), *French.* the third estate; common people.

**tie tack,** a decorative pin for holding a necktie in place, the point of which pierces the tie and shirt and is gripped by a small button on the inside.

**tie-up** (tī′up′), *n.* **1** the action of stopping work or action on account of a strike, storm, or accident: *The heavy snowstorm caused a tie-up of traffic.* **SYN**: halt. **2** *Informal.* a connection; relation: *There is no tie-up between the two business firms.* **3** a place for mooring a boat. **4** *U.S. Dialect.* a place for tying up or stabling cattle. **5** (in wrestling) a coming to grips while in a standing position; clinch.

**tiff**[1] (tif), *n., v.* —***n.*** **1** a little quarrel: *a boy and a girl ... having a bit of a tiff* (Arnold Bennett). **2** a slight outbrust of temper or ill humor.
—***v.i.*** **1** to have a little quarrel. **2** to be slightly peevish; be in a huff.
[origin uncertain]

**tiff**[2] (tif), *n.* a little drink, as of punch, beer, or other mild liquor. [probably imitative]

**tiff**[3] (tif), *v.i. British.* to lunch; tiffin. [< British slang *tiffing,* verbal noun of *tiff* to sip, drink.]

**tif|fa|ny** (tif′ə nē), *n., pl.* **-nies. 1** a thin, transparent silk. **2** a gauzy muslin. [< Old French *tifinie* Epiphany < Latin *theophania* theophany, Epiphany; allusion is uncertain]

**tif|fin** (tif′ən), *n., v.i., v.t. British.* lunch. [Anglo-Indian, probably < *tiffing;* see etym. under **tiff**[3].]

**tig** (tig), *v.*, **tigged, tig|ging,** *n.* —***v.i.*** *Scottish.* **1** to give light or playful touches; trifle; dally. **2** to interfere or meddle.
—***v.t.*** to touch in the game of tag.
—***n.*** **1** *Scottish.* a touch or tap. **2** the children's game of tag. **3** *British Informal.* a quarrel: *The spectacle of a man in a tig, even of two men in a tig, is not as a rule wholly entertaining* (Punch).
[probably variant of *tick*[1]]

***tiger**
definition 1a

***ti|ger** (tī′gər), *n.* **1a** a large, fierce, flesh-eating mammal of Asia that has dull-yellow fur striped with black. It belongs to the cat family and to the same genus as the lion, jaguar, and leopard. **b** any one of various related animals, such as the jaguar of South America or the leopard of South Africa. **c** any animal of similar appearance, such as the thylacine or Tasmanian wolf. **2** *Figurative.* a fierce, cruel, grasping, or bloodthirsty person. **3** a figure of a tiger, used as a badge or crest: *the Tammany tiger, the Princeton tiger.* **4** *U.S. Informal.* an extra yell at the end of a cheer: *Let's have three cheers and a tiger!* **5** *U.S. Slang.* the game of faro. **6** *Obsolete.* a boy in livery acting as groom or footman.
**buck** (or **fight**) **the tiger,** *U.S. Slang.* **a** to play

**Pronunciation Key:** hat, āge, cãre, fär; let, ēqual, tėrm; it, īce; hot, ōpen, ôrder; oil, out; cup, pu̇t, rüle; child; long; thin; ᴛʜen; zh, measure; ə represents **a** in about, **e** in taken, **i** in pencil, **o** in lemon, **u** in circus.

faro: *A third amused the company by informing them as to the luck he had that day bucking the tiger* (Police Gazette). **b** (in faro and roulette) to play against the bank: *bucking the tiger, which we wouldn't advise any one to do* (Rocky Mountain News).
**ride a tiger**, to attempt to use something that one may not be able to control and so endanger oneself: *De Gaulle's insistence on the prolongation of nationalism [did] not extend to the economic sphere ... There [were] uncertainties: one may wonder whether he [expected] to ride the German economic tiger, and how* (Manchester Guardian).
[partly Old English *tigras,* plural < Latin *tigris;* partly < Old French *tigre,* learned borrowing from Latin *tigris* < Greek *tigris*] —**ti′ger|like′**, *adj.*

**tiger beetle**, an active, flying beetle that preys on other insects. Its larvae live in tunnels in sandy soil and catch insects that come near. See picture under **beetle**[1].

**tiger cat**, **1** any one of several wildcats smaller than a tiger, but similar in markings and ferocity, such as the margay, ocelot, or serval. **2** a domestic cat with cross stripes like those of a tiger.

**ti|ger-eye** (tī′gər ī′), *n.* = tiger's-eye.

**tiger fish**, a ferocious, freshwater fish of southeastern Africa, having sharp teeth that slant backward and resembling a shark but smaller.

**ti|ger|ish** (tī′gər ish), *adj.* like a tiger; fierce; cruel; bloodthirsty. —**ti′ger|ish|ly**, *adv.* —**ti′ger|ish|ness**, *n.*

**tiger lily**, **1** a tall lily that has nodding, dull-orange flowers spotted with black. It is native to eastern Asia. The tiger lily produces bulblets in the axils of the leaves. **2** any one of various other lilies with similar flowers.

**tiger mosquito**, = aëdes.

**tiger moth**, any one of a group of moths having brightly colored, striped or spotted wings and a hairy body.

**tiger salamander**, either of two large salamanders of North America with tigerlike stripes on the back. Some tiger salamanders retain the gills of the larval stage, spending their adult lives in water.

**ti|ger's-eye** (tī′gərz ī′), *n.* a golden-brown stone with a changeable luster, composed chiefly of quartz colored by iron oxide, and used as a gem.

**tiger shark**, a large, voracious shark of the warmer parts of the Atlantic and Pacific oceans having yellow streaks on its grayish-black body; leopard shark.

**tiger's milk**, a drink made with dried milk, soybean oil, and various protein and vitamin concentrates, sold as a health food.

**tiger snake**, a poisonous snake of Australia, having a brownish body with crossbands of different colors.

**tiger swallowtail**, a large yellow, swallowtailed butterfly streaked with black, common in the United States.

**tight** (tīt), *adj., adv., n.* —*adj.* **1** firm; held firmly; packed or put together firmly: *a tight grip, a tight knot.* **SYN**: close, compact. **2** drawn; stretched: *a tight canvas, a tight cable.* **3** fitting closely; fitting too closely: *tight clothing. Since she gained weight, her skirt was a tight fit.* **SYN**: snug, close-fitting. **4** *Dialect.* well-built; trim; neat: *For she is such a smart little craft ... a bright, little, tight, little ... slim little craft* (W. S. Gilbert). **5** not letting water, air, or gas in or out: *a tight boat. The tight roof kept rain from leaking in.* **6** not wasteful of words; terse; concise: *tight writing, a tight style.* **7** *Informal, Figurative.* hard to deal with or manage; difficult: *a tight corner, to have tight going for a few years. His lies got him in a tight place.* **8** *Informal.* almost even; close: *It was a tight race.* **9a** hard or expensive to get; scarce: *Money for mortgages is tight just now.* **b** characterized by scarcity or eager demand: *a tight money market.* **10** *Figurative.* strict; severe: *to rule with a tight hand.* **11** *Informal.* stingy; close-fisted: *A miser is tight with his money.* **SYN**: parsimonious. **12** *Slang.* drunk; tipsy; intoxicated: *If you get tight, the policemen are told to take you home rather than to prison* (Time). **13** *Obsolete.* **a** competent; capable. **b** alert; lively.
—*adv.* firmly; closely; securely: *The rope was tied too tight. ... holding tight on with both hands* (Dickens). *He ... shut his lips tight* (Joseph Conrad).
—*n. U.S. Informal.* a tight place; position of difficulty: *He will work all day, He will work all night, He will work much harder when he gets in a tight* (Gene Roberts).
**in the tight**, *British.* in close formation or play, as in Rugby: *Instead of being pushed, Cambridge themselves now did the pushing, and they had an advantage in the tight until their numbers were reduced* (London Times).
**sit tight**. See under **sit**.
**tights**, a close-fitting garment, usually covering the lower part of the body and legs, worn by acrobats and dancers, and as women's apparel.
**up tight**, *Slang.* in a state of anxiety; tense; keyed-up: *A 21-year-old hippie ... said that the East Villagers are "up tight and frightened"* (New York Times).
[apparently alteration of Middle English *thight,* perhaps < Scandinavian (compare Old Icelandic *thēttr* watertight)] —**tight′ly**, *adv.* —**tight′ness**, *n.*
—*Syn. adj.* **2 Tight, taut** mean drawn or stretched so as not to be loose or slack. **Tight**, the more general word, applies to anything drawn over or around something so firmly that there is no looseness: *You need a tight string around that package.* **Taut** emphasizes stretching until the thing described would break, snap, or tear if pulled more tightly, and is used chiefly as a nautical or mechanical term or to describe strained nerves or muscles: *The covering on a drum must be taut.*

**-tight**, *combining form.* not allowing the passage of ______, as in *airtight, watertight.*

**tight|en** (tī′tən), *v.t.* to make tight or tighter: *He tightened his belt.* —*v.i.* to become tight or tighter: *The rope tightened as I pulled on it.* —**tight′en|er**, *n.*

**tight end**, *Football.* an end who lines up close to the tackle.

**tight-fist|ed** or **tight|fist|ed** (tīt′fis′tid), *adj.* somewhat miserly; stingy; close-fisted. **SYN**: parsimonious. —**tight′-fist′ed|ness, tight′fist′edness**, *n.*

**tight|ish** (tī′tish), *adj.* **1** rather tight or close-fitting: *tightish trousers.* **2** *Figurative.* somewhat difficult.

**tight-knit** (tīt′nit′), *adj.* intimately connected; close-knit: *a tight-knit community.*

**tight-laced** (tīt′lāst′), *adj.* **1** tightly laced. **2** = strait-laced.

**tight-lipped** (tīt′lipt′), *adj.* **1** keeping the lips firmly together. **2** saying little or nothing. **SYN**: taciturn.

**tight-mouthed** (tīt′mouᴛʜd′, -moutht′), *adj.* **1** = close-mouthed. **2** = tight-lipped.

**tight|rope** (tīt′rōp′), *n., adj.* —*n.* **1** a rope or cable stretched tight and raised above the ground, on which acrobats perform. **2** *Figurative.* a difficult or dangerous situation: *The middle-aged man in a new career is on a tightrope between asking too many questions and asking too few* (London Times).
—*adj.* of, having to do with, or done on a tightrope.
**walk a tightrope**, to maneuver in a difficult or dangerous situation: *The West has walked a tightrope on Trieste since then, trying to keep both Italy's and Yugoslavia's friendship and say nothing to alienate either* (Wall Street Journal).

**tights** (tīts), *n.pl.* See under **tight**.

**tight squeeze**, a difficult situation; narrow escape.

**tight|wad** (tīt′wod′), *n. Slang.* a stingy person; skinflint: *I don't want to be a tightwad but after all, a dollar is a dollar* (Sinclair Lewis). [American English < *tight* + *wad*[1] roll of money]

**tight|wire** (tīt′wīr′), *n.* a wire tightrope: *A thoroughly trained circus performer, he can walk the tightwire or the slack wire* (Time).

**tig|lic acid** (tig′lik), a poisonous, unsaturated liquid or crystalline acid obtained from croton oil, used in medicine. *Formula:* $C_5H_8O_2$ [< New Latin *tiglium* species name of the croton-oil plant < Medieval Latin *tiglia, tilli*]

**ti|glon** (tī′glon, -glən), *n.* an offspring of a tiger and a lioness. [< *tig*(er) + *l*(i)*on*]

**ti|gon** (tī′gon, -gən), *n.* = tiglon. [< *tig*(er) + (li)*on*]

**Ti|gré** (ti grā′), *n.* one of the two Semitic languages spoken in the north of Ethiopia. The other is Tigrinya.

**ti|gress** (tī′gris), *n.* **1** a female tiger. **2** *Figurative.* a fierce, cruel woman.

**ti|grine** (tī′grin, -grīn), *adj.* like a tiger, especially in coloring or marking. [< Latin *tigrīnus* < *tigris;* see etym. under **tiger**]

**Ti|gri|nya** (ti grē′nyə), *n.* a Semitic language spoken in the north of Ethiopia.

**ti|grish** (tī′grish), *adj.* = tigerish.

**tike** (tīk), *n.* = tyke.

**ti|ki** (tē′kē), *n.* **1** a Polynesian deity, regarded as the creator of man. **2** an image of it in wood or stone. [< Maori *tiki*]

**til**[1] (til, tēl), *n.* = sesame. Also, **teel**. [< Hindi *til* < Sanskrit *tila* sesamum plant]

**til**[2] (tēl), *n.* = tilde.

**ti|la|pi|a** (ti lā′pē ə), *n.* any of a genus of freshwater cichlid fishes important as a source of food in Africa and Asia. [< New Latin *Tilapia*]

**til|bu|ry** (til′bər ē), *n., pl.* **-ries**. a light, two-wheeled carriage without a top, fashionable in the early 1800's. [< *Tilbury,* a British coach designer of the 1800's]

∗**til|de** (til′də), *n.* **1** a diacritical mark used over *n* in Spanish when it is pronounced *ny,* as in *cañon* (kä nyōn′). **2** the same mark, used over certain Portuguese vowels to indicate that they are nasal, as in *São* (souɴ). The Portuguese name for this mark is *til.* **3** (in the pronunciations in this book) a mark used over *a* to show that it is pronounced as in *fare* (fãr). [< Spanish *tilde,* ultimately < Latin *titulus* title. See etym. of doublets **title, tittle, titer.**]

∗**tilde**
definitions 1, 2

cañon
Spanish

São Paolo
Portuguese

**tile** (tīl), *n., v.,* **tiled, til|ing**. —*n.* **1a** a thin piece of baked clay, often glazed and decorated, used for covering roofs, paving floors, lining walls, and ornamenting. **b** any one of various similar thin pieces of plastic, rubber, linoleum, or cement, used for similar purposes. **2** any thin, flat playing piece used in various games, such as mah-jongg and Scrabble. **3** a baked clay pipe for draining lands and roads. **4** tiles; tiling. **5** *Informal.* a stiff hat; high silk hat: *Afore the brim went, it was a very handsome tile* (Dickens).
—*v.t.* to put tiles on or in; build, cover, or decorate with tiles: *to tile a bathroom floor.*
[Old English *tigele,* ultimately < Latin *tēgula,* related to *tegere* cover] —**tile′like′**, *adj.*

**tile|fish** (tīl′fish′), *n., pl.* **-fish|es** or (*collectively*) **-fish**. a large, colorful marine food fish of northern waters. The upper part of its side is bluish or olive-green dotted with small yellow spots, blending into yellowish or rose on the lower part.

**til|er** (tī′lər), *n.* a person who makes or lays tiles.

**tile|work** (tīl′wėrk′), *n.* colored tiles with geometric or arabesque designs, used especially in architecture to decorate mosque walls and domes.

**til|i|a|ceous** (til′ē ā′shəs), *adj.* belonging to the basswood family of plants. [< New Latin *Tiliaceae* the basswood family (< Latin *tiliāceus,* adjective < *tilia* the linden, or lime tree) + English *-ous*]

**til|ing** (tī′ling), *n.* **1** tiles collectively. **2** the work of covering with or laying tiles. **3** anything consisting of or covered with tiles.

**till**[1] (til), *prep., conj.* —*prep.* **1** up to the time of; before; until: *The child played till eight.* **2** *Especially Scottish.* to or unto; as far as.
—*conj.* up to the time when; until: *Walk till you come to a white house.*
[Old English *til* < Scandinavian (compare Old Icelandic *til* < *-tili,* as in *aldertili* life's end)]
▶ **till, until**. These two words are not distinguishable in meaning. *Till* is more usual except at the beginning of sentences: *Until he went to college, he never had thought of his speech. He had never thought of his speech till [or until] he went to college.*

**till**[2] (til), *v.t., v.i.* to cultivate (land), as by plowing, harrowing, and manuring; cultivate; plow: *Farmers till the land before planting.* [Old English *tilian* cultivate, tend, work at; (originally) strive after, probably ultimately < *till* fixed point, goal] —**till′a|ble**, *adj.*

**till**[3] (til), *n.* **1** a small drawer for money, usually under or behind a counter: *A cash register is sometimes called a till.* **2** *Informal.* any place or thing that contains or stores money: *Do we have enough in the till for a vacation?* **SYN**: coffer. [origin uncertain]

**till**[4] (til), *n.* **1** glacial drift or deposit of stiff clay, gravel, sand, and boulders. **2** *British.* a stiff clay. [origin unknown]

**till|age** (til′ij), *n.* **1** the cultivation of land. **SYN**: agriculture, husbandry. **2** the fact or condition of being tilled. **3a** tilled or plowed land. **b** crops growing on it.

**til|land|si|a** (ti land′zē ə), *n.* any one of a large group of herbaceous plants of the pineapple family, found in tropical and subtropical America, most of which grow on trees for support, such as the Spanish moss. [< New Latin *Tillandsia* < Elias *Tillands,* 1640-1693, a Swedish professor of medicine and botanist]

**till|er**[1] (til′ər), *n.* a bar or handle at the stern used to turn the rudder in steering a boat. See picture under **sailboat**. [< Anglo-French *teiler,* Old French *telier* (originally) weaver's beam, learned borrowing from Medieval Latin *telarium* < Latin *tēla* web, loom]

**till|er**[2] (til′ər), *n.* a person who tills land; farmer. [Middle English *tiliere* < Old English *tilian* till[2] + *-ere* -er[1]]

**till|er**[3] (til′ər), *n., v.* —*n.* **1** *Dialect.* a shoot that springs from the root or base of the original stalk. **2** *Dialect.* a young tree; sapling.
—*v.i.* to sprout new shoots from the root or base

of the original stalk, as corn and certain other plants do.
[probably Old English *tealgor, telgra* a shoot (especially, a root sucker) < *telga* branch, twig]

**til|lite** (til′īt), *n.* a sedimentary rock composed of glacial till compacted into hard rock. [< *till*[4] + *-ite*[1]]

**til|ly seed** (til′ē), the seed of the croton. [apparently < French *tilli* < Medieval Latin; see etym. under **tiglic acid**]

**tilt**[1] (tilt), *v., n.* —*v.t.* **1** to cause to slope or slant; lean; tip: *You tilt your head forward when you bow. You tilt your cup when you drink.* **2** to point or thrust (a lance). **3** to rush at; charge. **4** to forge or hammer with a heavy pivoted hammer.
—*v.i.* **1** to be tilted; slope; slant; lean; tip: *This table tilts.* **2** to rush, charge, or fight with lances; joust. Knights used to tilt on horseback.
—*n.* **1a** the act of tilting: *One small tilt upset the lamp.* **b** the condition of being tilted; sloping position; slope; slant: *His hat had a smart tilt. The chair stood at a tilt.* **2** in the Middle Ages: **a** a fight between two men on horseback with lances, who charged at each other and tried to knock each other off the horse; joust. **b** the exercise of riding with a lance or the like at a mark, such as the quintain. **3** a sport in which opponents stand on a canoe or log and try to knock each other off with wooden poles. **4** *Figurative.* **a** a sharp thrust, as if with a weapon: *He used the occasion for sprightly tilts at his Labour and Liberal opponents* (Manchester Guardian Weekly). **b** a dispute or quarrel: *The two writers had a number of tilts in print.* **5** = seesaw. **6** = tilt hammer.
**at full** (or **high**) **tilt**, at full speed or power: *The park's artificial waterfall .. was cascading at full tilt* (New Yorker).
**tilt at**, to attack; fight; protest against: *I'm too discreet To run amuck and tilt at all I meet* (Alexander Pope).
[Middle English *tilten* push over, fall over, apparently unrecorded Old English *tieltan* < *tealt* unsteady] —**tilt′a|ble**, *adj.* —**tilt′er**, *n.*

**tilt**[2] (tilt), *n., v.* —*n.* an awning or canopy, as over a boat or wagon.
—*v.t.* to cover with a tilt or tilts.
[Middle English *telte* a covering of coarse cloth, variant of *tilde* and *telde,* Old English *geteld*]

**tilt|board** (tilt′bôrd′, -bōrd′), *n.* an apparatus used especially in the study of kinesthetic senses, consisting of a horizontal board, pivoted at the center upon a transverse axis in such a way that the subject, lying at full length upon it, may be tilted up or down; tilt table.

**tilt cart**, = tipcart.

**tilth** (tilth), *n.* **1** the condition of being tilled: *a garden in bad tilth, to put a field into good tilth.* **2** the cultivation of land; tillage. **3** tilled land. [Old English *tilth* < *tilian* till[2]]

**tilt hammer**, a heavy hammer used especially in forging, alternately tilted up and allowed to drop.

**tilt|me|ter** (tilt′mē′tər), *n.* a clinometer used by seismologists to detect and measure a tilt in the earth's surface. [< *tilt*[1] + *-meter*]

**tilt roof**, a roof with a generally semicircular section inside and out, like a canopy over a wagon.

**tilt table**, = tiltboard.

**tilt-top table** (tilt′top′), = tip table.

**tilt-wing** (tilt′wing′), *adj.* (of an aircraft) having wings which can be tilted upwards for vertical take-off and landing.

**tilt|yard** (tilt′yärd′), *n.* a place where tilting with lances was done.

**Tim.**, Timothy (referring to either of two books of the New Testament).

**ti|ma|rau** (tē′mə rou′), *n.* = tamarau.

**tim|bal** (tim′bəl), *n.* **1** = kettledrum. **2** a vibrating membrane like a drumhead, by which a shrill or chirping sound is produced, as in the cicada and certain other insects. Also, **tymbal**. [< Middle French *timbale,* alteration of *tamballe,* alteration of Spanish *atabal* Moorish drum < Arabic *aṭ-ṭabl* the drum. Compare etym. under **atabal**.]

**tim|bale** (tim′bəl), *n.* **1** chopped meat, fish, or vegetables, prepared with a sauce and cooked in a mold. **2** a cup-shaped mold of pastry containing various ingredients, often cooked by frying.
[< French *timbale* (originally) timbal (because of the resemblance)]

**tim|ber** (tim′bər), *n., v., adj.* —*n.* **1** wood used for building and making things. Houses, ships, and furniture are made from timber. SYN: lumber. **2** a large, sturdy piece of wood used in building: *Heavy timbers supported the floor above.* Beams and rafters are timbers. **3** a curved piece forming a rib or frame of a ship. **4** growing trees; wooded land; forests: *Half of his land is covered with timber.* SYN: timberland. **5a** trees providing wood suitable for use in building: *to mark timber for felling. Canada is rich in timber.* **b** logs, green or cured, cut from such trees: *a vessel loaded with timber from Sweden.* **6** *British.* **a** a piece of lumber larger than 4½ inches by 6 inches in cross section. **b** lumber. **7** *Figurative.* worth or value as a person; quality; character: *The country needs more men of his timber.*
—*v.t.* to cover, support, build, or furnish with timber.
—*adj.* **1** made or consisting of wood; wooden. **2** of or for timber.
**shiver my timbers**, a mock oath attributed to sailors: *I won't thrash you ... Shiver my timbers if I do* (Frederick Marryat).
[Old English *timber* a building; building material, trees suitable for building]

**timber cruiser**, *U.S.* a man who estimates the amount of timber ready to be felled on a tract of timberland.

**tim|bered** (tim′bərd), *adj.* **1** made of or furnished with timber; covered or supported with logs or beams. **2** covered with growing trees; forested: *the timbered slopes of the Rockies* (Theodore Roosevelt).

**tim|ber|head** (tim′bər hed′), *n. Nautical.* **1** the top part of a rib or frame, rising above the deck, and serving for belaying ropes, etc. **2** a bollard or upright post similar to this in placement and use.

**timber hitch**, a hitch or knot used to fasten a rope around something, such as a spar or post. See picture under **hitch**.

**tim|ber-hitch** (tim′bər hich′), *v.t.* to make fast with a timber hitch.

**tim|ber|ing** (tim′bər ing), *n.* **1** building material of wood, especially logs and beams. **2** timbers. **3** work made of timbers.

**tim|ber|land** (tim′bər land′), *n.* **1** land covered with trees that are, or will be, useful for timber. **2** any land with many trees; forest; woods.

**timber line**, or **tim|ber|line**[1] (tim′bər līn′), *n.* the line on mountains and in polar regions beyond which trees will not grow because of the cold; tree line.

**tim|ber-line** or **tim|ber|line**[2] (tim′bər līn′), *adj.* of or having to do with the timber line.

**tim|ber|man** (tim′bər mən), *n., pl.* **-men**. *Mining.* a man who prepares and takes care of the timbers used for supports.

**timber rattlesnake**, a large rattlesnake found in most of the United States from the Mississippi Valley eastward; banded rattlesnake.

**timber tree**, a tree yielding wood suitable for building or construction.

**timber wolf**, a large gray, black, or white wolf of northern and western North America, Europe, and Asia; gray wolf; lobo.

**tim|ber|work** (tim′bər wėrk′), *n.* work made with timbers, especially logs and beams.

**tim|bre** (tim′bər, tam′-), *n.* **1** *Music.* the quality in sounds, regardless of their pitch or volume, by which a certain voice, instrument, or condition can be distinguished from other voices, instruments, or conditions. Because of differences in timbre, identical notes played on a violin, an oboe, and a trumpet can be distinguished from one another. **2** *Phonetics.* the quality in the resonance of a sound, distinct from loudness and pitch, that gives it its identity. [< Old French *timbre* hemispherical bell without a clapper; heraldic crest, seal or stamp; (originally) a drum, timbrel, ultimately < Greek *týmpanon* kettledrum. See etym. of doublets **timpani**, **tympan**, **tympanum**.]

**tim|brel** (tim′brəl), *n.* a tambourine or similar instrument. [diminutive form of Middle English *timbre* a timbrel, (kettle) drum < Old French *timbre;* see etym. under **timbre**]

**tim|breled** or **tim|brelled** (tim′brəld), *adj.* accompanied by the playing of timbrels.

***time**
definition 14a

***time** (tīm), *n., v.,* **timed**, **tim|ing**, *adj.* —*n.* **1** all the days there have been or ever will be; the past, present, and future. Time is measured in years, months, days, hours, minutes, and seconds. ... *a rose-red city half as old as time* (John William Burgon). *Time present and time past Are both perhaps present in time future* (T. S. Eliot). **2** a part of time: *A minute is a short time. A long time ago people lived in caves. Remember that time is money* (Benjamin Franklin). **3a** a period of time; epoch; era; age: *in the time of the Stuart kings of England.* **b** a period of life; years of living; lifetime: *achievements that will outlast our time.* **c** a period in the existence of the world; unit of geological chronology. **4a** any specified or defined period; period in question: *They were with us the whole time.* **b** time that is or was present; prevailing period: *to change with the times.* **5** a term of imprisonment, enlistment, apprenticeship, or the like: *to complete one's time.* **6** a long time: *What a time it took you!* **7a** some point in time; particular point in time; hour of the clock: *The time the game begins is two o'clock. What time is it right now? At what time do you go to bed?* **b** a particular season; date or span of the calendar: *Summer is the time of hot weather. Autumn is a good time of year to be in the country.* **8** the right part or point of time: *It is time for us to be going. It is time to eat dinner.* **9** occasion; chance; opportunity: *to bide one's time. This time we will succeed. Now's your time to strike! She got the right answer every time.* **10** a way of reckoning time: *sidereal time, solar time, standard time, daylight-saving time.* **11** the conditions of a certain period; condition, such as of life or affairs: *Wars and lack of work bring hard times.* **12** an amount of time required or desired; available time: *I need time to rest. I could multiply witness upon witness ... if I had time* (John Ruskin). **13** an experience during a certain time or on a certain occasion: *Everyone had a good time at the party. The wounded soldier had a bad time for three hours.* **14** *Music.* **a** the rate of movement in music, denoted by a fraction (time signature), the numerator indicating the number of beats to the measure, and the denominator indicating the time value of the note receiving one beat; rhythm: *to beat time.* See picture below. **b** the characteristic rhythm, form, and style of a particular class of compositions; tempo: *waltz time, march time.* **c** the time value or length of a note or rest. **15** the rate of movement in poetry. **16a** the amount of time that one has worked or should work: *His normal time is 8 hours a day.* **b** the pay for a period of work: *to collect one's time. Pay was due to him—'time' as it was called* (Owen Wister). **c** the rate of pay: *We offer straight time for work up to 40 hours and time and a half for Saturdays.* **17** spare time; leisure: *to have time to read, to find time for hobbies.* **18** one of the three unities (unity of time). **19** *Prosody.* a unit or a group of units in metrical measurement, especially a short syllable or mora. **20** *Military.* a rate of stepping; pace: *to march in quick time.* **21a** the period of gestation. **b** the natural ending of gestation; time of giving birth. *Abbr:* t.
—*v.t.* **1** to measure the time of: *to time a worker on a new job. He timed the horse for each half mile.* **2** to fix, set, or regulate the length of in time: *to time an exposure correctly.* **3** to set, regulate, or adjust: *to time an alarm clock, to time all the clocks in an office according to the radio.* **4a** to do at regular times; do in rhythm with; set the time of: *The dancers time their steps to the music.* **b** to mark the rhythm or measure of, as in music. **c** to fix or assign the metrical quantity of (a syllable) or the length of (a note). **5** to choose the moment or occasion for: *The demonstrators timed their march through the business section so that most shoppers would see them. The lady timed her entrance so well that she went in when the prince did.*
—*v.i.* to keep time; sound or move in unison or harmony: *Timing to their stormy sounds, his stormy lays are sung* (John Greenleaf Whittier). *Beat, happy stars, timing with things below* (Tennyson).
—*adj.* **1** of or having to do with time. **2** provided with a clocklike mechanism: *a time lock.* **3** having to do with purchases to be paid for at a future date or dates. **4** *Commerce.* payable at a specified future date or at a certain length of time after presentation.
**about time**, at or near the proper time: *It's about time to go home. It's about time you came!*
**against time**, so as to finish before a certain time: *We are in a race against time in our efforts to rescue the trapped men. ... A man who ... was often ... compelled to write against time for his living* (Algernon Charles Swinburne).
**at a time**, at one time; simultaneously: ... *an utter aversion to speaking to more than one man at a time* (Spectator).
**at the same time**, **a** at one time; not before or after: *In two of Shakespeare's tragedies are introduced, at the same time, instances of counterfeit madness and of real* [*madness*] (London Mirror). **b** while saying this; however; nevertheless: *Give them my best wishes. At the same time I must say I do not envy the girl* (John Strange Winter).
**at times**, now and then; once in a while: *Most people have, at times, wished to have power.*
**behind the times**, old-fashioned; out-of-date: *A newspaper cannot afford to be behind the times.*
**bide one's time**, to wait for a good chance: *a bitter heart that bides its time* (Robert Browning).

**Pronunciation Key:** hat, āge, cãre, fär; let, ēqual, tėrm; it, īce; hot, ōpen, ôrder; **oi**l, **ou**t; cup, pu̇t, rüle; **ch**ild; lo**ng**; **th**in; **ŧh**en; **zh**, measure; **ə** represents **a** in about, **e** in taken, **i** in pencil, **o** in lemon, **u** in circus.

**buy time**, to gain time, as by stalling or postponing; put off or delay a course of action: *The Africans ... are not here to buy time while their governments operate behind the scenes, the way Western diplomats are* (New Yorker).
**do** (or **serve**) **time**, *Informal.* to be imprisoned as a criminal: *a man doing time for bank robbery.*
**fill in the time**, to occupy oneself during a period of inaction: *He filled in the time of waiting by reading a magazine.*
**for the time being**, for the present; for now: *The baby is asleep for the time being. The member for Nuneaton undertakes to stay in Parliament for the time being* (Manchester Guardian Weekly).
**from time to time**, now and then; once in a while: *From time to time we visit my uncle's farm. Statesmen are bound to make mistakes from time to time* (Manchester Guardian Weekly).
**have the time of one's life**, to enjoy oneself to the utmost: *You could tell by his voice that he was having the time of his life out there* (New York Times).
**in good time**, **a** at the right time: *Every true-hearted follower shall, in good time, arrive at the desired goal* (James Gilmour). **b** soon; quickly: *My aunt wants to be back in good time* (Punch).
**in no time**, shortly; before long: *We hurried and reached the boys in no time.*
**in time**, **a** after a while: *I think that in time we may win.* **b** soon enough: *Will the groceries arrive in time to cook for supper? [He] ... returned ... in time to assume the custody of the seal in September 1238* (English Historical Review). **c** in the right rate of movement in music, dancing, or marching: *They were trained to march in time.*
**keep time**, **a** to go correctly: *My watch keeps good time.* **b** to measure or record time or the rate of speed: *He kept time at the race with his stop watch.* **c** to sound or move at the right rate: *The marchers kept time to the music.*
**kill time**, *Informal.* to spend time so as to bring it to an end, as in activities of merely passing interest or entertainment: *He did not want to stay and filled in the puzzle "only to kill time"* (New York Times).
**make time**, to go with speed: *We'll have to make time to catch that early train.*
**mark time**, **a** to move the feet as in marching, but without advancing: *The soldiers marked time until the sergeant gave the order to march.* **b** *Figurative.* to suspend progress temporarily: *Others plan on marking time for a couple of years for another stab at Congress* (Wall Street Journal). **c** *Figurative.* to go through motions without accomplishing anything: *He's bored with his job, and merely marking time at it.*
**once upon a time**, long ago; once: *Once upon a time there were gods only, and no mortal creatures* (Benjamin Jowett).
**on time**, **a** at the right time; not late: *my endeavors to get the family out of the house and into our pew on time* (Scribner's Magazine). **b** with time in which to pay; on credit: *Like all young marrieds starting from ... scratch, my niece bought an apartment full of expensive furniture on time, a TV set on time, and a car on time* (Goodman Ace).
**out of time**, after the prescribed period has elapsed; too late: *Counsel for the respondent took a preliminary objection that the appeal was out of time* (Law Times).
**pass the time away**, to occupy oneself during the day: *She passed the time away by knitting.*
**take one's time**, to be in no hurry; proceed slowly; dally: *[He] does this in his last paragraph, I know, but he certainly takes his time getting there* (New Yorker).
**take time by the forelock**, to plan ahead; do things in plenty of time; anticipate: *We must take time by the forelock; for when it is once past, there is no recalling it* (Jonathan Swift).
**tell time**, *U.S.* to read the clock; know what time it is by the clock: *to teach a child to tell time.*
**time after time** or **time and again**, again and again: *Time after time we have warned you. The importance of the vote in helping Negroes gain equality has been shown time and again in recent years* (New York Times).
**time of life**, age: *a foolish thing to do at his time of life.*
**time out of mind**, beyond memory or record: *The barber's shop in a country town has been, time out of mind, the grand office of intelligence* (Richard Graves).
**times**, multiplied by: *Four times three is twelve. Twenty is five times as much as four.*
**time was**, there was a time; at one time; once: *Time was when we had a national style* (John T. Micklethwaite).
[Old English *tīma*]

**time and a half**, payment for overtime work at one and a half times the usual rate of pay.

**time and motion study**, an examination by an efficiency expert of the manner and time taken to do a job to find out if there is a quicker and easier way to do it; time study.

**time ball**, a ball suspended on a pole on top of an observatory or other tall building for the purpose of indicating an exact moment of mean time, such as noon, by dropping from the top to the bottom of the pole, usually by the closing of an electric circuit at the predetermined moment.

**time belt**, = time zone.

**time bill**, a bill to be paid at the future time stated in the bill.

**time bomb**, **1** a bomb that can be set to go off at a certain time. **2** *Figurative.* something that may blow up destructively at some future time: *The real time bombs in the constitution were the clauses that gave the Turkish [minority] the right to veto the ... legislative proposals of the Greek [majority]* (Maclean's).

**time buyer**, a person employed by an advertising agency to buy radio and television air time.

**time capsule**, **1** a container of things sealed to preserve a record of a civilization or some aspect of it: *A torpedo-shaped time capsule containing current news and literature in microfilm form, and also many objects of everyday use, was buried at the New York World's Fair of 1939-1940.* **2** a time-release capsule.

**time|card** (tīm′kärd′), *n.* **1** a card for recording the amount of time that a person works. **2** = timetable.

**time charter**, **1** a contract for the hiring of a ship, or part of a ship, for a certain period of time, usually to carry cargo: *Most recent time charters have been for the next 8 to 10 months* (Wall Street Journal). **2** the terms of such a contract. **3** a document embodying such a contract.

**time clock**, a clock with a device to record the time when workers arrive and leave or to release locks on the doors of bank vaults or other mechanisms.

**time-con|sum|er** (tīm′kən sü′mər), *n.* something that is time-consuming.

**time-con|sum|ing** (tīm′kən sü′ming), *adj.* taking up much or too much time: *a time-consuming and expensive process.*

**time deposit**, a deposit in a bank that must remain for a definite period of time, or can be withdrawn only after the depositor has given an advance notice to the bank.

**time depth**, *Anthropology.* the period of internal development or continuity of a culture, language, or the like.

**time dilation**, a slowing down or stretching out of time for a speeding object as its velocity increases relative to another object traveling at a different velocity: *One consequence of the special theory of relativity is that rate of time flow is not the same in two coordinate systems moving relative to one another. This phenomenon, known as time dilation, accounts for the slowing down of high-velocity natural clocks as recorded by a stationary observer* (New Scientist).

**time discount**, an amount deducted from an invoice price for payment within a given time.

**time draft**, a draft to be paid at the future time stated in the draft.

**timed-re|lease** (tīmd′ri lēs′), *adj.* = time-release.

**time exposure**, **1** the exposure of a photographic film or plate for a certain time, longer than a half second. **2** a photograph taken in this way.

**time frame**, the time in which something occurs or is planned to occur: *I cannot share that view if it means a crash program with a rigid time frame, like Apollo* (John H. Glenn, Jr.). *His policy clashes with ours because he is operating in a different time frame* (Henry A. Kissinger).

**time fuze** or **fuse**, a fuze that will burn for a certain time, used to set off a charge of explosive.

**time-hon|ored** (tīm′on′ərd), *adj.* honored, revered, or respected because old and established: *Giving gifts at Christmas is a time-honored custom.* SYN: venerable.

**time-hon|oured** (tīm′on′ərd), *adj. Especially British.* time-honored.

**time immemorial**, **1** a date or period in time beyond memory or historic record; age or year before the beginning of known chronology: *a tradition observed from time immemorial.* **2** *Law.* a time beyond legal memory. In England it is fixed by law as time before 1189, the beginning of the reign of Richard I.

**time|keep|er** (tīm′kē′pər), *n.* **1** a measurer of time; person or thing that keeps time; timer: *The factory timekeeper keeps account of the hours of work done. My watch is an excellent timekeeper. A timekeeper at a horse race or track meet measures and records the minutes and seconds taken by the winner and other contestants.* **2** a person who beats time in music.

**time|keep|ing** (tīm′kē′ping), *n.* **1** the work or duties of a timekeeper. **2** the measuring or recording of time.

**time killer**, *Informal.* **1** a pastime: *Touch football is a favorite time killer* (Time). **2** a person seeking to pass the time away.

**time killing**, *Informal.* the act of passing the time away; diversion: *Some of it is time killing for the lonely and some of it is refreshment for the intellectually hungry* (Harper's).

**time lag**, the amount of time between two related events one of which is usually the result of or dependent upon the other: *What fascinated me was the time lag between the issue of my instructions to the ship and the ship's response* (Joyce Warren).

**time-lapse** (tīm′laps′), *adj.* of or by means of time-lapse photography: *an arrangement for showing a bean plant growing by time-lapse movies* (Science News Letter).

**time-lapse photography**, the use of motion pictures to take a sequence of photographs at regular intervals to make a condensed record of a process that is too long to watch or too slow for the mind and the eye to observe.

**time|less** (tīm′lis), *adj.* **1** never ending; eternal. SYN: unending. **2** referring to no special time. **3** *Archaic.* untimely; unseasonable. —**time′less|ly**, *adv.* —**time′less|ness**, *n.*

**time limit**, a time at which something must be done or completed: *We were not working to a rigid syllabus or preparing for an examination; there was no time limit and hence there was a certain leisurely and even playful atmosphere* (New Scientist).

**time loan**, a loan with a fixed date for payment.

**time lock**, **1** a lock controlled by clockwork so that when locked it cannot be unlocked before the expiration of a certain interval of time. **2** = time recording lock.

**time|ly** (tīm′lē), *adj.*, **-li|er**, **-li|est**, *adv.* —*adj.* **1** at the right time; opportune: *The timely arrival of the firemen prevented the fire from destroying the building.* **2** *Archaic.* early.
—*adv.* **1** at the right time; opportunely; seasonably. **2** *Archaic.* early; soon. —**time′li|ness**, *n.*
—*Syn. adj.* **1 Timely, opportune** mean well-timed or especially suited to the time or occasion. **Timely** describes something perfectly suited to the time or circumstance, coming or happening just when it will be most useful or valuable: *Sunday's paper contained a timely article on wise buying and foolish spending.* **Opportune** describes either the moment or occasion most favorable for doing something, or an event or action happening or done at exactly the right and most advantageous moment: *The invitation came at an opportune moment.*

**time machine**, an imaginary machine for carrying passengers back and forth in time.

**time measure**, a system of units used in measuring time. *Examples:* 60 seconds = 1 minute; 60 minutes = 1 hour; 24 hours = 1 day; 7 days = 1 week; 4 weeks, or 28, 29, 30, or 31 days = 1 month; 12 months, or 365 or 366 days = 1 year.

**time money**, = time loan.

**time note**, a note to be paid at the future time stated in the note.

**ti|me|o Da|na|os et do|na fe|ren|tes** (tim′ē ō dan′ā ōs et dō′nə fə ren′tēz), *Latin.* I fear the Greeks even when bringing gifts.

**time of day**, **1** the hour or exact time as shown by the clock. **2** a point or stage in any course or period. **3** *Informal, Figurative.* **a** the current state of affairs. **b** the current fashion; latest thing.
**give one the time of day**, to pay attention to; acknowledge: *He's just an engineer; if we were home the Secretary of State wouldn't give him the time of day* (Harper's).
**know the time of day**, to be aware of the current state of affairs; know what is going on or what is fashionable: *"She knows the time of day," said the other* (Ouïda).
**pass the time of day**, to exchange words in greeting; converse with briefly in passing: *Instead of closing the Vatican gardens when he takes a walk, the new Pope will often pause and pass the time of day with workmen, gardeners, and such* (Harper's).

**tim|e|ous** (tī′məs), *adj.* = timely. —**time′ous|ly**, *adv.*

**time out**, or **time-out** (tīm′out′), *n.* **1** a period when play is suspended during the course of a game, at the request of one team, a player, an umpire, or other official, or a coach. **2** any period of suspension of activity; respite: *to take time out from work to smoke a cigarette.*

**time|piece** (tīm′pēs′), *n.* a clock or watch, or any other instrument for measuring and recording the passage of time.

**time|pleas|er** (tīm′plē′zər), *n.* = timeserver.

**tim|er** (tī′mər), *n.* **1** a person or thing that times; timekeeper. **2** a device for indicating or recording intervals of time, such as a stop watch. **3** a clockwork device for indicating when a certain period of time has elapsed or for automatically turning on or off an appliance or mechanism at a preset time: *Many stoves have timers for baking.* **4** an automatic device in an internal-combustion engine that causes the spark for igniting the charge to occur just at the time required.

**time recording lock**, a time lock which can be opened with any of several keys. When unlocked, it registers the number of the key and the time that the lock was opened.

**time-re|lease** (tīm′ri lēs′), *adj.* made to be released in the body at intervals of time so as to extend the medicinal effect over a long period: *a time-release medicine, drug, or capsule.*

**time reversal**, *Physics.* the principle that if the order in which a sequence of events occurs is reversed, the same sequence will occur again but in reverse order: *Time reversal ... says in effect that a motion-picture film of any process should show the system appearing to obey the same laws of physics whether the film is run forward or backward* (Scientific American).

**time-re|verse** (tīm′ri vėrs′), *v.t.*, **-versed, -vers|ing.** *Physics.* to reverse the order of (a sequence of events): *Because gravity is a one-way force, ... it might be supposed that the motions of bodies under the influence of gravity could not be time-reversed* (Martin Gardner).

**time-re|vers|i|ble** (tīm′ri vėr′sə bəl), *adj. Physics.* capable of being time-reversed: *All the fundamental laws of physics, including relativity and quantum mechanics, are time-reversible* (Science News).

**times** (tīmz), *n.pl.* See under **time.**

**time|sav|er** (tīm′sā′vər), *n.* a person or thing that saves time.

**time|sav|ing** (tīm′sā′ving), *adj.* that reduces the time previously required to do something: *a time-saving appliance or idea.*

**time scale**, any sequence of events used as a measure of the length or duration of a period of time: *an atomic time scale, the evolutionary time scale.*

**time|serv|er** (tīm′sėr′vər), *n.* a person who shapes his conduct to conform with the opinions of the time or of the persons in power, especially for selfish reasons. SYN: opportunist.

**time|serv|ing** (tīm′sėr′ving), *adj., n.* — ***adj.*** shaping one's conduct to conform with the opinions of the time or of persons in power, especially for selfish reasons.
— ***n.*** the act or conduct of a timeserver.

**time-share** (tīm′shãr′), *v.,* **-shared, -shar|ing.** — ***v.i.*** (of a computing system or program) to allocate divisions of the total operating time to two or more functions. — ***v.t.*** to share the operations of (a time-sharing computer or program).

**time-shared** (tīm′shãrd′), *adj.* of or having to do with time-sharing: *a time-shared central computer.*

**time-shar|ing** (tīm′shãr′ing), *n.* **1** the simultaneous use by many persons at remote locations of a single central computer whose speed in processing data is greater than the combined speed of all the users. **2** the occupancy of a dwelling, such as a condominium at a resort, for a guaranteed period of time each year, determined by the percentage of shares one owns in the dwelling: *Time-sharing ... can offer the advantages of a vacation home without the large initial investment or steady upkeep* (Time).

**time sheet**, a sheet for recording the amount of time that a person works.

**time-shift** (tīm′shift′), *n.* deviation from strict chronological order, as in a narrative: *His books are filled with bewildering time-shifts* (Newsweek).

**time signature**, *Music.* a sign showing the time of a piece. It is usually put at the beginning or where the time changes. See picture under **time.**

**time slot**, the position of a television or radio program in the daily schedule of programs.

**time spirit**, the spirit of the time or period; Zeitgeist.

**Times Roman**, a printing type of the old style, widely used in textbooks and reference books, originally designed for the London *Times.*

**time study**, = time and motion study.

**time|ta|ble** (tīm′tā′bəl), *n., v.,* **-bled, -bling.** — ***n.*** **1** a schedule showing the times when trains, ships, buses, airplanes, or other public conveyances come and go: *I would sooner read a timetable or a catalogue than nothing at all* (W. Somerset Maugham). **2** any list or schedule of the times things are to be done or happen.
— ***v.t.*** *British.* to set a timetable for; put on a timetable: *Musically talented children ... will be separately timetabled to give full scope for their abilities* (London Times).

**time-test|ed** (tīm′tes′tid), *adj.* proven by repeated tests over a long period of time.

**time trial**, a race in which the contestants perform and are timed individually instead of at the same time. Most ski races and some bicycle, automobile, and horse races are time trials.

**time-tried** (tīm′trīd′), *adj.* = time-tested.

**time value**, the duration of a musical tone in relation to the tempo involved.

**time warp**, a distortion or suspension in the continuity of time: *Science-fiction writers, stymied by the laws of physics, turn to such literary devices as time warps to make interstellar travel possible* (Time). *Haiti is like a sustained hallucination imposed upon a time warp* (Harper's).

**time-wast|er** (tīm′wās′tər), *n.* a person or thing that wastes time.

**time-wast|ing** (tīm′wās′ting), *adj.* using time to no value or purpose: *a time-wasting method.*

**time|work** (tīm′wėrk′), *n.* work paid for by the hour, day, or week.

**time|work|er** (tīm′wėr′kər), *n.* a worker paid by the hour, day or week.

**time|worn** (tīm′wôrn′, -wōrn′), *adj.* **1** worn by long existence or use: *timeworn steps.* **2** worn out by use; trite: *a timeworn excuse.* **3** very old; ancient; antiquated: *a timeworn superstition.*

**time zone**, a geographical region within which the same standard time is used. The world is divided into 24 time zones beginning and ending with the International Date Line.

**tim|id** (tim′id), *adj.* **1** easily frightened; shy: *The timid child was afraid of the dark. Deer are timid animals.* **2** characterized by or indicating fear: *a timid reply.* [< Latin *timidus* < *timēre* to fear] — **tim′id|ly,** *adv.* — **tim′id|ness,** *n.*
— *Syn.* **1 Timid, cowardly** mean afraid to do or try something hard or risky. **Timid** implies lack of self-confidence in facing any situation: *He does not like his job, but is too timid to try to find another.* **Cowardly** implies lack of moral character or strength in the presence of danger or trouble: *Leaving his wife because she was hopelessly sick was a cowardly thing to do.*

**ti|mid|i|ty** (tə mid′ə tē), *n.* a being timid; timid behavior; shyness.

**tim|ing** (tī′ming), *n.* **1a** the arrangement or regulation of the time or speed of the parts of anything to get the greatest possible effect: *the timing of an actor in responding to a cue, the timing of the release of a new play.* **b** the effect produced. **2** *Sports.* the physical and mental coordination necessary to achieve the greatest effect by a throw, blow, stroke, or other maneuver: *the timing of a stroke in tennis.* **3** the measurement of time: *the timing of a runner.*

**timing chain**, a chain by which the camshaft and accessory shafts of an engine are driven.

**ti|moc|ra|cy** (tī mok′rə sē), *n., pl.* **-cies.** **1** a form of government in which love of honor is the dominant motive of the rulers (used in this sense by Plato). **2** a form of government in which the ownership of property is a requirement for holding office (used in this sense by Aristotle). [< Medieval Latin *timocratia* < Greek *tīmokratiā* < *tīmē* valuation; honor + *-kratiā* a rule, reign < *kratein* to rule]

**ti|mo|crat|ic** (tī′mə krat′ik), *adj.* of or having to do with timocracy.

**ti|mo|crat|i|cal** (tī′mə krat′ə kəl), *adj.* = timocratic.

**Ti|mon** (tī′mən), *n.* **1** the hero of Shakespeare's play *Timon of Athens,* noted for his dislike of mankind. **2** a hater of mankind; misanthrope.

**tim|or|ous** (tim′ər əs), *adj.* **1** easily frightened; timid: *The timorous rabbit ran away.* SYN: fearful, fearsome. **2** characterizing or indicating fear: *a timorous approach to reality.* [< Old French *temerous, timoureus* < Medieval Latin *timorosus* < Latin *timor, -ōris* fear] — **tim′or|ous|ly,** *adv.* — **tim′or|ous|ness,** *n.*

**tim|o|thy** (tim′ə thē), *n.,* or **timothy grass**, a kind of coarse grass with long, cylindrical spikes, often grown for hay. See picture under **grass family.** [American English, apparently < *Timothy* Hanson, who cultivated it in America around 1720]

**Tim|o|thy** (tim′ə thē), *n.* **1** a disciple of the Apostle Paul. **2** either of the books of the New Testament (I Timothy and II Timothy) written as letters by the Apostle Paul to Timothy. *Abbr:* Tim.

**tim|pa|ni** (tim′pə nē), *n., pl. of* **tim|pa|no.** kettledrums. Also, **tympani.** [< Italian *timpani,* plural of *timpano* < Latin *tympanum.* See etym. of doublets **timbre, tympan, tympanum.**]

**tim|pa|nist** (tim′pə nist), *n.* a person who plays the kettledrums. Also, **tympanist.**

**tim|pa|no** (tim′pə nō), *n.* singular of **timpani.**

***tin** (tin), *n., adj., v.,* **tinned, tin|ning.** — ***n.*** **1** a metallic chemical element that shines like silver but is softer and cheaper. Tin is easily worked and has a low melting point. It is used in plating metals to prevent corrosion and in making alloys such as bronze, pewter, and Britannia metal. **2** thin sheets of iron or steel coated with tin; tin plate. **3** any can, box, pan, or other container made of or plated with tin: *a pie tin.* **4** *British.* a can: *to buy two tins of peas.* **5** *Slang.* money; cash.
— ***adj.*** made of or plated with tin: *a tin bucket.*
— ***v.t.*** **1** to cover or plate with tin. **2** *British.* to put up in tin cans or tin boxes; can: *to tin peas.* [Old English *tin*]

***tin**
definition 1

| symbol | atomic number | atomic weight | oxidation state |
|---|---|---|---|
| Sn | 50 | 118.69 | 2,4 |

**tin|a|mou** (tin′ə mü), *n.* any one of various birds of South and Central America and Mexico that look somewhat like a quail or grouse and have a body structure similar to the rhea. [< French *tinamou* < Carib (South America) *tinamu*]

**tin|cal** (ting′käl, -kôl, -kəl), *n.* crude borax, found in lake deposits in Tibet, Iran, and certain other Asian countries. [< Malay *tingkal* < Sanskrit *tankana*]

**tin can**, **1** = can[2] (def. 1). **2** *U.S. Naval Slang.* a destroyer. [(def. 2) because of the relatively thin armor plate]

**tinct** (tingkt), *adj., n., v.* — ***adj.*** *Archaic.* tinged; flavored: *lucent syrops tinct with cinnamon* (Keats).
— ***n.*** *Archaic.* tint; tinge.
— ***v.t.*** *Obsolete.* **1** to tinge; tint. **2** to tincture. [< Latin *tīnctus,* past participle of *tingere* tinge. See etym. of doublets **taint, tint[1].**]

**tinct.**, tincture.

**tinc|to|ri|al** (tingk tôr′ē əl, -tōr′-), *adj.* of, having to do with, or used in dyeing or coloring. [< Latin *tinctōrius* (< *tinctor* dyer < *tingere* to dye) + English *-al[1]*]

**tinc|ture** (tingk′chər), *n., v.,* **-tured, -tur|ing.** — ***n.*** **1** a solution of medicine in alcohol or in a mixture that is chiefly of alcohol: *tincture of iodine.* **2** *Figurative.* a trace; tinge; flavor: *His stern face showed for a moment a slight tincture of amusement.* SYN: whit, soupçon. **3** *Figurative.* a color; tint: *Her usually pale cheeks showed a faint tincture of pink.* **4** *Heraldry.* any one of the colors, furs, or metals used or represented in coats of arms. **5** *Alchemy.* a supposed spiritual principle or immaterial substance whose character or quality may be infused into material things, which are then said to be tinctured; quintessence, spirit, or soul of a thing. **6** *Obsolete.* a dye or pigment.
— ***v.t.*** **1** to give a trace or tinge to: *Everything he says is tinctured with conceit.* **2** to color; tint. [< Latin *tīnctūra* < *tingere;* see etym. under **tinge**]

**tin|der** (tin′dər), *n.* **1** anything that catches fire easily. **2** a material used to catch fire from a spark: *Before matches were invented people carried a box containing tinder, flint, and steel.* [Old English *tynder*]

**tin|der|box** (tin′dər boks′), *n.* **1** a box for holding tinder, flint, and steel for making a fire. **2** a very inflammable thing. **3** *Figurative.* a very excitable person.

**tine[1]** (tīn), *n.* **1** a sharp, projecting point or prong: *the tines of a fork.* **2** a pointed branch of a deer's antler. [Old English *tind*]

**tine[2]** (tīn), *v.,* **tint, tin|ing.** *Especially Scottish.*
— ***v.t.*** to have or enjoy no longer; lose.
— ***v.i.*** to be lost or destroyed; perish. Also, **tyne.** [Middle English *tinen* to fail; lose, ruin < Scandinavian (compare Old Icelandic *tȳna*)]

**tin|e|a** (tin′ē ə), *n.* any one of various contagious skin diseases caused by fungi, especially ringworm. [< Latin *tinea* a gnawing worm, moth]

**tin|e|al** (tin′ē əl), *adj.* of or having to do with tinea.

**tin ear**, *Informal.* **1a** inability to perceive small differences in sounds. **b** = tone-deafness. **c** a tone-deaf person. **2** = cauliflower ear.

**tin|e|id** (tin′ē id), *adj., n.* — ***adj.*** of or having to do with a family of clothes moths whose larvae are very destructive to woolen fabrics.
— ***n.*** a tineid moth.
[< New Latin *Tineidae* the family name < *Tinea* the genus name < Latin *tinea* worm, moth]

**tin fish**, *Slang.* a torpedo.

**tin|foil** (tin′foil′), *n., adj.* — ***n.*** Also, **tin foil. 1** a very thin sheet of tin, or of an alloy of tin and lead, used as a wrapping for candy, tobacco, or similar articles. **2** tin hammered or rolled into a thin sheet and coated with mercury, used for backing mirrors and other purposes.
— ***adj.*** of, made of, or wrapped in tinfoil.

**ting[1]** (ting), *v., n.* — ***v.i., v.t.*** to make or cause to make a clear ringing sound.
— ***n.*** a clear ringing sound.
[ultimately imitative]

**Pronunciation Key:** hat, āge, cãre, fär; let, ēqual, tėrm; it, īce; hot, ōpen, ôrder; **oi**l, **ou**t; cup, pu̇t, rüle; **ch**ild; lo**ng**; **th**in; **ᴛʜ**en; **zh**, measure; ə represents **a** in about, **e** in taken, **i** in pencil, **o** in lemon, **u** in circus.

**ting²** (ting), *n.* = thing².
**ting-a-ling** (ting′ə ling′), *n.* a clear, ringing sound, as of a small bell.
**tinge** (tinj), *v.,* **tinged, tinge|ing** or **ting|ing,** *n.* —*v.t.* **1** to color slightly: *A drop of ink will tinge a glass of water.* **2** *Figurative.* to add a trace of some quality to; change a very little: *Her remarks were tinged with envy. Sad memories tinged their present joy.*
—*n.* **1** a slight coloring or tint: *There is a tinge of red in her cheeks.* **2** *Figurative.* a very small amount; trace: *She likes just a tinge of lemon in her tea. There was a tinge of blame in his voice.*
[< Latin *tingere* to dye, color. Compare etym. under **taint, tinct, tint.**] —**ting′er,** *n.*
**tin|gis fly** (tin′jis), any one of a group of small, delicate, heteropterous insects whose wings and body are covered with a lacy network of lines; lacebug. [< New Latin *Tingis* the genus name]
**tin|gle** (ting′gəl), *v.,* **-gled, -gling,** *n.* —*v.i.* **1a** to have a feeling of thrills or a pricking, stinging feeling: *He tingled with excitement on his first airplane trip. Her ears were tingling with cold after ice-skating on the pond.* **b** to smart; blush: *cheeks tingling with shame.* **2** to be thrilling; pass with a thrill: (*Figurative.*) *The newspaper story tingled with excitement.* (*Figurative.*) *Every note ... tingled through his huge frame* (Thackeray). **3** to tinkle; jingle.
—*v.t.* to cause to tingle; cause to feel thrills or a pricking, stinging feeling: *Shame tingled his cheeks.*
—*n.* **1** a feeling of thrills or a pricking, stinging feeling: *The cold caused a tingle in my fingers and ears.* **2** a tinkle; jingle.
[probably originally a variant of *tinkle*] —**tin′gler,** *n.* —**tin′gling|ly,** *adv.*
**tin god,** an inferior or mediocre person who assumes an autocratic or omnipotent role: *People like that* [*become*] *tin gods in the neighborhood—people known for their habitual lawlessness* (New York Times).
**tin hat,** *Slang.* a metal helmet of the type worn by the British and American soldiers in World War I.
**tin|horn** (tin′hôrn′), *adj., n. Slang.* —*adj.* cheap and showy; noisy and pretentious; pretending to be wealthy, skillful, or influential, but lacking what is required: *a tinhorn lawyer.*
—*n.* a tinhorn person.
**tink** (tingk), *v., n.* —*v.i.* to make a short, light, metallic sound; clink.
—*n.* a tinking sound.
[Middle English *tinken;* imitative]
**tink|er** (ting′kər), *n., v.* —*n.* **1** a man who mends pots, pans, kettles, and other metal household articles, usually wandering from place to place. **2** *Figurative.* unskilled or clumsy work; activity that is rather useless. **3** a person who does such work. **4** any one of various fishes or birds, such as a small or young mackerel, a silversides, or a kind of auk.
—*v.t.* to mend, patch, or repair, especially in an unskilled or clumsy way.
—*v.i.* **1** to work in an unskilled or clumsy way: *The boys were tinkering with the clock and broke it.* **2** *Figurative.* to work or keep busy in a rather useless way; putter: *to tinker with a radio, to tinker with an idea.*
[Middle English *tynekere,* perhaps ultimately < *tin,* or *tink* to mend pots, solder] —**tink′er|er,** *n.*
**tinker's damn** or **dam,** something worthless or useless: *He doesn't care a tinker's damn what others think.*
**tin|kle** (ting′kəl), *v.,* **-kled, -kling,** *n.* —*v.i.* **1** to make short, light, ringing sounds: *Little bells tinkle.* **2** to move or flow with a tinkling sound.
—*v.t.* **1** to cause to tinkle. **2a** to make known, call attention to, or express by tinkling: *The little clock tinkled out the hours.* **b** to summon or attract by tinkling.
—*n.* a series of short, light, ringing sounds: *the tinkle of sleigh bells.*
[perhaps frequentative < Middle English *tinken* to ring, jingle; apparently ultimately imitative]
**tin|kling** (ting′kling), *adj., n.* —*adj.* that tinkles or jingles.
—*n.* **1** a tinkling noise. **2** a blackbird of Jamaica that makes a tinkling sound. —**tin′kling|ly,** *adv.*
**tin|kly** (ting′klē), *adj.* **1** full of tinkles; characterized by tinkling: *a tinkly toy. The tinkly temple bells* (Rudyard Kipling). **2** sounding weak, cheap, or childish: *a tinkly tune, a tinkly title, tinkly sentiments.*
**tin liz|zie** (liz′ē), *U.S. Slang.* a very old car, such as a Model T or the like; jalopy.
**tin|man** (tin′mən), *n., pl.* **-men. 1** a man who works with tin; tinsmith. **2** a dealer in tinware.
**tinned** (tind), *adj.* **1** covered or coated with tin. **2** put up or preserved in tins; canned.
**tin|ner** (tin′ər), *n.* **1** a person who works with tin; tin-plater; tinsmith. **2** *British.* a canner (of food). **3** a person who works in a tin mine.
**tin|ni|tus** (ti nī′təs), *n.* a ringing or hissing sensation in the ears, due to a defect of the auditory nerve. [< Latin *tinnītus, -ūs* < *tinnīre* to ring, tinkle]
**tin|ny** (tin′ē), *adj.,* **-ni|er, -ni|est. 1** of, containing, or yielding tin. **2** like tin in looks, sound, or taste: *These sardines have a tinny flavor.* **3** *Fine Arts.* hard; metallic. —**tin′ni|ly,** *adv.* —**tin′ni|ness,** *n.*
**tin opener,** *British.* can opener.
**tin-pan** (tin′pan′), *adj.* like tin; tinny.
**Tin Pan Alley** or **tin pan alley, 1** a district frequented by musicians, songwriters, and song publishers, especially such a district in New York City, between 14th and 42nd Streets, that became the center of music publishing in the United States. **2** musicians, songwriters, and song publishers as a group or industry, especially in the United States.
**tin-pan|ny** (tin′pan′ē), *adj.* **1** = tin-pan. **2** characteristic of Tin Pan Alley and the music it produces.
**tin pants,** *U.S.* lined canvas trousers soaked in paraffin to make them waterproof, formerly worn especially by lumbermen, fishermen, and hunters.
**tin plate,** thin sheets of iron or steel coated with tin. Ordinary tin cans are made of tin plate.
**tin-plate** (tin′plāt′), *v.t.,* **-plat|ed, -plat|ing.** to plate or coat (sheets of iron or steel) with tin.
**tin-plat|er** (tin′plā′tər), *n.* a workman who makes tin plates.
**tin-pot** (tin′pot′), *adj.* suggesting a tin pot in worth; of inferior quality; small-time; paltry: *Trujillo had been the model for every tin-pot, medal-jingling dictator that ever rifled a Latin American treasury* (Time).
**tin pyrites,** = stannite.
**tin|sel** (tin′səl), *n., adj., v.,* **-seled, -sel|ing** or (*especially British*) **-selled, -sel|ling.** —*n.* **1** glittering copper, brass, or some other metal, in thin sheets, strips, or threads. Tinsel is used to trim Christmas trees. **2** *Figurative.* anything showy but having little value: *That poverty of ideas which had been hitherto concealed under the tinsel of politeness* (Samuel Johnson). **3** a thin cloth of silk or wool woven with threads of gold, silver, or copper: *She wore a beautiful dress of gold tinsel.*
—*adj.* of or like tinsel; showy but not worth much.
—*v.t.* **1** to trim with tinsel. **2** *Figurative.* to make showy or gaudy; cover the defects with or as if with tinsel.
[apparently short for Middle French *estincelle* spark < Vulgar Latin *stincilla,* alteration of Latin *scintilla.* See etym. of doublets **scintilla, stencil.**] —**tin′sel|like′,** *adj.*
**tin|sel|ly** (tin′sə lē), *adj.* **1** of or like tinsel. **2** showy without real worth; tawdry.
**tin|smith** (tin′smith′), *n.* a person who works with tin; maker or repairer of tinware; tinman; tinner.
**tin soldier, 1** a toy soldier made of tin. **2** a person who plays at being a soldier.
**tin spirit,** a solution of tin in acid used as a mordant in dyeing.
**tin|stone** (tin′stōn′), *n.* = cassiterite.
**tint¹** (tint), *n., v.* —*n.* **1** a color or variety of a color; hue: *The picture was painted in several tints of blue.* **2** a delicate or pale color. **3** a variety of a color produced by mixing it with white. **4** a preparation for coloring hair. **5a** *Engraving.* an even and uniform shading produced by a series of fine parallel lines. **b** *Printing.* a light-colored background, as for an illustration.
—*v.t.* to put a tint on; color slightly: *The walls were tinted gray.*
[alteration of *tinct* < Latin *tīnctus, -ūs* a dyeing < *tingere* to dye, tinge. See etym. of doublets **taint, tinct.**] —**tint′er,** *n.*
**tint²** (tint), *v.* the past tense and past participle of **tine².**
**tin|tin|nab|u|lar** (tin′tə nab′yə lər), *adj.* = tintinnabulary.
**tin|tin|nab|u|lar|y** (tin′tə nab′yə ler′ē), *adj.* of or having to do with bells or bell ringing; like a bell. [< Latin *tintinnābulum* bell (< *tintinnāre* jingle, ring < *tinnīre* to resound, tinkle) + English *-ary*]
**tin|tin|nab|u|la|tion** (tin′tə nab′yə lā′shən), *n.* the ringing of bells: *The tintinnabulation that so musically wells From the bells* (Edgar Allan Poe). [American English < Latin *tintinnābulum* bell + English *-ation*]
**tint|y** (tin′tē), *adj.* **1** full of tints. **2** tinted or colored, as a painting.
**tin|type** (tin′tīp′), *n.* a photograph in the form of a positive taken on a sensitized sheet of enameled tin or iron; ferrotype. [American English < *tin* + *type*]
**tin|ware** (tin′wãr′), *n.* articles made of or lined with tin, such as dippers or pans.
**tin white,** bluish white; silvery white. —**tin′-white′,** *adj.*
**tin|work** (tin′wėrk′), *n.* work done in tin or with tin.
**tin|works** (tin′wėrks′), *n.pl.* (*sing. in use*). a place where tin is mined or tinware is made.
**ti|ny** (tī′nē), *adj.,* **-ni|er, -ni|est,** *n.* —*adj.* very small; wee: *a tiny baby chicken. She settled in two tiny rooms* (W. Somerset Maugham). *From the hugest nebula to the tiniest atom* (James Harvey Robinson). SYN: little, minute, microscopic.
—*n.* something tiny; a tiny child: *just like when you were a tiny* (John Galsworthy).
[Middle English *tine;* origin uncertain] —**ti′ni|ly,** *adv.* —**ti′ni|ness,** *n.*
**-tion,** *suffix added to verbs to make nouns.* **1** the act or process of ___ing: *Addition = the act or process of adding.*
**2** the condition of being ___ed: *Exhaustion = the condition of being exhausted.*
**3** the result of ___ing; thing that was ___ed: *Reflection = the result of reflecting.*
**4** thing or process that is ___ing, as in *affliction, attraction.*
[< Latin *-tiō, -ōnis* < *-t-,* stem ending of past participle + *-iō,* a noun suffix; or alteration of Old French *-cion* < Latin *-tiō*]
**tip¹** (tip), *n., v.,* **tipped, tip|ping.** —*n.* **1** the end part; end; point; top: *the tips of the fingers or toes, the tip of a hill or a baseball bat.* SYN: extremity. **2** a small piece put on the end of something: *a new tip for a billiard cue, shoes with steel tips. Buy rubber tips to put on the legs of a stool.* **3** = wing tip (def. 1).
—*v.t.* **1** to put a tip or tips on; furnish with a tip: *spears tipped with steel.* **2** to cover or adorn at the tip: *mountains tipped with snow. Sunlight tips the steeple.* **3** (in bookbinding) to paste or attach (special color pages or other inserts) within or at the binding edge of a signature: *an art book with many color plates tipped in.*
**tip²** (tip), *v.,* **tipped, tip|ping,** *n., adj.* —*v.t.* **1** to cause to have a slanting or sloping position; slope; slant: *She tipped the table toward her.* SYN: tilt, incline, lean. **2** to upset; overturn: *He tipped over his glass of water.* SYN: capsize. **3** to take off (a hat) in greeting: *Father tipped his hat to the children's teacher when he met her on the street.* **4** to empty out; dump: *She tipped the money in her purse onto the table.*
—*v.i.* **1** to slant; slope. SYN: tilt, incline, lean. **2** to upset; overturn. SYN: capsize.
—*n.* **1** the act of tipping or tilting; slope; slant: *There is such a tip to that table that everything slips off it.* **2** a place where vehicles, such as open railroad cars and trucks, are tipped and their contents dumped, as into the hold of a ship.
—*adj.* that empties itself by tipping: *a tip car, truck, or wagon.*
[Middle English *typpen;* origin uncertain]
**tip³** (tip), *n., v.,* **tipped, tip|ping.** —*n.* **1** a small present of money in return for service; gratuity: *He gave the waiter a tip.* **2** a piece of secret or confidential information: *I had a tip that the black horse would win the race.* **3** a useful hint or suggestion: *a tip on how to save money, a tip on removing stains from clothing. Father gave me a helpful tip about pitching the tent where trees would shade it.*
—*v.t.* **1** to give a small present of money to: *Did you tip the porter?* **2** to give secret or confidential information to. **3** *Slang.* to let have; give: *He tipped me an impudent wink* (Washington Irving).
—*v.i.* to give a tip or tips.
**tip off,** *Informal.* **a** to give secret or confidential information to: *They tipped me off about a good bargain.* **b** to warn: *Someone tipped off the criminal, and he escaped before the police arrived.*
[origin uncertain]
**tip⁴** (tip), *n., v.,* **tipped, tip|ping.** —*n.* **1** a light, sharp blow; tap. **2** *Sports.* **a** a glancing blow. **b** a ball so hit: *a foul tip.*
—*v.t.* **1** to hit lightly and sharply; tap. **2** *Sports.* to hit (a ball) lightly with the edge of the bat; hit with a glancing blow.
[origin uncertain. Compare Low German *tippen* poke, touch lightly. Probably related to **tip¹.**]
**ti palm** (tē), any one of various Asian shade trees and shrubs; ti².
**tip and run,** a form of cricket in which the batsman must run for every hit.
**tip-and-run** (tip′ən run′), *adj. British.* characterized by fleeing immediately after attacking; hit-and-run.
**tip|burn** (tip′bėrn′), *n.* a disease of potato, lettuce, and other plants in which excessive heat, humidity, or air pollution causes the tips of the leaves to turn brown.
**tip|cart** (tip′kärt′), *n.* a cart that can be tipped endways or sideways for dumping.
**tip|cat** (tip′kat′), *n.* **1** a game in which a short piece of wood (the cat), tapering at both ends, is hit with a stick so as to spring up, and then is hit to a distance by the same player. **2** the tapered piece of wood used in this game; cat.
**tiph|i|a** (tif′ē ə), *n.* a digger wasp common in the eastern United States. [< New Latin *Tiphia* the genus name < Greek *tiphē* a kind of insect]
**ti|pi** (tē′pē), *n., pl.* **-pis.** = tepee.

**tip-in** (tip′in′), *n.* a scoring shot in basketball made by tipping a rebounding ball into the basket; tap-in.

**tip|off** or **tip-off** (tip′ôf′, -of′), *n. Informal.* **1** a piece of secret or confidential information. **2** a warning. **3** a tipping off.

**tip|pa|ble**[1] (tip′ə bəl), *adj.* that can be tipped, tilted, or overturned. [< *tip*[2] + *-able*]

**tip|pa|ble**[2] (tip′ə bəl), *adj.* that can be tipped, or given a gratuity. [< *tip*[3] + *-able*]

**-tipped**, *combining form.* having a ___tip: *Cork-tipped = having a cork tip.*

**tip|per** (tip′ər), *n.* a person who gives a tip or tips: *a good tipper, a cheap tipper.*

***tip|pet** (tip′it), *n.* **1** a scarf for the neck and shoulders, usually with the ends hanging down in front. **2** a long, narrow, hanging part of a hood, sleeve, or scarf. **3** a band of silk or other material worn around the neck with its ends hanging down in front, worn by certain clergymen. [probably diminutive form of *tip*[1]]

***tippet** definition 2

**tip|ple**[1] (tip′əl), *v.*, **-pled, -pling,** *n.* **— *v.t., v.i.*** to drink (alcoholic liquor) often or too much: *I took to the bottle and tried to tipple away my cares* (Washington Irving).
**— *n.*** an alcoholic liquor; strong drink.
[origin uncertain. Compare Norwegian *tipla* drip, tipple.]

**tip|ple**[2] (tip′əl), *n. U.S.* **1** a mechanism by which freight cars and mining carts are tipped and emptied. **2** a place where such vehicles are emptied by tipping, as in a coal yard or at or near a mine shaft. [American English apparently < *tip*[2]]

**tip|ple**[3] (tip′əl), *v.t., v.i.,* **-pled, -pling.** *Dialect.* to tip over. [frequentative of *tip*[2]]

**tip|pler**[1] (tip′lər), *n.* a habitual drinker of alcoholic liquor.

**tip|pler**[2] (tip′lər), *n.* **1** a person or thing that tips over. **2** a mechanism for tipping and emptying; tipple. **3** a kind of tumbler pigeon.

**tip|py** (tip′ē), *adj.,* **-pi|er, -pi|est.** *Informal.* liable to tip, upset, or tilt: *a tippy canoe, a tippy table.*

**tip|py-toe** (tip′ē tō′), *n., v.i.,* **-toed, -toe|ing,** *adj., adv. Informal.* tiptoe.

**tip sheet,** *Informal.* a bulletin or newsletter furnishing tips for use in betting, speculation, etc.

**tip|si|fy** (tip′sə fī), *v.t.,* **-fied, -fy|ing.** to make tipsy; intoxicate slightly.

**tip|staff** (tip′staf′, -stäf′), *n., pl.* **-staves** or **-staffs. 1** a staff tipped or capped with metal, formerly carried as a badge of office by constables, bailiffs, and other officers of the law. **2** an official who carried such a staff. **3** an attendant or crier in a court of law.

**tip|ster** (tip′stər), *n. Informal.* a person who makes a business of furnishing private or secret information for use in betting, speculation, etc. [< *tip*[3] a hint + *-ster*]

**tip|stock** (tip′stok′), *n.* the movable tip or fore-end of a gunstock, situated under the barrel.

**tip|sy** (tip′sē), *adj.,* **-si|er, -si|est. 1** tipping easily; unsteady; tilted. **2** somewhat intoxicated, but not thoroughly drunk: *He was so tipsy that he wept upon my shoulder* (Robert Louis Stevenson). [probably < *tip*[2]] **— tip′si|ly,** *adv.* **— tip′si|ness,** *n.*

**tip table,** a small table with a hinged top that can be tipped down when the table is out of use.

**tip|toe** (tip′tō′), *n., v.,* **-toed, -toe|ing,** *adj., adv.*
**— *n.*** the tips of the toes.
**— *v.i.*** to go or walk on the tips of the toes; step lightly: *She tiptoed quietly up the stairs.*
**— *adj.*** **1** on tiptoe. **2** *Figurative.* silent; stealthy. **3** *Figurative.* eager; expectant. **4** tripping; dancing.
**— *adv.*** on tiptoe: *I stood tiptoe upon a little hill* (Keats).
**on tiptoe, a** on one's toes: *to stand or walk on tiptoe.* **b** *Figurative.* eager: *The children were on tiptoe for vacation to begin.* **c** *Figurative.* in a secret manner: *He followed his cousin on tiptoe* (Thomas Hughes).

**tip|top** (tip′top′), *n., adj., adv.* **— *n.* 1** the very top; highest point or part. **2** *Figurative.* the highest pitch or degree; the finest or best; acme.
**— *adj.*** **1** at the very top or highest point. **2** *Informal, Figurative.* first-rate; excellent: *He is a tiptop man and may be a bishop* (George Eliot).
**— *adv.*** extremely well; superlatively: *His work is going along tiptop.*

**tip|top|per** (tip′top′ər), *n. Informal.* a tiptop person or thing.

**tip-up** (tip′up′), *adj., n.* **— *adj.*** designed to tip or tilt up, as a seat when not occupied: *Inside, most cars have ... poor seat anchorage, dangerous tip-up seats* (Sunday Times).
**— *n.*** **1** a tip-up seat: *theater with ... fixed tip-ups to seat 700* (Punch). **2** anything that tips or tilts up.

**ti|rade** (tī′rād, tə rād′), *n., v.,* **-rad|ed, -rad|ing.**
**— *n.*** **1** a long, vehement speech. **SYN:** harangue. **2** a long, scolding speech. **SYN:** diatribe. **3** a passage or section in a poem dealing with a single theme or idea.
**— *v.i.*** to utter or write a tirade; inveigh or declaim vehemently: *They tirade against the influence of dogma* (R. B. Vaughan).
[< French *tirade* speech; a continuation; a drawing out < Italian *tirata* a drawing out < *tirare* to shoot < Vulgar Latin *tirāre*]

**ti|rage** (ti räzh′), *n.* a printing or impression of a book. [< French *tirage* < Old French *tirer* to draw; origin uncertain]

**ti|rail|leur** (tē rä yœr′), *n.* a soldier trained as a skirmisher and sharpshooter. [< French *tirailleur* < Old French *tirer* shoot; (originally) draw a bow; origin uncertain]

**tire**[1] (tīr), *v.,* **tired, tir|ing,** *n.* **— *v.t.* 1** to make weary; lower or use up the strength of: *The long walk tired her. He tired his eyes by too much reading.* **SYN:** exhaust, fatigue, fag. **2** to wear down the patience, interest, or appreciation of, especially because of dullness or excess: *Monotonous filing tired the office boy.* **SYN:** jade, satiate, bore. **— *v.i.*** to become weary: *The old lady tires easily. The teacher tired of answering foolish questions. You think I shall tire of her!* (George Bernard Shaw).
**— *n.*** *Dialect or Informal.* tiredness; fatigue.
**tire out,** to make very weary: *William, tired out by the voyage ... determined to land in an open boat* (Macaulay).
[Old English *tēorian*]

***tire**[2] (tīr), *n., v.,* **tired, tir|ing. — *n.* 1** a hooplike band of rubber or other material on the rim of the wheel of an automobile, bicycle, motorcycle, truck, trailer, or airplane. Some rubber tires have inner tubes for holding air; others hold the air in the tire itself or are made of solid rubber. **2** a band of iron or steel fitted on the rim of a wheel, as of a wagon or railroad car.
**— *v.t.*** to furnish with a tire or tires. Also, *British,* **tyre.**
[apparently < *tire*[3] covering]

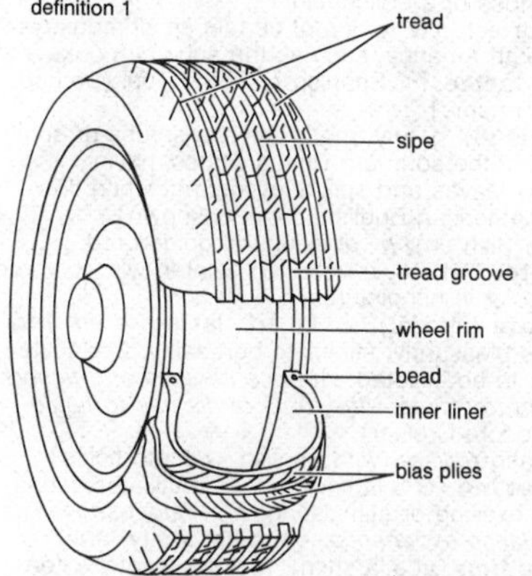


***tire**[2] definition 1

**tire**[3] (tīr), *n., v.,* **tired, tir|ing.** *Archaic.* **— *n.* 1** attire; apparel; raiment. **2** a covering or ornament for a woman's head; headdress: *She ... braided the hair of her head, and put a tire on it* (Judith 10:3).
**— *v.t.*** to attire or adorn.
[short for *attire*]

**tire cord,** rayon, fiberglass, polyester, or nylon yarn corded and coated with rubber to reinforce the casing of a pneumatic tire.

**tired** (tīrd), *adj.* **1** weary; wearied; fatigued; exhausted: *The team was tired, but each boy continued to play as hard as he could. (Figurative.) His suit always looked a bit tired after he had worn it all week.* **2** sick (of); impatient (with): *Oh, you make me tired!* (Sinclair Lewis). [originally, past participle of *tire*[1]] **— tired′ly,** *adv.* **— tired′ness,** *n.*
**— *Syn.* 1 Tired, weary, exhausted** mean drained of strength, energy, or power of endurance. **Tired** is the general word: *I am tired, but I must get back to work.* **Weary** means feeling worn out and unable to go on: *Weary shoppers wait for buses and streetcars.* **Exhausted** implies without enough energy left to be able to go on: *Exhausted by near starvation and bitter winds, the man lay in a stupor.*

**-tired,** *combining form.* having ___tires: *A rubber-tired vehicle = a vehicle having rubber tires.*

**tire|less** (tīr′lis), *adj.* **1** never becoming tired; requiring little rest: *a tireless worker.* **SYN:** indefatigable. **2** never stopping; unceasing: *tireless efforts.* **— tire′less|ly,** *adv.* **— tire′less|ness,** *n.*

**tire|man** (tīr′man′, -mən), *n., pl.* **-men.** a person who manufactures or deals in tires.

**Ti|re|si|as** (tī rē′sē əs, -shē-; tə-), *n. Greek Legend.* a seer of Thebes who saw Athena bathing. She blinded him for it, but in compensation gave him a staff to serve as eyes, understanding of birds' language, and prophetic vision.

**tire|some** (tīr′səm), *adj.* tiring; not interesting; boring: *a tiresome speech.* **SYN:** wearisome, irksome. **— tire′some|ly,** *adv.* **— tire′some|ness,** *n.*
**— *Syn.* Tiresome, tedious** mean tiring or boring, or both. **Tiresome** implies being dull and uninteresting: *Our neighbor is good-hearted, but I find her tiresome.* **Tedious** implies being too long, slow, or repetitious: *Weeding a garden is tedious work.*

**tire|wom|an** (tīr′wu̇m′ən), *n., pl.* **-wom|en.** *Archaic.* a lady's maid. [< *tire*[3] + *woman*]

**tir|ing glass** (tīr′ing), *Archaic.* a mirror used in dressing, combing the hair, and other grooming.

**tiring house,** (formerly) a small structure in which actors dressed for the stage: *an Elizabethan tiring house.*

**tiring room,** *Archaic.* a dressing room, especially in a theater. [< *attiring room*]

**tirl** (tėrl), *v., n. Scottish.* **— *v.t., v.i.*** to thrill; quiver.
**— *n.*** a thrill; tremor.

**tirl|ing pin** (tėr′ling), *Scottish.* a door knocker.

**ti|ro** (tī′rō), *n., pl.* **-ros.** = tyro.

**Ti|ro|le|an** (tə rō′lē ən), *adj., n.* = Tirolese. Also, **Tyrolean.**

**Tir|o|lese** (tir′ə lēz′, -lēs′), *adj., n.* **— *adj.*** of or having to do with the Tirol, a region in the Alps, chiefly in Austria and partly in Italy, or its inhabitants.
**— *n.*** a native or inhabitant of the Tirol. Also, **Tyrolese.**

**Ti|ro|ni|an** (tī rō′nē ən), *adj.* of or having to do with Tiro, the learned freedman and amanuensis of Cicero, who introduced a system of shorthand used by the ancient Romans.

**tir|ra|lir|ra** (tir′ə lir′ə), *n.* **1** the note of the lark. **2** a similar sound uttered as an exclamation of delight or gaiety. [imitative]

**tis** (tēz), *n.* plural of **ti**[2].

**'tis** (tiz), it is: *That he is mad, 'tis true ... And pity 'tis 'tis true* (Shakespeare).

**ti|sane** (ti zan′; *French* tē zȧn′), *n.* a decoction used or to be used as medicine: *an herb tisane.* [< Middle French *tizanne* < Latin *ptisana* < Greek *ptisánē* peeled barley; drink of barley water < *ptíssein* to peel, winnow]

**Tish|ah B'Ab** or **Tish|ah b'Ab** (tish′ä bə äv′, bäv′), a Jewish fast day, the ninth day of Ab, in remembrance of the destruction of the first Temple by the Babylonians in 587 B.C. and the destruction of the second Temple by Titus in A.D. 70. [< Hebrew *tish'āh bĕ'ābh*]

**Tish|ri** (tish′rē), *n.* the first month of the Jewish civil year or the seventh of the ecclesiastical year, corresponding to October and sometimes part of September. [< Hebrew *tishrī* < Babylonian *tashritu*]

**Ti|siph|o|ne** (ti sif′ə nē), *n. Greek Mythology.* one of the three Furies or Erinyes (Alecto and Megaera being the other two).

**tis|sue** (tish′ü), *n., v.,* **-sued, -su|ing. — *n.* 1** *Biology.* the masses of cells forming the parts of animals or plants. Tissue is formed of similar cells which perform a particular function. *The teacher showed pictures of muscle tissues, brain tissues, and skin tissues.* **2** a thin, light, or delicate cloth: *Her dress was of silk tissue.* **3** *Figurative.* a web; network: *Their whole story was a tissue of lies.* **4** = tissue paper. **5** a thin, soft, absorbent paper used especially as a handkerchief, to wipe the face, or as toilet paper.
**— *v.t.*** **1** to make into a tissue; weave. **2** to clothe or adorn with tissue.
[< Old French *tissu,* (originally) past participle of *tistre* to weave < Latin *texere.* Compare etym. under **textile, texture.**]

**tissue culture, 1** the technique or process of keeping bits of animal tissue alive and growing in

**Pronunciation Key:** hat, āge, cãre, fär; let, ēqual, tėrm; it, īce; hot, ōpen, ôrder; oil, out; cup, pu̇t, rüle; child; long; thin; ŧhen; zh, measure; ə represents **a** in about, **e** in taken, **i** in pencil, **o** in lemon, **u** in circus.

a sterile, nutrient medium. **2** the tissue growing within this medium.
**tissue paper**, a very thin, soft, unsized paper, used for wrapping, covering things, making carbon copies of letters, and in other ways.
**tissue respiration**, = internal respiration.
**tissue typing**, a procedure for determining the compatibility of tissues of donor and recipient in a transplant operation.
**tit**[1] (tit), *n.* **1** = titmouse. **2** any one of certain other small birds. **3** a runty or worthless horse; nag. **4** *Slang.* a girl or young woman of loose character; hussy; minx. [compare Old Icelandic *tittr* titmouse; small peak, pin]
**tit**[2] (tit), *n.* a nipple; teat. [Old English *titt.* See related etym. at **teat.**]
**tit**[3] (tit), *n. Obsolete.* a blow. [apparently variant of earlier *tip for tap*]
**tit.**, title.
**Tit.**, Titus (book of the New Testament).
**Ti|tan** (tī′tən), *n., adj.* —*n.* **1** *Greek Mythology.* **a** one of a family of giants who ruled the world before the gods of Mount Olympus. They were the children of Uranus (Heaven) and Gaea (Earth). Prometheus and Atlas were Titans. **b** the sun god, Helios (Sol), son of the Titan Hyperion. **2** the largest satellite of Saturn, the only satellite in the solar system known to have an atmosphere. **3** Also, **titan**. a person or thing having enormous size, strength, power, or intellect; giant.
—*adj.* Also, **titan**. **1** of or having to do with the Titans. **2** very powerful; gigantic; huge.
**ti|tan|ate** (tī′tə nāt), *n.* a salt or ester of titanic acid.
**Ti|tan|esque** (tī′tə nesk′), *adj.* of or like a Titan; titanic.
**Ti|tan|ess** (tī′tə nis), *n.* **1** a female Titan. **2** Also, **titaness**. a giantess.
**ti|ta|ni|a** (tī tā′nē ə), *n.* **1** titanium dioxide; titanic oxide. **2** a synthetic gem as brilliant but not as hard as a diamond, made by heating titanic oxide at a very high temperature.
**Ti|ta|ni|a** (ti tā′nē ə, tī-), *n.* the queen of the fairies and wife of Oberon in medieval legends. She is a main character in Shakespeare's *A Midsummer Night's Dream.*
**ti|tan|ic**[1] (tī tan′ik, ti-), *adj.* of or containing titanium, especially with a valence of four. [< *titan*(ium) + *-ic*]
**ti|tan|ic**[2] (tī tan′ik), *adj.* **1** Also, **Titanic**. having great size, strength, power, or intellect; gigantic; huge; colossal: *titanic energy. Here once, through an alley Titanic, Of cypress I roamed* (Edgar Allan Poe). **2 Titanic**, of or like the Titans: *The figure of Napoleon was Titanic* (Thomas Carlyle). —**Ti|tan′i|cal|ly**, *adv.*
**titanic acid**, **1** = titanic oxide. **2** any one of several weak acids derived from titanic oxide.
**titanic oxide**, a compound, the dioxide of titanium, occurring in nature in rutile, anatase, and brookite, or prepared artificially as a white powder. It is used in paints and dyes. *Formula:* $TiO_2$
**ti|tan|if|er|ous** (tī′tə nif′ər əs), *adj.* containing or yielding titanium. [< *titani*(um) + *-ferous*]
**Ti|tan|ism** (tī′tə niz əm), *n.* the spirit or quality typical of the Titans, especially that of revolt against the established order, defiance of convention, or the like.
**ti|tan|ite** (tī′tə nīt), *n.* a mineral, a silicate and titanite of calcium, occurring in igneous rocks; sphene. *Formula:* $CaTiSiO_5$ [< German *Titanit* < *Titanium* titanium + *-it* -ite[1]]
***ti|ta|ni|um** (tī tā′nē əm, ti-), *n.* a strong, lightweight, silver-gray metallic chemical element occurring in rutile, ilmenite, brookite, and various other minerals. It is highly resistant to corrosion and is used in making steel and other alloys for missiles and jet engines. [< German *Titanium* < Latin *Tītan* Titan]

***titanium**

| symbol | atomic number | atomic weight | oxidation state |
|---|---|---|---|
| Ti | 22 | 47.90 | 2,3,4 |

**titanium dioxide**, = titanic oxide.
**titanium oxide**, any oxide of titanium, especially titanic oxide.
**titanium tetrachloride**, a colorless liquid with a sharp acid odor, used in the production of titanium metal from the ore. When combined with water or moist air, it yields titanic oxide. In the presence of ammonia and moist air it yields a dense white smoke used for smoke screens and skywriting. *Formula:* $TiCl_4$
**ti|tan|o|saur** (tī′tə nə sôr), *n.* = Titanosaurus.
**Ti|tan|o|sau|rus** (tī′tə nə sôr′əs), *n.* any one of a genus of large herbivorous dinosaurs present in the Cretaceous period, especially in South America. [< New Latin *Titanosaurus* the genus name < Greek *Tītân* a Titan + *saûros* lizard]
**ti|tan|o|there** (tī′tə nə thir), *n.* an extinct, hoofed mammal like a rhinoceros, with a long, broad skull, very small brain, and a pair of horns over the nose. Its remains were found in the Tertiary formations of North America. [< Greek *tītáno-* (< *Tītân* a Titan) + *thērion* beast]
**ti|tan|ous** (tī tan′əs, tī′tə nəs), *adj.* containing titanium, especially with a valence of three.
**tit|bit** (tit′bit′), *n.* = tidbit. [variant of *tidbit*]
**ti|ter** (tī′tər, tē′-), *n. Chemistry.* **1** the weight of a pure substance which is contained in, would react with, or would be equivalent to, a unit volume of a reagent solution, usually expressed in milligrams of solute per milliliter of solution. **2** the amount of a standard solution necessary to produce a certain result in titration. Also, *especially British,* **titre**. [< French, Old French *titre,* proportions in alloyed metal; quality, (originally) inscription, learned borrowing from Latin *titulus.* See etym. of doublets **tilde, title, tittle.**]
**tit|fer** (tit′fər), *n. British Slang.* **1** a derby hat; bowler. **2** any hat. [short for *tit for tat,* rhyming slang for *derby hat*]
**tit for tat**, blow for blow; like for like: *She hasn't the courage to give him tit for tat* (Maria Edgeworth). [perhaps alteration of earlier *tip for tap* blow for blow]
**tith|a|ble** (tī′ᴛʜə bəl), *adj.* subject to the payment of tithes: *tithable land.*
**tithe** (tīᴛʜ), *n., v.,* **tithed, tith|ing.** —*n.* **1** a tenth part; one tenth. **2** a very small part; fraction. **3** any small tax or levy.
—*v.t.* **1** to put a tax of a tenth on. **2** to pay a tithe on. **3** to exact or collect a tithe from.
—*v.i.* to give one tenth of one's income to the church or to charity.
**tithes**, a tax or donation of one tenth of the yearly produce of land, animals, and personal work, paid for the support of the church and the clergy: *The whole tithes of the diocese were then paid to the bishop* (Richard Burn).
[Old English *tēotha* tenth]
**tithe barn**, (in Great Britain) a barn built formerly to hold the tithes received by a parson or parish church.
**tith|er** (tī′ᴛʜər), *n.* **1** a payer or a receiver of tithes. **2** a supporter of a system of ecclesiastical tithes.
**tithes** (tīᴛʜz), *n.pl.* See under **tithe**.
**tith|ing** (tī′ᴛʜing), *n.* **1** the payment or exacting of tithes. **2** one tenth given to the church; tithe. **3a** a company of ten householders in the old system of frankpledge in England. **b** an administrative unit in parts of rural England, descended from this system.
**tith|ing|man** (tī′ᴛʜing mən), *n., pl.* **-men**. a former town officer in England whose duties were like those of a policeman.
**ti|ti**[1] (ti tē′), *n.* any one of certain small monkeys of South America, such as the squirrel monkey. Also, **teetee**. [< Spanish *tití* < the Tupi (perhaps Brazil) name]
**ti|ti**[2] (tē′tē), *n.* any one of several shrubs or small trees of the southern United States, having glossy leaves and spikes of fragrant white flowers. [American English; origin unknown]
**ti|tian** (tish′ən), *n., adj.* auburn; golden red. [< *Titian,* 1487?-1576, a Venetian painter, who favored this color in his pictures]
**tit|il|late** (tit′ə lāt), *v.,* **-lat|ed, -lat|ing.** —*v.t.* **1** to excite pleasantly; stimulate agreeably. **2** = tickle.
—*v.i.* to be titillated: *At once his ears and fingers began to titillate—the roots of his hair to tingle* (Theodore Dreiser).
[< Latin *tītillāre* (with English *-ate*[1]) to tickle]
**tit|il|lat|ing** (tit′ə lā′ting), *adj.* that titillates; pleasantly exciting or stimulating: *a titillating sensation, a titillating experience.* —**tit′il|lat′ing|ly**, *adv.*
**tit|il|la|tion** (tit′ə lā′shən), *n.* **1** pleasant excitement; agreeable stimulation: *Thrills and titillations from games of hazard* (Thomas Hardy). **2** the act or fact of tickling.
**tit|il|la|tive** (tit′ə lā′tiv), *adj.* tending to titillate; titillating.
**tit|il|la|tor** (tit′ə lā′tər), *n.* a person or thing that titillates.
**tit|il|la|to|ry** (tit′ə lə tôr′ē, -tōr′-), *adj.* having to do with or characterized by titillation.
**tit|i|vate** (tit′ə vāt), *v.t., v.i.,* **-vat|ed, -vat|ing.** *Informal.* to dress up; make smart; spruce up; prink. Also, **tittivate**. [earlier *tiddivate,* perhaps < *tidy* + a pretended classical ending] —**tit′i|va′tion**, *n.*
**tit|lark** (tit′lärk′), *n.* a small bird somewhat like a lark; pipit. [< *tit*[1] + *lark*[1]]
**ti|tle** (tī′təl), *n., adj., v.,* **-tled, -tling.** —*n.* **1a** the name of a book, poem, play, picture, song, or the like: *"Goldilocks and the Three Bears" is the title of a famous story for little children.* SYN: See syn. under **name**. **b** a printing of this at the beginning of a book. **c** = title page. **d** a descriptive heading or caption, as of a chapter or section of a book. **e** any of the credits, lines of dialogue, or other printed material appearing on the screen in a motion picture or television program. **2** a name showing rank, occupation, or condition in life. King, duke, lord, countess, captain, doctor, professor, Madame and Miss are titles. **3** any descriptive or distinctive name: *Horatio in Shakespeare's Hamlet deserved the title of a true friend.* **4** a first-place position; championship: *He won the heavyweight title.* **5a** a legal right to the possession of property. **b** the legal evidence, especially a document, showing such a right. When a house is sold, the seller gives title to the buyer. **c** all of the things that make up legal ownership. **d** a subdivision of a statute or law book. **e** the descriptive or formal heading of a legal document, statute, or the like. **f** the heading that names the cause of or right to the action. **6** a recognized right; claim: *What title does he have to my gratitude?* **7** *Ecclesiastical.* **a** evidence of an assured benefice, or of a definite source of income, required by a bishop before he ordains a candidate. **b** any one of the principal Roman Catholic churches of Rome whose incumbents are cardinals. **8** *Obsolete.* **a** an inscription placed on or over an object, giving its name or describing it. **b** a placard hung up in a theater giving the name of the piece and other information.
—*adj.* **1** of or for a title: *a title search.* **2** (of an essay, poem, story, or the like) giving name to the whole collection or book: *The name of this book of poems is "Crossroads;" the title poem is the first poem in the volume.* **3** of a size or kind used in printing titles: *a title letter or type.*
—*v.t.* **1** to call by a title; term. **2** to furnish with a title; name; entitle.
[< Old French *title,* learned borrowing from Latin *titulus* inscription (in Late Latin, title of a book). See etym. of doublets **tilde, titer, tittle.**]
▶ **titles.** In formal usage the titles of books, long poems, plays published as separate volumes, and the names of magazines and newspapers are underlined or, in print, appear in italics. Capitals are used for the first and last words, for all nouns, pronouns, verbs, adjectives, and adverbs, and for prepositions of more than five letters: *Smarter and Smoother; Marching On; Life Behind Bars; Romeo and Juliet; National Geographic Magazine.* Titles of short stories, short poems, songs, essays, and magazine articles are usually put in quotation marks: "My Old Kentucky Home"; "Atomic Power in Tomorrow's World."
**ti|tled** (tī′təld), *adj.* having a title, especially a title of rank: *She married a titled nobleman.*
**title deed**, a document showing that a person owns certain property.
**ti|tle|hold|er** (tī′təl hōl′dər), *n.* the holder of a championship; champion: *the heavyweight titleholder.*
**title page**, the page at the beginning of a book that gives the title, the author's or editor's name, and usually the name of the publisher and his address.
**title role** or **part**, the part or character for which a play, motion picture, opera, operetta, or other dramatic work is named. Hamlet and Othello are title roles.
**ti|tlist** (tī′tlist), *n.* = titleholder.
**tit|mouse** (tit′mous′), *n., pl.* **-mice**. any one of a family of small birds with short bills and mostly gray feathers, related to the nuthatches and found in nearly all parts of the world: *The chickadee is the most common North American titmouse* (Arthur A. Allen). [Middle English *titemose* < *tit* titmouse + Old English *māse* titmouse; influenced by *mouse*]
**Ti|to|ism** (tē′tō iz əm), *n.* the principles and practices of Marshal Tito (born 1892), Yugoslav premier, especially the stressing of a form of Communism that places national above international interests and does not conform to the policies of the Soviet Union.
**Ti|to|ist** (tē′tō ist), *adj., n.* —*adj.* of or having to do with Titoism. —*n.* a supporter of Titoism.
**ti|trant** (tī′trənt), *n.* the substance added in titration.
**ti|trate** (tī′trāt, tit′rāt), *v.,* **-trat|ed, -trat|ing,** *n.* —*v.t., v.i.* to analyze or be analyzed by titration.
—*n.* a solution to be analyzed by titration.
[< French *titrer* (with English *-ate*[1]) < *titre;* see etym. under **titer**]
**ti|tra|tion** (tī trā′shən, ti-), *n.* the process of determining the amount of some substance present in a solution by measuring the amount of a different solution of known strength that must be added to complete a chemical change.
**ti|tra|tor** (tī′trā tər, tit′rā-), *n.* an instrument used in titration.
**ti|tre** (tī′tər, tē′-), *n. Especially British.* titer.
**ti|tri|met|ric** (tī′trə met′rik), *adj.* of or having to do with measurement by titration: *titrimetric analysis.*
**ti|trim|e|try** (tī trim′ə trē), *n.* measurement by titration.

**tit-tat-toe** (tit′tat tō′), *n.* = tick-tack-toe.

**tit|ter** (tit′ər), *v., n.* —***v.i.*** to laugh in a half-restrained manner, because of nervousness or silliness; giggle. —***n.*** the act of tittering; tittering laugh. —**tit′ter|er**, *n.* —**tit′ter|ing|ly**, *adv.*

**tit|tie** (tit′ē), *n. Scottish Informal.* titty.

**tit|ti|vate** (tit′ə vāt), *v.,* **-vat|ed, -vat|ing.** *Informal.* titivate.

**tit|ti|va|tion** (tit′ə vā′shən), *n. Informal.* titivation.

**tit|tle** (tit′əl), *n.* **1** a very little bit; particle; whit. **2** a small stroke or mark over a letter in writing or printing. The dot over the letter *i* is a tittle. **3** a very small part, originally of something written: *one jot or one tittle shall in no wise pass from the law* (Matthew 5:18). [< Medieval Latin *titulus* diacritical mark, vowel point, point of a letter < Latin, title, superscription. See etym. of doublets **tilde, titer, title.**]

**tit|tle-tat|tle** (tit′əl tat′əl), *n., v.i., v.t.,* **-tled, -tling.** = gossip. [varied reduplication of *tattle*] —**tit′tle-tat′ler**, *n.*

**tit|tup** (tit′əp), *v.,* **-tuped, -tup|ing** or (*especially British*) **-tupped, -tup|ping**, *n.* —***v.i.*** **1** to walk in an affected or prancing manner. **2** (of a horse or other animal) to canter or gallop easily; prance; caper. **3** (of a boat) to toss with abrupt or jerky movements.
—***n.*** prancing, frolicking behavior; frisk; caper.

**tit|tup|y** (tit′ə pē), *adj. British.* **1** tittuping; prancing or lively: *Barbara Windsor's tittupy Cockney ... maid is amusing* (Manchester Guardian Weekly). **2** shaky or unsteady, as furniture.

**tit|ty** (tit′ē), *n., pl.* **-ties.** *Scottish Informal.* sister (referring to a young woman or girl).
[probably imitation of infantile pronunciation of *sissie* sister]

**tit|u|bate** (tich′ů bāt), *v.i.,* **-bat|ed, -bat|ing.** **1** to stagger; totter; stumble. **2** *Figurative.* to falter in speaking; stammer. [< Latin *titubāre*]

**tit|u|ba|tion** (tich′ů bā′shən), *n.* an unsteady gait or a tottering, associated with spinal and cerebral disorders. [< Latin *titubātiō, -ōnis* < *titubāre* to stagger]

**tit|u|lar** (tich′ə lər, tit′yə-), *adj., n.* —***adj.*** **1** in title or name only; nominal: *He is a titular prince without any power.* **2** having a title; titled. **3** having to do with a title. **4a** of or having to do with certain Roman Catholic churches called titles. **b** deriving title from a see (now only nominal): *a titular bishop.*
—***n.*** **1** a person or clergyman who holds a title. **2** a person or thing from which a title or name, especially of a church, is taken.
[< Latin *titulus* (see etym. under **title**)]

**tit|u|lar|ly** (tich′ə lər lē, tit′yə-), *adv.* with respect to title; nominally.

**tit|u|lar|y** (tich′ə ler′ē, tit′yə-), *adj., n., pl.* **-lar|ies.** = titular.

**Ti|tus** (tī′təs), *n.* **1** a convert and companion of Saint Paul. **2** an epistle of the New Testament written to Titus by Saint Paul. Full title, *The Epistle of Paul to Titus.*

**Ti|u** (tē′ü), *n.* the Teutonic god of war and of the sky, identified with the Norse god Tyr.

**Tiv** (tiv), *n., pl.* **Tiv** or **Tivs.** **1** a member of an agricultural people of central Nigeria. **2** the language of this people, related to Efik and Bantu.

**tiv|y** (tiv′ē), *v.,* **tiv|ied, tiv|y|ing,** *interj.* —***v.i.*** to rush headlong, as a hunter on horseback.
—***interj.*** tantivy. [short for *tantivy*]

**tizz** (tiz), *n. Slang.* a very excited state; tizzy. [back formation < *tizzy*¹]

**tiz|zy¹** (tiz′ē), *n., pl.* **-zies.** *Slang.* a very excited state; dither. [origin uncertain]

**tiz|zy²** (tiz′ē), *n., pl.* **-zies.** *British Slang.* a sixpenny piece; sixpence. [origin unknown]

**tk.**, **1** track. **2** truck.

**T.K.O., TKO** (no periods), or **t.k.o.**, technical knockout (in boxing).

**Tl** (no period), thallium (chemical element).

**T.L.** or **TL** (no periods), trade-last.

**Tla|loc** (tlä lok′), *n.* the Aztec rain god, probably the oldest god in the Aztec pantheon.

**T.L.C.** or **TLC** (no periods), **1** *Informal.* tender loving care: *Babies who get T.L.C. probably will be better able to stand stresses and less likely to develop heart trouble ... when they grow up than babies not so gently handled* (Science News Letter). **2** thin-layer chromatography.

**Tlin|git** (tling′git), *n., pl.* **-git** or **-gits.** **1** a member of a group of Indian tribes living on the coast of British Columbia and southern Alaska. **2** a linguistic group comprising the languages of these tribes. It is a branch of the Na-Dene stock.

**t.l.o.**, total loss only (a condition of marine insurance covering the total destruction of a vessel).

**TLP** (no periods), transient lunar phenomena: ... *the so-called TLPs, elusive reddish glows which have been recorded in certain areas* (*notably that of the brilliant crater Aristarchus and the huge walled plain Alphonsus* (New Scientist and Science Journal).

**t.m.**, true mean.

**Tm** (no period), thulium (chemical element).

**TM** (no periods), Transcendental Meditation: *Readers were most interested in the Eastern religions and practices—TM, Yoga, and Zen* (National Review).

**T-man** (tē′man′), *n., pl.* **-men.** *Informal.* an agent or investigator of the United States Treasury. [American English; abbreviation for *Treasury man*]

**T-maze** (tē′māz), *n.* a maze used in experimental psychology, consisting of one or more sections shaped like a T, at the intersection of which the subject has to choose whether to go right or left.

**tme|sis** (tmē′sis), *n. Grammar.* the separation of the elements of a compound word or a phrase by the interposition of another word or words, as *chit and chat* for *chit-chat; to us-ward* (II Peter 3:9) for *toward us.* [< Late Latin *tmēsis* < Greek *tmêsis* (originally) a cutting < *témnein* to cut]

**TMV** (no periods), tobacco mosaic virus.

**tn.**, **1** ton. **2** town.

**Tn** (no period), thoron (chemical isotope).

**TN** (no periods), Tennessee (with postal Zip Code).

**tng.**, training.

**TNT** (no periods) or **T.N.T.**, a pale yellow to dark brown solid used as an explosive in hand grenades, torpedoes, etc.; trinitrotoluene. *Formula:* $CH_3C_6H_2(NO_2)_3$

**to** (tü; *unstressed* tů, tə), *prep., adv.* —***prep.*** **1** in the direction of; toward: *Go to the right. Stand with your back to the wall.* **2** as far as; until: *wet to the skin, from dawn to dusk, faithful to the end. The apple is rotten to the core. The captain stayed with his ship to the end.* **3** for the purpose of; for use with; for: *a means to an end, a horse bred to the plow. Mother soon came to the rescue.* **4** toward or into the position, condition, or state of: *He went to sleep.* **5** so as to produce, cause, or result in: *To her horror, the beast approached. To my amazement, he jumped.* **6** into: *She tore the letter to pieces.* **7** by: *a fact known to few.* **8** along with; with: *We danced to the music.* **9** compared with: *The score was 9 to 5.* **10** in agreement with: *Going without food is not to my liking.* **11** as seen or understood by: *a symptom alarming to the doctor. To my mind, the situation is not yet hopeless.* **12** belonging with; of: *the key to my room.* **13** in honor of: *The soldiers drank to the king.* **14** on; against: *Fasten it to the wall.* **15** about; concerning: *What did she say to that?* **16** included, contained, or involved in: *four apples to the pound, a book without much to it.* **17** *To* is used to show action toward: *Give the book to me. Speak to her.* **18** *To* is used with the infinitive form of verbs: *I like to read. The birds began to sing. To err is human; to forgive ... divine* (Alexander Pope).
—***adv.*** **1** forward: *You're wearing your cap wrong side to.* **2** together; touching; closed: *The door slammed to.* **3** to action or work: *We turned to gladly.* **4** to consciousness: *She came to.*
**to and fro**, first one way and then back again; back and forth: *And the Lord said unto Satan, Whence comest thou? Then Satan answered ... From going to and fro in the earth* (Job 1:7).
[Old English *tō*]

**t.o.**, an abbreviation for the following:
**1** table of organization.
**2** traditional orthography.
**3** turn over.
**4** turnover.

**T/O** (no periods), table of organization.

***toad** (tōd), *n.* **1** a small amphibian without a tail, somewhat like a frog, that lives most of the time on land rather than in water. Toads, which are found in gardens, have a rough, brown skin that suggests a lump of earth. *Toads have shorter legs and are generally more clumsy than frogs* (W. Frank Blair). **2** any tailless amphibian; any frog. **3** any one of certain other animals, such as the horned toad. **4** *Figurative.* a disgusting or contemptible person or thing. [Middle English *tode,* Old English *tāde, tādige*]

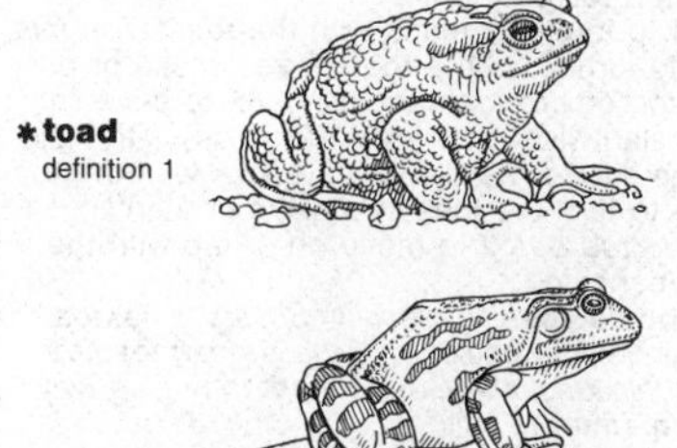

***toad** definition 1

frog

**toad|eat|er** (tōd′ē′tər), *n.* a fawning flatterer; sycophant; toady. [originally, a charlatan's attendant who pretended to eat toads, so his master might "cure" him of their poison]

**toad|eat|ing** (tōd′ē′ting), *n., adj.* —***n.*** fawning flattery; sycophancy.
—***adj.*** = sycophantic.

**toad|fish** (tōd′fish′), *n., pl.* **-fish|es** or (*collectively*) **-fish.** **1** any one of a family of fishes with large, thick heads, wide mouths, and slimy skin without scales, found near the bottom of tropical and temperate oceans. **2** = puffer (def. 2).

**toad|flax** (tōd′flaks′), *n.* **1** a common weed of the figwort family with yellow-and-orange flowers; butter-and-eggs; flaxweed. **2** any other plant of the same genus.

**toad-in-the-hole** (tōd′in ᴛʜə hōl′), *n. British.* a dish consisting of meat baked in batter.

**toad spit** or **spittle**, a frothy secretion found on plants, exuded by the nymphs of certain insects; cuckoo spit.

**toad|stone** (tōd′stōn′), *n.* any one of various stones or stonelike objects once believed to have been formed in the head or body of a toad, formerly worn as jewels or amulets.

**toad|stool** (tōd′stül′), *n.* **1** any one of various fungi, especially the agarics, that have a round, disklike top and a slender stalk, and grow on decaying vegetable matter; mushroom. **2** any poisonous mushroom. **3** any one of various other fungi, such as a puffball or morel.

**toad|y** (tō′dē), *n., pl.* **toad|ies**, *v.,* **toad|ied, toad|y|ing.** —***n.*** **1** a fawning flatterer; sycophant. **2** a humble dependent.
—***v.i.*** to be or act like a toady.
—***v.t.*** to fawn upon; flatter.
[perhaps alteration of *toadeater*]

**toad|y|ish** (tō′dē ish), *adj.* of or like a toady. —**toad′y|ish|ly**, *adv.*

**toad|y|ism** (tō′dē iz əm), *n.* the action or behavior of a toady; interested flattery; mean servility.

**to-and-fro** (tü′ən frō′), *adj., n.* —***adj.*** = back-and-forth.
—***n.*** a back-and-forth movement; *She, like some wild creature newly-caged, commenced a to-and-fro* (Tennyson).

**toast¹** (tōst), *n., v.* —***n.*** a slice or slices of bread browned by heat. [< verb]
—***v.t., v.i.*** **1** to brown by heat: *We toasted the bread.* **2** to heat thoroughly: *He toasted his feet before the open fire.*
[< Old French *toster* < Vulgar Latin *tostāre* < Latin *torrēre* to parch]

**toast²** (tōst), *n., v.* —***n.*** **1a** a person whose health is proposed and drunk: *"The King" was the first toast drunk by the officers.* **b** an event, institution, or sentiment in honor of which a group is requested to drink. **2** a popular or celebrated person, especially a beautiful or socially prominent woman: *The young pianist was the toast of the town.* **3** the act of drinking to the health of a person or thing. **4** a call on another or others to drink to some person or thing.
—***v.t.*** to take a drink and wish good fortune to; drink to the health or in honor of: *The men toasted the general. We toasted Grandfather by lifting our glasses, smiling at him, and drinking a little.* —***v.i.*** to drink toasts.
[< *toast*¹, from the use of spiced toast to flavor drinks]

**toast|er¹** (tōs′tər), *n.* **1** an electric appliance for toasting, especially bread. **2** a person who toasts something.

**toast|er²** (tōs′tər), *n.* a person who proposes or joins in a toast.

**toast|mas|ter** (tōst′mas′tər, -mäs′-), *n.* **1** a person who presides at a dinner and introduces the speakers. **2** a person who proposes toasts.

**toast|mis|tress** (tōst′mis′tris), *n.* a woman toastmaster.

**toast|y** (tōs′tē), *adj.,* **toast|i|er, toast|i|est.** **1** of or like toast; having a slightly burnt flavor. **2** *Figurative.* comfortably warm: *a trim hip-length jacket—toasty wool fleece in a very bright plaid—with a snug turtle neck* (New Yorker).

**tob** (tōb), *n.* = tobe.

**Tob.**, Tobit.

**to|bac|co** (tə bak′ō), *n., pl.* **-cos** or **-coes.** **1a** the prepared leaves of certain plants, used for smoking or chewing or as snuff. **b** one of these plants. Tobacco is native to tropical America and is now widely grown in many parts of the world. It belongs to the nightshade family. **2** things made from or containing these leaves, such as cigars and cigarettes: *That shop sells all kinds of tobacco.* **3** the smoking of a pipe, cigars, or cigarettes, or the chewing of tobacco leaves: *He* *gave up tobacco for the sake of his children.* [alteration of earlier *tabaco* < Spanish < Arawak (Haiti) *tabako* a Y-shaped pipe for inhaling smoke through the nostrils; also, a small cigar of rolled tobacco leaves]

**tobacco heart**, a heart disorder characterized by a rapid or irregular pulse, caused by excessive use of tobacco.

**tobacco hornworm.** = tobacco worm.

**to|bac|co|man** (tə bak′ō man′, -mən), *n., pl.* **-men.** a man engaged in the business of producing or selling tobacco.

**tobacco mosaic**, a mosaic disease of the tobacco plant, caused by a virus which attacks the leaves, producing spots, curling, and shrinking.

**tobacco mosaic virus**, the virus that causes tobacco mosaic, a disease of the tobacco plant. *Abbr:* TMV (no periods).

**to|bac|co|nist** (tə bak′ə nist), *n.* **1** a dealer in tobacco. **2** the business of such a person.

**Tobacco Road** or **tobacco road**, *U.S.* a rundown, depressed rural area, especially in the Southern United States where poor whites live. *Her childhood was spent ... in dreary sawmill towns at the dead ends of Tobacco Road* (Time). [< *Tobacco Road,* a novel by Erskine Caldwell (1932) dealing with a family of poor whites in the cotton-growing region of Georgia]

**tobacco worm**, the large, green caterpillar of either of two species of hawk moths, having white markings and a hornlike process near the end of the body. It feeds on tobacco, tomato, and related plants.

**To|ba|go|ni|an** (tō′bə gō′nē ən), *n.* a native or inhabitant of Tobago, an island in the West Indies.

**to-be** (tə bē′), *adj.* that is yet to be or to come; future: *to-be biologists. A wide selection of articles for the mother-to-be.*

**tobe** (tōb), *n.* a length of cotton cloth worn as an outer garment by natives of northern and central Africa. Also, **tob, thob.** [< Arabic *thawb*]

**To|bi|as** (tə bī′əs), *n.* **1** in the Douay Bible: **a** = Tobit (def. 2). **b** the book of Tobit, included in the canon. **2** the son of Tobit, hero of the Apocryphal book of Tobit.

**To|bit** (tō′bit), *n.* **1** a book of the Protestant Old Testament Apocrypha, included in the canon of the Roman Catholic Bible as Tobias. *Abbr:* Tob. **2** an Israelite exile in Nineveh.

**to|bog|gan** (tə bog′ən), *n., v.* —*n.* a long, narrow, flat sled with its front curved upward and without runners.
—*v.i.* **1** to slide downhill on a toboggan. **2** *Informal, Figurative.* to decline sharply and rapidly in value.
[American English < Canadian French *tabagane* < Algonkian (probably Micmac) *tobâkun*] —**to·bog′gan|er**, *n.*

**to|bog|gan|ist** (tə bog′ə nist), *n.* a person who toboggans.

**to|by¹** (tō′bē), *n., pl.* **-bies.** *U.S. Slang.* a long, slender, cheap cigar. [American English; origin unknown]

***To|by** or **to|by²** (tō′bē), *n., pl.* **-bies.** a small, fat jug or mug in the form of a fat man wearing a long coat and three-cornered hat, used for drinking ale or beer. [< *Toby,* a proper name, short for *Tobias*]

***Toby**

**Toby jug** or **mug** = Toby.

**toc|ca|ta** (tə kä′tə), *n., pl.* **-tas.** *Music.* a composition for the piano, organ, or harpsichord, using full chords and running passages, often intended to exhibit the technique of the performer. [< Italian *toccata* (literally) a touching, noun use of past participle of *toccare;* ultimately imitative]

**To|char|i|an** (tō kãr′ē ən, -kär′-), *n., adj.* —*n.* **1** an extinct Indo-European language or group of languages of which records from about 600 A.D. have been discovered in Turkestan. **2** one of the people of Central Asia who spoke this language.
—*adj.* of or having to do with this language or people. Also, **Tokharian.**

**toch|er** (toн′ər), *n., v. Scottish.* —*n.* a dowry.
—*v.t.* to furnish with a tocher; dower.
[< early Scottish Gaelic and Middle Irish *tochar* dowry, portion < Old Irish *to-chuirim* I assign]

**to|col|o|gy** (tō kol′ə jē), *n.* = obstetrics. Also, **tokology.** [< Greek *tókos* offspring (< *tiktein* give birth to) + English *-logy*]

**to|coph|er|ol** (tō kof′ə rōl, -rol), *n.* any one of four closely related alcohols associated with, or one of the components of, vitamin E, important as an antisterility factor in the diet, present in wheat germ and certain other vegetable oils, milk, and lettuce and other plant leaves. [< Greek *tókos* offspring + *phérein* to bear, produce + English *-ol¹*]

**toc|sin** (tok′sən), *n.* **1** an alarm sounded by ringing a bell or bells; warning signal: *the tocsin of the soul—the dinner-bell* (Byron). **2** a bell used to sound an alarm: *Oh, what a tocsin has she for a tongue* (Walter de la Mare). [< Middle French *tocsin* < Provençal *tocasenh* < *tocar* to strike, touch + *senh* bell, bell note < Late Latin *signum* bell, ringing of a bell < Latin, sign]

**tod¹** (tod), *n. British Slang.*
**on one's tod**, by oneself; on one's own; alone: *Francis Chichester went off on his tod around the world* (Punch).
[< *Tod* Sloane, an English jockey of the 1800's, from rhyming slang phrase "on one's Tod Sloane" (on one's own; alone)]

**tod²** (tod), *n. Scottish.* **1** a fox. **2** *Figurative.* a crafty person: *Take care of the old tod; he means mischief* (Robert Louis Stevenson). [origin uncertain]

**tod³** (tod), *n.* **1** an old British unit of weight, usually for wool, equal to about 28 pounds: *a tax of five ... shillings upon the exportation of every tod of wool* (Adam Smith). **2** a bushy mass, especially of ivy. [Middle English *todde.* Perhaps related to East Frisian *todde* bundle]

**To|da** (tō′də), *n., pl.* **-da** or **-das.** **1** a member of a Dravidian people of southern India and Ceylon (Sri Lanka) whose culture centers on the care and cult of the buffalo: *Amongst the Toda, several men, usually brothers, share the wife* (Manchester Guardian Weekly). **2** the language of this people.

**to|day** or **to-day** (tə dā′), *n., adv.* —*n.* **1** this day: *Today is Sunday.* **2** *Figurative.* the present time or age: *The popular writers of today can well become the old masters of tomorrow* (Listener).
—*adv.* **1** on or during this very day: *What are you doing today?* **2** *Figurative.* at the present time; now; nowadays: *Many girls wear their hair short today.*
[Old English *tō dæge* on (the) day]
► **Today** (like *tonight* and *tomorrow*) is rarely hyphenated now.

**tod|dle** (tod′əl), *v.,* **-dled, -dling,** *n.* —*v.i.* to walk with short, unsteady steps, as a baby does: *When his health enabled him to toddle abroad* (Thackeray).
—*n.* a toddling way of walking.
[origin unknown]

**tod|dler** (tod′lər), *n.* a child just learning to walk.

**tod|dy** (tod′ē), *n., pl.* **-dies.** **1** a drink made of whiskey, brandy, rum, or other alcoholic liquor, with hot water, sugar, and spices. **2** a beverage made from the fermented sap of an East Indian palm. [alteration of *tarrie* < Hindustani *tāṛī* palm sap < *tāṛ* palm tree < Sanskrit *tālī* palm tree]

**toddy palm**, any palm with sap that can be used for toddies.

**to-do** (tə dü′), *n., pl.* **-dos.** *Informal.* a fuss; bustle: *to make a great to-do over nothing.*

**to|dy** (tō′dē), *n., pl.* **-dies.** any one of various small, brilliantly colored, insect-eating birds of the West Indies, related to the motmots and kingfishers. [< French *todier* < New Latin *Todus* the genus name, special use of Latin *todus* a small bird]

**toe** (tō), *n., v.,* **toed, toe|ing.** —*n.* **1a** one of the five end parts of the human foot. **b** a corresponding part in a vertebrate animal. **2** the part of a stocking, shoe, or slipper, that covers the toes: *to have a hole in the toe of a sock.* **3** the forepart of a foot or hoof. **4** anything like a toe or the toes in shape or position: *the toe and heel of a golf club.* **5** a part of a machine placed vertically in a bearing, or a part projecting from a shaft, rod, or belt. **6** the part beyond the point of a frog in a railroad track.
—*v.t.* **1** to touch or reach with the toes: *Toe this line.* **2** to furnish with a toe or toes; make or put a new toe on: *to toe a stocking.* **3a** to drive (a nail) in slantwise. **b** to fasten (boards) with nails driven in such a way. **4** to hit or kick with the toe.
—*v.i.* **1** to turn the toes in walking or standing: *to toe in, to toe out.* **2** to move on or tap with the toes in dancing.
**dig in one's toes**, *Especially British.* to take a firm or inflexible position: *If the African leaders dig in their toes, the Government may give way* (London Times).
**on one's toes**, ready for action; alert: *Leading the Youth Symphony of New York,* [*he*] *offered a program fit to keep a top professional orchestra on its toes* (New York Times).
**step** (or **tread**) **on one's toes**, to offend or annoy one: *... stepping on the toes of vested interests* (Bulletin of Atomic Scientists).
**stub one's toe**, to fumble; blunder: *The scientist as the visionary bungler stubbing his toe over the most obvious facts of life certainly has his counterpart in everyday experience* (Wall Street Journal).
**toe to toe**, facing one another at close quarters: *to fight it out toe to toe.*
[Old English *tā*] —**toe′like′**, *adj.*

**toe|board** (tō′bôrd′, -bōrd′), *n.* **1** a board for the feet to rest upon, as on the floor of an automobile; floorboard. **2** a board marking the limit of the thrower's run in putting the shot and similar feats.

**toe|cap** (tō′kap′), *n.* a caplike piece of leather or metal covering the toe of a shoe or boot.

**toe crack**, a sand crack on the front of a horse's hoof.

**toed** (tōd), *adj.* **1** driven into wood, etc., on a slant: *a toed nail.* **2** fastened with nails driven in this way: *a toed board.*

**-toed**, *combining form.* having ____ toes: *Three-toed = having three toes.*

**toe dance**, a dance or dancing on the tips of the toes, usually with special slippers, as in ballet.

**toe-dance** (tō′dans′, -däns′), *v.i.,* **-danced, -danc|ing.** to do a toe dance; be a toe dancer.

**toe dancer**, a person who does a toe dance, especially a professional dancer.

**toe|hold** (tō′hōld′), *n.,* or **toe hold**, **1a** a small crack, projection, or ridge, just large enough for the toes in climbing: *a cliff without a toehold.* **b** the position of being supported by a toehold. **2** *Figurative.* any means of entering, overcoming, or expanding. **3** a hold in wrestling in which the opponent's foot is held and twisted.

**toe-in** (tō′in′), *n.* a slight inward tilt of the wheels of an automobile, trailer, or similar vehicle.

**toe|less** (tō′lis), *adj.* having no toes.

**toe|nail** (tō′nāl′), *n., v.* —*n.* **1** the nail growing on a toe. **2** a nail driven on a slant.
—*v.t.* to fasten with toed nails; toe.

**toe-out** (tō′out′), *n.* a slight outward tilt of the wheels of an automobile, trailer, or other vehicle.

**toe|piece** (tō′pēs′), *n.* = toecap.

**toe ring**, **1** a ring worn on the toe. **2** a stout ferrule on the end of a cant hook.

**toe|shoe** (tō′shü′), *n.* a ballet shoe reinforced at the toe for toe-dancing.

**toe strap**, a strap which passes over the toes and helps to hold a sandal, ski, snowshoe, or the like on one's foot, or gives one a firm footing or hold and prevents slipping.

**toff** (tôf, tof), *n. British Slang.* **1** a stylishly dressed man; swell; dandy. **2** a well-to-do person; nob. [perhaps alteration of *tuft,* formerly a gentleman commoner at Oxford who wore a gold tassel in his cap]

**tof|fee** (tôf′ē, tof′-), *n., pl.* **-fees.** a hard, chewy candy; taffy. [variant of *taffy*]

**tof|fee-nosed** (tôf′ē nōzd′, tof′-), *adj. British Slang.* conceited; pompous; stuck-up.

**tof|fy** (tôf′ē, tof′-), *n., pl.* **-fies.** = toffee.

**toft** (tôft, toft), *n.* **1** *British Dialect.* a homestead. **2** a knoll or hillock. [Old English *toft* < Scandinavian (compare Old Icelandic *topt* ground attached to a house)]

**to|fu** (tō′fü), *n.* = bean curd. [< Japanese *tōfu*]

**tog** (tog), *n., v.,* **togged, tog|ging.** *Informal.* —*n.* a garment.
—*v.t., v.i.* to clothe; dress (out, up).
**togs**, clothes: *"Look at his togs, Fagin!" said Charley ... "Look at his togs!—Superfine cloth, and the heavy swell cut!"* (Dickens).
[apparently short for *togmans,* an obsolete thieves' cant word, perhaps ultimately < Latin *toga* toga]

***to|ga** (tō′gə), *n., pl.* **-gas, -gae** (-jē). **1** a loose outer garment worn in public by men who were citizens of ancient Rome, especially in time of peace. **2** any similar loose outer garment. **3** *Figurative.* a robe of office: *the toga of royalty.* [< Latin *toga,* related to *tegere* to cover]

***toga**
definition 1

**to|gaed** (tō′gəd), *adj.* wearing a toga or togas.

**to|gat|ed** (tō′gā tid), *adj.* **1** = togaed. **2** Latinized: *togated words or language.* **3** stately; majestic. [< Latin *togātus* wearing a toga < *toga* (see etym. under **toga**) + English *-ed²*]

**to|ga vi|ri|lis** (tō′gə və rī′lis), *Latin.* the toga of manhood. It was an all-white toga worn by Roman boys from 14 to 17 years of age.

**to|geth|er** (tə geŧʜ′ər), *adv., adj.* —*adv.* **1a** with each other; in company: *to eat together. They were standing together. The girls were walking together.* **b** with united action; in cooperation: *to work together for peace.* **2** into one gathering, company, mass, or body: *to come together as friends. The pastor called the parish together. The woman will sew these pieces together and make a dress.* **3** at the same time; at once: *rain and snow falling together. You cannot have day and night together.* **4** without a stop or break; on end; continuously: *She reads for hours together. He worked for several days and nights together.* **5** taken or considered collectively: *This one costs more than all the others together.*
—*adj. U.S. Slang.* free of confusion or anxiety; mentally and emotionally stable: *Friends were saying that she was happier, more together, than she had been in some time* (New Yorker).
**together with,** along with: *The mayor, together with his financial advisors, has been working hard on the budget. Simon ... entered Persia, together with Thaddeus* (John Jackson).
[Old English *tōgædere* < *tō* to + *gædere* together. See related etym. at **gather.**]
▶ **together with.** Adding *together with* to a singular subject does not change the grammatical number of the subject. Formal English uses a singular verb to agree with the singular subject: *The general, together with his staff, is dining here tonight.* Informal English, however, often uses a plural verb, treating the construction as a compound subject: *The coach together with his players are attending a banquet.*

**to|geth|er|ness** (tə geŧʜ′ər nis), *n.* the condition of being close together or united, especially in family or social activities: *The American family is expected to revel in close communal existence, what one national magazine idealises as "togetherness"* (London Times).

**Tog|gen|burg** (tog′ən bėrg), *n.* any one of a breed of goats, originally from Switzerland, raised for their milk, and having brown hair and a light stripe down each side of the face. [< *Toggenburg,* a district in Switzerland]

**tog|ger|y** (tog′ər ē), *n., pl.* **-ger|ies.** *Informal.* garments; clothes.

**tog|gle** (tog′əl), *n., v.,* **-gled, -gling.** —*n.* **1** a pin, bolt, or rod put through a loop in a rope or a link of a chain to keep it in place, to hold two ropes together, or to serve as a hold for the fingers. **2a** = toggle joint. **b** a device furnished with a toggle joint.
—*v.t.* to furnish or fasten with a toggle.
[apparently variant of earlier *tuggle* to catch, entangle]

***toggle bolt,** a bolt whose nut is flanged to work a spring and spread out when the bolt has gone through a wall or other surface. It is used to support heavy objects hanging on thin walls.

***toggle bolt**

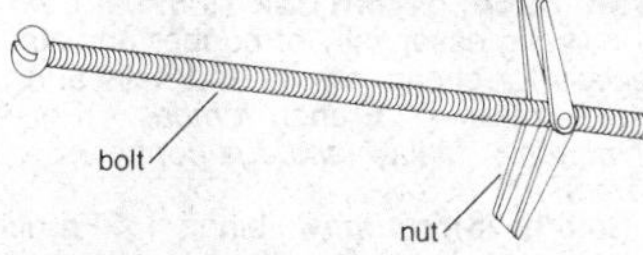


**toggle iron,** a harpoon with a pivoted crosspiece near the point, instead of fixed barbs.

**toggle joint,** a kneelike joint that transmits pressure at right angles. It has two arms that are hinged together at an angle. A force applied at the hinge, causing the angle to straighten, produces a much greater force at the ends of the arms.

**toggle switch,** an electric switch with a projecting lever that is pushed through a small arc to open or close the circuit. The common light switch is a toggle switch.

**To|go|land|er** (tō′gō lan′dər), *n.* a native or inhabitant of the former German protectorate of Togoland, in western Africa on the Gulf of Guinea, of which a part is now the Republic of Togo and part incorporated in Ghana.

**To|go|lese** (tō′gō lēz′, -lēs′), *adj., n., pl.* **-lese.** —*adj.* of or having to do with Togo or the former Togoland or their people. —*n.* a native or inhabitant of Togo or the former Togoland.

**togs** (togz), *n.pl.* See under **tog.**

**togue** (tōg), *n., pl.* **togues** or (*collectively*) **togue.** (in Canada, especially the Maritimes) lake trout. [< Canadian French *togue* < Algonkian]

**to|he|ro|a** (tō′hə rō′ə), *n.* an edible green marine clam of New Zealand. [< Maori *toheroa*]

**to|hu-bo|hu** (tō′hü bō′hü), *n.* chaos; confusion. [< Hebrew *thōhū wa bhōhu* emptiness and desolation, translated in Genesis 1:2 as "without form and void"]

**toil[1]** (toil), *n., v.* —*n.* **1** hard work; labor: *to succeed only after years of toil.* **SYN:** drudgery, travail, effort, exertion. See syn. under **work. 2** a spell of hard work; laborious task: *All the day's long toil is past* (Thomas Hood). **3** something made or done by hard work: *the toil Of dropping buckets into empty wells* (William Cowper). **4** *Archaic.* a fighting; strife.
—*v.i.* **1** to work hard; labor: *to toil with one's hands for a living.* **SYN:** drudge, slave. **2** to move with difficulty, pain, or weariness: *Carrying heavy loads, they toiled up the mountain.* —*v.t.* to bring, make, or obtain by hard work or effort.
[< Anglo-French *toil* turmoil, contention < *toiler* to agitate, stir up, Old French *toeillier* drag about, make dirty < Latin *tudiculāre* stir up < Latin *tudicula* olive press < *tudes* mallet, related to *tundere* to pound]

**toil[2]** (toil), *n.* a net; snare: *A lion was caught in the toil.*
**toils,** something like a net or snare: *The fly was caught in the toils of the spider. The thief was caught in the toils of the law.*
[< Old French *toile* and *teile* hunting net; cloth; web < Latin *tēla* web, related to *texere* to weave]

**toile** (twäl), *n.* a sheer linen and silk cloth. [< Old French *toile* linen cloth, canvas; see etym. under **toil[2]**]

**toile de Jouy** (twäl′də zhwē′), a cotton or linen cloth having colored patterns on a light-colored background. [< French *toile de Jouy* (literally) cloth of Jouy < *Jouy-en-Josar,* a town in France]

**toil|er** (toi′lər), *n.* a person who toils; hard worker; laborer.

**toi|let** (toi′lit), *n., adj., v.* —*n.* **1** a bathroom or lavatory. **2** a porcelain bowl with a seat attached and with a drain at the bottom connected with a tank of water to flush the bowl clean; water closet. Waste matter from the body is disposed of in a toilet. **3** the process of dressing. Washing, bathing, combing the hair, and putting on one's clothes are all parts of one's toilet. *She made a hurried toilet.* **4** a set of toilet articles. **5** = dressing table. **6a** a person's dress; costume. **b** the manner or style of dressing. **7** *Surgery.* the cleansing of a part after an operation.
—*adj.* of or for the toilet. Combs and brushes are toilet articles.
—*v.i., v.t.* to perform one's toilet; get dressed: *He rose from bed, toileted, and had breakfast.*
[originally, a cover for the clothes, especially in hairdressing < French *toilette* < *toile* toil[2]]

**toilet paper,** a soft, absorbent, cleansing paper, usually rolled up, for use in a lavatory.

**toi|let|ry** (toi′lə trē), *n., pl.* **-ries.** soap, face powder, perfume, or other articles for the toilet.

**toi|lette** (toi let′; *French* twȧ let′), *n.* = toilet (defs. 3, 6). [variant of *toilet*]

**toi|let-train** (toi′lit trān′), *v.t.* to give toilet training to. [back formation < *toilet training*]

**toilet training,** the training of a child to control his bladder and bowel movements and to use the toilet.

**toilet water,** a fragrant liquid, not so strong as perfume, used in or after bathing or after shaving.

**toil|ful** (toil′fəl), *adj.* characterized by or involving hard work; laborious; toilsome. —**toil′ful|ly,** *adv.*

**toil|less** (toil′lis), *adj.* free from toil.

**toils** (toilz), *n.pl.* See under **toil[2]**.

**toil|some** (toil′səm), *adj.* requiring hard work; laborious; wearisome; tiring: *We made a long, toilsome climb up the mountain.* **SYN:** fatiguing, onerous. —**toil′some|ly,** *adv.* —**toil′some|ness,** *n.*

**toil|worn** (toil′wôrn′, -wōrn′), *adj.* worn by toil; showing the effects of toil.

**to|ing and fro|ing** (tü′ing ən frō′ing), a moving to and fro; restless activity; bustle; fuss: *The toing and froing about the biological dangers of fallout continues* (New Scientist).

**toise** (toiz), *n.* an old French linear measure equal to 1.949 meters or 6.395 English feet. [< Middle French *toise,* Old French *teise* < Late Latin *tēsa* (*brachia*) outstretched arms < Latin *tendere* to stretch]

**to|ka|mak** (tō′kə mak), *n.* a device for producing controlled thermonuclear power, in which highly ionized gas is confined in an endless tube by magnetic fields generated by electric currents outside the tube and inside the gas itself: *Recently the tokamaks have produced plasmas nearer to fusion conditions than any other devices have been able to do* (Science News). [< Russian *tokamak*]

**To|kay** (tō kā′), *n.* **1** a rich, sweet Hungarian wine, golden in color. **2** any one of various wines made elsewhere in imitation of this. **3** the large, firm, reddish, sweet grape from which such wine is made, used also as a table grape. [< *Tokay,* a town in Hungary, where it was originally made]

**toke** (tōk), *n. U.S. Slang.* a puff on a cigarette, especially a marijuana cigarette: *He sits down on the steps in front of the sheriff's place, lights up, and takes a few tokes* (New Yorker). [probably short for *token* (i.e. partial smoke, mere taste)]

**to|ken** (tō′kən), *n., adj.* —*n.* **1a** a mark or sign (of something): *Black is a token of mourning.* **SYN:** symbol. See syn. under **mark. b** something that serves to prove; evidence: *His actions are a token of his sincerity.* **SYN:** symbol. See syn. under **mark. c** a characteristic mark or indication: *the tokens of a good horse, the tokens of a disease.* **SYN:** symbol. See syn. under **mark. 2** a sign of friendship; keepsake: *She received many birthday tokens.* **SYN:** memento, memorial. **3** a piece of metal, stamped for a higher value than the metal is worth. Tokens are used on some buses and trains instead of money. **4** a piece of metal or plastic indicating a right or privilege: *This token will admit you to the swimming pool.* **5** something that is a sign of genuineness or authority; password. **6** *Archaic.* a signal.
—*adj.* having only the appearance of; serving as a symbol; nominal; partial: *a token payment, a token resistance, a token fleet.*
**by the same token,** for the same reason; in the same way; moreover: *to receive letters from people whom they do not know, and are, by the same token, never likely to know* (Phyllis Dare).
**in token of,** as a token of; to show: *He sits down in token of submission* (George Bernard Shaw).
[Old English *tācen* sign, mark. See related etym. at **teach.**]

**token economy,** a system of reinforcement in behavior therapy using rewards of metal or plastic tokens for appropriate behavior. The recipient may exchange the tokens for privileges, such as food, free time, or books, according to their value in the token economy: *The goals of token economy ... are to promote behaviors necessary for effective personal functioning, not only in an institutional or school environment, but also in natural settings* (Ralph Brocas, W. G. Johnson).

**to|ken|ism** (tō′kə niz əm), *n. U.S.* a policy or practice of pretending to fulfill one's obligations with token efforts or gestures, especially towards eliminating racial segregation and discrimination.

**token payment,** a nominal payment made to acknowledge an obligation or agreement.

**To|khar|i|an** (to kär′ē ən, -kär′-), *n., adj.* = Tocharian.

**to|kol|o|gy** (tō kol′ə jē), *n.* = tocology.

**to|ko|no|ma** (tō′kə nō′mə), *n.* an alcove in a Japanese house for the decorative display of scrolls, prints, and flowers. [< Japanese *toko-no-ma*]

**to|la** (tō′lä), *n.* (in India) a unit of weight equal to 180 grains troy. [< Hindi *tola* < Sanskrit *tulā* weight < *tul* to weigh]

**to|lan** (tō′lan), *n.* a colorless crystalline, unsaturated hydrocarbon produced synthetically. *Formula:* $C_{14}H_{10}$ [< *tol*(uene) + *-an*(e)]

**to|lane** (tō′lān), *n.* = tolan.

**tol|booth** (tōl′büth′, -büŧʜ′), *n. Scottish.* a town prison; jail. Originally, the cells were under the town hall. Also, **tollbooth.** [Middle English *tolbothe* < *toll* toll[2] + *bothe* booth]

**tol|bu|ta|mide** (tol byü′tə mīd), *n.* a sulfonamide drug taken orally as a substitute for insulin in the treatment of mild diabetes. *Formula:* $C_{12}H_{18}N_2O_3S$ [< *tol*(u) + *but*(yric) + *amide*]

**told** (tōld), *v.* the past tense and past participle of **tell:** *You told me that last week. We were told to wait.*
**all told,** including all; in all; altogether: *a cost of $250 all told.*

**tole[1]** or **tôle** (tōl), *n.* lacquered and enameled metalware used in the 1700's, imitated today especially in trays and lamps. It often has a dark green or black field with gilt designs on it. [< French *tôle* plate work, sheet iron, probably dialectal variant of *table;* see etym. under **table**]

**tole[2]** (tōl), *v.t.,* **toled, tol|ing.** = toll[3].

**To|le|do** (tə lē′dō; *Spanish* tō lā′ŧʜō), *n.* a sword of fine temper made in Toledo, Spain, or elsewhere in imitation of this.

**tol|er|a|bil|i|ty** (tol′ər ə bil′ə tē), *n.* tolerable quality or condition; tolerableness.

**tol|er|a|ble** (tol′ər ə bəl), *adj.* **1** that can be endured; bearable; endurable: *a tolerable burden. The pain has become tolerable.* **SYN:** sufferable, supportable. **2** fairly good; not bad; passable: *She is in tolerable health.* **SYN:** mediocre, ordinary, indifferent. [< Latin *tolerābilis* bearable; able to bear < *tolerāre;* see etym. under **tolerate**] —**tol′er|a|ble|ness,** *n.*

**tol|er|a|bly** (tol′ər ə blē), *adv.* **1** in a tolerable manner. **2** moderately.

**tol|er|ance** (tol′ər əns), *n.* **1** a willingness to be patient toward people whose opinions or ways differ from one's own. **SYN:** forbearance. See syn. under **toleration. 2** the power of enduring or resisting the action of a drug, poison, or other, usually harmful, substance. **3** the action of tolerating; toleration: *The principal's tolerance of their repeated bad behavior surprised us.* **4a** an allowable amount of variation from a standard weight or fineness in the minting of coins. **b** an allowable amount of variation in the dimensions of a machine or part. **5** *Obsolete.* endurance.

**tol|er|ant** (tol′ər ənt), *adj.* **1** willing to let other people do as they think best; willing to endure beliefs and actions of which one does not approve: *A free nation is tolerant toward all religious beliefs.* **2** able to endure or resist the action of a drug, poison, or other, usually harmful, substance. **— tol′er|ant|ly,** *adv.*

**tol|er|ate** (tol′ə rāt), *v.t.,* **-at|ed, -at|ing. 1** to allow; permit: *The teacher won't tolerate any disorder. A nation at war will not tolerate treason. A free nation tolerates all religions.* **2** to bear; endure; put up with: *They tolerated the grouchy old man only out of kindness.* **3** to endure or resist the action of (a drug, poison, or other, usually harmful, substance): *He is one of those people who cannot tolerate penicillin.* [< Latin *tolerāre* (with English *-ate*[1]), related to *tollere* to bear]
**— tol′er|a′tor,** *n.*

**tol|er|a|tion** (tol′ə rā′shən), *n.* **1** a willingness to put up with beliefs and actions of which one does not approve. **2** the recognition of a person's right to worship as he thinks best without loss of civil rights or social privileges; freedom of worship.
**— *Syn.* 1, 2 Toleration, tolerance** mean permitting others to do, say, or think as they wish. **Toleration** implies putting up with actions, beliefs, or people one does not like or approve of because of indifference or a desire to avoid conflict: *Toleration of dishonest officials encourages corruption.* **Tolerance** implies being willing to let others think, live, or worship according to their own beliefs and to refrain from judging harshly or with prejudice: *Through tolerance we learn to understand people.*

**tol|er|a|tion|ist** (tol′ə rā′shə nist), *n.* a person who supports or advocates toleration, especially in religious matters.

**tol|er|a|tive** (tol′ə rā′tiv), *adj.* tending to tolerate or be tolerant; permissive.

**tole|ware** (tō′wãr′), *n.* = tole[1].

**tol|i|dine** (tol′ə dēn, -din), *n.* a base, a toluene derivative, found in several isomeric forms, one of which is used in the manufacture of dyestuffs. Another is important in testing for chlorine in public water supplies. *Formula:* $C_{14}H_{16}N_2$

**toll**[1] (tōl), *v., n.* **— *v.t.* 1** to cause to sound with single strokes slowly and regularly repeated: *Bells were tolled all over the country at the President's death.* **2** to call or announce by tolling.
**— *v.i.*** to sound with single strokes slowly and regularly repeated: *Any man's death diminishes me because I am involved in mankind; And therefore never send to know for whom the bell tolls; it tolls for thee* (John Donne).
**— *n.* 1** a stroke or sound of a bell being tolled. **2** the act or fact of tolling.
[perhaps special use of *toll*[3] to pull]

**toll**[2] (tōl), *n., v.* **— *n.* 1** a tax or fee paid for some right or privilege: *We pay a toll when we use that bridge.* **2** the right to collect tolls. **3** a charge for a certain service. There is a toll on long-distance telephone calls. **4** *Figurative.* something paid, lost, suffered, or otherwise taken away or exacted: *Automobile accidents take a heavy toll of human lives.* **5** a charge for the transport of goods by railway or canal. **6** (formerly) a part of the grain or flour taken by a miller in payment for grinding.
**— *v.t.*** to collect tolls from; take as toll. **— *v.i.*** to take or collect toll; exact or levy toll.
[Old English *toll,* variant of *toln,* apparently < Vulgar Latin *tolōnīum,* for Latin *telōnīum* < Greek *telōneîon* tollhouse < *telṓnēs* tax collector < *télos* tax]

**toll**[3] (tōl), *v.t. Dialect.* **1** to attract; entice; allure. **2** to lure (animals such as ducks) by arousing curiosity; decoy. Also, **tole.** [Middle English *tollen, tullen,* apparently related to Old English *-tyllan* draw, as in *betyllan* to lure]

**toll|a|ble** (tō′lə bəl), *adj.* subject to the payment of toll.

**toll|age** (tō′lij), *n.* **1** = toll. **2** the exaction or payment of toll.

**toll bar,** a barrier, especially a gate, across a road or bridge, where tolls are collected.

**toll|booth** (tōl′büth′, -bü**th**′), *n.* **1** a booth or gate at which tolls are collected before or after going over a bridge, toll road, or turnpike or through a tunnel. **2** *Scottish.* a tolbooth.

**toll bridge,** a bridge at which a toll is charged.

**toll call,** a long-distance telephone call, for which a higher rate is charged than for a local call.

**toll collector, 1** a person who collects the tolls, as on a turnpike or bridge. **2** a device for collecting tolls, such as a turnstile with a slot into which a coin is dropped.

**toll|er**[1] (tō′lər), *n.* **1** a person who tolls a bell. **2** a bell for tolling.

**toll|er**[2] (tō′lər), *n.* a dog trained to decoy ducks.

**tol|ley** (tol′ē), *n.* a marble used to shoot at marbles; taw or shooter. [origin unknown]

**toll|gate** (tōl′gāt′), *n.* **1** a gate at a road, bridge, or other barrier where tolls are collected. **2** = tollbooth.

**toll|gath|er|er** (tōl′ga**th**′ər ər), *n.* = toll collector.

**toll|house** (tōl′hous′), *n.* = tollbooth.

**toll|keep|er** (tōl′kē′pər), *n.* a person who collects the toll at a tollgate or tollhouse; toll collector.

**toll line,** a line for long-distance telephone calls.

**toll|man** (tōl′man′), *n., pl.* **-men.** = toll collector.

**toll road,** a road on which tolls are charged; turnpike.

**toll station,** a place where tolls are collected, such as a tollhouse or tollgate.

**toll television,** = subscription television.

**toll|way** (tōl′wā′), *n.* a toll road; turnpike.

**Tol|stoy|an** (tol stoi′ən), *adj.* of or having to do with the Russian novelist Leo Tolstoy (1828-1910), his writings, or his philosophy.

**Tol|tec** (tol′tek), *n., adj.* **— *n.*** a member of an Indian people who lived in central Mexico from about 900 to 1200 A.D., before the Aztecs, and influenced their culture and that of the Mayas.
**— *adj.*** of or having to do with the Toltecs.

**Tol|tec|an** (tol tek′ən), *adj.* = Toltec.

**to|lu** (tō lü′), *n.,* or **tolu balsam,** a fragrant balsam obtained from the bark of a tropical South American tree of the pea family, used in medicine and perfume. [< Spanish *tolú* < (*Santiago de*) *Tolú,* a city in Colombia, where it was originally obtained]

**tol|u|ate** (tol′yu̇ āt), *n.* a salt or ester of toluic acid.

**tol|u|ene** (tol′yu̇ ēn), *n.* a colorless, flammable liquid obtained from coal tar and petroleum. It is used as a solvent and for making explosives, dyes, and saccharin. Toluene is an aromatic hydrocarbon, with a smell like that of benzene. *Formula:* $C_7H_8$ [< *tolu*(ol) + *-ene*]

**to|lu|ic acid** (tə lü′ik, tol′yu̇-), a colorless carboxylic acid homologous with benzoic acid, found in four isomeric forms, derived from toluene or xylene. *Formula:* $C_8H_8O_2$

**tol|u|ide** (tol′yu̇ īd, -id), *n.* any of a group of compounds homologous with the anilides. The toluides are toluidine derivatives formed by replacement of the hydrogen in the amino radical with an acid radical.

**to|lu|i|dide** (tə lü′ə dīd, -did), *n.* = toluide.

**to|lu|i|dine** (tə lü′ə dēn, -din), *n.* a compound analogous to aniline, found in three isomeric forms. Toluidine is a toluene derivative used especially in making dyes. *Formula:* $C_7H_9N$

**tol|u|ol** (tol′yu̇ ōl, -ol), *n.* toluene, especially the form used commercially. [< German *Toluin* (< *tolu;* see etym. under **tolu**) + English *-ol*[2]]

**tol|u|yl** (tol′yu̇ əl), *n.* a univalent radical, $C_7H_7CO$-, occurring in toluic acid. [< *tolu*(ol) + *-yl*]

**tol|yl** (tol′əl), *n.* a univalent hydrocarbon radical, $C_7H_7$-, occurring in toluene. [< *tol*(u) + *-yl*]

**tom** or **Tom**[1] (tom), *n.* **1** a male cat; tomcat. **2** the male of various other animals: *Our Thanksgiving turkey was a tom.* [< *Tom,* used as a type name for a common man]

**Tom**[2] (tom), *n., v.,* **Tommed, Tom|ming.** *U.S.* **— *n.*** an Uncle Tom; a Negro who seeks to please or cooperate with whites (used in an unfriendly way): ... *a black social worker obviously of the middle class, but no Tom because his hair is semi-natural* (Harper's).
**— *v.i.*** Also, **Tom it.** to be or act like an Uncle Tom: *"She was an absolutely direct black woman. No Tomming, not a shade of the phony to her"* (John Hammond). *In Mr. Wright's view, the whole gamut of Negro behavior ... involves one form or another of "Tomming it": being like Uncle Tom* (New York Times).

***tomahawk**

***tom|a|hawk** (tom′ə hôk), *n., v.* **— *n.*** a light ax used by North American Indians as a weapon and a tool.
**— *v.t.*** to strike, kill, or wound with a tomahawk.
**bury the tomahawk,** to stop fighting; make peace: *Will the time never come when we may honorably bury the tomahawk?* (Congressional Globe).
[American English < Algonkian (probably Powhatan) *tamahack* a striking instrument]

**tom|al|ley** (tom′al′ē), *n.* the liver of the lobster, regarded as a delicacy. It turns green when cooked. [apparently < Carib *taumali* (originally) the inner part of a crab]

**to|man** (tə män′), *n.* **1** in Iran and Turkey: **a** ten thousand. **b** military division of 10,000 men. **2** an Iranian gold coin, not now in circulation, equal to 10 krans or 10,000 dinars. **3** an Iranian money of account equivalent to 10 krans. [< Persian *tuman*]

**Tom and Jer|ry** (jer′ē), *U.S.* a hot drink made of rum, sugar, beaten eggs, spices, and water or milk. [< two chief characters in *Life in London,* by Pierce Egan, 1772-1849]

**to|marc|tus** (tə märk′təs), *n.* an extinct mammal of the late Miocene, believed to be the ancestor of dogs, wolves, foxes, and jackals. It had a wedge-shaped head, long, low body, thick coat, and long, furry tail. [< New Latin *Tomarctus*]

**to|mat|i|dine** (tə mat′ə dēn, -din), *n.* a steroid alkaloid derived from tomatin, used in the synthesis of progesterone and testosterone, and in the treatment of certain fungous diseases. *Formula:* $C_{27}H_{45}NO_2$

**to|mat|in** (tə mat′in), *n.* an alkaloid extract of the juice of the tomato plant, used in antibiotics for the treatment of certain skin and stomach diseases, and as the source of tomatidine. *Formula:* $C_{50}H_{83}NO_{21}$

**tom|a|tine** (tom′ə tēn), *n.* the crystalline form of tomatin.

**to|ma|to** (tə mā′tō, -mä′-), *n., pl.* **-toes. 1** a juicy, slightly acid fruit, eaten as a vegetable. Most tomatoes are red when ripe, but some kinds are yellow. *A tomato is technically called a berry.* **2** the plant it grows on. It is a spreading, strong-smelling plant with hairy leaves and stems, and small, yellow flowers. The tomato belongs to the nightshade family. **3** any related plant. **4** *U.S. Slang.* a girl or woman, especially one who is good-looking.
[alteration of earlier *tomate* < Spanish < Nahuatl *tomatl*]

**tomato catchup,** a catchup made with tomatoes, onions, salt, sugar, and spices.

**tomato fruit worm,** the bollworm or corn earworm; a moth larva which feeds on tomatoes and parts of other plants.

**tomb** (tüm), *n., v.* **— *n.* 1** a grave, vault, mausoleum, or other place for a dead body, often above ground: *The greedy sea, The mighty tomb of mariners and kings* (William Morris). **2** *Figurative.* death.
**— *v.t.*** to put in a tomb; shut up in a tomb; entomb; bury.
[< Anglo-French *tumbe,* Old French *tombe* < Late Latin *tumba* < Greek *týmbos* burial mound]
**— tomb′less,** *adj.* **— tomb′like′,** *adj.*

**tom|bac, tom|back,** or **tom|bak** (tom′bak), *n.* an alloy consisting essentially of copper and zinc, used especially for cheap jewelry and bells and gongs. Also, **tambac.** [< French *tombac* < Portuguese *tambaca* < Malay *tambāga* copper < Sanskrit *tāmrāka*]

**tom|bo|la** (tom′bə lə), *n. British.* bingo. [< French *tombola* < Italian < *tombolare* turn a somersault, tumble]

**tom|bo|lo** (tom′bə lō), *n., pl.* **-los.** a sand bar which connects an island to the mainland or to another island. [< Italian *tombolo* < Latin *tumulus;* see etym. under **tumulus**]

**tom|boy** (tom′boi′), *n.* a girl who likes to play games supposedly suited to boys; boisterous, romping girl.

**tom|boy|ish** (tom′boi′ish), *adj.* like or characteristic of a tomboy: *tomboyish games or activities.*
**— tom′boy|ish|ly,** *adv.* **— tom′boy|ish|ness,** *n.*

**tomb|stone** (tüm′stōn′), *n.* a stone or other marker that marks a tomb or grave, usually having an inscription; gravestone: *mossy, tumble-down tombstones, one with a skull and crossbones upon it* (H. G. Wells).

**tom|cat** (tom′kat′), *n.* a male cat.

**tom|cod** (tom′kod′), *n.* any one of various small saltwater fishes related to and resembling the cod. [American English < *tom* + *cod*[1]]

**Tom Collins,** *U.S.* a cold drink made of gin, lemon or lime juice, sugar, and carbonated water. [compare etym. under **Collins**]

**Tom, Dick, and Harry,** people in general; everyone: *He was not the hearty pre-election politician who runs around greeting every Tom, Dick, and Harry* (Canada Month).

**tome** (tōm), *n.* **1** a book, especially a large, heavy book: *She directed Sir Arthur Helps to bring out a collection to the Prince's speeches and addresses, and the weighty tome appeared in 1862*

(Lytton Strachey). 2 *Obsolete.* a volume forming part of a larger work.
[< Middle French *tome,* learned borrowing from Latin *tomus* < Greek *tómos* (originally) piece cut off < *témnein* to cut]

**to|men|tose** (tō men′tōs, tō′men-), *adj.* 1 *Anatomy.* fleecy; flaky. 2 *Botany.* closely covered with down or matted hair.
[< New Latin *tomentosus* < Latin *tōmentum* cushion stuffing]

**to|men|tum** (tō men′təm), *n., pl.* **-ta** (-tə). 1 *Botany.* a soft down consisting of longish, soft, entangled hairs, pressed close to the surface.
2 *Anatomy.* a downy covering, especially the flocculent inner surface of the pia mater, consisting of numerous minute vessels entering the brain and spinal cord.
[< New Latin *tomentum* < Latin *tōmentum* cushion stuffing]

**tom|fool** (tom′fül′), *n., adj.* **—*n.*** a silly fool; stupid person; dolt.
**—*adj.*** very foolish.
[< *Tom Fool,* a personification of stupidity]

**tom|fool|er|y** (tom′fü′lər ē), *n., pl.* **-er|ies.** silly, foolish, or absurd behavior; nonsense.

**Tom|ism** (tom′iz əm), *n. U.S.* the attitude or behavior of an Uncle Tom; Uncle Tomism: *If Tomism was evident, so was a determined effort by Negro doctors to achieve equal status with white physicians* (Time).

**Tom|my** or **tom|my** (tom′ē), *n., pl.* **-mies.** 1 *Informal.* a British soldier, especially a private soldier. 2 *British Slang.* **a** a heavy, dark bread formerly supplied as rations to the enlisted men in the British army; brown tommy. **b** a loaf or chunk of any bread. **c** food or provisions carried by workmen each day. **d** provisions supplied to workmen under the truck system. **e** a store run by the employer, where vouchers given to workers instead of money wages can be exchanged for goods; tommy shop; truck shop. [< *Tommy,* apparently originally personified as *Tommy Brown* (for brown bread)]

**Tommy At|kins** (at′kinz), *Informal.* a British soldier.
[< *Thomas Atkins,* name used in the sample forms for privates given in the official regulations of the British Army from 1815 on]

**Tommy gun** or **tommy gun,** *Informal.* a Thompson submachine gun.

**Tom|my-gun** or **tom|my-gun** (tom′ē gun′), *v.t.,* **-gunned, -gun|ning.** to shoot with a Tommy gun: *He and his aide were ambushed and Tommy-gunned to death by four young officers* (Time).

**Tom|my-gun|ner** or **tom|my-gun|ner** (tom′ē gun′ər), *n.* a person skilled in operating a Tommy gun.

**tom|my|rot** (tom′ē rot′), *n. Slang.* nonsense; rubbish; foolishness. **SYN:** bosh, twaddle.

**to|mo|gram** (tō′mə gram), *n.* a photograph made by tomography.

**to|mo|graph** (tō′mə graf, -gräf), *n.* an X-ray machine used in tomography.

**to|mog|ra|phy** (tə mog′rə fē), *n. Medicine.* X-ray photography of a structure in a certain layer of tissue in the body, in which images of structures in other layers are eliminated. [< Greek *tómos* a cutting, section + English *-graphy*]

**to|mor|row** or **to-mor|row** (tə môr′ō, -mor′-), *n., adv.* **—*n.*** 1 the day after today; the morrow: *One today is worth two tomorrows* (Benjamin Franklin). 2 *Figurative.* the future: *She has a real right to call herself a citizen of tomorrow* (Manchester Guardian Weekly).
**—*adv.*** 1 on or for the day after today. 2 *Figurative.* very soon.
[Middle English *to morowe,* Old English *tō morgen* < *tō* to + *morgen* morn]
▶ See **today** for usage note.

**tom|pi|on** (tom′pē ən), *n.* = tampion.

**Tom Thumb,** 1 a diminutive hero popular in English folk tales. He was no bigger than his father's thumb. 2 anything that is very small; any dwarf. 3 a petty or insignificant person.

**Tom Tiddler's ground,** 1 a children's game in which one player guards a marked-off area over which the other players run and from which he chases them until he catches one who will take his place. 2 a place or area in which easy profits can be made: *What saddens me is the thought of all the fellows in my circle who have got on this Tom Tiddler's ground without putting me wise* (Sunday Times). 3 = no man's land.

**tom|tit** (tom′tit′), *n.* 1 a small bird, especially a titmouse. 2 *British Dialect.* any one of various other small birds, such as the wren and the tree creeper. [< *tom* + *tit*[1]]

***tom-tom** (tom′tom′), *n., v.,* **-tommed, -tom|ming.** **—*n.*** 1 a drum usually beaten with the hands. Tom-toms are used to dance to and for sending signals in Africa and among the American Indians. They were originally used in the East Indies. 2 a monotonous, rhythmic beat.
**—*v.i., v.t.*** to beat on a tom-tom.
[< Hindustani *tam-tam;* probably ultimately imitative]

***tom-tom**
definition 1

**-tomy,** *combining form.* 1 surgical incision or operation, as in *tracheotomy, lobotomy.*
2 a cutting or casting off: *Autotomy = a casting off of part of the body.*
[< Greek *-tomíā* a cutting]

***ton[1]** (tun), *n.* **1a** a measure of weight equal to 2,000 pounds or 907.18 kilograms, standard in the United States and Canada; short ton. **b** a measure of weight equal to 2,240 pounds or 1,016.05 kilograms, standard in Great Britain; long ton. **c** = metric ton (1,000 kilograms). **2** a measure of volume that varies with the thing measured; freight ton. It is about equal to the space occupied by a ton's weight of the particular stuff. Thus a ton of stone is 16 cubic feet or 0.4528 cubic meter; a ton of lumber is 40 cubic feet or 1.1320 cubic meters; a ton of wheat is 20 bushels or 70.4766 liters. **3a** a unit of measure of the internal capacity of a ship; 100 cubic feet or 2.830 cubic meters; register ton. **b** a unit of measure of the carrying capacity of a ship; 40 cubic feet or 1.1320 cubic meters; shipping ton. **c** a unit of measure of the weight by volume of water a ship will displace; 35 cubic feet (the volume of a long ton of seawater) or 0.9905 cubic meter; displacement ton. *Abbr:* tn. **4** a unit of refrigeration equal to the amount of heat needed (200 B.T.U.'s per minute) to melt one short ton of ice in 24 hours. **5** *Slang.* a motorcycle speed of 100 miles per hour. [spelling variant of *tun*[1]]

***ton[1]**
definitions 1a, 1b, 1c

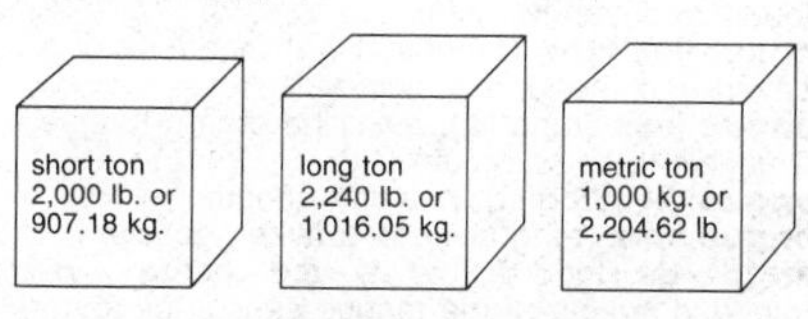


**ton[2]** (tôN), *n.* the prevailing fashion; style. [< French *ton* manner, learned borrowing from Latin *tonus.* See etym. of doublets **tone, tune.**]

**ton|al** (tō′nəl), *adj.* 1 of or having to do with tones or tone. 2 characterized by tonality: *tonal music.*

**tonal center,** *Music.* a note around which a passage, movement, or composition is based; tonic.

**ton|al|ist** (tō′nə list), *n.* 1 a painter who aims at effect through color harmonization rather than by contrasts. 2 a composer whose music is characterized by tonality rather than atonality.

**to|nal|ite** (tō′nə līt), *n.* a granular igneous rock, a variety of diorite, containing quartz and biotite. [< *Tonale,* a pass in the Tyrol, where it is found]

**to|nal|i|ty** (tō nal′ə tē), *n., pl.* **-ties.** 1 *Music.* **a** the relation, or sum of relations, of the chords and tones of a scale to the tonic or keynote. **b** a key or system of tones. **c** any stressing of a particular tone as the basis of a passage, movement, or composition. 2 the color scheme of a painting, etc.

**ton|al|ly** (tō′nə lē), *adv.* with respect to tone.

**to-name** (tü′nām′), *n. Scottish.* 1 a name added to another name; surname; nickname. 2 a name added to a first or given name and surname to distinguish a person from others having the same name; by-name. [Old English *tō-nama* < *tō* to + *nama* name]

**ton|do** (ton′dō), *n., pl.* **-di** (-dē), **-dos.** 1 a painting in circular form. 2 a carved relief in circular form.
[< Italian *tondo* (literally) plate < *tondo* round, ultimately < Latin *rotundus;* see etym. under **round, rotund**]

**tone** (tōn), *n., v.,* **toned, ton|ing.** **—*n.*** 1 any sound considered with reference to its quality, pitch, strength, or source: *angry tones, gentle tones, the deep tone of an organ.* 2 quality of sound: *Her voice was silvery in tone.* 3 *Music.* **a** a sound of definite pitch and character. **b** the difference in pitch between two notes; whole step. C and D are one tone apart. **c** any one of the nine melodies or tunes in Gregorian music, used in singing the Psalms; Gregorian tone. 4 *Figurative.* a manner of speaking or writing: *a moral tone. We disliked the haughty tone of her letter.* 5 *Figurative.* **a** spirit; character; style: *A tone of quiet elegance prevails in her home.* **b** mental or emotional state; mood; disposition: *These hardy exercises produce also a healthful tone of mind and spirits* (Washington Irving). 6 normal healthy condition; vigor: *He exercised regularly to keep his body in tone.* 7 the degree of firmness or tension normal to the organs or tissue when healthy. 8 a proper responsiveness to stimulation. 9 the effect of color and of light and shade in a picture: *a painting with a soft green tone.* **10a** the quality given to one color by another color: *blue with a greenish tone.* **b** a shade of color: *The room is furnished in tones of brown.* 11 *Linguistics.* **a** the pitch of the voice as it is high or low, or as it rises and falls, regarded as a distinctive feature of a language. **b** any one of the tonal levels distinctive in a language: *Mandarin Chinese has four phonemic tones.* **c** the pronunciation characteristic of a particular person, group of people, or area; accent. 12 *Phonetics.* **a** the sound produced by the vibration of the vocal cords; voice. **b** the stress or emphasis on a syllable.
**—*v.i.*** to harmonize: *This rug tones in well with the wallpaper and furniture.*
**—*v.t.*** 1 to change the tone of: **a** to soften or change the color or value contrasts in (a painting or photograph). **b** *Photography.* to alter the color of (a print), especially from gray to some other color. 2 to give a tone to; give the proper or desired tone to (a musical instrument); tune. 3 to utter with a musical or other tone; intone.
**tone down,** to soften; moderate: *to tone down one's voice, tone down the colors in a painting.*
**tone up,** to give more sound, color, or vigor to; strengthen: *Bright curtains would tone up this dull room.*
[< Latin *tonus* < Greek *tónos* vocal pitch, raising of voice; (originally) a stretching, taut string, related to *teínein* to stretch. See etym. of doublets **tune, ton[2].**]

**-tone,** *combining form.* having ___ tones or colors: *Two-tone = having two colors.*

**tone arm,** the movable arm of a phonograph, holding the needle and pickup.

**tone cluster,** a large number of musical notes played together, especially on the piano, to produce a dense and dissonant effect.

**tone color,** *Music.* timbre.

**-toned,** *combining form.* having a ___tone: *Sweet-toned = having a sweet tone.*

**tone-deaf** (tōn′def′), *adj.* not able to distinguish between different musical tones. **—tone′-deaf′-ness,** *n.*

**to|ne|la|da** (tō′nə lä′də; *Spanish* tō′nä lä′ᴛʜä; *Portuguese* tü′nə lä′ᴛʜə), *n.* a unit of weight equal to about 2,029 pounds in Spain and most of South America and to about 1,749 pounds in Brazil. [< Spanish and Portuguese *tonelada* < *tonel* cask, tun, ancient ship measure < Old French *tonel,* (diminutive) < *tonne* large tun, cask]

**tone language,** a language in which different tones are used to distinguish words that are otherwise identical. Chinese and some Bantu languages are tone languages.

**tone|less** (tōn′lis), *adj.* 1 without modulation or expression: *a toneless voice, a toneless reading.* 2 dull: *a toneless color.* 3 without tone; soundless; mute. **—tone′less|ly,** *adv.* **—tone′less-ness,** *n.*

**to|neme** (tō′nēm), *n. Linguistics.* a unit of tone in a tone language. Northern Mandarin has four tonemes; high or even, rising, dipping, and falling.
[< *tone* + *-eme,* as in *phoneme*]

**to|ne|mic** (tō nē′mik), *adj. Linguistics.* of or having to do with a toneme.

**tone painting,** 1 the art of musical description or suggestion, as in instrumental music. 2 such a composition, characteristic of most program music.

**tone poem,** = symphonic poem.

**tone poet,** a composer of symphonic poems.

**ton|er** (tō′nər), *n.* a person or thing that tones.

**tone row,** *Music.* the arrangement or succession of tones in a twelve-tone composition; twelve-tone row.

**to|net|ic** (tō net′ik), *adj.* of or having to do with tones, tone languages, or tonetics.

**to|net|ics** (tō net′iks), *n.* the linguistic study of tones in speech.

**to|nette** (tō net′), *n.* a small plastic wind instru-

---

**Pronunciation Key:** hat, āge, cãre, fär; let, ēqual, tėrm; it, īce; hot, ōpen, ôrder; oil, out; cup, pu̇t, rüle; child; long; thin; ᴛʜen; zh, measure; ə represents **a** in about, **e** in taken, **i** in pencil, **o** in lemon, **u** in circus.

ment somewhat like a recorder, used mainly to teach music to young or beginning students.

**ton|ey** (tō′nē), *adj.*, **ton|i|er**, **ton|i|est.** = tony.

**tong**[1] (tông, tong), *n.* **1** a Chinese association or club. **2** a secret Chinese organization or club in the United States. [American English < Chinese *t'ang, t'ong* (originally) meeting hall]

**tong**[2] (tông, tong), *v.t.* to grasp, gather, hold, or handle with tongs: *to tong clams, oysters, or logs.* — ***v.i.*** to use tongs; work with tongs. — **tong′er**, *n.*

**ton|ga** (tong′gə), *n.* (in India) a light, small, two-wheeled carriage or cart. [< Hindi *tāṅgā*]

**Ton|gan** (tong′gən), *adj., n.* — ***adj.*** of or having to do with Tonga, a country made up of a group of islands northeast of New Zealand in the South Pacific, its people, or their language.
— ***n.*** **1** a native or inhabitant of Tonga. **2** their Polynesian language.

**tong|man** (tông′mən, tong′-), *n., pl.* **-men. 1** a person whose occupation is the catching of oysters with tongs; tonger. **2** a member of a Chinese tong.

**tongs** (tôngz, tongz), *n.pl.* **1** a tool with two arms that are joined by a hinge, pivot, or spring, for seizing, holding, or lifting: *He changed the position of the burning log with the tongs.* **2** a tool for curling hair. [Old English *tong* + *-s*[1]]

***tongue** (tung), *n., v.,* **tongued, tongu|ing.** — ***n.*** **1a** the movable fleshy organ in the mouth. The tongue is used in tasting and swallowing and, by people, for talking. Most vertebrate animals have tongues. **b** a similar organ or part in an invertebrate animal. **c** an animal's tongue used for food: *Father likes cold beef tongue and salad.* **2** the power of speech; speech: *Have you lost your tongue? Give thy thoughts no tongue* (Shakespeare). **3** *Figurative.* a way of speaking; speech; talk: *Beware of that man's flattering tongue.* **4a** the language of a people: *the English tongue.* **b** the speech of a particular class or locality; dialect. **c** language: *a book written in one's native tongue. For he that speaketh in an unknown tongue speaketh not unto men, but unto God: for no man understandeth him* (I Corinthians 14:2). **5** something shaped or used like a tongue: *Tongues of flame leaped from the fire.* **6** the strip of leather under the laces of a shoe or boot. **7** a narrow strip of land running out into water. **8** a hinged pin, as of a buckle or brooch. **9** a long wooden bar attached to the front axle of a carriage or wagon, and extending between the horses or other animals that are harnessed to it; pole. See picture above. **10** a projecting strip along the edge of a board for fitting into a groove in the edge of another board. **11** the pointer of a dial or balance. **12** a movable piece inside a bell that swings against it, producing a sound; clapper. **13** the vibrating reed or the like in a musical instrument. **14** the short, movable rail of a switch in a railroad or other track. It is tapered at the end to pick up and guide the wheels passing over it when the switch is closed. See picture above. **15** *Machinery.* a projecting flange, rib, or strip for any purpose.
— ***v.t.*** **1** to modify the tones of (a flute, cornet, or other wind instrument) with the tongue. **2a** to provide with a tongue. **b** to join (boards) by fitting a tongue into a groove. **3** to touch with the tongue or with a tongue: *The horse tongued the bit.* **4** *Figurative.* to scold: *Falstaff tongued the barmaid for spilling the ale.* **5** to utter; pronounce; voice: *What avails ... to tongue mute misery* (Joel Barlow).
— ***v.i.*** **1** to use the tongue. **2** to modify the tones of an instrument by tonguing. **3** to talk volubly; prattle: *Quiet, ye tonguing gossips!* **4** to project, as a strip of land or ice. **5** to throw out jets, as of flame or light.
**at one's tongue's end**, in readiness for saying or reciting at any time: *to have names or dates at one's tongue's end.*
**give tongue**, to bay, as hounds do at the sight of game: *Coonhounds and other breeds give tongue when trailing game.*
**give tongue to**, to express: *He gave tongue to his feelings.*
**hold one's tongue**, to keep still: *"Hold your tongue while I'm speaking!" said father.*
**on one's tongue**, almost or ready to be spoken: *The words had been on his tongue all the evening* (Edith Wharton).
**on** (or **at**) **the tip of one's tongue**, on the point of being spoken; ready to be spoken: *His name is on the tip of my tongue, but I can't seem to remember it. She had arguments at the tip of her tongue* (Daniel Defoe).
**wag one's tongue**, to chatter; gossip: *Every one who owed him a grudge would eagerly begin to wag his tongue* (William H. Dixon).
**with (one's) tongue in (one's) cheek**, with sly humor; not to be taken seriously or literally; in a mocking manner: *He spoke with tongue in cheek when he said he enjoyed doing all that homework. He enjoys needling the wrong kind of reader by occasionally overwriting with his tongue in his cheek* (Punch).
[Old English *tunge*] — **tongue′like′**, *adj.*

***tongue**
definitions 9, 14

tongue

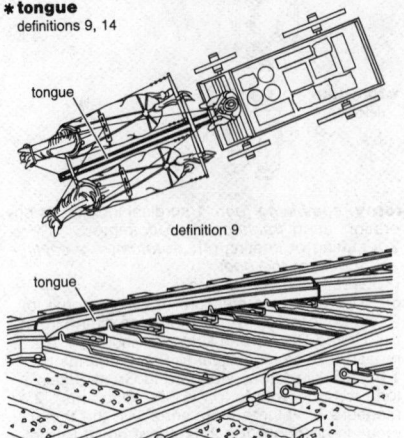

definition 9

tongue

definition 14

**tongue-and-groove joint** (tung′ən grüv′), a joint made by fitting a projecting strip along the edge of one board into a groove cut along the edge of another board, as in matchboard.

**-tongued**, *combining form.* having a ___ tongue or tongues: *Many-tongued = having many tongues.*

**tongue depressor**, a thin blade of wood used to hold down the tongue in an examination of the mouth and throat.

**tongue graft**, *Horticulture.* a whip graft.

**tongue-in-cheek** (tung′in chēk′), *adj.* not to be taken seriously or literally; mockingly ironical or satirical: *All the stories are ... amusing, mildly racy, and acted with a tongue-in-cheek seriousness that adds up to a rib of Hollywood* (Time).

**tongue-lash** (tung′lash′), *v.i., v.t.* to reprove loudly or severely; scold.

**tongue-lash|ing** (tung′lash′ing), *n.* a loud or severe reprimand; a scolding.

**tongue|less** (tung′lis), *adj.* **1** having no tongue. **2** unable to speak; mute.

**tongue|let** (tung′lit), *n.* a little tongue.

**tongue|ster** (tung′stər), *n.* a talker; gossip.

**tongue-tie** (tung′tī′), *n., v.,* **-tied, -ty|ing.** — ***n.*** impeded motion of the tongue caused by abnormal shortness of the frenum of the tongue.
— ***v.t.*** to make (a person) unable to speak, because of amazement, fear, or timidity, or other emotional or physical handicap: *The ligaments, which tongue-tied him, were loosened* (Charles Lamb).

**tongue-tied** (tung′tīd′), *adj.* **1** having the motion of the tongue hindered, usually because of abnormal shortness of the fold of membrane on the underside of the tongue. **2** *Figurative.* **a** unable to speak, especially because of shyness or embarrassment; speechless; silent: *to be tongue-tied with rage.* **b** reserved; reticent.

**tongue twister**, a phrase or sentence that is difficult to say quickly without a mistake. *Example:* She sells seashells at the seashore.

**tongue-twist|ing** (tung′twis′ting), *adj.* of or like a tongue twister; difficult to say quickly and rapidly: *tongue-twisting lyrics.*

**tongue worm**, **1** any one of a group of small tongue-shaped parasites which reach the adult stage in the nasal passages and sinuses of animals. **2** a small, soft-bodied sea animal; hemichordate.

**tongue|y** (tung′ē), *adj.* **1** *Informal.* talkative; loquacious; garrulous. **2** of or like a tongue; produced by the tongue; lingual.

**tongu|ing** (tung′ing), *n. Music.* the process or result of modifying or interrupting the tone by rapidly repeated strokes of the tongue, in playing a wind instrument.

**ton|ic** (ton′ik), *n., adj.* — ***n.*** **1a** a medicine or remedy supposed to stimulate or tone up the body. Cod-liver oil and sassafras tea are tonics. **b** anything that gives strength, invigorates, or braces: *The clean country air was a tonic to the tourists.* **2** *Music.* the first note or fundamental tone of a scale; keynote. See picture under **dominant**. **3** *Phonetics, Obsolete.* a voiced sound. **4** *U.S.* flavored carbonated water: *celery tonic.* [< adjective]
— ***adj.*** **1a** restoring to health and vigor; giving strength; bracing: *The mountain air is tonic.* **b** *Figurative.* refreshing to the mind or spirit: *Since most bands playing Chicago at the time were of the Dixieland persuasion, to hear Lombardo's restrained melodies over the air was a strange and tonic experience for many residents of the region* (New Yorker). **2a** having to do with muscular tension. **b** characterized by continuous contraction of the muscles: *a tonic convulsion.* **3** *Music.* **a** having to do with a tone or tones. **b** of or based on a keynote: *a tonic chord.* **4** *Linguistics.* **a** of or having to do with tone or accent in speaking. **b** (of a language) using tone distinctively. **5** *Phonetics.* **a** stressed; accented. **b** (formerly) voiced. **6** of or having to do with the effect of color, or of light and shade, in a picture.
[< Greek *tonikós* of stretching < *tónos* tension; see etym. under **tone**]

**tonic accent**, **1** accent given to a syllable in pronunciation as distinct from written accent. **2** accent featuring pitch rather than loudness.

**ton|i|cal|ly** (ton′ə klē), *adv.* **1** as a tonic. **2** in a tonic manner.

**to|nic|i|ty** (tō nis′ə tē), *n.* **1** tonic quality or condition. **2** the property of possessing bodily tone, especially the normal state of partial contraction of a resting muscle; tonus.

**tonic sol-fa**, a system of teaching music, especially sight singing, that emphasizes tonality or key relationship. The seven notes of any major scale are sung to the sol-fa syllables, with *do* always denoting the tonic or keynote, and the remaining syllables indicating the relation to it of the other notes of the scale.

**tonic spasm**, a prolonged contraction of a muscle or muscles without relaxation for some time.

**to|night** or **to-night** (tə nīt′), *n., adv.* — ***n.*** the night of of this day; this night. *Tonight is cold.*
— ***adv.*** **1** on or during this very night: *It's cold tonight.* **2** on or during the night following this day: *Do you think it will snow tonight?* **3** *Obsolete or Dialect.* on or during the night just past; last night.
[Old English *tō niht*]
► See **today** for usage note.

**to|nite**[1] (tō′nīt), *n.* an explosive consisting of guncotton and barium nitrate, used in blasting or in small bombs. [< Latin *tonāre* to thunder + English *-ite*[1]]

**to|nite**[2] (tə nīt′), *n., adv. Informal.* tonight.

**ton|ka bean** (tong′kə), **1** the black, fragrant, almond-shaped seed of any of various large trees of the pea family, of Brazil, Guiana, and adjacent regions, used in snuff and perfumes. **2** any one of these trees. [probably < Tupi]

**ton|kin** (ton′kin′), *n.* a high grade of bamboo, used for ski and fishing poles. [< *Tonkin*, a former French protectorate in Indochina, now in North Vietnam]

**Ton|kin|ese** (ton′kə nēz′, tong′-, tông′-; -nēs′), *n., pl.* **-ese**, *adj.* — ***n.*** **1** a native or inhabitant of Tonkin, a former French protectorate in northern Indochina, now part of North Vietnam. **2** the Vietnamese dialect of the Tonkinese.
— ***adj.*** of or having to do with Tonkin, its people, or their dialect.

**ton mile**, **1** one ton of freight carried a distance of one mile, a unit of measurement in transportation statistics: *Ton miles of freight moved by trucks today are four times greater than before the war* (New York Times). **2** a unit of measurement in estimating automobile economy. The loaded weight of the car in tons is multiplied by the miles traveled, and divided by the number of gallons of gasoline consumed.

**tonn.**, tonnage.

**ton|nage** (tun′ij), *n.* **1a** the carrying capacity of a ship, expressed in tons of 100 cubic feet. A ship of 50,000 cubic feet of space for freight has a tonnage of 500 tons. **b** the amount of a commodity or other cargo shipped, loaded, unloaded, or in storage, expressed in tons of 40 cubic feet. **2** the total amount of shipping in tons; ships considered with reference to their carrying capacity or together with their cargoes. **3** a duty or tax on ships for each ton of cargo, as at a wharf or on a canal. **4** weight in tons.

**tonne** (tun), *n. British.* a metric ton; 1,000 kilograms: *Each tonne of fuel yields about two kilogrammes of plutonium* (New Scientist). [variant of *ton*[1]]

**ton|neau** (tu nō′), *n., pl.* **-neaus** or **-neaux** (-nōz′). **1** the rear part of an automobile body, with seats for passengers and its own doors. **2** an automobile body having such a rear part. **3** = metric ton. [< French *tonneau* (literally) cask < *tonne* cask < a Germanic word]

**ton|neaued** (tu nōd′), *adj.* having a tonneau.

**-tonner**, *combining form.* something that weighs ___ tons: *A 48,000-tonner = a ship that weighs 48,000 tons.*

**ton|o|graph** (ton′ə graf, -gräf; tō′nə-), *n.* = tonometer.

**ton|o|graph|ic** (ton′ə graf′ik, tō′nə-), *adj.* = tonometric.

**to|nog|ra|phy** (tə nog′rə fē), *n.* = tonometry.

**to|nom|e|ter** (tō nom′ə tər), *n.* **1** an instrument, especially a tuning fork or a graduated set of tuning forks, for determining the pitch of tones. **2** an instrument for measuring the tension of the eyeball, or for measuring blood pressure within the blood vessels. **3** *Chemistry.* an instrument for measuring strains within a liquid, or for measuring vapor pressure. [(def. 1) < Latin *tonus* tone + English *-meter;* (defs. 2, 3) < Greek *tónos* tension]

**ton|o|met|ric** (ton′ə met′rik, tō′nə-), *adj.* **1** of or with a tonometer. **2** of or having to do with tonometry.

**to|nom|e|try** (tō nom′ə trē), *n.* measurement with a tonometer.

**to|no|plast** (tōn′ə plast, ton′ō-), *n.* a thin membrane that surrounds the vacuole of a plant cell: *The chlorophyll is protected from the enzyme by a tonoplast* (John McPhee). [< Greek *tónos* tension + English *-plast*]

**ton|qua bean** (tong′kə), = tonka bean.

***ton|sil** (ton′səl), *n.* either of the two oval masses of glandular tissue on the sides of the throat, just back of the mouth. [< Latin *tōnsillae,* plural, related to *tōlēs* goiter]

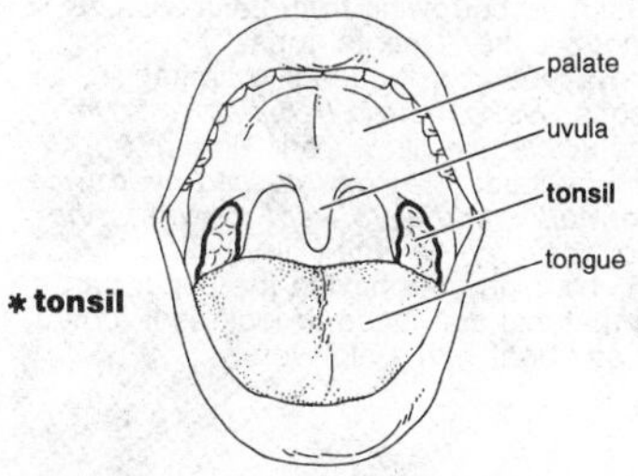

***tonsil**

**ton|sil|lar** or **ton|sil|ar** (ton′sə lər), *adj.* of or having to do with the tonsils.

**ton|sil|lec|to|my** (ton′sə lek′tə mē), *n., pl.* **-mies.** the surgical removal of the tonsils. [< *tonsil* + *-ectomy*]

**ton|sil|lit|ic** (ton′sə lit′ik), *adj.* of or affected with tonsillitis.

**ton|sil|li|tis** (ton′sə lī′tis), *n.* inflammation of the tonsils. [< Latin *tōnsillae* tonsils + English *-itis*]

**ton|sil|lo|scope** (ton sil′ə skōp), *n.* an instrument for examining the tonsils.

**ton|sil|lo|scop|ic** (ton sil′ə skop′ik), *adj.* of or with a tonsilloscope.

**ton|sil|lot|o|my** (ton′sə lot′ə mē), *n., pl.* **-mies.** the surgical removal of all or part of a tonsil. [< Latin *tōnsillae* tonsils + Greek *-tomiā* a cutting]

**ton|so|ri|al** (ton sôr′ē əl, -sōr′-), *adj.* of or having to do with a barber or his work (often used humorously). [< Latin *tōnsōrius* having to do with a *tōnsor, -ōris* barber < *tondēre* shear, shave] — **ton|so′ri|al|ly,** *adv.*

***ton|sure** (ton′shər), *n., v.,* **-sured, -sur|ing.** — *n.* **1** the act or process of clipping the hair, or shaving the head or a part of the head, required of a person entering the priesthood in some churches or an order of monks. **2** the shaved part of the head of a priest or monk. **3** the state of being so shaved.
— *v.t.* to shave the head of, especially as a religious ritual.
[< Latin *tōnsūra* < *tondēre* shear, shave]

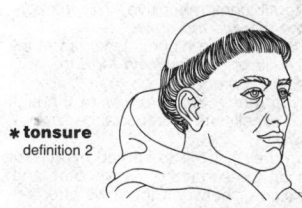

***tonsure**
definition 2

**ton|sured** (ton′shərd), *adj.* having undergone tonsure, especially ecclesiastical tonsure.

**ton|tine** (ton′tēn, ton tēn′), *n., adj.* — *n.* **1** a system of annuity or insurance in which subscribers share a fund. The shares of survivors increase as members die, until the last gets all that is left. **2** the total of money involved in such a system. **3** the share or right of each member in such system. **4** the members as a group.
— *adj.* of, having to do with, or like a tontine: *a tontine policy.*
[< French *tontine* < Lorenzo *Tonti,* an Italian banker who introduced it into France around 1653]

**ton-up** (tun′up′), *adj. British Slang.* **1** traveling in motorcycles at high or reckless speeds; doing a ton: *ton-up boys.* **2** having to do with or used by ton-up boys: *a ton-up road, black-leather ton-up outfits.*

**to|nus** (tō′nəs), *n.* **1** = tonicity; bodily or muscular tone. **2** a tonic spasm. [< Latin *tonus* < Greek *tónos* tension, tone]

**ton|y** (tō′nē), *adj.,* **ton|i|er, ton|i|est.** *Slang.* high-toned; fashionable; stylish. [< *ton*[2] + *-y*[1]]

***To|ny** (tō′nē), *n., pl.* **-nys.** an award presented annually in the United States for outstanding achievements in the theater: *The Tonys have been distributed annually since 1947 as a memorial to Antoinette Perry, the* [*theatrical*] *wing's wartime chairman* (New York Times). [< *Tony,* nickname of *Antoinette* Perry, 1888-1946, an American actress]

***Tony**

**too** (tü), *adv.* **1** in addition; also; besides: *The dog is hungry, and very thirsty too. We, too, are going away.* **2** more than what is proper or enough: *My dress is too long for you. He ate too much. The summer passed too quickly.* **3** very; exceedingly: *I am only too glad to help.* [spelling variant of *to,* Old English *tō* to, too]

**took** (tůk), *v.* the past tense of **take**: *She took the car an hour ago.*

**tool** (tül), *n., v.* — *n.* **1** a knife, hammer, saw, shovel, or any instrument used in doing work: *a carpenter's tools. Most boys like to work with tools.* (*Figurative.*) *They ... make use of similitudes ... and other tools of oratory* (Thomas Hobbes). **2** anything used like a tool, constituting an instrument of work: *Books are a scholar's tools.* **3** *Figurative.* a person or group used by another like a tool: *He is the tool of the party boss.* **4a** a part of a machine that cuts, bores, smooths, or otherwise fashions something. **b** the whole of such a machine. **5** *Law.* any implement or apparatus needed to carry on one's business or profession: *tools of trade.* **6a** a small stamp or roller used to impress designs on book covers. **b** the design so impressed.
— *v.t.* **1** to work or shape with a tool or tools; use a tool on: *He tooled beautiful designs in the leather with a knife.* **2** to ornament with a tool: *to tool a book cover.* **3** to provide or equip (a factory or other establishment) with tools. **4** *Informal.* to drive (a vehicle) in a certain way: *to tool a car smoothly down the street.*
— *v.i.* **1** to work with a tool or tools, as in bookbinding. **2** to equip a factory or other establishment with tools. **3** *Informal.* to drive in a vehicle: *to tool through the town.*
**down tools,** *British.* to lay down one's tools; stop working: *to down tools for the holiday.*
[Old English *tōl*] — **tool′er,** *n.*
— *Syn. n.* **1 Tool, implement** mean an instrument or other article used in doing work. **Tool** means an instrument or simple device especially suited or designed to make doing a particular kind of work easier, but applies particularly to something held and worked by the hands in doing manual work: *Plumbers, mechanics, carpenters, and shoemakers need tools.* **Implement** is a general word meaning a tool, instrument, utensil, or mechanical device needed to do something: *Hoes and tractors are agricultural implements.*

**tool box,** or **tool|box** (tül′boks′), *n.* a box in which tools and sometimes small parts and accessories are kept.

**tool|hold|er** (tül′hōl′dər), *n.* **1** a detachable handle used with different tools. **2** a device for holding the tool of a machine in position for work.

**tool house,** = toolshed.

**tool|ing** (tü′ling), *n.* **1** work done with a tool. **2** ornamentation made with a tool: *leather tooling.* **3** the assembly of machine tools in a factory.

**tool|mak|er** (tül′mā′kər), *n.* **1** a machinist who makes, repairs, and maintains machine tools. **2** any maker of tools: *Prehistoric men were the first toolmakers.*

**tool|mak|ing** (tül′mā′king), *n., adj.* — *n.* the work of a toolmaker.
— *adj.* that is a toolmaker; involved in making tools.

**tool pusher,** *Slang.* the person in charge of drilling operations at an oil well.

**tool|room** (tül′rüm′, -rům′), *n.* a department in a machine shop in which tools are made, kept, and handed out to the workers.

**tool|shed** (tül′shed′), *n.* a building in which tools are kept.

**tool subject,** an educational subject taught for its usefulness in other fields, not for its own sake, such as arithmetic and spelling.

**toom** (tüm), *adj., v. Scottish.* — *adj.* empty.
— *v.t.* to empty.
[Old English *tōm*]

**toon** (tün), *n.* **1** a tree of the mahogany family of the East Indies and Australia, that yields a red wood like mahogany, but softer and lighter. **2** the wood itself, used for furniture and cabinetwork. [< Hindi *tun, tūn* < Sanskrit *tunna*]

**toot**[1] (tüt), *n., v.* — *n.* the sound of a horn, whistle, or wind instrument; short blast: *The factory gives three toots of the whistle at noon.*
— *v.i.* **1** to give forth a short blast of sound: *He heard the train whistle toot three times.* **2** to sound or blow a whistle, horn, or wind instrument. **3** (of a grouse) to utter its call. — *v.t.* to sound (a horn, whistle, or wind instrument) in short blasts.
[probably ultimately imitative] — **toot′er,** *n.*

**toot**[2] (tüt), *n. U.S. Slang.* a spree, especially a drinking spree: *to go on a toot.* [earlier, a large drink < obsolete *toot,* verb, to drink copiously; origin unknown]

***tooth** (tüth), *n., pl.* **teeth,** *v.* — *n.* **1a** one of the hard, bonelike parts in the mouth, used for biting and chewing. Animals use their teeth as weapons of attack or defense. Teeth are attached in a row to each jaw. A tooth in man and most vertebrates is usually composed of dentin surrounding a hollow filled with pulp, through which run blood vessels and nerves, and coated at the root with cementum and at the crown and exposed parts with enamel. **b** any one of certain hard parts or processes in the mouth or digestive tract of invertebrates. **2** something like a tooth. Each one of the projecting parts of a comb, saw, file, rake, harrow, or fork is a tooth. **3** one of the series of projections, as on the rim of a gearwheel or pinion, that engage with others to transmit or convert motion; cog. **4** *Figurative.* a taste; liking: *to have no tooth for fruit.* **5** *Figurative.* a hurtful, gnawing, or destructive power: *'gainst the tooth of time* (Shakespeare). **6** *Botany.* **a** one of the delicate, pointed processes surrounding the mouth of the spore case in mosses, that together form the peristome. **b** one of the projections at the margin of certain leaves or petals.
— *v.t.* **1** to furnish with teeth; put teeth on. **2** to cut teeth on the edge of; indent.
— *v.i.* = interlock.
**tooth and nail** (or **claw**), with all one's force; fiercely: *to fight or resist tooth and nail.*
[Old English *tōth*] — **tooth′like′,** *adj.*

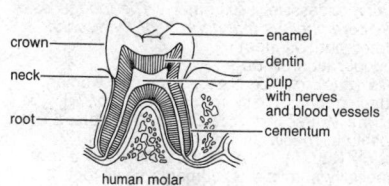

***tooth**
definition 1a

crown
neck
root
enamel
dentin
pulp with nerves and blood vessels
cementum
human molar

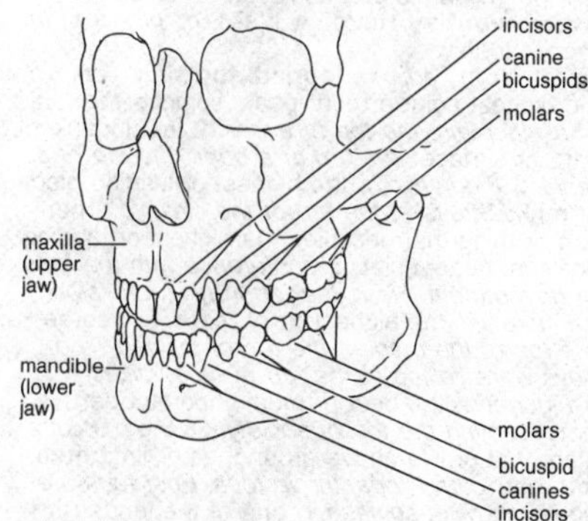


**tooth|ache** (tüth′āk′), *n.* a pain in a tooth or the teeth.

**toothache tree** = prickly ash. [because the bark produces a cooling sensation when chewed, and acts as an anesthetic for toothache]

---

**Pronunciation Key:** hat, āge, cãre, fär; let, ēqual, tėrm; it, īce; hot, ōpen, ôrder; oil, out; cup, půt, rüle; child; long; thin; ᴛʜen; zh, measure;
ə represents **a** in about, **e** in taken, **i** in pencil, **o** in lemon, **u** in circus.

**tooth|brush** (tüth′brush′), *n.* a small, stiff brush for cleaning the teeth.

**tooth|brush|ing** (tüth′brush′ing), *n., adj.* —***n.*** the act or process of cleaning one's teeth with a toothbrush: *It was clear that toothbrushing alone was not the only factor in promoting oral hygiene* (John Roper).
—***adj.*** of or having to do with toothbrushing: *toothbrushing technique.*

**toothbrush mustache**, a small, bristly mustache.

**toothed** (tütht, tüᴛʜd), *adj.* **1** having teeth. **2** notched: *the toothed surface of a gear.*

**toothed whale**, a whale or related sea mammal with true teeth in one or both jaws, such as the sperm whale, narwhal, bottlenose, dolphin, or porpoise.

**tooth|less** (tüth′lis), *adj.* without teeth: *a toothless old man.*

**toothless whale**, a whale or related sea mammal that has horny plates of whalebone in place of teeth, as the right whale, gray whale, humpback and sulphur-bottom; whalebone whale.

**tooth ornament**, *Architecture.* a projecting ornament of a pyramidal or flowerlike form, often repeated in a series in a hollow molding; dogtooth.

**tooth|paste** (tüth′pāst′), *n.* a paste used in cleaning the teeth. [American English]

**tooth|pick** (tüth′pik′), *n.* a small, pointed piece of wood, plastic, or sharpened quill for removing bits of food from between the teeth.

**tooth|pow|der** (tüth′pou′dər), *n.* a powder used in cleaning the teeth.

**tooth shell**, **1** the long, tubular, toothlike shell of a scaphopod. **2** = scaphopod.

**tooth|some** (tüth′səm), *adj.* **1** pleasing to the taste; tasty. **SYN:** savory, delicious. **2** *Figurative.* pleasing to the sight; pretty; comely: *a toothsome girl.* —**tooth′some|ly**, *adv.* —**tooth′some|ness**, *n.*

**tooth|wort** (tüth′wėrt′), *n.* **1** a European and Asian parasitic herb of the figwort family with a rootstock that is covered with toothlike scales. **2** any one of a group of plants of the mustard family having toothlike projections upon its creeping rootstock.

**tooth|y** (tü′thē), *adj.,* **tooth|i|er, tooth|i|est.** **1** showing many teeth prominently: *a toothy smile.* **2** having teeth. —**tooth′i|ly**, *adv.*

**too|tle** (tü′təl), *v.,* **-tled, -tling,** *n.* —***v.i.*** to toot continuously; produce a succession of toots.
—***v.t.*** to play by tooting; toot steadily.
—***n.*** the act of tootling.
[frequentative of *toot*[1]]

**too|tler** (tüt′lər), *n.* **1** a person or thing that tootles. **2** *Figurative.* a writer of verbiage or twaddle.

**too-too** (tü′tü′), *adj., adv.* —***adj.*** excessive; extreme: *The piece is nowhere; but my frocks are too-too!* (Mrs. A. Kennard).
—***adv.*** excessively; extremely: *The too-too painfully ceremonious manners ... of the French* (Notes and Queries).
[reduplication of *too*]

**toots** (tüts), *n. U.S. Slang.* **1** a girl or woman. **2** darling; dear. [back formation < *tootsie*]

**toot|sie** (tüt′sē), *n. U.S. Slang.* **1** = toots. **2** a prostitute. [origin uncertain]

**toot|sy** (tüt′sē), *n., pl.* **-sies.** *Informal.* **1** a foot, especially a child's or woman's small foot. **2** a toe. [< children's pronunciation of *footsie*]

**toot|sy-woot|sy** (tüt′sē wüt′sē), *n., pl.* **-sies.** *Informal.* tootsy.

**top**[1] (top), *n., adj., v.,* **topped, top|ping.** —***n.*** **1** the highest point or part; peak; summit: *the top of a mountain, the top of a tree.* **2** the upper end, part, or surface: *the top of a book, the top of a table.* **3** *Figurative.* **a** the highest or leading place or rank: *She is at the top of the class.* **b** a person or thing that occupies the highest or leading position; head; chief: *a conference with the tops of government. He is the top in his profession.* **4** *Figurative.* the highest point, pitch, or degree: *the top of the market, the top of fashion. The boys were yelling at the top of their voices.* **5** *Figurative.* the best or most important part: *a hotel serving the top of society.* **6a** the part of a plant that grows above ground, as distinct from the root: *carrot tops, turnip tops. Beet tops are somewhat like spinach.* **b** one of the tender tips of branches or shoots. **7** the head, especially the crown of the head: *a shaved top.* **8** the cover, as of a container or vehicle; lid; cap: *a top for a kettle, a new top for an automobile, the top of a can.* **9** the upper part of a shoe or boot. **10** a bunch of hair, fibers, or the like; tuft; crest. **11a** a platform around the top part of a lower mast on a ship. The top serves as a foothold for sailors and as a means of extending the upper rigging. **b** a similar part of the superstructure of a warship, for firing light guns and observation. **12a** the highest card of a suit in a hand. **b** the highest score made on a particular hand by any team at duplicate bridge. **c** an ace or a king. **13** a stroke above the center of a ball in golf. **14** a bundle of combed wool prepared for spinning; sliver. **15** a tent used as a covering for a circus or other performance. **16** the first half of an inning in baseball: *the top of the seventh.* **17** *Chemistry.* the part in a distillation that volatilizes first.
—***adj.*** **1** having to do with, situated at, or forming the top: *the top shelf of a cupboard.* **2** *Figurative.* highest in degree; greatest: *The runners set off at top speed. We pay top prices for used cars.* **3** *Figurative.* chief; foremost: *top honors.*
—***v.t.*** **1** to put a top on: *I will top the box.* **SYN:** cap. **2a** to be on top of; be at the top of; crown: *A church tops the hill.* **b** to be or form the top of: *A steeple tops the church.* **3** to reach the top of: *Call me when you see a gray car topping the hill.* **4** to rise high; rise above: *The sun topped the horizon.* **5** *Figurative.* to be higher than; be greater than: *That bid tops the best I can afford.* **6** *Figurative.* to do or be better than; surpass; outdo; excel: *His story topped all the rest.* **7** in golf: **a** to hit (a ball) above center. **b** to make (a stroke) in this way: *She topped her drive.* **8** to cut off the top part of (a plant); crop; prune: *to top a tree.* **9** *Chemistry.* (in distillation) to remove the part that volatilizes first; skim. **10** to treat (material or fabric) with a final dye to improve the color.

**blow one's top**, *Slang.* **a** to lose one's temper; get very excited: *It is no secret that he often resents criticism, ... and that he blows his top from time to time* (Harper's). **b** to become insane: *A prisoner blew his top and tried to kill one of the guards.*

**from top to toe**, **a** from head to foot: *She was dressed in brown from top to toe.* **b** *Figurative.* completely: *[They were] English from top to toe* (James Russell Lowell).

**off** (or **out of**) **the top of one's head**, *Informal.* without consideration; in an impromptu manner; spontaneously: *The Bishop was such an easy mark for criticism, and the comments of his detractors had been so abundant, making so many points (some of them off the top of their heads), and yet the congregation at large had been so nearly silent* (New Yorker).

**on top**, with success; with victory: *We have the best players, so our team will come out on top.*

**on top of**, **a** in addition to: *On top of everything else, it's raining* (Manchester Guardian Weekly). **b** *Figurative.* in control of: *The conductor was always on top of the music, keeping it alive and moving* (New York Times). **c** *Figurative.* following closely: *Hot on top of [him] came Hyndman, struggling to [pass] his ... opponent* (London Times).

**on top of the world**, *Informal.* **a** in a foremost or outstanding position: *A new plan to spread the fruit of scientific research was aimed at putting Britain "on top of the world"* (London Times). **b** in a very happy or successful state: *The new champion is on top of the world. Wearing beautiful clothes made her feel on top of the world.*

**over the top**, **a** over the front of a trench to make an attack: *Some fellows asked our captain when we were going over the top* (War Illustrated). **b** *Figurative.* over a goal or quota: *The salesman who goes over the top this month will get a bonus.*

**top and tail**, *British.* to take off both ends of; pull off the greens and roots of (as turnips, carrots, or beets): *A gentleman ... was topping and tailing gooseberries for wine* (L. M. Hawkins).

**top off**, **a** to complete; finish; end: *The market has been broadly hinting that the longlived business boom is topping off* (Wall Street Journal). **b** *Figurative.* to put the finishing touch to: *to top off dinner with a fine cigar.*

**top of the morning**, a very good morning (used as a greeting): *Captain, my darling, the top of the morning to you!* (Charles J. Lever).

**top out**, **a** to reach the top; end: *Real estate values across the country generally topped out during the past year, according to a survey* (Wall Street Journal). **b** to complete the skeleton structure of (a building being erected): *The building has been topped out and brickwork now is under way* (New York Times).

**top up**, to refill: *The terphenyl undergoes slow decomposition in the reactor, and has to be topped up at the rate of 1 or 2 per cent per day* (New Scientist).

[Old English *topp*]

—***Syn.*** *n.* **1, 3 Top, summit, crown** mean the highest point or part of something. **Top** is the general word: *It is now easy to drive to the top of the mountain.* (*Figurative.*) *She was at the top of her career after being elected senator.* **Summit** means the topmost point, and when used figuratively means the highest level attainable: *The road does not go to the summit.* (*Figurative.*) *At last he attained the summit of his ambition.* **Crown** applies especially to a rounded top: *There is snow on the crown of the mountain.* When used figuratively, *crown* means the highest degree of perfection or completion or highest state or quality: *A Nobel prize is the crown of success.*

**top**[2] (top), *n.* a toy that spins on a point, sometimes by the rapid unwinding of a string wound around it. Mechanical tops are powered by a spring.
**sleep like a top**, to sleep soundly: *No noisy window [air conditioning] units ... you sleep like a top* (New Yorker).
[origin uncertain. Compare Old High German *topf*, Old French *topoie.*]

**top-**, *combining form.* the form of **topo-** before vowels, as in *topectomy.*

**to|paz** (tō′paz), *n.* **1** a hard mineral that occurs in crystals of various forms and colors. It is a compound of aluminum, silica, and fluorine. Transparent yellow, pink, and brown varieties of topaz are used as gems. **2** a yellow variety of sapphire or quartz, used as a gem. **3** either of two South American hummingbirds that have bright feathers. **4** a clear, light brown with a trace of yellow. [Middle English *topace,* or *topaze* < Old French *topace,* learned borrowing from Latin *topazus* < Greek *tópazos* the "Oriental topaz"]

**top banana**, *Slang.* **1** the leading comedian, as in burlesque: *He is the top banana. He is, indeed, the whole film* (New York Times). **2** a leader in any field: *[He] was passed over twice for ... promotion and word went round that he would never be top banana* (Time).

***top boot**, **1** a high boot having the upper part of different material and made to look as if turned down. **2** any boot with a high top.

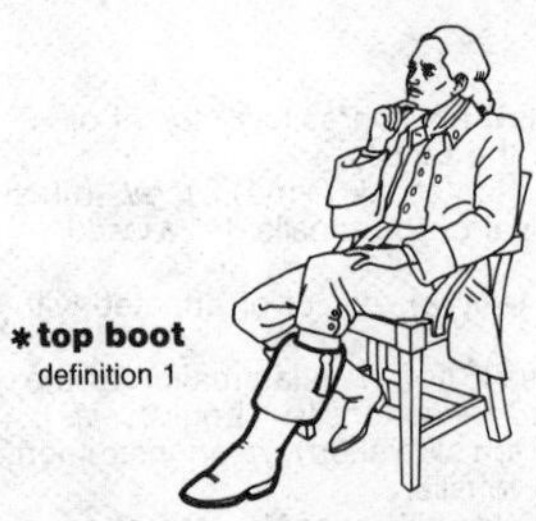

***top boot**
definition 1

**top-boot|ed** (top′bü′tid), *adj.* wearing top boots.

**top brass**, *U.S. Slang.* **1** high-ranking military officers: *How long will this careless attitude of some of the troops be tolerated by the top brass?* (Time). **2** high officials: *the assembled top brass of the government* (Harper's).

**top|coat** (top′kōt′), *n.* **1** a lightweight overcoat. **2** a loose overcoat.

**top cover**, **1** air cover at high altitude for a military force or flying mission: *Saberjets that were flying top cover for the reconnaissance craft* (New York Times). **2** the airplanes making up such protection.

**top cross**, *Genetics.* the offspring produced when a variety is crossed with one inbred line.

**top dog**, **1** the dog uppermost or on top in a fight. **2** *Informal, Figurative: Norway has been top dog of the whaling business for more than half a century* (Wall Street Journal).

**top-down** (top′doun′), *adj. Informal.* from the top down; covering all; comprehensive: *The manager's work in the store is top-down.*

**top drawer**, *Informal.* the highest level, as of importance or excellence: *a family in the top drawer of Washington society.*

**top-drawer** (top′drôr′), *adj. Informal.* of the highest level, as of excellence or importance: *a top-drawer musical.*

**top-dress** (top′dres′), *v.t.* **1** to spread manure or other fertilizer on the surface of (a piece of land), as before planting or between the rows after planting. **2** to put crushed rock on (a road).

**top-dress|ing** (top′dres′ing), *n.* **1** fertilizer applied to the surface and not worked in. **2** crushed rock or gravel put on a road without working it in. **3** the application of such material.

**tope**[1] (tōp), *v.,* **toped, top|ing.** —***v.t.*** to drink (alcoholic liquor) to excess or as a habit.
—***v.i.*** to be a toper.
[perhaps < obsolete *tope,* interjection, used in drinking, apparently in sense "done!," for accepting a toast or a wager < French *toper* < Spanish *topar* accept a wager; (originally) collide; imitative]

**tope**[2] (tōp), *n.* any one of several species of small sharks. [origin uncertain]

**tope**[3] (tōp), *n.* an ancient, dome-shaped monument in Buddhist countries for preserving relics or commemorating some event. [< Hindi *tōp,* perhaps < Pali *thūpo,* ultimately < Sanskrit *stūpa.* See etym. of doublet **stupa.**]

**tope**[4] (tōp), *n.* (in India) a clump, grove, or plantation of trees. [< Tamil *tōppu*]

**top-ech|e|lon** (top′esh′ə lon), *adj.* high-ranking; of a high level of command or authority: *top-echelon administrators.*

**to|pec|to|mize** (tə pek′tə mīz), *v.t.*, **-mized, -miz-ing.** to perform a topectomy on.

**to|pec|to|my** (tə pek′tə mē), *n., pl.* **-mies.** a surgical incision into the cortex of the brain to relieve the symptoms of psychosis. [< *top-* + *-ectomy*]

**to|pee** (tō pē′, tō′pē), *n.* a helmet made of pith to protect the head against the sun. Also, **topi.** [Anglo-Indian < Hindi *topī*, perhaps related to *top* helmet or hat]

**top|er** (tō′pər), *n.* a person who drinks alcoholic liquor too much or as a habit.

**top flight**, the highest level or rank: *In the top flight of Britain's Quality Cars—at £2,645* (Sunday Times).

**top-flight** or **top|flight** (top′flīt′), *adj. Informal.* excellent; first-rate; foremost: *The prophet Ezekiel was a top-flight scientific observer and recorder of important meteorological phenomena* (Science News).

**top|full** (top′fu̇l′), *adj.* full to the top; brimful.

**top|gal|lant** (top′gal′ənt; *Nautical* tə gal′ənt), *n., adj.* —*n.* the mast or sail next above the topmast. It is the third section of a mast above the deck.

—*adj.* **1** of or belonging to a topgallant; next above the topmast. **2** (of a deck, rail, or other structure) situated above a corresponding adjacent part: *topgallant forecastle.* **3** *Figurative.* lofty; grand; first-rate: *To have a new planet swim into one's ken ... this is topgallant delight* (Clifton Fadiman).

[< *top*[1] + *gallant* (because it makes a brave or gallant show in comparison with the other rigging)]

**top gear**, *British.* high gear.

**top-grade** (top′grād′), *adj.* of the highest grade or quality: *top-grade steers.*

**toph** (tōf), *n.* = tophus.

**top|ham|per** (top′ham′pər), *n.* **1a** the upper masts, sails, and rigging, on a ship. **b** all the spars and rigging above the deck. **2** any unnecessary weight or rigging aloft or on the deck; hamper.

***top hat**, a tall, black silk hat worn by men in formal clothes; high hat.

***top hat**

**top-hat** (top′hat′), *adj. Informal.* high-class; top-drawer: *top-hat executives.*

**top-hat|ted** (top′hat′id), *adj.* wearing a top hat.

**tophe** (tōf), *n.* = tophus.

**top-heav|y** (top′hev′ē), *adj.* **1** too heavy at the top. **2** liable to fall or fail as from too great weight above; unstable. **3** *Figurative.* overcapitalized, as a business corporation. **4** *Figurative.* having too many officials of high rank: *a department top-heavy with full professors.* —**top′-heav′i-ness**, *n.*

**To|phet** or **To|pheth** (tō′fit), *n.* **1** hell; Gehenna. **2** a place in the valley of Hinnom, near Jerusalem, where human sacrifices were offered to Moloch. It was later used as a garbage dump and came to symbolize the place of eternal torment. [< Hebrew *tōpheth*]

**top-hole** (top′hōl′), *adj. British Slang.* first-rate; top-notch.

**to|phus** (tō′fəs), *n., pl.* **-phi** (-fī). **1** a small, hard, chalklike growth in the tissues and joints of the feet and hands, and around the teeth, and other structures, in severe cases of gout; chalkstone. **2** = tufa. [< Latin *tōphus,* variant of *tōfus* loose stones. Compare etym. under **tufa.**]

**to|pi**[1] (tō pē′, tō′pē), *n.* = topee.

**to|pi**[2] (tō′pē), *n.* a large African antelope related to the hartebeest. [origin uncertain. Compare Swahili *tope.*]

**to|pi|ar|y** (tō′pē er′ē), *adj., n., pl.* **-ar|ies.** —*adj.* **1** trimmed or clipped into ornamental shapes: *topiary shrubs and trees.* **2** of or having to do with such trimming: *topiary art.*

—*n.* **1** topiary art. **2** a topiary garden.

[< Latin *topiārius* < *topia* ornamental gardening < Greek *tópia,* plural of *tópion* (originally) a field (diminutive) < *tópos* place]

**top|ic** (top′ik), *n.* **1** a subject that people think, write, or talk about: *Newspapers discuss the topics of the day. The main topics at Mother's party were gardening and clothes.* **SYN:** See syn. under **subject. 2** a short phrase or sentence used in an outline to give the main point, as of a part of a speech or writing. **3** *Rhetoric and Logic.* a class of considerations or arguments suitable for debate or discourse. **4** a general rule or maxim.

[singular of *topics* < Latin *topica* < Greek (*tà*) *topiká,* a work by Aristotle of logical and rhetorical generalities or commonplaces; *topiká* < *tópoi* commonplaces; (literally) plural of *tópos* place]

**top|i|cal** (top′ə kəl), *adj., n.* —*adj.* **1** of or having to do with topics of the day; of current or local interest: *topical news.* **2** of or having to do with a topic or topics: *Some books have topical outlines for each chapter.* **3a** of or having to do with a place or locality; local. **b** limited or applied to a certain spot or part of the body; not general.

—*n.* one of the stamps in a stamp collection based on a topic or theme, such as airplanes or world's fairs: *Nobody collects miscellaneously anymore. Let me show you some of my topicals* (Scientific American). —**top′i|cal|ly**, *adv.*

**top|i|cal|i|ty** (top′ə kal′ə tē), *n., pl.* **-ties. 1** the quality of being topical: *I think there are some situations that a writer dare not turn into adventure stories without running the risk of opportunistic topicality* (Paul Pickrel). **2** a topical reference or allusion: *The only thing wrong with the operas is Gilbert's outrageous puns and outdated topicalities* (Sunday Times).

**topic sentence**, a general introductory statement that announces or summarizes the idea of a paragraph or paragraphs. *Examples:* Philosophy has two important aims. Let us now discuss the contribution of engineering to medicine. There are many theories of economics.

**top|i|nam|bour** (top′ə nam′bər), *n.* = Jerusalem artichoke. [< French *topinambour,* alteration of Middle French *tompinambou,* (originally) the name of a tribe in Brazil]

**top kick**, *U.S. Slang.* **1** a top or first sergeant. **2** a person in authority; leader; boss. [< *top*[1] + *-kick,* as in *side-kick*]

**top|knot** (top′not′), *n.* **1** a knot or tuft of hair on the top of the head of a person or animal. **2** a plume or crest of feathers on the head of a bird. **3a** a knot or bow of ribbon worn by women as a headdress. **b** a bow of ribbon worn in a lace cap.

**top|less** (top′lis), *adj.* **1** having no top; immeasurably high: *The abysses we skirted ... seemed bottomless, and the mountain itself topless* (New Yorker). **2a** lacking an upper part or piece: *a topless bathing suit.* **b** wearing a topless garment: *a topless dancer.* **c** employing waitresses or entertainers who wear topless garments: *a topless bar.* **3** lofty; exalted: *Topless honours be bestowed on thee* (George Chapman). —**top′less-ness**, *n.*

**top-lev|el** (top′lev′əl), *adj. Informal.* at the highest level, as of authority, rank, or quality: *a top-level committee meeting.*

**top line**, the headline of a newspaper or other publication.

**top-line** (top′līn′), *adj. Informal.* of the highest rank or quality; leading; foremost; headline.

**top-lin|er** (top′lī′nər), *n. Informal.* a person or thing that is top-line; at the head, or in the first or principal place.

**top|loft|y** (top′lôf′tē, -lof′-), *adj. Informal.* lofty in character or manner; high and mighty; haughty; pompous; pretentious. —**top′loft′i|ly**, *adv.* —**top′-loft′i|ness**, *n.*

**top|mak|er** (top′mā′kər), *n.* a person who makes or deals in woolen or worsted tops.

**top making**, the process of making woolen or worsted tops on a machine by combing the sliver to make the fibers lie parallel to one another.

**top|man** (top′mən), *n., pl.* **-men.** *Nautical.* a man stationed for duty in a top.

**top|mast** (top′mast′, -mäst′; *Nautical.* top′məst), *n.* the second section of a mast above the deck; a smaller mast fixed at the top of a lower mast.

**top minnow**, or **top|min|now** (top′min′ō), *n., pl.* **-nows** or (*collectively*) **-now.** any one of various small, soft-finned fishes that feed on the surface of the water and bring forth their young alive.

**top|most** (top′mōst), *adj.* highest; uppermost: *the topmost branches of a tree.*

**top-notch** or **top|notch** (top′noch′), *adj. Informal.* first-rate; best possible: *a top-notch show, a top-notch storyteller.* **SYN:** supreme, incomparable.

**top|notch|er** (top′noch′ər), *n. Informal.* a first-rate person or thing.

**topo-**, *combining form.* place: *Toponym* = *a place name.* Also, **top-** before vowels. [< Greek *tópos*]

**top-of-the-world** (top′əv ᴛʜə wėrld′), *adj.* of or having to do with the north polar regions.

**topog.**, **1** topographical. **2** topography.

**top|o|graph** (top′ə graf, -gräf), *n.* an X-ray photograph of the surface features of an object, such as a crystal.

**to|pog|ra|pher** (tə pog′rə fər), *n.* **1** an expert in topography. **2** a person who accurately describes the surface features of a place or region.

**top|o|graph|ic** (top′ə graf′ik), *adj.* = topographical.

**top|o|graph|i|cal** (top′ə graf′ə kəl), *adj.* of or having to do with topography: *topographical features.* —**top′o|graph′i|cal|ly**, *adv.*

**topographical** or **topographic map**, a map that shows elevations as well as the positions of mountains, rivers, and other features, often in color and with contour lines.

**to|pog|ra|phy** (tə pog′rə fē), *n., pl.* **-phies. 1** the science of making an accurate and detailed description or drawing of places or their surface features. **2** a detailed description or drawing of the surface features of a place or region. **3** the surface features of a place or region. The topography of a region includes hills, valleys, streams, lakes, bridges, tunnels, and roads. **4** the surface features of any object or structure: *the topography of a quartz crystal, the topography of the brain.*

[< Late Latin *topographia* < Greek *topographíā* < *topográphos* topographer < *tópos* place + *gráphein* to write]

**top|o|log|ic** (top′ə loj′ik), *adj.* = topological.

**top|o|log|i|cal** (top′ə loj′ə kəl), *adj.* of or having to do with topology. —**top′o|log′i|cal|ly**, *adv.*

**to|pol|o|gist** (tə pol′ə jist), *n.* an expert in topology.

**to|pol|o|gy** (tə pol′ə jē), *n.* **1** the topographical study of a particular locality in order to learn the relationship between its topography and its history. **2** the anatomy of a certain area of the body. **3** *Geometry.* the study of the properties of figures or solids that are not normally affected by changes in size or shape. **4** the surface structure or arrangement of parts of any object: *the topology of a microelectronic device, the topology of a plant cell.*

**top|o|nym** (top′ə nim), *n.* **1a** a place name; regional name. **b** a name derived from the name of a place or location. **2** *Obsolete.* any area of the body of an animal, as distinguished from any organ. [< *top-* + dialectal Greek *ónyma* name]

**top|o|nym|ic** (top′ə nim′ik), *adj.* of or having to do with toponymy.

**top|o|nym|i|cal** (top′ə nim′ə kəl), *adj.* = toponymic.

**to|pon|y|mist** (tə pon′ə mist), *n.* a person who studies place names.

**to|pon|y|my** (tə pon′ə mē), *n.* **1** the place names of a country or district as a subject of study. **2** *Obsolete.* the naming or the names of areas of the body.

**to|pos** (tō′pos), *n., pl.* **-poi** (-poi). a commonplace notion; stereotyped expression. [< Greek *tópos* place; (in rhetoric) a commonplace]

**top-out** (top′out′), *n.* the completion of the skeleton structure of a building being erected: *Theoretically, a top-out can occur at any part of the working day, but, frankly, contractors like to arrange things so it falls toward the end of the afternoon* (New Yorker).

**top|per** (top′ər), *n.* **1** *Informal.* a top hat. **2** *Informal.* a topcoat. **3** a loose-fitting, short, usually lightweight coat, worn by women. **4** *Informal.* something that tops or surpasses the preceding thing or things: *The story has a topper. A pause and Mr. King hammers home the topper: "He's frostbitten"* (New York Times). **5** *Especially British Informal.* an excellent, first-rate person or thing. **6** a person or thing that tops.

**top|ping** (top′ing), *n., adj.* —*n.* **1** anything forming the top of something. **2** something put on the top of anything to complete it, especially a garnish, sauce, or icing put on food. **3** the cutting off of the top (of a tree or plant). **4a** the forelock of the hair of the head. **b** the forelock of a horse or other animal. **c** the crest of a bird. **d** the erect tassel of a Scottish cap. **e** the head (a humorous use). **5** the distillation of crude oil to separate it into its fractions.

—*adj.* **1** *Especially British Informal.* excellent; first-rate. **2a** chief; principal. **b** fine; pretty (often used ironically). **3** *Obsolete.* that exceeds in height; surpassingly high.

**toppings**, branches or stems cut off in topping trees or plants: *to use toppings to make a fire.*

**topping lift**, *Nautical.* a rope used to support or raise the outer end of a spanker boom or a lower studdingsail boom.

**top|ple** (top′əl), *v.*, **-pled, -pling.** —*v.i.* **1** to fall forward; tumble down: *The chimney toppled over on the roof.* **2** to lean or hang over in an unsteady way: *beneath toppling crags.* **SYN:** teeter.

—*v.t.* to throw over or down; overturn: *The wind toppled the tree. The wrestler toppled his opponent.* [< *top*[1], verb + *-le*]

**Pronunciation Key:** hat, āge, cãre, fär; let, ēqual, tėrm; it, īce; hot, ōpen, ôrder; **oi**l, **ou**t; cup, pu̇t, rüle; **ch**ild; lo**ng**; **th**in; **ᴛʜ**en; **zh**, measure;
**ə** represents **a** in about, **e** in taken, **i** in pencil, **o** in lemon, **u** in circus.

**top-pri|or|i|ty** (top′prī ôr′ə tē, -or′-), *adj.* having the highest priority: *Education must be a top-priority program in every government.*

**top-qual|i|ty** (top′kwol′ə tē), *adj.* of the highest or best quality: *Its heartening feature is that the few top-quality papers are going up in circulation even though they may raise their prices a bit from time to time* (New Yorker).

**top-rank** (top′rangk′), *adj.* of the highest rank or recognition: *top-rank musicians.*

**top-ranked** (top′rangkt′), *adj.* given the highest rank or rating.

**top-rank|ing** (top′rang′king), *adj.* holding the highest rank or rating.

**top-rat|ed** (top′rā′tid), *adj.* holding the highest rating.

**top round**, a cut of meat from the inside of a round of beef. See picture under **beef**[1].

**tops** (tops), *adj., n. Slang.* —*adj.* of the highest degree in quality or excellence.
—*n.* **the tops**, an excellent or outstanding person or thing: *That teacher is the tops.*

**TOPS** (tops), *n.* thermoelectric outer planet spacecraft: *As early as 1968, NASA began working on TOPS . . . a craft that could undertake a journey of 3 billion miles through the asteroid belt to the farthest planet, Pluto* (Science News).

**top|sail** (top′sāl′; *Nautical* top′səl), *n.* **1** a sail attached to a yard on a topmast of a square-rigged ship; upper topsail or lower topsail. **2** a square sail on the topmast of certain schooners, especially on the foremast. **3** = gaff-topsail.

**top secret**, *U.S.* a most important and highly guarded secret.

**top-se|cret** (top′sē′krit), *adj. U.S.* of utmost secrecy; extremely confidential: *intelligence from top-secret sources.*

**top-seed|ed** (top′sē′did), *adj.* given the best position in a seeded list, as in a tennis or other tournament; top-ranked.

**top-sell|ing** (top′sel′ing), *adj. Informal.* best-selling.

**top sergeant**, *U.S. Informal.* the first sergeant of a military company; top kick.

**top shell**, any of a group of marine mollusks with a spiral, regularly conical, shell.

**top|side** (top′sīd′), *n., adv., adj.* —*n.* **1** Also, **topsides. a** the upper part of a ship's side, especially the part above the water line. **b** the upper part of a ship, especially the part above the main deck, as distinct from the engine room, hold, etc. **2** *British.* the outer side of a round of beef. **3** the upper side or highest level of anything.
—*adv.* **1** to, toward, or on the bridge or upper deck: *The captain ordered the crew topside.* **2** on the top; in the highest position: *to sit topside at the table.*
—*adj.* **1** of the topside; situated on the topside: *a topside cabin, a topside officer.* **2** *Informal.* of the highest level or position: *"Wherever we went, we met topside people," Rockefeller said* (New Yorker).

**topside sounder**, any one of a series of artificial satellites designed jointly by the United States and Canada to obtain data on the ionosphere by measuring the reflected signals of radio waves beamed down into the atmosphere.

**top|soil** (top′soil′), *n., v.* —*n.* **1** the upper part of the soil; surface soil: *Farmers need rich topsoil for their crops.* **2** loam or other earth from or in this part of the soil, usually consisting of sand, clay, and decayed organic matter: *a load of good topsoil.*
—*v.t.* **1** to remove the topsoil from (land). **2** to cover with topsoil.

**top|spin** (top′spin′), *n.* a forward rolling motion given to a ball in the direction of its flight or roll, as in tennis or billiards. A baseball pitcher who throws a drop gives the ball topspin to make it curve down. *His game, emphasizing tricky forehand topspin and an undersliced backhand, still had an unorthodox look* (Newsweek).

**Top|sy** (top′sē), *n. Informal.*
**grow like Topsy**, to grow or expand rapidly; burgeon: *The tax relationship between the provincial and dominion governments has grown like Topsy* (Canada Month).
[< *Topsy*, a little slave girl in Harriet Beecher Stowe's *Uncle Tom's Cabin*]

**top|sy-tur|vy** (top′sē tėr′vē), *adv., adj., n., pl.* **-vies.** —*adv.*, *adj.* **1** upside down. **2** *Figurative.* in confusion or disorder: *Her room was always topsy-turvy because she never put anything away. A lively child is a godsend, even if she turns the whole house topsy-turvy* (Harriet Beecher Stowe).
—*n.* confusion; disorder.
[earlier *topsi-tervy*, probably ultimately < *top*[1] + obsolete *terve* overturn, related to Old English *tearflian* roll over] —**top′sy-tur′vi|ly**, *adv.* —**top′sy-tur′vi|ness**, *n.*

**top|sy-tur|vy|dom** (top′sē tėr′vē dəm), *n.* a state of affairs or a place in which everything is topsy-turvy.

**top weight**, the horse carrying the heaviest weight in a race.

**top-weight|ed** (top′wā′tid), *adj.* (of a horse) carrying the heaviest weight as a handicap in a race.

***toque** (tōk), *n.* **1** a hat or (formerly) bonnet or cap without a brim, or with a very small brim, worn by women. **2** a round cap or bonnet, especially of velvet, usually with a plume, formerly worn by men and women. **3** = tuque. [< Middle French *toque*, perhaps < Spanish *toca*, or Portuguese *touca* kerchief, coif, perhaps < Basque *taika* kind of cap, or perhaps < Arabic *ṭāq* < Persian]

definition 1

***toque** definitions 1, 2

definition 2

**to|quil|la** (tō kē′yä, -kēl′yä), *n.* **1** the jipijapa, whose palmlike leaves are used for Panama hats. **2** the fiber or leaves of the jipijapa. [< Spanish *toquilla* (diminutive) < *toca;* see etym. under **toque**]

**tor** (tôr), *n.* a high, rocky, or craggy hill, knoll, etc. [Old English *torr*, apparently < Celtic (compare Welsh *twr* heap, pile, Gaelic *tòrr* conical hill, burial mound)]

**to|rah** (tôr′ə, tōr′-), *n., pl.* **to|roth** or **to|rahs.** in Jewish usage: **1** Also, **Torah. a** the Old Testament. **b** the Mosaic law; Pentateuch: *to study the torah, to read the Torah in the synagogue.* **c** a parchment scroll on which the Pentateuch is written: *to take a torah out of the ark.* **d** the body of Jewish teachings and traditions, including the Talmud and later rabbinical commentaries and codes. **2a** any instruction, law, or judicial decision. **b** divine revelation, as manifested in judicial decisions. [< Hebrew *tōrāh* (literally) instruction, law]

**tor|bern|ite** (tôr′bər nīt), *n.* a mineral, a hydrated phosphate of uranium and copper, found in bright-green, tabular crystals; chalcolite. It is a minor ore of uranium. *Formula:* $CuU_2P_2O_{12} \cdot 12H_2O$ [< German *Torbernit* < *Torbernus*, a Latinization of *Torbern* Bergman, 1735-1784, a Swedish chemist + German *-it* - ite[1]]

**torc** (tôrk), *n.* = torque (def. 3).

**torch** (tôrch), *n., v.* —*n.* **1a** a light to be carried around or stuck in a holder on a wall. A piece of pinewood, or anything that burns easily, makes a good torch. *The Statue of Liberty holds a torch.* SYN: firebrand. **b** a lamp carried or supported on a pole. **2** a device for producing a very hot flame, used especially to burn off paint, to solder metal, and to melt metal, such as an acetylene torch or blowtorch. **3** *British.* a flashlight. **4** *Figurative.* something thought of as a source of enlightenment or guidance: *the torch of civilization, the torch of liberty.* SYN: lodestar.
—*v.t.* **1** to furnish, or light, with a torch: (*Figurative.*) *we sit, watching sunlight torch the wooded west* (New York Times). **2** (in plastering) to point the inside joints of (slating) with a mixture of lime and hair.
—*v.i.* **1** to flare like a torch; rise like smoke from a torch: *"Law! how them clouds torch up, we shall have rain"* (James Halliwell). **2** *U.S.* to catch fish, or hunt, by torchlight.
**carry a** (or **the**) **torch**, *Slang.* **a** to be in love, especially without being loved in return: *He has been carrying the torch for her for months.* **b** to crusade (for); campaign (for a cause): *Oddly enough, it is Coronel's younger brother, Rafael, who is carrying the torch for a new Mexican art* (Saturday Review).
**hand on the torch**, to pass on the tradition; continue or perpetuate the custom, practice, or belief: *Those* [*sonnets*] *handed on the torch of courtly love for good and ill to the Elizabethans* (C. C. Abbott).
[< Old French *torche* (originally) a twisted thing; a torch formed of a wick dipped in wax, probably < Vulgar Latin *torca* < Latin *torquēre* to twist] —**torch′like′**, *adj.*

**torch|bear|er** (tôrch′bãr′ər), *n.* **1** a person who carries a torch. **2** *Figurative.* a leader of a cause or movement; standardbearer: *Local 3 has made itself the torchbearer in labor's drive for a shorter work week* (Atlantic).

**torched** (tôrcht), *adj.* furnished with or lighted by torches.

**tor|chère** (tôr′shãr′), *n.* a tall, ornamental candlestick or lamp stand. [< French *torchère* < Old French *torche;* see etym. under **torch**]

**torch|fish** (tôrch′fish′), *n., pl.* **-fish|es** or (*collectively*) **-fish.** a deep-sea fish with a dorsal spine carrying a shiny bulb like a torch above the head.

**torch|light** (tôrch′līt′), *n., adj.* —*n.* the light of a torch or torches.
—*adj.* carrying or lighted by torchlights: *torchlight parades the night before football games* (Harper's).

**tor|chon lace** (tôr′shon), **1** a handmade linen lace with loosely twisted threads in simple, open patterns. **2** a machine-made imitation of this in linen or cotton. [< French *torchon* dish or dust cloth < Old French *torche;* see etym. under **torch**]

**torch singer**, a singer of torch songs: *So began a four-year career as a torch singer, which took her into the spotlights of Manhattan's flossiest nightclub* (Time).

**torch song**, a sad love song, especially of unrequited love: *singing in deep and straightforward tones, a collection of old-time torch songs* (New Yorker).

**torch|wood** (tôrch′wůd′), *n.* **1** any one of various resinous woods for making torches. **2** a tree yielding such wood.

**torch|y** (tôr′chē), *adj.,* **torch|i|er, torch|i|est.** of, having to do with, or characteristic of a torch song or a torch singer: *Pop tunes of a torchy temper, sung with a fine ear for theatrical effect* (Time).

**tore**[1] (tôr, tōr), *v.* the past tense of **tear**[2]: *She tore her dress on a nail yesterday.*

**tore**[2] (tôr, tōr), *n. Architecture, Geometry.* torus. [< Middle French *tore*, learned borrowing from Latin *torus.* See etym. of doublet **torus.**]

**tor|e|a|dor** (tôr′ē ə dôr), *n.* a man who fights a bull in an arena; bullfighter, especially one mounted on a horse (a term no longer used in Spanish bullfighting). [< Spanish *toreador* < *torear* to fight in a bullfight < *toro* bull < Latin *taurus*]

***toreador pants**, snug-fitting trousers ending at mid-calf, worn by women.

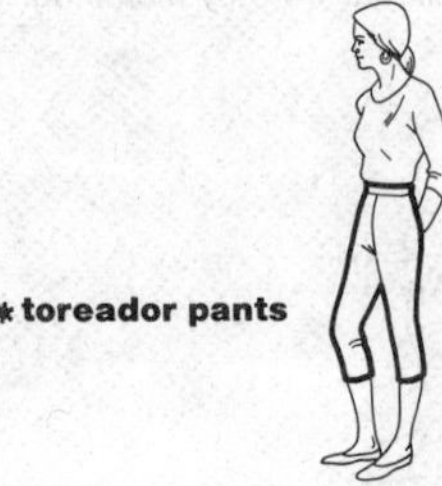

***toreador pants**

**to|re|ro** (tō rā′rō), *n., pl.* **-re|ros** (-rā′rōs). a bullfighter who is not mounted, such as a matador or a banderillero. [< Spanish *torero* < *torear;* see etym. under **toreador**]

**to|reu|tic** (tə rü′tik), *adj.* of or having to do with the ancient art of working in metal or ivory, including embossing, chasing, and working in relief. [< Greek *toreutikós* < *toreúein*, variant of *torneúein* to work in relief, chase < *tórnos* a carpenter's tool or lathe]

**to|reu|tics** (tə rü′tiks), *n.* the toreutic art.

**to|ri** (tôr′ī, tōr′-), *n.* plural of **torus.**

**tor|ic** (tôr′ik, tōr′-), *adj.* **1** of or having to do with a toric lens. **2** *Geometry.* of or having to do with a torus; shaped like a torus.

**toric lens**, an optical lens with a surface forming a part of a geometrical torus, used in eyeglasses because it refracts differently in different meridians.

***to|ri|i** (tôr′ē ē, tōr′-), *n., pl.* **-ri|i.** a gateway at the entrance to a Japanese Shinto shrine, built of two uprights and two crosspieces. [< Japanese *torii* < *tori* bird + *i* a roost (because the structure was a roosting spot for birds)]

***torii**

**to|ril** (tō rēl′), *n.* an enclosed stall where the bull is kept before a bullfight. [< Spanish *toril*]

**tor|ment** (*v.* tôr ment′; *n.* tôr′ment), *v., n.* —*v.t.* **1** to cause very great pain to: *Severe headaches tormented him. Like a hedgehog rolled up the*

*wrong way Tormenting himself with his prickles* (Thomas Hood). **2** to worry or annoy very much: *She torments everyone with silly questions.* **SYN**: tease, plague, harrass. **3** = torture. [Middle English *turmenten* < Old French *tormenter,* and *turmenter* < *torment;* see the noun]
—*n.* **1** a cause of very great pain: *A bad burn can be a torment. Instruments of torture were torments.* **2** very great pain; agony; torture: *years Dark with torment and with tears* (Emily Brontë). *He suffered torments from his aching teeth.* **SYN**: anguish, misery, distress. **3** a cause of great worry or annoyance.
[Middle English *turment* torture, pain; torsion machine < Old French *torment,* learned borrowing from Latin *tormentum* twisted sling, rack, related to *torquēre* to twist]
—*Syn. v.t.* **1 Torment, torture** mean to cause physical or mental pain. **Torment** implies repeated punishment or incessant harassment: *He is tormented by a racking cough.* **Torture** implies the infliction of acute and protracted suffering: *The civilized nations do not believe in torturing prisoners.*

**tor|ment|er** (tôr men′tər), *n.* = tormentor.

**tor|men|til** (tôr′men təl), *n.* a low European and Asian herb of the rose family, with yellow flowers having four petals, and a strongly astringent root used in medicine, tanning, and dyeing; bloodroot. [< Old French *tormentille,* learned borrowing from Medieval Latin *tormentilla,* apparently (diminutive) < Latin *tormentum;* see etym. under **torment** (because it supposedly relieved the gripes)]

**tor|ment|ing** (tôr men′ting), *adj.* that torments. —**tor|ment′ing|ly,** *adv.* —**tor|ment′ing|ness,** *n.*

**tor|men|tor** (tôr men′tər), *n.* **1** a person or thing that torments. **2** a curtain or flat on either side of the stage at the front, filling the space between the proscenium arch and the scenery and blocking the audience's view into the wings. **3** a screen covered with special material and used in motion-picture studios to prevent echo in sound recording. Also, **tormenter.**

**tor|men|tress** (tôr men′tris), *n.* a woman tormentor.

**torn** (tôrn, tōrn), *v.* the past participle of **tear**[2]: *They have torn up the plants by the roots. His coat was old and torn.*

**tor|nad|ic** (tôr nad′ik), *adj.* of or like a tornado: *The tornadic winds raked 12 square blocks in Galveston, demolishing houses and strewing debris* (Wall Street Journal).

**tor|na|do** (tôr nā′dō), *n., pl.* **-does** or **-dos. 1a** an extremely violent and destructive whirlwind. A tornado extends down from a mass of dark clouds as a whirling funnel and moves over the land in a narrow path. **b** any extremely violent windstorm. **2** a violent, whirling squall occurring during the summer on the west coast of Africa. **3** *Figurative.* any violent outburst: *a tornado of anger. In the fifteenth century a last tornado of nomadism arose in Western Turkestan* (H. G. Wells). **4** *Obsolete.* a violent thunderstorm of the tropical. Atlantic, with torrential rain. [probably alteration of Spanish *tronada* < *tronar* to thunder < Latin *tonāre;* apparently influenced by Spanish *tornar* to turn, twist < Latin *tornāre*]

**tornado lantern,** = hurricane lamp.

**tor|nil|lo** (tôr nil′ō, -nē′yō), *n., pl.* **-los.** = screw bean. [American English < American Spanish *tornillo* (in Spanish, a screw, diminutive) < *torno* a turn < *tornar* to turn < Latin *tornāre*]

**to|ro** (tō′rō), *n.* a bull, especially one used in bullfighting. [< Spanish *toro* < Latin *taurus*]

**to|roid** (tôr′oid, tōr′-), *n. Geometry.* **1** a surface described by the revolution of any closed plane curve about an axis in its own plane. **2** the solid enclosed by such a surface. [< *tor(e)*[2] + *-oid*]

**to|roi|dal** (tô roi′dəl, tō-), *adj.* of, having to do with, or characteristic of a toroid: *In this twisted toroidal field the effect of particle drift is much reduced* (Scientific American). —**to|roi′dal|ly,** *adv.*

**To|ron|to|ni|an** (tə ron′tō′nē ən, tor′on-), *n.* a native or inhabitant of Toronto, Canada.

**to|rose** (tôr′ōs, tōr′-; tô rōs′, tō-), *adj.* **1** *Botany.* cylindrical, with bulges or constrictions at intervals; swelling in knobs at intervals. **2** bulging; protuberant; knobbed: *torose muscles.* [< Latin *torōsus* bulging, brawny < *torus* a torus, bulge]

**to|roth** (tô rōth′, tō-), *n.* a plural of **torah.**

***tor|pe|do** (tôr pē′dō), *n., pl.* **-does,** *v.,* **-doed, -do|ing.** —*n.* **1** a large, cigar-shaped shell that contains explosives and travels through water by its own power. Torpedoes are sent under water from a submarine, surface vessel, or low-flying aircraft to blow up enemy ships. **2** an underwater mine, shell, or other device that explodes when hit. **3** an explosive device put on a railroad track that makes a loud noise for a signal when a wheel of the engine runs over it. **4** a firework consisting of an explosive and gravel wrapped in thin paper. It makes a bang when it is thrown against something hard. *Children used to play with torpedoes on the Fourth of July.* **5** *U.S.* an explosive enclosed in a tube and set off in an oil well to renew or increase the flow. **6** *U.S.* (formerly in military use) any one of various encased charges of explosive, especially an underground mine. **7** a fish that can give an electric shock; electric ray. **8** *Slang.* a hired gunman. **9** *U.S. Slang.* hero sandwich.
—*v.t.* **1** to attack, hit, or destroy with a torpedo or torpedoes. **2** to set off a torpedo in or against. **3** *Figurative.* to bring completely to an end; destroy: *to torpedo a peace conference.*
[< Latin *torpēdō* the electric ray (a fish); (originally) numbness (because of the ray's effect) < *torpēre* be numb or torpid] —**tor|pe′do|like′,** *adj.*

***torpedo**
definition 1

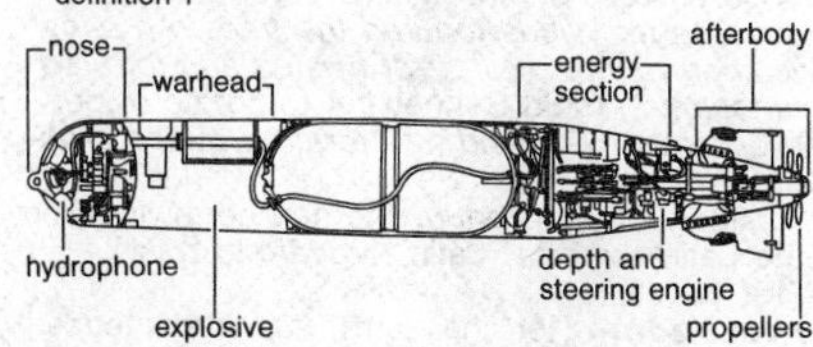


**torpedo boat,** a small, fast warship used for attacking with torpedoes.

**tor|pe|do-boat destroyer** (tôr pē′dō bōt′), a ship larger, faster, and more heavily armed than a torpedo boat, used to destroy torpedo boats.

**torpedo body,** a style of automobile body in which all side surfaces including fenders are flush.

**tor|pe|do|man** (tôr pē′dō man′), *n., pl.* **-men.** a U.S. Navy warrant officer in charge of the maintenance and repair of torpedoes and submarine equipment.

**torpedo plane,** an airplane for carrying and releasing self-propelled torpedoes.

**torpedo tube,** a tube through which a torpedo is sent out, as from a submarine or torpedo boat, either by an explosive charge or by compressed air.

**tor|pid**[1] (tôr′pid), *adj.* **1** dull, inactive, or sluggish: *It is a man's own fault ... if his mind grows torpid in old age* (Samuel Johnson). **SYN**: lethargic, apathetic. **2** not moving or feeling; dormant. Animals that hibernate become torpid in winter. **3** = numb. [< Latin *torpidus* < *torpēre* be numb] —**tor′pid|ly,** *adv.* —**tor′pid|ness,** *n.*

**tor|pid**[2] (tôr′pid), *n.* **1** an eight-oared, clinker-built boat rowed in the Lent races at Oxford. **2** a member of the crew of such a boat.
**torpids,** the Lent races at Oxford: *A suggestion of cancelling the torpids was defeated* (London Times).
[< earlier *torpid*[1] (*boat*) the second boat of a college (because it was slower than the varsity boat)]

**tor|pid|i|ty** (tôr pid′ə tē), *n., pl.* **-ties.** torpid condition.

**tor|por** (tôr′pər), *n.* **1** torpid condition or quality; apathy; lethargy; listlessness; dullness: *My calmness was the torpor of despair* (Charles Brockden Brown). **SYN**: stupor. **2** the absence or suspension of movement or feeling, as of a hibernating animal; dormancy. [< Latin *torpor, -ōris* < *torpēre* be numb]

**tor|por|if|ic** (tôr′pə rif′ik), *adj.* causing torpor.

**tor|quate** (tôr′kwit, -kwāt), *adj. Zoology.* ringed with hair or feathers around the neck; collared. [< Latin *torquātus* wearing a torque < *torquēs;* see etym. under **torque**]

**torque** (tôrk), *n., v.,* **torqued, torqu|ing.** —*n.* **1** a force causing rotation or torsion. **2** *Physics.* the moment of a system of forces causing rotation: *The power produced by an automobile engine consists of speed and torque.* **3** a necklace of twisted metal: *The ancient Gauls and Britons wore torques.* **4** *Optics.* the rotational effect produced by certain liquids or crystals on the plane of polarization of plane-polarized light passing through them.
—*v.t., v.i.* to apply torque to an axle, bolt, wheel, or the like.
[< Latin *torquēs* twisted neck chain < *torquēre* to twist] —**torqu′er,** *n.*

**torque converter** or **convertor,** a hydraulic device for altering the torque and speed delivered by a driving shaft to the ratio required by a driven shaft. Certain automobiles with automatic transmission use torque converters.

**torqued** (tôrkt), *adj.* twisted; convoluted; formed like a torque.

**Tor|que|ma|da** (tôr′kə mä′də), *n.* an intolerant and cruel inquisitor or prosecutor. [< *Torquemada,* 1420-1498, a leader in the Spanish Inquisition]

**tor|ques** (tôr′kwēz), *n. Zoology.* a ringlike band or marking around the neck of an animal, as of hair or feathers of a special color or texture; collar. [< Latin *torquēs;* see etym. under **torque**]

**torr** (tôr), *n., pl.* **torr.** a unit of pressure equivalent to the amount of pressure that will support a column of mercury one millimeter high; 1/760 of an atmosphere; 1333.22 microbars. [< Evangelista *Torr*(icelli), 1608-1647, an Italian mathematician and physicist]

**tor|re|fac|tion** (tôr′ə fak′shən, tor′-), *n.* **1** the act or process of torrefying. **2** the state of being torrefied.

**tor|re|fy** (tôr′ə fī, tor′-), *v.t.,* **-fied, -fy|ing.** to dry or parch with heat; dry out; roast: *torrefied drugs, torrefied metallic ores.* **SYN**: bake. [< Latin *torrēfacere* < *torrēre* to parch + *facere* make]

**Tor|rens system** (tôr′ənz, tor′-), a system of registering titles of real estate, designed to simplify the transfer of land, used especially in the British Commonwealth and in Europe. [< Sir Robert R. *Torrens,* 1814-1884, an Irish-born Australian politician, who introduced it in South Australia in 1858]

**tor|rent** (tôr′ənt, tor′-), *n., adj.* —*n.* **1** a violent, rushing stream of water: *The mountain torrent dashed over the rocks.* **2** a heavy downpour: *The rain came down in a torrent during the thunderstorm.* **3** *Figurative.* any violent, rushing stream; flood: *a torrent of lava from a volcano, a torrent of abuse, a torrent of questions.* **SYN**: inundation.
—*adj.* rushing like a torrent; torrential.
[< Latin *torrēns, -entis* a rushing stream; boiling; (originally) present participle of *torrēre* to parch]

**tor|ren|tial** (tô ren′shəl, to-), *adj.* of, caused by, or like a torrent: *torrential rains,* (*Figurative.*) *a torrential flow of words.* **SYN**: raging, tumultuous. —**tor|ren′tial|ly,** *adv.*

**Tor|ri|cel|li's law** or **theorem** (tôr′ə sel′ēz, -chel′-), a principle in hydrodynamics which states that the velocity with which a liquid flows through an opening in a container equals the velocity of a body falling from the surface of the liquid to the opening. [< Evangelista *Torricelli,* 1608-1647, an Italian mathematician and physicist, who developed the principle]

**tor|rid** (tôr′id, tor′-), *adj.* **1** very hot; burning; scorching: *torrid weather. July is usually a torrid month.* **2** exposed or subject to great heat: *torrid deserts.* **3** *Figurative.* very ardent; passionate: *a torrid love scene.* [< Latin *torridus* < *torrēre* to parch] —**tor′rid|ly,** *adv.* —**tor′rid|ness,** *n.*

**tor|rid|i|ty** (tô rid′ə tē, to-), *n.* extreme heat.

**Tor|ri|do|ni|an** (tôr′ə dō′nē ən), *n., adj. Geology.* —*n.* the sedimentary Pre-Cambrian sandstone occurring in northwestern Scotland.
—*adj.* of or having to do with this sandstone.
[< Loch *Torridon,* Scotland]

**Torrid Zone,** the very warm region between the two Temperate Zones and bounded by the tropic of Cancer and the tropic of Capricorn; the tropics. The equator divides the Torrid Zone. *Most of Brazil is in the Torrid Zone.*

**tor|ri|fac|tion** (tôr′ə fak′shən, tor′-), *n.* = torrefaction.

**tor|ri|fy** (tôr′ə fī, tor′-), *v.t.,* **-fied, -fy|ing.** = torrefy.

**tor|sade** (tôr säd′), *n.* **1** a twisted fringe, cord, or ribbon, used as an ornament in headdresses and curtains. **2** a carved or molded ornament like this. [< French *torsade* < Old French *tors* twisted, ultimately < Latin *torquēre* to twist]

**tor|sel** (tôr′səl), *n.* = tassel[2].

**tor|si|bil|i|ty** (tôr′sə bil′ə tē), *n.* **1** the capability of being twisted. **2** the tendency to straighten out after being twisted.

**tor|sion** (tôr′shən), *n.* **1** the act or process of twisting. **2** the condition of being twisted. **3** the twisting or turning of a body by two equal and opposite forces. **4** the tendency of a twisted object to straighten out. [< Old French *torsion,* learned borrowing from Late Latin *torsiō, -ōnis* torture, torment < Latin *tortiō, -ōnis* < *torquēre* to twist] —**tor′sion|less,** *adj.*

**tor|sion|al** (tôr′shə nəl), *adj.* of, having to do with, or resulting from torsion: *torsional rubber spring suspension.* —**tor′sion|al|ly,** *adv.*

**torsion balance,** an instrument for measuring small, horizontal forces by the amount of torsion they cause in a wire.

**torsion bar,** a type of suspension used in an automobile, resembling a coiled spring that has been straightened out into a rod. When the automobile goes over a bump, the shock is absorbed along the line of the bar by a series of twisting motions.

**torsk** (tôrsk), *n., pl.* **torsks** or (*collectively*) **torsk.**

---

**Pronunciation Key:** hat, āge, cãre, fär; let, ēqual, tėrm; it, īce; hot, ōpen, ôrder; oil, out; cup, pu̇t, rüle; child; long; thin; ᴛʜen; zh, measure; ə represents a in about, e in taken, i in pencil, o in lemon, u in circus.

1 = cusk (def. 1). 2 = cod[1] (def. 1). [< Scandinavian (compare dialectal Norwegian *torsk,* or *tosk*)]

**tor|so** (tôr′sō), *n., pl.* **-sos, -si** (-sē). **1** the trunk of the human body. **2** the trunk or body of a statue without any head, arms, or legs. **3** *Figurative.* something left mutilated or unfinished. [< Italian *torso* (originally) stalk, stump < Vulgar Latin *tursus,* for Latin *thyrsus* stalk < Greek *thýrsos*]

**tort** (tôrt), *n. Law.* any wrong, harm, or injury for which the injured party has the right to sue for damages in a civil court, with the exception of a breach of contract: *Torts include someone's trespassing on your land or using your idea for a movie script* (Harry Kalven, Jr.). [< Old French *tort* < Medieval Latin *tortum* injustice < Latin *torquēre* turn awry, twist]

**tor|te** (tôr′tə, tôrt), *n., pl.* **tor|ten** (tôr′tən), **tor|tes.** **1** a rich cake made with beaten egg whites, nuts, fruit, and little flour. **2** a cake with thin layers of custard, sometimes preserved fruit, and chocolate. [< German *Torte* < Late Latin *tōrta* flat cake]

**tor|tel|li|ni** (tôr′tə lē′nē), *n.pl.* small, round pieces of dough filled with chopped meat and cooked in boiling water. [< Italian *tortellini,* ultimately < Late Latin *tōrta* flat cake]

**tort|fea|sor** (tôrt′fē′zər), *n. Law.* a person who is guilty of a tort; wrongdoer. [< Old French *tortfesor, tortfaiseur,* < *tort* tort + *faiseur* doer < *fais-,* stem of *faire* do < Latin *facere*]

**tor|ti|col|lis** (tôr′tə kol′is), *n.* a muscular disorder in which the neck is twisted and the head turned to one side; wryneck. [< New Latin *torticollis* < Latin *torquēre* to twist + *collum* neck]

**tor|tile** (tôr′təl), *adj.* **1** twisted; coiled; winding. **2** that can be twisted. [< Latin *tortilis* < *torquēre* to twist]

**tor|til|la** (tôr tē′yə), *n.* a thin, flat, round cake made of corn meal, commonly eaten in Spanish America. It is baked on a flat surface and served hot. [American English < American Spanish *tortilla* (diminutive) < Spanish *torta* cake < Late Latin, round loaf < Latin *torquēre* to twist]

**tor|tious** (tôr′shəs), *adj. Law.* having to do with, like, or involving a tort. [earlier, injurious, hurtful < Anglo-French *torcious,* apparently < Old French *torsion,* or *tortion;* see etym. under **torsion**; influenced by English *tort*]

**tor|tive** (tôr′tiv), *adj. Archaic.* twisting; twisted; tortuous. [< Latin *tortīvus* < *torquēre* to twist]

**tor|toise** (tôr′təs), *n., pl.* **-tois|es** or **-toise.** **1a** a turtle living only on land, especially in dry regions. Tortoises have stumpy legs and a high, arched shell. **b** any turtle. **2** *Figurative.* a very slow person or thing. [alteration of Middle English *tortuca* < Medieval Latin, also *tortua,* variant of Vulgar Latin *tartarūca* hellish beast of Tartary; the symbol for heretics; spelling influenced by Latin *tortus* twisted (because of the shape of its feet)]

**tortoise beetle,** a small beetle shaped somewhat like a tortoise.

**tortoise shell,** **1** the mottled, yellow-and-brown shell of some turtles, especially the hawksbill turtle. It is much used for combs and ornaments. **2** any one of several butterflies spotted with yellow and black. **3** = tortoise-shell cat.

**tor|toise-shell** (tôr′təs shel′), *adj.* **1** made of tortoise shell. **2** mottled like a tortoise shell.

**tortoise-shell cat,** a domestic cat with mottled colors like those of tortoise shell.

**tortoise-shell turtle,** = hawksbill turtle.

**tor|to|ni** (tôr tō′nē), *n.* **1** a rich ice cream or mousse, often containing pieces of almond and maraschino cherries. **2** = biscuit tortoni. [< *Tortoni,* the name of an Italian ice-cream manufacturer in Paris during the early 1800's]

**tor|tri|cid** (tôr′trə sid), *adj., n.* — *adj.* of or belonging to a family of small, thick-bodied moths.
— *n.* a tortricid moth.
[< New Latin *Tortricidae* the family name < *Tortrix, -icis* genus name (literally) twister, ultimately < Latin *torquēre* twist (because of the habit of the larvae of rolling leaves up)]

**tor|trix** (tôr′triks), *n.* = tortricid.

**tor|tu|os|i|ty** (tôr′chu̇ os′ə tē), *n., pl.* **-ties.** **1** the quality or condition of being tortuous; twistedness; sinuosity. **2** a twisted or crooked part, passage, or thing. **3** a twist, bend or crook in something.

**tor|tu|ous** (tôr′chu̇ əs), *adj.* **1** full of twists, turns, or bends; twisting; winding; crooked: *We found the river's course very tortuous. We wind through tortuous ravines* (John Tyndall). **SYN**: sinuous, serpentine, zigzag, circuitous. **2** *Figurative.* not direct or straightforward; mentally or morally crooked: *Liars use tortuous reasoning to keep from doing what they don't want to do.* **3** *Geometry.* having no two successive parts in the same plane: *a tortuous curve.* [< Latin *tortuōsus* < *tortus, -ūs* a twisting < *torquēre* to twist] — **tor′tu|ous|ly,** *adv.* — **tor′tu|ous|ness,** *n.*

**tor|ture** (tôr′chər), *n., v.,* **-tured, -tur|ing.** — *n.* **1** the act or fact of inflicting very severe pain. Torture was formerly used to make people give evidence about crimes, or to make them confess. **2a** a very severe pain or suffering; agony: *She suffered tortures from a toothache.* **SYN**: anguish, misery, distress. **b** a cause of severe pain or suffering: *The sight of his sick brother was torture to him.* **3** *Figurative.* a violent and continuous twisting, pushing, or shaking that taxes a thing to the limit: *the torture of a boat by pounding waves.*
— *v.t.* **1** to cause very severe pain or suffering to; torment: *That cruel boy tortures animals. The fear of failure tortured him.* **SYN**: rack, persecute, distress. See syn. under **torment.** **2** *Figurative.* to twist the meaning or form of: *to torture a word, sentence, or idea.* **SYN**: strain, distort, pervert. **3** *Figurative.* to strain, twist, or force out of its natural form: *Winds tortured the trees. An early Victorian room ... full ... of twisted and tortured mahogany* (Arnold Bennett). **4** to puzzle or perplex greatly: *Her mind was tortured by the problem.*
[< Middle French *torture,* learned borrowing from Late Latin *tortūra* < Latin *torquēre* to twist]
— **tor′tur|er,** *n.*

**tor|ture|some** (tôr′chər səm), *adj.* characterized by or causing torture; extremely painful or distressing: *torturesome dreams.*

**tor|tur|ing** (tôr′chər ing), *adj.* that causes anguish; torturous: *torturing jealousy.* — **tor′tur|ing|ly,** *adv.*

**tor|tur|ous** (tôr′chər əs), *adj.* full of, involving, or causing torture; tormenting. **SYN**: excruciating. — **tor′tur|ous|ly,** *adv.*

**tor|u|la** (tôr′ə lə, -yə-; tor′-), *n., pl.* **-lae** (-lē), or **torula yeast,** a yeast rich in vitamins and minerals, grown in a medium made from waste products as of papermaking and fruit canning, and used as a supplement in animal and poultry feeds, and in pharmaceuticals. [< New Latin *torula,* feminine (diminutive) < Latin *torus* torus]

**to|rus** (tôr′əs, tōr′-), *n., pl.* **to|ri.** **1** *Architecture.* a large, convex molding, commonly forming the lowest member of the base of a column; tore. It resembles the astragal, but is much larger. **2** *Botany.* the receptacle of a flower. **3** *Anatomy.* a smooth, rounded swelling; protuberant part; ridge. **4** *Geometry.* **a** a doughnut-shaped surface described by the revolution of a conic section, especially a circle, about a line in the same plane as, but not intersecting, the circle; tore. **b** the solid enclosed by such a surface; tore. [< Latin *torus* (originally) cushion, swelling. See etym. of doublet **tore[2]**.]

**To|ry** (tôr′ē, tōr′-), *n., pl.* **-ries,** *adj.* — *n.* **1** a member of a British political party that favored royal power and the established church and opposed change. Strictly speaking, there has been no Tory party in Britain since about 1832, although members of the Conservative Party are often called Tories. **2** a member of the Conservative Party in Canada. **3** an American who favored British rule over the colonies at the time of the American Revolution; Loyalist. **4** Also, **tory.** a very conservative person. **5** Also **tory.** **a** an Irish outlaw in the 1600's. **b** any armed Irish Roman Catholic or Royalist.
— *adj.* Also, **tory.** of or having to do with Tories or tories: *Tory policy, a Tory convention.*
[< Irish *tōraidhe,* persecuted person; later, Irishmen dispossessed by the English in the 1600's; (originally) pursuer < Old Irish *tóirighim* I pursue]

**To|ry|ism** (tôr′ē iz əm, tōr′-), *n.* **1** a being a Tory. **2** the doctrines or behavior of a Tory.

**tosh** (tosh), *n. British Slang.* bosh; nonsense: *You can't deal with all the tosh if you are going to do justice to the good films* (Sunday Times). [origin uncertain. Compare etym. under **bosh.**]

**Tosk** (tosk), *n.* **1** an Albanian living south of the Shkumbin River. **2** the dialect spoken by such a person.

**toss** (tôs, tos), *v.,* **tossed** or **tost, toss|ing,** *n.* — *v.t.* **1** to throw lightly with the palm upward; cast; fling: *She tossed the ball to the baby.* **SYN**: See syn. under **throw.** **2** to throw about; pitch about: *The ship is tossed by the waves.* **3** to lift or move quickly; throw upward: *She tossed her head. The inexperienced bullfighter was tossed by the bull.* **4** to shake up or about, especially in order to mix the ingredients: *to toss a salad.* **5** *Figurative.* to disturb; agitate; disquiet. **6** *Informal.* to throw (a party or other social gathering).
— *v.i.* **1** to throw, pitch, or move about. **2** to throw a coin or some object in the air to decide something by the side that falls upward: *Let's toss to see who pays the bill.* **3** to throw oneself about in bed; roll restlessly: *He tossed in his sleep all night.* **4** to fling oneself: *He tossed out of the room in anger.*
— *n.* **1** the distance to which something is or can be tossed. **2** a throw; tossing. **3** a pitching about. **4** a throw of a coin to decide something by the side that falls upward, or a decision made by this: *A toss of a coin decided who should play first.* **5** *Obsolete, Figurative.* agitation; commotion.
**toss off, a** to do or make quickly and easily: *He tossed off a poem. Archer ... usually tossed off half a dozen papers with his morning coffee* (Edith Wharton). **b** to drink all at once: *He tossed off a glass of milk.*
[perhaps < Scandinavian (compare dialectal Norwegian *tossa* to strew)] — **toss′a|ble,** *adj.* — **toss′er,** *n.*

**toss bombing,** = loft-bombing.

**tos|sel** (tôs′əl, tos′-), *n.* = tassel[2].

**toss|pot** (tôs′pot′, tos′-), *n.* a heavy drinker; toper; drunkard.

**toss-up** or **toss|up** (tôs′up′, tos′-), *n.* **1** the act of tossing a coin to decide something. **2** *Informal.* an even chance: *It's a toss-up whether or not he'll accept.*

**tost** (tôst, tost), *v.* a past tense and a past participle of **toss.**

**tos|ta|da** (tôs tä′ᴛʜä), *n.* a tortilla fried in deep fat until it becomes crisp. [< Mexican Spanish *tostada,* ultimately < Latin *torrēre* parch. Compare etym. under **toast.**]

**tot[1]** (tot), *n.* **1** a little child. **2** *Especially British.* **a** a small portion of drink; dram. **b** a small quantity of anything. [origin uncertain. Compare Middle English *totte* fool, Danish *tommel-tot* Tom Thumb.]

**tot[2]** (tot), *v.,* **tot|ted, tot|ting,** *n. Informal.* — *v.t.* to find the total or sum of; add or sum (up): *to tot up a bill.* — *v.i.* to amount (to). — *n.* the total of an addition; sum. [shortening of *total*]

**tot.,** total.

**TOT** (no periods), time on target; time over target: *The TOT ... for both raids was 3:45* P.M. (New York Times).

**to|tal** (tō′təl), *adj., n., v.,* **-taled, -tal|ing** or (*especially British*) **-talled, -tal|ling.** — *adj.* **1** being or making up a whole; whole; entire: *The total cost of the house and land will be $25,000.* **SYN**: See syn. under **whole.** **2** complete; absolute; utter: *He is a total failure. The lights went out and we were in total darkness.*
— *n.* the whole amount; sum: *Our expenses reached a total of $100. Add the different sums to get the total.* **SYN**: aggregate.
— *v.t.* **1** to find the sum of; add: *Total that column of figures.* **2** to reach an amount of; amount to: *The money spent yearly on chewing gum totals millions of dollars.* **3** *U.S. Slang.* to wreck beyond repair; destroy totally: *An accident serious enough to "total" a car generally "totals" the occupants as well* (Scientific American).
— *v.i.* **1** to amount (to). **2** *U.S. Slang.* to be wrecked beyond repair; be totally destroyed: *The car almost totaled in the crash.*
[< Medieval Latin *totalis* < Latin *tōtus* all]

**total abstinence,** a complete refraining from drinking alcoholic liquor.

**total depravity,** the theological doctrine of the total unfitness of man for his moral purpose on earth until the stain of original sin is removed by his spiritual rebirth through the influence of the Spirit of God.

**total eclipse,** an eclipse of the sun or moon in which the whole of the disk is obscured.

**total heat,** *Physics.* the quantity of heat required to raise a unit mass of a liquid from a standard or convenient temperature, usually its freezing point, to a given temperature, and then to turn it into vapor at that temperature under constant pressure.

**to|tal|ism** (tō′tə liz əm), *n.* any system or philosophy of absolute control over individuals by the state. [short for *totalitarianism*]

**to|tal|i|tar|i|an** (tō tal′ə tãr′ē ən), *adj., n.* — *adj.* of or having to do with a government controlled by one political group which supresses all opposition, often with force, and which controls many aspects of people's lives. A totalitarian government usually regulates what goods are produced by industry, what radio and television programs are broadcast, what books the people may read, and other severe controls on private life. Nazi Germany and Fascist Italy had totalitarian systems of government. *In a totalitarian state the goal is to serve the needs of an expanding industrial order and the complexities of a bureaucratic government* (Science News Letter).
— *n.* a person in favor of totalitarian principles.
[< *total* + (author)*itarian*]

**to|tal|i|tar|i|an|ism** (tō tal′ə tãr′ē ə niz′əm), *n.* the system, principles, or methods of a totalitarian government: *Nothing is worse than the practice of totalitarianism because nothing that free men do is half so dangerous as the evils which inevitably follow in totalitarianism's wake* (K. F. Pople). **SYN**: autocracy, dictatorship.

**to|tal|i|tar|i|an|ize** (tō tal′ə tãr′ē ə nīz), *v.t.,* **-ized, -iz|ing.** to make totalitarian; put under totalitarian control: *All these schemes can only end by further ... socializing, regimenting, and eventually totalitarianizing our economy* (Newsweek).

**to|tal|i|ty** (tō tal′ə tē), *n., pl.* **-ties.** **1** the total number or amount; total; whole. **2** the quality or condition of being total; entirety. **3a** total obscuration of the sun or moon in an eclipse. **b** the time or duration of this.

**to|tal|i|za|tor** (tō′tə lə zā′tər), *n.* an apparatus for registering totals of operations or measurements, especially one used for pari-mutuel betting at horse races.

**to|tal|ize** (tō′tə līz), *v.t.,* **-ized, -iz|ing.** to make total; combine into a total. —**to′tal|i|za′tion,** *n.*

**to|tal|iz|er** (tō′tə lī′zər), *n.* **1** something that totalizes, such as an adding machine. **2** = totalizator.

**to|tal|ly** (tō′tə lē), *adv.* wholly; entirely; completely; altogether: *We were totally unprepared for a surprise attack.*

**total recall,** the ability to recall things to mind with absolute accuracy: *Summoning his talent for something very like total recall, he began an account of the long ride* (Truman Capote).

**total theater,** a play or other stage production emphasizing theatrical techniques and effects: *He sees in them total theater in which music, words, book, movement, decor blend into a seamless whole* (New York Times).

**total war,** war in which all the resources of a nation, such as manpower, industry, and raw materials, are used in the national interest, and in which attack is made not only on the armed forces of the enemy, but also (subject to certain limitations) on all its civilian people and property.

**to|ta|quine** (tō′tə kwēn, -kwin, -kēn, -kin), *n.* a mixture of alkaloids from certain kinds of cinchona, sometimes used against malaria as a substitute for quinine. [< Latin *tōtus* all (the series of alkaloids of quinine) + English *qu*(inine) + *-ine*[2]]

**to|ta|ra** (tō′tər ə, tō tär′-), *n.* a New Zealand timber tree, a variety of podocarpus, valued for its reddish wood. [< Maori *tótāra*]

**tote**[1] (tōt), *v.,* **tot|ed, tot|ing,** *n. Informal.* —*v.t.* to carry; haul.
—*n.* **1** the act of carrying or hauling. **2** the distance of this; haul: *a long tote.* **3** = tote bag. [American English; origin uncertain] —**tot′er,** *n.*

**tote**[2] (tōt), *v.t.,* **tot|ed, tot|ing.** *U.S. Informal.* Usually, **tote up.** to add up; total: *Columnists and others toted up the pluses and minuses* (New York Times). [short for *total*]

**tote**[3] (tōt), *n. Informal.* a totalizator.

**tote bag,** *U.S.* a large handbag somewhat like a shopping bag in shape and size: *Buyer Babs whips her order book out of what she calls a tote bag, but which to male eyes looks more like a Pony Express letter pouch* (Wall Street Journal).

**tote board,** *Informal.* the display board of a totalizator on which the odds and results of horse races are flashed: *Watching the tote board as it recorded the wagering ... was as fascinating as watching the race* (New Yorker).

**tote box,** *U.S.* a box or container for carrying or storing materials: *Smaller orders are drawn from bins in tote boxes* (Wall Street Journal).

**to|tem** (tō′təm), *n.* **1** (among American Indians) a natural object, often an animal, taken as the emblem of a tribe, clan, or family: *The clan usually considers the totem holy and prays to it. Sometimes the group considers the totem as an ancestor of the clan* (Fred Eggan). **2** the image of a totem. Totems are often carved and painted on poles. **3** *Figurative.* any venerated object: *Someone has suggested that every community has its totems and its taboos* (Emory S. Bogardus). [American English < Algonkian (probably Ojibwa) *ototeman* (literally) his sibling kin]

**to|tem|ic** (tō tem′ik), *adj.* **1** of a totem; having to do with totems. **2** having a totem or totems.
—**to|tem′i|cal|ly,** *adv.*

**to|tem|ism** (tō′tə miz əm), *n.* the use of totems to distinguish tribes, clans, or families.

**to|tem|ist** (tō′tə mist), *n.* a person who belongs to a clan having a totem.

**to|tem|is|tic** (tō′tə mis′tik), *adj.* of or having to do with totemism or totemists.

***totem pole**

***totem pole** or **post,** a pole carved and painted with representations of totems, erected by the Indians of the northwestern coast of North America, especially in front of their houses.

**To|ten|tanz** (tô′tən tänts′), *n. German.* dance of death; danse macabre.

**tote road,** a rough, temporary road for carrying goods to or from a settlement or camp: *I followed the tote road into the woods* (Atlantic).

**toth|er** or **t'oth|er** (tuᴛʜ′ər), *adj., pron. Dialect.* the other. [Middle English *the tother,* misdivision of *that other* the other]

**to|ti|dem ver|bis** (tot′ə dem vėr′bis), *Latin.* in so many words; in these very words.

**to|ti|pal|mate** (tō′tə pal′māt, -mit), *adj.* having all four toes completely webbed, as a pelican. [< Latin *tōtus* whole + English *palmate*]

**to|ti|pal|ma|tion** (tō′tə pal mā′shən), *n.* the condition of being totipalmate.

**to|tip|o|tence** (tō tip′ə təns), *n.* the quality of being totipotent.

**to|tip|o|ten|cy** (tō tip′ə tən sē), *n.* = totipotence.

**to|tip|o|tent** (tō tip′ə tənt), *adj. Biology.* capable of developing into a complete organism: *a totipotent cell.* [< Latin *tōtus* whole + English *potent*]

**to|tis vi|ri|bus** (tō′tis vir′ə bəs), *Latin.* with all one's powers.

**to|to cae|lo** (tō′tō sē′lō), *Latin.* **1** as far apart as the poles; diametrically opposite. **2** (literally) by the whole heavens.

**tot|ter** (tot′ər), *v., n.* —*v.i.* **1** to stand or walk with shaky, unsteady steps: *The old man tottered across the room.* **SYN:** wobble, stagger, reel. **2** to be unsteady; shake as if about to fall or collapse: *Babies totter as they walk.* (*Figurative.*) *The Roman Empire took about 200 years to totter and fall.* **3** to shake; tremble.
—*n.* a tottering: *I ... had his bend in my shoulders, and his totter in my gait* (Samuel Johnson). [Middle English *toteren* swing back and forth on a rope, perhaps < Scandinavian (compare dialectal Norwegian *totra* to quiver)] —**tot′ter|er,** *n.*

**tot|ter|ing** (tot′ər ing), *adj.* that totters. —**tot′ter|ing|ly,** *adv.*

**tot|ter|y** (tot′ər ē), *adj.* tottering; shaky. **SYN:** unsteady, wobbly.

**Toua|reg** (twä′reg), *n., pl.* **-regs** or **-reg.** = Tuareg.

**tou|can** (tü′kan, tü kän′), *n.* a bright-colored bird of tropical America, with an enormous beak. Toucans feed on fruit. They comprise a family of birds. [< French *toucan* < Tupi (Brazil) *tucana*]

**Tou|can** (tü′kan, tü kan′), *n., genitive* **Tou|ca|nis.** a southern constellation. [< *toucan*]

**tou|can|et** (tü′kə net′), *n.* a small green toucan that breeds at high altitudes, found from Mexico to Peru. [< *toucan* + *-et*]

**Tou|ca|nis** (tü kā′nis), *n.* the genitive of **Toucan.**

**touch** (tuch), *v., n.* —*v.t.* **1** to put the hand, finger, or some other part of the body on or against and feel: *She touched the pan to see whether it was still hot.* **2** to put (one thing) against another; make contact with: *He touched the post with his umbrella.* **3** to be against; come against: *Your sleeve is touching the butter. Water touched the dock.* **4a** to border on: *a country that touches the mountains on the north.* **b** *Geometry.* to be tangent to. **5** to strike lightly or gently: *to touch a doorbell. She touched the strings of the harp.* **SYN:** tap. **6** to injure slightly: *The flowers were touched by the frost.* **7** *Figurative.* to affect with some feeling: *The poor woman's sad story touched our hearts.* **SYN:** move. **8** to affect in some way by contact: *a metal so hard that a file cannot touch it.* **9** to wound; hurt: *No soldiers were touched in the skirmish.* **10** to play (an air). **11** to make slightly insane or crazy: *to be touched in the head.* **12** *Figurative.* to have to do with; concern: *The matter touches your interest. The new law does not touch his case.* **13** *Figurative.* to speak of; deal with; refer to; treat lightly: *Our conference touched many points.* **14** to take or taste; handle; use: *The tired man couldn't touch a bit of dinner. He won't touch liquor or tobacco.* **15** *Figurative.* to have to do with in any way; be a party to: *I won't touch that business —it's crooked.* **16** to come up to; reach: *His head almost touches the ceiling. The mercury touched 90 degrees.* **17** to stop at; visit in passing: *The ship touched many ports.* **18** *Slang, Figurative.* **a** to borrow from: *to touch a friend for a dollar.* **b** to get by underhanded means; steal. **19** *Figurative.* to compare with; rival: *No one in our class can touch her in music.* **20** *Figurative.* to mark slightly or superficially, as with some color: *a sky touched with pink.* **21** to mark, draw, or delineate, as with strokes of the brush or pencil. **22** to mark (metal) as of standard purity, with an official stamp, after it has been tested. **23** to lay the hand upon (a diseased person) for the cure of scrofula, as formerly practiced by French and English sovereigns.
—*v.i.* **1** to put the hand, finger, or some other part of the body on or against something: *These glasses are delicate—don't touch!* **2** to come or be in contact: *Our hands touched.* **3** to arrive and make a brief stop: *Most ships touch at that port.* **4** *Figurative.* to speak or write briefly or in passing. **5** to approach closely; verge. [< Old French *touchier* hit, knock < Vulgar Latin *toccāre* strike (as a bell). Compare etym. under **toccata.**]
—*n.* **1** the act of touching or condition of being touched: *A bubble bursts at a touch. The touch of the cold water made her shiver.* **2a** the sense by which a person perceives things by feeling, handling, or coming against them: *The blind develop a keen touch. Some wool is rough to the touch.* **b** the feeling caused by touching something; feel: *Worms and fish have a slimy touch.* **3** the act of coming or condition of being in contact: *the touch of their hands.* **4** *Figurative.* a slight amount; little bit: *a touch of sarcasm, a touch of salt. We had a touch of frost.* **SYN:** trace, tinge, shade, dash. **5a** a light, delicate stroke with a brush, pencil, or pen: *The artist finished my picture with a few touches.* **b** any light stroke or blow. **6** *Figurative.* a detail in any artistic work: *a story with charming poetic touches.* **7** *Figurative.* a close relation of communication, agreement, sympathy, or interest: *Mental patients often lose touch with daily life.* **8a** the act or manner of playing a musical instrument or striking the keys on the keyboard of a machine: *a typist's uneven touch. The girl playing the piano has an excellent touch.* **b** the way the keys of a musical instrument or machine work: *a piano with a stiff touch.* **9** *Figurative.* **a** a distinctive manner or quality; skill in style: *The work showed an expert's touch.* **b** a mental or moral perception or feeling: *a delicate, intellectual touch.* **10** a slight attack: *a touch of fever.* **11a** an official mark or stamp, as put on gold or silver to show it has been tested and is of standard fineness. **b** a die, stamp, or punch for impressing such a mark. **c** the quality or fineness so tested and indicated. **12** *Figurative.* quality, kind, or sort: *friends of noble touch.* **13** any testing or test; trial; criterion: *to put a new product to the touch.* **14** any series of less than a complete set of changes in change ringing. **15** *Slang, Figurative.* **a** a borrowing or getting money from a person. **b** money borrowed or gotten. **c** a person borrowed or to be borrowed from: *He is a soft touch.* **16** *Rugby, Soccer.* the part of the field, including the sidelines, lying outside the field of play.
**in touch,** in a close relation of communication, agreement, sympathy, or interest: *She kept in touch with her family while she was overseas. A newspaper keeps one in touch with the world.*
**out of touch,** lacking close relation of communication, agreement, sympathy, or interest: *The old man was completely out of touch with the youngsters and their ways.*
**touch down, a** to land an aircraft; land: *The pilot touched down at a small country airfield.* **b** *Rugby.* to touch the ground with (the ball) behind the opposing team's goal line: *A young member of the visiting pack was able to touch down a try in the follow-up* (London Times).
**touch off, a** to cause to go off; fire: *The only delay ... is due to a fear that a dispatch of the troops will touch off the magazine* (London Daily Chronicle). **b** *Figurative:* *to touch off a riot.*
**touch on** (or **upon**), **a** to treat lightly; mention: *Our conversation touched on many subjects.* **b** to concern; relate to: *an event that touches on her career.* **c** to come close to: *a sermon that touches on heresy.*
**touch up,** to change a little; improve: *to touch up a play. He touched up a photograph.*
[< Old French *touche* a blow, hit < *touchier;* see the verb] —**touch′a|ble,** *adj.* —**touch′er,** *n.*

**touch and go, 1** an uncertain, risky, or precarious situation: *It was touch and go whether the wounded man would live or die.* **2** the act of touching for an instant and at once quitting; something done quickly or instantaneously.

**touch-and-go** (tuch′ən gō′), *adj.* uncertain; risky; precarious.

**touch|back** (tuch′bak′), *n.* the act of touching the football to the ground by a player behind his own goal line when the impetus of the ball came from the other team. No points are scored.

**touch dancing,** dancing in which the partners hold each other and usually move in a series of complementary steps: *Touch dancing is back, and with it a new demand for formal instruction in a genre less sensuously described as ballroom dancing* (Jane Davison).

**touch|down** (tuch′doun′), *n.* **1** the act of a player in putting the football on the ground behind the

---

**Pronunciation Key:** hat, āge, cãre, fär; let, ēqual, tėrm; it, īce; hot, ōpen, ôrder; **oi**l, **ou**t; cup, pu̇t, rüle; **ch**ild; lo**ng**; **th**in; **ᴛʜ**en; **zh**, measure; ə represents **a** in about, **e** in taken, **i** in pencil, **o** in lemon, **u** in circus.

opponents' goal line. **2** the score of six points made in this way. **3** the act of landing an aircraft, especially the moment of first contact with the ground: *The pilot made an unexpected touchdown because of engine trouble.*

**tou|ché** (tü shā'), *n., interj.* — ***n.*** a touch, as by the weapon of an opponent in fencing.
— ***interj.*** an exclamation acknowledging an effective point in an argument or a clever reply.
[< French *touché,* past participle of *toucher* < Old French *touchier;* see etym. under **touch**, verb]

**touched** (tucht), *adj.* **1** *Informal.* not quite normal mentally; slightly crazed; daft. **2** *Figurative.* stirred emotionally; moved: *He was touched by our concern for his welfare.*

**touch football**, a game having rules similar to those of football except that the person carrying the ball is touched rather than tackled. The players usually have little or no protective equipment and the teams often consist of fewer than eleven players.

**touch|hole** (tuch'hōl'), *n.* (formerly) a small opening in a gun or cannon through which the gunpowder inside was set on fire.

**touch|ing** (tuch'ing), *adj., prep.* — ***adj.*** arousing tender feeling or sympathy: *"A Christmas Carol" is a touching story.* **SYN**: moving, pathetic.
— ***prep.*** concerning; about: *He asked many questions touching my house and school.* — **touch'ing|ly**, *adv.* — **touch'ing|ness**, *n.*

**touch judge**, *Rugby.* an umpire who marks when and where the ball goes into touch.

**touch|less** (tuch'lis), *adj.* **1** lacking the sense of touch. **2** *Figurative.* intangible.

**touch|line** (tuch'līn'), *n. Rugby, Soccer.* the boundary of the playing field on either side; sideline.

**touch-me-not** (tuch'mē not'), *n.* **1** any one of a group of plants whose ripe seed pods burst open when touched; impatiens; jewelweed. **2** *Obsolete.* the squirting cucumber.

**touch|stone** (tuch'stōn'), *n.* **1** a smooth, fine-grained, black stone used to test the purity of gold or silver by the color of the streak made on the stone by rubbing it with the metal. **2** *Figurative.* any means of testing: *Adversity is the touchstone of friendship. An era ... in which success is the only touchstone of merit* (Anthony Trollope). *Calamity is man's true touchstone* (Beaumont and Fletcher). **SYN**: test, criterion, standard.

**touch system**, the system of touch-typing.

**touch-tone** (tuch'tōn'), *adj.* having or using push buttons in place of a rotary dial that activate a system of distinct tones at a central to call a telephone number: *a touch-tone telephone, a touch-tone dial or panel.*

**touch-type** (tuch'tīp'), *v.i.,* **-typed**, **-typ|ing**. to type on a typewriter by the sense of touch alone, without having to look at the keyboard: *In writing it, he can already touch-type and, for note-taking, will learn Braille* (Time).

**touch-up** (tuch'up'), *n., adj.* — ***n.*** the act or process of touching up; retouching: *Acting as color guinea pigs, ... they keep coming back for touch-ups* (Walter Carlson).
— ***adj.*** of or for touching up: *touch-up dabs of paint, a touch-up kit.*

**touch|wood** (tuch'wu̇d'), *n.* **1** wood decayed by fungi so that it catches fire easily, used as tinder; punk. **2** a fungus found on old tree trunks, used as tinder; amadou.

**touch|y** (tuch'ē), *adj.,* **touch|i|er**, **touch|i|est**. **1** apt to take offense at trifles; too sensitive: *He is tired and very touchy this afternoon.* **SYN**: tetchy. **2** requiring skill in handling; ticklish; precarious: *Relations can be very touchy if one's friends are quarreling.* **SYN**: risky. **3** very sensitive to the touch. **4** catching fire very readily.
— **touch'i|ly**, *adv.* — **touch'i|ness**, *n.*

**tough** (tuf), *adj., adv., n., v.* — ***adj.*** **1** bending without breaking: *Leather is tough; cardboard is not.* **2** hard to cut, tear, or chew: *The steak was so tough I couldn't eat it.* **3** stiff; sticky: *tough clay.* **4** strong; hardy: *a tough plant. Donkeys are tough little animals and can carry big loads.* **SYN**: sturdy, stout. **5** hard; difficult: *a tough job. Dragging the load uphill was tough work for the horses.* **SYN**: laborious, arduous. **6** hard to bear; bad; unpleasant: *A spell of tough luck discouraged us.* **SYN**: trying. **7** *Figurative.* **a** hard to influence; firm: *a tough mind.* **SYN**: steadfast, persistent. **b** stubborn; obstinate: *a tough customer.* **8** *Figurative.* severe; violent; strenuous: *Football is a tough game.* **9** *U.S.* rough; disorderly: *He lived in a tough neighborhood.*
— ***adv.*** *Informal.* in a tough manner: *[He] talked tough about America's ideal approach to Communists* (New York Times).
— ***n.*** *U.S.* a rough person; rowdy: *A gang of toughs attacked the policeman.*
— ***v.t.*** Usually, **tough (it) out**, *U.S. Informal.* to resist or endure (pressure, hardship, or trouble); hold out without yielding: *His announced determination to tough it out whatever the cost brought him [no] real surcease from the gathering crisis* (Newsweek).
[Old English *tōh*] — **tough'ly**, *adv.* — **tough'ness**, *n.*

**tough|en** (tuf'ən), *v.t.* to make tough or tougher: *He toughened his muscles by doing exercises.*
— ***v.i.*** to become tough or tougher: *His muscles finally toughened.* — **tough'en|er**, *n.*

**tough|ie** (tuf'ē), *n. Slang.* **1** a tough thing: *It's a great old hotel ... but a real toughie to run* (Canada Month). **2** a rough person; tough: *In the City of Angels today, the toughie's uniform is a leather jacket* (Newsweek).

**tough|ish** (tuf'ish), *adj.* somewhat tough.

**tough-mind|ed** (tuf'mīn'did), *adj.* having firm convictions; not easily influenced or diverted by sentiment; hard-boiled: *The nation's purchasing agents are a tough-minded, down-to-earth group of business men* (Newsweek). — **tough'-mind'ed|ly**, *adv.* — **tough'-mind'ed|ness**, *n.*

**tough sledding**, *Informal.* a difficult time: *House dresses as a rule sell better when more expensive lines have tough sledding* (New York Times).

**tough spot**, *Informal.* a difficult position.

**tough|y** (tuf'ē), *n., pl.* **tough|ies**. = toughie.

**tou|jours** (tü zhür'), *adv. French.* always.

**tou|jours gai** (tü zhür' gā'), *French.* always gay; forever happy.

**tou|jours per|drix** (tü zhür' per drē'), *French.* **1** too much of a good thing. **2** (literally) always partridge.

**Tou|louse** (tü lüz'), *n.* a variety of domestic goose with a large head, short beak, and gray upper parts. [< *Toulouse,* a city in southern France]

**toun|gya** (toung'gyə), *n.* = taungya.

**tou|pee** (tü pā'), *n.* **1** a wig or patch of false hair worn by men to cover a bald spot; hairpiece. **2** a curl or lock of false hair formerly worn on the top of the head as a crowning feature of a periwig. [variant of obsolete *toupet* < French, tuft of hair, forelock < Old French *toupe* tuft, perhaps < Germanic (compare Middle Low German *top, toup*). Compare etym. under **top**[1].]

**tour** (tu̇r; *for n. 3 also* tour), *v., n.* — ***v.i.*** **1** to travel from place to place: *Many Americans tour by car every summer.* **2** *Theater.* to travel from town to town fulfilling engagements.
— ***v.t.*** **1** to travel through: *Last year they toured Mexico.* **2** to walk around in: *to tour the museum. The children toured the ship.* **3** *Theater.* to take (a play or other show or a lecture series) on tour.
[< noun]
— ***n.*** **1** the act of traveling around from place to place; long journey: *The family made a tour through Europe.* **2** a short journey; walk around: *a tour of the boat. Our class made a tour of the historic old battlefield.* **3** a period or turn of military or other activity at a certain place or station; tour of duty: *a soldier away on a tour overseas. We ... present this petition with the one plea that [he] be not returned for yet a third tour as Chief Justice to this Colony* (London Times).
**on tour**, touring: *The show was on tour traveling around the country giving performances in a number of different places.*
[< Old French *tour,* probably back formation from *tors* < *torner, tourner* to turn < Latin *tornāre* < *tornus* turner's wheel, lathe < Greek *tórnos.* See related etym. at **turn**.]

**tou|ra|co** (tu̇r'ə kō), *n., pl.* **-cos**. any one of various large African birds with brilliant feathers and a crest, related to the cuckoo. Also, **turakoo**. [perhaps < West African native name]

**tour|bil|lion** (tür bil'yən), *n.* **1** a kind of firework that spins in a spiral as it rises. **2** a whirling mass or system; vortex. **3** = whirlwind. [alteration of Middle English *turbilloun* < Old French *torbillon,* apparently < Latin *turbō, -inis* whirlwind]

**tour|bil|lon** (tür bē yôN'), *n.* = tourbillion. [< French *tourbillon* < Old French *torbillon*]

**tour de force** (tür' də fôrs'), *pl.* **tours de force** (tür' də fôrs'). **1** a notable feat of strength, skill, or ingenuity. **2** something done that is merely clever or ingenious: *His later work showed that his first novel was little more than a tour de force.* [< French *tour de force* (literally) feat of strength]

**tour d'ho|ri|zon** (tür' dô rē zôN'), *French.* **1** a general review: *A student beginning to read a course in French literature at a university will find it [a book] helpful as an initial tour d'horizon* (Manchester Guardian). **2** (literally) tour of the horizon.

**tou|relle** (tu̇ rel'), *n.* = turret. [< French *tourelle* (diminutive) < *tour* a tower]

**tour en l'air** (tür' äN ler'), *French.* (in ballet) a complete turn in the air after the dancer springs straight up.

**tour|er** (tu̇r'ər), *n. Especially British.* a touring car.

**tour|ing** (tu̇r'ing), *adj.* of or for tourists or making tours: *a touring guide.*

**touring car**, an open automobile with a folding top and no glass side windows, for four or more passengers.

**tour|ism** (tu̇r'iz əm), *n.* **1** the act or practice of touring or traveling for pleasure. **2** the business of serving tourists: *In many parts of the world tourism is providing the fastest growing source of dollars which in turn provide new funds for local investment in industries* (Wall Street Journal). **3** tourists as a group.

**tour|ist** (tu̇r'ist), *n., adj.* — ***n.*** **1** a person traveling for pleasure: *Each year many tourists go to Canada.* **SYN**: excursionist. **2** = tourist class.
— ***adj.*** **1** of or for tourists: *tourist accommodations, the tourist business.* **2** of or based on tourist class: *First-class summer-rate fare is now $792; tourist rate $522* (Newsweek).

**tourist camp**, *U.S.* a camp or building providing such accommodations as tourists need.

**tourist class**, **1** the least expensive class of accommodations, as on a ship or airplane. **2** a class of accommodations on some railroads that offers certain first-class or Pullman facilities at a lower rate.

**tourist court**, *U.S.* a motel.

**tourist home**, *U.S.* a house with rooms for rent to tourists.

**tour|is|tic** (tu̇ ris'tik), *adj.* of or for tourists; having to do with tourism: *For Sardinians, traditional costumes are daily dress and not a holiday or touristic get-up* (Atlantic). — **tour|is'ti|cal|ly**, *adv.*

**tourist trap**, an establishment that overcharges tourists.

**tour|ist|y** (tu̇r'ə stē), *adj. Informal.* like a tourist or tourists: *There was also a gaggle of housewives from Exurbia, Conn., [and] two more couples looking as touristy as we did* (Maclean's).

**tour je|té** (tür zhə tā'), *French.* a high turning leap in ballet: *The steps are modern and functional with never a tour jeté, never an entrechat* (Time).

**tour|ma|line** (tu̇r'mə lin, -lēn), *n.* a semi-precious colored mineral found in deposits of coarse granite. Tourmaline is a silicate of boron and aluminum with varying amounts especially of calcium and sodium, and may be black, brown, red, pink, green, blue, or yellow. The transparent varieties are used in jewelry. Also, **turmaline**. [< French *tourmaline* < Singhalese *tòramalli* a carnelian]

**tour|na|ment** (tėr'nə mənt, tu̇r'-), *n.* **1** a contest of many persons in some sport or game in which the competitors play a series of games: *a golf tournament, a chess tournament, a bridge tournament.* **2a** a medieval contest between groups of knights on horseback who fought each other with blunted weapons, according to certain rules, for a prize. **b** a meeting at which knightly contests, exercises, and sports took place. **c** the activities at such a meeting. **3** *Figurative.* any contest of strength or skill.
[Middle English *turnement* < Old French *torneiement* < *torneier* to tourney]

**tour|ne|dos** (tu̇r'nə dō'), *n., pl.* **-dos** (-dō'). one of several small slices cut from the center of the fillet of beef. [< French *tournedos*]

**tour|ney** (tėr'nē, tu̇r'-), *n., pl.* **-neys**, *v.,* **-neyed**, **-ney|ing**. — ***n.*** = tournament.
— ***v.i.*** to take part in a tournament.
[< Old French *tornei* < *torneier* to tourney < Vulgar Latin *tornidiāre* < Latin *tornus;* see etym. under **tour**]

**✱tour|ni|quet** (tu̇r'nə ket, -kā; tėr'-), *n.* a device for stopping bleeding by compressing a blood vessel, such as a bandage around a limb tightened by twisting with a stick, a pad pressed down by a screw, or an inflated rubber tube. [< French *tourniquet* < Old French *tourner* to turn]

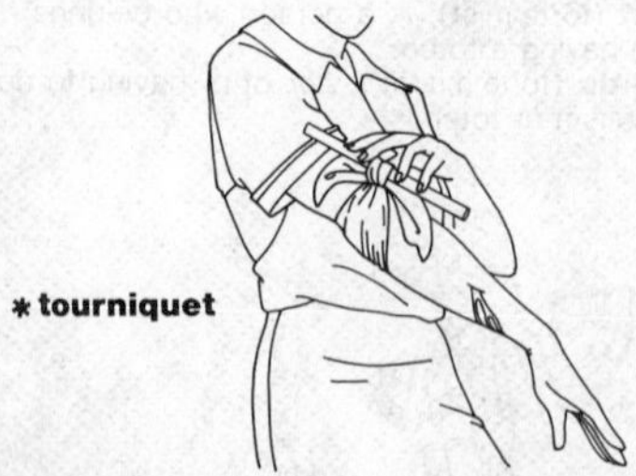

**✱tourniquet**

**tour|nure** (tu̇r nyu̇r'; *French* tür nyr'), *n.* **1** turn, contour, or form. **2** figure; appearance; bearing. [< French *tournure* < Old French *tourner* to turn]

**tour of duty**, **1** a period or turn of military duty at a certain place or station. **2** any spell of work; shift.

**touse** (touz), *n., v.,* **toused**, **tous|ing**. *Dialect.*
— ***n.*** **1** rough or noisy play. **2** a commotion; fuss.
— ***v.t.*** to tousle.
[Middle English *-tousen,* in *betousen* to touse;

origin uncertain. See related etym. at **tease**, **toss**.]

**tous frais faits** (tü fre fe′), *French.* all expenses paid.

**tou|sle** (tou′zəl), *v.*, **-sled, -sling,** *n.* — ***v.t.*** to put into disorder; make untidy; muss: *The baby tousled his mother's hair.* **SYN**: dishevel, rumple.
— ***n.*** a disordered mass: *hair or sheets in a tousle.* Also, **touzle**.
[< *tous*(e) + *-le.* Compare etym. under **tussle**.]

**tous-les-mois** (tü′lā mwä′), *n.* **1** a starch obtained from the edible rootstocks of a West Indian canna, used in baby food and cocoa. It is like arrowroot. **2** the plant itself. [< French (West Indies) *tous-les-mois* (literally) all the months; probably by folk etymology < *toloman* the name of the plant, perhaps < the native name]

**tout** (tout), *v., n. Informal.* — ***v.t.*** **1** to try to get (customers, jobs, votes, or other recognition of acceptance). **2** *U.S.* to urge betting on (a race horse) by claiming to have special information. **3** *Especially British.* to spy out (information about race horses) for use in betting. **4** to praise highly and insistently.
— ***v.i.*** to engage in touting; be a tout.
— ***n.*** **1** a person who touts. **2** a thieves' scout or watchman.
[earlier, spy on, Middle English *tuten* to peep, peer; origin uncertain]

**tout à fait** (tü tȧ fe′), *French.* entirely; completely; wholly; quite.

**tout à vous** (tü tȧ vü′), *French.* wholly yours; sincerely yours.

**tout com|pren|dre, c'est tout par|don|ner** (tü kôɴ präɴ′drə, se tü pȧr dô nā′), *French.* to understand all is to forgive all.

**tout court** (tü kür′), *French.* in short; briefly; simply.

**tout de suite** (tüt swēt′), *French.* **1** at once. **2** consecutively.

**tout en|sem|ble** (tü täɴ säɴ′blə), *French.* **1** the general effect of the various parts, as of a work of art, taken as a whole. **2** (literally) all together.

**tout|er** (tou′tər), *n.* a person who touts; tout.

**tout le monde** (tü lə môɴd′), *French.* the whole world; everyone.

**tou|zle** (tou′zəl), *v.t.*, **-zled, -zling,** *n.* = tousle.

**to|va|rish, to|va|rich,** or **to|va|risch** (tə vä′rish), *n.* = comrade. [< Russian *tovarishch*]

**tow**[1] (tō), *v., n.* — ***v.t.*** to pull, as by a rope or chain: *to tow a car from a ditch to a garage. The tug is towing three barges.* **SYN**: haul, drag, tug, draw. — ***v.i.*** to move by towing or being towed: *The ship towed out of port. We towed up as far as ... our boats would swim* (Daniel Defoe).
— ***n.*** **1** the act of towing or condition of being pulled along by a rope or chain: *The launch had the sailboat in tow.* **2** what is towed, such as a ship taken in tow or a string of boats or barges being towed: *Each tug had a tow of three barges.* **3** the rope, chain, cable, or the like, used for towing; towline. **4** that which tows, especially a ship that tows; tugboat; tug. **5** = ski tow.
**in tow, a** in one's company or charge: *Arizona Democrat Morris "Mo" Udall ... happened by with three constituents in tow* (Harper's). **b** under one's care or influence: *The boy had his little brother in tow for the day.*
[Old English *togian* drag] — **tow′a|ble**, *adj.*

**tow**[2] (tō), *n., adj.* — ***n.*** **1** the fiber of flax, hemp, or jute prepared for spinning by scutching. **2** the coarse, broken fibers, as of flax and hemp, that are separated in hackling: *This string is made of tow.*
— ***adj.*** made of tow.
[Old English *tōw-* spinning, as in *tōwlīc* fit for spinning, perhaps related to Old Icelandic *tō* unworked fiber]

**tow**[3] (tō), *n. Scottish.* a rope; halter. [perhaps < Scandinavian (compare Old Icelandic *tog* rope, cable, or *taug* string, rope)]

**TOW** (tō), *n.* a United States antitank guided missile: *The TOW missile can be used offensively from jeeps or armed cars* (Drew Middleton). [< *t*(ube-launched), *o*(ptically tracked), *w*(ire-guided)]

**tow|age** (tō′ij), *n.* **1** a charge for towing. **2** the act or process of towing or being towed. [< Medieval Latin *towagium*]

**to|ward** (*prep.* tôrd, tōrd, tə wôrd′; *adj.* tôrd, tōrd), *prep., adj.* — ***prep.*** **1** in the direction of: *He walked toward the north.* **2** turned or directed to; facing: *to lie with one's face toward the wall.* **3a** with respect to; about; concerning; regarding: *What is the senator's attitude toward foreign aid?* **b** against: *Do you have any malice toward him?* **4** shortly before; near: *It must be toward four o'clock.* **5** as a help to; for: *Will you give something toward our new hospital? The United Nations' work is toward peace.*
— ***adj.*** **1** about to happen; impending; imminent. **2** in progress; going on; being done. **3** *Archaic.* promising, hopeful, or apt.
[Old English *tōweard* < *tō* to + *-weard* -ward]

**to|ward|li|ness** (tôrd′lē nis, tōrd′-; tō′ərd-), *n. Archaic.* a readiness to do or learn; aptness; docility.

**to|ward|ly**[1] (tôrd′lē, tōrd′-; tō′ərd-), *adj. Archaic.* **1** ready to do or learn; docile. **2** promising; advantageous; propitious. [< *toward* + *-ly*[2]]

**to|ward|ly**[2] (tôrd′lē, tōrd′-; tō′ərd-), *adv. Archaic.* **1** in a docile manner; willingly; obligingly. **2** promisingly. [< *toward* + *-ly*[1]]

**to|wards** (tôrdz, tōrdz, tə wôrdz′), *prep.* = toward.

**tow|a|way** (tō′ə wā′), *n., adj. U.S.* — ***n.*** the action of towing away and impounding an illegally parked car. — ***adj.*** of or having to do with towaways: *a towaway zone.*

**tow|boat** (tō′bōt′), *n.* a tugboat, especially one with a flat bottom, used on a river.

**tow car,** = tow truck.

**tow|el** (tou′əl), *n., v.*, **-eled, -el|ing** or (*especially British*) **-elled, -el|ling.** — ***n.*** a piece of cloth or paper for wiping and drying something wet. We have hand towels, bath towels, and dish towels.
— ***v.t.*** to rub or dry with a towel: *to towel oneself.*
— ***v.i.*** to rub or dry oneself with a towel: *On one of the long sides of the pool ..., the instructor was toweling off lustily* (Atlantic).
**throw** (or **toss**) **in the towel,** *Informal.* to admit defeat: *The city made futile efforts to work out a peace formula before the strike deadline, but officials finally tossed in the towel at 6:45 P.M. and confessed that a tie-up was certain* (New York Times).
[Middle English *towele, towaille* < Old French *toaille* < Medieval Latin *toacula* < Germanic (compare Middle High German *twahele*)]

**tow|el|ing** (tou′ə ling), *n.* material used for towels, especially cotton.

**tow|el|ling** (tou′ə ling), *n. Especially British.* toweling.

**tow|er** (tou′ər), *n., v.* — ***n.*** **1** a high structure. A tower may stand alone or form part of a church, castle, or other building. Some towers are forts or prisons, others are used for storing water, watching for fires, or controlling the landing and taking off of aircraft. **SYN**: spire, steeple, turret. **2** a means of defense or protection. **SYN**: citadel, fortress, stronghold. **3** *Figurative.* a person or thing that is like a tower in some way: *a tower of strength.*
— ***v.i.*** to rise or stand high up: *The boy towered over his baby brother. The World Trade Center towers over all the other buildings in Manhattan.*
[partly Old English *torr* < Latin *turris;* partly Middle English *ture,* or *tour* < Old French *tur,* and *tour* < Latin] — **tow′er|like′**, *adj.*

**tower block,** *British.* a very tall residential or office building.

**tow|ered** (tou′ərd), *adj.* **1** having a tower or towers. **2** ornamented or defended with towers: *towered battlements.* **3** rising like a tower.

**tow|er|ing** (tou′ər ing), *adj.* **1** very high; lofty: *a towering mountain peak.* **2** very tall: *a towering basketball player.* **3** *Figurative.* very great: *towering ambition. Making electricity from atomic power is a towering achievement.* **4** *Figurative.* very violent: *towering rage.* — **tow′er|ing|ly**, *adv.*

**tow|er|man** (tou′ər mən), *n., pl.* **-men.** **1** *U.S.* a man in charge of a signal box on a railway. **2** a man who operates the control tower of an airport.

**Tower of Babel**. See under **Babel**.

**tower of silence**, a platform on which the Parsis of India place the bodies of their dead for the vultures to eat. It is built over a deep pit and is usually not higher than 30 feet.

**tower wagon**, a wagon having a platform that can be raised or lowered for use in repairing overhead wires or the like.

**tow|er|y** (tou′ər ē), *adj.* **1** having towers. **2** towering; lofty.

**tow|head** (tō′hed′), *n.* **1** a person having very light or pale-yellow hair. **2** a head of light-colored hair. [< *tow*[2] + *head*]

**tow|head|ed** (tō′hed′id), *adj.* having very light or pale-yellow hair.

**tow|hee** (tō′hē, tou′-), *n.*, or **towhee bunting**, any one of various American finches related to the sparrows but larger, such as the Oregon towhee of western North America and the red-eyed towhee, also called chewink or ground robin, of eastern North America. [American English; apparently imitative of its call]

**tow|line** (tō′līn′), *n.* a line, rope, chain, or the like, for towing.

**town** (toun), *n., adj.* — ***n.*** **1** a large group of houses and other buildings, smaller than a city but larger than a village: *a growing town, an abandoned town. Do you live in a town or in the country?* **2** any large place with many people living in it: *Chicago is my favorite town.* **3** the people of a town: *The whole town was having a holiday.* **4** the part of a town or city where the stores and office buildings are: *Let's go into town.* **5** the particular town or city under consideration: *to be in town, to have to leave town.* **6** *U.S.* **a** (in some states) a municipal corporation with less elaborate organization and powers than a city. **b** (in New England) a local administrative unit similar to a township, forming a division of a county and exercising self-government through town meetings. **c** (in other states) = township. **7** *British.* any village or hamlet: *a market town.*
— ***adj.*** **1** of, having to do with, or characteristic of a town or towns; urban: *town life, town government.* **2** of or belonging to a certain town: *the town clock.*
**go to town,** *Informal.* **a** to achieve success: *In Europe, he really went to town with his personal diplomacy; his friends were in the capitals of the Western, "civilized" world* (New Yorker). **b** to do or go through thoroughly: *The hungry boys really went to town on the pie.*
**on the town, a** on a pleasure tour of a city: *The group of tourists went out on the town.* **b** supported by a town; on charity: *the unemployed who had been a long time on the town.*
**paint the town red,** *Slang.* to go on a wild spree or party; celebrate in a noisy manner: *Mere horseplay; it is the cowboy's method of painting the town red, as an interlude in his harsh monotonous life* (Century Magazine).
[Old English *tūn* enclosure; enclosed land with its buildings; a village]

**town and gown**, the townspeople and the academic community.

**town-bred** (toun′bred′), *adj.* born and raised in a town rather than in the country.

**town car**, **1** an automobile with the driver's seat separated from the passengers by a partition; limousine. **2** an automobile designed for low speed and short range, for use on city streets.

**town clerk**, an official who keeps the records of a town.

**town crier**, a person in former times who called out the news and made announcements on the streets of a city or town.

**town|ee** (tou nē′), *n. Informal.* a townsman.

**town father**, one of the officials or leading citizens of a town.

**town gas**, *British.* gas piped to the buildings of a village or town.

**town hall**, a building belonging to a town, used for the town's business, and often also as a place for public meetings.

**town|house** (toun′hous′), *n.* **1** = town hall. **2** a town prison or poorhouse.

**town house**, **1** a house in town, belonging to a person who also has a house in the country. **2** one of a group of houses, each sharing a common wall with the next house; row house.

**town|ie** (tou′nē), *n.* = towny.

**town|ish** (tou′nish), *adj.* **1** of or having to do with a town or city; urban. **2** characteristic of the town as distinguished from the country; having the manners or habits of town dwellers.

**town|land** (toun′lənd), *n.* a division of a parish in Ireland; township.

**town|let** (toun′lit), *n.* a little town.

**town meeting**, **1** a general meeting of the inhabitants of a town. **2** a meeting of the qualified voters of a town in New England for the transaction of public business.

**town planner**, a person who is in charge of directing the work of town planning.

**town planning**, regulation of the development of a town especially by controlling the location of buildings, parks, and streets, and the type of occupancy permitted in various areas.

**town|scape** (toun′skāp), *n.* a scene or view of a town, whether pictured or natural. [< *town* + *-scape*]

**Town|send's solitaire** (toun′zəndz), a songbird of western North America related to the thrush and resembling a mockingbird, having a gray body with a white ring around the eye. [< John Kirk *Townsend,* 1809-1851, an American ornithologist]

**Townsend's warbler**, a warbler of western North America with yellow and black markings about the head and breast.

**towns|folk** (tounz′fōk′), *n.pl.* the people of a town; townspeople: *Townsfolk gathered to see the fire.*

**town|ship** (toun′ship), *n.* **1** (in the United States and Canada) a part of a county having certain powers of local government, such as responsibility for schools, poor relief, and maintenance of the roads. *Abbr:* twp. **2** (in United States surveys of public land) a region or district six miles square, made up of 36 sections. **3** in English history: **a** a local administrative division of a large

---

**Pronunciation Key:** hat, āge, cãre, fär; let, ēqual, tėrm; it, īce; hot, ōpen, ôrder; oil, out; cup, pu̇t, rüle; child; long; thin; ᴛʜen; zh, measure; ə represents **a** in about, **e** in taken, **i** in pencil, **o** in lemon, **u** in circus.

parish, containing a village, and usually having its own church. **b** a manor, parish, or division of a hundred, as a territorial division. **c** the inhabitants of such a community as a group. [Old English *tūnscipe* < *tūn* town + *-scipe* -ship]

**town|site** (toun′sīt′), *n.* **1** the site of a town. **2** (in the United States and Canada) a tract of land set apart by law to be occupied by a town, usually surveyed and laid out with streets, etc.

**towns|man** (tounz′mən), *n., pl.* **-men.** **1** a person who lives or has been raised in a town. **2** a person who lives in one's own town; fellow citizen. **3** a selectman of any one of certain New England towns.

**towns|peo|ple** (tounz′pē′pəl), *n.pl.* the people of a town; townsfolk.

**towns|wom|an** (tounz′wu̇m′ən), *n., pl.* **-wom|en.** **1** a woman who lives in a town. **2** a woman who lives in one's own town.

**town talk**, **1** the common talk or gossip of a town. **2** the subject of gossip.

**town|ward** (toun′wərd), *adv., adj.* toward the town: *On Sunday evenings in the fall the cars roll back townward* (Harper's).

**town|wards** (toun′wərdz), *adv.* = townward.

**town|y** (tou′nē), *n., pl.* **town|ies.** **1** *Informal.* a townee. **2** a citizen of a town, as contrasted with a student or teacher at a college there.

**tow|path** (tō′path′, -päth′), *n.* a path along the bank of a canal or river for use in towing boats.

**tow|rope** (tō′rōp′), *n.* a rope, hawser, cable, or the like, used in towing.

**tow target**, an object towed behind a plane for target practice by antiaircraft weapons or fighter planes.

**tow truck**, a truck equipped with apparatus to tow away wrecked or disabled cars; wrecker.

**tow|y** (tō′ē), *adj.* of or like tow.

**tox.**, toxicology.

**tox|ae|mi|a** (tok sē′mē ə), *n.* = toxemia.

**tox|ae|mic** (tok sē′mik), *adj.* = toxemic.

**tox|a|phene** (tok′sə fēn), *n.* a powerful insecticide derived from camphene and chlorine, used chiefly against cotton and forage crop parasites, but not on fruits or vegetables, for it cannot be washed off easily. *Formula:* $C_{10}H_{10}Cl_8$ [< *tox*(ic) + (cam)*phene*]

**tox|e|mi|a** (tok sē′mē ə), *n.* blood poisoning, caused by toxins, especially a form in which the toxins produced by pathogenic bacteria enter the bloodstream from a local lesion and are distributed throughout the body. Also, **toxaemia.** [< *tox*(ic) + *-emia*]

**tox|e|mic** (tok sē′mik), *adj.* **1** of or having to do with toxemia. **2** suffering from toxemia.

**tox|ic** (tok′sik), *adj.* **1** of, having to do with, or caused by a toxin or poison: *a toxic illness.* **2** poisonous: *toxic plants. Fumes from an automobile are toxic. It is relatively easy to find a chemical which, when tested in the glasshouse, is more toxic to one species than another* (New Scientist). **SYN:** noxious. [< Late Latin *toxicus* < Latin *toxicum* poison < Greek *toxikón* (*phármakon*) (poison) for use on arrows < *tóxon* bow] —**tox′i|cal|ly**, *adv.*

**tox|i|cal** (tok′sə kəl), *adj.* = toxic.

**tox|i|cant** (tok′sə kənt), *adj., n.* —*adj.* poisonous; toxic.
—*n.* **1** = poison. **2** = intoxicant. [< Medieval Latin *toxicans, -antis,* present participle of *toxicare* to poison < Late Latin *toxicus;* see etym. under **toxic**]

**tox|i|ca|tion** (tok′sə kā′shən), *n.* = poisoning.

**tox|ic|i|ty** (tok sis′ə tē), *n., pl.* **-ties.** toxic or poisonous quality; poisonousness: *Plants are convenient means of assessing the toxicity of smog* (Scientific American).

**tox|i|co|den|drol** (tok′sə kō den′drol), *n.* a nonvolatile, poisonous oil found in poison ivy, oak, and sumac. It can be washed off with alcohol but not with water. [< Greek *toxikón* poison (see etym. under **toxic**) + *déndron* tree + English *-ol*[2]]

**tox|i|co|gen|ic** (tok′sə kə jen′ik), *adj.* **1** producing toxins or poisons. **2** caused by toxins or poisons. [< Greek *toxikón* poison (see etym. under **toxic**) + English *-gen* + *-ic*]

**toxicol.**, **1** toxicological. **2** toxicology.

**tox|i|co|log|i|cal** (tok′sə kə loj′ə kəl), *adj.* of or having to do with toxicology. —**tox′i|co|log′i|cal|ly**, *adv.*

**tox|i|col|o|gist** (tok′sə kol′ə jist), *n.* an expert in toxicology.

**tox|i|col|o|gy** (tok′sə kol′ə jē), *n.* the science that deals with poisons and their effects, antidotes, detection, etc. [< Greek *toxikón* poison (see etym. under **toxic**) + English *-logy*]

**tox|i|co|sis** (tok′sə kō′sis), *n., pl.* **-ses** (-sēz). a diseased condition caused by a poison. [< New Latin *toxicosis* < Greek *toxikón* poison (see etym. under **toxic**) + *-ōsis* -osis]

**tox|i|gen|e|sis** (tok′sə jen′ə sis), *n.* the creation or production of toxins.

**tox|i|gen|ic** (tok′sə jen′ik), *adj.* creating or producing toxins.

**tox|in** (tok′sən), *n.* any poison formed by an animal or plant organism as a product of its metabolism, especially one of those produced by bacteria. The symptoms of a disease caused by bacteria, such as diphtheria and scarlet fever, are due to toxins. The body reacts to some toxins by producing antitoxins. [< *tox*(ic) + *-in*]

**tox|in-an|ti|tox|in** (tok′sən an′tē tok′sən), *n.* a mixture of a toxin with enough of the corresponding antitoxin to almost neutralize it, used formerly to immunize against diphtheria.

**tox|i|pho|bi|a** (tok′sə fō′bē ə), *n.* an abnormal fear of being poisoned.

**tox|oid** (tok′soid), *n.* a toxin, as of diphtheria or tetanus, specially treated so that it will lose its poisonous quality but still cause antitoxins to be produced when injected into the body. [< *tox*(in) + *-oid*]

**tox|oph|i|lite** (tok sof′ə līt), *n.* a person who is very fond of archery. [apparently < *Toxophilus,* probably coined by Roger Ascham, 1515-1568, an English scholar and writer, as the title of his book on archery; (literally) lover of the bow (< Greek *tóxon* bow + *phílos* loving) + *-ite*[1]]

**tox|oph|i|lit|ic** (tok sof′ə lit′ik), *adj.* of or having to do with archers or archery.

**tox|oph|i|ly** (tok sof′ə lē), *n.* the practice of, or liking for, archery.

**tox|o|plas|ma** (tok′sə plaz′mə), *n., pl.* **-ma** or **-mas.** the parasitic protozoan that causes toxoplasmosis. [< New Latin *Toxoplasma* the genus name < Greek *toxikón* poison + *plásma* plasm, plasma]

**tox|o|plas|mic** (tok′sə plaz′mik), *adj.* of or having to do with toxoplasma or toxoplasmosis.

**tox|o|plas|mo|sis** (tok′sə plaz mō′sis), *n.* a disease attacking people, dogs, cats, and other animals, caused by a protozoan. Children develop an inflammation of the brain and spinal cord; adults develop a condition similar to Rocky Mountain spotted fever. [< New Latin *toxoplasmosis* < *toxoplasma* + *-osis*]

**toy** (toi), *n., adj., v.* —*n.* **1** something for a child to play with; plaything. Dolls are toys; so are small wagons, colored rubber balls, and wooden building blocks. **2** *Figurative.* a thing that has little value or importance: *a toy, a thing of no regard* (Shakespeare). *Love and all his pleasures are but toys* (Thomas Campion). **SYN:** trifle, knickknack, trinket. **3** any small thing, especially any one of certain breeds of very small animals. There are toy dogs and toy pigeons. **4** *Scottish.* a close-fitting cap of linen or wool, with flaps coming down to the shoulders, formerly worn by lower-class women. **5** *Obsolete.* **a** amorous sport; dalliance. **b** a light caress. **6** *Obsolete.* an antic; trick.
—*adj.* **1** of, made as, or like a toy: *The boy ran a toy car along the floor.* **2** small; miniature in size: *a toy poodle.*
—*v.i.* to amuse oneself; play; trifle: *She toyed with her beads. Don't toy with matches.*
[Middle English *toye* playing, sport; origin uncertain] —**toy′like′**, *adj.*

***toy dog**, a very small dog, especially one belonging to a certain breed. Some toy dogs are related to larger dogs, such as poodles, spaniels, and terriers. Others belong to separate breeds, such as the Chihuahua.

***toy dog**

**toy dog** (toy poodle)

standard poodle

**to-year** (tə yir′), *adv. Dialect.* this year. [< *to* on + *year.* Compare etym. under **today, tonight.**]

**toy|land** (toi′land′), *n.* an imaginary place inhabited by toy characters and full of romantic adventure.

**toy|mak|er** (toi′mā′kər), *n.* **1** a manufacturer of toys. **2** a craftsman of toys: *Vladimir was not only a great clown; he was also a great scholar, painter, musician, toymaker* (Niccolò Tucci).

**toy|man** (toi′mən), *n., pl.* **-men.** a maker or seller of toys.

**toy Manchester terrier**, a small variety of Manchester terrier, weighing up to 12 pounds.

**to|yo** (tô′yō), *n.* **1** a straw made of rice paper, used for women's hats. **2** a hat made of such straw. [< Japanese *toyo*]

**to|yon** (tō′yən), *n.* a shrub of the rose family found on the Pacific coast of North America, whose evergreen leaves and scarlet berries look much like holly. [American English < American Spanish *tollón,* perhaps < an American Indian name]

**toy|shop** (toi′shop′), *n.* a shop where toys or playthings are sold.

**tp.**, township.

**t.p.**, title page.

**TPI** (no periods), treponema pallidum immobilization (designating a test for the presence of syphilis).

**tpk.**, turnpike.

**TPN** (no periods) or **T.P.N.**, triphosphopyridine nucleotide.

**T.P.O.**, traveling post office.

**tr.**, an abbreviation for the following:
1 trace.
2 transfer.
3 transitive.
4a translated. **b** translation. **c** translator.
5 transpose.
6 treasurer.

**T.R.**, Theodore Roosevelt, President of the United States, 1901-1909.

**tra|be|a** (trā′bē ə), *n.* a toga with horizontal purple stripes, worn as a robe of state by consuls, augurs, and some other officials in ancient Rome. [< Latin *trabea*]

**tra|be|ate** (trā′bē it, -āt), *adj.* = trabeated.

**tra|be|at|ed** (trā′bē ā′tid), *adj. Architecture.* **1** constructed with beams; having a lintel or entablature, instead of an arch: *a trabeated doorway.* **2** of or having to do with this type of construction.

**tra|be|a|tion** (trā′bē ā′shən), *n.* **1** construction with a lintel or entablature. **2** something constructed in this way. [< Latin *trabs, trabis* beam + English *-ation*]

**tra|bec|u|la** (trə bek′yə lə), *n., pl.* **-lae** (-lē). **1** a structure in an animal or plant like a small beam or bar. **2** *Botany.* a projection extending across the cell cavity in the ducts of some plants, or across the cavity of the sporangium in mosses. [< Latin *trabecula* (diminutive) < *trabs, trabis* beam]

**tra|bec|u|lar** (trə bek′yə lər), *adj.* **1** of or having to do with a trabecula. **2** forming or formed by trabeculae.

**tra|bec|u|late** (trə bek′yə lit, -lāt), *adj.* having a trabecula or trabeculae.

**trace**[1] (trās), *n., adj., v.,* **traced, trac|ing.** —*n.* **1** a mark or sign of the former existence, presence, or action of something; vestige: *The explorers found traces of an ancient city* (*Figurative.*) *In countries where all trace of the limited monarchy of the middle ages had long been effaced* (Macaulay). **2a** a footprint or other mark left by the passage of a person, animal, or thing; track: *We saw traces of rabbits and squirrels on the snow.* **b** a beaten path, as through a wild region; trail; track: *the Natchez Trace.* **3** *Figurative.* a very small amount; little bit: *There was not a trace of color in her cheeks. The trace of rainfall in the desert is too small to be measured.* **4a** a line or figure marked out or drawn; tracing, drawing, or sketch of something. **b** the line made by a self-recording instrument such as a cardiograph or seismograph. **5** *Chemistry.* an indication of an amount of some constituent in a compound, usually too small to be measured. **6** *Psychology.* an engram. **7** *Obsolete.* the way or path which anything takes. [< Old French *trace* < *tracier;* see the verb]
—*adj. Chemistry.* consisting of a trace; too small to be measured: *a trace compound, trace gases, a chemical found in trace amounts in the body. Uranium is the most highly concentrated trace metal found in the miners' lungs* (Franklin J. Tobey, Jr.). See **trace element.**
—*v.t.* **1** to follow by means of marks, tracks, or signs: *to trace deer. The dog traced the fox to its den. The counterfeit money was traced to a foreign printer.* **2** *Figurative.* to follow the course, development, or history of: *to trace the meanings of a word. He traced the river to its source. The Aldens trace their family back three hundred years to John Alden, one of the Pilgrims.* **3** *Figurative.* to find signs or proof of; observe; discover: *I could never trace in her one spark of jealousy* (Robert Louis Stevenson). **4** to draw an outline of; mark out; draw; sketch: *The spy traced a plan of the fort.* **5** to copy by following the lines of with a pencil or pen: *He put thin paper over the map and traced it.* **6** to decorate with tracery. **7** to write, especially by forming the letters carefully or laboriously: *The old man seized the pen and traced his name* (Francis M.

Crawford). **8** to copy, impress, or imprint with a tracer. **9** to record in the form of a curving, wavy, or broken line, as a cardiograph or seismograph does. **10** *Obsolete.* to pass along or over; traverse.

**— *v.i.*** **1** to trace the origin or history of something; go back in time. **2** *Obsolete.* to make one's way; go; proceed; travel.

[< Old French *trasser,* and *tracier* < Vulgar Latin *tractiāre* < Latin *tractus, -ūs* a drawing < *trahere* to drag]

**— *Syn.* *n.* 1 Trace, vestige** mean a mark or sign of what has existed or happened. **Trace** applies to any noticeable indication left by something that has happened or been present: *The campers removed all traces of their fire.* **Vestige** applies particularly to an actual remnant of something that existed in the past: *Some of our common courtesies are vestiges of very old cultural customs. They have discovered vestiges of an ancient civilization.*

**trace²** (trās), *n.* **1** either of the two straps, ropes or chains by which an animal pulls a wagon, carriage, or other vehicle. **2** = connecting rod.

**kick over the traces,** to throw off controls or restraints; become unruly: *I could not help thinking that Mr. Finney might produce something really worth listening to if he could kick over the traces of the serial system of composition* (New Yorker).

[new singular of Middle English *trays,* collective plural < Old French *traiz,* plural of *trait* < Latin *tractus, -ūs* a drawing, a track < *trahere* to drag, draw. See etym. of doublets **tract¹, trait, tret.**]

**trace|a|bil|i|ty** (trā′sə bil′ə tē), *n.* the fact or property of being traceable.

**trace|a|ble** (trā′sə bəl), *adj.* **1** that can be traced. **2** *Figurative.* attributable: *The engine's failure was traceable to an oil leak.* **— trace′a|ble|ness,** *n.* **— trace′a|bly,** *adv.*

**trace element,** a chemical element, especially a metallic one, used in small amounts by an organism but considered necessary to the organism's proper functioning; minor element. The trace elements include copper, cobalt, magnesium, manganese, and zinc.

**trace|less** (trās′lis), *adj.* leaving or showing no traces. **— trace′less|ly,** *adv.*

**trac|er** (trā′sər), *n.* **1** a person or thing that traces, especially a person whose business is tracing missing persons or property. **2** a machine for making tracings, as of drawings and plans. **3** an inquiry sent from place to place to trace a missing person, article, letter, parcel, or other lost item: *We'll put out a tracer on your stolen car.* **4a** a burning substance put in a tracer bullet to show its course. **b** = tracer bullet. **5** *Chemistry.* an element or atom, usually radioactive, that can be traced and observed as it passes through a body, plant, or other system in order to study biological processes or chemical reactions within the system.

**tracer bullet, 1** a bullet with a substance in it that burns when the bullet is fired, leaving a trail that can be followed with the eye. **2** a shell containing such a substance.

**trac|er|ied** (trā′sər ēd, trās′rēd), *adj.* ornamented with tracery: *a traceried window.*

**✱trac|er|y** (trā′sər ē, trās′rē), *n., pl.* **-er|ies. 1** ornamental work or designs consisting of very fine lines, as in certain kinds of embroidery. **2** a pattern of intersecting bars or a plate with leaflike decorations in the upper part of a Gothic window, in the ribs of a vault, in carved panels, and in plasterwork. [< *trac*(e)¹, verb + *-ery*]

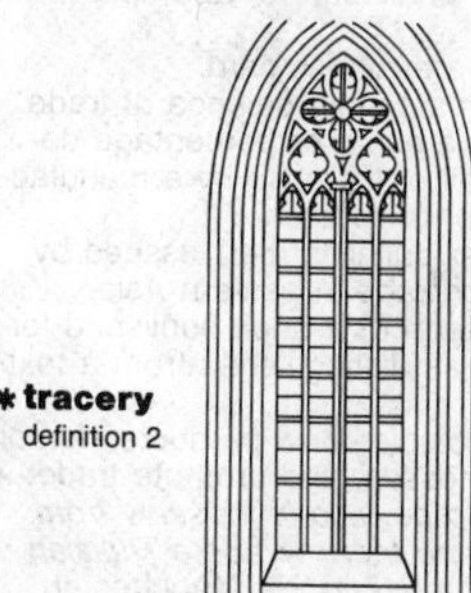

**✱tracery** definition 2

**tra|che|a** (trā′kē ə, trə kē′-), *n., pl.* **tra|che|ae** (trā′kē ē, trə kē′-), **tra|che|as. 1** the tube in air-breathing vertebrates extending from the larynx to the bronchi, by which air is carried to and from the lungs; windpipe. See picture under **chest. 2** *Zoology.* one of the air-carrying tubes of the respiratory system of insects and other arthropods. **3** *Botany.* **a** a duct in the xylem of a vascular plant, formed by a row of cells (tracheids) that have lost their intervening partitions and have become a single long canal permitting the passage of water and dissolved minerals. Tracheae are covered with various markings or thickenings, the spiral being the common type. **b** one of these cells. [< Medieval Latin *trachea* (*arteria*) trachea (artery), for Late Latin *trāchīa* < Greek *trācheîa artēríā* windpipe; (literally) rough air vessel]

**tra|che|al** (trā′kē əl, trə kē′-), *adj.* of or having to do with the trachea.

**tra|che|ar|y** (trā′kē er′ē, trə kē′ə rē), *adj. Botany.* of or having to do with tracheae or tracheids.

**tra|che|ate** (trā′kē āt, -it; trə kē′it), *adj., n. Zoology.* **— *adj.*** having tracheae.

**— *n.*** a tracheate arthropod.

**tra|che|id** (trā′kē id), *n. Botany.* an elongated, more or less lignified cell with thick, perforated walls, that serves to carry water and dissolved minerals through a plant, and provides support. Tracheids form an essential element of the xylem of vascular plants. [< German *tracheide* < *Trachea* trachea]

**tra|che|i|dal** (trə kē′ə dəl, trā′kē ī′-), *adj.* of, having to do with, or like tracheids.

**tra|che|i|tis** (trā′kē ī′tis), *n.* inflammation of the windpipe. [< New Latin *tracheitis* < *trachea* trachea + *-itis* -itis]

**tra|che|o|bron|chi|al** (trā′kē ō brong′kē əl), *adj.* having to do with the trachea and the bronchi.

**tra|che|ole** (trā′kē ōl), *n.* one of the tiny branches of the trachea of an insect.

**tra|che|o|scop|ic** (trā′kē ə skop′ik), *adj.* of or having to do with tracheoscopy.

**tra|che|os|co|pist** (trā′kē os′kə pist), *n.* a person skilled in tracheoscopy.

**tra|che|os|co|py** (trā′kē os′kə pē), *n., pl.* **-pies.** examination of the interior of the trachea, as with a laryngoscope.

**tra|che|ot|o|mist** (trā′kē ot′ə mist), *n.* a surgeon who performs a tracheotomy.

**tra|che|ot|o|my** (trā′kē ot′ə mē), *n., pl.* **-mies.** surgical incision into the trachea. [< *trachea* + Greek *-tomiā* a cutting]

**tra|chle** (trä′ʜəl), *v.t.,* **-chled, -chling.** *Scottish.* **1a** to dishevel. **b** to disorder or injure by trampling. **2a** to exhaust. **b** *Figurative.* to distress. Also, **trauchle.** [origin uncertain. Compare Flemish *tragelen* to go with difficulty, dialectal Swedish *traggla* to worry.]

**tra|cho|don** (trā′kə don), *n.* = trachodont.

**tra|cho|dont** (trā′kə dont), *n.* a very large dinosaur with a broad, flat skull, lower jaws like a duck's bill, and as many as 2,000 teeth. Some kinds had webbed feet. [< Greek *trāchýs* rough + *odoús, odóntos* tooth]

**tra|cho|ma** (trə kō′mə), *n.* a contagious inflammation of the mucous membrane of the eyeball and eyelids, caused by a virus. Trachoma is common in the Orient and sometimes causes blindness. [< Late Latin *trāchōma* < Greek *trāchōma* roughness < *trāchýs* rough]

**tra|chom|a|tous** (trə kom′ə təs, -kō′mə-), *adj.* of or affected with trachoma.

**tra|chyte** (trā′kīt, trak′īt), *n.* a light, volcanic rock with a rough surface, consisting of feldspars and augite or biotite. [< French *trachyte* < Greek *trāchýs* rough, or < *trāchýtēs, -ētos* roughness]

**tra|chyt|ic** (trə kit′ik), *adj.* (of rock) having densely packed prisms of feldspar lying parallel to each other.

**trac|ing** (trā′sing), *n.* **1** a copy of something made by putting thin paper over it and following the lines of it with a pencil or pen. **2** a line made by marking or drawing. **3** one of a series of lines or marks made by an electrical apparatus, such as a lie detector, electrocardiograph, or electroencephalograph, that records waves or impulses.

**tracing paper,** a thin, almost transparent paper for tracing or copying an original design.

**track** (trak), *n., v.* **— *n.*** **1** a double line of metal rails for cars to run on. A railroad line has tracks. **2** a mark left by anything: *The dirt road showed many automobile tracks.* **3** a footprint: *We saw bear and deer tracks near the camp.* **4a** a path; trail; rough road: *A track runs through the woods to the farmhouse.* **b** a line of travel or motion: *the track of an eagle to a mountain nest, the track of a comet or hurricane.* **5** *Figurative.* a way of doing or acting: *to go on in the same track year after year.* **6** a course for running or racing: *a trotting track.* **7a** contests in running, jumping, throwing, and similar sports performed around or inside a track: *My older brother has gone out for track this year.* **b** track-and-field sports as a group: *Sprinters, polevaulters, and shot-putters are engaged in track.* **8** *Figurative.* a sequence or succession of events or thoughts: *My pen goes in the track of my thoughts* (Edmund Burke). **9** *U.S.* a class or course of study arranged by grouping students according to their ability or aptitude. **10** the groove or channel of a phonograph record or magnetic tape which contains the actual recording. **11** the trace or mark left in a cloud chamber or on a photographic plate by the passage of an electrified subatomic particle. **12** the distance between the front or rear wheels of an automobile or other vehicle. **13** the arrangement of linked steel treads by which a tank, bulldozer, or caterpillar tractor is driven forward. **14** *Obsolete.* a vestige; trace.

**— *v.t.*** **1** to follow, as by means of footprints, marks, or smell: *The hunter tracked the bear and killed it.* **2** to trace in any way: *to track down a criminal.* **3** to find and follow (a track or course). **4** to make one's way through or over; traverse. **5** *U.S.* **a** to make footprints or other marks on: *Don't track up the floor with your muddy feet.* **b** to bring into a place on one's feet: *He tracked mud into the house.* **6** to follow and plot the course of, as by radar. **7** to provide (trains) with tracks. **8** to tow (a vessel) from the shore.

**— *v.i.*** **1** to follow a track or trail. **2a** (of wheels) to run in the same track; be in alignment. **b** (of opposite wheels or runners) to be a certain distance apart.

**in one's tracks,** *Informal.* right where one is; on the spot: *The squirrel froze in its tracks when it saw the boys. The rifle was fired ... and he fell dead in his tracks* (R. Carlton).

**jump the track,** to run off the rails suddenly; derail without warning: *The train jumped the track.*

**keep track of,** to keep within one's sight, knowledge, or attention: *The noise made it difficult for me to keep track of what you said.*

**lose track of,** to fail to keep track of: *When on vacation, it is easy to lose track of what day it is.*

**make tracks,** *Informal.* **a** to go very fast; run away: *We saw a bear and made tracks for home.* **b** *Figurative.* to make rapid progress: *Considering that she started with $5,000 ... Miss Capriotti is making tracks* (New York Times).

**off the beaten track, a** a remote; little used: *Airlines fly into primarily rural areas off the beaten track of the big trunk airlines linking the nation's major cities* (Wall Street Journal). **b** *Figurative.* not what might be expected; unusual: *This novel has a surprise ending that is definitely off the beaten track.*

**off the track,** off the right or proper course; off the subject; wrong: *The speaker was a long way off the track.*

**on the track,** on the right or proper course; on the subject; right: *"If they use some sense in managing their ... farms they will probably get back on the track," says one U.S. farm expert here* (Wall Street Journal).

**the wrong side of the tracks,** *U.S.* the poor or run-down section of a town or city; slums: *There are plenty of children from the wrong side of the tracks whose test scores surpass the average* (Saturday Review).

[< Middle French *trac,* probably < Germanic (compare Middle Low German *trecken* to draw, pull)]

**track|age** (trak′ij), *n.* **1** all the tracks of a railroad; lines of track: *10,000 miles of single trackage.* **2** the right of one railroad to use the tracks of another. **3** the fee for this. [American English]

**track and field,** the sports or events of running, jumping, vaulting, and throwing, as a group. A track-and-field meet includes races and the pole vault, shot-put, high jump, and long jump, on a field, usually in the center of the track. **— track′-and-field′,** *adj.*

**tracked** (trakt), *adj.* having tracks like those of a caterpillar tractor: *Troops are learning to cross the frozen tundra with tracked weasels and big-tired snowmobiles* (Time).

**track|er** (trak′ər), *n.* **1** a person or thing that tracks or trails. **2** an apparatus for tracking objects moving in the air, such as radar. **3** a person or device that tracks or tows a vessel.

**tracker dog,** a bloodhound or other dog trained to track; trackhound.

**track|hound** (trak′hound′), *n.* = tracker dog.

**track|ing** (trak′ing), *n.* **1** the action of following, trailing, or tracing the movements of something: *They intensified their tracking of the swirling tropical storms that have ripped a path of destruction up the east coast of the United States* (William P. Schenk). **2** *U.S.* the grouping of students of a school on the basis of the track system: *Tracking can be a useful educational device if tests are frequently administered and if movement from one track to another is made easy* (New York Times).

**tracking shot,** (in motion pictures and television) a shot taken from a moving dolly.

**tracking station,** one of a series of stations set up to track part of the orbit of a satellite: *Seven-*

---

**Pronunciation Key:** hat, āge, cãre, fär; let, ēqual, tėrm; it, īce; hot, ōpen, ôrder; oil, out; cup, půt, rüle; child; long; thin; ᴛʜen; zh, measure; ə represents **a** in about, **e** in taken, **i** in pencil, **o** in lemon, **u** in circus.

*teen minutes after launching, its first radio signals beeped to the tracking station in Manchester, England* (Time).

**track|lay|er** (trak′lā′ər), *n.* a railroad worker who lays track.

**track|lay|ing** (trak′lā′ing), *n.* the laying of railway track.

**track|less** (trak′lis), *adj.* **1** without a track. **2** without paths or trails: *The region near the South Pole is a trackless wilderness.*

**trackless trolley**, = trolley bus.

**track|man** (trak′mən), *n., pl.* **-men. 1** a railroad worker who lays, inspects, or repairs tracks. **2** = trackwalker. **3** an athlete who participates in track-and-field events: *Fullbacks can run the hundred-yard dash as fast as trackmen* (New Yorker).

**track meet**, a series of contests in running, jumping, throwing, and similar events: *to run a relay race in a track meet.*

**track race**, a race around a track, especially as distinguished from a road race: *an automobile track race.*

**track record**, **1** the record of speed set by a contestant at a particular distance and track. **2** *Figurative.* the record of performance made by a person, business, or another group or individual in a particular field or endeavor: *A modern university president is expected to have practical vision, a good track record in administration, and national prominence as a scholar* (Atlantic).

**track shoe**, a light, leather shoe worn by trackmen. On a cinder or dirt track shoes with sharp spikes in the sole are used; on a board track the shoes have no spikes.

**track|side** (trak′sīd′), *n., adj.* **—*n.*** the area adjacent to a railway track: *Dozens of commuters were leaping out of their trains on to the trackside and walking to the nearest station* (London Times).
**—*adj.*** of, having to do with, or located on the trackside: *a trackside rail, trackside equipment.*

**track suit**, a heavy, fleece-lined suit worn especially by track-and-field athletes to keep warm before and after exercise.

**track system**, *U.S.* an educational system in which students are grouped according to ability or aptitude as shown in standardized tests: *Among the most publicized recommendations were that widespread busing be adopted ... and that track systems, setting levels of the curriculum for slow students and gifted students, be eliminated* (New York Times).

**track|walk|er** (trak′wô′kər), *n.* a railroad worker who walks along railroad tracks to inspect a certain section.

**track|way** (trak′wā′), *n.* a path beaten by the feet of passers; track.

**tract**[1] (trakt), *n.* **1** a stretch of land or water; area; extent: *A tract of desert land has little value to farmers.* **SYN**: expanse. **2a** a system of related parts or organs in the body. The stomach and intestines are parts of the digestive tract. **b** a bundle of nerve fibers, or one pathway of the central nervous system. **3** a period of time. **4** an anthem consisting of verses from the Bible, sung in the Roman Catholic Mass instead of the alleluia from Septuagesima to Easter Eve. **5** *Obsolete.* course (of time); duration. [< Latin *tractus, -ūs* track, course, space, duration; (literally) a drawing out or hauling < *trahere* to drag. See etym. of doublets **trace**[2], **trait**, **tret**.]

**tract**[2] (trakt), *n.* **1** a little book or pamphlet on a religious or political subject. **SYN**: homily. **2** any little book or pamphlet. [apparently short for Latin *tractātus* a handling; see etym. under **tractate**]

**trac|ta|bil|i|ty** (trak′tə bil′ə tē), *n.* the quality of being tractable; manageableness; docility.

**trac|ta|ble** (trak′tə bəl), *adj.* **1** easily managed or controlled; easy to deal with; docile: *a tractable child. Dogs are more tractable than cats.* **SYN**: compliant, manageable. **2** easily handled or worked: *Tractable metals can be hammered and shaped or rolled into thin sheets.* **SYN**: malleable. [< Latin *tractābilis* < *tractāre;* see etym. under **treat**] **—trac′ta|ble|ness**, *n.*

**trac|ta|bly** (trak′tə blē), *adv.* in a tractable manner; manageably.

**Trac|tar|i|an** (trak tãr′ē ən), *n., adj.* **—*n.*** an adherent of Tractarianism.
**—*adj.*** of or belonging to the Tractarians; having to do with Tractarianism.

**Trac|tar|i|an|ism** (trak tãr′ē ə niz′əm), *n.* a system of religious opinion published at Oxford between 1833 and 1841 in a series of papers that opposed the liberalizing tendencies within the Church of England and favored High-Church doctrines; Oxford movement; Puseyism. [< *tract*[2] + *-arian* + *-ism*]

**trac|tate** (trak′tāt), *n.* a tract; treatise. [< Latin *tractātus, -ūs* a handling, treatise; treatment < *tractāre* to treat, handle]

**trac|tile** (trak′təl), *adj.* that can be drawn out in length; ductile.

**trac|til|i|ty** (trak til′ə tē), *n., pl.* **-ties.** the quality or property of being tractile.

**trac|tion** (trak′shən), *n.* **1a** the action of drawing or pulling. **b** the fact or condition of being drawn. **2** the act of drawing or pulling loads along a road or track. **3** the kind of power used for this. Electric traction is used on subways and some railroads. **4** friction between a body and the surface on which it moves, enabling the body to move without slipping: *Wheels slip on ice because there is too little traction.* **5** *Medicine.* the action of pulling or drawing a muscle, organ, or other structure, especially as a surgical technique for healing a fracture, dislocation, or as a corrective process. [< Medieval Latin *tractio, -onis* a drawing out < Latin *trahere* to drag]

**trac|tion|al** (trak′shə nəl), *adj.* of or having to do with traction.

**traction engine**, a steam locomotive or tractor used for pulling wagons, plows, and the like, along roads or over fields rather than on tracks.

**trac|tive** (trak′tiv), *adj.* drawing or pulling; used for drawing or pulling.

***trac|tor** (trak′tər), *n.* **1** an engine that moves on wheels or two endless belts of linked steel plates, used for pulling wagons and plows, cultivating crops, excavation and grading, and the like. **2** a powerful truck having a gasoline or diesel engine, a short body, and a cab for the driver, used for pulling a freight trailer along the highway. **3a** an airplane with the propeller or propellers in front of the wings. **b** the propeller of such an airplane. [< Medieval Latin *tractor* something that pulls < Latin *trahere* to drag] **—trac′tor|like′**, *adj.*

***tractor**
definitions 1, 2

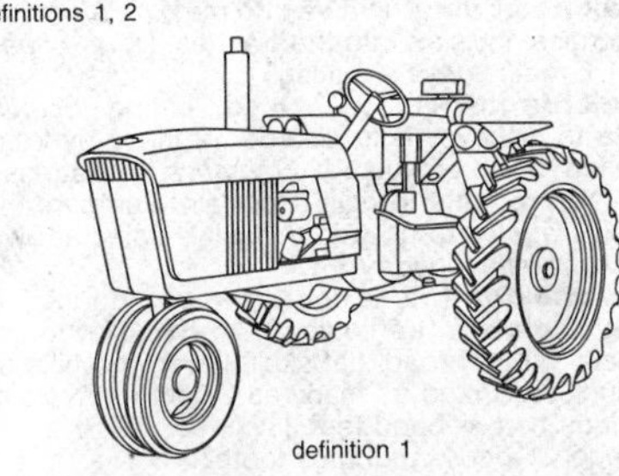

definition 1

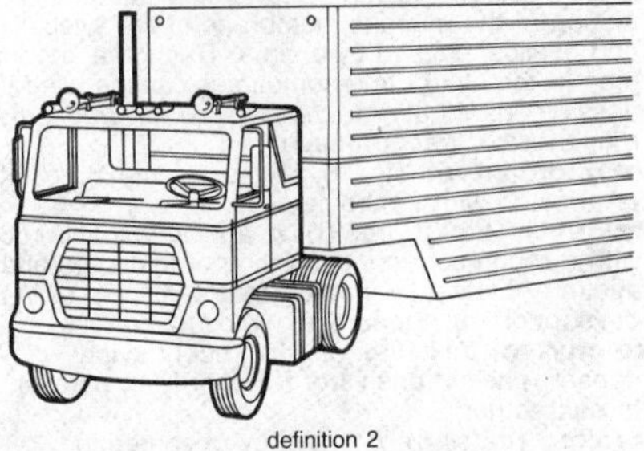

definition 2

**tractor airplane**, = tractor (def. 3a).

**tractor propeller**, = tractor (def. 3b).

**trac|tor-trail|er** (trak′tər trā′lər), *n.* a large highway freight vehicle consisting of a tractor and a detachable trailer.

**tractor train**, a train of vehicles pulled by a tractor.

**trad** (trad), *adj. British Informal.* traditional: *trad music, trad religion.*

**trade** (trād), *n., v.,* **trad|ed, trad|ing,** *adj.* **—*n.*** **1** the act or process of buying and selling; exchange of goods; commerce: *wholesale trade, retail trade, domestic trade. The United States has much trade with foreign countries.* **2** an exchange: *room and board in trade for doing the chores, an even trade.* **3** *Informal.* a bargain or business deal: *He made a good trade.* **4** a kind of work; business, especially one requiring skilled mechanical work: *the carpenter's trade, the plumber's trade, the weaver's trade.* **SYN**: occupation, craft, profession. **5** the people in the same kind of work or business: *the book trade. Carpenters, plumbers, and electricians are all members of the building trade.* **6** *Informal.* customers: *That store has a lot of trade.* **7** *Obsolete.* a regular course, as of action or movement. **8** *Obsolete.* a course; way; path. **9** *Obsolete.* dealings.
**—*v.i.*** **1** to buy and sell; exchange goods; be in commerce: *Some American companies trade all over the world. The early settlers traded with the Indians. Some speculators trade heavily in wheat and corn futures.* **SYN**: barter. **2** to make an exchange: *If you don't like your book, I'll trade with you.* **SYN**: swap. **3** to bargain; deal. **4** to be a customer: *I have traded at that grocery store for years.*
**—*v.t.*** to exchange: *to trade seats. I traded a stick of gum for a ride on her bicycle.*
**—*adj.*** **1** having to do with, used in, or characteristic of trade: *trade goods.* **2** of or having to do with a trade or occupation: *a trade guild.* **3** used as a means of communication in trading: *trade jargon.*
**the trades, a** the trade winds: *We caught the southeast trades and ran before them for nearly three weeks* (Richard Henry Dana). **b** *Informal.* trade journals or newspapers: *You can't possibly know what's going on unless you read the trades* (Time).
**trade down**, *Informal.* to buy or sell goods of a lower price or grade: *The stores traded down during the slow season.*
**trade in**, to give (an automobile, refrigerator, television set, or other appliance) as payment or part payment for something, especially for a newer model: *Yes, I can trade in your old refrigerator irrespective of condition for one of these luxurious models* (Cape Times).
**trade off**, to get rid of by trading: *to see what chance I could find to trade off my ax handles* (J. Downing).
**trade on** (or **upon**), to take advantage of; make use of for one's own ends: *He had no ability and had to trade on his friend's influence to get a job. They ... still trade on the fears and fancies of their fellows* (Edward Clodd).
**trade up**, *Informal.* to buy or sell goods of a higher rather than lower price or grade: *The decision to trade up was prompted by demand evidenced by upper income customers* (Wall Street Journal).
[< Middle Dutch or Middle Low German *trade* trade, track, course (apparently originally, of a trading ship). See related etym. at **tread**.]
**—*Syn.*** *n.* **1 Trade, commerce** mean the buying and selling or exchanging of goods or other commodities. **Trade** applies to the actual buying and selling, or exchange, of commodities: *The Government has drawn up new agreements for trade with various countries.* **Commerce**, a more general term, includes both trade and transportation, especially as conducted on a large scale between different states or countries: *The Interstate Commerce Commission sets the rates railroads charge for freight.*

**trade|a|ble** (trā′də bəl), *adj.* that can be traded: *stamps tradeable for merchandise.*

**trade acceptance**, a bill of exchange drawn by the seller of goods on the purchaser for the price of the goods, and payable in cash. The acknowledgment is written across its face by the purchaser.

**trade agreement**, **1** an agreement to promote trade between two or more nations: *The ... countries are about to enter upon their first trade agreement as a unit* (New York Times). **2** a contract between an employer and a labor union covering the conditions of employment for the length of the contract.

**trade area**, = trading area.

**trade association**, an association to promote trade, usually of firms within one industry or a group of closely related industries.

**trade balance**, the difference between the value of all the imports and that of all the exports of a country; balance of trade.

**trade barrier**, anything that hinders or restricts international trade, such as tariffs, or embargoes.

**trade book**, a book published for and sold to the general public.

**trade card**, *British.* a business card.

**trade deficit**, an unfavorable balance of trade.

**trade discount**, an amount or percentage deducted from the retail or list price by a manufacturer for a wholesaler or retailer.

**trade dollar**, a silver dollar formerly issued by the United States for trade in eastern Asia.

**trade edition**, the form of a book published for general distribution, as distinguished from a text edition.

**trade fair**, a fair to display new products, demonstrate industrial processes, and promote trade: *A British trade fair is to be held in Moscow from May 19 to June 4, and there will be a Russian fair in London from July 7 to 29* (Manchester Guardian).

**trade gap**, an unfavorable balance of trade; trade deficit.

**trade-in** (trād′in′), *n., adj.* **—*n.*** an automobile, refrigerator, television set, or other appliance given or accepted as payment or part payment for something, especially for a newer model.
**—*adj.*** having to do with such an item or such a means of paying: *We make this exceptional bonus trade-in offer because we need used cars for customers we have waiting* (Cape Times).

**trade-last** (trād′last′, -läst′), *n. Informal.* a compliment paid to a person without his knowledge but overheard by an acquaintance, who offers to tell it to the person involved in return for a compliment about himself. *Abbr:* T.L.

**trade magazine**, = trade journal.

**trade|mark** or **trade-mark** (trād′märk′), *n., v.* —*n.* **1** a mark, picture, name, word, symbol, or letters owned and used by a manufacturer or merchant to distinguish his goods from the goods of others. The registration and protection of trademarks now are provided for by law. **SYN**: brand. **2** *Figurative.* a distinctive mark or characteristic of some person or thing: *... that certainty of judgment which, we all know, is the trademark of the modern critic* (Irving Howe). *The use of emotive language is the trademark of propaganda* (Listener).
—*v.t.* **1** to distinguish by means of a trademark. **2** to register the trademark of.

**trade mission**, a group of businessmen sent by their government to a foreign country to negotiate trade agreements: *An Argentine trade mission traveling behind the Iron Curtain signed up to buy $27 million worth of oil drilling equipment* (Wall Street Journal).

**trade name**, **1** a name used by a manufacturer or merchant for some article that he sells. **2** a special name used for anything by those who buy and sell it. **3** the name under which a company does business.

**trade-name** (trād′nām′), *v.t.*, **-named, -nam|ing.** to give a trade name to; register under a trade name: *to trade-name a drug.*

**trade-off** (trād′ôf′, -of′), *n.* an even or fair exchange: *There would have to be at least implicit trade-offs giving higher prices to industry and higher real wages and salaries to employees* (London Times).

**trade pact**, = trade agreement.

**trade paper**, a newspaper published by or for some special trade or business.

**trad|er** (trā′dər), *n.* **1** a person who trades; merchant: *The trappers sold furs to traders.* **2** a ship used in trading. **3a** a member, as of a stock exchange or commodity exchange, who trades for himself and not as an agent of another or others. **b** a speculator, as in stocks or commodities.

**trade rat**, = pack rat (def. 1).

**trade route**, a route followed by traders or trading ships: *In ancient times, southern Arabia grew rich because it lay along important trade routes between Europe, Asia, and Africa* (William Spencer).

**trades** (trādz), *n.pl.* See under **trade**.

**trad|es|can|ti|a** (trad′es kan′shē ə), *n.* any one of a group of perennial American herbs; spiderwort. [< New Latin *Tradescantia* the genus name < John *Tradescant,* died about 1638, a British naturalist and gardener to Charles I]

**trade school**, a school where a trade or trades are taught.

**trade secret**, information about a commercial product kept secret to prevent competitors from duplicating the product: *A trade secret may consist of any formula, pattern, device ... which is used in one's business* (New Yorker).

**trades|folk** (trādz′fōk′), *n.pl.* = tradespeople.

**trades|man** (trādz′mən), *n., pl.* **-men. 1** a person engaged in trade; merchant; storekeeper; shopkeeper. **2** *Dialect.* a person skilled in a particular trade. [< *trade's* + *man.* Compare etym. under **salesman.**]

**trades|peo|ple** (trādz′pē′pəl), *n.pl.* people engaged in trade; storekeepers; shopkeepers.

**trades union**, or **trades-un|ion** (trādz′yün′yən), *n. Especially British.* a trade union.

**trades unionism**, or **trades-un|ion|ism** (trādz′-yün′yə niz əm), *n. Especially British.* trade unionism.

**trades unionist**, or **trades-un|ion|ist** (trādz′-yün′yə nist), *n. Especially British.* trade unionist.

**trades|wom|an** (trādz′wu̇m′ən), *n., pl.* **-wom|en.** a woman engaged in trade.

**trade union**, or **trade-un|ion** (trād′yün′yən), *n.* **1** an association of workers in any trade or craft to protect and promote their interests. **2** any labor union; union.

**trade unionism**, or **trade-un|ion|ism** (trād′-yün′yə niz əm), *n.* **1** the system of having trade unions. **2** the principles or practices of trade unions.

**trade unionist**, or **trade-un|ion|ist** (trād′yün′-yə nist), *n.* **1** a member of a trade union. **2** a supporter of trade unionism.

**trade wind**, **1** a wind blowing steadily toward the equator from about 30 degrees north latitude or from about 30 degrees south latitude. North of the equator, it blows from the northeast; south of the equator, from the southeast. **2** *Obsolete.* any wind that blows steadily in the same direction at sea. [< *trade* in obsolete sense of "habitual course"]

**TRADIC** (trā′dik), *n.* a transistor digital computer (a small transistorized computer used to make rapid calculation, such as in aerial navigation and gunnery, to meet the demands of supersonic flight).

**trad|ing area** (trā′ding), the area in which a manufacturer, distributor, or retailer conducts business regularly and profitably; trade area.

**trading bank**, (in Australia) a commercial bank.

**trading post**, **1** a store or station of a trader or trading company, especially in unsettled country. Some trading posts exist in the southwestern United States, where Indians sell or exchange products for food, clothing, and farm equipment. **2** any one of a number of posts or booths on the floor of a stock exchange which serves as the headquarters for transactions in certain specific stocks.

**trading stamp**, = stamp (def. 2).

**tra|di|tion** (trə dish′ən), *n.* **1** the handing down of beliefs, opinions, customs, and stories, such as from parents to children, especially by word of mouth or by practice: *She has been bred up ... by a very worldly family, and taught their traditions* (Thackeray). **2** what is handed down in this way: *According to the old tradition, the first American flag was made by Betsy Ross.* **SYN**: folklore, legend. **3a** (in Jewish theology) the unwritten laws and doctrines, or any of them, believed to have been received by Moses from God and handed down orally from generation to generation. **b** (in Christian theology) the unwritten precepts and doctrines, or any one of them, held to have been received from Jesus and his apostles and handed down orally since then. **4** *Law.* the delivery of something material to another; transfer. **5** the delivery, especially oral delivery, of information or instruction. **6** *Obsolete.* **a** a giving up; surrender. **b** betrayal. [< Latin *trāditiō, -ōnis* < *trādere* hand down < *trāns-* over + *dare* give. See etym. of doublet *treason.*] —**tra|di′tion|less,** *adj.*

**tra|di|tion|al** (trə dish′ə nəl, -dish′nəl), *adj.* **1** of tradition; handed down by tradition: *Shaking hands upon meeting is a traditional custom.* **SYN**: legendary. **2** according to tradition; conforming to earlier styles or customs: *traditional furniture. An Egyptian architect has designed a traditional building, with fountains for washing before worshipping* (Manchester Guardian). **3** customary: *A Memorial Day parade is traditional in almost every town.* —**tra|di′tion|al|ly,** *adv.*

**tra|di|tion|al|ism** (trə dish′ə nə liz′əm, -dish′nə-liz-), *n.* **1** adherence to the authority of tradition, especially in matters of religion, morality, and custom. **2** a philosophical system according to which all religious knowledge is derived from divine revelation and received by traditional instruction.

**tra|di|tion|al|ist** (trə dish′ə nə list, -dish′nə-), *n., adj.* —*n.* a traditionalistic person.
—*adj.* = traditionalistic.

**tra|di|tion|al|is|tic** (trə dish′ə nə lis′tik, -dish′nə-), *adj.* **1** of or having to do with traditionalists or traditionalism. **2** adhering to tradition.

**tra|di|tion|al|ize** (trə dish′ə nə līz, -dish′nə), *v.t.*, **-ized, -iz|ing.** to make traditional: *to traditionalize a habit or practice.*

**traditional logic**, = Aristotelian logic.

**tra|di|tion|ar|y** (trə dish′ə ner′ē), *adj., n., pl.* **-ar-ies.** —*adj.* = traditional.
—*n.* = traditionist.

**tra|di|tion|ist** (trə dish′ə nist), *n.* **1** a person who accepts or maintains the authority of tradition. **2** a person who records, preserves, or hands down tradition.

**trad|i|tive** (trad′ə tiv), *adj.* = traditional. [apparently < earlier French *traditive,* ultimately < Latin *trādere;* see etym. under **tradition**]

**tra|duce** (trə düs′, -dyüs′), *v.t.*, **-duced, -duc|ing.** to speak evil of (a person) falsely; slander. **SYN**: defame, malign, vilify, asperse, calumniate. [earlier, to alter, change over, transport < Latin *trādūcere* parade in disgrace; (originally) lead along, across, transfer < *trāns-* across + *dūcere* to lead] —**tra|duce′ment,** *n.* —**tra|duc′er,** *n.*

**tra|duc|tion** (trə duk′shən), *n.* **1** *Logic.* the transfer or transition from one classification or order of reasoning to another. **2** the act of traducing or maligning. **3** *Obsolete.* a translation, as into another language. **4** *Obsolete.* a transmission by generation. **5** *Obsolete.* a bringing over, transferring, or transmitting. [< Latin *trādūctiō, -ōnis* < *trādūcere;* see etym. under **traduce**]

**traf|fic** (traf′ik), *n., v.*, **-ficked, -fick|ing.** —*n.* **1** people, automobiles, wagons, ships, or the like, coming and going along a way of travel: *Police control the traffic in large cities.* **2** the act or process of buying and selling; commerce; trade: *traffic by sea.* **3a** the business done by a railroad line, steamship line, airline, or bus line; number of passengers or amount of freight carried. **b** the revenue from this. **4** the total amount of business done by any company or industry within a certain time. **5** the transportation of goods and merchandise for the purpose of trade: *ships of traffic.* **6** *Figurative.* dealings; association: *Traffic with criminals is dangerous. An extensive traffic in stolen goods* (George Borrow).
—*v.i.* **1** to carry on trade; buy and sell; exchange: *The men trafficked with the natives for ivory.* **2** to have illicit dealings: *to traffic in narcotics.*
—*v.t.* **1** to come and go along (a way of travel); traverse: *a lightly trafficked road.* **2** to carry on trade in; buy and sell: *to traffic illicit merchandise.*
[< Middle French *trafficque* < Italian *traffico* < *trafficare* < *tras-* across (< Latin *trāns-*) + *ficcare* shove, poke, ultimately < Latin *fīgere* fix, set] —**traf′fic|less,** *adj.*

**traf|fic|a|bil|i|ty** (traf′ə kə bil′ə tē), *n.* suitability for traffic or passage to and fro.

**traf|fic|a|ble** (traf′ə kə bəl), *adj.* suitable for traffic or passage to and fro.

**traf|fi|ca|tor** (traf′ə kā′tər), *n. British.* a turn indicator on an automobile; turn signal. [< *traffic* + (indic)*ator*]

***traffic circle**, a junction of several roads in which the merging traffic goes around a central circle in one direction only; rotary.

***traffic circle**

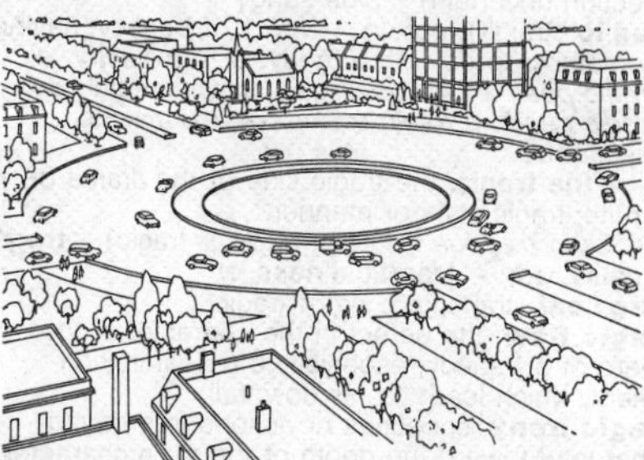

**traffic cop**, *Informal.* a policeman who directs the traffic of motor vehicles and pedestrians.

**traffic court**, a court which administers the laws regulating the actions of drivers on public roads and streets.

**traffic engineer**, an engineer who specializes in traffic engineering.

**traffic engineering**, a branch of civil engineering dealing with highway design and the efficient control of vehicular traffic.

**traffic island**, a safety zone in the center of a traffic circle or between lanes of traffic.

**traffic jam**, an overcrowding of vehicles in an area, hindering or stopping free movement.

**traf|fic-jammed** (traf′ik jamd′), *adj.* having much traffic; crowded with vehicles: *It was hot and muggy that June evening on Detroit's traffic-jammed Belle Isle Bridge* (Newsweek).

**traf|fick|er** (traf′ə kər), *n.* **1** a person who buys and sells; trader, merchant, or dealer: *... an itinerant trafficker in broken glass and rags* (George Eliot). **2** a person who carries on underhand or illicit dealings: *Clandestine manufacture of morphine ... near opium-growing areas of the Far East and Middle East indicated a network of well-organized international traffickers* (Harry J. Anslinger).

**traffic light**, a set of electric lights used for signaling at a corner or intersection to control traffic; stoplight. Usually, a red light ("stop") and a green light ("go") are flashed automatically every so many seconds or minutes.

**traffic pattern**, **1** the positions of aircraft above an airport before landing or after take-off, as assigned by the control tower. **2** the use of streets and roads, especially at certain turns and often by a particular type of driver, such as truckers or commuters.

**traffic sign**, a sign along a street or road indicating speed limits, directions, right or left turns, and hazards.

**traffic signal**, = traffic light.

**traffic ticket**, a summons issued to a motorist for a violation of a traffic law.

**traffic warden**, *British.* an official who controls vehicular traffic and parking.

**trag.**, **1** tragedy. **2** tragic.

**trag|a|canth** (trag′ə kanth), *n.* **1** a sticky substance obtained from certain Old-World shrubs or herbs of the pea family, used for stiffening cloth and for giving firmness to pills and lozenges;

---

**Pronunciation Key:** hat, āge, cãre, fär; let, ēqual, tėrm; it, īce; hot, ōpen, ôrder; oil, out; cup, pu̇t, rüle; **ch**ild; lo**ng**; **th**in; **ᴛʜ**en; **zh**, measure; ə represents **a** in about, **e** in taken, **i** in pencil, **o** in lemon, **u** in circus.

gum tragacanth. **2** any one of these shrubs. [< Latin *tragacantha* < Greek *tragákantha* (literally) goat's-thorn < *trágos* goat + *ákantha* thorn]

**tra|ge|di|an** (trə jē′dē ən), *n.* **1** an actor in tragedies. **2** a writer of tragedies: *Under this curled marble ... sleepe, rare tragedian, Shakespeare, sleepe alone* (John Donne). [< Old French *tragediane* < *tragedie* tragedy]

**tra|ge|di|enne** (trə jē′dē en′), *n.* an actress in tragedies. [< French *tragédienne,* feminine of *tragédien,* Old French *tragediane* tragedian < *tragedie* tragedy]

**trag|e|dy** (traj′ə dē), *n., pl.* **-dies. 1** a serious play having an unhappy ending. In classical drama a tragedy showed the conflict of man with fate or the gods and the unhappy ending brought about by some weakness or error on the part of the central character. Sophocles' *Oedipus* and Shakespeare's *Hamlet* are tragedies. **2a** the branch of drama that includes such plays. **b** the art or theory of writing or presenting such plays. **3** a novel, long poem, or other literary work, similar to a tragic play. **4** *Figurative.* a very sad or terrible happening; calamity or disaster: *The father's death was a tragedy to his family.* **SYN**: catastrophe. [< Medieval Latin *tragedia* < Latin *tragoedia* < Greek *tragōidiā* < *trágos* goat (connection uncertain) + *ōidē* song]

**trag|ic** (traj′ik), *adj., n.* **—*adj.* 1** of tragedy; having something to do with tragedy: *a tragic actor, a tragic poet.* **2** *Figurative.* very sad; dreadful: *a tragic death, a tragic event.* **SYN**: calamitous, disastrous.
**—*n.* the tragic,** the tragic side of the drama or of life; tragic style or manner.
[< Latin *tragicus* < Greek *tragikós* tragic] **—trag′i|cal|ly,** *adv.* **—trag′i|cal|ness,** *n.*

**trag|i|cal** (traj′ə kəl), *adj.* = tragic.

**tragic flaw,** the defect in the character of the hero of a tragedy, especially a defect in judgment, which leads to his downfall.

**tragic irony,** speeches or actions in a tragedy that lead toward the doom of the main character, unknown to him but known by the audience.

**trag|i|com|e|dy** (traj′i kom′ə dē), *n., pl.* **-dies. 1** a play having both tragic and comic elements. Shakespeare's *The Merchant of Venice* is a tragicomedy. **2** an incident or situation in which serious and comic elements are blended. [< Middle French *tragicomédie* < Latin *tragicōmoedia,* reduction of *tragicocōmoedia* < *tragicus* (see etym. under **tragic**) + *cōmoedia.* Compare etym. under **comedy.**]

**trag|i|com|ic** (traj′i kom′ik), *adj.* having both tragic and comic elements: *The clown is a tragicomic universal, the image of man himself, a sad and ridiculous creature, the gaiety of his tinsel earthly surroundings mocked by his godly consciousness of sin* (Newsweek).

**trag|i|com|i|cal** (traj′i kom′ə kəl), *adj.* = tragicomic.

**trag|o|pan** (trag′ə pan), *n.* any one of a group of brilliantly colored Asian pheasants, the male having a pair of upright, fleshy horns on the head. [< New Latin *Tragopan* the genus name < Latin *tragopān* < a reputed Ethiopian bird < Greek *tragópān* < *trágos* goat + *pân* Pan]

**tra|gus** (trā′gəs), *n., pl.* **-gi** (-jī). the bulge that partially conceals the external opening of the ear. [< Latin *tragus* < Greek *trágos* (originally) goat (because of the bunch of hairs on it)]

**tra|hi|son des clercs** (trá hē sôɴ′ dā klerk′), *French.* intellectual treason; abandonment of intellectual principles.

**traik** (trāk), *v.i., n. Scottish.* stroll. [origin uncertain. Compare Swedish *tråka* to tug, drudge.]

**trail** (trāl), *n., v.* **—*n.* 1** a path across a wild or unsettled region: *the Oregon Trail. The scouts followed mountain trails for days.* **2a** a track or smell: *The dogs found the trail of the rabbit.* **b** a mark left where something has been dragged or has passed along: *the trail of a snail or a snake.* **3** anything that follows along behind: *As the car sped down the road, it left a trail of dust behind it.* **4** the train of a skirt or gown. **5** the lower end of a gun carriage, which rests or slides on the ground when the carriage is unlimbered. **6** the command or position of trail arms. [< verb]
**—*v.t.* 1** to follow the trail or track of; hunt by track or smell; track: *to trail a bear, to trail a thief. The dogs trailed the rabbit.* **2a** to follow along behind; follow: *The dog trailed its master constantly.* **b** to follow in a long, uneven line: *The campers trailed their leader down the mountainside.* **3a** to pull, drag, or draw along behind: *The child trailed a toy horse after him. She trailed her gown through the mud.* **b** to draw along wearily or with difficulty: *The bird trailed its broken wing.* **4** to carry or bring by or as if by dragging: *to trail snow into a house.* **5** to bring or have floating after itself: *a car trailing dust.* **6** to lengthen in time; protract. **7a** *U.S.* to make a path by treading down (grass or other growth). **b** to mark out (a trail or track). **8** to bring, hold, or carry (a rifle or lance) at trail arms.
**—*v.i.* 1** to draw along behind; be pulled along behind; drag: *Her dress trails on the ground.* **2** to hang down or float loosely from something. **3** to grow along: *Poison ivy trailed by the road.* **4** to go along slowly, idly, or with difficulty, as if dragged along: *The children trailed to school.* **5** to move or float from and after something moving, as dust or smoke. **6** to extend in a long, uneven line; straggle: *refugees trailing from their ruined village.* **7** to follow, fall, or lag behind, as in a race. **8** to follow a trail, track, or scent. **9** to pass little by little: *Her voice trailed off into silence.*
**blaze the trail,** to pioneer or prepare the way for something new: *The Treaty blazes the trail to full-scale political federation in Western Europe* (London Times).
**hit the trail,** *U.S.* **a** to set out; depart: *Men can pass out the church door, shoulder their packs ..., and unconcernedly hit the trail to the lower* [*regions*] (Outing). **b** *Slang.* to go away at once; get out: *The sheriff ordered the suspicious-looking stranger to hit the trail.*
[< Old North French *trailler* to tow, ultimately < Latin *trāgula* dragnet] **—trail′less,** *adj.*

***trail arms, 1** the military command to bring or hold a weapon at the side with the butt nearly on the ground and the muzzle tilted forward. **2** the position in the manual of arms in which a weapon in thus held.

***trail arms**
definition 2

**trail|bas|ton** (trāl′bas′tən), *n.* one of a class of lawless ruffians in England against whom ordinances were issued in the 1300's. [< Anglo-French *traille-baston* (literally) one who trails or carries a cudgel < *traille,* imperative of *trailler* to trail + *baston* stick]

**trail bike,** a lightweight, rugged motorcycle for use on rough terrain: *Anyone hoping to escape the filth and din of cities for the quiet beauty of our woods, mountains, or deserts is ... greeted by the rattling snarl of trail bikes, dune buggies, and the like* (Time).

**trail|blaz|er** (trāl′blā′zər), *n.* a person or thing that pioneers or prepares the way to something new: *In the field of art, he has been a veritable trailblazer* (Saturday Review).

**trail|blaz|ing** (trāl′blā′zing), *adj.* that prepares or shows the way, especially to something new; innovating; pioneering: *trailblazing projects or exploits. He has written five trailblazing books on education* (Time).

**trail|break|er** (trāl′brā′kər), *n.* = trailblazer.

**trail|er** (trā′lər), *n., v.* **—*n.* 1** a cargo vehicle to be pulled along the highway. There are small two-wheeled trailers pulled by automobiles, and large trailers pulled by trucks, especially by trucks that lack bodies of their own. **2** a vehicle fitted up for people to live in and usually pulled by a automobile; house trailer. **3** a trailing plant or branch; vine that grows along the ground. **SYN**: creeper, runner. **4** a person or animal that follows a trail; tracker. **5** a few scenes shown to advertise a forthcoming motion picture or television program.
**—*v.i.*** to travel in a trailer: *If you're camping or trailering, you have nothing to worry about clear across the province* (Maclean's).
**—*v.t.*** to take by trailer: *They fade into the sunset ... in pickup trucks, with their trusty horses comfortably trailered on behind* (Time).

**trail|er|a|bil|i|ty** (trā′lə rə bil′ə tē), *n.* the condition of being trailerable.

**trail|er|a|ble** (trā′lə rə bəl), *adj.* that can be used or lived in as a trailer.

**trailer camp,** = trailer court.

**trailer coach,** a trailer used as a place to live.

**trailer court,** a site equipped with running water, electricity, and other facilities, for accommodating automobile trailers: *The families began to cultivate the little twelve-by-fifty foot plots of ground allotted to them in the trailer court* (Harper's).

**trail|er|ite** (trā′lə rīt), *n.* a person who travels or lives in a house trailer: *Trailerites, of course, buy less furniture and kitchen appliances than most householders* (Newsweek).

**trailer park,** = trailer court.

**trail|er|ship** (trā′lər ship′), *n.* a ship designed to carry loaded truck trailers as cargo.

**trail|er|ship|ping** (trā′lər ship′ing), *n.* the work or business of shipping by trailership.

**trail|ing arbutus** (trā′ling), = arbutus (def. 1).

**trailing edge,** the rearward edge of an airfoil or propeller blade.

**trail rope, 1** a rope trailed on the ground to check the speed of a balloon. **2** = prolonge.

**train** (trān), *n., v.* **—*n.* 1** a connected line of railroad cars moving along together: *A very long freight train of 100 cars rolled by.* **2** a line, as of people, animals, wagons, or trucks, moving along together; caravan: *The early settlers crossed the continent by wagon train.* **SYN**: row, chain, file, procession. **3** a collection of vehicles, animals, and men accompanying an army to carry supplies, baggage, ammunition, or any equipment or materials. **4** a part that hangs down and drags along behind: *The train of a lady's gown.* **5** something that is drawn along behind; trailing part; tail: *the train of a peacock, the train of a comet.* **6** a group of followers; retinue: *the king and his train, a train of admirers.* **7** *Figurative.* **a** a series; succession; sequence: *A long train of misfortunes overcame the hero.* **b** an order of succession; continuous course: *Now where was I when you interrupted? I seem to have lost my train of thought.* **c** a succession of results or conditions following some event: *The flood brought starvation and disease in its train.* **8** a line of gunpowder that acts as a fuze to fire a charge or mine. **9** a series of connected parts, such as wheels and pinions, through which motion is transmitted in a machine. **10** *Physics.* a series of wave cycles, pulses, etc., such as one caused by a short periodic disturbance. [< Old French *train* < *trainer;* see the verb]
**—*v.t.* 1** to bring up; rear; teach: *He trained his sons to respect their parents and teachers.* **SYN**: educate. **2** to make skillful by teaching and practice: *to train people as nurses.* **3** to discipline and instruct (an animal) to be useful, be obedient, perform tricks, race, or otherwise respond to command: *to train a horse. Saint Bernard dogs were trained to hunt for travelers lost in the snow.* **4** to make fit for a sport by proper exercise and diet: *to train a boxer.* **5** to bring into a particular position; make grow in a particular way: *Train the vine around this post.* **6** to aim, point, or direct: *to train cannon upon a fort.* **7** to trail or drag. **8** *Archaic.* to allure; entice; take in.
**—*v.i.* 1** to be trained; undergo training. **2** to train some person, group, or thing. **3** to make oneself fit, as by proper exercise and diet: *to train for a prizefight. Runners train for races.*
**in train,** in proper order, arrangement, or sequence; in process: *Arrangements are also in train for us to borrow a further $500 million from the American Export-Import Bank* (Sunday Times).
[< Old French *trainer* < Vulgar Latin *tragīnāre* < *tragere,* for Latin *trahere* drag, draw] **—train′a|ble,** *adj.*

**train|a|bil|i|ty** (trā′nə bil′ə tē), *n.* the ability to be trained: *The authors concluded that trainability in most occupations may be reasonably well predicted* (E. G. Williamson).

**train|band** (trān′band′), *n.* an organized group of trained citizen soldiers not in the regular army, such as existed in England in the 1500's, 1600's, and 1700's. [short for earlier *trained band*]

**train|bear|er** (trān′bãr′ər), *n.* a person who holds up the train of a robe or gown, especially one appointed to attend a sovereign on a ceremonial occasion.

**train case,** a small case for carrying the essential articles needed for travel by train.

**trained** (trānd), *adj.* **1** formed or made proficient by training; educated; practiced: *a trained eye, a trained teacher.* **2** having a train: *a trained skirt.*

**trained nurse,** = graduate nurse.

**train|ee** (trā nē′), *n.* **1** a person who is receiving training, especially for a particular kind of work, such as in a company or for the government. **2** *U.S.* a person undergoing basic training in a branch of the armed forces, especially in the Army.

**train|ee|ship** (trā nē′ship), *n.* **1** the condition or time of being a trainee. **2** the position or sum of money given to a trainee: *He also urged the establishment by the Public Health Service of traineeships for graduate nurses* (New York Times).

**train|er** (trā′nər), *n.* **1** a person or thing that trains, especially a person who trains or prepares people, horses, or other animals, for athletic or sporting competition. *He is an animal trainer for the circus.* **SYN**: coach. **2** an aircraft used in training pilots. **3** a member of a gun's crew on a ship who brings the gun or turret laterally to the correct direction.

**train|ing** (trā′ning), *n., adj.* **—*n.* 1** practical edu-

cation in some art, profession, or occupation: *training for teachers.* SYN: schooling, discipline. **2** the development of strength and endurance, as by proper diet and exercise: *physical training.* SYN: practice. **3** good condition maintained by exercise, diet, and care: *The athlete kept in training by not overeating and not smoking.* SYN: fitness.
—***adj.*** that trains; of or for training: *training exercises.*

**training camp**, **1** a military camp for basic training. **2** a camp where boxers or other athletes train and practice before the regular playing season or a match.

**training college**, *British.* a college for training persons for some particular profession, especially one for training teachers.

**training school**, **1** a school for giving training in some art, profession, or skill: *a training school for teachers or nurses, a training school for mechanics.* **2** a house of correction for young offenders or criminals: *At least two of the state training schools for delinquent boys, the New York State Training School for Boys in 1937 and the Illinois Training School for Boys, have tried using foster homes for the placement of certain children committed to them* (Clyde B. Vedder).

**training ship**, a ship equipped and used for practical training in seamanship.

**training table**, a special dining table or tables set aside for athletes in training, usually providing a special diet.

**train|load** (trān′lōd′), *n.* as much as a train can hold or carry: *It has a positive significance for railways in extreme climates, where maximum permitted trainloads have to be reduced in winter* (New Scientist).

**train|man** (trān′mən), *n., pl.* **-men**. **1** a brakeman or railroad worker in a train crew, of lower rank than a conductor. **2** any member of a train crew other than the engineer and fireman.

**train|mas|ter** (trān′mas′tər, -mäs′-), *n.* an official of a railroad line who directs trains through a railroad division or the switching operations in a terminal, station, or yard.

**train oil**, oil obtained from the blubber of whales, especially the right whale, seals, and certain fishes. [< obsolete *trane,* or *train* train oil < Middle Low German *trâne* or Middle Dutch *traen* exuded oil; apparently (originally) teardrop]

**train shed**, a large, open structure for sheltering railroad trains, especially one covering the tracks and adjacent platforms at a station or terminal.

**train|sick** (trān′sik′), *adj.* sick because of a train's motion. —**train′sick′ness**, *n.*

**train|time** (trān′tīm′), *n.* the scheduled time of a train's departure.

**traipse** (trāps), *v.,* **traipsed, traips|ing**, *n. Informal.* —***v.i.*** to walk about aimlessly, carelessly, or needlessly: *The idle boys went traipsing through the streets, looking for something exciting to do.*
—***v.t.*** to walk or tramp over; tread: *The idle boys traipsed the streets looking for excitement.*
—***n.*** a traipsing. Also, **trapes**.
[origin unknown]

**trait** (trāt, *especially British* trā), *n.* **1** a quality of mind or character; distinguishing feature; characteristic: *Courage, love of fair play, and common sense are desirable traits. This reliance on authority is a fundamental primitive trait* (James Harvey Robinson). SYN: See syn. under **feature**. **2** a stroke, as of wit, skill, or cunning. [< Middle French *trait* < Latin *tractus, -ūs* a draft, a drawing, a drawing out; line drawn, feature < *trahere* to drag. See etym. of doublets **trace²**, **tract¹**, **tret**.]

**trai|tor** (trā′tər), *n., adj.* —***n.*** **1** a person who betrays his country or ruler: *Benedict Arnold became a traitor by helping the British during the American Revolution. He is a traitor and betray'd the state* (Byron). **2** a person who betrays a trust, a duty, or a friend: *Judas Iscariot, which was . . . the traitor* (Luke 6:16). SYN: turncoat, renegade.
—***adj.*** = traitorous.
[< Anglo-French, Old French *traitour* < Latin *trāditor, -ōris* < *trādere* transmit < *trāns-* over + *dare* give]

**trai|tor|ess** (trā′tər is), *n.* = traitress.

**trai|tor|ous** (trā′tər əs), *adj.* **1** like a traitor; treacherous; faithless. SYN: disloyal, false, perfidious. **2** having to do with or of the nature of treason. —**trai′tor|ous|ly**, *adv.* —**trai′tor|ous|ness**, *n.*

**trai|tress** (trā′tris), *n.* a woman traitor.

**tra|ject** (*v.* trə jekt′; *n.* traj′ekt), *v., n.* —***v.t.*** **1** to throw across; cast over: *A persistent temptation to administer the sacramental wafer to his parishioners' lips by standing back two or three feet and trajecting it in a lovely arc over his left shoulder* (J. D. Salinger). **2** to transmit (as thoughts or words).
—***n.*** **1** a way or place for crossing over; means of passage; route: *The motorcade followed the logical traject: straight along Main Street* (Time). **2** an act of crossing over; passage: *During the whole traject I met with no living thing* (Edmund O'Donovan).
[< Latin *trājectus,* past participle of *trājicere* < *trāns-* across + *jacere* to throw]

**tra|jec|tion** (trə jek′shən), *n. Archaic.* the act of trajecting or fact of being trajected.

***tra|jec|to|ry** (trə jek′tər ē, -trē), *n., pl.* **-ries**. **1** a curved path, as of a projectile, comet, or planet. **2** *Geometry.* a curve or surface that passes through a given set of points or intersects a given series of curves or surfaces at a constant angle. [< Medieval Latin *trajectorius* for throwing across < Latin *trājectus;* see etym. under **traject**]

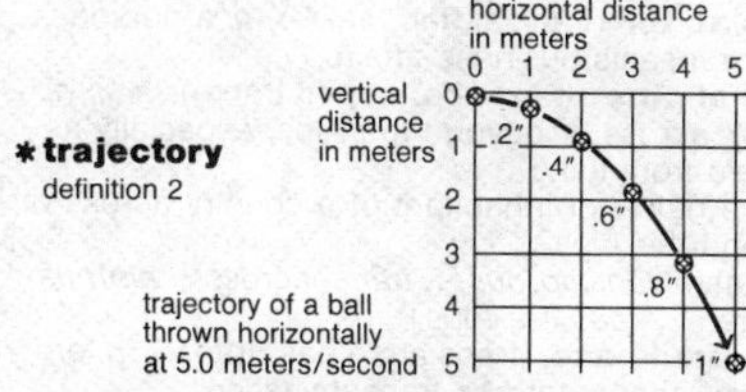


***trajectory**
definition 2

**tra-la-la** (trä′lä lä′), *interj.* a gay utterance sung as a musical phrase or representing a short instrumental flourish.

**tral|a|ti|tious** (tral′ə tish′əs), *adj.* **1** transferred; metaphorical or figurative, as words or meanings. **2** repeated by one person after another, as a statement. **3** handed down from one generation to another. [< Latin *trālātītius,* variant of *trālātīcius* (with English *-ous*) for *trānslāticus* < *trānslātus;* see etym. under **translate**]

**tram¹** (tram), *n., v.,* **trammed, tram|ming**. —***n.*** **1** *British.* a streetcar. **2** = tramway. **3** a truck or car for carrying loads in mines. **4** an overhead or suspended carrier traveling on a cable.
—***v.t.*** **1** to carry (coal, ore, or the like) by a tram or trams. **2** to push (a car or truck) to and from the shaft in a mine.
[originally, Scottish *tram,* the beams or shafts of a barrow or sledge; barrow or truck body. Compare Middle Dutch or Middle Low German *trame* beam.]

**tram²** (tram), *n.* silk thread consisting of two or more single strands loosely twisted together, used for the woof, especially in weaving fine silk goods and velvet. Also, **trame**. [earlier *tramme* mechanical contrivance; plot < French *trame,* Old French *traime* cunning device, plot; (originally) woof < Latin *trāma* woof]

**tram³** (tram), *n., v.,* **trammed, tram|ming**. —***n.*** **1** an instrument used in drawing ellipses. **2** (of machinery) the correct position or adjustment of one part to another: *in tram, out of tram.* **3** = trammel.
—***v.t.*, *v.i.*** to adjust, measure, or align with a tram or trammel.
[short for *trammel*]

**tram|car** (tram′kär′), *n.* **1** *British.* a streetcar. **2** *Mining.* a tram.

**trame** (tram), *n.* = tram².

**tram|line** (tram′līn′), *n.* = tramway.

**tram|mel** (tram′əl), *n., v.,* **-meled, -mel|ing** or **-melled, -mel|ling**. —***n.*** **1** a net to catch fish, birds, and other small animals, especially a net made of two or three layers, one of which is fine-meshed. In a trammel net, the fish strike the fine layer and carry it through the large one or ones, forming pockets in which they are caught. **2** a hook, bar, or chain in a fireplace to hold pots and kettles over the fire. **3** an instrument for drawing ellipses; tram. **4** a gauge used in adjusting and aligning mechanical parts. **5** a shackle for controlling the motions of a horse and making him amble; hobble.
—***v.t.*** **1** to hinder; restrain. SYN: fetter, hamper, impede. **2** to catch in or as if in a trammel; entangle.
**trammels**, anything that hinders or restrains: *A large bequest freed the artist from the trammels of poverty.*
[< Old French *tramail* < Medieval Latin *trimaculum* < Latin *tri-* three + *macula* mesh] —**tram′mel|er, tram′mel|ler**, *n.*

**tra|mon|ta|na** (trä′môn tä′nä), *n.* the north wind, as blowing over Italy or the Mediterranean from across the Alps. [< Italian *tramontana;* see etym. under **tramontane**]

**tra|mon|tane** (trə mon′tān, tram′ən-), *adj., n.* —***adj.*** **1** being or situated beyond the mountains, especially beyond the Alps as viewed from Italy; having to do with the other side of the mountains. **2** (of the wind) coming across or from beyond the mountains, especially blowing over Italy from beyond the Alps. **3** = foreign.
—***n.*** **1** a person who lives beyond the mountains, especially beyond the Alps. **2** a foreigner. **3** any cold wind from a mountain range.
[< Italian *tramontana* north wind, polestar; in plural, foreigners < Latin *trānsmontānus* beyond the mountains < *trāns-* across + *mōns, montis* mountain]

**tramp** (tramp), *v., n.* —***v.i.*** **1** to walk heavily: *He tramped across the floor in his heavy boots.* **2** to step heavily (on); trample: *He tramped on the flowers.* **3** to go on foot; walk: *The hikers tramped through the mountains. We tramped through the streets.* **4** to walk steadily; march: *The hikers tramped mile after mile.* **5** to go or wander as a tramp.
—***v.t.*** **1** to step heavily on; trample upon. **2** to travel on or through on foot: *to tramp the streets, to tramp the city day after day.*
—***n.*** **1** the sound of a heavy step or steps: *The steady tramp of marching feet.* **2** a long, steady walk; march; hike: *The friends took a tramp together over the hills.* **3** a person who wanders about, living by begging, doing odd jobs, or the like: *A tramp came to the door and asked for food.* SYN: vagabond, hobo, vagrant, beggar. **4** a freight ship without a regular route or schedule, that takes a cargo when and where it can; tramp steamer. **5a** an iron or steel plate worn under the shoe or boot to protect it, especially in digging and climbing. **b** an iron or steel plate with spikes, worn on a shoe or boot to give a firm foothold on ice. **6** *Informal.* a woman or girl of low morals: *Ladies don't fight with their fists in the street like common tramps* (Louise Meriwether).
[perhaps < Low German or Flemish *trampen* to stamp, tread] —**tramp′er**, *n.*

**tram|ple** (tram′pəl), *v.,* **-pled, -pling**, *n.* —***v.t.*** **1** to tread heavily on; crush: *The herd of wild cattle trampled the farmer's crops.* **2** *Figurative.* to treat cruelly, harshly or scornfully.
—***v.i.*** to tread or walk heavily; stamp.
—***n.*** the act or sound of trampling; tramp: *We heard the trample of many feet.*
**trample on** (or **upon**), to treat with scorn, harshness, or cruelty: *The dictator trampled on the rights of the people. Wit tramples upon rules* (Samuel Johnson). —**tram′pler**, *n.*

***tram|po|line** (tram′pə lēn′, tram′pə lin), *n.* a piece of canvas or other sturdy fabric stretched on a metal frame, used for tumbling and acrobatics in gymnasiums and circuses. [< Italian *trampolino* < *trampoli* stilts < Low German *trampeln* trample]

***trampoline**

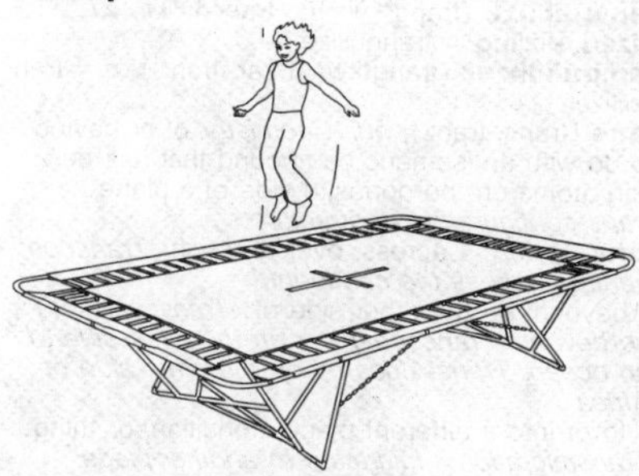

**tram|po|lin|er** (tram′pə lē′nər, tram′pə lə-), *n.* = trampolinist.

**tram|po|lin|ing** (tram′pə lē′ning, tram′pə lə-), *n.* the act or sport of using or performing on a trampoline.

**tram|po|lin|ist** (tram′pə lē′nist, tram′pə lə-), *n.* a person who uses or performs on a trampoline.

**tramp steamer** or **ship**, a freighter that takes a cargo when and where it can; tramp.

**tram|road** (tram′rōd′), *n.* **1** a road or track of parallel lines of wood, stone, or iron rails, for trams or wagons in a mining area. **2** a railroad in a mine.

**tram|way** (tram′wā′), *n.* **1** *British.* a track for streetcars. **2a** a track or roadway for carrying ores from mines. **b** *U.S.* a cable or system of cables on which suspended cars carry ore.

**trance¹** (trans, träns), *n., v.,* **tranced, tranc|ing**. —***n.*** **1** a condition somewhat like sleep, in which the mind seems to have left the body: *a hypnotic trance.* SYN: coma. **2** a dazed or stunned condition. **3** a dreamy or absorbed condition which is like a trance: *The old man sat before the fire in a trance, thinking of his past life.* **4** a high emotion; rapture. SYN: ecstasy.
—***v.t.*** to throw into or hold in a trance; enchant: *I trod as one tranced in some rapturous vision* (Shelley). SYN: entrance.

**Pronunciation Key:** hat, āge, cãre, fär; let, ēqual, tėrm; it, īce; hot, ōpen, ôrder; **oi**l, **ou**t; cup, pu̇t, rüle; **ch**ild; lo**ng**; **th**in; ᴛʜen; **zh**, measure; ə represents **a** in about, **e** in taken, **i** in pencil, **o** in lemon, **u** in circus.

[< Old French *transe* fear of coming evil < *transir* be numb with fear; (originally) die, pass on < Latin *trānsīre* cross over < *trāns-* across + *īre* go] — **trance′like′**, *adj.*

**trance²** (trans, träns), *n. Scottish.* a passageway. [origin uncertain]

**tranc|ed|ly** (tran′sid lē, trän′-), *adv.* in a trance-like manner; as if in trance.

**tran|gam** (trang′gəm), *n. Archaic.* a trinket or toy; knickknack; gewgaw. [origin uncertain]

**tran|ny** (tran′ē), *n., pl.* **-nies**. *British Informal.* a transistor radio. [< *tran*(sistor) + *-y*²]

**tran|quil** (trang′kwəl, tran′-), *adj.*, **-quil|er**, **-quil-est** or (*especially British*) **-quil|ler**, **-quil|lest**. calm; peaceful; quiet; free from agitation or disturbance: *the tranquil morning air.* **SYN**: placid, serene, undisturbed. [< Latin *tranquillus* < *trāns-* (intensive) + a root related to *quiēs* quiet] — **tran′-quil|ly**, *adv.* — **tran′quil|ness**, *n.*

**tran|quil|ise** (trang′kwə līz, tran′-), *v.t., v.i.*, **-ised**, **-is|ing**. *Especially British.* tranquilize.

**Tran|quil|ite** (trang′kwə līt), *n.* a compound of titanium, iron, and magnesium, found in lunar rock samples obtained from the Sea of Tranquility. [< Sea of *Tranquil*(ity) + *-ite*¹]

**tran|quil|i|ty** (trang kwil′ə tē, tran-), *n.* = tranquillity.

**tran|quil|i|za|tion** (trang′kwə lə zā′shən, tran′-), *n.* **1** the act or process of tranquilizing. **2** the state of being tranquilized.

**tran|quil|ize** (trang′kwə līz, tran′-), *v.*, **-ized**, **-iz-ing**. — *v.t.* to make calm, peaceful, or quiet; make tranquil; calm; soothe: *Although "The Maltese Falcon" at long last settled Huston professionally, it did not tranquilize his personal life* (Newsweek). **SYN**: pacify, compose, allay, still. — *v.i.* to become tranquil.

**tran|quil|iz|er** (trang′kwə lī′zər, tran′-), *n.* any one of various drugs for reducing physical or nervous tension, lowering blood pressure, or bringing into balance certain other conditions of the body; ataractic.

**tran|quil|iz|ing agent** or **drug** (trang′kwə lī′-zing, tran′-), = tranquilizer.

**tran|quil|lise** (trang′kwə līz, tran′-), *v.*, **-lised**, **-lis|ing**. *Especially British.* tranquilize.

**tran|quil|li|ty** (trang kwil′ə tē, tran-), *n.* tranquil condition; calmness; peacefulness; quiet: *Public tranquillity is shattered during revolution.* **SYN**: stillness.

**tran|quil|lize** (trang′kwə līz, tran′-), *v.t., v.i.*, **-lized**, **-liz|ing**. = tranquilize.

**tran|quil|liz|er** (trang′kwə lī′zər, tran′-), *n.* = tranquilizer.

**trans** (trans, tranz), *adj. Chemistry.* of or having to do with an isomeric compound that has certain atoms on the opposite side of a plane: *a trans configuration or structure.*

**trans-**, *prefix.* **1** across; over; through: *Transcontinental = across the continent.*
**2** beyond; on the other side of: *Transcend = to go beyond. Transoceanic = on the other side of an ocean. Trans-African = on the other side of Africa.*
**3** to or into a different place, condition, or thing: *Transmigration = migration to another place. Transform = to form into another condition.*
**4** *Chemistry.* having certain atoms on the opposite side of a plane: *a trans-isomeric compound.*
[< Latin *trāns*, preposition]

**trans.**, an abbreviation for the following:
**1** transactions.
**2** transferred.
**3** transitive.
**4a** translated. **b** translation. **c** translator.
**5** transportation.

**trans|act** (tran zakt′, -sakt′), *v.t.* to attend to; carry on (business); manage; do: *He transacts business daily. A lawyer will transact many affairs connected with the purchase of a home.* **SYN**: perform, conduct. — *v.i.* to carry on business; have dealings; deal. [< Latin *trānsāctus*, past participle of *trānsigere* accomplish < *trāns-* through + *agere* to drive]

**trans|ac|ti|nides** (trans ak′tə nīdz), *n.pl.* the series of chemical elements whose atomic numbers extend beyond the actinides, from element 104 through element 112.

**trans|ac|ti|nide series** (trans ak′tə nīd), = transactinides.

**trans|ac|tion** (tran zak′shən, -sak′-), *n.* **1** the carrying on of any kind of business: *The store manager attends to the transaction of important matters himself.* **2** a piece of business: *A record is kept of every transaction of the firm.* **SYN**: proceeding, deal, matter, affair. **3** *Psychology.* any event or situation that is determined by a person's perception or participation rather than by external factors.
**transactions**, a record of what was done at the meetings of a society, club, or other group: *What the club says has an audience far beyond Manchester, because its transactions are sent to libraries in this country and to American libraries, including Harvard, the Library of Congress, and the main library in New York* (Manchester Guardian). *Abbr:* trans.
[< Latin *trānsāctiō, -ōnis* < *trānsigere*; see etym. under **transact**]

**trans|ac|tion|al** (tran zak′shə nəl, -sak′-), *adj.* of or having to do with a transaction. — **trans|ac′-tion|al|ly**, *adv.*

**transactional analysis**, a form of psychoanalysis that deals with various levels on which a person functions in his relation to others and attempts to integrate or harmonize these levels within the personality. — **transactional analyst**.

**trans|ac|tor** (tran zak′tər, -sak′-), *n.* a person who transacts business affairs.

**trans|al|pine** (tranz al′pīn, -pin; trans-), *adj., n.* — *adj.* across or beyond the Alps, especially as viewed from Italy.
— *n.* a native or inhabitant of a country across or beyond the Alps.
[< Latin *trānsalpīnus* < *trāns-* across + *alpīnus* Alpine < *Alpēs* the Alps]

**trans|am|i|nase** (trans am′ə nās, tranz-), *n.* an enzyme that catalyzes transamination.

**trans|am|i|na|tion** (trans am′ə nā′shən, tranz-), *n.* the reversible transfer of an amino group from one compound to another.

**trans-An|de|an** (trans′an dē′ən, tranz′-; trans an′-dē ən, tranz-), *adj.* across or beyond the Andes, especially as viewed from Argentina or some other country east of the Andes.

**trans|arc|tic** (trans ärk′tik, -är′tik; tranz-), *adj.* across or beyond the arctic or north polar region.

**trans|at|lan|tic** (trans′ət lan′tik, tranz′-), *adj.* **1** crossing the Atlantic: *a transatlantic flight, a transatlantic cable.* **2** on the other side of the Atlantic, as viewed from either side: *a transatlantic ally.* — **trans′at|lan′ti|cal|ly**, *adv.*

**trans|ca|len|cy** (trans kā′lən sē), *n.* the property of being transcalent.

**trans|ca|lent** (trans kā′lənt), *adj.* freely permitting the passage of heat. [< *trans-* + Latin *calēns, -entis*, present participle of *calēre* be warm]

**trans|cau|ca|sian** (trans′kô kā′zhən, -shən; -kazh′ən, -kash′-), *adj.* across or beyond the Caucasus Mountains.

**Trans|cau|ca|sian** (trans′kô kā′zhən, -shən; -kazh′ən, -kash′-), *adj., n.* — *adj.* of or having to do with Transcaucasia, a region of the southwestern Soviet Union, in and south of the Caucasus Mountains.
— *n.* a native or inhabitant of Transcaucasia.

**trans|ceiv|er** (trans sē′vər, tran-), *n. Electronics.* a combined transmitter and receiver. [< *trans*-(mitter) + (re)*ceiver*]

**tran|scend** (tran send′), *v.t.* **1** to go beyond the limits or powers of; exceed; be above: *The grandeur of Niagara Falls transcends words.* **2** to be higher or greater than; surpass; excel: *The speed of airplanes transcends that of any previous form of transportation.* **3** (of God) to be above and independent of (the physical universe).
— *v.i.* to be superior or extraordinary.
[< Latin *trānscendere* < *trāns-* beyond + *scandere* to climb]

**tran|scend|ence** (tran sen′dəns), *n.* the condition of being transcendent.

**tran|scend|en|cy** (tran sen′dən sē), *n.* = transcendence.

**tran|scend|ent** (tran sen′dənt), *adj.* **1** going beyond ordinary limits; excelling; superior; extraordinary. **SYN**: unequaled, unrivaled, peerless, supreme. **2** above and independent of the physical universe. **3** *Philosophy.* **a** transcending the Aristotelian categories or predicaments, especially as considered by the medieval scholastics. **b** (in Kantian philosophy) not realizable in human experience. — **tran|scend′ent|ly**, *adv.* — **tran-scend′ent|ness**, *n.*

**tran|scen|den|tal** (tran′sen den′təl), *adj., n.* — *adj.* **1** transcendent; surpassing; excelling. **2** supernatural. **3a** explaining material things as products of the mind that is thinking about them; idealistic. **b** implied in and necessary to human experience. **4** beyond the limits of ordinary human experience; obscure; incomprehensible; fantastic: *an unmeaning and transcendental conception* (Benjamin Jowett). **5** = transcendentalist. **6** *Mathematics.* not capable of being the solution of a polynomial equation with rational coefficients. $\pi$ is a transcendental number.
— *n. Mathematics.* a transcendental term, quantity, or number. — **tran′scen|den′tal|ly**, *adv.*

**tran|scen|den|tal|ism** (tran′sen den′tə liz əm), *n.* **1** transcendental quality, thought, language, or philosophy. **2** any philosophy based upon the doctrine that the principles of reality are to be discovered by a study of the processes of thought, not from experience. Kant's *Critique of Pure Reason* was a chief source of transcendentalism. **3** the religious and philosophical doctrines of Ralph Waldo Emerson and others in New England in the middle 1800's, which emphasized the importance of individual inspiration and had an important influence on American thought and literature. **4** obscurity; incomprehensibility; fantasy.

**tran|scen|den|tal|ist** (tran′sen den′tə list), *n., adj.* — *n.* a person who believes in transcendentalism: *Emerson and Thoreau were transcendentalists.*
— *adj.* of or having to do with transcendentalism.

**tran|scen|den|tal|ize** (tran′sen den′tə līz), *v.t.*, **-ized**, **-iz|ing**. to make transcendental; idealize.

**transcendental meditation**, **1** a Hindu system of meditation designed to produce a relaxed state of consciousness intermediate between wakefulness and sleep: *The practice of transcendental meditation leads to greatly reduced physiological activity, indicative of an "inner calm"* (Gary E. Schwartz). **2 Transcendental Meditation**, a trademark for such a system of meditation. *Abbr:* TM

**tran|scen|sion** (tran sen′shən), *n.* = transcendence. [< Late Latin *trānscensiō, -ōnis* < Latin *trānscendere* to transcend]

**trans|con|ti|nen|tal** (trans′kon tə nen′təl, tranz′-), *adj.* **1** crossing a continent: *a transcontinental railroad.* **2** on the other side of a continent.

**trans|cor|ti|cal** (trans kôr′tə kəl, tranz-), *adj.* crossing the cortex of the brain.

**tran|scribe** (tran skrīb′), *v.*, **-scribed**, **-scrib|ing**. — *v.t.* **1a** to copy in writing or in typewriting: *to transcribe an ancient manuscript.* **b** to write out, as in ordinary letters, words, or characters: *The account of the trial was transcribed from the stenographer's shorthand notes.* **2** to set down in writing or print: *His speech was transcribed in the newspapers, word for word.* **3** *Music.* to arrange (a composition) for a different voice or instrument. **4** to make a recording or phonograph record of (as a program or music) for playing back or broadcasting. **5** *Phonetics.* to record (speech) in a system of phonetic symbols; represent (a speech sound) by a phonetic symbol. **6** *Genetics.* to form or synthesize (a nucleic acid molecule or molecules) by transferring genetic information from a template: *to transcribe DNA into messenger RNA, to transcribe RNA from DNA.* — *v.i.* to broadcast a phonograph record.
[< Latin *trānscrībere* < *trāns-* over + *scrībere* write] — **tran|scrib′er**, *n.*

**tran|script** (tran′skript), *n., v.* — *n.* **1** a written or typewritten copy: *The club's secretary prepared several transcripts of minutes of the meeting.* **2** *Law.* a copy of a legal record. **3** a copy or reproduction of anything: *The college wanted a transcript of the student's high-school record.*
— *v.t. Genetics.* = transcribe.
[< Latin *trānscriptum*, neuter past participle of *trānscrībere*; see etym. under **transcribe**]

**tran|scrip|tase** (tran skrip′tās), *n.* an enzyme that promotes genetic transcription: *The transcription processes, and the replication of DNA and of viral RNA, could be understood in terms of three distinctive enzymes: DNA-replicase, transcriptase, and RNA-replicase* (Joshua Lederberg). [< *transcript*(ion) + *-ase*]

**tran|scrip|tion** (tran skrip′shən), *n.* **1** the act or process of transcribing; copying. **2** a transcript; copy. **3** *Music.* the arrangement of a composition for a different instrument or voice. **4a** the act or process of recording something, especially music, on a phonograph record or tape for use in broadcasting. **b** the act or fact of broadcasting such a record. **5** *Phonetics.* a written representation of speech in a system of phonetic symbols. **6** *Genetics.* the process of forming a nucleic acid molecule by using a template of another molecule: *Gene transcription, whereby enzyme reactions mediate the synthesis of RNA molecules from DNA templates, has been investigated mostly in microbial organisms* (Nature).

**tran|scrip|tion|al** (tran skrip′shən əl), *adj.* of, having to do with, or occurring in transcription: *a transcriptional error.* — **tran|scrip′tion|al|ly**, *adv.*

**tran|scrip|tive** (tran skrip′tiv), *adj.* **1** of or having to do with transcribing, copying, or reproducing. **2** of or like a transcript.

**trans|cul|tur|al** (trans kul′chər əl, tranz-), *adj.* **1** common to all cultures: *transcultural phenomena.* **2** cutting across cultures; intercultural: *transcultural activities.*

**trans|cur|rent** (trans kėr′ənt, tranz-), *adj.* extending or running across. [< Latin *trānscurrēns, -entis*, present participle of *trānscurrere* < *trāns-* across + *currere* to run] — **trans|cur′rent|ly**, *adv.*

**trans|duce** (trans düs′, -dyüs′; tranz-), *v.t.*, **-duced**, **-duc|ing**. to convert (energy) from one form to another, as from heat energy to electric energy: *Industrial measurement and control systems ... integrate fluctuating light, velocity, flow, and other factors which can be transduced to electrical current* (Science). [< Latin *trānsdūcere* < *trāns-* across + *dūcere* to lead. Compare etym. under **traduce**.]

**trans|duc|er** (trans dü′sər, -dyü′-; tranz-), *n.* any device for converting energy from one form to another. A microphone, which converts sound into electric energy, is a transducer.

**trans|duc|tion** (trans duk′shən, tranz-), *n.* **1** *Biology.* **a** the transfer of a gene or chromosome particle from one cell to another. **b** such a transfer conducted by a bacterial virus in the cells of bacteria. **2** *Physics.* the conversion of energy from one form to another: *Transduction occurs when a loudspeaker changes electrical into acoustical energy.*

**trans|earth** (tranz ėrth′), *adj.* outside of or beyond the orbit of the earth (used especially of a spacecraft): *a transearth trajectory.*

**tran|sect** (*v.* tran sekt′; *n.* tran′sekt′), *v., n.* **—*v.t.*** to cut across; divide by passing across.
**—*n.*** **1** a cross section of the vegetation of an area, usually that part growing along a long, narrow strip: *For the botanist a brisk 15 miles between, say, Mumbles Head to Rhossili Bay in Glamorganshire is an eventful transect, abounding in rare flora* (New Scientist). **2** a representation of such a cross section.
[< *trans-* + Latin *sectus,* past participle of *secāre* to cut]

**tran|sec|tion** (tran sek′shən), *n.* the act or process of transecting; cross section.

**trans|el|e|ment** (tranz el′ə mənt, trans-), *v.t.* to transform the elements of.

***tran|sept** (tran′sept), *n.* **1** the shorter part of a cross-shaped church. **2** either end of this part. [< Medieval Latin *transeptum,* ultimately < Latin *trāns-* across + *saeptum* fence]

***transept**
definition 1

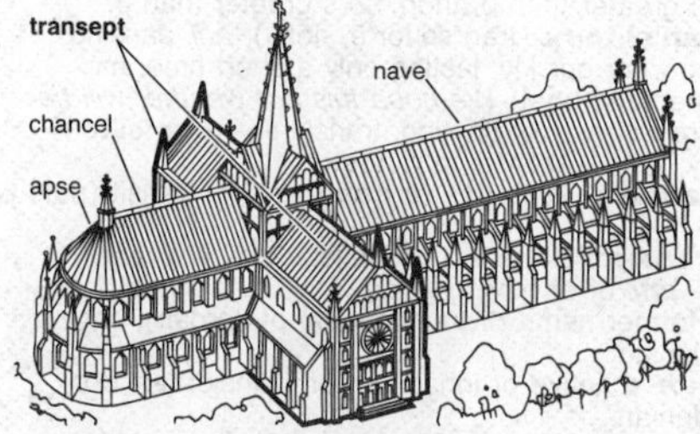


**tran|sep|tal** (tran sep′təl), *adj.* of, having to do with, or like a transept. **—tran|sep′tal|ly,** *adv.*

**trans|e|unt** (tran′sē ənt), *adj.* passing outward; producing an effect outside; transient: *a transeunt action.* [< Latin *trānsiēns, transeuntis;* see etym. under **transient**]

**transf.,** transferred.

**trans|fash|ion** (trans fash′ən), *v.t.* = transform.

**trans|fer** (*v.* trans fėr′, trans′fėr; *n.* trans′fėr), *v.,* **-ferred, -fer|ring,** *n.* **—*v.t.*** **1a** to take or remove from one person or place to another; hand over: *This farm has been transferred from father to son for generations. Please have my trunks transferred to the Union Station. The clerk was transferred to another department.* **b** to take or pass on from one condition to another: *The new meanings on many words have been ones transferred from literal to figurative uses.* **2** to convey (a drawing, design, or pattern) from one surface to another, as to a lithographic stone, earthenware, or glass, by any one of various special means or processes: *You transfer the embroidery design from the paper to cloth by pressing it with a warm iron.* **3** to make over (a title, right, or property) by deed or legal process: *to transfer a bond by endorsement.* **—*v.i.*** **1** to change from one public vehicle, such as a bus, train, or airplane, to another. **2** to change from one place, position, or condition to another: *The student transferred from the state university to a college nearer his home.*
**—*n.*** **1** the act of transferring or fact of being transferred: *The transfer of money by bank check is very common today.* **2** a writing, drawing, or pattern printed from one surface onto another, as in lithography or photography. **3** a ticket allowing a passenger to continue his journey on another bus, train, or airline. **4** a point or place for transferring. **5** the making over to another of title, right, or property by deed or legal process. **6a** the act of turning the ownership of a share of stock or registered bond over to someone else. **b** a document ordering this. **7** a person or thing transferred. **8** = transfer of training.
[< Latin *trānsferre* < *trāns-* across + *ferre* to bear]

**trans|fer|a|bil|i|ty** (trans′fər ə bil′ə tē, trans fėr′-), *n.* the quality of being transferable.

**trans|fer|a|ble** (trans fėr′ə bəl, trans′fər-), *adj.* **1** that can be transferred. **2** that can be made over to another; negotiable: *The currencies of most countries were still not freely convertible into dollars but they were made transferable over a steadily increasing area* (Samuel S. Shipman).

**trans|fer|al** (trans fėr′əl), *n.* transference; transfer.

**trans|fer|ase** (trans′fə rās), *n.* any one of various enzymes that transfer a radical from one molecule to another, such as transaminase and kinase.

**transfer case,** a box of gears which in a motor vehicle with four-wheel drive divides the driving power between the two drive shafts.

**transfer cell,** a specialized plant cell which exchanges dissolved substances with its surroundings and transfers them across the plant membranes.

**trans|fer|ee** (trans′fə rē′), *n.* **1** a person who is transferred or removed, as from one place, position, or grade to another. **2** *Law.* the person to whom a transfer of title, right, or property is made.

**trans|fer|ence** (trans fėr′əns, trans′fər-), *n.* **1** the act or process of transferring or condition of being transferred. **2** *Psychoanalysis.* a revival of emotions previously experienced and repressed, as toward a parent, with a new person as the object.

**trans|fer|en|tial** (trans′fə ren′shəl), *adj.* of or having to do with transference.

**transfer factor,** a substance believed to transfer immunity to disease from one person to another. It has been isolated from white blood cells and is smaller than an antibody or protein cell. *Transfer factor ... can apparently, when given to people suffering from immune deficiency diseases, transfer to them the immunological status of the donor* (New Scientist and Science Journal).

**transfer machine,** a grouping of simpler machines to produce a larger machine that functions as a unit, for automatically performing a series of operations, passing the work along from one machine to the next.

**transfer of training,** *Psychology, Education.* the transfer of some knowledge or skill acquired in one activity or field to a new or different activity or field. Transfer of training may help a person learn something new or it may interfere with and hinder him from learning it.

**trans|fer|or** (trans fėr′ər), *n. Law.* the person who makes a transfer of title, right, or property.

**transfer paper,** any one of various kinds of specially prepared paper for transferring drawings, designs, photographs, or printing and writing.

**transfer payment,** money spent by government or business without any return in the form of goods or services: *Such transfer payments as Social Security and veterans' benefits increased only slightly* (Wall Street Journal).

**transfer printing, 1** any process of printing by transfer. **2** a method of decorating pottery by applying to the ware impressions taken on paper from a copperplate engraving.

**trans|fer|ra|ble** (trans fėr′ə bəl, trans′fər-), *adj.* = transferable.

**trans|fer|rer** (trans fėr′ər), *n.* a person or thing that transfers.

**trans|fer|rin** (trans fer′in, tranz-), *n.* an iron-bearing protein of the blood plasma. [< *trans-* + Latin *ferr*(*um*) iron + English *-in*]

**transfer RNA,** a form of ribonucleic acid that delivers amino acids to the ribosomes during protein synthesis; soluble RNA: *There is at least one transfer RNA for each of the 20 common amino acids* (Scientific American). *Each transfer RNA is a relatively small molecule with less than 100 nucleotides in its chain, and all of the transfer RNA's have a similar sequence of nucleotides at the two ends of the chain* (Claude A. Villee, Jr.). *Abbr:* tRNA (no periods).

**transfer table,** = traverse table (def. 1).

**transfer tax,** a tax levied, usually in the form of a stamp tax, upon the transfer of real estate, documents, securities, and other property.

**Trans|fig|u|ra|tion** (trans fig′yə rā′shən), *n.* **1** the change in the appearance of Christ on the mountain (in the Bible, Matthew 17:2; Mark 9:2-3). **2** the church festival on August 6 in honor of this. [< Latin *trānsfigūrātiō, -ōnis* < *trānsfigūrāre;* see etym. under **transfigure**]

**trans|fig|u|ra|tion** (trans fig′yə rā′shən), *n.* a change in form or appearance; transformation. [< *Transfiguration*]

**trans|fig|ure** (trans fig′yər), *v.t.,* **-ured, -ur|ing. 1** to change in form or appearance; transform: *New paint and furnishings had transfigured the old house.* **2** *Figurative.* to change so as to glorify; exalt; idealize. [< Latin *trānsfigūrāre* < *trāns-* across + *figūra* figure]

**trans|fi|nite** (trans fī′nīt), *adj., n. Mathematics.* **—*adj.*** beyond or surpassing any finite number or magnitude: *a transfinite cardinal number.*
**—*n.*** a transfinite number.

**trans|fix** (trans fiks′), *v.t.* **1** to pierce through: *The hunter transfixed the lion with a spear. An arrow ... transfixed him* (Scott). **2** to fasten or fix by piercing through with something pointed; impale. **3** *Figurative.* to make motionless or helpless (as with amazement, terror, or grief). [< Latin *trānsfīxus,* past participle of *trānsfīgere* < *trāns-* through + *fīgere* to fix, fasten]

**trans|fix|ion** (trans fik′shən), *n.* the action of transfixing or state of being transfixed.

**trans|flu|ent** (trans′flü ənt), *adj.* flowing or running across or through. [< Latin *trānsfluēns, -entis,* present participle of *trānsfluere* < *trāns-* across + *fluere* to flow]

**trans|form** (*v.* trans fôrm′; *n.* trans′fôrm′), *v., n.* **—*v.t.*** **1** to change in form or appearance: *The blizzard transformed the bushes into mounds of white.* **2** to change in condition, nature, or character: *The witch transformed men into pigs. To Samarcand ... we owe the art of transforming linen into paper* (Cardinal Newman). **3** to change (one form of energy) into another. A generator transforms mechanical energy into electricity. **4** to change (an electric current) into one of higher or lower voltage, from alternating to direct current, or from direct to alternating current. **5** *Mathematics.* to change (a figure, term, or the like) to another differing in form but having the same value or quantity.
**—*v.i.*** to be transformed; change: *A tadpole transforms into a frog.*
**—*n.*** **1** *Mathematics.* an expression derived from another by changing a figure, term, etc., without changing its quantity or value. **2** *Linguistics.* a sentence derived from a kernel sentence by one or more transformations.
[< Latin *trānsformāre* < *trāns-* across + *formāre* to form < *forma* form] **—trans|form′a|ble,** *adj.*
**—*Syn.*** *v.t.* **1, 2 Transform, transmute, convert** mean to change the form, nature, substance, or state of something. **Transform** suggests a thoroughgoing or fundamental change in the appearance, shape, or nature of a thing or person: *Responsibility transformed him from a careless boy into a capable leader.* **Transmute** suggests a complete change in nature or substance, especially to a higher kind: *He thus transmuted disapproval into admiration.* **Convert** suggests a change from one state or condition to another, especially for a new use or purpose: *to convert boxes into furniture.*

**trans|for|ma|tion** (trans′fər mā′shən), *n.* **1** the act or process of transforming or state of being transformed: *the transformation of a caterpillar into a butterfly, the transformation of a thief into an honest man.* SYN: metamorphosis. **2** *Mathematics.* **a** the operation of changing a figure, term, or the like to another differing in form but having the same value or quantity. **b** the result of such an operation; transform. **3** *Linguistics.* the rearrangement of the elements of a sentence to produce an equivalent or more complex sentence. *Example:* John hit him. He was hit by John. Has John been hitting him? **4** a form of genetic transmission in which DNA passes out of a cell into the chromosome of another: *In bacterial transformation a bit of DNA penetrates the boundary of a bacterial cell and becomes incorporated into the cell's genetic apparatus* (Scientific American). **5** a wig worn by women.

**trans|for|ma|tion|al** (trans′fər mā′shə nəl), *adj. Linguistics.* having to do with or using transformations: *transformational rules.*

**transformational grammar,** a grammatical system in which sentence structures are derived by transformation: *Transformational grammar* [*assures*] *that language consists of irreducible kernel utterances, plus transformational laws, plus lexicon* (Harper's).

**trans|for|ma|tion|al|ism** (trans′fər mā′shə nə liz′əm), *n.* the linguistic theory or study concerned with transformations and transformational grammar.

**trans|for|ma|tion|al|ist** (trans′fər mā′shə nə list), *n.* a follower or advocate of transformationalism: *The school of transformationalists contends that language is an innate, instinctively acquired facility; the study of it should start with sentences, then try to discern the rules by which a sentence conveys its meaning* (Time).

**trans|form|a|tive** (trans fôr′mə tiv), *adj.* tending or serving to transform.

**trans|form|er** (trans fôr′mər), *n.* **1** a person or thing that transforms. **2** a device for changing an alternating electric current into one of higher or lower voltage by electromagnetic induction. The first is called a step-up transformer, and the second a step-down transformer.

---

**Pronunciation Key:** hat, āge, cãre, fär; let, ēqual, tėrm; it, īce; hot, ōpen, ôrder; **oi**l, **ou**t; cup, pu̇t, rüle; **ch**ild; lo**ng**; **th**in; ᴛʜen; **zh**, measure; **ə** represents **a** in about, **e** in taken, **i** in pencil, **o** in lemon, **u** in circus.

**transform fault**, *Geology.* a deep fault forming a steplike pattern on the edge of a plate and indicating the path of the plate: *Global analysis has established that the big shears called transform faults are the zones along which crustal plates glide as they separate* (New Scientist and Science Journal).

**trans|form|ism** (trans fôr′miz əm), *n. Biology.* **1** the doctrine that species transform into other species by descent with modification through many generations. **2** such transformation itself. **3** any form of the doctrine of evolution of species.

**trans|form|ist** (trans fôr′mist), *n.* an advocate of transformism.

**trans|fus|a|ble** (trans fyü′zə bəl), *adj.* = transfusible.

**trans|fuse** (trans fyüz′), *v.t.*, **-fused**, **-fus|ing.** **1** to pour (a liquid) from one container into another. **2** to transfer (blood) from the veins of one person or animal to those of another. **3** to inject (a solution) into a blood vessel. **4** *Figurative.* to infuse; instill: *The speaker transfused his enthusiasm into the audience.* [< Latin *trānsfūsus,* past participle of *trānsfundere* < *trāns-* across + *fundere* to pour] —**trans|fus′er,** *n.*

**trans|fus|i|ble** (trans fyü′zə bəl), *adj.* that can be transfused.

**trans|fu|sion** (trans fyü′zhən), *n.* **1** the act or fact of causing to pass from one container or holder to another. **2** the transfer of blood from one person or animal to another: *The injured man had lost so much blood that he needed an immediate transfusion. Transfusions are often given to patients after surgery.* [< Latin *trānsfūsiō, -ōnis* < *trānsfūsus;* see etym. under **transfuse**]

**transfusion cell**, a thin-walled plant cell that permits the passage of water to adjacent tissues.

**trans|gress** (trans gres′, tranz-), *v.i.* to break a law or command; sin (against). **SYN**: trespass, offend. —*v.t.* **1** to go contrary to; sin against. **SYN**: violate, break. **2** to go or pass beyond (a limit or bound); exceed: *His manners transgressed the bounds of good taste.* [< Latin *trānsgressus,* past participle of *trānsgredī* go beyond < *trāns-* across + *gradī* to step]

**trans|gres|sion** (trans gresh′ən, tranz-), *n.* **1** the act of transgressing; breaking a law, command, or duty; sin: *a transgression of a law, to commit a grave transgression.* **SYN**: violation, offense, fault, misdeed, trespass. **2** *Geology.* the spread of the sea over the land along a subsiding shoreline, producing an overlap by deposition of new strata upon old. [< Latin *trānsgressiō, -ōnis* (originally) a going over < *trānsgredī;* see etym. under **transgress**]

**trans|gres|sive** (trans gres′iv, tranz-), *adj.* transgressing; inclined to transgress; involving transgression. —**trans|gres′sive|ly,** *adv.*

**trans|gres|sor** (trans gres′ər, tranz-), *n.* a person who transgresses; sinner: *The way of transgressors is hard* (Proverbs 13:15).

**tran|shape** (tran shāp′), *v.t.*, **-shaped**, **-shap|ing.** = transshape.

**tran|ship** (tran ship′), *v.t., v.i.*, **-shipped**, **-shipping.** = transship. —**tran|ship′ment,** *n.* —**tranship′per,** *n.*

**trans|hu|man** (trans hyü′mən), *adj.* = superhuman.

**trans|hu|mance** (trans hyü′məns), *n.* the seasonal migration under the care of shepherds of herds and flocks between regions of different climates. [< French *transhumance* < *transhumer* to migrate seasonally < Spanish *trashumar* < Latin *trāns-* across + *humus* ground, soil]

**trans|hu|mant** (trans hyü′mənt), *adj.* migrating between regions of different climates: *transhumant flocks.*

**tran|sience** (tran′shəns), *n.* = transiency.

**tran|sien|cy** (tran′shən sē), *n.* the quality or condition of being transient; transitoriness: *Oliver ... didn't love life, because he hadn't the animal Epicurean faculty of enjoying it in its arbitrariness and transiency* (Atlantic).

**tran|sient** (tran′shənt), *adj., n.* —*adj.* **1** passing quickly or soon; not lasting; fleeting: *Joy and sorrow are often transient.* **SYN**: transitory, evanescent, momentary, ephemeral. See syn. under **temporary.** **2a** passing through and not staying long: *a transient guest in a hotel.* **b** *U.S.* serving transient guests or customers: *a transient hotel.* **3** *Music.* introduced in passing but not necessary to the harmony: *a transient modulation.* **4** = transeunt.
—*n.* **1** a visitor, boarder, customer, or student, who stays for a short time or a customer who does not return: *This hotel does not accept transients.* **2** *Electronics.* **a** a sudden surge of voltage or current, especially in a system of sound amplification or reproduction. **b** a sudden sound of short duration resulting from or accompanying such a surge.
[< Latin *trānsiēns, transeuntis,* present participle of *trānsīre* to go across < *trāns-* across + *īre* to go. Compare etym. under **transeunt.**] —**tran′sient|ly,** *adv.* —**tran′sient|ness,** *n.*

**tran|sil|i|ence** (tran sil′ē əns), *n.* an abrupt passing from one thing to another.

**tran|sil|i|ent** (tran sil′ē ənt), *adj.* leaping or passing from one thing or condition to another. [< Latin *trānsiliēns, -entis,* present participle of *trānsilīre* < *trāns-* across + *salīre* to leap]

**trans|il|lu|mi|nate** (trans′i lü′mə nāt, tranz′-), *v.t.*, **-nat|ed**, **-nat|ing.** to cause light to pass through (an organ or part) as a means of medical diagnosis.

**trans|il|lu|mi|na|tion** (trans′i lü′mə nā′shən, tranz′-), *n.* the act or process of transilluminating.

**trans|il|lu|mi|na|tor** (trans′i lü′mə nā′tər), *n.* a device used to transilluminate a part of the body.

**trans|i|re** (trans ī′rē), *n.* a permit issued by a custom house to let merchandise pass through the port. [< Latin *trānsīre* to go across; see etym. under **transient**]

**trans|i|sonde** (tran′sə sond), *n.* = transosonde.

**trans|isth|mi|an** (trans is′mē ən, tranz-), *adj.* passing or extending across an isthmus.

**tran|sis|tor** (tran zis′tər), *n. Electronics.* a small crystal device containing semiconductors such as germanium or silicon, that controls the flow of electricity in computers, radios, television sets, and other electronic equipment. Transistors can strengthen an electric current, create a vibrating current, or turn themselves and other devices off and on. *The transistor's small size and low power requirements make it an electronic engineer's dream gadget* (Watson Davis). [< *tran-* (sfer) + (re)*sistor*]

**tran|sis|tor|ise** (tran zis′tə rīz), *v.t.*, **-ised**, **-is|ing.** *Especially British.* transistorize.

**tran|sis|tor|i|za|tion** (tran zis′tər ə zā′shən), *n.* an equipping or reducing in size with transistors.

**tran|sis|tor|ize** (tran zis′tə rīz), *v.t.*, **-ized**, **-iz|ing.** to equip or reduce in size with transistors.

**transistor radio**, a usually small, battery-powered radio equipped with transistors: *the music which came from a transistor radio in* [*his*] *pocket* (Manchester Guardian).

***trans|it** (tran′sit, -zit), *n., v.*, **-it|ed**, **-it|ing.** —*n.* **1a** the act of carrying or state of being carried across or through: *The goods were damaged in transit.* **b** the act or process of carrying people from one place to another by trains, buses, or other conveyances: *All transit systems are crowded during the rush hours.* **2** the act or fact of passing across or through: *Transit across the icy little bridge was dangerous.* **3** a transition or change, especially the passage from this life to the next by death. **4** an instrument used in surveying to measure horizontal and vertical angles; a theodolite with a telescope that can be rotated through a full circle. **5** *Astronomy.* **a** the apparent passage of a heavenly body across the meridian of a place, or through the field of a telescope. **b** the passage of a heavenly body across the disk of a larger one.
—*v.t.* **1** to pass across or through; traverse; cross. **2** to turn (the telescope of a transit) around its horizontal transverse axis to point in the opposite direction.
—*v.i.* to pass through or over or across.
[< Latin *trānsitus, -ūs* < *trānsīre;* see etym. under **transient**]

***transit**
definition 4

**transit circle**, an astronomical instrument consisting of a telescope carrying a finely graduated circle, used for observing the transit of a heavenly body across the meridian.

**transit duty**, a duty paid on goods passing through a country.

**transit instrument**, **1** *Astronomy.* a telescope mounted with its east-west axis fixed so that it can move only in the plane of the local meridian, used to find the time of transit of a heavenly body. **2** = transit (def. 4).

**tran|si|tion** (tran zish′ən), *n.* **1** a change or passing from one condition, place, thing, activity, or topic to another: *Lincoln's life was a transition from poverty to power. The time between two distinct periods of history, art, or literature is called a period of transition. Abrupt transitions in a book confuse the reader.* **2** *Music.* **a** a passing from one key to another; modulation. **b** a passage linking one section, subject, or other part of a composition with another. [< Latin *trānsitiō, -ōnis* < *trānsīre;* see etym. under **transient**]

**tran|si|tion|al** (tran zish′ə nəl), *adj.* **1** of transition; of change from one more or less fixed condition to another; intermediate: *The "transitional" style incorporates features of both traditional and modern furniture types* (Wall Street Journal). **2** *Printing.* having some of the characteristics of both old style and modern: *Cheltenham is a transitional type face.* —**tran|si′tion|al|ly,** *adv.*

**tran|si|tion|ar|y** (tran zish′ə ner′ē), *adj.* = transitional.

**transition element** or **metal**, any one of a number of metallic chemical elements with an incomplete inner electron shell. Silver and gold are transition elements.

**tran|si|tive** (tran′sə tiv), *adj., n.* —*adj.* **1** of or having to do with a verb, either active or passive, taking a direct object. In "Bring me my coat" and "Raise the window," *bring* and *raise* are transitive verbs. **2** = transitional. **3** *Mathematics, Logic.* of or having to do with transitivity.
—*n.* a transitive verb. *Abbr:* trans.
[< Late Latin *trānsitīvus* < Latin *trānsīre;* see etym. under **transient**] —**tran′si|tive|ly,** *adv.* —**tran′si|tive|ness,** *n.*
▶ See **verb** for usage note.

**tran|si|tiv|i|ty** (tran′sə tiv′ə tē), *n.* **1** the condition of being transitive: *The idea of transitivity eludes seven-year-olds* (Time). **2** *Mathematics, Logic.* a relation such that if it holds between A and B and between B and C, it must also hold between A and C. *Example:* If 12 is greater than 6 and 6 is greater than 3, then 12 is greater than 3.

**tran|si|to|ry** (tran′sə tôr′ē, -tōr′-), *adj.* passing soon or quickly; lasting only a short time; momentary; brief: *We hope this hot weather will be transitory.* **SYN**: fleeting, transient. —**tran′si|to′rily,** *adv.* —**tran′si|to′ri|ness,** *n.*

**transit theodolite** or **compass**, = transit (def. 4).

**Trans|jor|da|ni|an** (trans′jôr dā′nē ən), *adj., n.* —*adj.* of or having to do with Transjordan (former name of the kingdom of Jordan); Jordanian.
—*n.* a native or inhabitant of Transjordan; Jordanian.

**transl.**, **1** translated. **2** translation.

**trans|lat|a|bil|i|ty** (trans lā′tə bil′ə tē, tranz-), *n.* translatable quality or condition.

**trans|lat|a|ble** (trans lā′tə bəl, tranz-), *adj.* that can be translated. —**trans|lat′a|ble|ness,** *n.*

**trans|late** (trans lāt′, tranz-; trans′lāt, tranz′-), *v.*, **-lat|ed**, **-lat|ing.** —*v.t.* **1** to change from one language into another: *to translate a book from French into English.* **2** to change into other words. **SYN**: paraphrase, render. **3** *Figurative.* **a** to explain the meaning of; interpret. **b** to express (one thing) in terms of another: *to translate words into actions.* **4** to change from one place, position, or condition to another: *She was translated to the fairy palace in a second.* **SYN**: transfer, transport. **5** to take to heaven without death: *By faith Enoch was translated that he should not see death* (Hebrews 11:5). **6** to remove (a bishop) from one see to another. **7** to remove (a bishop's see) from one place to another. **8** *Physics.* to move (a body) from one point or place to another without rotation. **9** to retransmit (a telegraphic message), as by a relay. **10** *Genetics.* to use (genetic information in messenger RNA) to direct the formation of amino acid in protein synthesis: *In this way, the transfer-RNA molecules act as "translating devices," translating a codon at one end into an amino acid at the other* (Isaac Asimov). **11** *Archaic.* to enrapture: *their souls, with devotion translated* (Longfellow).
—*v.i.* **1** to change something from one language or form of words into another. **2** to bear translation; allow to be translated: *Many foreign expressions do not translate well into English.*
[< Latin *trānslātus,* past participle of *trānsferre;* see etym. under **transfer**]

**trans|la|tion** (trans lā′shən, tranz-), *n.* **1** the act of translating; change into another language: *the translation of the Bible from Hebrew into English.* **2** *Figurative.* a change from one position or condition to another: *the translation of a promise into a deed.* **3** the result of translating; version. The Latin translation of the Bible is called the Vulgate. *He would have the original and all the translations* (James Boswell). **SYN**: interpretation, rendering. *Abbr:* trans. **4** the automatic retransmission of a long-distance telegraph message by means of a relay. **5** *Physics.* motion in which there is no rotation; onward movement that is not rotary or reciprocating. **6** *Genetics.* the formation of amino acids from information contained in messenger RNA: *Translation is the process whereby the genetic information contained in m-RNA determines the linear sequence of amino* *acids in the course of protein synthesis. Translation occurs on ribosomes, complex particles in the cytoplasm* (Robert G. Eagon).

**trans|la|tion|al** (trans lā′shə nəl, tranz-), *adj.* of or having to do with translation.

**trans|la|tive** (trans lā′tiv, tranz-), *adj.* = translational.

**trans|la|tor** (trans lā′tər, tranz-; trans′lā-, tranz′-), *n.* a person who translates.

**trans|la|tor|ese** (trans lā′tər ēz, tranz-; trans′lā-, tranz′-; -ēs), *n.* the style of language or writing characteristic of translators.

**trans|la|to|ry** (trans′lə tôr′ē, -tōr′-; tranz′-), *adj. Physics.* consisting in onward motion, as distinct from rotation: *rotatory and translatory motion.*

**trans|la|tress** (trans lā′tris, tranz-), *n.* a woman translator.

**translit.**, transliteration.

***trans|lit|er|ate** (trans lit′ə rāt, tranz-), *v.t.*, **-at|ed, -at|ing.** to change (letters, words, syllables, or other language elements) into corresponding characters or elements of another alphabet or language: *to transliterate the Greek χ as ch and ϕ as ph, to transliterate Arabic words into English letters.* [< *trans-* + Latin *littera* letter]

***transliterate**

from Greek to English:
λεξικον = lexicon

from Arabic to English:
المناخ = almanac

**trans|lit|er|a|tion** (trans lit′ə rā′shən, tranz-), *n.* the act of transliterating; the rendering of letters, characters, syllables, or other language elements of one alphabet by equivalents in another.

**trans|lo|cate** (trans lō′kāt, tranz-), *v.t.*, **-cat|ed, -cat|ing. 1** to remove from one place to another; displace; dislocate. **2** *Botany.* to cause to undergo translocation.

**trans|lo|ca|tion** (trans′lō kā′shən, tranz′-), *n.* **1** *Botany.* the conduction of food from one part of a plant to another. **2** the fact or condition of being displaced; displacement.

**trans|lu|cence** (trans lü′səns, tranz-), *n.* translucent quality or condition.

**trans|lu|cen|cy** (trans lü′sən sē, tranz-), *n.* = translucence.

**trans|lu|cent** (trans lü′sənt, tranz-), *adj.* **1** letting light through, but not able to be seen through: *Frosted glass is translucent.* **2** *Archaic.* **a** transparent. **b** that shines through. [< Latin *trāns-lūcēns, -entis,* present participle of *trānslūcēre* < *trāns-* through + *lūcēre* to shine] —**trans|lu′cent|ly,** *adv.*

**trans|lu|cid** (trans lü′sid, tranz-), *adj.* = translucent. [< Latin *trānslūcidus* < *trānslūcēre* < *trāns-* through + *lūcēre* to shine]

**trans|lu|nar** (trans lü′nər, tranz-), *adj.* **1** = translunary. **2** outside of or beyond the orbit of the moon (used especially of a spacecraft): *The U.S.S.R. on April 7 launched Luna 14 into a parking orbit and then into a translunar trajectory* (Mitchell R. Sharpe).

**trans|lu|na|ry** (trans lü′nər ē, tranz-), *adj.* **1** situated beyond or above the moon; superlunary. **2** *Figurative.* celestial, rather than earthly; ideal; visionary: [*Marlowe*] *had in him those brave translunary things that the first poets had* (Michael Drayton). [< *trans-* + Latin *lūna* moon; patterned on *lunary*]

**trans|make** (trans māk′, tranz-), *v.t.*, **-made, -mak|ing.** to make into something different; reshape.

**trans|ma|rine** (trans′mə rēn′, tranz′-), *adj.* across or beyond the sea; overseas. [< Latin *trānsmarīnus* < *trāns-* across + *mare* sea]

**trans|me|di|al** (trans mē′dē əl, tranz-), *adj.* = transmedian.

**trans|me|di|an** (trans mē′dē ən, tranz-), *adj.* passing or lying across a median line, as of the body: *a transmedian muscle.*

**trans|mi|grant** (trans mī′grənt, tranz-), *n., adj.* —*n.* a person passing through a country or place on his way from his own country to a country in which he intends to settle.
—*adj.* transmigrating.
[< Latin *trānsmigrāns, -antis,* present participle of *trānsmigrāre;* see etym. under **transmigrate**]

**trans|mi|grate** (trans mī′grāt, tranz-), *v.i.*, **-grat|ed, -grat|ing. 1** (of the soul) to pass at death into another body. **2** to move from one place to another to settle there; migrate. [< Latin *trānsmigrāre* (with English *-ate*[1]) < *trāns-* across + *migrāre* to move]

**trans|mi|gra|tion** (trans′mī grā′shən, tranz′-), *n.* **1a** the passing of a soul at death into another body; metempsychosis. **b** the doctrine of reincarnation of the soul in a human or an animal body after death. Many people in India believe in the transmigration of souls. *That peculiar feeling ... of having once been someone else, which accounts for so much belief in the transmigration of souls* (John Galsworthy). **2** the going from one place to another to settle there; migration.

**trans|mi|gra|tor** (trans mī′grā tər, tranz-), *n.* a person or thing that transmigrates.

**trans|mi|gra|to|ry** (trans mī′grə tôr′ē, -tōr′-; tranz-), *adj.* having to do with transmigration; transmigrating.

**trans|mis|si|bil|i|ty** (trans mis′ə bil′ə tē, tranz-), *n.* the quality of being transmissible.

**trans|mis|si|ble** (trans mis′ə bəl, tranz-), *adj.* that can be transmitted: *Scarlet fever is a transmissible disease.*

***trans|mis|sion** (trans mish′ən, tranz-), *n.* **1** the act or fact of sending over; passing on; passing along; letting through: *the transmission of money by telegraph. Mosquitoes are the only means of transmission of malaria. Alphabetical writing made ... the transmission of events more easy and certain* (Samuel Johnson). **2a** the part of an automobile or other motor vehicle that transmits power from the engine to the rear axle or sometimes the front axle. **b** the sets of gears that determine the relative speed. **3** the passing through space of radio or television waves from a transmitting station to a receiving station or stations: *When transmission is good, even foreign radio stations can be heard.* **4** something transmitted. [< Latin *trānsmissiō, -ōnis* < *trānsmittere,* see etym. under **transmit**]

***transmission**
definition 2a

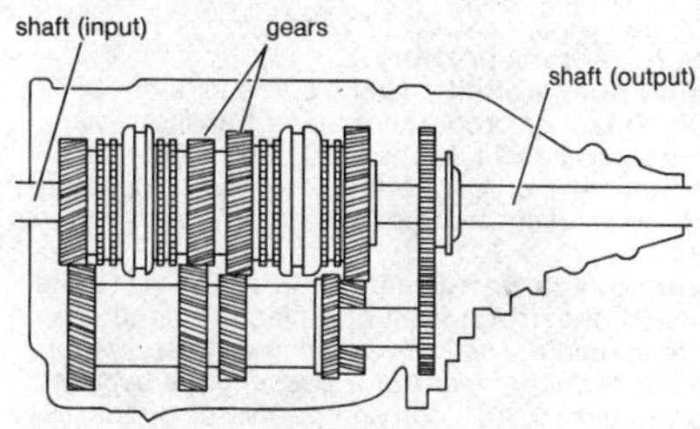


manual automobile transmission

**transmission electron microscope**, an electron microscope that transmits electrons through a specimen so that all the illuminated points of the image are produced at the same time.

**trans|mis|sive** (trans mis′iv, tranz-), *adj.* **1** transmitting; having to do with transmission. **2** obtained by transmission; transmitted; derived.

**trans|mis|siv|i|ty** (trans′mi siv′ə tē, tranz′-), *n.* the quality of being transmissible.

**trans|mis|som|e|ter** (trans′mi som′ə tər, tranz′-), *n.* an electronic apparatus that determines the degree of visibility, as on the runway of an airfield, by measuring the amount of light that comes through the atmosphere to a fixed point from a fixed transmitting point.

**trans|mit** (trans mit′, tranz-), *v.*, **-mit|ted, -mit|ting.** —*v.t.* **1** to send over; pass on; pass along; let through: *I will transmit the money by special messenger. Rats transmit disease.* **2** *Physics.* **a** to cause (light, heat, sound, or other form of energy) to pass through a medium. **b** to convey (force or movement) from one part of a body or mechanism to another. **c** to allow (light, heat, or other energy) to pass through; conduct: *Glass transmits light.* **3** to send out (signals, voices, music, or pictures) by means of radio or television or by wire. **4** *Figurative.* to pass on through inheritance: *The physical characteristics of a person may be transmitted to his children.*
—*v.i.* to send out signals by means of electromagnetic waves or by wire: *Some station is transmitting every hour of the day.*
[< Latin *trānsmittere* < *trāns-* across + *mittere* send]

**trans|mit|ta|ble** (trans mit′ə bəl, tranz-), *adj.* = transmissible.

**trans|mit|tal** (trans mit′əl, tranz-), *n.* **1** the act of transmitting; transmission. **2** something transmitted.

**trans|mit|tance** (trans mit′əns, tranz-), *n.* = transmittal.

**trans|mit|ter** (trans mit′ər, tranz-), *n.* **1** a person or thing that transmits something: *a disease transmitter.* **2** the part of a telegraph or telephone by which sound waves are converted to electrical impulses and sent to a receiver; sender. **3** an apparatus for sending out signals by means of radio or television; transmitting set. The term generally refers to the part of the broadcasting equipment that generates and modulates the radio waves, and sends them to the antenna to be sent out through space to a receiver.

**trans|mit|ti|ble** (trans mit′ə bəl, tranz-), *adj.* = transmissible.

**trans|mit|ting set** (trans mit′ing, tranz-), = transmitter.

**trans|mog|ri|fy** (trans mog′rə fī, tranz-), *v.t.*, **-fied, -fy|ing.** to change in form or appearance; transform in a surprising or grotesque manner: *Some had been models for the people Mr.* [*Thomas Hart*] *Benton ... transmogrified from stockbrokers and lawyers into poker players and Indian fighters in some of Mr. Benton's most famous works* (Wayne King). [perhaps a fanciful coinage] —**trans|mog′ri|fi|ca′tion,** *n.*

**trans|mon|tane** (trans mon′tān, tranz-), *adj.* beyond the mountains; tramontane.

**trans|moun|tain** (trans moun′tən, tranz-), *adj.* passing through or over a mountain: *a transmountain oil pipeline, a transmountain road.*

**trans|mun|dane** (trans mun′dān, tranz-), *adj.* beyond the world; beyond this world.

**trans|mu|ral** (trans myůr′əl, tranz-), *adj.* that is or passes beyond the walls of a city, institution, etc.

**trans|mut|a|bil|i|ty** (trans myü′tə bil′ə tē, tranz-), *n.* the quality of being transmutable.

**trans|mut|a|ble** (trans myü′tə bəl, tranz-), *adj.* that can be transmuted. —**trans|mut′a|ble|ness,** *n.* —**trans|mut′a|bly,** *adv.*

**trans|mu|ta|tion** (trans′myü tā′shən, tranz′-), *n.* **1** a change from one nature, substance, or form into another. **SYN:** alteration, transformation. **2** the transformation of one species into another; mutation. **3** *Chemistry, Physics.* a change from one atom into another atom of a different element, occurring naturally, as by radioactive disintegration, or artificially, as by bombardment with neutrons. **4** (in alchemy) the (attempted) conversion of a baser metal into gold or silver. **5** *Archaic.* a change of condition, attitude, etc.

**trans|mu|ta|tion|al** (trans′myü tā′shə nəl, tranz′-), *adj.* of or having to do with transmutation.

**trans|mute** (trans myüt′, tranz-), *v.*, **-mut|ed, -mut|ing.** —*v.t.* **1** to change from one nature, substance, or form into another: *We can transmute water power into electrical power.* **SYN:** convert. See syn. under **transform. 2** *Chemistry, Physics.* to subject to transmutation. —*v.i.* to undergo transmutation. [< Latin *trānsmūtāre* < *trāns-* thoroughly + *mūtāre* to change]

**trans|na|tion|al** (trans nash′ən əl, -nash′nəl; tranz-), *adj.* extending beyond national frontiers or bounds: *a transnational economy, a transnational culture.* —**trans|na′tion|al|ly,** *adv.*

**trans|nat|u|ral** (trans nach′ə rəl, -nach′rəl; tranz-), *adj.* that is beyond nature; supernatural.

**trans|na|ture** (trans nā′chər, tranz-), *v.t.*, **-tured, -tur|ing.** to change the nature of: *to transnature the human mind.*

**trans|o|cean** (trans ō′shən, tranz-), *adj.* = transoceanic.

**trans|o|ce|an|ic** (trans′ō shē an′ik, tranz′-), *adj.* **1** crossing the ocean. **2** on the other side of the ocean.

***tran|som** (tran′səm), *n.* **1** a small window over a door or other window, usually hinged for opening. **2** a crossbar separating a door from the window over it. **3** a horizontal bar across a window. **4** a window divided by a transom. **5** one of the beams or timbers attached across the sternpost of a ship between the two sides. **6a** the horizontal bar of a cross. **b** the transverse member of a gallows, a swing, or the like. [perhaps < Latin *trānstrum* (originally) crossbeam, related to *trāns* across]

***transom**
definition 1

**transom window**, **1** a window divided by a transom. **2** a window over the transom of a door.

**tran|son|ic** (tran son′ik), *adj.* having to do with or moving at speeds immediately below or above the speed of sound, or between 600 and 800 miles per hour. Also, **transsonic.**

**trans|o|sonde** (tran′sə sond), *n.* a transoceanic

**Pronunciation Key:** hat, āge, cãre, fär; let, ēqual, tėrm; it, īce; hot, ōpen, ôrder; oil, out; cup, pu̇t, rüle; child; long; thin; ᴛʜen; zh, measure; ə represents a in about, e in taken, i in pencil, o in lemon, u in circus.

balloon equipped with radiosonde for the transmission of meteorological data: *Cost of operating the constant-level balloons, called transosondes, can be as low as $75 for each wind reading* (Science News Letter). [< *transo*(ceanic) (radio)*sonde*]

**transp.**, transportation.

**trans|pa|cif|ic** (trans′pə sif′ik), *adj.* **1** crossing the Pacific: *a transpacific liner, a transpacific cable.* **2** on the other side of the Pacific: *a transpacific ally.*

**trans|par|ence** (trans pãr′əns), *n.* transparent quality or condition; transparency.

**trans|par|en|cy** (trans pãr′ən sē), *n., pl.* **-cies. 1** transparent quality or condition. **2** something transparent. **3** a picture, design, or the like, on glass, celluloid, or a photographic slide, made visible by light shining through from behind.

**trans|par|ent** (trans pãr′ənt), *adj.* **1** transmitting light so that bodies beyond or behind can be distinctly seen: *Window glass is transparent.* **SYN:** limpid, pellucid. **2** *Figurative.* **a** easily seen through or detected; obvious: *a transparent lie. The boy's transparent excuse didn't fool the teacher.* **SYN:** manifest, evident. **b** free from pretense or deceit; frank: *a person of transparent honesty. An ingenuous, transparent life* (Thomas Hardy). **SYN:** open, candid. **3** *Archaic.* shining through; penetrating: *Like to the glorious sun's transparent beams* (Shakespeare). [< Medieval Latin *transparens, -entis,* present participle of unrecorded *transparere* show light through < Latin *trāns-* through + *pārēre* appear] **— trans|par′ent|ly,** *adv.* **— trans|par′ent|ness,** *n.*

**Trans|par|ent** (trans pãr′ənt), *n.* an apple with a greenish white or pale yellow color.

**transparent fish,** = glass fish.

**trans|per|son|al** (trans pėr′sə nəl, -pėrs′nəl; tranz-), *adj.* beyond what is personal; transcending the personal.

**tran|spic|u|ous** (tran spik′yů əs), *adj.* **1** = transparent. **2** *Figurative.* easy to understand; plain; clear. [< New Latin *transpicuus* (with English *-ous*) < Latin *trānspicere* see through < *trāns-* through + *specere* look at]

**trans|pierce** (trans pirs′), *v.t.,* **-pierced, -pierc|ing.** to pass through; penetrate; pierce. [< *trans-* + *pierce,* patterned on French *transpercer,* alteration of *trespercier* < *tres-* (< Latin *trāns-* through) + *percier* to pierce]

**tran|spi|ra|tion** (tran′spə rā′shən), *n.* the action or process of transpiring, especially moisture in the form of vapor through a membrane or surface, as from the human body or from leaves or other parts of plants.

**tran|spir|a|to|ry** (tran spīr′ə tôr′ē, -tōr′-), *adj.* transpiring; having to do with transpiration.

**tran|spire** (tran spīr′), *v.,* **-spired, -spir|ing.** **— *v.i.* 1** to take place; happen; occur: *I heard later what transpired at the meeting.* **2** *Figurative.* to leak out; become known. **3** to pass off or send off moisture in the form of vapor through a membrane or surface, as from the human body or from leaves.

**— *v.t.*** to pass off or send off in the form of a vapor or liquid, as waste matter through the skin or moisture through the leaves of a plant.

[< Middle French *transpirer* < Latin *trāns-* through + *spīrāre* breathe]

**trans|plant** (*v.* trans plant′, -plänt′; *n.* trans′plant, -plänt), *v., n.* **— *v.t.* 1** to plant again in a different place: *We start the flowers indoors and then transplant them to the garden.* **2** to remove from one place to another; transport: *Many Scottish settlers were transplanted to the captured French colony of Nova Scotia by the British government.* **3** to transfer (skin, an organ, or other part) from one person, animal, or part of the body to another: *to transplant a kidney.*

**— *v.i.*** to bear moving to a different place: *Poppies do not transplant well and should be planted where they are to grow.*

**— *n.* 1a** the transferring of skin, an organ, or other part, from one person, animal, or part of the body to another: *a heart transplant.* **b** the part so transferred. **2** a seedling transplanted once or several times. **3** the transferring of bacterial organisms from one medium to another for culture.

[< Late Latin *trānsplantāre* < Latin *trāns-* across + *plantāre* to plant < *planta* a sprout]

**— trans|plant′er,** *n.*

**trans|plant|a|bil|i|ty** (trans plan′tə bil′ə tē, -plän′-), *n.* the quality of being transplantable.

**trans|plant|a|ble** (trans plan′tə bəl, -plän′-), *adj.* that can be transplanted.

**trans|plant|ate** (trans plan′tāt, -plän′-), *n.* an organ or section of tissue that has been or is to be transplanted, especially from one person to another; transplant.

**trans|plan|ta|tion** (trans′plan tā′shən, -plän-), *n.* **1** the act or process of transplanting or condition of being transplanted. **2** something that has been transplanted.

**trans|po|lar** (trans pō′lər, tranz-), *adj.* across the north or south pole or polar region: *a transpolar flight.*

**tran|spond|er** (tran spon′dər), *n.* an electronic device that can receive a radar or other signal and automatically transmit a response.

**trans|po|ni|ble** (trans pō′nə bəl), *adj.* = transposable. [< Latin *trānspōnere* transpose (< *trāns-* across + *pōnere* to place) + English *-ible*]

**trans|pon|tine** (trans pon′tin, -tīn), *adj.* across or beyond a bridge, especially on the south side of the Thames in London. [< *trans-* + Latin *pōns, pontis* bridge + English *-ine*[1]. Compare earlier French *transpontin.*]

**trans|port** (*v.* trans pôrt′, -pōrt′; *n.* trans′pôrt, -pōrt), *v., n.* **— *v.t.* 1** to carry from one place to another: *Wheat is transported from the farms to the mills.* **SYN:** remove, convey. See syn. under **carry. 2** *Figurative.* to carry away by strong feeling: *She was transported with joy by the good news.* **3** to send away to another country as a punishment: *Years ago, England transported many of her criminals to Australia.* **SYN:** banish, deport. **4** = kill.

**— *n.* 1** the action of carrying from one place to another; transporting: *Trucks are much used for transport of freight.* **2** a ship used to carry soldiers, equipment, supplies, and the like. **3** an aircraft that transports passengers, mail, or freight. **4** a system of transportation; transit. **5** *Figurative.* a very strong feeling: *a transport of joy or rage.* **6** a transported convict.

[< Latin *trānsportāre* < *trāns-* across + *portāre* carry] **— trans|port′er,** *n.*

**trans|port|a|bil|i|ty** (trans pôr′tə bil′ə tē, -pōr′-), *n.* the fact or property of being transportable.

**trans|port|a|ble** (trans pôr′tə bəl, -pōr′-), *adj.* **1** that can be transported. **2** involving, or liable to, punishment by transportation: *a transportable offense.*

**trans|por|ta|tion** (trans′pər tā′shən), *n.* **1a** the action of carrying from one place to another; transporting: *The railroad allows transportation for a certain amount of a passenger's baggage.* **b** the business of carrying people or goods: *Railroads, trucks, bus lines, and airlines are all engaged in transportation. Without transportation, our modern society could not exist.* **2** the condition of being transported. **3** Also, **Transportation.** the department of the United States government in charge of transportation. It was established in 1966. **4** a means of transport. **5** the cost of transport; ticket for transport. **6** the act or fact of sending away to another country as a punishment: *a set of rascals and rebels whom transportation is too good for* (Dickens).

**trans|por|ta|tion|al** (trans′pər tā′shən əl), *adj.* of, belonging to, or having to do with transportation.

**trans|port|ee** (trans′pôr tē′, -pōr-), *n.* **1** a transported convict. **2** an animal that has been transported from its habitat.

***trans|port|er bridge** (trans pôr′tər, -pōr′-), a bridge carrying a suspended platform or car which travels from bank to bank of the waterway to transport the traffic. It is built high enough not to interfere with navigation.

***transporter bridge**

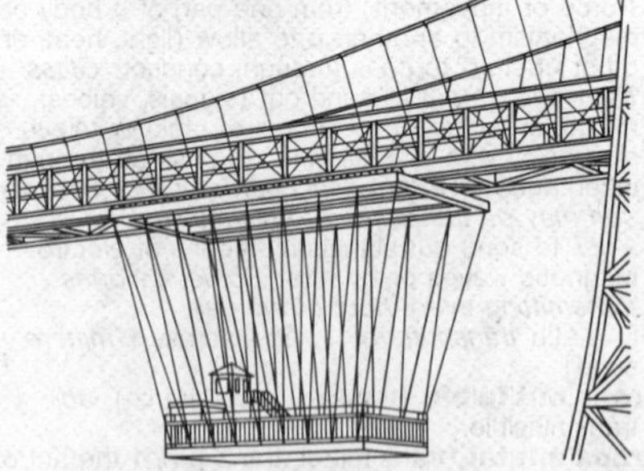

**trans|pos|a|bil|i|ty** (trans pō′zə bil′ə tē), *n.* the quality of being transposable.

**trans|pos|al** (trans pō′zəl), *n.* = transposition.

**trans|pose** (trans pōz′), *v.,* **-posed, -pos|ing,** *n.* **— *v.t.* 1** to change the position or order of; interchange: *Transpose the two colors to make a better design.* **2** to change the usual order of (letters, words, or numbers) *Example:* Then *comes he* with *horses many* the *road along. He transposed the numbers and mistakenly wrote 19 for 91.* **3** *Music.* to change the key of (a composition). **4** to transfer (a term) to the other side of an algebraic equation, changing plus to minus or minus to plus. *Abbr:* tr. **5** *Archaic.* to transform; transmute; convert: *Things base and vile ... Love can transpose to form and dignity* (Shakespeare).

**— *n.*** *Mathematics.* a matrix formed by transposing the rows and columns of a given matrix.

[< French *transposer* < *trans-* across + *poser* to put. Compare etym. under **pose**[1].] **— trans|pos′a|ble,** *adj.* **— trans|pos′er,** *n.*

**trans|po|si|tion** (trans′pə zish′ən), *n.* **1** the action of transposing or condition of being transposed. **2** *Music.* a composition transposed into a different key.

**trans|po|si|tion|al** (trans′pə zish′ə nəl), *adj.* of or involving transposition.

**transposition system,** a cryptographic system in which the letters of the plaintext are rearranged in a certain order.

**trans|pos|i|tive** (trans poz′ə tiv), *adj.* characterized by transposition.

**trans|ra|cial** (trans rā′shəl, tranz-), *adj.* across racial boundaries: *transracial marriage, transracial adoption of children.*

**trans|sex|u|al** (trans sek′shů əl), *n., adj.* **— *n.*** a person who is anatomically of one sex but who desires to belong to the opposite sex, especially by undergoing surgery to change his or her sexual organs.

**— *adj.*** of or having to do with transsexuals or transsexualism: *a transsexual operation.*

**trans|sex|u|al|ism** (trans sek′shů ə liz′əm), *n.* the condition of being a transsexual.

**trans|shape** (trans shāp′), *v.t.,* **-shaped, -shap|ing.** to change into another shape or form; transform. Also, **transhape.**

**trans|ship** (trans ship′), *v.t., v.i.,* **-shipped, -ship|ping.** to transfer from one ship, train, car, or other conveyance to another. Also, **tranship.**

**trans|ship|ment** (trans ship′mənt), *n.* a transshipping. Also, **transhipment.**

**trans|ship|per** (trans ship′ər), *n.* a person who transships. Also, **transhipper.**

**trans|son|ic** (trans son′ik), *adj.* = transonic.

**tran|sub|stan|tial** (tran′səb stan′shəl), *adj.* **1** changed or changeable from one substance to another. **2** of or having to do with transubstantiation. **— tran′sub|stan′tial|ly,** *adv.*

**tran|sub|stan|ti|ate** (tran′səb stan′shē āt), *v.,* **-at|ed, -at|ing. — *v.t.* 1** to change (bread and wine) into the body and blood of Christ. **2** to transmute or transform (any substance).

**— *v.i.*** to become transubstantiated.

**tran|sub|stan|ti|a|tion** (tran′səb stan′shē ā′shən), *n.* **1** a changing of one substance into another; transmutation. **2** in Christian theology: **a** the changing of the bread and wine of the Eucharist into the substance of the body of Christ, only the appearance of the bread and wine remaining. **b** the doctrine that this change occurs, held by the Roman Catholic and Eastern Churches. [< Medieval Latin *transubstantiatio, -onis* < *transubstantiare* to transmute < Latin *trāns-* over + *substantia* substance]

**tran|su|date** (tran′sů dāt), *n.* = transudation (def. 2).

**tran|su|da|tion** (tran′sů dā′shən), *n.* **1** the passing off or oozing out of a liquid through the pores of a substance; transuding. **2** a liquid that has transuded. [< *trans-* + Latin *sūdātiō, -ōnis* a sweating < *sūdāre* to sweat]

**tran|su|da|to|ry** (tran sü′də tôr′ē, -tōr′-), *adj.* transuding; characterized by transudation.

**tran|sude** (tran süd′), *v.i., v.t.* **-sud|ed, -sud|ing.** to ooze through or out like sweat; exude through pores. [< French *transuder* < Latin *trāns-* through, across + *sūdāre* to sweat]

**trans|u|ra|ni|an** (trans′yů rā′nē ən), *adj.* of or characteristic of a transuranic element.

**trans|u|ran|ic element** (trans′yů ran′ik), any one of a group of radioactive chemical elements whose atomic numbers are higher than that of uranium (92). The group includes neptunium, plutonium, americium, curium, berkelium, californium, einsteinium, fermium, mendelevium, nobelium, and lawrencium.

**trans|u|ra|ni|um element** (trans′yů rā′nē əm), *n.* = transuranic element.

**Trans|vaal|er** (trans vä′lər, tranz-), *n.* a native or inhabitant of the Transvaal, a province in the Republic of South Africa.

**trans|val|u|a|tion** (trans′val yů ā′shən), *n.* a change of values; revaluation.

**trans|val|ue** (trans val′yü), *v.t.,* **-ued, -u|ing.** to change the value of.

**trans|vase** (trans vās′, tranz-), *v.t.,* **-vased, -vas|ing.** to pour from one vessel into another. [< French *transvaser* < Latin *trāns-* across + *vās* vessel]

**trans|ver|sal** (trans vėr′səl, tranz-), *adj., n.* **— *adj.*** lying or passing across; transverse.

**— *n.*** a line intersecting two or more other lines. [< Medieval Latin *transversalis* < Latin *trānsversus;* see etym. under **transverse**] **— trans|ver′sal|ly,** *adv.*

**trans|verse** (trans vėrs′, tranz-; trans′vėrs, tranz′-), *adj., n.* **— *adj.* 1** lying or passing across; placed crosswise; crossing from side to side: *transverse beams.* **2** *Geometry.* of or having to do with the axis of a conic section that passes

through the foci. **3** having a mouth or opening on the side: *a transverse flute.*
—*n.* **1** something transverse. **2** *Geometry.* a transverse axis; the longer axis of an ellipse.
[< Latin *trānsversus,* past participle of *trānsvertere* < *trāns-* across + *vertere* to turn] —**trans·verse′ly**, *adv.*

**transverse arch**, an arch formed by bones across the ball of the foot; metatarsal arch.

**transverse colon**, the part of the large intestine that crosses under the liver. See diagram under **intestine**.

**transverse process**, a process projecting laterally from a vertebra.

**transverse vibrations**, *Physics.* periodic disturbances in which the particles of the medium move at right angles to the direction of propagation.

**transverse wave**, *Physics.* a wave in which the individual particles of the medium move at right angles to the direction of the wave's propagation.

**trans|vert|er** (trans vėr′tər, tranz-), *n.* a device for changing alternating electric current of low voltage into direct current of high voltage or for changing direct current of high voltage into alternating current of low voltage. [< *trans*(former) + (con)*verter*]

**trans|ves|tism** (trans ves′tiz əm, tranz-), *n.* the practice of dressing in the clothing of the opposite sex: *The plot, with its elements of transvestism* (*Achilles is disguised as a girl because his father does not want him to be killed in the Trojan war*), *cannot avoid humor* (London Times). [< obsolete *transvest* to clothe in garments, especially of the opposite sex (< *trans-* + Latin *vestīre* to clothe)]

**trans|ves|tist** (trans ves′tist, tranz-), *n.* = transvestite.

**trans|ves|tite** (trans ves′tīt, tranz-), *n., adj.* —*n.* a person who has a desire to dress in the clothing of the opposite sex.
—*adj.* of or having to do with transvestism.

**trans|ves|tit|ism** (trans ves′tə tiz əm, tranz-), *n.* = transvestism.

**Tran|syl|va|ni|an** (tran′səl vā′nē ən, -vān′yən), *adj., n.* —*adj.* of or having to do with Transylvania, a region in western Romania, or its people.
—*n.* a native or inhabitant of Transylvania.

**trap¹** (trap), *n., v.,* **trapped, trap|ping.** —*n.* **1 a** device or means for catching animals. Most traps have a spring or snare which when touched seizes, kills, or imprisons the animal: *to set a trap for beaver or rats. The fishermen set out huge nets in circles as a fish trap.* **2** *Figurative.* **a** a trick or other means for catching someone off guard, as by making him show his guilt or reveal a secret: *The police set traps to make the thief confess.* **b** anything that attracts because it seems easy but proves to be difficult. **3a** = trap door. **b** the opening covered by a trap door. **4** anything that catches and keeps something else or prevents it from reacting with something else: *The atmosphere traps sunshine much as a greenhouse does* (James E. Miller). **5a** a device in a pipe, such as a bend, to catch small objects or to keep air, water, steam, or gas, from backing up. **b** a ventilation door in a mine. **6** = speed trap. **7** a light, two-wheeled carriage, such as a gig. **8** a device for throwing clay pigeons or tin cans into the air to be shot at. **9** = sand trap. **10a** a piece of wood, shaped like a shoe with a hollow at the heel and moving on a pivot, used in trapball. **b** = trapball. **11** = trap net. **12** *Slang.* the mouth: *Shut your trap!*
—*v.t.* **1** to catch in a trap: *The bear was trapped.* **SYN:** entrap, ensnare. **2** *Figurative.* to trick or catch (someone), especially by putting (him) off his guard: *The science teacher trapped his class by asking them "Which was heavier, a pound of nails or a pound of feathers?"* **3** to provide with a trap. **4** to stop and hold with a trap, as water, air, gas, or heat in a pipe.
—*v.i.* **1** to set traps for animals. **2** to make a business of catching animals in traps for their furs: *Some men make their living by trapping.* **3** to work a trap in trapshooting.
**traps**, a group of percussion instruments, such as cymbals, bells, gongs, maracas, castanets, triangles, and other instruments for sound effects: *You jazzmen, bang ... drums, traps* (Carl Sandburg).
[Old English *træppe* a snare, trap]
—*Syn. n.* **1, 2a Trap, snare** mean something that catches or is contrived to catch an animal or person. **Trap**, literally usually a mechanical device springing shut, figuratively suggests a situation deliberately set to catch someone by surprise and destroy him or trick him into doing or saying something: *Suspecting a trap, the detachment of soldiers withdrew.* **Snare**, literally a noose tightening around an animal's foot or neck, figuratively applies to a situation someone gets entangled in unawares, or a device to lure him into getting caught: *The detectives used marked money as a snare for the thief.*

**trap²** (trap), *v.,* **trapped, trap|ping,** *n.* —*v.t.* to cover or ornament with trappings.
—*n. Obsolete.* trappings for a horse.
**traps**, *Informal.* personal effects; baggage; belongings: *I packed my traps and went on shore* (Frederick Marryat).
[Middle English *trappe* saddle cloth, caparison; origin uncertain; perhaps alteration of Old French *drap,* or Medieval Latin *drappus*]

**trap³** (trap), *n. Geology.* basalt or other fine-grained, dark, igneous rock having a more or less columnar structure. [earlier *trapp* < Swedish < *trappa* stair < Low German (because of its appearance)]

**tra|pan** (trə pan′), *n., v.t.,* **-panned, -pan|ning.** *Archaic.* trepan². —**tra|pan′ner**, *n.*

***trap|ball** (trap′bôl′), *n.* **1** an old game in which a player strikes a trap to throw the ball into the air and then hits the ball to some distance. **2** the ball used in this game.

***trapball** definition 1

**trap cut**, = step cut.

**trap door**, **1** a door flush with the surface of a floor, ceiling, or roof. It opens on hinges or by sliding in grooves. **2** the opening covered by such a door.

**trap-door spider** (trap′dôr′, -dōr′), any one of a group of large, hairy spiders that live in underground burrows covered by hinged lids that open and shut like a trap door. It is a tarantula and lives in warm climates.

**trapes** (trāps), *v.i., v.t., n. Informal.* traipse.

**tra|peze** (tra pēz′), *n.* **1** a short, horizontal bar hung by ropes like a swing, used in performing acrobatic stunts and exercises in gymnasiums and circuses. **2** *Geometry.* a trapezium. **3** a loose, unbelted dress that flares from the shoulders to the hem: *Araminta is glimpsed through the rain wearing her off-the-peg trapeze in a giant cabbage rose print* (Punch). [< French *trapèze* < Late Latin *trapezium* < Greek *trapézion* an irregular quadrilateral; small table (diminutive) < *trápeza* table < *tetra-* four + *péza* foot. See etym. of doublet **trapezium.**]

**trapeze dress**, = trapeze.

**tra|pe|zi|form** (trə pē′zə fôrm), *adj.* shaped like a trapezium or trapezoid.

**tra|pez|ist** (tra pē′zist), *n.* a performer on the trapeze.

***tra|pe|zi|um** (trə pē′zē əm), *n., pl.* **-zi|ums, -zi|a** (-zē ə). **1a** a four-sided plane figure having no two sides parallel. **b** *British.* a trapezoid. **2** *Anatomy.* the greater multangular (bone). [< Late Latin *trapezium.* See etym. of doublet **trapeze.**]

**tra|pe|zi|us** (trə pē′zē əs), *n., pl.* **-zi|i** (-zē ī). *Anatomy.* each of a pair of large, flat, triangular muscles of the back of the neck and the upper part of the back and shoulders, together forming a somewhat diamond-shaped figure. [< New Latin *trapezius* < Late Latin *trapezium:* see etym. under **trapeze**]

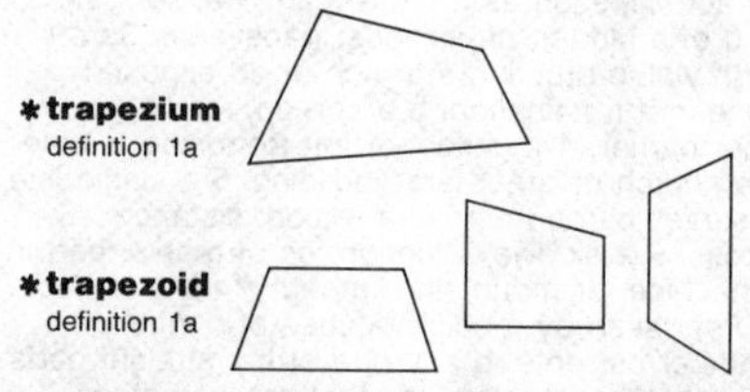
***trapezium** definition 1a

***trapezoid** definition 1a

***trap|e|zoid** (trap′ə zoid), *n., adj.* —*n.* **1a** a four-sided plane figure having two sides parallel and two sides not parallel. **b** *British.* a four-sided plane figure having no sides parallel; trapezium. **2** *Anatomy.* the lesser multangular (bone).
—*adj.* = trapezoidal.
[< New Latin *trapezöides* < Late Greek *trapezoidês* (in Greek, shaped like a trapezium) < Greek *trápeza* table + *eîdos* form]

**trap|e|zoi|dal** (trap′ə zoi′dəl), *adj.* in the form of a trapezoid.

**trap fishing**, fishing with a trap line or net.

**trap line**, **1** the route along which traps are set in trapping. **2** a line of baited fishing hooks to be anchored in place. **3** the filament in a spider's web that ensnares the prey.

**trap net**, an oblong net with one end in the shape of an inverted funnel, for catching fish.

**trap|per** (trap′ər), *n.* a person who traps, especially one who traps wild animals for their furs.

**trap|pings** (trap′ingz), *n.pl.* **1** ornamental coverings for a horse; caparisons. **2** things worn; ornaments: *the trappings of a king and his court, the trappings of a house at Christmas.* **3** outward appearances: *He had all the trappings of a cowboy, but he couldn't even ride a horse.* [< *trap*²]

**Trap|pist** (trap′ist), *n., adj.* —*n.* a monk belonging to an extremely austere branch of the Cistercian order established in 1664. The Trappists are vowed to almost complete silence and hard labor.
—*adj.* of or having to do with the Trappists.
[< French *trappiste* < the abbey *La Trappe* (< the village of *Soligny-la-Trappe,* in France) + *-iste* -ist]

**trap|rock** (trap′rok′), *n.* = trap³.

**traps** (traps), *n.pl.* See under **trap¹** and **trap².**

**trap|shoot|er** (trap′shü′tər), *n.* a person who shoots at clay pigeons thrown into the air.

**trap|shoot|ing** (trap′shü′ting), *n.* the sport of shooting at clay pigeons or other targets thrown or released from traps into the air.

**trap shot**, a half volley, especially in tennis.

**tra|pun|to** (trə pün′tō, -pün′-), *n.* embroidery in which a design outlined on one side is padded with cotton or yarn on the other side. [< Italian *trapunto* < Vulgar Latin *trapūnctus* < Latin *intrā* within + *pūnctum* a point, prick]

**trash¹** (trash), *n., v.* —*n.* **1** anything of little or no worth; worthless stuff; rubbish: *Please take the basket of trash to the garbage can.* **SYN:** debris, litter, refuse, garbage. **2** cheap and flashy writing, talk, etc.: *Many books and magazines are filled with cheap, sensational, and lurid trash.* **3** broken or torn bits, such as leaves, twigs, or husks: *Rake up the trash in the yard and burn it.* **4** *Figurative.* worthless or disreputable people; riffraff: *His father hated him travelling with trash like them* (Owen Wister). **5** the refuse of sugar cane after the juice has been pressed. **6** *Slang.* an act of vandalism.
—*v.t.* **1** to free from trash or refuse, especially to strip the outer leaves from (growing sugar cane) so it can ripen more quickly. **2** to treat or discard as worthless. **3** *Slang.* to vandalize: *Backstage at "Comes a Day" he got drunk and trashed his dressing room* (Time).
—*v.i. Slang.* to engage in vandalism: *Campus revolutionaries intent on destroying all freedom except their own are now turning to what they call 'trashing'—the setting of fires, hurling of rocks, smashing of windows* (New Yorker).
[< Scandinavian (compare dialectal Norwegian *trask,* and Old Icelandic *thraska* to rummage)]

**trash²** (trash), *n., v.* —*n.* **1** a leash for a dog. **2** anything that checks or restrains; hindrance.
—*v.t.* **1** to check by or as if by a trash or leash. **2** to hold back; restrain; hinder.
[origin uncertain]

**trash can**, a metal or plastic receptacle for the disposal of trash.

**trash|er** (trash′ər), *n. U.S. Slang.* a person who engages in vandalism.

**trash fish**, any fish that is not a food fish or a sport fish, especially any one of certain fishes, such as some kinds of hake, used to make fish meal: *A 6-in. saltwater trash fish, the alewife, ... monopolized the lakes* (Time).

**trash|man** (trash′man′, -mən), *n., pl.* **-men.** a man who collects and removes trash; garbageman.

**trash|y** (trash′ē), *adj.,* **trash|i|er, trash|i|est.** like or containing trash; worthless. —**trash′i|ly**, *adv.* —**trash′i|ness**, *n.*

**trass** (tras), *n.* a rock consisting largely of consolidated fragments of pumice or other volcanic material, used for making mortar or hydraulic cement. It is common along the Rhine. [< Dutch *tras,* earlier *tarasse,* ultimately < Vulgar Latin *terrācea.* Compare etym. under **terrace.**]

**trat|to|ri|a** (trät′tō rē′ä), *n., pl.* **-ri|e** (-rē′ā). an inexpensive Italian restaurant. [< Italian *trattoria*]

**trau|chle** (trä′ʜəl), *v.t.,* **-chled, -chling.** *Scottish.* trachle.

**trau|ma** (trô′mə, trou′-), *n., pl.* **-mas, -ma|ta** (-mə tə). **1** a physical wound; injury. **2** a psychic wound; emotional shock which has a lasting effect on the mind. **3** an abnormal physical or men-

**Pronunciation Key:** hat, āge, cãre, fär; let, ēqual, tėrm; it, īce; hot, ōpen, ôrder; oil, out; cup, pu̇t, rüle; child; long; thin; ᴛʜen; zh, measure; ə represents **a** in about, **e** in taken, **i** in pencil, **o** in lemon, **u** in circus.

tal condition produced by a wound, injury, or shock. [< Greek *traûma, -atos* wound]

**trau|mat|ic** (trô mat′ik, trou-), *adj.* **1** of, having to do with, or produced by a wound, injury, or shock: *a traumatic experience.* **2** for or dealing with the treatment of wounds, injuries, or shock. [< Late Latin *traumaticus* < Greek *traumatikós* of a wound < *traûma, -atos* wound, trauma] — **trau-mat′i|cal|ly,** *adv.*

**traumatic neurosis,** any neurosis brought on by an injury or severe shock.

**trau|ma|tism** (trô′mə tiz əm, trou′-), *n.* **1** any abnormal condition caused by a trauma. **2** a trauma or wound.

**trau|ma|tize** (trô′mə tīz, trou′-), *v.t.,* **-tized, -tiz-ing.** to wound or injure (the mind or part of the body); produce a trauma in. — **trau′ma|ti|za′tion,** *n.*

**trau|ma|to|log|i|cal** (trô′mə tə loj′ə kəl, trou′-), *adj.* of or having to do with traumatology: *A number of burns units and traumatological institutes were established* (Manchester Guardian Weekly).

**trau|ma|tol|o|gy** (trô′mə tol′ə jē, trou′-), *n.* the scientific study of traumas or physical injuries.

**trav.,** **1** travel or travels. **2** traveler.

**trav|ail** (trav′āl), *n., v.* — *n.* **1** toil; labor. **2** *Figurative.* **a** trouble, hardship, or suffering: *It was a time of great travail. Faint and sick with travail and fear* (Jeremy Taylor). **b** severe pain; agony; torture. **3** the labor and pain of childbirth.
— *v.i.* **1** to toil; labor. **2** to suffer the pains of childbirth; be in labor.
[< Old French *travail* < Late Latin *trepālium* torture device, ultimately < Latin *tri-* three + *pālus* stake]

**trave** (trāv), *n. Dialect.* **1a** a crossbeam. **b** a part of a ceiling, etc., between crossbeams. **2** a frame or enclosure for keeping a restive horse to be shod. [(def. 1) < Old French *trave* < Latin *trabs, trabis* beam; (def. 2) probably short for Old French *entrave* a fetter]

**trav|el** (trav′əl), *v.,* **-eled, -el|ing** or **-elled, -el-ling,** *n.* — *v.i.* **1** to go from one place to another; journey: *to travel across the country. She is traveling in Europe this summer. He travels the fastest who travels alone* (Rudyard Kipling). **2** to go from place to place selling things: *He travels for a large firm.* **3** to move; proceed; pass: *Light and sound travel in waves.* **4** to walk or run: *A deer travels far and fast when chased.* **5** to move in a fixed course, as some pieces of mechanism do.
— *v.t.* **1** to pass through or over: *to travel a road.* **2** to walk or run along or over: *narrow ledges traveled only by mountain goats.*
— *n.* **1** the act or fact of going in trains, ships, cars, and the like, from one place to another; journeying: *to spend a summer in travel. She loves travel.* **2** movement in general. **3** the length of stroke, movement in one direction, or the distance of such movement of a part of a machine. **travels, a** journeys: *Soon after we find him on his travels in Italy* (Samuel Taylor Coleridge). **b** a book about one's experiences, visits, or observations while traveling: *We possess the travels of a native of ... India in the fourth century* (Mountstuart Elphinstone).
[variant of *travail* in its sense of "labor, fatigue"]

**trav|el|a|ble** (trav′ə lə bəl, trav′lə-), *adj.* that can be traveled over: *Icy roads are not travelable.* Also, **travellable.**

**travel agency** or **bureau,** a business that arranges trips, tickets, hotel reservations, and other appointments for travelers.

**travel agent,** a person who arranges for travel accommodations and appointments in a travel agency.

**trav|el|a|tor** (trav′ə lā′tər), *n.* a moving platform or sidewalk operating like a conveyor belt to carry pedestrians between certain points. [patterned on *escalator*]

**trav|eled** (trav′əld), *adj.* **1** that has done much traveling; experienced in travel: *Gulliver was a traveled man.* **2** much used by travelers: *a well-traveled road.* **3** *Geology.* moved to a distance from the original site: *a traveled boulder. Also,* **travelled.**

**trav|el|er** (trav′ə lər, trav′lər), *n.* **1** a person or thing that travels. **2** a traveling salesman; commercial traveler. **3** a piece of mechanism constructed to move in a fixed course. **4** a sales slip that a customer takes with him for the recording of two or more purchases in different parts of a store. **5** *Nautical.* **a** an iron ring or thimble running freely on a rope, rod, or spar. **b** the rope, rod, or spar on which such a ring slides. Also, **traveller.**

**traveler's check,** a check issued by a bank or other institution for a specified amount and signed by the buyer, who may use it as cash by signing it again in the presence of a witness, such as a clerk in a store or hotel.

**trav|el|er's-tree** (trav′ə lərz trē′, trav′lərz-), *n.* a large palmlike plant of the banana family native to Madagascar, so called because the base of its large leaf holds water a passer-by may drink.

**trav|el|ing** (trav′ə ling, trav′ling), *adj.* **1** that goes from place to place: *a traveling circus, a traveling preacher.* **2** of or for travel; used on a journey: *traveling expenses, a traveling bag, a traveling clock.* **3** going along with a traveler: *a traveling companion.* **4** made to move in a fixed course: *a traveling sidewalk.* Also, **travelling.**

**traveling crane,** any crane for moving loads from one place to another, such as a bridge crane.

**traveling salesman,** a person whose work is going from place to place selling things for a company.

**traveling wave,** *Physics.* a wave in which the particles of the medium move with the wave and gain energy from the wave, so that they continuously overtake each other.

**trav|el|ing-wave tube** (trav′ə ling wāv′, trav′-ling-), a vacuum tube to amplify microwaves through a coil of wire. The electric field produced in the wire interacts with a beam of electrons to make the microwave stronger.

**trav|el|la|ble** (trav′ə lə bəl, trav′lə-), *adj.* = travelable.

**trav|el|la|tor** (trav′ə lā′tər), *n.* = travelator.

**trav|elled** (trav′əld), *adj.* = traveled.

**trav|el|ler** (trav′ə lər, trav′lər), *n.* = traveler.

**trav|el|ling** (trav′ə ling, trav′ling), *adj.* = traveling.

**travelling post office,** *British.* a railroad car in which mail in transit is sorted and classified.

**trav|e|log** or **trav|e|logue** (trav′ə lôg, -log), *n.* **1** a lecture describing travel, usually accompanied by pictures, or films. **2** a motion picture depicting travel. [American English < *trave(l)* + *-logue,* as in *dialogue*]

**trav|els** (trav′əlz), *n.pl.* See under **travel.**

**travel sickness,** = motion sickness.

**trav|ers|al** (trav′ər səl, trə vėr′-), *n.* the action of traversing or fact of being traversed; traverse.

**trav|erse** (*v., adv.* trav′ərs, trə vėrs′; *n., adj.* trav′ərs), *v.,* **-ersed, -ers|ing,** *n., adj., adv.* — *v.t.* **1** to pass across, over, or through: *We traversed the desert by truck.* **2** to go to and fro over or along (a place, etc.); cross: *The Duke traversed the apartment ... in much agitation* (Scott). **3** to lie, extend, or stretch across; cross; intersect: *Deeply worn footpaths ... traversing the country* (Washington Irving). **4** to ski or climb diagonally across (a slope). **5** *Figurative.* to read, examine, or consider carefully: *A field too wide to be fully traversed* (Daniel Webster). **6** to move sideways or turn from side to side: *The climber traversed a long horizontal crack in the face of the mountain slope.* **7** to turn (as a cannon or surveyor's transit) to the right or left. **8** *Figurative.* to go counter to; oppose; hinder; thwart. **9** *Law.* to contradict or to deny formally in pleading. To traverse an indictment means to deny or disagree with an indictment. To traverse an office means to deny the validity of an inquest of office (a writ of inquiry into a question of property of the British Crown). **10** *Nautical.* to secure (a yard) fore and aft.
— *v.i.* **1** to move, pass, or go across or back and forth; cross. **2** (in the manège) to move or walk crosswise, as a horse that throws his croup to one side and his head to the other. **3** to turn on or as if on a pivot; swivel. **4** to ski or climb diagonally across a slope. **5** to move sideways, especially across the face of rock in mountain climbing. **6** (in fencing) to glide the blade along that of the opponent's foil, toward the hilt, while applying pressure.
— *n.* **1** the act of traversing; a passing across, over, or through; crossing. **2** something put or lying across, such as a crossbeam, transom, or rung of a ladder; crosspiece; transverse. **3a** an earth wall protecting a trench or an exposed place in a fortification. **b** a screen, railing, or other barrier. **4** a gallery or loft from side to side in a church or other large building. **5** a single line of survey carried across a region; distance across. **6** a sideways motion, as of a ship, part in a machine, or mountain climbers. **7a** the zigzag course taken by a ship because of contrary winds or currents. **b** any one of the straight parts of such a course. **8** a line that crosses other lines. **9** a passage or way by which to cross: *This traverse may the poorest take Without oppress of toll* (Emily Dickinson). **10** *Figurative.* an obstacle; hindrance; opposition. **11a** a changing of the direction of a gun to the right or left. **b** the amount of such change. **12** *Law.* a formal denial of something alleged to be a fact by the opposing side.
— *adj.* lying, passing, or extending across; cross; transverse: *the traverse part of a cross.*
— *adv. Obsolete.* across; crosswise; traversely.
[< Old French *traverser* < Late Latin *trānsversāre* < Latin *trānsversus;* see etym. under **transverse**] — **trav′ers|a|ble,** *adj.* — **trav′ers|er,** *n.*

**traverse jury,** *Law.* = petit jury.

**traverse table,** **1** a platform moving sideways on wheels, used on a railroad to shift cars from one set of rails to another parallel to it; transfer table. **2** a table used in navigation to determine the difference of latitude and departure corresponding to any given course and distance.

**trav|er|tine** (trav′ər tin, -tēn), *n.* a white or light-colored form of limestone deposited by springs, especially hot springs and used as building material: *The Vivian Beaumont Theater is a ... playhouse of travertine and glass* (New York Times). [< Italian *travertino,* variant of *tivertino* < Latin *tīburtīnus* < *Tībur,* an ancient town of Latium (now Tivoli)]

**trav|es|ty** (trav′ə stē), *n., pl.* **-ties,** *v.,* **-tied, -ty-ing.** — *n.* **1** any treatment or imitation that makes a serious thing seem ridiculous: *The trial was a travesty of justice, since the judge and jury were prejudiced.* **2a** an imitation of a serious literary work or subject, done in such a way as to make it seem ridiculous. Travesty is a form of literary burlesque. **b** writing of this kind: *to be skilled in travesty.*
— *v.t.* to make (a serious subject or matter) ridiculous; imitate in an absurd or grotesque way.
[(originally) adjective < French *travesti* disguised, past participle of *travestir* to disguise < Latin *trāns-* over + *vestīre* to dress < *vestis* garment. Compare etym. under **transvestism.**]

***tra|vois** (trə voi′), *n., pl.* **-vois.** a vehicle without wheels used by North American Plains Indians, consisting of two long poles harnessed at one end to a horse or dog and trailing on the ground at the other, with crossbars, a platform, or a net for carrying loads. [American English < Canadian French *travois,* a pronunciation of *travails* spaces between the two bars in which a horse runs, plural of French *travail,* perhaps ultimately < Latin *trabs, trabis* beam. Compare etym. under **trave.**]

***travois**

**tra|voise** (trə voiz′), *n., pl.* **-vois|es.** = travois.

**trawl** (trôl), *n., v.* — *n.* **1** a large, strong net dragged along the bottom of the sea, used in commercial fishing, dredging for deep-sea scientific specimens, or the like. **2** a strong line supported by buoys and having many short lines with baited hooks attached to it.
— *v.i.* **1** to fish with a net by dragging it along the bottom of the sea: *to trawl for herring.* **2** to fish with a line supported by buoys and having many hooks attached. **3** = troll (def. 1).
— *v.t.* **1** to catch (fish) with a trawl or trawls. **2** = troll (defs. 1, 2). — **trawl′a|ble,** *adj.*

***trawl|er** (trô′lər), *n.* **1** a boat used in trawling. **2** a person who trawls.

***trawler**
definition 1

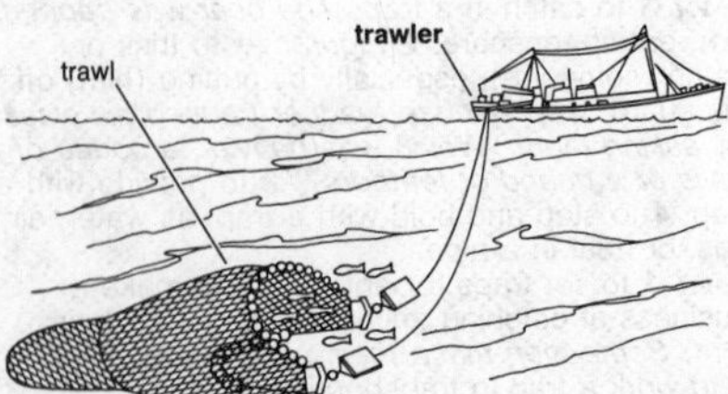


**trawl|er|man** (trô′lər man′, -mən), *n., pl.* **-men.** a man who fishes with a trawl or works on a trawler.

**trawl line,** = trawl (*n.* def. 2).

**trawl net,** = trawl (*n.* def. 1).

**tray** (trā), *n.* **1** a flat, shallow holder or container with a low rim around it: *The waiter carried the dishes on a tray.* **2** a tray with dishes of food on it: *The nurse brought a breakfast tray to the sick man.* **3** a shallow box that fits into a trunk or cabinet: *Our dentist keeps his instruments in trays.* **4** *Dialect.* any one of various shallow open vessels. [Old English *trēg*]

**tray agriculture,** = hydroponics.

**tray|ful** (trā′fůl), *n., pl.* **-fuls.** as much or as many as a tray will hold.

**treach|er|ous** (trech′ər əs), *adj.* **1** not to be trusted; not faithful; disloyal: *The treacherous soldier carried reports to the enemy.* **SYN**: traitorous, perfidious. **2** *Figurative.* having a false appearance of strength or security; not reliable; deceiving: *Thin ice is treacherous.* **SYN**: deceptive, unstable. —**treach′er|ous|ly**, *adv.* —**treach′er-ous|ness**, *n.*

**treach|er|y** (trech′ər ē), *n., pl.* **-er|ies.** **1** a breaking of faith; betrayal of trust; treacherous behavior; deceit: *King Arthur's kingdom was destroyed by treachery.* **SYN**: See syn. under **disloyalty**. **2** = treason. [< Old French *trecherie,* and *tricherie* < *trechier,* and *trichier* to cheat, perhaps < Germanic. Compare etym. under **trick**.]

**trea|cle** (trē′kəl), *n.* **1** *British.* molasses, especially that produced during the refining of sugar. **2** *Figurative.* anything too sweet or cloying, especially excessive sentimentality: *Hortense Calisher ... concocted something far richer and immeasurably rarer than the usual dreadful treacle of youthful domestic odyssey* (Time). **3** *Obsolete.* a sovereign remedy; panacea. **4** *Obsolete.* an antidote for poison or poisonous bites. [< Old French *triacle* antidote < Latin *thēriaca* < Greek *thēriakḗ* (*antídotos*) (antidote against) poisonous reptiles < *thḗrion* (diminutive) < *thḗr* beast. See etym. of doublet **theriaca**.]

**trea|cly** (trē′klē), *adj.* **1** sweet or sticky like treacle: *"Open your mouth," she said pouring out the treacly liquid* (Punch). **2** *Figurative.* excessively sweet or sentimental; sugared; honeyed: *Mrs. Snow has written a pleasant, better than usual, not too treacly life of the man* (Scientific American). —**trea′cli|ness**, *n.*

**tread** (tred), *v.,* **trod** or (*Archaic*) **trode, trod|den** or **trod, tread|ing,** *n.* —*v.i.* **1** to set the foot down; walk; step: *They trod through the meadow.* **2** to step heavily (on or upon); trample: *Don't tread on the flower beds.* **3** (of male birds) to copulate.
—*v.t.* **1** to put the foot or feet on; walk on or through; step on: *to tread the streets.* **2** to press under; trample on; crush: *to tread grapes to make wine. Tread out the fire before you go away.* **3** to make, form, or do by walking: *Cattle had trodden a path to the pond.* **4** *Figurative.* to follow; pursue: *to tread the path of virtue.* **5** *Figurative.* to treat with cruelty; oppress. **6** (of male birds) to copulate with (the hen).
—*n.* **1** the act or sound of treading: *We heard the tread of marching feet.* **2** a way of walking; step: *The fat lady walks with a heavy tread. Were it ever so airy a tread, My heart would hear her and beat* (Tennyson). **3a** the part of stairs or a ladder that a person steps on: *The stair treads were covered with rubber to prevent slipping.* See picture under **staircase**. **b** the width of a step from front to back, measured between risers. **4a** the part of a wheel or tire that touches the ground: *The treads of rubber tires are grooved to improve traction.* **b** the pattern left by the grooves or ridges in a tire: *The new tire left a deep tread in the snow.* **5** the part of a rail or rails that the wheels touch. **6** either of the endless belts of linked steel plates on which a caterpillar tractor, bulldozer, or tank moves. **7** the distance between opposite wheels of an automobile. **8** the sole of the foot or of a shoe. **9** the cicatricle or chalaza of an egg. **10** = footprint.
**treads,** injuries at the coronet of a horse's foot, caused by the shoe on the opposite foot or on the foot of the adjacent horse in a team: *A quittor ... arises often from treads* (J. Bartlet).
[Old English *tredan*] —**tread′er**, *n.*

**trea|dle** (tred′əl), *n., v.,* **-dled, -dling.** —*n.* **1** a lever or pedal worked up and down by the foot to operate a machine: *the treadle of a sewing machine.* **2** *British.* a pedal of a bicycle.
—*v.i.* to work a treadle. —*v.t.* to operate (a machine) by working a treadle.
[probably Old English *tredel* step, stair < *tredan* to tread]

***treadmill**
definition 1

***tread|mill** (tred′mil′), *n.* **1** an apparatus to turn something by having a person or animal walk on the moving steps of a wheel or of a sloping, endless belt. **2** *Figurative.* any wearisome or monotonous round of work or life: *a kind of mental treadmill, where you are perpetually climbing, but never rise an inch* (Scott).

**treads** (tredz), *n.pl.* See under **tread**.

**treas.,** **1** treasurer. **2** treasury.

**trea|son** (trē′zən), *n.* **1** the action of being false to one's country or ruler. Helping the enemies of one's country is treason. According to the United States Constitution, "Treason against the United States shall consist only in levying war against them or in adhering to their enemies, giving them aid and comfort" (Article 3, Section 3). An act against any individual does not constitute treason. **SYN**: See syn. under **disloyalty**. **2** the betrayal of a trust, duty, friend, or institution; treachery: *and in trust I have found treason* (Queen Elizabeth I of England). [< Anglo-French *treson* < Latin *trāditiō, -ōnis.* See etym. of doublet **tradition**.]

**trea|son|a|ble** (trē′zə nə bəl, trēz′nə-), *adj.* of treason; involving treason; traitorous. —**trea′son-a|ble|ness**, *n.*

**trea|son|a|bly** (trē′zə nə blē, trēz′nə-), *adv.* in a treasonable manner.

**trea|son|ous** (trē′zə nəs, trēz′nəs), *adj.* = treasonable. —**trea′son|ous|ly**, *adv.*

**treas|ure** (trezh′ər, trā′zhər), *n., v.,* **-ured, -ur-ing.** —*n.* **1** wealth or riches stored up; valuable things: *The pirates buried treasure along the coast. The palace contains treasures.* **2** *Figurative.* any thing or person that is much loved or valued: *The silver teapot was the old lady's chief treasure. The human heart has hidden treasures* (Charlotte Brontë).
—*v.t.* **1** to value highly; cherish; prize: *She treasures that doll more than all her other toys.* **2** *Figurative.* to put away for future use; store up: *The patient search and vigil long Of him who treasures up a wrong* (Byron). **SYN**: hoard.
[< Old French *tresor* < Latin *thēsaurus.* See etym. of doublet **thesaurus**.] —**treas′ur|a|ble**, *adj.*

**treasure house**, any place that contains something valuable: *The sea is a treasure house of minerals and food.*

**treasure hunt**, **1** a search for something of value. **2** a game, the winner being the one who first finds what has been hidden.

**treas|ur|er** (trezh′ər ər, trā′zhər-), *n.* a person in charge of money. The treasurer of a club, society, corporation, or government body pays its bills. *Abbr:* treas.

**treas|ur|er|ship** (trezh′ər ər ship, trā′zhər-), *n.* the position or term of office of a treasurer.

**Treasure State**, a nickname for Montana.

**treas|ure-trove** (trezh′ər trōv′, trā′zhər-), *n.* **1** money, jewels, or other treasure that a person finds, especially if the owner of it is not known. **2** (in English law) gold or silver, money, bullion, or other valuable objects found hidden in the ground or other place, the owner of it not known. **3** *Figurative.* any valuable discovery. [< Anglo-French *tresor trove* treasure found; *trove,* past participle of *trover* find]

**treas|ur|y** (trezh′ər ē, trā′zhər-), *n., pl.* **-ur|ies.** **1** a building, room, or other place where money or valuables are kept for security. **2** money owned; funds: *We voted to pay for the party out of the club treasury.* **3** Also, **Treasury.** the department of the government that has charge of the income and expenses of a country. The Treasury of the United States collects federal taxes, mints money, supervises national banks, enforces narcotics laws, and prevents counterfeiting. **4** a place where treasure is kept. **5** *Figurative.* a place where anything valuable is kept or found; book or person thought of as a valued source: *a treasury of modern poetry, a treasury of wisdom.*

**treasury bill**, an instrument of credit issued by a government when money is needed.

**treasury note**, a note or bill issued by the Treasury of the United States and receivable as legal tender for all debts.

**treasury of merits**, the more than abundant store of merits of Christ, the Virgin Mary, and the saints which, according to the Roman Catholic Church, forms the treasury from which the Church may grant indulgences.

**Treas|ur|ys** (trezh′ər ēz, trā′zhər-), *n.pl. U.S.* bonds or other securities issued by the treasury.

**treat** (trēt), *v., n.* —*v.t.* **1** to act or behave toward; deal with: *Father treats our new car with care. We must treat our elders with respect.* **2** to think of; consider; regard: *He treated his mistake as a joke.* **3** to deal with to relieve or cure: *The dentist is treating my toothache.* **4** to deal with to bring about some special result: *to treat a metal plate with acid in engraving.* **5** to deal with; discuss: *This magazine treats the progress of medicine.* **6** to express in literature or art; represent: *The author treats the characters of his story so that you feel you know them.* **7** to give food, drink, or amusement to: *He treated his friends to a soda, and they treated him to a movie.* **SYN**: regale, feast.
—*v.i.* **1** to pay the cost of a treat or entertainment: *I'll treat today.* **2** to deal with a subject. **3** to discuss terms; arrange terms: *Messengers came to treat for peace.* **SYN**: negotiate.
—*n.* **1** a gift of food, drink, or amusement: *"This is my treat," she said.* **2** anything that gives pleasure; pleasure; delight: *Being in the country is a treat to her. It was a treat to see the joy in her face.*
**treat of,** to deal with the subject of; discuss: *"The Medical Journal" treats of the progress of medicine.*
[Middle English *tretien* < Old French *traitier* < Latin *tractāre* (originally) drag violently, handle (frequentative) < *trahere* to drag] —**treat′er**, *n.*

**treat|a|ble** (trē′tə bəl), *adj.* that can be treated; suitable to be treated: *a treatable disease.*

**trea|tise** (trē′tis), *n.* **1** a book or other writing dealing with some subject. A treatise is more formal and systematic than most books or writings. *Never literary attempt was more unfortunate than my Treatise of Human Nature. It fell dead-born from the press* (David Hume). **2** *Archaic.* a story; tale; narrative; description. [Middle English *tretis* < Anglo-French *tretiz* < Old French *traitier;* see etym. under **treat**]

**treat|ment** (trēt′mənt), *n.* **1** the act or process of treating: *My cold won't respond to treatment.* **2** a way of treating: *This cat has suffered from bad treatment.* **3** a thing done or used to treat something else such as a disease. **4** a detailed outline of a proposed motion picture, television script, or the like.

**trea|ty** (trē′tē), *n., pl.* **-ties.** **1a** an agreement, especially one between nations, signed and approved by each nation: *The settlers broke many of the treaties the government made with the Indians.* **b** the document embodying such an agreement: *The peace treaty was signed in Paris.* **2** *Archaic.* **a** a negotiation: *The treaty was conducted very orderly* (Benjamin Franklin). **b** any agreement; covenant; compact. **c** entreaty; persuasion; request. [< Old French *traite,* or *traitie* < Latin *tractātus* discussion < *tractāre;* see etym. under **treat**]

**treaty Indian**, *U.S. and Canada.* a member of a tribe or group of Indians who live on reserves and receive treaty money and other rights.

**treaty money**, *U.S. and Canada.* an annual payment made by the government to treaty Indians.

**treaty port**, any one of various ports in China, Japan, and Korea, formerly required by treaty to be kept open to foreign commerce.

**tre|ble** (treb′əl), *adj., v.,* **-bled, -bling,** *n.* —*adj.* **1** three times as much or as many; triple: *His salary is treble mine.* **2** *Music.* of, having to do with, or for the treble; soprano: *a treble voice.* **3** high-pitched; shrill: *treble tones.*
—*v.t., v.i.* **1** to make or become three times as much or as many; triple: *He trebled his money by buying a dog for $5 and selling it for $15.* **2** *Obsolete.* to sing the treble part.
—*n.* **1** *Music.* **a** the highest part in harmonized composition; soprano. **b** a voice, singer, or instrument that takes this part. **c** the highest-pitched and smallest bell of a peal in change ringing. **2** a shrill, high-pitched voice, sound, or note.
[< Old French *treble* < Latin *triplus.* See etym. of doublet **triple**.]

***treble clef**, a symbol in music indicating that the pitch of the notes on a staff is above middle C; G clef.

***treble clef**

**treble staff**, a staff in music with the treble clef.

**tre|bly** (treb′lē), *adv.* three times; triply.

**treb|u|chet** (treb′yu̇ shet), *n.* a machine of war used in the Middle Ages for hurling stones or other objects, somewhat like a catapult. [< Old French *trebuchet* < *trebuchier* to stumble, fall < *tres* over (< Latin *trāns*) + *buc* trunk of the body < Germanic (compare Frankish *būk* belly, Old High German *būh*)]

**tre|cen|tist** (trā chen′tist), *n.* **1** an admirer of Ital-

**Pronunciation Key:** hat, āge, cãre, fär; let, ēqual, tėrm; it, īce; hot, ōpen, ôrder; oil, out; cup, pu̇t, rüle; child; long; thin; ᴛʜen; zh, measure; ə represents a in about, e in taken, i in pencil, o in lemon, u in circus.

ian art and literature of the trecento. **2** a follower of the style of the trecento.

**tre|cen|to** (trā chen′tō), *n.* the 1300's, with reference to Italy, and especially to the Italian art and literature of that period.
[< Italian *trecento,* short for *mille trecento* one thousand three hundred]

**tre|de|cil|lion** (trē′di sil′yən), *n.* **1** (in the U.S., Canada, and France) 1 followed by 42 zeros. **2** (in Great Britain and Germany) 1 followed by 78 zeros. [< Latin *tredecim* thirteen (< *tres* three + *decem* ten) + English *-illion,* as in *million*]

**tree** (trē), *n., v.,* **treed, tree|ing.** —*n.* **1** a large plant with a woody trunk, often having branches and leaves at some distance from the ground and living for more than two years, usually for many years. **2** any plant that resembles a tree in form or size, such as the banana and plantain. **3** a piece or structure of wood for some special purpose, such as a shoe tree or clothes tree, a beam, or the wooden handle of a tool. **4** anything like a tree with its branches. A family tree is a diagram with branches, showing how the members of a family are descended and related. **5** a treelike mass of crystals forming from a solution. **6** *Archaic.* a gallows. **7** *Archaic.* the cross on which Christ was crucified. **8** *Scottish.* a staff; cudgel.
—*v.t.* **1** to chase up a tree; force to take refuge in a tree: *The cat was treed by a dog. The hiker was treed by a bull.* **2** to furnish with a tree (such as a beam, bar, wooden handle): *to tree the roof of a coal mine, to tree a spade or a pick.* **3** to stretch or shape (a shoe or boot) on a tree. **4** *Informal, Figurative.* to put into a difficult position.
—*v.i.* **1** to take refuge in a tree. **2** to assume a treelike or branching form.
**bark up the wrong tree**, to pursue the wrong object or use the wrong means to attain it: *If you think to run a rig on me, you have made a mistake ... and barked up the wrong tree* (Thomas C. Haliburton)
**up a tree**, *Informal.* in a difficult position: *He was deploring the dreadful predicament in which he found himself, a house full of old women ... "Reg'larly up a tree, by jingo!" proclaimed the modest boy, who could not face the gentlest of her sex* (Thackeray).
[Old English *trēo*] —**tree′less**, *adj.* —**tree′like′**, *adj.*

**tree asp**, any one of a group of poisonous African snakes, such as the mamba.

**tree belt** = shelter belt.

**tree celandine**, = plume poppy.

**tree climber** = mudskipper.

**tree crab**, = coconut crab.

**tree creeper**, any one of various small birds that creep up and down the branches of trees and bushes looking for food, as the brown creeper.

**tree cricket**, a kind of noisy cricket that is pale green to black in color and lays its eggs in rows on twigs and plant stems.

**treed** (trēd), *adj.* planted or covered with trees; wooded: *treed slopes.*

**tree diagram**, *Linguistics.* a diagram of a sentence or phrase in which the components are shown as subdividing branches of the main structure.

**tree duck**, a duck of the southern United States and tropical America that nests in trees, usually far from water. It flies and feeds mainly at night.

**tree farm**, *Especially U.S.* a place where trees are grown as a business.

**tree fern**, a fern of tropical and subtropical regions that grows to the size of a tree, with a woody, trunklike stem and fronds at the top.

**tree frog**, any one of various small, tree-dwelling frogs with sticky disks or suckers on their toes that enable them to climb trees, such as the spring peeper; tree toad; hyla.

**tree|hop|per** (trē′hop′ər), *n.,* or **tree hopper**, any one of a group of insects that live in trees and have mouth parts adapted to sucking. Some treehoppers are very small and oddly shaped, and can leap long distances.

**tree house**, a platform, with or without sides and roof, built in a tree, now usually a playhouse.

**tree line**, = timber line.

**tree|lined** (trē′līnd′), *adj.* with trees lining the side or sides: *a treelined village street.*

**tre|en** (trē′ən, trēn), *n., pl.* **-en**, *adj.* —*n.* woodenware, especially bowls, dishes, or the like; treenware.
—*adj.* wooden: *a treen paten of ancient date* (Athenaeum).
[Old English *trēowen* made of wood < *trēo* tree]

**tree|nail** (tren′əl, trun′-; trē′nāl′), *n.* a round pin of hard, dry wood for fastening timbers together. Also, **trenail, trunnel.** [Middle English *trenayl* < *tree* wood + *nail* nail]

**tree of heaven**, = ailanthus.

**tree of knowledge**, the tree in Eden whose fruit, though forbidden, was eaten by Adam and Eve through the tempting of the serpent; knowledge of good and evil (in the Bible, Genesis 2:9, 16-17; 3:1-7).

**tree of life**, **1** a tree in the center of Eden whose fruit gave immortality (in the Bible, Genesis 2:9; 3:22). **2** a tree in the heavenly Jerusalem, the leaves of which were for the healing of the nations (in the Bible, Revelation 22:2). **3** = arbor vitae.

**tree otter** = tayra.

**tree peony**, a variety of slow-growing peony, originally from western China, having showy white or rose-colored flowers which grow on woody stems from three to four feet high; mountain peony.

**Tree Planters' State**, a nickname for Nebraska.

**tree ring**, = annual ring.

**tree-rip|ened** (trē′rī′pənd), *adj.* allowed to ripen on the tree: *tree-ripened oranges.*

**tree shrew**, any one of a group of squirrellike, insect-eating mammals that live in trees, found in India, Borneo, and other areas of southeastern Asia.

**tree sparrow**, **1** a sparrow with reddish-brown crown and a dark spot on the breast, that nests in northern North America and winters in the United States. **2** a European sparrow related to the English sparrow.

**tree squirrel**, = squirrel (def. 1).

**tree surgeon**, an expert in tree surgery.

**tree surgery**, the care and treatment of trees, especially of diseased or damaged trees by filling cavities, cutting away parts, and feeding.

**tree swallow**, a North American swallow with a bluish or bluish-green back and a white breast, that nests in a hole in a tree or in a birdhouse.

**tree toad**, = tree frog.

**tree|top** (trē′top′), *n.* the top or uppermost part of a tree.

**tref** (trāf), *adj.* forbidden by Jewish law; not kosher: *Pork and clams are tref foods.* [< Yiddish *treyf* < Hebrew *ṭrēphāh* (literally) that which is torn (see Leviticus 17:15) < *ṭāraf* to tear]

***tre|foil** (trē′foil), *n.* **1** a plant having threefold leaves. Trefoils belong to the pea family. The clover, black medic, and tick trefoil are trefoils. **2** an ornament like a threefold leaf. [< Anglo-French *trifoil* < Latin *trifolium* three-leaved plant < *tri-* three + *folium* leaf. See etym. of doublet **trifolium.**]

***trefoil**
definitions 1, 2

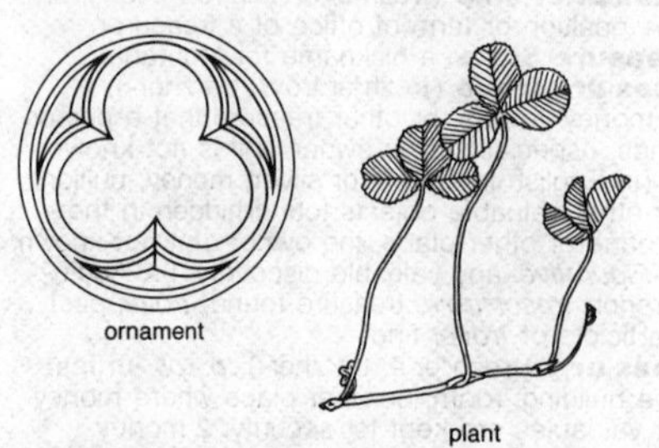


**tre|foiled** (trē′foild), *adj.* of or having ornaments shaped like threefold leaves.

**tre|ha|lose** (trē′hə lōs), *n.* a white crystalline sugar obtained from trehala, various fungi, and yeast. *Formula:* $C_{12}H_{22}O_{11}$

**treil|lage** (trā′lij), *n.* a lattice or trellis to support vines and other climbing plants. [< earlier French *treillage* < *treille* trellised arbor; latticework < Latin *tricla,* earlier *trichila* arbor, summerhouse, short for *triclīnium*]

**trek** (trek), *v.,* **trekked, trek|king,** *n.* —*v.i.* **1** to travel slowly; travel; migrate: *The pioneers trekked across the great western plains by covered wagon.* **2** *Informal, Figurative.* to go; proceed: *to trek down to the office.* **3** (in South Africa) to travel by ox wagon.
—*v.t.* (in South Africa) to draw (a vehicle or load), as an ox does.
—*n.* **1** the action of trekking; journey: *It was a long trek over the mountains.* **2** a stage of a journey between one stopping place and the next. **3** (in South Africa) the act or fact of traveling in a group, as pioneers into undeveloped country.
[< Afrikaans *trek,* verb < Dutch *trekken* to march, journey; (originally) to draw, pull]

**trek|ker** (trek′ər), *n.* a person who treks.

**trel|lis** (trel′is), *n., v.* —*n.* **1** a frame of light strips of wood or metal crossing one another with open spaces in between; lattice, especially one supporting growing vines. **2** a summerhouse or other structure with sides of lattice, used as a shady retreat in summer.
—*v.t.* **1** to furnish with a trellis; enclose with lattice: *to trellis a porch.* **2** to support or train (vines) on a trellis. **3** *Figurative.* to cross or interweave as in a trellis.
[< Old French *trelis* < Vulgar Latin *trilīcius* < Latin *trilīx, -icis* triple-twilled < *tri-* three + *līcium* thread]

**trel|lis|work** (trel′is wėrk′), *n.* work made of crossed or interwoven strips with open spaces in between; trellis or trellises; latticework.

**trem|a|tode** (trem′ə tōd, trē′mə-), *n., adj.* —*n.* any one of various flatworms that live as parasites in or on other animals, such as a variety which infests the lungs of sheep and a variety that lives in the blood vessels of man, causing schistosomiasis; fluke. Trematodes have suckers and sometimes hooks.
—*adj.* of or belonging to the trematodes.
[< New Latin *Trematoda* the class name < Greek *trēmatṓdēs* with holes; having a vent to the intestinal canal < *trêma, -atos* hole + *eîdos* form]

**trem|blant** (trem′blənt), *adj.* set on springs to make a trembling or vibrating motion: *a diamond tremblant brooch.*

**trem|ble** (trem′bəl), *v.,* **-bled, -bling,** *n.* —*v.i.* **1** to shake because of fear, excitement, weakness, cold, or other emotion or condition: *The old woman's hands trembled. Her voice trembled with emotion.* SYN: shiver, quake, shudder, quiver, vibrate. See syn. under **shake.** **2** *Figurative.* to feel fear, anxiety, or other emotion: *Don't go out in that storm—I tremble for your safety.* **3** to move gently: *The leaves trembled in the breeze.*
—*v.t.* **1** to cause to tremble or shake: *joined by an old man who pumped his knees and trembled his hands* (New Yorker). **2** to utter tremulously or falteringly: *and trembling out prayers, and waiting to die* (Adah Menken).
—*n.* the action of trembling: *There was a tremble in her voice as she began to recite.*
**trembles, a** *U.S.* a disease of cattle and sheep in the western and central United States, caused by a poison in white snakeroot and rayless goldenrod, and characterized by weakness and trembling. **b** *U.S.* this disease transmitted to man especially in milk, cream, and butter; milk sickness. **c** any disease or condition characterized by an involuntary shaking, such as louping ill.
[< Old French *trembler* < Medieval Latin *tremulare* < Latin *tremulus;* see etym. under **tremulous**]

**trem|bler** (trem′blər), *n.* **1** a person or thing that trembles. **2** an automatic vibrating device which alternately makes and breaks an electric circuit.

**trem|bles** (trem′bəlz), *n.pl.* See under **tremble.**

**trem|bly** (trem′blē), *adj.* trembling; tremulous.

**trem|el|lose** (trem′ə lōs), *adj. Botany.* shaking like jelly; of a jellylike consistency, as certain fungi. [< New Latin *Tremella* the genus name (diminutive) < Latin *tremula,* feminine of *tremulus* + English *-ose*[1]; see etym. under **tremulous**]

**tre|men|dous** (tri men′dəs), *adj.* **1** dreadful; very severe; awful: *The army suffered a tremendous defeat.* SYN: frightful, horrible. **2** *Informal.* very great; enormous; immense: *a tremendous sum, a wrestler of tremendous strength. That is a tremendous house for a family of three.* **3** *Informal.* excellent; memorable; wonderful; extraordinary: *to have a tremendous time at a party.* [< Latin *tremendus* (with English *-ous*) to be trembled at, gerundive of *tremere* to tremble] —**tre|men′dous|ly**, *adv.* —**tre|men′dous|ness**, *n.*

**trem|o|lan|do** (trem′ə län′dō), *adj., adv., n., pl.* **-dos, -di** (dē). *Music.* —*adj., adv.* with a tremolo (a direction to perform a tremolo).
—*n.* a note or passage rendered with a tremolo.
[< Italian *tremolando,* present participle of *tremolare* tremble; warble < Medieval Latin *tremulare* < Latin *tremulus* tremulous]

**trem|o|lant** (trem′ə lənt), *adj., n.* —*adj.* having a tremulous or quavering sound, as certain organ pipes. —*n.* **1** an organ pipe having a tremolant sound. **2** = tremolo.
[< Italian *tremolante* < *tremolare;* see etym. under **tremolando**]

**trem|o|lite** (trem′ə līt), *n.* a white or gray mineral, a variety of amphibole, consisting chiefly of a silicate of calcium and magnesium, occurring in fibrous masses or thin-bladed crystals. *Formula:* $Ca_2Mg_5Si_8O_{22}(OH)_2$ [< *Tremola,* valley in the Swiss Alps]

***tremolo**
definition 1

***trem|o|lo** (trem′ə lō), *n., pl.* **-los**, *adj. Music.* —*n.* **1** a trembling or vibrating quality in musical tones. A tremolo in the voice is produced by a rapid alternation of tones. A bowed tremolo is produced on a violin, cello, viola, or bass by rapidly repeating a tone with fast up-and-down strokes of the bow. A fingered tremolo on a stringed instrument

is an effect very much like a trill or stroke. **2** a device in an organ to produce this quality.
—***adj.*** of or like a tremolo.
[< Italian *tremolo* < Latin *tremulus.* See etym. of doublet **tremulous.**]

**trem|or** (trem′ər), *n.* **1** an involuntary shaking or trembling: *a nervous tremor in the voice.* **SYN**: quaking, quivering. **2** *Figurative.* **a** a thrill of emotion or excitement. **b** a state of emotion or excitement: *He went about all day in a tremor of delight* (Dickens). **3** a shaking or vibrating movement. An earthquake is sometimes called an earth tremor. [< Latin *tremor* a trembling < *tremere* to tremble]

**trem|u|lant** or **trem|u|lent** (trem′yə lənt), *adj.* tremulous; trembling. [< Medieval Latin *tremulans, -antis,* present participle of *tremulare* < Latin *tremulus* tremulous]

**trem|u|lous** (trem′yə ləs), *adj.* **1** trembling; quivering; quavering: *the tremulous flutter of young leaves. The child's voice was tremulous with sobs.* **SYN**: shaking, vibrating. **2** timid; feeling or showing fear: *tremulous beliefs* (Lionel Johnson). *He was shy and tremulous in the presence of strangers.* **3** that wavers; shaky: *tremulous writing.* [< Latin *tremulus* (with English *-ous*) < *tremere* to tremble. See etym. of doublet **tremolo.**] —**trem′u|lous|ly,** *adv.* —**trem′u|lous-ness,** *n.*

**tre|nail** (tren′əl, trun′-; trē′nāl′), *n.* = treenail.

**trench** (trench), *n., v.* —***n.*** **1** a long, narrow ditch with earth, sandbags, logs, or other shield put up in front to protect soldiers against enemy fire and attack. **2** a deep furrow; ditch: *to dig a trench around a tent to drain off water.* **3** a long, narrow depression in the ocean floor: *the Acapulco trench off the Pacific coast of Central America.* **4** *Figurative.* a cut, scar, or deep wrinkle: *Witness these trenches made by grief and care* (Shakespeare). [< Old French *trenche* < *trenchier;* see the verb]
—***v.t.*** **1** to dig a trench or trenches in (the ground): *to trench the ground around a fort or camp.* **2** to surround with a trench; fortify with trenches: *The place which they had trenched, ditched, and fortified with ordnance* (Edward Hall). **3a** to cut up; slice. **b** to cut off. **c** to cut into. **d** to cut (one's way).
—***v.i.*** to dig ditches or trenches: (*Figurative.*) *Madam, I am bold to trench so far upon your privacy* (Philip Massinger).
**trenches,** a system of ditches built as a military defense line: *After World War I, the canard spread that France had even collected rent for the use of trenches on its soil* (Time).
**trench on** (or **upon**), **a** to trespass upon: *Though I squandered my own property, I have not trenched on yours* (Mrs. H. Wood). *This scheme ... may seem to trench on the liberty of individuals* (J. Robertson). **b** *Figurative.* to come close to; border on: *a remark that trenched closely on slander.*
**trench to** (or **unto**), *Obsolete.* to extend in effect to: *In law it is said the demise of the King, and a gift unto the King, without saying more, trenches to his successors* (Sir H. Finch).
[< Old French *trenchier* to cut, apparently ultimately < Latin *truncāre* lop off < *truncus* mutilated]

**trench|an|cy** (tren′chən sē), *n.* trenchant quality; sharpness: *With the same trenchancy of contract* (Robert Louis Stevenson).

**trench|ant** (tren′chənt), *adj.* **1** sharp; keen; cutting: *trenchant wit, a trenchant remark.* **2** vigorous and effective: *a trenchant policy.* **3** clear-cut; distinct: *in trenchant outline against the sky.* **4** *Archaic.* having a keen edge; sharp: *the trenchant blade* (Samuel Butler). [< Old French *trenchant,* present participle of *trenchier* to cut; see etym. under **trench,** verb] —**trench′ant|ly,** *adv.*

***trench coat,** a kind of belted raincoat with straps on the shoulders and cuffs. It is usually made of cotton gabardine or poplin.

***trench coat**

**trench|er**[1] (tren′chər), *n., adj.* —***n.*** **1a** a wooden platter on which meat or other food was formerly served and carved. **b** such a platter with the food on it. **2** *Obsolete.* a slice of bread used instead of a plate or platter. **3** *Obsolete.* a knife.
—***adj.*** of or having to do with a trencher.
[< Anglo-French *trenchour,* Old North French *trencheor* knife < Vulgar Latin *truncatōrium* place for cutting, slicing < Latin *truncāre* lop off; see etym. under **trench,** verb]

**trench|er**[2] (tren′chər), *n.* **1** a person who digs trenches. **2** *Obsolete.* a person who carves.

**trencher cap,** = mortarboard (def. 2). [< *trencher*[1] flat piece + *cap*]

**trench|er|man** (tren′chər mən), *n., pl.* **-men. 1** a person who has a hearty appetite; eater. **2** a hanger-on; parasite.

**trench|es** (tren′chiz), *n.pl.* See under **trench.**

**trench fever,** an infectious fever caused by a rickettsia and transmitted by lice. It affected many soldiers in the trenches during World War I.

**trench foot** or **feet,** a foot disease like frostbite, caused by prolonged exposure to cold and wet, chiefly affecting soldiers.

**trench frostbite,** = trench foot.

**trench knife,** a knife with a long, double-edged blade, for use in close combat.

**trench mortar,** a small mortar firing shells at high angles over short ranges.

**trench mouth, 1** a contagious, painful bacterial infection of the mouth, characterized by sores and ulcers on the lining of the gums, cheeks, and tongue, and often extending to the throat; Vincent's angina; Vincent's infection. **2** any inflammation of the mouth and gums.

**trench silo,** a silo made by digging a shallow, narrow ditch in the ground, filling it with silage, and then covering it with a sheet of heavy plastic.

**trench warfare,** hostilities carried on by means of or in trenches.

**trend** (trend), *n., v.* —***n.*** **1** the general direction; course: *The hills have a western trend.* **SYN**: See syn. under **direction. 2** the general course or drift; tendency: *a trend toward smaller cars. The trend of modern living is away from many old customs.* **SYN**: See syn. under **direction. 3** *Figurative.* fashion; style; vogue: *the latest trend in clothes, to set or spot a new trend.* [< verb]
—***v.i.*** **1** to have a general tendency; tend: *events that trend toward a reconciliation. Modern life trends toward less formal customs.* **2** to turn off or bend in a certain direction; run: *a road trending to the north.*
[Middle English *trenden* roll about, turn, Old English *trendan*]

**trend line,** a line on a graph representing a trend: *Despite some selective strengthening of prices in the chemical industry, the overall downward trend line will continue in 1965* (Wall Street Journal).

**trend|set|ter** (trend′set′ər), *n.* a person, or thing that establishes a new style or vogue.

**trend|set|ting** (trend′set′ing), *adj.* capable of setting a trend or fashion: *trendsetting ideas.*

**trend|y** (tren′dē), *adj., n., pl.* **trend|ies.** *British Informal.* —***adj.*** fashionable; stylish: *trendy ideas, a trendy design.*
—***n.*** a person who keeps up with the latest trends and fashions. —**trend′i|ly,** *adv.* —**trend′i-ness,** *n.*

**tren|tal** (tren′təl), *n.* a service of thirty Requiems said either on the same day or on different days. [< Old French *trental* < Medieval Latin *trentale,* ultimately < Latin *trīgintā* thirty]

**trente et qua|rante** (träɴ′ tā kȧ räɴt′), = rouge et noir. [< French *trente et quarante* (literally) thirty and forty (the winning and losing numbers)]

**tre|pan**[1] (tri pan′), *n., v.,* **-panned, -pan|ning.** —***n.*** **1** an early form of the trephine. **2** a boring instrument, used for sinking shafts.
—***v.t.*** **1** = trephine. **2** to bore through with a trepan; cut a disk out of with a trepan or similar tool.
[< Medieval Latin *trepanum* < Greek *trȳpanon* < *trȳpē* hole < *trȳpân* to bore]

**tre|pan**[2] (tri pan′), *n., v.,* **-panned, -pan|ning.** *Archaic.* —***n.*** **1** a person who entraps or decoys others to his advantage and their ruin or loss. **2** a trick; trap; snare.
—***v.t.*** **1** to entrap; ensnare. **2** to do out of; cheat; swindle. Also, **trapan.**
[earlier *trapan* < *trap*[1]; spelling influenced by *trepan*[1]]

**trep|a|na|tion** (trep′ə nā′shən), *n.* the operation of trepanning; trephination.

**tre|pang** (tri pang′), *n.* **1** the dried flesh of any one of several species of sea cucumbers, used in China and the East Indies for making soup; bêche-de-mer. **2** any one of these animals. [< Malay *tĕripang*]

**tre|pan|ner**[1] (tri pan′ər), *n.* a person who works with a trepan.

**tre|pan|ner**[2] (tri pan′ər), *n. Archaic.* a person who trepans; decoy; swindler.

**treph|i|na|tion** (tref′ə nā′shən), *n.* the operation of trephining.

**tre|phine** (tri fīn′, -fēn′), *n., v.,* **-phined, -phin-ing.** —***n.*** a cylindrical saw with a removable center pin, used to cut out circular pieces from the skull. —***v.t.*** to operate on with a trephine.
[earlier *trafine,* alteration of *trapan,* variant of *trepan*[1]; spelling influenced by Latin *trēs fīnēs* three ends]

**trep|id** (trep′id), *adj.* scared; perturbed; agitated. [< Latin *trepidus*]

**trep|i|dant** (trep′ə dənt), *adj.* trembling; agitated.

**trep|i|da|tion** (trep′ə dā′shən), *n.* **1** nervous dread; fear; fright. **2** the action or condition of trembling, especially of the limbs, as in palsy. **3** a vibrating movement; vibration. [< Latin *trepidātiō, -ōnis* < *trepidāre* to tremble, be afraid < *trepidus* alarmed, trepid]

**trep|o|ne|ma** (trep′ə nē′mə), *n., pl.* **-mas, -ma|ta** (-mə tə). any one of a genus of spirochetes parasitic in man and other warm-blooded animals including the bacteria that cause syphilis, relapsing fever, and yaws. [< New Latin *Treponema* the genus name < Greek *trépein* to turn + *nêma* thread, yarn < *neîn* to spin thread]

**trep|o|ne|mal** (trep′ə nē′məl), *adj.* of or having to do with treponemas.

**trep|o|ne|ma|to|sis** (trep′ə nē′mə tō′sis), *n., pl.* **-ses** (-sēz). a disease caused by a treponema. [< New Latin *treponematosis* < *Treponema* treponema + *-osis* -osis]

**trep|o|ne|ma|tous** (trep′ə nē′mə təs, -nem′ə-), *adj.* = treponemal.

**trep|o|neme** (trep′ə nēm), *n.* = treponema.

**tres|pass** (tres′pəs, -pas), *v., n.* —***v.i.*** **1a** to go on somebody's property without any right: *The farmer put up "No Trespassing" signs to keep hunters off his farm.* **SYN**: encroach, infringe, invade. See syn. under **intrude. b** *Law.* to commit any trespass. **2** *Figurative.* to go beyond the limits of what is right, proper, or polite: *I won't trespass on your kind hospitality any longer.* **SYN**: encroach, infringe, invade. See syn. under **intrude. 3** to do wrong; sin: ... *as we forgive those who trespass against us* (Lord's Prayer).
—***n.*** **1** the act or fact of trespassing: *Since the farmer had permitted them to fish in his pond the boys were not guilty of trespass.* **SYN**: encroachment, infringement. **2** a wrong; sin: *Forgive us our trespasses* (Lord's Prayer). **SYN**: transgression, offense. **3a** an unlawful act done by force against the person, property, or rights of another. **b** a legal action to recover damages for such an injury.
[< Old French *trespasser* to trespass < *tres-* across (< Latin *trāns-*) + *passer* to pass (< *pas* a step < Latin *passus, -ūs*). Compare etym. under **pace**[1].] —**tres′pass|er,** *n.*

**tres|pass|o|ry** (tres′pə sôr′ē, -sōr′-), *adj. Law.* having to do with or of the nature of a trespass: *trespassory intrusion.*

**tress** (tres), *n.* a lock, curl, or braid of hair, especially of a woman or girl.
**tresses, a** locks of long, flowing hair of a woman or girl: *A hat covered her golden tresses.* **b** long shoots or tendrils, rays of the sun, etc.: *luxuriant tresses of maidenhair fern* (Henry B. Tristram).
[< Old French *tresce,* and *trece* < Medieval Latin *trecia;* origin uncertain]

**tressed** (trest), *adj.* (of the hair) arranged in tresses; braided.

**tres|sel** or **tres|sle** (tres′əl), *n.* = trestle.

**tress|es** (tres′iz), *n.pl.* See under **tress.**

**tres|sure** (tresh′ər), *n. Heraldry.* a diminutive of the orle, consisting of a narrow band one fourth the width of the bordure, usually decorated with fleurs-de-lis. [< Old French *tressure* and *tresseor* hair band; braid < *tresser* to plait < *tresce* a plait; see etym. under **tress**]

**tres-tine** (tres′tīn′), *n.* the third tine from the base of an antler; royal antler. [< Latin *trēs* three + English *tine*]

**tres|tle** (tres′əl), *n.* **1** a framework similar to a sawhorse, used as a support especially for a tabletop or platform. **2a** a braced framework of timber, iron, or steel, used as a bridge to support railroad tracks or a road across a gap. It is usually made of uprights or slanting pieces with diagonal braces. **b** a bridge or the like having such a framework. [< Old French *trestel* crossbeam < Vulgar Latin *transtellum* < Latin *trānstrum* beam; see etym. under **transom**]

**trestle table,** a table made of boards laid upon trestles.

**tres|tle|tree** (tres′əl trē′), *n.* either of two horizontal, fore-and-aft timbers or bars secured to a masthead, one on each side, to support the crosstrees.

---

**Pronunciation Key:** hat, āge, cãre, fär; let, ēqual, tėrm; it, īce; hot, ōpen, ôrder; oil, out; cup, pu̇t, rüle; child; long; thin; ᴛʜen; zh, measure; ə represents **a** in about, **e** in taken, **i** in pencil, **o** in lemon, **u** in circus.

**tres|tle|work** (tres′əl wėrk′), *n.* **1** any structure or construction consisting of a trestle or trestles. **2** a support, bridge, or the like, made of such structures.

**tret** (tret), *n.* an allowance formerly made to purchasers on goods sold by weight, after deduction for tare. [< Anglo-French *tret,* Old French *trait* a pull of the scale < *traire* to pull, draw < Latin *trahere.* See etym. of doublets **trace**[2], **tract**[1], **trait.**]

**tre|val|ly** (trə väl′ē), *n., pl.* **-lies** or (*collectively*) **-ly.** a food fish of the carangoid family found in the waters around Australia. [origin uncertain]

**trews** (trüz), *n.pl. Scottish.* close-fitting trousers, or breeches combined with stockings, formerly worn by Irishmen and Scottish Highlanders, and still worn by certain Scottish regiments. [variant of earlier *trouse;* see etym. under **trousers**]

**trey** (trā), *n.* a card, die, domino, or throw of dice showing three spots; a three. [< Old French *trei* < Latin *trēs* three. See related etym. at **three.**]

**trey|fah** (trā′fə), *adj.* forbidden by Jewish law; not kosher; tref: *Orthodox Jews do not eat treyfah foods.* [< Yiddish *treyfe* < Hebrew *trēphāh;* see etym. under **tref**]

**t.r.f.**, tuned radio frequency.

**T.R.H.**, Their Royal Highnesses.

**tri-**, *combining form.* **1** having three ___: *Triangle* = (*a plane figure*) *having three angles. Trilogy* = *a group of three novels, plays, etc.*
**2** three ___s: *Trisect* = *to divide into three parts.*
**3** once every three ___; lasting for three ___: *Trimonthly* = *occurring once every three months.*
**4** containing three atoms, radicals, or other constituents of the substance specified, as in *trioxide, trisulfate.*
[< Latin, Greek *tri-;* < Latin *trēs, tria* or Greek *treîs, tría* three, or *trís* thrice]

**tri** (trī), *n. Informal.* a trimaran.

**tri|a|ble** (trī′ə bəl), *adj.* **1** that can be tested or proved. **2** *Law.* that can be tried in a court of law. [< Anglo-French *triable* < *trier* to try (legally), Old French, to cull; origin unknown] —**tri′a-ble|ness**, *n.*

**tri|ac|e|tate** (trī as′ə tāt), *adj., n.* —*adj.* having three acetate radicals in the molecule.
—*n.* **1** a triacetate compound. *Formula:* ($CH_3$-$COO$-$)_3$ **2** something made from it, especially a fiber or film made from a triacetate cellulose acetate.

**tri|ac|e|tin** (trī as′ə tin), *n.* an oily liquid found in cod-liver oil, butter, and other fats, or derived by the action of acetic acid on glycerol, used in treating athlete's foot and other fungous diseases, in making celluloid, as a fixative for perfumes, and as a solvent of basic dyes. *Formula:* $C_9H_{14}O_6$ [< *triacet*(ate) + *-in*]

**tri|ac|id** (trī as′id), *adj., n.* —*adj.* **1** (of a base or alcohol) having three hydroxyl (-OH) groups which may replace the hydrogen of an acid to form a salt or ester. **2** having three replaceable acid atoms of hydrogen per molecule.
—*n.* an acid of which one molecule contains three hydrogen atoms which may be replaced by basic atoms or groups.

*** tri|ad** (trī′ad, -əd), *n.* **1** a group or set of three, especially of three closely related persons or things. **SYN:** trio, trinity. **2** *Music.* a chord of three tones, especially one consisting of a given note (called the root) with its major or minor third and its perfect, augmented, or diminished fifth.
**3** *Chemistry.* an element, atom, or radical with a valence of three. [< Late Latin *trias, -adis* < Greek *triás, -ados* < *treîs* three]

*** triad**
definition 2

**tri|ad|ic** (trī ad′ik), *adj.* **1** of or having to do with a triad. **2** constituting a triad. **3** consisting of triads. **4** *Chemistry.* that is a triad; trivalent.

**tri|age** (trē äzh′; *especially for 1 and 2 also* trī′ij), *n.* **1** the act of sorting, as according to kind or quality. **2** something sorted out, as the broken coffee beans separated from the whole coffee in sorting. **3** the act or fact of assigning priorities according to urgency or expediency, especially in military and political planning and in the choice of giving medical treatment to casualties most likely to survive when only limited help is available: *In the West, there is increasing talk of triage, a commonsense if callous concept that teaches that when resources are scarce they must be used where they will do the most good* (Time).
[< Old French *triage* < *trier* to pick, cull]

**tri|ag|o|nal** (trī ag′ə nəl), *adj.* = triangular. [alteration of *trigonal;* patterned on *tetragonal*]

**tri|a junc|ta in u|no** (trī′ə jungk′tə in yü′nō), *Latin.* three joined in one (the motto of the Order of the Bath).

**tri|a|kai|dek|a|phobe** (trī′ə kī dek′ə fōb), *n.* a person having an abnormal fear of the number 13: *Attention, all triakaidekaphobes! Next Friday is, b-r-r-r, the 13th* (Family Weekly). Also, **triskaidekaphobe.**

**tri|a|kai|dek|a|pho|bi|a** (trī′ə kī dek′ə fō′bē ə), *n.* an abnormal fear of the number 13. [< Greek *triakaídeka,* neuter of *treiskaídeka* thirteen (< *treîs* three + *kaí* and + *déka* ten) + English *-phobia*] Also, **triskaidekaphobia.**

**tri|al** (trī′əl), *n., adj.* —*n.* **1** the act or fact of examining and deciding a civil or criminal case by a law court: *Many thieves are caught and brought to trial.* **2** the act or process of trying or testing; trying out; test: *to learn by trial and error. He gave the machine another trial to see if it would work. Democracy is on trial in the world on a more colossal scale than ever before* (Charles F. Dole). **3** the condition of being tried or tested; probation: *He is employed for two weeks on trial.* **4** trouble; hardship; affliction: *Her life has been full of trials—sickness, poverty, and loss of loved ones.* **SYN:** misfortune. **5** a cause of trouble or hardship: *to be a trial to one's parents.* **6** an attempt to do something; effort; endeavor: *I proposed to make a trial for landing if the weather should suit* (John Smeaton). **7** a preliminary competition in field or track events at a track meet.
—*adj.* **1** made, done, used, or taken as a try or test: *a trial model, a trial trip.* **2** that is on trial: *a trial employee.* **3** of or having to do with a trial in a law court: *trial testimony.*
[< Anglo-French *trial* < *trier* to try]
—***Syn.*** *n.* **2 Trial, test, experiment** mean the process of proving the quality or worth of something. **Trial** suggests the purpose of trying out a thing to find out how it works: *Give the car a trial.* **Test** applies to a thorough trial in which the thing tried is measured against a standard or standards: *The new model has been subjected to vigorous tests.* **Experiment** applies to a carefully controlled trial to find out something still unknown or to test conclusions reached: *Experiments indicate the new drug will cure infections.*

**trial and error**, **1** a method of learning by trying out different responses to a new situation until one response is successful. **2** a method of arriving at a desired result by repeated experiments until past errors are eliminated. —**tri′al-and-er′-ror**, *adj.*

**trial balance**, a comparison of the items on each side of a double-entry ledger, in which the sum of the debits should equal the sum of the credits. If they are not equal, there is an error.

**trial balloon**, **1** a small balloon launched to determine atmospheric conditions, especially direction and velocity of wind. **2** *Figurative.* a plan or project launched on a small scale to determine its acceptability to the general public or some particular group, body, or interest.

**trial by battle**, = trial by combat.

**trial by combat**, a trial in which victory in combat between two disputing parties decides a case.

**trial by jury**, a courtroom trial in which a jury decides the facts in a case instead of a judge or judges.

**trial by ordeal**, a trial in which innocence or guilt was determined by the effect of torture or some other danger.

**trial court**, a lower or district court in which the first hearing of a case is decided, as contrasted with an appellate court.

**trial horse**, a person, craft, or animal used as an opponent or competitor to keep another in practice especially while training for a race.

**tri|al|ism** (trī′ə liz əm), *n.* **1** the doctrine of three distinct, ultimate substances or principles. **2** a union of three countries or states.

**tri|al|ist** (trī′ə list), *n.* **1** *Sports.* a person who takes part in a trial or preliminary match. **2** an advocate or supporter of trialism.

**trial judge**, a judge who hears a case in a trial court.

**trial jury**, a jury consisting usually of 6 or 12 persons, chosen to decide a case in court; petit jury.

**trial lawyer**, a lawyer who specializes in presenting cases in court: *Clarence Darrow was one of America's greatest trial lawyers.*

**trial marriage**, companionate marriage for the purpose of testing the compatibility of the partners over a specific period of time.

**tri|a|logue** (trī′ə lôg, -log), *n.* a conversation or discussion between three persons or groups: *... a trialogue between a scientist, a scholar, and a teacher* (New Yorker). [< *tri-* + (di)*alogue*]

**trial run**, a preliminary or experimental test of performance.

**tri|am|cin|o|lone** (trī′əm sin′ə lōn), *n.* a steroid drug similar to cortisone, used in the treatment of arthritis, psoriasis, and other inflammatory conditions. *Formula:* $C_{21}H_{27}FO_6$ [< *tri-* + *am*(ino) + (ri)*cin* + (prednis)*olone*]

*** tri|an|gle** (trī′ang′gəl), *n.* **1** a plane figure having three sides and three angles. **2** something shaped like a triangle; any three-cornered body, object, or space. **3** a musical instrument consisting of a triangle of steel open at one corner, that is struck with a small steel rod. **4** *Figurative.* a group or set of three; triad: *Mrs. Dudeney's novel ... deals with the eternal triangle, which, in this case, consists of two men and one woman* (London Daily Chronicle). *The plots of these magazines almost always turn on love triangles* (New York Times). **5** a thin, flat, straight-edged object in the shape of a triangle, usually a right triangle. It is used with a T-square in drawing parallel, perpendicular, and diagonal lines. [< Latin *triangulum* < *tri-* three + *angulus* corner]

*** triangle**
definition 1

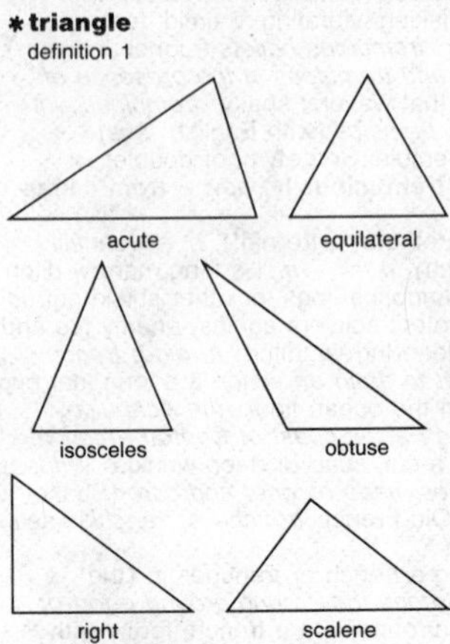


**triangle spider**, a spider that spins a triangular web in trees, which it springs on its prey by releasing one of the elastic threads.

**tri|an|gu|lar** (tri ang′gyə lər), *adj.* **1** shaped like a triangle; three-cornered. **2** *Figurative.* concerned with three persons, groups, or interests; three-sided. **3** constituting a triad or set of three; threefold. **4** having to do with or relating to a triangle. **5a** of or having to do with a pattern of organization formerly standard in the infantry and certain other combat branches of the armed forces of the United States and some other countries, in which a division consisted of three regiments, a regiment of three battalions, and so on. **b** characterized by such a pattern of organization. —**tri-an′gu|lar|ly**, *adv.*

**tri|an|gu|lar|i|ty** (trī ang′gyə lar′ə tē), *n.* the condition of being triangular; triangular form.

**tri|an|gu|late** (*v.* trī ang′gyə lāt; *adj.* trī ang′gyə-lit, -lāt), *v.,* **-lat|ed, -lat|ing,** *adj.* —*v.t.* **1** to mark out or divide into triangles. **2** to survey, measure, and map out (a region) by dividing (it) into triangles and measuring their angles and sides. **3** to find out by trigonometry: *to triangulate the height of a mountain.* **4** to make triangular; mark out or draw as a triangle.
—*adj.* **1** composed of or marked with triangles. **2** = triangular. —**tri|an′gu|late|ly**, *adv.*

**tri|an|gu|la|tion** (trī ang′gyə lā′shən), *n.* **1a** a survey or measurement done by means of trigonometry. **b** the series or network of triangles laid out for such measurement. **2** division into triangles.

**Tri|an|gu|li** (trī ang′gyə lī), *n.* gentive of **Triangulum.**

**Trianguli Aus|tra|lis** (ôs trā′lis), genitive of **Triangulum Australe.**

**Tri|an|gu|lum** (trī ang′gyə ləm), *n., genitive* **Tri|an-gu|li.** a northern constellation near Andromeda. [< Latin *triangulum;* see etym. under **triangle**]

**Triangulum Aus|tra|le** (ôs trā′lē), *genitive* **Tri-an|gu|li Aus|tra|lis.** a southern constellation near Centaurus.

**tri|ap|sal** (trī ap′səl), *adj.* = triapsidal.

**tri|ap|si|dal** (trī ap′sə dəl), *adj.* having three apses. [< *tri-* + Latin *apsis, -idis* apse + English *-al*[1]]

**tri|ar|chy** (trī′är kē), *n., pl.* **-ar|chies.** **1** a government by three persons. **2** three persons ruling jointly; triumvirate. **3** a group of three districts or states, each under its own ruler. [< Greek *triarchiā* < *tri-* three + *archiā* a rule]

**Tri|as** (trī′əs), *n.* the Triassic system or period.

**Tri|as|sic** (trī as′ik), *n., adj. Geology.* —*n.* **1** the earliest period of the Mesozoic era, before the Jurassic, characterized by the appearance of dinosaurs and primitive mammals, the domination of the earth by reptiles, and much volcanic activity. **2** the rocks formed during this period.

—*adj.* of or having to do with this period or its rocks.
[< German *Trias,* a certain series of strata containing three types of deposit < Late Latin *trias;* see etym. under **triad**]

**tri|at|ic stay** (trī at′ik), *Nautical.* **1** a stay, usually of wire, between the head of a topmast and the head of the lower section of the next mast toward the stern. **2** either of two ropes or cables, one attached to the head of the foremast and the other to the head of the mainmast, joined by a shackle and used in hoisting cargo from a hold. [origin uncertain]

**tri|a|tom|ic** (trī′ə tom′ik), *adj. Chemistry.* **1** containing three atoms; consisting of molecules each containing three atoms. **2** having three atoms or groups which can be replaced. **3** = trivalent.

**tri|ax|i|al** (trī ak′sē əl), *adj.* having three axes.

**tri|ax|i|al|i|ty** (trī ak′sē al′ə tē), *n.* triaxial condition.

**tri|a|zin** (trī′ə zin, trī az′in), *n.* = triazine.

**tri|a|zine** (trī′ə zēn, -zin; trī az′ēn, -in), *n.* **1** one of three isomeric compounds, each having a ring of three carbon atoms and three nitrogen atoms. *Formula:* $C_3H_3N_3$ **2** any one of various substances derived from these compounds. Some are used as pesticides and herbicides. [< *tri-* + *az*(o)- + *-ine*[2]]

**tri|a|zo|ic** (trī′ə zō′ik), *adj.* = hydrazoic.

**triazoic acid,** = hydrazoic acid.

**tri|a|zole** (trī′ə zōl, trī az′ōl), *n.* one of a group of four compounds, each having a ring of two carbon atoms and three nitrogen atoms. Triazoles are considered as pyrrole derivatives formed by the substitution of two nitrogen atoms for -CH groups. *Formula:* $C_2H_3N_3$

**trib.,** tributary.

**trib|ade** (trib′əd), *n.* a woman who is homosexual; Lesbian. [< Latin *tribas, -adis* < Greek *tribás, -ádos* < *tríbein* to rub]

**trib|al** (trī′bəl), *adj.* **1** of a tribe or tribes: *tribal customs.* **2** characteristic of a tribe. —**trib′al|ly,** *adv.*

**trib|al|ism** (trī′bə liz əm), *n.* **1** the condition of existing in separate tribes: *Touré tackled the tribalism that plagues all of Africa* (Time). **2** tribal relation, feeling, or loyalty.

**trib|al|ist** (trī′bə list), *n.* a person who favors or supports tribalism.

**trib|al|is|tic** (trī′bə lis′tik), *adj.* of or having to do with tribalism or tribalists.

**trib|al|ize** (trī′bə līz), *v.t.,* **-ized, -iz|ing.** to make or divide into tribes; give a tribal character to.

**tri|ba|sic** (trī bā′sik), *adj. Chemistry.* **1** (of an acid) having three hydrogen atoms which can be replaced by basic atoms or radicals. **2** having three atoms or radicals of a univalent metal. **3** containing three basic hydroxyl (-OH) radicals.

**tribe** (trīb), *n.* **1** a group of people united by race and customs under the same leaders; ethnic group: *America was once the home of many Indian tribes.* **SYN**: clan. **2a** a group of people forming a community and claiming descent from a common ancestor. **SYN**: clan. **b** any one of the twelve divisions of the ancient Hebrews, each claiming descent from a son of Jacob (in the Bible, Joshua 4:8): *the tribe of Judah, the ten lost tribes.* **3** a class or set of people; fraternity: *the tribe of artists, the whole tribe of gossips. Society is ... formed of two mighty tribes, the Bores and Bored* (Byron). **4** *Biology.* a group of related plants or animals ranking below a family or subfamily and usually containing at least one genus. **5** any group or series of animals or plants: *The feathered tribe is a name for birds.* **6** *Figurative.* a class, kind, group, or sort of things. **7** (in stock breeding) the descendants of a certain female animal through female offspring. **8** in ancient Rome: **a** one of the three divisions (Latins, Sabines, and Etruscans) of the Roman people. **b** (later) one of the 30 political divisions of the Roman people, increased to 35 in 241 B.C. **9** (in ancient Athens) the largest political subdivision; phyle. [< Latin *tribus, -ūs*]

**tribe|ship** (trīb′ship), *n.* **1** the condition of being a tribe. **2** the territory of a tribe.

**tribes|man** (trībz′mən), *n., pl.* **-men.** a member of a tribe, especially a man who is a member of a primitive tribe.

**tribes|peo|ple** (trībz′pē′pəl), *n.pl.* persons constituting a tribe; the members of a tribe.

**tribes|wom|an** (trībz′wu̇m′ən), *n., pl.* **-wom|en.** a woman belonging to a tribe.

**tri|bo|e|lec|tric** (trī′bō i lek′trik, trib′ō-), *adj.* of or having to do with triboelectricity.

**tri|bo|e|lec|tric|i|ty** (trī′bō i lek′tris′ə tē, -ē′lek-; trib′ō-), *n.* electricity produced by friction; static electricity. [< Greek *tríbos* a rubbing (< *tríbein* rub) + English *electricity*]

**tri|bo|log|i|cal** (trī′bə loj′ə kəl), *adj.* of or having to do with tribology. —**tri′bo|log′i|cal|ly,** *adv.*

**tri|bol|o|gy** (trī bol′ə jē), *n.* the study of friction, wear, and lubrication. [< Greek *tríbos* a rubbing (< *tríbein* to rub) + English *-logy*]

**tri|bo|lu|mi|nes|cence** (trī′bō lü′mə nes′əns; trib′ō-), *n.* the quality of emitting light under friction or violent pressure. [< Greek *tríbos* a rubbing (< *tríbein* rub) + English *luminescence*]

**tri|bom|e|ter** (trī bom′ə tər), *n.* an apparatus for measuring the force of friction in sliding surfaces. [< French *tribomètre* < Greek *tríbein* rub + *métron* measure]

**tri|brach** (trī′brak, trib′rak), *n. Greek and Latin Prosody.* a foot of three short or unstressed syllables. [< Latin *tribrachys* < Greek *tríbrachys* < *tri-* three + *brachýs* short]

**tri|brach|ic** (trī brak′ik, tri-), *adj.* **1** consisting of three short or unstressed syllables; constituting a tribrach. **2** having to do with a tribrach or tribrachs.

**tri|bro|mo|eth|a|nol** (trī brō′mō eth′ə nōl, -nol), *n.* a crystalline substance, used in solution as an anesthetic; Avertin. *Formula:* $C_2H_3Br_3O$ [< *tri-* + *bromo-* (< *bromine*) + *ethanol*]

**trib|u|late** (trib′yə lāt), *v.t.,* **-lat|ed, -lat|ing.** to trouble greatly; subject to tribulation; afflict. [< Latin *tribulāre* to oppress, press (with English *-ate*[1]); see etym. under **tribulation**]

**trib|u|la|tion** (trib′yə lā′shən), *n.* great trouble or misery; severe trial; affliction: *The early Christians suffered many tribulations. The fiery furnace of domestic tribulations* (Washington Irving). **SYN**: oppression, distress. [< Latin *trībulātiō, -ōnis* < *trībulāre* to oppress, press < *trībulum* threshing sledge, related to *terere* to rub]

**tri|bu|nal** (tri byü′nəl, trī-), *n.* **1** a court of justice; place of judgment or judicial assembly: *He was brought before the tribunal of seven judges for trial.* **SYN**: judicature. **2** the place where judges sit in a law court. **SYN**: bench. **3** *Figurative.* something by or in which judgment is given; judicial or deciding authority: *the tribunal of the polls, the tribunal of the press.* [< Latin *tribūnal* < *tribūnus;* see etym. under **tribune**[1]]

**trib|u|nate** (trib′yu̇ nit, -nāt), *n.* **1** = tribuneship. **2** government by tribunes. [< Latin *tribūnātus* < *tribūnus;* see etym. under **tribune**[1]]

**trib|une**[1] (trib′yün; *see usage note below*), *n.* **1** any one of various officials of ancient Rome. The tribune of the people was an official appointed by the plebeians to protect their rights and interests from arbitrary action by the patricians. A military tribune was one of six officers, each of whom in turn commanded a legion in the course of a year. **2** any person, especially a government official, who is appointed as a defender of the people or their rights. [< Latin *tribūnus* < *tribus, -ūs* tribe]

▶ **Tribune** in the name of a newspaper is often pronounced (tri byün′).

**trib|une**[2] (trib′yün), *n.* **1** a raised platform for a speaker. **SYN**: rostrum. **2** a raised area or gallery containing seats, especially in a church: *The church was crowded; not a chair nor a tribune vacant* (Benjamin Disraeli). **3** = apse. [< Italian *tribuna* tribunal < Latin *tribūnus;* see etym. under **tribune**[1]]

**trib|une|ship** (trib′yün ship), *n.* the position, duties, or term of office of a tribune.

**trib|u|ni|tial** or **trib|u|ni|cial** (trib′yə nish′əl), *adj.* of, having to do with, or characteristic of a tribune or his office or function. [< Latin *tribūnītius* (< *tribūnus;* see etym. under **tribune**[1]) + English *-al*[1]]

**tri|bu|ni|tian** or **tri|bu|ni|cian** (trib′yə nish′ən), *adj.* = tribunitial.

**trib|u|tar|y** (trib′yə ter′ē), *n., pl.* **-tar|ies,** *adj.* —*n.* **1** a stream that flows into a larger stream or body of water: *The Ohio River is one of the tributaries of the Mississippi River.* **2** a person or country that pays tribute. —*adj.* **1** flowing into a larger stream or body of water. **2** paying tribute; required to pay tribute. **3** paid or offered as tribute; of the nature of tribute. **4** *Figurative.* **a** contributing; helping. **b** subsidiary; auxiliary.

**trib|ute** (trib′yüt), *n.* **1** money paid by one nation to another for peace or protection, in acknowledgment of submission, or because of some agreement: *A large portion of the tribute was paid in money* (Edward Gibbon). **2** any forced payment: *The pirates demanded tribute from passing ships.* **3** the obligation or necessity of paying tribute; condition of being tributary: *Millions for defence but not a cent for tribute* (Robert G. Harper). **4** a tax or payment to raise money for tribute. **5** *Figurative.* an acknowledgment of thanks or respect; compliment: *Memorial Day is a tribute to our dead soldiers.* [< Latin *tribūtum* < *tribuere* to allot < *tribus, -ūs* tribe]

**tri|car|box|yl|ic acid** (trī kär′bok sil′ik), an organic compound containing three carboxyl groups.

**tricarboxylic acid cycle,** = Krebs cycle.

**tri|car|pel|lar|y** (trī kär′pə ler′ē), *adj. Botany.* having or consisting of three carpels.

**trice**[1] (trīs), *v.t.,* **triced, tric|ing. 1** to haul up and fasten with a rope: *to trice up a sail.* **2** to pull with an attached rope. [< Middle Dutch *trīsen* hoist < *trīse* pulley]

**trice**[2] (trīs), *n.* a very short time; moment; instant. **SYN**: twinkling.
**in a trice,** in an instant; instantly; immediately: *I'll open the gate in a trice. That structure which was so many years arearing was dashed ... in a trice* (James Howell).
[abstracted from phrase *at a trice* at a pull; see etym. under **trice**[1]]

**tri|cen|ni|al** (trī sen′ē əl), *adj.* **1** of or having to do with thirty years. **2** occurring every thirty years. [< Late Latin *trīcennium* thirty years (< Latin *triciēs* thirty times + *annus* year) + English *-al*[1]]

**tri|cen|te|nar|y** (trī sen′tə ner′ē, trī′sen ten′ər-; *especially British* trī′sen tē′nər ē), *adj., n., pl.* **-nar-ies.** = tercentenary.

**tri|cen|ten|ni|al** (trī′sen ten′ē əl, -ten′yəl), *adj., n.* = tercentenary.

**tri|ceps** (trī′seps), *n.* the large muscle at the back of the upper arm. It extends or straightens the arm. See picture under **arm**[1]. [< New Latin *triceps* three-headed < Latin *triceps, -cipitis* three-headed < *tri-* three + *caput, capitis* head]

***triceratops**

***tri|cer|a|tops** (trī ser′ə tops), *n.* a dinosaur of the Cretaceous period of western North America, with a huge skull, a large horn above each eye and a smaller horn on the nose, a large, bony collar extending from the neck, and a long and powerful tail. [< New Latin *Triceratops* the genus name < Greek *trikératos* three-horned + *ōps* face]

**trich-,** *combining form.* the form of **tricho-** before vowels, as in *trichiasis, trichite.*

**tri|chi|a|sis** (tri kī′ə sis), *n.* **1** an abnormal condition characterized by the turning in of the eyelashes. **2** a disease characterized by the presence of hairlike filaments in the urine. **3** a disease of the breasts occurring in women during lactation. [< New Latin *trichiasis* < Greek *trichíāsis* (originally) any hairy condition < *trichiân* be hairy < *thríx, trichós* a hair]

**tri|chi|na** (tri kī′nə), *n., pl.* **-nae** (-nē). a small, slender nematode worm whose adult form lives in the intestines and whose larva lives in the muscles of man, hogs, and various other animals, causing trichinosis. Trichinae usually get into the human body from pork which is infected with the larvae and is not cooked long enough to destroy them. [< New Latin *trichina* < Greek *trichínē,* feminine of *tríchinos* of or like hair < *thríx, trichós* a hair]

**trich|i|nel|la** (trik′ə nel′ə), *n., pl.* **-lae** (-lē). = trichina. [< New Latin *trichinella* (diminutive) < *Trichina* trichina]

**trich|i|ni|a|sis** (trik′ə nī′ə sis), *n.* = trichinosis.

**trich|i|nize** (trik′ə nīz), *v.t.,* **-nized, -niz|ing.** to infect with trichinae. —**trich′i|ni|za′tion,** *n.*

**trich|i|nosed** (trik′ə nōzd, -nōst), *adj.* affected with trichinosis; infected with trichinae.

**trich|i|no|sis** (trik′ə nō′sis), *n.* a disease characterized by headache, chills, fever, and soreness of muscles, caused by the presence of trichinae in the intestines and muscular tissues. [< New Latin *trichinosis* < *Trichina* trichina + *-osis* -osis]

**trich|i|not|ic** (trik′ə not′ik), *adj.* of or having to do with trichinosis.

**trich|i|nous** (trik′ə nəs), *adj.* of or having trichinosis; infected with trichinae.

**trich|ite** (trik′īt), *n.* a very minute, dark-colored, hairlike crystal occurring in some vitreous rocks. [< Greek *thríx, trichós* a hair + English *-ite*[1]]

**tri|chlo|rid** (trī klôr′id, -klōr′-), *n.* = trichloride.

**tri|chlo|ride** (trī klôr′īd, -id; -klōr′-), *n.* a chemical compound containing three atoms of chlorine combined with another element or radical.

**tri|chlo|ro|a|ce|tic acid** (trī klôr′ō ə sē′tik, -set′-ik; -klōr′-), a colorless, crystalline acid with a pungent odor, used in medicine as an astringent, in organic synthesis, and as a herbicide. *Formula:* $C_2HO_2Cl_3$

**Pronunciation Key:** hat, āge, cãre, fär; let, ēqual, tėrm; it, īce; hot, ōpen, ôrder; oil, out; cup, pu̇t, rüle; child; long; thin; ᴛʜen; zh, measure; ə represents **a** in about, **e** in taken, **i** in pencil, **o** in lemon, **u** in circus.

**tri|chlo|ro|eth|yl|ene** (trī klôr′ō eth′ə lēn, -klōr′-), *n.* a liquid derived from ethylene or acetylene, used in anesthesia, as a grease solvent for dry cleaning, and in chemical manufacturing. *Formula:* $C_2HCl_3$

**tricho-**, *combining form.* hair; hairs; hairlike: *Trichology* = *the study of hair. Trichosis* = *any disease of the hair.* Also, **trich-** before vowels. [< Greek *thríx, trichós* a hair]

**trich|o|car|pous** (trik′ə kär′pəs), *adj. Botany.* having hairy fruit. [< *tricho-* + Greek *karpós* fruit + English *-ous*]

**trich|o|cyst** (trik′ə sist), *n. Zoology.* one of the tiny stinging or grasping organs on the body of certain infusorians, consisting of a hairlike filament in a small sac.

**trich|o|cyst|ic** (trik′ə sis′tik), *adj.* **1** having to do with trichocysts. **2** having the character of trichocysts: *a trichocystic formation.*

**trich|o|gyne** (trik′ə jin, -jīn), *n.* a hairlike process forming the receptive part of the female reproductive organ in certain algae and fungi. [< *tricho-* + Greek *gynê* woman, female]

**trich|oid** (trik′oid), *adj.* resembling hair; hairlike.

**tri|chol|o|gist** (tri kol′ə jist), *n.* an expert in trichology.

**tri|chol|o|gy** (tri kol′ə jē), *n.* the study of the structure, functions, and diseases of the hair. [< *tricho-* + *-logy*]

**tri|chome** (trī′kōm, trik′ōm), *n.* an outgrowth from the epidermis of plants (a general term including hairs and prickles). [< Greek *trichōma, -atos* growth of hair < *thríx, trichós* a hair]

**tri|chom|ic** (tri kom′ik), *adj.* **1** of or having to do with a trichome. **2** like a trichome.

**trich|o|mon|a|cid|al** (trik′ō mon′ə sī′dəl, -mō′nə-), *adj.* destructive of trichomonads.

**trich|o|mon|a|cide** (trik′ō mon′ə sīd, -mō′nə-), *n.* a drug that destroys trichomonads.

**trich|o|mon|ad** (trik′ō mon′ad, -mō′nad), *n.* any one of a group of parasitic flagellate protozoans found in man and certain other animals, having several flagella and a tapering body. [< New Latin *Trichomonas, -adis* the genus name < Greek *thríx, trichós* a hair + Late Latin *monas* monad]

**trich|o|mo|ni|a|sis** (trik′ō mə nī′ə sis), *n.* the condition of being infected with the parasite trichomonad. Bovine trichomoniasis will cause miscarriage in cattle, and avian trichomoniasis is usually fatal in young chicks.

**tri|chop|ter|an** (tri kop′tər ən), *adj., n.* —*adj.* = trichopterous.
—*n.* a trichopterous insect; caddis fly.

**tri|chop|ter|ous** (tri kop′tər əs), *adj.* **1** having hairy wings. **2** belonging to an order of insects comprising the caddis flies. [< Greek *thríx, trichós* a hair + *pterón* wing + English *-ous*]

**tri|chord** (trī′kôrd), *n.* a musical instrument with three strings, as a form of lyre or lute. [< Greek *trichordos* having three strings < *tri-* three (< *treîs*) + *chordē* string]

**tri|cho|sis** (tri kō′sis), *n., pl.* **-ses** (sēz). any disease of the hair. [< *trich-* + *-osis*]

**trich|o|tom|ic** (trik′ə tom′ik), *adj.* **1** divided or dividing into three parts. **2** branching into three parts; giving off shoots by threes.

**tri|chot|o|mous** (trī kot′ə məs), *adj.* = trichotomic.

**tri|chot|o|my** (trī kot′ə mē), *n., pl.* **-mies. 1** division into three parts, classes, or categories; tripartite arrangement. **2** *Theology.* division into body, soul, and spirit. [< Greek *tricha* triple, triply (< *tri-* < *treîs* three) + *-tomiā* a cutting, division]

**tri|chro|ic** (trī krō′ik), *adj.* possessing the property of trichroism.

**tri|chro|ism** (trī′krō iz əm), *n.* the property of some crystals of exhibiting three different colors when viewed in three different directions. [< Greek *tríchroos* (< *tri-* three + *chrōā*, for *chroiā* skin, color of skin) + English *-ism*]

**tri|chro|mat** (trī′krō mat), *n.* a person who has trichromatic vision.

**tri|chro|mat|ic** (trī′krō mat′ik), *adj.* **1** having or showing three colors. **2** having to do with three colors. **3** using three colors, as in printing. **4** having to do with or characterized by vision in which all the primary colors can be seen.

**tri|chro|ma|tism** (trī krō′mə tiz əm), *n.* **1** the quality of being trichromatic. **2** the combination of three different colors, as in color photography. **3** vision in which all the primary colors can be seen; normal vision.

**tri|chro|mic** (trī krō′mik), *adj.* = trichromatic.

**tri-cit|y** (trī′sit′ē), *n., pl.* **-cit|ies,** *adj.* —*n.* **1** a group of three adjoining and mutually dependent cities. **2** a city in such a group: *Fine* [*industrial*] *facilities are ... already in existence in the tri-cities* (Scott R. Schmedel).
—*adj.* of, belonging to, or involving such a group of cities: *Calgary, Edmonton, and Red Deer studied the possibility of a tri-city project ... for a large thermoelectric system* (John E. Dutton).

**trick** (trik), *n., adj., v.* —*n.* **1** something done to deceive or cheat: *The false message was a trick to get him to leave the house.* **SYN**: ruse, subterfuge, artifice, stratagem. **2** a deceptive appearance; illusion: *Those two lines are really the same length, but a trick of the eyesight makes one of them look longer.* **3** a clever act; feat of skill, as in juggling or sleight of hand: *We enjoyed the tricks of the trained animals at the circus.* **SYN**: exploit, stunt. **4** the best way of doing or dealing with something; knack: *to learn the tricks of the trade. Mother certainly knows the trick of making pies.* **5** a piece of mischief; practical joke; prank: *Stealing John's lunch was a mean trick.* **6** a peculiar habit or way of acting; practice; mannerism: *He has a trick of pulling at his collar.* **7** the cards played in one round of a card game: *When in doubt, win the trick* (Edmund Hoyle). **8** a turn or period of duty on a job, especially at steering a ship. **9** *U.S. Informal.* a child, especially a young girl. **10** *U.S. Slang.* **a** the customer of a prostitute. **b** a transaction with a prostitute.
—*adj.* **1** of, like, or done as a trick or stunt: *trick riding, trick shooting.* **2** skilled in or trained to do tricks: *a trick dog.* **3** made or used for doing tricks: *a trick chair.* **4** (of a joint) tending to stiffen or weaken suddenly: *He had a trick knee, which made him sway slightly when he walked* (New Yorker).
—*v.t.* **1** to deceive by a trick; cheat: *We were tricked into buying a poor car. He was tricked out of his share of the reward. She was tricked into approving the scheme.* **SYN**: defraud, delude, cozen. See syn. under **cheat. 2** to dress: *She was tricked up in her mother's clothes.* —*v.i.* **1** to play tricks; trifle. **2** to practice trickery.
**do** (or **turn**) **the trick,** to do what one wants done; accomplish the purpose: *Pail of whitewash and box of paints will do the trick* (Punch).
**how's tricks?** *U.S. Informal.* how is everything? what are you dong? (used as a greeting): *My friend ..., brandishing his Martini glass across the room, called: "Hi, Eddie! How's tricks?"* (Alexander Frater).
**trick out, a** to dress up; ornament: *I must trick out my dwellings with something fantastical* (Scott). **b** *Figurative.* to disguise: *I mention it only as an example of the frivolous speculation tricked out to look like scholarship with which the Holmes cult defrauds the reading public* (Harper's).
[< Old North French *trique* < *trikier,* Old French *trichier* to trick, cheat, perhaps < Dutch *trekken* to draw, swindle] —**trick′er,** *n.* —**trick′less,** *adj.*

**trick|er|y** (trik′ər ē, trik′rē), *n., pl.* **-er|ies.** the use of tricks; deceitful conduct or practice; deception; cheating. **SYN**: artifice, stratagem, imposture, duplicity.

**trick|i|ly** (trik′ə lē), *adv.* in a tricky manner.

**trick|i|ness** (trik′ē nis), *n.* the quality of being tricky: *He went off chuckling at his own guile and trickiness* (Sunday Times).

**trick|ish** (trik′ish), *adj.* rather tricky. —**trick′ish|ly,** *adv.* —**trick′ish|ness,** *n.*

**trick|le** (trik′əl), *v.,* **-led, -ling,** *n.* —*v.i.* **1** to flow or fall in drops: *Tears trickled down her cheeks.* **SYN**: drip, dribble, ooze. **2** to flow in a very small stream: *The brook trickled through the valley. Salt trickled from a hole in the box.* **3** *Figurative.* to come, go, pass, or move forward slowly and unevenly: *An hour before the show started, people began to trickle into the theater.*
—*v.t.* to cause to flow in drops or in a small stream: *He trickled the water out of the bottle.*
—*n.* **1** a small flow or stream. **2** the act or fact of trickling.
[Middle English *triklen;* origin uncertain]

**trick|le-down** (trik′əl doun′), *adj. U.S.* of or based on the economic theory that money flowing into the economy, especially from the government, will stimulate growth by distribution through big business rather than by direct benefits, such as welfare payments or public works: *trickle-down economics.*

**trick|le-ir|ri|gate** (trik′əl ir′ə gāt), *v.t.,* **-gat|ed, -gat|ing.** to irrigate by slow application of water at designated intervals, usually with small-diameter hoses: *Vast areas in the Negev Desert of Israel are now trickle-irrigated* (Sylvan Wittwer).

**trick|let** (trik′lit), *n.* **1** a little trickle. **2** a small trickling stream.

**trick|ling filter** (trik′ling), a tank filled with crushed rocks on which sewage is distributed so that it comes in contact with bacteria that change the organic material in the sewage to less harmful substances as it trickles down through the layer of rocks.

**trick or treat, 1** the custom of going from door to door on Halloween dressed in costume and asking for treats of candy, fruit, and the like, by saying "trick or treat," practiced by children. **2** such a demand: *candies or pennies on hand to dole out to the oddly dressed midgets, doubling for goblins, who ring his doorbell and demand "trick or treat"* (Scientific American).

**trick-or-treat|er** (trik′ər trē′tər), *n.* a person who engages in trick-or-treating.

**trick-or-treat|ing** (trik′ər trē′ting), *n.* the act of demanding a trick or treat.

**trick|some** (trik′səm), *adj.* full of tricks; mischievous; frolicsome; playful.

**trick|ster** (trik′stər), *n.* a person who practices trickery; cheat; deceiver.

**trick|sy** (trik′sē), *adj.* **1** mischievous; playful; frolicsome: *a frolicsome and tricksy creature, full of wild fantastic humours* (W. H. Hudson). **2** tricky: *The chopping about has begun to seem tricksy and ornamental* (New Statesman). **SYN**: crafty, cunning. **3** spruce; smart. —**trick′si|ly,** *adv.* —**trick′si|ness,** *n.*

**trick|track** (trik′trak′), *n.* a variety of backgammon. Also, **trictrac.** [< French *trictrac;* ultimately imitative]

**trick|y** (trik′ē), *adj.,* **trick|i|er, trick|i|est. 1** full of tricks; characterized by trickery; deceiving; cheating: *A fox is trickier than a sheep.* **SYN**: deceptive, deceitful. **2** not doing what is expected; dangerous or difficult to deal with: *The back door has a tricky lock.* **3** skilled in performing clever tricks or dodges.

**tri|clad** (trī′klad), *n., adj.* = planarian. [< New Latin *Triclad*(*ida*) the order name < *tri-* + Greek *kládos* sprout, branch]

**tri|clin|ic** (trī klin′ik), *adj.* designating or belonging to a system of crystallization in which the three axes are unequal and obliquely inclined. See picture under **crystal.** [< *tri-* + Greek *klī́nein* bend, lean + English *-ic*]

**tri|clin|i|um** (trī klin′ē əm), *n., pl.* **-i|a** (-ē ə). **1** a couch or couches extending around three sides of a dining table, on which in ancient Rome the host and his guests reclined while eating, especially during a banquet or other formal meal. **2** a dining room containing such a couch or couches. [< Latin *triclīnium* < Greek *triklī́nion* (diminutive) < *tríklīnos* a (dining) room with three couches < *tri-* threefold, triply + *klī́nē* couch < *klī́nein* to lean, recline]

**tric|o|lette** (trik ə let′), *n.* a knitted fabric of rayon or silk, similar to jersey. [< *trico*(t) + *-lette,* as in *flannelette*]

**tri|col|or** (trī′kul′ər), *adj., n.* —*adj.* having three colors; three-colored.
—*n.* **1** the national flag of France adopted at the Revolution, consisting of equal vertical stripes of blue, white, and red. **2** any one of certain other flags consisting of three equal stripes or blocks each of a different color, such as that of Italy, which is green, white, and red.
[< French (*drapeau*) *tricolore* tricolored (flag)]

**tri|col|ored** (trī′kul′ərd), *adj.* having three colors: *a tricolored flag.*

**tri|col|our** (trī′kul′ər), *adj., n. Especially British.* tricolor.

**tri|con|o|dont** (trī kon′ə dont), *adj., n.* —*adj.* of or belonging to an extinct group of mammals that had molar teeth with three conical cusps and that are regarded as the most primitive of all known mammalian forms.
—*n.* a triconodont mammal.
[< New Latin *Triconodontidae* the family name < *tri-* + Latin *cōnus* cone + Greek *odoús, odóntos* tooth]

**tri|corn** (trī′kôrn), *adj., n.* —*adj.* having three horns or hornlike projections (applied especially to a cocked hat with the brim turned up on three sides).
—*n.* a tricorn hat.
[< French *tricorne* < Latin *tricornis* < *tri-* three + *cornū* horn]

**tri|corne** (trī′kôrn), *n.* a tricorn hat: *It was Washington who wore a tricorne; Napoleon wore a bicorne* (Atlantic).

**tri|cor|nered** (trī′kôr′nərd), *adj.* = three-cornered.

**tri|cor|po|rate** (trī kôr′pər it), *adj. Especially Heraldry.* having three bodies. [< Latin *tricorpor* (< *tri-* three + *corpus, -oris* body) + English *-ate*[1]]

**tri|cos|tate** (trī kos′tāt), *adj. Botany, Zoology.* having three ribs or riblike parts (costae). [< *tri-* + Latin *costa* rib + English *-ate*[1]]

**tri|cot** (trē′kō), *n.* **1** a knitted fabric of wool, cotton, rayon, nylon, or silk, made by hand or machine. **2** a kind of woolen cloth. **3** a close-fitting garment worn by ballet dancers. [< French *tricot* < Old French *tricoter* to stir, move about, variant of *estriquier,* probably < Low German *strikken* move about]

**tric|o|tine** (trik′ə tēn′), *n.* a kind of twilled woolen fabric. [< French *tricotine* < *tricot* tricot]

**tri|cres|yl phosphate** (trī kres′əl), a mixture of isomers derived from cresol and phosphorous oxychloride, used especially as a gasoline additive and plasticizer. *Formula:* $(CH_3C_6H_4O)_3PO$ *Abbr:* TCP (no periods).

**tri|crot|ic** (trī krot′ik), *adj.* (of a pulse or a tracing of it) having or showing a three-fold beat. [< Greek *trikrotos* rowed with a triple stroke (< *tri-* triply + *krótos* noise made by striking hands or feet) + English *-ic*]

**tri|cro|tism** (trī′krə tiz əm, trik′rə-), *n.* tricrotic condition.

**tric|trac** (trik′trak′), *n.* = tricktrack.

**tri|cus|pid** (trī kus′pid), *adj., n.* —*adj.* **1** having three points or cusps. **2** of or having to do with the tricuspid valve of the heart.
—*n.* **1** a tricuspid tooth. **2** = tricuspid valve.
[< Latin *tricuspis, -idis* three-pointed < *tri-* three + *cuspis* tip]

**tri|cus|pi|dal** (trī kus′pə dəl), *adj.* = tricuspid.

**tri|cus|pi|date** (trī kus′pə dāt), *adj.* three-pointed; tricuspid.

**tricuspid valve**, a valve of three segments opening from the right auricle into the right ventricle of the heart. It prevents blood from being forced back into the right auricle during contraction of the ventricles. See diagram under **heart**.

**tri|cy|cle** (trī′sə kəl, -sik′əl), *n., v.,* **-cled, -cling.** —*n.* **1** a small, light vehicle having three wheels, worked by pedals or handles. Children often ride tricycles. **2** a three-wheeled motorcycle.
—*v.i.* to ride a tricycle.
[< French *tricycle* < *tri-* three + *cycle,* ultimately < Greek *kýklos* ring, circle]

**tri|cy|cler** (trī′sə klər, -sik′lər), *n.* a person who rides on a tricycle; tricyclist.

**tri|cy|clic** (trī sī′klik, -sik′lik), *adj.* **1** passing through or having three cycles. **2** *Chemistry.* containing three rings of atoms in the molecule.

**tri|cy|clist** (trī′sə klist, -sik′list), *n.* a person who rides on a tricycle.

**tri|dac|tyl** (trī dak′təl), *adj.* having three digits (fingers, claws, toes, or the like) on each limb. [< Greek *tridáktylos* < *tri-* three, triple + *dáktylos* finger, toe]

**tri|dec|ane** (trī dek′ān), *n.* a colorless, liquid hydrocarbon of the methane series. *Formula:* $C_{13}H_{28}$
[< *tri-* + *dec-* ten + *-ane* (because it contains 13 atoms of carbon)]

***tri|dent** (trī′dənt), *n., adj.* —*n.* **1** a spear with three prongs, used for fishing. **2** a three-pronged spear that is the identifying attribute of Poseidon (Neptune) as the ancient Greek and Roman god of the sea. **3** a three-pronged spear that was one of the two weapons (the other being a net) of a retiarius in ancient Roman gladiatorial combat.
—*adj.* three-pronged.
[< Latin *tridēns, -dentis* < *tri-* three + *dēns* tooth]

***trident**
definitions 1, 2

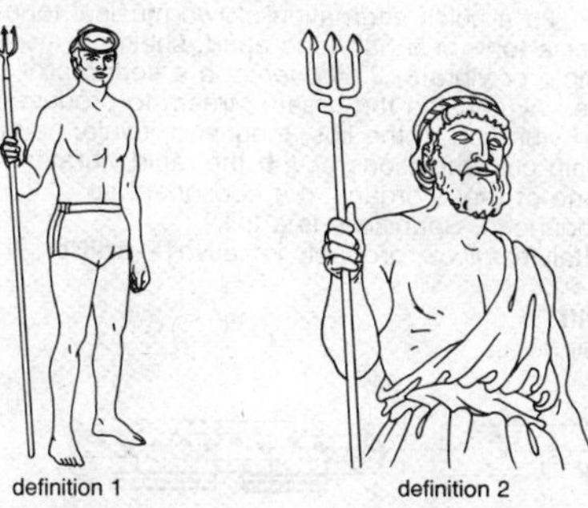

definition 1 — definition 2

**tri|den|tate** (trī den′tāt), *adj.* having three teeth or toothlike points; three-pronged: *tridentate teeth.*

**tri|den|tat|ed** (trī den′tā tid), *adj.* = tridentate.

**Tri|den|tine** (trī den′tin, -tīn; tri-), *adj.* **1** of or having to do with Trent, Italy (formerly Austria), or the Council of Trent. **2** conforming to the doctrine of the Council of Trent. [< Medieval Latin *Tridentinus* pertaining to *Tridentum,* the city of Trent, Italy]

**tri|di|men|sion|al** (trī′də men′shə nəl), *adj.* = three-dimensional.

**tri|di|men|sion|al|i|ty** (trī′də men′shə nal′ə tē), *n.* the condition or quality of having three dimensions; three-dimensionality.

**trid|u|um** (trij′ů əm), *n.* **1** a period of three days. **2** (in the Roman Catholic Church) a three days' period of prayer or devotion, usually preceding some feast. [< Latin *triduum* < *tri-* three + *diēs* day]

**trid|y|mite** (trid′ə mīt), *n.* a crystallized form of silica found in igneous rocks, usually in twinned groups of three crystals: *Tridymite occurs in small hexagonal tables, colorless and transparent* (James Dwight Dana). [< Greek *trídymos* threefold + English *-ite*[1]]

**tri|e|cious** (trī ē′shəs), *adj. Botany.* trioecious. —**tri|e′cious|ly,** *adv.*

**tried** (trīd), *adj., v.* —*adj.* **1** proved or tested by experience or examination; proven: *a person of tried abilities.* SYN: dependable, reliable, trustworthy. **2** (of fat) rendered. **3** *Obsolete.* freed from impurities; refined.
—*v.* the past tense and past participle of **try**: *I tried to call you. Have you tried calling again?*

**tried-and-true** (trīd′ən trü′), *adj.* tested and found to be true over a period of time; proven; dependable: *He believed in the tried-and-true American virtues of honesty, thrift, and opportunity* (Newsweek). *The producer—rather than speculate on something risky and new—sticks to a tried-and-true formula based on the successes of the past* (Harper's).

**tri|ene** (trī′ēn, trī ēn′), *n. Chemistry.* a compound having three double bonds. [< *tri-* + *-ene*]

**tri|en|ni|al** (trī en′ē əl), *adj., n.* —*adj.* **1** occurring every three years: *triennial elections.* **2** lasting three years.
—*n.* **1** an event that occurs every three years. **2** the third anniversary of an event.
[< Latin *triennium* (see etym. under **triennium**) + English *-al*[1]] —**tri|en′ni|al|ly,** *adv.*

**tri|en|ni|um** (trī en′ē əm), *n., pl.* **-en|ni|a** (-en′ē ə). a space or period of three years. [< Latin *triennium* < *tri-* three + *annus* year]

**tri|er** (trī′ər), *n.* a person or thing that tries.

**tri|er|arch** (trī′ə rärk), *n.* in ancient Greece: **1** the commander of a trireme. **2** (in Athens) a citizen who, singly or in conjunction with others, was charged with fitting out a trireme for the state. [< Latin *triērarchus* < Greek *triḗrarchos* < *triḗrēs* trireme + *archós* chief, leader]

**tri|er|ar|chic** (trī′ə rär′kik), *adj.* of or having to do with a trierarch or the trierarchy.

**tri|er|ar|chy** (trī′ə rär′kē), *n., pl.* **-chies. 1** the command over a trireme. **2** trierarchs collectively. **3** (in Athens) the system of requiring citizens to equip triremes for the state. [< Greek *triērarchiā* < *triḗrarchos;* see etym. under **trierarch**]

**tries** (trīz), *n., v.* —*n.* plural of **try.**
—*v.* the third person singular, present tense of **try**: *He always tries to do his best.*

**Tri|es|tine** (trē es′tēn), *adj., n.* —*adj.* of or having to do with Trieste, Italy: *Triestine dialects.*
—*n.* a native or inhabitant of Trieste.

**tri|e|ter|ic** (trī′ə ter′ik), *adj., n.* —*adj.* (in ancient Greece) occurring or held every third year (in the ancient reckoning, every alternate year), as certain festivals.
—*n.* a trieteric festival.
[< Latin *trietēricus* < Greek *trietērikós,* ultimately < *tri-* three + *étos* year]

**tri|eth|yl** (trī eth′əl), *adj. Chemistry.* containing three ethyl groups.

**tri|eth|yl|a|mine** (trī eth′ə lə mēn′, -lam′in), *n.* a colorless liquid with a strong smell like that of ammonia, used as a catalyst in organic reactions, as a solvent, and in certain propellants. *Formula:* $C_6H_{15}N$

**tri|eth|yl|ene melamine** (trī eth′ə lēn), a poisonous, crystalline compound used in manufacturing certain resins, in textile finishing, and as a drug in the treatment of malignant lymphomas and chronic leukemia. *Formula:* $C_9H_{12}N_6$

**triethylene phos|phor|a|mide** (fos′fə rə mīd′, -rə mid′; -ram′īd, -id), a drug used in the treatment of certain forms of carcinoma, malignant melanoma and lymphoma, and chronic leukemia; TEPA. *Formula:* $C_6H_{12}N_3OP$

**tri|fa|cial** (trī fā′shəl), *adj., n.* = trigeminal.

**tri|far|i|ous** (trī fãr′ē əs), *adj.* **1** threefold; triple. **2** in three rows. [< Latin *trifārius* (with English *-ous*)]

**tri|fec|ta** (trī fek′tə), *n. U.S.* a form of betting on a horse race in which the bettor picks the winners of the first, second, and third place in their order of finish. [American English < *tri-* three + (per)*fecta*]

**tri|fid** (trī′fid), *adj.* divided into three by clefts. [< Latin *trifidus* < *tri-* three, triply + *fid-,* a root of *findere* to split, cleave]

**tri|fi|lar** (trī fī′lər), *adj.* consisting of or furnished with three filaments or threads. [< *tri-* + Latin *fīlum* thread + English *-ar*]

**tri|fle** (trī′fəl), *n., v.,* **-fled, -fling.** —*n.* **1** a thing that is of little value or small importance: **a** a matter of little significance; trivial affair. SYN: triviality. **b** a small article of little intrinsic value; trinket; bauble; knickknack. **2** a small amount; little bit: *to move something a trifle to the right. I was a trifle late.* **3** an insignificant quantity or amount; very small amount of money: *The picture cost only a trifle.* **4** *Especially British.* a rich dessert made of sponge cake soaked in wine or liqueur, and served with whipped cream, custard, or fruit. **5** a kind of moderately hard pewter, used especially for beer mugs, containing a slightly greater proportion of lead than ordinary pewter.
—*v.i.* **1** to talk or act lightly, not seriously: *Don't trifle with serious matters. Stop trifling now—I want a serious answer.* **2** to play or toy (with); handle or finger a thing idly; fiddle or fidget: *He trifled with his pencil.* **3** to spend time idly or frivolously; waste time; dally: *Stop trifling and get to work.* SYN: dawdle, idle. —*v.t.* to spend (time, effort, or money) on things having little value; waste; fritter: *She had trifled away the whole morning.*
**trifles,** articles made of moderately hard pewter: *antique trifles.*
[< Old French *trufle* mockery (diminutive) < *truffe* deception; origin uncertain]
—*Syn. v.i.* **1 Trifle, dally** mean to treat a person or thing without seriousness. **Trifle,** the more general term, suggests treating too lightly something or someone that deserves seriousness or respect: *He is not a man to be trifled with.* **Dally** suggests the absence of any serious purpose or intent: *I have dallied with the idea of becoming a writer.*

**tri|fler** (trī′flər), *n.* a person who trifles; frivolous, shallow person.

**tri|fles** (trī′fəlz), *n.pl.* See under **trifle.**

**tri|fling** (trī′fling), *adj., n.* —*adj.* **1** having little value; not important; very small; paltry; insignificant: *The friends treated their quarrel as only a trifling matter. To a philosopher no circumstance, however trifling, is too minute* (Oliver Goldsmith). SYN: trivial, petty. **2** behaving idly or frivolously; shallow. SYN: foolish, vain.
—*n.* the act of a person who trifles. —**tri′fling|ly,** *adv.* —**tri′fling|ness,** *n.*

**tri|flu|o|ride** (trī flü′ə rīd, -ər id), *n.* a chemical compound containing three atoms of fluorine combined with another element or radical.

**tri|flu|ra|lin** (trī flü′rə lin), *n.* a yellowish-orange solid of low toxicity, used as a weedkiller. *Formula:* $F_3C_{13}H_{16}N_3O_4$

**tri|fo|cal** (trī fō′kəl, trī′fō′-), *adj., n.* —*adj.* having three focuses. Trifocal lenses have three sections of different focal length, one for near, one for intermediate (arm's length), and one for distant vision.
—*n.* a trifocal lens.
**trifocals,** a pair of eyeglasses having trifocal lenses: *old trifocals in a leather case.*
[< *tri-* + *focal;* patterned on *bifocal*]

**tri|foil** (trī′foil), *n.* = trefoil.

**tri|fo|li|ate** (trī fō′lē it, -āt), *adj.* **1** consisting of three leaves or leaflets (used chiefly, in the latter sense, of compound leaves, as a shortened form of *trifoliolate*). **2** having such leaves. Clover is trifoliate. [< *tri-* + Latin *foliātus* leaved < *folium* leaf]

**tri|fo|li|at|ed** (trī fō′lē ā′tid), *adj.* = trifoliate.

**trifoliate orange,** a Chinese orange tree with trifoliate leaves and a very acid, inedible, orange-like fruit. The trifoliate orange is grown as an ornament and as grafting stock for edible citrus fruits.

**tri|fo|li|o|late** (trī fō′lē ə lāt), *adj.* **1** consisting of three leaflets. **2** having leaves of this form; trifoliate.

**tri|fo|li|um** (trī fō′lē əm), *n.* any plant of a group of herbs of the pea family; clover. [< Latin *trifolium* three-layered grass, trefoil < *tri-* three + *folium* leaf. See etym. of doublet **trefoil.**]

**tri|fo|ri|um** (trī fôr′ē əm, -fōr′-), *n., pl.* **-fo|ri|a** (-fôr′ē ə, -fōr′-). a gallery or wall above a side aisle or transept in some large churches; the wall over the arches, occupying the space between the vaulting and roofs of the aisles, below the clerestory, usually consisting chiefly of an arcade, either blind or opening into a gallery. [< Medieval Latin *triforium* arcade, also, trefoil, apparently < Latin *tri-* three + *foris* door]

**tri|form** (trī′fôrm), *adj.* having a triple form; combining three different forms; formed or composed in three parts. [< Latin *triformis* < *tri-* three + *forma* form]

**tri|formed** (trī′fôrmd), *adj.* = triform.

**tri|fur|cate** (*adj.* trī fėr′kit, -kāt; *v.* trī fėr′kāt), *adj., v.,* **-cat|ed, -cat|ing.** —*adj.* divided into three branches like the prongs of a fork.
—*v.t., v.i.* to divide into three parts.
[< Latin *trifurcus* (< *tri-* three + *furca* a (two-pronged) fork) + English *-ate*[1]]

**tri|fur|cat|ed** (trī fėr′kā tid), *adj.* = trifurcate.

**tri|fur|ca|tion** (trī′fər kā′shən), *n.* **1** the state of being trifurcate. **2** a trifurcate shape, formation, or arrangement.

**trig**[1] (trig), *adj., v.,* **trigged, trig|ging.** —*adj.* **1** trim or neat in dress; smartly dressed. SYN: tidy, spruce. **2** smart; stylish: *Trotteur dresses with trig leather belts* (New Yorker). **3** strong; sound; well. **4** precise; exact. **5** smug.
—*v.t.* to make trim or smart: *He has rigged and trigged her with paint and spar* (Rudyard Kipling).
**trig out,** *Especially Scottish.* to dress or deck out: *She had gotten me into her room to see*

**Pronunciation Key:** hat, āge, cãre, fär; let, ēqual, tėrm; it, īce; hot, ōpen, ôrder; oil, out; cup, pu̇t, rüle; child; long; thin; ᴛʜen; zh, measure; ə represents **a** in about, **e** in taken, **i** in pencil, **o** in lemon, **u** in circus.

*that I was trigged out as I should be* (W. Beatty). [Middle English *trigg* trustworthy, steady, in firm condition < Scandinavian (compare Old Icelandic *tryggr* trusty, true)] — **trig'ly**, *adv.* — **trig'ness**, *n.*

**trig**[2] (trig), *n., v.,* **trigged, trig|ging.** — *n.* a wedge, block, or other obstacle used to keep a wheel, cask, or other round object from rolling.
— ***v.t.*** **1** to keep (a wheel or other round object) from rolling by a trig. **2** to support with a trig. [perhaps < Scandinavian (compare Old Icelandic *tryggja* to secure, make firm < *tryggr* firm, trusty)]

**trig**[3] (trig), *n. Informal.* trigonometry.

**trig.**, **1** trigonometric. **2** trigonometry.

**trig|a|mist** (trig'ə mist), *n.* **1** a person who has three wives or three husbands at the same time. **2** (formerly) a person who has been married three times. [< *trigam*(y) + *-ist*]

**trig|a|mous** (trig'ə məs), *adj.* **1** having three wives or three husbands at the same time; guilty of trigamy. **2** involving trigamy. **3** *Botany.* having male, female, and hermaphrodite flowers in the same head. [< Greek *trígamos* (with *-ous*) thrice married < *tri-* three + *gámos* wedding]

**trig|a|my** (trig'ə mē), *n.* the state or offense of having three wives or three husbands at the same time. [< Late Latin *trigamia* < Greek *trígamos;* see etym. under **trigamous**]

**tri|gas|tric** (trī gas'trik), *adj. Anatomy.* having three fleshy bellies, as certain muscles. [< *tri-* + Greek *gastḗr, gastrós* stomach, belly + *-ic*]

**tri|gem|i|nal** (trī jem'ə nəl), *adj., n.* — ***adj.*** of or denoting the fifth pair of cranial nerves, each of which divides into three branches having sensory and motor functions in the face.
— ***n.*** a trigeminal nerve.
[< Latin *trigeminalis* < Latin *trigeminus* born three at a birth < *tri-* three, triply + *geminus* born together]

**trigeminal neuralgia**, = tic douloureux.

**trig|ger** (trig'ər), *n., v.* — ***n.*** **1** the small lever pulled back by the finger in firing a gun. The trigger releases the hammer or other mechanism that fires the gun. **2** a lever that releases a spring when pulled or pressed and sets some mechanism in action. **3** *Figurative.* anything that sets off or initiates something else: *Received from a senate subcommittee a report that violent movies are potential triggers for juvenile delinquency* (Time).
— ***v.t.*** **1** to set off (an explosion): *A spark triggered the explosion. An A-bomb would be needed to "trigger" an H-bomb* (Joint Committee on Atomic Energy). **2** *Informal, Figurative.* to begin; start; initiate: *At present we cannot make rain. We can only trigger it off from suitable clouds* (Science News).
**quick on the trigger, a** quick to shoot: *He is reported so quick on the trigger, that all the other "shootists" in the country have an awe of him* (J. H. Beadle). **b** *Informal, Figurative.* quick to act or respond; mentally alert: *A born musical leader, fertile in ideas, quick on the trigger* (London Daily Chronicle).
[earlier *tricker* < Dutch *trekker* < *trekken* to pull]

**trigger finger**, the finger that presses the trigger of a gun, usually the forefinger.
**have an itchy trigger finger**, to be overanxious to shoot or gun down: *The fugitive was a reckless outlaw with the reputation of having an itchy trigger finger.*

**trig|ger|fish** (trig'ər fish'), *n., pl.* **-fish|es** or (*collectively*) **-fish.** any one of various plectognath fishes, having several strong spines on the dorsal fin.

**trigger guard**, a protective device enclosing the trigger of a firearm.

**trig|ger-hap|py** (trig'ər hap'ē), *adj. Informal.* inclined to shoot or attack at the slightest provocation; overly aggressive or belligerent: *This tiny community is being threatened by the high-spirited lawlessness of a lot of trigger-happy cowboys* (Sunday Times).

**trig|ger|man** (trig'ər man'), *n., pl.* **-men.** *Informal.* a gunman, especially a hired assassin.

**tri|glot** (trī'glot), *adj., n.* — ***adj.*** using or containing three languages; trilingual.
— ***n.*** a triglot book or edition.
[< *tri-* + Greek *glôtta* tongue]

**tri|glyc|er|ide** (trī glis'ə rīd, -ər id), *n.* any fatty compound of a group formed when three acid radicals replace the three hydrogen atoms of the -OH (hydroxyl) groups in glycerol: *Studies indicated that triglycerides may be a cause of coronary artery disease* (Science News Letter).

**tri|glyph** (trī'glif), *n.* a part of a Doric frieze between two metopes, consisting typically of a rectangular block with two vertical grooves and a half groove at each side. [< Latin *triglyphus* < Greek *tríglyphos* < *tri-* three + *glyphḗ* a carving < *glýphein* to carve]

**tri|glyph|ic** (trī glif'ik), *adj.* **1** having to do with a triglyph or triglyphs. **2** consisting of a triglyph or triglyphs. **3** containing three sets of characters or sculptures.

**tri|glyph|i|cal** (trī glif'ə kəl), *adj.* = triglyphic.

**tri|go** (trē'gō), *n.* = wheat. [< Spanish *trigo* < Latin *trīticum* wheat, related to *terere* to rub]

**tri|gon** (trī'gon), *n.* **1** in astrology: **a** a set of three signs of the zodiac, distant 120 degrees from each other, as if at the angles of an equilateral triangle; triplicity. **b** the aspect of two planets distant 120 degrees from each other; trine. **2** = trigonon. **3** = triangle. [< Latin *trigōnum* < Greek *trígōnon* triangle < *tri-* three + *-gōnos* angled < *gōniā* angle]

**trigon.**, **1** trigonometric. **2** trigonometry.

**trig|o|nal** (trig'ə nəl), *adj.* **1** (in astrology) of the nature of or having to do with a trigon. **2** (of a crystal) having triangular faces. **3** = triangular. — **trig'o|nal|ly**, *adv.*

**trig|o|nom|e|ter** (trig'ə nom'ə tər), *n.* an instrument for measuring sides and angles in a plane right triangle.

**trig|o|no|met|ric** (trig'ə nə met'rik), *adj.* of or having to do with trigonometry; based on or resulting from trigonometry: *trigonometric measurements.*

**trig|o|no|met|ri|cal** (trig'ə nə met'rə kəl), *adj.* = trigonometric.

**trig|o|no|met|ri|cal|ly** (trig'ə nə met'rə klē), *adv.* by or according to trigonometry.

**trigonometric function**, *Mathematics.* any one of the fundamental functions of an angle or arc that may be defined as ratios of the sides of a right triangle; circular function. The sine, cosine, tangent, cotangent, secant, and cosecant are trigonometric functions.

**trigonometric series**, *Mathematics.* an infinite series whose terms contain sines and cosines of angles.

**trig|o|nom|e|try** (trig'ə nom'ə trē), *n., pl.* **-tries.** **1** the branch of mathematics that deals with the relations between the sides and angles of triangles and the calculations based on these, particularly with certain functions, such as the sine, secant, and tangent. *Abbr:* trig. **2** a book on this subject. [< New Latin *trigonometria* < Greek *trígōnon* (see etym. under **trigon**) + *métron* a measure]

**tri|go|non** (trī gō'non), *n.* a kind of many-stringed psaltery or harp, triangular in form, originated by the ancient Greeks and borrowed by the Romans. [< Greek *trígōnon;* see etym. under **trigon**]

**trig|o|nous** (trig'ə nəs), *adj.* having three prominent angles, as a plant stem or ovary. [< Greek *trígōnos* (< *tri-* three + *gōniā* angle) + English *-ous*]

**tri|gram** (trī'gram), *n.* = trigraph.

**tri|graph** (trī'graf, -gräf), *n.* **1** a combination of three letters used to represent a single sound. The *eau* in *beau* is a trigraph. **2** any combination of three letters, such as may be used in a cryptogram. [< *tri-* + *-graph*]

**tri|graph|ic** (trī graf'ik), *adj.* having to do with a trigraph.

**tri|he|dral** (trī hē'drəl), *adj. Geometry.* **1** having, or formed by, three planes meeting at a point: *a trihedral angle.* **2** having, or formed by, three lateral planes: *a trihedral prism.* [< *tri-* + Greek *hédra* seat, base + English *-al*[1]]

***tri|he|dron** (trī hē'drən), *n., pl.* **-drons, -dra** (-drə). *Geometry.* a figure formed by three planes meeting at a point. [< *trihedr*(al) + *-on,* as in *polyhedron*]

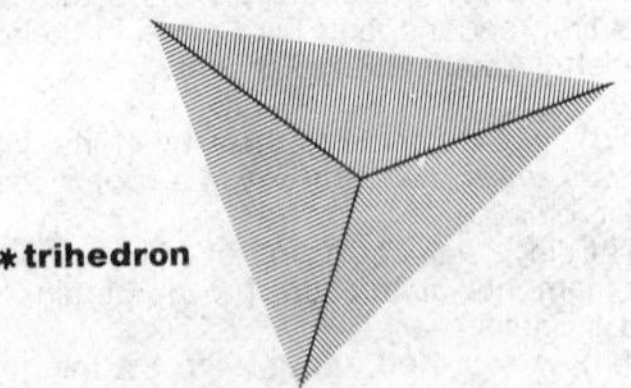

***trihedron**

**tri|hy|dric** (trī hī'drik), *adj.* = trihydroxy.

**tri|hy|drox|y** (trī'hī drok'sē), *adj. Chemistry.* having three hydroxyl (-OH) radicals.

**tri|i|o|do|thy|ro|nine** (trī ī'ə dō thī'rə nēn, -nin), *n.* an amino acid secreted by the thyroid gland or prepared synthetically, used in treating hypothyroid conditions. *Formula:* $C_{15}H_{12}I_3NO_4$ [< *tri-* + *iodo-* + *thyro*(id) + (ala)*nine*]

**tri|jet** (trī'jet'), *n., adj.* — ***n.*** an aircraft with three jet engines.
— ***adj.*** having three jet engines: *a trijet airbus.*

**tri|ju|gate** (trī'jù gāt; trī jü'git, -gāt), *adj. Botany.* (of a pinnate leaf) having three pairs of leaflets. [< Latin *trijugus* threefold]

**tri|ju|gous** (trī'jù gəs, trī jü'-), *adj.* = trijugate.

**trike** (trīk), *n. Informal.* a tricycle. [short for *tricycle*]

**tri|lat|er|al** (trī lat'ər əl), *adj.* **1** having three sides. **2** binding or involving three parties: *a trilateral agreement.* — **tri|lat'er|al|ly**, *adv.*

**tri|lat|er|al|ism** (trī lat'ər ə liz'əm), *n.* a policy of fostering close cooperation between three nations or regions, especially such a policy applied to Western Europe, Japan, and North America: *Trilateralism ... wants closer interaction, and, if possible, a united foreign front by the industrial nations of the non-Communist world* (Manchester Guardian). — **tri|lat'er|al|ist**, *n.*

**tri|lat|er|al|i|ty** (trī lat'ər al'ə tē), *n.* trilateral condition or quality.

**tri|lat|er|a|tion** (trī lat'ə rā'shən), *n.* (in surveying and mapping) the establishment of a network of triangles by measuring all sides of each, rather than one side and two angles as in triangulation.

**tril|by** (tril'bē), *n., pl.* **-bies.** = trilby hat.

**trilby hat**, a soft felt hat, especially one of the Homburg type, with a narrow brim and indented crown. [< *Trilby,* the heroine of the novel by George du Maurier, published in 1894]

**tri|lem|ma** (trī lem'ə), *n.* **1** a form of argument resembling the dilemma, but involving three alternatives instead of two. **2** a situation requiring a choice of one of three alternatives.

**tri|lin|e|ar** (trī lin'ē ər), *adj. Mathematics.* **1** of or involving three lines. **2** contained by three lines.

**tri|lin|gual** (trī ling'gwəl), *adj.* **1** able to speak three languages: *a trilingual person.* **2** using three languages: *Switzerland is a trilingual country.* **3** written or expressed in three languages: *a trilingual text.* [< Latin *trilinguis* trilingual (< *tri-* three + *lingua* language, tongue) + English *-al*[1]] — **tri|lin'gual|ly**, *adv.*

**tri|lit|er|al** (trī lit'ər əl), *adj., n.* — ***adj.*** **1** consisting of three letters. **2** consisting of three consonants.
— ***n.*** a triliteral word or root.

**tri|lit|er|al|ism** (trī lit'ər ə liz'əm), *n.* the use of triliteral roots, as in Semitic languages.

**tri|lith** (trī'lith), *n.* a prehistoric structure or monument consisting of two large, upright stones with another stone resting upon them like a lintel. [< Greek *trílithon,* neuter of *trílithos* of three stones < *tri-* three + *líthos* stone]

**tri|lith|ic** (trī lith'ik), *adj.* **1** having to do with a trilith. **2** of the nature of a trilith.

**tri|li|thon** (trī'lə thon), *n.* = trilith.

***trill**[1] (tril), *v., n.* — ***v.t., v.i.*** **1** to sound or speak with a tremulous, vibrating, high-pitched sound: *The child burst in, trilling with laughter* (Rudyard Kipling). **2** to sing with a tremulous vibration of sound: *to trill an aria. Some birds trill their songs.* **3** to play so as to make such a sound: *to trill on a flute.* **4** *Phonetics.* to pronounce with a trill: *He trilled his "r's" when he spoke.*
— ***n.*** **1** the act or sound of trilling: *the trill of a wren.* **2a** a quick alternation of two musical tones either a tone or a half tone apart; shake. **b** a tremolo or vibrato. **3** *Phonetics.* **a** a sound produced by causing the breath stream to produce rapid vibration of the lips, tongue, or uvula, as in certain pronunciations of *r.* **b** the rapid vibration of one of these organs. **c** a consonant so pronounced. Spanish *rr* is a trill.
[< Italian *trillare;* probably imitative] — **trill'er**, *n.*

***trill**[1]
definition 2a

**trill**[2] (tril), *v.t., v.i. Archaic.* to trickle. [perhaps < Scandinavian (compare Norwegian, Swedish *trilla* to roll, trundle)]

**tril|lion** (tril'yən), *n., adj.* **1** (in the U.S., Canada, and France) 1 followed by 12 zeros; one thousand billions. **2** (in Great Britain and Germany) 1 followed by 18 zeros; one billion billions. [Middle English *trillion* < *tri-* three; patterned on *million*]

**tril|lionth** (tril'yənth), *adj., n.* — ***adj.*** **1** being last in order of a series of a trillion. **2** being one of a trillion equal parts. — ***n.*** one of a trillion equal parts; the quotient of unity divided by a trillion.

**tril|li|um** (tril'ē əm), *n.* a plant with three leaves in a whorl, from the center of which rises a single flower; wake-robin. The leaves are short-stalked or stalkless, and the stem is unbranched. Trilliums comprise a genus of perennial herbs of the lily family. [< New Latin *trillium* < Latin *tri-* three]

**tri|lo|bal** (trī lō'bəl, trī'lə-), *adj.* = trilobate.

**tri|lo|bate** (trī lō'bāt, trī'lə-), *adj.* having or divided into three lobes: *a trilobate leaf.*

**tri|lo|bat|ed** (trī lō'bā tid), *adj.* = trilobate.

**tri|lobed** (trī'lōbd'), *adj.* = trilobate.

**tri|lo|bite** (trī'lə bīt), *n.* a small, extinct, marine arthropod of the Paleozoic era, with jointed legs and a body divided into three vertical lobes and many horizontal segments. Small fossil trilobites are widely found in various rocks. They are believed related to the crustaceans. [< New Latin *trilobita,* plural < Greek *tri-* three + *lobós* lobe]

**tri|lo|bit|ic** (trī′lə bit′ik), *adj.* **1** of or having to do with trilobites. **2** having the character of trilobites or affinity with them. **3** containing trilobites.

**tri|loc|u|lar** (trī lok′yə lər), *adj.* having three cells or compartments, as the capsule of a plant, or the heart of a reptile.

**tril|o|gy** (tril′ə jē), *n., pl.* **-gies. 1** a group of three novels which together form a related series, although each is complete in itself. **2** three plays, operas, or other works, written by the same person and more or less closely related in theme or subject. **3** a group of three tragedies by the same author, originally always closely related in subject, written for performance in series during the festival of Dionysus in ancient Athens. [< Greek *trilogiā* < *tri-* three + *lógos* story]

**trim** (trim), *v.,* **trimmed, trim|ming,** *adj.,* **trim|mer, trim|mest,** *n., adv.* **—*v.t.* 1** to make neat by cutting away parts: *The gardener trimmed the hedge. The barber trimmed my hair.* **2** to put in good order; tidy: *to trim up a room.* **3** to dress or shape (lumber): *The carpenter trimmed the lumber with a plane.* **4** to remove (parts that are not needed or not neat) by clipping, pruning, paring, or otherwise removing; cut: *to trim off dead branches, to trim dead leaves off plants;* (*Figurative.*) *to trim one's budget, to trim excess production.* **SYN:** clip, prune. **5** to decorate; adorn: *to trim a dress with braid. The children were trimming the Christmas tree.* **SYN:** deck, garnish. **6** to cause (a vessel) to float on an even keel by arranging the load carried. **7** to distribute or arrange (cargo, ballast, or people) in a vessel to make it float evenly. **8** to adjust the relative buoyancy of (a submarine) by taking or expelling water from tanks in the hull. **9** to balance (an aircraft) so that it maintains level flight with main controls in neutral positions. **10** to adjust (the controls of an aircraft) so as to bring this about. **11** to arrange (sails) to fit the direction of the wind and the course to be sailed. **12** *Figurative.* to change (opinions, positions, or the like) to suit circumstances. **13** *Informal, Figurative.* to defeat, especially overwhelmingly; beat. **14** *Informal, Figurative.* to cheat; fleece. **15** *Informal, Figurative.* to scold; rebuke. **16** *Obsolete.* to equip.

**—*v.i.* 1** to be or keep in balance, especially to assume a specified position in the water, owing to the distribution of cargo, ballast, or the amount of water in the tanks of a submarine. **2** to adjust sails to fit the direction of the wind and the course of the ship. **3** *Figurative.* to maintain a middle course or balance between opposing interests; adapt oneself to prevailing opinions, conditions, or the like.

**—*adj.* 1** in good condition or order; tidy and pleasing to the eye; neat: *A trim maid greeted us. The entire family works together to keep a trim house.* **SYN:** See syn. under **neat. 2** well designed and maintained: *a trim little ketch.* **3** *Obsolete.* pretty; handsome.

**—*n.* 1** proper condition: *Is our team in trim for the game?* **2** good order: *to put one's affairs in trim.* **3** condition; order: *that ship is in poor trim for a voyage.* **4** a clipping, paring, or dressing to make neat: *The hedge needs a trim. I asked the barber for a trim.* **5** trimming; decoration: *the trim on a dress.* **6** equipment; outfit. **7** the condition, manner, or degree of horizontal balance of a ship in the water. **8** the difference in the draft at the bow from that at the stern of a ship. **9** the fitness or readiness of a ship for sailing as affected by the cargo, masts, sails, and other distribution of weight. **10** the position or angle of the sails in relation to the direction of the wind. **11** the relative buoyancy of a submarine, controlled by taking in or expelling water from tanks in the hull: *to submerge to 100 feet and correct the trim.* **12** the attitude of an aircraft relative to the horizontal plane when it is balanced in flight at a particular altitude with regard to prevailing winds. **13** the visible woodwork inside a building, especially that around doors, windows, and other openings. **14** the woodwork on the outside of a building used as ornamentation or finish. **15** the upholstery, handles, and accessories inside an automobile. **16** the chrome, color scheme, and other decorations on the outside of an automobile. **17** a display in a store window; window display. **18** film that is trimmed away and discarded, as in editing.

**—*adv.*** *Archaic.* in a trim manner; neatly; accurately.

[probably Old English *trymman* strengthen, make ready] **—trim′ly,** *adv.* **—trim′ness,** *n.*

**tri|ma|ran** (trī′mə ran′), *n.* a sailboat with three hulls set side by side: *Trimarans ... make good family boats because they don't roll and heel in rough weather* (Maclean's). [< *tri-* + (cata)*maran*]

**tri|mer** (trī′mər), *n. Chemistry.* **1** a molecule formed by combining three identical smaller molecules. *Example:* $C_6H_6$ or $(C_2H_2)_3$ is a trimer formed by combining three molecules of $C_2H_2$. **2** a compound consisting of trimers. [< *tri-* + Greek *méros* part]

**trim|er|ous** (trim′ər əs), *adj.* **1** having or consisting of three parts. **2** characterized by three parts. **3** *Botany.* (of a flower) having three members in each whorl (generally written *3-merous*). **4** *Zoology.* having three segments to each tarsus, as certain insects. [< New Latin *trimerus* (with English *-ous*) < Greek *trimerḗs* < *tri-* three + *méros* part]

**tri|mes|ter** (trī mes′tər), *n.* **1** a period or term of three months. **2** a division (usually one third) of a school year. [< French *trimestre,* learned borrowing from Latin *trimēstris* of three months' duration < *tri-* three + *mēnsis* month]

**tri|mes|tral** (trī mes′trəl), *adj.* **1** consisting of or containing three months. **2** occurring or appearing every three months.

**tri|mes|tri|al** (trī mes′trē əl), *adj.* = trimestral.

**trim|e|ter** (trim′ə tər), *n., adj. Prosody.* **—*n.* 1** a line of verse having three metrical feet. *Example:* "Below/the light/house top." **2** a verse in Greek or Latin poetry containing three dipodies (six feet).

**—*adj.*** consisting of three feet or three dipodies. [< Latin *trimetrus* < Greek *trímetros* < *tri-* three + *métron* a measure]

**tri|meth|yl** (trī meth′əl), *adj. Chemistry.* having three methyl ($-CH_3$) radicals.

**tri|meth|yl|a|mine** (trī meth′ə lə mēn′, -lam′in), *n.* a colorless gas or liquid with a strong odor of ammonia, used in organic synthesis and as an insect attractant. *Formula:* $C_3H_9N$

**tri|met|ric** (trī met′rik), *adj.* **1** consisting of three measures; trimeter. **2** *Crystallography.* orthorhombic.

**tri|met|ri|cal** (trī met′rə kəl), *adj.* = trimetric.

**trimetric projection,** *Geometry.* the projection of a solid using different scales at arbitrarily chosen angles for its three dimensions.

**tri|met|ro|gon** (trī met′rə gon), *n.* a system of photographic mapping from the air, in which one camera photographs the area vertically and two obliquely, operating simultaneously at regular intervals. [< *tri-* + Greek *métron* measure + *gōniā* angle]

**trim|ma|ble** (trim′ə bəl), *adj.* that can be trimmed.

**trim|mer** (trim′ər), *n.* **1** a person or thing that trims: *a hat trimmer, a window trimmer, a hedge trimmer.* **2** *Figurative.* a person who changes his opinions, actions, or positions to suit the circumstances: *One of the trimmers who went to church and chapel both* (Thomas Hardy). **SYN:** timeserver. **3** a machine for trimming edges, as of lumber. **4** a long beam or timber to which the end of a header is attached in the frame around a window, chimney, or other opening.

**trim|ming** (trim′ing), *n., adj.* **—*n.* 1** anything used to trim or decorate; ornament; decoration: *trimmings for a Christmas tree, trimming for a dress.* **2** *Informal, Figurative.* a defeat, especially an overwhelming defeat; beating. **3** *Informal, Figurative.* a scolding. **4** the act of a person or thing that trims.

**—*adj.*** that trims.

**trimmings, a** parts cut away in trimming, clipping, paring, or pruning; scraps: *the trimmings of any game ... may be used for making the ... sauce* (Alexis Soyer). **b** *Informal.* additional or special items needed to make a festive meal or occasion: *a banquet with all the trimmings. We ate turkey with all the trimmings.*

**trimming tab,** an auxiliary surface hinged at the trailing edge of a control surface of an aircraft, used to make small adjustments in stabilizing flight.

**tri|mo|lec|u|lar** (trī′mə lik′yə lər), *adj. Chemistry.* of or made out of three molecules.

**tri|month|ly** (trī munth′lē), *adj.* occurring once every three months.

**tri|morph** (trī′môrf), *n. Crystallography.* **1** a trimorphic substance. **2** any one of its three different forms.

**tri|mor|phic** (trī môr′fik), *adj.* existing in or assuming three distinct forms; exhibiting trimorphism.

**tri|mor|phism** (trī môr′fiz əm), *n.* **1** the occurrence in three different forms of a crystalline substance. **2** *Zoology.* the occurrence of three forms distinct in color, size, structure, or function, in different individuals of a species. **3** *Botany.* the occurrence of three distinct forms of flowers, leaves, or other parts, on the same plant or in the same species. [< Greek *trímorphos* three-formed (< *tri-* three + *morphḗ* form) + English *-ism*]

**tri|mor|phous** (trī môr′fəs), *adj.* = trimorphic.

**tri|mo|tor** (trī′mō′tər), *n.* an airplane fitted with three motors: *The old Ford trimotor, the ... monoplane with the corrugated aluminum sides, was perhaps the first truly modern air transport* (Newsweek).

**trim size,** *Printing.* the size of the pages of a book after their edges have been trimmed; final size of a book's pages.

**Tri|mur|ti** (tri mür′tē), *n.* the three chief Hindu divinities (Brahma, Vishnu, and Siva) as a trinitarian unity, or threefold manifestation of the primary essence of divinity. [< Sanskrit *trimūrti* < *tri* three + *mūrti* shape]

**Tri|nac|ri|an** (tri nak′rē ən, trī-), *adj.* of Sicily; Sicilian. [< Latin *Trīnacria* Sicily]

**tri|nal** (trī′nəl), *adj.* composed of three parts; threefold; triple: *Trinal Unity* (Milton). [< Late Latin *trīnālis* < Latin *trīnus;* see etym. under **trine**]

**tri|na|ry** (trī′nər ē), *adj.* = ternary.

**trin|dle** (trin′dəl), *n., v.,* **-dled, -dling.** *Obsolete or Dialect.* **—*n.* 1** the wheel of a wheelbarrow. **2** any small wheel or caster; trundle. **3** something of rounded form, as a ball. **—*v.t., v.i.*** = trundle. [variant of Old English *trendel* a wheel, anything round, related to *trendan* to turn. Compare etym. under **trundle.**]

**trine** (trīn), *adj., n.* **—*adj.* 1** threefold; triple. **2** in astrology: **a** of or denoting the aspect of two heavenly bodies distant from each other 120 degrees, or the third part of the zodiac. **b** connected with or relating to this aspect, and therefore benign or favorable.

**—*n.* 1** a group of three; triad. **2** (in astrology) the trine aspect, supposed to be benign; trigon. [< Latin *trīnus* triple < *trēs, tria* three]

**Trine** (trīn), *n.* = Trinity. [< *trine*]

**trine immersion,** the immersion of a person three times in baptism, once in the name of each person of the Trinity.

**trin|gle** (tring′gəl), *n.* **1** a curtain rod. **2** any long, slender rod. **3** *Architecture.* a narrow, straight molding. [< Middle French *tringle,* Old French *tingle* beam; origin uncertain]

**Trin|i|dad|i|an** (trin′ə dad′ē ən), *adj., n.* **—*adj.*** of or having to do with Trinidad, an island in the West Indies near Venezuela, or its people.

**—*n.*** a native or inhabitant of Thinidad.

**Trin|i|tar|i|an** (trin′ə tãr′ē ən), *adj., n.* **—*adj.* 1** believing in the Trinity; orthodox in Christian belief. **2** of or having to do with the Trinity. **3** of or having to do with those who believe in the Trinity.

**—*n.* 1** a person who believes in the Trinity. **2** a friar or nun of the Roman Catholic Order of the Holy Trinity, a teaching and nursing fraternity originally founded in 1198 to ransom Christian captives from the Moslems.

[< New Latin *trinitarius* (< Latin *trīnitās;* see etym. under **Trinity**) + English *-an*]

**trin|i|tar|i|an** (trin′ə tãr′ē ən), *adj.* forming a trinity; consisting of or involving three in one; triple; threefold.

**Trin|i|tar|i|an|ism** (trin′ə tãr′ē ə niz′əm), *n.* the doctrine of Trinitarians; belief in the Trinity.

**tri|ni|tro|ben|zene** (trī nī′trō ben′zēn, -ben zēn′), *n.* a yellow, crystalline compound used as an explosive. *Formula:* $C_6H_3N_3O_6$ [< *tri-* + *nitro-* + *benzene*]

**tri|ni|tro|cre|sol** (trī nī′trō krē′sōl, -sol), *n.* a soluble, yellow, crystalline substance, used in the manufacture of certain antiseptics and explosives. *Formula:* $C_7H_5N_3O_7$

**tri|ni|tro|tol|u|ene** (trī nī′trō tol′yü ēn), *n.* a powerful explosive, known as TNT. *Formula:* $C_7H_5N_3O_6$ [< *tri-* three + *nitro-* + *tolu*(ol) + *-ene*]

**tri|ni|tro|tol|u|ol** (trī nī′trō tol′yü ōl, -ol), *n.* = trinitrotoluene.

**Trin|i|ty** (trin′ə tē), *n., pl.* **-ties. 1** the union of the Father, the Son, and the Holy Ghost in one divine nature; the triple person, separate but united, composed of these three persons; God: *the Holy Trinity.* **2** = Trinity Sunday. [< Old French *trinite,* learned borrowing from Latin *trīnitās* < *trīnus;* see etym. under **trine**]

**trin|i|ty** (trin′ə tē), *n., pl.* **-ties. 1** a group of three; triad. **2** the fact or state of being three. **3** a picture or sculpture of the Trinity, usually a symbol like the triangle or trefoil. [< *Trinity*]

**Trinity Season,** the season of the church year between Trinity Sunday and Advent Sunday.

**Trinity Sunday,** the eighth Sunday after Easter and the first after Pentecost, observed by Christians as a feast in honor of the Trinity.

**trin|ket** (tring′kit), *n., v.* **—*n.* 1** any small fancy article, bit of jewelry, or the like: *The baby played with the trinkets on her bracelet. There was nothing personal anywhere: no photographs, no books, no trinkets of any kind* (Graham Greene). **SYN:** knickknack. **2** a trifle: *The world's a jest and joy's a trinket* (James K. Stephens). **SYN:** bagatelle.

**—*v.i.*** to scheme secretly; intrigue: *to trinket with one's enemies.*

---

**Pronunciation Key:** hat, āge, cãre, fär; let, ēqual, tėrm; it, īce; hot, ōpen, ôrder; **oi**l, **ou**t; cup, pu̇t, rüle; **ch**ild; lo**ng**; **th**in; **ᴛʜ**en; **zh**, measure; ə represents **a** in about, **e** in taken, **i** in pencil, **o** in lemon, **u** in circus.

trinkets, *Obsolete.* the tools, implements, or tackle of an occupation; paraphernalia; accouterments: *The poorer sort of common soldiers have every man his leather bag or satchel well sewn together, wherein he packs up all his trinkets* (Richard Hakluyt).
[origin uncertain] —**trin′ket|er,** *n.*

**trin|ket|ry** (tring′kə trē), *n.* small articles of ornament; trinkets.

**trin|kum** (tring′kəm), *n. Dialect.* trinket. [alteration of *trinket*]

**tri|nod|al** (trī nō′dəl), *adj.* having three nodes or joints. [< Latin *trinōdis* (< *tri-* three + *nōdus* knot, node) + English *-al*[1]]

**tri|no|mi|al** (trī nō′mē əl), *n., adj.* —*n.* **1** *Algebra.* an expression consisting of three terms connected by plus or minus signs. $a + bx^2 - 2$ is a trinomial. **2** *Zoology, Botany.* a scientific name of an animal or plant consisting of three terms, the first indicating the genus, the second the species, and the third the subspecies or variety. *Malus prunifolia robusta* is a trinomial.
—*adj.* consisting of three terms.
[< *tri-* + *-nomial;* patterned on *binomial*] —**tri|no′mi|al|ly,** *adv.*

**tri|no|mi|al|ism** (trī nō′mē ə liz′əm), *n. Biology.* the trinomial system of nomenclature; the use of trinomial names.

**tri|nu|cle|o|tide** (trī nü′klē ə tīd, -nyü′-; -tid), *n.* a substance formed by the combination of three nucleotides; triplet: *Each amino acid can be coded by a trinucleotide containing three specific bases* (Albert L. Lehninger).

**tri|o** (trē′ō), *n., pl.* **tri|os.** **1a** a piece of music for three voices or instruments. **b** a group of three singers or players performing together. **c** the second or subordinate division of a scherzo, march, minuet, or other dance movement, usually in a different key or style. The main division is usually repeated after it. **2** any group of three: *a trio of rusted tools bound by a funereal ribbon* (Esquire). [< Italian *trio* < *tre* three < Latin *trēs, tria* three]

**tri|ode** (trī′ōd), *n.* a vacuum tube containing three elements, commonly a cathode, anode (plate), and control grid. [< *tri-* + *-ode,* as in *cathode*]

**tri|oe|cious** (trī ē′shəs), *adj. Botany.* designating a genus or other group in which male, female, and hermaphrodite flowers occur, each on different plants. Also, **triecious.** [< New Latin *Trioecia* the order name < Greek *tri-* three + *oîkos* house] —**tri|oe′cious|ly,** *adv.*

**tri|oi|cous** (trī oi′kəs), *adj.* = trioecious.

**tri|ol** (trī′ōl), *n.* a trihydroxy alcohol, such as glycerol. [< *tri-* + *-ol*[1]]

**tri|o|let** (trī′ə lit), *n.* a poem having eight lines and only two rhymes. Lines 1, 4, and 7 are the same. Lines 2 and 8 are the same. [< Middle French *triolet* (diminutive) < *trio* three < Italian; see etym. under **trio**]

**Tri|o|nal** (trī′ə nəl), *n. Trademark.* a hypnotic resembling sulfonmethane, with highly toxic properties. *Formula:* $C_8H_{18}O_4S_2$ [< *tri-* + (sulph)*onal*]

**tri|o|nym** (trī′ə nim), *n.* a name consisting of three terms; trinomial. [< Greek *triṓnymos* having three names < *tri-* three + *ónyma* name]

**tri|ose** (trī′ōs), *n.* any of a class of sugars containing three atoms of carbon, and produced from glycerin by oxidation.

**tri|ox|id** (trī ok′sid), *n.* = trioxide.

**tri|ox|ide** (trī ok′sīd, -sid), *n. Chemistry.* an oxide containing three atoms of oxygen in each molecule.

**trip**[1] (trip), *n., v.,* **tripped, trip|ping.** —*n.* **1** the action of traveling about; journey, voyage, or excursion: *a trip to Europe, a short business trip.* **2** a journey or run made by a ship, train, airplane, or other conveyance, between two places, or to a place and back again (a round trip). **3** a stumble or misstep caused by striking the foot against an object. **4** the act of catching a person's foot to throw him down, especially in wrestling. **5** *Figurative.* a mistake or blunder; slip; lapse. **6** the act of stepping lightly and quickly; light, quick tread. **7a** a device that releases a catch, lever, or cog, in a machine. **b** a projecting part, catch, or the like which comes into contact with another part so as to start or stop a movement. **c** the act of starting or stopping a movement in this way. **8** *Slang.* **a** the mental state or experience induced by hallucinogenic drugs, such as LSD: *a psychedelic trip, a bad trip, an acid trip.* **b** any overly stimulating or exhilarating state or experience: *The students … once accused him of being on a Machievallian power trip* (New Yorker). **c** any experience: *You may feel something with the audience, but what they feel with you—that's another trip* (Barry Melton). [< verb]
—*v.i.* **1** to strike the foot against something so as to stagger or fall; stumble: *to trip over a toy. He tripped on the stairs.* **2** *Figurative.* to make a mistake; do something wrong; be inconsistent or inaccurate, as in a statement; err: *He tripped on that difficult question.* **3** to take light, quick steps; move with a light, quick tread: *The children were tripping down the path to meet us.* SYN: skip, caper. **4** to tilt or tip up. **5** to move past or be released by the pallet, as a cog on an escapement wheel of a watch or clock. **6** to journey. **7** *Slang.* Often, **trip out.** to experience the hallucinatory effects of LSD or other psychedelic drug: *Dr. Jekyll tripped out on a mysterious powder and ended up as the nefarious Mr. Hyde* (Science News).
—*v.t.* **1** to cause to stumble or fall: *The loose board on the stairs tripped me.* **2** *Figurative.* to cause to make a mistake or blunder: *Father tripped me by that question.* **3** to overthrow by catching in a mistake or blunder; outwit. **4** *Figurative.* to detect in an inconsistency or inaccuracy: *The examining board tripped him up several times.* **5** to perform (a dance) with a light, quick step. **6** to tread lightly and quickly. **7** *Nautical.* **a** to lift (an anchor) free of the bottom. **b** to turn (a yard) into a vertical position before lowering. **c** to lift (an upper mast) enough to remove the pin before lowering to the deck or into its housing. **8a** to release (a catch, lever, clutch, or the like), as by contact with a projection. **b** to operate, start, or set free (as a mechanism or weight) in this way.
[< Old French *tripper* strike with the feet < Germanic (compare Middle Dutch *trippen*)]
—*Syn. n.* **1 Trip, journey, voyage** mean a traveling from one place to another. **Trip** is the general word, often suggesting a run between two places, but not suggesting the length, purpose, manner, or means of travel: *It's only a half-hour's trip from here to the bank.* **Journey** suggests a long or tiring trip by land to a place for a definite purpose: *He decided to make the journey to Mexico by car.* **Voyage** suggests a long trip by water: *The voyage to the Islands will be restful.*

**trip**[2] (trip), *n.* a small group of certain animals: *a trip of goats or seals.* [origin uncertain]

**TRIP** (trip), *adj.* having to do with or designating a steel alloy of great strength and high ductility, produced by deformation of the steel at very high temperatures: *TRIP steel, the TRIP Process.* [< *Tr*(ansformation)-*I*(nduced) *P*(lasticity)]

**tri|pack** (trī′pak′), *n.* a pack of three films or plates in color photography, each sensitive to a different color, superimposed and exposed simultaneously.

**tri|part|ed** (trī pär′tid), *adj.* divided into three parts.

**tri|par|tite** (trī pär′tīt), *adj.* **1** divided into or composed of three parts; threefold; triple. **2** involving division into three parts. **3** *Botany.* divided into three parts nearly to the base: *a tripartite leaf.* **4** having three corresponding parts or copies, as an indenture drawn up between three persons or parties, each of whom preserves one of the copies. **5** made or shared by three parties: *a tripartite treaty between the United States, Great Britain, and France.* **6** consisting of or involving three parties: *a tripartite league.* [< Latin *tripartītus* < *tri-* three + *partītus,* past participle of *partīrī* to divide < *pars, partis* share, portion] —**tri|par′tite|ly,** *adv.*

**tri|par|ti|tion** (trī′pär tish′ən), *n.* **1** division into three parts. **2** partition among three. **3** *Obsolete.* arithmetical division by three.

**tripe** (trīp), *n.* **1** the walls of the first and second stomachs of an ox, steer, or cow, used as food. The first stomach or rumen is plain tripe, and the second or reticulum is honeycomb tripe. **2** *Informal, Figurative.* something foolish, worthless, or offensive; nonsensical rubbish; trash. [< Old French *tripe* entrails, perhaps ultimately < Arabic *tharb* suet]

**tri|pe|dal** (trī′pə dəl, trī pē′-; trip′ə-), *adj.* having three feet. [< Latin *tripedālis* of three feet (in length) < *tri-* three + *pēs, pedis* foot]

**tripe-de-roche** (trēp′də rôsh′), *n.* any one of various edible lichens of arctic subarctic, and north temperate regions. [< French *tripe-de-roche* (literally) rock tripe (because of its appearance)]

**tri|per|son|al** (trī pėr′sə nəl), *adj.* **1** consisting of or existing in three persons (used of the Godhead). **2** relating to the three persons of the Godhead.

**tri|pet|al|ous** (trī pet′ə ləs), *adj.* having three petals.

**trip|ham|mer** (trip′ham′ər), *n., adj.* —*n.* a heavy iron or steel block raised by machinery, tripped by a cam or other mechanism, and allowed to drop, used in foundries and machine shops.
—*adj.* of or like a triphammer, especially with regard to power of impact: *a triphammer blow.*

**tri|phen|yl** (trī fen′əl, -fē′nəl), *adj., n.* —*adj.* having three phenyl radicals in the molecule.
—*n.* a triphenyl compound. *Formula:* $(—C_6H_5)_3$

**tri|phen|yl|meth|ane** (trī fen′əl meth′ān, -fē′nəl-), *n.* a colorless hydrocarbon, used in the manufacture of many synthetic dyes. *Formula:* $C_{19}H_{16}$

**tri|phib|i|an** (trī fib′ē ən), *adj., n.* —*adj.* = triphibious. —*n.* a triphibious airplane.

**tri|phib|i|ous** (trī fib′ē əs), *adj.* **1** involving land, sea, and air forces in a single action. **2** operating on land, water, and in the air: *a triphibious vehicle or craft.* [< *tri-* + (am)*phibious*]

**tri|phos|phate** (trī fos′fāt), *n.* a substance whose molecule contains three phosphate ($PO_4$) radicals.

**tri|phos|pho|pyr|i|dine nucleotide** (trī fos′fō-pir′ə dēn), a coenzyme that speeds the oxidation of living plant and animal tissues. It is similar in function to diphosphopyridine nucleotide. *Formula:* $C_{21}H_{28}N_7O_{17}P_3$ *Abbr:* TPN (no periods).

**triph|thong** (trip′thông, trif′-; -thong), *n.* **1** a combination of three vowel sounds in one syllable. **2** = trigraph. [< *tri-,* patterned on *diphthong*]

**triph|thong|al** (trip thông′gəl, trif-; -thong′-), *adj.* of or like a triphthong.

**triph|y|line** (trif′ə lin, -lēn), *n.* = triphylite.

**triph|y|lite** (trif′ə līt), *n.* a phosphate of iron, manganese, and lithium, occurring in greenish-gray or bluish crystals. [< *tri-* three + Greek *phȳlḗ* tribe + English *-ite*[1] (because it has three bases)]

**tri|phyl|lous** (trī fil′əs), *adj. Botany.* having or consisting of three leaves. [< *tri-* + Greek *phýllon* leaf + English *-ous*]

**tri|pin|nate** (trī pin′āt), *adj. Botany.* triply pinnate (applied to a bipinnate leaf whose divisions are also pinnate). —**tri|pin′nate|ly,** *adv.*

**tri|pin|nat|ed** (trī pin′ā tid), *adj. Botany.* tripinnate.

**tri|plane** (trī′plān′), *n.* an airplane having three sets of wings, one above another.

**tri|ple** (trip′əl), *adj., n., v.,* **-pled, -pling.** —*adj.* **1** three times as much or as many; of three times the measure or amount; multiplied by three: *a triple portion of cake.* **2** having three parts; threefold: *a triple crown.* **3** consisting of or involving three parties.
—*n.* **1** a number or amount that is three times as much or as large: *Nine is the triple of three.* **2** a hit in baseball by which a batter gets to third base.
—*v.t.* to make three times as much or as many; multiply by three: *to triple one's income. My older brother has tripled the number of lawns he mows each week.* —*v.i.* **1** to become three times as much or as many: *His savings have tripled in the past twenty years.* **2** to serve three purposes; play three parts: *Chiffon middy ties can triple as scarves, stoles, and sashes* (New Yorker). **3** to hit safely for three bases in baseball.
[< Latin *triplus* < *tri-* three + *-plus* -fold. See etym. of doublet **treble.**]

**tri|ple-A** (trip′əl ā′), *adj.* of the highest financial rank: *a triple-A credit rating, triple-A securities.*

**triple bond,** *Chemistry.* a bond in which three pairs of electrons are shared between two atoms, characteristic of unsaturated compounds such as acetylene.

**triple counterpoint,** *Music.* a counterpoint with three parts, each of which is interchangeable with either of the other two parts.

**triple crown, 1** the tiara worn by the pope. **2** any group of three championships, honors, or other awards.

**Triple Crown,** *U.S.* first place in the Kentucky Derby, the Preakness, and the Belmont Stakes, races for three-year-old horses.

**tri|ple-deck|er** (trip′əl dek′ər), *n.* = three-decker.

**tri|ple-ex|pan|sion engine** (trip′əl ek span′-shən), a steam engine in which the steam passes into three cylinders in succession, so that the expansive force is used in three stages.

**tri|ple-head|er** (trip′əl hed′ər), *n.* three games played in the same sports arena one after another on the same day: *a basketball triple-header.*

**triple jump,** a track-and-field event consisting of a hop, a stride, and a jump; hop, skip, and jump. —**triple jumper.** —**triple jumping.**

**triple measure,** = triple time.

**tri|ple-nerved** (trip′əl nėrvd′), *adj. Botany.* of a leaf in which two principal nerves emerge from the middle one a little above its base.

**triple play,** a play in baseball that puts three base runners out.

**triple point,** *Physics.* the point at which the three phases (gas, liquid, and solid) of a substance exist in equilibrium.

**Triple Sec** or **triple sec,** = Cointreau. [< French *Triple Sec,* a trademark]

**tri|ple-space** (trip′əl spās′), *v.t., v.i.,* **-spaced, -spac|ing.** to leave two blank spaces between every line in typing.

**tri|plet** (trip′lit), *n.* **1** one of three children born at the same time from the same mother. **2** a group of three; trio. **3** *Music.* a group of three notes of equal value to be performed in the time of two. **4** three successive lines of poetry, usually rhyming and equal in length. **5** *Genetics.* any combination of three bases in the genetic code; codon: *nonsense triplets.* **6** *Nuclear Physics.* a group of three elementary particles with similar characteristics.

**triplets**, **a** three children at a birth: *Triplets may result from the formation of a pair of twins and the simultaneous development of an additional egg* (Sidonie M. Gruenberg). **b** three of a kind in certain card games: *He came up with a straight to beat my triplets.*

[< *triple;* perhaps patterned on *doublet*]

**tri|ple|tail** (trip′əl tāl′), *n.* a large food fish of warm seas, having long dorsal and anal fins which extend backward, appearing to be lobes of the tail.

**triple threat**, **1** a football player who can pass, kick, and run with the ball adeptly. **2** a person who has three skills or fields of competence.

— **tri′ple-threat′**, *adj.*

**triple time**, *Music.* **1** time in which each measure contains three beats, with the first beat accented. **2** the rhythm of this. Also, **triple measure**.

**triple tree**, *Archaic.* the gallows (with allusion to the two posts and crossbeam comprising it).

**tri|plets** (trip′lits), *n.pl.* See under **triplet**.

**tri|plex** (trip′leks, trī′pleks), *adj., n.* — *adj.* **1** triple; threefold. **2** having three floors or three apartments: *a triplex building.*

— *n.* **1** something triple or threefold. **2** *Music.* triple time or measure. **3** *U.S.* a triplex house or building: *a Park Avenue triplex.*

[< Latin *triplex, -plicis* < *tri-* three + *-plex, -plicis,* related to *plaga* flat(ness)]

**trip|li|cate** (*adj., n.* trip′lə kit; *v.* trip′lə kāt), *adj., n., v.,* **-cat|ed, -cat|ing.** — *adj.* triple; threefold.

— *n.* one of three things exactly alike, especially one of three copies of a document.

— *v.t.* **1** to multiply by three; make threefold; triple. **2** *Linguistics.* to form (a word) by triple repetition of an element.

**in triplicate**, in three copies exactly alike: *The constitutions were written in triplicate* (Walter Hook).

[< Latin *triplicātus,* past participle of *triplicāre* to triple < *triplex;* see etym. under **triplex**]

**trip|li|ca|tion** (trip′lə kā′shən), *n.* **1** the act or process of triplicating. **2** the fact of being triplicated. **3** something triplicated. **4** *Linguistics.* **a** the formation of a word by triple repetition of an element. **b** a word thus formed.

**tri|plic|i|ty** (tri plis′ə tē), *n., pl.* **-ties. 1** the quality or condition of being triple; threefold character or existence. **2** a triad; trio. **3** (in astrology) a combination of three of the twelve signs of the zodiac, each sign being distant 120 degrees from the other two; trigon.

**trip|lite** (trip′līt), *n.* a phosphate of iron and manganese containing fluorine, of a brown or blackish color. [< German *Triplit* < Greek *triploûs* threefold + German *-it* -ite[1] (because of its cleavage in three directions)]

**trip|lo|blas|tic** (trip′lə blas′tik), *adj.* having three germ layers, the ectoderm, the endoderm, and the mesoderm, as the embryos of vertebrates do. [< Greek *triplóos* triple + *blastós* germ, sprout]

**trip|loid** (trip′loid), *adj., n. Biology.* — *adj.* having three times the number of chromosomes characteristic of germ cells of the species.

— *n.* a triploid organism.

[< New Latin *triploides* < Greek *triplóos* triple]

**trip|loi|dy** (trip loi′dē), *n. Biology.* the state of having three times the number of chromosomes characteristic of germ cells of the species.

**tri|ply** (trip′lē), *adv.* in a triple manner; three times. **SYN:** trebly, thrice.

**tri|pod** (trī′pod), *n.* **1** a three-legged support or stand for a camera, telescope, transit, or other instrument. **2** a stool, table, or other article having three legs. **3** in ancient Greece and Rome: **a** a three-legged pot or cauldron. **b** an ornamental vessel on the pattern of this, often presented as a prize, or as a votive offering. [< Latin *tripūs, -podis* < Greek *trípous, -podos* (literally) three-footed < *tri-* three + *poús, podós* foot]

**trip|o|dal** (trip′ə dəl), *adj.* three-footed; three-legged.

**tri|pod|ic** (trī pod′ik), *adj.* designating a method of walking in which two legs on one side and one on the other move together, used by certain insects.

**trip|o|dy** (trip′ə dē), *n., pl.* **-dies.** *Prosody.* a group or verse of three feet. [< Greek *tripodíā* < *tripous, -podos* three-footed; see etym. under **tripod**]

**tri|po|lar** (trī pō′lər), *adj.* having three poles.

**trip|o|li** (trip′ə lē), *n.* any one of several light, soft earths or rocks, especially infusorial earth and rottenstone, used in polishing, etc. [< French *tripoli* < *Tripoli,* a city in Africa, where it was originally found]

**Tri|pol|i|tan** (tri pol′ə tən), *adj., n.* — *adj.* of or having to do with Tripoli, a region in northern Africa, now included in Libya, or its people.

— *n.* a native or inhabitant of Tripoli.

**Tri|pol|i|ta|ni|an** (tri pol′ə tā′nē ən, trip′ə lə-), *n., adj.* — *n.* a native or inhabitant of Tripolitania, a former province of Libya. — *adj.* of or having to do with Tripolitania or the Tripolitanians.

**trip|o|lite** (trip′ə līt), *n.* tripoli that is made up of the fossil remains of diatoms.

**tri|pos** (trī′pos), *n., pl.* **-pos|es. 1** (at Cambridge University) a final honors examination, especially in mathematics. **2** *Obsolete.* tripod. [originally (at Cambridge), an official who composed humorous commencement verses and joked with degree candidates (because of his tripod stool) < Greek *trípos,* variant of *trípous;* see etym. under **tripod**]

**trip|per** (trip′ər), *n.* **1** a person or thing that trips. **2** a device or mechanism that releases a catch in a machine, a railroad signal, or other mechanism. **3** *Especially British.* a person who takes a trip; tourist: *Fares will probably be a lot cheaper, perhaps cheap enough to tempt the week-end tripper* (Sunday Times). **SYN:** excursionist.

**trip|per|y** (trip′ər ē), *adj. Especially British.* like a tripper or trippers; touristy: *Venice in its most trippery and least attractive garb* ... (London Daily Express).

**trip|pet** (trip′it), *n.* a cam, projection, or other device intended to strike some object at regularly recurrent intervals. [< *trip,* verb]

**trip|ping** (trip′ing), *adj., n.* — *adj.* light and quick; light-footed; nimble.

— *n.* **1** the act of a person or thing that trips. **2** a light dance. — **trip′ping|ly**, *adv.*

**tripping line**, a line or cable used to trip (free from the bottom) an anchor.

**trip|tane** (trip′tān), *n.* a liquid motor fuel noted for its antiknock qualities. It is used chiefly in aviation gasolines, especially to provide additional power. [< *tri-* + *p*(en)*tane*]

**trip|ter|ous** (trip′tər əs), *adj. Botany.* having three wings or winglike expansions. [< *tri-* + Greek *pterón* wing + English *-ous*]

**Trip|tol|e|mus** or **Trip|tol|e|mos** (trip tol′ə məs), *n. Greek Mythology.* a favorite of Demeter, who revealed the secrets of agriculture to man.

**trip|tych** (trip′tik), *n.* **1** a set of three panels side by side, having pictures, carvings, or the like on them. The side panels are usually subordinate, and are hinged to fold over the central panel. Triptychs are commonly used or designed to be used as altarpieces. **2** a hinged, three-leaved writing tablet, used in ancient Greece and Rome. [< Greek *triptychos* three-layered < *tri-* three + *ptýx* fold]

**trip|tyque** (trip tēk′), *n.* an international pass through customs for temporarily importing an automobile, as for touring. [< French *triptyque* (literally) triptych]

**trip wire**, a wire which, when pulled releases a catch and starts a process, such as the explosion of a mine or the sounding of an alarm.

**tri|que|tral** (trī kwē′trəl), *adj.* of or having to do with the triquetrum.

**tri|que|trous** (trī kwē′trəs, -kwet′rəs), *adj.* three-sided; triangular. [< Latin *triquetrus* (with English *-ous*) three-cornered < *tri-* three + *-quetrus,* related to *quadra* square]

**tri|que|trum** (trī kwē′trəm), *n., pl.* **-tra** (-trə). a bone of the human carpus (wrist) in the proximal row of carpal bones; the cuneiform or pyramidal. [< New Latin *triquetrum,* neuter of Latin *triquetrus;* see etym. under **triquetrous**]

**tri|ra|di|ate** (trī rā′dē āt), *adj.* having or consisting of the rays; radiating in three directions from a central point. — **tri|ra′di|ate′ly**, *adv.*

**tri|ra|di|us** (trī rā′dē əs), *n., pl.* **-di|i** (-dē ī), **-di|us|es. 1** a junction of three lines at the base of each finger on the palm of the hand. **2** a tiny triangle formed in fingerprints by ridges meeting at the corners.

**tri|reg|num** (trī reg′nəm), *n.* the triple crown worn by the pope as a symbol of his position; tiara. [< Latin *tri-* three + *regnum* reign]

***trireme**

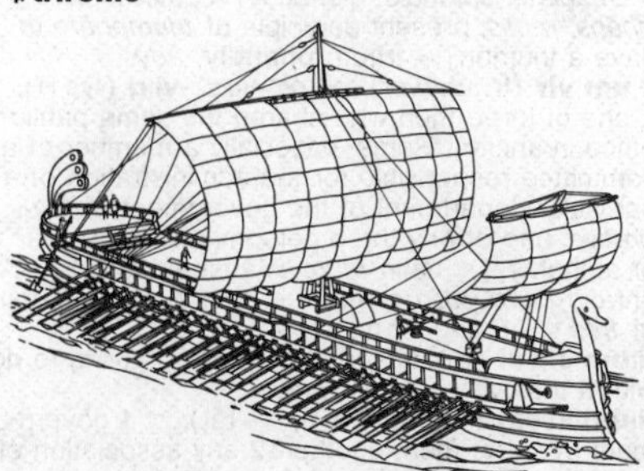

***tri|reme** (trī′rēm), *n., adj.* — *n.* a ship, usually a warship, with three rows of oars on each side, one above the other. Triremes were used in ancient Greece and Rome.

— *adj.* having three rows of oars.

[< Latin *trirēmis* < *tri-* three + *rēmus* oar]

**tri|sac|cha|rid** (trī sak′ər id), *n.* = trisaccharide.

**tri|sac|cha|ride** (trī sak′ə rīd, -ər id), *n.* any one of a class of carbohydrates, such as raffinose, which on hydrolysis yields three molecules of simply sugars (monosaccharides).

**tri|sect** (trī sekt′), *v.t.* **1** to divide into three parts. **2** to divide into three equal parts. [< *tri-* + Latin *sectus,* past participle of *secāre* to cut]

**tri|sec|tion** (trī sek′shən), *n.* **1** the division of a thing into three parts. **2** *Geometry.* the division of a straight line or an angle into three equal parts.

**tri|sec|tor** (trī sek′tər), *n.* a person or thing that trisects.

**tri|seme** (trī′sēm), *n., adj.* — *n.* a metrical foot consisting of three short syllables.

— *adj.* = trisemic.

[< Greek *trisēmos* < *tri-* three + *sêma, -atos* a sign]

**tri|se|mic** (trī sē′mik), *adj.* **1** having three morae or short syllables. **2** equivalent to three morae or short syllables.

**tri|sep|al|ous** (trī sep′ə ləs), *adj. Botany.* having three sepals.

**tri|sep|tate** (trī sep′tāt), *adj. Biology.* having three septa (partitions).

**tri|se|ri|al** (trī sir′ē əl), *adj.* **1** arranged in three series or rows. **2** *Botany.* having three floral whorls. [< *tir-* + *serial*]

**tri|shaw** (trī′shô), *n.* = pedicab. [< *tri*(cycle) + (rick)*shaw*]

**tris|kai|dek|a|phobe** (tris′kī dek′ə fōb), *n.* = triakaidekaphobe.

**tris|kai|dek|a|pho|bi|a** (tris′kī dek′ə fō′bē ə), *n.* = triakaidekaphobia. [< Greek *treiskaídeka* thirteen (< *treîs* three + *kaí* and + *déka* ten) + English *-phobia*]

**tris|kele** (tris′kēl), *n.* = triskelion.

**tris|kel|i|on** (tris kel′ē on), *n.* a symbolic figure consisting of three legs or lines radiating from a common center. [< New Latin *triskelion* < Greek *triskelês* three-legged < *tri-* three + *skélos* leg]

**tris|mic** (triz′mik, tris′-), *adj.* **1** of or having to do with lockjaw. **2** having lockjaw.

**tris|mus** (triz′məs, tris′-), *n.* = lockjaw. [< New Latin *trismus* < Greek *trismós,* alteration of *trigmós* a grating, grinding < *trízein* to creak, crack, grate]

**tris|oc|ta|he|dral** (tris ok′tə hē′drəl), *adj.* **1** bounded by twenty-four equal faces. **2** having to do with a trisoctahedron. **3** having the form of a trisoctahedron.

**tris|oc|ta|he|dron** (tris ok′tə hē′drən), *n., pl.* **-drons, -dra** (-drə). a solid bounded by twenty-four equal faces, every three of which correspond to one face of an octahedron. A trigonal trisoctahedron has twenty-four triangular faces and a tetragonal trisoctahedron has twenty-four quadrilateral or trapezoidal faces. [< Greek *tris-* (< *tris* thrice) + English *octahedron*]

**tri|so|di|um phosphate** (trī sō′dē əm), a crystalline compound used as a detergent, metal cleaner, and in the manufacture of paper and photographic developers. *Formula:* $Na_3PO_4$

**tri|some** (trī′sōm), *n. Biology.* a trisomic condition.

**tri|so|mic** (trī sō′mik), *adj. Biology.* diploid except for one chromosome which is triploid. [< *tri-* + Greek *sôma* body + English *-ic*]

**tri|so|my** (trī′sō mē), *n. Biology.* trisome.

**tri|sper|mous** (trī spėr′məs), *adj. Botany.* containing three seeds. [< *tri-* + Greek *spérma* seed + English *-ous*]

**tri|spor|ic** (trī spôr′ik, -spōr′-), *adj. Botany.* having three spores.

**tri|spor|ous** (trī spôr′əs, -spōr′-), *adj. Botany.* trisporic.

**trist** (trist), *adj. Archaic.* sad; sorrowful; melancholy. [< Old French *triste,* learned borrowing from Latin *trīstis* sad]

**Tris|tan** (tris′tən), *n.* = Tristram.

**tri-state** (trī′stāt′), *adj. U.S.* of, belonging to, or involving three adjoining states or the adjoining parts of three such states: *The* [*New Jersey*] *legislature refused to grant legal status to a tri-state transportation committee which had already been approved by New York and Connecticut* (Harper's).

**triste** (trēst), *adj. French.* sad; melancholy.

**tris|tesse** (três tes′), *n. French.* sadness; melancholy.

**tris|te|za** (tris tā′zə), *n.* a virus disease of citrus trees that attacks sweet orange, tangerine, and scions of certain other related trees grafted on the rootstocks of the sour orange. [< Spanish

**Pronunciation Key:** hat, āge, cãre, fär; let, ēqual, tėrm; it, īce; hot, ōpen, ôrder; oil, out; cup, pu̇t, rüle; child; long; thin; ᴛʜen; zh, measure; ə represents **a** in about, **e** in taken, **i** in pencil, **o** in lemon, **u** in circus.

and Portuguese *tristeza* grief, affliction < Latin *trīstitia* < *trīstis* sad]

**trist|ful** (trist′fəl), *adj. Archaic.* **1** sad; sorrowful. **2** dreary; dismal. —**trist′ful|ly**, *adv.*

**tris|tich** (tris′tik), *n.* the lines of verse forming a stanza or group. [< *tri-;* patterned on *distich*]

**tris|tich|ous** (tris′tə kəs), *adj.* **1** arranged in three rows or ranks. **2** characterized by three rows or ranks. **3** *Botany.* arranged in three vertical rows or ranks. [< Greek *tristichos* (with English *-ous*) < *tri-* three + *stíchos* row, line, stich]

**Tris|tram** (tris′trəm), *n.* one of the most famous knights of the Round Table in Arthurian legends. His love for Iseult, wife of King Mark, is the subject of many stories and poems and of an opera by Richard Wagner. Also, **Tristan**.

**tri|sty|lous** (trī stī′ləs), *adj. Botany.* having three styles.

**tri|sul|cate** (trī sul′kāt), *adj.* **1** *Botany.* having three sulci or grooves. **2** *Zoology.* divided into three digits, as a foot. [< Latin *trisulcus* having three clefts (< *tri-* tri- + *sulcus* furrow) + English *-ate*[1]]

**tri|sul|fid** or **tri|sul|phid** (trī sul′fid), *n.* = trisulfide.

**tri|sul|fide** or **tri|sul|phide** (trī sul′fīd, -fid), *n.* a compound containing three atoms of sulfur combined with another element or radical.

**tri|syl|lab|ic** (tris′ə lab′ik, trī′sə-), *adj.* having three syllables.

**tri|syl|lab|i|cal** (tris′ə lab′ə kəl, trī′sə-), *adj.* = trisyllabic.

**tri|syl|lab|i|cal|ly** (tris′ə lab′ə klē, trī′sə-), *adv.* as or in three syllables.

**tri|syl|la|ble** (tri sil′ə bəl, trī-), *n.* a word of three syllables. *Educate* is a trisyllable.

**trit.**, triturate.

**tri|tag|o|nist** (trī tag′ə nist, tri-), *n.* the third actor in an ancient Greek tragedy, next in importance after the deuteragonist. [< Greek *tritagōnistḗs* < *trítos* third + *agōnistḗs* combatant, actor]

**trit|a|nope** (trit′ə nōp, trī′tə-), *n.* a person who suffers from tritanopia.

**trit|a|no|pi|a** (trit′ə nō′pē ə, trī′tə-), *n.* a form of color blindness, the inability to distinguish violet, blue, green, and to some extent, yellow. [< New Latin *tritanopia* < Greek *trítos* third + *an-* without + *ôps* eye (referring to the lack of a third constituent of vision necessary for color awareness)]

**trit|a|no|pic** (trit′ə nō′pik, trī′tə-), *adj.* of or having to do with tritanopia: *tritanopic vision.*

**trite** (trīt), *adj.,* **trit|er, trit|est.** worn out by constant use or repetition; no longer new or interesting; commonplace; hackneyed: *"Cheeks like roses" is a trite expression.* **SYN:** stereotyped, banal, stale. [< Latin *trītus,* past participle of *terere* to rub] —**trite′ly**, *adv.* —**trite′ness**, *n.*

**tri|the|ism** (trī′thē iz əm), *n.* the belief in three Gods, especially the doctrine that the Father, the Son, and the Holy Ghost of the Christian Trinity are three distinct Gods. [< *tri-* + Greek *theós* god + English *-ism*]

**tri|the|ist** (trī′thē ist), *n., adj.* —*n.* a person who believes in tritheism.
—*adj.* = tritheistic.

**tri|the|is|tic** (trī′thē is′tik), *adj.* **1** of or having to do with tritheism. **2** believing in tritheism.

**tri|the|is|ti|cal** (trī′thē is′tə kəl), *adj.* = tritheistic.

**tri|thing** (trī′ᴛʜing), *n. Obsolete.* riding[2], an administrative division.

**trit|i|ate** (trit′ē āt, trish′-), *v.t.,* **-at|ed, -at|ing.** to mix, infuse, or coat with tritium.

**trit|i|ca|le** (trit′ə kā′lē), *n.* a highly productive and nutritious hybrid grain produced by crossing wheat and rye. [< Latin *trītic(um)* wheat + *(se)cāle* rye]

**trit|i|um** (trit′ē əm, trish′-), *n.* an isotope of hydrogen, three times as heavy as ordinary hydrogen. It is the explosive used in a hydrogen bomb. *Symbol:* T or $H^3$ [< New Latin *tritium* < Greek *trítos* third < *treîs* three]

**trit|o|ma** (trit′ə mə), *n., pl.* **-mas.** = red-hot poker. [< New Latin *Tritoma* the genus name < Greek *trítomos* thrice cut]

**Tri|ton** (trī′tən), *n.* **1a** *Greek Mythology.* a sea god, son of Poseidon and Amphitrite, having the head and body of a man and the tail of a fish and carrying a trumpet made of a conch shell. **b** (later) any one of a group of minor sea gods by whom Poseidon and the other major sea gods were served. **2** the larger of the two satellites of Neptune.

**tri|ton**[1] (trī′tən), *n.* **1** any one of a family of large marine gastropods, especially any one of a group having a brightly colored, spiral, trumpet-shaped shell. **2** the shell of such an animal. [< *Triton*]

**tri|ton**[2] (trī′ton), *n.* the nucleus of a tritium atom. [< *trit*(ium) + *-on,* as in *electron*]

**tri|tone** (trī′tōn′), *n. Music.* an interval consisting of three whole tones; augmented fourth. [< Greek *trítonos* < *tri-* three + *tónos* a tone]

**Tri|ton|ess** (trī′tə nis), *n.* a female Triton.

**triton's trumpet**, a triton shell used as a horn.

**trit|u|ra|ble** (trich′ər ə bəl), *adj.* capable of being triturated.

**trit|u|rate** (trich′ə rāt), *v.,* **-rat|ed, -rat|ing,** *n.*
—*v.t.* **1** to rub, crush, grind, or pound into fine particles or a very fine powder; pulverize. **2** *Archaic.* to masticate (food).
—*n.* **1** any substance that is ground into a very fine powder or fine particles. **2** *Pharmacology.* a trituration.
[< Late Latin *trīturāre* (with English *-ate*[1]) thresh < Latin *terere* to rub]

**trit|u|ra|tion** (trich′ə rā′shən), *n.* **1** the act or process of triturating. Trituration is a dry process, and thus distinguished from levigation. **2** *Pharmacology.* **a** a powder obtained by triturating 10 grams of a powdered drug or other substance, with 90 grams of powered lactose. **b** a powder produced, or medicine prepared by triturating.

**trit|u|ra|tor** (trich′ə rā′tər), *n.* **1** a person or thing that triturates. **2** an apparatus for grinding drugs to a powder.

**tri|tyl|o|dont** (trī til′ə dont), *n.* a small mammal-like reptile of the late Triassic and early Jurassic periods, having a long body and short legs, multiple bones in the lower jaw and cusped teeth. It is regarded as an evolutionary link between reptiles and mammals. [< New Latin *Tritylodon, -ontis* the genus name < Greek *tri-* + *týlos* knob + *odoús, odóntos* tooth (because their teeth had three rows of cusps)]

**tri|tyl|o|don|toid** (trī til′ə don′toid), *n., adj.* —*n.* = tritylodont.
—*adj.* of or having to do with the tritylodonts.

**tri|umph** (trī′umf), *n., v.* —*n.* **1** the act or fact of being victorious; victory: *final triumph over the enemy. But in ourselves are triumph and defeat* (Longfellow). **SYN:** conquest. See syn. under **victory**. **2** a notable success or achievement: *The conquest of outer space is one of the greatest triumphs of modern science.* **3** joy because of victory or success: *a smile of triumph. We welcomed the team home with cheers of triumph.* **SYN:** elation. **4** a procession in honor of a general of ancient Rome for an important victory over an enemy. **5** *Obsolete.* a spectacle or pageant, especially a tournament.
—*v.i.* **1** to gain victory; win success; prevail: *to triumph over adversity. Our team triumphed over theirs.* **SYN:** conquer. **2** to rejoice because of victory or success; exult; glory. **3** to celebrate a Roman triumph.
—*v.t. Obsolete.* to conquer.
**in triumph, a** triumphant: *to return, in triumph, with the spoils of victory.* **b** triumphantly: *He brought home the prize in triumph.*
[< Old French *triumphe,* learned borrowing from Latin *triumphus* < Greek *thríambos* a hymn to Dionysus] —**tri′umph|er**, *n.*

**tri|um|phal** (trī um′fəl), *adj.* **1** of or having to do with a triumph. **2** celebrating a victory; of the nature of a triumph: *a triumphal march.* —**tri|um′phal|ly**, *adv.*

**tri|um|phal|ism** (trī um′fə liz′əm), *n.* the preaching of ultimate victory over one's rivals or enemies, especially as an ideological doctrine or policy: *Nothing is surprising in the Communist triumphalism* (Manchester Guardian Weekly).

**tri|um|phal|ist** (trī um′fə list), *n., adj.* —*n.* a person who believes in triumphalism: *The favourite sport of the triumphalist was heretic hunting* (London Times).
—*adj.* of or having to do with triumphalism.

**tri|um|phant** (trī um′fənt), *adj.* **1** victorious or successful: *a triumphant army.* **2** rejoicing because of victory or success: *The winner spoke in triumphant tones to his defeated rival. O come all ye faithful, Joyful and triumphant* (Frederick Oakeley). **SYN:** jubilant, exultant. **3** = triumphal. **4** *Obsolete.* splendid; glorious. [< Latin *triumphāns, -antis,* present participle of *triumphāre* to have a triumph] —**tri|um′phant|ly**, *adv.*

**tri|um|vir** (trī um′vər), *n., pl.* **-virs, -vi|ri** (-və rī). **1** one of three men who shared the same public office in ancient Rome, especially a member of a committee responsible for the administration of a particular department of the government. **2** *Figurative.* one of any three persons sharing power or authority. [< Latin *triumvir,* abstracted from phrase *trium virōrum* of three men, genitive plural of *trēs* three and *vir* man]

**tri|um|vi|ral** (trī um′vər əl), *adj.* of or having to do with a triumvir or a triumvirate.

**tri|um|vi|rate** (trī um′vər it, -və rāt), *n.* **1** government by three men together. **2** any association of three in office or authority. **3** the position or term of office of a Roman triumvir. **4** *Figurative.* any group of three; trio. [< Latin *triumvirātus* < *triumvir;* see etym. under **triumvir**]

**Tri|um|vi|rate** (trī um′vər it, -və rāt), *n.* **1** the coalition of Pompey, Caesar, and Crassus; First Triumvirate. **2** the coalition of Octavian, Antony, and Lepidus; Second Triumvirate.

**tri|une** (trī′yün), *adj., n.* —*adj.* consisting of three in one, especially the Trinity: *the triune God.*
—*n.* any united group of three; triad. [< *tri-* + Latin *ūnus* one]

**Tri|une** (trī′yün), *n.* = Trinity.

**tri|u|ni|tar|i|an** (trī yü′nə tãr′ē ən), *n.* = Trinitarian.

**tri|u|ni|ty** (trī yü′nə tē), *n.* the fact or condition of being three in one.

**tri|va|lence** (trī vā′ləns, triv′ə-), *n.* the state or quality of being trivalent.

**tri|va|len|cy** (trī vā′lən sē, triv′ə-), *n., pl.* **-cies.** = trivalence.

**tri|va|lent** (trī vā′lənt, triv′ə-), *adj.* having a valence of three; tervalent.

**tri|valve** (trī′valv′), *adj.* having three valves, as certain shells.

**triv|et** (triv′it), *n.* **1** a small iron frame on short legs, usually three in number, for use under a hot dish to protect the surface of a table. **2** a three-legged stand for supporting a pot or kettle over coals in an open fireplace. **3** = tripod.
**as right as a trivet,** entirely or perfectly right (in allusion to a trivet's standing firm on its three legs): *"I hope you are well, sir." "Right as a trivet, sir," replied Bob Sawyer* (Dickens).
[Old English *trefet,* probably ultimately < Latin *tripūs, -podis* (see etym. under **tripod**); influenced by Latin *trifidus;* see etym. under **trifid**]

**triv|i|a** (triv′ē ə), *n. pl.* **1** things of little or no importance; trifles; trivialities. **2** plural of **trivium**. [< New Latin *trivia,* neuter plural of Latin *trivium* crossways; influenced by English *trivial*]

**triv|i|al** (triv′ē əl), *adj.* **1** not important; trifling; insignificant: *Your composition has only a few trivial mistakes.* **SYN:** paltry, slight, small, unimportant, inconsequential. **2** of or having to do with the trivium: *the trivial arts.* **3** *Biology.* (of a taxonomic designation) specific. **4** *Archaic.* not new or interesting; ordinary; commonplace: *the trivial round, the common task* (John Keble). [< Latin *triviālis* vulgar; (originally) of the crossways < *trivium* crossways < *tri-* three + *via* road, way]
—**triv′i|al|ly**, *adv.* —**triv′i|al|ness**, *n.*

**triv|i|al|ise** (triv′ē ə līz), *v.t.,* **-ised, -is|ing.** *Especially British.* trivialize.

**triv|i|al|ism** (triv′ē ə liz′əm), *n.* a triviality; trifle.

**triv|i|al|i|ty** (triv′ē al′ə tē), *n., pl.* **-ties. 1** trivial quality. **SYN:** unimportance, insignificance. **2** a trivial thing, remark, or affair; trifle: *completely engulfed in the trivialities of suburban life* (H. G. Wells).

**triv|i|al|ize** (triv′ē ə līz), *v.t.,* **-ized, -iz|ing.** to make trivial; render commonplace or trifling: *We trivialize Lent if we see it merely as a time for giving up smoking* (Manchester Guardian Weekly). —**triv′i|al|i|za′tion**, *n.*

**trivial name**, *Biology.* **1** the name added to a generic name to distinguish the species; specific name or epithet. **2** the common or vernacular name of a plant or animal.

**triv|i|um** (triv′ē əm), *n., pl.* **-i|a.** grammar, rhetoric, and logic, the first three of the seven liberal arts in ancient Rome and in the Middle Ages. The other four, the quadrivium, were arithmetic, music, geometry, and astronomy. [< Medieval Latin *trivium* (literally) a triple road or way < Latin; see etym. under **trivial**]

**tri|week|ly** (trī wēk′lē), *adv., n., pl.* **-lies,** *adj.*
—*adv.* **1** once every three weeks. **2** three times a week.
—*n.* newspaper or magazine published triweekly.
—*adj.* occurring or appearing triweekly.

**tRNA** (no periods), transfer RNA.

**Tro|ad|ic** (trō ad′ik), *adj.* of or having to do with ancient Troy and the civilization that flourished there. [< *Troad,* the region around the city of Troy + *-ic*]

**Tro|bri|and|er** (trō′brē ən dər, -an′-), *n.* a native or inhabitant of the Trobriand Islands, near New Guinea.

**tro|car** (trō′kär), *n.* a surgical instrument used to puncture cavities and draw fluid out, as in dropsy. Also, **trochar**. [< French *trocart,* for *troisquarts* (literally) three quarters < *trois* three (< Latin *trēs*) + *carre* side of a sword or knife (because of its triangular form)]

**tro|cha|ic** (trō kā′ik), *adj., n.* —*adj.* **1** consisting of trochees. **2** characterized by or based on trochees: *trochaic verse.* **3** of the nature of a trochee: *a trochaic foot.*
—*n.* **1** a trochaic poem or line of verse. **2** = trochee.
[< Latin *trochaicus* < Greek *trochāïkós* < *trochaîos;* see etym. under **trochee**]

**tro|chal** (trō′kəl), *adj. Zoology.* resembling a wheel, as the ciliated disk of a rotifer. [< Greek *trochós* a wheel (< *tréchein* to run) + English *-al*[1]]

**tro|chan|ter** (trō kan′tər), *n.* **1** a protuberance or process on the upper part of the thighbone of many vertebrates. **2** the second section of the leg of an insect. [< Middle French *trochanter* < Greek *trochantḗr, -ēros* protuberance on the thigh; earlier head of the femur; (literally) runner < *tréchein* to run]

**tro|char** (trō′kär), *n.* = trocar.
**tro|che** (trō′kē), *n.* a small medicinal tablet or lozenge, usually round and often sweetened, especially one to be dissolved in the mouth to medicate or sooth the throat: *cough troches.* [alteration of earlier *trochisk* < Middle French *trochisque*, learned borrowing from Medieval Latin *trochiscus* < Latin, small wheel < Greek *trochískos* (diminutive) < *trochós* wheel]
**tro|chee** (trō′kē), *n.* **1** a foot or measure in poetry consisting of two syllables, the first accented and the second unaccented or the first long and the second short. *Example:* "Sinǵ a / song of / sixṕence." **2** a long syllable followed by a short syllable in Greek or Latin verse. *Example: pātĕr.* [< Middle French *trochée,* learned borrowing from Latin *trochaeus* < Greek *trochaîos* (literally) running < *tréchein* to run]
**troch|el|minth** (trok′el minth), *n.* any invertebrate animal of a group including the rotifers and gastrotrichans. [< Greek *trochós* a wheel + English *helminth* (because of the shape)]
**tro|chil|ic** (trō kil′ik), *adj.* **1** having to do with rotary motion. **2** characterized by rotary motion. [< Greek *trochílos,* taken as *trochós* wheel + English *-ic*]
**tro|chil|ics** (trō kil′iks), *n.* the science of rotary motion.
**troch|i|lus** (trok′ə ləs), *n., pl.* **-li** (-lī). **1** any one of certain small European warblers. **2** = crocodile bird. **3** = hummingbird. [< Latin *trochilus* < Greek *trochílos* an Egyptian bird < *tréchein* to run]
**troch|le|a** (trok′lē ə), *n., pl.* **-le|ae** (-lē ē). *Anatomy.* a pulleylike structure or arrangement of parts with a smooth surface upon which another part glides, as the part of the humerus with which the ulna articulates. [< New Latin *trochlea* < Latin, pulley block < Greek *trochiliā* (diminutive) < *trochós* a wheel < *tréchein* to run]
**troch|le|ar** (trok′lē ər), *adj.* **1** *Anatomy.* **a** of, connected with, or forming a trochlea. **b** of or having to do with the trochlear muscle or trochlear nerve. **2** *Botany.* circular and narrowed in the middle, like the wheel of a pulley.
**trochlear muscle**, the superior oblique muscle of each eye.
**trochlear nerve**, either one of the fourth pair of cranial nerves innervating the trochlear muscle.
**tro|choid** (trō′koid), *n., adj.* — ***n.*** *Geometry.* a curve traced by a point on or connected with a circle which rolls on a straight line, or on the inside or outside of another circle (used especially in naval engineering).
— ***adj.*** **1** *Anatomy.* (of a pivot joint) having one bone turning upon another with a rotary motion. **2** *Zoology.* shaped like a top, as certain shells. [< Greek *trochoeidēs* round, wheel-shaped < *trochós* a wheel (< *tréchein* to run) + *eîdos* form]
**tro|choi|dal** (trō koi′dəl), *adj.* **1** having the form or nature of a trochoid. **2** of or having to do with trochoids. **3** = trochoid. — **tro|choi′dal|ly**, *adv.*
**troch|o|phore** (trok′ə fôr, -fōr), *n.* a free-swimming, ciliate larval form of most mollusks and of certain bryozoans, brachiopods, and marine worms. [< Greek *trochós* wheel (< *tréchein* to run) + English *-phore*]
**troch|o|sphere** (trok′ə sfir), *n.* = trochophore.
**tro|chus** (trō′kəs), *n.* a top shell, especially a large variety of the tropical Pacific having a valuable nacreous shell. [< New Latin *Trochus,* the genus name < Latin *trochus* hoop < Greek *trochós* wheel]
**trod** (trod), *v.* a past tense and a past participle of **tread**: *The path was trod by many feet.*
**trod|den** (trod′ən), *v.* a past participle of **tread**: *The cattle had trodden down the corn.*
**trode** (trōd), *v. Archaic.* a past tense of **tread.**
**trof|fer** (trof′ər), *n.* a lighting fixture in the shape of an inverted trough, used to enclose a fluorescent lamp or lamps. [apparently a blend of *trough* and *coffer*]
**trog|lo|dyte** (trog′lə dīt), *n.* **1** a cave dweller; cave man. **2** *Figurative.* a person thought to resemble a cave dweller, as: **a** one who lives in seclusion; hermit. **b** one of a degraded type or brutish nature, especially a dweller in a hovel or slum. **c** one who is extremely conservative in politics; a reactionary. **3** an anthropoid ape, such as a gorilla or chimpanzee. [< Latin *trōglodyta* < Greek *trōglodýtēs* < *trṓglē* a cave (< *trṓgein* gnaw) + *dýein* go in]
**trog|lo|dyt|ic** (trog′lə dit′ik), *adj.* of, having to do with, or characteristic of troglodytes.
**trog|lo|dyt|i|cal** (trog′lə dit′ə kəl), *adj.* = troglodytic.
**trog|lo|dyt|ism** (trog′lə dī tiz′əm), *n.* the condition of a troglodyte; the habit of living in caves.
**tro|gon** (trō′gon), *n.* any tropical or subtropical bird of a group having soft, brilliantly colored plumage. [< New Latin *Trogon* the genus name < Greek *trṓgōn,* present participle of *trṓgein* to gnaw]
***tro|ka** (troi′kə), *n.* **1** a Russian carriage, wagon, or sleigh, pulled by three horses harnessed abreast. **2** such a vehicle together with the horses pulling it. **3** (in Russia) a team of three horses. **4** *Figurative.* a triumvirate: *By the time Lenin died in 1924, Stalin was powerful enough to become with Zinoviev and Kamenev a member of the troika which seized power* (Newsweek). [< Russian *trojka* team of three horses abreast; any group of three; three, noun < *tri* three]

***troika** definition 2

**tro|i|lite** (trō′ə līt, troi′līt), *n.* a sulfide of iron found in meteorites: *Troilite is a good conductor of heat* (New Scientist). *Formula:* FeS [< Dominico *Troili,* an Italian scientist who in 1766 described a meteorite containing it + English *-ite*[1]]
**Troi|lus** (troi′ləs, trō′i-), *n.* **1** *Greek Legend.* a warrior, the son of King Priam of Troy. He was killed by Achilles. **2** *Medieval Legend.* this warrior represented as the lover of Cressida.
**troilus butterfly**, a large, spotted black butterfly of North America; spicebush swallowtail. [< *Troilus*]
**Tro|jan** (trō′jən), *adj., n.* — ***adj.*** **1** of or having to do with Troy, an ancient city in northwestern Asia Minor, or its people. **2** of or like that of a Trojan: *to do Trojan work.*
— ***n.*** **1** a person who was born or lived in Troy. **2** *Figurative.* a person who shows courage or energy; one who is vigorous and indomitable: *They all worked like Trojans.* **3** *Archaic.* **a** a roistering or dissolute fellow. **b** (in later use) a good fellow.
[< Latin *Trōjānus* < *Trōja* or *Trōia* Troy < Greek *Trōiā* < *Trōs,* its mythical founder]
**Trojan asteroids** or **group**, a group of asteroids that revolve to form an equilateral triangle with Jupiter and the sun. Most of them were named after heroes of the Trojan war.
**Trojan horse**, **1** *Greek Legend.* a huge wooden horse in which the Greeks concealed soldiers and brought them into Troy during the Trojan War; wooden horse. **2** *Figurative.* **a** an enemy group stationed inside of a country to sabotage its industry and defense preparations. **b** any group or thing that subverts or undermines from within: *Research ... is being described as the academic Trojan horse whose personnel have all but captured the city of the intellect* (Saturday Review).
**Trojan War**, *Greek Legend.* a ten-year war carried on by the Greeks against Troy, to get back Helen, wife of King Menelaus of Sparta, who was carried off by Paris, son of King Priam of Troy. It ended with the plundering and destruction of Troy.
**tro|land** (trō′lənd), *n.* a unit of measure of the retinal response to illumination. The illumination on the retina is one troland when a surface with a brightness of one candle per square meter is seen through an area of the pupil of one square millimeter. [< Leonard T. *Troland,* 1889-1932, an American psychologist and physicist]
**troll**[1] (trōl), *v., n.* — ***v.t.*** **1a** to sing (something) in a full, rolling voice. **b** to sing (something) in succession. When three people troll a round or catch, the soprano sings one line, the alto comes in next with the same line, and then the bass sings it, and so on, while the others keep on singing. **2** to draw (a line, baited hook, or lure) continuously through the water, especially from the stern of a moving boat. **3** to fish in (a body of water) by trolling. **4** *Obsolete.* to roll. **5** *Obsolete.* to entice; allure. **6** *Obsolete.* to move (the tongue) volubly. **7** *Obsolete.* to cause to pass from one to another; hand around among the company present.
— ***v.i.*** **1** to sing in a full, rolling voice; sing merrily or jovially. **2** to fish by trolling: *to troll for bass.* **3** *Obsolete.* to move nimbly, as the tongue in speaking; wag. **4** *Obsolete.* to ramble; saunter; stroll.
— ***n.*** **1** a song whose parts are sung in succession; round; catch: *"Three Blind Mice" is a well-known troll.* **2** a fishing lure, especially a spinning lure or spoon for trolling. **3** such a lure together with the line by which it is drawn through the water. **4** a fishing reel, especially one used for trolling.
[< Old French *troller* wander, search for game < Germanic (compare Middle High German *trollen* walk with short steps)] — **troll′er**, *n.*
**troll**[2] (trōl), *n.* an ugly dwarf or giant in Scandinavian folklore with supernatural powers, living underground or in caves. [< Scandinavian (compare Old Icelandic *troll* giant, fiend, demon)]
**trol|ley** (trol′ē), *n., pl.* **-leys**, *v.* — ***n.*** **1** a pulley at the end of a pole which moves against a wire to carry electricity to a streetcar or an electric engine. **2** = trolley car. **3** a pulley running on an overhead track, used to support and move a load. **4** a basket, carriage, or the like, suspended from a pulley which runs on an overhead track. **5** any one of several devices used to receive and convey current to a motor, such as a bow or shoe used in underground railways. **5** *British.* any one of various small carts, especially handcarts.
— ***v.t.*** to convey by trolley.
— ***v.i.*** to travel by trolley. Also, **trolly.**
**off one's trolley**, *U.S. Slang.* insane: *Among the minor issues with which he tries to cope are a psychology professor who goes off his trolley ... and the romantic confusions of his own youthful daughter* (Newsweek).
[probably < *troll*[1] to roll] — **trol′ley|er**, *n.*
**trolley bus** or **coach**, a passenger bus drawing power from an overhead electric wire by means of a trolley.
**trolley car**, a streetcar drawing power from an overhead wire by means of a trolley.
**trol|ley|man** (trol′ē man′), *n., pl.* **-men.** a man employed in operating a trolley car, as a motorman or a conductor.
**troll|mad|am** (trōl′mad′əm), *n.* an old game resembling bagatelle, played especially by women. [apparently alteration of French *troumadame*]
**trol|lop** (trol′əp), *n.* **1** an untidy or slovenly woman; slattern. **2** a morally loose woman; slut. **3** = prostitute. [probably < *troll*[1] in sense of "to trail, draggle"]
**Trol|lop|e|an** or **Trol|lop|i|an** (trə lop′ē ən, -lō′pē-), *adj.* having to do with, characteristic of, or like the English novelist Anthony Trollope (1815-1882) or his writings: *a Trollopian background of great houses and grouse moors* (Mollie Panter-Downes).
**trol|lop|y** (trol′ə pē), *adj.* like a trollop; slovenly; morally loose.
**trol|ly** (trol′ē), *n., pl.* **-lies**, *v.t., v.i.,* **-lied**, **-ly|ing.** = trolley.
**trom|ba** (trōm′bä), *n.* = trumpet. [< Italian *tromba*]
**tromba marina**, a large, medieval bowed instrument with one long gut string, fingered only to produce natural harmonics. [< Italian *tromba marina*]
**trom|bi|di|a|sis** (trom′bə dī′ə sis), *n.* the state of being infested with chiggers. [< New Latin *Trombidium* the chigger genus + English *-iasis*]
***trom|bone** (trom′bōn, trom bōn′), *n.* a large, brass wind musical instrument with a loud tone, consisting of a long, cylindrical tube bent twice upon itself, and expanding into a bell at one end. The U-shaped bend nearer the cup mouthpiece usually is a sliding piece for varying the length of the tube and thus produce different tones. Some trombones have valves instead of a slide. [< Italian *trombone* < *tromba* trumpet]

***trombone**

**trom|bon|ist** (trom′bō nist, trom bō′-), *n.* a person who plays the trombone.
**trom|mel** (trom′əl), *n. U.S.* a rotating cylindrical sieve used for washing and sizing ore. [< German *Trommel* a drum; any of various drum-shaped apparatuses; a sieve]
**tro|mom|e|ter** (trō mom′ə tər), *n.* an instrument for measuring or detecting very slight earthquake tremors. [< Greek *trómos* a trembling (< *trémein* tremble) + English *-meter*]

**Pronunciation Key:** hat, āge, cãre, fär; let, ēqual, tėrm; it, īce; hot, ōpen, ôrder; oil, out; cup, pu̇t, rüle; child; long; thin; ᴛʜen; zh, measure; ə represents **a** in about, **e** in taken, **i** in pencil, **o** in lemon, **u** in circus.

**tromp**[1] (tromp), *v. U.S. Informal.* —*v.i.* to move with heavy, noisy steps; tramp.
—*v.t.* **1** to pound; thump; stamp: *Satchmo mopped his brow, tromped his foot, lit into a two-beat tune* (Newsweek). **2** to trample: *If we've got to get out you go fast or you'll get tromped to death in the rush* (Maclean's). [perhaps blend of *tramp* and *stomp*]

**tromp**[2] (tromp), *n. Archaic.* trump[2].

**trompe** (tromp), *n.* an apparatus for producing a blast, as for a forge, in which water falling in a pipe carries air into a receiver, where it is compressed, and then led to the blast pipe. [< French, Old French *trompe;* see etym. under **trump**[2].]

**trompe-l'oeil** (trônp'lœ'yə), *n., adj.* —*n.* **1** an optical illusion, especially as an extreme style of realism in painting, sculpture, or architecture: *Trompe-l'oeil mimics architectural elements: startling, lifelike dwarfs open false doors; the long balconies missing from the palace facades are supplied in fresco in the interior* (New Yorker). **2a** something done in trompe-l'oeil. **b** a school of art emphasizing this.
—*adj.* of or in the style of trompe-l'oeil: *trompe-l'oeil perspective, a trompe-l'oeil painting, painter, or school.*
[< French *trompe-l'oeil* (literally) it deceives the eye]

**tron** (tron), *n. Scottish.* trone.

**-tron**, *suffix.* **1** having to do with electrons, as in *cryotron, magnetron.*
**2** a device for directing the movement of subatomic particles, as in *cyclotron, synchrotron.*
**3** a device for controlling physical conditions, as in *biotron, phytotron, climatron.*
[< Greek *-tron* device, instrument]

**tro|na** (trō'nə), *n.* a white, gray, or yellow mineral, a native hydrous sodium carbonate, used as a source of various sodium compounds. [< Swedish *trona* < Arabic *ṭrōn,* short for *naṭrūn* natron, soda]

**trone** (trōn), *n. Scottish.* a weighing machine, especially one for weighing merchandise in bulk. [< Old French *trone* < Latin *trutina* pair of scales < Greek *trytánē*]

**troop** (trüp), *n., v.* —*n.* **1** a group or band of persons: *a troop of boys.* **SYN:** crowd, throng. **2** a herd, flock, or swarm: *a troop of deer.* **3** a great number; lot; multitude. **4** a tactical unit of cavalry, especially armored cavalry, usually commanded by a captain. A troop corresponds to a company or battery in other branches of the army and consists of 80 to 200 men. *Abbr:* trp (no period). **5** a unit of Boy Scouts or Girl Scouts made up of 16 to 32 members, or two to four patrols. **6** *Obsolete.* a company of performers; troupe.
—*v.i.* **1** to gather in troops or bands; move or come together; flock; assemble: *The children trooped around the teacher.* **2** to walk; go; go away: *throngs trooping into a store. The young boys trooped off after the older ones.* **3** to associate (with).
—*v.t.* to carry (the colors) before a formation of troops as part of an official ceremony.
**troops**, soldiers: *a city filled with foreign troops. The government sent 1,500 troops to put down the revolt.*
[< Old French *troupe* < Late Latin *troppus* herd; origin uncertain]

**troop carrier**, **1** an aircraft or ship used to carry troops. **2** a half-track used to carry military personnel.

**troop|er** (trü'pər), *n.* **1** a soldier in the cavalry, especially one with the rank of private attached to a troop of cavalry. **SYN:** dragoon. **2** a mounted policeman. The state police of some states are called troopers, because they were originally organized as mounted troops. *Trooper* is used both generically and as a specific designation: *a New York state trooper, Trooper Jones.* **3** (in Australia) any mounted policeman. **4** a cavalry horse. **SYN:** charger. **5** = troopship. **6** = paratrooper.

**troop|i|al** (trü'pē əl), *n.* = troupial.

**troop|ing** (trü'ping), *n.* the transporting of troops.

**troops** (trüps), *n. pl.* See under **troop**.

**troop|ship** (trüp'ship'), *n.* a ship used to carry soldiers, especially one designed or modified for such use; transport.

**troost|ite** (trüs'tīt), *n.* a variety of willemite, with admixture of manganese, occurring in reddish hexagonal crystals. [< Gerard *Troost,* an American geologist of the 1800's + *-ite*[1]]

**trop** (trō), *adv. French.* too many; too much.

**trop.**, **1** tropic. **2** tropical.

**tro|pa|co|caine** (trō'pə kō kān', -kō'kān), *n.* a crystalline alkaloid obtained from dried coca leaves or made synthetically, used as a local anesthetic. *Formula:* $C_{15}H_{19}NO_2$ [< New Latin (A)*tropa* the belladonna plant + English *cocaine*]

**tro|pae|o|lin** (trō pē'ə lin), *n.* any one of a group of orange or yellow azo dyes, of complex composition, belonging to the class of sulfonic acids. [< *tropaeol*(um) + *-in* (because its color resembles that of certain species)]

**tro|pae|o|line** (trō pē'ə lin, -lēn), *n.* = tropaeolin.

**tro|pae|o|lum** (trō pē'ə ləm), *n., pl.* **-lums, -la** (-lə). any one of a group of native South American trailing or climbing herbs; nasturtium. [< New Latin *Tropaeolum* the genus name < Greek *trópaion;* see etym. under **trophy** (because its leaf resembles a shield, its flower a helmet)]

**tro|par|i|on** (trō pār'ē ən), *n., pl.* **-i|a** (-ē ə). in the Greek Church: **1** a short hymn. **2** a stanza of a hymn. [< Greek *tropárion* (diminutive) < *trópos* trope]

**trope** (trōp), *n.* **1** the use of a word or phrase in a sense different from its ordinary meaning; use of a figure of speech. **SYN:** metonymy. **2** a word or phrase so used; figure of speech; figurative language. *Example:* "All in a hot and *copper* sky, The *bloody* sun at noon." **3** (formerly, in the Western Church) a phrase, sentence, or verse interpolated into some part of the liturgy. **4** a subject heading. [< Latin *tropus* figure of speech < Greek *trópos* or *tropḗ* a turn(ing) < *trépein* to turn]

**tro|pe|o|lin** (trō pē'ə lin), *n.* = tropaeolin.

**tro|pe|o|line** (trō pē'ə lin, -lēn), *n.* = tropaeolin.

**troph|al|lax|is** (trof'ə lak'sis), *n., pl.* **-lax|es** (-lak'sēz). the reciprocal exchange of food among social insects: *[In] some groups of termites ... an adult worker caste takes charge of nest building and trophallaxis, or mutual feeding* (New Yorker). [< Greek *trophḗ* nourishment + *állaxis* exchange]

**troph|ic** (trof'ik), *adj.* of or having to do with nutrition: *trophic diseases, the trophic capacity of an ecosystem.* [< Greek *trophḗ* nourishment (< *tréphein* to feed) + English *-ic*] —**troph'i|cal|ly**, *adv.*

**troph|i|cal** (trof'ə kəl), *adj.* = trophic.

**trophic level**, *Ecology.* any one of the stages in the flow of food from one population of organisms to another: *The sequence of trophic levels in any ecosystem forms a food chain* (Clarence J. Hylander).

**tro|phied** (trō'fēd), *adj.* decorated with trophies: *trophied walls.*

**troph|o|blast** (trof'ə blast), *n.* a layer of cells external to the embryo in many mammals, having the function of supplying it with nourishment. [< Greek *trophós* feeder (< *tréphein* to feed) + *blastós* germ, sprout]

**troph|o|blas|tic** (trof'ə blas'tik), *adj.* of or having to do with the trophoblast.

**tro|phol|o|gy** (trō fol'ə jē), *n.* the branch of physiology that deals with nutrition. [< Greek *trophḗ* nourishment (< *tréphein* to feed) + English *-logy*]

**Tro|pho|ni|an** (trō fō'nē ən), *adj.* of or having to do with Trophonius, the legendary builder of the original temple of Apollo at Delphi, who after his death was worshipped as a god, and had a famous oracle in a cavern in Boeotia.

**tro|phop|a|thy** (trō fop'ə thē), *n.* any derangement of nutrition, especially of a tissue. [< Greek *trophḗ* nourishment (< *tréphein* to feed) + English *-pathy*]

**troph|o|plasm** (trof'ə plaz əm), *n. Biology.* **1** the nutritive protoplasm of a cell. **2** a constituent of the cytoplasm. [< Greek *trophḗ* nourishment (< *tréphein* to feed) + *plásma* something formed]

**troph|o|zo|ite** (trof'ə zō'īt), *n.* a sporozoan during its growing stage. [< Greek *trophḗ* nourishment (< *tréphein* to feed) + *zôion* animal + English *-ite*[1]]

**tro|phy** (trō'fē), *n., pl.* **-phies. 1** a spoil or prize of war or hunting, especially if kept or displayed as a memorial: *The hunter kept the lion's skin and head as trophies.* **2** any prize cup, or token, awarded to a victorious person or team: *The champion kept his tennis trophy on the mantelpiece.* **3** (in ancient Greece and Rome) a structure consisting of the captured arms, flags, or other spoils of a defeated enemy, hung on a tree or pillar on the field of battle or elsewhere as a memorial of victory. **4** any similar monument or memorial. **5** *Figurative.* anything serving as a remembrance; memento. **6** *Architecture.* a carved representation, as of a group of weapons. [< Middle French *trophée,* learned borrowing from Latin *trophaeum,* for *tropaeum* < Greek *trópaion* (things) of a defeat < *tropḗ* a rout; (originally) a turning of the enemy < *trépein* to turn]

**trop|ic** (trop'ik), *n., adj.* —*n.* **1** either of the two circles around the earth which represent the points farthest north and south at which the sun shines directly overhead. The tropic of Cancer is 23.45 degrees north of the equator; the tropic of Capricorn is 23.45 degrees south of the equator. **2** either of two circles in the celestial sphere, the limits reached by the sun in its apparent journey north and south. *Abbr:* trop.
—*adj.* of the tropics; belonging to the Torrid Zone; tropical: *the unwarning tropic gale* (John Greenleaf Whittier). (*Figurative.*) *the lost days of our tropic youth* (Bret Harte).
**tropics** or **Tropics**, the regions between the tropic of Cancer and the tropic of Capricorn; the zone between latitudes 23.45 degrees north or south or between 30 degrees north and south; the Torrid Zone. The hottest part of the earth is in the tropics. The tropics have no winter and, except at high altitudes, are almost always very warm. *The tropics are one vast garden* (Emerson).
[< Latin *tropicus* < Greek *tropikós* pertaining to a turn < *tropḗ* a turn, change < *trépein* to turn]

**trop|i|cal**[1] (trop'ə kəl), *adj., n.* —*adj.* **1** of the tropics; having to do with the tropics: *tropical studies.* **2** occurring in the tropics: *tropical diseases, a tropical depression that grows into a tropical storm.* **3** native to the tropics: *Bananas are tropical fruit.* **4** of or having to do with the tropics of Cancer and Capricorn, or either one. **5** *Figurative.* **a** like the climate of the tropics; very hot; burning or fervent. **SYN:** torrid, fiery. **b** like the growth in those parts of the tropics having abundant rainfall; luxuriant. **7** of or for tropical fish: *a tropical aquarium.*
—*n. Informal.* a man's lightweight suit for warm or hot weather: *Stay cool yet look neat in tropicals of "Dacron" polyester fiber and worsted* (New Yorker).
[< *tropic* + *-al*[1]] —**trop'i|cal|ly**, *adv.*

**trop|i|cal**[2] (trop'ə kəl), *adj.* **1** having to do with or involving a trope or tropes. **2** of the nature of a trope or tropes; metaphorical; figurative. [< Latin *tropicus* (see etym. under **tropic**) + English *-al*[1]]

**tropical fish**, any one of certain small, usually brightly colored fishes native to the tropics, commonly kept in home aquariums, such as the guppy, scalare, or swordtail.

**trop|i|cal|ize** (trop'ə kə līz), *v.t.,* **-ized, -iz|ing.** to make tropical; make suitable for tropical climates.

**tropical year**, = solar year.

**tropic bird**, any one of a genus of sea birds resembling the tern, found in tropical regions, swift in flight, and having webbed feet, varied coloration, and a pair of long central tail feathers.

**tropic of Cancer**. See under **tropic**.

**tropic of Capricorn**. See under **tropic**.

**trop|ics** or **Trop|ics** (trop'iks), *n.pl.* See under **tropic**.

**tro|pine** (trō'pēn, -pin), *n.* a poisonous, white, crystalline, basic alkaloid, obtained by the hydrolysis of atropine or hyoscyamine. *Formula:* $C_8H_{15}NO$ [< (a)*tropine*]

**tro|pism** (trō'piz əm), *n.* the tendency of an animal or plant to turn or move in response to a stimulus. [abstracted from *geotropism, heliotropism,* ultimately < Greek *tropḗ* a turning < *trépein* to turn]

**tro|pis|tic** (trō pis'tik), *adj.* of or having to do with a tropism.

**tro|po|col|la|gen** (trō'pō kol'ə jən), *n. Biochemistry.* a basic protein substance from which collagen is formed. [< Greek *trópos* a turning + English *collagen*]

**tro|po|e|las|tin** (trō'pō i las'tin), *n. Biochemistry.* a basic protein substance from which elastin is formed. [< Greek *trópos* a turning + *elastin*]

**trop|o|log|ic** (trop'ə loj'ik), *adj.* figurative or metaphorical: *tropologic interpretation.* —**trop'o|log'i|cal|ly**, *adv.*

**trop|o|log|i|cal** (trop'ə loj'ə kəl), *adj.* = tropologic.

**tro|pol|o|gy** (trō pol'ə jē), *n., pl.* **-gies. 1** the use of metaphor; figurative language. **2** the figurative rendition of a text. **3** the use of a Scriptural text to bring out a moral significance implied but not stated in its direct reading. [< Late Latin *tropologia* < Greek *tropologiā* < *trópos* a turning; see etym. under **trope**]

**tro|po|my|o|sin** (trō'pə mī'ə sin, trop'ə-), *n.* one of the major protein elements of muscle tissue.

**tro|po|pause** (trō'pə pôz), *n.* the area of atmospheric demarcation between the troposphere and the stratosphere.

**tro|poph|i|lous** (trō pof'ə ləs), *adj. Botany.* adapted to a climate which is alternately dry and moist or cold and hot. [< Greek *trópos* a turning (< *trépein* to turn) + *philos* (with English *-ous*) loving]

**trop|o|phyte** (trop'ə fīt), *n.* a plant which is adapted for growth in a climate which is alternately dry and moist or cold and hot, as the deciduous trees. [< Greek *tropḗ* a turning, change + *phytón* plant]

**trop|o|phyt|ic** (trop'ə fit'ik), *adj. Botany.* **1** of or having to do with a tropophyte. **2** like a tropophyte.

**tro|po scatter** (trō'pə), = tropospheric scatter.

**tro|po|sphere** (trō'pə sfir), *n.* the lowest region of the atmosphere, between the earth and the stratosphere, extending to about 10 miles above the earth's surface. Within the troposphere, there is a steady fall of temperature with increasing altitude. Turbulence of the air and most cloud formations occur in the troposphere. See diagram under **atmosphere**. [< French *troposphère* < Greek *tropḗ* a turn, a change + *sphaîra* sphere]

**tro|po|spher|ic** (trō'pə sfer'ik, -sfir'-), *adj.* of or having to do with the troposphere.

**tropospheric scatter**, a way of transmitting radio, television, and radiotelephone signals over long distances by bouncing the signals off the troposphere: *To the communications engineer the important fact is that for a route between 100 and 250 miles tropospheric scatter has unrivalled capacity* (New Scientist).

**trop|po** (trop′ō; *Italian* trôp′pō), *adv. Music.* too much; excessively. *Example: allegro ma non troppo,* fast, but not too fast. [< Italian *troppo* (literally) too much]

**trot¹** (trot), *v.,* **trot|ted, trot|ting,** *n.* —*v.i.* **1** to go at a gait between a walk and a run by lifting the right forefoot and the left hind foot at about the same time and then the other two feet in the same way: *Horses and some other four-legged animals trot.* **2** to ride or drive a horse at a trot. **3** *Figurative.* to run, but not fast; go briskly or busily: *The child trotted along after its mother.*
—*v.t.* **1** to ride or drive (a horse) at a trot; cause to trot: *The rider trotted his horse down the road.* **2** *Figurative.* to conduct or escort (a person to or around a place). **3** *Figurative.* to jog (a child) on one's knee.
—*n.* **1** the motion or gait of a trotting horse. In a slow trot there is always at least one foot on the ground, but in a fast trot all four feet may be momentarily off the ground at once. See picture under **gait**. **2** a slow running; brisk, steady movement. **3** the sound of trotting. **4** a single race in a program of harness racing. **5** *Informal.* **a** a toddling child; toddler. **b** a small or young animal. **6** *U.S. Slang.* a translation used by a student instead of doing the lesson himself; pony: *A lazy student can dispense with the original and use the English text as a trot* (New York Times Book Review).
**trot out,** *Informal.* to bring out for others to see: *Charles trots out his little bit of scientific nomenclature* (William De Morgan).
[< Old French *trotter* < Germanic (compare Old High German *trottōn*)]

**trot²** (trot), *n.* **1** one of the short lines suspended from a trotline. **2** = trotline. [origin unknown]

**trot³** (trot), *n.* an old woman (usually contemptuous); hag: *an old trot with ne'er a tooth in her head* (Shakespeare). [origin unknown]

**troth** (trôth, trōth), *n., v.* —*n. Archaic.* **1** faithfulness; fidelity; loyalty. **2** a promise. **3** truth. **4** betrothal.
—*v.t.* **1** to promise. **2** = betroth.
**in troth,** truly; verily: *In troth I think she would* (Shakespeare).
**plight one's troth, a** to promise to marry: *and thereto I plight thee my troth* (Book of Common Prayer). *These two young people loved, and plighted their troth* (Frederick Marryat). **b** to promise to be faithful; give one's word.
[Middle English *trowthe,* Old English *trēowth* good faith. See etym. of doublet **truth**.]

**troth|plight** (trôth′plīt′, trōth′-), *n., adj., v. Archaic.* —*n.* a solemn promise or engagement, especially of marriage; betrothal.
—*adj.* engaged; betrothed; affianced.
—*v.t.* to engage oneself to; betroth; affiance.

**trot|line** (trot′līn′), *n.* a long fishing line tied or anchored at one end and buoyed or tied at the other, from which short lines with baited hooks are suspended at regular intervals.

**Trots** (trots), *n., pl.* **Trots.** *Informal.* a Trotskyite.

**Trot|sky|ism** (trots′kē iz əm), *n.* the political principles or economic policy of Leon Trotsky, especially the doctrine that world-wide communist revolution must take precedence over everything else, even the growth and development of the Soviet Union. [< Leon *Trotsky,* 1879-1940, a leader in the Russian Revolution of 1917 + *-ism*]

**Trot|sky|ist** (trots′kē ist), *n., adj.* = Trotskyite.

**Trot|sky|ite** (trots′kē īt), *n., adj.* —*n.* a person who believes in or advocates Trotskyism; follower of Leon Trotsky. —*adj.* of or having to do with Trotskyism or Trotskyites.

**trot|ter** (trot′ər), *n.* **1** a horse that trots, especially one bred and trained for such a gait in harness racing: *At Roosevelt Raceway, the trotters and pacers are working out with the same diligence as the thoroughbreds* (New York Times). **2** a person who moves or goes about briskly and constantly.
**trotters,** the feet of a four-footed animal, especially a sheep or pig, used for food.

**trot|teur** (trô tœr′), *adj., n.* —*adj.* (of women's clothing) simple and tailored, and appropriate for outdoor use: *trotteur dresses.*
—*n.* a garment of this kind: *flannel trotteur done up with white piqué at the neckline and wrists* (New Yorker).
[< French *trotteur* (literally) trotter]

**trot|ting race** (trot′ing), a harness race using trotters.

**trot|toir** (trô twär′), *n.* = sidewalk. [< French *trottoir* < *trotter* to trot]

**trot|ty** (trot′ē), *adj.,* **-ti|er, -ti|est.** trotting; brisk.

**tro|tyl** (trō′təl, -tēl), *n.* = trinitrotoluene.

**trou|ba|dour** (trü′bə dôr, -dōr, -důr), *n.* one of a class of knightly lyric poets and composers mainly of southern France and northern Italy from the 1000's to the 1200's. The troubadours wrote mainly about love and chivalry and composed ecstatic, lyrical love songs. [< French *troubadour* < Old Provençal *trobador* < *trobar* to find; (probably earlier) to compose in verse, ultimately < Late Latin *tropus* song; musical mode < Greek *trópos* mode, style; see etym. under **trope**. See etym. of doublet **trouvère**.]

**trou|ble** (trub′əl), *n., v.,* **-bled, -bling.** —*n.* **1** pain and sorrow; distress; worry; difficulty: *a time of great trouble. That unhappy boy makes trouble for his baby sitters. So I was ready When trouble came* (A. E. Housman). SYN: anxiety, affliction. **2** an instance of this; distressing or vexatious circumstance, occurrence, or experience: *a life containing many troubles.* **3** a social disturbance; disorder: *political troubles.* **4** extra work; care; bother; effort: *Can't he at least take the trouble to write a note of thanks? Take the trouble to do careful work.* **5** a cause of inconvenience: *Is she a trouble to you?* **6** an illness; disease: *She has stomach trouble.*
—*v.t.* **1** to cause distress or worry to; disturb; worry: *That boy's poor grades trouble his parents. The lack of business troubled him.* **2** to distress (with something disagreeable and unwelcome); vex; annoy; bother: *to be troubled with poor eyesight.* SYN: afflict. **3** to cause extra work or effort to: *Don't trouble yourself to wash the dishes; you have done a full day's work already. May I trouble you to pass the sugar?* **4** to cause pain to; hurt; pain: *She is troubled by headaches. An abscessed tooth troubled me.* **5** to agitate or ruffle (as water or air), especially so as to make it cloudy or muddy: *For an angel went down ... into the pool, and troubled the water* (John 5:4).
—*v.i.* **1** to cause oneself inconvenience; take the trouble: *Don't trouble to come to the door; I can let myself in.* SYN: bother. **2** *Obsolete.* to be troubled.
**ask for trouble,** to court danger; be careless of one's welfare or safety: *Oh, Major Scobie, what made you write such a letter? It was asking for trouble* (Graham Greene).
**borrow trouble,** to worry about something before there is reason to: *Forget about it; why borrow trouble?*
[< Old French *truble, trouble* < *trubler, troubler* to trouble, disturb < Vulgar Latin *turbulāre* < Latin *turbula* (diminutive) < *turba* turmoil] —**trou′bling|ly,** *adv.*

**trou|bled** (trub′əld), *adj.* disturbed; disordered; agitated: *troubled thoughts, a troubled sleep, medicine for a troubled mind.* —**trou′bled|ly,** *adv.*

**troubled waters,** a situation or state of agitation or disquiet: *An inadvertent inquiry would have brought us into troubled waters* (George Musgrave).
**fish in troubled waters,** to take advantage of trouble or agitation to gain one's end: *The Mafia has at all times delighted in fishing in troubled waters* (New Yorker).

**trou|ble|mak|er** (trub′əl mā′kər), *n.* a person who often causes trouble for others: *The police arrest and arraign and deport suspected Red troublemakers before a lawyer can say habeas corpus* (Time).

**trou|ble|mak|ing** (trub′əl mā′king), *n., adj.* —*n.* the activities of a troublemaker.
—*adj.* making or causing trouble: *troublemaking gangs.*

**trou|bler** (trub′lər), *n.* a person or thing that troubles.

**trou|ble|shoot** (trub′əl shüt′), *v.,* **-shot** or **-shoot|ed, -shoot|ing.** *U.S.* —*v.i.* to work or serve as a troubleshooter.
—*v.t.* to deal with as a troubleshooter; eliminate trouble from: *How to troubleshoot your speedometer* (Popular Mechanics). *He established a Human Relation Advisory Commission to troubleshoot touchy racial problems* (Time).
[back formation < *troubleshooter* and *troubleshooting*]

**trou|ble|shoot|er** (trub′əl shü′tər), *n.* a person who discovers and eliminates causes of trouble, especially one trained or qualified to do so in a particular field or with a particular kind of apparatus: *He ... went wandering as an international banker and economic troubleshooter* (Time).

**trou|ble|shoot|ing** (trub′əl shü′ting), *n., adj.* —*n.* the work of a troubleshooter.
—*adj.* of or having to do with a troubleshooter or his work: *Sometimes he is sent elsewhere on troubleshooting errands of one sort or another* (Edward Newhouse).

**trou|ble|some** (trub′əl səm), *adj.* **1** causing trouble; annoying; full of troubles; distressing: *Bullies are troublesome people.* SYN: disturbing, vexatious, harassing, bothersome. **2** tiresome; difficult: *a troublesome process.* **3** *Obsolete.* disturbed; unsettled. —**trou′ble|some|ly,** *adv.* —**trou′ble|some|ness,** *n.*

**trouble spot,** a troublesome area or locality; place in which trouble is occurring or is likely to occur: *A high level of unemployment was the chief domestic economic trouble spot* (William B. Franklin).

**trou|blous** (trub′ləs), *adj.* **1** disturbed; unsettled; restless: *troublous times.* **2** tempestuous; stormy; violent: *a troublous sea.* **3** = troublesome.
—**trou′blous|ly,** *adv.* —**trou′blous|ness,** *n.*

**trou-de-loup** (trü′də lü′), *n., pl.* **trous-de-loup** (trü′də lü′). one of a series of pits having a pointed stake in the center, used to obstruct the progress of an enemy. [< French *trou-de-loup* (literally) wolf pit]

**trough** (trôf, trof), *n.* **1** a long, narrow, open container for holding food or water, especially for farm stock or other animals: *He led the horses to the watering trough.* SYN: manger. **2** something shaped like this: *The baker used a trough for kneading dough.* **3** a channel for carrying water; gutter: *A wooden trough under the eaves of the house carries off rain water.* SYN: conduit. **4** a long hollow between two ridges: *the trough between two waves or two hills.* SYN: furrow. See picture under **mountain**. **5** *Meteorology.* a long, narrow area of relatively low barometric pressure. **6** *Geology.* a basin-shaped depression; the lowest part of a synclinal fold. **7** *Figurative.* a low or lowest point: *They've also shown a slight tendency to lag at business-cycle peaks and troughs* (Wall Street Journal). [Old English *trog*]
—**trough′like′,** *adj.*

**trounce** (trouns), *v.t.,* **trounced, trounc|ing. 1** to beat or thrash. **2** to beat by way of punishment; inflict physical chastisement upon. **3** *Informal.* to defeat in a contest or match: *The victors trounced the losing team.* [origin uncertain]

**troupe** (trüp), *n., v.,* **trouped, troup|ing.** —*n.* a band or company, especially a group of actors, singers, dancers, acrobats, or other entertainers: *a troupe of strolling actors* (Henry James).
—*v.i.* to tour or travel with a troupe.
[American English < French *troupe* < Old French; see etym. under **troop**]

**troup|er** (trü′pər), *n.* **1** a member of a theatrical or other entertainment troupe. **2** an experienced entertainer, especially an actor (used as a term of praise). **3** any stalwart person.

**troup|i|al** (trü′pē əl), *n.* any American bird of a family including blackbirds, orioles, grackles, and cowbirds, but especially any tropical American oriole with bright plumage. Also, **troopial**. [< French *troupiale* < *troupe* flock < Old French; see etym. under **troop** (because they live in flocks)]

**trou|ser** (trou′zər), *adj., n.* —*adj.* of or belonging to a pair of trousers: *a trouser leg.*
—*n.* a pair of trousers.

**trou|sered** (trou′zərd), *adj.* wearing trousers.

**trou|ser|ing** (trou′zər ing), *n.* cloth for trousers.

**trouser part** or **role,** a male part performed by a woman in a play, opera, or the like: *Marcia Baldwin sang the trouser role of Stephano acceptably* (New Yorker).

**trou|sers** (trou′zərz), *n.pl.* **1** a two-legged, outer garment reaching from the waist to the ankles or to the knees, worn especially by men and boys. SYN: breeches, pants, knickerbockers, slacks. **2** the loose, baglike drawers or pantaloons that are a part of the native dress of both men and women in certain Moslem countries. **3** the lower part of any one of certain two-piece garments, especially pajamas. [< earlier *trouse* < Scottish Gaelic *triubhas,* probably < Old French *trebus* boot]
► See **pants** for usage note.

**trouser suit,** *British.* a pants suit.

**trous|seau** (trü sō′, trü′sō), *n., pl.* **trous|seaux** or **trous|seaus** (trü sōz′, trü′sōz). **1** a bride's outfit of clothes, linen, or the like. **2** *Obsolete.* a bundle. [< French *trousseau* (originally) bundle (diminutive) < *trousse* bundle < Old French *trousser* pack into a bundle; see etym. under **truss**]

**trout** (trout), *n., pl.* **trouts** or (*collectively*) **trout. 1** any one of certain food and game fishes of the same family as the salmon. Trout are found chiefly in cool, fresh waters, although some migrate from the sea to spawn, such as the rainbow trout or steelhead, the cutthroat trout, and the brown trout. **2** any one of a group of similar and related fishes, such as the Dolly Varden, the brook trout, and the lake trout. **3** any one of cer-

---

**Pronunciation Key:** hat, āge, cãre, fär; let, ēqual, tėrm; it, īce; hot, ōpen, ôrder; oil, out; cup, pu̇t, rüle; child; long; thin; ᴛʜen; zh, measure; ə represents **a** in about, **e** in taken, **i** in pencil, **o** in lemon, **u** in circus.

tain fishes which resemble a trout to some extent, such as the trout perch. [partly Old English *trūht* < Late Latin; partly < Old French *troite, truite* < Late Latin *tructa,* or *trocta,* probably < Greek *trṓktēs* a kind of fish (literally) gnawer < *trṓgein* to gnaw] —**trout′less**, *adj.* —**trout′like′**, *adj.*

**trout fly**, a fishing fly used in trout fishing.

**trout|let** (trout′lit), *n.* a little trout.

**trout lily**, the yellow dogtooth violet or adder's-tongue.

**trout|ling** (trout′ling), *n.* = troutlet.

**trout perch**, either of two North American fishes having certain striking similarities to both the trouts and the perches.

**trou|vaille** (trü vä′yə), *n.* something found unexpectedly; windfall; godsend. [< French *trouvaille* a find < *trouver* to find]

**trou|vère** (trü ver′), *n.* one of a class of poets who flourished in northern France from the 1000's to the 1300's, and whose works were chiefly epic in character. [< French *trouvère* < Old North French *trouvere* < *trouver* to compose, ultimately < Late Latin *tropus.* See etym. of doublet **troubadour.**]

**trou|veur** (trü vœr′), *n.* = trouvère.

**trove** (trōv), *n.* **1** something of value found; find; discovery: *delighted as a child at each new trove* (Rudyard Kipling). **2** a treasure. [< (treasure) *trove*]

**tro|ver** (trō′vər), *n. Law.* an action for the recovery of the value of personal property illegally converted by another to his own use. [noun use of Anglo-French, Old French *trouver* to find; see etym. under **trouvère**]

**trow** (trō), *v.i., v.t. Archaic.* to believe or think. [Old English *trēowian.* See related etym. at **troth, true, truth.**]

**trow|el** (trou′əl), *n., v.,* **-eled, -el|ing** or (*especially British*) **-elled, -el|ling.** —*n.* **1** a tool with a broad, flat blade, used for spreading or smoothing plaster or mortar. **2** a tool with a curved blade, used in gardening for loosening earth or taking up small plants.
—*v.t.* **1** to spread (a substance) or smooth (a surface) with or as if with a trowel; form or mold with a trowel. **2** to put, place, or move (something) with a trowel, especially thickly or clumsily: *to trowel mud into a hole;* (*Figurative.*) *to trowel praise.*
**lay it on with a trowel**, to be lavish or excessive in expression as of praise or apology: *Everyone likes flattery; and when you come to Royalty you should lay it on with a trowel* (Benjamin Disraeli).
[< Old French *troele, truele* < Late Latin *truella* a vessel (diminutive) < Latin *trua* a skimmer]
—**trow′el|er**, *especially British,* **trow′el|ler**, *n.* —**trow′el|like′**, *adj.*

**trowel bayonet**, a bayonet with a short and broad but sharp-pointed, trowellike blade, intended to serve also as an entrenching tool.

**trow|el|beak** (trou′əl bēk′), *n.* a broad-beaked bird, or broadbill, of Sumatra.

**troy** (troi), *adj., n.* —*adj.* in, of, or by troy weight. —*n.* = troy weight.
[apparently < Middle French *Troyes,* a city in France, former site of a fair, at which this weight may have been used]

**troy weight**, a standard system of weights used for gems and precious metals. One pound troy equals a little over four fifths of an ordinary pound. In the United States:
24 grains = 1 pennyweight or 1.55 grams
20 pennyweight = 1 ounce or 31.1035 grams
12 ounces or 5,760 grains = 1 pound or 373.24 grams
In Great Britain the ounce and decimal units of the ounce are used.

**trp** (no period), troop.

**tru|an|cy** (trü′ən sē), *n., pl.* **-cies.** the act or habit of playing truant; truant behavior.

**tru|ant** (trü′ənt), *n., adj., v.* —*n.* **1** a child who stays away from school without permission. **SYN**: absentee. **2** *Figurative.* a person who neglects duty or business. **SYN**: shirker.
—*adj.* **1** of or having to do with a truant: *a truant report.* **2** characteristic of a truant; lazy: *truant behavior.* **3** being a truant: (*Figurative.*) *The truant shepherd left his sheep.* **4** *Figurative.* wandering: *That truant dog won't stay home.*
—*v.i.* to be a truant, especially from school.
**play truant, a** to stay away from school without permission: *The boys played truant to go to see the parade.* **b** *Figurative.* to stay away from work or duties: *Several employees who often played truant were recently fired.*
[< Old French *truant* beggar, vagabond, probably < a Celtic word]

**truant officer**, *U.S.* an official whose job is to locate and return truants to school.

**tru|ant|ry** (trü′ən trē), *n., pl.* **-ries.** = truancy.

**truce** (trüs), *n., v.,* **truced, truc|ing.** —*n.* **1** the act of stopping fighting; peace for a short time: *A truce was declared between the two armies. There is never an instant's truce between virtue and vice* (Thoreau). **2** an agreement or treaty effecting this; armistice: *to sign a truce.* **3** *Figurative.* a rest from trouble or pain; respite from something irksome, painful, or oppressive: *The hot weather gave the old man a truce from rheumatism.*
—*v.i.* to make a truce.
[Middle English *trewes,* plural of *trewe,* Old English *trēow* faith, treaty. Compare etym. under **true.**]

**Truce of God**, a cessation of all active warfare, personal feuding, etc., such as was generally practiced on Sundays and holy days by Christians during the 1000's and 1100's.

**tru|cial** (trü′shəl), *adj.* of, having to do with, or bound by a truce (used especially in reference to a truce between the British government and certain sheikdoms in southeastern Arabia, made in 1853): *the trucial states.*

***truck**[1] (truk), *n., v., adj.* —*n.* **1** a motor vehicle designed primarily for the carrying of things rather than people, ranging in size from small vehicles used to carry tools or deliver parcels to large vehicles used to carry very heavy objects, such as furniture and commodities in bulk; motor truck. **2** a strongly built cart, wagon, or other vehicle used for a similar purpose. **3** a frame with two small wheels at the front and handles at the back, used for moving trunks and other heavy loads. **4** a strongly built, rectangular platform resting on four wheels, used to move heavy or bulky objects in a warehouse or factory. **5** any one of various small, light, four-wheeled conveyances used in stores, libraries, and other places, moved by pushing or pulling. **6** a frame that swivels, with two or more pairs of wheels, for supporting the front end of a locomotive or each end of a railroad car. **7** *British.* a flatcar, gondola, or other railroad freight car without a top. **8** a small wooden wheel or roller, such as was formerly used on gun carriages. **9** a wooden or metal disk or block at the top of a flagpole or mast with holes through which the ropes for hoisting a flag or pennant are passed.
—*v.t.* to carry or move on a truck or trucks: *to truck freight to the warehouse.* —*v.i.* **1** to drive a truck. **2** to engage in trucking goods, especially as a business; operate a trucking business. **3** to dance the trucking.
—*adj.* **1** of a truck. **2** for a truck; used on trucks: *a truck tire, a truck license.*
[perhaps < Latin *trochus* iron hoop < Greek *trochós* wheel < *tréchein* to run]

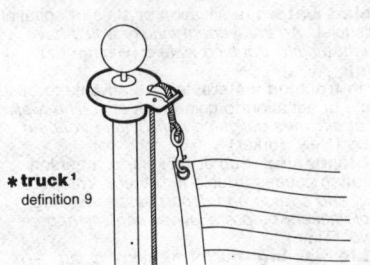

***truck**[1]
definition 9

**truck**[2] (truk), *n., v., adj.* —*n.* **1** vegetables raised for the market. **2** small articles of little value; odds and ends. **3** *Informal.* rubbish; trash. **4** *Informal.* dealings: *She has no truck with peddlers.* **5** exchange; barter. **6** the payment of wages in goods or kind, rather than in money. **7** the system or practice of such payment. [< verb]
—*v.t., v.i.* to give in exchange; barter: *Liberty's too often truck'd for Gold* (Daniel Defoe).
—*adj.* of truck; having to do with truck.
[Middle English *trukien* < Old North French *troquer* to barter, exchange < Medieval Latin *trocare;* origin uncertain]

**truck|age** (truk′ij), *n.* **1** the carrying of goods by a truck or trucks. **2** the charge for carrying by truck.

**truck crop**, *U.S.* a crop grown on a truck farm.

**truck|driv|er** (truk′drī′vər), *n.* a person who drives a truck; trucker.

**truck|er**[1] (truk′ər), *n.* **1** a person who drives a truck. **2** a person who owns a business that carries goods by truck.

**truck|er**[2] (truk′ər), *n.* **1** *U.S.* a person who grows garden produce for market; truck farmer. **2** a barterer; bargainer.

**truck farm** or **garden**, a farm where vegetables are raised for market.

**truck farmer** or **gardener**, a person who operates a truck farm.

**truck farming** or **gardening**, the business of operating a truck farm.

**truck|ing**[1] (truk′ing), *n.* **1** the act or business of carrying goods or articles on a truck or trucks. **2** = truckage. **3** a slow, shuffling cakewalk, danced with the index finger of one hand pointed upward. **4** *U.S. Slang.* the act of walking or marching, especially for a cause: *One poster taped on the wall ... bears the caption: Let's Keep On Truckin'* (Saturday Review).

**truck|ing**[2] (truk′ing), *n.* the raising of vegetables for market; truck farming.

**truck|le**[1] (truk′əl), *v.,* **-led, -ling.** —*v.i.* **1** to give up or submit tamely; be servile: *That man got his position by truckling to his superiors and flattering them.* **SYN**: cringe, fawn. **2** *Obsolete.* to trundle. —*v.t. Obsolete.* to trundle. [< *truckle bed,* formerly used by servants and inferiors]

**truck|le**[2] (truk′əl), *n.* **1** a small wheel, especially a grooved wheel of a pulley. **2** *Dialect.* a small roller; caster. **3** = trundle bed. [< Anglo-French *trocle* < Latin *trochlea* < Greek *trochileiā́;* see etym. under **trochlea**]

**truckle bed**, = trundle bed.

**truck|ler** (truk′lər), *n.* a person who truckles or acts with servility.

**truck|ling|ly** (truk′ling lē), *adv.* in a truckling manner.

**truck|load** (truk′lōd′), *n.* as much or as many as a truck can carry: *truckloads of fish.*

**truck|man** (truk′mən), *n., pl.* **-men.** a man who drives a truck; trucker.

**truck shop** or **store**, a store at which vouchers given to workers can be exchanged for goods.

**truck system**, the system of paying wages in goods or kind, rather than in money.

**truck tractor**, a motor truck consisting of a cab and engine, used to pull a truck trailer; tractor.

**truck trailer**, a trailer designed to be pulled by a motor truck, especially by a truck tractor.

**truc|u|lence** (truk′yə ləns, trü′kyə-), *n.* the quality or condition of being truculent: **a** fierceness and cruelty; brutal harshness. **b** belligerent or defiant quality: *There was a jaunty truculence in the President's voice as he spelled out what the order would mean* (Reporter).

**truc|u|len|cy** (truk′yə lən sē, trü′kyə-), *n.* = truculence.

**truc|u|lent** (truk′yə lənt, trü′kyə-), *adj.* **1** fierce, savage, or violent: *a truculent bully, to be in a truculent mood, a truculent defense of one's rights.* **SYN**: brutal. **2** brutally harsh or scathing: *a truculent remark, truculent satire. Voltaire is never either gross or truculent* (Viscount Morley). **3** belligerent or defiant. **4** *Obsolete.* (of a disease) very dangerous; deadly. [< Latin *truculentus* < *trux, trucis* fierce] —**truc′u|lent|ly**, *adv.*

**trudge** (truj), *v.,* **trudged, trudg|ing,** *n.* —*v.i.* **1** to go on foot; walk. **2** to walk heavily, wearily, or with effort, but steadily and persistently: *Let's ... shoulder our bundles and trudge along* (Louisa May Alcott). **3** *Figurative: to trudge through a dull book.* **SYN**: plod. —*v.t.* to travel (a distance) by trudging; trudge along or over.
—*n.* **1** the act of trudging; hard or weary going; plodding. **2** a hard or weary walk: *It was a long trudge up the hill.* **3** a person who trudges; trudger.
[origin unknown]

**trudg|en stroke**, or **trudg|en** (truj′ən), *n.* a swimming stroke in which the arms, alternately, are raised over the head and brought down and back parallel with the body, usually done with a scissors kick similar to the breaststroke. [< John *Trudgen,* 1852-1902, a British swimmer, who introduced the stroke from Argentina]

**trudg|er**[1] (truj′ər), *n.* a person who trudges.

**trudg|er**[2] (truj′ər), *n.* a swimmer who uses the trudgen stroke.

**true** (trü), *adj.,* **tru|er, tru|est,** *n., v.,* **trued, tru-ing** or **true|ing,** *adv.* —*adj.* **1** agreeing with fact; not false: *It is true that 6 and 4 are 10. The story he told is true; he did not make it up.* **SYN**: See syn. under **real.** **2** real; genuine: *true gold, true kindness.* **3** faithful; loyal: *a true patriot, my truest friend, true to your promises.* **SYN**: constant, staunch. **4** agreeing with a standard; right; proper; correct; exact; accurate: *a true voice, true to type. This is a true copy of my letter.* **5** representative of the class named: *A sweet potato is not a true potato.* **6** rightful; lawful: *the true heir to the property.* **7** *Figurative.* reliable; sure: *a true sign.* **8** accurately formed, fitted, or placed: *a true angle.* **9** steady, as in direction or force; unchanging: *The arrow made a true course through the air.* **10** *Archaic.* truthful. **11** = honest.
—*n.* **1** that which is true. **2** exact or accurate formation, position, or adjustment: *A slanting door is out of true.*
—*v.t.* to make true; shape, place, or make, as in the exact position, place, or form required: *If the combination is a lens, it must be trued* (Hardy and Perrin).
—*adv.* **1** in a true manner; truly; exactly: *His words ring true.* **2** in agreement with the ancestral type: *to breed true.*

**come true**, to happen as expected; become real: *To pack up fragments of a dream, Part of which comes true* (Shelley).
**true up**, to make true; shape, place, or make, as in the exact position, place, or form required: *The clerks, figuring that the weapons had been damaged during the trip over ... trued up quite a number of blades* (New Yorker).
[Middle English *trewe,* Old English *trēowe.* Compare etym. under **troth, truth.**] – **true′ness**, *n.*

**true bill**, a bill of indictment found by a grand jury to be supported by enough evidence to justify hearing the case.

**true blue**, **1** an especially nonfading blue dye or coloring matter. **2** the blue taken as their badge by the Scottish Covenanters of the 1600's. **3** a Scottish Covenanter. **4** the faith of the Scottish Covenanters; Presbyterianism.

**true-blue** (trü′blü′), *adj.* staunch and unwavering, as in one's faith or beliefs; unchanging; loyal: *If you're true-blue, you'll keep the promise you've made. Tom's true-blue. He won't desert* (Mark Twain). SYN: faithful.

**true-born** or **true|born** (trü′bôrn′), *adj.* born of a pure stock; legitimately born; having the sterling qualities associated with such descent: *a true-born nobleman.*

**true-false** (trü′fôls′), *adj.* having to do with or containing statements which must be marked as either true or false: *a true-false test, true-false questions.*

**true-heart|ed** or **true|heart|ed** (trü′här′tid), *adj.* **1** faithful; loyal. **2** honest; sincere.

**true level**, an imaginary line or plane perpendicular at all points to the plumb line.

**true-life** (trü′līf′), *adj.* **1** of or belonging to life; not fictitious; real-life; actual: *a true-life hero.* **2** = true-to-life.

**true|love** (trü′luv′), *n.* **1** a faithful lover; loyal sweetheart. **2** a person to whom love is pledged; eternal sweetheart; beloved: *My truelove hath my heart and I have his* (Philip Sidney). **3** the herb Paris, whose whorl of four leaves with a single flower or berry in the midst suggests the figure of a truelove knot.

**truelove knot**, a complicated bowknot, not easily untied, used as a token or symbol of eternal love.

**true-lov|er's knot** (trü′luv′ərz), = truelove knot.

**true|pen|ny** (trü′pen′ē), *n., pl.* **-nies**. *Archaic.* an honest person; trustworthy fellow.

**true ribs**, ribs which articulate with the sternum or breastbone, in man the first seven pairs.

**true time**, mean time; solar time.

**true-to-life** (trü′tə līf′), *adj.* consistent with, exactly agreeing with, or faithful to life; realistic: *true-to-life illustrations. He ... gives an entertaining and true-to-life account of how an orchestra does its work* (Manchester Guardian).

**true viper**, a poisonous, Old-World snake, that has no pit between the eye and nostrils.

**true vocal cords**, the lower pair of vocal cords, which produce the sound of voice.

**truf|fle** (truf′əl, trü′fəl), *n.* **1** a fungus that grows underground and is valued as food. It has a black, warty exterior and varies in size between that of a walnut and that of a potato. Truffles are native to central and southern Europe. **2** a soft, creamy chocolate candy, often filled with finely ground filberts. [< Old French *truffe* < Old Provençal *truffa* < Late Latin *tūfera,* alteration of Latin *tūber* tuber[1]]

**truf|fled** (truf′əld, trüf′-; trü′fəld), *adj.* cooked, garnished, or stuffed with truffles.

**truffle hound**, a dog or pig trained to find truffles by their scent.

**trug** (trug), *n. British.* **1** a shallow, oblong basket made of wooden strips, used especially for carrying fruit and vegetables. **2** a shallow, wooden tray or pan to hold milk. **3** a tray or hod for mortar. **4** an old local measure for wheat equal to two thirds of a bushel. [perhaps dialect variant < *trough*]

**tru|ism** (trü′iz əm), *n.* a statement that almost everybody knows is true; self-evident truth, especially one that has been needlessly repeated, such as "Health is a blessing." *The original thought of one age becomes the truism of the next* (Henry Hallam). SYN: axiom.

**tru|is|tic** (trü is′tik), *adj.* having the character of a truism; trivially self-evident.

**trull** (trul), *n.* a prostitute; strumpet. [< German *Trulle* fat, sloppy female; prostitute]

**tru|ly** (trü′lē), *adv.* **1** in a true manner; exactly; rightly; faithfully: *Tell me truly what you think.* **2** in fact; really; genuinely: *It was truly a beautiful day.* **3** indeed; verily.

**Tru|man Doctrine** (trü′mən), a declaration made by President Harry S Truman in 1947, that the United States would intervene and help free nations resist "attempted subjugation by armed minorities or by outside pressure."

**tru|meau** (trü mō′; *French* trʏ mō′), *n., pl.* **-meaux** (-mōz′; *French* -mō′). **1** a portion of wall between two openings, as doors or windows. **2** a central pier dividing a wide doorway, as in medieval churches. **3** a mirror or any piece of decorative work covering the space between two openings or above a mantelpiece or the like. [< French *trumeau;* origin uncertain]

**trump**[1] (trump), *n., v.* – *n.* **1a** any playing card of a suit that during the play of a hand ranks higher than the other suits: (*Figurative.*) *He did not object ... to Gladstone's always having the ace of trumps up his sleeve, but only to his pretence that God had put it there* (Henry Labouchere). **b** Often, **trumps**. the suit itself: *Martin, if dirt were trumps, what hands you would have* (Charles Lamb). **2** *Informal, Figurative.* a fine, dependable person; first-rate fellow.
– *v.t.* **1** to take (a trick or card of another suit) with a trump. **2** *Figurative.* to be better than; surpass; beat. – *v.i.* **1** to play a card of the suit that is trump when another suit has been led. **2** to win a trick with a trump.
[alteration of *triumph* < French *triomphe*]

**trump**[2] (trump), *n., v.* – *n.* **1** *Archaic.* **a** a trumpet. **b** the sound of a trumpet. **2** *Scottish, Northern Irish.* a jew's-harp. Also, **tromp**.
– *v.i., v.t. Archaic.* to trumpet.
[< Old French *trompe,* perhaps < Germanic (compare Old High German *trumpa, trumba*). Compare etym. under **trombone**.]

**trump**[3] (trump), *v.t.* to make (up) in order to deceive; fabricate: *to trump up new excuses, to trump up false charges against a person.* SYN: concoct, falsify. [perhaps special use of *trump*[1], or < French *tromper* to deceive]

**trump card**, **1** any card in the suit of trumps; trump. **2** *Figurative.* anything decisive held in reserve for use at a critical time: *The government can count on the support of the military, a possible trump card in any showdown* (Wall Street Journal).

**trumped-up** (trumpt′up′), *adj.* made up in order to deceive; fabricated; spurious: *The Old Mafia leader had to be tried on a trumped-up charge, for lack of anything better* (Norman Lewis).

**trump|er|y** (trum′pər ē, trump′rē), *n., pl.* **-er|ies**, *adj.* – *n.* something showy, but without value; worthless ornaments; useless stuff; rubbish; nonsense. SYN: frippery, trash.
– *adj.* showy but without value; trifling; worthless; useless; nonsensical. SYN: trashy.
[< Old French *tromperie* < *tromper* to deceive]

**∗trumpet**
definition 1a

trumpet

resembling a trumpet:

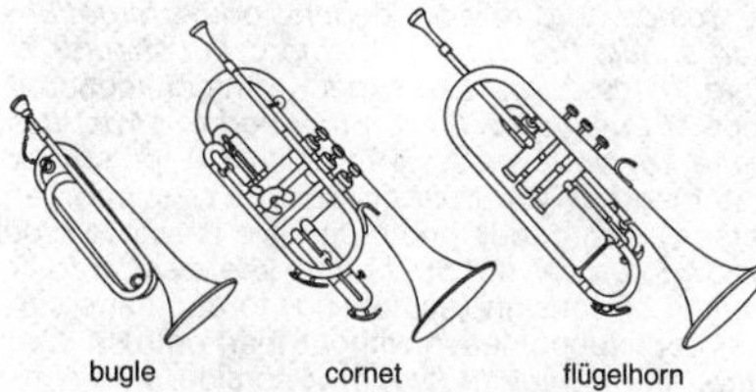
bugle cornet flügelhorn

**∗trum|pet** (trum′pit), *n., v.* – *n.* **1a** a brass wind musical instrument that has a bright, powerful tone, consisting of a tube commonly curved or bent upon itself once or twice, with a cup-shaped mouthpiece at one end and a flaring bell at the other end. **b** a powerful reed organ stop with a tone resembling that of a trumpet. **c** = trumpeter. **2** a thing shaped like a trumpet: *The deaf old lady has an ear trumpet to help her hearing.* **3** a sound like that of a trumpet, especially the loud cry of certain animals, such as the elephant.
– *v.i.* **1** to blow a trumpet. **2** to make a sound like a trumpet: *The elephant trumpeted.*
– *v.t.* **1** to sound on a trumpet. **2** to utter with a sound like that of a trumpet. **3** *Figurative.* to announce or publish as if by sound of trumpet; proclaim loudly or widely: *She will trumpet the news all over town.*
**blow one's own trumpet**, *Especially British.* to sound one's own praises; boast; brag: *There is still some British feeling that there is something slightly disreputable about selling and promoting, about getting out and blowing our own trumpet* (Brendan M. Jones).
[< Old French *trompette* (diminutive) < *trompe;* see etym. under **trump**[2]] – **trum′pet|like′**, *adj.*

**trumpet creeper**, any one of a group of woody climbing plants of the bignonia family, especially a native of the southern United States having clusters of large, scarlet, trumpet-shaped flowers and pinnate leaves; Virginia trumpet flower; trumpet vine. See picture under **bignonia family**.

**trum|pet|er** (trum′pə tər), *n.* **1** a person who blows or plays a trumpet. **2** a soldier who blows calls on a trumpet; bugler. **3** a large wild swan of western North America with a clear and shrill call. **4** any one of a family of South American birds having long legs and necks, related to and resembling the cranes. **5** a variety of domestic pigeon having a shell-shaped crest and heavily feathered feet.

**trumpeter swan**, = trumpeter (def. 3).

**trumpet flower**, **1** any one of certain plants with large or showy, trumpet-shaped flowers, especially the trumpet creeper and the trumpet honeysuckle. **2** the flower of one of these plants.

**trumpet honeysuckle**, a North American honeysuckle, grown for its large, handsome tubular flowers, which are red on the outside and yellowish within; coral honeysuckle.

**trumpet marine**, = tromba marina.

**trumpet narcissus**, a kind of daffodil with a single blossom at the end of each stalk.

**trum|pets** (trum′pits), *n., pl.* **-pets**. any one of various pitcher plants of the southern United States, with leaves shaped like a trumpet.

**trum|pet-shaped** (trum′pit shāpt′), *adj.* tubular, with one end dilated.

**trumpet tree**, = trumpetwood.

**trumpet vine**, = trumpet creeper.

**trum|pet|weed** (trum′pit wēd′), *n.* any one of various eupatoriums, especially: **a** = thoroughwort (def. 1). **b** = joe-pye weed.

**trum|pet|wood** (trum′pit wu̇d′), *n.* a West Indian and South American tree of the mulberry family, whose hollow stems and branches are used for wind instruments.

**trun|cate** (trung′kāt), *v.,* **-cat|ed**, **-cat|ing**, *adj.* – *v.t.* to cut off a part of; cut short: (*Figurative.*) *In the end, my adventure ... was unexpectedly truncated* (New Yorker).
– *adj.* **1** cut off; blunt as if cut off; abrupt: *the truncate leaf of the tulip tree.* **2** having no apex, as some spiral shells.
[< Latin *truncāre* (with English *-ate*[1]) < *truncus* trunk] – **trun′cate|ly**, *adv.*

**trun|cat|ed** (trung′kā tid), *adj.* **1** (of a crystal) having its angles or edges cut off or replaced by a plane face. **2** (of an edge or angle) cut off or replaced by a plane face. **3** = truncate.

**truncated cone** or **pyramid**, a cone or pyramid whose apex or vertex is cut off by a plane.

**trun|ca|tion** (trung kā′shən), *n.* **1** the act of truncating. **2** the state of being truncated. **3** a truncated part. **4** *Crystallography.* the replacement of an angle (or edge) by a crystalline face.

**trun|cheon** (trun′chən), *n., v.* – *n.* **1** a stick cut and shaped for use as a weapon; short club: *a policeman's truncheon.* SYN: cudgel. **2** a staff of office or authority; baton: *a herald's truncheon.* SYN: mace. **3** a length cut from a plant, especially one used for grafting or planting. **4** *Obsolete.* the stem of a tree. **5** *Obsolete.* the shaft of a spear.
– *v.t.* to beat with a truncheon; club.
[< Old French *tronchon* < Vulgar Latin *trunciō, -ōnis* < Latin *truncus* stem, trunk]

**trun|dle** (trun′dəl), *v.,* **-dled**, **-dling**, *n.* – *v.t.* **1** to roll along; push along on a wheel or wheels: *The workman trundled a wheelbarrow full of cement.* **2** to cause to rotate; twirl; spin; whirl. **3** *British Informal, Cricket.* to make (a bowl).
– *v.i.* **1** to move or be moved by trundling. **2** to whirl; revolve. **3** *British Informal, Cricket.* to bowl: [*He*] *is reported to be the best of his type now trundling* (Punch). [probably < Old French *trondeler* roll < Germanic (compare Middle High German *trendeln* to turn, rotate < *trendel* top)]
– *n.* **1** the act of trundling or rolling; rolling along: *Our caboose took up again its easy trundle* (Owen Wister). **2** a small wheel, roller, or revolving disk, especially a small but massive wheel adapted for supporting a heavy weight; caster. **3** = trundle bed. **4a** = lantern pinion. **b** one of its staves. **5** *Obsolete.* a low cart or wagon on small wheels. [perhaps alteration of earlier *trendle,* Old English *trendel* ring, disk]

**trundle bed**, a low bed moving on small wheels;

**Pronunciation Key:** hat, āge, cãre, fär; let, ēqual, tėrm; it, īce; hot, ōpen, ôrder; oil, out; cup, pu̇t, rüle; **ch**ild; lo**ng**; **th**in; ᴛʜen; **zh**, measure; ə represents **a** in about, **e** in taken, **i** in pencil, **o** in lemon, **u** in circus.

truckle bed. It can be pushed under a regular bed when not in use.

**trun|dler** (trun′dlər), *n.* **1** a person who trundles. **2** *British Informal, Cricket.* a bowler.

**trun|dle|tail** (trun′dəl tāl′), *n. Archaic.* a low-bred dog; mongrel; cur.

**trunk** (trungk), *n., adj., v.* —*n.* **1** the main stem of a tree, as distinct from the branches and the roots; bole; stock. **2** *Figurative.* the main part of anything: *The American colonies broke away from the trunk of the British Empire during the Revolution.* **3** a large box, usually with a hinged cover, for holding clothes and other articles when traveling. **4** an enclosed compartment in an automobile for storing baggage, a spare tire, tools, and similar things. **5** a human or animal body without the head, arms, and legs. **6** the thorax of an insect. **7** the main body of a blood vessel, nerve, or similar structure, as distinct from its branches. **8** an elephant's snout. **9** = trunk line. **10** a telephone circuit between two central offices or exchanges, used to make connections between individual subscribers. **11a** the shaft of a column. **b** the dado or die of a pedestal. **12** *Nautical.* **a** a large, enclosed shaft passing through the decks between the bulkheads of a vessel, as for coaling, loading, and ventilation. **b** a watertight casing in a boat or ship, such as the vertical box above the slot for the centerboard. **c** the part above deck of a cabin that is partly above and partly below deck. **13** any one of various boxlike passages for light, air, water, or solid objects, usually made of or lined with boards; wooden shaft, conduit, or chute. **14** the piston rod of a trunk engine.
—*adj.* **1** main; chief: *a trunk highway.* **2** of or having to do with a trunk line, principal artery, channel, or the like. **3** of or having to do with a trunk engine: *a trunk piston.*
—*v.t.* to shut up or enclose in a trunk or casing.
**trunks, a** very short pants or breeches worn by swimmers, boxers, acrobats, and other athletes: *Black velvet trunks cover his* [*the wrestler's*] *hips and thighs* (Archibald Gunter). **b** = trunk hose.
[< Latin *truncus* (originally) mutilated] —**trunk′like′,** *adj.*

**trunk|back** (trungk′bak′), *n.* a large sea turtle of tropical waters; leatherback.

**trunk call,** *British.* a long-distance telephone call: *It has extended the period for cheap rate trunk calls ...* (Economist).

**trunked** (trungkt), *adj.* having a trunk.

**trunk engine,** any one of various reciprocating internal-combustion or steam engines having a piston rod or piston open at one end and tubular. The tubular opening is large enough to permit a connecting rod connected directly to make its lateral motion within the diameter of the opening.

**trunk|fish** (trungk′fish′), *n., pl.* **-fish|es** or (*collectively*) **-fish.** any one of a family of plectognath fishes of tropical seas, having the body encased in bony, armorlike plates, so that only the appendages can be moved.

**trunk|ful** (trungk′fu̇l), *n., pl.* **-fuls.** as much or as many as a trunk will hold: *a trunkful of old books.*

∗**trunk hose,** full, baglike breeches reaching halfway down the thigh, or lower, worn in the 1500's and early 1600's.

∗**trunk hose**

**trunk line, 1** the main line of a railroad, canal, or other system connecting important commercial areas with each other or with the sea. **2** any main line, as between telephone exchanges.

**trunk|load** (trungk′lōd′), *n.* as much or as many as a trunk can hold or carry.

**trunks** (trungks), *n.pl.* See under **trunk.**

**trun|nel** (trun′əl), *n.* = treenail.

**trun|nion** (trun′yən), *n.* **1** either of the two round projections from the barrel of certain cannons, one on each side, which support it on its carriage and act as a pivot in elevation. **2** either of any similar pair of opposite supporting pins or pivots. **3** a single projecting pivot. [< Middle French *trognon* trunk < Latin *truncus;* influenced by Old French *moignon* stump of an amputated limb]

**trun|nioned** (trun′yənd), *adj.* provided with trunnions.

**truss** (trus), *v., n.* —*v.t.* **1** to tie; fasten; bind: *to truss up a bundle of plants. We trussed the burglar and called the police.* **2** to fasten the wings or legs of (a fowl or small animal) with skewers or twine in preparation for cooking: *Mother trussed up the turkey before roasting it.* **3** to support (a roof, bridge, or other structure) with trusses; strengthen or hold together with trusses. **4** *Archaic.* to fasten or tighten (a garment). **5** *Obsolete.* to bundle or pack.
—*n.* **1** a framework of beams or other supports usually connected in a series of triangles and used to form a support for a roof or bridge. **2** a bandage or pad used for support, especially one equipped with a belt and used to support a hernia. **3** a bundle; pack. **4** a bundle of hay or straw, especially (in England) a bundle weighing 56 pounds of old hay, or 60 pounds of new hay, or 36 pounds of straw. **5** a compact cluster or head of flowers of any kind, growing upon one stalk, such as an umbel or corymb. **6** *Nautical.* an iron fitting at the center of a heavy lower yard by which it is fastened to the mast. **7** *Architecture.* a large corbel or modillion.
[< Old French *trusser, trousser,* perhaps ultimately < Late Latin *torcere,* for Latin *torquēre* to twist] —**truss′er,** *n.*

**truss bridge,** a bridge supported wholly or chiefly by trusses.

**truss|ing** (trus′ing), *n.* **1** the timbers, girders, or other supports, forming a truss. **2** a brace or support consisting of a truss or trusses. **3** trusses collectively. **4** the act or process of strengthening or supporting with a truss or trusses.

**trust** (trust), *n., adj., v.* —*n.* **1** a firm belief in the honesty, truthfulness, justice, or power of a person or thing; faith: *A child puts trust in his parents.* SYN: confidence, credence, reliance. **2** a person or thing trusted: *God is our trust.* **3** confident expectation or hope: *Our trust is that she will soon be well.* **4** something managed for the benefit of another; something committed to one's care: *The house is a trust which he holds for his dead brother's children.* **5** the obligation or responsibility imposed on one in whom confidence or authority is placed: *He will be faithful to his trust.* SYN: charge, commission, duty, office. **6** the condition of one in whom trust has been placed; being relied on: *A guardian is in a position of trust.* **7** keeping; care: *The farm was left in the caretaker's trust.* **8** confidence in the ability or intention of a person to pay at some future time for goods or services; business credit. **9** *Law.* **a** a confidence reposed in a person by making him nominal owner of property, which he is to hold, use, or dispose of for the benefit of another. **b** an estate or other financial holding committed to a trustee or trustees. **c** the right of a person to enjoy the use or profits of property held in trust for him. **10** an illegal combination of businessmen or companies having a central committee to control the production and price of some commodity and to eliminate or reduce competition: *a steel trust.*
—*adj.* **1** managing property for an owner. A trust company undertakes to manage property for anyone. **2a** of or having to do with a trust or trusts. **b** held in trust.
—*v.t.* **1** to believe firmly in the honesty, truth, justice, or power of; have faith in: *He is a man to be trusted.* **2** to rely on; depend on: *A forgetful man should not trust his memory, but should write things down.* **3** to expect with confidence; hope: *I trust you will soon feel better. I trust this is the key you wanted.* **4** to believe (a person or statement): *if you trust my story.* **5** to supply (a person) with goods on credit; give business credit to: *The butcher will trust us for the meat.* **6** to commit or consign (something) to another's care with confidence; leave without fear; entrust: *Can I trust the money to him?* SYN: confide. **7** to confide or entrust something to the care of; invest: *Can I trust him with a large sum of money?* **8** to allow to go somewhere or do something without misgiving or fear of consequences.
—*v.i.* **1** to have faith (in); believe: *Trust in God.* **2** to hope (for). **3** to sell on credit.
**in trust,** as something taken charge of for another: *His sealed commission, left in trust with me* (Shakespeare).
**on trust, a** with confidence without investigation or evidence: *I am content to be beloved on trust for what I feel* (Byron). **b** on business credit; with payment later: *My master lived on trust at an alehouse* (Samuel Johnson).
**trust to,** to rely or depend on: *to trust to luck.*
[< Scandinavian (compare Old Icelandic *traust*)] —**trust′a|ble,** *adj.* —**trust′er,** *n.* —**trust′less,** *adj.*

**trust|a|bil|i|ty** (trus′tə bil′ə tē), *n.* trustable quality; credibility; reliability.

**trust|bust|er** (trust′bus′tər), *n. U.S.* a Federal official who breaks up, or tries to break up, business trusts and enforce the antitrust laws.

**trust|bust|ing** (trust′bus′ting), *n., adj. U.S.* —*n.* the activities of a trustbuster: *The politics of a flurry of trustbusting in an election year isn't lost on Justice Department politicians* (Wall Street Journal).
—*adj.* breaking up, or trying to break up companies combined to restrain competition.

**trust company,** a bank or other business concern that takes charge of the property of others and also often engages in other financial activities normally performed by banks.

**trust deed,** a deed to property, held in trust to secure payment of a debt. It is in the nature of a mortgage.

**trus|tee** (trus tē′), *n., v.,* **-teed, -tee|ing.** —*n.* **1** a person or one of a group of persons responsible for the property or the affairs of another person or of an institution, business firm, or the like: *A trustee will manage the children's property until they grow up. The Youth of a nation are the trustees of Posterity* (Benjamin Disraeli). SYN: steward. **2** *U.S.* a person who holds property attached from a debtor.
—*v.t.* **1** *U.S.* to attach by garnishment. **2** to turn over to the care of a trustee or trustees.

**trustee process,** *U.S., Law.* the attachment of property or rights by garnishment.

**trus|tee|ship** (trus tē′ship), *n.* **1** the position of a trustee. **2** the administration by a country of a trust territory, approved by the United Nations, usually with the idea that the trust territory will be developed toward self-government or independence. **3** = trust territory.

**trust|ful** (trust′fəl), *adj.* ready to confide; ready to have faith; trusting; believing: *That trustful boy would lend money to any of his friends. Trustful birds have built their nests* (Robert Bridges). SYN: confiding, credulous, unsuspicious, naive.
—**trust′ful|ly,** *adv.* —**trust′ful|ness,** *n.*

**trust fund,** money, property, or other valuables held in trust by one person for the benefit of another.

**trust|ing** (trus′ting), *adj.* that trusts; trustful: *a man of trusting nature.* —**trust′ing|ly,** *adv.* —**trust′ing|ness,** *n.*

**trust territory,** any one of various territories, regions, or small countries, administered for the United Nations by various countries, especially former colonial possessions or League of Nations mandates in Africa, Asia, or the Pacific.

**trust|wor|thy** (trust′wėr′ŧʜē), *adj.* that can be depended on or trusted; deserving confidence; reliable: *a trustworthy guide, a trustworthy report. The memory strengthens ... and becomes trustworthy as you trust it* (Thomas De Quincey). SYN: dependable, faithful. See syn. under **reliable.**
—**trust′wor′thi|ly,** *adv.* —**trust′wor′thi|ness,** *n.*

**trust|y** (trus′tē), *adj.,* **trust|i|er, trust|i|est,** *n., pl.* **trust|ies.** —*adj.* **1** that can be depended on; trustworthy; reliable: *The master left his money with a trusty servant.* **2** = trustful.
—*n.* **1** a prisoner who is given special privileges or responsibilities because of his good behavior. **2** any person or thing that is trustworthy. —**trust′i|ly,** *adv.* —**trust′i|ness,** *n.*

**truth** (trüth), *n., pl.* **truths** (trüŧʜz, trüths). **1** that which is true: *to speak truth. Is he telling the truth?* **2** the fact or facts; matter or circumstance as it really is: *to suspect the truth.* **3** a fixed or established principle, law, or the like; proven doctrine; verified hypothesis: *a basic scientific truth. It is the customary fate of new truths to begin as heresies and to end as superstitions* (Thomas H. Huxley). *All great truths begin as blasphemies* (George Bernard Shaw). **4** that which is true, real, or actual, in a general or abstract sense; reality: *to find truth in God.* **5** the quality or nature of being true, exact, honest, sincere, or loyal: *His friends his truth proclaim* (John Dryden). **6 Truth,** God (in the belief of Christian Scientists).
**in truth,** in fact; truly; really; verily: *These people pretend to blame him, whereas in truth they ought only to blame themselves* (Daniel Defoe).
[Old English *trēowth* < *trēowe* true. See etym. of doublet **troth.**] —**truth′less,** *adj.*

**truth drug,** = truth serum.

**truth|ful** (trüth′fəl), *adj.* **1** disposed to tell, or habitually telling, the truth; free from deceitfulness: *a truthful child.* SYN: veracious, honest, candid. **2** telling the truth; correct in statement: *a truthful witness.* **3** conforming to truth; factually accurate: *You can count on him for a truthful report of the accident.* SYN: exact, correct. —**truth′ful|ly,** *adv.* —**truth′ful|ness,** *n.*

**truth serum,** any one of various drugs, especially thiopental sodium or scopolamine, under the influence of which a person will reveal inner thoughts or emotions.

**truth set,** = solution set.

**truth table,** a table that lists all possible combinations of true and false values that can be assigned to a proposition. Truth tables are designed to show logical relationships and are used in mathematics, logic, and computer engineering.

**truth-val|ue** (trüth′val′yü), *n.* the truth or falseness of a proposition.

**try** (trī), *v.,* **tried, try|ing,** *n., pl.* **tries.** —*v.i.* **1** to make an attempt or effort; endeavor; attempt: *He tried hard but could not succeed.* **2** to make an experiment.
—*v.t.* **1** to attempt to do or accomplish: *He tried to do the work. It seems easy until you try it.* **2** to experiment on or with; make a trial of: *Try this candy and see if you like it.* **3** to find out about; put to the proof; test: *We try each car before we sell it.* **4** to investigate in a law court: *The man was tried and found guilty of robbery.* **5** to settle by test or investigation. **6** to subject to trials; afflict: *Job was greatly tried.* **7** to put to severe test; strain: *Her mistakes try my patience.* **8** to make pure by melting or boiling; render: *The lard was tried in a big kettle.* **SYN:** purify, refine, assay. **9** to shave or smooth the surface of, so as to fit with or to an adjoining surface, especially by planing. **10** to ascertain the truth or right of (as a matter or a quarrel) by test or endeavor.
—*n.* **1** an attempt; endeavor; effort: *Each boy had three tries at the high jump.* **2** a trial; test; experiment. **3** a play in Rugby scoring three points, made by holding the ball on or beyond the opponents' goal line.
**try on,** to put on to test the fit or looks of (a garment): *She tried on her new dress.*
**try out, a** to test the effect or result of: *The new rules have been but partially tried out* (New York Evening Post). **b** to test to find out about; sample: *Picked pilots of proved experience ... volunteer to try out new types* (Aeroplane). **c** to undergo a test or trial to determine fitness: *He tried out for the hockey team. One recent afternoon we watched [them] pass judgment on the merits of a couple of hundred dancers and showgirls who were assembled to try out for the weekly program* (New Yorker). **d** to separate (fat, grease, or the like, from a substance) by roasting, boiling, or steaming: *The whalers tried out the blubber in a large pot.*
**try over,** *Especially British.* to go through by way of experiment: *Let's try it over before we decide.*
[< Old French *trier* to cull; origin uncertain]
—*Syn. v.i.* **1 Try, attempt, endeavor** mean to make an effort to or at. **Try** is the general word: *I tried to see him.* **Attempt,** a more formal word, suggests making a great effort or trying hard: *I attempted to obtain an interview.* **Endeavor,** also formal, suggests both great effort and greater obstacles to be overcome: *The United Nations is endeavoring to establish peace.*
▶ **try and** or **try to.** The standard English idiom is *try to,* not *try and: Let us try to* (not *try and*) *get permission.*

**try|ing** (trī′ing), *adj.* hard to endure or bear; annoying; distressing: *a trying day, a trying person.* **SYN:** severe, difficult, vexing. —**try′ing|ly,** *adv.*

**trying plane,** a type of large plane used in trying a surface.

**try|ma** (trī′mə), *n., pl.* **-ma|ta** (-mə tə). a fruit resembling a drupe, but formed from an originally compound ovary, and having a fleshy or fibrous outer covering (epicarp) which ultimately dehisces, as in the walnut and hickory; a kind of drupaceous nut. [< New Latin *tryma* < Greek *tryma* hole < *tryein* wear through by rubbing]

**try-on** (trī′on′, -ôn′), *n.* the act of trying on a garment.

**try|out** (trī′out′), *n. Informal.* **1** a test made to determine fitness for a specific purpose; experimental trial. **2** a selective trial to eliminate contestants or candidates not sufficiently capable to compete: *Olympic tryouts. Tryouts for the school play will be held next week.* **3** the showing of a play before the opening. [American English]

**tryp|a|no|so|ma** (trip′ə nə sō′mə), *n.* = trypanosome.

**tryp|a|no|so|mal** (trip′ə nə sō′məl), *adj.* **1** of or having to do with trypanosomes. **2** caused by trypanosomes.

**tryp|a|no|so|mat|ic** (trip′ə nō sō mat′ik), *adj.* = trypanosomal.

**tryp|a|no|some** (trip′ə nə sōm, tri pan′ə-), *n.* any one of a group of minute, parasitic, flagellate protozoans inhabiting the blood of vertebrates, usually transmitted by blood-sucking insects or leeches and causing serious diseases, such as African sleeping sickness and nagana. [< New Latin *Trypanosoma* < Greek *trypanon* a borer, auger (< *trȳpân* to bore) + *sôma* a body]

**tryp|a|no|so|mi|a|sis** (trip′ə nō sō mī′ə sis), *n.* diseases caused by infection by trypanosomes.

**tryp|ars|am|ide** (trip′ärs am′id, -īd; trip är′sə mid, -mīd), *n.* a crystalline drug used to treat syphilis and sleeping sickness. *Formula:* $C_8H_{10}O_4N_2As\cdot Na\cdot \frac{1}{2}H_2O$

**try pot,** a large iron pot used by whalers to remove the oil from blubber by cooking.

**tryp|sin** (trip′sən), *n.* **1** an enzyme in the juice secreted by the pancreas, that aids in digestion by changing proteins into peptones by hydrolysis. **2** any enzyme having a similar function. [< German *Trypsin* < Greek *trîpsis* a rubbing (< *tribein* rub) + German *-in* (originally obtained by rubbing the pancreas with glycerine)]

**tryp|sin|o|gen** (trip sin′ə jən), *n.* an inactive form of the pancreatic enzyme trypsin, converted into trypsin by enterokinase in the small intestine.

**tryp|ta|mine** (trip′tə mēn), *n.* a crystalline substance closely related to serotonin, formed in the tissues from tryptophan. Formula: $C_{10}H_{12}N_2$

**tryp|tic** (trip′tik), *adj.* having to do with trypsin.

**tryp|to|phan** (trip′tə fan), *n.* a colorless, solid, essential amino acid formed from proteins by the digestive action of trypsin. *Formula:* $C_{11}H_{12}N_2O_2$ [< *tryptic* + Greek *phaínein* to appear]

**tryp|to|phane** (trip′tə fān), *n.* = tryptophan.

**try|sail** (trī′sāl′; *Nautical* trī′səl), *n.* a small triangular or four-sided sail attached to a gaff, on the foremast, mainmast, or a small extra mast, and used in stormy weather; spencer.

**trysail mast,** a small mast behind the foremast, on which a trysail is set.

**try square,** an instrument consisting of two straight pieces attached at right angles to each other, used for drawing right angles or for testing the squareness of anything.

**tryst** (trist, trīst), *n., v.* —*n.* **1** an appointment or engagement to meet at a certain time and place, especially one made by lovers. **2** an appointed meeting. **3** a place of meeting by appointment or engagement; rendezvous. **4** *Scottish.* a market or fair, especially for cattle.
—*v.i. Especially Scottish.* to make an agreement (to do something with a person), especially to fix a time and place of meeting (with someone).
—*v.t. Especially Scottish.* **1** to engage with (a person) to meet at a given place and time; agree to meet. **2** to fix (a time or place). [< Old French *triste;* origin uncertain] —**tryst′er,** *n.*

**tryst|ing place** (tris′ting, trīs′-), an appointed meeting place; place where a tryst is to be kept.

**tsa|di** or **tsa|de** (tsä′dē, -dā), *n.* = sadhe.

**tsar** (zär, tsär), *n.* = czar.

**tsar|dom** (zär′dəm, tsär′-), *n.* = czardom.

**tsar|e|vitch** (zär′ə vich, tsär′-), *n.* = czarevitch.

**tsa|rev|na** (zä rev′nə, tsä-), *n.* = czarevna.

**tsa|ri|na** (zä rē′nə, tsä-), *n.* = czarina.

**tsar|ism** (zär′iz əm, tsär′-), *n.* = czarism.

**tsar|ist** or **Tsar|ist** (zär′ist, tsär′-), *adj., n.* = czarist.

**tsa|rit|za** or **tsa|rit|sa** (zä rēt′sə, tsä-), *n.* = czarina.

**tses|se|be** (sas′ə bē), *n., pl.* **-bes** or (*collectively*) **-be.** = sassaby.

**tset|se fly,** or **tset|se** (tset′sē), *n.* any one of a group of two-winged African flies that suck the blood of mammals and transmit disease. One kind transmits the parasite that causes sleeping sickness, and another kind carries a disease of horses and other domestic animals. See picture at **fly**[1]. Also, **tzetze fly, tzetze.** [< Bantu word]

**tsetse fly disease,** = nagana.

**T. Sgt.,** technical sergeant.

**TSH** (no periods) or **T.S.H.,** thyroid stimulating hormone; thyrotropin.

**Tshi** (chwē, chē), *n., pl.* **Tshi** or **Tshis.** = Twi.

**Tshi|lu|ba** (chi lü′bə), *n.* a Bantu language used widely in the Congo as a lingua franca.

**T-shirt** (tē′shėrt′), *n.* **1** a light, close-fitting knitted shirt with short sleeves and no collar, worn for sports or as part of a dress or suit when decorated with colorful designs: *For work or casual lunches, ... the ensemble can be worn with Klein's buff T-shirt* (Time). **2** an undershirt like this. **3** a collarless polo shirt. Also, **tee shirt.** [because of the shape]

**Tsim|shi|an** (tsim′shē ən), *n., adj.* —*n.* **1** a member of an American Indian tribe of the northwestern coast of British Columbia. **2** the language of this tribe, related to Penutian. —*adj.* of or having to do with the Tsimshians or their language.

**tsp.,** **1** teaspoon or teaspoons. **2** teaspoonful.

**T square,** a T-shaped ruler used for making lines, especially parallel lines. The shorter arm slides along the edge of the drawing board which serves as a guide. See picture under **set square.**

**T-strap** (tē′strap′), *n., adj.* —*n.* a woman's shoe with a vertical center strap that fastens to another strap around the ankle. —*adj.* having such straps: *T-strap sandals or pumps.*

**tsu|na|mi** (tsü nä′mē), *n.* an oceanic tidal wave caused by a submarine earthquake. [< Japanese *tsunami* < *tsu* harbor + *nami* wave]

**tsu|na|mic** (tsü nä′mik), *adj.* of or having to do with a tsunami.

**tsu|tsu|ga|mu|shi disease** (tsü tsü′gə mü′shē), = scrub typhus. [< Japanese *tsutsugamushi* the bug that transmits the disease < *tsutsuga* disease + *mushi* insect]

**tsu|tsu|mu** (tsü tsü′mü), *n.* the Japanese art of packaging: *About two hundred examples of tsutsumu, ... in which simple materials such as bamboo and paper are used to create ingenious wrappings for everyday articles* (New Yorker). [< Japanese *tsutsumu* package, bundle]

**Tswa|na** (tswä′nə, chwä′-), *n., pl.* **-na** or **-nas.** **1** any one of the Bantu people of Botswana; Bechuana. **2** the language of this people; Setswana.

**T Tauri star,** any one of a group of very distant, variable stars found between clouds of dust and gas, usually associated with nebulae. [< *T Tauri,* a star in the constellation *Taurus,* the prototype of these stars]

**T-time** (tē′tīm′), *n.* the moment at the end of the countdown when a rocket or missile is launched. [short for *Take-off time*]

**TTS** (no periods), teletypesetter.

**Tu** (no period), thulium (chemical element). The accepted abbreviation today is *Tm.*

**Tu.,** Tuesday.

**T.U.,** trade union or trade unions.

**tu|an** or **Tu|an** (tü än′), *n.* a title of respect, equivalent to sir, master, or lord in certain areas of southeastern Asia: *they called him Tuan Jim: as one might say—Lord Jim* (Joseph Conrad). [< Malay *tuan*]

**Tua|reg** (twä′reg), *n., pl.* **-regs** or **-reg.** **1** a Moslem nomad of the Sahara speaking a Hamitic language of the Libyan or Berber group. **2** this language. Also, **Touareg.**

**tu|a|ta|ra** (tü′ə tä′rə), *n.* a large lizardlike reptile of New Zealand, the only surviving member of a prehistoric order of reptiles; sphenodon. [< Maori *tuatara*]

**tu|a|te|ra** (tü′ə tā′rə), *n.* = tuatara.

**tu|ath** (tü′ə), *n.* an Irish tribal group or territorial division during the time the Celts gained control of Ireland. [< Irish *tuath*]

**tub** (tub), *n., v.,* **tubbed, tub|bing.** —*n.* **1** a large, open container for washing or bathing. **2** = bathtub. **3** *Informal.* a bath: *He takes a cold tub every morning.* **4** a round, wooden container for holding butter, lard, or something similar, in bulk, especially one made of staves and hoops. **SYN:** firkin, kit. **5** as much as a tub can hold; contents of a tub. **6** a thing or person resembling a tub, especially in clumsy squatness of line or bulkiness of form: **a** *Informal.* a clumsy, slow boat or ship, especially one which is too broad in proportion to its length. **b** *Slang.* a fat person. **7** a small cask or keg containing about four gallons, especially of brandy, rum, or other liquor (a smugglers' term). **8a** a car for carrying ore in a mine; tram. **b** a bucket or box in which coal or ore is sent up from or conveyed in a mine. **c** the lining of a mine shaft.
—*v.t.* **1** to wash or bathe in a tub. **2** to put or pack in a tub. **3** to plant in a tub.
—*v.i.* to be washed or bathed in a tub.
[compare Middle Dutch *tubbe* (originally) a vessel with two handles]

***tuba**[1]
definition 1

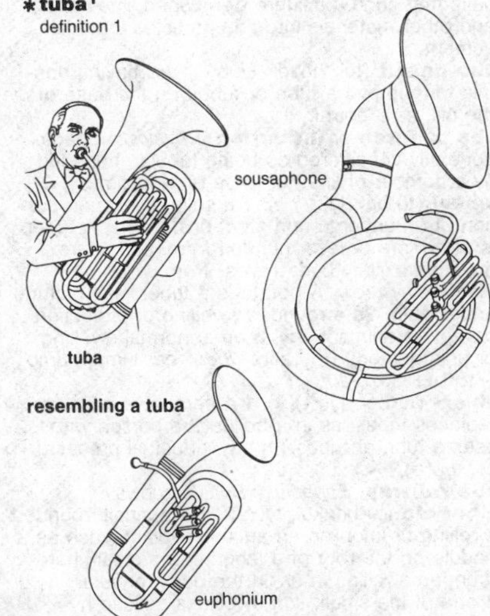


***tu|ba**[1] (tü′bə, tyü′-), *n., pl.* **-bas, -bae** (-bē). **1** a large, brass wind musical instrument that is low in pitch; bass horn. **2** a very powerful, 8-foot, organ reed stop. **3** a long, straight war trumpet of the ancient Romans. [< Latin *tuba* war trumpet]

**Pronunciation Key:** hat, āge, cãre, fär; let, ēqual, tėrm; it, īce; hot, ōpen, ôrder; oil, out; cup, pu̇t, rüle; child; long; thin; ᴛʜen; zh, measure; ə represents a in about, e in taken, i in pencil, o in lemon, u in circus.

**tu|ba**[2] (tü′bä, tü bä′), *n.* an alcoholic drink of the Philippines, made of the fermented sap of the coconut palm. [< Malay *tuba*]

**tub|al** (tü′bəl, tyü′-), *adj., n.* —*adj.* **1** of or having to do with a tube. **2** occurring in a tube, especially a Fallopian tube: *tubal pregnancy.*
—*n.* a Fallopian tube.

**Tu|bal-cain** (tü′bəl kān′, tyü′-), *n.* a pioneer in making things out of iron and brass (in the Bible, Genesis 4:22).

**tubal tonsil**, a mass of lymphoid tissue at the entrance of the Eustachian tube.

**tu|bate** (tü′bāt, tyü′-), *adj. Botany.* **1** forming a tube; tubiform. **2** having a tube or tubes.

**tub|ba|ble** (tub′ə bəl), *adj.* that can be bathed or put in a tub.

**tub|ber** (tub′ər), *n.* **1** a person who makes tubs; cooper. **2** a person who uses a tub in any industrial process. **3** a person who tubs; bather.

**tub|bing** (tub′ing), *n.* a bath; washing.

**tub|by** (tub′ē), *adj.,* **-bi|er, -bi|est.** **1** shaped like a tub; short and fat; stout or broad in proportion to height or length; corpulent: *a short, tubby fellow.* SYN: chunky. **2** having a sound like that of an empty tub when struck. —**tub′bi|ness**, *n.*

**tub chair**, *British.* a barrel chair.

**tube** (tüb, tyüb), *n., v.,* **tubed, tub|ing.** —*n.* **1** a long pipe of metal, glass, rubber, plastic, or other material. Tubes are used especially to carry or contain a liquid or gas. **2** a small cylinder of thin, easily bent metal with a cap that screws on the open end, used for holding toothpaste, shaving cream, paint, or some similar material. **3** = inner tube. **4** a pipe or tunnel through which something is sent, especially by means of compressed air. **5** a railroad tunnel, especially one bored through rock or under a body of water: *the Hudson tubes.* **6** *Especially British Informal.* a subway. **7** anything like a tube, especially any one of certain tubular or cylindrical animal organs: *the Eustachian tube, the bronchial tubes.* **8** an electron or vacuum tube. **9** *Botany.* the lower united portion of a gamopetalous corolla or a gamosepalous calyx. **10** *Physics.* tube of force. **11** *Informal.* television, especially a television set.
—*v.t.* **1** to furnish or fit with a tube or tubes; insert a tube in. **2** to pass through or enclose in a tube. **3** to make tubular.
[< Latin *tubus* tube, pipe] —**tube′like′**, *adj.*

**tube foot**, one of the many tubular organs of locomotion of a starfish, sea urchin, or other echinoderm.

**tube|less tire** (tüb′lis, tyüb′-), a pneumatic tire with butyl rubber bonded directly to the inside of the casing, sealing the tire to the rim of the wheel and eliminating the need for a separate inner tube: *Some tubeless tires are designed to seal themselves if punctured* (Donald G. Keen).

**tube mill**, a crushing and grinding machine consisting of a cylinder containing thousands of steel balls that grind a mixture of crushed limestone and other materials into fine particles to make cement.

**tube-nosed** (tüb′nōzd′, tyüb′-), *adj.* having nostrils formed into a tube or tubes on the base of the bill, as a petrel.

**tube of force** or **induction**, *Physics.* a space, generally considered as being tubular, bounded by a number of lines of force or induction.

**tu|ber**[1] (tü′bər, tyü′-), *n.* **1** a solid, thickened portion of an underground stem or rhizome. A tuber is of a more or less rounded form, and bears modified axillary buds (eyes) from which new plants may grow. A potato is a tuber. See picture under **bulb**. **2a** a rounded swelling or projecting part in an animal body. **b** an abnormal swelling or enlargement. [< Latin *tūber, -eris* lump, bump] —**tu′ber|like′**, *adj.*

**tub|er**[2] (tü′bər, tyü′-), *n.* **1** a person who fits or replaces tubes, as in a boiler. **2** a person who uses a tube or tubes (in any industrial process). [< *tub*(e) + *-er*[1]]

**tube railway**, *Especially British.* subway.

**tu|ber|cle** (tü′bər kəl, tyü′-), *n.* **1** a small, rounded swelling or knob on an animal or plant, such as a nodule on the root of a legume. **2** a small, hard, rounded swelling in or on the body; nodule. **3** one of the small, soft swellings caused by tuberculosis. **4** a knob (tuberculum costae) near the head of a rib at the point of articulation with the transverse process of a vertebra. [< Latin *tūberculum* small swelling, pimple (diminutive) < *tūber* lump]

**tubercle bacillus**, the bacillus that causes tuberculosis.

**tu|ber|cled** (tü′bər kəld, tyü′-), *adj.* characterized by or affected with tubercles.

**tu|ber|cu|lar** (tü bėr′kyə lər, tyü-), *adj., n.* —*adj.* **1** of or having to do with tuberculosis: *tubercular symptoms.* **2** having tuberculosis; tuberculous. **3** having tubercles. **4** having to do with tubercles. **5** characterized by tubercles.
—*n.* a tuberculous person. —**tu|ber′cu|lar|ly**, *adv.*

**tu|ber|cu|late** (tü bėr′kyə lit, -lāt; tyü-), *adj.* **1** having or affected with tubercles. **2** tubercular; tuberculous. [< New Latin *tuberculatus* < Latin *tūberculum;* see etym. under **tubercle**]

**tu|ber|cu|lat|ed** (tü bėr′kyə lā′tid, tyü-), *adj.* **1** = tuberculate. **2** characterized by tubercles.

**tu|ber|cu|la|tion** (tü bėr′kyə lā′shən, tyü-), *n.* **1** the formation of tubercles. **2** the disposition or arrangement of tubercles. **3** a growth or set of tubercles.

**tu|ber|cule** (tü′bər kyül, tyü′-), *n. Botany.* a tubercle; nodule.

**tu|ber|cu|lin** (tü bėr′kyə lin, tyü-), *n.* a liquid substance prepared from the proteins of the tubercle bacillus, or products of these proteins. Tuberculin is used in the diagnosis and treatment of tuberculosis, especially in children and animals. [< German *Tuberkulin* < Latin *tūberculum;* see etym. under **tubercle**]

**tu|ber|cu|line** (tü bėr′kyə lin, -lēn; tyü-), *n.* = tuberculin.

**tuberculin test**, a test to determine the presence of tuberculosis, made by injecting tuberculin into the skin.

**tu|ber|cu|lize** (tü bėr′kyə līz, tyü-), *v.t.,* **-lized, -liz|ing.** **1** to affect with tubercles; infect with tuberculosis; make tuberculous. **2** to treat with tuberculin. —**tu|ber′cu|li|za′tion**, *n.*

**tu|ber|cu|loid** (tü bėr′kyə loid, tyü-), *adj.* resembling tuberculosis or a tubercle.

**tu|ber|cu|lo|sis** (tü bėr′kyə lō′sis, tyü-), *n.* a disease that can affect any organ or part of the body, but most often the lungs, characterized by an inflammation or the formation of tubercles on the tissues, and caused by the tubercle bacillus. Tuberculosis of the lungs was formerly called consumption. *Abbr:* TB (no periods). [< New Latin *tuberculosis* < Latin *tūberculum* (see etym. under **tubercle**) + New Latin *-osis* -osis]

**tu|ber|cu|lous** (tü bėr′kyə ləs, tyü-), *adj.* **1** of or having to do with tuberculosis. **2** having tuberculosis. **3** = tubercular. —**tu|ber′cu|lous|ly**, *adv.*

**tube|rose**[1] (tüb′rōz′, tyüb′-), *n.* a plant with a spike of creamy-white, very fragrant flowers shaped like funnels. The tuberose grows from a bulb or tuber and belongs to the agave family. [< Latin *tūberōsa,* feminine of *tūberōsus;* see etym. under **tuberous**; often taken as if < *tube* + *rose*]

**tu|ber|ose**[2] (tü′bə rōs, tyü′-), *adj.* = tuberous.

**tu|ber|os|i|ty** (tü′bə ros′ə tē, tyü′-), *n., pl.* **-ties.** **1** the quality or condition of being tuberous. **2** a rounded knob or swelling. **3** a large, irregular protuberance of a bone, especially for the attachment of a muscle or ligament.

**tu|ber|ous** (tü′bər əs, tyü′-), *adj.* **1** bearing tubers: *a tuberous plant.* **2** of or like a tuber or tubers. **3** of the nature of tubers or abnormal swellings. **4** covered with rounded knobs or swellings. [< Latin *tūberōsus* < *tūber, -eris* lump]

**tuberous root**, *Botany.* a true root (usually one of a cluster) thickened so as to resemble a tuber, but bearing no buds, as in the lesser celandine and the dahlia.

**tu|ber|ous-root|ed** (tü′bər əs rü′tid, tyü′-; -rüt′id), *adj. Botany.* having a tuberous root or roots.

**tube|worm** (tüb′wėrm′, tyüb′-), *n.* any worm of a group of annelids that live in hard, flexible tubes. Some worms make these tubes of their own calcareous secretions; others glue together sandy or stony grit.

**tub|ful** (tub′fu̇l), *n., pl.* **-fuls.** as much or as many as a tub will hold.

**tu|bic|o|lous** (tü bik′ə ləs, tyü-), *adj. Zoology.* inhabiting a tube, as a mollusk with a tubular shell, an annelid with a tubular case, or a spider which spins a tubular web. [< Latin *tubus, -ī* tube + *colere* inhabit + English *-ous*]

**tu|bi|corn** (tü′bə kôrn, tyü′-), *adj.* hollow-horned; cavicorn. [< Latin *tubus, -ī* tube + *cornū* horn]

**tu|bi|fex** (tü′bə feks, tyü′-), *n., pl.* **-fex** or **-fex|es.** a small red worm that lives inside a tube and is often found in muddy waters. Tubifex are much used as food for aquarium fish. [< New Latin *Tubifex* the genus name < Latin *tubus, -ī* tube + *facere* to make, do]

**tu|bi|form** (tü′bə fôrm, tyü′-), *adj.* having the form of a tube; tube-shaped; tubular. [< Latin *tubus, -ī* tube + *forma* form]

**tub|ing** (tü′bing, tyü′-), *n.* **1** material in the form of a tube: *rubber tubing.* **2** tubes collectively. **3** a piece of tube. **4** the act of furnishing with a tube or tubes.

**tu|bo|cu|ra|rine** (tü′bō kyü rä′rēn, -rin; tyü′-), *n.* an alkaloid derived from the South American vine that yields curare, used as a muscle relaxant and antispasmodic. *Formula:* $C_{38}H_{44}N_2O_6Cl_2{\cdot}5H_2O$ [< Latin *tubus* tube + English *curare* + *-in* (because the curare is packed in tubes)]

**Tu B'She|bat** (tü′bish bät′), a Jewish arbor day celebrated on the 15th day of Shebat (the fifth month of the Jewish year, beginning in January). [< Hebrew *tu* (< *t,* the ninth letter of the alphabet + *u,* the sixth letter) + *bə* in + *Shəbaṭ* Shebat]

**tub thumper**, *Informal.* **1** a speaker or preacher who for emphasis thumps the desk or pulpit; a violent or declamatory speaker or orator. **2** *U.S.* a spokesman or press agent.

**tub thumping**, *Informal.* **1** loud and emotional oratory; declamatory speaking. **2** *U.S. Informal.* sensational advertising or publicity; ballyhoo: *Each year, to the accompaniment of much tub thumping, they pour out a stream of new models designed to make the old ones seem obsolete* (New Yorker).

**tub-thump|ing** (tub′thum′ping), *adj. Informal.* ranting; loud and emotional; declamatory: *tub-thumping oratory.*

**tu|bu|lar** (tü′byə lər, tyü′-), *adj.* **1** shaped like a tube; round, hollow, and open at one or both ends. **2** that is a tube; consisting of a tube: *a tubular corolla or calyx.* **3** of or having to do with a tube or tubes. **4** constructed with or consisting of a number of tubes: *a tubular boiler.* **5** performed by means of a tube or tubes. **6** *Medicine.* of or denoting a high-pitched respiratory murmur that sounds as if made through a tube. [< Latin *tubulus* (diminutive) < *tubus* tube, pipe + English *-ar*] —**tu′bu|lar|ly**, *adv.*

**tu|bu|late** (*adj.* tü′byə lit, -lāt; tyü′-; *v.* tü′byə lāt, tyü′-), *adj., v.,* **-lat|ed, -lat|ing.** —*adj.* = tubular.
—*v.t.* **1** to form into a tube. **2** to furnish with a tube. [< Latin *tubulātus* < *tubulus;* see etym. under **tubule**]

**tu|bu|la|tion** (tü′byə lā′shən, tyü′-), *n.* **1** the formation of a tube or tubule. **2** the disposition or arrangement of a set of tubes.

**tu|bule** (tü′byül, tyü′-), *n.* a small tube, especially a minute tubular structure in an animal or plant body: *the uriniferous tubules of the kidney.* See picture under **nephron**. [< French *tubule,* learned borrowing from Latin *tubulus* (diminutive) < *tubus* tube, pipe]

**tu|bu|li|flo|rous** (tü′byə lə flôr′əs, -flōr′-; tyü′-), *adj. Botany.* having all the perfect flowers of a head with tubular corollas, as certain composites. [< Latin *tubulus, -ī* tubule + *flōs, flōris* flower]

**tu|bu|lin** (tü′byə lin, tyü′-), *n.* globular protein that is the basic structural unit of microtubules: *Microtubules from any kind of eukaryotic flagella and cilia are composed of related proteins called tubulin* (Scientific American). [< *tubule* + *-in*]

**tu|bu|lose** (tü′byə lōs, tyü′-), *adj.* = tubular.

**tu|bu|lous** (tü′byə ləs, tyü′-), *adj.* **1** = tubular. **2** *Botany.* having florets shaped like tubes. [< New Latin *tubulosus* < Latin *tubulus;* see etym. under **tubule**]

**tu|bu|lure** (tü′byə lər, tyü′ ), *n.* a short tube, or projecting opening for the insertion of a tube, in a retort or receiver. [< French *tubulure* < *tubule;* see etym. under **tubule**]

**T.U.C.** or **TUC** (no periods), *British.* Trades Union Congress (the federation of the largest and most important trade unions).

**tu|chun** (dü′jyn′), *n.* the title of the military head of a province in China, during the period 1916-1923. [< Chinese (Pekingese) *tu-chün* (literally) overseer of troops]

**tuck**[1] (tuk), *v., n.* —*v.t.* **1** to thrust or put (an object) into some narrow space or into some out-of-the-way place: *She tucked her purse under her arm. He tucked the letter into his pocket. The little cottage is tucked away under the hill.* **2** to thrust the edge or end of (a garment, covering, or the like) closely into place: *Tuck your shirt in. He tucked a napkin under his chin.* **3** to cover snugly: *Tuck the child in bed.* **4** to pull or gather (up) in a fold or folds; fold or turn up: *The man tucked up his sleeves before washing his hands.* **5** to sew a fold in (a garment) for trimming or to make it shorter or tighter: *The baby's dress was beautifully tucked with tiny stitches.* —*v.i.* **1** to sew a tuck or tucks. **2** to draw together; contract.
—*n.* **1** a fold sewed down with stitches parallel to the line of the fold, made to shorten or ornament a garment: *The dress was too big, so Mother put a tuck in it.* **2** the act of tucking. **3** a tucked piece, part, or position. **4** *U.S. Dialect.* heart; spirit: *I've got the stuff here that'll take the tuck out of him* (Mark Twain). **5** the part of a ship where the after ends of the outside planks or plates come together, at or just beneath the sternpost. **6** the position assumed by a diver while in the air in executing a somersault, in which the knees are folded under the chest and the ankles are grasped in the hands. **7** *British Slang.* food, especially delicacies such as candy and pastry: *Parents at home and abroad. Let us send your child's tuck each week ... anywhere in U.K.* (London Times).
**tuck away** (or **in**), *Slang.* to eat or drink heartily; consume with gusto: *to tuck away a big meal.*
[Middle English *tukken* gather up, pluck out; stretch (cloth); earlier, upbraid, Old English *tūcian* disturb, chastise, torment]

**tuck**[2] (tuk), *n. Archaic.* a rapier. [perhaps variant

of obsolete *stock* < Old French *estoc,* ultimately < Germanic (compare Old High German *stoc* staff, stick, tree trunk)]

**tuck³** (tuk, tük), *n., v. Especially Scottish.* **—n.** a blow, stroke, or tap: *a tuck of drum.* [< verb] **—v.t., v.i.** to beat the drum. [< Old North French *touker,* Old French *toucher;* see etym. under **touch**]

**Tuck** (tuk), *n.* **Friar,** the jolly friar of Robin Hood's band.

**tuck|a|hoe** (tuk′ə hō), *n.* the edible food-storage body (sclerotium) of an underground fungus occurring on the roots of trees in the southern United States. [American English, apparently < Algonkian (Powhatan) *p'tŭkweu* it is round]

**tuck box,** *British Slang.* a box in which schoolchildren keep the food brought or sent from home.

**tucked** (tukt), *adj.* **1** drawn up, as in folds; sewed in or ornamented with tucks. **2** *Informal or Dialect.* cramped, as in position or space. **3** *Dialect.* wearied or exhausted.

***tuck|er¹** (tuk′ər), *n.* **1** a piece of muslin, lace, or other material worn by women around the neck or over the chest in the 1600's and 1700's. **2** a chemisette or dicky. **3** a person or thing that tucks. **4** a device on a sewing machine for making tucks. **5** *Australian Slang.* food; a meal. [< *tuck¹*, verb]

***tucker¹**
definition 1

**tuck|er²** (tuk′ər), *v.t. Informal.* to tire; weary; exhaust.
**tucker out,** to make utterly exhausted; wear out: *She's clean tuckered out, and kind o' discouraged* (Harriet Beecher Stowe).
[American English; origin uncertain. Compare *tucked* worn out, exhausted.]

**tucker bag,** *Australian Slang.* a bag for carrying food.

**tuck|et** (tuk′it), *n. Archaic.* a flourish on a trumpet, especially as a marching signal for cavalry. [see related etym. at **tuck³**]

**tuck|in** (tuk′in′), *n. British Slang.* a hearty meal; feast: *One good tuckin won't give you an ulcer* (Scottish Sunday Express). [< *tuck¹* eatables + *-in*]

**tuck-in** (tuk′in′), *adj., n.* **—adj.** that can or should be tucked in: *a tuck-in blouse or shirt.*
**—n.** an edge or end to be tucked in, as of a garment.

**tuck|shop** (tuk′shop′), *n. British Slang.* a shop that sells pastry, candy, and other delicacies, especially to schoolboys: *Arm in arm ... the two friends went down to the tuckshop for tea* (Punch).

**Tu|dor** (tü′dər, tyü′-), *n., adj.* **—n. 1** a member of the royal family that ruled England from 1485 to 1603. Henry VII, Henry VIII, Edward VI, Mary I, and Elizabeth I were Tudors. **2** a person who lived in England under the Tudors.
**—adj. 1** of or having to do with the English Gothic style of architecture developed during the reign of the Tudors. It was characterized by flat arches, shallow moldings, and elaborate paneling. The principal development was in domestic architecture, typified by the large manor house with regular plan, inner courts, and many windows, gables, and chimneys. **2** of or having to do with the Tudors.

**Tudor arch,** a flat, pointed arch.

**Tu|dor|esque** (tü′də resk′, tyü′-), *adj.* **1** of or resembling Tudor style in art or architecture: *a Tudoresque hotel.* **2** of or having to do with the Tudors.

**tu|e|bor** (tü ē′bôr, tyü-), *Latin.* I will defend (one of Michigan's mottoes).

**Tues.,** Tuesday.

**Tues|day** (tüz′dē, -dā; tyüz′-), *n.* the third day of the week, following Monday. *Abbr:* Tues., Tu. [Old English *Tīwesdæg* day of Tiu (god of war), translation of Late Latin *Martis diēs* day of Mars (the planet)]

**tu|fa** (tü′fə, tyü′-), *n.* **1** any one of various porous rocks formed of powdery matter consolidated and often stratified, especially a form of limestone deposited by springs. **2** = tuff. [< Italian *tufo* < Latin *tōfus.* See etym. of doublet **tuff.**]

**tu|fa|ceous** (tü fā′shəs, tyü-), *adj.* of the nature of or resembling tufa.

**tuff** (tuf), *n.* a rock produced by the consolidation of volcanic ash and other volcanic fragments: *Nuclear devices have been exploded ... in a spongy, volcanic rock called tuff* (Wall Street Journal). [< Middle French *tuf* < Italian *tufo* tufa. See etym. of doublet **tufa.**]

**tuff|a|ceous** (tu fā′shəs), *adj.* **1** having the properties of volcanic tuff. **2** composed of volcanic tuff.

**tuf|fet** (tuf′ət), *n.* a bunch of grass; tuft. [alteration of *tuft*]

**tuft** (tuft), *n., v.* **—n. 1** a bunch of hairs, feathers, grass, or other soft and flexible things, held together at one end: *My billy goat has a tuft of hair on his chin.* **2** a clump of bushes, trees, or other plants. **3** a cluster of threads sewn tightly through a mattress or comforter so as to keep the padding in place. **4** a button by which such a cluster is attached. **5** a gold tassel formerly worn on the cap by titled undergraduates at Oxford and Cambridge. **6** *Slang.* the wearer of such a tassel.
**—v.t. 1** to furnish with a tuft or tufts; put tufts on. **2** to divide into tufts.
**—v.i.** to form a tuft or tufts; grow in tufts.
[alteration of Middle English *tuffe,* perhaps < Old French *touffe* < Late Latin *tūfa* helmet crest]

**tuft|ed** (tuf′tid), *adj.* **1** furnished with a tuft or tufts: *a tufted quilt.* **2** having a tuft of feathers on the head; crested. **3** formed into a tuft or tufts.

**tufted duck,** an Old-World crested duck. The male has mostly black plumage.

**tufted titmouse,** a titmouse of the eastern United States, bluish-gray with white and rust underparts, and a crest.

**tuft|er** (tuf′tər), *n.* **1** a hunting dog trained to drive deer out of cover. **2** a person who tufts mattresses and cushions.

**tuft|hunt|er** (tuft′hun′tər), *n. Especially British.* a person who tries to become acquainted with persons of rank and title.

**tuft|hunt|ing** (tuft′hun′ting), *n., adj.* **—n.** the practice of a tufthunter: *He had kept the letters sent him by the many notable figures of the time whom he "collected" in his long career of tufthunting* (Richard D. Altick).
**—adj. 1** that is a tufthunter. **2** that is characteristic of a tufthunter.

**tuft|y** (tuf′tē), *adj.* **1** abounding in tufts or knots. **2** growing in tufts.

**tug** (tug), *v.,* **tugged, tug|ging,** *n.* **—v.t. 1** to move by pulling forcibly; pull with force or effort; drag; haul: *We tugged the boat in to shore.* **SYN:** See syn. under **pull. 2** to pull at with force; strain at: *to tug at a jammed window until it opens.* **SYN:** See syn. under **pull. 3** to pull or push by tugboat.
**—v.i. 1** to pull with force or effort; pull hard; strain (at): *to tug at a jammed window. The child tugged at his mother's hand.* **2** *Figurative.* to strive hard; toil; labor; struggle.
**—n. 1** an act or the act of tugging; hard pull: *a sudden tug on the line. The baby gave a tug at her mother's hair.* **2** *Figurative.* a hard strain, struggle, effort, or contest. **3** = tugboat. **4** either of two straps, ropes, or chains by which a horse pulls a wagon, cart, or carriage; trace. See picture under **harness. 5** *U.S.* a rope.
[Middle English *toggen* to pull playfully. See related etym. at **tow¹**.]

**tug|boat** (tug′bōt′), *n.* a small, powerful boat used to pull or push a barge or barges, to tow large ships into berths, and do other jobs of towing or hauling; towboat.

**tug|boat|man** (tug′bōt′mən), *n., pl.* **-men.** a man who works on a tugboat: *Against union advice, Liverpool tugboatmen decided to continue their strike* (London Times).

**tug|ger** (tug′ər), *n.* **1** a person who tugs or pulls with force. **2** *Informal.* a person who pulls in a tug of war.

**tug|ging|ly** (tug′ing lē), *adv.* with tugging.

**tu|ghrik** (tü′grik), *n., pl.* **-ghriks** or **-ghrik.** = tugrik.

**tug|man** (tug′mən), *n., pl.* **-men.** = tugboatman.

**tug of war,** or **tug-of-war** (tug′əv wôr′, tug′ə-), *n., pl.* **tugs-of-war. 1** a contest between two teams pulling at opposite ends of a rope, each trying to drag the other over a line marked between them. **2** *Figurative.* any hard struggle, especially for a decision or supremacy; stubbornly fought contest: *Rural-urban tug of war ... characterizes most Louisiana elections* (Wall Street Journal).

**tu|grik** (tü′grik), *n., pl.* **-griks** or **-grik.** the unit of money of the Mongolian People's Republic (Outer Mongolia), equal to 100 mongos. [< Mongolian *tugrik*]

**tu|i** (tü′ē), *n.* a New Zealand bird having dark plumage with white neck feathers; parson bird. [< Maori *tui*]

**tuille** (twēl), *n.* **1** one of the two or more plates of steel hanging below the tasses in a suit of armor. **2** the lowermost part of the tasses. [Middle English *toile* < Middle French *teuille,* Old French *tuile* (literally) plaque, tile < Latin *tēgula*]

**tu|i|tion** (tü ish′ən, tyü-), *n.* **1** money paid for instruction: *Her yearly tuition is $1,000.* **2** the act of teaching a pupil or pupils; teaching; instruction: *He pays for his daughter's tuition at college.* **3** *Obsolete.* **a** a safekeeping; custody. **b** guardianship. [< Latin *tuitiō, -ōnis* protection < *tuērī* watch over]

**tu|i|tion|al** (tü ish′ə nəl, tyü-), *adj.* of or having to do with tuition.

**tu|i|tion|ar|y** (tü ish′ə ner′ē, tyü-), *adj.* = tuitional.

**Tu|ku|lor** (tü′kü lér′), *n., pl.* **-lor.** a member of a Moslem Negroid people of Senegal, closely related to the Fulani.

**tu|la|re|mi|a** or **tu|la|rae|mi|a** (tü′lə rē′mē ə), *n.* an infectious disease of wild rabbits, rodents, and of certain birds, caused by a bacterium and sometimes transmitted to people by insect and tick bites or by the handling of infected animals, causing an intermittent fever that lasts several weeks; rabbit fever. [< New Latin *tularemia* < *Tulare,* a county in California + *-emia* -emia]

**tu|la|re|mic** or **tu|la|rae|mic** (tü′lə rē′mik), *adj.* of or having to do with tularemia.

**tu|la work** (tü′lə), = niello (def. 2). [< *Tula,* a town in Russia, where it is made]

**tu|le** (tü′lē), *n.* either of two large bulrushes abundant in lowlands along riversides in California and neighboring regions. [American English < Mexican Spanish *tule* < Nahuatl *tullin*]

**tu|lip** (tü′lip, tyü′-), *n.* **1** any one of certain plants that grow from bulbs and have large, cup-shaped, showy flowers of various colors and markings. Tulips comprise a genus of the lily family. Most tulips bloom in the spring. See picture under **lily family. 2** the flower or bulb of any of these plants. [< obsolete Dutch *tulipa* < French *tulipe* < Turkish *tülbent* gauze, muslin < Persian *dulband* turban. See etym. of doublet **turban.**]

**tulip ear,** an erect or pricked ear in dogs.

**tu|lip-eared** (tü′lip ird′, tyü′-), *adj.* prick-eared, as a dog.

**tulip poplar,** = tulip tree.

**tulip tree, 1** a large North American tree of the magnolia family, with greenish-yellow flowers, resembling large tulips, and truncate leaves; yellow poplar; whitewood. Its soft wood is much used in cabinetwork. **2** any one of certain other trees whose flowers resemble tulips.

**tu|lip|wood** (tü′lip wu̇d′, tyü′-), *n.* **1** the soft, light-colored wood of the tulip tree, used especially for cabinetwork; whitewood; white poplar. **2** any one of various other varicolored and striped woods. **3** any tree producing such wood.

**tulle** (tül), *n.* a thin, fine net, usually of silk, used for veils and trimming ladies' finery. [< *Tulle,* a town in France, where it was first made]

**tul|li|bee** (tul′ə bē), *n., pl.* **-bees** or (*collectively*) **-bee.** any one of a group of fishes of the Great Lakes area, related to the whitefishes. [American English < Canadian French *toulibi* < Algonkian (Cree, Ojibwa) *otonabi* mouth water < *oton* mouth + *abi* water (because of the watery flesh of this fish)]

**tul|war** (tul′wär), *n.* a kind of saber used by the peoples of northern India. [< Hindi *talwār*]

**tum|ble** (tum′bəl), *v.,* **-bled, -bling,** *n.* **—v.i. 1** to fall headlong or in a helpless way, as from stumbling or violence; be precipitated: *The child tumbled down the stairs.* **2** to fall prone; fall (down) to the ground. **3** to stumble by tripping (over an object). **4** (of a building or structure) to fall in ruins; collapse. **5** *Figurative.* to fall rapidly in value, amount, or price (used especially of stocks). **6** to roll or throw oneself about in a restless way; toss: *The sick child tumbled restlessly in his bed.* **7** to roll about on the ground, or in the water or air; pitch; wallow. **8** to move in a hurried or awkward way; proceed hastily, without apparent order or premeditation: *He tumbled out of bed. The occupants tumbled out of the burning building. Tumble into bed and go to sleep* (Charles J. Lever). **9** to perform leaps, springs, somersaults, or other feats of agility, without the aid of gymnasium apparatus. **10** *Obsolete.* to dance with posturing, balancing, and contortions.
**—v.t. 1** to throw over or down; cause to tumble: *The strong winds tumbled a tree in our yard.* **2** to turn over; disorder; rumple; muss: *to tumble bedclothes.* **3** to polish in a tumbling box or tumbler.
**—n. 1** an act of tumbling; a fall by tumbling: *The tumble hurt him badly.* **2** an acrobatic leap, spring, somersault or similar feat: *to perform tumbles.* **3** tumbled condition; confusion; disorder: *His desk was a complete tumble of papers.*
[Middle English *tumbelen* (frequentative) < Old English *tumbian* to dance about]

**Pronunciation Key:** hat, āge, cãre, fär; let, ēqual, tėrm; it, īce; hot, ōpen, ôrder; oil, out; cup, pu̇t, rüle; child; long; thin; ᴛʜen; zh, measure; ə represents **a** in about, **e** in taken, **i** in pencil, **o** in lemon, **u** in circus.

**tum|ble|bug** (tum′bəl bug′), *n.* any one of various beetles that roll up a ball of dung in which to lay their eggs.

**tum|ble-down** (tum′bəl doun′), *adj.* ready to fall down; not in good condition; dilapidated: *a tumble-down shack.* **SYN**: rickety, ramshackle.

**tum|ble-dry** (tum′bəl drī′), *v.t., v.i.,* **-dried, -dry|ing.** to dry in a tumble dryer.

**tumble dryer** or **drier**, a dryer in which hot air is blown through the clothes while they are tumbled inside a revolving barrel; tumbler.

**tum|ble|dung** (tum′bəl dung′), *n.* = tumblebug.

**tum|bler** (tum′blər), *n.* **1** a person who performs leaps, springs, somersaults, and other feats; acrobat. **2** a drinking glass without a stem, and with a heavy, flat bottom. **3** the contents of such a glass: *to drink a tumbler of water.* **4** the part of a lock that must be moved from a certain position in order to release the bolt. The tumbler is kept in position by a spring and has projections which drop into notches in the bolt and hold it until lifted by the proper key. **5** the part of a gunlock that forces the hammer forward when the trigger is pulled. **6** a kind of domestic pigeon that performs aerial acrobatics including backward somersaults while in flight; roller. **7** a toy figure with a low center of gravity and rounded base, that rocks when touched but rights itself. **8a** a revolving box or barrel in which things are polished; tumbling box. **b** a person who operates such an apparatus. **9** any one of a breed of dogs similar to small greyhounds, formerly used to catch rabbits. **10** a part in an automobile transmission that moves a gear into place. **11** a piece projecting from a shaft and actuating a cam or other device. **12** = tumble dryer. **13** *Dialect.* tumbrel.

**tum|bler|ful** (tum′blər fu̇l), *n., pl.* **-fuls.** a quantity sufficient to fill a tumbler.

**tum|ble|weed** (tum′bəl wēd′), *n.* a plant, growing in the western United States, that breaks off from its roots and is blown about by the wind, scattering its seeds. The amaranth and bugseed are two kinds. [American English < *tumble* + *weed*]

**tum|bling box** or **barrel** (tum′bling), a revolving box or barrel, used for polishing small objects, especially of metal, by shaking them about with abrasives.

**tum|brel** or **tum|bril** (tum′brəl), *n.* **1** any one of various two-wheeled carts, especially: **a** a cart used for hauling and dumping manure on a farm, collecting garbage, and carrying other loads. **b** such a cart used to carry prisoners to the guillotine during the French Revolution. **c** a covered cart formerly used to carry ammunition, tools, and spare parts, especially one belonging to a particular battery or other artillery unit. **2** an instrument of punishment of former times, especially a ducking stool. [probably < Old French *tumberel, tomberel* dump cart < *tomber* (let) fall or tumble, probably < a Germanic word]

**tu|me|fa|cient** (tü′mə fā′shənt, tyü′-), *adj.* producing or tending to produce swelling. [< Latin *tumefaciēns, -entis,* present participle of *tumefacere;* see etym. under **tumefy**]

**tu|me|fac|tion** (tü′mə fak′shən, tyü′-), *n.* **1** the act or process of swelling. **2** the condition of being swollen. **3** a swollen part. [< French *tuméfaction* < Latin *tumefacere;* see etym. under **tumefy**]

**tu|me|fy** (tü′mə fī, tyü′-), *v.t., v.i.,* **-fied, -fy|ing.** = swell. [< Latin *tumefacere* < *tumēre* to swell + *facere* make]

**tu|mes|cence** (tü mes′əns, tyü-), *n.* **1** the condition of swelling; growing tumid; tumefaction. **2** a swollen part or tumor; intumescence.

**tu|mes|cent** (tü mes′ənt, tyü-), *adj.* **1** becoming swollen; swelling. **2** somewhat tumid. [< Latin *tumēscēns, -entis,* present participle of *tumēscere* begin to swell < *tumēre* to swell] —**tu|mes′cent|ly,** *adv.*

**tu|mid** (tü′mid, tyü′-), *adj.* **1** characterized by swelling; enlarged; swollen. **2** *Figurative.* swollen with big words; pompous; turgid; bombastic: *His letters were tumid, formal and affected* (William E. H. Lecky). **3** = teeming. [< Latin *tumidus* < *tumēre* swell] —**tu′mid|ly,** *adv.* —**tu′mid|ness,** *n.*

**tu|mid|i|ty** (tü mid′ə tē, tyü-), *n.* **1** the quality or condition of being tumid or swollen. **2** a pompous or bombastic style; turgidness; fustian.

**tum|my** (tum′ē), *n., pl.* **-mies.** *Informal.* the stomach or abdomen: *Flat tummies and fetching contours need exercises as rigorous as a prizefighter's workout* (Maclean's). [< children's pronunciation of *stomach*]

**tu|mor** (tü′mər, tyü′-), *n.* **1** an abnormal growth in or on some part of the body that may be benign or malignant. Tumors exhibit laws of growth independent of the surrounding tissue and are characterized by gradual development. Some tumors are thought to be caused by viruses. **2** a swollen part; swelling. **3** *Obsolete.* a swollen condition. [< Latin *tumor, -ōris* < *tumēre* to swell] —**tu′mor|like′,** *adj.*

**tu|mor|i|gen|ic** (tü′mər ə jen′ik, tyü′-), *adj.* producing tumors, especially cancerous tumors: *a tumorigenic agent or substance.*

**tu|mor|i|ge|nic|i|ty** (tü′mə rə jə nis′ə tē, -tyü′-), *n.* tumor-producing tendency or capacity.

**tu|mor|ous** (tü′mər əs, tyü′-), *adj.* **1** of or having to do with a tumor or tumors. **2** having a tumor or tumors.

**tu|mour** (tü′mər, tyü′-), *n. Especially British.* tumor.

**tump** (tump), *n. British Dialect.* **1** a hillock; mound. **2** a clump of trees, grass, etc., especially one marking or forming a dry spot in a bog or fen. **3** a heap (of anything); pile. [origin unknown]

***tump|line** (tump′līn′), *n. U.S. and Canada.* a strap across the forehead and over the shoulders, used to carry loads on the back, especially by American Indians. [perhaps < Algonkian (compare Massachusetts *tâmpān* pack strap)]

***tumpline**

**tu|mu|lar** (tü′myə lər, tyü′-), *adj.* **1** having to do with a mound or tumulus. **2** consisting of a mound or tumulus. [< Latin *tumulus* (see etym. under **tumulus**) + English *-ar*]

**tu|mu|lar|y** (tü′myə ler′ē, tyü′-), *adj.* **1** = tumular. **2** having to do with a tomb; sepulchral: *a tumulary stone.*

**tu|mu|lose** (tü′myə lōs, tyü′-), *adj.* full of little hills or knobs. [< Latin *tumulōsus* hilly < *tumulus;* see etym. under **tumulus**]

**tu|mu|lous** (tü′myə ləs, tyü′-), *adj.* = tumulose.

**tu|mult** (tü′mult, tyü′-), *n.* **1** noise or uproar; commotion: *The sailors' voices could not be heard above the tumult of the storm.* **2** a violent disturbance or disorder: *The shout of "Fire!" caused a tumult in the theater. The tumult and the shouting dies* (Rudyard Kipling). **3** a riot; insurrection: *There is much bloodshedding in Spain ... and violent wars and tumults* (George Borrow). **SYN**: brawl, outbreak. **4** *Figurative.* a great disturbance of mind or feeling; confusion or excitement: *The quarrel left her in a tumult.* [< Latin *tumultus, -ūs,* related to *tumēre* to swell]

**tu|mul|tu|ar|y** (tü mul′chu̇ er′ē, tyü-), *adj.* **1** disposed to or marked by riotous tumult or public disorder. **2** of the nature of riotous tumult or public disorder.

**tu|mul|tu|ous** (tü mul′chu̇ əs, tyü-), *adj.* **1** characterized by or causing tumult; very noisy or disorderly; violent: *a tumultuous celebration. Fifty feet from the door a dozen headlights illuminated a bizarre and tumultuous scene* (F. Scott Fitzgerald). **SYN**: boisterous, turbulent. **2** *Figurative.* greatly disturbed; agitated and confused: *tumultuous emotions.* **3** large and violent; rough; stormy: *Tumultuous waves beat upon the rocks.* [< Latin *tumultuōsus* < *tumultus, -ūs;* see etym. under **tumult**] —**tu|mul′tu|ous|ly,** *adv.* —**tu|mul′tu|ous|ness,** *n.*

**tu|mu|lus** (tü′myə ləs, tyü′-), *n.,pl.* **-lus|es, -li** (-lī). a mound of earth, especially one marking the site of an ancient grave; barrow. [< Latin *tumulus* < *tumēre* to swell]

**tun**[1] (tun), *n.* **1** a large cask or barrel, usually for liquids, especially wine, ale, or beer. **2** a former measure of capacity of wine, liquor, and some other liquids, equal to eight barrels or 252 gallons. [Old English *tunne*]

**tun**[2] (tün), *n.* a year in the calendar of the Mayas, consisting of 360 days. [< Mayan *tun*]

**tu|na**[1] (tü′nə), *n., pl.* **tu|nas** or (*collectively*) **tu|na.** **1** a large sea fish, closely related to the mackerel, having coarse oily flesh that is widely used as food; tunny; horse mackerel. It is valued as a game fish. **2** any one of several similar or related fishes. **3** the flesh of the tuna. Tuna tastes somewhat like chicken. [American English < American Spanish *tuna* < Spanish *atún* < Arabic *tun* < Latin *thunnus;* see etym. under **tunny**] —**tu′na-like′,** *adj.*

**tu|na**[2] (tü′nə), *n.* **1** any one of several prickly pears, especially a treelike pear of tropical America with an edible fruit. **2** the fruit itself. [< Spanish *tuna* < Arawak (Haiti)]

**tun|a|bil|i|ty** (tü′nə bil′ə tē, tyü′-), *n.* the quality or condition of being tunable. Also, **tuneability.**

**tun|a|ble** (tü′nə bəl, tyü′-), *adj.* **1** that can be tuned. **2a** in tune. **b** *Figurative.* concordant. **3** *Archaic.* harmonious; tuneful; melodious. Also, tuneable. —**tun′a|ble|ness,** *n.* —**tun′a|bly,** *adv.*

**tuna fish,** = tuna[1].

**tun|dish** (tun′dish), *n.* a funnel-shaped receptacle used especially in brewing and casting steel and other metals. [< *tun*[1] + *dish*]

**tun|dra** (tun′drə), *n.* **1** a vast, level, treeless plain in the arctic regions. The ground beneath the surface of the tundras is frozen even in summer. Much of Alaska and northern Canada is tundra. **2** any one of various tracts and areas similar to this, as certain plateaus in the Andes and elsewhere. [< Russian *tundra*]

**tundra vole,** a small meadow mouse of the tundras of western Alaska.

**tundra wolf,** = arctic wolf.

**tune** (tün, tyün), *n., v.,* **tuned, tun|ing.** —*n.* **1** a piece of music; rhythmical succession of musical tones; air or melody: *A tune is more lasting than the voice of the birds* (Padraic Colum). *To see her is a picture, To hear her is a tune* (Emily Dickinson). **2** a musical setting of a psalm or hymn, usually in four-part harmony, to be used in public worship: *hymn tunes.* **3** the proper pitch: *The piano is out of tune. He can't sing in tune.* **4** agreement in pitch, unison, or harmony: *to keep a violin in tune with one's piano.* **5** *Figurative.* **a** harmony or agreement (with some person or thing): *A person out of tune with his surroundings is unhappy.* **b** proper condition: *a horse in good tune.* **6** *Figurative.* frame of mind; mood or manner; tone. **7** agreement or harmony in vibrations other than those of sound. **8** *Obsolete.* a sound or tone.

—*v.t.* **1** to adjust to the proper pitch; put in tune: *A man is tuning the piano.* **2** to adapt (the voice or a song or other piece of music) to a particular tone or to the expression of a particular feeling or subject. **3** to adapt or adjust so as to be in harmony. **4** *Figurative.* to bring into a proper or desirable state or mood or into a condition for producing an effect: *to tune public opinion.* **5** *Figurative.* to bring into harmony or accord; attune. **6** *Archaic.* to utter or express musically. **7** *Archaic.* to play upon (an instrument).

—*v.i.* **1** to give forth a musical sound; sound: *In came a fiddler—and tuned like fifty stomachaches* (Dickens). **2** to sing or sound in tune; be in tune; be in harmony; harmonize. **3** *Figurative.* to accord.

**call the tune,** to declare authoritatively what will be or what will happen; dictate: *Dow recognized that when the bears were calling the tune, it was time to be long, not on stocks, but on money* (Wall Street Journal).

**change one's tune,** to change one's way of speaking or attitude; speak or act differently: *He'll soon change his tune.*

**dance to one's tune,** to follow one's lead; act according to one's wishes: *He has lost control of Congress as completely as he had it dancing to his tune three years ago* (Atlantic).

**sing another** (or **different**) **tune,** to speak or act in a very different manner; change one's tune: *I imagine he would sing a different tune if the bluecoats ever get to Richmond* (George A. Henty).

**to the tune of,** *Informal.* in the amount or sum of: *Britian has been in the red on international trade to the tune of £28 million a month* (Manchester Guardian Weekly).

**tune in,** to adjust a radio or television set to receive (what is wanted): [*He*] *jots down such entries as "Dworshak Symphony #2," a reminder to tune it in on the radio* (New York Times). **b** *Figurative.* to be attuned: *... a genuine gift for tuning in to the spirit of the times* (Punch).

**tune out, a** to adjust a radio or television set to get rid of (a signal or interference that is unwanted): *The operator ... has it in his power to tune out either of these two stations* (J. A. Fleming). **b** *Figurative.* to ignore or be oblivious to: *Mothers have a way of tuning out the noise of screaming children.*

**tune up, a** to bring musical instruments to the same pitch; put in tune: *The band began to tune up, and a general feeling of expectation pervaded the building* (Violet Jacob). **b** to put (a motor, racing vessel, engine, or other mechanism) into the best working order: *The system is functioning properly—tuned up, properly greased and oiled* (New York Times). **c** *Informal, Figurative.* to begin to play, sing, cry, or otherwise make noise: *I have heard an old cow tune up in like manner* (John Millais). [variant of *tone*]

**tune|a|bil|i|ty** (tü′nə bil′ə tē, tyü′-), *n.* = tunability.

**tune|a|ble** (tü′nə bəl, tyü′-), *adj.* = tunable. —**tune′a|ble|ness,** *n.* —**tune′a|bly,** *adv.*

**tuned-in** (tünd′in′, tyünd′-), *adj. Slang.* smart; alert; up-to-date: *the very latest toy for a tuned-in young man: an enormous bike* (Listener).

**tune|ful** (tün′fəl, tyün′-), *adj.* **1** musical; melodious: *That canary has a tuneful song.* **SYN**: euphonious. **2** producing musical sounds. —**tune′ful|ly,** *adv.* —**tune′ful|ness,** *n.*

**tune|less** (tün′lis, tyün′-), *adj.* **1** without tune; not musical; unmelodious: *The tuneless yet sweet humming of the low, worn voice* (Elizabeth Gaskell). SYN: unmusical. **2** giving no sound or music. —**tune′less|ly**, *adv.*

**tun|er** (tü′nər, tyü′-), *n.* **1** a person who tunes pianos, organs, or other musical instruments. **2** a device for adjusting a radio set to accept a given frequency and reject other frequencies: *an FM tuner.*

**tune|smith** (tün′smith′, tyün′-), *n. U.S. Informal.* a composer of popular music; songwriter.

**tune-up** (tün′up′, tyün′-), *n. U.S.* **1** a series of checks and adjustments made on parts of an engine to put it into efficient order. **2** a game, match, race, or other contest of lesser importance preparatory to a major contest; warm-up: *The Daniels fight was to have been the first of two tune-ups for the Valdez bout* (New York Times).

**tung nut** (tung), the seed of the tung tree, yielding tung oil.

**tung oil**, a poisonous oil obtained from the seeds of the tung tree and related trees of the spurge family; chinawood oil; Japanese wood oil. It is much used in varnishes for its drying quality. [< Chinese (Pekingese or Cantonese) *t'ung-yu* tung oil]

**tung|state** (tung′stāt), *n.* a salt or ester of a tungstic acid.

***tung|sten** (tung′stən), *n.* a heavy, steel-gray chemical element found only in certain rare minerals; wolfram; wolframium. Its melting point (3,410 degrees centigrade) is higher than that of any other metal. Tungsten is added to steel to make it harder, stronger, and more elastic. It is also used in making electric light-bulb filaments, surgical instruments, and automobile parts. [< Swedish *tungsten* < *tung* heavy + *sten* stone]

***tungsten**

| symbol | atomic number | atomic weight | oxidation state |
|---|---|---|---|
| W | 74 | 183.85 | 6 |

**tungsten carbide**, an extremely hard substance, a compound of tungsten and carbon, used in the tips of high-speed cutting tools and in mining and petroleum drills. Carboloy is a form of tungsten carbide.

**tung|sten|ic** (tung sten′ik), *adj.* **1** of or having to do with tungsten. **2** obtained from tungsten.

**tungsten lamp**, an incandescent electric lamp whose filament is made of metallic tungsten.

**tungsten steel**, a hard, heat-resistant steel containing tungsten: *Machine tools of tungsten steel do not lose their hardness or their sharp cutting edges even if they are red-hot when used* (George L. Bush).

**tung|stic** (tung′stik), *adj.* **1** of tungsten. **2** containing tungsten, especially with a valence of five or of six.

**tungstic acid**, **1** a yellow powder, a hydrate of tungstic trioxide, used in making textiles and plastics. *Formula:* $H_2WO_4$ **2** any one of various acids formed by the hydration of the trioxide of tungsten.

**tung|stite** (tung′stīt), *n.* a yellow or yellowish-green mineral; tungsten trioxide, usually occurring in powdery form and the chief source of tungsten. *Formula:* $WO_3$

**tung tree**, a tree of the spurge family, native to China and cultivated in other areas, from which tung oil is obtained.

**Tun|gus** (tůn gůz′), *n., pl.* **-gus|es** or **-gus**, *adj.* —*n.* **1** a member of any one of a group of Mongolian tribes of Tungusic speech, including the Manchus. **2** the language of this people.
—*adj.* Tungusic.
[< the native name]

**Tun|gus|i|an** (tůn gůz′ē ən), *adj.* = Tungusic.

**Tun|gus|ic** (tůn gůz′ik), *n., adj.* —*n.* a linguistic family of Siberia and Manchuria, including Tungus and Manchu.
—*adj.* **1** of or having to do with the Tunguses or their language. **2** of or denoting the linguistic family to which Tungus and Manchu belong.

**Tun|guz** (tůn gůz′), *n., pl.* **-guz|es** or **-guz**, *adj.* = Tungus.

***tu|nic** (tü′nik, tyü′-), *n.* **1** a garment like a shirt or gown, worn by both men and women in ancient Greece and Rome. Tunics usually reached to the knees. **2** any garment like this. **3** a woman's garment, usually belted, extending below the waist or over the skirt. **4** a short, close-fitting coat reaching below the waist but never below the thighs, worn by soldiers, policemen, and some other uniformed personnel. **5** a natural covering of integument of a plant, animal, or part. **6** a membranous sheath enveloping or lining an organ of the body; tunica. **7** = tunicle (def. 1). [< Latin *tunica*]

**tu|ni|ca** (tü′nə kə, tyü′-), *n., pl.* **-cae** (-sē). *Anatomy.* a covering or enveloping membrane or fold of tissue. [< New Latin *tunica* < Latin *tunica* tunic]

**Tu|ni|ca** (tü′nə kə, tyü′-), *n., pl.* **-ca** or **-cas**. **1** a member of an American Indian tribe that formerly lived along the Yazoo River in Mississippi and was noted for its alliance with the French in the 1700's in fighting against neighboring tribes. **2** the language of this tribe.

**tu|ni|cate** (tü′nə kit, -kāt; tyü′-), *adj., n.* —*adj.* **1** *Botany.* made up of concentric layers. An onion is a tunicate bulb. **2** *Zoology.* having a tunic or outer covering. **3** belonging to the tunicates.
—*n. Zoology.* any one of a subphylum of small sea chordates, including the ascidians and allied forms, characterized by a saclike body enclosed in a tough, leathery membrane, with a single or double opening through which the water enters and leaves the pharynx; sea squirt.
[< Latin *tunicātus*, past participle of *tunicāre* clothe with a tunic < *tunica* tunic]

**tu|ni|cat|ed** (tü′nə kā′tid, tyü′-), *adj.* = tunicate.

**tu|ni|cle** (tü′nə kəl, tyü′-), *n.* **1** a vestment worn by subdeacons and bishops over the alb at the Eucharist. **2** *Obsolete.* an integument or enclosing membrane; tunic. [< Latin *tunicula* (diminutive) < *tunica* tunic]

**tun|ing fork** (tü′ning, tyü′-), a small steel instrument with two prongs, used in tuning musical instruments. When struck, it vibrates at a fixed, constant, known rate and so makes a musical tone of a certain pitch.

**tuning pin** or **peg**, one of the pegs around which the strings of a stringed musical instrument are passed and which can be turned by the player to change the pitch of the note that each string produces.

**Tu|ni|sian** (tü nish′ən, tyü-; -nē′shən), *adj., n.* —*adj.* of or having to do with the North African country of Tunisia or its inhabitants.
—*n.* a native or inhabitant of Tunisia.

**Tun|ku** (tůng′kü), *n.* the Malayan title of Prince: *the Malaysian Premier, Tunku Abdul Rahman* (Scotsman). Also, **Tenku**. [< Malay *tunku*]

**tun|nage** (tun′ij), *n. Obsolete.* tonnage.

**tun|nel** (tun′əl), *n., v.,* **-neled, -nel|ing** or **-nelled, -nel|ling**. —*n.* **1** an underground passageway, as for automobiles, trains, or persons on foot: *The railroad passes under the mountain through a tunnel.* **2** any one of certain other subterranean passageways or borings, such as one for the passage of water or sewage. **3** a nearly horizontal passageway in a mine (often used loosely for any drift or level). **4** a passageway dug into the earth by an animal as a means of getting into or out of its burrow. **5** the burrow itself. **6** *Obsolete, Dialect.* a funnel. **7** *Obsolete.* the shaft or flue of a chimney.
—*v.i.* to make a tunnel; excavate a passageway (through some body or substance): *A mole tunneled in the ground around the terrace. The workmen are tunneling under the river.*
—*v.t.* **1** to make a tunnel through or under: *to tunnel a hill or river.* **2** to make (one's way or a way) by digging. **3** *Obsolete.* to form into or like a tube or pipe.
[< Old French *tonnelle* tunnel, net, *tonel* cask < *tonne;* see etym. under **tun**¹] —**tun′nel|er, tun′nel|ler**, *n.* —**tun′nel|like′**, *adj.*

**tunnel diode**, *Electronics.* a very small semiconductor that uses less power and achieves high frequency faster than a transistor, and is relatively insensitive to temperature changes and nuclear radiation: *The tunnel diode is so named because of the manner in which electrons seem to "tunnel" through the device with the speed of light* (Wall Street Journal).

**tunnel kiln**, = continuous kiln.

**tunnel of love**, a dark, winding tunnel or waterway in a carnival or amusement park, through which couples ride in small cars or boats.

**tunnel vision**, a disorder of the eyes in which the range of vision is contracted, so that only objects in the direct line of sight are seen clearly.

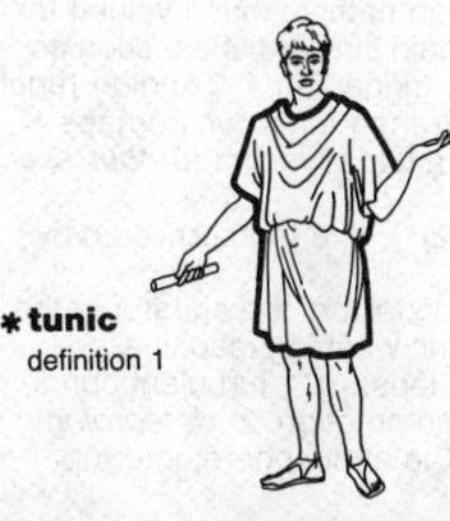

***tunic**
definition 1

**tun|ny** (tun′ē), *n., pl.* **-nies** or (*collectively*) **-ny**. **1** = tuna¹. **2** any one of certain related fishes. [apparently alteration of Old French *thon* < Old Provençal < Latin *thunnus*, or *thynnus* < Greek *thýnnos*, perhaps < Hebrew *tannīn*]

**tu|nu** (tü′nü), *n.* **1** the latex of a Nicaraguan tree, coagulated and boiled for the use as a gum base in making chewing gum. **2** the tree itself. [< American Spanish (Nicaragua) *tunu*]

**tup** (tup), *n., v.,* **tupped, tup|ping**. —*n.* **1** a male sheep; ram. **2** an object that strikes, as the head of a steam hammer or the falling weight of a pile driver. —*v.t.* (of a ram) to copulate with.
[origin uncertain. Compare Swedish *tupp* cock¹.]

**Tu|pa|ma|ro** (tü′pə mä′rō), *n., pl.* **-ros**. a member of an extreme left-wing guerrilla organization in Uruguay, known for acts of terrorism: *Uruguay's Tupamaros take their name from Tupac Amaru, a Peruvian Indian who led a revolt against the Spanish in Peru in the 18th century* (Sunday Times).

**tu|pe|lo** (tü′pə lō, tyü′-), *n., pl.* **-los**. **1** a large, North American tree that belongs to the same family as the sour gum, whose flowers are used for making honey; cotton gum. **2** its light, soft but tough wood. Tupelo is used for furniture, pulpwood, crates, and boxes. [American English, apparently < Algonkian *ito* tree + *opilwa* swamp]

**tupelo gum**, = tupelo.

**Tu|pi** (tü pē′), *n., pl.* **-pis** or **-pi**. **1** a member of a group of Indian tribes of the Tupi-Guarani linguistic stock in Brazil, Paraguay, and Uruguay. **2** their language, constituting the northern branch of the Tupi-Guarani linguistic stock.

**Tu|pi|an** (tü pē′ən), *adj.* **1** of or having to do with the Tupi Indians. **2** of or having to do with the Tupi-Guarani linguistic stock.

**Tu|pi-Gua|ra|ni** (tü pē′gwä′rä nē′), *n.* **1** a native linguistic stock of central South America, occurring particularly along the lower Amazon, and consisting principally of Tupi, the northern branch, and Guarani, the southern branch. **2** = Tupi (def. 1).

**tu|pik** (tü′pik), *n.* a hut or tent of animal skins in which Eskimos live during the summer: *When they move from the winter igloo to the summer tupik, they escape the dirt* (White and Renner). [< Eskimo *tupik*]

**Tu|pi|nam|ba** (tü′pə nam′bə), *n., pl.* **-ba** or **-bas**. a member of any one of several extinct tribes of Tupi Indians who lived in the coastal forests of Brazil and practiced cannibalism.

**tup|pence** (tup′əns), *n.* = twopence.

**tup|pen|ny** (tup′ə nē), *adj.* = twopenny.

**tuque** (tük, tyük), *n.* a kind of knitted cap tapered and closed at both ends, with one end tucked into the other to form the cap, originally worn especially by French-Canadian trappers and farmers, but now also widely by skiers, skaters, and others engaged in winter sports. [< Canadian French variant of French, Middle French *toque* cap; see etym. under **toque**]

**tu quo|que** (tü kwō′kwē, tyü), *Latin.* thou, too; you're the same (a retort accusing one's accuser of the same charge that he has made): *Much of the "managed news" debate has been conducted in a tu quoque manner* (Columbia University Forum).

**tu|ra|koo** (tůr′ə kü), *n.* = touraco.

**Tu|ra|ni|an** (tů rā′nē ən, tyů-), *adj., n.* —*adj.* **1** (originally) of, having to do with, or denoting a group or supposed family of languages, including all or nearly all Asian languages that are neither Indo-European nor Semitic. **2** (later) = Ural-Altaic.
—*n.* **1** a member of any one of the peoples that speak Turanian or Ural-Altaic languages. **2** the so-called Turanian languages, collectively.
[< Persian *Tūrān*, a district north of Oxus River, probably < a Turkic word]

***turban**
definition 1

***tur|ban** (tėr′bən), *n., v.* —*n.* **1** a scarf wound around the head or around a cap, worn originally by Moslem men, but now worn also by Sikhs and certain others who are of Asian origin but not of the Moslem faith. **2** any headdress like this, such as a big handkerchief tied around the head: *The woman wore a bright-colored turban.* **3** a small

**Pronunciation Key:** hat, āge, cãre, fär; let, ēqual, tėrm; it, īce; hot, ōpen, ôrder; **oi**l, **ou**t; cup, pu̇t, rüle; **ch**ild; lo**ng**; **th**in; **ŦH**en; **zh**, measure; **ə** represents **a** in about, **e** in taken, **i** in pencil, **o** in lemon, **u** in circus.

hat with little or no brim, worn by women and children.
—*v.t.* to envelop with a turban: (*Figurative.*) *My hat is off to them— with the lengths of surgical gauze currently turbaning my brow, I can't wear it anyway* (Peter DeVries).
[< obsolete French *turbant,* or Portuguese *turbante* < Turkish *tülbent* muslin, gauze < Persian *dulband.* See etym. of doublet **tulip.**]

**tur|baned** (tėr′bənd), *adj.* wearing a turban.

**tur|ba|ry** (tėr′bər ē), *n., pl.* **-ries. 1** land where turf or peat may be dug for fuel; peat bog.
**2** *Law.* the right to cut turf or peat for fuel on a common or on another's land. [< Anglo-French *turberie,* Old French *tourberie* < *tourbe* a peat turf < Germanic (compare Low German *turf* or *turv*)]

**tur|bel|lar|i|an** (tėr′bə lãr′ē ən), *n., adj.* —*n.* any one of a class of flatworms, including the planarians, which inhabit fresh or salt water or damp earth. They have external cilia which produce minute whirls in the water.
—*adj.* belonging to the turbellarians.
[< New Latin *Turbellaria* the class name (< Latin *turbellae,* plural, a bustle, stir; (literally) little crowd < *turba* crowd, disturbance) + English *-an*]

**tur|beth** (tėr′bith), *n.* = turpeth.

**tur|bid** (tėr′bid), *adj.* **1** not clear; cloudy; muddy: *a turbid river.* **2** thick; dense; dark: *turbid air or smoke.* **3** *Figurative.* confused or disordered: *a turbid imagination. Clear writers, like fountains, do not seem so deep as they are; the turbid look the most profound* (Walter S. Landor). [< Latin *turbidus* < *turba* turmoil, crowd] —**tur′bid|ly,** *adv.* —**tur′bid|ness,** *n.*

**tur|bi|dim|e|ter** (tėr′bə dim′ə tər), *n.* an instrument for determining the turbidity of liquids, such as a nephelometer. [< Latin *turbidus* (see etym. under **turbid**) + English *-meter*]

**tur|bi|di|met|ric** (tėr′bə də met′rik), *adj.* **1** of or having to do with a turbidimeter. **2** of or having to do with turbidimetry. —**tur′bi|di|met′ri|cal|ly,** *adv.*

**tur|bi|dim|e|try** (tėr′bə dim′ə trē), *n.* the act or process of determining the turbidity of liquids with a turbidimeter.

**tur|bi|dite** (tėr′bə dīt), *n. Geology.* **1** sediment deposited by turbidity currents. **2** a rock formed from this sediment.

**tur|bid|i|ty** (tėr bid′ə tē), *n.* the condition of being turbid: *Water beetles provide clues to the acidity and turbidity of water* (New Scientist).

**turbidity current,** *Geology.* an underwater stream of silt, mud, or the like, usually along the bottom of a slower-moving body of water.

**tur|bi|nal** (tėr′bə nəl), *adj., n.* —*adj.* shaped like a top; turbinate.
—*n.* a turbinate bone.
[< Latin *turbō, -inis* top², whirling object or motion, related to *turba* turmoil]

**tur|bi|nate** (tėr′bə nit, -nāt), *adj., n.* —*adj.*
**1** shaped like a spinning top or inverted cone: *a turbinate shell.* **2** of, having to do with, or denoting certain scroll-like, spongy bones of the nasal passages in higher vertebrates.
—*n.* **1** a turbinate shell. **2** a turbinate bone.
[< Latin *turbinātus* < *turbō, -inis* whirling object or motion]

**tur|bi|nat|ed** (tėr′bə nā′tid), *adj.* = turbinate.

**tur|bi|na|tion** (tėr′bə nā′shən), *n.* a toplike or turbinate form.

***turbine**
definition 1

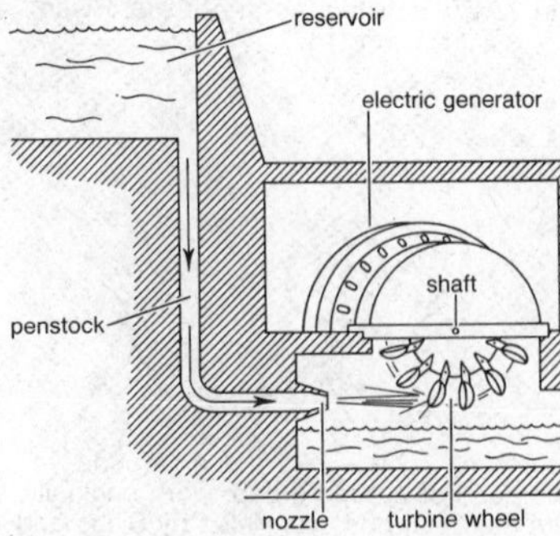

reservoir
electric generator
shaft
penstock
nozzle
turbine wheel

***tur|bine** (tėr′bin, -bīn), *n.* **1** an engine or motor in which a wheel with vanes is made to revolve by the force of water, steam, or air. Turbines are often used to turn generators that produce electric power. **2** any one of various rotary engines or motors, or any wheel, operating on a principle similar to this, such as the water wheel. [< French *turbine,* learned borrowing from Latin *turbō, -inis* whirling object or motion, related to *turba* turmoil, crowd]

**turbine generator,** = turbogenerator.

**tur|bit** (tėr′bit), *n.* any one of a breed of domestic pigeons having a stout, rounded body, a short beak, and a ruffle or frill on the neck and breast. [apparently < Latin *turbō* top²; see etym. under **turbine** (because of its plump, round build)]

**tur|bith** (tėr′bith), *n.* = turpeth.

**tur|bo** (tėr′bō), *n., pl.* **-bi|nes** (-bə nēz) *for 1,* **-bos** *for 1 and 2.* **1** a turbinate shell. **2** *Informal.* a turbine.

**turbo-,** *combining form.* **1** a machine coupled to a turbine which drives it: *Turbogenerator = a generator coupled to and driven by a turbine.*
**2** a machine that is a turbine: *Turbomotor = a motor that is a turbine.* [< *turbine*]

**tur|bo|al|ter|na|tor** (tėr′bō ôl′tər nā′tər, -al′-), *n.* an alternating-current generator connected to and driven by a turbine.

**tur|bo|car** (tėr′bō kär′), *n.* an automobile powered by a turbine.

**tur|bo|charge** (tėr′bō chärj′), *v.t.,* **-charged, -charg|ing.** to equip or operate with a turbocharger.

**tur|bo|charg|er** (tėr′bō chär′jər), *n.* a supercharger operated by a turbine driven by exhaust gases from the engine.

**tur|bo-com|pound engine** (tėr′bō kom′pound), a turbosupercharged aircraft engine.

**tur|bo|cop|ter** (tėr′bō kop′tər), *n.* a helicopter powered by a gas turbine. The fastest turbocopters can fly more than 200 miles an hour.

**tur|bo|drill** (tėr′bō dril′), *n.* a high-speed drill for boring oil or gas wells, in which the bit is rotated inside the well by a turbine powered by mud or water.

**tur|bo|e|lec|tric** (tėr′bō i lek′trik), *adj.* of or having to do with an electric generator driven by a turbine: *turboelectric power or machinery.*

**tur|bo|fan** (tėr′bō fan′), *n.,* or **turbofan engine,** a turbojet in which a fan forces low-pressure air through ducts into the hot turbine exhaust at the pressure of the turbine exhaust; fan-jet.

**tur|bo|gen|er|a|tor** (tėr′bō jen′ə rā′tər), *n.* a generator that produces electrical power by means of a steam or gas turbine.

**tur|bo|jet** (tėr′bō jet′), *n.* **1** Also, **turbojet engine.** a jet engine having a turbine-driven air compressor which supplies a continuous, high-pressure flow of air to the burners. **2** an aircraft having such an engine.

**tur|bo|pause** (tėr′bō pôz′), *n.* an area in which atmospheric turbulence ceases, especially such an area at the base of the thermosphere: *At the so-called turbopause this mixing [of gases] effectively ceases and the helium is released. Thus, if the turbopause falls in altitude, more helium rises to the upper atmosphere* (New Scientist). *Important to an understanding of the [Venusian] atmosphere is the turbopause, apparently about 144 km above the surface* (Science News).

**tur|bo|prop** (tėr′bō prop′), *n.* **1** Also, **turboprop engine.** an adaptation of the turbojet in which a propeller, driven by a turbine, provides most of the thrust; propjet. Some additional thrust is provided by the ejection of exhaust gases from the rear. **2** an aircraft having such an engine.

**tur|bo|pump** (tėr′bō pump′), *n.* a turbine-driven pump, especially that component of a rocket engine which regulates thrust.

**tur|bo-ram|jet** (tėr′bō ram′jet′), *n.* **1** Also, **turboramjet engine.** a type of turbojet in which there is a secondary combustion of fuel behind the turbine to produce exhaust gases at a higher temperature than the turbine can withstand. **2** an aircraft having such an engine.

**tur|bo|su|per|charge** (tėr′bō sü′pər chärj′), *v.t.,* **-charged, -charg|ing.** to equip or operate with a turbosupercharger.

**tur|bo|su|per|charg|er** (tėr′bō sü′pər chär′jər), *n.* a type of supercharger for an aircraft engine, operated by a turbine driven by the exhaust gases from the engine. With a turbosupercharger piston engines can operate at higher altitudes than would otherwise be possible.

**tur|bot** (tėr′bət), *n., pl.* **-bots** or (*collectively*) **-bot. 1** a large European flatfish, much valued for food. **2** any one of certain similar fishes, such as certain flounders. **3** = triggerfish. [< Anglo-French *turbut,* variant of Old French *tourbout,* perhaps < Scandinavian (compare Old Swedish *törnbut* < *törn* thorn + *but* butt)]

**tur|bo|train** (tėr′bō trān′), *n.* a train powered by turbine engines.

**tur|bu|la|tor** (tėr′byə lā′tər), *n.* the agitator in the tub or tank of an electric washing machine.

**tur|bu|lence** (tėr′byə ləns), *n.* **1** turbulent condition; disorder; tumult; commotion. **2** *Meteorology.* an eddying motion of the atmosphere, interrupting the flow of wind.

**tur|bu|len|cy** (tėr′byə lən sē), *n.* = turbulence.

**tur|bu|lent** (tėr′byə lənt), *adj.* **1** causing disturbance or commotion; disorderly; unruly; violent: *a turbulent nature. A turbulent mob rushed into the store.* **SYN:** boisterous, uproarious. **2** characterized by violent disturbance or commotion; violently disturbed or agitated; troubled: *turbulent times, muddy, turbulent water.* **SYN:** tumultuous.
**3** stormy; tempestuous: *turbulent weather.* **4** *Obsolete.* disturbing. [< Latin *turbulentus* < *turba* turmoil, crowd] —**tur′bu|lent|ly,** *adv.*

**turbulent flow,** flow in a fluid characterized by constant changes in direction and velocity at any particular point. See diagram under **fluid flow.**

**Tur|co** (tėr′kō), *n., pl.* **-cos.** a native soldier of a former body of light infantry commanded by French officers in the French service in Algeria. [< French *Turco* < Italian or Spanish *turco* Turk]

**Turco-,** *combining form.* a variant of **Turko-.**

**Tur|co|man** (tėr′kə mən), *n., pl.* **-mans.** = Turkoman.

**Tur|co|phil** (tėr′kə fil), *n.* = Turkophile.

**Tur|co|phile** (tėr′kə fil, -fīl), *n.* = Turkophile.

**tur|di|form** (tėr′də fôrm), *adj.* having the form or appearance of a thrush; thrushlike. [< Latin *turdus, -ī* thrush + English *-form*]

**tur|dine** (tėr′dīn, -din), *adj.* of or belonging to the true thrushes. [< New Latin *Turdinae* the subfamily name < Latin *turdus* thrush]

**tu|reen** (tù rēn′), *n.* a deep, covered dish, for serving soup and other foods at the table. It usually has two handles and an opening in the cover for the handle of a dipper. [alteration of French *terrine* earthen vessel < *terrin,* adjective, earthen, ultimately < Latin *terrēnus* of the earth < *terra* earth]

**turf** (tėrf), *n., pl.* **turfs** or **turves,** *v.* —*n.* **1** the upper surface of the soil covered with grass and other small plants, including their roots and the soil clinging to them; sod. **2** a piece of this: *We cut some turfs from a field and covered a bare spot in the lawn with them.* **3** peat, especially a slab or block of peat dug for use as fuel. **4** *U.S. Slang, Figurative.* **a** a city block or district regarded as the exclusive territory of a gang: *They had, he maintained, entered forbidden Dragon "turf" . . . and made threatening gestures* (Newsweek). **b** any area or territory belonging to someone: *Texans pay no mind to the upstart claim . . . that their turf is merely a smaller, baked Alaska* (Atlantic).
—*v.t.* to cover with turf or sod.
**the turf, a** a place where horses race: *Have you any horses on the turf?* (Edward G. Bulwer-Lytton). **b** horse racing: *Already there was among our nobility and gentry a passion for the amusements of the turf* (Macaulay).
[Old English *turf*] —**turf′less,** *adj.*

**-turfed,** *combining form.* having ______ turf: *Short-turfed = having short turf.*

**turf|en** (tėr′fən), *adj.* **1** consisting or made of turf. **2** covered with turf; turfy.

**turf|ite** (tėr′fīt), *n. Informal.* a frequenter of the turf or horse races; turfman.

**turf|man** (tėrf′mən), *n., pl.* **-men.** a person interested or engaged in horse racing.

**turf|y** (tėr′fē), *adj.,* **turf|i|er, turf|i|est. 1** covered with turf; grassy. **2** like turf. **3** like peat; full of peat. **4** of or having to do with horse racing.
—**turf′i|ness,** *n.*

**tur|gent** (tėr′jənt), *adj. Obsolete.* turgid. [< Latin *turgēns, -entis,* present participle of *turgēre* to swell]

**tur|ges|cence** (tėr jes′əns), *n.* **1** the act or fact of swelling. **SYN:** turgidness. **2** a swollen condition. **SYN:** distention.

**tur|ges|cen|cy** (tėr jes′ən sē), *n.* = turgescence.

**tur|ges|cent** (tėr jes′ənt), *adj.* becoming swollen; growing bigger; swelling. [< Latin *turgēscēns, -entis,* present participle of *turgēscere* begin to swell < *turgēre* to swell]

**tur|gid** (tėr′jid), *adj.* **1** puffed out; swollen; bloated; distended. **2** *Figurative.* using long words and elaborate constructions; bombastic; inflated; pompous; grandiloquent: *turgid, scholarly harangues* (Baron Charnwood). [< Latin *turgidus* < *turgēre* to swell] —**tur′gid|ly,** *adv.* —**tur′gid|ness,** *n.*

**tur|gid|i|ty** (tėr jid′ə tē), *n.* **1** turgid condition or quality; tumidity. **2** *Figurative.* bombast; pomposity: *Turgidity, and a false grandeur of diction* (Joseph Warton).

**tur|gite** (tėr′jīt), *n.* a hydrous oxide of iron, allied to limonite but containing less water. [< *Turginsk,* a mine in the Ural Mountains, where it was found + *-ite*¹]

**tur|gor** (tėr′gər, -gôr), *n.* **1** the normal, tense condition of living plant and animal cells, capillaries, and the like, caused by the pressure of the water or other fluid within. **2** the condition or quality of being turgescent or turgid; turgidity. [< Late Latin *turgor* a swelling up < Latin *turgēre* to swell]

**Tu|ring machine** (tůr′ing, tyůr′-), an ideal automatic computer that is capable of performing an infinite number of any type of calculation. [< Alan M. *Turing,* 1912-1954, a British mathematician, who first described such a machine in 1936]

**tu|ri|on** (tůr′ē ən, tyůr′-), *n. Botany.* a scaly shoot growing from a subterranean bud and becoming a new stem, as in the asparagus. [< Latin *turiō, -ōnis*]

**Turk** (tėrk), *n.* **1** a person born or living in Turkey, especially a Moslem who lives in Turkey. **2** a member of the dominant ethnic group of Turkey; Osmanli or Ottoman. **3** a member of any group of people speaking a Turkic language. **4** a person who fits the Christian conception of the Turk when Turkey was the spearhead of Islam in Europe; a cruel, barbarous person; tyrant. **5** *Figurative.* a very bad-tempered or unmanageable man. **6** a Turkish horse, especially any one of a breed of horses related to the Arabian horse, from at least one of which most modern race horses are descended. **7** *Historical.* any Moslem; Saracen. [< Old French *Turc* < Medieval Latin *Turcus* < Medieval Greek *Toûrkos* < Persian *turk* < a native Turkic name]

**Turk.**, **1** Turkey. **2** Turkish.

**★turkey** definition 1

**★tur|key** (tėr′kē), *n., pl.* **-keys.** **1** either of two large wild American birds with a bare head and neck and brown plumage, related to the pheasants. Turkeys nest on the ground and fly only short distances. One variety lives in Mexico and Central America; the other in eastern America. **2** any one of various domesticated birds developed from the wild turkey and raised for food. Many domesticated turkeys have white plumage. **3** the flesh of the turkey, used for food. **4** *Archaic.* any one of certain birds somewhat resembling a turkey. **5** *Slang.* a play, motion picture, or other creative work that is a hopeless failure; flop. **6** *Bowling.* three strikes in a row. **7** *Obsolete.* the guinea fowl.
**talk turkey,** *Informal.* to talk frankly and bluntly: *With the U.S. ... preparing to talk turkey with Red leaders, the political opportunity is obvious* (Time).
[earlier *turkey cock* (originally) a guinea fowl, apparently imported by way of Turkey; later confused with the American bird]

**turkey buzzard**, a vulture commonly found in South and Central America and the southern United States, and Canada, having a bare, reddish head and dark plumage.

**Turkey carpet**, **1** a carpet manufactured in or imported from Turkey made in one piece of richly colored wools, without any imitative pattern, and having a deep pile cut so as to resemble velvet. **2** any carpet made in imitation of this style.

**turkey cock**, **1** a male turkey. **2** *Figurative.* a strutting, conceited person.

**turkey fish**, = lionfish.

**turkey fly**, a small black fly that infests poultry in the southern United States.

**Turkey red**, **1** a brilliant and permanent red color produced in cotton cloth by means of alizarin or (formerly) madder in combination with oil or fat and an aluminum mordant. **2** a cotton fabric having this color.

**turkey shoot**, *U.S.* a contest in marksmanship in which turkeys or other moving targets are used.

**turkey trot**, a ballroom dance resembling the one-step, with swinging up-and-down movements, popular in the early 1900's.

**tur|key-trot** (tėr′kē trot′), *v.i.,* **-trot|ted, -trot|ting.** to dance the turkey trot.

**turkey vulture**, = turkey buzzard.

**turkey wing**, a marine bivalve mollusk with a thick, boat-shaped shell.

**Turkey work**, Turkish tapestry work or an imitation of it.

**Tur|ki** (tùr′kē), *adj.* **1** of or having to do with two typical groups of Turkic languages (East Turki and West Turki) spoken in the areas of Turkey and south Asia. **2** of or having to do with the peoples speaking them. [< Persian *Turkī* Turkish < *turk* a Turk]

**Tur|kic** (tėr′kik), *adj., n.* — ***adj.*** **1** of or having to do with a branch of the Ural-Altaic language family spoken in Turkey and south central Asia and comprised of Eastern Turki or Uigur, and West Turki or Seljuk and Osmanli, Kirghiz, Nogai, and Yakut. **2** = Turkish.
— ***n.*** the Turkic group of languages.

**Turk|ish** (tėr′kish), *adj., n.* — ***adj.*** of or having to do with Turkey, a country in western Asia and southeastern Europe, Turks, or their language.
— ***n.*** the Turkic language of the Turks. *Abbr:* Turk.

**Turkish bath**, a kind of bath in which the bather is kept in a room heated by steam until he sweats freely, then is bathed and massaged, and then takes a cold shower.

**Turkish crescent**, a jingling device used in military bands; Jingling Johnny.

**Turkish delight** or **paste**, a jellylike candy made, usually in cubes dusted with powdered sugar, of sugar, water, gelatin, and flavoring.

**Turkish pound**, a Turkish gold coin; the Turkish lira. Symbol: £T.

**Turkish rug**, an Oriental rug or carpet made in Turkey.

**Turkish tobacco**, a dark, very fragrant tobacco raised in Turkey, Greece, and neighboring regions of the eastern Mediterranean, used especially in cigarettes.

**turkish** or **Turkish towel**, a thick cotton towel with a long nap made of uncut loops.

**turkish** or **Turkish toweling**, material for Turkish towels.

**Turk|ism** (tėr′kiz əm), *n.* **1** Turkish institutions, ways, and beliefs. **2** *Obsolete.* Islam.

**Turk|man** (tėrk′mən), *n., pl.* **-men.** **1** a native or inhabitant of the Turkmen Soviet Socialist Republic in western Asia. **2** a native or inhabitant of Turkey; Turk.

**Turk|men** (tėrk′men), *n.* **1** an East Turkic language of Turkestan, a region in central Asia. **2** plural of **Turkman**.

**Turk|me|ni|an** (tėrk mē′nē ən), *adj.* of or having to do with Turkomans.

**Turkmen rug**, an Oriental rug or carpet made in Turkestan.

**Turko-**, *combining form.* Turkey or Turkish: *Turkophile = an admirer of Turkey, Turkish methods, or the like.* Also, **Turco-**. [< French, Italian *Turco-* < Medieval Latin *Turcus;* see etym. under **Turk**]

**Tur|ko|man** (tėr′kə mən *for 1;* tėrk′mən *for 2*), *n., pl.* **-mans.** **1** a member of any one of various nomadic and pastoral Turkic tribes inhabiting the region about the Aral Sea and parts of Iran and Afghanistan. **2** the Turkic language of this people; Turkmen. Also, **Turcoman**. [< Persian *turkumān* one like a Turk < *turk* + *māndan* to resemble]

**Tur|ko|phil** (tėr′kə fil), *n.* = Turkophile.

**Tur|ko|phile** (tėr′kə fīl, -fil), *n.* a person who greatly admires or favors Turkey, Turkish methods, policies of government, institutions, and the like. [< *Turko-* + *-phile*]

**Tur|ko-Ta|tar** (tėr′kō tä′tər), *adj., n.* = Turkic.

**Turk's-cap lily** (tėrks′kap′), either of two lilies with nodding flowers whose petals turn sharply backward.

**Turk's-head** (tėrks′hed′), *n.* a type of ornamental knot tied by winding small cord around a larger rope, used especially by sailors.

**tur|ma|line** (tėr′mə lin, -lēn), *n.* = tourmaline.

**tur|mer|ic** (tėr′mər ik), *n.* **1** a yellow powder prepared from the aromatic rhizome of an East Indian plant, used as a seasoning, as a yellow dye, and formerly in medicine as a stimulant. Turmeric is one of the ingredients in curry powder. **2** the plant itself. Tumeric belongs to the ginger family. **3** its rhizome. **4** any one of several similar plants, such as the bloodroot. **5** any one of several similar products. [variant of earlier *tarmaret* turmeric < Middle French *terre-mérite* < Medieval Latin *terra merita* (literally) worthy earth < Latin *terra* earth + *merere* to deserve, be worth]

**turmeric paper**, unsized paper tinged a yellow color with a solution of turmeric, used as a test for alkalis, which turn it brown, or for boric acid, which turns it reddish-brown.

**tur|moil** (tėr′moil), *n.* **1** a condition of agitation or commotion; disturbance; tumult: *Six robberies in one night put our village in a turmoil.* **2** *Obsolete.* harassing labor; toil. [origin uncertain]

**turn** (tėrn), *v., n.* — ***v.t.*** **1** to cause to move around as a wheel does; rotate: *I turned the crank three times.* **2** to do by turning; open, close, make lower, higher, tighter, or looser by moving around: *She turned the key in the lock.* **3** to perform by revolving: *to turn a somersault.* **4** to give a new direction to: *to turn a searchlight on a person. He turned his steps to the north.* **5** to change in position or direction; invert; reverse: *to turn a page, to turn one's face, to turn the soil in plowing, to turn a garment inside out, to turn a stream;* (*Figurative.*) *to turn a problem in one's mind.* **6** to change for or to a worse condition; make sour; spoil; taint; ferment: *Hot weather turns milk.* **7** to change so as to make; render: *The bitter cold turned him blue.* **8** to shape, especially into a rounded form on a lathe. **9** *Figurative.* to give form to; shape, form, or fashion artistically or gracefully: *He can turn pretty compliments.* **10** to change from one language or form of expression to another; translate; render: *Turn this sentence into Latin.* **11** *Figurative.* to put out of order; unsettle; distract: *Too much praise turned his head.* **12** to cause or command to go; drive; send: *to turn a person from one's door.* **13** to cause to go aside or retreat; drive back; stop; repel: *to turn a blow, to turn an attacker;* (*Figurative.*) *to turn a criticism.* **14** *Figurative.* to direct (thoughts, desire, speech, or action to, toward, or away from something): *to turn one's efforts to a new job. He turned his thoughts toward home.* **15** *Figurative.* to apply, as to some use or purpose; make use of; employ: *to turn everything to advantage, to turn money to good use.* **16** to move to the other side of; go around; get beyond: *to turn the corner.* **17** *Figurative.* to pass or get beyond (a particular age, time, or amount): *a man turning sixty.* **18** *Figurative.* to make antagonistic; prejudice: *to turn friends against friends.* **19** *Figurative.* to cause to recoil: *His argument was turned against himself.* **20** to change the color of: *Fall turned the leaves.* **21** to make sick; cause (the stomach) to reject food; nauseate: *The sight of blood turned his stomach.* **22** to give a curved or crooked form to; bend; twist. **23** to bend back (the edge of a sharp instrument) so as to make it useless for cutting. **24** to change, transform, or convert (into or to): *to turn rain into snow.* **25** to exchange for; get something else instead of; convert (into or to): *to turn stock into cash.* **26** *Obsolete.* to convert. **27** *Obsolete, Figurative.* to pervert.
— ***v.i.*** **1** to move around as a wheel does; rotate; revolve: *The merry-go-round turned.* **2** to move part way around in this way: *A door turns on hinges. The key turned in the lock. Turn on your back.* **3a** to take a new direction or the opposite direction: *The road turns to the left here. The wind turned. She turned and walked away. It is time to turn and go home. All faces turned toward him.* **SYN:** shift, veer. **b** *Nautical.* to beat to windward; tack. **4** to change and become; change: *She turned pale. Water turns to ice.* **5** to become sour or tainted: *That milk has turned.* **6** to change color: *The leaves turn in the fall.* **7** *Figurative.* to take up an attitude of opposition: *The people turned against their leader.* **8** *Figurative.* to change one's position in order to attack or resist: *The worm will turn.* **9** to adopt a different religion. **10** to become sick. **11** *Figurative.* to have a sensation as of whirling; become dizzy: *The height made her head turn.* **12** to assume a curved form; become blunted by bending. **13** to work with a lathe. **14** *Archaic.* to desert, as to another side or party.
[partly Old English *turnian* < Latin *tornāre* turn on a lathe < *tornus* lathe < Greek *tórnos;* partly < Old French *torner* < Latin. See related etym. at **tour**.]
— ***n.*** **1** a motion like that of a wheel: *At each turn the screw goes in further.* **SYN:** revolution, rotation. **2a** a change of direction; act of turning aside from one's course; deflection: *a turn of the eye. A turn to the left brought him in front of us.* **b** a change to the opposite direction; reversal: *the turn of the tide.* **c** *Figurative.* direction; tendency; drift; trend: *What turn did the discussion take?* **3** a place or point where there is a change in direction: *a turn in the road.* **4** *Figurative.* a change in affairs, conditions, or circumstances: *Matters have taken a turn for the worse. The sick man has taken a turn for the better.* **5** *Figurative.* the time at which such a change takes place: *the turn of the year, the turn of a fever.* **6a** a distinctive or particular style: *a happy turn of expression.* **b** form; mold; cast: *the turn of her arms.* **7a** a single coil or twist; one round in a coil of rope: *Give that rope a few more turns around the tree.* **b** the condition of being twisted or direction in which something is twisted. **8** a time or chance to do anything, which comes round to each individual in succession; opportunity: *It is his turn to read. My turn comes after yours.* **9a** a spell or bout of action: *Take a turn at the oars.* **b** *Especially British.* one of the performances or acts in a variety show. **10** *Figurative.* a deed; act: *One good turn deserves another.* **11a** a stroke or spell of work; job; performance: *a hand's turn.* **b** *British.* the time during which one workman or body of workmen is at work in alternation with another or others; shift. **12** *Figurative.* natural inclination, disposition, or bent; aptitude: *He has a turn for mathematics.* **13** a walk, drive, or ride: *to take a turn in the garden. We all enjoyed a turn in the park before dinner.* **14** a spell of dizziness, faintness, or the like.

**Pronunciation Key:** hat, āge, cãre, fär; let, ēqual, tėrm; it, īce; hot, ōpen, ôrder; **oi**l, **ou**t; cup, pu̇t, rüle; **ch**ild; lo**ng**; **th**in; **ŧh**en; **zh**, measure; ə represents **a** in about, **e** in taken, **i** in pencil, **o** in lemon, **u** in circus.

15 *Informal, Figurative.* a momentary shock; nervous shock: *to give someone a bad turn.* 16 *Figurative.* requirement; need; exigency; purpose: *This will serve your turn.* 17 *Music.* a grace note consisting of a principal tone with those above and below it. In the common type, the tone above precedes, and that below follows, the principal tone. In the inverted turn, the tone below precedes and that above follows. In either case, the principal tone is repeated at the end, and sometimes also precedes. 18 a prescribed movement in military drill by which a column or other formation changes direction to the right or left. 19 a complete transaction in stocks, bonds, or other property.

**at every turn**, on every occasion; without exception; constantly: *Traveling through England we kept meeting Americans at every turn.*

**by turns**, one after another in regular succession; successively; in rotation: *The lost campers slept by turns, to keep a fire going.*

**in turn**, in proper order; in due course or succession: *Each should go in turn. He that shuts Love out, in turn shall be shut out from Love* (Tennyson).

**out of turn**, **a** not in proper order: *You played out of turn.* **b** not appropriately; at the wrong time: *to speak out of turn.*

**take turns**, to act one after another in proper order; alternate: *They took turns watching the baby.*

**to a turn**, exactly to just the right degree: *meat done to a turn.*

**turn** (or **turn and turn**) **about**, one after another in proper order: *We took it turn and turn about to sit up and rock the baby* (Elizabeth Gaskell).

**turn around**, to change or reverse completely: *Many of the ... radicalized students appear determined not to destroy the system but to turn it around* (New York Times). *The market in any security will often turn around in the middle of the day* (Wall Street Journal).

**turn away**, **a** to refuse entrance or admission: *The stadium was so full that thousands of fans had to be turned away.* **b** *Figurative.* to refuse or dismiss; reject: *Those who came to him to borrow money were never turned away.*

**turn down**, **a** to fold down: *to turn down the covers on the bed.* **b** to bend downward: *He turned down the brim of his hat.* **c** to place with face downward: *The played cards were solemnly turned down* (George Fenn). **d** to refuse to accept; reject: *to turn down a plan.* **e** *U.S. Informal.* to reject the plan or request of: *to turn a person down.* **f** (1) to lower by turning something: *to turn down the gas.* (2) to lower or decline: *The stock market turned down after brisk trading had inflated prices.*

**turn in**, **a** to turn and go in: *I turned in at your house to see you.* **b** to point (toes) inward: *His feet turn in; he's pigeon-toed.* **c** *Informal.* to go to bed: *It's late and I'm going to turn in now.* **d** to give back: *A soldier turns in his rifle when he leaves the army.* **e** to exchange: *to turn in an old washing machine for a new model.* **f** to hand over; deliver: *to turn in finished work.* **g** to inform on: *to turn in a suspect.*

**turn loose**, to free from restraint and allow to go where, or do as, one will: *to turn a prisoner loose.*

**turn off**, **a** to stop the flow of; shut off: *Is the tap turned off or do I hear the water dripping? She did not turn the gas off at the meter* (Leslie Keith). **b** to put out (a light): *Turn off the lamp as you leave.* **c** to discharge: *Pay him his wages and turn him off* (Oliver Goldsmith). **d** to do: *to turn off a job. The German official or man of business is always appalled at the quantity of work his compeer can turn off in a given time* (Granville Hall). **e** to turn aside: *Where with noise the waters ... turn off with care, for treacherous rocks are nigh* (John Norris). **f** *Slang, Figurative.* to lose or cause to lose interest, liking, or enthusiasm: *We now judge candidates as much by their lack of offensiveness* (*who will turn off the fewest people*) *as by their appeal* (Saturday Review).

**turn on**, **a** to start the flow of; put on: *He turned on the gas in his back room to an unusual brightness* (Harriet Martineau). **b** to put on (a light): *Turn on the flashlight.* **c** to attack; resist; oppose: *The man turned on his pursuer.* **d** *Figurative.* to depend on: *The success of the picnic turns on the weather. The election will turn on this one point.* **e** *Figurative.* to be about; have to do with: *The conversation turned on literature.* **f** *Slang.* to take or cause to take a narcotic; get high on a drug: *A female addict who was sweet on John told others that the two of them had "turned on" together* (Maclean's). **g** *Slang, Figurative.* to arouse interest, liking, or enthusiasm; excite or stimulate: *The hero also must touch people's emotions. In modern jargon, that means someone who "turns people on"* (Time).

**turn out**, **a** to put out; shut off: *Turn out that big spotlight.* **b** to let go out: *to turn the cows out.* **c** to drive out; expel: *The noisy boys were turned out.* **d** to come out; go out: *Everyone turned out for the circus.* **e** to make; produce: *The author turns out two novels in a year.* **f** to equip; fit out: *to be smartly turned out in a new suit.* **g** *Figurative.* to come about in the end; result: *How did the game turn out? The deal turned out successfully.* **h** *Figurative.* to come to be; become: *She turned out a successful lawyer.* **i** *Figurative.* to be found or known; prove: *He turned out to be the son of an old friend.* **j** *Informal.* to get out of bed: *The next morning on turning out, I had the first glimpse of old England* (Washington Irving).

**turn over**, **a** to give; hand over; transfer: *to turn over a job to someone.* **b** *Figurative.* to think carefully about; consider in different ways: *to turn over an idea in one's mind.* **c** to buy and later sell; use in business: *Will he be able to turn over all of those cameras this year?* **d** to invest and get back (capital): *Some capital is turned over ten times in a year.* **e** to do business to the amount of (a specified sum): *a store turning over $200,000 yearly.* **f** to convert to different use: *That house ... is turned over for a shelter to sheep* (William Lithgow). **g** to start (an engine): *He pushed the starter to turn over the motor.*

**turn to**, **a** to refer to: *He took up a local paper and turned to the list of visitors* (K. S. Macquoid). **b** to go to for help: *You are the one man ... that I should turn to in such a time* (Clark Russell). **c** to get busy; set to work: *I found that no time was allowed for daydreaming, but that we must turn to at the first light* (Richard Henry Dana).

**turn up**, **a** to make (a lamp) burn more brightly: *Turn up the gas a little, I want to go on reading* (Rudyard Kipling). **b** to make (a radio, television set, record player, or other audio equipment) louder; increase the volume of: *Turn up the radio so I can hear it better.* **c** to fold up or over, especially so as to shorten: *to turn up a hem.* **d** to turn and go up: *She turned up the corridor to the left.* **e** to direct or be directed upward: *She turned up her eyes in horror at the idea.* **f** *Figurative.* (1) to appear: *An old friend has turned up.* (2) to be found; reappear: *The lost keys turned up.* **g** *Figurative.* to happen: *Something will turn up to save the hero.*

[partly < Anglo-French *tourn,* Old French *tour* tour, turn; (originally) a lathe < Latin *tornus* (see the verb); partly < the verb]

—*Syn. v.i.* **1 Turn, revolve, rotate** mean to move around in a circle. **Turn** is the general and common word for such motion about an axis or center: *That wheel turns freely now.* In science, a distinction is regularly made between **rotate**, to move on an axis, and **revolve**, to move in a circle around a center: *The earth rotates once every 24 hours. The earth revolves around the sun once a year.* This distinction is not, however, observed in ordinary usage. Otherwise, a *revolver* would be called a *rotater* and an engine's speed would be measured in *rotations per minute* rather than *revolutions per minute.*

**turn|a|ble** (tėr′nə bəl), *adj.* that can be turned.

**turn|a|bout** (tėr′ə bout′), *n.* **1** a change to an opposite position, view, or course; reversal: *The turnabout did not come out of a feeling of charity. It was purely a business proposition* (Newsweek). **2** the act or an act of turning about, especially of turning so as to face the other way. **3** a person or thing that does this. **4** *U.S.* a merry-go-round.

**turn|a|round** (tėrn′ə round′), *n.* **1** a reversal: *Most economists agree that there will be no strong turnaround in the economy until business starts building up its inventories again* (Time). **2** the time that a ship spends in a port before the outgoing voyage; turnround: *With a minimum reorganization the quick loading and turnaround will save us at least 20% on handling alone* (Wall Street Journal). **3** a place for a vehicle to turn around: *Build us a road with a turnaround at the farther end* (New Yorker).

**turn|back** (tėrn′bak′), *n., adj.* —*n.* **1** a person who retreats or gives up an enterprise; quitter. **2** that part of anything that is folded or turned back: *He spread his hands on his chest, and touched the turnback of the sheet, and then the blanket* (New Yorker).

—*adj.* that is folded back: *a turnback collar, a turnback brim.*

**turn|buck|le** (tėrn′buk′əl), *n.* a link or sleeve with a swivel at one end and an internal screw thread at the other, or with an internal screw thread at each end. Turnbuckles are used for connecting metal rods, wires, and regulating their length or tension.

**turn|coat** (tėrn′kōt′), *n.* a person who changes his party or principles; renegade; apostate. **SYN:** traitor.

**turn|down** (tėrn′doun′), *adj., n.* —*adj.* that is or can be turned down; folded or doubled down: *a turndown collar.*

—*n.* **1** the action of turning down; rejection: *turndowns on loan applications* (Wall Street Journal). **2** a decline; downturn: *Finance companies and commercial paper dealers ascribe the turndown in rates to recent declines in short-term borrowing costs on Treasury bills* (Wall Street Journal).

**turned comma** (tėrnd), *Printing.* an inverted comma above the line, such as is used (as one of a pair or singly) at the beginning of a quotation.

**turned-on** (tėrnd′on′, -ôn′), *adj.* very smart, stylish, or up-to-date; switched-on: *turned-on fashions. It's a compelling, immediate, turned-on book* (Saturday Review).

**turn|er**[1] (tėr′nər), *n.* **1** a person or thing that turns. **2** a person who forms things or shapes a substance on a lathe: *a turner of metal spindles, a turner of wood.* [Middle English *turner* < *turnen* to turn]

**turn|er**[2] (tėr′nər), *n.* **1** a member of a Turnverein. **2** a member of one of the gymnastic societies from which the modern Turnverein derives, instituted in Germany by F. L. Jahn (1778-1852). [< German *Turner* < *turnen* perform gymnastics < French *tourner* < Old French *torner;* see etym. under **turn**, verb]

**Tur|ner|esque** (tėr′nə resk′), *adj.* in or resembling the style of the English landscape painter Joseph M. W. Turner (1775-1851): *The sun ... was going down in an explosive, Turneresque brilliance above the sand hillocks* (New Yorker).

**Turner's syndrome**, a cogenital condition in which sexual development and general growth are retarded. [< Henry H. *Turner,* born 1892, an American physician]

**turn|er|y** (tėr′nər ē), *n., pl.* **-er|ies. 1** the art or work of a turner. **2** objects fashioned on the lathe; turner's work. **3** a place where articles are made on a lathe; turner's workshop.

**turn|hall** (tėrn′hôl′), *n.* the building, or part of a building, used by an American Turnverein. [American English < German *Turnhalle* gymnastic hall < *Turner* (see etym. under **turner**[2]) + *Halle* hall]

**turn-in** (tėrn′in′), *n.* act of turning in; return.

**turn indicator**, **1** a gyroscopic device that indicates in degrees per unit of time any turning movement about the vertical axis of an airplane. **2** one of the lights on the front and rear, and sometimes the sides, of a motor vehicle for signaling turns; turn signal.

**turn|ing** (tėr′ning), *n.* **1** a movement about an axis or center; rotation. **2** a place or point where a road, path, or other way turns, or turns off. **3** the act or art of shaping things on a lathe. **4** *Figurative.* shaping, molding, or fashioning (of an epigram or literary work).

**turning point**, **1** a point at which a notable or decisive change takes place; critical point; crisis: *The Battle of Gettysburg was a turning point in the Civil War.* **2** a temporary bench mark in surveying, the exact elevation of which is determined in leveling before the instrument is advanced, as a starting point for determining its height after resetting.

**tur|nip** (tėr′nəp), *n.* **1** a large, fleshy, roundish root of either of two plants, eaten as a vegetable. **2** one of these plants. Turnips are biennial plants of the mustard family. [earlier *turnepe,* probably ultimately Middle English *turn* turn (from its rounded shape) + *nepe* turnip, neep, Old English *nǣp* < Latin *nāpus* < Greek *nâpy*]

**tur|nix** (tėr′niks), *n.* any small, three-toed, quail-like bird of a group related to the bustards, found in southern Europe, northern Africa, and Australia. [< New Latin *Turnix* the genus name < Latin *cōturnīx* quail]

**turn|key** (tėrn′kē′), *n., pl.* **-keys**, *adj.* —*n.* a person who has charge of the keys of a prison, jail, or the like; keeper of a prison; jailer.

—*adj.* of or having to do with supplying a complete product by contract, especially in the building trades, where on the day the contractor completes the job the owner merely need turn the key of the door: *The company unwisely signed some "turnkey" contracts to supply complete plants at a fixed fee* (Time).

**turn|off** (tėrn′ôf′, -of′), *n.* a place at which a road, path, or other way turns off to another.

**turn of the century**, the period marking the end of the nineteenth and the beginning of the twentieth century: *The possession of any kind of bath with running water was, until the turn of the century, something to brag about* (Punch).

**turn-on** (tėrn′on′, -ôn′), *n. Slang.* excitement; stimulation.

**turn|out** (tėrn′out′), *n.* **1** a gathering of people; assemblage: *There was a good turnout at the picnic.* **2** the quantity produced, as by an industry, shop, or machine; total product; output; yield. **3** a wide place in a narrow road, where vehicles can pass. **4** a similar place in a canal. **5** a railroad siding. **6** the way in which somebody or something is equipped; equipment; outfit. **7** a horse or horses and carriage; driving equipage. **8** the action of turning out. **9** *Especially British.* **a** a strike. **b** a worker on strike; striker. **10** the act of getting out (of bed or a barracks). **11** a call to duty, especially during one's period of rest. **12** *Ballet.* a position in which the legs are completely turned outward, the feet forming a straight line with heels together.

**turn|o|ver** (tėrn′ō′vər), *n., adj.* —*n.* **1** the act of turning upside down; overturn; upset. **2** the number of people hired to replace workers who leave or are dismissed. **3** the amount of changing from one job to another; rate at which new workers are hired: *Employers wish to reduce labor turnover.* **4** the paying out and getting back of the money involved in a business transaction: *The store reduced prices to make a quick turnover.* **5** the number of times this takes place in a given period of time. **6** the total amount of business done in a given time: *He made a profit of $6,000 on a turnover of $90,000.* **7** *Especially British Slang.* a shifting of votes, transfer of allegiance, or the like, from one party, group, or faction to another. **8** a small pie made by putting a filling on half of a crust and folding the other half over it.
—*adj.* **1** having a part that turns over: *a turnover collar.* **2** that turns or is turned over.

**turnover tax**, **1** a tax paid on every sale of a given commodity: *Far more important are the so-called turnover taxes leveled at every stage of the production process* (Wall Street Journal). **2** *British.* a tax on gross volume of sales.

**turn|pike** (tėrn′pīk′), *n.* **1** Also, **turnpike road.** a road that has, or used to have, a gate where toll is paid; toll road. **2** a gate where a toll is paid; tollgate: (*Figurative.*) *I consider supper as a turnpike through which one must pass in order to get to bed* (Oliver Edwards). **3** any main highway. **4** *Obsolete.* a turnstile. [< *turn* + *pike*[2] a sharp point (referring to a spiked barrier across a road, turning on a vertical axis)]

**turn|plate** (tėrn′plāt′), *n. Especially British.* a turntable for locomotives.

**turn|round** (tėrn′round′), *n.* = turnaround.

**turn signal**, = turn indicator.

**turn|sole** (tėrn′sōl′), *n.* **1** any one of various plants whose flowers or leaves turn so as to follow the sun, especially the heliotrope and (formerly) the sunflower. **2** an annual herb of the spurge family, growing in the Mediterranean region, formerly valued for the blue dyestuff which it yields. **3** a deep-purple dye obtained from this plant. [< Middle French *tournesol* < *tourner* to turn (< Old French *torner*; see etym. under **turn**) + Latin *sōl, sōlis* sun]

**turn|spit** (tėrn′spit′), *n.* **1** a person, animal, or thing that turns roasting meat on a spit. **2** any one of a breed of small, long-bodied, short-legged dogs originally kept and trained especially as turnspits.

**turn|stile** (tėrn′stīl′), *n.* a post with bars that turn, set in an entrance or exit. The bars are turned to let one person through at a time. Some turnstiles are used to prevent a person's entrance, such as into a theater or onto a subway platform, until he has paid a charge.

**turn|stone** (tėrn′stōn′), *n.* either of two small migratory shore birds of the Old and New Worlds, that turn over stones to get at the worms and insects beneath them.

**turn|ta|ble** (tėrn′tā′bəl), *n.* **1** the round, revolving platform of a phonograph upon which records are placed. **2** a revolving platform used for turning things around. A turntable with a track is used for turning locomotives around.

**turntable ladder**, an aerial ladder that can be rotated as desired on a turntable mounted on a truck.

**turn|up** (tėrn′up′), *adj., n.* —*adj.* that is turned up or turns up.
—*n.* **1** the turned-up part of anything, especially of a garment. **2** *British.* a trouser cuff. **3** *Cribbage.* the first card selected after the crib has been dealt; starter.

**Turn|ver|ein** or **turn|ver|ein** (tůrn′fer īn′), *n.* any one of certain fraternal organizations of gymnasts in Germany, in the United States, and elsewhere in regions of considerable German immigration; athletic club. [< German *Turnverein* < *turnen* to exercise (see etym. under **turner**[2]) + *Verein* club]

**tur|pen|tine** (tėr′pən tīn), *n., v.,* **-tined, -tin|ing.** —*n.* **1** a mixture of oil and resin obtained especially by tapping any of certain pine trees. **2** a volatile oil obtained from this mixture by distilling; oil or spirits of turpentine. Turpentine is used in mixing paints and varnishes and in medicine. *Formula:* $C_{10}H_{16}$
—*v.t.* **1** to treat, mix, or smear with turpentine. **2** to obtain crude turpentine from (trees). [alteration of Middle English *terebentine* < Old French < Latin *terebinthina* (*rēsīna*) terebinth (resin) < Greek (*rhētínē*) *terebinthínē*. Compare etym. under **terebinth.**]

**tur|pen|tin|ic** (tėr′pən tin′ik), *adj.* having to do with or containing turpentine.

**tur|pen|tin|ous** (tėr′pən tī′nəs), *adj.* = turpentinic.

**tur|peth** (tėr′pith), *n.* **1** a preparation of the roots of an Asian plant of the morning-glory family, similar to jalap, formerly used as a cathartic. **2** the plant itself. **3** its root. **4** Also, **turpeth mineral.** a basic mercuric sulfate obtained as a lemon-yellow powder, formerly used as a cathartic. *Formula:* $HgSO_4 \cdot 2HgO$ Also, **turbeth, turbith.** [alteration of Old French *turpet* < Persian *turbid* < Arabic *turbath*]

**tur|pi|tude** (tėr′pə tüd, -tyüd), *n.* shameful character; wickedness; baseness: *He could laugh over the story of some ingenious fraud ... and seem insensible to its turpitude* (Edward G. Bulwer-Lytton). **SYN:** depravity, villainy. [< Latin *turpitūdō, -inis* < *turpis* vile]

**turps** (tėrps), *n. Informal.* turpentine.

**tur|quoise** (tėr′koiz, -kwoiz), *n., adj.* —*n.* **1** a clear, soft blue or greenish-blue stone. Turquoise is semiprecious almost opaque or sometimes translucent. It consists of copper and hydrous phosphate of aluminum. **2** Also, **turquoise blue.** a sky blue or greenish blue, like that of the turquoise.
—*adj.* sky-blue or greenish-blue.
[< Old French (*pierre*) *turqueise* Turkish (stone)]

**tur|ret** (tėr′it), *n.* **1** a small tower, often on the corner of a building. **2** a rounded addition to an angle of a building, sometimes beginning at some height above the ground, and frequently containing a spiral staircase. **3** a low, armored structure which revolves and within which guns are mounted. The big guns of battleships are mounted in turrets. The heavy gun of a tank is mounted in a turret which, now usually, makes up the entire upper portion of the tank. **4** a gunner's station in a military aircraft, usually enclosed by a domelike structure of strong, transparent plastic projecting from the fuselage. A turret contains a single heavy machine gun, or set of machine guns. **5** an attachment especially on a lathe or drill to hold cutting tools. **6** a tall tower on wheels, formerly used to scale the walls of castles and forts. [< Old French *touret* (diminutive) < *tour* tower < Latin *turris* < Greek *týrsis*] —**tur′ret|less,** *adj.*

**turret camera**, a motion-picture camera with a plate for holding lenses that can be rotated to a position in front of the shutter.

**tur|ret|ed** (tėr′ə tid), *adj.* **1** having a turret or turrets. **2** *Zoology.* having whorls in the form of a long spiral: *turreted shells.*

**tur|ret|head** (tėr′it hed′), *n.* turret (an attachment to a lathe).

**turret lathe**, a lathe fitted with a turret.

**tur|ri|cal** (tėr′ə kəl), *adj.* of or like a turret.

**tur|ric|u|late** (tə rik′yə lit, -lāt), *adj.* = turreted. [< Latin *turricula* (diminutive) < *turris* tower + English *-ate*[1]]

**tur|ric|u|lat|ed** (tə rik′yə lā′tid), *adj.* = turreted.

**tur|ri|lite** (tėr′ə līt), *n.* any one of a group of fossil cephalopods allied to the ammonites but having a long, spiral, turreted shell, found in Cretaceous formations. [< New Latin *Turrilites* the genus name < Latin *turris* tower + New Latin *-lites* -lite]

**tur|rum** (tėr′əm), *n.* a large carangoid fish found in the waters around Australia. [< a native Australian name]

***turtle**[1]

green sea turtle

tortoise

***tur|tle**[1] (tėr′təl), *n., pl.* **-tles** or (*collectively*) **-tle,** *v.,* **-tled, -tling.** —*n.* **1** a reptile having a toothless, horny beak and a soft body enclosed in a hard shell, into which many kinds can draw their heads and legs. Turtles live in fresh or salt water or on land; those living on land are often called tortoises. **2** a marine turtle, as distinguished from one of a kind living in fresh water or on land. **3** the flesh of turtles, especially the terrapin, used as food.
—*v.i.* to catch or seek to catch turtles.
**turn turtle**, to turn bottom side up; capsize: *An engine and two trucks had turned turtle on the embankment* (London Daily News).
[< French *tortue* tortoise; influenced by *turtle*[2] turtledove]

**tur|tle**[2] (tėr′təl), *n. Archaic.* turtledove. [Old English *turtle, turtla* < Latin *turtur*]

**tur|tle|back** (tėr′təl bak′), *n.* **1** Also, **turtle deck.** an arched frame built over the deck of a steamer at the bow, and often at the stern also, as a protection against damage from heavy seas. **2** the back (carapace) of a turtle.

**tur|tle|dove** (tėr′təl duv′), *n.* **1** a kind of small, slender, graceful dove, noted for its soft cooing and the affection that the mates seem to have for each other. **2** *U.S. Dialect.* any one of various doves of other groups, such as the North American mourning dove. [< *turtle*[2] + *dove*[1]]

**turtle grass**, **1** a marine plant of the West Indies with long, narrow, grasslike leaves. **2** = eelgrass (def. 1).

**tur|tle|head** (tėr′təl hed′), *n.* any plant of a group of North American perennial herbs of the figwort family; snakehead.

**turtle neck**, or **tur|tle|neck**[1] (tėr′təl nek′), *n.* **1** a round, high, closely fitting collar on a sweater or knitted shirt, usually turned down over itself when the garment is worn. **2** a sweater or knitted shirt with such a collar.

**tur|tle-neck** or **tur|tle|neck**[2] (tėr′təl nek′), *adj.* having a turtle neck: *a turtle-neck sweater.*

**turtle peg**, a prong fastened to a pole or cord used for harpooning large turtles, especially marine turtles.

**tur|tler** (tėr′tlər), *n.* a person or a vessel engaged in catching turtles.

**tur|ton clam** (tėr′tən), a very tiny yellowish clam of the North Atlantic. [< William *Turton,* 1762-1835, an English conchologist]

**turves** (tėrvz), *n.* a plural of **turf.**

**Tus|can** (tus′kən), *adj., n.* —*adj.* **1** of or having to do with Tuscany, a district in central Italy, its people, or their dialect. **2** *Architecture.* denoting or belonging to the simplest of the five classical orders, developed by the Romans, and similar in its proportions to the Doric, but having plain, round columns and no decoration.
—*n.* **1** a native or inhabitant of Tuscany. **2** the dialect of Tuscany, regarded as the classical and standard form of Italian.

**Tus|ca|ro|ra** (tus′kə rôr′ə, -rōr′-), *n., pl.* **-ra** or **-ras.** a member of a tribe of Iroquoian Indians that lived in colonial North Carolina and now live in New York State and Ontario.

**tusch|e** (tüsh′ə), *n.* a greasy liquid used for drawing or painting in lithography and as a resist in etching and silk-screen. [< German *Tusche* < *tuschen* to apply color < French *toucher* to touch]

**tush**[1] (tush), *interj., n., v.* —*interj., n.* an exclamation expressing impatience, contempt, or disappointment: *Tush! we have nothing to fear* (Hawthorne). —*v.i.* to make the sound of "tush."

**tush**[2] (tush), *n. Archaic.* **1** a tusk. **2** a canine tooth, especially of a horse. [Middle English *tusch,* Old English *tusc.* See related etym. at **tooth.**]

**tush|er|y** (tush′ər ē), *n., pl.* **-er|ies.** a style of writing, especially in historical novels, characterized by excessive use of affected archaisms and other expressions, such as "tush!": *In this witty and urbane story, quite free from romantic tushery, a scholarly author shows us the third century from an unfamiliar point-of-view* (Punch).

**Tu|si** (tü′sē), *n., pl.* **-si** or **-sis.** = Watusi.

**tusk** (tusk), *n., v.* —*n.* **1** a very long, pointed, projecting tooth. Elephants, walruses, and wild boars have two tusks; narwhals usually have only one tusk. **2** any tooth or part resembling a tusk. **3** a bevel or sloping shoulder on a tenon, used in woodworking for additional strength.
—*v.t.* **1** to wound with a tusk; gore. **2** to root or dig (up) or tear (off) with the tusks.
[Middle English *tusk,* Old English *tusc, tux;* see etym. under **tush**[2]] —**tusk′less,** *adj.* —**tusk′like′,** *adj.*

**tusked** (tuskt), *adj.* having tusks.

**tusk|er** (tus′kər), *n.* an animal, especially a male animal, having well-developed tusks, such as a

**Pronunciation Key:** hat, āge, cãre, fär; let, ēqual, tėrm; it, īce; hot, ōpen, ôrder; **oi**l, **ou**t; cup, pu̇t, rüle; **ch**ild; lo**ng**; **th**in; **ᴛʜ**en; **zh**, measure; **ə** represents **a** in about, **e** in taken, **i** in pencil, **o** in lemon, **u** in circus.

full-grown elephant, walrus, or wild boar.
**tusk shell**, = tooth shell.
**tusk tenon**, (in woodworking) a tenon with a tusk or tusks.
**tusk|y** (tus′kē), *adj.* having tusks.
**tus|sah** or **tus|sa** (tus′ə), *n.* **1** Also, **tussah silk**. a coarse, tan silk made especially in India. **2** an Asian silkworm that makes the cocoons that go into the making of tussah. [earlier *tessar* < Hindi *tasar* shuttle < Prakrit *tasara* < Sanskrit *trasara* shuttle]
**tus|sal** (tus′əl), *adj.* of or having to do with a cough. [< Latin *tussis* cough + English *-al*[1]]
**tus|sar** or **tus|ser** (tus′ər), *n.* = tussah.
**Tus|si** (tü′sē), *n., pl.* **-si** or **-sis**. = Watusi.
**tus|sie-mus|sie** (tus′ē mus′ē), *n. Archaic.* a nosegay. [origin uncertain]
**tus|sis** (tus′is), *n. Medicine.* a cough. [< Latin *tussis*]
**tus|sive** (tus′iv), *adj.* **1** having to do with a cough. **2** caused by a cough. [< Latin *tussis* cough + English *-ive*]
**tus|sle** (tus′əl), *v.,* **-sled, -sling,** *n.* — ***v.i.*** to struggle or wrestle; scuffle: *The boys tussled over the hat.*
— ***n.*** a vigorous or disorderly conflict; severe struggle or hard contest: *The cold war, then, is not a short, sharp tussle* (Manchester Guardian). [apparently variant of *tousle*]
**tus|sock** (tus′ək), *n.* **1** a tuft of growing grass, sedge, or the like. **2** a tuft or bunch of hair or feathers. [origin unknown]
**tussock caterpillar**, the larva of a tussock moth.
**tus|socked** (tus′əkt), *adj.* **1** covered with tussocks. **2** formed into tussocks.
**tussock moth**, any one of a family of dull-colored moths whose larvae have thick tufts of hair along the back, such as the gypsy moth.
**tus|sock|y** (tus′ə kē), *adj.* **1** abounding in tussocks. **2** forming tussocks.
**tus|sor, tus|sore,** or **tus|sur** (tus′ər), *n.* = tussah.
**tut** (tut), *interj., n., v.,* **tut|ted, tut|ting.** — ***interj.,*** ***n.*** an exclamation of impatience, contempt, or rebuke.
— ***v.i., v.t.*** to say or exclaim "tut" in contempt, rebuke, or impatience (of): *There was much tutting and disgusted head shaking on this afternoon* (Robin Marlar). Also, **tut-tut**. [imitative]
**tu|tee** (tü′tē′, tyü′-), *n.* a person being tutored.
**tu|te|lage** (tü′tə lij, tyü′-), *n.* **1** the office or function of a guardian; guardianship; protection. **2** instruction. **3** the condition of being in the charge of a guardian or tutor. [< Latin *tūtēla* a watching (< *tuērī* to watch) + English *-age*]
**tu|te|lar** (tü′tə lər, tyü′-), *adj.* = tutelary.
**tu|te|lar|y** (tü′tə ler′ē, tyü′-), *adj., n., pl.* **-lar|ies.** — ***adj.*** **1** having the position of guardian, especially protecting or watching over a particular person, place, or thing: *a tutelary saint.* **2** of a guardian; protective: *a tutelary charm. Great acts of tutelary friendship* (William Ewart Gladstone).
— ***n.*** a tutelary saint, spirit, divinity, etc. [< Latin *tūtēlārius* < *tūtēla* protection, watching; see etym. under **tutelage**]
**tu|te|nag** or **tu|te|nague** (tü′tə nag, tyü′-), *n.* **1** a whitish alloy of chiefly zinc, copper, and nickel. **2** = zinc. [< Portuguese *tutenaga* < Marathi *tuttināg* < Tamil *tuttanāgam* impure zinc, probably < Sanskrit *tuttha* blue vitriol + *nāga* tin, lead]
**tu|tor** (tü′tər, tyü′-), *n., v.* — ***n.*** **1** a person who is attached to a household or employed by a family as a private teacher: *Those rich children had tutors instead of going to school.* **2** a person (not necessarily professionally connected with a college, university, or school) engaged by students to help them prepare for examinations. **3** *U.S.* a teacher below the rank of instructor at a college or university. **4** a college official in an English university to whom students are assigned for advice and supervision. **5** (in Roman, civil, and Scots law) the guardian of a person legally incapable of managing his own affairs, especially a child under the age of puberty.
— ***v.t.*** **1** to give special or individual instruction to; teach; instruct: *She was tutored at home during her long illness.* **2** to instruct under discipline; school: *The world, however it may be taught, will not be tutored* (Shakespeare). **3** to admonish or reprove. **4** *Obsolete.* to take care or charge of.
— ***v.i.*** **1** *Informal.* to be taught by a tutor; study under a tutor: *He is tutoring in algebra.* **2** to act as tutor.
[< Latin *tūtor, -ōris* guardian < *tuērī* watch over]
**tu|tor|age** (tü′tər ij, tyü′-), *n.* **1** = tutorship. **2** the cost of educational tutoring.
**tu|tor|ess** (tü′tər is, tyü′-), *n.* a woman tutor.
**tu|to|ri|al** (tü tôr′ē əl, -tōr′-; tyü-), *adj., n.* — ***adj.*** **1** of or having to do with a tutor: *tutorial fees.* **2** exercised by a tutor: *tutorial authority.* **3** using tutors: *a tutorial system of private education.*
— ***n.*** a period of individual instruction given in some colleges by a tutor to either a single student or a small group: *The smallness of the tutorial encourages maximum participation* (Benjamin Fine).
**tutorial system**, **1** an educational system, usually at college level, in which each student is assigned, as one of a group, to a tutor, who advises and directs him. **2** an educational system, at any level, in which each student is taught individually or as one of a small group.
**tu|tor|ship** (tü′tər ship, tyü′-), *n.* the position, rank, or duties of a tutor.
**tu|toy|er** (tʏ twȧ yā′), *v.t.* to treat as an intimate; address with familiarity. [< French *tutoyer* < *tu,* familiar address for *vous* you + *toi* yourself]
**Tut|si** (tüt′sē), *n., pl.* **-si** or **-sis**. = Watusi.
**tut|ta** (tüt′tä), *adj. Music.* the feminine of **tutto**.
**tut|ti** (tü′tē; *Italian* tüt′tē), *adj., n., pl.* **-tis**. *Music.* — ***adj.*** **1** all; all (voices or instruments) together. **2** written for or performed by all voices or instruments together. — ***n.*** a passage or movement performed by all voices or instruments together. [< Italian *tutti* all < Vulgar Latin *totti,* for Latin *tōtī,* plural of *tōtus* all. Compare etym. **total**.]
**tut|ti-frut|ti** (tü′tē frü′tē), *n., adj.* — ***n.*** **1** a preserve of mixed fruits. **2** ice cream or another confection containing a variety of fruits or fruit flavorings.
— ***adj.*** flavored with or containing mixed fruits. [American English < Italian *tutti frutti* all fruits]
**tut|to** (tüt′tō), *adj. Music.* all; entire. [< Italian *tutto* < Vulgar Latin *tottus,* for Latin *tōtus* all]
**tut-tut** (tut′tut′), *interj., n., v.,* **-tut|ted, -tut|ting.** — ***interj., n.*** = tut. — ***v.i., v.t.*** to say or exclaim "tut-tut" in contempt, rebuke, or impatience (of).
**tut|ty** (tut′ē), *n.* a crude oxide of zinc found adhering in flakes to the flues of smelting furnaces, used chiefly as a polishing powder. [< Old French *tutie* < Arabic *tūtiyā* oxide of zinc, perhaps < Sanskrit *tuttha* blue vitriol]
***tu|tu**[1] (tü′tü; *French* tʏ tʏ′), *n.* a very short, full, stiff skirt worn by a ballet dancer. [< French *tutu,* alteration of *cucu,* infantile reduplication of *cul* rump < Latin *cūlus*]

***tutu**[1]

**tu|tu**[2] (tü′tü), *n. Hawaiian.* grandma; grandpa.
**tu|um** (tü′əm, tyü′-), *pron. Latin.* thine; that which is thine.
**Tu|vin|i|an** (tü vin′ē ən), *n.* **1** a member of a Turkic people living in Tuva (formerly Tannu Tuva), in central Asia, between Siberia and Outer Mongolia. **2** the language of this people.
**tu-whit** (tu̇ hwit′), *v.i.,* **-whit|ted, -whit|ting.** to hoot, as an owl.
**tu-whit tu-whoo** (tu̇ hwit′ tu̇ hwü′), an imitation of the call of an owl: *Then nightly sings the staring owl tu-whit to-whoo—a merry note* (Shakespeare).
**tux** (tuks), *n. Informal.* a tuxedo.
**tux|e|do** or **Tux|e|do** (tuk sē′dō), *n., pl.* **-dos** or **-does**. **1** a man's suit for semiformal evening wear, with a tailless coat, usually black with satin lapels. **2** the coat of such a suit; dinner coat or jacket. [American English < earlier *tuxedo coat* < *Tuxedo* Park, N.Y., where reputedly first worn]
**tux|e|doed** (tuk sē′dōd), *adj.* dressed in a tuxedo or tuxedos.
**tu|yère** (twē yãr′, twir), *n.* an opening through which the blast of air is forced into a blast furnace or forge. [< French *tuyère* < Old French *toiere* < a Germanic word]
**TV** (no periods), **1** television. **2** terminal velocity.
**TVA** (no periods) or **T.V.A.**, Tennessee Valley Authority (a United States government organization for developing the resources of the Tennessee River Valley, started in 1933).
**TV dinner**, a frozen meal on a tray ready to be heated and served.
**TVP** (no periods), *Trademark.* textured vegetable protein (an engineered food made from processed soybeans): *TVP and ground meat will soon be sold in most markets as "soy patties" or "fortified burgers"* (Harriet Van Horne).
**T.V.R.**, *Physics.* temperature variation of resistance.
**twa** (twä), *n., adj. Scottish.* two.
**Twa** (twä), *n., pl.* **Twa** or **Twas**. a member of a pygmoid people of Rwanda and Burundi, in east central Africa.
**Twad.**, Twaddell (hydrometer).
**Twad|dell** (twod′əl), *n.* a hydrometer used for densities greater than that of water, the excess of density above unity being found by multiplying the number of divisions (degrees) of the scale by 5 and dividing by 1,000. [< the name of the inventor]
**twad|dle** (twod′əl), *n., v.,* **-dled, -dling.** — ***n.*** **1** silly, feeble, tiresome talk or writing: *garrulous twaddle of old men on club sofas* (William B. Maxwell). **2** *Obsolete.* a person who talks or writes twaddle.
— ***v.i., v.t.*** to talk or write in a silly, feeble, tiresome way.
[alteration of *twattle,* variant of *tattle*]
**twad|dler** (twod′lər), *n.* a person who talks or writes twaddle.
**twain** (twān), *n., adj. Archaic.* two: *This visible Iron Curtain has slashed the city of Berlin in twain* (Wall Street Journal). [Old English *twēgen* two]
**twang** (twang), *n., v.* — ***n.*** **1** a sharp, ringing sound, such as is produced when a tense string is sharply plucked or suddenly released: *The bowstring made a twang when I shot the arrow.* **2** a sharp, nasal tone: *the twang of a Yankee farmer.*
— ***v.t.*** **1** to cause to make a sharp, ringing sound. **2** to play, pluck, or shoot with a twang: *He twanged an arrow into the target.* **3** to speak (words) with a sharp, nasal tone.
— ***v.i.*** **1** to make a sharp, ringing sound: *The banjos twanged.* **2** to shoot with a bow. **3** (of an arrow) to leave the bowstring with a twang. **4** to speak with a sharp, nasal tone.
[imitative]
**twan|gle** (twang′gəl), *n., v.,* **-gled, -gling.** — ***n.*** a continuous or repeated resonant sound, usually lighter or thinner than a twang; jingle.
— ***v.i.*** to twang lightly; jingle.
[apparently frequentative of *twang,* verb]
**twang|y** (twang′gē), *adj.,* **twang|i|er, twang|i|est.** having a twang: *a twangy banjo* (Harper's).
— **twang′i|ness**, *n.*
**Twan|kay** (twang′kā), *n.,* or **Twankay tea**, a kind of green tea, originally one consisting solely of leaves from a particular part of China, but later simply a designation of a blend of leaves of a particular size. [< Cantonese *t'wen-k'ai*]
**'twas** (twoz, twuz; *unstressed* twəz), it was: *"'Twas the night before Christmas."*
**tway|blade** (twā′blād′), *n.* any one of a group of terrestrial orchids, having two nearly opposite broad leaves springing from the stem or the root. [< earlier *tway* two, Middle English *tweien* (see etym. under **twain**) + *blade*]
**tweak** (twēk), *n., v.* — ***v.t., v.i.*** to seize and pull with a sharp jerk and twist: *to tweak a person's ear.*
— ***n.*** a sharp pull and twist; twitch; pluck.
[variant of *twick,* Old English *twiccian* to pluck. See related etym. at **twitch**.]
**twee** (twē), *adj. British Slang.* sweet; cute: *You look very twee tonight* (Punch). [< child's pronunciation of *sweet*]
**tweed** (twēd), *n.* **1** a woolen cloth with a rough surface. Tweed is sometimes made of wool and cotton, and usually has two or more colors. **2** a suit, jacket or other coat, or skirt made of this fabric.
**tweeds**, clothes made of tweed: *We do look disreputable enough in our rough tweeds* (George Fenn).
[apparently misreading of *tweel,* Scottish variant of *twill;* probably influenced by the name of the river *Tweed*]
**tweed|ed** (twē′did), *adj.* dressed in tweeds; wearing tweedy clothes: ... *elegantly tweeded women shoppers* (Manchester Guardian).
**twee|dle** (twē′dəl), *v.i.,* **-dled, -dling.** *Especially British Dialect and Scottish.* **1** to produce thin or shrill, modulated sounds by playing on a fiddle, bagpipe, or the like. **2** to pipe or whistle, as a bird. [apparently imitative]
**twee|dle|dum and twee|dle|dee** (twē′dəl-dum′ ən twē′dəl dē′), two things or parties that are identical or nearly identical. [< *tweedle* + *-dum, -dee,* suffixes suggesting musical notes; originally applied to a pair of musicians]
**tweeds** (twēdz), *n.pl.* See under **tweed**.
**tweed|y** (twē′dē), *adj.* **1** consisting of or like tweed: *a tweedy jacket.* **2** characterized by or given to wearing tweeds. — **tweed′i|ness**, *n.*
**'tweel** (twēl), *adv. Scottish.* atweel.
**tween** (twēn), *n. U.S.* a boy or girl between childhood and adolescence, especially between the ages of 10 and 13: *The youngsters choose ... games ... tailored to the various levels of teens, tweens, and tots* (Marion K. Sanders). [short for *between*]
**'tween** (twēn), *prep. Archaic.* between.
**tween-deck** (twēn′dek′), *adj.* being or lodging

between decks of a ship: *tween-deck passengers, tween-deck cabins.*

**tween|y** (twē′nē), *n., pl.* **tween|ies.** *British.* a between maid.

**tweet** (twēt), *n., interj., v.* — ***n., interj.*** **1** the note of a young bird: *We heard the "tweet, tweet" from a nest in the tree.* **2** any similar sound.
— ***v.i.*** to utter a tweet or tweets.
[imitative]

**tweet|er** (twē′tər), *n.* a high-fidelity loudspeaker for reproducing the higher frequency sounds, usually those above 6,000 cycles per second. [< *tweet* + *-er*[1]]

**tweeze** or **tweese** (twēz), *v.,* **tweezed, tweez|ing,** *n.* — ***v.t.*** to pull out with tweezers: *Hairs which spoil the line should be tweezed out* (Sunday Times).
— ***n.*** *Obsolete.* **1** a case of small instruments, as of a surgeon. **2** tweezers.
[earlier *tweese,* plural of *twee* < Old French *etui* a keeping safe < Old French *estuier* to keep. Compare etym. under **etui.**]

**tweez|er** (twē′zər), *n.* = tweezers.

**tweez|ers** (twē′zərz), *n.pl.* small pincers for pulling out hairs and picking up small objects. [alteration of *tweeze;* see etym. under **tweeze**]

**twelfth** (twelfth), *adj., n.* **1** next after the 11th; last in a series of 12: *Lincoln's birthday comes on February twelfth.* **2** one, or being one, of 12 equal parts: *Two is a twelfth of twenty-four.*

**Twelfth-day** (twelfth′dā′), *n.* the twelfth day after Christmas, January 6, the festival of the Epiphany, marking the traditional close of the Christmas season.

**Twelfth-night** (twelfth′nīt′), *n.* the evening (or sometimes the eve) of Twelfth-day or Epiphany, often celebrated as the end of the Christmas festivities.

**Twelfth|tide** (twelfth′tīd′), *n.* **1** the festive time of Twelfth-day and Twelfth-night. **2** = Twelfth-day.

**twelve** (twelv), *n., adj.* — ***n.*** **1** one more than 11; 12. A year has twelve months. **2** a set of twelve things.
— ***adj.*** one more than 11; 12.
[Old English *twelf*]

**Twelve** (twelv), *n.* **the,** = Twelve Apostles.

**Twelve Apostles,** the twelve disciples and associates of Jesus (Peter, James, John, Andrew, Thomas, James the Less, Jude, Philip, Bartholomew, Matthew, Simon, and Judas), who were chosen as His Apostles.

**twelve|fold** (twelv′fōld′), *adj., adv.* — ***adj.*** **1** twelve times as much or as many. **2** having 12 parts.
— ***adv.*** twelve times as much or as many.

**twelve|mo** (twelv′mō), *n., pl.* **-mos,** *adj.* = duodecimo.

**twelve|month** (twelv′munth′), *n.* a period of twelve months; year.

**twelve-note** (twelv′nōt′), *adj. British.* twelve-tone.

**Twelve Tables,** the early code of Roman law, drawn up in 451 and 450 B.C., containing the most important rules and serving as a basis for later legislation.

**twelve-tone** (twelv′tōn′), *adj.* **1** of or having to do with a system of atonal music, established by Arnold Schönberg in 1924, which is based on all twelve semitones of the chromatic scale in an arbitrarily selected order without any tone center (tonic). **2** using such a system: *a twelve-tone composer.* [translation of German *Zwölfton (musik)*]

**twelve-tone row,** = tone row.

**twen|ti|eth** (twen′tē ith), *adj., n.* **1** next after the 19th; last in a series of 20. **2** one, or being one, of 20 equal parts.

**twen|ty** (twen′tē), *n., pl.* **-ties,** *adj.* two times ten; 20. [Old English *twēntig*]

**twen|ty|fold** (twen′tē fōld′), *adj., adv.* — ***adj.*** **1** twenty times as much or as many. **2** having 20 parts.
— ***adv.*** twenty times as much or as many.

**twen|ty-four|mo** (twen′tē fôr′mō′, -fōr′-), *n., adj.* — ***n.*** **1** a size of a book, or of its pages, made by folding a sheet of paper twenty-four times. *Abbr:* 24mo or 24°. **2** a book having pages of this size.
— ***adj.*** of this size; having pages of this size.
[< *twenty-four* + *-mo,* as in *decimo*]

**twen|ty|ish** (twen′tē ish), *adj.* about twenty years old; looking twenty years of age: *a twentyish young man.*

**twen|ty-one** (twen′tē wun′), *n.* a gambling game in which the players draw cards from the dealer in trying to come as close to a count of twenty-one (in adding the spots on the cards) as possible without going past it; blackjack; vingt-et-un. [American English; translation of French *vingt-et-un,* the card game]

**twen|ty-three** (twen′tē thrē′), *interj.,* or **twenty-three skiddoo,** *U.S. Slang.* be off; go away; get out.

**twen|ty-twen|ty** or **20/20 vision** (twen′tē-twen′tē), the vision of the normal human eye, being that which can distinguish a character 1/3 inch in diameter from a distance of 20 feet. For vision less acute than this, the latter figure is a multiple of 20 and the amount by which the character seen exceeds 1/3 inch, taken as an arithmetical base of 1. For example, an eye which can distinguish only characters ten times this size at 20 feet is said to have 20/200 vision.

**twen|ty-two** (twen′tē tü′), *n.* a .22 caliber rifle or pistol.

**'twere** (twėr; *unstressed* twər), it were.

**twerp** (twėrp), *n. Slang.* a stupid, undesirable, or inferior person.

**twi-,** *prefix.* two; in two ways; double; twice, as in *twilight.* [Old English *twi-* two-, double]

**Twi** (twē), *n., pl.* **Twi** or **Twis. 1** a member of the chief tribe of Ghana. **2** the language of this tribe, a Sudanic dialect of Kwa. Also, **Tshi.**

**twi|bill** or **twi|bil** (twī′bil′), *n.* a battle-ax having a double-edged head. [Old English *twibill* < *twi-* two-, double + *bill* ax, sword, bill[3]]

**twice** (twīs), *adv.* **1** two times; on two occasions: *twice a day, twice in a lifetime. They say, an old man is twice a child* (Shakespeare). **2** two times in number, amount, or value: **a** two times as much as; double of: *twice two is four.* **b** in a twofold degree; two times as much; doubly: *twice as much. It's as large as life and twice as natural* (Lewis Carroll). [Middle English *twies, twiges,* Old English *twiga* twice + adverbial genitive *-es*]

**twice-born** (twīs′bôrn′), *adj.* **1** born twice; reincarnated. **2** that has experienced a second, spiritual birth; regenerate. **3** of or having to do with the three upper Hindu castes, the boys of which undergo spiritual rebirth in an initiation ceremony.

**twice-laid** (twīs′lād′), *adj.* **1** (of a rope) woven of strands of used rope. **2** *Figurative.* made from leftovers, scraps, or remnants.

**twic|er** (twī′sər), *n.* a person who does two things, especially (in England) a typographer who works at both composition and presswork.

**twicet** (twīst), *adv. U.S. Dialect.* twice.

**twice-told** (twīs′tōld′), *adj.* **1** told twice: *Life is as tedious as a twice-told tale* (Shakespeare). **2** *Figurative.* told many times before; hackneyed; trite.

**twid|dle** (twid′əl), *v.,* **-dled, -dling,** *n.* — ***v.t.*** **1** to cause to rotate lightly or delicately; twirl: *to twiddle one's pencil.* **2** to adjust or bring into some place or condition by twirling or handling lightly. **3** *Figurative.* to play with idly or absently.
— ***v.i.*** **1** to be busy about trifles; trifle. **2** to move in a twirling manner; turn about in a light or trifling way.
— ***n.*** a twirl; twist.
**twiddle one's thumbs.** See under **thumb.**
**twiddle with** (or **at**), to turn, twirl, or play with idly or absently: *Even in the midst of his terror he began mechanically to twiddle with his hair* (Thackeray).
[origin uncertain] — **twid′dler,** *n.*

**twid|dly** (twid′lē), *adj.* **1** twirling; twisting. **2** *Figurative.* trifling; trivial: *twiddly talk.*

**twi|er** (twī′ər), *n.* = tuyère.

**twi|fold** (twī′fōld′), *adj. Archaic.* twofold; double. Also, **twyfold.** [Old English *twifeald* < *twi-* two + *-feald* -fold]

**twig**[1] (twig), *n.* **1** a slender shoot of a tree or other plant; very small branch: *Dry twigs are good to start a fire with.* **2** a small branching division of a blood vessel or nerve. [Old English *twigu,* plural of *twig* twig] — **twig′less,** *adj.*

**twig**[2] (twig), *v.,* **twigged, twig|ging.** *British Informal.* — ***v.t.*** **1** to understand; comprehend. **2** to look at; watch. **3** to perceive; discern.
— ***v.i.*** to understand.
**twig on,** to catch on; understand: *to twig on to a fact or situation.*
[originally underworld slang, perhaps < Scottish Gaelic *tuig,* Irish *tuigim* I perceive, understand]

**twig**[3] (twig), *n. Obsolete.* style; fashion.

**twig blight,** *U.S.* a disease of the apple and quince.

**twig borer,** an insect larva which injures the tender twigs of certain trees, especially fruit trees.

**twig gall,** an abnormal enlargement of a twig, due to the action of insects, fungi, or bacteria.

**twigged** (twigd), *adj.* having twigs.

**twig|gy** (twig′ē), *adj.,* **-gi|er, -gi|est.** of, having to do with, or resembling a twig or twigs; slender; slim: *a twiggy girl.*

**twi|light** (twī′līt′), *n., adj.* — ***n.*** **1** the faint light reflected from the sky before the sun rises and after it sets. **2** the period during which this prevails, especially from sunset to dark night. **3** any faint light resembling twilight. **4** *Figurative.* a condition or period just after or just before full development, glory, understanding, or other state.
— ***adj.*** **1** of or having to do with twilight: *the twilight hour.* **2** like that of twilight: (*Figurative.*) *the old man's twilight years.* **3** seen or done in the twilight.
[Middle English *twilight* < *twi-* two-, double + *light*[1]]

**twi|light|ed** (twī′lī′tid), *adj.* = twilit.

**Twilight of the Gods,** the final destruction of the world and the gods in the battle with evil; Ragnarok; Götterdämmerung.

**twilight sleep,** a semiconscious condition produced by the hypodermic injection of scopolamine and morphine, administered to lessen the pains of childbirth. [translation of German *Dämmerschlaf*]

**twilight zone,** an area not clearly defined or limited, as that between day and night: (*Figurative.*) *Meanwhile, the party and its members, while increasingly circumscribed as to what they can and cannot do, will remain in a twilight zone of legality* (New York Times).

**twi|lit** (twī′lit′), *adj.* **1** lit by or as if by twilight: *a twilit afternoon.* **2** *Figurative.* not clearly defined; uncertain: *twilit moods, a twilit allegory.*

**twill** (twil), *n., v.* — ***n.*** **1** a cloth woven in raised diagonal lines by passing the woof threads over one and under two or more warp threads. Serge is a twill. **2** a diagonal line or pattern formed by such weaving.
— ***v.t.*** to weave (cloth) in this way.
[variant of Middle English *twile,* Old English *twilī,* half-translation (with *twi-*) of Latin *bilix, -īcis* with a double thread < *bi-* two + *licium* thread]

**'twill** (twil), it will.

**twilled** (twild), *adj.* woven in raised diagonal lines.

**twin**[1] (twin), *n., adj., v.,* **twinned, twin|ning.** — ***n.*** **1** one of two children or animals born at the same time to the same mother. Twins sometimes look just alike. **2** *Figurative.* one of two persons or things very much or exactly alike. **3** a composite crystal consisting of two crystals, usually equal and similar, united in reversed positions with respect to each other. **4** a composite crystal consisting of more than two.
— ***adj.*** **1** being twins; born at the same birth: *twin sisters.* **2** being a twin: *Have you met my twin sister?* **3** *Figurative.* being two persons or things which are very much alike or closely associated; forming a pair or couple: *twin engines, twin stars. Twin candlesticks stood on the shelf.* **4** *Figurative.* being one of two things very much or exactly alike: *a twin engine.* **5** *Figurative.* having two like or closely related parts: *Body and spirit are twins: God only knows which is which* (Algernon Charles Swinburne). **6** *Crystallography.* of or like a twin. **7** *Biology.* growing or occurring in pairs. **8** *Obsolete.* consisting of two; twofold; double.
— ***v.i.*** **1** to give birth to twins: *Two more ewes have twinned* (Thomas Hardy). **2** to be born at the same birth (with). **3** *Figurative.* to be coupled or joined.
— ***v.t.*** **1** to conceive or bring forth as twins, or as a twin (with another). **2** *Figurative.* to join closely; couple; pair. **3** to unite (crystals) so as to form a twin. **4** *Figurative.* to be or provide a counterpart to; match.
[Old English *twinn*]

**twin**[2] (twin), *v.t., v.i.,* **twinned, twin|ning.** *Scottish.* to twine; separate.

**twin bed,** a single bed that is one of a matching pair, usually 74 inches long and 39 inches wide.

**twin|ber|ry** (twin′ber′ē, -bər-), *n., pl.* **-ries. 1** = partridgeberry. **2** a North American shrub, a honeysuckle, whose yellowish-red flowers are subtended by purplish involucres.

**twin bill,** = double-header (def. 1).

**twin|born** (twin′bôrn′), *adj.* born a twin or twins; born at the same birth.

**twin cities,** a pair of cities on opposite banks of a river, lake, or other division.

**twin double,** in horse racing: **1** a combination bet in which the better attempts to pick the winners in four specified races. **2** these four races.

**twine**[1] (twīn), *n., v.,* **twined, twin|ing.** — ***n.*** **1** a strong thread or string made of two or more strands twisted together. **2** the action of twisting; twisting together. **3** a twisted thing, especially: **a** a twist or turn in the course of anything; coil; convolution. **b** *Figurative.* a tangle; knot; snarl. **c** a twining or trailing stem or spray of a plant.
— ***v.t.*** **1** to twist together: *She twined holly into wreaths.* **2** to form or make by twisting together: *to twine a wreath.* **3** to wrap, wind, or encircle: *to twine a rope around a post. The child twined her arms about her mother's knees.* **4** to insert (one thing in or into another) with a twisting or sinuous movement.

---

**Pronunciation Key:** hat, āge, cãre, fär; let, ēqual, tėrm; it, īce; hot, ōpen, ôrder; oil, out; cup, pu̇t, rüle; child; long; thin; ᴛʜen; zh, measure; ə represents a in about, e in taken, i in pencil, o in lemon, u in circus.

— ***v.i.*** **1** to wind or wrap around: *The vine twines around the tree.* **2** to extend or proceed in a winding manner; meander. **3** (of a serpent) to crawl sinuously.
[Old English *twīn.* See related etym. at **twist.**]
**twine²** (twīn), *v.t., v.i.,* **twined, twin|ing.** *Scottish.* to put separate; disjoin. [variant of *twin²*, verb]
**twin-en|gine** (twin′en′jin), *adj.* having or powered by two engines: *a twin-engine airliner, twin-engine transport.*
**twin-en|gined** (twin′en′jind), *adj.* = twin-engine.
**twin|er** (twī′nər), *n.* **1** a person or thing that twines. **2** a twining plant.
**twin|flow|er** (twin′flou′ər), *n.* either of two slender, creeping evergreen plants of the honeysuckle family, one found in Europe and the other found in America, with pairs of fragrant, pink or white flowers borne on long, thin stems.
**twinge** (twinj), *n., v.,* **twinged, twing|ing.** — ***n.*** **1** a sharp, pinching pain, often a momentary, local one: *a twinge of rheumatism.* **SYN**: ache, cramp. **2** *Figurative: a twinge of remorse.* **SYN**: pang. **3** *Obsolete.* a tweak; pinch. [< verb]
— ***v.i.*** to feel such pain.
— ***v.t.*** **1** to affect (the body or mind) with such pain. **2** *Obsolete.* to tweak.
[Old English *twengan* to pinch]
**twi-night** (twī′nīt′), *adj. U.S. Baseball.* starting late in the afternoon and continuing at night under lights: *a twi-night double-header.* [< *twi*(light)-*night*]
**twi-night|er** (twī′nī′tər), *n. U.S. Baseball.* a twi-night double-header.
**twink¹** (twingk), *n., v.* — ***n.*** **1** a winking of the eye. **2** the time taken by this: *in a twink, with a twink.* **3** a twinkle or sparkle.
— ***v.i.*** **1** to twinkle; sparkle. **2** *Obsolete.* to wink; blink.
[Middle English *twinken;* see etym. under **twinkle**]
**twink²** (twingk), *v.t.* to cause to clink; chink: *Oh, twink the viol and toot the flute* (Frank Sullivan).
— ***v.i.*** *Obsolete.* to clink; chink.
[probably imitative]
**twin|kle** (twing′kəl), *v.,* **-kled, -kling,** *n.* — ***v.i.*** **1** to shine with quick little gleams; sparkle; glitter: *The stars twinkled. His eyes twinkled when he laughed.* **SYN**: scintillate. **2** to move quickly, especially up and down, to and fro, or in and out: *The dancer's feet twinkled.* **3** *Archaic.* **a** to close and open the eye or eyes quickly (voluntarily or involuntarily); blink. **b** to make a signal by this means; wink.
— ***v.t.*** to cause to twinkle.
— ***n.*** **1** a twinkling; sparkle; gleam; scintillation: *He has a merry twinkle in his eye.* **2** a quick motion. **3** a quick motion of the eye; wink; blink. **4** the time it takes to wink: *in the twinkle of an eye.*
[Old English *twinclian* (apparently frequentative) < unrecorded Old English *twincan* twink¹]
— **twin′kler,** *n.*
**twin|kling** (twing′kling), *n., adj.* — ***n.*** **1** a little, quick gleam. **2** a very brief period; instant; moment. **3** *Obsolete.* a winking.
— ***adj.*** that twinkles: *twinkling eyes.*
**in the twinkling of an eye,** in an instant: *we shall all be changed, In a moment, in the twinkling of an eye* (I Corinthians 15:51-52).
— **twin′kling|ly,** *adv.*
**twin|kly** (twing′klē), *adj.* full of twinkles; twinkling: *a twinkly Christmas card.*
**twin lamb disease,** = pregnancy disease.
**twin|leaf** (twin′lēf′), *n.* a North American herb of the barberry family, whose leaves are each divided into two leaflets.
**twinned** (twind), *adj.* **1** born two at one birth; twin. **2** united, as two crystals. **3** consisting of two crystals united, so as to form a twin.
**twin|ning** (twin′ing), *n.* **1** the bearing of twins. **2** *Figurative.* close union or combination; coupling. **3** the union of two or more crystals so as to form a twin.
**Twins** (twinz), *n.pl.* a constellation and the third sign of the Zodiac; Gemini.
**twin-screw** (twin′skrü′), *adj.* equipped with two screw propellers, which revolve in opposite directions.
**twin|set** (twin′set′), *n.* a matching cardigan and sweater.
**twin|ship** (twin′ship), *n.* **1** the condition of being twin, or a twin. **2** the relation of a twin or twins.
**twire** (twīr), *v.i.,* **twired, twir|ing.** *Archaic or Dialect.* **1** to glance shyly or slyly; peep; peer: *Which maids will twire ... 'tween their fingers thus!* (Ben Jonson). **2** *Figurative.* to twinkle; wink: *When sparkling stars twire not, thou gild'st the even* (Shakespeare). [origin uncertain]
**twirl** (twėrl), *v., n.* — ***v.t.*** **1** to revolve rapidly; spin; whirl: *to twirl a baton.* **2** to turn around and around idly: *He twirled his umbrella as he walked.* **3** to twist; curl. **4** to flourish. **5** *Informal.* to pitch in baseball.
— ***v.i.*** **1** to be twirled. **2** *Informal.* to be the pitcher in baseball; pitch: *to twirl for three innings.*
— ***n.*** **1** a twirling; spin; whirl; turn: *a twirl in a dance.* **2** a twist; curl: *a twirl of hair.* **3** a flourish: *He signed his name with many twirls.*
[origin uncertain] — **twirl′er,** *n.*
**twirp** (twėrp), *n.* = twerp.
**twist** (twist), *v., n.* — ***v.t.*** **1** to turn with a winding motion; revolve; rotate: *to twist a key in a lock, to twist the steering wheel of a car. She twisted her ring on her finger.* **2** to wind; coil: *to twist braids of hair around the head.* **3** to wind together; entwine; interweave: *This rope is twisted from many threads. She twisted flowers into a wreath.* **SYN**: intertwine. **4** *Figurative.* to connect closely together; associate intimately: *Nor twist our Fortunes with your sinking fate* (John Dryden). **5** to give a spiral form to. **6** to curve; crook; bend: *to twist a piece of wire into a loop.* **7a** to force out of shape or place; contort: *trees twisted by wintry blasts. His face was twisted with pain.* **b** to sprain or wrench: *to twist an ankle.* **8** *Figurative.* to change the meaning of; distort: *Don't twist what I say into something different.* **9** *Figurative.* to distort the purpose or intent of; pervert: *to seek to twist the law to one's own advantage.* **10** *Figurative.* to mix (something up); confuse; confound: *They had twisted up the story* (H. Rider Haggard). **11** to make (a ball) go around while moving in a curved direction. **12** *Cricket.* to impart spin to (the ball) in bowling, so that it travels in a curve or jumps to the side on the rebound.
— ***v.i.*** **1** to turn around: *She twisted in her seat to see what was happening behind her.* **2** to have a winding shape or course; wind; meander; curve; bend: *The path twists in and out among the rocks.* **3** to spin; twirl: *leaves that twist and turn in the air.* **4** to wind together. **5** to move with a spin, as a curve in baseball or a billiard ball with english. **6** *Cricket.* to be twisted in bowling; travel in a curve or jump to the side on the rebound. **7** to dance the twist.
[< noun]
— ***n.*** **1** a curve; crook; bend: *to know every twist in the road. It is full of twists.* **2** a spiral line or pattern: *The tusks ... have a larger twist ... towards the smaller end* (Oliver Goldsmith). **3** a spin; twirl. **4** the act or process of twisting or condition of being twisted. **5** alteration of shape such as is caused by turning the ends of an object in opposite directions: *a girder with a bad twist.* **6** anything given shape by twisting in its manufacture, especially: **a** a small loaf or roll made of a twisted piece of dough: *a twist of bread.* **b** pipe tobacco wound or braided into ropelike form: *bring me up a pennyworth of twist* (Scott). **7** the twisting given to yarn in spinning. **8** a cord, thread, or strand made of two or more strands twisted together: *A twist of gold was round her hair* (Tennyson). **9** a strong, tightly twisted silk thread, used especially for tailoring and millinery. **10** a strong, tightly twisted cotton yarn, used for the warp in weaving. **11** *Figurative.* a peculiar bias or inclination: *His answer showed a mental twist.* **12** *Figurative.* an unexpected variation: *A new twist in the plot kept the audience in suspense. [The senator] gave a quite unforeseen twist to the American election tonight by renouncing his aspirations to Democratic nomination for the presidency* (London Times). **13** a wrench; sprain: *to suffer a painful twist of the elbow.* **14** torsional strain or stress; torque. **15** the amount or degree of spiral grooving (rifling) in the barrel of a gun: *a rifle with great twist.* **16a** a lateral spin imparted to a ball in throwing or striking it. **b** a ball thus spun. **17** a dance in two-beat rhythm, with strong swinging movements from side to side.
[earlier, anything made up of two elements, Old English *-twist,* as in *mæsttwist* mast rope, stay. See related etym. at **twine¹**.]
**twist|a|ble** (twis′tə bəl), *adj.* that can be twisted.
**twist dive,** a dive in which the diver twists before entering the water.
**twist drill,** a type of drill for metal having one or more deep spiral grooves around the body.
**twist|ed** (twis′tid), *adj.* **1** formed by or as by twisting strands together: *a twisted cord, twisted columns.* **2** bent by twisting; forced awry; distorted. **3** *Figurative.* perverted; warped: *a twisted mind. Hitler had a twisted personality.* **4** bent spirally; spiral. — **twist′ed|ly,** *adv.*
**twisted heath,** a dense shrub having small rosy-purple, bell-shaped flowers; Scotch heath. It is native to western Europe and a member of the heath family.
**twist|er** (twis′tər), *n.* **1** a person or thing that twists. **2** a person whose occupation is to twist together the ends of the yarns of the new warp to those of that already woven. **3** a mechanical device for spinning yarns, and the like. **4** a ball spinning as it moves, such as a curve in baseball or a break in cricket. **5** *Informal.* a whirling windstorm; whirlwind; tornado; cyclone.
**twist|ing** (twis′ting), *adj., n.* — ***adj.*** that twists; turning; winding: *the twisting streets of an old section of the city.*
— ***n.*** the practice of persuading a person to cancel or lapse an insurance policy so that the insurer may replace it with another policy, usually issued by a different company and of less value to the policyholder. — **twist′ing|ly,** *adv.*
**twist|y** (twis′tē), *adj.* full of twists and turns; winding: *a twisty road.*
**twit¹** (twit), *v.,* **twit|ted, twit|ting,** *n.* — ***v.t.*** to jeer at; reproach; taunt; tease: *The boys twitted me because I would not fight.*
— ***n.*** a reproach; taunt.
[earlier *twite,* short for *atwite,* Old English *æt-wītan* < *æt* at + *wītan* blame]
**twit²** (twit), *n. British Informal.* a very stupid person; nitwit: *"What do you think I'm doing, you loudmouthed twit," she said* (Sunday Times). [short for *nitwit*]
**twitch** (twich), *v., n.* — ***v.i., v.t.*** **1** to move with a quick jerk: *The child's mouth twitched as if she were about to cry.* **2** to pull with a sudden tug or jerk; pull (at): *She twitched the curtain aside.*
— ***n.*** **1** a slight, involuntary movement of a muscle or a quick, jerky movement of some part of the body. **2** a short, sudden pull or jerk: *He felt a twitch at his watch chain.* **SYN**: tug. **3** a sharp pain; twinge.
[Middle English *twicchen,* related to Old English *twiccian* to pluck] — **twitch′er,** *n.* — **twitch′ing|ly,** *adv.*
**twitch grass,** = couch grass. [earlier *twitch,* alteration of *quitch* (grass)]
**twitch|y** (twich′ē), *adj.* **1** having a tendency to twitch; jerky: *Faces peculiarly swollen, and twitchy about the nose* (Dickens). **2** *Figurative.* nervous; fidgety; irritable: *He was getting twitchy now ... before a dog race* (New Yorker).
— **twitch′i|ness,** *n.*
**twite** (twīt), *n.* a linnet found in hilly and moorland districts of northern Great Britain and Europe. [imitative]
**twit|ter¹** (twit′ər), *n., v.* — ***n.*** **1** a succession of light sounds made by birds. **2** a brief or muffled giggle; titter. **3** *Figurative.* an excited condition; flutter: *My nerves are in a twitter when I have to sing in public. In a twitter of indignation ...* (Thackeray).
— ***v.i.*** **1** to utter a succession of light sounds: *Birds begin to twitter just before sunrise. Swallows and martins skimmed twittering about the eaves* (Washington Irving). **2** to sing, talk, or chatter rapidly in a small or tremulous voice. **3** to titter; giggle. **4** *Figurative.* to tremble, as with excitement, eagerness, or fear; be in a flutter.
— ***v.t.*** to utter or express by twittering.
[probably ultimately imitative] — **twit′ter|er,** *n.*
**twit|ter²** (twit′ər), *v.t. Dialect.* to twit; tease.
**twit|ter|ing** (twit′ər ing), *adj.* **1** chirping lightly and tremulously. **2** *Figurative.* in a flutter; trembling; quivering: *[He was] hardly able to come downstairs for twittering knees* (Robert Louis Stevenson). — **twit′ter|ing|ly,** *adv.*
**twit|ter|y** (twit′ər ē), *adj.* apt to twitter or tremble; fluttering; shaky.
**'twixt** or **twixt** (twikst), *prep.* betwixt; between.
**two** (tü), *n., pl.* **twos,** *adj.* — ***n.*** **1** one more than one; 2: *Three may keep a secret if two of them are dead* (Benjamin Franklin). **2** a set of two persons or things: *Count the class by twos.* **3** a playing card, throw of the dice, domino, or a billiard ball or other playing piece, with two spots or a "2" on it; deuce.
— ***adj.*** one more than one; 2.
**in two,** in two parts or pieces: *At its full stretch as the tough string he drew, Struck by an arm unseen, it burst in two* (Alexander Pope).
**put two and two together,** to form an obvious conclusion from the facts: *Putting two and two together ... it was not difficult to guess who the expected Marquis was* (Thackeray).
[Old English *twā,* feminine of *twēgen* two. Compare etym. under **twain.**]
**two-bag|ger** (tü′bag′ər), *n. Slang.* a two-base hit in baseball; double.
**two-base hit** (tü′bās′), a hit in baseball where the ball goes far enough for the batter to reach second base; double.
**two-beat** (tü′bēt′), *adj.* of or having to do with jazz in which two beats of the four in every bar are accented: *two-beat rhythms.*
**two-bit** (tü′bit′), *adj. U.S. Slang.* **1** worth a quarter of a dollar: *There's a man ... always got a good story and a two-bit cigar for you* (Sinclair Lewis). **2** *Figurative.* cheap; worthless: *I admit that two-bit judge is short on ritual sense* (Saturday Evening Post).
**two bits,** *Slang.* a quarter of a dollar: *It was a nickel a ride for pedestrians; two bits for a load of hay* (Maclean's).
**two-by-four** (tü′bī fôr′, -fōr′), *adj., n.* — ***adj.***

1 measuring two inches or feet by four inches or feet. 2 *Informal, Figurative.* **a** small; narrow; limited: *a two-by-four room.* **b** small in mind or outlook; petty: *a two-by-four political hanger-on.*
—*n.* a piece of lumber formerly four inches wide by two inches thick. Two-by-fours are now about 1¾ inches by 3⅝ inches and are used especially in building.

**two cents' worth**, *U.S. Slang.* a statement of opinion or point of view: *He is an expert chairman, keeping the discussion firmly to the point and yet giving each speaker the feeling that he is getting in his two cents' worth* (New Yorker).

**two cultures**, Usually, **the two cultures**. the arts and humanities, or social sciences, on one hand, and the physical sciences and engineering technology on the other, viewed as two distinct and often conflicting cultures in modern society: *The conference called on UNESCO to convene a worldwide conference that might be instrumental in narrowing the gap between the two cultures* (New Scientist). [< *The Two Cultures and the Scientific Revolution,* title of a celebrated lecture delivered by the English writer C. P. Snow in 1959 at Cambridge University]

**two-cy|cle** (tü'sī'kəl), *adj., n.* —*adj.* **1** completing a series of operations in two cycles or strokes, as an internal-combustion engine. **2** of or having to do with a two-cycle engine.
—*n.* a cycle of two strokes in an internal-combustion engine.

**two-di|men|sion|al** (tü'də men'shə nəl), *adj.* **1** having only two dimensions. **2** *Figurative.* lacking depth; superficial: *The inherent weakness of the American Western novel, according to students of that popular literary theme, is that it is two-dimensional* (Newsweek). —**two'-di|men'sion|al|ly**, *adv.*

**two-di|men|sion|al|i|ty** (tü'də men'shə nal'ə tē), *n.* the quality or condition of being two-dimensional.

**two-edged** (tü'ejd'), *adj.* **1** having two edges, especially having two cutting edges, one on each side of the blade; cutting both ways: *a two-edged sword.* **2** *Figurative.* effective either way; double-edged, especially: **a** that supports or may be used in support of either side: *a two-edged argument.* **b** that may be reversed or sharply altered in order to achieve a purpose: *two-edged policy.*

**two-faced** (tü'fāst'), *adj.* **1** having two faces. **2** *Figurative.* deceitful; hypocritical. —**two'-fac'ed|ly**, *adv.* —**two'-fac'ed|ness**, *n.*

**two|fer** (tü'fər), *n. U.S. Slang.* **1a** a pair of theater tickets sold for roughly the price of one. **b** a coupon for obtaining such tickets. **2** any item sold at two for the price of one: *twofer cigars.* [alteration of *two for*]

**two-fist|ed** (tü'fis'tid), *adj. Informal.* **1** having two fists and able to use them: *a two-fisted cowboy.* **2** *Figurative.* strong; vigorous: *a two-fisted attack on crime. You tell him that no two-fisted enterprising Westerner would have New York for a gift* (Sinclair Lewis). **3** *Figurative.* such as appeals to persons of simple and virile taste: *a two-fisted romance of the high seas.*

**two|fold** (tü'fōld'), *adj., adv.* —*adj.* **1** two times as much or as many; twice as great; double. **2** having two parts; dual: *a twofold shipment, part coming now and the rest later.*
—*adv.* two times as much or as many; doubly.

**two-forked** (tü'fôrkt'), *adj.* having two dimensions or branches like the prongs of a fork; bifurcate; dichotomous: (*Figurative.*) *a two-forked argument.*

**two-four** (tü'fôr', -fōr'), *adj.* (of a musical time or rhythm) with two quarter notes to a measure.

**2,4-D** (tü'fôr'dē', -fōr'-), *n.* a poisonous, crystalline substance used to kill weeds. *Formula:* $C_8H_6Cl_2O_3$ [< *2,4-d*(ichlorophenoxyacetic acid)]

**2,4,5-T** (tü'fôr'fīv'tē', -fōr'-), *n.* a poisonous, crystalline substance used to kill weeds. [< *2,4,5-t*(richlorophenoxyacetic acid)]

**two-gun** (tü'gun'), *adj.* carrying or skillful in using two guns at the same time: *a two-gun cowboy.*

**two-hand|ed** (tü'han'did), *adj.* **1** having two hands. **2** using both hands equally well; ambidextrous. **3** *Figurative.* skillful with the hands; dexterous. **4** involving the use of both hands; requiring both hands to wield or manage: *a two-handed sword.* **5** requiring two persons to operate: *a two-handed saw.* **6** engaged in or played by two persons: *a two-handed game.* **7** *Obsolete.* big; bulky; strapping. —**two'-hand'ed|ness**, *n.*

**two-high** (tü'hī'), *adj.* of or having to do with a rolling mill having two rollers, one over the other, or with the rollers themselves.

**two-mast|er** (tü'mas'tər, -mäs'-), *n.* any sailing vessel with two masts.

**two-mind|ed** (tü'mīn'did), *adj.* vacillating between two intentions; having ambivalent or conflicting attitudes: *He is two-minded about going to the party without a formal invitation.*

**two-name** (tü'nām'), *adj. Banking.* signed by two people: *a two-name note.*

**two-name paper**, *Banking.* negotiable papers such as bills or notes, signed by two people, usually a maker and an endorser, both of whom are held liable.

**two|ness** (tü'nis), *n.* the quality of being two; duality; doubleness.

**two-o-cat** or **two-o'-cat** (tü'ō'kat'), *n.* a ball game similar to one-o-cat, but with two batters on a side instead of one.

**two old cat**, = two-o-cat.

**two-part time** (tü'pärt'), *Music.* a time or rhythm with two, or a multiple of two, beats to the measure.

**two-par|ty system** (tü'pär'tē), the condition or system of political balance that has prevailed historically in the United States, Great Britain (since the 1600's), and certain other countries, especially in the English-speaking world, under which normally in any particular election one or the other of two (although not necessarily always the same two) major political parties is certain to win.

**two|pence** (tup'əns), *n.* **1** two British pennies; two pence. **2** a British silver coin worth two pence (since 1662 minted only on special occasions). **3** a British copper coin worth two pence (minted in the reign of George III). Also, **tuppence**.

**two|pen|ny** (tup'ə nē), *adj.* **1** worth, costing, or amounting to twopence. **2** *Figurative.* of very little value; paltry; trifling; worthless. Also, **tuppenny**.

**two-phase** (tü'fāz'), *adj. Electricity.* diphase.

**two-piece** (tü'pēs'), *adj., n.* —*adj.* consisting of two parts made to be worn together: *a two-piece dress, a two-piece bathing suit.*
—*n.* a two-piece garment.

**two-piec|er** (tü'pē'sər), *n.* a two-piece garment.

**two-ply** (tü'plī'), *adj.* having two thicknesses, folds, layers, or strands.

**two-port** (tü'pôrt', -pōrt'), *adj.* **1** having two ports. **2** of or having to do with a type of two-cycle internal-combustion engine, common in marine use, in which the crankcase admission port of the three-port type of engine is dispensed with, and for it is substituted a kind of suction valve leading to the crankcase.

**two|score** (tü'skôr', -skōr'), *adj.* forty.

**two-seat|er** (tü'sē'tər), *n.* a car or airplane with a seat for two persons: *The tiny two-seater has a two-cycle, two-cylinder engine* (Wall Street Journal).

**two-sid|ed** (tü'sī'did), *adj.* having two sides; bilateral: (*Figurative.*) [*Theirs*] *was a two-sided friendship* (Scientific American). —**two'-sid'ed|ness**, *n.*

**two|some** (tü'səm), *n., adj.* —*n.* **1** a group of two people; two persons together. **2a** a game or match, especially in golf, in which two play. **b** the players.
—*adj.* played by two players, especially two golfers.
[< *two* + *-some*²]

**two-step** (tü'step'), *n., v.,* **-stepped, -step|ping.** —*n.* **1** a ballroom dance in march or polka rhythm, performed with sliding steps. **2** music for it.
—*v.i.* to dance the two-step.

**two-suit|er** (tü'sü'tər), *n.* **1** a man's suitcase that holds two suits and accessories: *His two-suiter ... was adorned with the baggage tags of many airlines* (New Yorker). **2** a hand in bridge containing two suits with at least five cards in each.

**two-thirds rule** (tü'thėrdz'), *U.S.* a former rule of the Democratic Party which required the vote of two-thirds of the delegates at a convention to nominate a candidate for the presidency.

**two-time**¹ (tü'tīm'), *v.t.,* **-timed, -tim|ing.** *Slang.* **1** to be unfaithful to in love. **2** to betray or be disloyal to; deceive; double-cross.

**two-time**² (tü'tīm'), *adj.* having performed, occurred, or been given twice: *I'm a two-time loser* (New York Times).

**two-tim|er** (tü'tī'mər), *n. U.S. Slang.* a person who is disloyal or unfaithful.

**two-tim|ing** (tü'tī'ming), *adj. U.S. Slang.* disloyal; unfaithful; deceitful.

**two-toed sloth** (tü'tōd'), any one of a group of sloths of tropical South and Central America having two toes on the forefeet. See picture under **sloth**.

**two-tone** (tü'tōn'), *adj.* having two colors or shades of color: *a two-tone station wagon, two-tone shoes.*

**two-toned** (tü'tōnd'), *adj.* = two-tone.

**'twould** (twůd; *unstressed* twəd), it would.

**two-up** (tü'up'), *n.* a game in which players bet on whether two pennies tossed up will fall heads or tails.

**two-way** (tü'wā'), *adj.* **1** moving or allowing movement in two directions: *two-way traffic, a two-way street.* **2** *Figurative.* going both ways; extending in two directions: *a two-way relationship.* **3** used in two ways or for two purposes: *a two-way radio for receiving and transmitting messages. There are seventeen two-way mirrors enabling students to watch doctor and patient without bothering the patient* (New York Times). **4** consisting of or involving two persons or groups: *a two-way race for senator, a two-way alliance.* **5** having to do with or designating a valve or cock with two outlets which may act together or alternately. **6** *Mathematics.* capable of varying in two ways: *a two-way progression.*

**two-wheel|er** (tü'hwē'lər), *n.* a bicycle or other vehicle running on two wheels: *The age at which a youngster can handle a two-wheeler, or "real bike," varies* (Sidonie M. Gruenberg).

**twp.** or **Twp.**, township.

**T.W.U.**, Transport Workers' Union.

**TWX** (no periods), teletypewriter exchange.

**twy|fold** (twī'fōld'), *adj. Archaic.* twifold.

**TX** (no periods), Texas (with postal Zip Code).

**-ty**¹, *suffix added to numbers.* ___ tens; ___ times ten: *Seventy = seven tens,* or *seven times ten.* [Old English *-tig*]

**-ty**², *suffix added to adjectives to form nouns.* the fact, quality, or condition of being ___: *Safety = the condition* or *quality of being safe.* Also, **-ity**. [Middle English *-tee, -tie* < Old French *-te* < *-tet* < Latin *-tās, -tātis*]

**Ty.**, territory.

**Ty|che** (tī'kē), *n. Greek Mythology.* the goddess of fortune, identified with the Roman goddess Fortuna.

**ty|coon** (tī kün'), *n.* **1** *Informal.* an important person in a (specified) business or industry; one having great wealth and power: *a financial tycoon, a gathering of shipping tycoons.* **2** a person of equivalent importance in any (specified) realm: *a political tycoon, a labor tycoon.* **3** the title given by foreigners to the former hereditary commanders in chief of the Japanese army; shogun. [< Japanese *taikun* < Chinese *tai* great + *kiun* lord]

**Ty|di|des** (ti dī'dēz), *n. Greek Legend.* Diomedes.

**ty|ee** (tī'ē), *n.* **1** a person of distinction; leader; chief. **2** = chinook salmon. [< Chinook jargon]

**tyg** (tig), *n.* a large, flat-bottomed drinking cup with two or more handles. [origin unknown]

**ty|ing** (tī'ing), *v.* the present participle of **tie**: *He is tying his shoes.*

**tyke** (tīk), *n.* **1** *Informal.* **a** a mischievous or troublesome child. **b** any child: *a friendly little tyke.* **2** *Scottish.* **a** a mongrel dog; cur. **b** any dog. **3** *Scottish.* a low fellow. Also, **tike**. [< Scandinavian (compare Old Icelandic *tīk* bitch)]

**ty|lo|sin** (tī lō'sən), *n.* an antibiotic derived from a strain of streptomyces found in Thailand, used to treat bacterial infections in cattle, swine, dogs, and other animals. *Formula:* $C_{45}H_{77}NO_{17}$ [probably < *tylosis* + *-in*]

**ty|lo|sis** (tī lō'sis), *n., pl.* **-ses** (-sēz). **1** *Botany.* a growth from a cell wall into the cavity of woody tissue: *In some woods the parenchyma cells, before they die, push bladderlike outgrowths called tyloses into the vessels, blocking them and making water conduction impossible* (New Scientist). **2** *Medicine.* **a** an inflammatory disease in which the eyelids become thick and hard around the edges. **b** a disease of the mucous membrane of the lips and mouth, characterized by whitish spots. [< Greek *týlōsis* formation of a callus < *týlē* callus]

**tym|bal** (tim'bəl), *n.* = timbal.

**tymp** (timp), *n.* (in some blast furnaces) the top portion or crown of the opening in front of the hearth.

**tym|pan** (tim'pən), *n.* **1** a stretched membrane, or a sheet or plate of some thin material, in an apparatus. **2** an appliance in a printing press, often consisting of a thickness of paper, cloth, cardboard, or the like, placed between the platen or impression cylinder and the paper to be printed, so as to soften and equalize the pressure. **3** *Architecture.* tympanum. **4** *Music, Archaic.* a kettledrum. [Old English *timpanum* < Latin *tympanum* < Greek *týmpanon.* See etym. of doublets **timbre, timpani, tympanum.**]

**tym|pa|nal** (tim'pə nəl), *adj.* = tympanic.

**tym|pa|ni** (tim'pə nē), *n., pl. of* **tympano**. timpani; kettledrums.

**tym|pan|ic** (tim pan'ik), *adj.* **1a** of or having to do with the eardrum. **b** of or in the middle ear: *the tympanic cavity.* **2** having to do with a drum. **3** like a drum.

**tympanic bone**, (in mammals) a bone supporting the eardrum and enclosing the passage of the external ear.

**tympanic membrane**, = eardrum.

**tym|pa|nism** (tim'pə niz əm), *n.* = tympanites.

---

**Pronunciation Key:** hat, āge, cãre, fär; let, ēqual, tėrm; it, īce; hot, ōpen, ôrder; oil, out; cup, půt, rüle; child; long; thin; ᴛʜen; zh, measure; ə represents **a** in about, **e** in taken, **i** in pencil, **o** in lemon, **u** in circus.

**tym|pa|nist** (tim′pə nist), *n.* = timpanist.

**tym|pa|ni|tes** (tim′pə nī′tēz), *n.* distention of the wall of the abdomen by gas or air. [< Late Latin *tympanītēs* < Greek *tympanītēs* < *týmpanon* drum; see etym. under **tympanum**]

**tym|pa|nit|ic** (tim′pə nit′ik), *adj.* **1** having to do with tympanites. **2** of the nature of tympanites.

**tym|pa|ni|tis** (tim′pə nī′tis), *n.* inflammation of the tympanum or middle ear.

**tym|pa|no** (tim′pə nō), *n., pl.* **-ni.** = timpano. [< Italian *timpano*]

**tym|pa|no|plas|ty** (tim′pə nō plas′tē), *n.* an operation to repair a damaged eardrum. [< *tympanum* + *-plasty*]

***tympanum**
definition 4b

***tym|pa|num** (tim′pə nəm), *n., pl.* **-nums, -na** (-nə). **1** = eardrum. **2** the middle part of the ear, consisting of a cavity in the temporal bone; middle ear. **3** the diaphragm in a telephone. **4** *Architecture.* **a** the vertical recessed face of a pediment, enclosed by the cornices, usually triangular and often adorned with sculpture. **b** a slab or wall between an arch and the horizontal top of a door or window below. **5** a drum, especially a kettledrum; tympano. **6** the stretched membrane of a drum; drumhead. [< Medieval Latin *tympanum* < Latin, drum < Greek *týmpanon* < *týptein* to beat, strike. See etym. of doublets **timbre, timpani, tympan.**]

**tym|pa|ny** (tim′pə nē), *n., pl.* **-nies. 1** tympanites. **2** an abnormal swelling or tumor of any kind. **3** *Figurative.* **a** a swelling, as of pride or arrogance; condition of being inflated or puffed up. **b** bombast. [< Medieval Latin *tympanias* < Greek *tympanías* < *týmpanon;* see etym. under **tympanum**]

**Tyn|dall beam** (tin′dəl), the visible path of a light beam that enters a colloid and is scattered by colloidal particles in the Tyndall effect. [< John *Tyndall,* 1820-1893, an English physicist]

**Tyndall effect,** the scattering of light in different colors by the particles of a colloid: *The bluish appearance of a light beam passing through something like a soap solution is called the "Tyndall effect"* (G. Gamow).

**Tyn|dar|e|us** (tin dar′ē əs), *n. Greek Legend.* a Spartan king, husband of Leda and father by her of Clytemnestra.

**tyne**[1] (tīn), *v.,* **tyned** or **tynt, tyn|ing.** *Especially Scottish.* tine[2].

**tyne**[2] (tīn), *n. Obsolete.* tine[1].

**typ., 1** typographer. **2a** typographic. **b** typographical. **3** typography.

**typ|al** (tī′pəl), *adj.* **1** of the nature of or answering to a type or pattern; representative; typical. **2** having to do with or relating to a type or symbol; symbolic; emblematic.

**type** (tīp), *n., adj., v.,* **typed, typ|ing.** —*n.* **1** a kind, class, or group alike in some important way: *three types of local government. Small pox of the most malignant type* (Macaulay). **2** kind; sort; order: *I don't like that type of work.* **3** a person or thing having the characteristics of a kind, class, or group; representative specimen; example; illustration: *The Tahitians are considered ... as the type of the whole Polynesian race* (James C. Prichard). **SYN:** prototype. **4** a perfect example of a kind, class, or group; model; pattern; exemplar: *He is a fine type of schoolboy. The Republican form of government is the highest form of government; but, because of this, it requires the highest type of human nature* (Herbert Spencer). **SYN:** prototype. **5** the general form, style, or character of some kind, class, or group: *She is above the ordinary type of politician.* **6** *Biology.* **a** a general plan or structure characterizing a group of animals, plants, or other organisms. **b** a genus, species, or other group which most perfectly exhibits the essential characters of its family or group, and from which the family or group is usually named. **7a** the inherited characteristics of an animal or breed which fit it for a certain use: *dairy or beef type.* **b** an animal or breed having such characteristics. **8a** a piece of metal or wood having on its upper surface a raised letter, figure, or other character, for use in printing; letter (used with an article and having a plural): *a type, the types.* **b** a collection of such pieces (used without article or plural): *to set the manuscript for a book in type.* **c** a printed character or characters: *small or large type.* **9** *Mathematics.* **a** the simplest of the equivalent forms of a series of transformations, as *10* in *10, 2(3+2), ≡100.* **b** a standard form. **10** a group of persons or substances which have certain physiological characteristics, functions, or properties in common, such as a blood type. **11a** a piece similar to a printing type on a typewriter or like machine. **b** such types collectively. **12** a figure, inscription, or design on either side of a coin or medal. **13** something having symbolical significance; symbol; emblem. **14** something that foreshadows something to come (the antitype); a prefigurement. **15** a person, object, or event in the Old Testament regarded as foreshadowing a corresponding reality of the new dispensation. **16** a distinguishing mark or sign.
—*adj.* **1** of, having to do with, or relating to a type: *a type specimen, a type animal.* **2** for a type or types, especially printing types (collectively): *type matter, type composition.* **3** using or dealing with printing types (collectively): *a type caster.* **4** making printing types (collectively).
—*v.t.* **1** to write with a typewriter; typewrite: *to type a letter asking for a job.* **2** to be the type or symbol of; symbolize; typify. **3** to be the pattern or model for. **4** to find out the type of; classify: *to type a person's blood.* **5** to foreshadow as a type; prefigure. **6** = typecast.
—*v.i.* to write with a typewriter; typewrite.
[< Latin *typus* < Greek *týpos* dent, impression < *týptein* to strike, beat]
► **type, type of.** The standard English idiom is *type of: this type of* (not *type*) *letter.*

**type bar, 1** each of the movable bars carrying the letters or characters in a typewriter. **2** a line of type cast in a solid bar, as by a linotype.

**type|case** (tīp′kās′), *n.* a flat, compartmented box for holding sorted printing type.

**type|cast** (tīp′kast′, -käst′), *v.t.,* **-cast, -cast|ing. 1** to cast (an actor) in a role that seems to suit his appearance and personality: *He is also a dignified, patriarchal-looking man, practically typecast for the role of a great composer* (New Yorker). **2** to cast repeatedly in the same role: *to become typecast as a politician.*

**type cutter,** a person who engraves the dies or punches from which printing types are cast.

***type face, 1** the printing surface of a plate or piece of type. **2** the style of the printing surface of the type, especially its thickness, serifs, and other characteristics.

***type face**
definition 2

**type founder,** a person who casts or makes metal printing type.

**type founding,** the art or process of manufacturing movable metallic types used by printers.

**type foundry,** a place where printing types are manufactured.

**type genus,** *Biology.* the genus from which the name of the family or subfamily is taken, theoretically, the genus most perfectly exhibiting the family characteristics.

**type-high** (tīp′hī′), *adj. Printing.* of the standard height of type (in the United States, 0.9186 inch; in Great Britain, 0.9175 inch).

**type metal,** an alloy of lead and antimony, sometimes with tin, of which printing types are cast; metal.

**type page,** the part of a page covered by type or letterpress.

**typ|er** (tī′pər), *n.* **1** a person or thing that types; a person who does typewriting. **2** = typewriter.

**type|script** (tīp′skript′), *n.* a typewritten manuscript.

**type|set** (tīp′set′), *v.t.,* **-set, -set|ting.** to set (copy) in printing type.

**type|set|ter** (tīp′set′ər), *n.* **1** a person who sets type for printing; compositor. **2** a machine that sets type for printing.

**type|set|ting** (tīp′set′ing), *n., adj.* —*n.* the act, art, or process of setting type for printing; composition.
—*adj.* used or adapted for setting type: *a typesetting machine.*

**type species,** *Biology.* the species from which the name of the genus is taken, theoretically, the species most perfectly exhibiting the generic characteristics; genotype.

**type specimen,** *Biology.* an individual or specimen from which the description of the species or subspecies has been prepared and upon which the specific name has been based.

**type|write** (tīp′rīt′), *v.t., v.i.,* **-wrote, -writ|ten, -writ|ing.** to write with a typewriter; type: *to typewrite a letter, to know how to typewrite.*

**type|writ|er** (tīp′rī′tər), *n.* **1** a machine for writing which reproduces letters similar to those of printers. When the keys of a typewriter keyboard are struck, they are pressed against an inked ribbon and a sheet of paper. See picture under **keyboard. 2** = typist. **3** *Printing.* a style of type that resembles that of a typewriter.

**type|writ|ing** (tīp′rī′ting), *n.* **1** the act or art of using a typewriter: *to study typewriting.* **2** work done on a typewriter: *His typewriting is very accurate.*

**type|writ|ten** (tīp′rit′ən), *adj., v.* —*adj.* written with a typewriter: *a typewritten letter.*
—*v.* the past participle of **typewrite:** *Your letter was typewritten and mailed yesterday.*

**type|wrote** (tīp′rōt′), *v.* the past tense of **typewrite.**

**typh|lit|ic** (tif lit′ik), *adj.* **1** having to do with typhlitis. **2** of the nature of typhlitis. **3** affected with typhlitis.

**typh|li|tis** (tif lī′tis), *n.* inflammation of the cecum. [< New Latin *typhlitis* < Greek *typhlón* the cecum + New Latin *-itis* -itis]

**typh|lol|o|gy** (tif lol′ə jē), *n.* the science dealing with blindness. [< Greek *typhlós* blind + *-logy*]

**typh|lo|sis** (tif lō′sis), *n.* = blindness. [< Greek *typhlōsis* < *typhloûn* make blind < *typhlós* blind]

**typh|lo|sole** (tif′lə sōl), *n.* a ridge or fold extending along the inner wall of the intestine and partly dividing the intestinal cavity in lampreys, mollusks, and worms. [< Greek *typhlós* blind + *sōlên* channel]

**Ty|pho|e|an** (tī fō′ē ən), *adj.* **1** of or having to do with Typhoeus. **2** characteristic of Typhoeus.

**Ty|pho|eus** (tī fō′yüs), *n. Greek Mythology.* a monster with a hundred serpents' heads each with a terrible voice, slain by Zeus's thunderbolt, and buried in Tartarus under Mount Etna.

**ty|pho|gen|ic** (tī′fə jen′ik), *adj.* **1** causing typhoid fever. **2** causing typhus.

**ty|phoid** (tī′foid), *adj., n.* —*adj.* **1** of or having to do with typhoid fever. **2** like or characteristic of typhoid fever. **3** affected with typhoid fever. **4** like typhus, as a stuporous state in certain fevers.
—*n.* = typhoid fever. [< *typhus*]

**ty|phoi|dal** (tī foi′dəl), *adj.* **1** having to do with typhoid fever. **2** characteristic of or resembling typhoid fever.

**typhoid bacillus,** a bacillus that causes typhoid fever.

**typhoid fever,** an infectious, often fatal, disease with intestinal inflammation and sometimes hemorrhage, fever, nosebleed, enlargement of the spleen, eruptions of the skin, disorder of the bowels, and sometimes stupor; enteric fever. It is caused by the typhoid bacillus, which is spread by contaminated food, drink, and clothing. People can be inoculated against typhoid fever.

**ty|phoi|din** (tī foi′din), *n.* a substance made from typhoid bacilli, used to test for the presence of typhoid.

**Typhoid Mary,** *U.S. Informal.* **1** a carrier of a communicable disease: *There is a cure for the menace to the public of Typhoid Marys* (Science News Letter). **2** *Figurative.* a carrier or transmitter of anything harmful or evil. [< the name given to a New York City cook who was a carrier of typhoid fever]

**ty|pho|ma|lar|i|al** (tī′fō mə lãr′ē əl), *adj.* (of a fever) having the characteristics of both typhoid fever and malaria.

**Ty|phon** (tī′fon), *n. Greek Mythology.* **1** a monster, the son of Typhoeus. **2** Typhoeus. **3** the Greek name for Set, the Egyptian god of evil.

**ty|phon|ic** (tī fon′ik), *adj.* like a whirlwind or tornado.

**ty|phoon** (tī fün′), *n.* **1** a violent cyclone or hurricane occurring in the western Pacific, chiefly during the period from July to October. **2** a violent storm or tempest occurring in Asia, especially in or near India. **3** any violent storm: *My coursers ... outstrip the Typhoon* (Shelley). [< Cantonese *tai-fung* big wind; influenced by Greek *typhôn, -ônos* whirlwind; (originally) the mythological father of the winds]

**ty|phous** (tī′fəs), *adj.* of or having to do with typhus.

**ty|phus** (tī′fəs), *n.,* or **typhus fever,** an acute, infectious disease characterized by high fever, extreme weakness, dark-red spots on the skin, and stupor or delirium. It is caused by a rickettsia carried by fleas, lice, ticks, or mites. [< New Latin *typhus* < Greek *tŷphos* stupor caused by fever; (originally) smoke < *tŷphein* to smoke]

**typ|ic** (tip′ik), *adj.* = typical.

**typ|i|cal** (tip′ə kəl), *adj.* **1** being a type; representative: *a typical American home. The typical Thanksgiving dinner consists of turkey, cranberry sauce, several vegetables, and mince or pumpkin pie.* **SYN**: illustrative. **2** of or having to do with a type or representative specimen; characteristic: *the hospitality typical of the frontiersman, the swiftness typical of a gazelle.* **SYN**: distinctive. **3** symbolical; emblematic. **4** *Biology.* that is the type of the genus, family, or other group. [< Medieval Latin *typicalis* figurative, symbolic < Latin *typicus* typic < *typus;* see etym. under **type**]
— **typ′i|cal|ness**, *n.*

**typ|i|cal|i|ty** (tip′ə kal′ə tē), *n.* the quality or character of being typical.

**typ|i|cal|ly** (tip′ə klē), *adv.* **1** in a typical manner. **2** to a typical degree. **3** characteristically; ordinarily.

**typ|i|fi|ca|tion** (tip′ə fə kā′shən), *n.* the act of typifying or condition of being typified.

**typ|i|fy** (tip′ə fī), *v.t.*, **-fied, -fy|ing.** **1** to be a symbol of: *The Statue of Liberty typifies the American tradition of freedom. The lamb typifies Christ's sacrifice.* **2** to have the common characteristics of; exemplify: *Daniel Boone typifies the pioneer.* **3** to indicate beforehand. — **typ′i|fi′er**, *n.*

**typ|ist** (tī′pist), *n.* **1** a person who operates a typewriter; person trained in typewriting: *to be a good typist.* **2** a person whose occupation is typing: *a part-time typist.*

**ty|po** (tī′pō), *n., pl.* **-pos**. *Informal.* a typographical error.

**typo.**, or **typog.**, **1** typographer. **2a** typographic. **b** typographical. **3** typography.

**ty|pog|ra|pher** (tī pog′rə fər), *n.* = printer (def. 1).

**ty|po|graph|ic** (tī′pə graf′ik), *adj.* = typographical.

**ty|po|graph|i|cal** (tī′pə graf′ə kəl), *adj.* **1** of or having to do with printing or typing. **2** produced or expressed in print or by typing: *typographical symbols. "Catt" and "hoRse" contain typographical errors.* — **ty′po|graph′i|cal|ly**, *adv.*

**ty|pog|ra|phy** (tī pog′rə fē), *n.* **1** the art, practice, or process of printing with type; work of setting and arranging type and of printing from it. **2** the arrangement, appearance, or style of printed matter. *Abbr:* typo., typog. [< Medieval Latin *typographia* < Greek *týpos* type + *-graphíā* writing, -graphy]

**ty|po|log|i|cal** (tī′pə loj′ə kəl), *adj.* of or having to do with typology. — **ty′po|log′i|cal|ly**, *adv.*

**ty|pol|o|gist** (tī pol′ə jist), *n.* a person skilled in typology.

**ty|pol|o|gy** (tī pol′ə jē), *n. Archaeology.* **1** the classification of remains and specimens. **2** the study of the evolution of types of tools, weapons, and ornaments. [< Greek *týpos* type + English *-logy*]

**ty|po|script** (tī′pō skript′), *n.* = typescript.

**ty|poth|e|tae** (tī poth′ə tē, ti-; tī′pə thē′-), *n.pl.* printers (used in the names of professional associations). [< New Latin *typothetae* < Greek *týpos* type + New Latin *-thetae,* for Greek *-thétai,* plural of *-thétēs,* an agent noun suffix]

**Tyr** (tir), *n.* a Norse god of war and victory, son of Odin, identified with the Teutonic god Tiu. Also, **Tyrr**.

**ty|ra|mine** (tī′rə mēn, tir′ə-; tī ram′in, tə-), *n.* a colorless, crystalline amine produced by bacterial action or by the decarboxylation of tyrosine, found in mistletoe, ripe cheese, and putrefied animal tissue. *Formula:* $HOC_6H_4CH_2CH_2NH_2$

**ty|ran|nic** (tə ran′ik, tī-), *adj.* = tyrannical. [< Latin *tyrannicus* < Greek *tyrannikós* < *týrannos* tyrant]

**ty|ran|ni|cal** (tə ran′ə kəl, tī-), *adj.* **1** of or having to do with a tyrant. **2** like a tyrant; arbitrary; cruel; unjust: *Charles I of England was a tyrannical king.* **SYN**: despotic, dictatorial. — **ty|ran′ni|cal|ly**, *adv.* — **ty|ran′ni|cal|ness**, *n.*

**ty|ran|ni|cide[1]** (tə ran′ə sīd, tī-), *n.* the act of killing a tyrant. [< Latin *tyrannicīdium* < *tyrannus* tyrant + *-cīdium* act of killing, -cide[2]]

**ty|ran|ni|cide[2]** (tə ran′ə sīd, tī-), *n.* a person who kills a tyrant. [< Latin *tyrannicīda* < *tyrannus* tyrant + *-cīda* killer, -cide[1]]

**tyr|an|nize** (tir′ə nīz), *v.*, **-nized, -niz|ing.** — *v.i.* **1** to use power cruelly or unjustly; behave like a tyrant: *Those who are strong should not tyrannize over those who are weak.* **2** to rule as a tyrant; be a tyrant.
— *v.t.* **1** to rule cruelly; oppress: *The embittered man tyrannized his family.* (*Figurative.*) *Poverty, which doth so tyrannize ... and generally depress us* (Robert Burton). **2** to rule over as a tyrant.
— **tyr′an|niz′er**, *n.*

**ty|ran|no|saur** (ti ran′ə sôr, tī-), *n.* = tyrannosaurus.

***tyrannosaurus**

***ty|ran|no|sau|rus** (ti ran′ə sôr′əs, tī-), *n.* a huge, prehistoric, flesh-eating dinosaur that lived in North America and walked on its two hindlimbs. It existed in the late Cretaceous period. [< New Latin *Tyrannosaurus* the genus name < Greek *týrannos* tyrant + *saûros* lizard]

**tyr|an|nous** (tir′ə nəs), *adj.* acting like a tyrant; cruel or unjust; arbitrary; tyrannical: *It is excellent To have a giant's strength, but it is tyrannous To use it like a giant* (Shakespeare). (*Figurative.*) *The Stamp Act seemed tyrannous to the colonists.* — **tyr′an|nous|ly**, *adv.*

**tyr|an|ny** (tir′ə nē), *n., pl.* **-nies.** **1** cruel or unjust use of power: *The boy ran away to sea to escape his father's tyranny.* [*The Americans*] *snuff the approach of tyranny in every tainted breeze* (Edmund Burke). *Where laws end, tyranny begins* (William Pitt). **SYN**: oppression, harshness, despotism. **2** an instance of this; tyrannical act: *The colonists rebelled against the king's tyrannies.* (*Figurative.*) *Bad laws are the worst sort of tyranny* (Edmund Burke). **3** the government, position, rule, or term of office of an absolute ruler. **4** a state ruled by a tyrant. [< Late Latin *tyrannia* < Greek *tyranníā* < *týrannos* tyrant]

**ty|rant** (tī′rənt), *n.* **1** a person who uses his power cruelly or unjustly; one who treats those under his control tyrannically; despot: *A good teacher is never a tyrant. Necessity is the argument of tyrants; it is the creed of slaves* (William Pitt). **2** a king or other ruler who uses his power unjustly or cruelly; despotical ruler; cruel master. **3** an absolute ruler, as in ancient Greece, who owed his office to usurpation. Some tyrants of Greek cities were mild and just. [< Old French *tyrant,* earlier *tyran,* learned borrowing from Latin *tyrannus* < Greek *týrannos* tyrant (def. 3)]

**tyrant flycatcher**, any one of a family of American flycatchers, such as the kingbird, phoebe, and least flycatcher.

**tyre** (tīr), *n., v.*, **tyred, tyr|ing.** *British.* tire[2].

**Tyr|i|an** (tir′ē ən), *adj., n.* — *adj.* **1** of or having to do with Tyre, an ancient seaport in Phoenicia. **2** made in ancient Tyre. **3** = Tyrian-purple.
— *n.* a native or inhabitant of ancient Tyre.
[< Latin *Tyrius* (< Greek *Tyriós* < *Týros* Tyre)]

**Tyrian purple**, **1** Also, **Tyrian dye**. a deep crimson or purple dye used by the ancient Greeks, Romans, and certain other Mediterranean peoples. It is known to have been obtained from various shellfish, but the exact formula for it is now unknown. It was primarily because of the high cost of obtaining Tyrian purple that the possession of purple cloth was evidence in ancient times of royalty or wealth. **2** a bluish red.

**Tyr|i|an-pur|ple** (tir′ē ən pėr′pəl), *adj.* of the color Tyrian purple; bluish-red.

**ty|ro** (tī′rō), *n., pl.* **-ros**. a beginner in learning or doing anything; novice: *Much practice changed the tyro into an expert.* Also, **tiro**. **SYN**: neophyte. [< Late Latin *tyro,* variant of Latin *tīrō* recruit]

**ty|ro|ci|din** (tī′rə sī′din), *n.* = tyrocidine.

**ty|ro|ci|dine** (tī′rə sī′dēn, -din), *n.* an antibiotic containted in tyrothricin, obtained from a soil bacterium. [< *tyro*(sine) + *-cide*[1] + *-ine*[2]]

**Ty|ro|le|an** (tə rō′lē ən), *adj., n.* = Tirolese.

**Tyr|o|lese** (tir′ə lēz′, -lēs′), *adj., n.* = Tirolese.

**Ty|ro|li|an** (tə rō′lē ən, tī-), *adj., n.* = Tirolese.

**Ty|ro|lienne** (tē rô lyen′), *n.* **1** a dance of Tirolese peasants, in ¾ time. **2** a song for it, or in its style, featuring the yodel. [< French *tyrolienne,* feminine of *tyrolien* Tirolese < *Tyrol* Tirol]

**ty|ro|sin** (tī′rə sin, tir′ə-), *n.* = tyrosine.

**ty|ro|sin|ase** (tī′rō sə nās, tir′ō-), *n.* an enzyme present in vegetable and animal tissues. It converts tyrosine into melanin and similar pigments by oxidation.

**ty|ro|sine** (tī′rə sēn, -sin, tir′ə-), *n.* a white, crystalline amino acid produced by the hydrolysis of a number of proteins, such as casein. It is a constitutent of cheese. *Formula:* $C_9H_{11}NO_3$ [< German *Tyrosin* < Greek *tȳrós* cheese + German *-in*]

**ty|ro|thri|cin** (tī′rə thrī′sin, -thris′in), *n.* a substance made up of the antibiotics gramicidin and tyrocidine, obtained from a soil bacterium, and used in treating localized infections. [< New Latin *Tyrothrix, -icis* former genus name of the bacterium + English *-in*]

**Tyrr** (tir), *n.* = Tyr.

**Tyr|rhe|ni|an** (tə rē′nē ən), *adj.* = Etruscan. [< Latin *Tyrrhenus* of or having to do with the *Tyrrheni* Etruscans]

**tyu|ya|mu|nite** (tyü′yə mü′nīt), *n.* a mineral found chiefly with and very similar to carnotite. [< *Tyuya Muyun,* in southeastern Turkestan, where it is mined as a uranium ore]

**tzad|dik** (tsä′dik), *n., pl.* **tsad|dik|im** (tsä dē′kim), *n.* = zaddik.

**tzar** (zär, tsär), *n.* = czar.

**tzar|e|vitch** (zär′ə vich, tsär′-), *n.* = czarevitch.

**tza|rev|na** (zä rev′nə, tsä-), *n.* = czarevna.

**tza|ri|na** (zä rē′nə, tsä-), *n.* = czarina.

**tzar|ism** (zär′iz əm, tsär′-), *n.* = czarism.

**tzar|ist** or **Tzar|ist** (zär′ist, tsär′-), *adj., n.* = czarist.

**tza|rit|za** (zä rēt′sə, tsä-), *n.* = czarina.

**tzet|ze fly**, or **tzet|ze** (tset′sē), *n.* = tsetse fly.

**tzi|gane** or **Tzi|gane** (tsē gän′), *n., adj.* — *n.* **1** a kind of fast folk dance, performed originally by the Hungarian Gypsies. **2** the music for such a dance. **3** a Hungarian Gypsy.
— *adj.* of or having to do with a tzigane.
[< French *tzigane* < German *Tzigan* < Hungarian *cigány*]

**Tzi|ga|ny** (tsi′gä nē), *n., adj.* = tzigane.

**tzim|mes** (tsim′is), *n.* **1** a casserole or stew made from a sweetened combination of carrots and other vegetables and fruits. **2** *U.S. Slang.* an uproar; commotion: *He would stage a big ceremony in Cawnpone, with painted elephants and sword swallowers and the whole tzimmes* (New Yorker). [< Yiddish *tsimes*]

**tzi|tsis** (tsi′tsis), *n.pl.* = zizith.

**Tzom Ge|dal|iah** (tsōm′ gə däl′yə), = Fast of Gedaliah. [< Hebrew *tsōm gədalyāh*]

***U¹** or **u** (yü), *n., pl.* **U's** or **Us, u's** or **us. 1** the 21st letter of the English alphabet. There are two *u's* in *usual.* **2** any sound represented by this letter.
**3** (used as a symbol for) the 21st, or more usually the 20th of a series (either *I* or *J* being omitted).

**U²** (yü), *n., pl.* **U's**. anything shaped like the letter U.

**U³** (yü), *adj., n. Especially British Informal.* —*adj.* upper-class; sophisticated; cultured: *The upper classes ... do not "take a bath"; the U version is "have one's bath"* (Time).
—*n.* a person or thing that is upper-class.
[< *u*(pper class)]

**U⁴** (ü), *n.* a Burmese title of respect that precedes a man's name: *U Thant.*

**u.,** 1 and (German, *und*). **2** uncle. **3** university. **4** upper.

**U** (no period), an abbreviation or symbol for:
1 *Mathematics.* universe.
2 *Education.* unsatisfactory (used as a grade).
3 uracil.
4 uranium (chemical element).
5 *U.S.* a mark on a packaged product indicating that it has been certified as kosher by the Union of Orthodox Hebrew Congregations.

**U.,** 1 uncle. **2** union. **3** university. **4** upper.

**U-235**, the isotope of uranium having a mass number of 235. It makes up about 0.7 per cent of naturally occurring uranium. It is a source of atomic energy.

**U-238**, the isotope of uranium having a mass number of 238. It makes up about 99 per cent of all naturally occurring uranium.

**U-239**, the isotope of uranium having a mass number of 239, formed by the bombardment of U-238 with neutrons.

**ua|ka|ri** (wä kär′ē), *n., pl.* **-ris.** = ouakari.

**UAM** (no periods), underwater-to-air missile.

**u|a ma|u ke e|a o ka a|i|na i ka po|no** (ü′ä mä′ü kä ā′ä ō kä ä′ē nä ē kä pō′nō), *Hawaiian.* the life of the land is perpetuated in righteousness (the motto of Hawaii).

**U.A.R.** or **UAR** (no periods), United Arab Republic.

**UAW** (no periods) or **U.A.W.**, United Automobile Workers.

**U|ban|gi** (yü bang′gē, ü bäng′-), *n., pl.* **-gis,** *adj.* —*n.* a female member of the Sara, an African Negro tribe near the Ubangi River in the Central African Republic. Many of the Ubangis wear flat wooden disks in their pierced lips.
—*adj.* of or characteristic of the Ubangis.

**Ü|ber|mensch** (Y′bər mensh′), *n., pl.* **-men|schen** (-men′shən). *German.* superman.

**u|ber|ri|ma fi|des** (yü ber′ə mə fī′dēz), *Latin.* the fullest faith: *Uberrima fides ... is the principle on which the whole of insurance is based* (J. R. L. Anderson).

**u|bi|ca|tion** (yü′bə kā′shən), *n.* the state of having place or local relation; location.

**u|bi|e|ty** (yü bī′ə tē), *n.* **1** condition in respect of place or location; local relationship. **2** the quality of occupying a position in space; objective reality. [< New Latin *ubietas* < Latin *ubi* where]

**u|bi|qui|none** (yü′bə kwi nōn′, -kwin′ōn; yü bik′wə-nōn), *n.* any one of a group of quinones that assist oxidation and reduction within cells, especially by serving as electron or hydrogen carriers between the flavoproteins and the cytochromes in the mitochondria of various cells; coenzyme Q. [blend of *ubiqui*(tous) and *quinone*]

**u|biq|ui|tous** (yü bik′wə təs), *adj.* that is everywhere at the same time; present everywhere: *It is through the ubiquitous donkey that Athens keeps in touch with the countryside* (Atlantic). **SYN:** omnipresent. —**u|biq′ui|tous|ly**, *adv.* —**u|biq′ui|tous|ness**, *n.*

**u|biq|ui|ty** (yü bik′wə tē), *n.* **1** the fact or capacity of being everywhere at the same time; omnipresence, especially in reference to Christ. **2** the ability to be everywhere at once. [< New Latin *ubiquitas* < Latin *ubīque* everywhere < *ubi* where]

**u|bi su|pra** (yü′bī sü′prə), *Latin.* where above; in the place mentioned above.

**U-boat** (yü′bōt′), *n.* **1** a German submarine. U-boats were first used to torpedo enemy ships during World War I. **2** any submarine. [half-translation of German *U-Boot,* short for *Unterseeboot* undersea boat]

**U bolt**, a bolt shaped like a U, each prong of which is threaded at the end to receive a nut.

**U-bomb** (yü′bom′), *n.* = uranium bomb.

**u.c., uc.,** or **uc** (no periods), upper case; a capital letter or capital letters (especially as an instruction to a typist, typesetter, or type founder).

**U.C.,** 1 Upper Canada. **2** United Church.

**UCLA** (no periods), University of California (Los Angeles division).

**U.C.V.**, United Confederate Veterans.

**u|dal** (yü′dəl), *n., adj.* —*n.* land in Orkney and Shetland held by the old native form of freehold tenure.
—*adj.* of or having to do with this form of freehold tenure; allodial: *In Scotland land was held according to the feudal system, in Orkney according to the udal system* (John Gunn).
[< Scandinavian (compare Old Icelandic *ōthal* property held by inheritance)]

**U.D.C.**, United Daughters of the Confederacy.

**ud|der** (ud′ər), *n.* the downward-hanging bag of cows, female goats, or certain other animals from which milk comes. The udder contains the milk-producing glands and has protruding teats through which milk can be drawn. [Middle English *udder,* Old English *ūder*]

**UDI** (no periods) or **U.D.I.**, unilateral declaration of independence (originally referring to the declaration proclaimed by the British self-governing territory of Southern Rhodesia on November 11, 1965).

**Ud|murt** (üd′mürt), *n.* **1** a Finnic people living in Russia in the Volga Valley. **2** their language; Votyak.

**u|do** (ü′dō), *n.* a plant grown chiefly in Japan and China for its edible young shoots. [< Japanese *udo*]

**u|dom|e|ter** (yü dom′ə tər), *n.* = rain gauge. [< Latin *ūdus* wet + English *-meter*]

**u|do|met|ric** (yü′də met′rik), *adj.* **1** having to do with a udometer. **2** made by means of a udometer.

**u|dom|e|try** (yü dom′ə trē), *n.* the measurement of rain by the use of a udometer.

**UDT** (no periods), Underwater Demolition Team (a unit of frogmen in the United States Navy).

**UFO** (yü′ef′ō′, yü′fō), *n., pl.* **UFO's** or **UFOs.** = flying saucer. [< *u*(nidentified) *f*(lying) *o*(bject)]

**u|fo|log|i|cal** (yü′fə loj′ə kəl), *adj.* of or having to do with ufology: *The ufological definition of a flap is a concentration of sightings in a small area within a short period* (New Yorker).

**u|fol|o|gist** (yü fol′ə jist), *n.* a person who tracks down flying saucers; enthusiast or devotee of ufology: *This only increased ufologists' conviction that the Air Force was hiding vital evidence* (Sunday Times).

**u|fol|o|gy** (yü fol′ə jē), *n.* the practice or hobby of tracking flying saucers. [< *UFO* + *-logy*]

**UFT** (no periods) or **U.F.T.**, United Federation of Teachers.

**UFWOC** (no periods), United Farm Workers Organizing Committee (a union of farmworkers in California established in 1966).

**U|gan|dan** (yü gan′dən), *adj., n.* —*adj.* of or having to do with Uganda, a country in eastern Africa, or its people.
—*n.* a native or inhabitant of Uganda.

**U|ga|rit|ic** (yü gə rit′ik, ü-), *adj., n.* —*adj.* of or having to do with Ugarit, an ancient city on the coast of Syria, its people, or its language.
—*n.* the Canaanite language of Ugarit, akin to Phoenician and Hebrew.

**UGC** (no periods) or **U.G.C.**, University Grants Commission (of Great Britain).

**ugh** (ug, u), *interj.* an exclamation expressing disgust, horror, or strong distaste. [probably imitative]

**ug|li** (ug′lē), *n., pl.* **-lis** or **-lies.** a Jamaican tangelo widely grown in the West Indies. [alteration of *ugly* (fruit); because of its wrinkled and mottled skin]

**ug|li|fi|ca|tion** (ug′lə fə kā′shən), *n.* the process of uglifying or disfiguring.

**ug|li|fy** (ug′lə fī), *v.t.,* **-fied, -fy|ing.** to make ugly; disfigure: *Especially since the year 1914 every single change in the English landscape has either uglified it or destroyed its meaning or both* (London Times). [< *ugly* + *-fy*]

**ug|li|ly** (ug′lə lē), *adv.* in an ugly manner.

**ug|li|ness** (ug′lē nis), *n.* **1** the quality or condition of being ugly; ugly appearance: *Of all these bereft, Nothing but pain and ugliness were left* (Keats). **2** an ugly thing or feature.

**ug|ly** (ug′lē), *adj.,* **-li|er, -li|est,** *n., pl.* **-lies.** —*adj.* **1** very unpleasant to look at: *an ugly house, an ugly face.* **2** loathsome; vile, especially: **a** very bad or disagreeable; offensive; nasty: *an ugly smell, an ugly task.* **b** morally offensive or repulsive; base: *ugly language, an ugly act of treason.* **3** likely to cause trouble; threatening; dangerous: *ugly clouds. The wound looked sore and ugly. Death is the ugly fact which Nature has to hide* (Alexander Smith). **4** *Informal.* very ill-natured; cross; bad-tempered; quarrelsome: *an ugly dog, an ugly temper, an ugly customer.*
—*n.* an ugly person or thing: *Peers and judges, beauties and uglies—they were all in the highest spirits* (Pall Mall Gazette).
[< Scandinavian (compare Old Icelandic *uggligr* dreadful < *uggr* fear)]
—*Syn. adj.* **1 Ugly, unsightly, homely** mean not pleasing in appearance. **Ugly,** the strongest of the three, means positively unpleasant or offensive in appearance: *There are two ugly, gaudy lamps in the room.* **Unsightly** means unpleasing to the sight through carelessness or neglect: *Trains approach the station through an unsightly section of the city.* **Homely** means lacking in beauty or attractiveness, but does not suggest unpleasant or disagreeable qualities: *A homely child often develops into an attractive adult.*

**ugly American**, an American living abroad who presents an unflattering image of Americans, especially by his insensitivity to the culture of other peoples. [< *The Ugly American,* a book of stories, published in 1958, about Americans in southeastern Asia, written by Eugene Burdick and William Lederer]

**ugly duckling**, a young person, especially a girl, who lacks beauty, charm, or grace but later develops some or all of these qualities to a surpassing degree. [< the *ugly duckling,* a swan in a story by Hans Christian Andersen, that is hatched by a duck and sneered at by the ducklings until it suddenly grows into the beauty and grace of an adult swan]

**U|gri|an** (ü′grē ən, yü′-), *n., adj.* —*n.* **1** a member of an ethnic group which includes the Magyars and certain peoples of western Siberia. **2** their languages, as a division of Finno-Ugric; Ugric.
—*adj.* of or having to do with the Ugrians or their division of Finno-Ugric.

**U|gric** (ü′grik, yü′-), *n., adj.* —*n.* a division of the Finno-Ugric linguistic family that includes Hungarian, Ostyak, and Vogul.
—*adj.* Ugrian.

**U|gro-Al|ta|ic** (ü′grō al tā′ik, yü′-), *adj., n.* = Ural-Altaic.

**U|gro-Finn|ic** (ü′grō fin′ik, yü′-), *adj., n.* = Finno-Ugric.

**ug|some** (ug′səm, ůg′-), *adj. Scottish.* horrible; loathsome. [Middle English *ugsome* < *uggen* to fear, loathe < Scandinavian (compare Old Icelandic *ugga*) + *-some*¹]

**UHF** (no periods), **U.H.F.,** or **uhf** (no periods), ultrahigh-frequency (of or having to do with the electromagnetic spectrum between 300 and 3,000 megahertz).

**uh-huh** (u hu′), *interj.* a sound made to indicate that one is listening to, or agrees with, what is being said.

**uh|lan** (ü′län, ü län′), *n.* **1** a mounted soldier of a type first known in Europe in Poland, armed with a lance. **2** a member of the heavy cavalry in the former German army. [< German *Ulan, Uhlan* < Polish *ułan* < Turkic *oglan* boy]

**u|hu|ru** (ü hü′rü), *n. Swahili.* freedom.

**Ui|gur** or **Ui|ghur** (wē′gůr), *n., adj.* —*n.* **1** a member of the eastern branch of the Turkic people, prominent in central Asia from the 700's to the 1100's, now the majority of the population in Sinkiang, a region in western China. **2** their Turkic language.
—*adj.* = Uigurian.

**Ui|gu|ri|an** or **Ui|ghu|ri|an** (wē gůr′ē ən), *adj.*

***U¹**
definition 1

Script letters look like examples of fine penmanship. They appear in many formal uses, such as invitations to social functions.

Handwritten letters, both manuscript or printed (left) and cursive (right), are easy for children to read and to write.

Roman letters have *serifs* (finishing strokes) adapted from the way Roman stonecutters carved their letters. This is *Times Roman* type.

Sans-serif letters are often called *gothic.* They have lines of even width and no serifs. This type face is called *Helvetica.*

Between roman and gothic, some letters have thick and thin lines with slight flares that suggest serifs. This type face is *Optima.*

Computer letters can be sensed by machines either from their shapes or from the magnetic ink with which they are printed.

1 of or having to do with the Uigurs. 2 used by the Uigurs.

**Ui|gu|ric** or **Ui|ghu|ric** (wē gu̇r′ik), *adj.* = Uigurian.

**u|in|ta|ite** or **u|in|tah|ite** (yü in′tə īt), *n. Mineralogy.* gilsonite. [American English < the *Uinta* Mountains, Utah, where deposits are found + *-ite*[1]]

**u|in|ta|there** (yü in′tə thir), *n.* a primitive mammal of the Eocene epoch in North America, having a long skull with three pairs of horns, similar in appearance and size to a small elephant. It had stout legs and round feet, and, in the male, a pair of tusks projecting downward from the upper jaws. [< the *Uinta* Mountains, Utah, where remains were found + Greek *thērion* wild animal]

**UIS** (no periods), Unemployment Insurance Service.

**uit|land|er** or **Uit|land|er** (oit′lan′dər, īt′-; *Dutch* œ′it län′dər), *n.* (in South Africa) a foreigner, especially a British settler in the Orange Free State and Transvaal in the late 1800's and early 1900's. [< Afrikaans *uitlander* < *uit* out + *land* land + *-er* -er[1]]

**UJA** (no periods), United Jewish Appeal.

**u|ja|ma|a** (ü′jä mä′ä), *n.* a program of introducing socialism in rural areas of Tanzania, based on cooperation between tribal communities: *Ujamaa is to be substituted for the blood and language kinship of the tribes* (Harper's). [< Swahili *ujamaa* relationship, brotherhood]

**u|ji fly** (ü′jē), a dipterous insect of Japan whose larva is parasitic on silkworms. [< Japanese *uji* a worm]

**U.K.** or **UK** (no periods), United Kingdom.

**UKAEA** (no periods) or **U.K.A.E.A.**, United Kingdom Atomic Energy Authority.

**u|kase** (yü kās′, yü′kās), *n.* 1 an official decree, having the force of law, issued by a Russian czar or his government. 2 *Figurative.* any proclamation or order of a final or arbitrary nature; decree by authority. [< Russian *ukaz* < *ukazat′* to show, decree]

**uke** (yük), *n. Informal.* ukulele.

**u|ki|yo-e** (yü kē′yô ā′), *n.* a style of Japanese painting and printmaking showing scenes from ordinary life, prevalent from the 1600's to the 1800's. [< Japanese *ukiyo-e* < *ukiyo* world life + *e* picture]

**Ukr.**, Ukraine.

**U|krain|i|an** (yü krā′nē ən, -krī′-), *adj., n.* —*adj.* of or having to do with the Ukraine, a republic in the Soviet Union, its people, or their language. —*n.* 1 a native or inhabitant of the Ukraine. 2 the Slavic language spoken in the Ukraine; Little Russian.

***u|ku|le|le** (yü′kə lā′lē; *Hawaiian* ü′kü lā′lā), *n.* a small guitar having four strings. [American English < Hawaiian *'ukulele* (literally) leaping flea < *'uku* flea + *lele* to fly, leap, or jump; the word was originally a nickname for a British army officer of the 1800's who popularized the instrument in Hawaii]

***ukulele**

**UL** (no periods) or **U.L.**, Underwriters' Laboratories.

**u|la|ma** (ü′lə mä′), *n.* = ulema.

**ul|cer** (ul′sər), *n.* 1 an open sore on the skin, or within the body, on a mucous membrane. It sometimes discharges pus. 2 *Figurative.* any corrupting influence, such as a moral sore spot or other corroding element. [< Latin *ulcus, ulceris*]

**ul|cer|ate** (ul′sə rāt), *v.t., v.i.,* **-at|ed, -at|ing.** 1 to affect or be affected with an ulcer: *An ulcerated stomach may be very painful.* 2 to form or be formed into an ulcer. [< Latin *ulcerāre* (with English *-ate*[1]) < *ulcus* ulcer]

**ul|cer|a|tion** (ul′sə rā′shən), *n.* 1 the act or process of ulcerating or condition of being ulcerated. 2 an ulcer or ulcers.

**ul|cer|a|tive** (ul′sə rā′tiv, -sər ə-), *adj.* 1 caused by or causing ulceration: *ulcerative colitis.* 2 like an ulceration.

**ul|cered** (ul′sərd), *adj.* ulcerated.

**ul|cer|ous** (ul′sər əs), *adj.* 1 having or affected with an ulcer or ulcers; exhibiting ulceration. 2 having the nature of ulcers. 3 like an ulcer; characteristic of ulcers. —**ul′cer|ous|ly,** *adv.* —**ul′cer|ous|ness,** *n.*

**-ule,** *suffix.* small; little, as in *ferule, granule, veinule.* [< Old French *-ule,* learned borrowing from Latin *-ulus, -ula, -ulum,* a diminutive suffix]

**u|le|ma** (ü′lə mä′), *n.* 1 any one of several bodies of Moslem officials, scholars in the religion and law of Islam, active within their separate countries as judicial bodies. 2 a Moslem theologian; scholar in Islamic law; mullah. Also, **ulama.** [< Turkish *ulema* < Arabic *'ulamā* learned men, plural of *'ālim* wise]

**u|lex|ite** (yü′lek sīt), *n.* a mineral, a hydrous sodium and calcium borate, occurring in loose, rounded masses of white, needle-shaped crystals that transmit light from one end to the other without being transparent. [< G. L. *Ulex,* a German chemist of the 1800's + *-ite*[1]]

**u|lig|i|nose** (yü lij′ə nōs), *adj.* 1 marshy; muddy; oozy. 2 (of animals and plants) living or growing in muddy places. [< Latin *ūlīginōsus* moist < *ūlīgō, -inis* moisture]

**u|lig|i|nous** (yü lij′ə nəs), *adj.* = uliginose.

**ul|lage** (ul′ij), *n.* 1 the quantity of wine, brandy, or other alcoholic liquor, by which a cask or bottle falls short of being completely full. 2 (originally) such a quantity lost by leakage or absorption, and required to be made good to the buyer. 3 the quantity of any commodity, such as grain or flour, by which a bag or other container falls short of being full; loss through spillage or sifting at the seams. [< Anglo-French *ulliage,* Old French *ouillage* < *ouillier, aouiller* fill a cask to the bunghole (or eye) < *a-* + *ueil* eye < Latin *oculus*]

**ul|ma|ceous** (ul mā′shəs), *adj.* belonging to the elm family of trees and shrubs. [< New Latin *Ulmaceae* the family name (< Latin *ulmus* elm) + English *-ous*]

**ul|na** (ul′nə), *n., pl.* **-nae** (-nē), **-nas.** 1 the thinner, longer bone of the forearm, on the side opposite the thumb. See picture under **arm**[1]. 2 a corresponding bone in the forelimb of a vertebrate animal. [< Latin *ulna* elbow]

**ul|nar** (ul′nər), *adj.* 1 of or having to do with the ulna. 2 in or supplying the part of the forearm near the ulna.

**ul|no|car|pal** (ul′nə kär′pəl), *adj.* of or having to do with the ulna and the wrist (carpus).

**ul|no|ra|di|al** (ul′nə rā′dē əl), *adj.* of or having to do with the ulna and the thicker and shorter bone of the forearm (radius).

**u|loid** (yü′loid), *adj.* resembling a scar: *a uloid mark on the skin.* [< Greek *oulḗ* scar + English *-oid*]

**U|lot|ri|chi** (yü lot′rə kī), *n.pl.* persons having woolly or kinky hair, as a division of mankind (proposed as an anthropological classification by Bory de St. Vincent and adopted in the classification of Thomas Henry Huxley). [< New Latin *Ulotrichi* the division name < Greek *oulóthrix, -trichos* woolly haired < *oûlos* curly + *thríx, trichós* hair]

**u|lot|ri|chous** (yü lot′rə kəs), *adj.* having woolly or kinky hair. [< New Latin *Ulotrichi* (see etym. under **Ulotrichi**) + English *-ous*]

**ul|pan** (ül′pän), *n., pl.* **ul|pa|nim** (ül′pä nēm′). an Israeli school for new immigrants, providing an intensive course of study in the Hebrew language. [< Modern Hebrew *ūlpan*]

**ul|ster** (ul′stər), *n.* a long, loose, heavy overcoat, often belted. Ulsters were originally made of frieze, or other heavy fabric, in Ulster, Ireland: *All superimposed upon their normal attire ... in winter an ulster or its equivalent* (London Times). [short for *Ulster overcoat* < *Ulster,* a region in northern Ireland]

**Ulster cycle**, the cycle of Irish legends in which the feats of the Red Branch are described. Its chief hero is Cuchulainn.

**Ul|ster|man** (ul′stər mən), *n., pl.* **-men.** a native or inhabitant of Ulster, a region in the northern part of Ireland.

**ult.**, 1a ultimate. b ultimately. 2 ultimo; of the past month: *your order of the 14th ult.*
► See **inst.** for usage note.

**ul|te|ri|or** (ul tir′ē ər), *adj.* 1 beyond what is seen or expressed; intentionally concealed or kept in the background; hidden: *an ulterior motive, an ulterior purpose.* 2 more distant; on the farther side. 3 further; later. [< Latin *ulterior,* comparative of root of *ultrā* beyond; see etym. under **ultra**] —**ul|te′ri|or|ly,** *adv.*

**ul|ti|ma** (ul′tə mə), *n.* the last syllable of a word. [< Latin *ultima* (*syllaba*) last syllable; see etym. under **ultimate**]

**ul|ti|ma|cy** (ul′tə mə sē), *n.* the state or character of being ultimate.

**ul|ti|ma ra|ti|o re|gum** (ul′tə mə rā′shē ō rē′gəm), *Latin.* 1 war; force of arms. 2 (literally) the final argument of kings.

**ul|ti|mate** (ul′tə mit), *adj., n.* —*adj.* 1 last possible; final, especially: a coming at the end: *Most people who drive too fast never consider that the ultimate result of their action might be a serious accident.* SYN: See syn. under **last**[1]. b beyond which there is no advance or progress: *the ultimate boundaries of human knowledge. Which shall have ultimate dominion, Dream, or dust?* (Don Marquis). SYN: See syn. under **last**[1]. 2 that is an extremity; beyond which there is nothing at all; extreme: *the ultimate limits of the universe.* 3a fundamental; basic; elemental: *an ultimate particle of matter. Hard work is the ultimate source of success. The ultimate check to population appears then to be want of food* (Thomas Malthus). b original: *The ultimate source of life has not been discovered.* 4 than which there is nothing greater; greatest possible: *He gave his life and thereby paid the ultimate price. Described as the ultimate weapon, against which there is no defense* (Newsweek). 5 beyond which breaking, shearing, distortion, or other fundamental change is certain or very probable; that is a quantitative maximum: *metal plate able to take an ultimate stress of 4,500 pounds per square inch.* —*n.* an ultimate point, result, fact, or other extreme condition or final place.
**the Ultimate,** God; the Ultimate Reality: *belief in the Ultimate.*
[< Medieval Latin *ultimatus,* past participle of *ultimare* < Italian, bring to an end < Latin *ultimāre* come to an end < *ultimus* last, superlative of root of *ultrā* beyond; see etym. under **ultra**] —**ul′ti|mate|ness,** *n.*

**ultimate analysis**, *Chemistry.* a form of analysis in which the quantity of each element in a compound is determined.

**ul|ti|mate|ly** (ul′tə mit lē), *adv.* in the end; finally.

**Ultimate Reality**, = God.

**ultimate strength**, *Physics.* 1 the inherent resistance in a piece of material equal but opposed to the ultimate stress. 2 the load necessary to produce fracture.

**ultimate stress**, *Physics.* the stress necessary to break or crush a piece of material.

**ul|ti|ma Thu|le** (ul′tə mə thü′lē), 1 the farthest north. 2 the farthest limit or point possible. 3 the utmost degree attainable. [< Latin *ultima Thūlē;* see etym. under **ultimate**. Compare etym. under **Thule**.]

**ul|ti|ma|tism** (ul′tə mə tiz′əm), *n.* an uncompromising attitude or tendency; extremism in opinion or belief.

**ul|ti|ma|tis|tic** (ul′tə mə tis′tik), *adj.* characterized by ultimatism; extremist.

**ul|ti|ma|tum** (ul′tə mā′təm), *n., pl.* **-tums, -ta** (-tə). 1 a final proposal or statement of conditions, acceptance of which is required under penalty of ending a relationship, negotiations, etc., or of punitive action: *This follows the ETU's [Electrical Trade Union's] reply to the congress' ultimatum that five of the union members should be debarred from office* (Manchester Guardian). 2 the final terms presented by one party in an international negotiation, rejection of which may lead to the breaking off of diplomatic relations or sometimes to a declaration of war. 3 something unanalyzable or fundamental: *certain ultimata of belief not to be disturbed in ordinary conversation* (Oliver Wendell Holmes). [< New Latin *ultimatum,* neuter of Medieval Latin *ultimatus;* see etym. under **ultimate**]

**ul|ti|mo** (ul′tə mō), *adv.* in or of last month. *Abbr:* ult. [< Medieval Latin *ultimo* (*mense*) in the course of last (month)]

**ul|ti|mo|bran|chi|al body** or **gland** (ul′tə mō brang′kē əl), a small organ near the thyroid glands of most vertebrates, believed to be derived from the last of several embryonic pouches of the gills or pharynx. It secretes a hormone that regulates the level of calcium in body fluids. [< Latin *ultimus* last + English *branchial*]

**ul|ti|mo|gen|i|ture** (ul′tə mō jen′ə chər), *n. Law.* the right or principle by which the youngest inherits or succeeds. [< Latin *ultimus* last (see etym. under **ultimate**); patterned on *primogeniture*]

**ulto.**, ultimo.

**ul|tra** (ul′trə), *adj., n.* —*adj.* beyond what is usual; very; excessive; extreme.
—*n.* a person who holds extreme views or urges extreme measures: *In 1871, a group of ultras in the Quebec Conservative party published ... an authoritarian and reactionary guide for the electors* (Maclean's).
[< Latin *ultrā* beyond, properly ablative feminine of unrecorded *ulter* beyond]

**ultra-**, *prefix.* 1 beyond the _____; on the other side of the _____: *Ultraviolet = beyond the violet.*
2 going beyond the limits, or province, of _____: *Ultramundane = going beyond the limits of the mundane.*
3 extremely _____: *Ultramodern = extremely modern.*

---

**Pronunciation Key:** hat, āge, cãre, fär; let, ēqual, tėrm; it, īce; hot, ōpen, ôrder; oil, out; cup, pu̇t, rüle; child; long; thin; ᴛʜen; zh, measure; ə represents a in about, e in taken, i in pencil, o in lemon, u in circus.

[< Latin *ultra-* < *ultrā* beyond; see etym. under **ultra**]

▶ The meaning of each of the words in the following list is found by substituting *very, excessively,* or *unusually* for *ultra-*.

**ultra-ambitious** **ultrafashionable**
**ultraconfident** **ultraloyal**
**ultracredulous** **ultramechanical**
**ultrademocratic** **ultramodest**
**ultraexclusive** **ultrarefined**

**ul|tra|ba|sic** (ul′trə bā′sik), *adj. Geology.* extremely rich in base-forming elements and poor in silica: *ultrabasic rocks.*

**ul|tra|cen|trif|u|gal** (ul′trə sen trif′ə gəl, -yə-), *adj.* of or by means of an ultracentrifuge. —**ul′tra-cen|trif′u|gal|ly,** *adv.*

**ul|tra|cen|trif|u|ga|tion** (ul′trə sen trif′ə gā′shən, -yə-), *n.* a subjecting or being subjected to the action of an ultracentrifuge.

**ul|tra|cen|tri|fuge** (ul′trə sen′trə fyüj), *n., v.,* **-fuged, -fug|ing.** —*n.* a centrifuge that can spin at very high speed, for measuring the molecular weights of solutes and determining the size of particles.
—*v.t.* to subject to the action of an ultracentrifuge.

**ul|tra|clean** (ul′trə klēn′), *adj.* maintaining a high level of cleanliness, especially under germfree conditions in laboratories: *Ultraclean technology can ... make possible new products and procedures that otherwise would be unachievable* (Science Journal).

**ul|tra|cold** (ul′trə kōld′), *adj.* extremely or unreasonably low in temperature; excessively cold: *Superconducting materials have been tested in the high vacuum and ultracold conditions they would meet in space* (Science News Letter).

**ul|tra|con|serv|a|tism** (ul′trə kən sėr′və tiz əm), *n.* extreme opposition to innovation or change; unreasonable conservatism.

**ul|tra|con|serv|a|tive** (ul′trə kən sėr′və tiv), *adj., n.* —*adj.* conservative in the extreme; excessively conservative.
—*n.* a person who is extremely conservative.

**ul|tra|crit|i|cal** (ul′trə krit′ə kəl), *adj.* excessively critical; overcritical.

**Ul|tra|fax** (ul′trə faks′), *n. Trademark.* a way of printing pictures or the like by radio or television transmission.

**ul|tra|fiche** (ul′trə fēsh′), *n., pl.* **-fich|es, -fiche** (-fēsh′). a strip of microfilm containing extremely reduced images of printed matter: *Ultrafiches of the photochromic microimage process store up to 4,000 pages on a 4 in. by 6 in. film and provide complete industrial data compilations on a pocket scale* (London Times). [< *ultra-* + (micro)-*fiche*]

**ul|tra|fil|tra|tion** (ul′trə fil trā′shən), *n.* = reverse osmosis.

**ul|tra|fine** (ul′trə fīn′), *adj.* extremely fine: *A photographic plate with ultrafine grains ... would require a prohibitively long exposure to photograph faint stars* (Julian Huxley).

**ul|tra|gas|e|ous** (ul′trə gas′ē əs), *adj. Physics.* **1** (of matter) being in the form of a highly rarefied gas with peculiar electrical and other properties, as that in a vacuum tube exhausted to one millionth of an atmosphere. **2** of or having to do with such matter: *the most rarefied form of matter — an ultragaseous condition of it* (William Ralph Inge).

**ul|tra|high** (ul′trə hī′), *adj.* of the highest degree; extremely high: *The chemical explodes unless kept at ultracold temperatures and ultrahigh pressures* (Science News Letter).

**ul|tra|high-fre|quen|cy** (ul′trə hī′frē′kwən sē), *adj.* = UHF.

**ul|tra|ism** (ul′trə iz əm), *n.* **1** doctrines or beliefs of an extremist, especially a political extremist. **2** an action, or group of actions, exemplifying such doctrines or beliefs.

**ul|tra|ist** (ul′trə ist), *n., adj.* —*n.* an extremist.
—*adj.* = ultraistic.

**ul|tra|is|tic** (ul′trə is′tik), *adj.* tending to extremes in opinions or practice.

**ul|tra|left** (ul′trə left′), *adj., n.* —*adj.* of or belonging to the extreme left in politics; extremely liberal or radical.
—*n.* **the ultraleft,** extreme leftists as a body or movement: *The ultraleft found its voice by ... joining cause with irate farmers fighting eviction from their farmlands* (New Scientist and Science Journal).

**ul|tra|left|ist** (ul′trə lef′tist), *n. adj.* —*n.* an extreme leftist: *As an ultraleftist, of course, We would hardly expect a warm welcome from as revisionist a country as the Soviet Union* (Time).
—*adj.* = ultraleft.

**ul|tra|lib|er|al** (ul′trə lib′ər əl, -lib′rəl), *adj., n.* —*adj.* holding very liberal views, especially in politics.
—*n.* an ultraliberal person or group.

**ul|tra|maf|ic** (ul′trə maf′ik), *adj.* = ultrabasic.

**ul|tra|ma|rine** (ul′trə mə rēn′), *n., adj.* —*n.* **1** Also, **ultramarine blue.** a deep blue. **2** a blue pigment, originally made from powdered lapis lazuli. **3** a similar blue pigment, prepared artificially by grinding together a mixture of kaolin, sulfur, soda ash, and charcoal. **4** any one of certain other pigments prepared artificially.
—*adj.* **1** deep-blue. **2** beyond or across the sea, especially beyond or across the Mediterranean or some part of it. SYN: overseas.
[< Medieval Latin *ultramarinus* < Latin *ultrā* beyond + *mare* sea (referring to Asia, the overseas source of lapis lazuli)]

**ul|tra|mi|cro** (ul′trə mī′krō), *adj.* = ultramicroscopic.

**ul|tra|mi|cro|chem|i|cal** (ul′trə mī′krō kem′ə-kəl), *adj.* of or having to do with ultramicrochemistry.

**ul|tra|mi|cro|chem|ist** (ul′trə mī′krō kem′ist), *n.* an expert in ultramicrochemistry.

**ul|tra|mi|cro|chem|is|try** (ul′trə mī′krō kem′ə-strē), *n.* microchemistry that deals with microgram quantities.

**ul|tra|mi|cro|fiche** (ul′trə mī′krə fēsh′), *n., pl.* **-fich|es, -fiche** (-fēsh′). = ultrafiche.

**ul|tra|mi|crom|e|ter** (ul′trə mī krom′ə tər), *n.* a very finely calibrated micrometer.

**ul|tra|mi|cro|scope** (ul′trə mī′krə skōp), *n.* a powerful instrument for making visible particles too small to be seen in an ordinary microscope, by means of light thrown on the object from one side, over a dark background.

**ul|tra|mi|cro|scop|ic** (ul′trə mī′krə skop′ik), *adj.* **1** too small to be seen with an ordinary microscope. **2** having to do with an ultramicroscope. —**ul′tra|mi′cro|scop′i|cal|ly,** *adv.*

**ul|tra|mi|cro|scop|i|cal** (ul′trə mī′krə skop′ə kəl), *adj.* = ultramicroscopic.

**ul|tra|mi|cros|co|py** (ul′trə mī kros′kə pē, -mī′-krə skō′-), *n.* the art or practice of using the ultramicroscope.

**ul|tra|mi|cro|tome** (ul′trə mī′krə tōm), *n.* an instrument used to cut extremely thin sections of tissues for examination by an electron microscope.

**ul|tra|mil|i|tant** (ul′trə mil′ə tənt), *adj.* militant to an extreme.

**ul|tra|min|i|a|ture** (ul′trə min′ē ə chər, -min′ə-chər), *adj.* done or made on an extremely small scale; smaller than miniature: *With continued research it should be possible ... to extend ultraminiature circuits and instruments to higher performance levels* (Scientific American).

**ul|tra|min|i|a|tur|ize** (ul′trə min′ē ə chə rīz, -min′-ə chə-), *v.t.,* **-ized, -iz|ing.** to reduce to ultraminiature size. —**ul′tra|min′i|a|tur|i|za′tion,** *n.*

**ul|tra|mod|ern** (ul′trə mod′ərn), *adj.* modern to the greatest possible degree; extremely modern: *ultramodern furniture.*

**ul|tra|mod|ern|ism** (ul′trə mod′ər niz əm), *n.* modernism to the greatest possible degree.

**ul|tra|mod|ern|ist** (ul′trə mod′ər nist), *n.* a person who is ultramodern, especially in ideas and tastes.

**ul|tra|mod|ern|is|tic** (ul′trə mod′ər nis′tik), *adj.* in an ultramodern style or fashion.

**ul|tra|mon|tane** (ul′trə mon′tān), *adj., n.* —*adj.* **1** beyond the mountains; transmontane. **2** south of the Alps; Italian. **3** supporting the absolute authority of the pope in matters of faith and morals when he speaks as the head of the Roman Catholic Church.
—*n.* **1** a person living south of the Alps. **2** one of a party of the Roman Catholic Church maintaining the absolute authority of the pope in matters of religious faith and ecclesiastical discipline.
[< Medieval Latin *ultramontanus* < Latin *ultrā* beyond + *mōns, montis* mountain]

**ul|tra|mon|ta|nism** (ul′trə mon′tə niz əm), *n.* the doctrine of absolute papal supremacy.

**ul|tra|mon|ta|nist** (ul′trə mon′tə nist), *n.* a person belonging to the ultramontane party; promoter of ultramontanism.

**ul|tra|mun|dane** (ul′trə mun′dān), *adj.* **1** beyond the world; beyond the limits of the known universe. **2** beyond this present life. [< Latin *ultrā-mundānus* < Latin *ultrā* beyond + *mundus* world]

**ul|tra|na|tion|al** (ul′trə nash′ə nəl, -nash′nəl), *adj.* = ultranationalistic.

**ul|tra|na|tion|al|ism** (ul′trə nash′ə nə liz′əm, -nash′nə liz-), *n.* extreme nationalism.

**ul|tra|na|tion|al|ist** (ul′trə nash′ə nə list, -nash′-nə-), *adj., n.* —*adj.* = ultranationalistic.
—*n.* an adherent of ultranationalism: *In the area of foreign policy, most ultraconservatives are ultranationalists* (Harper's).

**ul|tra|na|tion|al|is|tic** (ul′trə nash′ə nə lis′tik, -nash′nə-), *adj.* of ultranationalism or ultranationalists; extremely nationalistic: *Since internationalism is highly characteristic of science, no science can prosper under ultranationalistic regimes locked behind a closed door or iron curtain* (Bulletin of Atomic Scientists).

**ul|tra-Or|tho|dox** (ul′trə ôr′thə doks), *adj.* of or belonging to the extreme or ultrareligious wing of Orthodox Judaism.

**ul|tra|phys|i|cal** (ul′trə fiz′ə kəl), *adj.* beyond or transcending what is physical.

**ul|tra|pure** (ul′trə pyůr′), *adj.* more than pure; containing no visible or microscopic impurities: *ultrapure antiserum, ultrapure germanium.*

**ul|tra|rad|i|cal** (ul′trə rad′ə kəl), *adj., n.* —*adj.* excessively radical, especially in politics.
—*n.* a person who is extremely radical.

**ul|tra|red** (ul′trə red′), *adj.* = infrared.

**ul|tra|re|li|gious** (ul′trə ri lij′əs), *adj.* religious in the extreme; excessively religious.

**ul|tra|right|ist** (ul′trə rī′tist), *n., adj.* —*n.* a person who holds to an extremely conservative point of view, especially in politics. —*adj.* **1** holding such a point of view. **2** of or having to do with those who hold such a point of view.

**ul|tra|short** (ul′trə shôrt′), *adj.* **1** very short: *an ultrashort skirt.* **2** having a wave length of 10 meters or less: *ultrashort radio waves.*

**ul|tra|son|ic** (ul′trə son′ik), *adj.* of or having to do with ultrasound or ultrasonics; supersonic: *Ultrasonic generators produce sound waves to clean miniature parts* (New York Times). [< *ultra-* + Latin *sonus* sound + English *-ic*] —**ul′tra|son′i-cal|ly,** *adv.*

**ul|tra|son|ics** (ul′trə son′iks), *n.* the science that deals with or investigates the energy generated by sound waves of 20,000 or more vibrations per second; supersonics.

**ul|tra|son|o|gram** (ul′trə son′ə gram), *n.* a recording or tracing made by an ultrasonograph.

**ul|tra|son|o|graph** (ul′trə son′ə graf, -gräf), *n.* an instrument using ultrasonic waves to penetrate tissue and make recordings of abnormalities.

**ul|tra|so|nog|ra|phy** (ul′trə sə nog′rə fē), *n.* the use of an ultrasonograph to detect abnormalities in the body.

**ul|tra|so|nol|o|gist** (ul′trə sə nol′ə jist), *n.* a specialist in the use of ultrasonic devices in medical research and diagnosis.

**ul|tra|sound** (ul′trə sound′), *n.* sound above a frequency of 20,000 vibrations per second; ultrasonic sound: *Williams irradiated a solution of virus with high-frequency sound waves. When he dried the solution and photographed the result, he found that the ultrasound had broken the viruses into little bits* (Scientific American).

**ul|tra|struc|tur|al** (ul′trə struk′chər əl), *adj.* of or having to do with ultrastructure.

**ul|tra|struc|ture** (ul′trə struk′chər), *n.* a structure with extremely fine details, invisible to an ordinary microscope: *Particular attention is being paid to the ultrastructure of neurosecretory systems in crustaceans and in vertebrates, using the electron microscope* (New Scientist).

**Ul|tra|suède** (ul′trə swād′), *n. Trademark.* a synthetic, washable fabric that resembles suede: *Ultrasuède contained 60 percent polyester and 40 percent nonfibrous polyurethane* (Georgia Dulles).

**ul|tra|trop|i|cal** (ul′trə trop′ə kəl), *adj.* **1** outside of the tropics. **2** warmer than the tropics; very hot.

**ul|tra|vi|o|let** (ul′trə vī′ə lit), *adj., n.* —*adj.* **1** of or having to do with the invisible part of the spectrum whose rays have wavelengths shorter than those of the violet end of the visible spectrum and longer than those of the X rays: *ultraviolet light.* **2** of or having to do with the ultraviolet rays. Ultraviolet rays are present in sunlight and are important in healing and forming vitamins.
—*n.* the part of the spectrum comprising these rays. *Abbr:* UV (no periods).

**ultraviolet rays,** the invisible rays in the part of the spectrum beyond the violet. They are present in sunlight and light from sun lamps, and are used for healing, forming vitamins, and as sterilizers and disinfectants. Ultraviolet rays are more refrangible than violet rays as diffracted by a grating.

**ul|tra vi|res** (ul′trə vī′rēz), going beyond the powers granted by authority or by law: *His Lordship made a declaration in this action that the expulsion of the plaintiff ... was invalid and ultra vires* (London Times). [< New Latin *ultra vires* (literally) beyond the power < Latin *ultrā* beyond, *vīrēs,* plural of *vīs, vīris* strength, force]

**ul|tra|vi|rus** (ul′trə vī′rəs), *n.* a virus which can go through the finest bacterial filters. [< *ultra*(microscopic) *virus*]

**u|lu** (ü′lü), *n.* a type of knife used by the Eskimos, made of metal or chipped stone, with a flat curved blade, especially for cutting blubber: *The ulu remains the ideal instrument for skinning seal* (Harper's). [< Eskimo *ulu*]

**ul|u|lant** (yül′yə lənt, ul′-), *adj.* = howling. [< Latin *ululāns, -antis,* present participle of *ululāre;* see etym. under **ululate**]

**ul|u|late** (yül′yə lāt, ul′-), *v.i.,* **-lat|ed, -lat|ing. 1** to howl, as a dog or wolf does. **2** to lament loudly. [< Latin *ululāre* (with English *-ate*[1]) howl]

**ul|u|la|tion** (yül′yə lā′shən, ul′-), *n.* **1** a howl or wail. **2** the act of howling or wailing.

**U|lys|se|an** (yü lis′ē ən), *adj.* **1** of or having to do with Ulysses. **2** resembling Ulysses, as in craft or deceit, or in extensive wanderings. **3** characteristic of Ulysses.

**U|lys|ses** (yü lis′ēz), *n.* **1** *Greek Legend.* a king of Ithaca and hero of the Trojan War, known for his wisdom and shrewdness. Ulysses, who was called Odysseus by the Greeks, is the hero of Homer's *Odyssey,* which tells about his adventures. **2** a novel by James Joyce, published in 1922.

**um** (əm), *interj.* a low sound used especially to express hesitation and doubt. [imitative. Compare etym. under **hum.**]

**U|may|yad** (ü mī′ad), *n., pl.* **-yads, -ya|des** (-ə dēz). = Omayyad.

***um|bel** (um′bəl), *n.* a flower cluster in which stalks nearly equal in length spring from a common center, as in parsley. Their summits form a level or slightly curved surface. A simple umbel has only one set of rays, as in the ginseng; in a compound umbel the pedicels or rays each bear an umbel of flowers, as in the carrot and dill. [< Latin *umbella* parasol (diminutive) < *umbra* shade]

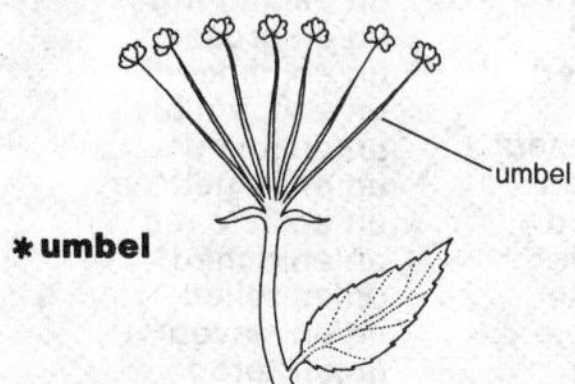


***umbel**

**um|bel|lar** (um′bə lər), *adj.* = umbellate.

**um|bel|late** (um′bə lit, -lāt), *adj. Botany.* **1** of or like an umbel. **2** having umbels; forming an umbel or umbels. **— um′bel|late|ly,** *adv.*

**um|bel|lat|ed** (um′bə lā′tid), *adj.* = umbellate.

**um|bel|let** (um′bə lit), *n.* = umbellule.

**um|bel|li|fer** (um bel′i fər), *n.* any plant of the parsley family. [< New Latin *umbellifer;* see etym. under **umbelliferous**]

**um|bel|lif|er|ous** (um′bə lif′ər əs), *adj. Botany.* **1** bearing an umbel or umbels: *The parsley and carrot are umbelliferous.* **2** belonging to the parsley family. [< New Latin *umbellifer* (< Latin *umbella* parasol + *ferre* to bear) + English *-ous*]

**um|bel|lu|late** (um bel′yə lit, -lāt), *adj. Botany.* having or arranged in umbellules.

**um|bel|lule** (um′bəl yül, um bel′-), *n. Botany.* a small or partial umbel; an umbel formed at the end of one of the primary pedicels or rays of a compound umbel. [< New Latin *umbellula* (diminutive) < Latin *umbella;* see etym. under **umbel**]

**um|ber**[1] (um′bər), *n., adj., v.* **— *n.* 1** a heavy, brown earth that is any one of various mixtures of clay and iron oxide, principally of alumina, iron oxide, and magnesium oxide. In its natural state it is used as a brown pigment called raw umber. After heating it becomes reddish brown and is called burnt umber. **2** a brown or reddish brown, like either of these pigments.
**— *adj.*** brown or reddish-brown.
**— *v.t.*** to stain or paint with umber; make of a brown color.
[< Italian (*terra di*) *ombra* (earth of) shade; *ombra* < Latin *umbra* shadow]

**um|ber**[2] (um′bər), *n.* **1** = grayling. **2** Also, **umber bird.** = umbrette. [< Old French *umbre* < Latin *umbra,* perhaps the same word as *umbra* shadow]

**um|ber|y** (um′bər ē), *adj.* **1** of or having to do with umber. **2** of the color of umber; dark brown.

**um|bil|ic** (um bil′ik), *n.* a point on a surface where the radii of curvature are all equal and a sphere osculates the surface.

**um|bil|i|cal** (um bil′ə kəl), *adj., n.* **— *adj.* 1** of or having to do with the navel or umbilical cord. **2** situated near the navel or the umbilical cord. **3** formed, placed, or shaped like a navel or umbilical cord: *The Chapter-house is large, supported as to its arched roof by one umbilical pillar* (Daniel Defoe).
**— *n.*** = umbilical cord.
[< Medieval Latin *umbilicalis* < Latin *umbilīcus* navel]

**umbilical cord, 1** a cordlike structure that connects the navel of an embryo or fetus with the placenta of the mother. It carries nourishment to the fetus and carries away waste. **2** *Figurative.* something that binds or unites closely; strong bond or tie: *He could never break the umbilical cord which held him to nature* (Emerson). **3** an electric cable, fuel line, or the like, connected to a missile on its launching site and released just before launching. **4** any long cord or cable by which a person or thing remains connected to a spacecraft, ship, the ground, or other surface.

**umbilical hernia,** hernia of the intestine at the navel; exomphalos.

**um|bil|i|cate** (um bil′ə kit, -kāt), *adj.* **1** navel-shaped. **2** having an umbilicus or navel.

**um|bil|i|cat|ed** (um bil′ə kā′tid), *adj.* = umbilicate.

**um|bil|i|ca|tion** (um bil′ə kā′shən), *n.* **1** a central depression resembling a navel. **2** the condition of being umbilicate.

**um|bil|i|cus** (um bil′ə kəs, um′bə lī′-), *n., pl.* **-ci** (-sī). **1** *Anatomy.* the navel; depression or scar on the middle of the abdomen, marking the spot where the umbilical cord was attached. **2** *Biology.* a small depression or hollow suggestive of a navel, such as the hilum of a seed. [< Latin *umbilīcus* navel]

**um|bil|i|form** (um bil′ə fôrm), *adj.* like a navel.

**um|ble pie** (um′bəl), *Obsolete.* a pie made from umbles; humble pie: *Mrs. Turner ... did bring us an umble pie hot out of her oven* (Samuel Pepys). [< *umbles*]

**um|bles** (um′bəlz), *n.pl. Obsolete.* the heart, liver, lungs, and other edible internal parts of an animal, especially of a deer; numbles. [variant of *numbles*]

**um|bo** (um′bō), *n., pl.* **um|bo|nes** (um bō′nēz), **um|bos. 1** a projection or knob, often pointed, near or at the center of a shield. **2** any elevation resembling this, as in the eardrum. **3** *Zoology.* the oldest and most protuberant portion of a bivalve mollusk shell, located near the hinge. [< Latin *umbō, -ōnis* boss of a shield, knob, projection, related to *umbilīcus* navel]

**um|bo|nal** (um′bə nəl), *adj.* = protuberant.

**um|bo|nate** (um′bə nit, -nāt), *adj.* **1** having an umbo or boss. **2** like an umbo or boss.

**um|bo|nat|ed** (um′bə nā′tid), *adj.* = umbonate.

**um|bo|na|tion** (um′bə nā′shən), *n.* **1** umbonate formation. **2** = umbo.

**um|bon|ic** (um bon′ik), *adj.* = umbonal.

***um|bra** (um′brə), *n., pl.* **-brae** (-brē), **-bras. 1** the completely dark shadow cast, as by the earth or moon, during an eclipse. **2** the dark inner or central part of a sunspot. **3** shade; shadow. [< Latin *umbra*]

***umbra**
definition 1

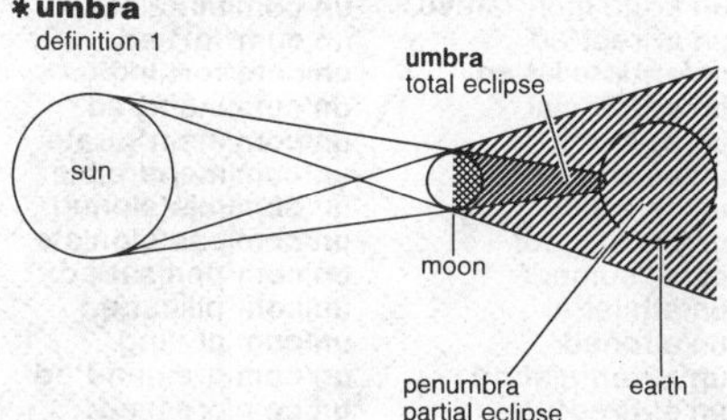


**um|brage** (um′brij), *n.* **1** suspicion that one has been slighted or injured; feeling offended; resentment: *Unless my pacific disposition was displeasing, nothing else could have given umbrage* (George Washington). SYN: offense, pique. **2** the foliage of trees or vines, providing shade: *at the foot of some tree of friendly umbrage* (Charlotte Brontë). **3** *Archaic.* a faint likeness; shadowy outline or indication. **4** *Obsolete.* shade; shadow.
**take umbrage,** to take offense; feel insulted or resentful: *He took umbrage at the criticism.*
[< Old French *ombrage* < Latin *umbrāticum,* neuter of *umbrāticus* shadowy < *umbra* shade]

**um|bra|geous** (um brā′jəs), *adj.* **1** likely to take offense; easily insulted. **2** revealing or displaying umbrage; offended; insulted. **3** giving shade; shady. **4** covered over or surrounded by that which cuts off light; somewhat dark; shaded. **— um|bra′geous|ly,** *adv.* **— um|bra′geous-ness,** *n.*

**um|bral** (um′brəl), *adj.* of or having to do with an umbra: *the umbral shadow of an eclipse.*

**um|brel|la** (um brel′ə), *n., adj.* **— *n.* 1** a light, portable, folding frame covered with cloth or plastic, used as a protection against rain or sun. **2** *Figurative: This is just short of the total 256 million bushels put under the Federal price umbrella for the entire season last year* (Wall Street Journal). **3** the gelatinous disk- or bowl-shaped body of a jellyfish; bell.
**— *adj.* 1** resembling an umbrella. **2** *Figurative: Within this large umbrella framework it should be possible to work out the necessary system of nuclear control* (Listener). *Therapies based on conditioning and learning theory* [*are*] *grouped under the umbrella term "behaviour therapy"* (New Scientist). SYN: general, comprehensive.
[< Italian *ombrella, ombrello* < *ombra* shade < Latin *umbra*] **— um|brel′la|like′,** *adj.*

**umbrella ant,** = leaf-cutter ant.

**umbrella bird,** any one of a group of tropical American birds, such as a kind that is black with a crest of long, curved feathers resembling an umbrella; dragoon bird.

**umbrella leaf,** a North American plant of the barberry family, having either a large umbrellalike leaf on a stout petiole, or a flowering stem with two similar but smaller leaves.

**umbrella palm,** a palm of the Solomon Islands, with pinnate leaves, grown for ornament in Florida and California.

**umbrella pine,** a tall, evergreen tree of the taxodium family, shaped like an umbrella, with tufts of stiff, leaflike petioles resembling pine needles. It is native to Japan but is grown in many parts of the world for shade. *Long ago we had spent a week in June at San Sebastian to cool off under the umbrella pines from the heat of Madrid* (Alice B. Toklas).

**umbrella plant,** an African plant of the sedge family, having several stems with umbrella-shaped clusters of leaves at the top. The umbrella plant is commonly grown in greenhouses as a potted plant.

**umbrella tent,** a tent made like an umbrella. The covered frame of an umbrella tent consists of ribs attached radially to a central staff or rod that supports the tent.

**umbrella tree, 1** an American magnolia tree having long leaves in clusters radiating from the ends of the branches, suggesting umbrellas. **2** any one of several other trees whose leaves or habit of growth resemble a shape suggesting an open umbrella.

**um|brel|la|wort** (um brel′ə wėrt′), *n.* any one of a group of chiefly American herbs, having opposite leaves, and flower-containing involucres in loose, terminal panicles; four-o'clock.

**um|brette** (um bret′), *n.* an African and Arabian wading bird with deep-brown plumage, related to the storks and herons; umber; umber bird. [< French *umbrette* < New Latin *umbretta* < Latin *umbra* shade]

**Um|bri|an** (um′brē ən), *adj., n.* **— *adj.* 1** of or belonging to Umbria, an ancient region in central and northern Italy, or its people. **2** of or having to do with the Italic dialect of ancient Umbria.
**— *n.* 1** a native or inhabitant of the modern district of Umbria. **2** a member of an Italic people who lived in ancient Umbria. **3** the Italic dialect, closely related to Oscan, spoken in ancient Umbria.

**um|brif|er|ous** (um brif′ər əs), *adj.* giving shade; umbrageous: *whiling away an afternoon lying under the umbriferous bows of an old elm.* [< Latin *umbrifer* (< *umbra* shade + *ferre* to bear) + English *-ous*] **— um|brif′er|ous|ly,** *adv.*

**um|bril** (um′brəl), *n.* the visor of a helmet. [variant of earlier *umbrel* < Old French *ombrel* shade, ultimately < Latin *umbra*]

**um|brous** (um′brəs), *adj.* lying in the shade; shadowed. [< Latin *umbrōsus* (with English *-ous*) < *umbra* shade]

**Um|bun|du** (əm bün′dü), *n., pl.* **-du** or **-dus. 1** a member of a Bantu people of central Angola. **2** the language of this people.

***u|mi|ak** or **u|mi|ack** (ü′mē ak), *n.* an open Eskimo boat made of skins covering a wooden or bone frame and worked by paddles. The umiak is very much broader and usually longer than a kayak. It is used especially by the women of a family or group of families to bring back the meat killed by the men and to transport a family and its possessions from place to place. Also, **oomiac, oomiak.** [< Eskimo *umiaq* an open skin boat]

***umiak**

***um|laut** (ům′lout), *n., v.* **— *n.* 1** the partial assimilation of a vowel to another vowel in a preceding or following syllable. **2** a change in vowel sound in the Germanic languages because of the influ-

**Pronunciation Key:** hat, āge, cãre, fär; let, ēqual, tėrm; it, īce; hot, ōpen, ôrder; oil, out; cup, pu̇t, rüle; child; long; thin; ᴛʜen; zh, measure; ə represents a in about, e in taken, i in pencil, o in lemon, u in circus.

ence of another vowel in the following syllable, now generally lost but responsible for such pairs as English *man-men, foot-feet,* and *gold-gild* where the vowels of *men, feet,* and *gild* are the result of umlaut. **3** a vowel that is the result of such a change. **4** the sign used to indicate such a vowel, especially in German, as in *Göring,* also written *Goering.*
— ***v.t.*** **1** to modify by umlaut. **2** to write (a vowel) with an umlaut.
[< German *Umlaut* < *um* about (altering) + *Laut* sound]

***umlaut**
definition 4

Käse=cheese
König=king
Küche=kitchen

**ump** (ump), *n., v. Slang.* — ***n.*** an umpire: *For Americans everywhere, there is no thrill like being there when the ump yells, "Play ball!"* (Time).
— ***v.i., v.t.*** to umpire: *Who's going to ump the game?*

**umph¹** (umf), *interj., n.* = humph.

**umph²** (ümf), *n.* = oomph.

**um|pir|age** (um′pīr ij, -pə rij), *n.* **1** the act of umpiring or arbitrating. **2** the office or power of an umpire or arbiter. **3** the decision of an umpire or arbiter.

**um|pire** (um′pīr), *n., v.,* **-pired, -pir|ing.** — ***n.*** **1** a person who rules on the plays in a game and who sees that the rules are not broken: *The umpire called the ball a foul.* **SYN**: referee. **2** a person chosen to settle a dispute; arbiter, especially one whose decisions are binding on both or all parties to the dispute. **SYN**: judge, arbitrator, mediator.
— ***v.t.*** to act as an umpire in (a game or dispute).
— ***v.i.*** to act as an umpire.
[Middle English *owmpere,* by misdivision < *a noumpere* a third man < Old French *nomper,* odd, not even < *non* not (< Latin) + *per* equal < Latin *pār*]

**um|pire|ship** (um′pīr ship), *n.* the office of an umpire; arbitrament; umpirage.

**ump|teen** (ump′tēn′), *adj. Informal.* of a great but indefinite number; being one of a long series; countless: *There have been umpteen versions of The Three Musketeers and none of 'em ever lost money* (Time).

**ump|teenth** (ump′tēnth′), *adj. Informal.* being the last of a great but indefinite number or of a long series: *the umpteenth version of Beauty and the Beast* (New York Times).

**ump|ti|eth** (ump′tē ith), *adj.* = umpteenth.

**ump|ty** (ump′tē), *adj. Informal.* of an indefinite number; many; umpteen: *umpty months, umpty times.*

**ump|ty-umpth** (ump′tē umpth′), *adj. U.S. Informal.* umpteenth.

**UMT** (no periods), Universal Military Training.

**UMTS** (no periods), Universal Military Training Service or System.

**UMW** (no periods) or **U.M.W.**, United Mine Workers.

**un** (un, ən), *n., pron. Dialect.* one: *"It [a rose] smells very sweet," he said; "those striped uns have no smell"* (George Eliot).

**un-¹**, *prefix.* **1** *with adjectives and adverbs.* not _____: *Unchanged = not changed. Unequal = not equal. Unjustly = not justly.*
**2** *with nouns.* the opposite of _____: *Uncooperation = the opposite of cooperation. Ungodliness = the opposite of godliness.*
[Old English *un-*]
► **un-**. Although this dictionary lists hundreds of words, only a fraction of the possible number of words are entered, since *un-* is a prefix freely used in forming new words, chiefly adjectives and nouns. The meaning of each of the words in the following list is found by substituting *not* for *un-*. See also **in-¹** and **a-⁴** for usage notes.

**un′a|bat′a|ble**
**un′a|bat′ing**
**un′ab|bre′vi|at′ed**
**un′a|bet′ted**
**un′a|bid′ing**
**un′a|bid′ing|ly**
**un′a|bol′ished**
**un′ab|rupt′**
**un|ab′sent**
**un′ab|solv′a|ble**
**un′ab|solved′**
**un′ab|sorbed′**
**un′ac|cen′tu|at′ed**
**un′ac|cept′ed**
**un′ac|cli′mat|ed**
**un′ac|cli′ma|tized**
**un′ac|com′plish|a|ble**
**un′ac|count′ed**
**un′ac|cu′mu|lat′ed**
**un′ac|cused′**
**un′a|chiev′a|ble**
**un′a|chieved′**
**un′ac|quit′ted**
**un|ac′tu|at′ed**
**un′ad|dict′ed**
**un′ad|journed′**
**un′ad|just′a|ble**
**un′ad|just′ed**
**un′ad|mir′ing**
**un′ad|mit′ta|ble**
**un′ad|mit′ted**
**un′ad|mon′ished**
**un′a|dopt′a|ble**
**un′a|dopt′ed**
**un′a|dored′**
**un′ad|van|ta′geous**
**un|ad′ver|tised**
**un′aes|thet′ic**
**un′aes|thet′i|cal**
**un′af|fec′tion|ate**
**un′af|flict′ed**
**un′af|front′ed**
**un|aged′**
**un|ag|glu′ti|nat′ed**
**un|ag′gra|vat′ed**
**un′ag|gres′sive**
**un|aimed′**
**un|aired′**
**un′a|larmed′**
**un′a|larm′ing**
**un′al|ien|at′ed**
**un′a|like′**
**un′al|le′vi|at′ed**
**un|al′lo|cat′ed**
**un′al|lot′ted**
**un′al|low′a|ble**
**un|al′pha|bet|ized**
**un|al′ter|ing**
**un′a|mazed′**
**un′am|biv′a|lent**
**un′a|mend′ed**
**un|am′pli|fied**
**un′an|a|lyt′ic**
**un|an′a|lyz′a|ble**
**un|an′a|lyzed**
**un|an′chored**
**un′an|nealed′**
**un|an′no|tat′ed**
**un′an|nounced′**
**un′a|noint′ed**
**un′an|tic′i|pat′ed**
**un|anx′ious**
**un′a|pol′o|get′ic**
**un′ap|plaud′ed**
**un′ap|plied′**
**un′ap|point′ed**
**un′ap|pre′ci|a′tion**
**un′ap|prov′ing**
**un|arched′**
**un′ar|gu|men′ta|tive**
**un′ar|rest′ed**
**un′ar|tic′u|lat′ed**
**un′ar|ti|fi′cial**
**un′as|sert′ed**
**un′as|so′ci|at′ed**
**un′as|soiled′**
**un′as|suaged′**
**un′as|sumed′**
**un′ath|let′ic**
**un′a|toned′**
**un′at|ten′u|at′ed**
**un′at|tired′**
**un′at|tract′ed**
**un|au′dit|ed**
**un′a|waked′**
**un|awed′**
**un|bait′ed**
**un|banked′**
**un|bast′ed**
**un|bel′li|cose**
**un′bel|lig′er|ent**
**un|bend′a|ble**
**un′be|spok′en**
**un′be|trayed′**
**un′be|trothed′**
**un′be|wailed′**
**un|billed′**
**un|blanched′**
**un|blend′ed**
**un|boiled′**
**un|bombed′**
**un|boned′**
**un|bor′rowed**
**un|both′ered**
**un|bound′a|ble**
**un|bowd′ler|ized**
**un|branch′ing**
**un|brand′ed**
**un|breath′a|ble**
**un|bridge′able**
**un|bridged′**
**un-Brit′ish**
**un|broached′**
**un|bruised′**
**un|brushed′**
**un|budg′et|ed**
**un|bur′nished**
**un|but′tered**
**un|but′tressed**
**un|cal′cined**
**un|cal′cu|lat′ed**
**un|cal′cu|lat′ing**
**un|cal′en|dered**
**un|cap′i|tal|ized**
**un|cap′tioned**
**un|car′bu|ret′ed**
**un|card′ed**
**un|car′ing**
**un|cas′trat|ed**
**un|catch′a|ble**
**un|caught′**
**un|cau′tious**
**un|cel′e|brat′ed**
**un|cen′sored**
**un|cen′sured**
**un|cen′tered**
**un′cer|e|mo′ni|al**
**un|cham′bered**
**un|chas′tened**
**un′chas|tised′**
**un|check′a|ble**
**un|cher′ished**
**un|chew′a|ble**
**un|chewed′**
**un|chic′**
**un|chilled′**
**un|chol′er|ic**
**un|chopped′**
**un|cho′sen**
**un|chris′tened**
**un|chron′i|cled**
**un|churned′**
**un|cit′ed**
**un|clar′i|fied**
**un|classed′**
**un|clas′sic**
**un|clas′si|cal**
**un|cleansed′**
**un|cleav′a|ble**
**un|climb′a|ble**
**un|climbed′**
**un|clois′tered**
**un|cloyed′**
**un′co|ag′u|lat′ed**
**un|coat′ed**
**un|cod′ed**
**un|cod′i|fied**
**un′co|erced′**
**un|col′lared**
**un′col|lect′a|ble**
**un′col|lect′i|ble**
**un|col′o|nized**
**un|combed′**
**un′com|bin′a|ble**
**un|com′fort|ed**
**un|com′fort|ing**
**un′com|mand′ed**
**un′com|mem′o|rate**
**un′com|mend′a|ble**
**un′com|mis′sioned**
**un′com|pas′sion|ate**
**un|com′pen|sat′ed**
**un|com′pli|cat′ed**
**un′com|ply′ing**
**un′com|pre|hend′ed**
**un′com|pressed′**
**un|com′pro|mised**
**un′com|put′ed**
**un′com|put′er|ized**
**un|com′rade|ly**
**un′con|ceal′a|ble**
**un′con|ced′ed**
**un′con|cert′ed**
**un′con|cil′i|at′ed**
**un′con|clud′ed**
**un′con|densed′**
**un′con|ferred′**
**un′con|fessed′**
**un′con|fid′ing**
**un′con|form′ing**
**un′con|fut′ed**
**un′con|geal′a|ble**
**un′con|gealed′**
**un′con|gest′ed**
**un′con|sci|en′tious**
**un′con|soled′**
**un′con|sol′i|dat′ed**
**un|con′so|nant**
**un|con′sti|tut′ed**
**un′con|strict′ed**
**un′con|struct′ed**
**un′con|struc′tive**
**un′con|sult′ed**
**un′con|sumed′**
**un′con|tam′i|nat′ed**
**un′con|tem′plat′ed**
**un′con|tend′ing**
**un′con|tract′ed**
**un′con|trite′**
**un′con|tro|ver′sial**
**un′con|tro|vert′i|ble**
**un′con|vened′**
**un′con|vict′ed**
**un′con|vinced′**
**un|cooled′**
**un|cor′dial**
**un|corked′**
**un|cor′re|lat′ed**
**un|cor′set|ed**
**un|court′ed**
**un|cowed′**
**un′cre|a′tive**
**un|cred′it|ed**
**un|crip′pled**
**un|crit′i|ciz′a|ble**
**un|crowd′ed**
**un|crush′a|ble**
**un|crys′tal|line**
**un|crys′tal|liz′a|ble**
**un|crys′tal|lized**
**un|cur′dled**
**un|cured′**
**un|curled′**
**un|cur′rent**
**un|cursed′**
**un′cur|tailed′**
**un|cur′tained**
**un|cush′ioned**
**un|cus′tom|ar′y**
**un|cut′ta|ble**
**un|dan′gered**
**un|dan′ger|ous**
**un|dat′a|ble**
**un|daugh′ter|ly**
**un|daz′zled**
**un|dealt′**
**un′de|bat′a|ble**
**un′de|cayed′**
**un′de|cay′ing**
**un′de|ceived′**
**un′de|ci′phered**
**un′de|clared′**
**un′de|com|posed′**
**un|dec′o|rat′ed**
**un|ded′i|cat′ed**
**un′de|duc′i|ble**
**un′de|fac′a|ble**
**un′de|feat′a|ble**
**un′de|feat′ed**
**un|de|fen′si|ble**
**un′de|flect′ed**
**un′de|formed′**
**un′de|grad′ed**
**un′de|lay′a|ble**
**un′de|layed′**
**un′de|lin′e|at′ed**
**un′de|liv′er|a|ble**
**un′de|liv′ered**
**un′de|lud′ed**
**un|de′mar|cat′ed**
**un|dem′on|strat′ed**
**un′de|nied′**
**un′de|nounced′**
**un′de|plored′**
**un′de|posed′**
**un′de|put′ed**
**un′de|rived′**
**un|der′o|gat′ing**
**un′de|rog′a|to′ry**
**un′de|scend′ed**
**un′de|scrib′a|ble**
**un′de|scrip′tive**
**un|des′ig|nat′ed**
**un′de|sist′ing**
**un′de|spair′ing**
**un′de|stroyed′**
**un′de|tach′a|ble**
**un′de|tached′**
**un′de|voured′**
**un′di|ag|nosed′**
**un′dif|fused′**
**un′di|lat′ed**
**un|dipped′**
**un′dis|band′ed**
**un′dis|closed′**
**un′dis|con|cert′ed**
**un′dis|cord′ant**
**un′dis|cour′aged**
**un′dis|cred′it|ed**
**un′dis|crim′i|na|tive**
**un′dis|guis′a|ble**
**un′dis|heart′ened**
**un′dis|il|lu′sioned**
**un′dis|man′tled**
**un′dis|mem′bered**
**un′dis|missed′**
**un′dis|patched′**
**un′dis|pelled′**
**un′dis|sect′ed**
**un′dis|sem′bling**
**un′dis|sem′i|nat′ed**
**un′dis|so′ci|at′ed**
**un′dis|tilled′**
**un′dis|tort′ed**
**un′dis|traught′**
**un′dis|tressed′**
**un|doc′tored**
**un|dog|mat′ic**
**un′do|mes′tic**
**un|dom′i|nat′ed**
**un|dou′bled**
**un|drained′**
**un|dram′a|tized**
**un|dried′**
**un|drilled′**
**un|dug′**
**un|dumped′**
**un|dust′ed**
**un′ec|cle′si|as′tic**
**un′e|clipsed′**
**un|ed′i|fied**
**un′ef|faced′**
**un′e|lat′ed**
**un′e|lec′tri|fied**
**un|el′e|vat′ed**
**un′e|lim′i|nat′ed**
**un′e|luc′i|dat′ed**
**un′e|man′ci|pat′ed**
**un′em|balmed′**
**un′em|bel′lished**
**un′em|bit′tered**
**un′em|brace′a|ble**
**un′e|mend′a|ble**
**un′e|mend′ed**
**un′em|phat′ic**
**un′em|pow′ered**
**un|emp′tied**
**un′en|coun′tered**
**un′en|cour′aged**
**un′en|dan′gered**
**un′en|dorsed′**
**un′en|fran′chised**
**un′en|gag′ing**
**un′en|grossed′**
**un′en|hanced′**
**un′en|joy′a|ble**
**un′en|joyed′**
**un′en|larged′**
**un′en|liv′ened**
**un′en|riched′**
**un′en|rolled′**
**un′en|slaved′**
**un|en′tered**
**un′en|tic′ing**
**un′en|ti′tled**
**un′e|nu′mer|at′ed**
**un|en′vy|ing**
**un′e|quipped′**
**un′e|rased′**
**un′e|rect′ed**
**un′e|rot′ic**
**un′e|rupt′ed**
**un′es|cort′ed**
**un′es|tab′lished**
**un′es|teemed′**
**un′es|thet′ic**
**un|es′ti|mat′ed**
**un-Eu′ro|pe′an**
**un′e|val′u|at′ed**
**un′e|vict′ed**
**un′ex|ag′ger|at′ed**
**un′ex|alt′ed**
**un′ex|am′ined**
**un|ex′ca|vat′ed**
**un′ex|change′a|ble**
**un′ex|cit′a|ble**
**un′ex|clud′ed**
**un′ex|cused′**
**un|ex′er|cised**
**un′ex|ert′ed**
**un′ex|haust′ed**
**un′ex|ot′ic**
**un′ex|pand′ed**
**un′ex|pend′a|ble**
**un′ex|pend′ed**
**un|ex′pi|at′ed**
**un′ex|plic′it**
**un′ex|ploit′ed**
**un′ex|port′a|ble**
**un′ex|port′ed**
**un′ex|punged′**
**un′ex|ten′u|at′ed**
**un′ex|ter′mi|nat′ed**
**un′ex|tin′guished**
**un|fad′ed**
**un|fall′en**
**un|fan′cy**
**un|fas′tened**
**un′fa|tigued′**
**un|fa′vored**
**un|fazed′**
**un|fear′ing**
**un|fed′er|at′ed**
**un′fe|lic′i|tous**
**un|fes′tive**
**un|filled′**
**un|filmed′**
**un|find′a|ble**
**un|fired′**
**un′flam|boy′ant**
**un|flat′tened**
**un|flat′tered**
**un|fla′vored**
**un|flawed′**
**un|flick′er|ing**
**un|flood′ed**

un|flus′tered
un|fo′cused
un′for|bear′ing
un|ford′a|ble
un|for′est|ed
un′for|get′ful
un′for|get′ting
un|for′mi|da|ble
un′for|sak′en
un|found′
un′fra|ter′nal
un|freed′
un|freez′a|ble
un-French′
un|fre′quent|ly
un|fright′ened
un|fro′zen
un|furred′
un′gain|say′a|ble
un|gal′va|nized
un|gar′ri|soned
un|gir′dled
un|giv′en
un|gla′ci|at′ed
un|glad′dened
un|glo′ri|fied
un|glossed′
un|glued′
un|gowned′
un|grad′u|at′ed
un|graft′ed
un|grained′
un|grant′ed
un|ground′
un|grouped′
un′guar|an|teed′
un|guess′a|ble
un|gummed′
un|hailed′
un|halved′
un|ham′mered
un|hand′i|capped
un|har′assed
un|harm′ing
un|har′nessed
un|har′rowed
un|har′vest′ed
un|haunt′ed
un|heal′a|ble
un|healed′
un|heal′ing
un|helped′
un|hemmed′
un|hes′i|tant
un|hit′
un|hulled′
un|hur′ry|ing
un|husked′
un|hy′phen|at′ed
un|hy′phened
un′i|de|al|is′tic
un′il|lu′mined
un|il′lus|trat′ed
un′im|bued′
un|im′i|tat′ed
un|im′mu|nized
un′im|pair′a|ble
un|im′pli|cat′ed
un′im|preg′nat|ed
un′im|pres′sive
un′im|pris′oned
un′in|au′gu|rat′ed
un′in|ci′sive
un′in|clined′
un′in|clud′ed
un|in′cu|bat′ed
un′in|dem′ni|fied
un′in|dent′ed
un′in|den′tured
un|in′dexed
un|in′di|cat′ed
un′in|dict′a|ble
un′in|dict′ed
un′in|dorsed′
un′in|dus′tri|al|ized
un′in|dus′tri|ous
un′in|fect′ed
un′in|fec′tious
un′in|fest′ed
un′in|flu|en′tial
un′in|fringed′
un′in|quir′ing
un′in|struc′tive
un|in′su|lat′ed
un′in|sur′a|ble
un′in|tel|lec′tu|al
un′in|ter′po|lat′ed
un′in|ter′pret|ed
un′in|terred′
un′in|tim′i|dat′ed
un′in|tox′i|cat′ed
un′in|vad′ed
un′in|vert′ed
un′in|vest′ed
un′in|ves′ti|gat′ed
un′in|voked′
un′in|volved′
un|i′roned
un′ir|ra′di|at′ed
un|ir′ri|gat′ed
un|is′sued
un|jack′et|ed
un|jad′ed
un|joined′
un|joy′ous
un|judged′
un′ju|di′cial
un|killed′
un|kin′dled
un|kink′
un|kissed′
un|knead′ed
un|knot′ted
un|knowl′edge|a|ble
un|ko′sher
un|la′beled
un|laced′
un|lac′quered
un|lad′en
un|lashed′
un|lat′ticed
un|laud′a|ble
un|learn′a|ble
un|les′sened
un|let′
un|le′thal
un|lev′ied
un|lib′er|al
un′li|bid′i|nous
un|life′like′
un|lift′a|ble
un|lik′a|ble
un|like′a|ble
un|liked′
un|lined′
un|liq′ue|fi′a|ble
un|lit′er|ar′y
un|lit′tered
un|liv′a|ble
un|lived′
un|live′ly
un|lobed′
un|lov′a|ble
un|lov′er|like′
un|loy′al
un|lu′bri|cat′ed
un′lux|u′ri|ous
un|ly′ing
un|mag′ni|fied
un|mailed′
un′main|tain′a|ble
un′ma|li′cious
un|malt′ed
un|man′a|cled
un|man′ful
un|man′gled
un|man′i|fest
un|man′i|fest′ed
un|man′nish
un′man|u|fac′tur|a|ble
un|mapped′
un|mar′ket|ed
un|mar′tial
un′ma|te′ri|al|is′tic
un′ma|ter′nal
un|mat′ted
un′ma|tured′
un′me|chan′i|cal
un|mech′a|nized
un|me′di|at′ed
un|meek′
un|meet′a|ble
un|mel′an|chol′y
un|melt′a|ble
un|melt′ed
un|mem′or|a|ble
un|men′aced
un|mend′a|ble
un|mend′ed
un|men′sur|a|ble
un|men′tion|a|bly
un|mer′ry
un′met|a|phys′i|cal
un|me′tered
un|met′ri|cal
un|mil′i|tant
un′mil|i|ta|ris′tic
un|milked′
un|milled′
un|mined′
un|min′is|tered
un|mint′ed
un′mi|rac′u|lous
un|mirth′ful
un|missed′
un′mis|tak′en
un|mix′a|ble
un|mod′ern|ized
un|mod′u|lat′ed
un|mold′ed
un|mol′li|fied
un|mol′ten
un|mon′i|tored
un|moot′ed
un|mort′gaged
un|mo′ti|vat′ed
un|mot′tled
un|mud′dled
un|muf′fled
un|mussed′
un|mut′ed
un′mys|te′ri|ous
un|mys′ti|fied
un|nailed′
un|na′tion|al|ized
un|nau′ti|cal
un′ne|ces′si|tat′ed
un|need′ed
un|net′ted
un|notched′
un|note′wor′thy
un|nour′ish|ing
un′nu|mer′i|cal
un′o|beyed′
un′o|bliged′
un′o|blig′ing
un′o|blit′er|at′ed
un′ob|scured′
un′ob|tained′
un′ob|trud′ing
un|ob′vi|ous
un′oc|ca′sioned
un′of|fend′ed
un|of′fered
un|of′fi|cered
un|o′pen|a|ble
un′op|pressed′
un|o′ri|ent|ed
un′or|nate′
un|os′si|fied
un|ox′i|dized
un|ox′y|gen|at′ed
un|pac′i|fied
un|pad′ded
un|paged′
un|pained′
un|paint′a|ble
un|paint′ed
un|pan′eled
un|pa′pered
un|par′a|phrased
un′pa|ren′tal
un|part′ed
un′par|tic′u|lar|ized
un|par′ti|san
un′par|ti′tioned
un|past′ed
un|pas′teur|ized
un|patched′
un′pa|trolled′
un|pa′tron|ized
un|pa′tron|iz′ing
un′pe|dan′tic
un|pe′nal|ized
un|pen′e|trat′ed
un′per|fect′ed
un′per|fumed′
un|per′me|at′ed
un′per|suad′ed
un′pe|rused′
un′phil|an|throp′ic
un′phil|o|log′i|cal
un′pho|net′ic
un|pho′to|graphed
un′pic|tur|esque′
un|pig′ment|ed
un|pin′ioned
un|plait′ed
un|planned′
un|plas′tered
un|plat′ed
un|played′
un|pleat′ed
un|pledged′
un|plight′ed
un|ploughed′
un|plowed′
un|po′lar|ized
un′po|lem′ic
un′po|lit′i|cal
un|pol′y|mer|ized
un|pon′dered
un|pop′u|lat′ed
un′por|tend′ed
un′por|ten′tious
un′por|tray′a|ble
un|posed′
un|pos′ing
un′pos|sessed′
un′post|pon′a|ble
un|poured′
un|pow′ered
un|praised′
un′pre|dict′ed
un′pre|oc′cu|pied
un′pre|served′
un|pres′sured
un|pres′sur|ized
un′pre|sumed′
un|primed′
un′pro|bat|ed
un|probed′
un|proc′essed
un|proc′tored
un′pro|cur′a|ble
un′pro|cured′
un′pro|fessed′
un′pro|fess′ing
un|pro′grammed
un′pro|mot′ed
un|proph′e|sied
un′pro|pi′ti|at′ed
un|propped′
un′pro|tect′a|ble
un′pro|test′ed
un′pro|test′ing
un′pro|vok′ing
un|pub′lish|a|ble
un|pul′ver|ized
un|punched′
un|punc′tu|at′ed
un|pur′chas|a|ble
un|pu′ri|fied
un|pur′sued′
un′pur|su′ing
un|quaffed′
un|quail′ing
un|quak′ing
un|qual′i|fy′ing
un|quar′an|tined
un|quar′ried
un|quar′tered
un|quelled′
un|quenched′
un|quiv′er|ing
un|quot′ed
un|ranked′
un|ran′somed
un|rat′ed
un|ra′tioned
un|rav′aged
un|razed′
un|reach′a|ble
un|reaped′
un′re|buked′
un′re|called′
un′re|ceiv′a|ble
un′re|cep′tive
un′re|cip′ro|cat′ed
un′re|clined′
un′re|clin′ing
un′re|cord′a|ble
un′re|cruit′ed
un|rec′ti|fied
un′re|deem′a|ble
un′re|dressed′
un′re|duced′
un|reel′a|ble
un′re|flect′ed
un′re|flec′tive
un′re|formed′
un′re|freshed′
un′re|fresh′ing
un′re|frig′er|at′ed
un′re|fund′ed
un′re|fus′a|ble
un′re|fut′ed
un|re′gal
un′re|gard′ful
un|reg′i|ment′ed
un′re|gret′ted
un′re|hearsed′
un′re|im|bursed′
un′re|in|forced′
un′re|ject′ed
un|rel′ished
un|rem′e|died
un′re|mit′ta|ble
un|ren′der|a|ble
un|ren′dered
un′re|nounced′
un′re|nowned′
un|rent′a|ble
un′re|peat′a|ble
un′re|peat′ed
un′re|pent′ing
un′re|placed′
un′re|ply′ing
un′re|port′ed
un′re|proach′able
un′re|proached′
un′re|pro|duc′i|ble
un′re|pu′di|at′ed
un′re|quired′
un′re|scind′ed
un′re|sent′ed
un′re|sent′ful
un′re|signed′
un′re|sist′ant
un′re|source′ful
un′re|spect′ful
un′re|spond′ing
un|rest′ed
un′re|stored′
un′re|strain′a|ble
un′re|sumed′
un′re|tired′
un′re|touched′
un′re|tract′ed
un′re|treat′ing
un′re|trieved′
un′re|turned′
un′re|view′a|ble
un′re|viewed′
un′re|vised′
un′rev|o|lu′tion|ar′y
un′rhe|tor′i|cal
un|rhymed′
un|rhyth′mic
un|ribbed′
un|rich′
un|ri′fled
un|right′a|ble
un|right′ed
un|rig′or|ous
un|rimed′
un|rinsed′
un|ris′en
un|roast′ed
un|roped′
un|rouged′
un|rubbed′
un|rum′pled
un|rust′ed
un|sac′ri|ficed
un|sad′dled
un|sa′lut′ed
un|sam′pled
un|sapped′
un|sat′ed
un|sa′ti|at′ed
un|sa′ti|at′ing
un|sat′is|fi′a|ble
un|sav′a|ble
un|saved′
un|sa′vored
un|sawn′
un|say′a|ble
un|scab′bard|ed
un|scaled′
un|scan′na|ble
un|scared′
un|scar′i|fied
un|scat′tered
un|scent′ed
un|scep′ti|cal
un|sched′uled
un|schol′ar|like′
un|scorched′
un|scored′
un|scorned′
un|scourged′
un|scraped′
un|scrubbed′
un|scru′ti|nized
un|sealed′
un|seamed′
un|seat′ed
un|sec′ond|ed
un|seg′re|gat′ed
un|seiz′a|ble
un′se|lect′ed
un′se|lec′tive
un′sen|sa′tion|al
un|sen′si|tive
un|sen′si|tized
un|sen′su|ous
un|sep′a|rat′ed
un|served′
un|sewed′
un|sewn′
un|sex′u|al
un|sharp′
un|sharp′ened
un|shat′tered
un|shaved′
un|sheathed′
un|shelled′
un|shield′ed
un|shift′ing
un|shock′a|ble
un|shocked′
un|short′ened
un|showed′
un|show′y
un|shroud′ed
un|shrunk′
un|shuf′fled
un|shunt′ed
un|shut′tered
un|si′lenced
un|sim′i|lar
un|sim′pli|fied
un|sim′u|lat|ed
un|singed′
un|skep′ti|cal
un|slacked′
un|slack′ened
un|slaugh′tered
un|sliced′
un|smeared′
un|smoked′
un|smooth′
un|smoothed′
un|smudged′
un|snagged′
un|snob′bish
un|soaked′
un|so′ber
un|sold′
un|sol′dier|like′
un|sol′dier|ly
un′so|lid′i|fied
un|sol′u|ble
un|solv′a|ble
un|soothed′
un|sor′did
un|sound′ed
un|soured′
un|sowed′
un|sown′
un|spe′cial|ized
un|spec′u|la′tive
un|spelled′
un|spiced′
un|splashed′
un|split′
un|spoil′a|ble
un|spoilt′
un|spon′sored
un|sprayed′
un|sprin′kled
un|squan′dered
un|squash′a|ble
un|squeam′ish
un|squeezed′
un|squelched′
un|stain′a|ble
un|stalked′
un|starched′
un|starred′
un|stat′ed
un|stemmed′
un|ster′i|lized
un|stif′fened
un|stig′ma|tized
un|stim′u|lat|ed
un|stim′u|lat|ing
un|stirred′
un|stitched′
un|stocked′
un|stopped′
un|stop′pered
un′stra|te′gic
un|stren′u|ous
un|stripped′
un|stung′
un|styl′ish
un′sub|mit′ted
un′sub|mit′ting
un′sub|scribed′
un|sub′si|dized
un|sug′ared
un′sug|ges′tive
un|sum′moned
un|sunk′
un′su|per|sti′tious
un′su′per|vised
un|sur′faced
un′sur|prised′
un′sur|ren′dered
un′sur|ren′der|ing
un|swal′low|a|ble
un|swal′lowed
un|swol′len
un|syn′chro|nized

**Pronunciation Key:** hat, āge, cãre, fär; let, ēqual, tėrm; it, īce; hot, ōpen, ôrder; oil, out; cup, pu̇t, rüle; child; long; thin; ᴛʜen; zh, measure; ə represents a in about, e in taken, i in pencil, o in lemon, u in circus.

**un|sys′tem|a|tized**
**un|tab′u|lat′ed**
**un|tact′ful**
**un|tagged′**
**un|tan′gled**
**un|ta′pered**
**un|tapped′**
**un|tax′a|ble**
**un|tend′ed**
**un|ter′ri|fied**
**un|teth′ered**
**un|thatched′**
**un|thawed′**
**un′the|at′ri|cal**
**un|thought′ful**
**un|thwart′ed**
**un|tilt′ed**
**un|tinc′tured**
**un|toil′ing**
**un|to′taled**
**un|trad′ed**
**un′tra|di′tion|al**
**un′trans|act′ed**
**un′trans|ferred′**
**un′trans|mit′ted**
**un′trans|port′ed**
**un′trans|posed′**
**un|trapped′**
**un|treas′ured**
**un|treat′ed**
**un|trem′bling**
**un|trust′ing**
**un|tucked′**
**un|tune′ful**
**un|twilled′**
**un|twist′ed**
**un|typ′i|cal**
**un′un|der|stood′**
**un|us′a|ble**
**un|u′ti|liz′a|ble**
**un|u′ti|lized**
**un|vac′il|lat′ing**
**un|val′i|dat′ed**
**un|vault′ed**
**un|vaunt′ed**
**un|veiled′**
**un|ven′tured**
**un|ver′bal|ized**
**un|vi′a|ble**
**un′vic|to′ri|ous**
**un|vin′di|cat′ed**
**un|vi′o|lent**
**un|vis′it|ed**
**un|vi′sored**
**un|vis′u|al|ized**
**un|vi′tal**
**un|vit′ri|fied**
**un|vo′cal|ized**
**un|vol′a|til|ized**
**un|vouched′**
**un|vul′can|ized**
**un|walled′**
**un|wan′ing**
**un|want′ed**
**un|warmed′**
**un|waste′ful**
**un|wast′ing**
**un|watched′**
**un|waxed′**
**un|wear′a|ble**
**un|weath′ered**
**un|weld′ed**
**un|wet′ted**
**un|whet′ted**
**un|whipt′**
**un|wife′like′**
**un|wife′ly**
**un|winc′ing**
**un|win′dowed**
**un|with′er|a|ble**
**un|wom′an|like′**
**un|won′**
**un|wood′ed**
**un|wor′ried**
**un|wound′**
**un|wo′ven**
**un|wreathed′**
**un|wrin′kled**
**un|youth′ful**
**un|zoned′**

**un-²**, *prefix with verbs.* to do the opposite of ______: *Unfasten = to do the opposite of fasten. Undress = to do the opposite of dress.* [Old English *un-, on-*]
▶ **Un-** is used freely to form verbs, and other examples are:

**un|bag′**
**un|bale′**
**un|ban′dage**
**un|bot′tle**
**un|box′**
**un|clamp′**
**un|kink′**
**un|nail′**
**un|peel′**
**un|rust′**
**un|shade′**
**un|shift′**
**un|thick′en**
**un|web′**

**UN** (no periods) or **U.N.**, United Nations: **a** a worldwide organization established in 1945 and devoted to establishing world peace, to promoting economic and social welfare through special agencies, and to creating cultural understanding between nations. It has over 130 members. Its headquarters are in New York City. **b** the nations that belong to this organization.

**un|a|bashed** (un′ə basht′), *adj.* not embarrassed, ashamed, or awed; bold; open: *The unabashed nationalism of these aims has aroused the fiercest opposition* (Harper's). SYN: forward. —**un′a·bash′ed|ly**, *adv.*

**un|a|bat|ed** (un′ə bā′tid), *adj.* not abated or lessened.

**un|a|ble** (un ā′bəl), *adj.* not able; lacking ability or power (to): *A little baby is unable to walk or talk.* SYN: incapable, unfit.

**un|a|bridged** (un′ə brijd′), *adj.* not shortened or condensed; complete: *an unabridged book.*

**un|ac|a|dem|ic** (un′ak ə dem′ik), *adj.* not academic; unconventional, as in literature or art.

**un|ac|cent|ed** (un ak′sen tid, un′ak sen′-), *adj.* not pronounced with force; not accented; not stressed. In *unattended* the second and fourth syllables are unaccented.

**un|ac|cept|a|ble** (un′ak sep′tə bəl), *adj.* not acceptable; unsatisfactory; displeasing; not welcome: *All of the children had behavior problems severe enough to make them socially unacceptable.* (Science News Letter). —**un′ac|cept′a|ble·ness**, *n.* —**un′ac|cept′a|bly**, *adv.*

**un|ac|com|mo|dat|ed** (un′ə kom′ə dā′tid), *adj.* **1** not provided (with): *a few persons still unaccommodated with rooms for the night.* **2** without accommodation or accommodations: *to leave no one unaccommodated.*

**un|ac|com|mo|dat|ing** (un′ə kom′ə dā′ting), *adj.* not accommodating or obliging: *She even liked his rugged manners and his rough, unaccommodating speech* (Lytton Strachey).

**un|ac|com|pa|nied** (un′ə kum′pə nēd), *adj.* **1** not accompanied; alone. SYN: unattended. **2** *Music.* without instrumental accompaniment.

**un|ac|com|plished** (un′ə kom′plisht), *adj.* **1** not accomplished. **2** incomplete; without accomplishments.

**un|ac|count|a|ble** (un′ə koun′tə bəl), *adj.* **1** that cannot be accounted for or explained; inexplicable: *He had an unaccountable foreboding that all was not right* (Frederick Marryat). SYN: incomprehensible. **2** that cannot be held to account; not responsible (for): *An insane person is unaccountable for his actions.* —**un′ac|count′a|ble|ness**, *n.*

**un|ac|count|a|bly** (un′ə koun′tə blē), *adv.* in a manner that cannot be accounted for; strangely: *The chartered jet was roaring down the Orly runway on take-off. Unaccountably, it failed to lift* (Time).

**un|ac|count|ed-for** (un′ə koun′tid fôr′), *adj.* not accounted for or explained: *an unaccounted-for loss of customers.*

**un|ac|cred|it|ed** (un′ə kred′ə tid), *adj.* not accredited; not received; not authorized: *an unaccredited minster or consul.*

**un|ac|cus|tomed** (un′ə kus′təmd), *adj.* **1** not accustomed (to): *a man unaccustomed to public life. Polar bears are unaccustomed to hot weather.* SYN: unused. **2** not familiar; unusual or strange: *unaccustomed surroundings. He was unaccustomed to the routine of his new job.*

**un|ac|knowl|edged** (un′ak nol′ijd), *adj.* not acknowledged; unrecognized; unavowed; unnoticed.

**u|na cor|da** (ü′nə kôr′də), *Music.* using the soft pedal; with the soft pedal depressed. [< Italian *una corda* (literally) one string (because in early pianos the soft pedal shifted the hammers so that they could strike only one string)]

**una corda pedal**, *Music.* soft pedal.

**un|ac|quaint|ance** (un′ə kwān′təns), *n.* lack of acquaintance or familiarity; lack of knowledge; ignorance.

**un|ac|quaint|ed** (un′ə kwān′tid), *adj.* not acquainted. —**un′ac|quaint′ed|ness**, *n.*

**un|ac|quir|a|ble** (un′ə kwīr′ə bəl), *adj.* not acquirable; not to be acquired or gained. —**un′ac|quir′a|ble|ness**, *n.*

**un|ac|quired** (un′ə kwīrd′), *adj.* **1** not acquired. **2** naturally belonging; innate.

**un|act|a|ble** (un ak′tə bəl), *adj.* not capable of being acted (on the stage): *"The Cenci" is no more unactable than "Titus Andronicus" or other of Shakespeare's lesser tragedies which, when they have been put on the stage, have turned out to contain wonderful dramatic matter* (Manchester Guardian).

**un|act|ed** (un ak′tid), *adj.* **1a** not acted or carried out in action; unperformed: *The fault unknown is as a thought unacted* (Shakespeare). **b** not acted (on or upon); undisturbed: *I wish you to peruse it alone and unacted upon by any extraneous influence* (Theodore E. Hook). **2** not performed on the stage: *His plays went unacted for many years.*

**un|a|dapt|a|ble** (un′ə dap′tə bəl), *adj.* not adaptable.

**un|a|dapt|ed** (un′ə dap′tid), *adj.* not adapted; unsuited; unfitted. —**un′a|dapt′ed|ness**, *n.*

**un|ad|dressed** (un′ə drest′), *adj.* not addressed; bearing no address, as a letter.

**un|ad|mired** (un′ad mīrd′), *adj.* not admired; not regarded with affection or respect; not admirable.

**un|a|dorned** (un′ə dôrnd′), *adj.* not adorned; without ornament or embellishment; plain: (*Figurative.*) *unadorned truth. Loveliness Needs not the foreign aid of ornament But is when unadorned adorned the most* (James Thomson).

**un|a|dul|ter|at|ed** (un′ə dul′tə rā′tid), *adj.* not adulterated; pure: *unadulterated flour.* [*She*] *is an unadulterated delight in the principal role of this fantasy* (New Yorker).

**un|ad|ven|tur|ous** (un′əd ven′chər əs), *adj.* not adventurous; not bold or resolute.

**un|ad|vis|a|ble** (un′əd vī′zə bəl), *adj.* = inadvisable.

**un|ad|vised** (un′əd vīzd′), *adj.* **1** not advised; without advice. **2** not prudent or discreet; rash: *It is too rash, too unadvis'd too sudden* (Shakespeare). SYN: imprudent, unwise. **3** = ill-advised.

**un|ad|vis|ed|ly** (un′əd vī′zid lē), *adv.* in an indiscreet manner; without careful consideration; rashly.

**un|ad|vis|ed|ness** (un′əd vī′zid nis), *n.* the character of being unadvised; imprudence; rashness; indiscretion.

**UNAEC** (no periods), United Nations Atomic Energy Commission.

**un|af|fect|ed¹** (un′ə fek′tid), *adj.* not affected; not influenced; unchanged: *Many of these birds seem unaffected by climate* (Alfred R. Wallace). SYN: unmoved, unimpressed. [< *un-*¹ + *affected*¹] —**un′af|fect′ed|ly**, *adv.* —**un′af|fect′ed|ness**, *n.*

**un|af|fect|ed²** (un′ə fek′tid), *adj.* simple and natural; without affectation; straightforward; sincere: *easy, unaffected manners* (Jane Austen). SYN: unpretentious, artless. [< *un-*¹ + *affected*²] —**un′af|fect′ed|ly**, *adv.* —**un′af|fect′ed|ness**, *n.*

**un|af|fil|i|at|ed** (un′ə fil′ē ā′tid), *adj.* not affiliated or associated with; independent: *an unaffiliated labor union, candidate, or radio station.*

**un|a|fraid** (un′ə frād′), *adj.* not afraid; fearless: *The menace of the years finds, and shall find, me unafraid* (William Ernest Henley).

**un|aid|ed** (un ā′did), *adj.* not aided; without help.

**un|al|ien|a|ble** (un āl′yə nə bəl, -ā′lē ə-), *adj.* that cannot be given away or taken away; inalienable: *We hold these truths to be self-evident, that all men are created equal, that they are endowed by their Creator with certain unalienable Rights, that among these are Life, Liberty and the pursuit of Happiness* (Declaration of Independence).

**un|a|ligned** (un′ə līnd′), *adj.* = nonaligned.

**un|a|live** (un′ə līv′), *adj.* **1** not alive. **2** *Figurative.* not awake or sensitive (to): *Dry, mechanical theorists, unalive to sentiment and fancy* (Leigh Hunt).

**un|al|layed** (un′ə lād′), *adj.* **1** not allayed. **2** *Obsolete.* unalloyed.

**un|al|lied** (un′ə līd′), *adj.* not allied; unrelated.

**un|al|loyed** (un′ə loid′), *adj.* that is itself alone; not mixed with or qualified by anything else: (*Figurative.*) *unalloyed generosity.*

**un|al|lur|ing** (un′ə lu̇r′ing), *adj.* **1** not tempting or enticing. **2** not charming; unattractive: *The catalogue is far from handsome, what with poor photographs, crude color, and unalluring typography* (New Yorker).

**un|al|ter|a|ble** (un ôl′tər ə bəl), *adj.* that cannot be altered; not changeable; permanent in nature; fixed: *an unalterable policy.* SYN: immutable. —**un|al′ter|a|ble|ness**, *n.*

**un|al|ter|a|bly** (un ôl′tər ə blē), *adv.* in a way that cannot be changed; permanently: *They recognized that they were now unalterably committed to the meeting, whatever its results might be* (New York Times).

**un|al|tered** (un ôl′tərd), *adj.* not altered; unchanged.

**un|am|big|u|ous** (un′am big′yu̇ əs), *adj.* not ambiguous; unequivocal; plain; clear. —**un′am|big′u|ous|ly**, *adv.*

**un|am|bi|tious** (un′am bish′əs), *adj.* not ambitious; unaspiring; unpretending; modest: *Those who ... pass their days in unambitious indolence* (James Boswell).

**un-A|mer|i|can** (un′ə mer′ə kən), *adj.* not characteristic of or proper to America or the United States; foreign or opposed to the American character, usages, or standards.
▶ See **anti-American** for usage note.

**un-A|mer|i|can|ism** (un′ə mer′ə kə niz′əm), *n.* **1** un-American character, belief, or activity. **2** an un-American custom or trait.

**un|a|mi|a|ble** (un ā′mē ə bəl), *adj.* not amiable; ill-natured; ungracious.

**un|a|mused** (un′ə myüzd′), *adj.* not amused; not entertained; not cheered by diversion or relaxation: *Instead of being unamused by trifles, I am, as I well know I should be, amused by them a great deal too much* (Sydney Smith).

**un|a|mus|ing** (un′ə myü′zing), *adj.* not amusing. —**un′a|mus′ing|ly**, *adv.*

**un|a|neled** (un′ə nēld′), *adj. Archaic.* without having received extreme unction: *to die unaneled.* [< *un-*¹ + *anele* give extreme unction to + *-ed*²]

**un|an|i|mat|ed** (un an′ə mā′tid), *adj.* **1** not animated; not possessed of life. **2** not enlivened; not having spirit; dull; inanimate.

**u|na|nim|i|ty** (yü′nə nim′ə tē), *n.* complete accord or agreement; being unanimous. SYN: harmony.

**u|nan|i|mous** (yü nan′ə məs), *adj.* **1** in complete accord or agreement; mutually agreed: *The children were unanimous in their wish to go to the beach.* **2** showing complete accord; concurred in by all: *She was elected president of her class by a unanimous vote.* [< Latin *ūnanimus* (with English *-ous*) < *ūnus* one + *animus* mind] —**u|nan′i|mous|ness**, *n.*

**u|nan|i|mous|ly** (yü nan′ə məs lē), *adv.* with complete agreement; without a single opposing vote: *The Committee then voted unanimously to send the bill to the Senate floor* (Wall Street Journal).

**un|an|swer|a|ble** (un an′sər ə bəl), *adj.* **1** that cannot be answered; not admitting of any answer or reply: *an unanswerable argument. What remarks he could have made—sarcastic, bitter, unanswerable* (Arnold Bennett). **2** that cannot be disproved: *an unanswerable proof.* SYN: irrefutable, irrefragable. —**un|an′swer|a|ble|ness**, *n.* —**un|an′swer|a|bly**, *adv.*

**un|an|swered** (un an′sərd), *adj.* **1** not answered; not replied to. **2** not proved false or incorrect; not refuted: *an unanswered argument.* **3** not returned.

**un|ap|palled** (un′ə pôld′), *adj.* not appalled; not daunted; fearless; dauntless.

**un|ap|par|ent** (un′ə par′ənt), *adj.* **1** not apparent; obscure: *Bitter actions of despite, too subtle and too unapparent for law to deal with* (Milton).

2 not visible: *The Zoroastrian definition of poetry, mystical, yet exact, "apparent pictures of unapparent natures"* (Emerson).

**un|ap|peal|a|ble** (un′ə pē′lə bəl), *adj.* **1** (of a case) not subject to appeal to a higher court. **2** (of a judge or a sentence or decision) that cannot be appealed against.

**un|ap|peal|ing** (un′ə pē′ling), *adj.* unattractive; devoid of interest or attraction: *Without some correlative understanding in the spectator, Titian's work ... must be utterly dead and unappealing to him* (John Ruskin). **—un′ap|peal′ing|ly,** *adv.*

**un|ap|peas|a|ble** (un′ə pē′zə bəl), *adj.* not to be appeased; implacable; insatiable: *unappeasable hatred.* **—un′ap|peas′a|bly,** *adv.*

**un|ap|peased** (un′ə pēzd′), *adj.* not appeased.

**un|ap|pe|tiz|ing** (un ap′ə tī′zing), *adj.* not appetizing. **—un|ap′pe|tiz′ing|ly,** *adv.*

**un|ap|pre|ci|at|ed** (un′ə prē′shē ā′tid), *adj.* not appreciated; not properly valued or esteemed.

**un|ap|pre|ci|at|ing** (un′ə prē′shē ā′ting), *adj.* not appreciating; unappreciative: *drudging at low rates for unappreciating booksellers* (Charles Lamb).

**un|ap|pre|ci|a|tive** (un′ə prē′shē ā′tiv, -shə tiv), *adj.* not appreciative; wanting in appreciation; inappreciative: *He was a cold-blooded, unappreciative stick* (Leonard Merrick).

**un|ap|pre|hend|ed** (un′ap ri hen′did), *adj.* **1** not apprehended; not taken. **2** not understood, perceived, or conceived of.

**un|ap|pre|hen|sive** (un′ap ri hen′siv), *adj.* **1** not apprehensive; not fearful or suspecting: *Careless of the common danger, and, through a haughty ignorance, unapprehensive of his own* (Milton). **2** not intelligent; not quick in perception or understanding: *Unlearned, unapprehensive, yet impudent* (Milton). **3** unconscious; not cognizant.

**un|ap|prised** (un′ə prīzd′), *adj.* not apprised; not previously informed: *You are not unapprised of the influence of this officer with the Indians* (Thomas Jefferson).

**un|ap|proach|a|bil|i|ty** (un′ə prō′chə bil′ə tē), *n.* the character or condition of being unapproachable.

**un|ap|proach|a|ble** (un′ə prō′chə bəl), *adj.* **1** very hard to approach; coolly aloof; distant: *an unapproachable manner, unapproachable seclusion.* **2** without an equal; unrivaled: *Rembrandt was an artist of unapproachable talent.* **SYN:** peerless, matchless. **—un′ap|proach′a|ble|ness,** *n.* **—un′ap|proach′a|bly,** *adv.*

**un|ap|proached** (un′ə prōcht′), *adj.* not approached; unrivaled.

**un|ap|pro|pri|at|ed** (un′ə prō′prē ā′tid), *adj.* not appropriated; not taken possession of; not assigned or allotted: *No contestant qualified, so the prize remained unappropriated.*

**un|ap|proved** (un′ə prüvd′), *adj.* not approved; not having received approval.

**un|apt** (un apt′), *adj.* **1** not fit or appropriate; unsuitable: *an unapt remark.* **2** not normally likely or inclined; not prone by habit or nature: *a mind unapt to wander.* **3** not skillful or dexterous; awkward; clumsy: *to be unapt with a hammer.* **4** not quick to learn; somewhat backward or stupid. **—un|apt′ly,** *adv.* **—un|apt′ness,** *n.*

**un|ar|gu|a|ble** (un är′gyů ə bəl), *adj.* that cannot be argued with or against; indisputable: *The proposition that talking is better than warring is unarguable* (Wall Street Journal).

**un|ar|gu|a|bly** (un ar′gyů ə blē), *adv.* indisputably: *Master Sergeant Kakuo Shimada was unarguably in command* (New Yorker).

**un|ar|gued** (un är′gyüd), *adj.* **1** not argued or debated. **2** not argued against.

**un|arm** (un ärm′), *v.t.* to take weapons or armor from; disarm: *To unarm his people of weapons, money, and all means whereby they may resist his power* (Sir Walter Raleigh). *—v.i.* **1** to lay down one's weapons. **2** to take off armor: *Unarm, unarm, and do not fight today* (Shakespeare).

**un|armed** (un ärmd′), *adj.* **1** without weapons or armor; not armed: *an unarmed man.* **SYN:** weaponless. **2** without horns, teeth, prickles, spines, or thorns.

**un|ar|mored** (un är′mərd), *adj.* not armored: *an unarmored cruiser.*

**un|ar|moured** (un är′mərd), *adj. Especially British.* unarmored.

**un|art|ful** (un ärt′fəl), *adj.* **1** not artful; artless; not having cunning; guileless; frank; genuine: *I'm sure unartful truth lies open in her mind* (John Dryden). **2** wanting in skill; inartistic.

**un|ar|tis|tic** (un′är tis′tik), *adj.* = inartistic.

**u|na|ry** (yü′nə rē), *adj. Mathematics.* singulary. [blend of Latin *ūnus* one and English *-nary,* as in *binary*]

**un|as|cer|tain|a|ble** (un′as ər tā′nə bəl), *adj.* not ascertainable; that cannot be certainly known, found out, or determined: *The percentage of American makes among small cars is unascertainable* (Harper's).

**un|as|cer|tained** (un′as ər tānd′), *adj.* not ascertained; not certainly known or determined.

**un|a|shamed** (un′ə shāmd′), *adj.* not ashamed; without shame.

**un|a|sham|ed|ly** (un′ə shā′mid lē), *adv.* in an unashamed manner; openly: *At the first run-through she had such power that a critical audience of theatrical professionals was sobbing unashamedly at the final line* (Time).

**un|asked** (un askt′, -äskt′), *adj.* not asked; unsolicited.

**un|as|pi|rat|ed** (un as′pə rā′tid), *adj.* not aspirated; pronounced without an aspirate.

**un|a|spir|ing** (un′ə spīr′ing), *adj.* not aspiring; unambitious. **—un′a|spir′ing|ly,** *adv.* **—un′a|spir′ing|ness,** *n.*

**un|as|sail|a|ble** (un′ə sā′lə bəl), *adj.* not assailable; safe from attack; incontestable. **—un′as|sail′a|bly,** *adv.*

**un|as|sailed** (un′ə sāld′), *adj.* not assailed or attacked.

**un|as|ser|tive** (un′ə sėr′tiv), *adj.* not insistent or forward; reserved in speech or actions: *With the little-known and unassertive Rodger in office, the executive committee would clearly have more authority* (Time). **—un′as|ser′tive|ness,** *n.*

**un|as|sign|a|ble** (un′ə sī′nə bəl), *adj.* not assignable.

**un|as|signed** (un′ə sīnd′), *adj.* not assigned.

**un|as|sim|i|la|ble** (un′ə sim′ə lə bəl), *adj.* that cannot be assimilated: *Major and sometimes marginal uglinesses ... seem unassimilable in art unless they are caricatured* (Louise Bogan).

**un|as|sim|i|lat|ed** (un′ə sim′ə lā′tid), *adj.* **1** not made to resemble; not brought into a relation of similarity. **2** *Physiology.* not united with and actually transformed into the fluid or solid constituents of the living body; not taken into the system as nutriment: *food still unassimilated.*

**un|as|sist|ed** (un′ə sis′tid), *adj.* not assisted; unaided.

**un|as|sum|ing** (un′ə sü′ming), *adj.* not putting on airs; modest: *The people of the village were delighted by the duke's unassuming manner.* **SYN:** humble, unaffected. **—un′as|sum′ing|ly,** *adv.* **—un′as|sum′ing|ness,** *n.*

**un|as|sured** (un′ə shůrd′), *adj.* **1** not assured; not sure, confident, or certain. **2** not securely or safely established. **3** not insured, as against loss.

**un|at|tached** (un′ə tacht′), *adj.* **1** not attached. **2** not connected or associated with a particular body, group, organization, or the like; independent. **3** not engaged or married.

**un|at|tain|a|ble** (un′ə tā′nə bəl), *adj.* not attainable; beyond the possibility of attainment; never to be attained or reached. **—un′at|tain′a|ble|ness,** *n.* **—un′at|tain′a|bly,** *adv.*

**un|at|tained** (un′ə tānd′), *adj.* not attained or reached.

**un|at|taint|ed** (un′ə tān′tid), *adj.* **1** not attainted legally. **2** *Archaic.* unsullied, unblemished, or without defect.

**un|at|tempt|ed** (un′ə temp′tid), *adj.* not attempted; not tried or essayed; not subjected to any attempt.

**un|at|tend|ed** (un′ə ten′did), *adj.* **1** without attendants; alone. **2** not accompanied. **3** not taken care of; not attended to.

**un|at|test|ed** (un′ə tes′tid), *adj.* not attested; not confirmed by witness or testimony.

**un|at|trac|tive** (un′ə trak′tiv), *adj.* not attractive; plain; homely. **—un′at|trac′tive|ly,** *adv.* **—un′at|trac′tive|ness,** *n.*

**u|nau** (yü nô′, ü nou′), *n.* = two-toed sloth. [< French *unau* < a Brazilian native name *unaü;* origin uncertain]

**un|aus|pi|cious** (un′ôs pish′əs), *adj.* = inauspicious.

**un|au|then|tic** (un′ô then′tik), *adj.* not authentic, reliable, or genuine.

**un|au|then|ti|cat|ed** (un′ô then′tə kā′tid), *adj.* not authenticated; not established as authentic.

**un|au|then|tic|i|ty** (un′ô then tis′ə tē), *n.* unauthentic character; want of authenticity.

**un|au|thor|i|ta|tive** (un′ə thôr′ə tā′tiv, -thor′-), *adj.* not authoritative; lacking authority. **—un′au|thor′i|ta′tive|ly,** *adv.* **—un′au|thor′i|ta′tive|ness,** *n.*

**un|au|thor|ized** (un ô′thə rīzd), *adj.* not authorized; not duly commissioned; not warranted by proper authority.

**un|a|vail|a|bil|i|ty** (un′ə vā′lə bil′ə tē), *n., pl.* **-ties. 1** the quality or condition of being unavailable: *Part of the reason for the slow progress with nucleic acids was the unavailability of pure material for analysis* (Scientific American). **2** that which is unavailable: *Faced with commitments, budget limitations, and unavailabilities, he will often make the fatal compromise* (New York Times).

**un|a|vail|a|ble** (un′ə vā′lə bəl), *adj.* **1** not available. **2** of no avail; ineffectual. **3** not suitable or ready for use. **—un′a|vail′a|ble|ness,** *n.*

**un|a|vail|ing** (un′ə vā′ling), *adj.* not successful; useless; futile: *unavailing efforts. The dog kept jumping at the high fence but his attempts to get out of the pen were unavailing.* **SYN:** ineffectual. **—un′a|vail′ing|ly,** *adv.*

**un|a|venged** (un′ə venjd′), *adj.* not avenged.

**un|a|void|a|ble** (un′ə voi′də bəl), *adj.* **1** that cannot be avoided; inevitable: *an unavoidable delay.* **SYN:** inescapable. **2** *Law, Archaic.* not liable to be voided. **—un′a|void′a|ble|ness,** *n.*

**un|a|void|a|bly** (un′ə voi′də blē), *adv.* because of something that cannot or could not be avoided or prevented; inevitably.

**un|a|vowed** (un′ə voud′), *adj.* not avowed; secret.

**un|a|vow|ed|ly** (un′ə vou′id lē), *adv.* in an unavowed manner; secretly.

**un|a|wak|ened** (un′ə wā′kənd), *adj.* not awakened.

**un|a|wak|en|ing** (un′ə wā′kə ning), *adj.* having no awakening: *stretched out ... in eternal, unawakening sleep* (W. H. Hudson).

**un|a|ware** (un′ə wãr′), *adj., adv.* *—adj.* **1** not aware; unconscious: *He was unaware of an approaching storm.* **2** reckless; rash: *And like the rest I grew desperate and unaware* (Shelley). *—adv. Poetic.* unawares. **—un′a|ware′ness,** *n.*

**un|a|wares** (un′ə wãrz′), *adv.* **1** without being expected; by surprise: *The police caught the burglar unawares. Age steals upon us unawares* (Matthew Prior). **SYN:** unexpectedly. **2** without knowing; unintentionally: *to approach danger unawares. Some have entertained angels unawares* **SYN:** unconsciously.

**un|backed** (un bakt′), *adj.* **1** not backed, helped, or supported; unaided. **2** not bet on. **3** *Archaic.* that has never been ridden; not yet broken to the bit, saddle, etc.

**un|bail|a|ble** (un bā′lə bəl), *adj.* not bailable; not admitting of bail, as an offense.

**un|baked** (un bākt′), *adj.* **1** not baked; not yet cooked by baking: *unbaked bread.* **2** *Figurative.* not mature; undeveloped.

**un|bal|ance** (un bal′əns), *n., v.,* **-anced, -anc|ing.** *—n.* lack of balance; unbalanced condition; imbalance. *—v.t.* to throw out of balance; disorder or derange.

**un|bal|anced** (un bal′ənst), *adj.* **1** not balanced. **2** *Figurative.* not entirely sane: *an unbalanced mind.* **3** not having credits equal to debts; not in balance: *an unbalanced account.*

**un|bal|last|ed** (un bal′ə stid), *adj.* **1** not ballasted. **2** *Figurative.* not properly steadied or regulated.

**un|band|ed** (un ban′did), *adj.* having no band, especially in the sense of being stripped of a band, or lacking one where one is needed: *Your bonnet unbanded* (Shakespeare).

**un|bap|tized** (un bap′tīzd), *adj.* not baptized.

**un|bar** (un bär′), *v.t., v.i.,* **-barred, -bar|ring. 1** to remove the bars from; unfasten the bolts of; unlock. **2** *Figurative.* to make possible entry into (a place) or progress along (a way); open up: *to unbar the channels of news.*

**un|barbed** (un bärbd′), *adj.* **1** not having a barb or barbs. **2** *Obsolete.* not shaved, sheared, or mowed.

**un|bar|bered** (un bär′bərd), *adj.* not barbered; unshaven; untrimmed.

**un|bat|ed** (un bā′tid), *adj.* **1** undiminished; unabated: *with unbated zeal* (Scott). **2** *Obsolete.* not blunted or dull: *a sword unbated* (Shakespeare).

**un|bathed** (un bāᵺd′), *adj.* **1** not bathed. **2** not wet.

**un|bear** (un bãr′), *v.t.,* **-bore, -borne** or **-born, -bear|ing.** to free (a horse) from the checkrein (bearing rein).

**un|bear|a|ble** (un bãr′ə bəl), *adj.* that cannot be endured; intolerable: *The pain from a severe toothache is almost unbearable.* **SYN:** insufferable. **—un|bear′a|ble|ness,** *n.*

**un|bear|a|bly** (un bãr′ə blē), *adv.* in an unbearable manner; intolerably.

**un|beard|ed** (un bir′did), *adj.* having no beard; beardless: *the yet unbearded grain* (John Dryden); *th' unbearded youth* (Ben Jonson).

**un|bear|ing** (un bãr′ing), *adj.* infertile; unproductive; barren: *Fruit trees must be continually lacerated to decrease the growth of unbearing wood* (C. R. Smith).

**un|beat|a|ble** (un bē′tə bəl), *adj.* that cannot be beaten, overcome, or surpassed: *The hand was unbeatable, declarer losing only one trick* (New York Times). *The immense strength-weight ratio of beryllium makes it unbeatable for aircraft*

**Pronunciation Key:** hat, āge, cãre, fär; let, ēqual, tėrm; it, īce; hot, ōpen, ôrder; **oi**l, **ou**t; cup, půt, rüle; **ch**ild; lo**ng**; **th**in; **ᵺ**en; **zh**, measure; ə represents **a** in about, **e** in taken, **i** in pencil, **o** in lemon, **u** in circus.

*structures* (New Scientist). *As unbeatable in retirement as he was at El Alamein, Monty scores a breakthrough on the autobiography front* (Time).

**un|beat|a|bly** (un bē′tə blē), *adv.* in an unbeatable manner: *unbeatably fast, unbeatably clever.*

**un|beat|en** (un bē′tən), *adj.* **1** not defeated or surpassed. **2** *Figurative.* not traveled; not trodden: *unbeaten paths.* **3** not struck, pounded, or whipped: *unbeaten eggs.*

**un|beau|ti|ful** (un byü′tə fəl), *adj.* not beautiful; plain; ugly: *Just south of Sennen there is another site, useful but unbeautiful, a caravan park owned by the National Trust* (Listener).

**un|be|com|ing** (un′bi kum′ing), *adj.* **1** not becoming; not appropriate: *unbecoming clothes.* **SYN**: inappropriate. **2** not fitting; not proper; unseemly: *unbecoming behavior.* **SYN**: unsuitable. —**un′be-com′ing|ly**, *adv.* —**un′be|com′ing|ness**, *n.*

**un|be|fit|ting** (un′bi fit′ing), *adj.* not befitting; unbecoming; unseemly. —**un′be|fit′ting|ly**, *adv.* —**un′be|fit′ting|ness**, *n.*

**un|be|friend|ed** (un′bi fren′did), *adj.* not befriended; not supported by friends; having no friendly aid: *Alas for Love! And Truth who wanderest lone and unbefriended* (Shelley).

**un|be|got|ten** (un′bi got′ən), *adj.* not begotten; not born.

**un|be|gun** (un′bi gun′), *adj.* **1** not yet begun. **2** *Obsolete.* having had no beginning; eternal.

**un|be|hold|en** (un′bi hōl′dən), *adj.* **1** not beheld; unseen. **2** not beholden; not under obligation (to).

**un|be|known** (un′bi nōn′), *adj.* **1** not known (to): *We arrived unbeknown to anyone.* **2** without the knowledge of others; in secrecy: *My love rose up so early and stole out unbeknown* (A. E. Housman).

**un|be|knownst** (un′bi nōnst′), *adj.* = unbeknown.

**un|be|lief** (un′bi lēf′), *n.* lack of belief, especially in matters of religious doctrine or faith: *Belief consists in accepting the affirmations of the soul; unbelief, in denying them* (Emerson).

—*Syn.* **Unbelief, disbelief** mean lack of belief. **Unbelief** suggests only lack of belief in something offered or held as true, with no positive feelings one way or the other: *Nowadays there is general unbelief in the idea that some people are witches.* **Disbelief** suggests a positive refusal to believe: *He expressed his disbelief in universal military training.*

**un|be|liev|a|ble** (un′bi lē′və bəl), *adj.* that is beyond belief; not unbelievable; incredible: *He told an unbelievable lie.*

**un|be|liev|a|bly** (un′bi lē′və blē), *adv.* beyond belief; incredibly: *The boy's grandfather is unbelievably old. The last decade has brought the introduction of unbelievably fine petunias* (New York Times).

**un|be|lieved** (un′bi lēvd′), *adj.* **1** not believed, credited, or trusted: *As I, thus wrong'd, hence unbelieved go* (Shakespeare). **2** = incredible.

**un|be|liev|er** (un′bi lē′vər), *n.* **1** a person who does not believe. **2** a person who does not believe in a particular religion. **3** a person who is skeptical of Christ's revelation or mission.

**un|be|liev|ing** (un′bi lē′ving), *adj.* **1** not believing; doubting: *an unbelieving smile.* **SYN**: skeptical, incredulous, suspicious, distrustful. **2** adhering to or inclined toward agnosticism or atheism; not religious. **3** not Christian; infidel; heathen. —**un′be-liev′ing|ly**, *adv.*

**un|be|loved** (un′bi luvd′), *adj.* not beloved.

**un|belt** (un belt′), *v.t.* **1** to remove (a sword) by unfastening the belt. **2** to remove a belt from. **3** *Obsolete.* to ungird; unbind.

**un|bend** (un bend′), *v.*, **-bent** or **-bend|ed, -bend-ing.** —*v.t.* **1** to remove the curves, bends, or wrinkles from; straighten: *a wire hard to unbend, to unbend the fingers.* **2** *Figurative.* to release from strain; cause to relax: *to unbend a bow. She unbent her mind afterwards—over a book* (Charles Lamb). **3** *Nautical.* **a** to untie or loosen (a rope) from its attachment. **b** to unfasten (a sail) from its spar or stay.

—*v.i.* **1** to become straight; straighten: *The wire was hard and it would not unbend.* **2** *Figurative.* to relax: *The judge unbent when he was at home and played games with his children.*

**un|bend|ing** (un ben′ding), *adj., n.* —*adj.* **1** not bending or curving; rigid. **2** *Figurative.* not yielding; stubborn; firm; inflexible: *an unbending attitude.*

—*n.* = relaxation. —**un|bend′ing|ly**, *adv.* —**un-bend′ing|ness**, *n.*

**un|ben|e|ficed** (un ben′ə fist), *adj.* not enjoying or having a benefice.

**un|ben|e|fit|ed** (un ben′ə fit′id), *adj.* having received no benefit or advantage.

**un|be|night|ed** (un′bi nī′tid), *adj.* not benighted; never visited by darkness.

**un|be|nign** (un′bi nīn′), *adj.* not benign; malignant.

**un|bent** (un bent′), *v., adj.* —*v.* a past tense and a past participle of **unbend**.

—*adj.* not bent or curved; unbowed: (*Figurative.*) *her unbent will's majestic pride* (John Greenleaf Whittier).

**un|be|ru|fen** (ün′be rü′fen), *interj. German.* **1** knock wood; hope misfortune will not happen. **2** (literally) uncalled (for).

**un|be|seem|ing** (un′bi sē′ming), *adj.* not beseeming; unbecoming.

**un|be|sought** (un′bi sôt′), *adj.* not besought; not sought by petition or entreaty.

**un|bi|ased** or **un|bi|assed** (un bī′əst), *adj.* not prejudiced; impartial; fair: *an unbiased witness, an unbiased opinion.* **SYN**: disinterested.

**un|bib|li|cal** (un bib′lə kəl), *adj.* not of, according to, or in the Bible: *The custom of representing Faith and Reason as opposites, is unbiblical and pernicious* (Edward White).

**un|bid** (un bid′), *adj.* = unbidden.

**un|bid|da|ble** (un bid′ə bəl), *adj.* **1** *British.* not to be commanded; not obedient: *The unbiddable spirit of perfection might come or it might not* (Paul Jennings). **2** (of a hand or suit in cards) not strong enough to justify a bid.

**un|bid|den** (un bid′ən), *adj.* **1** without invitation; not invited: *an unbidden guest.* **2** without being ordered; not commanded: *And beasts themselves would worship; camels knelt unbidden* (Tennyson).

**un|bind** (un bīnd′), *v.t.*, **-bound, -bind|ing.** to release from bonds or restraint; let loose; untie; unfasten. **SYN**: detach, loosen, free. [Old English *unbindan* < *un-* un-[2] + *bindan* to bind]

**un|bit|ted** (un bit′id), *adj.* **1** unbridled; unrestrained: *conflicts of unbitted nature with too rigid custom* (Robert Louis Stevenson). **2** freed of the bit: *an unbitted horse.*

**un|blam|a|ble** or **un|blame|a|ble** (un blā′mə-bəl), *adj.* not blamable; blameless. —**un|blam′a-ble|ness, un|blame′a|ble|ness**, *n.* —**un|blam′a-bly, un|blame′a|bly**, *adv.*

**un|blamed** (un blāmd′), *adj.* not blamed; free from censure; innocent: *So ... unblamed a life* (Ben Jonson).

**un|bleached** (un blēcht′), *adj.* not bleached; not made white by bleaching: *unbleached linen.*

**un|blem|ished** (un blem′isht), *adj.* not blemished; without blemish; spotless; flawless; unsullied: *unblemished integrity* (Macaulay).

**un|blenched** (un blencht′), *adj.* **1** = unflinching. **2** not soiled; unstained.

**un|blessed** or **un|blest** (un blest′), *adj.* **1** not favored or made happy; not blessed: *unblessed with children, unblessed by laughter.* **2** that has not been consecrated; not holy: *unblessed ground.* **3** deprived of or excluded from blessing or benediction: *And there his corpse, unblessed, is hanging still* (John Dryden). **4** unholy; evil; wicked. **5** unhappy; miserable; wretched.

**un|blink|ing** (un bling′king), *adj.* **1** not blinking; remaining open: *I can still see Mama watching him, her hand pressed tight across her mouth, her eyes wide and unblinking* (Atlantic). **2** *Figurative.* without flinching or wavering; steady: *He looks over his twelve Caesars, from Julius to Domitian, with a methodical eye, unblinking in the face of some of the most outrageous spectacles in history* (Newsweek). **3** *Figurative.* forthright; candid: *an unblinking study of two wild days in the dull, woolly middle-class lives of Mark and Antonia Painton* (New Yorker). —**un|blink′ing|ly**, *adv.*

**un|block** (un blok′), *v.t.* **1** to release from obstruction; remove the obstruction from: *to unblock a dam. London was once again the world antiques capital, with relaxed British trade restrictions unblocking the flow of merchandise to and from the highly esteemed London dealers* (Newsweek). **2** (in bridge) to permit (a suit in another hand) to be run: *By discarding his singleton ace of spades, the declarer unblocked dummy's spades.*

**un|blood|ied** (un blud′id), *adj.* not made bloody.

**un|blot|ted** (un blot′id), *adj.* **1** not blotted. **2** *Figurative.* not blotted out; not deleted; not erased.

**un|blown**[1] (un blōn′), *adj.* **1** not driven, tossed, or fanned by the wind: *... on fields of unblown mist* (Bayard Taylor). **2** not sounded, as a wind instrument: *The tents were all silent, the banners alone, the lances unlifted, the trumpet unblown* (Byron).

**un|blown**[2] (un blōn′), *adj.* **1** (of flowers) unopened; still in the bud: *The little flowers which we see unblown in the morning and withered at night* (Arthur Golding). **2** *Figurative.* not matured; young; inchoate: *How yet unripe we were, unblown, unhardened* (John Fletcher).

**un|blurred** (un blėrd′), *adj.* not blurred; distinct: *The sky was absolutely unblurred, and thick ... with stars* (Sabine Baring-Gould).

**un|blush|ing** (un blush′ing), *adj.* **1** not blushing or reddening. **2** *Figurative.* not unabashed; shameless: *unblushing servility.* **SYN**: unabashed, brazen, impudent. —**un|blush′ing|ly**, *adv.*

**un|boast|ful** (un bōst′fəl), *adj.* not boasting; unassuming; modest.

**un|bod|ied** (un bod′ēd), *adj.* **1** not having a body; incorporeal. **2** removed from the body; disembodied.

**un|bolt** (un bōlt′), *v.t., v.i.* to draw back the bolts of (a door, etc.); unbar; unlock: *to unbolt the gate.*

**un|bolt|ed**[1] (un bōl′tid), *adj.* not bolted or fastened; unlocked: *an unbolted door.*

**un|bolt|ed**[2] (un bōl′tid), *adj.* **1** not sifted: *unbolted flour.* **2** *Obsolete, Figurative.* rough and dirty; lacking any refinement; coarse: *I will tread this unbolted villain into mortar* (Shakespeare).

**un|bon|net** (un bon′it), *v.i.* to take off the bonnet; uncover the head, as in respect. —*v.t.* to take off the bonnet from.

**un|bon|net|ed** (un bon′ə tid), *adj.* wearing no bonnet or cap; bareheaded.

**un|booked** (un bu̇kt′), *adj.* not engaged; having no engagements: *There was not an unbooked day during the time, and the crowds were enormous and enthusiastic* (Maclean's).

**un|book|ish** (un bu̇k′ish), *adj.* **1** not bookish; not given to reading. **2** = unlearned.

**un|bore** (un bôr′, -bōr′), *v.* the past tense of **unbear**.

**un|born** (un bôrn′), *adj., v.* —*adj.* not yet born; still to come; of the future: *unborn generations.* —*v.* a past participle of **unbear**.

**un|borne** (un bôrn′, -bōrn′), *v.* a past participle of **unbear**.

**un|bos|om** (un bu̇z′əm, -bü′zəm), *v.t.* to reveal; disclose. —*v.i.* to speak frankly and at length: *the last person to whom he could unbosom* (George Meredith).

**unbosom oneself**, to tell or reveal one's thoughts, feelings, secrets, plans, or troubles: *to unbosom himself of his great secret* (Thackeray). [< *un-*[2] + *bosom*, verb] —**un|bos′om|er**, *n.*

**un|bot|tomed** (un bot′əmd), *adj.* = bottomless.

**un|bought** (un bôt′), *adj.* **1** not bought; not acquired by purchase. **2** not hired or bribed.

**un|bound**[1] (un bound′), *v.* the past tense and past participle of **unbind**.

**un|bound**[2] (un bound′), *adj.* not bound: *Unbound sheets of music were scattered about the room.* [< *un-*[1] + *bound*[1]]

**un|bound|ed** (un boun′did), *adj.* **1** not limited; very great; boundless: *the unbounded reaches of the universe. Unbounded courage and compassion join'd ... make the hero and the man complete* (Joseph Addison). **SYN**: infinite. **2** not kept within limits; not controlled.

**un|bowed** (un boud′), *adj.* **1** not bowed or bent. **2** *Figurative.* not forced to yield or submit; not subdued: *Under the bludgeonings of chance My head is bloody but unbowed* (William E. Henley).

**un|brace** (un brās′), *v.t.*, **-braced, -brac|ing. 1** to loosen or untie (as a band or belt); undo. **2** *Figurative.* to free (oneself, especially the heart or mind) from tension; relax. **3** to render feeble; weaken.

**un|braced** (un brāst′), *adj.* not braced.

**un|braid** (un brād′), *v.t.* to separate the strands of; unwind or unravel.

**un|branched** (un brancht′, -bräncht′), *adj.* not branched; not provided with branches.

**un|brave** (un brāv′), *adj.* cowardly; fearful: *He was a gentle man but strong and not unbrave* (Truman Capote). *All in all, they are pushing us toward a singularly unbrave new world* (Atlantic).

**un|break|a|ble** (un brā′kə bəl), *adj.* not breakable; not easily broken: *Some plastic phonograph records are unbreakable.*

**un|breathed** (un brēᴛʜd′), *adj.* not uttered or whispered; unspoken.

**un|bred** (un bred′), *adj.* not properly bred or brought up; ill-bred.

**un|breeched** (un brēcht′), *adj.* **1** not breeched; wearing no breeches: *a parcel of unbreeched heathen* (Herman Melville). **2** not yet wearing breeches, as a young boy.

**un|brib|a|ble** (un brī′bə bəl), *adj.* not bribable.

**un|bri|dle** (un brī′dəl), *v.t.*, **-dled, -dling. 1** to remove the bridle from (a horse). **2** *Figurative.* to free (a person or his faculties) from restraint: *The right approach to mathematics, then, is to unbridle the imagination* (Harper's).

**un|bri|dled** (un brī′dəld), *adj.* **1** not having a bridle on. **2** *Figurative.* not controlled; not restrained: *unbridled anger.*

**un|broke** (un brōk′), *adj.* = unbroken.

**un|bro|ken** (un brō′kən), *adj.* **1** not broken; whole: *an unbroken dish.* **SYN**: entire, intact. **2** not interrupted; continuous: *I had eight hours of unbroken sleep.* **3** not tamed; not yet broken, as to the bit and saddle: *an unbroken colt.* —**un|bro′-ken|ly**, *adv.* —**un|bro′ken|ness**, *n.*

**un|broth|er|ly** (un bruᴛʜ′ər lē), *adj.* not brotherly; not befitting a brother.

**un|buck|le** (un buk′əl), *v.*, **-led, -ling.** —*v.t.* **1** to

unfasten the buckle or buckles of: *A miser, who will not unbuckle his purse to bestow a farthing* (Scott). **2** to unfasten; detach.
– *v.i.* to unbend; become less stiff: (*Figurative.*) *Even the captain ... would unbuckle a bit and tell me of the fine countries he had visited* (Robert Louis Stevenson).

**un|budg|ing** (un buj′ing), *adj.* not budging; inflexible; unyielding: *What made the thing I saw so specially terrible to me was the metallic necessity, the unbudging fatality which governed it* (Herman Melville). – **un|budg′ing|ly**, *adv.*

**un|build** (un bild′), *v.t.*, **-built, -build|ing.** **1** to take apart; dismember. **2** to pull down; demolish.

**un|built**[1] (un bilt′), *adj.* not yet or ever built.

**un|built**[2] (un bilt′), *v.* the past tense and past participle of **unbuild**.

**un|bun|dle** (un bun′dəl), *v.t., v.i.*, **-dled, -dling.** to set separate prices for the parts of anything usually sold as a package: ... *IBM's decision to unbundle computer marketing so that it will eventually charge separately for computers and for the programs that make them work* (New Scientist).

**un|bur|den** (un bėr′dən), *v.t.* **1** to free from a burden. **2** *Figurative.* to relieve (one's mind or heart) by talking: *Tomorrow I die, and today I would unburden my soul* (Edgar Allan Poe). **3** *Figurative.* to throw off or disclose (something that burdens).

**un|bur|ied**[1] (un ber′ēd), *adj.* not buried.

**un|bur|ied**[2] (un ber′ēd), *v.* the past tense and past participle of **unbury**.

**un|burned** (un bėrnd′), *adj.* **1** not burned; not consumed or injured by fire. **2** not baked, as brick.

**un|burnt** (un bėrnt′), *adj.* = unburned.

**un|bur|y** (un ber′ē), *v.t.*, **-bur|ied, -bur|y|ing.** to take out of the place of burial; disinter; exhume.

**un|busi|ness|like** (un biz′nis līk′), *adj.* without system and method; not efficient.

**un|but|ton** (un but′ən), *v.t.* to unfasten the button or buttons of.

**un|but|toned** (un but′ənd), *adj.* **1** not buttoned; open: *an unbuttoned shirt or coat.* **2** *Figurative.* open and free; easy; casual: *He had had all too much of the unbuttoned, cozy, secure little world of the university* (New Yorker).

**U.N.C.** or **UNC** (no periods), United Nations Command.

**un|cage** (un kāj′), *v.t.*, **-caged, -cag|ing.** **1** to release from a cage. **2** *Figurative.* to release.

**un|called** (un kôld′), *adj.* not called; not summoned or invited: *to come uncalled.*

**un|called-for** (un kôld′fôr′), *adj.* **1** unnecessary and improper; impertinent: *an uncalled-for remark.* **2** not called for; not requested.

**un|can|celed** (un kan′səld), *adj.* not canceled.

**un|can|did** (un kan′did), *adj.* not candid; disingenuous.

**un|can|ny** (un kan′ē), *adj.* **1** strange and mysterious; weird; eerie: *The trees took uncanny shapes in the half darkness.* **SYN:** See syn. under **weird.** **2** so far beyond what is normal or expected as to have some special power: *Our teacher has an uncanny knack for solving math problems in his head.* **3** *Scottish.* **a** unpleasantly severe; painful. **b** unsafe; dangerous. – **un|can′ni|ly**, *adv.* – **un|can′ni|ness**, *n.*

**un|ca|non|i|cal** (un′kə non′ə kəl), *adj.* not belonging to the canon (of Scripture); not canonical: *The popular demand for uncanonical rites and offices is a good theme for meditation* (Manchester Guardian Weekly).

**un|cap** (un kap′), *v.t.*, **-capped, -cap|ping.** **1** to take the cap, top, or protective covering off of: *to uncap a bottle.* **2** to remove the hat from (the head, hair, or a person). **3** *Figurative.* to disclose or reveal: *to uncap a surprise or a secret.*

**un|ca|pa|ble** (un kā′pə bəl), *adj. Obsolete.* incapable.

**un|cared-for** (un kārd′fôr′), *adj.* not cared for or looked after; neglected.

**un|care|ful** (un kãr′fəl), *adj.* **1** careless: *Thus, all that we suspected as likely to happen under an uncareful program of disarmament did happen* (Bulletin of Atomic Scientists). **2** not taking any thought (of). **3** free from care; untroubled: *One of the ... most uncareful interludes of my life* (Hawthorne).

**un|car|pet|ed** (un kär′pə tid), *adj.* not carpeted.

**un|cart** (un kärt′), *v.t.* to remove or unload from a cart.

**un|case** (un kās′), *v.t.*, **-cased, -cas|ing.** **1** to take out of a case; remove the case or covering from; strip; uncover; lay bare. **2** *Figurative.* to disclose or reveal.

**un|cashed** (un kasht′), *adj.* **1** not exchanged for cash; unsettled: *an uncashed check.* **2** not yet played (said of a card certain to take a trick in bridge).

**un|cat|a|loged** or **un|cat|a|logued** (un kat′ə-lôgd, -logd), *adj.* not cataloged: *For the location of ... an uncatalogued item, your librarian has a ferret's nose* (Atlantic).

**un|cate** (ung′kāt, -kit), *adj.* hooked; uncinate. [< Latin *uncātus* < *uncus* hook]

**un|cath|o|lic** (un kath′ə lik, -kath′lik), *adj., n.* – *adj.* **1** not catholic or universal; limited: *Paradoxical indeed how many of us Catholics can be so uncatholic in our application of freedom* (Harper's). **2** not Roman Catholic.
– *n.* a person who is not a Roman Catholic.

**un|caused** (un kôzd′), *adj.* not caused; self-existent.

**un|ceas|ing** (un sē′sing), *adj.* not or never ceasing; continuous; constant: *unceasing labor, unceasing rain.* – **un|ceas′ing|ly**, *adv.*

**un|ce|les|tial** (un′sə les′chəl), *adj.* not celestial or heavenly; worldly; mundane: *any uncelestial envy or malice* (Anthony Trollope).

**un|cer|e|mo|ni|ous** (un′ser ə mō′nē əs), *adj.* **1** not ceremonious; informal. **2** not as courteous as would be expected; somewhat abrupt, peremptory, etc. – **un′cer|e|mo′ni|ous|ly**, *adv.* – **un′cer|e|mo′ni|ous|ness**, *n.*

**uncert.**, uncertain.

**un|cer|tain** (un sėr′tən), *adj.* **1** not known with certainty; not finally established; in doubt; dubious: *The election results were still uncertain.* **2** not sure; doubtful: *to be uncertain if a candidate will win. She came so late that she was uncertain of her welcome.* **3** likely to change; not to be depended upon; not reliable: *This dog has an uncertain temper.* **4** not constant; varying: *an uncertain flicker of light.* **5** not clearly identified, located, or determined; vague; indefinite: *an uncertain shape.* **6** not settled or fixed; indeterminate: *a job with an uncertain future.* **7** that may not happen. – **un|cer′tain|ness**, *n.*
– *Syn.* **1, 2 Uncertain, insecure** mean not sure in some way or about something. **Uncertain** implies not knowing definitely or surely about something or not having complete confidence in a thing, person, or oneself, and thus suggests the presence of doubt: *His plans for the summer are uncertain.* **Insecure** implies not being protected from or guarded against danger or loss, and suggests the presence of fear or anxiety: *Her position at the bank is insecure.*

**un|cer|tain|ly** (un sėr′tən lē), *adv.* in an uncertain manner: *He spoke slowly and uncertainly.* **SYN:** hesitatingly.

**un|cer|tain|ty** (un sėr′tən tē), *n., pl.* **-ties.** **1** uncertain quality or condition; doubt. **2** something uncertain.

**uncertainty principle**, the principle in quantum mechanics that certain coordinates of a single physical object, such as the position and velocity of an electron, can never be accurately determined simultaneously. Also, **Heisenberg uncertainty principle.**

**un|cer|tif|i|cat|ed** (un′sər tif′ə kā′tid), *adj.* not certificated; without certification.

**un|cer|ti|fied** (un sėr′tə fīd), *adj.* not certified; without certification.

**un|chain** (un chān′), *v.t.* to free from chains; let loose; set free: (*Figurative.*) *Until the spring Unchains the streams* (William Morris).

**un|chain|a|ble** (un chā′nə bəl), *adj.* incapable of being chained or held in restraint: (*Figurative.*) *We ... abide Unchainable as the dim tide* (William Butler Yeats).

**un|chained** (un chānd′), *adj.* not chained; unfettered; free.

**un|chal|lenge|a|ble** (un chal′ən jə bəl), *adj.* not capable of being challenged or opposed; certain; secure: *The Soviet Union is now most seriously challenging the supposedly unchallengable industrial might of the United States* (Time). *Mathematics could be saved from internal discord and from external pressures by becoming part of the unchallengeable science of logic* (Scientific American).

**un|chal|lenge|a|bly** (un chal′ən jə blē), *adv.* in an unchallengeable way; securely; indisputably: *Our freedom must be buttressed by a homogeny equally and unchallengeably free* (William Faulkner).

**un|chal|lenged** (un chal′ənjd), *adj.* not challenged; not called in question; not called to account.

**un|chanc|y** (un chan′sē, -chän′-), *adj. Scottish.* **1** not safe to meddle with; dangerous. **2** ill-timed. **3** ill-fated.

**un|change|a|ble** (un chān′jə bəl), *adj.* not changeable; that cannot be changed: *'Tis the immortal thought Whose passion still Makes of the unchanging The unchangeable* (Ford Madox Ford). **SYN:** immutable, unalterable, invariable. – **un|change′a|ble|ness**, *n.* – **un|change′a|bly**, *adv.*

**un|changed** (un chānjd′), *adj.* not changed; the same: *unchanged tradition.*

**un|chang|ing** (un chān′jing), *adj.* not changing; always the same. – **un|chang′ing|ly**, *adv.*

**un|chap|e|roned** (un shap′ə rōnd), *adj.* not chaperoned; without a chaperon.

**un|char|ac|ter|is|tic** (un′kar ək tə ris′tik), *adj.* not characteristic; not typical, natural, or usual in the particular instance: *With uncharacteristic mildness, he admitted that he had cut down his output* (Newsweek). – **un′char|ac|ter|is′ti|cal|ly**, *adv.*

**un|charge** (un chärj′), *v.t.*, **-charged, -charg|ing.** **1** to unload (a vessel). **2** to declare free of guilt; acquit.

**un|charged** (un chärjd′), *adj.* **1** not charged or loaded with powder or shot: *You have left me in a fair field standing, and in my hand an uncharged gun* (Francis J. Child). **2** not charged with electrical energy: *Ordinary matter does not exhibit electrical effects and is said to be ... neutral or uncharged* (Sears and Zemansky). **3** *Figurative.* not burdened (with): *The national desire* [*is*] *to be at any rate uncharged with responsibility* (Westminster Gazette). **4** not formally accused. **5** not subjected to a financial charge: *uncharged services.* **6** unassailed: *Open your uncharged ports* (Shakespeare).

**un|char|i|ta|ble** (un char′ə tə bəl), *adj.* not generous; not charitable; severe; harsh: *I hated them with the bitter, uncharitable condemnation of boyhood* (H. G. Wells). – **un|char′i|ta|ble|ness**, *n.*

**un|char|i|ta|bly** (un char′ə tə blē), *adv.* in an uncharitable manner; without charity.

**un|char|i|ty** (un char′ə tē), *n.* want of charity; uncharitable feeling.

**un|charm|ing** (un chär′ming), *adj.* lacking charm; unpleasant; disagreeable: *Old, uncharming Catherine* (John Dryden). [*His*] *contempt for women may strike some people as uncharming* (Punch).

**un|chart|ed** (un chär′tid), *adj.* not mapped; not marked on a chart.

**un|char|tered** (un chär′tərd), *adj.* **1** not chartered; without a charter: *an unchartered company.* **2** without license or regulation.

**un|char|y** (un chãr′ē), *adj.* not chary; not frugal; not careful; heedless.

**un|chaste** (un chāst′), *adj.* not chaste; not virtuous. – **un|chaste′ly**, *adv.*

**un|chas|ti|ty** (un chas′tə tē), *n.* lack of chastity; unchaste character; lewdness.

**un|checked** (un chekt′), *adj.* not checked; not restrained.

**un|cheer|ful** (un chir′fəl), *adj.* not cheerful: **a** sad; gloomy; melancholy. **b** not willing; grudging: *uncheerful service.*

**un|chiv|al|rous** (un shiv′əl rəs), *adj.* not chivalrous; ungallant. – **un|chiv′al|rous|ly**, *adv.*

**un|chris|tian** (un kris′chən), *adj.* **1** not Christian; heathen; pagan. **2** unworthy of Christians; at variance with Christian principles: *a demand ... that war might be declared unchristian* (John R. Green). **3** *Informal.* such as any civilized person would object to; barbarous: *to rout someone out of bed at a most unchristian hour.*

**un|church** (un chėrch′), *v.t.* **1** to expel from a church; deprive of church rights and privileges; excommunicate. **2** to refuse the name or character of church to.

**un|churched** (un chėrcht′), *adj., n.* – *adj.* **1** having no church. **2** excluded from a church. **3** not belonging to or affiliated with a church: *Surveys ... showed that more than half of the population of New York was unchurched* (New York Times).
– *n.* people who do not belong to or affiliate with a church; unchurched people, collectively: [*He*] *became even more convinced of the need to reach the nation's unchurched* (Time).

**un|church|ly** (un chėrch′lē), *adj.* not suitable or proper in or for a church: *unchurchly conduct.*

**un|ci** (un′sī), *n.* plural of **uncus.**

***uncial**
*adj.*, definition 2

The World Book Dictionary

***un|ci|al** (un′shē əl, -shəl), *n., adj.* – *n.* **1** an old style of writing, resembling modern capital letters but heavier and more rounded, found especially in Latin and Greek manuscripts from about the 300's to 800's A.D. **2** a letter in this style. **3** a manuscript written in this style or with such letters.
– *adj.* **1** of or having to do with this style or such letters. **2** written in this style or such letters. [< Late Latin *unciāles* (*litterae*) uncial (letters); the exact sense of *uncia* is not known] – **un′ci|al|ly**, *adv.*

**Pronunciation Key:** hat, āge, cãre, fär; let, ēqual, tėrm; it, īce; hot, ōpen, ôrder; oil, out; cup, pu̇t, rüle; child; long; thin; ᴛʜen; zh, measure; ə represents a in about, e in taken, i in pencil, o in lemon, u in circus.

**un|ci|form** (un′sə fôrm), *adj., n.* —*adj.* **1** hook-shaped. **2** *Anatomy.* denoting or having to do with the hamate bone, its hooklike process, or any similar hooklike process.
—*n. Anatomy.* the hamate bone.
[< New Latin *unciformis* < Latin *uncus* hook + *forma* form]

**unciform process**, *Anatomy.* **1** the process projecting from the palmar surface of the hamate bone. **2** a hook-shaped process of the ethmoid bone.

**un|ci|nal** (un′sə nəl), *adj.* = uncinate.

**un|ci|na|ri|a|sis** (un′sə nə rī′ə sis), *n.* = hookworm disease. [< New Latin *Uncinaria* the hookworm genus (< Latin *uncīnus* hook < *uncus* hook) + *-iasis*]

**un|ci|nate** (un′sə nit, -nāt), *adj.* bent at the end like a hook; hooked. [< Latin *uncīnātus* < *uncīnus* hook, barb (diminutive) < *uncus* hook]

**un|ci|nat|ed** (un′sə nā′tid), *adj.* = uncinate.

**un|ci|nus** (un sī′nəs), *n., pl.* **-ni** (-nī). any hook-shaped part or process. [< Latin *uncīnus* hook, barb]

**UNCIO** (no periods), United Nations Conference on International Organization.

**un|cir|cum|cised** (un sėr′kəm sīzd), *adj.* **1** not circumcised. **2** not Jewish; Gentile. **3** *Figurative.* heathen; pagan.

**un|cir|cum|ci|sion** (un′sėr kəm sizh′ən), *n.* **1** the condition of not being circumcised (in the Bible, Romans 2:25). **2** the Gentiles (in the Bible, Romans 2:26).

**un|civ|il** (un siv′əl), *adj.* **1** not civil; rude; impolite; discourteous: *I hope it's not uncivil to say that you ... ought to be in jail* (G. K. Chesterton). **SYN**: unmannerly. **2** = uncivilized. **SYN**: barbarian. —**un-civ′il|ly**, *adv.*

**un|civ|i|lized** (un siv′ə līzd), *adj.* not civilized; barbarous; savage: *The cave men of Europe were uncivilized hunters and fishermen of the Stone Age.*

**un|clad**[1] (un klad′), *adj.* not dressed; not clothed; naked. [< *un-*[1] + *clad*[1]]

**un|clad**[2] (un klad′), *v.* a past tense and past participle of **unclothe**.

**un|claimed** (un klāmd′), *adj.* not claimed.

**un|clar|i|ty** (un klar′ə tē), *n.* lack of clarity; indistinctness.

**un|clasp** (un klasp′, -kläsp′), *v.t.* **1** to unfasten. **2** to release from a clasp or grasp: *She clasped and unclasped her fingers while nervously waiting for the dentist.*
—*v.i.* **1** to unfasten. **2** to be released from a clasp or grasp: *I feel my feeble hands unclasp* (Longfellow).

**un|clas|si|fi|a|ble** (un klas′ə fī′ə bəl), *adj.* not classifiable.

**un|clas|si|fied** (un klas′ə fīd), *adj.* not classified.

**un|cle** (ung′kəl), *n., interj.* —*n.* **1** the brother of one's father or mother. See picture under **family tree**. **2** the husband of one's aunt. **3** *Informal.* an elderly man. **4** *Slang.* a pawnbroker.
—*interj. Informal.* I (or we) surrender!
**cry (holler** or **say) uncle**, *Informal.* to admit defeat; surrender: *The increasing desire of some businesses to cry uncle when the pinch is on* (Wall Street Journal).
[< Anglo-French *uncle*, Old French *oncle* < Latin *avunculus* one's mother's brother (diminutive) < *avus* (maternal) grandfather]

**un|clean** (un klēn′), *adj.* **1** not clean; dirty; soiled; filthy. **2** not pure morally; evil: *Woe is me! ... because I am a man of unclean lips* (Isaiah 6:5). **3** not ceremonially clean: *The Gentiles were no longer common or unclean* (Cardinal Newman). [Old English *unclǣne* < *un-* un-[1] + *clǣne* clean]
—**un|clean′ness**, *n.*

**un|cleaned** (un klēnd′), *adj.* not cleaned.

**un|clean|li|ness** (un klen′lē nis), *n.* lack of cleanliness; dirtiness; filthiness; foulness.

**un|clean|ly**[1] (un klen′lē), *adj.* not cleanly; unclean. [Old English *unclǣnlīc* < *un-* un-[1] + *clǣnlīc* cleanly[1]]

**un|clean|ly**[2] (un klēn′lē), *adv.* in an unclean manner. [Old English *unclǣnlīce* < *unclǣne* (see etym. under **unclean**) + *līce* -ly[1]]

**un|clear** (un klir′), *adj.* not clear; clouded; obscure; indistinct; uncertain: *unclear words, unclear penmanship.* —**un|clear′ly**, *adv.*

**un|cleared** (un klird′), *adj.* not cleared.

**un|clench** (un klench′), *v.t.* to open from a clenched condition: *to unclench one's fists.*
—*v.i.* to become opened from a clenched condition: *I saw her hands clench and unclench spasmodically* (W. Somerset Maugham).

**Uncle Sam**, *Informal.* the government or people of the United States. Uncle Sam is usually drawn in pictures as a tall, thin man with white chin whiskers, wearing a top hat, a blue swallow-tailed coat, and red-and-white striped pants: *Uncle Sam is rather despotic as to the disposal of my time* (Hawthorne). [American English, an expansion of US, initials of the United States]

**Uncle Tom**, **1** the central character of Harriet Beecher Stowe's antislavery novel *Uncle Tom's Cabin* (1851-52), a humble, pious, long-suffering Negro slave. **2** *U.S.* a Negro thought of as having the timid, servile attitude of a slave in his relations with whites (used in an unfriendly way).

**Un|cle-Tom** (ung′kəl tom′), *v.i.,* **-Tommed, -Tomming.** *U.S.* to act as an Uncle Tom. Also, **Tom**.

**Uncle Tomism**, *U.S.* a Negro attitude of compromise, gradualism, or half-hearted interest in the struggle to obtain full civil rights and abolish racial discrimination: *Negroes consider Uncle Tomism their most regressive trait* (Time). Also, **Tomism**.

**un|clinch** (un klinch′), *v.t., v.i.* = unclench.

**un|clip** (un klip′), *v.t.,* **-clipped, -clip|ping. 1** to remove a clip from. **2** to unfasten.

**un|cloak** (un klōk′), *v.t.* **1** to remove the coat from; divest of a cloak. **2** *Figurative.* to reveal; expose: *to uncloak a scoundrel.*
—*v.i.* to take off the cloak or outer garment.

**un|clog** (un klog′), *v.t.,* **-clogged, -clog|ging.** to free from a clog or from anything that clogs.

**un|close** (un klōz′), *v.t., v.i.,* **-closed, -clos|ing.** = open.

**un|closed** (un klōzd′), *adj.* **1** not closed: *His unclosed eye yet lowering on his enemy* (Byron). **2** not finished; not brought to a close. **3** *Figurative.* not balanced; not settled: *I don't love to leave any Part of the Account unclos'd* (Sir Richard Steele).

**un|clothe** (un klōᴛʜ′), *v.t.,* **-clothed** or **-clad, -cloth|ing. 1** to strip of clothes; undress. **2** *Figurative.* to lay bare; uncover.

**un|clothed** (un klōᴛʜd′), *adj.* not clothed; naked; bare.

**un|cloud|ed** (un klou′did), *adj.* not clouded; free from clouds; clear. —**un|cloud′ed|ness**, *n.*

**un|club|ba|ble** or **un|club|a|ble** (un klub′ə bəl), *adj.* unfit to be a member of a club; unsociable: *Sir John was a most unclubable man* (Samuel Johnson).

**un|clut|ter** (un klut′ər), *v.t.* to make uncluttered; make neat: *Our purpose is ... to unclutter the landscape* (Atlantic).

**un|clut|tered** (un klut′ərd), *adj.* in order; not littered; neat: *Greece is of all countries the most uncluttered* (Eleanor Perényi).

**un|co** (ung′kō), *adv., adj., n., pl.* **-cos.** *Scottish.*
—*adv.* remarkably; very; extremely.
—*adj.* **1** unknown, strange, or unusual: *It was an unco thing to bid a mother leave her ain house* (Scott). **2** remarkable, extraordinary, or great. **3** uncanny: *It was an unco place by night* (Robert Louis Stevenson).
—*n.* **1** something novel or strange. **2** a stranger. **3 uncos,** news.
[ultimately variant of *uncouth*]

**un|cock** (un kok′), *v.t.* to let down the hammer of (a firearm) gently from the position of cock, so as not to explode the charge.

**un|coil** (un koil′), *v.t., v.i.* = unwind.

**un|coined** (un koind′), *adj.* not coined; not minted.

**un|col|lect|ed** (un′kə lek′tid), *adj.* **1** not collected; not brought to one place; not received: *uncollected taxes, debts uncollected.* **2** *Figurative.* not having one's thoughts collected; not having control of one's mental faculties; not recovered from confusion, distraction, or wandering.

**un|col|ored** (un kul′ərd), *adj.* **1** not colored. **2** *Figurative.* not made to appear different from reality; open or undisguised; truthful or unbiased, as a statement or account; not influenced or affected by something. **3** plain or unadorned.

**un|com|bined** (un′kəm bīnd′), *adj.* not combined; separate.

**un|come|ly** (un kum′lē), *adj.* **1** not comely; wanting grace: *an uncomely person, uncomely dress.* **2** unseemly; unbecoming; unsuitable; indecent.

**un|com|fort|a|ble** (un kumf′tə bəl, -kum′fər-), *adj.* **1** not comfortable. **2** uneasy; restless. **3** disagreeable; causing discomfort: *His loyalty to the revolutionary principles made him conspicuous and extremely uncomfortable to the Bourbon Restoration* (Edmund Wilson). —**un|com′fort|a|ble|ness**, *n.*

**un|com|fort|a|bly** (un kumf′tə blē, -kum′fər-), *adv.* in a way that is not comfortable; with discomfort and uneasiness; disagreeably.

**un|com|mer|cial** (un′kə mėr′shəl), *adj.* **1** not commercial; not engaged in or connected with commerce. **2** not in accordance with the principles or methods of commerce. —**un′com|mer′cial|ly**, *adv.*

**un|com|mit|ted** (un′kə mit′id), *adj.* **1** not bound or pledged, as to a particular action, course, or group: *an uncommitted country.* **2** not committed to prison: *an uncommitted felon.*

**un|com|mon** (un kom′ən), *adj.* **1** rare; unusual: *uncommon kindness.* **2** remarkable; noteworthy: *uncommon good luck.* —**un|com′mon|ness**, *n.*

**un|com|mon|ly** (un kom′ən lē), *adv.* **1** rarely; unusually. **2** remarkably; especially: *She is an uncommonly good cook.*

**un|com|mu|ni|ca|bil|i|ty** (un′kə myü′nə kə bil′ə tē), *n.* the quality or condition of being uncommunicable.

**un|com|mu|ni|ca|ble** (un′kə myü′nə kə bəl), *adj.* = incommunicable.

**un|com|mu|ni|ca|tive** (un′kə myü′nə kā′tiv, -kə tiv), *adj.* not giving out any information, opinions, or advice; talking little; disposed to silence; reserved; reticent. **SYN**: taciturn. —**un′com|mu′ni-ca′tive|ness**, *n.*

**un|com|pan|ion|a|ble** (un′kəm pan′yə nə bəl), *adj.* not companionable or sociable: *an uncompanionable hermit.*

**un|com|pet|i|tive** (un′kəm pet′ə tiv), *adj.* **1a** that does not or will not compete: *an uncompetitive member firm, uncompetitive prices.* **b** not in accord with competition: *the uncompetitive spirit and traditions of Christmas.* **2** that discourages or prohibits competition. —**un′com|pet′i|tive|ly**, *adv.* —**un′com|pet′i|tive|ness**, *n.*

**un|com|plain|ing** (un′kəm plā′ning), *adj.* not complaining; not disposed to murmur; submissive. —**un′com|plain′ing|ly**, *adv.*

**un|com|plai|sant** (un′kəm plā′zənt, un kom′plə-zant), *adj.* not complaisant; not civil; not courteous.

**un|com|plet|ed** (un′kəm plē′tid), *adj.* not completed; unfinished.

**un|com|pli|a|ble** (un′kəm plī′ə bəl), *adj.* unready or unwilling to comply.

**un|com|pli|ant** (un′kəm plī′ənt), *adj.* = incompliant.

**un|com|pli|men|ta|ry** (un′kom plə men′tər ē), *adj.* not complimentary; unflattering; disparaging; derogatory.

**un|com|posed** (un′kəm pōzd′), *adj.* **1** not calm; disordered; excited: *sudden, uncomposed, and uncollected thoughts* (Edward Reynolds). **2** (of music) unwritten: *Schoenberg planned "Moses and Aaron" in three acts, but he left the last act uncomposed* (London Times).

**un|com|pound|ed** (un′kəm poun′did), *adj.* **1** not compounded; not mixed; simple. **2** not intricate or complicated.

**un|com|pre|hend|ing** (un′kom pri hen′ding), *adj.* not comprehending or understanding. —**un′com-pre|hend′ing|ly**, *adv.*

**un|com|pre|hen|si|ble** (un′kom pri hen′sə bəl), *adj. Obsolete.* incomprehensible.

**un|com|pre|hen|sion** (un′kom pri hen′shən), *n.* lack of understanding: *They might as well have come from different worlds, so striking is the uncomprehension between them* (Manchester Guardian).

**un|com|pro|mis|ing** (un kom′prə mī′zing), *adj.* unyielding; firm: *a stubborn, uncompromising person. His uncompromising attitude makes him very hard to deal with. The most honest, fearless and uncompromising republican of his time* (Macaulay). **SYN**: inflexible, rigid, inexorable. —**un|com′-pro|mis′ing|ly**, *adv.* —**un|com′pro|mis′ing|ness**, *n.*

**un|con|cealed** (un′kən sēld′), *adj.* not concealed; openly shown; manifest: *unconcealed scorn.*

**un|con|cern** (un′kən sėrn′), *n.* **1** lack of concern; freedom from care or anxiety; nonchalance. **2** lack of interest; indifference; apathy. **SYN**: See syn. under **indifference**.

**un|con|cerned** (un′kən sėrnd′), *adj.* **1** free from care or anxiety; nonchalant. **2** not interested; indifferent; apathetic. —**un′con|cern′ed|ly**, *adv.* —**un′con|cern′ed|ness**, *n.*

**un|con|demned** (un′kən demd′), *adj.* not condemned; not judged guilty; not disapproved; not pronounced criminal: *They have beaten us openly uncondemned* (Acts 16:37).

**un|con|di|tion|al** (un′kən dish′ə nəl, -dish′-nəl), *adj.* without conditions; absolute: *an unconditional refusal. The victorious general demanded unconditional surrender of the enemy.* **SYN**: unqualified, unrestricted.

**un|con|di|tion|al|ly** (un′kən dish′ə nə lē, -dish′-nə-), *adv.* without any conditions.

**un|con|di|tioned** (un′kən dish′ənd), *adj.* **1** without conditions; absolute. **2** = unconditional. **3** *Psychology.* **a** deriving from the innate nature of the organism as such; not learned; instinctive: *unconditioned behavior.* **b** that evokes a response without conditioning: *an unconditioned stimulus.* **4** accepted or promoted without condition: *an unconditioned student.* **5** *Philosophy.* of the nature of or deriving from that which is absolute in its nature and infinite in its extent; not dependent on or determined by antecedent conditions.

**unconditioned response** or **reflex**, *Psychology.* a response that occurs without specific learning or experience when a stimulus is presented. The knee jerk is an unconditioned reflex.

**un|con|fi|dent** (un kon′fə dənt), *adj.* lacking confidence; uncertain; hesitant; self-conscious: *an unconfident office boy.*

**un|con|fin|a|ble** (un′kən fī′nə bəl), *adj.* **1** that cannot be confined or restrained. **2** *Obsolete.* unbounded.

**un|con|fined** (un′kən fīnd′), *adj.* not confined; unrestricted; broad; unrestrained; free: *On with the dance! let joy be unconfined* (Byron).

**un|con|firmed** (un′kən fėrmd′), *adj.* not confirmed; without confirmation: *an unconfirmed report.*

**un|con|form|a|ble** (un′kən fôr′mə bəl), *adj.* **1** that does not conform. **2** *Geology.* having the relation of unconformity to underlying rocks.

**un|con|form|a|bly** (un′kən fôr′mə blē), *adv.* in an unconformable manner; so as not to be conformable.

***un|con|form|i|ty** (un′kən fôr′mə tē), *n., pl.* **-ties.** **1** lack of agreement; being inconsistent; nonconformity. **2** *Geology.* **a** a break in the continuity of strata, indicating an interruption of deposition. **b** the plane where such a break occurs.

***unconformity**
definition 2b

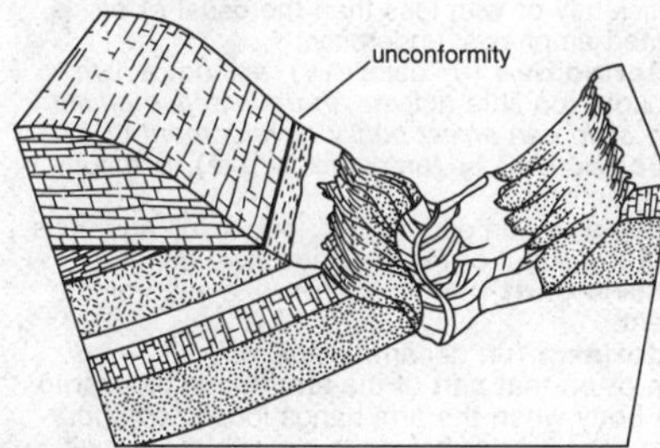


**un|con|fused** (un′kən fyüzd′), *adj.* **1** free from confusion or disorder. **2** not confused or embarrassed.

**un|con|geal** (un′kən jēl′), *v.i.* to thaw; melt.

**un|con|gen|ial** (un′kən jēn′yəl), *adj.* not congenial.

**un|con|nect|ed** (un′kə nek′tid), *adj.* **1** not connected; separated; distinct. **2** disconnected; incoherent.

**un|con|quer|a|ble** (un kong′kər ə bəl), *adj.* **1** that cannot be defeated: *Thou hast great allies; Thy friends are exultations, agonies, And love, and man's unconquerable mind* (Wordsworth). *I thank whatever gods may be For my unconquerable soul* (William E. Henley). SYN: invincible, insuperable, indomitable. **2** that cannot be brought under control: *un unconquerable temper. Romola ... shrank with unconquerable disgust from the shrill excitability of those illuminated women* (George Eliot). SYN: uncontrollable. — **un|con′quer|a|ble|ness,** *n.* — **un|con′quer|a|bly,** *adv.*

**un|con|quered** (un kong′kərd), *adj.* not conquered; not vanquished or subdued.

**un|con|scion|a|ble** (un kon′shə nə bəl), *adj.* **1** not influenced or guided by conscience: *an unconscionable liar. Sometimes the unconscionable editors will clip our paragraphs* (Washington Irving). SYN: unprincipled. **2** very great: *an unconscionable amount of snow. He waited an unconscionable time for her.* SYN: inordinate, unreasonable. — **un|con′scion|a|bly,** *adv.*

**un|con|scious** (un kon′shəs), *adj., n.* — *adj.* **1** not conscious, especially: **a** not in a conscious state; not able to feel or think: *unconscious from anesthetic. He was knocked unconscious when the car struck him.* **b** that is not a conscious being: *an unconscious force.* **2** not aware (of): *to be unconscious of danger. The general was unconscious of being followed by the spy.* SYN: oblivious, unmindful. **3** not meant; not intended; not done or felt consciously: *unconscious neglect.* **4** of or having to do with the part of the mind which cannot be drawn into consciousness. — *n.* Usually, **the unconscious.** that part of the mind containing thoughts and feelings, of which a person is not directly or fully aware; one's unconscious thoughts, desires, fears, or other emotions which may become groundless obsessions, compulsions, and other forms of abnormal behavior: *The unconscious is a special realm, with its own desires and modes of expression and peculiar mental mechanisms not elsewhere operative* (Sigmund Freud). SYN: subconscious. — **un|con′scious|ly,** *adv.* — **un|con′scious|ness,** *n.*

**un|con|se|crat|ed** (un kon′sə krā′tid), *adj.* not consecrated.

**un|con|sent|ing** (un′kən sen′ting), *adj.* not consenting; not yielding consent.

**un|con|sid|ered** (un′kən sid′ərd), *adj.* **1** not considered; not reflected on; not taken into consideration; not esteemed: *a snapper-up of unconsidered trifles* (Shakespeare). **2** unaccompanied by consideration or intention: *his own act of cool, nonchalant, unconsidered courage in a crisis* (Arnold Bennett).

**un|con|sid|er|ing** (un′kən sid′ər ing), *adj.* not considering; void of consideration; regardless.

**un|con|sol|a|ble** (un′kən sō′lə bəl), *adj.* = inconsolable.

**un|con|stant** (un kon′stənt), *adj.* = inconstant.

**un|con|sti|tu|tion|al** (un′kon stə tü′shə nəl, -tyü′-), *adj.* contrary to the constitution; not constitutional. — **un′con|sti|tu′tion|al|ly,** *adv.*

**un|con|sti|tu|tion|al|i|ty** (un′kon stə tü′shə nal′ə tē, -tyü′-), *n.* the fact or condition of being contrary to the constitution.

**un|con|strained** (un′kən strānd′), *adj.* **1** not constrained; not acting or done under compulsion; not subject to restraint: *unconstrained freedom.* **2** free from constraint or embarrassment; easy or unembarrassed: *Maggie's manner ... had been as unconstrained and indifferent as ever* (George Eliot).

**un|con|sum|mat|ed** (un kon′sə mā′tid), *adj.* not consummated; uncompleted; unfulfilled: *an unconsummated marriage.*

**un|con|test|ed** (un′kən tes′tid), *adj.* **1** not contested or disputed: *an uncontested will.* **2** indisputable; evident: *an uncontested fact.*

**un|con|tra|dict|a|ble** (un′kon trə dik′tə bəl), *adj.* that cannot be contradicted.

**un|con|tra|dict|ed** (un′kon trə dik′tid), *adj.* not contradicted or denied.

**un|con|trived** (un′kən trīvd′), *adj.* **1** not worked out beforehand; unplanned; unpremeditated: *uncontrived events.* **2** not artificial; natural; artless: *uncontrived mirth.*

**un|con|trol** (un′kən trōl′), *n.* lack of control.

**un|con|trol|la|bil|i|ty** (un′kən trō′lə bil′ə tē), *n.* the quality or condition of being uncontrollable; uncontrollableness: *What in the twenties was beyond government control because of the institutional uncontrollability of free capitalism, threatens ... to outgrow once again the controlling power of government* (New York Times).

**un|con|trol|la|ble** (un′kən trō′lə bəl), *adj.* not controllable; that cannot be controlled; not able to be checked or restrained; ungovernable: *His ... fierce and uncontrollable temper* (Samuel Richardson). — **un′con|trol′la|ble|ness,** *n.*

**un|con|trol|la|bly** (un′kən trō′lə blē), *adv.* in an uncontrollable manner; without being subject to control.

**un|con|trolled** (un′kən trōld′), *adj.* not controlled or governed; not restrained or checked.

**un|con|tro|vert|ed** (un kon′trə vėr′tid), *adj.* not controverted or disputed; not liable to be called in question.

**un|con|ven|tion|al** (un′kən ven′shə nəl), *adj.* not bound by or conforming to convention, rule, or precedent; free from conventionality. — **un′con|ven′tion|al|ly,** *adv.*

**un|con|ven|tion|al|i|ty** (un′kən ven′shə nal′ə tē), *n., pl.* **-ties.** the quality or condition of being unconventional; freedom from conventional restraints.

**un|con|vers|a|ble** (un′kən vėr′sə bəl), *adj.* not free in conversation; repelling conversation; not sociable; reserved.

**un|con|ver|sant** (un′kən vėr′sənt), *adj.* not conversant; not familiarly acquainted.

**un|con|vert|ed** (un′kən vėr′tid), *adj.* not converted.

**un|con|vert|i|ble** (un′kən vėr′tə bəl), *adj.* not convertible; that cannot be changed from one thing or form to another.

**un|con|vinc|ing** (un′kən vin′sing), *adj.* not convincing; open to doubt or disbelief: *an unconvincing argument, unconvincing testimony.* — **un′con|vinc′ing|ly,** *adv.* — **un′con|vinc′ing|ness,** *n.*

**un|cooked** (un kükt′), *adj.* not cooked; raw.

**un|cool** (un kül′), *adj. Slang.* lacking poise or sophistication; not cool: *"There are some very uncool people here—cats who come because they like a fight"* (Sunday Times).

**un|co|op|er|a|tion** (un′kō op′ə rā′shən), *n.* lack of cooperation.

**un|co|op|er|a|tive** (un′kō op′ə rā′tiv, -op′rə-), *adj.* not cooperative; unwilling to work with others: *The best constitution is useless when administered by disorderly, uncooperative individuals* (David Schoenbrun). — **un′co|op′er|a|tive|ly,** *adv.* — **un′co|op′er|a|tive|ness,** *n.*

**un|co|or|di|nat|ed** (un′kō ôr′də nā′tid), *adj.* lacking coordination; not working together; not in harmony: *the uncoordinated movements of a newborn baby.* — **un′co|or′di|nat′ed|ly,** *adv.*

**un|cop|i|a|ble** (un kop′ē ə bəl), *adj.* that cannot be copied.

**un|cork** (un kôrk′), *v.t.* **1** to pull the cork from. **2** *Informal, Figurative.* to let go; let loose; release: *The quarterback uncorked a long pass. These proposals immediately uncorked drives for action* (Wall Street Journal).

**un|cor|rect|a|ble** (un′kə rek′tə bəl), *adj.* irremediable; irreparable.

**un|cor|rect|ed** (un′kə rek′tid), *adj.* not corrected.

**un|cor|rob|o|rat|ed** (un′kə rob′ə rā′tid), *adj.* not corroborated; unconfirmed.

**un|cor|rupt** (un′kə rupt′), *adj.* not corrupt; not depraved; not perverted; incorrupt; pure: *an uncorrupt judgment, an uncorrupt text.*

**un|cor|rupt|ed** (un′kə rup′tid), *adj.* not corrupted; not debased; not vitiated; not depraved; not decomposed: *the common sense of readers uncorrupted with literary prejudices* (Samuel Johnson).

**un|coun|seled** (un koun′səld), *adj.* **1** not having counsel or advice. **2** *Obsolete.* wrongly counseled; led into error.

**un|count|a|ble** (un koun′tə bəl), *adj.* that cannot be counted; innumerable: *an uncountable number of stars.*

**un|count|ed** (un koun′tid), *adj.* **1** not counted; not reckoned. SYN: indefinite. **2** very many; innumerable. SYN: myriad.

**un|cou|ple** (un kup′əl), *v.t., v.i.,* **-pled, -pling.** to disconnect; unfasten: *They uncoupled two freight cars. The last two freight cars uncoupled and rolled to a stop.*

**un|cour|te|ous** (un kėr′tē əs), *adj.* not courteous; impolite; rude. SYN: discourteous. — **un|cour′te|ous|ly,** *adv.*

**un|court|ly** (un kôrt′lē, -kōrt′-), *adj.* not courtly; rude. — **un|court′li|ness,** *n.*

**un|couth** (un küth′), *adj.* **1** awkward; clumsy; crude; not refined: *an uncouth person, uncouth manners.* **2** unusual and unpleasant; strange: *the eerie and uncouth noises of the jungle.* [Old English *uncūth* < *un-* un-[1] + *cūth* known < *cunnan* to know] — **un|couth′ly,** *adv.* — **un|couth′ness,** *n.*

**un|cov|e|nant|ed** (un kuv′ə nən tid), *adj.* **1** not promised or secured by a covenant. **2** not in accordance with a covenant. **3** not bound by a covenant.

**un|cov|er** (un kuv′ər), *v.t.* **1** to remove the cover or covers from. **2** *Figurative.* to make known; reveal; expose. **3** to remove the hat, cap, or other head covering, of. — *v.i.* **1** to remove one's hat or cap in respect: *The men uncovered as the flag passed by.* **2** to remove a cover or covers.

**un|cov|ered** (un kuv′ərd), *adj.* **1** without a cover: *an uncovered pot of soup, an uncovered head.* **2** not protected by collateral or other security: *an uncovered note.*

**un|crate** (un krāt′), *v.t.,* **-crat|ed, -crat|ing.** to remove from a crate; unpack: *They were at work inside the individual pavilions, uncrating works of art* (New York Times).

**un|cre|ate** (un′krē āt′), *v.t.,* **-at|ed, -at|ing.** to undo the creation of; deprive of existence.

**un|cre|at|ed** (un′krē ā′tid), *adj.* **1** not created; not brought into existence. **2** existing without having been created.

**un|crit|i|cal** (un krit′ə kəl), *adj.* **1** not critical; not able or wanting to criticize. **2** wanting in acuteness of judgment or critical analysis: *an uncritical essay.* — **un|crit′i|cal|ly,** *adv.* — **un|crit′i|cal|ness,** *n.*

**un|cropped** (un kropt′), *adj.* **1** not cropped or plucked. **2** not cropped or cut, as the ears of a dog.

**un|cross** (un krôs′, -kros′), *v.t.* to change from a crossed position.

**un|crossed** (un krôst′, -krost′), *adj.* **1** not thwarted; not opposed. **2** not limited as regards cashability or negotiability by crossing. **3** not crossed; not canceled.

**un|crown** (un kroun′), *v.t.* to take the crown from; lower from high rank.

**un|crowned** (un kround′), *adj.* **1** not crowned; not having yet assumed the crown. **2** having royal power without being king or queen.

**UNCSAT** (no periods), United Nations Conference on Science and Technology.

**UNCTAD** (no periods), United Nations Conference on Trade and Development.

**unc|tion** (ungk′shən), *n.* **1** the action of anointing with oil, ointment, or the like, for medical purposes or as a religious rite: *The priest gave the dying man extreme unction.* **2** the oil, ointment, or the like, used for anointing. **3** *Figurative.* **a** something soothing or comforting: *the unction of flattery.* **b** a soothing, sympathetic, and persuasive quality in speaking. **4** *Figurative.* **a** fervor, especially religious fervor; earnestness. **b** affected earnestness or sentiment; smoothness and oiliness, as of language or manner. **5a** a divine or spiritual influence acting upon a person (in the Bible, I John 2:20). **b** the flowing of this influence. [< Latin *unctiō, -ōnis* < *unguere* to anoint]

**unc|tu|os|i|ty** (ungk′chü os′ə tē), *n.* **1** the quality of being unctuous. **2** = unction.

**Pronunciation Key:** hat, āge, cãre, fär; let, ēqual, tėrm; it, īce; hot, ōpen, ôrder; **oi**l, **ou**t; cup, pu̇t, rüle; **ch**ild; lo**ng**; **th**in; **ᴛʜ**en; **zh**, measure; ə represents **a** in about, **e** in taken, **i** in pencil, **o** in lemon, **u** in circus.

**unc|tu|ous** (ungk′chů əs), *adj.* **1** like an oil or ointment in texture; oily; greasy: *Oak, now black with time and unctuous with kitchen smoke* (Hawthorne). **2** *Figurative.* soothing, sympathetic, and persuasive; blandly ingratiating: **3** *Figurative.* **a** too smooth and oily: *the hypocrite's unctuous manner, an offensively unctuous speech.* **b** tending to or gushing with religious fervor or emotion, especially false or affected emotion; fervid in a shallow, sentimental way. **4** soft and clinging, but easily worked; rich in decayed organic matter, and containing more clay than sand: *an unctuous muck, ideal for celery.* **5** (of clay) very plastic; somewhat fat, as bentonite. [< Medieval Latin *unctuosus* < Latin *unctus, -ūs* anointment, anointing < *unguere* to anoint] —**unc′tu|ous|ly,** *adv.* —**unc′tu|ous|ness,** *n.*

**un|culled** (un kuld′), *adj.* **1** not gathered. **2** not separated; not selected.

**un|cul|ti|va|ble** (un kul′tə və bəl), *adj.* that cannot be tilled or cultivated.

**un|cul|ti|vat|ed** (un kul′tə vā′tid), *adj.* not cultivated; wild; undeveloped: (*Figurative.*) *an uncultivated mind.*

**un|cul|tured** (un kul′chərd), *adj.* not cultured.

**un|cum|bered** (un kum′bərd), *adj.* = unencumbered.

**un|cur|a|ble** (un kyůr′ə bəl), *adj.* = incurable.

**un|curb|a|ble** (un kėr′bə bəl), *adj.* that cannot be curbed or checked.

**un|curbed** (un kėrbd′), *adj.* not curbed: *uncurbed ambition.*

**un|cu|ri|ous** (un kyůr′ē əs), *adj.* **1** not curious or inquisitive; lacking curiosity; incurious. **2** not curious, odd, or strange.

**un|curl** (un kėrl′), *v.t., v.i.* to straighten out.

**un|cus** (ung′kəs), *n., pl.* **un|ci** (un′sī). *Biology.* a hooklike part or process. [< Latin *uncus*]

**un|cus|tomed** (un kus′təmd), *adj.* not passed through customs; with duty unpaid: *The police find him ... ninety dollars for having uncustomed goods in his possession* (Punch).

**un|cut** (un kut′), *adj.* **1** not cut, gashed, or wounded with a sharp-edged instrument; not having received a cut. **2** not cut down, mown, or clipped: *an uncut forest, uncut grass, an uncut hedge.* **3** not fashioned or shaped by cutting: *an uncut diamond.* **4** *Figurative.* not curtailed or shortened, as by editing: *an uncut novel or movie, an uncut performance of "Hamlet."* **5** not having the leaves cut open or the margins cut down: *an uncut book.*

**un|dam|aged** (un dam′ijd), *adj.* not damaged.

**un|damped** (un dampt′), *adj.* **1** not damped; not moistened. **2** not deadened; not checked or retarded in action. **3** *Figurative.* not depressed or discouraged. **4** *Physics.* not damped; not reduced gradually in amplitude.

**un|dat|ed** (un dā′tid), *adj.* not dated; not marked with a date, as a letter.

**un|daunt|ed** (un dôn′tid, -dän′-), *adj.* not afraid; not dismayed or discouraged; fearless; dauntless: *The captain was an undaunted leader.* **SYN:** intrepid. —**un|daunt′ed|ly,** *adv.* —**un|daunt′ed|ness,** *n.*

**un|dé** or **un|dée** (un′dā), *adj. Heraldry.* having the form of a wave or waves; wavy. [< Old French *unde* wave < Latin *unda*]

**un|dec|a|gon** (un dek′ə gon), *n. Geometry.* a polygon, especially a plane polygon, having eleven angles and eleven sides. [< Latin *ūndecim* eleven + English (dec)*agon*]

**un|de|ceiv|a|ble** (un′di sē′və bəl), *adj.* **1** that cannot be deceived; not subject to deception. **2** incapable of deceiving.

**un|de|ceive** (un′di sēv′), *v.t.,* **-ceived, -ceiv|ing.** to free (a person) from error, mistake, or deception; deliver from an erroneous idea or conception.

**un|de|cen|na|ry** (un′di sen′ər ē), *adj.* = undecennial.

**un|de|cen|ni|al** (un′di sen′ē əl, -sen′yəl), *adj.* **1** of or having to do with a period of eleven years. **2** occurring or observed every eleven years. [< Latin *ūndecim* eleven + *annus* year; patterned on English *decennial*]

**un|de|cent** (un dē′sənt), *adj.* = indecent.

**un|de|cid|ed** (un′di sī′did), *adj.* **1** not decided; not settled: *an undecided contest.* **2** not having one's mind made up: *I am undecided about which movie to see.* **SYN:** irresolute, wavering. —**un′de|cid′ed|ly,** *adv.* —**un′de|cid′ed|ness,** *n.*

**un|de|cil|lion** (un′də sil′yən), *n.* **1** (in the U.S., Canada, and France) 10 followed by 36 zeros. **2** (in Great Britain and Germany) 10 followed by 66 zeros. [< Latin *ūndecim* eleven + English *-illion,* as in *million*]

**un|de|ci|pher|a|ble** (un′di sī′fər ə bəl), *adj.* = indecipherable.

**un|decked** (un dekt′), *adj.* **1** not decked; not adorned. **2** not having a deck: *an undecked vessel or barge.*

**un|de|clin|a|ble** (un′di klī′nə bəl), *adj.* **1** *Grammar.* indeclinable. **2** *Obsolete.* not to be declined or avoided.

**un|de|clined** (un′di klīnd′), *adj.* **1** *Grammar.* not having cases marked by different terminations. **2** *Obsolete.* not deviating; not turned from the right way.

**un|de|com|pos|a|ble** (un′dē kəm pō′zə bəl), *adj.* not admitting of decomposition; that cannot be decomposed.

**un|de|faced** (un′di fāst′), *adj.* not defaced; not deprived of its form; not disfigured.

**un|de|fend|ed** (un′di fen′did), *adj.* **1** not defended; unprotected. **2** not assisted by legal defense, as a prisoner. **3** not contested, as a suit at law.

**un|de|filed** (un′di fīld′), *adj.* not defiled or polluted; pure or natural.

**un|de|fin|a|ble** (un′di fī′nə bəl), *adj.* = indefinable.

**un|de|fined** (un′di fīnd′), *adj.* **1** not defined or explained. **2** = indefinite.

**un|del|e|gat|ed** (un del′ə gā′tid), *adj.* not delegated; not deputed; not granted: *your assumption of undelegated power.*

**un|de|mand|ing** (un′di man′ding), *adj.* demanding nothing or very little: *an undemanding job, undemanding parents.*

**un|dem|o|crat|ic** (un′dem ə krat′ik), *adj.* not democratic; not in accordance with the principles of democracy. —**un′dem|o|crat′i|cal|ly,** *adv.*

**un|de|mon|stra|ble** (un′di mon′strə bəl), *adj.* = indemonstrable.

**un|de|mon|stra|tive** (un′di mon′strə tiv), *adj.* not demonstrative; not given to or characterized by open display or expression, as of the feelings; reserved. —**un′de|mon′stra|tive|ly,** *adv.* —**un′de|mon′stra|tive|ness,** *n.*

**un|de|ni|a|ble** (un′di nī′ə bəl), *adj.* **1** that cannot be disputed; not to be denied; certain; indisputable. **2** good beyond dispute; excellent. —**un′de|ni′a|ble|ness,** *n.*

**un|de|ni|a|bly** (un′di nī′ə blē), *adv.* beyond denial or dispute; certainly. **SYN:** unquestionably.

**un|de|nom|i|na|tion|al** (un′di nom′ə nā′shə nəl, -nāsh′nəl), *adj.* not connected with any particular religious sect.

**un|de|pend|a|bil|i|ty** (un′di pen′də bil′ə tē), *n.* unreliability; untrustworthiness.

**un|de|pend|a|ble** (un′di pen′də bəl), *adj.* not dependable; unreliable; untrustworthy. —**un′de|pend′a|ble|ness,** *n.*

**un|de|praved** (un′di prāvd′), *adj.* not depraved or corrupted.

**un|de|pre|ci|at|ed** (un′di prē′shē ā′tid), *adj.* not depreciated or lowered in value.

**un|de|pressed** (un′di prest′), *adj.* **1** not pressed down; not lowered; not sunk below the surface. **2** not depressed, dejected, or cast down: *disarmed but undepressed* (Byron).

**un|der** (un′dər), *prep., adv., adj.* —*prep.* **1** below; beneath: *The book fell under the table.* (*Figurative.*) *A general in the United States is under the President.* **2** below the surface of; *under the ground, under the sea.* **3** lower than; lower down than; not so high as: *He hit me under the belt.* **4** in such a position as to be covered, sheltered, or concealed by: *to sleep under a blanket. The moon is under a cloud.* **5** less than: *It will cost under ten dollars.* **6** during the rule, time, influence, or other condition, of: *England under the four Georges.* **7** in the position or condition of being affected by: *under the new rules. We learned a great deal under her teaching.* **8** because of: *under the circumstances. We cannot join your club under those conditions.* **9** according to: *under the law. The witness spoke under oath. The soldiers acted under orders.* **10** represented by: *under a new name.* **11** required or bound by: *You are not under any obligation to pay for merchandise that arrives damaged.* **12** with the authorization or sanction of: *under one's signature.* **13** included in a particular group, category, or class: *In this library, books on stamp collecting are listed under hobbies.*
—*adv.* **1** below; beneath: *The swimmer went under.* **2** in or to a lower place or condition.
—*adj.* lower, as in position, rank, degree, amount, or price: *the under level.*
[Old English *under*]
—*Syn. prep.* **1 Under, below, beneath** express a relation in which one thing is thought of as being lower than another. **Under** suggests being directly lower: *The toy is under the bed.* **Below** suggests being on a lower level, but not necessarily straight below nor without anyone or anything in between: *They live on one of the floors below us.* **Beneath** suggests being under and hence covered or hidden from view: *The letter was accidentally lost beneath the rug.*

**under-,** *prefix.* **1** on the underside; to a lower position; from a lower position; below; beneath: *Underline = to draw a line below. Underground = beneath the ground.*
**2** being beneath; worn beneath: *Underclothes = clothes worn beneath one's outer clothes.*
**3** lower or lower than: *Underlip = the lower lip. Underbid = to bid lower than.*
**4** lower in rank; subordinate: *Undersecretary = a secretary that is lower in rank.*
**5** not enough; not sufficiently: *Undernourished = not sufficiently nourished.*
**6** below normal: *Underweight = below normal weight.*
[< *under*]

**un|der|a|chieve** (un′dər ə chēv′), *v.i.,* **-chieved, -chiev|ing.** to fail to do schoolwork at the level of ability indicated by intelligence tests: *Two to three times as many boys underachieve in schools as do girls* (National Education Association Journal).

**un|der|a|chieve|ment** (un′dər ə chēv′mənt), *n.* a failure to achieve; lack of accomplishment, especially in schoolwork.

**un|der|a|chiev|er** (un′dər ə chē′vər), *n.* a pupil who fails to work at his level of ability.

**un|der|act** (un′dər akt′), *v.t., v.i.* to act (a part) insufficiently or with less than the usual or expected emphasis; underplay.

**un|der|ac|tive** (un′dər ak′tiv), *adj.* not active enough; too little active: *An underactive pituitary in a child can arrest bodily development* (Time).

**un|der|ac|tiv|i|ty** (un′dər ak tiv′ə tē), *n.* insufficient activity.

**un|der|age** (un′dər āj′), *adj.* not of full age; less than the usual or required age. **SYN:** minor.

**un|der|a|gent** (un′dər ā′jənt), *n.* a subordinate agent.

**un|der|arm** (un′dər ärm′), *adj., adv., n.* —*adj.* **1** in or on that part of the arm that is closest to the body when the arm hangs loose: *an underarm scar.* **2** of or having to do with the armpit. **3** for the armpit: *an underarm deodorant.* **4** = underhand.
—*adv.* with an underhand motion: *In softball a pitcher must throw underarm.*
—*n.* the part of the body under the arm, especially the armpit.

**un|der|bel|ly** (un′dər bel′ē), *n., pl.* **-lies. 1a** the lower part of the abdomen. **b** the part of a four-legged animal or of a reptile that is farthest from the spine. **2** *Figurative.* an unprotected or vulnerable part: *Winston Churchill [spoke] of an assault against the soft underbelly of Europe* (Atlantic).

**un|der|bid** (un′dər bid′), *v.,* **-bid, -bid|ding,** *n.* —*v.t.* **1** to offer to work or supply goods or services at a lower price than (another): *to underbid a competitor in seeking a contract to be awarded to the lowest bidder.* **2** to bid less than the full point value of: *to underbid a hand in bridge.*
—*v.i.* to bid less than another or less than the full value of something.
—*n.* an underbidding. —**un′der|bid′der,** *n.*

**un|der|bill** (un′dər bil′), *v.t.* to bill at less than the actual amount or value.

**un|der|bit** (un′dər bit′), *n. U.S.* an earmark to show ownership, made on the lower part of the ear of cattle.

**un|der|bod|ice** (un′dər bod′is), *n.* a bodice worn under an outer bodice.

**un|der|bod|y** (un′dər bod′ē), *n., pl.* **-bod|ies. 1** the underside of an animal's body. **2** the under portion of the body of a vehicle. **3** the part of a ship's hull below the water line.

**un|der|book** (un′dər bůk′), *v.t., v.i.* to make less reservations for accomodations than is possible (as in an airplane, ship, or hotel): *Aircraft would have been half full and hotels underbooked* (London Times). *Underbook and you lose money* (Scientific American).

**un|der|boss** (un′dər bôs′, -bos′), *n. U.S.* a member of the Mafia who ranks next below a boss or capo.

**un|der|branch** (un′dər branch′, -bränch′), *n. Obsolete.* a twig or branchlet.

**un|der|breath** (un′dər breth′), *n., adj.* —*n.* a low, subdued tone; whisper.
—*adj.* whispered.

**un|der|bred** (un′dər bred′), *adj.* **1** of inferior breeding or manners; coarse and vulgar; ill-bred: *a pert little obtrusive underbred creature* (Thackeray). **2** not of pure breed; not thoroughbred: *an underbred horse.*

**un|der|brush** (un′dər brush′), *n.* bushes, shrubs, and small trees growing under large trees in woods or forests. [American English < *under* + *brush*²]

**un|der|build** (un′dər bild′), *v.t.,* **-built, -build|ing. 1** to build under, as a means of strengthening or supporting; underpin: *to underbuild a pier.* **2** to build too little or too poorly.

**un|der|burn** (un′dər bėrn′), *v.t.,* **-burned** or **-burnt, -burn|ing.** to bake (brick, tile, or the like) insufficiently.

**un|der|but|ler** (un′dər but′lər), *n.* an assistant to a butler; one who works under a butler.

**un|der|buy** (un′dər bī′), *v.t.,* **-bought, -buy|ing. 1** to buy at less than the actual value or market price. **2** to buy for less than someone else. **3** to buy less of than one should.

**un|der|cap|i|tal|i|za|tion** (un′dər kap′ə tə lə zā′shən), *n.* the state of being undercapitalized.

**un|der|cap|i|tal|ize** (un′dər kap′ə tə līz), *v.t.*, **-ized, -iz|ing. 1** to supply with capital less than sufficient to operate efficiently or to carry out a program. **2** to issue stock or other securities to an amount small in proportion to assets and earnings.

**un|der|car|riage** (un′dər kar′ij), *n.* **1** the supporting framework, as of an automobile or carriage, on which the body is mounted or built. **2** the lower parts, often retractable, of an aircraft, by which it is supported on the ground or water; landing gear.

**un|der|cast** (un′dər kast′, -käst′), *n.* **1** an air passage cut through the rock or coal beneath the floor of a mine. **2** a layer of clouds beneath a flying airplane: *There's a black cloud of smoke coming up through the undercast* (Time).

**un|der|char|ac|ter|ize** (un′dər kar′ik tə rīz), *v.t.*, **-ized, -iz|ing.** to fail to develop the character or characters of: *The work as a whole was undercharacterized* (London Times). **—un′der|char′ac|ter|i|za′tion,** *n.*

**un|der|charge** (*v.* un′dər chärj′; *n.* un′dər chärj′), *v.*, **-charged, -charg|ing,** *n.* **—*v.t.*, *v.i.* 1** to charge (a person or persons) less than the established or a fair price; charge too little. **2** to undercharge a person or persons by (so much). **3** to load (a gun, shell, or area to be blasted) with an insufficient amount of explosive.
**—*n.* 1** a charge or price less than is proper or fair. **2** an insufficient charge or load.

**un|der|class** (un′dər klas′, -kläs′), *n.* a class of people having a low or the lowest status in society: *He could not ... relate to the black underclass or understand its impatience with a system that refused to recognize its legitimate demands* (Time). *The "underclass," especially its black elements, but also the Spanish speakers and the Appalachians, has begun to turn its desperation from a burden into a weapon* (Joseph G. Herzberg).

**un|der|class|es** (un′dər klas′iz, -kläs′-), *n.pl.* the freshman and sophomore classes.

**un|der|class|man** (un′dər klas′mən, -kläs′-), *n., pl.* **-men.** *U.S.* a freshman or sophomore; lowerclassman.

**un|der|clothe** (un′dər klōᴛʜ′), *v.t.*, **-clothed, -cloth|ing.** to provide with underclothing. [back formation < *underclothing*]

**un|der|clothed** (un′dər klōᴛʜd′), *adj.* not sufficiently clothed; not properly clad.

**un|der|clothes** (un′dər klōz′, -klōᴛʜz′), *n. pl.* = underwear.

**un|der|cloth|ing** (un′dər klō′ᴛʜing), *n.* = underwear.

**un|der|club** (un′dər klub′), *v.i.*, **-clubbed, -club|bing.** *Golf.* to use a club of insufficient power to gain the desired distance: *Many British players underclubbed here on Saturday, deceived by the change in weather* (London Times).

**un|der|coat** (un′dər kōt′), *n., v.* **—*n.* 1** a growth of short, fine hair under an animal's outer coat. **2** a coat of paint, varnish, or other substance, applied before the finishing coats; primer. **3a** a heavy, tarlike substance sprayed on the underneath parts of an automobile to protect them from water, dirt, and salt on the road. **b** a coating of this substance.
**—*v.t.*, *v.i.*** to apply or cover with an undercoat.

**un|der|coat|ing** (un′dər kō′ting), *n.* **1** = undercoat. **2** the process of applying an undercoat.

**un|der|cooked** (un′dər ku̇kt′, un′dər ku̇kt′), *adj.* not cooked enough; underdone.

**un|der|cool** (un′dər kül′), *v.t.* to cool below the normal freezing point; supercool.

**un|der|cov|er** (un′dər kuv′ər), *adj.* working or done in secret: *The jeweler was an undercover agent of the police.*

**un|der|croft** (un′dər krôft′, -kroft′), *n.* an underground vault or chamber; crypt, especially a crypt under a church or other place of worship.

**un|der|cur|rent** (un′dər kėr′ənt), *n.* **1** a current below the upper currents, or below the surface, as of a body of water or air: *Part of this air then returns as an undercurrent* (Thomas H. Huxley). **2** *Figurative.* an underlying tendency contrary to what is openly avowed or expressed: *There was an undercurrent of melancholy in Lincoln's humor.*

**un|der|cut** (*v.* un′dər kut′; *n., adj.* un′dər kut′), *v.*, **-cut, -cut|ting,** *n., adj.* **—*v.t.* 1** to cut under or beneath; cut away material from so as to leave a portion overhanging: *to undercut a stratum of rock.* **2** *Figurative.* to weaken; undermine: *The announcement ... was timed to undercut attempts ... to mobilize pressure against the Government* (New York Times). **3** to notch (the trunk of a tree, a large limb, or a timber or beam) so as to ensure falling in the desired direction or to prevent splitting. **4** *Figurative.* to sell or work, or offer to do so, for less than (another person or persons). **5** to hit (a ball) slightly below the center, causing it to have backspin, a short, high flight, and a minimum of roll or bounce, especially: **a** to hit (a golf ball) thus, as in getting out of a trap or making a short approach to a hole. **b** to hit (a tennis ball) thus, as in trapping one's opponent at the net.
**—*v.i.*** to undercut a person or thing.
**—*n.* 1** a cut, or a cutting away, underneath. **2** a notch cut in a tree to determine the direction in which the tree is to fall and to prevent splitting. **3** *Especially British.* a tenderloin or fillet of beef.
**—*adj.* 1** cut away underneath. **2** done by undercutting.

**un|der|de|vel|op** (un′dər di vel′əp), *v.i.* to be or become underdeveloped; fail to remain economically self-sufficient by losing or wasting capital and other resources: *Its GNP regularly declines from year to year. It is a developed country that is underdeveloping at speed* (Manchester Guardian Weekly). **—*v.t.*** to cause to underdevelop. [back formation < *underdeveloped*]

**un|der|de|vel|oped** (un′dər di vel′əpt), *adj.* **1** not normally developed: *an underdeveloped limb.* **2** poorly or insufficiently developed in production, technology, medicine, or standard of living: *The underdeveloped countries need trained workers.*

**un|der|de|vel|op|ment** (un′dər di vel′əp mənt), *n.* the fact or condition of being underdeveloped.

**un|der|do** (un′dər dü′), *v.i., v.t.*, **-did, -done, -do|ing.** to cook insufficiently.

**un|der|dog** (un′dər dôg′, -dog′), *n.* **1** the person having the worst of any struggle: *His early experience of poverty made him a champion of the underdog on every possible occasion* (London Times). **2** a contestant considered unlikely to win: *an outnumbered Army squad that had entered the contest a 4-point underdog* (New York Times). **3** the dog having the worst of a fight. [American English < *under-* + *dog*]

**un|der|done** (un′dər dun′, un′dər dun′), *adj., v.* **—*adj.*** not cooked enough; cooked very little.
**—*v.*** the past participle of **underdo.**

**un|der|dose** (*n.* un′dər dōs′; *v.* un′dər dōs′), *n., v.*, **-dosed, -dos|ing. —*n.*** an insufficient dose.
**—*v.t.*** to dose insufficiently; give too small a dose to.

**un|der|drain** (*v.* un′dər drān′; *n.* un′dər drān′), *v., n.* **—*v.t.*** to drain by means of drains placed under the ground.
**—*n.*** a drain placed under the ground.

**un|der|drain|age** (un′dər drā′nij), *n.* the drainage of land by drains buried in it.

**un|der|draw** (un′dər drô′), *v.t.*, **-drew, -drawn, -draw|ing. 1** to draw or represent inadequately. **2** to cover (the inside of a roof or floor) with boards or with lath and plaster. **3** to draw from (a bank account) so as to leave a reserve.

**un|der|drawers** (un′dər drôrz′), *n.pl. U.S.* = underpants.

**un|der|draw|ing** (un′dər drô′ing), *n.* an outline drawing put on a canvas, mural, or the like, prior to the application of paint: *the use of infrared radiation to examine the "underdrawings" of mediaeval European paintings* (New Scientist).

**un|der|dress** (*v.* un′dər dres′; *n.* un′dər dres′), *v., n.* **—*v.t.*, *v.i.*** to dress plainly or too plainly: *Well-dressed women often intentionally underdress.*
**—*n.* 1** a plain dress worn under an overdress or outer drapery. **2** = slip[1] (def. 2b).

**un|der|dressed** (un′dər drest′), *adj.* not dressed well or elaborately enough, as for a state occasion or an entertainment.

**un|der|drew** (un′dər drü′), *v.* the past tense of **underdraw.**

**un|der|drift** (un′dər drift′), *n.* a tendency under the surface of things; undercurrent.

**un|der|driv|en** (un′dər driv′ən), *adj. Machinery.* of or having to do with a driving mechanism in which the power is applied below the place where the work is done.

**un|der|earth** (un′dər ėrth′), *n., adj.* **—*n.*** the regions or matter below the surface of the earth.
**—*adj.*** underground; subterranean.

**un|der|eat|en** (un′dər ē′tən), *adj.* eaten away or eroded below: *an undereaten rock.*

**un|der|ed|u|cat|ed** (un′dər ej′ů kā′tid), *adj.* poorly or insufficiently educated: *By overemphasizing courses in "methodology" at the expense of regular academic subjects, they've produced a generation of undereducated teachers* (Wall Street Journal).

**un|der|ed|u|ca|tion** (un′dər ej′ů kā′shən), *n.* insufficient or inadequate education: *proposals for eradicating the undereducation and the ingrained economic distress of the Negro* (New York Times).

**un|der|em|pha|sis** (un′dər em′fə sis), *n.* insufficient emphasis; lack of stress.

**un|der|em|pha|size** (un′dər em′fə sīz), *v.t.*, **-sized, -siz|ing.** to emphasize insufficiently; not stress enough: *Basic research is still underemphasized in the United States* (Bulletin of Atomic Scientists).

**un|der|em|ployed** (un′dər em ploid′), *adj., n.* **—*adj.* 1** not sufficiently employed: **a** not put to the fullest or most profitable use: *Lastly, I proceed on the hope ... that full employment will mean just that and not a body of workers fully paid but underemployed* (Punch). **b** working only part of the time: *One fourth of the labor force is out of work or underemployed* (Time). **2** not employing or offering employment to enough people: *Some American railways, at the present time, are underemployed* (Wall Street Journal).
**—*n.*** underemployed people.

**un|der|em|ploy|ment** (un′dər em ploi′mənt), *n.* the quality or condition of being underemployed; insufficient or inadequate employment.

**un|der|e|quipped** (un′dər i kwipt′), *adj.* lacking the necessary equipment; poorly or inadequately equipped: *The great need of the city of New York ... is the swift rehabilitation of its underequipped and insufficiently used system of rapid mass transportation* (Lewis Mumford).

**un|der|es|ti|mate** (*v.* un′dər es′tə māt; *n.* un′dər es′tə mit, -māt), *v.*, **-mat|ed, -mat|ing,** *n.* **—*v.t.*, *v.i.*** to estimate at too low a value, amount, rate, or the like: *to underestimate the power of human endurance* (John Buchan). *Certainly she [Willa Cather] has been radically underestimated* (Manchester Guardian).
**—*n.*** an estimate that is too low.

**un|der|es|ti|ma|tion** (un′dər es′tə mā′shən), *n.* **1** the act or process of estimating at too low a rate. **2** the condition of being so estimated; undervaluation.

**un|der|ex|pose** (un′dər ek spōz′), *v.t.*, **-posed, -pos|ing. 1** to expose too little. **2** *Photography.* to expose (a film or negative) for a shorter time than required for the best results.

**un|der|ex|po|sure** (un′dər ek spō′zhər), *n.* too little or too short an exposure. Underexposure to light makes a photograph look dim.

**un|der|fall** (un′dər fôl′), *n.* the slope of a foothill.

**un|der|feed** (un′dər fēd′), *v.t., v.i.*, **-fed, -feed|ing. 1** to feed too little; not give enough food or fuel to: *An underfed nation is incapable of the endurance required of first-class soldiers* (William R. Inge). **2** to stoke with coal or other solid fuel from the bottom.

**un|der|fi|nanced** (un′dər fə nanst′, -fī-), *adj.* poorly or insufficiently financed: *Every time someone finds a new national need, understaffed, underfinanced schools are pressured to add new courses* (Harper's).

**un|der|fired** (un′dər fīrd′), *adj.* **1** not fired or baked enough. **2** supplied with fuel from below.

**un|der|floor** (un′dər flôr′, -flōr′), *v.t.* to floor below; make a lower floor for.

**un|der|flow** (un′dər flō′), *n.* a current flowing beneath the surface, or not in the same direction with the surface current, over a certain region; undercurrent.

**un|der|foot** (un′dər fůt′), *adv., adj.* **—*adv.* 1** under one's foot or feet; on the ground; underneath: *Katherine, that cap of yours becomes you not ... throw it underfoot* (Shakespeare). **2** in the way: *She complained that her six small children were always getting underfoot.*
**—*adj.*** lying under the foot or feet; downtrodden; abject.

**un|der|foot|ing** (un′dər fůt′ing), *n.* the ground under one's feet.

**un|der|frame** (un′dər frām′), *n.* a structure or framework which supports the body of a railroad car, truck, or other vehicle; a chassis: *In designing a 35-foot trailer, engineers usually allow three to five inches deflection space between the van and the underframe for spring compression* (Science News Letter).

**un|der|fur** (un′dər fėr′), *n.* the soft, fine hair under the outer coat of coarse hair of various mammals, such as beavers and some seals.

**un|der|gar|ment** (un′dər gär′mənt), *n.* a garment worn under another garment, especially next to the skin.

**un|der|gird** (un′dər gėrd′), *v.t.* to support or secure by a rope or the like passed beneath.

**un|der|glaze** (un′dər glāz′), *adj., n.* **—*adj.*** of or designating a decoration, color, or the like, put on a ceramic object, such as a piece of majolica, stoneware or china, before a more or less transparent glaze is applied.
**—*n.*** an underglaze color or decoration.

**un|der|go** (un′dər gō′), *v.t.*, **-went, -gone, -go|ing. 1** to go through; pass through; be subjected to; experience: *to undergo a complete alteration*

---

**Pronunciation Key:** hat, āge, cãre, fär; let, ēqual, tėrm; it, īce; hot, ōpen, ôrder; oil, out; cup, pu̇t, rüle; child; long; thin; ᴛʜen; zh, measure; ə represents a in about, e in taken, i in pencil, o in lemon, u in circus.

*in point of view. The town is undergoing many changes as more and more people are moving in.* **SYN**: See syn. under **experience**. **2** to bear the burden of; endure; suffer: *Soldiers undergo many hardships.* **SYN**: See syn. under **experience**.

**un|der|gone** (un′dər gôn′, -gon′), *v.* the past participle of **undergo**: *The town has undergone great change in the last five years.*

**un|der|grad** (un′dər grad′), *n. Informal.* an undergraduate: *Seton Hall, with fewer than 4,000 undergrads, is noted mainly for its basketball teams* (Time).

**un|der|grad|u|ate** (un′dər graj′ů it), *n., adj.* — ***n.*** a student in a college or university who has not yet received a degree.
— ***adj.*** **1** of or having to do with undergraduates. **2** for undergraduates. **3** like undergraduates. **4** that is an undergraduate.

**un|der|grad|u|ate|ship** (un′dər graj′ů it ship), *n.* the condition or standing of an undergraduate.

**un|der|grad|u|ette** (un′dər graj′ů et′), *n. British.* a girl or woman undergraduate; coed: *"It [Oxford] was a male community," says Mr. Waugh. "Undergraduettes lived in purdah"* (W. H. Auden).

**un|der|ground** (*adv.* un′dər ground′; *adj., n., v.* un′dər ground′), *adv., adj., n., v.* — ***adv.*** **1** beneath the surface of the ground: *The mole burrowed underground. Miners work underground.* **2** *Figurative.* **a** in secrecy or concealment; concealed from the eyes of the public or authorities; surreptitiously: *Spies work underground.* **b** into secrecy or concealment: *The thief went underground after the robbery.*
— ***adj.*** **1** being, working, or used beneath the surface of the ground; subterranean: *an underground passage.* **2** *Figurative.* **a** done or working secretly; concealed from the eyes of the public or some authority or authorities; secret; clandestine: *The revolt against the government was an underground plot. Many Soviet intellectuals continued to criticize government policy through underground publications, which the police were unable to suppress* (Ellsworth Raymond). **b** of or having to do with the secret underground of a country: *an underground headquarters. During the war he had been chosen, it was said, as the underground leader of a very wide area in the event of a successful German invasion* (Geoffrey Household). **3** *Figurative.* of or belonging to any group, organization, or movement outside the established society or culture: *the underground press, underground filmmakers, underground music, underground churches.*
— ***n.*** **1** a place or space beneath the surface of the ground. **2** *British.* a subterranean railroad; subway. **3** *Figurative.* a secret organization working to overthrow an unpopular government, especially during military occupation: *The French underground protected many American fliers shot down over France during World War II. We … fought side by side in the anti-Fascist underground* (Atlantic). **4** any group, organization, or movement whose activities are outside the established society or culture: *What these film makers, who proudly identify themselves as the "underground," profess to want is the freedom to create motion pictures in accordance with their own, intensely personal artistic visions, untrammeled by anything that has gone before* (Arthur Knight). *The Catholic "underground" has removed worship from the sanctuary entirely and transferred it to private homes* (New York Times).
— ***v.t.*** to place or lay underground: *The President's Conference on Natural Beauty specifically recommended widespread undergrounding of low voltage distribution lines* (New York Times). — **un′der|ground′er**, *n.*

**underground film** or **movie**, a motion picture made outside an ordinary commercial studio, usually at a low cost, and intended for a small or select audience: *"Love Song" is a low-pressure, small-scale, highly informal operation, more suggestive of underground movies or off-Broadway theater than … of commercial television* (New York Times).

**underground railroad**, **1** *U.S.* a system by which the opponents of slavery secretly helped fugitive slaves to escape to the free states or Canada before the Civil War. **2** a railroad running through tunnels under the ground or streets; subway.

**un|der|grown** (un′dər grōn′), *adj.* not fully grown; of low stature.

**un|der|growth** (un′dər grōth′), *n.* **1** = underbrush. **2** the shorter, finer hair underlying the outer hair of any one of various animals.

**un|der|hand** (un′dər hand′), *adj., adv.* — ***adj.*** **1** not open or honest; secret; sly. **2** done with the hand below the shoulder and the arm swung upward; underarm: *an underhand pitch.* **3** with the knuckles downward: *an underhand hold on a bat.*
— ***adv.*** **1** secretly; slyly. **2** in an underhand manner: *to throw a ball underhand.*

**un|der|hand|ed** (un′dər han′did), *adj.* **1** underhand; secret; sly: *an underhanded trick.* **SYN**: deceitful. **2** not having enough workers or helpers; short-handed: *an underhanded ship.* — **un′der|hand′ed|ly**, *adv.* — **un′der|hand′ed|ness**, *n.*

**un|der|head valve** (un′dər hed′), the intake or exhaust valve inside the cylinder of an L-head engine.

**un|der|housed** (un′dər houzd′), *adj.* having poor or inadequate housing: *Yugoslavia is underpopulated, underhoused, underfed* (Atlantic).

**un|der|hung** (un′dər hung′), *adj.* **1** resting on a track beneath, instead of being hung from above: *underhung sliding doors.* **2** (of the lower jaw) projecting beyond the upper jaw; undershot: *A bulldog has an underhung jaw.*

**un|der|in|sured** (un′dər in shůrd′), *adj.* not carrying enough insurance; insufficiently insured: *Not only are most houses undervalued, but … the contents are underinsured* (New York Times).

**un|der|jaw** (un′dər jô′), *n.* the lower jaw; mandible.

**un|der|jawed** (un′dər jôd′), *adj.* having a protruding lower jaw; undershot.

**un|der|keep|er** (un′dər kē′pər), *n.* an assistant keeper, as of a forest or park.

**un|der|kill** (un′dər kil′), *n.* an inability or unwillingness to overkill; an attacking with less force than is needed to destroy something: *Noting that "our legal tradition has special repugnance toward prior restraint," Harvard's Paul A. Freund maintained that "risk for risk, the law has opted for underkill in duels over publication"* (Time).

**un|der|laid** (un′dər lād′), *adj., v.* — ***adj.*** **1** supported, fitted, or supplied underneath (with something). **2** placed or built beneath; underlying.
— ***v.*** the past tense and past participle of **underlay**.

**un|der|lain** (un′dər lān′), *v.* the past participle of **underlie**.

**un|der|lap** (un′dər lap′), *v.t.,* **-lapped, -lap|ping.** to lap under; extend some way below: *The feathers of a bird's wing underlap each other.*

**un|der|lay**[1] (*v.* un′dər lā′; *n.* un′dər lā′), *v.,* **-laid, -lay|ing,** *n.* — ***v.t.*** **1** to lay or place (one thing) under another. **2** to provide with something laid underneath; raise or support with something laid underneath. **3** to coat or cover the bottom of.
— ***n.*** **1** something laid beneath. **2** *Printing.* a piece of paper, or a sheet with pieces pasted on it, laid under type to bring it to the proper height for printing.
[Old English *underlecgan* < *under-* under- + *lecgan* to lay]

**un|der|lay**[2] (un′dər lā′), *v.* the past tense of **underlie**.

**un|der|lay|er** (un′dər lā′ər), *n.* a lower layer; substratum.

**un|der|leaf** (un′dər lēf′), *n.* the under surface of a leaf.

**un|der|lease** (*n.* un′dər lēs′; *v.* un′dər lēs′), *n., v.t., v.i.,* **-leased, -leas|ing.** = sublease.

**un|der|let** (un′dər let′), *v.t.,* **-let, -let|ting.** *Especially British.* **1** to sublet. **2** to rent or lease for less than the amount actually worth or able to be obtained.

**un|der|lie** (un′dər lī′), *v.t.,* **-lay, -lain, -ly|ing.** **1** to lie under; be beneath; subtend. **2** *Figurative.* to be at the basis; form the foundation of, especially: **a** to give rise to; be the reason behind or origin of: *What underlies that remark?* **b** to give basic support to; be essential to. **3** *Finance.* to come before another (privilege or security) in time and order. **4** *Scottish.* to submit or be required to submit to (a punishment, charge, or law). [Old English *underlicgan* < *under-* under- + *licgan* lie[1]]

**un|der|life** (un′dər līf′), *n.* **1** life below the surface. **2** *Figurative.* a way of living apart and different from the life open to the common knowledge or view.

**un|der|line** (un′dər līn′, un′dər līn′), *v.,* **-lined, -lin|ing,** *n.* — ***v.t.*** **1** to draw a line or lines under; underscore: *In writing, we underline titles of books.* **2** *Figurative.* to make emphatic or more emphatic; emphasize.
— ***n.*** **1** a line drawn or printed under a word or passage. **2** the line of the lower part of the body of an animal, especially a sheep.

**un|der|lin|en** (un′dər lin′ən), *n.* linen (or cotton) undergarments.

**un|der|ling** (un′dər ling), *n.* a person of lower rank or position; inferior; subordinate (usually disparagingly): *The fault, dear Brutus, is not in our stars, But in ourselves, that we are underlings* (Shakespeare). [Old English *underling* < *under* under + *-ling* -ling]

**un|der|lin|ing**[1] (un′dər lī′ning), *n.* the inner lining of a garment.

**un|der|lin|ing**[2] (un′dər lī′ning), *n.* **1** the drawing of a line or lines under a word or passage. **2** the line or lines so drawn.

**un|der|lip** (un′dər lip′), *n.* the lower lip of a person, animal, or insect.

**un|der|load** (un′dər lōd′), *v.t.* to put an insufficient load on or in.

**un|der|look** (*v.* un′dər lůk′; *n.* un′dər lůk′), *v., n.* — ***v.t.*** **1** to look at from below. **2** to miss seeing by looking too low.
— ***n.*** a covert look; secret glance.

**un|der|look|er** (un′dər lůk′ər), *n.* a person who assists the manager of a mine and is in charge of the miners and workings.

**un|der|ly|ing** (un′dər lī′ing), *adj., v.* — ***adj.*** **1** lying under or beneath; subtending: *The stones That name the underlying dead* (Tennyson). **2** *Figurative.* forming the basis or foundation of; fundamental; basic; essential: *underlying facts.* **3** *Figurative.* not evident at first glance; present but not apparent except through careful scrutiny. **4** *Finance.* combing before another in time and order; having priority.
— ***v.*** the present participle of **underlie**.

**un|der|man** (un′dər man′), *v.t.,* **-manned, -man|ning.** to furnish with an insufficient number of men: *Our merchant ships are always undermanned* (Richard Henry Dana).

**un|der|manned** (un′dər mand′), *adj.* = understaffed.

**un|der|men|tioned** (un′dər men′shənd), *adj.* mentioned below or beneath.

**un|der|mill** (un′dər mil′), *v.t.* to mill (grain) without removing the bran coats: *Undermilled kernels have the brownish color of bran.*

**un|der|mine** (un′dər mīn′, un′dər mīn′), *v.t.,* **-mined, -min|ing.** **1** to make a passage or hole under; tunnel through or into; dig under: *to undermine a foundation. The soldiers undermined the wall.* **2** to wear away the foundations of; remove the underlying substance of: *The waves had undermined the cliff.* **3** *Figurative.* to weaken, injure, destroy, or ruin by secret or unfair means: *Some people tried to undermine the chairman's influence by spreading lies about him.* **SYN**: See syn. under **weaken**. **4** *Figurative.* to weaken or destroy gradually; sap: *Many severe colds had undermined the old lady's health.* **SYN**: See syn. under **weaken**.

**un|der|min|er** (un′dər mī′nər, un′dər mī′-), *n.* **1** a secret or insidious assailant or destroyer. **2** *Especially British.* a person who undermines; sapper.

**un|der|most** (un′dər mōst), *adj., adv.* at the very bottom; lowest.

**un|dern** (un′dərn), *n. British Dialect.* **1** the afternoon or evening. **2** a light meal, especially one taken in the afternoon. [< Middle English *undern* (originally) the third hour of the day, tierce, Old English]

**un|der|neath** (un′dər nēth′), *prep., adv., adj., n.* — ***prep.*** **1** beneath; below; under: *a cellar underneath a house. We can sit underneath this tree.* **2** under the power or control of; subject to: *underneath the yoke of Government* (Shakespeare). **3** *Archaic.* under the form or cover of.
— ***adv.*** **1** beneath what is on top; down below: *Someone was pushing up from underneath.* **2** beneath what is outermost: *to wear wool underneath.* **3** on the underside; at the bottom or base: *a house rotten underneath.*
— ***adj.*** lower; under.
— ***n.*** the lower part or surface.
[Old English *underneothan* < *under-* under + *neothan* below]

**un|der|note** (un′dər nōt′), *n.* a low or subdued note; undertone; suggestion: *an undernote of gaiety, an undernote of good sense.*

**un|der|nour|ish** (un′dər nėr′ish), *v.t.* to provide with less food than is necessary, as for growth, maintenance of vigor, or health; give insufficient nourishment to.

**un|der|nour|ished** (un′dər nėr′isht), *adj.* not sufficiently nourished; underfed.

**un|der|nour|ish|ment** (un′dər nėr′ish mənt), *n.* lack of nourishment; not having enough food.

**un|dern|song** (un′dərn sông′, -song′), *n. Ecclesiastical, Obsolete.* tierce. [< Old English *undernsang* < *undern* (originally) tierce; noon, forenoon + *sang* song]

**un|der|nu|tri|tion** (un′dər nü trish′ən, -nyü-), *n.* incomplete or imperfect nutrition; undernourishment: *It is economic unavailability which is the chief reason for the malnutrition and undernutrition which affects two out of three of the world's people* (New Scientist).

**un|der|oc|cu|pied** (un′dər ok′yə pīd), *adj.* **1** having fewer occupants than there is room for: *To find room in this way for the elderly and others needing small homes would release seriously underoccupied large houses for bigger families* (London Times). **2** having little to do; not sufficiently employed: *underoccupied people.*

**un|der|of|fi|cer** (*v.* un′dər ôf′ə sər, -of′-; *n.* un′dər ôf′ə sər, -of′-), *v., n.* — ***v.t.*** to furnish inadequately with officers.
— ***n.*** an officer of a lower grade.

**un|der|paid** (un′dər pād′), *v.* the past tense and past participle of **underpay.**

**un|der|paint|ing** (un′dər pān′ting), *n.* a plan for a painting, showing the outline, shadows or highlights, and sometimes the color scheme, painted on a canvas, mural, or the like: *He paints at times in such very thin washes that the underpainting often shows through, giving a streaky texture that is distracting* (New Yorker).

**un|der|pants** (un′dər pants′), *n.pl.* pants worn as an undergarment by men and women; drawers; underdrawers.

**un|der|part** (un′dər pärt′), *n.* **1** the part of an animal, plant, or any object, that lies below or underneath: *The tree swallow has pure white underparts.* **2** a secondary or subordinate part; minor role: *to play an underpart in a drama.*

**un|der|pass** (un′dər pas′, -päs′), *n.* a path underneath; road or other way under railroad tracks, another road, runway, or the like. [American English < *under-* + *pass*[2]]

**un|der|pay** (un′dər pā′), *v.t., v.i.,* **-paid, -pay|ing.** to pay too little.

**un|der|peo|pled** (un′dər pē′pəld), *adj.* = underpopulated.

**un|der|pin** (un′dər pin′), *v.t.,* **-pinned, -pin|ning.** **1** to support or strengthen (a building or other structure) from beneath, as with props, stones, or masonry: *to underpin a wall.* **2** to form or provide a base or fundamental support to (anything); support; prop: *The chromosome and the gene underpin the entire heredity of living beings.* (*Figurative.*) *The Constitution underpins all life in the United States.* **3** *Figurative.* to corroborate; vindicate.

**un|der|pin|ning** (un′dər pin′ing), *n.* **1** the materials or structure that give support from beneath, as to a building or wall: *an outside wall with new underpinning of poured concrete.* **2** a support; prop: (*Figurative.*) *Truth and justice are the underpinnings of law and order.*

**un|der|plant** (un′dər plant′, -plänt′), *v.t.* to plant (young trees) under an existing stand of trees.

**un|der|play** (un′dər plā′), *v.t., v.i.* = underact.

**un|der|plot** (un′dər plot′), *n.* a dramatic or literary plot subordinate to the principal plot, but connected with it; subplot.

**un|der|pop|u|lat|ed** (un′dər pop′yə lā′tid), *adj.* not sufficiently or well populated; having too small a population.

**un|der|pow|ered** (un′dər pou′ərd), *adj.* not sufficiently or well powered: *Early airships were underpowered* (New Scientist).

**un|der|price** (un′dər prīs′), *v.t.,* **-priced, -pric|ing.** **1** to price lower than the value: *to underprice a car or suit.* **2** to undercut in price: *to underprice a competitor.*

**un|der|print** (un′dər print′), *v.t.* to print (a photograph) with not enough depth or distinctness.

**un|der|priv|i|leged** (un′dər priv′ə lijd), *adj.* having fewer advantages than most people have, especially because of poor economic or social status: *an underprivileged nation, an underprivileged child.*

**un|der|prize** (un′dər prīz′), *v.t.,* **-prized, -priz|ing.** to prize too little; put a low value on; underestimate.

**un|der|pro|duce** (un′dər prə düs′, -dyüs′), *v.t.,* **-duced, -duc|ing.** to produce less than the usual amount or the amount needed: *In the Russian Republic, according to the State Planning Commission, meat will be underproduced by 40%* (Time).

**un|der|pro|duc|tion** (un′dər prə duk′shən), *n.* production that is less than normal or less than there is a demand for.

**un|der|pro|duc|tive** (un′dər prə duk′tiv), *n.* not producing enough; underproducing: *an underproductive industry, underproductive timberland.*

**un|der|pro|duc|tiv|i|ty** (un′dər prō′duk tiv′ə tē), *n.* insufficient or inadequate productivity.

**un|der|pro|mote** (un′dər prə mōt′), *v.t.,* **-mot|ed, -mot|ing.** *Chess.* to exchange (a pawn reaching the last rank) for a rook, bishop, or knight instead of a queen.

**un|der|pro|mo|tion** (un′dər prə mō′shən), *n.* *Chess.* an underpromoting or being underpromoted.

**un|der|proof** (un′dər prüf′), *adj.* having less alcohol than proof spirit does (in the United States, less than 50 per cent by volume).

**un|der|prop** (un′dər prop′), *v.t.,* **-propped, -prop|ping.** to prop underneath; support.

**un|der|quote** (un′dər kwōt′), *v.t.,* **-quot|ed, -quot|ing.** **1** to offer to sell something, such as merchandise or a commodity, at a lower price than (another or others); underbid. **2** to offer (something, such as merchandise or a commodity) for sale at a lower price than someone or anyone else.

**un|der|rate** (un′dər rāt′), *v.t.,* **-rat|ed, -rat|ing.** to rate or estimate too low; put too low a value on. **SYN:** underestimate.

**un|der|re|act** (un′dər rē akt′), *v.i.* to react with less force or intensity than the circumstances require: *They underreacted, allowing the march to become a mob and the mob to become milling looters* (Time). **—un′der|re|ac′tion,** *n.*

**un|der|re|port** (un′dər ri pôrt′, -pōrt′), *v.t.* **1** to cover (a news event) inadequately; underemphasize the importance of: *Africa is very much underrreported, even though it is making history every day* (Time). **2** to report (an amount) less than the actual: *The totals ... are so low as to suggest considerable underreporting* (Jean A. Flexner).

**un|der|rep|re|sen|ta|tion** (un′dər rep′ri zen tā′shən), *n.* inadequate or insufficient representation: *The city suffered from its underrepresentation in Congress.*

**un|der|rep|re|sent|ed** (un′dər rep′ri zen′tid), *adj.* represented inadequately or by less than a proper proportion: *Urban dwellers, who for decades have been underrepresented in state legislatures ...* (Atlantic).

**un|der|ripe** (un′dər rīp′), *adj.* not fully ripe; partly ripe.

**un|der|run** (*v.* un′dər run′; *n.* un′dər run′), *v.,* **-ran, -run, -run|ning,** *n.* **—*v.t.*** **1** to pass or move beneath. **2** to move along in a boat beneath (as a cable or net) to make an inspection or repair. **3** to run below capacity: *to underrun a power plant.*
**—*n.*** **1** = undercurrent. **2** the act or fact of underrunning. **3** an amount by which something is underrun.

**un|der|score** (*v.* un′dər skôr′, -skōr′; *n.* un′dər skôr′, -skōr′), *v.,* **-scored, -scor|ing,** *n.* **—*v.t.*** **1** = underline. **2** *Figurative.* emphasize.
**—*n.*** an underscored line.

**un|der|scrub** (un′dər skrub′), *n.* underbrush; undergrowth.

**un|der|sea** (*adj.* un′dər sē′; *adv.* un′dər sē′), *adj., adv.* **—*adj.*** being, done, working, or used beneath the surface of the sea: *an undersea cable, undersea exploration. The German submarine was the first dangerous undersea raider of World War II.*
**—*adv.*** = underseas.

**un|der|seas** (un′dər sēz′), *adv.* beneath the surface of the sea: *Submarines go underseas.*

**un|der|sec|re|tar|i|at** (un′dər sek′rə tãr′ē it, -at), *n.* **1** the office or position of an undersecretary. **2** the division of a government department administered by an undersecretary.

**un|der|sec|re|tar|y** (un′dər sek′rə ter′ē), *n., pl.* **-tar|ies.** **1** an official of a government department ranking just below the official who is at the head of it, or sometimes just below the official's deputy. **2** a subordinate secretary.

**un|der|sell** (un′dər sel′), *v.t.,* **-sold, -sell|ing.** **1** to sell things at a lower price than (someone else); sell for less than: *This store can undersell other stores because it sells in great volume.* **2** to sell (things, such as merchandise or commodities) at less than the actual value; sell at a loss. **—un′der|sell′er,** *n.*

**un|der|serv|ant** (un′dər sėr′vənt), *n.* a servant who does the simpler or lower tasks.

**un|der|set** (un′dər set′), *v.t.,* **-set, -set|ting.** **1** to provide or support with something set beneath; underpin; prop. **2** to set (a thing) under something else.

**un|der|sexed** (un′dər sekst′), *adj.* having little interest in or capacity for sexual activity.

**un|der|shap|en** (un′dər shā′pən), *adj.* = misshapen.

**un|der|sher|iff** (un′dər sher′if), *n.* a sheriff's deputy, especially one who acts when the sheriff is not able to act or when there is no sheriff.

**un|der|shirt** (un′dər shėrt′), *n.* a shirt worn next to the skin under other clothing. An undershirt is made of knitted cotton or the like, with or without sleeves.

**un|der|shoot** (un′dər shüt′), *v.,* **-shot, -shoot|ing.** **—*v.t.*** to shoot short of; shoot too low for: *to undershoot a target.*
**—*v.i.*** to shoot too short or low.

**un|der|shore** (un′dər shôr′, -shōr′), *v.t.,* **-shored, -shor|ing.** **1** to prop up or support with shores. **2** *Figurative.* to support; strengthen.

**un|der|shorts** (un′dər shôrts′), *n.pl.* underpants for men and boys; shorts.

**un|der|shot** (un′dər shot′), *adj., v.* **—*adj.*** **1** having the lower jaw or teeth projecting beyond the upper when the mouth is closed; underslung. **2** driven by water passing beneath: *an undershot water wheel.*
**—*v.*** the past tense and past participle of **undershoot.**

**un|der|shrub** (un′dər shrub′), *n.* **1** a small or low-growing shrub. **2** *Botany.* a plant having a shrubby base.

**un|der|side** (un′dər sīd′), *n.* **1** the surface lying underneath; bottom side: *The underside of the stone was covered with ants.* **2** *Figurative.* the hidden or gloomy side of anything: *... the grim underside of the affluent society* (John M. Muste). *He's well-versed in the dark underside of Gothic literature* (Eliot Fremont-Smith).

**un|der|sign** (un′dər sīn′, un′dər sīn′), *v.t.* to sign one's name at the end of (a letter or document); append one's signature to.

**un|der|signed** (un′dər sīnd′), *adj., n.* **—*adj.*** **1** having signed a letter or document; that is a signatory: *the undersigned persons.* **2** signed at the end of a letter or document: *the undersigned names.*
**—*n.*** **the undersigned,** the person or persons signing a letter or document: *I, the undersigned, ... am about to-day to lay down my life ... in defence of the Roman Catholic Church* (J. Stone).

**un|der|size** (un′dər sīz′), *adj.* = undersized.

**un|der|sized** (un′dər sīzd′), *adj.* smaller than the usual, required, or specified size: *An undersized fish has to be thrown back.*

**un|der|skirt** (un′dər skėrt′), *n.* a skirt worn under an outer skirt or overskirt.

**un|der|sleep** (un′dər slēp′), *v.i.,* **-slept, -sleep|ing.** to sleep less than is necessary.

**un|der|sleeve** (un′dər slēv′), *n.* a sleeve worn under an outer sleeve, especially an ornamental inner sleeve extending below the other.

**un|der|slung** (un′dər slung′, un′dər slung′), *adj.* **1** having the frame suspended below the axles: *an underslung vehicle.* **2** = undershot.

**un|der|soil** (un′dər soil′), *n.* = subsoil.

**un|der|sold** (un′dər sōld′), *v.* the past tense and past participle of **undersell.**

**un|der|song** (un′dər sông′, -song′), *n.* **1** a song that is sung softly along with another song, as an accompaniment such as was common in very old English music. **2** an underlying meaning; underlying element. [see etym. under **undernsong**]

**un|der|sparred** (un′dər spärd′), *adj. Nautical.* **1** having spars too small for the amount of sail needed. **2** having too few spars.

**un|der|spin** (un′dər spin′), *n.* a rolling motion in reverse to the direction of a ball; backspin. Underspin checks or reverses the forward motion of a ball when it strikes a surface.

**un|der|staffed** (un′dər staft′, -stäft′), *adj.* having too small a staff for one's needs and proper functioning; undermanned: *an understaffed hospital. The major problem is overcrowded and understaffed colleges and universities* (Science News Letter).

**un|der|stand** (un′dər stand′), *v.,* **-stood, -stand|ing.** **—*v.t.*** **1** to grasp the meaning of; know the meaning or idea of: *I don't understand that word. Now I understand the teacher's question.* **2** to grasp the meaning of the words, signs, or a line of reasoning, used by (a person): *What did he say? I couldn't understand him when he got into legal technicalities.* **3** to comprehend by knowing the meaning of the words used: *I can understand French if it is spoken slowly. A tongue no man could understand* (Tennyson). **4** to know well, especially: **a** to be able to explain, discuss, use, or experiment with: *to understand physics, to understand the techniques of writing.* **SYN:** See syn. under **know. b** to know how to deal with: *A good teacher understands children.* **SYN:** See syn. under **know. 5** to comprehend as a fact; grasp clearly; realize: *You understand, don't you, that I will be away for three weeks?* **6** to be informed; learn: *I understand that you are leaving town.* **7** to take as a fact; believe: *It is understood that you will come.* **8** to take as meaning; interpret: *How do you wish that remark to be understood? I understood your comment as approval of the plan. What are we to understand from his words?* **9** to supply in the mind. In "He hit the ball harder than I," the word *did* is understood after *I.*
**—*v.i.*** **1** to have or gain understanding or comprehension; get the meaning; grasp something with the mind: *Don't expect that fool ever to understand. I have told him three times, but he still doesn't understand.* **2** to have understanding; be sympathetic: *to expect a mother always to understand.* **3** to believe, assume, or infer: *He intends, as I understand, to leave tomorrow.* **4** *Obsolete.* to have or get knowledge or information; learn.
**understand each other,** to know each other's meaning and wishes; agree: *"You trust me," replied Leather, ... with a look as much as to say, "we understand each other"* (R. S. Surtees).
[Old English *understandan*]

**un|der|stand|a|bil|i|ty** (un′dər stan′də bil′ə tē), *n.* the quality of being understandable.

**un|der|stand|a|ble** (un′dər stan′də bəl), *adj.* that can be understood. **SYN:** comprehensible, intelligible.

---

**Pronunciation Key:** hat, āge, cãre, fär; let, ēqual, tėrm; it, īce; hot, ōpen, ôrder; oil, out; cup, put, rüle; child; long; thin; ᴛʜen; zh, measure; ə represents **a** in about, **e** in taken, **i** in pencil, **o** in lemon, **u** in circus.

**un|der|stand|a|bly** (un′dər stan′də blē), *adv.* in a manner that can be understood; conceivably: *an understandably appealing idea* (Wall Street Journal).

**un|der|stand|er** (un′dər stan′dər), *n.* **1** a person who understands; one who has knowledge or comprehension: *Some are pleased to be accounted understanders by others, and rest in such high words, as a badge of knowledge* (Richard Gilpin). **2** one who stands under: *short and muscular, like the understander in a human pyramid* (New Yorker).

**un|der|stand|ing** (un′dər stan′ding), *n., adj.* **—*n.*** **1** the act of one who understands, especially: **a** comprehension: *to have a clear understanding of the problem.* **b** knowledge: *a good understanding of what needs to be done.* **2** the power or ability to learn and know; intellect; intelligence: *the limited understanding of a child. Edison was a man of understanding.* **3** knowledge of each other's meaning and wishes: *a marriage based on true understanding.* **4** a mutual arrangement or agreement of an informal but more or less explicit nature: *You and I must come to an understanding.*
**—*adj.*** that understands or is able to understand; intelligent and sympathetic: *an understanding reply.* **—un′der|stand′ing|ly,** *adv.*

**un|der|state** (un′dər stāt′), *v.t., v.i.,* **-stat|ed, -stat|ing.** **1** to state too weakly, or less emphatically than one should; underemphasize: *to understate the facts, to understate one's position.* **2** to say less than the full truth about.

**un|der|stat|ed** (un′dər stā′tid), *adj.* played down for greater effect; restrained; low-key: *Her dancing is ... understated and delicate* (New Yorker). [*He*] *designed the understated modern interiors for the new shop* (New York Times).

**un|der|state|ment** (un′dər stāt′mənt, un′dər stāt′-), *n.* **1** a statement that expresses a fact too weakly or less emphatically than it should. Understatement is often used for humorous and other effects. *The designer used understatement to bring out subtle details in her dresses.* **SYN:** restraint. **2** a statement that says less than could be said truly.

**un|der|steer** (*v.* un′dər stir′; *n.* un′dər stir′), *v., n.* **—*v.i.*** to have an automobile turn less sharply on a curve than intended by the driver.
**—*n.*** **1** an act or instance of understeering. **2** a tendency to understeer: *When driven briskly, its excessive understeer called for a wrestler's muscles to pull the car around snaking curves* (London Times).

**un|der|stock** (un′dər stok′), *n.* the plant or part of a plant in which a graft is set.

**un|der|stood** (un′dər stu̇d′), *v., adj.* **—*v.*** the past tense and past participle of **understand**: *Have all of you understood today's lesson? I understood what he said.*
**—*adj.*** **1** agreed upon: *We gossip together, within understood limits, about our respective friends* (Midge Decter). **2** thoroughly known; comprehended: *a widely accepted and understood interpretation.* **3** implied; not expressed: *the understood sense of a word. The consent was for the most part an understood privilege.*

**un|der|sto|ry** (un′dər stôr′ē, -stōr′-), *n., pl.* **-ries.** the low layer of plants forming an underbrush or underwood.

**un|der|strap|per** (un′dər strap′ər), *n.* a subordinate; inferior; underling. [< *under-* + *strap,* verb + *-er*[1]]

**un|der|stra|tum** (un′dər strā′təm, -strat′əm), *n., pl.* **-stra|ta** (-strā′tə, -strat′ə), **-stra|tums.** an underlying stratum or layer; substratum.

**un|der|strength** (un′dər strengkth′, -strength′), *adj.* having too little strength; not up to the normal or required strength: *After Korea the Army gradually dwindled to 14 understrength divisions* (Time).

**un|der|stress** (un′dər stres′), *v.t.* to stress insufficiently; underemphasize: *His importance as a composer ... has tended to be understressed* (Listener).

**un|der|stroke** (un′dər strōk′), *v.t.,* **-stroked, -strok|ing.** to underline; underscore.

**un|der|struc|ture** (un′dər struk′chər), *n.* the base on which a structure rests or is built; foundation: *Underground erosion damaged the understructure of the building.* (*Figurative.*) *French money supports the whole understructure of the Tunisian economy* (Harper's).

**un|der|stud|y** (un′dər stud′ē), *n., pl.* **-stud|ies,** *v.,* **-stud|ied, -stud|y|ing.** **—*n.*** a person who can act as a substitute for an actor, actress, or any other regular performer: *Two of Notre Dame's touchdowns were scored by Worden's understudy, Tom McHugh* (New York Times).
**—*v.t.*** **1** to learn (a part) in order to be able to take the place of a regular performer if necessary. **2** to act as understudy to.
**—*v.i.*** to act as an understudy.

**un|der|suit** (un′dər süt′), *n.* a suit worn under or beneath another suit.

**un|der|sup|ply** (un′dər sə plī′; *n.* un′dər sə plī′), *v.,* **-plied, -ply|ing,** *n., pl.* **-plies.** **—*v.t.*** to supply insufficiently or inadequately: *If this should happen, the underdeveloped world will be even more desperately undersupplied with doctors* (Harper's).
**—*n.*** an insufficient or inadequate supply: *The total money market is tight, which means that there is an undersupply of lendable capital and an oversupply of potential borrowers* (New York Times).

**un|der|sur|face** (un′dər sėr′fis), *n.* the surface lying underneath; underside: *the undersurface of a leaf.*

**un|der|take** (un′dər tāk′), *v.,* **-took, -tak|en, -tak|ing.** **—*v.t.*** **1** to set about; try; attempt: *to undertake to reach home before dark.* **2** to set about to accomplish; take in hand; begin: *to undertake a journey.* **3** to agree to do; take upon oneself: *I will undertake to feed your dogs while you are away.* **4** to promise; guarantee: *I will undertake you shall be happy* (Henry Fielding). **5** *Archaic.* to accept the duty of attending to or looking after; take in charge. **6** *Obsolete.* to enter into combat with; engage.
**—*v.i.*** *Archaic.* to make oneself answerable, as for a person or fact; become surety: *I undertake For good Lord Titus' innocence* (Shakespeare).

**un|der|tak|er** (un′dər tā′kər *for 1;* un′dər tā′kər *for 2*), *n.* **1** a person who prepares the dead for burial and takes charge of funerals; mortician. **2** a person who undertakes something.

**un|der|tak|ing** (un′dər tā′king *for 1, 2, 4;* un′dər tā′king *for 3*), *n.* **1** something undertaken; task; enterprise: *a rash undertaking. My uncle engaged afterward in more prosperous undertakings* (Charlotte Brontë). *This is the very ecstasy of love, Whose violent property fordoes itself, And leads the will to desperate undertakings* (Shakespeare). **2** a promise; pledge; guarantee: *Three hundred pounds a year ... he proposed to pay her on an undertaking that she would never trouble him* (Thackeray). **3** the business of preparing the dead for burial and arranging funerals. **4** the act of one who undertakes any task or responsiblity.

**un|der|tax** (un′dər taks′), *v.t.* to tax insufficiently or inadequately.

**un|der|tax|a|tion** (un′dər tak sā′shən), *n.* insufficient or inadequate taxation: *Undertaxation of land helps speculators hold property out of use while they wait for a city's growth to raise its price* (Time).

**un|der|ten|ant** (un′dər ten′ənt), *n.* = subtenant.

**un|der-the-count|er** (un′dər ᴛʜə koun′tər), *adj.* offered or transacted under a counter; hidden and stealthy; secret; unauthorized; illegal: *under-the-counter literature, under-the-counter payoffs.*

**un|der-the-ta|ble** (un′dər ᴛʜə tā′bəl), *adj.* = under-the-counter.

**un|der|things** (un′dər thingz′), *n.pl.* = underclothes.

**un|der|thrust** (un′dər thrust′), *n., adj.* **—*n.*** *Geology.* **1** the forcing by compression of one rock mass under another, so as to produce a fault or fold. **2** the condition caused by such a forcing.
**—*adj.*** of or having to do with an underthrust: *an underthrust fault.*

**un|der|time** (*n., adv., adj.* un′dər tīm′; *v.* un′dər tīm′), *n., adv., adj., v.,* **-timed, -tim|ing.** **—*n.*** **1** time less than or below the regular hours. **2** wages for this period: *Would there not be merit in a scheme to pay undertime to workers?* (Atlantic).
**—*adv.*** less than or below the average hours: *He worked undertime this week and had to make it up.*
**—*adj.*** of or for undertime: *undertime pay.*
**—*v.t.*** to give too little time to: *to undertime a camera exposure.*

**un|der|tone** (un′dər tōn′), *n.* **1** a low or very quiet tone: *to talk in an undertone. He dropped his voice to a confidential undertone* (H. G. Wells). **2** a subdued color; color seen through other colors: *There was an undertone of brown beneath all the gold and crimson of autumn.* **3** *Figurative.* something beneath the surface; underlying quality, condition, or element: *an undertone of sadness in her gaiety.* **4** an underlying strength or weakness in the price level of any stock or commodity.

**un|der|took** (un′dər tu̇k′), *v.* the past tense of **undertake**: *He undertook more than he could do.*

**un|der|tow** (un′dər tō′), *n.* **1** any strong current below the surface of the water, moving in a direction different from that of the surface current. **2** the backward flow from waves breaking on a beach.

**un|der|trained** (un′dər trānd′), *adj.* insufficiently trained: *Undertrained and overworked sisters in parochial schools have taught hundreds of thousands of Catholic children* (Harper's).

**un|der|trick** (un′dər trik′), *n.* (in card games) a trick less than the number bid for or needed for game.

**un|der|trump** (un′dər trump′), in card games: **—*v.t.*** to play a trump to (a trick in which the lead is not trumps), lower than a trump already played by (another player).
**—*v.i.*** to play a lower trump than one already played to a trick.

**un|der|use** (un′dər yüz′), *v.t.,* **-used, -us|ing.** to use too little; underutilize: *The majority of playgrounds ... are grossly underused* (London Times).

**un|der|u|ti|lize** (un′dər yü′tə līz), *v.t.,* **-lized, -liz|ing.** to utilize insufficiently or wastefully: *Children from predominantly Negro and Puerto Rican schools can transfer to underutilized schools* (New York Times). **—un′der|u′ti|li|za′tion,** *n.*

**un|der|val|u|a|tion** (un′dər val′yu̇ ā′shən), *n.* too low a valuation.

**un|der|val|ue** (un′dər val′yü), *v.t.,* **-ued, -u|ing.** **1** to put too low a value on; underprize. **SYN:** underrate, underestimate, depreciate. **2** to esteem too little; appreciate insufficiently: *The Prince never committed the error of undervaluing the talents of his great adversary* (John L. Motley). **SYN:** underrate, underestimate, depreciate.

**un|der|vest** (un′dər vest′), *n.* an undershirt.

**un|der|vi|tal|ized** (un′dər vī′tə līzd), *adj.* insufficiently vitalized; lacking in vitality: *Much of the music sounded starved in emotion, undervitalized, and small-scale* (London Times).

**un|der|waist** (un′dər wāst′), *n.* a waist worn under another waist.

**un|der|wa|ter** (un′dər wôt′ər, -wot′-), *adj., adv.* **—*adj.*** **1** below the surface of the water. **2** made for use under the water: *A submarine is an underwater boat.* **3** situated below the water line of a ship.
**—*adv.*** below the surface of the water: *to swim underwater.*

**un|der|way** (un′dər wā′), *adv., adj.* **—*adv.*** going on; in motion; in progress: *The drive to raise money for the new library finally got underway. Normally, politicians have a pretty good idea once a campaign gets underway of who is likely to win* (Newsweek).
**—*adj.*** taking place while in motion or progress: *The student receives training in preparation for sea* [*and*] *underway procedures ... on a submarine* (Submarine Service, U.S. Naval Recruiting).

**un|der|wear** (un′dər wãr′), *n.* clothes worn under the outer garments, especially next to the skin; underclothes; underclothing.

**un|der|weight** (un′dər wāt′), *adj., n.* **—*adj.*** having too little weight; not up to the normal or required weight.
**—*n.*** weight that is not up to standard.

**un|der|went** (un′dər went′), *v.* the past tense of **undergo**: *Transportation underwent a great change with the development of the automobile.*

**un|der|whelm** (un′dər hwelm′), *v.t.* to create a feeling of indifference in; fail to excite or arouse enthusiasm: [*His*] *long, prepared speeches in more formal settings often underwhelm his audiences, but his peppy little talks followed by question periods show a perky platform style* (Time). [< *under-* + (over)*whelm*]

**un|der|wing** (un′dər wing′), *n., adj.* **—*n.*** one of the hind set of wings of an insect.
**—*adj.*** situated beneath the wing or wings: *underwing feathers.*

**underwing moth,** any one of a group of moths having brightly colored hind wings which are visible only in flight.

**un|der|wit** (un′dər wit′), *n.* a half-witted person; person who is stupid or feeble-minded.

**un|der|wit|ted** (un′dər wit′id), *adj.* = half-witted.

**un|der|wood** (un′dər wu̇d′), *n.* **1** = underbrush. **2** a quantity or stretch of woody undergrowth.

**un|der|wool** (un′dər wu̇l′), *n.* a fine, soft wool under the coarse outer hair of various mammals.

**un|der|work** (*n.* un′dər wėrk′; *v.* un′dər wėrk′), *n., v.,* **-worked** or **-wrought, -work|ing.** **—*n.*** **1** subordinate or inferior work. **2** secret or underhand work. **3** a structure placed under something; substructure.
**—*v.t.*** **1** to put insufficient work or labor on (something). **2** to exact insufficient work from. **3** to do the same work at a cheaper price than (another). **4** *Obsolete.* to injure or weaken by secret or insidious means; undermine.
**—*v.i.*** **1** to do less work than is required or suitable. **2** *Obsolete.* to work secretly or insidiously.

**un|der|world** (un′dər wėrld′), *n.* **1** the lower, degraded, or criminal part of human society; world of crime and vice. **2** the lower world; Hades: *The lord of the dark underworld, the king of the multitudinous dead, carried her* [*Persephone*] *off when ... she strayed too far from her companions* (Edith Hamilton). **3** *Archaic.* the earth as distinguished from heaven. **4** the opposite side of the earth; antipodes.

**un|der|world|ling** (un′dər wėrld′ling), *n. U.S. Informal.* a racketeer; gangster.

**un|der|write** (un′dər rīt′, un′dər rīt′), *v.*, **-wrote, -writ|ten, -writ|ing.** —*v.t.* **1a** to insure (property) against loss. **b** to sign one's name to (an insurance policy), thereby accepting the risk of insuring the person or thing specified against loss. **c** to assume liability for (a certain amount or risk) by way of insurance. **2** to write under (other written matter); sign one's name to (a document or written statement); be a signatory to. **3a** to agree to buy (all the stocks or bonds of a certain issue that are not bought by the public): *The bankers underwrote the steel company's bonds.* **b** to agree to buy (an entire issue of stocks or bonds). **4** to agree to meet the expense of: *to underwrite a person's education.*
—*v.i.* to carry on the business of insurance; be an underwriter.
[compare Old English *underwrītan,* translation of Latin *subscrībere*]

**un|der|writ|er** (un′dər rī′tər), *n.* **1** a person who underwrites an insurance policy or carries on an insurance business; insurer. **2** an official of an insurance company who determines the risks to be accepted, the premiums to be paid, and other conditions of an insurance agreement. **3** a person who underwrites (usually with others) an issue or issues of bonds, stocks, or other securities. *Abbr:* u/w (no periods).

**un|der|writ|ten** (un′dər rit′ən, un′dər rit′-), *v.* the past participle of **underwrite.**

**un|der|wrote** (un′dər rōt′, un′dər rōt′), *v.* the past tense of **underwrite.**

**un|der|wrought** (un′dər rôt′), *v.* underworked; a past tense and a past participle of **underwork.**

**un|de|scribed** (un′di skrībd′), *adj.* not described; not depicted, defined, or delineated: *an undescribed species.*

**un|de|served** (un′di zėrvd′), *adj.* not deserved or merited: *an undeserved reputation for wit* (Eden Phillpotts).

**un|de|serv|ed|ly** (un′di zėr′vid lē), *adv.* without desert, either good or evil; contrary to desert or what is merited: *athletic brutes whom undeservedly we call heroes* (John Dryden).

**un|de|serv|er** (un′di zėr′vər), *n.* an undeserving person; an unworthy person.

**un|de|serv|ing** (un′di zėr′ving), *adj.* not deserving or meriting. —**un′de|serv′ing|ly,** *adv.*

**un|de|signed** (un′di zīnd′), *adj.* not designed; unintentional.

**un|de|sign|ed|ly** (un′di zī′nid lē), *adv.* in an undesigned manner; without design or intention.

**un|de|sign|ing** (un′di zī′ning), *adj.* **1** having no selfish or ulterior designs; free from designing motives; disinterested. **2** simple and straightforward; not crafty.

**un|de|sir|a|bil|i|ty** (un′di zīr′ə bil′ə tē), *n.* the quality or condition of being undesirable.

**un|de|sir|a|ble** (un′di zīr′ə bəl), *adj., n.* —*adj.* **1** objectionable; disagreeable: *The drug was taken off the market because it had undesirable side effects on persons who used it.* **2** offensive to or subversive of the moral or social standards of an individual or group: *a gathering of criminals and other undesirable persons.*
—*n.* an undesirable person or thing. —**un′de|sir′a|ble|ness,** *n.*

**un|de|sir|a|bly** (un′di zīr′ə blē), *adv.* in an undesirable manner; contrary to what is desirable.

**un|de|sired** (un′di zīrd′), *adj.* not desired; unwelcome.

**un|de|tect|a|ble** (un′di tek′tə bəl), *adj.* that cannot be detected.

**un|de|tect|ed** (un′di tek′tid), *adj.* not detected; unperceived.

**un|de|ter|mi|na|ble** (un′di tėr′mə nə bəl), *adj.* = indeterminable.

**un|de|ter|mined** (un′di tėr′mənd), *adj.* indefinite; indeterminate.

**un|de|terred** (un′di tėrd′), *adj.* not deterred.

**un|de|vel|op|a|ble** (un′di vel′ə pə bəl), *adj.* that cannot be developed: *He's scheduled to take an embassy in an underdeveloped* (*and probably undevelopable*) *country* (Harper's).

**un|de|vel|oped** (un′di vel′əpt), *adj.* **1** not fully grown; immature. **2** not put to full use: *the underdeveloped natural resources of a country.*

**un|de|vi|at|ing** (un dē′vē ā′ting), *adj.* not deviating; not departing from a line of procedure; unvarying; uniform: *a course of undeviating rectitude* (Oliver Goldsmith). —**un|de′vi|at′ing|ly,** *adv.*

**un|de|vout** (un′di vout′), *adj.* not devout; having no devotion.

**un|did** (un did′), *v.* the past tense of **undo:** *He undid his shoes. The fire in the artist's studio undid many years of work.*

**un|dies** (un′dēz), *n.pl. Informal.* articles of women's underclothing.

**un|dif|fer|en|ti|at|ed** (un′dif ə ren′shē ā′tid), *adj.* not differentiated; without clear qualities or distinctive characteristics: *undifferentiated growth of cells. They discovered that both wheat and cotton cloth were "undifferentiated" products—that is, each grain of wheat, each bolt of calico, was like any other grain or bolt* (Wall Street Journal). *The typical student completes his college program with ... a hodgepodge of undifferentiated knowledge* (Carroll V. Newsom).

**un|di|gest|ed** (un′də jes′tid, -dī-), *adj.* **1** not digested in the stomach or intestines: *undigested food.* **2** not brought to a mature or proper condition by natural physical change: *undigested metals, undigested blood.* **3** *Figurative.* not understood or absorbed mentally: *undigested facts and figures* (Science News). **4** not properly arranged or regulated; chaotic; confused: *A crude and undigested mass of useless rubbish* (Manchester Examiner). *The whole was published in an undigested, incoherent, and sometimes self-contradictory paragraph* (Henry Hallam).

**un|di|gest|i|ble** (un′də jes′tə bəl, -dī-), *adj.* not digestible; indigestible.

**un|dig|ni|fied** (un dig′nə fīd), *adj.* not dignified; lacking in dignity. —**un|dig′ni|fied′ly,** *adv.*

**un|dig|ni|fy** (un dig′nə fī), *v.t.,* **-fied, -fy|ing.** to deprive of dignity; make undignified.

**un|di|lut|ed** (un′də lü′tid, -dī-), *adj.* not diluted or weakened.

**un|di|lu|tion** (un′də lü′shən, -dī-), *n.* an undiluted state.

**un|di|min|ish|a|ble** (un′də min′i shə bəl), *adj.* not diminishable; not subject to lessening or decrease: *Character is of a stellar and undiminishable greatness* (Emerson).

**un|di|min|ished** (un′də min′isht), *adj.* not diminished or lessened; of full size, amount, strength, or intensity; unabated.

**un|di|min|ish|ing** (un′də min′i shing), *adj.* not diminishing.

**un|dimmed** (un dimd′), *adj.* not dimmed, as a light or the eyes.

**un|di|nal** (un dē′nəl), *adj.* **1** of or having to do with an undine. **2** of or having to do with the belief in undines.

**un|dine** (un dēn′, un′dēn), *n.* a female water spirit, who, according to legend, might acquire a soul by marrying a mortal and bearing a child: *She looks, in her moments of ... loveliness, like an undine sighing in the Seine* (Time). [< New Latin *Undina* < Latin *unda* wave]

**un|dip|lo|mat|ic** (un′dip lə mat′ik), *adj.* not tactful: *an undiplomatic question, undiplomatic behavior.*

**un|dip|lo|mat|i|cal|ly** (un′dip lə mat′ə klē), *adv.* in an undiplomatic manner; tactlessly.

**un|di|rect|ed** (un′də rek′tid, -dī-), *adj.* **1** not directed toward some end or on some course; lacking guidance: *undirected energies, undirected children.* **2** not directed to some person or place; lacking an address: *an undirected letter.*

**un|dis|cerned** (un′də zėrnd′, -sėrnd′), *adj.* not discerned; unperceived.

**un|dis|cern|i|ble** (un′də zėr′nə bəl, -sėr′-), *adj.* indiscernible; imperceptible.

**un|dis|cern|ing** (un′də zėr′ning, -sėr′-), *adj.* not discerning; lacking discernment. —**un′dis|cern′ing|ly,** *adv.*

**un|dis|charged** (un′dis chärjd′), *adj.* **1** not dismissed; not freed from obligation: *Hold still in readiness and undischarged* (Ben Jonson). **2** not fulfilled; not carried out; unexecuted: *an undischarged duty.*

**un|dis|ci|plin|a|ble** (un dis′ə plin′ə bəl), *adj.* that cannot be disciplined: *a thin, nervous colonel in the undisciplined and seemingly undisciplinable Congolese Army* (New York Times).

**un|dis|ci|plined** (un dis′ə plind), *adj.* not disciplined; without proper control; untrained. **SYN:** wild, uncontrolled.

**un|dis|cov|er|a|ble** (un′dis kuv′ər ə bəl, -kuv′rə-), *adj.* not discoverable; not to be discovered, learned, or found out. —**un′dis|cov′er|a|bly,** *adv.*

**un|dis|cov|ered** (un′dis kuv′ərd), *adj.* not discovered; not found or known by discovery: *The undiscover'd country from whose bourn No traveller returns* (Shakespeare).

**un|dis|crim|i|nat|ing** (un′dis krim′ə nā′ting), *adj.* not discriminating; making no distinctions; lacking discrimination. —**un′dis|crim′i|nat′ing|ly,** *adv.*

**un|dis|cussed** (un′dis kust′), *adj.* not discussed; not argued or debated.

**un|dis|guised** (un′dis gīzd′), *adj.* **1** not disguised. **2** *Figurative.* unconcealed; open; plain; frank: *undisguised fear, gratitude, or delight.* —**un′dis|guis′ed|ly,** *adv.*

**un|dis|hon|ored** (un′dis on′ərd), *adj.* not dishonored; not disgraced.

**un|dis|mayed** (un′dis mād′), *adj.* not dismayed; undaunted.

**un|dis|pensed** (un′dis penst′), *adj.* **1** not dispensed. **2** not freed from obligation.

**un|dis|persed** (un′dis pėrst′), *adj.* not dispersed; not scattered.

**un|dis|posed** (un′dis pōzd′), *adj.* **1** not disposed (of): *goods remaining undisposed of.* **2** *Obsolete.* **a** indisposed. **b** disinclined.

**un|dis|put|a|ble** (un′dis pyü′tə bəl, un dis′pyə-), *adj.* indisputable; incontestable.

**un|dis|put|ed** (un′dis pyü′tid), *adj.* not disputed; not doubted: *Thou say'st an undisputed thing In such a solemn way* (Oliver Wendell Holmes). **SYN:** uncontested. —**un′dis|put′ed|ly,** *adv.*

**un|dis|sem|bled** (un′di sem′bəld), *adj.* not dissembled; open; undisguised; unfeigned.

**un|dis|si|pat|ed** (un dis′ə pā′tid), *adj.* not dissipated or scattered.

**un|dis|so|lute** (un dis′ə lüt), *adj.* not dissolute; not indulging in evil or foolish pleasures.

**un|dis|solv|a|ble** (un′di zol′və bəl), *adj.* not dissolvable; insoluble; indissoluble.

**un|dis|solved** (un′di zolvd′), *adj.* not dissolved.

**un|dis|tin|guish|a|ble** (un′dis ting′gwi shə bəl), *adj.* that cannot be distinguished; indistinguishable.

**un|dis|tin|guished** (un′dis ting′gwisht), *adj.* not distinguished: **a** not set apart; commonplace: *Though undistinguished from the crowd By wealth or dignity* (William Cowper). **b** not seen; not noticed: *Finding herself undistinguished in the dusk* (Jane Austen).

**un|dis|tract|ed** (un′dis trak′tid), *adj.* not distracted; not perplexed by contrariety or variety of thoughts, desires, or concerns.

**un|dis|trib|ut|ed** (un′dis trib′yə tid), *adj.* not distributed.

**undistributed middle term,** *Logic.* a middle term which does not include its whole class (*all* or *none*) in either the first or the second premise of a syllogism. It makes the syllogism invalid. *Example:* The middle term "men" or "man" is not distributed to include "all men" or "no man" in: All poets are men; my husband is a man; my husband is a poet.

**un|dis|turbed** (un′dis tėrbd′), *adj.* not disturbed; not troubled; calm. **SYN:** unruffled. —**un′dis|turb′ed|ly,** *adv.*

**un|di|ver|si|fied** (un′də vėr′sə fīd, -dī-), *adj.* not diversified; without variety.

**un|di|vert|ed** (un′də vėr′tid, -dī-), *adj.* **1** not diverted; not turned aside. **2** not amused; not entertained or pleased.

**un|di|vest|ed** (un′də ves′tid, -dī-), *adj.* not divested; not stripped or deprived (of).

**un|di|vid|ed** (un′də vī′did), *adj.* **1** not divided; not separated into parts; not separated or parted from each other, or one from another; not portioned out or distributed; complete: *The teacher asked for our undivided attention.* **2** *Botany.* not cleft, lobed, or branched. —**un′di|vid′ed|ly,** *adv.* —**un′di|vid′ed|ness,** *n.*

**undivided profits,** net profits remaining after the payment of dividends, as by a bank or corporation.

**un|di|vorced** (un′də vôrst′, -vōrst′), *adj.* not divorced; not separated.

**un|di|vulged** (un′də vuljd′), *adj.* not divulged; not revealed or disclosed; secret.

**un|do** (un dü′), *v.t.,* **-did, -done, -do|ing.** **1** to unfasten and open; unloose and remove the wrapping of: *"Please undo the package," she said.* **2** to untie: *to undo a knot. I undid the string.* **3** to do away with; cause to be as if never done; cancel or reverse; rescind: *What's done, cannot be undone* (Shakespeare). **SYN:** annul. **4** to bring to ruin; spoil; destroy: *The workmen mended the road, but a heavy storm undid their work. Curse on his virtues! they've undone his country* (Joseph Addison). **5** to unlock the mystery of; explain; solve. [Old English *undōn* < *un-* un-[2] + *dōn* to do] —**un|do′er,** *n.*

**un|do|a|ble** (un dü′ə bəl), *adj.* that cannot be done: *Schoenberg himself once said that the opera is undoable* (Time).

**un|dock** (un dok′), *v.t.* **1** to take (a ship) out of a dock. **2** to separate (a spacecraft) from another in space: *Conrad undocked Gemini and used his thrusters to back slowly away from the Agena* (Time).
—*v.i.* to come out of docking: *Cosmos 212 and 213 docked, coasted and undocked in orbit automatically* (Science News).

**un|doc|tri|naire** (un dok′trə nãr′), *adj.* not doctrinaire; not dogmatic: *The London group showed the same undoctrinaire attitude which allowed free room for experiment without being tied to a particular theory* (London Times).

**un|doc|u|ment|ed** (un dok′yə men′tid), *adj.* **1** without official papers: *an undocumented alien.* **2a** without real proof; not supported by facts: *undocumented evidence, undocumented charges.*

**Pronunciation Key:** hat, āge, cãre, fär; let, ēqual, tėrm; it, īce; hot, ōpen, ôrder; oil, out; cup, pu̇t, rüle; child; long; thin; ŦHen; zh, measure; ə represents a in about, e in taken, i in pencil, o in lemon, u in circus.

**b** without references or sources: *an undocumented book.*

**un|do|ing** (un dü′ing), *n.* **1** a bringing to ruin; spoiling; destroying; ruin. **2** a cause of destruction or ruin: *Gambling was his undoing. Drink was this man's undoing.* **3** a reversing of the effect of something; annulment; cancellation. **4** an untying; unfastening.

**un|do|mes|ti|cat|ed** (un′də mes′tə kā′tid), *adj.* **1** not domesticated; not accustomed to a family life. **2** not tamed, as an animal.

**un|done**[1] (un dun′), *adj.* **1** not done; not finished: *Nought done, the Hero deem'd, While ought undone remained* (Matthew Prior). SYN: uncompleted. **2** ruined: *Whichever way I turn I am undone* (Dickens). SYN: destroyed. **3** untied, unfastened. [< Middle English *undon* < *un-* un-[1] + *don* done]

**un|done**[2] (un dun′), *v.* the past participle of **undo**.

**un|dou|ble** (un dub′əl), *v.t., v.i.,* **-bled, -bling.** to straighten out; unclench.

**un|doubt|ed** (un dou′tid), *adj.* not doubted; accepted as true; beyond dispute; indisputable.

**un|doubt|ed|ly** (un dou′tid lē), *adv.* beyond doubt; certainly.

**un|doubt|ing** (un dou′ting), *adj.* **1** not doubting; assured; confident. **2** believing; credulous. — **un-doubt′ing|ly,** *adv.*

**UNDP** (no periods), United Nations Development Program.

**un|dra|mat|ic** (un′drə mat′ik), *adj.* not dramatic; lacking dramatic effectiveness. — **un′dra|mat′i-cal|ly,** *adv.*

**un|drape** (un drāp′), *v.t.,* **-draped, -drap|ing.** to strip of drapery; bare.

**un|draped** (un drāpt′), *adj.* not draped; without drapery.

**un|draw** (un drô′), *v.t.,* **-drew, -drawn, -draw|ing.** to draw back or away; pull open: *She undrew the curtain.*

**un|drawn** (un drôn′), *adj., v.* — ***adj.*** not drawn.
— ***v.*** the past participle of **undraw**.

**un|dread|ed** (un dred′id), *adj.* not dreaded; not feared.

**un|dreamed** (un drēmd′), *adj.* not dreamed; undreamed-of: *undreamed wealth, undreamed success.*

**un|dreamed-of** (un drēmd′uv′, -ov′), *adj.* never thought of, even in the imagination: *undreamed-of advances in medicine. There we find processes whose regularity makes it possible to measure time with undreamed-of accuracy* (Scientific American).

**un|dreamt** (un dremt′), *adj.* = undreamed.

**un|dreamt-of** (un dremt′uv′, -ov′), *adj.* = undreamed-of.

**un|dress** (*v.* un dres′; *n.* un′dres′, un dres′; *adj.* un′dres′), *v., n., adj.* — ***v.t.*** **1** to take the clothes off of; divest of garments; disrobe; strip. **2** to strip of ornament. **3** to remove the dressing from (a wound).
— ***v.i.*** to take off one's clothes; strip; disrobe.
— ***n.*** **1** loose, informal dress. **2** clothes proper for ordinary, everyday wear, as distinguished from those worn on formal or ceremonial occasions. **3** lack of clothing; nakedness.
— ***adj.*** of, having to do with, or designating clothes proper for ordinary, everyday wear: *an undress uniform.*

**un|dressed** (un drest′), *adj.* **1** not dressed; unclothed. **2** of or of the nature of suede: *undressed leather.*

**un|drew** (un drü′), *v.* the past tense of **undraw**.

**un|drink|a|ble** (un dring′kə bəl), *adj.* not drinkable.

**un|drunk** (un drungk′), *adj.* **1** not swallowed by drinking; not drunk: *In Soviet embassies and legations around the world huge supplies of vodka went undrunk, caviar uneaten* (Time). **2** not intoxicated.

**und so wei|ter** (ůnt zō vī′tər), *German.* and so forth. *Abbr:* usw.

**un|due** (un dü′, -dyü′), *adj.* **1** not fitting; improper; inappropriate; unsuitable: *He made rude, undue remarks about those around him.* **2** not right; unjustifiable; illegal. **3** too great; too much; excessive: *A miser gives undue importance to money.* **4** not properly owing or payable.

**undue influence,** *Law.* control over another, making him do in important affairs what he would not do of his free will.

**un|du|lan|cy** (un′jə lən sē, -dyə-), *n.* wavy state or character.

**un|du|lant** (un′jə lənt, -dyə-), *adj.* that undulates; waving; wavy: *undulant drapery.*

**undulant fever,** a disease characterized by intermittent or sometimes continuous fever, disorders of the bowels, enlarged spleen, weakness, anemia, and pain in the joints; brucellosis; Malta fever; Mediterranean fever; Rock fever. It is caused by infection with bacteria usually transmitted by contact with infected cattle, goats, and hogs, or by consumption of raw milk or milk products.

**un|du|late** (*v.* un′jə lāt, -dyə-; *adj.* un′jə lit, -lāt; -dyə-), *v.,* **-lat|ed, -lat|ing,** *adj.* — ***v.i.*** **1** to move in or in the manner of waves; rise and fall or come and go with a wavelike motion: *undulating water.* (*Figurative.*) *Tall spire from which the sound of cheerful bells Just undulates upon the list'ning ear* (William Cowper). **2** to have a wavy form or surface: *undulating hair, an undulating prairie.*
— ***v.t.*** **1** to cause to move in or in the manner of waves. **2** to give a wavy form or surface to. [< Late Latin *undula* wavelet (diminutive) < Latin *unda* wave + English *-ate*[1]]
— ***adj.*** = wavy[1].
[< Latin *undulātus* diversified as with waves < *unda* wave]

**un|du|lat|ed** (un′jə lā′tid, -dyə-), *adj.* = undulate.

**un|du|lat|ing** (un′jə lā′ting, -dyə-), *adj.* **1** that undulates; having a wavy motion: *undulating hair. The undulating and tumultuous multitude* (Jeremy Bentham). **2** having a form or surface resembling a series of waves: *an undulating prairie. The country became more undulating* (Samuel Butler). — **un′du|lat′ing|ly,** *adv.*

**un|du|la|tion** (un′jə lā′shən, -dyə-), *n.* **1** a wavelike motion; undulating. **2** a wavy form. **3** one of a series of wavelike bends, curves, swellings, or other patterns. **4** *Physics.* a wavelike motion in air or other medium, as in the propagation of sound or light; vibration; wave.

**un|du|la|to|ry** (un′jə lə tôr′ē, -tōr′-; -dyə-), *adj.* undulating; wavy.

**undulatory theory,** *Physics.* the theory that light is propagated in undulatory movements or waves; wave theory.

**un|du|lous** (un′jə ləs, -dyə-), *adj.* characterized by undulations or waves; wavy.

**un|du|ly** (un dü′lē, -dyü′-), *adv.* **1** in an undue manner; improperly. **2** to an undue degree; too much; excessively: *unduly harsh, unduly optimistic.*

**un|du|pli|cat|ed** (un dü′plə kā′tid, -dyü′-), *adj.* **1** not having a duplicate or duplicates: *an unduplicated set of records.* **2** not repeated or matched: *an unduplicated performance.*

**un|du|ti|ful** (un dü′tə fəl, -dyü′-), *adj.* not dutiful; not properly obedient or submissive. — **un|du′ti-ful|ly,** *adv.* — **un|du′ti|ful|ness,** *n.*

**un|dyed** (un dīd′), *adj.* not dyed; of the natural color.

**un|dy|ing** (un dī′ing), *adj.* that never dies; deathless; immortal; eternal: *undying beauty, a dog's undying love for its master.* SYN: perpetual, everlasting. — **un|dy′ing|ly,** *adv.* — **un|dy′ing|ness,** *n.*

**un|dy|nam|ic** (un′dī nam′ik), *adj.* not dynamic; not energetic, forceful, or active: *an undynamic personality. California was only a feeble, undynamic outpost of the Spanish Empire* (New Yorker).

**un|earned** (un ėrnd′), *adj.* **1** not earned by labor or service; not worked for: *an unearned gift of nature.* **2** not earned by merit; not deserved; unmerited: *unearned punishment.* **3** *Baseball.* scored because of a defensive error or errors: *The Phils tallied two runs, both unearned, in the fourth* (New York Times).

**unearned income,** income from investments as contrasted with wages.

**unearned increment,** an increase in the value of property from natural causes, as from growth of population, rather than from the labor, improvements, or expenditures made by the owner.

**un|earth** (un ėrth′), *v.t.* **1** to dig out of the earth; exhume: *to unearth a skeleton.* **2** to disclose by the removal of earth: *to unearth a buried city.* **3** to force out of a hole or burrow by or as if by digging: *to unearth a woodchuck.* **4** *Figurative.* **a** to find out and make public; disclose; reveal: *to unearth a plot.* **b** to look for and find; discover: *to unearth the answer to a problem.*

**un|earth|li|ness** (un ėrth′lē nis), *n.* the character or state of being unearthly.

**un|earth|ly** (un ėrth′lē), *adj.* **1** not of this world; supernatural: *an unearthly being. In after years, when she looked back upon them a kind of glory, a radiance as of an unearthly holiness, seemed to glow about these golden hours* (Lytton Strachey). **2** strange; weird; ghostly: *the unearthly wails that sometimes come from the demons* (Santha Rama Rau). **3** *Informal.* abnormal or unnatural; extraordinary; preposterous: *to rise at an unearthly hour.*

**un|ease** (un ēz′), *n.* = uneasiness.

**un|eas|i|ly** (un ē′zə lē), *adv.* in an uneasy manner; restlessly; apprehensively.

**un|eas|i|ness** (un ē′zē nis), *n.* lack of ease or comfort; restlessness; anxiety.

**un|eas|y** (un ē′zē), *adj.,* **-eas|i|er, -eas|i|est.** **1** mentally uncomfortable; disturbed; anxious; apprehensive; restless: *to be uneasy about a decision.* **2** physically uncomfortable; restless: *uneasy sleep.* **3** not conducive to ease or comfort; somewhat precarious: *an uneasy peace.* **4** characterized by absence of ease or comfort: *The benches were hard and uneasy. One or two uneasy sofas* (H. G. Wells). **5** not easy in manner; stiff; awkward.

**un|eat|a|ble** (un ē′tə bəl), *adj.* not eatable; unfit to be eaten: *The English country gentleman galloping after a fox—the unspeakable in full pursuit of the uneatable* (Oscar Wilde).

**un|eat|en** (un ē′tən), *adj.* not eaten.

**un|eath** (un ēth′), *adj. Obsolete.* not easy; difficult. [Old English *unēathe* < *un-* un-[1] + *ēathe* easy]

**un|e|co|nom|ic** (un′ē kə nom′ik, -ek ə-), *adj.* not economic; expensive; unprofitable: *The railways are compelled to operate uneconomic lines* (Canada Month).

**un|e|co|nom|i|cal** (un′ē kə nom′ə kəl, -ek ə-), *adj.* not economical. — **un′e|co|nom′i|cal|ly,** *adv.*

**UNEDA** (no periods), United Nations Economic Development Administration.

**un|ed|i|ble** (un ed′ə bəl), *adj.* = inedible.

**un|ed|i|fy|ing** (un ed′ə fī′ing), *adj.* not edifying; not elevating or beneficial morally.

**un|ed|it|ed** (un ed′ə tid), *adj.* not edited; not changed in any way: *an unedited speech.*

**un|ed|u|ca|ble** (un ej′ů kə bəl), *adj.* not capable of being educated; ineducable: *Industry finds it ... difficult to offer employment to uneducated and especially to uneducable young people* (Charles S. Ryckman).

**un|ed|u|cat|ed** (un ej′ů kā′tid), *adj.* not educated; not taught or trained. SYN: See syn. under **ignorant**.

**un|ed|u|ca|tion|al** (un′ej ů kā′shə nəl), *adj.* not furthering education or the development of the mind.

**UNEF** (no periods), United Nations Emergency Force.

**un|ef|fec|tu|al** (un′ə fek′chů əl), *adj. Obsolete.* ineffectual.

**un|e|lect|ed** (un′i lek′tid), *adj.* not elected; not chosen: *unelected for salvation.*

**un|em|bar|rassed** (un′em bar′əst), *adj.* not embarrassed or flustered; not confused; composed: *She was frank and unembarrassed toward him, without a trace of boldness or overfamiliarity* (Edgar Maass).

**un|em|bod|ied** (un′em bod′ēd), *adj.* **1** not embodied or materialized. **2** not having a body; incorporeal.

**un|em|broi|dered** (un′əm broi′dərd), *adj.* not embroidered; without embroidery: *an unembroidered speech.*

**un|e|mo|tion|al** (un′i mō′shə nəl), *adj.* not emotional; impassive: *an unemotional tone of voice, an unemotional observer.* — **un′e|mo′tion|al|ly,** *adv.*

**un|em|ploy|a|bil|i|ty** (un′əm ploi′ə bil′ə tē), *n.* the quality or condition of being unemployable: *Hence, educational inadequacies lead to lack of training, unemployability, etc.* (New York Times).

**un|em|ploy|a|ble** (un′em ploi′ə bəl), *adj., n.*
— ***adj.*** that cannot be employed, especially that cannot be employed to work because of a physical or mental impediment.
— ***n.*** a person who is unemployable.

**un|em|ployed** (un′em ploid′), *adj., n.* — ***adj.*** **1** not employed; not in use: *an unemployed skill.* **2** not having a job; having no work: *an unemployed person.* **3** earning no interest or dividends; not loaned or invested: *unemployed capital.*
— ***n.*** **the unemployed,** people out of work: *Some of the unemployed sought aid from the government. The employed and the unemployed, taken together, constitute the labour force* (Leon E. Truesdell).

**un|em|ploy|ment** (un′em ploi′mənt), *n.* lack of employment; being out of work.

**unemployment compensation,** *U.S.* payment under a system by which eligible workers are guaranteed a small weekly income during a limited period of involuntary unemployment.

**unemployment insurance,** a government insurance program, supported by employer-paid taxes, which provides income for a limited period of time to eligible workers who are involuntarily unemployed.

**un|en|closed** (un′en klōzd′), *adj.* not enclosed; not shut in or surrounded, as by a fence or wall.

**un|en|cum|bered** (un′en kum′bərd), *adj.* not encumbered; free from encumbrance.

**un|en|deared** (un′en dird′), *adj.* not attended with endearment.

**un|end|ed** (un en′did), *adj.* endless; infinite.

**un|end|ing** (un en′ding), *adj.* continuing; not ending; having no end; endless; ceaseless; eternal. — **un|end′ing|ly,** *adv.* — **un|end′ing|ness,** *n.*

**un|en|dowed** (un′en doud′), *adj.* not endowed; without an endowment.

**un|en|dur|a|ble** (un′en důr′ə bəl, -dyůr′-), *adj.* **1** not endurable; unbearable; intolerable; insufferable: *unendurable pain, an unendurable braggart.* **2** that cannot endure; unenduring. — **un′en|dur′a-bly,** *adv.*

**un|en|dur|ing** (un′en dùr′ing, -dyùr′-), *adj.* that does not endure; fleeting: *the unenduring clouds* (Wordsworth).

**un|en|force|a|ble** (un′en fôr′sə bəl, -fōr′-), *adj.* not enforceable; that cannot be enforced: *The [Chilean] President's hesitancy to legalize the bill was based on the belief that the law would be unenforceable* (Miguel Jorrín).

**un|en|forced** (un′en fôrst′, -fōrst′), *adj.* not enforced.

**un|en|gaged** (un′en gājd′), *adj.* not engaged.

**un-Eng|lish** (un ing′glish), *adj.* **1** not English; foreign or opposed to the English as in character, spirit, or usages. **2** not in accordance with the usages of the English language.

**un|en|light|ened** (un′en lī′tənd), *adj.* not enlightened; without intellectual or moral enlightenment; benighted; ignorant.

**un|en|light|en|ing** (un′en lī′tə ning), *adj.* not instructive or informative.

**un|en|tan|gled** (un′en tang′gəld), *adj.* not entangled; not complicated; not perplexed: *unentangled through the snares of life* (Samuel Johnson).

**un|en|ter|pris|ing** (un en′tər prī′zing), *adj.* not enterprising; lacking enterprise.

**un|en|ter|tain|ing** (un′en tər tā′ning), *adj.* not entertaining or amusing.

**un|en|thralled** (un′en thrôld′), *adj.* not enslaved; not reduced to thralldom.

**un|en|thu|si|as|tic** (un′en thü′zē as′tik), *adj.* not enthusiastic; without enthusiasm.

**un|en|thu|si|as|ti|cal|ly** (un′en thü′zē as′tə klē), *adv.* in an unenthusiastic manner.

**un|en|vi|a|ble** (un en′vē ə bəl), *adj.* not enviable; not such as to excite envy.

**un|en|vi|a|bly** (un en′vē ə blē), *adv.* so as not to be enviable.

**un|en|vied** (un en′vēd), *adj.* not envied; exempt from the envy of others.

**un|en|vi|ous** (un en′vē əs), *adj.* not envious; free from envy.

**UNEP** (yü′nep), *n.* the United Nations Environmental Program.

**un|e|qual** (un ē′kwəl), *adj., n.* —*adj.* **1** not the same in amount, size, number, value, merit, degree, or rank: *unequal sums of money, unequal achievements.* **2a** not balanced; not well matched: *an unequal marriage.* **b** not fair; one-sided: *an unequal contest.* **3** not enough; not sufficient; not adequate: *His strength was unequal to the task.* **SYN**: inadequate. **4** not regular; not even; variable: *unequal vibrations.*
—*n.* a person or thing that is not equal to another: *In social standing the two men were considered as unequals.* —**un|e′qual|ly**, *adv.* —**un|e′qual|ness**, *n.*

**un|e|qualed** (un ē′kwəld), *adj.* **1** that has no equal or superior; matchless: *unequaled beauty, unequaled speed.* **2** not equaled; unmatched.

**un|eq|ui|ta|ble** (un ek′wə tə bəl), *adj.* inequitable; unfair; unjust.

**un|eq|ui|ta|bly** (un ek′wə tə blē), *adv.* inequitably; unfairly; unjustly.

**un|e|quiv|o|ca|bly** (un′i kwiv′ə kə blē), *adv.* unequivocally: *The law unequivocably bars discriminatory state taxation* (Wall Street Journal).

**un|e|quiv|o|cal** (un′i kwiv′ə kəl), *adj.* **1** containing no trace of doubt or ambiguity; clear and straightforward in meaning or purpose; blunt and plain; clear: *unequivocal hostility, an unequivocal refusal.* **2** not inclined to temporize, compromise, or equivocate; speaking frankly and bluntly. —**un′e|quiv′o|cal|ly**, *adv.* —**un′e|quiv′o|cal|ness**, *n.*

**un|err|ing** (un ėr′ing, -er′-), *adj.* **1** that does not err, especially: **a** free of error; exactly right; certain; sure: *unerring aim.* **b** *Figurative.* making no mistakes; not going or leading astray; infallible: *an unerring guide.* **2** corresponding exactly to some standard or goal: *unerring precision.* —**un|err′ing|ly**, *adv.* —**un|err′ing|ness**, *n.*
► For a note on the pronunciation, see **err**.

**un|es|cap|a|ble** (un′es kā′pə bəl), *adj.* not escapable; not to be escaped or avoided; inescapable.

**un|es|cap|a|bly** (un′es kā′pə blē), *adv.* in an unescapable manner.

**UNESCO** or **U|nes|co** (yü nes′kō), *n.* the United Nations Educational, Scientific, and Cultural Organization (an independent organization related to and recognized by the United Nations as one of its specialized agencies).

**un|es|sayed** (un′e sād′), *adj.* not essayed; unattempted.

**un|es|sen|tial** (un′ə sen′shəl), *adj., n.* —*adj.* not essential; not of prime importance; nonessential.
—*n.* something not essential.

**un|eth|i|cal** (un eth′ə kəl), *adj.* not ethical; not in accordance with the rules for right conduct or practice. —**un|eth′i|cal|ly**, *adv.*

**un|e|van|gel|i|cal** (un′ē van jel′ə kəl, -ev ən-), *adj.* not evangelical; not in accord with the Gospels: *unevangelical doctrines.*

**un|e|ven** (un ē′vən), *adj.* **1** not level, flat, or smooth; having an irregular or broken surface; somewhat bumpy: *uneven ground.* **SYN**: rough, rugged, jagged. **2** not equal: *an uneven contest.* **3** not uniform or regular; changeable; inconsistent: *His work is of uneven quality.* **4** not straight or parallel. **5** that cannot be divided by 2 without a remainder; odd: *1, 3, 5, 7, and 9 are uneven numbers.* [Old English *unefen* unequal < *un-* un-[1] + *efen* equal, even] —**un|e′ven|ly**, *adv.* —**un|e′ven|ness**, *n.*

**uneven bars** or **uneven parallel bars**, parallel bars set at different heights, used in gymnastics.

**un|e|vent|ful** (un′i vent′fəl), *adj.* without important or striking occurrences: *a lazy, uneventful day in the country; laborious, uneventful years* (H. G. Wells). —**un′e|vent′ful|ly**, *adv.* —**un′e|vent′ful|ness**, *n.*

**un|e|volved** (un′i volvd′), *adj.* not evolved; undeveloped.

**un|ex|act|ing** (un′eg zak′ting), *adj.* not exacting; requiring little; easy.

**un|ex|am|pled** (un′eg zam′pəld, -zäm′-), *adj.* having no equal or like; without precedent or parallel; without anything like it: *Thanking you for your unexampled kindness* (Jane Austen). **SYN**: unprecedented.

**un|ex|celled** (un′ek seld′), *adj.* not excelled; unsurpassed.

**un|ex|cep|tion|a|ble** (un′ek sep′shə nə bəl), *adj.* beyond criticism; wholly admirable. **SYN**: faultless, irreproachable. —**un′ex|cep′tion|a|ble|ness**, *n.* —**un′ex|cep′tion|a|bly**, *adv.*

**un|ex|cep|tion|al** (un′ek sep′shə nəl), *adj.* **1** not exceptional; ordinary. **2** admitting of no exception. —**un′ex|cep′tion|al|ly**, *adv.*

**un|ex|cit|ed** (un′ek sī′tid), *adj.* not excited; calm.

**un|ex|cit|ing** (un′ek sī′ting), *adj.* not exciting; quiet; tame; dull.

**un|ex|e|cut|ed** (un ek′sə kyü′tid), *adj.* **1** not executed. **2** *Obsolete.* unemployed; inactive.

**un|ex|pect|ant** (un′ek spek′tənt), *adj.* not expectant; not expecting, looking for, or eagerly waiting for something. —**un′ex|pect′ant|ly**, *adv.*

**un|ex|pect|ed** (un′ek spek′tid), *adj.* not expected; not anticipated: *an unexpected difficulty, a sudden and unexpected change in the weather. We had an unexpected, but welcome, visit from our grandmother last week.* —**un′ex|pect′ed|ly**, *adv.* —**un′ex|pect′ed|ness**, *n.*
—*Syn.* **Unexpected, sudden** mean coming, happening, done, or made without advance warning or preparation. **Unexpected** emphasizes the lack of foreknowledge or anticipation: *The President made an unexpected visit to the city.* **Sudden** emphasizes the haste and absence of forewarning: *His decision to go was sudden.*

**un|ex|pe|ri|enced** (un′ek spir′ē ənst), *adj.* = inexperienced.

**un|ex|pert** (un′ek spėrt′), *adj.* = inexpert. —**un′ex|pert′ly**, *adv.*

**un|ex|pired** (un′ek spīrd′), *adj.* not expired; not having come to an end; having still some time to run, as a lease.

**un|ex|plain|a|ble** (un′ek splā′nə bəl), *adj.* not explainable; inexplicable.

**un|ex|plained** (un′ek splānd′), *adj.* not explained.

**un|ex|plod|ed** (un′ek splō′did), *adj.* not exploded.

**un|ex|plored** (un′ek splôrd′, -splōrd′), *adj.* not explored.

**un|ex|posed** (un′ek spōzd′), *adj.* not exposed.

**un|ex|pressed** (un′ek sprest′), *adj.* not expressed; unuttered.

**un|ex|press|i|ble** (un′ek spres′ə bəl), *adj.* = inexpressible.

**un|ex|pres|sive** (un′ek spres′iv), *adj.* **1** = inexpressive. **2** *Obsolete.* ineffable: *So Lycidas ... hears the unexpressive nuptial Song* (Milton). —**un′ex|pres′sive|ly**, *adv.* —**un′ex|pres′sive|ness**, *n.*

**un|ex|pur|gat|ed** (un eks′pər gā′tid), *adj.* not expurgated.

**un|ex|tend|ed** (un′ek sten′did), *adj.* **1** not extended or stretched out. **2** not having extension; occupying no assignable space: *a spiritual, that is, an unextended substance* (John Locke).

**un|ex|tin|guish|a|ble** (un′ek sting′gwi shə bəl), *adj.* = inextinguishable.

**un|face|a|ble** (un fā′sə bəl), *adj.* not to be faced or approached: *It was as if, by dwelling on these little things, she found relief from the contemplation of the appalling, unfaceable fact that was facing her* (New Yorker).

**un|fad|a|ble** (un fā′də bəl), *adj.* incapable of fading, withering, or perishing.

**un|fad|ing** (un fā′ding), *adj.* not or never fading; always fresh or bright. —**un|fad′ing|ly**, *adv.* —**un|fad′ing|ness**, *n.*

**un|fail|ing** (un fā′ling), *adj.* **1** never failing or giving way, especially: **a** never tiring or flagging; tireless: *unfailing hope.* **b** always ready when needed; constant in nature; loyal: *an unfailing friend.* **2** never running short; endless; continual; unceasing: *an unfailing supply of water.* **3** sure; certain; infallible: *an unfailing proof.* —**un|fail′ing|ly**, *adv.* —**un|fail′ing|ness**, *n.*

**un|fair** (un fãr′), *adj.* **1** not fair or equitable; unjust: *an unfair decision by an umpire, to have an unfair advantage.* **SYN**: partial, prejudiced, biased, one-sided. **2** not right or proper; dishonest: *unfair business practices. It was unfair of him to trick his little brother into giving him all the candy.* [< Old English *unfæger* not beautiful or comely < *un-* un-[1] + *fæger* fair] —**un|fair′ly**, *adv.* —**unfair′ness**, *n.*

**unfair list**, *U.S.* a list of employers who refuse to hire union members or violate union conditions.

**un|faith** (un fāth′), *n.* want of faith: *Unfaith in aught is want of faith in all* (Tennyson).

**un|faith|ful** (un fāth′fəl), *adj.* **1** not faithful, especially: **a** not true to duty or one's promises; faithless: *an unfaithful servant.* **b** not true to the vows of matrimony; adulterous: *an unfaithful husband.* **SYN**: false, disloyal, inconstant. **2** not following the original; not exact; not accurate: *an unfaithful translation.* —**un|faith′ful|ly**, *adv.* —**un|faith′fulness**, *n.*

**un|fal|ter|ing** (un fôl′tər ing), *adj.* not faltering; unhesitating; unwavering: *sustained and soothed by an unfaltering trust* (William Cullen Bryant). —**un|fal′ter|ing|ly**, *adv.*

**un|fa|mil|iar** (un′fə mil′yər), *adj.* **1** not well known; unusual; strange: *That face is unfamiliar to me.* **2** not acquainted: *The class was unfamiliar with the Greek language.* —**un′fa|mil′iar|ly**, *adv.*

**un|fa|mil|iar|i|ty** (un′fə mil′yar′ə tē), *n.* lack of familiarity.

**un|fan|cied** (un fan′sēd), *adj.* **1** unimagined: *unfancied joys.* **2** not liked or favored: *He was beaten decisively by unfancied horses on Saturday* (London Times).

**un|fash|ion|a|ble** (un fash′ən ə bəl, -fash′nə-), *adj.* not fashionable; not in good style. —**un|fash′ion|a|ble|ness**, *n.*

**un|fash|ion|a|bly** (un fash′ə nə blē, -fash′nə-), *adv.* in an unfashionable manner; not in accordance with fashion: *Both bade, me welcome, and if they thought I was unfashionably early, they said nothing* (Maclean's).

**un|fash|ioned** (un fash′ənd), *adj.* **1** not modified by art; not molded. **2** not having a regular form; shapeless.

**un|fas|ten** (un fas′ən, -fäs′-), *v.t., v.i.* to undo; untie; loosen; open.

**un|fas|tid|i|ous** (un′fas tid′ē əs), *adj.* not fastidious; easily pleased: *Irony, indignation, amusement, an unfastidious acceptance of people—all these ... make up this very personal account* (Manchester Guardian Weekly). —**un′fas|tid′i|ous|ness**, *n.*

**un|fa|thered** (un fä′ᴛʜərd), *adj.* **1** born out of wedlock; illegitimate. **2** *Figurative.* of obscure or dubious origin: *an unfathered rumor.*

**un|fa|ther|ly** (un fä′ᴛʜər lē), *adj.* not fatherly; unbefitting a father.

**un|fath|om|a|ble** (un faᴛʜ′ə mə bəl), *adj.* **1** not fathomable; too deep to be measured. **2** *Figurative.* too mysterious to be understood; impenetrable by the mind; inscrutable; incomprehensible.

**un|fath|omed** (un faᴛʜ′əmd), *adj.* **1** not measured. **2** *Figurative.* not understood.

**un|fa|vor|a|ble** (un fā′vər ə bəl, -fāv′rə-), *adj.* **1** not favorable; contrary to what is desired or needed; adverse: *unfavorable weather for a trip, an unfavorable review of a play.* **2** conducive to bad rather than good; harmful: *an unfavorable environment.* **3** not pleasing: *an unfavorable appearance.* —**un|fa′vor|a|ble|ness**, *n.*

**un|fa|vor|a|bly** (un fā′vər ə blē, -fāv′rə-), *adv.* in an unfavorable manner; so as not to countenance or promote; in a manner to discourage.

**un|feared** (un fird′), *adj.* **1** not feared; not dreaded. **2** *Obsolete.* not afraid; not daunted; intrepid.

**un|fea|si|ble** (un fē′zə bəl), *adj.* not feasible; impracticable; infeasible.

**un|feath|ered** (un feᴛʜ′ərd), *adj.* not provided with feathers; featherless.

**un|fea|tured** (un fē′chərd), *adj.* **1** without features; featureless: *the starless, unfeatured night* (Robert A. Vaughan). **2** *Informal.* not featured; not given prominence to: *an unfeatured motion picture.*

**un|fed** (un fed′), *adj.* not fed; having taken no food.

**un|feel|ing** (un fē′ling), *adj.* **1** not kind or compassionate; hard-hearted; cruel: *a cold, unfeeling person, an unfeeling remark. Can it be? That men should live with such unfeeling souls?* (Ben

**Pronunciation Key:** hat, āge, cãre, fär; let, ēqual, tėrm; it, īce; hot, ōpen, ôrder; **oi**l, **ou**t; cup, pu̇t, rüle; **ch**ild; lo**ng**; **th**in; ᴛʜen; **zh**, measure; ə represents **a** in about, **e** in taken, **i** in pencil, **o** in lemon, **u** in circus.

Jonson). SYN: unsympathetic. **2** not able to feel; without sensory power or capacity; insensible: *an unfeeling statue for his wife* (William Cowper). —**un|feel′ing|ly**, *adv.* —**un|feel′ing|ness**, *n.*

**un|feigned** (un fānd′), *adj.* not feigned; sincere; real: *unfeigned anger, unfeigned joy.* SYN: unaffected, true, genuine.

**un|feign|ed|ly** (un fā′nid lē), *adv.* really; sincerely; truly: *He pardoneth and absolveth all those who truly repent, and unfeignedly believe in His holy Gospel* (Book of Common Prayer).

**un|fel|lowed** (un fel′ōd), *adj.* without a fellow; unmatched; unequaled: *In his meed he's unfellowed* (Shakespeare).

**un|felt** (un felt′), *adj.* not felt or perceived.

**un|fem|i|nine** (un fem′ə nin), *adj.* not feminine; unwomanly.

**un|fenced** (un fenst′), *adj.* **1** having no fence; not fenced in: *Spreading afar and unfenced o'er the plain* (Longfellow). **2** *Figurative.* without protection, guard, or security; defenseless.

**un|fer|ment|ed** (un′fər men′tid), *adj.* not fermented.

**un|fer|tile** (un fėr′təl), *adj.* = infertile.

**un|fer|ti|lized** (un fėr′tə līzd), *adj.* not fertilized.

**un|fet|ter** (un fet′ər), *v.t.* **1** to remove fetters from; unchain. **2** *Figurative.* make free; liberate.

**un|fet|tered** (un fet′ərd), *adj.* **1** not fettered. **2** *Figurative.* free from restraint: *unfettered imagination.*

**un|filed** (un fīld′), *adj.* **1** not rubbed or polished with a file; not burnished. **2** not put away in a file, as papers.

**un|fil|i|al** (un fil′ē əl), *adj.* not filial; unbecoming from a child to a parent; not observing the obligations of a child to a parent.

**un|fil|tered** (un fil′tərd), *adj.* not filtered.

**un|fin|ished** (un fin′isht), *adj.* **1** not finished; not complete: *unfinished homework, an unfinished symphony.* **2** without some special finish; not polished; rough: *unfinished stone, unfinished furniture.* **3** not processed after coming off the loom: *unfinished fabric.*

**un|fished** (un fisht′), *adj.* not fished in: *The main reason why unfished waters are most productive, is that they are then more plentifully stocked* (Charles A. Johns).

**un|fit** (un fit′), *adj., v.,* **-fit|ted, -fit|ting.** —*adj.* **1** not fit; not suitable. **2** not good enough; unqualified. **3** not adapted.
—*v.t.* to make unfit; spoil. —**un|fit′ly**, *adv.* —**unfit′ness**, *n.*

**un|fit|ted** (un fit′id), *adj.* **1** not fitted; unsuited; unfit. **2** not fitting the body tightly; loose, as a coat or suit: *an unfitted jacket.*

**un|fit|ting** (un fit′ing), *adj.* not fitting; unbecoming: *an unfitting remark.* —**un|fit′ting|ly**, *adv.* —**un|fit′ting|ness**, *n.*

**un|fix** (un fiks′), *v.t.* **1** to loosen; detach; unfasten. **2** *Figurative.* to unsettle.

**un|fixed** (un fikst′), *adj.* **1** not fixed; not firmly set. **2** *Figurative.* not settled or determined; variable or uncertain.

**un|flag|ging** (un flag′ing), *adj.* not weakening or failing: *unflagging strength, unflagging efforts.* —**un|flag′ging|ly**, *adv.*

**un|flap|pa|bil|i|ty** (un flap′ə bil′ə tē), *n. Informal.* imperturbability: *Unflappability and golf are almost traditional attributes of Conservative leaders* (Punch).

**un|flap|pa|ble** (un flap′ə bəl), *adj. Informal.* not easily excited, confused, or alarmed; imperturbable: *His unflappable poise was buttressed by arctic sarcasm* (Time).

**un|flap|pa|bly** (un flap′ə blē), *adv. Informal.* imperturbably.

**un|flat|ter|ing** (un flat′ər ing), *adj.* not flattering; uncomplimentary. —**un|flat′ter|ing|ly**, *adv.*

**un|fledged** (un flejd′), *adj.* **1** too young to fly; not having full-grown feathers: *an unfledged crow.* **2** *Figurative.* undeveloped; immature or inexperienced: *This Society of unfledged Statesmen* (Joseph Addison).

**un|flesh|ly** (un flesh′lē), *adj.* not in or of the flesh; supernatural; spiritual.

**un|flinch|ing** (un flin′ching), *adj.* not drawing back from difficulty, danger, or pain; firm; resolute: *unflinching courage or resolve.* —**un|flinch′ing|ly**, *adv.*

**un|flur|ried** (un flėr′ēd), *adj.* not flurried; without excitement or confusion: *He replaced his cap and continued his unflurried way* (Manchester Guardian).

**un|foiled** (un foild′), *adj.* not vanquished; not defeated; not baffled.

**un|fold** (un fōld′), *v.t.* **1** to open the folds of; open up; spread out: *to unfold a napkin.* **2** to cause to be no longer bent, coiled, or interlaced; unbend and straighten out: *to unfold one's arm.* **3** *Figurative.* to develop or bring forth the parts or elements of so as to reveal the actual nature or dimensions; lay open to be seen or understood; reveal; show; explain: *to unfold the plot of a story. Briefly and plainly I unfolded what I proposed* (Samuel Butler). **4** = unwrap. **5** to let go; release. —*v.i.* to open up or cut; spread out or expand; develop: *Buds unfold into flowers.* [Old English *unfealdan* < *un-* un-[2] + *fealdan* to fold[1]] —**un|fold′er**, *n.*

**un|fold|ment** (un fōld′mənt), *n.* an unfolding; development.

**un|for|bid** (un′fər bid′), *adj. Dialect.* unforbidden.

**un|for|bid|den** (un′fər bid′ən), *adj.* not forbidden.

**un|forced** (un fôrst′, -fōrst′), *adj.* **1** not forced; not compelling; willing. **2** *Figurative.* natural; spontaneous.

**un|fore|bod|ing** (un′fôr bō′ding, -fōr-), *adj.* not foretelling; not telling the future; giving to omens.

**un|fore|known** (un′fôr nōn′, -fōr-), *adj.* not previously known of foreseen.

**un|fore|see|a|ble** (un′fôr sē′ə bəl, -fōr-), *adj.* not foreseeable; that cannot be forseen: *an unforeseeable delay.* —**un′for|see′a|ble|ness**, *n.* —**un′fore|see′a|bly**, *adv.*

**un|fore|see|ing** (un′fôr sē′ing, -fōr-), *adj.* not foreseeing; without foresight.

**un|fore|seen** (un′fôr sēn′, -fōr-), *adj.* not known beforehand; unexpected: *hoping for some unforeseen turn of fortune* (George Eliot). —**un′foreseen′ness**, *n.*

**un|fore|told** (un′fôr tōld′, -fōr-), *adj.* not predicted or foretold.

**un|for|feit|ed** (un fôr′fə tid), *adj.* not forfeited; maintained; not lost.

**un|forged** (un fôrjd′, -fōrjd′), *adj.* not forged or counterfeit; genuine.

**un|for|get|ta|ble** (un′fər get′ə bəl), *adj.* that can never be forgotten: *To smell the unforgettable, unforgotten River smell* (Rupert Brooke).

**un|for|get|ta|bly** (un′fər get′ə blē), *adv.* in an unforgettable manner.

**un|for|giv|a|ble** (un′fər giv′ə bəl), *adj.* not to be forgiven; unpardonable.

**un|for|giv|a|bly** (un′fər giv′ə blē), *adv.* in an unforgivable manner; to an unforgivable degree: *unforgivably bad or rude.*

**un|for|giv|en** (un′fər giv′ən), *adj.* not forgiven.

**un|for|giv|ing** (un′fər giv′ing), *adj.* not forgiving; not disposed to forgive; implacable. —**un′for|giv′ing|ly**, *adv.* —**un′for|giv′ing|ness**, *n.*

**un|for|got|ten** (un′fər got′ən), *adj.* not forgotten.

**un|formed** (un fôrmd′), *adj.* **1** without definite or regular form; shapeless: *an unformed lump of clay.* **2** *Figurative.* not yet shaped by process of growth or schooling; undeveloped: *an unformed mind.* **3** not formed or made; uncreated: *the yet unformed forefather of mankind* (Byron). **4** *Biology.* unorganized.

**un|for|mu|lat|ed** (un fôr′myə lā′tid), *adj.* not formulated.

**un|forth|com|ing** (un fôrth′kum′ing, -fōrth′-), *adj.* not responsive or obliging; unaccommodating: *the unforthcoming stiff-upper-lip, monosyllabic Englishman* (Newsweek).

**un|for|ti|fied** (un fôr′tə fīd), *adj.* not fortified.

**un|for|tu|nate** (un fôr′chə nit), *adj., n.* —*adj.* **1** having, bringing, or accompanied by bad luck; not lucky: *an unfortunate person, an unfortunate venture.* **2** not suitable; not fitting: *an unfortunate choice of words. The child's outburst of temper was an unfortunate thing for the guest to see.*
—*n.* **1** an unfortunate person. **2** a fallen woman; prostitute. **3** *Irish.* a congenital idiot; halfwit.
—**un|for′tu|nate|ly**, *adv.* —**un|for′tu|nate|ness**, *n.*

**un|fos|sil|if|er|ous** (un′fos ə lif′ər əs), *adj.* bearing or containing no fossils: *The rocks of Scotland are, as a whole, unfossiliferous* (Archibald Geikie).

**un|fought** (un fôt′), *adj.* not fought: *If they march along unfought withal* (Shakespeare).

**un|found|ed** (un foun′did), *adj.* **1** without foundation; without reason; unwarranted; baseless: *an unfounded complaint.* **2** not establish. —**unfound′ed|ly**, *adv.* —**un|found′ed|ness**, *n.*

**un|framed** (un frāmd′), *adj.* **1** not provided with a frame; not put into a frame: *an unframed picture.* **2** not formed; not constructed; not fashioned.

**un|fran|chised** (un fran′chīzd), *adj.* not franchised.

**un|fraught** (un frôt′), *adj.* not fraught; not filled with a load or burden; unloaded.

**un|free** (un frē′), *adj.* not free.

**un|free|dom** (un frē′dəm), *n.* the state of being unfree; want of freedom: *the struggle against injustice and unfreedom* (London Times).

**un|freeze** (un frēz′), *v.,* **-froze, -fro|zen, -freez|ing.** —*v.t.* **1** to thaw; loosen: *The company had unfrozen hundreds of pipes by this method* (London Times). (*Figurative.*) *He could not unfreeze himself into hospitality* (George W. Thombury). **2** to free from control or restrictions: *The urgent requirement on Capitol Hill is to unfreeze poverty programs, not stall them* (New York Times). **3** to release (money) for spending: *The Defense Department hopes to unfreeze over $10 billion of funds for new military procurement* (Wall Street Journal).
—*v.i.* to thaw; loosen: [*He*] *wanted to know if the weather would unfreeze sufficiently for him to drive to Idlewild the next day* (New Yorker).

**un|fre|quent** (un frē′kwənt), *adj.* not frequent; not common; infrequent.

**un|fre|quent|ed** (un′fri kwen′tid), *adj.* not frequented; seldom visited; rarely entered or used.

**un|friend|ed** (un fren′did), *adj.* without friends: *a raw and unfriended youth* (William Godwin). —**un|friend′ed|ness**, *n.*

**un|friend|li|ness** (un frend′lē nis), *n.* the quality of being unfriendly; lack of kindness; disfavor.

**un|friend|ly** (un frend′lē), *adj., adv.* —*adj.* **1** not friendly; hostile. SYN: See syn. under **hostile.** **2** not favorable: *unfriendly stars.*
—*adv.* in an unfriendly manner.

**un|frock** (un frok′), *v.t.* **1** to deprive (a priest or minister) of his office: *It is not the unfrocking of a priest ... that will make us a happy nation* (Milton). **2** to take away a frock from.

**un|fruit|ful** (un frūt′fəl), *adj.* **1** not fruitful; producing no offspring; barren: *an unfruitful marriage.* **2** *Figurative.* producing nothing worthwhile; not productive; unremunerative: *an unfruitful line of inquiry.* SYN: unproductive. —**un|fruit′ful|ly**, *adv.* —**un|fruit′ful|ness**, *n.*

**un|ful|filled** (un′fu̇l fild′), *adj.* not fulfilled.

**un|func|tion|al** (un fungk′shə nəl), *adj.* not functional; impractical: *There is a certain amount of shoddy, unfunctional, and ugly furniture on sale* (London Times).

**un|fund|ed** (un fun′did), *adj.* not funded; floating: *an unfunded debt.*

**un|fun|ny** (un fun′ē), *adj.* not funny; lacking humor: *an unfunny joke.*

**un|furl** (un fėrl′), *v.t., v.i.* to spread out; shake out; unfold: *The crew unfurled the sail.*

**un|fur|nish** (un fėr′nish), *v.t.* to strip of furnishings or furniture; dismantle.

**un|fur|nished** (un fėr′nisht), *adj.* not furnished; without furniture.

**un|fur|rowed** (un fėr′ōd), *adj.* not furrowed; not formed into drills or ridges; smooth: *an unfurrowed field.*

**un|fused** (un fyüzd′), *adj.* **1** not fused or melted. **2** not blended or united.

**un|fuss|i|ly** (un fus′ə lē), *adv.* in an unfussy manner.

**un|fuss|y** (un fus′ē), *adj.* not fussy: *Mr. Davis, whose editing is exacting and unfussy, deserves our gratitude* (New Yorker).

**un|gag** (un gag′), *v.t.,* **-gagged, -gag|ging.** to remove a gag from: *Once in the room, they ungagged their hostage.*

**un|gained** (un gānd′), *adj.* not yet gained; unpossessed.

**un|gain|ful** (un gān′fəl), *adj.* not producing gain; unprofitable.

**un|gain|li|ness** (un gān′lē nis), *n.* the condition or character of being ungainly; ungainly appearance; awkwardness; clumsiness.

**un|gain|ly** (un gān′lē), *adj., adv.* —*adj.* ungraceful in form or motion; awkward; clumsy: *The boy's long arms and large hands give him an ungainly appearance.* SYN: uncouth. See syn. under **awkward.**
—*adv.* in an ungainly manner; awkwardly.
[Middle English *ungaynly*, adverb, threateningly, improperly < *un-*[1] not + *gainly* fitting, graceful, perhaps < Scandinavian (compare Old Icelandic *ūgegnlig, ōgegnlig* improperly, obstinate < *ūgegn* unreasonable)]

**un|gal|lant** (un gal′ənt), *adj.* not gallant; unchivalrous. —**un|gal′lant|ly**, *adv.*

**un|galled** (un gôld′), *adj.* unhurt; not galled; uninjured.

**un|gar|nished** (un gär′nisht), *adj.* **1** not garnished or furnished; unadorned. **2** not properly provided or equipped.

**un|gar|tered** (un gär′tərd), *adj.* **1** not held by garters, as the hose or socks. **2** not having or wearing garters.

**un|gath|ered** (un gaᴛʜ′ərd), *adj.* **1** not gathered together; not culled; not picked; not collected. **2** having to do with printed sheets that have been folded, but not gathered in regular order for binding.

**un|gear** (un gir′), *v.t.* **1** to strip of gear. **2** to throw out of gear.

**un|gen|er|os|i|ty** (un jen′ə ros′ə tē), *n.* the quality or condition of being ungenerous; lack of kindness or compassion: *Even in victory ..., there was a certain ungenerosity to the fallen antagonist* (Sunday Times).

**un|gen|er|ous** (un jen′ər əs), *adj.* **1** not generous; meanly grasping or cruel. **2** small-minded and cowardly. —**un|gen′er|ous|ly**, *adv.*

**un|gen|ial** (un jēn′yəl), *adj.* **1** not favorable to natural growth: *ungenial air, ungenial soils.* **2** not kindly; unpleasant; disagreeable; harsh; unsympathetic: *an ungenial disposition.* **3** not congenial; not suited or adapted.

**un|gen|teel** (un′jen tēl′), *adj.* (of persons or manners) not genteel; impolite; rude.

**un|gen|tle** (un jen′təl), *adj.* not gentle; harsh; rough. – **un|gen′tle|ness,** *n.*

**un|gen|tle|man|li|ness** (un jen′təl mən lē nis), *n.* the character of being ungentlemanly.

**un|gen|tle|man|ly** (un jen′təl mən lē), *adj.* not gentlemanly; not befitting a gentleman; ill-bred; impolite; rude: *It's only if a man's a gentleman that he won't hesitate to do an ungentlemanly thing* (W. Somerset Maugham).

**un|gift|ed** (un gif′tid), *adj.* not gifted; not endowed with natural gifts.

**un|gird** (un gėrd′), *v.t.* **1** to unfasten or take off the belt or girdle of; unbelt. **2** to loosen, to take off, by unfastening a belt or girdle. [Old English *ongyrdan* < *on-* un-[2] + *gyrdan* to gird[1]]

**un|girt** (un gėrt′), *adj.* **1** ungirded: *Now in the ungirt hour, now ere we blink and drowse, Mithras, also a soldier, keep us true to our vows* (Rudyard Kipling). **2** not braced up or pulled together; loose and shapeless: *an ungirt appearance or style.*

**un|giv|ing** (un giv′ing), *adj.* not bringing gifts.

**un|glam|or|ous** (un glam′ər əs, -glam′rəs), *adj.* not glamorous; without charm: *[He] begged Lennie to change his unglamorous name so that his way to success would not be blocked* (Time). – **un|glam′or|ous|ly,** *adv.*

**un|glazed** (un glāzd′), *adj.* **1** not provided with glass, as a window. **2** not coated or covered with a glaze, as earthenware.

**un|glove** (un gluv′), *v.,* **-gloved, -glov|ing.** – ***v.t.*** to remove a glove or gloves from: *She ungloved her right hand and signed the papers.*
– ***v.i.*** to take off a glove or gloves: *The gentleman ungloved and shook hands with his rival.*

**un|gloved** (un gluvd′), *adj.* not gloved; without a glove or gloves.

**un|glue** (un glü′), *v.t.,* **-glued, -glu|ing.** to separate or open (something fastened with or as with glue).
**come unglued,** *U.S. Informal.* to fall apart; crumble: *He lives in a development house that is coming unglued* (Harper's). (*Figurative.*) *"The only thing that keeps me from coming unglued is ... the prospect of teaching in the near future"* (New York Times).

**un|god|li|ly** (un god′lə lē), *adv.* in an ungodly manner; impiously; wickedly.

**un|god|li|ness** (un god′lē nis), *n.* the quality of being ungodly; lack of godliness; impiety; wickedness; sinfulness: *For the wrath of God is revealed from heaven against all ungodliness* (Romans 1:18).

**un|god|ly** (un god′lē), *adj.* **1** not devout; not religious; impious. **SYN:** irreligious. **2** not conforming with the law or will of God; wicked; sinful. **3** *Informal, Figurative.* **a** very annoying; distressing; irritating: *an ungodly noise.* **b** outrageous; dreadful; shocking: *to pay an ungodly price.* **c** unbelievable: *to eat an ungodly amount.*

**un|got|ten** (un got′ən), *adj.* **1** not acquired, gained, or won. **2** = unbegotten.

**un|gov|ern|a|ble** (un guv′ər nə bəl), *adj.* impossible to control; very hard to control or rule; unruly: *an ungovernable temper.* **SYN:** See syn. under **unruly.** – **un|gov′ern|a|ble|ness,** *n.* – **un|gov′ern|a|bly,** *adv.*

**un|gov|erned** (un guv′ərnd), *adj.* not governed; not brought under government or control; unrestrained; unbridled.

**un|gown** (un goun′), *v.t.* **1** to divest or strip of a gown. **2** to deprive of the clerical office.

**un|graced** (un grāst′), *adj.* not graced; not favored; not honored: *Ungraced, without authority or mark* (Ben Jonson).

**un|grace|ful** (un grās′fəl), *adj.* not graceful; not elegant or beautiful; clumsy; awkward. – **ungrace′ful|ly,** *adv.* – **un|grace′ful|ness,** *n.*

**un|gra|cious** (un grā′shəs), *adj.* **1** not polite; discourteous; rude: *an ungracious remark.* **2** unpleasant; disagreeable; displeasing. **3** *Archaic.* ungraceful. – **un|gra′cious|ly,** *adv.* – **un|gra′cious|ness,** *n.*

**un|grad|ed** (un grā′did), *adj.* not graded; not arranged in grades or classes: *an ungraded school.*

**un|gram|mat|i|cal** (un′grə mat′ə kəl), *adj.* not in accordance with, or not observing, the rules of grammar or standard usage. – **un′gram|mat′i|cal|ly,** *adv.*

**un|grasp|a|ble** (un gras′pə bəl, -gräs′-), *adj.* that cannot be grasped or fully understood: *How ungraspable is the fact that real men ever did fight in real armour* (Mark Twain).

**un|grate|ful** (un grāt′fəl), *adj.* **1** not grateful; not thankful: *an ungrateful person.* **2** displaying lack of gratitude: *an ungrateful silence.* **3** unpleasant; disagreeable; distasteful: *an ungrateful task.* – **ungrate′ful|ly,** *adv.* – **un|grate′ful|ness,** *n.*

**un|grat|i|fied** (un grat′ə fīd), *adj.* not gratified; not satisfied; not indulged.

**un|ground|ed** (un groun′did), *adj.* without foundation; without reasons; unfounded.

**un|grudg|ing** (un gruj′ing), *adj.* not grudging; willing; hearty; liberal. – **un|grudg′ing|ly,** *adv.*

**un|gual** (ung′gwəl), *adj.* **1** of or having to do with a nail, claw, or hoof. **2** shaped like a nail, claw, or hoof. **3** having a nail, claw, or hoof. [< Latin *unguis* nail, claw, hoof + English *-al*[1]]

**un|guard** (un gärd′), *v.t.* **1** to deprive of a guard or guards; lay open to attack. **2** (in card games) to leave (a possible winning card) unprotected by playing a lower card of the same suit.

**un|guard|ed** (un gär′did), *adj.* **1** without a guard or guards; not protected: *an unguarded camp.* **2** not properly thoughtful or cautious; careless: *In an unguarded moment, she gave away the secret.* – **un|guard′ed|ly,** *adv.* – **un|guard′ed|ness,** *n.*

**un|guent** (ung′gwənt), *n.* a healing ointment for sores, burns, and scrapes; salve. [< Latin *unguentum* < *unguere* to anoint]

**un|guen|tar|y** (ung′gwən ter′ē), *adj.* **1** of or having to do with unguents. **2** suitable for unguents. **3** like unguents.

**un|gues** (ung′gwēz), *n.* plural of **unguis.**

**un|guessed** (un gest′), *adj.* not arrived at or attained by guess or conjecture; unsuspected.

**un|guic|u|lar** (ung gwik′yə lər), *adj.* **1** of or having to do with a nail or claw. **2** bearing a nail or claw. [< Latin *unguiculus* (see etym. under **unguiculate**) + English *-ar*]

**un|guic|u|late** (ung gwik′yə lit, -lāt), *adj., n.* – ***adj.*** **1** having nails or claws, as distinguished from hoofed animals and cetaceans. **2** *Botany.* having a clawlike base: *unguiculate petals.*
– ***n.*** a mammal that has nails or claws.
[< New Latin *unguiculatus* < Latin *unguiculus* (diminutive) < Latin *unguis* hoof, claw, nail]

**un|guic|u|lat|ed** (ung gwik′yə lā′tid), *adj.* = unguiculate.

**un|guid|ed** (un gī′did), *adj.* **1** not guided; not conducted: *a stranger unguided and unfriended* (Shakespeare). **2** *Figurative.* not regulated; ungoverned: *the accidental, unguided motions of blind matter* (John Locke).

**un|guif|er|ous** (ung gwif′ər əs), *adj.* bearing a nail, claw, or hoof. [< Latin *unguis* (see etym. under **unguis**) + English *-ferous*]

**un|guilt|y** (un gil′tē), *adj.* not guilty; innocent.

**un|gui|nous** (ung′gwə nəs), *adj. Obsolete.* oily; fatty; greasy. [< Latin *unguinōsus* < *unguen, -inis* ointment < *unguere* to anoint]

**un|guis** (ung′gwis), *n., pl.* **-gues** (-gwēz). **1** a nail, claw, or hoof. **2** *Botany.* the narrow, clawlike base of certain petals, by which they are attached to the receptacle; ungula. [< Latin *unguis* hoof, claw, nail]

***un|gu|la** (ung′gyə lə), *n., pl.* **-lae** (-lē). **1** a hoof. **2** a claw or nail. **3** *Botany.* an unguis (def. 2). **4** *Geometry.* a cylinder, cone, or other solid figure, the top part of which has been cut off by a plane oblique to the base. [< Latin *ungula* (diminutive) < *unguis* nail, claw, hoof]

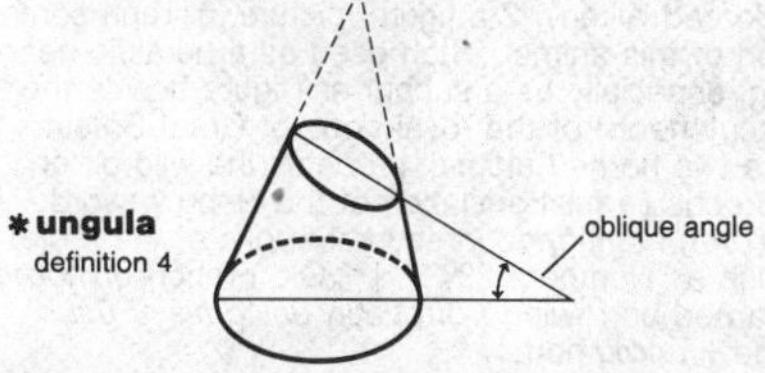

***ungula** definition 4

**un|gu|lar** (ung′gyə lər), *adj.* of or having to do with a hoof, claw, or nail.

**un|gu|late** (ung′gyə lit, -lāt), *adj., n.* – ***adj.*** **1a** having hoofs. **b** hoof-shaped. **2** of or belonging to the group of mammals that have hoofs, including the ruminant animals, horses, rhinoceroses, elephants, pigs, and Old-World conies.
– ***n.*** a mammal that has hoofs. Horses, cows, sheep, and deer are ungulates.
[< Latin *ungulātus* < *ungula;* see etym. under **ungula**]

**un|guled** (ung′gyüld, -gyəld), *adj. Heraldry.* (of animals) having the hoofs or claws of a different tincture from the body. [< Latin *ungula* ungula + English *-ed*[2]]

**un|gu|li|grade** (ung′gyə lə grād), *adj.* walking on the tips of the digits. [< New Latin *unguligradus* < Latin *ungula* claw (see etym. under **ungula**) + *gradī* to step]

**un|hack|neyed** (un hak′nēd), *adj.* **1** not hackneyed; not trite, commonplace, or stale. **2** not habituated or experienced: *one unhackneyed in the ways of intrigue* (Scott).

**un|hair** (un hãr′), *v.t., v.i.* **1** to divest of or lose the hair. **2** to remove the hair from (a hide or skin) as a preliminary to tanning.

**un|hal|low** (un hal′ō), *v.t.* **1** to deprive of a holy or sacred character. **2** to profane.

**un|hal|lowed** (un hal′ōd), *adj.* **1** not made holy; not sacred. **2** wicked; sinful; evil.

**un|ham|pered** (un ham′pərd), *adj.* not hampered; unimpeded.

**un|hand** (un hand′), *v.t.* to let go; take the hands from; set free; release.

**un|hand|i|ly** (un han′də lē), *adv.* in an unhandy manner; awkwardly; clumsily.

**un|hand|i|ness** (un han′dē nis), *n.* the condition or character of being unhandy; want of dexterity; clumsiness.

**un|han|dled** (un han′dəld), *adj.* **1** not handled; not touched. **2** not treated or managed. **3** not accustomed to being used; not trained or broken in: *youthful and unhandled colts* (Shakespeare).

**un|hand|some** (un han′səm), *adj.* **1** not good-looking; plain; ugly. **2** ungracious; discourteous; unseemly; mean. **3** not generous; meanly petty or small. – **un|hand′some|ly,** *adv.* – **un|hand′some|ness,** *n.*

**un|hand|y** (un han′dē), *adj.* **1** not easy to handle or manage: *an unhandy tool.* **2** not skillful in using the hands: *an unhandy workman.*

**un|hanged** (un hangd′), *adj.* not hanged; not punished by hanging: *There goes an unhanged rogue!*

**un|hap|pi|ly** (un hap′ə lē), *adv.* **1** not happily; in an unhappy manner; miserably: *to live unhappily.* **2** to one's misfortune; unfortunately: *Unhappily I missed seeing him.* **3** in an unsuitable or inappropriate way; not aptly.

**un|hap|pi|ness** (un hap′ē nis), *n.* **1** the fact or condition of being unhappy; sadness; sorrow: *We are erecting a first line of defense against personal maladjustment and unhappiness* (New York Times). **2** bad luck; misfortune: *It is our great unhappiness, when any calamities fall upon us, that we are uneasy and dissatisfied* (William Wake).

**un|hap|py** (un hap′ē), *adj.,* **-pi|er, -pi|est.** **1** without gladness; sad; sorrowful: *an unhappy face.* **2** miserable in lot or circumstances; unlucky: *an unhappy life, an unhappy accident.* **3** not appropriate; not suitable to the occasion or purpose: *an unhappy selection of colors.* **SYN:** unsuitable. **4** *Obsolete.* mischievous; naughty: *Beat him well, he's an unhappy boy* (Beaumont and Fletcher).

**un|hard|ened** (un här′dənd), *adj.* not hardened; not indurated.

**un|harmed** (un härmd′), *adj.* not harmed; uninjured; sound; intact.

**un|harm|ful** (un härm′fəl), *adj.* not harmful; harmless. – **un|harm′ful|ly,** *adv.*

**un|har|mo|ni|ous** (un′här mō′nē əs), *adj.* = inharmonious.

**un|har|ness** (un här′nis), *v.t.* **1** to take harness off from (a horse or other draft animal); free from harness or gear. **2a** to take armor off from (a person). **b** to take (armor) off from a person.
– ***v.i.*** to remove harness or gear.

**un|hasp** (un hasp′), *v.t.* to loose the hasp of.

**un|hast|y** (un hās′tē), *adj.,* **-hast|i|er, -hast|i|est.** not hasty; not precipitate; not rash; deliberate; slow.

**un|hat** (un hat′), *v.,* **-hat|ted, -hat|ting.** – ***v.t.*** to remove the hat from.
– ***v.i.*** to take off one's hat, as in respect.

**un|hatched**[1] (un hacht′), *adj.* (of a bird or egg) not hatched; undeveloped.

**un|hatched**[2] (un hacht′), *adj.* **1** not hatched or marked with cuts or lines. **2** not scratched or injured.

**UNHCR** (no periods), United Nations High Commissioner for Refugees.

**un|health|ful** (un helth′fəl), *adj.* bad for the health. – **un|health′ful|ly,** *adv.* – **un|health′ful|ness,** *n.*

**un|health|i|ly** (un hel′thə lē), *adv.* in an unhealthy manner.

**un|health|i|ness** (un hel′thē nis), *n.* **1** lack of health; sickness. **2** a condition causing disease or harmful to health.

**un|health|y** (un hel′thē), *adj.,* **-health|i|er, -health|i|est.** **1** not possessing good health; not well: *an unhealthy child.* **SYN:** sickly, frail, ill, diseased. **2** coming from or showing poor health: *an unhealthy paleness.* **3** hurtful to health; unwholesome; unhealthful: *an unhealthy climate.* **SYN:** unsanitary, unhygienic. **4** morally or spiritually harmful.

**un|heard** (un hėrd′), *adj.* **1** not perceived by the ear; not heard: *unheard melodies. The warning shout was unheard.* **2** without being given a hearing; not listened to: *to condemn a person unheard.* **3** not heard of; unknown: *Nor was his name unheard ... In ancient Rome* (Milton).

**un|heard-of** (un hėrd′uv′, -ov′), *adj.* **1** that was

**Pronunciation Key:** hat, āge, cãre, fär; let, ēqual, tėrm; it, īce; hot, ōpen, ôrder; **oil, out;** cup, pu̇t, rüle; **ch**ild; lo**ng**; **th**in; ᴛʜen; **zh,** measure; **ə** represents **a** in about, **e** in taken, **i** in pencil, **o** in lemon, **u** in circus.

never heard of; unknown: *Electric lights were unheard-of 200 years ago.* **2** not known before; unprecedented: *unheard-of prices. The rude little girl spoke to her mother with unheard-of impudence.*

**un|heat|ed** (un hē′tid), *adj.* not heated; without heat.

**un|heed|ed** (un hē′did), *adj.* not heeded; disregarded; unnoticed.

**un|heed|ful** (un hēd′fəl), *adj.* heedless; unmindful.

**un|heed|ing** (un hē′ding), *adj.* not heeding; unheedful: *Through the unheeding many he did move, A splendour among shadows* (Shelley).

**un|helm** (un helm′), *v.t. Archaic.* to deprive of the helm or helmet.

**un|help|ful** (un help′fəl), *adj.* **1** affording no aid. **2** unable to help oneself; helpless.

**un|her|ald|ed** (un her′əl did), *adj.* not heralded; not announced beforehand.

**un|he|ro|ic** (un′hi rō′ik), *adj.* not heroic.

**un|hes|i|tat|ing** (un hez′ə tā′ting), *adj.* prompt; ready. —**un|hes′i|tat′ing|ly,** *adv.*

**un|hewn** (un hyün′), *adj.* **1** not hewn; not shaped or fashioned by hewing. **2** *Figurative.* rough; unpolished.

**un|hid|den** (un hid′ən), *adj.* not hidden or concealed; open; manifest.

**un|hin|dered** (un hin′dərd), *adj.* not hindered; unimpeded.

**un|hinge** (un hinj′), *v.t.,* **-hinged, -hing|ing. 1** to take (a door) off its hinges. **2** to remove the hinges from. **3** *Figurative.* to separate from something; detach: *Minds that have been unhinged from their old faith* (George Eliot). **4** *Figurative.* to make unbalanced or disordered; unsettle; upset; disorganize: *Trouble has unhinged this poor man's mind.*

**un|hired** (un hīrd′), *adj.* not hired.

**un|his|tor|ic** (un′his tôr′ik, -tor′-), *adj.* **1** not famous or important in history: *an unhistoric event.* **2** = unhistorical.

**un|his|tor|i|cal** (un′his tôr′ə kəl, -tor′-), *adj.* **1** not in accordance with history: *The thoroughly unhistorical way in which these few subjects are dealt with* (James S. Northcote). **2** not having actually happened. **3** not acquainted with the facts of history: *Perhaps the unhistorical prophet had in mind some confused idea* (William G. Palgrave). —**un′his|tor′i|cal|ly,** *adv.* —**un′his|tor′i|cal|ness,** *n.*

**un|hitch** (un hich′), *v.t.* **1** to free (a horse, mule, or other animal) from being hitched; unloose the hitchings of. **2** to unloose and make free; unfasten; detach: *The boy unhitched the wagon from his bicycle so he could ride faster.*

**un|hive** (un hīv′), *v.t.,* **-hived, -hiv|ing.** to drive from or as from a hive.

**un|ho|li|ly** (un hō′lə lē), *adv.* in an unholy manner.

**un|ho|li|ness** (un hō′lē nis), *n.* the character or condition of being unholy; lack of holiness.

**un|ho|ly** (un hō′lē), *adj.,* **-li|er, -li|est. 1** not holy; profane. **2** ungodly; wicked; sinful. **3** *Informal, Figurative.* not seemly; dreadful; fearful: *to charge an unholy price.* [Old English *unhālig* < *un-* un-[1] + *hālig* holy]

**un|ho|mo|ge|ne|ous** (un′hō mə jē′nē əs), *adj.* not homogeneous; heterogeneous.

**un|hon|ored** (un on′ərd), *adj.* not regarded with respect or reverence; not famed or renowned; not given marks of esteem.

**un|hood** (un hu̇d′), *v.t.* **1** to strip of something that conceals; unmask; unveil. **2** *Falconry.* to take the hood from the eyes of (a hawk).

**un|hook** (un hu̇k′), *v.t.* **1** to loosen from a hook. **2** to undo by loosening a hook or hooks. —*v.i.* to become unhooked; become undone.

**un|hoped** (un hōpt′), *adj.* not hoped or looked for.

**un|hoped-for** (un hōpt′fôr′), *adj.* not expected; in addition to or beyond what is anticipated: *an unhoped-for blessing.*

**un|hope|ful** (un hōp′fəl), *adj.* not hopeful; leaving no room for hope; hopeless.

**un|horse** (un hôrs′), *v.t.,* **-horsed, -hors|ing. 1** to throw from a horse's back; cause to fall from a horse: *When hurdles and brush fences have to be cleared, the jumpers are in danger of spilling and their riders of being unhorsed* (New York Times). **2** *Figurative.* to destroy the power or defenses of; dislodge; overthrow; discomfit: *Douglas* [*is*] *completely unhorsed by an alarm clock in his hand which will not stop jangling* (Newsweek). **3** to deprive of a horse.

**un|hos|tile** (un hos′təl), *adj.* **1** not hostile; friendly. **2** not having to do with an enemy. **3** not caused by an enemy.

**un|housed** (un houzd′), *adj.* not housed; houseless.

**un|hou|seled** (un hou′zəld), *adj.* not having had the Eucharist administered: *He died, unhouseled, in his sins* (Robert Southey).

**un|hou|selled** (un hou′zəld), *adj. Especially British.* unhouseled.

**un|hu|man** (un hyü′mən), *adj.* **1** not human; destitute of human qualities. **2** = inhuman.

**un|hu|mor|ous** (un hyü′mər əs, -yü′-), *adj.* not humorous; unamusing: *Unfortunately,* [*he*] *seems to have forgotten that the most unhumorous thing a humorist can do is to lose his sense of humor* (Time).

**un|hung** (un hung′), *adj.* **1** not suspended; not hung. **2** not hanged; unhanged.

**un|hur|ried** (un hėr′id), *adj.* not hurried; without haste; leisurely: *an unhurried stroll in the park, an unhurried examination of the evidence.* —**un|hur′ried|ly,** *adv.*

**un|hurt** (un hėrt′), *adj.* not hurt; not harmed: *The driver was unhurt though his car had been completely destroyed in the accident.*

**un|hurt|ful** (un hėrt′fəl), *adj.* not hurtful; harmless. —**un|hurt′ful|ly,** *adv.*

**un|husk** (un husk′), *v.t.* to free from or as from a husk.

**un|hy|gi|en|ic** (un′hī jē en′ik, -jē′nik), *adj.* not hygienic; unhealthful; insanitary. —**un′hy|gi|en′i|cal|ly,** *adv.*

**uni-,** *prefix.* one; a single; having, or made of, only one: *Unicellular = having one cell.* [< Latin *ūnus* one]

**U|ni|at** (yü′nē at), *n., adj.* —*n.* a member of any Eastern church that is in communion with the Roman Catholic Church and acknowledges the supremacy of the pope but keeps its own liturgy. —*adj.* of or having to do with such a church or its members.
[< Russian *uniat* < obsolete Polish *uniata,* variant of *unita* < Latin *ūnīre* unite < *ūnus* one]

**U|ni|ate** (yü′nē it, -āt), *n., adj.* = Uniat.

**u|ni|ax|i|al** (yü′nē ak′sē əl), *adj.* **1** having one optic axis: *a uniaxial crystal.* **2** *Botany.* having but one axis, as when the primary stem of a plant does not branch and terminates in a flower.

**u|ni|cam|er|al** (yü′nə kam′ər əl), *adj.* having only one house in a lawmaking body. Nebraska has a unicameral legislature.

**UNICEF** or **U|ni|cef** (yü′nə sef), *n.* United Nations Children's Fund (an agency of the United Nations, established in 1946 under the name *United Nations International Children's Emergency Fund* to provide food and medical supplies to children and mothers through member nations).

**u|ni|cel|lu|lar** (yü′nə sel′yə lər), *adj.* having one cell only. The ameba is a unicellular animal.

**unicellular animals,** protozoans.

**u|ni|col|or** (yü′nə kul′ər), *adj.* of a single color; monochromatic.

**u|ni|col|ored** (yü′nə kul′ərd), *adj.* = unicolor.

**u|ni|col|or|ous** (yü′nə kul′ər əs), *adj.* = unicolor.

***u|ni|corn** (yü′nə kôrn), *n.* **1** an imaginary animal like a horse but having a single, long, spiral horn in the middle of its forehead and the tail of a lion. Unicorns are often mentioned in medieval fables and legends. *Neighing far off on the haunted air, The unicorns come down to the sea* (Conrad Aiken). **2** a figure, picture, or representation of this animal, often used as a heraldic bearing, especially as a supporter (figure beside the escutcheon) of the royal arms of Great Britain. **3** a two-horned animal, probably the wild ox or aurochs (a mistranslation of the Hebrew word *re'em*), mentioned in several books of the Bible, such as Numbers 23:22. [< Old French *unicorne,* learned borrowing from Latin *ūnicornis* < *ūnus* one + *cornū* horn]

***unicorn**
definition 1

**unicorn fish,** a filefish of West Indian and other warm seas, with a hornlike spine upon the head.

**unicorn plant,** an annual plant of the temperate parts of North America, whose pod ends in two long, curved beaks; double-claw.

**u|ni|cos|tate** (yü′nə kos′tāt), *adj. Botany.* denoting a leaf which has one large vein, the midrib, running down the center. [< *uni-* + Latin *costa* rib + English *-ate*[1]]

**u|ni|cus|pid** (yü′nə kus′pid), *adj., n.* —*adj.* having only one cusp, as an incisor or canine tooth. —*n.* a unicuspid tooth.

***u|ni|cy|cle** (yü′nə sī′kəl), *n.* a vehicle consisting of a frame mounted on a single wheel, propelled by pedaling, used especially by acrobats and circus performers. [< *uni-* + *-cycle,* as in *bicycle*]

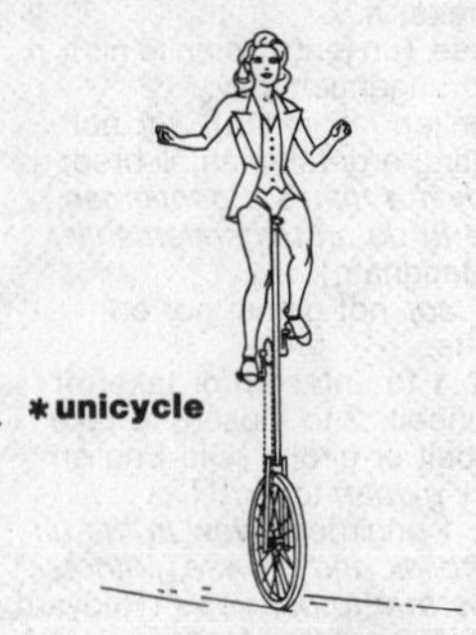
***unicycle**

**u|ni|cy|clist** (yü′nə sī′klist), *n.* a person who rides a unicycle, especially as a circus performer.

**un|i|de|aed** (un′ī dē′əd), *adj.* without imagination or wit; stupid and dull: *wretched, unideaed girls* (Samuel Johnson).

**un|i|de|al** (un′ī dē′əl), *adj.* **1** not ideal: **a** unimaginative; realistic; material. **b** coarse. **2** having no ideas; destitute of ideas, thoughts, or mental action.

**un|i|den|ti|fi|a|ble** (un′ī den′tə fī′ə bəl), *adj.* that cannot be identified.

**un|i|den|ti|fied** (un′ī den′tə fīd), *adj.* not identified; not recognized.

**unidentified flying object,** = flying saucer.

**u|ni|di|men|sion|al** (yü′nə də men′shə nəl), *adj.* having only one dimension; varying in only one way.

**un|id|i|o|mat|ic** (un′id ē ə mat′ik), *adj.* not idiomatic: *His words in English and German were clear and well matched to his tone, though German vowels sometimes sounded raw and unidiomatic* (London Times). —**un′id|i|o|mat′i|cal|ly,** *adv.*

**u|ni|di|rec|tion|al** (yü′nə də rek′shə nəl, -dī-), *adj.* in only one direction. A unidirectional microphone is sensitive to sounds from only one direction. *unidirectional radio waves.* —**u′ni|di|rec′tion|al|ly,** *adv.*

**UNIDO** (no periods), United Nations Industrial Development Organization.

**u|ni|far|i|ous** (yü′nə fãr′ē əs), *adj.* single; in one row. [< *uni-* + *-farious,* as in *bifarious*]

**u|ni|fi|a|ble** (yü′nə fī′ə bəl), *adj.* able to be brought together into a single body or mass; capable of unification.

**u|nif|ic** (yü nif′ik), *adj.* making one; forming unity; unifying. [< *uni-* + *-fic*]

**u|ni|fi|ca|tion** (yü′nə fə kā′shən), *n.* **1** formation into one unit; union: *the unification of many states into one nation.* **2** a making or being made more alike; reduction to a uniform system: *The traffic laws of the different states need unification.* **3** the result of this; state of being unified.

**u|ni|fi|ca|tion|ist** (yü′nə fə kā′shə nist), *n.* an advocate of unification.

**u|ni|fied field theory** (yü′nə fīd), any theory seeking to unify different physical theories or laws, especially a theory developed by Albert Einstein in which electric, magnetic, and gravitational phenomena are treated as parts or phases of a single process.

**u|ni|fi|er** (yü′nə fī′ər), *n.* a person or thing that unifies.

**u|ni|fi|lar** (yü′nə fī′lər), *adj.* having, suspended by, or using a single thread or fiber: *a unifilar magnetometer.* [< *uni-* + Latin *fīlum* thread + English *-ar*]

**u|ni|flo|rous** (yü′nə flôr′əs, -flōr′-), *adj.* having or bearing only one flower. [< New Latin *uniflorus* (with English *-ous*) < Latin *ūnus* uni- + *flōs, flōris* flower]

***u|ni|fo|li|ate** (yü′nə fō′lē it, -āt), *adj.* **1** having one leaf. **2** = unifoliolate.

***unifoliate**
definition 1

**u|ni|fo|li|o|late** (yü′nə fō′lē ə lāt), *adj.* **1** (of a leaf) compound in structure but having only one leaflet, as in the orange. **2** (of a plant) having such leaves.

**u|ni|form** (yü′nə fôrm), *adj., n., v.* —*adj.* **1** always the same; not changing: *to follow a uniform policy, to maintain a uniform temperature*

*throughout a house. The earth turns around at a uniform rate.* SYN: See syn. under **even. 2** all alike; not varying: *uniform hedges before all the houses. All the bricks have a uniform size.* **3** not mixed or blended: *lawns of a uniform green.* **4** free from quantitative fluctuation or variation; regular; even: *a uniform flow of water, a uniform pace.* SYN: See syn. under **even. 5** in accordance or agreement with one another; conforming to one standard, rule, or pattern: *uniform answers.*
*—n.* the distinctive clothes worn by the members of a group. Soldiers, policemen, and nurses wear uniforms so they can be easily recognized.
*—v.t.* to clothe or furnish with a uniform or uniforms.
[< Latin *ūniformis* < *ūnus* one + *forma* form]
**—u′ni|form′ly,** *adv.* **—u′ni|form′ness,** *n.*

**U|ni|form** (yü′nə fôrm), *n. U.S.* a code name for the letter *u,* used in transmitting radio messages.

**u|ni|formed** (yü′nə fôrmd), *adj.* **1** wearing a uniform; in uniform: *a uniformed soldier, a uniformed policeman.* **2** having a uniform: *the army and other uniformed services.*

**u|ni|form|i|tar|i|an** (yü′nə fôr′mə tãr′ē ən), *adj., n.* *—adj.* of or having to do with uniformitarianism or uniformitarians.
*—n.* an adherent of uniformitarianism.

**u|ni|for|mi|tar|i|an|ism** (yü′nə fôr′mə tãr′ē ə niz′əm), *n.* the theory that geological change is caused by a gradual process rather than sudden upheaval.

**u|ni|form|i|ty** (yü′nə fôr′mə tē), *n., pl.* **-ties. 1** uniform condition or character; sameness throughout. **2** something that is uniform: *Little by little the plain came into view, a vast green uniformity, forlorn and tenantless* (Francis Parkman).

**u|ni|fy** (yü′nə fī), *v.t., v.i.,* **-fied, -fy|ing.** to make or form into one; bring or come together; unite: *Several small states were unified into one nation.* [< Late Latin *ūnificāre* < Latin *ūnus* one + *facere* to make]

**u|ni|ju|gate** (yü′nə jü′git, -gāt; yü nij′ə gāt), *adj.* (of a pinnate leaf) having only one pair of leaflets. [< *uni-* + *jugate*]

**u|ni|lat|er|al** (yü′nə lat′ər əl), *adj.* **1** of, on, or affecting one side only: *unilateral disarmament.* **2** having all parts arranged on one side of an axis; turned to one side; one-sided. **3** *Law.* (of a contract or other instrument) affecting one party or person only; done by one side only; putting obligation on one party only. **4** concerned with or considering only one side of a matter. **5** *Sociology.* related or descended on only one side. **6** *Phonetics.* articulated with an opening on one side only: *unilateral L.* **—u′ni|lat′er|al|ly,** *adv.*

**u|ni|lat|er|al|ism** (yü′nə lat′ər ə liz′əm), *n.* belief in or adoption of a unilateral policy, especially in disarmament.

**u|ni|lat|er|al|ist** (yü′nə lat′ər ə list), *adj., n.* *—adj.* of or having to do with unilateralism or unilateralists.
*—n.* an adherent of unilateralism.

**u|ni|lin|e|ar** (yü′nə lin′ē ər), *adj.* **1** following a single, straight line of development: *unilinear progress.* **2** *Sociology.* following only one line of descent; unilateral.

**u|ni|lin|gual** (yü′nə ling′gwəl), *adj.* speaking or using only one language: *A dream of a unilingual State of the Marathi-speaking peoples became a reality* (Times of India). **—u′ni|lin′gual|ly,** *adv.*

**u|ni|lin|gual|ism** (yü′nə ling′gwə liz əm), *n.* the use of only one language, especially as the official language of a country.

**un|il|lu|mi|nat|ed** (un′i lü′mə nā′tid), *adj.* **1** not illuminated; not lighted; dark. **2** *Figurative.* ignorant.

**un|il|lu|mi|nat|ing** (un′i lü′mə nā′ting), *adj.* unenlightening: *The moments of action are smothered in a fog of unilluminating metaphor* (London Times).

**un|il|lu|sioned** (un′i lü′zhənd), *adj.* free from illusions; uncolored by illusion.

**u|ni|lobed** (yü′nə lōbd), *adj.* having or consisting of only one lobe.

**u|ni|loc|u|lar** (yü′nə lok′yə lər), *adj.* having or consisting of only one chamber or cell.

**un|i|mag|i|na|ble** (un′i maj′ə nə bəl), *adj.* that cannot be imagined or thought of; undreamed-of; inconceivable: *On every side now rose rocks which in unimaginable forms lifted their black and barren pinnacles* (Shelley). **—un′i|mag′i|na|ble|ness,** *n.*

**un|i|mag|i|na|bly** (un′i maj′ə nə blē), *adv.* in an unimaginable manner; inconceivably: *an unimaginably bad performance. The farthest galaxies we can see are unimaginably remote.*

**un|i|mag|i|na|tive** (un′i maj′ə nə tiv), *adj.* lacking imagination; literal; prosaic: *an unimaginative person, proposal, or performance.* **—un′i|mag′i|na|tive|ly,** *adv.* **—un′i|mag′i|na|tive|ness,** *n.*

**un|i|mag|ined** (un′i maj′ənd), *adj.* not imagined; never conceived even in imagination: *unimagined riches.*

**un|im|paired** (un′im pãrd′), *adj.* not impaired: *unimpaired eyesight. Strong for service still and unimpaired* (William Cowper).

**un|im|pas|sioned** (un′im pash′ənd), *adj.* not impassioned; not influenced by passion; calm; tranquil.

**un|im|peach|a|bil|i|ty** (un′im pē′chə bil′ə tē), *n.* the character of being unimpeachable or blameless.

**un|im|peach|a|ble** (un′im pē′chə bəl), *adj.* **1** free from fault, flaw, or error; not able to be doubted or questioned: *an unimpeachable fact, an unimpeachable source. When Parliament met, the leaders of both the parties in both the Houses made speeches in favour of the Prince, asserting his unimpeachable loyalty to the country* (Lytton Strachey). **2** blameless; irreproachable: *an unimpeachable reputation.*

**un|im|peach|a|bly** (un′im pē′chə blē), *adv.* in an unimpeachable manner; blamelessly.

**un|im|peached** (un′im pēcht′), *adj.* not impeached; not called in question.

**un|im|ped|ed** (un′im pē′did), *adj.* not impeded or hindered.

**un|im|plored** (un′im plôrd′, -plōrd′), *adj.* not implored; not solicited.

**un|im|por|tance** (un′im pôr′təns), *n.* unimportant nature or quality.

**un|im|por|tant** (un′im pôr′tənt), *adj.* not important; insignificant; trifling.

**un|im|pos|ing** (un′im pō′zing), *adj.* **1** not imposing; not commanding respect. **2** not enjoining as obligatory; voluntary.

**un|im|pressed** (un′im prest′), *adj.* not impressed.

**un|im|press|i|ble** (un′im pres′ə bəl), *adj.* not impressible; not susceptible; apathetic.

**un|im|pres|sion|a|ble** (un′im presh′ə nə bəl), *adj.* not impressionable; not easily impressed or influenced.

**un|im|proved** (un′im prüvd′), *adj.* **1** not improved; not turned to account; not cultivated. **2** not increased in value by betterments or improvements, as real property.

**un|in|closed** (un′in klōzd′), *adj.* = unenclosed.

**un|in|cor|po|rat|ed** (un′in kôr′pə rā′tid), *adj.* not incorporated.

**un|in|cum|bered** (un′in kum′bərd), *adj.* = unencumbered.

**un|in|flam|ma|ble** (un′in flam′ə bəl), *adj.* not inflammable.

**un|in|flect|ed** (un′in flek′tid), *adj.* not inflected; not subject to inflection: *uninflected languages.*

**un|in|flu|enced** (un in′flü ənst), *adj.* not influenced; not affected; not persuaded or moved; free from bias or prejudice.

**un|in|form|a|tive** (un′in fôr′mə tiv), *adj.* not giving information; not instructive: *It does not, however, follow that the truths of logic are of no use simply because they are uninformative* (Scientific American).

**un|in|formed** (un′in fôrmd′), *adj.* **1** not informed: **a** uninstructed, uneducated, or ignorant. **b** without information on some matter. **2** not endowed with life or spirit.

**un|in|hab|it|a|ble** (un′in hab′ə tə bəl), *adj.* not inhabitable; unfit to be inhabited: *an uninhabitable desert or slum.*

**un|in|hab|it|ed** (un′in hab′ə tid), *adj.* not lived in; without inhabitants: *an uninhabited wilderness.*

**un|in|hib|it|ed** (un′in hib′ə tid), *adj.* unrestrained; open; free: *an uninhibited person, uninhibited laughter.* **—un′in|hib′it|ed|ly,** *adv.*

**un|i|ni|ti|ate** (un′i nish′ē it, -āt), *n.* a person who has not been initiated: *Croquet upon the island "lawn" ... was a pastime to be shunned by the uninitiate* (Alexander Woollcott).

**un|i|ni|ti|at|ed** (un′i nish′ē ā′tid), *adj.* **1** not introduced into acquaintance with something. **2** not having been admitted, as into a society.

**un|in|jured** (un in′jərd), *adj.* not injured; not damaged; unharmed.

**un|in|quis|i|tive** (un′in kwiz′ə tiv), *adj.* not inquisitive; not curious to search or inquire; indisposed to seek information.

**un|in|scribed** (un′in skrībd′), *adj.* not inscribed; having no inscription.

**un|in|spect|ed** (un′in spek′tid), *adj.* not examined or investigated, especially by an official inspector.

**un|in|spired** (un′in spīrd′), *adj.* not inspired; dull; tiresome: *uninspired writing.*

**un|in|spir|ing** (un′in spīr′ing), *adj.* not giving or arousing inspiration: *an uninspiring teacher, an uninspiring book.* **—un′in|spir′ing|ly,** *adv.*

**un|in|struct|ed** (un′in struk′tid), *adj.* **1** not instructed; not educated. **2** not informed on some matter. **3** not furnished with instructions, directions, or orders.

**un|in|sured** (un′in shůrd′), *adj.* not insured; without insurance.

**un|in|te|grat|ed** (un in′tə grā′tid), *adj.* not integrated; not subjected to a process of integration.

**un|in|tel|li|gence** (un′in tel′ə jəns), *n.* lack of intelligence; ignorance; unwisdom.

**un|in|tel|li|gent** (un′in tel′ə jənt), *adj.* **1** not endowed with intelligence, as an inanimate object. **2** deficient in intelligence; dull; stupid. **3** *Obsolete.* having no knowledge (of). **—un′in|tel′li|gent|ly,** *adv.*

**un|in|tel|li|gi|bil|i|ty** (un′in tel′ə jə bil′ə tē), *n.* the quality or condition of being unintelligible.

**un|in|tel|li|gi|ble** (un′in tel′ə jə bəl), *adj.* that cannot be understood; not intelligible: *There was so much static on the radio that the program was unintelligible.* **—un′in|tel′li|gi|ble|ness,** *n.*

**un|in|tel|li|gi|bly** (un′in tel′ə jə blē), *adv.* in an unintelligible manner; so as not to be understood.

**un|in|tend|ed** (un′in ten′did), *adj.* not intended.

**un|in|ten|tion|al** (un′in ten′shə nəl), *adj.* not intentional; not acting with intention; not done on purpose: *an unintentional snub.* **—un′in|ten′tion|al|ly,** *adv.*

**un|in|ter|est** (un in′tər ist, -trist), *n.* disinterest: *The Senator gives an emphatic show of uninterest in such speculation* (New York Times).

**un|in|ter|est|ed** (un in′tər is tid, -tris-; -tə res′-), *adj.* **1** showing or having no interest, especially: **a** paying no attention; inattentive; apathetic; unconcerned (in): *an uninterested expression.* **b** not interested (in); indifferent: *to be uninterested in politics.* **2** having no financial interest (in); not a partner, shareholder, or the like. **3** *Obsolete.* disinterested.
► See **disinterested** for usage note.

**un|in|ter|est|ing** (un in′tər is ting, -tris-; -tə res′-), *adj.* not interesting; not arousing any feeling of interest. **—un|in′ter|est|ing|ly,** *adv.* **—un|in′ter|est|ing|ness,** *n.*

**un|in|ter|mit|ted** (un′in tər mit′id), *adj.* not intermitted; continuous.

**un|in|ter|mit|ting** (un′in tər mit′ing), *adj.* not intermitting; continuing. **—un′in|ter|mit′ting|ly,** *adv.*

**un|in|ter|pret|a|ble** (un′in tėr′prə tə bəl), *adj.* that cannot be interpreted.

**un|in|ter|rupt|ed** (un′in′tə rup′tid), *adj.* without interruption; continuous. **—un′in|ter|rupt′ed|ly,** *adv.*

**un|in|tox|i|cat|ing** (un′in tok′sə kā′ting), *adj.* not intoxicating.

**u|ni|nu|cle|ate** (yü′nə nü′klē it, -nyü′-), *adj.* having a single nucleus: *a uninucleate cell.*

**un|in|vent** (un′in vent′), *v.t.* to do away with; cause to be as if never invented: *It may not be possible to uninvent the motor car, but it should not prove difficult to limit its numbers and its uses* (Manchester Guardian).

**un|in|vent|ed** (un′in ven′tid), *adj.* **1** not invented. **2** not found out.

**un|in|ven|tive** (un′in ven′tiv), *adj.* not inventive; not having the power of inventing, discovering, or contriving: *In every company there is ... the inventive class of both men and women, and the uninventive or accepting class* (Emerson). **—un′in|ven′tive|ly,** *adv.* **—un′in|ven′tive|ness,** *n.*

**un|in|vit|ed** (un′in vī′tid), *adj.* not invited; without an invitation.

**un|in|vit|ing** (un′in vī′ting), *adj.* not inviting; unattractive: *The prospect of a long and damaging fight is uninviting* (Manchester Guardian). **—un′in|vit′ing|ly,** *adv.*

* **un|ion** (yün′yən), *n., adj.* *—n.* **1** the action of uniting: *the union of hydrogen and oxygen in water.* **2** the state of being united: *The United States was formed by the union of thirteen former British colonies. All your strength is in your union* (Longfellow). **3** a group, as of people or states, united for some special purpose: *a credit union, a customs union, the Pan American Union. The American colonies formed a union.* SYN: combination, consolidation, fusion, coalition, confederation, league, merger. **4** a group of workers, joined together to protect and promote their interests; labor union; trade union. **5** = marriage. **6** a flag, or part of one, that is an emblem of union. The blue rectangle with stars in the American flag is the union. **7** a building set aside by an institution for social gatherings, plays, and dances. **8** any one of various devices for connecting parts of machinery or apparatus, especially a piece to join pipes or tubes together; coupling. **9** *Mathematics.* a set including all the members which belong to either or both of two sets without repeating any members; join. *Example:* If set A = {1, 2, 3, 4} and set B = {4, 5, 6}, then the union of the two sets is {1, 2, 3, 4, 5, 6}. **10** a fabric woven of two or more different yarns, especially one containing cotton and another yarn. **11** *Especially British.* **a** a number of parishes united for the administration of the poor laws. **b** a workhouse maintained by such parishes.
*—adj.* having to do with or belonging to a labor

**Pronunciation Key:** hat, āge, cãre, fär; let, ēqual, tėrm; it, īce; hot, ōpen, ôrder; oil, out; cup, pu̇t, rüle; child; long; thin; ᴛʜen; zh, measure; ə represents a in about, e in taken, i in pencil, o in lemon, u in circus.

union: *union goods, union workers, union rules. The two union dancers had been supplemented by a dancer ... and ... no one seemed to know whether she was union or not* (Renata Adler).
[< Latin *ūniō, -ōnis* < *ūnus* one; unity; a uniting]
—***Syn.*** *n.* **1, 2 Union, unity** mean a forming or being one. **Union** emphasizes the joining of two or more things, people, or groups to form a whole, or the state of being joined together as a unit: *The Constitution of the United States replaced the Articles of Confederation in order to form a more perfect union of the states than had existed before.* **Unity** emphasizes the oneness of the whole thus formed: *The strength of any group is in its unity.*

***union** definition 9

symbol

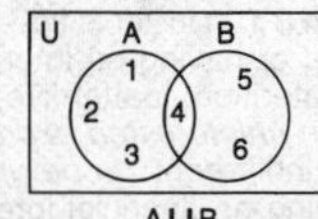

A∪B

**Un|ion** (yün′yən), *n., adj.* —*n.* **1a** the United States of America: *My paramount object is to save the Union, and not either to save or destroy slavery* (Abraham Lincoln). *The Constitution ... looks to an indestructible Union composed of indestructible States* (Salmon P. Chase). **b** those states that supported the federal government of the United States during the Civil War. **2** *British.* the United Kingdom.
—***adj.*** of or having to do with the Union: *Union soldiers. Early in the summer of 1861 he espoused the Union cause* (Nathaniel P. Langford).
[< *union*]

**union card**, a card indicating membership in the labor union by which it is issued.

**Union Congress of Soviets**, the former name of the Supreme Soviet.

**union down**, (of a flag or ensign) displaying the union at the lower corner next to the staff, instead of in its normal position (a flag hoisted in this way forming a signal of distress or of mourning): *There was an ensign, union down, flying at her main gaff* (Joseph Conrad).

**Union Flag**, *British.* = Union Jack (def. 1).

**union huck**, a kind of huckaback, or towel fabric, made of both cotton and linen. The cotton threads run lengthwise and the linen ones crosswise.

**u|ni|on|id** (yü′nē on′id), *n.* any member of a large and widely distributed family of freshwater mollusks, especially numerous in the United States, whose developing larvae are parasitic on fish. [< New Latin *Unionidae* the family name < Latin *ūniō, -ōnis* a single large pearl; (originally) union]

**un|ion|ism** (yün′yə niz əm), *n.* **1** the principle of union. **2** adherence to a union. **3** the system, principles, or methods of labor unions; trade unionism.

**Un|ion|ism** (yün′yə niz əm), *n.* adherence to the federal union of the United States, especially at the time of the Civil War.

**un|ion|ist** (yün′yə nist), *n.* **1** a person who promotes or advocates union. **2** a member of a labor union.

**Un|ion|ist** (yün′yə nist), *n.* **1** a supporter of the federal government of the United States during the Civil War. **2** a person who opposed the political separation of Ireland from Great Britain, before the establishment of the Irish Free State.

**un|ion|is|tic** (yün′yə nis′tik), *adj.* **1** having to do with or relating to unionism or unionists. **2** promoting union.

**un|ion|i|za|tion** (yün′yə nə zā′shən), *n.* the action of unionizing or state of being unionized.

**un|ion|ize** (yün′yə nīz), *v.,* **-ized, -iz|ing.** —***v.t.*** **1** to form into a labor union: *The first big drive of the new organization will be to unionize white collar workers* (Wall Street Journal). **2** to organize under a labor union; bring under the rules of a labor union.
—***v.i.*** to join in a labor union.

**Union Jack**, **1** the national flag of the United Kingdom, formed by combining the crosses of the patron saints of England, Scotland, and Ireland on the blue ground of the banner of Saint Andrew; British national ensign. **2** (originally) a ship's flag patterned on this. **3** a ship's flag of any one of various other countries, especially that of the United States.

**union jack**, any small flag, especially a ship's jack, which shows the symbol of union of a national flag. The United States union jack has 50 white stars against a blue background.

**union label**, a label on a manufactured product to show that union members worked on it according to union rules. Union labels are registered as trademarks.

**un|ion-made** (yün′yən mād′), *adj.* made or produced by unionized labor: *He smoked union-made cigarettes* (New Yorker).

**union security**, the part of a labor contract that provides for the security of union members, including such items as the union shop, preferential shop, and checkoff.

**union shop**, **1** a business establishment that by agreement employs only members of a labor union but may hire nonmembers provided they join the union within a specified period. **2** a business establishment that follows procedures agreed upon with a labor union in all matters concerning employment.

**union suit**, a suit of underwear in one piece.

**u|ni|o|vu|lar** (yü′nē ō′vyə lər), *adj.* derived from a single ovum: *Uniovular twins are identical twins.* [< *uni-* + *ovul*(e) + *-ar*]

**u|nip|a|rous** (yü nip′ər əs), *adj.* **1** bearing or producing one egg or one offspring at a birth. **2** *Botany.* developing a single axis at each branching: *a uniparous cyme.* [< New Latin *uniparus* < Latin *ūnus* one + *parere* to bear]

**u|ni|per|son|al** (yü′nə pėr′sə nəl), *adj.* **1** consisting of or existing as a single person. **2** (of a verb) impersonal.

**u|ni|pet|al|ous** (yü′nə pet′ə ləs), *adj. Botany.* having but one petal.

**u|ni|pla|nar** (yü′nə plā′nər), *adj.* **1** lying or taking place in one plane. **2** confined to one plane: *uniplanar motion.*

**u|ni|pod** (yü′nə pod), *n., adj.* —*n.* a stool, frame, or stand with one leg.
—***adj.*** having only one leg.
[< *uni-* + Greek *poús, podós* foot]

**u|ni|po|lar** (yü′nə pō′lər), *adj.* **1** having a single pole. **2** *Physics.* **a** produced by or proceeding from one magnetic or electric pole. **b** having or operating by means of one magnetic pole. **3** *Anatomy.* having or confined to only one fibrous process: *the unipolar nerve cells of the spine and cranium.*

**u|ni|po|lar|i|ty** (yü′nə pō lar′ə tē), *n.* unipolar quality or state.

**u|nique** (yü nēk′), *adj.* **1** having no like or equal; being the only one of its kind; standing alone in comparison with others; unrivaled; unparalleled: *a unique person or work. He discovered a unique specimen of rock in the cave. The astronaut described his experience as unique. That which gives to the Jews their unique position among the nations is what we are accustomed to regard as their Sacred History* (Spectator). **SYN:** unmatched, unequaled. **2** single; sole; solitary: *He despised play. His unique wish was to work* (Arnold Bennett). **3** *Informal.* very uncommon or unusual; rare; remarkable: *Her style of singing is rather unique. The most unique fabric service in the whole wide world* (House and Garden). [< Middle French *unique,* learned borrowing from Latin *ūnicus* single, sole < *ūnus* one] —**u|nique′ly**, *adv.* —**u|nique′ness**, *n.*

**u|niq|ui|ty** (yü nik′wə tē), *n.* = uniqueness.

**un|i|reme** (yü′nə rēm), *n.* a galley with only one row of oars on each side, used in ancient Greece and Rome. [< *uni-* + *-reme,* as in *trireme*]

**u|ni|sep|tate** (yü′nə sep′tāt), *adj. Biology.* having but one septum or partition.

**u|ni|se|ri|al** (yü′nə sir′ē əl), *adj.* arranged in a single series or row.

**u|ni|se|ri|ate** (yü′nə sir′ē it, -āt), *adj.* **1** = uniserial. **2** *Biology.* consisting of a single row of cells: *a uniseriate hair or filament.*

**u|ni|sex** (yü′nə seks′), *adj., n.* —***adj.*** designed or suitable for both sexes; not distinguishing or discriminating between males and females: *"Unisex" clothes were advertised from the walls of London's subway, and the psychological implications of unisex were eagerly discussed* (Phyllis W. Heathcote). *Garbed in loose-fitting tunics and trousers, the Chinese have a unisex look* (New York Times).
—***n.*** the quality or condition of being unisex or the same for both sexes: *the rise of unisex in fashions and in jobs.*
[< *uni-* + *sex*]

**u|ni|sexed** (yü′nə sekst′), *adj.* not distinguishable by sex: *In the background busy young men and women, sartorially unisexed, were laying out the ground plans* (Punch).

**u|ni|sex|u|al** (yü′nə sek′shu̇ əl), *adj.* **1** that is not a hermaphrodite; having the essential reproductive organs of only one sex. **2** *Botany.* diclinous. **3** having to do with one sex. **4** restricted to one sex. **5** of or having to do with unisex. —**u′ni|sex′u|al|ly**, *adv.*

**u|ni|sex|u|al|i|ty** (yü′nə sek′shu̇ al′ə tē), *n.* unisexual condition or quality.

**u|ni|son** (yü′nə sən, -zən), *n., adj.* —*n.* **1** harmonious combination or union; concord; agreement: *that unison of sense which marries sweet sound with the grace of form* (Keats). **2** agreement in pitch of two or more sounds, tones, voices, or instruments. **3** the state of sounding at the same pitch, as performed by different voices or instruments. **4** the relation of two tones of the same pitch considered as an "interval"; prime. **5** a combination of tones or melodies one or more octaves apart, as performed by male and female voices.
—***adj.*** **1** *Music.* **a** characterized by two or more tones having the same pitch, or pitches an even octave or octaves apart, or both, sounding together: *unison music, a unison phrase or passage.* **b** done in unison; producing unison music; *unison playing or singing.* **c** (of strings) tuned to the identical pitch. **2** (of sounds in general) sounding as one; in unison; unisonous. **3** done in unison; performed together as one: *a unison movement, unison marching, unison bowing.*
**in unison**, as one; together: *to act in unison. The feet of marching soldiers move in unison. The children sang "Happy Birthday" in unison.*
[< Medieval Latin *unisonus* sounding the same < Late Latin *ūnisonus* in immediate sequence in the scale, monotonous < Latin *ūnus* one + *sonus* sound]

**u|nis|o|nal** (yü nis′ə nəl), *adj.* = unisonous.

**u|nis|o|nance** (yü nis′ə nəns), *n.* = unison.

**u|nis|o|nant** (yü nis′ə nənt), *adj.* = unisonous.

**u|nis|o|nous** (yü nis′ə nəs), *adj.* rendered, or composed to be rendered, in unison or in octaves.

**u|nit** (yü′nit), *n., adj.* —*n.* **1** a single thing or person; individual member or part (of a group or number of things or individuals): *to regard husband and wife as the primary units of the family.* **2** any group of things or persons considered as one; division or section: *The family is a social unit.* **3** one of the individuals or groups of which a whole is composed: *The body consists of units called cells. The world ... so terrible in the mass, is so ... pitiable in its units* (Thomas Hardy). **4** a standard value, quantity, or amount, used as a basis for measuring: *A foot is a unit of length; a pound is a unit of weight.* **5** a part of a machine or other apparatus that has one specific purpose: *the storage unit of a computer.* **6a** the amount of a drug, vaccine, serum, or other agent, necessary to produce a specified effect: *international units of vitamins.* **b** the amount necessary to produce a specified effect upon a particular animal or upon animal tissues: *a rat growth unit.* **7** the smallest whole number; one; 1. **8** *Mathematics.* a single magnitude or number considered as the base of all numbers. **9** *Especially U.S.* a certain number of hours of classroom attendance and the accompanying outside work, used especially in computing credits and fees. **10** any one of the basic administrative and tactical groups or divisions of an armed force, forming part of a larger group or division.
—***adj.*** **1a** of, having to do with, or equivalent to a unit: *a unit measure, a unit weight, a circuit of unit resistance.* **b** consisting of, containing, or forming a unit or units: *a unit dose of medicine, the unit consumption of wheat per year.* **2** having the distinct or individual existence of a unit; individual: *All things in the exterior world are unit and individual; ... the mind contemplates these unit realities as they exist* (Cardinal Newman).
[alteration of *unity;* patterned on *digit*]

**Unit.**, Unitarian.

**u|nit|age** (yü′nə tij), *n.* detailed statement of the quantity making up a unit of measure.

**UNITAR** (no periods), United Nations Institute for Training and Research.

**u|ni|tar|i|an** (yü′nə tãr′ē ən), *n.* a person who believes in unity or centralization, as in government.

**U|ni|tar|i|an** (yü′nə tãr′ē ən), *n., adj.* —*n.* **1** a person who accepts the moral teachings of Jesus, but does not believe that he was divine; Christian who denies the doctrine of the Trinity. **2** a member of a Christian group or sect holding this doctrine and stressing individual religious freedom and the independence of each local congregation.
—***adj.*** **1** of or having to do with Unitarians or their doctrines. **2** characteristic of Unitarians or their doctrines. **3** adhering to Unitarianism.

**U|ni|tar|i|an|ism** (yü′nə tãr′ē ə niz′əm), *n.* the doctrines or beliefs of Unitarians.

**u|ni|tar|y** (yü′nə ter′ē), *adj.* **1** of or having to do with a unit or units. **2** of, based upon, or directed toward unity: *a unitary policy of government.* **3** under one control; unified; centralized: *a unitary government.* **4** like that of a unit; used as a unit. **5** of the nature of a unit; undivided or indivisible; single; separate.

**unit card**, a card in a library's card catalog, duplicated to serve as a unit for other cards, to which only a heading has to be added. The cards of the Library of Congress are used as unit cards.

**unit cell**, the basic building block of a crystal, consisting of the smallest group of molecules, atoms, or ions repeated over and over to make

up the crystal's geometric pattern.
**unit character**, a trait caused by one gene, or by a group of inseparable genes; a Mendelian character.
**unit circle** or **sphere**, *Mathematics.* a circle or sphere whose radius is one unit of distance.
**u|nite**[1] (yü nīt′), *v.*, **u|nit|ed, u|nit|ing.** —*v.t.* **1** to join together; make one; combine: *to unite bricks with mortar in a wall.* SYN: merge, consolidate, unify, couple. See syn. under **join. 2** to bring together; amalgamate or consolidate into one body; join, as in action, interest, opinion, or feeling: *to unite one's forces against an enemy. Several firms were united to form one company.* **3** to join by a mutual agreement or other formal bond; cause to become a union: *to unite a man and woman in marriage.* **4** to have or exhibit in union or combination: *a child uniting his father's temper and his mother's red hair.*
—*v.i.* to join in action; be united: *The class united in singing "America."* SYN: merge, consolidate, unify, couple. See syn. under **join.**
[< Latin *ūnītus,* past participle of *ūnīre* < *ūnus* one]
**u|nite**[2] (yü′nīt, yü nīt′), *n.* an English gold coin, issued by James I after the union of England and Scotland, originally worth 20 shillings. [< obsolete *unite,* adjective, united < Latin *ūnītus;* see etym. under **unite**[1] (because of the union of the crowns of Scotland and England in 1603)]
**u|nit|ed** (yü nī′tid), *adj.* **1** made one; joined; combined; unified. **2** having to do with or produced by two or more persons or things; joint: *united efforts.* **3** that harmonizes or agrees; in concord. —**u|nit′ed|ly,** *adv.*
**United Brethren**, an American Protestant denomination, founded in the early 1800's, Methodist in polity and Arminian in doctrine.
**United Church**, a Canadian Christian church formed in 1924-1925 as a union of Methodists, Presbyterians, and Congregationalists.
**United Church of Christ**, the union of the Congregational Christian Churches and the Evangelical and Reformed Church.
**United Empire Loyalist**, any one of a group of British colonists in America who emigrated to Canada during and after the Revolutionary War because they chose to remain British subjects; Loyalist.
**United Greeks**, the members of Christian communities which retain the liturgy, rites, etc., of the Greek or Eastern Church but are united to or in communion with the Church of Rome.
**United Nations**, **1** = UN. **2** the nations that fought against Germany, Italy, and Japan in World War II.
**United Nations Conference on International Organization**, a conference held in San Francisco from April 25 to June 26, 1945, to write a charter based on the Dumbarton Oaks proposals.
**United Nations Day**, October 24, commemorating the date in 1945 when the UN was officially established.
**United Nations Relief and Rehabilitation Administration**, = UNRRA.
**United States**, **1** a federation or union of states constituting a distinct, sovereign country, usually with territorial integrity: *the United States of Brazil.* **2** the United States of America. *Abbr:* U.S.
**u|nit|er** (yü nī′tər), *n.* a person or thing that unites; uniting agency or quality.
**unit factor**, *Biology.* a gene or a group of inseparable genes, causing the inheritance of a unit character.
**u|ni|ties** (yü′nə tēz), *n.pl.* See under **unity.**
**u|ni|tion** (yü nish′ən), *n.* = union. [< Late Latin *ūnītiō, -ōnis* < *ūnīre;* see etym. under **unite**[1]]
**u|ni|tive** (yü′nə tiv), *adj.* having or tending toward union. [< Late Latin *ūnītīvus* < Latin *ūnīre;* see etym. under **unite**[1]]
**u|ni|tize** (yü′nə tīz), *v.t.*, **-tized, -tiz|ing. 1** to make into or reduce to a unit; make as one: *The Rambler's unitized frame construction, in which body and frame are welded into a single unit ...* (Time). **2** to make a unit of; treat as an independent unit. —**u′ni|ti|za′tion,** *n.*
**unit magnetic pole**, the unit of magnetism exhibited by a magnetic pole which repels a like pole at a unit distance of one centimeter with a force of one dyne, or at a unit distance of one foot with a force of one pound.
**unit noun**, = count noun.
**unit pricing**, a method of pricing foods or other merchandise by showing both the total price and the cost per pound, ounce, or other agreed-upon unit of measure.
**unit rule**, *U.S.* a rule which requires that members of a delegation at a convention cast their votes in a body for the candidate preferred by the majority of the delegation.
**unit train**, a freight train which operates as a permanent unit, without uncoupling and reassembly of cars.
**unit trust**, = fixed trust.
**u|ni|ty** (yü′nə tē), *n., pl.* **-ties. 1** the fact, quality, or condition of being one; oneness; singleness, especially: **a** by nature or definition: *divine unity. A circle has more unity than a row of dots. A nation has more unity than a group of tribes.* **b** by union; unification: *unity in marriage, the unity of allies.* SYN: See syn. under **union. 2** a union of parts forming a complex whole; undivided whole, as distinct from its parts. **3** concord between two or more persons; harmony: *Brothers and sisters should live together in unity.* **4** the number one (1). **5** a quantity or magnitude regarded as equivalent to one (1) in calculation, measurement, or comparison. **6** oneness of effect; choice and arrangement of material (for a composition, book, picture, statue or other creation) to secure a single effect.
**the unities**, *Drama.* the three principles of the French classical dramatists, derived from Aristotle, that require a play to have one plot (unity of action) occurring on one day (unity of time) and in one place (unity of place): *the unities, Sir ... are ... a kind of a universal dovetailedness with regard to place and time* (Dickens).
[< Anglo-French *unité,* learned borrowing from Latin *ūnītās, -ātis* < *ūnus* one]
**univ.**, **1a** universal. **b** universally. **2** university.
**Univ.**, **1** Universalist. **2** University.
**UNIVAC** or **U|ni|vac** (yü′nə vak), *n. Trademark.* an electronic computer which uses a binary numbering system. [< *Univ*(ersal) *A*(utomatic) *C*(omputer)]
**u|ni|va|lence** (yü′nə vā′ləns, yü niv′ə-), *n.* a univalent quality or condition.
**u|ni|va|len|cy** (yü′nə vā′lən sē, yü niv′ə-), *n.* = univalence.
**u|ni|va|lent** (yü′nə vā′lənt, yü niv′ə-), *adj.* **1** *Chemistry.* having a valence of one; monovalent. **2** *Biology.* single (applied to a chromosome which lacks, or does not unite with, its homologous chromosome during synapsis).
***u|ni|valve** (yü′nə valv), *n., adj.* —*n.* **1** any mollusk having a shell consisting of one piece: *Snails are univalves.* **2** its shell.
—*adj.* **1** having a shell consisting of one piece. **2** composed of a single piece: *a univalve shell.*

***univalve**
definition 2

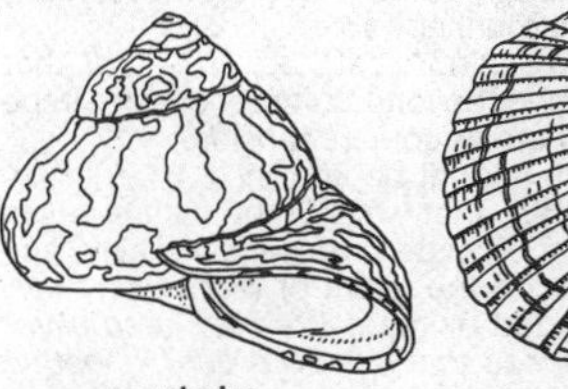


**u|ni|valved** (yü′nə valvd), *adj.* = univalve.
**u|ni|val|vu|lar** (yü′nə val′vyə lər), *adj.* = univalve.
**u|ni|ver|sal** (yü′nə vėr′səl), *adj., n.* —*adj.* **1a** of all; belonging to all; concerning all; shared by all: *Food is a universal need. Kings are not born; they are made by universal hallucination* (George Bernard Shaw). **b** coming from all; shared in by all: *a universal protest.* **c** understood or used by all: *the universal language of love.* **2** existing everywhere: *The law of gravity is universal. Sickness and disease are universal; they occur in every country of the world.* **3** covering a whole group, as of persons, things, or cases; general: *universal adult suffrage.* **4** accomplished in all, or many, subjects; wide-ranging: *a universal genius, universal knowledge.* **5** constituting, existing as, or regarded as a complete whole; complete; entire; whole: *the universal cosmos.* **6** adaptable as to different sizes, angles, or kinds of work. **7** *Philosophy, Logic.* asserting or denying something of every member of a class; generic: *"All men are mortal" is a universal proposition.* **8** *Mathematics.* having to do with a universe of objects or numbers; comprising all the elements under consideration: *a universal set.* **9** capable of operating from either alternating-current or direct-current power lines: *a universal motor, a universal television receiver.*
—*n.* **1** *Philosophy, Logic.* **a** that which is predicated or asserted of all the individuals or species of a class or genus; universal proposition. **b** a general term or concept; abstraction: *The common man is a universal.* **2** something universal, especially a person or thing that is universally powerful or current: *He made their pride, pity, love, anguish, glory, and endurance into universals* (Newsweek). **3** = universal joint.
[< Latin *ūniversālis* < *ūniversus;* see etym. under **universe**] —**u′ni|ver′sal|ness,** *n.*
**universal coupling**, = universal joint.
**universal donor**, a blood donor who has type O blood, that can be given safely in transfusion to a person of any blood type.
**universal gravitation**, gravitation conceived as a property of all matter in the universe.
**u|ni|ver|sal|ism** (yü′nə vėr′sə liz əm), *n.* **1** the quality of being universal; universality: *This is ... the universalism of Jesus Himself ... He belongs to humanity, not to Israel* (Andrew M. Fairburn). **2** the quality of having considerable knowledge of or interest in a great range of subjects. **3** love or concern for all humanity. **4** the doctrine of the unification of the world, as by establishing one religion, nationality, or economy for all mankind.
**U|ni|ver|sal|ism** (yü′nə vėr′sə liz əm), *n.* the doctrine or beliefs of Universalists.
**u|ni|ver|sal|ist** (yü′nə vėr′sə list), *n., adj.* —*n.* a person who believes in or practices universalism. —*adj.* **1** = universalistic. **2** of or having to do with universalism or universalists.
**U|ni|ver|sal|ist** (yü′nə vėr′sə list), *n., adj.* —*n.* **1** a Christian who believes that all people will finally be saved. **2** a member of a Christian church holding the belief that all people will finally be saved. The Universalists merged with the Unitarians in 1961. —*adj.* of or having to do with Universalists or their doctrines.
**u|ni|ver|sal|is|tic** (yü′nə vėr′sə lis′tik), *adj.* universal in scope or character: *a broad universalistic concept.*
**u|ni|ver|sal|i|ty** (yü′nə vėr sal′ə tē), *n., pl.* **-ties.** the quality of being universal.
**u|ni|ver|sal|i|za|tion** (yü′nə vėr′sə lə zā′shən), *n.* the act or process of making universal or general; generalization.
**u|ni|ver|sal|ize** (yü′nə vėr′sə līz), *v.t.*, **-ized, -iz|ing.** to render universal; make generally or universally applicable: *Civilization requires a different kind of education to survive, one that humanizes rather than mechanizes man, and one that universalizes rather than nationalizes community* (Saturday Review).
***universal joint**, a joint or coupling between two shafts that allows or provides for movement or turning in almost any direction, especially a coupling for transmitting power from one shaft to another when they are not in line, as between the transmission and drive shaft of an automobile.

***universal joint**

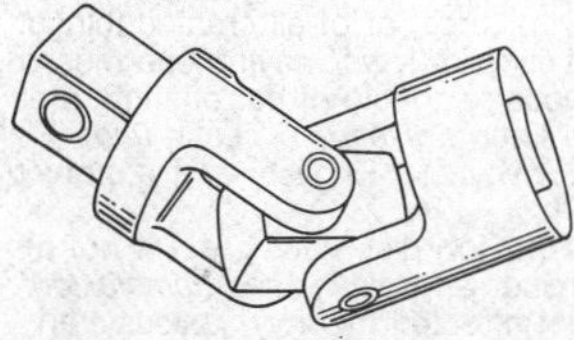

**universal language**, **1** a language created artificially for use throughout the world. Esperanto, Interlingua, and Volapük are three well-known universal languages. **2** *Figurative.* something that can be understood by all: *Love and laughter are universal languages.*
**u|ni|ver|sal|ly** (yü′nə vėr′sə lē), *adv.* **1** in every instance; without exception. **2** = everywhere.
**universal man**, a man skilled in many fields of knowledge; Renaissance man. [translation of Italian *uomo universale*]
**Universal Military Training** or **universal military training**, a system in which every qualified man receives a general military training when he reaches a certain age.
**Universal Product Code**, *U.S.* code on the labels of supermarket products in a computerized system of checkout and inventory: *The Universal Product Code ... is the coded symbol of lines and spaces now on the labels of about 60 per cent of the products in markets* (New York Post). *Abbr:* UPC (no periods).
**universal recipient**, a person having type AB blood, that can receive safely a transfusion of any blood type.
**universal solvent**, **1** a hypothetical substance, especially the alkahest, that dissolves everything. **2** a substance that dissolves all or nearly all metals or classes of metals. **3** water (because it can dissolve many compounds).
**universal suffrage**, suffrage extended to all the adult men and women of a country other than those disqualified by law.
**universal time**, = Greenwich Time. *Abbr:* u.t.
**u|ni|verse** (yü′nə vėrs), *n.* **1** Also, **Universe.** the

**Pronunciation Key:** hat, āge, cãre, fär; let, ēqual, tėrm; it, īce; hot, ōpen, ôrder; **oil**, **out**; cup, pu̇t, rüle; **ch**ild; lo**ng**; **th**in; **ᴛʜ**en; **zh**, measure; ə represents **a** in about, **e** in taken, **i** in pencil, **o** in lemon, **u** in circus.

whole of existing things; everything there is; cosmos, especially: **a** the whole of reality, as the creation of the Deity: *She had ... The quest of hidden knowledge, and a mind To comprehend the universe* (Byron). *Roaming in thought over the Universe, I saw the little that is Good steadily hastening towards immortality* (Walt Whitman). **b** the whole of observed or hypothesized physical reality; physical universe: *Our world is but a small part of the universe. The Egyptian's conception of the universe was ... anthropomorphic: the goddess of the heavens, Nut, arched her starry body over the solid Earth and let the ship of the Sun glide over her back* (Rudolf Thiel). **2** the world, especially as the abode of mankind; earth: *Who all our green and azure universe Threatenedst to muffle round with black destruction* (Shelley). **3** *Mathematics, Logic.* the set of all objects being considered at one time. The universe might be the set of all natural numbers, the numbers from 0 through 10, all animals, or the animals on a farm. *Abbr:* U (no period). **4** *Statistics.* the total number of items from which a sample is selected; population. [< Latin *ūniversum,* (originally) adjective, whole, turned into one, neuter of *ūniversus* < *ūnus* one + *vertere* to turn]

**universe of discourse**, *Logic.* all the objects or ideas to which an argument or discussion refers.

**u|ni|ver|si|ty** (yü′nə vėr′sə tē), *n., pl.* **-ties. 1** an institution of learning of the highest grade. A university usually has several schools, as of law, medicine, theology, teaching, and business. In the United States it also includes a college of liberal arts and a graduate school or schools, and is empowered to confer various degrees. *Abbr:* Univ. **2** a building or buildings occupied by a university. [< Anglo-French *universite,* learned borrowing from Medieval Latin *universitas, -atis* university < Late Latin *ūniversitās, -ātis* corporation, society < Latin, aggregate, whole < *ūniversus;* see etym. under **universe**]

**university extension**, the extending of the advantages of university instruction to adults who are not enrolled as university students, by means of lectures at convenient centers and sometimes also by classwork, homework, and correspondence.

**u|ni|ver|sol|o|gist** (yü′nə vėr sol′ə jist), *n.* an expert in universology.

**u|ni|ver|sol|o|gy** (yü′nə vėr sol′ə jē), *n.* the science of the universe, or of all created things.

**u|niv|o|cal** (yü niv′ə kəl), *adj.* having one meaning only; not equivocal; capable of but one interpretation. [< Late Latin *ūnivocus* (< Latin *ūnus* one + *vōx, vōcis* voice) + English *-al*[1]] — **u|niv′o|cal|ly**, *adv.*

**un|jaun|diced** (un jôn′dist, -jän′-), *adj.* **1** not affected by jaundice: *an unjaundiced complexion.* **2** *Figurative.* not affected by envy, jealousy, anger, or the like: *His description of the poverty program* [*was*] *all too true; and his strength and courage and unjaundiced eye beautifully evident throughout* (Harper's).

**un|jeal|ous** (un jel′əs), *adj.* not jealous; not suspicious or mistrustful.

**un|jelled** (un jeld′), *adj.* not jelled; without a definite form; not fixed: *Its communal character gives the impression of being sketchy, not filled out, unjelled* (New Yorker).

**un|joint** (un joint′), *v.t.* to take apart the joints of; dismember.

**un|joint|ed** (un join′tid), *adj.* **1** having no joints, nodes, or articulations; inarticulate. **2a** unjoined. **b** *Figurative.* disjointed; disconnected.

**un|joy|ful** (un joi′fəl), *adj.* joyless; unpleasant: *this unjoyful set of people* (Sir Richard Steele).

**un|just** (un just′), *adj.* in opposition to what is morally right; not just; not fair. — **un|just′ly**, *adv.* — **un|just′ness**, *n.*

**un|jus|ti|fi|a|ble** (un jus′tə fī′ə bəl), *adj.* that cannot be justified; not defensible or right: *an unjustifiable act. Nor is it unjustifiable to hold that those who owe a superior allegiance to a foreign Government ... have therefore forfeited the privilege of working for their own Government* (New York Times). — **un|jus′ti|fi′a|ble|ness**, *n.*

**un|jus|ti|fi|a|bly** (un jus′tə fī′ə blē), *adv.* in a manner that cannot be justified or vindicated: *unjustifiably severe. The organization was launched to an accompaniment of unjustifiably high hopes* (Wall Street Journal).

**un|jus|ti|fied** (un jus′tə fīd), *adj.* **1** not proved to be right or proper; unwarranted: *unjustified claims or accusations. The action of the strikers was unjustified.* **2** *Theology.* not brought into a state of justification; still subject to sin or the penalty of sin.

**un|jus|ti|fi|ed|ly** (un jus′tə fī′id lē), *adv.* in an unjustified manner; to an unjustified degree: *It is possible that the Soviet leaders ... however unjustifiedly ... fear attack from the West* (Times Of India).

**un|keeled** (un kēld′), *adj.* not having a keel: *unkeeled sepals.*

**un|kempt** (un kempt′), *adj.* **1** not combed; matted or disheveled: *unkempt hair.* **2** not properly cared for; neglected; untidy: *the unkempt clothes of a tramp.* [Middle English *unkembed* < *un-* un-[1] + *kempt, kembed,* Old English *cembed* combed, past participle of *cemban* to comb] — **un|kempt′ness**, *n.*

**un|kenned** (un kend′), *adj. Scottish.* unknown; strange.

**un|ken|nel** (un ken′əl), *v.,* **-neled, -nel|ing** or (*especially British*) **-nelled, -nel|ling.** — ***v.t.* 1** to let (a hound or hounds) out of the kennel. **2** *Figurative.* to force or drive out from hiding or concealment; bring to light: *to unkennel this knavery* (London Times).
— ***v.i.*** to be unkenneled.

**un|kept** (un kept′), *adj.* **1** not kept; not retained; not preserved. **2** not sustained, maintained, or tended.

**un|kind** (un kīnd′), *adj.* not kind; lacking kindness or compassion; harsh; cruel. **SYN:** unsympathetic, ungracious. — **un|kind′ness**, *n.*

**un|kind|li|ness** (un kīnd′lē nis), *n.* the character of being unkindly; unkindness; unfavorableness.

**un|kind|ly** (un kīnd′lē), *adj., adv.* — ***adj.*** harsh; unkind; unfavorable: *the bleak, unkindly air* (Hawthorne).
— ***adv.*** in an unkind way; harshly.

**un|king|ly** (un king′lē), *adj.* not kingly; not befitting a king; not royal.

**un|knelled** (un neld′), *adj.* not having the bell tolled for one at death or funeral; untolled: *Without a grave, unknell'd, uncoffin'd and unknown* (Byron).

**un|knight|li|ness** (un nīt′lē nis), *n.* the character of being unknightly.

**un|knight|ly** (un nīt′lē), *adj., adv.* — ***adj.*** not knightly; unworthy of a knight; not like a knight.
— ***adv.*** in a manner unbecoming to a knight.

**un|knit** (un nit′), *v.t., v.i.,* **-knit|ted** or **-knit, -knit|ting. 1** to untie or unfasten (a knot, tangle, or bond). **2** to ravel out (something knitted); unravel. **3** to smooth out (something wrinkled): *He unknit his black brows* (Charlotte Brontë). [Old English *uncnyttan* < *un-* un-[2] + *cnyttan* to knit]

**un|knot** (un not′), *v.t.,* **-knot|ted, -knot|ting.** to bring out of a knotted state; free from knots; untie.

**un|know|a|bil|i|ty** (un′nō ə bil′ə tē), *n.* the quality or state of being unknowable.

**un|know|a|ble** (un nō′ə bəl), *adj., n.* — ***adj.*** that cannot be known; beyond comprehension, especially beyond human comprehension.
— ***n.*** that which cannot be known.
**the Unknowable**, that which is by nature beyond man's knowing; ultimate or essential reality, as something outside the realm of that which may be comprehended by man: *We may keep alive the consciousness that it is alike our highest wisdom and our highest duty to regard that through which all things exist as the Unknowable* (Herbert Spencer).
— **un|know′a|ble|ness**, *n.*

**un|know|ing** (un nō′ing), *adj., n.* — ***adj.*** not knowing; ignorant or unsuspecting: *an unknowing child.*
— ***n.*** = ignorance.
**the unknowing**, those who do not know or are ignorant: *The pillars would not be recognized immediately by the unknowing as timber* (London Times).
— **un|know′ing|ly**, *adv.* — **un|know′ing|ness**, *n.*

**un|known** (un nōn′), *adj., n.* — ***adj.*** not known; not familiar; strange; unexplored: *an unknown language. Lewis and Clark explored the unknown country beyond the western frontier. How many ages hence Shall this our lofty scene be acted o'er, In states unborn and accents yet unknown!* (Shakespeare). **SYN:** obscure, nameless, unrenowned.
— ***n.* 1** a person or thing that is unknown: *a political unknown. The diver descended into the unknown.* **2** *Mathematics.* an unknown quantity.
**the Unknown**, something great and unknown or mysterious: *God, the Unknown.*

**unknown quantity**, *Mathematics.* a quantity whose value is to be found, usually represented by a letter from the last part of the alphabet, such as *x, y,* or *z.*

**Unknown Soldier**, an unidentified soldier killed in combat and buried with honors in a prominent place in his country as a memorial to all the unidentified dead of his country: *The tomb of the American Unknown Soldier is in the Arlington National Cemetery near Washington.*

**UNKRA** (no periods), United Nations Korean Reconstruction Agency.

**un|la|bored** (un lā′bərd), *adj.* **1** not produced by labor or toil: *Unlabored harvests shall the fields adorn* (John Dryden). **2** not cultivated by labor; not tilled. **3** spontaneous; voluntary; natural. **4** not cramped or stiff; easy; free: *an unlabored style.*

**un|la|boured** (un lā′bərd), *adj. Especially British.* unlabored.

**un|lace** (un lās′), *v.t.,* **-laced, -lac|ing. 1** to undo the lace of. **2** to free or relieve of clothing or an article of clothing, especially of clothing that is held on by a lace or laces; undress.

**un|lade** (un lād′), *v.t., v.i.,* **-lad|ed, -lad|en** or **-lad|ed, -lad|ing.** = unload.

**un|la|dy|like** (un lā′dē līk′), *adj.* not ladylike; not like or befitting a lady.

**un|laid** (un lād′), *adj., v.* — ***adj.* 1** not laid or placed; not fixed: *The first foundations of the world being yet unlaid* (Richard Hooker). **2** not allayed; not pacified: *Blue meagre hag or stubborn unlaid ghost, That breaks his magic chains at curfew time* (Milton). **3** not laid out, as a corpse. **4** *Nautical.* untwisted, as the strands of a rope.
— ***v.*** the past tense and past participle of **unlay**.

**un|la|ment|ed** (un′lə men′tid), *adj.* not lamented; whose loss is not deplored; not moaned; unwept: *Thus let me live, unseen, unknown, Thus unlamented let me die* (Alexander Pope).

**un|lash** (un lash′), *v.t.* **1** to detach or release by undoing a lashing. **2** to undo or untie (a lashing).

**un|latch** (un lach′), *v.t.* to unfasten or open by lifting a latch. — ***v.i.*** to become or be able to be thus unfastened.

**un|laun|dered** (un lôn′dərd, -län′-), *adj.* not laundered.

**un|law|ful** (un lô′fəl), *adj.* **1** contrary to law; against the law; prohibited by law; not lawful; forbidden; illegal. **2** = illegitimate. — **un|law′ful|ly**, *adv.* — **un|law′ful|ness**, *n.*

**unlawful assembly**, *Law.* the meeting of three or more persons to commit an unlawful act, or to carry out some purpose in such manner as to give reasonable ground for apprehending a breach of the peace in consequence of it.

**un|lay** (un lā′), *v.,* **-laid, -lay|ing.** — ***v.t.*** to untwist (a rope) into separate strands.
— ***v.i.*** to untwist; unravel: *an unlaid rope.*

**un|lead|ed** (un led′id), *adj.* **1** (of type) set without leads between the lines; solid. **2** not weighted, covered, or furnished with lead. **3** = nonleaded.

**un|learn** (un lėrn′), *v.t.* **1** to get rid of (ideas, habits, or tendencies); give up knowledge of; forget. **2** to cause (a person) to unlearn something; teach not to do or to do the opposite of what has been taught.

**un|learn|ed** (un lėr′nid *for 1, 3;* un lėrnd′ *for 2*), *adj.* **1** not educated; ignorant: *an audience of unlearned laymen. The man was unlearned and could not write his name.* **2a** not learned: *an unlearned lesson.* **b** known without being learned: *an untaught, unlearned, but nevertheless real appreciation of beauty. Being able to suck is an unlearned habit of babies.* **3** not showing education: *an unlearned comment.*

**un|learn|ed|ly** (un lėr′nid lē), *adv.* in an unlearned manner; so as to exhibit ignorance; ignorantly.

**un|leased** (un lēst′), *adj.* not leased.

**un|leash** (un lēsh′), *v.t.* **1** to release from a leash: *to unleash a dog.* **2** *Figurative.* to let loose: *to unleash one's temper.*

**un|leav|ened** (un lev′ənd), *adj.* not leavened. Unleavened bread is made without yeast.

**un|led** (un led′), *adj.* **1** not led; without guidance. **2** in command of one's faculties.

**un|less** (ən les′, un-), *conj., prep.* — ***conj.*** if it were not that; if not: *We shall go unless it rains.*
— ***prep.*** except: *Nor ever was he known ...* [*to*] *Curse, unless against the Government* (John Dryden).
[Middle English *onlesse* < *on* + *lesse,* that is, on a less condition (than)]

**un|les|soned** (un les′ənd), *adj.* untaught; untutored: *an unlesson'd girl, unschool'd, unpractised* (Shakespeare).

**un|let|tered** (un let′ərd), *adj.* **1** not educated; unlearned. **2** not able to read or write; illiterate.

**un|lev|el** (un lev′əl), *adj., v.,* **-eled, -el|ing** or (*especially British*) **-elled, -el|ling.** — ***adj.*** not level; uneven.
— ***v.t.*** to make not level or uneven.

**un|li|censed** (un lī′sənst), *adj.* **1** not licensed; having no license. **2** done or undertaken without license; unauthorized.

**un|licked** (un likt′), *adj.* **1** not licked. **2** not brought to the proper shape or condition by or as by licking. **3** *Figurative.* crude, rough, or unpolished.

**unlicked cub**, a crude or unmannerly young person: *You know, Polly, what an unlicked cub I was when I married you* (Besant and Rice).

**un|light|ed** (un lī′tid), *adj.* **1** not lighted; not illuminated. **2** not kindled or ignited.

**un|like** (un līk′), *adj., prep.* — ***adj.* 1** having little or no resemblance one to the other; not like; different; dissimilar: *The two problems are quite unlike.* **SYN:** diverse. **2** different in size or number; unequal: *unlike weights.* **3** *Archaic.* unlikely.
— ***prep.*** different from: *to act unlike others.*

**un|like|li|hood** (un līk′lē hu̇d), *n.* = improbability.

**un|like|li|ness** (un līk′lē nis), *n.* **1** the condition of being unlikely or improbable; improbability. **2** the condition of being unlike; dissimilarity.

**un|like|ly** (un līk′lē), *adj.* **1** not likely; not probable: *That horse is unlikely to win the race.* **2** not likely to succeed: *an unlikely undertaking.*

**un|like|ness** (un līk′nis), *n.* the condition of being unlike; difference.

**un|lim|ber** (un lim′bər), *v., n.* — *v.t.* **1** to detach (a gun) from a limber or towing apparatus in preparation for firing. **2** *Figurative.* to make or get (anything) ready for action or use: *to unlimber one's muscles.*
— *v.i.* to prepare for action.
— *n.* the act or procedure of unlimbering a gun.

**un|lim|it|ed** (un lim′ə tid), *adj.* **1** without limits; boundless. **2** not restrained; not restricted: *a government of unlimited power.* **3** *Mathematics.* indefinite. — **un|lim′it|ed|ness,** *n.*

**unlimited policy,** an insurance policy which covers every type of a certain risk or contingency.

**un|link** (un lingk′), *v.t.* **1** to undo two or more links of (a chain). **2a** to detach or set free by unfastening a link or chain. **b** *Figurative.* to detach or set free by undoing something that acts as a link or chain. — *v.i.* to become unlinked; part; separate.

**un|liq|ue|fied** (un lik′wə fīd), *adj.* not dissolved; unmelted.

**un|liq|ui|dat|ed** (un lik′wə dā′tid), *adj.* not liquidated; not settled: *unliquidated debts or claims.*

**un|list|ed** (un lis′tid), *adj.* **1** not on a or the usual list: *an unlisted telephone number.* **2** not in the official list of securities that can be traded in a stock exchange.

**un|lit** (un lit′), *adj.* not lit; unlighted.

**un|live** (un liv′), *v.t.,* **-lived, -liv|ing.** to reverse, undo, or annul (past life or experience).

**un|load** (un lōd′), *v.t.* **1** to remove (a load): *to unload cargo.* **2** to take the load from: *to unload a ship.* **3** *Figurative.* to get rid of; unburden oneself of: *She began to unload her troubles onto her mother.* **4** to remove the load or charge from (a firearm). **5** to remove (the shell or charge) from a firearm. **6** to dispose of or sell out, especially in large quantities: *to unload stock.* — *v.i.* to be or become unloaded: *The ship is unloading.* — **un|load′er,** *n.*

**un|lo|cat|ed** (un lō′kā tid), *adj.* **1** not located or placed. **2** *U.S.* (of land) not surveyed and marked off: *The disposal of the unlocated lands will hereafter be a valuable source of revenue, and an immediate one of credit* (Alexander Hamilton).

**un|lock** (un lok′), *v.t.* **1** to open the lock of: *to unlock a door.* **2** to open (anything firmly closed). **3** *Figurative.* to disclose; reveal: *to unlock one's heart, to unlock one's inmost thoughts. Science has unlocked the mystery of the atom.* — *v.i.* to be or become unlocked.

**un|locked** (un lokt′), *adj.* not locked: *an unlocked door.*

**un|looked-for** (un lu̇kt′fôr′), *adj.* unexpected; unforeseen: *this unlooked-for danger* (William Godwin).

**un|loose** (un lüs′), *v.t.,* **-loosed, -loos|ing.** to let loose; set free; release: (*Figurative.*) *Something ... seems to have ... unloosed her tongue* (Joseph Conrad).

**un|loos|en** (un lü′sən), *v.t.* = unloose.

**un|love** (un luv′), *v.t.,* **-loved, -lov|ing.** to cease to love.

**un|loved** (un luvd′), *adj.* not loved.

**un|love|li|ness** (un luv′lē nis), *n.* **1** ungraciousness; lack of the qualities which attract love. **2** lack of beauty or attractiveness; plainness of feature or appearance.

**un|love|ly** (un luv′lē), *adj.,* **-love|li|er, -love|li|est.** **1** without beauty or charm; unpleasing in appearance. **2** unpleasant; objectionable; disagreeable.

**un|lov|ing** (un luv′ing), *adj.* not loving; without love. — **un|lov′ing|ly,** *adv.* — **un|lov′ing|ness,** *n.*

**un|luck|i|ly** (un luk′ə lē), *adv.* in an unlucky manner; by ill luck; unfortunately; unhappily.

**un|luck|i|ness** (un luk′ē nis), *n.* the character or condition of being unlucky.

**un|luck|y** (un luk′ē), *adj.,* **-luck|i|er, -luck|i|est.** **1** not lucky; unfortunate: *an unlucky person, an unlucky choice.* **SYN:** unsuccessful, ill-fated. **2** bringing bad luck; ill-omened; inauspicious: *an unlucky day.*

**un|made** (un mād′), *v., adj.* — *v.* the past tense and past participle of **unmake.**
— *adj.* not made; not yet made: *an unmade bed.*

**un|maid|en|li|ness** (un mā′dən lē nis), *n.* the character or state of being unmaidenly.

**un|maid|en|ly** (un mā′dən lē), *adj.* not maidenly; unbefitting a maiden.

**un|mail|a|ble** (un mā′lə bəl), *adj.* not mailable; that cannot be mailed.

**un|make** (un māk′), *v.t.,* **-made, -mak|ing.** **1** to undo the making of; cause to be no longer in being: *The British people will have made a bad bargain, which they will be able to unmake only at great cost* (Manchester Guardian Weekly). **2** *Figurative.* to bring to nothing; undo; destroy; ruin: *The machine unmakes the man* (Emerson). **3** to deprive of rank or station; depose.

**un|mal|le|a|bil|i|ty** (un mal′ē ə bil′ə tē), *n.* unmalleable condition or quality.

**un|mal|le|a|ble** (un mal′ē ə bəl), *adj.* not malleable.

**un|man** (un man′), *v.t.,* **-manned, -man|ning.** **1** to deprive of the qualities of a man, such as courage or fortitude; weaken or break down the spirit of: *He was unmanned by fear.* **2** to deprive of virility; emasculate. **3** to deprive of the attributes of man; make no longer human. **4** to deprive of men: *to unman a ship.*

**un|man|age|a|ble** (un man′ə jə bəl), *adj.* not manageable; intractable; unruly; incapable of being handled: *an unmanageable horse.* — **un|man′age|a|ble|ness,** *n.* — **un|man′age|a|bly,** *adv.*

**un|man|like** (un man′līk′), *adj.* **1** unlike man in form or appearance. **2** unbecoming a man as a member of the human race; inhuman; brutal. **3** unsuitable to a man; effeminate; childish.

**un|man|li|ness** (un man′lē nis), *n.* the character of being unmanly; effeminacy.

**un|man|ly** (un man′lē), *adj.,* **-man|li|er, -man|li|est.** **1** not manly; weak; cowardly; effeminate: *'Tis unmanly grief* (Shakespeare). **2** dishonorable; degrading.

**un|manned** (un mand′), *adj.* **1** deprived of courage; made weak or timid. **2** emasculated; castrated. **3** without a complement of men; lacking a crew, garrison, or other organized group. **4** without human beings; lacking people; unpopulated. **5** *Falconry.* not tamed.

**un|man|nered** (un man′ərd), *adj.* **1** not affected or pretentious; simple and straightforward. **2** = unmannerly. — **un|man′nered|ly,** *adv.*

**un|man|ner|ly** (un man′ər lē), *adj., adv.* — *adj.* having bad manners; rude; discourteous: *He called them untaught knaves, unmannerly* (Shakespeare). **SYN:** impolite.
— *adv.* with bad manners; rudely. — **un|man′ner|li|ness,** *n.*

**un|man|u|fac|tured** (un′man yə fak′chərd), *adj.* **1** not made up; still in its natural state, or only partly prepared for use: *Fiber is unmanufactured before it is made into thread. Thread is unmanufactured before it is woven into cloth.* **2** *Figurative.* not simulated: *unmanufactured grief.*

**un|ma|nured** (un′mə nu̇rd′), *adj.* **1** not manured; not enriched by manure. **2** *Obsolete.* untilled; uncultivated.

**un|marked** (un märkt′), *adj.* **1** not marked; having no mark. **2** unobserved; not regarded; undistinguished; not noted: *He mix'd, unmark'd, among the busy throng* (John Dryden).

**un|mar|ket|a|ble** (un mär′kə tə bəl), *adj.* not marketable; unsalable.

**un|marred** (un märd′), *adj.* not marred or injured: *He had displayed indiscreet valor by provoking Neal, then by sticking his hitherto unmarred face in the way of Big Tom's flying knuckles* (Time).

**un|mar|riage|a|ble** (un mar′ə jə bəl), *adj.* **1** not fit to be married. **2** too young for marriage.

**un|mar|ried** (un mar′ēd), *adj.* not married; single. **SYN:** unwed.

**un|mar|ry** (un mar′ē), *v.,* **-ried, -ry|ing.** — *v.t.* to dissolve the marriage of; divorce.
— *v.i.* to become freed from a marriage.

**un|mask** (un mask′, -mäsk′), *v.i.* to remove a mask or disguise: *The guests unmasked at midnight.* — *v.t.* **1** to take off a mask or disguise from. **2** *Figurative.* to show the real nature or being of; expose: *to unmask a hypocrite. We unmasked the plot.* **3** to remove something that hides (a gun or guns) and begin firing: *to unmask a battery of howitzers.*

**un|mas|tered** (un mas′tərd, -mäs′-), *adj.* **1** not subdued; not conquered. **2** not conquerable: *He cannot his unmaster'd grief sustain* (John Dryden).

**un|match|a|ble** (un mach′ə bəl), *adj.* that cannot be matched or equaled: *an unmatchable color, an unmatchable voice.* **SYN:** incomparable; peerless.

**un|match|a|bly** (un mach′ə blē), *adv.* in an unmatchable manner: *His poems are like pebbles—slight and worn, but also unmatchably freaked, hard, compact, accurate* (Manchester Guardian Weekly).

**un|matched** (un macht′), *adj.* not matched; matchless; unequaled.

**un|mat|ed** (un mā′tid), *adj.* not mated; not paired.

**un|mean|ing** (un mē′ning), *adj.* **1** without meaning or significance; meaningless: *unmeaning words.* **2** empty of feeling or thought; without expression or sense; vacant: *an unmeaning stare.* — **un|mean′ing|ly,** *adv.* — **un|mean′ing|ness,** *n.*

**un|meant** (un ment′), *adj.* not intended; accidental.

**un|meas|ur|a|ble** (un mezh′ər ə bəl, -mā′zhər-), *adj.* immeasurable: *Their unmeasurable vanity* (Ben Jonson).

**un|meas|ured** (un mezh′ərd, -mā′zhərd), *adj.* **1** not measured; unlimited; measureless. **2** not restrained; intemperate: *Lord Melbourne and the Court were attacked by the Tory press in unmeasured language* (Lytton Strachey). **SYN:** excessive, unrestrained.

**un|med|i|tat|ed** (un med′ə tā′tid), *adj.* not meditated; not prepared by previous thought; unpremeditated.

**un|meet** (un mēt′), *adj.* not fit; not proper; unsuitable. **SYN:** unbecoming, unseemly. [Old English *unmǣte* < *un-* un-[1] + *gemǣte* suitable, meet] — **un|meet′ly,** *adv.* — **un|meet′ness,** *n.*

**un|me|lo|di|ous** (un′mə lō′dē əs), *adj.* not melodious; wanting melody; harsh.

**un|men|tion|a|ble** (un men′shə nə bəl, -mensh′nə-), *adj., n.* — *adj.* that cannot be mentioned; not fit to be spoken about.
— *n.* something unmentionable.

**unmentionables, a** underwear (often humorous in use): *a manufacturer of unmentionables.* **b** (in the 1800's) trousers: *The knees of the unmentionables ... began to get alarmingly white* (Dickens).
— **un|men′tion|a|ble|ness,** *n.*

**un|men|tioned** (un men′shənd), *adj.* not mentioned.

**un|mer|ce|nar|y** (un mėr′sə ner′ē), *adj.* not mercenary; not working or acting for money only.

**un|mer|chant|a|ble** (un mėr′chən tə bəl), *adj.* not merchantable; unfit for sale.

**un|mer|ci|ful** (un mėr′si fəl), *adj.* having no mercy; showing no mercy; cruel. **SYN:** pitiless, inhuman, merciless. — **un|mer′ci|ful|ly,** *adv.* — **un|mer′ci|ful|ness,** *n.*

**un|merge** (un mėrj′), *v.t.,* **-merged, -merg|ing.** to separate; dissolve: *Under the proposed law, the agency could unmerge corporations that had already consolidated* (New York Times).

**un|mer|it|ed** (un mer′ə tid), *adj.* not merited; undeserved.

**un|mer|it|ing** (un mer′ə ting), *adj.* not meriting; undeserving.

**un|mer|i|to|ri|ous** (un′mer ə tôr′ē əs, -tōr′-), *adj.* undeserving of reward or praise; unworthy: *There are a variety of unmeritorious occupations* (Frederick W. Faber).

**un|met** (un met′), *adj.* **1** not met; not encountered: *his yet unmet friend.* **2** not satisfied; unfulfilled: *unmet needs.*

**un|met|alled** (un met′əld), *adj. Especially British.* not covered with a surface, as of crushed stone, cinders, or asphalt: *an unmetalled road.*

**un|me|thod|i|cal** (un′mə thod′ə kəl), *adj.* not methodical.

**un|mew** (un myü′), *v.t. Poetic.* to set free; release. [< *un-*[2] + *mew*[3]]

**un|mil|i|tar|y** (un mil′ə ter′ē), *adj.* not according to military rules or customs; not of a military character.

**un|mind|ful** (un mīnd′fəl), *adj.* not mindful; heedless; careless; regardless: *He went ahead despite our warning and unmindful of the results.* — **un|mind′ful|ly,** *adv.* — **un|mind′ful|ness,** *n.*

**un|min|gled** (un ming′gəld), *adj.* not mingled; unmixed; pure.

**un|mis|tak|a|ble** (un′mis tā′kə bəl), *adj.* that cannot be mistaken or misunderstood; clear; plain; evident: *unmistakable signs of illness.* **SYN:** manifest. — **un′mis|tak′a|ble|ness,** *n.*

**un|mis|tak|a|bly** (un′mis tā′kə blē), *adv.* in an unmistakable manner.

**un|mi|ter** (un mī′tər), *v.t.* to deprive of a miter; depose from the rank of bishop.

**un|mit|i|ga|ble** (un mit′ə gə bəl), *adj.* not mitigable; not to be softened, lessened, or moderated: *unmitigable rage.*

**un|mit|i|ga|bly** (un mit′ə gə blē), *adv.* in an unmitigable manner.

**un|mit|i|gat|ed** (un mit′ə gā′tid), *adj.* **1** not softened or lessened in severity or intensity: *unmitigated harshness, the unmitigated glare of sun on snow.* **SYN:** unallayed. **2** *Figurative.* unqualified or absolute: *an unmitigated fraud.* **SYN:** sheer, utter. — **un|mit′i|gat′ed|ly,** *adv.*

**un|mi|tre** (un mī′tər), *v.t.,* **-tred, -tring.** *Especially British.* unmiter.

**un|mixed** or **un|mixt** (un mikst′), *adj.* not mixed; pure: *Marriage is not an unmixed blessing. Good never comes unmixed* (James Russell Lowell).

**un|mod|er|at|ed** (un mod′ə rā′tid), *adj.* **1** not having a moderator: *unmoderated debate.* **2** not moderated, slowed, or reduced: *unmoderated neutrons.*

**un|mod|ern** (un mod′ərn), *adj.* not modern; old-

**Pronunciation Key:** hat, āge, cãre, fär; let, ēqual, tėrm; it, īce; hot, ōpen, ôrder; oil, out; cup, pu̇t, rüle; child; long; thin; ᴛʜen; zh, measure; ə represents **a** in about, **e** in taken, **i** in pencil, **o** in lemon, **u** in circus.

fashioned: *He makes such surprisingly unmodern things as hourglasses* (Punch).
**un|mod|i|fi|a|ble** (un mod′ə fī′ə bəl), *adj.* not modifiable; that cannot be modified.
**un|mod|i|fied** (un mod′ə fīd), *adj.* not modified; not altered in form; not qualified in meaning; not limited or circumscribed.
**un|mod|ish** (un mō′dish), *adj.* not modish; not according to custom or fashion; not stylish; unfashionable. —**un|mod′ish|ly,** *adv.*
**un|moist|ened** (un moi′sənd), *adj.* not made moist or humid; not wetted; dry.
**un|mold** (un mōld′), *v.t.* to remove from a mold: *Unmold the gelatin and place it face down on a plate.*
**un|mo|lest|ed** (un′mə les′tid), *adj.* not molested; free from molestation; undisturbed. —**un′mo|lest′ed|ly,** *adv.*
**un|mon|eyed** (un mun′ēd), *adj.* not having money; moneyless: *I wish that unmoneyed fans ... didn't have to climb to the top ten rows of the upper level to find an unreserved seat* (New Yorker).
**un|moor** (un mu̇r′), *v.t.* **1** to release (a ship) from moorings or anchorage. **2** to raise one anchor of (a ship) when moored by two. —***v.i.*** to become free of moorings.
**un|mor|al** (un môr′əl, -mor′-), *adj.* neither moral nor immoral; not perceiving or involving right and wrong. —**un|mor′al|ly,** *adv.*
**un|mo|ral|i|ty** (un′mə ral′ə tē), *n.* the absence of morality; unmoral character.
**un|mor|tise** (un môr′tis), *v.t.,* **-tised, -tis|ing.** to disconnect, remove, or separate (a mortised part or joint).
**un|moth|er|ly** (un muᴛʜ′ər lē), *adj.* not resembling or not befitting a mother.
**un|mount|ed** (un moun′tid), *adj.* **1** not mounted; not on horseback: *unmounted troops.* **2** not fixed on or in a support, backing, setting, or the like: *an unmounted photograph.*
**un|mourned** (un môrnd′, -mōrnd′), *adj.* not mourned or lamented.
**un|mov|a|ble** (un mü′və bəl), *adj.* = immovable. **SYN:** stationary.
**un|moved** (un müvd′), *adj.* **1** not moved; unshaken; firm. **2** not disturbed; calm; indifferent: *to be unmoved by someone's tears.*
**un|mov|ing** (un mü′ving), *adj.* not moving; motionless. —**un|mov′ing|ly,** *adv.*
**un|mown** (un mōn′), *adj.* not mowed or cut down.
**un|muf|fle** (un muf′əl), *v.,* **-fled, -fling.** —***v.t.*** to strip of or free from something that muffles: *to unmuffle the face.*
—***v.i.*** to throw off something that muffles.
**un|mur|mur|ing** (un mėr′mər ing), *adj.* not murmuring; uncomplaining. —**un|mur′mur|ing|ly,** *adv.*
**un|mu|si|cal** (un myü′zə kəl), *adj.* **1** not musical; not melodious or harmonious; harsh or discordant in sound. **2** not fond of or skilled in music. —**un|mu′si|cal|ly,** *adv.* —**un|mu′si|cal|ness,** *n.*
**un|mu|si|cal|i|ty** (un′myü zə kal′ə tē), *n.* the quality of being unmusical; lack of musicality: *Dances of poverty-stricken invention and striking unmusicality were performed by dancers obviously more willing than able* (Clive Barnes).
**un|muz|zle** (un muz′əl), *v.t.,* **-zled, -zling. 1** to take off a muzzle from (a dog or other animal). **2** *Figurative.* to free from restraint; allow to speak or write freely: *to unmuzzle the press.*
**un|muz|zled** (un muz′əld), *adj.* not muzzled; without a muzzle.
**un|nam|a|ble** or **un|name|a|ble** (un nā′mə bəl), *adj.* that cannot be named; indescribable: *a cloud of unnameable feeling* (Edgar Allan Poe).
**un|named** (un nāmd′), *adj.* **1** having no name; not called or known by any name; nameless. **2** not mentioned by name: *throwing the burden on some unnamed third person* (George Meredith).
**un|nat|u|ral** (un nach′ər əl, -nach′rəl), *adj.* **1** not natural; not normal; not what is usual or to be expected; abnormal: *unnatural weather for the time of year. The cold war ... is not unnatural* (Manchester Guardian). **SYN:** unusual, irregular, strange. **2** horrible; shocking; not according to natural feeling or decency. **3** synthetic; not derived from nature; artificial. **4** perverted or depraved: *Murder most foul, But this most foul, strange and unnatural* (Shakespeare). —**un|nat′u|ral|ly,** *adv.* —**un|nat′u|ral|ness,** *n.*
**un|nat|u|ral|ized** (un nach′ər ə līzd, -nach′rə-), *adj.* not naturalized.
**un|nav|i|ga|bil|i|ty** (un nav′ə gə bil′ə tē), *n.* the quality or state of being unnavigable.
**un|nav|i|ga|ble** (un nav′ə gə bəl), *adj.* not navigable; not admitting of navigation: *an unnavigable river.*
**un|nav|i|gat|ed** (un nav′ə gā′tid), *adj.* not navigated; not passed over in ships or other vessels; not sailed on or over.
**un|nec|es|sar|i|ly** (un nes′ə ser′ə lē, un′nes ə-sãr′-), *adv.* in an unnecessary manner; without necessity; needlessly; superfluously: *to be unnecessarily suspicious, to spend money unnecessarily.*
**un|nec|es|sar|y** (un nes′ə ser′ē), *adj.* not necessary; needless: *unnecessary haste.* —**un|nec′es-sar′i|ness,** *n.*
**un|need|ful** (un nēd′fəl), *adj.* not needful; not wanted; needless; unnecessary.
**un|ne|go|tia|ble** (un′nē gō′shə bəl), *adj.* not negotiable.
**un|neigh|bor|ly** (un nā′bər lē), *adj.* not neighborly; not kindly, friendly, or sociable. —**un-neigh′bor|li|ness,** *n.*
**un|neigh|bour|ly** (un nā′bər lē), *adj. Especially British.* unneighborly.
**un|nerve** (un nėrv′), *v.t.,* **-nerved, -nerv|ing.** to deprive of nerve, firmness, or self-control: *The sight of blood unnerves her.*
**un|nerv|ing|ly** (un nėr′ving lē), *adv.* in a manner or to a degree that is unnerving: *He had unnervingly piercing eyes* (Scientific American).
**un|nest** (un nest′), *v.t.* to turn out of or as if out of a nest; dislodge: *The earth on its softly-spinning axle never jars enough to unnest a bird or wake a child* (Henry W. Warren).
**un|neu|tral** (un nü′trəl, -nyü′-), *adj.* not neutral; partial; one-sided: *It is in vain to remind her how very unneutral her armed neutrality is* (Earl Malmesbury).
**un|not|ed** (un nō′tid), *adj.* **1** not noted; not observed; not heeded; not regarded; unmarked. **2** not marked or shown outwardly.
**un|no|tice|a|ble** (un nō′tə sə bəl), *adj.* not noticeable; not such as to attract notice. —**un|no′tice-a|ble|ness,** *n.* —**un|no′tice|a|bly,** *adv.*
**un|no|ticed** (un nō′tist), *adj.* not noticed; not observed or heeded; not receiving any notice or attention; unperceived: *No more fiendish punishment could be devised ... than that one should ... remain absolutely unnoticed* (William James).
**un|num|bered** (un num′bərd), *adj.* **1** not numbered; not counted. **2** too many to count; innumerable: *There are unnumbered fish in the ocean.* **SYN:** myriad.
**un|nur|tured** (un nėr′chərd), *adj.* not nurtured; not educated; untrained; rough.
**UNO** (no periods) or **U.N.O.,** United Nations Organization.
**un|ob|jec|tion|a|ble** (un′əb jek′shə nə bəl), *adj.* not objectionable; not liable to objection. —**un′ob-jec′tion|a|ble|ness,** *n.* —**un′ob|jec′tion|a|bly,** *adv.*
**un|ob|li|gat|ed** (un ob′lə gā′tid), *adj.* **1** not set aside or used for a certain purpose: *Congress had directed that no more than $200,000,000 should be carried over unobligated into the new fiscal year* (New York Times). **2** having no obligations: *The listener, the grown-up, free-riding, unobligated listener, is thrilled, I think, to have it thrown at him* (New Yorker).
**un|ob|nox|ious** (un′əb nok′shəs), *adj.* **1** not obnoxious; not offensive or hateful. **2** not liable; not subject; not exposed to something: *Some apart, In quarters unobnoxious to such chance* (Wordsworth).
**un|ob|serv|a|bil|i|ty** (un′əb zėr′və bil′ə tē), *n.* the quality or condition of being unobservable: *The unobservability of absolute motion was rather a postulate of physics than the result of any particular structure of matter* (Norbert Wiener).
**un|ob|serv|a|ble** (un′əb zėr′və bəl), *adj., n.* —***adj.*** that cannot be observed; imperceptible; unnoticeable: *Two of them sat together on the steel plates of the deck ... facing forward, and the third faced them from a low seat ... unobservable from the bridge* (New Yorker).
—***n.*** something that cannot be observed or perceived by the senses.
**un|ob|serv|ant** (un′əb zėr′vənt), *adj.* **1** not observant; not taking notice; not quick to notice or perceive. **2** disregardful, as of rules or customs.
**un|ob|served** (un′əb zėrvd′), *adj.* not observed; not noticed; disregarded: *Am I alone, And unobserved? I am* (William S. Gilbert). **SYN:** unheeded, unnoticed.
**un|ob|serv|ing** (un′əb zėr′ving), *adj.* not observing; unobservant.
**un|ob|struct|ed** (un′əb struk′tid), *adj.* not obstructed; not blocked, impeded, or hindered; open or clear: *a wide, unobstructed view of the hills.* —**un′ob|struct′ed|ly,** *adv.*
**un|ob|tain|a|ble** (un′əb tā′nə bəl), *adj.* not obtainable.
**un|ob|tru|sive** (un′əb trü′siv), *adj.* not obtrusive; modest; inconspicuous: *Poetry should be ... unobtrusive, a thing which enters into one's soul and does not startle it* (Keats). —**un′ob|tru′sive-ly,** *adv.* —**un′ob|tru′sive|ness,** *n.*
**un|oc|cu|pied** (un ok′yə pīd), *adj.* **1** not occupied; vacant: *an unoccupied house, an unoccupied parking space.* **2** not in action or use; idle: *an unoccupied mind.*
**un|of|fend|ing** (un′ə fen′ding), *adj.* not offending; inoffensive: *Who ... could have thought of harming a creature so simple and so unoffending?* (Scott).
**un|of|fen|sive** (un′ə fen′siv), *adj.* = inoffensive.
**un|of|fi|cial** (un′ə fish′əl), *adj.* not official; without official character or authority. —**un′of|fi′cial|ly,** *adv.*
**un|of|fi|cious** (un′ə fish′əs), *adj.* not officious; not forward or intermeddling.
**un|oiled** (un oild′), *adj.* not oiled; free from oil.
**un|o|pen** (un ō′pən), *adj.* not open.
**un|o|pened** (un ō′pənd), *adj.* not opened; closed.
**un|op|er|at|ed** (un op′ə rā′tid), *adj.* **1** not operated on: *On the third day the bandage was removed from my unoperated eye* (Harper's). **2** that is not being operated: *Because of the strike, our elevator is unoperated.*
**un|op|posed** (un′ə pōzd′), *adj.* not opposed; meeting no opposition.
**un|or|dained** (un′ôr dānd′), *adj.* **1** not ordained. **2** *Obsolete.* inordinate.
**un|or|dered** (un ôr′dərd), *adj.* **1** not put in order; disordered; unarranged: *Side by side with the official defined science there appeared a popular science, vague, undisciplined, unordered, and yet extremely influential* (Oscar Handlin). **2** not ordered or commanded: *He volunteered his services, unordered.*
**un|or|di|nar|y** (un ôr′də ner′ē), *adj.* not common; rare; unusual: *Here are three excellent and unordinary travel books* (Eliot Fremont-Smith).
**un|or|gan|ized** (un ôr′gə nīzd), *adj.* **1** not formed into an organized or systematized whole. **2** not organized into a labor union or unions: *unorganized workers.* **3** lacking the characteristics of a living body; not being a living organism; unformed.
**unorganized ferment,** any one of certain compounds of organic origin, such as diastase or pepsin, which cause a substance to ferment.
**un|o|rig|i|nal** (un′ə rij′ə nəl), *adj.* **1** not original. **2** having no origin.
**un|or|na|men|tal** (un′ôr nə men′təl), *adj.* not ornamental.
**un|or|na|ment|ed** (un ôr′nə men′tid), *adj.* not ornamented; unadorned; not decorated; plain: *[He] was wearing an unornamented uniform and amber sunglasses* (New Yorker).
**un|or|tho|dox** (un ôr′thə doks), *adj.* not orthodox; heterodox; heretical.
**un|or|tho|dox|y** (un ôr′thə dok′sē), *n., pl.* **-dox-ies.** the quality or state of being unorthodox; heresy.
**un|os|ten|ta|tious** (un′os ten tā′shəs), *adj.* not ostentatious; not showy or pretentious; inconspicuous; modest. —**un′os|ten|ta′tious|ly,** *adv.* —**un′os|ten|ta′tious|ness,** *n.*
**un|owned** (un ōnd′), *adj.* **1** not owned; having no known owner; not claimed. **2** not avowed; not acknowledged as one's own; not admitted as done by oneself; unconfessed: *unowned faults.* [< *un-*[1] + *own* + *-ed*[2]]
**un|pa|cif|ic** (un′pə sif′ik), *adj.* unpeaceful; quarrelsome; belligerent: *East and West ought to be persuaded ... that it is in their mutual interest to sign a kind of test ban agreement not to use space for unpacific purposes* (New Scientist).
**un|pack** (un pak′), *v.t.* **1** to take out (things packed in a box, trunk, or other container): *He unpacked his clothes.* **2** to take things out of: *to unpack a trunk.* —***v.i.*** to take out things packed: *to start unpacking.* —**un|pack′er,** *n.*
**un|paid** (un pād′), *adj.* not paid: *His unpaid bills amounted to $200.*
**un|paid-for** (un pād′fôr′), *adj.* not paid for: *rustling in unpaid-for silk* (Shakespeare).
**un|pain|ful** (un pān′fəl), *adj.* not painful; giving no pain: *An easy and unpainful touch* (John Locke).
**un|paired** (un pãrd′), *adj.* not paired.
**un|pal|at|a|bil|i|ty** (un′pal ə tə bil′ə tē), *n.* the quality or condition of being unpalatable: *Experimental birds had learned to associate color pattern with unpalatability* (Science News Letter).
**un|pal|at|a|ble** (un pal′ə tə bəl), *adj.* not agreeable to the taste; distasteful; unpleasant: *unpalatable advice* (Washington Irving). **SYN:** unappetizing, unsavory. —**un|pal′at|a|ble|ness,** *n.* —**un|pal′at-a|bly,** *adv.*
**un|par|al|leled** (un par′ə leld), *adj.* having no parallel; unequaled; matchless: *an unparalleled achievement, an event unparalleled in modern history.* **SYN:** unmatched, unrivaled.
**un|par|don|a|ble** (un pär′də nə bəl), *adj.* not pardonable; that cannot be pardoned: *an unpardonable offense or mistake, an unpardonable offender. According to the Bible, the sin of blasphemy against the Holy Ghost is the unpardonable sin.* —**un|par′don|a|ble|ness,** *n.*
**un|par|don|a|bly** (un pär′də nə blē), *adv.* beyond pardon or forgiveness: *to be unpardonably rude.*
**un|par|doned** (un pär′dənd), *adj.* not pardoned.
**un|par|don|ing** (un pär′də ning), *adj.* not pardoning.

**un|park** (un pärk′), *v.t., v.i.* **1** to remove (an automobile or other vehicle) from a parking place: *Like the young housewife in Vancouver who found a parking spot all right, but couldn't unpark because other cars fore and aft were snubbed up so tight against hers* (Maclean's). **2** to remove (a space satellite or vehicle) from a parking orbit.

**un|par|lia|men|ta|ri|ly** (un′pär lə men′tər ə lē, -men′trə-), *adv.* in an unparliamentary manner.

**un|par|lia|men|ta|ri|ness** (un′pär lə men′tər ē-nis, -men′trē-), *n.* the quality or state of being unparliamentary.

**un|par|lia|men|ta|ry** (un′pär lə men′tər ē, -men′trē), *adj.* not in accordance with parliamentary practice, procedure, or usage.

**un|passed** (un past′, -päst′), *adj.* **1** not passed or ratified: *The unfinished business included unpassed appropriations for mutual security and public works* (Time). **2** not crossed: *unpassed barriers.*

**un|pas|sioned** (un pash′ənd), *adj.* free from passion; dispassionate: *Rupert Brooke wrote of the unpassioned beauty of a great machine* (London Times).

**un|pat|ent|a|ble** (un pat′ən tə bəl), *adj.* not patentable: *The better mousetraps of today ... are often unpatentable* (New Yorker).

**un|pat|ent|ed** (un pat′ən tid), *adj.* not patented; not protected by patent.

**un|pathed** (un patht′, -pätht′), *adj.* pathless; trackless: *unpathed waters* (Shakespeare).

**un|pa|tri|ot|ic** (un′pā trē ot′ik), *adj.* not patriotic.

**un|pa|tri|ot|i|cal|ly** (un′pā trē ot′ə klē), *adv.* in a manner that is unpatriotic: *accused of unpatriotically stabbing the Foreign Secretary in the back in the course of international negotiations* (Time).

**un|pa|tri|ot|ism** (un pā′trē ə tiz′əm), *n.* the quality or state of being unpatriotic.

**un|pat|terned** (un pat′ərnd), *adj.* having no pattern or design: *unpatterned fabric, unpatterned verse.*

**un|paved** (un pāvd′), *adj.* not paved.

**un|pay|a|ble** (un pā′ə bəl), *adj.* **1** that cannot be paid: *The picture often turns out to be a flop, leaving a wake of unpaid and unpayable debts* (Atlantic). **2** yielding no return; unprofitable; unremunerative: *The wildcat oil well was abandoned as unpayable.*

**un|peace** (un pēs′), *n.* lack of peace or quiet; constant movement: *The unpopular thesis that the secret of happiness lies in unpeace of mind, that is, fairly continuous, useful mental activity* (Atlantic).

**un|peace|a|ble** (un pē′sə bəl), *adj.* not peaceable; quarrelsome: *Away, unpeaceable dog, or I'll spurn thee hence!* (Shakespeare).

**un|peace|ful** (un pēs′fəl), *adj.* not pacific or peaceful; unquiet; disturbed.

**un|ped|i|greed** (un ped′ə grēd), *adj.* not distinguished by a pedigree.

**un|peg** (un peg′), *v.t.,* **-pegged, -peg|ging.** **1** to disengage from a peg. **2** to loosen, detach, or dismember (anything) by withdrawal of a peg or pegs. **3** to discontinue control of the rise or fall of the price of (something): *Government bonds were unpegged a year ago, and interest rates started rising* (Time).

**un|pen** (un pen′), *v.t.,* **-penned, -pen|ning.** to release from or as from a pen.

**un|pen|nied** (un pen′ēd), *adj.* not pennied; penniless.

**un|pen|sioned** (un pen′shənd), *adj.* **1** not pensioned; not rewarded by a pension: *an unpensioned soldier.* **2** not kept in pay; not held in dependence by a pension.

**un|peo|ple** (un pē′pəl), *v.,* **-pled, -pling,** *n.* **—*v.t.*** to deprive of people; depopulate.
**—*n.*** people who have lost their individuality: *They are so devoid of romance or passion they're like the unpeople at the end of "1984"* (New Yorker).

**un|peo|pled** (un pē′pəld), *adj.* **1** without inhabitants; not inhabited. **2** deprived of people; depopulated.

**un|per|ceiv|a|ble** (un′pər sē′və bəl), *adj.* not perceivable; imperceptible.

**un|per|ceived** (un′pər sēvd′), *adj.* not perceived; unnoticed.

**un|per|ceiv|ing** (un′pər sē′ving), *adj.* not perceiving.

**un|per|cep|tive** (un′pər sep′tiv), *adj.* lacking or incapable of perception or discrimination: *an unperceptive mind, an unperceptive reader.* **—un′per|cep′tive|ness,** *n.*

**un|per|fo|rat|ed** (un pėr′fə rā′tid), *adj.* **1** not perforated. **2** (of a postage stamp) not perforated at the edges; imperforate.

**un|per|form|a|ble** (un′pər fôr′mə bəl), *adj.* not performable; undoable: *Though the composer grandly pronounced Tristan "the greatest musical drama of all time," opera houses in Dresden, Berlin, Vienna, and Munich rejected it as unperformable* (Time).

**un|per|formed** (un′pər fôrmd′), *adj.* **1** not performed; not done; not executed; not fulfilled: *an unperformed promise.* **2** not represented on the stage; unacted: *The play remained unperformed.*

**un|per|ish|a|ble** (un per′i shə bəl), *adj.* not perishable; imperishable.

**un|per|ish|ing** (un per′i shing), *adj.* not perishing; lasting; durable.

**un|per|plexed** (un′pər plekst′), *adj.* **1** free from perplexity or complication; simple: *simple, unperplexed proposition* (John Locke). **2** not perplexed; not harassed; not embarrassed: *This [man] throws himself on God, and unperplexed Seeking shall find him* (Robert Browning).

**un|per|son** (un pėr′sən), *n., v.* **—*n.*** a political or other public figure who has lost his importance or influence and has been relegated to an inferior or inconsequential status, especially in a totalitarian state: *Famous men and women in all walks of life have been ruthlessly turned, as in George Orwell's chilling novel "1984," from persons into unpersons* (New York Times).
**—*v.t.*** to cause to become an unperson: *"The Fierce and Beautiful World," by Andrei Platonov, unpersoned under Stalin* (Manchester Guardian Weekly).

**un|per|suad|a|ble** (un′pər swā′də bəl), *adj.* that cannot be persuaded or influenced by motives urged.

**un|per|sua|sive** (un′pər swā′siv), *adj.* not persuasive; unable to persuade. **—un′per|sua′sive|ly,** *adv.* **—un′per|sua′sive|ness,** *n.*

**un|per|turbed** (un′pər tėrbd′), *adj.* not perturbed; free from perturbation; undisturbed; calm; composed: *Still with unhurrying chase And unperturbed pace* (Francis Thompson). **—un′per|turb′ed|ly,** *adv.* **—un′per|turb′ed|ness,** *n.*

**un|per|vert|ed** (un′pər vėr′tid), *adj.* not perverted; not wrested or turned to a wrong sense or use.

**un|phil|o|soph|ic** (un′fil ə sof′ik), *adj.* = unphilosophical.

**un|phil|o|soph|i|cal** (un′fil ə sof′ə kəl), *adj.* not philosophical. **—un′phil|o|soph′i|cal|ly,** *adv.*

**un|phys|i|cal** (un fiz′ə kəl), *adj.* **1** not physical; immaterial; incorporeal. **2** not in accordance with the laws of physics: *an unphysical theory of motion.* **—un|phys′i|cal|ly,** *adv.*

**un|phys|i|o|log|i|cal** (un′fiz ē ə loj′ə kəl), *adj.* not sound or proper physiologically; not in accordance with the laws of physiology: *Fasting is an unphysiological and potentially dangerous practice if continued for more than a few days* (Harper's). **—un′phys|i|o|log′i|cal|ly,** *adv.*

**un|pick** (un pik′), *v.t.* to pick or take out (stitches, sewing, or threads); pick out the stitches in (a garment or other sewing work).

**un|picked** (un pikt′), *adj.* **1** not picked; not chosen or selected. **2** unplucked; ungathered: *unpicked fruit.* **3** not picked or opened with an instrument: *an unpicked lock.*

**un|pierced** (un pirst′), *adj.* not pierced; not penetrated.

**un|pile** (un pīl′), *v.,* **-piled, -pil|ing.** **—*v.t.*** **1** to remove from a pile or heap: *to unpile wood and stack it.* **2** to cause to be no longer in a pile: *to unpile canned goods.* **3** to take (a pile or heap) apart.
**—*v.i.*** to be disengaged from a pile.

**un|pi|lot|ed** (un pī′lə tid), *adj.* unguided through dangers or difficulties.

**un|pin** (un pin′), *v.t.,* **-pinned, -pin|ning.** **1** to take out a pin or pins from. **2** to loosen, detach, or dismember (anything) by withdrawal of a pin or pins; unfasten: *The mother unpinned the baby's bib after he finished eating.* **3** to undo the dress by unpinning; undress: *who had the honor to pin and unpin Lady Bellaston* (Henry Fielding).

**un|pit|ied** (un pit′ēd), *adj.* not pitied.

**un|pit|y|ing** (un pit′ē ing), *adj.* not pitying; without pity: *The unpitying waters flowed over our prostrate bodies* (Herman Melville). **—un|pit′y|ing|ly,** *adv.*

**un|placed** (un plāst′), *adj.* **1** not assigned to, or set in, a definite place: *She is now an unsheltered and unplaced person* (Manchester Guardian). **2** not appointed to a place or office: *The other fifteen were to be unplaced noblemen and gentlemen of ample fortune* (Macaulay). **3** not among the first three finishers in a horse race: *After being unplaced in his first start, he won his next ten races* (New Yorker).

**un|plagued** (un plāgd′), *adj.* not plagued; not harassed; not tormented; not afflicted.

**un|plait** (un plāt′), *v.t.* to bring out of a plaited state; unbraid, as hair.

**un|plant|a|ble** (un plan′tə bəl, -plän′-), *adj.* that cannot be planted: *The company also owns in Florida another 10,509 acres of unplanted and in most cases unplantable land* (Wall Street Journal).

**un|plant|ed** (un plan′tid, -plän′-), *adj.* **1** not planted; of spontaneous growth. **2** not cultivated; unimproved.

**un|play|a|ble** (un plā′ə bəl), *adj.* that cannot be played or played on: *In its 24 years the concerto has gained something of a reputation for being unplayable* (Time). *Hours of heavy rain had rendered the Lawns ground unplayable* (London Times).

**un|pleas|ant** (un plez′ənt), *adj.* not pleasant; disagreeable; displeasing: *A ... damp, moist, unpleasant body* (Dickens). **SYN:** objectionable, obnoxious. **—un|pleas′ant|ly,** *adv.*

**un|pleas|ant|ness** (un plez′ənt nis), *n.* **1** unpleasant quality. **2** something unpleasant. **3** *Figurative.* a quarrel.

**un|pleas|ant|ry** (un plez′ən trē), *n., pl.* **-ries.** = unpleasantness.

**un|pleased** (un plēzd′), *adj.* not pleased; displeased.

**un|pleas|ing** (un plē′zing), *adj.* not pleasing; not such as to please. **—un|pleas′ing|ly,** *adv.* **—un|pleas′ing|ness,** *n.*

**un|pleas|ur|a|ble** (un plezh′ər ə bəl), *adj.* not giving pleasure; disagreeable: *Many of our waking hours pass irksome and insipid, unprofitable to others, and unpleasurable to ourselves* (Abraham Tucker).

**un|pleas|ure** (un plezh′ər), *n.* lack of pleasure; displeasure: *I don't like to use any words that might give you unpleasure* (Samuel Taylor Coleridge).

**un|pli|a|ble** (un plī′ə bəl), *adj.* not pliable.

**un|pli|ant** (un plī′ənt), *adj.* **1** not pliant; not easily bent; stiff. **2** *Figurative.* not readily yielding the will; not compliant.

**un|plucked** (un plukt′), *adj.* not plucked; not pulled or torn away: *an unplucked chicken.*

**un|plug** (un plug′), *v.t.,* **-plugged, -plug|ging.** **1** to remove the plug or stopper from; unstopper; uncork. **2** to free from any obstruction; open: *Unplug your ears and listen to me. Apparently satisfied now that rock-bottom prices have been reached many cautious investors have unplugged their money to buy municipals* (Wall Street Journal). **3** to disconnect by removing the plug from an electric outlet: *to unplug a lamp.*

**un|plumbed** (un plumd′), *adj.* **1** not plumbed; not fathomed; not measured; of unknown depth: *unplumbed seas.* (*Figurative.*) *the unplumbed depths of a person's character.* **2** having no plumbing. **3** not encased or sealed in lead.

**un|po|et|ic** (un′pō et′ik), *adj.* not poetic; prosaic; matter-of-fact. **—un′po|et′i|cal|ly,** *adv.*

**un|po|et|i|cal** (un′pō et′ə kəl), *adj.* = unpoetic.

**un|point|ed** (un poin′tid), *adj.* **1** not having a point; not sharp. **2** *Figurative.* having no point or sting; wanting point or definite aim or purpose. **3** not punctuated. **4** not having the vowel points or marks: *an unpointed manuscript in Hebrew or Arabic.* **5** *Obsolete.* having the points unfastened: *an unpointed doublet.*

**un|poised** (un poizd′), *adj.* not poised; not balanced.

**un|po|liced** (un′pə lēst′), *adj.* not supervised or regulated by an agency charged with maintaining the law or the terms of a treaty agreement: *There is no suggestion that the unpoliced test ban be indefinitely continued* (Bulletin of Atomic Scientists).

**un|pol|ished** (un pol′isht), *adj.* **1** not polished: *unpolished stone.* **2** *Figurative.* without polish; rough; unrefined; rude: *unpolished manners.*

**un|pol|i|tic** (un pol′ə tik), *adj.* not politic; impolitic.

**un|polled** (un pōld′), *adj.* not polled, especially not voting or not cast at the polls: *an unpolled voter or vote.*

**un|pol|lut|ed** (un′pə lü′tid), *adj.* not polluted; undefiled; clean; pure.

**un|pop|u|lar** (un pop′yə lər), *adj.* not popular; not generally liked, accepted, or used; disliked: *an unpopular candidate.* **—un|pop′u|lar|ly,** *adv.*

**un|pop|u|lar|i|ty** (un′pop yə lar′ə tē), *n.* the condition of being unpopular; lack of popularity. **SYN:** disfavor.

**un|pos|sess|a|ble** (un′pə zes′ə bəl), *adj.* that cannot be possessed: *He did a paper on "The Unpossessable Loved One in Troubadour Poetry"* (New Yorker).

**un|post|ed**[1] (un pōs′tid), *adj.* not bearing signs against trespassing: *He does not mind hunters on the unposted parts of his land.*

**un|post|ed**[2] (un pōs′tid), *adj.* not having a fixed station or appointment. [< *un-*[1] + *post*[2] + *-ed*[2]]

**un|post|ed**[3] (un pōs′tid), *adj.* **1** not sent or delivered by mail: *I stand with an unposted letter before the box of the general post office* (Time). **2** *Informal.* not informed.

**un|prac|ti|cal** (un prak′tə kəl), *adj.* not practical;

**Pronunciation Key:** hat, āge, cãre, fär; let, ēqual, tėrm; it, īce; hot, ōpen, ôrder; oil, out; cup, pu̇t, rüle; child; long; thin; ᴛʜen; zh, measure; ə represents a in about, e in taken, i in pencil, o in lemon, u in circus.

impractical; lacking practical usefulness or wisdom; visionary. —**un|prac′ti|cal|ly**, *adv.* —**un-prac′ti|cal|ness**, *n.*

**un|prac|ti|cal|i|ty** (un′prak tə kal′ə tē), *n., pl.* **-ties. 1** the character of being unpractical. **2** something that is not practical.

**un|prac|ticed** or **un|prac|tised** (un prak′tist), *adj.* **1** not familiarized or skilled by practice; not expert; inexperienced: *Unpractic'd he to fawn or seek for power, By doctrines fashion'd to the varying hour* (Oliver Goldsmith). **2** not used, done, or accepted, especially: **a** not put into practice; untried. **b** no longer current in practice.

**un|prec|e|dent|ed** (un pres′ə den′tid), *adj.* having no precedent; never done before; never known before: *unprecedented devotion to duty. An unprecedented event in history took place in 1961, when a human being traveled for the first time in outer space.* **SYN**: unexampled, new. —**un-prec′e|dent′ed|ly**, *adv.*

**un|pre|cise** (un′pri sīs′), *adj.* not precise; lacking precision or definiteness; inexact. —**un′pre|cise′-ly**, *adv.* —**un′pre|cise′ness**, *n.*

**un|pre|dict|a|bil|i|ty** (un′pri dik′tə bil′ə tē), *n.* the quality or condition of being unpredictable: *He had an increasing unpredictability of temper and a reputation for violent outbursts that had cost him several good friends* (New Yorker). *The history of the steam engine has been marked by this machine's endearing unpredictability* (Manchester Guardian).

**un|pre|dict|a|ble** (un′pri dik′tə bəl), *adj., n.* —*adj.* that cannot be predicted; uncertain or changeable: *All the children were emotionally unstable, unpredictable, and unadaptable* (Science News Letter).
—*n.* something unpredictable; an uncertainty: *Other unpredictables, such as a switch in Government regulations for the [year's] crop, also could change the outlook* (Wall Street Journal).

**un|pre|dict|a|bly** (un′pri dik′tə blē), *adv.* in an unpredictable manner: *Prices fluctuate unpredictably from sale to sale* (Punch).

**un|preg|nant** (un preg′nənt), *adj. Obsolete.* unapt; unfit: *This deed ... makes me unpregnant And dull to all proceedings* (Shakespeare).

**un|prej|u|diced** (un prej′ə dist), *adj.* **1** without prejudice; not biased; fair; impartial: *an unprejudiced observer.* **SYN**: disinterested. **2** not impaired: *an unprejudiced right of appeal.* **SYN**: unimpaired.

**un|pre|med|i|tat|ed** (un′prē med′ə tā′tid), *adj.* not premeditated; not planned in advance; undesigned. —**un′pre|med′i|tat′ed|ly**, *adv.*

**un|pre|med|i|ta|tion** (un′prē med′ə tā′shən), *n.* absence of premeditation.

**un|pre|pared** (un′pri pãrd′), *adj.* **1** not made ready; not worked out ahead: *an unprepared speech.* **SYN**: impromptu, improvised. **2** not ready: *a person unprepared to answer.* —**un′pre|par′ed-ly**, *adv.* —**un′pre|par′ed|ness**, *n.*

**un|pre|pos|sess|ing** (un′prē pə zes′ing), *adj.* not prepossessing; unattractive: *Unprepossessing ... in feature, gait and manners ... these poor fellows formed a class apart* (Samuel Butler). —**un′-pre|pos|sess′ing|ly**, *adv.* —**un′pre|pos|sess′-ing|ness**, *n.*

**un|pre|scribed** (un′pri skrībd′), *adj.* not prescribed; not authoritatively laid down; not appointed.

**un|pre|sent|a|ble** (un′pri zen′tə bəl), *adj.* not presentable; not suitable for being introduced into company; not fit to be seen.

**un|pressed** (un prest′), *adj.* **1** not pressed. **2** *Figurative.* not enforced.

**un|pre|sum|ing** (un′pri zü′ming), *adj.* not presuming; modest; humble; unpretentious.

**un|pre|sump|tu|ous** (un′pri zump′chu̇ əs), *adj.* not presumptuous or arrogant; humble; submissive; modest.

**un|pre|tend|ing** (un′pri ten′ding), *adj.* = unpretentious. —**un′pre|tend′ing|ly**, *adv.*

**un|pre|ten|tious** (un′pri ten′shəs), *adj.* not pretentious; unassuming; modest. —**un′pre|ten′-tious|ly**, *adv.* —**un′pre|ten′tious|ness**, *n.*

**un|pret|ty** (un prit′ē), *adj.* **1** without beauty or charm; plain; unattractive: *The only girl in the picture is obliged to look ... clinical and unpretty* (Brendan Gill). **2** disagreeable; ugly: *The tougher Novak has an unpretty side* (Time). *Things are coming to a most unpretty pass* (Punch).

**un|pre|vail|ing** (un′pri vā′ling), *adj.* of no force; unavailing; vain.

**un|pre|vent|a|ble** (un′pri ven′tə bəl), *adj.* that cannot be prevented.

**un|pre|vent|ed** (un′pri ven′tid), *adj.* **1** not prevented; not hindered. **2** *Obsolete.* not preceded by anything.

**un|priced** (un prīst′), *adj.* **1** not having a price assigned: *merchandise still unpriced.* **2** beyond price; priceless.

**un|priest|ly** (un prēst′lē), *adj.* not priestly; not befitting a priest.

**un|prince|ly** (un prins′lē), *adj.* not princely; not becoming a prince.

**un|prin|ci|pled** (un prin′sə pəld), *adj.* lacking good moral principles; not upright or ethical; bad. **SYN**: See syn. under **unscrupulous.** —**un|prin′ci-pled|ness**, *n.*

**un|print|a|ble** (un prin′tə bəl), *adj., n.* —*adj.* not fit or proper to be printed.
—*n.* a word, expression, cartoon or other matter, that is unprintable: *Maine writers have lamented that so much of what is said up and down the coast runs to unprintables* (John Gould).

**un|print|a|bly** (un prin′tə blē), *adv.* in a word or words not fit to be printed.

**un|print|ed** (un prin′tid), *adj.* not, or not yet, printed.

**un|priv|i|leged** (un priv′ə lijd), *adj.* not privileged; not enjoying a particular privilege, liberty, or immunity.

**un|priz|a|ble** (un prī′zə bəl), *adj. Obsolete.* **1** worth little or nothing. **2** priceless.

**un|prized** (un prīzd′), *adj.* not prized or valued.

**un|pro|duced** (un′prə düst′, -dyüst′), *adj.* not yet produced, as a playwright or his work: *He had written several stage and television plays, all unproduced* (Saturday Review).

**un|pro|duc|tive** (un′prə duk′tiv), *adj.* not productive. —**un′pro|duc′tive|ly**, *adv.* —**un′pro|duc′-tive|ness**, *n.*

**un|pro|duc|tiv|i|ty** (un′prō duk tiv′ə tē), *n.* the quality or state of being unproductive.

**un|pro|faned** (un′prə fānd′), *adj.* not profaned or desecrated; not polluted or violated.

**un|pro|fes|sion|al** (un′prə fesh′ə nəl, -fesh′nəl), *adj., n.* —*adj.* **1** contrary to professional etiquette; unbecoming in members of a profession: *It would be unprofessional for a doctor to speak publicly of a patient's personal problems.* **2** not having to do with or connected with a profession. **3** not belonging to a profession.
—*n.* a person who is not a professional: *The secret of his failure in politics ... is that he was really an unprofessional* (New York Times). —**un′-pro|fes′sion|al|ly**, *adv.*

**un|prof|it|a|bil|i|ty** (un′prof ə tə bil′ə tē), *n.* the quality or state of being unprofitable: *The milk and fishing industries were on the verge of unprofitability* (London Times).

**un|prof|it|a|ble** (un prof′ə tə bəl), *adj.* not profitable; producing no gain or advantage: *They proved the most idle and unprofitable [months] of my life* (Edward Gibbon). **SYN**: fruitless. —**un-prof′it|a|ble|ness**, *n.*

**un|prof|it|a|bly** (un prof′ə tə blē), *adv.* in an unprofitable manner; without profit, gain, benefit, advantage, or use; to no good purpose or effect: *unprofitably travelling towards the grave* (Wordsworth).

**un|prof|it|ed** (un prof′ə tid), *adj.* not having profit or gain; profitless.

**un|pro|gres|sive** (un′prə gres′iv), *adj.* not progressive; conservative; backward. —**un′pro-gres′sive|ly**, *adv.* —**un′pro|gres′sive|ness**, *n.*

**un|pro|hib|it|ed** (un′prō hib′ə tid), *adj.* not prohibited; not forbidden; lawful.

**un|pro|ject|ed** (un′prə jek′tid), *adj.* not planned; not projected.

**un|pro|lif|ic** (un′prə lif′ik), *adj.* not fertile or productive; unfruitful.

**un|prom|is|ing** (un prom′ə sing), *adj.* not promising; not appearing likely to turn out well. —**un-prom′is|ing|ly**, *adv.*

**un|prompt|ed** (un promp′tid), *adj.* not prompted; not dictated; not urged or instigated.

**un|pro|nounce|a|ble** (un′prə noun′sə bəl), *adj.* that cannot be pronounced; not pronounceable; difficult to pronounce: *With unpronounceable awful names* (Bret Harte).

**un|pro|nounced** (un′prə nounst′), *adj.* not pronounced; not uttered.

**un|prop|er** (un prop′ər), *adj.* not proper; not correct, right, or respectable: *His equally unproper brother ... shocked purists in the 1930's by building a flat-topped house in Ipswich* (Time).

**un|prop|er|tied** (un′prop′ər tēd), *adj.* not propertied; not owning property.

**un|pro|pi|ti|a|ble** (un′prə pish′ē ə bəl), *adj.* that cannot be propitiated.

**un|pro|pi|tious** (un′prə pish′əs), *adj.* not propitious; not favorable; inauspicious: *On the other hand, unpropitious as the times may be, it is safe to assume that there will be large numbers of serious and talented writers* (Saturday Review). —**un′pro|pi′tious|ly**, *adv.* —**un′pro|pi′tious-ness**, *n.*

**un|pro|por|tion|ate** (un′prə pôr′shə nit), *adj.* not proportionate; disproportionate.

**un|pro|por|tioned** (un′prə pôr′shənd), *adj.* not proportioned; not suitable.

**un|pro|posed** (un′prə pōzd′), *adj.* not proposed; not offered for acceptance, adoption, or the like.

**un|pros|per|ous** (un pros′pər əs), *adj.* not prosperous; unfortunate; unsuccessful. —**un|pros′per-ous|ly**, *adv.* —**un|pros′per|ous|ness**, *n.*

**un|pro|tect|ed** (un′prə tek′tid), *adj.* not protected. —**un′pro|tect′ed|ness**, *n.*

**un|prov|a|ble** (un prü′və bəl), *adj.* that cannot be proved; indemonstrable: *For many years I have been intrigued by a largely unprovable hypothesis about the coexistence of Homo sapiens and Neanderthal man* (Scientific American).

**un|proved** (un prüvd′), *adj.* not proved.

**un|prov|en** (un prü′vən), *adj.* unproved: *That politics has a bearing on business confidence is unproven* (Esquire).

**un|pro|vid|ed** (un′prə vī′did), *adj.* **1** not provided; not furnished or supplied. **2** not furnished or supplied with something: *assailants ... unprovided with regular means of attack* (Alexander W. Kinglake).

**un|pro|vid|ed-for** (un′prə vī′did fôr′), *adj.* not provided for.

**un|pro|voked** (un′prə vōkt′), *adj.* not provoked; without provocation. —**un′pro|vok′ed|ly**, *adv.*

**un|pruned** (un pründ′), *adj.* not pruned; not lopped or trimmed.

**un|pub|li|cized** (un pub′lə sīzd), *adj.* not made public; not given publicity: *But, almost unpublicized, another mass escape from behind the Iron Curtain has been going on* (Newsweek).

**un|pub|lished** (un pub′lisht), *adj.* **1** not published, especially not issued in print: *an unpublished manuscript.* **2** that has not yet had a work in print: *an unpublished poet.* **3** not generally known: *a man of great but unpublished generosity.* **4** *Law.* designating a literary work which, at the time of registration, has not been made available to the public by general distribution or reproduction in salable form.

**un|puck|er** (un puk′ər), *v.t.* to straighten out from a puckered condition.

**un|punc|tu|al** (un pungk′chu̇ əl), *adj.* not punctual; tardy: *a vague, unpunctual star* (Rupert Brooke). —**un|punc′tu|al|ly**, *adv.*

**un|punc|tu|al|i|ty** (un′pungk chu̇ al′ə tē), *n.* the quality or state of being unpunctual.

**un|pun|ish|a|ble** (un pun′i shə bəl), *adj.* not punishable; not capable or deserving of being punished.

**un|pun|ished** (un pun′isht), *adj.* not punished.

**un|pure** (un pyu̇r′), *adj.,* **-pur|er, -pur|est.** not pure; impure.

**un|purged** (un pėrjd′), *adj.* **1** not purified. **2** *Figurative.* not cleared from moral defilement or guilt.

**un|pur|posed** (un pėr′pəst), *adj.* not intended; not designed.

**un|qual|i|fied** (un kwol′ə fīd), *adj.* **1** not qualified; not fitted: *He is unqualified to be President.* **SYN**: incompetent. **2** not modified, limited, or restricted in any way: *unqualified praise.* **SYN**: unconditional. **3** complete; absolute: *an unqualified failure.* **SYN**: unmitigated. —**un|qual′i|fied′ly**, *adv.* —**un|qual′i-fied′ness**, *n.*

**un|quan|ti|fi|a|ble** (un kwon′tə fī′ə bəl), *adj.* that is not measurable or easily calculable: *The bulletin attributed the growth of exports to "good luck"—a somewhat unquantifiable factor* (London Times).

**un|quan|ti|fied** (un kwon′tə fīd), *adj.* not quantified; not measured: *According to these criteria, unquantified observations and studies receive little respect* (Saturday Review).

**un|quench|a|ble** (un kwen′chə bəl), *adj.* that cannot be quenched or extinguished: *an unquenchable thirst,* (*Figurative.*) *unquenchable zeal.* **SYN**: inextinguishable.

**un|quench|a|bly** (un kwen′chə blē), *adv.* in an unquenchable manner; so as to be unquenchable.

**un|ques|tion|a|ble** (un kwes′chə nə bəl), *adj.* **1** beyond dispute or doubt; certain: *Size is an unquestionable advantage in a basketball player. Having a school diploma is an unquestionable advantage to a person who is looking for a good job.* **2** accepted without question; unexceptionable: *unquestionable doctrine.* —**un|ques′tion|a-ble|ness**, *n.*

**un|ques|tion|a|bly** (un kwes′chə nə blē), *adv.* beyond dispute or doubt; certainly.

**un|ques|tioned** (un kwes′chənd), *adj.* **1** not questioned. **2** not inquired into; not examined. **3** not disputed; unquestionable.

**un|ques|tion|ing** (un kwes′chə ning), *adj.* not questioning, disputing, or objecting. —**un|ques′-tion|ing|ly**, *adv.*

**un|qui|et** (un kwī′ət), *adj.* **1** not at rest; agitated; restless: *to pass an unquiet night.* **2** disturbed; uneasy: *an unquiet mind.* **3** causing or likely to cause trouble, disturbance, or upset: *an unquiet populace.* —**un|qui′et|ly**, *adv.* —**un|qui′et|ness**, *n.*

**un|quot|a|ble** (un kwō′tə bəl), *adj.* not quotable.

**un|quote** (un kwōt′), *v.i.,* **-quot|ed, -quot|ing.** to mark the end of a quotation (used especially in the phrase *quote ... unquote* to indicate the beginning and end of a spoken quotation): *After the religious songs, quote/unquote, there is always a* *thunderous pause* (New Yorker).

**U.N.R.** or **UNR** (no periods), Union for the New Republic (French, *Union pour la Nouvelle République*); a French political organization favoring the policies of former President de Gaulle.

**un|raised** (un rāzd′), *adj.* **1** not elevated. **2** not abandoned: *an unraised siege.*

**un|raked** (un rākt′), *adj.* **1** not raked. **2** not raked together; not raked up. **3** *Obsolete.* not sought or acquired by effort, as by raking.

**un|rat|i|fied** (un rat′ə fīd), *adj.* not ratified; unsanctioned.

**un|rav|el** (un rav′əl), *v.*, **-eled, -el|ing** or (*especially British*) **-elled, -el|ling.** — *v.t.* **1** to separate the threads or strands of; pull apart: *The kitten unraveled Grandma's knitting.* **2** *Figurative.* to bring out of a tangled state; work out the problems of; solve: *The detective unraveled the mystery.* **SYN**: untangle, resolve.
— *v.i.* **1** to come apart: *This sweater is unraveling at the elbow.* **2** to come out of a tangled state.

**un|ra|zored** (un rā′zərd), *adj.* = unshaven.

**un|reached** (un rēcht′), *adj.* not reached; not attained to.

**un|re|act|ed** (un′rē ak′tid), *adj.* that has not taken part in a chemical reaction: *The liquid withdrawn from the reaction vessels contains a higher proportion of unreacted raw materials because some of the incoming liquid finds its way to the outlet before it has time to react* (New Scientist).

**un|re|ac|tive** (un′rē ak′tiv), *adj.* that cannot take part in a chemical reaction: *Work has been carried out to develop ... crucibles coated on the inside with an unreactive ceramic* (New Scientist).

**un|read** (un red′), *adj.* **1** not read: *an unread book.* **2** not instructed by reading; not having read much: *an unread person.*

**un|read|a|bil|i|ty** (un′rē də bil′ə tē), *n.* the quality or state of being unreadable; lack of readability: *The essays themselves ... are marred, some of them to the point of unreadability, by the dreadful jargon of the specialist* (New Scientist).

**un|read|a|ble** (un rē′də bəl), *adj.* **1** that cannot be read or deciphered; illegible: *an unreadable manuscript.* **2** not suitable or fit for reading; not worth reading: *a dull, unreadable book.*

**un|read|i|ly** (un red′ə lē), *adv.* in an unready manner: **a** unpreparedly. **b** not promptly; not quickly. **c** awkwardly.

**un|read|i|ness** (un red′ē nis), *n.* the character of being unready.

**un|read|y** (un red′ē), *adj.* **1** not ready; not prepared. **2** not prompt or quick; slow. **3** *Obsolete or Dialect.* not dressed or fully dressed.

**un|re|al** (un rē′əl), *adj.* lacking reality or substance; not real; imaginary; fanciful. **SYN**: fictitious. — **un|re′al|ly**, *adv.*

**un|re|al|is|tic** (un′rē ə lis′tik), *adj.* not realistic: *an unrealistic play or novel, an unrealistic education. The President said that it would be unrealistic to expect a miraculous ending of the "cold war" as a result of the conference* (New York Times).

**un|re|al|is|ti|cal|ly** (un′rē ə lis′tə klē), *adv.* in a manner that is unrealistic: *Well known is Boswell's account of how Johnson unrealistically thought he could complete it* [*dictionary*] *in three years' time* (New York Times).

**un|re|al|i|ty** (un′rē al′ə tē), *n., pl.* **-ties. 1** lack of reality or substance; imaginary or fanciful quality. **2** impractical or visionary character or tendency; impracticality. **3** something without reality; something unreal.

**un|re|al|iz|a|ble** (un rē′ə lī′zə bəl), *adj.* not realizable.

**un|re|al|ized** (un rē′ə līzd), *adj.* not realized.

**un|rea|son** (un rē′zən), *n.* **1** absence of reason; indisposition or inability to act or think rationally; irrationality: *in some mood of cantankerous unreason* (George Gissing). **2** that which is contrary to or devoid of reason; absurdity.

**un|rea|son|a|ble** (un rē′zə nə bəl, -rēz′nə-), *adj.* **1** not reasonable: **a** not acting in accordance with reason or good sense; not reasonable, as in conduct or demands: *a capricious, unreasonable child.* **b** not in accordance with reason; irrational: *The little boy was very timid and had an unreasonable fear of the dark. The unreasonable* [*man*] *persists in trying to adapt the world to himself. Therefore all progress depends on the unreasonable man* (George Bernard Shaw). **2** not moderate; exorbitant: *$75 is an unreasonable price for a pair of shoes.* **3** not endowed with reason: *an unreasonable lunatic.* — **un|rea′son|a|ble|ness**, *n.*

**un|rea|son|a|bly** (un rē′zə nə blē, -rēz′nə-), *adv.* **1** in a way that is not reasonable; contrary to reason; foolishly: *to act or behave unreasonably.* **2** extremely; immoderately: *A miser is unreasonably stingy.*

**un|rea|soned** (un rē′zənd), *adj.* not reasoned or based on reasoning.

**un|rea|son|ing** (un rē′zə ning, -rēz′ning), *adj.* **1** not reasoning; not using reason; irrational: *I cannot traffic in the trade of words with that unreasoning sex* (Samuel Taylor Coleridge). **SYN**: reasonless. **2** deriving from or yielding to the emotions or instincts without intervention of reason or good sense: *to be the victim of blind, unreasoning terror.* — **un|rea′son|ing|ly**, *adv.*

**un|re|buk|a|ble** (un′ri byü′kə bəl), *adj.* not deserving rebuke; not open to censure.

**un|re|call|a|ble** (un′ri kô′lə bəl), *adj.* **1** that cannot be called back, revoked, or annulled; irrevocable: *You can develop sufficient assurance in the system so that you would do everything short of an unrecallable commitment* (Manchester Guardian). **2** that cannot be remembered: *Many days of our childhood are unrecallable.*

**un|re|ceipt|ed** (un′ri sē′tid), *adj.* not receipted.

**un|re|ceived** (un′ri sēvd′), *adj.* **1** not taken; not come into possession. **2** not embraced or adopted.

**un|reck|oned** (un rek′ənd), *adj.* not reckoned, computed, counted, or summed up.

**un|re|claim|a|ble** (un′ri klā′mə bəl), *adj.* = irreclaimable.

**un|re|claimed** (un′ri klāmd′), *adj.* **1** not brought to a domestic state; not tame: *a savageness in unreclaimed blood* (Shakespeare). **2** not reformed; not called back from vice to virtue: *a sinner unreclaimed.* **3** not brought into a state of cultivation, as desert or wild land.

**un|rec|og|niz|a|ble** (un rek′əg nī′zə bəl), *adj.* not recognizable. — **un|rec′og|niz′a|bly**, *adv.*

**un|rec|og|nized** (un rek′əg nīzd), *adj.* not recognized.

**un|rec|om|mend|ed** (un′rek ə men′did), *adj.* not recommended; not favorably mentioned.

**un|rec|om|pensed** (un rek′əm penst), *adj.* not recompensed.

**un|rec|on|cil|a|ble** (un rek′ən sī′lə bəl), *adj.* = irreconcilable.

**un|rec|on|ciled** (un rek′ən sīld), *adj.* not reconciled.

**un|re|con|struct|ed** (un′rē kən struk′tid), *adj.* **1** stubborn, as in adherence to standards or practices of an earlier day or previous regime or institution; unashamedly and tenaciously loyal to that which has been overthrown or superseded. **2** *U.S. History.* not yet subjected to the Reconstruction: *an unreconstructed area.* **3** *U.S.* not reconciled to the Reconstruction: *an unreconstructed Southerner.*

**un|re|cord|ed** (un′ri kôr′did), *adj.* not recorded.

**un|re|count|ed** (un′ri koun′tid), *adj.* not recounted; not related or recited.

**un|re|cov|er|a|ble** (un′ri kuv′ər ə bəl, -kuv′rə-), *adj.* **1** that cannot be recovered, found, restored, or obtained again. **2** not obtainable from a debtor; irrecoverable. **3** that cannot recover; incurable; irremediable.

**un|re|deemed** (un′ri dēmd′), *adj.* **1** not recalled by payment of what is due: *unredeemed bonds.* **2** not taken out of pawn. **3** not fulfilled: *an unredeemed promise.* **4** not ransomed; not delivered or rescued. **5** not saved spiritually. **6** not remedied or relieved by any countervailing quality or feature; unmitigated: *unredeemed ugliness* (Thomas Carlyle).

**un|reel** (un rēl′), *v.t., v.i.* to unwind from or as if from a reel.

**un|reeve** (un rēv′), *v.*, **-rove** or **-reeved, -reeving.** *Nautical.* — *v.t.* to draw (rope) back as through a block or thimble.
— *v.i.* **1** (of a rope) to become unreeved. **2** to draw back a reeved rope.

**UNREF** (no periods), United Nations Refugee Emergency Fund.

**un|re|fined** (un′ri fīnd′), *adj.* **1** not purified. **2** not free from coarseness or vulgarity; lacking nice feeling, taste, or sensibilities.

**un|re|flect|ing** (un′ri flek′ting), *adj.* unthinking; thoughtless. — **un′re|flect′ing|ly**, *adv.*

**un|re|form|a|ble** (un′ri fôr′mə bəl), *adj.* not reformable; that cannot be reformed or amended.

**un|re|gard|ed** (un′ri gär′did), *adj.* **1** not heeded or noticed; disregarded. **2** not valued or esteemed.

**un|re|gen|er|a|cy** (un′ri jen′ər ə sē), *n.* unregenerate condition; enmity toward God; wickedness.

**un|re|gen|er|ate** (un′ri jen′ər it), *adj.* **1** not born again spiritually; not turned to the love of God. **2** not disposed to reform or repent; stubborn and hardened, as in wickedness or crime; wicked; bad. — **un′re|gen′er|ate|ly**, *adv.* — **un′re|gen′er|ate|ness**, *n.*

**un|re|gen|er|at|ed** (un′ri jen′ə rā′tid), *adj.* = unregenerate.

**un|reg|is|tered** (un rej′ə stərd), *adj.* not registered.

**un|reg|u|lat|ed** (un reg′yə lā′tid), *adj.* not regulated: *The proposals ... prevent diversion of freight traffic to private, unregulated truck carriers* (Wall Street Journal).

**un|re|lat|ed** (un′ri lā′tid), *adj.* not related. — **un′re|lat′ed|ness**, *n.*

**un|re|laxed** (un′ri lakst′), *adj.* **1** not relaxed. **2** not made loose or slack. **3** not slackened or abated.

**un|re|lax|ing** (un′ri lak′sing), *adj.* not relaxing or slackening: *a time of unrelaxing effort* (John Morley).

**un|re|lent|ing** (un′ri len′ting), *adj.* **1** not giving way to feelings of kindness or compassion; merciless; cruel: *an unrelenting enemy.* **SYN**: unyielding, obdurate, relentless. See syn. under **inflexible. 2** not slackening or relaxing in severity, harshness, or determination: *unrelenting anger.* **3** not slowing down: *an unrelenting pace.* — **un′re|lent′ing|ly**, *adv.* — **un′re|lent′ing|ness**, *n.*

**un|re|li|a|bil|i|ty** (un′ri lī′ə bil′ə tē), *n.* lack of reliability.

**un|re|li|a|ble** (un′ri lī′ə bəl), *adj.* not reliable; not to be depended on; irresponsible. **SYN**: uncertain. — **un′re|li′a|ble|ness**, *n.*

**un|re|li|a|bly** (un′ri lī′ə blē), *adv.* in an unreliable manner.

**un|re|liev|a|ble** (un′ri lē′və bəl), *adj.* not relievable.

**un|re|lieved** (un′ri lēvd′), *adj.* not relieved: *unrelieved monotony, the unrelieved hardships of pioneer life.*

**un|re|liev|ed|ly** (un′ri lē′vid lē), *adv.* without relief or mitigation: *The tempo is funereal, and throughout the mood is unrelievedly austere* (Time).

**un|re|li|gious** (un′ri lij′əs), *adj.* **1** = irreligious. **2** not connected with religion; nonreligious; secular: *The popular poetry ... became profane, unreligious, at length in some part, irreligious* (Henry H. Milman).

**un|re|mark|a|ble** (un′ri mär′kə bəl), *adj.* unworthy of remark or notice; not notable or striking: *But how did he make the jump from these unremarkable poems to the later work?* (Punch).

**un|re|marked** (un′ri märkt′), *adj.* not remarked; not noticed: *The unremarked phenomenon of Herbert Hoover is that he* [*had*] *been so long out of a regular job and* [*had*] *kept himself so busy* (Time).

**un|re|mem|ber|a|ble** (un′ri mem′bər ə bəl), *adj.* not rememberable; forgettable: *The smallest flint spark, in a world all black and unrememberable, will be welcome* (Thomas Carlyle).

**un|re|mem|bered** (un′ri mem′bərd), *adj.* not remembered; forgotten: *little nameless, unremembered acts Of kindness and of love* (Wordsworth).

**un|re|mem|ber|ing** (un′ri mem′bər ing), *adj.* not remembering; having no memory or recollection: *She went her unremembering way* (Francis Thompson).

**un|re|mit|ted** (un′ri mit′id), *adj.* **1** not remitted; not pardoned, forgiven, or canceled. **2** not slackened or abated: *Our exertions to discover him are unremitted* (Mary Shelley).

**un|re|mit|ting** (un′ri mit′ing), *adj.* never stopping; not slackening or relaxing; maintained steadily: *unremitting vigilance. Driving in heavy traffic requires unremitting attention.* **SYN**: unceasing, incessant, constant. — **un′re|mit′ting|ly**, *adv.*

**un|re|morse|ful** (un′ri môrs′fəl), *adj.* feeling no remorse; unpitying; remorseless.

**un|re|mov|a|ble** (un′ri mü′və bəl), *adj.* that cannot be removed; fixed; irremovable.

**un|re|moved** (un′ri müvd′), *adj.* **1** not removed; not taken away. **2** *Figurative.* firm; unshaken.

**un|re|mu|ner|at|ed** (un′ri myü′nə rā′tid), *adj.* not remunerated; without remuneration.

**un|re|mu|ner|a|tive** (un′ri myü′nə rā′tiv, -nər ə-), *adj.* not remunerative; not affording remuneration; unprofitable. — **un′re|mu′ner|a′tive|ness**, *n.*

**un|re|newed** (un′ri nüd′, -nyüd′), *adj.* **1** not made anew: *an unrenewed lease.* **2** not regenerated; not born of the Spirit: *an unrenewed heart.* **3** not renovated; not restored to freshness.

**un|rent** (un rent′), *adj.* not rent; not torn asunder.

**un|rent|ed** (un ren′tid), *adj.* not rented.

**un|re|paid** (un′ri pād′), *adj.* not repaid; not compensated; not recompensed; not requited: *a kindness unrepaid.*

**un|re|pair** (un′ri pãr′), *n.* lack of repair; disrepair; dilapidation.

**un|re|pair|a|ble** (un′ri pãr′ə bəl), *adj.* that cannot be repaired; irreparable.

**un|re|paired** (un′ri pãrd′), *adj.* not repaired.

**un|re|peal|a|ble** (un′ri pē′lə bəl), *adj.* not repealable; irrevocable.

**un|re|pealed** (un′ri pēld′), *adj.* not repealed.

**un|re|pent|ance** (un′ri pen′təns), *n.* the state of being unrepentant or impenitent; impenitence.

**un|re|pent|ant** (un′ri pen′tənt), *adj.* not repentant; impenitent. — **un′re|pent′ant|ly**, *adv.*

**Pronunciation Key:** hat, āge, cãre, fär; let, ēqual, tėrm; it, īce; hot, ōpen, ôrder; oil, out; cup, pu̇t, rüle; child; long; thin; ᴛʜen; zh, measure; ə represents a in about, e in taken, i in pencil, o in lemon, u in circus.

**un|re|pent|ed** (un′ri pen′tid), *adj.* not repented of.
**un|re|pin|ing** (un′ri pī′ning), *adj.* not repining; uncomplaining. —**un′re|pin′ing|ly,** *adv.*
**un|re|plen|ished** (un′ri plen′isht), *adj.* not replenished; not filled; not adequately supplied.
**un|rep|re|sent|a|tive** (un′rep ri zen′tə tiv), *adj.* not representative; failing to represent adequately; not typical.
**un|rep|re|sent|ed** (un′rep ri zen′tid), *adj.* not represented.
**un|re|pressed** (un′ri prest′), *adj.* not repressed; unrestrained.
**un|re|priev|a|ble** (un′ri prē′və bəl), *adj.* that cannot be reprieved.
**un|re|prieved** (un′ri prēvd′), *adj.* not reprieved; not respited.
**un|re|prov|a|ble** (un′ri prü′və bəl), *adj.* not reprovable; not deserving reproof; without reproach; not liable to be justly censured.
**un|re|proved** (un′ri prüvd′), *adj.* **1** not reproved; not censured. **2** not liable to reproof or blame. **3** *Obsolete.* not disproved.
**un|re|quest|ed** (un′ri kwes′tid), *adj.* not requested; not asked.
**un|re|quit|a|ble** (un′ri kwī′tə bəl), *adj.* that cannot be requited; unreturnable: *Britain owes an unrequitable debt to the work of the famous Temporary National Economic Committee* (Manchester Guardian Weekly).
**un|re|quit|ed** (un′ri kwī′tid), *adj.* not requited; without requital or return: *unrequited love.*
**un|re|serve** (un′ri zėrv′), *n.* freedom from reserve; candor; frankness: *questions which he will answer with perfect unreserve* (Samuel Butler).
**un|re|served** (un′ri zėrvd′), *adj.* **1** not restrained in action or speech; frank; open. **2** not restricted, limited, or qualified; without reservation. —**un′re-serv′ed|ness,** *n.*
**un|re|serv|ed|ly** (un′ri zėr′vid lē), *adv.* **1** in an unreserved manner; frankly; openly. **SYN:** straightforwardly. **2** without reservation or restriction. **SYN:** fully.
**un|re|sist|ed** (un′ri zis′tid), *adj.* **1** not resisted; not opposed. **2** *Obsolete.* irresistible.
**un|re|sist|ing** (un′ri zis′ting), *adj.* not resisting; not making resistance; submissive. —**un′re|sist′-ing|ly,** *adv.*
**un|re|solv|a|ble** (un′ri zol′və bəl), *adj.* that cannot be resolved: *I have in the past accused him of both hubris and loss of self-respect, but the paradox is not unresolvable* (Joseph Wood Krutch).
**un|re|solved** (un′ri zolvd′), *adj.* **1** not resolved; not determined. **2** not solved; not cleared: *unresolved doubt.* **3** not separated into its constituent parts: *an unresolved nebula.* **4** not reduced to a state of solution.
**un|re|spect|a|ble** (un′ri spek′tə bəl), *adj.* not respectable; disreputable; dishonorable.
**un|res|pit|ed** (un res′pə tid), *adj.* **1** not respited: *Unrespited, unpitied, unreprieved, Ages of hopeless end* (Milton). **2** *Obsolete.* admitting no pause or intermission.
**un|re|spon|sive** (un′ri spon′siv), *adj.* not responsive or inclined to respond. —**un′re|spon′sive-ness,** *n.*
**un|rest** (un rest′), *n.* **1** lack of ease and quiet; restlessness. **SYN:** inquietude, uneasiness. **2** agitation or disturbance amounting almost to rebellion. **SYN:** disquiet.
**un|rest|ful** (un rest′fəl), *adj.* **1** not restful or at rest; restless. **2** not affording or promoting rest.
**un|rest|ing** (un res′ting), *adj.* not resting; continually in motion or action; restless: *life's unresting sea* (Oliver Wendell Holmes).
**un|re|strained** (un′ri strānd′), *adj.* **1** not kept in check or under control: *unrestrained laughter.* **2** not subjected to restraint: *unrestrained freedom, an unrestrained movement.* **3** free from restraint of manner; easy; natural: *an unrestrained greeting.* —**un′re|strain′ed|ly,** *adv.*
**un|re|straint** (un′ri strānt′), *n.* lack of restraint.
**un|re|strict|ed** (un′ri strik′tid), *adj.* not restricted; without limitation. —**un′re|strict′ed|ly,** *adv.*
**un|re|tard|ed** (un′ri tär′did), *adj.* not retarded; not delayed, hindered, or impeded.
**un|re|ten|tive** (un′ri ten′tiv), *adj.* not retentive.
**un|re|turn|a|ble** (un′ri tėr′nə bəl), *adj.* that cannot be returned; impossible to be repaid.
**un|re|vealed** (un′ri vēld′), *adj.* not revealed; not disclosed.
**un|re|venged** (un′ri venjd′), *adj.* not revenged.
**un|re|versed** (un′ri vėrst′), *adj.* not reversed; not annulled by a counter decision; not revoked; unrepealed.
**un|re|voked** (un′ri vōkt′), *adj.* not revoked; not recalled; not annulled.
**un|re|ward|ed** (un′ri wôr′did), *adj.* not rewarded; unrequited: *unrewarded kindness.*
**un|re|ward|ing** (un′ri wôr′ding), *adj.* not rewarding; not affording a reward: *an image of serfs destined to poverty and endless unrewarding work* (Scientific American).
**un|rhyth|mi|cal** (un riᴛʜ′mə kəl), *adj.* not rhythmical; irregular in rhythm.
**un|rid|dle** (un rid′əl), *v.t.,* **-dled, -dling.** to work out the answer to (as a puzzling matter, mystery, or riddle); solve: *The riddle ... was now unriddled* (Edgar Allan Poe).
**un|rig** (un rig′), *v.t.,* **-rigged, -rig|ging. 1** to dismantle and remove the rigging of (a ship). **2** to take apart and remove (a scaffold or mechanical equipment); dismantle. **3** *Archaic or Dialect.* to undress.
**un|rigged** (un rigd′), *adj.* without rigging; not rigged.
**un|right|eous** (un rī′chəs), *adj.* **1** not morally righteous or upright; wicked; sinful. **SYN:** unprincipled, iniquitous. **2** not justly due; undeserved. [Old English *unrihtwīs* < *un-* un-[1] + *rihtwīs.* Compare etym. under **righteous.**] —**un|right′eous|ly,** *adv.* —**un|right′eous|ness,** *n.*
**un|right|ful** (un rīt′fəl), *adj.* **1** not rightful; unjust; not consonant with justice. **2** not having right; not legitimate.
**un|rip** (un rip′), *v.t.,* **-ripped, -rip|ping. 1** to open up or detach by or as if by ripping; tear or pull open or off. **2** to lay open by slicing; slit.
**un|ripe** (un rīp′), *adj.,* **-rip|er, -rip|est. 1** not ripe; not matured by growth; green: *an unripe peach.* **2** not fully developed or grown; immature. **3** *Obsolete.* (of death) too early; premature. —**un|ripe′-ness,** *n.*
**un|rip|ened** (un rī′pənd), *adj.* not ripened; not matured.
**un|ri|valed** (un rī′vəld), *adj.* having no rival; without an equal; matchless; peerless. **SYN:** incomparable.
**un|robe** (un rōb′), *v.t., v.i.,* **-robed, -rob|ing.** to divest or be divested of a robe or robes; undress; disrobe: *The King ... unrobed, took his seat ... and listened ... to the debate* (Macaulay).
**un|roll** (un rōl′), *v.t.* **1** to open or spread out (something rolled). **SYN:** unfold, unfurl. **2** to lay open or spread out so as to be seen; display. **3** *Obsolete.* to strike from a roll; remove from a roster: *If I make not this Cheat bring out another ... let me be unrolled* (Shakespeare). —*v.i.* to become opened or spread out.
**un|ro|man|tic** (un′rō man′tik), *adj.* not romantic; prosaic; practical; commonplace. —**un′ro|man′ti-cal|ly,** *adv.*
**un|roof** (un rüf′, -rŭf′), *v.t.* to pull or pluck off the roof or upper covering of: *They ... unroofed a great part of the building* (Alexander W. Kinglake).
**un|roofed** (un rüft′, -rŭft′), *adj.* not provided with a roof.
**un|root** (un rüt′, -rŭt′), *v.t.* to uproot. —*v.i.* to be uprooted.
**un|rough** (un ruf′), *adj.* not rough; unbearded; smooth.
**un|round** (un round′), *v.t. Phonetics.* **1** to decrease or eliminate the lip rounding in the pronunciation of (a normally rounded sound). **2** to spread (the lips) during articulation.
**un|round|ed** (un roun′did), *adj. Phonetics.* pronounced without rounding of the lips, as the vowels in *sit* and *sat.*
**un|rove** (un rōv′), *adj., v.* —*adj. Nautical.* unreeved.
—*v.* a past tense and a past participle of **unreeve.**
**UNRRA** (un′rə), *n.* United Nations Relief and Rehabilitation Administration (an international agency established in 1943 to provide food, clothing, medical supplies, and other needs to redeveloping nations devastated by war).
**un|ruf|fled** (un ruf′əld), *adj.* **1** not ruffled; smooth. **2** not disturbed; calm: *with contented mind and unruffled spirit* (Anthony Trollope). **SYN:** serene, unperturbed. —**un|ruf′fled|ness,** *n.*
**un|ruled** (un rüld′), *adj.* **1** not kept under control; not governed. **2** not marked with lines: *unruled paper.*
**un|ru|li|ness** (un rü′lē nis), *n.* the condition of being unruly; disregard of restraint; turbulence: *the unruliness of men.*
**un|ru|ly** (un rü′lē), *adj.,* **-li|er, -li|est. 1** hard to rule or control, especially: **a** not manageable; ungovernable; unmanageable: *an unruly horse, a disobedient and unruly boy, an unruly lock of hair.* **b** disorderly; lawless; turbulent: *an unruly mob, an unruly section of a country.* **2** stormy; tempestuous: *an unruly sea.*
—*Syn.* **1 Unruly, ungovernable** mean hard or impossible to control. **Unruly** means not inclined to obey or accept discipline and suggests getting out of hand and becoming disorderly, contrary, or obstinately willful: *The angry mob became unruly.* **Ungovernable** means incapable of being controlled or restrained, either because of never having been subjected to rule or direction or because of escape from it: *One of the circus lions had always been ungovernable.*
**UNRWA** (no periods) or **U.N.R.W.A.,** United Nations Relief and Works Agency (originally for Palestine refugees in the Near East).
**un|sad|dle** (un sad′əl), *v.t.,* **-dled, -dling. 1** to take the saddle off (a horse). **2** to cause (a person) to fall from a horse; throw; unhorse.
**un|safe** (un sāf′), *adj.,* **-saf|er, -saf|est.** not safe; dangerous. **SYN:** perilous, hazardous, precarious. —**un|safe′ly,** *adv.* —**un|safe′ness,** *n.*
**un|safe|ty** (un sāf′tē), *n.* **1** dangerous quality; lack of safety. **2** *Archaic.* the state of being in danger; peril.
**un|said** (un sed′), *adj., v.* —*adj.* not said or uttered: *All he had meant to say remained unsaid. It's better to leave bitter remarks unsaid.*
—*v.t.* the past tense and past participle of **unsay.**
**un|saint|ly** (un sānt′lē), *adj.* **1** not saintly; not like a saint. **2** not befitting a saint.
**un|sal|a|bil|i|ty** or **un|sale|a|bil|i|ty** (un sā′lə bil′ə tē), *n.* not being of a salable condition or quality: *Unsaleability is almost the hallmark ... of quality in writing* (Logan Pearsall Smith).
**un|sal|a|ble** or **un|sale|a|ble** (un sā′lə bəl), *adj.* not salable; not meeting a ready sale. —**un|sal′-a|ble|ness, un|sale′a|ble|ness,** *n.*
**un|sal|a|ried** (un sal′ər id), *adj.* not salaried; not paid, or not provided with, a fixed salary.
**un|salt|ed** (un sôl′tid), *adj.* not salted; fresh.
**un|sanc|ti|fied** (un sangk′tə fīd), *adj.* not sanctified; unhallowed; unholy.
**un|sanc|ti|mo|ni|ous** (un′sangk tə mō′nē əs), *adj.* not making a show of holiness; not putting on airs of sanctity: [*This*] *unsanctimonious appreciation of the Bible story has some witty and winning scenes* (New York Times).
**un|sanc|tioned** (un sangk′shənd), *adj.* not sanctioned; not ratified; not approved.
**un|san|i|tar|y** (un san′ə ter′ē), *adj.* not sanitary; bad for the health; unhealthful. —**un|san′i|tar′i-ness,** *n.*
**un|sa|ti|a|ble** (un sā′shē ə bəl, -shə bəl), *adj.* incapable of being satiated or appeased; insatiable.
**un|sat|is|fac|to|ri|ly** (un′sat is fak′tər ə lē), *adv.* in an unsatisfactory manner.
**un|sat|is|fac|to|ry** (un′sat is fak′tər ē), *adj.* not satisfactory; not good enough to satisfy; inadequate. —**un′sat|is|fac′to|ri|ness,** *n.*
**un|sat|is|fied** (un sat′is fīd), *adj.* not satisfied; not gratified to the full; not contented: *His evasive answers to our questions left us unsatisfied.*
**un|sat|is|fy|ing** (un sat′is fī′ing), *adj.* not satisfying; insufficient to meet the desires; inadequate: *an unsatisfying meal.* —**un|sat′is|fy′ing|ly,** *adv.* —**un|sat′is|fy′ing|ness,** *n.*
**un|sat|u|rate** (un sach′ər it, -ə rāt), *n.* an unsaturated compound.
**un|sat|u|rat|ed** (un sach′ə rā′tid), *adj.* **1** not saturated; able to absorb or dissolve an additional quantity of a substance. **2** *Chemistry.* having a double or triple bond and one or more free valences so that another atom or radical may be taken on without the liberation of other atoms, radicals, or compounds (used of an organic compound, such as acetylene).
**unsaturated radical,** *Chemistry.* an organic radical having a double or triple bond which joins two atoms of carbon.
**un|sat|u|ra|tion** (un′sach ə rā′shən), *n.* the state of being unsaturated.
**un|sa|vor|y** (un sā′vər ē, -sāv′rē), *adj.* **1** unpleasant in taste or smell; distasteful: *a most unsavory medicine.* **2** *Figurative.* morally unpleasant; offensive or dubious: *an unsavory reputation.* **3** tasteless; insipid. —**un|sa′vor|i|ly,** *adv.* —**un|sa′vor|i-ness,** *n.*
**un|say** (un sā′), *v.t.,* **-said, -say|ing.** to take back (something said or written); withdraw (a statement); retract.
**un|scal|a|ble** (un skā′lə bəl), *adj.* not scalable; not to be climbed: *the unscalable side of a mountain* (Joseph Conrad).
**un|scanned** (un skand′), *adj.* not scanned; not measured; not computed.
**un|scarred** (un skärd′), *adj.* not scarred, as from a wound; having no scars.
**un|scathed** (un skāᴛʜd′), *adj.* not harmed; uninjured: *He escaped unscathed from the car wreck.*
**un|schol|ar|ly** (un skol′ər lē), *adj.* **1** not scholarly; lacking scholarly qualities or attainments. **2** unbefitting a scholar. —**un|schol′ar|li|ness,** *n.*
**un|schooled** (un sküld′), *adj.* not schooled; not taught; not disciplined.
**un|sci|en|tif|ic** (un′sī ən tif′ik), *adj.* **1** not in accordance with the facts or principles of science: *an unscientific notion. This assumption is unscientific* (Samuel Butler). **2** not acting in accordance with the facts or principles of science: *an unscientific farmer.* —**un′sci|en|tif′i|cal|ly,** *adv.*
**un|scoured** (un skourd′), *adj.* not scoured; not cleaned by rubbing: *an unscoured sink.*
**un|scram|ble** (un skram′bəl), *v.t.,* **-bled, -bling. 1** to reduce from confusion to order; bring out of

a scrambled condition: *to unscramble one's neglected affairs. After the wind died down, he picked up and unscrambled the papers that had blown on the floor.* **2** to restore to the original condition; make no longer scrambled: *to unscramble a coded radio message.*

**un|scram|bler** (un skram′blər), *n.* **1** a person or thing that unscrambles: *They were also, however, expert unscramblers* (Harper's). **2** a device which unscrambles special broadcasts: *Its figure did not include about $80 for the cost of installation of an unscrambler for subscription TV receivers* (New York Times).

**un|scratched** (un skracht′), *adj.* not scratched; not torn.

**un|screened** (un skrēnd′), *adj.* **1** not screened; not covered; not sheltered; not protected. **2** not passed through a screen; not sifted: *unscreened coal.* **3** not made into, or adapted for, a motion picture: *The story is as yet unscreened.*

**un|screw** (un skrü′), *v.t.* **1** to take out the screw or screws from. **2** to detach or remove by doing this: *to unscrew a bracket from the wall.* **3** to loosen or take off by turning; untwist: *to unscrew an electric bulb.* —*v.i.* to be able to be or become unscrewed: *This light bulb won't unscrew.*

**un|script|ed** (un skrip′tid), *adj. British.* delivered or presented without a script.

**un|scrip|tur|al** (un skrip′chər əl), *adj.* not scriptural; not in accordance with the Scriptures. —**un-scrip′tur|al|ly,** *adv.*

**un|scru|pu|lous** (un skrü′pyə ləs), *adj.* not careful about right or wrong; without principles or conscience: *The unscrupulous boy cheated on the test.* —**un|scru′pu|lous|ly,** *adv.* —**un|scru′pu-lous|ness,** *n.*

—*Syn.* **Unscrupulous, unprincipled** mean without regard for what is morally right. **Unscrupulous** implies a willful disregard of moral principles: *He would stoop to any unscrupulous trick to avoid paying his bills.* **Unprincipled** implies a lack of moral principles: *He is so unprincipled that when I explained my scruples to him it was obvious he didn't know what I was talking about.* The distinction is roughly parallel to the difference between *immoral* and *amoral.*

**un|sculp|tured** (un skulp′chərd), *adj.* **1** not sculptured; not covered with sculpture or markings. **2** *Zoology.* without elevated or impressed marks on the surface; smooth.

**un|seal** (un sēl′), *v.t.* **1** to break or remove the seal of: *to unseal a letter or a jar.* **2** *Figurative.* to cause to open in speech: *The threat of punishment unsealed her lips.*

**un|seam** (un sēm′), *v.t.* **1** to undo the seam or seams of. **2** to rip lengthwise: (*Figurative.*) *Till he unseam'd him from the nave to the chops* (Shakespeare).

**un|search|a|ble** (un sėr′chə bəl), *adj.* not to be searched into; that cannot be understood by searching; mysterious: *the unsearchable and secret aims Of nature* (Robert Bridges). **SYN:** inscrutable.

**un|search|a|bly** (un sėr′chə blē), *adv.* in an unsearchable manner; inscrutably.

**un|searched** (un sėrcht′), *adj.* not searched.

**un|sea|son|a|ble** (un sē′zə nə bəl, -sēz′nə-), *adj.* **1** not suitable to or characteristic of the season: *an unseasonable snowstorm.* **2** coming at the wrong time; not timely: *an unseasonable suggestion.* **SYN:** inopportune, untimely. —**un|sea′son|a-ble|ness,** *n.*

**un|sea|son|a|bly** (un sē′zə nə blē, -sēz′nə-), *adv.* in an unseasonable manner; at an inappropriate or awkward time.

**un|sea|son|al|ly** (un sē′zə nə lē, -sēz′nə-), *adv.* = unseasonably.

**un|sea|soned** (un sē′zənd), *adj.* **1** not matured, dried, hardened, or prepared by due seasoning: *unseasoned lumber.* **2** not inured to a climate, service, work, or mode of life; inexperienced. **3** not tested and approved by time: *unseasoned securities.* **4** not flavored with seasoning: *unseasoned food.* **5** *Obsolete.* unseasonable.

**un|seat** (un sēt′), *v.t.* **1** to remove from office: *to unseat a congressman, to unseat a government.* **2a** to displace from a seat. **b** to dislodge from its base: *to unseat a boiler.* **3** to throw (a rider) from the saddle.

**un|sea|wor|thi|ness** (un sē′wėr′ᴛʜē nis), *n.* the state of being unseaworthy.

**un|sea|wor|thy** (un sē′wėr′ᴛʜē), *adj.* not seaworthy.

**un|sec|tar|i|an** (un′sek tãr′ē ən), *adj.* not sectarian; not confined to or dominated by any particular sect; free from sectarian character or aims.

**un|sec|tar|i|an|ism** (un′sek tãr′ē ə niz′əm), *n.* the character of being unsectarian; freedom from sectarianism; unprejudiced attitude in religious matters.

**un|sec|u|lar** (un sek′yə lər), *adj.* not secular or worldly.

**un|se|cured** (un′si kyůrd′), *adj.* **1** not secured. **2** not insured against loss, as by a bond or pledge: *unsecured debts.*

**un|see|a|ble** (un sē′ə bəl), *adj.* that cannot be seen; invisible: *To see things unseeable, as St. Paul heard things unutterable* (Daniel Defoe).

**un|seed|ed** (un sē′did), *adj.* **1** not seeded; not sown. **2** not having or bearing seed: *an unseeded plant.* **3** not ranked in a tournament: *an unseeded player.*

**un|see|ing** (un sē′ing), *adj.* **1** not perceiving; unobservant: *We drive to work along a familiar route unseeing and lost in thought* (Scientific American). **2** = blind. —**un|see′ing|ly,** *adv.*

**un|seem|li|ness** (un sēm′lē nis), *n.* the character of being unseemly; uncomeliness; indecency; indecorum; impropriety.

**un|seem|ly** (un sēm′lē), *adj.,* **-li|er, -li|est,** *adv.* —*adj.* not seemly; not proper; not suitable: *to flee with unseemly haste, a joke of a rather unseemly nature. Laughing out loud in church is unseemly.* **SYN:** unbecoming, unfit, improper. —*adv.* improperly; unsuitably.

**un|seen** (un sēn′), *adj.* **1** not seen; overlooked by the eye; unnoticed: *an unseen error.* **SYN:** unobserved. **2** not able to be seen; invisible: *an unseen spirit.*

**un|seg|ment|ed** (un seg′men tid), *adj.* not segmented.

**un|seized** (un sēzd′), *adj.* **1** not seized; not apprehended; not taken. **2** *Law.* not possessed; not put in possession.

**un|self-con|scious** (un′self kon′shəs), *adj.* not self-conscious; uninhibited; natural; spontaneous: *Children and animals make the best movie actors ... because they are unself-conscious and unable to fake* (Harper's). —**un′self-con′scious|ly,** *adv.* —**un′self-con′scious|ness,** *n.*

**un|self|ish** (un sel′fish), *adj.* not selfish; caring for others; generous. **SYN:** charitable, liberal. —**un-self′ish|ly,** *adv.* —**un|self′ish|ness,** *n.*

**un|sell** (un sel′), *v.t.,* **-sold, -sell|ing.** *Informal.* to talk out of; persuade not to buy, accept, or undertake something: *Dad unsold me on the idea of going to Seattle this summer.*

**un|sell|a|ble** (un sel′ə bəl), *adj.* that no one will buy; that cannot be sold; unsalable: *The house which was to provide the mainstay of the trust ... was proving unsellable* (New Yorker).

**un|sent** (un sent′), *adj.* not sent; not dispatched; not transmitted: *an unsent letter.*

**un|sent-for** (un sent′fôr′), *adj.* not summoned or ordered: *unsent-for guests.*

**un|sen|ti|men|tal** (un′sen tə men′təl), *adj.* not sentimental; hard-headed; practical; matter-of-fact. —**un′sen|ti|men′tal|ly,** *adv.* —**un′sen|ti-men′tal|ness,** *n.*

**un|se|ri|ous** (un sir′ē əs), *adj.* not serious: *But however serious or unserious the latest warning may be ... there is no doubt that the Chinese wish it to be seriously regarded* (Manchester Guardian Weekly). —**un|se′ri|ous|ly,** *adv.*

**un|serv|ice|a|ble** (un sėr′və sə bəl), *adj.* not serviceable; not satisfactory for service or use; not durable. —**un|serv′ice|a|ble|ness,** *n.*

**un|serv|ice|a|bly** (un sėr′və sə blē), *adv.* not in a serviceable manner; not serviceably.

**un|serv|iced** (un sėr′vist), *adj.* **1** not kept fit for service. **2** not provided with service of any kind.

**un|set**[1] (un set′), *adj.* **1** not in a setting; not mounted: *an unset ruby.* **2** not fixed or settled: *unset cement.*

**un|set**[2] (un set′), *v.t.,* **-set, -set|ting.** to put out of place; undo the setting of: *to unset the hair.*

**un|set|tle** (un set′əl), *v.,* **-tled, -tling.** —*v.t.* to make unstable; cause to become disordered; disturb; shake; weaken: (*Figurative.*) *The shock unsettled her mind.* **SYN:** disorder, upset, disconcert. —*v.i.* to become unstable.

**un|set|tled** (un set′əld), *adj.* **1** not in the proper condition or order; disordered; disturbed: *Our house is still unsettled;* (*Figurative.*) *an unsettled mind.* **2** not fixed or firmly established; unstable: *an unsettled government.* **3** liable to change; uncertain: *The weather is unsettled.* **4** not adjusted or disposed of: *an unsettled estate, an unsettled bill.* **5** not determined or decided: *an unsettled question.* **6** not populated; not inhabited: *Some parts of the world are still unsettled.* **SYN:** uninhabited. —**un|set′tled|ness,** *n.*

**un|set|tle|ment** (un set′əl mənt), *n.* **1** the act of unsettling. **2** the state of being unsettled; unsettled or disturbed condition of affairs: *The continuing unsettlement was a call to him that ... he had still a portion of the Lord's work to do* (John Morley). *Uncertainty as to the scope of the new program added unsettlement in futures* (Wall Street Journal). **3** an area or region that has not been definitely settled: *It is in the temporary communities and the amorphous unsettlements that conformity and anxiety breed* (Manchester Guardian).

**un|set|tling** (un set′ling), *adj.* upsetting; disturbing; disconcerting: *In its quiet, pleasant way this is a most unsettling book* (Saturday Review). —**un|set′tling|ly,** *adv.*

**un|sev|ered** (un sev′ərd), *adj.* not severed; not parted or sundered; not disjoined or separate.

**un|sew** (un sō′), *v.t.,* **-sewed, -sewed** or **-sewn, -sew|ing. 1** to undo the sewing of (a garment or other material); remove the stitches from. **2** to unwrap or set free by the removal of stitches.

**un|sex** (un seks′), *v.t.* to deprive of the attributes of one's sex, especially to deprive of womanly character: *Come, you spirits ... unsex me* (Shakespeare).

**un|shack|le** (un shak′əl), *v.t.,* **-led, -ling.** to remove the shackles from; set free. **SYN:** unfetter.

**un|shad|ed** (un shā′did), *adj.* **1** without shade: *an unshaded lawn.* **2** not screened by a shade: *an unshaded light bulb.* **3** without shades or gradations of light or color: *an unshaded drawing.*

**un|shad|owed** (un shad′ōd), *adj.* **1** not shadowed; not darkened or obscured. **2** *Figurative.* free from gloom.

**un|shak|a|ble** or **un|shake|a|ble** (un shā′kə-bəl), *adj.* not shakable; that cannot be shaken; firm: (*Figurative.*) *The rule of unshakeable falsehood and established tyranny ... was the basis of Orwell's terrible prophecy* (New Statesman).

**un|shak|a|bly** or **un|shake|a|bly** (un shā′kə-blē), *adv.* in an unshakable manner.

**un|shak|en** (un shā′kən), *adj.* not shaken; firm: *unshaken courage, an unshaken resolve, an unshaken belief in Santa Claus.* **SYN:** resolute, unwavering.

**un|shamed** (un shāmd′), *adj.* not shamed; not ashamed; not abashed.

**un|shape** (un shāp′), *v.t.,* **-shaped, -shap|ing.** *Archaic, Figurative.* to put out of shape or order; derange: *This deed unshapes me quite* (Shakespeare).

**un|shaped** (un shāpt′), *adj.* **1** lacking distinctive shape; formless: *an unshaped thought.* **2** not yet in final shape; rough and unfinished: *unshaped timber.* **3** of an ugly shape; misshapen.

**un|shape|li|ness** (un shāp′lē nis), *n.* unshapely quality or condition.

**un|shape|ly** (un shāp′lē), *adj.* not shapely; unpleasing in shape; ill-formed: *a foot, unshapely and huge* (Charles Brockden Brown). *The wrong of unshapely things is a wrong too great to be told; I hunger to build them anew* (William Butler Yeats).

**un|shap|en** (un shā′pən), *adj.* unshaped: (*Figurative.*) *this blind trust in some unshapen chance* (George Eliot).

**un|shared** (un shãrd′), *adj.* not shared; not partaken or enjoyed in common.

**un|shav|en** (un shā′vən), *adj.* not shaven.

**un|sheathe** (un shēᴛʜ′), *v.t.,* **-sheathed, -sheath-ing. 1** to draw (a sword, knife, or the like) from a sheath: *People ... as ready to draw a knife on you as a cat was to unsheathe its claws* (W. H. Hudson). **2** to bring or put forth from a covering.

**un|shed** (un shed′), *adj.* not shed: *unshed tears.*

**un|shell** (un shel′), *v.t.* **1** to take out of the shell. **2** to remove or release, as from a shell.

**un|shel|tered** (un shel′tərd), *adj.* not sheltered; without shelter.

**un|ship** (un ship′), *v.,* **-shipped, -ship|ping.** —*v.t.* **1** to put off or take off from a ship; discharge; unload: *to unship a cargo or passengers.* **2** to remove from the proper place for use: *to unship an oar or a mast.*

—*v.i.* **1** to be discharged or unloaded: *Such other cargo as was ... unshipping at the pier* (Dickens). **2** to be or become detached: *The boat's rudder unshipped and caused the boat to capsize* (Pall Mall Gazette).

**un|shirk|a|ble** (un shėr′kə bəl), *adj.* that cannot be shirked: *our unshirkable responsibility ... to world peace* (Time).

**un|shirt|ed** (un shėr′tid), *adj. Informal.* unadorned; unreserved; plain: *Unlike his father who gave him unshirted hell in earthy language, Kennedy* [*did*] *not normally use profanity but he* [*could*] *be devastatingly cutting* (Harper's).

**un|shod** (un shod′), *adj.* without shoes.

**un|shorn** (un shôrn′, -shōrn′), *adj.* not shorn; not sheared or clipped; unshaven: *an unshorn beard. The unshorn fields, boundless and beautiful ... The Prairies* (William Cullen Bryant).

**un|shown** (un shōn′), *adj.* not shown; not exhibited.

**un|shrink|a|ble** (un shring′kə bəl), *adj.* not shrinkable; not liable to shrink: *unshrinkable flannels.*

**un|shrink|ing** (un shring′king), *adj.* not shrinking: **a** not drawing up or contracting. **b** not drawing

---

**Pronunciation Key:** hat, āge, cãre, fär; let, ēqual, tėrm; it, īce; hot, ōpen, ôrder; **oi**l, **ou**t; cup, půt, rüle; **ch**ild; lo**ng**; **th**in; ᴛʜen; **zh**, measure; ə represents **a** in about, **e** in taken, **i** in pencil, **o** in lemon, **u** in circus.

back or recoiling; unflinching; firm. —**un|shrink'ing|ly**, *adv.*

**un|shriv|en** (un shriv'ən), *adj.* not shriven: *How about the souls unshriven, the infants unbaptized?* (Time).

**un|shroud** (un shroud'), *v.t.* to remove the shroud from; divest of something that shrouds; uncover; unveil.

**un|shunned** (un shund'), *adj.* not shunned; not avoided.

**un|shut** (un shut'), *v.t.*, **-shut**, **-shut|ting.** to open.

**un|shut|ter** (un shut'ər), *v.t.* to remove the shutters from; open the shutters of: *Merchants yesterday were beginning to unshutter their stores* (Wall Street Journal).

**un|sick|er** (un sik'ər), *adj. Scottish.* not to be counted on; uncertain; insecure.

**un|sift|ed** (un sif'tid), *adj.* **1** not sifted: *unsifted flour.* **2** *Figurative.* not critically examined; untried: *unsifted evidence.*

**un|sight** (un sīt'), *v., adj.* —*v.t.* to deprive of sight; make unable to see: *He is an impeccable jumper usually, and it is possible that he was unsighted* (London Times).
—***adj.*** without inspection or examination.
**unsight unseen,** (originally, *unsight, unseen*) without seeing or examining in advance; sight unseen: *Comtesse Cosel's diamonds, which certainly nobody will buy here unsight unseen* (Lord Chesterfield).

**un|sight|ed** (un sī'tid), *adj.* **1** not sighted or seen. **2** not furnished with, or not directed by means of, a sight or sights: *an unsighted firearm.*

**un|sight|li|ness** (un sīt'lē nis), *n.* the condition of being unsightly; disagreeableness to the sight; ugliness; deformity.

**un|sight|ly** (un sīt'lē), *adj.* ugly or unpleasant to look at: *an unsightly old shack. His cluttered room was an unsightly mess.* See syn. under **ugly.**

**un|signed** (un sīnd'), *adj.* not signed.

**un|sing|a|ble** (un sing'ə bəl), *adj.* not singable; not suited or adapted for being sung.

**un|sink|a|ble** (un sing'kə bəl), *adj.* not sinkable.

**un|sis|ter|ly** (un sis'tər lē), *adj.* not like a sister; unbecoming a sister.

**un|sized** (un sīzd'), *adj.* not sized; not coated or treated with size.

**un|skilled** (un skild'), *adj.* **1** not skilled; not trained; not expert: *unskilled in athletics.* **2** not involving or requiring skill: *unskilled labor.* **3** having no special skill; not trained in any craft, trade, or the like: *Unskilled workers usually earn less than skilled workers.*

**un|skill|ful** or **un|skil|ful** (un skil'fəl), *adj.* **1** displaying lack of skill; awkward; clumsy. **2** lacking in skill; unskilled. —**un|skill'ful|ly, un|skil'ful|ly,** *adv.* —**un|skill'ful|ness, un|skil'ful|ness,** *n.*

**un|slaked** (un slākt'), *adj.* **1** unsatisfied; unappeased: *unslaked thirst.* **2** not slaked: *unslaked lime.* **3** = unrelaxed.

**un|sleep|ing** (un slē'ping), *adj.* **1** not sleeping. **2** *Figurative.* ever wakeful.

**un|sling** (un sling'), *v.t.*, **-slung, -sling|ing. 1** to free from being slung, especially to make no longer slung across the shoulder or back: *to unsling a rifle.* **2** to remove the slings from (as a yard or cask) on a ship; release from the hoisting slings.

**un|slum** (un slum'), *v.t.*, **-slummed, -slum|ming.** to rebuild, renovate, or otherwise get rid of (a slum or slum buildings): [*She*] *blasts the urban renewal projects that would destroy the character of cherished neighborhoods in an effort to unslum them* (Saturday Review).

**un|slum|ber|ing** (un slum'bər ing), *adj.* never sleeping or slumbering; always watching or vigilant.

**un|smart** (un smärt'), *adj.* not clever, witty, or stylish; not smart.

**un|smil|ing** (un smī'ling), *adj.* not smiling; grave; serious. —**un|smil'ing|ly,** *adv.*

**un|smirched** (un smércht'), *adj.* not stained; not soiled or blacked; clean.

**un|snag** (un snag'), *v.t.*, **-snagged, -snag|ging.** to remove or release from a snag.

**un|snap** (un snap'), *v.t.*, **-snapped, -snap|ping.** to unfasten the snap or snaps of.

**un|snarl** (un snärl'), *v.t.* **1** to remove the snarls from. **2** *Figurative.* to straighten up (a confused or perplexing thing); untangle.

**un|soaped** (un sōpt'), *adj.* not soaped; unwashed: *The unsoaped of Ipswich brought up the rear* (Dickens).

**un|so|cia|bil|i|ty** (un'sō shə bil'ə tē), *n.* unsociable nature or behavior; lack of friendliness.

**un|so|cia|ble** (un sō'shə bəl), *adj.* **1** not sociable; not associating easily with others: *an unsociable hermit, an ill-tempered, unsociable old man.* **2** discouraging or repelling those who seek to be sociable: *unsociable behavior.* **3** incompatible: *very incongruous and unsociable ideas* (Samuel Johnson). —**un|so'cia|ble|ness,** *n.*

**un|so|cia|bly** (un sō'shə blē), *adv.* in an unsociable manner; with reserve.

**un|so|cial** (un sō'shəl), *adj.* not social; unsociable: *an unsocial, taciturn disposition* (Jane Austen). *He was now no longer gloomy and unsocial* (Samuel Johnson). —**un|so'cial|ly,** *adv.* —**un|so'cial|ness,** *n.*

**un|soft|ened** (un sôf'ənd, -sof'-), *adj.* not softened.

**un|soiled** (un soild'), *adj.* **1** not soiled; not smirched. **2** *Figurative.* unsullied; clean.

**un|sold** (un sōld'), *v.* the past tense and past participle of **unsell.**

**un|sol|der** (un sod'ər), *v.t.* **1** to separate (something joined by solder). **2** *Figurative.* to break up; divide; dissolve.

**un|so|lic|it|ed** (un'sə lis'ə tid), *adj.* not solicited; unasked; unsought: *spontaneous and unsolicited praise.*

**un|so|lic|i|tous** (un'sə lis'ə təs), *adj.* not solicitous; unconcerned; indifferent. —**un'so|lic'i|tous|ness,** *n.*

**un|sol|id** (un sol'id), *adj.* **1** not having the properties of a solid; liquid or gaseous. **2** *Figurative.* not sound, substantial, or firm; empty; weak; vain; ill-founded.

**un|solved** (un solvd'), *adj.* not solved, explained, or cleared up.

**un|son|sy** (un son'sē), *adj. Scottish.* **1** unlucky. **2** ill-omened. **3** not handsome; plain. [< *un-*[1] + *sonsy*]

**un|so|phis|ti|cate** (un'sə fis'tə kāt, -kit), *n.* an unsophisticated person.

**un|so|phis|ti|cat|ed** (un'sə fis'tə kā'tid), *adj.* not sophisticated; simple; natural; artless. **SYN:** naive. —**un'so|phis'ti|cat'ed|ness,** *n.*

**un|so|phis|ti|ca|tion** (un'sə fis'tə kā'shən), *n.* unsophisticated condition or quality; simplicity; artlessness. **SYN:** naturalness.

**un|sort|ed** (un sôr'tid), *adj.* **1** not sorted; not arranged or put in order; not assorted or classified. **2** *Obsolete.* ill-sorted; ill-chosen.

**un|sought** (un sôt'), *adj.* not sought; not looked for; not asked for; unsolicited: *unsought advice, an unsought compliment.*

**un|sound** (un sound'), *adj.* **1** not in good condition; not sound: *A diseased mind or body is unsound. Unsound walls are not firm. An unsound business is not reliable.* **2** not based on truth or fact; not valid: *an unsound doctrine, an unsound theory.* **3** not deep; not restful; disturbed: *an unsound sleep.* —**un|sound'ly,** *adv.* —**un|sound'ness,** *n.*

**un|span** (un span'), *v.t.*, **-spanned, -span|ning.** to remove (horses or other beasts of burden) from their traces; detach (an animal) from a vehicle: *An enthusiastic audience had unspanned the horses from a beloved singer's coach and had drawn it through the town themselves* (Isak Dinesen).

**un|spar|ing** (un spãr'ing), *adj.* **1** not sparing; very generous; lavish; liberal: *to distribute gifts with unsparing hand.* **SYN:** bountiful. **2** not merciful; severe; ruthless: *unsparing justice, to forgive others but be unsparing of oneself.* **SYN:** rigorous, unmerciful. —**un|spar'ing|ly,** *adv.* —**un|spar'ing|ness,** *n.*

**un|speak** (un spēk'), *v.t.*, **-spoke, -spo|ken, -speak|ing.** to retract (a statement); unsay.

**un|speak|a|ble** (un spē'kə bəl), *adj.* **1** that cannot be expressed in words; indescribable: *unspeakable joy, an unspeakable loss.* **2** so bad that it is not spoken of; bad or objectionable beyond description: *unspeakable manners.* —**un|speak'a|ble|ness,** *n.*

**un|speak|a|bly** (un spē'kə blē), *adv.* in a manner or degree that cannot be expressed; beyond words; extremely: *unspeakably vile.* **SYN:** inexpressibly, unutterably.

**un|speak|ing** (un spē'king), *adj.* not speaking; lacking power of speech.

**un|spe|cif|ic** (un'spi sif'ik), *adj.* not specific; indefinite; vague.

**un|spec|i|fied** (un spes'ə fīd), *adj.* not specified; not specifically or definitely named or stated: *an unspecified wage.*

**un|spec|tac|u|lar** (un'spek tak'yə lər), *adj.* not spectacular; modest: *The Council of Europe has provided a broad European forum where many far-reaching if unspectacular achievements have been hammered out* (Bulletin of Atomic Scientists). —**un'spec|tac'u|lar|ly,** *adv.*

**un|spent** (un spent'), *adj.* not spent; not expended; not used up or exhausted; still active or effective.

**un|sphere** (un sfir'), *v.t.*, **-sphered, -spher|ing.** to remove (as a star or spirit) from its place or realm of existence: *to unsphere the stars* (Shakespeare).

**un|spilled** (un spild'), *adj.* not spilled; not shed.

**un|spilt** (un spilt'), *adj.* = unspilled.

**un|spir|i|tu|al** (un spir'ə chù əl), *adj.* not spiritual; carnal; worldly.

**un|spoiled** (un spoild'), *adj.* **1** not ruined or marred. **2** not impaired in character, or deprived of the original or natural excellences, as by excessive indulgence.

**un|spoke** (un spōk'), *v.* the past tense of **unspeak.**

**un|spo|ken** (un spō'kən), *adj., v.* —***adj.*** not spoken; unuttered.
—***v.*** the past participle of **unspeak.**

**un|sport|ing** (un spôr'ting, -spōr'-), *adj.* not sporting; unsportsmanlike: *He was not a nice man; he had beaten Inchcape Jones at tennis, with a nasty, unsporting serve* (Sinclair Lewis). —**un|sport'ing|ly,** *adv.*

**un|sports|man|like** (un spôrts'mən līk', -spōrts'-), *adj.* not sportsmanlike; unbefitting a sportsman; not fair or honorable.

**un|spot|ted** (un spot'id), *adj.* **1** without moral stain; pure; unblemished: *an unspotted reputation.* **2** having no spots.

**un|sprung** (un sprung'), *adj.* **1** not sprung: *an unsprung trap.* **2** having no springs: *an unsprung wagon.* **3** *Obsolete.* not sprouted: *unsprung seed.*

**un|squared** (un skwãrd'), *adj.* not squared.

**un|sta|ble** (un stā'bəl), *adj.* **1** not stable; not firmly fixed: **a** easily moved or shaken; likely to break down: *an unstable mind.* **SYN:** unsettled. **b** easily overthrown: *an unstable government.* **SYN:** unsettled. **2** not firm or solid; insecure: *unstable footing.* **3** somewhat precarious; unsteady: *an unstable equilibrium.* **4** not constant; apt to change or alter; variable; wavering: *unstable hopes, an unstable nature.* **SYN:** fickle. **5** easily decomposed; readily changing into other compounds, or into elements: *an unstable chemical compound.* **6** capable of decay; radioactive: *an unstable nuclear particle.* —**un|sta'ble|ness,** *n.* —**un|sta'bly,** *adv.*

**unstable element,** *Chemistry.* an element which decomposes because of its radioactive nature; a radioactive element which changes into a radioactive isotope.

**un|stack** (un stak'), *v.t.* to bring out of a stacked condition; take a stack of (something) down or apart: *to unstack hay.*

**un|stained** (un stānd'), *adj.* **1** not stained; without stain or spot. **2** *Figurative.* unsullied; stainless.

**un|stamped** (un stampt'), *adj.* not stamped; not bearing a stamp.

**un|stand|ard|ized** (un stan'dər dīzd), *adj.* not standardized.

**un|state** (un stāt'), *v.t.*, **-stat|ed, -stat|ing. 1** to deprive of rank or status. **2** to deprive of the character of a state.

**un|states|man|like** (un stāts'mən līk'), *adj.* not statesmanlike; unlike or unbefitting a statesman.

**un|stead|fast** (un sted'fast, -fäst), *adj.* **1** not steadfast; not firmly fixed. **2** not firm, as in purpose, resolution, or faith; inconstant; irresolute. —**un|stead'fast|ly,** *adv.* —**un|stead'fast|ness,** *n.*

**un|stead|i|ly** (un sted'ə lē), *adv.* in an unsteady manner; without steadiness.

**un|stead|i|ness** (un sted'ē nis), *n.* the state or character of being unsteady.

**un|stead|y** (un sted'ē), *adj.*, **-stead|i|er, -stead|i|est,** *v.*, **-stead|ied, -stead|y|ing.** —***adj.*** **1** not steady; shaky: *an unsteady voice, an unsteady flame.* **2** likely to change; not reliable: *an unsteady mind, unsteady winds.* **3** not regular in habits.
—***v.t.*** to deprive of steadiness; make unsteady: *I was quite unsteadied by all that had fallen out* (Robert Louis Stevenson).

**un|steel** (un stēl'), *v.t.* to soften: *Why then should this enervating pity unsteel my foolish heart?* (Samuel Richardson).

**un|step** (un step'), *v.t.*, **-stepped, -step|ping.** to remove (a mast, especially a lower mast) from its step.

**un|stick** (un stik'), *v.t.*, **-stuck, -stick|ing.** to make no longer stuck; loosen or free (that which is stuck).

**un|stiff|en** (un stif'ən), *v.t.* to remove the stiffness from; make limber again; loosen up.

**un|stint|ed** (un stin'tid), *adj.* not stinted; plentiful. —**un|stint'ed|ly,** *adv.*

**un|stint|ing** (un stin'ting), *adj.* ungrudging; lavish; liberal: *The critics were unstinting in their praise of the youthful conductor* (New York Times). —**un|stint'ing|ly,** *adv.*

**un|stock|inged** (un stok'ingd), *adj.* not wearing stockings.

**un|stop** (un stop'), *v.t.*, **-stopped, -stop|ping. 1** to remove the stopper from (a bottle or other container or tube); uncork. **2** to free from any obstruction; open: *The ears of the deaf shall be unstopped* (Isaiah 35:5). **3** to pull out a stop or stops of (an organ).

**un|stop|pa|ble** (un stop'ə bəl), *adj.* that cannot be stopped: *The opening words of the chairman for the day were drowned by ... an apparently unstoppable record player* (Sunday Times).

**un|stop|pa|bly** (un stop'ə blē), *adv.* in an unstoppable manner.

**un|stop|per** (un stop'ər), *v.t.* **1** to remove the

stopper from; uncork: *There, on the dressing table, was an abandoned glass of brandy, an unstoppered bottle of cologne* (New Yorker). **2** to free from any obstruction.

**un|sto|ried** (un stôr′ēd, -stōr′-), *adj.* not yet celebrated in story or history: *To the land vaguely realizing westward, But still unstoried, artless, unenhanced* (Robert Frost).

**un|strained** (un strānd′), *adj.* **1** not under strain or tension; not forced; natural. **2** not separated or cleared by straining.

**un|strap** (un strap′), *v.t.,* **-strapped, -strap|ping.** to take off or loosen the strap or straps of (a trunk, box, or other container).

**un|strat|i|fied** (un strat′ə fīd), *adj.* not deposited in strata: *unstratified rock.*

**un|stressed** (un strest′), *adj.* not stressed; unaccented. In *upward,* the second syllable is unstressed.

**un|stri|at|ed** (un strī′ā tid), *adj.* not striated; nonstriated: *unstriated muscle.*

**un|strik|a|ble** (un strī′kə bəl), *adj.* that cannot be legally subjected to a strike by workers: *The government speedily passed legislation declaring certain services such as the courts and the cable office to be essential and therefore unstrikable* (C. G. Lindo).

**un|string** (un string′), *v.t.,* **-strung, -string|ing.** **1** to take off or loosen the string or strings of: *to unstring a guitar.* **2** to take from a string: *to unstring pearls.* **3** *Figurative.* to weaken the nerves of; make nervous: *I'm told getting married unstrings some men* (Owen Wister).

**un|striped** (un strīpt′), *adj.* not striped; nonstriated, as muscular tissue.

**un|struc|tured** (un struk′chərd), *adj.* not structured or organized; lacking a definite structure: *Discussions were unstructured* (Science News Letter).

**un|strung** (un strung′), *adj., v.* —*adj.* **1** with strings loose, broken, or missing: *an unstrung guitar.* **2** *Figurative.* weakened in the nerves; nervous. **SYN:** upset, shaken. —*v.* the past tense and past participle of **unstring.**

**un|stuck** (un stuk′), *v.* the past tense and past participle of **unstick.**

**un|stud|ied** (un stud′ēd), *adj.* **1** not labored or artificial; natural: *simple and unstudied manners.* **2** not an object of study; not studied. **3** not having studied; unversed (in): *unstudied in Latin. I ... was not unstudied in those authors which are most commended* (Milton).

**un|stuffed** (un stuft′), *adj.* not stuffed; not crowded.

**un|sub|dued** (un′səb düd′, -dyüd′), *adj.* not subdued; unconquered.

**un|sub|mis|sive** (un′səb mis′iv), *adj.* not submissive; unyielding. —**un′sub|mis′sive|ly,** *adv.* —**un′sub|mis′sive|ness,** *n.*

**un|sub|stan|tial** (un′səb stan′shəl), *adj.* **1** not based or founded on fact; flimsy; slight; unreal: *these deep but unsubtantial meditations* (Edward Gibbon). *Nor build on unsubstantial hope thy trust* (Robert Southey). **2** lacking in substance: *a rather unsubstantial meal.* **3** not of a material substance; intangible: *to man's purer unsubstantial part* (Robert Bridges). —**un′sub|stan′tial|ly,** *adv.*

**un|sub|stan|ti|al|i|ty** (un′səb stan′shē al′ə tē), *n., pl.* **-ties.** **1** the condition or quality of being unsubstantial. **2** an unsubstantial or illusive thing.

**un|sub|stan|ti|at|ed** (un′səb stan′shē ā′tid), *adj.* not substantiated; not established by evidence: *an unsubstantiated statement.*

**un|sub|stan|ti|a|tion** (un′səb stan′shē ā′shən), *n.* the act or fact of depriving of substantiality.

**un|sub|tle** (un sut′əl), *adj.* not subtle; coarse; blunt: *He was rugged, unsubtle, passionately sincere and consistent; a headstrong dynamic man of narrow vision and inflexible purpose* (Manchester Guardian Weekly).

**un|sub|tly** (un sut′lē), *adv.* coarsely; bluntly: *[He] has developed his unsubtly sensational theme into a big, slick composition* (Time).

**un|suc|cess** (un′sək ses′), *n.* lack of success; failure.

**un|suc|cess|ful** (un′sək ses′fəl), *adj.* **1** not fortunate or successful; having no success: *an unsuccessful businessman, an unsuccessful show. Their marriage was unsuccessful.* **2** useless; ineffectual; futile: *The attempts to save the victim's life were unsuccessful.* **SYN:** unavailing. —**un′suc|cess′ful|ly,** *adv.* —**un′suc|cess′ful|ness,** *n.*

**un|suf|fer|a|ble** (un suf′ər ə bəl), *adj. Obsolete.* insufferable; intolerable.

**un|suit|a|bil|i|ty** (un′sü tə bil′ə tē), *n.* the quality or state of being unsuitable; unfitness, inappropriateness.

**un|suit|a|ble** (un sü′tə bəl), *adj.* not suitable; unfit; inappropriate: *She danced in a highly unsuitable manner* (New Yorker). **SYN:** incongruous. —**un|suit′a|ble|ness,** *n.*

**un|suit|a|bly** (un sü′tə blē), *adv.* in an unsuitable manner.

**un|suit|ed** (un sü′tid), *adj.* not suited; unfit: *That shy dog is unsuited for a family with children.*

**un|sul|lied** (un sul′ēd), *adj.* not sullied; unsoiled; spotless; stainless; pure; untarnished: (*Figurative.*) *The intransigents risked the destruction of the Church in order to keep doctrine unsullied* (Manchester Guardian Weekly).

**un|sung** (un sung′), *adj.* **1** not sung: *an unsung note.* **2** *Figurative.* not honored or celebrated, especially by song or poetry: *unsung heroes. Here ... not a mountain rears its head unsung* (Thomas Carlyle).

**un|sunned** (un sund′), *adj.* **1** not exposed to the sun; not lighted by the sun; dark. **2** *Figurative.* not cheered; gloomy.

**un|sup|port|a|ble** (un′sə pôr′tə bəl, -pōr′-), *adj.* = insupportable.

**un|sup|port|ed** (un′sə pôr′tid, -pōr′-), *adj.* not supported; not upheld; not sustained; not maintained; not countenanced; not aided.

**un|sup|pressed** (un′sə prest′), *adj.* not suppressed; not held or kept under; not subdued; not quelled; not put down: *unsuppressed laughter, unsuppressed rebellion.*

**un|sure** (un shůr′), *adj.,* **-sur|er, -sur|est.** not sure; uncertain: *What's to come is still unsure* (Shakespeare). —**un|sure′ly,** *adv.* —**un|sure′ness,** *n.*

**un|sur|mount|a|ble** (un′sər moun′tə bəl), *adj.* = insurmountable.

**un|sur|pass|a|ble** (un′sər pas′ə bəl, -päs′-), *adj.* not surpassable; that cannot be surpassed.

**un|sur|pass|a|bly** (un′sər pas′ə blē, -päs′-), *adv.* in an unsurpassable manner or degree; so as not to be surpassed: *At his worst, he is unsurpassably tedious* (Observer).

**un|sur|passed** (un′sər past′, -päst′), *adj.* not or never surpassed; unexcelled: *As a chamber group they [the Budapest String Quartet] stand unsurpassed* (New Yorker).

**un|sur|pris|ing** (un′sər prī′zing), *adj.* not surprising; expected: *An unsurprising feature of the special new volume: 5,300 of the distinguished women declined to tell their ages* (Newsweek). —**un′sur|pris′ing|ly,** *adv.*

**un|sus|cep|ti|ble** (un′sə sep′tə bəl), *adj.* not susceptible; unimpressionable.

**un|sus|pect|ed** (un′sə spek′tid), *adj.* **1** not suspected; clear of or not under suspicion: *an imperious old dame, not unsuspected of witchcraft* (Hawthorne). **2** not thought of; not imagined to exist: *an unsuspected danger.* **3** not surmised. —**un′sus|pect′ed|ly,** *adv.*

**un|sus|pect|ing** (un′sə spek′ting), *adj.* not suspecting; having no suspicion; unsuspicious: *the unsuspecting victim.* —**un′sus|pect′ing|ly,** *adv.* —**un′sus|pect′ing|ness,** *n.*

**un|sus|pi|cious** (un′sə spish′əs), *adj.* **1** not suspicious; without suspicion; unsuspecting: *to visit them openly as if unsuspicious of any hostile design* (Francis Parkman). **2** not inclined to suspicion or distrust: *an unsuspicious nature.* **3** not such as to excite suspicion. —**un′sus|pi′cious|ly,** *adv.* —**un′sus|pi′cious|ness,** *n.*

**un|sus|tain|a|ble** (un′sə stā′nə bəl), *adj.* not sustainable; not to be supported, maintained, upheld, or corroborated.

**un|sus|tained** (un′sə stānd′), *adj.* not sustained; not maintained; not upheld.

**un|swathe** (un swāŧʜ′), *v.t.,* **-swathed, -swath|ing.** to divest of that which swathes or covers; unwrap.

**un|sway|a|ble** (un swā′ə bəl), *adj.* not to be swayed or influenced.

**un|swayed** (un swād′), *adj.* not swayed.

**un|swear** (un swãr′), *v.t., v.i.,* **-swore, -sworn, -swear|ing.** to retract (something sworn or asserted); abjure; recant.

**un|sweet|ened** (un swē′tənd), *adj.* not sweetened.

**un|swept** (un swept′), *adj.* not swept.

**un|swerv|ing** (un swėr′ving), *adj.* **1** not swerving; undeviating. **2** *Figurative.* unwavering; firm. —**un|swerv′ing|ly,** *adv.*

**un|sworn** (un swôrn′, -swōrn′), *adj., v.* —*adj.* **1** not bound by an oath; not having taken an oath: *an unsworn witness.* **2** not solemnly pronounced or taken. —*v.* the past participle of **unswear.**

**un|sym|met|ri|cal** (un′si met′rə kəl), *adj.* not symmetrical; lacking symmetry; asymmetrical. —**un′sym|met′ri|cal|ly,** *adv.*

**un|sym|me|try** (un sim′ə trē), *n.* lack of symmetry.

**un|sym|pa|thet|ic** (un′sim pə thet′ik), *adj.* not sympathetic; without sympathy. —**un′sym|pa|thet′i|cal|ly,** *adv.*

**un|sym|pa|thiz|ing** (un sim′pə thī′zing), *adj.* not sympathizing; unsympathetic.

**un|sym|pa|thy** (un sim′pə thē), *n.* lack of sympathy.

**un|sys|tem|at|ic** (un′sis tə mat′ik), *adj.* not systematic; without system; not methodical. —**un′sys|tem|at′i|cal|ly,** *adv.*

**un|tack** (un tak′), *v.t.* to unfasten (something tacked); loose or detach by removing a tack or tacks.

**un|taint|ed** (un tān′tid), *adj.* not tainted; free from taint.

**un|tak|en** (un tā′kən), *adj.* not taken.

**un|tal|ent|ed** (un tal′ən tid), *adj.* not talented; not gifted; not accomplished or clever.

**un|talked-of** (un tôkt′ov′, -uv′), *adj.* not talked or spoken about; not made the subject of talk.

**un|tam|a|ble** or **un|tame|a|ble** (un tā′mə bəl), *adj.* not tamable; tameless: (*Figurative.*) *an untamable tongue.* —**un|tam′a|ble|ness, un|tame′a|ble|ness,** *n.*

**un|tame** (un tām′), *adj.,* **-tam|er, -tam|est.** not tame; wild.

**un|tamed** (un tāmd′), *adj.* **1** not tamed; not domesticated: *the untamed beauty of mountains.* **2** = unsubdued.

**un|tan|gle** (un tang′gəl), *v.t.,* **-gled, -gling.** **1** to take the tangles out of; disentangle. **2** *Figurative.* to straighten out or clear up (anything confused or perplexing).

**un|tanned** (un tand′), *adj.* not tanned.

**un|tar|nished** (un tär′nisht), *adj.* **1** not tarnished; of unimpaired luster. **2** *Figurative.* unstained or unsullied.

**un|tast|ed** (un tās′tid), *adj.* not tasted.

**un|taught** (un tôt′), *adj., v.* —*adj.* **1** not taught; not educated: *an untaught child.* **2** known without being taught; learned naturally: *untaught wisdom. That untaught innate philosophy* (Byron). —*v.* the past tense and past participle of **unteach.**

**un|taxed** (un takst′), *adj.* not taxed; exempt from taxation.

**un|teach** (un tēch′), *v.t.,* **-taught, -teach|ing.** **1** to cause (a person) to forget or discard previous knowledge. **2** to remove from the mind (something known or taught) by different teaching.

**un|teach|a|ble** (un tē′chə bəl), *adj.* not teachable; indocile. —**un|teach′a|ble|ness,** *n.*

**un|tech|ni|cal** (un tek′nə kəl), *adj.* not technical.

**un|tem|pered** (un tem′pərd), *adj.* not tempered: *untempered steel,* (*Figurative.*) *untempered behavior.*

**un|ten|a|ble** (un ten′ə bəl), *adj.* not tenable; indefensible: (*Figurative.*) *the untenable proposition that London is as hot as Calcutta* (Thackeray). —**un|ten′a|ble|ness,** *n.*

**un|ten|ant|ed** (un ten′ən tid), *adj.* not tenanted; not occupied by a tenant.

**un|ten|der** (un ten′dər), *adj.* not tender; unfeeling: *So young, and so untender?* (Shakespeare).

**un|tent|ed** (un ten′tid), *adj. Archaic.* not probed or dressed: *an untented wound.* [< *un-*[1] + *tent*[2] in obsolete sense "to probe" + *-ed*[2]]

**Un|ter|mensch** (ůn′tər mensh′), *n., pl.* **-men|schen** (-men′shən). *German.* a person regarded as less than human; a subhuman: *Only a century ago, the workers were widely regarded as Untermenschen, subspecies fortunate to live in their hovels, to eat bread and enjoy long hours in foul mines, mills and factories* (Punch).

**un|test|ed** (un tes′tid), *adj.* not tested; untried.

**un|teth|er** (un teŧʜ′ər), *v.t.* to loose from a tether.

**un|thanked** (un thangkt′), *adj.* **1** not thanked; not repaid with acknowledgments. **2** not received with thankfulness.

**un|thank|ful** (un thangk′fəl), *adj.* **1** = ungrateful. **2** not appreciated; thankless: *One of the most unthankful offices in the world* (Oliver Goldsmith). —**un|thank′ful|ly,** *adv.* —**un|thank′ful|ness,** *n.*

**un|think** (un thingk′), *v.,* **-thought, -think|ing.** —*v.t.* to put out of the mind: *to unthink unpleasant thoughts.* —*v.i.* to end or reverse one's thoughts or ideas: *to learn to unthink as well as to think.*

**un|think|a|bil|i|ty** (un′thing kə bil′ə tē), *n.* the quality or condition of being unthinkable: *Genuine determinism occupies a totally different ground; not the impotence but the unthinkability of free will is what it affirms* (William James).

**un|think|a|ble** (un thing′kə bəl), *adj., n.* —*adj.* **1** not thinkable; that cannot be imagined; inconceivable: *the unthinkable infinitude of time* (George Bernard Shaw). **2** not to be thought of or considered: *All wars are really unthinkable till you're in the middle of them* (John Buchan). —*n.* something unthinkable: *In the present crisis a delicate course has to be steered between two unthinkables* (New York Times).

**un|think|a|bly** (un thing′kə blē), *adv.* unimaginably; inconceivably: *... this recollecting of things utterly and unthinkably past* (Shirley Hazzard).

**Pronunciation Key:** hat, āge, cãre, fär; let, ēqual, tėrm; it, īce; hot, ōpen, ôrder; oil, out; cup, pův, rüle; **ch**ild; lo**ng**; **th**in; **ŧʜ**en; **zh**, measure; **ə** represents **a** in about, **e** in taken, **i** in pencil, **o** in lemon, **u** in circus.

**un|think|ing** (un thing′king), *adj.* **1** not thinking; thoughtless; careless; heedless: *a pert unthinking coxcomb* (Tobias Smollett). **2** showing little or no thought: *blind, unthinking anger.* **3** not having the faculty of thought; unable to think. —**un|think′ing|ly**, *adv.*

**un|thought** (un thôt′), *adj., v.* —*adj.* not thought; not conceived or considered.
—*v.* the past tense and past participle of **unthink**.

**un|thought-of** (un thôt′ov′, -uv′), *adj.* not imagined or considered.

**un|thread** (un thred′), *v.t.* **1** to take the thread out of: *to unthread a needle.* **2** to unravel: (*Figurative.*) *Who can ... unthread the rich texture of Nature and Poetry?* (Charles Lamb). **3** *Figurative.* to find one's way through.

**un|thrift** (un thrift′), *n., adj.* —*n.* **1** lack of thrift. **2** a thriftless person.
—*adj. Archaic.* unthrifty: *this mad, unthrift world* (James Russell Lowell).

**un|thrift|y** (un thrif′tē), *adj.,* **-thrift|i|er, -thrift|i|est. 1** wasteful; lavish. **2** not thriving or flourishing; lacking vigor or promise in growth: *a border of unthrifty grass* (Hawthorne). *Moderate infestations cause sheep to be unthrifty and subject to other diseases* (Tracy I. Storer). —**un|thrift′i|ly**, *adv.* —**un|thrift′i|ness**, *n.*

**un|throne** (un thrōn′), *v.t.,* **-throned, -thron|ing.** to depose; dethrone.

**un|ti|di|ly** (un tī′də lē), *adv.* in an untidy manner.

**un|ti|di|ness** (un tī′dē nis), *n.* the character or condition of being untidy; lack of neatness; slovenliness.

**un|ti|dy** (un tī′dē), *adj.,* **-di|er, -di|est.** not neat; not in order; in disorder: *an untidy house.* **SYN:** disorderly, slovenly, littered.

**un|tie** (un tī′), *v.,* **-tied, -ty|ing.** —*v.t.* **1** to loosen; unfasten; undo; unbind: *to untie a knot. She was untying bundles.* **2** to make free; release: *to untie a horse.* **3** *Figurative.* to make clear; explain (a problem). **4** *Figurative.* to clear away (a difficulty); resolve (a dispute).
—*v.i.* to become, or be able to be, untied.
[Old English *untīgan* < *un-* un-[2] + *tīgan* to tie]

**un|tied** (un tīd′), *adj.* **1** not tied; free from any fastening or bond. **2** *Obsolete.* morally unrestrained; dissolute.

**un|til** (ən til′, un-), *prep., conj.* —*prep.* **1** up to the time of: *It was cold from November until April.* **2** before: *not to rest until victory. She did not leave until morning.*
—*conj.* **1** up to the time when: *He waited until the sun had set.* **2** before: *He did not come until the meeting was half over.* **3** to the degree or place that: *She worked until she was too tired to do more.*
[Middle English *untill* < *un-* up to (see etym. under **unto**) + *till*[1]]
▶ See **till**[1] for usage note.

**un|till|a|ble** (un til′ə bəl), *adj.* that cannot be tilled or cultivated.

**un|tilled** (un tild′), *adj.* not tilled or cultivated: *Most will come home to partially or totally destroyed villages, to weed-grown, untilled fields* (Time).

**un|time|li|ness** (un tīm′lē nis), *n.* the character of being untimely; unseasonableness: *the untimeliness of temporal death* (Jeremy Taylor).

**un|time|ly** (un tīm′lē), *adj.,* **-li|er, -li|est,** *adv.* —*adj.* **1** at a wrong time or season; unseasonable: *an untimely refusal. Snow in May is untimely.* **2** too early or too young; too soon: *to die at the untimely age of 18.*
—*adv.* too early or young; too soon: *His death came untimely at 18.*

**un|time|ous** (un tī′məs), *adj. Scottish.* untimely; unseasonable.

**un|tim|ous** (un tī′məs), *adj. Scottish.* untimeous.

**un|tinged** (un tinjd′), *adj.* **1** not tinged; not stained; not discolored. **2** not infected.

**un|tipped**[1] (un tipt′), *adj.* not furnished with a tip: *an untipped cane, untipped cigarettes.*

**un|tipped**[2] (un tipt′), *adj.* not presented with a gratuity.

**un|tired** (un tīrd′), *adj.* not tired; not exhausted.

**un|tir|ing** (un tīr′ing), *adj.* tireless; unwearying: *untiring energy, an untiring runner, untiring efforts to succeed.* **SYN:** indefatigable. —**un|tir′ing|ly**, *adv.*

**un|ti|tled** (un tī′təld), *adj.* **1** having no title; not named: *an untitled piece of music.* **2** not distinguished by a title: *an untitled nobleman.* **3** not of titled rank: *the gentry and other untitled classes.* **4** lacking lawful right; not entitled (to rule): *an untitled tyrant* (Shakespeare).

**un|to** (un′tü; *before consonants often* un′tə), *prep.* to: *The soldier was faithful unto death. Not even continents can live unto themselves* (New York Times). [Middle English *unto* < *un-* up to (< Scandinavian; compare Old Icelandic *und*) + *to* to]

**un|told** (un tōld′), *adj.* **1** not told; not revealed: *an untold secret, untold heroism.* **2** too many or too much to be counted; innumerable; countless: *to spend untold millions. There are untold stars in the sky.* **3** very great; immense: *untold wealth. Wars do untold damage.*

**un|torn** (un tôrn′, -tōrn′), *adj.* not torn; not rent or forced asunder.

**un|touch|a|bil|i|ty** (un′tuch ə bil′ə tē), *n.* **1** untouchable quality or condition. **2** the condition or character of being an untouchable.

**un|touch|a|ble** (un tuch′ə bəl), *adj., n.* —*adj.* **1** that cannot be touched, especially: **a** not composed of a material substance; not tangible; immaterial. **b** out of reach; unattainable. **c** *Figurative.* unique of its kind; unparalleled. **2** that must not be touched, especially: **a** that defiles if touched, especially if eaten or drunk. **b** that is defiled by the touch of a human hand, foot, etc. **3** suffering from leprosy; leprous.
—*n.* **1** a Hindu belonging to the lowest caste in India, whose touch supposedly defiled members of higher castes. Strictly, untouchables are beneath caste. Under the constitution of the Republic of India discrimination is forbidden and the term has been replaced in official use by the phrase "Scheduled Caste." **2** any person divested of caste; outcaste. **3** *Figurative.* any person rejected by his social group; social outcast; pariah. **4** *Figurative.* a thing or idea that is troublesome or risky to deal with: *The President and his aides [were] preparing for the Herculean task of trying to cut back that political untouchable known as veterans benefits* (Wall Street Journal).

**un|touched** (un tucht′), *adj.* not touched: *The cat left the milk untouched. The last topic remained untouched.* (*Figurative.*) *The miser was untouched by the poor man's story.*

**un|to|ward** (un tôrd′, -tōrd′; -tō′ərd), *adj.* **1** contrary to what is desired; not propitious; unfavorable: *an untoward wind, untoward weather.* **SYN:** inconvenient. **2** characterized as by misfortune or calamity; unlucky; unfortunate: *an untoward accident.* **3** difficult to manage, restrain, or control; perverse; stubborn; willful: *The untoward child made things difficult for her baby sitter.* **SYN:** intractable, refractory, contrary. **4** *Obsolete.* awkward; clumsy; ungraceful. [< *un-*[1] + *toward*] —**un|to′ward|ly**, *adv.* —**un|to′ward|ness**, *n.*

**un|trace|a|ble** (un trā′sə bəl), *adj.* that cannot be traced or followed.

**un|traced** (un trāst′), *adj.* **1** not traced; not followed. **2** not marked by footsteps. **3** not marked out.

**un|tracked** (un trakt′), *adj.* **1** not tracked; not marked by footsteps; pathless: *an untracked wilderness.* **2** not followed by tracking.

**un|tract|a|ble** (un trak′tə bəl), *adj.* **1** not tractable; intractable. **2** *Obsolete.* difficult; rough.

**un|trained** (un trānd′), *adj.* not trained; without discipline or education: *Babies have untrained minds.*

**un|tram|meled** (un tram′əld), *adj.* not hindered; not restrained; free. **SYN:** unimpeded.

**un|trans|fer|a|ble** (un′trans fėr′ə bəl), *adj.* that cannot be transferred or passed from one to another.

**un|trans|lat|a|ble** (un′trans lā′tə bəl), *adj.* **1** that cannot be translated. **2** not fit to be translated. —**un′trans|lat′a|bly**, *adv.*

**un|trans|lat|ed** (un′trans lā′tid), *adj.* not translated.

**un|trav|eled** (un trav′əld), *adj.* **1** not having traveled, especially to distant places; not having gained experience by travel. **2** not traveled through or over; not frequented by travelers: *an untraveled road.*

**un|trav|ers|a|ble** (un trav′ər sə bəl, -trə vėr′-), *adj.* not traversable.

**un|trav|ersed** (un trav′ərst, -trə vėrst′), *adj.* not traversed.

**un|tread** (un tred′), *v.t.,* **-trod, -trod|den** or **-trod, -tread|ing.** to retrace (one's steps).

**un|treat|a|ble** (un trē′tə bəl), *adj.* that cannot be treated; unsuitable for treatment: *Difficult to detect, the condition used to be untreatable, and usually caused death before age 20* (Time).

**un|tried** (un trīd′), *adj.* **1** not tried or proven by use; not tested: *an untried plan. What is conservatism? Is it not adherence to the old and tried, against the new and untried?* (Abraham Lincoln). **2** without being given, or not yet given, a trial in court: *to condemn a man untried, an untried case.*

**un|trim** (un trim′), *v.t.,* **-trimmed, -trim|ming.** to deprive of trimming.

**un|trimmed** (un trimd′), *adj.* **1** not trimmed; not decorated with trimming. **2** not clipped or pruned: *his ... untrimmed hair and beard* (Scott).

**un|trod** (un trod′), *adj., v.* —*adj.* not trodden.
—*v.* the past tense and a past participle of **untread.**

**un|trod|den** (un trod′ən), *adj., v.* —*adj.* not trodden: *an untrodden forest.* (*Figurative.*) *Some untrodden region of my mind* (Keats).
—*v.* a past participle of **untread**.

**un|trou|bled** (un trub′əld), *adj.* not troubled; undisturbed; tranquil; calm.

**un|trou|ble|some** (un trub′əl səm), *adj.* not troublesome; giving no trouble: *The progress of industry is gradually affording other modes of investment almost as safe and untroublesome* (John Stuart Mill).

**un|true** (un trü′), *adj.,* **-tru|er, -tru|est. 1** not true to the facts; false; incorrect: *She attributes qualities and characteristics to them that are often obviously untrue* (Saturday Review). **2** not faithful; faithless; disloyal. **3** not true to a standard or rule; not exact; inaccurate: *Whose hand is feeble or his aim untrue* (William Cowper). **SYN:** inexact. [Old English *untrēowe* < *un-* un-[1] + *trēowe* true] —**un|true′ness**, *n.*

**un|tru|ly** (un trü′lē), *adv.* **1** in an untrue manner; incorrectly; falsely. **2** inexactly; not in a true course.

**un|truss** (un trus′), *v.t.* **1** to unfasten; loose from a truss. **2** = undress.

**un|trust|ful** (un trust′fəl), *adj.* **1** not trustworthy. **2** not trustful.

**un|trust|wor|thy** (un trust′wėr′ᴛʜē), *adj.* not trustworthy; unreliable: *He was both skillfully smooth and totally untrustworthy* (Newsweek). —**un|trust′wor′thi|ness**, *n.*

**un|trust|y** (un trus′tē), *adj.,* **-trust|i|er, -trust|i|est.** not trusty; not worthy of confidence; unfaithful.

**un|truth** (un trüth′), *n.* **1** lack of truth; falsity. **2** a lie; falsehood. **3** *Archaic.* lack of loyalty; faithlessness. [Old English *untrēowth* < *un-* un-[1] + *trēowth* truth]

**un|truth|ful** (un trüth′fəl), *adj.* **1** not truthful; contrary to the truth; untrue: *an untruthful rumor.* **2** not telling the truth: *an untruthful child.* —**un|truth′ful|ly**, *adv.* —**un|truth′ful|ness**, *n.*

**un|tuck** (un tuk′), *v.t.* to undo or free from being tucked up, under, or in.

**un|tuft|ed** (un tuf′tid), *adj.* without tufts or projecting bunches, as of scales or hairs.

**un|tun|a|ble** (un tü′nə bəl, -tyü′-), *adj.* **1** that cannot be tuned or brought to the proper pitch. **2** not harmonious; discordant; not musical.

**un|tune** (un tün′, -tyün′), *v.t.,* **-tuned, -tun|ing. 1** to make no longer in tune; render inharmonious. **2** *Figurative.* to disorder; upset; discompose.

**un|tuned** (un tünd′, -tyünd′), *adj.* not tuned.

**un|turned** (un tėrnd′), *adj.* not turned.

**un|tu|tored** (un tü′tərd, -tyü′-), *adj.* not tutored; not educated; untaught: *the untutored many* (Jeremy Bentham).

**un|twine** (un twīn′), *v.t., v.i.,* **-twined, -twin|ing.** = untwist.

**un|twist** (un twist′), *v.t.* to undo or loosen (something twisted); unravel: *He untwisted the tangled strands of the rope.*
—*v.i.* to become untwisted.

**un|urged** (un ėrjd′), *adj.* not urged; of one's own accord; unsolicited; voluntary.

**un|used** (un yüzd′ *for 1 and 2; for 3, before the word "to,"* un yüst′), *adj.* **1** not being used; not in use: *unused space, an unused room.* **2** never having been used; still new or clean: *unused drinking cups, an unused car.* **3** not accustomed: *The doctor's hands were unused to labor.*

**un|u|su|al** (un yü′zhü əl), *adj.* not usual; beyond the ordinary; not in common use; uncommon; rare. **SYN:** strange, singular. —**un|u′su|al|ness**, *n.*

**un|u|su|al|ly** (un yü′zhü ə lē), *adv.* in an unusual manner; uncommonly; rarely.

**un|ut|ter|a|ble** (un ut′ər ə bəl), *adj.* **1** that cannot be expressed in words; unspeakable; indescribable: *General nuclear war, apparently, signals unutterable destruction* (Bulletin of Atomic Scientists). **2** that cannot be pronounced; unpronounceable.

**un|ut|ter|a|bly** (un ut′ər ə blē), *adv.* in a way or to a degree that cannot be expressed or described in words; unspeakably.

**un|ut|tered** (un ut′ərd), *adj.* not uttered.

**un|vac|ci|nat|ed** (un vak′sə nā′tid), *adj.* **1** not vaccinated. **2** having never been successfully vaccinated.

**un|val|ued** (un val′yüd), *adj.* **1** not valued; not appraised. **2** not esteemed or prized. **3** *Obsolete.* that cannot be valued; of inestimable value: *thy unvalued book* (Milton).

**un|van|quished** (un vang′kwisht), *adj.* not conquered; not overcome.

**un|var|ied** (un vãr′ēd), *adj.* not varied; not diversified; not changed or altered.

**un|var|nished** (un vär′nisht), *adj.* **1** not varnished. **2** *Figurative.* plain; unadorned: *the unvarnished truth.*

**un|var|y|ing** (un vãr′ē ing), *adj.* not varying or changing; steady; constant; uniform. —**un|var′y|ing|ly**, *adv.*

**un|veil** (un vāl′), *v.t.* **1** to remove a veil from. **2** to remove any covering from; uncover: *to unveil a statue. The sun broke through the mist and unveiled the mountains.* **3** *Figurative.* to disclose; reveal: *to unveil a secret.* —*v.i.* to become unveiled; take off one's veil; reveal oneself: *The princess unveiled.*

**un|veil|ing** (un vā′ling), *n.* **1** the act or fact of uncovering or revealing; disclosure: *the unveiling of a secret, the unveiling of a new work of art.* **2** the act or ceremony of removing the covering from a statue or monument: *So heavy and persistent was the downpour that the unveiling had to be put off for an hour* (Manchester Guardian). **3** the removal of a veil.

**un|vent|ed** (un ven′tid), *adj.* not vented; not uttered; not opened for utterance or emission.

**un|ven|ti|lat|ed** (un ven′tə lā′tid), *adj.* not ventilated.

**un|ve|ra|cious** (un′və rā′shəs), *adj.* not veracious; untruthful.

**un|ve|rac|i|ty** (un′və ras′ə tē), *n.* lack of veracity; untruth; falsehood.

**un|ver|i|fi|a|ble** (un ver′ə fī′ə bəl), *adj.* not verifiable.

**un|ver|i|fied** (un ver′ə fīd), *adj.* not verified.

**un|versed** (un vėrst′), *adj.* not versed; unskilled.

**un|vexed** (un vekst′), *adj.* not vexed; not troubled; not disturbed; not agitated or disquieted: *A country life unvexed with anxious cares* (John Dryden).

**un|vi|o|lat|ed** (un vī′ə lā′tid), *adj.* **1** not violated; not injured. **2** not broken; not transgressed.

**un|vi|ti|at|ed** (un vish′ē ā′tid), *adj.* not vitiated; not corrupted; pure.

**un|vo|cal** (un vō′kəl), *adj.* **1** not vocal. **2** = taciturn.

**un|voice** (un vois′), *v.t.*, **-voiced, -voic|ing.** *Phonetics.* to stop the vibration of the vocal cords in pronouncing (a normally voiced sound); pronounce without voice: *The "z-" sound at the end of "news" is often unvoiced in the compound "newspaper".*

**un|voiced** (un voist′), *adj.* **1** not spoken; not expressed in words. **2** *Phonetics.* voiceless; devoiced: *"S" in "sit" and "f" in "fit" represent unvoiced sounds.*

**un|voic|ing** (un voi′sing), *n. Phonetics.* the act of stopping the vibration of the vocal cords in pronouncing a normally voiced sound.

**un|wak|ened** (un wā′kənd), *adj.* not wakened; not roused from sleep: (*Figurative.*) *unwakened passion.*

**un|war|i|ly** (un wãr′ə lē), *adv.* in an unwary manner; incautiously; unguardedly.

**un|war|i|ness** (un wãr′ē nis), *n.* the character or condition of being unwary.

**un|war|like** (un wôr′līk′), *adj.* **1** not fit for war; not military. **2** not used to war.

**un|warned** (un wôrnd′), *adj.* not warned; not cautioned.

**un|warped** (un wôrpt′), *adj.* **1** not warped. **2** unbiased; impartial.

**un|war|rant|a|ble** (un wôr′ən tə bəl, -wor′-), *adj.* **1** not justifiable or defensible; improper: *an unwarrantable conjecture.* **2** without legal warrant; not permitted; illegal. —**un|war′rant|a|ble|ness,** *n.* —**un|war′rant|a|bly,** *adv.*

**un|war|rant|ed** (un wôr′ən tid, -wor′-), *adj.* **1** not warranted; not assured or certain; not guaranteed as to fulfillment, reliability, or quality. **2** not authorized or justified: *unwarranted interference.* —**un|war′rant|ed|ly,** *adv.*

**un|war|y** (un wãr′ē), *adj.*, **-war|i|er, -war|i|est.** not wary; not cautious; careless; unguarded. **SYN:** indiscreet.

**un|washed** (un wosht′, -wôsht′), *adj., n.* —*adj.* **1** not washed; not cleansed by water. **2** not washed by waves or flowing water.
—*n.* **the (great) unwashed,** the lower classes of the people; rabble: *Gentlemen, there can be but little doubt that your ancestors were the great unwashed* (Thackeray).

**un|wast|ed** (un wās′tid), *adj.* **1** not wasted or lost by extravagance; not lavished away; not dissipated. **2** not consumed or diminished by time, violence, or other means. **3** not devastated; not laid waste. **4** not emaciated, as by illness.

**un|watch|ful** (un woch′fəl, -wôch′-), *adj.* not vigilant.

**un|wa|tered** (un wôt′ərd, -wot′-), *adj.* **1** freed from water; drained: *an unwatered mine.* **2** not watered; undiluted; unmoistened. **3** not supplied with water; not given water to drink.

**un|wa|ver|ing** (un wā′vər ing), *adj.* not wavering; steadfast; firm: *an unwavering line of conduct.* —**un|wa′ver|ing|ly,** *adv.*

**un|weak|ened** (un wē′kənd), *adj.* not weakened; not enfeebled.

**un|weaned** (un wēnd′), *adj.* **1** not weaned. **2** *Figurative.* not withdrawn or disengaged.

**un|wea|ried** (un wir′ēd), *adj.* **1** not weary; not tired. **2** never growing weary; indefatigable; tireless.

**un|wea|ry** (un wir′ē), *adj.*, **-ri|er, -ri|est,** *v.*, **-ried, -ry|ing.** —*adj.* not weary.
—*v.t.* to relieve of weariness; refresh after fatigue.

**un|wea|ry|ing** (un wir′ē ing), *adj.* not wearying; not growing weary or tired; untiring: *unwearying efforts.* —**un|wea′ry|ing|ly,** *adv.*

**un|weave** (un wēv′), *v.t.*, **-wove, -wo|ven, -weav|ing.** to undo, take apart, or separate (something woven); unravel.

**un|webbed** (un webd′), *adj.* **1** not webbed. **2** not web-footed.

**un|wed** (un wed′), *adj.* = unmarried.

**un|wed|ded** (un wed′id), *adj.* not wedded; unmarried.

**un|weed|ed** (un wē′did), *adj.* not weeded; not cleared of weeds.

**un|weighed** (un wād′), *adj.* **1** not weighed; not having the weight ascertained. **2** *Figurative.* not considered and examined; not pondered.

**un|weight** (un wāt′), *v.t.* to remove or reduce the weight from: *to unweight silk. He bounces, and unweights his skis* (New Yorker).

**un|wel|come** (un wel′kəm), *adj.* not welcome; not gladly received; not wanted: *The bees were unwelcome guests at our picnic.* —**un|wel′come|ly,** *adv.* —**un|wel′come|ness,** *n.*

**un|well** (un wel′), *adj.* not in good health; ailing; ill; sick.

**un|wept** (un wept′), *adj.* **1** not wept for; not mourned: *unwept, unhonour'd and unsung* (Scott). **2** not shed: *unwept tears.*

**un|whipped** (un hwipt′), *adj.* not whipped; not punished.

**un|whole|some** (un hōl′səm), *adj.* **1** not wholesome, especially: **a** not good for the body; not physically wholesome; unhealthful: *a damp, unwholesome climate. A diet consisting mainly of candy is unwholesome.* **b** not good for the mind or spirit; not morally wholesome: *unwholesome literature, unwholesome companions.* **2** not in good health; unhealthy. —**un|whole′some|ly,** *adv.* —**un|whole′some|ness,** *n.*

**un|wield|i|ly** (un wēl′də lē), *adv.* in an unwieldy manner; cumbrously.

**un|wield|i|ness** (un wēl′dē nis), *n.* the condition of being unwieldy.

**un|wield|y** (un wēl′dē), *adj.* **1** hard to handle or manage, because of size, shape, or weight; bulky and clumsy: *an unwieldy weapon. The armor worn by knights seems unwieldy to us today.* **SYN:** unmanageable, cumbersome. **2** not graceful; clumsy; awkward: *a fat, unwieldy man.*

**un|willed** (un wild′), *adj.* not intended; involuntary; unintentional.

**un|will|ing** (un wil′ing), *adj.* **1** not willing or ready; not consenting. **SYN:** reluctant, averse, loath. **2** not freely or willingly granted or done: *an unwilling acceptance of necessity. The unwilling admiration of his enemies* (Macaulay). **SYN:** reluctant, averse, loath. —**un|will′ing|ly,** *adv.* —**un|will′ing|ness,** *n.*

**un|wind** (un wīnd′), *v.*, **-wound, -wind|ing.** —*v.t.* **1** to wind off or uncoil; take from a spool, ball, or the like. **2** *Figurative.* to disentangle.
—*v.i.* **1** to become unwound. **2** *Figurative.* to relax: *To unwind from his work, Dykstra likes to raise flowers ... in the garden of his Georgian colonial home* (Time).
[Old English *unwindan* unwrap (clothes) < *un-* un-[2] + *windan* to wind]

**un|wink|ing** (un wing′king), *adj.* **1** not winking; not shutting the eyes. **2** *Figurative.* not ceasing to wake or watch; vigilant.

**un|wis|dom** (un wiz′dəm), *n.* absence of wisdom; foolishness; stupidity: *It appears that one officer present knew of the unwisdom of the course adopted, but he was so junior that he did not dare to tell his superiors about it* (Norbert Wiener).

**un|wise** (un wīz′), *adj.*, **-wis|er, -wis|est.** not wise; not showing good judgment; foolish: *It is unwise to delay going to the doctor if you are sick.* **SYN:** imprudent, indiscreet. [Old English *unwīs* < *un-* un-[1] + *wīs* wise] —**un|wise′ly,** *adv.*

**un|wish** (un wish′), *v.t.* **1** to take back or cancel (a wish). **2** to make or seek to make not existent by wishing.

**un|wished** (un wisht′), *adj.* not wished; undesired; unwelcome.

**un|wished-for** (un wisht′fôr′), *adj.* = unwished.

**un|with|ered** (un wiᴛʜ′ərd), *adj.* not withered or faded.

**un|with|er|ing** (un wiᴛʜ′ər ing), *adj.* not liable to wither or fade.

**un|wit|nessed** (un wit′nist), *adj.* not witnessed; not attested by witnesses; wanting testimony.

**un|wit|ting** (un wit′ing), *adj.* **1** not knowing; unaware; unconscious: *to be unwitting of danger.* **2** unintentional: *an unwitting insult.*

**un|wit|ting|ly** (un wit′ing lē), *adv.* not knowingly; unconsciously; not intentionally.

**un|wom|an|li|ness** (un wům′ən lē nis), *n.* unwomanly character or state.

**un|wom|an|ly** (un wům′ən lē), *adj.* not womanly; unbecoming in a woman; unfeminine: *a woman clad in unwomanly rags* (Thomas Hood).

**un|wont|ed** (un wōn′tid, -wun′-), *adj.* **1** not customary; not usual: *an unwonted task, unwonted anger. The unwonted jollity that brightened the faces of the people* (Hawthorne). **2** not accustomed; not used: *Then Juno ... from his unwonted hand received the goblet* (William Cowper). —**un|wont′ed|ly,** *adv.* —**un|wont′ed|ness,** *n.*

**un|wooed** (un wüd′), *adj.* not wooed.

**un|work|a|bil|i|ty** (un′wėr kə bil′ə tē), *n.* the quality or condition of being unworkable: *It may have taken a disaster to prove the unworkability of the scheme* (Wall Street Journal).

**un|work|a|ble** (un wėr′kə bəl), *adj.* **1** that cannot be worked. **2** unmanageable; impracticable: *an unworkable scheme.*

**un|worked** (un wėrkt′), *adj.* not worked; not developed or exploited, as a field of operations.

**un|work|ing** (un wėr′king), *adj.* not working; doing no work.

**un|work|man|like** (un wėrk′mən līk′), *adj.* not workmanlike; not like or befitting a workman.

**un|world|li|ness** (un wėrld′lē nis), *n.* the condition of being unworldly.

**un|world|ly** (un wėrld′lē), *adj.* **1** not caring much for the things of this world, such as money, pleasure, and power: *a gentle, unworldly clergyman.* **2** not of the world; spiritual; supernatural.

**un|worn** (un wôrn′, -wōrn′), *adj.* **1** not worn. **2** not impaired by wear.

**un|wor|shiped** or **un|wor|shipped** (un wėr′shipt), *adj.* not worshiped; not adored.

**un|wor|thi|ly** (un wėr′ᴛʜə lē), *adv.* **1** in a way that is not worthy or honorable; shamefully. **2** not according to one's merits.

**un|wor|thi|ness** (un wėr′ᴛʜē nis), *n.* the condition or character of being unworthy.

**un|wor|thy** (un wėr′ᴛʜē), *adj.*, **-thi|er, -thi|est,** *n., pl.* **-thies.** —*adj.* **1** not worthy; not deserving: *Such a silly story is unworthy of belief.* **2** not befitting or becoming; unsuitable; unfit; unbecoming: *a gift not unworthy of a king.* **3** deserving of contempt; base; shameful; dishonorable: *unworthy conduct.* **SYN:** ignoble, discreditable. **4** lacking value or merit; worthless.
—*n.* an unworthy person: *The worthies of England being your subject, you have mingled many unworthies among them* (Thomas Fuller).

**un|wound** (un wound′), *v.* the past tense and past participle of **unwind:** *Mother unwound the ball of string.*

**un|wound|ed** (un wün′did), *adj.* not wounded.

**un|wove** (un wōv′), *v.* the past tense of **unweave.**

**un|wo|ven** (un wō′vən), *v.* the past participle of **unweave.**

**un|wrap** (un rap′), *v.*, **-wrapped, -wrap|ping.**
—*v.t.* to remove the wrapping or wrappings from; open.
—*v.i.* to become opened.

**un|wreathe** (un rēᴛʜ′), *v.t.*, **-wreathed, -wreath|ing.** to bring out of a wreathed condition; untwist; untwine.

**un|wrin|kle** (un ring′kəl), *v.*, **-kled, -kling.** —*v.t.* to smooth the wrinkles from.
—*v.i.* to become smooth.

**un|writ|a|ble** (un rī′tə bəl), *adj.* that cannot be written; not suitable or fit for writing: *They insist that ... the nineteenth-century novel ... is impossible, over and done with, certainly unwritable, and maybe unreadable* (New Yorker).

**un|writ|ten** (un rit′ən), *adj.* **1** not written; oral; verbal: *an unwritten order.* **2** not yet written. **3** understood or customary, but not actually expressed in writing: *the unwritten code of a gentleman. Great Britain has an unwritten Constitution.* **4** not written on; blank.

**unwritten law, 1** law that is based on custom or on decisions of judges, rather than on written commands, decrees, statutes, and other written records; (English) common law. **2** the principle that a person who commits certain crimes, especially those which avenge personal or family honor, is entitled to lenient treatment.

**un|wrought** (un rôt′), *adj.* not wrought; not worked or elaborated into a finished product.

**un|wrung** (un rung′), *adj.* not pinched; not galled.

**un|yield|ing** (un yēl′ding), *adj.* not yielding; not giving in; firm; obstinate: *The crippled man learned to walk again because of his unyielding determination. Such is the unyielding nature of his reasoning* (Manchester Guardian). —**un|yield′ing|ly,** *adv.* —**un|yield′ing|ness,** *n.*

**un|yoke** (un yōk′), *v.*, **-yoked, -yok|ing.** —*v.t.* **1** to free from a yoke: *to unyoke oxen.* **2** to make separate; disconnect; disjoin.
—*v.i.* to remove a yoke.

**un|zeal|ous** (un zel′əs), *adj.* not zealous; destitute of zeal.

**Pronunciation Key:** hat, āge, cãre, fär; let, ēqual, tėrm; it, īce; hot, ōpen, ôrder; **oil, out;** cup, půt, rüle; **ch**ild; lo**ng**; **th**in; **ᴛʜ**en; **zh**, measure; **ə** represents **a** in about, **e** in taken, **i** in pencil, **o** in lemon, **u** in circus.

tute of fervor, ardor, or zeal.

**un|zip** (un zip′), *v.t., v.i.,* **-zipped, -zip|ping.** to open or unfasten a zipper or something held by a zipper: *He squatted on his tiny legs to unzip his overshoes* (Atlantic). *When unzipped, the case front drops open and makes the binoculars available for immediate use* (Science News Letter).

**U. of S. Afr.,** (formerly) Union of South Africa.

**uo|mo u|ni|ver|sa|le** (wō′mō ü′nē ver sä′lā), *Italian.* universal man.

**up** (up), *adv., prep., adj., n., v.,* **upped, up|ping.** —***adv.*** **1** from a lower to a higher place or condition; to, toward, or near the top: *The bird flew up.* **2** in a higher place or condition; on or at a higher level: *We stayed up in the mountains several days.* **3** from a smaller to a larger amount: *Prices have gone up.* **4** to or at any point, place, or condition that is considered higher: *He lives up north.* **5** above the horizon: *The sun came up.* **6** in or into an erect position: *Stand up.* **7** out of bed: *Please get up before you are too late.* **8** thoroughly; completely; entirely: *The house burned up.* **9** at an end; over: *Your time is up now.* **10** in action or into being: *Don't stir up trouble.* **11** together: *Add these up.* **12** to or in an even position; not behind: *to catch up in a race. Keep up with the times.* **13** in or into view, notice, or consideration: *to bring up a new topic.* **14** in or into a state as of tightness: *Shut the bird up in his cage.* **15** into storage or a safe place; aside; by: *Squirrels lay up nuts for the winter.* **16** at bat in baseball: *He went up four times in the game.* **17** apiece; for each one: *The score at the half was ten up.*

—***prep.*** **1** to a higher place on or at a higher place in: *The cat ran up the tree.* **2** to, toward, or near the top of: *They climbed up a hill.* **3** along; through: *She walked up the street.* **4** toward or in the inner or upper part of: *We sailed up the river. He lives up state.*

—***adj.*** **1** advanced; forward. **2** going or pointed upward: *an up trend.* **3** above the ground or horizon: *The sun is up. The wheat is up.* **4** out of bed: *On Christmas morning the children were up at dawn.* **5** to or in an even position; not behind. **6** near; close. **7** with much knowledge or skill. **8** at bat in baseball: *He was up four times in the game.* **9** ahead of an opponent by a certain number: *We are three games up.*

—***n.*** **1** an upward movement, course, or slope. **2** a piece of good luck. **3** *U.S. Slang.* upper (def. 3).

—***v.t.*** to put up: *They upped the price of eggs.*

**on the up and up, a** *Informal.* increasing; rising; improving: *Attendances and sales at recent exhibitions of the Royal Academy have been on the up and up* (London Times). **b** *Slang.* honest; legitimate: *"All my books are open and on the up and up," he declared* (New York Times).

**up against,** *Informal.* facing as a thing to be dealt with: *First, we are up against a dynamic opponent whose strident anti-Americanism will not soon die away* (New Yorker).

**up and doing,** busy; active: *If the Labor party's supporters had been up and doing, the party's losses would not have been so great* (New York Times).

**up and down,** here and there; at various points; in many or different places throughout an area: *There are many fine examples of reinforced concrete storage bunkers up and down the country* (London Times).

**up for, a** a candidate for: *to be up for senator, be up for reelection.* **b** on trial in a court of law for: *He is up for robbery.*

**up to, a** as far or as high as: *up to one's elbows in work.* **b** till; until: *up to the present day.* **c** reaching the limit of; fulfilling: *work not up to expectations.* **d** doing; about to do: *She is up to some mischief. This may be true of Cage's trick, for it loses its point once we know what he is up to* (New Yorker). **e** equal to; capable of doing: *up to a task. Do you feel up to going out so soon after being sick?* **f** plotting; scheming: *What are you up to?* **g** before (a person) as a duty or task to be done: *[The President] hasn't yet shown public concern about the dispute, but ultimately it may be up to him to determine the Government's policy* (Wall Street Journal).

[Old English *ūpp* and *uppe*]

**up-,** *prefix.* up, as in *upland, upkeep, uphold, upstart, upbeat, uplifted, upstanding, uprising.* [< Old English *ūp-*. See related etym. at **up.**]

**up.,** upper.

**u.p.,** under proof.

**UP** (no periods) or **U.P.,** (formerly) United Press. Now, **UPI** (no periods).

**U.P.,** Union Pacific Railroad.

**up-an|chor** (up′ang′kər), *v.i.* to weigh or heave up the anchor: *Once the cargo is on board the captain will up-anchor* (New York Times).

**up-and-com|er** (up′ən kum′ər), *n.* an up-and-coming person or thing: *The very best of the Beatles' music was an expression of sheer delight at being a tightly-knit group of attractive young up-and-comers* (Sunday Times).

**up-and-com|ing** (up′ən kum′ing), *adj.* **1** on the way to prominence or success; promising; active; alert; enterprising: *an up-and-coming singer or politician, a small but up-and-coming college. One reason up-and-coming riders are scarce is that the big stables aren't trying to develop them any more* (New Yorker). **2** gaining or rising in importance: *These three aluminum applications are among the more unusual of the jobs lately undertaken by this up-and-coming metal* (Wall Street Journal).

**up-and-down** (up′ən doun′), *adj.* **1a** occurring alternately upward and downward: *The flapping of an insect's wings is no mere up-and-down motion* (Scientific American). **b** alternately rising and falling; presenting variations comparable to movement up and down: *The upsurge in farmer benefits will be temporary ... since an up-and-down trend appears every time the act is extended to a new group* (Wall Street Journal). **2** perpendicular; erect: *up-and-down stripes.*

**U|pan|i|shad** (ü pan′ə shad), *n.* any one of a group of ancient Sanskrit Vedic philosophical commentaries. [< Sanskrit *upaniṣad* (literally) a sitting down near]

**U particle,** an elementary particle belonging to the same class as the electron and mu-meson, but having a mass twice as great as that of proton; a heavy lepton: *Among the exotic new particles found in collisions of electrons and positrons are the U particles ..., heavy members of the lepton family* (Science News). [< *U*(nknown)]

**u|pas** (yü′pəs), *n.* **1** a large, tropical Asian tree of the mulberry family, whose poisonous milky sap is used in making a poison for arrows. **2** the sap itself. **3** a climbing plant of Java, a variety of strychnos, whose poisonous sap is also used in making a poison for arrows. **4** its sap. [< Malay *upas* poison]

**up|bear** (up bãr′), *v.t.,* **-bore, -borne, -bear|ing.** to bear up; raise aloft; support; sustain: *When other actors faltered ... Julie upbore them* (Time). —**up|bear′er,** *n.*

**up|beat** (up′bēt′), *n., adj.* —***n.*** **1** *Music.* **a** an unaccented beat in a measure, especially one preceding a downbeat: *[He] began with the upbeat, an open-string quarter-note G, and I recognized the dearly familiar beginning of Opus 18, No. 4* (New Yorker). **b** the upward gesture of the conductor's hand to indicate this beat. **2** *Figurative.* an upswing; upturn; revival: *The economy lags behind last autumn's boom—but it's on the upbeat* (Wall Street Journal).

—***adj.*** **1** upward; rising: *an upbeat cycle, an upbeat mood.* **2** *Informal, Figurative.* hopeful; optimistic; buoyant: *a motion picture with an upbeat ending.*

**up|bind** (up bīnd′), *v.t.,* **-bound, -bind|ing.** to bind up.

**up|blaze** (up blāz′), *v.i.,* **-blazed, -blaz|ing.** to blaze up; shoot up, as a flame.

**up|blown** (up blōn′), *adj.* blown up; inflated; puffed up.

**up|bore** (up bôr′, -bōr′), *v.* the past tense of **upbear.**

**up|borne** (up bôrn′, -bōrn′), *adj., v.* —***adj.*** borne up; raised aloft; supported.

—***v.*** the past participle of **upbear.**

**up|bound¹** (up′bound′), *adj., adv.* upward bound; in an upward direction.

**up|bound²** (up bound′), *v.* the past tense and past participle of **upbind.**

**up-bow** (up′bō′), *n.* a stroke toward the handle or lower end of the bow in playing a violin, cello, or the like.

**up|braid** (up brād′), *v.t.* to find fault with; blame; reprove: *to upbraid a person for his errors. The captain upbraided the guards for falling asleep.* **SYN:** reproach, censure. See syn. under **scold.** [Old English *ūpbregdan* reproach (with) < *ūp-* up- + *bregdan* to weave, braid] —**up|braid′er,** *n.*

**up|braid|ing** (up brā′ding), *n., adj.* —***n.*** a severe reproof; scolding. —***adj.*** full of reproach; reproving. —**up|braid′ing|ly,** *adv.*

**up|brake** (up brāk′), *v. Archaic.* a past tense of **upbreak.**

**up|break** (up brāk′), *v.,* **-broke** or (*Archaic*) **-brake, -bro|ken** or (*Archaic*) **-broke, -break|ing,** *n.* —***v.i.*** to break or force a way upward; come to the surface; appear.

—***n.*** a breaking or bursting up; an upburst.

**up|breathe** (up brēᴛʜ′), *v.t.,* **-breathed, -breath|ing.** *Obsolete.* to breathe up or out; exhale.

**up|bred** (up bred′), *v.* the past tense and past participle of **upbreed.**

**up|breed** (up′brēd′), *v.t.,* **-bred, -breed|ing.** to improve the quality of by mating with superior strains or breeds: *The technique of artificial insemination helps a farmer with poor herds to upbreed his herd only by slow stages* (Time).

**up|bring|ing** (up′bring′ing), *n.* care and training given to a child while growing up; bringing-up; rearing: *to devote care to the upbringing of one's children.*

**up|broke** (up brōk′), *v.* **1** a past tense of **upbreak.** **2** *Archaic.* a past participle of **upbreak.**

**up|bro|ken** (up brō′kən), *v.* a past participle of **upbreak.**

**up|build** (up bild′), *v.t.,* **-built, -build|ing.** to build up. —**up|build′er,** *n.*

**up|built** (up bilt′), *v.* the past tense and past participle of **upbuild.**

**up|burst** (up′bėrst′), *n.* a burst upward; an uprush.

**UPC** (no periods), Universal Product Code.

**up|cast** (up′kast′, -käst′), *adj., n.* —***adj.*** turned or directed upward.

—***n.*** **1** the act of casting or state of being cast upward. **2** something that is cast or thrown up, such as in digging a trench or pit. **3** the shaft by which the ventilating air of a mine is returned to the surface.

**up|caught** (up kôt′, -kot′), *adj.* caught or seized up.

**up|chuck** (up′chuk′), *v.t., v.i. Informal.* to vomit.

**up|climb** (up klīm′), *v.t., v.i.,* **-climbed** or (*Archaic*) **-clomb, -climb|ing.** to climb up.

**up|clomb** (up klōm′), *v. Archaic.* a past tense and past participle of **upclimb.**

**up|coil** (up koil′), *v.t., v.i.* = coil.

**up|com|ing** (up′kum′ing), *adj.* forthcoming; approaching; impending: *the upcoming semester.*

**up|con|vert** (up′kən vėrt′), *v.t.* to change by means of an upconverter: *A laser beam can be used to upconvert infrared light to visible light* (New Yorker).

**up|con|vert|er** (up′kən vėr′tər), *n.* a converter from one form of radiant energy to another: *An upconverter ... can produce a three-dimensional color image from infrared waves* (Science News).

**up|coun|try** (up′kun′trē), *n., pl.* **-tries,** *adv., adj.* —***n.*** the interior of a country: *The upcountry is sparsely settled.*

—***adv.*** toward, in, or into the interior of a country: *He went hunting upcountry in hopes of finding more game.* —***adj.*** of or in the interior of a country: *an upcountry village.*

**up|curl** (up kėrl′), *v.t., v.i.* to curl up: *Here are Thumbelina's shoes ... with toes upcurled like the roofs of pagodas* (Punch).

**up|cur|rent** (up′kėr′ənt), *n.* a rising current of air; updraft: *The wind was producing a strong upcurrent as it hit this slope, and a few of the larger birds were taking advantage of it to do some soaring* (Manchester Guardian).

**up|curve** (up′kėrv′), *n.* an upward curve; upswing: *He's on the upcurve of his political fortunes* (Time).

**up|curved** (up′kėrvd′), *adj.* curved upward; recurved.

**up|date** (*v.* up dāt′; *n.* up′dāt′), *v.,* **-dat|ed, -dat|ing,** *n.* —***v.t.*** to bring up to date; make no longer or relatively less out of date: *Though their curriculum is continuously updated, many cadets ... would like to see things tougher* (Harper's).

—***n.*** **1** a piece of information that modifies previous data used in the operation of a computer, spacecraft, or other device; any current or updated information: *the reentry update of a spacecraft.* **2** an act of updating: *to vote for an update of a Congressional bill.* **3** something or someone updated: *The men ... were updates of ... the characters in Scott Fitzgerald's "May Day"* (Atlantic).

**up-do** (up′dü′), *n.* a hairdo in which the hair is swept upwards and piled on top of the head.

**up|draft** (up′draft′, -dräft′), *n.* an upward movement of air, wind, or gas: *He parachuted from a plane at 2,500 feet over Alabama, but a thunder storm updraft lifted him to 3,000 feet* (Wall Street Journal).

**updraft carburetor,** a carburetor below the intake manifold in a motor vehicle.

**up|draught** (up′draft′, -dräft′), *n. Especially British.* updraft.

**up|drawn** (up drôn′), *adj.* drawn up.

**up|end** (up end′), *v.t., v.i.* to set on end; stand on end: *If you upend the box it will take less space.*

**up|field** (up′fēld′), *adv., adj.* (in soccer, Rugby, and other field games) in or towards the opposing team's goal: *to kick the ball upfield* (adv.), *an upfield kick* (adj.).

**up|flare** (up′flãr′), *n.* an upward flare.

**up|flow** (up′flō′), *v., n.* —***v.i.*** to flow up.

—***n.*** **1** an upward flow. **2** something that flows up.

**up|fold** (up fōld′), *v.t.* to fold up; fold together.

**up-front** (up′frunt′), *adj. U.S. Informal.* not concealed; direct; forthright: *an up-front attitude toward racism. The up-front public business he had to do ... was done for him by his surrogates* (Newsweek).

**up|furled** (up fėrld′), *adj.* furled or rolled up; upfolded.

**up|gath|er** (up gaᴛʜ′ər), *v.t.* to gather up or together; contract.

**up|go|ing** (up′gō′ing), *adj.* going up; moving upward.

**up|grade** (up′grād′), *n., adv., adj., v.,* **-grad|ed, -grad|ing.** *—n.* **1** an upward slope or incline. **2** the act or fact of increasing, as in strength, power, or value; improvement.
*—adv.*, *adj.* uphill; upward.
*—v.t.* **1** to raise, as the status or rating of; raise to a higher position with a higher salary: *to upgrade a job, to upgrade an employee.* **2** to sell (a product of lesser worth) as a substitute for a product of greater worth, charging the higher price.
**on the upgrade,** increasing, as in strength, power, or value; rising; improving: *The growing company's sales are on the upgrade.*

**up|grew** (up grü′), *v.* the past tense of **upgrow.**

**up|grow** (up grō′), *v.i.,* **-grew, -grown, -grow|ing.** to grow up.

**up|grown** (up grōn′), *v.* the past participle of **upgrow.**

**up|growth** (up′grōth′), *n.* **1** the process of growing up; development: *To be ashamed with ... noble shame is the very germ and first upgrowth of all virtue* (Charles Kingsley). **2** something that has grown or is growing up.

**up|gush** (up gush′), *v., n. —v.i.* to gush up.
*—n.* an upward gush.

**up|heap** (up hēp′), *v.t.* to pile or heap up; accumulate.

**up|heav|al** (up hē′vəl), *n.* **1a** the act or fact of heaving up. **b** the state of being heaved up. **2** *Figurative.* a sudden or violent agitation; great turmoil: *with post-war social upheaval at its height* (Manchester Guardian). *Tension stayed high in a country torn by a full year of upheaval* (Newsweek). **3** *Geology.* **a** the act or fact of raising above the original level, especially by rapid earth movements. **b** the state of being raised above the original level.

**up|heave** (up hēv′), *v.,* **-heaved** or **-hove, -heav|ing.** *—v.t.* to heave up; lift up; raise: *land upheaved by volcanic forces.* *—v.i.* = rise.

**up|held** (up held′), *v.* the past tense and past participle of **uphold:** *The higher court upheld the lower court's decision.*

**up|hill** (*adj., n.* up′hil′; *adv.* up′hil′), *adj., adv., n.* *—adj.* **1** up the slope of a hill; upward: *It is an uphill road all the way.* **2** situated on high ground; elevated: *an uphill pasture.* **3** *Figurative.* difficult: *an uphill fight.*
*—adv.* upward: *We walked a mile uphill.*
*—n.* an upward slope; ascent.

**uphill orbit,** the orbit of a rocket or satellite in which it must pull against the sun's gravitational force.

**up|hold** (up hōld′), *v.t.,* **-held, -hold|ing. 1** to give support to; confirm: *The principal upheld the teacher's decision.* SYN: sustain. See syn. under **support. 2** to hold up; not let down; keep from falling; support: *Walls uphold the roof. We uphold the good name of our school.* **3** to sustain on appeal; approve: *The higher court upheld the decision of the lower court.* **—up|hold′er,** *n.*

**up|hol|ster** (up hōl′stər), *v.t.* **1** to provide (chairs or sofas) with coverings, cushions, springs, or stuffing. **2** to furnish (a room), as with curtains and rugs. [American English; back formation < *upholsterer*]

**up|hol|ster|er** (up hōl′stər ər), *n.* a person whose business is to cover furniture and provide it with cushions, springs, and stuffing, and sometimes also to furnish and put in place curtains and rugs. [alteration of earlier *upholdster* tradesman < *uphold* + *-ster*]

**upholsterer bee,** any one of various bees which cut small, regularly-shaped pieces of leaves or flower petals to use as a lining for their cells.

**up|hol|ster|y** (up hōl′stər ē, -hōl′strē), *n., pl.* **-ster|ies. 1** the coverings for chairs or sofas; cushions, springs, and stuffing for furniture. **2** the business of upholstering.

**up|hove** (up hōv′), *v.* a past tense and past participle of **upheave.**

**u|phroe** (yü′frō, -vrō), *n. Nautical.* euphroe.

**UPI** (no periods), United Press International (an independent news-gathering agency that distributes news, photographs, and feature stories to its subscribers).

**up|jew|el|ing** (up′jü′ə ling), *n.* the addition of jewel bearings to imported watch movements brought in with jewels missing under lower customs duties.

**up|keep** (up′kēp′), *n.* **1** the act of keeping or condition of being kept up or in good repair; maintenance: *the upkeep of a house.* **2** the cost of operating and repair: *The upkeep of a yacht is very expensive.*

**up|land** (up′lənd, -land′), *n., adj. —n.* **1** elevated or hilly ground; high land. **2** *Archaic.* upcountry.
*—adj.* of high land; living, growing, or situated on high land: *upland flowers, upland meadows.*
**uplands,** a hilly or mountainous region or section: *the uplands of the American West.*

**upland cotton,** a type of cotton having a short staple, much grown in the United States.

**upland cress,** = winter cress.

**up|land|er** (up′lən dər, -lan′-), *n.* **1** an inhabitant of the uplands. **2** = upland plover.

**upland plover,** a large American sandpiper frequenting upland fields and pastures.

**upland rice,** rice that grows where there is much rain. Upland rice needs no irrigation.

**up|lands** (up′ləndz, -landz′), *n.pl.* See under **upland.**

**up|lift** (*v.* up lift′; *n.* up′lift′), *v., n. —v.t.* **1** to lift or move up; raise; elevate: *At thy voice her pining sons uplifted Their prostrate brows* (Shelley). **2** to exalt emotionally or spiritually: *to uplift the mind and soul by prayer.* **3** to raise socially or economically; improve the status of. **4** to raise morally or intellectually; improve the quality of.
*—n.* **1** the act of lifting up. **2** emotional or spiritual exaltation. **3** social or moral improvement or effort toward it: *Now you look here! The first thing you got to understand is that all this uplift ... and settlement work and recreation is nothing in God's world but the entering wedge for socialism* (Sinclair Lewis). **4** *Geology.* an upward heaving of the earth's surface, especially one which is very slow: *Uplift ... turns sea bottoms into land* (Carroll Lane Fenton). **—up|lift′er,** *n.*

**up|lift|ment** (up lift′mənt), *n.* = uplift.

**up|link** (up′lingk′), *n.* the communications connection for the transmission of signals from a ground station to a spacecraft or satellite: *Oscar 6 [an amateur artificial satellite] received signals in the 145.9-146.0 MHz range (uplink) and retransmitted them at 29.45-29.55 MHz (downlink)* (Morgan W. Godwin).

**up|look|ing** (up′lu̇k′ing), *adj.* looking up; aspiring.

**up|ly|ing** (up′lī′ing), *adj.* **1** = elevated. **2** (of land) upland.

**up|man|ship** (up′mən ship), *n. Informal.* one-upmanship: *Upmanship is the art of being one up on all the others* (London Times).

**up|most** (up′mōst), *adj.* = uppermost.

**up|on** (ə pon′, -pôn′), *prep., adv. —prep.* = on: *He stood upon the ladder.*
*—adv. Obsolete.* **1a** on the surface. **b** on one's person. **2** thereafter; thereupon.
[< *up* + *on*]

**up|per** (up′ər), *adj., n. —adj.* **1** that is the higher of two: **a** higher in position or location: *the upper lip, an upper berth.* **b** higher in rank, office, or station; superior: *the upper grades in school, the upper classes.* **2** above the bottom or other point: *the upper notes of a singer's voice, the upper floors of an office building.* **3** consisting of those members of a legislative body who are usually less subject to direct control by voters and are comparatively few in number: *the upper branch of a legislature.* **4** *Geology.* **a** Usually, **Upper.** being or relating to a later division of a period, system, or the like; more recent: *Upper Cambrian.* **b** lying nearer the surface and formed later than others of its group, type, or class: *an upper stratum.* **5** farther from the sea or nearer to the source: *the upper reaches of a river.* **6** that covers or clothes a part of the body above the waist, especially the chest or shoulders: *an upper garment.* **7** *Archaic.* worn over another; outer.
*—n.* **1** the part of a shoe or boot above the sole. **2** *Informal.* an upper berth. **3** *U.S. Slang.* a stimulant drug: *... an excessive number of amphetamine tablets and assorted other "uppers"* (Harper's). **4** *U.S., Archaic.* a cloth gaiter.
**on one's uppers,** *Informal.* **a** with the soles of one's shoes worn out: *to walk on one's uppers.* **b** *Figurative.* very shabby or poor: *I'm on my uppers ... I want money* (R. Marsh).
**uppers,** *U.S.* an upper set of false teeth: *The short upper lip ... makes him look like he doesn't have his uppers in* (Time).

**upper air** or **atmosphere,** the stratosphere and ionosphere.

**upper bound,** *Mathematics.* a number which is higher than or equal to a given function.

**up|per-brack|et** (up′ər brak′it), *adj.* of a higher bracket, rank, or level: *As to income, 10 per cent of the total population is rated upper-bracket* (New York Times).

**Upper Carboniferous,** *Geology.* the name outside of North America for the Pennsylvanian period of Carboniferous time.

**upper case,** **1** capital letters. *Abbr:* u.c. **2** *Printing.* a frame in which types for capital letters are kept for hand setting.

**up|per-case** (up′ər kās′), *adj., v.,* **-cased, -cas|ing.** *Printing. —adj.* **1** in capital letters. **2** capital: *an upper-case letter.* **3** kept in or having to do with the upper case.
*—v.t.* to print in capital letters.

**up|per-class** (up′ər klas′, -kläs′), *adj.* **1** of, having to do with, or included in the upper class: *upper-class society.* **2** of or having to do with the junior and senior classes in a college or school.

**upper class,** **1** a class of society above the middle class, having the highest social and economic status. The upper class includes the aristocracy, the gentry, and those with the highest incomes and the most power in society. **2** the junior and senior classes in schools and colleges.

**up|per|class|man** (up′ər klas′mən, -kläs′-), *n., pl.* **-men.** a junior or senior in a college or school.

**upper crust,** **1** *Informal.* the upper classes: *The St. Louis upper crust had looked down their noses at the fair as mere vulgar show and noise* (Harper's). **2** the upper layer of pastry on a pie.

**up|per-crust** (up′ər krust′), *adj. Informal.* of or having to do with the upper classes.

***up|per|cut** (up′ər kut′), *n., v.,* **-cut, -cut|ting.** *Boxing. —n.* a swinging blow with the fist directed upward from beneath; punch that is delivered at a sharp upward angle: *a short uppercut to the jaw.*
*—v.t., v.i.* to strike with or deliver such a blow.

***uppercut**

**upper hand,** advantage that is or is likely to prove decisive; control; mastery: *Do what the doctor says or that cold may get the upper hand.*

**Upper House** or **upper house,** the more restricted branch of a lawmaking body that has two branches, made up of members who are less numerous and (usually) less subject to direct control by the voters. The House of Lords is the Upper House of the British Parliament.

**up|per|most** (up′ər mōst), *adj., adv. —adj.* **1** highest; topmost: *the uppermost reaches of the Amazon.* **2** having the most force or influence; most prominent.
*—adv.* **1** in, at, or near the top. **2** first: *The safety of her children was uppermost in the mother's mind.*

**upper register,** *Music.* the upper range of a voice or instrument.

**up|pers** (up′ərz), *n.pl.* See under **upper.**

**upper stage,** a second or later stage of a multistage rocket. **—up′per-stage′,** *adj.*

**up|per|stock** (up′ər stok′), *n.* a high stocking worn by men in the 1500's with netherstocks.

**upper story** or **storey,** *Humorous.* the head as the seat of the mind or intellect; brain; wits: *He's not overburthen'd i' th' upper storey* (George Eliot).

**upper transit,** *Astronomy.* the passage of a heavenly body across the upper part of a celestial meridian.

**upper works,** *Nautical.* the parts of a ship which are above the surface of the water when it is loaded for a voyage.

**up|per|world** (up′ər wėrld′), *n.* the respectable portion of society; overworld.

**up|piled** (up pīld′), *adj.* piled up; upheaped.

**up|ping** (up′ing), *n.* the nicking of the upper part of the beak of a swan to indicate its ownership, especially (in Great Britain) its ownership by the sovereign. [< *up,* verb + *-ing*[1]]

**up|pish** (up′ish), *adj.* **1** *Informal.* somewhat arrogant, self-assertive, or conceited. **2** *British.* upward: *an uppish stroke of the ball.* [< *up,* adverb + *-ish*] **—up′pish|ly,** *adv.* **—up′pish|ness,** *n.*

**up|pi|ty** (up′ə tē), *adj. U.S. Informal.* uppish: *Where she came from, horsewhips were still widely used on uppity servants* (New Yorker). [American English, probably < *uppi*(sh) + *-ty,* as in *haughty*] **—up′pi|ty|ness,** *n.*

**up|raise** (up rāz′), *v.t.,* **-raised, -rais|ing.** to lift up; raise.

**up|rate** (up′rāt′), *v.t.,* **-rat|ed, -rat|ing. 1** to increase the rate of: *The investment grants will be uprated by 5 per cent during the next two years* (London Times). **2** to increase, as in power or efficiency; improve: *The uprated Saturn 1 booster*

---

**Pronunciation Key:** hat, āge, cãre, fär; let, ēqual, tėrm; it, īce; hot, ōpen, ôrder; oil, out; cup, pu̇t, rüle; child; long; thin; ᴛʜen; zh, measure; ə represents **a** in about, **e** in taken, **i** in pencil, **o** in lemon, **u** in circus.

[*had*] *almost 140,000 pounds of added thrust in the first stage alone* (Science News).

**up|rear** (up rir′), *v.t.* to lift up; raise. — *v.i.* to be lifted up.

**up|right** (up′rīt′, up rīt′), *adj., adv., n., v.* — ***adj.*** **1** standing, sitting, or set up straight; erect: *an upright post, a person upright in a chair, a ladder upright against a house, a glass upright on its base.* **2** *Figurative.* morally good; honest; righteous: *a thoroughly honest and upright person.*
— ***adv.*** straight up; in a vertical position: *Hold yourself upright. Man walks upright on two feet.*
— ***n.*** **1** a vertical or upright position. **2** something standing erect; vertical part or piece. **3** = upright piano. **4** *U.S.* one of the goal posts in football.
— ***v.t.*** to raise to an upright position: *to upright a rowboat.*
[Old English *upriht*] — **up′right′ly**, *adv.* — **up′right′ness**, *n.*
— ***Syn.*** *adj.* **1 Upright, erect** mean straight up. **Upright** literally means standing up straight on a base or in a position that is straight up and down, not slanting: *After the earthquake not a lamp or chair was upright.* **Erect** means held or set upright, not stooping or bent: *At seventy she is still erect.*

**upright piano**, a rectangular piano having vertical strings behind the keyboard.

**up|rise** (*v.* up rīz′; *n.* up′rīz′), *v.,* **-rose, -ris|en, -ris|ing,** *n.* — ***v.i.*** **1** to rise up; rear. **2** to slope upward; ascend. **3** to get up; arise. **4** to increase as in volume or amount.
— ***n.*** a rising up; upward rise.

**up|ris|en** (up riz′ən), *v.* past participle of **uprise**.

**up|ris|ing** (up′rī′zing, up rī′-), *n.* **1** a revolt; rebellion: *a popular uprising against tyranny.* **2** the act of rising up. **3** an upward slope; ascent.

**up|riv|er** (up′riv′ər), *adj., adv.* — ***adj.*** **1** belonging to or situated farther up, or toward the upper end of, a river: *The upriver jetty on the River Thames at Battersea ... is a particularly interesting structure* (London Times). **2** leading or directed toward the source of a river: *to move upriver freight.*
— ***adv.*** toward or in the direction of the source of a river: *When salmon go upriver to spawn their stomachs contract and their throats shrink so that they lose all desire to return to their sea feeding grounds* (Manchester Guardian).

**up|roar** (up′rôr′, -rōr′), *n.* **1** a noisy disturbance; tumult. **SYN**: commotion. **2** a loud, confused noise; tumultuous sound; clamor: *to hear a sudden uproar in the next room, the thunderous uproar of a passing train.* **SYN**: See syn. under **noise**.
**in an uproar**, in a state of great disturbance or confusion; commotion: *Thus it was at Alcamo, where the streets seemed to be in an uproar till after midnight* (Leigh Hunt).
[< Dutch *oproer*, or Middle Low German *oprōr* insurrection, tumult; influenced by English *roar*]

**up|roar|i|ous** (up rôr′ē əs, -rōr′-), *adj.* **1** making an uproar; noisy and disorderly; clamorous: *an uproarious crowd.* **2** loud, confused, and unrestrained: *uproarious laughter.* — **up|roar′i|ous|ly**, *adv.* — **up|roar′i|ous|ness**, *n.*

**up|roll** (up rōl′), *v.t.* to roll up.

**up|root** (up rüt′, -ru̇t′), *v.t.* **1** to tear or pull up by the roots: *The storm uprooted many trees.* **2** *Figurative.* to tear away, remove, or displace completely: *Famine uprooted many families from their homes in Ireland during the 1840's.* — **up-root′|er**, *n.*

**up|root|al** (up rü′təl, -ru̇t′əl), *n.* **1** the act of uprooting. **2** the state of being uprooted.

**up|root|ed|ness** (up rü′tid ness, -ru̇t′id-), *n.* the quality or state of being uprooted: (*Figurative.*) *The chief peculiarity of the adolescent's existence is its ... phase of transition from childhood to manhood, a phase of uprootedness and drastic change* (Harper's).

**up|rose** (up rōz′), *v.* the past tense of **uprise**.

**up|rouse** (up rouz′), *v.t.,* **-roused, -rous|ing.** to rouse up; arouse; awake.

**up|rush** (up′rush′), *v., n.* — ***v.i.*** to rush upward: *It gets a forward push by leaning its tail fluke against the uprushing water of the wave* (Scientific American).
— ***n.*** an upward rush or flow: *the sizzling uprush of a rocket* (New Yorker).

**ups-and-downs** (ups′ən dounz′), *n.pl.* **1** changes, as in fortune or success; vicissitudes: *the ups-and-downs of a millionaire and a chauffeur's daughter who find themselves in love* (New Yorker). **2** alternations, as in condition or quality; vagaries; variations: *The cycle of ups-and-downs in film-making will always be with us, for its root is in human restlessness* (Saturday Review).

**up|scale** (up′skāl′), *adj. U.S.* well above the average in income and education: *an upscale readership. The size and character—young and "upscale"—of the* [*Monty*] *Python audience inevitably attracted the interest of the commercial networks* (New Yorker).

**up|set** (*v.* up set′; *n.* up′set′; *adj.* up set′, up′set′), *v.,* **-set, -set|ting,** *n., adj.* — ***v.t.*** **1** to tip over; cause to capsize; overturn: *He upset the milk pitcher. Moving about in a boat may upset it.* **2** to disturb greatly; disorder: *Rain upset our plans for a picnic. The shock upset her nerves.* **3a** to defeat unexpectedly in a contest: *The independent candidate upset the mayor in the election.* **b** *Figurative.* to overthrow; defeat: *to upset a will, to upset an argument.* **4** to shorten and thicken (a metal bar, rivet, or the like) by hammering on the end, especially when heated. **5** to shorten (as a metal tire) while resetting.
— ***v.i.*** to be or become upset.
— ***n.*** **1** the act or fact of tipping over; overturn: *The upset of the wheelbarrow caused all the dirt to spill over the ground.* **2** a great disturbance; disorder: *The fire caused an upset in the office.* **3** an unexpected defeat in a contest: *The hockey team suffered an upset.* **4** a swage or other tool used for upsetting. **5** a bar or rod end, rivet, or the like, which is upset.
— ***adj.*** **1** tipped over; overturned; capsized: *an upset boat.* **2** greatly disturbed; disordered: *an upset stomach, an upset mind.*
— ***Syn.*** *v.t.* **1 Upset, overturn** mean to cause to tip over. **Upset** implies a toppling from an upright or stable position: *He accidentally kicked the table and upset the vase of flowers.* **Overturn** often suggests a more violent action which leaves the object upside down or on its side: *The collision overturned both cars.*

**upset forging**, forging in which a heated bar, bolt, or the like is thickened at one end to form a head, usually by forcing it horizontally into a die.

**upset price**, the lowest price at which a thing offered for sale, especially at auction, will be sold.

**up|set|ta|ble** (up set′ə bəl), *adj.* capable of being upset; easily upset.

**up|set|ter** (up set′ər), *n.* a person, thing, or event that upsets: *The volunteer driver of the hackney coach ... and the involuntary upsetter of the whole party* (Dickens).

**up|set|ting** (up set′ing), *adj.* greatly disturbing; causing disorder: *It was upsetting to have to wait so long for the bus.* — **up|set′ting|ly**, *adv.*

**up|shift** (up′shift′), *v., n.* — ***v.t., v.i.*** to shift from a lower to a higher gear.
— ***n.*** a shifting from a lower to a higher gear.

**up|shoot** (up′shüt′), *n.* **1** a shooting up; something that shoots up. **2** a curve thrown in baseball, which shoots or bends up as it approaches home plate.

**up|shot** (up′shot′), *n.* **1** conclusion; result; outcome: *The upshot of the argument was a fist-fight.* **SYN**: issue. **2** the essential facts involved in an argument. [< the fact that (originally) it was the last shot in an archery match < *up-* + *shot,* noun]

**up|side** (up′sīd′), *n.* the upper side; top part or surface.
**upside down, a** having what should be on top at the bottom: *The slice of buttered bread fell upside down on the floor.* **b** *Figurative.* in or into complete disorder: *She turned the room upside down searching for a letter. The room was upside down.*
[alteration of earlier *up so down*]

**up|side-down cake** (up′sīd′doun′), a cake made of batter poured over fruit, baked, and served bottom up.

**up|side|down|ness** (up′sīd′doun′nis), *n.* the state of being topsy-turvy: (*Figurative.*) [*He*] *is not original if that means turning accepted views upside down for the sake of the upsidedownness* (Manchester Guardian Weekly).

***up|si|lon** (yüp′sə lon), *n.* **1** the 20th letter of the Greek alphabet corresponding to the English U, u, or Y, y. **2** *Nuclear Physics.* an elementary particle that is six times as heavy as a proton, produced by bombarding beryllium nuclei with high-energy protons: *The lifetime of the upsilons is too fleeting to be detected, and their properties are inferred from their decay products* (Science News). [< Greek (*tò*) *y psīlón* (literally) bare *y* (that is, distinguished from *oi*, which had the same pronunciation)]

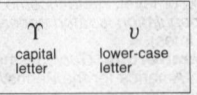

| ***upsilon** definition 1 | Υ capital letter | υ lower-case letter |
|---|---|---|

**up|slope** (up′slōp′), *adv.* upward toward the top of a slope.

**upslope fog**, a fog formed by the cooling of stable moist air as it moves from lower to higher elevations.

**up|soar** (up sôr′, -sōr′), *v.i.* to soar aloft; mount up.

**up|sprang** (up sprang′), *v.* a past tense of **upspring**.

**up|spring** (*v.* up spring′; *n.* up′spring′), *v.,* **-sprang** or **-sprung, -sprung, -spring|ing,** *n.*
— ***v.i.*** **1** to spring up from the soil or into being. **2** to leap to one's feet; rise suddenly.
— ***n.*** **1** the act of upspringing. **2** an upward jump; spring into the air.

**up|sprung** (up sprung′), *v.* a past tense and the past participle of **upspring**.

**up|stage** (up′stāj′), *adv., adj., n., v.,* **-staged, -stag|ing.** — ***adv.*** toward or at the back of the stage, which was formerly higher than the front; away from the footlights: *to walk upstage.*
— ***adj.*** **1** toward or at the back of the stage: *upstage furniture.* **2** having to do with the back part of the stage. **3** *Informal, Figurative.* haughty; aloof; supercilious.
— ***n.*** the back part of a stage.
— ***v.t.*** **1** to draw attention away from (an actor) by doing something upstage or in back of him, or by forcing him to face away from the audience. **2** *Figurative: ... a style of house design so original and so lavish that it tends to upstage most of the public architecture* (Maclean's). **SYN**: outdo, outshine. **3** *Figurative.* to treat rudely or curtly; snub: *He is likely to be insulted by the box-office attendant, ... upstaged by the usher* (Time).

**up|stairs** (up′stãrz′), *adv., adj., n.* — ***adv.*** **1** up the stairs: *The boy ran upstairs.* **2** on or to an upper floor: *She lives upstairs.* **3** *Informal, Figurative.* to or in a place or rank of greater authority, higher status, or the like. **4** *Informal, Figurative.* to or at a high or higher altitude, especially in an aircraft: *to avoid a storm by going upstairs.*
— ***adj.*** on an upper floor: *He is waiting in an upstairs hall.*
— ***n.*** the upper floor or floors: *to hear a cry from upstairs. The small cottage has no upstairs.*
**kick upstairs**, *Informal.* to promote (a person) to a higher but less powerful or important position: *Instead of retiring their conservative old president the corporation kicked him upstairs to Chairman of the Board.*

**up|stand** (up′stand′), *n. British.* an upstanding thing; an upright structure or part.

**up|stand|ing** (up stan′ding), *adj.* **1** standing up; erect: *short, upstanding hair.* **2** straight and tall; well-grown: *a healthy, upstanding plant. Two upstanding, pleasant children* (W. Somerset Maugham). **3** *Figurative.* honorable; upright: *a fine, upstanding young man.*

**up|start** (up′stärt′), *n., adj., v.* — ***n.*** **1** a person who has suddenly risen from a humble position to wealth, power, or importance, especially one who is considered to lack the manners, taste, knowledge, or the like, requisite for or becoming to his position; parvenu. **2** an unpleasant and conceited person who puts himself forward too much. **3** *Figurative: a culture compared with which that of the West is a mere upstart.*
— ***adj.*** **1** suddenly risen from a humble position to wealth, power, or importance: *He dreaded their upstart ambition* (Edward Gibbon). **2** conceited; self-assertive.
— ***v.i.*** to rise suddenly up, out, or into view. — ***v.t.*** to cause to rise suddenly up, out, or into view.

**up|state** (up′stāt′), *adj., adv., n. U.S.* — ***adj.*** of the part of a state away from and usually north of the principal city: *upstate New York.*
— ***adv.*** to, toward, or in an upstate area: *to drive upstate.* — ***n.*** an upstate area or part.

**up|stat|er** (up′stā′tər), *n.* a person born in, living in, or from an upstate area.

**up|stream** (up′strēm′), *adv., adj.* against the current of a stream; up a stream: *It is hard to paddle upstream* (adv.). *They stopped at an upstream camping site* (adj.).

**up|stretched** (up′strecht′), *adj.* stretched or extended upward: *an upstretched arm.*

**up|stroke** (up′strōk′), *n.* **1** an upward stroke, as of a pen or pencil. **2** a stroke delivered upwards: *the upstroke of a piston.*

**up|surge** (*n.* up′sérj′; *v.* up sérj′), *n., v.,* **-surged, -surg|ing.** — ***n.*** **1** an upward turn or trend; rise; upturn: *an upsurge in grain production. Business and consumer credit has provided much of the steam behind this year's economic upsurge* (New York Times). **2** an upward surge; uprise: *The upsurge in Asia, the most important political event in the world today, is fundamentally a revolt against hunger and poverty* (Scientific American).
— ***v.i.*** **1** to surge upward: *The fountain upsurged.* **2** to undergo an upsurge: *Production upsurged.*

**up|sur|gence** (up′sér′jents), *n.* = upsurge.

**up|sweep** (*v.* up swēp′; *n.* up′swēp′), *v.,* **-swept, -sweep|ing,** *n.* — ***v.t.*** to cause to be upswept.
— ***v.i.*** to be upswept.
— ***n.*** an upswept thing, part, or arrangement.

**up|swell** (up swel′), *v.i.,* **-swelled, -swelled** or **-swol|len, -swell|ing.** to swell up.

***up|swept** (up′swept′), *adj., v.* — ***adj.*** **1** curving or slanting upward, especially in a smooth or regular line: *a dog with an upswept jaw.* See picture above on next page. **2** brushed upward to or toward the crown of the head: *an upswept coiffure.*

— ***v.*** the past tense and past participle of **upsweep**.

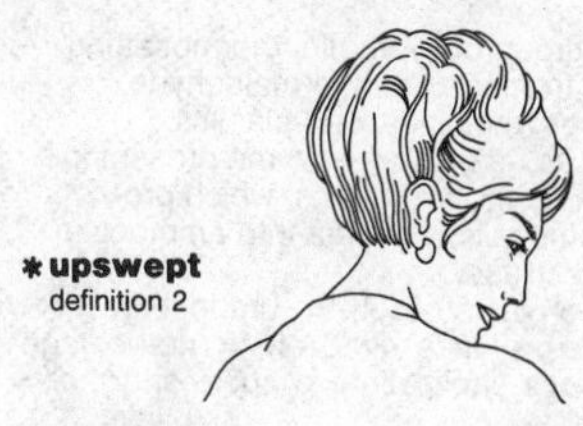

***upswept**
definition 2

**up|swing** (*n.* up′swing′; *v.* up swing′), *n., v.,* **-swung, -swing|ing.** —***n.*** **1** an upward swing; movement upward: *the upswing of a golf club before driving.* **2** *Figurative.* a marked improvement; strong advance.
— ***v.i.*** to undergo an upswing.

**up|swol|len** (up swō′lən), *v.* a past participle of **upswell**.

**up|swung** (up swung′), *v.* the past tense and past participle of **upswing**.

**up|sy-dai|sy** (up′sē dā′zē), *interj.* an exclamation made to a child on helping it stand up from a fall or when raising it in the arms.

**up|take** (up′tāk′), *n.* **1** a ventilating shaft for the upward discharge of foul air or fumes. **2** a line or flue through which a boiler discharges into the smokestack, funnel, or chimney. **3** absorption; ingestion: *Patient research work has been carried out ... on all aspects of the subject—the effect of diet, of mineral uptake during the period in which the teeth are being formed* (New Scientist). **4** *Informal.* the act of lifting or raising; taking upward.
**on** (or **in**) **the uptake,** *Informal.* in understanding and response; in perceptive ability: *quick on the uptake.*

**up|tear** (up tãr′), *v.t.,* **-tore, -torn, -tear|ing.** to tear up.

**up-tem|po** (up′tem′pō), *adj.* of rapid or increasing tempo: *They play ballads, blues and up-tempo numbers* (Saturday Review).

**up|throw** (*n.* up′thrō′; *v.* up thrō′), *n., v.,* **-threw, -thrown, -throw|ing.** —***n.*** **1** *Geology.* an upward dislocation of a mass of rock, generally due to faulting; upheaval; uplift. **2** an upward throw or cast.
— ***v.t.*** to throw upwards; toss or fling up: *Fifty tons of water were upthrown* (Byron).

**up|thrust** (*n.* up′thrust′; *v.* up thrust′), *n., v.* —***n.*** **1** an upward push. **2** *Geology.* an upward movement of part of the earth's crust.
— ***v.t.*** to push up, as in an upthrust: *The region as a whole consists of a geological anticline, ... upthrust by an outer ripple of those same Miocene foldings that formed the Alps and the Himalayas* (New Scientist).

**up|tick** (up′tik′), *n.* **1** a price higher than that of the immediately preceding one, paid as the condition of a short sale on a stock exchange. **2** the sale so made.

**up|tight** (up′tīt′), *adj. Slang.* **1** very uneasy or apprehensive; anxious: *Sometimes you can get so uptight about your disadvantages that you ignore your advantages* (Ralph Ellison). **2** nervous; tense; irritable: *When [she] left New York for India she was hassled and really uptight* (Maclean's). **3** strictly conventional or formal; straitlaced: *In black with a white collar, he could be impersonating an uptight Calvinist parson* (Melvin Maddocks). — **up′tight′ness,** *n.*

**up|tilt** (up tilt′), *v.t.* to tilt up.

**up-to-date** (up′tə dāt′), *adj.* **1** extending to the present time; based on or inclusive of the latest facts, data, or other information: *an up-to-date record, an up-to-date textbook.* **2** having modern equipment, utilizing the latest techniques, and the like; not obsolescent: *an up-to-date store, an up-to-date factory.* **3** keeping up with the times in style or ideas; modern. — **up′-to-date′ness,** *n.*

**up|tore** (up tôr′, -tōr′), *v.* the past tense of **uptear**.

**up|torn** (up tôrn′, -tōrn′), *v.* the past participle of **uptear**.

**up-to-the-min|ute** (up′tə ᴛʜə min′it), *adj.* latest; most recent; up-to-date: *up-to-the-minute news, styles, or equipment.*

**up|town** (*adv.* up′toun′; *adj., n.* up′toun′), *adv., adj., n.* —**adv., adj.** to or in the upper part or away from the main business section of a town or city: *to go uptown* (adv.); *an uptown store* (adj.).
—***n.*** the upper part or part away from the business section of a town or city: *a quiet section of uptown.*

**up|trend** (up′trend′), *n.* an upward tendency or trend; inclination to rise, become better, or grow larger.

**up|turn** (*v.* up tėrn′; *n.* up′tėrn′), *v., n.* —***v.t., v.i.*** **1** to turn or face up. **2** to turn or roll over, so as to face down. **3** *Obsolete.* to overturn.
—***n.*** **1** an upward turn. **2** *Figurative.* an improvement: *As business improved, his income took an upturn.*

**up|turned** (up tėrnd′, up′tėrnd), *adj.* **1** turned or facing upward. **2** turned over; overturned. **3** turned up at the end.

**UPU** (no periods) or **U.P.U.,** Universal Postal Union (an international organization to improve postal services, affiliated with the United Nations).

**u|pu|poid** (yü′pyə poid), *adj.* **1** resembling the hoopoe. **2** belonging to a family of Old-World nonpasserine birds including the hoopoes. **3** having to do with this family. [< New Latin *Upupidae* the family name < Latin *upupa* hoopoe]

**up|val|u|a|tion** (up′val yů ā′shən), *n.* an upvaluing of a country's currency.

**up|val|ue** (up′val′yü), *v.t., v.i.,* **-ued, -u|ing.** to fix a higher legal value on (currency that has depreciated) in relation to gold: *If the franc were devalued and the Deutsche mark upvalued, French food prices in francs would rise proportionately overnight and German food prices in marks would fall proportionately* (Listener).

**up|waft|ed** (up waf′tid, -wäf′-), *adj.* borne up; carried aloft with a waving or undulatory motion: *a kite upwafted by the breeze.*

**up|ward** (up′wərd), *adv., adj.* —**adv. 1** to or toward a higher place; up: *to fly upward. He climbed upward in the tree till he reached the apple.* **2** in the higher or highest position; uppermost: *to store baskets with the bottoms upward.* **3** to or toward a higher rank, amount, age, or the like: *to move upward in life.* **4** to or into the latter or current part of life; onward in years: *to work from the age of 16 upward. From ten years of age upward she had studied French.* **5** to or toward the source: *We traced the river upward.* **6** to or toward the upper or topmost part: *to rot from the base upward.* **7** above; more: *to demobilize soldiers of 35 and upward, hotel rooms at $10 and upward. Children of twelve years and upward must pay full fare.*
—**adj.** directed or moving toward a higher place; in a higher position: *an upward flight; an upward course* (Shakespeare).
**upward of,** more than: *Repairs to the car will cost upward of $100.*
[Old English *upweard*] — **up′ward|ness,** *n.*

**up|ward|ly** (up′wərd lē), *adv.* in an upward manner or direction; upward.

**up|ward-mo|bile** (up′wərd mō′bəl, -mō bēl′), *adj.* characterized by upward mobility: ... *a typical upward-mobile professional couple in their thirties or forties* (Scientific American).

**upward mobility,** the tendency or drive to rise from a lower to a higher economic or social class: *Upward mobility is an unfortunate drive in one who hopes to be an artist* (Pauline Kael).

**up|wards** (up′wərdz), *adv.* = upward.
**upwards of,** more than; upward of: *Its optimum length worked out to upwards of seventy feet* (Fortune).

**up|warp** (up′wôrp′), *v., n. Geology.* —**v.t., v.i.** to fold or bend in an anticlinal or upward manner.
—***n.*** an upwarped condition or area.

**up|well** (up wel′), *v.i.* to well or shoot up.

**up|well|ing** (up wel′ing), *n.* the action of shooting or welling up, especially the rising of nutrient-laden waters from the ocean depths to the surface: *It would obviously be worthwhile to stimulate upwelling artificially, not only because of the probability of high fish yields ...* (Scientific American).

**up|whirl** (up hwėrl′), *v.t., v.i.* to whirl upward.

**up|wind** (up′wind′), *adv., adj.* into the wind; against the wind; in the direction from which the wind is blowing: *to sail a boat upwind* (adv.); *the upwind side of the island* (adj.).

**up|wreathe** (up rēᴛʜ′), *v.i.,* **-wreathed, -wreathed** or (*Archaic*) **-wreath|en, -wreath|ing.** to wreathe upward, or rise with a curling motion, as smoke.

**up|wreath|en** (up rē′ᴛʜən), *v. Archaic.* a past participle of **upwreathe**.

**ur-,** *prefix.* original or earliest, as in *ur-performance, urtext.* [< German *Ur-* primitive, original]

**Ur** (no period), (formerly) uranium (chemical element). Now, **U** (no period).

**u|ra|cil** (yůr′ə səl), *n.* a substance present in nucleic acid in cells. It is one of the pyrimidine bases of ribonucleic acid or RNA, corresponding to thymine in DNA. *RNA is a giant molecule built up of nucleotides containing ribose sugar and any one of four bases: adenine, uracil, guanine or cytosine* (Scientific American). *Formula:* $C_4H_4N_2O_2$ *Abbr:* U (no period). [< *ur*(ea) + *ac*(etic) + *-il,* variant of *-yl*]

**u|rae|mi|a** (yů rē′mē ə), *n.* = uremia.

**u|rae|mic** (yů rē′mik), *adj.* = uremic.

***u|rae|us** (yů rē′əs), *n.* a stylized representation of the sacred asp of ancient Egypt, used especially in the formal headdress of royal persons as a symbol of sovereignty, typically with the forepart of the asp reared and projecting out from the forehead. [< Latin *ūraeus* < Greek *ouraîos* < *ourâ* tail]

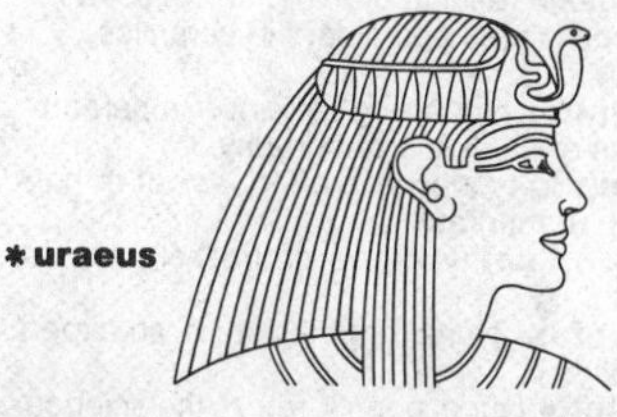

***uraeus**

**U|ral** (yůr′əl), *adj.* of or having to do with the Ural Mountains or the Ural River.

**U|ral-Al|ta|ic** (yůr′əl al tā′ik), *adj., n.* —***adj.*** **1** of or having to do with a large group of languages spoken in eastern Europe and northern Asia, comprising the Uralic and Altaic families. **2** of the region including the Ural and Altaic Mountains, or the people living there.
—***n.*** the Ural-Altaic language group.

**U|ra|li|an** (yů rā′lē ən), *n., adj.* —***n.*** = Uralic.
—***adj.*** **1** = Ural. **2** = Uralic.

**U|ral|ic** (yů ral′ik), *adj., n.* —***adj.*** **1** of or having to do with a family of languages that includes Finno-Ugric and Samoyed. **2** of the Ural Mountains or the people living in or near them.
—***n.*** the Uralic family of languages; Uralian.

**u|ral|ite** (yůr′ə līt), *n.* a mineral, pyroxene altered to hornblende. [< German *Uralit* < the *Ural* Mountains + *-it* -ite[1]]

**u|ral|it|ic** (yůr′ə lit′ik), *adj. Mineralogy.* **1** having the characters of uralite in a greater or less degree. **2** containing, or consisting wholly or in part of, uralite.

**u|ra|nal|y|sis** (yůr′ə nal′ə sis), *n., pl.* **-ses** (-sēz). = urinalysis.

**U|ra|ni|a** (yů rā′nē ə), *n. Greek Mythology.* **1** the Muse of astronomy. **2** an epithet of Aphrodite (Venus). [< Latin *ūrania* < Greek *Ouraníā,* (originally) feminine of *ouraniós* heavenly < *ouranós* heaven. Compare etym. under **Uranus.**]

**U|ra|ni|an** (yů rā′nē ən), *adj.* of or having to do with the planet Uranus.

**u|ran|ic**[1] (yů ran′ik), *adj. Chemistry.* **1** of uranium. **2** containing uranium, especially with a valence of six.

**u|ran|ic**[2] (yů ran′ik), *adj.* of or having to do with the heavens; celestial; astronomical. [< Late Latin *ūranus* (< Greek *ouranós*) + English *-ic*]

**u|ra|nide** (yůr′ə nīd), *n.* a transuranic element.

**u|ra|nif|er|ous** (yůr′ə nif′ər əs), *adj.* containing or yielding uranium.

**u|ran|i|nite** (yů ran′ə nīt), *n.* a black uranium mineral, occurring as crystals, or in veins, when it is called pitchblende. *Formula:* $UO_2$ [< *uran*(ium) + *-in* + *-ite*[1]]

**u|ra|nite** (yůr′ə nīt), *n.* a group of minerals, including autunite and torbernite, composed largely of uranium phosphate. [< German *Uranit* < *Uranus,* the planet, which had been discovered shortly before this group + *-it* -ite[1]]

**u|ra|nit|ic** (yůr′ə nit′ik), *adj.* **1** of or having to do with uranite. **2** containing uranite.

***u|ra|ni|um** (yů rā′nē əm), *n.* a white, radioactive metallic chemical element that weighs more than any other element in nature. Uranium occurs naturally in combination in pitchblende, carnotite, and certain other minerals. Naturally occurring uranium contains three isotopes of mass numbers 234, 235, and 238. Certain isotopes of uranium can sustain efficient chain reaction and are for this reason used as sources of atomic energy and in the atomic bomb. [< New Latin *uranium* < *Uranus,* the planet + *-ium,* a suffix meaning "element"]

***uranium**

| symbol | atomic number | mass number | oxidation state |
|---|---|---|---|
| U | 92 | 238 | 3,4,5,6 |

**uranium 235,** = U-235.

**uranium 238,** = U-238.

**uranium bomb,** an atomic bomb that derives its force from the splitting of uranium atoms.

**uranium dioxide,** a highly refractory, black, crystalline dioxide of uranium, used in ceramics, pigments, photographic chemicals, and as a nu-

**Pronunciation Key:** hat, āge, cãre, fär; let, ēqual, tėrm; it, īce; hot, ōpen, ôrder; **oil, out**; cup, půt, rüle; **ch**ild; lo**ng**; **th**in; ᴛʜen; **zh,** measure; **ə** represents **a** in about, **e** in taken, **i** in pencil, **o** in lemon, **u** in circus.

clear fuel element. *Formula:* $UO_2$

**uranium oxide**, any one of various oxides of uranium obtained from uranium ores, especially uranium dioxide and uranium trioxide.

**uranium trioxide**, a red or yellow powder that is an intermediate in refining uranium and is used in making various glazes and colors in ceramics. *Formula:* $UO_3$

**u\|ra\|nog\|ra\|pher** (yůr′ə nog′rə fər), *n.* a person who practices or studies uranography.

**u\|ra\|no\|graph\|ic** (yůr′ə nə graf′ik), *adj.* of or having to do with uranography.

**u\|ra\|no\|graph\|i\|cal** (yůr′ə nə graf′ə kəl), *adj.* = uranographic.

**u\|ra\|nog\|ra\|phist** (yůr′ə nog′rə fist), *n.* an expert in uranography.

**u\|ra\|nog\|ra\|phy** (yůr′ə nog′rə fē), *n.* the science of describing and mapping the heavens and the position of the heavenly bodies. Also, **ouranography**. [< Greek *ouranographíā* < *ouranós* the heavens, sky + *gráphein* to draw]

**u\|ra\|no\|log\|i\|cal** (yůr′ə nə loj′ə kəl), *adj.* of or having to do with uranology.

**u\|ra\|nol\|o\|gy** (yůr′ə nol′ə jē), *n., pl.* **-gies. 1** = astronomy. **2** an astronomical treatise. [< Late Latin *ūranus* the heavens, sky (< Greek *ouranós*) + English *-logy*]

**u\|ra\|nom\|e\|try** (yůr′ə nom′ə trē), *n., pl.* **-tries. 1** a map or description of the heavens showing the stars with names, magnitudes, relative positions, and various other data. **2** the measurement of stellar distances. [< Late Latin *ūranus* the heavens (< Greek *ouranós*) + English *-metry*]

**u\|ra\|nous** (yůr′ə nəs), *adj.* **1** of uranium. **2** containing uranium, especially with a valence of four.

***U\|ra\|nus** (yů rā′nəs, yůr′ə-), *n.* **1** *Greek Mythology.* a god who represented heaven. Uranus was the husband or son of Gaea (Earth), the father of the Titans, the Cyclopes, and the Furies, and the original ruler of the world. He was eventually overthrown by his son Cronus, the youngest of the Titans, at Gaea's instigation in revenge for Uranus' imprisoning his children in Tartarus. **2** one of the larger planets in the solar system and the seventh in distance from the sun. See diagram under **solar system**. [< Late Latin *Ūranus,* the god < Greek *Ouranós* (literally) the heavens, sky]

***Uranus** definition 2

symbol

**u\|ra\|nyl** (yůr′ə nəl), *n.* a bivalent radical, $UO_2$—, existing in many compounds of uranium, and forming salts with acids. [< *uran*(ium) + *-yl*]

**u\|ra\|nyl\|ic** (yůr′ə nil′ik), *adj.* **1** of or having to do with uranyl. **2** containing uranyl.

**u\|rase** (yůr′ās, -āz), *n.* = urease.

**u\|rate** (yůr′āt), *n.* a salt of uric acid. [< French *urate* < *urique* uric + *-ate* -ate²]

**urb** (ėrb), *n. U.S.* an urban or metropolitan area: *The growth of American suburbia, fed by the yearning for a home of one's own, raises problems for urb and suburb alike* (New York Times Magazine). [abstracted from *urban* and *suburb*]

**ur\|ban** (ėr′bən), *adj.* **1** that is or has the essential characteristics of a city or town: *an urban community, an urban center.* **2** of or having to do with cities and towns: *urban planning.* **3** living in a city or cities: *urban population. Most people who live in apartments are urban dwellers.* **4** characteristic of cities: *urban life.* **5** accustomed to or inclined toward cities: *a man still urban after 20 years in the country.* [< Latin *urbānus* < *urbs* city]

**urban district**, (in England, Wales, and Northern Ireland) a subdivision of a county, often containing several towns or cities, governed by a local council but not having the charter of a borough.

**ur\|bane** (ėr bān′), *adj.* **1** having the elegance of manner, refinement of taste, or sophisticated polish formerly rare outside of the city; courteous, refined, or elegant: *urbane manners.* **2** smoothly polite; suave: *an urbane scoundrel.* [< Latin *urbānus* (originally) urban. See related etym. at **urban.**] —**ur\|bane′ly**, *adv.* —**ur\|bane′ness**, *n.*

**urban guerrilla**, **1** a revolutionary who uses guerrilla tactics in the cities to spread terror and undermine the government. **2** an organized band of urban guerrillas.

**urban homesteading**, a program of the U.S. government to restore run-down urban areas by offering ownership of abandoned or neglected housing in return for repairing a building to suitable condition and living in it for a specified length of time: *Urban homesteading offers abandoned or foreclosed housing, free or at nominal cost, to those agreeing to rehabilitate and occupy it over a given period* (Joseph P. Fried).

**ur\|ban\|ise** (ėr′bə nīz), *v.t.,* **-ised, -is\|ing.** *Especially British.* urbanize.

**ur\|ban\|ism** (ėr′bə niz əm), *n.* **1** urban character or life. **2** the study of urban life. **3** the development of urban areas; urbanization.

**ur\|ban\|ist** (ėr′bə nist), *n.* = city planner.

**ur\|ban\|is\|tic** (ėr′bə nis′tik), *adj.* of or having to do with urbanists or urbanism. —**ur′ban\|is′ti\|cal\|ly**, *adv.*

**ur\|ban\|ite** (ėr′bə nīt), *n.* a dweller in a city: *Suburbanites and urbanites have successfully sought relief from the political monopoly of legislative power long exercised by America's rural minorities* (Atlantic).

**ur\|ban\|i\|ty** (ėr ban′ə tē), *n., pl.* **-ties. 1** the character or quality of being urbane; courtesy, refinement, or elegance: *When we think of Athens we think . . . of urbanity and clarity and moderation in all things* (James H. Robinson). **2** smooth politeness. **3** the character or condition of being urban. **urbanities**, civilities; courtesies: *She smiled and murmured urbanities* (Leonard Merrick). [< Latin *urbānitās* < *urbānus;* see etym. under **urban**]

**ur\|ban\|i\|za\|tion** (ėr′bə nə zā′shən), *n.* the process of making or becoming urban.

**ur\|ban\|ize** (ėr′bə nīz), *v.t., v.i.,* **-ized, -iz\|ing.** to make or become urban: *to urbanize an area.*

**ur\|ban\|oid** (ėr′bə noid), *adj.* having the characteristics of a large city: *I use "kakotopia" as the opposite of "utopia," to describe a misplanned and ugly urbanoid place* (Lewis Mumford).

**ur\|ban\|ol\|o\|gist** (ėr′bə nol′ə jist), *n.* an expert in urbanology.

**ur\|ban\|ol\|o\|gy** (ėr′bə nol′ə jē), *n.* the study of cities and their problems: *Just as the word urbanology is a cross between Latin and Greek, the science— or is it an art?— is a mélange of many disciplines* (Time).

**urban renewal**, improvement of urban areas by removing slums and converting them into attractive living or industrial areas: *The heart of downtown Denver has been torn out in the name of urban renewal, with one old-fashioned block of Larimer Street left to preserve its memory* (New York Times).

**urban sprawl**, the uncontrolled growth of a city over the countryside: *The automobile has brought another consequence that tends to be overlooked but is no less serious: by fostering "urban sprawl" it has in effect isolated much of the population* (Scientific American).

**ur\|bi\|cul\|ture** (ėr′bə kul′chər), *n.* the care of cities and city people; urban interests.

**ur\|bi et or\|bi** (ėr′bī et ôr′bī), *Latin.* to the city (Rome) and to the world; to mankind (used especially in the publication of papal bulls).

**ur\|ce\|o\|late** (ėr′sē ə lit, -lāt), *adj.* shaped like a pitcher; swelling out like a pitcher and contracted at the orifice, as a calyx. [< New Latin *urceolatus* < Latin *urceolus* (diminutive) < *urceus* pitcher]

**ur\|chin** (ėr′chən), *n.* **1** a poor, ragged child: *Urchins played in the street. . . . ragged urchins . . . peeping through the railings* (John L. Motley). **2** a mischievous boy. **3** a small boy. **4** = sea urchin. **5** *Archaic.* an elf. **6** *Archaic or Dialect.* a hedgehog. [Middle English *urchun* hedgehog < Old French *irechon* < Latin *ērīcius* < *ēr, ēris;* (the term was applied to persons because of a belief that goblins took the shape of a hedgehog)]

**urd** (ėrd), *n.* a bean, a variety of the mung bean, largely cultivated throughout India; black gram. [< Hindustani *urd*]

**Urd** (ůrd), *n. Norse Mythology.* one of the three Norns or goddesses of fate, a giantess representing the past.

**Ur\|du** (ůr′dü, ėr′-; ůr dü′, ėr-), *n.* Moslem form of Hindustani, spoken in India and Pakistan, using Arabic and Persian loan words and the Arabic alphabet. Urdu is the official language of Pakistan. [< Hindustani (*zaban-i-*) *urdū* (language of) camp < Persian; *urdū,* ultimately < Turkic *ordu* army, or Tartar *urda.* Compare etym. under **horde.**]

**-ure**, *suffix added to verbs to form nouns.* **1** the act or fact of____ing: *Failure = the act of failing.*
**2** the condition of being____ed: *Pleasure = the condition of being pleased.*
**3** the result of being ____ed: *Exposure = the result of being exposed.*
**4** something that ____s: *Legislature = something that legislates.*
**5** a thing that is____ed: *Disclosure = a thing that is disclosed.*
**6** other special meanings, as in *procedure, sculpture, denture.*
[< French *-ure* < Latin *-ūra,* or directly < Latin]

**u\|re\|a** (yů rē′ə, yůr′ē ə), *n.* a substance found in the urine of mammals and in other body fluids as a product of protein metabolism, or produced synthetically; carbamide. In nature it is a crystalline, nitrogenous solid. Synthesized urea is used in making adhesives and plastics and in fertilizers and medicine. *Formula:* $CH_4N_2O$ [< New Latin *urea* < French *urée* < *urine*]

**u\|re\|a-for\|mal\|de\|hyde resins** (yů rē′ə fôr mal′də hīd, yůr′ē-), = urea resins.

**u\|re\|al** (yů rē′əl, yůr′ē-), *adj.* **1** of or relating to urea. **2** containing urea.

**urea resins**, a group of synthetic, thermosetting resins obtained from urea and formaldehyde, used in adhesives, moldings, and plastics.

**u\|re\|ase** (yůr′ē ās, -āz), *n.* an enzyme present in various bacteria, fungi, and beans, which promotes the decomposition of urea into ammonium carbonate. Also, **urase**.

**u\|re\|di\|al stage** (yů rē′dē əl), = uredostage.

**u\|re\|din\|i\|al stage** (yůr′ə din′ē əl), = uredostage.

**u\|re\|din\|i\|o\|spore** (yůr′ə din′ē ə spôr, -spōr), *n.* = uredospore.

**u\|re\|din\|i\|um** (yůr′ə din′ē əm), *n., pl.* **-i\|a** (-ē ə). = uredium.

**u\|re\|di\|um** (yů rē′dē əm), *n., pl.* **-di\|a** (-dē ə). *Botany.* a pustule bearing uredospores, formed by certain rust fungi. [< *ured* (o) + New Latin *-ium,* a diminutive suffix]

**u\|re\|do** (yů rē′dō), *n.* **1** = urticaria. **2** = uredostage. [< Latin *ūrēdō, -inis* itch, blight < *ūrere* to burn]

**u\|re\|do\|so\|rus** (yů rē′də sôr′əs, -sōr′-), *n., pl.* **-so\|ri** (-sôr′ī, -sōr′-). = uredium.

**u\|re\|do\|spore** (yů rē′də spôr, -spōr), *n. Botany.* a one-celled, orange or brownish spore produced by certain rust fungi. Uredospores appear in the summer after the aeciospores and before the teliospores, and reproduce and extend the fungus rapidly.

**u\|re\|do\|stage** (yů rē′də stāj′), *n.,* or **uredo stage**, *Botany.* the phase in the life cycle of certain rust fungi in which uredospores are produced.

**u\|re\|id** (yůr′ē id), *n.* = ureide.

**u\|re\|ide** (yůr′ē īd, -id), *n.* a derivative of urea containing acid radicals, as urethane.

**u\|re\|mi\|a** (yů rē′mē ə), *n.* an abnormal condition resulting from the accumulation in the blood of waste products that should normally be eliminated in the urine. Nephritis is a frequent cause of uremia. Also, **uraemia**. [< New Latin *uremia* < Greek *oûron* urine + *haîma* blood]

**u\|re\|mic** (yů rē′mik), *adj.* **1** of or having to do with uremia: *Uremic poisoning can result from too much urea in the blood.* **2** suffering from uremia.

**u\|re\|o\|tel\|ic** (yůr′ē ō tel′ik), *adj.* having urea as the main constituent of nitrogenous waste. Mammals are ureotelic. [< *urea* + Greek *télos* end + English *-ic*]

**u\|re\|sis** (yů rē′sis), *n. Medicine.* urination. [< New Latin *uresis* < Greek *oúresis* urination]

**u\|re\|ter** (yů rē′tər, yůr′ə-), *n.* a duct that carries urine from a kidney to the bladder or the cloaca. See diagram under **kidney**. [< Greek *ourētḗr, -ēros* < *oureîn* to urinate < *oûron* urine]

**u\|re\|ter\|al** (yů rē′tər əl), *adj.* of or having to do with a ureter.

**u\|re\|ter\|ec\|to\|my** (yů rē′tə rek′tə mē), *n., pl.* **-mies.** surgical removal of the ureter. [< *ureter* + *-ectomy*]

**u\|re\|ter\|ic** (yůr′ə ter′ik), *adj.* = ureteral.

**u\|re\|than** (yůr′ə than′, yů reth′an), *n.* **1** a compound derived from urethane. **2** = urethane.

**u\|re\|thane** (yůr′ə thān′, yů reth′ān), *n.* **1** a strong, fire-resistant plastic resin made in rigid or flexible form and widely used as insulation and as a binder, filler, and stiffener; polyurethane. **2** any ester of carbamic acid. **3** a colorless or white crystalline compound, used in medicine and in organic synthesis. *Formula:* $C_3H_7NO_2$ [< French *uréthane* < *urée* (see etym. under **urea**) + *-thane*]

**urethane foam**, a foam derived from polyurethane, used especially for padding and filters.

**u\|re\|thra** (yů rē′thrə), *n., pl.* **-thrae** (-thrē), **-thras**. the duct in most mammals through which urine is discharged from the bladder, and, in males, through which the semen is also discharged. See diagram under **kidney**. [< Late Latin *ūrethra* < Greek *ourḗthra* < *oureîn* urinate; see etym. under **ureter**]

**u\|re\|thral** (yů rē′thrəl), *adj.* of or having to do with the urethra.

**u\|re\|threc\|to\|my** (yůr′ə threk′tə mē), *n., pl.* **-mies**. surgical removal of all or a part of the urethra. [< *urethra* + *-ectomy*]

**u\|re\|thrit\|ic** (yůr′ə thrit′ik), *adj.* affected with urethritis.

**u\|re\|thri\|tis** (yůr′ə thrī′tis), *n.* inflammation of the urethra.

**u\|re\|thro\|scope** (yů rē′thrə skōp), *n.* an instrument for examining the urethra. [< *urethra* + *-scope*]

**u\|re\|thros\|co\|py** (yůr′ə thros′kə pē), *n.* examination of the urethra with a urethroscope.

**u\|re\|throt\|o\|my** (yůr′ə throt′ə mē), *n., pl.* **-mies**. surgical correction of a stricture of the urethra. [< *urethra* + *-tomy*]

**u\|ret\|ic** (yů ret′ik), *adj.* of or having to do with urine; diuretic. [< Late Latin *ūrēticus* < Greek *ourētikós* < *oureîn* urinate; see etym. under **ureter**]

**urge** (ėrj), *v.*, **urged, urg|ing,** *n.* —*v.t.* **1** to push, force, or drive forward or onward: *The rider urged on his tired horse with whip and spurs. Hunger urged him to steal.* **SYN**: press, incite. **2** to cause to hasten or gather speed; accelerate the pace of; speed up: *to urge a trotting horse into a gallop.* **3** to try to persuade with arguments; ask or request earnestly; plead with; entreat: *We urged them to stay for dinner.* **4** to press the need of; plead or argue earnestly for; recommend strongly: *The superintendent of schools urged a larger budget for education. His doctor urges a change of climate. Motorists urged better roads.* **5** to press upon the attention; refer to often and with emphasis: *to urge a claim, to urge an argument.* **6** to use, work, or employ briskly or diligently: *and urge The strokes of the inexorable scourge* (Shelley).
—*v.i.* **1** to be or act as an impelling force: *Fear urges, reason exhorts* (David Hume). **2** to present arguments or statements for or against something.
—*n.* **1** a driving force or impulse: *The urge of hunger made him beg. Always the procreant urge of the world* (Whitman). **2** the act of urging.
[< Latin *urgēre*]

**ur|gence** (ėr′jəns), *n.* = urgency.

**ur|gen|cy** (ėr′jən sē), *n., pl.* **-cies.** **1** the condition or fact of being urgent; need for immediate action or attention; urgent situation: *A house on fire is a matter of great urgency. Anxiety to secure the future blunts attention to the urgencies of the present* (John Morley). **2** insistence; persistence.

**ur|gent** (ėr′jənt), *adj.* **1** demanding immediate action or attention; pressing; important: *an urgent duty, an urgent message.* **SYN**: imperative, necessary. **2** insistent; persistent. **SYN**: importunate. [< Latin *urgēns, -entis,* present participle of *urgēre* to urge] —**ur′gent|ly,** *adv.*

**-uria,** *combining form.* a state (usually abnormal or morbid) of the urine due to the presence of ___, as in *albuminuria, glycosuria, pyuria.* [< New Latin *-uria* < Greek *-ouria* < *oûron* urine]

**U|ri|ah** (yů rī′ə), *n.* a Hittite soldier in David's army, the husband of Bathsheba. David arranged for Uriah to be killed in battle so that he could marry Bathsheba (in the Bible, II Samuel 11:2-27).

**u|ri|al** (ůr′ē əl), *n.* a wild sheep of southern Asia, usually reddish-brown, and somewhat like the bighorn. Also, **oorial.** [< a native name]

**u|ric** (yůr′ik), *adj.* **1** of or having to do with urine. **2** found in urine. [probably < French *urique* < *urine* urine]

**uric acid,** a white, crystalline acid, only slightly soluble in water, found in the urine of man, certain animals, reptiles, and birds. It is formed as a waste product of the metabolism of purines. *Formula:* $C_5H_4N_4O_3$

**u|ri|case** (yůr′ə kās), *n.* a liver enzyme in lower mammals that breaks down uric acid into allantoin before excretion. The presence of uricase prevents the formation of uric acid in the joints. [< *uric* + *-ase*]

**u|ri|co|sur|ic** (yůr′ə kō sůr′ik), *adj.* aiding or stimulating the passing of uric acid.

**u|ri|co|tel|ic** (yůr′ə kō tel′ik), *adj.* having uric acid as the main constituent of nitrogenous waste. Birds and snakes are uricotelic. [< *uric* (acid) + Greek *télos* end + English *-ic*]

**u|ri|dine** (yůr′ə din, -dēn), *n.* a white powder, a nucleoside of uracil, present in ribonucleic acid. *Formula:* $C_9H_{12}N_2O_6$

**U|ri|el** (yůr′ē əl), *n.* one of the archangels in Hebrew and Christian tradition.

**U|rim** (yůr′im), *n.pl.* (in the Old Testament) objects whose nature is not known but which were used in connection with the breastplate of the high priest and which served some oracular purpose (usually in the phrase *Urim and Thummim,* as in Exodus 28:30, but sometimes alone, as in Numbers 27:21). [< Hebrew *'urim,* plural, perhaps < *'or* light]

**u|ri|nal** (yůr′ə nəl), *n.* **1** a container for urine, now especially a plumbing fixture designed for use by men or boys. **2** a room, building, or other place for urinating. [< Late Latin *ūrīnal* chamber pot, ultimately < Latin *ūrīna* urine]

**u|ri|nal|y|sis** (yůr′ə nal′ə sis), *n., pl.* **-ses** (-sēz). a chemical analysis of a sample of urine. By means of urinalysis doctors can detect certain diseases, such as diabetes. Also, **uranalysis.**

**u|ri|nar|y** (yůr′ə ner′ē), *adj., n., pl.* **-nar|ies.** —*adj.* **1** of or having to do with urine. **2** like urine. **3** of or having to do with the organs that secrete and discharge urine. **4** affecting or occurring in these organs.
—*n.* **1** = urinal. **2** *Obsolete.* a reservoir for keeping urine, etc., to be used as manure.

**urinary bladder,** = bladder.

**urinary calculus,** a stone formed in any part of the urinary passages; urolith.

**u|ri|nate** (yůr′ə nāt), *v.i.,* **-nat|ed, -nat|ing.** to discharge urine from the body. [< Medieval Latin *urinare* (with English *-ate*[1]) < Latin *ūrīna* urine]

**u|ri|na|tion** (yůr′ə nā′shən), *n.* the act of discharging urine.

**u|ri|na|tive** (yůr′ə nā′tiv), *adj.* provoking the flow of urine; diuretic.

**u|rine** (yůr′ən), *n.* the fluid that is excreted by the kidneys as a waste product of the body. Human urine goes through the ureters into the bladder and is then discharged from the body through the urethra. Normal human urine is amber in color and slightly acid and has a specific gravity of about 1.02. [< Latin *ūrīna,* related to Greek *oûron*]

**urine analysis,** = urinalysis.

**u|ri|nif|er|ous** (yůr′ə nif′ər əs), *adj.* conveying urine.

**u|ri|no|gen|i|tal** (yůr′ə nō jen′ə təl), *adj.* = urogenital.

**u|ri|nom|e|ter** (yůr′ə nom′ə tər), *n.* an instrument for measuring the specific gravity of urine.

**u|ri|nose** (yůr′ə nōs), *adj.* = urinous.

**u|ri|nous** (yůr′ə nəs), *adj.* **1** of or having to do with urine or containing urine. **2** resembling urine in color, odor, etc.

***urn** (ėrn), *n.* **1** a vase with a foot or pedestal. Urns were used in Greece and Rome to hold the ashes of the dead. **2** a place of burial; grave; tomb. **3** a coffeepot or teapot with a faucet near the bottom, used for making or serving coffee or tea at the table. **4** *Botany.* the hollow vessel in which the spores of a moss are produced. [< Latin *urna* a vessel of burned clay < *ūrere* to burn]

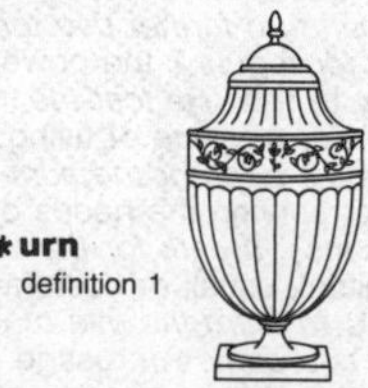

***urn**
definition 1

**uro-**[1], *combining form.* urine; urinary: *Urogenous = secreting urine.* [< Greek *oûron*]

**uro-**[2], *combining form.* tail; posterior part, as in *urochord, uropod.* [< Greek *ourā́* tail]

**u|ro|can|ic acid** (yůr′ə kan′ik), an acid that is a product of the metabolism of histidine, found in dog's urine and also in the human epidermis, where it is thought to absorb and dissipate harmful ultraviolet rays. *Formula:* $C_6H_6N_2O_2$ [< *uro-*[1] + Latin *canis* dog + English *-ic*]

**u|ro|chord** (yůr′ə kôrd), *n. Zoology.* the notochord of an ascidian larva, usually limited to the caudal region. [< *uro-*[2] + *chord*[2]]

**u|ro|chor|dal** (yůr′ə kôr′dəl), *adj.* **1** provided with a urochord. **2** of or having to do with the urochord or larvae having urochords.

**u|ro|chrome** (yůr′ə krōm), *n.* the yellow pigment which colors urine. [< *uro-*[1] + *chrōma* color]

**u|rochs** (yůr′oks), *n.* = aurochs.

**u|ro|dele** (yůr′ə dēl), *adj., n.* —*adj.* belonging to an order of amphibians which retain the tail throughout life, including the salamanders and newts.
—*n.* a urodele amphibian.
[< New Latin *Urodela* the former order name < Greek *ourā́* tail + *dêlos* visible]

**u|ro|gen|i|tal** (yůr′ə jen′ə təl), *adj.* having to do with the urinary and genital organs; urinogenital.

**u|rog|e|nous** (yů roj′ə nəs), *adj.* **1** secreting or producing urine. **2** obtained from or present in urine. [< *uro-*[1] + *-gen* + *-ous*]

**u|rog|ra|phy** (yů rog′rə fē), *n., pl.* **-phies.** the examination of the urinary tract, kidneys, bladder, etc., by means of X rays or the like. [< *uro-*[1] + *-graphy*]

**ur|o|ki|nase** (yůr′ō kī′nās, -kin′ās), *n.* a protein enzyme that dissolves blood clots: *Urokinase* [*is*] *found as a trace in human urine* (New York Times). [< *uro-*[1] + *kinase*]

**u|ro|lith** (yůr′ə lith), *n.* = urinary calculus.

**u|ro|li|thi|a|sis** (yůr′ə li thī′ə sis), *n. Medicine.* the formation of urinary calculi; lithiasis occurring in the urinary tract.

**u|ro|lith|ic** (yůr′ə lith′ik), *adj.* of or having to do with a urinary calculus.

**u|ro|log|ic** (yůr′ə loj′ik), *adj.* = urological.

**u|ro|log|i|cal** (yůr′ə loj′ə kəl), *adj.* of or having to do with urology or the urinary tract.

**u|rol|o|gist** (yů rol′ə jist), *n.* an expert in urology.

**u|rol|o|gy** (yů rol′ə jē), *n.* the branch of medicine dealing with the urogenital tract in the male or the urinary tract in the female and their diseases. Also, **ourology.** [< *uro-*[1] + *-logy*]

**u|ron|ic acid** (yů ron′ik), any one of a group of chemical compounds found in urine and in mucopolysaccharides, formed by oxidation of the primary alcohol groups of sugars. Galacturonic acid and glucuronic acid are common uronic acids. [< Greek *oûron* urine + English *-ic*]

**u|ro|pod** (yůr′ə pod), *n.* an abdominal appendage of an arthropod, especially one of the last pair of paddlelike appendages of a lobster. [< *uro-*[2] + Greek *poús, podós* foot]

**u|ro|pyg|i|al** (yůr′ə pij′ē əl), *adj., n.* —*adj.* of or having to do with the uropygium.
—*n.* a tail feather, especially a large tail feather.

**uropygial gland,** a large gland opening on the backs of many birds at the base of the tail, with an oily secretion used in preening the feathers; preen gland; oil gland.

**u|ro|pyg|i|um** (yůr′ə pij′ē əm), *n.* the rump of a bird, which bears the tail feathers. [< Medieval Latin *uropygium* < Greek *ouropýgion* < *ourā́* tail + *pygḗ* rump]

**u|ro|scop|ic** (yůr′ə skop′ik), *adj.* having to do with the inspection of urine in the diagnosis and treatment of disease.

**u|ros|co|pist** (yů ros′kə pist), *n.* a person who makes a specialty of urinary examinations.

**u|ros|co|py** (yů ros′kə pē), *n., pl.* **-pies.** the examination of the urine, especially as a means of diagnosis. Also, **ouroscopy.** [< New Latin *uroscopia* < Greek *oûron* urine + *-scopia* -scopy]

**u|ro|style** (yůr′ə stīl), *n. Zoology.* the posterior unsegmented portion of the vertebral column in certain fishes and amphibians. [< *uro-*[2] + Greek *stŷlos* pillar]

**U|rot|ro|pin** (yů rot′rə pin), *n. Trademark.* a colorless, crystalline substance prepared by the action of ammonia on formaldehyde, used chiefly as a urinary antiseptic. *Formula:* $C_6H_{12}N_4$ [< *uro-*[1] + Greek *-tropos* a turning + English *-in*]

**u|ro|xan|thin** (yůr′ə zan′thin), *n.* = indican (def. 2). [< German *Uroxanthin* < Greek *oûron* urine + German *Xanthin* xanthin]

**ur-per|form|ance** (ůr′pər fôr′məns), *n.* the original performance, especially of a musical composition: *The BBC ... are offering the symphonies in urtext and* (*as far as may be*) *in ur-performance—that is, with original mistakes uncorrected* (Manchester Guardian Weekly).

**Ur|sa** (ėr′sə), *n. Astronomy.* **1** Ursa Major. **2** Ursa Minor.

**Ur|sae Ma|jor|is** (ėr′sē mə jō′ris), genitive of **Ursa Major.**

**Ur|sae Mi|nor|is** (ėr′sē mi nō′ris, -nôr′-), genitive of **Ursa Minor.**

**Ursa Major,** *genitive* **Ur|sae Ma|jor|is.** the most prominent northern constellation, shaped somewhat like a bear with an enormous tail, and including the seven stars of the Big Dipper, two of which (the Pointers) point toward the North Star (Polaris); Great Bear. See picture under **constellation.** [< Latin *Ursa Major* (literally) larger bear]

**Ursa Minor,** *genitive* **Ur|sae Mi|nor|is.** the northern constellation, shaped somewhat like a bear, that includes the seven stars of the Little Dipper, with the North Star (Polaris) at the end of its handle (or at the tip of the Little Bear's tail); Little or Lesser Bear; Cynosure. See picture under **constellation.** [< Latin *Ursa Minor* (literally) smaller bear]

**ur|si|form** (ėr′sə fôrm), *adj.* having the form or appearance of a bear. [< Latin *ursus* bear + English *-form*]

**ur|sine** (ėr′sīn, -sin), *adj.* **1** of or having to do with a bear; bearlike: *noted for ursine manners* (Robert Southey). **2** covered with stiff hairlike processes: *ursine caterpillars.* [< Latin *ursīnus* < *ursus* bear]

**ursine dasyure,** = Tasmanian devil.

**ursine howler,** a red howler or howling monkey of Brazil.

**ur|son** (ėr′sən), *n.* the porcupine of forest regions of northern and western North America, of large size with short spines and long hairs. [< Canadian French *ourson* (diminutive) < French *ours* bear < Latin *ursus*]

**Ur|spra|che** (ůr′shprä′ʜə), *n.* an original or parent language, especially proto-Germanic or Indo-European, reconstructed by comparison of common forms in cognate languages. [< German *Ursprache* < *ur-* primitive + *Sprache* language]

**Ur|su|line** (ėr′sə lin, -līn; -syə-), *n., adj.* —*n.* a member of a Roman Catholic order of women, founded by Saint Angela Merici in 1535 for the teaching of girls and the care of the sick and needy.
—*adj.* of or having to do with this order.
[< New Latin *Ursulinae,* feminine plural < Saint *Ursula*]

**ur|text** (ůr′tekst′), *n.* the original text, especially of a musical composition: *This is the last word*

**Pronunciation Key:** hat, āge, cãre, fär; let, ēqual, tėrm; it, īce; hot, ōpen, ôrder; oil, out; cup, půt, rüle; child; long; thin; ᴛʜen; zh, measure; ə represents a in about, e in taken, i in pencil, o in lemon, u in circus.

*on Feuerfest, unless someone produces an ur-text containing Strauss's own marginalia on the subject* (Saturday Review).

**ur|ti|ca|ceous** (ėr′tə kā′shəs), *adj.* belonging to a family of dicotyledonous herbs, shrubs, and trees, many of which, such as the nettle, are covered with stinging hairs. [< New Latin *Urticaceae* the family name (< *Urtica* the genus name < Latin *urtīca* nettle, probably < *ūrere* to burn) + English *-ous*]

**ur|ti|car|i|a** (ėr′tə kãr′ē ə), *n.* = hives. [< New Latin *urticaria* < Latin *urtīca* nettle; see etym. under **urticate**]

**ur|ti|car|i|al** (ėr′tə kãr′ē əl), *adj.* **1** of or having to do with urticaria. **2** like urticaria. **3** affected with urticaria.

**ur|ti|cate** (ėr′tə kāt), *v.*, **-cat|ed, -cat|ing.** —*v.t.* **1** to sting with or as if with nettles. **2** to whip (a benumbed or paralyzed limb) with nettles to restore sensation or circulation. —*v.i.* to sting as or like a nettle. [< Medieval Latin *urticare* (with English *-ate*[1]) < Latin *urtīca* nettle, probably < *ūrere* to burn]

**ur|ti|ca|tion** (ėr′tə kā′shən), *n.* **1** the act or process of urticating, especially in medicine. **2** a pricking sensation suggestive of stinging with nettles.

**Uru.**, Uruguay.

**u|ru|bu** (ü′rü bü′), *n.* the black vulture or carrion crow, ranging from Argentina to the southern United States. [< Tupi (Brazil) *urubú*]

**U|ru|guay|an** (yůr′ə gwā′ən, -gwī′-), *adj., n.* —*adj.* of or having to do with Uruguay or its people. —*n.* a native or inhabitant of Uruguay.

**u|rus** (yůr′əs), *n.* = aurochs (def. 2). [< Latin *ūrus* < Germanic (compare Old High German *ūr*)]

**u|ru|shi|ol** (ü rü′shē ol, -ōl), *n.* a poisonous, pale, oily liquid derived from catechol. It is the active irritant principle in poison ivy, and is used in making lacquer and for tests as an allergen. *Formula:* $C_{21}H_{32}O_2$ [< Japanese *urushi* lacquer + English *-ol*[2]]

**us** (us; *unstressed* əs), *pron. Objective case of* **we**: *We learn; the teacher helps us. Please bring us food. Mother went with us to the theater. Please don't forsake us.* [Old English *ūs*]

**u.s.**, *Latin.* **1** ubi supra. **2** ut supra.

**US** (no periods), the United States.

**U.S.**, **1** the United States. **2** United States Supreme Court Reports.

**U.S.** or **U.S. No.**, United States Highway: *to turn left on U.S. 40 and follow it into the city.*

**U.S.A.** or **USA** (no periods), **1** Union of South Africa. **2** United States Army. **3** United States of America.

**us|a|bil|i|ty** (yü′zə bil′ə tē), *n.* a being usable. Also, **useability.**

**us|a|ble** (yü′zə bəl), *adj.* **1** that can be used; capable of use. **2** fit or proper to be used; suitable for use. Also, **useable.** —**us′a|ble|ness**, *n.*

**USAC** (no periods) or **U.S.A.C.**, United States Auto Club.

**USAF** (no periods) or **U.S.A.F.**, United States Air Force.

**USAFI** (no periods), United States Armed Forces Institute.

**USAFR** (no periods) or **U.S.A.F.R.**, United States Air Force Reserve.

**us|age** (yü′sij, -zij), *n.* **1** way or manner of using; treatment: *This car has had rough usage.* **2** a long-continued practice; customary use; habit; custom: *Travelers should learn many of the usages of the countries they visit.* **3** the customary way of using words: *a person familiar with American usage. The usage of the best writers and speakers determines what is good English.* **4** an instance of such use: *a new usage.* [< Anglo-French, Old French *usage,* ultimately < Latin *ūsus, -ūs*; see etym. under **use**, verb]

**USAID** (no periods), United States Agency for International Development.

**us|ance** (yü′zəns), *n.* **1** *Commerce.* the time (varying between different places) allowed for the payment of foreign bills of exchange. **2** income in any form derived from the ownership of any kind of wealth. [< Old French *usance* < Vulgar Latin *ūsāre,* see etym. under **use**, verb]

**USAR** (no periods) or **U.S.A.R.**, United States Army Reserve.

**Us|beg** (us′beg), *n.* = Uzbek.

**Us|bek** (us′bek), *n.* = Uzbek.

**U.S.C.**, **1** United States Code. **2** United States of Colombia. **3** University of Southern California.

**U.S.C.A.**, United States Code Annotated.

**USCC** (no periods), United States Commercial Company.

**USCG** (no periods) or **U.S.C.G.**, United States Coast Guard.

**USCGR** (no periods) or **U.S.C.G.R.**, United States Coast Guard Reserve.

**USCGS** (no periods) or **U.S.C. & G.S.**, United States Coast and Geodetic Survey.

**U.S.C. Supp.**, United States Code Supplement.

**USDA** (no periods) or **U.S.D.A.**, United States Department of Agriculture.

**use** (*v.* yüz; *n.* yüs), *v.*, **used, us|ing,** *n.* —*v.t.* **1** to put into action or service; utilize: *We use our legs in walking. We use spoons to eat soup. He used a knife to cut the meat.* **2** to employ or practice actively; exercise, especially habitually or customarily: *to use one's knowledge, authority, or judgment.* **3** to employ (as words and phrases); say; utter: *to use bad grammar.* **4** to act toward in a certain way; treat: *He used us well. Use others as you would have them use you.* **5** to consume or expend by using: *to use most of the available funds, to use water for irrigation. He uses tobacco. Most of the money you gave me has been used.* **6** to avail oneself of; put to one's own purposes: *May I use your telephone?*

—*v.i. Archaic.* to go frequently to a place; frequent: *But we be only sailormen That use in London town* (Rudyard Kipling).

[< Old French *user* < Vulgar Latin *ūsāre* < Latin *ūsus, -ūs* act of using < *ūtī* to use]

—*n.* **1** the act of using: *the use of tools, the use of a catalyst in a chemical process.* SYN: employment, application, utilization. **2** the condition of being used: *methods long out of use.* **3** the quality of being useful; usefulness; advantage or benefit: *a thing of no practical use. There is no use in crying over spilled milk.* SYN: utility. **4** a purpose that a thing is used for: *to find a new use for something.* **5a** the way of using: *a proper use of one's time, a poor use of a material.* **b** employment or usage resulting in or causing wear, damage, or the like. **6** need or occasion for using; necessity; demand: *We found no further use for it. A hunter often has use for a gun.* **7** the power or capacity of using; ability to use: *He lost the use of his hand.* **8** the right or privilege of using: *He had the use of his friend's boat for the summer.* **9** the fact or quality of serving the needs or ends (of a person or persons): *a park for the use of all the people.* **10a** habitual, usual, or customary practice; custom; habit: *to learn the use of the sea. It was his use to rise early.* SYN: usage, wont. **b** the distinctive ritual and form of service, or any liturgical form, of a particular church, diocese, province, or other segment: *Sarum use, Roman use.* **11** *Law.* **a** the act or fact of employing, occupying, possessing, or holding property so as to derive benefit from it. **b** the right of a beneficiary to the benefit or profits of land or tenements to which another has legal title in trust for the beneficiary. **c** a trust vesting title to real property in someone for the benefit of another.

**have no use for, a** not to need or want: *You may have the book; I have no use for it any longer.* **b** *Informal, Figurative.* to dislike: *The Marquis had ... spoken in French, and the Captain had no use for that language* (H. S. Merriman).

**in use,** being used: *All the fashionable phrases and compliments now in use* (Richard Steele).

**make use of, a** to put in use; use; utilize; employ: *She made much use of milk in her cooking.* **b** to take advantage of: *Perhaps she had only made use of him as a convenient aid to her intentions* (Thomas Hardy).

**put to use,** to use; employ: *If you can put to use that old bicycle, you may have it. Every moment may be put to some use* (Lord Chesterfield).

**used to, a** accustomed to: *used to hardships. Eskimos are used to cold weather.* **b** was or were accustomed to; formerly did: *He used to come at 10 o'clock, but now he comes at noon.*

**use up,** to consume or expend entirely: *to use up the available funds. We have used up our sugar.*

[< Old French *us,* masculine, and *use,* feminine < Latin *ūsus;* see the verb]

—*Syn. v.t.* **1 Use, employ, utilize** mean to put into action or service for some purpose. **Use,** the general and common word, suggests any kind of purpose when applied to things but a selfish purpose when applied to persons: *He uses a typewriter for his schoolwork. He uses his friends to get ahead.* **Employ** suggests a special purpose: *That architect frequently employs glass brick.* **Utilize** suggests a practical purpose: *She utilizes every scrap of food.*

► **used to.** Before *to, used* is commonly pronounced (yüst) or (yüs).

**use|a|bil|i|ty** (yü′zə bil′ə tē), *n.* = usability.

**use|a|ble** (yü′zə bəl), *adj.* = usable. —**use′a|ble|ness,** *n.*

**used** (yüzd; yüst, yüs, *for 3, when immediately preceding "to"*), *adj.* **1** that has been used: **a** not new; that has belonged to someone else; second-hand: *a used car.* **b** not clean or fresh: *to remove used towels from a rack.* **2** that is used; in use; utilized: *a seldom used room.* **3** accustomed; usual; customary.

**used to.** See under **use.**

**used up,** *Informal.* tired out; thoroughly exhausted: [*He was*] *barefooted ... ; cleaned out to the last real, and completely used up* (Richard H. Dana).

**used-up** (yüzd′up′), *adj.* **1** *Informal.* thoroughly exhausted by physical exertion; tired out. **2** worn out or made useless, as by hard work, age, or dissipation: [*He*] *is by now a wholly dissipated, used-up drunk, his last reserves gone with the death of his mother* (Time). **3** reduced, exhausted, or consumed by using; depleted: *Underground salt domes and used-up oil wells are being considered* (Newsweek).

**use|ful** (yüs′fəl), *adj.* **1** of use; helpful: *a useful suggestion. She made herself useful about the house.* **2** giving or able to give service; serviceable; usable: *an old but still useful pair of shoes.* —**use′ful|ly,** *adv.* —**use′ful|ness,** *n.*

**use|less** (yüs′lis), *adj.* of no use; worthless: *a useless person, a useless effort. A television set would be useless without electricity.* —**use′less|ly,** *adv.* —**use′less|ness,** *n.*

—*Syn.* **Useless, ineffectual** mean having or being of no value for a purpose. **Useless** implies having no practical value under the circumstances: *An electric toaster is useless to a camper in the woods.* **Ineffectual** implies having no means to accomplish a purpose or having no effect whatever: *Her attempts to become friends again after the quarrel were ineffectual.*

**us|er** (yü′zər), *n.* **1** a person or thing that uses: *a constant user of the telephone, a heavy user of raw cotton.* **2** *Law.* **a** a right to use or enjoy property. **b** the use or enjoyment of property, or of the right to it.

**USES** (no periods), United States Employment Service.

**use tax** (yüs), *U.S.* state tax on goods purchased outside the state and later brought in.

**U.S.G.A.** or **USGA** (no periods), United States Golf Association.

**USGS** (no periods) or **U.S.G.S.**, United States Geological Survey.

**USHA** (no periods) or **U.S.H.A.**, United States Housing Authority.

**U-shaped** (yü′shāpt′), *adj.* having the shape of the letter U.

**U|shas** (ü′shəs, ů shäs′), *n.* the ancient Indian (Vedic) goddess of the dawn. [< Sanskrit *Ushas*]

**ush|er** (ush′ər), *n., v.* —*n.* **1** a person who shows people to their seats in a church, theater, or public hall. **2** *U.S.* a male friend of the bride or groom serving as an usher at a wedding. **3** *Especially British.* a person who has charge of the door and admits people to a hall or chamber, now especially one who is an official of or employed by a court or college. **4** *British.* an assistant teacher in an English school: *My companion was a schoolmaster and ... the youth, one of the bigger boys or the usher* (Charles Lamb).

—*v.t.* **1** to conduct or guide; escort; show: *The host ushered the visitors to the door.* **2** to go or come before; precede to announce the coming of: (*Figurative.*) *the stars that usher evening* (Milton).

**usher in,** to inaugurate; introduce: *a winter ushered in by cold rains.*

[< Anglo-French *uissier* < Vulgar Latin *ustiārius* doorkeeper < *ustium,* variant of Latin *ōstium* door, related to *ōs, ōris* mouth]

**ush|er|ette** (ush′ə ret′), *n.* a girl or woman usher.

**USIA** (no periods) or **U.S.I.A.**, United States Information Agency.

**USIS** (no periods) or **U.S.I.S.**, United States Information Service.

**U.S.L.T.A.** or **USLTA** (no periods), United States Lawn Tennis Association.

**USM** (no periods), United States Marine or Marines.

**U.S.M.**, **1** United States Mail. **2** United States Marine or Marines.

**U.S.M.A.** or **USMA** (no periods), United States Military Academy.

**USMC** (no periods) or **U.S.M.C.**, United States Marine Corps.

**USMCR** (no periods) or **U.S.M.C.R.**, United States Marine Corps Reserve.

**USN** (no periods) or **U.S.N.**, United States Navy.

**U.S.N.A.** or **USNA** (no periods), **1** United States National Army. **2** United States Naval Academy.

**us|ne|a** (us′nē ə), *n.* any lichen of a group, commonly found as a pendulous, grayish or yellowish, mosslike growth on trees or rocks in temperate or cool climates. [< New Latin *Usnea* the genus name, ultimately < Arabic, or Persian *ushnah* moss]

**USNG** (no periods) or **U.S.N.G.**, United States National Guard.

**us|nic acid** (us′nik), a yellow, crystalline substance derived from lichens, used as an antibiotic. *Formula:* $C_{18}H_{16}O_7$ [< *usn*(ea) + *-ic*]

**USNR** (no periods) or **U.S.N.R.**, United States Naval Reserve.

**USO** (no periods), United Service Organizations.

**USOE** (no periods), United States Office of Education.

**USOM** (no periods), United States Operations Mission.
**U.S.P.** or **USP** (no periods), United States Pharmacopeia.
**U.S.Pharm.**, United States Pharmacopeia.
**U.S.P.H.S.** or **USPHS** (no periods), United States Public Health Service.
**U.S.P.O.**, United States Post Office.
**us|que** (us′kwē), *n.* = usquebaugh.
**us|que ad a|ras** (us′kwē ad ā′ras), *Latin.* even to the altars; up to the point where one's religion intervenes.
**us|que|baugh** or **us|que|bae** (us′kwē bô, -bä), *n. Obsolete.* whiskey. [< Irish, and Scottish Gaelic *uisge beatha* (literally) water of life]
**USS** (no periods), United States Ship, Steamer, or Steamship.
**U.S.S.**, **1** United States Senate. **2** United States Ship, Steamer, or Steamship.
**U.S.S.C.**, United States Supreme Court.
**USSFA** (no periods), United States Soccer Football Association.
**U.S.S.R.** or **USSR** (no periods), Union of Soviet Socialist Republics.
**USTS** (no periods), United States Travel Service (an agency of the Department of Commerce).
**us|tu|late** (*v.* us′chə lāt; *adj.* us′chə lit, -lāt), *v.*, **-lat|ed, -lat|ing,** *adj. Obsolete.* **— *v.t., v.i.*** to scorch.
**— *adj.*** browned or blackened by or as if by scorching.
[< Latin *ustulāre* (with English *-ate*[1]) to burn (frequentative) < *ūrere* to burn]
**us|tu|la|tion** (us′chə lā′shən), *n.* **1** *Pharmacology.* the roasting or drying of moist substances in preparation for pulverizing. **2** *Obsolete.* the burning of wine.
**usu.**, **1** usual. **2** usually.
**u|su|al** (yü′zhü əl), *adj.* commonly seen, used, or happening; in common use; customary; ordinary: *Snow is usual in the Rocky Mountains during winter. My little brother's usual bedtime is 8 P.M.*
**as per usual,** *Informal.* as usual: *I shall accompany him, as per usual* (William S. Gilbert).
**as usual,** in the usual manner; at the usual time; as is customary: *We met, as usual, on the way to school. Our conversation opened, as usual, upon the weather* (John Dryden).
[< Late Latin *ūsuālis* < Latin *ūsus;* see etym. under **use,** verb] **— u′su|al|ness,** *n.*
**— *Syn.* Usual, customary** mean often or commonly seen or found, especially in a certain place or at a given time. **Usual** applies to something of expected occurrence or of familiar nature or quality: *This is the usual weather at this time of year.* **Customary** applies to something that is according to the regular practices or habits of a particular person or group: *I stayed up long past my customary bedtime.*
**u|su|al|ly** (yü′zhü ə lē), *adv.* according to what is usual; commonly; ordinarily; customarily: *We usually eat dinner at 6 P.M.*
**u|su|cap|tion** (yü′zyü kap′shən, -syü-), *n. Law.* the acquisition of the title or right to property by the uninterrupted and undisputed possession of it in good faith for a certain term prescribed by law. [< Old French *usucaption,* learned borrowing from Medieval Latin *usucaptio, -onis,* variant of Latin *ūsūcapiō, -ōnis* < *ūsūcapere* to acquire ownership by prescription]
**u|su|fruct** (yü′zyü frukt, -syü-), *n., v.* **— *n.*** the legal right to use another's property and enjoy the advantages of it without injuring or destroying it.
**— *v.t.*** to hold or make subject to usufruct.
[< Latin *ūsūfrūctū,* ablative of *ūsus-frūctus,* earlier *ūsus* (*et*) *frūctus* use (and) enjoyment]
**u|su|fruc|tu|ar|y** (yü′zyü fruk′chü er′ē, -syü-), *adj., n., pl.* **-ar|ies. — *adj.*** **1** of or having to do with a usufruct. **2** like a usufruct.
**— *n.*** a person who has the usufruct of property.
[< Late Latin *ūsūfrūctuārius* < Latin *ūsūfrūctus* < *ūsus-frūctus;* see etym. under **usufruct**]
**u|su|rer** (yü′zhər ər), *n.* **1** a person who lends money at an extremely high or unlawful rate of interest. **2** *Obsolete.* a person who lends money at interest; moneylender. [< Anglo-French *usurer,* Old French *usurier* < Late Latin *ūsūrārius* moneylender < Latin, adverb, at interest, for use < *ūsūra* use, noun < *ūtī* to use]
**u|su|ri|ous** (yü zhu̇r′ē əs), *adj.* **1** taking extremely high or unlawful interest for the use of money. **2** characterized by or involving usury: *Fifty per cent is a usurious rate of interest.* **3** of or having to do with usury. **— u|su′ri|ous|ly,** *adv.* **— u|su′ri-ous|ness,** *n.*
**u|surp** (yü zėrp′, -sėrp′), *v.t.* to seize and hold (power, position, or authority) by force or without right: *The king's wicked brother tried to usurp the throne.* **SYN:** appropriate, arrogate, assume. **— *v.i.*** to act as a usurper; commit usurpation.
[< Old French *usurper* < Latin *ūsūrpāre* seize possession of (for use) < *ūsū,* ablative of *ūsus* (see etym. under **use,** verb) + *rapere* seize]
**— u|surp′er,** *n.* **— u|surp′ing|ly,** *adv.*
**u|sur|pa|tion** (yü′zər pā′shən, -sər-), *n.* the act of usurping; seizing and holding of the place or power of another by force or without right: *the usurpation of the throne by a pretender.*
**u|su|ry** (yü′zhər ē), *n., pl.* **-ries. 1** the lending of money at an extremely high or unlawful rate of interest. **2** an extremely high or unlawful rate of interest. **3** *Obsolete.* **a** interest. **b** the fact or practice of lending money at interest. [< Medieval Latin *usuria,* alteration of Latin *ūsūra;* see etym. under **usurer**]
**U.S.V.**, United States Volunteers.
**usw.** or **u.s.w.**, and so forth; etc. (German, *und so weiter*).
**USWA** (no periods), United Steelworkers of America.
**ut** (ut, üt), *n. Music.* the syllable originally used for the keynote of the scale, now commonly called do. [< Latin *ut* (literally) that. See etym. under **gamut.**]
**u.t.** or **U.T.**, universal time.
**Ut.**, Utah (not official).
**UT** (no periods), Utah (with postal Zip Code).
**U|tah|an** (yü′tô ən, -tä-), *adj., n.* **— *adj.*** of or having to do with the state of Utah or its inhabitants.
**— *n.*** a native or inhabitant of Utah.
**Utah effect** (yü′tô, -tä), *Nuclear Physics.* the increase in the number and energy of mu-mesons within successively deeper levels of the earth's surface: *The record of more than 200,000 mumesons in the last three years shows an anomaly, the so-called Utah effect. The proportion of mu mesons arriving from vertical directions is higher than it should be and rises as the depth below the earth's surface* (*and therefore the energy of the mu mesons*) *increases* (Science News). [< *Utah,* the state (because the effect was discovered in underground experiments performed in a silver mine at Park City, Utah)]
**ut dict.** (ut), as directed (Latin, *ut dictum*).
**Ute** (yüt, yü′tē), *n., pl.* **Ute** or **Utes. 1** a member of a group of American Indian tribes now living in Utah, Colorado, and New Mexico. **2** their Shoshonean language. [American English < Shoshonean (Ute) *Ute,* said to mean "person, people"]
**u|ten|sil** (yü ten′səl), *n.* **1** a container or implement used for practical purposes: *eating utensils.* Pots, pans, kettles, and mops are kitchen utensils. **2** an instrument or tool used for some special purpose; implement. Pens and pencils are writing utensils. [< Old French *utensile,* learned borrowing from Medieval Latin, noun use of neuter of Latin *ūtēnsilis* usable, that may be used < *ūtī* to use]
**u|ter|al|gi|a** (yü′tə ral′jē ə), *n.* uterine pain. [< New Latin *uteralgia* < Latin *uterus* womb + Greek *álgos* pain]
**u|ter|ec|to|my** (yü′tə rek′tə mē), *n., pl.* **-mies.** surgical removal of the uterus; hysterectomy. [< *uter*(us) + *-ectomy*]
**u|ter|ine** (yü′tər in, -tə rīn), *adj.* **1** of or having to do with the uterus. **2** in the region of the uterus. **3** having the same mother, but a different father. Uterine brothers are half brothers born of the same mother. [< Late Latin *uterīnus* < Latin *uterus* uterus]
**u|ter|us** (yü′tər əs), *n., pl.* **-ter|i** (-tə rī). **1** the organ of the body in female mammals that holds and nourishes the young until birth; womb. It is an enlarged and thickened section of an oviduct. See diagram under **Fallopian tubes. 2** a corresponding part in lower animals. [< Latin *uterus* womb, belly]
**Ut|gard** (üt′gärd), *n.* = Jotunheim.
**U|ther** (yü′thər), *n.* or **Uther Pendragon,** a king of ancient Britain in Arthurian legends, the father of King Arthur and husband of Igraine.
**u|tile**[1] (yü′təl), *adj.* having utility; useful. [< Old French *utile,* learned borrowing from Latin *ūtilis* < *ūtī* to use]

***utilidor**

**u|tile**[2] (yü′tīl), *n.* a large mahogany tree of western and central Africa whose durable wood is much used for furniture frames. [< New Latin (*Entandrophragma*) *utile,* the botanical name]
***u|til|i|dor** (yü til′ə dôr), *n.* a system in Canada of elevated and insulated conduits carrying water and steam to communities situated on the permafrost. [< *utility;* perhaps patterned on *humidor*]
**u|ti|lise** (yü′tə līz), *v.t.,* **-lised, -lis|ing.** *Especially British.* utilize.
**u|til|i|tar|i|an** (yü til′ə tãr′ē ən), *adj., n.* **— *adj.*** **1** of or having to do with utility. **2** aiming at usefulness rather than beauty or style. **3** of, having to do with, or adhering to utilitarianism.
**— *n.*** an adherent of utilitarianism.
**u|til|i|tar|i|an|ism** (yü til′ə tãr′ē ə niz′əm), *n.* **1** the doctrine or belief that the greatest good of the greatest number should be the purpose of human conduct, especially as proposed by Jeremy Bentham. **2** the doctrine or belief that actions are good if they are useful.
**u|til|i|ty** (yü til′ə tē), *n., pl.* **-ties,** *adj.* **— *n.*** **1** usefulness; power to satisfy people's wants: *A fur coat has more utility in winter than in summer.* **2** a useful thing. **3** a company that performs a public service; public utility. Railroads, bus lines, and gas and electric companies are utilities. **4** *Philosophy.* the greatest happiness of the greatest number. **5** a low grade of meat, usually from older animals, as classified by the United States Department of Agriculture. **6** (in Australia) a motor vehicle with a variety of uses.
**— *adj.*** **1** used for various purposes: *a utility shed in the yard, a utility infielder.* **2** of low grade, usually from older animals: *utility beef.*
**utilities,** shares of stock issued by a public utility company: *Utilities managed to edge up 0.08%* (Wall Street Journal).
[< Old French *utilite,* learned borrowing from Latin *ūtilitās* < *ūtilis* usable < *ūtī* to use]
**utility man,** a member of a theatrical company, a baseball team, or other group or team, who is expected to serve in any capacity necessary.
**utility pole,** a high wooden pole sunk in the ground, supporting lines or cables carrying electric or telephone wires.
**utility room,** a room in a house for a furnace or water heater, or for a washing machine and other appliances, especially in a house with no basement.
**u|ti|liz|a|ble** (yü′tə lī′zə bəl), *adj.* that can be utilized.
**u|ti|li|za|tion** (yü′tə lə zā′shən), *n.* **1** the act of utilizing. **2** the fact or state of being utilized.
**u|ti|lize** (yü′tə līz), *v.t.,* **-lized, -liz|ing.** to make use of; put to some practical use: *The cook will utilize the leftover ham bone to make soup.* **SYN:** See syn. under **use. — u′ti|liz′er,** *n.*
**ut in|fra** (ut in′frə), *Latin.* as below.
**u|ti pos|si|de|tis** (yü′tī pos′ə dē′tis), the principle of international law under which a belligerent or belligerents may be confirmed by treaty or other formal agreement in possession of all territory controlled at the close of active hostilities. [< Late Latin *utī possidētis* (literally) as you possess]
**ut|most** (ut′mōst), *adj., n.* **— *adj.*** **1** greatest possible; greatest; highest: *a state of the utmost confusion. Sunshine is of the utmost importance to health.* **2** most remote; farthest; extreme: *the utmost reaches of the universe. She walked to the utmost edge of the cliff.*
**— *n.*** the most that is possible; extreme limit: *He enjoyed himself to the utmost at the circus.*
[alteration of Old English *ūtemest* < *ūte* outside + *-mest* -most]
**U|to-Az|tec|an** (yü′tō az′tek ən), *adj., n.* **— *adj.*** of, denoting, or having to do with a widespread American Indian linguistic stock that includes Shoshonean, Piman, and Nahuatl.
**— *n.*** this linguistic stock. [< *Ute* + *Aztecan*]
**U|to|pi|a** (yü tō′pē ə), *n.* **1** an ideal commonwealth where perfect justice and social harmony existed, as described in *Utopia,* by Sir Thomas More. **2** the island on which this commonwealth existed. **3** = utopia. [< New Latin *Utopia* < Greek *oú* not + *tópos* place]
**u|to|pi|a** (yü tō′pē ə), *n.* **1** an ideal place or state with perfect laws: *the wildest promises of an earthly utopia the day after tomorrow* (William R. Inge). **2** a visionary, impractical system of political or social perfection: *averse to all enthusiasm, mysticism, utopias and superstition* (William E. H. Lecky). [< *Utopia*]
**U|to|pi|an** (yü tō′pē ən), *adj., n.* **— *adj.*** of or like Utopia. **— *n.*** an inhabitant of Utopia.
**u|to|pi|an** (yü tō′pē ən), *adj., n.* **— *adj.*** **1** of or like a utopia. **2** visionary; impractical: *Many ... are infused with a passionate utopian faith that it* [*the*

**Pronunciation Key:** hat, āge, cãre, fär; let, ēqual, tėrm; it, īce; hot, ōpen, ôrder; oil, out; cup, pu̇t, rüle; child; long; thin; ᴛʜen; zh, measure; ə represents **a** in about, **e** in taken, **i** in pencil, **o** in lemon, **u** in circus.

*Party] is to redeem mankind* (Manchester Guardian).
—*n.* **1** an ardent but impractical reformer; extreme and visionary idealist: *The weakness of utopians in America is their insistence on being "realistic"* (Saturday Review). **2** an inhabitant of a utopia.
**u|to|pi|an|ism** (yü tō′pē ə niz′əm), *n.* **1** the ideas, beliefs, and aims of utopians. **2** any ideal schemes for the improvement of life or social conditions.
**utopian socialism**, a form of socialism, advocated by Johann G. Fichte, François M. C. Fourier, Robert Owen, and others, which would not be achieved by revolution but by moral and rational persuasion based on the examples of model socialist communities. — **utopian socialist.**
**u|to|pism** (yü tō′piz əm), *n.* = utopianism.
**u|to|pist** (yü tō′pist), *n.* = utopian.
**u|to|pis|tic** (yü′tō pis′tik), *adj.* having to do with or characteristic of utopians or utopianism.
**u|tri|cle** (yü′trə kəl), *n.* **1** a small sac or baglike body, such as a cell filled with air in a seaweed. **2** a thin seed vessel resembling a bladder. **3** the larger of the two membranous sacs in the labyrinth of the inner ear, the saccule being the smaller. [< Latin *ūtriculus* (diminutive) < *ūter, ūtris* skin bag, skin bottle]
**u|tric|u|lar** (yü trik′yə lər), *adj.* **1** of or having to do with a utricle. **2** like a utricle. **3** having or composed of a utricle or utricles.
**u|tric|u|late** (yü trik′yə lit, -lāt), *adj.* = utricular.
**u|tric|u|li|tis** (yü trik′yə lī′tis), *n.* inflammation of a utricle, as of the inner ear.
**u|tric|u|lus** (yü trik′yə ləs), *n., pl.* **-li** (-lī). = utricle. [< Latin *ūtriculus* utricle]
**ut su|pra** (ut sü′prə), *Latin.* as above.
**ut|ter[1]** (ut′ər), *adj.* **1** complete; total; absolute: *utter surprise, utter darkness, utter defeat.* **SYN**: entire, unqualified, sheer. **2** that is such to an extreme degree; out-and-out: *an utter fool.* [Old English *ūterra* outer]
**ut|ter[2]** (ut′ər), *v.t.* **1** to speak; make known; express: *the last words he uttered, to utter one's thoughts.* **SYN**: deliver, articulate. **2** to give forth; give out; emit: *She uttered a cry of pain.* **3** to put (especially counterfeit money or forged checks) into circulation. **4** *Obsolete.* **a** to issue or publish: *an order ... that the ... translation of Tindal ... should not be uttered either by printer or bookseller* (John Strype). **b** to issue or offer for sale or barter; vend: *Such ... drugs I have; but Mantua's law Is death to any he that utters them* (Shakespeare).
[Middle English *utteren,* ultimately < Old English *ūt* out] — **ut′ter|er,** *n.*
**ut|ter|a|ble** (ut′ər ə bəl), *adj.* that can be uttered: *He was so frightened as to be unable to make an utterable cry.*

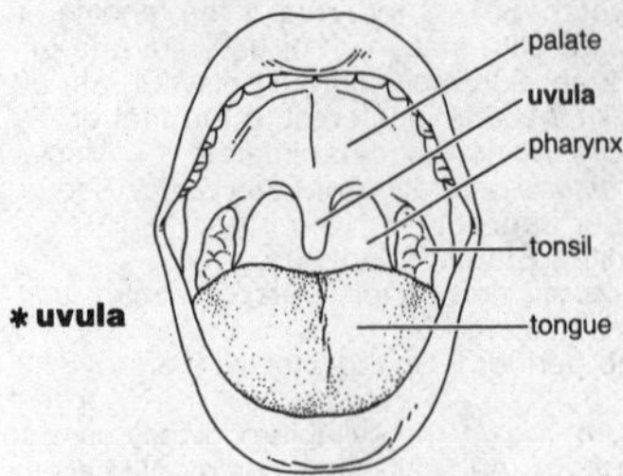

***uvula**

**ut|ter|ance[1]** (ut′ər əns), *n.* **1** the act or fact of uttering; expression in words or sounds: *The child gave utterance to his grief.* **2** a way of speaking: *a man of polished utterance. Stammering hinders clear utterance.* **3** something uttered; spoken word or words: *The utterance died on his lips as his father came into the room.* **4** the action of putting into circulation counterfeit money, forged checks, or bogus securities; uttering. **5** *Obsolete.* the disposal of goods by sale or barter; vending. [< *utter*[2] + *-ance*]
**ut|ter|ance[2]** (ut′ər əns), *n.* the utmost extremity, as of life or strength; bitter end. [< Old French *oultrance* < *oultrer* pass beyond < *oultre* beyond < Latin *ultrā*]
**ut|ter|ing** (ut′ər ing), *n. Law.* the act of intentionally putting counterfeit money, forged checks, or bogus securities, into circulation.
**ut|ter|ly** (ut′ər lē), *adv.* completely; totally; absolutely: *I fail utterly to see why* (Winston Churchill).
**ut|ter|most** (ut′ər mōst), *adj., n.* = utmost.
**ut|ter|ness** (ut′ər nis), *n.* the state of being utter; completeness.
**U-tube** (yü′tüb′, -tyüb′), *n.* a tube shaped like the letter U, used in chemistry experiments, etc.
**U-turn** (yü′tėrn′), *n.* a U-shaped turn made by a motor vehicle to reverse its direction.
**U.U.**, Ulster Unionist.
**UV** (no periods), **1** ultrahigh vacuum. **2** ultraviolet.
**u|va grass** (ü′və), a tropical American ornamental grass with tall, plumelike flower clusters. [< American Spanish *uva*]
**u|va|rov|ite** (ü vä′rə fīt), *n.* an emerald-green variety of garnet containing chromium. *Formula:* $Ca_3Cr_2Si_3O_{12}$ [< Count S.S. *Uvarov,* 1786-1855, president of St. Petersburg Academy + *-ite*[1]]
**u|ve|a** (yü′vē ə), *n.* **1** the posterior, colored surface of the iris of the eye. **2** the middle, vascular coat of the eye, composed of the iris, choroid membrane, and the ciliary muscle and process. [< Medieval Latin *uvea* < Latin *ūva* grape]
**u|ve|al** (yü′vē əl), *adj.* of or relating to the uvea.
**u|ve|it|ic** (yü′vē it′ik), *adj.* **1** affected with uveitis. **2** resembling uveitis.
**u|ve|i|tis** (yü′vē ī′tis), *n.* inflammation of the uvea. [< *uve*(a) + *-itis*]
**u|ve|ous** (yü′vē əs), *adj.* **1** resembling a grape or a bunch of grapes. **2** = uveal. [< Medieval Latin *uveus* (with English *-ous*) < Latin *ūva* grape]
***u|vu|la** (yü′vyə lə), *n., pl.* **-las, -lae** (-lē). the small piece of flesh hanging down from the soft palate in the back of the mouth. [< Late Latin *ūvula* (diminutive) < Latin *ūva* (originally) grape]
**u|vu|lar** (yü′vyə lər), *adj., n.* —*adj.* **1** of or having to do with the uvula. **2** *Phonetics.* **a** pronounced or sounded with vibration of the uvula: *Another pronunciation of Danish "r" is as a uvular trill.* **b** pronounced or sounded with the extreme back of the tongue raised toward or against the uvula: *One pronunciation of Danish "r" is as a uvular fricative.*
—*n. Phonetics.* a uvular sound.
**u|vu|li|tis** (yü′vyə lī′tis), *n.* inflammation of the uvula. [< *uvul*(a) + *-itis*]
**u|vu|lot|o|my** (yü′vyə lot′ə mē), *n., pl.* **-mies**. the surgical removal of the whole or a part of the uvula. [< *uvul*(a) + *-tomy*]
**U/W** or **u/w** (no periods), underwriter.
**ux.**, wife (Latin, *uxor*).
**ux|o|ri|al** (uk sôr′ē əl, -sōr′-), *adj.* **1** of or having to do with a wife. **2** like that of a wife; wifely: *uxorial affection.* **3** = uxorious. [< Latin *uxor, -ōris* wife + English *-ial*]
**ux|or|i|cid|al** (uk sôr′ə sī′dəl, -sōr′-), *adj.* **1** of or having to do with uxoricide. **2** tending to uxoricide.
**ux|or|i|cide[1]** (uk sôr′ə sīd, -sōr′-), *n.* a person who kills his wife. [< Latin *uxor, -ōris* wife + English *-cide*[1]]
**ux|or|i|cide[2]** (uk sôr′ə sīd, -sōr′-), *n.* the act of killing one's wife. [< Medieval Latin *uxoricidium* < Latin *uxor, -ōris* wife + *-cīdium* -cide[2]]
**ux|or|i|lo|cal** (uk sôr′ə lō′kəl, -sōr′-), *adj. Anthropology.* having the focus in the home of the wife's family; matrilocal: *uxorilocal residence, an uxorilocal culture.* [< Latin *uxor, -ōris* wife + *locus* place + English *-al*[1]]
**ux|o|ri|ous** (uk sôr′ē əs, -sōr′-), *adj.* excessively or foolishly fond of one's wife. [< Latin *uxōrius* (with English *-ous*) < *uxor, -ōris* wife] — **ux|o′ri|ous|ly,** *adv.* — **ux|o′ri|ous|ness,** *n.*
**Uz** (uz), *n.* the home of Job (in the Bible, Job 1:1).
**Uz|beg** (uz′beg), *n.* = Uzbek.
**Uz|bek** (uz′bek), *n.* **1** a member of a highly civilized Turkic people of Turkestan. **2** their Turkic language. Also, **Usbeg, Usbek.**

**✱V¹** or **v** (vē), *n., pl.* **V's** or **Vs, v's** or **vs. 1** the 22nd letter of the English alphabet. There are two *v*'s in *vivid.* **2** any sound represented by this letter, usually a voiced labiodental fricative, as in *valve.* **3** (used as a symbol for) the 22nd or more usually the 21st (of an actual or possible series, either I or J being omitted). **4** the Roman numeral for 5. **5** *Informal.* a five-dollar bill.

**V²** (vē), *n., pl.* **V's.** anything shaped like the letter V: *I saw the fish make his V toward the conch bait* (Edward Weeks).

**v** (no period), volt.

**v.**, an abbreviation for the following:
1 of (German, *von*).
2 see (Latin, *vide*).
3 valve.
4 verb.
5 verse.
6 version.
7 versus.
8 vice-, as in *v.p.* for *vice-president.*
9 vocative.
10 voice.
11 volt.
12 voltage.
13 volume.

**V** (no period), an abbreviation for the following:
1 vanadium (chemical element).
2 *Mathematics.* vector.
3 velocity.
4 Victory (a symbol of the Allies during World War II).
5 volt.

**V.**, **1** Venerable. **2** Victoria. **3** Viscount. **4** Volunteer.

**V-1** (vē′wun′), *n.* a pulsejet flying bomb used by the Germans in World War II in June, 1944; buzz bomb. [abbreviation of German *Vergeltungswaffe eins* vengeance-weapon one]

**V-2** (vē′tü′), *n.* a rocket bomb used by the Germans in World War II after June, 1944. [abbreviation of German *Vergeltungswaffe zwei* vengeance-weapon two]

**V-8** (vē′āt′), *n.* = V-8 engine.

**✱V-8 engine**, an automobile engine in the shape of a V, with four cylinders on each of the two cylinder heads, opposite each other, instead of all eight cylinders in a single line.

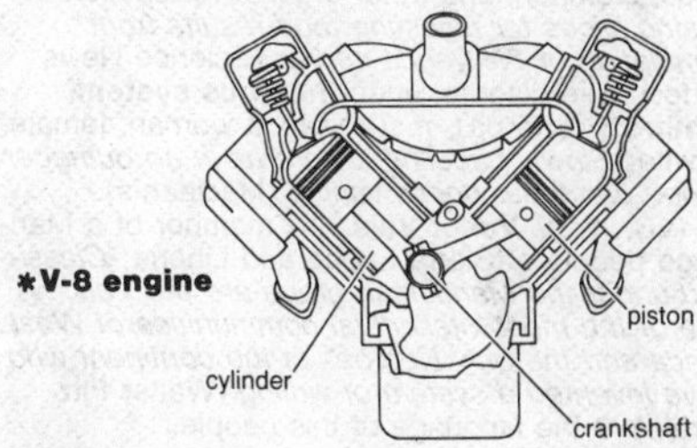


**✱V-8 engine**

**va** (no periods), volt-ampere.

**v.a.**, active verb.

**Va.**, the state of Virginia.

**VA** (no periods), **1** Veterans Administration (an independent agency of the U.S. government, established July 21, 1930, to administer veteran's benefits, such as pensions, hospital care, education, and insurance). **2** Virginia (with postal Zip Code).

**V.A.**, an abbreviation for the following:
1 Veterans Administration.
2 Vicar Apostolic.
3 Vice-Admiral.
4 *British.* Royal Order of Victoria and Albert.

**vac** (no period), **1** vacation. **2** vacuum.

**vac.**, vacation.

**va|ca** (vä′kə), *n.* a West Indian fish related to the grouper and sea bass. [< Cuban Spanish *vaca*]

**va|can|cy** (vā′kən sē), *n., pl.* **-cies. 1** the state of being vacant; emptiness: *the stark vacancy of the arctic landscape.* SYN: See syn. under **empty. 2** an unoccupied position: *The retirement of two policemen made two vacancies in our police force.* **3** the state of being or becoming unoccupied: *the vacancy of the bishopric.* SYN: expressionless, meaningless, inane. **4** an empty space: *The great arch ... with the lofty vacancy beneath it* (Hawthorne). **5** a room, space, or apartment for rent: *There was a vacancy in the motel. There are many vacancies in the parking lot when the stores are closed.* **6** a deficiency: *a vacancy in the scheme of knowledge.* **7** lack of thought or intelligence; emptiness of mind: *More absolute vacancy I never saw upon the countenances of human beings* (Samuel Butler). **8** freedom, as from work or activity; idleness: *Much time squandered upon trifles, and more lost in idleness and vacancy* (Samuel Johnson). **9** *Obsolete.* an interval of leisure time.

**va|cant** (vā′kənt), *adj.* **1** not occupied: *a vacant chair, a vacant house.* **2** empty; not filled: *a vacant space.* **3** empty of thought or intelligence: *a vacant smile.* **4** free, as from work or business: *vacant time.* [< Latin *vacāns, -antis,* present participle of *vacāre* be empty] —**va′cant|ly**, *adv.* —**va′cant|ness**, *n.*

**va|cate** (vā′kāt), *v.,* **-cat|ed, -cat|ing.** —*v.t.* **1** to go away from and leave empty or unoccupied; make vacant: *They will vacate the house at the end of the month.* **2** to leave (a position or office) empty or unoccupied by death, resignation, or retirement: *His office was automatically vacated when he was judged guilty.* **3** to make legally void; annul; cancel: *All former agreements were vacated by this contract.* —*v.i.* **1** to go away; leave. **2** to give up possession or occupancy, as of a house. **3** to give up a position or office. [< Latin *vacāre* (with English *-ate*¹) be empty]

**va|ca|tion** (vā kā′shən), *n., v.* —*n.* **1** a time of rest and freedom from work; freedom from school, business, or other duties; holiday: *a short vacation at the seashore. Our school has a spring vacation each year.* **2** the act of vacating: *Immediate vacation of the premises was demanded.*
—*v.i.* to take a vacation or holiday: *We vacationed in the Hawaiian Islands.*
[< Latin *vacātiō, -ōnis* < *vacāre* have time; be free, empty] —**va|ca′tion|er**, *n.*

**va|ca|tion|ist** (vā kā′shə nist), *n.* a person who is taking a vacation.

**va|ca|tion|land** (vā kā′shən land′), *n.* a place with many scenic attractions, lodging, and amusement for vacationists.

**va|ca|tion|less** (vā kā′shən lis), *adj.* without a vacation.

**vac|ci|nal** (vak′sə nəl), *adj.* **1** of or having to do with vaccine. **2** caused by vaccination.

**vac|ci|nate** (vak′sə nāt), *v.,* **-nat|ed, -nat|ing.** —*v.t.* **1** to inoculate with a vaccine as a protection against a disease. Children who are vaccinated against measles, whooping cough, diphtheria, and tetanus are made immune to these diseases. **2** to inoculate with the modified virus of cowpox as a protection against smallpox. —*v.i.* to perform or practice vaccination.
[< *vaccin*(e) + *-ate*¹]

**vac|ci|na|tion** (vak′sə nā′shən), *n.* **1** the act, practice, or process of vaccinating: *Vaccination has made smallpox a very rare disease.* **2** the scar where vaccine was injected.

**vac|ci|na|tion|ist** (vak′sə nā′shə nist), *n.* a person who believes in or advocates vaccination.

**vac|ci|na|tor** (vak′sə nā′tər), *n.* **1** a person who vaccinates. **2** an instrument used in performing vaccination.

**vac|cine** (vak′sēn, -sin), *n., adj.* —*n.* **1** any preparation, especially one of bacteria or viruses of a particular disease, used to inoculate a person in order to prevent or lessen the effects of that disease: *Most modern vaccines consist of dead or weakened germs which cause the body to produce antibodies that can later fight off any natural infection by the fully virulent organism* (Judith Randal). **2** the virus causing cowpox, prepared for use in preventive inoculation against smallpox.
—*adj.* **1a** of or having to do with a vaccine: *The vaccine test was the most extensive field experiment ever undertaken, and its evaluation was an exceedingly complex task* (Scientific American). **b** used in vaccine. **c** connected with vaccination. **2** characteristic of cowpox. **3** relating to cows: *vaccine medical knowledge.*
[< Latin *vaccīnus* of or from cows < *vacca* cow]

**vac|ci|nee** (vak′sə nē′), *n.* a person who has been vaccinated: *It was of cardinal importance to show that the [rubella] virus does not spread from vaccinees to pregnant women* (Donald N. Medearis, Jr.).

**vaccine point**, a sharp-pointed instrument used in vaccinating.

**vac|cin|i|a** (vak sin′ē ə), *n.* = cowpox. [< New Latin *vaccinia* < Latin *vaccīnus;* see etym. under **vaccine**]

**vac|cin|i|a|ceous** (vak sin′ē ā′shəs), *adj.* belonging to a group of plants usually placed in the heath family, including the blueberry, huckleberry, and cranberry. [< New Latin *Vaccineaceae* the family name (< *Vaccinium* the typical genus < Latin *vaccīnium* blueberry; (originally) hyacinth) + English *-ous*]

**vac|cin|i|al** (vak sin′ē əl), *adj.* of or having to do with cowpox.

**vac|ci|ni|za|tion** (vak′sə nə zā′shən), *n.* a thorough method of vaccination in which repeated inoculations are made until immunity is established.

**vac|ci|no|ther|a|py** (vak′sə nō ther′ə pē), *n.* treatment of disease by means of vaccines.

**vac|il|lant** (vas′ə lənt), *adj.* vacillating; wavering.

**vac|il|late** (vas′ə lāt), *v.i.,* **-lat|ed, -lat|ing. 1** to waver in mind or opinion: *A vacillating person finds it hard to make up his mind.* SYN: hesitate. **2** to move first one way and then another; waver. SYN: oscillate, sway. [< Latin *vacillāre* (with English *-ate*¹)]

**vac|il|lat|ing** (vas′ə lā′ting), *adj.* **1** tending to hesitate or be uncertain; characterized by hesitation or uncertainty: *A vacillating person finds it hard to make up his mind.* **2** unsteady; swaying. —**vac′il|lat′ing|ly**, *adv.*

**vac|il|la|tion** (vas′ə lā′shən), *n.* **1** the action or quality of wavering in mind or opinion: *His constant vacillation made him an unfit administrator.* **2** unsteadiness; swaying.

**vac|il|la|tor** (vas′ə lā′tər), *n.* a person who vacillates or wavers: *[He] is essentially a vacillator, a man who shrinks from unpleasant decisions* (Wall Street Journal).

**vac|il|la|to|ry** (vas′ə lə tôr′ē, -tōr′-), *adj.* = vacillating.

**vac|u|a** (vak′yu̇ ə), *n.* a plural of **vacuum.**

**vac|u|ate** (vak′yu̇ āt), *v.t.,* **-at|ed, -at|ing. 1** to create a vacuum in. **2** *Obsolete.* to make empty. **3** *Obsolete.* to annul; nullify. **4** *Obsolete.* to clear out or discharge. [< Latin *vacuāre* (with English *-ate*¹)]

**vac|u|a|tion** (vak′yu̇ ā′shən), *n.* the act of emptying; evacuation.

**va|cu|i|ty** (va kyü′ə tē), *n., pl.* **-ties. 1** emptiness. **2** an empty space; vacuum. **3** emptiness of mind; lack of ideas or intelligence: *In indolent vacuity of thought* (William Cowper). **4** something foolish or stupid: *an undue preoccupation with the vacuities which society has invented* (Arnold Bennett). **5** an absence or lack (of something specified). [< Latin *vacuitās* < *vacuus* vacuous]

**vac|u|o|lar** (vak′yu̇ ə lər), *adj.* = vacuolated.

**vac|u|o|late** (vak′yu̇ ə lāt), *adj.* = vacuolated.

**vac|u|o|lat|ed** (vak′yu̇ ə lā′tid), *adj.* provided with one or more vacuoles.

**vac|u|o|la|tion** (vak′yu̇ ə lā′shən), *n.* **1** the formation of vacuoles. **2** vacuolated condition.

**vac|u|ole** (vak′yu̇ ōl), *n.* **1** a tiny cavity in the protoplasm of a living cell, containing fluid. See picture under **cell. 2** (formerly) any very small cavity in organic tissue. [< French *vacuole* < Latin *vacuus* empty]

**vac|u|ous** (vak′yu̇ əs), *adj.* **1** showing no thought or intelligence; stupid; foolish: *the vacuous smile of an idiot; a vacuous, solemn snob* (Thackeray). SYN: fatuous. **2** having no meaning or direction; idle; indolent: *a vacuous life.* **3** empty (of matter or anything solid or tangible). [< Latin *vacuus* (with English *-ous*)] —**vac′u|ous|ly**, *adv.* —**vac′u|ous|ness**, *n.*

**vac|u|um** (vak′yu̇m, vak′yu̇ əm), *n., pl.* **vac|u|ums** or (*except for def. 6*) **vac|u|a**, *adj., v.* —*n.* **1** an empty space without even air in it. **2** an enclosed space from which almost all the air or other gas has been removed, especially to permit ex-

**✱V¹**
definition 1

Script letters look like examples of fine penmanship. They appear in many formal uses, such as invitations to social functions.

Handwritten letters, both manuscript or printed (left) and cursive (right), are easy for children to read and to write.

Roman letters have *serifs* (finishing strokes) adapted from the way Roman stonecutters carved their letters. This is *Times Roman* type.

Sans-serif letters are often called *gothic.* They have lines of even width and no serifs. This type face is called *Helvetica.*

Between roman and gothic, some letters have thick and thin lines with slight flares that suggest serifs. This type face is *Optima.*

Computer letters can be sensed by machines either from their shapes or from the magnetic ink with which they are printed.

perimentation without atmospheric distortion. **3** an empty space; void: (*Figurative.*) *Her husband's death left a vacuum in her life.* **4** the condition or amount of loss in atmospheric pressure within a space. **5a** emptiness. **b** *Figurative.* something that needs filling; hiatus; gap: *a political vacuum.* **c** *Figurative.* a condition of seclusion or apartness from others: *to live in a vacuum.* **6** = vacuum cleaner.
—***adj.*** **1** of or having to do with a vacuum: *a vacuum gauge.* **2** producing a vacuum: *a vacuum fan.* **3** using a vacuum: *vacuum canning.* **4** entirely or partially exhausted of air (or other gas): *a vacuum tube.* **5** using suction: *vacuum ventilation.* **6** using gas pressures that are lower than atmospheric pressure, as in various processes.
—***v.t.*** **1** to clean with a vacuum cleaner: *Mother vacuums the rugs on Thursday.* **2** to use any vacuum device on.
—***v.i.*** to use a vacuum cleaner: *She is a tidy housekeeper who contends that "nothing can clear the mind like vacuuming"* (Time).
[< Latin *vacuum,* neuter of *vacuus* empty]

***vacuum bottle** or **flask**, a bottle or flask made with a vacuum between its inner and outer walls so that its contents remain hot or cold for long periods of time; thermos bottle.

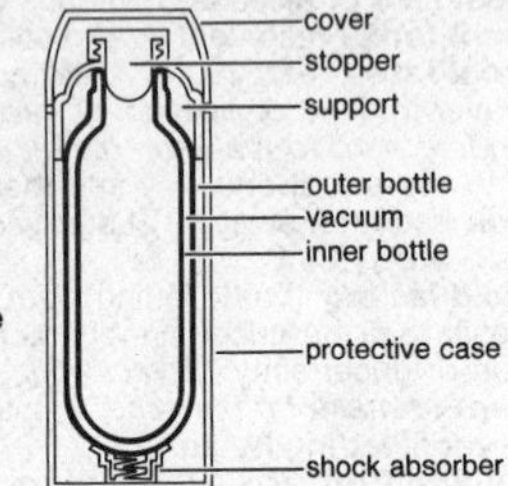

***vacuum bottle**

**vacuum cleaner**, an apparatus for cleaning carpets, rugs, floors, and often furniture and curtains, by suction.

**vacuum cleaning**, the act of cleaning with a vacuum cleaner.

**vacuum fan**, a fan that operates by suction, used to ventilate an enclosed area.

**vacuum gauge**, a form of pressure gauge for indicating the internal pressure or the amount of vacuum in a container.

**vac|u|um|ize** (vak′yu̇ mīz, vak′yu̇ ə-), *v.,* **-ized, -iz|ing.** —***v.t.*** to produce a vacuum in (a container, chamber, or other enclosed area).
—***v.i.*** to produce a vacuum.

**vacuum melting**, a method of melting metals or alloys in a sealed furnace to prevent atmospheric oxidation, remove gaseous impurities, and improve purity and physical properties: *To produce stronger and more ductile steel, 17 U.S. companies have adopted another new innovation called vacuum melting* (Time).

**vac|u|um-packed** (vak′yu̇m pakt′, vak′yu̇ əm-), *adj.* **1** packed in an airtight can, jar, or other container, to keep fresh: *vacuum-packed coffee.* **2** having had all or most of the air removed before sealing: *vacuum-packed cans.*

**vacuum pump**, **1** a pump or device by which a partial vacuum can be produced. **2** a pump in which a partial vacuum is utilized to raise water.

**vacuum sweeper**, = vacuum cleaner.

***vacuum tube**, a sealed glass tube or bulb from which almost all the air has been removed, and into which electrodes from outside project; electron tube. A vacuum tube consists typically of a cathode or filament, that emits electrons, an anode or plate that receives the electrons and a grid, between the cathode and anode, that controls the flow of electrons. Vacuum tubes were once widely used in radio and television sets, photoelectric cells, and other devices to control the flow of electric currents.

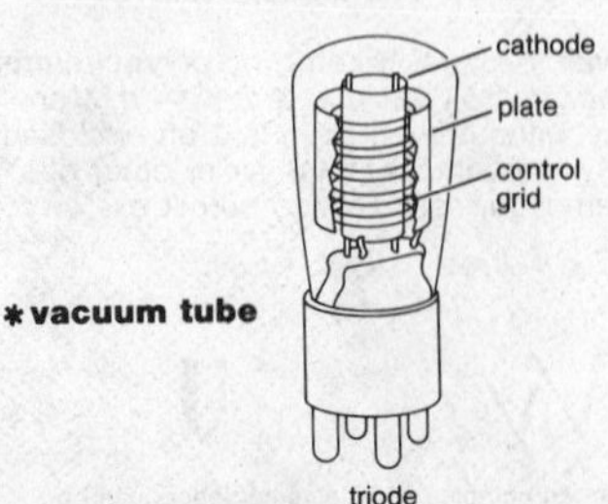

***vacuum tube**

**vacuum valve**, *Especially British.* vacuum tube.

**vacuum ventilation**, a system in which the vitiated air is drawn out of the space to be ventilated, and is replaced by the fresh air coming in from the outside because of the decreased pressure.

**V.A.D.** or **VAD** (no periods), Voluntary Aid Detachment.

**va|de me|cum** (vā′dē mē′kəm), **1** anything a person carries about with him because of its usefulness. **2** a book for ready reference; manual; handbook: *[His] tax guide alone has sold more than thirteen million copies in its eighteen years as the taxpayer's vade mecum* (Harper's). [< Medieval Latin *vade mecum* < Latin imperative of *vādere* go + *mēcum* with me]

**V. Adm.**, Vice-Admiral.

**va|dose** (vā′dōs), *adj. Geology.* having to do with or occurring in the unsaturated area between the earth's surface and the water table: *the vadose zone. The descending vadose water dissolves the soluble minerals and carries them in solution down into the zone of saturation* (White and Renner). [< Latin *vadōsus* shallow < *vadum* a ford]

**vae vic|tis** (vē vik′tis), *Latin.* woe to the vanquished.

**vag|a|bond** (vag′ə bond), *n., adj., v.* —***n.*** **1** an idle wanderer; wanderer; tramp. **SYN**: vagrant, nomad, hobo. **2** a good-for-nothing person; rascal. **SYN**: rogue.
—***adj.*** **1** wandering: *the Crow chieftain and his vagabond warriors* (Washington Irving). *The Gypsies lead a vagabond life.* **2** shiftless; disreputable; good-for-nothing: *a vagabond tramp.* **SYN**: worthless. **3** moving hither and thither; drifting: *vagabond winds.* **4** *Figurative.* not subject to control or restraint; roving; straying: *vagabond thoughts, a short book well-suited to vagabond habits.*
—***v.i.*** to roam or wander about like a vagabond: *the delights and tribulations of vagabonding around the Gulf* (Sunset).
[< Middle French *vagabond,* learned borrowing from Latin *vagābundus* < *vagārī* to wander < *vagus* roving]

**vag|a|bond|age** (vag′ə bon′dij), *n.* **1** the fact or condition of being a vagabond; idle wandering: *the vagabondage of the Gypsies.* (*Figurative.*) *to indulge in literary vagabondage.* **SYN**: vagrancy. **2** vagabonds collectively: *rural vagabondage.*

**vag|a|bond|ish** (vag′ə bon′dish), *adj.* having to do with or characteristic of a vagabond.

**vag|a|bond|ism** (vag′ə bon diz′əm), *n.* the ways or habits of a vagabond; vagabondage.

**vag|a|bond|ize** (vag′ə bon dīz), *v.i.,* **-ized, -iz|ing.** to wander as or like a vagabond; roam at will.

**va|gal** (vā′gəl), *adj.* of or having to do with the vagus nerve: *In 20 more or less sedentary men a 6- to 12-week period of vigorous physical retraining restored the vagal tone toward normal* (Science News Letter).

**va|gar|i|ous** (və gãr′ē əs), *adj.* having vagaries; whimsical; capricious; erratic: *Bozzy's vagarious search for a wife, described in the previous volume, has succeeded, and for the moment at least he is well-behaved* (Time). —**va|gar′i|ous|ly**, *adv.*

**va|gar|y** (və gãr′ē, vā′gər-), *n., pl.* **-gar|ies.** **1** an odd fancy; extravagant notion: *the vagaries of a dream.* **SYN**: whim, fantasy. **2** an odd action; caprice; freak: *the vagaries of women's fashions.* **SYN**: fad. [probably < Latin *vagārī* to wander < *vagus* roving]

**V-a|gent** (vē′ā′jənt), *n.* any one of a class of extremely toxic nerve gases, including GB and VX.

**va|gi** (vā′jī), *n.* plural of **vagus**.

**vag|ile** (vaj′əl, -īl), *adj. Zoology.* characterized by vagility; able to move around: *vagile organisms.* [< Latin *vagus* roving + English *-ile,* as in *sessile*]

**va|gil|i|ty** (və jil′ə tē), *n. Zoology.* the condition of being able or free to move around; mobility: *The ability of insects to cross oceans depends on their habits and vagility in immature and adult stages* (Science).

**va|gi|na** (və jī′nə), *n., pl.* **-nas, -nae** (-nē). **1a** the membranous passage in female mammals that leads from the uterus to the vulva or external opening. **b** a similar part in certain other animals. **2** a sheathlike part, organ, or covering; sheath or theca. **3** *Botany.* the sheath formed around a stem by the lower parts of some leaves, such as those of the tulip. [< Latin *vagīna* (originally) sheath, scabbard]

**vag|i|nal** (vaj′ə nəl, və jī′-), *adj.* **1** of, having to do with, or affecting the vagina of a female mammal. **2** of, resembling, or serving as a sheath; thecal. —**vag′i|nal|ly**, *adv.*

**vag|i|na|lec|to|my** (vaj′ə nə lek′tə mē), *n., pl.* **-mies.** = vaginectomy.

**vag|i|nate** (vaj′ə nit, -nāt), *adj.* **1** having a vagina or sheath; invaginate. **2** like a sheath.

**vag|i|nec|to|my** (vaj′ə nek′tə mē), *n., pl.* **-mies.** **1** excision of the vagina. **2** surgical removal of the membrane around the testes. [< *vagin*(a) + *-ectomy*]

**vag|i|nis|mus** (vaj′ə niz′məs), *n.* a spasm or contraction of the vagina, usually prolonged and painful. [< New Latin *vaginismus* < Latin *vagina* + *-ismus* -ism]

**vag|i|ni|tis** (vaj′ə nī′tis), *n.* inflammation of the vagina. [< New Latin *vaginitis* < Latin *vagīna* (see etym. under **vagina**) + New Latin *-itis* inflammation, -itis]

**va|got|o|my** (və got′ə mē), *n., pl.* **-mies.** the surgical separation of the vagus nerve. [< *vag*(us nerve) + *-tomy*]

**va|go|to|ni|a** (vā′gə tō′nē ə), *n.* excessive activity of the vagus nerve, affecting the normal function of the heart, stomach, and other organs. [< New Latin *vagotonia* < *vagus* + Greek *tónos* tone]

**va|go|ton|ic** (vā′gə ton′ik), *adj.* having to do with vagotonia.

**va|gran|cy** (vā′grən sē), *n., pl.* **-cies.** **1** a wandering idly from place to place without proper means or ability to earn a living: *The tramp was arrested for vagrancy.* **2** the act of wandering. **3** a vagrant act or idea; wandering or disgressing, as in mind, opinion, or thought: *Conscience helps to check the vagrancies of the heart.* **4** an instance or occasion of wandering or roaming; rambling journey; straying.

**va|grant** (vā′grənt), *n., adj.* —***n.*** **1** an idle wanderer; tramp. **2** a wanderer.
—***adj.*** **1** a wandering without proper means of earning a living: *a town overrun with vagrant beggars.* **2a** *Figurative.* moving in no definite direction or course; wandering: *vagrant thoughts.* **b** leading a wandering or nomadic life; ranging or roaming from place to place: *a vagrant tribe of Indians.* **3** of or having to do with a vagrant: *vagrant habits.*
[perhaps alteration of Anglo-French *wacrant* (< a Germanic word); influenced by French *vagant* straying < Latin *vagārī* to wander] —**va′grant|ly**, *adv.*

**va|grom** (vā′grəm), *adj. Archaic.* vagrant. [alteration of *vagrant*]

**vague** (vāg), *adj.,* **va|guer, va|guest.** **1** not definitely or precisely expressed: *His vague statement confused them. He gave a vague assent.* **SYN**: ambiguous. See syn. under **obscure**. **2** indefinite; indistinct: *a vague feeling.* **3** indistinctly seen or perceived; formless; obscure; shadowy: *In a fog everything looks vague.* **SYN**: hazy. **4** lacking clarity or precision: *a vague personality.* **5** devoid of expression: *his mild, vague old eyes* (Booth Tarkington). [< Old French *vague,* learned borrowing from Latin *vagus* wandering. See etym. of doublet **vagus**.] —**vague′ly**, *adv.*

**vague|ness** (vāg′nis), *n.* the quality or condition of being vague; indefiniteness: *Vagueness should not be invoked when a precise answer is possible* (Bernard DeVoto).

**va|gus** (vā′gəs), *n., pl.* **va|gi.** = vagus nerve. [< New Latin *vagus* < Latin, wandering. See etym. of doublet **vague**.]

**vagus nerve**, either of the tenth pair of cranial nerves, extending from the brain to the heart, lungs, stomach, and other organs: *Production of gastric juices for digesting food results from stimulation of the vagus nerves* (Science News Letter). See diagram under **nervous system**.

**va|hi|ne** (vä hē′nā), *n. Tahitian.* a woman, female, or wife: *Slowly paddling toward us in an outrigger canoe came our host's vahine* (Maclean's).

**Vai** (vī), *n., pl.* **Vai** or **Vais.** **1** a member of a Mandingo people of Sierra Leone and Liberia: *Classified under the Mandingan group are the Vais, one of the most intellectual communities of West Africa and the only Negroes in the continent who have invented a system of writing* (Walter Fitzgerald). **2** the language of this people.

**vail**[1] (vāl), *Archaic.* —***v.t.*** **1** to lower; cause or allow to fall. **2** to take off; doff.
—***v.i.*** to yield; bow.
[< Old French *valer,* or short for Middle English *avalen* < Old French *avaler* < *a val* downhill < Latin *ad vallem* to the valley. Compare etym. under **avalanche**.]

**vail**[2] (vāl), *n. Archaic.* money given to a servant or attendant, especially by a guest on his departure from his host's home. [< Old French *vaille-,* stem of *valoir* be of worth < Latin *valēre.* Compare etym. under **avail**.]

**vain** (vān), *adj., n.* —***adj.*** **1** having too much pride in one's looks, ability, or achievements: *She is vain of her beauty.* **SYN**: conceited, egotistical. **2** of no use; without effect or success; producing no good result; unsuccessful; fruitless: *I made vain attempts to reach her by telephone.* **3** of no value or importance; worthless; empty: *a vain boast.* **4** without sense or wisdom; foolish; senseless: *unruly and vain talkers* (Titus 1:10).
—***n.*** **in vain**, without effect or success: *The hunter who had lost his way shouted in vain, for no one could hear him.*
**take a name in vain.** See under **name**.
[< Old French *vein, vain* < Latin *vānus* idle, empty] —**vain′ness**, *n.*
—***Syn.*** *adj.* **2 Vain, futile** mean without effect or

success. **Vain** describes thinking, action, and effort that fails to accomplish a given result: *The principal made another vain appeal for better equipment in the high-school laboratories.* **Futile** adds and emphasizes the idea of being incapable of producing the result, and often suggests that the attempt is useless or unwise: *Without microscopes and other essential equipment, attempts to teach science were futile.*

**vain|glo|ri|ous** (vān′glôr′ē əs, -glōr′-), *adj.* excessively proud or boastful; extremely vain: *a vainglorious confidence prevailed ... among the Spanish cavaliers* (Washington Irving). SYN: vaunting, arrogant, conceited. —**vain′glo′ri|ous|ly,** *adv.* —**vain′glo′ri|ous|ness,** *n.*

**vain|glo|ry** (vān′glôr′ē, -glōr′-), *n., pl.* **-ries. 1** an extreme pride in oneself; boastful vanity. **2** worthless pomp or show: *What needs these Feasts, pomps and vainglories?* (Shakespeare). SYN: ostentation. [< *vain* + *glory,* translation of Medieval Latin *vana gloria*]

**vain|ly** (vān′lē), *adv.* **1** in vain. **2** with conceit. SYN: arrogantly.

**vair** (vãr), *n.* **1** a gray-and-white squirrel fur used for lining and trimming the robes of nobles in the 1200's and the 1300's. **2** its representation in heraldry by small, shield-shaped figures alternately silver and azure. [< Old French *vair,* oblique of *vairs* < Latin *varius* variegated. See etym. of doublet **various.**]

**Vaish|na|va** (vīsh′nə və), *n.* = Vishnuvite. [< Sanskrit *vaiṣṇava* of Vishnu < *viṣṇu* Vishnu]

**Vaish|na|vism** (vīsh′nə viz əm), *n.* = Vishnuism.

**Vais|ya** (vīs′yə), *n.* a member of the mercantile and agricultural caste among the Hindus. [< Sanskrit *Vaiśya* < *viś* settlement; people]

**vai|vode** (vī′vōd), *n.* = voivode.

**va|keel** (və kēl′), *n.* **1** (in India) an agent or representative, especially of a person of political importance, as an ambassador or special commissioner at a court. **2** a native attorney in a court of law. [< Hindustani *vakīl*]

**va|kil** (və kēl′), *n.* = vakeel.

**val.,** **1** valuation. **2** value.

***val|ance** (val′əns), *n.* **1** a short, decorative drapery over the top of a window. **2** a short curtain, such as one hanging from the canopy of a bed or from the mattress to the floor: *An iron bedstead (no valance of course), and hair mattress* (Florence Nightingale). [probably < unrecorded Anglo-French *valance* < Old French *avaler* to descend; see etym. under **vail¹**]

***valance**
definitions 1, 2

**val|anced** (val′ənst), *adj.* provided or furnished with a valance: *an old ... chair, valanced, and fringed around with worsted bobs* (Laurence Sterne).

**Val|div|i|a** (val div′ē ə), *adj.* of, having to do with, or belonging to a culture that flourished on the northern coast of Ecuador about 3000 B.C., noted for the similarity of its pottery to that of the Jomon culture of Japan. [< *Valdivia,* a fishing village in northern Ecuador, where remains of this culture were discovered in 1954]

**Val|div|i|an** (val div′ē ən), *n., adj.* —*n.* a member of the people who produced the Valdivia culture: *The newcomers from Japan began to instruct the Valdivians, who were such apt students that their pottery soon equaled ... that of distant Kyushu* (Science News Letter).
—*adj.* = Valdivia.

**vale¹** (vāl), *n.* **1** valley: *o'er vale and mountain* (Wordsworth). **2** the world regarded as a place of sorrow or tears, or the scene of life: *my dear friends and brethren in this vale of tears* (Thackeray). [< Old French *val* < Latin *vallis*]

**va|le²** (vā′lē, vä′lā), *interj., n.* —*interj.* good-by; farewell.
—*n.* **1** a good-by; a farewell: *I am going to make my vales to you for some weeks* (Shakespeare). **2** a farewell greeting, letter, or gift.
[< Latin *valē,* imperative of *valēre* to fare well]

**val|e|dic|tion** (val′ə dik′shən), *n.* **1** the action of bidding farewell: *Their last valediction, thrice uttered by the attendants, was ... very solemn* (Sir Thomas Browne). **2** = farewell. [< Latin *valedictus,* past participle of *valedīcere* bid farewell (< *valē* be well! + *dīcere* to say) + English *-ion*]

**val|e|dic|to|ri|an** (val′ə dik tôr′ē ən, -tōr′-), *n.* the student who gives the farewell address at the graduation of his class. The valedictorian is usually the student who ranks highest in his class. [American English < *valedictory* + English *-ian*]

**val|e|dic|to|ry** (val′ə dik′tər ē, -dik′trē), *n., pl.* **-ries,** *adj.* —*n.* a farewell address, especially at the graduating exercises of a school or college.
—*adj.* bidding farewell: *Sir Winston treated the House of Commons to a stunning valedictory performance* (Newsweek).

**va|lence** (vā′ləns), *n.* **1** *Chemistry.* **a** the capacity of an atom or radical to combine with other atoms or radicals, determined by the number of electrons that an atom will lose, add, or share when it reacts with other atoms. Elements whose atoms lose electrons, such as hydrogen and the metals, have a positive valence. Elements whose atoms add electrons, such as oxygen and other nonmetals, have a negative valence. **b** a unit of valence: *Oxygen has two valences.* **2** *Biology.* **a** the ability of serums and other organic substances to interact or produce a certain effect. **b** the ability of chromosomes to unite with or produce a certain effect upon each other. [< Latin *valentia* strength, capacity < *valēns, -entis,* present participle of *valēre* be strong]

**valence electron,** an electron in the outer shell of an atom. In a chemical change, the atom gains, loses, or shares such an electron in combining with another atom or atoms to form a molecule.

**Va|len|ci|a orange,** or **Va|len|ci|a** (və len′shē ə, -shə), *n.* a thin-skinned, yellowish-brown orange that ripens during the summer, grown chiefly in California and Florida. [< *Valencia,* a seaport and former colony in Spain]

**Va|len|ci|ennes lace,** or **Va|len|ci|ennes** (və-len′sē enz′; *French* vȧ läɴ syen′), *n.* a fine lace in which the pattern and background are made together of the same threads, originally made at Valenciennes, France, but now made elsewhere.

**va|len|cy** (vā′lən sē), *n., pl.* **-cies.** = valence.

**-valent,** *combining form.* having valence, as in *trivalent.* [< Latin *valēns;* see etym. under **valence**]

**val|en|tine** (val′ən tīn), *n.* **1** a greeting card or small gift sent on Valentine's Day, February 14. **2a** a sweetheart chosen on this day: *I am also this year my wife's Valentine, and it cost me £5; but that I must have laid out if we had not been Valentines* (Samuel Pepys). **b** any sweetheart. [< Saint *Valentine* < Late Latin *Valentīnus,* a proper name]

**Valentine Day,** = Valentine's Day.

**Valentine's Day,** February 14, the day on which valentines are exchanged; Saint Valentine's Day.

**Val|en|tin|i|an** (val′ən tin′ē ən), *adj., n.* —*adj.* of or having to do with Valentinus, a Gnostic leader who taught at Rome in the middle of the 100's A.D.; of or belonging to the Gnostic system or sect instituted by him.
—*n.* a follower of Valentinus; Valentinian Gnostic.

**Val|en|tin|i|an|ism** (val′ən tin′ē ə niz′əm), *n.* the system of doctrines maintained by the Valentinians.

**val|er|ate** (val′ə rāt), *n.* a salt of valeric acid.

**va|le|ri|an** (və lir′ē ən), *n.* **1** a strong-smelling drug used to quiet the nerves, prepared from the roots of the common variety of valerian. **2** any one of a group of perennial herbs, cultivated for its medicinal root. Heliotrope, a kind of valerian, has small pinkish or white flowers and is often grown in gardens. [< Old French *valeriane* or < Medieval Latin *valeriana* < Latin, adjective, probably ultimately < *valēre* be strong, of worth]

**va|le|ri|a|na|ceous** (və lir′ē ə nā′shəs), *adj.* belonging to a family of dicotyledonous herbs or shrubs typified by the valerian. [< New Latin *Valerianaceae* the family name (< *Valeriana* the typical genus < Medieval Latin *valeriana;* see etym. under **valerian**) + English *-ous*]

**va|le|ri|a|nate** (və lir′ē ə nāt), *n.* a salt of valeric acid.

**va|le|ri|an|ic** (və lir′ē an′ik), *adj.* = valeric.

**valerianic acid,** = valeric acid.

**va|ler|ic** (və ler′ik, -lir′-), *adj.* **1** of, obtained from, or related to the plant valerian. **2** of or having to do with valeric acid or one of the acids isomeric with it.

**valeric acid, 1** an organic acid present in valerian roots or produced synthetically, having a pungent odor and used in making perfumes, in flavoring, and in medicine. *Formula:* $C_5H_{10}O_2$ **2** any one of several acids with the same formula. [short for *valerianic* < *valerian*]

***val|et** (val′it, -ā; va lā′), *n., v.* —*n.* **1** a servant who takes care of a man's clothes and gives him personal service: *No man is a hero to his valet* (Marquise de Sévigné). SYN: manservant. **2** a worker in a hotel who cleans or presses clothes and performs similar personal services. **3** a rack or stand for holding a coat, trousers, hat, or other clothing.
—*v.t., v.i.* to wait upon or serve as a valet.
[< Old French *valet,* variant of *vaslet* (originally) a squire (probably diminutive) < *vasal* vassal. Compare etym. under **varlet.**]

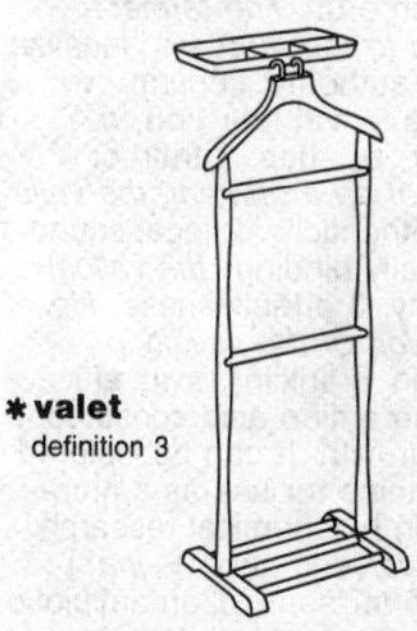

***valet**
definition 3

**va|let de cham|bre** (vȧ le′ də shäɴ′brə), *pl.* **va-lets de cham|bre** (vȧ le′ də shäɴ′brə). a man's personal servant; valet. [< French *valet de chambre* (literally) chamber servant]

**val|e|tu|di|nar|i|an** (val′ə tü′də nãr′ē ən, -tyü′-), *n., adj.* —*n.* **1** a person in weak health; chronic invalid: *Having been a valetudinarian all his life, without activity of mind or body, he was a much older man in ways than in years* (Jane Austen). **2** a person who thinks he is ill when he is not; hypochondriac.
—*adj.* **1** = sickly. **2** thinking too much about the state of one's health.
[< Latin *valētūdinārius* sickly (< *valētūdō, -inis* good or bad health < *valēre* be strong) + English *-an*]

**val|e|tu|di|nar|i|an|ism** (val′ə tü′də nãr′ē ə niz′-əm, -tyü′-), *n.* valetudinarian condition or habits; invalidism.

**val|e|tu|di|nar|y** (val′ə tü′də ner′ē, -tyü′-), *n., pl.* **-nar|ies,** *adj.* = valetudinarian.

**val|gus** (val′gəs), *n., adj.* —*n.* a form of clubfoot or talipes in which the foot is turned outward.
—*adj.* **1** (of the bones, especially in the foot, knee, and hip) characterized by the abnormal position of turning outward. **2** = knock-kneed.
[< New Latin *valgus* knock-kneed < Latin, bow-legged]

**Val|hal|la** (val hal′ə), *n.* **1** *Norse Mythology.* the hall where the souls of heroes slain in battle feast with the god Odin. **2** *Figurative: Neither Pitt nor Peel lives in my Valhalla* (Lord Acton). Also, **Walhalla.** [< New Latin *Valhalla* < Old Icelandic *valhöll, valhall* < *valr* those slain in battle + *höll, hall* hall]

**va|li** (vä lē′), *n.* the governor general of a Turkish vilayet. [< Turkish *vali* < Arabic *wālī*]

**val|iance** (val′yəns), *n.* **1** bravery; valor; valiancy: *When our affright was over we ... set out afresh with double valiance* (Elizabeth Gaskell). **2** *Archaic.* a courageous act or deed. [< Anglo-French *valiance,* Old French *vaillance* < *valiant, vaillant;* see etym. under **valiant**]

**val|ian|cy** (val′yən sē), *n.* = valiance.

**val|iant** (val′yənt), *adj., n.* —*adj.* **1** having courage; brave; courageous: *a valiant soldier.* **2** showing courage; heroic: *a valiant deed.*
—*n.* a brave or courageous person: *Wealth ... is the possession of the valuable by the valiant* (John Ruskin). *Cowards die many times before their deaths; The valiant never taste of death but once* (Shakespeare).
[< Anglo-French, Old French *vaillant, valiant,* present participle of *valeir* (originally) be strong < Latin *valēre*] —**val′iant|ly,** *adv.* —**val′iant|ness,** *n.*

**val|id** (val′id), *adj.* **1** supported by facts or authority; sound or true: *a valid argument, proof, or*

**Pronunciation Key:** hat, āge, cãre, fär; let, ēqual, tėrm; it, īce; hot, ōpen, ôrder; **oi**l, **ou**t; cup, pu̇t, rüle; **ch**ild; lo**ng**; **th**in; **ᴛʜ**en; **zh**, measure; **ə** represents **a** in about, **e** in taken, **i** in pencil, **o** in lemon, **u** in circus.

*assertion.* **2** having force in law; legally binding: *A contract made by an insane person is not valid.* **3** having force; holding good; effective: *Illness is a valid excuse for being absent from work.* **4** *Archaic.* **a** strong; powerful. **b** = healthy. **c** sane. [< Latin *validus* strong < *valēre* be strong] —**val′id|ly,** *adv.* —**val′id|ness,** *n.*

—*Syn.* **1 Valid, sound, cogent** mean convincing with respect to truth, rightness, or reasoning. **Valid** implies being based on truth or fact and supported by correct reasoning: *His objections to the plan on the basis of cost are valid.* **Sound** implies having a solid foundation of truth or right and being free from defects or errors in reasoning: *The author has sound views on opportunities today.* **Cogent** implies being so valid or sound as to be convincing: *He gives cogent advice to young people.*

**val|i|date** (val′ə dāt), *v.t.,* **-dat|ed, -dat|ing. 1** to make valid; give legal force to: *The farmer's deed validated his claim to the land.* SYN: legalize. **2** to support by facts or authority; confirm. SYN: corroborate, substantiate. —**val′i|da′tion,** *n.*

**va|lid|i|ty** (və lid′ə tē), *n., pl.* **-ties. 1** truth or soundness: *the validity of an argument, the validity of an excuse.* SYN: authenticity. **2** legal soundness or force; being legally binding: *the validity of a contract.* SYN: legality. **3** effectiveness: *He had ... too high an opinion of the validity of regular troops* (Benjamin Franklin). SYN: efficacy.

**val|ine** (val′ēn, -in), *n.* an amino acid constituent of protein, essential to growth. It can be isolated by hydrolysis of fish proteins for use as a nutrient, in medication, and in biochemical research. *Formula:* $C_5H_{11}NO_2$ [< *val*(eric acid) + *-ine*[2]]

**val|i|no|my|cin** (val′ə nō mī′sən), *n.* an antibiotic substance that activates the movement of ions in cells, derived from a species of streptomyces. *Formula:* $C_{54}H_{90}N_6O_{18}$ [< *valine* + (strepto)*mycin*]

**va|lise** (və lēs′), *n.* a traveling bag to hold clothes and other personal articles or to hold special equipment, such as that used by a doctor. SYN: portmanteau, suitcase. [< French *valise* < Italian *valigia;* origin uncertain]

**Va|li|um** (vā′lē əm), *n. Trademark.* diazepam, a tranquilizer.

**Val|kyr** (val′kir), *n.* = Valkyrie.

**Val|kyr|i|an** (val kir′ē ən), *adj.* of or relating to the Valkyries.

**Val|kyr|ie** (val kir′ē, val′kər ē), *n. Norse Mythology.* one of the twelve handmaidens of Odin, who ride through the air and hover over battlefields, choosing the heroes who are to die in battle and afterward leading them to Valhalla. Also, **Walkyrie.** [earlier *Valkyria* < Old Icelandic *valkyrja* < *valr* those slain in battle + *kyrja* chooser < *kjōsa* to choose]

**val|la** (val′ə), *n.* plural of **vallum.**

**Val lace** (val), = Valenciennes lace.

**val|late** (val′āt), *adj.* surrounded by a ridge or elevation; having a surrounding ridge or elevation. [< Latin *vallātus,* past participle of *vallāre* to surround with a rampart < *vallum* rampart < *vallus* stake]

**val|lat|ed** (val′ā tid), *adj.* surrounded with or as with a rampart or wall.

**val|la|tion** (va lā′shən), *n.* a trench; rampart. [< Late Latin *vallātiō, -ōnis* < Latin *vallāre;* see etym. under **vallate**]

**val|lec|u|la** (və lek′yə lə), *n., pl.* **-lae** (-lē). **1** *Anatomy.* a furrow or fissure. **2** *Botany.* a groove or channel. [< New Latin *vallecula* < Late Latin *vallicula* depression (diminutive) < Latin *vallis* valley, furrow]

**val|lec|u|lar** (və lek′yə lər), *adj.* **1** of or like a vallecula. **2** having a vallecula or valleculae.

**val|lec|u|late** (və lek′yə lāt), *adj.* = vallecular.

*** val|ley** (val′ē), *n., pl.* **-leys. 1** lowland between hills or mountains and usually having a river or stream flowing along its bottom. SYN: vale, dale, glen, dell. See picture below. **2** a wide region of generally flat, low country drained by a great river system: *the Mississippi Valley.* **3** any hollow or structure like a valley, especially a trough between waves. **4** *Figurative.* a place or condition marked by depression, darkness, or sorrow: *a valley of tears. Yea, though I walk through the valley of the shadow of death, I will fear no evil* (Psalms 23:4). **5** *Architecture.* a depression formed by the meeting of two sloping sides of a roof, or a roof and a wall; gutter. [< Old French *valee,* earlier *vallede* < *val* vale[1] < Latin *vallis*] —**val′ley|like′,** *adj.*

**valley fever,** a lung disease caused by a fungus, affecting people in hot, dusty areas; coccidioidomycosis: *The long, hot summer apparently cannot completely destroy the soil fungus that causes valley fever in humans* (Science News Letter).

**valley flat,** a low, level deposit of sediment in the channel of a stream: *Gradually, by undermining and caving the valley wall on one side and depositing on the other, the stream produces the broad valley flat of old age* (Finch and Trewartha).

**valley glacier,** a glacier that occupies a mountain valley, as in the Alps and the mountains of the western United States.

**valley mahogany,** = feather tree.

**val|lis|ne|ri|a|ceous** (val′is nir′ē ā′shəs), *adj.* belonging to the frogbit family of aquatic plants. [< New Latin *Vallisneriaceae* the family name < Antonio *Vallisneri,* 1661-1730, an Italian naturalist]

**val|lum** (val′əm), *n., pl.* **-la.** a wall or rampart of earth, sods, or stone, erected as a permanent means of defense, especially one of those constructed by the Romans in northern England and central Scotland: *He would walk round the ancient vallum ... and wonder at the mechanical skill which could have moved such ponderous masses* (John Lubbock). [< Latin *vallum* rampart; see etym. under **vallate**]

**Va|lois** (val′wä), *n., adj.* —*n.* a French royal house that ruled from 1328 to 1589, between the Capetians and Bourbons.

—*adj.* of or having to do with Valois, a medieval district in northern France, or the Valois family.

**va|lo|ni|a** (və lō′nē ə), *n.* the large acorn cups of the valonia oak, used especially in tanning and dyeing. [< Italian *vallonia* < New Greek *balánia,* plural of *baláni* acorn < Greek *bálanos*]

**valonia oak,** an oak of Greece and Asia Minor.

**val|or** (val′ər), *n.* bravery; courage: *The Virginia troops showed great valor.* (George Bancroft). SYN: prowess, intrepidity. [< Old French *valour* < Medieval Latin *valor* < Latin *valēre* be strong]

**val|or|i|za|tion** (val′ər ə zā′shən), *n. U.S.* the actual or attempted maintenance of certain prices for a commodity by a government. [American English < *valor,* in obsolete sense of "value" + *-ize* + *-ation;* perhaps patterned on Portuguese *valorização* < *valor* worth, price]

**val|or|ize** (val′ə rīz), *v.t., v.i.,* **-ized, -iz|ing. 1** to assign a value to. **2** *U.S.* to regulate the price of by valorization.

***valley**
definition 1

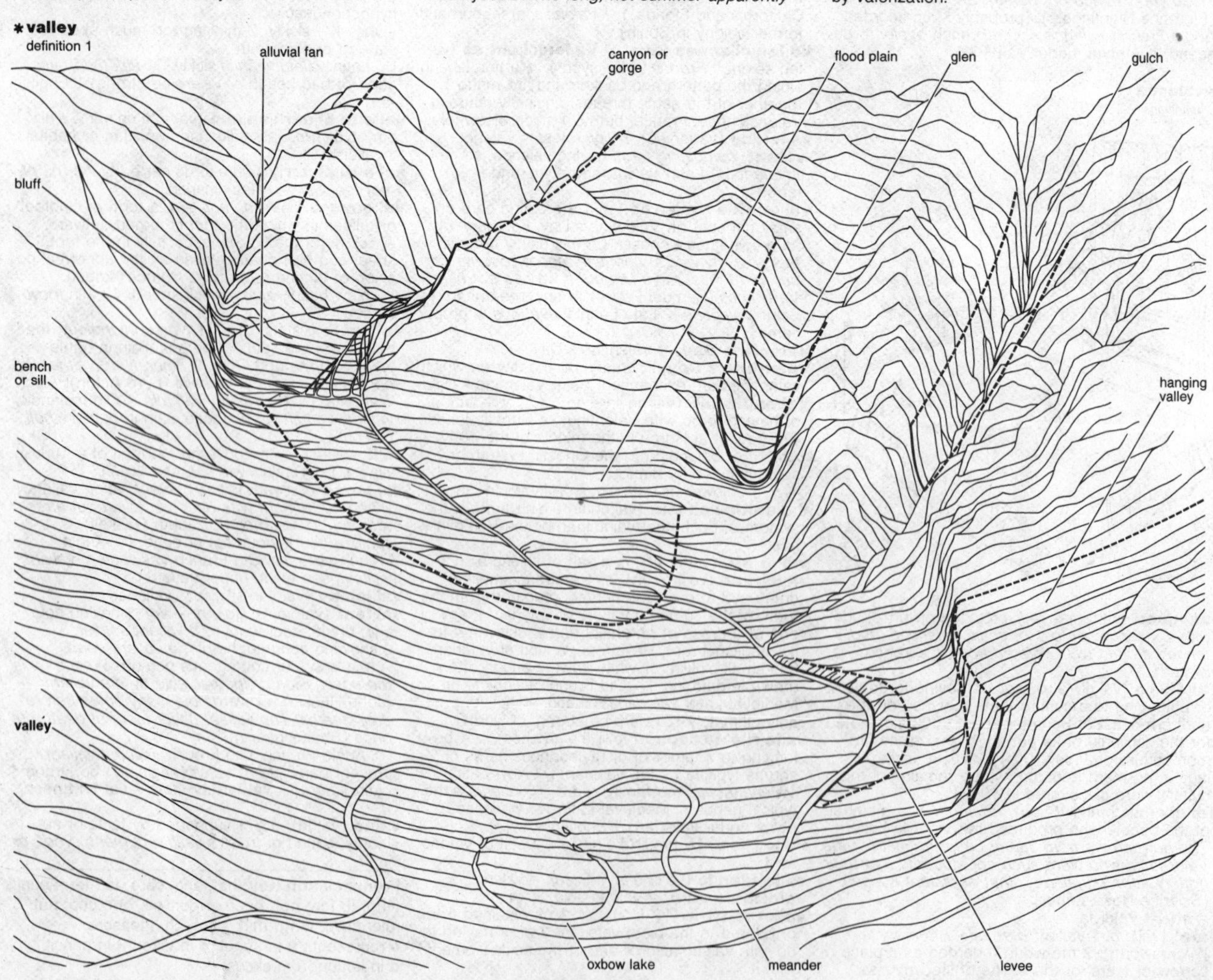

**val|or|ous** (val′ər əs), *adj.* **1** having courage; valiant; brave; courageous: *that host of valorous men who ... had fought so strenuous a fight for freedom* (John Morley). **2** showing courage. [< Middle French *valeureux* (with English *-ous*) < Old French *valeur,* earlier *valour;* see etym. under **valor**] —**val′or|ous|ly,** *adv.* —**val′or|ous|ness,** *n.*

**val|our** (val′ər), *n. Especially British.* valor.

**Val|po|li|cel|la** (väl′pō lē chel′ä), *n.* an Italian red table wine. [< *Valpolicella,* a valley in northern Italy]

**Val|sal|va maneuver** (val sal′və), the action of forcibly blowing through the nose while keeping the mouth and nostrils closed, performed by pilots and astronauts especially after descent to open the Eustachian tube and prevent the pain caused by reduced pressure within the middle ear. It is also used in medicine to test the openness of the Eustachian tube; if open, air will pass into the middle ear. [< Antonio Maria *Valsalva,* 1666-1723, an Italian anatomist, who first described it]

**valse** (väls), *n., v.,* **valsed, vals|ing.** —*n.* = waltz. —*v.i.* to waltz.
[< French *valse* < German *Walzer* waltz]

**val|u|a|ble** (val′yu̇ ə bəl, -yə bəl), *adj., n.* —*adj.* **1** having value; being worth something: *a valuable ring, a valuable old family Bible.* **2** having great value because of some special trait or quality: *a valuable tool, valuable information, a valuable friend.* **3** that can have its value measured.
—*n.* Usually, **valuables,** articles of value: *She keeps her jewelry and other valuables in a safe.*
—**val′u|a|ble|ness,** *n.*
—*Syn. adj.* **2 Valuable, precious** mean worth much. **Valuable** applies to anything costly, very useful, or highly esteemed: *He has a valuable stamp collection.* **Precious** applies to anything very valuable, especially to something that is irreplaceable: *The original Declaration of Independence is a precious document kept in Washington.*

**val|u|a|bly** (val′yu̇ ə blē, -yə-), *adv.* **1** with valuable or precious articles. **2** in a valuable manner; so as to be valuable or highly useful.

**val|u|ate** (val′yu̇ āt), *v.t.,* **-at|ed, -at|ing.** to estimate the value of; evaluate; appraise. [back formation < *evaluation*]

**val|u|a|tion** (val′yu̇ ā′shən), *n.* **1** value estimated or determined: *The jeweler's valuation of the necklace was $10,000.* **2** an estimating or determining the value of something: *She asked for a valuation of the collection.* **3** an appreciation or estimation of anything in respect to excellence or merit: *I believe it is difficult to find any two persons who place an equal valuation on any virtue* (Henry Fielding). [< Old French *valuation* < *valuer* to value]

**val|u|a|tion|al** (val′yu̇ ā′shə nəl), *adj.* of or having to do with valuation.

**val|u|a|tor** (val′yu̇ ā′tər), *n.* a person who estimates or determines the value of things, especially one appointed or licensed to do so; appraiser.

**val|ue** (val′yü), *n., v.,* **-ued, -u|ing.** —*n.* **1** the real worth; proper price: *They bought the house for less than its value.* **2** high worth; excellence, usefulness, or importance: *the value of education, the value of milk as a food.* **3** the power to buy: *The value of the dollar lessened from 1960 to 1970.* **4** an equivalent or adequate return: *We hardly could be said to have received value for our money.* **5** an estimated worth: *He placed a value on his furniture.* **6** meaning, effect, or force: *the value of a symbol.* **7** the number or amount represented by a symbol: *The value of XIV is fourteen.* **8** the relative length of a tone in music indicated by a note. **9** *Phonetics.* **a** a special quality of sound in speech. **b** a speech sound equivalent to a letter or a phonetic symbol: *The symbol* ᴛʜ *represents the value of "th" in "then."* **10a** the degree of lightness or darkness of a color, especially in a painting, in relation to other colors and sometimes to black and white; hue; tone: *A certain quantity of cold colours is necessary to give value and lustre to the warm colours* (Joshua Reynolds). **b** the relationship and effect of an object, spot of color, shadow, or other feature, to a whole painting.
—*v.t.* **1** to rate at a certain value or price; estimate the worth of; appraise: *The land is valued at $5,000.* **2** to think highly of; regard highly: *We all value our teacher's opinion of our work.* **3** to consider with respect to worth, excellence, usefulness, or importance.
**values,** *Sociology.* the established ideals of life; objects, customs, ways of acting, and the like, that the members of a given society regard as desirable: *Man lives by values; all his enterprises and activities ... make sense only in terms of some structure of purposes which are themselves values in action* (Will Herberg).
[< Old French *value,* originally past participle of *valeir* be worth < Latin *valēre*] —**val′u|er,** *n.*
—*Syn. v.t.* **2 Value, appreciate, esteem** mean to think highly of a person or thing. **Value** means to think highly of because of worth, importance, or some other quality: *I value your friendship.* **Appreciate** implies a valuing based on knowledge, sound judgment, or insight: *His classmates do not appreciate him.* **Esteem** means to think highly of because of warm or respectful regard: *The professor is esteemed by all his colleagues.*

**val|ue-add|ed tax** (val′yü ad′id), a sales tax based on the increase in value or price of a product at each stage in its manufacture and distribution. The cost of the tax is added to the final price and is eventually paid by the consumer. *Many European countries have a value-added tax, a kind of national sales levy that pounds up prices on everything from shoelaces to plumbing repairs* (Time). *Abbr:* VAT (no periods). Also, **added-value tax.**

**val|ued** (val′yüd), *adj.* **1** having its value estimated or determined. **2** regarded highly.

**valued policy,** a policy obliging an insurance company to pay the full face value of the policy in case of total loss, even though the insured property was not worth the full amount.

**value engineer,** a person who is trained or skilled in value engineering.

**value engineering, 1** the analysis as of a product or process to determine the least expensive method of design and production. **2** the modification as of a product or process as a result of such an analysis.

**value judgment,** an assessment of someone or something in terms of personal values, such as whether he or it is good or bad, worthwhile or troublesome; a subjective judgment or appraisal: *Stories about celebrities are only made meaningful through our superimposition of a ... psychological value judgment which relates the subject's adventures to cause-and-effect experience as the reader himself has observed it* (Harper's).

**val|ue|less** (val′yü lis), *adj.* without value; worthless: *Many quick judgments are valueless.* —**val′ue|less|ness,** *n.*

**val|ues** (val′yüz), *n. pl.* See under **value.**

**va|lu|ta** (vä lü′tä), *n.* **1** the fixed value of a nation's currency in terms of a foreign currency. **2** the fixed rate of exchange between a nation's currency and a specified foreign currency. [< Italian *valuta* (literally) value, originally past participle of *valere* be worth < Latin *valēre*]

**val|val** (val′vəl), *adj.* = valvular.

**val|var** (val′vər), *adj.* = valvular.

**val|vate** (val′vāt), *adj.* **1** furnished with, or opening by, a valve or valves. **2** serving as or resembling a valve. **3** *Botany.* **a** meeting without overlapping, as the parts of certain buds do. **b** united by the margins only, and opening as if by valves, as the capsules of regularly dehiscent fruits and certain anthers do. **c** composed of or characterized by such an arrangement of parts.
[< Latin *valvātus* having folding doors < *valvae,* plural, folding door; see etym. under **valve**]

*****valve** (valv), *n., v.,* **valved, valv|ing.** —*n.* **1** a movable part that controls the flow of a liquid or gas through a pipe or out of an enclosed space by opening or closing the passage. A faucet contains a valve. **2** a part of the body that works like a valve. The valves of the heart are membranes that control the flow of blood into and out of the heart. **3** one of the two or more parts of hinged shells like those of oysters and clams, or the whole shell when it is in one piece, as in snails. **4** *Botany.* **a** one of the halves or sections formed when a seed vessel bursts open. **b** a section that opens like a lid when an anther opens. **c** either of the halves of the shell of a diatom. **5** *Electronics.* **a** any device permitting the passage of electric current in one direction only. **b** *Especially British.* a vacuum tube or electron tube. **6** *Music.* a device in certain brass wind instruments, such as trumpets and French horns, connected with subsidiary loops of tubing, for changing the pitch of a tone by changing the length and direction of the column of air. There are two types of valves, the piston and the rotary cylinder. **7** a door or gate controlling the flow of water in a sluice. **8** *Archaic.* either one of the halves or leaves of a double or folding door.
—*v.t.* **1** to control the flow of (a liquid, gas, or stream of electrons) by a valve. **2** to discharge (gas) from a balloon by opening a valve. **3** to furnish with a valve or valves.
—*v.i.* **1** to make use of a valve or valves. **2** to open a valve of a balloon in order to descend.
[< Latin *valva* one of a pair of folding doors; leaf of a door] —**valve′like′,** *adj.*

**valve|gear** (valv′gir′), *n.* a mechanism which regulates the motions of the valves of an engine or other mechanical apparatus.

**valve-in-head engine** (valv′in hed′), an internal-combustion engine that has both intake and exhaust valves in the cylinder head.

**valve|less** (valv′lis), *adj.* having no valve.

**valve|let** (valv′lit), *n.* a small valve; valvule.

**valve port,** the opening uncovered by a valve in the cylinder block or head of a gasoline engine.

**valve seat,** the rim of the valve port on which the valve rests when closed, made of specially hardened steel inserts.

**val|vu|la** (val′vyə lə), *n., pl.* **-lae** (-lē). *Anatomy.* a valve or valvule. [< Medieval Latin *valvula;* see etym. under *valvule*]

**val|vu|lar** (val′vyə lər), *adj.* **1** of, having to do with, or affecting a valve or valves, especially the valves of the heart. **2** having the form or function of a valve. **3** furnished with a valve or valves; working by valves.

**val|vule** (val′vyül), *n.* a small valve; valvelet. [< French *valvule,* learned borrowing from Medieval Latin *valvula* (diminutive) < Latin *valva;* see etym. under **valve**]

**val|vu|li|tis** (val′vyə lī′tis), *n.* inflammation of a valve, especially of a valve of the heart. [< New Latin *valvulitis* < *valvula* + *-itis* inflammation, -itis]

**vam|brace** (vam′brās), *n.* defensive armor for the forearm. [alteration of earlier *vantbrace* < Anglo-French *vantbras,* short for *avantbras* < *avant* before + *bras* arm]

**va|moose** (va müs′), *v.t., v.i.,* **-moosed, -moos|ing.** *U.S. Slang.* to go away quickly. [American English < Spanish *vamos* let's go]

**va|mose** (va mōs′), *v.t., v.i.,* **-mosed, -mos|ing.** *U.S. Slang.* vamoose.

*****valve**
definitions 1, 6

gate valve:

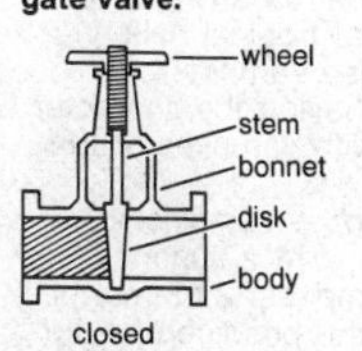

closed

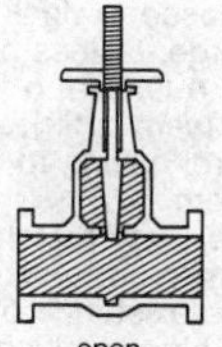
open

globe valve:

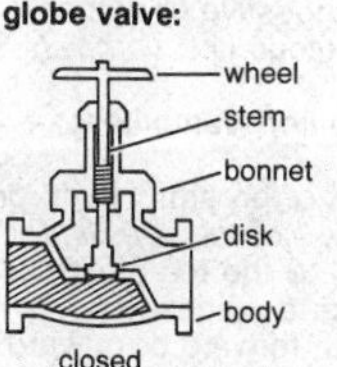

closed

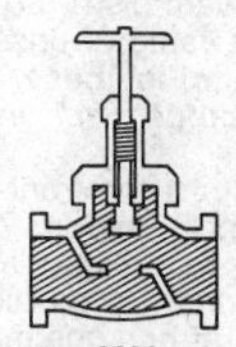
open

check valve:

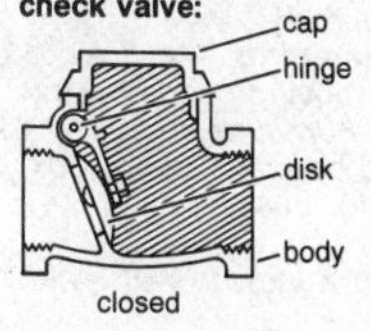

closed

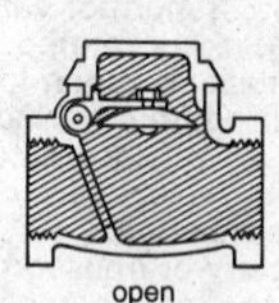
open

definition 6

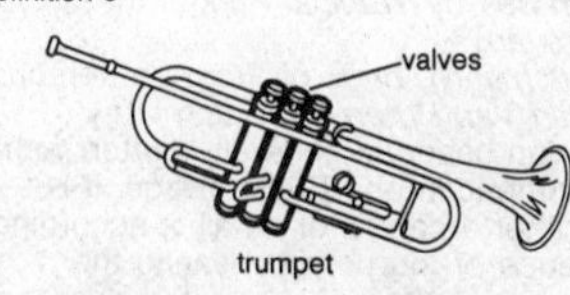

trumpet

**vamp**[1] (vamp), *n., v.* —*n.* **1** the upper front part of a shoe or boot. **2** a piece or patch added to an old thing to make it look new. **3** anything that is patched up or restored by a vamp; patchwork. **4** *Music.* a simple accompaniment, usually an improvised series of chords.
—*v.t.* **1** to furnish (footwear) with a vamp; repair (a shoe or boot) with a new vamp. **2** to make (an old thing) look new; patch up. **3** *Figurative.* to put together (a book or composition) out of old materials; compile; compose. **4** to improvise in a simple or crude way to (an accompaniment, song, or melody). —*v.i. Music.* to improvise an accompaniment: *I got a banjo, you know, and I vamp a bit* (H. G. Wells).
**vamp up, a** to make (something old) appear new: *The women of the town* [*were*] *vamped up for show with paint, patches, plumpers, and eve-*

**Pronunciation Key:** hat, āge, cãre, fär; let, ēqual, tėrm; it, īce; hot, ōpen, ôrder; oil, out; cup, pu̇t, rüle; child; long; thin; ᴛʜen; zh, measure;
ə represents **a** in about, **e** in taken, **i** in pencil, **o** in lemon, **u** in circus.

*ry external ornament that art can administer* (Samuel Johnson). **b** to make up to deceive: *to vamp up a worthless accusation.*
[short for Old French *avanpie* < *avant* before + *pie* foot < Latin *pēs, pedis*] —**vamp′er**, *n.*

**vamp²** (vamp), *n., v. Slang.* —***n.*** an unscrupulous flirt; adventuress.
—***v.t.*** to flirt with (a man) for the purpose of extortion.
—***v.i.*** to flirt with a man in order to extort from him. [short for *vampire*] —**vamp′er**, *n.*

**vamp horn**, any one of several, variously shaped, valveless horns used in churches in the 1700's and 1800's to amplify the singing or speaking voice.

**vamp|i|ness** (vam′pē nis), *n.* a vampish quality or condition: *The varnished vampiness of Greta Garbo* (Sunday Express).

**vam|pire** (vam′pīr), *n.* **1** a corpse supposed to come to life at night and leave its grave and suck the blood of people while they sleep.
**2** *Figurative.* **a** a person who preys ruthlessly on others. **b** a woman who flirts with men to get money or to please her vanity. **c** an actress known for playing the part of a beautiful woman who is ruthless and vain. **3** = vampire bat. **4** a trap door with two leaves closed by a string and used for sudden disappearances from the stage.
[< French *vampire* < German *Vampir* < Slavic (compare Serbian *vampir*)]

**vampire bat**, **1** any one of several groups of bats of South and Central America that pierce the skin of animals with their sharp teeth and drink the blood as it flows. **2** any one of several large bats of South and Central America, incorrectly supposed to drink blood. **3a** any one of a group of large, tailless bats of tropical Asia, Africa, and Australia. **b** = false vampire.

**vam|pir|ic** (vam pir′ik), *adj.* having the character of a vampire; having to do with vampires or the belief in them.

**vam|pir|ish** (vam′pīr ish), *adj.* = vampiric.

**vam|pir|ism** (vam′pīr iz əm), *n.* **1** a superstitious belief in the existence of vampires. **2** the act or practice of bloodsucking. **3** the practice of extortion or preying on others.

**vamp|ish** (vam′pish), *adj.* suggestive or characteristic of a vamp or unscrupulous flirt: *vampish wiles.* —**vamp′ish|ness**, *n.*

**vamp|y** (vam′pē), *adj.*, **vamp|i|er, vamp|i|est.** = vampish.

**van¹** (van), *n.* **1** the front part of an army, fleet, or other advancing group: *Thou, like the van, first took'st the field* (Henry King). **2** the foremost part of, or the foremost position in, a company or procession of persons moving forward or onward. **3** *Figurative.* = vanguard (defs. 2, 3): *to be in the van of industrial nations, to lead the van of modern painting.* [short for *vanguard*]

**van²** (van), *n., v.,* **vanned, van|ning.** —***n.*** **1** a covered truck or wagon for moving goods or animals, opening from behind: *Furniture is usually moved in a van.* **2** a railroad baggage car or boxcar. **b** a lightweight vehicle for business and delivery; pickup truck.
—***v.t.*** to carry or transport in a van: *to van race horses from track to track.*
—***v.i.*** to travel by van: *On race days he vans to the track from nearby Tropical Park* (Time).
[short for *caravan*]

**van³** (van; *Dutch* vän), *prep.* of; from (in personal names): *Martin Van Buren.* [< Dutch *van*]
► **Van** in foreign usage is generally written with a small *v;* in American and British usage, it is written with either a capital or small *v,* according to the preference of the person bearing the name.

**van⁴** (van), *n.* **1** *Dialect.* a basket or shovel used to catch tossed grain as the chaff is blown away by the wind. **2** *Poetic.* a wing: *As bats at the wired window of a dairy, They beat their vans* (Shelley). **3** a sail of a windmill. [probably dialectal variant of *fan¹*]

**van|a|date** (van′ə dāt), *n.* a salt or ester of vanadic acid.

**va|na|di|ate** (və nā′dē āt), *n.* = vanadate.

**va|nad|ic** (və nad′ik, -nā′dik), *adj.* **1** of, derived from, or having to do with vanadium. **2** containing vanadium, especially with a valence of three or of five.

**vanadic acid**, any one of a group of acids known only in the form of their salts (vanadates), and considered hydrates, such as vanadium pentoxide, $V_2O_5$.

**va|nad|i|nite** (və nad′ə nīt), *n.* a mineral consisting of a vanadate and chloride of lead, occurring in brilliant crystals of various colors. *Formula:* $Pb_5ClV_3O_{12}$

**va|na|di|ous** (və nā′dē əs), *adj.* = vanadous.

***va|na|di|um** (və nā′dē əm), *n.* a very hard, silver-white metallic chemical element occurring in certain iron, lead, and uranium ores, such as vanadinite, and used especially in making various strong alloys of steel. [< New Latin *vanadium* < Old Icelandic *Vanadīs,* a name of the Scandinavian goddess Freya (because it was found in iron by a Swedish chemist)]

***vanadium**

| symbol | atomic number | atomic weight | oxidation state |
|---|---|---|---|
| V | 23 | 50.942 | 2,3,4,5 |

**vanadium pentoxide**, a yellowish-brown crystalline compound used as a catalyst in oxidation reactions, as a developer in photography, in textile dyeing, and in making certain inks. *Formula:* $V_2O_5$

**vanadium steel**, **1** a steel containing some vanadium (from 0.10 to 0.20 per cent) to make it tougher and harder. **2** a steel containing vanadium, chromium, and various other elements.

**van|a|dous** (van′ə dəs), *adj.* **1** of or having to do with vanadium. **2** containing vanadium, especially with a valence of two or of three.

**Van Al|len belt** (van al′ən), = Van Allen radiation belt.

***Van Allen radiation belt**, either of two broad bands of intense radiation surrounding the earth, consisting of charged particles which are apparently held by the earth's magnetic field. [< James A. *Van Allen,* born 1914, an American physicist, who discovered them in 1958]

***Van Allen radiation belt**

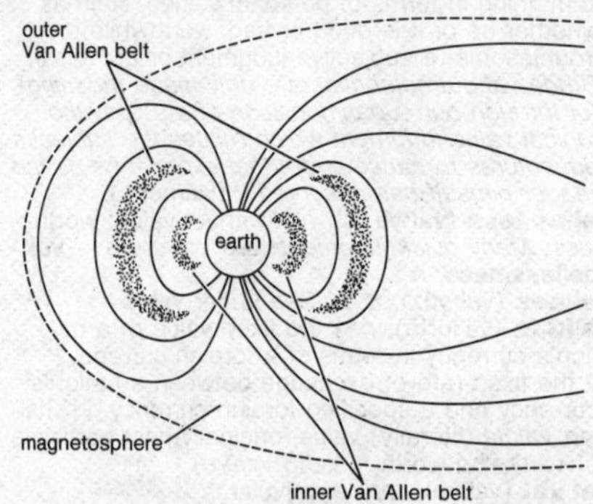


**va|nas|pa|ti** (və nes′pə tē), *n.* a hydrogenated fat made in India from vegetable oils and used as a butter substitute. [< Hindustani *vanaspati*]

**van|co|my|cin** (van′kō mī′sin), *n.* an antibiotic derived from a microorganism found in Indonesian and Indian soil, used against staphylococcal and other infections. [< *vanco-* (origin uncertain) + *-mycin,* as in *streptomycin*]

**Van|cou|ver|ite** (van kü′və rīt′), *n.* a native or inhabitant of Vancouver, a seaport in British Columbia, Canada.

**van|da** (van′də), *n.* any one of a genus of orchids native to tropical Asia, having large, showy flowers, borne in racemes. [< New Latin *Vanda* the genus name < Sanskrit *vandā* a kind of parasitic plant]

**Van|dal** (van′dəl), *n., adj.* —***n.*** a member of a Germanic tribe that invaded western Europe in the 300's and 400's, and ravaged Gaul, Spain, and northern Africa. In A.D. 455 the Vandals took Rome.
—***adj.*** of or having to do with the Vandals.
[< Late Latin *Vandalus* < a Germanic tribal name]

**van|dal** (van′dəl), *n., adj.* —***n.*** a person who destroys or damages beautiful or valuable things on purpose.
—***adj.*** **1** destructive. **2** characterized by vandalism or lack of culture; vandalistic.
[< *Vandal* (because of the wanton destruction they carried out)]

**Van|dal|ic** (van dal′ik), *adj.* **1** Often, **vandalic.** characteristic of Vandals; destructive; vandalistic. **2** of, having to do with, or consisting of Vandals.

**van|dal|ise** (van′də līz), *v.t.,* **-ised, -is|ing.** *Especially British.* vandalize.

**van|dal|ism** (van′də liz əm), *n.* **1** the action of destroying or damaging beautiful or valuable things on purpose. **2** conduct, spirit, or actions characteristic of the Vandals in respect to culture, especially hostility toward culture. **3** a vandalistic act.

**van|dal|is|tic** (van′də lis′tik), *adj.* **1** characterized by or given to vandalism. **2** of, having to do with, or consisting of Vandals.

**van|dal|ize** (van′də līz), *v.t.,* **-ized, -iz|ing.** to destroy willfully or senselessly. —**van′dal|i|za′tion,** *n.*

**van|dal|ous** (van′də ləs), *adj.* vandalistic; destructive. —**van′dal|ous|ly,** *adv.*

**Van de Graaff generator** or **accelerator** (van′ də graf′), an apparatus used to produce electric potentials of very high voltages, for accelerating charged particles used in bombarding nuclei; electrostatic generator. [< Robert *Van de Graaff,* 1901-1967, an American physicist]

**van der Waals forces** (van′ dər wôlz′), *Physical Chemistry.* the relatively weak forces of attraction existing between atoms or molecules, caused by the interaction of varying dipoles. [< Johannes *van der Waals,* 1837-1923, a Dutch physicist]

**Van|dyke** (van dīk′), *adj., n.* —***adj.*** of or having to do with Anton Van Dyck (1599-1641), a Flemish painter, or the style of dress, coloring, or other features characteristic of his portraits.
—***n.*** Often, **vandyke.** **1** = Vandyke beard. **2** = Vandyke collar. **3a** one of a number of deep-cut points on the border or fringe of an article of dress. **b** a notched or deeply indented border, edging, or formation: (*Figurative.*) *a vandyke of bays and promontories.*
[< *Vandyke,* Anglicized spelling of *Van Dyck*]

***Vandyke beard**, a short, close-cut, pointed beard.

***Vandyke beard**

**Vandyke brown**, **1** any of various dark-brown pigments, consisting of mixtures of iron oxide and lampblack or other organic substances. **2** a dark-brown pigment used by Anton Van Dyck. Its composition is uncertain.

***Vandyke collar** or **cape**, a wide collar or shoulder covering with a lace or linen border having deep points indenting the edge.

***Vandyke collar**

**van|dyked** (van dīkt′), *adj.* cut or shaped at the edge with deep indentations; zigzagged: *a vandyked border, a wall with a vandyked top.*

**vane** (vān), *n.* **1a** a flat piece of metal, or some other device, fixed upon a spire or other high object in such a way as to move with the wind and indicate its direction; weather vane; weathercock. **b** a similar device on the masthead of a boat, consisting of a cloth on a wooden frame. **2** a blade of a windmill, ship's propeller, or the like. **3** a blade, wing, or similar projection attached to an axis, wheel, rocket, or the like, to guide or somehow affect movement. **4** the flat, soft part of a feather; web. See picture under **feather.** **5** any one of the feathers fastened to the back end of an arrow to give it accuracy in flight. **6** *Surveying.* **a** a target. **b** a sight, as on a quadrant or compass. [dialectal variant of Middle English *fane,* Old English *fana* banner]

**vaned** (vānd), *adj.* furnished with a vane or vanes.

**vane|less** (vān′lis), *adj.* having no vane.

**va|nes|sa** (və nes′ə), *n., pl.* **-sas.** any one of a group of butterflies, the members of which have the outer margin of the forewings more or less notched, as the red admiral. [< New Latin *Vanessa* the genus name]

**van|ette** (və net′), *n.* a small motor van.

**vang** (vang), *n.* either of two ropes used for steadying the gaff of a fore-and-aft sail. [apparently variant of *fang*]

**van|guard** (van′gärd′), *n.* **1** the front part of an army; soldiers marching ahead of the main part of an army to clear the way and guard against surprise. **2** *Figurative.* **a** the foremost or leading position, usually in intellectual and political movements or social reforms. **b** the leaders of a movement, especially persons who experiment or work with new ideas. [Middle English *vantgarde* < Old French *avangarde* < *avant* before (< Vulgar Latin *abante* < Latin *ab* from + *ante* before) + *garde* guard. Compare etym. under **avant-garde.**]

**van|guard|ism** (van′gär′diz əm), *n.* = avant-gardism.

**van|guard|ist** (van′gär′dist), *n.* = avant-gardist.

***va|nil|la** (və nil′ə), *n., pl.* **-las. 1** a flavoring used in candy, ice cream, or perfume; vanilla extract. **2** any one of a group of tropical American climbing orchids especially a species that yields the beans used to make this flavoring. **3** = vanilla bean. [< New Latin *Vanilla* the genus name < Spanish *vainilla,* Old Spanish (originally) little pod (diminutive) < *vaina* < Latin *vagīna* sheath]

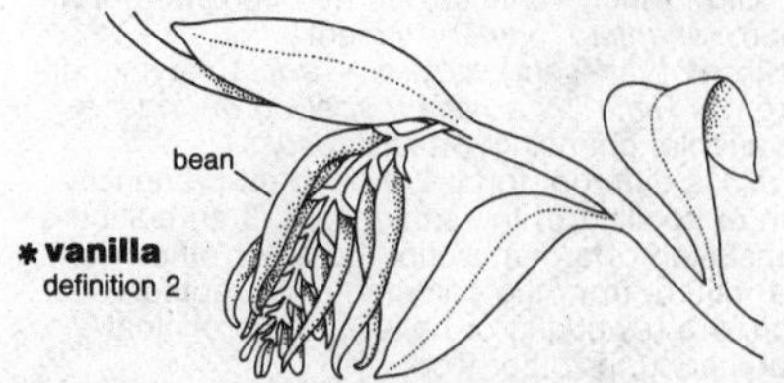


***vanilla**
definition 2

**vanilla bean**, the long, slender pod of the vanilla plant, used in making vanilla flavoring.

**vanilla extract**, a flavoring extract made from the vanilla bean and used in candy, ice cream, and perfumes.

**va|nil|lic** (və nil′ik), *adj.* of or obtained from vanilla or vanillin.

**van|il|lin** (van′ə lin, və nil′in), *n.* a white crystalline compound constituting the odoriferous principle of vanilla, obtained from the vanilla bean or made synthetically, used as a flavoring, in perfumery, and in making paper pulp. *Formula:* $C_8H_8O_3$

**van|il|line** (van′ə lin, -lēn; və nil′in, -ēn), *n.* = vanillin.

**Va|nir** (vä′nir), *n. Norse Mythology.* an early race of gods, including Frey, Freya, and Njorth, who preceded the Aesir.

**van|ish** (van′ish), *v., n.* —*v.i.* **1** to disappear, especially suddenly: *The sun vanished behind a cloud.* **SYN:** See syn. under **disappear. 2** to pass away; cease to be: *Dinosaurs have vanished from the earth.* **3** *Mathematics.* to become zero.
—*v.t.* to cause to disappear; remove from sight: *... a far more effective trick than her own proposed feat of vanishing a man or woman without the use of drops or drapes* (Edwin O'Connor).
—*n. Phonetics.* the brief end sound of phonemes.
[short for Old French *esvaniss-,* stem of *esvanir* < Vulgar Latin *exvānīre,* for Latin *ēvānēscere* < *ex-* out + *vānēscere* vanish < *vānus* empty]
—**van′ish|er,** *n.*

**van|ish|ing cream** (van′i shing), a facial cream to protect the skin or serve as a base for face powder or other cosmetics.

**van|ish|ing|ly** (van′i shing lē), *adv.* in a vanishing manner; imperceptibly: *The neutrino is uncharged, has a vanishingly small mass, and has been found to spiral in a left-handed manner* (Science News Letter).

***vanishing point, 1** the point toward which receding parallel lines seem to converge. **2** *Figurative.* a point at which anything disappears or comes to an end: *His income had reached the vanishing point.*

***vanishing point**
definition 1

**van|ish|ment** (van′ish ment), *n.* **1** the act of vanishing or disappearing: *the overnight vanishment of our "way of life"* (Wall Street Journal). **2** the state of having vanished.

**van|i|to|ry** (van′ə tôr′ē, -tōr′-), *n., pl.* **-ries. 1** a bathroom fixture combining a washbasin and dressing table. **2 Vanitory,** a trademark for this fixture. [< *vani*(ty), def. 7 + (lava)*tory*]

**van|i|tous** (van′ə təs), *adj.* full of vanity; vain: *French criticism ... instructs without wounding any but the vanitous person* (George Meredith).

**van|i|ty** (van′ə tē), *n., pl.* **-ties. 1a** too much pride in one's looks, ability, or accomplishments: *The girl's vanity made her look in the mirror often.* **SYN:** conceit, egotism, self-esteem. **b** an instance of this; worthless pleasure or display: *In spite of her small vanities, Margaret had a sweet ... nature* (Louisa M. Alcott). **2** a lack of real value; worthlessness: *the vanity of wealth.* **3** a useless, idle, or worthless thing: *I had forsaken the vanities of the world* (Thomas Malory). **4** a thing of which one is vain: *She was my Vanity, and oh All other vanities how vain!* (Coventry Patmore). **5** a lack of effect or success: *It is vanity to waste our days in blind pursuit of knowledge* (Sir Thomas Browne). **6** = vanity case. **7** a dressing table, usually fitted with a mirror. [< Old French *vanite,* learned borrowing from Latin *vānitās, -ātis* < *vānus* empty]

**vanity case**, a small handbag used by women to carry cosmetics and other toilet articles.

**Vanity Fair**, any place or scene, such as the world, a great city, or the world of fashion, regarded as given over to vain pleasure or empty show. [< *Vanity Fair,* the fair described in John Bunyan's *Pilgrim's Progress,* symbolizing the world of vain pleasure or empty show]

**vanity press** or **publisher**, a publishing house that publishes books at the expense of the authors.

**vanity surgery**, plastic surgery to improve the appearance, for example by face-lifting, reshaping the nose, or removing fat from the abdomen.

**van|load** (van′lōd′), *n.* as much as a van can hold or carry: *In Madison Square Garden, huge, fragrant vanloads of flowers were unloaded* (Time).

**van|man** (van′mən), *n., pl.* **-men.** a man who drives or works on a van.

**van|ner** (van′ər), *n. Mining.* **1** a person who separates ore. **2** an apparatus for separating ores. [< *van*[4] + *-er*[1]]

**van|quish** (vang′kwish, van′-), *v.t.* **1a** to conquer, defeat, or overcome in battle or conflict. **SYN:** See syn. under **defeat. b** to overcome or subdue (a person) by other than physical means: *though vanquished, he could argue still* (Oliver Goldsmith). **2** to subdue, overcome, or put an end to (a feeling or state of things); suppress: *to vanquish fear.* [Middle English *vencusen* < Old French *vencus,* past participle of *veintre,* and Middle English *venquisshen,* probably influenced by Old French *vainquiss-,* stem of *vainquir,* both Old French verbs < Latin *vincere* to conquer]
—**van′quish|er,** *n.*

**van|quish|a|ble** (vang′kwi shə bəl), *adj.* that can be vanquished.

**van|quished** (van′kwisht), *adj., n.* —*adj.* defeated or overcome in conflict or battle; conquered.
—*n.* the person, group, army, feeling, or state of things, defeated, subdued, or conquered: *Yet we recognize that another world war in the age of atomic and thermonuclear weapons would be an unparalleled disaster for victor and vanquished alike* (Bulletin of Atomic Scientists).

**van|quish|ment** (vang′kwish mənt), *n.* the act of vanquishing or overcoming.

**van|tage** (van′tij, vän′-), *n.* **1** a better position or condition; advantage: *a station of vantage for introducing him to the public favor* (Thomas De Quincey). **2** *British.* advantage; the first point scored in a tennis game after deuce. [short for Middle English *avantage* advantage]

**vantage ground**, = vantage point.

**vantage point, 1** a superior position that gives a person an advantage, as in combat or an argument: *If the manor were attacked, the tower would become a vantage point from which defending archers could pick off attackers who were floundering across the ditch* (Scientific American). **2** *Figurative: The picture he provides of these years is a truthful one, but he gives the impression of looking back from some remote vantage point in order to extract from these fateful events the grim lesson of the spiritual agony of those who endured them* (Atlantic).

**van|ward** (van′wərd), *adj., adv.* toward or in the front; forward. [< *van*[1] + *-ward*]

**vap|id** (vap′id), *adj.* **1** without much life or flavor; tasteless; dull; flat: *table-beer, guiltless of hops and malt, vapid and nauseous* (Tobias Smollett). **2** *Figurative.* lacking interest, zest, or animation; lifeless; insipid: *vapid conversation.* [< Latin *vapidus,* related to *vapor* vapor] —**vap′id|ly,** *adv.* —**vap′id|ness,** *n.*

**va|pid|i|ty** (va pid′ə tē), *n., pl.* **-ties. 1** flatness of flavor; insipidity. **2** *Figurative.* a lifeless, uninteresting, or dull remark, idea, or feature.

**va|por** (vā′pər), *n., v.* —*n.* **1** moisture that can be seen, such as steam from boiling water or fog or mist: *the vapor of the morning mist.* **2** a gas formed when a solid or liquid substance is sufficiently heated. A *gas* is a substance that at ordinary temperatures and pressures exists in the gaseous state, while a *vapor* is the gaseous form of a substance that normally exists in a solid or liquid form. *We could smell the gasoline vapor as the gas tank of the car was being filled.* **3** *Figurative.* something without substance; empty fancy: *A man to whom Earth and all its glories are in truth a vapor and a dream* (Thomas Carlyle). **4a** a substance, such as alcohol, mercury, or benzoin, that has been changed into vapor for use as in medicine or industry. **b** a mixture of a vaporized substance and air, as in an internal-combustion engine. **c** the emission or exhalation of such mixtures or of any substance in gaseous form.
—*v.t.* **1** to cause to rise or ascend in the form of a vapor: *Then, upon a gentle heat, vapor away all the spirit of wine* (Francis Bacon). **2** to give (a person) the vapors; depress or bore. **3** to boast; swagger; brag.
—*v.i.* **1** to rise, ascend, or pass off as vapor. **2** to give or send out vapor, steam, or gas; emit vapors or exhalations. **3** *Figurative.* to use blustering or grandiloquent language; brag, swagger, or boast: *Strutting and vaporing about his own pretensions* (William Hazlitt). Also, *especially British,* **vapour.**
**the vapors,** *Archaic.* low spirits; hypochondria, hysteria, or other nervous disorder: *I had sent for him in a fit of the vapors* (Stanley J. Weyman).
**vapors, a** exhalations once considered in medical circles to be injurious to the health, and to originate especially in the stomach: *vapors from an empty stomach* (Daniel Defoe). **b** a condition once supposed to be caused by the presence of such exhalations: *She had a headache, vapors. They are over* (George Meredith).
[< Latin *vapor, -ōris*] —**va′por|er,** *n.*

**va|por|a|ble** (vā′pər ə bəl), *adj.* that can be converted into vapor.

**va|po|rar|i|um** (vā′pə rãr′ē əm), *n., pl.* **-rar|i|ums, -rar|i|a** (-rãr′ē ə). an apartment or bath equipped for the application of the vapor of water to the body; vapor bath. [< New Latin *vaporarium* < Latin *vapor, -ōris* vapor]

**vapor barrier**, a material used to prevent or eliminate condensation and penetration of moisture into a structure: *A new vapor barrier for building construction ... is made in thin sheets of a pliable material known as polyethylene* (New York Times).

**vapor bath, 1** an application of the vapor of water to the body in a close apartment or place. **2** = vaporarium.

**va|por|es|cence** (vā′pə res′əns), *n.* the process of changing into vapor.

**va|por|es|cent** (vā′pə res′ənt), *adj.* changing into vapor; vaporizing.

**va|po|ret|to** (vä′pô rät′tō), *n., pl.* **-ti** (-tē). *Italian.* a small steamboat used to carry passengers along a certain route on a canal or canals, especially in Venice: *He stepped with her onto a vaporetto bound from St. Mark's to the Lido* (New Yorker).

**va|por|if|ic** (vā′pə rif′ik), *adj.* **1** associated or connected with, producing or causing, vaporization: *vaporific sublimation.* **2** = vaporous. [< Latin *vapor, -ōris* vapor, steam + *facere* to make]

**va|por|im|e|ter** (vā′pə rim′ə tər), *n.* an instrument for measuring vapor pressure or volume.

**va|por|ing** (vā′pər ing), *adj., n.* —*adj.* **1** talking pretentiously or boastfully; bragging: *a vaporing little man.* **2** pretentious and foolishly boastful: *vaporing talk.* **3** = vaporous.
—*n.* boastful talk; pretentious or ostentatious behavior. —**va′por|ing|ly,** *adv.*

**va|por|ise** (vā′pə rīz), *v.t., v.i.,* **-ised, -is|ing.** *Especially British.* vaporize.

**va|por|ish** (vā′pər ish), *adj.* **1** like vapor. **2** abounding in vapor: *a vaporish cave.* **3** dim or obscure because of the presence of vapor; vapory: *the vaporish moon.* **4** *Figurative.* in low spirits; depressed; dejected: *Lady Lyndon, always vaporish and nervous ... became more agitated than ever* (Thackeray). **5** *Figurative.* having to do with or connected with low spirits: *vaporish fears.* —**va′por|ish|ness,** *n.*

**va|por|iz|a|ble** (vā′pə rī′zə bəl), *adj.* that can be vaporized: *The entire prescription is not large, for the more readily vaporizable material has evanesced during the years of simmering* (Matthew Luckiesh).

**va|por|i|za|tion** (vā′pər ə zā′shən), *n.* **1** the process of changing, or of being changed, into vapor. **2** the rapid conversion of water into steam with the application of heat, as in a boiler. **3** *Medicine.* treatment with vapor.

**va|por|ize** (vā′pə rīz), *v.,* **-ized, -iz|ing.** —*v.t.* to change into vapor by the application of heat, re-

**Pronunciation Key:** hat, āge, cãre, fär; let, ēqual, tėrm; it, īce; hot, ōpen, ôrder; oil, out; cup, pu̇t, rüle; child; long; thin; ᴛʜen; zh, measure; ə represents a in about, e in taken, i in pencil, o in lemon, u in circus.

duction of pressure, or other means; cause to evaporate: *The sun's heat vaporizes the water of the ocean.*
—*v.i.* to pass off in vapor; become vaporous: *On the journey some of the liquid will vaporize ...; but this is not expected to exceed more than one-half per cent a day* (New York Times).

**va|por|iz|er** (vā′pə rī′zər), *n.* **1** a device for converting a liquid into vapor or mist, such as an atomizer or an apparatus that releases steam into a room for medicinal purposes: *There are many preparations that claim to break up respiratory congestion when dissolved in a vaporizer* (Sidonie M. Gruenberg). **2** a device in the carburetor of an internal-combustion engine for turning liquid fuel into a fine mist.

**vapor lamp**, an electric lamp that uses a vapor or gas instead of a wire filament to produce light, used chiefly for street and highway lighting: *The more modern ... vapor lamps contain sodium or mercury gas, and provide more light than ordinary electric lights* (Pyke Johnson).

**va|por|less** (vā′pər lis), *adj.* lacking or free from vapor.

**vapor lock**, an interruption in the flow of fuel in a gasoline engine, occurring when excessive heat vaporizes the gasoline in the fuel line or carburetor, causing the engine to stall: *Vapor lock occurs most frequently during long, steep climbs on hot days, or when slowing suddenly after a hard drive* (Willard Rogers).

**va|por|ole** (vā′pə rōl), *n.* a medicinal preparation, such as a volatile drug for inhalation, enclosed in a thin glass capsule, to be broken for use.

**va|por|os|i|ty** (vā′pə ros′ə tē), *n.* vaporous quality.

**va|por|ous** (vā′pər əs), *adj.* **1** full of vapor; misty: *vaporous atmosphere.* **2** covered or obscured with vapor: *vaporous hills.* **3** like vapor. **4** *Figurative.* soon passing; worthless: *vaporous dreams of grandeur.* **5** thin and gauzelike: *a vaporous fabric.* **6** *Figurative.* vague; fanciful; frothy: *vaporous imaginations* (Francis Bacon). **7** characteristic of vapor: *matter in a vaporous or gaseous state.* —**va′por|ous|ly**, *adv.* —**va′por|ous|ness**, *n.*

**vapor pressure** or **tension**, *Physics.* the pressure exerted by a vapor in an enclosed space when the vapor is in equilibrium with its liquid or solid at any specified temperature: *The vapor pressure in the container of sea water is lower than in the flask of pure water, because its water molecules, being bound to salt ions, do not evaporate as easily* (Scientific American).

**vapor trail**, the condensation of water vapor in the exhaust fumes from any aircraft engine, especially those of jet planes and rockets at high altitudes; contrail.

**va|por|y** (vā′pər ē), *adj.* = vaporous.

**va|pour** (vā′pər), *n., v.t., v.i. Especially British.* vapor.

**va|pour|ize** (vā′pə rīz), *v.t., v.i.*, **-ized, -iz|ing.** *Especially British.* vaporize.

**vap|u|la|tion** (vap′yə lā′shən), *n. Obsolete.* a flogging or thrashing. [< Latin *vāpulāre* to flog + English *-ation*]

**vap|u|la|to|ry** (vap′yə lə tôr′ē, -tōr′-), *adj. Obsolete.* of or having to do with vapulation.

**va|que|ro** (vä kãr′ō), *n., pl.* **-ros.** *Spanish America and Southwestern United States.* a cowboy, a herdsman, or a cattle driver. [American English < American Spanish *vaquero* < Spanish, cowherd < *vaca* cow < Latin *vacca* cow. Compare etym. under **buckaroo.**]

**var.,**
1 variant.
2 variation.
3 variety.
4 various.

**VAR** (no periods), visual-aural range (a VHF radio-signaling device for both visual and aural reception, used as a navigational aid).

**va|ra** (vä′rä), *n.* **1** a measure of length used in Spain, Portugal, and Latin America, usually about 33 inches, but varying from about 32 to about 43 inches. **2** this measure squared, used as a unit of area. [< Spanish and Portuguese *vara* yardstick, rod < Latin *vāra* forked pole < *vārus* bent (in)]

**va|rac|tor** (və rak′tər), *n.* a type of semiconducting diode whose capacitance varies with the applied voltage. [probably < *var*(iable cap)*ac*(i)*tor*]

**Va|ran|gi|an** (və ran′jē ən), *n., adj.* —*n.* **1** one of the Scandinavian rovers who overran parts of Russia, establishing a dynasty there under Rurik in the 800's, and reached Constantinople in the 900's. **2** = Varangian Guard.
—*adj.* of or having to do with the Varangians.
[< Medieval Latin *Varangus* < Medieval Greek *Várangos* < Old Russian *varegŭ* < Scandinavian (compare Old Icelandic *Væringi*, apparently originally, a pledged ally < *vār* plighted faith) + English *-ian*]

**Varangian Guard**, the bodyguard of later Byzantine emperors, recruited from the Varangians and, later, from Anglo-Saxons.

***var|gue|no** (vär gān′yō, -gā′nō), *n., pl.* **-nos.** an antique Spanish type of cabinet or desk, consisting of a box-shaped body mounted on columns or a stand, and having the front hinged at the lower edge so as to afford, when let down, a surface for use in writing. [< Spanish *vargueño*, said to be < *Vargas*, a village near Toledo, Spain]

***vargueno**

**var|i|a** (vãr′ē ə), *n.pl.* a miscellaneous collection, especially of essays, stories, poems, and the like. [< New Latin *varia* < Latin, neuter plural of *varius* various]

**var|i|a|bil|i|ty** (vãr′ē ə bil′ə tē), *n.* **1** the fact or quality of being variable; changeableness: *The adaptability of man was not, according to Darlington, a matter of individual flexibility or plasticity, but rather one of the genetic variability of the race* (Graham Phillips DuShane). **2** the tendency to vary.

**var|i|a|ble** (vãr′ē ə bəl), *adj., n.* —*adj.* **1** apt to change; changeable; uncertain: *variable winds. The weather is more variable in New York than it is in California.* **SYN**: unsteady, unstable, fluctuating, wavering, mutable. **2** likely to shift from one opinion or course of action to another; inconsistent: *a variable frame of mind.* **SYN**: fickle. **3** that can be varied, changed, or modified: *Adjustable curtain rods are of variable length.* **SYN**: alterable. **4** *Biology.* deviating, as from the normal or recognized species, variety, or structure. **5** likely to increase or decrease in size, number, amount, or degree; not remaining the same or uniform: *a constant or variable ratio. The so-called variable costs—prices for story rights, producer, director, scriptwriter, and stars—are, if you want a good product, the least amenable to trimming* (Sunday Times).
—*n.* **1** a thing or quality that varies: *Temperature and rainfall are variables.* **SYN**: inconstant. **2** *Mathematics.* **a** a quantity that can assume any of the values in a given set of values. **b** a symbol representing this quantity. **3** a shifting wind. **4** = variable star.
**the variables**, the region between the northeast and the southeast trade winds: *The meeting of the two opposite currents [of wind] here produces the intermediate space called the ... variables* (Arthur Young).
—**var′i|a|ble|ness**, *n.*

**variable annuity**, an annuity in which part of the premium is invested in bonds and the remainder in common stocks, giving the holder an income that varies with the earnings of the stocks.

**variable geometry**, = variable sweep.

**var|i|a|ble-pitch propeller** (vãr′ē ə bəl pich′), an aircraft propeller whose pitch can be changed while rotating.

**variable star**, a star that varies periodically in brightness or magnitude.

**variable sweep**, a design that allows the angle of aircraft wings to be adjusted so as to give the best conditions for various phases of flight.

**var|i|a|ble-sweep wing** (vãr′ē ə bəl swēp′), an aircraft wing that can be adjusted in flight; swing-wing. It is set perpendicular to the fuselage during take-off and landing and swung backward when high speeds are reached.

**variable time fuse**, = proximity fuse.

**Variable Zone**, = Temperate Zone.

**var|i|a|bly** (vãr′ē ə blē), *adv.* in a variable manner; changeably; inconstantly.

**Var|i|ac** (vãr′ē ak), *n. Trademark.* an autotransformer which varies and controls voltage, made of a single layer of wire wound on an iron core.

**va|ri|a lec|ti|o** (vãr′ē ə lek′shē ō), *pl.* **va|ri|ae lec|ti|o|nes** (vãr′ē ē lek′shē ō′nēz). *Latin.* a variant reading.

**var|i|ance** (vãr′ē əns), *n.* **1** a difference; disagreement: *variances in the spelling of proper names.* **2** a difference or discrepancy between two legal statements or documents, as between a writ and a complaint or between evidence and an accusation, sufficient to make them ineffectual. **3** a disagreeing or falling out; discord; quarrel: *to yield without variance.* **4** a varying; change; variation: *a mean daily variance in temperature of eleven degrees.* **5** *Statistics.* the square of the standard deviation. **6** *Physical Chemistry.* the number of conditions, such as temperature or pressure, which must be fixed in order that the state of the system may be defined; degree of freedom of a system.
**at variance, a** in a condition of disagreement; differing; conflicting: *The politician's actions are at variance with his promises.* **b** in a condition of discord or dissension: *at variance with the neighbors.*
[< Old French *variance*, learned borrowing from Latin *variantia* < *variāns* variant]

**var|i|ant** (vãr′ē ənt), *adj., n.* —*adj.* **1** varying; different: *"Rime" is a variant spelling of "rhyme."* **2** variable; changing: *variant results.*
—*n.* **1** a different form. **2** a different pronunciation or spelling of the same word. **3** an edition or translation of a manuscript, book, or other work, that differs from the common or accepted version. **4** a reworking or revising of an original story, song, or other work.
[< Latin *variāns, -antis*, present participle of *variāre* change, vary]

**var|i|ate** (vãr′ē āt), *n. Statistics.* the size or value of a particular character in one specimen; random variable. [back formation < *variation*]

**var|i|a|tion** (vãr′ē ā′shən), *n.* **1** the fact of varying; change: *variations in color, marked variations of dialect.* **2** the act of changing: *There was no variation in his expression, whatever his mood.* **3** the amount of change: *There was a variation of 30 degrees in the temperature yesterday.* **4** a varied or changed form. **5** *Music.* **a** a tune or theme repeated with changes in rhythm or harmony; a change, modification, or embellishment by which on repetition the theme appears in a new but still recognizable form. **b** one of a series of such modifications upon a theme. **6** *Biology.* **a** a deviation of an animal or plant from type; deviation or divergence in the structure, character, or function of an organism from those typical of or usual in the species or group or from those of the parents. **b** an animal or plant showing such deviation or divergence. **7** *Astronomy.* the deviation of a heavenly body, such as the moon, from its average orbit or motion. **8** *Mathematics.* one of the different ways in which the members of any group or set may be combined. **9** *Geography, Aeronautics.* the angular difference between geographic north and magnetic north from any point. [< Old French *variation*, learned borrowing from Latin *variātiō, -ōnis* < *variāre* to vary]

**var|i|a|tion|al** (vãr′ē ā′shə nəl), *adj.* of or having to do with variation, especially in its biological senses.

**var|i|cat|ed** (var′ə kā′tid), *adj.* having varices, as a shell.

**var|i|ca|tion** (var′ə kā′shən), *n.* **1** the formation of a varix. **2** a set or system of varices.

**var|i|cel|la** (var′ə sel′ə), *n.* = chicken pox. [< New Latin *varicella* (diminutive) < *variola*; see etym. under **variola**]

**var|i|cel|lar** (var′ə sel′ər), *adj.* of or relating to varicella.

**var|i|cel|late** (var′ə sel′āt), *adj.* marked with or having small varices, as some shells. [< *varices* + Latin *-ella*, a diminutive suffix + Engish *-ate*[1]]

**var|i|cel|loid** (var′ə sel′oid), *adj.* resembling varicella or chicken pox: *varicelloid smallpox.* [< *varicell*(a) + *-oid*]

**var|i|ces** (vãr′ə sēz), *n.* plural of **varix.**

**var|i|co|cele** (var′ə kō sēl), *n.* a varicose condition of the veins of the spermatic cord. [< Latin *varix, -icis* dilated vein + Greek *kḗlē* tumor]

**var|i|col|ored** (vãr′ē kul′ərd), *adj.* **1** having various colors; variegated in color: *varicolored tropical birds.* **2** *Figurative.* different; diverse; diversified: *His varicolored accounts of the accident puzzled the police.* [< Latin *varius* various + English *colored*]

**var|i|col|oured** (vãr′ē kul′ərd), *adj. Especially British.* varicolored.

**var|i|cose** (var′ə kōs), *adj.* **1** abnormally swollen or enlarged; cirsoid: *In advanced cases of varicose veins, bluish knotty lumps form along the vein* (Hyman S. Rubinstein). **2a** having to do with, affected with, or caused by varicose veins. **b** designed to remedy or be used in the treatment of varicose veins. **3** *Biology.* resembling a varix. [< Latin *varicōsus* < *varix, -icis* dilated vein]

**var|i|cosed** (var′ə kōst), *adj.* = varicose.

**var|i|co|sis** (var′ə kō′sis), *n.* **1** the formation of varicose veins or varices. **2** = varicosity. [< New Latin *varicosis* < Latin *varix, -icis* dilated vein + New Latin *-osis* -osis]

**var|i|cos|i|ty** (var′ə kos′ə tē), *n., pl.* **-ties. 1** the quality or condition of being varicose or abnormally swollen. **2** a varicose part; varix.

**var|i|cot|o|my** (var′ə kot′ə mē), *n., pl.* **-mies.** the surgical removal of a varicose vein. [< Latin *varix, -icis* dilated vein + Greek *-tomiā* a cutting]

**var|ied** (vãr′ēd), *adj.* **1** of different sorts or kinds;

having variety: *a varied assortment of candies.* **2a** characterized by, presenting, or having different forms: *varied shadows at twilight. And changing like that varied gleam is our inconstant shape* (Scott). **b** changed; altered. **3** having different colors (used especially in the names of birds or animals): *the varied bunting.* —**var′ied|ly**, *adv.* —**var′ied|ness**, *n.*

**varied thrush**, a thrush of western North America, similar to a robin but with a black band across the breast.

**var|i|e|gate** (vãr′ē ə gāt, vãr′i gāt), *v.t.*, **-gat|ed, -gat|ing.** **1** to vary in appearance; mark, spot, or streak with different colors. **2** to give variety to. SYN: diversify. [< Latin *variegāre* (with English *-ate*[1]) < *varius* various + *agere* to drive, make]

**var|i|e|gat|ed** (vãr′ē ə gā′tid, vãr′i gā′-), *adj.* **1** varied in appearance; marked with patches or spots of different colors; many-colored; varicolored: *Pansies are usually variegated.* SYN: mottled, dappled. **2** *Figurative.* having variety; diverse. —**var′i|e|gat′ed|ly**, *adv.*

**var|i|e|ga|tion** (vãr′ē ə gā′shən, vãr′i gā′-), *n.* **1** the condition or quality of being variegated; varied coloring. **2** the act or process of making varied in character.

**var|i|e|ga|tor** (vãr′ē ə gā′tər, vãr′i gā′-), *n.* a person or thing that variegates.

**var|i|er** (vãr′ē ər), *n.* a person who varies.

**va|ri|e|tal** (və rī′ə təl), *adj., n.* —*adj.* of, having to do with, or constituting a variety.
—*n.* a kind of wine made almost entirely from one variety of grape and bearing its name: *His winery is the only one in the state to make varietals ... like Diana, Elvira, Delaware, or Niagara* (Harper's). —**va|ri′e|tal|ly**, *adv.*

**va|ri|e|ty** (və rī′ə tē), *n., pl.* **-ties. 1** the fact, quality, or condition of being varied; lack of sameness; difference or variation: *Variety is the spice of life. The variety of her moods kept us guessing.* **2** a number of different kinds: *The store has a great variety of toys.* **3** a kind or sort: *Which variety of cake do you prefer?* **4a** a division of a species. **b** a plant or animal differing from those of the species to which it belongs in some minor but permanent or transmissible particular. **5** a group of domestic animals or cultivated plants whose modifications have been produced by artificial selection: *a variety of hybrid tea rose.* **6** *Especially British.* vaudeville. [< Latin *varietās* < *varius* various]
—*Syn.* **2 Variety, diversity** mean a number of things of different kinds or qualities. **Variety** emphasizes absence of sameness in form or character, and applies to a number of related things of different kinds or to a number of different things of the same general kind: *A teacher has a wide variety of duties.* **Diversity** emphasizes unlikeness, complete difference, in nature, form, or qualities: *A person who has traveled widely has a diversity of interests.*

**variety meats**, various organs of animals, such as the heart, liver, and kidneys, sold as extra parts, fancy meats, or meat sundries.

**variety show**, **1** an entertainment featuring different kinds of acts, such as songs, dances, acrobatic feats, and comic skits; vaudeville. **2** a theatrical entertainment produced on radio or television and having the characteristics of vaudeville: *The variety show has won wide popularity because of its high-powered dancing, acrobatic, musical, and wise-cracking performers* (Emory S. Bogardus).

**variety store**, *U.S.* a store that sells a large variety of low-priced goods; dime store.

**var|i|form** (vãr′ə fôrm), *adj.* varied in form; having various forms. [< Latin *varius* various + English *-form*]

**var|i|hued** (vãr′ə hyüd′), *adj.* = varicolored.

**var|i|o|cou|pler** (vãr′ē ō kup′lər), *n. Electricity.* a kind of transformer having within the primary coil a secondary coil that can be rotated to adjust the mutual inductance. [< Latin *varius* various + English *coupler*]

**va|ri|o|la** (və rī′ə lə), *n.* = smallpox. [< Medieval Latin *variola* < Late Latin, any rash, measles; pustule < Latin *varius* various, spotted]

**va|ri|o|lar** (və rī′ə lər), *adj.* = variolous.

**var|i|o|late** (vãr′ē ə lāt), *v.t.*, **-lat|ed, -lat|ing.** to inoculate with the virus of smallpox. [< *variol*(a) + *-ate*[1]]

**var|i|o|la|tion** (vãr′ē ə lā′shən), *n.* inoculation with the virus of smallpox.

**var|i|ole** (vãr′ē ōl), *n.* **1** a marking or depression resembling the pit left by smallpox; foveola. **2** a spherulitic concretion of a variolite. [< *variola,* in sense of "pustule, pockmark" (because of its shape)]

**var|i|o|lite** (vãr′ē ə līt), *n.* a diabasic rock embedded with spherulites that give it a pock-marked appearance when weathered. [< Medieval Latin *variola* pockmark, pustule + English *-ite*[1] (because of its granular surface)]

**var|i|o|lit|ic** (vãr′ē ə lit′ik), *adj.* having to do with, resembling, or containing variolite.

**var|i|o|loid** (vãr′ē ə loid), *adj., n.* —*adj.* having to do with or resembling variola or smallpox.
—*n.* a mild form of variola or smallpox, occurring usually in those who are partially protected by vaccination or have had smallpox.
[< New Latin *varioloides* < Medieval Latin *variola* (see etym. under **variola**) + New Latin *-oides* -oid]

**va|ri|o|lous** (və rī′ə ləs), *adj.* **1** of, having to do with, or characteristic of variola or smallpox. **2** affected with or suffering from variola or smallpox. **3** having marks like the scars of variola or smallpox; pitted.

**var|i|om|e|ter** (vãr′ē om′ə tər), *n.* **1** an instrument for comparing the intensity of magnetic forces, especially the magnetic force of the earth at different points. **2** *Electricity.* an apparatus consisting of a coil of insulated wire connected in series with and designed to turn inside a similar coil and so to vary the inductance. **3** an instrument used in an airplane, especially a glider, for showing the rate at which it rises or descends, usually in units of 100 feet a minute. [< Latin *varius* various + *-meter*]

**var|i|o|rum** (vãr′ē ôr′əm, -ōr′-), *n., adj.* —*n.* **1** an edition of a book, especially of a classic, that has the comments and notes of several editors, critics, or other commentators. **2** an edition of a book containing variant versions of the text.
—*adj.* of or like a variorum.
[< Latin (*ēditiō cum notīs*) *variōrum* (edition with notes) of various people; genitive plural masculine of *varius* various]

**var|i|ous** (vãr′ē əs), *adj.* **1** differing from one another; different: *There have been various opinions as to the best way to raise children.* SYN: diverse, diversified. **2** several; many: *We have looked at various houses, but have decided to buy this one.* **3** many-sided; varied: *lives made various by learning.* **4** varying; changeable: *apparel as gaudy as it is various.* [< Latin *varius* (with English *-ous*). See etym. of doublet **vair.**] —**var′i|ous|ness**, *n.*
▶ It is not always possible to distinguish between senses 1 and 2, as the meaning often blends into *many different.*

**var|i|ous|ly** (vãr′ē əs lē), *adv.* **1** in different ways; with variation or variety; differently: *He began to use burlap as a medium, sewing together variously weathered pieces and stretching two or three thicknesses on a frame* (Newsweek). **2** *U.S.* at different times: *to live variously in town and in the country.*

**var|is|cite** (var′ə sīt), *n.* a mineral, a hydrous aluminum phosphate, occurring in bright-green, crystalline or kidney-shaped crusts. *Formula:* $AlPO_4 \cdot 2H_2O$ [< Latin *Variscia,* a part of Saxony + English *-ite*[1] (because it was found there)]

**var|i|sized** (vãr′ē sīzd′), *adj.* varying in size: *One floor lamp appeared to be a tank with several varisized periscopes emerging from the top* (Evelyn Rose). [< Latin *varius* various + English *-sized*]

**va|ris|tor** (və ris′tər), *n.* a type of semiconducting resistor whose resistance varies with the applied voltage. [< *vari*(able *resi*)*stor*]

**var|i|type** (vãr′ē tīp), *v.,* **-typed, -typ|ing.** —*v.t.* to set with a Varityper.
—*v.i.* to operate a Varityper.

**Var|i|typ|er** (vãr′ē tī′pər), *n. Trademark.* a composing machine like a typewriter but with changeable type faces.

**var|i|typ|ist** (vãr′ē tī′pist), *n.* a person who operates a Varityper.

**va|ri|um et mu|ta|bi|le sem|per fe|mi|na** (vãr′ē əm et myü tab′ə lē sem′pər fem′ə nə), *Latin.* ever a fickle and changeable thing is woman.

**var|ix** (vãr′iks), *n., pl.* **var|i|ces. 1a** an abnormal dilation or enlargement of a vein or artery, usually accompanied by tortuous development; varicose vein or artery. **b** the diseased condition characterized by this. **2** a longitudinal elevation or swelling on the surface of a shell. [< Latin *varix, -icis* dilated vein]

**var|let** (vär′lit), *n. Archaic.* **1** a low, mean fellow; rascal: *a little contemptible varlet, without the least title to birth, person, wit* (Jonathan Swift). **2a** a man or boy acting as an attendant or servant; groom. **b** an attendant on a knight or other person of military importance. [< Old French *varlet,* variant of *vaslet* (originally) squire, young man (diminutive) < Old French *vasal* vassal]

**var|let|ry** (vär′lə trē), *n. Archaic.* a number or crowd of attendants or rascals; varlets: *Shall they hoist me up, And show me to the shouting varletry Of censuring Rome?* (Shakespeare).

**var|mint** or **var|ment** (vär′mənt), *n. Dialect.* **1** vermin. **2** an objectionable animal or person: *skunks, weasels, and such-like varments.* [variant of *vermin*]

**var|na** (vär′nə), *n.* any one of the four main castes or classes of Hindu society: *The varnas were the priests* (*Brahmans*), *the warriors* (*Kshatriyas*), *the merchants* (*Vaisyas*), *and the servitors* (*Sudras*) (New Yorker). [< Sanskrit *varna* color; caste]

**var|nish** (vär′nish), *n., v.* —*n.* **1a** a thin, transparent liquid that gives a smooth, hard, glossy, and durable or ornamental surface on wood, metal, or the like. Varnish is made from substances like resin dissolved in oil, turpentine, or alcohol. **b** any one of various natural or synthetic substances having a similar use. **2** the smooth, hard surface made by this liquid when it dries: *The varnish on the table has been scratched.* **3** a glossy or lustrous appearance: *ivy glistening with leaves of high varnish. A cloudy and rainy day takes the varnish off the scenery.* **4** *Figurative.* a false or deceiving appearance; a pretense: *She covers her selfishness with a varnish of good manners.*
—*v.t.* **1a** to put varnish on; coat with varnish. **b** to smear or stain with some substance similar to varnish. **2** to embellish or adorn; improve the appearance of (something). **3** *Figurative.* to give a false or deceiving appearance to: *to varnish over the truth with a lie.*
[Middle English *vernich* < Old French *vernis, verniz* < Medieval Latin *vernix, vernica* odorous resin < Late Greek *verenīkē* < Greek *Berenīkē,* an ancient city in Libya] —**var′nish|er**, *n.*

**var|nish|ing day** (vär′ni shing), a day before the opening of an exhibition, when exhibitors have the privilege of retouching and varnishing their pictures already hung; vernissage.

**varnish tree**, any one of several trees yielding a resinous substance used as a varnish or lacquer, especially a Japanese and Chinese tree of the cashew family.

**va|room** (və rüm′, -ru̇m′), *n., v.* —*n.* the sound made by the engine of a speeding sports car or racing car.
—*v.i., v.t.* to go or travel at great speed, making such a sound: *varooming through town in a new 350-h.p. Corvette Sting Ray* (Time). Also, **vroom.** [imitative]

**var|sal** (vär′səl), *adj. Dialect.* **1** universal; whole: *the varsal world.* **2** single; individual: *not a varsal thing, every varsal soul.* [shortened and altered < *universal*]

**var|si|ty** (vär′sə tē), *n., pl.* **-ties,** *adj.* —*n.* the most important team in a given sport in a university, college, or school.
—*adj.* of or having to do with such a team.
[variant of earlier *versity* < (uni)*versity*]

**var|so|via|na** (vär′sō vyä′nə), *n.* **1** a dance which originated in the 1800's, in imitation of the mazurka, polka, and redowa. **2** the music for this dance, in triple meter and slow, with a strong accent on the first beat of every second measure.
[< Italian *Varsoviana,* feminine of *Varsoviano* of Warsaw < *Varsovia* Warsaw]

**var|so|vienne** (vär′sō vyen′), *n.* = varsoviana. [< French *Varsovienne,* feminine of *Varsovien* of Warsaw]

**var|ta|bed** (vär′tə bəd), *n.* a member of an order of clergy in the Armenian Church. [< Armenian *vartabed*]

**Var|u|na** (var′u̇ nə, vur′-), *n. Hindu Mythology.* the supreme god of the heavens and judge of the earth. [< Sanskrit *Varuṇa*]

**var|us** (vãr′əs), *n., adj.* —*n.* a form of clubfoot or talipes in which the foot is turned inward.
—*adj.* **1** (of the bones, especially in the foot, knee, and hip) characterized by the abnormal position of turning inward. **2** = bowlegged.
[< New Latin *varus* foot turned inward < Latin *vārus* knock-kneed, bent in]

**varve** (värv), *n. Geology.* any stratified layer of sediment deposited within one year, used in determining the lapse of time in dating geological phenomena: *Radiocarbon dating of tree rings and clay varves on lake bottoms will permit scientists to determine solar cycles even before 220 B.C.* (Science News Letter). [< Swedish *varv* layer]

**varved** (värvd), *adj.* deposited in varves.

**var|y** (vãr′ē), *v.,* **var|ied, var|y|ing.** —*v.t.* **1** to make different; change: *The driver can vary the speed of an automobile.* SYN: alter, modify, diversify. **2** to give variety to (something); introduce changes into (something): *to vary one's style of writing.* **3** *Music.* to repeat (a tune or theme) with changes and ornament.
—*v.i.* **1** to be different; differ: *Stars vary in brightness.* SYN: disagree, deviate. **2** to undergo change or alteration; become different; show dif-

ferences: *The weather varied between cloudy and bright.* **3** *Mathematics.* to undergo or be subject to a change in value according to some law: *to vary inversely as the cube of y.* **4** *Biology.* to exhibit or be subject to variation, as by natural or artificial selection.
[< Old French *varier* < Latin *variāre* < *varius* varied, spotted, various] — **var′y|ing|ly**, *adv.*

**var|y|ing hare** (vãr′ē ing), = snowshoe hare.

**vas** (vas), *n., pl.* **va|sa** (vā′sə). **1** a duct or vessel conveying blood, lymph, or other fluid through the body. **2** a tube or conduit in a plant. [< Latin *vās, vāsis* vessel. See etym. of doublet **vase**.]

**va|sal** (vā′səl), *adj.* having to do with or connected with a vas or vasa.

**vas|cu|lar** (vas′kyə lər), *adj.* **1a** having to do with, made of, or provided with vessels that carry blood, lymph, or other body fluid. **b** affecting the vascular system. **2a** having a vascular structure that carries sap. **b** having the form of or consisting of tubes. [< New Latin *vascularis* < Latin *vāsculum* (diminutive) < *vās* vessel] — **vas′cu|lar|ly**, *adv.*

**vascular bundle**, *Botany.* a strand of vascular tissue consisting mostly of xylem and phloem. It is the structural unit of the stele in vascular plants.

**vascular cylinder**, *Botany.* stele.

**vas|cu|lar|i|ty** (vas′kyə lar′ə tē), *n.* a vascular form or condition.

**vas|cu|lar|ize** (vas′kyə lə rīz), *v.t., v.i.,* **-ized, -iz|ing.** to make or become vascular. — **vas′cu|lar|i|za′tion**, *n.*

**vascular plant**, *Botany.* a plant in which the structure is made up in part of vascular tissue or vessels. Vascular plants comprise the spermatophytes and pteridophytes.

**vascular ray**, *Botany.* medullary ray.

**vascular system**, **1** *Zoology.* the vessels and organs that carry and circulate the blood and lymph. **2** *Botany.* the vascular tissue in a plant.

**vascular tissue**, *Botany.* the tissue in a vascular plant, consisting essentially of phloem and xylem, which carries the sap throughout the plant.

**vas|cu|la|ture** (vas′kyə lə chůr, -chər), *n.* the system or arrangement of blood vessels in the body or any part of the body: *The migration of the germ cells takes place at first through the vasculature* (Science Journal). [< *vascula*(r) + *-ture,* as in *musculature*]

**vas|cu|li|tis** (vas′kyə lī′tis), *n.* inflammation of a vessel, especially a blood vessel. [< New Latin *vasculitis*]

**vas|cu|lose** (vas′kyə lōs), *n., adj.* — *n.* the principal constituent of the vascular tissue in plants.
— *adj.* = vascular.

**vas|cu|lous** (vas′kyə ləs), *adj.* = vascular.

**vas|cu|lum** (vas′kyə ləm), *n., pl.* **-lums, -la** (-lə). **1** a long, oval, tin box for carrying newly-collected botanical specimens. **2** *Botany.* a pitcher-shaped leafy structure; ascidium. [< Latin *vāsculum* (diminutive) < *vās* vessel]

**vas de|fe|rens** (vas def′ə renz), *pl.* **va|sa de|fe|ren|ti|a** (vā′sə def′ə ren′shē ə). the excretory duct that conveys semen from the testicle to the urethra. [< New Latin *vas deferens* < Latin *vās* vessel, *dēferēns* carrying down, present participle of *dēferre* < *dē-* down + *ferre* carry]

**vase** (vās, vāz; *especially British* väz), *n.* a holder or container used chiefly for ornament or for holding flowers. In ancient times vases were used for religious or sacrificial purposes. [< French *vase,* learned borrowing from Latin *vās, vāsis* vessel. See etym. of doublet **vas**.] — **vase′like′**, *adj.*

**vas|ec|to|my** (va sek′tə mē), *n., pl.* **-mies**. the surgical removal of part or all of the vas deferens, usually for the purpose of producing sterility. [< Latin *vās* vessel + Greek *ektomē* a cutting out]

**vas ef|fe|rens** (vas ef′ə renz), *pl.* **va|sa ef|fe|ren|ti|a** (vā′sə ef′ə ren′shē ə). **1** any one of a number of small ducts conveying semen from the testicle to the epididymis. **2** a lymphatic vessel leading from a lymph gland. [< New Latin *vas efferens* < Latin *vās* vessel, *efferēns* carrying out, present participle of *efferre* < *ex-* out + *ferre* carry]

**Vas|e|line** (vas′ə lēn, -lin), *n. Trademark.* a soft, greasy, yellow or whitish substance made from petroleum, used as a healing ointment or as a lubricant; petrolatum. [American English; coined < German *Wasser* water + Greek *élaion* oil + English *-ine*[1]]

**Vash|ti** (vash′tē, -tī), *n.* the queen of Persia banished by King Ahasuerus when she disobeyed his command to come before him and his royal guests (in the Bible, Esther 1:10-22).

**vaso-**, *combining form.* blood vessel; vascular system: *Vasoconstrictor = a drug, nerve, etc., that constricts blood vessels.* [< Latin *vās, vāsis* vessel]

**vas|o|ac|tive** (vas′ō ak′tiv), *adj.* acting on the blood vessels, especially by constricting or dilating them: *A vasoactive peptide, perhaps responsible for the local swellings, has been isolated from plasma from patients during attacks* (Chester A. Alper).

**vas|o|con|stric|tion** (vas′ō kən strik′shən), *n.* constriction of the blood vessels, especially by the action of a nerve or a drug.

**vas|o|con|stric|tive** (vas′ō kən strik′tiv), *adj.* serving to constrict blood vessels; vasoconstrictor: *a vasoconstrictive drug, a vasoconstrictive nerve.*

**vas|o|con|stric|tor** (vas′ō kən strik′tər), *n., adj.* — *n.* something that constricts blood vessels, such as a nerve or a drug.
— *adj.* constricting blood vessels.

**vas|o|de|pres|sor** (vas′ō di pres′ər), *n.* a drug that lowers blood pressure by artificially relaxing the blood vessels: *A wide variety of vasodepressors of varying effectiveness have now been offered to the physician* (Morris Fishbein).

**vas|o|dil|a|ta|tion** (vas′ō dil′ə tā′shən, -dī′lə-), *n.* dilatation of the blood vessels, especially by the action of a nerve or a drug.

**vas|o|di|lat|ing** (vas′ō dī lā′ting, -də-), *adj.* = vasodilator.

**vas|o|di|la|tion** (vas′ō dī lā′shən, -də-), *n.* = vasodilatation.

**vas|o|di|la|tor** (vas′ō dī lā′tər, -də-), *n., adj.* — *n.* something that dilates blood vessels, such as a nerve or a drug.
— *adj.* dilating blood vessels.

**vas|o|mo|tor** (vas′ō mō′tər), *adj.* of or having to do with the nerves and nerve centers that regulate the size of blood vessels and so govern circulation.

**vas|o|pres|sin** (vas′ō pres′in), *n.* **1** a pituitary hormone that contracts small blood vessels, raises blood pressure, and reduces the excretion of urine by the kidneys. **2** a synthetic form of this hormone used as an antidiuretic in the treatment of diabetes insipidus; Pitressin. [< *vasopress*(or) + *-in*]

**vas|o|pres|sor** (vas′ō pres′ər), *adj., n.* — *adj.* of or having to do with the constriction of blood vessels: *The life-saving vasopressor drugs, used to combat shock after a heart attack, conserve the blood supply to heart and brain at the expense of other less sensitive organs in the body* (Science News Letter).
— *n.* a hormone or drug that constricts blood vessels.

**vas|o|spasm** (vas′ō spaz′əm), *n.* constriction of blood vessels; vasoconstriction.

**vas|sal** (vas′əl), *n., adj.* — *n.* **1** in the European feudal system: **a** a person who held lands from a lord or a superior, to whom in return he gave help in war or some other service. A great noble could be a vassal of the king and have many other men as his vassals. **b** a tenant in fee; retainer. **2a** a person who holds a position similar to that of a feudal vassal. **b** a person in the service of another; servant. **c** *Figurative.* a person completely subject to some influence: *The feeble vassals of wine and anger and lust* (Tennyson). *To You, O Goddess of Efficiency, Your happy vassals bend the reverent knee* (Samuel Hoffenstein). **3** a bondman; slave.
— *adj.* **1** like that of a vassal; subject; subordinate: *vassal princes, a vassal nation.* **SYN**: dependent. **2** of, having to do with, or like a vassal: *an oath of vassal loyalty.*
[< Old French *vassal* < Medieval Latin *vassallus* retainer < *vassus* < Celtic (compare Old Irish *foss* servant)]

**vas|sal|age** (vas′ə lij), *n.* **1a** the condition of being a vassal. **b** the homage, allegiance, or service due from a vassal to his lord or superior. **c** the land held by a vassal. **2a** dependence; servitude. **b** *Figurative.* subjection to some influence: *the vassalage of strength to the demands of intellect.* **3** a body or group of vassals.

**vas|sal|ize** (vas′ə līz), *v.t.,* **-ized, -iz|ing.** to make a vassal or vassals of.

**vas|sal|ry** (vas′əl rē), *n.* a body of vassals.

**vast** (vast, väst), *adj., n.* — *adj.* **1** of great area; of immense extent; extensive: *Texas and Alaska cover vast territories.* **SYN**: immense, tremendous, colossal. **2** of large dimensions; of very great size; huge; massive: *vast forms that move fantastically* (Edgar Allan Poe). **SYN**: immense, tremendous, colossal. **3** very great in amount, quantity, or number: *A billion dollars is a vast amount of money. It is a building with a vast collection of chambers and galleries.* **SYN**: immense, tremendous, colossal. **4** *Figurative.* unusually large or comprehensive in grasp or aims: *the vast and various affairs of government.*
— *n.* **1** an immense space: *her return to the unconscious vast* (Eden Philpotts). **2** *Dialect.* a very great number or amount: *They had heard a vast of words* (Robert Louis Stevenson).
[< Latin *vastus* immense, empty] — **vast′ness**, *n.*

**vas|ti|tude** (vas′tə tüd, -tyüd), *n.* **1** the quality of being vast; immensity. **2** unusual largeness. **3** a vast extent or space. [< Latin *vastitūdō* < *vastus* vast]

**vas|ti|ty** (vas′tə tē), *n., pl.* **-ties**. **1** vastness; immensity; vastitude: *The huge vastity of the world* (Philemon Holland). **2** wasteness; desolation; void: *Nothing but emptiness and vastity* (Thomas Nashe). [< Latin *vastitās, -ātis* < *vastus* vast]

**vast|ly** (vast′lē, väst′-), *adv.* **1** to a vast extent or degree; immensely: *an explosion vastly more rapid and powerful.* **2** exceedingly; extremely; very: *new housing projects vastly superior to the old slums.*

**vast|y** (vas′tē, väs′-), *adj.* vast; immense: *I can call spirits from the vasty deep* (Shakespeare).

**vat** (vat), *n., v.,* **vat|ted, vat|ting.** — *n.* **1** a barrel, cask, tank, or other large container for liquids: *a vat of dye.* **2** a large container, often wooden, for fermenting beer, cider, or the like. **3** a container for collecting and evaporating sea water to extract its salt. **4a** a container for holding a liquid used in dyeing. **b** a liquid in which a vat dye is made soluble by treatment with an alkaline reducing agent.
— *v.t.* to place, store, or treat in a vat.
[Middle English dialectal variant of *fat*[2], Old English *fæt*]

**Vat.**, Vatican.

**VAT** (no periods), value-added tax.

**vat dye** or **color**, a dye, such as indigoid, that is insoluble in water and is made soluble by treatment with an alkaline reducing agent. Vat dyes are resistant to fading.

**vat-dyed** (vat′dīd′), *adj.* dyed with vat dyes: *vat-dyed goods.*

**vat|ful** (vat′fůl), *n., pl.* **-fuls**. the quantity that a vat will hold.

**vat|ic** (vat′ik), *adj.* of, having to do with, or characteristic of a prophet or seer; prophetic; inspired: *I believe Norman MacCaig's reputation—made slowly and quietly, without any vatic posturing—will prove a durable one* (Manchester Guardian Weekly). [< Latin *vātēs, -is* prophet + English *-ic*]

**Vat|i|can** (vat′ə kən), *n., adj.* — *n.* **1a** the collection of buildings grouped about the palace of the pope, built upon the Vatican Hill in Rome. **b** the artistic or literary treasures preserved there; the Vatican galleries or library. **2** the government, office, or authority of the pope.
— *adj.* of or having to do with the Vatican or its library.
[< Latin *Vāticānus* (*mōns*) Vatican (hill), one of the hills in ancient Rome on which the palace of the pope was later built]

**Vatican Council**, **1** Also, **Vatican I.** the twentieth ecumenical council of the Roman Catholic Church, which met at the Vatican, in 1869 and was indefinitely suspended in 1870. **2** Also, **Vatican II.** the twenty-first ecumenical council, which met at the Vatican from 1962 to 1965, and was, in effect, a continuation of Vatican I.

**Vat|i|can|ism** (vat′ə kə niz′əm), *n.* the doctrine of absolute papal infallibility and supremacy.

**Vat|i|can|ist** (vat′ə kə nist), *n.* a devoted adherent of the pope and believer in Vaticanism.

**vat|i|cide**[1] (vat′ə sīd), *n.* the act of killing a prophet. [< Latin *vātēs, -is* prophet + English *-cide*[2]]

**vat|i|cide**[2] (vat′ə sīd), *n.* a person who kills a prophet. [< Latin *vātēs, -is* prophet + English *-cide*[1]]

**va|tic|i|nal** (və tis′ə nəl), *adj.* of the nature of or characterized by prophecy; prophetic.

**va|tic|i|nate** (və tis′ə nāt), *v.t., v.i.,* **-nat|ed, -nat|ing.** to prophesy; predict. [< Latin *vāticinārī* (with English *-ate*[1]) < *vāticinus* prophetic < *vātēs, -is* seer] — **va|tic′i|na′tion**, *n.* — **va|tic′i|na′tor**, *n.*

**vau|de|ville** (vô′də vil, vōd′vil), *n.* **1** a theatrical entertainment featuring a variety of acts. Vaudeville consists of songs, dances, acrobatic feats, short plays, and trained animals. **2** a play or stage performance of light character, interspersed with songs. **3** a light popular song, commonly of a satirical or topical nature. [< French *vaudeville,* earlier *vau de ville,* alteration of Middle French (*chanson du*) *Vau de Vire* (song of the) valley of Vire in Calvados, Normandy; first applied to the songs of Olivier Basselin, a poet of the 1400's who lived there]

**vau|de|vil|lian** (vô′də vil′yən, vōd vil′-), *n., adj.* — *n.* a person who performs in or writes songs, sketches, or other entertainment, for vaudeville: *The pros peddle their skill with the peripatetic energy of old-time vaudevillians* (Time).
— *adj.* of or having to do with vaudeville: *In these, and the like, he shows a special flair for vaudevillian humor* (Winthrop Sargeant).

**Vau|dois** (vō dwä′), *n.pl.* = Waldenses. [< Middle French *Vaudois* < Medieval Latin *Valdensis* Waldenian]

* **vault**[1] (vôlt), *n., v.* — *n.* **1a** an arched masonry or concrete structure built so that the parts support each other, serving as a roof or covering over a

space; series of arches. **b** an arched roof or ceiling. **c** *Figurative.* something like an arched roof, especially the sky: *Heaven's ebon vault, Studded with stars* (Shelley). **2** an underground cellar or storehouse: *He went into the inner vault where he kept his choicest wines* (Samuel Butler). **3** a place for storing valuable things and keeping them safe. Vaults are often made of steel. *A paper currency is employed when there is no bullion in the vaults* (Emerson). **4a** an arched space under the floor of a church; crypt. **b** a place for burial: *to be buried in the family vault.* **5** a natural cavern or cave. **6** *Anatomy.* an arched structure, especially the skull.
—*v.t.* **1** to make in the form of a vault: *The roof was vaulted.* **2** *Figurative.* to set or extend like a vault: *Hateful is the dark-blue sky Vaulted o'er the dark-blue sea* (Tennyson). **3** to cover with a vault.
[<Old French *voulte, vaulte* <Vulgar Latin *volvita,* noun use of *volvitus,* for Latin *volūtus,* feminine past participle of *volvere* to roll] —**vault′-like′**, *adj.*

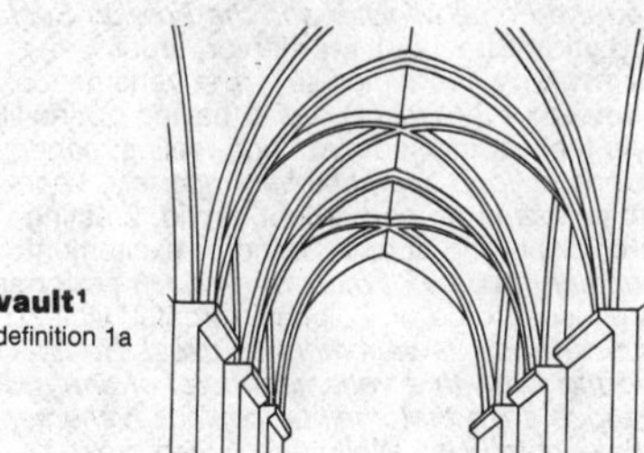
**∗vault¹**
definition 1a

**vault²** (vôlt), *v., n.* —*v.t.* **1** to jump or leap over by using a pole or the hands: *He vaulted the fence.* **2** to mount (a horse) by leaping. —*v.i.* to jump or leap: *He vaulted over the wall.*
—*n.* **1** the act of vaulting; jump; leap. **2** the leap of a horse in the manège; curvet.
[alteration (influenced by *vault*¹) of Middle French *volter* <Old French <Italian *voltare* <*volta* < Vulgar Latin *volvita;* see etym. under **vault¹**] —**vault′er**, *n.*
**vault|ed** (vôl′tid), *adj.* **1** in the form of a vault; arched: *a vaulted ceiling.* **2** built or covered with a vault: *a vaulted room.* **SYN:** domed. **3** having vaults or underground passages: *the vaulted catacombs.*
**vault|ing¹** (vôl′ting), *n.* **1** a vaulted structure. **2** vaults collectively. **3** the art, practice, or operation of constructing vaults.
**vault|ing²** (vôl′ting), *adj., n.* —*adj.* **1** that vaults or leaps, especially in an overzealous manner: (*Figurative.*) *vaulting ambition.* **2** used in or for vaulting.
—*n.* the act of leaping with a vault.
**vaulting horse**, = side horse.
**vault of heaven**, = sky.
**vault|y** (vôl′tē), *adj.* like a vault; arched.
**vaunt** (vônt, vänt), *v., n.* —*v.t.* to boast of (something); talk vaingloriously: *Charity vaunteth not itself* (I Corinthians 13:4).
—*v.i.* to brag or boast; use boastful language: *He talked little, never vaunted* (William Temple).
—*n.* a boasting assertion or speech; brag: *Vainglorious men are : .. the slaves of their own vaunts* (Francis Bacon).
[<Old French *vanter* <Late Latin *vānitāre* < Latin *vānāre* to utter empty words <*vānus* idle, empty]
**vaunt-cour|i|er** (vônt′kůr′ē ər, vänt′-), *n.* **1** a person or thing sent in advance to prepare for or announce the approach of another; forerunner. **2** *Obsolete.* one of the soldiers or horsemen sent before an army or body of troops; an advance guard; scout. [short for Old French *avant-coureur* (literally) forerunner <*avant* forward + *coureur* courier]
**vaunt|ed** (vôn′tid, vän′-), *adj.* boasted or bragged of; highly praised: *the vaunted triumphs of civilization.*
**vaunt|er** (vôn′tər, vän′-), *n.* **1** a boaster or braggart. **2** a person who boastfully asserts or praises something.
**vaunt|ful** (vônt′fəl, vänt′-), *adj. Archaic.* boastful.
**vaunt|ing** (vôn′ting, vän′-), *adj.* that vaunts; boasting; bragging; boastful. —**vaunt′ing|ly**, *adv.*
**vaunt|y** (vôn′tē, vän′-), *adj. British Dialect and Scottish.* boastful; proud; vain.
**v. aux.**, auxiliary verb.
**Vaux's swift** (vôk′səz), a swift of western North America resembling the chimney swift. [<William S. *Vaux,* 1811-1882, an American naturalist]
**vav** (vôv, väv), *n.* the sixth letter of the Hebrew alphabet. Also, **waw.** [<Hebrew *vāv* ]
**vav|a|sor** (vav′ə sôr, -sōr), *n.* a vassal ranking below a baron, holding land and having other vassals under him in the European feudal system: *vavasors subdivide again to vassals* (John L. Motley). [<Old French *vavassour* <Medieval Latin *vasvassor,* apparently reduction of phrase *vassi vassorum* vassals of vassals. Compare etym. under **varlet**, **valet.**]
**vav|a|sour** (vav′ə sůr), *n.* = vavasor.
**va|ward** (vā′wôrd′), *n. Obsolete.* vanguard: *We that are in the vaward of our youth* (Shakespeare). [variant of *vanward* <earlier *vantward,* short for *avantward* <Old North French, Old French *avant-garde;* see etym. under **vanguard**]
**vb.**, **1** verb. **2** verbal.
**V-belt** (vē′belt′), *n.* a belt for running on a pulley with a V-shaped groove, used as the fan belt in automobiles to connect the crankshaft with the fan and generator, and also used to connect a motor to a tool, such as a saw.
**V-block** (vē′blok′), *n.* a block of metal cut in the shape of the letter V on one side, used for holding cylindrical objects in machining.
**V-bomb** (vē′bom′), *n.* **1** a German robot bomb of World War II; V-1. **2** a German rocket bomb of World War II; V-2.
**V-bomb|er** (vē′bom′ər), *n.* a British military aircraft capable of carrying nuclear weapons.
**V.C.** or **VC** (no periods), an abbreviation for the following:
**1** Veterinary Corps.
**2** Vice-Chairman.
**3** Vice-Chancellor.
**4** Vice-Consul.
**5** Victoria Cross.
**6** Vietcong.
**v.d.**, various dates.
**VD** (no periods) or **V.D.**, venereal disease.
**V-Day** (vē′dā′), *n.* the day (December 31, 1946) of the presidential proclamation marking the complete victory of the Allied Forces in World War II. [< *v*(ictory)]
**VDT** (no periods), video display terminal.
**VDU** (no periods), visual display unit (of a computer).
**VE** (no periods), vesicular exanthema.
**Ve|a|dar** (vē′ə där), *n.* the intercalary month of the Jewish calendar, inserted after Adar during the Hebrew leap years; Adar Sheni. [<Hebrew *vəadhār* (literally) and Adar; second Adar]
**∗veal** (vēl), *n.* **1** the flesh of a calf, used for food. **2** a calf, especially as killed or intended for food. [<Anglo-French *vel,* Old French *veel, veal,* earlier *vedel* <Latin *vitellus* (diminutive) <*vitulus* calf, perhaps in the sense of "yearling," related to *vetus* year, weather]

**∗veal**
definition 1

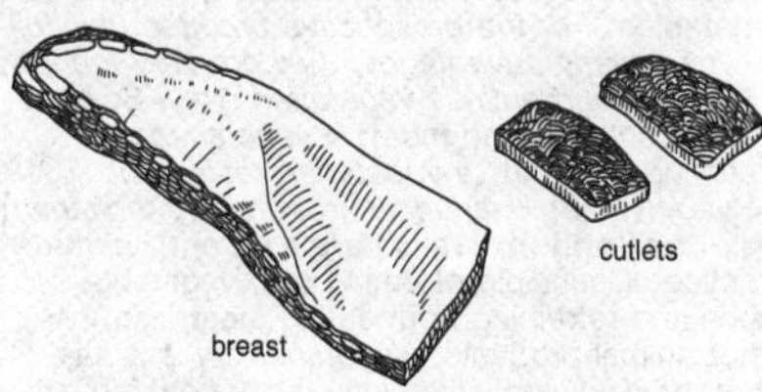


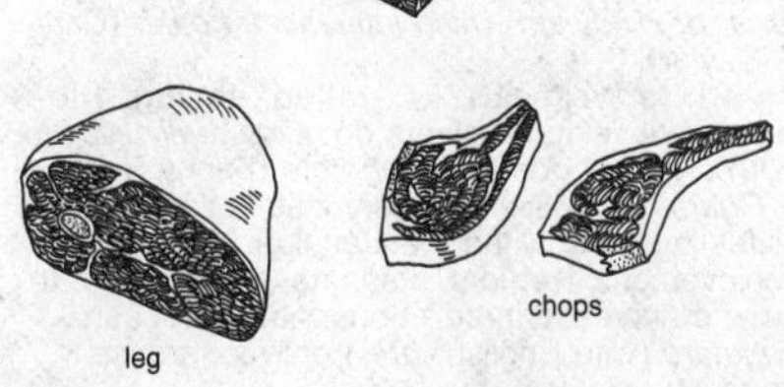


**veal|er** (vē′lər), *n. U.S.* a milk-fed calf under 12 weeks old.
**veal|y** (vē′lē), *adj.* **1** like or suggesting veal; having the appearance of veal. **2** *Figurative.* immature.
**vec|tion** (vek′shən), *n. Medicine.* the act of conveying disease germs. [<Latin *vectiō, -ōnis* a carrying, conveyance <*vehere* carry]
**vec|to|graph** (vek′tə graf, -gräf), *n.* a photograph composed of two superimposed images that give a three-dimensional impression when viewed through polarizing lenses.
**∗vec|tor** (vek′tər), *n., v.* —*n.* **1** *Mathematics.* **a** a quantity involving direction as well as magnitude. **b** a line, such as an arrow, representing both the direction and magnitude of some force. The length of the line indicates the magnitude of the force. **2** a mosquito, tick, or other organism that transmits disease germs. **3** *Astronomy.* radius vector.
—*v.t.* **1** to guide (a pilot, aircraft, or missile) from one point to another within a given time by means of a vector: *He vectored the pilot back to the base.* **2** *Figurative.* to carry or direct toward a particular point or on a particular course: *Decades ago Wegener proposed that the drift of the continents was vectored by forces he termed Westwanderung (westward drift) and Polarfluchtkraft (flight from the poles)* (Scientific American). [<Latin *vector* carrier <*vehere* carry]

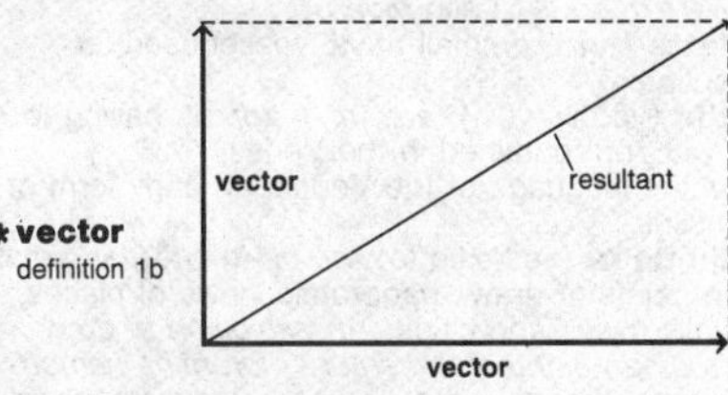

**∗vector**
definition 1b

**vec|tor|car|di|o|gram** (vek′tər kär′dē ə gram), *n.* a tracing of the direction and magnitude of the electrical forces in the heart.
**vec|tor|car|di|o|graph** (vek′tər kär′dē ə graf, -gräf), *n.* an instrument for making a vectorcardiogram, similar to the electrocardiograph but using more electrodes to record both direction and magnitude of the heart's electrical forces.
**vec|tor|car|di|o|graph|ic** (vek′tər kär′dē ə graf′-ik), *adj.* having to do with, made by, or diagnosed with a vectorcardiograph.
**vec|tor|car|di|og|ra|phy** (vek′tər kär′dē og′rə-fē), *n.* the science or technique of using a vectorcardiograph.
**vector field**, a set of vectors each of whose values depend upon a certain point from which the vectors radiate, composing a region of space.
**vec|to|ri|al** (vek tôr′ē əl, -tōr′-), *adj.* of or having to do with a vector or vectors: *Another new instrument being installed at Palomar is a vectorial recorder which photographs a pattern of the earth's surface motion in two dimensions* (Science News Letter).
**vec|to|ri|al|ly** (vek tôr′ē ə lē, -tōr′-), *adv.* in a vectorial manner.
**vector meson**, any one of a class of elementary particles with masses greater than 1200 million electron volts, including the omega, phi, and rho mesons: *The discovery of vector mesons ... has been essential for understanding nuclear forces and for interpreting nuclear spectra* (Science).
**vector product**, *Mathematics.* cross product.
**vec|tu|rist** (vek′chər ist), *n.* a person who collects transportation tokens. [<Latin *vectūra* conveyance (<*vehere* carry) + English *-ist*]
**Ve|da** (vā′də, vē′-), *n.* any one or all of the four collections of sacred Hindu writings in an early form or dialect of Sanskrit. They include *Rig-Veda* or hymns, *Sama-Veda* or chants, *Yajur-Veda* or sacred formulas, and *Atharva-Veda,* later and more superstitious hymns. [<Sanskrit *vēda* (sacred) knowledge <*vid* to know; (literally) to have perceived]
**Ve|da|ic** (vā dā′ik, vē-), *adj., n.* —*adj.* = Vedic. —*n.* the language of the Veda, an early form of Sanskrit.
**Ve|da|ism** (vā′də iz əm, vē′-), *n.* the system of religious beliefs and practices contained in the Vedas.
**ve|da|li|a** (və dā′lē ə, -dāl′yə), *n.* an Australian ladybug widely used to combat scale insects. It was originally introduced from Australia to California to prevent scale insects from destroying citrus groves. [<New Latin *Vedalia,* a variant of *Rodolia* the genus name; origin unknown]
**Ve|dan|ta** (vi dän′tə, -dan′-), *n.* a leading system of Hindu philosophy founded on the Vedas, and concerned with the relation of the universe and the human soul to the Supreme Spirit. [<Sanskrit *vēdanta* <*vēda* (see etym. under **Veda**) + *anta* the end]
**Ve|dan|tic** (vi dän′tik, -dan′-), *adj.* of the Vedanta.
**Ve|dan|tism** (vi dän′tiz əm, -dan′-), *n.* the doctrines or system of the Vedanta.
**Ve|dan|tist** (vi dän′tist, -dan′-), *n.* a person versed in the doctrines of the Vedanta.
**V-E Day** (vē′ē′), the day of the Allied victory in Europe in World War II, May 8, 1945.
**Ved|da** or **Ved|dah** (ved′ə), *n.* a member of a primitive race of Sri Lanka, an island just off southern India. [<Singhalese *veddā* hunter, archer]
**Ved|doid** (ved′oid), *n., adj.* —*n.* a member of a group of Asian people represented by the Vedda of Sri Lanka, and regarded as intermediate between the Caucasian and Australian types.
—*adj.* of or having to do with Veddoids.

**Pronunciation Key:** hat, āge, cãre, fär; let, ēqual, tėrm; it, īce; hot, ōpen, ôrder; **oi**l, **ou**t; cup, pu̇t, rüle; **ch**ild; lo**ng**; **th**in; **ᴛʜ**en; **zh**, measure; ə represents **a** in about, **e** in taken, **i** in pencil, **o** in lemon, **u** in circus.

**ve|dette** (vi det′), *n.* **1** a mounted sentry stationed in advance of the outposts of an army. **2** = vedette boat. Also, **vidette**. [< French *vedette* < Italian *vedetta* sentry post, outlook (alteration of *veletta* < Spanish *vela* watch, vigil) < *vedere* to see < Latin *vidēre*]

**vedette boat**, a small naval vessel used for scouting.

**Ve|dic** (vā′dik, vē′-), *adj., n.* —*adj.* of, having to do with, or contained in the Vedas.
—*n.* the language of the Vedas, an early form of Sanskrit.

**ved|u|tis|ta** (ved′ə tis′tə), *n., pl.* **-ti** (-tē). an artist who paints or draws panoramic views of places, usually towns and cities: *An exhibition of drawings by an eighteenth-century Florentine named Giuseppe Zocchi, who ... was a vedutista, or depicter of views* (New Yorker). [< Italian *vedutista* < *veduta* a painting or drawing of a place, (literally) a view + *-ista* -ist]

**vee** (vē), *n., adj.* —*n.* **1** the letter V or v. **2** anything shaped like a V. **3** *Informal.* a five-dollar bill.
—*adj.* = V-shaped.

**vee|na** (vē′nə), *n.* = vina[1].

**Veep** (vēp), *n. Slang.* the Vice-President of the United States. [American English < pronunciation of *V.P.,* abbreviation of *Vice President*]

**veep** (vēp), *n. Slang.* a vice-president. [< *Veep*]

**veer**[1] (vir), *v., n.* —*v.i.* **1** to change in direction; shift; turn: *The wind veered to the south. The talk veered to ghosts.* **2** *Nautical.* **a** to change course, especially to turn the head away from the wind. **b** to alter course by swinging the stern to windward so as to sail another tack.
—*v.t.* to turn (something); change the direction of: *We veered our boat.*
—*n.* a change of direction; shift; turn: *The car made a sudden veer to the left.* **SYN**: deviation.
[< Middle French *virer;* origin uncertain]

**veer**[2] (vir), *v.t.* **1a** to let out (any line or rope); allow to run out gradually. **b** to let out or pay out (a cable). **2** to allow (as a boat or buoy) to drift away or out by letting out line attached to it.
[compare Middle Dutch *vieren* to slacken]

**veer|ing** (vir′ing), *n., adj.* —*n.* the act or fact of changing course or direction: *the veering of his opinions from day to day kept his supporters in a dither.* —*adj.* vacillating; variable; changeful.
—**veer′ing|ly**, *adv.*

**veer|y** (vir′ē), *n., pl.* **veer|ies**. a thrush of northeastern North America with tawny head, back, and tail and a faintly spotted white breast; Wilson's thrush; tawny thrush. [American English; probably imitative of its note]

**veg** (vej), *n.,* or **veg.**, *Especially British Informal.* vegetable or vegetables: *meat with two watery veg and currant roll* (Manchester Guardian).

**Ve|ga** (vē′gə), *n.* a bluish-white star, the brightest star in the constellation Lyra and in the summer sky. [< Medieval Latin *Vega* < Arabic (*al-Nasr al-*) *Wāqi′* (the) falling (vulture); the constellation Lyra]

**veg|an** (vej′ən), *n., adj. British.* —*n.* a strict vegetarian: *The true ... vegan excludes all animal protein from his diet, and he may even forego articles of clothing and household equipment of animal origin* (New Scientist).
—*adj.* strictly vegetarian: *It is difficult for a vegan diet not to result in deficiencies* (J. G. Sutherland).
[< *veg*(etari)*an*]

**veg|e|ta|ble** (vej′tə bəl, vej′ə-), *n., adj.*
—*n.* **1** a plant whose fruit, seeds, shoots or stems, leaves, roots, or other parts are used for food. Peas, corn, lettuce, tomatoes, and beets are vegetables. **2** the part of such a plant which is used for food. **3** any plant; living organism belonging to the vegetable kingdom. **4** *Figurative.* a person who lives a vegetative existence; dull, passive person: *It describes particularly the mental deprivations intended to turn intelligent men into vegetables* (Manchester Guardian Weekly).
—*adj.* **1** of plants; having something to do with plants: *vegetable substances, vegetable life, the vegetable kingdom.* **2** of or made from vegetables: *vegetable soup, a vegetable dinner.*
**3** *Figurative.* like that of a vegetable; uneventful; dull: *a vegetable existence.* **4** living and growing in the manner of a plant or organism having the lowest form of life; vegetative.
[< Middle French *vegetable,* learned borrowing from Late Latin *vegetābilis* vivifying, refreshing < Latin *vegetāre* enliven, arouse < *vegetus* vigorous]

**vegetable beefsteak**, = liver fungus.

**vegetable butter**, a fixed vegetable oil, solid at ordinary temperatures.

**vegetable fat**, fat derived from vegetables or vegetable oils: *The main sources of edible oils and fats are vegetable fats* (London Times).

**vegetable ivory**, **1** the hard endosperm or albumen of the ivory nut, resembling ivory in hardness, color, and texture, used especially for ornamental work and buttons. **2** the hard brown shell of the coquilla nut, used similarly.

**vegetable kingdom**, that division of the natural world which includes all plants; plant kingdom.

**vegetable lamb**, = tartarian lamb.

**vegetable marrow**, an oblong squash with a green skin that turns light yellow, used especially in Great Britain as a vegetable; marrow.

**vegetable oil**, any oil obtained from the fruit or seeds of plants, such as olive oil, peanut oil, corn oil, and linseed oil, used in cooking, medicines, and paints, and for lubrication: *Sunflower seed production is being boosted to provide more vegetable oil* (Wall Street Journal).

**vegetable oyster**, a vegetable with a root that tastes somewhat like an oyster; salsify.

**vegetable parchment**, = parchment paper.

**vegetable silk**, a cottonlike fiber borne on the seeds of a Brazilian tree of the bombax family, used especially for stuffing cushions.

**vegetable tallow**, a fatty substance obtained from various plants, used in making candles, soap, and lubricants.

**vegetable wax**, a wax or waxlike substance obtained from plants or vegetable growths.

**veg|e|ta|blize** (vej′tə blīz, vej′ə-), *v.,* **-blized, -bliz|ing.** —*v.i.* to be or live like a vegetable; lead a monotonous existence; vegetate.
—*v.t.* to convert to a vegetable substance.

**veg|e|ta|bly** (vej′tə blē, vej′ə-), *adv.* in the manner of a vegetable or plant.

**veg|e|tal** (vej′ə təl), *adj.* **1** of, like, or derived from plants or vegetables. **2** of or having to do with the vegetable kingdom. **3a** characterized by, exhibiting, or producing plant life and growth. **b** *Obsolete, Figurative.* insensible; insensitive; irrational: *All creatures, vegetal, sensible, and rational* (Robert Burton).
[< Medieval Latin *vegetalis* < Late Latin *vegetāre* to grow; see etym. under **vegetate**]

**veg|e|tal|i|ty** (vej′ə tal′ə tē), *n.* vegetable character or quality.

**vegetal pole**, = vegetative pole.

**veg|e|tant** (vej′ə tənt), *adj.* **1** giving life and vigor; invigorating. **2** vegetating; vegetable; vegetal. [< Latin *vegetāns, -antis,* present participle of *vegetāre* enliven < *vegetus* vigorous]

**veg|e|tar|i|an** (vej′ə tãr′ē ən), *n., adj.* —*n.* a person who eats only vegetable foods and refrains from eating meat, fish, or some other animal products, especially one who does so on the basis of principle: *Most vegetarians exclude meat from their diet, but eat butter, cheese, eggs, and milk* (Willard J. Jacobson).
—*adj.* **1** eating vegetables but no meat. **2** devoted to or advocating vegetarianism. **3** living on vegetables: *For the prospective breeder, chinchillas have many advantages; they are very friendly, odourless, and entirely vegetarian* (New Scientist). **4** containing no meat: *a vegetarian diet.*
**5** serving no meat: *a vegetarian restaurant.*
[< *veget*(able) + *-arian,* as in *agrarian, trinitarian*]

**veg|e|tar|i|an|ism** (vej′ə tãr′ē ə niz′əm), *n.* the practice or principle of eating only vegetable foods and refraining from eating meat, fish, or other animal products: *Vegetarianism is a basic tenet of Hinduism which influences health* (Carl E. Taylor).

**veg|e|tate** (vej′ə tāt), *v.i.,* **-tat|ed, -tat|ing.** **1** to grow or develop as plants do: *One really lives nowhere; one does but vegetate* (Fanny Burney).
**2** *Figurative.* to live with very little action, thought, or feeling; exist without material or intellectual achievement. **SYN**: loaf, stagnate. **3** *Pathology.* to grow or increase in size abnormally. [< Latin *vegetāre* (with English *-ate*[1]) enliven, arouse < *vegetus* lively, vigorous]

**veg|e|tat|ed** (vej′ə tā′tid), *adj.* provided with vegetation or plant life.

**veg|e|ta|tion** (vej′ə tā′shən), *n.* **1** plant life; growing plants: *There is not much vegetation in deserts.* **2** the act or process of vegetating; growth of plants. **3** *Figurative.* an existence similar to that of a vegetable; dull, empty, or stagnant life.
**4** *Pathology.* an abnormal growth occurring on some part of the body.

**veg|e|ta|tion|al** (vej′ə tā′shə nəl), *adj.* of or having to do with vegetation: [*He*] *studied vegetational areas throughout the world and recognized the role of precipitation in determining the various vegetational types* (Harbaugh and Goodrick).

**veg|e|ta|tive** (vej′ə tā′tiv), *adj.* **1** growing as plants do: *a weed so vegetative as to infest the whole land.* **2** of plants or plant life: *a vegetative season.* **3** *Botany.* concerned with growth and development rather than reproduction. The roots, stems, and leaves of plants are vegetative organs. **4** causing or promoting growth in plants; productive; fertile: *vegetative mold.* **5** of or having to do with the unconscious or involuntary functions of the body: *the vegetative processes of the body, such as growth and repair.* **6** *Figurative.* having very little action, thought, or feeling.
—**veg′e|ta′tive|ly**, *adv.* —**veg′e|ta′tive|ness**, *n.*

**vegetative multiplication**, **1** artificially induced asexual reproduction by which cuttings, branches, and other parts are made to grow independently of the parent plant. **2** = vegetative reproduction.

**vegetative pole**, the part of an egg's surface located opposite to the animal pole and usually containing the principal mass of yolk.

**vegetative reproduction**, asexual reproduction, as by means of budding and fission.

**ve|gete** (və gēt′), *adj. Rare.* healthy; vigorous: *a vegete countenance, a vegete mind.* [< Latin *vegetus*]

**veg|e|tism** (vej′ə tiz əm), *n.* vegetal condition or quality.

**veg|e|tive** (vej′ə tiv), *adj., n.* —*adj.* = vegetative.
—*n. Obsolete.* **1** a vegetable or plant. **2** a vegetable cultivated for food.

**ve|he|mence** (vē′ə məns), *n.* vehement nature or quality; strong feeling; forcefulness; violence: *The two brothers argued loudly and with vehemence. For eighteen months the controversy raged; while the Queen, with persistent vehemence, opposed the Prime Minister and the Foreign Secretary* (Lytton Strachey). **SYN**: fervor, ardor.

**ve|he|men|cy** (vē′ə mən sē), *n.* = vehemence.

**ve|he|ment** (vē′ə mənt), *adj.* **1** having or showing strong feeling; caused by strong feeling; eager; passionate: *loud and vehement quarrels, vehement partisanship.* **SYN**: ardent, fervid. **2** acting with or displaying strong feeling or excitement: *a vehement devotee of modern music.* **3** performed with unusual force or violence; forceful; violent: *applause twice as vehement as usual. He finished the job with a vehement burst of energy. I announce a life that shall be copious, vehement, spiritual, bold* (Walt Whitman). **4** with great strength or violence: *vehement deluges of rain.*
[< Latin *vehemēns, -entis* impetuous, headlong; carried away, related to *vehere* to carry] —**ve′hement|ly**, *adv.*

**ve|hi|cle** (vē′ə kəl), *n.* **1a** any means of carrying, conveying, or transporting: *The rockets launched to carry astronauts to the moon are space vehicles.* **b** a carriage, wagon, sled, train, automobile, or other conveyance having wheels or runners and used on land. **2** *Figurative.* a means or medium by which something is communicated, shown, or done: *Language is the vehicle of thought.* **3** the means by which a substance or property, such as sound or heat, is conveyed or transmitted from one point to another. **4** a substance serving as a means for easier use or application of another substance mixed with it: **a** a liquid into which pigment is mixed to apply color to a surface: *Linseed oil is a vehicle for paint.*
**b** a medium, especially a liquid, in which strong or unpalatable drugs or medicines are administered. [< Latin *vehiculum* (diminutive) < *vehere* to carry]

**ve|hic|u|lar** (vi hik′yə lər), *adj.* **1** of or having to do with vehicles: *vehicular traffic, vehicular accidents, a vehicular tunnel.* **2** of the nature of or serving as a vehicle: *All language is vehicular and ... is good for conveyance* (Emerson).

**veil** (vāl), *n., v.* —*n.* **1** a piece of very thin material worn, especially by women, to protect or hide the face, or as an ornament, now especially worn attached to a hat: *a bridal veil.* **2** a piece of linen, or the like, worn as part of a nun's headdress, and falling over the head and shoulders.
**3** *Figurative.* **a** the secluded life of a nun. **b** the vows made by a woman either as a novice, when she takes the white veil, or as a nun, when she pronounces the irrevocable vows and assumes the black veil. **4** *Figurative.* anything that screens or hides: *a veil of deception. A veil of clouds hid the sun.* **5** a piece of fabric serving as a curtain or hanging. **6** *Biology.* a veillike membrane or membranous appendage or part, serving as a cover or screen; velum. **7** *Dialect.* a caul.
—*v.t.* **1a** to cover with a veil: *a woman closely veiled. Moslem women used to veil their faces before going into public.* **b** to enclose or hang with a veil or curtain. **2** to bestow the veil of a nun upon (a woman). **3** *Figurative.* to cover, screen, or hide: *Fog veiled the shore. The spy veiled his plans in secrecy. The most barefaced action seeks to veil itself under some show of decency* (William H. Prescott). **SYN**: conceal, mask.
—*v.i.* **1** to put on or wear a veil. **2** *Photography.* to become dark; darken.
**take the veil**, to become a nun: *She never took the veil, but lived and died in severe seclusion, and in the practice of the Roman Catholic religion* (Scott).
[< Anglo-French *veil* < Latin *vēla,* plural (taken as feminine singular) of *vēlum* curtain, (sail) covering. See etym. of doublets **velum**, **voile**.]
—**veil′like′**, *adj.*

**veiled** (vāld), *adj.* **1** covered with or wearing a veil: *the veiled figure of a ghost.* **2** *Figurative.*

a concealed, covered, or hidden, as if by a veil: *a magician's veiled hand.* **b** not clearly expressed; not openly declared or stated: *a veiled threat, veiled insults.*

**veil|ing** (vā′ling), *n.* **1** = veil. **2** material for veils. **3** *Figurative.* the action or fact of covering or concealing with a veil or of becoming blurred or dimmed as if covered by a veil.

**veiling luminance**, the dissipation of light by water: *When one is driving in a fog at night, the headlights seem unable to penetrate the fog because so much of their light is scattered back to the eye by tiny droplets of water. The same phenomenon, known as veiling luminance, makes it difficult to use artificial light to see under water* (Scientific American).

**veil|less** (vāl′lis), *adj.* without a veil.

**veil|tail** (vāl′tāl′), *n.* any one of a variety of goldfish having long, translucent fins.

***vein** (vān), *n., v.* —*n.* **1a** one of the blood vessels or tubes that carry the blood to the heart from all parts of the body. **b** any blood vessel. **2** the rib of a leaf; one of the strands or bundles of vascular tissue forming the principal framework of a leaf; nerve or nervure. **3** one of the ribs that strengthen the wing of an insect. **4a** a small natural channel within the earth through which water trickles or flows. **b** a flow of water through such a channel: *a vein of water.* **5** *Geology.* **a** a crack or seam in rock filled with a material, especially metallic ore, different from the containing rock. **b** a deposit, as of ore or coal, having a more or less regular development in length, width, and depth; lode: *a vein of copper.* **6** a streak or stream of a different material or texture from the main substance: *a vein of gristle in the meat.* **7** any streak or marking of a different shade or color in wood, marble, or glass.
**8** *Figurative.* a strain or blend of some quality in conduct, writing, speech, or other activity: *a vein of criticism, comedy written in a witty vein.*
**9** *Figurative.* a special character or disposition; state of mind; mood: *a vein of cruelty, a joking vein. In the midst of a vein of thought ... I was interrupted* (Washington Irving).
—*v.t.* **1** to mark (with lines or streaks) in a manner suggesting veins. **2** to cover with, spread out over, or run through (something) the way veins do: *Many rivers vein the lowlands.*
[< Old French *veine* < Latin *vēna*] —**vein′er**, *n.* —**vein′like′**, *adj.*

elm leaf

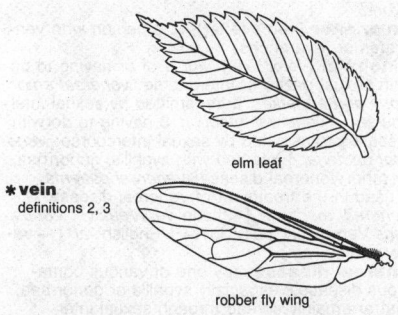

***vein**
definitions 2, 3

robber fly wing

**veined** (vānd), *adj.* having or showing veins: *veined marble, a veined leaf.*

**vein|ing** (vā′ning), *n.* the formation or arrangement of veins or veinlike markings on or in something.

**vein|less** (vān′lis), *adj.* having no veins.

**vein|let** (vān′lit), *n.* **1** a small vein; venule. **2** *Botany.* a branch or subdivision of a vein or venule: *The veins divide and subdivide, making a network, and are so distributed that no part of the mesophyll is far removed from one or more veinlets* (Fred W. Emerson).

**vein|ous** (vā′nəs), *adj.* **1** full of, marked with, or having to do with veins. **2** (of blood) venous.

**vein|stone** (vān′stōn′), *n.* stone or earth composing a vein and containing ore; gangue; matrix.

**vein|ule** (vā′nyül), *n.* a small vein; venule. [< French *veinule, venule,* learned borrowing from Latin *vēnula* (diminutive) < *vēna* vein. See etym. of doublet **venule**.]

**vein|u|let** (vā′nyə lit), *n.* = veinule.

**vein|y** (vā′nē), *adj.,* **vein|i|er, vein|i|est. 1a** of, having to do with, or full of veins, especially blood vessels. **b** having prominent veins. **2** *Geology.* covered with or crossed by veins having different substance or structure. **3** marked by veins of color. **4** *Botany.* having many veins: *veiny leaves.*

**vei|tchi** (vā′chē), *n.* a small-flowered variety of Cape jasmine, grown as a potted plant. [< (*Gardenia*) *Veitchii* the variety name < James *Veitch,* an English horticulturist of the 1900's, who introduced it]

**vel.**, vellum.

**ve|la** (vē′lə), *n.* plural of **velum.**

**ve|la|men** (və lā′mən), *n., pl.* **-lam|i|na** (-lam′ə-nə). **1** *Botany.* the thick, outer, spongy tissue consisting of several layers of cells, covering the aerial roots of epiphytic orchids. **2** *Anatomy.* a membranous covering or partition; velum. [< Latin *vēlāmen, -inis* < *vēlāre* to cover < *vēlum* covering]

**vel|a|men|tous** (vel′ə men′təs), *adj.* of or like a membrane or membranous covering.

**ve|lar** (vē′lər), *adj., n.* —*adj.* **1** of or having to do with a velum, especially the soft palate: *Velar closure ... is the closure of the oral passage by the tongue against the lower surface of the velum* (Henry A. Gleason, Jr.). **2** *Phonetics.* pronounced with the back of the tongue raised toward or against the soft palate; dorsal. *G* in *goose* has a velar sound, *g* in *geese* does not.
—*n.* *Phonetics.* a velar sound.
[< Latin *vēlāris* < *vēlum* covering]

**ve|lar|i|um** (və lãr′ē əm), *n., pl.* **-i|a** (-ē ə). a large awning used in ancient Rome to cover a theater or amphitheater as a protection against sun or rain. [< Latin *vēlārium* < *vēlum* covering]

**ve|lar|ize** (vē′lə rīz), *v.t.,* **-ized, -iz|ing.** *Phonetics.* to pronounce (a sound) or modify (a nonvelar sound) by giving it velar articulation. The second *l* in *lull* is often slightly velarized. —**ve′lar|i|za′tion**, *n.*

**ve|late** (vē′lāt), *adj. Biology.* having a veil or velum. [< Latin *vēlātus* veiled, past participle of *vēlāre* to cover < *vēlum* veil]

**Vel|cro** (vel′krō), *n. Trademark.* a fastener, as for clothing or carpeting, made usually of a strip of minute nylon hooks that penetrate and catch in a closely woven strip of nylon loops.

**veld** or **veldt** (velt, felt), *n.* the open, grass-covered plains of southern Africa, often with bushes but with very few trees. [< Afrikaans *veld* < Dutch, earlier *veldt* field]

**veld|schoen** or **veldt|schoen** (velt′shůn′, felt′-), *n., pl.* **-schoens, -schoen|en** (-skůn′ən). = velschoen.

**ve|le|ta** (və lē′tə), *n.* a round dance for couples, popular in the early 1900's. [< Spanish *veleta* weather vane]

**ve|li|ger** (vē′lə jər), *n.* **1** the embryonic stage of a mollusk when it has a ciliate swimming membrane or velum. **2** the embryo in that stage. [< Latin *vēlum* covering + *-ger* bearing < *gerere* to bear]

**vel|i|ta|tion** (vel′ə tā′shən), *n.* **1** a light encounter with the enemy; patrol action; skirmish. **2** *Figurative.* an argument, controversy, or debate; dispute: *He returned to Germany in 1948 after an inconclusive velitation with the Un-American Activities Committee* (New Yorker). [< Latin *vēlitātiō, -ōnis* < *vēlitārī* to skirmish < *vēles, -itis;* see etym. under **velites**]

**ve|li|tes** (vē′lə tēz), *n.pl.* light-armed soldiers used as skirmishers in the Roman armies. [< Latin *vēlitēs,* plural of *vēles,* probably related to *vēlōx* swift]

**vel|le|i|ty** (və lē′ə tē), *n., pl.* **-ties. 1** the fact or quality of wishing or desiring, without any action, effort, or resolve toward obtaining fulfillment. **2** a mere wish or slight inclination, without accompanying action or effort: *He perceived ... that every wish, every velleity of his had only to be expressed to be at once Victoria's* (Lytton Strachey). [< Medieval Latin *velleitas* < Latin *velle* to wish]

**vel|li|cate** (vel′ə kāt), *v.,* **-cat|ed, -cat|ing.** *Medicine.* —*v.t.* *Obsolete.* to pluck, nip, pinch, or tear (the body) with small, sharp points.
—*v.i.* to twitch or move convulsively.
[< Latin *vellicāre* (with English *-ate*[1]) < *vellere* to pluck (out), twitch]

**vel|li|ca|tion** (vel′ə kā′shən), *n.* **1** the act of twitching or causing to twitch. **2** a twitching or convulsive movement of a muscular fiber.

**vel|li|ca|tive** (vel′ə kā′tiv), *adj.* having the power of vellicating, plucking, or twitching.

**vel|lum** (vel′əm), *n., adj.* —*n.* **1** the finest kind of parchment, usually prepared from the skins of calves, kids, or lambs, once used instead of paper for books. Some very expensive books are still bound in vellum. **2** a manuscript, testimonial, or degree written or printed on vellum. **3a** any superior quality of parchment: *vegetable vellum.* **b** paper or cloth imitating vellum. A college diploma is usually made of vellum.
—*adj.* made of or resembling vellum.
[Middle English *velym* < Old French *vellin* < *veel* calf; see etym. under **veal**]

**ve|lo|ce** (vā lō′chā), *adv., adj. Music.* with very rapid tempo; presto. [< Italian *veloce* swift < Latin *vēlōx, -ōcis*]

**vel|o|cim|e|ter** (vel′ə sim′ə tər), *n.* any one of various devices for measuring velocity or speed, as an instrument for measuring the initial velocity of a projectile or a ship's log: *The National Bureau of Standards has developed ... a velocimeter that automatically measures the speed of sound in the sea to depths as great as 300 feet and plots the result as a function of depth or time* (Science). [< Latin *vēlōx, -ōcis* swift + English *-meter*]

**ve|loc|i|pede** (və los′ə pēd), *n.* **1** a child's tricycle. **2a** an early bicycle which the rider straddled and propelled with a walking motion pushing his feet alternately on the ground; walk-along. **b** any one of the early bicycles or tricycles propelled by pressure from the rider's feet upon pedals usually attached to the front wheel. **3** a railroad handcar. [< French *vélocipède* < Latin *vēlōx, -ōcis* swift + *pēs, pedis* foot]

**ve|loc|i|ty** (və los′ə tē), *n., pl.* **-ties,** *adj.* —*n.*
**1** quickness of motion; speed; swiftness; rapidity: *to fly with the velocity of a bird.* [*The flood*] *burst on them ... whirling great trees and fragments of houses past with incredible velocity* (Charles Reade). SYN: celerity. **2** rate of motion in a particular direction: *The velocity of light is about 186,282 miles per second.* SYN: pace. **3** the absolute or relative rate of operation or action: *The rate at which boiled water loses temperature is the velocity of cooling.*
—*adj.* of or having to do with the rapidity or rate of motion or action: *velocity ratio.*
[< Latin *vēlōcitās* < *vēlōx, -ōcis* swift]

**ve|lo|drome** (vē′lə drōm), *n.* a building having a track for bicycle and motorcycle racing: *The other night a hot-blooded throng went to the velodrome to watch the British cyclists merely rehearse* (Newsweek). [< French *vélodrome* < *vélo,* short for *vélocipède* (see etym. under **velocipede**) + Greek *drómos* a running]

**ve|lom|e|ter** (və lom′ə tər), *n.* = velocimeter.

**Vel|on** (vē′lon), *n. Trademark.* a synthetic fiber derived from petroleum and brine, used in drapery and upholstery materials, shoe fabrics, and industrial cloth.

**ve|lour** or **ve|lours** (və lůr′), *n.* a fabric like velvet, with a pile surface on one side and a plain or satin weave on the other, used for making upholstery material, draperies, coats, jackets, and hats. [< French *velours* velvet < Old French *velour, velous* < Old Provençal *velos* < noun use of Latin adjective *villōsus* < *villus* shaggy hair]

**ve|lou|té** (və lü tā′), *n., adj.* —*n.* a smooth, creamy, white sauce made from meat stock.
—*adj.* made with meat stock, flour, and fat. [< French *velouté* (literally) velvety < *velours;* see etym. under **velour**]

**velouté sauce**, = velouté.

**vel|schoen** (vel′skůn′, fel′-), *n., pl.* **-schoens, -schoen|en** (-skůn′ən). (in South Africa) a light shoe made of untanned hide: *From the shapeless roof of his hat to the soft, handmade velschoens he was the human counterpart of the desert* (Harper's). Also, **veldschoen, veldtschoen.** [< Afrikaans *velschoen* < Dutch *vel* hide[2] + *schoen* shoe]

**ve|lum** (vē′ləm), *n., pl.* **-la. 1** a membrane or membranous covering or partition resembling a veil. **2** the soft palate: *Above and behind the velum is the nasal pharynx opening into the cavity of the nose which acts as a resonance chamber* (Simeon Potter). **3** any one of several membranes connected to or in the brain. **4** a membranous structure or covering in certain fungi. **5** a ciliated membrane which covers the veliger of a mollusk, serving as an organ of swimming or locomotion: *The free-swimming young teredo hangs in the water from a velum, an extraordinary mobile structure that looks like an animated umbrella and functions as an organ of locomotion* (Scientific American). [< Latin *vēlum* covering, sail. See etym. of doublets **veil, voile.**]

**ve|lure** (və lůr′), *n., v.,* **-lured, -lur|ing.** —*n.* **1** a soft material like velvet. **2** a soft pad of silk or plush, used for smoothing and giving a luster to silk hats.
—*v.t.* to brush or dress (a hat) with a velure.
[earlier, velvet < Old French *velour;* see etym. under **velour**]

**ve|lu|ti|nous** (və lü′tə nəs), *adj. Biology.* having a hairy surface resembling velvet in texture. [< New Latin *velutinus* (with English *-ous*) < Medieval Latin *velutum,* ultimately < Latin *villus* shaggy hair]

**vel|vet** (vel′vit), *n., adj., v.* —*n.* **1** a cloth with a thick, short, soft pile on one side. Velvet may be made of silk, rayon, cotton, nylon, or some combination of these. In weaving velvet the warp is pulled over a needle, making loops that are cut (cut velvet) or uncut (pile velvet). **2** something

**Pronunciation Key:** hat, āge, cãre, fär; let, ēqual, tėrm; it, īce; hot, ōpen, ôrder; **oi**l, **ou**t; cup, půt, rüle; **ch**ild; lo**ng**; **th**in; **ᴛʜ**en; **zh**, measure; **ə** represents **a** in about, **e** in taken, **i** in pencil, **o** in lemon, **u** in circus.

like velvet in softness or appearance. **3** the furry skin that covers the growing antlers of a deer. **4** *Slang.* clear profit or gain: *Whatever equity the family may build up in the house, no matter how slowly it grows, will be taken as so much velvet* (Wall Street Journal). **5** *Slang.* money won through gambling.
—*adj.* **1** made of velvet: *She wore a velvet hat.* **2** covered with velvet. **3** smooth or soft like velvet; velvety: *velvet petals. Our kitten has soft, velvet paws.*
—*v.t.* to cover with or as if with velvet; cause to resemble velvet: *The back wall is to be velveted in absorbent fiberglass* (Time).
**on velvet**, *Slang.* in a position of ease or advantage; in an advantageous or prosperous condition: *Before that we were on velvet; but the instant he appeared everything was changed* (Benjamin Disraeli).
**to the velvet**, to the good: *Before the whistle blew for dinner I was several hundred to the velvet* (K. McGaffey).
[< Medieval Latin *velvetum,* ultimately < Latin *villus* tuft of hair] —**vel'vet|like'**, *adj.*

**velvet ant**, any one of a group of hymenopterous burrowing insects with soft, hairy coverings, resembling ants and wasps, common in the southern United States.

**velvet bean**, an annual leguminous climbing plant, with a stem sometimes 50 feet long, used especially in the southern United States for its fertilizing value and as hay.

**vel|vet-bean caterpillar** (vel'vit bēn'), a dull-green to dark-brown caterpillar, the larva of an American noctuid moth, that feeds on soybeans, velvet beans, peanuts, and similar plants.

**velvet carpet**, a carpet having the loops of the pile cut like Wilton.

**vel|vet|ed** (vel'və tid), *adj.* covered with or clad in velvet.

**vel|vet|een** (vel'və tēn'), *n., adj.* —*n.* a fabric resembling velvet, made of cotton or of silk and cotton.
—*adj.* made of velveteen.
**velveteens**, trousers or knickers made of this fabric: *He ... thought of the fine times coming, when he would ... wear velveteens* (Charles Kingsley).

**vel|vet|eened** (vel'və tēnd'), *adj.* dressed in velveteen.

**vel|vet|leaf** (vel'vit lēf'), *n.* any one of various plants with soft, velvety leaves, such as the Indian mallow and the pareira brava.

**velvet osier**, any one of various willows with flexible stems used for baskets, wickerwork, and furniture.

**velvet sponge**, a horse sponge found off the coasts of Cuba, Honduras, and the Bahamas, used for rough cleaning work.

**vel|vet-voiced** (vel'vit voist'), *adj.* having a deep, rich, mellow voice: *Velvet-voiced contralto Marian Anderson has played to capacity houses at all stops* (Time).

**vel|vet|y** (vel'və tē), *adj.* **1** smooth and soft like velvet. **2** smooth and soft to the taste.

**Ven.**, **1** Venerable. **2** Venice.

**ve|na** (vē'nə), *n., pl.* **ve|nae** (vē'nē). *Anatomy.* a vein. [< Latin *vēna*]

**ve|na ca|va** (vē'nə kā'və), *pl.* **ve|nae ca|vae** (vē'nē kā'vē). either of two large veins that empty blood from the upper and lower halves of the body into the right auricle of the heart. See diagram under **heart**. [< Latin *vēna cava* empty vein]

**ve|nal** (vē'nəl), *adj.* **1** willing to sell one's services or influence basely; open to bribes; corrupt: *Venal judges are a disgrace to a country.* **2** influenced or obtained by bribery: *venal conduct.* [< Latin *vēnālis* < *vēnum*, accusative, thing that is for sale] —**ve'nal|ly**, *adv.*

**ve|nal|i|ty** (vē nal'ə tē), *n.* the quality of being venal: *France and the rest of the world were treated to the spectacle of one set of collaborators trying another set of collaborators with all the venom and venality they could bring to their task* (Observer).

**ve|nat|ic** (vē nat'ik), *adj.* of, having to do with, or devoted to hunting. [< Latin *vēnāticus* < *vēnārī* to hunt]

**ve|nat|i|cal** (vē nat'ə kəl), *adj.* = venatic.

**ve|nat|i|cal|ly** (vē nat'ə klē), *adv.* in the chase; in hunting.

**ve|na|tion** (vē nā'shən), *n.* **1** the arrangement of the veins in the blade of a leaf or in an insect's wing; nervation. **2** these veins collectively. [< Latin *vēna* vein + English *-ation*]

**ve|na|tion|al** (vē nā'shə nəl), *adj.* of or having to do with venation.

**vend** (vend), *v.t.* **1** to sell; peddle: *He vends fruit from a cart.* **2** *Figurative.* to put forward (an opinion, lie, or other statement).
—*v.i.* to be sold; find a market or purchaser. [< Latin *vendere* < *vēnum dare* offer for sale]

**Ven|da** (ven'də), *n., pl.* **-das**. **1** a member of an agricultural group of tribes living in northern South Africa. **2** the Bantu language of the tribes.

**ven|dace** (ven'dās), *n., pl.* **-dac|es** or (*collectively*) **-dace**. **1** a small whitefish found in certain lakes in Scotland. **2** a closely related species found in England. [apparently < Old French *vendese, vendoise*]

**ven|dage** (ven'dij), *n.* the harvesting of grapes; vintage. [< Old French *vendange;* see etym. under **vintage**]

**ven|dange** (väɴ däɴzh'), *n. French.* vendage.

**Ven|de|an** (ven dē'ən), *n.* an inhabitant of La Vendée, in western France, who took part in the insurrection of 1793 against the French Republic.

**vend|ee** (ven dē'), *n. Especially Law.* the person to whom a thing is sold; buyer.

**Ven|dé|miaire** (väɴ dā myer'), *n.* the first month of the French revolutionary calendar, extending from September 22nd to October 21st. [< French *Vendémiaire* < Latin *vendēmia* grape gathering]

**vend|er** (ven'dər), *n.* **1** a seller, especially a peddler or person who sells on the street; vendor: *a flower vender.* **SYN**: hawker. **2** = vending machine.

**ven|det|ta** (ven det'ə), *n.* **1** a feud in which a murdered or injured person's relatives try to take revenge on the wrongdoer or his relatives; blood feud. A vendetta may sometimes be carried on from one generation to another. **2** any prolonged or bitter feud: *What made the case so obnoxious ... was the implication that British police were being used to aid a political vendetta in another country* (Bulletin of Atomic Scientists). [< Italian *vendetta* < Latin *vindicta* revenge, related to *vindex, -icis* protector, avenger < *vindicāre;* see etym. under **vindicate**]

**ven|det|tist** (ven det'ist), *n.* a person who takes part in or carries on a vendetta.

**ven|deuse** (väɴ dœz'), *n. French.* a saleswoman: *Although customers can change materials, it is wise to take the advice of the vendeuse on this* (London Times).

**vend|i|bil|i|ty** (ven'də bil'ə tē), *n.* salable quality; quality of being marketable.

**vend|i|ble** (ven'də bəl), *adj., n.* —*adj.* **1** salable; marketable: *Spoiled food is not vendible.* **2** *Figurative:* *the vendible favors of some city officials.* **SYN**: corrupt, venal.
—*n.* a salable thing. —**vend'i|bly**, *adv.*

**vend|ing machine** (ven'ding), a machine from which one obtains candy, stamps, or other small articles when a coin is dropped in.

**ven|di|tion** (ven dish'ən), *n.* the act of selling or peddling; sale. [< Latin *venditiō, -ōnis* < *vendere* to sell]

**ven|dor** (ven'dər), *n.* a seller; peddler: *The narcotics vendor is one of society's most dangerous enemies.* [< Anglo-French *vendor,* earlier *vendour* < *vendre* to sell < Latin *vendere;* see etym. under **vend**]

**ven|due** (ven dü', -dyü'), *n.* a public sale or auction. [< Dutch *vendu* < Middle French *vendue* sale < *vendre* to sell; see etym. under **vend**]

**ve|neer** (və nir'), *v., n.* —*v.t.* **1a** to cover (wood) with a thin layer of finer wood or other material to produce an elegant or polished surface: *The cabinetmaker veneered the pine desk with mahogany.* **b** to glue together (thin layers of wood) to make plywood. **2** *Figurative.* to cover (anything) with a layer of something else to give an appearance of superior quality: *A rogue in grain veneer'd with sanctimonious theory* (Tennyson).
—*n.* **1a** a thin layer of wood or other material used in veneering: *The panel had a veneer of gold and ivory.* **b** one of the thin layers of wood used in making plywood. **2** *Figurative.* a surface appearance or show: *a veneer of culture. A veneer of pity hid his real meanness. Their treachery was hidden by a veneer of friendship.*
[earlier *fineer, faneer* < German *fournieren* < French *fournir* furnish] —**ve|neer'er**, *n.*

**ve|neer|ing** (və nir'ing), *n.* **1** the art or process of applying veneer. **2** any thin material applied or used as a veneer. **3** the covering or surface formed by a veneer. **4** *Figurative.* a mere surface appearance or show; outward pretense: *It was not long before his veneering of good will wore through.*

**ven|e|na|tion** (ven'ə nā'shən), *n.* the act or process of poisoning, especially through a bite, sting, or the like: *... venenation by venoms that are capable of producing local histolysis such as those of pit vipers and some spiders* (Science). [< Latin *venēnum* poison + English *-ation*]

**ven|e|nose** (ven'ə nōs), *adj.* poisonous; venomous. [< Late Latin *venēnōsus* < Latin *venēnum* poison + *-ōsus* -ose[1]]

**ven|e|punc|ture** (ven'ə pungk'chər, vē'nə-), *n.* = venipuncture.

**ven|er|a|bil|i|ty** (ven'ər ə bil'ə tē), *n.* the fact or quality of being venerable: *At 57, he was approaching venerability in the eyes of party workers clamoring for younger leadership* (Newsweek).

***Venetian architecture**

**ven|er|a|ble** (ven'ər ə bəl), *adj.* **1** worthy of reverence; deserving respect because of age, character, or importance: *a venerable priest, venerable customs, the venerable ruins of Athens and Rome.* **2** designating an archdeacon of the Anglican Church (used as a title of respect). **3** (in the Roman Catholic Church) designating a person recognized as having attained a degree of virtue but not yet recognized as beatified or canonized: *the Venerable Bede.* [< Latin *venerābilis* < *venerārī;* see etym. under **venerate**] —**ven'er|a|ble|ness**, *n.*

**ven|er|a|bly** (ven'ər ə blē), *adv.* in a venerable manner; so as to excite reverence.

**ven|er|ate** (ven'ə rāt), *v.t.,* **-at|ed, -at|ing.** to regard with deep respect; revere: *He venerates his father's memory. Holy writers, and such whose names are venerated to all posterity* (Sir Thomas Browne). **SYN**: honor, esteem. [< Latin *venerārī* (with English *-ate*[1]) < *Venus, -eris* (goddess of) love]

**ven|er|a|tion** (ven'ə rā'shən), *n.* **1** a feeling of deep respect; reverence: *veneration for learning, to hold one's grandfather in veneration.* **2** the act of showing respect and reverence: *An important teaching of Confucius was veneration of one's ancestors.* **3** the condition of being venerated: *Such veneration seems strange to the Western World.*

**ven|er|a|tor** (ven'ə rā'tər), *n.* a person who venerates or reverences.

**ve|ne|re|al** (və nir'ē əl), *adj.* **1** of or having to do with sexual desire or intercourse: *venereal emotions and appetites.* **2** transmitted by sexual intercourse: *a venereal infection.* **3** having to do with diseases transmitted by sexual intercourse: *venereal bacteria.* **4** infected with syphilis, gonorrhea, or other venereal disease: *venereal patients.* **5** used in the treatment of venereal disease: *a venereal medicine.* [< Latin *venereus* (< *Venus, -eris* Venus; originally, love) + English *-al*[1]] —**ve|ne're|al|ly**, *adv.*

**venereal disease**, any one of various contagious diseases, especially syphilis or gonorrhea, that are mainly spread through sexual intercourse; social disease. *Abbr:* V.D. or VD

**ve|ne|re|an** (və nir'ē ən), *adj.* **1** inclined to the service of Venus or to sexual desire: *For certain I am venerean in feeling* (Chaucer). **2** amorous; wanton: *There's nothing wrong with Sir Thomas Urquhart's "venerean ecstasy"* (Anthony Burgess). **3** of the planet Venus; Venusian. [< Latin *venereus* (see etym. under **venereal**) + English *-an*]

**ve|ne|re|ol|o|gist** (və nir'ē ol'ə jist), *n.* a person who treats or studies venereal diseases.

**ve|ne|re|ol|o|gy** (və nir'ē ol'ə jē), *n.* the branch of medicine dealing with venereal diseases. [< *venerea*(l) + *-logy*]

**ven|er|er** (ven'ər ər), *n. Archaic.* a huntsman. [< *vener*(y)[2] + *-er*[2]]

**ven|er|y**[1] (ven'ər ē), *n.* the practice or pursuit of sexual pleasure; gratification of sexual desire. [< Latin *Venus, -eris* Venus; (originally) love + English *-y*[3]]

**ven|er|y**[2] (ven'ər ē), *n. Archaic.* the practice or sport of hunting; the chase. [< Old French *venerie* < *vener* to hunt < Latin *vēnārī*]

**ven|e|sec|tion** (ven'ə sek'shən), *n.* the opening of a vein to let blood; phlebotomy: *Venesection was practiced by barbers in the Middle Ages.* Also, **venisection.** [< Medieval Latin *venaesectio, -onis* < Latin *vēnae*, genitive of *vēna* vein + *sectiō, -ōnis* a cutting, section]

**Ven|e|ti** (ven'ə tī), *n.pl.* an ancient people of northeastern Italy who spoke Venetic. [< Latin *Veneti*]

**Ve|ne|tian** (və nē'shən), *adj., n.* —*adj.* of or having to do with Venice, a city on the northeastern coast of Italy, or its people.

—*n.* **1** a person born or living in Venice. **2** Also, **venetian.** *Informal.* a Venetian blind. **3** a closely woven, twilled woolen fabric, used especially for dresses, suits, and coats.
**Venetians,** a heavy tape or braid used especially on Venetian blinds.

∗**Venetian architecture,** the style of medieval architecture elaborated in Venice, Italy, combining elements from the Byzantine, Italian, and transalpine European styles, into a new style of high decorative quality and originality. See picture opposite on preceding page.

∗**Venetian blind,** a window blind made of many horizontal wooden, steel, or aluminum slats. The blind can be raised or lowered, or the slats can be tilted so that they open or overlap, to regulate the light that is allowed in.

∗**Venetian blind**

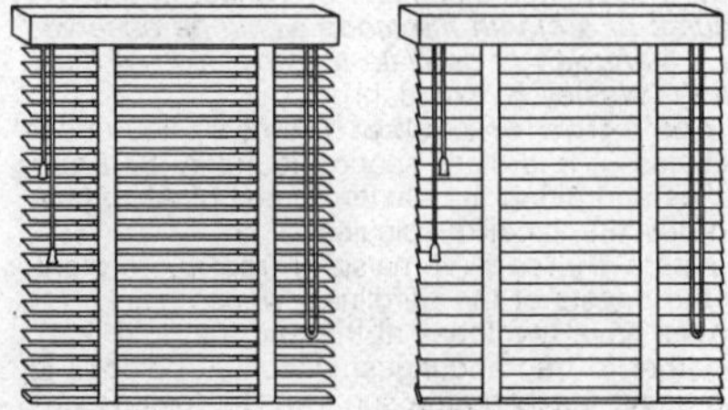

**ve|ne|tianed** (və nē′shənd), *adj.* furnished with Venetian blinds.

**Venetian glass, 1** a very fine, delicate, brittle kind of glass originally manufactured near Venice, Italy. **2** an article made of this.

**Venetian painting,** the style of painting distinguished by its mastery and brilliance of coloring, originating in and near Venice, Italy, in the 1400's and reaching its climax in the 1500's: *Those rugged, swart, bald-headed old fisher apostles, with their coppery bare shoulders, are as emblematic of Venetian painting as the sensuous, pensive Madonna with whom they fraternize* (New Yorker).

**Venetian red, 1** a red pigment consisting of a mixture of iron oxide and calcium sulfate, produced synthetically. **2** a dark red with a tinge of orange.

**Ve|ne|tians** (və nē′shənz), *n.pl.* See under **Venetian.**

**Venetian school,** a group of predominantly Italian artists of the 1400's and 1500's who worked in the style of Venetian painting.

**Ve|net|ic** (və net′ik), *n., adj.* —*n.* an ancient Indo-European language of northeastern Italy, regarded by some scholars as an Italic dialect, known only from inscriptions dating from the 400's B.C. to the 100's B.C.
—*adj.* of or having to do with Venetic or the Veneti.
[< Latin *Veneticus* of the Veneti < *Veneti*]

**Venez.,** Venezuela.

**Ven|e|zue|lan** (ven′ə zwē′lən, -zwā′-), *adj., n.* —*adj.* of or having to do with Venezuela, a country in South America, or its people: *Venezuelan oil interests.*
—*n.* a native or inhabitant of Venezuela.

**venge** (venj), *v.t.,* **venged, veng|ing.** *Archaic.* to avenge; revenge. [< Old French *vengier* < Latin *vindicāre;* see etym. under **vindicate**]

**venge|ance** (ven′jəns), *n.* **1** punishment in return for a wrong; revenge: *He swore vengeance against the men who murdered his father.* SYN: retribution. **2** the inflicting of injury or punishment in return for a wrong; avenging oneself or another: *Vengeance is mine; I will repay* (Romans 12:19).
**with a vengeance, a** with great force or violence: *It started sprinkling at three o'clock and by six o'clock it was raining with a vengeance.* **b** to an unusual extent; much more than expected: *When rebuked for rudeness, he turned polite with a vengeance.*
[< Anglo-French *vengeaunce,* Old French *vengeance* < *vengier* to venge]

**venge|ful** (venj′fəl), *adj.* **1** seeking vengeance; inclined to avenge oneself; vindictive: *vengeful enemies.* **2** arising from or showing a strong desire for vengeance: *vengeful hate.* **3** inflicting vengeance; serving as an instrument of vengeance: *rebellion's vengeful talons* (Samuel Johnson). —**venge′ful|ly,** *adv.* —**venge′ful|ness,** *n.*

**ve|ni|al** (vē′nē əl, vēn′yəl), *adj.* **1** that may be forgiven; not very wrong or sinful; wrong but pardonable. **2** of an unimportant nature; excusable; trivial: *a venial fault. If they do nothing, 'tis a venial slip* (Shakespeare).
[< Latin *veniālis* < *venia* forgiveness, related to *Venus* Venus; (originally) love] —**ve′ni|al|ly,** *adv.* —**ve′ni|al|ness,** *n.*

**ve|ni|al|i|ty** (vē′nē al′ə tē), *n.* the quality of being venial.

**venial sin,** (in the Roman Catholic Church) a sin not destroying the soul because it is minor or, if grave, due to inadvertence or not willfully committed.

**ven|in** (ven′in), *n. Biochemistry.* any one of a group of poisonous substances present in the venom of snakes, toads, and scorpions. [< *ven*(om) + *-in*]

**ven|i|punc|ture** (ven′ə pungk′chər, vē′nə-), *n.* the piercing of a vein, especially with a hypodermic needle for removing blood. Also, **venepuncture.** [< Latin *vēna* vein + English *puncture*]

**ve|ni|re** (və nī′rē), *n. Law.* a writ issued to a sheriff requiring him to summon persons to serve on a jury. [< Latin *venīre faciās* that you may cause (him) to come]

**venire fa|ci|as** (fā′shē as), = venire.

**ve|ni|re|man** (və nī′rē mən), *n., pl.* **-men.** *Law.* a person summoned to serve on a jury by a writ of venire. [American English < *venire* (facias) + *man*]

**ven|i|sec|tion** (ven′ə sek′shən), *n.* = venesection.

**ven|i|son** (ven′ə sən, -zən), *n.* **1** the flesh of a deer, used for food; deer meat. **2** (formerly) the flesh of any animal killed by hunting, especially a deer, boar, hare, or other game animal. **3** *Archaic.* any beast or wild animal killed by hunting. [< Old French *venesoun* < Latin *vēnātiō, -ōnis* a hunting < *vēnārī* to hunt]

**venison bird,** (in Canada) = Canada jay.

**Ve|ni|te** (vi nī′tē), *n.* **1** the 95th Psalm (94th in the Vulgate), recited as a canticle at matins or morning prayer. **2** a musical setting (usually a chant) of this. [< Latin *venīte* come ye! (the first word in the Latin version)]

**ve|ni, vi|di, vi|ci** (vē′nī vī′dī vī′sī; wā′nē wē′dē wē′kē), *Latin.* I came, I saw, I conquered (a report of victory at Zela made by Julius Caesar to the Roman Senate).

∗**Venn diagram** (ven), a diagram using circles and rectangles to represent various types of mathematical sets and to show the relationship between them. In a Venn diagram, separate sets may be represented by two or more separate circles, and overlapping sets by two or more overlapping circles. [< John *Venn,* 1834-1923, an English logician]

∗**Venn diagram**

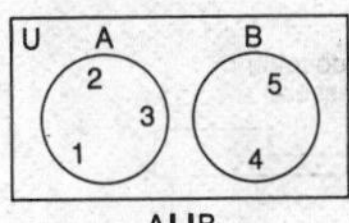

A∪B
separate sets

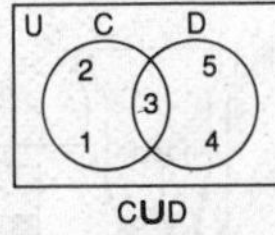

C∪D
overlapping sets

**ve|no|gram** (vē′nə gram), *n.* an X-ray photograph of a vein, after it has been injected with an opaque substance. [< Latin *vēna* vein + English *-gram*]

**ve|no|graph|ic** (vē′nə graf′ik), *adj.* of or having to do with venography.

**ve|nog|ra|phy** (vē nog′rə fē), *n.* the science or technique of making venograms; radiography of a vein or veins.

**ven|om** (ven′əm), *n., v.* —*n.* **1a** the poison of some snakes, spiders, scorpions, lizards, and similar animals. Venom is injected into their prey as by biting or stinging. **b** any sort of poison. **2** *Figurative.* bitterness; spite; malice: *Her enemies had learned to fear the venom of her tongue. She hated the rich old tyrant and spoke of him with the utmost venom.* SYN: rancor, hate, malignity.
—*v.t.* to put venom in or on (something); make venomous; envenom: (*Figurative.*) *to venom a refusal with contempt.*
[< Old French *venim,* variant of *venin* < Vulgar Latin *venīmen,* for Latin *venēnum* poison] —**ven′om|er,** *n.*

**ven|om|less** (ven′əm lis), *adj.* without venom: **a** *Boa constrictors are venomless snakes.* **b** *Figurative: Her venomless reply took any sting out of her refusal.*

**ven|o|mol|o|gy** (ven′ə mol′ə jē), *n.* the study of venoms, including the treatment of venomous bites and stings. —**ven′o|mol′o|gist,** *n.*

**ven|om|ous** (ven′ə məs), *adj.* **1** poisonous: *a venomous bite. Rattlesnakes are venomous.* **2** *Figurative.* spiteful; malicious; embittered: *a venomous attack. The stings and venomous stabs of public contumely* (Hawthorne). SYN: malignant. —**ven′om|ous|ly,** *adv.* —**ven′om|ous|ness,** *n.*

**ve|nose** (vē′nōs), *adj.* **1** *Botany.* having numerous veins or a branching network, as a leaf. **2** venous. [< Latin *vēnōsus* < *vēna* vein]

**ve|nos|i|ty** (vē nos′ə tē), *n.* venous or venose quality or condition.

**ve|nous** (vē′nəs), *adj.* **1** of or having to do with a vein or veins; venose. **2** contained in the veins. Venous blood is dark red after having given up oxygen and become charged with carbon dioxide. **3** having or appearing to have veins: *the venous wings of insects.* [< Latin *vēna* vein + English *-ous*] —**ve′nous|ly,** *adv.* —**ve′nous|ness,** *n.*

**vent**[1] (vent), *n., v.* —*n.* **1** a hole or opening, especially one serving as an outlet: *He used a pencil to make air vents in the box top so his frog could breathe.* SYN: orifice. **2** a way out; outlet: (*Figurative.*) *His great energy found vent in hard work.* SYN: escape. **3** *Figurative.* free expression: *She gave vent to her grief in tears.* SYN: effusion. **4** *Zoology.* the excretory opening at the end of the digestive tract, especially in birds, fishes, amphibians, and reptiles. **5** the small opening in the barrel of a gun by which fire is communicated to the powder; touchhole. **6** an adjustable opening for indirect ventilation, such as a small, often oblong or triangular, window in an automobile.
—*v.t.* **1** to let out; express freely: *He vented his anger on the dog.* **2** to make a vent in: *to vent an attic through the roof.* SYN: tap.
[partly < Middle French *vent* wind < Latin *ventus;* partly short for Middle French *évent* vent, ultimately < Latin *ex-* out + *ventus* wind]

**vent**[2] (vent), *n.* an opening or slit in a garment, especially in the back of a coat.
[dialectal variant of Middle English *fente* < Middle French, slit, split < Old French *fendre* to split < Latin *findere*]

**vent|age** (ven′tij), *n.* **1** a small hole, especially for the escape or passage of air; vent. **2** a hole in a wind instrument for controlling the pitch of the tone; finger hole.

**ven|tail** (ven′tāl), *n.* **1** the lower, movable part on the front of a helmet of armor. **2** the whole movable part on a helmet including the visor. Also, **aventail.** [< Old French *ventaille* (originally) air hole in a helmet < *vent* wind, air < Latin *ventus;* see etym. under **vent**[1]]

**ven|ter**[1] (ven′tər), *n.* **1a** the abdomen; belly. **b** the part of lower forms of animal life corresponding to the belly in function or position. **2a** the belly of a bone. **b** *Obsolete.* the thick, fleshy part of a muscle. **3** *Obsolete.* the abdomen, thorax, and head. **4** *Law.* one of two or more wives as sources of one's offspring. **5a** the womb as a source of one's birth or origin. **b** *Obsolete.* a mother in relation to her children. [< Latin *venter, ventris* womb, paunch]

**vent|er**[2] (ven′tər), *n.* **1** a person or thing that vents or gives vent. **2** a person who utters or publishes a statement or doctrine, especially such a statement of an erroneous or otherwise objectionable nature.

**ven|ti|duct** (ven′tə dukt), *n.* a duct or passage bringing cool or fresh air into an apartment or place. [< Latin *ventus* wind + English *duct*]

**ven|ti|la|ble** (ven′tə lə bəl), *adj.* that can be ventilated: *An enclosed bathroom must be made ventilable through a duct and fan to the outside of a building.*

**ven|ti|late** (ven′tə lāt), *v.t.,* **-lat|ed, -lat|ing. 1** to change the air in: *We ventilate a room by opening windows.* **2** to expose to fresh air so as to keep in, or restore to, good condition: *to ventilate bedding.* **3** to purify by fresh air: *The lungs ventilate the blood.* **4** (of air) to blow on, pass over, or circulate through so as to purify or freshen. **5** *Figurative.* to make known publicly; discuss openly: *He was glad of an opportunity of ventilating his grievance* (W. H. Hudson). **6** to furnish with a vent or opening for the escape of air or gas. **7** *Rare.* to fan or winnow (corn or other grain).
[< Latin *ventilāre* (with English *-ate*[1]) to fan, agitate by air < *ventus* wind]

**ven|ti|la|tion** (ven′tə lā′shən), *n.* **1** a change of air; act or process of supplying with fresh air: *The amount of air required for proper ventilation varies, depending on ... the number of people* (Merl Baker). SYN: aeration. **2** a means of supplying fresh air: *Ventilation is required in modern house plans.* **3** a purifying by fresh air: *Air conditioning systems supply regulated temperatures and ventilation.* **4** *Figurative.* an open discussion in public: *The ventilation of one's family affairs is in poor taste.*

**ven|ti|la|tive** (ven′tə lā′tiv), *adj.* of or having to do with ventilation; producing or promoting ventilation.

---

**Pronunciation Key:** hat, **ā**ge, c**ã**re, f**ä**r; let, **ē**qual, t**ė**rm; it, **ī**ce; h**o**t, **ō**pen, **ô**rder; **oi**l, **ou**t; cup, p**u̇**t, r**ü**le; **ch**ild; lo**ng**; **th**in; **ᴛʜ**en; **zh**, measure; **ə** represents **a** in about, **e** in taken, **i** in pencil, **o** in lemon, **u** in circus.

**ven|ti|la|tor** (ven′tə lā′tər), *n.* **1** any apparatus or means, such as an opening, shaft, air conditioner, or fan, for changing or improving the air in a room, airplane, or any enclosed space: *A kitchen ventilator does more to make life comfortable than any other single piece of household equipment* (New Yorker). **2** a person or thing charged with ventilating some enclosure, especially a bee that fans air into a hive with its wings. **3** *Figurative.* a person or thing that brings some matter to public notice.

**ven|ti|la|to|ry** (ven′tə lə tôr′ē, -tōr′-), *adj.* **1** of or having to do with ventilation; provided with ventilation. **2** of or having to do with oxygenation of the blood in the lungs: *Cigarette smoking is associated with a reduction in ventilatory function* (Science News Letter).

**vent|less** (vent′lis), *adj.* having no vent or outlet.

**Ven|tôse** (väɴ tōz′), *n.* the sixth month of the French revolutionary calendar, extending from February 19th to March 20th. [< French *Ventôse,* learned borrowing from Latin *ventōsus* windy < *ventus* wind]

**ven|trad** (ven′trad), *adv. Anatomy.* toward the belly or ventral side of the body. [< Latin *venter, ventris* belly + *ad* toward]

**ven|tral** (ven′trəl), *adj., n.* —*adj.* **1** of, having to do with, or situated in or on the abdomen; abdominal: *To ... shake ... with a silent, ventral laughter* (George Eliot). **2** of, having to do with, or situated on or near the surface or part opposite the back. **3** *Botany.* of or belonging to the anterior or lower surface, as of a carpel.
—*n.* **1** = ventral fin. **2** *Entomology.* an abdominal segment. [< Late Latin *ventrālis* < Latin *venter, ventris* belly, paunch]

**ventral fin,** = pelvic fin.

**ven|tral|ly** (ven′trə lē), *adv.* in a ventral position or direction; on or toward the abdomen.

**ven|tri|cle** (ven′trə kəl), *n.* **1** either of the two lower chambers of the heart that receive blood from the auricles and force it into the arteries. See diagram under **heart. 2** any one of a series of connecting cavities in the brain: *These* [*ideas*] *are begot in the ventricle of memory* (Shakespeare). **3** any hollow organ or cavity in an animal body, now chiefly confined to a space between the true and false vocal cords. [< Latin *ventriculus* (diminutive) < *venter, ventris* belly]

**ven|tri|cose** (ven′trə kōs), *adj.* **1** *Biology.* swelling out in the middle, or on one side; protuberant. **2** having an unusually or abnormally large abdomen; big-bellied. [< New Latin *ventricosus* < Latin *venter, ventris* belly]

**ven|tri|cous** (ven′trə kəs), *adj.* = ventricose.

**ven|tric|u|lar** (ven trik′yə lər), *adj.* **1** of, having to do with, or like a ventricle. **2** having to do with the stomach; abdominal; ventral. **3** swelling out; distended.

**ventricular fibrillation,** a heart condition in which the ventricle muscles quiver spasmodically and are unable to pump blood regularly.

**ven|tric|u|log|ra|phy** (ven trik′yə log′rə fē), *n.* a method of examining the ventricles of the head with X rays after removing the cerebral fluid and replacing it with air or an opaque medium. [< Latin *ventriculus* (see etym. under **ventricle**) + English *-graphy*]

**ven|tric|u|lus** (ven trik′yə ləs), *n., pl.* **-li** (-lī). **1a** the stomach or digestive cavity of certain insects, fish, and reptiles. **b** the gizzard in birds. **2** the body cavity of a sponge. [< Latin *ventriculus;* see etym. under **ventricle**]

**ven|tri|lo|qui|al** (ven′trə lō′kwē əl), *adj.* **1** having to do with ventriloquism. **2** using ventriloquism. —**ven′tri|lo′qui|al|ly,** *adv.*

**ven|tril|o|quism** (ven tril′ə kwiz əm), *n.* the art or practice of speaking or uttering sounds with the lips still so that the voice seems to come from some source other than the speaker. [< *ventriloquy* (< Medieval Latin *ventriloquium* < Latin *ventriloquus* ventriloquist < *venter, ventris* belly + *loquī* speak) + English *-ism*]

**ven|tril|o|quist** (ven tril′ə kwist), *n.* a person skilled in ventriloquism, especially a performer who uses a puppet with whom he pretends to carry on a conversation.

**ven|tril|o|quis|tic** (ven tril′ə kwis′tik), *adj.* **1** of or having to do with ventriloquism. **2** using or practicing ventriloquism.

**ven|tril|o|quize** (ven tril′ə kwīz), *v.i., v.t.,* **-quized, -quiz|ing.** to speak or utter as a ventriloquist.

**ven|tril|o|quous** (ven tril′ə kwəs), *adj.* of, having to do with, resembling, or using ventriloquism.

**ven|tril|o|quy** (ven tril′ə kwē), *n.* = ventriloquism.

**ven|tro|dor|sal** (ven′trō dôr′səl), *adj.* = dorsoventral.

**ven|tro|lat|er|al** (ven′trō lat′ər əl), *adj. Anatomy.* of, having to do with, or affecting both ventral and lateral parts: *the ventrolateral area of the thalamus.*

**ven|tro|me|di|al** (ven′trō mē′dē əl), *adj. Anatomy.* of, having to do with, or affecting both ventral and medial parts: *the ventromedial region of the hypothalamus.*

**ven|ture** (ven′chər), *n., v.,* **-tured, -tur|ing.** —*n.* **1** a risky, daring, or dangerous undertaking: *His courage was equal to any venture.* **SYN:** enterprise, adventure, risk. **2** a speculation to make money: *A lucky venture in oil stock has made him a rich man.* **3** something risked, especially in a commercial enterprise or speculation; stake: *to lose an entire venture on the stock market.* **4** *Obsolete.* the chance or risk of incurring harm or loss; danger; peril.
—*v.i.* **1** to dare to come, go, or proceed: *They ventured out on the thin ice and fell through.* **SYN:** See syn. under **dare. 2** to attempt or undertake something difficult or dangerous without assurance of success: *to venture on an arctic expedition.* **3** to guess (at): *to venture at a reason.*
—*v.t.* **1** to expose to risk or danger: *Men venture their lives in space exploration.* **2** to run or take the risk of (something dangerous or harmful): *to venture battle in the night, to venture a jail sentence by a crusade against a law.* **3** to dare to say or make: *to venture a sly joke at matrimony. She ventured an objection.* **4** to dare when embarrassment, rejection, or rebuff might follow: *No one ventured to interrupt the speaker.* **5** *Archaic.* to take the risk of sending: *to venture goods to a distant country.*
**at a venture,** at random; by chance: *'Tis possible that I may several times by guess, or at a venture, hit upon it* (William Whiston).
[short for *aventure,* an earlier form of *adventure*]

**venture capital,** = risk capital.

**ven|tur|er** (ven′chər ər), *n.* **1** a person who ventures; adventurer. **2** a commercial speculator or trader.

**ven|ture|some** (ven′chər səm), *adj.* **1** inclined to take risks; rash; daring: *Venturesome boys hung from rooftops* (Time). **SYN:** adventurous, bold. **2** of the nature of or involving risk; risky; hazardous: *A trip to the moon is a venturesome journey.* —**ven′ture|some|ly,** *adv.* —**ven′ture|some|ness,** *n.*

***ven|tu|ri** (ven tůr′ē), *n.,* or **venturi tube,** a short, narrow section of a tube in a carburetor or similar device, which lowers the pressure and increases the speed of the air or liquid flowing through it. [< Giovanni B. *Venturi,* 1746-1822, an Italian physicist]

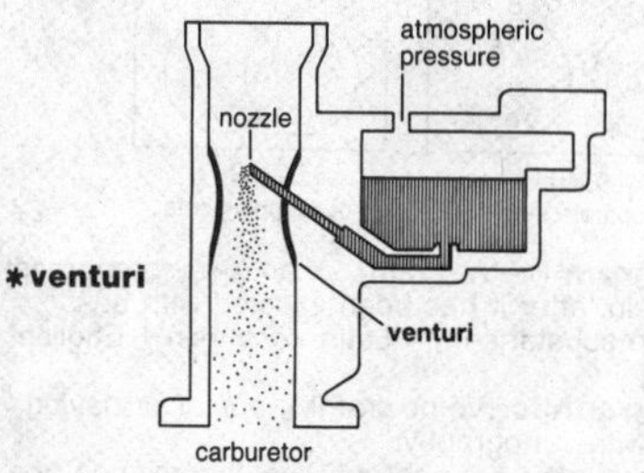


***venturi**

**ven|tur|ous** (ven′chər əs), *adj.* **1** bold; daring; adventurous; rash. **2** risky; dangerous. —**ven′tur|ous|ly,** *adv.* —**ven′tur|ous|ness,** *n.*

**ven|ue** (ven′yü), *n.* **1** *Law.* **a** the place or neighborhood of a crime or cause of action. **b** the place where the jury is summoned and the case tried: *The prisoner's lawyer asked for a change of venue because the county was so prejudiced against the prisoner.* **c** the statement on an indictment or complaint designating the place for trial. **d** the statement indicating where and before whom an affidavit was sworn. **2** the scene of a real or supposed action or event, especially in a novel or other literary work.
[< Old French *venue* coming < *venir* to come < Latin *venīre* ]

**ven|u|lar** (ven′yə lər), *adj.* marked with veins; veined. [< *venul*(e) + *-ar*]

**ven|ule** (ven′yül), *n.* **1** a small vein, especially one that begins at the capillaries and connects them with the larger veins. **2** a small vein in the wing of an insect; nervule. [< Latin *vēnula* (diminutive) < *vēna* vein. See etym. of doublet **veinule.**]

**ven|u|lose** (ven′yə lōs), *adj.* full of venules.

**ven|u|lous** (ven′yə ləs), *adj.* = venulose.

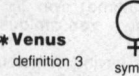

***Venus** definition 3

symbol

***Ve|nus** (vē′nəs), *n.* **1** the Roman goddess of love and beauty. The Greeks called her Aphrodite. **2** a very beautiful woman: *the Venus of the village.* **3** the sixth largest planet in the solar system and the second in distance from the sun. Venus is the brightest planet in the solar system and the one that comes closest to the earth. See diagram under **solar system. 4** any one of a group of bivalve mollusks having a thick, ridged shell. **5** a style of sans-serif printing type. **6** *Alchemy.* copper.

**Ve|nus|berg** (vē′nəs bėrg; *German* vā′nůs berk), *n.* in the legends of Tannhäuser, the site of the caverns where Venus held her pagan court. [< *Venusberg,* a mountain in central Germany, between Eisenach and Gotha]

**Ve|nus'-hair** (vē′nəs hãr′), *n.* = Venus's-hair.

**Ve|nu|si|an** (və nü′sē ən, -nyü′-), *adj., n.* —*adj.* of or having to do with the planet Venus: *The little that astronomers can see suggests that the Venusian atmosphere has neither oxygen nor water* (Time).
—*n.* a supposed inhabitant of Venus: *In the course of a month the moon would be observed by a Venusian to oscillate to either side of the earth* (Wasley S. Krogdahl).

**Ve|nus's-flow|er-bas|ket** (vē′nə siz flou′ər bas′kit, -bäs′-), *n.* a glass sponge found in the East Indies and along the eastern coast of Asia, having delicate, lacelike spicules.

**Ve|nus's-fly|trap** (vē′nə siz flī′trap′), *n.* a plant of the coasts of the Carolinas, whose hairy leaves have two lobes at the end that fold together to trap and ingest insects. It belongs to the same family as the sundew. See picture under **carnivorous.** [American English < *Venus*]

**Ve|nus's-gir|dle** (vē′nə siz gėr′dəl), *n.* a long, transparent, ribbonlike ctenophore that lives in tropical seas.

**Ve|nus's-hair** (vē′nə siz hãr′), *n.* a maidenhair fern with blackish stipes (frond petioles).

**Venus's-shoe** (vē′nə siz shü′), *n.* = lady's-slipper.

**Ve|nu|tian** (və nü′shən, -nyü′-), *adj., n.* = Venusian. [< *Venus;* patterned on *Martian*]

**ven|ville** (ven′vil), *n.* a special form of tenure in certain English parishes, by which the tenants enjoy certain privileges in the use of the forest. [origin uncertain]

**ver.,** **1** verse or verses. **2** versus.

**ve|ra|cious** (və rā′shəs), *adj.* **1** truthful: *The testimony of the two veracious and competent witnesses* (Dickens). **2** true: *veracious testimony.* [< Latin *vērāx, -ācis* (with English *-ous*) < *vērus* true] —**ve|ra′cious|ly,** *adv.* —**ve|ra′cious|ness,** *n.*

**ve|rac|i|ty** (və ras′ə tē), *n., pl.* **-ties. 1** truthfulness: *the unquestioned veracity of a judge. Any fool may write a most valuable book ... if he will only tell us what he heard and saw with veracity* (Thomas Gray). **2** truth: *Falsehoods and veracities are separated by so very thin a barrier* (William Stubbs). **3** correctness; accuracy: *to test the veracity of a scientific instrument. Narratives where historical veracity has no place* (Samuel Johnson). **SYN:** exactitude, precision. [< Medieval Latin *veracitas* < Latin *vērāx;* see etym. under **veracious**]

**ve|ran|da** or **ve|ran|dah** (və ran′də), *n.* a large porch along one or more sides of a house; piazza. [< Hindustani *varandā,* or < Portuguese *varanda* railing] —**ve|ran′da|like′,** *adj.*

**ve|ran|daed** or **ve|ran|dahed** (və ran′dəd), *adj.* furnished with a veranda or verandas: *We drove ... to register in the administration building, a verandaed cottage like all the other dwellings of the settlement* (Atlantic).

**ve|ra|tri|a** (və rā′trē ə, -rat′rē-), *n.* = veratrine.

**ve|rat|ric acid** (və rat′rik), a white crystalline acid present in the seeds of the sabadilla, and also produced by the decomposition of veratrine. *Formula:* $C_9H_{10}O_4$ [< Latin *vērātrum* hellebore]

**ve|rat|ri|din** (və rat′rə din), *n.* = veratridine.

**ve|rat|ri|dine** (və rat′rə dēn, -din), *n.* **1** an amorphous alkaloid present in the seeds of the sabadilla. *Formula:* $C_{36}H_{51}NO_{11}$ **2** = veratrine (def. 1).

**ver|a|trin** (ver′ə trin), *n.* = veratrine.

**ver|a|tri|na** (ver′ə trī′nə), *n.* = veratrine.

**ver|a|trine** (ver′ə trēn, -trin), *n.* **1** a poisonous mixture containing veratridine and other alkaloids extracted from the seeds of the sabadilla, used medicinally as an ointment, especially for the relief of rheumatism and neuralgia. **2** = veratridine (def. 1). Also, **veratria.** [< French *vératrine* < Latin *vērātrum* hellebore + French *-ine*[2]]

**ver|a|trize** (ver′ə trīz), *v.t.,* **-trized, -triz|ing.** to drug, poison, or treat with veratrine.

**ve|ra|trum** (və rā′trəm), *n.* any one of a group of plants of the lily family, especially the American hellebore, whose dried roots and stem are used in drugs, as for the treatment of hypertension and nausea. [< Latin *vērātrum* hellebore]

**verb** (vėrb), *n.* **1** a word that tells what is or what is done. *Do, eat, sit, be, go, think,* and *know* are verbs. A verb serves to connect a subject with a predicate. Verbs may be inflected for person, tense, voice, and mood. English verbs are classified as transitive or intransitive. *Abbr:* v. **2** the

part of speech or form class to which such words belong. [< Latin *verbum* (originally) word]
▶ **Verbs.** A verb that takes an object (or is used in the passive voice) is said to be transitive: *He washed the car. The car was washed quickly.* A verb that does not take an object is intransitive: *He slept soundly.* Many verbs in English are used both ways, usually with some distinction in meaning. Transitive: *He wrote two books.* Intransitive: *She cannot write.*

**ver|bal** (vėr′bəl), *adj., n., v.,* **-balled, -bal|ling.** —*adj.* **1** in words; of words: *A description is a verbal picture.* **2** expressed in spoken words; oral: *a verbal promise, a verbal message.* **3** having to do with or affecting words only, rather than things, realities, or context: *a verbal correction not affecting the idea in the sentence.* **4** word for word; literal: *a verbal translation from the French.* SYN: verbatim. **5a** having to do with a verb. Two common verbal endings are *-ed* and *-ing.* **b** derived from a verb: *a verbal adjective.* **c** resembling a verb in function or meaning.
—*n.* **1** a word, particularly a noun or adjective, derived from a verb. Gerunds and participles are verbals. **2** *Linguistics.* a word or group of words that functions as a verb. **3** *Especially British Slang.* an alleged admission of guilt by a defendant at the time of arrest: *I am very troubled by the danger that a man may be convicted on verbals, to use the slang, which he never uttered at all* (Lord Chief Justice Widgery).
—*v.t. Especially British Slang.* to induce or cause to make an admission of guilt at the time of arrest: *He said ... that he had been verballed before by the police and that on this occasion he would on no account make any statement* (London Times).
[< Latin *verbālis* < *verbum;* see etym. under **verb**]
▶ See **oral** for usage note.

**verbal auxiliary,** = auxiliary verb.

**ver|bal|ism** (vėr′bə liz əm), *n.* **1** a verbal expression, word or phrase. **2** too much attention to mere words. SYN: literalism. **3** a stock phrase or formula in words with little meaning.

**ver|bal|ist** (vėr′bə list), *n.* **1** a person who is skilled in the use or choice of words. **2** a person who pays too much attention to mere words.

**ver|bal|is|tic** (vėr′bə lis′tik), *adj.* of or having to do with verbalists; characterized by verbalism or verbalisms. —**ver′bal|is′ti|cal|ly,** *adv.*

**ver|bal|i|za|tion** (vėr′bə lə zā′shən), *n.* **1** expression in words: *Language can best be thought of as a systematized code of signals involving verbalization* (London Times). **2** the use of too many words. SYN: verbosity, verboseness, verbiage, wordiness. **3** the act of changing to a verb.

**ver|bal|ize** (vėr′bə līz), *v.,* **-ized, -iz|ing.** —*v.t.* **1** to express in words: *New subjects [who were] shown these pictures usually found them helpful in clarifying their feelings and verbalizing their experiences* (Scientific American). **2** *Grammar.* to change (a noun or other word usually functioning as another part of speech) into a verb.
—*v.i.* to use too many words; be wordy. —**ver′bal|iz′er,** *n.*

**ver|bal|ly** (vėr′bə lē), *adv.* **1** in words: *to explain verbally.* **2** in spoken words; orally: *a contract verbally agreed upon. The boy who was deaf and dumb could not reply verbally but used signs.* **3** word for word: *to translate French verbally. The child reported the conversation verbally.* **4** in regard to words only: *verbally intelligible.* **5** as a verb; having the function of a verb: *Breast is used verbally in "The boat breasts the wave."*

**verbal noun, 1** a noun derived from a verb. **2** an infinitive or gerund functioning as a noun but retaining such characteristics of a verb as being modified by adverbs and taking objects. *Example: To dance* (infinitive) gracefully is fun. *Dancing* (gerund) a polka can be strenuous.
▶ See **gerund** for usage note.

**ver|ba|tim** (vėr bā′tim), *adv., adj., n.* —*adv.* word for word; in exactly the same words: *His speech was printed verbatim in the newspaper.* SYN: literally, exactly.
—*adj.* **1** corresponding with or following an original, word for word: *The newspaper gave a verbatim report of the President's speech.* **2** of a person who writes or repeats an original, word for word: *verbatim reporters in the Turkish Assembly* (Manchester Guardian).
—*n.* a full or word-for-word report, especially of a speech: *a court reporter taking down a verbatim.* [< Medieval Latin *verbatim* < Latin *verbum* word]

**ver|ba|tim et lit|te|ra|tim** (vėr bā′tim et lit′ə rā′tim), *Latin.* word for word and letter for letter.

**ver|be|na** (vər bē′nə), *n.* any one of certain low-growing garden plants with elongated or flattened spikes of flowers of various colors; vervain. [< Latin *verbēna* leafy branch. See etym. of doublet **vervain.**]

**ver|be|na|ceous** (vėr′bə nā′shəs), *adj.* belonging to the verbena family of plants. [< New Latin *Verbenaceae* the family name (< *Verbena* the genus < Latin *verbēna;* see etym. under **verbena**) + English *-ous*]

**verbena family,** a group of dicotyledonous trees, shrubs, and herbs of tropical or subtropical regions, having characteristics very similar to those of the mint family. The family includes the verbena, lantana, and teak.

**ver|bi|age** (vėr′bē ij), *n.* the use of too many words; abundance of useless words or words hard to understand: *a contract full of legal verbiage.* SYN: prolixity, diffuseness. [< French *verbiage* < Middle French *verbier* to chatter < *verbe* word < Latin *verbum*]

**ver|bi|cide**[1] (vėr′bə sīd), *n.* the perversion of a word from its proper meaning: *Oliver Wendell Holmes referred to punning as verbicide.* [< Latin *verbum* word + English *-cide*[2]]

**ver|bi|cide**[2] (vėr′bə sīd), *n.* a person who perverts a word from its proper meaning: *a habitual verbicide.* [< Latin *verbum* word + English *-cide*[1]]

**ver|bid** (vėr′bid), *n. Grammar, Linguistics.* verbal.

**ver|bi|fy** (vėr′bə fī), *v.t.,* **-fied, -fy|ing.** to convert (a noun or other word usually functioning as another part of speech) into a verb; use as a verb; verbalize.

**ver|big|er|a|tion** (vėr bij′ə rā′shən), *n. Psychology, Medicine.* the frequent or obsessive repetition of the same word or phrase in a seemingly meaningless fashion: *The law of causation extends to the most incoherent acts and even verbigerations in insanity* (Sigmund Freud). [< Latin *verbigerātus* (past participle of *verbigerāre* to talk, chat < *verbum* word + *gerere* carry on) + English *-ion*]

**verb|less** (vėrb′lis), *adj.* having no verb.

**ver|bose** (vėr bōs′), *adj.* using too many words; wordy: *a verbose and confused writer, a style verbose to the brink of tediousness.* SYN: See syn. under **wordy.** [< Latin *verbōsus* < *verbum* word] —**ver|bose′ly,** *adv.* —**ver|bose′ness,** *n.*

**ver|bos|i|ty** (vėr bos′ə tē), *n., pl.* **-ties. 1** the use of too many words; wordiness: *verbosity of writing.* **2** an instance of this: *A ... rhetorician [Gladstone], inebriated with the exuberance of his own verbosity* (Benjamin Disraeli).

**ver|bo|ten** (vėr bō′tən; *German* fer bō′tən), *adj.* absolutely forbidden by authority; prohibited: *The Department of Commerce has made public a list of seven hundred previously verboten items that American exporters may now ship to the Soviet bloc of nations without a special license* (New Yorker). [< German *verboten*]

**verb. sap., verbum sap.,** or **verbum sat.,** verbum sapienti sat est.

**ver|bum sa|pi|en|ti sat est** (vėr′bəm sap′ē en′tī sat est), *Latin.* a word to the wise is sufficient.

**ver|bum sat sa|pi|en|ti** (vėr′bəm sat sap′ē en′tī), = verbum sapienti sat est.

**ver|dan|cy** (vėr′dən sē), *n., pl.* **-cies. 1** greenness: *the verdancy of the forest.* **2** *Figurative.* inexperience: *the verdancy of youth.*

**Ver|dan|de** or **Ver|dan|di** (vėr dan′dē), *n. Norse Mythology.* one of the three Norns or goddesses of fate, an elf representing the present.

**ver|dant** (vėr′dənt), *adj.* **1** green: *verdant hills. The fields are covered with verdant grass.* **2** *Figurative.* inexperienced: *verdant newcomers.* [< *verd*(ure) + *-ant*] —**ver′dant|ly,** *adv.*

**verd an|tique** or **verde antique** (vėrd′an tēk′), **1** an ornamental variety of marble consisting chiefly of serpentine mixed with calcite and dolomite, used especially by the Romans for interior decoration; serpentine marble. **2** a green porphyry. **3** = verdigris (def. 1). [< obsolete French *verd antique* < Old French *verd* (see etym. under **verdure**), *antique* antique]

**ver|der|er** or **ver|der|or** (vėr′dər ər), *n.* (in English law) a judicial officer responsible for enforcing the law in royal forests and directing their maintenance. [< Anglo-French *verderer,* alteration of *verder* < Late Latin *viridārius* < Latin *viridis* green < *virēre* be green, verdant]

**Ver|di|an** (vār′dē ən), *adj., n.* —*adj.* of, having to do with, or characteristic of Giuseppe Verdi (1813-1901), Italian composer, or his operas: *A sure command of the Italian text and a strong feeling for Verdian line* (Saturday Review).
—*n.* an admirer or lover of Verdi's operas.

**ver|dict** (vėr′dikt), *n.* **1** the decision of a jury: *The jury returned a verdict of "Not Guilty."* **2** *Figurative.* **a** a judgment given by some body or authority acting as or like a jury: *Might we not render some such verdict as this?—'Worthy of death but not unworthy of love'* (Hawthorne). **b** any decision or judgment: *the verdict of history, the verdict of the public.* [alteration (influenced by Medieval Latin *veredictum*) of Middle English *verdit* < Anglo-French < Old French *ver* true (< Latin *vērus*) + *dit,* past participle of *dire* to speak < Latin *dīcere*]

**ver|di|gris** (vėr′də grēs, -gris), *n.* **1** a green or bluish coating, usually of a carbonate of copper, that forms on brass, copper, or bronze when exposed to the air for long periods of time. **2** a green or bluish-green poisonous compound obtained by the action of acetic acid on thin plates of copper, used as a pigment, in dyeing, and in insecticides; basic acetate of copper. **3** *Chemistry.* a bluish-green poisonous compound used especially in making synthetic rubber and textiles; normal acetate of copper. *Formula:* $C_4H_6CuO_4 \cdot H_2O$ [< Old French *vert de Grece* (literally) green of Greece; confused with Old French *gris* gray]

**ver|di|grised** (vėr′də grēst, -grist), *adj.* coated with verdigris: *A forlorn, verdigrised statue of Dante ... will overlook a music and art center rivaling any in the world* (Newsweek).

**ver|din** (vėr′dən), *n.* a small, yellow-headed titmouse of Mexico and the southwestern United States; goldtit. [American English < French *verdin* the yellowhammer, perhaps < Old French *verd* green < Latin *viridis* < *virēre* be green]

**ver|di|ter** (vėr′də tər), *n.* **1** one of two pigments usually obtained by grinding azurite (blue verditer) or malachite (green verditer), and consisting of basic carbonate of copper; bice. **2** *Obsolete.* verdigris. [< Old French *verd de terre* (literally) green of earth < Latin *viridis* green and *terra* land]

**ver|dure** (vėr′jər), *n.* **1** fresh greenness. **2** a fresh growth of green grass, plants, or leaves. **3** *Figurative.* a fresh or flourishing state or condition; vigor: *the verdure of youth.* [< Old French *verdure* < *verd* green < Latin *viridis* < *virēre* be green, verdant]

**ver|dured** (vėr′jərd), *adj.* covered with verdure or green vegetation; verdant.

**ver|dure|less** (vėr′jər lis), *adj.* lacking vegetation; bleak; bare.

**ver|dur|ous** (vėr′jər əs), *adj.* **1a** rich and plentiful; flourishing and green. **b** covered with rich, green vegetation: *verdurous vegetation.* **2a** of or having to do with verdure or green vegetation. **b** *Figurative.* consisting of verdure; fresh. —**ver′dur|ous|ness,** *n.*

**Ver|ein** (fer īn′), *n. German.* society; association; club.

**Ve|rel** (və rel′), *n. Trademark.* an acrylic fiber resembling wool.

**verge**[1] (vėrj), *n., v.,* **verged, verg|ing.** —*n.* **1** the point at which something begins or happens; edge; rim; brink: *The country is on the verge of civil war. His business if on the verge of ruin.* **2** a limiting edge, margin, or bound of something; border: *the verge of a cliff,* (*Figurative.*) *the verge of reason and propriety.* (*Figurative.*) *Give us the eyes to see Over the verge of the sundown The beauty that is to be* (Bliss Carman). **3a** a belt or strip at the edge of something: *verges of grassy fringes.* **b** the space within a boundary or limiting border: (*Figurative.*) *a little verge for religious contemplation.* **4a** a rod or staff carried as an emblem of authority: *the Bishops's gold verge.* **b** *Obsolete.* a rod or wand held by a new tenant or vassal swearing loyalty to the lord of a manor. **5** (in English history) the area extending twelve miles around the royal court, subject to the jurisdiction of the Lord High Steward. **6** *Architecture.* **a** that part of a sloping roof which projects over the gable. **b** the shaft of a column. **7** the lever or spindle in the escapement of a watch having pallets on the end that lock and release the scape wheel. **8** *U.S.* the part of a linotype machine carrying the pawls by which the matrices are released.
—*v.i.* to be on the verge; be on the border; border (on): *Fifth Avenue verges on Central Park.* (*Figurative.*) *His talk was so poorly prepared that it verged on the ridiculous.* (*Figurative.*) *Your generosity must have verged on extravagance* (Charlotte Brontë).
—*v.t.* to pass along the border or edge of; skirt.
[< Old French *verge* < Latin *virga* staff. See etym. of doublet **virga.**]

**verge**[2] (vėrj), *v.i.,* **verged, verg|ing.** to tend; incline: *She was plump, verging toward fatness.* [< Latin *vergere*]

**ver|ger** (vėr′jər), *n.* **1** a person who takes care of a church; sexton. **2** an official who carries a rod, staff, or similar symbol of office before the dignitaries of a cathedral, church, or university. [< Middle French *verger* < *verge;* see etym. under **verge**[1]]

**ver|ger|ship** (vėr′jər ship), *n.* the position, charge, or office of a verger.

**Ver|gil|i|an** (vėr jil′ē ən), *adj.* = Virgilian.

**ver|glas** (ver glä′), *n.* a hard thin surface of ice over snow: *Verglas ... is formed by precisely the*

**Pronunciation Key:** hat, āge, cãre, fär; let, ēqual, tėrm; it, īce; hot, ōpen, ôrder; oil, out; cup, pu̇t, rüle; child; long; thin; ᴛʜen; zh, measure; ə represents **a** in about, **e** in taken, **i** in pencil, **o** in lemon, **u** in circus.

*right heaviness of rain falling onto a good bed of snow under precisely the right temperature* (Peter Gzowski). [< French *verglas* < Old French *verre-glaz* < *verre* glass + *glaz* ice]

**ve|rid|i|cal** (və rid′ə kəl), *adj.* telling the truth; truthful; veracious: *to convert Homer into a veridical historian.* [< Latin *vēridicus* (< *vērum* truth + *dīcere* to speak) + English *-al*¹] —**ve|rid′i-cal|ly**, *adv.*

**veridical hallucination**, a hallucination coincident with, corresponding to, or representing real events or persons: *Veridical hallucinations ... do, in fact, coincide with some crisis in the life of the person whose image is seen* (Frederic W. H. Myers).

**ve|rid|i|cal|i|ty** (və rid′ə kal′ə tē), *n.* truthfulness; veracity.

**ver|i|est** (ver′ē ist), *adj.* utmost: *the veriest nonsense.* **SYN**: uttermost.

**ver|i|fi|a|bil|i|ty** (ver′ə fī′ə bil′ə tē), *n.* the quality of being verifiable: *The honest moralizer labels his statements personal assertions, and he renounces any claim to verifiability* (James B. McMillan).

**ver|i|fi|a|ble** (ver′ə fī′ə bəl), *adj.* that can be checked or tested and proved to be true. —**ver′-i|fi′a|ble|ness**, *n.*

**ver|i|fi|a|bly** (ver′ə fī′ə blē), *adv.* in a verifiable way; so as to be capable of proof.

**ver|i|fi|ca|tion** (ver′ə fə kā′shən), *n.* **1** proof by evidence or testimony: *verification of the facts.* **SYN**: confirmation. **2** a demonstration of truth or correctness by facts or circumstances: *to await the verification of time.* **SYN**: confirmation. **3** *Law.* an affidavit added to testimony or a statement by the pleading party declaring that his allegations are true.

**ver|i|fi|er** (ver′ə fī′ər), *n.* a person or thing that verifies.

**ver|i|fy** (ver′ə fī), *v.t.*, **-fied, -fy|ing.** **1** to prove (something) to be true; confirm: *to verify a theory with examples. The driver's report of the accident was verified by two women who had seen it happen.* **SYN**: substantiate, corroborate, authenticate. **2** to find out the truth of; test the correctness of; check for accuracy; make sure of: *You can verify the spelling of a word by looking in a dictionary.* **3** *Law.* **a** to testify or affirm to be true, formally or upon oath. **b** to declare that one's allegations are true. [< Old French *verifier,* learned borrowing from Medieval Latin *verificare* < Latin *vērus* true + *facere* to make]

**ver|i|ly** (ver′ə lē), *adv. Archaic.* in truth; truly; really. [< *very* + *-ly*¹]

**ver|i|sim|i|lar** (ver′ə sim′ə lər), *adj.* appearing true or real; probable. **SYN**: likely. [< Latin *vērisimilis* (see etym. under **verisimilitude**) + English *-ar;* probably patterned on *similar*] —**ver′i-sim′i|lar|ly**, *adv.*

**ver|i|si|mil|i|tude** (ver′ə sə mil′ə tüd, -tyüd), *n.* **1** an appearance of truth; resemblance to reality; closeness to fact; probability: *Stories must have verisimilitude to interest people.* **2** something having merely the appearance of truth: *They are, in truth, but shadows of fact—verisimilitudes, not verities* (Charles Lamb). [< Latin *vērisimilitūdō, -inis* < *vērisimilis* like truth < *vērus* true + *similis* like]

**ver|i|si|mil|i|tu|di|nous** (ver′ə sə mil′ə tü′də nəs, -tyü′-), *n.* having verisimilitude; verisimilar.

**ver|ism** (vir′iz əm), *n.* the literary or artistic style practiced or advocated by verists; rigid adherence to truth and reality in literature and art. [< Italian *verismo*]

**ver|is|mo** (vār ēs′mō, -ēz′-), *n.* **1** = verism. **2** the veristic style of Italian opera at the turn of the century: *"Cavalleria Rusticana" is the first flaring excitement of verismo, the style which sought to root Italian opera in everyday life* (London Times). [< Italian *verismo* < *vero* true + *-ismo* -ism]

**ver|ist** (vir′ist), *n., adj.* —*n.* a person who believes in or practices the rigid representation of truth and reality in literature or art, especially the use of everyday materials rather than the mythical, legendary, or heroic.

—*adj.* = veristic.

**ve|ris|tic** (və ris′tik), *adj.* of or having to do with verists or verism; rigidly adhering to truth and reality.

**ver|i|ta|ble** (ver′ə tə bəl), *adj.* **1** true, real, or actual: *veritable proof of honesty. The author himself, the veritable and only genuine author* (Arnold Bennett). **2** having all the qualities or attributes of the specified person or thing: *The salesman is a veritable fox.* **3** *Obsolete.* in accordance with the truth or fact, as statements. [< Anglo-French, Old French *veritable* < *verite* verity, learned borrowing from Latin *vēritās;* see etym. under **verity**] —**ver′i|ta|ble|ness**, *n.*

**ver|i|ta|bly** (ver′ə tə blē), *adv.* in truth; truly; really; actually.

**ver|i|tism** (ver′ə tiz əm), *n. U.S.* verism. —**ver′i-tist**, *n., adj.*

**ver|i|tis|tic** (ver′ə tis′tik), *adj.* = veristic.

**ver|i|ty** (ver′ə tē), *n., pl.* **-ties.** **1** truth: *denying the verity of my experiments* (Benjamin Franklin). *In sober verity I will confess a truth to thee* (Charles Lamb). **2** a true statement, fact, opinion, or doctrine; a truth: *Beliefs that were accepted as eternal verities* (James Henry Robinson). **3** = reality. [< Latin *vēritās* < *vērus* true]

**ver|juice** (vėr′jüs′), *n., adj.* —*n.* **1** an acid liquor made from the juice of crab apples, unripe grapes, or other sour fruits, formerly much used in cooking or for medicinal purposes. **2** *Figurative.* sourness, as of temper, expression, or remark.

—*adj.* = verjuiced.

[< Old French *verjus* < *verd* green (< Latin *viridis*) + *jus* juice < Latin *jūs, jūris*]

**ver|juiced** (vėr′jüst′), *adj.* of or having to do with verjuice; sour.

**ver|krampte** (fər krämp′tə), *n.* a member of the conservative faction of the National Party in South Africa favoring rigid policies toward black Africans. [< Afrikaans *verkrampte* (literally) cramped (one)]

**ver|lig|te** (fər liH′tə), *n.* a member of the liberal faction of the National Party in South Africa favoring moderate policies toward black Africans. [< Afrikaans *verligte* (literally) enlightened (one)]

**ver|meil** (vėr′məl), *n., adj.* —*n.* **1** silver, bronze, or copper coated with gilt. **2** the color vermilion.

—*adj.* **1** of or like vermeil: *vermeil knives and forks.* **2** of the color vermilion.

[< Old French *vermeil* < Latin *vermiculus* (diminutive) < *vermis* worm]

**ver|mi|an** (vėr′mē ən), *adj.* **1** belonging or having to do with a former primary division of the animal kingdom comprising wormlike forms. **2** = wormlike. [< New Latin *Vermes* (< Latin *vermis* worm) + English *-ian*]

**ver|mi|cel|li** (vėr′mə sel′ē, -chel′-), *n.* a mixture of flour and water, shaped into long, slender, solid threads thinner than spaghetti. [< Italian *vermicelli* (literally) little worms, plural of *vermicello* (diminutive) < *verme* worm < Latin *vermis*]

**ver|mi|cid|al** (vėr′mə sī′dəl), *adj.* destroying worms; having the effect of a vermicide.

**ver|mi|cide** (vėr′mə sīd), *n.* any substance or drug that kills worms, especially parasitic intestinal worms. [< Latin *vermis* worm + English *-cide*¹]

**ver|mic|u|lar** (vėr mik′yə lər), *adj.* **1** of, having to do with, or characteristic of a worm or worms. **2** like a worm in nature, form, or method of movement. **3** like the wavy track of a worm. **4** marked with close, wavy lines. **5** = worm-eaten. [< Medieval Latin *vermicularis* < Latin *vermiculus* (diminutive) < *vermis* worm] —**ver|mic′u|lar|ly**, *adv.*

**ver|mic|u|late** (*adj.* vėr mik′yə lāt, -lit; *v.* vėr mik′yə lāt), *adj., v.,* **-lat|ed, -lat|ing.** —*adj.* **1** vermicular; sinuous: (*Figurative.*) *Subtile, idle, unwholesome, and, (as I may term them) vermiculate questions* (Francis Bacon). **2** having tortuous excavations as if eaten by worms.

—*v.t.* to ornament with winding and waving lines like the track of a worm.

—*v.i.* to become worm-eaten.

[< Latin *vermiculārī* (with English *-ate*¹) < *vermiculus* (diminutive) < *vermis* worm]

**ver|mic|u|la|tion** (vėr mik′yə lā′shən), *n.* **1** the fact or condition of being infested with or eaten by worms. **2** a marking or boring made by, or resembling the track of, a worm: *The face of the boards is ... eaten into innumerable vermiculations* (Thomas Hardy). **3** *Obsolete.* peristaltic movement.

**ver|mi|cule** (vėr′mə kyül), *n.* **1** a little worm. **2** a small wormlike creature or object. [< Latin *vermiculus* (diminutive) < *vermis* worm]

**ver|mic|u|lite** (vėr mik′yə līt), *n.* a mineral, hydrous micaceous silicate of aluminum, iron, and magnesium, occurring in small foliated scales. It is used as a filler in paint and concrete and as a soil conditioner and insulator. [American English < Latin *vermiculus* (diminutive) < *vermis* worm + *-ite*¹ (because of its appearance when heated by a blowpipe)]

**ver|mi|form** (vėr′mə fôrm), *adj.* shaped like a worm; long, thin, and more or less cylindrical. [< New Latin *vermiformis* < Latin *vermis* worm + *forma* form]

**vermiform appendix**, a slender tube, closed at one end, growing out of the large intestine in the lower right-hand part of the abdomen; appendix. Appendicitis is inflammation of the vermiform appendix.

**vermiform process**, *Anatomy.* **1** the median lobe of the cerebellum. **2** the vermiform appendix.

**ver|mi|fuge** (vėr′mə fyüj), *n., adj.* —*n.* a medicine to expel worms from the intestines.

—*adj.* causing the expulsion of worms from the intestines.

[< Latin *vermis* worm + *fugāre* cause to flee]

**ver|mil|ion** (vər mil′yən), *n., adj., v.* —*n.* **1** a bright red. **2a** a bright-red coloring matter consisting of mercuric sulfide; cinnabar. **b** any one of various other bright-red coloring matters.

—*adj.* bright-red; scarlet: *The black strokes of writing thereon looked like the twigs of a winter hedge against a vermilion sunset* (Thomas Hardy).

—*v.t.* to color or paint with vermilion: (*Figurative.*) *A blush vermilioned her face.*

[Middle English *vermeylion, vermilloun* < *vermeil* < Old French; see etym. under **vermeil**]

**vermilion flycatcher**, a flycatcher found from the southwestern United States to Argentina. The male has a vermilion crown, throat, and breast.

**ver|min** (vėr′mən), *n. pl. or sing.* **1** small animals that are troublesome or destructive. Fleas, lice, bedbugs, rats, and mice are vermin. **2** *British.* animals or birds that destroy game or poultry in game preserves. **3** *Figurative.* a very unpleasant and troublesome or vile person or persons. [< Anglo-French *vermin* < Vulgar Latin *vermīnum* < Latin *vermis* worm]

**ver|mi|nate** (vėr′mə nāt), *v.i.,* **-nat|ed, -nat|ing.** to breed vermin; become infested with parasitic vermin.

**ver|mi|na|tion** (vėr′mə nā′shən), *n.* **1** the breeding, growth, or production of vermin, especially parasitic vermin. **2** the condition of being infested with parasitic vermin.

**ver|min|i|cide** (vər min′ə sīd), *n.* a preparation for killing vermin: *During the summer months verminicide became a necessary item in the bazar* (Blackwood's Magazine).

**ver|min|ous** (vėr′mə nəs), *adj.* **1** infested with or full of vermin, especially parasitic vermin. **2** (of diseases) caused by, due to, or characterized by the presence of parasitic vermin or intestinal worms. **3** consisting of or having to do with vermin. **4** *Figurative.* like vermin; very unpleasant; vile. —**ver′min|ous|ly**, *adv.* —**ver′min|ous|ness**, *n.*

**ver|miv|o|rous** (vėr miv′ər əs), *adj.* eating worms; feeding on worms, as certain birds. [< Latin *vermis* worm + *vorāre* devour + English *-ous*]

**Ver|mont|er** (vər mon′tər), *n.* a native or inhabitant of the state of Vermont.

**Ver|mont|ese** (vər mon′tēz′, -tēs′), *n., pl.* **-ese,** *adj.* —*n.* = Vermonter.

—*adj.* of or belonging to Vermont: *Our Vermontese housewives are not a little vain of their knowledge in making homemade wines* (Ira Allen).

**ver|mouth** (vər müth′, vėr′müth), *n.* a white wine, either dry (pale yellow) or sweet (usually reddish-brown), flavored with wormwood or other herbs and used as a liqueur or in cocktails. [< French *vermouth* < German *Wermuth* wormwood]

**ver|na|cle** (vėr′ni kəl), *n.* = vernicle.

**ver|nac|u|lar** (vər nak′yə lər), *n., adj.* —*n.* **1** a native language; language used by the people of a certain country or place: *a sixteenth century Saxon of peasant and mining stock, handling a vernacular which has at no period been remarkable for refinement* (C. V. Wedgewood). *Turns of speech that showed they had been that instant translated from the vernacular* (Rudyard Kipling). **2a** everyday language; informal speech. **b** a vernacular word or idiom. **3** *Figurative.* the language of a particular profession, trade, or other group: *There are many strange words in the vernacular of lawyers.* **4** the common name of a plant or animal, not its scientific name, such as *black-eyed Susan* for *Rudbeckia serotina.*

—*adj.* **1** used by the people of a certain country or district; native: *English is our vernacular tongue.* **2** of or in the native language, rather than a literary or learned language. **3** of, having to do with, or forming part of the native language. **4** (of arts or features of these) native or peculiar to a certain country or locality: *the vernacular style of architecture.* **5** of or designating the common informal name given to a plant or animal. **6** *Obsolete.* (of a disease) endemic.

[< Latin *vernāculus* domestic, native (< *verna* home-born slave) + English *-ar*] —**ver|nac′u|lar-ly**, *adv.*

**ver|nac|u|lar|ism** (vər nak′yə lə riz′əm), *n.* **1** a vernacular word, idiom, or mode of expression. **2** the use of the vernacular.

**ver|nac|u|lar|ist** (vər nak′yə lər ist), *n.* a vernacular writer; person who writes in the language of the people or country: *There was ample material ... which in the hands of a vernacularist of genius could produce a play as striking as "Strife"* (Glasgow Herald).

**ver|nac|u|lar|i|za|tion** (vər nak′yə lər ə zā′shən), *n.* the action of making, or fact of being made, vernacular or native to a language: *Thousands of words ... on their first appearance, or revival, as candidates for vernacularization, must have met* *with repugnance* (Fitzedward Hall).

**ver|nac|u|lar|ize** (vər nak′yə lə rīz), *v.t.*, **-ized, -iz-ing.** to make vernacular; express in or translate into the vernacular: *The author undoubtedly felt under obligation to vernacularize his style* (Sidney Ditzion).

**ver|nal** (vėr′nəl), *adj.* **1a** of spring; having to do with or coming in spring: *a grass of vernal green, vernal flowers, vernal months.* **b** like spring; suggesting spring: *vernal rain.* **2** *Figurative.* youthful: *Everyone admired the young girl's vernal freshness.* [< Latin *vernālis* < *vernus* of spring < *vēr, vēris* spring] —**ver′nal|ly,** *adv.*

**Ver|nal** (vėr′nəl), *n. U.S.* a winter-hardy, wilt-resistant variety of alfalfa.

**vernal equinox,** the equinox that occurs about March 21.

**ver|nal|i|za|tion** (vėr′nə lə zā′shən), *n.* the act or process of vernalizing: *Vernalization consists of the transformation of winter cereals into spring varieties by chilling and soaking the seeds* (Laurence H. Snyder).

**ver|nal|ize** (vėr′nə līz), *v.t.*, **-ized, -iz|ing.** to cause (a plant) to bloom and bear fruit early by subjecting the seed or bulb to a very low temperature; jarovize.

**ver|na|tion** (vėr nā′shən), *n. Botany.* the arrangement or formation of the leaves of plants or fronds of ferns in the bud, with reference to their folding, coiling, and other such characteristics; foliation. [< New Latin *vernatio, -onis* < Latin *vernāre* bloom, renew foliage, as in spring < *vernus* of spring < *vēr, vēris* spring]

**Ver|ner's law** (vėr′nərz), a statement by the Danish linguist Karl Verner in 1877, explaining certain apparent exceptions to Grimm's law, by showing that the Germanic voiceless fricatives became voiced between voiced sounds unless the syllable preceding them bore the accent in Indo-European.

**ver|neuk** (ver nük′), *v.t.* (in South Africa) to cheat; humbug; swindle: *How Hendrich enjoyed verneuking the Boer* (Cape Monthly Magazine). [< Afrikaans *verneuk*]

**ver|ni|cle** (vėr′ni kəl), *n.* = veronica[1] (def. 2). Also, **vernacle.** [< Old French *vernicle,* variant of *veronicle, veronique* < Medieval Latin *Veronica;* see etym. under **veronica**[1]]

**ver|ni|cose** (vėr′nə kōs), *adj. Botany.* having a shiny surface as if freshly varnished. [< New Latin *vernicosus* < Medieval Latin *vernix* varnish]

*****ver|ni|er** (vėr′nē ər, -nir), *n., adj.* —*n.* **1** a small movable scale for measuring a fractional part of one of the divisions of the fixed scale of astronomical, surveying, or other mathematical instruments to which it is attached; vernier scale. **2** an auxiliary device used to obtain fine adjustments or measurements with another device or mechanism. **3** = vernier engine.

—*adj.* furnished with a vernier: *a vernier caliper, compass, or transit.*

[< Pierre *Vernier,* 1580-1637, a French mathematician]

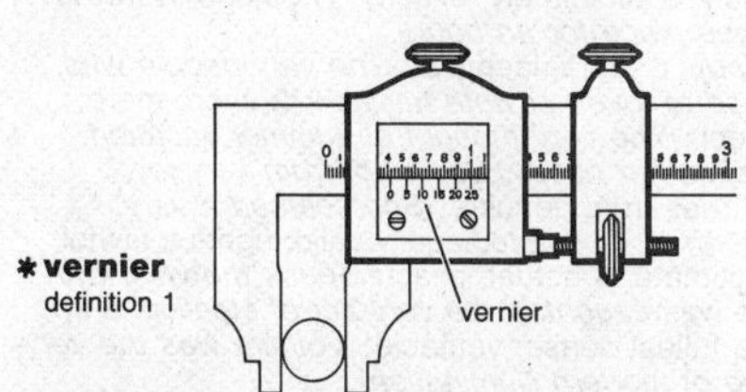


*** vernier**
definition 1

**vernier engine** or **rocket,** a small auxiliary rocket engine used for minute adjustments in velocity or trajectory, such as before a spacecraft soft-lands or docks: *On Jan. 9, 1968, following a 66-hour flight, a large retrorocket and three smaller vernier rockets slowed Surveyor VII from 6,000 to 3 mph* (William J. Cromie).

**vernier scale,** = vernier.

**ver|nis Mar|tin** (ver nē′ mȧr taɴ′), a clear, brilliant lacquer used in decoration, as of carriages, furniture, and fans. [< French *vernis Martin* (literally) Martin varnish < a family of French artificers in the 1700's]

**ver|nis|sage** (ver nē sȧzh′), *n.* **1** the opening or first showing of an art exhibition: *It was the first time in history that the Vatican had staged a one-man show, or that an artist had been thus honored by the presence of the Pope at his vernissage* (Newsweek). **2** = varnishing day. [< French *vernissage* < Old French *vernis;* see etym. under **varnish**]

**ver|nix** (vėr′niks), *n.* a fatty substance covering the skin of the fetus, to prevent its softening by the amniotic fluid. [< New Latin *vernix* (*caseosa*) (literally) cheesy varnish < Medieval Latin *vernix* varnish, and Latin *caseus* cheese]

**vernix ca|se|o|sa** (kā′sē ō′sə), = vernix.

**Ver|o|nal** (ver′ə nəl, -nôl), *n. Trademark.* barbital. [< German *Veronal* < *Verona,* Italy, where the inventor was going when he proposed the name of the product]

**Ver|o|nese** (ver′ə nēz′, -nēs′), *adj., n.* —*adj.* of or having to do with Verona, a city in northern Italy, or its people.

—*n.* a native or inhabitant of Verona.

**ve|ron|i|ca**[1] (və ron′ə kə), *n.* **1** any one of a group of plants of the figwort family; speedwell. **2a** Often, **Veronica.** the sudarium or handkerchief, preserved as a relic at St. Peter's, Rome, and alleged to be the original with which Saint Veronica wiped the face of Christ as He went to Calvary and on which the likeness of Christ's features remained. **b** a cloth or ornament bearing a representation of Christ's face. **c** the likeness or representation of Christ's face on such a cloth or ornament. [< Medieval Latin *Veronica,* the saint < Greek *Berenīkē*]

**ve|ron|i|ca**[2] (və ron′ə kə), *n.* a maneuver in bullfighting, in which the matador slowly turns with the cape without moving his feet as the bull rushes toward him: *Cordobano tried a series of curtailed and unsatisfactory veronicas, but the bull had excellent brakes and no acceleration whatever, which made the passes extremely dangerous* (Atlantic). [< Spanish *veronica* < *Veronica,* the saint]

**ver|ru|ca** (ve rü′kə), *n., pl.* **-cae** (-sē). **1** *Medicine.* a wart. **2** *Zoology.* a wartlike growth or prominence. [< Latin *verrūca* wart; excrescence on a stone]

**ver|ru|ca|no** (ver′ə kä′nō), *n. Geology.* a stratified conglomerate found in the Alps. [< Italian *verrucano* < Mount *Verruca,* near Pisa, Italy]

**ver|ru|cose** (ver′u̇ kōs), *adj.* **1** *Medicine.* covered with or full of verrucae or warts. **2** *Botany.* studded with small wartlike swellings or protuberances. [< Latin *verrūcosus* < *verrūca;* see etym. under **verruca**]

**ver|ru|cos|i|ty** (ver′u̇ kos′ə tē), *n., pl.* **-ties. 1** verrucose condition. **2** = wart.

**ver|ru|cous** (ver′u̇ kəs), *adj.* = verrucose.

**ver|ru|ga** (ve rü′gə), *n.* a Peruvian skin disease characterized by warty growths and often fatal, caused by a bacillus transmitted by the sand fly. [< Spanish *verruga peruviana* < Latin *verrūca;* see etym. under **verruca**]

**vers** (no period), *Trigonometry.* versed sine.

**ver|sal** (vėr′səl), *adj. Archaic.* varsal.

**ver|sant**[1] (vėr′sənt), *adj.* familiar; conversant; versed: *thoroughly versant in the law, a person versant with many languages.* [< Latin *versans, -antis,* present participle of *versāre, versāri* turn over (frequentative) < *vertere* to turn]

**ver|sant**[2] (vėr′sənt), *n.* **1** the slope, side, or descent of a mountain or mountain chain. **2** the area or region covered by a slope. [< French *versant,* noun use of present participle of Middle French *verser* to (make) turn < Latin *versāre* (frequentative) < *vertere* to turn]

**ver|sa|tile** (vėr′sə təl), *adj.* **1** able to do many things well: *Theodore Roosevelt was a versatile man; he was successful as a statesman, soldier, sportsman, explorer, and author.* **SYN:** many-sided. **2** *Zoology.* **a** turning forward or backward: *the versatile head of certain insects, the versatile toe of an owl.* **b** freely moving up and down or from side to side: *versatile antennae.* **3** *Botany.* attached at or near the middle so as to swing freely: *a versatile anther.* **4a** changeable; variable: *a versatile taste in reading.* **b** fickle; inconstant: *a versatile, impressionable woman.* [< Latin *versātilis* turning < *versāre* to turn (frequentative) < *vertere* to turn] —**ver′sa|tile|ly,** *adv.* —**ver′sa|tile|ness,** *n.*

**ver|sa|til|i|ty** (vėr′sə til′ə tē), *n., pl.* **-ties. 1** the ability to do many things well: *the versatility of your genius* (Frederick Marryat). **2** the quality of being changeable; fickleness. **3** diversity of nature or character; variety of application. **4** the ability to turn about as if on a pivot.

**vers de so|cié|té** (ver′ də sô syā tā′), light, graceful, entertaining poetry, such as to appeal to polite society. [< French *vers de société* (literally) society verse]

**verse**[1] (vėrs), *n., v.,* **versed, vers|ing.** —*n.* **1** poetry; lines of words usually with a regularly repeated accent and often with rhyme. Verse is sometimes distinguished from poetry by its lighter or more frivolous content and greater emphasis on structure. **2** a single line of poetry: *And he wrote for them wonderful verses that swept the land like flame* (Rudyard Kipling). *Abbr:* vs. **3** a group of lines or short portion in poetry or song; stanza: *Sing the first verse of "America."* **4** a type of poetry; meter: *blank verse, iambic verse.* **5** a short division of a chapter of the Bible. **6** a certain amount of poetry considered as a whole; poetry of a particular author: *the minstrel verse* (Scott).

—*v.i., v.t.* = versify.

**cap verses,** to follow one quotation with another in turn, especially as a game in which each verse (usually from the classics) begins with the same letter with which the last ended: *He thinks the Roman poets good for nothing but for boys to cap verses* (The English Theophrastus).

[partly Old English *vers;* partly < Old French *vers;* both < Latin *versus, -ūs* (originally) row, furrow < *vertere* turn around]

▶ **verse.** A full line or more of verse quoted in a paper should be lined off and written exactly as it is in the original. It should be indented from the left margin and, if very short, far enough not to leave a conspicuous blank at its right. No quotation marks are used.

**verse**[2] (vėrs), *v.t.,* **versed, vers|ing.** to make experienced or conversant; train; instruct: *to verse oneself in the classics.* [back formation < *versed*[1]]

**versed**[1] (vėrst), *adj.* experienced; practiced; skilled; conversant: *Our doctor is well versed in medicine.* **SYN:** proficient, acquainted. [< past participle of obsolete *verse* turn over (in the mind) < Latin *versāre* (frequentative) < *vertere* to turn]

**versed**[2] (vėrst), *adj. Mathematics.* turned; reversed. [< Latin *versus,* past participle of *vertere* to turn + English *-ed*[2]]

**verse drama,** a drama written in verse: *A new verse drama, "Hogan's Goat," ... proved to be an absorbing tragedy of Irish political life in late 19th-century Brooklyn* (John W. Gassner).

**versed sine,** *Trigonometry.* unity minus the cosine of an angle. *Abbr:* vers (no period).

**verse|let** (vėrs′lit), *n.* a little verse; small or trifling poem: *The pages of this time are crammed with squibs and verselets invaluable to later biographers of the illustrious obscure* (Punch). [< *verse*[1] + *-let*]

**verse|mak|er** (vėrs′mā′kər), *n.* a maker of verses; versifier.

**verse|man** (vėrs′mən), *n., pl.* **-men.** a man who makes or writes verses; versifier.

**Ver|sene** (vėr sēn′), *n. Trademark.* a white powdery compound, a chelate, used as a water softener and in the treatment of lead poisoning. *Formula:* $C_{10}H_{12}N_2Na_4O_8$

**vers|er** (vėr′sər), *n.* = versifier.

**vers|et** (vėr′sət), *n.* **1** a short verse of poetry or prose, especially one from the Bible, the Koran, or other such document: *Despite [his] dismissal of tradition, he must be aware that these versets ... are very much in a tradition* (Harper's). **2** a short piece of organ music suitable for use as an interlude or short prelude in a church service.

**ver|si|cle** (vėr′sə kəl), *n.* **1** a little verse. **2** one of a series of short sentences said or sung by the minister during services, to which the people make response. [< Latin *versiculus* (diminutive) < *versus;* see etym. under **verse**[1]]

**ver|si|col|or** (vėr′sə kul′ər), *adj.* = versicolored.

**ver|si|col|ored** (vėr′sə kul′ərd), *adj.* **1** changing or varying in color; iridescent. **2** of various colors; variegated. [< Latin *versus* turned, past participle of *vertere* to turn + English *colored*]

**ver|sic|u|lar** (vėr sik′yə lər), *adj.* of, having to do with, or consisting of versicles or verses, especially of the Bible. [< Latin *versiculus* (see etym. under **versicle**) + English *-ar*[1]]

**ver|si|fi|ca|tion** (vėr′sə fə kā′shən), *n.* **1a** the act or process of making verses. **b** the art or theory of making verses. **2** the form or style of poetry or verse; metrical structure. **3** an adaptation in verse of something: *His epigrams are versifications of his own jokes.*

**ver|si|fied** (vėr′sə fīd), *adj.* written or composed in verse.

**ver|si|fi|er** (vėr′sə fī′ər), *n.* **1** a person who makes verses; poet. **2** = poetaster.

**ver|si|fy** (vėr′sə fī), *v.,* **-fied, -fy|ing.** —*v.i.* to make or compose verses: *Miss Arton can versify handsomely enough, and bring things to a happy finish where the necessity of passion does not prohibit sense* (Atlantic).

—*v.t.* **1** to tell in verse; deal with in verse form. **2** to turn (prose) into poetry; rewrite in verse form.

[< Old French *versifier,* learned borrowing from Latin *versificāre* < *versus* (see etym. under **verse**[1]) + *facere* to make]

**ver|sine** or **ver|sin** (vėr′sīn), *n. Trigonometry.* versed sine.

**ver|sion** (vėr′zhən, -shən), *n.* **1** one particular statement, account, or description given by one person or source: *Each of the three girls gave her own version of the quarrel.* **2** a special form or variant of something: *a Scottish version of the Christmas tree.* **3** a translation from one language to another: *the King James version of the*

---

**Pronunciation Key:** hat, āge, cãre, fär; let, ēqual, tėrm; it, īce; hot, ōpen, ôrder; oil, out; cup, pu̇t, rüle; child; long; thin; ᴛʜen; zh, measure; ə represents **a** in about, **e** in taken, **i** in pencil, **o** in lemon, **u** in circus.

*Bible.* **4** *Obstetrics.* the manipulation or manual turning of the fetus in the uterus so as to facilitate delivery. **5** an abnormal turning of the uterus so that its axis is deflected without being bent upon itself. [< Latin *versiō, -ōnis* (originally) a turning < *vertere* to turn]

**ver|sion|al** (vėr′zhə nəl, -shə-), *adj.* of or having to do with a version.

**ver|si|tron** (vėr′sə tron), *n.* a device that can detect slight temperature changes at great distances: *He told how a versitron could be attached to a radar set, increasing the radiated power of the transmitter 1,000 times* (Science News Letter). [< Latin *versus,* past participle of *vertere* to turn + English *-tron,* as in *electron*]

**vers li|bre** (ver lē′brə), *French.* free verse; verse that follows no fixed metrical form: *His rhythms became more individual as he moved away from conventional metres toward a kind of patterned vers libre* (Louise Bogan).

**vers li|brist** (ver lē′brist), a person who writes free verse. [< French *vers-libriste*]

**ver|so** (vėr′sō), *n., pl.* **-sos** (-sōz). **1** *Printing.* the back of a leaf in a manuscript or printed book; the left-hand page of an open book. **2** the reverse side, as of a coin or medal. [< Latin *versō (foliō)* a turned (leaf), ablative neuter of *versus,* past participle of *vertere* to turn]

**verst** (vėrst), *n.* a Russian measure of length equal to 0.66288 miles or 1.067 kilometers. [< Russian *versta*]

**ver|sus** (vėr′səs), *prep.* **1** against: *The most exciting game was Harvard versus Yale.* **2** as the alternative of; as compared or contrasted with: *federal versus state control of education. Abbr:* v., ver., or vs. [< Latin *versus* turned toward, past participle of *vertere* to turn]

► **Versus** is used especially in legal documents and the like, to denote an action by one party against another: *the State versus Smith,* or in sports writing to signify two contestants: *Army versus Navy.*

**vert** (vėrt), *n.* **1** in English forest law: **a** everything bearing green leaves in a forest. **b** the right to cut green trees or shrubs in a forest. **2** *Heraldry.* the green color in a coat of arms. [< Old French *vert, verd* green < Latin *viridis* < *virēre* be green]

**vert.,** vertical.

**ver|te|bra** (vėr′tə brə), *n., pl.* **-brae** (-brē), **-bras.** **1** one of the bones of the backbone or spinal column. In man and higher animals a vertebra consists typically of a somewhat cylindrical central body (centrum) and arch (neural arch) supporting seven processes, the whole forming an opening for the passage of the spinal cord. **2** the vertebral column; spine or backbone. [< Latin *vertebra* (originally) any joint, a turning place < *vertere* to turn]

**ver|te|bral** (vėr′tə brəl), *adj., n.* —*adj.* **1** of, having to do with, or situated on or near a vertebra or the vertebrae; spinal. **2** of the nature of a vertebra. **3** composed of vertebrae. **4** having vertebrae; backboned.
—*n.* a vertebral artery or vein. —**ver′te|bral|ly,** *adv.*

**vertebral column,** = backbone.

**ver|te|brate** (vėr′tə brit, -brāt), *n., adj.* —*n.* an animal that has a backbone. Fishes, amphibians, reptiles, birds, and mammals are vertebrates. Technically, vertebrates comprise a subphylum of chordates having a segmented spinal column and a brain case or cranium. *Vertebrates characteristically have a red blood pigment, rich in iron, known as haemoglobin, which combines readily with oxygen* (Mary Sears).
—*adj.* **1** having a backbone. **2** of, belonging to, or having to do with the vertebrates.
[< New Latin *Vertebrata* the subphylum name < Latin *vertebrātus* jointed < *vertebra;* see etym. under **vertebra**]

**ver|te|brat|ed** (vėr′tə brā′tid), *adj.* **1** having a spinal column; vertebrate. **2** consisting of or provided with vertebrae. **3** *Figurative.* constructed in a manner suggestive of vertebrae.

**ver|te|bra|tion** (vėr′tə brā′shən), *n.* division into segments like those of the spinal column: vertebrate formation.

**ver|tex** (vėr′teks), *n., pl.* **-tex|es** or **-ti|ces.** **1** the highest point of something, especially a hill or structure; top. SYN: apex, summit. **2** *Anatomy.* the top or crown of the head, especially in man, the part lying between the occiput and the sinciput. **3** *Astronomy.* the point in the heavens directly overhead; zenith. **4** *Mathematics.* **a** the point opposite to and farthest from the base of a triangle, pyramid, or other figure having a base. **b** the point where the two sides of an angle meet. See diagram under **angle**[1]. **c** any point of intersection of the sides of a polygon or the edges of a polyhedron. **d** the point in a curve or surface at which the axis meets it. **5** *Optics.* the point, at the center of a lens, where the axis cuts the surface. [< Latin *vertex, -icis* highest point; (originally) a whirl, whirling < *vertere* to turn]

***ver|ti|cal** (vėr′tə kəl), *adj., n.* —*adj.* **1** straight up and down; perpendicular to a level surface or to the plane of the horizon; upright. A person standing straight is in a vertical position. **2** of or at the highest point; of the vertex. **3** directly overhead; at the zenith: *a vertical sighting.* **4** so organized as to include many or all stages in the production or distribution of some manufactured product: *a vertical union, vertical trusts.* **5** *Botany.* **a** having a position at right angles to the plane of the axis, body, or other supporting surface, as the blade of a leaf. **b** in the direction of the stem or axis; lengthwise. **6** of or having to do with the sounds forming harmony, especially in a homophonic composition.
—*n.* **1** a vertical line, plane, position, direction, or part. **2** = vertical angle. **3** a vertical beam or other part in a truss.
[< Late Latin *verticālis* < *vertex, -icis* highest point, vertex] —**ver′ti|cal|ly,** *adv.* —**ver′ti|cal|ness,** *n.*

***vertical**
definition 1

vertical
horizontal

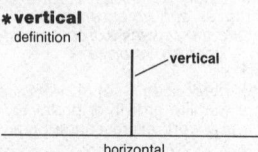

**vertical angle,** *Geometry.* **1** an opposite angle. **2** the angle opposite the base of a triangle or polygon.

**vertical circle,** *Astronomy.* any great circle of the celestial sphere perpendicular to the plane of the horizon, passing through the zenith and nadir.

**vertical divestiture,** the act or fact of limiting a conglomerate company's holdings in related businesses by law, such as forcing an oil company to limit its holdings in the oil industry to exploration and drilling or refining or marketing.

**vertical envelopment,** attack by airplanes or paratroops, usually combined with operations by ground forces, in an effort to cut off or encircle the enemy.

**vertical file,** **1** a file of pamphlets, circulars, charts, bulletins, newspaper clippings, and the like, about topics of current interest, maintained by a library or other organization for quick or easy reference. **2** a cabinet for such a file.

**vertical integration,** = vertical merger.

**ver|ti|cal|i|ty** (vėr′tə kal′ə tē), *n.* **1a** the condition of being vertical; vertical position. **b** perpendicular quality: *the verticality of a building.* **2** *Astronomy.* the fact of being directly overhead or at the zenith.

**ver|ti|cal|i|za|tion** (vėr′tə kə lə zā′shən), *n.* = vertical integration.

**vertical merger,** a merger of companies that are each other's suppliers or customers, as distinguished from a horizontal merger.

**vertical take-off,** a take-off by an aircraft directly upward.

**vertical union,** a labor union whose membership includes the workers of an entire industry rather than those employed at a particular craft or task; industrial union.

**ver|ti|ces** (vėr′tə sēz), *n.* a plural of **vertex.**

**ver|ti|cil** (vėr′tə sil), *n.* a whorl or circle of leaves, hairs, and other parts, growing around a stem or central point. [< Latin *verticillus* whorl (diminutive) < *vertex* vertex]

**ver|ti|cil|las|ter** (vėr′tə si las′tər), *n. Botany.* a determinate inflorescence in which the flowers are arranged in a seeming whorl, consisting in fact of a pair of opposite axillary, usually sessile, cymes, as in many plants of the mint family. [< Latin *verticillus* (see etym. under **verticil**) + *-aster,* a diminutive suffix]

**ver|tic|il|late** (vėr tis′ə lāt, -lit; vėr′tə sil′āt), *adj.* **1** forming verticils or whorls: *verticillate leaves or flowers.* **2** *Obsolete.* having leaves, flowers, and other parts arranged or produced in circles or whorls around the stem. [< New Latin *verticillatus* < Latin *verticillus;* see etym. under **verticil**] —**ver|tic′il|late|ly,** *adv.*

**ver|tic|il|lat|ed** (vėr tis′ə lā′tid), *adj.* = verticillate.

**ver|tic|il|la|tion** (vėr tis′ə lā′shən), *n.* **1** the formation of verticils. **2** a vertical or verticillate form or structure.

**ver|ti|cil|li|um** (vėr′tə sil′ē əm), *n.* **1** a disease of cotton, tomatoes, hops, and other plants, caused by a soil fungus that attacks the entire plant through the roots; verticillium wilt. **2** the fungus causing this disease: *Verticillium is likely to be present in all old agricultural soils in which potatoes and tomatoes have been grown* (Sunset). [< New Latin *Verticillium* genus of the fungus < Latin *verticillus;* see etym. under **verticil**]

**verticillium wilt,** = verticillium.

**ver|tic|i|ty** (vėr tis′ə tē), *n. Obsolete.* a tendency to turn towards a vertex or pole, especially as exhibited by a magnetic needle. [< Latin *vertex, -icis* vertex + English *-ity*]

**ver|tig|i|nate** (vėr tij′ə nāt′), *v.i.,* **-nat|ed, -nat|ing.** to turn round, spin, or rush dizzily: *Finding where the car is parked once one descends and ceases to vertiginate becomes a real problem* (New York Times). *Surely never did argument vertiginate more* (Samuel Taylor Coleridge).

**ver|tig|i|nous** (vėr tij′ə nəs), *adj.* **1** whirling; rotary; revolving: *the vertiginous action of a gyroscope.* **2** affected with or suffering from vertigo; dizzy: *At the edge of the cliff she grew vertiginous and hastily retreated.* **3** of the nature of or having to do with vertigo; likely to cause vertigo. **4** *Figurative.* fickle; unstable. [< Latin *vertīginōsus* suffering from dizziness < *vertīgō, -inis;* see etym. under **vertigo**] —**ver|tig′i|nous|ly,** *adv.* —**ver|tig′i|nous|ness,** *n.*

**ver|ti|go** (vėr′tə gō), *n., pl.* **ver|ti|goes, ver|tig|i|nes** (vėr tij′ə nēz). **1** an abnormal condition characterized by a feeling that the person, or the objects around one, are whirling in space, and by a tendency to lose equilibrium and consciousness; dizziness; giddiness: *Vertigo is caused by changes of the blood supply in the head.* **2** *Veterinary Medicine.* the staggers in horses, the sturdy or gid in sheep, or a similar disease in dogs. [< Latin *vertīgō, -inis* dizziness; (originally) a turning round < *vertere* to turn]

**ver|tim|e|ter** (vėr tim′ə tər), *n.* an instrument that measures the rate of climb or descent of an aircraft.

**ver|ti|port** (vėr′tə pôrt′, -pōrt′), *n.* a small airport for aircraft that can take off and land vertically; VTOLport. [< *verti*(cal take-off) + (air)*port*]

**ver|tu** (vėr tü′, vėr′tü), *n.* = virtu.

**Ver|tum|nus** (vər tum′nəs), *n.* the Roman god of spring, guardian of gardens and orchards, and husband of Pomona. Also, **Vortumnus.** [< Latin *Vertumnus* (literally) self-changing < *vertere* to turn]

**ver|vain** (vėr′vān), *n.* any verbena, especially any species bearing spikes of small white, bluish, or purple flowers, such as a common European species and a common American species. [< Old French *verveine, vervainne* < Latin *verbēna* leafy bough. See etym. of doublet **verbena.**]

**verve** (vėrv), *n.* **1** enthusiasm; energy; vigor; spirit; liveliness: *full of verve and enjoyment of life.* **2a** intellectual vigor or energy, especially as expressed or shown in literary productions; liveliness of ideas and expression. **b** *Obsolete.* talent in writing. [< French *verve,* Old French, a fancy, caprice, perhaps < Vulgar Latin *verva* < Latin *verba,* in sense of "whimsical words"]

**ver|vet** (vėr′vit), *n.* a small African monkey of a grayish-green color, one of the guenons. [< French *vervet,* probably fusion of *vert* green + *(gri)vet* a grivet]

**ver|y** (ver′ē), *adv., adj.,* **ver|i|er, ver|i|est.** —*adv.* **1** much; greatly; extremely: *The sunshine is very hot in July.* SYN: exceedingly, surpassingly, excessively. **2** absolutely; exactly: *He stood in the very same place for an hour.*
—*adj.* **1** same; identical: *The very people who used to love her hate her now.* **2** even; mere; sheer: *The very thought of summer vacation makes her happy. She wept from very joy.* **3a** real; true; genuine: *She seemed a very queen.* **b** *Obsolete.* legally valid; rightful; lawful; legitimate. **4** actual; exact: *Speak the very truth. He was caught in the very act of stealing.* **5** in the fullest sense; veritable: *Voltaire was the very eye of modern illumination.*
[< Anglo-French *verrai,* Old French *verai* < Vulgar Latin *vērācus,* for Latin *vērāx, -ācis* < *vērus* true]

► The use of **very,** in place of *very much* or *much,* to modify past participles, as in *He was very annoyed by the letter,* is regarded as nonstandard. This is not true when the participles function as simple attributive or predicate adjectives: *a very pleased look. He was very tired.*

**very high frequency** or **Very High Frequency,** = VHF.

**Very light,** a colored flare fired from a pistol at night as a signal: *The commissioner was to reveal his position on the ground by firing a purple Very light into the sky* (New Yorker). [< Edward *Very,* 1847-1910, an American naval officer, who invented it]

**very low frequency** or **Very Low Frequency,** = VLF.

**Very pistol,** a pistol used to discharge a Very light: *The Very pistol works somewhat like a Roman candle. Both these and rockets are used in signaling* (Julius Roth).

**ve|si|ca** (və sī′kə), *n., pl.* **-cae** (-sē). **1** *Anatomy.* a bladder, especially the urinary bladder; sac. **2** *Botany.* vesicle. [< Latin *vēsīca* bladder, blister]

**ves|i|cal** (ves′ə kəl), *adj.* of or having to do with the bladder; formed in the urinary bladder.

**ves|i|cant** (ves′ə kənt), *n., adj.* —*n.* **1** something

that raises blisters, such as a mustard plaster; vesicatory. **2** any chemical agent causing burns, inflammation, and destruction of the internal or external tissue of the body.
—***adj.*** causing or effective in producing blisters, as a medical application; vesicatory.
[< New Latin *vesicans, -antis,* present participle of *vesicare* to raise blisters < Latin *vēsīca* blister]

***vesica pis|cis** (pis′is), a pointed oval figure, formed properly by the intersection of the arcs of two equal circles each of which passes through the center of the other, frequently used in ecclesiastical architecture and art, often to enclose a sacred figure, as that of Christ or the Virgin. [< Latin *vēsīca piscis* (literally) bladder of or like a fish]

***vesica piscis**

**ves|i|cate** (ves′ə kāt), *v.,* **-cat|ed, -cat|ing.** *Medicine.* —***v.t.*** to cause blisters on; blister.
—***v.i.*** to become blistered.
[< Latin *vēsīca* blister + English *-ate*[1]]

**ves|i|ca|tion** (ves′ə kā′shən), *n. Medicine.* **1** the formation, development, or result of blistering. **2** a blister or group of blisters.

**ves|i|ca|to|ry** (ves′ə kə tôr′ē, -tōr′-), *adj., n., pl.* **-ries.** —***adj.*** that can raise blisters.
—***n.*** = vesicant.

**ves|i|cle** (ves′ə kəl), *n.* **1** a small bladder, cavity, sac, or cyst, especially one filled with fluid. A blister is a vesicle in the skin. **2** *Botany.* a small bladder or air cavity resembling a bladder. **3** *Geology.* a small spherical or oval cavity in igneous rock produced by the presence of bubbles of gas or vapor during the rock's solidification. [< Latin *vēsīcula* (diminutive) < *vēsīca* bladder, blister]

**ve|sic|u|lar** (və sik′yə lər), *adj.* **1** of or having to do with a vesicle or vesicles, especially the air cells of the lungs: *vesicular breathing.* **2** like a vesicle; bladderlike. **3** having vesicles. [< New Latin *vesicularis* < Latin *vēsīcula,* see etym. under **vesicle**] —**ve|sic′u|lar|ly,** *adv.*

**vesicular exanthema,** a contagious virus disease of swine in which blisters appear above the hoof, between the toes, and on the snout and nostrils. It is caused by eating decayed garbage and is similar to foot-and-mouth disease in cattle.

**vesicular stomatitis,** a noncontagious virus disease of cattle, horses, and hogs, in which small superficial ulcers form on the mucous membrane of the mouth. It is spread by mosquitoes and other insects.

**ve|sic|u|late** (*v.* və sik′yə lāt; *adj.* və sik′yə lit, -lāt), *v.,* **-lat|ed, -lat|ing,** *adj.* —***v.t., v.i.*** to make or become vesicular; develop vesicles (in).
—***adj.*** = vesiculated.

**ve|sic|u|lat|ed** (və sik′yə lā′tid), *adj.* **1** full of or having small cavities or air cells. **2** of the nature of a vesicle or vesicula. **3** *Medicine.* covered with vesicles.

**ve|sic|u|la|tion** (və sik′yə lā′shən), *n.* the formation of vesicles, especially on the skin.

**ve|sic|u|lose** (və sik′yə lōs), *adj.* full of vesicles; vesiculated.

**ve|sic|u|lous** (və sik′yə ləs), *adj.* = vesiculose.

**Ves|per** (ves′pər), *n.* the planet Venus, when it appears as the evening star. [< Latin *Vesper* evening star]

**ves|per** (ves′pər), *n., adj.* —***n.*** **1** an evening prayer, hymn, or service; vespers. **2** an evening bell. **3** *Obsolete.* the evening.
—***adj.*** **1** of, belonging to, or occurring in the evening: *the vesper hours.* **2** Sometimes, **Vesper.** of, used at, or having to do with vespers.
[< Old French *vespre,* variant of *vespres;* see etym. under **vespers**]

**ves|per|al** (ves′pər əl), *n.* **1** a book containing the psalms, chants, anthems, and prayers, with their music, used at vespers. **2** a cover used over the altar cloth between services.

**vesper bell,** the bell that summons to vespers or evensong.

**vesper mouse,** = white-footed mouse.

**ves|pers** or **Ves|pers** (ves′pərz), *n.pl.* **1** a church service held in the late afternoon or early evening; evensong. **2a** the sixth of the seven canonical hours. **b** the office or service for this hour, following nones, and said in late afternoon or evening. **c** (in the Roman Catholic Church) the evening service, often said before a public assembly on Sundays and holy days. [partly < Old French *vespres* < Medieval Latin; partly < Medieval Latin *vesperae,* for Latin, plural of *vespera* evening]

**vesper sparrow,** a North American sparrow resembling the song sparrow but with its outer tail feathers white; grass finch.

**ves|per|til|i|o|nid** (ves′pər til′ē ə nid), *n., adj.* —***n.*** any one of a group of widely distributed insect-eating bats of the temperate regions, such as the myotis, pipistrel, hoary bat and evening bat.
—***adj.*** of or having to do with these bats.
[< New Latin *Vespertilionidae* the family name < Latin *vespertīliō, -ōnis* a bat < *vesper* evening]

**ves|per|til|i|o|nine** (ves′pər til′ē ə nīn, -nin), *adj.* of or having to do with the vespertilionids. [< Latin *vespertīliō, -ōnis* a bat (< *vesper* evening) + *-ine*[1]]

**ves|per|ti|nal** (ves′pər tī′nəl), *adj.* = vespertine.

**ves|per|tine** (ves′pər tin, -tīn), *adj.* **1** of or having to do with the evening; occurring in the evening: *vespertine hours.* **2a** *Zoology.* flying or appearing in the early evening. Bats and owls are vespertine animals. **b** *Botany.* opening in the evening, as some flowers do. **3** descending toward the horizon in the evening: *a vespertine planet or star.* [< Latin *vespertīnus* < *vesper* evening]

**ves|pi|ar|y** (ves′pē er′ē), *n., pl.* **-ar|ies.** a nest or colony of social wasps. [< Latin *vespa* wasp; patterned on *apiary*]

**ves|pid** (ves′pid), *n., adj.* —***n.*** a member of a widely distributed family of insects that includes hornets, yellow jackets, and certain wasps; vespid wasp. Some vespids live in colonies like bees and ants, others are solitary.
—***adj.*** belonging to or having to do with this family.
[< New Latin *Vespidae* the family name < *Vespa* the typical genus < Latin *vespa* wasp]

**vespid wasp,** = vespid.

**ves|pi|form** (ves′pə fôrm), *adj.* = wasplike. [< Latin *vespa* wasp + *forma* form]

**ves|pine** (ves′pīn, -pin), *adj.* of or having to do with wasps; wasplike. [< Latin *vespa* wasp + English *-ine*[1]]

**ves|sel** (ves′əl), *n.* **1a** any large boat; ship, especially one larger than a canoe or rowboat, designed or equipped for conveying passengers and cargo: *Ocean liners and other vessels are usually docked by tugboats.* **b** *Law.* any floating structure. **2** = airship. **3** a hollow holder or container. Cups, bowls, pitchers, bottles, barrels, and tubs are vessels. **4** a tube carrying blood, lymph, or other fluid in the body. Veins and arteries are blood vessels. **5** *Botany.* **a** one of the rows or chains of cells, an essential element of the xylem of plants, that have lost their intervening partitions and have become a long continuous canal permitting the passage of water and dissolved minerals; trachea or duct. **b** = pericarp. **6** *Figurative.* a person regarded as a container of some quality or as made for some purpose (used chiefly in Biblical expressions): *a vessel of wrath, the weaker vessel.* [< Old French *vessel* < Latin *vascella,* plural (taken as feminine singular) of *vascellum* (diminutive) < *vās, vāsis* vessel] —**ves′sel|like′,** *adj.*

**vest** (vest), *n., v.* —***n.*** **1** a short, buttoned, sleeveless garment worn by men or boys under a suit coat or a jacket. **2** a similar garment or part of a dress bodice made to resemble the front of a vest, worn by women. **3a** *British.* an undershirt. **b** an undershirt specifically for a woman. **4** a man's knee-length, sleeveless garment introduced by Charles II to be worn beneath the coat. **5a** a loose outer garment worn by men in Eastern countries or in ancient times; robe or gown. **b** a similar garment worn by women. **6** an ecclesiastical vestment. **7** *Archaic.* clothing; garment. [< Old French *veste* < Italian *vesta, veste* < Latin *vestis* garment]
—***v.t.*** **1a** to clothe, robe, or dress (another person or oneself), especially in ecclesiastical vestments or for a ceremony: *The vested priest stood before the altar.* **b** to cover or drape (an altar). **2** to furnish with powers, authority, rights, or functions: *Congress is vested with the power to declare war.* **3** to put in the possession or control of a person or persons: *The management of the hospital is vested in a board of trustees.*
—***v.i.*** **1** to become vested; pass into possession; descend or devolve on a possessor: *The right of the crown vests upon his heir.* **2** to dress in ecclesiastical vestment.

**close to the vest,** with great care and cunning so as to avoid all possible risks: *Modern chess masters, like modern generals, play ... close to the vest ..., stressing logistic planning and minutely synchronized attacks* (Newsweek).
[< Old French *vestir* < Latin *vestīre* (literally) clothe < *vestis* garment] —**vest′like′,** *adj.*

**Ves|ta** (ves′tə), *n.* **1** the Roman goddess of the hearth, the hearth fire, and the household. The Greeks called her Hestia. A sacred fire, guarded by the vestal virgins, was always kept burning in the temple of Vesta. **2** *Astronomy.* one of the asteroids or minor planets revolving in an orbit between Mars and Jupiter. It is 240 miles in diameter and the only asteroid visible to the naked eye. [< Latin *Vesta*]

**ves|ta** (ves′tə), *n.* **1** a kind of short friction match: *The Skipper scratched a vesta and lit the brass student lamps at either end of the table* (Atlantic). **2** *British.* a kind of wax match. [< *Vesta*]

**ves|tal** (ves′təl), *n., adj.* —***n.*** **1** one of the vestal virgins. **2** a chaste woman; virgin: *She was the most ... jovial of old vestals, and had been a beauty in her day* (Thackeray). **3** = nun[1] (def. 1).
—***adj.*** **1** of or having to do with a vestal; suitable for a vestal. **2** pure; chaste.

**Ves|ta|li|a** (ves tā′lē ə, -tāl′yə), *n.pl.* an ancient Roman festival honoring Vesta, celebrated in June. [< Latin *Vestālia* < *Vesta*]

**vestal virgin** or **Vestal Virgin,** one of the virgin priestesses of the Roman goddess Vesta. Six vestal virgins tended an undying fire in honor of Vesta at her temple in ancient Rome.

**vest|ed** (ves′tid), *adj.* **1** placed in the possession or control of a person or persons; fixed; settled: *a vested privilege, vested rights.* **2** clothed, robed, or dressed, especially in church garments: *a vested choir.* **3** including a vest; three-piece: *a vested suit.*

**vested interest,** **1** an interest in something that may be lost by change, especially a commitment to a cause, institution, or the like, based on self-interest: *a vested interest in labor, a vested interest in segregation. The U.S. has a deep vested interest in Venezuela's political stability* (Newsweek). **2** a person or group that stands to lose by change: *The fulfillment of many of these obligations will mean stepping on the toes of vested interests in both scientific and military spheres* (Bulletin of Atomic Scientists). **3** a legally established title to real or personal property.

**vested right,** a legally established right to present and prospective enjoyment of a property.

**vested rights,** rights to pension benefits even if an employee leaves a company before the retirement age; vesting: *Vested rights ... will vary with different types of plans, and are made available ... on the basis of years of service, age, or length of participation in the pension program* (New York Times).

**vest|ee** (ves tē′), *n.* an ornamental vest worn by women as an insert on a dress bodice or between the open edges of a blouse or jacket; dickey. [American English < *vest* + *-ee*]

**ves|ti|ar|y** (ves′tē er′ē), *adj., n., pl.* **-ar|ies.** —***adj.*** of or having to do with clothes or dress.
—***n.*** **1** a room or building, especially in a monastery or other large establishment, for keeping and storing vestments, clothes, or coats; cloakroom or wardrobe. **2** a vestry of a church.
[< Old French *vestiarie, vestiaire,* learned borrowings from Latin *vestiārium* clothes chest, neuter of *vestiārius* of clothing < *vestis* garment]

**ves|tib|u|lar** (ves tib′yə lər), *adj.* of, having to do with, or serving as a vestibule.

**ves|tib|u|late** (ves tib′yə lāt, -lit), *adj.* **1** *Zoology.* having a vestibule. **2** = vestibular.

**ves|ti|bule** (ves′tə byül), *n., v.,* **-buled, -bul|ing.** —***n.*** **1a** a passage, hall, or chamber immediately between the outer door and the inside of a building; antechamber, entrance hall, or lobby. **b** an enclosed or covered area in front of the main entrance of ancient Greek and Roman buildings; forecourt. **2** the enclosed platform and entrance at one or both ends of a railroad passenger car, serving as a passage from one car to another. **3** a cavity or hollow that leads to another (usually larger or more important) cavity. The vestibule of the ear is the central cavity of the inner ear. See diagram under **ear**[1].
—***v.t.*** **1** to replace the open platforms, once universal on railroad trains, by vestibules. **2** to couple (railroad cars).
[< Latin *vestibulum*]

**vestibule school,** the training department in an industrial plant, teaching new employees the skills necessary to do their work.

**vestibule train,** a railroad train composed of cars with vestibules.

**ves|tige** (ves′tij), *n.* **1** all that remains; slight remnant; trace: *A blackened, charred stump was a vestige of a fire. Ghost stories are vestiges of a*

**Pronunciation Key:** hat, āge, cãre, fär; let, ēqual, tėrm; it, īce; hot, ōpen, ôrder; **oi**l, **ou**t; cup, pu̇t, rüle; **ch**ild; lo**ng**; **th**in; **ᴛʜ**en; **zh**, measure; **ə** represents **a** in about, **e** in taken, **i** in pencil, **o** in lemon, **u** in circus.

*former widespread belief in ghosts.* **SYN**: mark. See syn. under **trace**. **2** *Biology.* a part, organ, or kind of behavior, that is no longer fully developed or useful but performed a definite function in an earlier stage of the existence of the same organism or in lower preceding organisms. **3** *Rare.* a footprint or track. [< French *vestige,* learned borrowing from Latin *vestīgium* footprint]

**ves|tig|i|al** (ves tij′ē əl), *adj.* **1** remaining as a vestige. **2** *Biology.* no longer fully developed or useful. — **ves|tig′i|al|ly,** *adv.*

**ves|tig|i|um** (ves tij′ē əm), *n., pl.* **-i|a** (-ē ə). **1** *Biology.* a part, organ, or kind of behavior that is no longer fully developed or useful; vestige. **2** *Obsolete.* a vestige in general. [< Latin *vestīgium* footprint, trace]

**ves|ti|men|ta|ry** (ves′tə men′tər ē), *adj.* of or having to do with clothes or dress, especially ecclesiastical garments: *The rest of the men ... were in white tie, hatless and gloveless, and with no white carnation—an omission that would have constituted vestimentary impropriety in the old days of the Third Republic* (New Yorker).

**vest|ing[1]** (ves′ting), *n.* cloth for making vests.

**vest|ing[2]** (ves′ting), *n.* = vested rights.

**vest|less** (vest′lis), *adj.* without a vest.

**vest|ment** (vest′mənt), *n.* **1a** one of the garments worn by clergymen, their assistants, the choristers, or other functionaries, in performing sacred duties or on some special occasion. It is often indicative of the wearer's rank or the ceremony being performed. **b** one of the garments worn by clergymen at the Eucharist, especially the chasuble. **2** a garment, especially a robe or gown, worn by an official on a ceremonial occasion. **3** *Figurative.* something that covers like a garment; covering: *the green vestment of the meadow.* [< Old French *vestment,* alteration of Latin *vestimentum* < *vestīre* to clothe < *vestis* garment]

**vest|men|tal** (vest′mən təl), *adj.* = vestimentary.

**vest-pock|et** (vest′pok′it), *adj.* **1** able to fit in a vest pocket: *a vest-pocket radio.* **2** very small: *a vest-pocket industry, a vest-pocket park.*

**ves|try** (ves′trē), *n., pl.* **-tries. 1** a room, part of a church, or building attached to a church, where vestments, and often the sacred vessels, altar equipment, and parish records are kept; sacristy. **2** a similar place used for Sunday school and prayer meetings; chapel. **3** (in the Church of England and the Protestant Episcopal Church of America) an elected committee of church members that helps the church-wardens to manage church business. **4** (in parishes of the Church of England) a meeting of the parishioners on church business. [Middle English *vestrye,* perhaps < unrecorded Anglo-French *vesterie* < Old French *vestir* to vest, clothe + -(*e*)*rie* -ery]

**ves|try|man** (ves′trē mən), *n., pl.* **-men.** a member of a committee that helps manage church business.

**vestry room,** a room forming the vestry of a church.

**ves|tur|al** (ves′chər əl), *adj.* of or having to do with vesture or clothing.

**ves|ture** (ves′chər), *n., v.,* **-tured, -tur|ing.** — *n.* **1** clothing; garments: *Pharaoh ... arrayed him in vestures of fine linen* (Genesis 41:42). **2** *Figurative.* a covering: *a suitable vesture for ideas.* **3** *British Law.* everything that grows on, covers, or is a product of the land, except trees.
— *v.t.* to put clothing or vesture on; robe; vest.
[< Old French *vesture* < Late Latin *vestītūra* decoration < Latin *vestīre* to clothe < *vestis* garment]

**ves|tur|er** (ves′chər ər), *n.* **1** a person who is in charge of the vestments worn in church. **2** a person who assists the treasurer of a collegiate church or cathedral.

**Ve|su|vi|an** (və sü′vē ən), *adj., n.* — *adj.* of, having to do with, or resembling Mount Vesuvius, a volcano southeast of Naples, Italy; volcanic.
— *n.* **1** Sometimes, **vesuvian.** (formerly) a kind of match with a sputtering flame used especially for lighting cigars and pipe tobacco. **2** = vesuvianite.

**ve|su|vi|an|ite** (və sü′vē ə nīt), *n.* a mineral, a silicate of aluminum, calcium, iron, and magnesium, sometimes with other elements, occurring in massive or, more frequently, in square crystals of various colors; idocrase. [< *Vesuvian* (< *Vesuvius,* a volcano near Naples, Italy) + *-ite*[1]]

**vet[1]** (vet), *n., v.,* **vet|ted, vet|ting.** *Informal.* — *n.* = veterinarian.
— *v.t.* **1** to submit to examination or treatment by a veterinarian: *to vet a sick calf. I'd as soon vet a hippopotamus for nerves as you* (John Buchan). **2** *Figurative.* to subject to careful examination; scrutinize; check; test: *Every application for membership is carefully vetted, in such a way as to make it nearly impossible for anyone with no experience of fair business to enter it* (Economist).
— *v.i.* to practice veterinary medicine.

**vet[2]** (vet), *n., adj. Informal.* a veteran. [American English, short for *veteran*]

**vet.,** **1** veteran. **2a** veterinarian. **b** veterinary.

**ve|tan|da** (vē tan′də), *n.pl.* things to be forbidden. [< Latin *vetanda,* neuter plural gerundive of *vetāre* forbid]

**vetch** (vech), *n.* **1** any one of a group of climbing herbs, species of which are much grown as food for cattle and sheep; tare. Vetches belong to the pea family. **2** any one of several related plants, such as the milk vetch. **3** the beanlike fruit of certain of these plants. [< Old North French *veche* < Latin *vicia*]

**vetch bruchid,** a small weevil that lives in and destroys the green seed of some vetches.

**vetch|ling** (vech′ling), *n.* any one of a group of vetchlike herbs of the pea family, especially a common meadow weed.

**veter.,** veterinary.

**vet|er|an** (vet′ər ən, vet′rən), *n., adj.* — *n.* **1** a person who has been in one of the armed services for a long time and who has had much experience in war; old soldier, sailor, or airman. **2a** a person who has served in the armed forces: *There are millions of American veterans from the second World War and the Korean and Vietnam wars.* **b** *U.S. Law.* a former member of any branch of the military service who meets the requirements for the extension of some benefit or privilege provided by law to honorably discharged servicemen. **3** a person who has had much experience in some position or occupation: *He is a veteran in the printing trade.*
— *adj.* **1** having had much experience in war: *Veteran troops fought side by side with new recruits.* **2** grown old in service; having had much experience: *a veteran farmer.* **3** old; long-continued: *veteran wines.*
[< Latin *veterānus* of old (that is, long) experience < *vetus, -eris* old]

**Vet|er|ans Day** (vet′ər ənz, vet′rənz), *U.S.* a legal holiday observed on November 11, the anniversary of the end of World War I, to honor all United States veterans. From 1971 to 1978 it was celebrated on the fourth Monday in October. Until 1954 it was called *Armistice Day.*

**vet|er|i|nar|i|an** (vet′ər ə nãr′ē ən, vet′rə-), *n.* a doctor or surgeon who treats animals; doctor of veterinary medicine.

**vet|er|i|nar|y** (vet′ər ə ner′ē, vet′rə-), *adj., n., pl.* **-nar|ies.** — *adj.* of or having something to do with the medical or surgical treatment of animals.
— *n.* = veterinarian. [< Latin *veterīnārius* < *veterīnus* having to do with beasts of burden, probably < *vetus, veteris* old (good for nothing else)]

**veterinary medicine,** the branch of medicine that deals with the causes, prevention, and medical or surgical treatment of diseases and injuries in animals, especially in domestic animals.

**vet|i|ver** (vet′ə vər), *n.* **1** the fibrous aromatic roots of an East Indian grass grown in the tropics and the southern United States. They are made into mats and screens and yield vetiver oil; cuscus. **2** the plant itself. [< French *vétiver* < Tamil *veṭṭivēru* (literally) root dug up < *vēr* root]

**vetiver oil,** a fragrant oil derived from vetiver, used in making perfumes and soaps.

**ve|to** (vē′tō), *n., pl.* **-toes,** *adj., v.,* **-toed, -to|ing.**
— *n.* **1** the right or power of a president or governor to reject bills passed by a lawmaking body: *The President has the power of veto over bills passed in Congress.* **2** the right or power of one branch or part of a government to forbid or prevent an action of another branch or part. **3** the right or power of any one member of an official body to prevent some action proposed by that body, especially in the United Nations Security Council: *a categorical demand for a veto-ridden three-man administrative control council* (Manchester Guardian). **4** the use of any such rights or powers: *The governor's veto kept the bill from becoming a law.* **5** a statement of the reasons for disapproval of a bill passed by the legislature. **6** any power or right to prevent action through prohibition. **7** a refusal of consent; prohibition: *Our plan met with three vetoes—from Father, Mother, and our teacher.*
— *adj.* having to do with a veto: *veto power.*
— *v.t.* **1** to reject (a legislative measure) by a veto: *The President has vetoed two bills during this session of Congress.* **2** to inhibit or prevent some action proposed by a group or council. **3** to refuse to consent to: *My parents vetoed my plan to buy a motorcycle.*
[< Latin *vetō* I forbid, first person singular present of *vetāre* (used by Roman tribunes of the people in opposing senatorial or executive measures)] — **ve′to|er,** *n.*

**vet|tu|ra** (vet tü′rä), *n., pl.* **-re** (-rā). a kind of four-wheeled carriage used in Italy. [< Italian *vettura* < Latin *vectūra* carriage < *vehere* carry]

**vet|tu|ri|no** (vet′tü rē′nō), *n., pl.* **-ni** (-nē). in Italy: **1** a person who lets out or drives a vettura. **2** = vettura. [< Italian *vetturino* < *vettura;* see etym. under **vettura**]

**vex** (veks), *v.t.* **1** to anger by trifles; annoy; provoke: *The child's rude remarks vexed his father.* **2** to harass by aggression or interference with peace or quiet: *With such compelling cause to grieve As vexes the household peace* (Tennyson). **3** to worry; distress deeply; trouble: *Uncertainty as to the justice of his decision vexed the judge.* **4** to disturb by causing movement or commotion; agitate: *Cape Hatteras is much vexed by storms.* **5** to discuss or debate at excessive length. **6** to subject to or affect with pain or suffering: *to vex the slave with torture.*
— *v.i.* to feel annoyed, unhappy, or distressed.
[< Middle French *vexer,* learned borrowing from Latin *vexāre*]

**vex|a|tion** (vek sā′shən), *n.* **1** the action of vexing or fact of being vexed: *His face showed his vexation at the delay.* **SYN**: irritation, exasperation, annoyance, chagrin. **2** a thing that vexes: *Rain on Saturday was a vexation to the children.*

**vex|a|tious** (vek sā′shəs), *adj.* **1** vexing; annoying: *a vexatious interruption of an interesting conversation.* **2** *Law.* brought with insufficient grounds for the purpose of causing trouble to the defendant: *a vexatious action.* — **vex|a′tious|ly,** *adv.* — **vex|a′tious|ness,** *n.*

**vexed** (vekst), *adj.* **1** annoyed; irritated; distressed. **2** kept in a disturbed or unquiet state; troubled; harassed: *the vexed affair of Northern Ireland.* **3** subjected to physical force or strain; tossed about; agitated: *the vexed waters of the lake.*

**vex|ed|ly** (vek′sid lē), *adv.* with vexation; with a sense of annoyance or vexation.

**vex|ed|ness** (vek′sid nis), *n.* vexation; annoyance.

**vexed question,** a question causing difficulty and debate: *The situation of little magazines is so bound up with vexed questions of cultural economics and with wider questions about writing in modern societies that little can be said about it* (Peter Levi).

**vex|il** (vek′səl), *n.* = vexillum.

**vex|il|la** (vek sil′ə), *n.* plural of **vexillum.**

**vex|il|lar** (vek′sə lər), *adj.* **1** *Botany, Zoology.* of or having to do with the vexillum. **2** (in ancient Rome) of or having to do with an ensign or standard.

**vex|il|lar|y** (vek′sə ler′ē), *adj., n., pl.* **-lar|ies.**
— *adj.* **1** *Biology.* of or having to do with a vexillum. **2** of or having to do with an ensign or standard.
— *n.* in ancient Rome: **a** one of the oldest class of army veterans serving under a special standard. **b** a standardbearer.
[< Latin *vexillārius,* noun use of adjective *vexillum* a standard; see etym. under **vexillum**]

**vexillary estivation,** *Botany.* a mode of estivation in which the exterior petal, as in the case of the vexillum, is largest and encloses and folds over the other petals.

**vex|il|late** (vek′sə lāt, -lit), *adj. Biology.* having a vexillum or vexilla.

**vex|il|lol|o|gist** (vek′sə lol′ə jist), *n.* a person who studies flags.

**vex|il|lol|o|gy** (vek′sə lol′ə jē), *n.* the study of flags: *Vexillology is not normally a very vexed subject. It concerns the design, making and history of flags* (Daily Telegraph). [< Latin *vexillum* a flag or banner + English *-logy*]

**vex|il|lum** (vek sil′əm), *n., pl.* **-la. 1** a square flag or banner carried by ancient Roman troops. **2** a body of troops grouped under such a flag or banner. **3** *Botany.* the large upper external petal of a papilionaceous flower. **4** *Zoology.* the web or vane of a feather. [< Latin *vexillum,* perhaps related to *vehere* to convey, or to *vēla* sail, covering]

**vex|ing** (vek′sing), *adj.* that vexes; annoying: *It is vexing to have to wait a long time for anyone.* — **vex′ing|ly,** *adv.*

**vext** (vekst), *adj.* = vexed.

**v.f.** or **VF** (no periods), **1** video frequency. **2** voice frequency.

**VFO** (no periods), variable frequency oscillator.

**V force,** a British airborne patrol for defense and warning against nuclear attack: *The V force ... at its maximum was believed to have numbered about 180 aircraft* (London Times).

**VFR** (no periods), visual flight rules.

**VFW** (no periods) or **V.F.W.,** Veterans of Foreign Wars (an association of veterans of the U.S. armed forces who have taken part in wars in foreign countries).

**v.g.,** for example (Latin, *verbi gratia*).

**V.G.,** vicar-general.

**V-girl** (vē′gėrl′), *n. U.S. Slang.* a girl or woman who follows or consorts with servicemen in wartime; a wartime camp follower.

**VHF** (no periods), **V.H.F.,** or **vhf** (no periods), very high frequency (of or having to do with the electromagnetic spectrum between 30 and 300 megahertz, especially with reference to radio and television transmission and reception).

**v.i.**, **1** intransitive verb. **2** see below (Latin, *vide infra*).

**Vi** (no period), virginium (chemical element).

**VI** (no periods), Virgin Islands (in postal Zip Code).

**V.I.**, Virgin Islands.

**vi|a** (vī′ə, vē′-), *prep.* by way of; by a route that passes through or over: *We are going from New York to California via the Panama Canal.* [< Latin *viā*, ablative of *via* way]

**vi|a|bil|i|ty** (vī′ə bil′ə tē), *n.* **1** the ability to keep alive; quality or condition of being viable: (*Figurative.*) *Many in Seoul ... asked whether it should not be accepted that economic viability without unification was impossible* (Manchester Guardian). **2** *Biology.* the ability to live in certain conditions of environment, such as climatic or geographical conditions.

**vi|a|ble** (vī′ə bəl), *adj.* **1** able to keep alive: *a viable animal or plant.* **2** fit to live in; livable: *a viable community. Only controlled disarmament can make a viable world in the nuclear age* (Stuart Chase). **3** *Figurative.* that can work or be put to use; workable: *a viable program, a viable economy.* **SYN:** vigorous, active. **4** sufficiently developed to maintain life outside the uterus: *a viable infant.* **5** *Botany.* capable of living and growing: *a viable spore or seed.* [< French *viable* < *vie* life < Latin *vīta*]

**vi|a|bly** (vī′ə blē), *adv.* in a viable manner.

**vi|a cru|cis** (vī′ə krü′sis), *Latin.* **1** a way marked by suffering and torment like that of Jesus: *the via crucis of a war orphan.* **2** (literally) the way of the cross.

**vi|a dol|o|ro|sa** (vī′ə dol′ə rō′sə), *Latin.* **1** a road or course of suffering and torment; via crucis. **2** (literally) the sorrowful way. [< *Via Dolorosa,* the road in Jerusalem taken by Jesus from the hall of judgment to Calvary]

***vi|a|duct** (vī′ə dukt), *n.* **1** a bridge for carrying a road or railroad, as over a valley, a part of a city, or a river. A viaduct consists of a series of narrow arches of masonry or reinforced concrete supported by high piers, or of steel with short spans supported by towers. **2** any bridge, as over a road, railroad, or canal. [< Latin *via* road + English *-duct,* as in *aqueduct*]

***viaduct**
definition 1

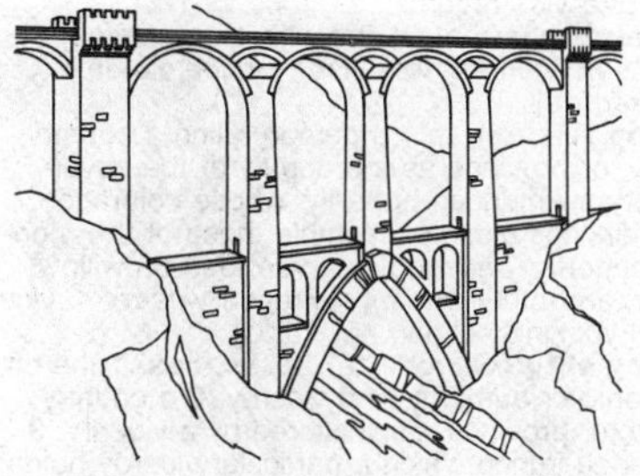

**vi|a|graph** (vī′ə graf, -gräf), *n.* an instrument that indicates the resistance due to grades, inequalities of surface, or the like, that a roadway presents to a wheeled vehicle running over it. [< Latin *via* road + English *-graph*]

**vi|al** (vī′əl), *n., v.,* **-aled, -al|ing** or (*especially British*) **-alled, -al|ling.** —*n.* **1** a small glass or plastic bottle for holding medicines, liquids, or the like; phial. **2** *Figurative.* a store or accumulation (of wrath, indignation, or other feeling) poured out upon an offender, victim, or other object (originally in allusion to the seven vials full of the wrath of God mentioned in Revelation 15:7 and 16:1-17): *For one so patient and good, he had a very large vial of indignation, and on occasion poured it out right heartily over all injustice* (W. G. Blaikie).
—*v.t.* to put, keep, or store in a vail.
[Middle English *viole, vial,* variant of *fiol* phial]

**vi|a me|di|a** (vī′ə mē′dē ə), *Latin.* a middle way; intermediate course (especially applied to the Anglican Church as standing halfway between the Roman Catholic and Protestant beliefs).

**vi|and** (vī′ənd), *n.* an article of food.
**viands,** articles of choice food: *When I demanded of my friend what viands he preferred, He quoth: "A large cold bottle, and a small hot bird"* (Eugene Field).
[< Anglo-French *viaunde,* Old French *viande* < Vulgar Latin *vīvanda,* for Late Latin *vīvenda* things for living < Latin, to be lived, neuter plural gerundive of *vīvere* to live]

**vi|at|ic** (vī at′ik), *adj.* = viatical. [< Latin *viāticus* of a journey < *via* way]

**vi|at|i|cal** (vī at′ə kəl), *adj., n.* —*adj.* of or having to do with a road or way; relating to a journey.
—*n.* **viaticals,** articles used or carried along in traveling, especially military baggage: *His back would have been bent ... under the weight of armour and viaticals which Titus carried with him easily and far* (Walter Savage Landor).

**vi|at|i|cum** (vī at′ə kəm), *n., pl.* **-ca** (-kə), **-cums.** **1** Holy Communion given to a person who is dying or in danger of death. **2** supplies or money for a journey. **3** supplies and transportation or money given to a public official of ancient Rome traveling on state business. [< Latin *viāticum* provision for a journey, noun use of neuter adjective, of a journey < *via* road, journey. See etym. of doublet **voyage.**]

**vi|a|tor** (vī ā′tər), *n., pl.* **vi|a|tor|es** (vī′ə tôr′ēz, -tōr′-), **1** a traveler; wayfarer. **2** a servant of certain magistrates of ancient Rome, one of whose duties was to deliver summonses. [< Latin *viātor, -ōris* < *via* way]

**vibes** (vībz), *n.pl.* **1** *Informal.* a vibraphone: *to play the vibes.* **2** *Slang.* vibrations (def. 5): *"There were wonderful vibes from the people," he [the conductor] said as the orchestra headed home. "I could feel them in the small of my back"* (Time).

**vib|ist** (vī′bist), *n. Informal.* a person who plays the vibes; vibraphonist.

**vi|brac|u|la** (vī brak′yə lə), *n.* plural of **vibraculum.**

**vi|brac|u|lar** (vī brak′yə lər), *adj.* **1** of, having to do with, or caused by vibracula. **2** having vibracula.

**vi|brac|u|loid** (vī brak′yə loid), *adj.* resembling a vibraculum or vibracula.

**vi|brac|u|lum** (vī brak′yə ləm), *n., pl.* **-la.** *Zoology.* one of the long, slender, whiplike, movable appendages or organs of certain bryozoans. [< New Latin *vibraculum* < Latin *vibrāre* to shake, oscillate]

**vi|bra|harp** (vī′brə härp′), *n.* = vibraphone.

**vi|bra|harp|ist** (vī′brə här′pist), *n.* = vibraphonist.

**vi|brance** (vī′brəns), *n.* = vibrancy.

**vi|bran|cy** (vī′brən sē), *n.* the quality or condition of being vibrant: (*Figurative.*) *Athens is vibrant; the merit of his book is that it communicates this sense of vibrancy* (New York Times).

**vi|brant** (vī′brənt), *adj., n.* —*adj.* **1** characterized by or exhibiting vibration; resounding; resonant. **2a** moving or quivering rapidly; vibrating: *a vibrant tongue, a vibrant string.* **b** *Figurative.* vibrating or thrilling something (with): *The stock exchange was vibrant with speculation.* **3** *Figurative.* throbbing, as with vitality or enthusiasm: *a vibrant personality.* **4** *Obsolete.* **a** agitated with anger or emotion. **b** moving or acting with rapidity or energy. **5** *Phonetics.* voiced.
—*n. Phonetics.* a vibrant sound.
[< Latin *vibrāns, -antis,* present participle of *vibrāre* to vibrate, shake] —**vi′brant|ly,** *adv.*

**vi|bran|te** (vē brän′tā), *adv., adj.* with a vibrating effect; pulsing or agitating. [< Italian *vibrante* < *vibrare* vibrate < Latin *vibrāre*]

**vi|bra|phone** (vī′brə fōn), *n.* a musical instrument similar to the xylophone, consisting of metal bars and electrically operated resonators that produce rich, vibrant tones. [< *vibra*(te) + *-phone*]

**vi|bra|phon|ist** (vī′brə fō′nist), *n.* a person who plays a vibraphone.

**vi|brate** (vī′brāt), *v.,* **-brat|ed, -brat|ing.** —*v.i.* **1a** to move rapidly to and fro: *A snake's tongue vibrates when he sticks it out. A piano string vibrates and makes a sound when a key is struck.* **SYN:** quiver, shake, tremble, throb. **b** *Physics.* to swing to and fro or otherwise move in an alternating or reciprocating motion by disturbing the equilibrium of the particles in an elastic body. **c** to swing to and fro; oscillate: *a vibrating pendulum.* **2** to be moved; quiver. **3** *Figurative.* to move or oscillate as between extreme conditions or opinions; fluctuate; vacillate. **4** *Figurative.* to thrill: *Their hearts vibrated to the speaker's stirring appeal.* **5a** to continue to be heard; strike; sound; resound: *The clanging vibrated in my ears.* **b** to circulate, move, pass, or pierce by vibration (about, through, to): *The mournful sound of the tolling bell vibrated through the air.*
—*v.t.* **1** to cause to move to and fro or up and down; set in vibration: *Virginian rattlesnakes ... swiftly vibrating and shaking their tails* (John Evelyn). **2** to measure by moving to and fro: *A pendulum vibrates seconds.* **3a** to send out, give forth, or emit (as light or sound) by vibration: (*Figurative.*) *to vibrate sympathy.* **b** *Obsolete.* to launch or hurl (as a thunderbolt or sentence). [< Latin *vibrāre* (with English *-ate*[1]) to shake]

**vi|bra|tile** (vī′brə təl, -tīl), *adj.* **1** that can vibrate or be vibrated. **2** having a vibratory motion. **3** having to do with or characterized by vibration.

**vi|bra|til|i|ty** (vī′brə til′ə tē), *n.* the property or condition of being vibratile; disposition to vibration or oscillation.

**vi|bra|tion** (vī brā′shən), *n.* **1a** a rapid or, sometimes, continuous movement to and fro or up and down; quivering or swaying motion; vibrating: *The passing buses shake the house so much that we feel the vibration.* **b** an instance of this; quiver; tremor: *The vibration of the ground during an earthquake is terrifying. The vibrations of deathless music* (Edgar Lee Masters). **2a** the act of moving or swinging to and fro, especially of a pendulum or other suspended body, across a position of equilibrium; oscillation: (*Figurative.*) *The words arose within him, and stirred innumerable vibrations of memory* (George Eliot). **b** a single swing or oscillation. **3** *Physics.* **a** the rapid alternating or reciprocating motion back and forth, or up and down, produced in the particles of an elastic body or medium by the disturbance of equilibrium. When the reciprocating movement is comparatively slow, such as that of a pendulum, the term *oscillation* is commonly used, while the term *vibration* is generally confined to a motion with rapid reciprocations or revolutions. **b** a single movement of this kind. **4** *Figurative.* the action or fact of vacillating or varying conduct or opinion; change or swinging around: *a great vibration of opinion* (George Bancroft). **5** Usually, **vibrations,** *pl. Slang, Figurative.* a feeling or sense of what others are thinking or feeling (supposedly from electric vibrations emanating from their minds); vibes: *"I never worried that I wouldn't see him [a dog] after he escaped, because I was sending out real strong vibrations to get him back"* (New Yorker).

**vi|bra|tion|al** (vī brā′shə nəl), *adj.* of, having to do with, or of the nature of vibration: *The lower the musical tone, the smaller is the number of vibrational cycles a second* (Simeon Potter). —**vibra′tion|al|ly,** *adv.*

**vi|bra|tion|less** (vī brā′shən lis), *adj.* free from vibration.

**vi|bra|tion-proof** (vī brā′shən prüf′), *adj.* that will not vibrate: *Vibration-proof buildings near the jet runways will soon be required.*

**vi|bra|ti|un|cle** (vī brā′shē ung′kəl), *n.* a slight vibration: *The English physician-philosopher David Hartley ... 200 years ago suggested that ideas were represented in the brain as vibrations and vibratiuncles* (Scientific American). [a diminutive form of *vibration*]

**vi|bra|tive** (vī′brə tiv), *adj.* vibrating; vibratory.

**vi|bra|to** (vē brä′tō), *n., pl.* **-tos,** *adv. Music.* —*n.* a vibrating or pulsating effect produced in the human voice or on stringed and wind instruments by a wavering of pitch, for shading or expressive purposes: [*Her*] *voice, a young, clear one with an agreeable vibrato, floats along prettily* (New Yorker).
—*adv.* with much vibration of tone.
[< Italian *vibrato* < *vibrare* vibrate < Latin *vibrāre*]

**vi|bra|tor** (vī′brā tər), *n.* **1** a thing that vibrates. **2** any one of various appliances, instruments, or parts that have or cause a vibrating motion or action: **a** a hammer, such as one in an electric bell, that vibrates. **b** one of the vibrating reeds of an organ. **3** an electrical device used to massage a part of the body: *Electric vibrators are used on the scalp to stimulate circulation.* **4** *Electricity.* **a** an apparatus for setting a given component in vibration by means of continual impulses. **b** a device for causing oscillations.

**vi|bra|to|ry** (vī′brə tôr′ē, -tōr-), *adj.* **1a** vibrating or easily vibrated: *a vibratory set of strings.* **b** capable of vibration: *a tuning fork is vibratory.* **2** of or having to do with vibration: *vibratory motion.* **3** causing or producing vibration: *a vibratory current of electricity.* **4** of the nature of, characterized by, or consisting of vibration: *Periodic oscillation is vibratory.*

**vib|ri|o** (vib′rē ō), *n., pl.* **-ri|os.** any one of a genus of short, curved bacteria, often shaped like a comma, spiral, or S, and characterized by lively motion, such as the species that causes Asiatic cholera. [< New Latin *Vibrio* the genus name < Latin *vibrāre* to vibrate]

**vib|ri|oid** (vib′rē oid), *adj.* resembling a vibrio.

**vibrioid body,** *Botany.* any one of various cylindrical bodies present in the outer layers of the cytoplasm of certain algae and fungi.

**vib|ri|on|ic** (vib′rē on′ik), *adj.* of, having to do with, or caused by vibrios or vibriosis: *vibrionic abortion in cattle and sheep.* [< New Latin *Vibrio, -onis* the genus Vibrio + English *-ic*]

**vib|ri|o|sis** (vib′rē ō′sis), *n.* a disease of cattle and sheep caused by a species of vibrio and characterized by abortion or infertility. [< *vibrio* + *-osis*]

**vi|bris|sa** (vī bris′ə), *n., pl.* **-bris|sae** (-bris′ē). **1** *Anatomy.* a hair growing in a nostril. **2** *Zoology.*

---

**Pronunciation Key:** hat, āge, cãre, fär; let, ēqual, tėrm; it, īce; hot, ōpen, ôrder; oil, out; cup, pu̇t, rüle; child; long; thin; ᴛʜen; zh, measure; ə represents a in about, e in taken, i in pencil, o in lemon, u in circus.

one of the long, bristlelike, tactile organs growing upon the upper lip and elsewhere on the head of most mammals; a whisker, as of a mouse. **3** *Zoology.* one of the special set of long, slender, bristlelike feathers that grow in a series along each side of the rictus (gape of the mouth) of many birds, such as flycatchers and goatsuckers. The vibrissae entangle the legs and wings of insects, and thus diminish or prevent their struggling when caught. [< Late Latin *vibrissae,* plural < Latin *vibrāre* to vibrate]

**vi|bro|graph** (vī′brə graf, -gräf), *n.* an instrument for recording vibrations: *Vibrographs installed in the rooms of the temples provided the criteria for the mode of excavation used* (New Scientist). [< Latin *vibrāre* vibrate + English *-graph*]

**vi|bron|ic** (vī bron′ik), *adj.* of or having to do with electronic vibrations: *vibronic spectra.* [< *vibr-*(ation) + (electr)*onic*]

**vi|bro|scope** (vī′brə skōp), *n.* an instrument for observing or for registering vibrations. [< Latin *vibrāre* to vibrate + English *-scope*]

**vi|bur|num** (vī bėr′nəm), *n.* **1** any one of several shrubs or small trees having showy clusters of white or pinkish flowers, such as the snowball, withe rod, and dockmackie. Viburnums comprise a genus of the honeysuckle family and are native to the Northern Hemisphere. **2** the dried bark of certain species, used in medicine. [< Latin *vīburnum*]

**vic|ar** (vik′ər), *n.* **1** in the Church of England: **a** the minister of a parish, who is paid a salary by the man to whom the tithes are paid. **b** a person acting as parish priest in place of the actual rector. **2** in the Protestant Episcopal Church: **a** a clergyman in charge of a chapel in a parish. **b** a clergyman acting for a bishop, in a church where the bishop is rector or in a mission. **3** in the Roman Catholic Church: **a** a clergyman who represents the pope or a bishop. **b** the Pope, as the earthly representative of God or Christ. **4** a person acting in place of another, especially in administrative functions; representative; vicegerent. [< Anglo-French *vikere, vicare,* Old French *vicaire,* learned borrowing from Latin *vicārius* (originally) substituted < *vicis* change, alteration. See etym. of doublet **vicarious.**]

**Vi|car|a** (vī kar′ə), *n. Trademark.* a woollike synthetic fiber made from zein, a protein abstracted from corn: *Vicara ... is used in blends with wool and synthetics to produce knit and woven fabrics having the soft, lofty feeling of cashmere* (William D. Appel).

**vic|ar|age** (vik′ər ij), *n.* **1** the residence or household of a vicar: *She goes to every service at the church, but is not a frequenter of the vicarage* (J. W. R. Scott). **2** the position, office, or duties of a vicar. **3** the salary paid to a vicar.

**vicar apostolic**, *pl.* **vicars apostolic.** in the Roman Catholic Church: **a** a missionary or titular bishop stationed either in a country where no episcopal see has yet been established, or in one where the succession of bishops has been interrupted. **b** (formerly) a bishop, archbishop, or other ecclesiastic with delegated authority from the pope.

**vic|ar|ate** (vik′ə rāt, -ər it), *n.* a parish or district under the jurisdiction of a vicar; vicariate.

**vicar capitular**, a clergyman in the Roman Catholic Church who administers a diocese in the absence of a bishop.

**vicar choral**, an assistant to the canons or prebendaries of the Church of England in the parts of public worship performed in the chancel or choir, especially in connection with the music.

**vic|ar|ess** (vik′ər is), *n.* **1** the Roman Catholic sister ranking immediately beneath the abbess or mother superior in a convent: *In 1931 she was elected vicaress* (*second in command*), *and in 1935 she spent a year traveling as Mother Mary Joseph's deputy* (Time). **2a** the wife of a Protestant Episcopal vicar. **b** a woman vicar in the Protestant Episcopal Church.

**vicar fo|rane** (fə rān′), an ecclesiastic dignitary or parish priest in the Roman Catholic Church appointed by a bishop to exercise a limited jurisdiction in a particular town or district of his diocese. [*forane* < Late Latin *forāneus* living outside. Compare etym. under **foreign.**]

**vic|ar-gen|er|al** (vik′ər jen′ər əl, -jen′rəl), *n., pl.* **vic|ars-gen|er|al. 1** (in the Roman Catholic Church) a deputy of a bishop or an archbishop, assisting him in the administration of a diocese. **2** (in the Church of England) an ecclesiastical officer, usually a layman, who assists a bishop or the Archbishop of Canterbury or York in legal or jurisdictional matters.

**vi|car|i|al** (vī kãr′ē əl, vi-), *adj.* **1** of or belonging to a vicar or vicars. **2** holding the office of a vicar. **3** delegated, as duties or authority; vicarious.

**vi|car|i|ate** (vī kãr′ē it, āt; vi-), *n.* **1a** the office or authority of a vicar. **b** a district in the charge of a vicar. **2a** a political office held by a person as deputy for another. **b** the exercise of delegated authority by a person or governing body. **c** a district under the rule of a deputy governor.

**vi|car|i|ous** (vī kãr′ē əs, vi-), *adj.* **1** done or suffered for others: *vicarious work, vicarious punishment.* **2** felt by sharing in the experience of another: *The invalid received vicarious pleasure from reading travel stories.* **3** taking the place of another; doing the work of another: *a vicarious agent.* **4** delegated: *vicarious authority.* **5** based upon the substitution of one person for another: *this vicarious structure of society, based upon what others do for us.* **6** *Physiology.* denoting the performance by or through one organ of functions normally discharged by another, as for example in vicarious menstruation. [< Latin *vicārius* (with English *-ous*) substituted < *vicis* a turn, change, substitution. See etym. of doublet **vicar.**] —**vi|car′i|ous|ly,** *adv.* —**vi|car′i|ous|ness,** *n.*

**vicarious menstruation**, bleeding from some part other than the uterus at the time of and instead of menstruation.

**vic|ar|ly** (vik′ər lē), *adj.* having to do with, appropriate to, or resembling a vicar, especially in dress.

**Vicar of Bray**, a person who changes his principles or opinions to suit the time or circumstances. [< a *vicar of Bray* in the 1500's, in Berkshire, England, who is said to have held his office in this way]

**Vicar of Christ**, (in the Roman Catholic Church) the pope, as standing in the place of and acting for Christ.

**vic|ar|ship** (vik′ər ship), *n.* the office or position of a vicar.

**vice[1]** (vīs), *n.* **1** an evil, immoral, or wicked habit or tendency: *Lying and cruelty are vices.* **2** evil; wickedness: *There is never an instant's truce between virtue and vice* (Thoreau). **SYN:** sin, iniquity, depravity, corruption. **3** a moral fault or defect; bad habit; flaw in character or conduct: *So for a good old-gentlemanly vice, I think I must take up with avarice* (Byron). *Ferocity and insolence were not among the vices of the national character* (Macaulay). **4** a mechanical defect in action or procedure; imperfection in the construction, arrangement, or constitution of a thing. **5** a physical defect or blemish; imperfection or weakness in some part of the system. **6** any one of several bad habits or tricks of horses, such as bolting or shying. **7** Also, **Vice.** a buffoon, often named for some vice, who supplied the comic relief in English morality plays. [< Old French *vice,* learned borrowing from Latin *vitium*]

**vice[2]** (vīs), *n., v.t.,* **viced, vic|ing.** = vise.

**vi|ce[3]** (vī′sē), *prep.* instead of; in the place of; in succession to. [< Latin *vice,* adverb; properly ablative of *vicis* a turn, change]

**vice-**, *prefix.* one who acts in place of another; substitute; deputy; subordinate: *Vice-president = a person who acts in the place of a president. Vice-consul = a subordinate consul.* [< Late Latin *vice-* < Latin *vice* vice[3]]

**vice-ad|mi|ral** (vīs′ad′mər əl), *n.,* or **vice admiral**, a naval officer ranking next below an admiral and next above a rear admiral. *Abbr:* V.Adm.

**vice-ad|mi|ral|ty** (vīs′ad′mər əl tē), *n., pl.* **-ties,** or **vice admiralty**, the rank or position of a vice-admiral.

**vice-chair|man** (vīs′chãr′mən), *n., pl.* **-men.** a person who substitutes for the regular chairman, or acts as his assistant: *In the absence of the chairman, the vice-chairman presided over the meeting.*

**vice-chan|cel|lor** (vīs′chan′sə lər, -chän′-), *n.* **1** a person who substitutes for the regular chancellor or acts as his assistant. **2** an officer of a university, acting for the chancellor, and in fact the chief administrative officer. **3** *Law.* a judge in a court of equity who assists the chancellor (presiding judge).

**vice-chan|cel|lor|ship** (vīs′chan′sə lər ship, -chän′-), *n.* **1** the office or dignity of a vice-chancellor. **2** the term of office of a vice-chancellor.

**vice-con|sul** (vīs′kon′səl), *n.* a person next in rank below a consul. He acts as his assistant or substitute or, in more remote areas, his agent. *Abbr:* V.C.

**vice-con|su|lar** (vīs′kon′sə lər), *adj.* of or having to do with a vice-consul.

**vice-con|su|late** (vīs′kon′sə lit), *n.* = vice-consulship.

**vice-con|sul|ship** (vīs′kon′səl ship), *n.* **1** the office or duties of a vice-consul. **2** the term of office of a vice-consul.

**vice|ge|ral** (vīs′jir′əl), *adj.* of or having to do with a vicegerent.

**vice|ge|ren|cy** (vīs′jir′ən sē), *n., pl.* **-cies. 1** the position or administration of vicegerent. **2** a district or province ruled by a vicegerent.

**vice|ge|rent** (vīs′jir′ənt), *n., adj.* —*n.* **1** a person appointed by a king or other ruler to act in his place or exercise his powers, authority, or administrative duties: *He was trusted by the sultan as the faithful vicegerent of his power* (Edward Gibbon). **2** a person who takes the place of another in the discharge of some office or duty; deputy.
—*adj.* **1** taking the place or performing the functions of another. **2** characterized by delegated power: *Under his great Vicegerent reign abide ... For ever happy* (Milton).
[< Medieval Latin *vicegerens, -entis* < Latin *vice* instead (of) + *gerere* to manage]

**vice|less** (vīs′lis), *adj.* free from vice.

**vice|like** (vīs′līk′), *adj. Especially British.* viselike.

**vic|e|nar|y** (vis′ə ner′ē), *adj.* **1** having to do with or consisting of twenty. **2** *Mathematics.* having 20 for the base: *a vicenary scale.* [< Latin *vīcēnārius* of twenty < *vīcēnī* twenty each < *vīgintī* twenty]

**vi|cen|ni|al** (vī sen′ē əl, -sen′yəl), *adj.* **1** of or for twenty years. **2** occurring once every twenty years. [< Latin *vīcennium* twenty-year period (< stem of *vīciēs* twenty times + *annus* year) + English *-al*[1]]

**vice-pre|mier** (vīs′pri mir′, -prē′mē ər), *n.* a deputy or assistant premier; an official ranking immediately below a premier: *This would be another promotion for Muñoz Grandes, who was named vice-premier in a Cabinet change in July 1962* (Bruce B. Solnick).

**Vice Pres.**, Vice-President.

**vice-pres|i|den|cy** (vīs′prez′ə dən sē, -prez′-dən-), *n.* the position of vice-president.

**vice-pres|i|dent** (vīs′prez′ə dənt, -prez′dənt), *n.* an officer next in rank to the president, who takes the president's place when necessary. If the President of the United States dies, resigns, or is removed from office, the Vice-President becomes President. The Vice-President of the United States takes part in cabinet meetings at the President's invitation, and is the president of the Senate. *Abbr:* V.P.

**vice-pres|i|den|tial** (vīs′prez ə den′shəl), *adj.* of or having to do with the vice-president.

**vice|re|gal** (vīs′rē′gəl), *adj.* of or having to do with a viceroy. —**vice′re′gal|ly,** *adv.*

**vice-re|gen|cy** (vīs′rē′jən sē), *n., pl.* **-cies. 1** the office or duties of a vice-regent. **2** the term of office of a vice-regent.

**vice-re|gent** (vīs′rē′jənt), *n., adj.* —*n.* a person who takes the place of the regular regent whenever necessary; deputy regent.
—*adj.* of, having to do with, or occupying the position of a vice-regent.

**vice|reine** (vīs′rān), *n.* the wife of a viceroy. [< French *vicereine* < *vice* vice[3] + *reine* queen < Latin *rēgīna*]

**vice|roy** (vīs′roi), *n.* **1** a person ruling a country, colony, or province as the deputy of the sovereign. **2** an American butterfly, whose coloration and markings closely resemble those of the monarch butterfly, and whose larvae feed on willow, poplar, and other trees. [< French *vice-roi* < *vice* vice[3] + *roi* king < Latin *rēx, rēgis*]

**vice|roy|al|ty** (vīs′roi′əl tē), *n., pl.* **-ties. 1** the office, rank, or authority of a viceroy. **2** a country, colony, or province administered by a viceroy. **3** the period during which a particular viceroy holds office.

**vice|roy|ship** (vīs′roi ship), *n.* the dignity, office, or jurisdiction of a viceroy; viceroyalty.

**vice squad**, *U.S.* a police squad responsible for enforcing laws against gambling and other vices: *In Detroit, a vice squad broke up a dice game, smashed dice tables and chairs, carted the players off to jail* (Time).

**vi|ce ver|sa** (vī′sē vėr′sə, vīs), the other way round; conversely; *John blamed Michael, and vice versa* (*Michael blamed John*). [< Latin *vice versa* < *vice* vice[3] + *vertere* to turn]

**Vich|y** (vish′ē), *n.* = Vichy water.

**Vich|y|ite** (vish′ē īt), *n.* a supporter of the government of unoccupied France from July, 1940 to November, 1942, and its policy of collaboration with the Nazis. [< *Vichy,* the capital of unoccupied France + *-ite*[1]]

**Vi|chys|sois** (vē shē swä′), *adj., n.* —*adj.* **1** of or having to do with the city of Vichy in central France. **2** of or supporting the Vichyite government: *Later still as Nuncio in Paris, he defended the accused Vichyssois bishops* (London Times).
—*n.* **1** a native or inhabitant of the city of Vichy. **2** = Vichyite.
[< French *vichyssois* of *Vichy*]

**vi|chys|soise** (vish′ē swäz′), *n.* a creamy potato-and-leek soup, sprinkled with chives served cold: *Vichyssoise is unquestionably a good soup and a great help in hot weather* (New Yorker). [< French *vichyssoise,* feminine, ultimately < *Vichy,* a city in France, near where the originator of the soup was born]

**Vi|chys|soise** (vē shē swäz′), *n. French.* the feminine of **Vichyssois.**

**Vichy water**, **1** a natural mineral water from springs at Vichy, France, containing sodium bicarbonate and other salts, used in the treatment of digestive disturbances, gout, and other ailments. **2** a natural or artificial water of similar composition.

**vic|i|nage** (vis′ə nij), *n.* **1a** surrounding district; neighborhood; vicinity: *to know well the people in his own vicinage.* **b** the people living in a certain district or neighborhood: *an to his thought the whole vicinage was haunted by her* (George Eliot). **2** the fact of being or living close to another or others; nearness; proximity. [< Old French *vicenage, voisinage* < *voisin* < Latin *vīcīnus,* see etym. under **vicinity**]

**vic|i|nal** (vis′ə nəl), *adj.* **1** neighboring; adjacent; near. **2** = local. **3** of or like a vicinal plane. [< Latin *vīcīnālis* < *vīcīnus;* see etym. under **vicinity**]

**vicinal plane,** *Mineralogy.* a subordinate plane in crystal whose position varies little from that of the fundamental plane which it replaces.

**vicinal way** or **road,** a local road, as distinguished from a highway; crossroad.

**vi|cin|i|ty** (və sin′ə tē), *n., pl.* **-ties. 1** the region near or about a place; neighborhood; surrounding district: *There are no houses for sale in this vicinity. He knew many people in New York and its vicinity.* **2** nearness in place; being close: *The vicinity of the apartment to his office was an advantage on rainy days.* SYN: propinquity, proximity. **in the vicinity of,** in the neighborhood of; near or close to: *a park in the vicinity of town,* (*Figurative.*) *a boat costing in the vicinity of $1,000.* [< Latin *vīcīnitās* < *vīcīnus* neighbor, neighboring < *vīcus* quarter, village, habitation]

**vi|cious** (vish′əs), *adj.* **1** evil; wicked: *vicious and weak conduct, a dictator's vicious love of power. The criminal led a vicious life.* **2** having bad habits or a bad disposition; fierce; savage: *a vicious horse, the vicious temper of the wicked witch.* **3** spiteful; malicious: *I won't listen to such vicious gossip.* **4** *Informal, Figurative.* unpleasantly severe: *a vicious headache.* **5** not correct; having faults: *This argument contains vicious reasoning. Oliver's Latin was vicious and scanty* (John Morley). **6** *Logic.* faulty, in the manner of a vicious circle. **7** *Obsolete.* foul; impure; noxious. **8** *Obsolete.* (of a part or function of the body) diseased; irregular. [< Anglo-French *vicious,* Old French *vicieux,* learned borrowing from Late Latin *viciōsus,* for Latin *vitiōsus* < *vitium* fault, vice[1]] **—vi′cious|ly,** *adv.* **—vi′cious|ness,** *n.*

**vicious circle, 1** two or more undesirable things, each of which keeps causing the other. **2** *Logic.* **a** false reasoning that uses one statement to prove a second statement when the first statement really depends upon the second for proof. **b** an inconclusive form of definition, in which two or more undefined terms or their equivalents are used to define each other. **3** *Pathology.* an abnormal process in which one disease or condition causes a second disease that then aggravates the first.

**vi|cis|si|tude** (və sis′ə tüd, -tyüd), *n.* **1** a change in circumstances or fortune: *The vicissitudes of life may suddenly make a rich man very poor.* **2** a change; variation; mutation: *the whirlpool of political vicissitude* (Hawthorne). **3** regular change: *the vicissitude of day and night.* [< Latin *vicissitūdō, -inis* < *vicissim* changeably < *vicis* a turn, change]

**vi|cis|si|tu|di|nar|y** (və sis′ə tü′də ner′ē, -tyü′-), *adj.* marked by alternation; coming alternately or by turns.

**vi|cis|si|tu|di|nous** (və sis′i tü′də nəs, -tyü′-), *adj.* subject to or experiencing changes of fortune or circumstances.

**Vick|ers test** (vik′ərz), a method of determining the hardness of metals by indenting them with a diamond pyramid under a specified load and measuring the size of the indentation. It is especially useful for thin samples. [< the *Vickers* Works, a British industrial firm]

**vi|comte** (vē kôNt′), *n. French.* viscount.

**vi|com|tesse** (vē kôN tes′), *n. French.* viscountess.

**vi|con|ti|el** (vī kon′tē əl), *adj. Law.* (in English history) of or having to do with a sheriff or a viscount. [< Anglo-French *vicontiel* < *viconte* viscount]

**vic|tim** (vik′təm), *n.* **1a** a person or animal sacrificed, injured, or destroyed: *victims of war, victims of an accident.* **b** a person who suffers some hardship or loss: *a victim of poverty.* **c** a person who dies or suffers as a result of voluntarily undertaking some enterprise or pursuit: *a victim of overwork.* **2** *Figurative.* a person badly treated or taken advantage of; dupe: *the victim of a swindler.* **3** a person or animal killed and offered as a sacrifice to a god. [< Latin *victima*] **—vic′tim|less,** *adj.*

**vic|tim|ise** (vik′tə mīz), *v.t.,* **-ised, -is|ing.** *Especially British.* victimize.

**vic|tim|iz|a|ble** (vik′tə mī′zə bəl), *adj.* that can be victimized.

**vic|tim|ize** (vik′tə mīz), *v.t.,* **-ized, -iz|ing. 1** to make a victim of; cause to suffer. **2** to cheat; swindle; defraud. **3** to put to death as or like a sacrificial victim; slaughter. **—vic′tim|i|za′tion,** *n.*

**vic|tim|iz|er** (vik′tə mī′zər), *n.* a person who victimizes another or others.

**vic|tim|ol|o|gist** (vik′tə mol′ə jist), *n.* a specialist in victimology.

**vic|tim|ol|o|gy** (vik′tə mol′ə jē), *n.* the study of victims and their roles in the crimes committed against them.

**vic|tor** (vik′tər), *n., adj.* **—*n.*** a winner; conqueror: *They see nothing wrong in the rule that to the victor belong the spoils of the enemy* (William Marcy).
**—*adj.*** victorious; triumphant: *Despite thy victor sword ... thou art a traitor* (Shakespeare).
[< Latin *victor, -ōris* < *vincere* to conquer]

**Vic|tor** (vik′tər), *n. U.S.* a code name for the letter *v,* used in transmitting radio messages.

**Victor Charlie,** *U.S. Military Slang.* **1** a Vietcong guerrilla. **2** the Vietcong. [< *Victor Charlie,* the communications code name for *V.C.,* abbreviation of *Vietcong*]

*** vic|to|ri|a** (vik tôr′ē ə, -tōr′-), *n.* **1** a low, four-wheeled carriage with a folding top and a seat for two passengers. A victoria has a raised seat in front for the driver. **2** an open automobile with a folding top covering the rear seat only. **3** any one of a small genus of South American water lilies with huge, strong, circular leaves often six feet or more in diameter, and a solitary flower, usually 12 to 14 inches in diameter, that changes from white to pink or red on the second day it is open. [< French *victoria* < *Victoria,* 1819-1901, Queen of England]

***victoria**
definitions 1, 2

definition 1

definition 2

**Vic|to|ri|a** (vik tôr′ē ə, -tōr′-), *n.* **1** any one of a breed of hogs bred primarily for lard. **2** a butterfly of the Solomon Islands, one of the largest in the world, with a wingspread of over nine inches.

**Victoria Cross,** a bronze Maltese cross awarded to members of the British armed forces as a decoration for remarkable valor during battle. [< Queen *Victoria*]

**Victoria Day,** a national holiday in Canada falling on the Monday before May 24, birthday of Queen Victoria, formerly celebrated as Empire Day.

*** Vic|to|ri|an** (vik tôr′ē ən, -tōr′-), *adj., n.* **—*adj.*** **1** of or having to do with the reign or time of Queen Victoria of England (1837-1901): *the Victorian age.* **2** having characteristics considered typical of Victorians, such as prudishness, bigotry, and conventionality.
**—*n.*** **1** a person, especially an author, who lived during the reign of Queen Victoria. **2** an article of furniture, piece of clothing, or other thing of style, from or identified with the time of Queen Victoria.

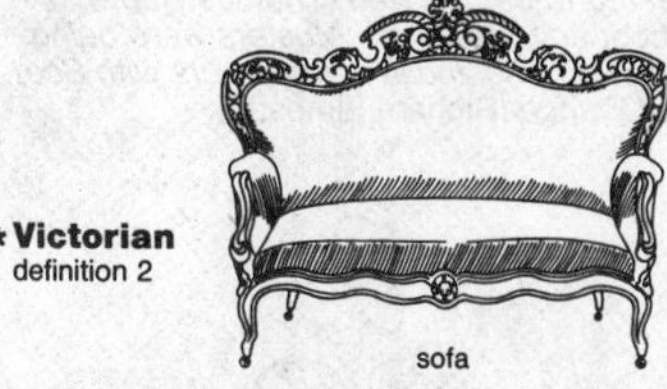

***Victorian**
definition 2

sofa

**Vic|to|ri|a|na** (vik tôr′ē ä′nə, -an′ə, -ā′nə; -tōr′-), *n.pl.* furniture, clothing, books, art, music, and facts, belonging to the Victorian period: *There are visions of interiors crammed with Victoriana, of walls hung with holy pictures and framed diplomas* (New Yorker).

**Victorian age,** the period during the reign of Queen Victoria of England, from 1837 to 1901, marked by scientific and literary achievements.

**Vic|to|ri|an|ism** (vik tôr′ē ə niz′əm, -tōr′-), *n.* **1** the ideas, beliefs, morals, way of living, and other standards common during the reign of Queen Victoria. **2** a novel, piece of furniture, building, or other work, characteristic of the Victorian age.

**Vic|to|ri|an|ize** (vik tôr′ē ə nīz, -tōr′-), *v.t.,* **-ized, -iz|ing.** to make Victorian in style or outlook: *to Victorianize a historic monument, to Victorianize education.* **—Vic|to′ri|an|i|za′tion,** *n.*

**Vic|to|ri|an|ly** (vik tôr′ē ən lē, -tōr′-), *adv.* in a Victorian manner: *The tone and manner of this song were Victorianly simple* (Chamber's Journal).

**vic|to|ri|ous** (vik tôr′ē əs, -tōr′-), *adj.* **1** having won a victory; conquering: *a victorious team, a victorious army.* **2** of or having something to do with victory; ending in victory: *a victorious war.* **—vic|to′ri|ous|ly,** *adv.* **—vic|to′ri|ous|ness,** *n.*

**vic|to|ry** (vik′tər ē, vik′trē), *n., pl.* **-ries. 1** the defeat of an enemy in combat, battle, or war. **2** the advantage or superiority gained in defeating the enemy or an opponent in battle; triumph gained by force of arms. **3** success in any contest, struggle, or enterprise; supremacy, superiority, or triumph in any effort: *The game ended in a victory for our school. Health alone is victory* (Thomas Carlyle). [< Latin *victōria* < *victor, -ōris* victor]
**—*Syn.*** **1, 2, 3 Victory, conquest, triumph** mean success in a contest or struggle. **Victory** applies to success in any kind of contest or fight: *We celebrated the victory of our football team.* **Conquest** emphasizes absolute control of the defeated: *the Spanish conquest of Peru. Some day we may complete the conquest of disease.* **Triumph** applies to a glorious victory or conquest: *The Nineteenth Amendment was a triumph for the suffragists.*

**victory garden,** (in World War II) a vegetable garden cultivated to help in the wartime effort to produce more food.

**Victory girl,** *U.S. Slang.* V-girl.

**Victory Medal,** a bronze decoration awarded at the end of World War I and World War II to all men and women who served in the U.S. armed forces during either war.

**Victory note,** a note of the Victory Liberty Loan issue, put forth by the U.S. Government in May, 1919, after the cessation of fighting in World War I, to provide funds for meeting obligations connected with the war.

**victory ribbon,** a service ribbon worn in place of the Victory Medal.

**Victory ship,** a cargo ship similar to a Liberty ship, built during World War II.

**vic|tress** (vik′tris), *n.* a female victor or conqueror.

**vic|trix** (vik′triks), *n.* = victress.

**vic|tro|la** (vik trō′lə), *n.* **1 Victrola.** *Trademark.* a kind of phonograph. **2** any phonograph, especially one having a motor whose spring is wound up with a crank. [American English < the *Victor* Talking Machine Company]

**vict|ual** (vit′əl), *n., v.,* **-ualed, -ual|ing** or **-ualled, -ual|ling. —*n.*** **victuals,** food or provisions, especially for human beings: *There was ... decking of the hall in the best hangings ... ; cooking of victuals, broaching of casks* (Charles Kingsley).
**—*v.t.*** to supply with food or provisions, especially with enough to last for some time: *The captain victualed his ship for the voyage.*
**—*v.i.*** **1** to take on a supply of food or provisions: *The ship will victual before sailing.* **2** to eat or feed: *sheep victualing on new grass.*
[spelling alteration (influenced by Latin) of Middle English *vitaylle* < Old French *vitaille* < Latin *victūalia,* neuter plural of *victūalis* of food < *victus, -ūs* food, sustenance < *vīvere* to live]

**vict|ual|age** (vit′ə lij), *n.* = victuals.

**vict|ual|er** (vit′ə lər), *n.* **1** a person who supplies food or provisions, as to a ship or an army. **2a** a tavernkeeper or innkeeper. **b** a person who sells food and drink. **3** a ship that carries provisions for other ships or for troops.

**vict|ual|ler** (vit′ə lər), *n.* = victualer.

**vict|ual|less** (vit′əl lis), *adj.* lacking food.

**vi|cu|gna** (vi kün′yə), *n.* = vicuña.

**vi|cu|ña** or **vi|cu|na** (vi kün′yə, -kyü′nə), *n.* **1** a wild, ruminant mammal of South America, related to and resembling the llama, having soft, delicate wool. **2** a soft cloth made from this wool, or from some substitute, used especially for coats. [< Spanish *vicuña* < the Quechua (Peru) name]

**vid.,** see (Latin, *vide*).

**vi|dame** (vē dȧm′), *n.* **1** (in French feudal use) the deputy or representative of a bishop in tem-

**Pronunciation Key:** hat, āge, cãre, fär; let, ēqual, tėrm; it, īce; hot, ōpen, ôrder; oil, out; cup, pu̇t, rüle; child; long; thin; ᴛʜen; zh, measure; ə represents **a** in about, **e** in taken, **i** in pencil, **o** in lemon, **u** in circus.

poral affairs, holding a fief from him. **2** a French minor title of nobility. [<Middle French *vidame* < Old French *visdame* <Medieval Latin *vicedominus* <Latin *vice* vice³ + *dominus* lord, master]

**Vi|dar** (vē′där), *n. Norse Mythology.* a strong, silent god of the Aesir, son of Odin, and the guardian of the forest or of peace.

**vi|de** (vī′dē), *v. Latin.* see; refer to; consult (a word indicating reference to something stated elsewhere): *The French Communist Party and press* (*vide the . . . affair of Picasso's posthumous portrait of Stalin*) *have repeatedly got themselves into hot water* (New Yorker).

**vi|de an|te** (vī′dē an′tē), *Latin.* see before this.

**vi|de in|fra** (vī′dē in′frə), *Latin.* see below.

**vi|de|li|cet** (və del′ə set), *adv.* that is to say; namely. *Abbr:* viz. [<Latin *vidēlicet,* for *vidēre licet* it is permissible to see]
▶See **viz.** for usage note.

**vid|e|o** (vid′ē ō), *adj., n.* **—*adj.*** of or used in the transmission or reception of images in television.
**—*n.*** = television. [<Latin *videō* I see, first person singular present of *vidēre* to see]

**video art,** a form of art based especially on the creation of videotapes of abstract or representational compositions.

**video cartridge** or **cassette,** a cartridge of film or videotape for use on a television set converted to show film or tape.

**vid|e|o|disc** (vid′ē ō disk′), *n.,* or **video disc,** a disc for recording sounds and images for use in television sets in the same way video cartridges are used.

**video display terminal,** a computer terminal with a cathode-ray tube.

**video game,** a game played by a special electronic unit that converts a television set into a display screen for points, lines, and dots of light that can be manipulated by twisting knobs to simulate games, such as tennis, hockey, and soccer.

**vid|e|o|gen|ic** (vid′ē ə jen′ik), *adj.* televising very well: *a videogenic face.*

**vid|e|o|ize** (vid′ē ō īz), *v.t.,* **-ized, -iz|ing.** to convert for use on television.

**vid|e|o|phone** (vid′ē ō fōn′), *n.* a telephone combined with a television camera and screen so people talking on the telephone can see each other; Picturephone; viewphone.

**vid|e|o|play|er** (vid′ē ō plā′ər), *n.* a television set that replays programs recorded on videotape and inserted into it.

**video recorder,** = videotape recorder.

**vid|e|o|tape** (vid′ē ō tāp′), *n., v.,* **-taped, -tap|ing.**
**—*n.*** a wide magnetized tape with tracks for recording and reproducing both sound and picture, especially for television.
**—*v.t.*** to record on videotape.

**videotape recorder,** a device for recording sounds and images on videotape: *Videotape recorders can be adjusted to turn on TV sets and record favorite programs* (Time).

**vid|e|o|tel|e|phone** (vid′ē ō tel′ə fōn), *n.* = videophone.

**vi|de post** (vī′dē pōst), *Latin.* see after.

**vi|de su|pra** (vī′dē sü′prə), *Latin.* see above.

**vi|dette** (vi det′), *n.* = vedette.

**vi|de ut su|pra** (vī′dē ut sü′prə), *Latin.* see as (given) above.

**vid|i|con** (vid′ə kon), *n.* a small pickup tube for a television camera: *The key of the camera is a . . . pickup tube, called a vidicon, which is only one inch in diameter and six inches long* (Science News Letter). [<Latin *vidēre* to see]

**vi|du|i|ty** (vi dü′i tē, -dyü′-), *n.* the condition or time of being a widow; widowhood. [<Old French *viduite,* <Latin *viduitās* <*vidua* widow]

**vie** (vī), *v.,* **vied, vy|ing.** **—*v.i.*** to strive for superiority; contend in rivalry; compete: *candidates vying for office. The children vie with each other to be first in line.* **—*v.t.*** **1** *Archaic.* to try to outdo in competition or rivalry; strive or contend; bandy (with): *to vie retorts with an opponent in debate.* **2** *Obsolete.* to hazard, stake, or bet (a sum or some article) on a hand of cards.
[short for Middle French *envier* increase the stake, Old French, challenge, invite <Latin *invītāre* invite, provoke. See etym. of doublet **invite.**] **—vi′er,** *n.*

**vie de bo|hème** (vē′də bô em′), *French.* Bohemian life; the unconventional life of artists, writers, and the like, especially in Paris: *Diderot followed his own advice and lived the . . . vie de bohème, made up of much talk, not enough food and more than enough love* (Time).

***vielle** (vyel), *n.* **1** one of the large, early forms of the medieval viol: *A series of performances with solo singer, vielles, recorders, lute, drums, in the now increasingly familiar manner of the musical explorers into older music* (Harper's). **2** = hurdy-gurdy. [<French *vielle,* Old French *viele;* origin uncertain]

**Vi|en|na sausage** (vē en′ə), a small sausage or frankfurter, often sold in cans; wienerwurst.

**Vi|en|nese** (vē′ə nēz′, -nēs′), *adj., n., pl.* **-nese.**
**—*adj.*** of or having to do with Vienna, the capital of Austria, or its people.
**—*n.*** **1** a person born or living in Vienna. **2** a dialect of German spoken in Vienna.

**vier|kleur** (fēr′klœr′), *n.* the flag of the old Transvaal Republic in South Africa. [<Afrikaans, Dutch *vierkleur* four-color <Dutch *vier* four + kleur color]

**Viet** (vyet), *n., adj. U.S. Informal.* **—*n.*** a Vietnamese. **—*adj.*** Vietnamese.

**vi et ar|mis** (vī′ et är′mis), *Latin.* by force of arms; by sheer force.

**Vi|et|cong** (vē et′kông′, vē′et-; vē et′kong′, vē′-et-), *n., adj.,* or **Viet Cong,** **—*n.*** **1** the Communist guerrilla force in South Vietnam. **2** a member of this force.
**—*adj.*** of or having to do with the Vietcong.

**Vi|et|minh** (vē et′min′, vē′et min′), *n.,* or **Viet Minh, 1** the Communist party in Indochina.
**2** a member of this party.

**Vi|et|nam|esé** or **Vi|et-Nam|ese** (vē et′nä mēz′, -mēs′), *adj., n., pl.* **-ese.** **—*adj.*** of or having to do with Vietnam, a country in southeastern Asia or its people.
**—*n.*** **1** a person born or living in Vietnam. **2** the Austro-Asiatic language spoken in Vietnam; Annamese.

**Vi|et|nam|ize** (vē et′nə mīz), *v.t.,* **-ized, -iz|ing.** to put under Vietnamese control. **—Vi|et′nam|i|za′tion,** *n.*

**Vi|et|nik** (vē et′nik), *n. U.S. Slang.* an opponent of American involvement in the war in Vietnam. [<*Viet*(nam) + *-nik*]

**vieux jeu** (vyœ zhœ′), *French.* **1** an old game. **2** an old-fashioned thing; something out-of-date. **3** *Figurative.* old-fashioned; out-of-date. *The festival was going to be largely vieux jeu by Western standards* (Harper's).

**view** (vyü), *n., v.* **—*n.*** **1** the act of seeing; sight: *It was our first view of the ocean.* **SYN:** look, survey, inspection, scrutiny. **2** the power of seeing; range of the eye: *A ship came into view.* **3** a thing seen; scene: *The view from our house is beautiful.* **4** a drawing, painting, print, photograph, or other picture of some scene: *Various views of the mountains hung on the walls.* **5** visual appearance or aspect: *Of stateliest view* (Milton). **6** *Figurative.* a mental picture or impression; idea: *This book will give you a general view of the way pioneers lived.* **SYN:** notion, conception. **7** *Figurative.* a way of looking at or considering a matter or question; opinion: *Children take a different view of school from that of their teachers. What are your views on the subject?* **SYN:** See syn. under **opinion. 8** *Figurative.* an aim; intention; purpose: *It is my view to leave tomorrow.* **9** *Figurative.* a prospect; expectation; outlook: *with no view of success.* **10** *Figurative.* a general account of something; survey: *The title is: "A View of Modern Art."*
**—*v.t.*** **1** to see; look at: *They viewed the scene with pleasure.* **SYN:** behold, witness, survey, examine, scan. **2** to look at carefully; inspect: *to view specimens under a microscope.* **3** *Figurative.* to consider; regard: *The plan of reducing school hours was not viewed favorably by the teachers.*
**in view, a** in sight: *As the noise grew louder, the airplane came in view.* (*Figurative.*) *He had no other job in view.* **b** *Figurative.* under consideration or attention: *Try to keep the teacher's advice in view as you try to improve your work.* **c** *Figurative.* as a purpose or intention: *Keep probability in view* (John Gay). **d** *Figurative.* as a hope or expectation: *Then, too, he had his uncle's bequest in view.*
**in view of,** a considering; because of: *In view of the fact that he is the best player on the team, he should be the captain. In view of the readiness she showed to second my search, all was, or appeared to be, forgiven* (Thomas Hope). **b** in prospect or anticipation of: *Musters were being taken through England in view of wars with Scotland and France* (Richard Simpson).

***vielle** definition 1

**on view,** to be seen; open for people to see: *The exhibit is on view from 9 A.M. to 5 P.M. He shall be on view in the drawing room before dinner* (Mary E. Braddon).
**take a dim view of,** to look upon or regard with disapproval, doubt, pessimism, or the like: *President Eisenhower and his assistants* [*took*] *a dim view of the old American custom of having beauty queens pictured with the President* (Tuscaloosa News).
**with a view to, a** with the purpose or intention of; with the hope of effecting or accomplishing: *He worked hard after school with a view to earning money for a new bicycle. The tendency is more and more to promote individual effort with a view to individual comfort* (Arthur Helps). **b** with regard to: *War may be considered with a view to its causes and its conduct* (William Paley). **c** in view of: *With a view to his approaching nuptials, Lord Castleton presented him with a handsome service of plate* (Eleanor Sleath).
[<Anglo-French *vewe* view, Old French *veüe,* noun use of feminine past participle of *veoir* to see <Latin *vidēre*]
**—*Syn.*** n. **3 View, scene** mean something which can be seen. **View** applies to what is within the range of vision of someone looking from a certain point: *That new building spoils the view from our windows.* **Scene** applies to those elements which make up a landscape, with little regard to where they are seen from: *We have a fine view of the mountain scene.*

**view|a|bil|i|ty** (vyü′ə bil′ə tē), *n.* the quality of being viewable: [*The television show*] *had won virtually every TV award and maintained a rare reputation for high production standards and general viewability* (Newsweek).

**view|a|ble** (vyü′ə bəl), *adj.* **1** worth viewing; pleasant to view: *Limited but decidedly viewable television was being produced in Britain during the last pre-war years* (New York Times). **2** exposed to view; visible: *Viewable ant colonies . . . aren't particularly new* (Wall Street Journal).

**view camera,** a large, adjustable-focus camera with bellows between the plate and a replaceable lens, used especially for portraits and architectural pictures.

**view|er** (vyü′ər), *n.* **1** a person who views, especially one who views television: *Many viewers, I have no doubt, will learn much from these programmes about the nerve-racking business of being interviewed by top people* (Punch). **2** a person appointed to examine or inspect something, especially by a law court. **3** an overseer, manager, or superintendent of a coal mine. **4** *Photography.* a device that magnifies and sometimes illuminates slides placed in it for viewing.

**view|er|ship** (vyü′ər ship), *n.* the television viewing audience: *The book will receive not only a wide readership . . . but also a wide viewership. The BBC has filmed* [*it*] *as a 13-part TV series* (Time).

**view|find|er** (vyü′fīn′dər), *n.,* or **view finder,** any device attached to or built in a camera for determining how much of a given scene is being photographed or televised.

**view halloo, hallo,** or **halloa,** the shout given by a huntsman on seeing a fox break cover.

**view|i|ness** (vyü′ē nis), *n.* the character or state of being viewy.

**view|ing** (vyü′ing), *n.* the act of a viewer, especially of a television viewer: *Americans take their viewing so seriously that more than one-fourth have their set repaired or replaced within four hours* (Time).

**view|less** (vyü′lis), *adj.* **1** that cannot be seen; invisible. **2** lacking a view or prospect. **3** *Figurative.* without views or opinions. **—view′less|ly,** *adv.*

**view|phone** (vyü′fōn′), *n.* = videophone.

**view|point** (vyü′point′), *n.* **1** a place from which one looks at something. **2** *Figurative.* an attitude of mind; point of view: *A heavy rain that is good from the viewpoint of farmers may be bad from the viewpoint of tourists.*

**view window,** = picture window.

**view|y** (vyü′ē), *adj.* **1** inclined to be impractical or visionary: *a viewy freshman, a viewy theory.* **2** *Slang.* attractive in appearance; showy.

**vi|ga** (vē′gə), *n. Southwestern U.S.* a beam that supports the roof in Indian and Spanish types of houses. [<Spanish *viga* beam, rafter]

**vi|gent** (vī′jənt), *adj.* flourishing; prosperous: *Durham College . . . after several changes of fortune is now vigent as Trinity College* (J. Wall). [<Latin *vigens, -entis,* present participle of *vigēre* to thrive]

**vi|ges|i|mal** (vī jes′ə məl), *adj.* **1** = twentieth. **2** in or by twenties. [<Latin *vīgēsimus,* variant of *vīcēnsimus* twentieth <*vīcēnī* twenty each <*vīgintī* twenty]

**vi|gi|a** (vi jē′ə), *n.* an indication given on a hydrographic chart of the presence of a rock, shoal, or the like, dangerous to navigation. [<Spanish *vigía* shoal; a lookout <Latin *vigilia;* see etym. under **vigil**]

**vig|il** (vij′əl), *n.* **1** the act of keeping awake during the usual hours of sleep for some purpose; act of watching; watch: *All night the mother kept vigil over the sick child.* **2** a night spent in prayer. **3** the eve, or the day and night, before a solemn religious festival or holy day, especially when observed as a fast. **4** wakefulness or a period of wakefulness due to inability to sleep: *Worn out by the labours and vigils of many months* (Macaulay).
**vigils,** the devotions, prayers, or services said or sung on the night before a religious festival: *I have seen the sublime Cathedral of Amiens on the night of Allhallows, when the vigils ... were sung there* (Kenelm E. Digby).
[< Old French *vigile,* learned borrowing from Latin *vigilia* < *vigil, -ilis* watchful, awake, related to *vigēre* be lively, in full possession of one's powers]

**vig|i|lance** (vij′ə ləns), *n.* **1** watchfulness, alertness, or caution: *Constant vigilance is necessary in order to avoid accidents in driving. The cat watched the mousehole with vigilance.* **2** *Pathology.* abnormal wakefulness; sleeplessness; insomnia.

**vigilance committee,** *U.S.* **1** a self-appointed and unauthorized group of citizens to maintain order and punish criminals in a community where law enforcement is imperfectly or insufficiently organized. In the 1800's, vigilance committees were common in frontier territories of the United States. **2** (formerly) a self-appointed organization of Southern white citizens whose aim was to intimidate, suppress, and terrorize Negroes, abolitionists, and carpetbaggers.

**vig|i|lant** (vij′ə lənt), *adj.* keeping steadily on the alert; attentively or closely observant; watchful, wide-awake, or cautious: *The dog kept vigilant guard over the baby.* SYN: wary, sharp. See syn. under **watchful.** [< Latin *vigilāns, -antis* watching, present participle of *vigilāre* keep watch < *vigil* watchful; see etym. under **vigil**] —**vig′i|lant|ly,** *adv.* —**vig′i|lant|ness,** *n.*

**vig|i|lan|te** (vij′ə lan′tē), *n. U.S.* a member of a vigilance committee. [American English < Spanish *vigilante* (literally) watchman < Latin *vigilāns;* see etym. under **vigilant**]

**vig|i|lan|tism** (vij′ə lan′tiz əm), *n.* the policies or actions of a vigilante or vigilance committee: *Langdon Street is identified ... with anti-intellectual vigilantism* (Harper's).

**vig|ils** (vij′əlz), *n.pl.* See under **vigil.**

**vi|gin|ten|ni|al** (vī′jin ten′ē əl), *adj.* occurring once in twenty years: *[The planets'] vigintennial conjunction is due a few months hence* (Glasgow Herald). [< Latin *vīgintī* twenty + English *-ennial,* as in *biennial*]

**vi|gin|til|lion** (vī′jin til′yən), *n., adj.* **1** (in the U.S., Canada, and France) 1 followed by 63 zeros. **2** (in Great Britain and Germany) 1 followed by 120 zeros. [< Latin *vīgintī* twenty + English *-illion,* as in *million*]

**vi|gne|ron** (vē nyə rôN′), *n.* a cultivator of grapevines; winegrower: *[He] told me about the wonderful year of 1893, when conditions had been so favorable that the vignerons were able to start picking grapes on August 16th* (New Yorker). [< French *vigneron* < *vigne* vine]

**vi|gnette** (vin yet′), *n., v.,* **-gnet|ted, -gnet|ting.** —*n.* **1** a decorative design on a page of a book, especially on or just before the title page, or at the beginning or end of a chapter. **2** a literary sketch; short verbal description: *"Dinner at Eight" in its original state is an episodic work, really a series of vignettes of the guests at the party and their relationship to each other* (New York Times). **3a** an engraving, drawing, photograph, or the like, that shades off gradually at the edge. **b** any picture or view of small, pleasing, and delicate proportion. **4** *Obsolete.* a decorative ornamentation of vine leaves, branches, and tendrils, as in architecture.
—*v.t.* **1** to make a vignette of. **2** to finish (a photograph or portrait) in the manner of a vignette.
[< French *vignette* < Old French (diminutive) < *vigne* vine < Latin *vīnea* < *vīnum* wine]

**vi|gnet|ter** (vin yet′ər), *n.* **1** a device for producing photographic vignettes. **2** = vignettist.

**vi|gnet|tist** (vin yet′ist), *n.* an artist or engraver who produces vignettes.

**vig|or** (vig′ər), *n.* **1a** active physical strength or force; flourishing physical condition: *A brief rest restored the traveler's vigor.* **b** the time or condition of greatest activity or strength, especially in the life of a person; healthy energy or power: *The vigor of a person's body lessens as he grows old.* **2** *Figurative.* mental activity, energy, or power; moral strength or force: *the vigor of a personality. The principal argued with vigor that the new school should have a library.* **3** *Figurative.* a powerful or active force of conditions, qualities, or agencies; intensity of effect, especially in artistic or literary works: *A succinct style lends vigor to writing.* **4a** strong or energetic action, especially in administration or government. **b** the use or exercise of power and action by a ruler or government official. **5** *Figurative.* legal or binding force; validity: *a law in full vigor.* Also, *especially British,* **vigour.** [< Anglo-French *vigour,* learned borrowing from Latin *vigor, -ōris* < *vigēre* be lively, thrive]

**vig|or|ish** (vig′ər ish), *n. U.S. Slang.* **1** the percentage of money from bets kept by a bookmaker as his commission or profit: *Despite the small vigorish, bookmakers find baseball their No. 1 sport* (Time). **2** the interest collected by a loan shark. [apparently < Russian *vyigrysh* winnings]

**vi|go|ro|so** (vē′gō rō′sō), *adj. Music.* vigorous; with energy. [< Italian *vigoroso* < *vigore* vigor (< Latin *vigor;* see etym. under **vigor**) + *-oso* -ose[1]]

**vig|or|ous** (vig′ər əs), *adj.* **1** full of vigor; strong and active in body and mind; full of strength or active force: *He keeps himself vigorous by taking exercise. At forty-five he was so vigorous that he made his way to Scotland on foot* (John R. Green). **2** characterized by, done with, or acting with vigor or energy; energetic: *Doctors wage a vigorous war against disease.* **3** *Figurative.* powerful; forcible: *an able, vigorous and well-informed statesman* (Edmund Burke). *His vigorous understanding and his stout English heart* (Macaulay). —**vig′or|ous|ly,** *adv.* —**vig′or-ous|ness,** *n.*
—*Syn.* **1 Vigorous, strenuous** mean having or showing active strength or energy. **Vigorous** emphasizes being full of healthy physical or mental energy or power and displaying active strength or force: *The old man is still vigorous and lively.* **Strenuous** emphasizes having a constant driving force and continuous energetic activity: *A diving champion leads a strenuous life.*

**vig|our** (vig′ər), *n. Especially British.* vigor.

**vi|ha|ra** (və hä′rə), *n.* a Buddhist temple or monastery. [< Sanskrit *vihāra*]

**Vi|king** or **vi|king** (vī′king), *n.* one of the daring Scandinavian pirates who raided the coastal towns and river ports of Europe from the 700's to the 900's A.D., often establishing settlements there. The Vikings were great warriors and explorers who conquered parts of England, France, Russia, and other countries and explored distant lands that may have included North America. [< Old Icelandic *vīkingr*]

**vil.,** village.

**vi|la** (vē′lä, -lə), *n., pl.* **-las** or **-le** (-lā). a nymph or fairy of the woods, fields, and streams in Slavic folklore, often described as deciding the destiny of newborn children and warning people that they are about to die. [< Serbo-Croatian *vila*]

**vi|la|yet** (vē′lä yet′), *n.* one of the provinces or main governmental divisions of Turkey. Also, **eyalet.** [< Turkish *vilâyet* < Arabic *wilāyat* < *wālī* governor]

**vile** (vīl), *adj.,* **vil|er, vil|est. 1** very bad: *a vile absurdity. The weather today was vile—rainy, windy, and cold.* **2** foul; disgusting; obnoxious: *A vile smell hung in the air around the garbage dump.* **3** evil; low; immoral: *vile habits, vile language, a vile criminal.* SYN: See syn. under **base. 4** poor; mean; lowly: *The king's son stooped to the vile tasks of the kitchen.* **5** of little worth or account; trifling: *the vile weeds in the field.* [< Anglo-French, Old French *vile* < Latin *vīlis* cheap; base, common] —**vile′ly,** *adv.* —**vile′ness,** *n.*

**vil|i|fi|ca|tion** (vil′ə fə kā′shən), *n.* the action of vilifying or fact of being vilified: *She defends her lovers from the vilification of the chroniclers* (Atlantic).

**vil|i|fi|er** (vil′ə fī′ər), *n.* a person who vilifies or defames.

**vil|i|fy** (vil′ə fī), *v.t.,* **-fied, -fy|ing. 1** to speak evil of; revile; slander: *Dissatisfied men are apt to vilify whatever government is in power.* SYN: disparage, defame. **2** *Obsolete.* **a** to lower in worth or value. **b** to make morally vile; degrade. **c** to dirty or defile. **3** *Obsolete.* to regard as worthless; despise. [< Late Latin *vīlificāre* < Latin *vīlis* vile + *facere* to make]

**vil|i|pend** (vil′ə pend), *v.t.* **1** to regard as having little value or consequence; treat contemptuously: *A youth ... vilipends the conversation and advice of his seniors* (Scott). **2** to speak with contempt; abuse; vilify: *to vilipend a rival.* [< Latin *vīlipendere* < *vīlis* vile, cheap + *pendere* to consider; (literally) weigh] —**vil′i|pend′er,** *n.*

**vill** (vil), *n.* **1** a territorial unit under the European feudal system, corresponding to the modern township. **2** = village. [< Anglo-French *vill,* Old French *ville* country house, village < Latin *vīlla*]

**vil|la** (vil′ə), *n., adj.* —*n.* **1a** a house in the country or suburbs, sometimes at the seashore. A villa is usually a large or elegant residence. *Magnificent villas are found throughout Italy.* **b** (originally) a country estate, including the land, residence, barns, and other farm buildings. **2** any house, usually in the suburbs.
—*adj.* of, having to do with, or like a villa: *villa style.*
[< Italian *villa* < Latin *vīlla,* perhaps related to *vicus* village]

**vil|la|dom** (vil′ə dəm), *n.* **1** suburban villas or their residents collectively. **2** *Figurative.* a smug, narrow-minded, and moderately prosperous suburban society.

**Vil|la|fran|chi|an** (vil′ə fran′chē ən), *n., adj.* —*n.* the early part of the Pleistocene: *[His] estimated date of 1.6 million years for the Pleistocene was the Pleistocene as then defined, and not the Pleistocene including the whole of the Villafranchian* (New Scientist).
—*adj.* of the early Pleistocene: *Villafranchian fauna.*
[< *Villefranche,* a village in southeastern France; form influenced by Italian name *Villafranca*]

**vil|lage** (vil′ij), *n., adj.* —*n.* **1a** a group of houses, usually smaller than a town, and often comprising a small municipality with limited corporate powers. **b** any group of people living together in separate, and usually rude, dwellings: *an Indian village.* **2** the people of a village; villagers: *The whole village turned out to watch the parade.* **3** a group or cluster of prairie dog burrows, often extending over a large area and having several thousand inhabitants.
—*adj.* of, having to do with, characteristic of, or living in a village; rural; rustic: *village schools.*
[< Old French *village* < Latin *vīllāticum,* noun use of neuter adjective, having to do with a villa < *vīlla* villa; see etym. under **villa**] —**vil′lage|like′,** *adj.*

**village community,** a primitive economic and political unit, consisting of a group of families living close together and owning the surrounding land more or less in common, as formerly existed in early England, Russia, Germany, India, and some other countries, and out of which many historians believe the modern political state evolved.

**village green,** *U.S.* the grassy open area of a New England village or town; the common.

**vil|lage|less** (vil′ij lis), *adj.* having no village.

**vil|lag|er** (vil′ə jər), *n.* a person who lives in a village.

**vil|lage|y** or **vil|lag|y** (vil′ə jē), *adj.* characteristic of or somewhat like a village: *"I love this neighborhood," she says. "It's so informal and villagey"* (New York Times). *The East End is very villagy* (London Times).

**vil|lag|i|za|tion** (vil′ə jə zā′shən), *n.* (in parts of South Africa and Asia) the placement of land under the control of villages.

**vil|lain** (vil′ən), *n.* **1** a very wicked person; scoundrel; knave: *The villain stole the money and cast the blame on his friend.* SYN: miscreant, reprobate, malefactor. **2** a playful name for a mischievous person. **3a** a character in a play, novel, or other work, whose evil motives or actions form an important element in the plot. **b** an actor who regularly plays parts of this nature. **4** = villein. [< Anglo-French, Old French *villain, vilein* < Medieval Latin *villanus* farmhand < Latin *vīlla* country house; see etym. under **villa**]

**vil|lain|age** (vil′ə nij), *n.* = villeinage.

**vil|lain|ess** (vil′ə nis), *n.* a woman villain.

**vil|lain|ize** (vil′ə nīz), *v.,* **-ized, -iz|ing.** —*v.t.* **1** to make villainous; debase or degrade: *Those writings which villainize mankind have a pernicious tendency towards propagating and protecting villainy* (Edmund Law). **2** to treat or revile as villainous or as a villain: *Our "best writers" villainize computers, automation, and the rest, while our publicists respond by concealing the new technology behind humanized images* (New York Times).
—*v.i.* to play the villain; act as a villain.

**vil|lain|ous** (vil′ə nəs), *adj.* **1** very wicked; depraved: *a villainous crew of pirates.* **2** deserving condemnation; marked by depravity; immoral: *a villainous act.* **3** characteristic of a villain; offensive; profane: *a villainous, low oath* (Robert Louis Stevenson). **4** *Figurative.* extremely bad; vile: *villainous weather.* —**vil′lain|ous|ly,** *adv.* —**vil′lain-ous|ness,** *n.*

**vil|lain|y** (vil′ə nē), *n., pl.* **-lain|ies. 1** great wickedness: *There was no manifest villainy about this woman* (New Yorker). SYN: baseness, rascality, infamy. **2** a very wicked act; crime. **3** *Obsolete.* **a** villeinage. **b** a base or morally degraded condition.

**vil|lan|age** (vil′ə nij), *n.* = villeinage.

**vil|la|nel|la** (vil′ə nel′ə), *n., pl.* **-nel|las, -nel|le**

**Pronunciation Key:** hat, āge, cãre, fär; let, ēqual, tėrm; it, īce; hot, ōpen, ôrder; oil, out; cup, pu̇t, rüle; child; long; thin; ᴛʜen; zh, measure; ə represents **a** in about, **e** in taken, **i** in pencil, **o** in lemon, **u** in circus.

(-nel′ā). **1a** an unaccompanied Italian part song of a light and rustic nature, forerunner of the madrigal. **b** a light, less contrapuntal madrigal. **2** a brisk, gay air, or the old rustic dance accompanying it. [< Italian *villanella;* see etym. under **villanelle**]

**vil|la|nelle** (vil′ə nel′), *n.* a fixed form of pastoral or lyric poetry normally consisting of 19 lines with two rhymes, written in five three-line stanzas (tercets) and a final quatrain: *A dainty thing's the villanelle, Sly, musical, a jewel in rhyme* (William E. Henley). [< Middle French *villanelle* < Italian *villanella* rustic < *villano* peasant, rustic < Medieval Latin *villanus;* see etym. under **villain**]

**Vil|la|no|van** (vil′ə nō′vən), *adj.* of or having to do with the early Iron Age in Italy, dating from about 1000 B.C.: *an eighth-century B.C. Villanovan ... handle in the form of a stylized bull with a smaller one on its back* (London Times). [< *Villanova,* a town in Italy, where remains of the age were found]

**vil|lat|ic** (vi lat′ik), *adj.* of or having to do with a villa or farm; rural; rustic: *tame, villatic fowl* (Milton). [< Latin *vīllāticus* < *vīlla* country house, village]

**-ville,** *combining form. U.S. Slang.* in a state of; being in or from: *He's Despairville, see, ... and he's fed up with humanity* (S. J. Perelman). *I just finished it* [*a book*] *and all I can say is like War and Peaceville* (Bruce Jay Friedman). [< *-ville,* place name suffix, as in *Nashville, Louisville*]

**vil|lein** (vil′ən), *n.* one of a class of half-free peasants in the European feudal system in the Middle Ages; villain. A villein was under the control of his lord, but in his relations with other men had the rights of a freeman. [Middle English variant of *villain*]

**vil|lein|age** or **vil|len|age** (vil′ə nij), *n.* **1** the fact or state of being a villein. **2** the conditions under which a villein held his land. Also, **villainage, villanage.** [< Anglo-French, Old French *villenage* < *vilein* (see etym. under **villain**) + *-age* -age]

**vil|li** (vil′ī), *n. pl. of* **vil|lus. 1** tiny, hairlike parts growing out of a membrane, especially those of the small intestine. The villi aid in absorbing certain substances. **2** *Botany.* the long, straight, soft hairs that cover the fruit, flowers, and other parts of certain plants. [< Latin *villi,* plural of *villus* tuft of hair, related to *vellere* to pluck]

**vil|li|form** (vil′ə fôrm), *adj.* having the form of villi; so shaped, numerous, slender, and closely set as to resemble the plush or pile of velvet, as the teeth of certain fishes.

**vil|li|no** (və lē′nō), *n., pl.* **-ni** (-nē). a small country house or villa, usually with a garden. [< Italian *villino* (diminutive) < *villa;* see etym. under **villa**]

**vil|lose** (vil′ōs), *adj.* = villous.

**vil|los|i|ty** (vi los′ə tē), *n., pl.* **-ties. 1** villous condition. **2** a villous formation, surface, or coating. **3** a number of villi together. **4** a villus.

**vil|lous** (vil′əs), *adj.* **1** having villi; covered with villi, especially covered with long, soft hairs, as parts of certain plants are. **2** like villi. [< Latin *villōsus* shaggy < *villus;* see etym. under **villi**] —**vil′lous|ly,** *adv.*

**vil|lus** (vil′əs), *n.* singular of **villi.**

**vim** (vim), *n.* force; energy; vigor: *The campers were full of vim after a good night's sleep.* [American English, apparently < Latin *vim,* accusative of *vīs* force]

**vi|ma|na** (vi mä′nə), *n.* (in India) a pyramidal tower, built in stories, surmounting the shrine of a temple. [< Sanskrit *vimāna*]

**vi|men** (vī′mən), *n., pl.* **vim|i|na** (vim′ə nə). *Botany.* a long, flexible shoot of a plant; twig. [< Latin *vīmen, -inis* twig, osier]

**vim|ful** (vim′fəl), *adj.* full of vim or vigor: *Valladolid ... retains the vimful life of a capital* (Glasgow Herald).

**vim|i|nal** (vim′ə nəl), *adj.* **1** of a vimen. **2** producing vimina.

**Vim|i|nal** (vim′ə nəl), *n.* one of the seven hills on which the city of Rome was built.

**vi|min|e|ous** (vi min′ē əs), *adj.* **1** *Botany.* producing long, flexible shoots or twigs. **2** made of pliable twigs or wickerwork. [< Latin *vīmineus* (with English *-ous*) < *vīmen, -inis* twig, osier]

**v. imp.,** impersonal verb.

**vi|na**[1] (vē′nə), *n.* a four- or five-stringed Hindu musical instrument of ancient origin, consisting of a long, fretted, bamboo finger board, and having a gourd at each end for resonance. Also, **veena.** [< Sanskrit *vīṇā*]

**vi|na**[2] (vī′nə), *n.* plural of **vinum.**

**vi|na|ceous** (vī nā′shəs), *adj.* **1** belonging to wine or grapes. **2** red, like wine; wine-colored. [< Latin *vīnāceus* (with English *-ous*) < *vīnum* wine]

**vin|ai|grette** (vin′ə gret′), *n., adj.* —*n.* **1** a small ornamental bottle or box usually containing a sponge charged with smelling salts or the like. Also, **vinegarette. 2** = vinaigrette sauce.
—*adj.* served with vinaigrette sauce: *Hofmann had also stirred up ... pickled whale flippers, and walrus flippers vinaigrette* (New Yorker).
[< French *vinaigrette* < Old French *vinaigre;* see etym. under **vinegar**]

**vinaigrette sauce,** a sauce made of vinegar, oil, and herbs, used on cold meats or vegetables.

**vi|nal**[1] (vī′nəl), *adj.* of, produced by, or originating in wine: *vinal spirits, vinal energy.* [< Latin *vīnālis* < *vīnum* wine]

**vi|nal**[2] (vī′nəl), *n.* any one of a group of synthetic fibers with high resistance to fungi and mildew, used for fishing nets, bathing suits, rainwear, and the like. Vinals are long-chain polymers composed of measured units of vinyl alcohol and acetal. [< *vin*(yl) *al*(cohol)]

**vi|nasse** (vi nas′), *n.* the dregs remaining after distilling liquor or pressing wine. [< French *vinasse,* probably < Provençal *vinassa* < Latin *vīnācea* grapeskin; (originally) adjective, feminine of *vīnāceus;* see etym. under **vinaceous**]

**Vin|a|ya** (vin′ə yə), *n.* (in Hinayana Buddhism) the body of monastic rules of discipline. [< Sanskrit *Vinaya*]

**vin blanc** (vaN blän′), *French.* white wine.

**vin|blas|tine** (vin blas′tēn), *n.* an alkaloid derived from the periwinkle of Madagascar, used in the treatment of leukemia and lymphoma. *Formula:* $C_{46}H_{58}N_4O_9$ [< *vin*(caleuko)*blastine*]

**vin|ca** (ving′kə), *n.* = periwinkle. [< New Latin *Vinca,* the genus name < Latin (*per*)*vinca* periwinkle]

**vin|ca|leu|ko|blas|tine** (ving′kə lü′kō blas′tēn), *n.* = vinblastine. [< *vinca* + *leuko-* + *blast-* + *-ine*[2]]

**Vin|cen|tian** (vin sen′shən), *adj., n.* —*adj.* of or having to do with the French priest St. Vincent de Paul (1581?-1660) or with certain religious associations of which he was the founder or patron: *Vincentian Fathers, a Vincentian missionary.* —*n.* a member of an order of Roman Catholic missionary priests founded by St. Vincent de Paul in France in 1625; Lazarist.

**Vin|cent's angina** (vin′sənts), an inflammation of the mucous membranes of the throat and mouth, characterized by the formation of ulcers and a false membrane at the back of the throat and tonsils; trench mouth. Vincent's angina is caused by fusiform bacteria usually found together with spirochetes. [< Jean *Vincent,* 1862-1950, a French physician, who described it]

**Vincent's infection** or **stomatitis,** = Vincent's angina.

**vin|ci|bil|i|ty** (vin′sə bil′ə tē), *n.* the state or character of being vincible; capability of being conquered.

**vin|ci|ble** (vin′sə bəl), *adj.* easily overcome, defeated, or vanquished; conquerable: *a vincible army, a vincible argument.* [< Latin *vincibilis* < *vincere* to conquer] —**vin′ci|ble|ness,** *n.*

**vin|cit om|ni|a ve|ri|tas** (vin′sit om′nē ə ver′ə-tas), *Latin.* truth conquers all things.

**vin|cris|tine** (vin kris′tēn), *n.* an alkaloid derived from the periwinkle of Madagascar and similar to vinblastine, used in combination with steroids to treat acute leukemia. *Formula:* $C_{46}H_{56}N_4O_{10}$ [< *vin*(ca) + Latin *crista* crest + English *-ine*[2]]

***vin|cu|lum** (ving′kyə ləm), *n., pl.* **-la** (-lə). **1** a bond of union; tie: (*Figurative.*) *the vinculum linking cause and effect.* **2** *Mathematics.* a straight line or brace drawn over several terms to show that they are to be considered together, as in $c \cdot \overline{a+b}$, meaning ca + cb. [< Latin *vinculum* bond < *vincīre* to bind]

***vinculum**
definition 2

$$c \cdot \overline{a+b}$$
ca + cb

$$3 \cdot \overline{4+5} = 27$$
3 x (4 + 5) = 27

**vin|cu|lum ma|tri|mo|ni|i** (ving′kyə ləm mat′rə-mō′nē ī), *Latin.* the bond of matrimony.

**vin d'hon|neur** (vaN′ dô nœr′), **1** wine drunk on a special occasion in honor of a visitor, especially a local wine that is saved for such an occasion. **2** the ceremony at which this is offered. **3a** a cocktail party: *After the ceremony General Gruenther and his staff gave a vin d'honneur for the German representatives* (London Times). **b** = cocktail. [< French *vin d'honneur* wine of honor]

**vin|di|ca|ble** (vin′də kə bəl), *adj.* that can be vindicated; justifiable.

**vin|di|cate** (vin′də kāt), *v.t.,* **-cat|ed, -cat|ing. 1** to clear from suspicion, dishonor, or any charge of wrongdoing: *The verdict of "not guilty" vindicated him.* SYN: exculpate. **2** to defend successfully against opposition; uphold; justify: *The heir vindicated his claim to the fortune.* **3** to assert a claim to; take possession of. **4** *Obsolete.* to avenge, punish, or retaliate. **5** *Obsolete.* to make or set free; deliver or rescue (from). [< Latin *vindicāre* (with English *-ate*[1]) to set free; avenge, claim, probably < *vim,* accusative of *vīs* force + *dīcere* to say]

**vin|di|ca|tion** (vin′də kā′shən), *n.* the act of vindicating or state of being vindicated; defense; justification.

**vin|dic|a|tive** (vin dik′ə tiv, vin′də kā′-), *adj.* **1** tending to vindicate; justifying. **2** *Obsolete.* vindictive. [< Medieval Latin *vindicativus* < Latin *vindicāre;* see etym. under **vindicate**]

**vin|di|ca|tor** (vin′də kā′tər), *n.* a person who vindicates; one who justifies, maintains, or defends.

**vin|di|ca|to|ry** (vin′də kə tôr′ē, -tōr′-), *adj.* **1** serving to vindicate or justify; defensive. **2** avenging; punitive; retaliatory.

**vin|dic|tive** (vin dik′tiv), *adj.* **1** wanting revenge; bearing a grudge: *He is so vindictive that he never forgives anybody.* SYN: revengeful, spiteful. **2** showing a strong tendency toward revenge: *Vindictive acts rarely do much good.* SYN: revengeful, spiteful. [< Latin *vindicta* revenge (< *vindicāre* vindicate) + English *-ive*] —**vin|dic′tive|ly,** *adv.* —**vin|dic′tive|ness,** *n.*

**vin du pa|ys** (vaN′ dʏ pā ē′), *French.* **1** locally produced wine: *Most rosés are vin du pays and should be drunk where they grow and when they're young* (Atlantic). **2** (literally) wine of the country.

**vine** (vīn), *n.* **1** any plant with a long, slender stem that grows along the ground, or that climbs by attaching itself to a wall, tree, or other support. Melons and pumpkins grow on vines. Ivy is a vine. **2** the stem of any trailing or climbing plant. **3** = grapevine.
**wither on the vine,** to end prematurely or fruitlessly; abort: *An enterprise that does not attract customers soon withers on the vine* (William Henry Chamberlin).
[< Old French *vine* < Latin *vīnea* vine, vineyard < *vīnum* wine. See related etym. at **wine.**]
—**vine′like′,** *adj.*

**vin|e|al** (vin′ē əl, vī′nē-), *adj.* of or having to do with vines or wine: *vineal aroma, vineal exports.* [< Latin *vīneālis* < *vīnea* vine + *-ālis* -al]

**vine borer,** the larva of any one of certain beetles and moths, that bores into the wood or root of vines and is often very destructive.

**vine-clad** (vīn′klad′), *adj.* clad or covered with vines.

**vined** (vīnd), *adj.* **1** having leaves like those of a vine; ornamented with vine leaves: *wreathed and vined and figured columns* (Henry Wotton). **2** separated from the pod or vine: *Most vegetables, including vined peas, are air-dried* (London Times).

**vine|dress|er** (vīn′dres′ər), *n.* a person who prunes, trains, and cultivates vines, especially grapevines.

**vin|e|gar** (vin′ə gər), *n., v.* —*n.* **1** a sour liquid produced by the fermenting of cider, wine, beer, ale, malt, or the like, consisting largely of dilute, impure acetic acid. Vinegar is used in salad dressing and in flavoring or preserving food. **2** a preparation made by macerating a drug in dilute acetic acid and filtering. **3** *Figurative.* speech or temper of a sour or acid character: *several little sprinklings of wordy vinegar* (Dickens).
—*v.t.* to treat with vinegar; put vinegar in or on.
[< Old French *vinaigre,* or *vinagre* < *vin* wine (< Latin *vīnum*) + *aigre,* and *egre* sour < Latin *ācer, ācris*] —**vin′e|gar|like′,** *adj.*

**vinegar eel** or **worm,** a minute nematode worm found commonly in vinegar.

**vin|e|gar|ette** (vin′ə gə ret′), *n.* = vinaigrette. [alteration (influenced by *vinegar*) of *vinaigrette*]

**vinegar fly,** a fruit fly that is attracted by fermentation and develops in pickles, jam, and decaying fruit.

**vin|e|gar|ish** (vin′ə gər ish), *adj.* somewhat like vinegar; sourish: [*The*] *Bishop of London ... had some vinegarish afterthoughts about the meeting of the World Council of Churches last year* (Newsweek).

**vin|e|gar|oon** (vin′ə gə rün′), *n.* a large whip scorpion of the southwest United States, mistakenly believed to be poisonous, and, when alarmed, having an odor like that of vinegar. [American English, alteration of American Spanish *vinagrón* < Spanish *vinagre* vinegar]

**vin|e|gar|y** (vin′ə gər ē, -grē), *adj.* of or like vinegar; sour: *This salad dressing has a vinegary taste.* (*Figurative.*) *That cross, old woman has a vinegary disposition.*

**vine|less** (vīn′lis), *adj.* having no vines.

**vine|let** (vīn′lit), *n.* a young vine.

**vin|er** (vī′nər), *n.* a machine for harvesting and shelling peas: *a mobile viner.*

**vin|er|y** (vī′nər ē), *n., pl.* **-er|ies. 1a** a hothouse for the cultivation of grapevines; grapery. **b** *Obsolete.* a vineyard. **2** vines collectively.

**vine|yard** (vin′yərd), *n.* **1** a place planted with grapevines. **2** *Figurative.* a field or sphere of activity, especially religious work.

**vine|yard|ing** (vin′yər ding), *n.* the cultivation of vineyards.

**vine|yard|ist** (vin′yər dist), *n.* a person who engages in growing vines.

**vingt-et-un** (vaɴ′tā œɴ′), *n.* = twenty-one. [< French *vingt-et-un* (literally) twenty-one]

**vi|nic** (vī′nik), *adj.* of, obtained, or derived from wine or alcohol. [< Latin *vīnum* wine + English *-ic*]

**vin|i|cul|tur|al** (vin′ə kul′chər əl), *adj.* of or having to do with viniculture. – **vin′i|cul′tur|al|ly**, *adv.*

**vin|i|cul|ture** (vin′ə kul′chər), *n.* the cultivation of grapes for the production of wine. [< Latin *vīnum* wine + *cultūra* culture]

**vin|i|cul|tur|ist** (vin′ə kul′chər ist), *n.* a person who cultivates grapes for the production of wine.

**vi|nif|e|ra** (vī nif′ə rə), *adj.* having to do with or designating the chief species of grapes used in Europe to make the finest wines, transplanted to California, South America, Africa, and Australia. [< New Latin (*Vitis*) *vinifera* the species name < Latin *vīnifer* wine-producing, viniferous]

**vi|nif|er|ous** (vī nif′ər əs), *adj.* yielding or producing wine. [< Latin *vīnifer* (< *vīnum* wine) + English *-ous*]

**vin|i|fi|ca|tion** (vin′ə fə kā′shən), *n.* the process of making wine; conversion of the juice of grapes or the like into wine by fermentation. [< Latin *vīnum* wine + English *-fication*]

**vin|i|fi|ca|tor** (vin′ə fə kā′tər), *n.* an apparatus for collecting alcoholic vapor that rises from fermenting grape juice in making wine.

**vin|i|fy** (vin′ə fī), *v.t.*, **-fied, -fy|ing.** to make wine from; convert the juice of (grapes or the like) into wine by fermentation. [< Latin *vīnum* wine + English *-fy*]

**vi|no** (vē′nō), *n.* **1** = wine. **2** an alcoholic liquor consisting of the fermented leaves and sap of the coconut and the talipot palm, drunk in the Philippines, Guam, and western Mexico. [< Spanish and Italian *vino* wine]

**vin|ol|o|gy** (vi nol′ə jē, vī-), *n.* the study of wines; oenology. [< Latin *vīnum* wine + English *-logy*]

**vin|om|e|ter** (vi nom′ə tər, vī-), *n.* an instrument for measuring the alcoholic strength or the purity of wine. [< Latin *vīnum* wine + English *-meter*]

**vin or|di|naire** (vaɴ ôr dē ner′), a low-priced wine (usually red) ordinarily served at meals in France and elsewhere. [< French *vin ordinaire* (literally) ordinary wine]

**vi|nos|i|ty** (vī nos′ə tē), *n.* **1** the quality or condition of being vinous. **2** fondness for, or addiction to, wine. [< Latin *vīnōsitās* wine flavor < *vīnōsus* full of wine, addicted to wine < *vīnum* wine]

**vi|nous** (vī′nəs), *adj.* **1** of, like, or having to do with wine. **2** caused by drinking wine. **3** addicted to wine. **4** red, like wine; having a wine-colored tinge. [< Latin *vīnōsus* < *vīnum* wine] – **vi′nous|ly**, *adv.*

**vin ro|sé** (vaɴ rō zā′), *French.* rosé.

**vin rouge** (vaɴ rüzh′), *French.* red wine.

**vint**[1] (vint), *v.t.* to make (vintage wine): *I wouldn't give a straw for the best wine that was ever vinted after it had lain here a couple of years* (Anthony Trollope). [back formation < *vintner* or *vintage*]

**vint**[2] (vint), *n.* a Russian card game resembling auction bridge. [< Russian *vint*]

**vin|ta** (vēn′tä), *n.* a kind of dugout or canoe with outriggers, used in the Philippines, especially by the Moros. [< Visayan *binta*]

**vin|tage** (vin′tij), *n., adj., v.,* **-taged, -tag|ing.** – ***n.*** **1** the wine from a certain crop of grapes. Some vintages are better than others. **2** a year's crop of grapes. **3** the year in which a particular wine, especially one of outstanding quality, was produced. **4** the gathering of grapes for making wine. **5** the season of gathering grapes and making wine. **6** *Figurative.* the output of anything at some particular time; something which was fashionable or popular during an earlier season: *Her old hat was of the vintage of 1940.* **7** *Figurative.* age, especially old age: *Hamlin's staging respects the play's vintage* (Howard Taubman).
– ***adj.*** **1** of outstanding quality; choice: *vintage wines.* **2** *Figurative.* of antique or classic style or excellence: *a vintage thoroughbred, a vintage Rolls-Royce engine.* **3** *Figurative.* out-of-date; old-fashioned: *a vintage streetcar.*
– ***v.t.*** to make (wine) from gathered grapes; vint: *Marne, where the true sparkling champagne is vintaged* (Pall Mall Gazette).
[< Anglo-French *vintage,* alteration of Old French *vendange* < Latin *vīndēmia* < *vīnum* wine + *dēmere* take off < *dē-* away + *emere* to take]

**vin|tag|er** (vin′tə jər), *n.* a person who gathers grapes for making wine; laborer at the vintage.

**vintage year**, **1** a year in which a particular outstanding wine was produced. **2** a year distinguished for some particular accomplishment.

**vint|ner** (vint′nər), *n.* **1** a dealer in wine; wine merchant. **2** a maker of wine; wine manufacturer. *When Prohibition came, the vintners either ground out tons of grape juice or sadly closed down their presses and let their plump grapes wrinkle up into raisins* (Time). [alteration of Middle English *vinter* < Anglo-French *vineter* < Medieval Latin *vinetarius* < Latin *vīnum* wine]

**vi|num** (vī′nəm), *n., pl.* **-na.** *Pharmacology.* wine, as an ingredient in prescriptions or other medicinal substances. [< Latin *vīnum*]

**vin|y** (vī′nē), *adj.,* **vin|i|er, vin|i|est. 1** of, like, or having to do with vines. **2** abounding in or covered with vines; bearing or producing vines.

**vi|nyl** (vī′nəl), *n., adj.* – ***n.*** a univalent radical regarded as an ethylene derivative. Vinyl is made into various tough synthetic plastics or resins used in floor coverings, toys, molded articles, and phonograph records. *Formula:* $CH_2$:CH-
– ***adj.*** of, denoting, or containing this radical.
[< Latin *vīnum* wine + English *-yl*]

**vinyl acetate**, a colorless liquid readily polymerized by heat, oxygen, or light, to form polyvinyl acetate and other resins. *Formula:* $C_4H_6O_2$

**vi|nyl|a|cet|y|lene** (vī′nəl ə set′ə lēn, -lin), *n.* a colorless liquid, the dimer of acetylene, used as an intermediate in manufacturing neoprene. *Formula:* $C_4H_4$

**vinyl alcohol**, an ethylene derivative, an alcohol, which polymerizes to form polyvinyl alcohol (the only form in which it is known). *Formula:* $C_2H_4O$

**vinyl chloride**, a colorless, inflammable gas or liquid used in the manufacture of plastics, as a refrigerant, and in organic synthesis. *Formula:* $C_2H_3Cl$

**vi|nyl|i|dene** (vī nil′ə dēn), *n., adj.* – ***n.*** a bivalent radical, regarded as an ethylene derivative. *Formula:* $CH_2$:C-
– ***adj.*** of, denoting, or containing this radical.

**vinylidene chloride**, a compound, an ethylene derivative, readily polymerized to form polyvinylidene chloride. *Formula:* $C_2H_2Cl_2$

**vinylidene fluoride**, a colorless gas used in making synthetic rubber. *Formula:* $C_2H_2F_2$

**vinylidene resin**, any one of a group of thermoplastic, synthetic resins produced by polymerizing a compound, such as vinylidene chloride, that contains the radical vinylidene; polyvinylidene resin.

**Vi|nyl|ite** (vī′nə līt), *n. Trademark.* any one of a group of thermoplastic, synthetic resins used in making adhesives, moldings, and phonograph records.

**vinyl plastic**, = vinyl resin.

**vinyl polymer**, any one of a group of compounds formed by the polymerization of compounds that contain the radical vinyl.

**vinyl resin**, any one of a group of thermoplastic, synthetic resins produced by polymerizing a compound, such as vinyl acetate, that contains the vinyl radical; polyvinyl resin. Vinyl resins are much used for adhesives, floor coverings, toys, molded articles, phonograph records, and surface coatings.

**vin|yon** (vin′yon), *n.* a synthetic fiber similar to nylon, produced from soft coal and brine, and used in industrial fabrics and elastic garments. [< *Vinyon,* a trademark]

***viol**
definition 1

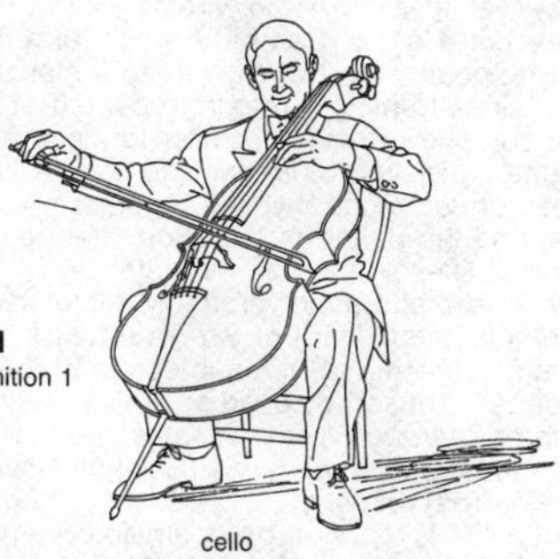

cello

viola da gamba

viola d'amore

***vi|ol** (vī′əl), *n.* **1** any one of several stringed musical instruments played with a bow, distinguished from the violin by its deeper ribs, flat back, sloping shoulders, number of strings (usually six), and originally fretted neck. Viols, used chiefly in the 1500's and 1600's, have been superseded by instruments of the violin type. **2** = double bass. [< Old French *viole,* and *vielle* < Medieval Latin *vitula.* Perhaps related to **fiddle**. See etym. of doublet **viola**[1].]

**vi|o|la**[1] (vē ō′lə, vī-), *n.* **1** a musical instrument shaped like a violin, but slightly larger; tenor or alto violin. A viola has four strings tuned a fifth below a violin. It is held like a violin while being played. **2** a string-toned organ stop, usually of 8-foot pitch, sometimes 4-foot or 16-foot pitch, and similar to the gamba; viola d'orchestre. [< Italian *viola* < Medieval Latin *vitula.* See etym. of doublet **viol.**]

**vi|o|la**[2] (vī′ə lə, vī ō′-), *n.* **1** any one of a group of low, herbaceous plants, including the violets and pansies, that bear single white, yellow, purple, or variegated flowers, especially any one of several hybrid garden plants distinguished from the pansy by a more delicate and uniform coloring of the flowers. **2** a small, perennial garden pansy. [< New Latin *Viola* the genus name < Latin *viola* violet]

**vi|o|la|bil|i|ty** (vī′ə lə bil′ə tē), *n.* capability of being violated.

**vi|o|la|ble** (vī′ə lə bəl), *adj.* that can be violated or broken: *... an abiding conviction that this country is not really violable* (Bulletin of Atomic Scientists). [< Latin *violābilis* < *violāre;* see etym. under **violate**] – **vi′o|la|ble|ness**, *n.* – **vi′o|la|bly**, *adv.*

**vi|o|la|ceous** (vī′ə lā′shəs), *adj.* **1** belonging to a family of dicotyledonous herbs and shrubs or small trees typified by the violet. **2** of a violet color; purplish-blue. [< Latin *violāceus* (with English *-ous*) violet-colored < *viola* viola, violet] – **vi′o|la′ceous|ly**, *adv.*

**vi|o|la da brac|cio** (vē ō′lə dä brät′chō), an old stringed instrument of the viol family, held like a violin, and corresponding to the modern viola. [< Italian *viola da braccio* (literally) viol for the arm]

**vi|o|la da gam|ba** (vē ō′lə dä gäm′bä), **1** an old stringed instrument of the viol family, held on or between the legs, and corresponding to the modern cello; a bass viol. **2** a string-toned open organ stop, usually of 8-foot pitch, and sometimes 16-foot or 4-foot pitch. [< Italian *viola da gamba* (literally) viol for the leg; (see etym. under **viola**[1]); *gamba* < Late Latin, leg]

**vi|o|la d'a|mo|re** (vē ō′lə dä mō′rā), **1** a viol with seven sympathetic strings of metal, in addition to seven gut strings on the finger board, with a sweet delicate tone. **2** a string-toned open organ stop of 8-foot or 16-foot pitch. [< Italian *viola d'amore* (literally) viol of love]

**vi|o|la d'or|ches|tre** (vē ō′lə dôr kes′trə), = viola[1] (def. 2).

**vi|o|late** (vī′ə lāt), *v.t.,* **-lat|ed, -lat|ing. 1** to break (a law, rule, agreement, promise, or instructions); act contrary to; fail to perform: *Speeding violates the traffic regulations. He violated the law and was arrested by the police.* **2** to break in upon; disturb: *to violate someone's privacy. The sound of automobile horns violated the usual calm of Sunday morning.* **3** to treat with disrespect or contempt: *The soldiers violated the church by using it as a stable.* SYN: dishonor. **4** to trespass on; infringe on: *to violate the right of free speech.* **5** to use force against (a woman or girl); rape. **6** *Obsolete.* to assail or abuse (a person). [< Latin *violāre* (with English *-ate*[1]), probably < *vīs* violence, strength]

**vi|o|la|tion** (vī′ə lā′shən), *n.* **1** the use of force; violence. **2** the action of breaking (a law, rule, agreement, promise, or instructions): *He was fined $10 for his violation of the traffic laws.* SYN: infringement, infraction, breach. **3** an interruption or disturbance (as of sleep or privacy). **4** treatment (of a holy thing) with disrespect or contempt. **5** ravishment; rape. [< Latin *violātiō, -ōnis* < *violāre;* see etym. under **violate.**]

**vi|o|la|tive** (vī′ə lā′tiv), *adj.* tending to violate; causing or involving violation.

**vi|o|la|tor** (vī′ə lā′tər), *n.* a person who violates.

**vi|o|lence** (vī′ə ləns), *n.* **1** rough force in action: *He slammed the door with violence.* **2** rough or harmful action or treatment: *the violence of war. The dictator ruled with violence.* **3** harm; injury: *It would do violence to her principles to work on Sunday.* **4** *Law.* **a** the unlawful use of physical force to injure or damage persons or property. **b** intimidation by threatening such use of force. **c** an instance of using such force or intimidation. **5** strength, as of action or feeling; fury; passion. **6** the improper treatment or use of a word; distortion of meaning or application. **7** rape. [< Anglo-French, Old French *violence,* learned borrowing from Latin *violentia* impetuosity, vehe-

---

**Pronunciation Key:** hat, āge, cãre, fär; let, ēqual, tėrm; it, īce; hot, ōpen, ôrder; **oi**l, **ou**t; cup, pu̇t, rüle; **ch**ild; lo**ng**; **th**in; **ᴛʜ**en; **zh**, measure; **ə** represents **a** in about, **e** in taken, **i** in pencil, **o** in lemon, **u** in circus.

mence < *violēns, -entis;* see etym. under **violent**]

**vi|o|lent** (vī′ə lənt), *adj.* **1** acting or done with strong, rough force: *a violent blow, violent exercise, a violent storm.* **SYN**: fierce, furious. **2** caused by strong, rough force: *a violent death.* **3** showing or caused by very strong feeling or action: *violent language, a violent rage.* **SYN**: vehement. **4** very great; severe; extreme: *a violent pain, violent heat, a violent headache.* **5** that tends to distort meaning. [< Latin *violentus,* for earlier *violēns, -entis* < *vīs* force. Compare etym. under **violate**.] —**vi′o|lent|ly**, *adv.*

**vi|o|les|cent** (vī′ə les′ənt), *adj.* tinged with violet. [< *viol*(a)² + *-escent*]

**vi|o|let** (vī′ə lit), *n., adj.* —*n.* **1** a small plant with purple, blue, yellow, or white flowers. Many common violets grow wild and bloom in the spring. See picture under **bird's-foot violet**. **2** the flower of any of these plants. Some violets are very fragrant. The violet is the state flower of Illinois, New Jersey, Rhode Island, and Wisconsin. **3** any one of several similar but unrelated plants or their flowers (used with a qualifying word): *the dogtooth violet.* **4** a bluish purple like that of certain violets. Violet is red and blue mixed, lying at the end of the color spectrum and having a wavelength shorter than about 4,000 angstroms.
—*adj.* bluish-purple.
[< Old French *violette* (diminutive) < *viole* viola, violet < Latin *viola*] —**vi′o|let|like′**, *adj.*

**vi|o|let-green swallow** (vī′ə lit grēn′), a swallow of western North America with greenish back, wings, and crown and pure white underparts.

**violet rays**, **1** the shortest rays of the spectrum that can be seen, having wavelengths of about 3,850 angstroms. **2** (incorrectly) ultraviolet rays.

**violet shift**, *Astronomy.* a shift of the light of stars, nebulae, and other heavenly bodies, toward the violet end of the spectrum.

**violet wood**, = kingwood.

***vi|o|lin** (vī′ə lin′), *n.* **1** a musical instrument with four strings played with a bow. It has the highest pitch of the stringed instruments. **2** a person who plays the violin, especially in an orchestra. [< Italian *violino* (diminutive) < *viola* viola¹]

***violin**
definition 1

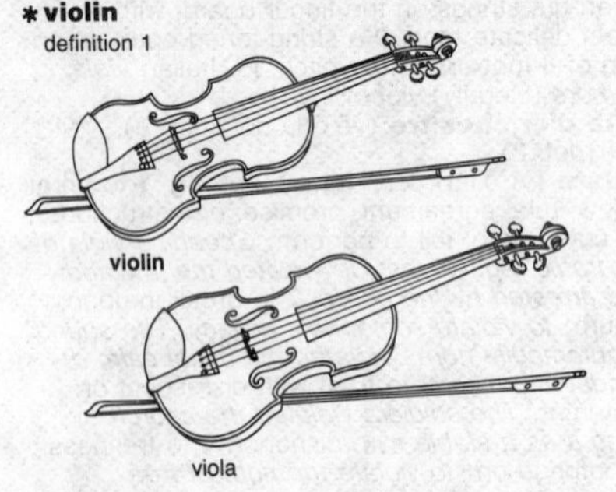


**vi|o|lin|ist** (vī′ə lin′ist), *n.* a person who plays the violin.

**vi|o|lin|is|tic** (vī′ə lə nis′tik), *adj.* **1** of or characteristic of a violinist: *violinistic mannerisms.* **2** belonging to or characteristic of a violin: *The point of the music, in the main, is violinistic cleverness in a pleasing vein* (Atlantic). —**vi′o|lin|is′ti|cal|ly**, *adv.*

**vi|ol|ist** (vī′ə list; vē ō′list), *n.* a person who plays the viol or the viola.

**vi|o|lon|cel|list** (vī′ə lən chel′ist, vē′-), *n.* = cellist.

**vi|o|lon|cel|lo** (vī′ə lən chel′ō, vē′-), *n., pl.* **-los.** a stringed musical instrument like a violin, but very much larger; cello. [< Italian *violoncello* (diminutive) < *violone;* see etym. under **violone**]

**vi|o|lo|ne** (vē′ə lō′nā), *n.* **1** = double bass. **2** a string-toned open labial organ stop of 16-foot pitch, played by the pedals. [< Italian *violone* (originally, augmentative) < *viola* viola¹, viol]

**vi|o|my|cin** (vī′ō mī′sin), *n.* a purple crystalline antibiotic derived from a soil microorganism and related to streptomycin, used in the treatment of tuberculosis. *Formula:* $C_{18}H_{31-33}N_9O_8$ [< *vio*(let) + *-mycin,* as in *streptomycin*]

**vi|os|ter|ol** (vī os′tə rōl, -rol), *n.* a preparation of ergosterol containing a form of vitamin D which has been activated by exposure to ultraviolet light. It is used as a medicine to prevent or cure rickets. [< (ultra)*vio*(let) + (ergo)*sterol*]

**VIP** (no periods) or **V.I.P.**, *Informal.* very important person: *Almost any time a Washington VIP needs medical attention, one of the two big military hospitals is likely to be picked for his care* (Time).

***vi|per** (vī′pər), *n., adj.* —*n.* **1** any one of a group of poisonous Old World snakes with a pair of large, hollow fangs and often having a thick, heavy body, including the adder of Great Britain and other parts of Europe, and the puff adder of Africa. **2** = pit viper. **3** any one of certain other poisonous or supposedly poisonous snakes. **4** *Figurative.* a spiteful, treacherous person: *Loan sharks are vipers of the poor.*
—*adj.* extremely bitter; spiteful; venomous: *the viper talk of old maids.*
[< Latin *vīpera* < *vīvus* alive + *parere* bring forth, bear] —**vi′per|like′**, *adj.*

***viper**
definition 2

**vi|per|fish** (vī′pər fish′), *n., pl.* **-fish|es** or (*collectively*) **-fish.** a small, elongate deep-sea fish with very long, sharp teeth and photophores along the sides.

**vi|per|ine** (vī′pər in, -pə rīn), *adj.* = viperous.

**vi|per|ish** (vī′pər ish), *adj.* like a viper; viperous: (*Figurative.*) *the quick and viperish tongue of a spiteful old lady.*

**vi|per|ous** (vī′pər əs), *adj.* **1** of or having to do with a viper or vipers. **2** like a viper. **3** *Figurative.* spiteful; treacherous: *the viperous tongue of an old gossip.* —**vi′per|ous|ly**, *adv.* —**vi′per|ous|ness**, *n.*

**viper's bugloss**, a prickly weed with showy, blue flowers; blueweed.

**vi|ra** (vir′ə), *n., pl.* **-ras.** a type of lively folk dance and song of Portugal, done with a clicking of fingers. [< Portuguese *vira* (literally) a turning]

**Vir|a|co|cha** (vir′ə kō′chə), *n.* the chief god of the Incas.

**vi|ra|go** (və rā′gō), *n., pl.* **-goes** or **-gos.** **1** a violent, bad-tempered, or scolding woman; termagant. **SYN**: vixen, shrew. **2** *Archaic.* a strong, vigorous, and heroic woman; amazon. [< Latin *virāgo* a manlike (or warrior) woman < *vir* man]

**vi|ral** (vī′rəl), *adj.* **1** of or having to do with a virus. **2** characterized by a virus. **3** caused by a virus: *an important therapeutic reagent against viral infections* (New Scientist). —**vi′ral|ly**, *adv.*

**viral hepatitis**, a contagious viral disease with inflammation of the liver, and usually jaundice; infectious hepatitis; serum hepatitis.

**vi|re|lai** (vēr le′), *n. French.* virelay.

**vir|e|lay** (vir′ə lā), *n.* **1** an old French form of short lyric poem with two rhymes to a stanza, the first two lines forming a refrain, repeated at intervals. **2** any one of several similar forms, especially one consisting of longer and shorter lines, the lines of each kind rhyming together in a stanza, and the rhyme of the short lines repeated in the long lines of the following stanza. [< Old French *virelai,* alteration (probably influenced by Old French *lai* lay, lyric) of *vireli* a refrain]

**vi|re|mi|a** (vī rē′mē ə), *n.* an infection of the bloodstream caused by a virus: *Finally the virus is absorbed through lymph vessels into the blood, thus producing viremia* (Science News Letter). [< *vir*(us) + *-emia*]

**vir|e|o** (vir′ē ō), *n., pl.* **-e|os.** a small, olive-green songbird that eats insects; greenlet. The North American black-capped vireo, red-eyed vireo, yellow-throated vireo, white-eyed vireo, blue-headed vireo, and warbling vireo are six kinds. [American English < Latin *vireō, -ōnis* a kind of bird; perhaps, the greenfinch < *virēre* be green]

**vir|e|o|nine** (vir′ē ə nīn, -nin), *adj.* of, having to do with, resembling, or related to a vireo.

**vi|res** (vī′rēz), *n. Latin.* plural of **vis**.

**vi|res|cence** (vī res′əns), *n.* **1** the action or fact of turning or becoming green; greenness. **2** *Botany.* the abnormal assumption of a green color by organs, such as petals, that are normally white or colored other than green.

**vi|res|cent** (vī res′ənt), *adj.* turning green; tending to a green color; greenish. [< Latin *virēscēns, -entis,* present participle of *virēscere* turn green < *virēre* be green]

**vir|ga** (vėr′gə), *n. Meteorology.* streamers of rain or snow falling from a cloud, but dissipated before they reach the ground. [< Latin *virga* a twig, streak (in the heavens); colored stripe. See etym. of doublet **verge**¹.]

**vir|gate**¹ (vėr′git, -gāt), *adj.* **1** long, slender, and straight; rodlike. **2** *Botany.* producing a large number of small twigs. [< Latin *virgātus* of a twig, streak < *virga* twig]

**vir|gate**² (vėr′git, -gāt), *n.* an old English unit of measure for land, usually ¼ of a hide or about 30 acres. [< Medieval Latin *virgata* (*terra*) a measure of land, feminine of Latin *virgātus* (see etym. under **virgate**¹); translation of Old English *gierd-land* (literally) yard-land]

**Vir|gil|i|an** (vėr jil′ē ən), *adj.* of, having to do with, or suggestive of Virgil (70-19 B.C.), the Roman poet, or his poetry. Also, **Vergilian.**

**vir|gin** (vėr′jən), *n., adj.* —*n.* **1** a woman, especially a young one, who has not had sexual intercourse. **2** an unmarried woman, especially a young woman or girl; maiden. **3** Also, **Virgin.** a picture or image of the Virgin Mary. **4** *Figurative.* an unmarried woman, distinguished by piety or steadfastness in religion, especially one vowed to lifelong chastity. **5** a man, especially a young one, who has not had sexual intercourse. **6** a female animal that has not copulated. **7** *Zoology.* a female insect that produces fertile eggs by parthenogensis.
—*adj.* **1** of or having to do with a virgin; suitable for a virgin: *virgin modesty.* **2** being a virgin or virgins; chaste. **3** composed or consisting of virgins. **4** *Figurative.* pure; spotless. Virgin snow is newly fallen snow. **5** *Figurative.* not yet used: *virgin soil, a virgin forest.* **6** free or clear of something. **7** found pure or uncombined in nature; native: *virgin gold.* **8** *Figurative.* **a** used for the first time: *a virgin sword.* **b** being the first attempt; initial. **9** obtained directly from the ore or as a first product from smelting: *virgin metal.* **10** obtained from the first pressing, without the application of heat: *virgin olive oil.* **11** *Zoology.* reproducing by parthenogenesis.
[< Old French *virgine,* learned borrowing from Latin *virgō, -inis*]

**Vir|gin** (vėr′jən), *n.* **1** = Virgin Mary. **2** a constellation and the sixth sign of the zodiac; Virgo. [< *virgin*]

**vir|gin|al**¹ (vėr′jə nəl), *adj.* **1** of or suitable for a virgin; maidenly; chaste. **2** *Figurative.* fresh; pure; unsullied; untouched. **3** *Zoology.* parthenogenetic. [< Latin *virginālis* < *virgō, -inis* virgin, maiden] —**vir′gin|al|ly**, *adv.*

***vir|gin|al**² (vėr′jə nəl), *n.* **1** a small harpsichord or spinet set in a rectangular box without legs. It was much used in England in the 1500's and 1600's. **2** any harpsichord or spinet. [apparently < *virginal*¹]

***virginal**²
definition 1

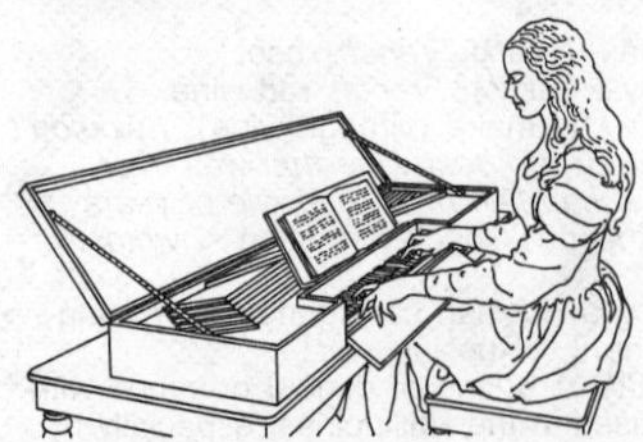

**vir|gin|al|ist** (vėr′jə nə list), *n.* a person who plays the virginal.

**virgin birth**, **1** Also, **Virgin Birth.** the doctrine that Jesus was the Son of God and was miraculously conceived by and born to the Virgin Mary. **2** *Zoology.* parthenogenesis.

**vir|gin|hood** (vėr′jən hu̇d), *n.* = virginity.

**Vir|gin|ia** (vər jin′yə), *n. Roman Legend.* a maiden slain by her father to preserve her from the lust of one of the decemvirs.

**Virginia bluebell**, = Virginia cowslip.

**Virginia cowslip**, a smooth perennial herb of the borage family, native to the eastern United States, with clusters of bell-shaped, blue flowers.

**Virginia creeper**, an American climbing, woody vine having leaves with five leaflets and bluish-black berries that are not good to eat; woodbine; American ivy. Virginia creeper belongs to the grape family.

**Virginia deer**, = white-tailed deer.

**Virginia fence** or **Virginia rail fence**, a fence made of rails laid zigzag; snake fence.

**Virginia ham**, a dark red or brown hickory-smoked ham with a rich, salty flavor, originally made in the state of Virginia.

**vir|gin|ia|my|cin** (vər jin′yə mī′sən), *n.* an antibiotic derived from a species of streptomyces, used chiefly against infections by Gram-positive bacteria. *Formula:* $C_{28}H_{36}N_3O_8$ [< New Latin (*Streptomyces*) *virginiae* a species of streptomyces + *-mycin,* as in *streptomycin*]

**Vir|gin|ian** (vər jin′yən), *adj., n.* —*adj.* **1** of or having to do with the state of Virginia or its people. **2** of or having to do with an Algonkian language formerly spoken by Indians in eastern

Virginia, North Carolina, and Maryland.
—*n.* a native or inhabitant of Virginia.

**Virginia opossum**, the common opossum of the eastern United States.

**Virginia pine**, the scrub pine of the eastern United States.

**Virginia rail**, a small reddish-brown rail with a long, slender bill. It lives in the freshwater marshes of central and eastern North America.

**Virginia reel**, an American folk dance in which the partners form two lines facing each other and perform a number of dance steps; reel. The Virginia reel usually comprises three distinct parts, the second of which is like the reel of Ireland and the Scottish Highlanders.

**Virginia snakeroot**, a birthwort of eastern North America, whose rhizome is used as a stimulant or tonic.

**Virginia trumpet flower**, = trumpet creeper.

**vir|gin|i|bus pu|er|is|que** (vər jin′ə bəs pyü′ə-ris′kwē), *Latin.* for maidens and boys.

**Vir|gi|nis** (vėr′ji nis), *n.* the genitive of **Virgo** (the constellation).

**Virgin Islander**, a native or inhabitant of any of the Virgin Islands.

**vir|gin|i|ty** (vər jin′ə tē), *n.* **1a** the state or condition of a virgin; maidenhood. **b** a condition that presumes a state of chastity; spinsterhood. **2** *Figurative.* the condition of being virgin; purity; freshness.

**vir|gin|i|um** (vər jin′ē əm), *n.* the former name of francium. *Symbol:* Vi (no period). [American English <New Latin *virginium* <the state of *Virginia* + *-ium*, a suffix meaning "element"]

**Virgin Mary**, Mary, the mother of Jesus and the wife of Joseph.

**Virgin Queen**, Queen Elizabeth I (1533-1603) of England.

**vir|gin's-bow|er** (vėr′jənz bou′ər), *n.* any one of various climbing species of clematis, bearing clusters of small white flowers, such as a common American and a European species.

**virgin wool**, wool that has not been previously processed.

**Vir|go** (vėr′gō), *n., genitive* (def. 1) **Vir|gi|nis**. **1** a constellation on the celestial equator between Leo and Libra, containing the bright white star Spica and seen by ancient astronomers as having the rough outline of a woman; Virgin. **2** the sixth sign of the zodiac, which the sun enters about August 22; Virgin. **3** a person born under this sign. [<Latin *Virgō* (literally) maiden]

**vir|gu|late** (vėr′gyə lit, -lāt), *adj.* shaped like a small rod.

***vir|gule** (vėr′gyül), *n.* a thin, sloping or upright line used between two words to indicate that the meaning of either word pertains, as in *and/or,* or as part of an abbreviation, as in *c/o;* diagonal. [< Latin *virgula* punctuation mark, twig; (diminutive) <*virga* rod, virga]

***virgule**

/ p/o=purchase order

**vi|ri|cid|al** (vī′rə sī′dəl), *adj.* destructive to viruses: *a viricidal compound.* Also, **virucidal**.

**vi|ri|cide** (vī′rə sīd), *n.* a substance that destroys viruses. Also, **virucide**. [<*virus* + *-cide*[1]]

**vir|id** (vir′id), *adj.* green; verdant: *The virid brilliance of the grass in the locust grove* (New Yorker). [<Latin *viridis* green]

**vir|i|des|cence** (vir′ə des′əns), *n.* the quality of being viridescent.

**vir|i|des|cent** (vir′ə des′ənt), *adj.* somewhat green; greenish. [<Late Latin *viridēscēns, -entis,* present participle of *viridēscere* turn green < Latin *viridāre* <*viridis* green <*virēre* be green]

**vi|rid|i|an** (və rid′ē ən), *n., adj.* —*n.* a clear bluish-green coloring matter, a hydrated chromic oxide.
—*adj.* green; verdant.
[<Latin *viridis* green + English *-an*]

**vi|rid|i|ty** (və rid′ə tē), *n.* **1** the quality or state of being green; greenness; verdancy. **2** *Figurative.* innocence; inexperience. [<Latin *viriditās* < *viridis* green <*virēre* be green]

**vir|i|do|gris|e|in** (vir′ə dō gris′ē in), *n.* a crystalline antibiotic derived from a species of streptomyces, used against Gram-positive bacteria and certain fungi. *Formula:* $C_{44}H_{62}N_8O_{10}$ [<Latin *viridis* green + *griseus* gray + English *-in*]

**vir|ile** (vir′əl), *adj.* **1** of, belonging to, or characteristic of a man; manly; masculine. **2** full of manly strength or masculine vigor. **3** having to do with or capable of procreation. **4** *Figurative.* vigorous; forceful. [<Latin *virīlis* <*vir* man]

**vir|il|ism** (vir′ə liz əm), *n.* an abnormal condition in any female, in which certain male secondary sex characteristics appear, as abnormally heavy facial hair or a large Adam's apple.

**vi|ril|i|ty** (və ril′ə tē), *n., pl.* **-ties**. **1** manly strength; masculine vigor. **2** manhood. **3** *Figurative.* vigor; forcefulness.

**vir|il|i|za|tion** (vir′ə lə zā′shən), *n.* the acquiring of secondary male characteristics.

**vir|il|ize** (vir′ə līz), *v.t., v.i.,* **-ized, -iz|ing**. to cause to acquire secondary male characteristics.

**vir|i|lo|cal** (vir′ə lō′kəl), *adj. Anthropology.* having the focus in the home of the husband's family; patrilocal. [<Latin *vir* man + *locus* place]

**vi|ri|on** (vī′rē on, vir′ē-), *n.* a mature virus particle, consisting of RNA or DNA enclosed in a protein shell. The virion is the infectious form of a virus. [<*virus* + *-on*]

**virl** (vėrl), *n. Scottish.* a ferrule.

**vi|ro|gene** (vī′rō jēn′), *n.* a virus-producing gene: *The virogene can code for transforming protein, internal and external viral antigens, polymerases, and other enzymes that go into the making of a complete virus* (Science). [< *virus* + *gene*]

**vi|roid** (vī′roid), *n., adj.* —*n.* an ultramicroscopic form existing in living organisms that is capable of either becoming a virus or giving rise to viruses by mutation.
—*adj.* **1** of a viroid: *a viroid mutant, a viroid ancestor.* **2** = viral.

**vir|o|la** (vir′ə lə), *n.* a South American tree related to the nutmeg, having a hard, reddish-brown wood. [<New Latin *Virola* the genus name]

**vi|ro|log|ic** (vī′rə loj′ik), *adj.* = virological.

**vi|ro|log|i|cal** (vī′rə loj′ə kəl), *adj.* of or having to do with virology: *The most practical results so far of virological research are vaccines* (Time). —**vi′ro|log′i|cal|ly**, *adv.*

**vi|rol|o|gist** (vī rol′ə jist), *n.* an expert in virology: *Top virologists . . . are focusing their powerful electron microscopes on suspected cancer viruses* (Wall Street Journal).

**vi|rol|o|gy** (vī rol′ə jē), *n.* the branch of medicine that deals with viruses and virus diseases: *Virology . . . includes some of the most destructive and crippling diseases known to man* (Scientific American).

**vi|rol|y|sin** (vī rol′ə sin), *n.* an enzyme produced in a healthy cell by a virus, and responsible for the spread of the virus to other cells: *Virolysin . . . causes an explosion of the cell wall thus spreading the infection* (Science News Letter).

**vi|ro|sis** (vī rō′sis), *n., pl.* **-ses** (-sēz). any disease caused by a virus.

**v. irr.**, irregular verb.

**vir|tu** (vėr tü′, vėr′tü), *n.* **1** excellence or merit in an object of art because of its workmanship, rarity, antiquity, or the like. **2** objects of art; choice curios. **3** a taste for objects of art or curios; knowledge of, or interest in, the fine arts. Also, **vertu**. [<Italian *virtù* excellence <Latin *virtus.* See etym. of doublet **virtue**.]

**vir|tu|al** (vėr′chü əl), *adj.* **1** being something in effect, though not so in name; for all practical purposes; actual; real: *The battle was won with so great a loss of soldiers that it was a virtual defeat. He is the virtual president, though his title is secretary.* **2** *Optics.* **a** of or having to do with an image formed when the rays from each point of the object diverge as if from a point beyond the reflecting or refracting surface. A virtual image cannot be placed on a screen. **b** having to do with or designating a focus forming such an image. **3** having inherent qualities or virtues which exert a powerful influence on other objects. [< Medieval Latin *virtualis* <Latin *virtus;* see etym. under **virtue**]

**vir|tu|al|i|ty** (vėr′chü al′ə tē), *n.* the condition or quality of being virtual.

**vir|tu|al|ly** (vėr′chü ə lē), *adv.* in effect, though not in name; actually; really: *If you travel by jet plane, Los Angeles and New York are virtually neighbors. The factory worker, virtually imprisoned and broken in will by submission to his machines, . . . envies the worker at a trade* (Edmund Wilson).

**vir|tue** (vėr′chü), *n.* **1** moral excellence; goodness: *Her virtue is shown in her many good deeds.* **SYN:** uprightness, integrity. See syn. under **goodness**. **2** a particular moral excellence, such as one of the four cardinal virtues or the three theological or Christian virtues: *Justice and kindness are virtues.* **3** a good quality; merit: *He praised the virtues of the small car.* **4** the quality of being chaste; purity: *a woman of great virtue.* **SYN:** chastity. **5** the power to produce good results; potency; efficacy: *There is little virtue in that medicine.* **6** *Obsolete.* manliness.

**by (or in) virtue of**, because of; on account of; relying on: *The king then assumed the power in virtue of his prerogative* (Daniel Webster).

**make a virtue of necessity**, to do willingly what must be done anyway: *Making a virtue of necessity, I put the best face I could upon it, and went about the work she set me upon* (William Hughes).

**virtues**, the seventh of the nine orders of angels in medieval theology: *Troops of powers, virtues, cherubims, . . . are chanting praises to their heavenly king* (Francis Quarles).

[Middle English *vertu,* and *virtu* <Anglo-French, Old French *vertu* <Latin *virtus* moral strength; manliness; virile force <*vir* man. See etym. of doublet **virtu**.]

**vir|tue|less** (vėr′chü lis), *adj.* devoid of virtue; without excellence or merit; bad.

**vir|tues** (vėr′chüz), *n.pl.* See under **virtue**.

**vir|tu|o|sa** (vėr′chü ō′sə), *n., pl.* **-sas**. a woman virtuoso. [<Italian *virtuosa,* feminine of *virtuoso*]

**vir|tu|ose** (vėr′chü ōs′), *adj.* having the characteristics of a virtuoso; of or having to do with virtuosos.

**vir|tu|os|ic** (vėr′chü os′ik, -ō′sik), *adj.* showing the artistic qualities and skills of a virtuoso: *a virtuosic performance.* —**vir′tu|os′i|cal|ly**, *adv.*

**vir|tu|os|i|ty** (vėr′chü os′ə tē), *n., pl.* **-ties**. **1** the character or skill of a virtuoso. **2a** interest or taste in the fine arts, especially of a trifling, dilettante nature. **b** excessive attention to technique, or to the production of special effects, especially in music. **3** lovers of the fine arts.

**vir|tu|o|so** (vėr′chü ō′sō), *n., pl.* **-sos, -si** (-sē), *adj.* —*n.* **1** a person skilled in the techniques of an art, especially in playing a musical instrument. **2** a person who has a cultivated appreciation of artistic excellence; connoisseur. **3** a student or collector, as of objects of art, curios, or antiquities. **4** *Obsolete.* a person who pursues special investigations or has a general interest in the arts or sciences; learned person; scientist or scholar.
—***adj.*** showing the artistic qualities and skills of a virtuoso; virtuosic: *virtuoso singing. The play is built around Sir Alec's virtuoso performance as Dylan* (Maclean's).
[<Italian *virtuoso* learned person; of exceptional worth <Late Latin *virtuōsus;* see etym. under **virtuous**]

**vir|tu|o|so|ship** (vėr′chü ō′sō ship), *n.* the occupation or pursuits of a virtuoso.

**vir|tu|ous** (vėr′chü əs), *adj.* **1** good; moral; righteous: *virtuous conduct, a virtuous life.* **SYN:** upright, worthy. **2** chaste; pure: *a virtuous maiden.* **3** *Archaic.* having inherent, natural virtue or power, often of a magic or supernatural nature; endowed with potent medicinal powers beneficial in healing. [<Anglo-French, Old French *vertuous,* learned borrowing from Late Latin *virtuōsus* <*virtus, -ūs* virtue] —**vir′tu|ous|ly**, *adv.* —**vir′tu|ous|ness**, *n.*

**vir|tu|te et ar|mis** (vər tü′tē et är′mis, vər tyü′-tē), *Latin.* by valor and arms (the motto of Mississippi).

**vi|ru|cid|al** (vī′rə sī′dəl), *adj.* = viricidal.

**vi|ru|cide** (vī′rə sīd), *n.* = viricide.

**vir|u|lence** (vir′yə ləns, vir′ə-), *n.* **1** the quality of being very poisonous or harmful; deadliness: *the virulence of a rattlesnake's bite.* **2** *Figurative.* intense bitterness or spite; violent hostility.

**vir|u|len|cy** (vir′yə lən sē, vir′ə-), *n.* = virulence.

**vir|u|lent** (vir′yə lənt, vir′ə-), *adj.* **1** very poisonous or harmful; deadly: *a virulent poison.* **SYN:** noxious. **2** characterized by a rapid and severe malignant or infectious condition: *a virulent disease.* **3** able to cause a disease by breaking down the protective mechanisms of the host: *a virulent microorganism.* **4** *Figurative.* intensely bitter or spiteful; violently hostile: *virulent abuse. Enemies as virulent as ever* (Gouverneur Morris). **SYN:** acrimonious. [Latin *vīrulentus* <*vīrus* poison; see etym. under **virus**] —**vir′u|lent|ly**, *adv.*

**vir|u|lif|er|ous** (vir′yə lif′ər əs, vir′ə-), *adj.* carrying or causing infection: *viruliferous leafhoppers.* [< *virul*(ent) + *-ferous* ]

**vi|rus** (vī′rəs), *n.* **1** any one of a group of substances that cause certain infectious diseases. Viruses are composed of protein and nucleic acid. They are smaller than ordinary bacteria and cannot be seen through most microscopes. They are dependent upon living tissue for their reproduction and growth. Most viruses are filterable and cause such diseases in man as rabies, polio, chicken pox, and the common cold. **2** = virus disease. **3** the poison produced in a person or animal suffering from an infectious disease. **4** the venom emitted by a poisonous animal. **5** *Figurative.* something that poisons the mind or morals; corrupting influence: *the virus of prejudice.* [< Latin *vīrus* poison; sap of plants; any slimy liquid] —**vi′rus|like′**, *adj.*

**virus disease**, any disease caused by a virus, such as tobacco mosaic or influenza.

**virus hepatitis**, = viral hepatitis.

**Pronunciation Key:** hat, āge, cãre, fär; let, ēqual, tėrm; it, īce; hot, ōpen, ôrder; oil, out; cup, pu̇t, rüle; child; long; thin; ᴛʜen; zh, measure;
ə represents **a** in about, **e** in taken, **i** in pencil, **o** in lemon, **u** in circus.

**virus pneumonia**, = primary atypical pneumonia.

**virus X**, an infection or disease of uncertain nature, sometimes resembling influenza.

**vis** (vis), *n., pl.* **vi|res.** *Latin.* force; power.

**Vis.**, 1 Viscount. 2 Viscountess.

**vi|sa** (vē′zə), *n., v.,* **-saed, -sa|ing.** *—n.* an official signature or endorsement upon a passport, showing that it has been examined and approved and that the bearer may enter a country or pass through it. A visa is granted by the consul or other representative of the country to which a person wishes to travel.
*—v.t.* to examine and sign (a passport or other document). Also, **visé**.
[< French *visa,* learned borrowing from Latin (*carta*) *vīsa* (paper) that has been verified, that is, seen; feminine of *vīsus,* past participle of *vidēre* to see] **—vi′sa|less,** *adj.*

**vis|age** (viz′ij), *n.* **1** the face: *a dark visage, a grim visage, a visage of despair. A visage ... looking no fresher than an apple that has stood the winter* (George Eliot). **SYN**: See syn. under **face**. **2** *Figurative.* an appearance or aspect: *to recall the visage of autumn.* [< Old French *visage* < *vis* face, appearance < Latin *vīsus, -ūs* a look < *vidēre* to see]

**vis|aged** (viz′ijd), *adj.* having a visage: *visaged in sorrow* (Horace Bushnell).

**-visaged**, *combining form.* having a ___ visage: *Grim-visaged = having a grim visage.*

**vi|sa|giste** (vē zȧ zhēst′), *n.* an expert in applying facial cosmetics; cosmetologist. [< French *visagiste* < *visage* face, visage + *-iste* -ist]

**vis-à-vis** (vē′zə vē′), *adv., adj., prep., n., pl.* **vis-à-vis** (vē′zə vēz′, -vē′). *—adv., adj.* face to face; opposite: *We sat vis-à-vis* (adv.). *The usual position in modern dancing is vis-à-vis* (adj.).
*—prep.* **1** face to face with; opposite to. **2** in relation to; in comparison with; over against: *He looked poor and shabby vis-à-vis his well-dressed companion. The President is responsible vis-à-vis Congress for his cabinet.*
*—n.* **1** a person or thing that is opposite: *New York is the center of commerce as its vis-à-vis, Washington, is of government.* **2** a light carriage for two persons sitting face to face. **3** an S-shaped seat built so that two people can sit on it facing each other; tête-à-tête.
[< French *vis-à-vis* (literally) face to face; *vis* < Old French; see etym. under **visage**]

**Vi|sa|yan** (vi sä′yən), *n.* **1** a member of a large native people in the Philippines. **2** the Malay language of this people. Also, **Bisayan.**

**Visc.**, 1 Viscount. 2 Viscountess.

**vis|ca|cha** (vis kä′chə), *n.* either of two large burrowing rodents of South America, related to the chinchillas. Also, **vizcacha.** [< Spanish *viscacha* < Quechua (Peru) *huiscacha*]

**vis|cer|a** (vis′ər ə), *n.pl. of* **vis|cus. 1** the soft internal organs of the body, especially of the abdominal cavity. The heart, stomach, liver, intestines, and kidneys are viscera. **2** the intestines. [< Latin *vīscera,* neuter plural of *vīscus*]

**vis|cer|al** (vis′ər əl), *adj.* **1** of, having to do with, or in the region of the viscera. **2** affecting the viscera: *a visceral disease.* **3** consisting of or of the nature of viscera. **4** *Figurative.* touching deeply; affecting inward feelings; not mental or rational: *visceral reactions.* **SYN**: irrational, emotional. **5** crude; blunt: *a visceral description of prison life.* **—vis′cer|al|ly,** *adv.*

**vis|cer|o|gen|ic** (vis′ər ə jen′ik), *adj.* originating in the viscera or in visceral processes: *viscerogenic hunger, viscerogenic needs.*

**vis|cer|o|pto|sis** (vis′ər ə tō′sis), *n.* a slipping down of the abdominal viscera. [< *viscera* + *ptosis*]

**vis|cer|o|ton|ic** (vis′ər ə ton′ik), *n., adj.*
*—n.* = endomorph.
*—adj.* = endomorphic.
[< *viscera* + *ton*(us) + *-ic*]

**vis|cid** (vis′id), *adj.* **1** thick and sticky like heavy syrup or glue; sticky; glutinous; adhesive; viscous. **SYN**: mucilaginous. **2** *Botany.* covered with a sticky secretion: *viscid leaves.* [< Late Latin *viscidus* < Latin *viscum* birdlime] **—vis′cid|ly,** *adv.* **—vis′cid|ness,** *n.*

**vis|cid|i|ty** (vi sid′ə tē), *n.* **1** the quality of being viscid or sticky; viscidness. **2** a viscid substance or collection of substances.

**vis|co|e|las|tic** (vis′kō i las′tik), *adj.* having the properties of viscosity and elasticity.

**vis|co|e|las|tic|i|ty** (vis′kō i las′tis′ə tē, -ē′las-), *n.* the quality or condition of being viscoelastic.

**vis|coid** (vis′koid), *adj.* of a viscid or viscous nature. [< *visc*(ous) + *-oid*]

**vis|coi|dal** (vis koi′dəl), *adj.* = viscoid.

**vis|com|e|ter** (vis kom′ə tər), *n.* = viscosimeter.

**vis|co|met|ric** (vis′kō met′rik), *adj.* = viscosimetric.

**vis|com|e|try** (vis kom′ə trē), *n.* = viscosimetry.

**vis|cose¹** (vis′kōs), *n., adj.* *—n.* a thick, sticky substance made by treating cellulose with caustic soda and carbon disulfide. Viscose is used in manufacturing rayon and cellophane, for sizing, and for other purposes.
*—adj.* having to do with or made from viscose.
[< Latin *viscum* birdlime + English *-ose²* (because it is a syruplike material)]

**vis|cose²** (vis′kōs), *adj. Obsolete.* viscous; viscid. [< Late Latin *viscōsus.* Compare etym. under **viscous.**]

**vis|co|sim|e|ter** (vis′kō sim′ə tər), *n.* an instrument for measuring the viscosity of liquids. [< *viscosi*(ty) + *-meter*]

**vis|co|si|met|ric** (vis′kō sə met′rik), *adj.* of or having to do with a viscosimeter.

**vis|co|sim|e|try** (vis′kō sim′ə trē), *n.* the measurement of the viscosity of liquids.

**vis|cos|i|ty** (vis kos′ə tē), *n., pl.* **-ties. 1** the condition or quality of being viscous. **2** *Physics.* **a** the resistance of a fluid to the motion of its molecules among themselves. **b** the ability of a solid or semisolid to change its shape gradually under stress.

**vis|count** (vī′kount), *n.* **1** an English nobleman, ranking next below an earl and above a baron. A viscount is usually the eldest son of an earl, holding the title of viscount during his father's lifetime. **2** a person administering a district as the deputy or representative of an earl, especially a sheriff or high sheriff in England. **3** the son or younger brother of a count in a Continental country. [< Anglo-French *viscount* < Medieval Latin *vicecomes, -itis* < *vice-* vice- + Latin *cōmes, -itis* companion. Compare etym. under **count².**]

**vis|count|cy** (vī′kount sē), *n., pl.* **-cies.** the title, rank, or dignity of a viscount.

**vis|count|ess** (vī′koun tis), *n.* **1** the wife or widow of a viscount. **2** a lady equal in rank to a viscount.

**vis|count|ship** (vī′kount ship), *n.* = viscountcy.

**vis|count|y** (vī′koun tē), *n., pl.* **-count|ies. 1** = viscountcy. **2** the office or jurisdiction of a viscount, or the territory under his rule.

**vis|cous** (vis′kəs), *adj.* **1** thick like heavy syrup or glue; sticky; viscid. **2** *Physics.* having the property of viscosity. [< Late Latin *viscōsus* < *viscum* birdlime] **—vis′cous|ly,** *adv.* **—vis′cous|ness,** *n.*

**Visct.**, 1 Viscount. 2 Viscountess.

**vis|cus** (vis′kəs), *n.* singular of **viscera.**

*__vise__ (vīs), *n., v.,* **vised, vis|ing.** *—n.* a tool having two jaws opened and closed by a screw, used to hold an object firmly while work is being done on it.
*—v.t.* to hold, press, or squeeze with a vise: (*Figurative.*) *He usually has a cigar butt vised in his teeth* (Time). Also, *especially British,* **vice.**
[Middle English *vyse* any apparatus driven by screws; screw-shaped < Old French *vis* screw < Vulgar Latin *vītium* < Latin *vītis* tendril of a vine] **—vise′like′,** *adj.*

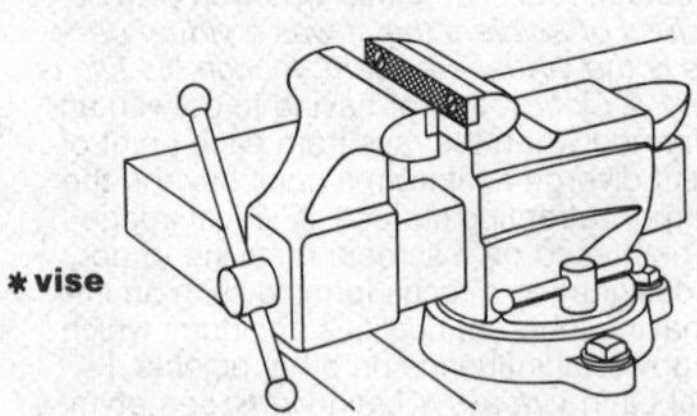

*__vise__

**vi|sé** (vē′zā), *n., v.t.,* **-séed, -sé|ing.** = visa. [< French *visé,* past participle of *viser* < *visa;* see etym. under **visa**]

**Vish|nu** (vish′nü), *n.* the name of one of the three chief deities of Hinduism (Brahma, the creator, Vishnu, the preserver, and Siva, the destroyer), identified by his worshipers with the supreme deity and regarded as the preserver of the world. Of Vishnu's ten appearances on earth in human form (avatars), nine have already occurred. The most important reincarnations, Krishna and Rama, are specially honored. [< Sanskrit *viṣṇu,* probably < root *vis-* to make, do]

**Vish|nu|ism** (vish′nü iz əm), *n.* the worship of Vishnu; Vaishnavism.

**Vish|nu|ite** (vish′nü īt), *n.* = Vishnuvite.

**Vish|nu|vite** (vish′nü vīt), *n.* a worshiper or adherent of Vishnu; Vaishnava. [< Sanskrit *vaiṣṇava* of Vishnu + English *-ite¹*]

**vis|i|bil|i|ty** (viz′ə bil′ə tē), *n., pl.* **-ties. 1** the condition or quality of being visible; capability of being seen. **2a** the condition of light or atmosphere with reference to the distance at which things can be clearly seen: *In a fog the visibility is very poor.* **b** the greatest distance at which objects are visible, especially to the naked eye or, sometimes, radar; range of vision: *Fog and rain decreased visibility to about 50 feet.* **3** a visible thing or object: *Men are visibilities; ghosts are not.* **4** the ratio of the luminous flux of a specified wavelength to the radiation that produces it.

**vis|i|ble** (viz′ə bəl), *adj., n.* *—adj.* **1a** that can be seen: *The shore was barely visible through the fog.* **SYN**: distinct. **b** that can be converted, often from one of various forms of energy, into electrical energy in order to be made visible: *heartbeat made visible with an electrocardiograph.* **2** that can be seen under certain particular conditions: *The eclipse of the moon was visible at midnight.* **3** *Figurative.* readily evident; apparent; obvious: *A tramp has no visible means of support.* **SYN**: manifest, perceptible.
*—n.* **1** something seen; visible thing. **2** *Genetics.* a mutation easily seen by examination: *We know how many of the genetical effects are ... dominant visibles which affect the offspring, or recessive visibles which affect later generations of irradiated flies* (C. Auerbach).
[< Latin *vīsibilis* < *vidēre* to see] **—vis′i|ble|ness,** *n.*

**visible light**, light consisting of electromagnetic waves that can be seen, as contrasted with ultraviolet and infrared waves that are invisible: *Visible light occupies less than one octave of the spectrum of electromagnetic waves* (W. C. Vaughan).

**visible spectrum**, the part of the spectrum that can be seen, appearing as a band of colors merging through continuous hues into each other from red to violet.

**visible speech**, a system of phonetic notation invented by Alexander Melville Bell (1819-1905) as an aid for teaching the deaf to speak, consisting of conventionalized diagrams of the organs of speech in position to utter various sounds.

**vis|i|bly** (viz′ə blē), *adv.* **1** so as to be visible. **2** *Figurative.* plainly; evidently: *After the hike over the mountain the boys were visibly weary.*

**Vis|i|goth** (viz′ə goth), *n.* a member of the western division of the Goths. The Visigoths plundered Rome in A.D. 410, and formed a monarchy in France and northern Spain about A.D. 418. [< Late Latin *Visigothī* < Germanic; taken as "western Goths." Compare etym. under **Ostrogoths.**]

**Vis|i|goth|ic** (viz′ə goth′ik), *adj.* of or having to do with the Visigoths.

**vis|ile** (viz′əl, vizh′-), *n. Psychology.* a person in whose mind visual images are predominant, or especially distinct; visualizer. [< Latin *vīsus, -ūs* sight; see etym. under **visual**]

**vi|sion** (vizh′ən), *n., v.* *—n.* **1** the power of seeing; sense of sight: *The old man wears glasses because his vision is poor.* **SYN**: eyesight. **2** the act or fact of seeing; sight: *The vision of the table loaded with food made our mouths water.* **3** the power of perceiving by imagination or by clear thinking: *the vision of a prophet, a man of great vision.* **SYN**: discernment. **4** something seen in the imagination, in a dream, in one's thoughts, or the like: *The beggar had visions of great wealth.* **SYN**: fantasy. **5** a phantom. **6** something that is very beautiful, such as a person or scene.
*—v.t., v.i.* **1** to see in a vision. **2** to show in a vision.
[< Anglo-French *visiun,* Old French *vision,* learned borrowing from Latin *vīsiō, -ōnis* < *vidēre* to see]

**vi|sion|al** (vizh′ə nəl), *adj.* **1** connected or concerned with, relating to, or based upon, a vision or visions: *a visional theory explaining the phenomenon of hallucinations.* **2** of the nature of, part of, or seen or occurring in, a vision; visionary; unreal. **—vi′sion|al|ly,** *adv.*

**vi|sion|ar|y** (vizh′ə ner′ē), *n., pl.* **-ar|ies,** *adj.* *—n.* **1** a person who is not practical; person given to imagining or dreaming; dreamer. **2** a person who has visions of unknown or future things: *Many great scientists have been visionaries.*
*—adj.* **1** not practical; dreamy: *She is a visionary girl; she spends her time daydreaming.* **2** not practicable; fanciful: *Forty years ago most people would have regarded plans for an atomic power plant as visionary.* **3** of or belonging to a vision; seen in a vision; imaginary: *The visionary scene faded and he awoke. The danger was not entirely visionary.* **4** having visions; able to have visions. **—vi′sion|ar′i|ness,** *n.*

**vi|sion|less** (vizh′ən lis), *adj.* **1** without vision; blind. **2** having no vision of unseen things; lacking higher insight or inspiration: *visionless leadership.*

**vi|sion-mix** (vizh′ən miks′), *v.i.* to combine or blend different camera shots in motion pictures or television. **—vi′sion-mix′er,** *n.*

**vision phone**, *Especially British.* videophone.

**vis|it** (viz′it), *v., n.* *—v.t.* **1** to go to see; come to see: *to visit a church or museum. Would you like to visit New Orleans?* **2** to make a call on or stay with for social or other reasons; be a guest of: *to visit the sick. I shall visit my aunt next week.* **3** to go or come to see, to inspect, or to examine officially or as a professional duty: *The doctor visits his patients when they are unable to come to his office. The inspector visits the factory once a* month. **4** to go to; come to; come upon; afflict: *The poor old man was visited by many troubles.* **5** to send upon; inflict: *to visit one's anger on someone.* **6** to punish; avenge: *So the sins of my mother should be visited upon me* (Shakespeare).

—*v.i.* **1** to pay a call; make a stay; be a guest: *to visit in the country.* **2** *Informal.* to talk or chat. **3** to inflict punishment or take vengeance.

—*n.* **1** the act of going or coming to a place, as for sightseeing or pleasure: *a visit to a foreign country.* **2** the act of going or coming to a person or place for the purpose of inspection, examination, or treatment: *a visit to the dentist.* **3** a stay as a guest: *to make or return a visit. My aunt paid us a visit last week.* **4** *Informal.* an informal talk; chat. **5** *Maritime Law.* the act of a naval officer boarding a vessel belonging to a neutral state to ascertain its nationality and cargo.

[<Latin *vīsitāre* come to inspect (frequentative) <*vīsere* look at well (intensive) <*vidēre* to see]

**vis|it|a|ble** (viz′ə tə bəl), *adj.* **1** that can be visited; suitable for or deserving of a visit: *The tropics are visitable only during the winter.* **2** subject to official visits or inspections, as by authorities.

**Vis|i|tan|dine** (viz′ə tan′dēn), *n.* a nun belonging to the Order of the Visitation, dedicated to teaching and care of the sick. [<French *Visitandine* < Latin *vīsitand-*, gerundial stem of *vīsitāre* to visit]

**vis|it|ant** (viz′ə tənt), *n., adj.* —*n.* **1** a visitor; guest. **2** a migratory bird temporarily frequenting a particular locality.

—*adj.* paying a visit or visits; visiting.

**vis|it|a|tion** (viz′ə tā′shən), *n.* **1** the act of visiting. **SYN:** visit, call. **2** the act of visiting for the purpose of making an official inspection or examination. A nation at war has the right of visitation of neutral ships; that is, the right to inspect their cargoes. **3** a punishment or reward sent by God; severe affliction, blow, or trial, regarded as an instance of divine dispensation. **4** the fact of some violent or destructive agency or force falling upon a people, country, or other group or place: *the visitation of the plague.* **5** *Zoology.* the appearance of animals or birds at a place in unusual numbers or at an unusual time.

**Vis|it|a|tion** (viz′ə tā′shən), *n.* **1** the visit paid by the Virgin Mary to Elizabeth, her cousin and the mother of John the Baptist (in the Bible, Luke 1:39-56). **2** a church festival commemorating this, celebrated on July 2. [<*visitation*]

**vis|it|a|tion|al** (viz′ə tā′shə nəl), *adj.* of or having to do with a visitation.

**vis|it|a|to|ri|al** (viz′ə tə tôr′ē əl, -tōr′-), *adj.* **1** having to do with, involving, or implying official visitation. **2** having or exercising the power or authority of visitation.

**vis|it|ing card** (viz′ə ting), **1** a small card bearing a person's name, to be left or presented on paying a visit; calling card. **2** a card issued to a visitor at some institution, military base, or other place, allowing him entry.

**visiting fireman,** *U.S. Slang.* **1** a visiting dignitary or official accorded special treatment, as by being given a reception, guided tour, or the like: *The U.S. Information Service still had to round up 70 more cars from embassy and military sources for the rest of the visiting firemen* (Wall Street Journal). **2** a vacationer or tourist supposed to be a liberal spender: *our local sightseeing guides, whose very livelihood depends on distinguishing at first glance a visiting fireman from a . . . resident* (Newsweek). **3** any member of a visiting group: *Tuesday, the squad plays a team of visiting firemen* (New Yorker).

**visiting nurse,** a registered nurse employed by a community, a hospital, or a social-service agency to go to the homes of patients needing medical care and take part in other public-health programs.

**visiting professor,** a professor on a leave of absence or in retirement who is invited by a college or university to deliver a special course of lectures.

**visiting teacher,** a schoolteacher trained in social work who visits the homes of sick or disabled pupils to instruct them.

**vis|i|tor** (viz′ə tər), *n.* **1** a person who visits or is visiting; guest: *The museum has many visitors.* **2** an animal or bird that frequents certain areas at regular seasons.

—*Syn.* **1 Visitor, guest** mean someone who comes to stay somewhere or with someone. **Visitor,** the general word, applies to anyone, regardless of the length of his stay or his reason for coming: *Visitors from the East arrived last night.* **Guest** emphasizes the idea of being entertained, and applies especially to someone invited to come or stay: *They usually entertain their guests at the club.*

**vis|i|to|ri|al** (viz′ə tôr′ē əl, -tōr′-), *adj.* **1** = visitatorial. **2** capable of or having to do with visiting.

**vis|i|tress** (viz′ə tris), *n.* **1** a female visitor. **2** a woman who makes charitable visits to the poor.

**vi|sive** (viz′iv), *adj. Archaic.* having to do with sight or the power of seeing; visual. [<Medieval Latin *visivus* <Latin *vidēre* to see]

**vis ma|jor** (vis mā′jər), **1** *Latin.* a superior or overpowering force. **2** *Law.* a superior force that cannot be resisted, sometimes releasing one from the obligation to fulfill a contract. [<Latin *vīs major* (literally) greater force]

**vi|sor** (vī′zər), *n., v.* —*n.* **1** the movable front part of a helmet, lowered to cover the face, or the upper section of this part, the lower being the ventail. See picture under **armor.** **2** the brim of a cap, part that sticks out in front to protect the eyes from the sun. **3** a shade that can be lowered from above to the inside of a car windshield to shield the eyes from the sun. **4** *Figurative.* an outward appearance that hides something different under it; mask; disguise: *to conceal hatred under a visor of friendliness.*

—*v.t.* to cover up with or as if with a visor; protect: *Franny, looking at him, now had a hand visored over her eyes* (J. D. Salinger). Also, **vizor.** [Middle English *viser* <Anglo-French *viser,* Old French *visiere* <*vis* face; see etym. under **visage**]

**vi|sored** (vī′zərd), *adj.* furnished or covered with a visor.

**vi|sor|less** (vī′zər lis), *adj.* having no visor.

**vis|ta** (vis′tə), *n.* **1** a view seen through a narrow opening or passage: *The opening between the two rows of trees afforded a vista of the lake.* **2** such an opening or passage itself: *a shady vista of elms.* **3** *Figurative.* **a** a mental view: *Education should open up new vistas.* **b** an extended view of a long period of time or series of events, experiences, or the like: *the dim vista of centuries.*

[<Italian *vista* a view, noun use of feminine past participle of *vedere* to see <Latin *vidēre*]

**VISTA** or **Vis|ta** (vis′tə), *n.* Volunteers in Service to America (an antipoverty agency of the United States government, established in 1964 to send volunteers to work and help in depressed areas of the country).

***vista dome,** a glass dome enclosing the upper level of a railroad observation car and providing a view of the scenery.

***vista dome**

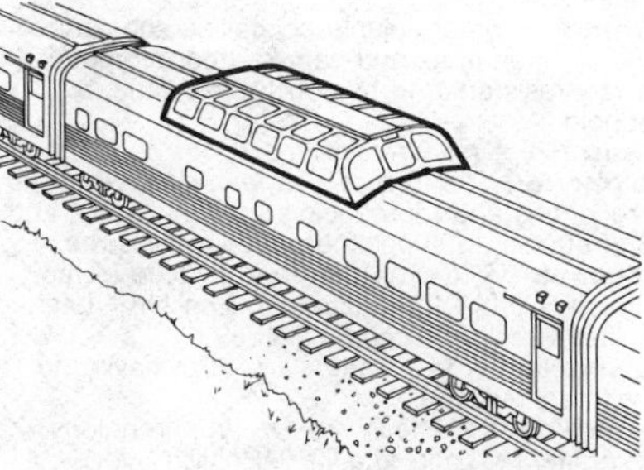

**vis|taed** (vis′təd), *adj.* **1** placed or arranged so as to make a vista or avenue. **2** provided with vistas. **3** *Figurative.* seen as if in prospect by the imagination.

**vis|ta|less** (vis′tə lis), *adj.* lacking any vista or prospect.

**vis|u|al** (vizh′ü əl), *adj., n.* —*adj.* **1** of sight; having something to do with sight or vision: *Being near-sighted is a visual defect.* **2** having the function of producing vision: *the visual rods in the eye.* **3** received through the sense of sight; performed or produced by means of vision: *visual impressions or sensations, a visual test.* **4** that can be seen; perceptible; visible: *visual colors.* **5** of vision and light in relation to each other; optical: *the visual focus of a lens. Telescopes and microscopes are visual instruments.* **6** *Figurative.* of the nature of a mental vision; produced or occurring as a picture in the mind: *to form a visual image of the author's description.*

—*n.* **1a** a rough layout of an advertisement. **b** the part of an advertisement that contains pictures and designs: *A good ad is a fortunate melding of visual and words* (Walter Carlson). **2** = visualist.

**visuals,** a film or part of a film without a sound track: *The program consists of a live lecture with visuals plus film clips* (Harper's).

[<Late Latin *vīsuālis* <Latin *vīsus, -ūs* sight, a look <*vidēre* to see] —**vis′u|al|ly,** *adv.*

**visual acuity,** distinctness of vision; the ability of the eye to perceive and distinguish an image.

**visual aid,** any device or means for aiding the learning process through the sense of sight, such as a chart, diagram, motion picture, or filmstrip.

**visual arts,** the arts that appeal through the sense of sight, including painting, photography, sculpture, architecture, landscape design, furniture, ceramics, jewelry, and textile design.

**visual binary,** a binary or double star that can be seen as two stars with a telescope and sometimes with the unaided eye.

**visual double,** = visual binary.

**visual education,** the use of visual aids in teaching.

**visual field,** = field of vision.

**visual flight,** *Aeronautics.* a flight in which the pilot navigates on the basis of observed bodies of land or water; contact flight.

**visual instrument,** an electronic keyboard instrument for producing patterns of different colors on a screen, played by itself or as an accompaniment to music.

**vis|u|al|ise** (vizh′ü ə līz), *v.t., v.i.,* **-ised, -is|ing.** *Especially British.* visualize.

**vis|u|al|ist** (vizh′ü ə list), *n.* a person who thinks, remembers, or imagines in terms of sight.

**vis|u|al|iz|a|ble** (vizh′ü ə lī′zə bəl), *adj.* that can be visualized: *The electron microscope . . . made many virus particles visualizable* (Time).

**vis|u|al|i|za|tion** (vizh′ü ə lə zā′shən), *n.* **1** the act or fact of visualizing. **2** a thing visualized.

**vis|u|al|ize** (vizh′ü ə līz), *v.,* **-ized, -iz|ing.** —*v.t.* **1** to form a mental picture of: *to visualize a friend's face when he is away, to visualize the scene of a battle.* **2** to make visible.

—*v.i.* to form a mental picture of something invisible, absent, or abstract.

**vis|u|al|iz|er** (vizh′ü ə lī′zər), *n.* **1** a person who visualizes or has the ability to form mental images of invisible things or abstractions. **2** *Psychology.* a person whose mental images are mainly visual.

**visual pollution,** the defacement of the environment or surroundings by litter, graffiti, billboards, run-down or ugly buildings, and unsightly building projects: *The chief weapon in the arsenal of those fighting visual pollution here is a law that restricts the type, size, number and placement of roadside advertising signs* (New York Times).

**visual purple,** *Biochemistry.* a purplish-red protein present in the rods of the retina of the eye, that, in the presence of light, is bleached to form a yellow pigment (visual yellow); rhodopsin. Visual purple, in turn, decomposes to form colorless substances and vitamin A. Visual purple is considered an important factor in vision, especially night vision.

**vis|u|als** (vizh′ü əlz), *n.pl.* See under **visual.**

**visual yellow,** = retinene.

**vis|u|o|spa|tial** (vizh′ü ō spā′shəl), *adj.* of the field of vision, especially as it involves the relationships of space and configuration of the objects seen: *Psychological testing has repeatedly shown that girls are in general better at verbal skills, whereas boys are better at visuospatial skills (such as jigsaw puzzles)* (London Times).

**vis vi|va** (vis vī′və), **1** *Latin.* a living or active force. **2** the energy of motion or of a moving thing; kinetic energy.

**vi|ta** (vī′tə), *n., pl.* **vi|tae** vī′tē). **1** *Latin.* life. **2** a biography. [<Latin *vīta* life, related to *vīvere* to live]

**vi|ta|ceous** (vī tā′shəs), *adj.* belonging to the grape family. [<New Latin *Vitaceae* the family name (<Latin *vītis* vine, tendril) + English *-ous*]

**vi|ta|glass** (vī′tə glas′, -gläs′), *n.* **1** a glass that allows the passage of a large part of the ultraviolet rays of the sunlight. **2 Vitaglass,** a trademark for this glass.

**vi|tal** (vī′təl), *adj., n.* —*adj.* **1** of life; having something to do with life; exhibited by living things: *vital energy. Growth and decay are vital processes.* **2** necessary to life: *Eating is a vital function. The heart is a vital organ.* **3** *Figurative.* very necessary; very important; basic; essential: *a vital question. The education of young people is vital to the future of our country. Voting is a vital function of citizens in a democracy. Drainage of the swamp was considered vital to the welfare of the community.* **SYN:** fundamental. **4** causing death, failure, or ruin: *a vital wound, a vital blow to an industry.* **SYN:** mortal. **5** having life; living; animate. **6** full of life and spirit; lively: *What a vital boy he is— never idle, never dull.* **SYN:** vigorous. **7** being that immaterial force that is present in living things and by which they are animated and maintained: *the vital spark.*

—*n.* **vitals, a** the parts or organs necessary to life. The brain, heart, lungs, and stomach are vitals. *A slight wound; though it pierced his body, it*

**Pronunciation Key:** hat, āge, cãre, fär; let, ēqual, tėrm; it, īce; hot, ōpen, ôrder; oil, out; cup, pu̇t, rüle; child; long; thin; ᴛʜen; zh, measure; ə represents **a** in about, **e** in taken, **i** in pencil, **o** in lemon, **u** in circus.

... *missed the vitals* (John Fletcher). **b** *Figurative.* the essential parts or features of anything; essentials: *If the vitals were preserved, I should not differ for the rest* (Thomas Burton).
[< Latin *vītālis* < *vīta* life, related to *vīvere* to live] —**vi′tal|ly**, *adv.* —**vi′tal|ness**, *n.*

**vital capacity**, the amount of air that the lungs can hold when breathing in as deeply as possible and then exhaling.

**vital force** or **principle**, the animating force in animals and plants; the principle upon which the phenomena of life are supposed to depend.

**vi|tal|ise** (vī′tə līz), *v.t.*, **-ised, -is|ing.** *Especially British.* vitalize.

**vi|tal|ism** (vī′tə liz əm), *n.* the doctrine that the behavior of a living organism is, at least in part, due to a vital principle that cannot possibly be explained by physics and chemistry.

**vi|tal|ist** (vī′tə list), *n.* an adherent of the doctrine of vitalism.

**vi|tal|is|tic** (vī′tə lis′tik), *adj.* of or like vitalism or vitalists: *Until recently, investigation of the central cerebral processes has been confined to the experimental psychologist who, all too frequently in the last resort, seeks the aid of vitalistic postulates* (George M. Wyburn).

**vi|tal|i|ty** (vī tal′ə tē), *n., pl.* **-ties. 1** vital force; power to live: *Her vitality was lessened by illness.* **2** something having vital force. **3** *Figurative.* the power to endure and act: *the vitality of Shakespeare's sonnets. America has great vitality.* **4** *Figurative.* strength or vigor of mind or body; energy: *There is little vitality in his weak efforts to cope with his problems.*

**vi|tal|i|za|tion** (vī′tə lə zā′shən), *n.* **1** the act or process of vitalizing. **2** the condition of being vitalized.

**vi|tal|ize** (vī′tə līz), *v.t.*, **-ized, -iz|ing. 1** to give life to. **2** *Figurative.* **a** to put vitality or vigor into; make more energetic, lively, or enterprising. **b** to present (a literary or artistic idea) in a lifelike manner.

**vi|tal|iz|er** (vī′tə lī′zər), *n.* a person or thing that vitalizes.

**Vi|tal|li|um** (vī tal′ē əm), *n. Trademark.* an alloy consisting essentially of cobalt and chromium, used especially in bone surgery.

**vi|tals** (vī′təlz), *n.pl.* See under **vital.**

**vital statistics, 1** statistics that give facts about births, deaths, marriages, divorces, sicknesses, and other events affecting the population of a country, state, or other community. **2** *Informal* (*chiefly in humorous use*). a woman's bust, waist, and hip measurements: *His wife's vital statistics* [*in the metric system*] *will trun out to be 92-61-92 instead of 36-24-36* (New Scientist).

**vi|ta|mer** (vī′tə mər), *n.* any substance in the diet of an animal that can produce the same effect a vitamin does. Vitamers vary from species to species. [< *vita*(min) + (iso)*mer*]

**vi|tam im|pen|de|re ve|ro** (vī′tam im pen′də rē vir′ō), *Latin.* to devote (one's) life to truth.

**vi|ta|min** or **vi|ta|mine** (vī′tə min), *n., adj.* —*n.* any one of certain special substances necessary for the normal growth and proper nourishment of the body, found especially in milk, butter, raw fruits and vegetables, brewers' yeast, the outside part of wheat, and cod-liver oil. Lack of vitamins in food causes such diseases as rickets and scurvy, as well as general poor health.
—*adj.* of or containing vitamins: *He protected himself against a vitamin deficiency by taking vitamin tablets.*
[< Latin *vīta* life + English *amine* (because it was originally thought to be an amine derivative)]

**vitamin A**, a vitamin found in milk, butter, cod-liver oil, egg yolk, liver, green and yellow vegetables, etc., and also synthesized in the body. Vitamin A increases the resistance of the body to infection and prevents night blindness. Vitamin A is a fat-soluble alcohol. It exists in two known forms, $A_1$ (*Formula:* $C_{20}H_{30}O$) and $A_2$ (*Formula:* $C_{20}H_{28}O$).

**vitamin $B_1$**, = thiamine.

**vitamin $B_2$**, = riboflavin.

**vitamin $B_6$**, = pyridoxine.

**vitamin $B_{12}$**, a vitamin containing cobalt, found especially in liver, milk, and eggs; extrinsic factor. It is active against pernicious anemia. *Formula:* $C_{63}H_{90}N_{14}O_{14}PCo$

**vitamin $B_c$**, = folic acid.

**vitamin B complex**, a group of water-soluble vitamins including thiamine (vitamin $B_1$), riboflavin (vitamin $B_2$), nicotinic acid, pyridoxine (vitamin $B_6$), pantothenic acid, inositol, para-aminobenzoic acid (vitamin $B_x$), biotin (vitamin H), choline, and folic acid (vitamin $B_c$), which are found in high concentration in yeast and liver.

**vitamin $B_t$**, a vitamin found chiefly in meat, liver, and milk, essential to the growth of the meal worm and certain insects but not to higher animals or man; carnitine. *Formula:* $C_7H_{15}NO_3$

**vitamin $B_x$**, = para-aminobenzoic acid.

**vitamin C**, a vitamin found in citrus fruits, tomatoes, and leafy green vegetables; ascorbic acid; cevitamic acid. Vitamin C prevents and cures scurvy. *Formula:* $C_6H_8O_6$

**vitamin D**, a vitamin found in cod-liver oil, milk, and egg yolk, that is necessary for the growth and health of bones and teeth. Vitamin D prevents rickets. It exists in several related forms, including $D_2$ (calciferol), $D_3$, and $D_4$. Vitamin D is a fat-soluble vitamin, produced by irradiating ergosterol and other sterols.

**vitamin $D_2$**, = calciferol.

**vitamin $D_3$**, the natural form of vitamin D, found in fish-liver oils, irradiated milk, and all irradiated animal foodstuffs; sunshine vitamin. *Formula:* $C_{27}H_{44}O$

**vitamin $D_4$**, a vitamin produced by irradiating a form of ergosterol. *Formula:* $C_{28}H_{46}O$

**vitamin E**, a pale-yellow liquid, fat-soluble vitamin found in wheat germ, oil, milk, lettuce and other plant leaves, that is necessary for some reproductive processes and aids in preventing abortions. Lack of vitamin E is associated with sterility. *Formula:* $C_{29}H_{50}O_2$

**vitamin G**, = riboflavin.

**vitamin H**, the former name of biotin.

**vi|ta|min|ic** (vī′tə min′ik), *adj.* of, having to do with, or containing vitamins.

**vi|ta|min|ise** (vī′tə mə nīz), *v.t.*, **-ised, -is|ing.** *Especially British.* vitaminize.

**vi|ta|min|ize** (vī′tə mə nīz), *v.t.*, **-ized, -iz|ing.** to furnish with vitamins: *Many stores specialize in "health foods," which are supposed to be mineralized and vitaminized and to have special nutritional virtues* (Consumer Reports Buying Guide). —**vi′ta|min|i|za′tion**, *n.*

**vitamin K**, a vitamin found in green leafy vegetables, alfalfa, putrefied fish meal, egg yolk, and tomatoes, that promotes clotting of the blood and prevents hemorrhaging. It exists in several related forms, the best known ones being vitamin $K_1$ and $K_2$.

**vitamin $K_1$**, a vitamin present in green plants, used in the formation of prothrombin. *Formula:* $C_{31}H_{46}O_2$

**vitamin $K_2$**, a vitamin found in fish meal and in microorganisms. *Formula:* $C_{41}H_{56}O_2$

**vitamin L**, a vitamin found in beef liver (vitamin $L_1$) and yeast (vitamin $L_2$) that promotes normal lactation.

**vitamin P**, a water-soluble crystalline substance found in citrus fruits and paprika, that promotes capillary resistance to hemorrhaging; citrin; bioflavonoid.

**vitamin PP**, = nicotinic acid.

**Vi|ta|phone** (vī′tə fōn), *n. Trademark.* a device for recording and reproducing speech, music, and sound effects, to supplement moving pictures.

**vi|ta|scope** (vī′tə skōp), *n.* an early type of motion-picture projector. [American English < Latin *vīta* life + English *-scope*]

**vi|ta|scop|ic** (vī′tə skop′ik), *adj.* of or having to do with a vitascope.

**vi|ta|tive|ness** (vī′tə tiv nis), *n.* (in phrenology) love of life. [< Latin *vīta* life + English *-ive* + *-ness*]

**vit|el|lar|i|um** (vit′ə lãr′ē əm), *n., pl.* **-i|ums, -i|a** (-ē ə). the gland of the ovary which secretes the vitellus of the egg in certain invertebrates, especially worms. [< Latin *vitellus* egg yolk + *ārium* a place for]

**vi|tel|lin** (vi tel′ən, vī-), *n.* a protein contained in the yolk of eggs. [< Latin *vitellus* egg yolk; (literally) little calf (diminutive) < *vitulus* calf + English *-in*]

**vi|tel|line** (vi tel′in, vī-), *adj., n.* —*adj.* **1** of or having to do with the yolk of an egg. **2** deep-yellow with a tinge of red; colored like the yolk of an egg.
—*n.* an egg yolk.
[< Medieval Latin *vitellinus* < Latin *vitellus;* see etym. under **vitellin**]

**vitelline duct**, = yolk stalk.

**vitelline membrane**, the transparent membrane enclosing an egg yolk.

**vi|tel|lo|gen|e|sis** (vī tel′ō jen′ə sis), *n.* the formation of vitellus or yolk. [< New Latin *vitellogenesis* < Latin *vitellus* + *genesis*]

**vi|tel|lus** (vi tel′əs, vī-), *n.* the yolk of an egg. [< Latin *vitellus* egg yolk; (literally) little calf]

**vi|ti|ate** (vish′ē āt), *v.t.*, **-at|ed, -at|ing. 1** to impair or injure the quality of; spoil; pollute: *Pollution from smoke and dust vitiates the air. Sewage vitiated the stream. His illness vitiated his chances of success. The abridgment vitiated the original text.* **2a** to destroy the legal force or authority of; invalidate: *The contract was vitiated because one person signed under compulsion.* **b** to make (an argument, theory, proof, or the like) unconvincing or doubtful: *Uncontrolled experiment vitiated my theory.* [< Latin *vitiāre* (with English *-ate*[1]) < *vitium* fault, vice]

**vi|ti|a|tion** (vish′ē ā′shən), *n.* **1** the act of vitiating. **2** the fact or state of of being vitiated.

**vi|ti|a|tor** (vish′ē ā′tər), *n.* a person or thing that vitiates.

**vi|tic|o|lous** (vī tik′ə ləs), *adj. Biology.* growing or living upon the grapevine, as certain fungi and insects. [< Latin *vītis* vine + *colere* to inhabit + English *-ous*]

**vit|i|cul|tur|al** (vit′ə kul′chər əl, vī′tə-), *adj.* of or having to do with viticulture.

**vit|i|cul|ture** (vit′ə kul′chər, vī′tə-), *n.* **1** the cultivation of grapes. **2** the science of grape cultivation. [< Latin *vītis* vine + English *culture*]

**vit|i|cul|tur|er** (vit′ə kul′chər ər, vī′tə-), *n.* = viticulturist.

**vit|i|cul|tur|ist** (vit′ə kul′chər ist, vī′tə-), *n.* a person whose business is viticulture; grape grower.

**vit|i|li|go** (vit′ə lī′gō), *n.* a skin disease characterized by the lessening or loss of pigment, in which smooth, whitish patches of various shapes and sizes appear, especially on the parts of the body exposed to the sun. [< Latin *vitilīgō, -inis,* related to *vitium* fault, vice]

**Vi|ton** (vī′ton), *n. Trademark.* a synthetic rubber resistant to the corrosive effects of acids, alkalis, fuels, and hydrocarbon solvents at very high temperatures.

**vit|rain** (vit′rān), *n.* a narrow glossy band in bituminous coal, composed chiefly of the decayed cell walls of tree trunks and limbs. [< Latin *vitrum* glass + English *-ain,* as in *fusain*]

**vit|re|os|i|ty** (vit′rē os′ə tē), *n.* the state or quality of being vitreous.

**vit|re|ous** (vit′rē əs), *adj., n.* —*adj.* **1** of or like glass; resembling glass, as in brittleness, composition, or luster; glassy: *vitreous china.* **2** having to do with glass: *earthenware with a vitreous coating.* **3** made from glass: *vitreous tableware.* **4** having to do with the vitreous humor.
—*n.* = vitreous humor.
[< Latin *vitreus* (with English *-ous*) of glass, glassy < *vitrum* glass] —**vit′re|ous|ly**, *adv.* —**vit′re|ous|ness**, *n.*

**vitreous electricity**, electricity produced by rubbing glass with silk; positive electricity.

**vitreous humor**, the transparent, jellylike substance that fills the eyeball behind the lens: *The vitreous humor helps hold the retina, or visual sense cells, in place* (Science News Letter). See diagram under **eye.**

**vitreous silica**, = quartz glass.

**vi|tres|cence** (vi tres′əns), *n.* the state of becoming glassy, or of growing to resemble glass.

**vi|tres|cent** (vi tres′ənt), *adj.* tending to become glass; that can be turned into glass; glassy. [< Latin *vitrum* glass + English *-escent*]

**vi|tres|ci|ble** (vi tres′ə bəl), *adj.* that can be vitrified; vitrifiable.

**vit|ric** (vit′rik), *adj.* of the nature of or having to do with glass or any glasslike material. [< Latin *vitrum* glass + English *-ic*]

**vit|ri|fac|tion** (vit′rə fak′shən), *n.* = vitrification.

**vit|ri|fac|ture** (vit′rə fak′chər), *n.* the manufacture of glass. [< Latin *vitrum* glass + English (manu)*facture*]

**vit|ri|fi|a|bil|i|ty** (vit′rə fī′ə bil′ə tē), *n.* the property of being vitrifiable.

**vit|ri|fi|a|ble** (vit′rə fī′ə bəl), *adj.* that can be vitrified or changed into glass: *Flint and alkalis are vitrifiable.*

**vit|ri|fi|ca|tion** (vit′rə fə kā′shən), *n.* **1** the process of making or becoming glass or a glasslike substance. **2** something vitrified.

**vit|ri|form** (vit′rə fôrm), *adj.* having the structure or appearance of glass; vitreous; glasslike. [< Latin *vitrum* glass + English *-form*]

**vit|ri|fy** (vit′rə fī), *v.*, **-fied, -fy|ing.** —*v.t.* to change into glass or something like glass, especially by fusion due to heat.
—*v.i.* to become changed into glass or something like glass.
[< Middle French *vitrifier* < *vitre* glass, learned borrowing from Latin *vitrum* + Middle French *-fier* to make < Latin *facere*]

**vit|rine** (vit′rin), *n.* a glass case or cabinet for displaying articles; showcase: *some remarkable inkwells for gentlemen's desks, the likes of which are not often seen outside a museum vitrine* (New Yorker). [< French *vitrine* < *vitre* glass, learned borrowing from Latin *vitrum*]

**vit|ri|nel|lid** (vit′rə nel′id), *n.* any one of a group of very small sea snails found in many parts of the world, having tiny, translucent, helical shells. [< New Latin *Vitrinellidae* the family name, ultimately < Latin *vitrum* glass]

**vit|ri|ol** (vit′rē əl), *n., v.*, **-oled, -ol|ing** or (*especially British*) **-olled, -ol|ling.** —*n.* **1** = sulfuric acid. **2** any one of certain sulfates of metals, characterized by a glassy appearance, such as a sulfate of copper (blue vitriol), iron (green vitriol or copperas), or zinc (white vitriol). **3** *Figurative.* intense or bitter feeling; very sharp speech or severe criticism. SYN: acerbity, mordancy.
—*v.t.* **1** *Metallurgy.* to subject to the action of dilute sulfuric acid; pickle. **2** *Figurative.* to injure (a

person) by means of vitriol.
[< Medieval Latin *vitriolum* < Latin *vitrum* glass (because of the glassy appearance of the sulfate)]

**vit|ri|o|late** (vit′rē ə lāt), *v.t.*, **-lat|ed, -lat|ing.** to change into a vitriol: *to vitriolate iron sulfide.*

**vit|ri|ol|ic** (vit′rē ol′ik), *adj.* **1** of or containing vitriol. **2** derived from or like vitriol. **3** *Figurative.* bitterly severe; sharp; scathing: *vitriolic criticism.* **SYN**: caustic. — **vit′ri|ol′i|cal|ly,** *adv.*

**vit|ri|ol|ize** (vit′rē ə līz), *v.t.*, **-ized, -iz|ing. 1** to convert into or treat with vitriol. **2** *Figurative.* to injure (a person) by means of vitriol, as by throwing it in one's face; vitriol. — **vit′ri|ol|i|za′tion,** *n.*

**Vi|tru|vi|an** (vi trü′vē ən), *adj.* of, having to do with, or in the style of Vitruvius, a Roman architect and writer who lived in the first century B.C.

***vit|ta** (vit′ə), *n., pl.* **vit|tae** (vit′ē). **1** a headband or fillet, especially as used by the ancient Greeks and Romans as a decoration of sacred things or persons. **2** *Botany.* one of a number of elongated, club-shaped canals or tubes for oil, occurring in the fruit of most plants of the parsley family. **3** *Zoology, Botany.* a band or stripe of color. [< Latin *vitta* fillet (for the head); chaplet]

***vitta**
definition 1

**vit|tate** (vit′āt), *adj.* **1** provided with or having a vitta or vittae. **2** *Zoology, Botany.* striped longitudinally.

**vit|tles** (vit′əlz), *n.pl. Informal or Dialect.* food; provisions: *... beer and vittles provided by the management* (New York Times). [variant of *victuals*]

**vit|u|line** (vich′ə līn, -lin), *adj.* belonging to, having to do with, or resembling a calf or veal. [< Latin *vitulīnus* of a calf < *vitulus* calf]

**vi|tu|per|ate** (vī tü′pə rāt, -tyü′-), *v.t., v.i.*, **-at|ed, -at|ing.** to scold very severely; find fault with in abusive words; revile. **SYN**: abuse. [< Latin *vituperāre* (with English *-ate*[1]) < *vitium* fault, vice + *parāre* to prepare, make]

**vi|tu|per|a|tion** (vī tü′pə rā′shən, -tyü′-), *n.* **1** bitter abuse in words; very severe scolding: *a campaign of vituperation against ones enemies.* **SYN**: objurgation, castigation. **2** vituperative or abusive language.

**vi|tu|per|a|tive** (vī tü′pə rā′tiv, -tyü′-), *adj.* abusive; reviling: *vituperative language. The candidate launched a vituperative attack on his political opponents.* **SYN**: opprobrious. — **vi|tu′per|a′tive|ly,** *adv.*

**vi|tu|per|a|tor** (vī tü′pə rā′tər, -tyü′-), *n.* a person who vituperates; reviler.

**vi|va**[1] (vē′və), *interj., n., pl.* **-vas.** — ***interj.*** (long) live (the person or thing named).
— ***n.*** a shout of applause or good will.
[< Italian *viva* may he live < *vivere* to live < Latin *vīvere.* See related etym. at **vivat, vive.**]

**vi|va**[2] (vī′və), *n., pl.* **-vas,** *v.*, **-vaed, -va|ing.** *British Informal.* — ***n.*** an oral examination; viva voce: *Immediately he began to put me through a moderately stiff viva* (C. P. Snow).
— ***v.t.*** to subject to an oral examination; examine viva voce.
[short for *viva voce*]

**vi|va|ce** (vē vä′chā), *adj., adv. Music.* — ***adj.*** lively; brisk.
— ***adv.*** in a lively manner.
[< Italian *vivace* < Latin *vīvāx, -ācis.* See etym. of doublet **vivacious.**]

**vi|va|cious** (vī vā′shəs, vi-), *adj.* **1** lively; sprightly; animated; gay: *a vivacious disposition or manner, a vivacious puppy.* **SYN**: jaunty, breezy. **2** *Obsolete.* remaining alive for a long time; long-lived. [< Latin *vīvāx, -ācis* (with English *-ous*) lively, long-lived < *vīvere* to live. See etym. of doublet **vivace.**] — **vi|va′cious|ly,** *adv.* — **vi|va′cious|ness,** *n.*

**vi|vac|i|ty** (vī vas′ə tē, vi-), *n., pl.* **-ties. 1** liveliness; gaiety; sprightliness; animation. **2** something vivacious or lively, such as an act, expression, or scene. [< Latin *vīvācitās* < *vīvāx;* see etym. under **vivacious**]

**vi|van|dière** (vē vän dyer′), *n.* a woman who formerly accompanied French regiments or Continental armies, selling food and liquor to the troops; sutler. [< Middle French *vivandière* < Medieval Latin *vivenda* victuals, supplies; (literally) noun use of neuter plural gerundive of Latin *vīvere* to live. Compare etym. under **viand.**]

**vi|var|i|um** (vī vãr′ē əm), *n., pl.* **-i|ums, -i|a** (-ē ə). a place in which living animals or plants are kept under circumstances simulating their natural state, either as objects of interest or for the purpose of scientific study, especially a small indoor enclosure for animals or plants. [< Latin *vīvārium* fish pond, enclosure for live game < *vīvere* to live + *-ārium* a place for]

**vi|vat** (vī′vat), *interj., n.* a shout of acclamation wishing long life, as to a ruler or a popular favorite. [< French *vivat* may he live < Latin *vīvat* < *vīvere* to live]

**vi|va vo|ce** (vī′və vō′sē), **1** by word of mouth; orally; oral: *Shall we vote viva voce or by ballot? The class was given a viva voce examination.*
**2** an oral examination, especially a supplementary one to written examinations given in British universities. [< Late Latin *vīvā vōce* (literally) by living voice; ablative of Latin *vīva vōx* oral statement]

**vi|vax malaria** (vī′vaks), a common, persistent form of malaria in which the attacks occur about every 48 hours and may recur after months or years of inactivity. [< New Latin *vivax* the species name of the mosquito that transmits the disease]

**vive** (vēv), *interj.* (long) live (the person or thing named): *"Vive la république" means "Long live the republic."* [< French *vive,* imperative of *vivre* to live < Latin *vīvere*]

**vive la ba|ga|telle** (vēv′ lä bȧ gȧ tel′), *French.* (long) live frivolity!

**vive le roi** (vēv′ lə rwȧ′), (long) live the king! [< French *vive le roi*]

**vi|ver|rid** (vī ver′id, vi-), *adj., n.* = viverrine.

**vi|ver|rine** (vī ver′īn, -in; vi-), *adj., n.* — ***adj.*** of or having to do with the civet cat or any related mammal, such as the mongoose and the genet.
— ***n.*** any animal of the same family as the civet cat.
[< New Latin *viverrinus* < Latin *vīverra* ferret]

**vi|vers** (vē′vərz), *n.pl. Scottish.* food; provisions; eatables. [< Middle French *vivres,* plural of *vivre* food; noun use of infinitive, live < Latin *vīvere*]

**vives** (vīvz), *n.* inflammation and hard swelling of the submaxillary glands of a horse. [< Old French *vives* < Medieval Latin *vivae,* plural < Arabic *ad-dība*]

**vi|ve va|le|que** (vī′vē və lē′kwē), *Latin.* live and be well or strong.

**Vi|vi|an** or **Vi|vi|en** (viv′ē ən), *n.* an enchantress, known as the Lady of the Lake, who was hostile to King Arthur and imprisoned Merlin by one of his own magic spells.

**viv|i|an|ite** (viv′ē ə nīt), *n.* a phosphate of iron, usually occurring in crystals of blue and green color. *Formula:* $Fe_3(PO_4)\cdot 8H_2O$ [< J. G. *Vivian,* an English mineralogist of the 1900's + *-ite*[1]]

**viv|id** (viv′id), *adj.* **1** strikingly bright; brilliant; strong and clear: *vivid coloring. Dandelions are a vivid yellow.* **2** lively; full of life: *a vivid personality, a vivid picture. Her description of the party was so vivid that I almost felt I had been there.* **SYN**: animated. **3** strong and distinct: *a vivid impression, a vivid sensation. I had a vivid memory of the fire.* **SYN**: keen. **4** very active or intense: *vivid interest, vivid indignation, a vivid imagination.* [< Latin *vīvidus* < *vīvus* alive] — **viv′id|ly,** *adv.* — **viv′id|ness,** *n.*

**vi|vif|ic** (vī vif′ik), *adj.* animating; enlivening; vivifying. [< Latin *vīvificus* < *vīvus* alive + *-ficus* -fic]

**viv|i|fi|ca|tion** (viv′ə fə kā′shən), *n.* **1** the act of vivifying. **2** the condition of being vivified.

**viv|i|fi|er** (viv′ə fī′ər), *n.* a person or thing that gives life.

**viv|i|fy** (viv′ə fī), *v.*, **-fied, -fy|ing.** — ***v.t.*** **1** to give life or vigor to; quicken; animate: *to vivify the desert by irrigation.* **2** *Figurative.* to make more vivid, brilliant, or striking; enliven: *to vivify an idea with wit.*— ***v.i.*** to acquire life; become alive.
[< Latin *vīvificāre* < *vīvus* alive + *facere* to make]

**viv|i|par|i|ty** (viv′ə par′ə tē), *n.* the quality of being viviparous.

**vi|vip|a|rous** (vī vip′ər əs), *adj.* **1** bringing forth live young, rather than eggs. Dogs, cats, cows, human beings and most mammals, and some other animals are viviparous. **2** *Botany.* **a** reproducing from seeds or bulbs that germinate while still attached to the parent plant. **b** = proliferous. [< Latin *vīviparus* (with English *-ous*) < *vīvus* alive + *parere* give birth to, bear] — **vi|vip′a|rous|ly,** *adv.* — **vi|vip′a|rous|ness,** *n.*

**viv|i|sect** (viv′ə sekt, viv′ə sekt′), *v.t.* to operate on (a living animal); perform vivisection upon.
— ***v.i.*** to practice vivisection. [back formation < *vivisection*]

**viv|i|sec|tion** (viv′ə sek′shən), *n.* **1** the act or practice of operating on living animals for scientific study or experimentation. [< Latin *vīvus* alive + English *section*]

**viv|i|sec|tion|al** (viv′ə sek′shə nəl), *adj.* of or having to do with vivisection. — **viv′i|sec′tion|al|ly,** *adv.*

**viv|i|sec|tion|ist** (viv′ə sek′shə nist), *n.* **1** a person who practices vivisection; vivisector. **2** a person who favors or defends the scientific practice of vivisection.

**viv|i|sec|tor** (viv′ə sek′tər), *n.* a person who practices vivisection.

**vix|en** (vik′sən), *n.* **1** a female fox. **2** *Figurative.* a bad-tempered or quarrelsome woman; shrew. **SYN**: termagant. [unrecorded Old English *fyxen,* feminine of *fox* fox] — **vix′en|ly,** *adj., adv.*

**vix|en|ish** (vik′sə nish), *adj.* ill-tempered; scolding. — **vix′en|ish|ly,** *adv.* — **vix′en|ish|ness,** *n.*

**Vi|yel|la** (vī yel′ə), *n. Trademark.* a soft, lightweight cloth that is a blend of cotton and wool.

**viz.,** that is to say; namely (Latin, *videlicet*): *There are four seasons, viz., spring, summer, fall, and winter.*
► **Viz.** is used mainly in formal or technical writing, and is usually read "namely."

**viz|ard** (viz′ərd), *n.* **1** = visor. **2** a mask to conceal the face. **3** *Figurative.* an outward appearance or show; disguise. [alteration of earlier *vizer* visor]

**viz|ard|ed** (viz′ər did), *adj.* disguised with or wearing a mask.

**viz|ca|cha** (vis kä′chə), *n.* = viscacha.

**vi|zier** or **vi|zir** (vi zir′), *n.* a high government official in Moslem countries, especially in the former Turkish empire; minister of state. [< Turkish *vezir* < Arabic *wazīr* (originally) porter; one who bears the burden of office; a viceroy < *wazara* he carried]

**vi|zier|ate** or **vi|zir|ate** (vi zir′āt), *n.* the office, state, or authority of a vizier.

**vi|zier|i|al** or **vi|zir|i|al** (vi zir′ē əl), *adj.* of, having to do with, or issued by a vizier.

**vi|zier|ship** or **vi|zir|ship** (vi zir′ship), *n.* the office or authority of a vizier.

**vi|zor** (vī′zər), *n., v.t.* = visor.

**Vizs|la** or **vizs|la** (vēz′lä; *Hungarian* vēzh′lä), *n.* a short-haired, Hungarian hunting dog with a deep rust- or gold-colored coat, and docked tail; Hungarian pointer. [< *Vizsla,* a village in Hungary]

**V-J Day** (vē′jā′), the date of the Allied victory over Japan in World War II, either August 14, 1945 (the surrender of Japan) or September 2, 1945 (the signing of the formal surrender on the U.S.S. Missouri).

**VL** (no periods), Vulgar Latin.

**VLA** (no periods), very large array (of antennas).

**Vlach** (vlak), *n., adj.* = Walachian.

**vlaie** (vlī, flī; vlā, flā), *n. U.S.* vlei (def. 2).

**VLDL** (no periods), very low density lipoprotein: *When the diet contains large amounts of saturated fats ..., the liver makes more VLDLs and LDLs, which promote atherosclerosis* (New York Times).

**vlei** or **vley** (vlī, flī; vlā, flā), *n.* **1** (in South Africa) a small lake; a large pool of water: *I came full in view of the vley or pool of water beside which I had been directed to encamp* (R. G. Cumming). **2** *U.S.* Also, **vlaie, vly.** a swamp or marsh; a pond or creek: *Have you reason to believe that an attempt was made to fire the Owl Vlaie?* (Harper's). [< Afrikaans *vlei* < Dutch *vallei.* See related etym. at **valley.**]

**VLF** (no periods), **V.L.F.,** or **vlf** (no periods), very low frequency (of or having to do with the electromagnetic spectrum below 30 kilohertz, especially in radio transmission and reception).

**vly** (vlī, flī), *n. U.S.* vlei (def. 2).

**V-Mail** (vē′māl′), *n.* a service using microfilm in transmitting letters to and from members of the U.S. armed forces overseas during World War II. [< *V*(ictory)]

**V.M.D.,** Doctor of Veterinary Medicine (Latin, *Veterinariae Medicinae Doctor*).

**v.n.,** neuter verb.

**V-neck** (vē′nek′), *n.* the neck of a sweater, dress, or shirt in the shape of a V.

**V-necked** (vē′nekt′), *adj.* having a V-neck: *The overblouse is ... V-necked* (New Yorker).

**VOA** (no periods), Voice of America.

**vo-ag** (vō′ag′), *n. U.S. Informal.* **1** vocational agriculture. **2** a teacher or advocate of vocational agriculture.

**voc.,** vocative.

**vocab.,** vocabulary.

**vo|ca|ble** (vō′kə bəl), *n., adj.* — ***n.*** a word, especially as heard or seen without consideration of its meaning.— ***adj.*** that can be uttered.
[< Latin *vocābulum* < *vocāre* to call]

**vo|cab|u|lar** (vō kab′yə lər), *adj.* of or having to do with vocabulary or words.

**vo|cab|u|lar|y** (vō kab′yə ler′ē), *n., pl.* **-lar|ies.**
**1** the stock of words used, as by a person, group

**Pronunciation Key:** hat, āge, cãre, fär; let, ēqual, tėrm; it, īce; hot, ōpen, ôrder; oil, out; cup, pu̇t, rüle; child; long; thin; ᴛʜen; zh, measure; ə represents **a** in about, **e** in taken, **i** in pencil, **o** in lemon, **u** in circus.

of people, or profession: *Reading will increase your vocabulary. The vocabulary of science has grown tremendously in the past 20 years.* **2** a list of words, usually in alphabetical order, with their meanings, especially such a list at the back of a foreign-language text or grammar; glossary: *There is a vocabulary at the back of our French book.* **3** all the words of a language. **4** *Figurative.* the stock of characteristic expressions of any person or thing: *As a choreographer Mr. Kidd inclines to a limited vocabulary of broad, angular movement* (New York Times). *The ... alarm substances are only part of the ants' chemical vocabulary* (Scientific American). [< Medieval Latin *vocabularius* < Latin *vocābulum;* see etym. under **vocable**]

**vocabulary entry**, **1** a word, term, or item entered in a vocabulary. **2** any word or phrase in alphabetical order and defined in a dictionary, or any related word listed for identification under the word from which it is derived.

**vo|cal** (vō′kəl), *adj., n.* —*adj.* **1** of the voice; having to do with the voice or speaking: *vocal power, vocal talents, a vocal message. The tongue is a vocal organ.* **2** made with the voice: *I like vocal music better than instrumental.* **3** having a voice; giving forth sound: *Men are vocal beings. The zoo was vocal with the roar of lions.* **4** *Figurative.* **a** aroused to speech; inclined to talk freely: *He became vocal with anger.* SYN: articulate. **b** active, especially in making known policy, desires, or other goals: *a very vocal minority group.* **5** *Phonetics.* **a** of, having to do with, or like a vowel; vocalic. **b** voiced.
—*n.* **1** a vocal sound. All vowels are vocals. **2** the part of music, or of a musical composition, that is to be sung: *... the evolution in subtlety of the jazz vocal* (Atlantic).
[< Latin *vōcālis* < *vōx, vōcis* voice. See etym. of doublet **vowel**.]

***vocal cords**, two pairs of membranes in the throat, projecting into the cavity of the larynx. The lower pair (inferior or true vocal cords) can be pulled tight or let loose to help make the sounds of the voice. The upper pair (superior or false vocal cords) do not directly aid in producing voice.
► The variant **vocal chords** is also used, especially in Great Britain. Since either term is likely to give a mistaken notion of the structure it designates, some phoneticians prefer *vocal lips* or *vocal folds.*

***vocal cords**

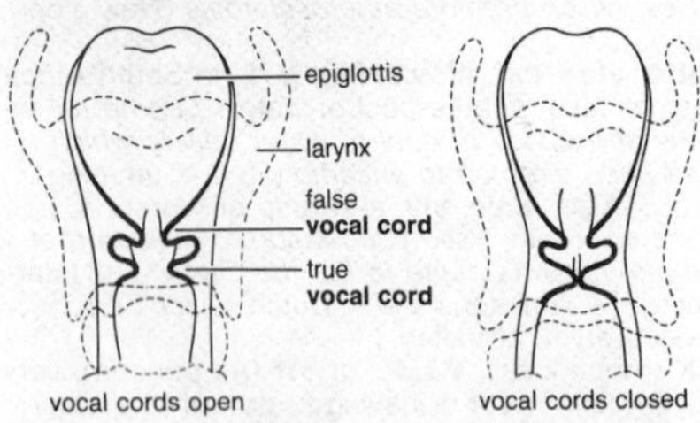


**vo|cal|ic** (vō kal′ik), *adj., n.* —*adj.* **1** of, having to do with, or like a vowel. **2** having many vowel sounds.
—*n. Linguistics.* a vowel sound or group of sounds. —**vo|cal′i|cal|ly**, *adv.*

**vo|cal|ise**¹ (vō′kə līz), *v.t., v.i.,* **-ised, -is|ing.** *Especially British.* vocalize.

**vo|ca|lise**² (vō′kə lēz′), *n.* a musical composition for a singer, usually without words, designed either as an exercise or for public performance. [< French *vocalise*]

**vo|cal|ism** (vō′kə liz əm), *n.* **1a** the art of using the voice or vocal organs in speaking. **b** the act, art, or techniques of singing. **2** *Phonetics.* **a** the vowel system of a dialect, language, or group of languages. **b** the variation or range that vowels have in a certain context. **c** a vocal sound or articulation.

**vo|cal|ist** (vō′kə list), *n.* = singer.

**vo|cal|i|ty** (vō kal′ə tē), *n.* the quality of being vocal.

**vo|cal|i|za|tion** (vō′kə lə zā′shən), *n.* **1** the act of vocalizing. **2** the fact of being vocalized.

**vo|cal|ize** (vō′kə līz), *v.,* **-ized, -iz|ing.** —*v.t.* **1** to form into voice; utter or sing: *to vocalize old camp songs.* **2** to make vocal: *The dog vocalized his pain in a series of long howls.* (*Figurative.*) *The speaker vocalized the feeling of the entire group.* **3** *Phonetics.* **a** to change into a vowel; use as a vowel. Some people vocalize the *r* in *four.* **b** to voice. **4** to insert vowels or vowel symbols in (as an Arabic or Hebrew text).
—*v.i.* **1a** to use the voice; speak, sing, shout, or hum. **b** to sing with one vowel sound for many notes. **2** *Phonetics.* **a** to become vocalized. **b** to vocalize speech sounds.

**vo|cal|iz|er** (vō′kə lī′zər), *n.* a person who vocalizes.

**vo|cal|ly** (vō′kə lē), *adv.* **1** in a vocal manner; with the voice; out loud: *The child vocally demanded a toy.* **2** verbally; orally. **3** in song; by means of singing: *Here is a moving musical work that cannot be carried as a piece of theatre by its music alone, either vocally or orchestrally* (Wall Street Journal). **4** having to do with vowels or vowel sounds.

**vo|ca|tion** (vō kā′shən), *n.* **1a** a particular occupation, business, profession, or trade: *She chose teaching as her vocation. Medicine is my brother's vocation.* SYN: métier. **b** the persons who are engaged in the same business or profession: *a new law affecting the entire vocation.* **2a** an inner call or summons to perform a specific function or fill a certain position, especially of a spiritual nature, such as devoting one's life to the ministry. **b** a divine call to a state of union or salvation with God or Christ. [< Latin *vocātiō, -ōnis* (literally) a calling < *vocāre* to call]
► **Vocation, avocation.** *Vocation* applies to one's regular occupation, the way he earns his living. *Avocation* applies to a kind of work one does in his spare time, a hobby: *Bookkeeping is his vocation and photography is his avocation.*

**vo|ca|tion|al** (vō kā′shə nəl, -kāsh′nəl), *adj.* **1** of or having to do with some occupation, business, profession, or trade. **2** of or having to do with studies or training for some occupation, business, profession, or trade: *Vocational agriculture is taught to students who plan to become farmers.* —**vo|ca′tion|al|ly**, *adv.*

**vocational counselor**, a person who gives vocational guidance.

**vocational education**, any program of education designed to train a person for a particular occupation, business, profession, or trade.

**vocational guidance**, professional advice given in schools or specialized agencies on the basis of tests and interviews, to help a person choose the occupation for which he is best suited.

**vo|ca|tion|al|ism** (vō kā′shə nə liz′əm, -kāsh′nə-), *n.* belief in, or emphasis on, vocational education, especially in schools and collges: *Vocationalism ... demands of education only that it prepare students for a job immediately after graduation* (Newsweek).

**vo|ca|tion|al|ize** (vō kā′shə nə līz, -kāsh′nə-), *v.t.,* **-ized, -iz|ing.** to design or adjust to vocational ends; make vocational: *Our science faculties have yielded to the pressures of industrial demand for their product and to student demand for good jobs and high salaries, and have vocationalized their instruction* (Bulletin of Atomic Scientists).

**vocational nurse**, = practical nurse.

**vocational school**, an educational institution, usually at the secondary-school level, where training is given in various vocations or trades, such as printing, stenography, or mechanics.

**voc|a|tive** (vok′ə tiv), *adj., n.* —*adj.* **1** *Grammar.* showing the person or thing spoken to. **2** of, having to do with, or characteristic of calling or addressing.
—*n.* **1** the vocative case. **2** a word in that case. *Domine,* "O, Lord" is the vocative of the Latin *dominus. Abbr:* voc. **3** an appeal or call for help. [< Latin *vocātīvus* < *vocāre* to call] —**voc′a|tive|ly**, *adv.*

**vo|ces** (vō′sēz), *n. Latin.* plural of **vox**.

**vo|cif|er|ance** (vō sif′ər əns), *n.* a noisy or clamorous shouting.

**vo|cif|er|ant** (vō sif′ər ənt), *adj., n.* —*adj.* shouting; crying; vociferating.
—*n.* a noisy person; one who vociferates.
[< Latin *vōciferāns, -antis,* present participle of *vōciferārī;* see etym. under **vociferate**]

**vo|cif|er|ate** (vō sif′ə rāt), *v.t., v.i.,* **-at|ed, -at|ing.** to cry out loudly or noisily; shout; clamor. [< Latin *vōciferārī* (with English *-ate*¹) < *vōx, vōcis* voice + *ferre* to bear]

**vo|cif|er|a|tion** (vō sif′ə rā′shən), *n.* a vociferating; noisy oratory; clamor. SYN: outcry.

**vo|cif|er|a|tor** (vō sif′ə rā′tər), *n.* a person or thing that vociferates; clamorous or noisy shouter.

**vo|cif|er|ous** (vō sif′ər əs, -sif′rəs), *adj.* **1** loud and noisy; shouting; clamoring: *a vociferous person, vociferous cheers. The incensed crowd became more vociferous.* SYN: clamorous, thundering. **2** of the nature of, or characterized or accompanied by, loud speech or heated assertions: *vociferous hatred.* [< Latin *vōciferārī* (see etym. under **vociferate**) + English *-ous*] —**vo|cif′er|ous|ly**, *adv.* —**vo|cif′er|ous|ness**, *n.*

**vo|cod|er** (vō′kō′dər), *n.* an electronic device that breaks down and transmits a message in garbled elements consisting of buzzes and hisses of different pitch, frequency, and strength to a receiving apparatus that reconstructs the original message. [< *vo*(ice) + *coder*]

**vo|coid** (vō′koid), *n., adj. Phonetics.* —*n.* any sound having a vowellike character.
—*adj.* having a vowellike character: *a vocoid sound or articulation.* [< *voc*(al) + *-oid*]

**VODER** (no periods), voice operation demonstrator.

**vod|ka** (vod′kə), *n.* an alcoholic liquor, distilled from potatoes, rye, barley, or corn. [< Russian *vodka* (diminutive) < *voda* water]

**vod|ka|ti|ni** (vod′kə tē′nē), *n., pl.* **-nis.** a martini made with vodka in place of gin. [< *vodka* + (mar)*tini*]

**vo|dun** (vō dün′), *n.* = voodooism. [< Haitian Creole *vodun* < Ewe *vodū* divinity]

**voe** (vō), *n.* (in the Shetland and Orkney Islands) a narrow inlet of the sea: *Over headland, ness and voe—The Coastwise Lights of England watch the ships of England go!* (Rudyard Kipling). [< Scandinavian (compare Icelandic *vāgr* bay)]

**vo-ed** (vō′ed′), *n. U.S. Informal.* vocational education.

**voet|gang|er** (fu̇t′gäng′ər), *n.* an immature, wingless locust of South Africa, highly destructive to crops. [< Afrikaans *voetganger* (literally) walker, pedestrian]

**voet|sak** (fu̇t′sak), *interj. Afrikaans.* be off; begone.

**vogue** (vōg), *n., adj.* —*n.* **1** the fashion: *Hoop skirts were in vogue many years ago.* SYN: mode. **2** popularity or acceptance: *That song had a great vogue at one time.* SYN: favor, approval.
—*adj.* fashionable; voguish: *a vogue phrase, vogue attitudes.*
[< Anglo-French *vogue* success, course; (literally) a rowing < Old French *voguer* to row < Italian *vogare*]

**vo|gueish** (vō′gish), *adj.* = voguish. —**vo′gueish|ly**, *adv.* —**vo′gueish|ness**, *n.*

**vogue word**, a word currently in vogue: *In recent years "camp" ... has been expropriated from the critic's vocabulary to become a vogue word* (Nathan Cohen). *"Planning" has now clearly become a vogue word for people of all political persuasions* (London Daily Telegraph).

**vo|guey** (vō′gē), *adj. Informal.* in vogue or popular for the time being: *Color-pale, tasteful, and a bit voguey ... paintings at the Hugo Gallery* (New York Times).

**vo|guish** (vō′gish), *adj.* in vogue or popular for the time being; fashionable: *Current trends suggest ... that even Mister* (*and indeed Miss*) *may ultimately be abandoned, for the voguish style of address now is simply by name: John Brown or Jane Brown straight* (Manchester Guardian Weekly). —**vo′guish|ly**, *adv.* —**vo′guish|ness**, *n.*

**Vo|gul** (vō′gu̇l), *n.* **1** a Finno-Ugric language of western Siberia. **2** any of the people speaking this language, related to the Votyaks.

**voice** (vois), *n., v.,* **voiced, voic|ing.** —*n.* **1** a sound or sounds made through the mouth, especially by people in speaking, singing, or shouting: *The voices of the children could be heard coming from the playground.* **2a** the sounds naturally made by a single person in speech or other utterance, often regarded as characteristic of the person and distinguishing him from others: *to recognize someone's voice.* **b** the quality or condition of the voice: *a low, gentle, loud, or angry voice, to be in good voice.* **3** the power to make sounds through the mouth: *His voice was gone because of a sore throat.* **4** anything like speech or song: *the voice of the wind, the voice of the bells.* **5** *Music.* **a** a musical sound made by the vocal cords and resonated by several head and throat cavities; tones made in singing. **b** ability as a singer: *to have a voice. That choir girl has no voice.* **c** a singer: *a choir of fifty voices.* **d** a part of a piece of music for one kind of singer or instrument. **6** *Figurative.* anything likened to speech that conveys impressions to the mind or senses: *the voice of one's conscience, the voice of duty.* **7** expression: *They gave voice to their joy.* **8** an expressed opinion, choice, or wish: *His voice was for compromise.* **9** the right to express an opinion or choice: *Have we any voice in this matter at all?* **10** the means or agency by which something is expressed, represented, or revealed: *Poetry is the voice of imagination* (H. Reed). **11** *Grammar.* a form of the verb that shows whether its subject is active or passive. **12** *Phonetics.* a sound uttered with vibration of the vocal cords, not with mere breath. **13** *Obsolete.* **a** a general or common talk; rumor. **b** reputation; fame.
—*v.t.* **1** to speak or utter (a word or sound): *to voice a cry.* **2** to express: *They voiced their approval of the plan.* **3** *Phonetics.* to utter with a sound made by vibration of the vocal cords: *"Z" and "v" are voiced; "s" and "f" are not.* **4** *Music.* **a** to regulate the tone of (an organ, etc.). **b** to write the parts of for one kind of singer or instrument.

**in voice**, in condition to sing or speak well: *You*

*know very well ... that I am not in voice* [*for singing*] *to-day* (Oliver Goldsmith).
**lift up** (or **raise**) **one's voice, a** to cry out loudly: *And it came to pass, when the angel of the Lord spake these words unto all the children of Israel, that the people lifted up their voice, and wept* (Judges 2:4). **b** *Figurative.* to protest; complain: *But London did not raise its voice against the crimes* (London Times).
**with one voice**, unanimously: *All the members demanded with one voice who it was who was charged with the crime* (M. Pattison).
[< Old French *vois,* and *voiz* < Latin *vōx, vōcis*] —**voic′er**, *n.*

▶ **Voice** (*n.* def. 11). When the subject of a verb is the doer of the action or is in the condition named by its verb, the verb is said to be in the active voice: *The congregation sang "Abide with Me." They will go swimming. Our side had won. My friend's father gave us a ride. We rested an hour.* When the subject of a verb receives the action, the verb is in the passive voice: *"Abide with Me" was sung by the congregation. My friend and I were given a ride by his father. The pit was dug fully eight feet deep. They were caught.*

**voice box**, the box-shaped cavity in the throat containing the vocal cords; larynx.

**voice coil**, (in a sound system) a coil of thin wire wound about a cylinder in the loudspeaker cone. Electrical impulses passing through the wire make it vibrate, causing the cone to vibrate and produce sound.

**voiced** (voist), *adj.* **1** spoken or expressed: *voiced criticism.* **2** *Phonetics.* uttered with vibration of the vocal cords, as any vowel or such consonants as *b, d,* and *g;* sonant. —**voic′ed·ness**, *n.*

**-voiced**, *combining form.* having a ___ voice: *Low-voiced = having a low voice.*

**voice|ful** (vois′fəl), *adj.* **1a** having a voice or the power to speak. **b** having the power to produce or make loud sounds: *the voiceful sea.* **2** involving much speech or argument; vocal: *voiceful criticism.* —**voice′ful|ness**, *n.*

**voice|less** (vois′lis), *adj.* **1** having no voice; lacking the power of speech; dumb; silent. **2** not expressed or uttered; unspoken: *voiceless indignation.* **3** lacking any voice or singing ability. **4** having no voice or vote, as in the control of something. **5** *Phonetics.* spoken without vibration of the vocal cords, as the English consonants *p, t,* and *k;* surd. —**voice′less|ly**, *adv.* —**voice′less|ness**, *n.*

**Voice of America**, an international broadcasting service of the United States government, used to give overseas listeners a picture of American life, culture, and aims.

**voice operation demonstrator**, a keyboard device that imitates the sounds of human speech.

**voice-o|ver** (vois′ō′vər), *n., adv.* —*n.* the voice of a narrator, commentator, or announcer speaking offscreen in a motion-picture film or television program: *The only dialogue is an announcer's voice-over* (Time).
—*adv.* in a voice-over; speaking without being seen: *It's all done voice-over, except for the flashbacks* (New Yorker).

**voice part**, *Music.* one of the parts or melodies for a voice or instrument in a harmonic or contrapuntal composition.

**voice pipe**, = speaking tube.

***voice|print** (vois′print′), *n.* a spectrographic record of the distinctive sound patterns formed by a person's voice: *Voiceprints, just as fingerprints, appear to be unique and almost unchangeable* [*and*] *may eventually take their place with fingerprints as a positive means of identification* (New York Times).

voiceprint of the word "you"

**voice|print|er** (vois′prin′tər), *n.* an instrument for producing voiceprints.

**voice|print|ing** (vois′prin′ting), *n.* the science or technique of making and using voiceprints, especially for the purpose of identifying voices.

**voice throwing**, = ventriloquism.

**voice vote**, a vote, as on a motion or bill, taken by saying "aye" or "yes" or by saying "nay" or "no" when called upon: *Passage came on a voice vote with a scattering of "ayes" and with no "nay" heard* (Wall Street Journal).

**voic|ing** (voi′sing), *n.* **1** the act of a person or thing that voices. **2** the regulating or obtaining of the correct quality of tone, especially of an organ.

**void** (void), *n., adj., v.* —*n.* **1** an empty space; vacuum. **2** *Figurative.* a feeling of emptiness or great loss: *The death of his dog left an aching void in the boy's heart.* **3** a space, gap, or opening, such as that left in a wall for a window or another wall. **4** emptiness; vacancy. **5** the state of holding no cards of a suit in a hand, as in bridge or pinochle.
—*adj.* **1** empty; vacant: *a void space.* **2a** without legal force or effect; not binding in law: *A contract made by a twelve-year-old boy would be void.* SYN: invalid, null. **b** that can be declared to have no legal force; voidable. **3** without effect; useless. **4** having no incumbent or holder: *The position of secretary is void.*
—*v.t.* **1** to make of no legal force or effect. SYN: invalidate, nullify. **2** to empty out (contents); evacuate (excrement); discharge. **3** *Archaic.* **a** to empty or clear (a room, place, receptacle, etc.) of something. **b** to free or rid of something. **4** *Obsolete.* to leave (a place).
—*v.i.* to empty the bowels or bladder.
**void of**, devoid of; without; lacking: *His words were void of sense.*
[< Old French *voide,* feminine of *voit* < Vulgar Latin *vocitus* < *vocuus,* for Latin *vacuus* empty] —**void′er**, *n.* —**void′ly**, *adv.* —**void′ness**, *n.*

**void|a|ble** (voi′də bəl), *adj.* **1** capable of being made or declared void; that can be either voided or confirmed: *The contract was voidable by either party after twelve months.* **2** capable of being given up. —**void′a|ble|ness**, *n.*

**void|ance** (voi′dəns), *n.* **1** the act or process of emptying out the contents of something. **2** the act of making legally void; invalidation; annulment. **3a** removal from a benefice. **b** a vacancy, especially of an ecclesiastical office.

**void|ed** (voi′did), *adj.* **1** having a part cut out, leaving a void or vacant space. **2** made void or empty. **3** *Heraldry.* having a part cut out to make the field visible with only the edge remaining.

**voi|là** (vwȧ lȧ′), *interj. French.* see there; behold.

**voi|là tout** (vwȧ lȧ tü′), *French.* that's all.

**voile** (voil), *n.* a very thin cloth of silk, nylon, rayon, wool, or cotton, with an open weave, used for dresses, curtains, and trimmings. [< French *voile* < Old French *veile* (originally) veil < Vulgar Latin *vēla,* feminine < Latin, neuter plural of *vēlum* covering. See etym. of doublets **veil, velum.**]

**voir dire** (vwär dir′), *Law.* **1** an oath administered in a preliminary examination to a proposed witness or juror by which he swears to answer truthfully questions regarding his competence. **2** such a preliminary examination. [< Old French *voir* truth (< Latin *vēra,* adverbial use of neuter plural of *verus*), and *dire* to say < Latin *dīcere*]

**voi|ture** (vwȧ tʏr′), *n., pl.* **voi|tures** (vwȧ tʏr′). a carriage or conveyance; vehicle. [< French *voiture* < Latin *vectūra* act of transporting < *vehere* carry]

**voi|tu|rette** (vwȧ tʏ ret′), *n., pl.* **voi|tu|rettes** (vwȧ tʏ ret′). a small motor vehicle. [< French *voiturette* (diminutive) < *voiture* voiture]

**voi|vode** (voi′vōd), *n.* in Slavic countries: **1** the title of various rulers and governing or administrative officials in southeastern Europe, as (formerly) the princes of Wallachia and Moldavia. **2** the leader of an army. Also, **vaivode.** [< Rumanian *voivod* < Bulgarian *vojvoda* < Slavic *voi* warriors + *voditi* to lead]

**voix cé|leste** (vwä sā lest′), **1** a soft-toned organ stop of 8-foot pitch having two sets of pipes, one tuned slightly sharper, thus producing a tremulous, wavering tone. **2** a soft flute stop like a dulciana. [< French *voix céleste* (literally) heavenly voice < Latin *vōx, vōcis* voice, and *caelestis* heavenly < *caelum* heaven]

**vol** (vol), *n. Heraldry.* two wings expanded and joined at the base. [< French *vol* flight < *voler* to fly < Latin *volāre*]

**vol.**, **1** volcano. **2** volume.

**Vo|lans** (vō′lanz), *n., genitive* **Vo|lan|tis.** a southern constellation near Argo. [< Latin *Volāns, -antis* (literally) flying, present participle of *volāre* to fly]

**vo|lant** (vō′lənt), *adj.* **1** flying; able to fly: *volant birds.* **2** represented in heraldry as flying. **3** nimble; quick: *the volant fingers of the pianist.* [probably < Middle French *volant,* present participle of *voler* to fly < Latin *volāre* to fly. See etym. of doublet **volante.**]

**vo|lan|te** (vō län′tā), *adj. Music.* moving lightly and rapidly; flying. [< Italian *volante* (literally) flying, present participle of *volare* to fly < Latin *volāre.* See etym. of doublet **volant.**]

**Vo|lan|tis** (vō lan′tis), *n.* the genitive of **Volans.**

**Vo|la|pük** or **Vo|la|puk** (vō′lə pʏk), *n.* an artificial language for international use, based chiefly on English, Latin, German, and other European tongues, invented about 1879 by Johann Martin Schleyer, a German priest. [< Volapük *Volapük* < *vol,* reduction of English *world* + *pük,* reduction of English *speak,* or German *Sprache* language]

**Vo|la|pük|er** or **Vo|la|puk|er** (vō′lə pʏ′kər), *n.* = Volapükist.

**Vo|la|pük|ist** or **Vo|la|puk|ist** (vō′lə pʏ′kist), *n.* **1** a person who is skilled in Volapük. **2** an advocate of the adoption of Volapük as a universal language.

**vo|lar**[1] (vō′lər), *adj.* of or having to do with the palm of the hand or the sole of the foot; palmar. [< Latin *vola* hollow of the palm or sole + English *-ar*]

**vo|lar**[2] (vō′lər), *adj.* used in flying. [< Latin *volāre* to fly + English *-ar*]

**vol|a|tile** (vol′ə təl), *adj., n.* —*adj.* **1** evaporating rapidly at ordinary temperatures; changing into vapor easily: *Gasoline is volatile.* **2** *Figurative.* changing rapidly from one mood or interest to another; fickle; frivolous: *He has a volatile disposition and can change from merry to sad very quickly.* SYN: capricious, mercurial. **3** changeable; unstable: *Some volatile stocks were on the active list* (Wall Street Journal). **4** likely to break out into violence; explosive: *a volatile temper. Riots erupted in Kerala, a politically volatile and troubled southern state* (Norman D. Palmer). **5** *Figurative.* readily vanishing or disappearing; transient: *volatile dreams.* **6** that can fly; flying; volant.
—*n.* **1** a volatile matter or substance. **2** a winged creature, such as a bird or a butterfly: *As to the volatiles of this country, there are turkeys ... parrots, woodquists* (John Davies).
[< Latin *volātilis* flying < *volāre* to fly] —**vol′a·tile|ness**, *n.*

**volatile oil**, an oil that vaporizes quickly.

**volatile salt**, **1** = sal volatile. **2** a solution containing it.

**vol|a|til|ise** (vol′ə tə līz), *v.i., v.t.,* **-ised, -is|ing.** *Especially British.* volatilize.

**vol|a|til|i|ty** (vol′ə til′ə tē), *n.* volatile quality or condition.

**vol|a|til|iz|a|ble** (vol′ə tə lī′zə bəl), *adj.* that can be volatilized.

**vol|a|til|ize** (vol′ə tə līz), *v.,* **-ized, -iz|ing.** —*v.i.* to change into vapor; evaporate.
—*v.t.* to make volatile; cause to evaporate or disperse in vapor. —**vol′a|til|i|za′tion**, *n.*

**vol|a|til|iz|er** (vol′ə tə lī′zər), *n.* an apparatus for volatilizing.

**vo|la|tion** (vō lā′shən), *n.* the act of flying; faculty or power of flight, especially of birds.

**vo|la|tion|al** (vō lā′shə nəl), *adj.* of or having to do with volation or the faculty of flight.

**vol-au-vent** (vô′lō väN′), *n.* a kind of pie having a shell of very light puff paste filled with a preparation of meat, fish, etc., in a sauce. [< French *vol-au-vent* (literally) flight in the wind]

**vol|can|ic** (vol kan′ik), *adj., n.* —*adj.* **1** of or caused by a volcano; having to do with volcanoes: *a volcanic eruption.* **2** discharged from, or produced or ejected by, a volcano or volcanoes; consisting of materials produced by igneous action. **3** characterized by the presence of volcanoes: *volcanic country.* **4** *Figurative.* like a volcano; liable to break out violently: *a volcanic temper.*
—*n.* volcanic rock or lava: *lunar volcanics.* —**vol·can′i|cal|ly**, *adv.*

**volcanic ash**, finely pulverized lava thrown out of a volcano in eruption: *The Romans used a mixture of volcanic ash and slaked lime to build the Colosseum and the Pantheon* (Science News Letter).

**volcanic bomb**, a piece of molten lava, often very large and hollow, thrown out of a volcano in eruption.

**volcanic cone**, a hill around the rim of a volcano, consisting chiefly of matter thrown out during eruptions.

**volcanic dust**, very fine particles of lava thrown out of a volcano, sometimes carried very high and to great distances by the wind.

**volcanic glass**, a natural glass produced by the very rapid cooling of lava; obsidian.

**vol|can|ic|ity** (vol′kə nis′ə tē), *n.* volcanic state or quality; volcanic activity; volcanism.

**volcanic neck**, a mass of hardened volcanic rock, or magma, that has been thrust upward into a volcanic cone by subterranean pressure and may remain upright after erosion has stripped away the surrounding material. See diagram under **mountain.**

**volcanic rock**, rock formed by volcanic action; lava.

**volcanic tuff**, compressed volcanic ash.

---

**Pronunciation Key:** hat, āge, cãre, fär; let, ēqual, tėrm; it, īce; hot, ōpen, ôrder; oil, out; cup, pu̇t, rüle; child; long; thin; ᴛʜen; zh, measure; ə represents **a** in about, **e** in taken, **i** in pencil, **o** in lemon, **u** in circus.

**vol|can|ism** (vol′kə niz əm), *n.* the phenomena connected with volcanoes and volcanic activity: *Some of the chains of crater pits must have their origin in a type of volcanism, perhaps in lava flows of matter liquefied by the impact* (Atlantic). Also, **vulcanism.**

**vol|can|ist** (vol′kə nist), *n.* a person who studies or is expert on volcanoes.

**vol|can|i|za|tion** (vol′kə nə zā′shən), *n.* the process of undergoing, or the state of having undergone, change by volcanic heat or action.

**vol|can|ize** (vol′kə nīz), *v.t.,* **-ized, -iz|ing.** to subject to or modify by volcanic action or heat.

***vol|ca|no** (vol kā′nō), *n., pl.* **-noes** or **-nos. 1** an opening or openings in the earth's crust at the top of and sometimes on the sides of a cone-shaped hill or mountain, connected to the interior of the earth by a funnel or crater through which steam, gases, ashes, rocks, and lava are forced out in periods of activity. **2** a cone-shaped hill or mountain around this opening, built up of the material that is forced out. **3** *Figurative.* **a** a violent feeling or suppressed passion: *a volcano of hatred.* **b** a condition of instability, such as that in which people or causes are likely to burst out violently at some time: *the social volcano below modern society.* [< Italian *volcano* < Latin *Vulcānus,* or *Volcānus* Vulcan]

***volcano**
definitions 1, 2

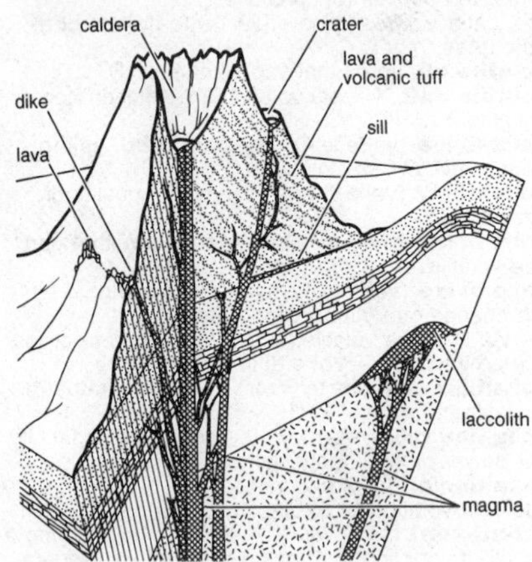


**vol|can|o|log|ic** (vol′kə nə loj′ik), *adj.* = volcanological.

**vol|can|o|log|i|cal** (vol′kə nə loj′ə kəl), *adj.* of or having to do with volcanology. Also, **vulcanological.**

**vol|can|ol|o|gist** (vol′kə nol′ə jist), *n.* an expert in volcanology: *The earth remains quiescent but the volcanologist is aware of a deep stirring* (New York Times). Also, **vulcanologist.**

**vol|can|ol|o|gy** (vol′kə nol′ə jē), *n.* the scientific study of volcanoes and volcanic phenomena. Also, **vulcanology.**

**vole¹** (vōl), *n.* any one of various rodents of the same family as rats and mice, usually of heavier build and having short limbs and tail, such as the redback vole and the meadow mouse. [abstracted < earlier *volemouse* < Norwegian *voll* field + English *mouse*]

**vole²** (vōl), *n.* a slam in playing cards. [< French *vole,* apparently < *voler* to fly < Latin *volāre*]

**vol|er|y** (vol′ər ē), *n., pl.* **-er|ies. 1** = aviary. **2** the birds kept in an aviary. [< French *volière* (< *voler* to fly) + English *-ery*]

**vol|i|tant** (vol′ə tənt), *adj.* **1** constantly moving about; flitting; flying. **2** characterized by flitting or flying to and fro. [< Latin *volitāns, -antis,* present participle of *volitāre* (frequentative) < *volāre* fly]

**vol|i|ta|tion** (vol′ə tā′shən), *n.* the act or power of flight; flying: *Pigeons in circular volitation, soaring gray, flapping white and then gray again, wheeled across the limpid, pale sky* (New Yorker). [< Medieval Latin *volitatio, -onis* < Latin *volitāre;* see etym. under **volitant**]

**vol|i|ta|tion|al** (vol′e tā′shə nəl), *adj.* of or having to do with volitation or flight.

**vo|li|tient** (vō lish′ənt), *adj.* exercising the will; willing. [< *voliti*(on) + *-ent*]

**vo|li|tion** (vō lish′ən), *n.* **1** the act of willing; decision or choice: *She went away of her own volition.* **SYN:** preference. **2** the power of willing: *The use of drugs has weakened his volition.* **3** = willpower. [< Medieval Latin *volitio, -onis* < Latin *vol-,* stem of *velle* to wish]

**vo|li|tion|al** (vō lish′ə nəl), *adj.* of or having to do with volition or the act of willing. – **vo|li′tion|al|ly,** *adv.*

**vo|li|tion|ar|y** (vō lish′ə ner′ē), *adj.* = volitional.

**vol|i|tive** (vol′ə tiv), *adj.* **1** of or having to do with volition or the will. **2** *Grammar.* expressing a wish or desire: *a volitive subjunctive.*

**Volks|deut|scher** (fôlks′doi′chər), *n., pl.* **-sche** (-chə). *German.* a German by birth or descent who is a citizen of another country.

**Volks|kam|mer** (fôlks′kä′mər), *n. German.* the People's Chamber, a legislative body in East Germany, consisting of 500 voting members elected by universal suffrage.

**Volks|lied** (fôlks′lēt′), *n., pl.* **Volks|lie|der** (fôlks′lē′dər). *German.* a folk song.

**Volks|po|li|zei** (fôlks′pô li tsī′), *n. German.* the People's Police, the police force in East Germany: *Truckloads of Red Army troops and squad cars crowded with Volkspolizei stood by* (Time).

**Volks|raad** (fôlks′rät′), *n. Afrikaans.* a legislative assembly or a house of parliament in South Africa: *It was therefore decreed by a resolution of the Volksraad that no additional natives should be allowed to take up their residence in the Colony* (C. Barter).

**Volks|schu|le** (fôlks′shü′lə), *n., pl.* **-len** (-lən). *German.* an elementary school: *At age six a child starts his schooling by attending a Volksschule, which provides a general education up to age fifteen* (New Scientist).

**vol|ley** (vol′ē), *n., pl.* **-leys,** *v.,* **-leyed, -ley|ing.**
–*n.* **1** a shower of stones, bullets, or other missiles: *A volley of arrows rained down upon the attacking knights.* **2** the discharge of a number of guns at once. **3** *Mining.* the simultaneous explosion of two or more blasts in the rock. **4** *Figurative.* a noisy, rapid outpouring or burst of many things at once: *a volley of angry words.* **5** in tennis: **a** the hitting or return of a ball before it touches the ground. **b** the flight of the ball in play before it has touched the ground. **6** (in soccer) a kick given the ball before it bounces on the ground. **7** (in cricket) a ball bowled so that it strikes the wicket before bouncing.
–*v.t.* **1** to discharge in a volley, or as if in a volley. **2** (in tennis) to hit or return (a ball in play) before it touches the ground. **3** (in soccer) to kick (the ball) before it bounces on the ground. **4** (in cricket) to bowl (a ball) that reaches the wicket before bouncing.
–*v.i.* **1** to be discharged in a volley: *Cannon volleyed on all sides.* **2** to sound together or continuously, as firearms, or in a way suggesting firearms. **3** to make a volley in tennis, soccer, or cricket.
[< Middle French *volee* flight < *voler* to fly < Latin *volāre*]

**vol|ley|ball** (vol′ē bôl′), *n.* **1** a game played by two teams of players with a large inflated ball and a high net. The players must hit the ball back and forth over the net with their hands without letting it touch the ground. **2** the ball used in this game.

**vol|ley|er** (vol′ē ər), *n.* a person who volleys, especially in tennis: *The backcourt or base line game is practically hopeless against a volleyer of any real skill* (New Yorker).

**vo|lost** (vō′lost), *n.* **1** a rural soviet (local governmental assembly in the Soviet Union). **2** (formerly) a small administrative division in Russia. [< Russian *volost′* < Old Russian *volostĭ* territory, rule, related to *voloděti* to rule]

**vol|plane** (vol′plān′), *v.,* **-planed, -plan|ing,** *n.*
–*v.i.* to glide downward in an airplane without using the motor.
–*n.* the act of doing this.
[earlier, a controlled dive < French *vol plané* gliding flight; *vol* < *voler* to fly < Latin *volāre; plané,* past participle of *planer* to glide < *plan* level, plane < Latin *plānus*]

**vol|plan|ist** (vol′plā′nist), *n.* a person who volplanes.

**vols.,** volumes.

**Vol|sci** (vol′sī), *n.pl.* an ancient, warlike people of eastern Latium, in southwestern Italy, subdued by the Romans in the 300's B.C. [< Latin *Volscī,* plural of *Volscus*]

**Vol|scian** (vol′shən), *adj., n.* –*adj.* of, having to do with, or belonging to the Volsci.
–*n.* the Italian dialect spoken by the Volsci, related to Umbrian.

**Vol|scians** (vol′shənz), *n.pl.* = Volsci.

**Vol|stead|ism** (vol′sted iz əm), *n.* the policy of prohibiting the production or sale of alcoholic liquor; prohibition.
[< Andrew J. *Volstead,* 1860-1947, a member of the U.S. House of Representatives, who sponsored the bill + *-ism*]

**Vol|sung** (vol′sung), *n., pl.* **-sungs.** *Norse Mythology.* **1** a powerful king, one of the heroes of the Volsunga Saga. **2** any member of a race of heroic warriors who were his descendants. [< Old Icelandic *Völsung*]

**Vol|sun|ga Saga** (vol′sung gə), an Icelandic prose legend of the Volsungs and Nibelungs, the equivalent of the German *Nibelungenlied,* the chief hero being Sigurd, son of Volsung. [< Old Icelandic *Völsunga saga* saga of the Volsungs]

**volt¹** (vōlt), *n.* the unit for measuring the force of electric energy. A volt is equal to the difference in potential needed to cause a current of one ampere to flow through a resistance of one ohm. *Abbr:* v. [< Alessandro *Volta,* 1745-1827, an Italian physicist, who devised the voltaic pile]

**volt²** (vōlt), *n.* **1** in the manège: **a** a circular movement executed by a horse. **b** a gait or maneuver made by a horse going sidewise round a center, with the head turned outward. **2** *Fencing.* a quick step or leap to escape a thrust. [(originally) verb < French *volter* < *volte* a turning < Italian *volta;* see etym. under **volta**]

**vol|ta** (vol′tə; *Italian* vôl′tä), *n., pl.* **-te** (-tā). **1** *Music.* a turn; a time. *Una volta* means once; *due volte* means twice. *Prima volta,* first time, marks the first ending of a movement to be repeated, and *seconda volta,* second time, marks the second time for the same movement. **2** a dance of the 1500's. [< Italian *volta,* noun use of feminine past participle of *volvere* to turn, roll < Latin]

**volt|age** (vōl′tij), *n.* the strength of electrical force, measured in volts. A current of high voltage is used in transmitting electric power over long distances. *Abbr:* v.

**voltage divider,** *Electricity.* a resistor with two terminals between which the current flows. A portion of the total voltage may be obtained by connecting at any point between the terminals.

**vol|ta|ic** (vol tā′ik), *adj.* **1** producing an electric current by chemical action. **2** of, having to do with, or caused by electricity produced by chemical action; galvanic. **3** Also, **Voltaic.** of, relating to, or discovered by Count Alessandro Volta, an Italian physicist. [< Alessandro *Volta* (see etym. under **volt¹**) + *-ic*]

**Vol|ta|ic** (vol tā′ik), *adj., n.* –*adj.* **1** of or having to do with Upper Volta, a country in western Africa, its people, or their culture. **2** of or belonging to the Gur language group.
–*n.* the Gur language group.

**voltaic battery, a** an electric battery composed of one or more voltaic cells. **2** = voltaic cell.

**voltaic cell,** an electric cell consisting of two electrodes, each of a different metal, connected by a wire and immersed in an electrolyte; galvanic cell. An electric current is produced in the wire by a chemical reaction between the electrolyte and one of the electrodes.

**voltaic couple,** (in a voltaic cell) the pair of (commonly) metallic substances that act as the source of the electric current when placed in the electrolyte.

**voltaic electricity,** electricity produced by a voltaic cell; electric current.

**voltaic pile,** = galvanic pile.

**Vol|tair|e|an** or **Vol|tair|i|an** (vol tãr′ē ən), *adj., n.* –*adj.* of or in the style of the French satirical and philosophical writer François Marie Arouet de Voltaire (1694-1778). –*n.* an admirer or imitator of Voltaire or his works.

**vol|ta|ism** (vol′tə iz əm), *n.* **1** the branch of electrical science that deals with the production of an electric current by the chemical action of a liquid on metals. **2** electricity thus produced. [< Alessandro *Volta* (see etym. under **volt¹**) + *-ism*]

**vol|tam|e|ter** (vol tam′ə tər), *n.* a device for measuring the quantity of electricity passing through a conductor by the amount of electrolytic decomposition it produces, or for measuring the strength of a current by the amount of such decomposition in a given time. [< *volta*(ic) + *-meter*]

**vol|ta|met|ric** (vol′tə met′rik), *adj.* having to do with or involving the use of a voltameter: *voltametric measurement.*

**volt|am|me|ter** (vōlt′am′mē′tər), *n.* **1** an instrument that can measure either volts or amperes. **2** = wattmeter. [< *volt¹* + *ammeter*]

**volt-am|pere** (vōlt′am′pir), *n.* a unit of electric measurement equivalent to the product of one volt and one ampere. For alternating currents it is a measure of apparent power; for direct currents it is a measure of power and equals one watt. *Abbr:* va (no periods).

**Vol|ta's pile** (vol′təz), = galvanic pile. [< Alessandro *Volta;* see etym. under **volt¹**]

**vol|te-face** (vôl′tə fäs′, volt fäs′), *n.* an about-face; reversal of judgment, belief, or policy: *Whatever the real explanation for the Chinese volte-face, it is unlikely that it will reverse the most significant result of the attack upon India* (London Times). [< French *volte-face* < Italian *volta faccia* < *volta* a turn (see etym. under **volta**) + *faccia* face < Latin *faciēs*]

**vol|ti** (vôl′tē), *v. imperative. Music.* turn; turn over (the page), more usually seen as *V.S.* (*volti subito*), turn over swiftly! [< Italian *volti,* imperative of *voltare* turn < Latin *voltāre,* or *volvitāre,* for Latin *volūtāre* < *volvere* to roll, turn]

**volt|me|ter** (vōlt′mē′tər), *n.* an instrument for measuring the number of volts between any two points in an electric circuit. [< *volt*[1] + *-meter*]

**vol|u|bil|i|ty** (vol′yə bil′ə tē), *n.* **1** the tendency to talk much; fondness for talking; garrulousness. **SYN**: loquacity, talkativeness. **2** a great flow of words. **SYN**: fluency. **3** the ability to revolve, roll, or turn round on an axis or center.

**vol|u|ble** (vol′yə bəl), *adj.* **1** ready to talk much; having the habit of talking much; fond of talking; talkative: *He is a voluble speaker.* **2** having a smooth, rapid flow of words: *a voluble oration.* **SYN**: See syn. under **fluent**. **3** *Botany.* twining; twisting. [earlier, moving easily < Latin *volūbilis* (originally) rolling < *volvere* to roll] —**vol′u|ble|ness**, *n.*

**vol|u|bly** (vol′yə blē), *adv.* in a voluble or fluent manner.

**vol|u|crar|y** (vol′yə krer′ē), *n., pl.* **-crar|ies.** a treatise on birds, of a kind written in the Middle Ages. [< Latin *volucris* bird + English *-ary*]

**vol|u|crine** (vol′yə krin, -krīn), *adj.* of or having to do with birds. [< Latin *volucris* bird + English *-ine*[1]]

✱**vol|ume** (vol′yəm), *n., adj., v.,* **-umed, -um|ing.** —*n.* **1** a collection of printed or written sheets bound together to form a book; book; tome: *We own a library of 500 volumes.* **2** a book forming part of a set or series: *You can find what you want to know in the ninth volume of this encyclopedia.* **3** a roll of parchment, papyrus, rice paper, or the like, containing written matter (the ancient form of a book); scroll. **4** *Figurative.* something comparable to a book, such as something that can be studied in the way that one studies a book. **5** space occupied, as measured in three dimensions; bulk, size, or dimensions expressed in cubic units: *The storeroom has a volume of 4,000 cubic feet.* **6** an amount; quantity: *the volume of business at a store for a particular period. Volumes of smoke poured from the chimneys of the factory.* **SYN**: See syn. under **size**. **7** the amount of sound; fullness of tone: *A pipe organ gives much more volume than a violin or flute. Abbr:* vol.
—*adj.* of or having to do with large amounts; in large amounts; bulk: *volume mailing, volume production of computers.*
—*v.i.* to rise or roll in a volume: *Smoke came voluming from the chimney.*
—*v.t.* to send up or pour out in volumes.
**speak volumes**, to express much; be full of meaning: *A pause ensued, during which the eyes of Zastrozzi and Matilda spoke volumes to each guilty soul* (Shelley).
[< Old French *volume,* learned borrowing from Latin *volūmen, -inis* book; roll of parchment, scroll < *volvere* to roll]
▶ See **book** for usage note.

✱**volume**
definition 5

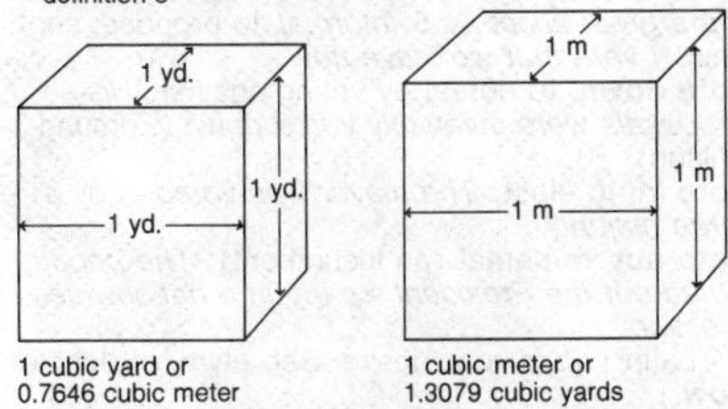


1 cubic yard or 0.7646 cubic meter

1 cubic meter or 1.3079 cubic yards

**vol|umed** (vol′yəmd), *adj.* **1** made into or filling a volume or volumes of a specified size or number: *The shelf contains the complete volumed works of Jefferson.* **2** formed into a rolling, rounded, or dense mass: *volumed smoke.*

**vo|lu|men** (və lü′mən), *n., pl.* **-mi|na** (-mə nə). a roll or scroll, as of parchment or similar material. [< Latin *volūmen;* see etym. under **volume**]

**vo|lu|me|ter** (və lü′mə tər), *n.* **1** any one of various instruments used to measure the volume of a gas or liquid directly or of a solid by displacement. **2** a kind of hydrometer. [< *volu*(me) + *-meter*]

**vol|u|met|ric** (vol′yə met′rik), *adj.* of or having to do with measurement by volume. —**vol′u|met′ri|cal|ly**, *adv.*

**vol|u|met|ri|cal** (vol′yə met′rə kəl), *adj.* = volumetric.

**volumetric analysis**, **1** quantitative chemical analysis in which the analyst determines the volume of a solution having a precisely known concentration, that is required to complete a specified chemical reaction. **2** the measurement of the volume of gases, as by an eudiometer.

**vo|lu|me|try** (və lü′mə trē), *n.* the measurement of volume; the use of volumeters.

**vo|lu|mi|nal** (və lü′mə nəl), *adj.* having to do with volume or cubic magnitude.

**vo|lu|mi|nos|i|ty** (və lü′mə nos′ə tē), *n.* the quality or state of being voluminous; copiousness.

**vo|lu|mi|nous** (və lü′mə nəs), *adj.* **1** forming or filling a large book or many books: *a voluminous report, the voluminous works of Sir Walter Scott.* **2** writing much: *a voluminous author or correspondent.* **3** of great size or volume; very bulky; large: *A voluminous cloak covered him from head to foot.* **4** full of or containing many coils, convolutions, or windings. [< Latin *voluminōsus* with many coils < Latin *volūmen, -inis;* see etym. under **volume**] —**vo|lu′mi|nous|ly**, *adv.* —**vo|lu′mi|nous|ness**, *n.*

**vol|un|tar|i|ly** (vol′ən ter′ə lē, vol′ən tãr′-), *adv.* of one's own choice; without force or compulsion: *Did you do that voluntarily, or did someone force you to do it by threats?* **SYN**: willingly.

**vol|un|tar|i|ness** (vol′ən ter′ē nis), *n.* the quality or state of being voluntary: *They assumed that socialism would bring ... a new attitude toward work, which would become a matter of joy and voluntariness* (Wall Street Journal).

**vol|un|ta|rism** (vol′ən tə riz′əm), *n.* **1** *Philosophy.* a theory or doctrine that regards the will (rather than the intellect) as the fundamental principle or dominant factor in the individual or in the universe. **2** = voluntaryism.

**vol|un|ta|rist** (vol′ən tər ist), *n.* an adherent of voluntarism or the voluntary principle in philosophy.

**vol|un|ta|ris|tic** (vol′ən tə ris′tik), *adj.* of or like voluntarism or voluntarists.

**vol|un|tar|y** (vol′ən ter′ē), *adj., n., pl.* **-tar|ies.**
—*adj.* **1** done, made, given, undertaken, or entered into, of one's own choice; not forced or compelled: *a voluntary contribution, to go into voluntary exile.* **2** maintained or supported by voluntary gifts: *a voluntary hospital, a voluntary church or school.* **3** acting of one's own free will or choice: *Voluntary workers built a road to the boys' camp.* **4** able to act of one's own free will: *People are voluntary agents.* **5a** done, given, or proceeding from the free or unconstrained will of a person: *a voluntary affidavit. The thief's confession was voluntary.* **b** acting or done without obligation or without receiving a valuable consideration: *a voluntary partition of land.* **c** deliberately intended; done on purpose, not by accident: *voluntary manslaughter. Voluntary disobedience will be punished.* **6** controlled by the will: *Talking is voluntary, breathing is only partly so.*
—*n.* **1** anything done, made, given, or entered into, of one's own free will. **2a** a piece of music, often improvised, played as a prelude. **b** an organ solo played before, during, or after a church service. **3** = volunteer.
[< Latin *voluntārius* < *voluntās* will < *vol-,* stem of *velle* to wish. See related etym. at **volunteer**.]
—*Syn. adj.* **1 Voluntary, spontaneous** mean done, made, given or entered into, without being forced or compelled. **Voluntary** emphasizes that it is done of one's own free will or choice: *The state is supported by taxes, the church by voluntary contributions.* **Spontaneous** emphasizes that it is done from natural impulse, without thought or intention: *The laughter at his jokes is never forced, but always spontaneous.*

**vol|un|tar|y|ism** (vol′ən ter′ē iz əm), *n.* **1** the principle or system under which churches, schools, and other institutions are supported by voluntary contributions or assistance, rather than by the state. **2** the principle or method of voluntary service: *military voluntaryism.*

**vol|un|tar|y|ist** (vol′ən ter′ē ist), *n.* a person who believes in or advocates voluntaryism, especially in religion.

**voluntary minority**, a national, religious, or racial group that chooses to remain a minority by preserving the traditions and customs of their forbears without assimilating with the majority.

**voluntary muscle**, = striated muscle.

**vol|un|teer** (vol′ən tir′), *n., v., adj.* —*n.* **1** a person who enters any service of his own choice; one who is not drafted: *Most soldiers are volunteers.* **2** a person who serves without pay. In some towns the firemen are volunteers. **3** *Law.* **a** a person who acts of his own free will in a transaction. **b** a person who receives property by a conveyance made without a valuable consideration. **4** a plant which grows from self-sown seed.
—*v.i.* **1** to offer one's services of one's own free will: *to volunteer for an expedition. As soon as war was declared, many men volunteered for the army.* **2** to offer of one's own free will: *He volunteered to carry the water.*
—*v.t.* **1** to offer (one's services or oneself) for some special purpose or enterprise. **2** to offer to do, undertake, give, or show (something) without being asked: *to volunteer a job or song.* **3** to tell or say voluntarily: *She volunteered the information.*
—*adj.* **1** of or made up of volunteers: *Our village has a volunteer fire department.* **2** serving as a volunteer: *That man is a volunteer fireman in this town.* **3** = voluntary. **4** growing from self-sown seed: *volunteer petunias.*
[earlier *voluntier* < French *volontaire* (originally) adjective < Latin *voluntārius.* See related etym. at **voluntary**.]

**volunteer army**, an army made up of volunteers instead of conscripts: *There remains a serious question as to whether a volunteer army would attract enough manpower to back up the U.S.'s worldwide commitments* (Time).

**vol|un|teer|ism** (vol′ən tir′iz əm), *n.* = voluntaryism.

**Volunteers of America**, an organization for religious reform and charity, similar to the Salvation Army, founded in 1896 by Ballington Booth, son of William Booth, the founder of the Salvation Army.

**Volunteer State**, a nickname for Tennessee.

**vo|lup|té** (vô lyp tā′), *n. French.* voluptuousness: *She had ... these sex attractions and talents—volupté, she had* (Saul Bellow).

**vo|lup|tu|ar|y** (və lup′chü er′ē), *n., pl.* **-ar|ies,** *adj.*
—*n.* a person who cares much for luxurious or sensual pleasures.
—*adj.* of or having to do with luxurious or sensual pleasures: *He leads a voluptuary life.*
[< Latin *voluptuārius,* earlier *voluptārius* < *voluptās* pleasure; see etym. under **voluptuous**]

**vo|lup|tu|ous** (və lup′chü əs), *adj.* **1** caring much for the pleasures of the senses. **2** giving pleasure to the senses: *voluptuous music.* **3** suggestive of sensual pleasure by fullness and beauty of form: *voluptuous loveliness.* [< Latin *voluptuōsus* < *voluptās* pleasure < *volupe* agreeable] —**vo|lup′tu|ous|ly**, *adv.* —**vo|lup′tu|ous|ness**, *n.*

✱**vo|lute** (və lüt′), *n., adj.* —*n.* **1** a spiral or twisted thing or form. **2** *Architecture.* a spiral or scroll-like ornament, especially one of those on Ionic, Corinthian, and Composite capitals. **3** *Zoology.* **a** a turn or whorl of a spiral shell. **b** any one of a group of gastropods that have a spiral shell.
—*adj.* **1** rolled up; spiral. **2** of machinery: **a** forming a spiral curve or curves: *a volute casing of a centrifugal pump.* **b** moving in a rotary, and usually also a lateral, way.
[< French *volute* < Italian *voluta* < Latin *volūta,* (originally) feminine past participle of *volvere* to roll. See related etym. at **volta**.]

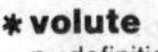
✱**volute**
*n.,* definitions 2, 3b

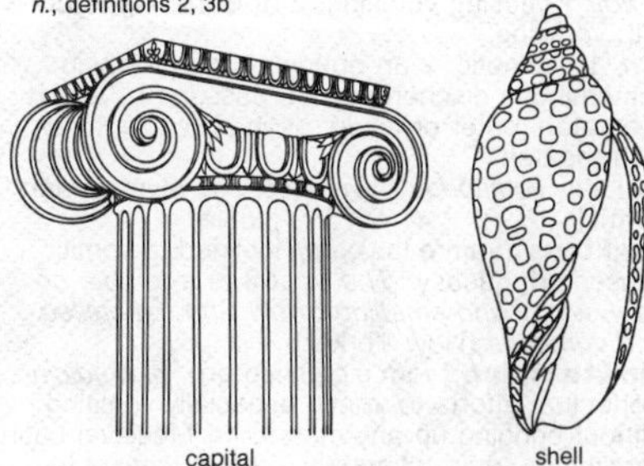


**vo|lut|ed** (və lü′tid), *adj.* having a coil, whorl, or volute: *a voluted shell.*

**volute spring**, a metal spring resembling a volute, commonly one consisting of a flat bar or ribbon coiled in a conical helix so as to be compressible in the direction of the axis about which it is coiled.

**vol|u|tin** (vol′yə tin), *n.* a granular substance in the cells of bacteria and yeast, that stains with basic dyes. [< New Latin *volutans* the species name of the bacteria in which it was found + English *-in*]

**vo|lu|tion** (və lü′shən), *n.* **1** a rolling or winding; twist; convolution; spiral turn; whorl. **2** a set of whorls, as of a spiral shell. [< Latin *volūtus,* past participle of *volvere* to roll + English *-ion*]

**vol|va** (vol′və), *n. Botany.* the membranous covering that completely encloses many fungi, especially mushrooms, in the early stage of growth. [< Latin *volva,* variant of *vulva;* see etym. under **vulva**]

**vol|vent** (vol′vənt), *n.* one of a series of pear-shaped cells on the tentacles of a hydra. The volvents release short, thick threads to capture small swimming animals by coiling about them. [< Latin *volvens, -entis,* present participle of *volvere* to roll (because of its coiled structure)]

**vol|vox** (vol′voks), *n.* any one of a group of fresh-water, green algae existing as spherical colonies

**Pronunciation Key:** hat, āge, cãre, fär; let, ēqual, tėrm; it, īce; hot, ōpen, ôrder; **oil**, **out**; cup, pu̇t, rüle; **ch**ild; lo**ng**; **th**in; **ᴛʜ**en; **zh**, measure; **ə** represents **a** in about, **e** in taken, **i** in pencil, **o** in lemon, **u** in circus.

of thousands of differentiated cells, and provided with cilia that enable them to roll over in the water. [< New Latin *Volvox* the genus name < Latin *volvere* to roll]

**vol|vu|lus** (vol′vyə ləs), *n. Medicine.* a twisting of the bowel so as to cause intestinal obstruction. [< New Latin *volvulus* (in Latin, small womb of an animal) < *volvere* to roll, turn]

**vo|mer** (vō′mər), *n.* **1** (in most vertebrates) a bone of the skull in or near the nose. **2** (in man) a bone forming a large part of the nasal septum (partition between the nostrils) and having the shape of a plowshare. [< Latin *vōmer, -eris* plowshare]

**vo|mer|ine** (vō′mər in, vom′ər-), *adj.* of or having to do with the vomer.

**vom|i|ca** (vom′ə kə), *n. Medicine.* **1** an ulcerous cavity or abscess, usually in the lungs. **2** the pus in such a cavity or abscess. [< Latin *vomica* boil, ulcer < *vomere* to eject, vomit]

**vom|it** (vom′it), *v., n.* —***v.i.*** **1** to throw up what has been eaten; expel the contents of the stomach through the mouth. **2** *Figurative.* to come out with force or violence.
—***v.t.*** **1** to bring up and eject through the mouth (swallowed food or drink). **2** *Figurative.* to throw out with force; throw up: *The chimneys vomited smoke.* **3** to cause (a person) to vomit.
—***n.*** **1** the act of vomiting. **2** the substance thrown up from the stomach by vomiting. **3** = emetic. **4** a disease marked by copious vomiting.
[< Latin *vomitus,* past participle of *vomere* spew forth, eject] —**vom′it|er,** *n.*

**vom|it|ing gas** (vom′ə ting), a gas that causes vomiting, coughing, and sneezing, used chiefly in breaking up riots; chloropicrin.

**vom|i|tive** (vom′ə tiv), *adj., n.* = emetic.

**vom|i|to** (vom′ə tō), *n.,* or **vomito negro,** black vomit, especially the black vomit of yellow fever. [< Spanish *vómito* (*negro*) (black) vomit < Latin *vomitus*]

**vom|i|to|ri|um** (vom′ə tôr′ē əm, -tōr′-), *n., pl.* **-to|ri|a** (-tôr′ē ə, -tōr′-). a passage providing entrance and exit in a theater, stadium, or other public place; vomitory: *the great vomitoria ... designed to handle the crowds in Pennsylvania Station* (Lewis Mumford). [< Latin *vomitōria,* plural < *vomere* spew forth, eject]

**vom|i|to|ry** (vom′ə tôr′ē, -tōr′-), *adj., n., pl.* **-ries.**
—***adj.*** **1** causing vomiting. **2** of or having to do with vomiting.
—***n.*** **1** = emetic. **2** an opening through which something is discharged. **3** a passage by which spectators enter or leave, as in an ancient Roman theater.
[< Latin *vomitōrius* < *vomitus;* see etym. under **vomit**]

**vom|i|tous** (vom′ə təs), *adj.* inclined to vomit; nauseated; queasy: *The boat was a terrible ordeal, windy and smelling of oil. She felt chilled and vomitous* (New Yorker).

**vom|i|tu|ri|tion** (vom′ə chu̇ rish′ən), *n. Medicine.* ineffectual efforts to vomit, especially vomiting without bringing up any matter. [< Medieval Latin *vomituritio, -onis,* ultimately < Latin *vomere* to vomit]

**vom|i|tus** (vom′ə təs), *n.* vomited matter; vomit: *They should take the child and a sample of the poison* (*the vomitus will serve in a pinch*) *to the hospital right away* (Time). [< Latin *vomitus;* see etym. under **vomit**]

**von** (fôn; *English* von), *prep. German.* from; of.
▶ **von** is used in German family names (originally before names of places or estates) as an indication of nobility or rank.

**V-one** (vē′wun′), *n.* = V-1.

**Von Gier|ke's disease** (gir′kəz), a metabolic condition in which excess glycogen causes an abnormal enlargement of the liver, kidneys, or other organ; glycogenosis. [< Edgar *von Gierke,* 1877-1945, a German pathologist]

**Von Jaksch's anemia** (yäk′shiz), a disease affecting young children, characterized by anemia and a swelling of the spleen. [< Rudolf *von Jaksch,* 1855-1947, a German physician]

**von Wil|le|brand's disease** (wil′ə brandz, vil′-), = pseudohemophilia. [< E. A. *von Willebrand,* 1870-1949, a German physician in Finland, who first described it]

**voo|doo** (vü′dü), *n., pl.* **-doos,** *adj., v.,* **-dooed, -doo|ing.** —***n.*** **1** a body of religious beliefs made up of mysterious rites and practices that include sorcery, magic, and conjuration. Voodoo came from Africa; belief in it still prevails in many parts of the West Indies and some parts of the United States. **2** a person who practices such magic. **3** a charm or fetish used in the practice of voodoo.
—***adj.*** of, having to do with, used in, or practicing voodoo.
—***v.t.*** to affect by voodoo sorcery, magic, or conjuration. Also, **voudou.**
[American English < Creole (Haiti) *voodoo* < Ewe *vodū* divinity]

**voo|doo|ism** (vü′dü iz əm), *n.* voodoo rites and practices; belief in or practice of voodoo as a superstition or form of sorcery; vodun.

**voo|doo|ist** (vü′dü ist), *n.* a believer in voodoo; practicer of voodoo.

**voo|doo|is|tic** (vü′dü is′tik), *adj.* of or having to do with voodooism.

**voor|lop|er** (fōr′lō′pər), *n. Afrikaans.* the native boy who guides the foremost pair of a team of oxen: *One of the drivers ... called to his voorloper to turn the cattle loose to graze* (Percy Fitzpatrick).

**voor|trek|ker** (fōr′trek′ər), *n. Afrikaans.* a pioneer, especially one of the Dutch who emigrated from the Cape of Good Hope region into the lands north of the Orange River about 1835-40.

**Vo|po** (fō′pō), *n.* **1** *no pl.* the East German People's Police; Volkspolizei. **2** *pl.* **-pos.** a member of Volkspolizei: *At the sector boundary I was stopped by a couple of Vopos* (New Yorker). [< German *Vopo* < *Vo*(lks)*po*(lizei) People's Police]

**VOR** (no periods), very high frequency omnidirectional range, a kind of radio range giving bearings in all directions from its transmitter: *VOR is able to utilize all the air space by sending out signals in every direction* (New York Times). [< *v*(ery high frequency) *o*(mnidirectional) *r*(ange)]

**vo|ra|cious** (və rā′shəs), *adj.* **1** eating much; greedy in eating; ravenous: *voracious sharks.* **SYN:** gluttonous. **2** *Figurative.* very eager; unable to be satisfied: *He is a voracious reader of history.* **SYN:** insatiable. [< Latin *vorāx, -ācis* greedy (with English *-ous*) < *vorāre* to devour] —**vo|ra′cious|ly,** *adv.* —**vo|ra′cious|ness,** *n.*

**vo|rac|i|ty** (və ras′ə tē), *n.* the quality or state of being voracious; voracious nature; voracious behavior. [< Latin *vorācitās* < *vorāx;* see etym. under **voracious**]

**Vor|la|ge** (fōr′lä′gə), *n.* a position in skiing in which the skier leans forward by bending at the ankles, without raising the heels from the skis. [< German *Vorlage* < *vor* before + *Lage* position]

**vor|spiel** (fōr′shpēl′), *n.* a prelude or overture. [< German *Vorspiel* < *vor* before + *Spiel* a play, a playing]

***vor|tex** (vôr′teks), *n., pl.* **-tex|es** or **-ti|ces. 1** a swirling mass of water that sucks in everything near it; whirlpool. **2** a violent whirl of air; cyclone; whirlwind. **3** a whirl or whirling mass of fire, flame, atoms, fluid, or vapor. **4** *Figurative.* a whirl of activity or other situation from which it is hard to escape: *The two nations were unwillingly drawn into the vortex of war.* **5** a supposed rotatory movement of cosmic matter round a center or axis, regarded in old theories, especially that of Descartes, as accounting for the origin or phenomena of the terrestrial and other systems. [< Latin *vortex, -icis,* variant of *vertex;* see etym. under **vertex**]

***vortex** definition 1

**vor|ti|cal** (vôr′tə kəl), *adj., n.* —***adj.*** of or like a vortex; moving in a vortex; whirling around: *vortical currents.*
—***n.*** a vortical motion. —**vor′ti|cal|ly,** *adv.*

**vor|ti|cel|la** (vôr′tə sel′ə), *n., pl.* **-cel|lae** (-sel′ē). any one of a genus of one-celled animals with a ciliate, bell-shaped body on a slender contractile stalk, often found attached to a plant or other object under water. [< New Latin *Vorticella* the typical genus (diminutive) < Latin *vortex* vortex]

**vor|ti|ces** (vôr′tə sēz), *n.* vortexes: a plural of **vortex.**

**vor|ti|cism** (vôr′tə siz əm), *n.* a movement in modern art and literature started in England about 1914 and chiefly supported by the poet Ezra Pound and the painter Wyndham Lewis. It emphasized that a work of art should have a point of central meaning obtained by reducing content to its simplest details, as in cubism. [< Latin *vortex, -icis* vortex + English *-ism*]

**vor|ti|cist** (vôr′tə sist), *n., adj.* —***n.*** a follower or exponent of vorticism: *The reviled ... Cubists, Futurists, Expressionists, Vorticists of today may be the honoured masters of tomorrow* (Observer).
—***adj.*** exhibiting or following the principles of vorticism: *A block away, at 105 Mulberry, a chicken and a ... rabbit have been painted, and a vorticist woman has been chalked* (New Yorker).

**vor|tic|i|ty** (vôr tis′ə tē), *n.* the condition of a fluid with respect to its vortical motion: *The National Weather Analysis Center ... provides the daily reports on winds, temperatures and vorticity as well as forecasts of Northern Hemisphere weather* (Science News Letter).

**vor|ti|cose** (vôr′tə kōs), *adj.* = vortical. [< Latin *vorticōsus* < *vortex, -icis* vortex] —**vor′ti|cose′ly,** *adv.*

**vor|tig|i|nous** (vôr tij′ə nəs), *adj.* **1** (of motion) vortical. **2** moving in a vortex; rushing in whirls or eddies. [< Latin *vortīgō, -inis,* variant of *vertīgō* (see etym. under **vertigo**) + English *-ous*]

**Vor|tum|nus** (vôr tum′nəs), *n.* = Vertumnus.

**vot|a|ble** (vō′tə bəl), *adj.* that can be voted for, against, or on.

**vo|ta|ress** (vō′tər is), *n.* a woman votary.

**vo|ta|rist** (vō′tər ist), *n.* = votary.

**vo|ta|ry** (vō′tər ē), *n., pl.* **-ries,** *adj.* —***n.*** **1** a person bound by vows to a religious life; monk or nun. **2** a person who is devoted to a particular religion or to some form of religious worship. **3** a person who is devoted to a particular pursuit, occupation, study, or interest; devotee: *He is a votary of golf.* **4** a devoted admirer or adherent to some person, cause, or institution. **SYN:** partisan.
—***adj.*** *Obsolete.* **1** consecrated by a vow. **2** of the nature of a vow.
[< Latin *vōtum* vow, noun use of neuter past participle of *vovēre* to vow + English *-ary*]

**vote** (vōt), *n., v.,* **vot|ed, vot|ing.** —***n.*** **1** a formal expression of a wish or choice on a proposal, motion, candidate for office, or other matter under discussion. A vote can be cast by a ballot or indicated by saying "aye" or "nay," holding up the hand, standing up, or otherwise. *The person receiving the most votes is elected.* **2** the right to give such an expression of opinion or choice. Children don't have the vote, and adult citizens can lose it by being convicted of certain crimes. **3** a ballot or other means by which a vote is cast or indicated: *More than a million votes were counted.* **4** what is expressed or granted by a majority of voters: *a vote of thanks. The vote for foreign aid was $50,000,000.* **5** votes considered together: *a light vote, the labor vote.* **6** a voter. **7** *Obsolete.* **a** a vow. **b** a prayer. **c** an ardent wish or desire.
—***v.i.*** to give or cast a vote: *He voted for the Democrats; she voted against them.*
—***v.t.*** **1** to support by one's vote: *to vote the Republican ticket.* **2** to elect, enact, establish, or ratify, by vote: *to vote a bill through Congress, vote a woman to the Senate.* **3** to pass, determine, or grant by vote: *Money for a new school was voted by the board.* **4** to declare, especially by general consent: *The children all voted the trip a great success.* **5** *Informal.* to propose; suggest: *I vote that we leave now.*
**vote down,** to defeat by voting against: *His proposals were invariably voted down* (Edmund Wilson).
**vote in,** to elect: *The mayor was voted in by a large majority.*
**vote out,** to defeat (an incumbent): *The people voted out the President's party in a nationwide election.*
[< Latin *vōtum* vow, desire. See etym. of doublet **vow.**]

**vote-get|ter** (vōt′get′ər), *n. Informal.* a person who is successful in getting votes; popular candidate: *He is a good senator and might make a good President, but unless he is able to prove himself an irresistible vote-getter he is unlikely to be given the chance to be one* (Manchester Guardian).

**vote|less** (vōt′lis), *adj.* having no vote; not entitled to vote: *So there arose a demand for someone who could speak officially for Alaska, a voteless delegate, such as every other territory had had from its beginnings* (Atlantic).

**vote of confidence, 1** a vote given by the majority of members in a parliament to the government or its chief representative, especially in a period of crisis, to indicate support of its policies: *The Government is asking for a vote of confidence* (London Times). **2** any expression of approval or support: *British and French officialdom, in a rare vote of confidence in U.S. diplomatic skill, admiringly agreed that Washington had handled Mikoyan adroitly* (Time).

**vot|er** (vō′tər), *n.* **1** a person who votes. **2** a person who has the right to vote: *Women have been voters in the United States only since 1920.* **SYN:** elector.

**vot|ing machine** (vō′ting), a mechanical device for registering and counting votes: *Voting machines have replaced the ballot box.*

**voting paper,** a paper on which a vote is recorded, especially as used in British parliamentary elections.

**voting trust**, 1 a method of restraining trade in which a board of trustees controls the affairs of a group of companies by obtaining the right to vote the stocks in each concern. 2 a method of centralizing control of a company, in which all or a majority of the stockholders relinquish their voting power to a board of trustees for a limited period of time.

**vo|tive** (vō′tiv), *adj.* **1** promised by a vow; given or done because of a vow: *votive offerings to the gods, a knight on his votive quest, to light a votive candle.* **2** made up or expressive of a vow, desire, or wish: *a votive prayer.* **3** (in the Roman Catholic Church) done or performed with special intention and not corresponding strictly to the established liturgical order. [< Latin *votīvus* < *vōtum* a vow] —**vo′tive|ly**, *adv.* —**vo′tive|ness**, *n.*

**vo|tress** (vō′tris), *n.* = votaress.

**Vo|ty|ak** (vō′tē ak, -tyäk), *n.* **1** a Finno-Ugric language, spoken in the eastern Soviet Union in Europe. **2** any of the people speaking this language; Udmurt.

**vouch** (vouch), *v., n.* —*v.i.* **1** to be responsible; give a guarantee (for): *I can vouch for the truth of the story. The principal vouched for the boy's honesty.* **2** to give evidence or assurance of a fact (for): *The success of the campaign vouches for the candidate's popularity.*
—*v.t.* **1** to guarantee (as a statement or document) to be true or accurate; confirm; bear witness to; attest. **2** to support or uphold with evidence; back with proof. **3** to support or substantiate (as a claim or title) by vouchers. **4** to cite, quote, or appeal to (as authority, example, or a passage in a book) in support or justification as of a view. **5** *Law.* to call into court to give warranty of title. **6** to sponsor or recommend (a person or thing); support; back. **7** *Archaic.* to call to witness.
—*n. Obsolete.* an assertion, declaration, or attestation of truth or fact.
[Middle English *vouchen* < Anglo-French *voucher*, Old French *vochier* < Latin *vocāre* call]

**vouch|ee** (vou chē′), *n.* a person who is vouched for by another.

**vouch|er¹** (vou′chər), *n.* **1** a person or thing that vouches for something. **2** a written evidence of payment; receipt. Canceled checks returned to a person from his bank are vouchers.

**vouch|er²** (vou′chər), *n.* in early English law: **a** a person summoned into court to give warranty of a title. **b** the act of summoning a person into court to give warranty of title. [< Anglo-French *voucher* a summoning, noun use of infinitive; see etym. under **vouch**]

**vouch|safe** (vouch sāf′), *v.*, **-safed, -saf|ing.** —*v.t.* **1** to be willing to grant or give; deign (to do or give): *The proud man vouchsafed no reply when we told him we had not meant to hurt his feelings.* **2** *Obsolete.* to guarantee as safe; secure; assure.
—*v.i.* to permit; grant; condescend; stoop. [< Middle English phrase *vouchen* (*it*) *safe* to guarantee it as safe]

**vouch|safe|ment** (vouch sāf′mənt), *n.* **1** the act of vouchsafing. **2** something vouchsafed.

**vou|dou** (vü′dü), *n., adj., v.* = voodoo.

**vouge** (vüzh), *n.* a type of weapon carried by foot soldiers in the Middle Ages, having an ax blade with a spear point at the top. [< French *vouge* < Old French *vouge*, or *veouge*, earlier *vedoge* < Late Latin (Gaul) *vidubium*, probably < Celtic (compare Middle Irish *fidbæ* sickle)]

**vous|soir** (vü swär′), *n.* one of the wedge-shaped pieces or sections that form part of an arch or a vault. See picture under **keystone.** [< French *voussoir* < Old French *vausoir* < Vulgar Latin *volsōrium* < Latin *volvere* to roll]

**vow** (vou), *n., v.* —*n.* **1** a solemn promise: *a vow of secrecy, a marriage vow.* **2** a promise made to God: *a nun's vows.* **3** a solemn declaration or affirmation; asseveration.
—*v.t.* **1** to make a vow to do, give, get, or the like: *to vow not to disclose a secret, to vow revenge. The knight vowed loyalty to the king.* **2** to dedicate, consecrate, or devote to some person or service: *to vow oneself to a life of service to God.* **3** to declare earnestly or emphatically: *I vowed never to leave home again.*
—*v.i.* to make a vow.
**take vows**, to become a member of a religious order: *The girl took vows to become a teaching nun.*
[< Anglo-French, Old French *vou* < Latin *vōtum*, noun use of past participle of *vovēre* to vow. See etym. of doublet **vote.**] —**vow′er**, *n.*

**vow|el** (vou′əl), *n., adj., v.*, **-eled, -el|ing** or (*especially British*) **-elled, -el|ling.** —*n.* **1** any speech sound produced by not blocking the breath with the lips, teeth, or tongue, with the vocal cords generally but not necessarily vibrating. A vowel can form a syllable by itself, as does the first syllable of *awful* (ô′fəl). The various vowel sounds are produced by modification of the shape of the oral chamber by movements of the tongue and lips. **2** a letter that stands for such a sound. English *a, e, i, o,* and *u* are vowels. *Y* is sometimes a vowel, as in *bicycle.*
—*adj.* of or having something to do with a vowel. *Voluntary* has four vowel sounds; *strength* has only one.
—*v.t.* **1** to supply with vowels or vowel points: *with pauses, cadence, and well-vowelled words* (John Dryden). **2** *Slang.* to pay (a creditor) with an I.O.U.: *Do not talk to me, I am voweled by the Count, and cursedly out of humour* (Sir Richard Steele).
—*v.i.* to utter or pronounce vowels: *Sir Maurice, vowelling imperially as the Sheldonian* (Sunday Times).
[< Old French *vouel* < Latin (*littera*) *vōcālis* sounding (letter) < *vōx, vōcis* voice. See etym. of doublet **vocal.**] —**vow′el|like′**, *adj.*

**vow|el|ize** (vou′ə līz), *v.t.*, **-ized, -iz|ing.** **1** to insert vowel symbols or points in: *to vowelize a Hebrew text.* **2** to pronounce like a vowel. **3** to modify by a vowel sound. —**vow′el|i|za′tion**, *n.*

**vow|el|less** (vou′əl lis), *adj.* having no vowel or vowels.

*__vowel point__, (in Hebrew, Arabic, and certain other Eastern writing systems) any of certain marks placed above or below consonants, or attached to them, to indicate vowels.

***vowel point**

**the Hebrew consonant, daleth**

dee deh day dah daw duh doh doo

**vox** (voks), *n., pl.* **vo|ces.** *Latin.* voice; sound; word; expression.

**vox an|gel|i|ca** (voks an jel′ə kə), = voix céleste. [< Latin *vōx* voice + *angelica*, feminine, angelic]

**vox bar|ba|ra** (voks bär′bər ə), a barbarous or outlandish word or phrase (commonly used of those terms in botany and zoology that are ostensibly New Latin, but which are neither Latin nor Greek, nor of classic derivation and formation, although they may be Latin and Greek hybrids). [< Latin *vōx* voice + *barbara*, feminine, (originally) non-Greek or Roman]

**vox et prae|te|re|a ni|hil** (voks′ et prē ter′ē ə nī′hil), *Latin.* a voice and nothing more; only sound.

**vox hu|ma|na** (voks hyü mā′nə), an organ reed stop of 8-foot, or occasionally 16-foot, pitch whose tones are intended to imitate those of the human voice. [< Latin *vōx* voice + *hūmāna*, feminine, human]

**vox pop** (voks′ pop′), popular opinion, especially as given on some current topic, often by a person who is stopped on the street and questioned by a television or radio reporter: *A few days ago, a BBC camera crew went round Washington collecting vox pops—close-ups of men in the street saying pithily what they think of things* (Listener). [shortened < *vox populi*]

**vox po|pu|li** (voks pop′yü lī), *Latin.* the voice or opinion of the people. *Abbr:* vox pop.

**voy|age** (voi′ij), *n., v.*, **-aged, -ag|ing.** —*n.* **1a** a journey or travel by water; cruise: *to make or take a voyage. We had a pleasant voyage to England.* **SYN:** See syn. under **trip. b** such a journey in which return is made to the starting point. **2** a journey or travel through the air or through space: *an airplane voyage, the earth's voyage around the sun.* **3** (formerly) a journey by either land or sea. **4** a written account of a voyage; book describing a voyage (often used in the plural in book titles). **5** the course of life (or some part of it), or the fate of persons after death: *the voyage of matrimony.* **6** *Obsolete.* an enterprise or undertaking.
—*v.i.* to make or take a voyage or voyages; go by sea or air: *Columbus voyaged across unknown seas.* —*v.t.* to cross or travel over; traverse: *Freighters voyage all the seas of the world.*
[< Old French *veiage*, and *voyage* < Latin *viāticum* provision for travel; (originally) of or for a journey. See etym. of doublet **viaticum.**]

**voy|age|a|ble** (voi′ə jə bəl), *adj.* that can be voyaged over; navigable.

**voy|ag|er** (voi′ə jər), *n.* a person who makes a voyage; traveler.

**vo|ya|geur** (vwä′yä zhœr′; *French* vwȧ yȧ zhœr′), *n., pl.* **-geurs** (-zhœrz′; *French* -zhœr′). a French Canadian or half-breed worker for the early fur-trading companies who transported men and supplies to and from remote places, especially by canoe through unsettled regions. [American English < Canadian French *voyageur* (in Middle French, a traveler) < *voyager* to travel < Old French *voyage*, see etym. under **voyage**]

**vo|yeur** (vwä′yœr′), *n.* a person who gets pleasure from watching the private acts of others without being seen by them; Peeping Tom. [< French *voyeur* < *voir* to see < Latin *vidēre*]

**vo|yeur|ism** (vwä yœr′iz əm), *n.* the practices of a voyeur.

**vo|yeur|is|tic** (vwä′yə ris′tik), *adj.* of or having to do with voyeurs or voyeurism: *a voyeuristic tendency.* —**vo′yeur|is′ti|cal|ly**, *adv.*

**V.P.** or **VP** (no periods), Vice-President.

**V-par|ti|cle** (vē′pär′tə kəl), *n.* a name originally given to nuclear particles that produced V-shaped tracks when passing through a cloud chamber, now identified as hyperons or heavy mesons.

**VRA** (no periods), Vocational Rehabilitation Administration.

**vrai|sem|blance** (vre säɴ bläɴs′), *n.* appearance of truth; likelihood; verisimilitude. [< French *vraisemblance* < *vrai* true + *semblance* appearance]

**V.Rev.**, Very Reverend.

**vroom** (və rüm′, -rům′; vrüm, vrům), *n., v.i., v.t.* = varoom.

**vrouw** (vrou; *South African* frou), *n.* **1** a woman; wife; lady. **2** Mrs. [< Dutch *vrouw*]

**vs.**, **1** versus. **2** verse.

**v.s.**, see above (Latin, *vide supra*).

**V.S.**, **1** Veterinary Surgeon. **2** *Music.* turn over swiftly (Italian, *volti subito*).

**V-shaped** (vē′shāpt′), *adj.* **1** shaped like the letter V: *Most of the modern jet airliners have V-shaped wings.* **2** like the letter V in cross section.

**V-sign** (vē′sīn′), *n.* **1** a sign indicating victory, especially in wartime, made by spreading out two fingers in the form of a V. **2** this sign used as an expression of peace; peace sign: *He had them rhythmically chanting "Peace Now!" and making the two-finger V-sign* (New Yorker).

**VSO** (no periods) or **V.S.O.**, Voluntary Service Overseas (a British government organization similar to the American Peace Corps).

**V.S.O.P.**, Very Superior Old Pale (applied to a brandy about 12 years old).

*__VSTOL__ (vē′stôl), *n.* vertical and short takeoff and landing (a type of aircraft combining the characteristics of VTOL and STOL).

***VSTOL**

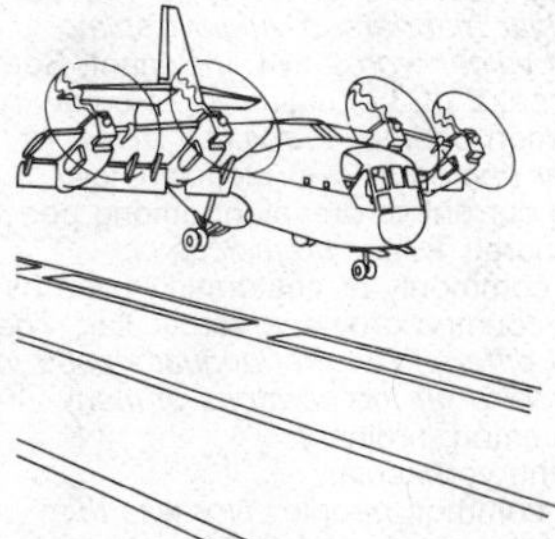

**v.t.**, transitive verb.

**Vt.**, Vermont.

**VT** (no periods), Vermont (with postal Zip Code).

**VT fuse** = proximity fuse. [< *v*(ariable) *t*(ime) *fuse*]

**VTO** (no periods), vertical take-off.

**VTOL** (vē′tôl), *n.* vertical take-off and landing (a type of aircraft other than a helicopter that can take off and land vertically).

**VTOL|port** (vē′tôl pôrt′, -pōrt′), *n.* = vertiport.

**V.T.R.** or **VTR** (no periods), videotape recorder.

**V-two** (vē′tü′), *n.* = V-2.

**vug, vugg,** or **vugh** (vug, vůg), *n. Mining.* a cavity; a hollow in a rock or lode, often completely lined with quartz. [< Cornish *vooga*, or *fuogo* cavern]

**vug|gy** or **vugh|y** (vug′ē, vůg′-), *adj. Mining.* full of cavities.

**Vul.**, Vulgate.

**Vul|can** (vul′kən), *n.* the Roman god of fire and metalworking, the husband of Venus. The Greeks called him Hephaestus.

**vul|ca|ni|an** (vul kā′nē ən), *adj.* **1** = volcanic. **2** having to do with metalworking. **3** *Especially British.* Plutonic.

**Vul|ca|ni|an** (vul kā′nē ən), *adj.* **1** having to do with, characteristic of, or made by Vulcan. **2** of or designating a type of volcano or eruption characterized by the ejection of dense clouds of ash and other particles of solid matter, with little or no lava.

---

**Pronunciation Key:** hat, āge, cãre, fär; let, ēqual, tėrm; it, īce; hot, ōpen, ôrder; oil, out; cup, pu̇t, rüle; child; long; thin; ᴛʜen; zh, measure; ə represents **a** in about, **e** in taken, **i** in pencil, **o** in lemon, **u** in circus.

**vul|can|ic|i|ty** (vul′kə nis′ə tē), *n.* = volcanicity.
**vul|can|ism** (vul′kə niz əm), *n.* volcanic phenomena; volcanism.
**vul|can|ist** (vul′kə nist), *n.* a person who believes there is volcanic activity in the moon's core; hot mooner.
**vul|can|ite** (vul′kə nīt), *n., adj.* —*n.* a hard, usually black substance made by heating rubber with a large amount of sulfur; ebonite; hard rubber. Vulcanite is used for combs, for shoe soles, for buttons, in electric insulation, and in many other ways.
—*adj.* made of this substance.
**vul|can|iz|a|ble** (vul′kə nī′zə bəl), *adj.* that can be vulcanized.
**vul|can|i|zate** (vul′kə nə zāt), *n.* a vulcanized material: *Rubber vulcanizates have remarkable strength* (Scientific American).
**vul|can|i|za|tion** (vul′kə nə zā′shən), *n.* the act or process of vulcanizing.
**vul|can|ize** (vul′kə nīz), *v.,* **-ized, -iz|ing.** —*v.t.* **1** to treat (rubber) with sulfur or a sulfur compound and heat it to make it more elastic and durable. Rubber is sometimes treated with a large amount of sulfur and intense heat in order to harden it, as in the preparation of vulcanite. **2** to repair (a rubber tire or tube) by using heat and chemicals to fuse the patch. **3** to treat (rubber) with sulfur or a sulfur compound, but without subjecting it to heat. **4** to treat (a substance) by an analogous process, as for hardening.
—*v.i.* to undergo the process of vulcanizing.
**vul|can|ized fiber** (vul′kə nīzd), **1** a tough, hard substance formed by compressing paper that has been treated with acids or zinc chloride. **2 Vulcanized Fiber.** a trademark for this substance.
**vul|can|iz|er** (vul′kə nī′zər), *n.* **1** a person who vulcanizes. **2** an apparatus that vulcanizes, especially that used in vulcanizing rubber.
**vul|can|o|log|i|cal** (vul′kə nə loj′ə kəl), *adj.* = volcanological.
**vul|can|ol|o|gist** (vul′kə nol′ə jist), *n.* = volcanologist.
**vul|can|ol|o|gy** (vul′kə nol′ə jē), *n.* = volcanology.
**vulg.,** **1** vulgar. **2** vulgarly.
**Vulg.,** Vulgate.
**vul|gar** (vul′gər), *adj., n.* —*adj.* **1** showing a lack of good breeding, manners, or taste; not refined; coarse; low: *vulgar manners, a vulgar display. The tramp used vulgar words.* SYN: inelegant. See syn. under **coarse**. **2** of, belonging to, or comprising the common people: *the vulgar mass, to be held in vulgar contempt.* SYN: plebeian, lowbrow, ignoble. **3** current or prevalent among people; popular; general: *vulgar prejudices or superstitions.* **4** commonly or customarily used by the people of a country; ordinary; vernacular: *The vulgar language differs from the language used in a court's judgment or in the sermons of many preachers.* **5** common; ordinary.
—*n. Obsolete.* the vernacular.
**the vulgar**, the common people: *Nor was this the suspicion of the vulgar alone; it seems to have been shared by the clergy* (Henry Hart Milman).
[< Latin *vulgāris* < *vulgus* the common people, multitude] —**vul′gar|ly**, *adv.* —**vul′gar|ness**, *n.*
**vulgar fraction**, = common fraction.
**vul|gar|i|an** (vul gãr′ē ən), *n.* **1** a vulgar person. **2** a rich person who lacks good breeding, manners, or taste.
**vul|gar|ise** (vul′gə rīz), *v.t.,* **-ised, -is|ing.** *Especially British.* vulgarize.
**vul|gar|ism** (vul′gə riz əm), *n.* **1** a word, phrase, or expression used only by ignorant or careless persons. In "You could of told me" and "I ain't mad at you," *could of* and *ain't* are vulgarisms. **2** vulgar character or action; vulgarity. **3** a vulgar expression; coarse or obscene word or phrase.
**vul|gar|i|ty** (vul gar′ə tē), *n., pl.* **-ties. 1** a lack of fineness of feeling; lack of good breeding, manners, or taste; coarseness: *Talking loudly on a train and chewing gum in church are signs of vulgarity.* **2** a thing done or said that shows vulgarity; vulgar act or word: *His vulgarities made him unwelcome in our home.*
**vul|gar|ize** (vul′gə rīz), *v.t.,* **-ized, -iz|ing. 1** to make vulgar or common; degrade or debase: *Signs and advertisements along a road often vulgarize the countryside.* **2** to make common or popular. —**vul′gar|i|za′tion**, *n.* —**vul′gar|iz′er**, *n.*
**Vulgar Latin**, the popular form of Latin, the main source of French, Spanish, Italian, and Portuguese; Popular Latin.
**Vul|gate** (vul′gāt), *n., adj.* —*n.* the Latin translation of the Bible used in the Roman Catholic Church. It is primarily a translation from the Hebrew, Greek, and Aramaic texts made by Saint Jerome about A.D. 405 but with subsequent revisions. *Abbr:* Vulg.
—*adj.* of or having to do with the Vulgate: *the Vulgate translation of a Hebrew word.*
[< Late Latin *vulgāta* (*ēditiō*) popular (edition); feminine past participle of *vulgāre* make public < *vulgus* the common people]
**vul|gate** (vul′gāt), *n., adj.* —*n.* the ordinary text of a work or author.
—*adj.* **1** ordinary or substandard in language. **2** having to do with the common or usual version of a literary work.
**the vulgate, a** common or colloquial speech: *"Here's a pretty mess," returned the pompous gentleman, descending to the vulgate* (J. E. Cooke). **b** substandard speech: *the vulgate of the backwoods country.*
[< *Vulgate*]
**vul|gus**¹ (vul′gəs), *n., pl.* **-gus|es.** the common people; the crowd. [< Latin *vulgus*]
**vul|gus**² (vul′gəs), *n., pl.* **-gus|es.** *British.* (in some public schools) a short set of Latin verses on a given subject to be memorized or written. [probably an alteration of *vulgars,* plural of *vulgar*]
**vul|ner|a|bil|i|ty** (vul′nər ə bil′ə tē), *n.* **1** *no pl.* vulnerable quality or condition; being open to attack or injury: *The Commission ... made a study of civil defense and the problems of the reduction of urban vulnerability* (Bulletin of the Atomic Scientists). **2** *pl.* **-ties.** a vulnerable part or place.
**vul|ner|a|ble** (vul′nər ə bəl), *adj.* **1** that can be wounded or injured; open to attack: *Pollution of its drinking water left the city vulnerable to disease. Achilles was vulnerable only in his heel.* **2** sensitive to criticism, temptations, or influences: *Most people are vulnerable to ridicule.* **3** having won one game toward a rubber in contract bridge and thus in the position where penalties and premiums are increased. [< Late Latin *vulnerābilis* wounding < Latin *vulnerāre* to wound < *vulnus, -eris* wound] —**vul′ner|a|ble|ness**, *n.*
**vul|ner|a|bly** (vul′nər ə blē), *adv.* in a vulnerable manner.
**vul|ne|rant om|nes, ul|ti|ma ne|cat** (vul′nərant om′nēz, ul′tə mə nē′kat), *Latin.* all (hours) wound, the final (one) kills (sometimes inscribed on clocks).
**vul|ner|ar|y** (vul′nə rer′ē), *adj., n., pl.* **-ar|ies.**
—*adj.* used for or useful in healing wounds; curative: *a vulnerary root.*
—*n.* a vulnerary plant or remedy: *The Indians taught the New England settlers about many vulneraries.*
**Vul|pec|u|la** (vul pek′yə lə), *n., genitive* **Vul|pec|u|lae.** a small northern constellation lying between Hercules and Pegasus; Little Fox. [< Latin *Vulpecula* (diminutive) < *vulpēs, -is* fox]
**Vul|pec|u|lae** (vul pek′yə lē), *n.* the genitive of **Vulpecula**.
**vul|pec|u|lar** (vul pek′yə lər), *adj.* of or having to do with a fox, especially a young fox; vulpine.
**vul|pi|cid|al** (vul′pə sī′dəl), *adj.* committing or taking part in, connected with, or of the nature of vulpicide.
**vul|pi|cide**¹ (vul′pə sīd), *n.* (in England) a person who kills a fox otherwise than by hunting with hounds. [< Latin *vulpēs, -is* fox + English *-cide*¹]
**vul|pi|cide**² (vul′pə sīd), *n.* (in England) the act of killing a fox otherwise than by hunting with hounds. [< Latin *vulpēs, -is* fox + English *-cide*²]
**vul|pine** (vul′pīn, -pin), *adj.* of or like a fox; cunning; sly. [< Latin *vulpīnus* < *vulpēs, -is* fox]
**vul|pi|nite** (vul′pə nīt), *n. Mineralogy.* a granular variety of anhydrite. [< *Vulpino,* Italy, where it is found + *-ite*¹]
**vul|ture** (vul′chər), *n.* **1** a large bird of prey related to the eagles, falcons, and hawks, that eats the flesh of dead animals. Vultures usually have featherless heads and necks, weak talons, and keen sight. They comprise two families, one of the Old World, that includes the griffon vulture, and the other of the New World, that includes the condor, the turkey buzzard or turkey vulture, and the black vulture. **2** *Figurative.* a person that preys upon another; greedy, ruthless person: *Misers, swindlers, and other vultures are not welcome here.* [< Latin *vultur, -uris*] —**vul′ture|like′**, *adj.*
**vul|tur|ine** (vul′chə rīn, -chər in), *adj.* of or having to do with vultures; resembling or characteristic of a vulture. [< Latin *vulturīnus* < *vultur, -uris* vulture]
**vul|tur|ous** (vul′chər əs), *adj.* characteristic of or resembling a vulture.
**vul|va** (vul′və), *n., pl.* **-vae** (-vē), **-vas.** the external genital organs of the female. [< Latin *vulva* womb; wrapper < *volvere* to roll, turn]
**vul|val** (vul′vəl), *adj.* of or having to do with the vulva.
**vul|var** (vul′vər), *adj.* = vulval.
**vul|vi|form** (vul′və fôrm), *adj.* **1** *Zoology.* shaped like the vulva of the human female. **2** *Botany.* shaped like a cleft with projecting edges.
**vul|vi|tis** (vul vī′tis), *n.* inflammation of the vulva.
**vum** (vum), *v.i.,* **vummed, vum|ming.** *U.S. Dialect.* to vow; swear: *I vum, it makes a man come all over uneasy* (New Yorker).
**vv.,** **1** verses. **2** violins.
**v.v.,** vice versa.
**VX** (no periods), the United States Army code name for a type of V-agent, a very lethal nerve gas.
**Vy|cor** (vī′kôr), *n. Trademark.* a nonporous glass composed of 96 per cent silica, very resistant to heat and chemicals, used for laboratory and industrial apparatus, and cooking and baking dishes.
**vy|gie** (vī′jē), *n.* any one of a large group of dicotyledonous, fleshy plants of the carpetweed family, found especially in South Africa, having white, yellow, or rose-colored flowers with unconnected petals. [< Afrikaans *vygie*]
**vy|ing** (vī′ing), *v., adj.* —*v.* the present participle of **vie**: *The boys are vying with each other for a position on the baseball team.*
—*adj.* that vies; competing; emulating. —**vy′ing|ly**, *adv.*

***W¹** or **w** (dub′əl yü), *n., pl.* **W's** or **Ws, w's** or **ws.** **1** the 23rd letter of the English alphabet. There are two *w*'s in *window.* **2** a speech sound representing this letter. **3** (used as a symbol for) the 23rd, or more usually the 22nd (of an actual or possible series, either *I* or *J* being omitted).
▶ The name of this letter ("double u") derives from the fact that originally it was written with two u's (uu) to represent its sound. As *u* and *v* were often used interchangeably, and *v* was used as a capital letter of *u* and as the symbol for what was considered the "consonant" sound of *u*, it was natural for later writers and printers to use the "VV" form in the initial position of such words as had the sound represented originally by "uu."
**W²** (dub′əl yü), *n., pl.* **W's.** anything shaped like the letter W.
**w** (no period), watt or watts.
**w.**, an abbreviation for the following:
**1** wanting.
**2** warden.
**3** watt or watts.
**4** week or weeks.
**5** weight.
**6a** west. **b** western.
**7a** wide. **b** width.
**8** wife.
**9** with.
**10** won.
**11** *Physics.* work.
**W** (no period), an abbreviation or symbol for the following:
**1** *Chemistry.* tungsten (German, *Wolfram*).
**2** watt or watts.
**3a** west. **b** western.
**4** *Physics.* work.
**5** W particle.
**W.**, an abbreviation for the following:
**1** Wales.
**2** warden.
**3** Washington.
**4** Wednesday.
**5** weight.
**6** Welsh.
**7a** west. **b** western.
**8** width.
**9** *Physics.* work.
**wa'** (wô, wä), *n. Scottish.* wall.
**WA** (no periods), Washington (with postal Zip Code).
**W.A.**, **1** West Africa. **2** Western Australia.
**Wa** (wä), *n., pl.* **Wa** or **Was. 1** a member of an aboriginal tribe of the Mon-Khmer linguistic family living in the jungles of northeastern Burma, chiefly in hill villages that can be entered only by tunnels. **2** the language of this people.
**WAAC** or **Waac** (wak), *n.* a member of the WAAC.
**WAAC** (no periods) or **W.A.A.C.**, **1** *U.S.* Women's Army Auxiliary Corps (the former name of the Women's Army Corps or WAC). **2** *British.* Women's Army Auxiliary Corps (a former name of the Women's Royal Army Corps or WRAC).
**WAAF** or **Waaf** (waf), *n.* a member of the WAAF.
**WAAF** (no periods) or **W.A.A.F.**, *British.* Women's Auxiliary Air Force (the former name of the Women's Royal Air Force or WRAF).
**wab** (wab, wäb), *n. Scottish.* web.
**wab|ble¹** (wob′əl), *v.i., v.t.,* **-bled, -bling,** *n.* = wobble.
**wab|ble²** (wob′əl), *n.* = warble².
**wab|bler** (wob′lər), *n.* = wobbler.
**wab|bling** (wob′ling), *adj.* = wobbling. — **wab′bling|ly,** *adv.*
**wab|bly** (wob′lē), *adj.,* **-bli|er, -bli|est.** = wobbly¹.
**WAC** or **Wac** (wak), *n.* a member of the WAC; woman in the U.S. Army other than a nurse.
**WAC** (no periods), *U.S.* Women's Army Corps.
**wack** (wak), *n. Slang.* an eccentric or crazy person: *Dear old wack, would you like to walk through the streets of the city tomorrow giving away money?* (Punch). [probably back formation < *wacky*]
**wack|e** (wak′ə), *n.* **1** a rock similar to sandstone, resulting from the decomposition of rocks in place. **2** a soft basaltic rock formed by a similar process. [< German *Wacke* pebbles and gravel in riverbeds < Middle High German, large stone < Old High German *waggo,* and *wacko* pebble]
**wack|y** (wak′ē), *adj.,* **wack|i|er, wack|i|est.** *Slang.* unconventional in behavior; eccentric; crazy. Also, **whacky.** [American English, perhaps < *whack* to beat; a blow + *-y*¹] — **wack′i|ly,** *adv.* — **wack′i|ness,** *n.*
**wad¹** (wod), *n., v.,* **wad|ded, wad|ding.** — *n.* **1** a small, soft mass: *He plugged his ears with wads of cotton.* **2** a tight roll; compact bundle or mass: *a wad of bills, a wad of crumpled paper, a wad of chewing gum.* **3** a round plug of leather, felt, cardboard, jute, or the like, used to hold the powder and shot in place in a gun or cartridge. **4** *Ceramics.* a small lump of fine clay used to cover inferior material, especially a strip doubled over the edge of a dish. **5** *Slang.* **a** a large bundle of paper money. **b** personal wealth; riches: *He made his wad in oil.* **6** *British Dialect.* a bundle of hay or straw, especially a small one.
— *v.t.* **1** to make into a wad; press into a wad: *He wadded up the paper and threw it onto the floor.* **2** to line (a garment) with padding; pad; quilt. **3** to pad for fullness; fill out with padding; stuff. **4a** to place a wad in (a gun barrel). **b** to hold (powder and shot) in place with a wad. **5** to fill (an opening) with a wad; stop up.
— *v.i.* **1** to become pressed into a wad. **2** to be formed into a wad easily; hold or stick together well.
**wads,** *Slang.* very much or many; a lot: *He will find them well padded by wads of extracts from second-hand authorities* (Saturday Review).
[origin uncertain. Compare Swedish *vadd,* Dutch *watte,* Medieval Latin *wadda.*]
**wad²** (wod), *n.* an impure, earthy ore of manganese. [origin unknown]
**wad³** (wäd, wəd), *v. Scottish.* would¹. [earlier *waude* < *walde,* dialectal variant of Old English *wolde* would]
**wad⁴** (wod), *n. Scottish.* **1** a pledge. **2** a hostage.
**in wad of,** as security for (a payment): *jewels held in wad of a sum owed.*
**to** (or **in**) **wad,** as a pledge or hostage: *to lay to wad one's land or valuables.*
[variant of obsolete *wed* a pledge, Old English *wedd.* See related etym. at **wed,** verb]
**wad⁵** (wod), *v.t., v.i.,* **wad|ded, wad|ding.** *Scottish.* to wed.
**wad|a|ble** (wā′də bəl), *adj.* that can be waded.
**wad|der** (wod′ər), *n.* **1** a person or thing that wads. **2** *Obsolete.* implement to wad a gun.
**wad|ding** (wod′ing), *n.* **1** a soft material for padding, stuffing, or packing, especially carded cotton in sheets. **2** any material for making wads for guns or cartridges. **3** any small mass or bundle; wad.
**wad|dle** (wod′əl), *v.,* **-dled, -dling,** *n.* — *v.i.* to walk with short steps and an awkward, swaying motion, as a duck does: *A very fat man waddled across the street.*
— *n.* **1** the act of waddling: *He made us laugh by imitating the waddle of a duck.* **2** an awkward, swaying gait.
[< *wade* to proceed + *-le*] — **wad′dler,** *n.*
**wad|dy¹** (wod′ē), *n., pl.* **-dies,** *v.,* **-died, -dy|ing.** — *n.* **1** a heavy war club used by the Australian aborigines. **2** (in Australia) a walking stick.
— *v.t.* to strike, injure, or kill with a waddy.
[probably native alteration of English *wood*¹, in sense "club"]
**wad|dy²** (wod′ē), *n., pl.* **-dies.** *Western U.S.* a temporary ranch hand, hired to punch cattle. [origin uncertain]
**wade** (wād), *v.,* **wad|ed, wad|ing,** *n.* — *v.i.* **1** to walk through water, snow, sand, mud, or anything that hinders free motion: *to wade across a brook, to wade through slush, to wade in muck.* **2** *Figurative.* to come or force one's way as if by wading: *To wade through slaughter to a throne* (Thomas Gray). **3** *Figurative.* to make one's way with difficulty: *to wade through a badly written letter. Must I wade through that dull book?* **4** *Obsolete.* to make one's way; proceed; go.
— *v.t.* to get across or pass through by wading; ford: *The soldiers waded the stream when they saw the bridge had been destroyed.*
— *n.* **1** the act of wading: *to go for a wade, a long wade to the other side.* **2** a shallow place in a stream; ford.
**wade in,** *Informal.* to thrust or throw oneself into the middle or thick of something and fight, work, or otherwise engage with vigor: (*Figurative.*) *to wade in and straighten out a dispute.*
**wade into,** *Informal.* **a** to make a vigorous attack on: *to wade into an opponent and knock him out.* **b** *Figurative.* to begin to work vigorously on: *to wade into a job and finish it quickly.*
[Old English *wadan* to proceed, go forward]
**wade|a|ble** (wā′də bəl), *adj.* = wadable.
**wad|er** (wā′dər), *n.* **1** a person or thing that wades. **2** a long-legged bird that wades about in shallow water, searching for food. Cranes, herons, storks, plovers, snipes, and sandpipers are waders.
**waders,** high, waterproof boots, used for wading: *Moving up the stream the fisherman stepped into a hole, dumping cold water into his waders.*
**wadge** (waj, woj), *n. British.* a lumpy bundle; wad: *[He] gave him a wadge of pound notes from his jacket pocket* (Sunday Times). [perhaps blend of *wad* and *wedge.* Compare **wodge.**]
**wa|di** (wä′dē), *n., pl.* **-dis** or **-dies. 1** a usually dry valley or ravine, especially in Arabia or North Africa, through which a stream flows during the rainy season. **2** the stream or torrent running through such a ravine. **3** = oasis. Also, **wady.** [< Arabic *wādī*]
**wad|ing** (wā′ding), *adj.* that wades: *a wading bird.*
**wading pool,** a small, shallow pool for children to wade in.
**wad|mal, wad|maal, wad|mol,** or **wad|moll** (wod′məl), *n.* a coarse woolen fabric formerly worn by country people in Northern Europe. [< Scandinavian (compare Old Icelandic *vathmāl,* probably ultimately < *vāth* cloth). See related etym. at **weed².**]
**wad|na** (wäd′nə), *v. Scottish.* would not. [< *wad*³ + *na*]
**wads** (wodz), *n. pl.* See under **wad¹.**
**wa|dy** (wä′dē), *n., pl.* **-dies.** = wadi.
**wae** (wā), *n. Obsolete.* woe.
**w.a.e.,** when actually employed.
**wae|suck** (wā′suk), *interj. Scottish.* woe is me! alas! (expressing grief or pity). [< *wae* + variant of *sake*¹]
**wae|sucks** (wā′suks), *interj.* = waesuck.
**waf** (waf, wäf), *adj., n. Scottish.* = waff².
**WAF** or **Waf** (waf), *n.* a member of the WAF; woman in the U.S. Air Force other than a nurse.
**WAF** (no periods), *U.S.* Women in the Air Force.
**Wafd** (woft), *n.,* or **Wafd Party,** the (Egyptian) National party. [< Arabic *wafd* delegation, deputation]
**Wafd|ist** (wof′tist), *n., adj.* — *n.* a member of the Wafd.
— *adj.* of or having to do with the Wafd or Wafdists.
**wa|fer** (wā′fər), *n., v.* — *n.* **1** a very thin cake or biscuit, sometimes flavored or sweetened. **2** the thin, round piece of unleavened bread used in celebrating Holy Communion or the Eucharist in certain churches, especially the Roman Catholic Church: *a consecrated wafer bearing the outline of a cross on its upper surface.* **SYN:** Host. **3** a thin piece of candy, chocolate, or medicine. **4** a piece of wax, gelatin, sticky paper, or dried paste, used as a seal or fastening. **5** a disk of thin paper, adhesive at the edges, or of some soluble substance, such as was formerly often used alone or as one of a pair to enclose a dose of a powder or other medicine for swallowing. **6** a tiny disk of silicon or ceramic material imprinted or engraved with one or more microcircuits.
— *v.t.* to seal or attach with a wafer or wafers: *to wafer a letter, to wafer a note to a window.*
[< Anglo-French *wafre* < Germanic (compare earlier Flemish *wāfer*). Compare etym. under **goffer, waffle¹.**] — **wa′fer|like′,** *adj.*
**wa|fer-thin** (wā′fər thin′), *adj.* very thin; wafery: (*Figurative.*) *The Democrats hold a majority in the lower house, the Republicans a wafer-thin majority in the State Senate* (Wall Street Journal).
**wa|fer|y** (wā′fər ē), *adj.* like a wafer; very thin.
**waff¹** (waf, wäf), *n., v. Scottish.* — *n.* **1** a waving movement; wave. **2a** a puff (of wind); gust. **b** a

***W**
definition 1

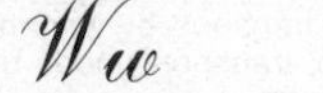

Script letters look like examples of fine penmanship. They appear in many formal uses, such as invitations to social functions.

Handwritten letters, both manuscript or printed (left) and cursive (right), are easy for children to read and to write.

Roman letters have *serifs* (finishing strokes) adapted from the way Roman stonecutters carved their letters. This is *Times Roman* type.

Sans-serif letters are often called *gothic.* They have lines of even width and no serifs. This type face is called *Helvetica.*

Between roman and gothic, some letters have thick and thin lines with slight flares that suggest serifs. This type face is *Optima.*

Computer letters can be sensed by machines either from their shapes or from the magnetic ink with which they are printed.

whiff (of perfume). **3** a slight attack (of illness); touch. **4** a passing view; glimpse. **5** an apparition; wraith.

—*v.t.* **1a** (of the wind) to cause (something) to move to and fro. **b** (of a bird) to move (the wings) in flight. **2** to direct a current of air against; fan.

—*v.i.* **1** to wave to and fro; flutter in the wind. **2** to produce a current of air by waving something to and fro.

**put out** (or **set forth**) **a waff**, to wave something as a signal: *When you are about half a mile from shore, as it were passing by the house ... set forth a waff* (Earl Cromarty).

[variant of *wave* to move, as with a fanning gesture, or with the wind]

**waff[2]** (waf, wäf), *adj., n. Scottish.* —*adj.* **1** of no account; worthless (used of a person or condition of life). **2a** (of an animal) wandering; stray. **b** (of a person) solitary.

—*n.* a waffie. Also, **waf**.

[variant of *waif*]

**Waf|fen S.S.** (vä′fən), an elite corps of troops in the Wehrmacht. [< German *Waffen S(chutz)-S(taffel)* (literally) weapons defense-staff]

**waff|ie** (waf′ē, wäf′ē), *n. Scottish.* a wandering, homeless person; vagabond. [< *waff*[2] + *-ie*]

**waf|fle[1]** (wof′əl), *n., adj.* —*n.* a cake made of batter and cooked until brown and crisp in a waffle iron that makes the cakes very thin in places, usually eaten while hot with butter and syrup: *to have waffles for breakfast.*

—*adj.* = wafflelike.

[American English < Dutch *wafel,* Middle Dutch *wāfel.* Compare etym. under **wafer**.]

**waf|fle[2]** (wof′əl), *v.,* **-fled, -fling,** *n. Especially British Informal.* —*v.i.* to talk incessantly or foolishly; prattle; engage in doubletalk: *It might be thought that a council of naturalists would be proof against any tendency to waffle* (Punch).

—*n.* foolish talk; nonsense; doubletalk.

[< dialectal *waff* to yelp, bark + *-le*]

**waffle iron**, a utensil in which waffles are cooked, consisting of two hinged griddles having square projections on the inside which make the ridges and very thin places in the waffle.

**waf|fle|like** (wof′əl līk′), *adj.* ridged or indented like a waffle or waffle iron; honeycombed: *Its wafflelike tread is designed to grip slick surfaces tenaciously* (Science News Letter).

**waffle weave**, a texture and appearance woven into a fabric, resembling small squares like those in a waffle. —**waf′fle-weave′**, *adj.*

**waf|fling** (waf′ling), *adj. Informal.* vague; indecisive; equivocal: *waffling excuses, a waffling statement.* [< *waffle*[2]]

**waf|fly** (wof′lē), *adj. Especially British Informal.* equivocal; waffling: *Too many people ... accused Mr. Grimond of going in for "vague and waffly talk"* (Manchester Guardian). [< *waffle*[2] + *-y*[1]]

**waft[1]** (waft, wäft), *v., n.* —*v.t.* **1** to carry over water or through air: *The waves wafted the boat to shore.* **2** *Figurative.* to transport or transfer very quickly or as if by magic: *to be wafted by plane from New York to London, to be wafted by sleep into the land of dreams.*

—*v.i.* **1** = float. **2** to blow gently; stir: *a wafting breeze.*

—*n.* **1** a breath or puff of air, wind, or scent: *A waft of fresh air came through the open window.* **2** a waving movement; wave: *a waft of the hand. And the lonely sea bird crosses With one waft of the wing* (Tennyson). **3** the act of wafting.

[apparently back formation < obsolete *wafter* a convoy ship < Dutch, Low German *wachter* a guard; (literally) watcher]

**waft[2]** (waft, wäft), *n., v.* —*n. Nautical.* **1** a flag hoisted or intended to be hoisted as a signal; signal flag. **2** the act of signaling by such a flag or flags.

—*v.t. Obsolete.* **1** to signal by a wave of the hand; direct, call, or warn, by waving. **2** to avert (one's eyes).

[probably alteration of *waff*[1]]

**waft[3]** (waft, wäft), *n. Scottish.* weft.

**waft|age** (waf′tij, wäf′-), *n.* **1** the act of wafting. **2** a means of wafting.

**waft|er** (waf′tər, wäf′-), *n.* **1** a person or thing that wafts. **2** a revolving fan or disk in a type of blower. [< *waft*[1] + *-er*[1]]

**waf|ture** (waf′chər, wäf′-), *n.* **1** the act of waving. **2a** the act of wafting. **b** a thing wafted. [< *waft*[1] and *waft*[2] + *-ure*]

**wag[1]** (wag), *v.,* **wagged, wag|ging,** *n.* —*v.t.* **1** to cause to wag: *The dog wagged its tail. Her high-borne turban'd head she wags and rolls her darkling eye* (Walt Whitman). **2** to move (the tongue) in talking, as in gossip or idle chatter.

—*v.i.* **1** to move from side to side or up and down: *an indignantly wagging finger. The dog's tail wagged back and forth.* **2** to move busily in talking: *a scandal that made tongues wag throughout the village.* **3** to sway as one moves or walks; waddle or totter. **4** *Especially British Informal.* to go away; depart.

—*n.* a wagging motion: *a wag of the tail. He said "no" with a wag of his head.*

[Middle English *waggen* < root of Old English *wagian* move backwards and forwards] —**wag′ger**, *n.*

**wag[2]** (wag), *n., v.,* **wagged, wag|ging.** —*n.* a person who is fond of making jokes or of clowning; jocular fellow; wit; joker. SYN: jester.

—*v.i. Especially British Slang.* to play truant: *to wag from school.*

[probably reduction of obsolete *waghalter* rogue, gallows bird < *wag*[1] + *halter*[1]]

**wage** (wāj), *n., v.,* **waged, wag|ing.** —*n.* **1a** an amount paid for work: *to get a day's wage for a day's work* (W. G. Clark). SYN: salary, pay, remuneration, stipend, compensation. **b** *Figurative.* something given in return; recompense; reward: *The gods give thee fair wage and dues of death* (Algernon Charles Swinburne). SYN: return. **2** *Obsolete.* a pledge; gage; bet. [< Old North French *wage,* Old French *gage* < Germanic (compare Gothic *ga-wadjon, wadi* pledge). Compare etym. under **wad[4]**, **wed**. See etym. of doublet **gage[1]**.]

—*v.t.* **1** to carry on: *Doctors wage war against disease.* SYN: prosecute. **2** *British Dialect.* to hire. **3** *Obsolete.* to pledge; gage; bet.

—*v.i. Obsolete.* to struggle; fight.

**wages, a** an amount paid for work: *His wages are $100 a week. Thus we have private individuals whose wages are equal to the wages of seven or eight thousand other individuals* (Thomas Carlyle). **b** *Figurative.* something given in return; reward; recompense: *The wages of poor eating is poor health. All Friends shall taste the wages of their virtue* (Shakespeare).

[< Old North French *wager* < *wage;* see etym. under the noun]

▶ See **salary** for usage note.

**wage drift**, *Economics.* an upward movement of wages resulting in an increase in average earnings over the official average wage rates of a country.

**wage earner**, **1** a person who works for wages. **2** a person who receives remuneration for work of any kind; one who is employed: *a family in which both husband and wife are wage earners.*

**wage freeze**, a fixing of wages and salaries, as by government decree: *In that situation, a wage freeze, whether voluntary or imposed by the Government, deals with a symptom of inflation rather than with inflation itself* (Wall Street Journal).

**wage hike**, an increase in wages; raise: *It was touched off by the government's offer of a 15 per cent wage hike in response to demands for more pay* (Wall Street Journal).

**wage|less** (wāj′lis), *adj.* that does not earn or receive wages: *the wageless efforts of the missionary.* —**wage′less|ness**, *n.*

**Wa|ge|ni|a** (wä gē′nē ə), *n. pl.* a tribe of fishermen in the Congo, who catch fish by lowering large wooden baskets or nets into the river.

**wage packet**, *British.* a pay envelope: *As yet it had not affected him where it hurts most—in his wage packet* (Manchester Guardian).

**wage pattern**, a specific wage scale regarded as a model or guide in determining the general wage scale of an industry or region: *The contracts under discussion set the warehouse wage pattern throughout Northern California* (Wall Street Journal).

**wage-price** (wāj′prīs′), *adj.* of or having to do with the relation of wages to prices: *So the wage-price spiral works not only vertically from wages to prices but horizontally from wages to other wages* (Atlantic).

**wage-push inflation** (wāj′pu̇sh′), *Economics.* the cost push resulting from inflationary wage increases: *Wage-push inflation got its strongest nudge in construction; union craftsmen wrung out raises averaging 17½%* (Time).

**wa|ger** (wā′jər), *n., v.* —*n.* **1** something staked on an uncertain event: *to double one's wager, to lose a wager. The wager of $10 on the black horse was promptly paid.* **2** the act of betting; bet: *to make a wager with a friend.* **3** a subject of betting. **4** a solemn undertaking; pledge. **5** *Obsolete.* a promising, especially to act or accept an outcome.

—*v.t., v.i.* **1** to bet; gamble: *to wager more than one can afford to lose* (v.t.). *He doesn't often wager* (v.i.). *I'll wager the black horse will win the race* (v.t.). **2** to offer to prove one's sureness or trust by wagering: *I'd wager my life on him* (v.t.). *I'll wager that you never hear from him again* (v.t.).

[< Anglo-French *wageure* < Old North French *wager* to wage < *wage;* see etym. under **wage**, noun] —**wa′ger|er**, *n.*

**wage rate**, the rate of pay assigned to a worker for a certain job or time spent in working; wage scale: *A number of wage agreements made in the last few months indicate that average wage rates are likely to rise by about 6 per cent* (Manchester Guardian).

**wager of battle**, (in feudal law) a challenge by a defendant to decide his guilt or innocence by single combat.

**wag|es** (wā′jiz), *n. pl.* See under **wage**.

**wage scale**, **1** the schedule of the various rates of pay for similar or related jobs, as in a particular industry. **2** the range of the wages paid by an employer.

**wage slave**, a worker whose labor and dependence on wages is regarded as a form of slavery: *These ... people tried to persuade them that they were downtrodden wage slaves being exploited by cynical capitalists* (Punch). —**wage slavery**.

**wage stop**, *British.* the principle or policy of not allowing an unemployed person to receive more money from public funds than he would earn while working: *The wage stop is the device used to stop families receiving more in social security payments than their normal income from full-time work* (London Times).

**wage-stop** (wāj′stop′), *v.t.,* **-stopped, -stopping.** *British.* to apply the wage stop to (an unemployed person): *Ninety per cent of the people wage-stopped under the ... ruling would be lifted back to full benefit* (Sunday Times).

**wage|work|er** (wāj′wėr′kər), *n.* a person who works for wages, especially as distinguished from a professional, clerical, or other salaried worker.

**wage|work|ing** (wāj′wėr′king), *n., adj.* —*n.* work done for wages.

—*adj.* doing work for wages.

**wag|ger|y** (wag′ər ē), *n., pl.* **-ger|ies.** **1** the act or habit of joking, playing pranks, or clowning; drollery; jocularity. **2** a joke: ... *they indulged in a hundred sports, jocularities, waggeries* (Thackeray). [< *wag*[2] + *-ery*]

**wag|gish** (wag′ish), *adj.* **1** fond of making jokes. SYN: jocular. **2a** of or characteristic of a wag: *a waggish look.* **b** done or made in a spirit of waggery or mischievous fun; funny; humorous: *a waggish remark.* SYN: prankish. —**wag′gish|ly**, *adv.* —**wag′gish|ness**, *n.*

**wag|gle** (wag′əl), *v.,* **-gled, -gling,** *n.* —*v.t., v.i.* to move quickly and repeatedly from side to side; wag.

—*n.* a waggling motion.

[< *wag*[1] + *-le.* Compare etym. under **wiggle**.]

**wag|gling|ly** (wag′ling lē), *adv.* with a waggle.

**wag|gly** (wag′lē), *adj.* waggling; unsteady.

**wag|gon** (wag′ən), *n. British.* wagon.

**Wag|gon|er** (wag′ə nər), *n.* = Wagoner.

**wag|gon|ette** (wag′ə net′), *n. Especially British.* wagonette.

**wag|gon-head|ed** (wag′ən hed′id), *adj. Especially British.* wagon-headed.

**Wag|ne|ri|an** (väg nir′ē ən), *adj., n.* —*adj.* of or having to do with Richard Wagner (1813-1883), German musical composer, or his music, theories, or musical style.

—*n.* an admirer of Richard Wagner's style or theory of music.

**Wag|ner|ism** (väg′nə riz əm), *n.* **1** Richard Wagner's theory and practice in the composition of music dramas, placing great stress upon the dramatic effect as well as the musical content, especially in the orchestra, thus departing from the earlier approach of the Italian opera, which consisted of arias and ensembles and stressed primarily the vocal parts. **2** the influence of Wagner's music and theories.

**Wag|ner|ite** (väg′nə rīt), *n.* = Wagnerian.

**wag|on** (wag′ən), *n., v.* —*n.* **1** a four-wheeled vehicle for carrying heavy loads, such as loads of farm produce or timber, or of military equipment or supplies. The body of a wagon is typically either a flat bed with removable boards at the sides or a boxlike enclosure with or without a top and drawn by a team of horses, mules, or oxen. See picture under **covered wagon**. **2** a somewhat similar vehicle but with canvas sides and top, used especially for the transport of persons and their possessions; covered wagon. **3** any one of various other four-wheeled vehicles, such as a baby carriage or a child's toy cart. **4** *Informal.* a station wagon. **5** a tray on wheels for serving food or drinks. **6** a rolling platform on which scenery is placed so that it may be moved quickly on and off the stage of a theater. **7** *British.* a railroad freight car: *a goods wagon, a coal wagon.* **8** *U.S. Slang.* a battleship; battlewagon. **9** *U.S. Slang.* an automobile: *to get some extra life out of the old wagon* (Wall Street Journal). **10** *Obsolete.* a chariot.

—*v.t.* to carry in wagons; transport by wagon.

—*v.i.* to travel in a wagon; transport goods by wagon. Also, *British,* **waggon**.

**hitch one's wagon to a star**, to have high hopes and ambitions; aim high: *He hitched his wagon to a star and worked hard to achieve success.*

**off the wagon**, *Slang.* back to drinking alcoholic liquor: *After the birth of his daughter, he had a night on the town and off the wagon to celebrate* (Canadian Saturday Night).
**on the wagon**, *Slang.* not drinking any alcoholic liquor; in or into a state of temperance: *"Roberta felt bad about her drinking. She wanted to stay on the wagon—we call it 'going on the wagon' when somebody stops drinking," Mrs. Moon said seriously* (New Yorker).
**the wagon**, *U.S. Informal.* a police patrol wagon; paddy wagon: *They waited for the wagon to haul the lawbreakers off to jail.*
[< Dutch *wagen.* See related etym. at **wain.**]
— **wag′on|less**, *adj.*

**Wag|on** (wag′ən), *n.* the Big Dipper; Charles's Wain. [< *wagon*]

**wagon boss**, a person in charge of a wagon train: *Alderman Griffin will need the qualities of a wagon boss in Apache country* (London Times).

**wag|on|er** (wag′ə nər), *n.* **1** a person who drives a wagon, especially for a livelihood. **2** *Obsolete.* the driver of a chariot (especially in mythology).

**Wag|on|er** (wag′ə nər), *n.* **1** the constellation Auriga. **2** the Big Dipper; Charles's Wain. [< *wagoner*]

**wag|on|ette** (wag′ə net′), *n.* a four-wheeled carriage, open or with a removable top, with a seat in front running crosswise and two lengthwise seats facing each other.

**wag|on-head|ed** (wag′ən hed′id), *adj. Architecture.* having a cylindrical ceiling, roof, or vault.

**wa|gon-lit** (vȧ gôN′lē′), *n., pl.* **wa|gons-lits** or **wagon-lits** (vȧ gôN lē′). (in Europe) a sleeping car. [< French *wagon-lit* < *wagon* railway coach (< English *wagon*) + *lit* bed < Latin *lectus*]

**wag|on|load** (wag′ən lōd′), *n.* the amount that a wagon can hold or carry: *There in the yard sat a wagonload of hay.*

**wagon master**, a person who has charge of one or more wagons, especially one commanding a wagon train.

**wagon train**, **1** a group of wagons traveling along in a line one after another, especially one carrying a company of settlers: *Wagon trains bound for the Far West used scouts to guide them through Indian territory.* **2** a convoy of wagons carrying military supplies; military supply train.

**wag|on|way** (wag′ən wā′), *n.* a road or track of parallel lines of wooden rails for horse-drawn wagons or carts, built especially formerly over muddy or rutted dirt roads.

**wag|some** (wag′səm), *adj.* = waggish.

**wag|tail** (wag′tāl′), *n.* **1** any one of various small birds that have a slender body with a long tail that they habitually move up and down, such as a species of Great Britain or either of the pipits of North America. **2** *U.S.* **a** one of the water thrushes. **b** the ovenbird.

**Wa|ha|bi** or **Wah|ha|bi** (wä hä′bē), *n., pl.* **-bis.** a member of a strict Moslem sect, founded in the 1700's and now dominant in Saudi Arabia, which adheres rigidly to the Koran as a guide, rejects all other writings except those of Mohammed's companions, denounces the worship of, or prayers to, the saints, and bars elaborate ritual, dress, or decoration. [< Arabic *Wahhābī* < ʿAbd al-*Wahhāb*, 1691-1787, a Moslem reformer]

**Wa|ha|bi|ism** (wä hä′bē iz əm), *n.* = Wahabism.

**Wa|ha|bism** or **Wah|ha|bism** (wä hä′biz əm), *n.* the doctrines, principles, or practices of the Wahabis.

**Wa|ha|bite** or **Wah|ha|bite** (wä hä′bīt), *n., adj.*
— *n.* an adherent of Wahabism; Wahabi.
— *adj.* of or having to do with Wahabis or Wahabism.

**wa|hi|ne** (wä hē′nā), *n. Hawaiian.* a woman; female; wife: *a muumuu-clad wahine.*

**wa|hoo**[1] (wä′hü, wä hü′), *n., pl.* **-hoos.** a North American shrub or small tree of the staff-tree family that has a purple fruit and scarlet seeds; burning bush. [American English < Siouan (Dakota) *wanhu* arrowwood]

**wa|hoo**[2] (wä′hü, wä hü′), *n., pl.* **-hoos.** any one of several North American trees: **a** a small species of elm. **b** a species of linden. **c** = cascara. [American English < Muskhogean *ûhawhu* the cork elm]

**wa|hoo**[3] (wä′hü, wä hü′), *n., pl.* **-hoos.** any one of various marine food and game fishes of warm waters related to the mackerel, with a long, narrow body and pointed snout; peto; queenfish. [American English; origin unknown]

**wa|hoo**[4] (wä′hü, wä hü′), *interj., n., pl.* **-hoos.** *U.S.* — *interj.* an exclamation or shout used to express unrestrained pleasure or to attract attention.
— *n.* a call or shout of "wahoo."

**wah-wah** (wä′wä), *adj., n. Music, especially Jazz.*
— *adj.* producing a wavering muted sound somewhat like the sound of a crying baby: *a wah-wah trumpet, wah-wah brass, an electronic wah-wah pedal.*
— *n.* a trumpet or trombone mute, or any similar device, for producing a wah-wah sound or effect. Also, **wa-wa.** [imitative]

**wai|a|ta** (wī′ə tə), *n., pl.* **-ta** or **-tas.** (in New Zealand) a native song: *In common with other waiata, "E Pa To Hau" uses as a formal principle the varied repetition of a basic melody* (Mervyn McLean). [< Maori *waiata* (literally) song]

**waif** (wāf), *n., adj.* — *n.* **1** a person without home or friends, especially a homeless or neglected child. **SYN**: foundling. **2** anything without an owner; stray thing or animal. **SYN**: estray. **3** *Nautical.* waft[2]. **4** *Obsolete.* (in English law) goods stolen and abandoned by a thief in his flight.
— *adj. Scottish.* **1** stray; wandering; homeless. **2** current (applied to a report or saying).
[< Anglo-French *waif,* probably < Scandinavian (compare Old Icelandic *veif* something waving, flapping, *veifa* to wave). See related etym. at **waive.**] — **waif′like′**, *adj.*

**wail** (wāl), *v., n.* — *v.i.* **1** to cry long and loud because of grief or pain: *The baby wailed.* **2** to make a mournful or shrill sound: *The wind wailed around the old house. The sirens were wailing for a total blackout* (Graham Greene). **3** to lament; mourn. **4** to cry out piteously (for): *a child wailing for its mother.*
— *v.t.* **1** to grieve for or because of; bewail. **2** to utter (as a wailing cry or bad news).
— *n.* **1a** a long cry of grief or pain: *Newborn babies begin their life with a wail.* **b** a sound like such a cry: *the wail of a hungry coyote, the wail of a siren.* **2** any prolonged, bitter complaining; whine. **3** the act of wailing: *Wail shook Earl Walter's house; His true wife shed no tear* (Elizabeth Barrett Browning).
[< Scandinavian (compare Old Icelandic *vǣla* < *vǣ* woe). See related etym. at **woe.**] — **wail′er**, *n.*

**wail|ful** (wāl′fəl), *adj.* **1** full of lamentation; sorrowful. **2** resembling a wail; plaintive. **3** producing plaintive sounds: *the wailful wind.* — **wail′ful|ly**, *adv.*

**wail|ing wall** (wā′ling), a place where one seeks or finds solace in times of sorrow or unhappiness: *She retired to her dressing table, which has served as a wailing wall for all the years of our marriage* (John Cheever). [< the *Wailing Wall,* a relic of the western wall of the Temple, in Jerusalem, at which Jews gather to pray and especially to lament the destruction of the Temple by the Romans in A.D. 70]

**wail|some** (wāl′səm), *adj.* **1** wailing; wailful. **2** *Obsolete.* that is to be bewailed.

**wain** (wān), *n. Archaic or Dialect.* a wagon, especially a farm wagon. [Old English *wægen.* See related etym. at **wagon.**]

**Wain** (wān), *n.* **the,** Charles's Wain (the Big Dipper).

**✱wain|scot** (wān′skət, -skot), *n., v.,* **-scot|ed, -scot|ing** or **-scot|ted, -scot|ting.** — *n.* **1** a lining of wood on the walls of a room. A wainscot usually has panels. **2** the lower part of the wall of a room when it is decorated differently from the upper part; dado. **3a** a straight-grained white oak of very good quality, such as was originally imported into England from Russia, Germany, and Holland, used especially for paneling rooms. **b** a board or piece of this.
— *v.t.* to line (the walls of a room), especially with wood: *a room wainscoted in oak.*
[perhaps < Middle Dutch or Middle Flemish *waghenscote* < *waghen* wagon + *scote* partition]

**✱wainscot**
definition 2

**wain|scot|ing** (wān′skə ting, -skot ing), *n.* **1** = wainscot. **2** material used for wainscots.

**wain|scot|ting** (wān′skə ting, -skot ing), *n.* = wainscoting.

**wain|wright** (wān′rīt′), *n.* a person who makes or repairs wagons. [< *wain* + *wright*]

**wair** (wār), *v.t. Scottish.* ware[3].

**waist** (wāst), *n.* **1** the part of a person's body between the ribs and the hips. **2** = waistline. **3a** a garment or part of a garment covering the body from the neck or shoulders to the hips; shirtwaist, blouse, or bodice. **b** (formerly) a child's undergarment to which a petticoat or underpants were buttoned. **4** a narrow middle part; narrowest part or section: *the waist of a violin, to cross the waist of the peninsula.* **5** the middle part of a ship, such as that between the forecastle and the quarterdeck of a sailing vessel, or between the forward and stern superstructure of an oil tanker. **6** the middle section of an airplane's fuselage, especially that of a bomber. **7** the slender part of the abdomen of various insects, such as wasps, ants, and some flies. [Middle English *wast,* perhaps unrecorded Old English *wæst.* See related etym. at **wax**[2] grow.]

**waist|band** (wāst′band′), *n.* a band around the waist: *the waistband of a skirt or a pair of trousers.* **SYN**: belt.

**waist|cloth** (wāst′klôth′, -kloth′), *n.* = loincloth.

**✱waist|coat** (wāst′kōt′, wes′kət), *n.* **1** *British.* a man's vest. **2** an elaborate garment, with or without sleeves, formerly worn by men, so as to show under the doublet.

**✱waistcoat**
definition 2

**waist|coat|ed** (wāst′kō′tid, wes′kə-), *adj.* provided with a waistcoat.

**waist|coat|ing** (wāst′kō′ting, wes′kə-), *n.* a material for making waistcoats.

**waist-deep** (wāst′dēp′), *adj., adv.* **1** of a depth sufficient to reach or cover a person's waist: *They decided to strike out down the slope through the waist-deep snow* (Time). **2** *Figurative: The French literary marketplace was waist-deep in a porridge of ideological dialectics and metaphysical jargon* (Atlantic). **SYN**: immersed.

**-waisted**, *combining form.* having a ______ waist: *Long-waisted = having a long waist.*

**waist|ing** (wās′ting), *n.* material for making waists or waistcoats.

**waist|less** (wāst′lis), *adj.* having no waist or waistline: *a waistless velvet tunic.*

**waist|line** (wāst′līn′), *n.* **1** an imaginary line around the body at the smallest part of the waist: *an expanding waistline.* **2** the place of smallest width in a woman's dress between the arms and the knees. **3** the line where the waist and skirt of a dress join.

**wait** (wāt), *v., n.* — *v.i.* **1a** to stop doing something or stay until someone comes or something happens: *Let's wait in the shade. The dog waited patiently just outside the door.* **SYN**: tarry, linger, remain, abide. **b** to defer or suspend, as speech or action; hold up going on (for): *Please be quiet and wait for me to finish. Time and tide wait for no man.* **2** to look forward; be expecting or ready: *The children wait impatiently for vacation.* **3** to be left undone; be put off: *That matter can wait until tomorrow unless you are planning to leave on your trip today.* **4** to act as a servant; change plates, pass food, or attend the wants of persons at table.
— *v.t.* **1** to wait for; await: *to wait one's chance, opportunity, turn, or time. Go wait me in the gallery* (Beaumont and Fletcher). **2** *Informal.* to delay or put off: *I'll be late; don't wait dinner for me.* **3** *Obsolete.* to accompany or attend as an escort; escort. **4** *Obsolete.* to be a consequence of; wait on or upon; follow.
— *n.* **1** the act or time of waiting: *a long wait between trains, a three-hour wait for dinner. He had a long wait at the doctor's office.* **2** the time of an audience's waiting between acts, or of an actor's waiting between appearances on stage. **3** *Obsolete.* a member of any of certain bands of musicians maintained by certain towns and cities. **4** *Obsolete.* a watchman or sentry; sentinel.
**lie in wait**, to stay hidden ready to attack: *Robbers lay in wait for the travelers. Huge piles of bones and tusks mark their camps beside the Don and other rivers in southern Russia, where they lay in wait for game migrating from winter to summer pastures* (New Scientist).
**wait for it**, *British.* wait till you hear this (used to prefigure a surprise): *But—wait for it—an unimpeachable scientific source maintains that Loch Ness is probably one of the most unpolluted*

**Pronunciation Key:** hat, āge, cãre, fär; let, ēqual, tėrm; it, īce; hot, ōpen, ôrder; **oi**l, **ou**t; cup, pu̇t, rüle; **ch**ild; lo**ng**; **th**in; **ᴛʜ**en; **zh**, measure; ə represents **a** in about, **e** in taken, **i** in pencil, **o** in lemon, **u** in circus.

*stretches of water in Britain* (Manchester Guardian Weekly).
**wait on** (or **upon**), **a** to be a servant to; fetch and carry for: *to wait on a sick child.* **b** to give one's attention to and try to fill the needs of (a customer): *Will you wait on me, please?* **c** to serve as a waiter or waitress: *to wait on three tables at once.* **d** to call on (a superior) to pay a respectful visit: *The victorious general waited upon the king. A deputation had waited upon Lords Salisbury, Redesdale, and Roxburghe* (Manchester Examiner). **e** to go with; result from: *And live a coward in thine own esteem, Letting I dare not, wait upon I would* (Shakespeare). **f** (of a hawk) to soar in circles over the head of the falconer, waiting for the game to be flushed: *Cressida is sooner or later going to have to wait on—be released for hunting* (New Yorker).
**wait out, a** to wait until the end of: *He and his wife started to wait out the war in a modest flat in Montmartre* (New Yorker). **b** *Baseball.* to refrain from swinging at the pitches of, in the hope of getting a base on balls: *to wait out a pitcher.*
**waits,** a group of singers and musicians who go about the streets singing and playing at Christmastime: *The sound of the waits ... breaks upon mid-watches of a winter night* (Washington Irving).
**wait up,** *Informal.* to stay out of bed (until the arrival of someone or something): *Did you wait up long? I'll wait up for him until midnight.*
[< Old French *waitier,* (originally) to watch < Germanic (compare Frankish *wahtôn,* Old High German *wahtēn*). See related etym. at **watch.**]
▶ **wait, await.** *Await* is now the more usual in the transitive sense, and *wait* the more usual in the intransitive: *We are eagerly awaiting your arrival. We can wait here until he comes.*

**wait-a-bit** (wāt′ə bit′), *n.* any one of various plants and shrubs that have thorns or hooked and clinging appendages, such as the greenbrier or various South African plants. [translation of Afrikaans *wag-n'-bietjie* < Dutch *wacht-een-beetje*]

**wait|er** (wā′tər), *n.* **1** a person who waits. **2** a man who waits on table in a hotel or restaurant. **SYN:** garçon. **3** a tray for carrying dishes. **SYN:** salver. **4** *Obsolete.* a watchman.

**wait|ing** (wā′ting), *adj., n.* —*adj.* **1** that waits: *The waiting crowd rushed to the train as soon as it was ready.* **2** used to wait in.
—*n.* the time that one waits.
**in waiting, a** in attendance, especially on a king, queen, prince, or princess: *Lady Pembroke is in waiting at Windsor* (R. Gale). **b** next due or listed, as for some duty or privileges in the British Army and Navy: *to be in waiting for overseas tour of duty.* —**wait′ing|ly,** *adv.*

**waiting game,** the tactic or strategy of not attempting to secure an advantage immediately, with a view to more effective action at a later stage: *Mr. Smith has ... to justify a "waiting game" to his more impetuous followers* (London Times).

**waiting list,** a list of persons waiting for appointments, selection for any purpose, or the next chance of obtaining something: *Few holiday bookings for trains and coaches are being cancelled, and these are quickly filled from long waiting lists* (London Times).

**waiting maid,** a woman servant, especially one in personal attendance on a lady.

**waiting man,** a man servant or attendant.

**waiting room,** a room for people to wait in, as in a railroad station or at a doctor's or dentist's office.

**waiting woman,** a woman servant or attendant.

**wait-list** (wāt′list′), *v.t.* to enter on a waiting list: *There are now three people wait-listed for every occupancy* (Time).

**wait|ress** (wā′tris), *n., v.* —*n.* a woman who waits on table in a hotel dining room or a restaurant.
—*v.i.* to be a waitress: *Waitressing in coffee bars can be interesting, but the work is hard* (Cape Times).

**waive** (wāv), *v.t.,* **waived, waiv|ing. 1** to give up (a privilege, right, or claim); do without; relinquish: *He ... is glad to waive the distinctions of rank* (Washington Irving). **SYN:** surrender, forgo, abandon. **2** to refrain from pressing (an objection or argument). **3** to decline to avail oneself of (an advantage); refuse to accept some provision in one's favor: *The lawyer waived the privilege of cross-examining the witness.* **4** to refrain from applying (a rule or law). **5** to put aside; defer: *I waive discussion of this today* (John Ruskin). [earlier, disclaim ownership; withdraw legal protection from < Anglo-French *weyver* to abandon < Scandinavian (compare Old Icelandic *veifa* to wave). See related etym. at **waif.**]

**waiv|er** (wā′vər), *n.* **1** a giving up of a right or claim; waiving. **SYN:** relinquishment, renunciation. **2** a written statement of this: *For $100, the injured man signed a waiver of all claims against the railroad.* **3** a condition in professional baseball and other sports in which the contract of a player to be released by a team is offered to the other clubs in the league at a fixed price. Only if the other teams decline the player may his contract be taken up by a team of another league. *Supposedly, a player, put up for waiver, carries a $10,000 price tag* (New York Times). [< Anglo-French *weyver,* noun use of infinitive; see etym. under **waive**]

**waiver of immunity,** the act or fact of a witness's giving up legal right to immunity from self-incrimination in a criminal case. Public officials under investigation are requested to give such a waiver.

**wai|wode** (wā′wōd), *n.* = voivode.

**wa|ka** (wä′kə), *n., pl.* **-ka** or **-kas.** a Japanese poem of 31 syllables; tanka. [< Japanese *waka*]

**wa|kan|da** (wä kän′dä), *n., pl.* **-das. 1** a spirit worshiped by the Sioux Indians as a force of nature with supernatural powers. **2** a supernatural or magic power believed by the Sioux Indians to be contained in every object and being. Also, **wakonda.** [American English < Siouan (Dakota) *wakanda* to reckon as holy < *wakan* a spirit; something sacred]

**Wa|kash|an** (wä kash′ən), *adj., n.* —*adj.* of or having to do with an American Indian linguistic stock of the northwest United States and British Columbia, including Nootka.
—*n.* this linguistic stock.

**wake¹** (wāk), *v.,* **waked** or **woke, waked** or (*Archaic and Dialect*) **wok|en, wak|ing,** *n.* —*v.i.* **1** to stop sleeping; become awake; awaken: *I usually wake at dawn. She wakes at seven every morning.* **SYN:** awake, waken, rouse, arouse. **2** to be awake; stay awake; not be asleep: *all his waking hours.* **3a** to become alive or active: *Bears wake up in the spring after a winter of hibernation. Flowers wake in the spring, too.* **b** *Figurative.* to be roused from mental inactivity; become alert (to). **c** to be restored to life; come back from the dead, or from a condition like that of death. **4** to keep a watch or vigil, especially over a corpse. **5** *Archaic.* to be or remain active; not be passive or dormant. **6** *Obsolete.* to carouse or revel late into the night.
—*v.t.* **1** to cause to stop sleeping: *The noise of the traffic always wakes the baby. Wake me up early.* **SYN:** awake, waken, rouse, arouse. **2a** *Figurative.* to make alive or active: *He needs some interest to wake him up.* **b** to restore to life; resurrect from the grave: *to wake the dead.* **3** to keep watch over (a dead body) until burial; hold a wake over. **4** to break (a silence); disturb.
—*n.* **1** the state of wakefulness: *the ghostly visions that haunt the borders between wake and sleep.* **2** an all-night watch beside the body of a dead person (now used chiefly among the Irish). **3** chiefly in England and Scotland: **a** an annual festival commemorating the completion and consecration of a church. **b** (especially in Lancashire and Yorkshire) an industrial worker's annual holiday. **c** *Obsolete.* any merrymaking; festival; fête. **4** *Obsolete.* any merrymaking; watch or solemn vigil. **5** *Obsolete.* the state of being awake.
[Old English *wacian* to become awake, and *wacan* to awake, arise] —**wake′like′,** *adj.* —**wak′ing|ly,** *adv.*
▶ In the eastern part of the United States, for which evidence is available, *woke* appears to be by far the more common form of the past tense in spoken use and to be spreading at the expense of *waked.*

**wake²** (wāk), *n.* **1** the track left behind a moving ship. **2** the track left behind any moving thing. **3** the air currents left by an airplane, missile, or other body in flight: *In the wake, masses of air coil themselves up into vortices or eddies* (O. G. Sutton).
**in the wake of,** following; behind; after: *floods coming in the wake of a hurricane, a dog following in the wake of its master.*
[probably < Middle Dutch *wak,* perhaps < Scandinavian (compare Norwegian *vok* a hole or channel in the ice)]

**wake|ful** (wāk′fəl), *adj.* **1** not able to sleep; restless: *A fever made him wakeful.* **2** without sleep: *a stormy wakeful night.* **3** *Figurative.* watchful: *a wakeful sentry.* **SYN:** alert, vigilant. **4** *Obsolete.* that rouses from sleep; awakening. —**wake′ful|ly,** *adv.* —**wake′ful|ness,** *n.*

**wake|less** (wāk′lis), *adj.* without waking; unbroken; undisturbed.

**wak|en** (wā′kən), *v.i., v.t.* = wake. [Old English *wæcnan,* or *wæcnian*] —**wak′en|er,** *n.*

**wak|en|ing** (wā′kə ning), *n.* the act of a person or thing that wakens; awakening.

**wak|er** (wā′kər), *n.* a person who wakes.

**wake|rife** (wāk′rīf), *adj. Scottish.* wakeful; vigilant. [< *wake¹* a waking, wakefulness + *rife*] —**wake′rife|ness,** *n.*

**wake-rob|in** (wāk′rob′ən), *n.* **1** *U.S.* any one of a group of plants with purple, pink, yellow, or white flowers and a disagreeable odor; trillium. **2** *British.* **a** the cuckoopint. **b** any one of several other arums, or plants closely related to the arums, such as the jack-in-the-pulpit. **c** *Dialect.* a purple European orchid.

**wake-up¹** (wāk′up′), *n. U.S. Dialect.* the flicker (bird). [apparently imitative]

**wake-up²** (wāk′up′), *n. Australian Slang.* a person who is alert and not easily fooled; a wide-awake person.

✱**wa|ki|za|shi** (wä kē′zä shē′), *n., pl.* **-shi.** a short sword worn by Japanese samurai with the cutting edge uppermost. [< Japanese *wakizashi*]

✱**wakizashi**

**wa|kon|da** (wä kon′dä), *n., pl.* **-das.** = wakanda.

**Wal.,** **1** Walachian. **2** Walloon.

**Walach.,** Walachian.

**Wa|la|chi|an** (wo lā′kē ən), *adj., n.* —*adj.* of or having to do with Walachia, a region in southern Romania, its people, or their language. —*n.* **1** a native or inhabitant of Walachia. **2** the language of the Walachians, a dialect of Romanian. Also, **Vlach, Wallachian.**

**Wal|den|ses** (wol den′sēz), *n.pl.* a Christian sect that arose about 1170 in southern France and in the 1500's joined the Reformation movement. [< Medieval Latin *Waldenses,* plural < *Waldensis,* Latinized name of Peter *Waldo,* a merchant at Lyons, France in the 1100's, who founded the sect]

**Wal|den|si|an** (wol den′sē ən, -shən), *adj., n.* —*adj.* of or having to do with the Waldenses.
—*n.* a member of the Waldenses.

**wald|grave** (wôld′grāv), *n.* **1** an officer having jurisdiction over a royal forest in medieval Germany. **2** any one of various former hereditary German noblemen, especially in the area of the lower Rhine, whose title derived from one of these officers. [< German *Waldgraf* < *Wald* woods + *Graf* count; perhaps spelling influenced by *margrave*]

**Wal|dorf salad** (wôl′dôrf), a salad made of diced apples, celery, nuts (usually walnuts), and mayonnaise. [American English < the old *Waldorf*-Astoria Hotel, in New York City]

**wale¹** (wāl), *n., v.,* **waled, wal|ing.** —*n.* **1** a ridge or streak raised on the skin by a stick or whip; welt; weal. **SYN:** wheal. **2a** a ridge in the weave of cloth, especially corduroy. **b** the texture of a cloth. **3** a ridge woven horizontally into a basket to strengthen it.
—*v.t.* **1** to raise a welt or welts on (the skin). **2** to weave with ridges. **3** to brace, strengthen, or protect with wales.
**wales,** a continuous line of thick outside planking on the sides of a wooden ship, as buffers or for reinforcement: *Such a pointblank* [*shot*] *would have torn off a streak of our wales* (James Fenimore Cooper).
[Old English *walu* mark of a lash, weal; raised line of earth or stone. Compare etym. under **channel², gunwale.**]

**wale²** (wāl), *n., v.,* **waled, wal|ing.** *Scottish.* —*n.* **1a** a choice. **b** the scope for choice; plurality of things to choose from. **2** what is chosen or selected as the best; choicest individual, kind, or specimen.
—*v.t.* to choose; pick out.
[< Scandinavian (compare Old Icelandic *val*)]

**Wal|er** (wā′lər), *n.* a horse imported from Australia, especially into India and from New South Wales. During the 1800's, many of the horses used by the British military, as mounts for cavalry and infantry officers, were Walers. [< New South *Wale*(s) + *-er²*]

**Wal|hal|la** (wol hal′ə), *n.* = Valhalla.

**wa|li** (wä′lē), *n.* **1** the governor of an Arab province. **2** a Moslem saint. [< Arabic *wālī*]

**walk** (wôk), *v., n.* —*v.i.* **1** to go on foot. In walking, a person always has one foot on the ground: *to learn to walk at the age of two, walk slowly backwards, walk to church. Walk down to the post office with me.* **2** to roam: *The ghost will walk tonight.* **3** to go slowly: *Please walk, do not run, to the nearest exit.* **4** to move or shake in a manner suggestive of walking: *Vibration from the traffic makes the dishes walk on the shelves.* **5**

to stroll, as for pleasure or exercise; take a walk or walks. **6** *Figurative.* to conduct oneself in a particular manner; behave; live: *to walk as a man among men. Walk humbly with thy God* (Micah 6:8). **7** *Baseball.* to go to first base after the pitcher has thrown four balls. **8** to take two or more steps with the ball in basketball without bouncing or dribbling it, and thus forfeit possession of it. **9** *Obsolete.* **a** to be in motion; move. **b** (of the tongue) to move briskly; wag.

*—v.t.* **1** to go over, on, or through: *to walk the empty rooms of a house. The captain walked the deck.* **2** to make, put, or drive by walking: *to walk off a headache.* **3** to cause to walk; make go step by step: *The rider walked his horse up the hill.* **4** to accompany or escort in walking; conduct on foot: *to walk a guest to the door.* **5** to help or force (a person) to walk: *Mr. Bucket has to take Jo by the arm ... and walk him on before him* (Dickens). **6** to traverse on foot in order to measure or examine; pace off or over: *to walk the back line of a piece of property.* **7** to move (a heavy object) in a manner suggestive of walking: *He walked his big trunk along the corridor.* **8** *Baseball.* to allow (a batter) to reach first base by pitching four balls. **9** to retain (the ball in basketball) for two steps or more without dribbling it.

*—n.* **1a** the act of walking, especially for pleasure or exercise: *We went for a walk in the country.* SYN: stroll, hike, tramp, promenade. **b** the pace of walking: *to slow down to a walk.* **2a** a distance to walk: *It is a long walk to school from here.* **b** a race in walking: *the 50-kilometer walk at the Olympic Games.* **3** a way of walking; gait: *We knew the man was a sailor from his rolling walk.* **4** a place for walking: **a** a path: *a long walk of aged elms* (Joseph Addison). *There are many pretty walks in the park.* **b** = sidewalk. **c** = ambulatory. **d** = ropewalk. **5** *Figurative.* a way of living: *A doctor and a street cleaner are in different walks of life.* **6** *Baseball.* a going to first base after four balls. **7** a race in which contestants must use a walking pace. **8a** a pen or other enclosed place; tract: *a poultry walk.* **b** a pasture or meadow, fenced or unfenced: *a sheepwalk.* **9** *Especially British.* a plantation of coffee, banana, or other trees, growing in straight rows with wide spaces between them. **10** *Especially British.* **a** the round or circuit, as of a tradesman, official, or postman. **b** the district traversed or served by such a person. **11** *British.* a division of forestland under the charge of a forester, ranger, or keeper: *a forest divided into five walks.* **12** *Obsolete.* a haunt; resort.

**take a walk**, to get out or depart; withdraw: *Backers ... warn wavering Republican leaders that conservatives will take a walk if the Senator fails to win the GOP race* (Wall Street Journal).

**walk all over**, to act without regard for; trample on; override: *Are you going to let that old ... banker walk all over you?* (S. E. White).

**walk around**, to bypass; circumvent: *The production code has largely dissolved, partly because some producers have walked around it and partly because the movies ... have had to find new themes* (Maclean's).

**walk away from**, **a** to progress much faster than: *Beaten by a banjo! ... If it had not been for the banjo I should have walked away from her* (Rhoda Broughton). **b** to go through or emerge from without damage or injury: *to walk away from an accident.*

**walk away with**, to gain possession of (something) by means of art, charm, or talent; steal: *Cesare Siepi as Mephistopheles walked away with the show* (Leonard Marcus).

**walk off with**, **a** to take; get; win: *to walk off easily with first prize.* **b** to steal: *She walked off with an expensive wrist watch.*

**walk on air**. See under **air**.

**walk out**, **a** to go on strike: *If denied what they consider a fair hearing, labour unionists resort to strikes. They lay down their tools and walk out* (Emory S. Bogardus). **b** to leave a room or a meeting suddenly: *The dissenting delegate walked out in protest.* **c** *Informal.* to go out with a person of the opposite sex; keep company; court: *To him, the business of walking out with a girl was miracle enough in itself* (New Yorker).

**walk out on**, *Informal.* to desert: *She walked out on him on account of his laziness.*

**walk over**, **a** to defeat easily and by a wide margin: *The candidate was so popular that he walked over his opposition to win the race for mayor.* **b** = walk all over.

**walk the plank**. See under **plank**.

**walk through**, (in the theater) to do a walk-through of: *to walk through a part or a play.*

**walk up**, to start (game birds) by beating up the ground with pointers or setters: *The coveys were far too wild at the end of October to be walked up* (Geoffrey Household).

**win in a walk**, *Informal.* to win without much effort: *If there had been an election, he would have won in a walk* (Time).

[Old English *wealcan* to toss]

*—Syn. v.i.* **1 Walk, stride, plod** mean to go on foot at a pace slower than a run. **Walk** is the general word: *I walked downstairs.* **Stride** means to walk with long steps, as in haste, annoyance, or self-importance, or with healthy energy: *He strode along briskly.* **Plod** means to walk heavily, slowly, and with effort: *The old horse plodded up the road.*

**Walk** (wôk), *n., v. —n.* a group dance in which the participants perform steps similar to walking: *The club plays recorded music and everyone does the Walk, much as they do it everywhere else around town, but with an added dash of salsa* (New York Post). *—v.i.* to dance the Walk.

**walk|a|bil|i|ty** (wôk′ə bil′ə tē), *n.* the quality or condition of being walkable.

**walk|a|ble** (wôk′ə bəl), *adj.* **1** that can be walked on: *walkable ice floes.* **2** suitable for walking: *walkable clothes.* **3** that may be walked: *a walkable distance.*

**walk|a|bout** (wôk′ə bout′), *n.* **1** (in Australia) a brief period of wandering in the bush. Aborigines take occasional leave from work to go on a walkabout. **2** a walking about; short trip or tour on foot.

**walk-along** (wôk′ə lông′, -long′), *n.* an early bicycle which the rider straddled and propelled with a walking motion, pushing his feet alternately on the ground; velocipede.

**walk|a|thon** (wôk′ə thon), *n. U.S. and Canada.* a walking marathon. [< *walk* + *-athon*, as in *marathon*]

**walk|a|way** (wôk′ə wā′), *n. Informal.* an easy victory. SYN: walkover.

**walk clerk**, a messenger employed by London banks in the 1600's to collect cash from other banks to cover credits.

**walk|down** (wôk′doun′), *n. U.S. Informal.* the slow approach of the hero and villain from opposite sides of a street just before the showdown, as in western movies.

***walk|er** (wô′kər), *n.* **1** a person who walks. **2** a framework on casters with a seat to support babies learning to walk; gocart. **3** a lightweight framework of legs and supporting bars for a crippled person to support himself while walking. **walkers, a** walking shorts: *The walkers ... are comfortable worsted in a cotton and dacron mixture* (New Yorker). **b** shoes used especially for walking: *five types of shoe: kickers, creepers, crawlers, trainers, and walkers—for children between the ages of one week and 10 years* (Wall Street Journal).

***walker**
definitions 2, 3

definition 2

definition 3

**walk|ie-look|ie** (wô′kē lu̇k′ē), *n.* a portable television camera; creepie-peepie: *The walkie-lookie ... did for the visual audience what the roving candid microphone had done for radio listeners* (Life).

**walk|ie-talk|ie** (wô′kē tô′kē), *n.* a small, portable receiving and transmitting radio set. It is powered by a battery and has a collapsible antenna. *So violent were the winds that the men could not speak with each other, though with a walkie-talkie they were able to communicate with the base camp 9,000 feet below* (Scientific American). Also, **walky-talky**.

**walk-in** (wôk′in′), *adj., n. —adj.* **1** large enough to walk into: *a walk-in pantry, a bedroom with walk-in closets.* **2** that can be entered directly from the street: *a walk-in studio apartment.* **3** that can be walked into without a previous appointment or arrangement: *a walk-in clinic.*

*—n. Informal.* **1** an easy or certain victory; sure thing; shoo-in: *Many Republicans say, privately, that next year's contest will be no walk-in for the Senator* (New York Times). **2** a walk-in apartment. **3** a person who joins of his own accord; volunteer: *The Marine Corps reports a similar spurt in walk-ins* (Wall Street Journal).

**walk|ing** (wô′king), *adj., n. —adj.* **1** of or having to do with a walk; going on foot: *a walking race or contest, a walking marathon.* **2** used mainly for walking: *walking shoes.* **3** that is pulled by a horse, mule, or other beast of burden, or a team, and has no seat for the driver, who walks behind: *a walking plow.* **4** that oscillates back and forth or up and down at its ends: *a walking beam.* **5** that moves or is able to be moved with a motion resembling walking: *a walking crane.* **6** in human form; living: *a walking dictionary, a walking library of contemporary fiction.*

*—n.* **1a** the act of going on foot; taking a walk. **b** the manner or style in which a person walks. **2** the condition of a path or road for walking on: *easy walking, icy walking.* **3** the sport of walking competitively for speed or against time, especially by the heel-and-toe method.

**walking bass** (bās), a short series of notes persistently played in the bass, each note of which is usually followed by the note an octave higher, as used in playing boogie-woogie.

**walking beam**, the beam (lever) of a steam engine.

**walking catfish**, a catfish of Asia that can crawl over ground by means of its tail and spiny fins and live on land for extended periods by taking in air through its auxiliary breathing apparatus: *An example of an imported species that became a dangerous threat to the freshwater ecology of the subtropical United States ... is Clarias batrachus, the "walking catfish"* (D. A. Brown).

**walking delegate**, a union official charged with traveling about on union business, as to represent the union in negotiations or to inspect working conditions.

**walking fern**, a fern whose fronds taper into a slender prolongation that frequently roots at the tip.

**walking fish**, a kind of sea robin that moves along the sea-bottom by using its highly developed thoracic fin rays.

**walking horse**, = Tennessee walking horse.

**walking leaf**, **1** any one of certain insects that have a leaflike appearance; leaf insect. **2** = walking fern.

**walk|ing-on** (wô′king on′, -ôn′), *adj.* of a walk-on: *a walking-on part.*

**walking papers**, *Informal.* a dismissal, as from a position.

**walking shorts**, shorts worn as for leisure or walking and similar to Bermuda shorts.

**walking staff**, a staff or long stick which a person carries for support or aid in walking.

**walking stick**, **1** a stick used in walking; cane. **2** any one of a group of mostly wingless insects related to the grasshoppers, having a body like a stick or twig; stick insect.

**walk-off** or **walk|off** (wôk′ôf, -of′), *n.* **1** the act of walking off: *The walk-off is the bittersweet image by which, undoubtedly, Chaplin wishes to be remembered* (Time). **2** an abrupt departure; walkout: *The 22 Springbok cricketers who held a two-minute walk-off at Newlands Ground ... in protest against apartheid* (Manchester Guardian Weekly). **3** something that marks a departure or withdrawal; a farewell: *Mr. Ellington's part consisted of his signature theme, "Take the 'A' Train" ... and, as a walkoff, another Ellington signature, "Things Ain't What They Used to Be"* (New York Times).

**walk-on** (wôk′on′, -ôn′), *n., adj. —n.* **1** a part in a play, movie, or other performance, in which the performer merely comes on and goes off the stage with little or no speaking. **2** a performer having such a part: *I started as a walk-on, and later played principal roles and became stage manager* (New Yorker).

*—adj.* **1** of a walk-on: *a walk-on part.* **2** appearing or performing on the stage: *a walk-on humorist.*

**walk|out** (wôk′out′), *n.* **1** a strike of workers: *Striking employees ... will go back to work tomorrow, fifty-seven days after their walkout* (New York Times). **2** a sudden departure from a room, meeting, or the like, usually as a form of protest. *France staged the walkout ... to protest an Assembly decision to debate nationalist claims in French Algeria* (Wall Street Journal).

**walk|o|ver** (wôk′ō′vər), *n. Informal.* **1** an easy victory; walkaway. **2** a race in which the winner is predetermined either because only one horse starts and can thus walk the course to win or because all starters belong to one owner.

**walk shorts**, = walking shorts.

**walk-through** (wôk′thrü′), *n.* **1** in the theater:

---

**Pronunciation Key:** hat, āge, cãre, fär; let, ēqual, tėrm; it, īce; hot, ōpen, ôrder; oil, out; cup, pu̇t, rüle; child; long; thin; ᴛʜen; zh, measure; ə represents **a** in about, **e** in taken, **i** in pencil, **o** in lemon, **u** in circus.

**a** a rehearsal at which lines are read and accompanied by actions, such as walking and sitting. **b** an initial or perfunctory rehearsal. **c** a walk-on part. **2** a television rehearsal without cameras, usually for the purpose of checking the cues.

**walk-up** (wôk′up′), *n., adj.* **—*n.*** **1** an apartment house or building having no elevator. **2** a room or apartment in such a building: *a third-floor walk-up.* **3** a start in horse racing in which the jockeys ride the horses as close as possible to the starting line before the signal to race.
**—*adj.*** of or in an apartment building having no elevator: *a walk-up apartment.*

**walk|way** (wôk′wā′), *n.* **1** a structure for walking: *an overhead steel walkway.* **2** a path; walk: *Built in mellow brickwork they are set well away from the road with private walkways* (Sunday Times).

**Wal|kyr** (wol′kir, vol′-), *n.* = Valkyr.

**Wal|kyr|ie** (wol kir′ē, vol-), *n.* = Valkyrie. [probably < *Valkyrie;* influenced by German *Walküre*]

**walk|y-talk|y** (wô′kē tô′kē), *n., pl.* **-talk|ies.** = walkie-talkie.

**wall**[1] (wôl), *n., v., adj.* **—*n.*** **1a** the side of a room or building, as between the floor or foundation and the ceiling or roof: *a brick outer wall, to paper a bedroom wall.* **b** the side part of any hollow thing: *the wall of a chimney, the wall of the stomach.* **c** the inside surface of any hollow thing: *to repair the walls of a furnace.* **2** a structure of stone, brick, or other material, built up to enclose, divide, support, or protect. Cities used to be surrounded by high walls to keep out enemies. *Our garden is surrounded by a stone wall.* **SYN:** partition. **3** a defensive rampart: *to dig in behind a wall of earth.* **4** *Figurative: a wall of flame, a wall of ignorance. The flood came in a wall of water twelve feet high. The soldiers kept their ranks a solid wall.*
**—*v.t.*** **1** to enclose, divide, protect, or fill with a wall or walls: *to wall in a house, to wall off a house from the road, to wall up a doorway,* (*Figurative.*) *to wall out the noise of the city.* **2** to shut within walls: (*Figurative.*) *a complete invalid walled up for years in his bed.*
**—*adj.*** **1** of or having to do with a wall or walls. **2** planted along and growing up a wall or walls.
**drive** (or **push**) **to the wall,** to make desperate or helpless; drive to the last extremity: *His creditors drove the bankrupt man to the wall. Being ... driven to the wall, Addington complied* (L. Harcourt).
**drive up the wall,** *Informal.* to annoy extremely; exasperate: [*The*] *five-year-old had been acting up ... and driving her father up the wall* (Maclean's).
**go over the wall,** *Slang.* to escape, as from prison: *He knew it was an unwritten law that an escape extinguished such a debt, and so he decided to go over the wall* (London Times).
**go to the wall, a** to give way; be defeated: *Sam and Mayford are both desperately in love with her, and one must go to the wall* (Henry Kingsley). **b** to give way or precedence (to something else): *Where political interests interfered family arrangements went to the wall* (Justin McCarthy). **c** to fail in business: *In Berlin a newspaper would very soon go to the wall if it did not present its subscribers with light entertainment* (Nineteenth Century).
**hang by the wall,** to hang up neglected; remain unused: *All the enrolled penalties Which have, like unscour'd armour, hung by the wall* (Shakespeare).
**jump** (or **leap**) **over the wall,** to leave one's church or religious order: *No one knows exactly how many religious have jumped over the wall —partly because it is so easy today for a priest, nun or brother simply to take a leave of absence and never return* (Time).
**the Wall, a** a wall of concrete and barbed wire, 26 miles long, built by East Germany in 1961 to divide East and West Berlin: *Thousands of grinning, gift-laden West Berliners swarmed through the Wall for their first reunions with eastern sector relatives since August 1961* (Time). **b** the remains of the western wall of Solomon's Temple in Jerusalem, known as the Wailing Wall: *An exaltation swept Israel at the thought that the Wall belonged to Jews once more* (New Yorker).
**up against a** (**blank, stone, brick,** or other kind of) **wall,** facing an obstacle that cannot be overcome; at a dead end: *His campaign against irresponsible bait advertisements ... had come up against a stone wall* (London Times).
**walls,** a series or system of defensive ramparts; encircling fortifications: *to raze the walls of a medieval city.*
**with** (or **having**) **one's back to the wall.** See under **back**[1].
[Old English *weall* rampart < Latin *vallum*]
**—wall′er,** *n.* **—wall′-like′,** *adj.*

**wall**[2] (wôl), *v.t., v.i. Especially U.S.* to roll (the eyes): *The boy's blue eyes were walling with fear* (Atlantic). [< Scottish *wawlen,* related to Middle English *wawil-*(*eghed*) wall(eyed)]

**wal|la** (wol′ə), *n.* = wallah.

**wal|la|ba** (wol′ə bə), *n.* a tropical tree of South America, with a hard, heavy, deep-red, resinous wood. [< Arawakan *wallaba*]

**wal|la|by** (wol′ə bē), *n., pl.* **-bies** or (*collectively*) **-by.** any one of various small or medium-sized kangaroos. Some wallabies are no larger than rabbits. See picture under **kangaroo**[1]. [< native Australian *wolabā,* or *wallibah*]

**Wal|lace|ism** (wol′ə siz əm, wôl′-), *n.* the policies associated with George C. Wallace (born 1919), governor of Alabama, especially opposition to racial integration and championship of states' rights in the South.

**Wal|lace|ite** (wol′ə sīt, wôl′-), *n.* a supporter or follower of Governor George C. Wallace or of Wallaceism.

**Wal|lace's Line** (wol′ ə siz, wôl′-), an imaginary line in the southwestern Pacific that divides the animal life of the Australian region from that of the Asian or Oriental region. [< Alfred Russel *Wallace,* 1823-1913, a British naturalist and explorer]

**Wal|la|chi|an** (wo lā′kē ən), *adj., n.* = Walachian.

**wal|lah** (wol′ə), *n. British Informal, originally Anglo-Indian.* **1** a person; chap; fellow. **2** a person or (sometimes) animal who does or is associated with some (specified) work, thing, or place. *Examples:* kitchen wallah = one who works in the kitchen; jungle wallah = one who dwells in the jungle. Also, **walla.** [< Anglo-Indian *-wālā,* as in *Dilliwālā* person of Delhi < Hindi *-vālā* of or having to do with, perhaps < Sanskrit *bāla* boy]

**wall arcade,** an arcade with columns built very close to the wall, as in some monasteries.

**wal|la|roo** (wol′ə rü′), *n.* a large kangaroo that has thick reddish or gray fur. [< native Australian *wolarū*]

**wall-at|tach|ment effect** (wôl′ə tach′mənt), = Coanda effect.

**wall|board** (wôl′bôrd′, -bōrd′), *n.* any one of various building materials, such as plasterboard or fiberboard, made by pressing wood pulp, plaster, or the like, into large, flat sheets. Wallboard is used instead of wood or plaster to make or cover inside walls.

**wall cloud,** = eyewall.

**wall creeper,** a small Old-World bird related to the nuthatch, that has bright plumage and that frequents rocky walls and slopes of alpine regions hunting for insects.

**walled** (wôld), *adj.* having walls: *a walled city, high-walled.*

**wal|let** (wol′it, wôl′-), *n.* **1** a small, flat leather case for carrying paper money, cards, etc., in one's pocket; folding pocketbook; billfold. **2** a bag for carrying food and small articles for personal use when on a journey. **3** *Obsolete.* something (in or on an animal's body) that hangs out and down; protuberant and pendulous growth. [Middle English *walet* pilgrim's scrip, knapsack; origin uncertain]

**wal|let|ful** (wol′it fu̇l, wôl′-), *n., pl.* **-fuls.** as much as a wallet contains; purseful.

**wall|eye** (wôl′ī′), *n.* **1** an eye having a whitish iris, so that it has little or no color. **2a** a turning of one or both eyes away from the nose, a form of strabismus. **b** an eye having such a condition, so as to show a large amount of white. **3** a large, staring eye. **4a** an eye having a white opacity in the cornea. **b** the white opacity; leucoma. **5** the condition of being walleyed. **6** any one of various fishes with large, staring eyes, especially the walleyed pike, the walleyed surf fish, the alewife or walleyed herring, or the walleyed pollack. [back formation < *walleyed*]

**wall|eyed** (wôl′īd′), *adj.* **1** having eyes that show much white and little color. **2** having one or both eyes turned away from the nose, so as to show much white. **3** having large, staring eyes, as some fishes do. **4** *Obsolete.* having glaring eyes (indicative of rage or jealousy). [Middle English *wawil-eghed* < Scandinavian (compare Old Icelandic *vagl-eygr* < *vagl* speck in the eye + *eygr* having eyes of a certain kind < *auga* eye)]

**walleyed herring,** = alewife.

**walleyed pike** or **perch,** a large, edible North American freshwater game fish, a pike perch, with large, staring eyes (in the southern United States also called *blowfish*).

**walleyed pollack,** a black North American pollack of the Pacific coast with large, prominent eyes.

**walleyed surf fish,** a black marine fish of the California coast with large, prominent eyes.

**wall fern,** the common polypody.

**wall|flow|er** (wôl′flou′ər), *n.* **1** *Informal.* a person, especially a girl or woman, who sits by the wall at a dance instead of dancing. **2a** a perennial plant with sweet-smelling yellow, orange, or red flowers, found growing on walls, cliffs, and the like. The wallflower belongs to the mustard family. **b** any one of various plants of a related group. **3** a desert shrub of the pea family of Australia.

**wall fruit,** fruit from trees or other plants trained to grow against a wall, as for protection or warmth.

**wall|hang|ing** (wôl′hang′ing), *n.* a tapestry used as a hanging on walls: *Italy, where magnificent silk wallhangings originated* (London Times).

**wal|lies** (wā′lēz), *n.pl.* See under **wally.**

**wall|ing** (wô′ling), *n.* **1** the making of walls; a furnishing or fortifying with a wall. **2** walls collectively; material for walls: *some of the best examples of drystone walling I have seen for a long time* (Manchester Guardian).

**wall-less** (wôl′lis), *adj.* having no wall.

**Wal|lo|ni|an** (wo lō′nē ən), *n., adj.* **—*n.*** the dialect of the Walloons; Walloon.
**—*adj.*** = Walloon.

**Wal|loon** (wo lün′), *n., adj.* **—*n.*** **1** any one of a group of people inhabiting chiefly the southern and southeastern parts of Belgium and adjacent regions in France. **2** their language, the French dialect of Belgium.
**—*adj.*** of or having to do with the Walloons or their language.
[< French *Wallon* < Medieval Latin *Wallo, -onis* < Germanic (compare Old English *wealh* foreigner, Celt). See related etym. at **Welsh.**]

**wal|lop**[1] (wol′əp), *v., n.* **—*v.t.*** *Informal.* **1** to beat soundly; thrash. **SYN:** flog. **2** to hit very hard; strike with a vigorous blow. **3** to defeat thoroughly, as in a game.
**—*v.i.*** **1** *Informal and Dialect.* to move clumsily or noisily; flounder; plunge. **2** *Especially Scottish.* to dangle, flap, or wobble. **3** *Obsolete.* to gallop.
**—*n.*** **1** *Informal.* a very hard blow: *The wallop knocked him down.* **2** *Informal.* the power to hit very hard blows. **3** *Informal and Dialect.* a heavy, clumsy, noisy movement of the body; floundering; lurching. **4** *Figurative, Informal.* strong force; power; impact: *... the wallop of vivid contemporary prints* (New York Times). *There is plenty of wallop in this album* (Bosley Crowther). **5** *British Slang.* beer: *a drink of wallop.* **6** *Obsolete.* a gallop.
**go** (**down**) **wallop,** *Informal and Dialect.* to fall noisily: *The horse tripped and the rider went down wallop.*
**pack a wallop,** *Informal.* to carry great force or power; have a strong impact: *Here's painstaking scholarship that packs a wallop* (Saturday Review).
[< Old North French *waloper,* Old French *galoper* to gallop, related to *galop* a gallop. See etym. of doublet **gallop.**]

**wal|lop**[2] (wol′əp), *v., n.* **—*v.i.*** to boil violently and with a noisy bubbling.
**—*n.*** *Obsolete.* the noisy bubbling of rapidly boiling water.
[perhaps special use of *wallop*[1]; perhaps imitative of the noise. Compare etym. under **pot-walloper.**]

**wal|lop|er** (wol′ə pər), *n. Dialect.* anything strikingly large or big; whopper.

**wal|lop|ing** (wol′ə ping), *n., adj. Informal.* **—*n.*** **1** a sound beating or thrashing. **2** a thorough defeat.
**—*adj.*** big; powerful; strong; whopping.

**wall oven,** an oven built into a wall or cabinet in a kitchen, bakery, or laboratory: *Kitchen equipment includes a ... built-in wall oven, dishwasher and a range* (New York Times).

**wal|low** (wol′ō), *v., n.* **—*v.i.*** **1** to roll about; flounder: *The pigs wallowed in the mud. The boat wallowed helplessly in the stormy sea.* **2** *Figurative.* to live contentedly in filth, wickedness, or other dissolute way of life, like a beast. **3** *Figurative.* to live or delight self-indulgently or luxuriously in some form of pleasure, manner of life, attitude, or emotion: *to wallow in wealth, wallow in sentimentality.* **4** to billow up or surge out; gush (from): *dense black smoke wallowing from the chimneys.*
**—*n.*** **1a** the act of wallowing: *a wallow in the mud.* **b** the condition of wallowing: (*Figurative.*) *to sink into a hopeless wallow of despair.* **2a** a muddy or dusty place where an animal wallows: *a hog wallow. There used to be many buffalo wallows on the prairies.* **b** a depression or hollow in such a place, caused by wallowing.
[Old English *wealwian* to roll] **—wal′low|er,** *n.*

**wall|paint|ing** (wôl′pān′ting), *n.* **1** the painting of the surface of a wall, or similar surfaces, with ornamental designs and figures, as seen in fresco and tempera. **2** a picture or design so painted.

**wall|pa|per** (wôl′pā′pər), *n., v.* **—*n.*** paper, usually printed with a decorative pattern in color, for pasting on and covering inside walls.
**—*v.t., v.i.*** to put wallpaper on (a wall) or on the walls of (a room, apartment, or house).

**wallpaper music,** recorded music piped into an office, restaurant, or the like, through a public-address system: *'Wallpaper music' ... the plastic,* *bland pop stuff that churns out as a comfy background you don't really have to notice* (Sunday Times).

**wall pellitory**, a low, bushy European variety of pellitory that grows upon or at the foot of old walls.

**wall pennywort**, = navelwort.

**wall plate**, 1 a timber (plate) placed horizontally in or along a wall, under the ends of girders, joists, or rafters, to distribute pressure. 2 a metal plate fastened to a wall or ceiling as a support or place of attachment for machinery, a bracket, anchor in a building, or heavy load.

**wall rock**, *Mining.* the rock forming the walls of a vein.

**wall rocket**, a yellow-flowered European plant of the mustard family, naturalized in North America.

**wall rue**, a small fern, a variety of spleenwort, that grows on walls and cliffs.

**walls** (wôlz), *n.pl.* See under **wall**.

**wall-sid|ed** (wôl′sī′did), *adj. Nautical.* (of a ship or vessel) having sides nearly perpendicular.

**Wall Street**, 1 a street in downtown New York City that is the chief financial center of the United States. 2 the money market or financiers of the United States.

**Wall Street|er** (strē′tər), a person who works on Wall Street or in the financial district around it: *Fraunces Tavern, at Broad and Pearl Streets ... a restaurant much favored by Wall Streeters with a sense of history* (New Yorker).

**wall tent**, a tent with perpendicular sides, usually rising two or three feet from the ground.

**wall-to-wall** (wôl′tə wôl′), *adj.* 1 covering the entire floor between opposite walls in both directions: *wall-to-wall carpeting.* 2 *Especially U.S., Figurative.* extending from one end or extreme to the other: [*The car*] *comes with a wall-to-wall front grille that conceals the headlights* (Time). *It is not easy to forsee an all-Europe computer manufacturer or a Continental wall-to-wall version of General Electric* (Harper's).

**wal|ly** (wā′lē), *adj., n., pl.* **-lies**. *Scottish.* —*adj.* 1 handsome; fine. 2 large; ample.
—*n.* a toy or trinket; gewgaw. Also, **waly**.
**wallies**, finery: *bonny wallies.*
[perhaps < *wale*[2] a choice + *-y*[1]]

**wal|ly|drag** (wā′lē drag, wol′ē-), *n. Scottish.* 1a a weak or runty person or animal. b the youngest (and often feeblest) of a family, brood, or litter. 2 a worthless, slovenly person, especially a woman.

**wal|ly|drai|gle** (wā′lē drā′gəl, wol′ē-), *n. Scottish.* wallydrag. [origin unknown]

***wal|nut** (wôl′nut, -nət), *n.* 1 a rather large, almost round nut with a division between its two halves and a hard, ridged surface. The meat of the walnut is eaten by itself or used in cakes and cookies. 2 any one of the trees that it grows on, especially the English or Persian walnut and the black walnut, much grown in north temperate regions for their nuts, their valuable wood, and as shade trees. 3 the wood of any of these trees. Some kinds of walnut are used in making furniture. 4 any one of several trees, or their fruits, that resemble the walnut. 5 *U.S. Dialect.* the shagbark (hickory) or its nut. 6 the brown color of polished black walnut. [Old English *wealhhnutu* < *wealh* foreign; Welsh (< Celtic tribal name *Volcae*) + *hnutu* nut. Compare etym. under **Welsh**.]

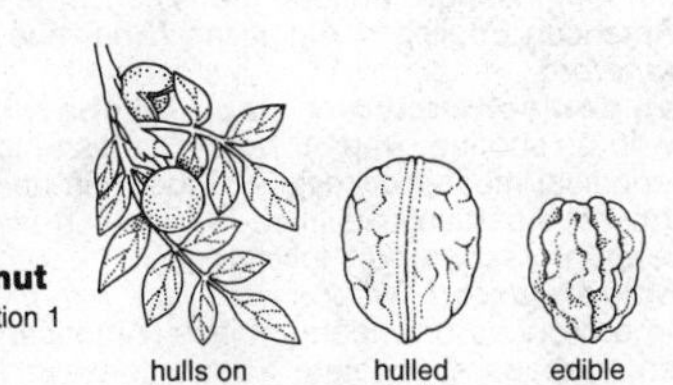

***walnut** definition 1

**walnut family**, a group of dicotyledonous, resinous trees and shrubs, found in north temperate regions. The family includes the walnut, hickory, and pecan.

**Wal|po|li|an** (wôl′pō′lē ən, wol′-), *adj., n.* —*adj.* 1 of or like the English author and letter writer Horace Walpole (1717-1797) or his writings. 2 of or like the English statesman and financier Sir Robert Walpole (1676-1745) or his political views.
—*n.* a follower or admirer of Horace Walpole or Sir Robert Walpole.

**Wal|pur|gis|nacht** (väl pu̇r′gis näʜt′), *n. German.* Walpurgis Night.

**Wal|pur|gis Night** (väl pu̇r′gis), the night of April 30; the feast of Saint Walpurgis, when, according to German legend, witches were supposed to hold revels with the Devil on a peak of the Harz Mountains. [translation of German *Walpurgisnacht*]

**wal|rus** (wôl′rəs, wol′-), *n., pl.* **-rus|es** or (*collectively for 1*) **-rus**, *adj.* —*n.* 1 a large sea animal of arctic regions, related to and resembling the seals, but having two long tusks. Walruses are valuable for their ivory tusks and blubber oil. Walrus hide is made into leather for suitcases, bags, etc. See picture under **seal**[2]. 2 *Slang, Figurative.* a very fat, clumsy person or animal.
—*adj.* 1 of or having to do with a walrus or walruses: *walrus hide, a walrus hunter.* 2 like a walrus: *a walrus face.*
[< Dutch *walrus*, or *walros* < *wal*(*visch*) whale + *ros* horse]

**walrus mustache**, a man's mustache that is very long and curves downward at the ends, so as to resemble somewhat the tusks of the male walrus.

**Wal|ter Mitty** (wôl′tər), = Mitty.

**Walter Mit|ty|ish** (mit′ē ish), = Mittyesque.

**waltz** (wôlts), *n., v., adj.* —*n.* 1 a smooth, even, gliding ballroom dance with three beats to the measure. In a waltz the couples make a complete turn to each measure (originally, rapidly and always in the same direction; now usually at a moderate pace and with changes of direction). 2 music for it. 3 *Slang, Figurative.* a thing accomplished with ease; something simple; breeze: *His bold putt from twenty-five feet hit the back of the cup, jumped up in the air, landed outside the cup, and toppled in. After that, it was a waltz* (New Yorker).
—*v.i., v.t.* 1 to dance a waltz. 2 *Figurative.* to move nimbly or quickly.
—*adj.* of, having to do with, or characteristic of the waltz as a dance, piece of music, or rhythm.
[< German *Walzer* < *walzen* to roll] —**waltz′er**, *n.* —**waltz′like′**, *adj.*

**waltz-length** (wôlts′length′), *adj.* midway to the calf in length: *Waltz-length gowns are meeting better acceptance than longer ones* (New York Times).

**waltz|time** (wôlts′tīm′), *n.* triple time; three-quarter time.

**waltz|y** (wôl′tsē), *adj.,* **waltz|i|er, waltz|i|est**. like a waltz; suggesting a waltz, as in quality or tempo: *The phrases are natural, even obviously waltzy at times* (London Times).

**wal|y**[1] (wā′lē, wô′-), *interj. Scottish.* an exclamation of sorrow. [probably < Old English *wā lā.* Compare etym. under **wellaway, woe**.]

**wal|y**[2] (wā′lē, wol′ē), *adj., n., pl.* **wal|ies**. *Scottish.* wally.

**wam|ble** (wom′əl, wam′-), *v.,* **-bled, -bling**, *n. Dialect.* —*v.i.* 1a to feel nausea. b (of the stomach or its contents) to be felt to roll about (in nausea). 2 to move unsteadily; stagger; totter; reel. 3 to turn and twist the body about; roll or wriggle (about, over, through).
—*n.* 1 a feeling of nausea. 2a an unsteady movement (of a person or thing). b a rolling or staggering gait.
[Middle English *wamelen;* origin uncertain. Compare Danish *vamle* be nauseated, Norwegian *vamla* to stagger.]

**wam|bly** (wom′lē, wam′-), *adj. Dialect.* 1 affected with nausea. 2 causing nausea. 3 shaky; tottering; unsteady.

**wame** (wām), *n. Scottish.* 1 the belly; abdomen. 2 the womb; uterus. [variant of *womb*]

**wam|mus** (wom′əs), *n.* = wamus.

**Wam|pa|no|ag** (wom′pə nō′ag), *n.* a member of an Indian tribe of southeastern Massachusetts at the time of the Pilgrims.

**wam|pee** (wom pē′), *n.* 1 the fruit of an Asian tree of the rue family, resembling the grape in size and taste, and growing in clusters. 2 the tree. [< Chinese *hwang-pī* < *hwang* yellow + *pī* skin]

**wamp|ish** (wom′pish, wam′-), *v.i., v.t. Scottish.* to wave or toss to and fro. [perhaps imitative]

***wam|pum** (wom′pəm, wôm′-), *n.* 1 beads made from shells, formerly used by North American Indians as money and for ornament. 2 *Slang.* money. [American English, short for *wampumpeag*]

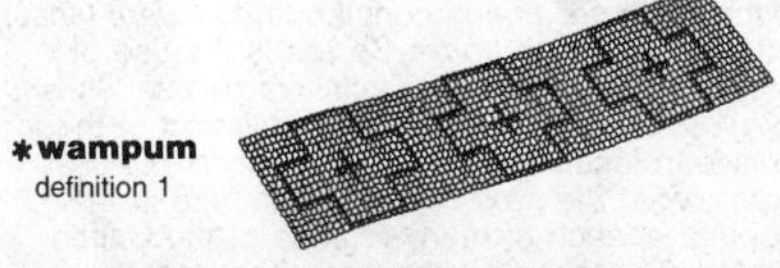
***wampum** definition 1

**wam|pum|peag** (wom′pəm pēg, wôm′-), *n.* 1 wampum made of white shells (less valuable than that made of black shells). 2 any wampum. [American English < Algonkian (probably Narragansett) *waⁿpaⁿpiak* string of white shell beads]

**wam|pus** (wom′pəs), *n.* = wamus.

**wa|mus** (wôm′əs, wom′-), *n. U.S.* 1 a type of cardigan (sweater). 2 an outer jacket of coarse, durable fabric. [American English < Dutch *wammeis*, earlier *wambuis* < Old North French *wambeis*, or *wambois* leather doublet]

**wan**[1] (won), *adj.,* **wan|ner, wan|nest**, *v.,* **wanned, wan|ning**. —*adj.* 1 lacking natural or normal color; pale: *Her face looked wan after her long illness.* SYN: See syn. under **pale**. 2 looking worn or tired; faint; weak: *The sick boy gave the doctor a wan smile.* 3 partially obscured; dim: *a wan moon behind scudding clouds, the wan sunlight of winter.* 4 lacking light or luster; dark-hued; dusky; gloomy. 5 *Obsolete.* sad; dismal.
—*v.i.* to grow wan: *His round cheek wans in the candlelight* (Walter de la Mare).
[Old English *wann* dark (in hue); lacking luster; leaden, pale gray] —**wan′ly**, *adv.* —**wan′ness**, *n.*

**wan**[2] (won), *v. Archaic or Scottish.* won, a past tense of **win**.

**wan|chanc|y** (won chan′sē, -chän′-), *adj. Scottish.* 1 unlucky; dangerous. 2 eerie; uncanny. [< obsolete *wanchance* misfortune < Old English *wan-* lacking + *chance* fortune]

**wand** (wond), *n.* 1 a slender stick or rod: *The magician waved his wand, and a rabbit popped out of his hat.* 2 *British.* a rod or staff carried as a sign of office, especially a tall, slender rod of white wood, sometimes of ebony or silver, carried erect by an officer of the royal household, a court of justice, etc., on occasions of ceremony. 3 *U.S.* a slat, six feet long and two inches wide, set up as a mark for shooting in archery, 100 yards away for men, 60 for women. 4 *Scottish.* a slender, pliant stick cut from a stem or branch of a shrub or young tree. 5 *Archaic.* a young shoot; slender stem of a shrub or tree; slender branch or twig. 6 *Obsolete.* a scepter. [< Scandinavian (compare Old Icelandic *vöndr*). Probably related to **wend, wind**[2].] —**wand′like′**, *adj.*

**wan|der** (won′dər), *v., n.* —*v.i.* 1 to move here and there without any special purpose: *to wander around a city or in the woods. We wandered through the stores, hoping to get ideas for his birthday present.* 2 to go from the right way; stray: *The dog wandered off and got lost.* (*Figurative.*) *She wanders away from her subject when she talks.* (*Figurative.*) *Don't let your attention wander.* 3 to follow an uncertain or irregular course; meander: *a driver who wanders all over the road.* 4 *Figurative.* to be unable to think sensibly; be delirious; be incoherent: *His mind wandered when he had a very high fever.* 5 *Figurative.* to fall into wickedness; be morally misled or corrupted.
—*v.t.* to go aimlessly on, over, in, or through; roam: *to wander the city streets.*
—*n.* an act of wandering; stroll.
[Old English *wandrian.* See related etym. at **wend, wind**[2].] —**wan′der|er**, *n.*
—*Syn.* *v.i.* 1, 2. **Wander, stray** mean to go from place to place more or less aimlessly or without a settled course. **Wander** emphasizes moving about without a definite course or destination: *We wandered through the fields, looking for wildflowers.* **Stray** emphasizes going beyond the usual or proper limits or away from the regular path or course, and often suggests getting lost: *Two of the children strayed from the picnic grounds.*

**wan|der|ing** (won′dər ing), *adj., n.* —*adj.* that moves from place to place; nomadic; roving: *wandering tribes, wandering herds of antelope.*
—*n.* the act of a person or thing that wanders: *Migration was at first characterized by aimless wandering, as in the case of primitive tribes moving up and down valleys in search of food for themselves and their flocks* (Emory S. Bogardus). —**wan′der|ing|ly**, *adv.*

**wandering albatross**, a large albatross, white with black wings, frequenting southern seas. It has the largest wingspread of any living bird.

**Wandering Jew**, a Jew in medieval legend who insulted Christ and was condemned to wander on earth till Christ's second coming.

**wandering Jew**, one of two trailing plants of the spiderwort family that grow and spread rapidly: **a** a variety native to eastern South America with white flowers. **b** a variety native to Mexico with white and purplish flowers. [< *Wandering Jew*]

**Wan|der|jahr** (vän′dər yär′), *n., pl.* **-jah|re** (-yä′rə). a year of travel, especially one taken before settling down to work. [< German *Wanderjahr* < *wandern* wander + *Jahr* year]

**wan|der|lust** (won′dər lust′), *n.* a strong desire to wander: *Her wanderlust led her all over the world.* [< German *Wanderlust* < *wandern* wander + *Lust* desire, longing]

**wan|der|oo** (won′də rü′), *n.* 1 = langur. 2 an In-

**Pronunciation Key:** hat, āge, cãre, fär; let, ēqual, tėrm; it, īce; hot, ōpen, ôrder; oil, out; cup, pu̇t, rüle; child; long; thin; ᴛʜen; zh, measure; ə represents **a** in about, **e** in taken, **i** in pencil, **o** in lemon, **u** in circus.

dian macaque monkey. [< Singhalese *wanteru,* probably < Sanskrit *vānara,* or *vanara* monkey < *vana* forest]

**wan|der|year** (wonʹdər yirʹ), *n.* = Wanderjahr. [translation of German *Wanderjahr*]

**wan|dle** (wänʹdəl), *adj. Scottish.* **1** (of a thing) flexible; supple. **2** (of a person) lithe, agile, or nimble. [apparently < *wand* in a Scottish sense of "supple rod"]

**wane** (wān), *v.,* **waned, wan|ing,** *n.* — ***v.i.*** **1** to lose size; become smaller; diminish: *The moon wanes after it has become full.* **2** to lose power, influence, or importance: *Many great empires have waned.* **SYN**: ebb. **3** to lose strength or intensity: *Their early enthusiasm was waning. The light of day wanes in the evening.* **SYN**: abate. **4** to draw to a close: *Summer wanes as autumn approaches.*
— ***n.*** **1** the act or process of waning. **SYN**: decrease, lessening. **2** the period of waning, especially the period of the decrease of the moon's visible surface. **3** the amount by which a plank or log falls short of a correctly squared shape.
**on** (or **in**) **the wane,** growing less; waning: *His power was on the wane. While overt anit-Catholicism had been on the wane for some years, there were, and still are, many people, including politicians, who benefit from religious divisions* (Manchester Guardian Weekly).
[Old English *wanian*]

**wane|y** (wāʹnē), *adj.* = wany.

**wan|gan** (wongʹgən), *n.* = wanigan.

**wan|gle¹** (wangʹgəl), *v.,* **-gled, -gling.** *Informal.* — ***v.t.*** **1** to manage to get by schemes, tricks, persuasion, or the like: *to wangle an interview with the president.* **2** to change (an account, report, or other datum) dishonestly for one's advantage. **SYN**: falsify, fake, counterfeit.
— ***v.i.*** **1** to make one's way through difficulties. **2** to obtain something by wangling; use irregular means to accomplish a purpose. [perhaps alteration of *waggle*] — **wanʹgler,** *n.*

**wan|gle²** (wangʹgəl), *v.,* **-gled, -gling.** *British Dialect.* — ***v.i.*** to be unsteady; shake; totter; walk unsteadily.
— ***v.t.*** to wiggle; jiggle. [perhaps alteration of *waggle;* influenced by *wankle*] — **wanʹgler,** *n.*

**wan|i|gan** (wonʹə gən), *n.* **1** a lumberman's chest or trunk. **2** a kind of boat used especially by loggers for carrying supplies and tools and as a houseboat. [American English < Algonkian (Abnaki) *waniigan* trap, a receptacle for stray objects]

***wan|ing** (wāʹning), *adj., n.* — ***adj.*** **1** (of the moon) becoming smaller gradually after the full moon. **2** decreasing or declining, as in importance, power, or influence. **3** declining, as in strength or intensity.
— ***n.*** **1** (of the moon) the periodic decrease in apparent size. **2** a decrease or decline, as in importance, power, or influence.

***waning**
definition 1

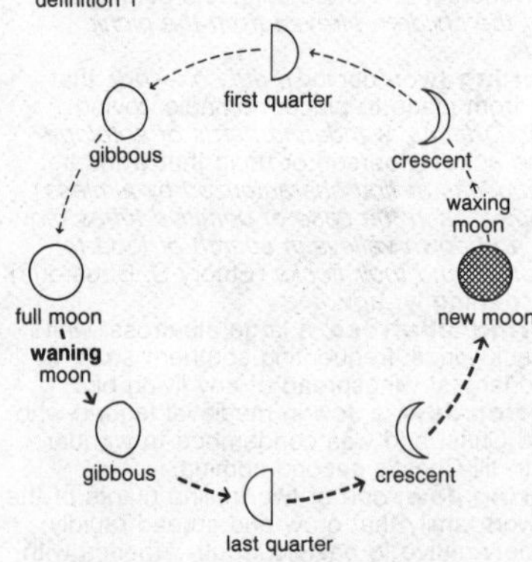

moon's phases as seen from the earth

**wan|ion** (wonʹyən), *n. Archaic.*
**with a** (**wild**) **wanion,** with a vengeance: *Come away, or I'll fetch thee with a wanion* (Shakespeare).
[alteration of Middle English *waniand,* present participle of *wanien,* Old English *wanian* wane, probably in phrase "in the waning moon," that is "in an unlucky hour"]

***Wan|kel engine,** or **Wan|kel** (wangʹkəl; *German* vänʹkəl), *n.* an internal-combustion engine in which the difference in shape of a triangular rotor revolving within a cylinder makes firing chambers that replace conventional pistons and cylinders: *Compared to like-rated conventional engines, the Wankel is 30-50% lighter and smaller, … operates on nonleaded fuel, and is very responsive to antipollution devices* (Frank A. Smith). [< Felix *Wankel,* born 1902, a German engineer, who invented it]

***Wankel engine**

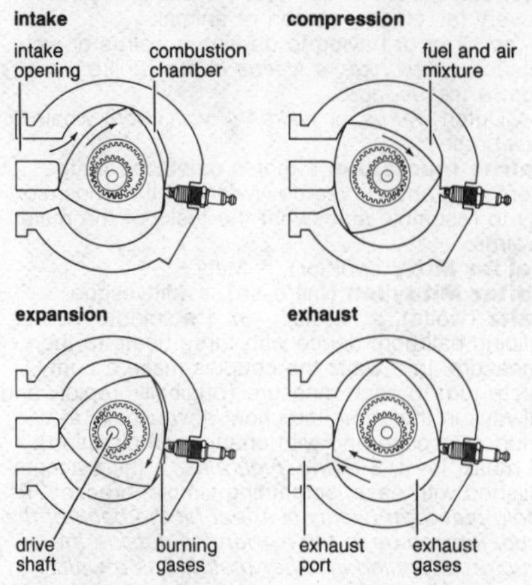


**wan|kle** (wangʹkəl), *adj. British Dialect and Scottish.* **1** unsteady; shaky; tottering. **2** uncertain; precarious. [Middle English *wankel,* Old English *wancol*]

**wan|ni|gan** (wonʹə gən), *n.* = wanigan.

**wan|nish** (wonʹish), *adj.* somewhat wan.

**wan|rest|ful** (won restʹfəl), *adj. Scottish.* restless. [Old English *wan-* lacking + *restful*]

**want** (wont, wônt), *v., n.* — ***v.t.*** **1** to feel that one needs or would like to have; wish for; wish: *The child wants his dinner. Mother wants more children. My brother wants to become an engineer.* **SYN**: desire, crave. **2** to be without; lack: *It sounds fine, but wants sense. The fund for a new church wants only a few hundred dollars of the sum needed.* **SYN**: See syn. under **lack**. **3** to need; require: *Plants want water. Your hands want washing.* **4** to wish to see, speak to, or use (a person): *Call me if you want me. He is the man we want for the job.* **5** to seek after to catch or arrest: *The escaped prisoner is wanted by the police.*
— ***v.i.*** **1** to need food, clothing, and shelter; be very poor: *Waste not, want not.* **2** to be lacking. [< Scandinavian (compare Old Icelandic *vanta* < *vant*); see the noun]
— ***n.*** **1** something desired or needed: *the selfish wants of a spoiled child. He is a man of few wants and is happy with simple pleasures. Food and water are primary wants of human life.* **2** the condition of being without something desired; lack: *a complete want of common sense. The plant died from want of water.* **SYN**: dearth, deficiency, scarcity, insufficiency. **3** a need: *to supply a long-felt want.* **SYN**: requirement, necessity. **4** a lack of food, clothing, or shelter; great poverty: *The old soldier is now in want.* **SYN**: destitution, privation, indigence, straits. See syn. under **poverty**.
**for want of,** because of the lack or absence of: *We sold the store for want of customers.*
**want for,** to be in need of; suffer a shortage of; lack: *to want for nothing.*
**want in,** *Informal.* to desire to enter or have a share in something: *That big advertiser liked the show and wanted in* (Walter Carlson).
**want out,** *Informal.* to desire to leave or take no part in something: *Despite his high standing with the boss, Gordon decided … that he wanted out* (Time).
**want to,** *Informal.* ought to: *You want to eat a balanced diet.*
[< Scandinavian (compare Old Icelandic *vant,* neuter of *vanr,* adjective, lacking)] — **wantʹa|ble,** *adj.*
▶ **a** The use of **want** followed by a noun clause with or without *that* is nonstandard: *I want* (*that*) *you should come home.* So too is the use of **want for** followed by an infinitive phrase: *I want for you to come home.* **b** The omission of the infinitive in locutions like *The cat wants out* or *I want off at the next corner* is common in the popular speech of many regions of the United States. This construction has often been ascribed to the influence of Pennsylvania German, but it appears to be largely of Scotch-Irish origin.

**wan't** (wont, wônt), *U.S. Dialect.* wasn't.
▶ See usage note under **wasn't**.

**want ad,** a small notice in a newspaper, stating that something, such as an employee or an apartment, is wanted; classified ad.

**want|age** (wonʹtij, wônʹ-), *n.* deficiency; shortage.

**want|er** (wonʹtər, wônʹ-), *n.* **1** a person who wants. **2** *Scottish and British Dialect.* a person who wants a wife or a husband.

**want|ing** (wonʹting, wônʹ-), *adj., prep.* — ***adj.*** **1** lacking; missing: *The machine had some of its parts wanting. A dollar of the price is still wanting. One volume of the set is wanting.* **2** not satisfactory; not coming up to a standard or need: *Some people are wanting in courtesy. The vegetables were weighed and found wanting.* **SYN**: deficient. **3** *British Dialect.* mentally defective; weak-minded.
— ***prep.*** without; less; minus; lacking: *a year wanting three days, a man wanting one leg.*

**want|less** (wontʹlis, wôntʹ-), *adj.* having no want; abundant; fruitful. — **wantʹless|ness,** *n.*

**wan|ton** (wonʹtən), *adj., n., v.* — ***adj.*** **1** reckless, heartless, or malicious: *That boy hurts animals from wanton cruelty.* **2** without reason or excuse: *a wanton attack, wanton mischief.* **SYN**: unjustified. **3a** not moral; not chaste: *a wanton person.* **SYN**: dissolute, licentious. **b** lewd; lascivious: *And dancing round him, with wanton looks and bare arms* (Edward G. Bulwer-Lytton). **4** frolicsome; playful: *a wanton breeze, a wanton child. Who for thy table feeds the wanton fawn* (Alexander Pope). **5** profuse in growth; luxuriant; rank: *On the wanton rushes lay you down* (Shakespeare). **6** not restrained: *a wanton mood. How does your tongue grow wanton in her praise* (Joseph Addison). **SYN**: extravagant, unrestrained. **7** *Obsolete.* luxurious; lavish.
— ***n.*** a wanton person, especially a woman.
— ***v.i.*** **1** to act in a wanton manner: *The wind wantoned with the leaves.* **2** to behave as a wanton. **3** (of plants) to grow in profusion; run riot.
— ***v.t.*** to waste foolishly; squander; dissipate: *With this money the King shall wanton away his time in pleasures* (Samuel Pepys).
[Middle English *wantowen* < Old English *wan-* not, lacking + *togen* brought up, past participle of *tēon* to bring] — **wanʹton|er,** *n.* — **wanʹton|ly,** *adv.* — **wanʹton|ness,** *n.*

**want|wit** (wontʹwitʹ, wôntʹ-), *n. Informal.* a person who lacks wit or sense; simpleton.

**wan|y** (wāʹnē), *adj.* **1** having a natural curve or bevel: *a plank with a wany edge.* **2** (of lumber) poor because of curved or beveled edges. Also, **waney.** [< *wane* + *-y¹*]

**wap¹** (wop, wap), *v.,* **wapped, wap|ping,** *n. Dialect.* — ***v.t.*** to throw quickly or with violence (down or to the ground).
— ***v.i.*** to knock (upon); strike (through).
— ***n.*** **1** a blow, knock, or thump. **2** *Scottish.* a sudden storm (of snow). **3** *Scottish.* a fight; quarrel.
[apparently imitative. Compare etym. under **whop**.]

**wap²** (wop, wap), *v.,* **wapped, wap|ping,** *n. Obsolete.* — ***v.t.*** to wrap.
— ***n.*** a turn of a string wrapped around something.
[origin unknown]

**wap|en|take** (wopʹən tāk, wapʹ-), *n.* (formerly, in certain northern and midland counties in England) a division of the county corresponding to the hundred of other counties. [Old English *wǣpentæc,* apparently (originally) the local assembly < Scandinavian (compare Old Icelandic *vāpnatak* (literally) taking of weapons)]

**wap|i|ti** (wopʹə tē), *n., pl.* **-tis** or (*collectively*) **-ti.** a large, reddish deer of western North America, with long, slender antlers; the American elk. [American English < Algonkian (Shawnee) *wapetee*]

**wap|pen|schaw|ing** or **wap|pen|shaw|ing** (wopʹən shôʹing, wapʹ-), *n.* (in Scottish history) a periodical muster or review of the men under arms in a particular district. [< Scottish *wapin* weapon + *schawing* showing]

**wap|per-jawed** (wopʹər jôdʹ), *adj. Informal.* having a crooked or undershot jaw. [American English, perhaps < obsolete *wapper* to waver]

**war¹** (wôr), *n., v.,* **warred, war|ring,** *adj.* — ***n.*** **1a** fighting carried on by armed force between nations or parts of a nation: *to repudiate war as a means of settling international disputes, to prepare for war.* **SYN**: warfare, hostilities. **b** an instance or particular period of this: *a veteran of two wars, to remember the dead on both sides in the last war.* **2** *Figurative.* any fighting or struggle; strife; conflict: *a trade war. Doctors carry on war against disease.* **3a** the occupation or art of fighting with weapons; military science: *Soldiers are trained for war.* **b** the division of a government responsible for the armed forces, military planning, budgets, and the like: *to appoint a new secretary of war.* **4** *Archaic.* a battle.
— ***v.i.*** **1** to make war; fight: *brother warring against brother, to war with an aggressor. Germany warred against France.* **2** *Figurative.* to carry on any struggle actively; contend; battle: *to war against all things mean or petty.*
— ***adj.*** **1** of or having to do with war: *war crimes.* **2** used in war: *war weapons.* **3** caused by war: *war casualties.*

**at war**, taking part in a war: *The United States was at war with Great Britain in 1812.* (*Figurative.*) *Teetotalers and moderate drinkers will probably be at war on this point ... as long as the world lasts* (Graphic).
**go to war**, **a** to enter into a state of war; start a war: *The aim of the nation in going to war is exactly the same as that of an individual in entering a court; it wants its rights, or what it alleges to be its rights* (James Mozley). **b** to go as a soldier or sailor in a war: *The minstrel boy to the war is gone* (Thomas Moore).
**make war**, to engage in war; fight a war: *Aristotle maintained the general right of making war upon barbarians* (William Paley).
[< Old North French *werre,* Old French *guerre* < Germanic (compare Old High German *werra*)]

**war²** (wär), *adj., adv., v.,* **warred, war|ring.** *Scottish.* —**adv., adj.** worse.
—*v.t.* to worst. Also, **waur.**
[< Scandinavian (compare Old Icelandic *verri,* adjective, and *verr,* adverb). See related etym. at **worse.**]

**war³** (wär), *v.t., v.i. Dialect.* ware².

**war⁴** (wär), *n. Obsolete.* ware¹.

**war baby**, **1** a child born in wartime; child of a soldier: *about 1965, when the greatest number of so-called war babies, born in the nineteen-forties,* [*were*] *of college age* (New Yorker). **2** *Informal.* **a** an industry that is stimulated by war or threat of war. **b** a stock or security of such an industry: *The war babies—copper, chemical, oil, rubber and steel issues—attracted most investor interest* (New York Times).

**War Between the States**, the American Civil War.

**war|ble¹** (wôr′bəl), *v.,* **-bled, -bling,** *n.* —*v.i.* **1** to sing with trills, quavers, or melodious turns: *Birds warbled in the trees.* **2** to make a sound like that of a bird warbling: *The brook warbled over its rocky bed.* **SYN:** purl, ripple. **3** *U.S.* yodel.
—*v.t.* **1** to sing with melodious runs, trills, quavers, or turns. **2** to express in or as if in song; sing.
—*n.* **1** a melodious song with trills and quavers. **2** any sound like warbling. **3** the act of warbling.
[< Old North French *werbler* < *werble* a flourish, melody < Germanic (compare Old High German *wirbel* a whirl)]

**war|ble²** (wôr′bəl), *n.* **1** a small, hard tumor, caused by the pressure of the saddle on a horse's back. **2** a small tumor or swelling on the back of cattle, deer, and some other animals, produced by the larva of the warble fly. **3** a warble fly, especially in its larval form. Also, **wabble.**
[origin uncertain. Compare obsolete Swedish *varbulde* boil.]

**war|bled** (wôr′bəld), *adj.* affected with or injured by warbles.

**warble fly**, any one of certain flies whose larvae burrow under the skin of cattle, deer, and other animals, forming warbles.

**war|bler** (wôr′blər), *n.* **1** a person or bird that warbles; singer; songster. **2** any one of several kinds of small songbirds, often brightly colored. The wood warblers include the redstart, water thrush, chat, yellow warbler, myrtle warbler, and ovenbird, among others. **3** any one of various small, plain-colored songbirds of the Old World, such as the blackcap and whitethroat.

**war|bling vireo** (wôr′bling), a small, plain-colored vireo that lives in high woodlands of North America and has a melodious warble.

**war bond**, *U.S.* a government bond issued in World War II.

***war bonnet**, a ceremonial headdress of skin set with feathers and often a long trailing piece with feathers, worn by certain North American Indians: *Indians ... with the long red streamers of their war bonnets reaching nearly to the ground* (John C. Frémont).

***war bonnet**

**war-born** (wôr′bôrn′), *adj.* produced or developed during war; resulting from a war: *The war-born alliance grew to greatness out of sheer necessity and through the personal relationships of Roosevelt and Churchill* (Atlantic).

**war bride**, the bride of a soldier or sailor in wartime.

**war chest**, a fund of money put aside to pay for the costs of some undertaking, especially a political campaign: *In the current campaign businessmen are actively at work in a traditional role for them in politics—raising money for party war chests* (Wall Street Journal).

**war cloud**, **1** a cloud of dust and smoke rising from a battlefield. **2** something that threatens war: *Markets fall into a well-known pattern when war clouds gather* (Economist).

**war club**, a heavy club used as a weapon.

**war college**, a school for teaching advanced military techniques to officers.

**war correspondent**, a person employed by a newspaper, magazine, or radio station to send news from overseas about a war, especially first-hand accounts of the fighting: *Stephen Crane was another great writer to gain fame as a war correspondent* (Gordon Sabine).

**war|craft** (wôr′kraft′, -kräft′), *n., pl.* **-craft. 1** any ship or aircraft used in war: *Still other jet and propellered warcraft provided close air support* (New York Times). **2** the science or art of war; cunning and skill in warfare.

**war crime**, a violation of the rules of warfare, especially any inhuman act against civilians or prisoners in time of war.

**war criminal**, a person convicted of committing a war crime: *Berlin's ancient Spandau Fortress* [*served*] *as a prison for Germany's most notorious war criminals* (Newsweek).

**war cry**, **1** a word or phrase shouted in fighting; battle cry. **2** any cry or slogan used in rallying people to a cause.

**ward** (wôrd), *n., v.* —*n.* **1** a division of a hospital or prison: **a** a section often a long room, of a hospital, accomodating several or many patients: *a children's ward, a charity ward.* **b** a single large room or group of rooms or cells, formerly comprising a section of a prison, especially in Great Britain. **2a** a district of a city or town, especially one represented by an alderman. **b** an administrative division of certain counties in northern England and Scotland; wapentake; hundred. **c** the people in any of these. **3** a small administrative district within the Mormon Church. It is part of a stake. **4a** a person, especially a child or insane person under the care of a guardian or of a court. **b** the status of such a person; legal guardianship. **c** any guardianship; custody. **5** guard: *The soldiers kept watch and ward over the castle.* **6a** any defensive movement or position in fencing; parry. **b** *Archaic.* any defensive movement, attitude, or position. **7a** any one of the slots or notches in a key that slide past projections inside the lock. **b** a corresponding projection or ridge in a lock. **8** in feudal law: **a** a lord's guardianship of the infant heir of a deceased tenant, including the control and use of the heir's lands until he came of age. **b** land given to the (Scottish) crown in payment for exemption from military service. **9** any one of certain fortified parts of a castle, especially: **a** an open area within or between the walls. See picture under **castle. b** *Obsolete.* a guarded entrance. **c** *Obsolete.* the part of a fortress entrusted to a particular officer and his men. **10** *Obsolete.* **a** a company, group, or detachment of watchmen. **b** any watchman; sentinel; guard. **c** a garrison. **11** *Obsolete.* **a** any one of the three parts (van, middle, rear) of an army on the march. **b** a separate part of an army led by a subordinate commander. [Old English *weard* a guarding, guard. Compare etym. under **ware².**]
—*v.t.* **1** to put into a ward, especially of a hospital. **2** *Archaic.* to keep watch over.
—*v.i. Archaic.* to parry blows; stand on the defensive.
**ward off**, **a** to keep away; turn aside: *to erect a fence to ward off dogs. The big stone barn had been ... equipped with hex signs to ward off ... cattle* (S. J. Perelman). **b** to prevent: *The telephone is his lifeline; through it he tries to ward off insanity and to forestall his collapse* (New Yorker).
[Old English *weardian* to guard. See related etym. at **guard.**] —**ward′less,** *adj.*

**-ward**, *suffix forming adverbs and adjectives.* tending or leading to ___; in the direction of ___; toward ___: *Homeward = in the direction of home. Backward = toward the back.* See also **-wards.** [Old English *-weard,* adjective and adverb suffix]
► When pairs like *downward-downwards, eastward-eastwards* exist, both are used as adverbs (or, in the case of *toward-towards,* as a preposition), but only the forms without *-s* occur as adjectives: *He fell forward*(*s*)*; a forward movement.* The adjectival form is the one usually employed as a noun: *looking to the westward.*

**war dance**, a dance of primitive tribes before going to war or to celebrate a victory.

**ward boss**, *U.S.* the political leader of a ward: *Jauntily,* [*he*] *moved among his hard-drinking guests, smiling and shaking hands like a ward boss* (Time).

**ward|ed** (wôr′did), *adj.* (of a key or lock) constructed with wards.

**ward|en¹** (wôr′dən), *n., v.* —*n.* **1** the official in charge of a prison; head keeper. **2** an official who enforces certain laws and regulations: *an air-raid warden.* **3** = game warden. **4** = fire-warden. **5** = churchwarden. **6** a person in charge of a place or its contents; keeper, guard, or custodian. **SYN:** watchman. **7** in England: **a** the head of certain schools or colleges; principal; master. **b** any one of the trustees of certain schools, hospitals, or guilds. **c** the superintendent of a port or market. **d** an officer holding any of certain positions of trust, now usually honorary or ceremonial, under the Crown: *Warden of the Cinque Ports.* **8** the chief official in a town or area in former times. **9a** the chief executive officer of a county in Canada. **b** the head of a borough in Connecticut. **c** a magistrate who is the chief government officer of a gold field in Australia. **10** = gatekeeper. **11** *Obsolete.* anyone who guards; protector; defender; guardian.
—*v.i.* to guard or protect as a game warden: *The wardening of Exmoor, for example, with its wide acres of moorland under rising pressure of visitors, is described as rudimentary* (Manchester Guardian Weekly).
[< Old North French *wardein,* Anglo-French *gardein.* See etym. of doublet **guardian.**]

**ward|en²** or **Ward|en** (wôr′dən), *n. Especially British.* a variety of winter cooking pear. [Middle English *wardon,* probably < unrecorded Anglo-French < *warder* to keep, Old French *garder.* Compare etym. under **guard.**]

**ward|en|ry** (wôr′dən rē), *n., pl.* **-ries.** the office or position of warden.

**ward|en|ship** (wôr′dən ship), *n.* the position or office of a warden.

**ward|er¹** (wôr′dər), *n.* **1** a guard or watchman. **SYN:** sentinel. **2** *British.* a warden or jailor. [< Anglo-French *wardere,* and *wardour,* Old North French *warder,* Old French *guarder.* Compare etym. under **guard.**]

**ward|er²** (wôr′dər), *n.* **1** (in early use) a staff or wand. **2** (later) the baton or truncheon carried as a symbol of office, command, or authority, especially as used to give the signal for the commencement or cessation of hostilities in a battle or tournament. [origin uncertain]

**ward|er|ship** (wôr′dər ship), *n.* **1** the office or position of warder. **2** the carrying out of the duties of a warder.

**ward heeler**, *Informal.* a follower of a political boss, who distributes literature, asks for votes, and does other minor tasks: *Back-benchers find it harder than ministers do to see the evil of patronage, and ward heelers find it hardest of all* (Maclean's).

**War|di|an case** (wôr′dē ən), a close-fitting case with glass sides and top for growing and transporting small ferns and other plants. [< Nathaniel B. *Ward,* 1791-1868, the English botanist who invented it + *-ian*]

**ward|mote** (wôrd′mōt), *n. British.* a meeting of the citizens of a ward, especially a meeting of the liverymen of a ward under the presidency of the alderman to discuss local affairs. [< *ward* + *mote,* as in *gemote*]

**ward|ress** (wôr′dris), *n.* a female warder in a prison.

**ward|robe** (wôrd′rōb′), *n.* **1a** a stock of clothes: *She is shopping for her spring wardrobe.* **SYN:** apparel, clothing. **b** *Figurative: More and more it makes sense to analyze a family's needs and provide a wardrobe of cars to meet them* (Wall Street Journal). **2** a room, closet, or piece of furniture for holding clothes. **3a** the department of a royal or noble household charged with the care of the wearing apparel. **b** the building in which the officers of this department conduct their business. [< Old North French *warderobe,* Old French *garderobe* < *guarder* to guard + *robe* gown, robe. Compare etym. under **guard, robe.**]

**wardrobe case**, a suitcase in which suits or dresses are carried on hangers to avoid wrinkling.

**wardrobe mistress**, a woman in charge of the professional wardrobe of an actress or of a theatrical company.

**wardrobe trunk**, a trunk designed to stand on end when opened, usually with hangers and drawers for clothes.

**ward|room** (wôrd′rüm′, -rům′), *n.* **1** the living and eating quarters for all the commissioned officers on a warship except the commanding officer.

**Pronunciation Key:** hat, āge, cãre, fär; let, ēqual, tėrm; it, īce; hot, ōpen, ôrder; oil, out; cup, pu̇t, rüle; child; long; thin; ᴛʜen; zh, measure; ə represents **a** in about, **e** in taken, **i** in pencil, **o** in lemon, **u** in circus.

2 these officers as a group.

**-wards**, *suffix forming adverbs.* in the direction of ___; toward ___: *Backwards = in the direction of or toward the back.* [Old English *-weardes,* adverbial suffix]

► See **-ward** for usage note.

**ward|ship** (wôrd′ship), *n.* **1a** guardianship over a minor or ward; guardianship; custody. **b** (in feudal law) the guardianship and custody of a minor with all profits accruing during his minority. **c** any guardianship; custody. **2** the condition of being a ward, or under a legal or feudal guardian.

**ward sister**, *British.* a nurse in charge of a hospital ward.

**ware**[1] (wãr), *n.* **1** a kind of manufactured thing; article for sale (now chiefly in compounds): *silverware and tinware.* **2** what anyone produces by his own effort and offers for sale: *the ware of a sculptor, short stories and other literary wares.* **3a** pottery or other ceramic objects: *porcelain ware. Delft is a blue-and-white ware.* **b** such objects in a raw or unfinished state: *The ware must be thoroughly dry before firing.*

**wares**, articles for sale; manufactured goods: *The peddler sold his wares from door to door.* [Old English *waru*]

**ware**[2] (wãr), *adj., v.,* **wared, war|ing.** *Archaic.* —*adj.* **1** aware. **2** watchful; vigilant. **3** prudent; sagacious; cunning. [Old English *wær* alert, wise] —*v.t., v.i.* to look out (for); beware (of). [partly Old English *warian* give heed; partly Old North French *warer* to guard; protect. See related etym. at **warn.**]

**ware**[3] (wãr), *v.t.,* **wared, war|ing.** *Scottish.* **1** to spend; lay out (money or goods in, on, upon). **2** *Figurative.* to squander or dissipate (as time, energy, or emotion); waste. [< Scandinavian (compare Old Icelandic *verja* lay out or invest money; originally, to clothe). See related etym. at **wear**[1].]

**ware|house** (*n.* wãr′hous′; *v.* wãr′houz′, -hous′), *n., v.,* **-housed, -hous|ing.** —*n.* **1** a place where goods are kept, especially in large quantities; storehouse. SYN: depot, depository, entrepôt. **2** *Especially British.* **a** a store where goods are sold wholesale. **b** a large retail establishment. —*v.t.* **1** to put or deposit in a warehouse, as for storage. **2** to place in a bonded warehouse, or in government or customhouse custody, to be kept until duties are paid.

**ware|house|man** (wãr′hous′mən), *n., pl.* **-men.** **1** a person who receives and stores the goods of others for pay, without assuming ownership, such as the owner of a warehouse. **2** a person who works in a warehouse.

**ware|hous|er** (wãr′hou′zər), *n.* = warehouseman.

**ware|hous|ing** (wãr′hou′zing), *n.* **1a** the depositing of goods, etc., in a warehouse: *The building, containing 6,000 square feet of space, will be used for manufacturing, warehousing, and distribution* (New York Times). **b** the money paid for the service of a warehouse. **2** a financial transaction in which a short-term lender, such as a commercial bank, extends credit on long-term investments, such as mortgages, to individuals or institutions, until the borrower is able to get a long-term lender, such as a savings bank or insurance company, to take over the loan.

**ware|room** (wãr′rüm′, -rům′), *n.* a room in which goods are shown and offered for sale.

**wares** (wãrz), *n.pl.* See under **ware**[1].

**war|fare** (wôr′fãr′), *n.* **1** war; fighting; armed conflict: *Modern warfare has moved away from the days when soldiers with rifles were the most important part of an army* (Payson S. Wild). **2** *Figurative.* any struggle or contest. [Middle English *werefare* < *werre* war, conflict + *fare* a going, Old English *faru* journey]

**war|far|in** (wôr′fər in), *n.* a highly potent drug used as an anticoagulant for humans, and as a rat poison. *Formula:* $C_{19}H_{16}O_4$ [< *W*(isconsin) *A*(lumni) *R*(esearch) *F*(oundation) + *-arin,* as in *coumarin*]

**war footing**, the condition or state of being engaged in or prepared, mobilized, and equipped for war.

**war game**, a training exercise that imitates war. It may be an exercise on a map or maneuvers with actual troops, weapons, and equipment.

**war-game** (wôr′gãm′), *v.,* **-gamed, -gam|ing.** —*v.t.* to develop or test (a plan, strategy, or the like) by means of a war game. —*v.i.* to engage in or play a war game: *Wargaming is the preoccupation of tens of thousands of mini-generals round the world* (Time). —**war′-gam′er,** *n.*

**war|hawk** (wôr′hôk′), *n. U.S.* a person who is eager for war. [< *War Hawk*]

**War Hawk** or **war hawk**, *U.S. History.* any one of a group of Congressmen, led by Henry Clay, who advocated going to war with Great Britain in the years 1810-12. [coined by Thomas Jefferson]

**war|head** (wôr′hed′), *n.* the forward part of a torpedo, ballistic missile, or rocket, that contains the explosive. By the attaching of the warhead the weapon is made ready (armed) for use. *A missile carrying an atomic warhead can speed 6,000 miles in 25 minutes, giving little opportunity for advance warning* (Leo A. Hoegh).

**war horse**, **1** a horse used in war; charger. **2** *Informal, Figurative.* **a** a person who has taken part in many wars, campaigns, or battles; veteran soldier, sailor, etc. **b** a veteran actor, politician, or other public figure. **c** any well-known, standard, and somewhat trite work of art or activity: *two old war horses—the grammar school play and the social studies project* (New York Times).

**war|i|ly** (wãr′ə lē), *adv.* cautiously; with care; in a wary manner: *The hikers climbed warily up the dangerous path. He hesitated warily before going into politics.* SYN: carefully, gingerly, heedfully.

**war|i|ness** (wãr′ē nis), *n.* caution; care: *He looked at her with the hopeful wariness of a puppy who isn't sure whether he has done wrong* (John Strange). SYN: vigilance, watchfulness.

**war|i|son** (war′ə sən), *n.* a war cry; battle cry. Also, **warrison.** [mistaken by Sir Walter Scott from Old English *warison* gift; wealth, treasure < Old North French, Old French *garison.* See etym. of doublet **garrison.**]

**wark**[1] (wärk), *n., v. Dialect.* —*n.* a pain; ache. —*v.i.* to ache; suffer pain. [Old English *wærc*]

**wark**[2] (wärk), *n., adj., v.i., v.t. Dialect.* work.

**war|less** (wôr′lis), *adj.* free or exempt from war; not engaging in war: *There is in many places a willingness to face war again, if that be necessary, rather than see the new hopes lost to warless conquest* (Wall Street Journal).

**war|like** (wôr′līk′), *adj.* **1** fit for war; ready for war; fond of war: *warlike tribes.* **2** courageous in war; valiant. **3** threatening war: *a warlike speech.* SYN: belligerent, hostile. **4** of or having to do with war: *warlike music.* SYN: martial. See syn. under **military.** —**war′like′ness,** *n.*

**war|lock** (wôr′lok), *n.* **1** = wizard. **2** = magician. SYN: sorcerer. [Old English *wǣrloga* devil, traitor; (literally) oath-breaker < *wǣr* covenant + *-loga* one who denies, related to *lēogan* to lie, dissemble]

**war lord** or **war|lord** (wôr′lôrd′), *n.* **1** a military commander or commander in chief, especially one who has sovereign authority in a particular country or region, whether conferred under law or usurped by force. **2** the military head of a province in China during the period 1916-1923; tuchun.

**war|lord|ism** (wôr′lôr′diz əm), *n.* the principles and practices of a war lord: *The United States Embassy ... hailed the ouster of General Thi as "a step toward political stability" and "a defeat for warlordism"* (New York Times).

**warm** (wôrm), *adj., adv., v., n.* —*adj.* **1** more hot than cold; having some heat; giving forth gentle heat: *a warm fire. She sat in the warm sunshine.* **2a** having a feeling of heat: *to be warm from running.* **b** producing such a feeling: *warm work.* **3** that makes or keeps warm: *We wear warm clothes in winter.* **4** subject to or characterized by the prevalence of a comparatively high temperature, or of moderate heat: *a warm climate, warm countries.* **5** having the degree of heat natural to living beings: *warm blood.* **6** *Figurative.* **a** having or showing affection, enthusiasm, or zeal: *a warm heart, warm regard, warm thanks, a warm welcome, a warm friend.* SYN: cordial, hearty, fervent, enthusiastic. **b** amorous or passionate. **7** *Figurative.* **a** easily excited: *a warm temper.* SYN: fiery, peppery. **b** showing irritation or anger: *warm language.* **8** *Figurative.* exciting; lively: *a warm dispute.* **9** fresh and strong: *a warm scent.* **10** *Informal.* near what one is searching for, as in games. **11** suggesting heat. Red, orange, and yellow are called warm colors. **12** *Informal, Figurative.* uncomfortable, unpleasant, or disagreeable: *to make things warm for a person.* **13** *Informal.* well-to-do; wealthy; rich. —*adv.* so as to be warm; warmly. —*v.t.* **1** to make warm, as by heating, exercise, or clothing; heat: *to warm a room.* **2** *Figurative.* to make cheered, interested, friendly, or sympathetic: *Her happiness warms my heart.* **3** *Figurative.* to make excited, enthusiastic, eager, or zealous: *He is warmed by his success.* —*v.i.* **1** to become warm. **2** *Figurative.* to become cheered, interested, friendly, or sympathetic: *The speaker warmed to his subject.* —*n. Informal.* the act or process of warming; heating.

**warm over**, *Informal.* to rehash: *The Mirror got the Bishop of Woolwich to warm over his controversial views* (Time).

**warm up**, **a** to heat or cook again: *She requests to have that little bit of sweetbread that was left, warmed up for the supper* (Dickens). **b** *Figurative.* to make or become more cheered, interested, or friendly; acquire zest: *She warmed up on the subject* (Harper's). **c** to practice or exercise for a few minutes before entering a game or contest or beginning to sing or play an instrument: *Actors could warm up before the curtain by, for instance, improvising the faculty party that takes place before Albee's "Virginia Woolf?" begins* (Manchester Guardian Weekly). **d** to run (a machine) before using it until it reaches its normal working condition: *We always warm up the car engine on cold mornings.* [Old English *wearm*] —**warm′er,** *n.* —**warm′ly,** *adv.* —**warm′ness,** *n.*

**war|mak|er** (wôr′mā′kər), *n.* = warmonger.

**war|mak|ing** (wôr′mā′king), *adj.* of or for making or waging war: *Our nation has enough power in its strategic retaliatory forces to bring near annihilation to the warmaking capacities of any country* (Newsweek).

**warm-blood|ed** (wôrm′blud′id), *adj.* **1** having warm blood or blood that stays about the same temperature regardless of the air or water around the animal. The normal body temperature of warm-blooded animals is between 98 degrees and 112 degrees Fahrenheit or about 40 degrees centigrade (Celsius). Cats and birds are warm-blooded; snakes and turtles are cold-blooded. **2** *Figurative.* with much feeling; eager; ardent. SYN: fervent, passionate. —**warm′-blood′ed-ness,** *n.*

**warmed-o|ver** (wôrmd′ō′vər), *adj.* **1** warmed again, as food that has become cold; reheated. **2** *Figurative: American televiewers are in for the largest helping of warmed-over fare in TV history this summer* (Newsweek). SYN: old, stale.

**war memorial**, a monument in memory of a battle or those killed in battle: *the marble war memorial, that the best local stonemason builds in the market place—set round with the green of living grass and with benches for widows* (Wolfgang Borchert).

**warm front**, the advancing edge of a warm air mass as it passes over and displaces a cooler one.

**warm-heart|ed** (wôrm′här′tid), *adj.* kind; sympathetic; friendly: *He was, by the account of such intimates as Secretary of State Frank B. Kellogg, "a warm-hearted, charming gentleman"* (Newsweek). SYN: kindly, tender. —**warm′-heart′ed|ly,** *adv.* —**warm′-heart′ed|ness,** *n.*

* **warm|ing pan** (wôr′ming), a covered pan with a long handle for holding hot coals, formerly used to warm beds.

* **warming pan**

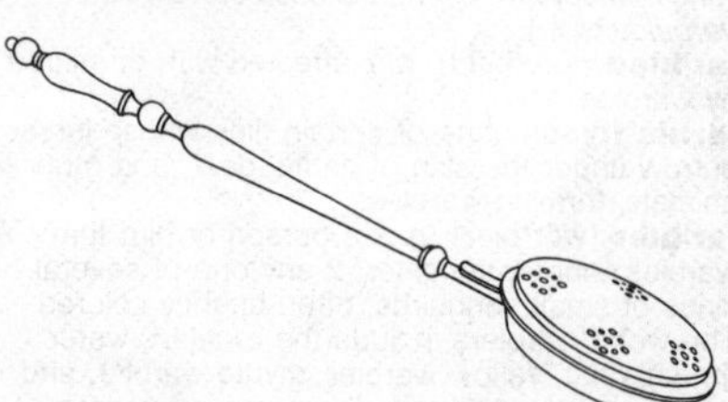

**warm|ing-up** (wôr′ming up′), *n.* a making or becoming warm or warmer; increase of warmth: *a warming-up of the weather.*

**warm|ish** (wôr′mish), *adj.* rather warm. SYN: lukewarm, tepid. —**warm′ish|ly,** *adv.* —**warm′ish-ness,** *n.*

**war|mon|ger** (wôr′mung′gər, -mong′-), *n.* a person who is strongly in favor of war or attempts to bring about war: *On May Days past ... the chunky rulers of Russia had hurled the condemnations at the U.S. warmongers and bellicosely pointed to their own armed strength in the square below and in the skies above* (Time).

**war|mon|ger|ing** (wôr′mung′gər ing, -mong′-), *n., adj.* —*n.* the acts or practices of a warmonger: *As the tension increased and Americans became more concerned about the war in Europe, the isolationists became extremely worried, and some of them accused Roosevelt of warmongering* (Gerald Johnson). —*adj.* of or having to do with a warmonger or warmongers.

**war|mouth** (wôr′mouth′), *n.* a large-mouthed, voracious, freshwater sunfish of the eastern and southern United States.

**warmth** (wôrmth), *n.* **1** the condition of being warm: *We enjoyed the warmth of the open fire.* **2** *Figurative.* warm or friendly feeling: *to greet a person with warmth.* **3** *Figurative.* liveliness of feelings or emotions; fervor: *She spoke with warmth of the natural beauty of the mountains.* SYN: zeal, ardor. **4** a glowing effect in painting, as produced by the use of reds and yellows.

**warm-up** (wôrm′up′), *n., adj.* —*n.* **1** the practice

or exercise taken for a few minutes before entering a game, contest, or performance: *My fingers felt cold, so I played some Bach, which is a very good warm-up* (New Yorker). **2** a period of running required for a machine to reach normal working condition before use: *Transistor radios require no warm-up. Four plane-makers ... have spent $2,742,000 on equipment to muffle the sound of jet warm-ups* (Newsweek). **3** a preliminary trial or session before the main contest, exhibition, or undertaking: *two wonderful pre-session warm-ups ... while the studio engineers were adjusting their equipment* (Saturday Review). *The observations planned this year ... at observatories all over the world will be a warm-up for the even closer approach two years from now* (Science News Letter).
— ***adj.*** for or as a warm-up; preliminary: *a warm-up run, a warm-up game before the season.*

**warn** (wôrn), *v.t.* **1** to give notice to in advance; put on guard (against danger, evil, or harm): *The clouds warned us that a storm was coming.* **2** to give notice to; inform: *The whistle warned visitors that the ship was ready to sail.* **SYN**: appraise, notify. **3** to give notice as to go or stay: *to warn off trespassers, to warn a child to remain in the house.* **4** to remind (of); counsel (against); admonish: *to warn a man of his duty, warn a driver against speeding.*
— ***v.i.*** to give a warning or warnings; sound an alarm.
[Old English *wearnian.* See related etym. at **ware**[2].] — **warn′er**, *n.*
— ***Syn.*** *v.t.* **1 Warn, caution** mean to give notice of possible or coming danger, harm, risk, or unpleasantness. **Warn** implies giving clear and firm notice, especially of an imminent or serious danger: *The children were warned not to speak to strangers.* **Caution** implies giving notice of a possible danger and advice about avoiding it: *Citrus growers are cautioned to protect the fruit from frost.*

**war neurosis**, = shell shock.

**warn|ing** (wôr′ning), *n., adj.* — ***n.*** **1** the action of putting on guard or giving notice: *death without warning.* **SYN**: admonition, advice. **2** something that warns; notice given in advance: *Let this experience be a warning to you to be more careful.* **SYN**: admonition, advice.
— ***adj.*** that warns. — **warn′ing|ly**, *adv.*

**warning coloration**, natural coloring or marking of an animal that serves to warn or alarm enemies.

**warning net**, any system or network of communications set up to give warning of aggressive enemy movements, such as those of enemy aircraft.

**war nose**, **1** the nose of a shell, which contains the detonator for the bursting charge. **2** = warhead.

**warn't** (wornt, wôrnt), *U.S. Dialect.* **1** wasn't. **2** weren't.

**war of liberation**, (in Communist parlance) warfare, especially guerrilla warfare, conducted against a government that is pro-Western or anti-Communist: *A Communist takeover in South Vietnam would be followed by similar "wars of liberation" in other countries* (New York Times).

**war of nerves**, a conflict in which tension is built up by intimidation, propaganda, or obstructive or delaying tactics rather than by use or threat of violence: *Both sides are digging in for a war of nerves with each determined to wait out the other to get the price it wants* (Wall Street Journal).

**War of Secession**, the American Civil War.

**warp** (wôrp), *v., n.* — ***v.t.*** **1** to bend, curve, or twist (an object) out of shape; permanently distort the shape of, as by shrinking or heating: *Age had warped and cracked the floor boards.* **2** *Figurative.* to make not as it should be; cause not to work as it should; mislead; pervert: *Prejudice warps our judgment.* **3** *Figurative.* **a** to pervert the meaning of (a statement); misrepresent. **b** to distort (a meaning purpose, or intention); misinterpret. **4** to move (as a ship) by taking up on ropes fastened to something fixed, such as a dock. **5** to bend or twist (a wing or airfoil) at the end or ends: *The aviator warped a wing tip to regain balance.* **6** to arrange (threads or yarn) so as to form a warp. **7** to improve the quality of (land) by flooding with a deposit of alluvial soil.
— ***v.i.*** **1** to become bent, curved, or twisted out of shape, by contraction or expansion, or both: *A steel girder may warp in a fire. This old board has warped so that it does not lie flat.* **2** *Figurative.* to be made not as it should be; be distorted, twisted, misled, or perverted: *There is our commission From which we would not have you warp* (Shakespeare). **3a** (of a ship) to be moved by warping. **b** (of the crew) to move a ship thus. **4** *Obsolete.* to leave one's proper route; swerve; stray (from). [Old English *weorpan* to throw, hit with a missile; twist]
— ***n.*** **1** the condition of being twisted; bend or twist; distortion: *a warp in wood that has dried unevenly.* **2** *Figurative.* a distortion of judgment; mental twist; bias. **3a** a rope fixed at one end and pulled upon to move a ship. **b** a rope attached to a net in trawl fishing. **c** a harpoon line attached to the main line in whaling. **4** the threads or yarn running lengthwise in a fabric. The warp is crossed by the woof. See picture under **loom**[1]. **5a** alluvial sediment; silt. **b** a rich bed or layer of this, made by artificial flooding.
**warp and woof**, fabric; structure: *Apartheid is woven deeply into the warp and woof of society as it is organized ... in South Africa* (New York Times).
[Old English *wearp* < *werp-*, root of *weorpan* to throw, warp] — **warp′er**, *n.*

**warp|age** (wôr′pij), *n.* **1** the act of warping or condition of being warped: *Lumber will be glued together in laminations for less warpage* (Science News Letter). **2** a charge for warping or hauling ships entering certain harbors.

**war paint**, **1** paint put on the face or body by North American Indians, members of some African tribes, and some other groups before going to war. **2** *Slang, Figurative.* **a** best clothes and finery; full dress; ornaments. **b** cosmetics; makeup.

**war party**, **1** a group of North American Indian warriors banded together for a fighting expedition. **2** a political party that favors war.

**war|path** (wôr′path′, -päth′), *n.* the way taken by a fighting expedition of North American Indians.
**on the warpath**, **a** at or ready for war: *The two enemy tribes are on the warpath again.* **b** *Figurative.* looking for a fight; angry: *A tremendous rapping at my door announced that Bobby was again on the warpath* (Mrs. J. H. Riddell).

**warp beam**, the roller or other apparatus in a loom around which the warp is wound.

**warp-knit|ted** (wôrp′nit′id), *adj.* (of fabrics) made by warp knitting.

**warp knitting**, knitting by machine using many threads of yarn in the direction of the length.

**war|plane** (wôr′plān′), *n.* an airplane used in war rather than for pleasure or commerce.

**warp-print|ed** (wôrp′prin′tid), *adj.* (of textiles) woven after a roller print design has been applied to the warp yarns only, using a filling yarn that is a solid color for unusual effects: *a warp-printed satin dress.*

**warp-proof** (wôrp′prüf′), *adj.* protected against warping: *The door, which has extruded aluminum frames, is said to be weather-resistant, shatter-proof, and warp-proof* (Science News Letter).

**warp sizing**, the application of a sizing solution to the warp yarns of a fabric before weaving, to increase strength and smoothness and add weight to the finished fabric.

**war|rant** (wôr′ənt, wor′-), *n., v.* — ***n.*** **1** that which gives a right; authority: *He had no warrant for his action.* **SYN**: sanction, authorization. **2** a written order giving authority for something: *a warrant for the payment of money. Canada's War Measures Act ... permits police to search and arrest without warrants and to deny bail* (Paul D. Stevens). **3** a good and sufficient reason: *to suspect a friend without warrant. He had no warrant for his hopes.* **4a** a document certifying something, especially to a purchaser; written guarantee. **b** any guarantee; certification; promise. **5** the official certificate of appointment issued to a non-commissioned officer in the army or navy. **6** a certificate giving the holder the right to buy a stated number of shares of stock of a corporation at a specific price. **7** *Especially British.* a receipt given to a person who has deposited goods in a warehouse, by assignment of which the title to the goods is transferred; warehouse receipt. **8** a person who answers for a fact; authoritative witness. **9** *Obsolete.* a person or thing that serves as guaranty; security.
— ***v.t.*** **1** to authorize: *The law warrants his arrest.* **SYN**: sanction. **2** to justify: *Nothing can warrant such rudeness.* **3** to give one's word for; guarantee; promise: *The storekeeper warranted the quality of the eggs.* **SYN**: assure. **4** to attest the truth or authenticity of; authenticate. **5a** to guarantee to (the purchaser of goods) the security of the title to the goods; guarantee to indemnify for loss. **b** to guarantee (a title) or guarantee the title to (a person) of granted property. **6** *Informal.* to assert as probable to the point of certainty; declare positively; certify: *I'll warrant he won't try that again.* **SYN**: affirm, attest.
[< Old North French *warant,* Old French *guarant;* see etym. under **warranty**]

**war|rant|a|bil|i|ty** (wôr′ən tə bil′ə tē, wor′-), *n.* the quality of being warrantable.

**war|rant|a|ble** (wôr′ən tə bəl, wor′-), *adj.* **1** that can be warranted; justifiable; defensible. **2** old enough to be hunted, as deer. — **war′rant|a|ble|ness**, *n.*

**war|rant|a|bly** (wôr′ən tə blē, wor′-), *adv.* in a warrantable manner; justifiably; defensibly.

**war|ran|tee** (wôr′ən tē′, wor′-), *n. Law.* a person to whom a warranty is made.

**war|rant|er** (wôr′ən tər, wor′-), *n.* a person who warrants.

**war|rant|less** (wôr′ənt lis, wor′-), *adj.* without warrant; unauthorized; unjustifiable: *warrantless invasion of privacy.*

**warrant officer**, **1** an officer in the armed forces who has received a certificate of appointment, but not a commission, ranking between commissioned officers and enlisted men. **2** any one of various subordinate officers in the United States Navy, such as a boatswain, carpenter, gunner, pay clerk, or torpedoman. **3** an officer of similar rank in the armed forces of certain other countries. *Abbr:* WO (no periods).

**war|ran|tor** (wôr′ən tər, wor′-; wôr′ən tôr′, wor′-), *n. Law.* a person who makes a warranty; guarantor.

**war|ran|ty** (wôr′ən tē, wor′-), *n., pl.* **-ties.** **1** a warrant or authorization; justification. **2a** a promise or pledge that something is what it is claimed to be; guarantee: *a warranty of the quality of the goods sold.* **b** a covenant annexed to a deed to land in which the seller guarantees that the title is good. In feudal law, the warranty given by a grantor of a freehold estate obliged him to give the grantee lands of equal value if the latter were evicted. **c** a promise or pledge made by the insured in an insurance contract, breach of which invalidates the policy. **d** a warrant or writ. **3** *Obsolete except Dialect.* an assurance; promise. [< Old North French *warantie,* Anglo-French *guarantie* < *warantir* to warrant < *warant,* Old French *guarant* warrant < Germanic (compare Middle Low German *warend,* and *warent,* present participle of *waren* to assure, protect). See etym. of doublet **guaranty.**]

**warranty deed**, a deed that contains a warranty that the title is good.

**war|ren** (wôr′ən, wor′-), *n.* **1a** a piece of ground filled with burrows, where rabbits live or are raised. **b** the rabbits living or raised there. **2** *Figurative.* a crowded district or building. **3** *English Law.* **a** a piece of land enclosed and preserved for breeding game or hunting small game. **b** a right to keep or hunt beasts and fowl of warren, such as hares, partridge, and woodcock. [< Anglo-French, Old North French *warenne,* probably < Germanic (compare the root *war-,* as in English *ward, ware*[2])]

**war|ren|er** (wôr′ə nər, wor′-), *n.* **1** a person who owns or rents a rabbit warren. **2** the keeper of a warren, especially: **a** a servant who has the charge of a rabbit warren. **b** an officer employed to watch over the game in a park or preserve.

**Warren hoe**, a hoe with a triangular-shaped blade. [perhaps < a proper name]

**war|ring** (wôr′ing), *n., adj.* — ***n.*** the act of waging war; fighting.
— ***adj.*** at war; antagonistic; hostile; conflicting: (*Figurative.*) *warring opinions.*

**war|ri|or** (wôr′ē ər, wor′-), *n., adj.* — ***n.*** a fighting man; experienced soldier.
— ***adj.*** belonging to or characteristic of a warrior; martial.
[< Old North French *werreieor* < *werreier* wage war < *werre;* see etym. under **war**[1]] — **war′ri|or-like′**, *adj.*

**war risk insurance**, term insurance issued by the U.S. government for members of the armed forces.

**war|ri|son** (war′ə sən), *n.* = warison.

**war room**, a room used at a military headquarters for briefings, film showings, and map displays, dealing with conditions at one or more theaters of operation.

**war|saw** (wôr′sô), *n.* a large grouper of the southeastern coast of the United States. [American English; alteration of Spanish *guasa*]

**war|ship** (wôr′ship′), *n.* any ship armed and manned for war, such as a destroyer, cruiser, or battleship.

**war|sle** (wär′səl), *v.,* **-sled, -sling,** *n. Scottish.* — ***v.i.*** **1** to wrestle; struggle. **2** to move with effort; flounder.
— ***v.t.*** to wrestle with (an adversary).
— ***n.*** **1** a wrestling bout. **2** *Figurative.* any struggle; tussle.
[alteration of Middle English *wrastlen;* see etym. under **wrestle**]

**war|sler** (wärs′lər), *n. Scottish.* wrestler.

**war|stle** (wär′səl), *v.i., v.t.,* **-stled, -stling,** *n. Scottish.* warsle. — **war′stler**, *n.*

---

**Pronunciation Key:** hat, āge, cãre, fär; let, ēqual, tėrm; it, īce; hot, ōpen, ôrder; oil, out; cup, pu̇t, rüle; child; long; thin; ᴛʜen; zh, measure; ə represents **a** in about, **e** in taken, **i** in pencil, **o** in lemon, **u** in circus.

**war surplus**, equipment, materials, clothing, and other supplies, no longer required by the military services, and usually disposed of by direct sale or auction.
**wart** (wôrt), *n.* **1** a small, hard, dry lump on the skin, caused by a virus. **2** a similar lump on a plant. **3** *Figurative.* any fault or blemish: *It is crucial to the future life and progress of our community to have a newspaper unafraid to comment and show us up, warts and all* (New Yorker). [Old English *wearte*] —**wart'like'**, *adj.*
**war tax**, a tax to provide money for a war.
**wart|ed** (wôr'tid), *adj.* having a wart or warts; verrucose.
**wart hog**, a wild hog of Africa that has two large tusks and large wartlike growths on each side of the face. See picture under **pig**[1].
**war|time** (wôr'tīm'), *n., adj.* —*n.* a time of war. —*adj.* of or having to do with a time of war; taking place during a time of war: *What the senators want is expert opinion as to whether ... production and missile development should be placed on a wartime footing at once* (Newsweek).
**war time**, *British.* double summer time.
**war-torn** (wôr'tôrn', -tōrn'), *adj.* disrupted, damaged, or destroyed by war: *The American people ... endorsed the government's economic aid and technical assistance to underdeveloped and war-torn countries of the postwar world* (Bulletin of Atomic Scientists).
**wart|y** (wôr'tē), *adj.,* **wart|i|er, wart|i|est.** **1** having warts. **2** covered with lumps like warts. **3** of or like a wart.
**warve** (wôrv), *n.* = wharve.
**war vessel**, = warship.
**war-wea|ri|ness** (wôr'wir'ē nis), *n.* war-weary condition or feeling: *The people of South Vietnam have been at war for ... years and war-weariness is deep in their bones* (New York Times).
**war-wea|ry** (wôr'wir'ē), *adj.* wearied of war and its hardships: *Some observers here think this might be acceptable to the war-weary rebels now as a basis for a cease-fire* (Wall Street Journal).
**war whoop**, **1** a war cry of American Indians. **2** *Figurative.* any war cry; shout of battle.
**war|y** (wãr'ē), *adj.,* **war|i|er, war|i|est.** **1** on one's guard against danger or deception: *a wary fox.* SYN: alert, vigilant, watchful, guarded. **2** cautious; careful: *He gave wary answers to all of the stranger's questions.* SYN: circumspect, prudent. See syn. under **careful**.
**wary of**, cautious about; careful about: *to be wary of driving in heavy traffic. He lied to me about my friend, and I've been wary of him ever since.*
**was** (woz, wuz; *unstressed* wəz), *v.* the 1st and 3rd person singular, past indicative of **be**: *Once there was a king. I was late to school yesterday. Was he late, too? The candy was eaten.* [Old English *wæs*]
► **Was** in the second person singular (*you was*), formerly common in standard English, is no longer in good use.
See **were** for another usage note.
**wa|sa|bi** (wä sä'bē), *n.* **1** a plant of the mustard family, cultivated in Japan for its roots, which taste like horseradish. **2** the grated root of this plant, served with raw fish in a Japanese meal. [< Japanese *wasabi*]
**wash** (wosh, wôsh), *v., n., adj.* —*v.t.* **1** to clean with water or other liquid: *to wash a floor, wash one's hands, wash clothes, wash dishes.* SYN: cleanse, rinse. **2** to remove (dirt, stains, paint, or the like) by or as if by scrubbing with soap and water: *Can you wash that spot out?* **3** *Figurative.* to make clean or free from guilt, corruption, or sin; purify: *washed from sin.* **4** to make wet; moisten thoroughly with water or other liquid: *The flowers are washed with dew.* **5** to flow over or past (the shore or coast); beat upon (walls, cliffs, or shore); lave: *a beach washed by waves.* **6** to carry (by a liquid): *Wood is often washed ashore by the waves.* **7** to wear (by water or any liquid): *The cliffs are being slowly washed away by the waves. Rain washed channels in the ground.* **8** to pass (a gas or gaseous mixture) through or over a liquid in order to remove impurities or to dissolve out some component. **9** to cover with color mixed with water or a watery liquid: *The house was washed white.* **10** to cover with a film of metal deposited from a solution: *to wash copper with silver.* **11a** to sift (earth, ore, or the like) by the action of water to separate valuable material, especially gold, from waste. **b** to separate (gold or other valuable mineral) in this way. **12** *Informal, Figurative.* to dismiss or reject from a school, course of study, or the like, as not qualified or able to be qualified.
—*v.i.* **1** to wash clothes: *Mother usually washes on Monday. She washes for a living.* **2** to wash oneself; wash one's face and hands: *He washed before eating dinner.* SYN: bathe. **3** to undergo washing without damage: *This material washes well.* **4** to be carried along or away by water or other liquid: *Cargo washed ashore. The topsoil washed away.* **5** to flow or beat with a lapping sound: *The waves washed upon the rock. The flood waters washed against the house.* **6** *Informal, Figurative.* to stand being put to the proof: *patriotism that won't wash. That argument won't wash.*
—*n.* **1** the act or process of washing: *to give a dog a wash.* **2** the condition of being washed: *This floor needs a good wash.* **3** a quantity of clothes or other articles washed or to be washed: *She hung the wash on the line.* **4** material carried by moving water and then deposited as sediment; alluvial deposit. A delta is formed by the wash of a river. **5a** the motion, rush, or sound of water: *We listened to the wash of the waves against the boat.* **b** wear or attrition caused by the action of water. **c** the action of rain and flowing water in wearing away or removing soil: *Even after a light rainfall a heavy wash of soil-laden water flows from the high ground into the wadis* (Scientific American). **6a** a tract of land sometimes overflowed with water and sometimes left dry; tract of shallow water; fen, marsh, or bog. **b** a shallow pool or stream formed by the overflow of a river. **7** *Western U.S.* the dry bed of an intermittent stream. **8** a liquid for a special use: *a hair wash, a mouthwash.* **9a** a broad, thin layer of water color laid on by a continuous movement of the brush, sometimes partly painted over with other colors while it is still damp. **b** a thin coat of water color or distemper spread over a wall or similar surface; preparation used for this purpose: *Pictures and fragments have ... been inset flush with the wall, which is covered with a honey-coloured wash* (Observer). **10a** waste liquid matter; liquid garbage: *The kitchen wash is given to the pigs.* **b** the fermented wort from which the spirit is extracted in distilling. **11** washy or weak liquid food. **12** a thin coat of metal. **13** earth, ore, or the like, from which gold or some other substance can be washed. **14a** the rough or broken water left behind by a moving ship. **b** a disturbance in air made by an airplane or any of its parts: *prop wash.*
—*adj.* that can be washed without damage: *a wash dress.*
**come out in the wash**, to be discovered in the end: *It all comes out in the wash, to mock the riddled corpses round Bapaume* (Sunday Times).
**wash down, a** to wash from top to bottom or from end to end: *to wash down the walls of a kitchen.* **b** *Figurative.* to swallow liquid along with or after (solid food) to help in swallowing or digestion: *After his dinner, he washed it all down with a cup of good hot tea.*
**wash out, a** to cleanse or rinse the interior of: *to wash out one's mouth. It is requisite that it* [*the bottle*] *be washed out after every experiment, the last two or three rinsings being made with distilled water* (Michael Faraday). **b** to rinse so as to remove soap or other substance from the fabric: *After soaping the dyed cloth she washed it out.* **c** *Figurative.* to lose color, body, or vigor: *Candidates should wear light blue or gray shirts because white washes out on the screen* (Time). **d** to carry or be carried away by water: *The rain washed out part of the pavement. The road washed out during the storm.* **e** *Informal, Figurative.* to cause to lose strength or vitality; wear out: *The old man was just about washed out ... when he died* (James T. Farrell). **f** *Informal, Figurative.* to finish; ruin: *The fire completely washed out his business.* **g** to call off because of rain: *The first two days of the original match were washed out* (London Times). **h** *Slang.* to fail and be released from a school, course of study, or training; flunk out: *He was absent so often that he finally washed out of school.*
**wash up, a** to wash one's hands and face, as before eating: *When they finished eating lunch, the children went to wash up.* **b** to wash the dishes: *His supper over, ... Ernana ... retired into the kitchen to wash up* (R. Bagot). **c** *Figurative.* to finish: *Everybody thought he was all washed up as an actor; then he made his big comeback.*
[Old English *wascan,* or *wæscan*]
**Wash.**, Washington.
**wash|a|bil|i|ty** (wosh'ə bil'ə tē, wôsh'-), *n.* the quality of being washable.
**wash|a|ble** (wosh'ə bəl, wôsh'-), *adj.* that can be washed without damage: *washable silk.*
**wash-and-wear** (wosh'ən wãr', wôsh'-), *adj.* specially treated to require little or no ironing after washing and drying: *wash-and-wear fabrics.*
**wash|ball** (wosh'bôl', wôsh'-), *n.* a ball of soap, sometimes perfumed or medicated, used for washing the hands and face, and for shaving.
**wash|ba|sin** (wosh'bā'sən, wôsh'-), *n.* a basin for holding water to wash one's face and hands.
***wash|board** (wosh'bôrd', -bōrd'; wôsh'-), *n., adj.* —*n.* **1** a board having ridges on it, used for rubbing the dirt out of clothes. **2** a baseboard or skirting board. **3a** a thin board extending upward from the gunwale of a boat as a guard against spray. **b** a similar guard on the sill of a port.
—*adj.* full of ridges or ruts: *a washboard road.*

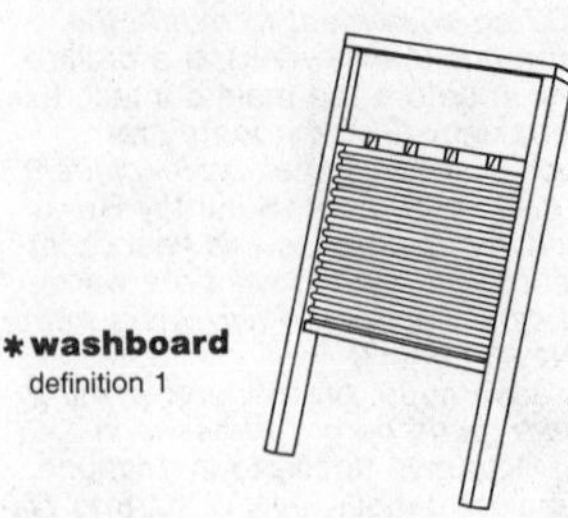
***washboard**
definition 1

**wash|boil|er** (wosh'boi'lər, wôsh'-), *n.* a large metal receptacle with a removable cover, for boiling clothes, table linen, and the like.
**wash bottle**, a glass flask having a stopper that is perforated by tubes, arranged so that by blowing in one tube the water or other liquid in the flask may be forced out in a small stream through another tube: *Wash bottles are used in laboratories, for washing precipitates on filters.*
**wash|bowl** (wosh'bōl', wôsh'-), *n.* a bowl to hold water to wash one's hands and face.
**wash|cloth** (wosh'klôth', -kloth'; wôsh'-), *n.* a small cloth for washing oneself. SYN: washrag.
**wash|day** (wosh'dā', wôsh'-), *n.* a day when clothes are washed.
**wash-down** (wosh'doun', wôsh'-), *n.* a washing from top to bottom or from end to end.
**wash drawing**, **1** a representation of an object produced by laying in the shades in washes, with merely the outlines and chief details in line. **2** the method of producing such representations.
**washed-out** (wosht'out', wôsht'-), *adj.* **1** lacking color; faded. **2** *Informal, Figurative.* lacking life, spirit, or vigor. **3** damaged by flood; eroded.
**washed-up** (wosht'up', wôsht'-), *adj. Informal.* **1a** done with; through, especially after having failed. **b** done for; finished. **2** fatigued.
**wash|er** (wosh'ər, wôsh'-), *n.* **1** a person who washes. **2** a machine that washes; washing machine. **3** a flat ring of metal, rubber, leather, or plastic with a hole in the middle. Washers are used with bolts or nuts, or to make joints tight, as in a water faucet. **4** a device for washing gases; scrubber.
**wash|er-dry|er** (wosh'ər drī'ər, wôsh'-), *n.* a machine that washes clothes and then dries them.
**wash|er|man** (wosh'ər mən, wôsh'-), *n., pl.* **men.** a man whose work is washing clothes.
**wash|er-up** (wosh'ər up', wôsh'-), *n. British.* a person who washes dishes; dishwasher.
**wash|er|wom|an** (wosh'ər wům'ən, wôsh'-), *n., pl.* **-wom|en.** a woman whose work is washing clothes; laundress.
**wash|er|y** (wosh'ər ē, wôsh'-), *n., pl.* **-er|ies.** a place where something is washed: *A pipe to take the coal from pit top to washery has been installed* (London Times).
**wash|e|ter|i|a** (wosh'ə tir'ē ə, wôsh'-), *n. British.* a self-service laundry or car wash. [patterned after *cafeteria*]
**wash-fast|ness** (wosh'fast'nis, wôsh'-; -fäst'-), *n.* the quality of not fading when washed: *finishes which increase wrinkle resistance and wash-fastness of dyes* (Wall Street Journal).
**wash goods**, washable fabrics.
**wash-hand basin** (wosh'hand', wôsh'-), *British.* a washbasin.
**wash|house** (wosh'hous', wôsh'-), *n.* a building or room for washing, especially for washing clothes.
**wash|ing** (wosh'ing, wôsh'-), *n., adj.* —*n.* **1** the act or action of cleaning with water: *to give a car, one's hands, or clothes, a good washing.* **2** the act of washing as part of an industrial process: *the washing of coal or ore.* **3** the act or action of washing away material; erosion by action of water: *to build a wall to prevent washing of soil from a bank.* **4a** clothes washed or to be washed at one time: *to do two washings before lunch.* **b** laundry: *to send washing to the laundry.* **5** a thin coat, as of a metal applied by electrolysis. **6** Sometimes, **washings. a** liquid that has been used to wash something. **b** matter removed in washing something: *washings of gold obtained from the earth.* **c** places containing soil, ore, or the like, from which metal is obtained by washing. **7** *Finance.* a manipulating of a security by means of a wash sale.
—*adj.* **1** for washing. **2** that washes.
**washing bear**, = raccoon. [because of its habit of putting its food into water before eating it]

**washing bottle**, = wash bottle.
**washing machine**, a machine that washes clothes, sheets, towels, and other things made of cloth.
**washing soda**, crystallized sodium carbonate, used in washing; sal soda.
**Wash|ing|to|ni|an** (wosh′ing tō′nē ən, wôsh′-), *n., adj.* —*n.* a native or inhabitant of Washington, D.C., or the state of Washington.
—*adj.* of or having to do with Washington, D.C., or the state of Washington.
**Wash|ing|to|ni|a|na** (wosh′ing tō′nē ä′nə, -an′ə, -ā′nə; wôsh′-), *n.pl.* a collection of objects, documents, books, facts, stories, or other memorabilia about or belonging to George Washington.
**Wash|ing|ton palm** (wosh′ing tən, wôsh′-), one of two fan palms growing in southern California and neighboring areas.
**Washington pie**, *U.S.* a layer cake with a jam, cream, or other filling.
**Washington's Birthday**, February 22, the anniversary of George Washington's birth, observed on the third Monday in February as a legal holiday in most states of the United States.
**Washington thorn**, a species of hawthorn native to the southern United States, with white flowers and scarlet fruit.
**wash|ing-up** (wosh′ing up′, wôsh′-), *n. British.* the act of washing dishes.
**washing-up bowl**, *British.* a dishpan.
**washing-up machine**, *British.* a dishwasher: *Labour-saving kitchen, including washing-up machine* (Sunday Times).
**wash leather**, chamois or the like, used for gloves.
**wash 'n' wear**, = wash-and-wear.
**Wa|sho** (wä′shō), *n., pl.* **-sho** or **-shos**. **1** a member of an Indian tribe near Lake Tahoe, in Nevada and California. **2** the Hokan language of this tribe.
**wash|out** (wosh′out′, wôsh′-), *n.* **1** the act or action of washing away earth, gravel, a road, bridge, or other structure, by water, as from very heavy rains or a flooding stream. **2** the hole, cavity, or break made by this. **3** *Informal, Figurative.* a person who is dismissed or rejected from a school, course of study, or training, as not qualified or able to be qualified; person who washes out. **4** *Informal, Figurative.* a failure; disappointment: *The party was a complete washout.*
**wash|pot** (wosh′pot′, wôsh′-), *n.* **1** a vessel used for washing, especially one's hands. **2** a vessel containing melted tin, into which iron plates are plunged to be converted into tin plate.
**wash|rack** (wosh′rak′, wôsh′-), *n.* a section of a service station, hangar, or other parking place, equipped for the quick washing of vehicles.
**wash|rag** (wosh′rag′, wôsh′-), *n.* = washcloth.
**wash|room** (wosh′rüm′, -rům′; wôsh′-), *n.* **1** a room where toilet facilities are provided; lavatory. **2** *Obsolete.* a laundry.
**wash sale**, *Finance.* a fictitious buying and selling of a security, now prohibited by law, as by two brokers at the same time for a single customer, to give an appearance of market activity and encourage outside participation in helping to raise or lower the price.
**wash|stand** (wosh′stand′, wôsh′-), *n.* **1** a bowl with pipes and faucets for running water to wash one's hands and face. **2** a stand for holding a basin and pitcher for washing.
**wash|trough** (wosh′trôf′, -trof′; wôsh′-), *n.* **1** a trough used for washing the hands and face. **2** a trough in which ore is washed; buddle.
**wash|tub** (wosh′tub′, wôsh′-), *n.* a tub used to wash or soak clothes in.
**wash-up** (wosh′up′, wôsh′-), *n.* the act or process of washing oneself: *One of the principal issues before and after the … settlement was the amount of time allotted employes for rest and wash-up* (Wall Street Journal).
**wash|wom|an** (wosh′wům′ən, wôsh′-), *n., pl.* **-wom|en**. = washerwoman.
**wash|y** (wosh′ē, wôsh′-), *adj.,* **wash|i|er, wash|i|est.** **1** too much diluted; weak; watery: *washy coffee.* **2** *Figurative.* lacking strength and stamina; feeble: *a washy style of writing or lecturing.* **3** lacking body; pale: *washy coloring.* **4** liable to sweat or scour after slight exertion: *a washy horse or cow.* **5** *Obsolete.* **a** having too much moisture; water-logged. **b** bringing moisture or rain: *a washy wind, washy weather.*
**was|n't** (woz′ənt, wuz′-), was not
▶ The form *wan't* (wont, wônt) for *wasn't* is particularly common in New England and in the coastal areas of the South Atlantic States. It occurs both in folk speech and in the usage of cultivated, but old-fashioned, speakers.
***wasp** (wosp, wôsp), *n.* a kind of insect that has a slender body and a powerful sting. Wasps belong to a group of insects, including the ants and the bees, that have four membranous wings, and mouthparts adapted for chewing. Wasps usually feed on other insects, spiders, and decaying animal matter. The social wasps, including the yellow jackets and hornets, build paper nests, though yellow jackets may nest in the ground. Solitary wasps, including the sand wasp and the mud wasp, build mud nests or tunnel into the ground, trees, or buildings. [Old English *wæps, wæsp.* See related etym. at **weave**.]

***wasp**

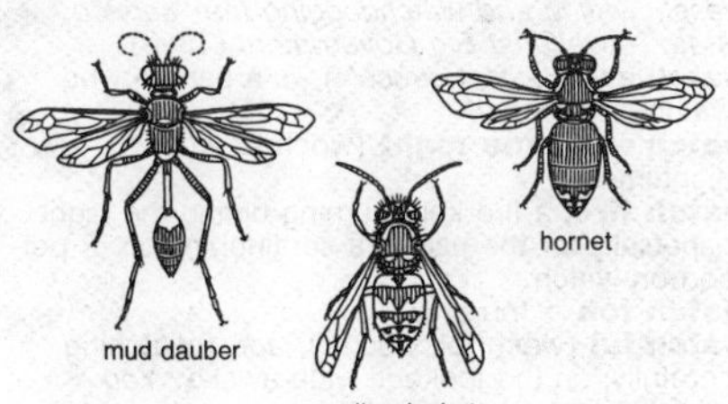


**WASP¹** or **Wasp¹** (wosp, wôsp), *n.* a member of the WASP (Women's Air Force Service Pilots).
**Wasp²** or **WASP²** (wosp, wôsp), *n., adj.* —*n.* a white Anglo-Saxon Protestant, especially one belonging to the group of middle- and upper-class Americans descended from British and northern European settlers who are regarded as the traditionally dominant or privileged group in America: *As they have been driven out of urban politics by the various minority ethnic groups, the WASPs have concentrated their activities in private associations and in community-chest drives, the symphony, the opera, and other forms of community culture* (Seymour Martin Lipset).
—*adj.* of or having to do with Wasps: *a Wasp community, the WASP mentality.*
[< *W*(hite) *A*(nglo-)*S*(axon) *P*(rotestant)]
**WASP³** (no periods), *U.S.* Women's Air Force Service Pilots (an organization formed in the early part of World War II, and dissolved in 1944).
**Wasp|dom** or **WASP|dom** (wosp′dəm, wôsp′-), *n.* the characteristics, beliefs, or attitudes of Wasps: *The foundation of WASP dominance in national politics and culture rested on the supposition that WASPdom was the true America* (Harper's).
**wasp|ish** (wos′pish, wôs′-), *adj.* **1** like a wasp; like that of a wasp. **2** *Figurative.* **a** bad-tempered; irritable: *a waspish person.* **SYN**: irascible, snappish, fractious. **b** marked or characterized by virulence or petulance; spiteful: *a waspish remark.*
—**wasp′ish|ly**, *adv.* —**wasp′ish|ness**, *n.*
**Wasp|ish** or **WASP|ish** (wos′pish, wôs′-), *adj.* belonging to or typical of Wasps: *She says that she hated the Waspish ambience of the school, but she had got a scholarship …, and she wanted to keep it* (New Yorker). *He was a Harvard Business School graduate, WASPish, attractive, crisp, alert, and formidably informed* (Atlantic). —**Wasp′ish|ly**, *adv.* —**Wasp′ish|ness**, *n.*
**wasp|like** (wosp′līk′, wôsp′-), *adj.* resembling a wasp, especially in structure, form, or movement; vespiform.
**wasp paper**, the papery substance made by paper wasps for their nests.
**wasp waist**, a very slender waist.
**wasp-waist|ed** (wosp′wās′tid, wôsp′-), *adj.* having a very slender waist.
**wasp|y** (wos′pē, wôs′-), *adj.,* **wasp|i|er, wasp|i|est.** wasplike; waspish.
**was|sail** (wos′əl, was′-), *n., v., interj.* —*n.* **1** a drinking party; revelry with drinking of healths. **2** spiced ale or other liquor drunk at a wassail. **3** a salutation wishing good health or good luck to a person, used especially in England in former times when drinking a toast. The reply is "Drink hail!" **4** *Obsolete.* a carol or song sung by wassailers.
—*v.i.* to take part in a wassail; revel.
—*v.t.* to drink to the health of; toast.
—*interj.* your health!
[Middle English *wassail* < Scandinavian (compare Old Icelandic *ves heill* be healthy!)]
**wassail bowl**, **1** a large bowl or cup containing the spiced ale drunk at a wassail; loving cup. **2** the ale itself; wassail.
**was|sail|er** (wos′əl ər, was′-), *n.* **1** a reveler. **2** a drinker of toasts.
**Was|ser|mann test** or **reaction**, or **Was|ser|mann** (wä′sər mən), *n.* a test for syphilis, made on a sample of a person's blood serum. [< August von *Wassermann,* 1866-1925, a German physician and bacteriologist, who invented the test]
**wast¹** (wost), *v. Archaic.* were. "Thou wast" means "you were."
**wast²** (wast, wāst), *n., adj., adv. Scottish.* west.
**wast|age** (wās′tij), *n.* **1** loss, such as by use, wear, decay, or leakage; waste. **2** the amount wasted; quantity lost.
**waste** (wāst), *v.,* **wast|ed, wast|ing,** *n., adj.* —*v.t.* **1** to make poor use of; spend uselessly; fail to get value or benefit from: *Though he had much work to do, he wasted his time doing nothing. Don't waste your money.* **SYN**: squander, dissipate. **2** to wear down little by little; destroy or lose gradually: *The sick man was wasted by disease. To … waste huge stones with little water drops* (Shakespeare). **SYN**: diminish. **3** to damage greatly; spoil; ruin; destroy: *The soldiers wasted the enemy's fields.* **4** *U.S. Slang.* to kill.
—*v.i.* **1** to be consumed or spent uselessly, extravagantly, or without adequate return. **2** to be used up or worn away gradually. **3** to pass away; be spent: *Time is wasting; let's get started.*
—*n.* **1** a poor use; useless spending; failure to get the most out of something: *a waste of goods, time, or effort, a waste of a man's ability. Buying that suit was a waste of money; it is already starting to wear out.* **2** useless or worthless material; stuff to be thrown away. Garbage or sewage is waste. **SYN**: trash, rubbish, refuse. **3** bare or wild land; desert; wilderness: *We traveled through treeless wastes.* **4a** a vast, dreary, desolate, or empty expanse or tract, as of water or snow-covered land. **b** a piece of land uncultivated or unused, producing little or no herbage or wood. **5** the act or fact of wearing down little by little; gradual destruction or decay: *Both waste and repair are constantly going on in our bodies.* **6a** destruction or devastation as caused by war, floods, and fires. **b** *Law.* an injury to an estate caused by an act or by neglect on the part of a tenant. **7** cotton or wool threads in bunches, used for cleaning machinery, or wiping off oil, grease, or the like. **8** *Physical Geography.* material derived by mechanical and chemical erosion from the land, carried by streams to the sea.
—*adj.* **1** thrown away as worthless or useless: *waste products, waste water, a pile of waste lumber.* **SYN**: rejected. **2** left over; not used: *waste food.* **3** not cultivated; that is a desert or wilderness; bare; wild. **SYN**: desolate, uninhabited. **4** in a state of desolation or ruin. **SYN**: devastated. **5** carrying off or holding refuse: *a waste drain.* **6** of no further use to, and therefore excreted by, an animal or human body.
**go to waste**, to be wasted: *There is not a particle of vapour in the universe that goes to waste* (H. Hunter).
**lay waste**, to damage greatly; destroy; ravage; devastate: *War laid waste the land.*
[< Old North French *waster,* Old French *guaster* < Latin *vāstāre* lay waste < *vāstus* vast, waste. Compare etym. under **devastate**.]
**waste|bas|ket** (wāst′bas′kit, -bäs′-), *n.* a basket or other container for wastepaper or other small or light items of dry trash.
**wast|ed** (wās′tid), *adj.* **1** spent unprofitably; squandered; misused: *wasted opportunities, a wasted life.* **2** worn; decayed: *The bones showed through the sick man's wasted body.* **3** laid waste; ravaged; ruined: *wasted buildings, a wasted land.* **4** *U.S. Slang.* killed. **5** *Archaic.* gone by; elapsed: *The remnant of his wasted span* (William Cowper).
**waste|ful** (wāst′fəl), *adj.* using or spending too much: *to be wasteful of water.* **SYN**: extravagant, prodigal, improvident. —**waste′ful|ly**, *adv.* —**waste′ful|ness**, *n.*
**waste|land** (wāst′land′, -lənd), *n.* **1** land in its natural, uncultivated state: *a barren wasteland covered with ice and snow.* **2** an area ruined by poor management or other excess: *an urban wasteland.*
**waste|lot** (wāst′lot′), *n. Canadian.* a vacant lot in a city, especially one neglected and left to run to weeds.
**waste|ness** (wāst′nis), *n.* the state of lying waste or being barren; desolation.
**waste|pa|per** (wāst′pā′pər), *n., adj.* —*n.* paper thrown away or to be thrown away as useless or worthless.
—*adj.* of or for wastepaper: *a wastepaper basket.*
**waste pipe**, a pipe for carrying off wastewater, or other waste matter, from any plumbing fixture except toilets.
**wast|er** (wās′tər), *n.* a person or thing that wastes; squanderer; spendthrift. **SYN**: prodigal.
**waste|wa|ter** (wāst′wôt′ər, -wot′-), *n.* water containing waste matter; sewage.
**wast|ing** (wās′ting), *adj., n.* —*adj.* **1** laying waste; devastating. **2** gradually destructive to the body:

---

**Pronunciation Key:** hat, āge, cãre, fär; let, ēqual, tėrm; it, īce; hot, ōpen, ôrder; oil, out; cup, půt, rüle; child; long; thin; ᴛʜen; zh, measure; ə represents **a** in about, **e** in taken, **i** in pencil, **o** in lemon, **u** in circus.

*a wasting disease.*
—*n.* gradual decay of life or organic tissue; gradual loss of strength and vitality: *The disease ... a progressive wasting of the muscles which causes helplessness* (Newsweek).
**wasting asset**, *Accounting.* any asset that progressively decreases in value through depletion or exhaustion, such as a mine, oil well, stand of timber, or other natural resource.
**wast|rel** (wās′trəl), *n.* **1** a waster; spendthrift. **2** an idle, worthless person; good-for-nothing. **3** something useless, inferior, or imperfect. [< *waster* + *-el*, a diminutive suffix]
**wat**[1] (wät, wot), *n. Scottish.* wet.
**wat**[2] (wät, wot), *v.t., v.i. Scottish.* to know; wot.
**wat**[3] (wät), *n.* Buddhist temple in Thailand: *Gaze at Bombay's ghats, wonder at wats in Bangkok* (New Yorker). [< Thai *wat*]
**wat**[4] (wät), *n.* a highly spiced, peppery vegetable stew made with or without meat, eaten in Ethiopia. [< a native name]
**watch** (woch, wôch), *v., n., adj.* —*v.i.* **1** to look carefully or attentively: *The medical students watched while the surgeon performed the operation.* **2** to look or wait (for) with care and attention; be very careful: *I watched for a chance to cross the street.* **3** to keep guard: *The sentry watched throughout the night.* **4** to stay awake for some purpose: *The nurse watches with the sick.* **5** to remain awake for devotional purposes; keep vigil.
—*v.t.* **1** to look at; observe with care or interest; view: *to watch people passing by, watch a play, watch an operation. Are you watching that show on television? We watched the kittens play.* **2** to look or wait for with care and attention: *to watch a good opportunity to do something.* **3** to keep guard over; tend: *a shepherd watching his flock. The police watched the prisoner. The dog was supposed to watch the little boy.* SYN: protect. **4** to keep in mental view; stay informed about: *to watch a person's career, to watch the stockmarket.*
—*n.* **1** the action of careful looking; attitude of attention: *Be on the watch for automobiles when you cross the street.* SYN: vigilance. **2** the action of protecting; guarding: *A man kept watch over the bank at night.* SYN: surveillance. **3a** a device for telling time, small enough to be carried in a pocket or worn on the wrist. Many watches are driven by springs or batteries. SYN: timepiece. **b** any device for indicating the passage of time, such as a ship's chronometer or a candle marked into sections, each of which requires a certain amount of time to burn. **4a** a person or persons kept to guard and protect: *The man's cry aroused the night watch, who came running to his aid.* SYN: watchman. **b** a period of time for guarding: *a watch in the night.* **c** *Archaic.* the duty or post of a guard or watchman: *to stand upon one's watch.* **5** the act of staying awake for some purpose. **6** *Nautical.* **a** the time of duty of one part (commonly one half) of a ship's crew. A watch usually lasts four hours. **b** the part of a crew on duty at the same time. **7** one of the periods into which the night was regularly divided in ancient time: three, and later four, among the Hebrews, four or five among the Greeks, four among the Romans.
—*adj.* of or for a watch (timepiece).
**watch it**, *U.S. Informal.* to be careful: *Watch it! You're spilling the soup!*
**watch out**, *Informal.* to look out; be on guard: *Watch out for cars when you cross the street. The ways of God are strange. You have to watch out for any chances that He gives you* (New Yorker).
**watch over**, to guard or supervise; protect or preserve, as from danger, harm, or error: *The eye of the rulers is required always to watch over the young* (Benjamin Jowett).
[Old English *wæccan*] —**watch′a|ble**, *adj.*
**watch and ward**, the old custom of watching by day and night in towns and cities, as in medieval times.
**keep watch and ward**, to keep constant vigilance by night and day: *Mrs. Pipchin had kept watch and ward over little Paul and his sister for nearly twelve months* (Dickens).
**watch|band** (woch′band′, wôch′-), *n.* a band of leather, metal, or cloth, to fasten a watch on the wrist.
**watch cap**, a snugly fitting cap of knitted blue wool worn by sailors on watch in cold weather, originally especially as part of their uniform by enlisted men in the U.S. Navy.
**watch|case** (woch′kās′, wôch′-), *n.* the outer covering for the works of a watch, usually not including the glass face.
**watch chain**, a chain attached to a watch and fastened to one's clothing or worn, especially by women, around the neck.
**watch|dog** (woch′dôg′, -dog′; wôch′), *n., adj., v.* **-dogged, -dog|ging.** —*n.* **1** a dog kept to guard property. **2** *Figurative.* a watchful guardian.
—*adj.* **1** having to do with or characteristic of a watchdog. **2** *Figurative.* organized or acting as a watchful guardian, especially against unlawful practices: *a Congressional watchdog committee, a watchdog group in civil liberties.*
—*v.t. Informal.* to guard vigilantly; watch carefully: *Pound spent ... his years at Harvard endlessly writing and watchdogging the "service state"—welfarist Big Government* (Time).
**watch|er** (woch′ər, wôch′-), *n.* a person who watches; observer.
**watch|es of the night** (woch′iz, wôch′-), = nighttime.
**watch fire**, a fire kept burning during the night, especially for the use of a sentinel, party, or person on watch.
**watch fob**, = fob chain.
**watch|ful** (woch′fəl, wôch′-), *adj.* **1** watching carefully; on the lookout; wide-awake: *You should always be watchful for cars when you cross the street.* **2** *Archaic.* **a** wakeful; sleepless. **b** (of time) passed in wakefulness. —**watch′ful|ly**, *adv.* —**watch′ful|ness**, *n.*
—*Syn.* **1** **Watchful, vigilant, alert** mean wide-awake and attentive or on the lookout. **Watchful** means paying close attention or keeping careful guard: *She is watchful of her health.* **Vigilant** means being especially and necessarily watchful: *Because the enemy was so close, they kept a particularly vigilant watch.* **Alert** means being wide-awake and ready for whatever may happen: *The alert driver avoided an accident.*
**watch glass**, **1** a thin, concave piece of glass used in laboratories as a receptacle for small objects under close examination. **2** = crystal (of a watch).
**watch guard**, a chain, cord, or ribbon for securing a watch when worn on the person.
**watch hand**, any one of the hands of a watch; the hour hand, minute hand, or second hand.
**watch|ing brief** (woch′ing, wôch′-), **1** a brief instructing a lawyer to observe proceedings on one's behalf. **2** *Figurative.* a watchful attitude; surveillance: *No less important is the utilisation section which regards itself as holding a watching brief for timber growers and traders by following developments in research* (New Scientist).
**watch|keep|er** (woch′kē′pər, wôch′-), *n.* **1** a person who keeps watch. **2** a person who serves as a member of a watch on board ship; an officer in charge of a watch.
**watch|mak|er** (woch′mā′kər, wôch′-), *n.* a person who makes and repairs watches.
**watch|mak|ing** (woch′mā′king, wôch′-), *n.* the business of making and repairing watches.
**watch|man** (woch′mən, wôch′-), *n., pl.* **-men.** a man who keeps watch; guard. A watchman is often employed to watch over property or a building while it is unoccupied or not in use. *A watchman guards the bank at night.*
**watch meeting**, a church service held at night, especially on the last night of the year until midnight.
**watch night**, **1** New Year's Eve, observed by Methodist and certain other churches with religious services which last until the arrival of the new year. **2** = watch meeting.
**watch pocket**, a small pocket for holding a watch.
**watch|tow|er** (woch′tou′ər, wôch′-), *n.* a tower or other high structure from which a watch is kept for enemies, fires, ships, or any approaching danger; lookout station.
**watch|word** (woch′wėrd′, wôch′-), *n.* **1** a secret word or short phrase that allows a person to pass a guard; password: *We gave the watchword, and the sentinel let us pass.* **2** *Figurative.* motto; slogan: *"Forward" is our watchword. His watchword is honor, his pay is renown* (Scott).
**wa|ter** (wô′tər, wot′-), *n., v., adj.* —*n.* **1** the liquid that fills the oceans, rivers, lakes, and ponds, and falls from the sky as rain. We use water for drinking and washing. Pure water is a transparent, colorless, tasteless, odorless compound of hydrogen and oxygen. It freezes at 32 degrees Fahrenheit or 0 degrees centigrade (Celsius), boils at 212 degrees Fahrenheit or 100 degrees centigrade (Celsius), and has its maximum density at 39 degrees Fahrenheit or 4 degrees centigrade (Celsius), one cubic centimeter weighing one gram. *Formula:* $H_2O$ **2** a liquid like water occurring in or discharged from the human body, especially: **a** tears: *a ... rap on the nose ... which brought the water into his eyes* (Dickens). **b** saliva: *the thought of ... oysters brought the water to his mouth* (W. S. Gilbert). **c** urine: *to void water.* **d** any one of various other bodily liquids, such as sweat or serum. **3a** any liquid preparation like water: *lavender water, barley water.* **b** *Pharmacology.* a saturated solution in water of some volatile or aromatic substance: *ammonia water.* **4a** a body of water; sea, lake, river, bay, sound, or the like: *to cross the water on a ferry.* **b** an underground flow or pool of water: *to strike water at 267 feet.* **5a** the water of a sea, river, lake, bay, sound, or the like, with reference to its relative depth or height: *to reach low water in August, to sail at high water.* **b** the depth of water, or of a body of water, with regard to suitability for navigation: *to sail in shallow water, to require 22 feet of water when loaded.* **6** the surface of a body of water: *to swim under the water.* **7** *Figurative.* the degree of clearness and brilliance of a precious stone. A diamond of the first water is a very clear and brilliant one. **8** a wavy marking, as on silk, mohair, or metal. **9** *Finance.* **a** additional shares or securities issued without a corresponding increase of capital or assets. **b** an inflationary quality; excess: *It has been suggested that there may be some water in current steel backlogs, meaning that many users may have placed orders some time ago hoping to beat the obviously forthcoming steel price increase* (New York Times). **10** = water color.
—*v.t.* **1** to sprinkle or wet with water: *to water grass, to water the streets.* **2a** to supply with drinking water: *to water cattle.* **b** to supply water to (as an army, ship, or engine); fill, as the tanks or reservoirs of: *He seized the town ... and watered his ship ... at the enemy's wells* (Charles Kingsley). **3** to supply (land, crops, or people and communities) with water: *Our valley is well watered by rivers and brooks.* **4** to weaken by adding water: *It is against the law to sell watered milk.* **5** to produce a wavy marking on (as silk) by sprinkling it with water and passing it through a calender. **6** *Finance.* to increase (as stock) by issue of additional shares or securities without a corresponding addition in capital or assets.
—*v.i.* **1a** to fill with water; flow with tears: *Strong sunlight makes your eyes water.* **b** to secrete abundant saliva, usually in anticipation of food: *The cake made the boy's mouth water.* **2** to drink water; get drinking water. **3** to take a supply of fresh water on board: *A ship waters before sailing.*
—*adj.* **1** of water; holding, storing, conveying, or distributing water: *a water jug, a water pipe, a water heater.* **2** done or used in or on water: *water sports.* **3** growing or living in or near water; having water as its habitat: *water plants, water insects.* **4** prepared with water; diluted with water; mixed with water: *water paint.* **5** at or near the edge of a body of water: *water frontage.* **6** associated with the water; having rule over water: *a water spirit, a water god.* **7** worked, driven, or powered by water.
**above water**, **a** above the surface of the water; not submerged; afloat: *Our Carpenter ... was lost for want of having fastened on somewhat that might have kept him above water* (J. Davies). **b** *Figurative.* out of trouble or difficulty, especially out of financial trouble or difficulty: *A number of struggling men, who have managed to keep above water during the bad seasons, must now go under* (Field, Farm, Garden).
**back water**, to order oarsmen to row in a reverse direction to give a boat sternway, or to the oarsmen on the port or starboard side only, to effect a quick turn: *The mate yelled to back water as the whale surfaced.*
**by water**, on a ship or boat: *to ship by water.*
**fish in troubled waters**. See under **troubled waters**.
**hold water**, to stand the test; be true, dependable, or effective: *I think these documents will hold water* (G. Allen). *"Brothers," said he, "the demand of Loggerhead will not hold water"* (Tobias Smollett).
**in deep water**, in trouble, difficulty, or distress: *Once he had been very nearly in deep water because Mrs. Proudie had taken it in dudgeon that a certain young rector, who had been left a widower, had a very pretty governess for his children* (Anthony Trollope).
**like water**, very freely: *to spend money like water.*
**like water off a duck's back**, without having any effect: *It had all passed off like water off a duck's back* (L. B. Walford).
**make water**, to take in water through leaks or over the side: *Almost simultaneously a similar SOS was received from the stricken Dutch vessel. It said: "Dutch vessel making water, require immediate assistance"* (New York Times).
**of the first water**, **a** of the highest degree: *That boy is a scamp of the first water.* **b** See under **water**, *n.* (def. 7).
**pour (throw** or **dash) cold water on**, to discourage by being indifferent or unwilling: *Father threw cold water on our plan to camp in the mountains because he thought it was dangerous. Congressmen ... have poured cold water on that plan* (Wall Street Journal).
**take (the) water**, **a** to go swimming: *I heard a*

*splash and saw a deer take the water 300 yards or so above me* (Scribner's Monthly). **b** to be launched: *The cruiser Kent ... took the water without a hitch* (Scotsman). **c** to embark; take ship: *For see, the Queen's barge lies at the stairs, as if her Majesty were about to take water* (Scott). **d** *Western U.S.* to leave abruptly; run away: *The fellow, who was really a coward, though nearly twice as big as myself, took water at once* (L. Roberts).
**take (the) waters**, to drink mineral water at a health resort, usually in a scheduled course of treatment: *He went to Hot Springs last winter to take the waters.*
**tread water**, **a** to keep oneself from sinking by moving the feet up and down: *Barely managing to breathe, he treaded water until the lifeguard pulled him out.* **b** *Figurative.* to be in a state of uncertainty; be unsettled: *The channel-tunnel discussions had acted as a negative influence, and ... British Railways had largely been treading water while awaiting the decision* (London Times).
**water down**, **a** to reduce in strength by diluting with water: *to water down whiskey.* **b** *Figurative: An amendment to almost the same effect—though somewhat watered down in wording—was promptly offered* (Newsweek). *How can the needs of the slow learner be met more adequately without stultifying and watering down the intellectual performance of brighter pupils?* (Atlantic).
**water over the dam**, something that is finished and cannot be changed or remedied: *Mr. Ferrers did not like talking about the past. "That's all water over the dam"* (New Yorker).
**waters**, **a** flowing water: *the broad waters of the Mississippi.* **b** water moving in waves; sea; high seas: *And hear the mighty waters rolling evermore* (Wordsworth). **c** flood water; floods: *The waters are out in Lincolnshire* (Dickens). **d** spring water; mineral water: *to drink the waters.* **e** the amniotic fluid: *The amnion, which encloses the amniotic fluid, is often called the bag of waters.*
[Old English *wæter*] —**wa′ter|er**, *n.*

**wa|ter|age** (wôt′ər ij, wot′-), *n.* **1** conveyance as by ship or boat; transport by water. **2** the charge or payment for this.

**water arum**, a plant of the arum family growing in moist woods and marshes, with greenish-yellow flowers that bloom in early spring and red berries; calla; marsh calla.

**water back**, a tanklike receptacle or reservoir for heating water, built into the back of a wood or coal stove.

**water bag**, **1** a bag of skin or leather used for holding or carrying water, especially in Oriental countries. **2** the reticulum of an animal. **3** the membranous sac filled with amniotic fluid; bag of waters. **4** = hot-water bottle.

**water bailiff**, *British.* an official responsible for the enforcement of bylaws relating to fishing waters.

**water ballet**, a rhythmic, synchronized dance performed by swimmers in the water; synchronized swimming.

**wa|ter-based** (wôt′ər bāst′, wot′-), *adj.* using water as the base, thinner, or emulsifying agent: *water-based paint.*

**water bath**, **1** a bath composed of water, rather than vapor. **2** *Chemistry.* a device for heating or cooling something by means of a surrounding medium of water.

**water bear**, a tardigrade organism; bear animalcule.

**Water Bearer**, Aquarius (def. 1).

**wa|ter-bear|ing** (wôt′ər bãr′ing, wot′-), *adj.* **1** (of a stratum) through which water percolates; holding water: *Because of substantial water-bearing fissures, considerable difficulties have been experienced since the start of mining operations* (London Times). **2** (of a country) producing water; not arid.

**water bed**, or **wat|er|bed** (wôt′ər bed′, wot′-), *n.* a bed with a mattress consisting of a water-filled vinyl bag and usually equipped with a temperature-control device: *And the waterbed ..., a kind of gigantic hot water bottle, must surely be the ultimate in nocturnal comfort* (New Scientist and Science Journal).

**water beech**, = American hornbeam.

**water beetle**, any one of various aquatic beetles having the legs broad and fringed so as to be well adapted for swimming, such as the diving beetle and whirligig beetle.

**water bird**, any bird that swims or wades in water; aquatic bird.

**water biscuit**, a cracker made of flour, shortening, and water.

**wa|ter|blink** (wôt′ər blingk′, wot′-), *n.* a spot of dull or dark color in the sky, due to reflection from open water beneath, seen in arctic regions.

**water blister**, a blister containing a clear, watery fluid derived from serum.

**water bloom**, a discoloration on a pond, lake, or other slow-moving body of water, produced by a sudden accumulation of algae or other microscopic plants or animals.

**water boa**, = anaconda (def. 1).

∗**water boatman**, any one of a family of water bugs with long, oarlike hind legs that enable them to move through the water at great speed; corixid.

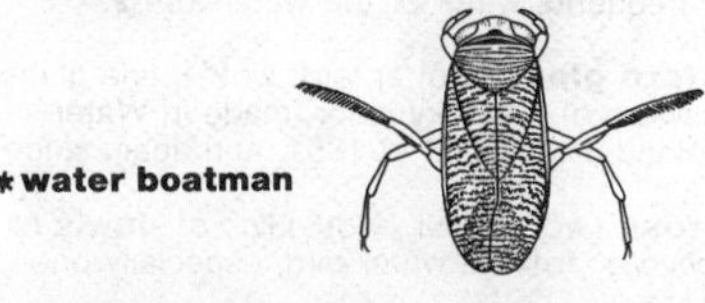

∗**water boatman**

**water boiler**, an atomic reactor that uses a uranyl salt in heavy water as its fuel and coolant to produce steam for electric power.

**water bomb**, a paper bag or other container filled with water, usually dropped by hand on a target below: *They received only a pelting by water bombs apparently thrown by irate office workers* (New York Times).

**wa|ter-borne** or **wa|ter|borne** (wôt′ər bôrn′, -bōrn′; wot′-), *adj.* **1** supported by water, especially so as to be clear of the ground or bottom upon which it has rested; floating; afloat. **2** conveyed by a ship, boat, or the like; transported by water.

**water bottle**, a bottle, bag, or other container for holding water.

**wa|ter-bound** (wôt′ər bound′, wot′-), *adj.* **1** shut in by water or floods: *While waterbound, it [a foraging party] was attacked by guerrillas* (New York Tribune). **2** solidified by rolling and watering: *Oiled gravel roads are a natural development of the water-bound macadam variety* (New Scientist).

**water boy**, a boy who supplies or distributes water to a group, such as soldiers or laborers: *He started as a water boy before World War I, toting water to thirsty construction workers* (New York Times).

**wa|ter|brain** (wôt′ər brān′, wot′-), *n.* = gid.

**water brash**, **1** a clear acid liquid that sometimes rises to the mouth with a heartburn. **2** a heartburn; pyrosis. [< *water* + *brash*¹]

**wa|ter|buck** (wôt′ər buk′, wot′-), *n., pl.* **-bucks** or (*collectively*) **-buck**. **1** either of two African antelopes that frequent rivers and marshes. **2** any one of several other antelopes of similar habits. [< Afrikaans *waterbok* < Dutch]

**water buffalo**, the common buffalo of Asia, especially of India and the Philippines; water ox. Water buffalo are commonly used as draft animals.

**water bug**, **1** any one of certain hemipterous insects that live in, on, or near the water, especially any one of several large bugs with flattened bodies, grasping front legs, and a poisonous bite. **2** = Croton bug.

**wa|ter-bus** (wôt′ər bus′, wot′-), *n., pl.* **-bus|es** or **-bus|ses**. a motorboat used to carry passengers along a certain route on a canal or waterway: *Part of the gondoliers' woe stems from the motorized water-bus* (San Francisco Chronicle).

**wa|ter-butt** (wôt′ər but′, wot′-), *n.* a large open cask set up on end to receive and store rain water.

**water cabbage**, = water lettuce.

**water cannon**, a large nozzle usually mounted on a truck to shoot water at high pressure, used especially in riot control: *Water cannon were brought in to break up the crowds* (Sunday Times).

**water carrier**, **1** a person or thing that transports passengers, goods, or animals, by water, instead of by land, railway, or air. **2** a man or animal that carries water, especially, in Oriental countries, a native who supplies an establishment or a number of troops with water. **3** a tank or other vessel for carrying water: *It is, therefore, necessary for fire brigades to have water carriers available* (Manchester Guardian Weekly). **4** an open channel for water, as in an irrigated meadow. **5** a rain cloud.

**Water Carrier**, = Aquarius (def. 1).

**water chestnut** or **caltrop**, **1** any one of a genus of aquatic plants of the evening-primrose family, whose nutlike fruit contains a single, large, edible seed, especially a species native to Eurasia that has become a troublesome weed in parts of the United States. **2** the fruit of any one of these plants. **3** a species of sedge, grown in the Far East for its edible tuber. **4** its tuber.

**water chinquapin**, **1** a North American water plant, a variety of nelumbo, that bears yellow flowers and edible, nutlike seeds. **2** its seed.

**wa|ter|chute** (wôt′ər shüt′, wot′-), *n.* **1** a gutter or channel for the overflow of water. **2** an artificial cascade for the amusement or exercise of sliding down the rapids in a boat or by swimming. Also, **water-shoot**.

**wa|ter-clear** (wôt′ər klir′, wot′-), *adj.* as clear as water; very clear: *Not from her did the young ones get those water-clear eyes* (Katherine Anne Porter).

**water clock**, an instrument for measuring time by the flow of water. A clepsydra is a water clock.

**water closet**, **1** a toilet flushed by water. **2a** a small room or enclosure containing such a toliet. **b** a room containing such a toilet and also a hand basin, shower or tub; bathroom. **3** any enclosed place for urination or defecation; privy; latrine. *Abbr:* w.c.

**water color**, or **wa|ter|col|or**¹ (wôt′ər kul′ər, wot′-), *n.* **1** a pigment to be mixed with water instead of oil. **2** the art or method of painting or drawing with water colors. **3** a picture painted with water colors.

**wa|ter-col|or** or **wa|ter|col|or**² (wôt′ər kul′ər, wot′-), *adj.* having to do with, used for, or made with water colors.

**wa|ter-col|or|ist** or **wa|ter|col|or|ist** (wôt′ər-kul′ər ist, wot′-), *n.* an artist who paints in water colors.

**water conversion**, the conversion of seawater into fresh water.

**wa|ter-cool** (wôt′ər kül′, wot′-), *v.t.* to reduce the heat produced as by combustion, friction, or radiation, by causing water to pass through a chamber or casing (water jacket) surrounding all or part of the mechanism of (an engine, motor, machine gun, or nuclear reactor).

**water cooler**, any device for cooling water, especially one used to dispense drinking water cooled by refrigeration.

**wa|ter|course** (wôt′ər kôrs′, -kōrs; wot′-), *n.* **1** a stream of water; river; brook. **2** the channel or bed of a stream of water: *In the summer many watercourses dry up.* **3** an artifical channel for the conveyance of water, such as an irrigation ditch.

**wa|ter|craft** (wôt′ər kraft′, -kräft′; wot′-), *n.* **1** activity or skill in water sports, such as boating or swimming. **2a** a ship or boat. **b** ships and boats collectively.

**water crake**, **1** = spotted crake. **2** = water ouzel.

**water crane**, a swinging pipe or other apparatus for supplying water from an elevated tank, as to locomotive tenders or watering carts.

**water cress**, or **wa|ter|cress** (wôt′ər kres′, wot′-), *n.* **1** a hardy plant that grows in water or near springs and small running streams, and has crisp, pungent leaves. It is a perennial belonging to the mustard family. **2** its leaves, used for salad and as a garnish. —**wa′ter-cress′**, *adj.*

**water crowfoot**, a kind of crowfoot or buttercup that grows in water and has deeply divided leaves and white or yellow flowers.

**water culture**, = hydroponics.

**water cure**, **1** treatment of disease by the use of water; hydropathy or hydrotherapy. **2** *Slang.* the forcing of water down a person's throat in such a quantity as to cause severe physical pain, through distention of the stomach, used as a means of torture.

∗**water cycle**, a cycle in nature whereby water evaporates from oceans, lakes, and other bodies of water, forms clouds that move over land areas, and is returned to those bodies of water in the form of rain and snow, the run-off from rain and snow, or as ground water; hydrologic cycle. See diagram below on next page.

**water deer**, a small deer without antlers, that frequents riverbanks in China and Korea. It resembles the musk deer.

**water dog**, **1** a dog that is trained or bred for swimming, especially one trained to retrieve game from the water. **2** *Informal.* a man thoroughly at home either on or in the water: **a** a sailor, especially an experienced one; sea dog. **b** a good swimmer. **3** *U.S.* the mud puppy.

**wa|ter|drop** (wôt′ər drop′, wot′-), *n.* **1** a drop of water: *The waterdrops shoot from the salad basket and fall like stars to the dreary wooden floor* (New Yorker). **2** a tear; teardrop: *Let not women's weapons, waterdrops, stain my man's cheeks* (Shakespeare).

**wa|tered** (wôt′ərd, wot′-), *adj.* **1** having a wavelike pattern or marking, such as that produced on a silk fabric by moisture and pressure, or that formed naturally or artificially on the surface of certain steels. **2** having a clouded appearance.

---

**Pronunciation Key:** hat, āge, cãre, fär; let, ēqual, tėrm; it, īce; hot, ōpen, ôrder; **oi**l, **ou**t; cup, pu̇t, rüle; **ch**ild; lo**ng**; **th**in; **ŦH**en; **zh**, measure; ə represents **a** in about, **e** in taken, **i** in pencil, **o** in lemon, **u** in circus.

**wa|tered-down** (wôt′ərd doun′, wot′-), *adj.* **1** diluted with water: *We half slept through the bread and butter with jam, and flat, icy, watered-down milk, totally unrelated to milk straight from a cow* (New Yorker). **2** *Figurative: The measure is a watered-down version of the bill the Senate had approved* (Wall Street Journal).

**watered stock**, **1** *U.S.* cattle given little water while being driven to market, and then given all the water thay can drink to increase their weight before weighing in. **2** shares or securities that have been increased without a corresponding increase in capital or assets.

***wa|ter|fall** (wôt′ər fôl′, wot′-), *n.* **1** a fall of water from a high place; cascade or cataract. **2a** = chignon. **b** a wave of hair falling down the neck below the chignon or net.

***waterfall**
definition 1

cascade

cataracts:

steep waterfall

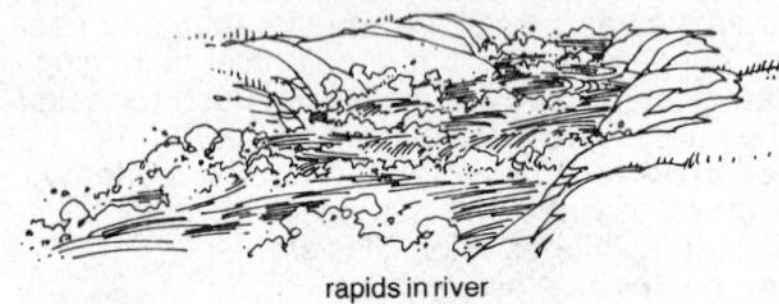

rapids in river

**wa|ter|fern** (wôt′ər fėrn′, wot′-), *n.* any fern of a group, growing in boggy places and wet woods, that forms tufts of large bipinnate fronds.

**wa|ter|find|er** (wôt′ər fīn′dər, wot′-), *n.* = dowser.

**water flea**, any one of an order of tiny freshwater crustaceans that swim with a skipping motion; daphnia. Water fleas are cladocerans.

**wa|ter|flood** (wôt′ər flud′, wot′-), *v., n.* —*v.t.* to subject (an oil field or well) to waterflooding. —*n.* a waterflooding operation.

**wa|ter|flood|ing** (wôt′ər flud′ing, wot′-), *n.* the act or process of pumping water underground into an oil field or oil well to force residual oil to the surface or toward producing wells.

**wa|ter|flow** (wôt′ər flō′, wot′-), *n.* the flow or current of water.

**wa|ter|fly** (wôt′ər flī′, wot′-), *n., pl.* **-flies. 1** any fly that frequents water or the waterside. **2** = stone fly.

**Wa|ter|ford glass** (wôt′ər fərd, wot′-), fine glass or glassware of a smoky color, made in Waterford, Ireland, from 1783 to 1851, and again since 1951.

**wa|ter|fowl** (wôt′ər foul′, wot′-), *n., pl.* **-fowls** or (*collectively*) **-fowl.** a water bird, especially one that swims.

**water frame**, a type of spinning machine powered by water, patented by Richard Arkwright in 1769.

**wa|ter|front** (wôt′ər frunt′, wot′-), *n., adj.* —*n.* **1** the part of a city beside a river, lake, or harbor. **2** land at the water's edge.
—*adj.* of or having to do with the waterfront, especially with its harbor activities.

**water gage**, = water gauge.

**water gap**, a mountain pass or gorge through which a stream flows. SYN: flume.

**water garden**, **1** a garden with a running brook at its center. **2** a garden for aquatic plants.

**water gas**, a poisonous gas consisting largely of carbon monoxide and hydrogen, made by passing steam through very hot coal or coke; blue gas. It is used for lighting when carbureted, and sometimes for fuel. —**wa′ter-gas′**, *adj.*

**water-gas tar** (wôt′ər gas′, wot′-), tar obtained as a by-product of the manufacture of water gas.

**water gate**, **1** a gate or gateway through which water passes. **2** a gate that controls the flow of water; sluice or floodgate. **3** a gate (as of a town or a castle) opening on water.

**Wa|ter|gate** (wôt′ər gāt′, wot′-), *n.* **1** a major political scandal involving illegal activities directed against political opponents of President Richard Nixon and subsequent attempts to cover up these activities: ... *the disclosures of misconduct in high places loosely defined as "Watergate"* (James A. Wechsler). **2** any similar misuse of the power of public office to discredit political opponents or for private gain: *If there is a British Watergate who will expose it and track it down?* (New Statesman). **3** any widespread public scandal: *The incident ... is being referred to in the scientific community as "a medical Watergate"* (New York Times). [< the *Watergate,* an apartment-house and office-building complex in Washington, D.C., where men connected with the Republican Committee for the Reelection of the President were arrested burglarizing Democratic National Committee headquarters]

**water gauge**, **1** any one of various apparatus for measuring quantity of water, as in a tank or boiler, or flow of water, as from or into a reservoir. **2** the part of such an apparatus by which measurement at a given moment is recorded, as a calibrated glass tube in which the level of water indicates the level inside a tank or boiler.

**water glass**, or **wa|ter|glass** (wôt′ər glas′, -gläs′; wot′-), *n.* **1a** a glass to hold water; tumbler. **b** *Obsolete.* a glass finger bowl. **2** an aqueous, jellylike, or powdery compound of sodium, silicon, and oxygen that solidifies when exposed to the air, used especially in soaps, in preserving eggs and wood, in cement manufacture, and in fireproofing wood, cloth, and paper; sodium silicate; soluble glass: *Water glass is* [*also*] *used in the purification of fats and oils, in refining petroleum and in the manufacture of silica gel* (George L. Bush). **3** an instrument for making observations beneath the surface of water, consisting of an open box or tube with a glass bottom. **4** = water clock. **5** = water gauge.

**water grass**, **1** any one of various grasses and grasslike plants growing in water. **2** *British Dialect.* water cress.

**wa|ter|ground** (wôt′ər ground′, wot′-), *adj.* ground between rotating stones by power provided by water: *waterground corn meal.*

**wa|ter|guard** (wôt′ər gärd′, wot′-), *n.* **1** a body of men employed by a custom house to watch ships in order to prevent smuggling or other violations of law. **2** a member of such a body.

**water gum**, **1** (in the United States) a tupelo. **2** (in Australia) any one of several trees of the myrtle family, growing in moist places.

**water gun**, = water pistol.

**water hammer**, **1** the concussion of water in a pipe when its flow is suddenly stopped, or when live steam is admitted. **2** the sound of this, typically a sharp thump or series of thumps.

**wa|ter-ham|mer** (wôt′ər ham′ər, wot′-), *v.i.* (of a pipe or system of pipes) to give off a sharp thump or series of thumps, from concussion of water or live steam.

**water hazard**, a stream, pond, or ditch filled with water on a golf course, intended as an obstacle.

**water haze**, a light-gray haze composed of small drops of water mixed with smoke or dust.

**water hemlock**, any one of a group of poisonous bog herbs of the parsley family, of north temperate regions that have finely divided leaves and white flowers, such as the spotted cowbane.

**water hen**, **1** = moor hen. **2** the coot of America.

**water hickory**, a hickory with bitter nuts, found in the southern United States.

**water hog**, = capybara.

**water hole**, **1** a hole in the ground where water collects; small pond; pool. **2** *Astronomy.* a part of the electromagnetic spectrum, considered the most likely band for use in extraterrestrial contact with earth. It is almost free of radio noise and radiates interstellar hydrogen and oxygen (elements that combine to form water). *Radio telescopes in each hemisphere would sweep along the galactic plane every few minutes, transmitting in a noise-free band, such as the so-called water hole* (New Scientist).

**water hyacinth**, a floating or rooting aquatic plant of the same family as the pickerelweed, with violet or blue flowers and ovate leaves that have inflated, bladderlike petioles, native to tropical South America, and cultivated elsewhere.

**water ice**, **1** *Especially British.* a frozen dessert made of fruit juice, sugar, and water; sherbet. **2** solid ice formed by the direct freezing of water, and not by the compacting of snow.

**wa|ter-inch** (wôt′ər inch′, wot′-), *n.* a unit equal to the quantity of water flowing in a given period, as one minute or 24 hours, through a circular opening one inch in diameter.

**wa|ter|ing** (wôt′ər ing, wot′-), *n., adj.* —*n.* the act of a person or thing that waters.
—*adj.* **1** (of eyes) discharging watery fluid; running. **2** (of the mouth) secreting saliva profusely in anticipation of appetizing food. **3** irrigating.

**watering can**, a can with a spout for sprinkling water on plants.

**watering cart**, a cart designed to carry water for watering plants or the streets.

**watering hole**, **1** = water hole. **2** *U.S. Informal.* a resort where there is bathing and boating; watering place. **3** *U.S. Slang.* **a** a popular or stylish night club, restaurant, or resort. **b** any popular or stylish public place or establishment: *a watering hole for artists or politicians.*

**watering place**, **1a** a resort with springs of mineral water. **b** a resort where there is bathing, boating. **2** a place where water may be obtained.

**watering pot**, = watering can.

**watering trough**, **1** a trough in which water is provided for domestic animals. **2** a long, shallow trough parallel to the rails, from which water is scooped by steam locomotives in passing.

**wa|ter|ish** (wôt′ər ish, wot′-), *adj.* = watery. —**wa′ter|ish|ly**, *adv.* —**wa′ter|ish|ness**, *n.*

**water jacket**, a casing with water in it, put around something to keep it cool or at a certain temperature.

**wa|ter|jack|et** (wôt′ər jak′it, wot′-), *v.t.* to enclose in or fit with a water jacket.

**wa|ter-jet** (wôt′ər jet′, wot′-), *adj.* operated by a stream of water sent out with force from a small opening: *a water-jet loom.*

**water jump**, an obstacle consisting of or including a body of water across which horses must jump in a steeplechase.

***water cycle**

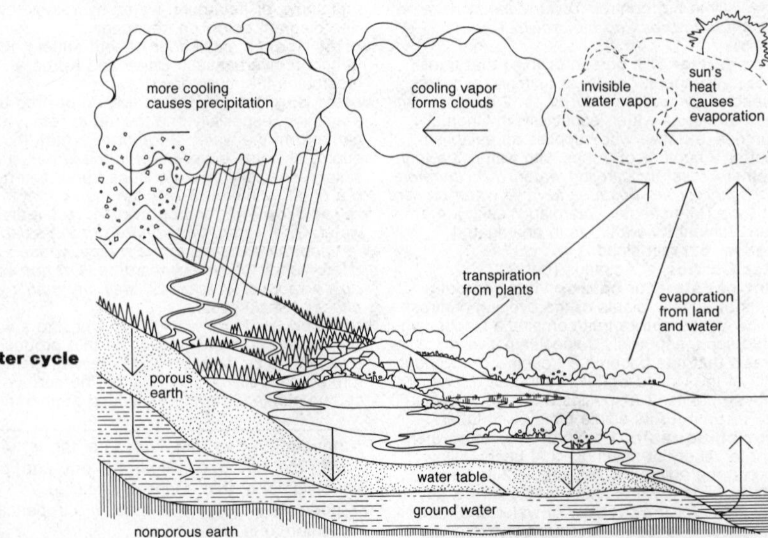

**wa|ter|leaf** (wôt′ər lēf′, wot′-), *n., pl.* **-leafs** or **-leaves.** any herb of a group of North America with clusters of white or purplish flowers.

**waterleaf family,** a group of dicotyledonous herbs having characteristics similar to those of the borage family and commonly cultivated as ornamentals. The family includes the waterleaf, baby blue-eyes, and tarbush.

**wa|ter|less** (wôt′ər lis, wot′-), *adj.* using or containing little or no water: *waterless cooking. We know that the moon is an airless, waterless world* (Atlantic). —**wa′ter|less|ly,** *adv.* —**wa′ter|less-ness,** *n.*

**water lettuce,** a common floating plant of the tropics with a rosette of rounded and downy leaves: *Water lettuce .. spends its life afloat, supported by spongy, air-filled tissue on the bottom surface of its leaves* (Scientific American).

**water level, 1a** the surface level of a stream, lake, or other body of water: *The water level of the pond rose after the heavy rains.* **b** the surface level of a body of static water, as in a tank, boiler, or cistern. **2** the plane below which the rock or soil is saturated with water; water table. **3** *Nautical.* water line. **4** an instrument for showing the level of fluid, in which water is used instead of alcohol.

**water lily, 1** a water plant having flat, floating leaves and showy, fragrant, white, pink, yellow, or blue flowers; pond lily; water nymph. A common North American variety has fragrant, white or pink flowers. **2** any other plant of the water-lily family. **3** any showy-flowered aquatic plant. **4** the flower of any one of these plants.

**wa|ter-lil|y family** (wôt′ər lil′ē, wot′-), a widely distributed group of dicotyledonous water plants that are herbs and are characterized by large floating leaves and showy flowers, such as the water lily, fanwort, lotus, and spatterdock.

**water line,** or **wa|ter|line** (wôt′ər līn′, wot′-), *n.* **1** the line where the surface of the water touches the side of a ship or boat. **2** any one of several lines marked on the hull of a ship to show the depth to which it sinks when unloaded, partly loaded, or fully loaded.

**wa|ter-log** (wôt′ər lôg′, -log′; wot′-), *v.t., v.i.,* **-logged, -log|ging.** to cause to be or to become water-logged.

**wa|ter-logged** (wôt′ər lôgd′, -logd′; wot′-), *adj.* **1** so full of water that it will barely float. **2** thoroughly soaked with water. **3** *Figurative.* bogged down: *water-logged in details.*

**Wa|ter|loo** (wôt′ər lü, wot′-; wôt′ər lü′, wot′-), *n.* **1** any decisive or crushing defeat: *to meet one's Waterloo.* **2** a cause of ruin or defeat; undoing: *Cicero's Waterloo ... was a woman* (S. K. Obereck). [< *Waterloo,* a town in Belgium, scene of Napoleon's final defeat in 1815]

**water main,** a large pipe for carrying water, especially one by which water is supplied, through smaller pipes, to many buildings or to various parts of a large building.

**wa|ter|man** (wôt′ər mən, wot′-), *n., pl.* **-men. 1** a man who works on a boat or among boats; boatman. **2** = oarsman.

**wa|ter|man|ship** (wôt′ər mən ship, wot′-), *n.* the art of a waterman; skill in rowing or managing boats.

**water marigold,** an aquatic composite herb of North America, having yellow flower heads and submerged, finely dissected leaves.

**wa|ter|mark** (wôt′ər märk′, wot′-), *n., v.* —*n.* a mark showing how high water has risen or how low it has fallen: *the high watermark of a river.* **2a** a distinguishing mark or design impressed in the substance of a sheet of paper during manufacture. It is usually barely visible except when the sheet is held against the light. **b** the metal design from which the impression is made, usually an ornamental figure of wire, fastened on the mold or dandy roll, pressure of which makes the paper thinner and more translucent at that point.
—*v.t.* **1** to put a watermark in. Some letter paper is watermarked. **2** to impress (a mark or design) as a watermark.

**water meadow,** a meadow kept fertile by the overflow of adjoining streams from time to time.

**wa|ter|mel|on** (wôt′ər mel′ən, wot′-), *n.* **1** a large, roundish or oblong fruit with red, pink, or yellow pulp with much sweet, watery juice, and a hard, green rind. It is good to eat. **2** the vine bearing this fruit. It is a slender, trailing vine belonging to the gourd family. See picture under **gourd family.**

**water meter,** an apparatus for measuring and recording the amount of water drawn from a water main, public water system, or well, by a particular user or group of users.

**water milfoil,** any perennial water plant of a group having very finely divided submerged leaves. See picture under **amphibian.**

**water mill,** a mill, especially a grist mill, whose machinery is run by water power.

**water mite,** = water spider.

**water moccasin, 1** a large, poisonous snake that lives in swamps and along streams in the southern United States; cottonmouth. It is a pit viper like the rattlesnake. **2** any one of various similar but harmless water snakes.

**water mold,** a fungus that lives in water or wet soil, feeding on decaying plants and animals, and sometimes parasitic on aquatic animals.

**water monitor,** a large monitor lizard found from India to northern Australia, usually near the banks of rivers and streams.

**water moth** = caddis fly.

**water motor,** any form of motor or engine that is operated by the kinetic energy, pressure, or weight of water, especially a small turbine or waterwheel fitted to a pipe supplying water, as for driving sewing machines or other light machinery.

**water mouse,** an Australian murine rodent.

**water nymph, 1** *Greek and Roman Mythology.* a nymph or goddess living in or associated with some body of water, such as a Naiad, Nereid, or Oceanid. **2** any one of a group of water plants; water lily.

**water oak, 1** an oak found especially along streams and in swamps in the southeastern United States. **2** any of several other American oaks.

**water of crystallization,** water that is present in chemical combination in certain crystalline substances. When the water is removed by heating, the crystals break up into a powder.

**water of hydration,** water that is present in chemical combination with some substance to form a hydrate; water of crystallization.

**water on the brain,** = hydrocephalus.

**water on the knee,** a painful swelling of the knee, caused by inflammation, infection, or injury of the cartilages or membranes of the knee joint; hydroarthrosis of the knee.

**water ouzel,** any one of a family of small water birds that are related to the thrushes, and swim and dive in deep water for food; dipper; ouzel; water crake.

**water ox,** = water buffalo.

**water parsnip,** any herb of a group of the parsley family that grows chiefly in watery places.

**water parting,** a watershed or divide.

**water pepper, 1** = smartweed. **2** any one of certain closely related plants.

**water pig,** a large aquatic rodent of South America; capybara.

**water pimpernel, 1** = brookweed. **2** the common pimpernel.

**water pipe, 1** a pipe through which water is conducted. **2** a hookah, narghile, or kalian.

**water pipit,** a variety of pipit of northern regions of both hemispheres.

**water pistol,** a toy pistol that shoots water taken in by suction; water gun; squirt gun.

**wa|ter|plane** (wôt′ər plān′, wot′-), *n., v.,* **-planed, -plan|ing.** —*n.* an airplane adapted for alighting on, ascending from, and traveling on the water; seaplane.
—*v.i.* to go or travel by waterplane: *We waterplaned along the main channels ... carrying food, blankets, and clothing to the villages* (Alex Hendry).

**water plant,** = hydrophyte.

**water plantain,** any one of a group of water plants, especially a species common in shallow water in north temperate regions, whose leaves suggest those of the plantain.

**water polo,** a game played in a swimming pool by two teams of seven swimmers who try to throw or push an inflated ball into the opponent's goal.

**wa|ter|pot** (wôt′ər pot′, wot′-), *n.* **1** a vessel, usually of earthenware, for holding water. **2** = watering can.

**water power, 1** the power from flowing or falling water. It can be used to drive machinery and generate electricity. **2** a fall or flow of water that can supply power. **3** the right or privilege of a mill to make use of this.

**water pox,** = chicken pox.

**water pressure,** pressure caused by the weight of water.

**wa|ter|proof** (wôt′ər prüf, wot′-), *adj., n., v.* —*adj.* that will not let water through; resistant to water: *An umbrella should be waterproof.*
—*n.* **1** a waterproof material. **2** a waterproof coat; raincoat.
—*v.t.* to make waterproof: *These hiking shoes have been waterproofed.*

**wa|ter|proof|er** (wôt′ər prü′fər, wot′-), *n.* **1** a person who makes something waterproof. **2** a waterproof material: *Invisible silicone waterproofers are extremely useful for porous brick or stone walls exposed to heavy driving rain* (London Times).

**wa|ter|proof|ing** (wôt′ər prü′fing, wot′-), *n.* **1** the act or process of making waterproof. **2** a substance, such as rubber or oil, used to make something waterproof.

**water pump, 1** a pump for raising water: [*He*] *stopped in the store to order a valve for the old water pump at his summer cottage* (Wall Street Journal). **2** any one of various devices for circulating water through the cooling system, as of an automobile.

**water purslane,** any one of several marsh plants resembling the purslane, such as two species of the evening-primrose family.

**water rail,** a gray and brownish rail with a long, mostly red bill, found in marshes of the Old World north of the tropics.

**water rat, 1** a rodent that lives on the banks of streams or lakes, especially a large vole of Great Britain. **2** = muskrat. **3** a water mouse of Australia. **4** *Slang. Figurative.* a person who is or poses as a sailor or longshoreman, but who lives by petty thievery, smuggling, and other dishonest work.

**wa|ter-re|pel|len|cy** (wôt′ər ri pel′ən sē, wot′-), *n.* the quality of repelling water or moisture: *Water-repellency is a handicap in garments that lie close to the skin* (Wall Street Journal).

**wa|ter-re|pel|lent** (wôt′ər ri pel′ənt, wot′-), *adj., n.* —*adj.* impervious to water or moisture: *The duck hunter's jacket has been copied in moss-green, water-repellent cotton poplin* (New Yorker).
—*n.* a chemical agent that makes something water-repellent.

**wa|ter-re|sist|ance** (wôt′ər ri zis′təns, wot′-), *n.* the quality of resisting the penetration of water.

**wa|ter-re|sist|ant** (wôt′ər ri zis′tənt, wot′-), *adj.* resisting the penetration of water: *His company's laboratories have turned out a tough, flexible, water-resistant film similar to cellophane* (Wall Street Journal).

**wa|ter|ret** (wôt′ər ret′, wot′-), *v.t.,* **-ret|ted, -ret-ting.** to ret (flax, hemp, or other grass crop) by soaking in soft water.

**water right,** a riparian right.

**water sapphire,** a variety of iolite. [translation of French *saphir d'eau*]

**wa|ter|scape** (wôt′ər skāp, wot′-), *n.* scenery consisting of water, or a picture of this.

**water scorpion,** any one of a family of large, aquatic, hemipterous insects that have a long, anal breathing tube.

**water screw,** a ship's propeller.

***wa|ter|shed** (wôt′ər shed′, wot′-), *n.* **1** the ridge between the regions drained by two different river systems. On one side of a watershed, rivers and streams flow in one direction; on the other side, they flow in the opposite direction. See picture below on next page. **2** the region drained by one river system. **3** *Forestry.* an area of sloping land down which water drains from rain or melted snow. **4** *Figurative.* a point at which a notable change takes place; turning point: *The two short papers ... mark a watershed in the intellectual history of mankind* (Science). [< *water* + *shed*[2], in the Scottish sense of "portion of land." Compare German *Wasserscheide.*]

**water shield, 1** a plant of the water-lily family having shield-shaped, floating leaves covered with a viscid, jellylike substance and small, dull-purple flowers. **2** any one of a group of allied plants, especially the fanwort.

**wa|ter-shoot** (wôt′ər shüt′, wot′-), *n.* = water-chute.

**water shrew,** either of two amphibious shrews of North America, with the hind feet fringed with hair for swimming and running across the water.

**wa|ter-sick** (wôt′ər sik′, wot′-), *adj.* (of land) unworkable and unproductive because of too much irrigation.

**wa|ter|side** (wôt′ər sīd′, wot′-), *n., adj.* —*n.* the land along the sea, a lake, a river, or other body of water.
—*adj.* **1** of, on, or at the waterside: *waterside flowers, waterside property.* **2** that works near the waterside or on the waterfront.

**wa|ter|sid|er** (wôt′ər sī′dər), *n. British.* a dock-side laborer.

**water ski,** one of a pair of skis used for gliding over water while being towed at the end of a rope by a motorboat.

**wa|ter-ski** (wôt′ər skē′, wot′-), *v.i.,* **-skied, -ski-ing.** to glide over the water on water skis: *Bronzed girls in Bikinis water-skied on the Mediterranean* (Newsweek). —**water skier, wa′ter-ski′er,** *n.*

**wa|ter-ski|ing** (wôt′ər skē′ing, wot′-), *n.* the sport of skiing with water skis.

---

**Pronunciation Key:** hat, āge, cãre, fär; let, ēqual, tėrm; it, īce; hot, ōpen, ôrder; oil, out; cup, pu̇t, rüle; child; long; thin; ᴛʜen; zh, measure;
ə represents a in about, e in taken, i in pencil, o in lemon, u in circus.

**wa|ter|skin** (wôt′ər skin′, wot′-), *n.* a vessel or bag of skin used for the storage or transportation of water.

**water snail**, **1** any one of a group of gastropods that live in or frequent water. **2** = Archimedean screw.

**water snake**, **1** any one of various nonpoisonous snakes that live in or frequent water. **2** any one of several other snakes that live in or frequent water.

**wa|ter-soak** (wôt′ər sōk′, wot′-), *v.t.* to soak thoroughly with water.

**water softener**, **1** a chemical added to hard water to remove dissolved mineral matter. **2** a device containing such a chemical attached to a water line to soften water coming from it.

**wa|ter-sol|u|bil|i|ty** (wôt′ər sol′yə bil′ə tē, wot′-), *n.* the quality of dissolving easily in water.

**wa|ter-sol|u|ble** (wôt′ər sol′yə bəl, wot′-), *adj.* that will dissolve in water: *water-soluble vitamins.*

**water spaniel**, a large spaniel with a heavy, curly coat, often trained to swim out for wild birds, such as ducks or geese, that have been shot down by hunters.

**water speedwell**, a common speedwell growing in wet places.

**water spider**, any one of various aquatic spiders, such as a European freshwater spider that makes a baglike nest opening downward beneath the surface of the water, so that it may be filled with air brought down in bubbles on the spider's body.

**wa|ter|splash** (wôt′ər splash′, wot′-), *n.* a shallow stream or ford crossing a road.

**wa|ter|spout** (wôt′ər spout′, wot′-), *n.* **1** a pipe that takes away or spouts water, especially one used to drain water from a roof. **2** a rapidly spinning column or cone of mist, spray, and water, produced by the action of a whirlwind over the ocean or a large lake. **3** *Obsolete.* a sudden, very heavy fall of rain; cloudburst.

**water sprite**, a sprite, nymph, or spirit, supposed to live in water, such as a Naiad, Nereid, or kelpie.

**water starwort**, any slender tiny-flowered herb of a group growing either in water or damp soil.

**water stone**, = hydrolite.

**water strider**, any long-legged bug of a family that walks on the surface of water and feeds on other insects.

**wa|ter-struck** (wôt′ər struk′, wot′-), *adj.* (of bricks) that have been dipped in water after leaving the mold and before firing.

**water supply**, **1** water for the use of a community or particular area. **2** the process of collecting and piping water for a community or particular area.

**water system**, **1a** reservoirs, wells, pipes, and other equipment, together with the persons responsible for them, by which water is provided to a city; physical plant and personnel of a water supply. **b** = water supply. **2** a river with all its tributary streams.

**water table**, **1** the level below which the ground is saturated with water. **2** *Architecture.* a projecting course, molding, or the like, sloping on top, to throw off rainfall.

**water thrush**, **1** any American warbler of a group usually found close to a running stream and resembling small thrushes, such as the Louisiana water thrush and the northern water thrush. **2** a European water ouzel.

**wa|ter|tight** (wôt′ər tīt′, wot′-), *adj.* **1** so tight that no water can get in or out. Ships are often divided into watertight compartments by watertight partitions. **2** *Figurative.* leaving no opening as for misunderstanding or criticism; perfect: *a watertight argument.* — **wa′ter|tight′ness**, *n.*

**water tower**, **1** a very tall structure for the storage of water, such as a standpipe, or that by which a tank cistern is supported, by means of which water may be supplied to a building or community at a constant pressure. **2** a fire-extinguishing apparatus used to throw water on the upper parts of tall buildings.

**wa|ter-tube boiler** (wôt′ər tüb′, -tyüb′; wot′-), a steam boiler in which the water circulates through tubes exposed to fire and the gases of combustion.

**water turbine**, a turbine which uses water from a dam, waterfall, or the like, for its motive power; turbine operated by the force of a current of water.

**water turkey**, a large, blackish bird with a long tail and snakelike neck, found in swampy areas of the southern United States and south through tropical America; snakebird; anhinga.

**water vapor**, water in a gaseous state, especially when fairly diffused, as it is in the air, and below the temperature of boiling, as distinguished from steam.

**wa|ter-vas|cu|lar** (wôt′ər vas′kyə lər, wot′-), *adj.* of or having to do with the water-vascular system.

**water-vascular system**, the system of water-filled canals connecting the tube feet of echinoderms.

**water wagon**, *U.S.* a truck or cart fitted with a large tank for carrying water.

**on the water wagon**, *Informal.* not drinking alcoholic liquor; in or into a state of temperance: *Spain took the pledge and got on the water wagon* (Wall Street Journal).

**wa|ter|ward** (wôt′ər wərd, wot′-), *adv.* toward the water: *The thoughts of the five million boat-owners throughout our land turn waterward* (Saturday Review).

**water wave**, **1** a wave set into wet hair with combs and dried with heat. **2** a wave of water.

**wa|ter-wave** (wôt′ər wāv′, wot′-), *v.t.*, **-waved, -wav|ing.** to arrange (hair) in a water wave.

**wa|ter|way** (wôt′ər wā′, wot′-), *n.* **1** a river, canal, or other body of water that ships can go on: *Seine River and its branches form the chief commercial waterway of France* (W. R. McConnell). **2** a channel for water. **3** a hollowed plank along either side of a ship's deck for draining off water through the scuppers.

**wa|ter|weed** (wôt′ər wēd′, wot′-), *n.*, or **water weed**, **1** any aquatic plant with inconspicuous flowers, such as the pondweed. **2** = elodea.

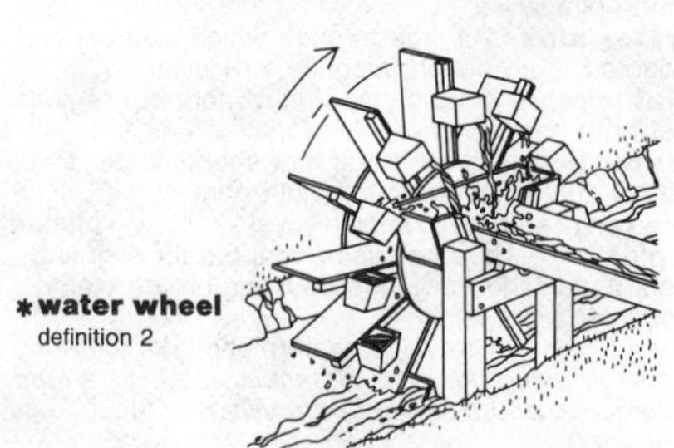

***water wheel** definition 2

***water wheel**, or **wa|ter|wheel** (wôt′ər hwēl′ wot′-), *n.* **1** a wheel turned with water and designed to drive machinery, such as that of a mill or pump. The grindstones of grain mills used to be run by water wheels. **2** a wheel for raising water, especially for irrigation purposes, by means of buckets or boxes fitted on its circumference.

**wa|ter-white** (wôt′ər hwīt′, wot′-), *adj.* colorless and transparent, as water or glass. — **wa′ter-white′ness**, *n.*

**water wings**, two waterproof bags filled with air and put under a person's arms to hold him afloat while he is learning to swim.

**water witch**, **1** waterfinder; dowser. **2** = grebe.

**water witching**, the practice of dowsing.

**wa|ter|work** (wôt′ər wėrk′, wot′-), *n. Obsolete.* **1** a pageant exhibited on the water. **2** waterworks.

**wa|ter|works** (wôt′ər wėrks′, wot′-), *n.pl. or sing.* **1** Also, **water works** (*often sing. in use*). **a** a system of pipes, reservoirs, water towers, pumps, and other equipment, for supplying a city or town with water. **b** a building with machinery for pumping water; pumping station. **2** *Slang.* a flow of tears, especially a sudden and violent flow. **3** *Obsolete.* an ornamental fountain or cascade.

**wa|ter|worn** (wôt′ər wôrn′, -wōrn′; wot′-), *adj.* worn or smoothed by the action of water: *water-worn pebbles rattling under the pounding surf.*

**wa|ter|y** (wôt′ər ē, wot′-), *adj.* **1** of water; connected with water. **2** full of water; wet: *watery soil.* **3a** indicating rain: *a watery sky.* **b** having much rain; rainy: *a watery summer.* **4** full of tears; tearful: *watery eyes.* **5** containing too much water: *watery soup.* **6** like water: *a watery discharge.* **7** *Figurative.* **a** pale or thin in color: *a watery blue.* **b** weak; insipid; ineffectual; vapid: *a watery but harmless story.* **8** in or under water: *A drowned person or a sunken ship goes to a watery grave.* — **wa′ter|i|ness**, *n.*

**WATS** (no periods), Wide Area Telephone Service (a system of unlimited long-distance telephone service for a flat monthly charge, used by business and industry).

**Wat|son-Crick** (wot′sən krik′), *adj.* of or having to do with various genetic concepts and hypotheses, such as the double helix and the central dogma, postulated by the American biologist James D. Watson (born 1928) and the English biologist Francis H. C. Crick (born 1916): ... *the so-called Watson-Crick Theory, which holds that all genetic traits are basically derived from the structure of a kind of master molecule in the chromosomes called deoxyribonucleic acid, or DNA* (New York Times).

**Watson-Crick model**, a model of the double-helical molecular structure of deoxyribonucleic acid; double helix.

**watt** (wot), *n.* a unit of electric power equal to the flow of one ampere under the pressure of one volt, to one joule or $10^7$ ergs per second, or to 1/746 horsepower: *My lamp uses 60 watts; my toaster uses 1,000 watts. Abbr:* w (no period). [< James *Watt*, 1736-1819, a Scottish engineer, who pioneered in the development of the steam engine]

**watt|age** (wot′ij), *n.* **1** the amount of electric power, measured in watts, especially kilowatts. **2** the power, in watts, necessary for the operation of an electrical appliance, motor, or the like.

**Wat|teau** (wä tō′; *French* vȧ tō′), *adj.* designating things associated with Antoine Watteau (1684-1721), a French painter, or his paintings, as style of dress and coloring.

***Watteau back**

***Watteau back**, an arrangement of the back of a dress with a broad pleat falling from the neck to the end of the skirt without being gathered in at the waist.

**watt-hour** (wot′our′), *n.* a measure of electrical energy or work, equal to the work done by one watt acting for one hour. *Abbr:* w.-hr.

***wattle¹** definition 1a

***wat|tle¹** (wot′əl), *n.* **1a** the bright-red flesh hanging down from the throat on the males of chickens, turkeys, or other domestic fowls and certain other birds. **b** a fleshy appendage below the throat of certain reptiles, such as the iguana. **c** the barbel of a fish. **2** *Slang.* a loose fold of skin hanging under a person's chin. [origin uncertain]

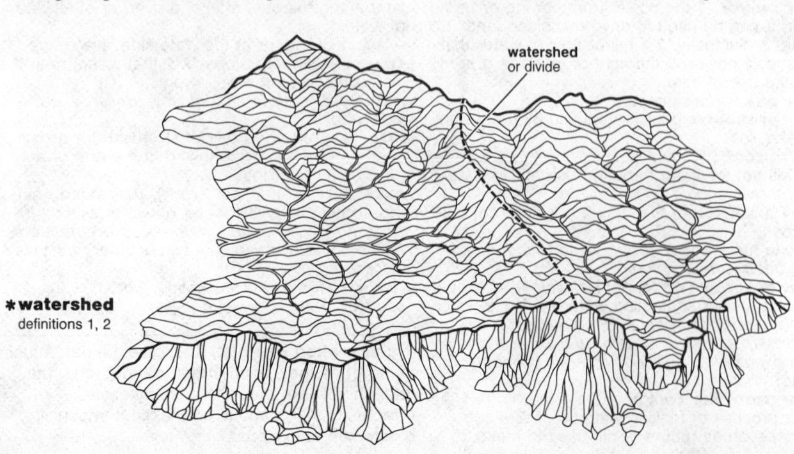


***watershed** definitions 1, 2

**wat|tle**[2] (wot′əl), *n., v.,* **-tled, -tling,** *adj.* —*n.* **1** Also, **wattles. a** sticks interwoven with twigs, branches, or reeds; framework of wicker: *a hut built of wattle.* **b** a framework of poles or rods for a thatched roof. **2** any one of various acacias of Australia, used to make wattles and in tanning. **3** *British Dialect.* **a** any stick, wand, rod, or twig. **b** a sheep hurdle made of wattle.
—*v.t.* **1** to make (a fence, wall, roof, hut, or barrier) of wattle. **2** to twist or weave together (twigs, branches, or reeds). **3** to bind together with interwoven twigs, branches, or reeds.
—*adj.* made or built of wattle.
[Old English *watol*]

**wattle and daub** or **dab,** *Especially British.* a building material consisting of wattle plastered with clay.

**wat|tle|bird** (wot′əl bėrd′), *n.* any one of certain Australian honey eaters that have wattles.

**wat|tled**[1] (wot′əld), *adj.* having wattles.

**wat|tled**[2] (wot′əld), *adj.* made or built of wattle; formed by interwoven twigs; interlaced.

**watt|less** (wot′lis), *adj. Electricity.* without watts or power (applied to an alternating current that differs in phase by 90 degrees from the electromotive force, or to an electromotive force that differs in phase by 90 degrees from the current).

**watt|me|ter** (wot′mē′tər), *n.* an instrument for measuring electric power in watts; voltammeter.

**watt-sec|ond** (wot′sek′ənd), *n.* a unit of electrical energy or work, equal to one watt maintained for one second.

**Wa|tu|si** or **Wa|tus|si** (wä tü′sē), *n., pl.* **-si** or **-sis.** a member of a people of central Africa, originally from Ethiopia, many of the men of which are over seven feet tall. Also, **Tusi, Tussi, Tutsi, Watutsi.**

**wa|tu|si** (wä tü′sē), *n., v.,* **-sied, -si|ing.** —*n.* a dance in two-beat rhythm, marked by vigorous, jerky movements of the arms and head.
—*v.i.* to dance the watusi.
[< *Watusi*]

**Wa|tut|si** (wä tüt′sē), *n., pl.* **-si** or **-sis.** = Watusi.

**waucht** (wäнt, wôнt), *n., v. Scottish.* —*n.* a copious draft.
—*v.t., v.i.* to drink at a gulp or in large drafts; drain (a goblet).
[perhaps variant of *quaff.* Compare etym. under **quaich.**]

**waught** (wäнt, wôнt), *n., v.* = waucht.

**waul** (wôl), *v., n.* —*v.i.* to wail, especially loudly and harshly.
—*n.* a howling cry; wail. Also, **wawl.**
[apparently imitative]

**waulk** (wôk), *v.t.* to shrink and thicken (woolen cloth) by soaking, heating, pounding, and rubbing. [apparently related to **walk**]

***wave** (wāv), *n., v.,* **waved, wav|ing.** —*n.* **1** a moving ridge or swell of water: *The raft rose and fell on the waves.* **2** any movement like this. **3** a body of water; sea. **4** *Figurative.* a swell, surge, or rush; sudden increase, as of some emotion, influence, or condition: *waves of invaders. The announcement brought a wave of enthusiasm. A trend is sometimes called "the wave of the future."* **5** a curve or series of curves: *waves in a girl's hair.* **6** = permanent wave. **7** a wavy line of color or texture, as on a watered fabric. **8** the act of waving, especially of something, as a signal: *a wave of the hand.* **9** *Physics.* a movement of particles by which energy is transferred from one place to another; vibration. Light, heat, and sound travel in waves. Waves are usually measured by their length, amplitude, velocity, and frequency. In a longitudinal wave, the motion of the particles is parallel to the direction in which the wave travels; in a transverse wave, it is perpendicular to the direction in which the wave travels. **10** a change of atmospheric pressure or temperature moving in a particular direction; heat wave or cold wave: *A wave of cold weather is sweeping over the country.*
—*v.i.* **1** to move as waves do; move up and down or back and forth; sway: *The tall grass waved in the breeze.* **SYN:** rock, fluctuate, undulate. **2** to be moved back and forth or up and down regularly, especially as a signal: *The lady's handkerchief waved in token of encouragement and triumph* (Edward G. Bulwer-Lytton). **3** to have a wavelike or curving form: *Her hair waves naturally.*
—*v.t.* **1** to cause (something) to sway or move back and forth or up and down: *The wind waved the flag. Wave your hand.* **2** to signal or direct by waving: *She waved him away. The policeman waved the speeding driver to the side of the road.* **3** to shake in the air; brandish: *I waved the stick at them.* **4a** to give a wavelike form or pattern to: *Some girls wave their hair.* **b** to give a wavelike appearance or texture to; water: *to wave silk.*

**make waves,** *U.S. Informal.* to cause disturbance; upset a normal course or routine: *This is the kind of broker you love to have working for you ... He makes no waves, runs up no extensive phone bills, keeps his major account supplied with gifts of wine, dinners, and tickets* (Atlantic).
[Old English *wafian*] —**wave′like′,** *adj.*
—*Syn. n.* **1 Wave, breaker, ripple** mean a moving ridge on the surface of water. **Wave** is the general term: *The little boat bobbed up and down on the waves.* **Breaker** applies to a heavy ocean wave that breaks into foam as it nears the shore or strikes rocks: *Our favorite sport is riding the breakers in.* **Ripple** applies to a tiny wave, such as one caused by the ruffling of a smooth surface by a breeze: *There is scarcely a ripple on the lake tonight.*

***wave**
*n.,* definition 9

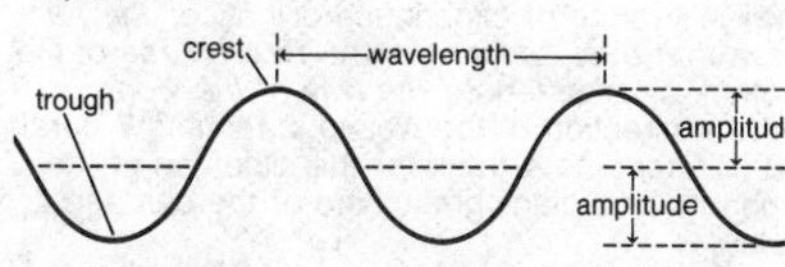


**longitudinal wave**

**transverse wave**

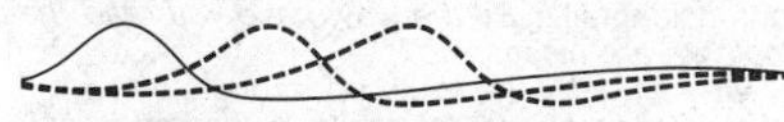

**WAVE** or **Wave** (wāv), *n.* a member of the WAVES; woman in the United States Navy other than a nurse.

**wave|band** (wāv′band′), *n.,* or **wave band,** a series of wavelengths of electromagnetic waves that fall between two given limits: *The honeyed tones of the announcers fill every waveband on local wireless sets* (London Times).

**wave cloud,** a cloud consisting of a series of long, narrow parallel bands resembling waves, produced by layers of air flowing one over another. Glider pilots look for wave clouds as indicators of air currents.

**waved** (wāvd), *adj.* **1** having a wave or waves. **2** having a wavy or undulating form or outline; marked with wavy lines; watered, as silk.

**waved whelk,** a whelk that grows up to 3 inches in length, found off the coasts of northern Europe and off the northeastern coast of North America.

**wave equation,** *Physics.* **1** a partial differential equation that is used to describe wave motion. **2** = Schrödinger wave equation.

**wave form, 1** the form assumed by a wave. **2** *Electricity.* the shape of the curve obtained by plotting the instantaneous values of an alternating current against time.

**wave front,** *Physics.* the continuous line or surface including all the points in space reached by a wave or vibration at the same instant in traveling through a medium.

**wave function,** a mathematical function in quantum mechanics describing the propagation of waves by an elementary particle.

**wave guide,** or **wave|guide** (wāv′gīd′), *n. Electronics.* a piece of hollow metal tubing, commonly rectangular or circular in cross section, or a dielectric cylinder, used to propagate ultrahigh-frequency electromagnetic waves.

**wave|length** (wāv′lengkth′, -length′), *n.,* or **wave length,** *Physics.* the distance between one peak or crest of a wave of light, sound, or other electromagnetic or mechanical energy, and the next corresponding peak or crest. The wavelengths of radio waves are measured in meters; the wavelengths of X rays are measured in billionths of an inch.

**on the same wavelength,** *Informal.* attuned to one another; in harmony or accord: *I was acceptable only on the grounds that I was on the same wavelength and played their kind of music* (London Times). *She and other designers on the same wavelength are busy proving "classics" doesn't have to mean dowdy* (New York Times).

**wave|less** (wāv′lis), *adj.* free from waves; undisturbed; still: *a strange and glassy, waveless sea.* —**wave′less|ly,** *adv.*

**wave|let** (wāv′lit), *n.* a little wave.

**wa|vel|lite** (wā′və līt), *n. Mineralogy.* hydrous phosphate of aluminum, found in globular aggregates with a radiating structure. *Formula:* $Al_3(OH)_3(PO_4)_2 \cdot 5H_2O$ [< William *Wavell,* died 1829, an English physician, who discovered it + *-ite*[1]]

**wave-me|chan|i|cal** (wāv′mə kan′ə kəl), *adj.* of or having to do with wave mechanics: *In the newer wave-mechanical picture of the atom the orbits are replaced by probability distribution of electrons* (W. D. Corner).

**wave mechanics,** *Physics.* a theory ascribing characteristics of waves to subatomic particles and attempting to interpret physical phenomena on this basis.

**wave|me|ter** (wāv′mē′tər), *n. Electricity.* an instrument used to measure the wavelength of electromagnetic waves.

**wave motion, 1** motion like that of waves in water, alternately concave and convex. **2** the forward undulating or vibrational motion of waves by which disturbance of equilibrium is transmitted.

**wave number,** (in a series of regularly fluctuating waves) the number of waves in one centimeter's length along the line of advance.

**wave offering,** an offering that was moved (waved) from left to right or vice versa by the priest when presented, and became the portion of the priests and their families (in the Bible, Exodus 29:27).

**wav|er**[1] (wā′vər), *n.* a person or thing that waves.

**wa|ver**[2] (wā′vər), *v., n.* —*v.i.* **1** to move to and fro; flutter. **2** to vary in intensity; flicker: *a wavering light.* **3** to grow fainter, then louder, or change pitch up and down fairly quickly; quaver, tremble, or pulsate: *a wavering voice.* **4a** to be undecided; hesitate: *Her choice wavered between the blue dress and the green one.* **SYN:** See syn. under **hesitate. b** to be undermined by doubt: *My courage wavered.* **SYN:** See syn. under **hesitate. 5** to become unsteady; begin to give way: *The battle line wavered and broke.* **6** *Obsolete.* to wander about; rove.
—*n.* the act of wavering.
[perhaps < *wave,* verb + *-er*[6]. Compare Old English *wæfre* unsteady.] —**wa′ver|er,** *n.* —**wa′ver|ing|ly,** *adv.*

**Wa|ver|ley** (wā′vər lē), *n.* **1** the first of a famous series of novels by Sir Walter Scott. **2** a pen name of Sir Walter Scott.

**wa|ver|y** (wā′vər ē), *adj.* wavering; unsteady; fluttering; tremulous: *high, wavery tenors.*

**WAVES** or **Waves** (wāvz), *n.pl.* a formerly distinct unit of the United States Navy comprising women volunteers. [< *W*(omen) *A*(ccepted for) *V*(olunteer) *E*(mergency) *S*(ervice)]

**wave set,** a preparation used before setting the hair to give it waves or make it stay curly.

**wave theory,** *Physics.* undulatory theory.

**wave train,** *Physics.* a group of waves sent out at successive intervals along the same path from a vibrating body.

**wave trap,** a device for eliminating an undesired radio signal by absorbing it in an extra circuit that can be tuned to the wave length of the signal.

**wa|vey** (wā′vē), *n., pl.* **-veys.** *Canadian.* the snow goose. Also, **wavy.** [< Cree *wehwew* goose]

**wav|y**[1] (wā′vē), *adj.,* **wav|i|er, wav|i|est. 1** having waves; having many waves: *wavy hair, a wavy line.* **2** moving with a wavelike motion. **3** (of ground or the surface of the country) rising and falling gently in a succession of rounded heights and hollows. **4** *Botany.* **a** undulating: *a leaf with a wavy margin.* **b** having an undulating margin.
—**wav′i|ly,** *adv.* —**wav′i|ness,** *n.*

**wa|vy**[2] (wā′vē), *n., pl.* **-vies.** = wavey.

**waw** (vôv, väv), *n.* = vav.

**wa-wa** (wä′wä), *adj., n.* = wah-wah.

**wawl** (wôl), *v.i., n.* = waul.

**wax**[1] (waks), *n., v., adj.* —*n.* **1a** a yellowish substance made by bees for constructing their honeycombs. Wax is hard when cold, but can be easily shaped when warm. **b** a similar substance made by various kinds of scale insects. **2** a substance like this, such as ozocerite or paraffin. Most of the wax used for candles or for keeping air from jelly is really paraffin. Sealing wax and the wax used by shoemakers for rubbing thread are other common waxes. **3** a compound containing wax for polishing floors, furniture, and other surfaces. **4** = earwax. **5** *Figurative.* a thing or person easily manipulated: *The poor fellow is wax in her hands.* **6** *Botany.* a waxlike secretion of certain plants: *Nature protects most plants, flowers, and fruits with a shield of wax* (George R. Greenbank). **7** *Slang.* a phonograph record: *The Dukes of Dixieland, familiar here only as performers on wax, tape, and the air, can now be seen by the naked eye* (New Yorker).
—*v.t.* **1** to treat with wax; rub, stiffen, or polish with wax or something like wax: *to wax leather or a mustache. We wax that floor once a month.*

**Pronunciation Key:** hat, āge, cãre, fär; let, ēqual, tėrm; it, īce; hot, ōpen, ôrder; oil, out; cup, pu̇t, rüle; child; long; thin; ᴛʜen; zh, measure; ə represents **a** in about, **e** in taken, **i** in pencil, **o** in lemon, **u** in circus.

**2** *Slang.* to make a phonograph recording of: *Artur Schnabel waxed the Beethoven piano sonatas* (New York Times).

—***adj.*** of wax; waxen.

[Old English *weax*] —**wax′er,** *n.* —**wax′like′,** *adj.*

**wax**$^2$ (waks), *v.i.,* **waxed, waxed** or **wax|en, wax-ing. 1** to grow bigger or greater; increase: *The moon waxes till it becomes full, and then wanes.* **2** to become: *to wax impatient. The party waxed merry.* [Old English *weaxan*]

**wax**$^3$ (waks), *n. Especially British Informal.* a fit of rage; angry condition: *to be in a wax.* [perhaps < phrase "to wax angry" < *wax*$^2$]

**wax bean,** a yellow string bean with a waxy appearance.

**wax|ber|ry** (waks′ber′ē, -bər-), *n., pl.* **-ries. 1a** = wax myrtle. **b** = bayberry. **c** = snowberry. **2** the fruit of any one of these.

**wax|bill** (waks′bil′), *n.* **1** any small bird of a group allied to the weaverbirds, with a white, pink, or red bill having a waxy appearance. **2** = Java sparrow.

**waxed paper,** = wax paper.

**wax|en** (wak′sən), *adj.* **1** of wax; made of wax: *For now my love is thaw'd; Which, like a waxen image 'gainst a fire Bears no impression of the thing it was* (Shakespeare). **2** *Figurative.* like wax; smooth, soft, and pale: *Her skin is waxen.* **3** covered or filled with wax. [< *wax*$^1$ + *-en*$^2$]

**wax gourd, 1** = tallow gourd. **2** its fruit.

**wax|ing** (wak′sing), *n.* **1** the coating of thread with wax before sewing. **2** a method of blacking, dressing, and polishing leather, to give it a finish. **3** the process of stopping out colors in batik.

**waxing moon,** the moon between the new moon and full moon.

**wax insect,** any scale insect of various species that secrete or produce wax.

**wax|jack** (waks′jak′), *n.* a device for melting sealing wax that was used in the 1700's, consisting of a length of wick wound around a spindle, with the part for burning fed through a small hole.

**wax|light** (waks′līt′), *n.* a candle, taper, or night light made of wax.

**wax moth,** a moth whose larvae feed on the honeycomb; bee moth.

**wax museum,** a museum of waxworks: *a traveling wax museum that would depict Canadian military history* (Maclean's).

**wax myrtle, 1** an evergreen shrub or tree of eastern North America, whose small berries are coated with wax that is used for candles; candleberry; waxberry. Wax myrtle is related to the sweet gale. **2** any one of certain related plants, such as the bayberry.

**wax palm, 1** an Andean pinnate-leaved palm. Its stem and leaves are the source of a resinous wax. **2** a Brazilian palmate-leaved palm whose young leaves are coated with wax; carnauba.

**wax paper,** paper coated with paraffin or other waxlike substance, used for moistureproof wrappings.

**wax|plant** (waks′plant′, -plänt′), *n.* any tropical Asian and Australian plant of a group of the milkweed family having shiny leaves and waxy flowers.

**wax tree,** any one of various trees yielding wax, such as a sumac of Japan, or the wax myrtle.

**wax|weed** (waks′wēd′), *n.* a small, purple-flowered, American plant of the loosestrife family that has a viscid down on the foliage.

**wax|wing** (waks′wing′), *n.* a small bird with a showy crest, smooth, brown plumage, and red markings (resembling bits of red sealing wax) on the tips of the wings, such as the cedar waxwing or cedarbird, and the Bohemian waxwing; chatterer.

**wax|work** (waks′wėrk′), *n.* a figure or figures made of wax.

**waxworks, a** an exhibition of figures made of wax, especially of figures representing celebrated or notorious characters. **b** the place of such an exhibition; wax museum.

**wax|work|er** (waks′wėr′kər), *n.* **1** a person who works in wax; a maker of waxwork. **2** a bee that produces wax.

**wax worm,** the larva of the wax moth.

**wax|y** (wak′sē), *adj.,* **wax|i|er, wax|i|est. 1** like wax. **2** made of wax; containing wax; waxen. **3** abounding in or covered with wax; waxed. **4** *Medicine.* characterized by or affected with the formation and deposit of an insoluble protein in tissues and organs. —**wax′i|ness,** *n.*

**way** (wā), *n., adv.* —*n.* **1** form or mode of doing; manner; style; fashion: *a new way of cooking, a new way of treating a disease. She is wearing her hair in a new way.* SYN: mode. **2** a method; means: *Doctors are using new ways of preventing disease.* **3** a point; feature; respect; detail: *The plan is bad in several ways.* **4** direction: *Look this way. Which way are you going?* **5** motion along a course: *The guide led the way.* **6** distance: *The sun is a long way off.* **7** a means of moving along a course; road; path; street; course: *The hunter found a way through the forest. She lives across the way.* SYN: route, highway, avenue, lane. **8a** space for passing or going ahead. **b** *Figurative.* freedom of action; scope; opportunity: *to find one's way clear to leave earlier than usual.* **c** *Law.* right of way. **9** Often, **ways,** habit; custom: *Don't mind his teasing; it's just his way.* **10** one's wish; will: *A spoiled child wants his own way all the time.* **11a** condition; state: *That sick man is in a bad way.* **b** *Informal.* a kind of work or business; occupation; calling: *in the steel way.* **12** movement forward; forward motion: *The ship slowly gathered way as it slid through the water.* SYN: progress, advance. **13** *Informal.* district; area; region: *He lives out our way.* **14** range of experience or notice: *the best idea that ever came my way.* **15** a course of life, action, or experience: *the way of the world.* **16** the direction of the weave in fabric. **17** parallel sills forming a track for the slides as of the uprights of a planing machine or the carriage of a lathe.

—***adv.*** *Informal.* **1** at or to a great distance; far: *The cloud of smoke stretched way out to the pier.* **2** at or to a great degree; much: *He is way behind the times. This dress is way too big for her.*

**all the way,** without reservation; completely: *The new principal asked the teachers and students to go all the way with him in improving the school.*

**by the way, a** while coming or going; on the road; during a journey: *We stopped by the way to eat.* **b** *Figurative.* in passing; in that connection; incidentally: *By the way, have you read the book we are discussing?*

**by way of, a** by the route of; through; via: *He went to India by way of Japan.* **b** *Figurative.* as; for; for the purpose of; to serve as: *a summary given by way of introduction. By way of an answer he just nodded.* **c** *Especially British.* making a profession of or having a reputation for (being or doing something): *He is by way of being a clever cartoonist.*

**come a long way,** to accomplish much; make great progress: *For a couple of country boys, they have come a long way in the business world.*

**come** (or **fall**) **one's way,** to happen to one: *That was a wonderful experience; I didn't expect it to fall my way.*

**every which way,** *Informal.* in all directions; in disorder: *children with hair and clothes every which way. Wires led every which way from the truck to the Mansion* (New Yorker).

**find one's way, a** to make one's way by observation, search, or inquiry: *He finally found his way home.* **b** to come to a place by natural course or by force of circumstances: *The river finds its way to the sea. The picture found its way to the auction room.*

**give way, a** to make way; retreat; yield: *to give way to superior forces. We have adhered to quality and not given way to the cry for the production of construction* (London Times). **b** to break down or fail, as health, strength, or one's voice: *His heart finally gave way and he died.* **c** to abandon oneself to emotion: *to give way to despair.* **d** *Finance.* to drop in value: *The dollar keeps giving way.*

**go a long way,** to help very much: *A little less preoccupation with ... sectional interests would go for a long, long way towards getting us out of the present economic mess* (Manchester Guardian Weekly).

**go out of the way,** to make a special effort: *The government still seems to be going out of its way to court unpopularity about money for the universities* (New Scientist).

**have a way with,** to be persuasive or successful with: *He had a way with and an eye for the ladies* (Time).

**in a way,** to some extent: *He is handsome in a way. In a way it's better you came late.*

**in the way,** being an obstacle, hindrance, or annoyance: *He is cast as an irritating gadfly, standing in the way of Lloyd George's efforts to win a peace that would give Germany its just due* (Saturday Review).

**in the way of, a** in a favorable position for doing or getting: *He put me in the way of a good investment.* **b** in the matter or business of; as regards: *We have a small stock in the way of hats.*

**(in) the worst way,** *Informal.* very much: *That poor family needs help in the worst way. He lacks experience in business but wants to succeed in it in the worst way.*

**know one's way around,** to be completely familiar with: [*They*] *really know their way around a roulette table* (Manchester Guardian Weekly).

**look the other way,** to turn aside so as not to see something; pretend unawareness: *What the statistics did not show was the thousands of times the police simply looked the other way* (Time).

**lose one's way,** not to know any longer where one is: *She lost her way in the streets of London.*

**make one's way, a** to go: *It was in despair of reaching Italy that the young scholar* [*Erasmus*] *made his way to Oxford* (John Green). **b** to get ahead; succeed: *He made his way rapidly in the world of finance.*

**make way, a** to give space for passing or going ahead; make room: *Automobiles must make way for a fire engine. If a young man sees his mother-in-law coming along the path, he must retreat into the bush and make way for her* (Gouldsbury and Sheane). **b** to move forward: *We lost our maintopmast, so that after the storm was over we could not make any way* (M. Bishop).

**no way,** *U.S. Informal.* under no circumstances: *None of these conditions will ever get any better.* (*"No way," as they keep saying ...*) (New Yorker).

**once in a way,** occasionally: *Now I like this kind of thing once in a way* (Anthony Trollope).

**on the way,** coming; getting closer: *Help is on the way. New machines to do farm work are on the way. The country is well on the way to industrialization.*

**out of the way, a** so as not to be an obstacle, hindrance, or annoyance: *We moved the fallen tree out of the way.* **b** far from where most people live or go: *The farm lies so much out of the way that we had a hard time finding it.* **c** out of reach; not in danger: *While the fight was going on, he tried to keep out of the way.* **d** to death: *to put an animal out of the way.* **e** *Figurative.* unusual; remarkable; strange: *Her abilities are not out of the way.* **f** *Figurative.* off the right path; improper; wrong: *Did you ever know me to do anything out of the way?* (William Dean Howells).

**pave the way,** to make ready; prepare: *Parents can do much in advance to pave the way for a smooth transition from home to camp for a child* (New York Times).

**pick one's way,** to move with great care and caution over treacherous ground or a difficult situation: *One has to crawl through narrow passages ... pick his way down sharp descents* (Scientific American).

**rub the right way,** to please; pacify: *It is impossible to rub him the right way when he is in such a state.*

**rub the wrong way,** to annoy; irritate: *They rub everybody the wrong way because of their clear implication that ... doctors are incompetent* (Bulletin of Atomic Scientists).

**see one's way,** to be willing or able: *He did not see his way clear to allow their names to remain upon the register* (Law Times).

**stroke the wrong way, a** to stroke (an animal) in a direction contrary to that in which the fur naturally lies: *The kitten doesn't mind being stroked the wrong way.* **b** *Figurative.* to ruffle or irritate (a person), as by going counter to his wishes: *Somebody's been stroking him the wrong way* (Anthony Trollope).

**take one's way,** to set out; go: *She took her way sadly and slowly down the pier* (Joseph Ashby-Sterry).

**under way,** going on; in motion; in progress: *The committee finally got its plans under way. ... their obstinate failure to recognize, even after it was well under way, the rise and domination of Prussia* (Edmund Wilson).

**ways,** timbers on which a ship is built and launched: *to slide a ship down the ways.*

[Old English *weg*]

—***Syn.*** *n.* **1, 2 Way, method, manner** mean mode or means. **Way** is the general word, sometimes suggesting a personal or special mode of doing or saying something: *She uses old ways of cooking.* **Method** applies to an orderly way, suggesting a special system of doing something or a definite arrangement of steps to follow: *He follows a new method of teaching reading.* **Manner** applies to a characteristic or particular method or way, much as the word *style* does: *He rides in the western manner.*

► **way, ways.** *Way,* meaning distance (def. 6), is standard; *ways* is nonstandard: *a long way* (not *ways*) *off.*

► The nautical phrase **under way** (*The ship is under way*) is sometimes written *under weigh* from the mistaken notion that it refers to the weighing of the anchor.

**wa|yang** (wä′yäng), *n.* a stylized Indonesian puppet play based on legend and performed to music, and sometimes with live actors. [< Javanese *wayang*]

**way|bill** (wā′bil′), *n.* a list of goods with a statement of where they are to go and how they are to get there.

**way|fare** (wā′fãr′), *v.i.,* **-fared, -far|ing.** to journey or travel, especially on foot. [back formation < *wayfaring*]

**way|far|er** (wā′fãr′ər), *n.* a traveler, especially one who travels on foot.

**way|far|ing** (wā′fãr′ing), *adj., n.* traveling; journeying. [Middle English *wayfaringe,* Old English *wayfarende* < *weg* way + *farende,* present participle of *faran* to fare]

**wayfaring tree,** 1 a European shrub or small tree of the honeysuckle family with dense cymes of small, white flowers, common along roadsides. 2 = hobblebush.

**way|go|ing** (wā′gō′ing), *n., adj. Scottish.* — ***n.*** a going away or leaving; departure.
— ***adj.*** departing; outgoing.

**way|laid** (wā′lād′, wā′lād′), *v.* the past tense and past participle of **waylay:** *I waylaid him when he entered the meeting.*

**Way|land** (wā′lənd), *n.,* or **Wayland the Smith,** a marvelously skilled smith, normally invisible but able to become visible under certain circumstances, so called in English folklore, but encountered as a standard figure in all early Germanic folklore.

**way|lay** (wā′lā′, wā′lā′), *v.t.,* **-laid, -lay|ing. 1** to lie in wait for; attack on the way: *Robin Hood waylaid travelers and robbed them.* **2** to stop (a person) on his way: *Newspaper reporters waylaid the famous actor and asked him many questions.* [< *way* + *lay*[1]; probably patterned on Middle Low German *wegelagen* < *wegelage* an ambush]
— **way′lay′er,** *n.*

**way|leave** (wā′lēv′), *n. Law.* **1** permission to make or use a way across private land. **2** payment for such permission.

**way|less** (wā′lis), *adj.* having no way or road; pathless; trackless.

**way|mark** (wā′märk′), *n.* a mark or sign set up along a way; guidepost; milestone.

**way-off** (wā′ôf′, -of′), *adj.* distant: *The way-off sound of children's voices* (New Yorker).

**way of life,** the habits of an individual, family, or community with respect to food, habitation, manners, or morals; lifeway: *The automobile changed the people's way of life in many lands* (Ernest W. Williams, Jr.).

**way of the cross, 1** the way or course followed by Christ in going to Calvary to be crucified. **2** a way or course marked by stations of the cross in commemoration of Christ's course. **3** the devotion of the stations of the cross.

**way-out** (wā′out′), *adj. Slang.* far-out.

**way point,** *U.S.* a stopping place on a route or during a journey.

**ways** (wāz), *n.pl.* See under **way**.

**-ways,** *suffix forming adverbs.* **1** in the direction or position of the ____: *Lengthways = in the direction of the length.*
**2** in ____ manner: *Anyways = in any manner.* [< *way* + *-s*[3]]

**ways and means, 1** ways of raising revenue for current governmental expenditures. **2** methods and resources that are at a person's disposal for effecting some object.

**way|side** (wā′sīd′), *n., adj.* — ***n.*** the edge of a road or path: *We ate lunch by the wayside.*
— ***adj.*** along the edge of a way or path: *We slept in a wayside inn.*
**go by the wayside,** to be put or left aside: *Several records went by the wayside during the session just ending, with Oct. 31 the banner day* (New York Times).

**way station,** *U.S.* a station between main stations, especially on a railroad or bus line.

**way-stop** (wā′stop′), *n.* a stop between main stations in the course of a journey.

**way train,** local train.

**way|ward** (wā′wərd), *adj.* **1** turning from the right way; disobedient; willful: *In a wayward mood, he ran away from home.* **SYN:** perverse, stubborn. **2** irregular; unsteady; erratic: *the wayward flight of some birds.* **3** *Obsolete.* untoward. — **way′ward|ly,** *adv.* — **way′ward|ness,** *n.*

**way|ward|en** (wā′wôr′dən), *n. Especially British.* a person elected to supervise highways, usually as a member of an official board.

**way|wi|ser** (wā′wī′zər), *n.* an instrument for measuring and indicating a distance traveled by road: *During the time that they were made and used waywisers were also known as hodometers, odometers, and perambulators* (London Times). [partial translation of German *Wegweiser* < *Weg* way + *Weiser* one that shows]

**way|worn** (wā′wôrn′, -wōrn′), *adj.* wearied or worn by traveling.

**wayz|goose** (wāz′güs′), *n., pl.* **-goos|es.** *British.* an annual festivity held in summer by the employees of a printing establishment, consisting of a dinner and usually an excursion into the country. [origin unknown]

**wa|zir** (wä zir′), *n.* = vizier.

**w.b.,** 1 warehouse book. 2 water ballast. 3 westbound.

**W.B.,** waybill.

**WBA** (no periods) or **W.B.A.,** World Boxing Association.

**w.c.,** 1 water closet. 2 without charge.

**W.C.,** 1 water closet. 2 Western-Central (a postal district in London).

**WCC** (no periods), World Council of Churches.

**W.C.T.U.** or **WCTU** (no periods), Woman's Christian Temperance Union.

**we** (wē; *unstressed* wi), *pron., pl. nom.; poss.,* **our** or **ours;** *obj.,* **us.** the 1st person nominative plural of **I. 1** the persons speaking: *We are glad to see you.* **2** the person speaking. An author, an editor, a king, or a judge sometimes uses *we* to mean *I.* **3** people in general, including the speaker. [Old English *wē*]
► **We** is frequently used as an indefinite pronoun in expressions like *we find, we sometimes feel,* to avoid passive and impersonal constructions.

**We|a** (wē′ə, wā′ə), *n., pl.* **We|a** or **We|as.** a member of a North American Indian tribe within the Miami, formerly living in Indiana.

**WEA** (no periods) or **W.E.A.,** Workers' Educational Association (of Great Britain).

**weak** (wēk), *adj.* **1** that can easily be broken, crushed, overcome, torn, or otherwise destroyed, ruined, or captured; not strong: *a weak chair, a weak foundation, weak defenses, a weak candidate, a weak link in a chain.* **2a** not having bodily strength or health: *The weak old man tottered as he walked.* **b** not functioning well; somewhat impaired: *weak eyes, weak hearing.* **3** lacking power, authority, or force: *a weak government, a weak law.* **4** *Figurative.* lacking moral strength or firmness: *a weak character. Their faith was weak.* **SYN:** irresolute. **5** *Figurative.* lacking mental power: *a weak mind.* **6a** lacking or poor in amount, volume, loudness, taste, or intensity: *a weak voice, a weak current of electricity.* **b** lacking in force or effectiveness: *a weak argument.* **7a** containing relatively little of the active ingredient or ingredients; not concentrated; diluted: *a weak solution of boric acid.* **b** of less than the normal or desired strength: *weak coffee. Weak wheat contains little gluten.* **8** lacking or poor in something specified: *She is still a little weak in spelling.* **9** inflected by additions of consonants to the stem, not by vowel change; regular. English weak verbs form the past tense and past participle by adding *-ed, -d,* or *-t. Example: want-wanted* (weak); *sing-sang-sung* (strong). **b** (of nouns and adjectives) inflected with a majority of endings with *-n,* as German *alten* in *zum alten Krug.* **10** *Phonetics.* **a** not stressed: *a weak syllable.* **b** not strong; light: *a weak accent.* **11** *Commerce.* of prices, especially on an exchange: **a** having a downward tendency; not firm. **b** characterized by a fluctuating or downward tendency: *a weak market. Industrials continue to be weak.* **12** *Prosody.* weakly stressed (especially of a word at the end of a line of poetry). **13** *Photography.* with the light and dark not strongly contrasted; thin: *a weak negative.* [Middle English *weke* < Scandinavian (compare Old Icelandic *veikr*)]
— ***Syn.* 1, 2 Weak, feeble, decrepit** mean lacking or inferior in strength, energy, or power. **Weak** is the general word: *She has weak ankles.* **Feeble** implies loss of strength from sickness or age, or, describing things, faintness or ineffectiveness: *He is too feeble to feed himself. She made a feeble effort to get to school on time.* **Decrepit** means worn out or broken down by age or long-continued use: *They have only one decrepit bed.*

**weak|en** (wē′kən), *v.t.* to make weak or weaker: *You can weaken tea by adding water.* — ***v.i.* 1** to grow or become weak or weaker. **2** to take a less firm attitude; give way: *We are almost to the top of the mountain; let's not weaken now.*
— **weak′en|er,** *n.*
— ***Syn.* *v.t.* Weaken, undermine, debilitate** mean to cause to lose strength, energy, or power. **Weaken** is the general word: *Poor organization weakened his argument.* **Undermine** means to weaken gradually by working secretly or treacherously: *Rumors undermined confidence in the company's stock.* **Debilitate** means to make (a person's constitution or mind) weak or feeble by damaging and taking away vitality or strength: *He was debilitated by disease.*

**weak|er sex** (wē′kər), women as a group; gentle sex.

**weaker vessel,** = woman (in the Bible, I Peter 3:7).

**weak|fish** (wēk′fish′), *n., pl.* **-fish|es** or (*collectively*) **-fish.** a spiny-finned saltwater food fish with a tender mouth, especially a species found along the Atlantic coast of the United States; squeteague. [American English < obsolete Dutch *weekvisch* soft fish]

**weak force,** = weak interaction.

**weak interaction,** an interaction between elementary particles that causes radioactive decay and involves little or no release of radioactive energy. The weak interaction controls the absorption and emission of neutrinos and is thought to control the coupling of fermions. Its hypothetical quantum is the W particle.

**weak|ish** (wē′kish), *adj.* somewhat weak.
— **weak′ish|ly,** *adv.* — **weak′ish|ness,** *n.*

**weak-kneed** (wēk′nēd′), *adj.* **1** having weak knees. **2** *Figurative.* yielding easily, as to opposition or intimidation.

**weak|ling** (wēk′ling), *n., adj.* — ***n.*** a weak person or animal.
— ***adj.*** weak; feeble.

**weak|ly** (wēk′lē), *adv., adj.,* **-li|er, -li|est.** — ***adv.*** in a weak manner.
— ***adj.*** weak; feeble; sickly. — **weak′li|ness,** *n.*

**weak mayor,** *U.S.* a mayor in a mayor-council type of government who has limited executive authority. A weak mayor appoints few or none of the city's administrative officials and has only limited control over them.

**weak-mind|ed** (wēk′mīn′did), *adj.* **1** having or showing little intelligence; feeble-minded. **2** lacking firmness of mind. — **weak′-mind′ed|ness,** *n.*

**weak|ness** (wēk′nis), *n.* **1** the quality or condition of being weak; lack of power, force, or vigor: *Weakness kept him in bed.* **2** a weak point; slight fault: *Putting things off is her weakness.*
**3** *Figurative.* **a** a fact or condition of liking that one is a little ashamed of; fondness: *a weakness for sweets.* **b** something for which one has such a liking.

**weak side, 1** the side of a person's character at which he is most easily influenced or affected.
**2** the side of a football formation away from which players have shifted.

**weak sister,** *U.S. Slang.* one that is helpless or cannot be depended upon, especially in time of stress; weakling.

**weak-willed** (wēk′wild′), *adj.* weak-minded; indecisive: *The Indian intruders were ... so feeble and weak-willed as to recoil from action even before Chinese troops could come on the scene* (Manchester Guardian Weekly).

**weal**[1] (wēl), *n.* **1** well-being; prosperity; happiness: *Good citizens act for the public weal.* **SYN:** welfare. **2** *Obsolete.* a state or community. **3** *Obsolete.* wealth; riches (often in *world, world's* or *worldly weal*). [Old English *wela* wealth; welfare]

**weal**[2] (wēl), *n.* a streak or ridge raised on the skin by a stick or whip; welt; wale; wheal. [variant of *wale*[1]]

**weald** (wēld), *n. British.* **1** open country. **2** woodland. [Old English *weald* woods, forest. See related etym. at **wold**[1].]

**Weald|en** (wēl′dən), *adj.* of or having to do with a series of deposits of the Lower Cretaceous in England. [< (the) *Weald,* an area in England + *-en*[2]]

**wealth** (welth), *n.* **1a** many valuable possessions; much money or property; riches: *a man of wealth, the wealth of a city.* **SYN:** prosperity, fortune. **b** the condition of having wealth; great material prosperity; affluence. **SYN:** prosperity, fortune. **2a** all things that have money value; resources: *The wealth of our country includes its mines and forests as well as its factories.*
**b** (more strictly) all material things that are capable of or adaptable to satisfying human wants, and are or can be made subject to ownership, whether private or public. **c** all such material things, and qualities or attributes of man, such as health or intelligence, that increase his ability to produce. **3** *Figurative.* a large quantity; abundance: *a wealth of hair, a wealth of words.* **SYN:** profusion. **4** *Obsolete.* well-being; weal. [< *weal*[1], or *well*[1]; perhaps patterned on *health* and *heal*]

**wealth tax,** *British.* a proposed annual tax on all of an individual's assets above a specified minimum, whether they produce income or not: *A wealth tax ... has the disadvantage of being extremely difficult to collect, as it is administratively equivalent to the imposition of estate duty on all wealthy people once a year* (London Times).

**wealth|y** (wel′thē), *adj.,* **wealth|i|er, wealth|i|est,** *n.* — ***adj.* 1** having wealth; rich: *a very wealthy man, a wealthy country.* **SYN:** See syn. under **rich.** **2** *Figurative.* abundant; copious: *a wealthy supply of wit, a verse wealthy in satirical allusions.*
— ***n.* the wealthy,** persons having wealth; rich people: *to curry favor with the wealthy.*
— **wealth′i|ly,** *adv.* — **wealth′i|ness,** *n.*

**Wealth|y** (wel′thē), *n., pl.* **Wealth|ies.** a bright-red, American variety of apple, ripening in autumn. [< *wealthy,* in the sense of "thriving"]

**wean**[1] (wēn), *v.t.* **1** to accustom (a child or young animal) to food other than its mother's milk.

**Pronunciation Key:** hat, āge, cãre, fär; let, ēqual, tėrm; it, īce; hot, ōpen, ôrder; oil, out; cup, pu̇t, rüle; child; long; thin; ᴛʜen; zh, measure;
ə represents **a** in about, **e** in taken, **i** in pencil, **o** in lemon, **u** in circus.

2 *Figurative.* to accustom (a person) to do without something; cause to turn away: *He was sent away to school to wean him from bad companions.* [Old English *gewenian,* and *āwenian* accustom (to do without)] —**wean′er,** *n.*

**wean**[2] (wēn, wē′ən), *n. Scottish.* a very young child; baby. [contraction of earlier *wee ane* wee one]

**wean|ling** (wēn′ling), *n., adj.* —*n.* a child or animal that has only recently been weaned.
—*adj.* recently weaned.

**weap|on** (wep′ən), *n., v.* —*n.* **1a** any object or instrument used in fighting. Swords, spears, arrows, clubs, guns, and shields are man-made weapons. **b** *Figurative.* any means of attack or defense: *to use truth as a weapon of freedom. Drugs are effective weapons against many diseases.* **2** any organ of a plant or animal used for fighting or for protection, such as claws, horns, teeth, and stings.
—*v.t.* to furnish with weapons or a weapon; arm: *ragged, shouting, weaponed with sticks, iron bars and brickbats* (Time).
[Old English *wǣpen*] —**weap′on|less,** *adj.*

**weap|on|eer** (wep′ə nir′), *n.* **1** a person who develops or produces weapons. **2** a person who activates a nuclear weapon.

**weap|on|eer|ing** (wep′ə nir′ing), *n.* the design or production of weapons: *Contemporary weaponeering is essentially a process of miniaturization; of packing more devastation into a smaller and more portable warhead* (Bulletin of Atomic Scientists).

**weap|on-grade** (wep′ən grād′), *adj.* surpassing the minimum standards set for materials to be used in nuclear weapons: *weapon-grade plutonium.*

**weap|on|ry** (wep′ən rē), *n.* **1** the developing and producing of weapons: *He pointed out that anything—the knowledge that two and two makes four—may play a part in atomic weaponry* (Harper's). **2** weapons collectively: *What the U.S. now needs to back up its broadened array of weaponry … is a more subtle set of concepts in diplomacy* (Time).

**weapons carrier,** a military vehicle for transporting weapons not part of its own equipment.

**weap|ons-grade** (wep′ənz grād′), *adj.* = weapon-grade.

**weapons system,** a missile, bomber, submarine, or other device required to carry a bomb or warhead to its target: *America's first successful long-range pilotless bomber [was] a major weapons system conceived and developed in peace-time* (Time).

**wear**[1] (wãr), *v.,* **wore, worn, wear|ing,** *n.* —*v.t.* **1** to have on the body: *We wear clothes.* **2** to use in one's costume or adornment, especially habitually: *to wear a beard, to wear a watch, to wear one's hair in a pony tail. She wears black since her husband died.* **3** *Figurative.* to have or show: *to wear a big smile. The gloomy old house wore an air of sadness.* **4** *Figurative.* to have as a quality or attribute; bear: *to wear one's honors modestly.* **5** (of a ship) to fly (a flag or colors). **6** to cause loss or damage to by using: *These shoes are badly worn.* **7** to make, as by rubbing, scraping, or washing away: *to wear a dress to rags, to wear a path across the grass. Walking wore a hole in my shoe.* **8** *Figurative.* to tire; weary: *She is worn with toil and care. Age, the common fate of all, has worn thy frame* (William Cullen Bryant). **9** to spend or pass: *to wear away the night in song.* **10** to bring (a person) gradually (into a habit or disposition).
—*v.i.* **1** to suffer loss or damage from being used: *This coat has worn to shreds.* **2a** to last long; give good service: *That coat has worn well.* **b** *Figurative.* to stand the test, as of experience, familiarity, or criticism: *a friendship that did not wear. A person wears well if you like him better the longer you know him.* **3** to pass or go gradually; grow or become in time: *His socks were beginning to wear thin in the heel. It became hotter as the day wore on.* **4** to be used up: *The pencil is worn to a stub. The paint wore off the house.* **5** *Obsolete.* to be in fashion; be worn.
—*n.* **1** the act of wearing or the fact of being worn: *Clothing for summer wear is being shown in the shops. This suit has been in constant wear for two years.* **2** things worn or to be worn; clothing: *The store sells children's wear.* **3** gradual loss or damage caused by use: *The rug shows wear.* **4** lasting quality; good service: *There is still much wear in these shoes.*
**wear down, a** to tire; weary: *Worn down by … loneliness, finally smashed by grief, the scholar's mind revolves all these things in a confusion which indicates the onset of death* (New Yorker). **b** to overcome by persistent effort: *The young Quaker strove to wear down malice by his patient and forgiving mood* (William Hepworth Dixon). **c** to reduce or erode, as by use or friction: *Running water wears down rocks with the help of particles of sand and gravel* (Ernest E. Wahlstrom).
**wear off,** to become less gradually; diminish: *The novelty soon wore off.*
**wear out, a** to wear until no longer fit for use: *The child needs new shoes; he has worn out his present pair.* **b** to use up: *He did not strike a blow till all the powers of diplomacy had been thoroughly worn out between himself and his rival* (Edward A. Freeman). **c** *Figurative.* to tire out; weary: *She is worn out by too much work. All that thinking about so many things can wear you out* (Harper's). **d** *Figurative.* to exhaust, destroy, or abolish by gradual loss or the lapse of time: *He stayed too late and wore out his welcome. Let me wither and wear out mine age in a … prison* (John Donne).
**wear thin, a** to weaken or decrease; wear out: *His patience began to wear thin during the long wait. [Her] aggressive ways have worn thin her welcome in many offices* (New York Times). **b** *Figurative.* to lose interest or appeal; become hackneyed: *A joke heard too often can wear thin. Popular airs of the time … tend to wear thin after a while* (Atlantic).
[Old English *werian*] —**wear′er,** *n.*
► In nonstandard English *wore* is extensively used as the past participle, as well as the past tense.

**wear**[2] (wãr), *v.,* **wore, worn, wear|ing,** *n.* —*v.t.* to turn (a ship) to sail with the wind at the stern in changing to the other tack, instead of turning the bow into the wind.
—*v.i.* to turn or be turned to sail with the wind at the stern in changing to the other tack.
—*n.* the act or process of wearing or turning a ship.
[apparently alteration of *veer*[1]]

**wear|a|bil|i|ty** (wãr′ə bil′ə tē), *n.* the quality or condition of being wearable; ability to stand wear: *Synthetic fabrics have attained new heights of fashion success, while working miracles of wearability* (New York Times).

**wear|a|ble** (wãr′ə bəl), *adj., n.* —*adj.* **1** that can be worn; suitable for being worn. **2** able to stand wear; lasting.
—*n.* **wearables,** something wearable; an article of apparel: *He … moved off with Mrs. Dutton's wearables and deposited the trunk containing them safely in the boat* (Scott).
—**wear′a|ble|ness,** *n.*

**wear and tear,** loss or damage caused by use.

**wea|ri|ful** (wir′ē fəl), *adj.* causing weariness; wearisome. —**wea′ri|ful|ly,** *adv.* —**wea′ri|ful|ness,** *n.*

**wea|ri|less** (wir′ē lis), *adj.* that does not weary or become weary. —**wea′ri|less|ly,** *adv.*

**wea|ri|ly** (wir′ə lē), *adv.* in a weary manner: *The tired old man walked slowly and wearily along the road.*

**wea|ri|ness** (wir′ē nis), *n.* weary condition or feeling: *After tramping all day the hikers were overcome with weariness.* SYN: fatigue, exhaustion.

**wear|ing** (wãr′ing), *adj.* **1** exhausting; tiring: *a very wearing trip, a wearing conversation.* **2** of or for wear; intended to be worn. —**wear′ing|ly,** *adv.*

**wearing apparel,** = clothes.

**wear|ish** (wãr′ish, wir′-), *adj. Dialect.* **1** tasteless; insipid; unsalted. **2a** sickly; feeble. **b** wizened; shriveled. Also, **wersh.** [origin uncertain. Compare Dutch *wars* disgusted, averse.]

**wea|ri|some** (wir′ē səm), *adj.* wearying; tiring; tiresome: *a long, boring, and wearisome tale.*
—**wea′ri|some|ly,** *adv.* —**wea′ri|some|ness,** *n.*

**wear-out** (wãr′out′), *n.* damage caused by use: *Stretch fabrics ease wear-out at the elbows, knees, and seat* (Time).

**wea|ry** (wir′ē), *adj.,* **-ri|er, -ri|est,** *v.,* **-ried, -ry|ing.** —*adj.* **1** tired; worn-out: *weary feet, a weary brain.* SYN: fatigued, exhausted, fagged. See syn. under **tired. 2** causing tiredness; tiring: *a weary wait.* **3** having one's patience, tolerance, or liking exhausted: *to be weary of excuses.*
—*v.t.* to make weary; fatigue; tire: *Walking up the hill wearied Grandfather.*
—*v.i.* **1** to become weary. **2** to long (for): *She is wearying for home.*
[Old English *wērig*] —**wea′ry|ing|ly,** *adv.*

**Weary Willie** or **Willy,** *British Slang.* a person of little strength or energy: *[He] said that Opposition members were a bunch of Weary Willies* (London Times).

**wea|sand** (wē′zənd), *n. Archaic.* **1** the windpipe. **2** the throat. [Old English *wāsend*]

**wea|sel**[1] (wē′zəl), *n., v.* —*n.* **1** a small, flesh-eating mammal related to the mink and skunk, with a long, slender, furry body and short legs. Weasels have keen sight and smell and are known for their quickness and slyness. They feed on rats, mice, birds, and other small animals, and eggs. The least weasel and short-tailed weasel are two kinds. The weasel is brown and white, except in northern regions where it turns white in winter and is called an ermine. **2** *Figurative.* a cunning, sneaky person.
—*v.t. Informal.* to deprive (a word or phrase) of its force or meaning; take away (the meaning) from a word or phrase.
—*v.i. Informal.* to use tricky actions or words; be evasive; hedge: *The accused man tried to weasel but after hearing the evidence admitted his part in the plot.*
**weasel out,** to escape or withdraw craftily or irresponsibly; evade duty, responsibility, or obligation: *They use any excuse to weasel out of a job.*
[Old English *weosule, wesle*] —**wea′sel|like′,** *adj.*

**wea|sel**[2] (wē′zəl), *n.* a military vehicle with a roofless, boxlike body that runs on treads for travel in snow, mud, sand, and other difficult terrain. [< *weasel*[1]]

**wea|sel|ing** (wē′zə ling), *n., adj. Informal.* —*n.* the use of tricky actions or words; equivocation: *precampaign weaseling.*
—*adj.* tricky; equivocating; evasive.

**wea|sel|ly** (wē′zə lē), *adj.* like a weasel; tricky; evasive.

**weasel word,** *U.S. Informal.* a word lacking in force or exact meaning, used to make a statement evasive or equivocal; ambiguous word or one used ambiguously: *"Standardization" is one of the subtlest, trickiest weasel words ever coined* (Atlantic).

**wea|sel-word|ed** (wē′zəl wėr′did), *adj. Informal.* worded in an evasive way: *mutual defense, a weasel-worded device for committing further follies by a more palatable name* (Wall Street Journal).

**wea|son** (wē′zən), *n. Archaic.* weasand.

**weath|er** (weᴛʜ′ər), *n., v., adj.* —*n.* **1** the condition of the air around and above a certain person or place; temperature, humidity, violence or gentleness of winds, presence or absence of precipitation, clearness or cloudiness, and other such atmospheric conditions: *the hot weather of summer. The weather is very windy today in Chicago.* **2a** windy, rainy, or stormy weather; the elements: *to protect a building against damage by the weather.* **b** the level of the atmosphere characterized by this: *to fly above the weather.*
—*v.t.* **1** to expose (anything) to the weather; wear, as by sun, rain, or frost; discolor thus: *Wood turns gray if weathered for a long time.* **2** *Figurative.* to go or come through safely: *to weather an economic depression. The ship weathered the storm.* **3** to sail to the windward of; pass safely around: *The ship weathered the cape.* **4** *Architecture.* to build (as a roof or top of a wall) on a slant so as to shed water.
—*v.i.* **1** to become discolored or worn as by air, rain, sun, or frost. **2** to resist exposure to the weather; endure; last.
—*adj.* toward the wind; of the side exposed to the wind; windward: *a ship's weather deck. It was very cold on the weather side of the ship.*
**under the weather,** *Informal.* sick; ailing: *They had been very well as a general thing, although now and then they might have been under the weather for a day or two* (Frank R. Stockton).
**weather in, a** to ground (an aircraft) because of bad weather: *Most of the planes were weathered in during the storm.* **b** to close (an airport or airfield) because of bad weather: *Santa Fe's airport was weathered in for several hours during the day* (New York Times).
**weather out, a** to shut out of a place because of bad weather: *So far as that other difficulty—the one about cargo vessels being weathered out of some bases for nine months—it strikes us that may have been something of a blessing* (Wall Street Journal). **b** to cancel or curtail because of bad weather: *the usual air show was weathered out* (Time).
[Old English *weder*]

**weath|er|a|bil|i|ty** (weᴛʜ′ər ə bil′ə tē), *n.* resistance to weathering: *A two-year … study on the effects of weathering on 20 different plastics … would provide a way to predict a plastic's weatherability* (Science News).

**weather balloon,** a balloon (often unmanned) in which instruments are carried for recording meteorological data of the upper air, used especially in weather forecasting.

**weather beam,** *Nautical.* the side of a ship toward the wind; weatherboard.

**weath|er-beat|en** (weᴛʜ′ər bē′tən), *adj.* worn or hardened by the wind, rain, and other forces of the weather: *an old seaman's weather-beaten face, a weather-beaten old barn.*

**weath|er|board** (weᴛʜ′ər bôrd′, -bōrd′), *n., v.* —*n.* **1** a thin board, thicker along one edge than along the other; clapboard. **2** *Nautical.* the side of a ship or boat toward the wind.
—*v.t., v.i.* to cover or protect with weather-

boards: *He was going to move his cabin into town and weatherboard it for more insulation* (John Dos Passos).

**weath|er|board|ing** (weᴛʜ′ər bôr′ding, -bōr′-), *n.* **1** a covering or surface consisting of weatherboards, as on a wall or roof. **2** weatherboards collectively.

**weath|er-bound** (weᴛʜ′ər bound′), *adj.* delayed by bad weather.

**weather breeder**, a fine, clear day, popularly supposed to betoken a coming storm.

**Weather Bureau**, a former division of the U.S. Department of Commerce that recorded and forecast the weather. It is now called the National Weather Service.

**weath|er-burned** (weᴛʜ′ər bėrnd′), *adj.* burned, scorched, or browned by the sun, wind, or other forces of the weather.

**weath|er|cast** (weᴛʜ′ər kast′, -käst′), *n.* a report on the weather which is broadcast on radio or television.

**weath|er|cast|er** (weᴛʜ′ər kas′tər, -käs′-), *n.* a person who gives weather reports on radio or television.

**weather cloth**, *Nautical.* a covering of canvas or tarpaulin used to protect boats or to shelter persons from wind and spray.

**weath|er|coat** (weᴛʜ′ər kōt′), *n. Especially British.* a coat that protects against wet or cold weather; stormcoat.

**weath|er|cock** (weᴛʜ′ər kok′), *n., v.* **—*n.*** **1** a device to show which way the wind is blowing, especially one in the shape of a rooster; weather vane. **2** *Figurative.* a person or thing that is changeable or inconstant, especially one who veers easily to conform to the prescribed attitudes or popular beliefs of the moment.
**—*v.i.*** to veer or vary like a weathercock: *It is easy enough to make a stable hovercraft which is capable of "weathercocking" quickly into the wind* (New Scientist).
**—*v.t.*** to provide with a weathercock; serve as a weathercock for: *weathercocked gables.*

**weath|er|con|di|tion** (weᴛʜ′ər kən dish′ən), *v.t.* to prepare or protect against all kinds of weather: *to weathercondition a cabin.*

**weath|ered** (weᴛʜ′ərd), *adj.* **1** worn, stained, or seasoned by the weather. **2** (of rocks) altered by the weather or other atmospheric influence. **3** *Architecture.* made sloping, so as to shed water: *a weathered sill.*

**weather eye**, **1** a careful and alert watch. **2** a device used for measuring and reporting meteorological conditions: *This coast-to-coast system of radar weather eyes* [*is*] *linked by teletype with a central computer* (Wall Street Journal). **3** = weather satellite.
**keep one's weather eye open**, to be on the lookout for possible danger or trouble: *The fishermen kept a weather eye open for bears as they moved upstream.*

**weather gauge**, *Nautical.* the position of a vessel, especially a sailing vessel, when it is windward of another, and thus able to make more advantageous use of the wind relative to the other in maneuvering.
**have** (or **keep) the weather gauge of, a** to be to windward of: *The rest ... entered as far as the place permitted and their own necessities, to keep the weather gauge of the enemy* (Sir Walter Raleigh). **b** to get the better of: *He has got the weather gauge of them, and for us to run down to them would be to run ourselves into the lion's mouth* (John M. Wilson).

**weather girl**, *U.S.* a woman weathercaster.

**weath|er|glass** (weᴛʜ′ər glas′, -gläs′), *n.* any one of several instruments designed to show the state of the atmosphere and predict the weather, such as a barometer, a baroscope, or a hygroscope.

**weath|er|ing** (weᴛʜ′ər ing), *n.* the destructive or discoloring action as of air, water, or frost, especially on rock or wood: *The weathering on the old boards from the barn gave them a beautiful gray cast.*

**weath|er|ize** (weᴛʜ′ə rīz), *v.t.*, **-ized, -iz|ing.** *U.S.* to insulate against cold weather, especially in order to conserve fuel: *Operation Open City helps the poor weatherize their homes and apartments and prevent wasting of fuel* (New York Times).
**—weath′er|i|za′tion,** *n.*

**weath|er|li|ness** (weᴛʜ′ər lē nis), *n.* (of ships and boats) weatherly character or qualities.

**weath|er|ly** (weᴛʜ′ər lē), *adj.* (of a sailing vessel) that can sail close to the wind; making very little leeway when close-hauled.

**weath|er|man** (weᴛʜ′ər man′), *n., pl.* **-men.** *Informal.* a man who forecasts the weather, now especially a meteorologist or other person who is employed particularly to do so.

**Weath|er|man** (weᴛʜ′ər mən), *n., pl.* **-men.** *U.S.* a member of a militant revolutionary youth organization active in the 1960's.

***weather map**, a map or chart showing temperature, barometric pressure, precipitation, direction and velocity of winds, and other atmospheric conditions over a wide area for a given time or period. See picture below.

**weather mark**, *Nautical.* a mark used in boat racing to indicate the direction from which the wind is blowing.

**weath|er|most** (weᴛʜ′ər mōst), *adj.* furthest to windward. [< *weather* + *-most*]

**weath|er|om|e|ter** (weᴛʜ′ə rom′ə tər), *n.* an instrument used to determine the ability of a paint to withstand exposure to various conditions of weather.

**weath|er|proof** (weᴛʜ′ər prüf′), *adj., v., n.* **—*adj.*** protected against rain, snow, or wind; able to stand exposure to all kinds of weather.
**—*v.t.*** to make weatherproof.
**—*n.*** *Especially British.* a raincoat. **—weath′er-proof′ness,** *n.*

**weather satellite**, an artificial earth satellite that measures and reports meteorological conditions, especially as an aid in long-range weather forecasting.

**Weather Service**, = National Weather Service.

**weather ship**, any one of a group of ships stationed at points in the North Atlantic for weather observation and reporting, maintained by the United States and other members of the International Civil Aviation Organization.

**weather side**, **1** *Nautical.* the side of a ship facing windward. **2** the side of a building, tree, pole, wall, or other structure, most exposed to injury from weather: *During winter storms they* [*the goats*] *found shelter in the numerous caves that rain, wind, and the Adriatic had gouged out of the weather side* (Atlantic).

**weather stain**, a stain or discoloration left or produced by the weather.

**weath|er-stained** (weᴛʜ′ər stānd′), *adj.* bearing weather stains.

**weather station**, a station where weather conditions are observed and recorded and, if it is manned, are usually forecast.

**weather strip**, = weather stripping.

**weath|er-strip** (weᴛʜ′ər strip′), *v.t.*, **-stripped, -strip|ping.** to fit or seal with weather stripping.

**weather stripping**, a narrow strip of cloth, metal, or a combination of the two, to fill or cover the space between a door or window and the casing, to keep out rain, snow, and wind.

**weather tide**, a tide running to windward, or in the direction opposite to that in which the wind is blowing.

**weath|er|tight** (weᴛʜ′ər tīt′), *adj.* so tight that it can stand exposure to all kinds of weather; weatherproof: *weathertight windows.*

***weather map**

**legend:**
1012 barometric pressure
cold front
warm front
○ clear
◑ partly cloudy
● cloudy
precipitation
wind speeds: (miles per hour)
1 - 3
4 - 7
8 - 12
13 - 18

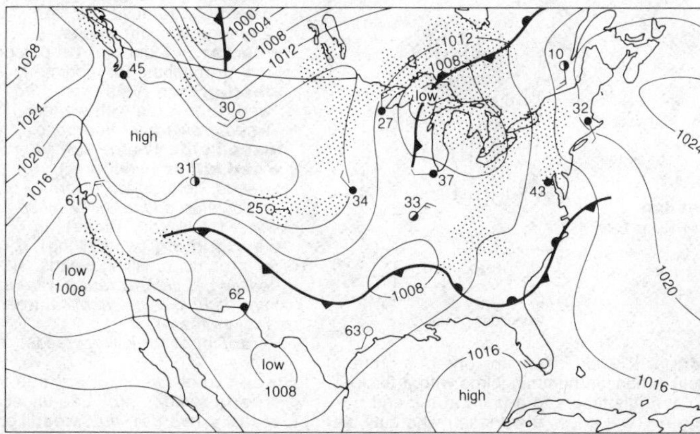


***weather vane**, a device to show which way the wind is blowing; vane; weathercock.

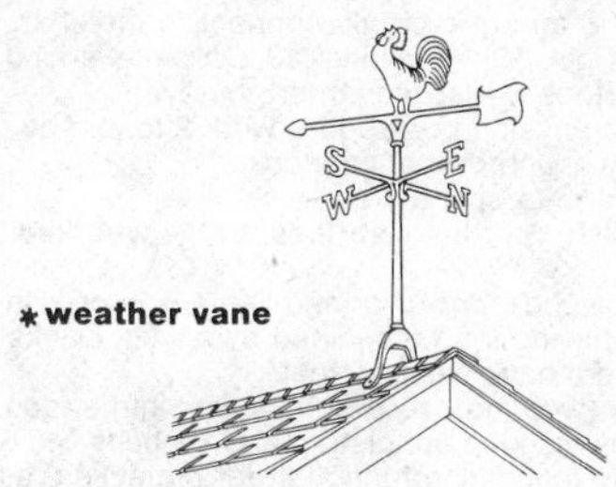

***weather vane**

**weath|er|vi|sion** (weᴛʜ′ər vizh′ən), *n.* the communication of weather information to aircraft pilots by a system of radar and television.

**weath|er|wise** (weᴛʜ′ər wīz), *adv.* with reference to weather.

**weath|er-wise** (weᴛʜ′ər wīz′), *adj.* **1** skillful in forecasting the changes of the weather. **2** skillful in forecasting changes in anything, such as the mood of the populace or political climate.

**weath|er|worn** (weᴛʜ′ər wôrn′, -wōrn′), *adj.* = weather-beaten.

**weath|er|y** (weᴛʜ′ər ē), *adj.*, **-er|i|er, -er|i|est.** changing like the weather; fitful: ... *the weathery dalliance of gnats* (Richard D. Blackmore).

**weave** (wēv), *v.*, **wove** or (*Rare*) **weaved, woven** or **wove, weav|ing,** *n.* **—*v.t.*** **1** to form (threads or strips) into a thing or fabric. People weave thread into cloth, straw into hats, and reeds into baskets. **2** to make (something) out of threads or strips: *She is weaving a rug. A spider weaves a web.* **3** *Figurative.* **a** to combine into a whole: *The author wove three plots together into one story.* **b** to make by combining parts: *The author wove a story from three plots.* **4** *Figurative.* to introduce into a connected whole: *to weave a melody into a musical composition.* **5** to make with care, by weaving: (*Figurative.*) *to weave a web of lies.* **6** *Figurative.* to direct in a twisting and turning course: *to weave one's way home, to weave a car in and out of traffic.*
**—*v.i.*** **1** to work with a loom. **2** to become woven or interlaced. **3** *Figurative.* to go by twisting and turning; move with a rocking or swaying motion: *a car weaving in and out of traffic.*
**—*n.*** a method or pattern of weaving: *Homespun is a cloth of coarse weave.*
[Old English *wefan*] **—weav′ing|ly,** *adv.*
▶As past participle, **wove** is chiefly used in certain technical terms like *wire-wove* and *wove paper.*

**weav|er** (wē′vər), *n.* **1** a person who weaves. **2** a person whose work is weaving. **3** = weaverbird.

**weav|er|bird** (wē′vər bėrd′), *n.* any one of a family of birds similar to finches, mostly of Asia, Africa, and Australia, that build elaborately woven nests. The whidah, English sparrow, and republican grosbeak are weaverbirds.

**weaver finch**, = weaverbird.

**weaver's hitch** or **knot**, = sheet bend.

**wea|zen** (wē′zən), *v.i., v.t., adj.* = wizen.

**web** (web), *n., v.*, **webbed, web|bing.** **—*n.*** **1** something woven. A spider spins a web. Some insect larvae also spin a fabric of delicate, silken threads. **2** a whole piece of cloth made at one time. It is called a web while being woven or after being taken from the loom. **3** *Figurative.* **a** anything like a web; something that ensnares or entangles: *His story was a web of lies.* **b** anything flimsy or fanciful. **4** *Figurative.* a complicated network: *a web of railroads.* **5a** the skin joining the toes of ducks, geese, other swimming birds, and certain other water animals. **b** a malformation of skin somewhat resembling this, between human fingers or toes. **c** *Anatomy.* connective tissue. **6a** the vane of a feather; series of barbs on each side of the shaft of a bird's feathers; vexillum. **b** the two series of barbs of a feather, collectively. **7** a thin metal sheet, especially between heavier or projecting parts. **8a** the vertical plate (or its equivalent) that connects the upper and lower lateral plates in a beam or girder. **b** one of these lateral plates or flanges. **9** *Papermaking.* **a** an endless belt of wire cloth working on rollers and carrying the pulp. **b** the sheet of pulp on this belt, in process of being made into paper. **c** a large roll of paper made in

**Pronunciation Key:** hat, āge, cãre, fär; let, ēqual, tėrm; it, īce; hot, ōpen, ôrder; oil, out; cup, pu̇t, rüle; child; long; thin; ᴛʜen; zh, measure; ə represents **a** in about, **e** in taken, **i** in pencil, **o** in lemon, **u** in circus.

this way, such as that used in a rotary press for printing newspapers. **10** *Architecture.* the masonry between the ribs of a ribbed vault. **11** *Machinery.* the arm of a crank, connecting the shaft and crank pin. **12** = webbing. **13** *Obsolete.* a kind of cataract, or similar growth on the eye.
— ***v.t.*** **1** to envelop or trap in a web. **2** to join by or as if by a web; twine; interlock.
— ***v.i.*** to form or spin a web.
[Old English *webb*] — **web′less**, *adj.* — **web′like′**, *adj.*

**webbed** (webd), *adj.* **1** formed like a web or with a web. **2** having the toes joined by a web. Ducks and beavers have webbed feet.

**web|bing** (web′ing), *n.* **1** cloth woven into strong, wide strips, used in upholstery and for belts. **2** the plain foundation fabric left for protection, as at the edge of some rugs. **3** anything forming a web. **4** the skin joining the toes, such as that of a duck's feet.

**web|by** (web′ē), *adj.* **1** consisting of or resembling a web: *webby fabric, a webby net.* **2** having a web; webbed: *the webby wings of a bat.*

**We|be|los** (wē′bə lōs, web′ə-), *n., pl.* **-los.** a cub scout of the highest rank. A Webelos is 10 years old and prepares to enter the Boy Scouts as a tenderfoot. [contraction of *We*('ll) *be lo*(yal) *s*(couts); originally coined as an imaginary tribal name < the initials of *wolf, bear, lion scouts* (the cub scout ranks)]

**we|ber** (vā′bər, wē′-), *n. Electricity.* **1** a unit of magnetic flux, equivalent to $10^8$ maxwells. **2** formerly: **a** = coulomb. **b** = ampere. **c** = maxwell. [< Wilhelm E. *Weber,* 1804-1891, a German physicist]

**web-fed** (web′fed′), *adj.* having the paper fed on a printing press from a continuous roll instead of in single sheets.

**web-fin|gered** (web′fing′gərd), *adj.* having the fingers united for a considerable part of their length by a fold of skin.

**web|foot** (web′fu̇t′), *n., pl.* **-feet. 1** a foot in which the toes are joined by a web. **2** a bird or animal having webbed feet.

**web-foot|ed** (web′fu̇t′id), *adj.* having the toes joined by a web.

**web offset**, offset printing by means of a web-fed rotary printing press: *In the U.S. the Christian Science Monitor became the first large-circulation daily to print by web offset* (W. P. Jaspert).

***web press**, a rotary printing press in which the paper is fed from a roll.

***web press**

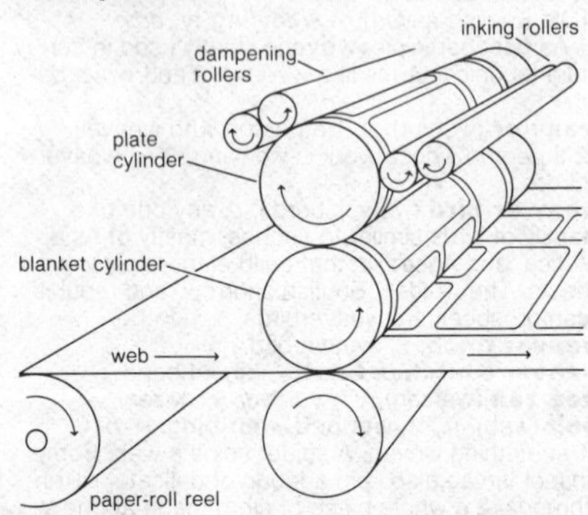


**web spinner**, any one of an order of small insects with chewing mouthparts and forelegs that have silk spinning organs; embiid. Web spinners live in underground tunnels lined with the silk which they spin.

**web|ster** (web′stər), *n. Obsolete.* a weaver.

**web-toed** (web′tōd′), *adj.* = web-footed.

**web-winged** (web′wingd′), *adj.* (of bats) having wings consisting of a large web or membrane supported and extended by the forelimbs and four elongated digits.

**web|work** (web′wėrk′), *n.* **1** the structural part or web of a textile pattern. **2** *Figurative.* network: *the webwork of the city's highways* (Time).

**web|worm** (web′wėrm′), *n.* any one of certain more or less gregarious caterpillars that spin large webs.

**Wechs|ler-Belle|vue Scale** (weks′lər bel′vyü), *Psychology.* a series of tests for adults or children, to determine intelligence and mental age. [< David *Wechsler,* born 1896, an American psychologist, who devised it at *Bellevue* Psychiatric Hospital, New York City]

**Wechsler test**, = Wechsler-Bellevue Scale.

**wecht** (weᴋʜt), *n. Scottish.* weight.

**wed** (wed), *v.,* **wed|ded, wed|ded** or **wed, wed-ding.** — ***v.t.*** **1a** = marry. **b** to unite in marriage; conduct the marriage ceremony for. **c** to give (a woman) in marriage. **2** *Figurative.* to unite or join closely. **3** *Figurative.* to be obstinately attached to (an opinion, one's own will, or a habit or faction). — ***v.i.*** to enter into marriage; marry.
[Old English *weddian* < *wedd* a pledge. Compare etym. under **wad⁴**, **wadset.**]

**we'd** (wēd; *unstressed* wid), **1** we had. **2** we should. **3** we would.

**Wed.**, Wednesday.

**wed|ded** (wed′id), *adj.* **1** joined in wedlock; married. **2** of or having to do with marriage or married persons; connubial: *wedded bliss.* **3** *Figurative.* united. **4** *Figurative.* devoted.

**Wed|dell seal** (wed′əl), a large, common hair seal of the antarctic regions. It lives mostly in the water and below the ice in winter. [< James *Weddell,* 1787-1834, an English navigator, who commanded antarctic sealing ships]

**wed|ding** (wed′ing), *n.* **1** a marriage ceremony with its attendant festivities. **SYN:** See syn. under **marriage. 2** an anniversary of this. A golden wedding is the fiftieth anniversary of a marriage. **3** *Figurative.* a close union or association; joining; combination; merger: *A chemical wedding between the element boron and organic substances promised industry a new family of compounds* (Science News Letter). [Old English *weddung* < *weddian* to wed]

**wedding cake**, a large, rich cake, usually arranged in tiers, covered with icing and decorated with sugar ornaments, cut and distributed to the guests at a wedding reception.

**wedding ring**, a ring of platinum, gold, or other precious metal, placed on the third finger of the left hand of the bride. In a double-ring ceremony, the bride places a ring on the bridegroom's finger.

**we|del** (vā′dəl), *v.i.* to ski by performing wedeln: *They wedeled down the 1,200-ft. slope or slammed through the slalom course* (Time). [back formation < *wedeln*]

**we|deln** (vā′dəln), *n., v.* — ***n.*** the act or technique of skiing downhill with fast, swiveling turns to the right and left while skis are kept parallel and close together.
— ***v.i.*** to ski in this manner; wedel: *The tests cover ... the first snowplow turn to how to hold a pole to wedeln in deep powder* (Newsweek).
[< German *wedeln* (literally) to wag]

***wedge** (wej), *n., v.,* **wedged, wedg|ing.** — ***n.*** **1** a piece of wood or metal, thick at one end and tapering to a thin edge at the other, used especially in splitting and separating. It is one of the simple machines. **2a** something shaped like a wedge: *a wedge of cheese or pie. Wild geese fly in a wedge.* **b** a cuneiform stroke or character of this shape. **3** *Figurative.* something used like a wedge: *to drive a wedge of suspicion between friends, to drive a wedge of tanks through the enemy line. Her grand party was an entering wedge into society.* **4** *Meteorology.* a long, narrow area of high pressure between two cyclonic systems. **5** a golf club used for high, short shots, especially lofting the ball out of traps and heavy grass: [*She*] *clinched the match with a 100-foot wedge shot* (New York Times). **6** a woman's short haircut that falls over the forehead and forms a triangle in the back.
— ***v.t.*** **1** to split or separate with or as if with a wedge or wedges. **2** to fasten or tighten with a wedge or wedges. **3** to thrust or pack in tightly; squeeze: *to wedge passengers into a subway train. He wedged himself through the narrow window. The man's foot was wedged between the rocks.* **4** *Ceramics.* to expel air bubbles from (clay) by cutting it into lumps or wedges and beating it.
— ***v.i.*** **1** to force a way or opening: *to wedge through a crowd.* **2** to become stuck or caught: *Two fat men wedged in a doorway.*
[Old English *wecg*] — **wedge′like′**, *adj.*

***wedge**
definitions 1, 2b

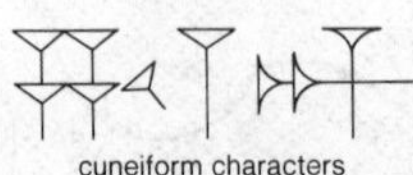
cuneiform characters

**wedge|bill** (wej′bil′), *n.* any one of a group of South American hummingbirds with a thick bill that abruptly tapers to a point at the end.

**wedg|er** (wej′ər), *n.* a workman who cuts clay into lumps or wedges and beats it to expel air bubbles.

**wedge-shaped** (wej′shāpt′), *adj.* shaped like a wedge; cuneate.

**wedge-tailed eagle** (wej′tāld′), a large, black eagle of Australia with tail feathers that taper to the shape of a wedge.

***wedg|ie** (wej′ē), *n.* a woman's shoe resembling a clog, with a thick, wedgelike piece forming a sole, all of which touches the ground, without the customary arched instep.

***wedgie**

**Wedg|wood** (wej′wu̇d), *n., adj. Trademark.* — ***n.*** a kind of English pottery, especially with a blue or black glaze and a design of white-colored Greek and Roman models in relief.
— ***adj.*** of or having to do with this kind of pottery: *Wedgwood ware.*
[< Josiah *Wedgwood,* 1730-1795, an English potter, who developed this kind of pottery and design]

**Wedgwood blue**, a shade of medium blue characteristic of Wedgwood ware.

**wedg|y** (wej′ē), *adj.* **1** formed or adapted to use as a wedge. **2** fitted for prying into or among.

**wed|lock** (wed′lok), *n.* **1** married state; marriage: *to be united in wedlock. The king's illegitimate son was born out of wedlock.* **2** *Obsolete.* the marriage ceremony; wedding. [Old English *wedlāc* marriage vow < *wedd* a pledge + *-lāc,* a noun suffix]

**Wednes|day** (wenz′dē, -dā), *n.* the fourth day of the calendar week, between Tuesday and Thursday. *Abbr:* Wed., W. [Old English *Wōdnesdæg* Woden's day < *Wōden* Woden; translation of Late Latin *Mercuriī diēs* day of Mercury]

**wee** (wē), *adj.,* **we|er, we|est,** *n.* — ***adj.*** very small; tiny.
— ***n.*** a little; bit; mite.
[Middle English *we,* variant of *wei* < Old English *wǣge* weight]

**weed¹** (wēd), *n., v.* — ***n.*** **1** a useless or troublesome plant: *Weeds choked out the vegetables and flowers in the garden.* **2a** *Figurative.* a useless or troublesome person or thing. **b** a useless animal, especially a horse unfit for racing or breeding. **c** *Figurative.* any very weak or malformed thing. **3** *Informal.* **a** a cigarette or cigar. **b** Also, **the weed.** tobacco. **c** marijuana. **4** *Archaic.* profusely growing wild plants; luxuriant underbrush.
— ***v.t.*** to take weeds out of: *Please weed the garden now.*
— ***v.i.*** **1** to take out weeds or anything like weeds. **2** *Figurative.* to clear anything of something harmful or useless.
**weed out, a** to free from what is useless or worthless: *Mother weeded out the old letters she wanted to save and threw the rest away.* **b** to remove as useless or worthless: *The general weeded out poor commanders.*
[Old English *wēod*] — **weed′like′**, *adj.*

**weed²** (wēd), *n.* **1** a black cloth band, worn on the arm or (sometimes) the hat of a man, as a token of mourning. **2** *Obsolete.* costume: *monastic weeds.* **3** *Archaic.* any garment.
**weeds,** mourning garments: *a widow's weeds.*
[Old English *wǣd,* or *wǣde* garment. Compare etym. under **wadmal.**]

**weed|ed** (wē′did), *adj.* **1** from which the weeds have been removed: *a freshly weeded garden.* **2** overgrown with weeds.

**weed|er** (wē′dər), *n.* **1** a person who weeds. **2** a tool or machine for digging up weeds.

**weed-grown** (wēd′grōn′), *adj.* overgrown with weeds; covered with weeds: *They stood in the weed-grown parade ground ...* (Time).

**weed|i|cide** (wē′də sīd), *n.* = weedkiller.

**weed|kill|er** (wēd′kil′ər), *n.* a chemical for killing weeds; herbicide: *Poison ivy plants can now be eradicated successfully by spraying with a weedkiller* (New York Times).

**weed|kill|ing** (wēd′kil′ing), *n., adj.* — ***n.*** the act or process of killing weeds: *Weeds ... could easily get life insurance were it not for the modern technique of chemical weedkilling* (R. N. Higinbotham).
— ***adj.*** of or for killing weeds: *weedkilling operations.*

**weed|less** (wēd′lis), *adj.* free from weeds.

**weeds** (wēdz), *n.pl.* See under **weed².**

**weed|y** (wē′dē), *adj.,* **weed|i|er, weed|i|est. 1** full of weeds: *a weedy garden.* **2** of or like a weed or weeds. **3** *Figurative.* **a** thin and lanky; gangling. **b** weak and underdeveloped; scrawny. —**weed′i|ly**, *adv.* —**weed′i|ness**, *n.*

**wee hours**, the early morning hours; small hours: *Beginning in the wee hours next Sunday, air coach passengers will be boarding the same swift DC-7's* (Wall Street Journal).

**week** (wēk), *n.* **1** seven days, one after another. **2** the time from Sunday through Saturday: *He is away most of the week but comes home on Sundays.* **3** the working days of this period, usually beginning on Monday and ending on Friday: *the banking week. A school week is usually five days. Abbr:* wk.

**Monday** (or **Tuesday**, and so on) **week**, the Monday (or Tuesday, and so on) one week from this Monday (or Tuesday, and so on): *Let us say Thursday week, dear—This is Saturday, so it is quite enough notice to give* (J. S. Winter).

**this day week**, one week from today: *Can you make it convenient to be there this day week?* (D. C. Murray).

**week in, week out**, week after week: *She sat on her rocking chair sewing, week in, week out.*

[Middle English *weke*, Old English *wice*, probably (originally) turn, a turning]

**week|day** (wēk′dā′), *n., adj.* —*n.* any day except Sunday or (now often) Saturday: *That store is open only on weekdays.*

—*adj.* of or on a weekday: *weekday church services.*

**week|days** (wēk′dāz′), *adv.* during every weekday; in the course of the week except the weekend.

**week|end** or **week-end** (wēk′end′), *n., adj., v.* —*n.* **1** Saturday and Sunday as a time for recreation, visiting, and other pastimes: *a weekend in the country.* **2** a house party occurring over a weekend, as at a college or university.

—*adj.* of or on a weekend: *a weekend job, the weekend traffic.*

—*v.i.* to spend a weekend: *to weekend with friends in the country.*

**week|end|er** (wēk′en′dər), *n.* a person who spends a weekend away from home: *Boating takes vacationists and weekenders off crowded highways* (New York Times).

**week|ends** or **week-ends** (wēk′endz′), *adv.* on or during the weekend: *We go fishing weekends.*

**week|long** (wēk′lông′, -long′), *adj.* continuing for a week; of a week's duration: *Concurrently, a weeklong series of meetings ... will be held in various auditoriums and meeting places* (New York Herald Tribune).

**week|ly** (wēk′lē), *adj., adv., n., pl.* **-lies**. —*adj.* **1** of a week; for a week; lasting a week. **2** done, happening, or appearing once a week or each week: *She writes a weekly letter to her grandmother.* **3** of or having to do with the working week or weekdays: *His weekly wage is $100.*

—*adv.* **1** once each week; every week. **2** by the week; on the basis of weeks.

—*n.* a newspaper or magazine published once a week.

**weekly bill**, = bill of mortality.

**week|night** (wēk′nīt′), *n., adj.* —*n.* any night of the week except Sunday or (now often) Saturday: *The theater is open every weeknight.*

—*adj.* of or on a weeknight: *weeknight concerts.*

**week|nights** (wēk′nīts′), *adv.* during every weeknight; every night of the week except those on the weekend.

**week of Sundays**, *Informal.* a period long enough to include seven Sundays; indefinitely long time.

**weel** (wēl), *adv., adj. Scottish.* well[1].

**ween** (wēn), *v.t., v.i. Archaic.* to think; suppose; believe; expect. [Old English *wēnan*]

**wee|nie** (wē′nē), *n. U.S. Informal.* a wiener; frankfurter.

**ween|sy** (wēn′sē), *adj.,* **-si|er, -si|est.** *Informal.* weeny; teensy.

**ween|y** (wē′nē), *adj.,* **ween|i|er, ween|i|est.** *Informal.* very small; little; tiny: *They sound like ... teachers who have grown a weeny bit tired of their energetic, articulate, expressive little charges* (New Yorker). [< *wee* + *-ny,* as in *teeny, tiny*]

**weep[1]** (wēp), *v.,* **wept, weep|ing,** *n.* —*v.i.* **1** to shed tears; cry: *to weep with sorrow or with rage. She wept for joy when she won the award.* **SYN**: sob. **2** to show sorrow or grief: *In some good cause ... To perish, wept for, honour'd, known* (Tennyson). **3** to shed water or moisture in drops. The stem of a plant, the soil, or a sore may be said to weep.

—*v.t.* **1** to shed tears for; mourn: *No poet wept him* (William Cowper). **SYN**: bewail. **2** to let fall in drops; shed: *She wept bitter tears.* **3** to spend in crying: *to weep one's life away.* **4** to shed (moisture or water) in drops; exude: *And trees weep amber on the banks of Po* (Alexander Pope).

—*n.* an oozing of moisture; sweating; exudation.

**the weeps**, *Informal.* a period or fit of weeping; cry (used especially in reference to women): *to have the weeps, to get over the weeps.*

[Old English *wēpan*]

**weep[2]** (wēp), *n.* = lapwing. [imitative of its cry]

**weep|er** (wē′pər), *n.* **1** a person who weeps. **2** a person hired to weep at funerals; professional mourner. **3** = capuchin (def. 1).

**weepers**, a conventional badge of mourning: *Our merry mourners clap bits of muslin on their sleeves, and these are called weepers* (Oliver Goldsmith).

**weep hole**, an opening through which water drips, as in a wall of a building, to let out accumulated moisture: *Even the building itself leaks; it has weep holes in the spandrels* (New Yorker).

**weep|ie** (wē′pē), *n. British Slang.* an overly emotional or sentimental book, film, play, or the like; tear-jerker: *Sunrise at Campobello [a motion picture], a strange throwback to the Forties, was a weepie about the last days of F. D. R.* (Listener).

**weep|ing** (wē′ping), *adj.* **1** that weeps. **2** having thin branches that arch over and hang down drooping: *a weeping shrub.* **3** dripping; rainy: *weeping weather, weeping skies.* —**weep′ing|ly**, *adv.*

**weeping birch**, a variety of the white birch of northern Europe and the northern United States having drooping branches.

**weeping cherry**, any one of various flowering cherry trees with drooping branches, native to Japan.

**weeping sinew**, *Informal.* a gathering of fluid in the synovial sheath of a tendon; ganglion.

**weeping willow**, a large willow tree native to eastern Asia and widely cultivated in Europe and America for ornament, distinguished by its long and slender drooping branches.

**weeps** (wēps), *n.pl.* See under **weep**.

**weep|y** (wē′pē), *adj.,* **weep|i|er, weep|i|est,** *n., pl.* **weep|ies.** —*adj.* **1** *Informal.* inclined to weep; tearful: *the bold dragoon sang ... with such pathos ... that his audience felt almost weepy* (George du Maurier). **2** *British Dialect.* exuding moisture; oozy; moist: *An old marlpit full of black water, where weepy, hairy moss hangs around the stumps of the willows and alders* (Rudyard Kipling).

—*n. British Slang.* weepie. —**weep′i|ly**, *adv.* —**weep′i|ness**, *n.*

**wee|ver** (wē′vər), *n.* any one of a group of small, edible marine fishes found along the coasts of Europe, Africa, and Chile, that have eyes directed upward and sharp poisonous spines. [probably < Old North French *wivre*, Old French *guivre* (originally) serpent, dragon (because of its venomous spines); see etym. under **wivern**]

**wee|vil** (wē′vəl), *n.* **1** a small beetle that has a long snout and feeds on plants. The larvae of the seed weevil and rice weevil feed inside of and destroy nuts, fruits, and grain; those of the sweet potato weevil live and feed in the stems or roots of plants. *Adult weevils are sometimes so small that they are hard to see* (R. E. Blackwelder). **2** any one of certain related small insects that damage stored grain. [Middle English *wevel* < Old English *wifel*]

**wee|vil|y** or **wee|vil|ly** (wē′və lē), *adj.* infested with weevils.

**weft** (weft), *n.* **1** the threads running from side to side across a fabric; woof. **2** something woven or spun, such as a web. [Old English *weft*, or *wefta* < *wefan* to weave]

**Wehr|macht** (ver′mäHt′), *n.* the armed forces of (Nazi) Germany. [< German *Wehrmacht* < *Wehr* defense; weapon + *Macht* power; might]

**wei|ge|la** (wī jē′lə, -gē′-), *n.* any one of a group of Asian shrubs of the honeysuckle family, species of which are often grown for their funnel-shaped white, red, or pink flowers. [< New Latin *Weigela* the genus name < Christian E. *Weigel,* 1748-1831, a German physician]

**weigh[1]** (wā), *v.t.* **1** to find out how heavy a thing is; measure the heaviness of by means of scales: *to weigh oneself, to weigh a bag of sugar.* **2** to measure by weight: *The grocer weighed out five pounds of apples.* **3** to bend by weight; burden: *The boughs of the apple tree are weighed heavily with fruit.* (*Figurative.*) *She is weighed with responsibilities beyond her capacity.* **4a** to hold in the hand or hands in order to estimate or compare the weight of. **b** to balance or fondle (an object or objects) as if doing this; hold and move gently up and down or tip from side to side: *to weigh one's hat in one's hands while waiting for someone to take it.* **5** *Figurative.* **a** to balance in the mind; consider carefully: *He weighed his words before speaking.* **SYN**: See syn. under **consider**. **b** to estimate in comparison: *weigh our sorrow with our comfort* (Shakespeare). **6** to lift up (a ship's anchor) from the bottom before sailing; hoist (anchor): *The ship weighed anchor and sailed away.* **7** *Obsolete.* to regard highly; esteem; value.

—*v.i.* **1** to have as a measure by weight: *to weigh 140 pounds. He weighs more than I do.* **2** *Figurative.* to have importance or influence; carry weight: *The amount of his salary does not weigh with him at all, because he is very rich.* **3** *Figurative.* to lie as a burden or worry; bear down: *Don't let that little mistake weigh upon your mind.* **4** to lift anchor.

**weigh down**, **a** to force or bend down by pressure of weight: *The porter's back was weighed down by the heavy loads he carried.* **b** *Figurative.* to burden; depress; oppress: *He was weighed down by his sorrows. The people were so weighed down by endless taxation that they finally rebelled.*

**weigh in**, **a** to verify the weight of (a jockey) after a horse race: *The Clerk of the Scales ... shall in all cases weigh in the riders of the horses, and report to the stewards any jockey not presenting himself to be weighed in* (Encyclopedia of Sports). **b** to determine the weight of (a boxer) before a fight, in accordance with restrictions on exceeding the limit for his class: *The contender was weighed in by members of the commissioner's staff.* **c** to be weighed in in this way: *Both boxers weighed in this afternoon* (Daily Express). *He was six feet four and weighed in at 135* (O. Henry).

**weigh in with**, *Informal.* to introduce or produce (something that is additional or extra): *[He] weighed in with some genially barbed compliments and a Latin quotation* (Punch).

**weigh on** (or **upon**), to be a burden to: *The London atmosphere weighs on me* (Jane Welsh Carlyle). *The silence began to weigh upon her* (J. L. Allen).

**weigh out**, **a** to verify the weight of (a jockey) before a horse race: *The stakeholder shall not allow a jockey to be weighed out for any horse until such horse's stake [shall] have been paid* (Encyclopedia of Sports). **b** to be weighed out in this way: *The rider of Musjid ... is said to have weighed in and weighed out with a whip weighing 7 or 9 lbs. and to have exchanged it for a lighter whip before and after the race* (J. Rice).

[Old English *wegan* weigh, lift, heft; bear]

—**weigh′er**, *n.*

**weigh[2]** (wā), *n.*

**under weigh**, under way: *She got under weigh with very little fuss, and came so near us as to throw a letter on board* (Richard H. Dana).

[spelling variant of *way;* influenced by *aweigh*]

► See **way** for a usage note.

**weigh|a|bil|i|ty** (wā′ə bil′ə tē), *n.* the capability of being weighed.

**weigh|a|ble** (wā′ə bəl), *adj.* that can be weighed. —**weigh′a|ble|ness**, *n.*

**weigh|a|bly** (wā′ə blē), *adv.* so as to be weighed.

**weigh|bridge** (wā′brij′), *n.* a weighing machine with a platform on which cattle, loaded carts, or trucks, and other large items are weighed.

**weigh-in** (wā′in′), *n.* **1** *Sports.* the act of weighing in, as in horse racing or boxing: *I got to the Stadium in plenty of time for the weigh-in* (New Yorker). **2** the act of checking baggage weight of a passenger before he boards a commercial airplane. **3** the act of weighing: *For junior: Weekly weigh-ins, and full-scale check-ups every twelve weeks* (Maclean's).

**weigh|ing machine** (wā′ing), any one of various machines for weighing.

**weigh|man** (wā′mən), *n., pl.* **-men.** a man whose work is weighing things.

**weigh|mas|ter** (wā′mas′tər, -mäs′-), *n.* **1** an official in charge of public scales. **2** a person in charge of weighing any product, as coal at a mine or produce at a cannery.

**weight** (wāt), *n., v.* —*n.* **1** how heavy a thing is; amount a thing weighs: *to find the weight of a feather or a rock. That man's weight is 175 pounds.* **2a** the quality that makes all things tend toward the center of the earth; heaviness; ponderability: *Gas has hardly any weight.* **b** the force with which a body is attracted to the earth or some other field of gravitation. The weight of a body is the product of the mass of the body and the acceleration of gravity and is expressed in such units as newton and dyne. **3a** a system of standard units used for expressing weight, such as avoirdupois weight or troy weight. **b** a unit of such a system. **c** a piece of metal or other substance, having a specific weight, used in weighing things: *a pound weight.* **4** a quantity that has a certain weight: *a half-ounce weight of gold dust, a ten-ton weight of coal.* **5** a heavy

**Pronunciation Key:** hat, āge, cãre, fär; let, ēqual, tėrm; it, īce; hot, ōpen, ôrder; **oi**l, **ou**t; cup, pu̇t, rüle; **ch**ild; lo**ng**; **th**in; **ᴛʜ**en; **zh**, measure; **ə** represents **a** in about, **e** in taken, **i** in pencil, **o** in lemon, **u** in circus.

thing, such as: **a** an object used to pull down, hold down, or flatten something: *to tie a weight on a fishing line. A weight keeps the papers in place.* **b** an object that balances by its weight; counterpoise: *a sash weight.* **c** an object that is raised by winding and affords power by its descent: *a clock with two weights.* **6** a load; burden: *The pillars support the weight of the roof.* **7** *Figurative.* the burden of care or responsibility; mental load: *the weight of high office. That's a great weight off my mind. She sank into despair under the weight of her troubles.* **8** *Figurative.* influence; importance; value: *a man of weight in his community, evidence of little weight. A wise person's opinion has great weight.* **9** *Figurative.* the greater or more influential portion: *the weight of public opinion.* **10** the relative heaviness of an article of clothing appropriate to the season's weather: *summer weight.* **11** *Statistics.* **a** a factor assigned to a number in a computation, as in determining an average, to make the number's effect on the computation reflect its importance. **b** the frequency of an item in a statistical compilation. **12** *Sports.* a metal ball thrown, pushed, or lifted in contests of strength. **13** the force, expressed in pounds, needed to pull a bow a given distance, such as the length of an arrow. **14** the total load that a horse must carry in a race, according to its handicap, as for age, sex, or type of race, including the jockey, the saddle, and any weights added to make up the total: *The Experimental Free Handicap ... will be contested by horses carrying the weights already assigned by the handicapper* (New York Times). **15** force; strength; impetus: *The sailing instructions give the length of the course as 60 sea miles. If there is enough weight in the wind it could be a fast race* (London Times). *Abbr:* wt.

*–v.t.* **1** to load down; burden: *a heavily weighted truck, a person weighted by care. Job was weighted with troubles.* **2** to add weight to; put weight on: *The elevator is weighted too heavily.* **3** to load (fabric or thread) with mineral to make it seem of better quality: *weighted silk.* **4** *Statistics.* to give a weight to: *a weighted average.* **5** *Skiing.* to direct all or most of the downward thrust onto: *to weight the left ski.*

**by weight**, measured by weighing: *The proportions of acid and water were equal by weight* (A. T. Thomson).

**carry weight**, to be of importance; count: *What he says carries much weight with me.*

**pull one's weight**, to do one's part or share: *In boating phraseology, he "pulled his weight" ...; he was not a mere passenger* (London Daily News).

**throw one's weight around** (or **about**), *Informal.* to make too much use of one's rank or position; assert one's importance improperly or excessively: *The varsity star became unpopular after he began to throw his weight around.*

[Middle English *weighte,* alteration (by analogy with *weigh*) of *wighte,* Old English *gewiht* < *wegan* weigh]

**weight density**, the weight of a substance per unit volume.

**weight-for-age** (wāt′fər āj′), *n.* the weight assigned to a race horse based on age, without regard to other considerations.

**weight|i|ly** (wā′tə lē), *adv.* in a weighty manner; heavily; ponderously; momentously; forcibly.

**weight|i|ness** (wā′tē nis), *n.* the quality or condition of being weighty: (*Figurative.*) *The weightiness of the problems the President faces causes men to age considerably while holding that high and lonely office.*

**weight|less** (wāt′lis), *adj.* **1** having little or no weight: *The reflection of the night glow ... lit the cherry trees ... and made their branches look as if they were smothered in weightless snow* (New Yorker). **2** being free from the pull of gravity: *Astronauts know what it is like to float in space in a weightless condition.* – **weight′less|ly**, *adv.* – **weight′less|ness**, *n.*

**weight lifter**, a person who lifts barbells, dumbbells, or other weights as a body-building exercise or in sports competition: *Weight lifters and other athletes are prime candidates for back trouble* (Harper's).

***weight lifting**, the lifting of barbells, dumbbells, or other weights, as a body-building exercise or in sports competition: *Eight or ten years ago, as a result of a program of weight lifting, he put an inch on his biceps in two weeks* (New Yorker). – **weight′-lift′ing**, *adj.*

**weight throw**, a sport in which a heavy metal ball at the end of a flexible cable is thrown competitively for distance: *In winning the weight throw Thomson gave a remarkable exhibition of consistency* (New York Times).

**weight thrower**, a person who competes in the weight throw: *Spring-legged sprinters, brawny weight throwers and durable distance runners gathered ... for the ... championships* (Time).

**weight-watch|er** (wāt′woch′ər, -wôch′-), *n.* a person who tries to control his weight by dieting; dieter: [*They*] *are not exactly the keenest weight-watchers in the world and hardly let a day go by without forking into the pasta* (Sunday Times). [< *Weight Watchers,* a trademark for an organization of dieters]

**weight|y** (wā′tē), *adj.,* **weight|i|er, weight|i|est.** **1** heavy; having much weight. SYN: ponderous. See syn. under **heavy**. **2** *Figurative.* too heavy; burdensome: *The old king could no longer deal with the weighty cares of state.* SYN: onerous. **3** *Figurative.* **a** important; influential: *a weighty speaker.* SYN: momentous. **b** convincing: *weighty arguments.*

**Weil's disease** (vīlz, wīlz), an infectious disease characterized by jaundice and fever; leptospirosis. [< Adolph *Weil,* 1848-1916, a German physician, who described it]

**Wei|ma|ra|ner** (vī′mə rä′nər, wī′-), *n.* any one of a breed of medium-sized gray dogs with a docked tail, bred in Germany as a hunting dog. [< German *Weimaraner* < *Weimar,* Germany]

**wei|ner** (wē′nər), *n. U.S.* a wiener.
► See usage note under **wiener**.

**weir** (wir), *n.* **1** a dam erected across a river to stop and raise the water, as for conveying a stream to a mill. **2** a fence of stakes or broken branches put in a stream or channel to catch fish. **3** an obstruction erected across a channel or stream to divert the water through a special opening in order to measure the quantity flowing. [Old English *wer*]

**weird** (wird), *adj., n.* – *adj.* **1** unearthly or mysterious; wild; strange: *The witches moved in a weird dance. They were awakened by a weird shriek.* **2** *Informal.* odd; fantastic; queer: *a rather weird pattern, answer, or person. The shadows made weird figures on the wall.* **3** *Archaic or Scottish.* having to do with fate or destiny.

*–n. Archaic or Scottish.* **1a** the power or agency by which events are predetermined; fate; destiny. **b** magical power; enchantment. **2** a witch, wizard, or soothsayer. **3a** what is fated to happen to a particular person, thing, or event; one's appointed lot or fortune. **b** an evil fate inflicted by supernatural power, especially by way of retribution. **4** what is destined or fated to happen; predetermined events collectively. **5a** a prophecy. **b** a supernatural occurrence. **c** an omen.

[Old English *wyrd* fate] – **weird′ly**, *adv.* – **weird′ness**, *n.*

*–Syn. adj.* **1 Weird, eerie, uncanny** mean mysteriously or frighteningly strange. **Weird** describes something that seems not of this world or due to something above or beyond nature: *All night weird cries came from the jungle.* **Eerie** suggests the frightening effect of something weird or ghostly or vaguely and evilly mysterious: *The light from the single candle made eerie shadows in the cave.* **Uncanny** suggests a strangeness that is disturbing because it seems unnatural: *I had an uncanny feeling that eyes were peering from the darkness.*

**weird|ie** (wir′dē), *n. Slang.* a person or thing regarded as weird, odd, or eccentric.

**weird|o** (wir′dō), *n., pl.* **-dos,** *adj. U.S. Slang.* – *n.* a weirdie: *The weirdo in this melodrama* [*is*] *a young man who kidnaps a girl* (New York Times). – *adj.* odd; eccentric; queer: *He is being blackmailed by a weirdo youth who carries out the pretense of being his son* (Time).

***weight lifting**

**Weirds** (wirdz), *n.pl.* = Fates.

**weird sisters** or **Weird Sisters**, **1** the Fates. **2** the witches in *Macbeth.*

**weird|y** (wir′dē), *n., pl.* **weird|ies.** = weirdie.

**Weis|mann|ism** (vīs′män iz əm), *n. Biology.* the theory of evolution and heredity propounded by August Weismann (1834-1914), a German biologist, especially his theory that germ plasm is the material basis of heredity and that acquired characters are not transmissible.

**Weiss** (vīs, wīs), *n. German.* an ornate style of printing type.

**weiss beer** (wīs; *German* vīs), very pale, highly effervescent beer, usually prepared from wheat. [half translation of German *Weissbier* white beer]

**we|jack** (wē′jak), *n.* = fisher (def. 1a). [American English; see etym. under **woodchuck**]

**we|ka** (wā′kä, wē′kə), *n.* any one of certain flightless birds of New Zealand. Wekas are rails about the size of a chicken, with short legs and brown plumage. [< Maori *weka;* probably imitative]

**welch** (welch, welsh), *v.i.* = welsh. – **welch′er**, *n.*

**Welch** (welch, welsh), *adj., n.* = Welsh.

**Welch|man** (welch′mən, welsh′-), *n., pl.* **-men.** = Welshman.

**wel|come** (wel′kəm), *v.,* **-comed, -com|ing,** *n., adj., interj.* – *v.t.* **1** to greet (a person) kindly; give a friendly reception to: *We always welcome guests at our house.* **2** to receive gladly: *We welcome new ideas.*

*–n.* **1** the act of welcoming or being welcomed; kind or friendly reception: *Our friends are always sure of a welcome here.* **2** a word or phrase expressing this; kindly greeting: *to voice a warm welcome.*

*–adj.* **1** gladly received: *a welcome letter, a welcome visitor, a welcome rest.* **2** gladly or freely permitted: *You are welcome to pick the flowers.* **3** free to enjoy courtesies or other offerings without obligation (used as a conventional response to *thanks*): *You are quite welcome.*

*–interj.* an exclamation of friendly greeting: *Welcome home! Welcome, everyone!*

**wear out one's welcome**, to visit a person too often or too long: *We decided not to visit them every Sunday lest we wear out our welcome.*

[alteration (perhaps influenced by *well*[1]) of Old English *wilcuma* (originally) desired guest < *willa* pleasure, desire + *cuma* a comer < *cuman* to come] – **wel′come|ly**, *adv.* – **wel′come|ness**, *n.*

► As a reply to "Thank you," **you're welcome** is usual in the United States and parts of northern England, while the southern and western English reply is normally another "Thank you."

**welcome mat**, **1** a doormat, especially one with the word "Welcome" on it: *One day she opened her front door, and there, lying across the welcome mat, was a man, sound asleep or dead drunk* (New Yorker). **2** *Informal, Figurative: Throughout all of Tidewater Virginia the welcome mat is out for industry seeking new locations* (Wall Street Journal).

**wel|com|er** (wel′kə mər), *n.* a person or thing that welcomes or greets.

**welcome wagon**, *U.S.* an organization that greets new residents by extending to them free promotion from local merchants.

**weld**[1] (weld), *v., n.* – *v.t.* **1** to join (pieces of metal, plastic, or other material) together by heating the parts that touch to the melting point, so that they flow together and become one piece in cooling. The heating may be either by a flame torch or an electric current and may include melting a similar metal or plastic into the joint. *He welded the broken rod.* **2** *Figurative.* to unite closely; join intimately or inseparably: *to weld nations into an alliance. Working together for a month welded them into a strong team. ... welding words into the crude mass from the new speech round him* (Browning). – *v.i.* to be welded or be capable of being welded: *Steel welds; wood does not. Cooper welds easily.*

*–n.* **1** welded joint or fitting. **2** the act of welding.

[alteration of *well*[2], in sense of "to boil"] – **weld′er**, *n.* – **weld′less**, *adj.*

**weld**[2] (weld), *n.* **1** a European mignonette, from which a yellow dye is obtained; dyer's-weed; yellowweed. **2** the dye. Also, **woald, wold, would.** [Middle English *welde,* and *wald,* probably unrecorded Old English *wealde.* Apparently related to **weald, wold**[1].]

**weld|a|bil|i|ty** (wel′də bil′ə tē), *n.* the quality or property of being weldable: *Columbium in stainless steel improved the alloy's weldability* (Science News Letter).

**weld|a|ble** (wel′də bəl), *adj.* that can be welded.

**weld|ing** (wel′ding), *n.* the process of joining with a weld.

***welding rod**, a metal rod melted into the joint of a weld to bond two pieces of metal.

***welding rod**
***welding torch**

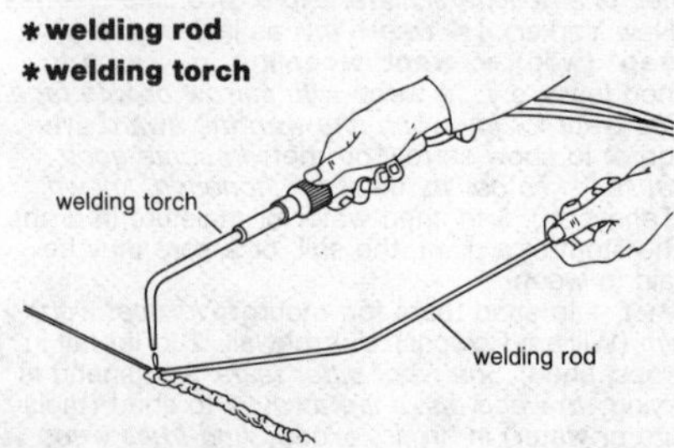


***welding torch**, a torch using gas as the source of heat for welding.

**weld|ment** (weld′mənt), *n.* an assembly of parts welded together: *Rohr pioneered the manufacture of stainless steel honeycomb structures and high-strength weldments* (Wall Street Journal).

**wel|fare** (wel′fãr′), *n., adj.* —*n.* **1** the condition of being well or doing well; health, happiness, and prosperity: *My uncle asked about the welfare of everyone in our family.* **2** = welfare work. **3** aid provided by the government to poor and needy people; relief: [*She*] *had been receiving forty dollars a month in welfare for herself and her four children* (New Yorker).
—*adj.* **1** receiving public financial assistance; being on welfare: *a welfare client, a welfare mother.* **2** having to do with or designed for the benefit of poor or needy people: *a government welfare program, federal welfare payments.*
**on welfare,** receiving aid from the government because of hardship or need; on relief: *The services and the programs of the city are to help the poor, whether they are actually on welfare or whether they are trying to support a family on the wages earned* (Atlantic).
[< earlier phrase *wel fare* < *wel* well + *fare* go]

**welfare fund,** a fund to provide benefits for workers, set up by a union from its own dues, or by an employer under terms of the Taft-Hartley Act.

**welfare state,** a state whose government provides for the welfare of its citizens, especially through social security, unemployment insurance, free medical treatment, and other such programs.

**welfare stater,** = welfare statist.

**welfare statism, 1** the condition of being a welfare state. **2** the principles and practices of a welfare state.

**welfare statist,** a supporter of the principles and practices of a welfare state. —**wel′fare-stat′ist,** *adj.*

**welfare work,** work done to improve the conditions of people who need help, carried on by government, private organizations, or individuals.

**welfare worker,** a person who does welfare work.

**wel|far|ism** (wel′fãr iz əm), *n.* the principles, practices, or condition of a welfare state: *He was marching ideologically in the spirit of the great wave of welfarism that inundated this state* (Newsweek). —**wel′far|ist,** *n., adj.*

**wel|i** (wel′ē), *n.* in Moslem countries: **1** a saint or holy man. **2** a tomb or shrine of a saint, commonly a domed structure. [< Arabic *walī,* or *welī* friend (of God), saint]

**wel|kin** (wel′kən), *n. Archaic.* the sky; vault of heaven. [Middle English *welken,* variant of *wolken,* Old English *wolcen* cloud]

**well**[1] (wel), *adv.,* **bet|ter, best,** *adj., interj.* —*adv.* **1** in a satisfactory, favorable, or good manner; all right: *The job was well done. Is everything going well at school?* **2a** thoroughly; fully: *a roast well done. Shake the medicine well before taking it.* **b** to a satisfactory or adequate degree; sufficiently; enough: *to be well fed.* **3** to a considerable degree; much; considerably: *The fair brought in well over a hundred dollars.* **4** in detail; intimately: *He knew the lesson well.* **5** fairly; reasonably: *I couldn't very well refuse to lend him the book. You can't very well argue today in favor of what you were against yesterday.*
—*adj.* **1** good; right; satisfactory: *All's well. It is well you came along.* **2** in good health: *Is he well enough to travel?* SYN: hale, sound, hearty. **3** desirable; advisable: *It is always well to start a bit early.*
—*interj.* an expression used to show mild surprise or agreement or just to fill in: *Well! Well! here she is. Well, I'm not sure.*
**as well, a** also; besides: *Marx had to fight the French Blanquists as well, on somewhat similar grounds* (Edmund Wilson). **b** equally: *He thought he might as well strive to promote his own needs* (J. E. T. Rogers).
**as well as, a** in addition to; besides: *It permits telling others who the actors are. as well as letting actors know a world beyond themselves* (Saturday Review). **b** as much as: *Thus the Government may understandably regard the US build-up as a source of provocation as well as protection* (Manchester Guardian Weekly).
**be** (or **get**) **well away,** *British.* to have made a good start or good progress: *From the drop* [*kick*] *Andrew got well away but Henry pulled him up* (Glasgow Herald).
[Old English *wel*]
► **a** Compound adjectives whose first element is **well** are normally hyphenated when used attributively and written as separate words in other uses: *a well-written book. The book was well written.* But those whose second element is a noun plus *-ed* (*well-intentioned*) and a few others, like *well-read,* are hyphenated in all positions. *Wellborn* is exceptional in being written solid. **b Well** is both adverb (*He plays well*) and adjective (*He looks well*). *To feel good* and *to feel well* are both standard English, the first implying a sense of satisfaction or elation, the second the absence of illness.
► See **good** for a usage note.

***well**[2] (wel), *n., v.* —*n.* **1** a hole dug or shaft bored in the ground to get water, oil, gas, or steam: *The farmer pumped all his water from a well with a windmill.* **2** *Figurative.* a spring, fountain, or other source; fount: *a well of everlasting love. A scholar is a well of ideas.* **3** something like a well in shape or use. The reservoir of a fountain pen is a well. **4** a shaft or opening for stairs or an elevator, extending upward through the floors of a building. **5** a compartment around a ship's pumps making them accessible for inspection and maintenance, and protecting them from damage. **6** a storage compartment for fish in the hold of a fishing boat, kept filled with water to keep the catch alive. **7** the space where the solicitors sit in English law courts, directly in front of the judge or judges. **8** the part of a meeting hall where the speaker's rostrum is: *... as he spoke from the well of the House* (Time). **9** a hollow part in a wing or fuselage of an aircraft into which a wheel of the landing gear is moved when the plane is airborne. **10** *Archaic.* **a** a spring (of water). **b** a pool fed by a spring. [Old English *welle, wielle* < stem of *weallan,* to boil]
—*v.i.* **1** to spring; rise: *Water wells from a spring beneath the rock.* (*Figurative.*) *Tears welled up in her eyes.* **2** to surge, gush, or billow: *Smoke welled out of the front window.*
—*v.t.* to send gushing up or pouring forth: *a spring welling up cool water.*
[Old English *wellan,* or *wiellan* (causative) < *weallan* to boil]

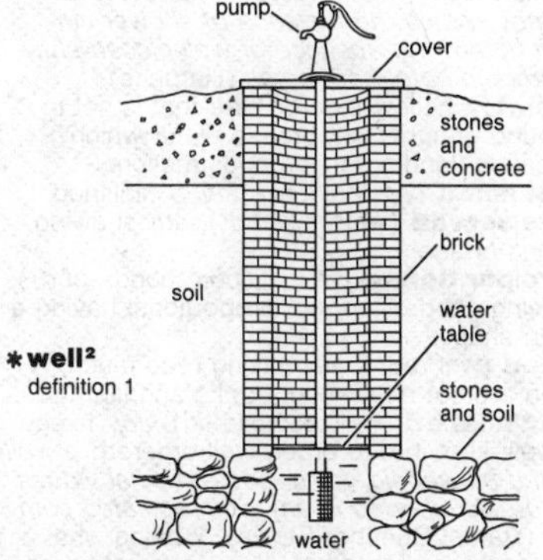

***well**[2] definition 1

**we'll** (wēl; *unstressed* wil), **1** we will. **2** we shall.

**well-act|ed** (wel′ak′tid), *adj.* **1** skillfully performed on the stage. **2** cleverly feigned or simulated.

**well|a|day** (wel′ə dā′), *interj. Archaic.* alas!; wellaway. [alteration of *wellaway;* influenced by *lackaday*]

**well-ad|ver|tised** (wel′ad′vər tīzd), *adj.* given much advertising or publicity: *A well-advertised brand recently cut its price ... and doubled sales* (Newsweek).

**well-ad|vised** (wel′ad vīzd′), *adj.* **1** prudent; careful; doing the wise or proper thing: *The inventor was no doubt well-advised in patenting his invention.* **2** based on wise counsel or careful consideration: *well-advised plans, a well-advised silence.*

**well-ap|point|ed** (wel′ə poin′tid), *adj.* having good furnishings or equipment.

**well|a|way** (wel′ə wā′), *interj. Archaic.* alas! [Old English *wei lā wei,* alteration of *wā lā wā* (literally) woe, lo! woe]

**well-bal|anced** (wel′bal′ənst), *adj.* **1** rightly balanced, adjusted, or regulated: *A well-balanced diet includes plenty of fruit and vegetables.* **2** *Figurative.* sensible; sane: *She has a well-balanced outlook on life.*

**well-be|haved** (wel′bi hāvd′), *adj.* showing good manners or conduct.

**well-be|ing** (wel′bē′ing), *n.* health and happiness; welfare.

**well-be|lov|ed** (wel′bi luv′id, -luvd′), *adj.* dearly beloved.

**well|born** (wel′bôrn′), *adj.* belonging to a good family; of good lineage.

**well-bred** (wel′bred′), *adj.* **1** well brought up; having or showing good manners; courteous. **2** of good breed or stock: *well-bred animals.*

**well-built** (wel′bilt′), *adj.* **1** put together well; solid; sturdy: *a well-built house.* **2** *Informal.* having a muscular, shapely, or coordinated build: *a well-built athlete, a well-built dancer.*

**well car,** a railroad flatcar with a depressed center section and additional wheels, for carrying heavy shipment.

**well-cho|sen** (wel′chō′zən), *adj.* carefully selected (used especially of words).

**well-con|nect|ed** (wel′kə nek′tid), *adj.* **1** thought out well; planned carefully: *a well-connected paragraph.* **2** of good family and connections.

**well-con|tent** (wel′kən tent′), *adj.* highly pleased or satisfied.

**well-cut** (wel′kut′), *adj.* tailored in the proper style or fashion.

**well deck,** an open space on the main deck of a ship, lying at a lower level between the forecastle and poop.

**well-de|fined** (wel′di fīnd′), *adj.* rightly, properly, or definitely marked; clearly defined or indicated; distinct: *well-defined limits, a well-defined style.*

**well-de|signed** (wel′di zīnd′), *adj.* designed or planned competently; arranged with skill: *a well-designed building, a well-designed scheme.*

**well-de|vel|oped** (wel′di vel′əpt), *adj.* **1** developed or worked out well: *The architect has a well-developed plan for remodeling our house.* **2** showing good development: *The athlete had a well-developed body.*

**well-di|rect|ed** (wel′də rek′tid, -dī-), *adj.* **1** aimed, guided, or addressed with skill and care. **2** conducted, led, or coached with skill and care: *The well-directed rioters who stormed the British embassy in Baghdad were ... symbols of the confusion and the turmoil in the Arab world* (Economist).

**well-dis|ci|plined** (wel′dis′ə plind), *adj.* **1** carefully trained; conditioned or ordered well: *a well-disciplined body or mind.* **2** having controls; following an established order and methods: *a relic of the past, when archaeology was a rich man's hobby rather than a well-disciplined subject* (New Scientist).

**well-dis|posed** (wel′dis pōzd′), *adj.* **1** favorably or kindly disposed: *The city government is well-disposed toward the project.* **2** = well-meaning. **3** rightly or properly disposed.

**well-do|er** (wel′dü′ər), *n.* a person who does deeds are good.

**well-do|ing** or **well|do|ing** (wel′dü′ing), *n., adj.* —*n.* the act or fact of doing right; good conduct or action.
—*adj.* acting well; doing what is right and satisfactory.

**well-done** (wel′dun′), *adj.* **1** performed well; skillfully done: *a well-done job, a well-done translation.* **2** thoroughly cooked: *a well-done steak.*

**well-dressed** (wel′drest′), *adj.* **1** fashionably dressed; in good taste. **2** properly cultivated, trimmed, cooked, or otherwise prepared.

**well-dress|ing** (wel′dres′ing), *n.* a traditional custom in the rural areas of England of decorating the wells at Whitsuntide.

**Wel|ler|ism** (wel′ə riz əm), *n.* an expression used by, or typical of, Sam Weller, a character in Charles Dickens's *Pickwick Papers. Example:* "It's over and can't be helped, and that's one consolation, as they always say in Turkey, ven they cuts the wrong man's head off."

**well-es|tab|lished** (wel′ə stab′lisht), *adj.* firmly established in being or acceptance: *a well-established belief, family, or business.*

**well-fa|vored** (wel′fā′vərd), *adj.* of pleasing appearance; good-looking.

**well-fa|voured** (wel′fā′vərd), *adj. Especially British.* well-favored.

**well-fed** (wel′fed′), *adj.* showing the result of good feeding: fat; plump.

**well field,** an area of land containing large amounts of water.

**well-fixed** (wel′fikst′), *adj. Informal.* well-to-do.

**well-formed** (wel′fôrmd′), *adj.* **1** rightly, properly, or finely formed; shapely: *a well-formed tree, a well-formed physique.* **2** *Linguistics.* conforming to given or established grammatical rules: *a well-formed sentence.* —**well′-form′ed|ness,** *n.*

**well-found** (wel′found′), *adj.* well supplied or equipped.

**well-found|ed** (wel′foun′did), *adj.* rightly or justly founded: *a well-founded faith in schools: well-founded suspicions.*

**well-groomed** (wel′grümd′), *adj.* well cared for; neat and trim.

**well-ground|ed** (wel′groun′did), *adj.* **1** based on good reasons; well-founded: *a well-grounded argument.* **2** thoroughly instructed in the fundamental principles of a subject: *to be well-grounded in mathematics.*

**well-grown** (wel′grōn′), *adj.* well-advanced in growth.

**well-han|dled** (wel′han′dəld), *adj.* accomplished or managed with skill and dexterity.

---

**Pronunciation Key:** hat, āge, cãre, fär; let, ēqual, tėrm; it, īce; hot, ōpen, ôrder; oil, out; cup, pu̇t, rüle; child; long; thin; ᴛʜen; zh, measure; ə represents **a** in about, **e** in taken, **i** in pencil, **o** in lemon, **u** in circus.

**well|head** (wel′hed′), *n.* **1** a spring of water. **2** the head or top of a well; site of a well: *the price of gas at the wellhead.* **3** *Figurative.* the chief source of fountainhead of anything.

**well-heeled** (wel′hēld′), *adj. U.S. Informal.* **1** well-to-do; prosperous: *A group of well-heeled oilmen are in the process of acquiring 5,000 acres of choice land between Dallas and Fort Worth for $10 million* (Time). **2** dressed well and giving the impression of having enough money to maintain oneself: *They are all well-heeled and live universally beyond their means* (Phyllis McGinley).

**well|hole** (wel′hōl′), *n.* **1** the hole or shaft of a well. **2** a well or shaft in a building, as for stairs or elevators. **3** an enclosed space within which a balancing weight rises and falls.

**well-in|formed** (wel′in fôrmd′), *adj.* **1** having reliable or full information on a subject: *a well-informed source.* **2** having information on a wide variety of subjects: *a well-informed librarian.*

***Wel|ling|ton boot**, or **Wel|ling|ton** (wel′ing tən), *n.* **1** a high boot covering the knee in front and cut away behind. **2** a somewhat shorter boot worn under the trousers. [< the first Duke of *Wellington,* 1769-1852, a British general, victor over Napoleon at Waterloo]

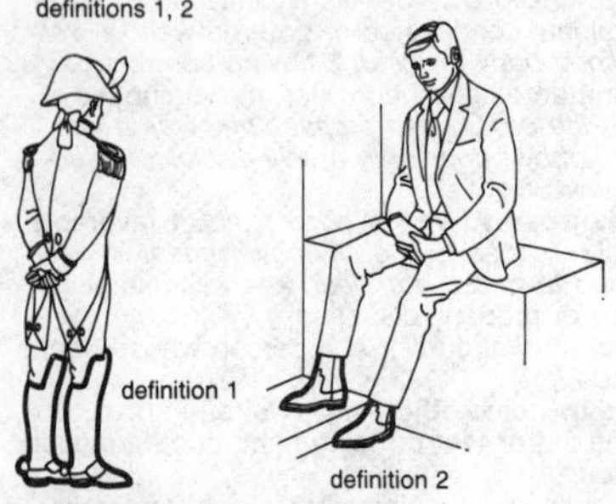

***Wellington boot**
definitions 1, 2

**Wel|ling|to|ni|an** (wel′ing tō′nē ən), *adj.* of, having to do with, or characteristic of the first Duke of Wellington: *There is a Wellingtonian vigor in his way of stating a case* (Nation).

**well-in|ten|tioned** (wel′in ten′shənd), *adj.* having or showing good intentions; well-meaning: *politicians who were clever and well-intentioned* (Baron Charnwood). *The climate in which English scientists went about their work was crammed full of confidence, socially well-intentioned, and, in a serious working sense, international* (C. P. Snow).

**well-judged** (wel′jujd′), *adj.* done with or resulting from good judgment; judicious: *Mr. Rattigan has had a remarkably well-judged shot at all this* (Manchester Guardian).

**well-kept** (wel′kept′), *adj.* **1** well cared for; carefully intended: *a well-kept house or garden.* **2** faithfully observed or guarded: *Undoubtedly all efforts will be made to preserve this deep and well-kept secret* (New York Times).

**well-knit** (wel′nit′), *adj.* **1** well joined or put together; closely linked or connected: *I found it an extremely well-knit and occasionally exciting work* (New Yorker). **2** strong and compact of build; well-developed; well-built: *As he approached, his well-knit figure was a picture of confidence.*

**well-known** (wel′nōn′), *adj.* **1** clearly or fully known: *reasons well-known to you.* **2** familiar: *to sing old, well-known songs.* **3** generally or widely known: *the well-known actor.*

**well log**, the log kept as a record of a well logging project.

**well logging**, the making of exploratory test borings in an underground mineral formation, and maintaining a record or log of what is found.

**well-made** (wel′mād′), *adj.* **1** skillfully made; sturdily built: *a well-made old desk.* **2** well-proportioned: *His ... well-made hind legs and ability make him a most desirable stallion* (London Times). **3** (of a play) having an ingeniously constructed plot but superficial in characters and ideas: *Sardou ... was a master of the well-made play, which emphasized plot construction* (John W. Gassner).

**well-man|nered** (wel′man′ərd), *adj.* having or showing good manners; polite; courteous: *The well-mannered child always remembered to say "please" and "thank you."*

**well-marked** (wel′märkt′), *adj.* clearly marked or distinguished; distinct.

**well-matched** (wel′macht′), *adj.* **1** that fit or go well together; harmonious: *They are a well-matched couple.* **2** of equal ability, strength, or other characteristics: *It was like the sixth or seventh round in a long championship fight between two well-matched heavyweights* (Time).

**well-mean|ing** (wel′mē′ning), *adj.* **1** having good intentions. **2** caused by good intentions.

**well-meant** (wel′ment′), *adj.* done or proceeding from good intentions: *a cold return for a well-meant kindness* (Scott). *They are well-meant proposals and they may succeed* (Manchester Guardian).

**well|ness** (wel′nis), *n.* the state of being well.

**well-nigh** (wel′nī′), *adv.* very nearly; all but entirely; almost.

**well-off** (wel′ôf′, -of′), *adj.,* or **well off, 1** in a good condition or position; favorably circumstanced. **2** fairly rich.

**well-oiled** (wel′oild′), *adj.* in good running condition; smooth; frictionless: *The President heads a well-oiled, relatively trouble-free Administration* (Time).

**well-or|dered** (wel′ôr′dərd), *adj.* ordered or arranged well; well-regulated: *a well-ordered method.*

**well-paid** (wel′pād′), *adj.* liberally rewarded or compensated: *When some comedian or wit told Queen Victoria jokes, they weren't supplied to him by six well-paid gag writers, but just occurred to him* (Newsweek).

**well-pay|ing** (wel′pā′ing), *adj.* giving a good salary or return: *It is appreciably below the ... average for such a well-paying industry* (Wall Street Journal).

**well-placed** (wel′plāst′), *adj.* **1** directed or aimed well: *One well-placed missile ... would destroy most of the tanks, trucks ... and other equipment* (Time). **2** holding a good social or official position: *That's from a well-placed Eastern European diplomat here* (Newsweek). **3** set in a good place or position; rightly or fitly placed; handy: *That would not explain the absence of shower curtains in hotels, the absence of well-placed shaving mirrors in hotel bathrooms* (Harper's).

**well point**, a hollow pipe or tube that is set in the ground to pump out ground water which could cause flooding during construction.

**well-pol|ished** (wel′pol′isht), *adj.* = polished.

**well-pre|served** (wel′pri zėrvd′), *adj.* showing few signs of age.

**well-pro|por|tioned** (wel′prə pôr′shənd, -pōr′-), *adj.* having good or correct proportions; having a pleasing shape.

**well-read** (wel′red′), *adj.* having read much; knowing a great deal about books and literature.

**well-reg|u|lat|ed** (wel′reg′yə lā′tid), *adj.* **1** regulated well; kept in due order; well-ordered: *a well-regulated household, mind, or life. Social virtues not to be disregarded in any well-regulated community* (Harriet Beecher Stowe). **2** being what a person or thing should be: *He was to return as any respectable, well-regulated prodigal ought to return—abject, broken-hearted, asking forgiveness* (Samuel Butler).

**well-round|ed** (wel′roun′did), *adj.* **1** having a properly rounded shape; well filled out: *But she grew up well-rounded, just the same, and at 15 ... she got a small part in a movie* (Newsweek). **2** *Figurative.* complete in all parts or respects: *a well-rounded education.*

**well-set** (wel′set′), *adj.* **1** fittingly or happily placed, fixed, or arranged: *a person well-set in his ways, an air of well-set distinction.* **2** strongly built; well-knit: *a handsome, well-set figure.* **3** *Cricket.* playing the bowling with ease: *a well-set batsman.*

**well shrimp**, a freshwater crustacean found in wells.

**Wells|i|an** (wel′zē ən), *adj.* of, having to do with, or characteristic of the writings of H. G. Wells (1866-1946), English author, especially his anticipation of future conditions.

**wells|ite** (wel′zīt), *n.* a mineral, a colorless to white, hydrous silicate of aluminum, barium, calcium, and potassium, occurring in crystals. [< Horace L. *Wells,* 1855-1924, an American chemist + *-ite*[1]]

**well-spo|ken** (wel′spō′kən), *adj.* **1** speaking well, fittingly, or pleasingly; polite in speech. **2** spoken well.

**well|spring** (wel′spring′), *n.* **1** the source of a stream or spring; fountainhead. **2** *Figurative.* the source of a supply that never fails.

**well-suit|ed** (wel′sü′tid), *adj.* suitable; convenient.

**well sweep**, a device used to draw water from a well, consisting of a long, tapering or weighted pole swung on a pivot and having a bucket hung on the smaller or lighter end.

**well-tem|pered** (wel′tem′pərd), *adj.* **1** *Music.* (of keyboard instruments) adjusted to the equal temperament. **2** having a good temper; controlled; mild: *and also see Mr. Dunn's well-tempered disquietude about a society that seems to be planning its own obsolescence* (New Yorker). **3** *Metallurgy.* brought to the right degree of hardness and elasticity.

**well-thought-of** (wel′thôt′ov′, -uv′), *adj.* highly respected; esteemed.

**well-thumbed** (wel′thumd′), *adj.* bearing marks of frequent handling: *They pore over ... well-thumbed pages as if touring their favorite market place* (Time).

**well-timed** (wel′tīmd′), *adj.* at the right time; timely: *a well-timed sermon.*

**well-to-do** (wel′tə dü′), *adj., n.* —*adj.* having enough money to live well; prosperous: *A well-to-do widow bought the big corner house.*
—*n.* **the well-to-do**, well-to-do persons: *No government is interested in putting up low-rent housing for the well-to-do* (Wall Street Journal).
—**well′-to-do′ness**, *n.*

**well-trav|eled** (wel′trav′əld), *adj.* **1** that has traveled far; experienced in travel: *an alert, well-traveled American.* **2** much traveled; carrying much traffic: *well-traveled airways.*

**well-turned** (wel′tėrnd′), *adj.* **1** turned or shaped well, as with rounded or curving form: *a well-turned ankle.* **2** *Figurative.* gracefully or happily expressed: *a well-turned compliment. A few well-turned paragraphs ... in the Bishop's most approved style* (John L. Motley).

**well-turned-out** (wel′tėrnd′out′), *adj.* dressed well; stylish: *But a man otherwise well-turned-out, who stretches his arms on the dinnertable ... is bound to feel a passing unease* (Punch).

**well-wish** (wel′wish′), *n.* a good wish: *Harry Truman, like Lyndon Johnson after him, had the well-wishes of everybody* (Vermont Royster).

**well-wish|er** (wel′wish′ər), *n.* a person who wishes well to a person, cause, or institution: *The well-wishers came around to congratulate the winning candidate.*

**well-wish|ing** (wel′wish′ing), *adj., n.* —*adj.* that wishes well to others; benevolent.
—*n.* **1** the act of wishing well to another. **2** an expression of good wishes.

**well-worn** (wel′wôrn′, -wōrn′), *adj.* **1** much worn by use: *a well-worn pair of shoes.* **2** *Figurative.* used too much; trite; stale; hackneyed: *He bored the neighbors with his well-worn jokes.*

**Wels|bach burner** (welz′bak, -bäk; *German* vels′bäн), a gas burner like a Bunsen burner, having an incombustible mantle which becomes incandescent and emits a brilliant light. [< K. Auer von *Welsbach,* 1858-1929, an Austrian chemist, who invented it]

**Welsbach mantle**, the gas mantle of a Welsbach burner, consisting of thorium oxide with a trace of cerium oxide around the flame.

**welsh** (welsh, welch), *v.i. Slang.* **1** to cheat by failing to pay a bet. **2** to evade the fulfillment of an obligation: *to welsh on a promise, to welsh on a business deal. Also,* **welch.** [origin uncertain]
—**welsh′er**, *n.*

**Welsh** (welsh, welch), *adj., n.* —*adj.* of or having to do with Wales, its people, or their Celtic language.
—*n.* **1** *pl. in use.* all the people of Wales. **2** their Celtic language. **3** any one of a certain breed of dairy cattle. Also, **Welch.**
[Old English *Welisc* < *Wealh* a Briton, foreigner < *Volcae,* the name of a Celtic tribe. Compare etym. under **Walloon, walnut.**]

**Welsh Black**, one of a breed of black, long-horned cattle raised for its high-quality beef.

**Welsh corgi** or **Corgi**, either of two breeds of Welsh working dogs having a long body, short legs, and a foxlike head. The Cardigan breed has rounded ears and a long tail, and the Pembroke breed has pricked ears and a short tail. [< Welsh *corgi* < *cor* dwarf + *ci* dog]

**Welsh|man** (welsh′mən, welch′-), *n., pl.* **-men.** a person born or living in Wales.

**Welsh|ness** (welsh′nis, welch′-), *n.* Welsh character or quality.

**Welsh pony**, a sturdy pony, originally from Wales, from 10 to 12 hands high, and weighing from 400 to 650 pounds.

**Welsh rabbit** or **rarebit**, a dish of cheese melted and cooked with milk or (often) beer or ale, eggs, and the like, and poured over toast or crackers; rarebit. It is served piping hot.
► **Welsh rabbit**, the original form, is a humorous coinage like *Cape Cod turkey* for codfish. The variant *Welsh rarebit* is the result of folk etymology.

**Welsh springer spaniel**, any one of a breed of red-and-white hunting dogs similar to the English springer spaniel, used for retrieving game on land or in water.

**Welsh terrier**, any one of a breed of black-and-tan, wiry-haired terriers, thought to be originally from Wales.

**welt** (welt), *n., v.* —*n.* **1** a strip of leather between the upper part and the sole of a shoe or boot. **2** a narrow strip of material or cord fastened on the edge or at a seam of a garment or upholstery, for trimming or strengthening. **3** a seam similar to a flat fell seam, used in tailoring. **4** any one of various ribs, flanges, or seams in which

one edge is lapped back for strength, used especially in leatherworking, blacksmithing, and metalwork. **5a** a streak or ridge made on the skin by a stick or whip; wale; wheal; weal. **b** a heavy blow. —*v.t.* **1** to put a welt or welts on. **2** *Informal.* to beat severely.
[Middle English *welte,* or *walte.* Perhaps related to **wale**[1].]

**Welt|an|schau|ung** (velt′än′shou′ůng), *n.* **1** a broad or comprehensive view of life. **2** a scheme or concept of human history, especially one by which a particular individual or group seeks to understand or explain things as they are, and possibly or probably may be, in order to be guided in forming a policy or program. [< German *Weltanschauung* (literally) world view < *Welt* world + *Anschauung* view, perception]

**Welt|an|sicht** (velt′än′ziнt), *n.* a special concept or particular interpretation of reality. [< German *Weltansicht* (literally) world view < *Welt* world + *Ansicht* view]

**wel|ter**[1] (wel′tər), *v., n.* —*v.i.* **1** to roll or tumble about; wallow. **2** to lie soaked; be drenched. **3** to be sunk or deeply involved (in). **4** to surge: *a weltering sea.*
—*n.* **1** a rolling or tumbling about. **2** a surging or confused mass: *All we saw was the welter of arms, legs, and bodies.* **3** commotion; confusion.
[< Middle Dutch, or Middle Low German *welteren*]

**wel|ter**[2] (wel′tər), *adj., n.* —*adj. Racing.* of or having to do with a race in which horses carry welterweights.
—*n. Informal.* a welterweight.
[< *welt* to thrash or whip + *-er*[1]]

**wel|ter|weight** (wel′tər wāt′), *n.* **1** a boxer who weighs more than 135 and less than 147 pounds. **2** a wrestler weighing between 147 and 160 pounds. **3** a weight of 28 pounds sometimes carried by a horse as a handicap in addition to that added for age.

**Welt|po|li|tik** (velt′pô li tēk′), *n.* world politics; international politics. [< German *Weltpolitik* < *Welt* world + *Politik* politics]

**Welt|schmerz** (velt′shmerts′), *n.* sorrow or pain caused by pondering the troubles of the world; pessimistic melancholy. [< German *Weltschmerz* (literally) world sorrow < *Welt* world + *Schmerz* sorrow]

**Wel|witsch|i|a** (wel wich′ē ə), *n., pl.* **-i|a.** a desert plant of southwestern Africa with a short, woody trunk and a single pair of green leaves, 2 or 3 feet wide and often twice as long, that spills over the top so that the plant resembles a giant mushroom. [< New Latin *Welwitschia* the genus name < Friedrich *Welwitsch,* 1807-1872, an Austrian botanist]

**wen**[1] (wen), *n.* a harmless cyst of the skin, especially on the scalp. It forms when the fatty matter secreted by a sebaceous gland collects inside of the gland. [Old English *wenn*]

**wen**[2] (wen), *n.* the name of an Old English runic letter functioning much as *w* does, and of the manuscript form of this in and early Middle English. [Old English *wen,* variant of *wyn* (literally) joy]

**wench** (wench), *n., v.* —*n.* **1** a girl or young woman. **2a** a woman servant: *a kitchen wench.* **b** any girl considered as belonging to the class of workers or peasants: *a buxom country wench.* **3** *Archaic.* a wanton woman.
—*v.i.* to seek out and consort with wenches.
[short for Middle English *wenchel* child, Old English *wencel,* probably related to *wancol* unsteady, weak. Compare etym. under **wankle.**] —**wench′er,** *n.*

**wend** (wend), *v.,* **wend|ed** or (*Archaic*) **went, wend|ing.** —*v.t.* to direct (one's way): *We wended our way home.*
—*v.i.* to go; travel.
[Old English *wendan*]

**Wend** (wend), *n.* one of a Slavic people living in Lusatia in central Germany; Sorb. [< German *Wende.* Compare Medieval Latin *Venedi.*]

**Wend|ic** (wen′dik), *adj.* = Wendish.

**wen|di|go** (wen′di gō), *n., pl.* **-gos** *for 1,* **-go** or **-goes** *for 2.* **1** an evil spirit of a cannibalistic nature in Algonkian mythology. **2** *Canadian.* the splake. [< Algonkian (Ojibwa) *weendigo* cannibal]

**Wend|ish** (wen′dish), *adj., n.* —*adj.* of or having to do with the Wends or their language; Sorbian.
—*n.* the Slavic language of the Wends.

**Wen|dy house** (wen′dē), *British.* a playhouse for a child: *A loud din arising from one Wendy house attracted the attention of the teacher* (Punch). [< the little house built around Wendy by Peter Pan in J. M. Barrie's play *Peter Pan*]

**wen|nish** (wen′ish), *adj.* **1** having the character or appearance of a wen. **2** affected with wens. [< *wen*[1] + *-ish*]

**wen|ny** (wen′ē), *adj.* = wennish.

**Wens|ley|dale** (wenz′lē dāl′), *n.* a variety of white cheese with blue veins.
[< *Wensleydale,* a district of Yorkshire, England, where the cheese is made]

**went** (went), *v.* the past tense of **go:** *I went home promptly after school.* [(originally) past tense of *wend*]
▶ In nonstandard English **went** is also used as the past participle: *I could have went yesterday.*

**wen|tle|trap** (wen′təl trap′), *n.* any one of a group or family of marine gastropods that have an elongated, white, spiral shell. [< Dutch *wenteltrap* winding staircase; spiral shell]

**wept** (wept), *v.* the past tense and past participle of **weep**[1]: *She wept for hours over the loss of her dog.*

**wer** (wėr, wer), *n.* = wergild.

**were** (wėr; *unstressed* wər), *v.* **1** the plural and 2nd person singular past indicative of **be:** *The children were playing in the park.* **2** the past subjunctive of **be:** *If I were rich, I would help the poor. Would you, if you were rich?*
**as it were,** in some way; so to speak: *She has thought fit, as it were, to mock herself* (Sir Richard Steele).
[Old English *wǣron*]
▶ **a** Subjunctive **were** is used in clauses stating conditions contrary to fact or not capable of being met (*If I were young again ...*) and conditions which are hypothetical but possible (*If he were to be chosen unanimously ...*). Sometimes the conjunction is omitted and the subject and verb are inverted: *Were I young again. ...* **b Were** is also used in noun clauses after *wish: I wish I were there.*
▶ See **was** for another usage note.

**we're** (wir), we are.

**were|gild** (wir′gild′, wer′-), *n.* = wergild.

**weren't** (wėrnt), were not.

**were|wolf** (wir′wůlf′, wėr′-), *n., pl.* **-wolves** (-wůlvz′). a person in folklore who has been changed into a wolf or who can change himself at times into a wolf, while retaining human intelligence. Also, **werwolf.** [Old English *werewulf,* probably < *wer* man + *wulf* wolf]

**wer|gild** (wėr′gild′, wer′-), *n.* (in early English and Germanic law) the price set upon a man according to his rank, paid to his relatives in cases of homicide and certain other crimes, to free the offender from further obligation or punishment. [Old English *wergeld,* or *weregild* (literally) man-compensation]

**wer|ner|ite** (wėr′nə rīt), *n.* any one of a group of minerals, silicates of aluminum, calcium, and sodium; scapolite. [< Abraham G. *Werner,* 1749?-1817, a German mineralogist + *-ite*[1]]

**wersh** (wersh), *adj. Scottish.* wearish.

**wert** (wėrt; *unstressed* wərt), *v. Archaic.* were. "Thou wert" means "you were."

**Wer|the|ri|an** or **Wer|te|ri|an** (ver tir′ē ən), *adj.* of or characteristic of Werther, the fictional character in Goethe's romance *The Sorrows of Young Werther;* morbidly sentimental: *An ancient lovelorn swain ... full of imaginary sorrows and Wertherian grief* (Anthony Trollope).

**Wer|ther|ism** (ver′tə riz əm), *n.* Wertherian character or quality; morbid sentimentality.

**wer|wolf** (wėr′wůlf′, wer′-), *n., pl.* **-wolves** (-wůlvz′). = werewolf.

**wes|kit** (wes′kit), *n. Informal.* a waistcoat; vest: *The Prime Minister wore a weskit that was not in startling colors but was less than sober raiment* (Harper's).

**Wes|ley|an** (wes′lē ən; *especially British* wez′lē-ən), *n., adj.* —*n.* **1** a follower of John Wesley (1703-1791), English clergyman who founded the Methodist Church. **2** = Methodist.
—*adj.* **1** of or having to do with John Wesley or his teaching. **2** of or having to do with the Methodist Church.

**Wes|ley|an|ism** (wes′lē ə niz′əm; *especially British* wez′lē ə niz′əm), *n.* the system of doctrines and church government of the Wesleyan Methodists.

**west** (west), *n., adj., adv.* —*n.* **1** the direction of the sunset; point of the compass to the left as one faces north. *Abbr:* W. or W (no period). **2** Also, **West.** the part of any country toward the west.
—*adj.* **1** toward the west; farther toward the west: *a west window. He took the west road.* **2** from the west: *a warm west wind.* **3** in the west; western: *west New York. The kitchen is in the west wing of the house.* **4** in or toward the part of a church furthest from the altar.
—*adv.* **1** toward the west; farther toward the west; westward: *Walk west three blocks.* **2** in the west: *The wind was blowing west.*
**west of,** farther west than: *Kansas is west of Pennsylvania.*
[Old English *west,* adverb, to the west, and *westan* from the west]
▶ A **west** or **westerly** wind carries a ship *east* or on an *easterly* course.

**West** (west), *n.* **1** the western part of the United States, especially the region west of the Mississippi River. **2** the countries in Europe and the Americas, as distinguished from those in Asia, especially southwestern Asia; Western Hemisphere and Europe; Occident. **3** the non-Communist nations, especially those of western Europe and America: *The problems dividing East and West should be discussed peacefully and soberly* (Manchester Guradian). **4** = Western Roman Empire. **5** one of the four players or positions in bridge.

**West Atlantic,** of or having to do with a branch of the Niger-Congo linguistic group spoken in West Africa, including Fulani and Wolof.

**west|bound** (west′bound′), *adj.* going west; bound westward.

**west by north,** the point of the compass or the direction, one point or 11 degrees 15 minutes to the north of west.

**west by south,** the point of the compass or the direction, one point or 11 degrees 15 minutes to the south of west.

**West End,** a fashionable section of London, England.

**west|er** (wes′tər), *v., n.* —*v.i.* **1** to move westward in its course; draw near the west. **2** to shift to the west.
—*n.* a wind or storm blowing from the west.

**west|er|ing** (wes′tər ing), *adj.* **1** that declines from the meridian toward the west (used chiefly of the sun when it is nearing the western horizon). **2a** that moves in a westward direction. **b** (of the wind) that shifts to the west.

**west|er|li|ness** (wes′tər lē nis), *n.* a westerly situation.

**west|er|ly** (wes′tər lē), *adj., adv., n., pl.* **-lies.**
—*adj., adv.* **1** toward the west. **2** from the west: *a westerly wind.*
—*n.* a wind that blows from the west.
**westerlies,** the prevailing westerly winds found in certain latitudes: *Between the westerlies and the trades are the horse latitudes* (Scientific American).
▶ See **west** for a usage note.

**west|ern** (wes′tərn), *adj., n.* —*adj.* **1** toward the west. **2** from the west. **3** of or in the west.
—*n.* **1** *Informal.* a story, motion picture, or television show about life in the western part of the United States, especially cowboy life. **2** a westerner or Westerner.
[Old English *westerne*]

**West|ern** (wes′tərn), *adj.* **1** of or in the West part of the United States. **2** of or in the countries of Europe and America, especially as contrasted with those of Asia. **3** of or in North and South America. **4** of or having to do with the non-Communist nations, especially those of western Europe and America: *In international affairs the conference supported neither the Western nor the Communist bloc* (Listener). **5** of or having to do with the Western Church. [< *western*]

**western Canada goose,** = white-cheeked goose.

**western catalpa,** a catalpa of the western United States, with light, soft, but durable wood, often cultivated as an ornamental tree and for its showy, white flowers; Shawneewood.

**Western Church, 1** the part of the Catholic Church that acknowledges the pope as its spiritual leader and follows the Latin Rite; Roman Catholic Church. **2** the Christian churches of Europe and America, as a group; western Christendom.

**Western civilization,** European and American civilization.

**western diamondback rattlesnake,** a large rattlesnake found from Arkansas and Texas to California and nearby Mexico.

**Western Empire,** = Western Roman Empire.

**West|ern|er** (wes′tər nər), *n.* **1** a person born or living in the western part of the United States. **2** a person who lives in the non-Communist West: *The French probably are happier than any other Westerners that the Soviet Union is willing to discuss a European settlement* (New York Times). [American English < *western* + *-er*[1]]

**west|ern|er** (wes′tər nər), *n.* **1** a person born or living in the western part of any country. **2** a person belonging to a people or country of Europe or America; Occidental. [< *Westerner*]

**western grebe,** a large black and white grebe of western North America; swan grebe.

**Western Hemisphere,** the half of the world that includes North and South America.

**western hemlock,** a large hemlock of the Pacific Northwest, used for lumber and pulp.

**west|ern|ise** (wes′tər nīz), *v.t.,* **-ised, -is|ing.**

**Pronunciation Key:** hat, āge, cãre, fär; let, ēqual, tėrm; it, īce; hot, ōpen, ôrder; oil, out; cup, půt, rüle; child; long; thin; ᴛʜen; zh, measure; ə represents **a** in about, **e** in taken, **i** in pencil, **o** in lemon, **u** in circus.

*Especially British.* westernize.

**west|ern|ism** (wes′tər niz əm), *n.* **1** Also, **Westernism.** methods, customs, or traits peculiar to Western nations: *To outward appearance, Japan's gloss of Westernism has deepened since the end of the Allied Occupation* (New York Times). **2** a word, idiom, custom, or manner peculiar to people or life in the western United States.

**west|ern|i|za|tion** or **West|ern|i|za|tion** (wes′tər nə zā′shən), *n.* the act or process of making western or Western in habits, customs, or character: *A certain amount of Westernization has been taking place in Soviet politics* (New Yorker).

**west|ern|ize** or **West|ern|ize** (wes′tər nīz), *v.t.*, **-ized, -iz|ing.** to make western or Western in habits, customs, or character: *Leningrad is as near to being Westernized as any Russian city can be without jukeboxes* (Punch). —**west′ern|iz′er, West′ern|iz′er,** *n.*

**western larch, 1** a large tree of North America with an orange-red, scaly bark, grown for its lumber; Oregon larch. **2** the wood of this tree.

**west|ern|most** (wes′tərn mōst), *adj.* farthest west; most westerly.

**Western Ocean,** (in classical times) the Atlantic Ocean, which was to the west of the world then known.

**Western omelet,** an omelet filled with diced ham, onions, and green peppers.

**western paper birch,** a variety of paper birch growing in western North America, eastern Canada, and New England.

**western red cedar,** an evergreen of the northwestern United States and western Canada, valued for its wood. It is a kind of arbor vitae.

***western roll,** a style of high jump in which the body is parallel to the crossbar at the height of the jump.

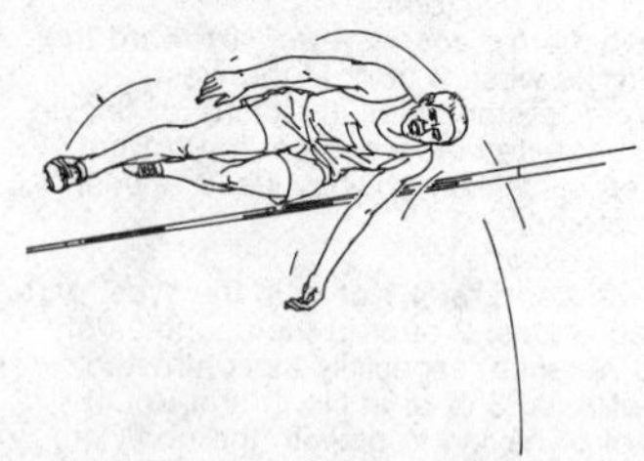

***western roll**

**Western Roman Empire,** the western part of the Roman Empire after its division in A.D. 395; Western Empire. It ended with the forced abdication of the last Roman emperor in 476.

**Western saddle,** a saddle with a high, curved pommel, to tie the end of a lariat to when roping cattle, so that the horse can pull against the steer; stock saddle. See picture under **saddle.**

**western sandpiper,** a small sandpiper that nests in Alaska and winters along the coasts of the United States south to northern South America.

**Western sandwich,** a sandwich filled with a mixture of fried eggs, diced ham, onions, and green peppers.

**western tanager,** a tanager of western North America, the male of which has yellow underparts, a red face, and black back, tail, and wings; Louisiana tanager.

**western X-disease,** a virus disease of peach and cherry trees, carried by a leaf hopper.

**western yellow pine, 1** = ponderosa pine. **2** = Jeffrey pine.

**western yew,** = Pacific yew.

**West German, 1** of or having to do with West Germany. **2** a native or inhabitant of West Germany.

**West Germanic,** the division of Germanic consisting of English, Frisian, Dutch, and German.

**West Highland white terrier,** a small, white terrier of a breed originating in Scotland.

**West Indian, 1** of or having to do with the West Indies, a group of islands in the Atlantic Ocean between Florida and South America. **2** a person born or living in the West Indies.

**West Indian cherry,** = acerola.

**West Indian corkwood,** a light, strong, porous wood; balsa.

**west|ing** (wes′ting), *n.* the distance westward covered by a ship on any westerly course; movement to the west.

**west|lin** (west′lin), *adj. Scottish.* western; westerly. [variant of earlier *westland,* adjective]

**Westm.,** Westminster.

**west|mark** (west′märk; *German* vest′märk′), *n.* the Deutsche mark of West Germany. [< German *Westmark* < *West* west + *Mark* mark[2]]

**West|min|ster** (west′min′stər), *n. British Informal.* Parliament, or the British government: *The danger facing Westminster is that once released from the current tensions of a spring election, it will relapse into somnolence* (Sunday Times). [< *Westminster,* the part of London that contains the Houses of Parliament]

**west-north|west** (west′nôrth′west′), *n., adj., adv.* —*n.* the point of the compass or the direction midway between west and northwest, two points or 22 degrees 30 minutes to the north of west.
—*adj., adv.* of, from, or toward the west-northwest.

**Wes|ton cell** (wes′tən), a cadmium-mercury electric cell used as a laboratory standard of voltage, producing a force of about 1.0190 volts. [< *Weston* Electrical Instrument Corp.]

**West|pha|li|an** (west fā′lē ən), *adj., n.* —*adj.* of or having to do with Westphalia, a western province of Prussia (formerly a duchy, later, with larger territory, a Napoleonic kingdom).
—*n.* a native or inhabitant of Westphalia.

**Westphalian ham,** a kind of hard smoked ham with a strong flavor, originally made in Westphalia.

**West Pointer,** a student or graduate of the U.S. Military Academy at West Point, N.Y.

**West Saxon, 1** a member of the division of the Saxons in England south of the Thames and westward from Surrey and Sussex. **2** the dialect of Old English used by the West Saxons. **3** of, having to do with, or characteristic of the West Saxons or their speech.

**west-south|west** (west′south′west′), *n., adj., adv.* —*n.* the point of the compass or the direction midway between west and southwest, two points or 22 degrees 30 minutes to the south of west.
—*adj., adv.* of, from, or toward the west-southwest.

**Wes|tral|ian** (wes trāl′yən), *adj., n.* —*adj.* of or having to do with Western Australia or its people.
—*n.* a native or inhabitant of Western Australia.

**West Virginian, 1** a native or inhabitant of West Virginia. **2** of or having to do with West Virginia.

**West|wall** (west′wôl′; *German* vest′väl′), *n.* = Siegfried Line. [< German *Westwall* < *west* West + *Wall* wall]

**west|ward** (west′wərd), *adv., adj., n.* —*adv.* toward the west; in a westerly direction: *Columbus sailed westward.*
—*adj.* toward, facing, or at the west; westerly; west: *The orchard is on the westward slope of the hill.*
—*n.* the direction or part which lies to the west; west.

**west|ward|ly** (west′wərd lē), *adj., adv.* **1** toward the west. **2** from the west.

**west|wards** (west′wərdz), *adv.* = westward.

**wet** (wet), *adj.,* **wet|ter, wet|test,** *v.,* **wet** or **wet|ted, wet|ting,** *n.* —*adj.* **1** covered, soaked, or sprinkled with water or other liquid: *wet hands, a wet sponge.* SYN: moist, damp. **2** watery; liquid: *Her eyes were wet with tears.* **3** not yet dry: *Don't touch, wet paint.* **4** rainy; drizzly; showery: *wet weather, a wet day.* **5** using, or performed by the use or presence of, water or other fluid, as chemical analysis. **6** preserved in syrup; bottled in a liquid. **7** *Informal.* having or favoring laws that permit the making and selling of alcoholic drinks: *a wet town or district.* **8** *British Slang.* **a** weak-willed; spineless. **b** overly sentimental; mawkish.
—*v.t.* **1** to make wet, moist, or damp: *Wet the cloth and wipe off the window.* **2** to pass urine in or on: *A child wets the bed, and no attempted medication has helped* (Saturday Review).
—*v.i.* **1** to become wet, moist, or damp: *Your good suit will wet in the rain unless you take a raincoat.* **2** to pass urine.
—*n.* **1** water or other liquid; moisture: *After the flooding our basement floor was covered with wet and slime.* **2** wetness; rain: *Come in out of the wet.* **3** *U.S. Informal.* a person who favors laws that permit the making and selling of alcoholic drinks. **4** *British Slang.* a spineless or mawkish person.
**all wet,** *Slang.* completely wrong or mistaken: *The weather forecast was all wet; instead of a storm, we had a sunny day.*
**wet behind the ears.** See under **ear**[1].
[Middle English *wett,* past participle of *weten* to wet, Old English *wǣtt,* for *wǣted,* past participle of *wǣtan* to make wet] —**wet′ly,** *adv.* —**wet′ness,** *n.*
—*Syn. v.t.* **1 Wet, drench, soak** mean to make very moist. **Wet** is the general word: *Wet the material well before applying soap.* **Drench** means to wet thoroughly, as by a pouring rain: *We were drenched by a sudden downpour.* **Soak** means to wet thoroughly by putting or being in a liquid for some time: *Soak the stained spot in milk.*

**wet|back** (wet′bak′), *n. U.S. Informal.* a Mexican who enters the United States illegally, especially by swimming or wading across the Rio Grande. [American English < *wet* + *back*[1]]

**wet bargain,** a bargain agreed upon by the parties drinking together.

**wet basin,** a dock at which a new ship is fitted out after launching.

**wet blanket,** a person or thing that has a discouraging or depressing effect. SYN: killjoy.

**wet-blan|ket** (wet′blang′kit), *v.t.* to throw a damper on; discourage; depress: *His gravity at birthday parties, surprise parties, didn't wet-blanket them* (J. D. Salinger).

**wet bob,** *British Slang.* a person who engages in water sports, such as rowing.

**wet brain,** an abnormal accumulation of watery fluid in the brain tissues, associated with acute alcoholism.

**wet bulb,** the one of the two thermometers of a psychrometer whose bulb is kept moistened during the period when humidity determinations are being made.

**wet-bulb thermometer** (wet′bulb′), **1** = wet bulb. **2** = psychrometer.

**wet cell,** *Electricity.* a cell having a liquid electrolyte.

**wet-clean** (wet′klēn′), *v.t.* to clean (clothes, rugs, or other objects) with water: *Customers send their suits back to London and ... have them wet-cleaned and pressed by hand* (Time).

**wet dock,** a dock or basin at a seaport furnished with gates, used where the withdrawal of the tide would otherwise leave a ship resting on the bottom, as in parts of England, to keep ships floating as at high tide, while loading or unloading.

**wet dream,** an involuntary emission of semen occurring during sleep along with a sexually exciting dream; nocturnal emission: *"Wet dreams" ... are a natural way of releasing excess semen* (Evelyn M. Duvall).

**wet fly,** an artificial fishing fly that is designed to sink below the surface of the water when cast.

**wet gas,** natural gas containing heavy hydrocarbons such as propane, butane, and pentane, that must be refined for use as gasoline.

**weth|er** (weᴛʜ′ər), *n.* a castrated ram. [Old English *wether*]

**wet lab** or **laboratory,** a laboratory in an underwater vessel or habitat, equipped with aquariums and other facilities for aquatic experiments.

**wet|land** (wet′land′), *n.* a swamp, marsh, or bog.

**wet milling,** a process of milling in which the grain is soaked and treated chemically before grinding. The principal products of wet milling are starch and oil.

**wet nurse,** a woman employed to suckle the infant of another.

**wet-nurse** (wet′nėrs′), *v.t.,* **-nursed, -nurs|ing. 1** to act as wet nurse to. **2** *Figurative.* to treat with special care; coddle; pamper: *We plan to wet-nurse the most promising little men to the point where they are good customers for* [*our*] *conventional banking operations* (Wall Street Journal).

**wet pack,** a blanket wet and wrung out and put on the body for medical purposes.

**wet plate,** *Photography.* a glass plate coated with wet sensitized collodion, formerly (and still occasionally) used, like the modern dry plate, for making pictures in a camera, so called because it must remain wet during the processes of sensitization, exposure, and development.

**wet pleurisy,** pleurisy in which fluid from blood vessels collects in the pleural cavity, often causing compression of the lung.

**wet rot,** decay in wood or timber caused by excessive moisture: *Wet rot is the destructive agent at work more or less on all telegraph poles* (Preece and Sivewright).

**wet steam,** steam in which water particles are held in suspension.

**wet strength,** the ability to hold together and not tear or break to pieces when wet, as of paper: *The product's wet strength is achieved through use of ... melamine resin, a chemical compound that binds paper fibers together much the way cement binds bricks* (Wall Street Journal).

**wet suit,** a skin-tight rubber suit worn especially by skin divers: *In wintertime he will don a ... wet suit and go right on surfing* (Peter Bart).

**wet sump,** a type of engine lubrication in which the oil supply is contained within the engine, in the bottom of the crankcase.

**wet|ta|bil|i|ty** (wet′ə bil′ə tē), *n.* wettable quality, property, or extent: *the wettability of a fabric.*

**wet|ta|ble** (wet′ə bəl), *adj.* that can be wetted without damage: *A wettable powder, the chemical is mixed with water and sprayed onto plants* (Science News Letter).

**wet|ter** (wet′ər), *n.* a person or thing that wets, such as a workman who dampens paper to be used in printing.

**wet|ting** (wet′ing), *n.* **1** the act of a person or thing that wets; sprinkling, dabbling, or drenching with water (especially rain) or the like. **2** something used to make a thing wet.
**wetting agent**, a substance capable of reducing surface tension so that a liquid will spread more easily on a surface.
**wet|ting-out agent** (wet′ing out′), = wetting agent.
**wet|tish** (wet′ish), *adj.* somewhat wet. SYN: damp, moist.
**wet wash**, *U.S.* clothes or linens that have been washed but not dried or ironed: *She hung the wet wash on the line to dry.*
**wet water**, water to which a detergent has been added to increase its penetrating quality, used in fighting fires.
**wet way**, *Chemistry.* the method of analysis in which the reactions are produced mostly in solutions and by the use of liquid reagents.
**we've** (wēv; *unstressed* wiv), we have.
**wey** (wā), *n.* a British unit of weight or measure, varying widely according to commodity and locality. [Old English *wǣge.* Compare etym. under **weigh**[1].]
**wf** (no periods) or **w.f.**, *Printing.* wrong font.
**WFTU** (no periods) or **W.F.T.U.**, World Federation of Trade Unions.
**w.g.**, wire gauge.
**W. Ger.**, West Germanic.
**wh.**, watt-hour.
**whack** (hwak), *n., v.* —*n.* **1** *Informal.* **a** a sharp, resounding blow. **b** the sound of this. **2** *Slang.* a portion, share, or allowance, especially a full share. **3** = wack.
—*v.t., v.i.* **1** to strike with a sharp, resounding blow: *The batter whacked the baseball out of the park.* **2** to beat or win in a contest. **3** *Slang.* to reduce; knock off: *Filling stations have whacked as much as a dime off their regular prices* (Wall Street Journal).
**have** (or **take**) **a whack at**, *Slang.* to make a trial or attempt at: *I'd like to have a whack at flying in a glider to see what it's like. Perhaps one should ... take a whack at reducing this appalling catalogue of ignorance* (New York Times).
**in whack**, *Slang.* in line; in proper order or condition: *Their members ... work toward a solution of the bedevilling problem of keeping prices and incomes in whack* (New Yorker).
**out of whack**, *Slang.* **a** not in proper condition; disordered: *Their stomachs are out of whack* (Sinclair Lewis). **b** out of proper condition; into disorder: *The space man's sense of balance would be thrown out of whack* (New Yorker).
**whack out**, *Slang.* to perform or produce vigorously: *a woman pianist at a concert grand, whacking out Bach as only the gentler sex can* (Manchester Guardian Weekly). *He has a second contract for six mysteries a year and somehow whacks out a short story every Monday, rain or shine* (Maclean's).
**whack up**, *Slang.* **a** to share; divide: *to whack up the loot.* **b** to increase: *The thinner rural areas will be forced to whack up the tax rates steeply for the distinctly unamused householders left therein* (New Yorker).
[imitative. Compare etym. under **thwack**.]
—**whack′er**, *n.*
**whacked** (hwakt), *adj. British Slang.* tired out; exhausted: *Let's sit the next one out—I'm whacked* (Punch).
**whack|i|ness** (hwak′ē nis), *n.* = wackiness.
**whack|ing** (hwak′ing), *adj. British Informal.* large; forcible.
**whack|y** (hwak′ē), *adj.,* **whack|i|er, whack|i|est.** = wacky.

***whale**[1]
definition 1

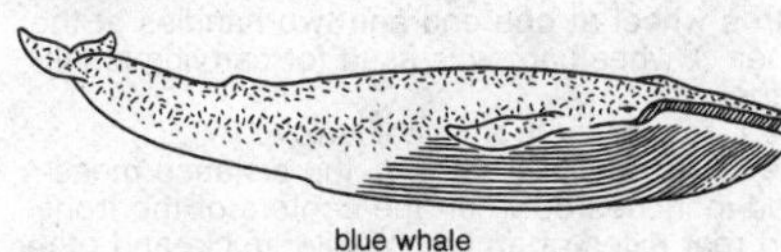

blue whale

**related to whales:**

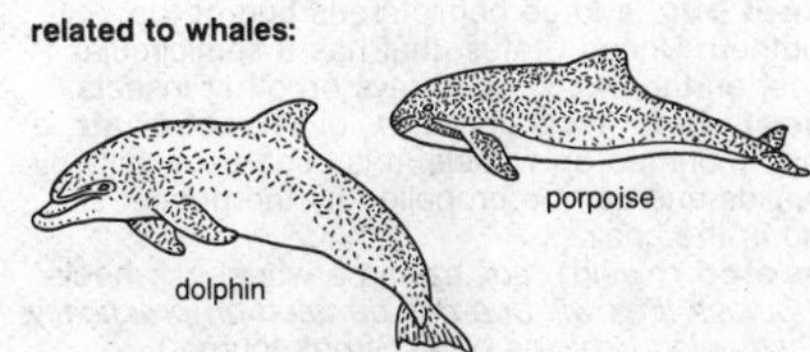

porpoise

dolphin

***whale**[1] (hwāl), *n., pl.* **whales** or (*collectively*) **whale,** *v.,* **whaled, whal|ing.** —*n.* **1** a mammal shaped like a huge fish and living in the sea. A whale has a broad, flat tail, forelimbs developed into flippers, no hind limbs, and a thick layer of fat under the skin. Men get oil and whalebone from whales. **2** *Informal, Figurative.* something very big, great, impressive, terrifying, or otherwise awesome or immense.
—*v.i.* to hunt and catch whales.
**a whale of**, *Informal.* a very excellent, large, or impressive kind of: *a whale of a party. One of Mr. Taylor's daughters got married recently and the guests ... had a whale of a time* (Manchester Guardian Weekly).
[Old English *hwæl*]
**whale**[2] (hwāl), *v.t.,* **whaled, whal|ing.** *Informal.* **1** to whip severely; beat; flog; thrash: *I caught Stockings trying to open the gate again, and I whaled him with a rope, and then tied the gate up* (Atlantic). **2** to hit hard. [apparently variant of *wale*[1], verb]
**whale|back** (hwāl′bak′), *n.* **1** a type of freighter with a rounded upper deck shaped like a whale's back, used especially on the Great Lakes. **2** any mass having the shape of the back of a whale.
**whale|bird** (hwāl′bėrd′), *n.* any one of various birds which inhabit the places where whales are found, or which feed on their oil or offal.
**whale|boat** (hwāl′bōt′), *n.* a long, narrow rowboat, with a pointed bow and stern, formerly much used in whaling, now used as a lifeboat.
**whale|bone** (hwāl′bōn′), *n.* **1** an elastic, horny substance growing in place of teeth in the upper jaw of certain whales and forming a series of thin, parallel plates; baleen. **2** a thin strip of this used for stiffening corsets and dresses.
**whalebone whale**, any one of a group of whales that yield whalebone, such as the right whale, finback, gray whale, and humpback; baleen whale.
**whale fishing**, the work or industry of taking whales; whaling.
**whale-head|ed stork** (hwāl′hed′id), = shoebill.
**whale line**, a long, strong rope attached to a harpoon.
**whale louse**, a barnacle or crustacean that is parasitic on whales.
**whale|man** (hwāl′mən), *n., pl.* **-men. 1** a man engaged in whaling. **2** a vessel engaged in whaling: *In most American whalemen the mast-heads are manned almost simultaneously with the vessel's leaving her port* (Herman Melville).
**whale|meat** (hwāl′mēt′), *n.* the flesh of the whale, used for food.
**whale oil**, oil obtained from the blubber of whales.
**whal|er** (hwā′lər), *n.* **1** a person who hunts whales. **2** a ship used for hunting and catching whales. **3** = whaleboat.
**whaler shark**, any one of various large, maneating sharks found off the coast of Australia.
**whal|er|y** (hwā′lər ē), *n., pl.* **-er|ies. 1** the industry of whaling or whale fishing. **2** an establishment for canning whalemeat.
**whale shark**, a very large, spotted, harmless shark of warm seas, often more than 50 feet long.
**whal|ing**[1] (hwā′ling), *n.* the hunting and catching of whales.
**whal|ing**[2] (hwā′ling), *n. Informal.* a sound whipping, thrashing, or beating.
**whal|ing**[3] (hwā′ling), *adj. Informal.* extraordinary or uncommonly big of its kind; whopping.
**whaling ship**, a ship used for hunting whales; whaler.
**whaling station**, a place where whale blubber is boiled to make oil, either on a factory ship or on shore.
**wham** (hwam), *n., interj., v.,* **whammed, whamming.** *Informal.* —*n., interj.* an exclamation or sound as of one thing striking hard against another: *Then, wham into the station* (New York Times).
—*v.t., v.i.* to hit with a hard, striking sound: *Other photographers, crowded out onto the deck, whammed their fists against the glass wall to catch her attention* (Time).
[imitative]
**wham|my** (hwam′ē), *n., pl.* **-mies.** *Slang.* the power or invocation of magic; jinx; hex: *The witch doctor, a thoroughly wrong sort, has put the whammy on him* (Atlantic). [< *wham*]
**whang**[1] (hwang), *n., v. Informal.* —*n.* a resounding blow or bang.
—*v.t., v.i.* to strike with a blow or bang.
[imitative]
**whang**[2] (hwang), *v.i. Scottish.* to throw, drive, pull, or push with force or with violent impact. [partly < *whang*[1]; partly < *whang*[3], verb, in earlier sense of "to lash with a thong"]
**whang**[3] (hwang), *n., v.* —*n. Scottish.* a large or thick slice, especially of cheese, bread, cake, or meat.
—*v.t.* to cut in large slices.
[variant of Scottish *thwang* thong]
**whang|ee** (hwang ē′), *n.* **1** a Chinese plant allied to the bamboo. **2** a cane made from it. [probably < Chinese *hwang* hard bamboo]
**whap** (hwop, wop), *v.t., v.i.,* **whapped, whap|ping,** *n.* = whop.
**whap|per** (hwop′ər), *n.* = whopper.
**wharf** (hwôrf), *n., pl.* **wharves** or **wharfs**, *v.* —*n.* **1** a platform built on the shore or out from the shore, beside which ships can load and unload; dock; pier. **2** any structure to which a vessel may tie in docking. **3** *Obsolete.* the bank of a river.
—*v.t.* **1** to furnish (a harbor) with a wharf or wharves. **2** to bring, place, or store (cargo) on a wharf. **3** to direct or steer (a ship) to a wharf.
—*v.i.* to tie up to a wharf; dock.
[Old English *hwearf* shore (where ships could tie up), related to *hweorfan* to turn]
**wharf|age** (hwôr′fij), *n.* **1** the use of a wharf for mooring a ship or storing and handling goods. **2** the fee or charge made for this. **3** wharves: *There are miles of wharfage in New York City.*
**wharf|ie** (hwôr′fē), *n. Australian.* a dockworker.
**wharf|in|ger** (hwôr′fin jər), *n.* a person who owns or has charge of a wharf. [alteration of earlier *wharfager* < *wharfage.* Compare etym. under **passenger**.]
**wharf rat**, **1** the common brown rat when living in or about a wharf. **2** *Informal, Figurative.* a man or boy, without regular or ostensible occupation, who loafs about wharves.
**wharf|side** (hwôrf′sīd′), *n., adj.* —*n.* the area on or at the side of a wharf.
—*adj.* on or at the side of a wharf: *a wharfside cafe.*
**Whar|ton's jelly** (hwôr′tənz), mucoid connective tissue which constitutes most of the bulk of the umbilical cord. [< Thomas *Wharton,* 1614-1673, an English anatomist]
**wharve** (hwôrv), *n.* **1** a small flywheel fixed on the spindle of a spinning wheel to maintain or regulate the speed. **2** a small pulley in a spinning machine for driving the spindle; whorl. [variant of earlier *wherve,* Old English *hweorfa* whorl of a spindle, related to *hweorfan* to whirl]
**wharves** (hwôrvz), *n.* a plural of **wharf.**
**what** (hwot, hwut; *unstressed* hwət), *pron., pl.* **what,** *adj., adv., n., interj., conj.* —**pron. 1** (as an interrogative pronoun) a word used in asking about people or things: *What is your name? What is the matter?* **2** *British Informal.* a word used as a (more or less) interrogative expletive, usually at the end of a sentence: *She is a clever girl, what?* **3** as a relative pronoun: **a** that which: *I know what you mean.* **b** whatever; anything that: *Do what you please.*
—**adj. 1** (as an interrogative adjective) a word used in asking questions about persons or things: *What time is it?* **2** as a relative adjective: **a** that which; those which: *Put back what money is left.* **b** whatever; any that: *Take what supplies you will need.* **3** (a word used to show surprise, doubt, anger, liking, dislike, or other feeling, or to add emphasis) how great; how remarkable: *What a mistake! What a pity that we missed you!*
—**adv. 1** how much; how: *What does it matter? What do we, as a nation, care about books?* (John Ruskin). **2** partly: *What with the wind and what with the rain, our walk was spoiled.* **3** (a word used to show surprise, doubt, anger, liking, dislike, or other feeling, or to add emphasis) how very: *What happy times we had together at the seashore last summer!* **4** *Obsolete.* **a** in what way or respect: *But alas, what can I help you?* (Miles Coverdale). **b** for what cause or reason; why: *What sit we then projecting Peace and War?* (Milton).
—*n.* the essence or substance of a thing in question: *In the relations between governments the how is generally at least as important as the what* (Atlantic).
—*interj.* a word used to show surprise, doubt, anger, liking, dislike, or other feeling, or to add emphasis: *What! Are you late again?*
—*conj. Dialect.* to the extent that; as much as; so far as: *to help one's friends what one can.*
**and what not**, and all kinds of other things: *She collected buttons, beads, bangles, and what not.*
**but what**. See under **but**[1].
**give one what for**, *Informal.* to give one something to cry, suffer, or be miserable for; punish; castigate: *The teacher gave the unruly boys what for.*
**so what**? See under **so**[1].
**what for**, why: *I can't imagine what she bought that silly hat for.*
**what have you**, *Informal.* anything else like this; and so on: *Wintertime there are no bears, no cars—but herds, coveys, schools and what have*

**Pronunciation Key:** hat, āge, cãre, fär; let, ēqual, tėrm; it, īce; hot, ōpen, ôrder; oil, out; cup, pu̇t, rüle; child; long; thin; ᴛʜen; zh, measure; ə represents **a** in about, **e** in taken, **i** in pencil, **o** in lemon, **u** in circus.

*you of elk, bison and deer* (New York Times).

**what if, a** what would happen if: *What if she told her husband how much her new dress really cost?* **b** what is the difference if: *What if it rains as long as we carry umbrellas?*

**what it takes,** *Informal.* whatever one needs to achieve success, such as ambition or intelligence: *As a student, he certainly has what it takes.*

**what of, a** what has happened to: *What of the book you were supposed to lend me?* **b** what is so important about: *Even if I miss the meeting, what of it?*

**what's what,** *Informal.* the true state of affairs; the important facts or skills: *When it comes to sports, he knows what's what. It takes time to find out what's what in a new job.*

**what's with,** *Informal.* what is the matter with: *Miss Flinch had already slammed the door. ... "What's with Miss Flinch?" I asked Louisa* (Harper's).

**what then?** what happens (or would happen) in that case? what of that? *If the diagnosis is not correct, what then?*

**what though,** what is the difference if: *What though the baby is small provided it is healthy?*

**what with,** in consequence of; considering: *They expect their partygoing to be somewhat curtailed what with the fair and the baby* (New York Times).

[Old English *hwæt*]

**what|cha|ma|call|it** (hwot′chə mə kôl′it, hwut′-), *n. Informal.* what-do-you-call-it.

**what-do-you-call-it** (hwot′də yə kôl′it, hwut′-), *n. Informal.* something whose name one forgets, does not know, or thinks not worth mentioning; thingumbob: *She forgot the word "orange" and kept telling me she was out of what-do-you-call-its* (Atlantic).

**what|e'er** (hwot ãr′, hwət-), *pron., adj.* = whatever.

**what|ev|er** (hwot ev′ər, hwət-), *pron., adj.* —***pron.*** **1** anything that: *Do whatever you like.* **2** no matter what: *Whatever happens, he is safe.* **3** (a word used for emphasis instead of *what*) what in the world: *Whatever do you mean?*

—***adj.*** **1** any that: *Ask whatever friends you like to the party.* **2** no matter what: *Whatever excuse he makes will not be believed.* **3** no matter who; at all: *Any person whatever can tell you the way to the old mill.*

**what-is-it** (hwot iz′it, hwət-), *n. Informal.* any curious, rare, or nameless object or contraption: *Others saw the what-is-it flying with others in a diamond-shaped formation* (New York Times). Also, **whatsis, whatsit.**

**what|not** (hwot′not′, hwut′-), *n.* **1** a stand with several shelves for books, ornaments, and curios. **2** a thing or person that may be variously named or described; nondescript.

**what's** (hwots, hwuts), **1** what is: *What's the latest news?* **2** what has: *What's been going on here lately?*

**what|sis** (hwot′sis, hwut′-), *n. Informal.* what-is-it.

**what|sit** (hwot′sit, hwut′-), *n. Informal.* what-is-it.

**what|so** (hwot′sō, hwut′-), *pron., adj. Archaic.* whatever: *Whatso thou wilt do with us, Our end shall not be piteous* (William Morris).

**what|so|e'er** (hwot′sō ãr′, hwut′-), *pron., adj.* whatsoever; whatever.

**what|so|ev|er** (hwot′sō ev′ər, hwut′-), *pron., adj.* whatever: *Whatsoever is troubling him?* (pron.). *The mayor got no support whatsoever for his program to build a new city hall* (adj.).

**whaup** (hwäp, hwôp), *n. Scottish.* the curlew. [probably imitative. Compare Old English *hwilpe* curlew.]

**wheal¹** (hwēl), *n.* **1** a ridge on the skin made by a blow, as of a whip; welt; weal. **2** a small swelling on the skin, often burning or itching. [variant of *weal²*]

**wheal²** (hwēl), *n. Obsolete.* a pimple or pustule. [Middle English *whele,* probably < Old English *hwelian* to suppurate. Compare etym. under **whelk².**]

**wheat** (hwēt), *n.* **1** the grain or seed of a common cereal grass, used to make flour. Its flour is the chief breadstuff in temperate countries. **2** the plant yielding this grain. It is closely related to barley and rye, and bears grains or seeds in dense, four-sided spikes that sometimes have awns (bearded wheat), and sometimes do not (beardless or bald wheat). Spring and summer wheat are planted in the spring; winter wheat is planted in the fall, maturing the next spring or summer. The various kinds comprise a genus of plants. See picture under **grass family.** [Old English *hwǣte*]

**wheat belt,** a region in which wheat is the leading crop.

**wheat bulb fly,** a European fly whose larva infests the stems of wheat.

**wheat|cake** (hwēt′kāk′), *n.* a pancake, especially if made of wheat flour; griddlecake; flapjack.

**wheat|ear** (hwēt′ir′), *n.* a small bird related to the thrushes and stonechat, brown with a black-and-white tail, that frequents open ground in the northern parts of North America, Europe, and Asia; fallow chat.

**wheat|en** (hwē′tən), *adj.* **1** made of the grain or flour of wheat, as bread made of the whole grain as distinct from white bread. **2** of or belonging to wheat as a plant.

**wheat germ,** a tiny, golden germ or embryo in the wheat kernel, separated in the milling of flour. It is rich in vitamins and is used as a cereal or food supplement.

**wheat|grass** (hwēt′gras′, -gräs′), *n.* any one of several wild, weedlike grasses, especially couch grass.

**wheat|land** (hwēt′land′), *n.* land on which wheat is grown or which is suitable for growing wheat.

**wheat|less** (hwēt′lis), *adj.* without wheat; characterized by refraining from the use of wheat: *wheatless days.*

**wheat rust, 1** any one of various fungi that attack the roots of wheat plants, and produce reddish rust marks on the stems and leaves. **2** a plant disease caused by such fungi.

***Wheat|stone bridge** (hwēt′stōn, -stən), an apparatus for measuring electrical resistance. It consists essentially of two arms of known resistance and an adjustable resistor, connected in circuit with the unknown resistor. [< Sir Charles *Wheatstone,* 1802-1875, a British physicist, who brought the invention to notice]

***Wheatstone bridge**

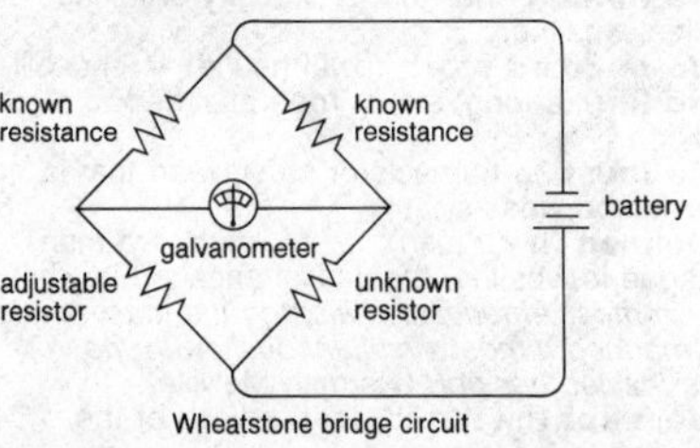

Wheatstone bridge circuit

**wheat|worm** (hwēt′wėrm′), *n.* a small nematode worm that causes a disease in wheat.

**whee** (hwē, wē), *interj., v.,* **wheed, whee|ing.** —***interj.*** an exclamation of joy or delight.

—***v.t. U.S. Slang.*** Usually, **whee up,** to fill with excitement of exuberance: *My first start against the White Sox meant so much to me ... I was all wheed up, feeling great* (Denny McLain).

**whee|dle** (hwē′dəl), *v.,* **-dled, -dling.** —***v.t.*** **1** to persuade by flattery, smooth words, or caresses; coax: *The children wheedled their mother into letting them go to the picnic.* **SYN:** cajole, blandish. **2** to get by wheedling: *They finally wheedled the secret out of him.*

—***v.i.*** to use soft, flattering words.

[origin uncertain. Compare Old English *wǣdlian* to beg; be poor < *wǣdl* poverty.] —**whee′dler,** *n.* —**whee′dling|ly,** *adv.*

***wheel** (hwēl), *n., v.* —***n.*** **1** a round frame that turns on a pin or shaft in its center. Wheels are used for moving vehicles and transmitting motion or power. **2a** any instrument, machine, apparatus, or other object shaped or moving like a wheel. A bicycle is often called a wheel. A ship's wheel is used in steering. Clay is shaped into dishes on a potter's wheel. **b** = steering wheel. **c** a contrivance shaped like a wheel on which, in former times, a person was stretched for torture or punishment while his limbs were broken by an iron bar: *Her niceness shines through her charmingly florid prose and it's evident in her clear disapproval of such practices as breaking slaves on the wheel merely because they'd tried to blow up Government House* (Harry Bruce). **3a** a firework that revolves on an axis while burning. **b** any circle or circular object; disk. **4** *Figurative.* any force thought of as moving or propelling: *the wheel of life. The wheels of government began to turn.* **5** a circling or circular motion or movement; revolution. **6** a military or naval movement by which troops or ships in line change direction while maintaining a straight line. **7** *U.S. Slang.* a person who manages affairs or personnel, as in a business; executive: *We have more trouble from company wheels trying to save a buck than we do with the little fellows* (Wall Street Journal). **8** a round frame of natural cheese in the form in which it is cured: *The 175 lb. wheels of Emmenthal—are the largest and heaviest cheeses in the world* (Punch). **9** = wheel of fortune. **10** a song's refrain.

—***v.i.*** **1** to turn: *He wheeled around suddenly.* **2** to turn or revolve about an axis or center, as a wheel does; rotate. **3** to turn to the right or left while in line. **4** *Figurative.* to change or reverse one's opinion, attitude, or course of action. **5** to move or perform in a curved or circular direction; circle: *gulls wheeling about.* **6a** to go along on or as if on wheels; proceed smoothly. **b** *Informal.* to ride a bicycle or tricycle.

—***v.t.*** **1** to turn (something) on or as if on a wheel or wheels; cause to revolve or rotate. **2** to cause (something) to move or perform in a curved or circular direction: *The rider wheeled his horse about.* **3** to move on wheels: *The workman was wheeling a load of bricks on a wheelbarrow.* **4** to furnish with a wheel or wheels. **5** *U.S.* to transmit (power or electricity): *The power company agreed to wheel electricity from the dam to the Co-ops* (Wall Street Journal).

**at the wheel, a** at the steering wheel: *You're at the wheel of a car that's sized for six-footers* (Newsweek). **b** *Figurative.* in control: *His father's death left him at the wheel of the firm.*

**lock the wheels** (or **brakes**), to apply the brakes of a vehicle hard enough to prevent the wheels from turning at all.

**wheel and deal,** *U.S. Slang.* to make deals, as in business or politics, in an aggressive, free-wheeling manner: *Unhampered by debates in press or Parliament,* [*it*] *can wheel and deal as it pleases, buying up surpluses here, dumping there* (Newsweek).

**wheels, a** machinery; system: *the wheels of industry or of justice.* **b** *U.S. Slang.* an automobile: *Guess what* [*she*] *was doing for wheels back in Washington ... a new 350-h.p. Corvette* (Time).

**wheels within wheels,** complicated circumstances, motives, influences, or forces: *There are wheels within wheels ... in the social world of Paris* (H. S. Merriman).

[Old English *hwēol, hweogl*]

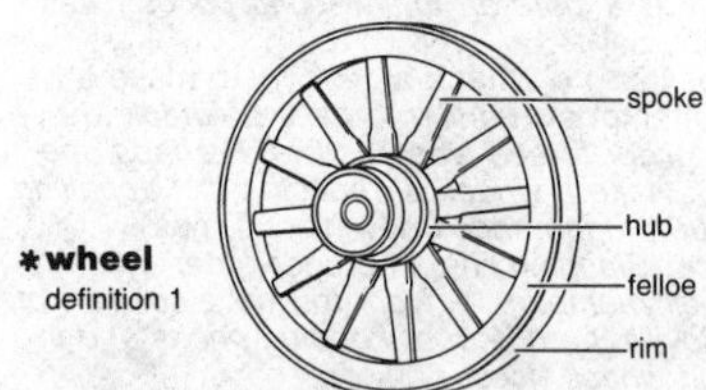

***wheel**
definition 1

***wheel and axle,** a device consisting of a cylindrical axle on which a wheel is fastened, used to lift weights by winding a rope onto the axle as the wheel is turned. It is a simple machine.

***wheel and axle**

**wheel animalcule** or **animal,** = rotifer.

**wheel barometer,** a barometer in which a float at the surface of the column of mercury is connected to the hand that indicates changes on the face of the instrument; weatherglass.

**wheel|bar|row** (hwēl′bar′ō), *n., v.* —***n.*** a frame with a wheel at one end and two handles at the other. A wheelbarrow is used for carrying small loads.

—***v.t.*** to convey in a wheelbarrow.

**wheel|base** (hwēl′bās′), *n.* the distance measured in inches between the centers of the front and rear axles of an automobile, truck, and other vehicles.

**wheel bug,** a large hemipterous bug of the southern United States, that has a semicircular crest on the thorax and preys on other insects.

**wheel|chair** (hwēl′chãr′), *n.,* or **wheel chair,** a chair mounted on wheels. It is used especially by invalids and can be propelled by the person sitting in the chair.

**wheeled** (hwēld), *adj.* having a wheel or wheels: *Tubeless tires will one day be used on practically all wheeled vehicles* (Wall Street Journal).

**wheel|er** (hwē′lər), *n.* **1** a person or thing that wheels. **2** a thing, such as a vehicle or a boat, that has a wheel or wheels: *a four-wheeler, side-wheeler.* **3** = wheel horse.

**wheel|er-deal|er** (hwē′lər dē′lər), *n. U.S. Slang.* a person who wheels and deals; aggressive, freewheeling operator.

**wheel horse**, 1 the horse in a team that is nearest to the wheels of the vehicle being pulled. 2 *Informal.* a person who works hard, long, and effectively. SYN: workhorse.

**wheel|house** (hwēl′hous′), *n.* a small, enclosed place on a ship to shelter the steering wheel and those who steer the ship; pilot house.

**wheel|ie** (hwē′lē), *n.* a stunt of riding a motorcycle or bicycle on one wheel: *"Doing a wheelie" ... means lifting the front wheel off the ground and balancing on the rear wheel alone* (New York Times).

**wheel|ing** (hwē′ling), *n.* 1 the act of a person or thing that wheels. 2 the condition of a roadbed with reference to passing over it on wheels.

**wheel|less** (hwēl′lis), *adj.* 1 without a wheel or wheels; having no wheels. 2 not adapted to wheeled vehicles.

**wheel lock**, an old gunlock of the firelock type, in which sparks were produced by a small serrated steel wheel wound on a spring so that it revolved against a piece of flint when released. It was superseded by the flintlock.

**wheel|man** (hwēl′mən), *n., pl.* **-men.** 1 a man who steers a ship; helmsman. 2 a man who attends to a wheel in some piece of mechanism. 3 *Informal.* a male cyclist.

**wheel of fortune**, 1 the revolving device that fortune is fabled to turn, emblematic of the vicissitudes of life. 2 a revolving wheel, used as a device for gambling in roulette. 3 = lottery wheel.

**wheels** (hwēlz), *n.pl.* See under **wheel**.

**wheels|man** (hwēlz′mən), *n., pl.* **-men.** = wheelman.

**wheel|spin** (hwēl′spin′), *n.* the spinning of the wheel of a vehicle without traction.

**wheel static**, static in an automobile radio produced by the rotation of the wheels.

**wheel window**, an ornamental circular window with radiating tracery or mullions more or less resembling the spokes of a wheel.

**wheel|work** (hwēl′wėrk′), *n.* a combination of wheels, especially gearwheels, as in a watch or other mechanism.

**wheel|wright** (hwēl′rīt′), *n.* a man whose work is making or repairing wheels, carriages, and wagons. [< *wheel* + *wright*]

**wheen** (hwēn), *adj., n. Scottish.* —*adj.* not many; few: *to carry a wheen parcels.*
—*n.* a fair number: *a wheen of toys on the floor.* [earlier Scottish *quheyn,* Old English *hwēne* somewhat; (originally) instrumental case of *hwōn* a few]

**wheeze** (hwēz), *v.,* **wheezed, wheez|ing,** *n.* —*v.i.* 1 to breathe with difficulty and a whistling sound. 2 to make a sound like this: *The old engine wheezed, but it didn't stop.*
—*v.t.* to utter with a sound of wheezing.
—*n.* 1 a whistling sound caused, or as if caused, by difficult breathing: *an asthmatic wheeze, the wheeze of an old engine.* 2 *Slang.* a funny saying or story, especially one made familiar by constant repetition; old or familiar joke, trick, or criticism. [probably < Scandinavian (compare Old Icelandic *hwǣsa* to hiss). Compare Old English *hwōsan* to cough.] —**wheez′er,** *n.* —**wheez′ing|ly,** *adv.*

**wheez|y** (hwē′zē), *adj.,* **wheez|i|er, wheez|i|est.** 1 wheezing: *The old dog was fat and wheezy.* 2 *Slang.* old and familiar; trite: [*His*] *interpretation of the Charlotte Brontë novel is a rather wheezy business* (New Yorker). —**wheez′i|ly,** *adv.* —**wheez′i|ness,** *n.*

**wheft** (hweft), *n. Nautical.* waft[2].

***whelk**[1] (hwelk), *n.* a sea snail with a long, spiral shell, especially a kind commonly used for food in Europe. There are two genera of whelks. [alteration of Middle English *welke,* or *wilke,* Old English *weoloc,* or *wioloc*]

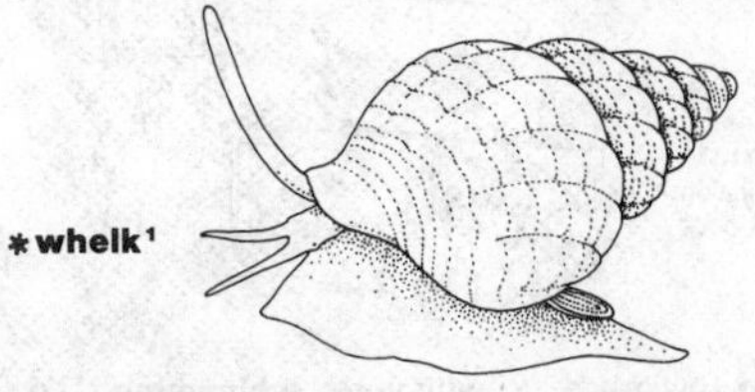

***whelk**[1]

**whelk**[2] (hwelk), *n.* a pimple or pustule. [Old English *hwylca* < *hwelian* to suppurate. Compare etym. under **wheal**[2].]

**whelm** (hwelm), *v.t.* 1 = overwhelm. SYN: overpower. 2 = submerge. SYN: immerse. [Middle English *whelmen* turn with the concave side down, probably fusion of Old English *-hwielfan* and *helmian* to cover]

**whelp** (hwelp), *n., v.* —*n.* 1 a puppy or cub; young dog or animal of prey, such as a young wolf, lion, tiger, bear, or seal. 2 *Figurative.* an impudent boy or young man. SYN: scamp. 3 *Machinery.* a one of the longitudinal projections on the barrel of a capstan or the drum of a windlass. b one of the teeth of a sprocket wheel.
—*v.i., v.t.* to give birth to (whelps). [Old English *hwelp*]

**when** (hwen; *unstressed* hwən), *adv., conj., pron., n.* —**adv.** at what time: *When does school close? When did I say such a thing?*
—*conj.* 1 at the time that: *His father died when he was a child. Stand up when your name is called.* 2 at any time that: *The dog comes when his name is called. He is impatient when he is kept waiting.* 3 at which time; and then: *The dog growled till his master spoke, when he gave a joyful bark. We were just leaving, when it began to snow.* 4 at or on which (preceded by *time, day,* or the like): *at the time when I wrote the story.* 5 in the, or any, case or circumstances in which: *Most confident, when palpably most wrong* (William Cowper). 6 although: *We have only three books when we need five.* 7 considering that; inasmuch as; since: *How can I help you when I don't know how to do the problems myself?*
—*pron.* what time; which time: *Since when have they had a car? He joined our company twenty years ago, since when he has risen to become its president.*
—*n.* the time or occasion: *the when and where of an event.*
**say when,** *Informal.* to call a halt to something; stop: [*He*] *never seems to know when to say when* (New York Times). [Old English *hwenne, hwaenne*]

**when|as** (hwen az′, hwən-), *conj. Archaic.* when; while; whereas.

**whence** (hwens), *adv., conj.* —**adv.** 1 from what place; from where: *Whence do you come?* 2 from what source or cause; from what: *Whence has he so much wisdom?* 3 from which: *Let them return to the country whence they came.*
—*conj.* from what place, source, or cause: *He told whence he came.*
**from whence,** whence (a pleonasm): *From whence have we derived that spiritual profit?* (Dickens). [Middle English *whennes* < Old English *hwanone* whence + adverbial genitive *-s*]

**whence|so|ev|er** (hwens′sō ev′ər), *conj., adv.* from whatever place, source, or cause.

**when|e'er** (hwen âr′, hwən-), *conj., adv.* = whenever.

**when|ev|er** (hwen ev′ər, hwən-), *conj., adv.* at whatever time; at any time that; when: *Please come whenever you wish* (conj.). *He played chess whenever possible* (adv.).

**when-is|sued** (hwen′ish′üd), *adj.* at such time as a stock or security is issued, referring to the trading that is permitted between the time a security is authorized and its actual issuance. If issuance does not take place, all prior trading in the security becomes invalid. *Over-the-counter trading, on a when-issued basis, began in New York as soon as the S.E.C. clearance was announced* (Wall Street Journal).

**when|so|ev|er** (hwen′sō ev′ər), *conj., adv.* at whatever time; whenever.

**where** (hwãr), *adv., conj., pron., n.* —**adv.** 1 in what place; at what place: *Where are they? Where do you live.* 2 to what place: *Where are you going?* 3 from what place: *Where did you get that story?* 4 in which; at which: *That is the house where I was born.* 5 to which: *the place where he is going.* 6 in or at which place: *I don't know where she is.* 7 in what way; in what respect: *Where is the harm in trying?*
—*conj.* 1 in the place in which; at the place at which: *Your coat is where you left it.* 2 in any place in which; at any place at which: *Use the salve where the pain is felt.* 3 any place to which: *I will go where you go.* 4 in or at which place: *They came to the town, where they stayed for the night.* 5 in the case, circumstances, or respect, in which: *Some people worry where it does no good.*
—*pron.* 1 what place; which place: *Where does he come from?* 2 the place in which: *This is where the bus stops.* 3 the point or situation at which: *This is where I come in. That's where you're making a mistake.*
—*n.* the place, locality, or scene: *the when and where of an event.*
**where away?** *Nautical.* what is the bearing? what direction? (used of an object, ship, or land, seen by the lookout): *"Sail ho!" shouted the lookout from the masthead. "Where away?" asked the officer on the deck.*
**where it's at,** *U.S. Slang.* the place of greatest activity, excitement, or interest: *Piscataway or Tahiti may be lovely places, but are they really where it's at these days?* (New Yorker). [Old English *hwǣr*]

**where|a|bout** (hwãr′ə bout′), *adv., conj., n.* = whereabouts.

**where|a|bouts** (hwãr′ə bouts′), *adv., conj., n.* —**adv., conj.** 1 near what place; where: *Whereabouts are my books? Whereabouts can I find a doctor? We did not know whereabouts we were.* 2 *Obsolete.* a about or around which. b concerning or in regard to which (used interrogatively or relatively).
—*n.* the place where a person or thing is: *Do you know her whereabouts? I've forgotten the whereabouts of his present home.*

**where|as** (hwãr az′), *conj., n., pl.* **-as|es.** —*conj.* 1 on the contrary; but; while: *Some children like school, whereas others do not.* 2 considering that; since (now only introducing a preamble or recital in a legal or other formal document): *"Whereas the people of the colonies have been grieved and burdened with taxes. ..."*
—*n.* a statement introduced by "whereas," especially the preamble of a formal document or something likened to this.

**where|at** (hwãr at′), *adv., conj.* at what; at which.

**where|by** (hwãr bī′), *adv., conj.* 1 by what; by which: *There is no other way whereby he can be saved.* 2a by, beside, or near what; in what direction. b by what means; how. c *Obsolete.* for what reason; why.

**wher|e'er** (hwãr âr′), *conj., adv.* = wherever.

**where|fore** (hwãr′fôr, -fōr), *adv., conj., n.* —**adv.** 1 for what reason? why? 2 for which reason; therefore; so.
—*conj.* for what reason; why.
—*n.* a reason; cause: *Can you understand the whys and wherefores of his behavior?* [Middle English *hwarfore* < *hwar* where + *fore* for, preposition]

**where|from** (hwãr from′, -frum′), *adv., conj.* from which; whence.

**where|in** (hwãr in′), *adv., conj.* in what; in which; how.

**where|in|so|ev|er** (hwãr in′sō ev′ər), *conj.* in whatsoever place, thing, respect, etc.

**where|in|to** (hwãr in′tü, hwãr′in tü′), *adv., conj.* into what; into which.

**where|ness** (hwãr′nis), *n.* the state or property of having place or local relation; ubication.

**where|of** (hwãr ov′, -uv′), *adv., conj.* of what; of which; of whom: *Does he realize whereof he speaks? Solomon knew whereof he spoke.*

**where|on** (hwãr on′, -ôn′), *adv., conj.* on which; on what: *Summer cottages occupy the land whereon the old farmhouse stood.*

**where|so** (hwãr sō′), *conj. Archaic.* wherever.

**where|so|e'er** (hwãr′sō âr′), *conj., adv.* wheresoever; wherever.

**where|so|ev|er** (hwãr′sō ev′ər), *conj., adv.* = wherever.

**where|through** (hwãr thrü′), *adv., conj.* through which.

**where|to** (hwãr tü′), *adv., conj.* 1 to what; to which; where: *He went to that place whereto he had been sent.* 2 for what purpose; why: *Whereto do you lay up riches?*

**where|un|der** (hwãr un′dər), *adv.* under which: *The Vietnamese have suggested the desirability of a change in Saigon whereunder the chief representative of France should be a civilian rather than a military commander* (New York Times).

**where|un|to** (hwãr un′tü, hwãr′un tü′), *adv., conj. Archaic.* whereto.

**where|up|on** (hwãr′ə pon′, -pôn′), *adv., conj.* 1 upon what; upon which: *We have a constitution whereupon the country runs its government.* 2 at which; after which: *We got into an argument, whereupon my father left the room.*

**wher|ev|er** (hwãr ev′ər), *conj., adv.* 1 to whatever place; in whatever place; where: *Sit wherever you like* (conj.). *He will be happy wherever he lives* (conj.). *He goes wherever he pleases* (adv.). 2 in any case, condition, or circumstances in which: *Let me know wherever you disagree.*

**where|with** (hwãr wiᴛʜ′, -with′), *adv., conj., pron., n.* —**adv., conj.** with what; with which: *Wherewith shall we be fed? He has no clothes wherewith to cover himself properly.*
—*pron.* that with which; the means by which: *How will he get wherewith to educate himself?*
—*n.* = wherewithal.

**where|with|al** (*n.* hwãr′wiᴛʜ ôl; *adv., conj.* hwãr′-wiᴛʜ ôl′), *n., adv., conj.* —*n.* means, supplies, or money needed: *Has she the wherewithal to pay for the trip?*
—**adv., conj.** *Archaic.* with what; with which; wherewith.

**wher|ry** (hwer′ē), *n., pl.* **-ries,** *v.,* **-ried, -ry|ing.**

---

**Pronunciation Key:** **h**a**t**, **ā**ge, **c**ã**re**, **f**ä**r**; **l**e**t**, **ē**qual, **t**ė**rm**; **i**t, **ī**ce; **h**o**t**, **ō**pen, **ô**rder; **oi**l, **ou**t; **c**u**p**, **p**u̇**t**, **r**ü**le**; **ch**ild; **l**o**ng**; **th**in; **ᴛʜ**en; **zh**, measure; **ə** represents **a** in about, **e** in taken, **i** in pencil, **o** in lemon, **u** in circus.

—*n.* 1 a light, shallow rowboat for carrying passengers and goods on rivers, especially in England. 2 a light rowboat for one person, used for racing. 3 *British.* any one of several types of larger boats, varying in different localities, such as a barge, a fishing boat, or a sailboat, used on rivers.
—*v.t.* to carry in or as if in a wherry.
[origin unknown]

**whet** (hwet), *v.,* **whet|ted, whet|ting,** *n.* —*v.t.* 1 to sharpen by rubbing; hone: *to whet a knife.* 2 *Figurative.* to make keen or eager; stimulate: *The smell of the food whetted my appetite. An exciting story whets your interest.* SYN: kindle, quicken.
—*n.* 1 the act of whetting; sharpening. 2 something that whets. 3 = appetizer. 4 *Dialect.* **a** the interval between two sharpenings, as of a scythe, during which the tool is used for cutting. **b** any occasion of work or action; turn.
[Old English *hwettan*] —**whet′ter,** *n.*

**wheth|er** (hweᴛʜ′ər), *conj., pron.* —*conj.* 1 *Whether* is used in expressing a choice or alternative: *It matters little whether we go or stay. I don't know whether to work or rest. His neighbors might well doubt whether it were more dangerous to be at war or at peace with him* (Macaulay). 2 either: *Whether sick or well, she is always cheerful. He was not sent a ticket, whether by accident or design.* 3 if: *I asked whether I might be excused.* 4 *Obsolete.* introducing a direct question expressing doubt between alternatives.
—*pron. Archaic.* which of two; whichever of the two (used both as an interrogative and as a relative): *Whether would ye? gold or field?* (Tennyson).
**whether or not** (or **no**). See under **not.**
[Middle English *whether* < Old English *hwether, hwæther*]
▶ See **if** for usage note.

**whet|stone** (hwet′stōn′), *n.* a stone for sharpening knives or tools, especially a shaped stone for giving a very fine edge after grinding.

**whew** (hwyü), *interj., n.* an exclamation of surprise, dismay, or relief: *Whew! it's cold!*
[imitative]

**whey** (hwā), *n.* the watery part of milk that separates from the curd when milk sours and becomes coagulated, or when cheese is made.
[Old English *hwǣg*]

**whey|ey** (hwā′ē), *adj.* of, like, or containing whey.

**whey|face** (hwā′fās′), *n.* 1 a person having a pale face. 2 a pale face; pallid visage.

**whey|faced** (hwā′fāst′), *adj.* having a white or pale face; pallid.

**which** (hwich), *pron., adj.* —*pron.* 1 (as an interrogative pronoun) a word used in asking questions about persons or things: *Which seems the best plan? Which is your car?* 2 as a relative pronoun: **a** a word used in connecting a group of words with some word in the sentence; the one or ones indicated by the antecedent: *Read the book which you have. He now has the dog which used to belong to his cousin. She drew on the windowpane a pattern with her ring, the outlines of which are still visible today.* **b** the one that; any that: *Here are three boxes. Choose which you like best.* 3 a thing that: *and, which is worse, you were late.*
—*adj.* 1 (as an interrogative adjective) a word used in asking questions about persons or things: *Which cities did you visit? Which student won the prize? Which books are yours?* 2 (as a relative adjective) a word used in connecting a group of words with some word in the sentence: **a** referring to something just mentioned: *It rain'd all night and all day ... during which time the ship broke in pieces* (Daniel Defoe). **b** referring to the one or ones specified: *Be careful which way you turn. Choose which books you like best.*
**which is which,** which is one and which is the other: *The twins look so alike that it is impossible to tell which is which.*
[Old English *hwilc, hwelc*]
▶ **which.** As a relative pronoun *which* refers to things and to groups of people regarded impersonally: *They returned for his ax which they had forgotten. The legislature which passed the act deserves most of the credit.*
▶ See **this** and **that** for usage notes.

**which|a|way** (hwich′ə wā′), *adv. U.S. Dialect.* in which direction; where.

**which|ev|er** (hwich ev′ər), *pron., adj.* 1 any one that; any that: *Whichever you take will be becoming* (pron.). *Buy whichever hat you like* (adj.). 2 no matter which: *Whichever side wins, I shall be satisfied* (adj.). *You will find deer crossings whichever road you take* (adj.).

**which|so|ev|er** (hwich′sō ev′ər), *pron., adj.* = whichever.

**whick|er** (hwik′ər, wik′-), *v., n.* —*v.i.* (of a horse) to whinny.
—*n.* a whinny: *The little boy was frightened by Dobbin's whicker.*
[probably imitative. Compare etym. under **nicker**[2].]
▶ In the Eastern States, for which evidence is available, **whicker** is found in southeastern and northeastern New England and is the favored term from the Chesapeake Bay south along the coast, including most of the Carolinas.

**whid** (hwid), *v.i.,* **whid|ded, whid|ding.** *Scottish.* to move nimbly without noise. [earlier, blast of wind, perhaps < Scandinavian (compare Old Icelandic *hvitha* a squall)]

**whid|ah** (hwid′ə), *n.* any one of certain African weaverbirds, the male of which grows long tail feathers during the breeding season; widow bird. The female lays its eggs in other birds' nests. Also, **whydah.** [alteration of *widow bird;* influenced by *Whidah* (now *Ouidah*), a town in Dahomey]

**whidah bird** or **finch,** = whidah.

**whiff** (hwif), *n., v.* —*n.* 1 a slight gust; puff; breath: *A whiff of fresh air cleared his head. Not a whiff of life left in either of the bodies* (Thomas Hardy). 2 a blow. 3 a slight smell; puff of air having an odor: *a whiff of garlic. A whiff of smoke blew in his face.* 4 a puff of tobacco smoke: *A whiff of his pipe encircled his head.* 5 *Figurative.* a slight trace: *a whiff of scandal.* 6 *Informal.* **a** a swing at a ball without hitting it, as in baseball or golf. **b** a strikeout in baseball.
—*v.i.* 1 to blow or move with or as if with a whiff or puff; puff. 2 to exhale or inhale whiffs or puffs, as when smoking tobacco. 3 *Informal.* to be struck out in baseball: *He got only three hits in 21 tries and tied an all-time Series record by whiffing eight times* (Newsweek).
—*v.t.* 1 to drive or carry by or as if by a whiff or puff; waft. 2 to inhale or exhale (air, smoke, or fumes) in whiffs or puffs. 3 to smoke (a pipe, cigarette, or cigar). 4 *Informal.* to strike out in baseball: *His peak strikeout effort was against Boston ... when he whiffed thirteen Red Sox* (New York Times).
[imitative; perhaps partly Middle English *wheffe* vapor, whiff, variant of *waff*[1]] —**whiff′er,** *n.*

**whif|fet** (hwif′it), *n.* 1 *Informal.* an insignificant person or thing. SYN: whipper-snapper. 2 a small dog. [American English, probably variant of *whippet;* perhaps influenced by *whiff*]

**whif|fle** (hwif′əl), *v.,* **-fled, -fling,** *n.* —*v.i.* 1 to blow in puffs or gusts. 2**a** (of the wind or a ship) to veer or shift (about). **b** *Figurative.* to back and fill; vacillate. 3 to blow lightly; scatter. —*v.t.* to blow or drive with or as if with a puff of air.
—*n.* 1 something light or insignificant; trifle. 2 a slight blast of air.
[apparently < *whiff* + *-le*]

**whif|fle|ball** (hwif′əl bôl′), *n.* 1 a lightweight, hollow, plastic ball with openings to catch the air and reduce its speed and distance of travel. Originally developed for golf practice in a confined area, whiffleballs are also made like a softball. 2 a game somewhat like baseball, played with such a ball.

**whif|fler**[1] (hwif′lər), *n.* 1 a person who whiffles, or shifts about, as in thought, opinion, or intention. 2 = trifler. [< *whiffl(e)* + *-er*[1]]

**whif|fler**[2] (hwif′lər), *n. Historical.* one of a body of attendants armed with a javelin, battle-ax, sword, or staff, and wearing a chain, employed to keep the way clear for a procession or at some public spectacle. [< obsolete *wifle* javelin, ax + *-er*[2]]

**whif|fle|tree** (hwif′əl trē′), *n.* the swinging, horizontal crossbar of a carriage or wagon, to which the traces of a harness are fastened; singletree. Also, **whippletree.** [American English, variant of *whippletree,* apparently < *whip* in sense of "move quickly to and fro" + *tree* a staff, wooden bar. Compare etym. under **whiffet.**]

**Whig** (hwig), *n., adj.* —*n.* 1 a member of a former political party in Great Britain that favored reforms and progress and opposed the Tory party. The Whigs were in favor of parliamentary rather than royal power. The Whig party existed from the late 1600's to the early 1800's and was succeeded by the Liberal Party. 2 an American colonist who opposed British rule over the colonies at the time of the Revolutionary War. 3 a member of a political party in the United States that was formed about 1832 in opposition to the Democratic Party. It favored high tariffs and a loose interpretation of the Constitution. It was succeeded by the Republican Party about 1855.
—*adj.* of or having to do with Whigs; like Whigs.
[short for *whiggamore* one of the people of western Scotland who marched on Edinburgh in 1648 to oppose the engagement entered into with Charles I of England against the followers of Oliver Cromwell, perhaps < dialectal *whig* to urge forward]

**Whig|ger|y** (hwig′ər ē), *n.* the principles or practices of Whigs.

**Whig|gish** (hwig′ish), *adj.* 1 of or having to do with Whigs; inclined to Whiggism. 2 like Whigs. —**Whig′gish|ly,** *adv.* —**Whig′gish|ness,** *n.*

**Whig|gism** (hwig′iz əm), *n.* the principles or practices of Whigs; Whiggery.

**whig|ma|lee|rie** or **whig|ma|lee|ry** (hwig′məlir′ē), *n., pl.* **-ries.** *Scottish.* 1 a fantastic notion; whim; crotchet. 2 a fanciful ornament or contrivance; knickknack. [origin uncertain]

**while** (hwīl), *n., conj., v.,* **whiled, whil|ing,** *prep.* —*n.* 1 a space of time; time: *quite a while. He kept us waiting a long while. The postman came a while ago.* 2 *Archaic.* a particular time at which something occurs or is done; occasion. 3 *Obsolete.* the time spent (and hence also the effort or labor expended) in doing something.
—*conj.* 1 during the time that; in the time that; in the same time that: *While I was speaking he said nothing. Summer is pleasant while it lasts.* 2 in contrast with the fact that; although: *While I like the color of the hat, I do not like its shape. Walnut is a hard wood, while pine is soft.* 3 *Dialect.* until.
—*v.t.* to pass or spend in some easy or pleasant manner: *The children while away many afternoons on the beach.*
—*prep. Archaic or Dialect.* until.
**between whiles,** at times; at intervals: *A sort of ... dashing (as it were) of waves, and between whiles, a noise like that of thunder* (George Berkeley).
**once in a while,** now and then: *We see him once in a while.*
**the while,** during the time; in the meantime: *They danced and sang the while. Top athletes will do their eight months of compulsory military training in these platoons and enjoy major mollycoddling the while* (Sports Illustrated).
**worth (one's) while,** worth (one's) time, attention, or effort: *If you help me with the painting, I'll make it worth your while—I'll pay you ten dollars.*
[Old English *hwīl,* noun]
—*Syn. v.t.* **While, beguile** mean to pass time pleasantly. **While,** followed by *away,* suggests spending a period of free time in as pleasant a way as possible under the circumstances: *He whiled away the hours on the train by talking to other passengers.* **Beguile** suggests charming away the tediousness of the time by doing something interesting: *A good book helped him to beguile the long hours of the journey.*
▶ **While,** as a subordinate conjunction, is used chiefly to introduce adverbial clauses of time: *They waited on the bank while he swam to the raft.* It is also used, rather weakly, in the sense of "although" or "but": *While the doctor did all he could, he couldn't save her. While* is occasionally used for *and: The second number was an acrobatic exhibition, while the third was a lady trapeze artist.*

**whiles** (hwīlz), *adv., conj. Archaic or Dialect.*
—*adv.* 1 sometimes. 2 in the meantime.
—*conj.* while.
[Old English *-hwīles* < *hwīl* while, noun + adverbial genitive *-s*]

**whi|lom** (hwī′ləm), *adj., adv. Archaic.* —*adj.* former: *a whilom friend.*
—*adv.* formerly; once.
[Old English *hwīlum* at times; dative plural of *hwīl* while, noun]

**whilst** (hwīlst), *conj.* = while. [< *whiles;* the *-t* is a later addition. Compare etym. under **amidst, amongst.**]

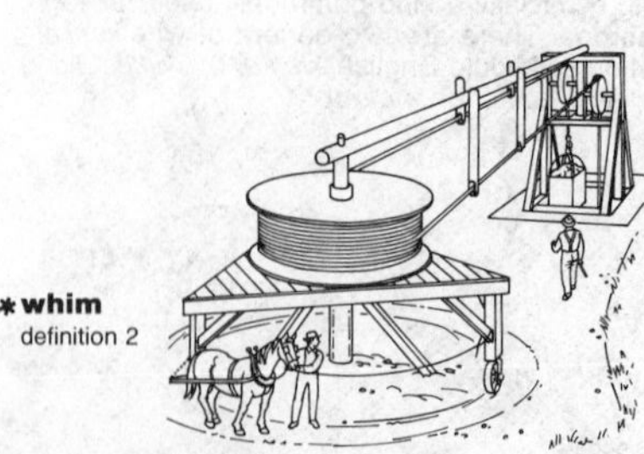

**✱whim**
definition 2

**✱whim** (hwim), *n., v.,* **whimmed, whim|ming.** —*n.* 1 a sudden fancy or notion; freakish or capricious idea or desire: *She has a whim for gardening but it won't last long.* SYN: whimsy. 2 *Mining.* a kind of capstan used especially for raising ore or water from mines. It has one or more radiating arms to which a horse or horses or other beast of burden may be yoked and by which it may be turned.
—*v.i.* to desire as a sudden fancy or notion: *piecework which could be used, ignored, changed, rewritten, or combined with the work of other writers as the producer willed or whimmed* (Harper's).

[perhaps < Scandinavian (compare Old Icelandic *hvim* unsteady look, *hvima* roll the eyes). Compare etym. under **whimwham**.]

**whim|brel** (hwim′brəl), *n.* a curlew of arctic regions; Hudsonian curlew. [probably < *whimp,* or *whimper* (because of its cry)]

**whim|per** (hwim′pər), *v., n.* — *v.i.* **1** to cry with low, broken, mournful sounds: *The sick child whimpered.* **2** to make a low, mournful sound. **3** *Figurative.* to complain in a peevish, childish way; whine: *to whimper for mercy.*
— *v.t.* to say with a whimper.
— *n.* a whimpering cry or sound.
[probably imitative. Compare German *wimmern.*]
— **whim′per|er,** *n.* — **whim′per|ing|ly,** *adv.*

**whim|sey** (hwim′zē), *n., pl.* **-seys.** = whimsy.

**whim|si|cal** (hwim′zə kəl), *adj.* **1** full of whims; having many odd notions or fancies: *a whimsical person. However absurd the story may sound when thus reduced, Garnett is much too fine an artist to be whimsical* (Newsweek). **SYN**: capricious, notional. **2** of or like a whim or whims; odd; fanciful: *a whimsical expression.* [< *whims*(y) + *-ic* + *-al*[1]] — **whim′si|cal|ly,** *adv.* — **whim′si|cal|ness,** *n.*

**whim|si|cal|i|ty** (hwim′zə kal′ə tē), *n., pl.* **-ties.** **1** whimsical character or quality. **SYN**: oddity, singularity. **2** a whimsical notion, speech, or act. **SYN**: whimsy.

**whim|sy** (hwim′zē), *n., pl.* **-sies,** *adj.* — *n.* **1** an odd or fanciful notion. **SYN**: vagary, caprice. **2** odd or fanciful humor; quaintness: *"Alice in Wonderland" is full of whimsy.* **SYN**: drollery. **3** something showing this. **4** = whim.
— *adj.* = whimsical.
[earlier, a whim, dizziness; probably < *whim*]

**whim|wham** (hwim′hwam′), *n. Archaic or Dialect.* **1** any odd or fanciful object or thing; gimcrack; trifle. **2** a fanciful notion; an odd fancy. [varied reduplication of *whim*]

**whin**[1] (hwin), *n.* a low, prickly shrub with yellow flowers, common on wastelands in Europe; furze. [perhaps < Scandinavian (compare Icelandic *hvingras* bent grass, Norwegian *hvine*)]

**whin**[2] (hwin), *n.* = whinstone. [origin uncertain]

**whin|chat** (hwin′chat′), *n.* a small, tan, European songbird, closely allied to the stonechat; furzechat. [< *whin*[1] + *chat*[1] a bird]

**whine** (hwīn), *v.,* **whined, whin|ing,** *n.* — *v.i.* **1** to make a low, complaining cry or sound: *The dog whined to go out with us.* **2** *Figurative.* to complain in a peevish, childish way: *Some people are always whining about trifles.*
— *v.t.* to say with a whine.
— *n.* **1** a low, complaining cry or sound. **2** *Figurative.* a peevish, childish complaint.
[Old English *hwīnan* to whiz (like an arrow)]
— **whin′er,** *n.* — **whin′ing|ly,** *adv.*

**whin|ey** (hwī′nē), *adj.,* **whin|i|er, whin|i|est.** = whiny.

**whing|ding** (hwing′ding′), *n., adj.* = wingding.

**whinge** (hwinj), *v.i.,* **whinged, whing|ing.** *British.* to whine: *A baby whinges in a tasselled pram* (Punch).

**whin|ny**[1] (hwin′ē), *n., pl.* **-nies,** *v.,* **-nied, -ny|ing.**
— *n.* the prolonged, rather soft or gentle, quavering sound that a horse makes.
— *v.i.* to utter a whinny or any sound like it.
— *v.t.* to express by such a sound.
[probably related to **whine**]
► In the eastern part of the United States, for which evidence is available, **whinny** is the favored term from Pennsylvania north. See also **whicker.**

**whin|ny**[2] (hwin′ē), *adj.* abounding in whin or furze. [< *whin*[1] + *-y*[1]]

**whin|stone** (hwin′stōn′), *n.* any one of various hard, fine-grained, dark-colored rocks, such as basalt, diabase, or dolerite.

**whin|y** (hwī′nē), *adj.,* **whin|i|er, whin|i|est.** whining; disposed to whine; fretful: *The baby was in a whiny mood.*

**whip** (hwip), *n., v.,* **whipped** or **whipt, whip|ping.**
— *n.* **1** a thing to strike or beat with, usually a stick with a lash at the end. Lawbreakers used to be punished with a whip. *It is cruel to use a whip to punish a child.* **SYN**: scourge, switch. **2** a stroke or blow with or as if with a whip. **3** a whipping or lashing motion. **4a** a member of a political party who controls and directs the other members in a lawmaking body, as by seeing that they attend meetings in which important votes will be taken, and finding out how the vote is likely to go; party whip. **b** *British.* a call made on members of a political party in a legislature to attend a given session or remain in attendance for it. **5a** the person who manages the hounds of a hunting pack. **b** a person who uses a driving whip; driver of horses; coachman. **6** a dessert made by beating cream, eggs, and other ingredients, into a froth and adding fruit or a flavoring: *prune whip.* **7** a simple kind of tackle or pulley, consisting of a single block with a rope through it, used for hoisting. **8** something that moves briskly, such as each of the vanes of a windmill. **9** any one of various mechanical parts that move as a whip does. **10** a vibrating spring for closing an electric circuit. **11** a ride in an amusement park on a chain of cars changing direction sharply: *Features of particular interest to children will be pony rides, a ferris wheel, merry-go-round, the whip* (New York Times).
— *v.t.* **1** to strike or beat with a whip; lash: *He whipped the horse to make it go faster.* **SYN**: scourge, flog, thrash, switch. **2** *Figurative.* to strike or beat as if with a whip: *the rain whipping the pavement* (Thackeray). **3** to move, put, or pull quickly and suddenly: *He whipped off his coat and whipped out his knife.* **4** to bring, get, make, or produce by or as if by whipping: *to whip the nonsense out of someone.* (*Figurative.*) *We'll whip the car into shape for the next race.* (*Figurative.*) *She whipped up a dress for the party at the last minute.* **5** *Figurative.* to rouse; incite; revive: *to whip up some enthusiasm.* **6** *Figurative.* to criticize or reprove with cutting severity. **7** *Informal.* to defeat in a fight or contest; vanquish: *The mayor whipped his opponents in the election.* **8** to summon (in, up) to attend, as the members of a political party in a legislative body, for united action. **9** to beat (cream, eggs, or other ingredients) to a froth. **10a** to sew with stitches passing over and over an edge; overcast. **b** to overcast the rolled edge of (a fabric) and draw it into gathers. **11a** to wind (a rope, stick, or spool) closely with thread or string. **b** to wind (cord, twine, or thread) in this way around something. **12** to fish upon: *to whip a stream.* **13** to hoist or haul with a rope and pulley.
— *v.i.* **1** to move suddenly and nimbly; start or go quickly; whisk; dart: *The thief whipped round the corner and escaped.* **2** to beat, flap, or thrash about as the lash of a whip does; swish. **3** to fish by casting with a motion like that of using a whip.
**whip in,** to keep from scattering: *to whip in the foxhounds.*
[Middle English *whippen,* probably < Middle Dutch and Middle Low German *wippen* to swing, move up and down, oscillate] — **whip′like′,** *adj.* — **whip′per,** *n.*

**whip|cord** (hwip′kôrd′), *n., adj.* — *n.* **1** a thin, tough, tightly twisted cord, sometimes used for or braided into the lashes of whips. **2** a closely woven, strong worsted cloth with diagonal ridges on it, used for suits and upholstery. **3** a kind of catgut.
— *adj.* taut, tough, or sinewy: *He was deeply tanned, middle-aged, and he had the whipcord conditioning of an athlete* (Saturday Review).

**whip|crack** (hwip′krak′), *n.* **1** the crack of a whip. **2** *Figurative: The words* [*need*] *more whipcrack of sharp, modern speech rhythms* (Sunday Times).

**whip graft,** *Horticulture.* a graft made by cutting the scion and stock in a sloping direction so as to fit each other, and by inserting a tongue on the scion into a slit in the stock; tongue graft.

**whip|graft** (hwip′graft′, -gräft′), *v.t. Horticulture.* to graft by cutting the scion and stock in a sloping direction and by inserting a tongue on the scion into a slit in the stock.

**whip grafting** or **graftage,** the act or method of making a whip graft.

**whip hand, 1** the hand (normally, the right hand) that holds the whip in driving. **2** *Figurative.* a position of control; advantage: *A clever person frequently gets the whip hand over others.* **SYN**: mastery.

**whip|lash** (hwip′lash′), *n., v.* — *n.* **1** the lash of a whip. **2** *Figurative: the whiplash of fear.* **3** Also, **whiplash injury.** an injury to the neck caused by a sudden jolt that snaps the head backward and then forward, as to a driver whose car is struck with force from behind.
— *v.t.* to beat or lash with a whiplash; treat harshly: (*Figurative.*) *For consumers, whiplashed the past couple of years by inflationary forces, the prospect of a price comedown … is welcome news* (Wall Street Journal). **SYN**: punish.

**whip|per-in** (hwip′ər in′), *n., pl.* **whip|pers-in.** **1** a huntsman's assistant who keeps the hounds from straying by driving them back with the whip into the main body of the pack. **2** *Historical.* a whip (def. 4a).

**whip|per-snap|per** or **whip|per|snap|per** (hwip′ər snap′ər), *n.* a young or insignificant person who thinks he is smart or important: *Don't pay any attention to that little whipper-snapper.* [apparently < *whip* + *-er*[1] + *snapper* a cracker of whips]

**whip|pet** (hwip′it), *n.* **1** a small, very swift dog that looks somewhat like a small greyhound, often used in racing. **2** Also, **whippet tank.** a small, relatively fast, lightly armored tank developed and used in World War I. **3** *Obsolete.* a nimble, diminutive person. [< *whip* + *-et*]

**whip|ping** (hwip′ing), *n.* **1a** a striking with or as if with a whip; flogging. **SYN**: flagellation. **b** *Figurative: The favored team got a good whipping from the underdogs.* **SYN**: defeat, beating. **2a** an arrangement of cord, twine, or the like, wound about a thing: *We fastened the broken rod with a whipping of wire.* **b** the act of overlaying or binding with cord, twine, or the like, wound closely round and round. **3** a beating to a froth or thickness: *Whipping is fast and easy when the cream is cold.* **4** the bending or springing motion of something held rigidly at one end: *the whipping of an antenna in a strong wind.* **5** an overcasting in sewing.

**whipping boy, 1** a person or thing that is the target of unmerited indignation or punishment; scapegoat. **2** a boy educated together with a young prince or royal personage in former times, and flogged in his stead when the prince committed a fault that was considered to deserve flogging.

**whipping cream,** = heavy cream.

**whipping post,** a post to which lawbreakers were tied to be whipped.

**whip|ple|tree** (hwip′əl trē), *n.* = whiffletree.

**whip|poor|will** (hwip′ər wil′, hwip′ər wil), *n.* a North American bird whose call sounds somewhat like its name. It is active at night or twilight. [American English; imitative]

**whip|py** (hwip′ē), *adj.,* **-pi|er, -pi|est.** **1** bending like a whip; flexible; springy: *With prestressed concrete we can make a whippy fishpole or a bouncy diving board* (Scientific American). **2** *Informal, Figurative.* pert; snappy; saucy: *The girl—long, thin and whippy—was instantly a-grin* (New Yorker).

**whip-round** (hwip′round′), *n.* British. a request for or a collection of contributions: *Thanks to a whip-round, the paupers are assured of ample supplies of beef, plum pudding, porter and snuff* (Punch).

**whip|saw** (hwip′sô′), *n., v., adj.* — *n.* a long, narrow saw with its ends held in a frame, used especially for curved work.
— *v.t.* **1** to cut with a whipsaw. **2** *U.S. Informal, Figurative.* **a** to defeat or cause to fail in two opposite ways at the same time: *Instances of selling in the decline before the election with the intention of buying back later were whipsawed* (Wall Street Journal). **b** to have or take the advantage of, as by playing one against the other: *A major problem for dozens of U.S. industries: they must either stand together or risk being whipsawed by unions* (Time). **3** to win at one turn or play (two bets from the same player), as in faro.
— *v.i.* **1** to bend back and forth; whip: *The next morning the 5-inch steel cable, worn by constant whipsawing, snapped* (Newsweek). **2** *Figurative.* to play one person, company, or group, against another: *Whipsawing is striking one company at a time, while permitting others to operate and thus adding to the pressure on the closed company* (Wall Street Journal).
— *adj.* of or characteristic of whipsawing: (*Figurative.*) *whipsaw tactics.*

**whip scorpion,** any one of a family of arachnids similar to the scorpions but having a slender, whiplike process on the abdomen and no sting.

**whip-shaped** (hwip′shāpt′), *adj.* shaped like the lash of a whip; long and slender; flagelliform.

**whip snake,** any one of various snakes whose long, slender form somewhat resembles a whip.

**whip|stall** (hwip′stôl′), *n., v.* — *n.* Also, **whip stall.** a stall in which the nose of an airplane falls suddenly downward, often just after the plane has slipped backward and downward along the angle of a sharp climb.
— *v.i.* to go into a whipstall.
— *v.t.* to cause (an airplane) to whipstall.

**whip|ster** (hwip′stər), *n. Archaic.* a whipper-snapper.

**whip|stitch** (hwip′stich′), *v., n.* — *v.t.* to sew with stitches passing over and over an edge; whip.
— *n.* the stitch made in whipstitching.

**whip|stock** (hwip′stok′), *n., v.* — *n.* **1** the handle of a whip. **2** a wedge-shaped tool used with the thick end down to deflect a drill from obstructions in oil-well drilling.
— *v.t., v.i.* to drill with a whipstock.

**whipt** (hwipt), *v.* whipped; a past tense and past participle of **whip.**

**whip-tailed lizard** (hwip′tāld′), any one of various lizards having a long, slender tail like a whiplash, with species widely distributed in North, Central, and South America.

**whip|worm** (hwip′wėrm′), *n.* a nematode worm,

**Pronunciation Key:** hat, āge, cãre, fär; let, ēqual, tėrm; it, īce; hot, ōpen, ôrder; oil, out; cup, pu̇t, rüle; child; long; thin; ᴛʜen; zh, measure; ə represents **a** in about, **e** in taken, **i** in pencil, **o** in lemon, **u** in circus.

often parasitic in the intestines of human beings, that has a stout posterior and slender anterior part, like a whipstock with a lash.

**whir** (hwėr), *n., v.,* **whirred, whir|ring.** *—n.* **1** a buzzing noise; noise that sounds like whir-r-r: *the whir of a small machine.* **2** *Figurative.* **a** commotion of mind or feeling; mental or nervous shock: *The news of her mother's illness put her in a whir.* **b** violent or rapid movement; rush; hurry.
*—v.i.* to move quickly or operate with a whir: *The motor whirs.*
*—v.t.* to carry or hurry along; move or stir with a whir: *A lasting storm, whirring me from my friends* (Shakespeare). Also, **whirr.**
[probably imitative. Compare Danish *hvirre* whirl.]

**whirl** (hwėrl), *v., n. —v.i.* **1** to turn or swing round and round; spin; gyrate: *The leaves whirled in the wind.* **2** to move round and round; circle; circulate: *We whirled about the room.* **3** to turn around or aside quickly; wheel. **4** to move or go quickly, on or as if on wheels. **5** *Figurative.* to feel dizzy or confused; reel: *The strong medicine made my head whirl.*
*—v.t.* **1** to cause to move round and round: *He whirled the club.* **2** to move or carry quickly: *We were whirled away in an airplane. The last red leaf is whirl'd away* (Tennyson). **3** *Obsolete.* to hurl; fling.
*—n.* **1** a whirling movement: *The dancer suddenly made a whirl.* **2** something that whirls or the part at which this takes place; eddy; vortex. **3** a dizzy or confused condition: *His thoughts are in a whirl.* **SYN:** vertigo. **4** *Figurative.* a rapid round of happenings, parties, or the like: *the endless whirl of the holiday season.*
**give** (something) **a whirl,** *Informal.* to try, test, or experiment with (something): *I'm going to give this new recipe a whirl. The Society decided to toss communism out the window and give capitalism a whirl* (Wall Street Journal).
[probably < Scandinavian (compare Old Icelandic *hvirfla,* related to *hverfa* to turn)] **—whirl'er,** *n.*

**whirl|a|bout** (hwėrl'ə bout'), *n., adj. —n.* **1** the act of whirling about. **2** something that whirls about, or is in a whirl.
*—adj.* characterized by whirling about.

**whirl|a|way** (hwėrl'ə wā'), *n., adj. —n.* a rapid, whirling or spiraling movement or course: *In the labor-hungry whirlaway of U.S. production, job discrimination has begun to melt* (Time).
*—adj.* moving or developing rapidly as if in a whirl: *a whirlaway bestseller.*

**whirl|ey|bird** (hwėr'lē bėrd'), *n. Informal.* whirlybird; a helicopter.

***whirl|i|gig** (hwėr'lē gig), *n.* **1a** a toy that whirls, twirls, or spins around. **b** *Obsolete.* a top[2]. **2** = merry-go-round. **3** *Figurative.* **a** anything that whirls: *the whirligig of politics.* **b** a whirling movement. **4** = whirligig beetle. **5** *Obsolete.* a fantastic notion; whim; crotchet. [< obsolete *whirly-,* combining form of *whirl* + *gig*[1] something that whirls]

***whirligig**
definition 1a

**whirligig beetle,** any one of a family of gregarious beetles that circle about on the surface of water. See picture under **beetle**[1].

**whirl|ing dervish** (hwėr'ling), = dancing dervish.

**whirl|pool** (hwėrl'pül'), *n.* **1** a current of water whirling round and round rapidly and violently; eddy or vortex of water: *The swimmer caught in the whirlpool had hard work to keep from drowning.* **2** anything like a whirlpool: *little whirlpools of snow, the cosmic whirlpool of the galaxies.* **3** *Figurative.* a whirl of confused or turbulent activity; vortex: *the whirlpool of war. What a whirlpool of contending feelings!* (Dickens).

**whirlpool bath,** a therapeutic bath in which a circular stream of water is directed against all or parts of the body, used especially in physical therapy.

**whirl|wind** (hwėrl'wind'), *n., adj. —n.* **1** a current of air whirling violently round and round; whirling windstorm; vortex of air. **SYN:** cyclone, tornado. **2** anything like a whirlwind: (*Figurative.*) *a whirlwind of activity.*
*—adj. Informal.* marked by great speed; fast; hasty: *a whirlwind tour. [He] married her after a whirlwind courtship* (Maclean's).
**reap the whirlwind,** to suffer disastrous consequences, especially as a result of recklessness or folly (in allusion to Hosea 8:7): *Now the B.B.C. appear to be reaping the whirlwind of their decision to ban ... the film* (London Times).
[< *whirl* + *wind*[1]; probably influenced by Scandinavian (compare Old Icelandic *hvirfilvindr*)]

**whirl|y** (hwėr'lē), *adj.,* **whirl|i|er, whirl|i|est,** *n., pl.* **whirl|ies.** *—adj.* that can whirl; whirling: *There are some dresses of red and white checked gingham with whirly skirts* (New Yorker).
*—n. Informal.* whirlwind (def. 1).

**whirl|y|bird** (hwėr'lē bėrd'), *n. Informal.* a helicopter.

**whirr** (hwėr), *n., v.i., v.t.* = whir.

**whir|ry** (hwėr'ē), *v.t., v.i.,* **-ried, -ry|ing.** *Scottish.* to hurry. [probably < *whir* + *-y,* as in *hurry*]

**whish** (hwish), *n., v. —n.* a soft, rushing sound, such as that of something moving rapidly through the air or over the surface of water; whiz; swish.
*—v.i.* to make such a rushing sound; whiz: *The lightning express-train whishes by a station* (Oliver Wendell Holmes).
*—v.t.* to drive or chase with a whish: *He whished the sheep forward.*
[imitative]

**whisht** (hwisht, wisht; *Scottish* hwusht), *interj., n., adj., v. Scottish and Irish. —interj.* an exclamation enjoining silence; hush!
*—n.* **1** a whisper. **2** (with negative) not a whisper; not the least utterance.
*—adj.* silent; quiet; still; hushed.
*—v.i.* to be silent; keep silence.
*—v.t.* to put to silence; silence; hush.
[variant of *whist*[2], interjection]

**whisk**[1] (hwisk), *v., n. —v.t.* **1** to sweep or brush (dust, crumbs, or the like) from a surface: *She whisked the crumbs from the table.* **2** to move (something or someone) quickly: *She whisked the letter out of sight. After his speech, the senator was whisked out of the building into his car.*
*—v.i.* to move quickly: *The mouse whisked into its hole at the sight of the cat.*
*—n.* **1** a light stroke of a whisk broom, or the like; quick sweep: *She brushed away the dirt with a few whisks of her broom.* **2** a light, quick movement; brief, rapid sweeping motion.
[< Scandinavian (compare Danish *viske* wipe, Swedish *viska* sweep off)]

***whisk**[2] (hwisk), *v., n. —v.t.* to beat or whip (cream, eggs, or other ingredients) to a froth, especially with a whisk. [< Scandinavian (compare Swedish *viska* to sponge, sweep off)]
*—n.* **1** a wire beater for eggs, cream, or other ingredients. **2** a small bundle of twigs, hair, straw, feathers, or the like, fixed on a handle, used for brushing or dusting. **3** = whisk broom.
[earlier, a bristle < Scandinavian (compare Norwegian *viske,* Swedish *viska* a besom, swab). See related etym. at **whisk**[1].]

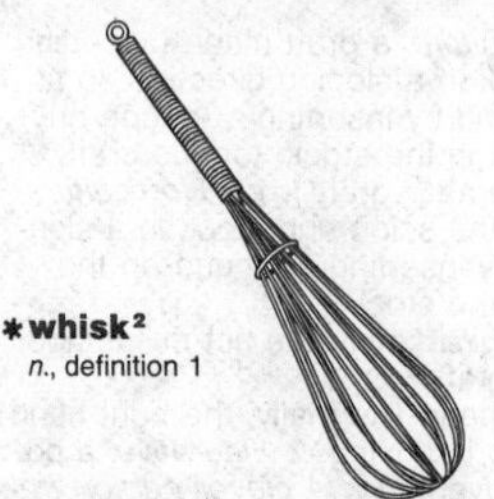

***whisk**[2]
*n.,* definition 1

**whisk broom,** a small broom for brushing clothes or upholstery.

**whisk|er** (hwis'kər), *n.* **1** one of the hairs growing on a man's face: *The old man's long beard was full of gray whiskers.* **2** one of the long, stiff hairs or bristles growing near the mouth of a cat, rat, bird, or other animal; vibrissa: *The cat's whiskers stuck out of both sides of its face.* **3** Also, **whisker boom.** *Nautical.* either of two wooden or iron spars extending laterally, one on each side of the bowsprit, to spread the guys of the jib or flying jib boom. **4** *Dialect.* something that whisks or is used for whisking. **5a** a microscopic crystal filament on the surface of a metal or other crystalline solid. **b** a very strong synthetic crystal filament; monocrystal. **6** *Figurative.* a very small amount or degree: *... missed the edge of the bat by a whisker* (Manchester Guardian).
**whiskers,** the hair growing on a man's face, especially that on his cheeks: *His whiskers ... squared off in a line which met the large stiff collar below at an angle of forty-five* (Besant and Rice).
[< *whisk*[2] + *-er*[1]] **—whisk'er|less,** *adj.*

**whisk|ered** (hwis'kərd), *adj.* **1** having whiskers: *a grave whiskered young man* (Arnold Bennett). **2** in the form of whiskers: *whiskered hair.*

**whisk|ers** (hwis'kərz), *n.pl.* See under **whisker.**

**whisk|er|y** (hwis'kər ē), *adj.* **1** having whiskers: *a ruddy, whiskery Englishman dressed in shorts* (Harper's). **2** *Figurative.* suggestive of whiskers and age; very old: *a whiskery saying or superstition.*

**whis|key** (hwis'kē), *n., pl.* **-keys,** *adj. —n.* **1** a strong, intoxicating liquor made from grain. Whiskey usually consists of from two fifths to one half alcohol by volume. In the United States, whiskey is made of corn or rye; in Scotland, Ireland, and Great Britain, whiskey is often made of malted barley. **2** a drink of whiskey.
*—adj.* of, having to do with, composed of, or like whiskey.
[short for obsolete *whiskybae,* variant of *usquebaugh* < Gaelic *uisge beatha* (literally) water of life. Compare etym. under **aqua vitae, usquebaugh.**]
▶ **whiskey, whisky.** The preferred spelling in the United States is *whiskey.* Outside of the United States, except in Ireland, the preferred form is *whisky.* Scotch made in the United States, however, is spelled *whisky* in imitation of the Scots' spelling.

**Whis|key** (hwis'kē), *n. U.S.* a code name for the letter *w,* used in transmitting radio messages.

**whiskey and soda,** a drink made with whiskey and carbonated water, served with or without ice; highball.

**whiskey sour,** a cocktail made with whiskey, lemon juice, and sugar shaken with ice, strained, and usually served with a slice of orange and a cherry.

**whis|ky** (hwis'kē), *n., pl.* **-kies,** *adj.* = whiskey.

**whis|ky-jack** (hwis'kē jak'), *n.* a jay, chiefly of northern North America, with plain grayish feathers; Canada jay. [American English; alteration of earlier *whisky-john* < Algonkian (Cree) *wiskatjân*]

**whisp** (hwisp), *n., v.t., v.i.* = wisp.

**whis|per** (hwis'pər), *v., n. —v.i.* **1a** to speak very softly and low. **b** to talk in this way, especially in another's ear, for the sake of secrecy or privacy. **2** *Figurative.* to talk quietly or secretly (usually implying hostility, malice, conspiracy, or gossip). **3** *Figurative.* to make a soft, rustling sound: *The wind whispered in the pines.*
*—v.t.* **1** to speak to in a whisper or low voice. **2** *Figurative.* to tell secretly or privately: *It is whispered that his business is failing.* **3** to utter without vibration of the vocal cords.
*—n.* **1a** a very soft, low spoken sound: *to converse in whispers.* **b** *Phonetics.* speech without vibration of the vocal cords; sound produced by the outgoing breath stream when the glottis is closed almost as much as for voice, but the vocal cords are tightened so that they do not vibrate, used in pronouncing the voiced sounds when whispering, the voiceless sounds being produced as in normal speech. **2** *Figurative.* something told secretly or privately: *the whispers of one's conscience. No whisper about having a new teacher has come to our ears.* **3** a whispered word, phrase, remark, or speech. **4** *Figurative.* a soft, rustling sound: *The wind was so gentle that we could hear the whisper of the leaves.*
[Old English *hwisprian*] **—whis'per|er,** *n.*

**whis|per|ing** (hwis'pər ing), *n., adj. —n.* the act of a person or thing that whispers.
*—adj.* **1** that whispers; speaking in a whisper. **2** *Figurative.* making a soft, rustling sound.
**—whis'per|ing|ly,** *adv.*

**whispering campaign,** a campaign of spreading rumors, insinuations, or the like, to discredit a person or group, as by whispered communication: *A whispering campaign started against electing any party member to the council* (Atlantic).

**whispering gallery, 1** a gallery, as that in St. Paul's Cathedral, London, so shaped that a whisper uttered at a certain point can be heard (by reflection and concentration of the sound) at a distant point, beyond the range of ordinary hearing. **2** any chamber or hollow place, such as a cave, having the same acoustic property.

**whis|per|ous** (hwis'pər əs), *adj.* = whispery.

**whis|per|y** (hwis'pər ē), *adj.* full of or characterized by whispers; resembling a whisper: *He leaned closer to catch the soft, whispery words his uncle spoke* (Harper's).

**whisp|y** (hwis'pē), *adj.,* **whisp|i|er, whisp|i|est.** = wispy.

**whist**[1] (hwist), *n.* a card game somewhat like bridge for two pairs of players. Auction and contract bridge developed from it. [alteration of earlier *whisk,* perhaps < *whisk*[1] (because the players whisked in the tricks), probably influenced by *whist*[2] (because of the silence required for the game)]

**whist**[2] (hwist), *interj., adj., adv., n., v. Archaic or Dialect. —interj.* hush! silence!
*—adj.* hushed; silent.
*—adv.* silently; quietly.
*—n.* silence.
*—v.i.* to be or become silent.
**hold one's whist,** to keep silence: *'Tis your brother that's ... askin' you to hold your whist*

(Michael MacDonagh). [imitative]

**whis|tle** (hwis′əl), *v.*, **-tled, -tling,** *n.* —*v.i.* **1** to make a clear, shrill sound by forcing breath through one's teeth or pursed lips: *The boy whistled and his dog ran to him quickly.* **2** to make any similar shrill sound: *The cardinal whistled from its nest.* **3** to blow a whistle: *The policeman whistled for the automobile to stop. Locomotives whistle at crossings.* **4** *Figurative.* to move or rush with a shrill sound: *In the winter blizzards the wind whistled around cracks of the drafty, old house.*

—*v.t.* **1** to produce or utter by whistling: *to whistle a tune.* **2** to call, direct, or signal by or as if by a whistle: *to whistle up a taxi.* **3** *Figurative.* to send or drive with a whistling or whizzing sound: *to whistle off a team of players, to whistle away fear.*

—*n.* **1** the sound made by whistling: (*Figurative.*) *the whistle of the wind.* **2** an instrument for making whistling sounds. The whistles used by factories, ships, and trains to signal or to warn are tubes through which air or steam is blown. **3** the act of whistling or blowing a whistle. **4** *Figurative.* a call; summons. **5** a simple flute with one end plugged.

**(as) clean as a whistle, a** neatly; without impediment or trouble; easily: *As the last seconds flitted painfully by, ... up went little McCalliog, a fleck of the head, and the ball was home clean as a whistle* (London Times). **b** completely and entirely clean; without fault or error: *The match, though tough, was as clean as a whistle and the injuries were just bad luck* (Michael Green).

**blow the whistle on,** *Informal.* **a** *Sports.* to penalize: *The referee blew the whistle on the hockey player for roughness.* **b** *Figurative.* to declare illegal or dishonest: *Congress finally blew the whistle on employers who discriminated in hiring workers.* **c** *Figurative.* to bring into the open; expose: *It was in the Greek hills that the West first blew the whistle on the spread of Communism* (Time).

**wet one's whistle,** *Informal.* to take a drink: *Let's ... wet our whistles, and so sing away all sad thoughts* (Izaak Walton).

**whistle for,** *Informal.* to go without; fail to get: *Without him* [*the Mayor*] *the city might still have been whistling for its fair and for its railway* (Manchester Guardian Weekly).

**whistle in the dark,** to try to be courageous or hopeful in a fearful or trying situation: [*He*] *said he was not whistling in the dark or crying alarms, but declared he had tremendous confidence that business is basically strong* (Wall Street Journal).

[Old English *hwistlian*]

**whis|tle|a|ble** or **whis|tla|ble** (hwis′ə lə bəl, hwis′lə-), *adj.* that can be or is suitable for whistling; tuneful: *whistleable tunes.*

**whis|tler** (hwis′lər), *n.* **1** a person or thing that whistles. **2** a large North American marmot resembling a woodchuck; mountain beaver. **3** any one of certain birds whose wings make a hissing sound when in flight, such as the goldeneye and widgeon. **4** a horse suffering from a defect of the respiratory system similar to the condition called "roaring." **5** *Physics.* a radio signal with a whistling sound rapidly decreasing in frequency and then usually rising again. It originates in a flash of lightning that may be thousands of miles away.

**Whis|tle|ri|an** (hwis lir′ē ən), *adj.* of or having to do with James McNeill Whistler (1834-1903), an American painter and etcher, or his style of painting.

**whistle stop,** *U.S. Informal.* **1** a small, little-known town along a railroad line at which a train stops only when signaled. **2** a stop at such a town or station for a brief appearance or speech, as in a political campaign tour: *When the campaign train stops in a city or town the general steps out on the rear platform, delivers his speech or, if it is truly a whistle stop, simply waves and grins* (Life).

**whis|tle-stop** (hwis′əl stop′), *adj., v.,* **-stopped, -stop|ping.** *U.S. Informal.* —*adj.* of, having to do with, or at a whistle stop: *whistle-stop speeches. The President plans a whistle-stop tour to the West Coast for early October* (New York Times).

—*v.i.* to make brief appearances or speeches at small towns or stations along a railroad, as in a political campaign tour: *Then I had a wonderful day whistle-stopping through the Central Valley of California* (New York Times).

—*v.t.* to make whistle stops across or through: *In a sort of swan song to the Democratic Party as its leader, he offered to whistle-stop the country for his successor* (Birmingham News).

**whis|tle-stop|per** (hwis′əl stop′ər), *n. U.S. Informal.* **1** a political candidate or speaker who makes whistle stops. **2** a whistle-stop campaign or trip.

**whis|tling** (hwis′ling), *n.; adj.* —*n.* **1** the act of a person or thing that whistles. **2** a defect of the respiratory system in which a horse breathes hard with a shrill sound.

—*adj.* **1** producing a whistle or whistling. **2** characterized by whistling. **3** sounding like a whistle. [Old English *hwistlung* < *hwistlian* to whistle]

—**whis′tling|ly,** *adv.*

**whistling buoy,** a type of buoy that produces a whistling noise.

**whistling swan,** a wild swan of Siberia and North America, that has white plumage and a small, yellow spot next to the eye, at the base of the bill.

**whit** (hwit), *n.* a very small bit; particle; jot: *The hikers were tired and didn't care a whit where they slept. The sick man is not a whit better.* **SYN:** mite, tittle. [apparently variant of *wight*[1]]

**Whit** (hwit), *adj. British.* Whitsun.

**white** (hwīt), *adj.,* **whit|er, whit|est,** *n., v.,* **whit-ed, whit|ing.** —*adj.* **1** having the color of snow or salt; reflecting light without absorbing any of the rays composing it. **2** approaching this color: *white bread.* **SYN:** milky, chalky. **3** pale: *She turned white with fear.* **SYN:** pallid, ashy. **4** light-colored: *white meat. White wine ranges in color from pale yellow to amber.* **5a** having a light-colored skin; not black, brown, red, or yellow; Caucasian. **b** controlled by or including only members of this race. **c** light; fair; blond. **6** silvery; gray: *a white beard. Grandmother has white hair.* **7** made or consisting of silver. **8** snowy: *a white winter.* **9** not written or printed upon; blank: *a white space.* **10** transparent and colorless: *white glass.* **11** chased or roughened so as to retain a light-gray color and lustrous appearance; not burnished: *white silverware.* **12** *Figurative.* spotless, pure; innocent. **13** *Informal, Figurative.* honorable; trustworthy; fair. **14** wearing white clothing: *a white friar.* **15** ultraconservative; reactionary; royalist. **16** *Figurative.* **a** good; beneficent: *white magic.* **b** propitious; favorable; auspicious. **17** being at white heat.

—*n.* **1** the color of snow, salt, or the paper on which this book is printed. It is the color of a surface that is nonselective in reflecting polychromatic light uniformly throughout the spectrum. The incident light when mixed in proper proportion is also said to be *white,* as is the reflected light. **2a** the quality of being white; white coloration or appearance; whiteness. **b** *Figurative.* whiteness as a symbol of purity, goodness, and truth. **3** a white coloring matter or pigment. **4a** Also, **whites.** white clothing: *attired in white, a sailor wearing his whites.* **b** white cloth. **5** something, or a part of something, that is white or light-colored: **a** the albumen surrounding the yolk of an egg. **b** the white part of the eyeball; sclera. **c** white wine. **d** Also, **whites.** *Printing.* any unprinted space. **6** a white person; person of the Caucasian race. **7** whiteness or fairness of skin or complexion. **8a** the central part of a butt in archery (formerly painted white). **b** a shot that hits this ring. **c** *Archaic.* a white target. **9** an ultraconservative; reactionary; royalist. **10** Often, **White.** an animal, especially a swine, of a species, breed, or variety white in color. **11** any one of a family of small to medium white butterflies, such as the cabbage white, having rounded wings, dark borders, and simple markings. Whites range throughout the Temperate Zone of North America. **12a** the light-colored pieces used in chess, checkers, backgammon, and some other games. **b** the player moving these pieces. Traditionally white moves first in chess and has the burden of winning or drawing chess problems.

—*v.t.* **1** to make white; whiten, whitewash, or bleach: *The windows of the jury bus were whited over ... so that no juror could glimpse the headline on street newsstands* (Time). **2** *Printing.* to space out (type).

**bleed white.** See under **bleed.**

**whites, a** the finest grade of white flour: *At a meeting of the London Flour Millers' Association ... the following prices were fixed ... whites, 31s.* (London Daily News). **b** = leucorrhea: *Among novices there is some difficulty in distinguishing the discharge of whites from that of blennorrhoea* (John M. Good).

[Old English *hwīt*]

**white admiral,** a butterfly with a dark green upper surface and white bands across its wings.

**white agate,** a white variety of chalcedony.

**white alkali, 1** a whitish crust formed on some alkaline soils by a mixture of salts. **2** soda ash that has been refined or purified.

**white ant,** = termite.

**white arsenic,** = arsenic trioxide.

**white ash,** a tall variety of ash of eastern North America; American ash.

**white backlash,** a hostile reaction on the part of whites to Negro demands for racial equality: *The removal of* Little Black Sambo *from the schools provoked some local white backlash* (Canadian Forum).

**white|bait** (hwīt′bāt′), *n., pl.* **-bait. 1** a young herring or sprat an inch or two long, used whole as food. **2** any one of certain similar fishes used as food.

**white|bark pine** (hwīt′bärk′), a low pine of the mountains of western North America with brown or creamy-white scales on the bark, and a fragrant resin. Its large, sweet seeds were eaten by the Indians.

**white bass,** a freshwater food fish of the Great Lakes region from Kansas to New York, silvery in color with blackish lines along the sides and yellow underneath; silver bass.

**white|beam** (hwīt′bēm′), *n.* a small European tree, with large leaves dark green on top and silvery white and silky on the underside, and a mealy fruit of a reddish color.

**white bear,** = polar bear.

**white|beard** (hwīt′bird′), *n.* a very old man.

**white bedstraw,** a species of bedstraw with white flowers, grown in Europe and eastern North America.

**white belt,** the lowest order in judo.

**white birch, 1** a common European birch that has a whitish bark. **2** = paper birch.

**white blood cell** or **corpuscle,** a colorless cell in the blood, formed chiefly in bone marrow, that destroys disease germs; white corpuscle; white cell; leucocyte. See picture under **corpuscle.**

**white book,** a book of official government reports bound in white.

**white-breast|ed nuthatch** (hwīt′bres′tid), a common nuthatch of North America with black crown and white underparts.

**white bryony,** a European species of bryony.

**white canon,** a Premonstratensian canon, so called from the white habit.

**white|cap** (hwīt′kap′), *n.* **1** a wave with a foaming white crest. **2** a person wearing or entitled to wear a white cap.

**white cast iron,** a silvery-white, hard, and brittle cast iron made by chilling heated cast iron.

**white cedar, 1** a coniferous evergreen tree of the cypress family, much like a cypress with pale-green or silvery needles, growing in swamps in the eastern United States. **2** its soft wood. **3** a common North American species of arbor vitae, grown in many varieties for ornament.

**white cell,** = white blood cell.

**white-cheeked goose** (hwīt′chēkt′), a dark-colored variety of Canada goose of the northern Pacific coast of North America; western Canada goose.

**white chocolate,** a creamy-white candy having the taste of chocolate but made without cacao.

**white clover,** a kind of clover with white flowers, common in fields and lawns.

**white coal,** water used as a source of power.

**white-col|lar** (hwīt′kol′ər), *adj.* of or having to do with clerical, professional, or business work or workers: *Most young Germans inevitably yearn for white-collar respectability* (Time).

**white corpuscle,** = white blood cell.

**white crab,** = sand crab.

**white crappie,** an edible freshwater bass of central and eastern North America, silvery with dark spots; white perch.

**white-crowned pigeon** (hwīt′kround′), a wild pigeon of the West Indies and the southern tip of Florida, having slate-colored plumage with a white crown.

**white-crowned sparrow,** a North American sparrow with a gray breast and black-and-white striped crown.

**whit|ed** (hwī′tid), *adj.* **1** covered or coated with white: *the whited desert.* **2** whitened; bleached: *whited linen.*

**white damp,** = carbon monoxide.

**white death,** *Informal.* heroin: *U.S. narcotics agents around the world ... are engaged in an escalating war against the "white death"* (Newsweek).

**white diarrhea,** pullorum disease in chickens.

**whited sepulcher,** a hypocrite (in the Bible, Matthew 23:27).

**white dwarf,** *Astronomy.* a white star of low luminosity, small size, and very great density.

**white elephant, 1** a whitish or pale-gray Indian elephant, considered holy in several Asian countries, such as Thailand (Siam) and Burma, and not used for work. **2** *Figurative.* anything that is expensive and troublesome to keep and take care of. **3** a possession that is no longer wanted by its owner.

**white elm,** a tall elm of eastern North America,

commonly planted as a shade tree; American elm.
**white-eye** (hwīt′ī′), *n.* **1** any one of various birds whose eyes have white or colorless irises. **2** any one of various small songbirds of tropical regions of the Old World, having a ring of white feathers around the eye.
**white-eyed vireo** (hwīt′īd′), a vireo of the eastern United States having white eyes ringed with yellow.
**white|face** (hwīt′fās′), *n., adj.* —*n.* **1a** makeup used to whiten the faces as of clowns and mimes: *A sad-eyed clown in whiteface trails behind a circus troupe* (Time). **b** a clown or mime in whiteface. **2** a white-faced animal, such as a Hereford.
—*adj.* of, having to do with, or in whiteface.
**white-faced** (hwīt′fāst′), *adj.* **1** pale; pallid: *a group of tired, undernourished, white-faced children.* **2** having a large patch of white or whitish hair between the muzzle and the top of the head: *a white-faced pony.*
**white-faced hornet**, a common American hornet, black with white face and markings.
**white feather**, **1** a symbol of cowardice (in allusion to the fact that a white feather in a gamecock's tail is a mark of inferior breeding). **2** = coward.
**show the white feather**, to act like a coward: *No one will defend him who shows the white feather* (Scott).
**white fir**, **1** any one of various firs, especially a large fir of the Rocky Mountains, having pale foliage and soft wood suitable for lumber. **2** = lowland fir.
**white|fish** (hwīt′fish′), *n., pl.* **-fish|es** or (*collectively*) **-fish**. **1** a food fish with white or silvery sides, related to the salmons and trouts, found in lakes and streams throughout the Great Lakes region. **2** any one of certain other white or silver fishes, such as the whiting, the menhaden, and the young bluefish. **3** = beluga (whale).
**white flag**, a plain white flag used as a sign of truce or surrender.
**white flax**, = gold-of-pleasure.
**white flight**, *U.S. Informal.* migration of white city residents to the suburbs to escape the effects of desegregation: *a busing plan for school desegregation will cause further "white flight" and decreased enrollment in public schools* (United Press).
**white fly**, any one of a group of flies with a long body and wings that are covered by a waxy, white dust. White flies attack many plants and citrus trees.
**white-foot|ed mouse** (hwīt′fu̇t′id), any one of a group of small North American mice with large ears and snow-white feet and underparts; vesper mouse; deer mouse.
**white fox**, **1** the arctic fox in its winter phase. **2** its fur, used for, on, or in coats and jackets, and as a stole.
**white friar** or **White Friar**, = Carmelite.
**white|front** (hwīt′frunt′), *n.* = white-fronted goose.
**white-front|ed goose** (hwīt′frun′tid), a grayish-brown goose with white on the front of the face, nesting in arctic regions of both hemispheres.
**white frost**, the white, feathery crystals of ice formed when water vapor in the air condenses at a temperature below freezing; hoarfrost; rime.
**white fuel**, water used as a source of power.
**white gasoline**, nonleaded gasoline.
**white gerfalcon**, the gyrfalcon during its white phase.
**white gold**, an alloy of gold and especially nickel, palladium, or platinum, sometimes with copper and zinc. White gold looks much like platinum and is used for jewelry.
**white goods**, **1** white household linens, such as sheets, pillowcases, towels, napkins, and tablecloths. **2** heavy household appliances such as stoves, refrigerators, and washing machines, often coated with white enamel.
**white gourd**, **1** = tallow gourd. **2** its fruit.
**white gum**, **1** any eucalyptus with a white or light-colored bark. **2** = sweet gum.
**white-haired boy** (hwīt′hãrd′), *Informal.* a favorite; fair-haired boy: *At the moment [he] is the white-haired boy of the London theatre* (New York Times).
**white hake**, a marine fish related to the hake.
**White|hall** (hwīt′hôl′), *n.* the British government or its policies. [< *Whitehall,* a London street adjacent to the Houses of Parliament, site of many government offices]
**white|head** (hwīt′hed′), *n.* a hard, white or yellow lump in the skin, produced by the retention of a sebaceous secretion; milium.
**white-head|ed** (hwīt′hed′id), *adj.* **1** having white hair, plumage, or other covering on the head. **2a** having white hair, especially from age. **b** having very light or fair hair; flaxen-haired.
**white-headed boy**, *Informal.* a fair-haired boy; favorite.
**white heart**, **1** a small delicate, perennial plant with flattened, heart-shaped flowers, growing in shady woods in the eastern United States and Canada; Dutchman's-breeches. **2** a disease of lettuce, caused by a virus.
**white heat**, **1** extremely great heat, at which metals and some other bodies give off a dazzling white light. **2** *Figurative.* a state of extremely great activity, excitement, or feeling.
**white heath**, a shrubby heath of southern Europe; brier.
**white hellebore**, **1** a European variety of false hellebore whose roots have medicinal properties. **2** = American hellebore.
**white heron**, **1** = great white heron. **2** = egret.
**white hole**, a hypothetical hole in outer space from which energy and stars and other heavenly matter emerge or explode.
**white hope**, **1** *Informal.* a person or thing expected to be a success: *the young American writer who, in the far off days of the middle nineteen-fifties, was regarded as the white hope of the medium* (Observer). *The great white hope for the German aircraft industry was the European airbus* (Sunday Times). **2** (perhaps originally) any white boxer who was thought capable of winning the heavyweight boxing championship from the American Negro boxer Jack Johnson between 1908 and 1915.
**white horehound**, = horehound (def. 1).
**white horse**, a white-topped wave; whitecap.
**white-hot** (hwīt′hot′), *adj.* **1** white with heat; extremely hot. **2** *Figurative.* very enthusiastic; excited; violent. **3** *Figurative.* that gives rise to excitement, enthusiasm, or violence: *The dues issue was a white-hot thing four years ago* (Wall Street Journal).
**White House**, **1** the official residence of the President of the United States, in Washington, D.C. **2** the office, authority, or opinion of the President of the United States.
**white hunter**, a white man employed to guide a safari.
**white ibis**, an ibis with white feathers, black wing tips, and red face and legs, found from the southern United States south to northern South America.
**white iron**, = tin.
**white iron pyrites**, = marcasite.
**white knight**, a political reformer or champion of a cause: ... *white knights dealing with the joint evils of corruption and reaction* (London Times).
**white lady**, *Slang.* cocaine.
**white lead**, **1** a heavy, white, poisonous, powdery compound, basic lead carbonate, used in making paint and in putty; ceruse. *Formula:* $PbCO_3$. **2** the putty or paste prepared by grinding this substance with oil (white lead in oil). **3** Also, **white lead ore**. = cerussite.
**white leather**, leather treated with salt and alum to retain its natural light color.
**white lie**, a lie about some small matter; polite or harmless lie.
**white light**, **1** the light which comes directly from the sun, and which has not been decomposed, as by refraction. **2** any light producing the same color or color sensation as direct sunlight.
**white lightning**, *U.S. Slang.* unaged, illegally distilled corn whiskey; moonshine.
**white line**, **1** a white (or yellow) stripe painted on a road or street, for the guidance of drivers of vehicles. **2** the flaky white layer in the wall of a horse's hoof.
**white-lipped peccary** (hwīt′lipt′), a large peccary with white markings on the face, living from Mexico south to Paraguay.
**white list**, *U.S.* a list of members of diplomatic households who are entitled to diplomatic immunity from the jurisdiction of courts.
**white-liv|ered** (hwīt′liv′ərd), *adj.* **1** cowardly. SYN: lily-livered. **2** pale; unhealthy looking; wan.
**white lupine**, an Old-World lupine with white flowers, much used in Europe as fodder.
**white|ly** (hwīt′lē), *adv.* so as to be or appear white; with a white color or aspect.
**white mahogany**, the wood of the primavera.
**white mangrove**, a tree or shrub of western Africa and tropical America as far north as Florida, with greenish-white flowers and a reddish bark rich in tannin.
**white man's burden**, the assumed duty of members of the Caucasian race to care for, educate, and govern the underdeveloped countries and uncivilized peoples of the world, especially of Asia and Africa.
► The phrase **White Man's Burden**, coined by Rudyard Kipling in his *From Sea to Sea* (1899), was felt by many to justify the cause of imperialism by reconciling it with Christian duty.
**white-marked moth** (hwīt′märkt′), a tussock moth common in the eastern United States. The female has no wings.
**white market**, the lawful buying and selling of any item in short supply or of ration coupons to prevent a black market from springing up: *To minimize racketeering, any rationing ought to be coupled with what has been called the "white market"—a kind of legal black market* (Time).
**white marlin**, a small marlin of Atlantic waters with a conspicuous lateral line.
**white matter**, whitish nerve tissue, especially in the brain and spinal cord, that consists chiefly of nerve fibers with myelin sheaths.
**white meat**, **1** any light-colored meat, such as veal or breast of chicken or turkey. **2** *Dialect.* dairy products.
**white metal**, **1** any one of several light-colored or white alloys, such as babbitt. **2** any one of several other alloys containing a large percentage of lead or tin.
**white mineral oil**, = mineral oil (def. 2).
**white mouse**, an albino strain of the common house mouse, bred for medical and biological research and sometimes for a pet.
**white mouth**, = thrush².
**white mulberry**, a mulberry native to China whose leaves are used for feeding silkworms.
**white mule**, *U.S. Slang.* raw, illegally distilled liquor; moonshine.
**white mullein**, a mullein covered with a thin, powdery down, growing in the eastern United States.
**white muscle disease**, a serious disease which affects lambs and calves by wasting of muscle tissue; stiff-lamb disease.
**white mustard**, a variety of mustard plant cultivated for its seeds, which are used for seasoning, and for its edible leaves.
**whit|en** (hwī′tən), *v.t.* to make white or whiter: *Sunshine helps to whiten clothes.* —*v.i.* to become white or whiter: *She whitened when she heard the bad news.* —**whit′en|er**, *n.*
—*Syn. v.t., v.i.* **Whiten, bleach, blanch** mean to make or become white, whiter, or lighter. **Whiten**, the more general word, particularly suggests applying or rubbing some substance on a surface: *The dentist used a powder to whiten my teeth.* **Bleach** implies exposure to sunlight and air or the use of chemicals: *You can bleach those handkerchiefs by leaving them out on the clothesline for several days.* **Blanch** implies turning white by some natural process: *Her cheeks were blanched by fear.*
**white-necked raven** (hwīt′nekt′), a raven with a ring of white feathers around the neck, found from Texas to southern California, and from western Kansas to Mexico.
**white|ness** (hwīt′nis), *n.* **1** white color or appearance: *the whiteness of milk.* **2a** lightness or fairness of complexion. **b** paleness; pallor. **3** a white substance: *to be covered with a whiteness.* **4** *Figurative.* spotless character or quality; purity: *He had kept the whiteness of his soul* (Byron).
**whit|en|ing** (hwī′tə ning), *n.* **1a** the act or process of making white; bleaching, whitewashing, tinning, or the like. **b** the fact or process of becoming white. **2** = whiting.
**white noise**, **1** the sound heard when the entire range of audible frequencies is produced at once, as in the operation of a jet engine. **2** an overlay of sound to cover up distracting or annoying noises; acoustic perfume.
**white oak**, **1** a large oak tree of eastern and central North America which has a light-gray or whitish bark and hard wood. **2** an oak of British and other European forests; durmast. **3** any one of various other oaks, such as the robur, a common species in Great Britain, or the roble, a shade tree of California and Mexico. **4** the wood of any of these trees.
**white oakum**, oakum made from clean rope, formerly used as dressings for wounds.
**white-on-white** (hwīt′on hwīt′, -ôn-), *n.* **1** a white cloth with a figured design in an off-white woven into it, used especially for shirts and blouses. **2** a shirt made of this cloth.
**white oryx**, a rare, very pale-colored oryx of Arabia.
**white|out** (hwīt′out′), *n.* **1** a condition in arctic and antarctic regions in which the sky, the horizon, and the ground become a solid mass of dazzling reflected light, obliterating all shadows and distinctions: *A whiteout can be more devastating than a blizzard, for the snow on the ground merges with a solid white overcast of clouds, with no visible point of junction* (John Brooks). **2** a temporary loss of vision resulting from this: *Travelers in Arctic snow on an overcast day, in fog, or under an unbroken sky may suffer not a blackout but a whiteout* (Science News Letter). **3** loss of view when snow blows across the path ahead.
**white paper**, **1a** paper of a white color. **b** blank paper, not written or printed upon. **2** a policy statement issued by the British government; command paper. **3** any official government report.

► The United States government does not use the term **white paper** officially, but certain U.S. documents are popularly referred to as white papers.

**white pelican**, a large pelican of western North America, mostly white with black flight feathers.

**white pepper**, a seasoning, less pungent than black pepper, made from the husked, dried, fully ripened berries of the pepper vine, a tropical climbing shrub.

**white perch**, **1** a small, silvery food fish of the eastern United States, found in both fresh and marine waters; silver perch. **2** = white crappie.

**white phosphorus**, the common form of phosphorus, in which it appears yellow and luminous in the dark.

**white pickerel**, = Chautauqua muskellunge.

**white pigweed**, a coarse weed of the goosefoot family with narrow, notched leaves; lamb's-quarters.

**white pine**, **1** a tall pine tree of eastern North America, valued for its soft, light wood. The white pine is the state tree of Maine and Michigan. See picture under **deciduous**. **2** the wood itself, much used for building. **3** any one of various similar pines.

**white pine blister rust**, a disease that destroys the tissues of white pines, caused by a fungus sheltered by currant plants.

**white-pine weevil** (hwīt′pīn′), a kind of weevil whose larvae feed on the new stems of the white pine and some other coniferous trees.

**white plague**, tuberculosis, especially of the lungs.

**white poplar**, **1** a large, spreading poplar, a native of Europe and Asia, whose deeply indented, roundish leaves have a silvery-white down on the undersurface; abele. **2a** = tulip tree. **b** its soft wood; tulipwood.

**white potato**, = potato (def. 2).

**white primary**, *U.S.* a primary election formerly held in some Southern states, in which only white persons were permitted to vote.

**white quebracho**, a South American tree of the dogbane family whose bark is used for tanning, and in medicine as a respiratory stimulant.

**white race**, the Caucasian race.

**white rat**, **1** an albino variety of the brown or Norway rat, used in laboratory experiments. **2** any albino rat.

**white room**, = clean room.

**white rose**, the emblem of the House of York.

**white rot**, **1** any one of several small herbaceous plants, such as the pennywort. **2** any one of various fungous plant diseases characterized by numerous white or grayish spots on the affected parts.

**white-rumped sandpiper** (hwīt′rumpt′), a small sandpiper that nests in arctic America and winters in southern South America. It reveals a conspicuous white rump when in flight.

**White Russian**, **1** a Russian living in the western part of the Soviet Union, north of the Ukraine; Byelorussian. **2** a Russian who recognized the former czarist government of Russia as the legal government of that country; Russian monarchist.

**white rust**, **1** a fungous disease of plants characterized by the eruption of white spores on the affected parts. **2** the fungus causing this.

**whites** (hwīts), *n.pl.* See under **white**.

**white sale**, a sale of white goods: *Merchants reported that January White Sales business was good* (New York Times).

**white sandalwood**, a variety of sandalwood cultivated in India, having a hard, fragrant wood used for construction and in making medicines, perfumes, and cosmetics.

**white sapphire**, a colorless variety of corundum or sapphire.

**white sauce**, a sauce made of milk, butter, and flour cooked together until thick and smooth, frequently with seasoning added.

**white shark**, = great white shark.

**white sheep**, = Dall sheep.

**white slave**, **1** a woman forced to be a prostitute. **2** a white person held as a slave. —**white′-slave′**, *adj.*

**white slaver**, a person whose business is white slavery.

**white slavery**, **1** the condition of a white slave or slaves. **2** the practice or business of a white slaver; traffic in white slaves.

**white-slav|ing** (hwīt′slā′ving), *n.* = white slavery.

**white|smith** (hwīt′smith′), *n.* **1** a worker in tin (white iron); tinsmith. **2** a person who finishes or polishes iron articles.

**white snakeroot**, a North American herb of the composite family, a variety of eupatorium with clusters of white flowers.

**white spruce**, **1** a spruce of northern North America with light-gray bark and unpleasant-smelling foliage. It may reach a height of 150 feet. **2** its light, strong wood, used for paper pulp and to make wooden containers.

**white squall**, a squall of wind without clouds.

**white stork**, the common European stork, also occurring in Africa and Asia, having white feathers with black on the wings.

**white sturgeon**, a sturgeon of the Pacific coast that is the largest American freshwater fish known, often growing to a length of 10 feet and a weight of more than 1000 pounds.

**white supremacist**, a believer in or supporter of white supremacy: *You cannot deal honestly with the question of race without infuriating the white supremacists in the South or the Negro liberals in the North* (Listener).

**white supremacy**, the belief that the white race is superior to and should have supremacy over all others, especially the Negro race: *Already the idea of white supremacy has a certain fustiness about it, which before long could make it a merely curious anachronism* (New Yorker).

**white|tail** (hwīt′tāl′), *n.* = white-tailed deer.

**white-tailed deer** (hwīt′tāld′), the common deer of eastern North America, white on the underside of the tail, known also in its summer coat as a red deer; Virginia deer. See picture under **deer**.

**white-tailed eagle**, a sea eagle of northern Europe with a white tail, closely related to the bald eagle.

**white-tailed gnu**, a gnu that ranges in color from brown to black and has a yellowish-white tail and a hairy face. It is almost extinct.

**white-tailed jack rabbit**, a jack rabbit of the northern and western plains of the United States whose fur turns white in winter.

**white-tailed kite**, a falconlike hawk with white tail and underparts, a variety of kite found from California and Texas south to Chile.

**white-tailed ptarmigan**, a ptarmigan that lives in the Rocky Mountains, ranging from central Alaska south to New Mexico.

**white|thorn** (hwīt′thôrn′), *n.* = English hawthorn.

**white|throat** (hwīt′thrōt′), *n.* **1** any one of certain European warblers, brown with a whitish throat and belly. **2** = white-throated sparrow.

**white-throat|ed** (hwīt′thrō′tid), *adj.* having a white throat.

**white-throated sparrow**, a large sparrow of eastern North America, brown with a white patch on the throat; peabody bird; whitethroat.

**white-throated swift**, a black and white swift (bird) found from British Columbia south through the western United States to Guatemala.

**white tie**, **1** a white bow tie, such as is worn by men in formal evening clothes. **2** formal evening clothes for men that include a white bow tie: *decreeing that all male guests appear in white tie* (New Yorker).

**white-tie** (hwīt′tī′), *adj.* of or having to do with a formal affair at which white ties are worn.

**white trash**, **1** poor whites, as a group (used in an unfriendly way). **2** a descendant or the descendants of poor whites, regardless of means (used in an unfriendly way).

**white turnip**, a kind of broad turnip with hairy leaves.

**white vitriol**, a white or colorless, crystalline substance used as an antiseptic, and for dyeing calico, and preserving wood; zinc sulfate. *Formula:* $ZnSO_4 \cdot 7H_2O$

**white vulture**, = Pharaoh's hen.

**white|wall** (hwīt′wôl′), *n.* an automobile tire with a white rim on the outer casing.

**white walnut**, **1** the butternut tree. **2** the wood of the butternut, used to make furniture.

**white|ware** (hwīt′wãr′), *n.* articles made of white pottery, earthenware, and porcelain, such as plumbing fixtures, dinnerware, and electrical insulators.

**white|wash** (hwīt′wosh′, -wôsh′), *n., v.* —*n.* **1** a liquid mixture of lime and water or of whiting, size, and water. It is used for whitening walls, woodwork, or other surfaces, as a substitute for paint. **2** *Figurative.* **a** the act of covering up faults or mistakes. **b** anything that covers up faults or mistakes. **3** *Informal.* a defeat in a game without a score for the loser; shut-out. **4** *Obsolete.* a cosmetic formerly used to make the skin fair.

—*v.t.* **1** to whiten with whitewash. **2** *Figurative.* to cover up the faults or mistakes of. **3** *Informal.* to defeat in a game without a score for the loser; shut out: *The faltering world champions meekly submitted to a 6-0 whitewashing ... at the Polo Grounds last night* (New York Times). —**white′-wash′er**, *n.*

**white water**, water with breakers or foam, as in shallows or rapids on the sea or a river.

**white wax**, *British.* paraffin.

**white|weed** (hwīt′wēd′), *n.* the common or oxeye daisy.

**white whale**, = beluga.

**white willow**, a tall ornamental willow with leaves whose underside appears white and silky.

**white|wing** (hwīt′wing′), *n. Informal.* a person employed to clean the streets and remove rubbish, especially an employee of a municipal department of sanitation (from the white uniforms now or formerly worn).

**white-winged crossbill** (hwīt′wingd′), a rose-colored crossbill of northern regions of both hemispheres, with white bars on the wings.

**white-winged dove**, a large dove of southern and western North America, with a white patch on each wing.

**white-winged junco**, a large junco with white tail feathers and two white bars on each wing. It nests in the Black Hills of South Dakota and winters in Colorado.

**white-winged scoter**, a blackish, North American sea duck with a large white patch on the rear edge of each wing.

**white wolf**, = arctic wolf.

**white|wood** (hwīt′wu̇d′), *n.* **1** any one of various trees with white or light-colored wood, such as the North American tulip tree and the North American linden or basswood. **2** the wood of any of these trees. **3** = cottonwood.

**white wreath aster**, a white-flowered aster of the eastern United States; heath aster; fall flower.

**Whit|ey** or **whit|ey** (hwī′tē), *n., pl.* **-ties.** (used in an unfriendly way) **1** the white man; white men collectively; white society. **2** a white man.

**whith|er** (hwiᴛʜ′ər), *adv., conj.* to what place; to which place; where. [Old English *hwider,* alteration of *hwæder;* apparently influenced by *hider* hither]

**whith|er|so|ev|er** (hwiᴛʜ′ər sō ev′ər), *adv., conj.* to whatever place; wherever.

**whith|er|ward** (hwiᴛʜ′ər wərd), *adv. Archaic.* **1a** toward or to what place; in what direction; whither. **b** toward what. **2a** whithersoever. **b** toward which.

**whith|er|wards** (hwiᴛʜ′ər wərdz), *adv.* = whitherward.

**whit|ing¹** (hwī′ting), *n., pl.* **-ings** or (*collectively*) **-ing. 1** a common European fish related to the cod, used for food. **2** = silver hake. **3** any one of certain spiny-finned, carnivorous fishes found along the Atlantic coast of the United States, used for food. [probably < Middle Dutch *wijting.* Compare Old English *hwītling* a kind of fish.]

**whit|ing²** (hwī′ting), *n.* a finely powdered white chalk. Whiting is used in making putty, whitewash, and silver polish. [apparently < *whit*(e) + *-ing*¹. Compare Old English *hwīting,* implied in *hwīting-melu* whiting meal.]

**whit|ish** (hwī′tish), *adj.* somewhat white; of a color inclining to or approaching white. —**whit′-ish|ness**, *n.*

**whit|leath|er** (hwit′leᴛʜ′ər), *n.* = white leather. [Middle English *whitlether* < *whit* white + *lether* leather]

**whit|low** (hwit′lō), *n.* an abscess on a finger or toe, usually near a nail; felon or agnail. [alteration of Middle English *whitflaw,* probably < *whit* white, Old English *hwīt* + *flawe,* related to *flake* a layer, covering]

**Whit|man|esque** (hwit′mə nesk′), *adj.* of, having to do with, or suggestive of Walt Whitman (1819-1892), an American poet, or his style of poetry: *The pretentiousness derives ... from a kind of Whitmanesque grandiosity that runs through the book* (New Yorker).

**Whit|mon|day** (hwit′mun′dē, -dā), *n.* the Monday after Whitsunday, a bank holiday in England.

**Whit|sun** (hwit′sən), *adj., n.* —*adj.* of, having to do with, or occurring at Whitsunday or Whitsuntide.

—*n.* = Whitsuntide.

[Middle English *whitsone,* misdivision of *whitsondei* Whitsunday, Old English *Hwīta Sunnandæg;* see etym. under **Whitsunday**]

**Whit|sun|day** (hwit′sun′dē, -dā; hwit′sən dā), *n.,* or **Whitsun Day**, the seventh Sunday after Easter; Pentecost. [Old English *Hwīta Sunnandæg* < *hwīt* white + *Sunnandæg* Sunday (probably because of the custom of wearing white baptismal robes on this day)]

**Whit|sun|tide** (hwit′sən tīd′), *n.,* or **Whitsun Tide**, the week beginning with Whitsunday, especially the first three days.

**whit|tle** (hwit′əl), *v.,* **-tled, -tling,** *n.* —*v.t.* **1** to cut shavings or chips from (wood) with a knife, usually for fun. **2** to shape (an object) with a knife; carve: *The old sailor whittled a boat for his friend.* **3** *Figurative.* to cut down or reduce gradually; trim: *to whittle costs. Production schedules can be whittled* (Wall Street Journal).

---

**Pronunciation Key:** hat, āge, cãre, fär; let, ēqual, tėrm; it, īce; hot, ōpen, ôrder; oil, out; cup, pu̇t, rüle; child; long; thin; ᴛʜen; zh, measure; ə represents **a** in about, **e** in taken, **i** in pencil, **o** in lemon, **u** in circus.

—*v.i.* to cut shavings from wood with a knife, as in making something or for idle amusement. [< noun]
—*n. Scottish.* a large knife.
**whittle down** (or **away**), to cut down little by little: *to whittle down expenses. These proposals were gradually whittled away during the talks* (Manchester Guardian Weekly).
[Middle English *whittel* a knife, variant of *thwittle,* ultimately < Old English *thwītan* to cut] —**whit′tler**, *n.*
**whit|tling** (hwit′ling), *n.* the act of a person or thing that whittles.
**whittlings**, chips or slivers cut off in whittling; shavings: *Litter of ... whittlings strewed the floor* (William Dean Howells).
**whit|y** (hwī′tē), *adj.* = whitish.
**whiz** or **whizz** (hwiz), *n., v.,* **whizzed, whiz|zing.** —*n.* **1a** a humming or hissing sound. **b** a swift movement producing such a sound. **2** *Slang.* **a** a very clever person; expert. **b** something skillful or appealing: *I did a whiz of a pantomime* (Atlantic).
—*v.i.* **1** to make a humming or hissing sound. **2** to move or rush swiftly with a whiz: *An arrow whizzed past his head.*
—*v.t.* to cause to whiz; hurl, shoot, or send swiftly with a whiz.
[imitative]
**whiz-bang** or **whizz-bang** (hwiz′bang′), *n., adj.* —*n.* **1** a shell fired in a flat trajectory at high velocity from a rifled piece of artillery of relatively small caliber, so that the sound of its explosion is heard almost simultaneously with the whizzing sound of its passage through the air. **2** a firework that makes a short, whizzing or buzzing sound and then explodes, intended to imitate the characteristic sound of such a shell. **3** *Informal.* anything strikingly noisy or noticeable.
—*adj. Informal.* strikingly good; first-rate: *Brown is a whiz-bang campaigner with a wide personal following* (Time).
**whiz kid**, *U.S. Slang.* **1** a child prodigy: *a musical whiz kid.* **2** a superior pupil. **3** a young man of outstanding intelligence and skill; whiz: *an accounting whiz kid. Fuzzy-cheeked whiz kids with computers telling battle-scarred dogfaces how to fight and win wars* (Wall Street Journal).
**whiz|zer** (hwiz′ər), *n.* **1** a person or thing that whizzes. **2** a machine for drying various articles or materials by the centrifugal force of rapid revolution.
**who** (hü; *unstressed relative* ü), *pron., poss.* **whose,** *obj.* **whom. 1** (as an interrogative pronoun) a word used in asking a question about a person or persons: *Who is your friend? Who told you? Who goes there?* **2** as a relative pronoun: **a** a word used in connecting a group of following words with some previous words in the sentence; person or persons indicated by the antecedent: *The girl who spoke is my best friend. We saw men who were working in the fields.* **b** the person who; any person who; one that; whoever: *Who is not for us is against us.*
**as who should** (or **would**) **say**, as if saying; as if one should say; as much as to say: *Sid beamed at Kips, as who should say, "You don't meet a character like this every dinnertime"* (H. G. Wells).
**who's who, a** which person is which; who each person is: *In such large and noisy parties as this, I can never tell who's who.* **b** which people are important: *As a society columnist it's her business to know who's who.* **c** a collection or gathering of important people: *The reviewing stand became a who's who of city and state politicians* (New York Times). **d** a reference book containing short biographies of important people: *a who's who of the theater. Crockford's Clerical Directory ... an ecclesiastical Who's Who* (Newsweek).
[Old English *hwā*]
► **Who** refers to people, to personified objects (a ship, a country), and occasionally to animals: *They have three dogs who always give us a big welcome.*
► See **that** for another usage note.
**WHO** (no periods) or **W.H.O.**, World Health Organization (an agency acting within the United Nations).
**whoa** (hwō, wō), *interj.* stop!; stand still!: *"Whoa there!" said the farmer to his team of horses.* [variant of obsolete *who,* interjection, variant of *ho*]
**who'd** (hüd), **1** who would: *Who'd have thought he could do such a thing!* **2** who had: *I was the one who'd seen him last.*
**who|dun|it** (hü dun′it), *n. Slang.* a story, motion picture, or play, dealing with crime, especially murder, and its detection. [spelling alteration of "who done it"]
**who|ev|er** (hü ev′ər), *pron.* **1** any person that; who: *Whoever wants the book may have it.* **2** no matter who: *Whoever else goes hungry, he won't.* **3** *Informal.* (as an interrogative pronoun implying perplexity or surprise) who: *Whoever could have done such a dreadful thing?*
► **a** In standard, written English **whoever** and **whomever** are used as subject and object respectively. In informal, spoken English, *whoever,* like *who,* frequently serves as either subject or object. **b** In *They gave tickets to whoever requested them,* the whole clause *whoever requested them* is the object of *to* and *whoever* is the subject of *requested.* In sentences of this type, *whomever* is sometimes substituted because of the mistaken notion that it is required by the preceding preposition.
**whole** (hōl), *adj., n.* —*adj.* **1** making up or being the full quantity, amount, extent, or number; entire: *to tell the whole story, to give a matter one's whole attention. He worked the whole day. He ate the whole melon. The whole state was hit by the hurricane.* **2** having all its parts or elements; complete; full: *He gave her a whole set of dishes.* **SYN**: perfect, intact. **3** not injured, broken, or defective: *He came out of the fight with a whole skin.* **SYN**: unimpaired, uninjured, unbroken. **4** in one piece; undivided: *The dog swallowed the meat whole.* **5** being fully or entirely such: *a whole brother or sister* (a son or daughter of both parents). **6** *Mathematics.* not fractional; integral: *a whole number.* **7a** well; healthy. **SYN**: hale, sound. **b** *Archaic.* restored to good health, as from disease, an injury, or a wound; well again. **c** *Obsolete.* (of a wound) healed.
—*n.* **1** all of a thing; the total: *Four quarters make a whole.* **SYN**: entirety, aggregate, sum. **2** something complete in itself; system: *the complex whole of civilization.*
**as a whole**, as one complete thing; altogether: *The public must be represented when the wage bargains are struck because the nation as a whole is an interested third party* (Manchester Guardian Weekly).
**on** (or **upon**) **the whole, a** considering everything; in sum: [*I*] *determined that the Alps were, on the whole, best seen from below* (John Ruskin). **b** in general; for the most part: *But on the whole the people of Coronation Street don't bother about the outside world* (Maclean's).
[spelling variant of Middle English *hole,* Old English *hāl.* See etym. of doublet **hale**[1]. See related etym. at **heal, holy.**] —**whole′ness**, *n.*
—*Syn. adj.* **1 Whole, total** mean consisting of and including all the parts or elements. **Whole** emphasizes that no element or part is left out or taken away: *The whole class was invited to the party.* **Total** emphasizes that every element or part is counted or taken in: *Her total income is more this year than last. Her total interest was riveted on the TV screen.*
**whole blood**, natural blood with none of the essential components removed.
**whole gale**, a wind with a velocity of 55 to 63 miles (89 to 102 kilometers) per hour on the Beaufort scale.
**whole|heart|ed** (hōl′här′tid), *adj.* earnest; sincere; hearty; cordial: *a wholehearted friend, wholehearted support. The returning soldiers were given a wholehearted welcome.* [American English < *whole;* perhaps patterned on *half-hearted*] —**whole′heart′ed|ly**, *adv.* —**whole′heart′ed|ness**, *n.*
**whole-hog** (hōl′hog′, -hôg′) *adj. Slang.* that goes the whole hog; thoroughgoing; unlimited: *Anything less than whole-hog public ownership would seem like backsliding* (New Yorker).
**whole-hog|ger** (hōl′hog′ər, -hôg′-), *n. Slang.* a person who goes the whole hog; one who does something thoroughly: *Temperamentally a whole-hogger, de Foucauld plunged into Trappist monasteries* (Manchester Guardian Weekly).
**whole|ly** (hō′lē, hōl′lē), *adv.* = wholly.
**whole-meal** (hōl′mēl′), *adj.* **1** made of the entire wheat grain kernels: *whole-meal flour.* **2** made of whole-meal flour.
**whole milk**, milk from which none of the natural constituents have been removed.
∗**whole note**, a note to be given as much time as four quarter notes; the longest duration of sound commonly encountered in music today; semibreve. It is the standard unit of time measurement in modern music notation.

∗**whole note**

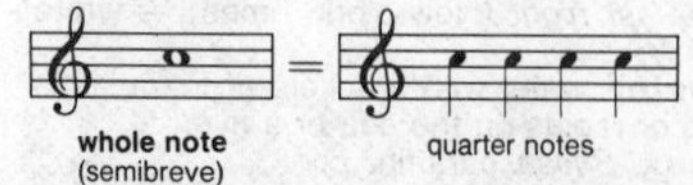

whole note (semibreve) = quarter notes

**whole number**, **1** a number denoting one or more whole things or units; integer. 1, 2, 3, 15, 106 are whole numbers; ½, ¾, and ⅞ are fractions; 1⅜, 2½, and 12⅔ are mixed numbers. **2** a positive integer or zero. The set of whole numbers is usually {0, 1, 2, 3, ...}, 0 sometimes being excluded.
∗**whole rest**, *Music.* a rest as long as a whole note.

∗**whole rest**

whole rest

**whole|sale** (hōl′sāl′), *n., adj., adv., v.,* **-saled, -sal|ing.** —*n.* the sale of goods in large quantities at a time, usually to storekeepers or others who will in turn sell them in small quantities to users: *They buy at wholesale and sell at retail.*
—*adj.* **1** in large lots or quantities: *The wholesale price of this coat is $22; the retail price is $30.* **2** selling in large quantities: *a wholesale merchant, a wholesale house, a wholesale fruit business.* **3** *Figurative.* broad and general; extensive and indiscriminate: *Avoid wholesale condemnation.* **SYN**: sweeping, unlimited.
—*adv.* in large lots or quantities; at or by wholesale: *to buy something wholesale.*
—*v.t.* to sell in large quantities: *They wholesale these jackets at $10 each. New car dealers are using their good trade-ins instead of wholesaling them* (Wall Street Journal).
—*v.i.* to be sold in large quantities: *Such jackets usually wholesale for much less.*
**by wholesale, a** in large quantities: *a commodity sold by wholesale.* **b** *Figurative.* in a large way and indiscriminately: *They despise a valuable book, and ... throw contempt upon it by wholesale* (Isaac Watts).
**wholesale price index**, *U.S.* a list of prices paid for a representative number of goods in various cities during a given month compared with average prices paid in a recent base period. It is compiled by the Bureau of Labor Statistics.
**whole|sal|er** (hōl′sā′lər), *n.* a wholesale merchant.
**whole snipe**, the common snipe of Europe.
**whole|some** (hōl′səm), *adj.* **1** good for the health; healthful: *Milk is a wholesome food.* **2** suggesting good health; healthy-looking: *She has a clean, wholesome face.* **SYN**: See syn. under **healthy. 3** good for the mind or morals; beneficial: *She reads only wholesome books.* **4** free from disease or taint: *Ere the wholesome flesh decay* (A. E. Housman). [spelling variant of Middle English *holsum* < *hol* whole + *-sum* -some[1]] —**whole′some|ly**, *adv.* —**whole′someness**, *n.*
**whole-souled** (hōl′sōld′), *adj.* = wholehearted.
**whole step**, *Music.* an interval of two half steps, and equal to one sixth of an octave, such as D to E, or E to F#; major second.
**whole-time** (hōl′tīm′), *adj. British.* full-time: *whole-time employment.*
**whole tone**, = whole step.
∗**whole-tone scale** (hōl′tōn′), *Music.* a scale proceeding in whole steps, dividing the octave into six equal parts, used in the first decade of the 1900's.

∗**whole-tone scale**

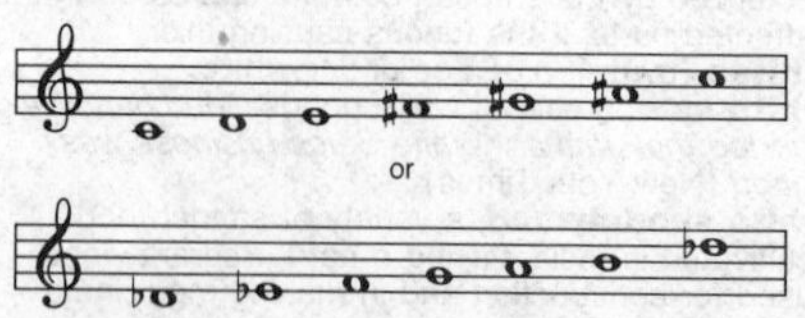


**whole-wheat** (hōl′hwēt′), *adj.* **1** made of the entire wheat kernel: *whole-wheat flour.* **2** made from whole-wheat flour: *whole-wheat bread.*
**whole-word method** (hōl′wėrd′), = word method.
**who|lism** (hō′liz əm), *n.* = holism.
**who|lis|tic** (hō lis′tik), *adj.* = holistic.
**who'll** (hül), **1** who will. **2** who shall.
**whol|ly** (hō′lē, hōl′lē), *adv.* **1** to the whole amount or extent; completely; entirely; totally; altogether: *to be wholly finished. The sick boy was wholly cured.* **SYN**: utterly. **2** as a whole; in its entirety; in full: *A man who can see truth at all, sees it wholly, and neither desires nor dares to mutilate it* (John Ruskin). **3** exclusively; solely: *A creature wholly given to brawls and wine* (Tennyson). **SYN**: only.
**whom** (hüm), *pron.* the objective case of **who.** what person; which person: *Whom do you like best? He does not know whom to believe. The girl to whom you spoke is my cousin.* [Old English *hwām,* dative of *hwā* who, and *hwæt* what]
**whom|ev|er** (hüm′ev′ər), *pron.* **1** whom; any person whom. **2** no matter whom.
► See **whoever** for usage note.
**whomp** (hwomp), *n., v. Informal.* —*n.* a loud out-

burst of sound: *the whomp and hiss of exploding firecrackers.*
— ***v.i.*** to hit or fall with such a sound; thump: *The Sunday edition of the New York Times ... whomped to the floor outside my apartment door* (New Scientist).
— ***v.t.*** **1** to beat or knock down with such a sound: *jailed and systematically whomped by the local police* (New York Times). **2** to defeat; drub: *The whomping the Republicans and we conservatives took in this past election hurts* (Wall Street Journal). Also, **whump**.
**whomp up,** *Informal.* to produce or accomplish quickly; knock up: *to whomp up a new sales approach, to whomp up a crisis.*
[imitative]

**whom|so** (hüm′sō′), *pron.* = whomever.

**whom|so|ev|er** (hüm′sō ev′ər), *pron.* = whomever; any person whom.

**whoop** (hüp, hwüp), *n., v., interj.* — ***n.*** **1** a loud cry or shout: *When land was sighted, the sailor let out a whoop of joy. The man gave a whoop of rage.* **2** such a cry or shout used by North American Indians as a signal or war cry (war whoop). **3** the loud, gasping sound made by a person with whooping cough after a fit of coughing. **4** the cry of an owl, swan, or crane; hoot. **5** *Informal, Figurative.* a bit; scarcely anything: *not worth a whoop. Who could possibly believe it or care two whoops?* (Atlantic).
— ***v.i.*** **1** to shout or call loudly. **2** to make the loud, gasping sound of a person when he has whooping cough. **3** to hoot, as an owl or crane does.
— ***v.t.*** **1** to utter with a whoop; express by whooping. **2** to call, urge, drive, or make fun of, with whoops or shouts: *to whoop dogs on.* (*Figurative.*) *The Senate whooped it through and sent it to the House* (Time).
— ***interj.*** a cry or shout to attract attention or to express excitement, encouragement, or surprise. Also, **hoop**.
**a whoop and a holler,** *U.S. Informal.* **a** a comparatively short distance: *Eudora Welty's characters have till now been found no farther than a whoop and a holler from Jackson, Natchez, or Vicksburg, Miss.* (New York Times). **b** a great to-do; hullabaloo: *The Republicans make a great whoop and a holler about the honesty of federal employees* (Harry S Truman).
**whoop it up,** *Slang.* **a** to make merry; revel; celebrate: *No one was happy except him, his wife, and two brothers, whooping it up in a Milwaukee hotel* (Manchester Guardian). **b** to act or work in a rousing way; support vigorously: *One of the most persistent clichés about democracy is that the thoughtless masses, being given their head, would run headlong to disaster by whooping it up for ... spending by the government while howling down the taxes* (Wall Street Journal).
[variant of *hoop*[2] (influenced by *who*) < Old French *houper* to cry out; probably ultimately imitative]

**whoop-de-do** or **whoop-de-doo** (hüp′dē dü′, hwüp′-, hwu̇p′-), *n. U.S. Informal.* noisy commotion or excitement; hullabaloo: *Despite all the whoop-de-do in the public press about it no one knows the real extent of juvenile delinquency* (Harper's). [extended < *whoop*]

**whoop|ee** (hü′pē, wu̇p′ē, hwü′pē, hwu̇p′ē), *interj., n.* — ***interj.*** an exclamation expressing unrestrained pleasure, joy, or excitement, or the intent to have a hilariously good time.
— ***n.*** **1** a cry of "whoopee." **2** noisy commotion, excitement, or revelry; hilarity.
**make whoopee,** to rejoice noisily or hilariously; have a good time: *When he received a raise in pay, he spent the weekend making whoopee.*
[< *whoop*]

**whoop|er** (hü′pər, hwü′-), *n.* **1** a person or animal that whoops. **2** = whooper swan. **3** = whooping crane.

**whooper swan**, an Old-World swan that has a whooping call.

**whoop|ing cough** (hü′ping, hu̇p′-), an infectious disease, usually of children, that causes fits of coughing that end with a loud, gasping sound (whoop); pertussis. Whooping cough is caused by bacteria which inflame the air passages.

**whooping crane**, a large white crane of North America with a red face and black wing tips, noted for its loud, trumpetlike call. Whooping cranes once ranged widely in the United States.

**whoop|la** (hüp′lä, hwüp′-, hwu̇p′-), *n.* = hoopla.

**whoops** (hwu̇ps, wu̇ps), *interj.* = oops.

**whoop-up** (hüp′up′, hwüp′-, hwu̇p′-), *n. U.S. Informal.* noisy commotion, excitement, or revelry: *Many were no doubt getting over the Saturday-night whoop-up, which in my time used to absorb most of the week's spending money* (New Yorker).

**whoosh** (hwu̇sh), *n., v., interj.* — ***n.*** a dull, soft, hissing sound like that of something rushing through the air: *The ... autos are away from the starting line, some with a whoosh, others at a more leisurely pace* (Wall Street Journal).
— ***v.i.*** to make, or move with, such a sound: *When the time comes that people whoosh across vast reaches of the Earth in rocket carriages* (Saturday Review). — ***v.t.*** to carry or move with such a sound: [*The plane*] *can whoosh 80 first-class passengers across the Atlantic at 550 miles per hour* (Wall Street Journal).
— ***interj.*** a sound made to describe a rushing through the air with a soft, hissing noise: *"At first it was a real little thing," he said, "then it caught in some of the blowing sawdust and—whoosh—up it went"* (New York Times).

**whop** (hwop, wop), *v.,* **whopped, whop|ping,** *n.* — ***v.t.*** **1** *Informal.* to strike with heavy blows; beat soundly; flog; belabor. **2** *Figurative.* to overcome; defeat utterly. **3** *Dialect.* to throw, take, or put violently and suddenly. — ***v.i.*** *U.S. Informal.* to flop: *to whop down in a chair.*
— ***n.*** *Informal.* an act of whopping; heavy blow or bump: *a sudden whop on the head.* Also, **whap, wop.**
[dialectal variant of *wap*[1]]

**whop|per** (hwop′ər), *n. Informal.* **1** something uncommonly large of its kind. **2** a big lie. Also, **whapper.** [< *whop* in sense of "to beat, overcome" + *-er*[1]]

**whop|ping** (hwop′ing), *adj. Informal.* very large of its kind; huge: *a whopping lie.* Also, **whapping.**

**whore** (hôr, hōr), *n., v.,* **whored, whor|ing.** — ***n.*** **1** = prostitute. **2** an unchaste woman.
— ***v.i.*** **1a** to have sexual intercourse with a whore or whores. **b** to be or act as a whore. **2** *Figurative.* to commit an act of idolatry; be guilty of unfaithfulness to the true God (in the Bible, Exodus 34:15). — ***v.t.*** *Obsolete.* to debauch (a woman).
[spelling variant of Middle English *hore,* Old English *hōre,* perhaps < Scandinavian (compare Old Icelandic *hōra*)]

**whore|dom** (hôr′dəm, hōr′-), *n. Archaic.* **1** the act of a whore. **2** fornication. **3** *Figurative.* (in the Bible) unfaithfulness to the true God; idolatry.

**whore|house** (hôr′hous′, hōr′-), *n.* = brothel.

**whore|mas|ter** (hôr′mas′tər, -mäs′-; hōr′-), *n.* = whoremonger.

**whore|mon|ger** (hôr′mung′gər, -mong′-; hōr′-), *n.* **1** = lecher. **2** = pander.

**whore|son** (hôr′sən, hōr′-), *adj., n. Archaic.* bastard. [Middle English *hores son,* or *hore son* whore's son]

**whor|ish** (hôr′ish, hōr′-), *adj. Obsolete.* lewd; unchaste. — **whor′ish|ly,** *adv.* — **whor′ish|ness,** *n.*

∗**whorl** (hwėrl, hwôrl), *n.* **1** a circle of leaves or flowers around the stem of a plant; verticil. **2** one of the turns of a spiral shell. **3** anything that circles or turns on or around something else, such as: **a** a convolution, coil, curl, or wreath. A person can be identified by the whorls of his fingerprints. **b** a type of fingerprint in which the ridges in the center make a turn through at least one complete circle. **c** one of the spiral curves in the cochlea of the ear. **4** = wharve. **5** a bowl of stone or baked clay, used in ancient hand spinning, in which a spindle was set to allow it to spin freely. [Middle English *whorle,* and *whorlwyl* flywheel or pulley on a spindle, apparently variants of *whirl.* Compare earlier Dutch *worvel,* and *wervel.*]

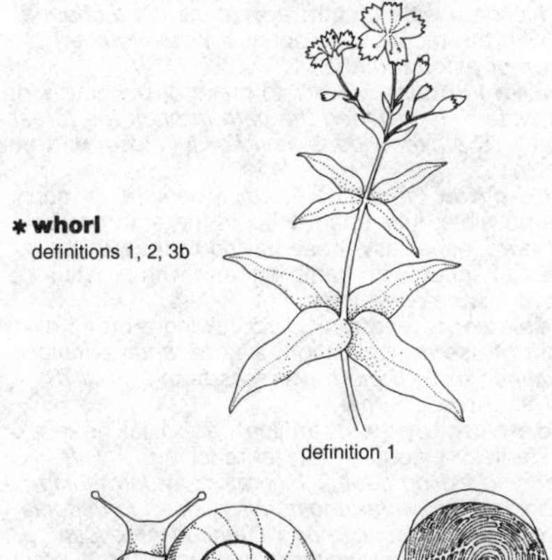

∗ **whorl**
definitions 1, 2, 3b

definition 1

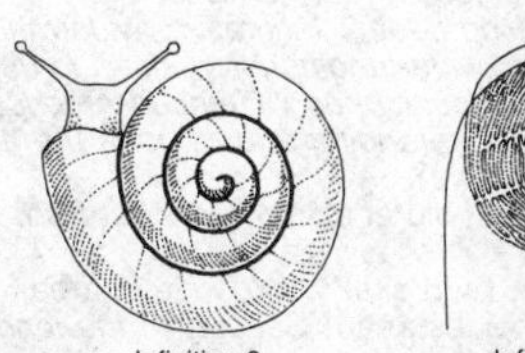

definition 2

definition 3b

**whorled** (hwėrld, hwôrld), *adj.* **1** having a whorl or whorls. **2** arranged in a whorl: *whorled petals.*

**whort** (hwėrt), *n.* **1** = whortleberry. **2** its fruit. [dialectal variant of obsolete *hurt.* Compare etym. under **huckleberry.**]

**whor|tle** (hwėr′təl), *n.* = whort.

**whor|tle|ber|ry** (hwėr′təl ber′ē), *n., pl.* **-ries. 1** a small, edible, black berry much like the blueberry, the fruit of any one of several European and Siberian shrubs of the heath family; bilberry. **2** the shrub that it grows on, of the same genus as the blueberry. **3** = huckleberry. [dialectal variant of *hurtleberry*]

**who's** (hüz), **1** who is: *Who's at the door?* **2** who has: *Who's been using my pen?*

**whose** (hüz), *pron.* **1** the possessive case of **who** and of **which.** of whom; of which: *a dog whose bark is loud. The girl whose work got the prize is the youngest in her class. Whose book is this? Hand me that book whose cover is frayed. A hamlet, inhabited by fishermen, whose humanity he had occasion to remember* (Oliver Goldsmith). **2** (historically) the possessive case of **what.**
[Middle English *whos, hwas,* Old English *hwæs,* genitive of *hwā* who; influenced in Middle English by nominative *wha*]
► The use of **whose** as a relative referring to a nonpersonal antecedent (*generators whose combined capacity ...* ), frequently condemned by prescriptive grammarians, has been thoroughly established for centuries, in both literary and general English. The equivalent construction, *of which,* often produces a stiff and clumsy sentence.

**whose|so|ev|er** (hüz′sō ev′ər), *pron. Archaic.* of any person whatsoever; whose.

**who|so** (hü′sō), *pron. Archaic.* whoever.

**who|so|ev|er** (hü′sō ev′ər), *pron.* anybody who; whoever.

**w.-hr** or **whr.,** watt-hour.

**whump** (hwump), *n., v.i., v.t.* = whomp.

**whup** (hwup), *v.t.,* **whupped, whup|ping.** *Dialect or Informal.* to beat soundly; whip; wallop: *The Bundawallop Workers were our deadliest rivals, a mean bunch who whupped us consistently* (Punch). [probably alteration of *whip*]

**why** (hwī), *adv., n., pl.* **whys,** *interj.* — ***adv.*** **1** for what reason, cause, or purpose; wherefore: *Why did you do it? I don't know why I did it.* **2** for which; because of which: *His laziness is the reason why he failed.* **3** the reason for which: *That is why she raised the question.*
— ***n.*** the cause, reason, or purpose: *I can't understand the whys and wherefores of his strange behavior.*
— ***interj.*** an expression of surprise, doubt, hesitancy, etc., or just to fill in: *Why, it's all gone! Why, yes, I will go with you if you wish.*
[Old English *hwȳ,* instrumental case of *hwā* who, and *hwæt* what]

**whyd|ah** (hwid′ə), *n.* = whidah.

**why|ev|er** (hwī ev′ər), *adv.* for whatever reason; why: *Laughter in your Church? Whyever not!* (London Times).

**w.i.,** when issued.

**WI** (no periods), Wisconsin (with postal Zip Code).

**W.I., 1** West Indian. **2** West Indies.

**wib|bly-wob|bly** (wib′lē wob′lē), *adj.* = wobbly.

**Wich|i|ta** (wich′ə tô), *n., pl.* **-ta** or **-tas. 1** a member of a tribe of Plains Indians formerly found in Kansas and now chiefly in Oklahoma. **2** the Caddoan language of this tribe.

**wick**[1] (wik), *n.* the part of an oil lamp or candle that is lighted. A wick is now usually a cord or tape of loosely twisted or woven cotton, immersed or enclosed except at one end in the oil or wax. The oil or melted wax is drawn up by the wick and burned. [Middle English *wicke, weke* < Old English *wice, wēoce*]

**wick**[2] (wik), *n.* a narrow opening in the course left between the stones of previous players in the game of curling. [< obsolete *wick,* verb, to drive a stone through the opening between two guards]

**wick|ed** (wik′id), *adj., n.* — ***adj.*** **1** bad; evil; sinful: *a wicked witch, wicked deeds, wicked words, a wicked heart.* **SYN:** ungodly, corrupt, depraved, vile, infamous, immoral. See syn. under **bad. 2** playfully sly; mischievous: *a wicked smile.* **3** *Informal.* unpleasant; severe: *a wicked task, a wicked smell, a wicked blow. A wicked snowstorm swept through the northern part of the state.* **4** savage; vicious: *The wicked mongrel fought for his life.* **5** *Informal.* very clever or effective; excellent: *He plays a wicked game of pinochle.*
— ***n.*** **the wicked,** wicked persons: *There must the wicked cease from their tyranny* (Coverdale). [Middle English *wicked,* earlier *wicke* wicked, perhaps related to Old English *wīcan* yield, give way, fall down] — **wick′ed|ly,** *adv.*

---

**Pronunciation Key:** hat, āge, cãre, fär; let, ēqual, tėrm; it, īce; hot, ōpen, ôrder; oil, out; cup, pu̇t, rüle; child; long; thin; ᴛʜen; zh, measure; ə represents **a** in about, **e** in taken, **i** in pencil, **o** in lemon, **u** in circus.

**wick|ed|ness** (wik′id nis), *n.* **1** the quality of being wicked; sinfulness. **SYN:** wrongdoing, turpitude. **2** a wicked thing or act. **SYN:** vice.

**wick|er** (wik′ər), *n., adj.* —*n.* **1** a slender, easily bent branch or twig, usually of willow, especially as used for making baskets and chairs; osier; withe. **2** twigs or branches woven together. Wicker is used in making baskets and furniture. **3** something made of wicker.
—*adj.* **1** made of wicker: *a wicker chair.* **2** covered with wicker.
[< Scandinavian (compare dialectal Swedish *vikker* branch of willow)]

**wick|er|work** (wik′ər wėrk′), *n.* **1** twigs or branches woven together; wicker. **2** objects made of wicker.

***wick|et** (wik′it), *n.* **1** a small door or gate: *The big door has a wicket in it.* **2** a small window or opening, usually having a grate or grill over it: *Buy your tickets at this wicket.* **3** a wire arch stuck in the ground in the game of croquet for the ball to be knocked through; hoop. **4a** either of the two sets of sticks at which the ball is bowled in cricket. They are placed at opposite ends of the playing pitch. Each wicket consists of three uprights (stumps) across which two small sticks (bails) are laid in grooves. The bowler's object is to strike the stumps, the batsman's to prevent the ball from hitting them. **b** the level space between these, especially with reference to its condition for bowling: *a fast wicket.* **c** the turn of a batsman. **d** the period during which two men bat together. **e** an incomplete (or unopened) inning for any batsman. **5** a small gate or valve for emptying the chamber of a canal lock, or in the chute of a water wheel for regulating the passage of water. **6** an entrance turnstile. [< Anglo-French *wiket,* perhaps ultimately < Scandinavian (compare Old Icelandic *vīkja* a move, turn)]

***wicket**
definitions 3, 4a

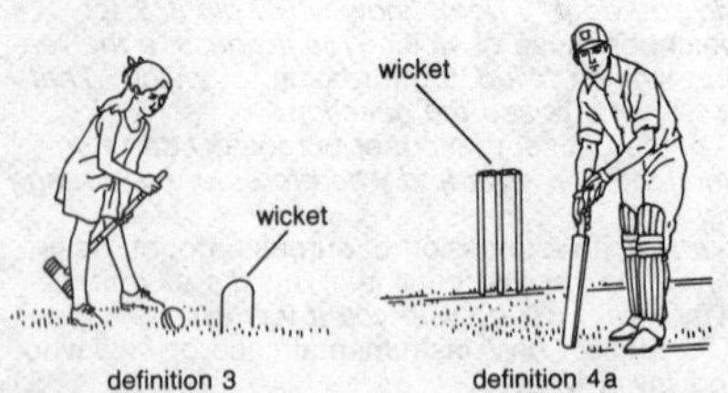

definition 3 definition 4a

**wick|et|keep|er** (wik′it kē′pər), *n.* the fielder in cricket who stands behind the wicket.

**wick|ing** (wik′ing), *n.* material for wicks.

**wick|i|up** (wik′ē up′), *n.* **1** an American Indian hut made of brushwood or covered with mats, formerly used by nomadic tribes in the West and Southwest. **2** *U.S.* any small hut or shanty. Also, **wikiup.** [American English < Algonkian (Sauk, or Fox) *wickĭyapi* lodge, dwelling]

**wic|o|py** (wik′ə pē), *n., pl.* **-pies. 1** = leatherwood. **2** any one of several willow herbs. **3** = basswood (def. 1). [American English < Algonkian (compare Massachusetts *wik′pi* stringy bark of basswood)]

**wid|der|shins** (wid′ər shinz), *adv. Scottish.* withershins.

**wid|dy**[1] or **wid|die** (wid′ē), *n., pl.* **-dies.** *Scottish.* **1** a band or rope, especially one made of intertwined osiers or the like. **2** a rope for hanging (used, like *gallows,* in various expressions alluding to hanging). [variant of earlier *withy* < *with*(e) + *-y*[1]]

**wid|dy**[2] (wid′ē), *n., pl.* **-dies.** *Dialect.* a widow. [variant of *widow*]

**wide** (wīd), *adj.,* **wid|er, wid|est,** *adv., n.* —*adj.* **1** filling more space from side to side than the usual thing of the same sort; not narrow; broad: *a wide street, a wide hall.* **2** extending a certain distance from side to side: *The door is three feet wide.* **3** extending a great distance; extensive; vast; great: *to go forth into the wide world. Columbus sailed across the wide ocean.* (*Figurative.*) *The opposing candidates had wide differences of opinion.* **4** full; ample; roomy: *wide shoes.* **5** *Figurative.* having great range; including many different things; extensive; comprehensive: *A trip around the world gives wide experience. Wide reading gives wide understanding of our times and places.* **6** far or fully open; distended: *The child stared with wide eyes.* **7** far from a named point, object, or target; too far or too much to one side: *His shot was wide of the target.* (*Figurative.*) *His guess was wide of the truth.* **8** *Phonetics.* uttered with the tongue relatively relaxed, as the vowel in *bid* or *bed;* lax. **9** having a big difference between the buying and selling prices of a security. **10** (of livestock feed) containing a proportionately small amount of protein.
—*adv.* **1** to a great or relatively great extent from side to side: (*Figurative.*) *opinions that are wide apart.* **2** over an extensive space or region: *to travel far and wide.* **3** to the full extent; fully: *Open your mouth wide. The gates stand wide open.* **4** aside; astray: *The arrow went wide.*
—*n.* **1** a wide space or expanse. **2** a ball bowled wide of the wicket in cricket, counting as a run for the batsman's side. **3** *Phonetics.* a wide vowel.
[Old English *wīd*] —**wide′ness,** *n.*
—*Syn. adj.* **3 Wide, broad** mean far or large across. **Wide** emphasizes the distance from one side to the other: (*Figurative.*) *a wide gap between knowledge and practice.* **Broad** emphasizes the expanse between the two sides: *Ships sail on the broad ocean.*

**wide-an|gle** (wīd′ang′gəl), *adj.* requiring the use of or made with a wide-angle lens: *a wide-angle shot.*

**wide-angle lens,** a lens of short focus, the field of which extends through a wide angle, used especially for photographing at short range.

**wide-a|wake** (wīd′ə wāk′), *adj., n.* —*adj.* **1** with the eyes wide open; fully awake. **2** *Figurative.* alert; keen; knowing: *A watchdog must be a wide-awake guard against danger.* **SYN:** sharp, acute.
—*n.* **1** = sooty tern. **2** Also, **wide-awake hat.** a soft felt hat with a broad brim and a low crown.
—**wide′-a|wake′ness,** *n.*

**wide ball,** a cricket ball bowled wide of the wicket; wide.

**wide|band** (wīd′band′), *adj. Electronics.* covering, transmitting, or receiving over a wide range of frequencies: *a wideband antenna, wideband magnetic tape.*

**wide boy,** *British Slang.* a young man of unscrupulous morals and manners; delinquent: *These young men rarely work and ... by their insulting behaviour, by creating nuisance or by causing wilful damage ... they build themselves a reputation for being wide boys whom nobody can control* (London Times).

**wide-brimmed** (wīd′brimd′), *adj.* having a wide brim: *a group of Pennsylvania Dutch in their black beards and wide-brimmed hats* (Horace Sutton).

**wide-eyed** (wīd′īd′), *adj.* **1** with the eyes wide open in wonder or surprise: *The children watched the rabbits with wide-eyed interest.* **2** *Figurative.* greatly surprised; astonished: *Many orthodox Moslem traditionalists just stared wide-eyed, stunned, and aghast at the appearance in public of Her Royal Highness ... unveiled and unashamed* (Time). **3** *Figurative.* simple; artless; innocent: *Readers of fiction in popular magazines think of the wide-eyed blonde as dumb* (Newsweek).

**wide-field** (wīd′fēld′), *adj.* encompassing a wide field of view or perspective: *Most satellite observers will also want a good low-power, wide-field telescope* (Scientific American).

**wide|ly** (wīd′lē), *adv.* to a wide extent: *a widely distributed plant, widely opened eyes. Figurative: a man who is widely known, to be widely read, two widely different accounts of a quarrel.* **SYN:** extensively.

**wide-mouthed** (wīd′mouᴛʜd′, -moutht′), *adj.* **1** having a wide mouth: *a wide-mouthed channel.* **2** with the mouth wide open: *a wide-mouthed look of astonishment.*

**wid|en** (wī′dən), *v.t., v.i.* to make or become wide or wider: *He widened the path through the forest* (v.t.). *The river widens as it flows* (v.i.). —**wid′en|er,** *n.*

**wide-o|pen** (wīd′ō′pən), *adj.* **1** opened as much as possible; fully open. **2** lax in the enforcement of laws, especially those having to do with the sale of liquor, with gambling, and with prostitution: *a wide-open town.*

**wide-range** (wīd′rānj′), *adj.* having a broad extent of use or application: *a wide-range antibiotic claimed to fight more diseases than penicillin* (Wall Street Journal).

**wide-rang|ing** (wīd′rān′jing), *adj.* **1** taking in a wide field; extending far; far-reaching: *a wide-ranging fishing fleet.* **2** *Figurative: wide-ranging conclusions, wide-ranging interests. It is undeniable that the Council has influenced American policy with wide-ranging effects upon the average citizen* (Harper's).

**wid|er|shins** (wid′ər shinz), *adv. Scottish.* withershins.

**wide-scale** (wīd′skāl′), *adj.* wide in area, extent, or degree; widespread: *Security in the long run requires that there be a universal reduction and control of the methods of wide-scale destruction* (Bulletin of Atomic Scientists). *In countries using wide-scale vaccination, the disease is already on the decline* (Time). *There has been no wide-scale general testing ... that would offer conclusive proof* (Atlantic).

**wide screen,** a screen for showing motion pictures that has greater width than height and is curved to give the illusion of realism. —**wide′-screen′,** *adj.*

**wide-spec|trum** (wīd′spek′trəm), *adj.* = broad-spectrum.

**wide|spread** (wīd′spred′), *adj.* **1** spread widely: *widespread wings.* **SYN:** outspread. **2** spread over a wide space: *a widespread flood.* **3** occurring in many places or among many persons far apart: *a widespread belief.*

**wide|spread|ing** (wīd′spred′ing), *adj.* = widespread.

**wide-wale** (wīd′wāl′), *adj.* (of cloth) having wide ridges or wales: *wide-wale corduroy.*

**widg|eon** (wij′ən), *n., pl.* **-eons** or (*collectively for 1*) **-eon. 1** any one of several kinds of wild ducks of fresh waters. A widgeon is slightly larger than a teal. The baldpate is a common American species. **2** *Obsolete.* a simpleton; ninny (applied to a person in allusion to the supposed stupidity of the bird). Also, **wigeon.** [origin unknown]

**widg|et** (wij′it), *n.* **1** *Informal.* a gadget. **2** *Air Force Slang.* a young gremlin. [alteration of *gadget*]

**wid|ish** (wī′dish), *adj.* somewhat wide: *The skirt is navy, and a series of widish tucks sweeps around it* (New Yorker).

**wid|ow** (wid′ō), *n., v., adj.* —*n.* **1** a woman whose husband is dead and who has not married again. **SYN:** relict. **2** a hand, or group of cards, not dealt to any player but capable of being used by a player who bids for it. **3** *Printing.* a word or group of words constituting less than a full line at the head of a column or page, generally considered to be typographically undesirable before widespread use of computer typesetting.
—*v.t.* **1** to make a widow or (rarely) widower of: *She was widowed when she was only thirty years old.* **2** *Figurative.* to deprive (of a valuable or highly prized possession, whether person, thing, or quality). **3** *Obsolete.* **a** to survive as a widow; become the widow of. **b** to endow with a widow's right.
—*adj.* that is a widow; widowed.
[Old English *widewe,* or *widuwe*]

**widow bewitched,** *Informal.* a grass widow.

**widow bird,** = whidah. [translation of New Latin *Vidua* the genus name < Latin *vidua* widow (because of its black plumage). Compare etym. under **whidah.**]

**wid|ow|er** (wid′ō ər), *n.* a man whose wife is dead and who has not married again.

**wid|ow|er|hood** (wid′ō ər hůd), *n.* the condition or time of being a widower.

**wid|ow|hood** (wid′ō hůd), *n.* the condition or time of being a widow.

**widow's cruse,** an inexhaustible supply (in allusion to II Kings 4:1-7, I Kings 17:8-16): *a widow's cruse of money and goods.*

**widow's mite,** a small amount of money given cheerfully by a poor person (in allusion to the widow's gift mentioned in Mark 12:42).

**widow's peak,** hair that grows or has the appearance of growing low and to a point on the forehead, traditionally supposed to presage early widowhood.

***widow's walk,** *U.S.* a balcony, on or near the roof of a house along a seacoast, giving a good view of the ocean. New England seafaring men used to build widow's walks on their houses to give their wives a place from which to watch for returning ships.

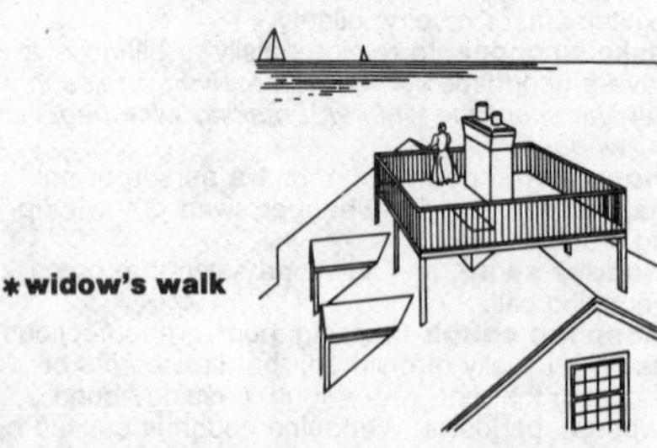
***widow's walk**

**widow's weeds,** the mourning clothes of a widow.

**width** (width, witth), *n.* **1a** how wide a thing is; distance across; breadth: *a plank 15 inches in width. The room is 12 feet in width.* **b** extent of opening; distance apart of the two parts of something, such as a pair of compasses. **2a** a piece of a certain width. **b** a piece extending the full breadth of the material: *Two widths of cloth will make the curtains.* **3** *Figurative.* freedom from narrowness; breadth: *width of mind, width of vision.* [< *wid*(e) + *-th,* as in *breadth*]

**width|way** (width′wā′, witth′-), *adv.* = widthwise.

**width|ways** (width′wāz′, witth′-), *adv.* = widthwise.

**width|wise** (width′wīz′, witth′-), *adv.* in the direction of the width; transversely.
**Wie|gen|lied** (vē′gən lēt′), *n., pl.* **-lie|der** (-lē′dər). *German.* a cradlesong; lullaby.
**wield** (wēld), *v.t.* **1a** to hold and use; manage; control: *to wield a hammer. A writer wields the pen. The people wield the power in a democracy.* **2** *Obsolete.* to govern; command. [Middle English *welden,* Old English *weldan*] —**wield′a|ble,** *adj.* —**wield′er,** *n.*
**wield|y** (wēl′dē), *adj.,* **wield|i|er, wield|i|est.** easily controlled or handled; manageable. [< *wield* + *-y*[1]; later, taken as back formation < *unwieldy*]
**wie|ner** (wē′nər), *n.* = frankfurter. [American English, short for *wienerwurst*]
▶ In popular usage, as on the signs in butchers' windows, the spelling *weiner* is not uncommon.
**wiener roast,** an informal, usually outdoor, party at which wieners are roasted.
**Wie|ner schnitzel** (vē′nər), a breaded veal cutlet, served with or without a garnish. [< German *Wiener Schnitzel* Viennese cutlet]
**wie|ner|wurst** (wē′nər wėrst′), *n. U.S.* **1** a frankfurter. **2** a Vienna sausage. [American English < German *Wiener Würstchen* Viennese sausages]
**wie|nie** (wē′nē), *n. U.S. Informal.* a wiener; frankfurter.
**wife** (wīf), *n., pl.* **wives. 1** a woman who has a husband; married woman. **2** *Archaic or Dialect.* a woman.
**take to wife,** to marry: *James had ... taken to wife the princess Mary of Modena* (Macaulay).
[Old English *wīf* woman, wife]
**wife|dom** (wīf′dəm), *n.* = wifehood.
**wife|hood** (wīf′hu̇d), *n.* the condition or time of being a wife.
**wife|less** (wīf′lis), *adj.* without a wife; unmarried. —**wife′less|ness,** *n.*
**wife|like** (wīf′līk′), *adj., adv.* —***adj.*** like that of a wife; wifely.
—***adv.*** in the manner of a wife.
**wife|ly** (wīf′lē), *adj.,* **-li|er, -li|est.** of a wife; like a wife; suitable for a wife. —**wife′li|ness,** *n.*
**wig** (wig), *n., v.,* **wigged, wig|ging.** —***n.* 1** an artificial covering of hair for the head. Women often wear wigs over their real hair for beauty or fashion. In former times men wore wigs over their real hair, and English judges and lawyers still wear them in court. *The bald man wore a wig.* **SYN**: peruke. **2** *U.S. Slang.* **a** a person's hair. **b** *Figurative.* the head or mind: *a big wig.*
—***v.t.* 1** to supply with, or cover with, a wig or wigs. **2** *Slang or Informal.* to rebuke; scold: *The teacher wigged him for not paying attention.* **3** *U.S. Slang.* to make excited or enthusiastic: *He used to be real wigged on Zen* (New Yorker).
—***v.i.*** *U.S. Slang.* to get excited or enthusiastic; flip: *teen-agers wigging over a rock music group.*
[short for *periwig*]
**wig|an** (wig′ən), *n.* a stout calico resembling canvas, used for stiffening parts of garments. [< *Wigan,* a city in Lancashire, England, where it was made originally]
**wig|eon** (wij′ən), *n.* = widgeon.
**wigged** (wigd), *adj.* wearing a wig.
**wig|ger|y** (wig′ər ē), *n., pl.* **-ger|ies. 1a** wigs or false hair collectively. **b** = wig. **2** the practice of wearing a wig. **3** *Figurative.* empty formality; red tape: *some wisdom amid ... mountains of wiggeries and folly* (Thomas Carlyle).
**wig|ging** (wig′ing), *n. Slang or Informal.* a rebuke; reprimand; scolding: *a well-deserved wigging.* [< *wig,* in slang sense of "a scolding" + *-ing*[1]]
**wig|gle** (wig′əl), *v.,* **-gled, -gling,** *n.* —***v.i.*** to move with short, quick movements from side to side; wriggle: *The restless child wiggled in his chair.* **SYN**: squirm, twist. —***v.t.*** to move with short, quick movements from side to side: *to wiggle a trunk across the floor.*
—***n.* 1** a wiggling movement. **2** fish or shellfish served in a white sauce with peas: *shrimp wiggle.*
[perhaps < Dutch, or Flemish *wiggelen* (frequentative) < *wiegen* to rock]
**wig|gler** (wig′lər), *n.* **1** a person or thing that wiggles. **2** the larva of a mosquito. **3** a fishing lure used in casting that zigzags across the water when drawn in.
**wig|gly** (wig′lē), *adj.,* **-gli|er, -gli|est. 1** wiggling. **2** wavy: *editorials ... printed in bold type surrounded by a wiggly border* (Sinclair Lewis).
**wig|gy** (wig′ē), *adj.,* **wig|gi|er, wig|gi|est. 1** wearing a wig; wigged. **2** *Figurative.* **a** extremely grave or formal. **b** *Slang.* very stylish; classy.
**wight**[1] (wīt), *n.* **1** *Archaic.* a human being; person. **2** *Obsolete.* any living being; creature. [Old English *wiht* any living creature. Compare etym. under **whit.**]
**wight**[2] (wīt), *adj. Archaic.* **1** strong and courageous; valiant. **2a** exercising strength; robust; stalwart. **b** powerful in effect; violent. **3** moving briskly or rapidly; nimble; swift. [Middle English *wihte* < Scandinavian (compare Old Icelandic *vīgt* in self-defense; neuter *vīgr* of fighting age]
**wig|let** (wig′lit), *n.* a small hairpiece, especially one added to a woman's hair.
**wig|mak|er** (wig′mā′kər), *n.* a person who makes or sells wigs.
**wig|wag** (wig′wag′), *v.,* **-wagged, -wag|ging,** *n.* —***v.t., v.i.* 1** to move to and fro; wag. **2** to signal by waving or holding a single flag or light in various positions according to a code. The three motions used in wigwagging represent a dot, a dash, and the end of a word or paragraph.
—***n.* 1** the act or system of signaling by wigwagging. **2** the message signaled.
[probably varied reduplication of *wag*[1]; perhaps influenced by *wiggle*] —**wig′wag′ger,** *n.*
***wig|wam** (wig′wom, -wôm), *n.* **1a** a hut used especially by the Algonkian Indians of the eastern woodlands of North America, made of bark, mats, or skins laid over a frame of poles: *In a strict sense, a wigwam is a dome-shaped wooden American Indian house, the skin structures ... being tepees* (New York Times). **b** any hut of poles covered with bark, mats, or skins, made by North American Indians, such as the tepee. **2** *U.S. Obsolete.* a large structure used for political conventions. [American English < Algonkian (compare Abnaki *wigwâm* a dwelling)]

definition 1a

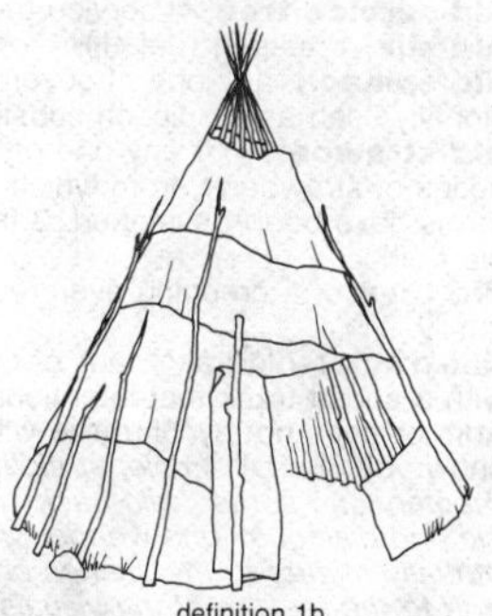

definition 1b

***wigwam**
definitions 1a, 1b

**Wig|wam** (wig′wom, -wôm), *n.* = Tammany Hall.
**Wiik|ite** (vē′kīt), *n.* a brownish-black or yellow mineral similar to euxenite found in Finland. It is a source of scandium. [< F. J. *Wiik,* a Finnish mineralogist + *-ite*[1]]
**wik|i|up** (wik′ē up′), *n.* = wickiup.
**wi|ki|wi|ki** (wē′kē wē′kē), *adv. Hawaiian.* quickly.
**wi|la|ya** (wi lä′yə), *n., pl.* **-yas, -yat.** a military district or zone in northern Africa. Also, **willaya.** [< Arabic *wilāya* < *waliya* administer]
**wil|co** (wil′kō), *interj.* will comply (used in radio transmission).
**wild** (wīld), *adj., n., adv.* —***adj.* 1** living or growing in the forests or fields; not tamed; not cultivated: *The tiger is a wild animal. The daisy is a wild flower.* **SYN**: undomesticated. **2** produced or yielded naturally, without the aid of man; uncultivated: *wild honey, wild cherries.* **3** with no people living in it; waste; desolate; desert: *a wild field, wild hills. Airplanes now fly from California to Europe over the wild region of the far north.* **SYN**: uninhabited. **4a** not civilized; savage: *He is reading about the wild tribes of ancient times in Europe.* **SYN**: barbarous. **b** fierce; ferocious; destructive: *a wild bull.* **5** *Figurative.* **a** not checked; not restrained: *a wild rush for the ball. The children wild in the streets* (Dickens). **b** resisting control or restraint; unruly or insubordinate; wayward or self-willed: *He has turned out very wild* (Jane Austen). **c** dissolute; dissipated: licentious: *wild living, to live a wild life. The wildest of libertines* (Macaulay). **6** *Figurative.* not in proper control or order: *wild hair.* **7** *Figurative.* boisterous: *wild laughter, wild shouts, wild boys.* **8** violently excited; frantic: *The injured animal was wild with rage.* **9a** violent: *a wild storm, wild winds. Wild waves came roaring onto the shore.* **b** out of one's wits; distracted; mad: *driven almost wild with pain.* **c** showing distraction or madness: *wild eyes.* **10** *Figurative.* **a** rash; crazy: *wild schemes.* **SYN**: reckless. **b** absurdly improbable; fantastic: *wild stories of riches.* **11** *Informal.* very eager: *wild to go home.* **SYN**: enthusiastic, excited. **12** *Figurative.* far from the mark: *a wild shot, a wild throw.* **13** *Figurative.* **a** unconventional, barbaric, or fanciful: *a wild tune or song.* **b** strange or fantastic in appearance: *a wild shape in the mist* (Elizabeth Barrett Browning). **14** of arbitrary denomination or suit: *In this card game deuces are wild.*
—***n.*** an uncultivated or desolate region or tract; waste; desert.
—***adv.*** in a wild manner; to a wild degree.
**run wild,** to live or grow without restraint: *Of all countries ... where the horse runs wild, Arabia produces the most beautiful breed* (Oliver Goldsmith). *The boy had run wild since his young mother's death* (Longman's Magazine).
**wild and woolly,** *U.S.* rough and uncivilized like the American West during frontier times; rough-and-tumble: *Clarke is a wild and woolly county, where bobcats roam the streets of its largest community* (Clarke County Democrat).
**wilds,** wild country: *Huge Forests ... and sandy perilous wilds* (Milton).
[Old English *wilde* in the natural state; undomesticated] —**wild′ly,** *adv.* —**wild′ness,** *n.*
**wild allspice,** = spicebush.
**wild anemone,** = pasqueflower.
**wild bergamot,** a plant of the mint family that grows in dry areas of the eastern United States. It has large pinkish-purple flowers.
**wild boar,** a wild hog of Europe, central and southwestern Asia, and northern Africa, generally considered as the ancestor of the domestic hog.
**wild brier, 1** = dog rose. **2** = sweetbrier. **3** any other uncultivated brier.
**wild canary, 1** = goldfinch. **2** = yellow warbler.
**wild-card** (wīld′kärd′), *adj.* **1** not affiliated, assigned, or limited; unrestricted: *at least one wild-card candidate who won't go through the primaries* (Harper's). *wild-card CD's ... sold to savers ... at whatever rate the issuer chooses to pay* (Time). **2** *U.S.* (of a sports team) qualifying for championship play-offs by winning an arbitrary play-off among second-place teams: *Cincinnati was the American Conference wild-card team, finishing 11-3 in the same conference with defending league champion Pittsburgh, which was 12-2* (Kevin M. Lamb).
**wild carrot,** a common weed of the parsley family, a native of Europe, Asia, and Africa, having a thin, woody, acrid root and clusters of lacy, white flowers; Queen Anne's lace. It is the origin of the cultivated carrot.
**wild|cat** (wīld′kat′), *n., adj., v.,* **-cat|ted, -cat|ting.** —***n.* 1** a wild animal like a common cat, but larger. The lynx, bobcat of North America, related cats of Europe and North Africa, or any of various servals, ocelots, and margays are wildcats. **2** *Figurative.* a fierce or savage person, especially a woman. **3** *Figurative.* **a** a risky or unsafe business undertaking. **b** a well drilled for oil or gas in a region where none has been found before. **4** *U.S. Informal.* a locomotive and its tender operating without other cars.
—***adj.* 1** not safe; wild; reckless: *a wildcat company. He lost all of his money by investing in wildcat stocks.* **2** of or denoting an illicit business or enterprise or its products. **3** running without control or without a schedule: *a wildcat engine.* **4** not authorized by proper union officials; precipitated by small groups or local unions: *a wildcat strike.*
—***v.t., v.i.*** to drill wells in regions not known to contain oil or gas. —**wild′cat′ter,** *n.*
**wildcat bank,** *U.S.* a bank that issued notes although it possessed little or no capital, before the passage of the National Bank Act of 1863.
**wild celery,** eelgrass, a freshwater plant growing in shallow ponds.
**wild chervil,** a variety of chervil that grows as a weed in parts of North America.
**wild columbine,** a columbine that bears red and yellow nodding flowers on rigid, slender stems.
**wild crocus,** = pasqueflower.
**wil|de|beest** (wil′də bēst′), *n., pl.* **-beests** or (*collectively*) **-beest.** = gnu. [< Afrikaans *wildebeest* wild beast]
**wil|der** (wil′dər), *Poetic or Archaic.* —***v.t.*** to bewilder. —***v.i.*** to lose one's way; be perplexed. [apparently < *wilderness,* on analogy of *wander.* Compare Middle Dutch *verwilderen.*]
**wil|der|ness** (wil′dər nis), *n.* **1a** a wild place; region with no people living in it. **SYN**: See syn. under **desert**[1]. **b** a waste or desolate region of any kind, such as the open sea or the arctic regions. **2** *Figurative.* a bewildering mass or collection: *a wilderness of streets.* **3** *Obsolete.* uncultivated condition; wildness. [Middle English *wildernesse*

**Pronunciation Key:** hat, āge, cãre, fär; let, ēqual, tėrm; it, īce; hot, ōpen, ôrder; **oi**l, **ou**t; cup, pu̇t, rüle; **ch**ild; lo**ng**; **th**in; **ŧh**en; **zh**, measure; **ə** represents **a** in about, **e** in taken, **i** in pencil, **o** in lemon, **u** in circus.

< *wilderne* wild (< Old English *wildēoren* like wild beasts < *wilde* wild + *dēor* animal) + *-ness* -ness]

**wilderness area**, *U.S.* an area of virgin land 100,000 acres or more in extent, set apart by law as a national park.

**wild-eyed** (wīld′īd′), *adj.* **1** having wild eyes; staring wildly or angrily. **2** *Figurative.* senseless; irrational: *wild-eyed bigots, wild-eyed notions.*

**wild fig**, = caprifig.

**wild|fire** (wīld′fīr′), *n.* **1** any one of certain substances easily set on fire whose flames could not be put out with water, formerly used in warfare. **2** any fire hard to put out. **3** sheet lightning without audible thunder; heat lightning. **4** = will-o'-the-wisp. **5** any one of various inflammatory, eruptive diseases, especially of sheep. **6** a bacterial wilt of tobacco plants. **7** *Obsolete.* erysipelas or a similar inflammatory, eruptive disease. **8** *Obsolete.* furious or destructive fire; conflagration.

**like wildfire**, very rapidly: *The news spread like wildfire. We can't keep up with the demand .... Sales are growing like wildfire* (Wall Street Journal).

**wild flax**, **1** = gold-of-pleasure. **2** = toadflax.

**wild flower**, or **wild|flow|er** (wīld′flou′ər), *n.* **1** any uncultivated flowering plant. **2** the flower of such a plant.

**wild fowl**, **1** birds ordinarily hunted, such as wild ducks or geese, partridges, quails, and pheasants. **2** any such bird.

**wild-fowl|er** (wīld′fou′lər), *n.* a hunter of wild fowl: *Wild-fowlers will find much to interest them in the display of duck decoys, which is believed to be one of the finest in existence* (New York Times).

**wild-fowl|ing** (wīld′fou′ling), *n.* the hunting of wild fowl for sport.

**wild ginger**, an aromatic herb of the birthwort family with heart-shaped leaves, common in moist areas of temperate North America; false coltsfoot.

**wild goose**, any undomesticated goose, such as the graylag of Great Britain or the Canada goose of North America.

**wild-goose chase** (wīld′güs′), **1** a useless search or attempt; foolish or hopeless quest. **2** an erratic course taken or led by one person (or thing) and followed (or that may be followed) by another.

**wild honeysuckle**, **1** any one of several uncultivated varieties of honeysuckle. **2** = pinxter flower.

**wild horse**, **1** an untamed horse. **2** a domestic horse run wild, or a wild descendant of such a horse.

**wild hyacinth**, **1** a plant, a camass, of eastern North America, bearing white or blue flowers. **2** = bluebell.

**wild indigo**, any one of a group of American perennial plants of the pea family, especially a yellow-flowered species whose root is used as a purgative; false indigo.

**wild|ing** (wīl′ding), *n., adj.* —*n.* **1** a plant or animal that is wild or grows without cultivation. **2a** a wild crab-apple tree. **b** its fruit. **3** a plant once cultivated but now growing wild; escape. **4** *Figurative.* any person or thing that deviates from or refuses to conform with the multitude or norm of its type. —*adj.* growing wild; wild.

**wild|ish** (wīl′dish), *adj.* somewhat wild.

**wild|land** (wīld′land′), *n.* land in its natural state; uncultivated land.

**wild leek**, = ramp³.

**wild lettuce**, any uncultivated species of lettuce growing as a weed, especially a prickly-stemmed European species with yellow flower heads.

**wild|life** (wīld′līf′), *n., adj.* —*n.* animals and plants in the natural state, especially as they exist in national parks or other lands in the public domain, under government programs of conservation; wild animals: *The forest ranger is familiar with most of the wildlife of his state. Widespread use of DDT in strong concentrations endangers human beings as well as wildlife* (Science News Letter).

—*adj.* of or for wildlife: *wildlife conservation.*

**wild|lif|er** (wīld′lī′fər), *n.* a person who strongly advocates the protection of wildlife.

**wild|ling** (wīld′ling), *n.* a wild plant or animal.

**wild madder**, **1** = madder (def. 1). **2** either of two bedstraws, especially the white bedstraw.

**wild mandrake**, = May apple.

**wild morning-glory**, = hedge bindweed.

**wild mustard**, = charlock.

**wild oats**, **1** Also, **wild oat**. any one of a group of grasses growing as weeds in meadows and other open areas, especially a tall grass resembling the cultivated oat. **2** *Figurative.* youthful dissipation.

**sow one's wild oats**, to indulge in youthful dissipation before settling down in life: *A young man must sow his wild oats and reform* (Frederick W. Robertson).

**wild olive**, **1** any one of various trees resembling the olive or bearing similar fruit. **2** the wild variety of the cultivated olive, having more or less thorny branches and small, worthless fruit; oleaster.

**wild pansy**, the common pansy, occurring as a weed, especially in grainfields and other open areas, with small flowers compounded of purple, yellow, and white; heartsease; Johnny-jump-up; love-in-idleness.

**wild parsley**, any one of several weeds of the parsley family, with foliage like that of the parsley.

**wild parsnip**, a weed of the parsley family, found in Europe and America, from which the cultivated parsnip originated.

**wild peach**, any one of a group of American trees or shrubs of the rose family, especially the cherry laurel.

**wild pink**, a catchfly or campion of eastern North America, with notched petals and white or pink flowers.

**wild pitch**, *Baseball.* a ball pitched out of control that the catcher cannot stop and that results in a base runner advancing.

**wild rice**, a North American aquatic grass, whose grain is used for food.

**wild rose**, any one of various roses that grow wild, such as the sweetbrier and dog rose.

**wild rubber**, rubber from trees growing wild, especially from a Brazilian species.

**wild rye**, any one of a group of grasses that resemble rye.

**wilds** (wīldz), *n.pl.* See under **wild**.

**wild sage**, = red sage.

**wild senna**, a plant growing in the eastern United States that is three or four feet high, has yellow flowers, and whose dried leaves are used as a laxative.

**wild service tree**, = service tree.

**wild silk**, = tussah (def. 1).

**wild spinach**, any one of several plants occasionally used as a spinach substitute.

**wild strawberry**, **1** any one of various wild varieties of strawberry, from which the cultivated forms have been developed. **2** their reddish, edible fruit.

**wild thyme**, a creeping evergreen of the mint family.

**wild-track** (wīld′trak′), *adj.* of or having to do with a sound track that intentionally diverges from or does not synchronize with the action shown on film: *A simple, straightforward commentary and some "wild-track" recording of music and dialogue* (*one wonders if the dialogue actually relates to the scenes one is witnessing*) *add to the realism of the visuals* (New Scientist).

**wild turkey**, any one of various nondomesticated American turkeys, especially one living in the woodlands of the eastern and southern United States and Mexico, which closely resembles the common domestic turkey that was developed from it.

**wild-type** (wīld′tīp′), *adj. Genetics.* of or belonging to the normal strain or ordinary type of an organism, as distinguished from a mutant strain or type: *a wild-type gene, a wild-type virus.*

**wild vanilla**, a perennial composite herb of the southeastern United States, whose leaves smell like vanilla.

**wild|wa|ter** (wīld′wôt′ər, -wot′-), *n.* water with strong currents; turbulent part of a stream: *a canoeing race in wildwater.*

**wild West** or **Wild West**, the western United States during pioneer days.

**wild|wood** (wīld′wu̇d′), *n.* trees growing in their natural state; forest.

**wild yam**, any one of several yams growing wild.

**wile** (wīl), *n., v.,* **wiled, wil|ing.** —*n.* **1** a trick to deceive; cunning way; ruse; stratagem: *The witch by her wiles persuaded the prince to go with her.* **2** subtle trickery; slyness; craftiness.

—*v.t.* to coax; lure; entice: *The sunshine wiled me from my work.*

**wile away**, to while away; pass easily or pleasantly: *I was reading a book tonight, to wile the time away* (Dickens).

[Middle English *wil* wile, trick. Ultimately related to **guile**.]

**wil|ful** (wil′fəl), *adj.* = willful. —**wil′ful|ness**, *n.*

**wil|ful|ly** (wil′fə lē), *adv.* = willfully.

**wil|ga** (wil′gə), *n.* an Australian tree of the rue family, yielding a hard, aromatic wood. [< a native Australian name]

**will¹** (wil; *unstressed* wəl), *v., pres. indic. sing., 1st and 3rd pers.* **will**, *2nd* **will** or (*Archaic*) **wilt**, *3rd* **will**, *pl.* **will**; *past tense sing. 1st and 3rd pers.* **would**, *2nd* **would** or (*Archaic*) **wouldst**, *pl.* **would**; *pp.* (*Obsolete*) **would** or **wold** (wōld); *imperative and infinitive lacking.*

—***auxiliary v.*** (with infinitive without *to*): **1** am going to; is going to; are going to: *They will come tomorrow.* **2** am willing to; is willing to; are willing to: *I will go if you do. People will read what is well written.* **3** be able to; can; may: *This pail will hold four gallons. One hour will be enough time to finish the work.* **4** must: *Don't argue with me; you will do it at once!* **5** do often or usually: *She will read for hours at a time.*

—***v.t., v.i.*** to wish, desire, want, or be willing: *We cannot always do as we will.*

[Old English *willan*]

▶ **will, shall**. The usage of *will* and *shall* is not uniform in English, differing mainly in formal English (where the rules of prescriptive grammarians are followed more or less consistently) and in informal English (where these rules are virtually ignored).

**1** *Formal usage.* **a** *Simple future. Shall* is used in the first person, *will* in the second and third:
First person: *I shall ask, we shall ask.*
Second person: *you will ask, you will ask.*
Third person: *he, she will ask, they will ask.*
In questions, *shall* is used in the first person, *will* in the third, and *shall* in the second, provided the expected answer contains *shall: Shall you go?*
Expected answer: *I shall* (not *will*) *go.*

**b** *Determination or obligation.* In declarative sentences, the use of *shall* and *will* is the reverse of that noted above:
First person: *I will ask, we will ask.*
Second person: *you shall ask, you shall ask.*
Third person: *he, she shall ask, they shall ask.*

**2** *Informal usage.* **a** *Simple future.* In writing as well as in speech, the prevailing use in the United States, and in many other parts of the English-speaking world, is *will* in all persons: *I will ask, you will ask, he will ask, ...* In questions, *shall* is usual in the first person, and *will* in the *second* and *third,* but practice is not consistent: *Shall I go? Will you go? What will he do with it?* In the negative, *won't,* rather than *shan't,* is usual: *Won't I look funny in that? What won't he think of next?* In contractions, *'ll* is used for *shall* and *will* (*I'll, you'll, he'll*). *Won't* is used for *will not* and *shan't* for *shall not.*

**b** *Determination or obligation.* In spoken English, determination is expressed by stressing *shall* (or *will*). In written English, there is a growing tendency to express it by using *shall* in all persons: *I, you, he, she, we, you, they shall ask.*

**will²** (wil), *n., v.,* **willed, will|ing.** —*n.* **1** the power of the mind to decide and do; deliberate control over thought and action: *A good leader must have a strong will. The will of man is by his reason swayed* (Shakespeare). **2** the act of choosing to do something, sometimes including also all deliberation that precedes making the choice; volition: *He strove to speak, but no voice answered his will* (George P. R. James). **3** purpose; determination: *a will to live, a will to win.* **SYN**: resolution, decision. **4** a wish; desire: *Thy will be done* (Lord's Prayer). *This boundless will to please* (A. E. Housman). **SYN**: inclination, preference, choice. **5** an order, command, or decree: *My will is law* (Tennyson). **6** what is chosen to be done; (one's or its) pleasure: *Leaving misrule and violence to work their will among men* (John Ruskin). **7a** a legal statement of a person's wishes about what shall be done with his property after he is dead. **b** the written document containing such a statement. **c** (formerly) a statement of a person's wishes regarding the disposal of his real property after his death, his personal property being disposed of by testament. **8** feeling toward another: *Most people feel good will toward their friends and ill will toward their enemies.* **9** *Obsolete.* carnal desire; lust. [Old English *will, willa*]

—*v.t.* **1** to decide by using the power of the mind; use the will: *She willed to keep awake.* **2** to determine; decide: *Fate has willed it otherwise.* **SYN**: purpose, intend. **3** to influence or try to influence by deliberate control over thought and action, as by hypnotism: *She willed the person in front of her to turn around.* **4** to give or dispose of by a will: *He willed all his property to his two daughters.* **SYN**: bequeath. **5** *Archaic.* to wish; desire. **6** *Archaic.* to request or entreat; command or decree.

—*v.i.* to use the will.

**against one's will**, unwillingly; in opposition to one's own inclination or to another's wish: *to force a child to eat against his will. He that complies against his will is of his own opinion still* (Samuel Butler).

**at will**, whenever or wherever one wishes: *to allow a President, in case of disability, to delegate whatever powers he thinks necessary to the Vice-President, and to terminate this voluntary delegation of power at will* (Newsweek).

**do the will of**, to obey: *to do the will of one's parents.*

**with a will**, with energy and determination: *He got to work with a will and cleaned out the attic.*

[Old English *willian* < *will,* noun] —**will′er**, *n.*

**will|a|ble** (wil′ə bəl), *adj.* that can be willed.

**wil|la|ya** (wi lä′yə), *n.* = wilaya.

**-willed**, *combining form.* having a ____ will: *Strong-willed = having a strong will.*
**wil|lem|ite** (wil′ə mīt), *n.* a mineral, a silicate of zinc, found in masses or hexagonal prisms of various colors from light greenish-yellow to red and black. It is a minor zinc ore. *Formula:* $Zn_2SiO_4$ [< German *Willemit* < *Willem I* William I, 1772-1843, king of the Netherlands + *-it* -ite[1]]
**wil|let** (wil′it), *n., pl.* **-lets** or (*collectively*) **-let.** a large, grayish North American wading bird, related to the snipes and sandpipers, that reveals a striking black-and-white pattern on the wings when in flight; duck snipe. [American English; imitative of its call]
**will|ful** (wil′fəl), *adj.* **1** wanting or taking one's own way; stubborn: *The willful child would not eat his supper.* **SYN**: obstinate, headstrong, perverse. **2** done on purpose; intended: *a willful murder, willful waste.* **SYN**: deliberate, intentional. Also, **wilful.** [< *will*[2] + *-ful*] — **will′ful|ness**, *n.*
**will|ful|ly** (wil′fə lē), *adv.* **1** by choice; voluntarily. **2** by design; intentionally. **3** selfishly; perversely; obstinately; stubbornly. Also, **wilfully.**
**wil|lies** (wil′ēz), *n.pl. Informal.* a spell of nervousness: *Bert gives me the willies the way he's always lookin' for trouble* (Jack London). [origin unknown]
**will|ing** (wil′ing), *adj.* **1** ready; consenting: *He is willing to wait.* **SYN**: disposed, inclined. **2** cheerfully ready: *a willing worker.* **3** freely done or offered; voluntary: *willing obedience.* **4** of, having to do with, or using the will; volitional. — **will′ing|ly**, *adv.* — **will′ing|ness**, *n.*
**wil|li|waw** (wil′ē wô), *n.* **1** *Especially Nautical.* a sudden, violent gust of wind moving down to the sea from mountains along the coast, such as one into the fiords of Tierra del Fuego or into the Strait of Magellan. **2** *Figurative.* any agitated state of affairs; storm; tempest; squall: *The President in press conference tried to head off a williwaw by insisting that Glennan's move was only part of a "study" in which the President himself would make the final ruling* (Time). [origin unknown]
**will-less** (wil′lis), *adj.* **1** lacking will or will power. **2** = involuntary.
**will-o'-the-wisp** (wil′ə ᴛʜə wisp′), *n.* **1** a flickering light appearing at night over marshy places; ignis fatuus; jack-o'-lantern. It is thought to be caused by combustion of marsh gas. **2** *Figurative.* a thing (rarely a person) that deceives or misleads by luring on: *Any scheme to get rich quickly is likely to be a will-o'-the-wisp. Through what extraordinary labyrinths this Love, this will-o'-the-wisp, guides his votaries* (Scott). [earlier *Will with the wisp*, apparently < *Will*, short for *William*, a proper name]
**will-o'-the-wisp|ish** (wil′ə ᴛʜə wis′pish), *adj.* of the nature of a will-o'-the-wisp.
**wil|low**[1] (wil′ō), *n., adj.* — *n.* **1** a tree or shrub with tough, slender branches and long, narrow leaves, such as the weeping willow. There are several kinds. The branches of most willows bend easily and are used to make furniture and baskets. Willows are widely distributed in temperate and cold regions. **2** the wood of any of these trees. **3** something made of willow, such as a cricket bat.
— *adj.* of or having to do with willow; made of the wood of the willow.
**wear the willow**, to be lovelorn: *You are quite wrong ... in supposing that I have any call ... to wear the willow* (Richard Blackmore).
[Middle English *wilwe*, variant of *wilghe*, Old English *welig*] — **wil′low|like′**, *adj.*
**wil|low**[2] (wil′ō), *n., v.* — *n.* a revolving cylindrical machine with spikes inside, used for opening and cleaning wool, cotton, and other fibers.
— *v.t.* to put (wool, cotton, and other fibers) through a willow.
[variant of *willy*]
**wil|low|er** (wil′ō ər), *n.* **1** a person or thing that willows. **2** = willow[2]. [< *willow*[2] + *-er*[1]]
**willow family**, a group of dicotyledonous shrubs and trees, bearing small flowers in aments or catkins. The family includes the willows and poplars.
**willow herb**, **1** any one of a genus of plants of the evening-primrose family that grow in moist places, and have long, narrow, willowlike leaves and long clusters of purple or white flowers; rosebay. **2** = purple loosestrife.
**willow oak**, an oak found in the eastern United States, having narrow, entire leaves resembling those of the willow.
**willow pattern**, a pattern of domestic crockery in blue, originally designed by Thomas Turner in the late 1700's, having willow trees as a prominent feature.
**willow ptarmigan**, a ptarmigan of arctic regions with brown body, white wings, and black tail. In winter the brown plumage becomes white.
**willow warbler**, a small woodland bird of Europe and the British Isles, about five inches long, greenish above, whitish below. It is related to the chiffchaff.
**willow ware**, crockery ware of a willow pattern.
**willow wren**, = willow warbler.
**wil|low|y** (wil′ō ē), *adj.* **1** like a willow; slender; supple; graceful. **SYN**: lithe, lissome. **2** having many willows.
**will|pow|er** (wil′pou′ər), *n.* strength of will; firmness: [*She*] *keeps her trim figure with lots of walking and willpower* (New York Times).
**will to power**, the drive to gain power and control, especially self-control, which, according to the philosophy of Friedrich Nietzsche, motivates all human behavior but is developed in its highest form in the superman.
**wil|ly** (wil′ē), *n., pl.* **-lies**, *v.,* **-lied, -ly|ing.** — *n.* = willow[2]. — *v.t.* = willow[2]. [Middle English *wile*, Old English *wilige* < *welig* willow[1]]
**wil|ly-nil|ly** (wil′ē nil′ē), *adv., adj.* — *adv.* **1** willingly or not; with or against one's wishes. **2** in a disordered manner; helter-skelter: *Books were piled willy-nilly in the attic.*
— *adj.* **1** undecided; vacillating. **2** that is such, or that takes place, whether one wishes or not: *a willy-nilly spinster; a willy-nilly current of sensations* (Tennyson).
[< early phrase *will I* (*he, ye*), *nill I* (*he, ye*); *nill* not will, Old English *nyllan* < *ne* not + *willan* will]
**wil|ly-wil|ly** (wil′ē wil′ē), *n., pl.* **-lies.** (in Australia) a violent windstorm or rainstorm. [perhaps < a native name]
**Wilms's tumor** (vilm′ziz), a painless tumor in the kidneys of very young children. [< Max *Wilms*, 1867-1918, a German surgeon, who described it]
**Wil|son chamber** or **Wilson cloud chamber** (wil′sən), a type of cloud chamber. [< C. T. R. *Wilson*, 1869-1959, a British physicist, who invented it]
**Wil|so|ni|an** (wil sō′nē ən), *adj.* of or having to do with Woodrow Wilson (1856-1924) or his policies or principles: *Wilsonian diplomacy, Wilsonian idealism.*
**Wil|so|ni|an|ism** (wil sō′nē ə niz′əm), *n.* the political doctrines or practices of Woodrow Wilson.
**Wil|son's bird of paradise** (wil′sənz), a bird of paradise with a scarlet back and a moss-green breast. It has a tuft of yellow feathers on the back of its neck that can be raised to form a halo. [< Alexander *Wilson*, 1766-1813, an American ornithologist]
**Wilson's disease**, a hereditary, degenerative disease in which a deficiency of ceruloplasmin causes copper to accumulate in the liver, brain, and other tissues; hepaticolenticular degeneration. [< Samuel A. K. *Wilson*, 1878-1937, an English neurologist]
**Wilson's petrel**, a petrel of the Antarctic and the Atlantic Ocean, black with a patch of white on the rump. [< Alexander *Wilson*, 1766-1813, an American ornithologist]
**Wilson's phalarope**, a phalarope that nests in central North America and winters in South America.
**Wilson's plover**, a brown and white plover of the southeastern United States with a black band across the breast.
**Wilson's snipe**, the American snipe.
**Wilson's thrush**, = veery.
**Wilson's warbler**, a small yellow and olive-green, black-capped warbler of North America.
**wilt**[1] (wilt), *v.i.* **1** to become limp and drooping; wither. **2** to lose strength, vigor, assurance, or determination. — *v.t.* to cause to wilt.
[variant of obsolete *welt*, alteration of *welk* to wither. Compare Middle Dutch *welken.*]
**wilt**[2] (wilt), *v. Archaic.* second person singular present of **will**[1]; will. "Thou wilt" means "you will."
**wilt**[3] (wilt), *n.* **1** Also, **wilt disease. a** any one of various fungous or bacterial plant diseases, characterized by the wilting of leaves and withering and drying out of the parts of the plant above the soil. Wilt is generally caused by interference with the passage of water through the plant. **b** an infectious disease of various caterpillars, which causes their bodies to liquefy. **2** the act of wilting. [special use of *wilt*[1]]
**Wil|ton** (wil′tən), *n.,* or **Wilton carpet** or **rug**, a kind of carpet or rug resembling Brussels carpet in weave but having the loops cut so as to produce a velvety surface. [< *Wilton*, a town in Wiltshire, England, where such carpets were made]
**Wilt|shire** (wilt′shir, -shər), *n.* **1** any one of an English breed of pure white sheep having long, spiraling horns. **2** = Wiltshire cheese. [< *Wiltshire*, a county in England]
**Wiltshire cheese**, a kind of Cheddar cheese with a sharp flavor, somewhat similar to Derby cheese.
**wil|y** (wī′lē), *adj.,* **wil|i|er, wil|i|est.** using subtle tricks to deceive; tricky; crafty; cunning; sly: *a wily thief, wily schemes. The wily fox got away. The wily subtleties and reflexes of man's thoughts* (Milton). **SYN**: artful, subtle, designing, insidious. [< *wil*(e) + *-y*[1]] — **wil′i|ly**, *adv.* — **wil′i|ness**, *n.*
**wim|ble** (wim′bəl), *n., v.,* **-bled, -bling.** — *n.* a tool for boring: **a** = gimlet. **b** = auger. **c** = brace and bit. **d** an instrument for boring in soft ground, or for extracting rubbish from a bore hole in mining.
— *v.t. Dialect.* to pierce with or as with a wimble; make (a hole) with a wimble.
[perhaps < Anglo-French *wimbel*, Old French *guimbel* < Middle Low German *wemel.* Compare etym. under **gimlet**[1].]
***wim|ple** (wim′pəl), *n., v.,* **-pled, -pling.** — *n.* **1** a cloth for the head arranged in folds about the head, cheeks, chin, and neck, worn by some nuns and formerly by other women. **2** *Archaic or Dialect.* **a** a fold or wrinkle. **b** a turn, winding, or twist. **c** a ripple or rippling in a stream. **3** *Scottish.* a crafty turn or twist; wile.
— *v.t.* **1a** to cover or muffle with a wimple. **b** *Figurative.* to veil. **2** to cause to ripple. **3** *Archaic.* to lay in folds: *to wimple a veil.*
— *v.i.* **1** to ripple. **2** *Archaic.* to lie in folds. **3** *Archaic or Dialect.* to move shiftily or unsteadily.
[Old English *wimpel*]

***wimple**
definition 1

**win**[1] (win), *v.,* **won** or (*Archaic*) **wan** (won), **won, win|ning,** *n.* — *v.i.* **1** to be successful over others; get victory or success: *We all hope our team will win. The tortoise won in the end.* **2** to succeed in making or finding one's way: *The army won through to the Mediterranean ports.*
— *v.t.* **1** to get victory or success in: *He won the race.* **2** to get by effort, ability, or skill; gain: *to win fame, win a prize.* **SYN**: secure, obtain, earn, attain. **3a** to gain the favor of: *The speaker soon won his audience.* **b** to gain the affection or love of, often gradually and increasingly: *to win new friends.* **c** *Figurative.* to prevail upon; influence; persuade; induce: *She could not win him, however, to any conversation* (Jane Austen). **4** to get the love of; persuade to marry. **5** to get to; reach, often by effort; arrive at: *to win the summit of a mountain.* **6** *Especially British.* **a** to get or extract (coal or ore) by mining. **b** to sink a shaft or make an excavation so as to reach (a vein or seam) and prepare it for working. **7** *Metallurgy.* to obtain (metal or other substance) from ore.
— *n.* **1** *Informal.* **a** the act or fact of winning; success; victory: *We had five wins and no defeats. It was our team's eighth win since the season began.* **b** Often, **wins.** gains; winnings: *His gambling losses exceeded his wins.* **2** *Sports.* first place, as in a horse race: *win, place, and show.*
**win out, a** to be victorious: *to win out over an opponent.* **b** *Figurative.* to succeed; prevail: *As long as a fellow's got some good horse sense ... he can win out in the law business* (A. McFaul).
**win over**, to prevail upon; persuade: *She has completely won Mother over to her side. The President had won over his audience again* (London Times).
[Middle English *winnen*, probably fusion of Old English *winnan* struggle (for); work (at), and *gewinnan* to win]
**win**[2] (win), *v.t.,* **winned, winned, win,** or **won, win|ning.** *Scottish.* **1** to dry (as hay, seed, turf, or wood). **2** = winnow. [perhaps < *win*[1]; influenced by *wind*[3]]
**wince**[1] (wins), *v.,* **winced, winc|ing,** *n.* — *v.i.* to draw back suddenly; flinch slightly: *I winced when the dentist's drill touched my tooth.* **SYN**: shrink, recoil.
— *n.* the act of wincing: *When he saw the wince, the dentist stopped drilling for a moment.*
[< unrecorded Anglo-French *wencir*, Old French *guencir*, and *guenchir* < Germanic (compare Old High German *winkan* move sidewards, sway)]
**wince**[2] (wins), *n.* a reel or roller placed over the division between two vats of dye in such a way that a fabric spread upon it may be lowered into either vat. [variant of *winch*[1]]

---

**Pronunciation Key:** hat, āge, cãre, fär; let, ēqual, tėrm; it, īce; hot, ōpen, ôrder; **oil**, **out**; cup, pu̇t, rüle; **ch**ild; lo**ng**; **th**in; **ᴛʜ**en; **zh**, measure; **ə** represents **a** in about, **e** in taken, **i** in pencil, **o** in lemon, **u** in circus.

**wince pits**, the vats over which a wince is placed.

***winch**[1] (winch), *n., v.* —*n.* **1** a machine for lifting or pulling, consisting of a drum around which a rope passes and a crank by which it is turned by hand or by an engine. **2** the crank of a revolving machine. **3** = wince[2]. **4** a fishing reel.
—*v.t.* to lift or pull by using a winch.
[Middle English *wynch*, Old English *wince*]
—**winch′er**, *n.*

***winch**[1] definition 1

**winch**[2] (winch), *v.i., n. Dialect.* wince; flinch.

**Win|ches|ter** (win′ches′tər, -chə stər), *n.*, or **Winchester rifle**, a kind of breechloading repeating rifle, having a tubular magazine under the barrel and a bolt operated by a lever, first made and used about 1866. [< Oliver F. *Winchester*, 1810-1880, an American manufacturer, who produced them]

**Winchester bushel**, a unit of dry measure equivalent to 2150.4 cubic inches (35.24 liters). [< *Winchester*, a city in southern England where the standard was originally deposited]

**winch|man** (winch′mən), *n., pl.* **-men.** a man who operates a winch.

**winc|ing** (win′sing), *adj.* that winces; flinching; recoiling. —**winc′ing|ly**, *adv.*

**wind**[1] (*n.* wind, *Archaic* wīnd; *v.* wind), *n., v.*, **wind|ed, wind|ing.** —*n.* **1** air in motion. The wind varies in force from a slight breeze to a strong gale. *The wind bends the branches.* **2** a strong wind; gale: *Winds blowing at ninety miles an hour toppled trees and cars. Blow, blow, thou winter wind! Thou art not so unkind As man's ingratitude* (Shakespeare). SYN: blast. **3** the direction or point of the compass from which the wind blows, especially one of the four cardinal points of the compass (the four winds). **4** air filled with some smell: *The deer caught wind of the hunter and ran off.* **5** *Figurative.* a current of air considered as driving a person or thing along, as conveying information, as striking upon a person or thing, or the like: *What wind blows you here? It's an ill wind that blows nobody good.* **6** air as used for sounding a musical instrument. **7** a wind instrument or the player on such an instrument. **8** a blast of air artificially produced, as by bellows, a fan, or a rapidly moving body: *the wind of a bullet.* **9** gas in the stomach or bowels. **10a** the power of breathing; breath: *A runner needs good wind.* **b** *Boxing Slang.* the pit of the stomach, where a blow checks the action of the diaphragm and takes away the breath. **11** *Figurative.* **a** empty, useless talk. **b** vanity; conceit.
—*v.t.* **1** to follow (an animal, person, or thing) by scent; smell. **2** to put out of breath; cause difficulty in breathing: *The fat man was winded by the climb up the steep hill.* **3** to let recover breath: *They stopped in order to wind their horses.* **4** to expose to wind or air; air.
—*v.i.* to sniff or scent game.
**before the wind**, in the direction toward which the wind is blowing: *We got before the wind to the Cape of Good Hope* (William Phillip).
**between wind and water**, **a** near the water line of a ship: *They ... had received a shot between wind and water, and the ship leaked very much* (William R. Chetwood). **b** *Figurative.* in a dangerous or vulnerable place: *The cynicism of his own reflection struck him between wind and water* (John Galsworthy).
**break wind**, to expel gas from the stomach or bowels.
**by the wind**, pointing as nearly as possible toward the direction from which the wind blows: *Having struck our sails, we did nothing but lie by the wind* (Thomas Washington).
**down (the) wind**, in the direction that the wind is blowing: *Down the wind she swims, and sails away* (William Cowper).
**get** (or **have**) **wind of**, to find out about; get a hint of: *Don't let Mother get wind of our plans to give her a surprise party. Because the police had wind of their plans for a park battle, the gangs met halfway between their homes and the park* (Harper's).
**haul on** (or **to**) **the wind**, to sail closer to the direction of the wind: *The Spanish fleet ... hauled to the wind on the larboard tack* (Horatio Nelson).
**in the eye** (or **teeth**) **of the wind**, directly agains the wind: *to sail in the eye of the wind.*
**in the wind**, happening or about to happen; impending: *There is nothing in the wind to justify fears that the "bad old days" are coming back* (Manchester Guardian Weekly).
**into the wind**, pointing toward the direction from which the wind is blowing: *You are tempted to turn into the wind and land* (Blackwood's Magazine).
**off the wind**, with the wind blowing from behind: *The Enterprise was again steered more off the wind* (Frederick Marryat).
**on the** (or **a**) **wind**, as nearly as possible in the direction from which the wind is blowing: *Clippers are fastest on the wind* (Richard Henry Dana).
**raise the wind**, *Informal.* **a** to raise money for a purpose: *Somebody, somehow will raise the wind that is needed—at least $80 millions all told* (Manchester Guardian Weekly). **b** to make a disturbance: *to raise the wind after being insulted.*
**run**(or **sail**) **close to the wind**, **a** *Nautical.* to sail with the ship pointed as nearly as possible in the direction from which the wind is blowing: *The only hope in the storm was to run close to the wind.* **b** *Figurative.* to just barely follow rules or laws: *In court he sailed so close to the wind as to risk disbarment.* **c** *Figurative.* to manage with close calculation or the utmost economy: *He realized that ... he was sailing rather close to the wind financially* (Theodore Dreiser).
**take** (or **knock**) **the wind out of one's sails**, to take away one's advantage, argument, or other good position, suddenly or unexpectedly: *Whether he can knock the wind out of the bubbling McKinley's sails remains to be seen* (London Times).
**the way the wind blows** (or **is blowing**), the tendency, turn, or condition of affairs: *Some indication of which way the wind is blowing can be seen in such new foundations as the institute of air and space law* (Sunday Times).
**to the wind**, to the point from which the wind blows: *Gascoigne went to the helm, [and] brought the boat up to the wind* (Frederick Marryat).
**twist in the wind**, to suffer in a state of uncertainty and suspense: *Everybody ... has taken it that, in fact, the Government was jolly well making you wait for the money; it was keeping you twisting in the wind, I think is the phrase* (Listener).
**up (the) wind**, with the wind blowing from in front: *Passing over the earths, he came away directly with his head up wind* (Sporting Magazine).
**winds**, **a** wind instruments, especially those in an orchestra, considered collectively. Trumpets, trombones, and French horns are brass winds. Clarinets, flutes, bassoons, and oboes are woodwinds. *The second movement begins with a slow fugue by the winds.* **b** the players on such instruments.
[Old English *wind*]
—*Syn. n.* **1 Wind, breeze** mean air in motion. **Wind** is the general word: *The wind is from the north.* **Breeze**, except as a technical term in meteorology, means a light, gentle wind, especially one that is cool or refreshing: *We nearly always have a breeze at night.*

**wind**[2] (wīnd), *v.*, **wound** or (*Archaic.*) **wind|ed, wind|ing**, *n.* —*v.i.* **1** to move this way and that; go in a crooked way; change direction; turn: *a bicycle winding through the crowded streets. A brook winds through the woods.* SYN: curve, crook, twist, bend. **2** to proceed in a roundabout or indirect manner: *to wind into power. I winded and winded ... till ... out comes the truth* (Maria Edgeworth). **3** to twist or turn around something; twine: *The vine winds around a pole.* **4** to be warped or twisted: *That board will wind.* **5** to be wound: *This clock winds easily.* **6** to move with a winding gait: *That horse winds.*
—*v.t.* **1** to fold, wrap, or place (about something): *to wind a scarf around one's neck. The mother wound her arms about the child.* **2** to cover (with something put, wrapped, or folded around): *The man's arm is wound with bandages.* **3** to roll into a ball or on a spool: *Grandma was winding yarn. Thread comes wound on spools.* **4** to make (some machine) go by turning some part of it: *to wind a clock.* **5** to haul or hoist by turning a winch, windlass, or the like. **6** to tighten the strings or pegs of (a musical instrument); tune. **7** to make (one's or its way) in a curved, crooked, or zigzagging course: *We wound our way through the crooked streets.* **8** *Figurative.* to insinuate (oneself in or into); worm: *to wind oneself into a position of importance.* **9** *Figurative.* to bend or turn at will; exercise control over.
—*n.* the act of winding; bend; turn; twist: *The road makes a wind to the south.*
**wind down**, *Informal.* **a** to reduce by degrees; bring or come gradually to an end: *to wind down space exploration. Now ... the war is supposed to be "winding down"* (New York Times). **b** *Figurative.* to relax; unwind: *to wind down tensions.*
**wind off**, to unwind: *Would you wind off some string for me? The thread winds off easily.*
**wind up**, **a** to end; settle; conclude: *The committee wound up its meeting in time for dinner.* **b** to make the swinging and twisting movements that a baseball pitcher makes just before pitching the ball: *The pitcher is winding up.* **c** to roll or coil; wind completely: *When the weight is down on the grandfather clock we have to wind it up* (Listener). **d** *Figurative.* to put into a state of tension, great strain, or intensity of feeling; excite: *Chicago exhibitors are all wound up about polypropylene* (New York Times). **e** *Informal, Figurative.* to come to a place or a circumstance: *to wind up exhausted. Emotionally unstable young people do wind up in the village* (Canadian Saturday Night).
[Old English *windan*]

**wind**[3] (wīnd, wind), *v.t., v.i.*, **wind|ed** or **wound, wind|ing.** **1** to sound by forcing the breath through; blow: *The hunter winds his horn.* **2** to blow (a blast, call, or note), as on a horn. [special use of *wind*[1]]

**wind|age** (win′dij), *n.* **1** the power of the wind to turn a missile from its course. **2** the distance that a missile is turned from its course by the wind. **3** a change in aim to compensate for windage, accomplished on a rifle by a slight lateral adjustment of the rear sight. **4** atmospheric disturbance produced by the passage of a bullet, shell, or other missile. **5** the part of a ship's surface affected by the action of wind. **6** the slight difference between the diameter of a bullet or shell, and of the bore of a gun of the same caliber, a necessary characteristic of certain smoothbore guns and rifled guns firing spherical shot.

**wind avalanche**, a mass of fine, dry snow that strong winds sweep down a mountainside.

**wind|bag** (wind′bag′), *n.* **1** *Slang.* a person who talks a great deal but does not say much. **2** the chest or body considered as a receptacle of breath (a humorous use). **3** a bag full of wind. **4** *Obsolete.* the bellows of an organ.

**wind bell** (wind), a bell or bell-like percussion instrument made of metal, glass, or ceramic, freely suspended so as to be sounded by the wind.

**wind-blown** (wind′blōn′), *adj.* **1** blown along or about by the wind. **2** cut short and brushed forward: *a wind-blown haircut.* **3** slanted or twisted in growth as a result of the prevailing winds: *wind-blown trees.*

**wind-borne** (wind′bôrn′, -bōrn′), *adj.* carried by the wind: *wind-borne seed or pollen.*

**wind|box** (wind′boks′), *n.* an airtight box which receives air under pressure from a bellows or similar source, and from which the air passes into a furnace, organ pipes, or similar apparatus.

**wind|break** (wind′brāk′), *n.* a shelter from the wind or something used to break the force of the wind. A row of trees is one kind of windbreak.

**wind|break|er** (wind′brā′kər), *n. U.S.* **1** a short sports jacket of nylon, wool, or leather, having a tight-fitting band at the waist and cuffs, used for outdoor wear. **2 Windbreaker.** a trademark for this jacket.

**wind-bro|ken** (wind′brō′kən), *adj.* (of horses) unable to breathe properly because of damage to the respiratory organs, and therefore unable to sustain hard work or move at a quick pace.

**wind burn** (wind), or **wind|burn** (wind′bėrn′), *n.* **1** a roughening or reddening of the skin caused by prolonged exposure to the wind. **2** any injury to leaves or bark caused by the wind.

**wind-burned** or **wind|burned** (wind′bėrnd′), *adj.* having a wind burn: *a wind-burned face.*

**wind|cheat|er** (wind′chē′tər), *n. Especially British.* a windbreaker (def. 1).

**wind|chest** (wind′chest′), *n.* = windbox.

**wind chill**, or **wind|chill** (wind′chil′), *n.* the combined cooling effect on the human body of air temperature and wind speed. If the air temperature is 10°F and the wind speed is 10 mph, the estimated wind chill is −9°F.

**windchill factor**, a factor determined by wind chill; chill factor.

**wind chimes**, small pieces of glass, metal, or wood, suspended to be sounded by the wind.

**wind cone** (wind), = wind sock.

**wind direction** (wind), the direction from which the wind is blowing, indicated by a weathercock.

**wind-down** (wīnd′doun′), *n.* a winding down; gradual reduction or suspension.

**wind|ed** (win′did), *adj.* **1** out of breath; breathless. **2** exposed to wind or air, especially spoiled or tainted by exposure to air.

**-winded**, *combining form.* being ____ of wind, or breath: *Short-winded = being short of wind, or breath.*

**wind|er¹** (wīn′dər), *n.* **1** a person or thing that winds. **2** an apparatus for winding thread, cable, or the like. **3** an operative employed in winding wool or other fiber. **4** a key for winding a jack, clock, or other mechanism. **5** *Obsolete.* a twining plant.
**winders**, winding steps in a staircase: *The best staircases are those without winders* (John C. Loudon).

**wind|er²** (wīn′dər, win′dər *for 1,* win′dər *for 2*), *n.* **1** a person who winds (blows) a wind instrument: *Winder of the horn, When snouted wild boars ... Anger our Huntsmen* (Keats). **2** *Informal, Figurative.* something that takes one's breath away, as a blow, a run, or a climb.

**wind erosion** (wind), the removal of topsoil by dust storms.

**wind|fall** (wind′fôl′), *n.* **1a** fruit blown down from a tree or vine by the wind. **b** a tree or trees blown down by the wind. **2** *Figurative.* an unexpected piece of good luck; unexpected acquisition or advantage: *We would urge great caution in any shifting and refunding of our bonding structure which might result in a windfall of profits to bondholders* (New York Times). **SYN:** godsend.

**wind|flaw** (wind′flô′), *n.* a sudden gust (of wind); flaw. [< *wind*¹ + *flaw*²]

**wind|flow|er** (wind′flou′ər), *n.* **1** = anemone. **2** = rue anemone. [translation of Latin *anemōnē* < Greek *anemṓnē*]

**wind|gall** (wind′gôl′), *n.* a soft tumor or swelling of the synovial bursa at the fetlock joint of a horse, once thought to contain air.

**wind|galled** (wind′gôld′), *adj.* having windgalls.

**wind gap** (wind), a depression in a mountain ridge not deep enough to give passage to a watercourse.

**wind gauge** (wind), = anemometer.

**wind harp** (wind), = aeolian harp.

**wind|hov|er** (wind′huv′ər), *n.* = kestrel. [< *wind*¹ + *hover* (because it hovers in the air with its head to the wind)]

**wind|ing** (wīn′ding), *n., adj.* —*n.* **1** the act of a person or thing that winds. **2** a bend; turn. **3** something that is wound or coiled. **4** *Electricity.* **a** a continuous coil of wire forming a conductor, as in a generator or motor. **b** the manner in which the wire is coiled: *a series winding.* **5** a faulty gait of a horse in which one leg tends to curve around another.
—*adj.* bending; turning. —**wind′ing|ly**, *adv.*

**winding frame**, a machine that winds yarn.

**winding sheet**, a cloth in which a dead person is wrapped for burial; shroud.

**wind instrument** (wind), a musical instrument sounded by blowing air into it, particularly one sounded by the breath of the player. French horns, flutes, and trombones are wind instruments.

**wind|jam|mer** (wind′jam′ər), *n.* **1** *Informal.* **a** a sailing ship, especially a square-rigged ship. **b** a member of its crew. **2** *U.S. Slang, Figurative.* a loquacious person; windbag. [American English < *wind*¹ + *jam*¹ + *-er*¹ (because sailors on steamships derided its capabilities)]

**wind|lass** (wind′ləs), *n., v.* —*n.* a machine for pulling or lifting things. A windlass is a kind of winch with a horizontal roller or beam, resting on supports, around which a rope, cable, or chain is wound, as to hoist water from a well or to raise an anchor. *Modern forms of the windlass include drums and cables of cranes and elevators* (Allen S. Hall, Jr.).
—*v.t., v.i.* to hoist or haul with a windlass.
[perhaps fusion of obsolete *windas* windlass < Anglo-French < Scandinavian (compare Old Icelandic *windāss* < *vinda* wind, turn + *āss* pole), and obsolete *windle* winding apparatus < Middle English *winden* wind, turn]

**win|dle** (win′dəl), *v.i.,* **-dled, -dling.** *Dialect.* **1** to move circularly or sinuously; meander; wind. **2** to wind thread, cable, or the like.

**wind|less** (wind′lis), *adj.* **1** free from wind; calm. **2** out of breath. —**wind′less|ness**, *n.*

**win|dle|straw** (win′dəl strô′), *n. Scottish.* **1** a dry, thin, withered stalk of grass. **2** *Figurative.* a person or thing of trifling worth or a flimsy nature. [Old English *windelstrēaw* dry grass stalk, type of grass, perhaps < *windel* a basket + *strēaw* straw]

**wind load** (wind), the amount of pressure from the force of the wind that a building can withstand.

**wind meter** (wind), = anemometer.

***wind|mill** (wind′mil′), *n., v.* —*n.* **1a** a mill or machine worked by the action of the wind upon a wheel of vanes or sails set around a horizontal shaft, usually mounted on a tall tower. Windmills are mostly used to pump water or grind grain. **b** the wheel on which the wind acts to drive such a mill. **2** any one of various objects that resemble a windmill in appearance or method of working, such as certain toys. **3** a small turbine on an airplane, exposed to and driven by the force of the air, used to operate various auxiliary mechanisms. **4** *Informal.* a helicopter.
—*v.i.* **1** to move one's arms or legs in a manner suggesting a windmill. **2** to rotate by the force of air acting upon it, without power from the engine: *With the engine dead, the prop was windmilling loosely in the air* (Time).
—*v.t.* **1** to move in a manner suggestive of a windmill: *Some of the jumpers windmilled their arms awkwardly in trying to keep their balance* (Time). **2** to cause to rotate by force of air, without engine power: *to windmill a propeller.*
**tilt at** (or **fight**) **windmills**, to attack imaginary enemies; expend one's energy in futile attacks on what cannot be overcome (in allusion to the story of Don Quixote tilting at windmills under the delusion that they were giants): *The whimsy* [*a play*] *will be about a gentle knight tilting at the windmills of government* (Wall Street Journal).

***windmill**
definition 1a

**wind motor** (wind), any machinery or motor using the force of the wind directly, including the ordinary windmills and apparatus of other construction.

**wind of change**, an irresistible movement toward political or economic change; social turmoil or upheaval: ... *the wind of change now sweeping through Africa* (Wall Street Journal).

**win|dow** (win′dō), *n., v.* —*n.* **1** an opening, as in a wall or roof of a building, boat, or car, to let in light or air, usually enclosed by a frame that holds a movable sash or sashes fitted with panes of glass: *a good view from the window. But, soft! what light through yonder window breaks?* (Shakespeare). **2** such an opening with the frame, sashes, and panes of glass. **3** the sashes and panes that fit such an opening: *to open the window.* **4** = windowpane: *to break a window.* **5** *Figurative.* **a** an opening like a window in shape or use, such as the transparent part of some envelopes through which the address is seen. **b** anything suggesting a window: *The window of my heart, mine eye* (Shakespeare). **6** *Aeronautics.* the conjunction of time and planetary position in a condition that permits successful space flight; launch window: *The Soviet and American vehicles flew to Venus close together because both were fired during one of the periodic windows for such shots* (New York Times). **7** a region of the electromagnetic spectrum, such as the radio region, whose radiation is not absorbed by the earth's atmosphere and is able to reach the earth: *One window is that portion called the visible spectrum through which the optical telescopes receive their information either by eye, photographic plate or photocell. The other window is that through which the aerials of the radio telescopes can operate* (New Scientist). **8** Also, **Window.** strips of metal foil dropped from airplanes to interfere with enemy radar indicators by reflecting the radar beams.
—*v.t.* to furnish with windows or openings likened to windows.
[< Scandinavian (compare Old Icelandic *vindauga* < *vindr* wind, gust + *auga* eye)] —**win′dow|less**, *adj.*

**window box**, **1** a container of wood, metal, or plastic, set on or fastened to a window sill, in which small plants may be grown. **2** one of the vertical shafts or boxes at each side of the frame of a double-hung window, that houses the cords and weights that counterbalance a sliding sash.

**window display**, the display of goods for sale in the window of a store to advertise its products and attract passers-by.

**win|dow-dress** (win′dō dres′), *v.t., v.i.,* **-dressed** or **-drest, -dress|ing.** to engage in, make use of, or subject to window dressing.

**window dresser**, a person employed to arrange in the windows of a store attractive displays of goods for sale.

**window dressing**, **1** the action of dressing a window with goods attractively displayed. **2** *Figurative.* a display made in such a manner as to give a favorable, often false, impression of the facts, such as the arrangement of a balance sheet so as to suggest that the business concerned is more prosperous than it is: *Although lacking the best-in-show competition that the officers of the club consider "window dressing," other dog show features are included* (New York Times).

**-windowed**, *combining form.* having a ___ window or windows: *Many-windowed = having many windows.*

**window envelope**, an envelope with an opening or transparent part in the front through which the address can be seen.

**window frame**, the supports built around a window sash or casement

**win|dow|pane** (win′dō pān′), *n.* a piece of glass in a window; pane.

**window sash**, a frame for the glass in a window.

**window seat**, a bench built into the wall of a room, under a window.

**window shade**, **1a** a sheet of opaque material wound on a roller, and unwound to cover a window. **b** the roller together with such a sheet, fastened especially at the top of a window frame. **2** any adjustable inside covering for a window.

**win|dow-shop** (win′dō shop′), *v.i.,* **-shopped, -shop|ping.** to look at articles in store windows without going in to buy anything.

**window shopper**, or **win|dow-shop|per** (win′dō shop′ər), *n.* a person who looks at articles in the windows of shops, instead of going in to do actual shopping.

**window sill**, or **win|dow|sill** (win′dō sil′), *n.* a piece of wood or stone across the bottom of a window.

**win|dow|y** (win′dō ē), *adj.* full of windows or openings.

**wind|pipe** (wind′pīp′), *n.* the passage by which air is carried from the throat to the lungs, in man situated in front of the esophagus; trachea. See picture under **bronchi**.

**wind-pol|li|nat|ed** (wind′pol′ə nā′tid), *adj.* fertilized by pollen carried by the wind; anemophilous.

**wind-pol|li|na|tion** (wind′pol′ə nā′shən), *n.* fertilization by pollen carried by the wind.

**wind|proof** (wind′prüf′), *adj.* resistant to wind; that will not let wind through: *Windproof clothing, as any hiker or climber will know, has a close weave and is expensive* (New Scientist).

**wind|puff** (wind′puf′), *n.* = windgall.

**wind pump**, a pump operated by a windmill.

**wind rose** (wind), *Meteorology.* a diagram indicating the relative frequency, force, and other factors of the winds from various directions at some given place.

**wind|row** (wind′rō′), *n., v.* —*n.* **1** a row of hay raked together to dry before being made into cocks or heaps. **2** any similar row, as of sheaves of grain, made for the purpose of drying, or a row of dry leaves, dust, or brush, swept together by the wind or the like. **3** a deep furrow for planting, especially one in which cut sugar-cane stalks are put and covered with earth.
—*v.t.* to arrange in a windrow or windrows; bring together in long rows.
[< *wind*¹ + *row*¹ (because it was set up to be dried by the wind)] —**wind′row′er**, *n.*

**winds** (windz), *n.pl.* See under **wind**¹.

**wind scale**, a system of numbers or words used to record the speed of the wind.

**wind|screen** (wind′skrēn′), *n. British.* windshield.

**wind shake**, **1** a flaw or crack in timber supposed to be due to a strain caused by the force of the wind. **2** such flaws or cracks collectively.

**wind-shak|en** (wind′shā′kən), *adj.* **1** (of timber) affected by wind shake. **2** shaken or agitated by the wind.

**wind|shield** (wind′shēld′), *n.* **1** a sheet of glass to keep off the wind. A windshield enables the driver of an automobile, locomotive, or airplane, to see the road, track, or other area ahead without being exposed to the rush of air caused by the forward movement of the vehicle. **2** a cover of light metal mounted on some explosive shells to reduce air resistance. [American English]

**windshield wiper**, a metal strip with a rubber insert attached to a rod that usually swings in an arc across the outside of a windshield to wipe away moisture.

**wind sock** or **sleeve** (wind), a cone-shaped sleeve mounted on a pole or the like, showing the direction of the wind; wind cone.

**Wind|sor** (win′zər), *n.* **1** the name of the British royal family since 1917. **2** = windsor bean.

**windsor bean**, = broad bean.

**Pronunciation Key:** hat, āge, cãre, fär; let, ēqual, tėrm; it, īce; hot, ōpen, ôrder; oil, out; cup, pu̇t, rüle; child; long; thin; ᴛʜen; zh, measure; ə represents **a** in about, **e** in taken, **i** in pencil, **o** in lemon, **u** in circus.

∗**Windsor chair**, a kind of comfortable wooden chair, with or without arms, having a spindle back, slanting legs, and a flat or slightly hollowed seat. Windsor chairs were much used in England and the American colonies in the 1700's. [< *Windsor* (officially *New Windsor*), a city in Berkshire, England, where it was first made]

∗**Windsor chair**

**Windsor knot**, 1 the knot of a Windsor tie. 2 a wide knot on any necktie.

**Windsor tie**, a wide necktie of soft silk, tied in a loose, double or triangular bow.

**wind sprint**, any short spell of running, rowing, swimming, or other activity, performed at top speed to develop breathing power and stamina.

**wind|storm** (wind′stôrm′), *n.* a storm with much wind but little or no rain.

**wind-suck|er** (wind′suk′ər), *n.* a horse given to crib-biting and wind sucking; crib-biter.

**wind sucking** (wind), a drawing in and swallowing of air, as in a horse that crib-bites. —**wind′-suck′ing**, *adj.*

**wind|surf|ing** (wind′sėr′fing), *n.* the sport of riding over water on a surfboard equipped with a sail. —**wind′surf′er**, *n.*

**wind|swept** or **wind-swept** (wind′swept′), *adj.* exposed to the full force of the wind: *a wind-swept hillside.*

**wind tee** (wind), *Aviation.* a weather vane in the form of a T, on or near a landing field.

**wind tunnel** (wind), a tunnel for testing the effects of wind and air pressure on aircraft, missiles, and the like, with air forced through at high speeds.

**wind-up** or **wind|up** (wīnd′up′), *n., adj.* —*n.* 1 a winding up; end; close; conclusion; finish. 2 the series of swinging and twisting movements of the arm and body made by a baseball pitcher just before pitching the ball.
—*adj.* 1 that must be wound up in order to work: *a wind-up toy, a wind-up motor.* 2 being the last; closing: *a wind-up game.*

**wind vane** (wind), = weather vane.

**wind|ward** (wind′wərd; *Nautical* win′dərd), *adv., adj., n.* —*adv.* toward the wind.
—*adj.* 1 on the side toward the wind; facing into the wind. 2 in the direction from which the wind is blowing; moving against the wind.
—*n.* 1 the side toward the wind. 2 the direction from which the wind is blowing.
**cast an anchor to windward**. See under **anchor**[1].
**get to windward of**, to gain an advantage over: *If I happen to have got to windward of the young woman, why, so much the better for me* (H. Rider Haggard).
**keep to windward of**, to keep out of the reach of: *He had developed the skill of keeping to windward of his creditors.*

**wind|way** (wind′wā′), *n.* 1 a ventilating passage in a mine; airway. 2 the access of the wind to a sailing vessel so as to give her freedom of passage. 3 the part of a flue pipe through which the air current is directed.

**wind|y** (win′dē), *adj.,* **wind|i|er, wind|i|est.** 1 having much wind: *a windy day, windy weather, the windy seas.* 2 exposed to or blown upon or through by the wind: *a windy street, the windy deck of a ship.* 3 of or consisting of wind: *March, departed with his windy rage* (William Basse). 4 like the wind in quality as of sound or swiftness: *her windy sighs* (Shakespeare). 5 causing gas in the stomach or intestines; flatulent. 6 *Figurative.* **a** made of wind; empty: *windy talk, a windy political speech.* **b** talking a great deal; voluble; loquacious. 7 *Scottish.* boastful. [Old English *windig* < *wind* wind[1], gust] —**wind′i|ly**, *adv.* —**wind′i|ness**, *n.*

**wine** (wīn), *n., v.,* **wined, win|ing.** —*n.* 1 the juice of grapes after it has fermented and contains alcohol, widely used as a beverage and also used in religious rites. Red wines are made by allowing the juice of dark-colored grapes to remain in contact with the skins while fermenting; white wines are made from light-colored grapes or from dark-colored grapes whose skins have been removed. Wines are also classified as sweet or dry, and still or sparkling. 2 the fermented juice of other fruits or plants, especially when used as a beverage: *currant wine, dandelion wine.* 3 the color of red wine. 4 *Figurative.* something that exhilarates or intoxicates like wine. 5 intoxication from drinking wine. 6 *British.* a party, especially of undergraduates, for drinking wine. 7 *Pharmacology.* a solution of a medicinal substance in wine; vinum.
—*v.t.* to entertain with wine: *to wine and dine someone.* —*v.i.* to drink wine.
**new wine in old bottles**, something new that is too strong to be held back by old forms (in the Bible in allusion to Matthew 9:17): *The younger generation sees itself as new wine in old bottles.*
[Old English *wīn,* ultimately < Latin *vīnum.* See related etym. at **vine**.] —**wine′less**, *adj.*

**wine|bib|ber** (wīn′bib′ər), *n.* a person who drinks much wine. [< *wine* + *bibber*]

**wine|bib|bing** (wīn′bib′ing), *n., adj.* —*n.* the habit of drinking wine to excess.
—*adj.* drinking much wine.

**wine card**, *Especially British.* wine list.

**wine cellar**, 1 a cellar where wine is stored. 2 a store or stock of wine.

**wine color**, purplish red.

**wine-col|ored** (wīn′kul′ərd), *adj.* of a dark purplish-red color.

**wine cooler**, a vessel in which one or more bottles of wine can be placed in ice.

**wine-fat** (wīn′fat′), *n. Archaic.* a vat or vessel in which grapes were trodden in making wine.

**wine gallon**, 1 a former British unit of liquid measure for wine, equal to the standard U.S. gallon. 2 the standard U.S. gallon; 231 cu. in. or 3.7853 liters.

**wine|glass** (wīn′glas′, -gläs′), *n.* a small drinking glass for wine, usually having a stem. Wine glasses range in capacity from about two to about six fluid ounces and vary in shape for different types of wine.

**wine|glass|ful** (wīn′glas′fu̇l, -gläs′-), *n., pl.* **-fuls.** about two fluid ounces (the amount held by a wineglass of the type normally used for sherry, port, and other fortified wines).

**wine|grow|er** (wīn′grō′ər), *n.* a person who raises grapes and makes vine.

**wine|grow|ing** (wīn′grō′ing), *n.* the cultivation of grapes to make vine.

**wine|house** (wīn′hous′), *n.* 1 a tavern where wine is drunk. 2 a firm of wine merchants.

**wine list**, a list of the wines that may be obtained at a restaurant.

**wine|mak|er** (wīn′mā′kər), *n.* = winegrower.

**wine measure**, an old British system of measure for wine.

**wine palm**, any one of various palms from whose sap wine is made.

**wine press**, 1 a machine for pressing the juice from grapes in making wine. 2 a vat in which grapes are trodden in the process of making wine.

**win|er|y** (wī′nər ē), *n., pl.* **-er|ies.** a place where wine is made. [American English < *win*(e) + *-ery*]

**Wine|sap** or **wine|sap** (wīn′sap′), *n.* a red, winter variety of apple, much cultivated in the United States. It is of medium size and slightly tart.

**wine|shop** (wīn′shop′), *n.* = winehouse.

**wine|skin** (wīn′skin′), *n.* a container made of the nearly complete skin especially of a goat or hog, used in some countries of southern Europe and Asia and South America for holding wine.

**wine|tast|er** (wīn′tās′tər), *n.* a person who judges the quality of wine by tasting it: *A wine-taster, savoring a fine wine, can sometimes guess from its bouquet not only the type of wine but also the vineyard from which it came and the year in which the grapes were grown* (Science News Letter).

**wine|y** (wī′nē), *adj.,* **win|i|er, win|i|est.** = winy.

**wing** (wing), *n., v.* —*n.* 1a one of the movable parts of a bird, insect, or bat used in flying, or a corresponding part in a bird or insect that does not fly. Birds have one pair of wings; insects usually have two pairs. **b** any similar structure, such as the parachute of a flying squirrel or one of the enlarged fins of a flying fish. 2 the wing of a bird or domesticated fowl used as food. 3a a winglike organ attributed to supernatural beings, such as angels and demons, and to fabulous creatures, such as dragons and griffins. **b** a figure or representation of a wing. **c** *Figurative.* something (inanimate or abstract) considered as flying or as carrying one swiftly along: *on the wings of time.* 4 anything like a wing in shape or use, such as one of the major lifting and supporting surfaces of an airplane, one of the vanes of a windmill, or the feather of an arrow. See picture under **airplane** at bottom of page. 5a a part that sticks out from the main part or body, especially the part of a building that projects sideways from the main part: *The house has a wing at each side.* **b** either of the longer sides of an outwork, by which it is joined to the main fortification. 6a either of the side portions of an army or fleet formed to the left or right of the main force when ready for battle. **b** an air force unit composed of two or more groups, and smaller than a command. 7a Often, **wings.** either of the spaces to the right or left of the stage of a theater, between the side scenes, out of sight of the audience. **b** any one of the side scenes on the stage. 8 a part of an organization holding certain views; faction. The liberals of a political party are called the left wing. 9 in ice hockey and some other team games: **a** one of the positions, or a player in such a position, on the right or left of the center, when facing the opponents' goal. **b** such a position or player on the forward line. 10 an outlying portion of a region. 11 a sidepiece projecting frontwards at the top of the back of an armchair. 12a either of the two side petals of a pealike flower; ala. **b** a leafy or membranous expansion or thin extension, as of a samara. 13 *Figurative.* a means of flight, travel, or passage. 14 the act or manner of flying; winged flight. 15 *Slang.* **a** an arm or a foreleg. **b** the throwing or pitching arm of a baseball player. 16 either part of a double door, screen, or the like, which may be folded or otherwise moved back. 17 *Anatomy.* the ala of the nose. 18 the part of the plowshare of a moldboard plow that extends sideways and cuts the bottom of the furrow. 19 *British.* a mudguard or fender over the wheel of an automobile, truck, carriage, or other vehicle.
—*v.t.* 1 to fly: *The bird wings its way south.* 2 to fly through, upon, or across. 3a to supply with wings. **b** to furnish (a building, etc.) with side parts or projections. 4 *Figurative.* to make able to fly; give speed to; hasten: *Terror winged his steps as the bear drew near.* 5 to convey by or as if by means of wings. 6 to let fly; send flying: *to wing an arrow in the sky.* 7 to wound in the wing or arm: *The bullet winged the bird but did not kill it.* 8 *Informal.* to disable (an airplane) by a shot. 9 to brush with a bird's wing. 10 *Theatrical Slang.* **a** to play (a part) with little preparation, by studying it in the wings or being prompted from the wings. **b** to improvise: *If you miss a cue you've got to wing it.*
—*v.i.* to take flight with or as if with wings.
**clip one's wings**, to curtail one's power: *His enemies ... had combined to clip his wings, and he had been removed from the key Ministry of the Interior to a more innocuous post* (Atlantic).
**in the wings**, just beyond public view; behind the scenes: *There are four announced Democratic candidates—and several others ... lurking in the wings* (New York Times).
**on (the) wing, a** flying; in flight: *The bird that flutters least is longest on the wing* (William Cowper). **b** *Figurative.* moving; active; busy: *I have been, since I saw you in town, pretty much on the wing, at Hampton, Twickenham, and elsewhere* (Thomas Gray). **c** *Figurative.* going away: *He's wild, and soon on wing, if watchful eyes come near* (John Dryden).
**take wing, a** to fly away: *And now, from the trees, from the earth all around them, the locusts were taking wing* (New Yorker). **b** *Figurative.* to depart: *I found a fellow who was in the same regiment with him, and knew this Mrs. Glasher before she took wing* (George Eliot).
**under the wing of**, under the protection or sponsorship of: *There liv'd Miss Cicely ... under the wing of an old maiden aunt* (Samuel Foote).
**wings**, insignia awarded by the U.S. Air Force to men who have qualified as pilots, navigators, etc.: *In their third and final year cadets ... are awarded their wings* (Observer).
[Middle English *wenge* < Scandinavian (compare Old Icelandic *vængr*)] —**wing′like′**, *adj.*

**wing and wing**, with two sails extended on opposite sides by booms, as a schooner or other fore-and-aft-rigged vessel sailing before the wind.

**wing|back** (wing′bak′), *n.* 1 an offensive back in football whose position is beyond and behind an end. 2 the position of a wingback.

**wingback formation**, an offensive formation in football in which the position of a back or the backs is a little beyond and behind either or both ends.

**wing|beat** (wing′bēt′), *n.* the stroke or sweep of the wings in flying: *the wingbeat of a bird.*

**wing bow** (bō), the feathers of a distinctive coloring at the bend of a bird's wing.

**wing case** or **cover**, either of a pair of thickened front wings that form a protective covering for the hind pair in certain insects; elytron. Beetles have wing cases.

**wing chair**, a comfortable upholstered chair with high sidepieces extending forward from the back, by which the head is supported and protected from drafts.

**wing collar**, a stand-up collar with the corners folded down, worn especially in men's formal dress.

**wing commander**, 1 the commander of a wing. 2 a commissioned officer in the Royal Air Force or Royal Canadian Air Force, equivalent to a lieutenant colonel in the United States Air Force.

**wing coverts**, the feathers concealing the bases of the flight feathers of a bird's wing.

**wing|ding** (wing′ding′), *n., adj. U.S. Slang.* — ***n.*** **1** a party or celebration, especially a lavish or noisy one. **2** something extraordinary; humdinger: *a wingding of a fight.* **3** a thing; device; gadget. — ***adj.*** festive, especially lavish or boisterous: *The big wingding Christmas parties for employees are definitely decreasing* (Wall Street Journal). Also, **whingding**.

**winged** (wingd; *especially poetic* wing′id), *adj.* **1** having wings, as a bird and a bat do. **2** having a part or parts resembling or analogous to a wing. **3** *Figurative.* swift; rapid: *a winged messenger.* **4** *Figurative.* lofty; elevated; sublime: *winged words.* **5** wounded or disabled in the wing or arm. **6** *Obsolete.* crowded with flying birds.

**winged elm**, a small North American species of elm having branches with corky projections.

**wing|er** (wing′ər), *n. Especially British.* a wing (def. 9).

**wing|fish** (wing′fish′), *n., pl.* **-fish|es** or (*collectively*) **-fish**. a flying fish, especially a flying gurnard.

**wing-foot|ed** (wing′fu̇t′id), *adj.* having or seeming to have wings on the feet; swiftly moving.

**wing|less** (wing′lis), *adj.* **1** having no wings. **2** having rudimentary wings. The ostrich and kiwi are wingless birds. — **wing′less|ness**, *n.*

**wing|let** (wing′lit), *n.* **1** a little wing. **2** = alula.

**wing loading** or **load**, the gross weight of a fully loaded airplane divided by the total square feet or other units of square measure of the wings and other supporting surfaces, not including the stabilizer and elevators.

**wing|man** (wing′man′, -mən), *n., pl.* **-men**. **1a** a pilot who flies at the side and to the rear of an element leader, usually in a two-plane or three-plane formation. **b** the airplane flown in this position. **2** *Sports.* a wing (def. 9).

**wing nut**, a nut with winged sides that can be turned with the thumb and a finger. See picture under **nut**.

**wing|o|ver** (wing′ō′vər), *n.* a maneuver of an airplane into a steep climb letting the nose drop sharply just before stalling and making a half roll, returning to normal flight in a reverse direction.

**wing rail**, (on a railroad track) an additional rail at a switch, laid so as to prevent the wheels from leaving the track.

**wing root**, the base of an airplane's wing, where it joins and is faired into the fuselage.

**wings** (wingz), *n.pl.* See under **wing**.

**wing shell**, **1** = stromb (so called from the winglike lip of the aperture). **2** any one of a family of various bivalves, characterized by winglike expansions of the hinge margin.

**wing shooting**, the practice of shooting birds that are in flight.

**wing|span** (wing′span′), *n.*, or **wing span**, the wingspread of an airplane, including ailerons projecting beyond the wing tips.

**wing spar**, the spar of a wing, as contrasted with that of any other airfoil.

**wing|spread** (wing′spred′), *n.* **1** the distance between the tips of the wings of a bird, bat, insect, or other such animal, when they are spread. **2** the distance between the tips of the wings of an airplane.

**wing tank**, a fuel tank in the wing of an airplane, or an auxiliary one attached to a wing.

**wing tip**, or **wing|tip** (wing′tip′), *n.* **1** the outer end of a wing, as of a bird, insect, or airplane. **2** an ornamental tip on a shoe which is carried back along the sides. **3** a shoe with such a tip.

**wing|wall** (wing′wôl′), *n.* a side of a floating dry dock with compartments for flooding to lower the dock.

**wing-wea|ry** (wing′wir′ē), *adj.* fatigued by prolonged flying.

**wing|y** (wing′ē), *adj.,* **wing|i|er, wing|i|est**. **1** having wings: *wingy insects.* **2** *Figurative.* soaring: *wingy thoughts.*

**wink**[1] (wingk), *v., n.* — ***v.i.*** **1a** to close the eyes and open them again quickly: *The bright light made him wink.* **b** to close and open again quickly: *His right eye winked.* **2** to close one eye and open it again quickly as a hint or signal: *Father winked at him to keep still.* **3** to twinkle: *The stars winked.*
— ***v.t.*** **1** to close (the eyes or an eye) and open quickly. **2** to move by winking: *to wink back tears.* **3** to give (a signal) or express (a message), as by a winking of the eye or a flashlight.
— ***n.*** **1** the act of winking. **2** a hint or signal given by winking: *a knowing wink.* **3** = twinkle. **4** a very short time: *He'll be here quick as a wink. I didn't sleep a wink.*
**forty winks**. See under **forty winks**.
**wink at**, to pretend not to notice: *Critics say the commission isn't doing much for the law when it finds a practice illegal and then announces it may wink at the violation* (Wall Street Journal).
[Old English *wincian*]

**wink**[2] (wingk), *n.* one of the small colored disks used in the game of tiddlywinks: *Winks (the ones you flick) must be either seven-eighths or five-eighths of an inch in diameter* (London Times). [< (tiddly)*wink*(s)]

**wink|er** (wing′kər), *n.* **1** a person or thing that winks. **2** *Informal.* **a** an eyelash. **b** an eye. **3** a blinder or blinker for a horse.
**winkers, a** *Slang.* the eyes: *As soon as my winkers are opened I am always blessed with one of your epistles* (Mary Delany). **b** blinkers: *He weareth a pair of winkers over his eyes like a mill horse* (William Fulke). **c** *Rare.* spectacles: *to look through a pair of winkers.*

**winker braces**, the part of a horse's harness that passes over the head below the ears and helps to hold the blinders on.

**win|kle**[1] (wing′kəl), *n.* a periwinkle or any one of certain other relatively large marine snails used for food. [short for *periwinkle*[2]]

**win|kle**[2] (wing′kəl), *v.t.,* **-kled, -kling**. *Especially British.* to dig (out); force; wrest: ... *to winkle out the hard core of Omani rebels from their last stronghold* (Manchester Guardian). [probably partly < *winkle*[1] and partly < German *Winkel* corner]

**win|kle|pick|er** (wing′kəl pik′ər), *n. British Slang.* a shoe with a sharply pointed toe: *Winklepickers, it seems, are doing much damage to the feet of Britain's young people* (Listener). [< *winkle*[1] + *picker*[1]]

**win|less** (win′lis), *adj.* without a win or victory; having lost every encounter thus far: *a winless season.*

**win|na|ble** (win′ə bəl), *adj.* capable of being won: *He ... is convinced that the war is not militarily winnable* (Time).

**Win|ne|ba|go** (win′ə bā′gō), *n., pl.* **-gos** or **-goes**. a member of an American Indian tribe speaking a Siouan language and living mostly in eastern Wisconsin.

**win|ner** (win′ər), *n.* a person or thing that wins: *The winner of the contest got a prize.* **SYN:** victor.

**winner's circle**, a small enclosure at a race track where the winning horse and jockey are given the award.

**Win|nie** (win′ē), *n.* an award presented annually in the United States for outstanding achievements in fashion design: *The American Fashion Critics' "Winnie" went to dress designer Donald Brooks* (Berta Mohr). (< *winn*(er) + *-ie*]

**win|ning** (win′ing), *adj., n.* — ***adj.*** **1** that wins: *a winning team, a winning tactic.* **2** having more victories than defeats. **3** *Figurative.* charming; attractive: *She has a very winning smile.*
— ***n.*** **1** the act of a person or thing that wins. **2** the process of obtaining metal from ore. **3** *Especially British.* **a** a shaft or pit which is being sunk to win (open) a bed of coal. **b** a portion of a coal field or mine ready for working.
**winnings**, what is won; money won: *One loss may be of more consequence to him, than all his former winnings* (John Dryden).
— **win′ning|ly**, *adv.* — **win′ning|ness**, *n.*

**win|ning|est** (win′ing ist), *adj. Informal.* winning or having won the most.

**winning gallery**, the opening on the back wall on the hazard side, farthest from the dedans or spectators' gallery, one of three winning openings in court tennis.

**winning opening**, any one of the three openings in the back walls of the court into which a ball is hit to score a point in court tennis; the dedans, winning gallery, or grille.

**winning post**, a post marking the finish line on a race track.

**win|nings** (win′ingz), *n.pl.* See under **winning**.

**Win|ni|peg|ger** (win′ə peg′ər), *n.* a native or inhabitant of Winnipeg, Canada.

**win|nock** (win′ək), *n. Scottish.* a window. [variant of *window;* perhaps influenced by Gaelic *uinneag*]

**win|now** (win′ō), *v., n.* — ***v.t.*** **1** to blow off the chaff from (grain); drive or blow away (chaff): *Farmers winnow rice to separate the rice hulls from the kernels* (Nelson E. Jodon). **2** *Figurative.* to sort out; separate; sift: *to winnow the facts from a wordy report, to winnow truth from lies.* **3** *Figurative.* to blow on or away, as the wind does in removing chaff from grain; scatter or disperse. **4** to fan (with wings); flap (wings). **5** to follow (a course) with flapping wings.
— ***v.i.*** **1** to blow chaff from grain. **2** to move with flapping wings; flutter.
— ***n.*** **1** a contrivance for winnowing grain. **2** the act of winnowing or a motion resembling it.
[Old English *windwian* < *wind* wind[1], gust]

**win|now|er** (win′ō ər), *n.* **1** a person who winnows. **2** a machine for winnowing grain.

**wi|no** (wī′nō), *n., pl.* **-nos**. *U.S. Slang.* an alcoholic addicted to wine.

**win|some** (win′səm), *adj.* **1** charming; attractive; pleasing: *a winsome girl, a winsome smile.* **2** *Dialect.* cheerful; joyous; gay. [Old English *wynsum* agreeable, pleasant < *wynn* joy + *-sum* -some[1]] — **win′some|ly**, *adv.* — **win′some|ness**, *n.*

**wint** (wīnt), *v. Scottish.* wound; the past tense of **wind**[2].

**win|ter** (win′tər), *n., adj., v.* — ***n.*** **1** the coldest of the four seasons; time of the year between fall and spring. In northern latitudes winter is reckoned astronomically as beginning about December 22 (the winter solstice) and ending about March 21 (the vernal equinox), and popularly as comprising the months of December, January, and February or (in British use) November, December, and January. In southern latitudes winter corresponds in calendar time to the northern summer. *His uncle and he would go toiling up the mountain side, sometimes striding over rutted, clay-caked, and frost-hardened roads, sometimes beating their way downhill ... smashing their way through the dry and brittle undergrowth of barren Winter* (Thomas Wolfe). **2** a year of life: *a man of eighty winters.* **3** *Figurative.* **a** the last period of life: *Father Mapple was in the hardy winter of a healthy old age* (Herman Melville). **b** a period of decline, dreariness, or adversity: *It was the best of times, it was the worst of times ... it was the spring of hope, it was the winter of despair* (Dickens).
— ***adj.*** **1** of, having to do with, or characteristic of winter: *winter weather, winter winds. The winter moon, brightening the skirts of a long cloud* (Tennyson). **2** for the winter: *winter clothes, winter sports.* **3** of the kind that may be kept for use during the winter: *winter apples.* **4** sown in the fall and harvested in the spring: *winter crops.*
— ***v.i.*** to pass or spend the winter: *Robins winter in the south.*
— ***v.t.*** to keep, feed, or manage during winter: *We wintered our cattle in the warm valley.*
[Old English *winter*] — **win′ter|er**, *n.*

**winter aconite**, any plant of a group of small Old-World herbs of the crowfoot family, whose bright-yellow flowers appear very early in the spring.

**winter apple**, **1** an apple that does not ripen till winter. **2** an apple that keeps well in winter.

**win|ter|ber|ry** (win′tər ber′ē), *n., pl.* **-ries**. any one of various North American hollies with berries, usually scarlet, that persist through the winter.

**win|ter|bloom** (win′tər blüm′), *n.* = witch hazel.

**win|ter|bourne** (win′tər bôrn′, -bōrn′, -bu̇rn′), *n.* an intermittent stream that flows only in winter or at long intervals, found especially in certain chalk and limestone regions of England. [< *winter* + *bourne*[1]]

**winter cress**, any one of a group of plants of the mustard family, especially a common European weed naturalized in North America and sometimes used in salads; upland cress; Swedish cress.

**winter crookneck**, a winter squash with a long, curved neck.

**win|ter|feed** (win′tər fēd′), *v.,* **-fed, -feed|ing**, *n.* — ***v.t.*** to feed or maintain (animals, etc.) during winter.
— ***n.*** food supplied to animals during winter.

**winter flounder**, a flounder of the coast of the eastern United States with the eyes on the right side of the head.

**win|ter|green** (win′tər grēn′), *n.* **1** a small, creeping, evergreen plant of North America with small, white, drooping flowers, bright-red berries, and aromatic leaves. An oil made from its leaves is used in medicine and candy. Wintergreen belongs to the heath family. The wintergreen is also called *checkerberry, spiceberry, teaberry,* and (incorrectly) *partridgeberry.* **2** this oil. **3** its flavor, or something flavored with it. **4** any other plant of the same group. **5** any one of a group of evergreen herbs, especially a woodland plant with roundish, drooping, white flowers; shinleaf. **6** any one of various low plants of an allied group; pipsissewa.

**wintergreen barberry**, a hardy evergreen barberry, originally from China, with spiny leaves and blue-black berries, used as an ornamental shrub.

**wintergreen oil**, = oil of wintergreen.

**winter gull**, = kittiwake.

**win|ter-har|dy** (win′tər här′dē), *adj.* able to withstand the effects of cold weather: *Plant breeders often search other countries for alfalfa plants that are winter-hardy* (C. H. Hanson).

**win|ter|ize** (win′tə rīz), *v.t.,* **-ized, -iz|ing**. **1** to make (a mechanism, especially an automobile)

---

**Pronunciation Key:** hat, āge, cãre, fär; let, ēqual, tėrm; it, īce; hot, ōpen, ôrder; **oi**l, **ou**t; cup, pu̇t, rüle; **ch**ild; lo**ng**; **th**in; **ᴛʜ**en; **zh**, measure; **ə** represents **a** in about, **e** in taken, **i** in pencil, **o** in lemon, **u** in circus.

ready for operation or use during the winter, as by putting antifreeze in the radiator and replacing a relatively heavy engine lubricant with a relatively light one. **2** to prepare (anything) for winter use or occupation: *to winterize a house.* —**win′ter|i|za′tion**, *n.*

**win|ter|kill** (win′tər kil′), *v., n. U.S.* —*v.t., v.i.* to kill by or die from exposure to cold weather: *The rosebushes were winterkilled.*
—*n.* death of a plant or animal due to exposure to cold weather.

**win|ter|less** (win′tər lis), *adj.* having no winter; without wintry weather.

**win|ter|ly** (win′tər lē), *adj.* **1** of, belonging to, or occurring in winter. **2** like winter or that of winter; cold and cheerless; wintry.

**winter melon**, a variety of muskmelon that keeps through part of the winter. It has a smooth skin and sweet flesh.

**winter Nel|is** (nel′is), a Belgian variety of medium-sized, greenish-red pear, widely cultivated in the United States. [< *Nelis,* a proper name]

**winter solstice**, **1** (for the Northern Hemisphere) the time when the sun is farthest south from the equator, about December 21 or 22.
**2** the point on the ecliptic farthest south of the celestial equator, which the sun reaches at this time. It was formerly in the constellation Cancer, but is now in Sagittarius. *Off the tip of the Archer's bow is the place of the winter solstice, where the sun is found about December 21* (Hubert J. Bernhard).

**winter squash**, any one of various squashes that have hard shells and may be stored through the winter, such as the Hubbard squash or the winter crookneck.

**win|ter|tide** (win′tər tīd′), *n. Archaic.* wintertime.
[Old English *wintertīd* < *winter* winter + *tīd* tide, time]

**win|ter|time** (win′tər tīm′), *n.* the season of winter; winter.

**winter wheat**, wheat planted in the autumn and ripening in the following spring or summer.

**winter wren**, a small, short-tailed wren of northern parts of the Northern Hemisphere.

**win|ter|y** (win′tər ē, -trē), *adj.,* **-ter|i|er, -ter|i|est.** = wintry.

**win|tle** (win′təl), *v.,* **-tled, -tling,** *n. Scottish.* —*v.i.* **1** to roll or swing from side to side. **2** to tumble, capsize, or be upset.
—*n.* a rolling or staggering movement.
[< earlier Flemish *windtelen* < *winden* to wind]

**win|try** (win′trē), *adj.,* **-tri|er, -tri|est. 1** of winter; of such a kind as occurs in winter; like winter: *wintry weather, a wintry sky.* SYN: hibernal.
**2** *Figurative.* not warm or friendly; chilly; cold: *a wintry smile, a wintry greeting, a wintry manner.*
**3** *Figurative.* **a** aged. **b** white with age; snowy: *wintry hair.* —**win′tri|ly**, *adv.* —**win′tri|ness**, *n.*

**Win|tu** (win′tü), *n., pl.* **-tu** or **-tus. 1** a member of a North American Indian tribe living in the region of Mount Shasta, in northern California. **2** the Copehan language of this tribe. **3** = Copehan.

**Win|tun** (win′tün), *n.* = Wintu.

**win|y** (wī′nē), *adj.,* **win|i|er, win|i|est.** tasting, smelling, or looking like wine.

**winze**[1] (winz), *n. Scottish.* an imprecation; curse.
[origin uncertain. Compare earlier Flemish *wensch.*]

**winze**[2] (winz), *n. Mining.* a shaft or an inclined passage connecting one level with another, but not rising to the surface. [earlier *winds,* perhaps < *wind*[2]]

**wipe** (wīp), *v.,* **wiped, wip|ing,** *n.* —*v.t.* **1** to rub (something) as with cloth or paper in order to clean or dry: *to wipe a table, wipe one's hands. We wipe our shoes on the mat. We wipe the dishes with a towel.* **2** to take (away, off, or up) by rubbing: *Wipe away your tears. She wiped off dust. I used a napkin to wipe up the spilled milk.* **3** to remove: *The rain wiped away the footprints.* (*Figurative.*) *Time had wiped her image from his memory.* **4** to rub or draw (something) over a surface, as for cleaning or drying. **5** to apply (a soft substance) by rubbing it on, as with a cloth or pad: *to wipe ointment on a burn.* **6a** to form or seal (a joint in lead pipe) by spreading solder with a leather or cloth pad. **b** to apply (solder) in this way.
—*n.* **1** the act of wiping clean or dry: *He gave his face a hasty wipe.* **2** *Informal.* a slashing or sweeping blow; swipe. **3** *Informal or Dialect.* a cutting remark; jeer; gibe. **4** *Slang.* a handkerchief. **5** *Machinery.* a cam or other wiper.
**wipe out, a** to destroy completely; obliterate; annihilate: *Whole cities were wiped out by the barbarians that swept over Europe. A vast slag heap slipped down a mountain to wipe out a school full of children* (Manchester Guardian Weekly). **b** to do away with; abolish: *Automation ... is wiping out about 40,000 unskilled jobs a week* (Saturday Review). **c** *Slang.* to fall off a surfboard, skis, or motorcycle or other moving vehicle: *There is no rhyme or reasoning with a wave. Once you are committed there is no way out except to make it or wipe out* (International Surfing Magazine).
[Old English *wīpian*]

**wipe-out** (wīp′out′), *n.* **1** *U.S. Slang.* a fall from an upright position on a surfboard, skis, or motorcycle or other moving vehicle: *Even when elated beginners go too fast and hit a bump, the worst that usually happens is a harmless wipe-out in soft snow* (Time). **2** *Informal.* a wiping out or being wiped out; total destruction or undoing: *the wipe-out of an army, the wipe-out of a business.*

**wip|er** (wī′pər), *n.* **1** a person who wipes, especially a member of the crew of a ship who is employed in the engine room to clean and polish machinery and fittings. **2a** a thing used for wiping: *a windshield wiper.* **b** *Slang.* a handkerchief. **3** *Electricity.* a moving piece that makes contact with the terminals of a device, such as a rheostat. **4** a projecting piece in a machine fixed on a rotating or oscillating part, and periodically communicating movement by a rubbing action to some other part; a cam, eccentric, or tappet, especially one serving to lift a hammer, stamper, valve rod, or other piece that in the intervals falls by its own weight.

**wir|a|ble** (wīr′ə bəl), *adj.* that can be wired.

**wire** (wīr), *n., adj., v.,* **wired, wir|ing.** —*n.*
**1** metal drawn out into a thin, flexible rod or fine thread. **2a** such metal as a material, as for fences. **b** a fence made of wire. **3** a piece, length, or line of such metal used for various purposes, such as a cross hair of an optical instrument. **4** a long piece of metal drawn out into a thread used for electrical transmission, as in electric lighting, telephones, and telegraphs.
**5** telegraph: *He sent a message by wire.* **6** *Informal.* a telegram: *The news of his arrival came in a wire.* **7** = wire netting. **8** Often, **wires. a** a metal bar of a cage. **b** *Music.* a metallic string of an instrument. **9** the finish line of a race course. **10** a metal snare for hares or rabbits. **11** a long, wiry, hairlike growth of the plumage of various birds.
—*adj.* made of or consisting of wire: *a wire fence.*
—*v.t.* **1** to furnish with a wire or wires: *to wire a house for electricity.* **2** to fasten with a wire or wires: *He wired the two pieces together.* **3** to fence (in) with wire. **4** to stiffen with wire; place on a wire. **5** to catch or trap in a wire snare. **6** *Informal.* to telegraph: *He wired a birthday greeting.* **7** to hit (a ball in croquet) so that it rests behind an arch and thus blocks another ball.
—*v.i. Informal.* to send a message by telegraph.
**down to the wire**, to the very last minute; to the end: *The World Series pursued its peculiar pattern down to the wire today* (New York Times).
**pull wires**, *Informal.* **a** to use secret influence to accomplish one's purpose: *He pulled wires to get his son a job.* **b** to direct the actions of others secretly: *The mayor used his influence to pull wires of local legislators and get votes for his programs.*
**under the wire**, just before it is too late: *The Trumbull Terrace, a building for refreshments, came in just under the wire and was ready for the first festival goers* (New York Times).
[Old English *wīr*] —**wire′like′**, *adj.* —**wir′er**, *n.*

**wire|bar** (wīr′bär′), *n.* a bar of copper or other refined metal, cast into a suitable form for drawing into wire.

**wire brush**, a brush with metal bristles, for cleaning surfaces of rust, paint, or other unwanted coating.

**wire cloth**, a fabric woven from wire, used for strainers. —**wire′-cloth′**, *adj.*

**wire coat**, a coat of rough, wiry hair, as of some dogs.

**wire cutter**, a tool for cutting wire.

**wire|danc|er** (wīr′dan′sər, -dän′-), *n.* a person who dances or performs acrobatic stunts on a taut wire high above the ground.

**wire|danc|ing** (wīr′dan′sing, -dän′-), *n.* the performance or work of a wiredancer.

**wire|draw** (wīr′drô′), *v.t.,* **-drew, -drawn, -drawing. 1** to draw out (metal) into wire. **2** to draw out (a material thing) to an elongated form; stretch; elongate. **3** *Figurative.* **a** to protract excessively; spin out. **b** to draw out to an extreme tenuity; attenuate. —**wire′draw′er**, *n.*

**wire|draw|ing** (wīr′drô′ing), *n.* **1** the art of drawing metal into wire. **2** *Figurative.* the act of drawing out an argument or a discussion to prolixity.

**wire|drawn** (wīr′drôn′), *adj., v.* —*adj.* **1** drawn out into a wire. **2** *Figurative.* treated with too much hairsplitting and refinement.
—*v.* the past participle of **wiredraw**.

**wire edge**, a thin, wirelike bur or thread of metal often formed at the edge of a cutting tool during the process of sharpening.

**wire entanglement**, an arrangement or system of barbed wire set up to impede enemy troops.

***wire gauge**, a device for measuring the diameter of wire, the thickness of metal sheets, or the like, usually a disk with notches of different sizes cut in its edge.

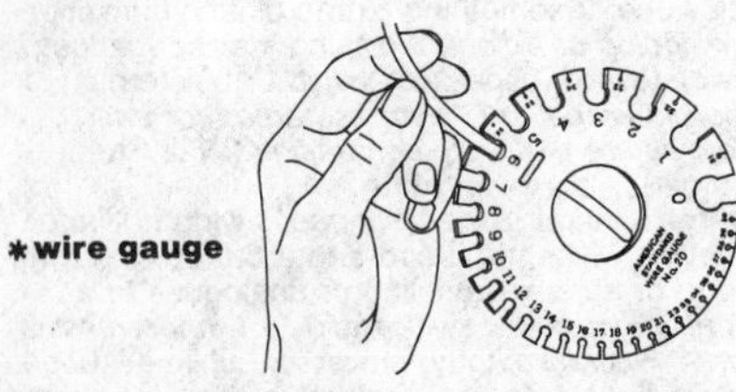

***wire gauge**

**wire gauze**, a fabric of very fine wire.

**wire glass**, glass in which wire is embedded to strengthen it.

**wire grass**, any one of various grasses having wiry stems or leaves, especially a slender Old-World meadow grass, naturalized in North America, and the yard grass.

**wire|hair** (wīr′hãr′), *n.* a fox terrier with a rough, wiry coat.

**wire-haired** (wīr′hãrd′), *adj.* having short, coarse, stiff hair: *a wire-haired fox terrier.*

**wire-haired pointing griffon**, a medium-sized hunting dog with a rough, stiff coat, used to point and retrieve game.

**wire-haired terrier**, = wirehair.

**wire house**, a brokerage firm that communicates with its branch offices by private telephone or telegraph.

**wire|less** (wīr′lis), *adj., n., v.* —*adj.* **1** using no wires; transmitting by radio waves instead of by electric wires. **2** *Especially British.* radio.
—*n. Especially British.* **1** a system of transmission by radio waves without the use of wires. **2a** radio. **b** a message sent by radio; radiogram.
—*v.t., v.i. Especially British.* to send or transmit by radio.

**wireless telegraphy** or **telegraph**, a system of telegraphy in which no conducting wire is used between the transmitting and receiving stations, the signals or messages being transmitted through space by means of electromagnetic waves.

**wireless telephone**, = radiotelephone.

**wireless telephony**, a system of telephony in which there are no conducting wires, the messages being transmitted by means of radio.

**wire|man** (wīr′mən), *n., pl.* **-men. 1** a man who puts electric wires in place and maintains them, as for a telegraph, telephone, electric lighting, or electric power system; lineman. **2** *Obsolete.* a man who makes or works in wire.

**wire nail**, a small, thin nail made from iron or steel wire, with a small head produced by compression of the end.

**wire netting**, a fabric of woven wire, used for screens for windows and doors.

**Wire|pho|to** (wīr′fō′tō), *n., pl.* **-tos.** *Trademark.* **1** a method for transmitting photographs by reproducing a facsimile through electric signals. **2** a photograph transmitted by this method.

**wire|pho|to** (wīr′fō′tō), *v.t.,* **-toed, -to|ing.** to transmit by Wirephoto. [< *Wirephoto*]

**wire|pull** (wīr′pu̇l′), *v.t., v.i. Informal.* to promote by wirepulling.

**wire|pull|er** (wīr′pu̇l′ər), *n. Informal.* a person who uses secret influence to accomplish his purposes. SYN: manipulator.

**wire|pull|ing** (wīr′pu̇l′ing), *n. Informal.* the use of secret influence to accomplish a purpose.

**wire recorder**, a device for recording and reproducing sound on a magnetized steel wire. The sound impulses from the microphone are magnetically impressed on the wire by an electromagnet. The sounds are reproduced as the magnetized wire moves past a receiver.

**wire recording**, a recording made on a wire recorder.

**wire rope**, rope or cable made of twisted strands of wire.

**wire service**, a news agency that gathers foreign and domestic news and photographs and distributes them to member newspapers and radio and television stations, such as the Associated Press (AP) and United Press International (UPI) in the United States.

**wire|smith** (wīr′smith′), *n.* a person who makes metal into wire.

**wire|spun** (wīr′spun′), *adj.* = wiredrawn.

**wire|tap** (wīr′tap′), *v.,* **-tapped, -tap|ping,** *n., adj.*
—*v.t.* **1** to record or obtain by wiretapping: *to wiretap a conversation.* **2** to attach an electronic device to (a telephone, telegraph, or their wires) to listen secretly to private conversations or to record information; tap.
—*v.i.* to tap a telephone or telegraph wire secretly to record or obtain information.

*—n.* Also, **wire tap**. **1** an instance of wiretapping: *to be guilty of a wiretap.* **2** the information obtained or recorded by wiretapping: *a conviction based on a wiretap.*

*—adj.* of or having to do with wiretapping or a wiretap: *wiretap evidence, a wiretap law. A wiretap center illegally operated by two detectives had been discovered ... by special agents of the New York Telephone Company* (New York Times). **—wire′tap′per**, *n.*

**wire|tap|ping** (wīr′tap′ing), *n., adj.,* or **wire tapping**. *—n.* the making of a secret connection with telephone, telegraph, or their wires, to listen to conversations or record information sent over them. Wiretapping is forbidden by law in many countries and states, except as specifically authorized by a qualified authority.

*—adj.* of or having to do with wiretapping: *a wiretapping system, wiretapping equipment. He faces trial on wiretapping charges in New York* (Wall Street Journal). *The two biggest wiretapping agencies in the U.S. are the FBI ... and the New York City Police Department* (Time).

**wire-walk|er** (wīr′wô′kər), *n.* an acrobat who walks and performs feats on a wire rope.

**wire-walk|ing** (wīr′wô′king), *n.* the act of walking or performing on a wire rope.

**wire|work** (wīr′wėrk′), *n.* **1** the making of wire. **2** work done in or made with wire.

**wireworks**, an establishment where wire is made or where wire goods are manufactured.

**wire|work|er** (wīr′wėr′kər), *n.* **1** = wiresmith. **2** *Informal.* a wirepuller.

**wire|worm** (wīr′wėrm′), *n.* **1** the slender, hard-bodied larva of certain beetles. Wireworms feed on the roots of plants and do much damage to crops. **2** = millipede. **3** = stomach worm.

**wire-wove** (wīr′wōv′), *adj.* **1** designating a fine grade of smooth paper, made on a mold of wire gauze, used especially for letter paper. **2** made of woven wire.

**wir|ing** (wīr′ing), *n., adj.* *—n.* **1** a system of wires for carrying an electric current, as in a switchboard or in a building. **2** the act of a person who wires.

*—adj.* **1** that wires: *a wiring crew.* **2** of, having to do with, or required for wiring: *a wiring plan, wiring equipment.*

**wir|ra** (wir′ə), *interj. Irish.* an exclamation of sorrow or lament. [< Irish *a Mhuire* (literally) O Mary]

**wir|y** (wīr′ē), *adj.,* **wir|i|er, wir|i|est**. **1** like wire: *wiry hair, a wiry coat of fur, wiry grass.* **2** lean, strong, and tough: *a man with a wiry build.* **3** made of wire. **4a** produced by or as if by the plucking or vibration of a wire: *wiry sounds.* **b** thin and metallic: *a wiry voice.* **—wir′i|ly**, *adv.* **—wir′i|ness**, *n.*

**wis** (wis), *v.t., v.i. Archaic.* to know (used only in *I wis*). [< *iwis* (erroneously understood as *I wis*) < Old English *gewiss* certain, sure]

**Wis.** or **Wics.**, Wisconsin.

**Wis|con|sin** (wis kon′sən), *adj.* of or having to do with the fourth period of glaciation in North America, beginning about 115,000 years ago and lasting about 95,000 years. [< *Wisconsin,* the state]

**Wis|con|sin|ite** (wis kon′sə nīt), *n.* a native or inhabitant of Wisconsin.

**Wisd.**, Wisdom of Solomon (Book of the Old Testament Apocrypha).

**wis|dom** (wiz′dəm), *n.* **1** knowledge and good judgment based on experience; being wise. **SYN**: sagacity, sapience. **2** wise conduct; wise words: *His wisdom guided us.* **SYN**: prudence, discretion. **3** scholarly knowledge: *Moses was learned in all the wisdom of the Egyptians* (Acts 7:22). **SYN**: learning, erudition. [Old English *wīsdōm* < *wīs* wise, smart + *-dōm* -dom]

**Wis|dom** (wiz′dəm), *n.* **1** a form of literature common to the ancient Egyptians, Syrians, and Mesopotamians, consisting chiefly of wise sayings, and exemplified by the Old Testament books of Proverbs, Job, and Ecclesiastes. **2** = Wisdom of Solomon.

**Wisdom of Jesus, Son of Si|rach** (sī′rak), = Ecclesiasticus.

**Wisdom of Solomon**, a philosophical book of the Old Testament Apocrypha, traditionally attributed to Solomon, included in the canon of the Roman Catholic Bible. *Abbr:* Wisd.

**wisdom tooth**, the back tooth on either side of each jaw, ordinarily appearing between the ages of 17 and 25.

**wise**[1] (wīz), *adj.,* **wis|er, wis|est**, *v.,* **wised, wis|ing**. *—adj.* **1** having or showing knowledge and good judgment: *a wise judge, wise advice, wise plans.* **2** having knowledge or information: *We are none the wiser for his explanation.* **3** learned; erudite; well-informed. **4** *Figurative.* brashly or impudently bold; arrogant; fresh. **5** *Archaic.* having knowledge of occult or supernatural things.

*—v.t., v.i.* **wise up**, *Slang.* **a** to inform or enlighten (a person): *You won't wise him up that I threw a spanner into the machinery?* (P. G. Wodehouse). **b** to become enlightened; gain awareness or understanding: *I wish you'd wise up about these things.*

**get wise**, *Slang.* to find out; understand; realize: *By the time they got wise they'd be paying off* (Harper's).

**wise to**, *Slang.* aware of; informed about: *to put someone wise to something.*

[Old English *wīs*] **—wise′ly**, *adv.* **—wise′ness**, *n.*

*—Syn. adj.* **1 Wise, sage** mean having or showing knowledge and good judgment. **Wise** implies having knowledge and understanding of people and of what is true and right in life and conduct, and showing sound judgment in applying such knowledge: *His wise father knows how to handle him.* **Sage** suggests deep wisdom based on wide knowledge, experience, and profound thought: *The old professor gave us sage advice we have never forgotten.*

**wise**[2] (wīz), *n.* way; manner; fashion; mode; style: *Though a good student, he is in no wise a scholar.* [Old English *wīse.* See related etym. at **guise**.]

**wise**[3] (wīz), *v.t.,* **wised, wis|ing**. *Scottish.* **1** to guide; direct. **2** to induce or entice (away, from). [Old English *wīsian.* See related etym. at **wise**[1].]

**-wise**, *suffix forming adverbs.* **1** in a ____ manner: *Likewise = in a like manner.*

**2** in a ____ ing manner: *Slantwise = in a slanting manner.*

**3** in the characteristic way of a ____; like a ____: *Clockwise = in the way the hands of a clock go.*

**4** in the direction of the ____: *Lengthwise = in the direction of the length.*

**5** in the ____ respect or case: *Otherwise = in the other respect.*

**6** special meanings, as in *sidewise.*

[< *wise*[2]]

► In popular jargon, and that of certain professions, **-wise** is often suffixed to polysyllabic nouns to form words for the occasion: *We have made a number of changes curriculumwise.*

**wise|a|cre** (wīz′ā′kər), *n.* **1** a person who thinks that he knows everything. **2** a learned person; sage (usually contemptuous or ironical, with implication of pedantry or impracticality). [half translation of Middle Dutch *wijssegger* soothsayer. Compare Middle High German *wīssager.*]

**wise|crack** (wīz′krak′), *n., v. Slang.* *—n.* a snappy comeback; smart remark.

*—v.i.* to make wisecracks: *An attendant directed me up a flight of stairs to an antechamber of the court, where I was soon joined by ... a half dozen defiant-looking youths, wisecracking to keep up their courage* (Maclean's). **—wise′-crack′er**, *n.*

**wise guy**, *Slang.* a person who pretends to know more than he really does; impudent or conceited fellow.

**wise|ling** (wīz′ling′), *n.* a pretender to wisdom; wiseacre: *This may well put to the blush those wiselings that show themselves fools in so speaking* (John Donne).

**wis|en|heim|er** (wī′zən hī′mər), *n. U.S. Slang.* a wise guy: *Scent of Mystery has been tagged by the Hollywood wisenheimers as "the first movie that ever smelled on purpose"* (Time). [< *wise*[1] + German *-enheimer,* as in *Oppenheimer*]

**wi|sent** (wē′zənt), *n.* = aurochs (def. 1). [< German *Wisent* < Old High German *wisunt.* Compare etym. under **bison**.]

**wish** (wish), *v., n.* *—v.t.* **1** to have a desire for; be glad to have or do; want: *to wish help, to wish money. I wish that it would snow tomorrow. Do you wish to go home?* **2** to feel or express a desire for (a person or thing to be as specified): *to wish oneself at home, to wish a speech were finished.* **3** to desire (something) for someone; have or express a hope for: *to wish someone good luck. I wish you a happy new year. We wished her good night. I don't wish him any harm.* **4** to request or command (a thing or action, or a person to do something): *Do you wish me to send her in now?*

*—v.i.* **1** to have a desire; express a hope; long (for): *He wished for a new house.* **2** to desire or hope for something, especially something good, for another: *to wish well to a friend.*

*—n.* **1** a wishing or wanting; desire or longing: *He had no wish to be king. What is your wish?* **2a** a saying of a wish: *She sends you best wishes for a happy new year.* **b** a request or command; entreaty: *He granted her slightest wish.* **3** a thing wished for: *She got her wish.*

**wish on**, *Informal.* to pass on to; foist on: *They wished the hardest job on me. Professor Henry's efforts to dissociate himself from the museum that Congress had wished on him did not meet with ... success* (New Yorker).

[Old English *wȳscan.* See related etym. at **ween**[1].] **—wish′er**, *n.*

*—Syn. v.t.* **1 Wish, desire** mean to long for something. **Wish** is the least emphatic word, sometimes suggesting only that one would like to have, do, or get a certain thing, sometimes suggesting a longing that can never be satisfied: *I wish I could go to Europe next year.* **Desire**, sometimes used as a formal substitute for *wish* or, especially, *want,* suggests wishing strongly for something and usually being willing or determined to work or struggle to get it: *She finally received the position she desired.*

**wish|a** (wish′ə), *interj. Irish.* an exclamation especially of surprise or regret: *But no sooner would the excursion be over than she would sigh, "Wisha, it would have been far better for me to have gone to the chapel and said my rosary"* (Atlantic).

**wish|bone** (wish′bōn′), *n.* the forked bone in the front of the breastbone in poultry and other birds; furcula. [< *wish* + *bone* (because of the custom of breaking it between two persons, one, usually the one with the longer end, getting his wish)]

**wish|ful** (wish′fəl), *adj.* having or expressing a wish; desiring; desirous. **—wish′ful|ly**, *adv.* **—wish′ful|ness**, *n.*

**wish fulfillment**, *Psychoanalysis.* indirect fulfillment of a frustrated wish, as through a daydream: *Every time that we fully understand a dream it proves to be a wish fulfillment* (Sigmund Freud).

**wishful thinker**, a person who engages in wishful thinking.

**wishful thinking**, a believing something to be true that one wishes or wants to be true.

**wish|ing cap** (wish′ing), a fabulous cap supposed to ensure fulfillment of any wish made by one wearing it.

**wishing well**, a well supposed to magically grant the wish of a person who throws a coin into it.

**wish-wash** (wish′wosh′, -wôsh′), *n.* a wishy-washy thing.

**wish|y-wash|y** (wish′ē wosh′ē, -wôsh′-), *adj.* **1** thin and weak; insipid; watery: *wishy-washy soup with no flavor.* **2** *Figurative.* feeble; weak; poor: *a wishy-washy excuse, a wishy-washy attitude.* [varied reduplication of *washy* thin, watery]

**wisp** (wisp), *n., v.* *—n.* **1** a small bundle; small bunch: *a wisp of hay.* **2** a small portion of anything; slight bit; shred; fragment: *a wisp of hair, a wisp of smoke.* **3** a little thing: *a wisp of a girl.* **4** a twisted bundle, as of hay or straw, or a twist of paper, especially when burned as a torch or used as kindling. **5** = will-o'-the-wisp. **6** = whisk broom.

*—v.t.* to twist into or as a wisp.

*—v.i.* to move or drift as a wisp of smoke or vapor.

[origin uncertain. Compare Frisian *wisp.*] **—wisp′-like′**, *adj.*

**wisp|ish** (wis′pish), *adj.* of the nature of or resembling a wisp; somewhat wispy: *As they went higher and higher, she looked out at the very white, wispish clouds* (New Yorker).

**wisp|y** (wis′pē), *adj.,* **wisp|i|er, wisp|i|est**. like a wisp; thin; slight: *A number of them are decorated with wispy feathers trailing down one cheek or over the forehead* (New Yorker).

**wist** (wist), *v. Archaic.* the past tense and past participle of **wit**[2]: *He wist not who had spoken.*

**Wis|tar|berg glass** (wis′tər bərg), a green glassware used especially in bottles, decorated with bands, swirls, and threads of applied glass, made in Wistarberg, New Jersey, in the 1700's; South Jersey glass.

**wis|tar|i|a** (wis tãr′ē ə), *n.* = wisteria.

**wis|te|ri|a** (wis tir′ē ə), *n.* a climbing shrub with large, drooping clusters of showy, purple, blue, or white flowers, especially the Chinese wisteria and the Japanese wisteria, species often grown to cover verandas and walls. Wisteria belongs to the pea family. See picture under **pea family**. [American English < New Latin *Wistaria* the genus name < Caspar *Wistar,* 1761-1818, an American anatomist]

► Although **wistaria** accords better with the name *Wistar,* **wisteria** is both the earlier and the more common form.

**wist|ful** (wist′fəl), *adj.* **1** longing; yearning: *A child stood looking with wistful eyes at the toys in the window.* **SYN**: wishful. **2** pensive; melancholy. **SYN**: musing, meditative. **3** *Obsolete.* closely attentive; intent. [< obsolete *wist,* back formation < *wistly* intently + *-ful;* origin uncertain] **—wist′ful|ly**, *adv.* **—wist′ful|ness**, *n.*

**wis|ti|ti** (wis tē′tē), *n.* a marmoset of South

America, often kept as a pet. Also, **ouistiti**. [probably imitative]

**wit**[1] (wit), *n.* **1** the power to perceive quickly and express cleverly ideas that are unusual, striking, and amusing: *His wit made even troubles seem amusing. Brevity is the soul of wit* (Shakespeare). **2** a person who is amusing by his striking or clever expression: *Go on joking, Ann. You're the wit of the family* (Thackeray). **3** a person noted for his brilliant or sparkling sayings, clever repartee, or the like. **4** understanding; mind; sense: *People with quick wits learn easily. The child was out of his wits with fright. That poor man hasn't wit enough to earn a living.* **SYN**: intelligence.

**at one's wit's** (or **wits'**) **end**, not knowing what to do or say; utterly perplexed: *What shall we do? is the doleful cry of men at their wits' end* (John Flavel).

**have** (or **keep**) **one's wits about one**, to be alert: *Have all your wits about you, ... you are nursing a viper in your bosom* (Benjamin H. Malkin).

**live by one's wits**, to get one's living by clever or crafty devices rather than by any settled occupation: *Living by his wits—which means by the abuse of every faculty that, worthily employed, raises man above the beasts* (Dickens).

[Old English *witt*. Ultimately related to **wit**[2].]

**—*Syn.*** **1 Wit, humor** mean power to see and express what is amusing or causes laughter. **Wit** applies to the sort of mental power that is quick in perceiving what is striking, unusual, or inconsistent and in expressing it in a clever and amusing manner: *Bernard Shaw was famous for his wit.* **Humor** applies to the ability to see and show with warm sympathy the things in life and human nature that are funny or absurdly out of keeping: *Her sense of humor eased her trouble.*

**wit**[2] (wit), *v.t., v.i., pres. 1st pers.* **wot**, *2nd pers.* **wost** (wost), *3rd pers.* **wot**, *pl.* **wit**; *pt. and pp.* **wist**; *pres. p.* **wit|ting**. *Archaic.* to know.

**to wit**, that is to say; namely: *To my son I leave all I own—to wit: my house, what is in it, and the land on which it stands.*

[Old English *witan*]

**wit|an** (wit′ən), *n.pl.* in Anglo-Saxon times: **1** the members of the national council (witenagemot). **2** the council itself. [modern revival of Old English *witan,* plural of *wita* council or (literally) one who knows < *witan* wit, know]

**witch** (wich), *n., v.* **—*n.*** **1** a woman supposed to have magic power. It was thought that witches generally used their power to do evil. *I have heard of one old witch changing herself into a pigeon* (John Rhys). **2** *Figurative.* **a** an ugly old woman; hag. **SYN**: crone. **b** *Informal.* a charming or fascinating girl or woman. **SYN**: charmer. **3** *Dialect.* a male practitioner of magic; magician; sorcerer; wizard. **4** *Mathematics.* witch of Agnesi.

**—*v.t.*** **1a** to use the power of a witch on; put a spell upon. **b** to bring, draw, put, or change by witchcraft. **2** *Figurative.* to charm; fascinate; bewitch. **SYN**: enthrall, captivate.

**—*v.i.*** to use a divining rod; dowse.

[Old English *wicce*]

**witch ball**, **1** a hollow ball of glass with loops and stripes of color, made in the 1700's to be hung in windows to ward off witches. **2** a similar ball of glass made in various colors during the 1800's for use as decorative stoppers on pitchers, jars, and vases.

**witch-broom** (wich′brüm′, -brům′), *n.,* or **witch broom**, = witches'-broom.

**witch|craft** (wich′kraft′, -kräft′), *n.* **1** what a witch does or is supposed to do; magic power or influence: *There are few superstitions which have been so universal as a belief in witchcraft* (Henry T. Buckle). **SYN**: sorcery. **2** *Figurative.* bewitching or fascinating attraction or charm.

**witchcrafts**, magic arts: *All these witchcrafts ceased after the coming of Christ* (Fynes Moryson).

**witch doctor**, a medicine man, especially in certain primitive societies.

**witch-elm** (wich′elm′), *n.* = wych-elm.

**witch|er|y** (wich′ər ē, wich′rē), *n., pl.* **-er|ies**. **1** witchcraft; magic. **2** *Figurative.* charm; fascination.

**witch|es'-be|som** (wich′iz bē′zəm), *n.* = witches'-broom.

**witches' brew**, **1** a strange or exotic concoction, such as witches were once supposed to brew: *A witches' brew of antifreeze and slurry was concocted to coat the wires that had been damaged* (New Yorker). **2** *Figurative.* a confused mixture; an awesome mess: *a real witches' brew of a race, complete with thunder, lightning, and enough rain to quench a volcano* (London Times). *... a witches' brew of ideas, objections, and counterproposals* (New York Times). Also, **witch's brew**.

**witch|es'-broom** (wich′iz brüm′, -brům′), *n.* **1** an abnormal growth on trees and shrubs, especially conifers, consisting of a dense mass of small, thin branches, caused chiefly by various fungi; hexenbesen. **2** a similar growth on the potato, caused by a virus.

**witches'** or **Witches' Sabbath**, a midnight meeting of demons, sorcerers, and witches, supposed in medieval times to have been held annually as a festival; Sabbat.

**witch|et|ty** (wich′ə tē), *n. Australian.* the larva of some species of longicorn beetles, eaten as food by the aborigines. [< a native name]

**witch grass**, **1** a North American panic grass having a brushlike panicle. **2** = couch grass. [American English, probably variant of *quitch grass*]

**witch hazel**, **1** a shrub or small tree of eastern North America that has yellow flowers in the fall or winter after the leaves have fallen; spotted alder; hamamelis. Witch hazel has leaves with straight veins and wavy edges. **2** a lotion for cooling and soothing the skin, made by steeping the bark and leaves of this shrub in alcohol; hamamelin. **3** any other plant of the same genus. Also, **wych-hazel**. [earlier *wyche hasill,* apparently < Old English *wice* wych-elm; taken as *witch,* noun]

**witch hunt**, or **witch-hunt** (wich′hunt′), *n.* **1** the action of hunting out and persecuting persons suspected of witchcraft. There were witch hunts in New England in the 1600's. **2** *Informal, Figurative.* the action of persecuting or defaming persons to gain political advantage: *He denounced the investigation as a "witch hunt" and invoked his constitutional right not to testify against himself* (Wall Street Journal).

**witch-hunt|er** (wich′hun′tər), *n. Informal.* a person who conducts a witch hunt.

**witch-hunt|ing** (wich′hun′ting), *n., adj. Informal.* **—*n.*** = witch hunt.

**—*adj.*** of or having to do with a witch hunt.

**witch|ing** (wich′ing), *adj., n.* **—*adj.*** **1** bewitching; magical. **2** *Figurative.* enchanting.

**—*n.*** **1** = witchcraft. **2** *Figurative.* enchantment; fascination. **—witch′ing|ly**, *adv.*

**witch|like** (wich′līk′), *adj.* having the nature of or resembling a witch: *Her eyes weren't witchlike, not black and beady and evil but large and milky blue and kind* (New Yorker).

**witch|man** (wich′mən), *n., pl.* **-men**. = witch doctor.

**witch moth**, any one of certain large, dark, noctuid moths.

**witch of A|gne|si** (ä nyā′zē), *Mathematics.* a plane cubic curve that is symmetrical about the y-axis and asymptotic to the x-axis, defined by the equation $4a^2\ (2a - y) = x^2y$. [translation of Italian *versiera di Agnesi* < *versiera* witch, versed sine + *di* of + Maria Gaetana *Agnesi,* 1718-1799, an Italian mathematician]

**witch's brew**, = witches' brew.

**witch|weed** (wich′wēd′), *n., pl.* **-weeds** or (*collectively*) **-weed**. a small weed of Africa and the United States belonging to the figwort family. It lives as a parasite on roots of corn and other grains.

**witch|y** (wich′ē), *adj.,* **witch|i|er, witch|i|est**. = witchlike.

**wite** (wīt), *n., v.,* **wit|ed, wit|ing**. *Scottish.* **—*n.*** **1** blame; reproach. **2** blameworthiness; fault.

**—*v.t.*** = blame. Also, **wyte**. [Old English *wītan* to blame]

**wit|e|na|ge|mot** or **wit|e|na|ge|mote** (wit′ə nə gə mōt′), *n.* the royal council of the Anglo-Saxons; assembly of the witan. [modern revival of Old English *witena gemōt* (literally) assembly of wise men < *witena,* genitive plural of *wita* councilor (see etym. under **witan**) + *gemōt* meeting]

**with** (wiᴛʜ, with), *prep.* **1** in the company of: *to sit with a friend. Come with me.* **2** among; into: *They will mix with the crowd.* **3** having, wearing, or carrying: *a book with a red cover. He is a man with ideas. She received a telegram with good news.* **4** by means of; by using: *to work with a machine. The man cut the meat with a knife.* **5** using; showing: *Work with care.* **6** as an addition to; added to: *Do you want sugar with your tea?* **7** including; and: *tea with sugar and lemon.* **8** in regard to: *We are pleased with the house.* **9** in relation to: *one day with another. They are friendly with us.* **10** in proportion to: *The army's power increases with its size.* **11** as a result of; because of; on account of: *eyes dim with tears. The man almost died with thirst. The child is shaking with cold.* **12** in the keeping or service of: *to leave a package with a friend. Leave the dog with me.* **13** in the region, sphere, experience, opinion, or view of: *It is summer with us while it is winter with the Australians. It is day with us while it is night with the Chinese. High taxes are unpopular with many people.* **14** at the same time as: *With this battle the war ended.* **15** in the same direction as: *to sail with the tide. The boat floated along with the current.* **16** on the side of; for: *to vote or side with someone. They are with us in our plans.* **17** from: *I hate to part with my favorite things.* **18** against: *The English fought with the Germans.* **19** receiving; having; being allowed: *I went with my parents' permission.* **20** in spite of; notwithstanding: *With all his size he was not a strong man.* **21** by (some response or reaction): *a suggestion received with silence, to interrupt with a laugh.* **22** in the course, process, or duration of: *to mellow with age.* **23** by adding, furnishing, filling, or the like, a material to something: *a ring set with diamonds.*

**with it**, *Slang.* **a** informed; up-to-date; hip: *[He] is one of the new school of BBC heads—frank, approachable, and in every way "with it"* (Manchester Guardian Weekly). **b** inspired or excited by something: *Faced with a work of modern art, [he] isn't "with it"* (Harper's).

**with that**. See under **that**, *pron.*

[Old English *with* against]

**—*Syn.*** **4 With, by, through** are used to connect to a sentence a word naming the agent that has performed an action or the means or instrument used to perform it. **With** is used to connect the word naming the instrument: *Write the letter with a pen.* **By** is used to connect the word naming the agent when it has not been named in the subject of the sentence, and sometimes to name the means: *The meat was taken by the dog. I travel by airplane.* **Through** is used to connect the word naming the means or the reason: *They ran through fear. We found out through him.*

**with-**, *prefix.* **1** away; back: *Withdraw = to draw back, withhold.*

**2** against; opposing: *Withstand = to stand against.*

**3** along with; alongside; toward, as in *withal, without, within.*

[Old English *with-,* related to *with* with]

**with|al** (wiᴛʜ ôl′, with-), *adv., prep. Archaic.* **—*adv.*** **1** with it all; as well; besides; also: *The lady is rich and fair and wise withal.* **SYN**: moreover, likewise. **2** at the same time; in spite of all; notwithstanding; nevertheless. **3** therewith: *Having spoiled the gods Of honours, crown withal thy mortal men* (Elizabeth Barrett Browning).

**—*prep.*** with: *Such eyes and ears as Nature had been pleased to endow me withal* (James Russell Lowell).

[Middle English *with alle* < *with* + *all*]

**with|draw** (wiᴛʜ drô′, with-), *v.,* **-drew, -drawn, -draw|ing**. **—*v.t.*** **1** to draw back; draw away: *He quickly withdrew his hand from the hot stove.* **2** to take back; remove: *He agreed to withdraw his charge of theft if they returned the money. We withdrew our savings from the bank. Worn-out money is withdrawn from use by the government.* **SYN**: recall, retract.

**—*v.i.*** **1** to draw back; draw away: *I withdrew from the discussion before it became an argument.* **2** to go away: *She withdrew from the room.* **SYN**: leave. See syn. under **depart**. **3** to demand the withdrawal as of a statement, motion, or proposal. [< *with-* away + *draw*]

**with|draw|a|ble** (wiᴛʜ drô′ə bəl, with-), *adj.* that can be withdrawn.

**with|draw|al** (wiᴛʜ drô′əl, with-), *n.* **1** a withdrawing or being withdrawn: *a withdrawal of money from a bank account.* **SYN**: retreat. **2a** the act of depriving or state of being deprived of the use of narcotic drugs: *Sudden withdrawal is the only procedure recognized and sanctioned by the Narcotics Bureau* (Wall Street Journal). **b** a condition of physical distress in an addict suddenly deprived of narcotic drugs.

**withdrawal symptom**, any one of various symptoms, such as profuse sweating and nausea, induced in a person addicted to a drug when he is deprived of that drug: *If morphine is withheld, gross homeostatic imbalances occur that cause the distressing effects known as withdrawal symptoms* (Scientific American).

**with|draw|ing room** (wiᴛʜ drô′ing, with-), *Archaic or Historical.* a drawing room.

**with|draw|ment** (wiᴛʜ drô′mənt, with-), *n.* = withdrawal.

**with|drawn** (wiᴛʜ drôn′, with-), *v., adj.* **—*v.*** the past participle of **withdraw**: *He was withdrawn from the game.*

**—*adj.*** **1** retiring; reserved; shy: *Overly sensitive persons are frequently withdrawn.* **2** isolated; secluded.

**with|drawn|ness** (wiᴛʜ drôn′nis, with-), *n.* withdrawn or retired character.

**with|drew** (wiᴛʜ drü′, with-), *v.* the past tense of **withdraw**: *The coach withdrew the player from the game when he was hurt.*

**withe** (wīᴛʜ, with, wiᴛʜ), *n., v.,* **withed, with|ing**. **—*n.*** **1** a willow twig. **2** any tough, easily bent twig or branch used for binding or tying, and sometimes for plaiting; withy. **3** a flexible handle of a tool, to prevent or lessen jarring of the wrist.

**—*v.t.*** *Dialect.* **1a** to bind with a withe or withes.

**b** *U.S.* to take (deer) with a noose made of withes. **2** to twist like a withe.
[Old English *withthe*]

**with|er** (wiᴛʜ′ər), *v.i., v.t.* **1** to lose or cause to lose freshness, vigor, or other lively quality; make or become dry and lifeless; dry up; fade; shrivel: *The hot sun withers grass* (v.t.). *Flowers wither after they are cut* (v.i.). *Old age had withered her face* (v.t.). **2** *Figurative.* to feel or cause to feel ashamed or confused: *to wither at the thought of a public rebuke* (v.i.). *She blushed under her aunt's withering look* (v.t.). [variant of Middle English *wydderen,* probably variant of *wederen* to weather. Compare etym. under **weather**, verb.]

**with|er|ing** (wiᴛʜ′ər ing), *adj.* **1** very destructive: *a withering blast of machine-gun fire.* **2** *Figurative.* very sarcastic or trenchant: *a withering remark.* —**with′er|ing|ly**, *adv.*

**with|er|ite** (wiᴛʜ′ə rīt), *n.* native barium carbonate, a rare white, gray, or yellowish mineral. *Formula:* $BaCO_3$ [< William *Withering,* 1741-1799, an English physician, who first described and analyzed it + *-ite*[1]]

**withe rod**, either of two North American shrubs of the honeysuckle family, varieties of viburnum, with tough, osierlike shoots and white or yellowish flowers.

**with|ers** (wiᴛʜ′ərz), *n.pl.* the highest part of a horse's or other animal's back, behind the neck. See picture under **horse**.
**wring one's withers**, to subject one to emotional stress, pain, or other torment; cause anguish; distress: *He wrings our withers in this, but perhaps he lacks the ability to awe us with the agonies of the soul* (Punch).
[apparently reduction of obsolete *widersome,* perhaps < Old English *wither* opposite, back]

**with|er|shins** (wiᴛʜ′ər shinz), *adv. Scottish.* **1** in a direction contrary to the apparent course of the sun (considered as unlucky or causing disaster). **2** *Obsolete.* in a direction opposite to the usual; in the wrong way. Also, **widdershins, widershins.** [earlier *widdershins* < Middle Low German *weddersinnes,* Middle High German *widersinnes* < *wider* against, opposed + *-sind* way, direction + *-es* -s[2]]

**with|held** (with held′, wiᴛʜ-), *v.* the past tense and past participle of **withhold**: *The boy wrongly withheld information about his friend, thinking he was protecting him.*

**with|hold** (with hōld′, wiᴛʜ-), *v.,* **-held, -hold|ing.** —*v.t.* **1** to refuse to give: *There will be no seal hunting if the government withholds permits.* **2** to hold back; keep back: *The dam broke as it was too weak to withhold the pressure of the rising water.* **SYN**: See syn. under **keep**.
—*v.i.* to refrain (from): *to withhold from spreading the news.*
[< *with-* back, away + *hold*[1]] —**with|hold′er**, *n.*

**with|hold|ing tax** (with hōl′ding, wiᴛʜ-), the part of a person's income tax that is deducted from his salary or wages by his employer on behalf of the government.

**with|hold|ment** (with hōld′mənt, wiᴛʜ-), *n.* the act of withholding.

**with|in** (wiᴛʜ in′, with-), *prep., adv., n.* —*prep.* **1** inside the limits of; not beyond; not more than: *to live within one's income, to be within sight. The task was within the man's power. He guessed my weight within five pounds.* **2** in or into the inner part of; inside of: *By the use of X rays, doctors can see within the body.* **3** *Figurative.* in the inner being, soul, or mind of: *And fire and ice within me fight* (A. E. Housman).
—*adv.* **1** in or into the inner part; inside: *The house had been painted within and without. The curtains were white without and green within.* **2** *Figurative.* in the inner being; in the being, soul, or mind; inwardly: *to keep one's grief within.*
—*n.* the inner part; interior; inside.
**from within**, from the inside of a person, place, or thing: *His regime is clearly being eroded from within* (New York Times).
[Old English *withinnan* < *with* with, against + *innan,* adverb, inside]

**with|in|doors** (wiᴛʜ in′dôrz′, -dōrz′; with-), *adv. Archaic.* indoors.

**with|in-named** (wiᴛʜ in′nāmd′, with-), *adj.* specified by name within this or that document, clause, or other piece of writing.

**with-it** (wiᴛʜ′it′, with′-), *adj. Slang.* up-to-date; keeping up with the latest trends or fashions; hip; in: *Etams ... set out to get with-it trendy clothes as quickly as possible on to the backs of the girls* (Scotsman). *The papier-mâché toe rings are very simple and very with-it* (Maclean's).
—**with′-it′ness**, *n.*

**with|out** (wiᴛʜ out′, with-), *prep., adv., conj., n.* —*prep.* **1** with no; not having; free from; lacking: *A cat walks without noise. I drink tea without sugar.* **2** so as to leave out, avoid, or neglect: *She walked past without noticing us.* **3** outside of; beyond: *Only those who lived without the city walls were able to save anything from the fire.*
—*adv.* **1** on the outside; outside: *The house is clean within and without.* **2** *Figurative.* outside of the inner being; with regard to external actions or circumstances; in relation to others: *at ease without and at peace within* (James Martineau). **3** lacking: *We must eat this or go without.*
—*conj. Dialect.* unless: *I will not come without you invite me.*
—*n.* the outer part; exterior; outside: *The wholeness of man encompasses both the without or physical* [*aspect*] *and the within* (New Scientist).
**from without**, from the outside of a person, place or thing: *An independent state, jealous of all interference from without* (Macauley). *Doors opened smartly from without* (Dickens).
[Old English *withūtan* < *with* with, against + *ūtan,* adverb, outside]
▶ **a Without** as a conjunction meaning "unless" (*He could not move without the Congress sent him supplies*), formerly common in both general and literary English, is now confined to nonstandard use. **b** For *without hardly* (or *scarcely*), see **hardly**.

**with|out|doors** (wiᴛʜ out′dôrz′, -dōrz′; with-), *adv. Obsolete.* outdoors.

**with|stand** (with stand′, wiᴛʜ-), *v.,* **-stood, -stand|ing.** —*v.t.* to stand against; hold out against; bear up under; resist; endure; oppose, especially successfully: *Explorers have to withstand hardships. These shoes will withstand much hard wear.* **SYN**: See syn. under **oppose**.
—*v.i.* to offer resistance or opposition; resist; endure. **SYN**: See syn. under **oppose**.
[Old English *withstandan* < *with-* against + *standan* to stand]

**with|stood** (with stůd′, wiᴛʜ-), *v.* the past tense and past participle of **withstand**: *The windows withstood the force of the blast and did not shatter.*

**with|y** (wiᴛʜ′ē, with′-), *n., pl.* **with|ies,** *adj.* —*n.* **1** a willow or osier. **2** a twig of willow or osier; withe. **3** a band or halter made of withes.
—*adj.* resembling a withe in flexibility.
[Old English *wīthig* < *withthe* withe + *-ig* -y[1]]

**wit|less** (wit′lis), *adj.* **1** lacking sense; stupid; foolish: *a witless person, a witless remark. Crossing the street without looking in both directions is a witless thing to do.* **SYN**: brainless. **2** not knowing; unaware: *to be witless of danger.* —**wit′less|ly**, *adv.* —**wit′less|ness**, *n.*

**wit|ling** (wit′ling), *n.* a person who fancies himself to be clever at repartee; would-be wit. [< *wit*[1] + *-ling*]

**wit|loof** (wit′lōf), *n.* = endive. [< Dutch *witloof* (literally) white leaf]

**wit|ness** (wit′nis), *n., v.* —*n.* **1** a person who saw something happen; spectator; eyewitness: *He made the remark in the presence of several witnesses.* **2** a person who takes an oath to tell the truth in a court of law: *Both the judge and the lawyers questioned the police witness.* **3a** evidence; testimony: *A person who gives false witness in court is guilty of lying under oath.* **b** a person or thing that furnishes evidence or proof of the thing or fact mentioned: (*Figurative.*) *Their tattered clothes were a witness of their poverty.* **4** a person who writes his name on a document to show that he saw the maker sign it; person selected to be present at some transaction in order to be able to testify that it occurred.
—*v.t.* **1** to see; perceive: *I witnessed the accident.* **2** to be the scene or setting of (a fact or event): *the years that witnessed the Industrial Revolution.* **3** to testify to; give evidence of: *Her whole manner witnessed her surprise.* **4** *Figurative.* to furnish evidence or proof of; betoken. **5** to sign (a document) as a witness: *The two servants witnessed his will.*
—*v.i.* to give evidence; bear witness; testify (to, against).
**bear witness**, to be evidence; give evidence; testify: *The results of the experiment bore witness to the scientist's theory. The girl's blushing bore witness to her embarrassment.*
[Old English *witnes* (originally) knowledge < *wit* wit, cleverness] —**wit′ness|er**, *n.*

**Wit|ness** (wit′nis), *n.* a member of Jehovah's Witnesses.

**witness box**, a rectangular enclosure in a British court occupied by a witness while giving evidence.

**witness chair**, a chair for a witness, especially on a witness stand.

**witness stand**, a place where a witness stands or sits to give evidence in a law court.

**wit|ster** (wit′stər), *n.* a person who is adept in making witticisms; wit.

**-witted**, *combining form.* having a ___ wit or wits: *Quick-witted = having a quick wit.*

**wit|ti|cism** (wit′ə siz əm), *n.* a witty remark. **SYN**: quip, mot.

**wit|ti|ly** (wit′ə lē), *adv.* in a witty manner; with wit.

**wit|ti|ness** (wit′ē nis), *n.* the character of being witty; quality of being ingenious or clever.

**wit|ting** (wit′ing), *adj., n.* —*adj.* done or acting consciously, and so with responsibility; not unwitting; intentional: *a witting aggressor, aggression, etc.*
—*n. Dialect.* **1** tidings; news. **2** notice; warning.

**wit|ting|ly** (wit′ing lē), *adv.* knowingly; intentionally. **SYN**: purposely, designedly.

**wit|tol** (wit′əl), *n. Archaic.* a man who is aware of and complaisant about the infidelity of his wife; contented cuckold. [Middle English *wetewold,* apparently < *weten* to wit, know + *-wold,* as in *cokewold* cuckold]

**wit|ty** (wit′ē), *adj.,* **-ti|er, -ti|est.** **1** full of wit; clever and amusing: *A witty person makes witty remarks.* **SYN**: facetious, droll. **2** *Dialect.* **a** intelligent; clever. **b** skillful; expert. [Old English *wittig* wise, clever < *witt* reasoning + *-ig* -y[1]]

**wit|wall** (wit′wôl), *n.* = green woodpecker. [< earlier German *Wittewal,* related to Middle Low German *wedewale.* See related etym. at **woodwall.**]

**wive** (wīv), *v.,* **wived, wiv|ing.** —*v.i.* to take a wife; get married; marry (with).
—*v.t.* **1** to take as a wife. **2** *Archaic.* to furnish with a wife.
[Old English *wīfian*]

**wi|vern** (wī′vərn), *n. Heraldry.* a two-legged, winged dragon with a long, barbed tail. Also, **wyvern.** [earlier *wiver,* special use of Middle English *wyver,* and *guivre* serpent, viper < Old North French *wivre,* Old French *guivre* < Latin *vīpera*]

**wives** (wīvz), *n.* plural of **wife**.

**wiz** (wiz), *n. Informal.* wizard: *He thinks he's such a wiz at cars, but he couldn't locate that squeak* (Sinclair Lewis).

**wiz|ard** (wiz′ərd), *n., adj.* —*n.* **1** a man supposed to have magic power; magician; sorcerer. **2** *Informal, Figurative.* a very clever person; expert: *to be a wizard at math. Edison was a wizard at invention.* **3** *Obsolete.* a wise man; sage (often contemptuous).
—*adj.* **1** = magic. **2** *British Slang.* very good or excellent: *a wizard time.*
[Middle English *wysard* < *wise* wise, smart + *-ard,* a noun suffix]

**wiz|ard|ly** (wiz′ərd lē), *adj.* of or like a wizard.

**wiz|ard|ry** (wiz′ər drē), *n.* **1** magic skill; magic. **SYN**: sorcery, witchcraft. **2** *Informal, Figurative.* great cleverness or expertise: *an astonishing record of administrative wizardry in industry* (David Levy).

**wiz|en** (wiz′ən, wē′zən), *v., adj.* —*v.i.* to dry up; shrivel; wither.
—*v.t.* to cause to wither or shrivel.
—*adj.* = wizened. Also, **weazen.**
[Old English *wisnian* dry up, shrivel.]

**wiz|ened** (wiz′ənd, wē′zənd), *adj.* dried up; withered; shriveled: *a wizened apple, a wizened face.* **SYN**: shrunken, wrinkled.

**wiz|en-faced** (wiz′ən fāst′, wē′zən-), *adj.* having a thin, shriveled face.

**wk.**, **1** week. **2** work.

**wks.**, **1** weeks. **2** works.

**w.l.**, **1** water line. **2** wave length.

**WLB** (no periods), War Labor Board.

**w. long.** or **W. long.**, west longitude.

**Wm.**, William.

**W.M.**, worshipful master (in Freemasonry).

**WMC** (no periods), War Manpower Commission.

**wmk.**, watermark.

**WMO** (no periods) or **W.M.O.**, World Meteorological Organization.

**WNW** (no periods) or **W.N.W.**, between west and northwest; west-northwest.

**wo** (wō), *n., interj.* = woe.

**w/o** (no periods), without.

**W.O.** or **WO** (no periods), **1** War Office. **2** warrant officer.

**woad** (wōd), *n.* **1** a European plant of the mustard family, formerly extensively cultivated for the blue dye furnished by its leaves; dyer's-weed; pastel. **2** the dye. [Old English *wād*]

**woad|ed** (wō′did) *adj.* dyed or colored blue with woad.

**woad|wax|en** (wōd′wak′sən), *n.* an Old-World yellow-flowered shrub of the pea family; dyeweed; dyer's-broom. Its flowers were formerly used as the source of a yellow dye. Also, **woodwaxen.** [alteration (influenced by *woad*) of *woodwaxen* < Old English *wuduweaxen,* oblique case of *wuduweaxe* < *wudu* wood, tree + *-weaxe,* related to *weaxan* to wax, grow]

**woald** (wōld), *n.* = weld[2].

**wob|ble** (wob′əl), *v.,* **-bled, -bling,** *n.* —*v.i.* **1** to move unsteadily from side to side: *A baby wob-*

**Pronunciation Key:** hat, āge, cãre, fär; let, ēqual, tėrm; it, īce; hot, ōpen, ôrder; **oi**l, **ou**t; cup, pủt, rüle; **ch**ild; lo**ng**; **th**in; ᴛʜen; **zh**, measure; **ə** represents **a** in about, **e** in taken, **i** in pencil, **o** in lemon, **u** in circus.

*bles when it begins to walk alone.* **2** to shake or quiver; tremble: *Soft jelly wobbles.* **3** *Figurative.* to be uncertain, unsteady, or changeable; waver.
— ***v.t.*** *Informal.* to cause to wobble.
— ***n.*** the act of wobbling; wobbling motion. Also, **wabble**.
[perhaps < Low German *wabbeln*]

**wobble pump**, a hand pump in an airplane by which fuel may be transferred from an auxiliary tank to a main tank, or to the engine or for use when the power pump fails.

**wob|bler** (wob′lər), *n.* **1** a person or thing that wobbles. **2** a person or animal that walks unsteadily. **3** *Figurative.* a person who wavers in his opinions. **4** spoon bait (because it wobbles when drawn across the water). Also, **wabbler**.

**wob|bli|ness** (wob′lē nis), *n.* the state of being wobbly: *We feel the wobbliness of a bear on roller skates* (Atlantic).

**wob|bling** (wob′ling), *adj.* that wobbles. Also, **wabbling**. — **wob′bling|ly**, *adv.*

**wob|bly**[1] (wob′lē), *adj.*, **-bli|er**, **-bli|est**. unsteady; shaky; wavering. Also, **wabbly**.

**wob|bly**[2] or **Wob|bly** (wob′lē), *n., pl.* **-blies**. *U.S. Slang.* a member or adherent of the Industrial Workers of the World (a federation of industrial unions active in the United States between about 1905 and 1918). [American English; origin unknown]

**wo|be|gone** (wō′bi gôn′, -gon′), *adj.* = woebegone.

**WOC** (no periods) or **W.O.C.**, *U.S.* **1** without compensation (said of a businessman working without pay as an expert for the federal government while drawing a salary from his firm). **2** such a businessman.

**Wo|den** or **Wo|dan** (wō′dən), *n.* the most important Anglo-Saxon god. The Scandinavians called him Odin. [modern revival of Old English *Wōden*. Compare etym. under **Odin, Wednesday**.]

**wodge** (woj), *n. British.* a lumpy, protuberant object: *A wodge in his left breast pocket* (Chamber's Journal). [perhaps alteration of *wedge*]

**woe** (wō), *n., interj.* — ***n.*** great grief, trouble, or distress: *Sickness and poverty are common woes. For never was a story of more woe Than this of Juliet and her Romeo* (Shakespeare). **SYN**: sorrow.
— ***interj.*** an exclamation of grief, trouble, or distress; alas! *"Woe! Woe is me!" the miserable beggar cried.* Also, **wo**.
**woe worth**, *Archaic.* a curse upon; cursed be: *Woe worth the day.*
[Old English *wā*, interjection]

**woe|be|gone** (wō′bi gôn′, -gon′), *adj.* **1** looking sad, sorrowful, or wretched. **2** *Obsolete.* beset with woe or woes. Also, **wobegone**. [< Middle English *wo bigon*, in phrase *me is wo begon* woe has beset me < *wo* woe + *begon* beset] — **woe′be|gone′ness**, *n.*

**woe|ful** (wō′fəl), *adj.* **1** full of woe; sad; sorrowful; wretched: *The lost little boy had a woeful expression.* **SYN**: mournful, distressed, miserable. **2** = pitiful. **3** of wretched quality. — **woe′ful|ly**, *adv.* — **woe′ful|ness**, *n.*

**wo|ful** (wō′fəl), *adj.* = woeful. — **wo′ful|ly**, *adv.* — **wo′ful|ness**, *n.*

**wog**[1] (wog), *n. British Slang.* a native of one of the former British colonies, especially in the Middle East (used in an unfriendly way). [origin uncertain]

**wog**[2] (wog), *n. Australian.* any germ, small insect, or grub. [origin uncertain]

**woi|wode** (woi′wōd), *n.* = voivode.

**wok** (wok), *n.* a Chinese metal pan with a round bottom, for frying. [< Cantonese *wok*]

**woke** (wōk), *v.* waked; a past tense of **wake**[1]: *He woke before we did.*
▶ See **wake**[1] for a usage note.

**wo|ken** (wō′kən), *v. Archaic and Dialect.* waked; a past participle of **wake**[1]: *He was woken by the sound of bells.*

**wold**[1] (wōld), *n.* **1** high, rolling country, bare of woods. **2** *Obsolete.* wooded upland. [Old English *wald* (originally) wooded country, a wood. See related etym. at **weald**.]

**wold**[2] (wōld), *n.* = weld[2].

**wold**[3] (wōld), *v. Obsolete.* a past participle of **will**[1].

***wolf** (wůlf), *n., pl.* **wolves**, *v.* — ***n.*** **1** a wild, meat-eating mammal somewhat like and related to the dog, usually with a long muzzle, high, pointed ears, and a bushy tail. Wolves sometimes kill livestock but rarely attack people. **2** the fur of any of these animals. **3** any animal in some way resembling a wolf, such as the thylacine (Tasmanian wolf) or the hyena. **4** any one of certain beetle or moth larvae that infest granaries. **5** *Figurative.* a cruel, greedy person. **6** *Slang.* a man who flirts with or tries to entice women; philanderer. **7** *Music.* **a** the harsh dissonant sound heard in some chords on the organ and other keyboard instruments when tuned by a system of unequal temperament. **b** a chord or interval characterized by such a sound. **c** a harsh sound due to faulty vibration in certain tones, the result of a defect in the instrument.
— ***v.t.*** to eat like a wolf; eat greedily or ravenously: *The starving man wolfed down the food.*
**cry wolf**, to give a false alarm: *People will stop believing a person who constantly cries wolf.*
**keep the wolf from the door**, to keep safe from hunger or poverty: *Business began to flag, and the most I could do was to keep the wolf from the door* (Peter Drake).
**throw to the wolves**, to abandon to a hostile enemy or force or to some unpleasant or ruinous condition: *Most farmers felt they had been thrown to the wolves when the government withdrew price supports.*
**wolf in sheep's clothing**, a person who hides harmful intentions or an evil character beneath an innocent or friendly exterior; hypocrite: *This tender lamb has been allowed to wander out ... while a wolf in sheep's clothing was invited into the* [*community*] (Anthony Trollope).
[Old English *wulf*] — **wolf′like′**, *adj.*

***wolf**
definition 1
timber wolf

**Wolf** (wůlf), *n.* **1** *no pl.* the southern constellation Lupus. **2** *pl.* **Wolves**. a cub scout of the second highest rank. Wolves are eight years old.

**wolf|ber|ry** (wůlf′ber′ē, -bər-), *n., pl.* **-ries**. a North American shrub of the honeysuckle family, allied to the snowberry, sometimes grown for its ornamental white berries.

**wolf child**, a child believed to have been raised by wolves or other animals: *Those who want to emphasize the importance of environment can quote as their extreme case wolf children* (Punch).

**wolf cub**, a member of the junior organization of Boy Scouts in Great Britain, corresponding to an American cub scout.

**wolf dog**, **1** any one of various large dogs formerly kept for hunting wolves. **2** a hybrid of a dog and a wolf.

**wolf eel**, the wolf fish of the North Pacific.

**wolf|er** (wůl′fər), *n.* a hunter of wolves; wolver.

**Wolff|i|an** (wůl′fē ən, vôl′-), *adj.* having to do with or first noted by Kaspar Friedrich Wolff (1733-1794), a German anatomist, physiologist, and embryologist.

**Wolffian body**, = mesonephros.

**Wolffian duct**, = mesonephric duct.

**wolf fish**, **1** any one of certain large, voracious marine fishes having numerous sharp teeth and edible flesh, related to the blennies. **2** = lancet fish.

**wolf|hound** (wůlf′hound′), *n.* a large dog of any one of various breeds once used in hunting wolves and other animals. The Irish wolfhound and the borzoi or Russian wolfhound are two kinds.

**wolf|ish** (wůl′fish), *adj.* **1** like a wolf; savage: *a wolfish-looking dog, wolfish cruelty.* **SYN**: rapacious. **2** greedy: *a wolfish appetite.* **3** of or having to do with a wolf or wolves. — **wolf′ish|ly**, *adv.* — **wolf′ish|ness**, *n.*

**wolf|kin** (wůlf′kin), *n.* a young wolf.

**wolf|ling** (wůlf′ling), *n.* = wolfkin.

**wolf pack**, **1** a pack of wolves. **2** (in World War II) a body of submarines acting in concert against enemy shipping, especially a body of German submarines using tactics such as are traditionally ascribed to wolves, as of harrying pursuit or mass assault at night.

**wolf|ram** (wůl′frəm), *n.* = tungsten. **2** = wolframite. [< German *Wolfram*, perhaps < *Wolf* wolf + *Rahm* cream, foam (in Middle High German, filth, soot) (because it was thought of inferior quality)]

**wolf|ram|ic** (wůl fram′ik), *adj.* = tungstic.

**wolf|ram|ite** (wůl′frə mīt), *n. Mineralogy.* an ore consisting of compounds of tungsten with iron, manganese, and oxygen, occurring in crystals or masses. It is an important source of tungsten. *Formula:* (Fe, Mn) $WO_4$ [< German *Wolframit* < *Wolfram* + *-it* -ite[1]]

**wolf|ra|mi|um** (wůl frā′mē əm), *n.* = tungsten. [< New Latin *wolframium* < *wolfram* wolfram + *-ium*, a suffix meaning "element"]

**wolfs|bane** or **wolf's-bane** (wůlfs′bān′), *n.* any one of several species of aconite, especially a European species with yellowish flowers, sometimes called monkshood.

**wolf|skin** (wůlf′skin′), *n.* the skin or pelt of a wolf.

**wolf spider**, any one of a family of large spiders with keen eyesight and strong legs and jaws, that stalk, rather than lie in wait for, their prey.

**wolf tooth**, a tiny tooth that grows in front of the molar of a horse, often interfering with the bit. Wolf teeth are usually removed.

**wolf whistle**, *Slang.* a whistle consisting of a high and a low note, made by a male in appreciation of an attractive female: *This is one of the recognized meeting places of the sexes in Birmingham, and wolf whistles have become an everyday sound* (London Times).

**wol|las|ton|ite** (wůl′ə stə nīt), *n. Mineralogy.* a native silicate of calcium, occurring as crystals or in massive form. *Formula:* $CaSiO_3$ [< William H. *Wollaston*, 1766-1828, a British physicist and chemist + *-ite*]

**Wo|lof** (wō′lof), *n., pl.* **-lof** or **-lofs**. **1** a member of a native tribe of Senegal and Gambia. **2** the West Atlantic language of this tribe.

**wolv|er** (wůl′vər), *n.* a person who hunts wolves; wolfer.

**wol|ver|ene** (wůl′və rēn′, wůl′və rēn), *n., pl.* **-enes** or (*collectively*) **-ene**. *Especially British.* wolverine.

**wol|ver|ine** (wůl′və rēn′, wůl′və rēn), *n., pl.* **-ines** or (*collectively*) **-ine**. **1** a clumsy, heavily built meat-eating mammal of northern North America, Europe, and Asia; carcajou. It is related to the weasel and badger. The wolverine has short legs and dark, shaggy fur. It is noted for its strength, ferocity, and stealth, and is called the glutton in Europe. **2** its fur. [earlier *wolvering*, perhaps < obsolete *wolver* a wolfish animal < *wolf*]

**Wol|ver|ine** (wůl′və rēn′, wůl′və rēn), *n.* a nickname for a native or inhabitant of Michigan.

**Wolverine State**, a nickname for Michigan.

**wolves** (wůlvz), *n.* plural of **wolf**.

**wolv|ish** (wůl′vish), *adj. Obsolete.* wolfish.

**wom|an** (wům′ən), *n., pl.* **wom|en**, *adj., v.*, **-anned**, **-an|ning** or **-aned**, **-an|ing**. — ***n.*** **1** a female human being. A woman is a girl grown up. **2** women as a group; the average woman; womankind: *The woman of today rarely has servants. When lovely woman stoops to folly* (Oliver Goldsmith). **3** woman's nature; womanliness. **4** a female servant or attendant: *The princess told her woman to wait outside.* **5** a wife. **6** a mistress; paramour.
— ***adj.*** **1** of a woman or women; feminine. **2** female (used especially with designations of occupation or profession, and in the plural with a plural noun, now often considered somewhat offensive): *a woman lawyer, women lawyers.*
— ***v.t.*** **1** to supply or staff with women: *a hospital womanned by intelligent nurses.* **2** to call (a person) "woman," especially derogatorily or jocularly: *She was annoyed by his womanning her constantly.* **3** *Obsolete.* **a** to cause to act like a woman. **b** to unite to or accompany by a woman.
[Middle English *womman*, earlier *wumman*, Old English *wimman*, alteration of *wīfman* < *wīf* woman + *man* human being]
— ***Syn.*** ***n.*** **1 Woman, lady, female** mean member of the feminine sex. **Woman** is the general word for an adult: *a married woman, a woman of high ideals.* **Lady** applies particularly to a woman of refinement or high social position: *the manners of a lady.* It is sometimes used to refer to any woman (*Ladies and gentlemen, let me introduce the next speaker*), often in an inconsistent connotation: *the lady I hire to clean my apartment.* **Female** applies to a person of any age, baby or child as well as adult. It emphasizes the sex and is largely confined to science and statistics: *The control group consists of 241 males and 246 females.*
▶ See **man** for usage note.

**wom|an-hat|er** (wům′ən hā′tər), *n.* a person who hates or dislikes women.

**wom|an|hood** (wům′ən hůd), *n.* **1** the condition or time of being a woman: *The little girl grew up to womanhood.* **2** the character or qualities of a woman; womanliness: *graceful womanhood.* **3** women as a group; womankind: *Joan of Arc was an honor to womanhood.*

**wom|an|ish** (wům′ə nish), *adj.* **1a** characteristic of a woman or women; womanly; feminine. **b** like a grown woman: *a womanish girl.* **2** like a woman; suitable for women rather than for men; womanlike; effeminate (now chiefly derogatory). — **wom′an|ish|ly**, *adv.* — **wom′an|ish|ness**, *n.*

**wom|an|i|ty** (wů man′ə tē), *n.* the normal disposition or character of womankind; womanliness: *Women did not enter—for example—economics to aerate that ... agglomeration of male abstractions with a little "womanity," but simply to prove they could be as abstract ... as anyone* (Werner Pelz). [< *woman* + *-ity*, patterned on *humanity*]

**wom|an|ize** (wům′ə nīz), *v.*, **-ized**, **-iz|ing**. — ***v.t.*** to make effeminate or weak; emasculate.
— ***v.i.*** *Informal.* to consort illicitly with women: *We*

*womanized, we cheated, and we stole* (Edmund Wilson).
**wom|an|iz|er** (wu̇m′ə nī′zər), *n. Informal.* a man who pursues or consorts illicitly with women.
**wom|an|kind** (wu̇m′ən kīnd′), *n.* women as a group.
**wom|an|less** (wu̇m′ən lis), *adj.* without a woman or women.
**wom|an|like** (wu̇m′ən līk′), *adj., adv.* —***adj.*** **1** like a woman; womanly. **2** womanish; effeminate (in derogatory use).
—***adv.*** in a manner characteristic of women; in a womanly fashion.
**wom|an|li|ness** (wu̇m′ən lē nis), *n.* womanly quality, character, or behavior.
**wom|an|ly** (wu̇m′ən lē), *adj.,* **-li|er, -li|est,** *adv.* —***adj.*** **1** like a woman. **2** as a woman should be; gentle, fine, and ladylike: *She has much womanly sympathy for those who need help.* **3** suitable for a woman; feminine: *Tennis is as much a womanly sport as it is a manly sport.*
—***adv.*** in a womanly manner.
**woman of the street,** a prostitute, especially a streetwalker.
**woman of the world,** a woman who knows people and customs, and is tolerant of both.
**wom|an|pow|er** (wu̇m′ən pou′ər), *n.* power supplied by the work of women: *Teaching or library work* [*are*] *two fields where skilled womanpower is most in demand* (New York Times).
**woman's rights,** social, political, and legal rights for women, equal to those of men.
**woman suffrage, 1** the political right of women to vote. **2** women's votes. —**wom′an-suf′frage,** *adj.*
**wom|an-suf|fra|gist** (wu̇m′ən suf′rə jist), *n.* a person who favors the right of women to vote.
**womb** (wüm), *n., v.* —***n.*** **1** the part of the body in mammals that holds, protects, and (usually) nourishes the young till birth; uterus. **2** *Figurative.* a place containing or producing anything: *to emerge from the womb of time.* **3** a hollow space or cavity, or something conceived as such, such as the depth of night. **4** *Obsolete.* the belly.
—***v.t.*** to enclose in a womb: (*Figurative.*) *She prayed in a church wombed in quiet* (James T. Farrell).
[Old English *wamb*] —**womb′like′,** *adj.*
**wom|bat** (wom′bat), *n.* a burrowing Australian mammal that looks like a small bear (in Australia also called badger). A female wombat has a pouch for carrying her young. [< native Australian name]
**womb|y** (wü′mē), *adj.* having a womblike cavity; hollow.
**wom|en** (wim′ən), *n.* plural of **woman.**
**wom|en|folk** (wim′ən fōk′), *n.pl.* = women.
**wom|en|folks** (wim′ən fōks′), *n.pl.* = women.
**wom|en|kind** (wim′ən kīnd′), *n.* = womankind.
**Women's Libber,** *Informal.* Women's Liberationist.
**Women's Liberation** or **Lib,** a movement of active feminists demanding equal rights with men in all areas of life: *Women's liberation is a development of possibly very great significance to the future of American society* (Harper's). *If it is any compensation for Women's Lib, … distinguished women Prime Ministers are ushered into the Diplomats' Gallery, which has always been a male preserve* (London Times).
**Women's Liberationist,** a member or supporter of Women's Liberation.
**women's room,** *U.S.* ladies' room.
**wom|er|a, wom|er|ah,** or **wom|mer|a** (wom′ər ə), *n.* a device used to throw spears by aborigines of Australia. Also, **woomera.** [< native Australian name]
**won**[1] (wun), *v.* a past tense and the past participle of **win:** *Which side won yesterday?*
**won**[2] (wun, wu̇n, wōn), *v.i. Scottish.* to dwell; live (in a place or with someone). [Old English *wunian* dwell, be accustomed]
**won**[3] (won), *n., pl.* **won. 1** the unit of money of North Korea equal to 100 jun. **2** the unit of money of South Korea, used until 1953 and reestablished in place of the hwan in 1962, equal to 100 chon. [< Korean *won*]
**won|der** (wun′dər), *n., v.* —***n.*** **1** a strange and surprising thing or event: *The Grand Canyon is one of the wonders of the world. He saw the wonders of the city. It is a wonder that he refused such a good offer.* **2** the feeling caused by what is strange and surprising: *The baby looked with wonder at the Christmas tree.* **SYN:** amazement.
—***v.i.*** **1** to feel wonder: *We wonder at the splendor of the stars.* **2** to be surprised or astonished: *I shouldn't wonder if he wins the prize.* **3** to be curious; wish to know or learn; speculate: *to wonder about his sudden departure.* **SYN:** ponder.
—***v.t.*** **1** to feel wonder at: *I wonder that you came at all.* **2** to be curious about; think about; wish to know: *I wonder what time it is. I wonder where she bought her new hat.*
**do** (or **work**) **wonders,** to do wonderful things; achieve or produce extraordinary results: *They've done wonders with that old house, making it look modern and elegant.*
**for a wonder,** as a strange and surprising thing: *For a wonder he was not seasick* (Charles Reade).
**no** (or **small**) **wonder,** it is not very surprising: *No wonder he is sick; he eats too much candy. Pa's miserable, and no wonder!* (Dickens). *If 'the great authorities differ' small wonder that weaker minds are in doubt* (H. L. Jackson).
[Old English *wundor*] —**won′der|er,** *n.*
**wonder boy,** a young man who is outstanding in his profession or field: *Dylan Thomas, the wild Welsh wonder boy, was the greatest lyric poet produced in this century* (Time).
**wonder child,** an unusually gifted or talented child; a child prodigy: *By reason of his marvellous piano playing, he was looked upon as a wonder child* (Catholic Magazine). [translation of German *Wunderkind*]
**wonder drug,** a drug notably successful in treating different diseases, especially an antibiotic; miracle drug.
**won|der|ful** (wun′dər fəl), *adj.* **1** causing wonder; marvelous; remarkable: *The works of God are wonderful. The explorer had wonderful adventures.* **2** surprisingly large, fine, excellent, or splendid: *We had a wonderful time at the party.* [Old English *wunderfull* (literally) full of wonder] —**won′der|ful|ly,** *adv.* —**won′der|ful|ness,** *n.*
—***Syn.*** **1 Wonderful, marvelous** mean causing wonder. **Wonderful** describes something so new and unfamiliar, out of the ordinary, beyond expectation, or imperfectly understood that it excites a feeling of surprise, admiration, puzzled interest, or, sometimes, astonishment: *The boys from New York saw some wonderful sights on their first trip across the continent.* **Marvelous** describes something so extraordinary, surprising, or astonishing that it seems hardly believable: *The machine that can translate from foreign languages is a marvelous scientific invention.*
**won|der|ing** (wun′dər ing), *adj.* that wonders. —**won′der|ing|ly,** *adv.*
**won|der|land** (wun′dər land′), *n.* a land or place full of wonders.
**won|der|less** (wun′dər lis), *adj.* destitute of wonder.
**won|der|ment** (wun′dər mənt), *n.* **1** wonder; surprise: *He stared at the huge bear in wonderment.* **2** an object of or a matter for wonder; wonderful thing.
**wonder metal,** a lightweight metal, such as titanium or zirconium, capable of withstanding great pressure, strain, and heat.
**won|der-strick|en** (wun′dər strik′ən), *adj.* overcome or very much affected by wonder or amazement.
**won|der-struck** (wun′dər struk′), *adj.* = wonder-stricken.
**won|der|work** (wun′dər wėrk′), *n.* **1** a marvelous or miraculous act or achievement. **2** a wonderful work or structure. [Old English *wundorweorc* < *wundor* wonder + *weorc* work]
**won|der-work|er** (wun′dər wėr′kər), *n.* a person who performs wonders or surprising things.
**won|der|work|ing** (wun′dər wėr′king), *adj.* doing wonders or surprising things.
**won|drous** (wun′drəs), *adj., adv.* —***adj.*** = wonderful.
—***adv.*** = wonderfully.
[alteration of Middle English *wonders* wondrous; genitive of *wonder* wonder] —**won′drous|ly,** *adv.* —**won′drous|ness,** *n.*
**won|ky** (wong′kē), *adj.,* **-ki|er, -ki|est.** *British Slang.* in poor condition or working order; likely to break down or collapse; unsound. [perhaps related to **wankle**]
**won|na** (wun′nə), *Scottish.* will not. [alteration of earlier *willna* < *will*[1] + *na*]
**wont** (wōnt, wunt), *adj., n., v.,* **wont, wont|ed** or **wont, wont|ing.** —***adj.*** accustomed: *He was wont to read the paper at breakfast.*
—***n.*** custom; habit: *She rose early, as was her wont.*
—***v.t.*** *Archaic.* to make (a person or his will or affections) used (to); accustom. —***v.i.*** *Archaic.* to be accustomed (to do something).
[Middle English *wuned* (originally) past participle of Old English *wunian* dwell, be accustomed. See related etym. at **won**[2].]
▶ Since **wont** has become relatively rare in spoken use, various spelling pronunciations have arisen, of which (wōnt) is the most common. The inherited pronunciation is (wunt).
**won't** (wōnt, wunt), will not. [contraction of Middle English *woll not* will not]
**wont|ed** (wōn′tid, wun′-), *adj.* **1** accustomed; customary; usual: *The cat was in its wonted place by the stove.* **SYN:** habitual. **2** *U.S.* made familiar with one's environment. —**wont′ed|ly,** *adv.* —**wont′ed|ness,** *n.*
**won ton** (won′ ton′), a thin soup containing dumplings made of noodle dough wrapped around meat. [< Chinese *wan t'an*]
**woo** (wü), *v.t.* **1** to make love to; seek to marry. **2** *Figurative.* to seek to win; try to get: *Some people woo fame; some woo wealth.* **3** to try to persuade; urge. —***v.i.*** **1** to make love; court. **2** to make solicitation or entreaty; sue (for).
**pitch woo,** *U.S. Slang.* to make love; court: (*Figurative.*) *The … man pitching woo at the apparently fickle fiefdoms of the Communist world* (New York Times).
[Old English *wōgian*]
**wood**[1] (wu̇d), *n., adj., v.* —***n.*** **1** the hard, fibrous substance beneath the bark of trees and shrubs; xylem: *With one swing of the axe he cut through the bark down to the wood.* **2** trees cut into boards or planks for use; lumber or timber: *The carpenter brought wood to build a garage.* **3** = firewood. **4** Often, **woods. a** a large number of growing trees; small forest: *The children go to the woods behind the farm for wild flowers and for nuts.* **b** an area covered by a forest or forests: *Many hunters go to the Maine woods.* **5** a thing made of wood. **6** a cask; barrel; keg: *wine drawn from the wood.* **7** *Printing.* woodcuts collectively or a woodcut. **8** *Music.* one of the woodwinds. **9** any one of several golf clubs having a wooden head. See picture under **golf club.**
—***adj.*** **1** made or consisting of wood; wooden: *a wood house.* **2** used to store or convey wood: *a wood box.* **3** dwelling or growing in woods: *wood moss.*
—***v.t.*** **1** to plant with trees. **2** to supply with wood, especially firewood.
—***v.i.*** Also, **wood up.** to get or take in a supply of wood for fuel: *We went on down the river, … stopping … occasionally to wood up* (Cecil Roberts).
**knock** (**on**) **wood, a** to hit a wooden object in the belief that this will prevent evil or misfortune: *"Right now," Egan said, doing so, "I'm knocking on wood"* (New York Times). **b** to hope that misfortune will not happen or recur: *Only accident I've ever been damaged in. Knock wood* (New Yorker).
**not to see the wood for the trees,** to lose the view of the whole in the multitude of details: *Garrick … bears no very distinct figure. One hardly sees the wood for the trees* (Walter Pater).
**out of the woods** (or **wood**), out of danger or difficulty: *When a patient reaches this stage* [*of convalescence*], *he is out of the woods* (Owen Wister).
**saw wood,** *Informal.* **a** to attend to one's own affairs: *Read what happened to Hannibal at Capua while the defeated Romans were busy sawing wood* (New York Evening Post). **b** to sleep heavily: *When he is sawing wood, he really snores.*
**touch wood,** to knock wood: *We haven't had too many people killed, touch wood* (New York Times).
**woods,** the woodwinds collectively of an orchestra or band: *The conductor signaled the strings to join the brasses and woods.*
[Old English *wudu,* earlier *widu*]
▶ **Woods** (def. 4), though plural in form, is usually singular (or collective) in meaning and is used both as a singular (*a woods*) and as a plural (*the woods are*).
**wood**[2] (wüd, wōd, wu̇d), *adj. Obsolete or Dialect.* **1** mad; demented. **2** furious; enraged. Also, **wud.** [Old English *wōd*]
**wood acid,** = wood vinegar.
**wood alcohol,** = methyl alcohol.
**wood anemone,** any one of various anemones growing wild in woods. The common wood anemone has a white flower in the spring. The wood anemone is commonly grown in rock gardens.
**wood ant, 1** a large ant which lives in the woods. **2** = termite.
**wood betony, 1** = betony. **2** an herb, a lousewort, of the figwort family, growing in eastern North America, and bearing spikes of yellow or reddish flowers.
**wood|bin** (wu̇d′bin′), *n.* a bin or box for firewood.
**wood|bind** (wu̇d′bīnd′), *n.* = woodbine.
**wood|bine** (wu̇d′bīn′), *n.* **1** a common European honeysuckle, a climbing shrub with pale-yellow, fragrant flowers. **2** any one of certain other honeysuckles. **3** = Virginia creeper. [Old English *wudubinde* any climbing plant < *wudu* wood + *binde* wreath. Compare etym. under **bine.** See related etym. at **bind.**]

---

**Pronunciation Key:** hat, āge, cãre, fär; let, ēqual, tėrm; it, īce; hot, ōpen, ôrder; **oi**l, **ou**t; cup, pu̇t, rüle; **ch**ild; lo**ng**; **th**in; **ŦH**en; **zh**, measure; ə represents **a** in about, **e** in taken, **i** in pencil, **o** in lemon, **u** in circus.

**wood block**, **1** a block of wood. **2** = woodcut, especially one made from wood sawed with the grain. —**wood′-block′**, *adj.*
▶ See **woodcut** for usage note.

**wood|bor|er** (wu̇d′bôr′ər, -bōr′-), *n.* an insect, crustacean, or mollusk that bores in wood: *The huge volumes of logs introduced into seawater provided ideal conditions for the breeding and growth of woodborers* (New Scientist).

**wood|box** (wu̇d′boks′), *n.* a box for firewood; woodbin.

**wood|carv|er** (wu̇d′kär′vər), *n.* a person who carves figures or other objects from wood.

**wood|carv|ing** (wu̇d′kär′ving), *n.* **1** some object, such as a figure, carved from wood. **2** the art or process of making woodcarvings.

**wood charcoal**, charcoal resulting from heating wood without enough air to burn it completely.

**wood|chat** (wu̇d′chat′), *n.* **1** a European shrike. **2** any one of certain Asian birds related to the thrush. [< *wood*[1] + *chat*[1] a bird]

**wood|chop|per** (wu̇d′chop′ər), *n.* a person who chops wood, especially one who chops down trees; lumberjack.

**wood|chuck** (wu̇d′chuk′), *n.* a thick-set North American mammal with short legs and a bushy tail; ground hog. It is a kind of marmot. Woodchucks grow fat in summer and sleep in their holes in the ground all winter. [American English, alteration (influenced by *wood*[1]) of *wejack* < Algonkian (Cree) *otchek*, or (Ojibwa) *otchig*, the name of the fisher, that is, the marten, transferred to the ground hog]

**wood coal**, **1** = lignite. **2** *Archaic.* charcoal.

**wood|cock** (wu̇d′kok′), *n., pl.* **-cocks** or (*collectively*) **-cock.** **1** a small game bird with short legs and a long, sensitive bill used to probe the ground for worms. It is related to the snipe. Woodcock are found in eastern North America and in Europe. **2** *Archaic.* a fool; simpleton (in allusion to the ease with which the woodcock is taken in a snare or net). [Old English *wuducoc* < *wudu* wood + *cocc* cock]

**wood|craft** (wu̇d′kraft′, -kräft′), *n.* **1** knowledge about how to get food and shelter in the woods; skill as in hunting, trapping, and finding one's way. **2** skill in working with wood.

**wood|crafts|man** (wu̇d′krafts′mən, -kräfts′-), *n., pl.* **-men.** a person skilled in woodcraft.

**wood|cut** (wu̇d′kut′), *n.* **1** an engraved block of wood to print from. **2** a print made from such a block.
▶ **Woodcut** in its broadest sense includes both *wood block* and *wood engraving.* In both, printing is by the relief method. In terms of black-and-white prints, the *wood-block* method produces black lines and masses against a white background, *wood engraving* the reverse. The strict technical distinction lies in the tools and the kind of block employed: in *wood block* knives and gouges are used on wood sawed with the grain; in *wood engraving* burins and sometimes punches are used on wood sawed across the grain.

**wood|cut|ter** (wu̇d′kut′ər), *n.* a man who cuts down trees or chops wood.

**wood|cut|ting** (wu̇d′kut′ing), *n., adj.* —*n.* **1** the act or work of cutting down trees for wood. **2** wood engraving.
—*adj.* **1** having to do with or used in woodcutting: *Foresters naturally expect their woodcutting saws to become blunter* (New Scientist). **2** of or having to do with the making of woodcuts.

**wood duck**, a North American duck with a large crest, short neck, and long tail, that builds its nest in hollow trees in the woods and frequents ponds and streams. The male is richly colored with green, blue, and purple upper feathers, and red, yellow, and white underparts.

**wood|ed** (wu̇d′id), *adj.* **1** covered with trees: *The house stood on a wooded hill.* **2** full of woods or forests: *a heavily wooded region.*

**wood|en** (wu̇d′ən), *adj.* **1** made of wood: *a wooden bench.* **2** *Figurative.* stiff as wood; awkward: *a wooden manner.* **3** *Figurative.* dull; stupid. —**wood′en|ly**, *adv.* —**wood′en|ness**, *n.*

**wood engraver**, a person skilled in wood engraving.

**wood engraving**, **1** the art or process of making woodcuts. **2** a woodcut, especially one made from wood sawed across the grain.
▶ See **woodcut** for usage note.

**wood|en|head** (wu̇d′ən hed′), *n.* a stupid person; blockhead.

**wood|en-head|ed** (wu̇d′ən hed′id), *adj. Informal.* dull; stupid. —**wood′en-head′ed|ness**, *n.*

**wooden horse**, **1** *Greek Legend.* a huge, hollow horse made of wood and filled with Greek soldiers, used, according to Virgil's *Aeneid,* as a ruse by the Greeks during the Trojan War; Trojan horse. After the Trojans took it into their city, the Greeks stole out during the night and let their army into Troy. **2** any one of various wooden frames or supports, especially one having four legs, such as a sawhorse. **3** an English bicycle of the early 1800's; hobbyhorse.

* **wooden Indian**, **1** a figure of an American Indian carved from a block of wood and brightly painted, often holding a tomahawk in one hand and cigars in the other, formerly often placed in front of a tobacco store as a means of identification and advertisement; cigar-store Indian. **2** *Informal, Figurative.* a silent and impassive person.

* **wooden Indian**
definition 1

**wooden nickel**, *U.S. Slang.* a worthless or fraudulent thing; wooden nutmeg: *You can't change the political system from above, because it produces leaders that are always trying to sell you wooden nickels* (New York Times).

**wooden nutmeg**, **1** an imitation nutmeg made of wood, an alleged article of manufacture in Connecticut for export. **2** *Figurative.* something fraudulent.

**wooden spoon**, **1** a spoon made of wood, especially one presented at a college or university to the lowest of those taking honors. **2** *Figurative.* the lowest position in any list or set.

**wooden tongue**, actinomycosis affecting the tongues of cattle, hogs, and sheep.

**wooden walls**, ships or shipping as a defensive force: *The old wooden walls of Britain, as the Fleet was called a century or so ago* (London Times).

**wood|en|ware** (wu̇d′ən wãr′), *n.* containers, utensils, and other household articles made of or carved from wood: *Tubs and rolling pins are woodenware.*

**wood fern**, any one of a genus of hardy ferns with dark green foliage and a shield-shaped covering of the spore cases, widely distributed throughout the world; shield fern.

**wood float**, a wooden trowel used to smooth or level concrete, plaster, or the like before it hardens.

**wood flour**, very fine sawdust, especially that made from pine wood for use as a surgical dressing, in plastics, and in dynamite.

**wood frog**, a common brown frog of damp woodlands of northern and eastern North America, with a black spot on each side of the face.

**wood grouse**, any one of various grouse inhabiting woods, such as the spruce grouse.

**wood hen**, = weka.

**wood|henge** (wu̇d′henj′), *n.* a prehistoric circular structure of wood, found in various places in England; a wooden henge: *The four largest henge monuments in England, each surrounded by earthworks measuring more than 1,000 feet in diameter, are Avebury and three woodhenges: Mount Pleasant* (*near Dorchester*), *Durrington Walls, and Marden* (*both on the River Avon*) (Scientific American).

**wood hoopoe**, any one of a group of African birds; irrisor.

**wood|house** (wu̇d′hous′), *n.* a house or shed in which wood is stored; woodshed.

**wood hyacinth**, an Old-World plant, a squill, having drooping, usually blue, flowers. It is also called bluebell, (in Scotland) harebell, and wild hyacinth.

**wood ibis**, a large white wading bird with a naked head and black and white wings, that inhabits tropical and subtropical America.

**wood|i|ness** (wu̇d′ē nis), *n.* woody quality or condition.

**wood|land** (*n.* wu̇d′land′, -lənd; *adj.* wu̇d′lənd), *n., adj.* —*n.* land covered with trees.
—*adj.* of the woods; having something to do with woods; living in the woods: *woodland sounds, woodland animals.*

**Wood|land** (wu̇d′lənd), *adj.* of or having to do with a stage of North American Indian culture dating from 500 B.C., characterized by large burial mounds, core tools and grooved axes, and simple pottery: *He traced the derivation of some of the ceramic styles in this region to Woodland cultures of North America* (New York Times).

**woodland caribou**, a large caribou of wooded areas of Canada and parts of the northwestern United States.

**wood|land|er** (wu̇d′lən dər), *n.* a person who lives in the woods.

**wood|lark** (wu̇d′lärk′), *n.* a European lark.

**wood|less** (wu̇d′lis), *adj.* without wood, timber, or woods; treeless.

**wood lice**, plural of **wood louse**.

**wood lily**, = orangecup lily.

**wood|lore** (wu̇d′lôr′, -lōr′), *n.* knowledge about the woods; woodcraft: *Four Explorer Scouts, lost while skiing during a blinding snowstorm ..., used woodlore and a single pack of matches to survive the night* (New York Times).

**wood lot**, or **wood|lot** (wu̇d′lot′), *n. Especially U.S.* a plot of land on which trees are grown and cut for firewood, timber, or pulp.

**wood louse**, **1** a small crustacean that has a flat, oval body and lives in decaying wood and damp soil; sow bug. Wood lice are isopods that live on land. **2** any one of certain small insects, such as termites, book lice, and mites, that live in the woodwork of houses.

**wood|man** (wu̇d′mən), *n., pl.* **-men.** **1** a man who cuts down trees for timber or fuel. SYN: woodcutter. **2** a person who takes care of trees; forester. **3** *Obsolete.* a person who lives in the woods. **4** *Obsolete.* person who hunts game in a wood or forest.

**wood|man|craft** (wu̇d′mən kraft′, -kräft′), *n.* the business or skill of a woodman.

**wood mice**, plural of **wood mouse**.

**wood mouse**, a deer mouse or other mouse that habitually lives in the woods.

**wood note**, or **wood-note** (wu̇d′nōt′), *n.* a musical sound made by a bird or animal of the forest.

**wood nym[illegible]**, **1** a nymph that lives in the woods; dryad or hamadryad. **2** a brown or grayish butterfly with yellow markings and round spots on its wings; satyr. **3** a moth that destroys grapevines. **4** any one of certain tropical American hummingbirds.

**wood oil**, = tung oil.

**wood opal**, wood that has become petrified in the form of opal.

**wood|peck|er** (wu̇d′pek′ər), *n.* a bird having a sharp, chisel-like bill for pecking holes in trees to get insects. Woodpeckers have long, sharp tongues for spearing insects, strong feet adapted for climbing tree trunks, and stiff tail feathers which serve as props. They usually have brightly colored plumage. The flicker, the redheaded woodpecker, the downy woodpecker, the hairy woodpecker, the three-toed woodpecker, and the ivory-billed woodpecker are some of the kinds of woodpeckers.

**wood pewee**, a small flycatcher of eastern North America with a plaintive call suggesting its name; pewee.

**wood pigeon**, **1a** a European pigeon with two whitish patches on the neck; ringdove. **b** any of several related pigeons. **2** a wild pigeon of western North America.

**wood|pile** (wu̇d′pīl′), *n.* a pile of wood, especially wood for fuel.

**wood pitch**, the dark residue yielded by wood tar on further distillation.

**wood|print** (wu̇d′print′), *n.* a print from an engraved or carved wood block; woodcut.

**wood pulp**, wood made into pulp by mechanical or chemical disintegration of wood fiber, used for making paper.

**wood pussy**, or **wood|puss|y** (wu̇d′pu̇s′ē), *n., pl.* **wood pussies** or **wood|puss|ies.** *U.S. Informal.* a skunk.

**wood|queest** or **wood|quist** (wu̇d′kwēst′), *n. British Dialect.* the wood pigeon or ringdove; queest.

**wood rabbit**, = cottontail.

**wood rat**, = pack rat.

**wood ray**, *Botany.* medullary ray.

**wood rosin**, rosin obtained from the stumps of pine trees by extraction and distillation.

**wood|ruff** (wu̇d′ruf), *n.* a low-growing herb of the madder family, with clusters of small white, pink, or bluish flowers and whorls of sweet-scented leaves. [Old English *wudurofe* < *wudu* wood + *-rofe,* meaning unknown]

**woods** (wu̇dz), *n.pl.* See under **wood**[1].

**wood screw**, a screw used in wood.

**wood|shed** (wu̇d′shed′), *n., v.,* **-shed|ded, -shed|ding.** —*n.* a shed for storing wood.
—*v.i. Jazz Slang.* to practice or rehearse playing a piece of music or a musical instrument.

**wood|shop** (wu̇d′shop′), *n.* a shop in which articles of wood are made or where woodworking is taught.

**wood shot**, **1** a shot in tennis, badminton, or other racket game, made off the wooden part of the racket instead of off the strings. A wood shot is usually considered legal. **2** a shot in golf hit with a wood. Wood shots are usually long.

**wood|si|a** (wu̇d′zē ə), *n.* any one of a group of delicate ferns growing in rocky places in temperate and cold regions. [< New Latin *Woodsia* the genus name < Joseph *Woods,* 1776-1864, a British botanist]

**wood|side** (wu̇d′sīd′), *n.* the side or border of woods or a forest: *a lonely spot by a woodside* (George R. Gissing).

**woods|man** (wu̇dz′mən), *n., pl.* **-men. 1** a man used to life in the woods and skilled in hunting, fishing, trapping, and other woodcraft. **2** a man whose work is cutting down trees; lumberman.

**woods|man|ship** (wu̇dz′mən ship), *n.* the condition or the skill of a woodsman; woodcraft.

**Wood's metal**, a fusible metal, an alloy of bismuth, lead, tin, and cadmium with a melting point between 60 and 75 degrees centigrade (Celsius), used for electric fuses and plugs, in automatic fire alarms and sprinkler systems, etc. [< Bertram *Wood,* born 1889, an American metals engineer]

**wood smoke**, smoke produced by a slow-burning wood fire and containing chemicals that slow the growth of microorganisms, especially used to preserve meat and fish.

**wood sorrel**, **1** any one of a group of plants with acid juice, usually having leaves composed of three heart-shaped leaflets and white, yellow, red, or pink flowers sometimes streaked with purple; oxalis. **2** = sheep sorrel.

**wood spirit**, **1** a spirit or imaginary being, fabled to dwell in or haunt woods. **2** = methyl alcohol.

**wood stork**, = wood ibis.

**wood sugar**, the dextrorotatory form of xylose.

**woods|y** (wu̇d′zē), *adj.,* **woods|i|er, woods|i|est.** of, having to do with, or characteristic or suggestive of the woods; sylvan. [American English < *woods* + *-y*[1]]

**wood tar**, a dark-brown, poisonous, sticky substance produced by the destructive distillation of wood, and containing resins and turpentine. It yields pyroligneous acid, creosote and oils, and a dark residue (wood pitch) on further distillation. Wood tar is used as a preservative on wood and rope, as a disinfectant, etc.

**wood thrush**, **1** a thrush with a white, spotted breast, common in the thickets and woods of eastern North America; bellbird; song thrush. It is noted for its sweet song. **2** = missel thrush (locally in England and Scotland).

**wood tick**, **1** any one of a family of ticks (acarids) found frequently in woods. **2** = deathwatch (def. 3).

**wood turner**, a person skilled in wood turning.

**wood turning**, the making of pieces of wood into various shapes by using a lathe.

**wood-turn|ing** (wu̇d′tėr′ning), *adj.* of or having to do with wood turning.

**wood vinegar**, a crude acetic acid; pyroligneous acid; wood acid.

**wood|wall** (wu̇d′wôl), *n. British Dialect.* the green woodpecker. Also, **witwall.** [< Middle Low German *wedewale* < *wede* wood + *wale,* meaning unknown. See related etym. at **witwall.**]

**wood warbler**, any one of a family of small American birds; warbler.

**wood|ward** (wu̇d′wərd), *n.* (formerly, in England) a forestkeeper or forester: *The woodward ... could claim every tree that the wind blew down* (John R. Green).

**wood|ware** (wu̇d′wãr′), *n.* articles made of wood.

**wood wasp**, **1** any one of various wasps that burrow in wood, as species of a family, the female of which excavates a cell in decayed wood as a place to deposit her eggs. **2** any insect of a family, the larvae of which burrow in the wood of trees.

**wood|wax** (wu̇d′waks′), *n. Obsolete.* woadwaxen.

**wood|wax|en** (wu̇d′wak′sən), *n.* = woadwaxen.

**wood|wind** (wu̇d′wind′), *n., adj.* —*n.* any one of the wind instruments of an orchestra which were originally made of wood, but are now often made of metal. Clarinets, flutes, oboes, and bassoons are woodwinds.

—*adj.* of or having to do with woodwinds.

**woodwinds, a** the wind instruments of an orchestra, such as the clarinet, flute, bassoon, and oboe. **b** the players on woodwinds.

**wood wool**, fine shavings made from pine wood, used as a surgical dressing, in plaster, and as an insulating material: *The roof construction has been changed to slabs of wood wool in place of boarding* (Science).

**wood|work** (wu̇d′wėrk′), *n.* things made of wood, especially the wooden parts inside of a house, such as doors, stairs, and moldings.

**come out of the woodwork,** *U.S. Informal.* to come out of hiding or from unknown places; come out of the blue: *We found speculators and gold hoarders coming out of the woodwork trying to buy gold in any shape, manner, or form* (New York Times).

**wood|work|er** (wu̇d′wėr′kər), *n.* a person who makes things of wood; worker in wood. **SYN:** carpenter.

**wood|work|ing** (wu̇d′wėr′king), *n., adj.* —*n.* the act or work of making or shaping things of wood: *A carpenter is skilled in woodworking.*

—*adj.* having to do with or used for woodworking: *a woodworking machine. The carpenter used woodworking tools.*

**wood|worm** (wu̇d′wėrm′), *n.* any worm or larva that is bred in wood or bores in wood.

**wood|y**[1] (wu̇d′ē), *adj.,* **wood|i|er, wood|i|est. 1** having many trees; covered with trees: *a woody hillside.* **2a** of the nature of or consisting of wood; ligneous. **b** of which wood is a constituent part; forming wood: *the woody parts of a plant.* **3** like wood; tough and stringy: *Turnips become woody when they are old.* **4a** of, having to do with, or situated in a wood. **b** *Obsolete.* belonging to, inhabiting, or growing in woods or woodland; sylvan.

**wood|y**[2] (wud′ē, wü′dē), *n., pl.* **wood|ies.** *Scottish.* widdy (rope). [variant of *widdy*[1]]

**wood|yard** (wu̇d′yärd′), *n.* a yard or enclosure in which wood is chopped, sawed, or stored, especially for use as fuel.

**woody nightshade**, = bittersweet.

**woo|er** (wü′ər), *n.* a person or animal that woos; suitor.

**woof**[1] (wu̇f), *n.* **1** the threads or yarn running from side to side across a loom, or those in a woven fabric which cross the warp; filling; weft. See picture under **loom**[1]. **2** fabric; cloth; texture. [earlier *wofe,* alteration (influenced by *wove*) of Middle English *ōf,* Old English *ōwef* < *ō-,* a prefix + *wefan* to weave. Compare etym. under **weft.**]

**woof**[2] (wu̇f), *n., v.* —*n.* the sound of a dog barking. —*v.i.* to make such a sound. [imitative]

**woof|er** (wu̇f′ər), *n.* a high-fidelity loudspeaker for reproducing sounds below the treble register. [apparently < *woof*[2] + *-er*[1]]

**woo|ing|ly** (wü′ing lē), *adv.* in the manner of wooing; invitingly.

**wool** (wu̇l), *n., adj.* —*n.* **1** the fine, soft, curly hair of sheep and some other animals such as the goat and alpaca. It is characterized by its property of felting due to the overlapping of minute surface scales. Sheep's wool is next to cotton in importance as a material for clothing. **2** short, thick, curly hair. **3** any one of various fine, fibrous substances, naturally or artificially produced, resembling wool. **4a** clothing or material made of wool: *We wear wool in cold weather.* **b** yarn made of wool, used for knitting, embroidery, and weaving; worsted. **5** a downy substance found on certain plants, or the furry hair of some insect larvae, such as the caterpillar. **6** = wool sponge.

—*adj.* **1** made of wool; woolen. **2** of or having to do with the manufacture, storage, transportation, or sale of wool or woolen goods.

**pull the wool over one's eyes,** *Informal.* to deceive or trick one: *I don't propose he shall pull the wool over my eyes* (William Dean Howells). [Old English *wull*] —**wool′like′,** *adj.*

**wool clip**, the quantity of raw wool produced annually; total amount of wool sheared in a year.

**wool|comb|er** (wu̇l′kō′mər), *n.* a person or thing that combs or cards wool.

**wooled** (wu̇ld), *adj.* covered with wool; with the wool still on; unshorn: *a wooled lamb, wooled sheepskins.*

**-wooled,** *combining form.* having ____ wool: *Fine-wooled = having fine wool.*

**wool|en** (wu̇l′ən), *adj., n.* —*adj.* **1** made of wool: *a woolen suit.* **2** of or having to do with wool or cloth made of wool; that makes things from wool: *a woolen mill.*

—*n.* yarn or cloth made of wool. The fibers in woolen lie in all directions, resulting in a soft, fuzzy surface.

**woolens,** cloth or clothing made of wool: *Mother puts our woolens in plastic bags every summer to protect them against moths. The exportation of Irish woolens to the colonies and to foreign countries was prohibited* (George Bancroft).

**wool fat**, the fatty coating on sheep's wool; lanolin.

**wool|fell** (wu̇l′fel′), *n.* a sheepskin with the fleece on it. [Middle English *wolle felle* < *wolle* wool + *felle* fell, skin]

**wool|gath|er** (wu̇l′gaᴛʜ′ər), *v.i.* to indulge in idle imagining or daydreaming: *My brain sometimes woolgathered or wandered, sometimes concentrated on ... problems* (Robert Kotlowitz). [back formation < *woolgathering*]

**wool|gath|er|er** (wu̇l′gaᴛʜ′ər ər), *n.* a daydreaming or absent-minded person.

**wool|gath|er|ing** (wu̇l′gaᴛʜ′ər ing, -gaᴛʜ′ring), *n., adj.* —*n.* **1** an absorption in thinking or daydreaming; absent-mindedness. **2** the gathering up of fragments of wool torn from sheep, as by bushes.

—*adj.* inattentive; absent-minded; dreamy.

**wool grease**, = wool fat.

**wool|grow|er** (wu̇l′grō′ər), *n.* a person who raises sheep for their wool.

**wool|grow|ing** (wu̇l′grō′ing), *adj., n.* —*adj.* producing sheep and wool.

—*n.* the raising of sheep for their wool.

**wool|hat** (wu̇l′hat′), *n., adj. U.S. Informal.* —*n.* a Southern farmer or back-country rustic: *The businessmen like him; so do the Republicans and the downstate woolhats* (Harper's).

—*adj.* of the Southern back-country region: *a woolhat politician.*

**wool|i|ness** (wu̇l′ē nis), *n.* = woolliness.

**woolled** (wu̇ld), *adj.* = wooled.

**wool|len** (wu̇l′ən), *adj., n.* = woolen.

**wool|li|ness** (wu̇l′ē nis), *n.* the quality or condition of being woolly.

**wool|ly** (wu̇l′ē), *adj.,* **-li|er, -li|est,** *n., pl.* **-lies.** —*adj.* **1** consisting of wool; fleecy: *the woolly coat of a sheep.* **2** of the nature, texture, or appearance of wool; like wool: *woolly hair, woolly clouds.* **3** covered with wool or something like it: *woolly sheep.* **4** *Figurative.* not clear; confused and hazy; muddled: *Both his thinking and his writing are woolly. The report ... is woolly in such a way that almost anything can be read into it, or out of it* (Manchester Guardian). **SYN:** vague, fuzzy, indistinct, unclear. **5** *U.S. Informal, Figurative.* rough and uncivilized like the Western part of the United States in frontier times (used especially in *wild and woolly*).

—*n.* **1** *Informal.* an article of clothing made from wool. Also, **wooly. 2** *Western U.S.* a sheep.

**woollies,** *Informal.* woolen underwear: *I can still feel the thrill of exchanging my prickly woollies for soft cool cotton* (Maclean's).

**woolly bear**, the hair-covered larva of a tiger moth. [because of its appearance]

**wool|ly-head|ed** (wu̇l′ē hed′id), *adj.* **1** having woolly hair on the head. **2** stupid; muddle-headed.

**woolly mammoth**, a large, extinct elephant formerly native to Europe and northern Asia, remains of which have been found in Siberia; hairy mammoth.

**woolly monkey**, a large monkey with thick, soft, dark fur that lives in the western Amazon Valley of South America.

**woolly rhinoceros**, an extinct two-horned rhinoceros with a thick woolly covering. Woolly rhinoceroses have been preserved where they fell into crevasses in deep ice.

**wool maggot**, the larva of the blowfly.

**wool|man** (wu̇l′mən), *n., pl.* **-men.** a dealer in wool; wool merchant.

**wool|pack** (wu̇l′pak′), *n.* **1** a large cloth bag for carrying wool. **2** a bundle or bale of wool. **3** a round, fleecy, cumulus cloud.

**wool|sack** (wu̇l′sak′), *n.* **1** a bag of wool. **2a** the cushion, a large cloth-covered bag of wool, on which the Lord Chancellor sits in the British House of Lords. **b** the office of Lord Chancellor.

**wool|shed** (wu̇l′shed′), *n.* a building or enclosure where sheep are sheared and their wool processed and stored.

**wool|skin** (wu̇l′skin′), *n.* a sheepskin with the fleece on it.

**wool|sort|er** (wu̇l′sôr′tər), *n.* a person who sorts wool, especially one skilled in dividing wool in lots according to length, fineness of fiber, and other characteristics.

**woolsorters' disease**, a form of anthrax attacking man and caused by the inhalation of dust contaminated with spores of a bacterium; pulmonary anthrax.

**wool sponge**, any one of certain tough, flexible horse sponges, important commercially, especially the sheepswool.

**wool stapler**, a merchant who buys wool from the producer, grades it, and sells it to the manufacturer.

**wool top**, fleece from the sheep's back, cleaned and combed into strands, not yet spun into yarn.

**wool wax**, = wool fat.

**wool|work** (wu̇l′wėrk′), *n.* needlework done with wool, as on canvas.

**wool|y** (wu̇l′ē), *adj.,* **wool|i|er, wool|i|est,** *n., pl.* **wool|ies.** = woolly.

**woo|mer|a** (wü′mər ə), *n.* = womera.

**woops** (wu̇ps), *interj.* = oops.

**woo|ra|li** (wü rä′lē), *n.* = curare. [< a Tupi word]

**woo|ra|ri** (wü rä′rē), *n.* = curare. [variant of *woorali, oorali*]

**wooz|y** (wü′zē, wu̇z′ē), *adj.,* **wooz|i|er, wooz|i|est.** *Informal.* **1** somewhat dizzy or weak; slightly ill: *to be just over an illness and still a little woozy. "Motion sickness"—the woozy feeling suffered by some troops while riding* (Baltimore Sun). **2** muddled; confused: *a mind woozy from fatigue.* **3** slightly drunk; tipsy. [probably a variant of *oozy*[2] muddy] —**wooz′i|ly,** *adv.* —**wooz′i|ness,** *n.*

---

**Pronunciation Key:** hat, āge, cãre, fär; let, ēqual, tėrm; it, īce; hot, ōpen, ôrder; **oi**l, **ou**t; cup, pu̇t, rüle; **ch**ild; lo**ng**; **th**in; **ᴛʜ**en; **zh,** measure; **ə** represents **a** in about, **e** in taken, **i** in pencil, **o** in lemon, **u** in circus.

**wop** (wop), *v.*, **wopped**, **wop|ping**, *n.* = whop.
**wops** (wops), *n. Dialect.* a wasp or hornet. [Old English *waps.* Compare etym. under **wasp**.]
**wor|ble** (wôr′bəl), *n.* the larva of a botfly, that infests squirrels. [variant of *warble*[2]]
**Worces|ter china** or **porcelain** (wu̇s′tər), a kind of china originating in Worcester, England.
**Worces|ter|shire** (wu̇s′tər shir, -shər), *n.*, or **Worcestershire sauce**, a highly seasoned sauce containing soy, vinegar, and other ingredients, originally made in Worcester, England.
**Worcs** (no period), Worcestershire.
**word** (wėrd), *n.*, *v.* —*n.* **1** a sound or a group of sounds that has meaning and is an independent unit of speech; vocable: *We speak words when we talk. A free form which is not a phrase is a word. A word, then, is a free form which does not consist entirely of ... lesser free forms; in brief, a word is a minimum free form* (Leonard Bloomfield). **2** the writing, or printing, that stands for a word. *Bat, bet, bit,* and *but* are words. *This page is filled with words. Proper words in proper places make the true definition of style* (Jonathan Swift). **3** a short talk: *May I have a word with you?* **SYN**: conversation. **4** speech: *He is honest in word and deed.* **SYN**: utterance. **5** a brief expression: *The teacher gave us a word of advice.* **6** a command; order: *His word was law.* **SYN**: bidding, behest. **7** a signal; watchword; password: *The word for tonight is "the King.".* **8** a promise: *The boy kept his word. I give you my word; I'll pay you back in a week. He's a man of his word and can be trusted completely.* **SYN**: pledge. **9** news; tidings; information: *No word has come from the battlefront. What's the good word today?* **SYN**: report. **10** a saying; proverb; maxim: *That well-known word which forbids the too accurate scanning of a present, 'One must not look a gift horse in the mouth'* (Richard C. Trench). **11** *Electronics.* any set of symbols or characters stored and transferred by computer circuits as a unit of meaning.
—*v.t.* to put into or express in words; phrase: *He worded his message clearly.*
**be as good as one's word**, to keep one's promise: *To be as good as my word, I bade Will to get me a rod* (Samuel Pepys).
**beyond words**, incapable of being expressed; indescribable; unutterable: *grief beyond words. Her kindness is beyond words.*
**by word of mouth**, by spoken words; orally: *He would rather tell him of this by word of mouth than by letter* (D. D. Murray).
**eat one's words**, to take back what one has said; retract: *The pretence that prices need not go up would ... compel some Ministers to eat their words once it became clear that prices had in fact moved* (Manchester Guardian Weekly).
**from the word go**, *Slang.* from the very beginning: *The whole thing prospered from the word go* (Maclean's).
**in a word**, briefly: *Man, in a word, is dependent on that which lies outside himself* (Brooke F. Westcott).
**in so many words**, literally; in precisely that number of words; in those very words: *The Lord Mayor had threatened in so many words to pull down the old London Bridge* (Dickens).
**mince words**, to avoid coming to the point, telling the truth, or taking a stand by using ambiguous or evasive words: *The teacher did not mince words in criticizing homework.*
**my word**! an expression of surprise: *My word! ... that something like a mob* (Rolf Boldrewood).
**not breathe a word**, not to tell anything; keep something silent or confidential: *Promise not to breathe a word of this to anyone.*
**of few words**, not given to much or lengthy speaking; taciturn; laconic: *Mr. Dubbley, who was a man of few words, nodded assent* (Dickens).
**of many words**, given to much or lengthy speaking; talkative; loquacious: *Not being a man of many words, [he] contented himself by stammering something about honour* (R. S. Surtees).
**on my word**, truly; assuredly; upon my word: *"I assure you, Major Scobie, on my word— ... on my word as a friend, the package contains nothing"* (Graham Greene).
**put in a (good) word for**, to say something on behalf of; recommend to the favor of another or others: *I would also like to put in a good word for the catering, this coming as a pleasant surprise to me* (Colin Howard).
**put words into one's mouth**, to change the meaning of or add to what someone is saying: *That is not all what I meant to say; please don't put words into my mouth.*
**take one at one's word**, to take one's words seriously and act accordingly: *He started out with a confession that he knew nothing about it, and, confessing so much, I take it that the Senate will take him at his word* (New Yorker).
**take one's word (for it)**, to believe one: *Take my word for it, there is nothing in it* (Sir Richard Steele).
**take the words out of one's mouth**, to anticipate what another was just going to say: *That's just what I had in mind; you took the words out of my mouth.*
**the last word**. See under **last word**.
**the Word, a** the Bible; the Scriptures or a part of them: *Read us a chapter out of the Bible. I am very low in my mind, and at such times I like to hear the word* (Henry Kingsley). **b** the message of the gospel: *to spread the Word.* **c** the Logos; the Son of God as a manifestation of God to mankind; second person of the Trinity: *In the beginning was the Word, and the Word was with God, and the Word was God* (John 1:1).
**upon my word**, truly; certainly; indeed: *Upon my word, I think the truth is the hardest missile one can be pelted with* (George Eliot).
**word for word**, in the exact words: *to repeat something word for word.*
**words, a** angry talk; quarrel; dispute: *to have words with a person. I had sharp words with him.* **b** the text of a song as distinguished from the notes; lyrics: *To the selfsame tune and words* (Shakespeare).
[Old English *word*]
**word accent**, = word stress.
**word|age** (wėr′dij), *n.* **1** words collectively. **2** quantity of words. **3** = verbiage. **4** = wording.
**word association**, *Psychology.* the act or process by which one or more words presented to a person are associated by him with another word or words, usually in quick succession.
**word association test**, a psychological test in which word association is used to evoke a subject's repressed thoughts or feelings or to determine the quality or rate of his verbal associations.
**word-blind** (wėrd′blīnd′), *adj.* suffering from word blindness.
**word blindness**, loss of the ability to read; alexia.
**word|book** (wėrd′bu̇k′), *n.* **1** a list of words, usually with explanations; dictionary. **SYN**: lexicon. **2** the libretto of an opera or other musical work.
**word class**, *Linguistics.* **1** part of speech. **2** form class.
**word element**, a combining form, prefix, suffix, or other element that by addition to a word modifies the word's meaning or use.
**word-for-word** (wėrd′fər wėrd′), *adj.* = verbatim.
**word-hoard** (wėrd′hôrd′, -hōrd′), *n.* a person's vocabulary. [Old English *wordhord*]
**word|i|ly** (wėr′də lē), *adv.* in a wordy manner; verbosely.
**word|i|ness** (wėr′dē nis), *n.* the quality of being wordy; verbosity.
**word|ing** (wėr′ding), *n.* a way of saying a thing; choice of words; use of words; phrasing: *Careful wording helps you make clear to others what you really mean.* **SYN**: See syn. under **diction**.
**word|less** (wėrd′lis), *adj.* **1** without words; silent; speechless. **2** not put into words; unexpressed. —**word′less|ly**, *adv.* —**word′less|ness**, *n.*
**word|lore** (wėrd′lôr′, -lōr′), *n.* **1** the study of words and their history; knowledge of words. **2** the words of a language and their history.
**word-mag|ic** (wėrd′maj′ik), *n.* the use of a word or name in the belief that its utterance will magically alter, influence, or dispel the thing mentioned or named.
**word|man** (wėrd′man′), *n.*, *pl.* **-men.** a man who deals with or has a command of words; a master of language: *Behind the derivations given in the dictionaries are stories that beguile wordmen and laymen alike* (Saturday Review).
**word method**, a way of teaching reading by learning words before teaching the letters; whole-word method.
**word|mon|ger** (wėrd′mung′gər, -mong′-), *n.* a person who deals in words, especially in pedantic or empty words: *The wordmongers who could clothe one shivering thought in a hundred thousand garments* (John Motley).
**word|mon|ger|ing** (wėrd′mung′gər ing, -mong′-), *n.* the act of dealing with words as a wordmonger does.
**Word of God**, = the Word.
**word of honor**, a solemn promise.
**word-of-mouth** (wėrd′əv mouth′), *adj.*, *n.* —*adj.* communicated by spoken words; oral.
—*n.* oral communication: *Chartercraft owners also rely on travel agents, word-of-mouth and advertising ... to drum up business* (Wall Street Journal).
**word order**, the arrangement of words in a sentence, clause, or phrase. In English, the usual word order for statements is subject plus predicate: *The boy hit the ball. The ball hit the fence.* Other word orders are chiefly rhetorical and poetic: *"Uneasy lies the head that wears a crown."* In English, with its relative absence of inflections, word order is the chief grammatical device for indicating the function of words and their relation to each other.
▶ **word order**. The order of words and of other locutions in a sentence is a fundamental part of English grammar and in addition contributes to some effects of style, especially emphasis. The work done in many languages by inflections (endings) is in English performed largely by function words (prepositions, auxiliary verbs, and so on) and by the word order.
**word painting**, **1** the art of describing or portraying in words; graphic, vivid, or colorful description. **2** the art of expressing musically the thoughts conveyed by the words of a song or other vocal piece. The word "heaven" may be expressed by ascending notes, the word "death" by falling tones.
**word-per|fect** (wėrd′pėr′fikt), *adj.* = letter-perfect.
**word picture**, a picture presented in words; graphic or vivid description.
**word|play** (wėrd′plā′), *n.* play of or upon words; repartee: *He is equally inventive off the stage, with a love for puns and wordplay* (Maclean's).
**word processing**, the use of automated office equipment to produce letters, reports, and other documents especially on a typewriter controlled by a computer tape: *Potential savings from word processing range from 15 to 40 percent in secretarial and typing costs alone* (General Services Administration Bulletin). —**word′-proc′ess|ing**, *adj.*
**words** (wėrdz), *n.pl.* See under **word**.
**word-sign** (wėrd′sīn′), *n.* any symbol or character that stands for a word. Word-signs in English are + for plus, $ for dollar, and F for Fahrenheit.
**word|smith** (wėrd′smith′), *n.* a person who deals with or has a command of words.
***word square**, a set of words of the same number of letters arranged in a square so as to read the same horizontally and vertically.

***word square**

P A S T E
A C T O R
S T O M A
T O M B S
E R A S E

**word stress**, the varying emphasis given to syllables of a word that affects the meaning of the word. *Example:* "This is a hard *project* (proj′ekt)," as compared with, "Let's *project* (prə jekt′) the movie on the screen." Also, **word accent**.
**Words|wor|thi|an** (wėrdz′wėr′thē ən, wėrdz′-wėr′-), *adj.*, *n.* —*adj.* of, having to do with, or characteristic of the English poet William Wordsworth (1770-1850) or his works.
—*n.* an admirer of Wordsworth.
**word|y** (wėr′dē), *adj.*, **word|i|er**, **word|i|est**. **1** using too many words; verbose. **2** consisting of or expressed in words; verbal (now used chiefly in *wordy war*).
—*Syn.* **1 Wordy, verbose** mean using more words than are necessary. **Wordy** is the general term: *a wordy discussion, a wordy sentence.* **Verbose** implies tiresome or pretentious wordiness often resulting in obscurity: *a verbose speaker, verbose jargon.*
**wore** (wôr, wōr), *v.* **1** the past tense of **wear**[1]: *He wore out his shoes in two months.* **2** the past tense of **wear**[2].
▶ See **wear**[1] for usage note.
**work** (wėrk), *n.*, *adj.*, *v.*, **worked** or **wrought**, **work|ing**. —*n.* **1** effort in doing or making something: *to stop work at five. Few people like hard work.* **2** something to do; occupation; employment: *She is looking for work. He went to work at sixteen.* **3** something made or done; result of effort: *the works of Dickens. The artist considers that picture to be his greatest work.* **SYN**: product, achievement, feat, deed. **4** a particular task, job, or undertaking: *to plan one's work for the day.* **5** that on which effort is put: *The dressmaker took her work out on the porch.* **6** *Physics.* the transference of energy from one body or system to another, causing motion of the body acted upon in the direction of the force producing it and against resistance. It is equal to the product of the force and the distance through which the force moves and is commonly expressed in ergs, kilogram-meters, or foot-pounds. *Abbr:* w. **7** the action, activity, or operation (of a person or thing), especially of a particular kind and with reference to result: *The medicine and suggestion have done their work.* **8** embroidery; needlework. **9a** an engineering structure. **b** a fortification. **10** material at any stage of manufacture or processing, as in a machine tool. **11** a froth produced

by fermentation during the process of making vinegar. *Abbr:* wk. **12** *Obsolete.* workmanship. See also **works.** [Old English *weorc*]

**— *adj.*** of, for, having to do with, or used in work: *a work routine.*

**— *v.i.*** **1** to do work; labor: *Most people must work for a living.* **SYN**: toil, drudge, strive. **2** to do work for pay; be employed: *She works at an airplane factory.* **3** to act; operate, especially effectively: *The radio will not work.* (*Figurative.*) *The plan worked well.* **SYN**: perform. **4** to move as if with effort: *The child's face worked as she tried to keep back the tears.* **5** to go slowly or with effort: *The ship worked to windward.* **6** to become (up, round, or loose): *The window catch has worked loose.* **7** to behave (in a specified way) while being kneaded, pressed, or shaped: *clay that works easily.* **8** to ferment: *Yeast makes beer work.* **9** to seethe, rage, or toss, as a stormy sea does. **10** to go in a particular direction in some operation: *to work from left to right, work toward the back.* **11** (of a ship) to strain so that the fastenings become slack. **12** *Machinery.* to move irregularly or unsteadily so as to become out of gear.

**— *v.t.*** **1** to put effort on: *He worked his farm with success.* **2a** to get ore, coal, or other mineral, from (a mine or quarry). **b** to get or obtain (ore, coal, or other mineral) from a mine or quarry. **3** to put into operation; use; manage: *puppets worked with wires, to work a scheme.* **SYN**: execute. **4** to bring about; cause; do: *to work a change.* (*Figurative.*) *The plan worked harm.* **SYN**: accomplish, effect. **5** to cause to do work: *He works his employees long hours.* **6** to carry on operations in (districts): *The salesman worked the Eastern states.* **7a** to form; shape; make: *He worked a piece of copper into a tray. He worked an essay into an article.* **SYN**: fashion, mold. **b** to make by needlework; sew, knit, embroider, or weave: *to work a pair of socks, work embroidery.* **8a** to treat or handle in making; knead; mix: *to work butter, work dough to mix it.* **b** to stretch, twist, or pull, to achieve a certain result: *to work rope to soften it.* **9a** to make, get, do, or bring about by effort: *The wounded man worked his way across the room on his hands and knees.* **b** to earn money to support: *He worked his way through college.* **10** *Figurative.* to influence; persuade: *to work men to one's will.* **11** *Figurative.* to move; stir; excite: *Don't work yourself into a temper.* **12** to solve: *Work all the problems on the page.* **13** *Slang, Figurative.* to use tricks on to get something: *to work a friend for a job.* **14** to cause (beer, cider, or other such liquid) to ferment.

**at work,** working; operating: *Officials were insisting until a few days ago that the deflationary forces already at work in the economy ... would be sufficient* (Manchester Guardian Weekly).

**make short work of,** to deal with quickly: *He watched enthusiastic samplers making short work of the cake* (New York Times).

**out of work,** having no job; unemployed: *the panic of '73, when there were a hundred and eighty thousand men out of work in New York State* (Edmund Wilson).

**work in,** to put in; insert: *A ... tale in which several particulars ... are worked in with a lofty contempt for chronology* (Edward A. Freeman).

**work off,** to get rid of, especially by continuous action or effort: *to work off a debt.*

**work on** or **upon, a** to try to persuade or influence: *He had many minds to work upon and to win over to his cause* (Edward A. Freeman). **b** to affect or influence: *The medicine finally worked on him.*

**work out, a** to plan; develop: *And they ... worked out with some precision the mechanics of a planned society* (Edmund Wilson). **b** to solve; find out: *This ought to be worked out on paper like a problem in mathematics* (Graham Greene). **c** to use up: *As soon as one tunnel was worked out, the miners dug another.* **d** to take exercise or give exercise to; practice: *I saw Barber work out in the gymnasium* (London Daily Express). **e** to accomplish: *O lift your natures up: ... work out your freedom* (Tennyson). **f** to proceed to a result; conclude: *It is ... impossible to tell ... how the situation in Ireland will work out* (Spectator). **g** to make its way out, especially from being embedded or enclosed: *The splinter worked out from his finger.*

**work out at,** to amount to (so much): *The permutations ... for each of these functions work out at the alarming figure of 49 million* (Manchester Guardian Weekly).

**work over, a** to do again or anew; repeat: *The old story was worked over for television.* **b** *U.S. Slang.* to beat up; rough up: *One of my buddies got into an argument with a couple of German sharpies in a restaurant ... They waited outside and worked him over good* (Newsweek).

**work up, a** to plan; develop: *Mártov had worked up a plan for persuading the German government to let them return through Germany* (Edmund Wilson). **b** *Figurative.* to stir up; arouse; excite: *It is never difficult for him to work himself up into a frenzy* (Manchester Guardian Weekly). **c** to ascend; advance: *The Torridge is in full flood, and plenty of salmon are working up to spawn* (London Daily Telegraph). *He was merely working up to a peroration* (Rudyard Kipling). **d** to make into something or prepare for the use by labor: *The raw and prepared material* [*silk*] *... is worked up in various ways* (Edmund Burke). **e** to subject (a patient) to a workup: *The interns spend many hours working up new hospital patients.*

[Old English *wyrcean,* verb]

**— *Syn.*** *n.* **1 Work, labor, toil** mean effort or exertion turned to making or doing something. **Work** is the general word, applying to physical or mental effort or to the activity of a force or machine: *pleasant work, a day's work. This lathe does the work of three of the older type.* **Labor** applies to hard physical or mental work: *That student's understanding of his subjects shows the amount of labor he puts into his homework.* **Toil,** a word with some literary flavor, applies to long and wearying labor: *The farmer's toil was rewarded with good crops.*

**work\|a\|bil\|i\|ty** (wėr′kə bil′ə tē), *n.* the quality of being workable; practicability; feasibleness.

**work\|a\|ble** (wėr′kə bəl), *adj.* **1** that can be worked. **2** that can be used or put into effect; practicable: *a workable plan.* **SYN**: feasible. **—work′a\|ble\|ness,** *n.*

**work\|a\|bly** (wėr′kə blē), *adv.* in a workable manner; so as to be workable.

**work\|a\|day** (wėr′kə dā′), *adj.* of or characteristic of working days; practical; commonplace; ordinary: *workaday clothes.* **SYN**: everyday.

**work\|a\|hol\|ic** (wėr′kə hôl′ik, -hol′-), *n.* a person having an obsessive need to work constantly, often as a way of avoiding social contact. [(coined by the American writer Wayne Oates) < *work* + a(lco)*holic*]

**work\|bag** (wėrk′bag′), *n.* a bag to hold the things that a person works with, especially a bag for sewing materials.

**work\|bas\|ket** (wėrk′bas′kit, -bäs′-), *n.* a basket to hold the things that a person works with, especially sewing materials.

**work\|bench** (wėrk′bench′), *n.* a table for working at, especially one at which a mechanic, carpenter, or other artisan works. A workbench is usually a sturdy, benchlike table specially designed for and fitted with certain accessories required to do a certain kind of work.

**work\|boat** (wėrk′bōt′), *n.* a boat used for work, such as a fishing boat: *workboats to carry out the steady stream of supplies needed by a drilling crew* (Listener).

**work\|book** (wėrk′bu̇k′), *n.* **1** a book containing outlines for the study of some subject, questions to be answered, and other exercises; book in which a student does parts of his written work. **2** a book containing rules for doing certain work. **3** a book for notes of work planned or work done.

**work\|box** (wėrk′boks′), *n.* a box to hold the materials and tools a person works with.

**work camp, 1** a summer camp for teenagers with a program of activities such as farming, building, and arts and crafts. **2** a prison camp where inmates do farm work, build roads, and other manual labor. **3** a camp where work is provided for unemployed youth.

**work\|day** (wėrk′dā′), *n., adj.* **—*n.*** **1** a day for work; day that is not Sunday or a holiday. **2** the part of a day during which work is done: *to put in a long workday.* **—*adj.*** = workaday.

**worked** (wėrkt), *adj.* ornamented with needlework, engraving, or the like; shaped, fashioned, or dressed for use or ornament.

**worked lumber,** dressed lumber that has a design cut in it for decoration or to make boards fit together.

**work\|er** (wėr′kər), *n.* **1** a person or thing that works. **SYN**: laborer, toiler, artisan, craftsman. **2** a person who works for wages; member of the working class. **3** an ant, bee, wasp, or other insect that works for its community and usually does not produce offspring. See pictures under **ant** and **bee**[1]. **4** *Printing.* an electrotype plate used for printing.

**worker** or **workers' participation,** the principle that organized labor should take part in the management of business; codetermination: *It is at the top level that workers' participation is most obviously practicable, and in Germany it is enforced by law in the coal and steel industries* (Anthony Sampson).

**work\|er-priest** (wėr′kər prēst′), *n.* (in France and some other European countries) a Roman Catholic priest who spends part of his time working, as in a factory, and living as an ordinary worker.

**work ethic,** *Sociology.* the attitude of a group or a society toward work, especially the attitude or belief that work is good for man and higher on society's scale of values than play or leisure.

**work\|fare** (wėrk′fãr′), *n.* a welfare program in which recipients of public welfare must work at assigned jobs or enlist in job training: *One of* [*his*] *programs is what he calls workfare; he has said that everybody ought to work for what he gets, that welfare ought to exist only for those who can't work or for whom no jobs can be made available* (Harper's). [< *work* + (wel)*fare*]

**work farm,** a farm to which young or minor lawbreakers are sent for a period of work or rehabilitation: *He has been caught tampering with a parking meter and sent off to a work farm* (Time).

**work\|fel\|low** (wėrk′fel′ō), *n.* a person engaged in the same work with another.

**work\|folk** (wėrk′fōk′), *n.pl.* working people, especially farm laborers.

**work\|folks** (wėrk′fōks′), *n.pl.* = workfolk.

**work force, 1a** the number of workers employed, as in an area, industry, or plant. **b** the number potentially available for such employment. **2** the group of workers in a specific plant or activity.

**work function,** the energy required to release an electron as it passes through the surface of a metal.

**work\|horse** (wėrk′hôrs′), *n., adj.,* or **work horse. —*n.*** **1** a horse used for labor, and not for showing, racing, or hunting. **2** *Figurative.* a very hard worker, especially one able to do many jobs or work long hours: *The bulldozer, workhorse of World War II, soon will get its biggest peacetime working orders ...* (New York Times).

**— *adj.*** of, having to do with, or like a workhorse: (*Figurative.*) *The freighter is the workhorse vessel whose deep holds and cluttered decks carry American-produced autos, machine tools, foodstuffs, and other cargoes all over the globe* (Wall Street Journal).

**work\|house** (wėrk′hous′), *n.* **1** a house of correction where petty criminals are kept and made to work. **2** *British.* **a** a house where very poor people are lodged and set to work. **b** (originally) a house established for the provision of work for the unemployed poor of a parish. **3** *Obsolete.* a place of regular work; workshop.

**work-in** (wėrk′in′), *n.* a form of protest demonstration in which a group of people report to work or study but disregard the rules and procedures which they normally follow.

**work\|ing** (wėr′king), *n., adj.* **—*n.*** **1** the method or manner of work; operation; action: *Do you understand the working of this machine? We bend to that, the working of the heart* (Shakespeare). **2** the performance of work or labor: *laws to prevent working on Sunday.* **3a** the manufacture, production, or preparation of something, often of something requiring skill. **b** the manner or style in which something is made; workmanship. **4** the act of performing work on something; management as of a machine, ship, or mine. **5** the putting into operation or carrying on, as of a scheme, system, or law. **6** the process of solving a mathematical problem. **7** a restless or agitated movement, as of the face or mouth, due to emotion. **8** gradual movement or progress, especially against resistance. **9** the act or process of fermenting, as of liquor.

**— *adj.*** **1** that works; *the working population, a working model of a helicopter.* **2** of, for, or used in working: *working hours, working clothes.* **3** used to operate with or by: *working expenses, a working majority.* **4** that can be arranged or accomplished; workable: *a working agreement, a working arrangement.* **5** providing a basis for further work: *a working hypothesis.* **6** moving convulsively, as the features from emotion. **7** fermenting: *working beer.*

**workings, a** operation; action: *the workings of the mind.* **b** the parts of a mine, quarry, or tunnel, where work is being or has been done: *A warning system ... for use at a colliery where methane was extracted from boreholes near the workings and piped to the surface* (Science News).

**working assets,** invested capital that is more or less available for use if needed.

**working capital, 1** the amount of capital necessary to run a business. **2** the amount by which current assets exceed current liabilities. **3** *Finance.* the capital of a business placed in liquid assets, as distinguished from buildings or other fixed assets.

**Pronunciation Key:** hat, **ā**ge, c**ã**re, f**ä**r; let, **ē**qual, t**ė**rm; **i**t, **ī**ce; h**o**t, **ō**pen, **ô**rder; **oi**l, **ou**t; cup, p**u̇**t, r**ü**le; **ch**ild; lo**ng**; **th**in; **ᴛʜ**en; **zh**, measure; **ə** represents **a** in about, **e** in taken, **i** in pencil, **o** in lemon, **u** in circus.

**working class**, the class of people who work for wages, especially manual and industrial workers.
**work|ing-class** (wėr′king klas′, -kläs′), *adj.* of, belonging to, or characteristic of the working class.
**working cylinder**, (in an internal-combustion engine) a cylinder in which the gas or vapor explodes.
**working day**, = workday.
**work|ing-day** (wėr′king dā′), *adj.* = workaday.
**working dog**, a dog bred or trained for useful work, such as herding animals, pulling sleds, assisting the blind, or guarding property. Collies and German shepherds are working dogs.
**working drawing**, a drawing, as of the whole or a part of a structure or machine, made to scale and in such detail with regard to dimensions and other description as to form a guide for the workmen in the construction of the object represented.
**work|ing|girl** (wėr′king gėrl′), *n.* **1** a girl who works. **2** a girl who works with her hands or with machines.
**work|ing|man** (wėr′king man′), *n., pl.* **-men. 1** a man who works. **2** a man who works with his hands or with machines.
**working papers**, documents, as a certificate of age, that permit a child to leave school and go to work.
**work|ings** (wėr′kingz), *n. pl.* See under **working**.
**working stroke**, (in engines) the stroke of the piston during which the working fluid performs its useful work, that is, drives the piston outward.
**working substance**, the substance, such as a working fluid, that operates an engine or other prime mover.
**work|ing-to-rule** (wėr′king tu̇ rül′), *n.* = work to rule.
**working week**, = workweek.
**work|ing|wom|an** (wėr′king wu̇m′ən), *n., pl.* **-wom|en. 1** a woman who works. **2** a woman who works with her hands or with machines.
**work|less** (wėrk′lis), *adj.* out of work; unemployed. — **work′less|ness**, *n.*
**work|load** (wėrk′lōd′), *n.* the amount of work carried by or assigned to a worker or position: *Mr. Eisenhower's heart attack ... increased the workload of the Vice President's office* (Wall Street Journal).
**work|man** (wėrk′mən), *n., pl.* **-men. 1** a man who works with his hands or with machines: *The plumbers, carpenters, and other workmen finished the new house quickly.* **2** = worker (def. 2).
**work|man|like** (wėrk′mən līk′), *adj., adv.* — ***adj.*** skillful; done well: *a neat, workmanlike job.* — ***adv.*** = skillfully.
**work|man|ly** (wėrk′mən lē), *adj., adv.* = workmanlike.
**work|man|ship** (wėrk′mən ship), *n.* **1** the art or skill of a worker or his work: *Good workmanship requires long practice.* **2** the quality or manner or work; craftsmanship: *His workmanship is obvious in everything he does.* **3** the work done: *Most agreements state the price of all workmanship.* **SYN**: performance, achievement.
**work|men's compensation** (wėrk′mənz), the compensation which, as specified by law, an employer must pay to a worker who is injured or contracts a disease as a result of his employment.
**work of art**, **1** a product of any of the arts, such as a painting, statue, or literary or musical work. **2** anything done or made with great skill or artistry.
**work of supererogation**, (in the Roman Catholic Church) a good work above and beyond what is prescribed for man by God, by which typically the lives of saints are characterized, but of which any human being is capable.
**work|out** (wėrk′out′), *n. Informal.* **1** a trial; test: *The mechanic gave the car a thorough workout after repairing it.* **SYN**: tryout. **2** exercise; practice: *He had a good workout running around the track before breakfast.*
**work|peo|ple** (wėrk′pē′pəl), *n. pl. Especially British.* people who work, especially those who work with their hands or with machines.
**work|piece** (wėrk′pēs), *n.* a piece of metal or other material that is being worked on in a manufacturing process.
**work|place** (wėrk′plās′), *n.* a place where one does his work; workshop.
**work|room** (wėrk′rüm′, -ru̇m′), *n.* a room where work is done: *Many workers were sewing in one of the large workrooms of the garment factory.*
**works** (wėrks), *n.pl.* **1** a factory or other place for doing some kind of work: *the Beloit Iron Works.* **2** the moving parts of a machine or device: *the works of a watch.* **3** buildings, bridges, docks, and other large industrial establishments: *He lives down behind the works where gas is stored.* **4a** actions: *good works.* **b** acts that are done to obey or accord with the law of God; moral actions, especially in contrast to *faith* or *grace* in the doctrine of justification.
**give (one) the works**, *U.S. Slang.* **a** to attack, criticize, or beat soundly; punish severely: *I asked to whom I should give the works and he said that we took no guff from anybody* (Ernest Cuneo). **b** to kill: *They gave Caesar the works in the Capitol* (Punch).
**in the works**, *Informal.* in the planning stage; upcoming: *The usual struggle over public housing and slum clearance legislation is in the works* (Newsweek).
**shoot the works**, *U.S. Slang.* to go to the limit; go all-out in something; use or spend completely: *She suddenly decides to shoot the works with the little fortune he left behind* (New Yorker).
**the works**, *U.S Slang.* everything: *He had all the paraphernalia ... that a German intellectual ought to have. Encyclopedias, dictionaries, books on medicine—the works* (New Yorker).
**works council**, *British.* a group of factory workers or other employees that consults with the employer on problems involving working conditions, wages, and the like.
**work|shop** (wėrk′shop′), *n.* **1** a shop or building where work is done. **2** a course of study, discussion, or work for a group of people working or studying on a special project: *a history workshop; ... intensive journalism workshops* (New York Times).
**work-shy** (wėrk′shī′), *adj.* not willing to work; idle: *He argues very logically against the view that immigrants are work-shy parasites* (Manchester Guardian Weekly).
**work song**, a song sung by a gang of workers in rhythm with the motions made during their work.
**work stoppage**, the action of stopping work within a company, plant, or industry, as caused by a strike or layoff.
**work study**, *British.* time and motion study.
**work|ta|ble** (wėrk′tā′bəl), *n.* a table to work at.
**work to rule**, *British.* **1** a form of slowdown used by labor to force concessions from management in which work is slowed down by the deliberate, punctilious observance of every working rule and regulation. **2** to slow down work by the punctilious observance of working rules.
**work|up** (wėrk′up′), *n.* a complete medical investigation of a person's illness: *They will insist that real and alleged mental patients be given a proper diagnostic workup by highly qualified physicians* (Atlantic).
**work-up** (wėrk′up′), *n. Printing.* the imprint of a quadrat, lead, or other piece that has worked up out of position so as to be unintentionally inked and printed.
**work|week** (wėrk′wēk′), *n.* the part of the week in which work is done, usually Monday through Friday.
**work|wom|an** (wėrk′wu̇m′ən), *n., pl.* **-wom|en. 1** a woman worker. **2** a woman who works with her hands or with machines.
**world** (wėrld), *n., adj.* — ***n.*** **1** the earth: *Ships can sail around the world.* **SYN**: See syn. under **earth**. **2** all of certain parts, people, or things of the earth: *women's world, the world of ideas. The New World is North America and South America. The Old World is Europe, Asia, and Africa. Fashionable people belong to the world of fashion. Ants are parts of the insect world. With no aspirations beyond the little world in which she moved* (Benjamin Disraeli). **3** all people; the human race; the public: *The whole world knows it. You know that these two parties still divide the world—Of those that want, and those that have* (Tennyson). **4** the things of this life and the people devoted to them: *Monks and nuns live apart from the world.* **5** any planet, especially when considered as inhabited: *"The War of the Worlds" is a book about creatures from Mars who wanted to conquer Earth.* **6** any time, condition, or place of life: *Heaven is in the world to come.* **7** all things; everything; the universe; cosmos. **8** a great deal; very much; large amount: *Sunshine does children a world of good. "I ... think the world of you, pal, even with all your faults"* (Saul Bellow).
— ***adj.*** **1** of the entire world: *the world champion in weight lifting, the world premiere of a motion picture, the world output of uranium.* **2** of all or most nations of the world; international: *a world congress of scientists. The UN is a world organization.* **3** worldly; world-wide: *Our outlook is a world outlook* (Maclean's).
**all the world and his wife**, everybody, male and female, especially everybody of any social pretensions: *Aunt Charlotte knows all the world and his wife* (Mrs. Humphry Ward).
**bring into the world**, to give birth to: *I was brought into the world on the 28th February* (Samuel Bamford).
**come into the world**, to be born: *He died ... six months before I came into the world* (Dickens).
**for all the world**, **a** for any reason, no matter how great: *I am sure I would not do such a thing for all the world* (Jane Austen). **b** in every respect; exactly: *He ... swung about his arms, for all the world as if he were going through the sword exercise* (Thomas Hardy).
**in the world**, **a** anywhere: *He was ... the most retiring man in the world* (Dickens). **b** at all; ever: *How in the world did you persuade the captain?* (Adeline D. T. Whitney).
**out of this world**, *Informal.* of which there is nothing like; great; wonderful; distinctive: *The cuisine is both American and Continental and is out of this world* (Time).
**the world, the flesh, and the devil**, the world with its interests, the flesh with its appetites, and the devil with his evil promptings, as the great sources of temptation and sin for mankind: *From all the deceits of the world, the flesh, and the devil, Good Lord, deliver us* (Book of Common Prayer).
**world without end**, eternally; forever: *Jesus Christ our Lord, to whom, with thee and the Holy Ghost, be all honor and glory, world without end. Amen* (Book of Common Prayer).
[Old English *worold,* earlier *weorold* literally, age of man]
**world-beat|er** (wėrld′bē′tər), *n. Especially U.S. Informal.* **1** a champion: *The race ... turned Dawn [a horse] into a world-beater* (Time). **2** a great success; smash hit: *His first picture wasn't a world-beater* (Wall Street Journal).
**World Calendar**, a proposed twelve-month calendar divided into four equal quarters, each totaling 91 days. An extra day is added each year and still another every leap year. *The World Calendar ... achieves the regular flow of seasons, days and years* (Elizabeth Achelis).
**world-class** (wėrld′klas′, -kläs′), *adj.* of international note or quality: *Ashkenazy ... showed himself a world-class accompanist* (Manchester Guardian Weekly).
**World Communion Sunday**, the first Sunday in October, on which a Communion service is held in many churches throughout the world to affirm Christian unity.
**World Cup**, **1** a series of soccer games between national teams from many countries to choose an international winning team, held every four years: *the opening match of the World Cup.* **2** the trophy awarded to the winner of this series.
**world-famed** (wėrld′fāmd′), *adj.* = world-famous.
**world-fa|mous** (wėrld′fā′məs), *adj.* famous the world over: *a world-famous writer.*
**world federalism**, a movement that advocates world government by a federation of all the nations of the world.
**world federalist**, an advocate of world federalism.
**world|ful** (wėrld′fəl), *n., pl.* **-fuls.** enough to fill the world: *To choose from a worldful of events is a difficult, exciting and sometimes painful business* (Time).
**world government**, a proposed government that would govern and serve everybody in the world, taking the place of individual governments: *World government ... is probably accepted by most thinking people today as a necessity at some time in the not too distant future* (Bulletin of Atomic Scientists).
**world island**, (in geopolitics) the land mass that constitutes Asia, Africa, and Europe.
**world line**, the path of an elementary particle through space and time: *The strong gravitational field of the collapsing star bends the "world lines," or space-time paths, of photons emitted by the star* (Scientific American).
**world|li|ness** (wėrld′lē nis), *n.* worldly ideas, ways, or conduct.
**world|ling** (wėrld′ling), *n.* a person who cares much for the interests and pleasures of this world. [< *world* + *-ling*]
**world|ly** (wėrld′lē), *adj.,* **-li|er, -li|est,** *adv.* — ***adj.*** **1** of this world; not of heaven: *worldly wealth, worldly knowledge, worldly ambition.* **SYN**: mundane. See syn. under **earthly**. **2a** caring much for the interests and pleasures of this world. **b** caring too much for such interests and pleasures. **3** = worldly-wise.
— ***adv.*** in a worldly manner; with a worldly intent or disposition.
**world|ly-mind|ed** (wėrld′lē mīn′did), *adj.* having or showing a worldly mind; caring much for the interests and pleasures of this world. — **world′ly-mind′ed|ly**, *adv.* — **world′ly-mind′ed|ness**, *n.*
**world|ly-wise** (wėrld′lē wīz′), *adj.* wise about the ways and affairs of this world. **SYN**: sophisticated, urbane. — **world′ly-wise′ness**, *n.*
**world ocean**, the continuous body of water that covers most of the earth's surface, made up of three great oceans—the Pacific, the Atlantic, and the Indian. The continents lie like islands in the world ocean.
**world power**, a nation having such military or

other power as to be able to exert a decisive influence on the course of world affairs: *The United States and Russia are two of the chief world powers in this part of the twentieth century.*
**world-re|nowned** (wėrld′ri nound′), *adj.* = world-famous.
**world series** or **World Series**, a series of baseball games played each fall between the winners of the two major-league championships, to decide the professional championship of the United States. The first team to win four games wins the series.
**world's fair**, an international exposition, with exhibits, as of arts, crafts, scientific developments, and products, from various countries.
**world-shak|er** (wėrld′shā′kər), *n.* a world-shaking person or event: *Goya is one of the great world-shakers* (London Times).
**world-shak|ing** (wėrld′shā′king), *adj.* of world-wide importance or effect; earth-shaking: *a world-shaking debate.*
**world soul** or **spirit**, the animating principle that informs the physical world.
**world-view** (wėrld′vyü′), *n.* view of life; Weltanschauung. [translation of German *Weltanschauung*]
**world war**, a war involving most of the major countries of the world, especially either one of the World Wars: *In the period between the world wars, military aircraft benefited from [many] design improvements* (Atlantic).
**World War**, **1** Usually, **World War I.** a war mainly in Europe and the Middle East, from July 28, 1914, to November 11, 1918; First World War; Great War. The United States, Great Britain, France, Russia, and their allies were on one side; Germany, Austria-Hungary, and their allies were on the other side. **2** Usually, **World War II.** a war in Europe, Asia, Africa, and elsewhere, from September 1, 1939, to August 14, 1945; Second World War. Great Britain, the United States, France, the Soviet Union, China, and their allies were on one side; Germany, Italy, Japan, and their allies were on the other side. *Abbr:* WW (no periods).
**world-wea|ri|ness** (wėrld′wir′ē nis), *n.* the condition of being tired of living.
**world-wea|ry** (wėrld′wir′ē), *adj.* weary of this world; tired of living.
**world-wide** or **world|wide** (wėrld′wīd′), *adj., adv.* —*adj.* spread throughout the world; extending over or involving the entire earth or its peoples: *the world-wide threat of atomic radiation. Gasoline now has world-wide use.*
—*adv.* all over the world: *to sell a product world-wide.* —**world′-wide′ly**, **world′wide′ly**, *adv.*
**world-wise** (wėrld′wīz′), *adj.* = worldly-wise.
**worm** (wėrm), *n., v.* —*n.* **1** a small, slender, crawling or creeping animal with no backbone. Most worms have soft bodies and no legs. The earthworms, flatworms, and roundworms are three kinds. **2** any one of various small, slender, crawling or creeping animals that resemble the true worms, such as a maggot, grub, or caterpillar, various crustaceans or mollusks (the shipworm), and the adult of some insects (the glowworm). **3** something like a worm in shape or movement, especially: **a** the thread of a screw. **b** a long, spiral or coiled tube of a still, in which the vapor is condensed. **c** a short, continuously threaded shaft or screw, the thread of which gears with the teeth of a toothed wheel. **d** an Archimedean screw or a device using the same principle. **4** *Figurative.* a person who deserves contempt, scorn, or pity. **5** *Figurative.* something that slowly eats away, or the pain or destruction it causes: *The worm of conscience still begnaw thy soul!* (Shakespeare). **6** the lytta, as of a dog. **7** *Anatomy.* the median lobe of the cerebellum; vermiform process.
—*v.t.* **1** to make (one's way) by creeping or crawling slowly, silently, or stealthily: *The soldier wormed his way toward the enemy's lines.* **2** *Figurative.* to get by persistent and secret means: *She tried to worm the secret out of me. He wormed himself into our confidence.* **3** to remove worms from: *to worm a dog.* **4** to remove a rod of cartilage (the lytta or worm) from the tongue of (a dog or other animal). **5** *Nautical.* to wind yarn, small rope, etc., spirally around (a rope or cable) so as to fill up the grooves between the strands and make the surface smooth for parceling or serving.
—*v.i.* **1** to move like a worm; crawl or creep slowly, silently, or stealthily: *He wormed under the high fence. The soldiers wormed through the tall grass toward the enemy's camp.* **2** *Figurative.* **a** to make one's way insidiously (into): *Already some of these riffraff are worming into it [a club]* (Booth Tarkington). **b** to wriggle (as out of trouble). **3** to look for or catch worms.
**worms**, a disease characterized by the presence of parasitic worms in the body, especially in the intestines; helminthiasis: *Our dog had worms, but he is fine now. A dose of santonin often produces results which will seem to justify a diagnosis of worms* (Patrick Manson).
[Old English *wurm*, variant of *wyrm*] —**worm′er**, *n.*
**worm-eat|en** (wėrm′ē′tən), *adj.* **1** eaten into by worms: *worm-eaten timbers.* **2** *Figurative.* worn-out; worthless; out-of-date.
**worm-eat|ing warbler** (wėrm′ē′ting), a dull-colored warbler of eastern North America with black stripes on its crown.
**wormed** (wėrmd), *adj.* damaged by worms; worm-eaten.
**worm fence**, = snake fence.
***worm gear**, **1** = worm wheel. **2** a worm wheel and an endless screw together. By a worm gear the rotary motion of one shaft can be transmitted to another.

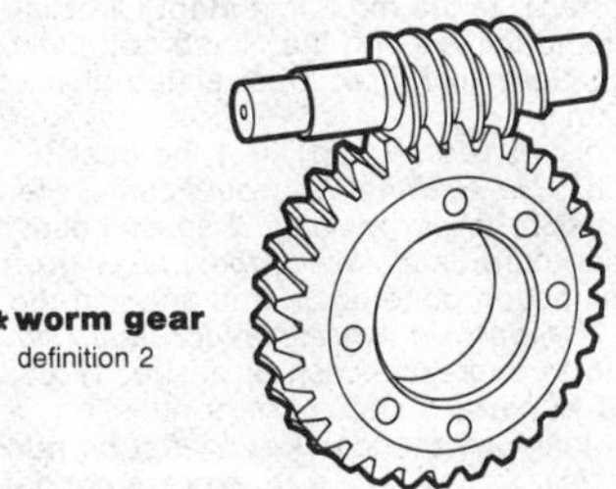

***worm gear**
definition 2

**worm|hole** (wėrm′hōl′), *n.* a hole made by a burrowing worm, larva, or insect: *wormholes in wood, an apple filled with wormholes.*
**worm|holed** (wėrm′hōld′), *adj.* having wormholes.
**worm|i|ness** (wėr′mē nis), *n.* the condition of being wormy.
**worm|like** (wėrm′līk′), *adj.* resembling a worm in, as structure, form, or movement; vermiform.
**worm lizard**, = amphisbaena.
**worm|root** (wėrm′rüt′, -rût′), *n.* = pinkroot.
**worms** (wėrmz), *n. pl.* See under **worm**.
**worm|seed** (wėrm′sēd′), *n.* **1** the dried flower heads of any one of various plants of the composite family, especially the Levant wormseed, used as a vermifuge. **2** the seeds of various goosefoots, used similarly. **3** one of these plants.
**worm's-eye** (wėrmz′ī′), *adj.* seen from below or very closely; narrow; detailed: *a worm's-eye view of city life.*
**worm shell**, **1** the shell of any one of a family of gastropod mollusks, in the young animal regularly conic and spiral, but later having whorls separate, and often crooked or contorted, with a wormlike appearance. **2** the animal itself.
**worm snake**, a small, harmless snake of the eastern United States that is commonly found under bark, logs, and stones and feeds mainly on earthworms.
**worm wheel**, a wheel with teeth that fit a revolving screw. —**worm′-wheel′**, *adj.*
**worm|wood** (wėrm′wůd′), *n.* **1** a bitter herb used in making medicine and in certain liquors, such as absinthe and some brands of vermouth. It is a woody perennial plant native to Europe. **2** any one of the genus of herbs or shrubs of the composite family to which the wormwood belongs, such as santonica, moxa, and tarragon; artemisia. Several kinds of wormwoods of the western United States are usually called sagebrush. **3** *Figurative.* something bitter or extremely unpleasant. [alteration (influenced by *worm* + *wood*[1]) of earlier *wermod*, Old English *wermōd.* Compare etym. under **vermouth.**]
**worm|y** (wėr′mē), *adj.*, **worm|i|er, worm|i|est.** **1** having worms; containing many worms: *wormy apples.* **2** damaged by worms; worm-eaten: *wormy wood.* **3a** resembling a worm; wormlike. **b** *Figurative: wormy, groveling ways.* **4** of or having to do with worms.
**worn** (wôrn, wōrn), *v., adj.* —*v.* **1** the past participle of **wear**[1]: *He has worn that suit for two years.* **2** the past participle of **wear**[2].
—*adj.* **1** damaged by long or hard wear or use: *a worn suit, worn rugs.* SYN: threadbare. **2** *Figurative.* tired and drawn; wearied: *a worn face.*
**worn-out** (wôrn′out′, wōrn′-), *adj.* **1** used until no longer fit for use. **2** *Figurative.* physically exhausted; very tired; completely fatigued.
**wor|ried** (wėr′id), *adj.* troubled; distressed: *He is also a worried man, worried that Britain may not succeed in adapting her institutions successfully to modern pressures* (St. Louis Post Dispatch).
**wor|ried|ly** (wėr′id lē), *adv.* in a manner showing worry; with worry.
**wor|ri|er** (wėr′ē ər), *n.* a person who worries.
**wor|ri|less** (wėr′ē lis), *adj.* free from worry.
**wor|ri|ment** (wėr′ē mənt), *n. Informal.* **1** a worrying. **2** worry; anxiety.
**wor|ri|some** (wėr′ē səm), *adj.* **1** causing worry. SYN: troublesome. **2** inclined to worry. SYN: apprehensive. —**wor′ri|some|ly**, *adv.* —**wor′ri|someness**, *n.*
**wor|rit** (wėr′it), *v.i., v.t., n. Dialect.* worry. [alteration of *worry*]
**wor|ry** (wėr′ē), *v.*, **-ried, -ry|ing,** *n., pl.* **-ries.** —*v.i.* **1** to feel anxious; be uneasy: *She worries about little things. She will worry if we are late.* **2** to pull or tear at an object with the teeth; shake, mangle, or bite an animal or object with the teeth.
—*v.t.* **1** to make anxious; trouble: *The problem worried him. Increasing anxieties about money have worried her* (George Eliot). **2** to annoy; bother; vex: *Don't worry me with so many questions.* **3** to seize and shake with the teeth; bite at; snap at: *A cat will worry a mouse.* **4** to harass, as if by repeated biting; harry by rough treatment or repeated attacks.
—*n.* **1** to an anxious, troubled, or uneasy state of mind; care: *Worry kept her awake.* SYN: anxiety, uneasiness, trouble. **2** a cause of trouble or care: *A mother of sick children has many worries.* **3** the act of seizing and shaking an animal or rag or other object.
**worry along** (or **through**), to manage somehow: *She must ... try to worry along without him* (William Dean Howells).
[Middle English *worien*, Old English *wyrgan* to strangle]
—*Syn. v.t.* **1 Worry, annoy, harass** mean to disturb or distress someone. **Worry** means to cause great uneasiness, care, or anxiety: *The change in his disposition and habits worries me.* **Annoy** means to irritate or vex, as by constant interference or repeated interruption: *The new girl annoys her fellow workers with too many foolish questions.* **Harass** means to annoy deeply and unceasingly: *He is harassed by business troubles and a nagging wife.*
**worry beads**, a string of beads played with for relaxation or distraction, originally chiefly in countries of the Middle East.
**wor|ry|ing** (wėr′ē ing), *adj.* causing worry; worrisome: *The continuous decline in the percentage of students achieving the necessary 'A' levels to enter university physics courses since the early 60s is worrying* (New Scientist). —**wor′ry|ing|ly**, *adv.*
**wor|ry|wart** (wėr′ē wôrt′), *n. U.S. Slang.* a person who worries too much.
**worse** (wėrs), *adj., comparative of* **bad**, *adv., n.*
—*adj.* **1** less well; more ill: *The patient is worse today.* **2** less good; more evil: *He is bad enough, but his brother is worse.* **3** more harmful, painful, regrettable, unpleasant, or unfavorable: *The accident could have been worse.* **4** more unattractive, unsuitable, faulty, incorrect, or ill-advised: *His pen was poor and his writing even worse.* **5** of lower quality or value; inferior: *The soil is worse in the valley.* **6** less fortunate or well off.
—*adv.* in a more severe or evil manner or degree: *It is raining worse than ever today.*
—*n.* that which is worse: *The weather has been bad enough, but from the looks of the sky we can expect even worse tonight.*
[Old English *wyrsa*]
**wors|en** (wėr′sən), *v.t.* to make worse. —*v.i.* to become worse.
**wors|er** (wėr′sər), *adj., adv.* = worse.
► **Worser** was a common variant of *worse* in the 1500's and 1600's but is now a nonstandard usage except as a literary survival (especially in phrases like the *worser part, sort,* or *half*).
**wor|set** (wėr′sit), *n., adj. Scottish.* worsted.
**wor|ship** (wėr′ship), *n., v.*, **-shiped, -ship|ing** or **-shipped, -ship|ping.** —*n.* **1** great honor and respect: *the worship of God, idol worship, fire worship.* SYN: reverence. **2** religious ceremonies or services in honor of God. Prayers and hymns are part of worship. *A church is a place for public worship.* **3** great love and admiration; adoration: *hero worship, the worship of wealth and power.* **4** an object of worship. **5** *British.* a title used in addressing certain magistrates and various others of high rank or position: *"Yes, your worship," he said to the judge.* **6** *Archaic.* **a** honorable character; honor; distinction; renown. **b** honorable or high rank or standing; importance; dignity.
—*v.t.* **1** to pay great honor and respect to: *People go to church to worship God.* SYN: revere, venerate. **2** to consider extremely precious; hold very dear; adore: *She worships her mother. A miser worships money. I worshiped the very ground she walked on* (Dickens).
—*v.i.* **1** to take part in a religious service. **2** to

**Pronunciation Key:** hat, āge, cãre, fär; let, ēqual, tėrm; it, īce; hot, ōpen, ôrder; oil, out; cup, půt, rüle; child; long; thin; ᴛʜen; zh, measure; ə represents **a** in about, **e** in taken, **i** in pencil, **o** in lemon, **u** in circus.

feel extreme adoration or devotion for a person or thing.
[Old English *worthscip,* variant of *weorthscipe* < *weorth* worth + *-scipe* -ship] —**wor′ship|er, wor′ship|per,** *n.* —**wor′ship|less,** *adj.*

**wor|ship|ful** (wėr′ship fəl), *adj.* **1** honorable: *We beg you, worshipful gentlemen, to grant our request.* **2** worshiping: *the worshipful eyes of a dog watching its master.* **3** deserving or capable of being worshiped. —**wor′ship|ful|ly,** *adv.* —**wor′ship|ful|ness,** *n.*

**worst** (wėrst), *adj., superlative of* **bad,** *adv., n., v.* —***adj.*** **1** least well; most ill: *This is the worst cold I ever had.* **2** least good; most evil: *He is the worst boy in school.* **3** of the lowest quality or value; least valuable, desirable, or successful: *the worst room in the hotel.*
—***adv.*** in the worst manner or degree: *This child acts worst when he is tired.*
—***n.*** that which is worst: *Yesterday was bad, but the worst is yet to come.*
—***v.t.*** to beat; defeat: *The hero worsted his enemies.*
**at (the) worst,** under the least favorable circumstances: *I thought ... that if a man played long enough he was sure to win ... or, at the worst, not to come off a loser* (Dickens).
**give (one) the worst of it,** to defeat (someone): *If the captain hadn't been sick, our team would not have been given the worst of it.*
**if worst comes to (the) worst,** if the very worst happens: *Even if worst comes to worst, I've got enough to live on for six months* (Dreiser).
**(in) the worst way.** See under **way.**
[Old English *wyrresta* < *wyrsa* worse + *-sta,* a superlative suffix]

**worst-case** (wėrst′kās′), *adj.* designed to accommodate the very worst eventualities under a given set of circumstances: *A large number of the "worst-case scenarios" put forward ... focus on the possibility that a new pathogenic form of the host bacterium might be created inadvertently by experimenters working with the novel gene-splicing technique* (Scientific American).

**wor|sted** (wu̇r′stid, wu̇s′tid), *n., adj.* —***n.*** **1** a firmly twisted thread or yarn made of long-stapled wool. **2** a cloth made from such thread or yarn. **3** a fine, soft woolen yarn for knitting, crocheting, and needlework.
—***adj.*** made of worsted.
[< *Worsted* (now *Worstead*), a town in England, where it was originally made]
▶ The (r) was lost from **worsted,** as from *Worcester,* in Early Modern English, but the letter representing it was retained in the spelling and now spelling pronunciation (wu̇r′stid), is generally heard.

**wort**[1] (wėrt), *n.* **1** the liquid made from malt which later becomes beer, ale, or other liquor when fermented. **2** any one of various similar infusions. [Old English *wyrt*]

**wort**[2] (wėrt), *n.* a plant, herb, or vegetable, used for food or medicine (chiefly in combination in plant names such as *liverwort, figwort*). [Middle English *wort,* earlier *wurt,* Old English *wyrt*]

**worth**[1] (wėrth), *adj., n.* —***adj.*** **1** good or important enough for; deserving: *The book is worth reading. New York is a city worth visiting.* **2** equal in value to: *This book is worth $5.00. That toy is worth little.* **3** having property, or income that amounts to: *The man is worth a million dollars.*
—***n.*** **1** merit; usefulness; importance: *We should read books of real worth.* **SYN**: See syn. under **merit. 2** value: *the worth of a house. She got her money's worth out of that coat.* **SYN**: See syn. under **merit. 3** the quantity that a certain amount will buy: *He bought a dollar's worth of stamps.* **4** excellence of character; personal merit. **5** *Archaic.* property; wealth. [Old English *weorth*]

**worth**[2] (wėrth), *v.i. Archaic.* to come to be; come about, happen. [Old English *weorthan* become, come about; (originally) to turn]

**wor|thi|ly** (wėr′ᴛʜə lē), *adv.* **1** in a worthy manner; honorably: *He fought worthily but he was no match for the champion.* **2** rightly; suitably; fittingly. **3** deservedly; justly.

**wor|thi|ness** (wėr′ᴛʜē nis), *n.* the quality or condition of being worthy; merit; excellence: *Nobody doubts the worthiness of a fire department.*

**worth|less** (wėrth′lis), *adj.* without worth; good-for-nothing; useless: *Throw those worthless, broken tools away.* **SYN**: valueless, trashy. —**worth′less|ly,** *adv.* —**worth′less|ness,** *n.*

**worth|while** or **worth-while** (wėrth′hwīl′), *adj.* worth time, attention, or effort; having real merit: *He ought to spend his time on some worthwhile reading.* **SYN**: valuable, useful. —**worth′while′ness, worth′-while′ness,** *n.*
▶ **Worthwhile** or **worth-while** is the form used before a noun: *a worthwhile undertaking.* As predicate complement it is written as two words: *It's hardly worth while.*

**wor|thy** (wėr′ᴛʜē), *adj.,* **-thi|er, -thi|est,** *n., pl.* **-thies.** —***adj.*** **1** having worth or merit: *a worthy opponent. Helping the poor is a worthy cause.* **2** deserving; meriting: *She helps the worthy poor.* **3** *Obsolete.* deserved or merited by default or wrongdoing; condign.
—***n.*** a person of great merit; admirable person: *The Wright brothers stand high among American worthies.*
**worthy of, a** deserving: *His courage was worthy of high praise. Bad acts are worthy of punishment.* **b** having enough worth for: *Your sentiments and conduct are worthy of the noble house you descend from* (Scott).

**wost** (wost), *v. Archaic. 2nd person singular of* **wit**[2]. know. "Thou wost" means "you know."

**wot** (wot), *v. Archaic. 1st and 3rd person singular of* **wit**[2]. know. "I wot" means "I know." "He wot" means "He knows." [Old English *wāt*]

**Wo|tan** (wō′tən), *n.* the most important Old High German god, identified with the Norse god Odin. [< Old High German *Wotan.* See related etym. at **Odin, Woden.**]

**would**[1] (wu̇d; *unstressed* wəd), *v.* **1** the past tense of **will**[1]: *He said that he would come. He would go in spite of our warning.* **2** special uses: **a** to express future time: *Would they never go?* **b** to express action done again and again in the past time: *The children would play for hours on the beach.* **c** to express a wish or desire: *Would I were rich!* **d** to make a statement or question more polite than *will* sounds: *Would that be fair? Would you help us, please?* **e** to express conditions: *If he would only try, he could do it.* [Old English *wolde,* past tense of *willan* to will]
▶ **a** The frequent misspelling **would of** for *would have* arises out of the fact that *have* and *of,* when completely unstressed, are pronounced identically. **b Would rather** is used to express a strong preference: *I would rather stay home than dance with him.*

**would**[2] (wōld), *n.* = weld[2].

**would-be** (wu̇d′bē′), *adj., n.* —***adj.*** **1** wishing or pretending to be: *a would-be actor.* **2** intended to be: *a would-be work of art.*
—***n.*** a person who wishes or pretends to be something: *The theatrical would-be hoped to get a starring role.*

**would|n't** (wu̇d′ənt), would not.

**wouldst** (wu̇dst), *v. Archaic. 2nd person singular past tense of* **will**[1]. would. "Thou wouldst" means "you would."

**Woulfe's apparatus** (wu̇lfs), a series of Woulfe's bottles with connecting tubes. [< Peter *Woulfe,* about 1727-1803, an English chemist]

**Woulfe's bottle,** a bottle or jar with two or three necks, used especially in washing gases and saturating liquids with gases.

**wound**[1] (wünd; *Archaic* wound), *n., v.* —***n.*** **1** a hurt or injury to a person or animal caused by cutting, stabbing, shooting, or other violence rather than disease: *The man has a knife wound in his arm.* **SYN**: laceration. **2** a similar injury, due to external violence, in any part of a tree or plant. **3** *Figurative.* any hurt or injury to feelings or reputation: *The loss of his job was a wound to his pride.*
—***v.t.*** **1** to injure by cutting, stabbing, shooting, or other violence; hurt; damage: *The hunter wounded the deer.* **2** *Figurative.* to injure in feelings or reputation: *Their unkind words wounded me.*
—***v.i.*** to inflict a wound or wounds; do harm or injury.
**lick one's wounds,** to try to recover one's strength or pride after an injury, defeat, or setback: *The theatre's director, who had fought for the play, deplored this decision and said he ... was going away for a day or two to lick his wounds* (Manchester Guardian Weekly).
[Old English *wund*]

**wound**[2] (wound), *v.* **1** a past tense and a past participle of **wind**[2]: *She wound the string into a tight ball. It is wound too loosely.* **2** winded; a past tense and a past participle of **wind**[3].

**wound|ed** (wün′did), *adj., n.* —***adj.*** **1** suffering from a wound or wounds: *Kay near him groaning like a wounded bull* (Tennyson). **2** *Figurative.* deeply pained or grieved: *The quiet of my wounded conscience* (Shakespeare).
—***n.* the wounded,** those who have received wounds; wounded people collectively: *The battlefield was strewn with the dead and the wounded.* —**wound′ed|ly,** *adv.*

**wound|less** (wünd′lis; *Archaic and Poetic* wound′lis), *adj.* without wounds.

**wound|wort** (wünd′wėrt′), *n.* any one of various plants formerly used for treating wounds, such as the comfrey or the kidney vetch.

**wove**[1] (wōv), *v.* a past tense and a past participle of **weave**: *The spider wove a new web after the first was destroyed.*
▶ See **weave** for usage note.

**wove**[2] (wōv), *n.* = wove paper.

**wo|ven** (wō′vən), *v.* a past participle of **weave**: *The cloth is closely woven.*

**wove paper,** a paper made on a mold of closely woven wire and having a plain surface or one finely marked by the mold.

**wow**[1] (wou), *interj., n., v.* —***interj.*** an exclamation, as of surprise, joy, or dismay.
—***n.*** **1** a bark or similar short, explosive sound. **2** = wail. **3** a slow rise and fall in the sound pitch of a phonograph, film, or tape recorder, caused by slight variations in the speed at which the recording is played.
—***v.i.*** to utter such a sound or sounds.
[imitative]

**wow**[2] (wou), *n., v. U.S. Slang.* —***n.*** an unqualified success; hit.
—***v.t.*** to overwhelm with delight or amazement: *He wanted to wow his classmates by the thoroughness of his research* (New York Times).
[American English, noun and verb use of *wow*[1]]

**wow|ser** (wou′zər), *n.* (in Australia) a person who is rigidly moral or proper, especially one who seeks to suppress whatever he disapproves of, however minor or petty; bigoted and puritanical person. [origin uncertain]

**wow|ser|ism** (wou′zə riz′əm), *n.* (in Australia) the practices of a wowser; puritanical intolerance.

**w.p., 1** weather permitting. **2** without prejudice.

**WP** (no periods), word processing.

**W.P.,** worthy patriarch (in Freemasonry).

**WPA** (no periods), Works Projects Administration (an agency of the U.S. Government established in 1935 as the *Works Progress Administration,* and abolished in 1942, to provide jobs especially in public works).

**W particle,** a hypothetical elementary particle that is the carrier, or quantum unit, of the weak interaction: *The so-called intermediate vector boson or W particle ... is important to certain theories of how the weak subnuclear force behaves* (Science News).

**WPB** (no periods), War Production Board.

**wpm** (no periods) or **w.p.m.,** words per minute: *A very fast typist can do 80 wpm.*

**WRAC** (no periods) or **W.R.A.C.,** *British.* Women's Royal Army Corps.

**wrack**[1] (rak), *n., v.* —***n.*** **1a** what remains afloat when a vessel is wrecked; wreckage. **b** *Dialect.* a wrecked vessel; wreck. **2** ruin; destruction. **3a** seaweed cast ashore by the waves or growing on the tidal seashore. **b** any one of several species of brown algae.
—***v.t.*** *Archaic or Dialect.* to wreck.
—***v.i.*** *Archaic or Dialect.* to be wrecked.
[probably < earlier Flemish *wrack* < Middle Low German *wrak* wreck < *wraken* shoot out, eject. Compare etym. under **rack**[2], **wreak.**]

**wrack**[2] (rak), *n.* = rack[4]. [spelling variant of *rack*[4]]

**wrack**[3] (rak), *v.t.* to hurt very much; torment: *... his body wracked with a succession of hot spells and chills* (James T. Farrell). [spelling variant of *rack*[1]]

**Wraf** or **WRAF** (raf, räf), *n. British.* a member of the WRAF.

**WRAF** (no periods) or **W.R.A.F.,** *British.* Women's Royal Air Force.

**wraith** (rāth), *n.* **1** the ghost of a person seen before or soon after his death. **2** a specter; ghost. **SYN**: apparition. [perhaps < Old English *wrāth* wroth, in sense of "angry person or spirit"] —**wraith′like′,** *adj.*

**wran|gle** (rang′gəl), *v.,* **-gled, -gling,** *n.* —***v.i.*** **1** to argue or dispute in a noisy or angry way; quarrel: *The children wrangled about who should sit in the front seat of the car.* **SYN**: squabble, brawl. **2** (formerly) to dispute or discuss publicly, as at a university for or against a thesis.
—***v.t.*** **1** to argue. **2** *Western U.S. and Canada.* to herd or tend (horses or cattle) on the range.
—***n.*** a noisy dispute; angry quarrel.
[perhaps < Low German *wrangeln.* See related etym. at **wring.**]

**wran|gler** (rang′glər), *n.* **1** a person who wrangles. **2** *Western U.S. and Canada.* a herder in charge of horses or cattle. **3** *British.* (at Cambridge University) a person winning high honors in mathematics as the result of the final examination (tripos).

**wrap** (rap), *v.,* **wrapped** or **wrapt, wrap|ping,** *n.* —***v.t.*** **1** to cover by winding or folding something around: *She wrapped herself in a shawl. She wrapped the child in a blanket.* **2** to wind, fold, or arrange (something about or around) as a covering: *to wrap one's arms about someone, wrap paper around a book.* **3** to cover with paper and tie up or fasten: *to wrap a book in tissue paper.* **4** *Figurative.* to cover; envelope; hide: *The mountain peak is wrapped in clouds. She sat wrapped in thought. The crime is wrapped in mystery.* **5** *Figurative.* to involve or infold (in a soothing state or condition): *The house is wrapped in slumbers* (Dickens). **6** to roll or fold up.
—***v.i.*** **1** to wrap oneself in a garment or other

covering. **2** to twine or circle around or about something.
—*n.* **1** Often, **wraps.** an outer garment for outdoor wear. Shawls, scarfs, coats, and furs are wraps. **2** = blanket.
**under wraps,** secret or concealed: *Plans for the new missile design were kept under wraps.*
**wrapped up in, a** devoted to; thinking mainly of: *He is so wrapped up in his work that he never sees his old friends any more.* **b** involved in; associated with: *I put mine* [*happiness*] *under your guardianship also, for mine is wrapped up in yours* (George P. R. James).
**wraps,** a cloak of secrecy or concealment: *Since the first major application of the new fuels probably will be military—as propellants for rockets or guided missiles—most of the research is shrouded in secrecy. But it's hard to keep the wraps completely over such developments* (Wall Street Journal).
**wrap up, a** to put on warmer or protective clothing: *He had to be wrapped up against the cold and further fortified by a cup of black coffee* (Annie F. Hector). **b** *Informal.* to conclude; finish: *By midnight he had wrapped up his report and gone to bed.* **c** *Informal.* to make assured in ending; clinch: *They wrapped up the game with three runs in the ninth.* **d** *U.S. Informal.* to summarize: *to wrap up the evening's news. The goal can be wrapped up in one word—quality!* (American Scholar).
[Middle English *wrappen.* Compare earlier Middle English *biwrabled* bewrapped.]

**wrap|a|round** (rap′ə round′), *adj., n.* —*adj.* **1** worn by drawing, folding, or shaping around: *a wraparound coat.* **2** curving around and along part of the sides: *a wraparound windshield.* **3** of or designating letterpress printing in which a thin, flexible plate is wrapped around the cylinder of a press. —*n.* a wraparound garment or object.

**wrap|page** (rap′ij), *n.* **1** the act of wrapping. **2** that in which something is wrapped.

**wrap|per** (rap′ər), *n.* **1** a person or thing that wraps: *a parcel wrapper.* **2** something in which something is wrapped; covering or cover: *Some magazines are mailed in paper wrappers.* **3** a woman's long, loose outer garment to wear in the house. **4** the leaf or leaves rolled around smaller leaves or pieces to form the outside layer of tobacco in a cigar.

**wrap|ping** (rap′ing), *n., adj.,* or **wrap|pings** (rap′ingz), *n.pl.* —*n.* paper, cloth, or the like, in which something is wrapped: *wrappings for Christmas gifts.*
—*adj.* used for wrapping: *wrapping paper.*

**wraps** (raps), *n.pl.* See under **wrap.**

**wrapt** (rapt), *v.* wrapped; a past tense and a past participle of **wrap.**

**wrap-up** (rap′up′), *n. Informal.* **1** the final item or summary of a news report. **2** any final report or summary: *Forums had been provided, enabling him to present a wrap-up of his views on major issues* (New York Times). **3** the final or decisive outcome; clincher; payoff: *Advertising is the wrap-up—the way to pay off all the thinking and planning that have come before* (Walter Carlson).

**wrasse** (ras), *n.* any one of a family of spiny-finned fishes of warm seas, especially a genus having thick, fleshy lips, powerful teeth, and usually a brilliant coloration. [perhaps < Cornish *gwrach*]

**wrath** (rath, räth; *especially British* rôth), *n., adj.* —*n.* **1** very great anger; rage. **SYN:** ire, fury, indignation, resentment. See syn. under **anger. 2** anger displayed in action (often in *wrath of God* or *day of wrath*): *The wrath of the stupid has laid waste the world quite as often as has the craft of the bright* (Time). —*adj.* = wrathful.
[Old English *wrǣththu*]

**wrath|ful** (rath′fəl, räth′-; *especially British* rôth′fəl), *adj.* very angry; feeling or showing wrath: *The wrathful lion turned on the hunters. His wrathful eyes flashed.* **SYN:** irate, furious, raging. —**wrath′ful|ly,** *adv.* —**wrath′ful|ness,** *n.*

**wrath|i|ly** (rath′ə lē, räth′-; *especially British* rô′thə lē), *adv.* with wrath or great anger; angrily.

**wrath|y** (rath′ē, räth′-; *especially British* rô′thē), *adj.,* **wrath|i|er, wrath|i|est.** = wrathful.

**wreak** (rēk), *v.t.* **1** to give expression to; work off (feelings, desires, or the like): *The cruel boy wreaked his bad temper on his dog.* **2** to inflict (vengeance or punishment): *Till vengeance had been wreaked for the wrongs suffered in life* (William Paley). **3** *Archaic.* to avenge. [Old English *wrecan.* See related etym. at **wrack**[1], **wreck.**] —**wreak′er,** *n.*

**wreath** (rēth), *n., pl.* **wreaths** (rēᴛʜz). **1** a ring of flowers or leaves twisted together. *Many people hang wreaths in the windows at Christmas.* **SYN:** garland. **2** something suggesting a wreath: *a wreath of smoke.* **SYN:** curl. [Old English *wrǣth,* related to *wrīthan* to writhe]

**Wreath** (rēth), *n.* the southern constellation Corona Australis.

**wreathe** (rēᴛʜ), *v.,* **wreathed, wreathed** or (*Archaic*) **wreath|en, wreath|ing.** —*v.t.* **1** to make into a wreath; twist: *The children wreathed flowers to put on the soldiers' graves.* **2** to decorate or adorn with wreaths; garland: *The inside of the schoolhouse was wreathed in holiday decorations.* **3** to make a ring around; encircle: *Mist wreathed the hills.* **4** to unite, form, or make by twining together; entwine; intertwine: *An eagle and a serpent wreathed in fight* (Shelley). **5** to envelop: *a face wreathed in smiles.*
—*v.i.* **1** to twist, coil, bend, or curve. **2** to move in rings: *The smoke wreathed upward.* [partly < Middle English *wrethen,* alteration of *writhen* writhe; influenced by *wreath*] —**wreath′er,** *n.*

**wreath|y** (rē′thē), *adj.* of the form of a wreath: *wreathy clouds, a wreathy vine.*

**wreck** (rek), *n., v.* —*n.* **1** partial or total destruction of a ship, building, train, automobile, or airplane: *The hurricane caused many wrecks. Reckless driving causes many wrecks on the highway.* **2** any destruction or serious injury: *Heavy rains caused the wreck of many crops.* **3** what is left of anything that has been destroyed or much injured: *The wrecks of six ships were cast upon the shore by the waves.* **4** *Figurative.* a person who has lost his health or money: *a wreck of his former self, a nervous wreck. He was a wreck from overwork.* **5** *Law.* goods or cargo cast up by the sea from a disabled or foundered vessel.
—*v.t.* **1** to cause the wreck of; destroy; ruin: *Robbers wrecked the mail train.* **2** *Figurative.* to cause to lose health or money. **3** to involve (a person) in a wreck. —*v.i.* **1** to be wrecked; suffer serious injury. **2** to act as wrecker.
[perhaps < Anglo-French *wrec* < Scandinavian (compare Old Icelandic *rek*). See related etym. at **rack**[4], **wreak.**]

**wreck|age** (rek′ij), *n.* **1** what is left by a wreck or wrecks: *The shore was covered with the wreckage of a ship.* **2** the act or process of wrecking or state of being wrecked: (*Figurative.*) *She wept at the wreckage of her hopes.*

**wreck|er** (rek′ər), *n.* **1** a person or thing that causes wrecks. **2** a person whose work is tearing down buildings. **3** a person, car, train, or machine that removes wrecks. **4** a person or ship that recovers wrecked or disabled ships or their cargoes. **5** a person who causes shipwrecks by showing false lights or signals on shore so as to plunder the wrecks.

**wrecker's ball,** a large steel ball attached to a crane, used for demolition: *The wrecker's ball will soon shatter the French Renaissance structure to clear the site for a 40-story office building* (New York Times).

**wreck|ful** (rek′fəl), *adj. Archaic.* causing or involving wreck, ruin, or destruction.

**wreck|ing** (rek′ing), *n., adj.* —*n.* **1** the act or business of a wrecker. **2** the act or business of salvaging a wreck or wrecks.
—*adj.* **1** used for or having to do with salvaging a wreck or wrecks: *a wrecking crane, a wrecking operation.* **2** engaged in salvaging a wreck or wrecks: *a wrecking company.*

**wrecking ball,** = wrecker's ball.

**wrecking bar,** a kind of crowbar with one or both ends bent, and forming a claw at one end and a wedge or a straight point at the other. See picture under **crowbar.**

**wrecking car,** a car provided with means and appliances for clearing wreckage, as from railroad tracks.

**wren** (ren), *n.* **1** a small brown or grayish songbird with rounded wings, a slender bill, and a short tail, often held erect, such as the house wren and the Carolina wren of North America. Wrens often build their nests near houses. **2** any one of certain similar birds. [Old English *wrenna*] —**wren′like′,** *adj.*

**Wren** or **WREN** (ren), *n. British Informal.* a member of the Women's Royal Naval Service (W.R.N.S.), made part of the regular navy in 1949. [spelling for pronunciation of *W.R.N.(S.)*]

***wrench** (rench), *n., v.* —*n.* **1** a tool to hold or turn nuts, bolts, pieces of pipe, or the like. **2** a violent twist or twisting pull: *The knob broke off when I gave it a sudden wrench.* **3** an injury caused by twisting: *He gave his ankle a wrench when he jumped off the ladder.* **4** *Figurative.* a source of grief or sorrow; pain: *It was a wrench to leave the old home.* **5** *Figurative.* distortion of the proper or original meaning, interpretation, or intention. [< verb]
—*v.t.* **1** to twist or pull violently: *I wrenched the knob off when I was trying to open the door. The policeman wrenched the gun out of the man's hand.* **SYN:** wring, wrest. **2** to injure by twisting: *He wrenched his back in wrestling.* **SYN:** strain, sprain. **3** to distress or pain greatly; rack: (*Figurative.*) *His spirit was wrenched with grief at the loss.* **4** *Figurative.* to twist the meaning of: *to wrench a Biblical text.* —*v.i.* to pull or tug (at something) with a twist or turn.
**throw a wrench into,** *Informal.* to disrupt; throw a monkey wrench into: [*He*] *consistently has tried to "throw a wrench into the works and interfere" with ... proposals to relax international tension* (Wall Street Journal).
[Old English *wrencan* twist] —**wrench′ing|ly,** *adv.*

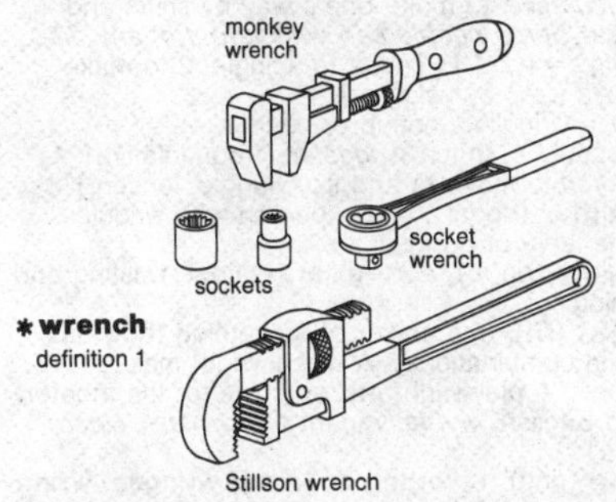


***wrench** definition 1

**wren-tit** (ren′tit′), *n.* a small, brownish bird somewhat resembling the wrens and the titmice, found in Oregon, California, and Baja California.

**wrest** (rest), *v., n.* —*v.t.* **1** to twist, pull, or tear away with force; wrench away: *After much pulling and tugging he wrested the stick from the jaws of the dog.* **2** to take by force: *The nobles wrested the power from the king.* **3** *Figurative.* to twist or turn from the proper meaning, use, or intention: *You wrest my words from their real meaning.* **4** *Figurative.* to obtain by extortion, persistence, or persuasion; wring: *to wrest a secret.*
—*n.* **1** the act of wresting; violent twist; wrench. **2** a key, wrench, or other implement for tuning certain stringed musical instruments, such as a harp, piano, or zither, by turning the wrest pins around which the ends of the strings are coiled.
[Old English *wrǣstan.* See related etym. at **wrist, writhe.**] —**wrest′er,** *n.*

**wres|tle** (res′əl), *v.,* **-tled, -tling,** *n.* —*v.t.* **1a** to try to throw or force (an opponent) to the ground. **b** to engage in (a wrestling match). **2** to contend with in wrestling or as if in wrestling: (*Figurative.*) *I have been wrestling this problem for an hour.*
—*v.i.* **1** to be a contestant in a wrestling match; grapple with an opponent and seek to throw him to the ground. **2** *Figurative.* to struggle: *We often wrestle with temptation.*
—*n.* **1** a wrestling match. **2** a struggle: (*Figurative.*) *The body politic ... straining every nerve in a wrestle for life or death* (Macaulay).
[Middle English *wrestlen, wrastlen,* unrecorded Old English *wrǣstlian* (frequentative) < *wrǣstan;* see etym. under **wrest**]

**wres|tler** (res′lər), *n.* **1** a person who wrestles, especially as a sport. **2** *Western U.S.* a person who throws cattle for the purpose of branding.

**wres|tling** (res′ling), *n.* a sport or contest in which each of two opponents tries to throw or force the other to the ground. The rules for wrestling do not allow using the fists or certain holds on the body.

**wrest pin,** a peg or pin around which the ends of the strings are coiled in a stringed musical instrument.

**wretch** (rech), *n.* **1** a very unfortunate or unhappy person. **2** a very bad person. **SYN:** scoundrel, villain, rogue. [Old English *wrecca* exile]

**wretch|ed** (rech′id), *adj.* **1** very unfortunate or unhappy. **2** very unsatisfactory; miserable: *a wretched hut.* **SYN:** pitiful, shabby. **3** very bad: *a wretched traitor.* **SYN:** despicable, base, mean. —**wretch′ed|ly,** *adv.* —**wretch′ed|ness,** *n.*
—***Syn.* 1 Wretched, miserable** mean very unhappy or deeply disturbed. **Wretched** suggests a state of unhappiness and extreme lowness of spirits marked by discouragement and hopelessness, as caused by sorrow, sickness, or worry: *He was wretched when he failed the examination again.* **Miserable** suggests a state of severe suffering or distress of mind, caused especially by conditions or circumstances such as poverty, humiliation, or misfortune: *After the loss of their savings and their home they felt too miserable to see their old friends.*

**wrick** (rik), *v.t., n.* strain; sprain. [apparently < Middle English *wricken* to twist]

**wried** (rīd), *v.* the past tense and past participle of **wry.**

**Pronunciation Key: h**a**t, ā**ge, c**ã**re, f**ä**r; l**e**t, **ē**qual, t**ė**rm; **i**t, **ī**ce; h**o**t, **ō**pen, **ô**rder; **oi**l, **ou**t; c**u**p, p**u̇**t, r**ü**le; **ch**ild; lo**ng**; **th**in; **ᴛʜ**en; **zh**, measure; **ə** represents **a** in about, **e** in taken, **i** in pencil, **o** in lemon, **u** in circus.

**wri|er** (rī′ər), *adj.* the comparative of **wry**.

**wri|est** (rī′ist), *adj.* the superlative of **wry**.

**wrig** (rig), *v.i., v.t.,* **wrigged, wrig|ging.** *Obsolete or British Dialect.* to wriggle. [variant of *wrick*]

**wrig|gle** (rig′əl), *v.,* **-gled, -gling,** *n.* — *v.i.* **1** to twist and turn; squirm; wiggle: *Children wriggle when they are restless.* **2** to move by twisting and turning: *A snake wriggled across the road.* **3** *Figurative.* to make one's way by shifts and tricks: *Some people can wriggle out of any difficulty.* — *v.t.* **1** to cause to wriggle. **2** to make (one's way) by wriggling.
— *n.* a wriggling motion or course.
[probably < Dutch *wriggelen* (frequentative) < *wrikken* to move to and fro, wriggle, loosen.]

**wrig|gler** (rig′lər), *n.* **1** a person who wriggles. **2** the larva of a mosquito.

**wrig|gly** (rig′lē), *adj.,* **-gli|er, -gli|est.** twisting and turning.

**wright** (rīt), *n.* a maker of something (now usually in combinations). A wheelwright makes wheels. A playwright makes plays for the theater. [Old English *wryhta,* variant of *wyrhta* < *weorc* work]

**wring** (ring), *v.,* **wrung** or (*Rare*) **wringed, wring|ing,** *n.* — *v.t.* **1** to twist with force; squeeze hard: *to wring clothes.* **2** to force by twisting or squeezing: *I wrung water from my wet bathing suit.* **3** *Figurative.* to get by force, effort, or persuasion: *to wring a promise from someone. The old beggar could wring money from anyone with his sad story.* **4** to clasp and hold firmly; press: *He wrung his old friend's hand in joy at seeing him.* **5** *Figurative.* to cause distress, pain, pity, or other sentiment in: *His soul was wrung with grief. Their poverty wrung his heart.* **6** to twist violently; wrench: *to wring a chicken's neck.* — *v.i.* to twist about in or as if in struggle or anguish; writhe.
— *n.* a twist or squeeze.
**wring out, a** to twist so as to force out water: *to wring out a towel. Wring out your wet bathing suit.* **b** to force out by twisting; squeeze out: *to wring out water.* (*Figurative.*) *to wring out tears in an effort to get sympathy.* **c** *Figurative.* to draw out by force or pressure; extract: *to wring out a confession.*
[Old English *wringan.* See related etym. at **wrangle.**] — **wring′a|ble,** *adj.*

**wring|er** (ring′ər), *n.* **1** a machine for squeezing water from clothes. **2** a person who wrings clothes or the like after washing. **3** a person or thing that wrings.
**put through the wringer,** *Informal.* to put through an ordeal; subject to severe stresses: *Students asking for loans are really put through the wringer* (Wall Street Journal).

**wring|ing-wet** (ring′ing wet′), *adj.* so wet that water may be wrung out.

**wrin|kle¹** (ring′kəl), *n., v.,* **-kled, -kling.** — *n.* **1** a ridge or fold; crease: *The old man's face has wrinkles. I must press the wrinkles out of this dress.* **2** *Figurative.* a difficulty, problem, or the like: *It will probably take a few more days or … weeks to get all the wrinkles ironed out and make the formal offer* (Wall Street Journal).
— *v.t.* to make a wrinkle or wrinkles in: *She wrinkled her forehead.* **SYN:** crease, crinkle.
— *v.i.* **1** to have wrinkles; acquire wrinkles: *This shirt will not wrinkle.* **2** to contract (as into smiles or a look of concern) by puckering.
[perhaps back formation < Middle English *wrynkled* winding, Old English *gewrinclod* winding (of a ditch)]

**wrin|kle²** (ring′kəl), *n. Informal.* **1** a useful hint or idea; clever trick. **2** a special or unusual technique, approach, or device; novelty: *The newest wrinkle in the $2.5 billion cosmetics business is a lotion that camouflages … creases* (Time). [perhaps special use of *wrinkle¹*]

**wrin|kly** (ring′klē), *adj.,* **-kli|er, -kli|est.** wrinkled. **SYN:** creased, puckered.

***wrist**
definition 3

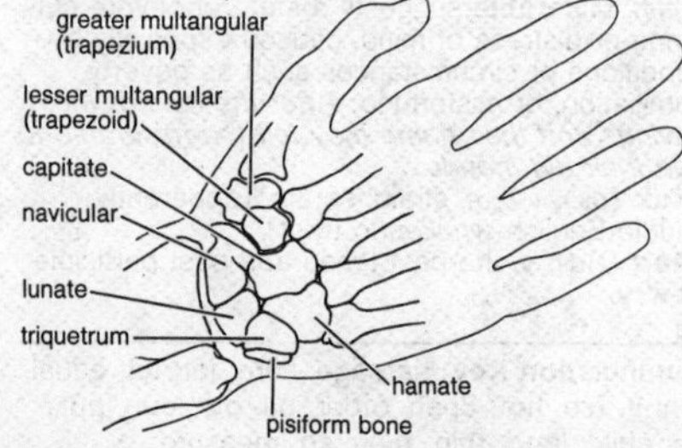


***wrist** (rist), *n., v.* — *n.* **1** the joint that connects the hand with the arm. **2** a corresponding joint or part of the forelimb of an animal. **3** the bones of this part; carpus. **4** the part of a glove, mitten, or garment covering the wrist. **5** = wrist pin.
— *v.t.* to move, send, or throw by a movement of the wrist: *Evans rounded off a hectic … few seconds by wristing the second rebound high over the bar* (London Times).
**slap on the wrist, a** See under **slap¹**. **b** *Informal.* to give a light scolding: *He can slap his own discipline on the wrist: "We* [*sociologists*] *find it easier to describe the limits of human conduct than the areas of freedom"* (New Yorker).
[Old English *wrist.* See related etym. at **wrest, writhe.**]

**wrist|band** (rist′band′), *n.* **1** the band of a sleeve fitting around the wrist. **2** a strap worn around the wrist, such as that of a wrist watch.

**wrist-drop** (rist′drop′), *n.,* or **wrist drop,** a disorder characterized by the inability to extend the hand and fingers, usually caused by a paralysis of the extensor muscles of the hand.

**wrist|er** (ris′tər), *n. U.S. Dialect.* a wristlet.

**wrist|let** (rist′lit), *n.* **1** a band worn around the wrist to keep it warm or for ornament. **2** = bracelet. **3** = handcuff.

**wrist|lock** (rist′lok′), *n.* a hold in wrestling in which one contestant grasps the wrist of the other and twists it so as to force his body in some desired direction.

**wrist pin,** a stud or pin projecting from the side of a crank, wheel, or the like, and forming a means of attachment to a connecting rod.

**wrist shot,** *Sports.* a shot or stroke in which the power is supplied mainly by the wrist instead of the arm. Wrist shots are often used in ice hockey, badminton, and golf.

**wrist watch,** or **wrist|watch** (rist′woch′, -wôch′), *n.* a small watch worn on a strap or bracelet around the wrist.

**wrist|work** (rist′wėrk′), *n.* flexure of the wrist, as in batting: *Shifting to an entirely new grip, which makes nonsense of all that preliminary wristwork, he speeds away* (Punch).

**wrist|y** (ris′tē), *adj.* performed by flexure of the wrist; marked by or skilled in wristwork: *wristy shots or strokes, a wristy play.*

**writ¹** (rit), *n.* **1** something written; piece of writing. The Bible is Holy Writ. **2a** a formal written order issued in the name of a court of law, government, or other authority, directing a person to do or not to do something: *The lawyer got a writ from the judge to release the man wrongly held in jail.* **b** (in early English law) any one of certain documents issued under seal in the form of a letter, in the king's name. [Old English *writ,* related to *wrītan* to write]

**writ²** (rit), *v. Archaic.* a past tense and a past participle of **write**: *The names are writ in gold.*
**writ large,** visibly enlarged or magnified: [*The*] *new Pay Tax is just old Income Tax writ large* (Punch). *The excitement the race generates is writ large* (New York Times).

**writ|a|tive** (rī′tə tiv), *adj.* disposed or inclined to write; given to writing: *Increase in years makes men more talkative, but less writative* (Alexander Pope).

**write** (rīt), *v.,* **wrote** or (*Archaic*) **writ, writ|ten** or (*Archaic*) **writ, writ|ing.** — *v.i.* **1** to make letters, words, or symbols with pen, pencil, or chalk, or on a hard or plastic surface with a sharp instrument: *He learned to write.* **2** to mark with letters or words: *Please write on both sides of the paper.* **3** to produce (a specified kind of) writing: *a pen that writes poorly, to write legibly or illegibly.* **4** to write a letter: *She writes to her mother every week.* **5** to be an author or writer: *to write for the stage, write about the stage. He writes for the magazines. But you cannot teach a man to write or to edit; if he has latent abilities in these areas, you can develop them; you cannot inject them as so much vaccine* (Harper's). **6** to work as a clerk, amanuensis, journalist, or other contributor of professional writing.
— *v.t.* **1a** to make (letters, words, or symbols) on paper, parchment, or the like, with a pencil, pen, or chalk; inscribe. **b** to carve, engrave, or incise (letters, words, or symbols) on a hard or plastic surface. **2** to put down the letters or words of: *Write your name and address.* **3** to give in writing; record: *She writes all that happens. She wrote that she was feeling better.* **4** to make (books, stories, articles, poems, letters, or the like); compose: *to write a sonnet.* **5** to write a letter to: *She wrote her parents that she would be home for New Year's.* **6** *Figurative.* to show plainly: *Fear is written on his face.* **7a** to fill in (a form) with writing: *to write a check.* **b** to draw up or draft (a document); put into proper written form: *to write one's will.* **8** to spell (a word or name) in a certain way in writing: *Many words written alike are pronounced differently.* **9** to cover or fill with writing; produce in writing: *to write three pages, write three copies.* **10** to release or print out (data) from the memory of a computer: *Millions of* [*magnetic*] *cores are used for very large computer memories … so that appropriate pulses can cause each core to absorb* (*"read"*) *or release* (*"write"*) *information bits* (New York Times).
**write down, a** to put into writing: *I will … write down all they say to me* (Sir Richard Steele). **b** to put a lower value on: *The properties produced so little that they were written down on Javelin's books to $1* (Wall Street Journal).
**write in, a** to insert (as a fact, statement, or punctuation) in a piece of writing: *The teacher wrote in corrections between the sentences on the paper.* **b** to send (a message) to a headquarters or other place in charge, in writing: *The customers … were not slow about writing in their suggestions* (Publishers' Weekly). **c** to cast a vote for an unlisted candidate by writing his name on a ballot: *to write in the candidate of one's choice, to write in a vote in a primary.*
**write off, a** to cancel: *The company wrote off the loss as a bad debt* (Law Times). **b** to note the deduction of for depreciation: *During the early life of a piece of equipment, the company bookkeeper could write off each year more of its value, and subtract that sum from taxable income* (Wall Street Journal). **c** *Figurative.* to give up; treat as if nonexistent: *The new blow … came at a time when his own … colleagues have, in effect, written him off and are looking for a way to dump him* (Wall Street Journal).
**write out, a** to put into writing: *Write out a check. We wrote out a contract.* **b** to write in full, especially from a rough draft: *He wrote out his speech and memorized it.* **c** *Figurative.* to exhaust one's resources or stock of ideas by excessive writing: *The author had … written himself out* (Scott).
**write up, a** to write a description or account of, especially a full or detailed account: *The reporter wrote up his interview with the mayor for the newspaper.* **b** to bring up to date in writing: *He … writes up the journal neglected for a week or two* (Longfellow). **c** to bring to public notice by writing, especially by praising in writing: *to write up a candidate.* **d** to put a higher value on: *It … is the policy of the bank to … "write up" such securities should they appreciate* (Sunday Times).
[Old English *wrītan* (originally) to scratch]
▶ **Wrote** as the past participle, found in the standard language in Early Modern English, is still widespread in the nonstandard dialects.

**write-down** (rīt′doun′), *n.* a reduction in the amount of an account, capital, or assets, as in an accounting record: *Everybody got scared that prices would be cut, and started using up their stocks to avoid big inventory write-downs* (Wall Street Journal).

**write-in** (rīt′in′), *adj., n.* — *adj.* of or having to do with a candidate who is not listed but who is voted for by having his name written in on a ballot: *a write-in candidate, a write-in vote, a write-in campaign.*
— *n.* a write-in candidate or vote: *There were no other candidates, no places for write-ins, nothing to mark* (Time).

**write-off** (rīt′ôf′, -of′), *n.* an amount written off or canceled, especially as a bad debt or a tax-deductible expense: *His profits were helped along through an accelerated write-off of his equipment for tax purposes* (Harper's). *The write-offs of $3,837,000 were for unabsorbed overhead in operating* (Wall Street Journal).

**writ|er** (rī′tər), *n.* **1** a person who writes or is able to write: *Was he the writer of that letter?* **2** a person whose occupation is writing; author: [*He*] *goes on to discuss a variety of authors whom he believes pass Emerson's test of a writer* (*"Talent alone cannot make a writer. There must be a man behind the book"*) (Wall Street Journal). **3** an attorney; lawyer (in Scots law).

**writer's block,** a psychological inability to write professionally: *After twenty years of … writer's block, he is back with his fourth novel* (Saturday Review).

**writer's cramp, palsy,** or **spasm,** pain and spasm of the muscles of the hand and fingers resulting from their excessive use in writing.

**write-up** (rīt′up′), *n.* **1** *Informal.* a written description or account: *to give a short write-up in the paper.* **2** *Accounting.* a writing up (of an asset).

**writhe** (rīᴛʜ), *v.,* **writhed, writhed** or (*Archaic*) **writh|en, writh|ing,** *n.* — *v.i.* **1** to twist and turn; twist about: *The snake writhed along the branch. The wounded man writhed in pain.* **2** *Figurative.* to suffer mentally; be very uncomfortable. — *v.t.* to twist or coil (something); bend by twisting.
— *n.* a writhing movement, as of the body or countenance; contortion.
[Old English *wrīthan.* See related etym. at **wrest, wrist.**]

**writh|en** (riᴛʜ′ən), *adj., v.* — *adj. Rare.* twisted; contorted.
— *v. Poetic.* writhed; a past participle of **writhe**.

**writh|er** (rī′ᴛʜər), *n.* a person who writhes or twists.

**writ|ing** (rī′ting), *n., adj.* —*n.* **1** the act of making letters, words, or symbols with pen, pencil, chalk, or the like: *For the period since the invention of writing (around 400 B.C.) there are records on clay, stone, metal, and paper giving precise dates for many events and clues to the relative dates of other events* (Frank Hole). **2** a written form: *an agreement in writing. Put your ideas in writing.* **3** handwriting; penmanship; chirography: *to recognize someone's writing. His writing is hard to read.* **4** something written (or typewritten), such as a letter, document, or inscription. **5a** a literary work; book, story, article, poem, or other literary production: *the writings of Benjamin Franklin or Charles Dickens.* **b** the profession or business of a person who writes.
—*adj.* **1** used to write with or on: *a writing tool, writing material.* **2** of or for writing: *a writing course, lesson, or exercise.* **3** that writes: *a writing clerk.*
**see** (or **read**) **the writing on the wall,** to perceive that something is coming to its end; see the handwriting on the wall: *He has seen the writing on the wall ... and is beating the inevitable by rapid expansion* (London Times).
**the Writings,** the Hagiographa; Kethubim.
**writing on the wall,** a portent of change or of doom; handwriting on the wall: *[When] Todd was overthrown as Rhodesia's Prime Minister ... it was the writing on the wall* (Canadian Saturday Night).

**writing desk,** **1** a desk or piece of furniture for use in writing, commonly with drawers and often pigeonholes for holding materials, papers, or the like. **2** a portable case for holding materials for writing, and affording when opened a surface to rest the paper on in writing.

**writing paper,** paper of a suitable kind and size for writing on: *The bulletin announcing the birth of the New Prince was written by hand on a sheet of red-crested palace writing paper in a gilded frame* (Manchester Guardian Weekly).

**writ of assistance,** a search warrant issued without naming the place to be searched, used by British customs officials before the American Revolution.

**writ of certiorari,** = certiorari.

**writ of error,** *Law.* an order to a court to send records of a proceeding to a superior or appellate court, so that the judgment may be examined for errors of law.

**writ of execution,** *Law.* a writ ordering a sheriff or other judicial officer to execute a judgment.

**writ of extent,** *Law.* a writ to recover debts due the crown.

**writ of privilege,** *Law.* a writ to release a privileged person, such as a member of Parliament, from custody when arrested in a civil suit.

**writ of prohibition,** *Law.* a writ from a higher court forbidding a lower court to proceed with a suit.

**writ of protection,** *Law.* a writ issued to a person required to attend court as witness, party, or juror, to secure him from arrest for a certain period of time.

**writ of right,** **1** (in early English law) either of two writs issued in cases concerning freehold property brought before manorial courts by feudal tenants. **2** *U.S.* a similar writ in common law for restoring real property to its rightful owner.

**writ|ten** (rit′ən), *v., adj.* —*v.* a past participle of **write**: *He has written a letter.*
—*adj.* **1** that is written; committed to writing: *Written English in our present alphabet is hardly fifteen hundred years old* (John S. Kenyon). **2** formulated in documents, codes, or printed works: *written laws.*

**W.R.N.S.,** *British.* Women's Royal Naval Service.

**wrnt.,** warrant.

**wrong** (rông, rong), *adj., adv., n., v.* —*adj.* **1** not right; bad; unjust; unlawful: *It is wrong to tell lies. Stealing is wrong.* SYN: wicked, reprehensible. **2a** not true; not correct; not what it should be: *He gave the wrong answer.* SYN: incorrect, inaccurate, erroneous, faulty. **b** judging, acting, or believing contrary to the facts; mistaken; in error: *I admit that I was wrong.* **3** not proper; not fit; unsuitable: *to get on the wrong bus. Heavy boots would be the wrong thing to wear for tennis.* SYN: improper, inappropriate, unfit. **4** in a bad state or condition; out of order; amiss: *Something is wrong with the car.* **5** not meant to be seen; less or least important: *Cloth often has a wrong side and a right side.*
—*adv.* in a wrong manner; in the wrong direction; badly; astray: *Tintoret ... may lead you wrong if you don't understand him* (Ruskin).
—*n.* **1** anything not right; wrong thing or action: *to know right from wrong. Two wrongs do not make a right.* SYN: evil, sin, misdemeanor. **2** injustice; injury; harm: *You do an honest man a wrong to call him a liar or a thief.* **3** *Law.* a violation of law; infringement on the rights of another resulting in damage or injury to him, especially a tort.
—*v.t.* **1** to do wrong to; treat unfairly; injure: *He forgave those who had wronged him.* SYN: harm, maltreat, abuse, oppress. **2** to discredit or dishonor, unjustly, as by statement or opinion; impute evil to undeservedly. **3** to cheat or defraud.
**go wrong, a** to turn out badly: *Everything went wrong today.* **b** to make a mistake: *You can't go wrong in buying this bargain.* **c** to stop being good and become bad: *Thus men go wrong ...; Bend the straight rule to their own crooked will* (William Cowper).
**in the wrong,** wrong: *I quarrelled with her last night. I was quite in the wrong* (Henry Kingsley).
[Old English *wrang,* apparently < Scandinavian (compare Old Icelandic *rangr* crooked)]
—**wrong′ly,** *adv.* —**wrong′ness,** *n.*

**wrong|do|er** (rông′dü′ər, rong′-), *n.* a person who does wrong.

**wrong|do|ing** (rông′dü′ing, rong′-), *n.* the action of doing wrong; bad acts; evil; wrong: *The thief was guilty of wrongdoing. The ruling indicated the Government could escape liability for the payment if its found wrongdoing was connected with the power contract* (Wall Street Journal).

**wrong font,** *Printing.* a correction used on proofs, to designate a character of the wrong size, style, or face. *Abbr:* w.f.

**wrong|ful** (rông′fəl, rong′-), *adj.* **1** wrong: *Cruelty is always a wrongful act.* **2a** that is contrary to law, statute, or established rule; unlawful; illegal: *Rebellion is a wrongful act unless the rebels win.* **b** having no legal right or claim. —**wrong′ful|ly,** *adv.* —**wrong′ful|ness,** *n.*

**wrong-head|ed** or **wrong|head|ed** (rông′hed′id, rong′-), *adj.* **1** wrong in judgment or opinion. **2** stubborn even when wrong. —**wrong′-head′ed|ly, wrong′head′ed|ly,** *adv.* —**wrong′-head′ed|ness, wrong′head′ed|ness,** *n.*

**wrong|o** (rông′ō, rong′-), *n., pl.* **wrong|os.** *Slang.* a wrongdoer; badman.

**wrote** (rōt), *v.* a past tense of **write**: *He wrote his mother a long letter last week.*
► See **write** for usage note.

**wroth** (rôth, roth), *adj.* very angry; wrathful: *As usual, the columnist for Lord Rothermere's London Evening News was wroth* (Time). [Old English *wrāth.* See related etym. at **wrath.**]

**wroth|y** (rôth′ē, roth′-), *adj.,* **wroth|i|er, wroth|i|est.** wrathful; angry: *I am writing letters, wrothy letters* (New Yorker).

**wrought** (rôt), *v., adj.* —*v.* worked; a past tense and a past participle of **work.**
—*adj.* **1** made; fashioned; formed: *The gate was wrought with great skill.* **2** formed with care; not rough or crude. **3** manufactured or treated; not in a raw state. **4** formed by hammering: *wrought metals.*

**wrought iron,** a tough, durable form of iron with little carbon in it. It is commonly produced from pig iron by puddling. It is malleable and soft enough to be forged and welded easily.
—**wrought′-i′ron,** *adj.*

**wrought-i|ron casting** (rôt′ī′ərn), **1** the operation of casting with mitis metal. **2** a casting of mitis metal.

**wrought-up** (rôt′up′), *adj.* stirred up; excited.

**wrung** (rung), *v.* a past tense and past participle of **wring**: *She wrung out the wet cloth and hung it up. Her heart is wrung with pity for the poor.*

**wry** (rī), *adj.,* **wri|er, wri|est,** *v.,* **wried, wry|ing.** —*adj.* **1** turned to one side; twisted: *a wry smile. She made a wry face to show her disgust.* **2a** (of words, thoughts, or an expression) contrary to that which is right, fitting, or just; wrong or ill-natured. **b** perverted, distorted, or twisted, especially in irony: *wry humor, a wry mind.* [< verb]
—*v.i.* = writhe. —*v.t.* **1** to twist or turn (as the body or neck) around or about; contort. **2** to twist out of shape, form, or relationship; contort.
[Old English *wrīgian* to turn; move, go] —**wry′ly,** *adv.* —**wry′ness,** *n.*

**wry|neck** (rī′nek′), *n.* **1** a twisted neck caused by unequal contraction of the muscles; torticollis. **2** a bird, related to the woodpeckers, that habitually twists its neck and head in a peculiar way. **3** *Informal.* a person who has wryneck.

**wry-necked** (rī′nekt′), *adj.* having wryneck (torticollis): *The wry-necked verger, his dues paid in the past to pain, has a speech that queries the physically agonized part of Christ's passion* (New Statesman).

**WSB** (no periods), Wage Stabilization Board.

**WSW** (no periods) or **W.S.W.,** between west and southwest.

**wt.,** weight.

**wud** (wu̇d), *adj. Scottish.* wood².

**wul|fen|ite** (wu̇l′fə nīt), *n. Mineralogy.* a molybdate of lead, found in brilliant crystals. *Formula:* $PbMoO_4$ [< German *Wulfenit* < Franz X. von *Wulfen,* 1728-1805, an Austrian scientist + *-it*]

**Wun|der|kind** or **wun|der|kind** (vu̇n′dər kint′, wun′-), *n., pl.* **-kin|der** (-kin′dər). a remarkably brilliant child; young prodigy: *Maazel ... is that rare specimen among musicians, a Wunderkind who not only grew up but matured* (Atlantic). [< German *Wunderkind* (literally) wonder child]

**wur|ley** (wėr′lē), *n., pl.* **-leys.** (in South Australia) a hut of the aborigines; native hut. [< native Australian name]

**Würm** (vu̇rm, wėrm; *German* vʏrm), *n. Geology.* the fourth glaciation of the Pleistocene in Europe. [< *Würm,* a lake in Germany]

**wurst** (wėrst, wu̇rst), *n.* = sausage. [< German]

**wurtz|ite** (wėrt′sīt), *n.* a native sulfide of zinc, a crystalline dimorph of sphalerite. *Formula:* ZnS [< Charles *Wurtz,* 1817-1884, French chemist]

**wuth|er** (wuᴛʜ′ər), *v., n. Scottish.* —*v.i.* **1** to blow with a roaring sound, as the wind; bluster. **2** to rush noisily; whiz. —*n.* a wuthering sound or movement: *the "wuther" of wind amongst trees* (Charlotte Brontë). [variant of Scottish *whither,* verb < Scandinavian (compare Norwegian *kvidra* to go with quick movements, related to *hvitha* squall of wind)]

**wuth|er|ing** (wuᴛʜ′ər ing), *adj., v. Scottish.* —*adj.* **1** that wuthers: *Hatless, his hair a little ruffled in the wuthering northern air, Mr. Macmillan today stepped out of the Westminster doldrums and into active politics* (Manchester Guardian Weekly). **2** (of a place) characterized by a wuthering sound or sounds: *Wuthering Heights* (Emily Brontë). —*v.* the present participle of **wuther.**

**WV** (no periods), West Virginia (with postal Zip Code).

**W.Va.,** West Virginia.

**W.V.S.** or **WVS** (no periods), *British.* Women's Voluntary Service.

**WW** (no periods) or **W.W.,** World War.

**WWW** (no periods), World Weather Watch (a program of the World Meteorological Organization which operates networks of weather stations throughout the world and uses satellites and computers to gather weather information).

**Wy.,** Wyoming.

**WY** (no periods), Wyoming (with postal Zip Code).

**Wy|an|dot** (wī′ən dot), *n.* **1** an American Iroquoian Indian of the Huron tribe or confederacy that once lived in the Middle Western United States. **2** Iroquoian language of the Wyandots.

**Wy|an|dotte** (wī′ən dot), *n.* any one of an American breed of medium-sized, hardy chickens, kept for the production of meat and eggs. [< *Wyandot* (because the tribe bred them)]

**wych-elm** (wich′elm′), *n.* **1** an elm tree found especially in northern and western Europe, having broader leaves and more spreading branches than the English elm. **2** its wood. Also, **witch-elm.** [< Old English *wice* wych-elm + *elm* elm]

**wych-ha|zel** (wich′hā′zəl), *n.* **1** = witch hazel. **2** = wych-elm.

**Wyc|liff|ite** or **Wyc|lif|ite** (wik′li fīt), *n., adj.* —*n.* a person who adhered to or propagated the religious tenets or doctrines of John Wycliffe (1320?-1384).
—*adj.* **1** of or having to do with Wycliffe or his followers. **2** that is a follower of Wycliffe.

**wyd|ah** (wid′ə), *n.* = whidah.

**wye** (wī), *n.* **1** the letter Y. **2** *Electricity.* a type of three-phase circuit arrangement. Three conductors are connected to three terminals in the form of the letter Y.

**wye level,** a surveying level with the telescope mounted on Y-shaped forks in which it can be rotated.

**Wyke|ham|i|cal** (wik′ə mə kəl), *adj.* of or having to do with Wykehamists.

**Wyke|ham|ist** (wik′ə mist), *n.* a student or alumnus of Winchester College in England, founded by William of Wykeham (1324-1404).

**wyle** (wīl), *v.t.,* **wyled, wyl|ing.** = wile.

**wy|lie|coat** (wī′lē kōt′, wil′ē-, wul′ē-), *n. Scottish.* **1** an undergarment in earlier use especially one worn under a doublet. **2** a petticoat. [origin uncertain]

**wynd** (wīnd), *n. Scottish.* an alley between houses; narrow lane or street: *It was up a wynd off a side street in St. Bride's that Jessie had her lodging* (Robert Louis Stevenson). [apparently variant of *wind*², noun]

**Wyo.,** Wyoming.

**Wy|o|ming|ite** (wī ō′ming īt), *n.* a native or inhabitant of the state of Wyoming.

**wyte** (wīt), *n., v.t.,* **wyt|ed, wyt|ing.** = wite.

**wythe** (wīᴛʜ, with, wiᴛʜ), *n., v.,* **wythed, wyth|ing.** = withe.

**wy|vern** (wī′vərn), *n.* = wivern.

**Pronunciation Key:** hat, āge, cãre, fär; let, ēqual, tėrm; it, īce; hot, ōpen, ôrder; oil, out; cup, pu̇t, rüle; child; long; thin; ᴛʜen; zh, measure; ə represents **a** in about, **e** in taken, **i** in pencil, **o** in lemon, **u** in circus.

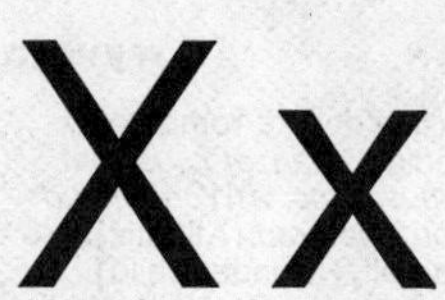

✱**X**[1] or **x**[1] (eks), *n., pl.* **X's** or **Xs**, **x's** or **xs**. **1** the 24th letter of the English alphabet: *There are very few words that begin with x.* **2** any sound represented by this letter. **3** used as a symbol for: **a** the 24th, or more usually the 23rd (of an actual or possible series, either *I* or *J* being omitted). **b** an unknown quantity (especially in algebraic equations, along with *y* and *z*). **c** times (the multiplication sign); by: *3 × 6 = 18; a box 14 × 20 inches.* **d** abscissa. **4** a term often used to designate a person, thing, agency, factor, or the like that has not yet been named or whose true name is unknown or withheld: *virus X, Mr. X.* **5** the Roman numeral for 10. **6** *Informal.* a ten-dollar bill.

**X**[2] (eks), *n., pl.* **X's**. anything shaped like the letter X: *The cyclone fence was formed of interlacing wire X's.*

**x**[2] (eks), *v.t.*, **x-ed** or **x'd**, **x-ing** or **x'ing**. **1** to cross out with or as if with an x or x's: *She x-ed out the last word in the sentence.* **2** to indicate or mark with an x: *He x-ed his answers in the little boxes on the test sheet.*

**X** (no period), a symbol used in the United States for motion pictures to which only adults are admitted.

**X** (no period), **1** Christ. **2** Christian. [< the Greek letter *X* chi, which begins the word *Christós* Christ]

**Xan|a|du** (zan′ə dü), *n., pl.* **-dus**. a large or stately mansion or the like; pleasure-dome: *The house is no Xanadu; ... there is something extravagantly not right about it* (Time). [allusion to the exotic place in Samuel Taylor Coleridge's *Kubla Khan*]

**xanth-**, *combining form.* the form of **xantho-** before vowels, as in *xanthoma.*

**xan|thate** (zan′thāt), *n. Chemistry.* a salt or ester of xanthic acid: *Xanthates are produced from wheat flour or corn starch. They're added to wood pulp. The resulting paper is eight times stronger than other types made from wood pulp alone* (Wall Street Journal).

**xan|the|in** (zan′thē in), *n.* the yellow water-soluble coloring matter of flowers. [< French *xanthéine* < Greek *xanthós* yellow + French *-ine* -ine[2]]

**xan|thene** (zan′thēn), *n.* a crystalline compound that is the basis of a group of mainly yellow dyes. It is formed by the reduction of xanthone. *Formula:* $C_{13}H_{10}O$

**xan|thic** (zan′thik), *adj.* **1** yellow (applied especially in botany to a series of colors in flowers passing from yellow through orange to red). **2** of or having to do with xanthin or xanthine.

**xanthic acid**, any one of a group of unstable acids having the general formula ROCSSH (in which R denotes a hydrocarbon radical), especially a colorless, oily liquid, $C_3H_6OS_2$, with a strong odor.

**xan|thin** (zan′thin), *n.* **1** the yellow nonwater-soluble coloring matter of flowers. **2** a yellow coloring matter obtained from madder. **3** = xanthine. [< German *Xanthin* < Greek *xanthós* yellow + German *-in* -in]

**xan|thine** (zan′thēn, -thin), *n.* a crystalline, nitrogenous substance, present in the urine, blood, liver, and muscle tissue, and also in various plants. *Formula:* $C_5H_4O_2N_4$

**xanthine oxidase**, an oxidizing enzyme that converts xanthine into uric acid.

**Xan|thip|pe** (zan tip′ē), *n.* a scolding woman; shrew. SYN: termagant, virago. Also, **Xantippe**. [< *Xanthippe,* who lived in the 400's B.C., the wife of Socrates]

**xan|thism** (zan′thiz əm), *n.* a condition, as of the skin, marked by an abnormal amount of yellow pigment: *All examples of albinism (whitening), melanism (darkening), xanthism (yellowing), or erythrism (reddening) are throwing light on genetic divergence as well as colour changes of a noncongenital kind* (New Scientist).

**xantho-**, *combining form.* yellow: *Xanthophyll = a yellow pigment.* Also, **xanth-** before vowels. [< Greek *xanthós* yellow]

**xan|tho|chro|ic** (zan′thə krō′ik), *adj.* = xanthochroid.

**xan|tho|chroid** (zan′thə kroid), *adj., n. Ethnology.* —*adj.* having yellow hair and pale complexion. —*n.* a xanthochroid person. [< New Latin *xanthochroi,* plural, xanthochroids as a group (coined by Thomas Huxley) < Greek *xanthós* yellow + *ōchrós* pale]

**xan|tho|ma** (zan thō′mə), *n.* a disease of the skin with yellowish patches: *An increased incidence of atherosclerosis has been observed in diseases ... such as xanthoma* (Science News Letter).

**xan|tho|ma|to|sis** (zan thō′mə tō′sis), *n.* a disease with soft, yellowish, tumorlike patches on the body, caused by an unbalanced cholesterol metabolism.

**xan|thom|a|tous** (zan thom′ə təs), *adj.* of or having to do with xanthoma.

**xan|tho|my|cin** (zan′thə mī′sin), *n.* an antibiotic obtained from streptomyces.

**xan|thone** (zan′thōn), *n.* a crystalline compound that is the basis of a group of naturally occurring yellow dyes. *Formula:* $C_{13}H_8O$

**xan|tho|phore** (zan′thə fôr, -fōr), *n.* a chromatophore containing a yellow pigment: *Unlike melanophores, the cells that carry the yellow pigment (xanthophores) do not increase or decrease in number in response to outside stimulation* (Scientific American).

**xan|tho|phyll** or **xan|tho|phyl** (zan′thə fil), *n.* **1** a yellow pigment related to carotene, present in green leaves and plants, and found especially in autumn leaves; lutein. It is thought to be a product of the decomposition of chlorophyll. *Formula:* $C_{40}H_{56}O_2$ **2** any one of various related yellow pigments. [< French *xanthophylle* < Greek *xanthós* yellow + *phýllon* leaf]

**xan|tho|phyl|lic** (zan′thə fil′ik), *adj.* having to do with or containing xanthophyll.

**xan|tho|phyl|lous** (zan′thə fil′əs), *adj.* = xanthophyllic.

**xan|tho|pro|te|ic** (zan′thō prō tē′ik), *adj.* having to do with xanthoprotein.

**xanthoproteic acid**, an acid that does not crystallize, resulting from the decomposition of albuminoids by nitric acid.

**xan|tho|pro|tein** (zan′thō prō′tēn), *n.* the yellow substance formed by the action of hot nitric acid on protein.

**xan|thop|ter|in** (zan thop′tər in), *n.* a yellow pigment found in the wings of butterflies. *Formula:* $C_6H_5N_5O_2$ [< *xantho-* + Greek *pterón* wing + English *-in*]

**xan|thous** (zan′thəs), *adj.* **1** = yellow. **2** of or having to do with peoples having yellowish, reddish, or light-brown hair. **3** of or having to do with peoples having a yellowish skin, such as the Mongolians: *It is true that the Greek and Roman writers do describe the various barbarous tribes of Europe ... representing some to be of the fair, or as it has been styled, xanthous complexion; others of the dark, or melanic* (T. Price). [< Greek *xanthós* yellow (with English *-ous*)]

**xanth|u|ren|ic acid** (zan′thù ren′ik), a yellowish, crystalline acid in the urine of those deficient in pyridoxine, and with an unbalanced metabolism of tryptophan. *Formula:* $C_{10}H_7NO_4$

**Xan|tip|pe** (zan tip′ē), *n.* = Xanthippe.

✱**x-ax|is** (eks′ak′sis), *n.* the horizontal axis in a system of rectangular coordinates, as on a chart or graph.

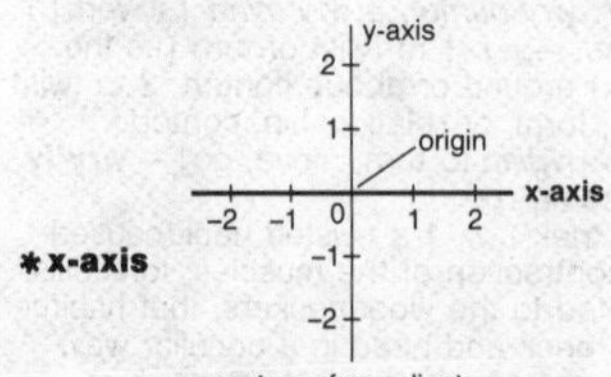

✱**x-axis**

system of coordinates

**X.C.** or **x.c.**, *Finance.* without coupon.

✱**X chromosome**, one of the two chromosomes that determine sex. A fertilized egg cell containing two X chromosomes, one from each parent, develops into a female.

✱**X chromosome**

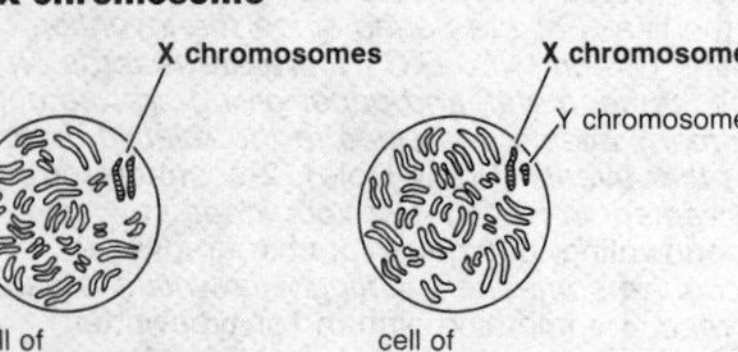


**x-cp.**, *Finance.* without coupon.

**X-C skiing**, *U.S.* cross-country skiing: *X-C skiing is being appreciated for the "total" sport it has become with multitudes of adherents* (Betsy Palmedo-Thompson).

**X.D., x.d.**, or **x-div.**, *Finance.* without dividend; ex-dividend.

**X-dis|ease** (eks′də zēz′), *n.* **1** = hyperkeratosis (def. 1). **2** a virus disease of peach trees with yellow and red patches on the leaves, and withered fruit. **3** any one of various diseases of unknown or uncertain cause.

**Xe** (no period), xenon (chemical element).

**xe|bec** (zē′bek), *n.* a small, three-masted vessel of the Mediterranean: *The sails of the xebec are in general similar to those of the polacre, but the hull is extremely different* (William Falconer). Also, **zebec**. [< French *chébec* < Italian *sciabecco* < Arabic *shabbāk*]

**xe|ni|a** (zē′nē ə), *n. Botany.* the action of pollen on the seed showing in the same generation the characteristics which result from pollination. [< New Latin *xenia* < Greek *xeníā* being a guest < *xénos* guest]

**xe|ni|al** (zē′nē əl), *adj.* having to do with hospitality, especially in ancient Greece. [< Greek *xeníā* (see etym. under **xenia**) + English *-al*[1]]

**xe|nic** (zē′nik), *adj.* having to do with or derived from a compound of xenon and another element or radical: *xenic acid.*

**xeno-**, *combining form.* **1** a stranger: *Xenophobia = fear of strangers.* **2** foreign, strange, as in *xenolith, xenomorphic.* [< Greek *xénos* guest]

**xen|o|di|ag|no|sis** (zen′ō dī′əg nō′sis), *n.* diagnosis of a disease by exposing the patient or his tissue to a vector, such as a mosquito, and then examining it for the presence of the infectious microorganism.

**xen|o|do|chei|on** (zen′ə dō kī′on), *n., pl.* **-chei|a** (-kī′ə). = xenodochium.

**xen|o|do|chi|um** (zen′ə dō kī′əm), *n., pl.* **-chi|a** (-kī′ə). (especially in the Middle Ages and ancient times) an inn; hotel: *I once spent eighteen hours in a suite in the Mark Hopkins Hotel and never saw the rest of this fabled Frisco xenodochium, for I snoozed out my entire stay* (Maclean's). [< Late Latin *xenodochīum* < Greek *xenodocheîon* < *xénos* guest, stranger + *déchesthai* to receive]

**xe|nog|a|mous** (zə nog′ə məs), *adj. Botany.* of or produced by cross-fertilization.

**xe|nog|a|my** (zə nog′ə mē), *n. Botany.* cross-fertilization.

**xen|o|gen|e|sis** (zen′ə jen′ə sis), *n. Biology.* **1** = alternation of generations. **2** the supposed production of offspring wholly and permanently unlike the parent. **3** = spontaneous generation.

**xen|o|ge|net|ic** (zen′ə jə net′ik), *adj. Biology.* of the nature of or having to do with xenogenesis.

**xen|o|gen|ic** (zen′ə jen′ik), *adj.* = xenogenetic.

**xe|nog|e|ny** (zə noj′ə nē), *n.* = xenogenesis.

**xen|o|graft** (zen′ə graft′, -gräft′), *n.* a graft of tissue taken from an individual of another species; heterograft.

**xen|o|lith** (zen′ə lith), *n.* a fragment of older rock embedded in an igneous mass: *A "xenolith" is simply a "stranger"—one not belonging to the rock system of the district* (T. Hannan).

**xen|o|lith|ic** (zen′ə lith′ik), *adj.* of or having to do with a xenolith.

**xen|o|ma|ni|a** (zen′ə mā′nē ə), *n.* a fondness for what is foreign: *a command of pure English, unadulterated by xenomania* (George Saintsbury).

**xen|o|mor|phic** (zen′ə môr′fik), *adj.* of rock having a form different from the normal form because of pressure. [< *xeno-* + Greek *morphē* form, shape] —**xen′o|mor′phi|cal|ly**, *adv.*

✱**X**

definition 1

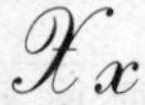

Script letters look like examples of fine penmanship. They appear in many formal uses, such as invitations to social functions.

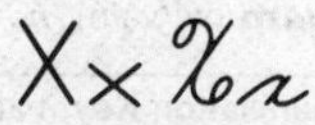

Handwritten letters, both manuscript or printed (left) and cursive (right), are easy for children to read and to write.

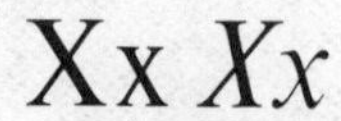

Roman letters have *serifs* (finishing strokes) adapted from the way Roman stonecutters carved their letters. This is *Times Roman* type.

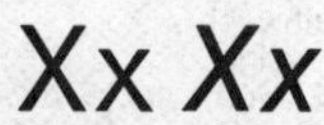

Sans-serif letters are often called *gothic.* They have lines of even width and no serifs. This type face is called *Helvetica.*

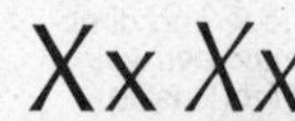

Between roman and gothic, some letters have thick and thin lines with slight flares that suggest serifs. This type face is *Optima.*

Computer letters can be sensed by machines either from their shapes or from the magnetic ink with which they are printed.

***xe|non** (zē′non, zen′on), *n.* a heavy, colorless, odorless, inert gaseous chemical element, present in very small quantities in the air. Xenon is used in filling flashbulbs and vacuum tubes. Xenon is obtained from liquid air, and it forms compounds with fluorine and oxygen. *There was the moment of crisis at the start of the first Hanford reactor when the chain reaction threatened to die off because of the unexpectedly high neutron-capture cross section of an isotope of xenon* (Bulletin of Atomic Scientists). [< Greek *xénon,* neuter of *xénos,* adjective, strange]

***xenon**

| symbol | atomic number | atomic weight |
|---|---|---|
| Xe | 54 | 131.30 |

**xen|o|phile** (zen′ə fīl), *n.* a person who is friendly toward foreign persons or things.

**xen|o|phil|i|a** (zen′ə fil′ē ə), *n.* friendship toward foreign persons or things: *American intellectuals themselves have debated the question ... with intermediate tinges of embarrassment, self-hate, xenophilia, and double-mindedness* (Manchester Guardian Weekly).

**xen|o|phobe** (zen′ə fōb), *n.* a person who fears or hates foreigners or strangers: *The vision of the melting pot, with its ideal of inclusiveness, has often been severely challenged by bigots and xenophobes of various stripe* (Atlantic).

**xen|o|pho|bi|a** (zen′ə fō′bē ə), *n.* a hatred or fear of foreigners or strangers: *The darkest cloud over the cultural landscape is that of steadily increasing xenophobia* (Atlantic).

**xen|o|pho|bic** (zen′ə fō′bik), *adj.* of or having to do with xenophobia: *A xenophobic view is taken in the Yemen of all foreigners* (Sunday Times). —**xen′o|pho′bi|cal|ly,** *adv.*

**xen|o|time** (zen′ə tīm), *n.* a yellowish-brown, natural phosphate of yttrium. It resembles zircon in form but is not as hard. *Formula:* $YPO_4$ [< *xeno-* + Greek *tīmḗ* honor]

**xer-,** *combining form.* the form of **xero-** before vowels, as in *xeric.*

**xer|arch** (zir′ärk), *adj. Ecology.* originating in dry habitats: *a xerarch plant succession.* [< *xer-* + Greek *archḗ* beginning]

**xe|ric** (zir′ik), *adj. Botany.* **1** lacking moisture: *xeric varieties of wheat.* **2** xerophytic. —**xe′ri|cal|ly,** *adv.*

**xero-,** *combining form.* dry: *Xeroderma* = *(a disease characterized by) dry skin. Xerophilous* = *adapted to a dry climate.* Also, **xer-** before vowels. [< Greek *xērós* dry]

**xe|ro|der|ma** (zir′ə dėr′mə), *n.* a disease characterized by dryness and discoloration of the skin. [< *xero-* + Greek *dérma* skin]

**xer|o|gram** (zir′ə gram), *n.* a xerographic copy.

**xe|ro|graph|ic** (zir′ə graf′ik), *adj.* of or having to do with xerography: *In the xerographic process the characters are optically projected onto the charged surface of a rotating selenium-coated drum* (Hugo Gernsback). —**xe′ro|graph′i|cal|ly,** *adv.*

**xe|rog|ra|phy** (zi rog′rə fē), *n.* **1** a dry printing process for making copies of letters, pictures, manuscripts, books, or other printed, written, or drawn material, by using electrically charged particles to make a positive photographic contact print. Paper is placed on a metal plate sprayed with electrons before exposure and dusted with black powder, and the image is transferred to the paper by heat. Xerography is used for printing such material as engineering drawings and ruled forms, and for making quick copies of office records and correspondence. *Other items that are speeded up by xerography are the budgets for circulation to directors, the minutes of board meetings and many other internal documents* (London Times). **2 Xerography,** a trademark for this process.

**xe|ro|ma** (zi rō′mə), *n.* = xerophthalmia.

**xe|ro|morph** (zir′ə môrf), *n.* a plant adapted to saltwater marshes or highly alkaline soils. [< *xero-* + Greek *morphḗ* form]

**xe|roph|a|gy** (zi rof′ə jē), *n., pl.* **-gies.** the practice of living on dry food, especially a form of abstinence in which only bread, herbs, salt, and water are consumed: *As for xerophagies, says Tertullian, they charge them with being a novel title for a pretended duty* (Frederic W. Farrar). [< Late Latin *xērophagia* < Greek *xērophagíā* < *xērós* dry + *phageîn* eat]

**xe|roph|i|lous** (zi rof′ə ləs), *adj.* adapted to a dry climate: *The cactus is a natural xerophilous plant.* [< *xero-* + Greek *phílos* (with English *-ous*) loving]

**xe|roph|i|ly** (zi rof′ə lē), *n.* the condition or character of being xerophilous.

**xe|roph|thal|mi|a** (zir′of thal′mē ə), *n.* an abnormal condition of mucous membrane of the eyeball, characterized by dryness and thickness, and often accompanied by night blindness or day blindness: *Malaria and yaws have been practically eliminated in central Java, but one now finds disquieting evidence of clinical malnutrition ... and xerophthalmia, the blindness of Vitamin A deficiency* (New Scientist). [< Greek *xērophthalmíā* < *xērós* dry + *ophthalmíā* eye disease < *ophthalmós* eye]

**xe|roph|thal|mic** (zir′of thal′mik), *adj.* having to do with or characterized by xerophthalmia.

**xe|ro|phyte** (zir′ə fīt), *n. Botany.* a plant that loses very little water and can grow in deserts or very dry ground. Cactuses, sagebrush, and century plants are xerophytes.

**xe|ro|phyt|ic** (zir′ə fit′ik), *adj. Botany.* of or having to do with a xerophyte: *This is at all times less frequented than the main beach, and here grow many xerophytic plants, and curlew and other wading birds here alight, where mud and sand mingle* (Manchester Guardian).

**xe|ro|phyt|i|cal|ly** (zir′ə fit′ə klē), *adv.* in the manner of a xerophyte.

**xe|ro|phyt|ism** (zir′ə fī tiz′əm), *n.* the quality or condition of being adapted to live in a very dry climate.

**xe|ro|ra|di|o|graph** (zir′ō rā′dē ə graf, -gräf), *n.* a picture made by xeroradiography.

**xe|ro|ra|di|og|ra|phy** (zir′ō rā′dē og′rə fē), *n.* a process of X-ray photography that uses an electrically charged metal plate instead of film: *A picture taken by xeroradiography can be developed in 15 seconds, without recourse to darkroom or wet chemicals* (New Scientist).

**xe|ro|sis** (zi rō′sis), *n. Medicine.* abnormal dryness, as of the skin or the eyeball. [< New Latin *xerosis* < Greek *xērōsis* a drying up < *xērós* dry + *-ōsis* -osis]

**xe|ro|ther|mic** (zir′ə thėr′mik), *adj. Biology.* both dry and hot: *a xerothermic environment.*

**xe|rot|ic** (zi rot′ik), *adj. Medicine.* **1** characterized by dryness; of the nature of xerosis. **2** having to do with xerosis.

**Xe|rox** (zir′oks), *n. Trademark.* **1** a dry process for making copies of letters, typewritten, printed, or drawn materials by using electrically charged particles instead of ink and pressure to transfer the original copy from a metal plate to paper: *Microfilm takes weeks and is costly. Positive photostat takes time. What about Xerox?* (Harper's). **2** a copying machine using this process.

**xe|rox** (zir′oks), *v.t., v.i.* to make copies by xerography: *We xeroxed thirty ... sample essays to be graded by all the teachers* (New Yorker).

**x-height** (eks′hīt′), *n. Printing.* **1** the height of the lower-case x. **2** the height of any lower-case letter without descenders or ascenders.

**Xho|sa** (kō′sə), *n., pl.* **-sa** or **-sas. 1** a member of a group of Bantu tribes living mainly in the Transkei, east of Cape Province, in South Africa. **2** the language of these tribes, closely related to Zulu. Also, **Xosa.**

***xi** (sī, zī, ksē), *n.* the 14th letter of the Greek alphabet, corresponding to English X, x. [< Greek *xî*]

***xi**

| Ξ | ξ |
|---|---|
| capital letter | lower-case letter |

**X.i.** or **x-i.,** *Finance.* ex interest.

**XI** (no periods), **1** the Roman numeral for 11. **2** *British Informal.* a team of eleven players, as in cricket: *The first XI, beaten by seven wickets* (Punch).

**x-int.,** *Finance.* ex interest.

**-xion,** *suffix. British.* a variant of **-tion,** as in *connexion.*

**xi particle,** a hyperon, either neutral or negative, present in cosmic rays and existing very briefly during a high-energy nuclear collision in a large atomic reactor: *If a nucleon is struck so violently that it loses two K-mesons, it changes into a xi particle, which thus differs from the original nucleon by two units of hypercharge* (Victor F. Weisskopf).

**xiph|i|oid** (zif′ē oid), *adj.* **1** resembling the swordfish. **2** belonging to the same family as the swordfish. [< Latin *xiphias* swordfish (< Greek *xiphías* < *xíphos* sword)]

**xiph|i|ster|nal** (zif′ə stėr′nəl), *adj.* = xiphoid.

**xiphisternal cartilage,** the cartilaginous lower end of the sternum; xiphisternum.

**xiph|i|ster|num** (zif′ə stėr′nəm), *n., pl.* **-na** (-nə). the posterior or lower part of the sternum of mammals (in man usually called *xiphoid cartilage*). [< New Latin *xiphisternum* < Greek *xíphos* sword + Latin *sternum* sternum]

**xiph|oid** (zif′oid), *adj., n. Anatomy.* —*adj.* **1** shaped like or resembling a sword; ensiform: *a xiphoid bone.* **2** of or having to do with the xiphisternum or xiphisternal cartilage.
—*n.* the xiphisternal or xiphoid cartilage. [< New Latin *xiphoides* < Greek *xiphoeidês* < *xíphos* sword + *eîdos* form]

**xi|phoi|dal** (zə foi′dəl), *adj.* = xiphoid.

**xiphoid cartilage** or **process,** the cartilaginous lower end of the sternum in man. See picture under **skeleton.**

**xiph|o|phyl|lous** (zif′ə fil′əs), *adj. Botany.* having sword-shaped or ensiform leaves. [< Greek *xíphos* sword + *phýllon* leaf]

**xiph|o|su|ran** (zif′ə sůr′ən), *adj., n.* —*adj.* of or belonging to an order of arthropods comprising the horseshoe crabs.
—*n.* a xiphosuran arthropod; horseshoe crab. [< New Latin *Xiphosura* the order name (< Greek *xíphos* sword + *ourā́* tail) + English *-an*]

**xiph|o|sure** (zif′ə sůr), *n.* = xiphosuran.

**X-ir|ra|di|ate** (eks′i rā′dē āt), *v.t.,* **-at|ed, -at|ing.** to subject to the action of X rays: *When the male gametes [of guinea pigs and mice] are heavily X-irradiated in post-spermatogonial stages the offspring show high incidences of dominant defects* (Bulletin of Atomic Scientists).

**X-ir|ra|di|a|tion** (eks′i rā′dē ā′shən), *n.* a subjection to X rays, as in the treatment of disease.

**xi zero,** a xi particle.

**X.L.** or **XL** (no periods), extra large.

**X|mas** (kris′məs), *n.* = Christmas. [< *X* Christ + (Christ)*mas*]

**Xn.,** Christian.

**Xnty.,** Christianity.

**X-o|gen** (eks′ō jən), *n. Astronomy.* an unidentified molecule detected through radio emission in the region of various constellations, including Orion and Sagittarius: *X-ogen's close correspondence with hydrogen cyanide leads to the conclusion that its structure has similarities with that of hydrogen cyanide* (Science News). [< *X*[1] (def. 4) + (hydr)*ogen*]

**Xo|sa** (kō′sə), *n., pl.* **-sa** or **-sas.** = Xhosa.

**XP** (kī′rō′, kē′-), the first two letters (*chi* and *rho*) of the Greek word ΧΡΙΣΤΟΣ (Christos, Christ), used as an abbreviation alone or in combination; Chi-Rho; Christogram.

**X particle,** = meson.

**X-ra|di|a|tion** (eks′rā dē ā′shən), *n.* **1** X rays: *Ultraviolet light from an atom electrically excited in a discharge tube might have the same frequency as low-voltage X-radiation* (Edgar N. Grisewood). **2** examination or treatment with X rays: *A special technique has been developed of very soft X-radiation to improve delicate photographic contrasts* (London Times).

**X-rat|ed** (eks′rā′tid), *adj. U.S.* **1** produced for exhibition or viewing by adult audiences; having an X rating: *an X-rated motion picture.* **2** *Informal.* **a** sexually explicit; pornographic: *X-rated books, an X-rated show.* **b** obscene: *X-rated street language.*

**X|ray** (eks′rā′), *n. U.S.* a code name for the letter *x,* used in transmitting radio messages.

***X ray**
definition 1

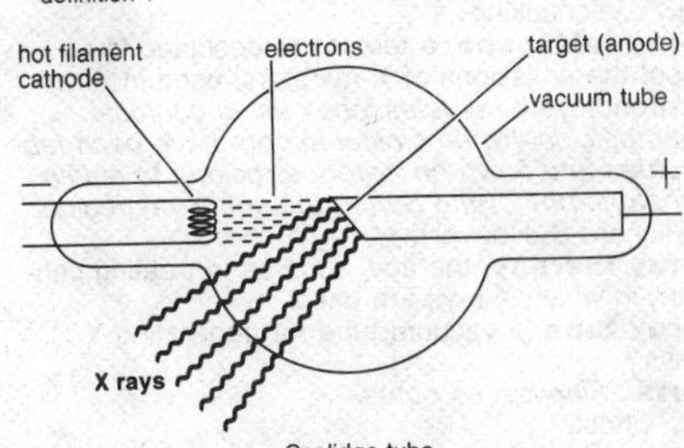


Coolidge tube

***X ray, 1** an electromagnetic ray having an extremely short wavelength that can go through substances that ordinary light cannot penetrate; roentgen ray. X rays are formed when a high-speed stream of electrons strikes a target, usually of metal, in a special kind of vacuum tube. X rays are used to locate breaks in bones, bullets lodged in the body, and other particles and malfunctions, and to diagnose and treat certain diseases. **2** a picture made by means of X rays. [half-translation of obsolete German *X-Strahlen* plural < *X,* in sense of "unknown" + *Strahl* ray, beam]
▶ **X ray** is usually written with a capital *X.* It is not hyphenated as a noun, but it is as a verb or

**Pronunciation Key:** hat, āge, cãre, fär; let, ēqual, tėrm; it, īce; hot, ōpen, ôrder; oil, out; cup, pủt, rüle; child; long; thin; ᴛʜen; zh, measure; ə represents **a** in about, **e** in taken, **i** in pencil, **o** in lemon, **u** in circus.

adjective: *to X-ray the chest, an X-ray examination.*

**X-ray** (eks′rā′), *v., adj.* — ***v.t.*** **1** to examine, photograph, or treat with X rays: *The doctor X-rayed my knee for broken bones.* **2** to subject to very close scrutiny; examine minutely: *The Republicans X-rayed the charge for legitimate political dynamite, and the Democrats prayed that it would pass* (Manchester Guardian Weekly).
— ***v.i.*** to use X rays: *If ... a doctor suspects tuberculosis, he may X-ray* (Time).
— ***adj.*** **1** of or having to do with X rays. **2** by X rays: *an X-ray examination of one's teeth.*

**X-ray astronomer**, a specialist in X-ray astronomy.

**X-ray astronomy**, **1** the study of X-ray stars: *X-ray astronomy ... can be carried out only from rockets and satellites sent above the atmosphere, since the atmosphere screens out the radiation* (New York Times). **2** the branch of astronomy dealing with this study.

**X-ray burster**, a stellar object that emits very short but intense pulses of X rays: *The new X-ray bursters ... flare up and die again in only a few seconds* (New Scientist).

**X-ray crystallography**, the study of the arrangement of atoms and molecules in crystals and chemical substances by X rays.

**X-ray diffraction**, the diffusion of X rays on contact with matter, with changes in radiation intensity as a result of differences in atomic structure within the matter. It is an important method of studying atomic and molecular structure and is used in X-ray crystallography. *... the techniques of X-ray diffraction, which have contributed so much to the understanding of the inner structure of metals and alloys* (F. A. Fox).

**X-ray microscope**, a microscope using X rays for studying the internal structure of metals, plastics, and other substances, and the interiors of minute organisms. It is capable of magnifying up to 1,500 diameters.

**X-ray photograph**, a photograph made by means of X rays.

**X-ray pulsar**, a pulsar that is the source of powerful X-ray emissions: *One of the most remarkable developments of X-ray astronomy was the ... discovery of an X-ray pulsar in the Crab Nebula* (Richard B. Hoover).

**X-ray source**, = X-ray star.

**X-ray spectrometer**, a spectrometer using X rays by which the chemical constituents of a substance are separated into their characteristic spectral lines for identification and determination of their concentration.

**X-ray spectrometry**, the use of an X-ray spectrometer; chemical analysis by means of an X-ray spectrometer.

**X-ray spectroscopy**, = X-ray spectrometry.

**X-ray star**, an astronomical source of X rays concentrated at a point; a celestial body that emits X rays: *The X-ray star is approximately 1,000 light-years away and ... radiates about 500 times more energy as X rays than as visible light* (E. L. Schücking).

**X-ray telescope**, a telescope designed to reflect the emissions of X-ray stars, used in X-ray astronomy: *X-ray telescopes using confocal paraboloidal-hyperboloidal mirrors have been fabricated and flown on Aerobee rockets to obtain photographs of the Sun in the soft X-ray region* (Richard B. Hoover).

**X-ray therapy**, therapy, such as in treating cancer, in which X rays are used.

**X-ray tube**, a vacuum tube for generating X rays.

**X-rts.**, *Finance.* ex rights.

**Xt.**, Christ.

**Xtian.**, Christian.

**Xty.**, Christianity.

**XV** (no periods), **1** the Roman numeral for 15. **2** *British Informal.* a team consisting of fifteen players, as in Rugby.

**xyl-**, *combining form.* the form of **xylo-** before vowels, as in *xylan, xylene.*

**xy|lan** (zī′lan), *n. Chemistry.* a yellow, gelatinous compound, a pentosan, found in woody tissue. It yields xylose when hydrolyzed. *One disadvantage of hardwoods over soft is that hardwood contains a higher percentage of xylan, a gummy substance that must be removed* (Science News Letter).

**xy|la|ry ray** (zī′lər ē), = medullary ray.

**xy|lem** (zī′lem), *n.* the tissue in a plant or tree. It consists of tissue that conveys upward by capillary attraction the water and dissolved minerals absorbed by the roots and provides support. It is the harder portion of a vascular bundle, and consists usually of tracheids, tracheae or vessels, woody fibers, and parenchyma. [< German *Xylem* < Greek *xýlon* wood + German *-em,* as in *Phloem* phloem]

**xylem ray**, a ray or plate of xylem between two medullary rays.

**xy|lene** (zī′lēn), *n.* any one of three isomeric, colorless, liquid hydrocarbons of the benzene series, obtained from petroleum, coal tar, or coal gas; xylol. Commercial xylene is a mixture of all three, and is used in making dyes, aviation gasoline, lacquers, and as a raw material for polyester fibers. *Formula:* $C_8H_{10}$

**xy|le|nol** (zī′lə nol, -nōl), *n.* any one of five isomeric, white, crystalline phenols obtained from coal tar. Commercial xylenol is a mixture of the isomers, used as a disinfectant, in solvents and pharmaceuticals, and in the manufacture of polyphenylene oxide. *Formula:* $C_8H_{10}O$

**xy|lic** (zī′lik, zil′ik), *adj. Chemistry.* of or having to do with any of several isomeric acids which are derivatives of xylene.

**xylic acid**, one of a group of six isomeric acids which are carboxyl derivatives of xylene. *Formula:* $C_9H_{10}O_2$

**xy|li|din** (zī′lə din, zil′ə-), *n.* = xylidine.

**xy|li|dine** (zī′lə dēn, -din; zil′ə-), *n.* any one of a group of six isomeric compounds which are amino derivatives of xylene, homologous with aniline. Commercial xylidine is an oily liquid composed of a mixture of five of these substances, and is used in making dyes. *Formula:* $C_8H_{11}N$ [< *xyl*(ene) + *-id* + *-ine*[2]]

**xylo-**, *combining form.* wood; woody: *Xylograph = a woodcut.* Also, **xyl-** before vowels. [< Greek *xýlon* wood]

**Xy|lo|cain** (zī′lə kān), *n. Trademark.* lidocaine.

**xy|lo|carp** (zī′lə kärp), *n. Botany.* a hard and woody fruit. [< *xylo-* + Greek *karpós* fruit]

**xy|lo|car|pous** (zī′lə kär′pəs), *adj. Botany.* having fruit which becomes hard and woody.

**xy|lo|gen** (zī′lə jən), *n. Botany.* **1** wood or xylem in a formative state. **2** lignin.

**xy|lo|graph** (zī′lə graf, -gräf), *n.* = woodcut.

**xy|log|ra|pher** (zī log′rə fər), *n.* an engraver on wood, especially one of the earliest wood engravers, as of the 1400's.

**xy|lo|graph|ic** (zī′lə graf′ik), *adj.* **1** of or having to do with xylography: *The woodcuts, if ... coarse from a xylographic point of view, are admirably characteristic* (Athenaeum). **2** cut in or on wood: *The xylographic picture is a good specimen of popular art* (Nation).

**xy|lo|graph|i|cal** (zī′lə graf′ə kəl), *adj.* = xylographic.

**xy|log|ra|phy** (zī log′rə fē), *n.* the art of engraving on wood, or of making prints from such engravings: *The forthcoming edition of the New Testament, illustrated with all the powers of modern xylography* (Saturday Review). [< French *xylographie* < Greek *xýlon* wood + French *-graphie* -graphy]

**xy|loid** (zī′loid), *adj.* **1** of or having to do with wood. **2** like wood; ligneous. [< Greek *xyloeidḗs* < *xýlon* wood + *eîdos* form]

**xy|lol** (zī′lōl, -lol), *n.* = xylene.

**xy|lol|o|gy** (zī lol′ə jē), *n.* the study of the structure of wood.

**xy|lo|nite** (zī′lə nīt), *n.* **1** a substance like celluloid made from pyroxylin: *Paper knives, hairpin boxes, and various other small articles ... made in xylonite look remarkably well when carved* (Eleanor Rowe). **2 Xylonite**, a trademark for this substance.

**xy|lo|phage** (zī′lə fāj), *n.* an insect, mollusk, or crustacean that eats or destroys wood.

**xy|loph|a|gous** (zī lof′ə gəs), *adj.* **1** feeding on wood, as some insect larvae. **2** boring into or destroying wood, as some mollusks and crustaceans. [< New Latin *xylophagus* (with English *-ous*) < Greek *xýlon* wood + *phageîn* to eat]

***xy|lo|phone** (zī′lə fōn, zil′ə-), *n.* a musical percussion instrument, consisting of two rows of wooden bars of varying lengths, which are sounded by striking with small wooden hammers.

***xylophone**

**resembling a xylophone:**

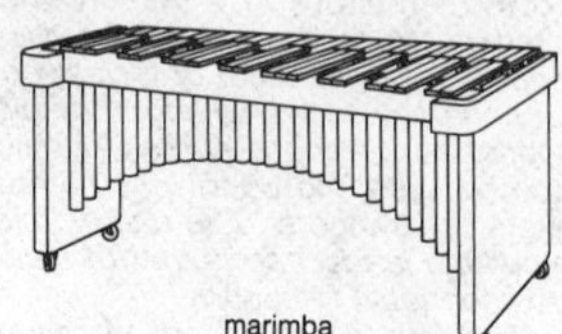

marimba

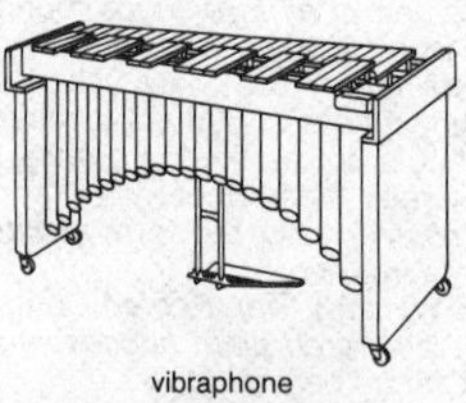

vibraphone

**xy|lo|phon|ist** (zī′lə fō′nist, zil′ə-; zī lof′ə-, zi-), *n.* a person who plays on a xylophone.

**xy|lo|rim|ba** (zī′lə rim′bə, zil′ə-), *n.* a lightweight marimba resembling a xylophone.

**xy|lose** (zī′lōs), *n.* a crystalline, pentose sugar present in woody plants. It is obtained from the decomposition of xylan, as in straw and corncobs, by the action of warm, dilute sulfuric acid. *Formula:* $C_5H_{10}O_5$

**xy|lot|o|mist** (zī lot′ə mist), *n.* a person skilled in xylotomy.

**xy|lot|o|mous** (zī lot′ə məs), *adj.* able to bore into or cut wood, as some insects.

**xy|lot|o|my** (zī lot′ə mē), *n.* the preparation of sections of wood, especially with a microtome, for examination with a microscope. [< *xylo-* + Greek *-tomiā* a cutting]

**xy|lyl** (zī′ləl), *n. Chemistry.* a univalent radical, part of xylene. *Formula:* $C_8H_9$-

**xy|lyl|ene** (zī′lə lēn), *n. Chemistry.* a bivalent radical part of xylene. *Formula:* -$C_8H_8$-

**xyst** (zist), *n.* **1** (among the ancient Greeks) a portico in a gymnasium where athletes exercised in winter. **2** (among the ancient Romans) a walk in a garden, between rows of trees. [< Latin *xystus* < Greek *xystós* polished (floor) < *xýein* to smooth]

**xys|tus** (zis′təs), *n.* = xyst.

**XYY syndrome**, a congenital disorder of males resulting from the presence of an extra male sex chromosome (XYY instead of XY) in the cells, and thought to be characterized by overaggressive behavior, low intelligence, and social inadequacy: *The XYY syndrome, a defect in sexual chromosomes, has, for instance, been linked to criminal behavior in some men* (Science News).

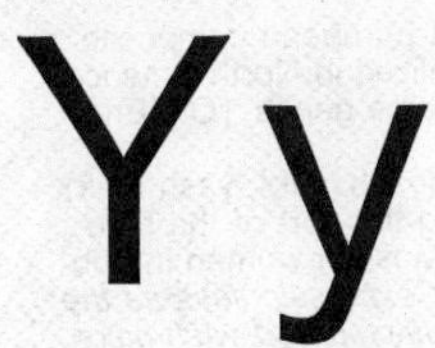

***Y¹** or **y** (wī), *n., pl.* **Y's** or **Ys, y's** or **ys. 1** the 25th letter of the English alphabet: *There are two y's in yearly and yesterday.* **2** any sound represented by this letter. **3** (used as a symbol for) the 25th, or more usually the 24th (of an actual or possible series, either *I* or *J* being omitted). **4** used as a symbol for unknown quantity, especially in algebraic equations.

**Y²** (wī), *n., pl.* **Y's. 1** anything shaped like the letter Y: *the Y of a wishbone. The piping branched out into a Y.* **2** a forked support for a Y-level or similar instrument.

**Y³** (wī), *n. Informal.* Y.M.C.A. or Y.W.C.A.; Y.M.H.A or Y.W.H.A.

**-y¹**, *suffix forming adjectives.* **1** (*added to nouns*) full of ___: *Bumpy = full of bumps.*
**2** (*added to nouns*) containing ___: *Salty = containing salt.*
**3** (*added to nouns*) having ___: *Cloudy = having clouds.*
**4** (*added to nouns*) characterized by ___: *Funny = characterized by fun.*
**5** (*added to adjectives*) somewhat ___: *Chilly = somewhat chill.*
**6** (*added to verbs*) inclined to ___: *Sleepy = inclined to sleep.*
**7** (*added to nouns*) resembling or suggesting ___: *Sugary = resembling or suggesting sugar.*
**8** In certain words, chiefly adjectives, such as *paly, steepy, stilly, vasty,* the addition of *-y* does not change the meaning.
[Old English *-ig*]

**-y²**, *suffix added to nouns to form other nouns.*
**1** small ___: *Dolly = a small doll.*
**2** dear ___: *Daddy = dear dad.*
[Middle English *-y*]

**-y³**, *suffix forming nouns.* **1** (*added to adjectives*) ___ condition or quality: *Jealousy = jealous condition or quality.*
**2** (*added to nouns*) condition or quality of being ___: *Victory = condition or quality of being a victor.*
**3** (*added to verbs*) activity of ___ing: *Delivery = activity of delivering. Entreaty = activity of entreating.*
[Middle English *-ye, -ie* < Old French *-ie* < Latin *-ia* < Greek *-ia*]

**y., 1** yard or yards. **2** year or years.

**Y** (no period), **1** yen (Japanese unit of money). **2** yttrium (chemical element). **3** yuan (Chinese unit of money).

**yab|ber** (yab′ər), *n., v. Especially in Australia:* —*n.* speech; language. —*v.i., v.t.* to talk. [apparently < native Australian *yabba* < a root *ya-* to speak]

**yab|bie** (yab′ē), *n.* a small freshwater crawfish of the Australian bush: *There are ... yabbies ... roasted on fire-heated stones for breakfast* (Punch). [< a native Australian name]

**yacht** (yot), *n., v.* —*n.* a boat for pleasure trips or racing, equipped with sails or engines, or both. —*v.i.* to sail or race on a yacht. [< earlier Dutch *jaght* < *jaghtship* pursuit ship] —**yacht′er,** *n.* —**yacht′less,** *adj.* —**yacht′like′,** *adj.*

**yacht chair,** a folding armchair with a canvas back and seat.

**yacht club,** a club of yachtsmen; a yachting organization.

**yacht|ing** (yot′ing), *n., adj.* —*n.* **1** the art of sailing a yacht. **2** the pastime of sailing on a yacht. —*adj.* **1** of yachting or yachts. **2** interested in yachting.

**yachts|man** (yots′mən), *n., pl.* **-men.** a person who owns or sails a yacht.

**yachts|man|ship** (yots′mən ship), *n.* skill or ability in handling a yacht.

**yachts|wom|an** (yots′wu̇m′ən), *n., pl.* **-wom|en.** a woman who owns or sails a yacht.

**yack** (yak), *v., n. Slang.* —*v.i., v.t.* to talk endlessly and foolishly; chatter: *We'll be in your hair all the time, yacking and quarrelling and everything* (New Yorker).
—*n.* endless, foolish talk: *Local stations are either full of yack or turn out gloom by the square yard* (Cape Times). Also, **yak.**
[imitative]

**yack|e|ty-yak** (yak′ə tē yak′), *v.i., v.t.,* **-yakked, -yak|king,** *n.* = yack. Also, **yakety-yak.**

**yaff** (yaf, yäf), *v., n. Scottish.* —*v.i.* to bark; yelp. —*n.* a bark or yelp. [imitative]

**yaf|fle** (yaf′əl), *n. Dialect.* the green woodpecker. [imitative of its cry]

**YAG** (yag), *n.* a synthetic garnet of yttrium and aluminum oxide, used especially to generate laser beams. [< *Y*(ttrium) *A*(luminum) *G*(arnet)]

**ya|ger** (yā′gər), *n.* = jaeger.

**Ya|gi** (yä′gē), *adj.* of, having to do with, or designating a powerful type of directional radio antenna or array that is like a dipole but with four conducting rods in a plane parallel to the ground. [< Hidetsugu *Yagi,* 1886–1976, a Japanese electrical engineer, who invented it]

**yah** (yä), *interj.* an exclamation of derision, disgust, defiance, or impatience. [imitative]

**Yah|gan** (yä′gən), *n., pl.* **-gans** or **-gan. 1** a member of a tribe of South American Indians of Tierra del Fuego, occupying the southernmost habitable region of the world. **2** their language.

**Ya|hoo** (yä′hü, yä hü′), *n.* a brute in human shape in Jonathan Swift's *Gulliver's Travels,* who works for a race of intelligent horses.

**ya|hoo** (yä′hü, yä hü′), *n.* a rough, coarse, or uncouth person: *She launches into a philippic against the yahoos who desecrate picnic sites* (New Yorker). [< *Yahoo*]

**ya|hoo|ism** (yä′hü iz əm, yä hü′-), *n.* a style or quality characteristic or suggestive of a yahoo.

**Yahr|zeit** (yär′tsīt′), *n. Judaism.* the yearly anniversary of the death of a parent or close relative, observed by saying kaddish and by the lighting of a memorial candle. [< Yiddish *yortsayt* (literally) a year's time]

**Yah|veh** or **Yah|ve** (yä′vā), *n.* = Yahweh.

**Yah|vism** (yä′viz əm), *n.* = Yahwism.

**Yah|vist** (yä′vist), *n.* = Yahwist.

**Yah|vis|tic** (yä vis′tik), *adj.* = Yahwistic.

**Yah|weh** or **Yah|we** (yä′wā), *n.* **1** a name of God in the Hebrew text of the Old Testament, often used by writers on the religion of the Hebrews; Jehovah. **2** the ancient god of the Hebrew tribes. Also, **Jahve, Jahveh.** [< Hebrew *Yahweh*]

**Yah|wism** (yä′wiz əm), *n.* **1** the ancient religion of the Hebrews. **2** the use of *Yahweh* as God's name. Also, **Jahvism, Jehovism.**

**Yah|wist** (yä′wist), *n., adj.* —*n.* the writer or writers of certain portions of the Old Testament, forming a separate source of the Hexateuch, characterized by the use of the name *Yahweh* for God. —*adj.* **1** = Yahwistic. **2** of or having to do with Yahwism: *The primitive Yahwist faith of Israel ... preached an afterlife* (Time). Also, **Jahvist, Jehovist.**

**Yah|wis|tic** (yä wis′tik), *adj.* **1** of or by the Yahwist. **2** using *Yahweh* as the name of God. Also, **Jahvistic, Jahwistic, Jehovistic.**

**yak¹** (yak), *n., pl.* **yaks** or (*collectively*) **yak.** a long-haired ox of Tibet and central Asia. The domesticated yak is raised for its meat, milk, and hair and is used as a beast of burden. [< Tibetan *gyak*]

**yak²** (yak), *v.i., v.t.,* **yakked, yak|king,** *n.* **1** = yack. **2** = yock.

**yak|e|ty-yak** (yak′ə tē yak′), *v.i., v.t.,* **-yakked, -yak|king.** = yack.

**Yak|i|ma** (yak′ə mä), *n., pl.* **-ma** or **-mas. 1** a member of a confederation of American Indian tribes living on a reservation in the Yakima Valley of south central Washington. **2** the Shahaptian language of this group of tribes.

**ya|ki|to|ri** (yä′kē tôr′ē, -tōr′ē), *n.* a Japanese dish of grilled or skewered chicken, usually boneless and served with soy sauce. [< Japanese *yakitori* < *yaki* grilled + *tori* chicken]

**yak|ka** (yak′ə), *n. Australian Slang.* hard work.

**yak lace,** heavy lace made from yak hair.

**yak|ow** (yak′ou), *n.* the offspring of a yak and a cow: *Baby yakow ... was bred to flourish in the uplands of Great Britain and eventually to provide inexpensive meat to residents of the U.K.* (John P. Jordan).

**Ya|kut** (yä küt′), *n., pl.* **-kuts. 1** a member of a Turkic people living in eastern Siberia. **2** the Turkic language of this people.

**ya|ku|za** (yə kü′zə), *n., pl.* **-za.** a Japanese gangster or mobster: *Corporations hire yakuza to police stockholders' meetings and intimidate any questioners* (New Yorker). [< Japanese *yakuza*]

**yale** (yāl), *n.* a fabulous beast with horns and tusks, resembling the two-horned rhinoceros: *The yale has the tail of an elephant and the jowls of a boar* (New York Times). [< Latin *eālē*]

**yam** (yam), *n.* **1** the starchy, tuberous root of various vines, much like the sweet potato. It is eaten as a vegetable. **2** any one of these vines, which grow in warm regions. **3** *U.S.* the sweet potato: *We often have candied yams with ham.* **4** *Scottish.* the potato. [< Spanish *ñame,* ultimately < Senegalese *nyami* eat]

**Yam|a|see** (yam′ə sē), *n., pl.* **-see** or **-sees.** a member of a Muskhogean tribe of American Indians formerly occupying the region of the lower Savannah River, the Georgia coast, and northern Florida. During the 1700's they merged with the Creek and Seminole Indians.

**Ya|ma|to** (yä′mä tō), *n., adj.* —*n.* **1** one of the legendary ancestors of the Japanese people, who migrated from the mainland in ancient times. **2** the Japanese people. —*adj.* of the Japanese, especially the legendary Japanese.

**ya|men** (yä′mən), *n.* **1** the official residence of a high Chinese official before 1912. **2** the headquarters of any department of the civil service in China. Also, **yamun.** [< Manchu *yamun* official residence, courthouse]

**yam|mer** (yam′ər), *v., n.* —*v.i.* **1** to whine or whimper. **2** to howl or yell: *These inflationary actions illustrate the Administration's policy: yammer against inflation, but actually let it ride* (Time). **3** = lament.
—*v.t.* to say in a querulous tone.
—*n.* the action of yammering.
[alteration (perhaps influenced by Middle Dutch *jammeren*) of Middle English *yomeren,* Old English *geōmrian* to lament < *geōmor* sorrowful]

**ya|mun** (yä′mən), *n.* = yamen.

**yang** (yang), *n.* the active principle or element in Chinese dualistic philosophy, representing the male qualities of light and heat, in constant interaction with its opposing principle (yin): *We have spent many a pleasant moment in the past, browsing among the packaged shark fins ... and contemplating the yang and the yin of things* (New Yorker). [< Chinese (Peking) *yang*]

**yank** (yangk), *v., n. Informal.* —*v.t., v.i.* to pull with a sudden motion; jerk; tug: *The dentist yanked the tooth. ... where a lifting foresail-foot is yanking at the sheet* (John Masefield).
—*n.* a sudden pull; jerk; tug: *He had to give the door a yank in order to open it.*
[origin uncertain]

**Yank** (yangk), *n., adj. Slang.* Yankee: *With all the publicity there has been, many authorities, Latin as well as Yank, also worry that expectations may be built too high* (Wall Street Journal).

**Yan|kee** (yang′kē), *n., adj.* —*n.* **1a** a native of New England. **b** a native of any one of the Northern states. **2** *Southern U.S.* a Northerner (often used in an unfriendly way). **3** a native or inhabitant of the United States; American. **4** *U.S.* a code name for the letter *y,* used in transmitting radio messages.
—*adj.* of or having to do with Yankees: *Yankee shrewdness.*
[American English, perhaps ultimately < Dutch *Jan Kees,* dialectal variant of *Jan Kaas* (literally) John Cheese, a nickname for Dutch and English settlers; the *-s* was taken in English as a plural ending]

**Yan|kee|dom** (yang′kē dəm), *n.* **1** Yankees collectively. **2** the region inhabited by Yankees.

**Yankee Doodle,** an American song, probably of English origin and taken over by the American soldiers in the Revolutionary War.

**Yan|kee|fied** (yang′kē fīd), *adj.* made or become like a Yankee; characteristic of a Yankee: *Japan is ... Yankeefied in more ways than one* (New York Voice).

**Yan|kee|ism** (yang′kē iz əm), *n.* **1** Yankee character or characteristics. **2** a Yankee peculiarity, as of speech. Saying *guess* for *think* is a Yankeeism.

**Yan|kee|land** (yang′kē land′), *n.* **1** New England: *Gift shop operators in Yankeeland bought cautiously at the fall giftware show here* [*Boston*] (Wall Street Journal). **2** the United States: *The*

***Y¹**
definition 1

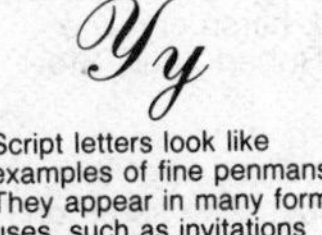

Script letters look like examples of fine penmanship. They appear in many formal uses, such as invitations to social functions.

Handwritten letters, both manuscript or printed (left) and cursive (right), are easy for children to read and to write.

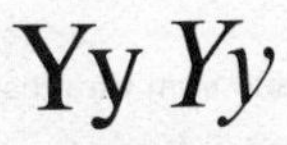

Roman letters have *serifs* (finishing strokes) adapted from the way Roman stonecutters carved their letters. This is *Times Roman* type.

Sans-serif letters are often called *gothic.* They have lines of even width and no serifs. This type face is called *Helvetica.*

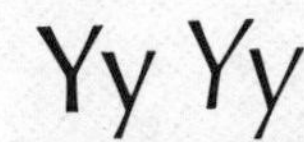

Between roman and gothic, some letters have thick and thin lines with slight flares that suggest serifs. This type face is *Optima.*

Computer letters can be sensed by machines either from their shapes or from the magnetic ink with which they are printed.

*Dominion populace of 16 million is less than one-tenth of Yankeeland's 169 million* (Wall Street Journal). **3** the northern part of the United States: *Don't you realize that these hillbillies are bringing the precious "Southern way of life" to unenlightened Yankeeland?* (Time).

**yan|ki** (yăng′kē), *n., adj.* = yanqui.

**yan|ni|gan** (yan′ə gən), *n. Baseball Slang.* a player not on the regular or starting team. [perhaps < U.S. dialect *young'un*]

**yan|qui** or **Yan|qui** (yăng′kē), *n., adj.* in Spanish America: **—*n.*** a citizen of the United States.
**—*adj.*** of the United States or its citizens: *This could be built up into the standard charge of "yanqui imperialism"* (Newsweek).
[< Spanish *yanqui* < English *Yankee*]

**Ya|o**[1] (yä′ō), *n., pl.* **Ya|o** or **Ya|os.** **1** a member of a people living chiefly in southwestern China, but also found in the mountains of northern Burma, Thailand, Laos, and Vietnam. **2** the language of this people.

**Ya|o**[2] (yä′ō), *n., pl.* **Ya|o** or **Ya|os.** **1** a member of a Bantu people of eastern Africa, living on the southeastern shores of Lake Nyasa. **2** the language of this people.

**yap** (yap), *n., v.,* **yapped, yap|ping.** **—*n.*** **1** a snappish bark; yelp. **2** *Slang, Figurative.* snappish, noisy, or foolish talk. **3** *Slang, Figurative.* a peevish or noisy person. **4** *Slang.* the mouth: *Those prissy college boys ... [are] scared speechless every time McAlmon opens his yap* (Atlantic).
**—*v.i.*** **1** to bark in a snappish way; yelp: *The little dog yapped at every stranger who came to the door.* **2** *Slang.* to talk snappishly, noisily, or foolishly. **3** *Slang.* to chatter or talk idly: *They're always yapping about life* (Philip Gibbs).
[imitative] **—yap′per,** *n.*

**Yap|ese** (ya pēz′, -pēs′), *n., pl.* **-ese,** *adj.* **—*n.*** a native or inhabitant of Yap, an island in the Pacific.
**—*adj.*** of or having to do with the island of Yap or its people.

**ya|pok** or **ya|pock** (yə pok′), *n.* a South and Central American water opossum, having webbed toes. [< French *yapok* < *Oyabok,* a river in French Guiana]

**yapp** (yap), *n., adj.* **—*n.*** a style of bookbinding in limp leather with overlapping edges or flaps.
**—*adj.*** of or having to do with this.
[< *Yapp,* the name of a London bookseller]

**yap|py** (yap′ē), *adj.,* **-pi|er, -pi|est.** inclined to yap or yelp; yapping: *a yappy dog.*

**ya|qo|na** (yä kō′nä), *n.* a traditional or ceremonial drink of the Fiji Islands, prepared from the dried roots of the kava. [< Fijian]

**Ya|qui** (yä′kē), *n., pl.* **-qui** or **-quis,** *adj.* **—*n.*** a member of a tribe of American Indians in northwestern Mexico and Arizona.
**—*adj.*** of this tribe of Indians.

**yar** (yär), *adj.* = yare (defs. 1 and 2).

**Yar|bor|ough** or **yar|bor|ough** (yär′bėr′ō; *especially British* yär′bər ə), *n.* a hand at whist or bridge with no card higher than a nine. [supposedly < an Earl of *Yarborough* who used to bet 1,000 to 1 against its occurrence]

**yard**[1] (yärd), *n., v.* **—*n.*** **1** a piece of ground near or around a house, barn, school, or other building: *You can play outside, but you must not leave the yard.* **2** a piece of enclosed ground for some special purpose or business: *a chicken yard.* **SYN**: court, enclosure. **3** a space with tracks where railroad cars are stored, shifted around, or serviced, or where new trains are made up: *His brother works in the railroad yards.* **4** an open area in a prison used for recreation by prisoners. **5** *Especially U.S. and Canada.* an area in which moose and deer gather for feeding during the winter.
**—*v.t.*** **1** to put into or enclose in a yard: *... to yard a flock of lambing ewes throughout the winter* (London Times). **2** to store in a yard: *to yard up wood.*
**—*v.i.*** to gather for winter feeding: *The area is full of game ... Deer yard in it* (New York Times).
**the Yard,** = Scotland Yard.
[Old English *geard* an enclosure]

**★yard**[2]
definition 1

**1 yard** = 3 feet or 36 inches

1 meter = 3.28 feet or 39.37 inches

1 foot = 12 inches

**★yard**[2] (yärd), *n.* **1** a measure of length equal to 36 inches or 3 feet, and equivalent to .9144 meter: *Mother bought three yards of blue cloth for curtains. The football player ran 40 yards for a touchdown. Abbr:* yd., y. **2** a long, slender beam or pole fastened across a mast, used to support a sail. See picture at **mast**[1]. **3** *Figurative, Informal.* a great length: *He ... could talk by the yard of what little he did know* (Wat Bradwood). *He had a face a yard long* (Henry James). **4** *Especially U.S. Slang.* 100 dollars: *"Would you like to make an easy five yards, Eddy?" asks the driver* (Maclean's). [Old English *gerd,* or *gierd* rod]

**Yard** (yärd), *n., pl.* **Yards** or **Yard.** *Slang.* (in southeast Asia) a Montagnard. [< the pronunciation of the last syllable of *Montagnard*]

**yard|age**[1] (yär′dij), *n.* **1** the service, use, or hire of a railroad yard or enclosure, as for storing freight or cattle. **2** the charge for such use.

**yard|age**[2] (yär′dij), *n.* **1** length in yards: *A high point of Nevers' college career was the 1925 Rose Bowl game against Notre Dame, in which he rolled up more yardage (134) than Notre Dame's famous Four Horsemen together* (Newsweek). **2** an amount measured in yards: *Textile executives contend the actual yardage of goods being sold, while not as good as they'd like, is "not bad"* (Wall Street Journal).

**yard|arm** (yärd′ärm′), *n.* either end of a long, slender beam or pole which supports a square sail.

**yard|bird** (yärd′bėrd′), *n. Slang.* **1** an army recruit: *The hero is a bemused, irreverent yardbird who gets himself and his officers into every kind of Army-life trouble* (Newsweek). **2** a member of any one of the armed forces, restricted to camp or given menial duties for breaking regulations.

**yard goods,** cloth cut to measure and sold by the yard: *There was no doubt that he had made a mistake in judgment in the autumn when he had ordered the yard goods for his spring line* (New Yorker).

**yard grass,** a kind of wire grass with flowering spikes, commonly found as a weed in backyards; dog's-tail.

**yard|land** (yärd′land′), *n.* an area of land held by a tenant in villeinage in early English manors, varying in different counties from 15 to 40 acres.

**yard line,** any one of the white lines that divide a football field every five yards.

**yard|man**[1] (yärd′mən), *n., pl.* **-men.** **1** a man who has charge of, or works in, a yard, such as a railroad yard. **2** = gardener.

**yard|man**[2] (yärd′mən), *n., pl.* **-men.** a sailor working on the yards of a ship.

**yard|mas|ter** (yärd′mas′tər, -mäs′-), *n.* the man in charge of a railroad yard.

**yard of ale, 1** a deep, slender glass for holding several pints of liquor: *Yards of ale are a specialty of the house* (Craig Claiborne). **2** the amount of liquor contained in such a glass.

**yard|stick** (yärd′stik′), *n.* **1** a stick one yard long, used for measuring; 36-inch ruler. **2** *Figurative.* any standard of judgment or comparison: *What yardstick do you use to decide whether your conduct is right or wrong? The food chains ... have shown a declining trend in those two critical yardsticks for at least five years* (Advertising Age). **SYN**: criterion, gauge.

**yard|wand** (yärd′wond′), *n. Especially British.* a yardstick.

**yare** (yãr), *adj., adv.* **—*adj.*** **1** alert, nimble, active, brisk, or quick. **2** (of a ship) easily steered or managed. **3** *Archaic.* **a** ready; prepared. **b** ready for use.
**—*adv.*** *Obsolete.* **1** readily; promptly. **2** well; thoroughly.
[Old English *gearu*] **—yare′ly,** *adv.*

**yarl** (yärl), *n.* = jarl.

**yar|mel|ke** (yär′məl kə), *n.* = yarmulka.

**Yar|mouth** (yär′məth), *adj. Geology.* of or having to do with the second interglacial stage in the topographical development of North America, beginning about 320,000 years ago. [< *Yarmouth,* a place in Iowa]

**Yarmouth bloater,** *British.* a herring that has been smoked but not salted. [< *Yarmouth,* a fishing town on the coast of Norfolk, in England]

**yar|mul|ka** or **yar|mul|ke** (yär′məl kə), *n.* a skullcap worn by Jewish men and boys, especially for prayer and ceremonial occasions. Also, **yarmelke.** [< Yiddish < Polish *yarmulka* a kind of hat or cap]

**yarn** (yärn), *n., v.* **—*n.*** **1** any spun thread, especially that prepared for weaving or knitting: *The woman knits stockings from yarn.* **2** *Informal, Figurative.* a story; tale: *The old sailor made up his yarns as he told them.*
**—*v.i.*** *Informal.* to tell stories: *Thomas was yarning and clowning* (Time).
[Old English *gearn* spun fiber]

**yarn-dyed** (yärn′dīd′), *adj.* made from yarn that was dyed before weaving.

**yar|o|vize** (yär′ə vīz), *v.t.,* **-vized, -viz|ing.** = jarovize (vernalize).

**yar|row** (yar′ō), *n.* **1** a common plant with finely divided leaves and close, flat clusters of white or pink flowers; milfoil. It is a European composite herb that has been naturalized in North America. **2** any other plant of the same genus. [Old English *gearwe*]

**yash|mak** or **yash|mac** (yäsh mäk′, yash′mak), *n.* a double veil concealing the part of the face below the eyes, worn by Moslem women in public: *Brown eyes, each pair expressionless as the last, peer from behind multi-coloured yashmaks* (Punch). [< Arabic *yashmaq*]

**yat|a|ghan** or **yat|a|gan** (yat′ə gan), *n.* a type of sword used by Moslems, having no guard for the hand and no crosspiece, but usually a large pommel on the end. Also, **ataghan.** [< Turkish *yatağan*]

**yat|ter** (yat′ər), *v., n.* **—*v.i.*** = chatter.
**—*n.*** = chatter: *The yatter over Prohibition died with Repeal* (Time).
[probably < *ya(p)* + *(cha)tter*]

**yaud** (yôd, yăd), *n. Scottish.* **1** an old mare. **2** a worn-out horse. [< Scandinavian (compare Old Icelandic *jalda* mare). Compare etym. under **jade**[2].]

**yaul** (yôl), *n.* = yawl[2].

**yauld** (yôd, yäd, yäld), *adj. Scottish.* **1** active; sprightly. **2** strong; vigorous.

**yaup** (yôp, yäp), *v.i., n. Informal.* yawp. **—yaup′er,** *n.*

**yau|pon** (yô′pon), *n.* a holly of the southern United States whose leaves have been used as a substitute for tea. Also, **yopon.** [American English < Siouan (Catawba) *yopún* (diminutive) < *yop* tree, shrub]

**yau|ti|a** (you tē′ä), *n.* **1** a tropical plant of the West Indies and South America whose starchy tuber is used for food. **2** = taro. [< American Spanish *yautía* < a native word]

**yaw** (yô), *v., n.* **—*v.i.*** **1** to turn from a straight course; go unsteadily. **2** (of an aircraft) to turn from a straight course by a motion about its vertical axis.
**—*v.t.*** to cause (a ship, aircraft, or missile) to yaw.
**—*n.*** **1** a movement from a straight course. **SYN**: deviation. **2** the amount of this.
[origin uncertain]

**yawl**[1] (yôl), *n.* **1** a type of boat rigged like a sloop, with a large mast near the bow and a short mast near the stern, usually aft of the rudder post. **2** a ship's boat rowed with four or six oars. [apparently < Dutch *jol*]

**yawl**[2] (yôl), *n., v.i., v.t. Dialect:* yowl; howl. [probably ultimately imitative. Compare Low German *jaulen.*]

**yaw|me|ter** (yô′mē′tər), *n.* an instrument for measuring the yaw of an aircraft.

**yawn** (yôn), *v., n.* **—*v.i.*** **1** to open the mouth wide because one is sleepy, tired, or bored: *The reader must not yawn, or yield to tickles in the throat, or tire of the tale in the middle* (London Times). **2** to open wide; gape: *The canyon yawned beneath our feet.* **—*v.t.*** **1** to utter with a yawn: *to yawn a reply.* **2** to cause by yawning.
**—*n.*** **1** the act of yawning: *A yawn is often contagious.* **2** something that yawns; a gaping opening; chasm. **3** *Figurative, Informal.* a tiresome person or thing; a bore: *He thought the cathedral a big yawn after the marvels of Burgos and Seville* (New Yorker).
[variant of Middle English *yonen,* Old English *geonian, ginian*] **—yawn′er,** *n.*

**yawn|ful** (yôn′fəl), *adj.* causing one to yawn; tiresome; tedious: *He writes at yawnful length about ... distortions of his positions as carried in the press, and at even greater length about what those positions really were* (Time). **—yawn′ful|ly,** *adv.*

**yawn|ing** (yô′ning), *adj.* **1** characterized by or producing yawns; yawny; yawnful: *The account of the character of Mr. Legge is the most yawning pamphlet I ever read* (John Wilkes). **2** opening or open wide: *a lofty pass ... surrounded by yawning precipices* (James Gilmour). **—yawn′ing|ly,** *adv.*

**yawn|y** (yô′nē), *adj.,* **yawn|i|er, yawn|i|est.** characterized by a yawn or yawns; inclined to yawning: *There were those first few unbelievable steps when you are nervously tired and yawny and must learn ... the easy rhythm* (Harper's).

**yawp** (yôp, yäp), *v., n. Informal.* **—*v.i.*** **1** to utter a loud, harsh cry: *I heard a ghostly, low-pitched yawping* (Gwyn Thomas). **2** *Figurative.* to speak foolishly: *What're you yawping about?* **3** to gape: *They stood yawping at the strangers.*
**—*n.*** **1** a loud, harsh cry: *The prevailing interest does not come from Ornette's yawps and squeals* (Saturday Review). **2** *Figurative.* speech or utterance likened to a loud, harsh cry: *the 'barbaric yawp' of Whitman* (Robert Louis Stevenson). Also, **yaup.**
[probably imitative] **—yawp′er,** *n.*

**yaws** (yôz), *n.pl.* a contagious disease of the tropics, characterized by raspberrylike sores on the skin, especially of the face, hands, and feet, and caused by a spirochete; frambesia: *Yaws is known the world over as a painful, crippling, and highly contagious disease that covers the body with sores and eventually eats away the outer flesh* (Time). [probably < Carib *yaya,* the native name for the disease]

***y-ax|is** (wī′ak′sis), *n.* the vertical axis in a system of rectangular coordinates, as on a chart or graph.

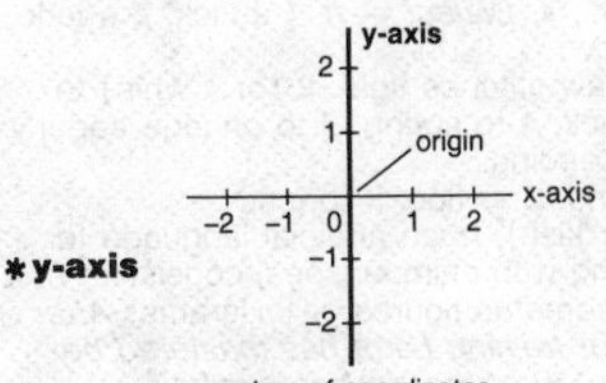

system of coordinates

***y-axis**

**Yaz|i|di** (yä′zə dē), *n., pl.* **-di** or **-dis.** = Yezidi.

**Yaz|oo** (ya′zü), *n., pl.* **-oo** or **-oos.** a member of an American Indian tribe that formerly lived along the Yazoo River in Mississippi.

**Yb** (no period), ytterbium (chemical element).

**Y.B.** or **YB** (no periods), yearbook.

**Y.C.,** Yacht Club.

**Y chromosome,** one of the two chromosomes that determine sex. A fertilized egg cell containing a Y chromosome develops into a male.

**y|clad** or **y-clad** (i klad′), *v. Archaic.* clad; clothed; a past participle of **clothe.** [Middle English *ycladde* < Old English *ge-,* past participial prefix + *clathod* clad]

**y|clept** or **y|cleped** (i klept′), *adj. Archaic.* called; named; styled. [Middle English *ycleped,* or *ycliped* < Old English *geclipod* named, past participle of *geclipian,* or *gecleopian* to speak, call]

**yd.,** yard or yards.

**yds.,** yards.

**ye¹** (yē; *unstressed* yi), *pron. pl. Archaic.* you: *If ye are thirsty, drink.* [Old English *gē*]

▶ Originally **ye** was the subject, **you** the object form. In Late Middle English *you* began to be used as subject and in the Early Modern period the two forms were extensively confused. Before 1700 *you* had become regular for both cases.

▶ See **thou¹** for another usage note.

**ye²** (ᴛʜē; *popularly* yē), *definite article.* an old way of writing the definite article "the."

▶ In Old and Middle English **the** was commonly written as **þe.** The early printers, who ordinarily did not have this consonant symbol (called "thorn") in their fonts, substituted *y* for it, but this was not intended to be read with the value of *y.*

**yea** (yā), *adv., n.* —***adv.*** **1** yes (used in agreeing with or assenting to something). **2** indeed; truly (used to introduce a sentence or clause). **3** *Archaic.* not only that, but also; moreover.
—***n.*** **1** an affirmative answer. **2** a vote or voter in favor of something.
[Old English *gēa,* or *gē*]

**yeah** (yeə), *adv. U.S. Informal.* yes: *"Yeah, that's right," said Buster* (New Yorker).

**yean** (yēn), *v.t., v.i.* (of a sheep or goat) to bring forth (young). [unrecorded Old English *geēanian.* Compare Old English *ēanian* to yean, *geēan* pregnant.]

**yean|ling** (yēn′ling), *n., adj.* —***n.*** the young of a sheep or goat; lamb or kid.
—***adj.*** very young or newborn.

**year** (yir), *n.* **1** 12 months or 365 days; January 1 to December 31. Leap year has 366 days. **2** 12 months reckoned from any point: *I will see you again a year from today. A fiscal year is a period of 12 months at the end of which the accounts of a government, business, or the like, are balanced.* **3** the part of a year spent in a certain activity: *Our school year is 9 months.* **4** the period of the earth's revolution around the sun: *The solar or astronomical year is 365 days, 5 hours, 48 minutes, 45.51 seconds.* **5** the time in which any planet completes its revolution around the sun. **6** the time it takes for the sun to make an apparent journey from a given star back to it again: *The sidereal year is 20 minutes, 23 seconds longer than the solar year.* **7** 12 lunar months, about 354 days long (lunar year). **8** a class or grade of a school or college: *He is in his sophomore year. Abbr:* yr.
**a year and a day,** *Law.* a period constituting a term for certain purposes, in order to insure that a full year is completed: *They shall lose the rights to the estate if they do not claim it within a year and a day of the death of the testator.*
**stricken in years,** advanced in years; old: *A man well stricken in years* (Anthony Trollope).
**year after year,** every year: *Winter fades into spring year after year.*
**year by year,** with each succeeding year; as years go by: *Be it your fortune, year by year, the same resource to prove* (William Cowper).
**year in, (and) year out,** always; continuously: *You see other girls having splendid times, while you grind, grind, year in and year out* (Louisa May Alcott).
**years, a** age (of a person): *young in years but old in experience, I hope to live to your years.* **b** a very long time: *I haven't seen him in years.* **c** age; period; times: *years of prosperity.* **d** *Archaic.* old age: *a man of (or in) years.*
[Old English *gēar*]

**year-a|round** (yir′ə round′), *adj.* = year-round.

**year|book** (yir′bu̇k′), *n.* a book or a report published every year. Yearbooks often report facts of the year. The graduating class of a school or college usually publishes a yearbook, with pictures of its members.

**year-by-year** (yir′bī yir′), *adv., adj.* from one year to another; with each succeeding year.

**year-end** (yir′end′), *n., adj.* —***n.*** **1** the end of the year. **2** *Informal.* a stock dividend given at the end of the year. —***adj.*** of or at the end of the year.

**year|ling** (yir′ling, yėr′-), *n., adj.* —***n.*** **1** an animal one year old: *Rustlers work in late fall and winter to pick up yearlings missed by the branding iron at roundup* (Newsweek). **2** a race horse in the second calendar year since it was foaled. **3** *U.S.* a cadet in the second year at a military academy.
—***adj.*** one year old: *a yearling colt.*

**year|long** (yir′lông′, -long′), *adj.* **1** lasting for a year. **2** lasting for years.

**year|ly** (yir′lē), *adj., adv.* —***adj.*** **1** once a year; in every year: *He takes a yearly trip to the mountains from his home in the city.* **2** lasting a year: *The earth makes a yearly revolution around the sun.* **3** for a year: *He is paid a yearly salary of $6,000.*
—***adv.*** once a year; in every year; annually: *That company sends out new calendars to its customers yearly.*

**yearn** (yėrn), *v.i.* **1** to feel a strong desire or longing; desire earnestly: *He yearns for home.* **SYN:** hanker, pine. **2** to feel pity; have tender feelings: *Her kind heart yearned for the starving, homeless children.* **SYN:** mourn, commiserate. [Old English *geornan,* or *giernan*]

**yearn|ful** (yėrn′fəl), *adj.* **1** full of yearning. **2** = sorrowful. —**yearn′ful|ly,** *adv.*

**yearn|ing** (yėr′ning), *n., adj.* —***n.*** **1** an earnest or strong desire; longing. **2** the condition of being moved with compassion.
—***adj.*** that yearns. —**yearn′ing|ly,** *adv.*

**year of grace,** a particular year of the Christian Era: *He departed the thirteenth of February in the year of grace 1163* (Richard Knolles). [translation of Medieval Latin *anno gratiae*]

**year-round** (yir′round′), *adj., adv.* throughout the year: *year-round residents.*

**year-round|er** (yir′roun′dər), *n. Informal.* a person who lives in a place all year long.

**years** (yirz), *n.pl.* See under **year.**

**year-to-year** (yir′tə yir′), *adj.* occurring or done from year to year.

**yea|say** (yā′sā′), *v.t., v.i.* to say yea (to); assent; agree; vote in the affirmative. —**yea′say′er,** *n.*

**yeast** (yēst), *n., v.* —***n.*** **1** the substance that causes dough for most kinds of bread to rise and that causes beer to ferment. Yeast consists of very small single-celled plants that grow quickly in a liquid containing sugar. **2** = yeast plant. **3** = yeast cake. **4** *Figurative.* an influence, element, or the like, that acts as a leaven. **5** foam; froth. **SYN:** spume. **6** fermentation; agitation.
—***v.i.*** to ferment; be covered with froth.
[Old English *gist*] —**yeast′like′,** *adj.*

**yeast bread,** bread baked with yeast.

**yeast cake,** flour or meal mixed with yeast and pressed into a small cake.

**yeast|i|ness** (yēs′tē nis), *n.* the quality or state of being yeasty.

**yeast plant,** any one of a group of minute, one-celled, ascomycetous fungi, which produce alcoholic fermentation in saccharine fluids.

**yeast|y** (yēs′tē), *adj.,* **yeast|i|er, yeast|i|est.** **1** of, containing, or resembling yeast. **2** frothy or foamy: *yeasty waves.* **3** *Figurative.* light or trifling; frivolous: *[He] writes what is probably the yeastiest scandal column printed anywhere* (Time).

**Yeats|i|an** (yā′tsē ən), *adj.* of or having to do with the Irish poet and playwright William Butler Yeats (1865-1939) or his writings: *Yeatsian lyricism.*

**yecch** (yuk, yuʜ), *interj. U.S. Informal.* an exclamation of disgust: *"You ask a guy today how the economy will be in three weeks and he'll say 'Yecch!' "* (Newsweek).

**yegg** (yeg), *n. U.S. Slang.* **1** a burglar who robs safes; safecracker. **2** any burglar. [American English; origin uncertain]

**yegg|man** (yeg′mən), *n., pl.* **-men.** = yegg.

**yeld** (yeld), *adj. Scottish.* **1** (of an animal) not able to bear young. **2** (of cattle) not yielding milk; dry. Also, **yell.** [Old English *gelde;* perhaps related to **geld¹**]

**yelk** (yelk), *n. Archaic.* yolk¹.

**yell¹** (yel), *v., n.* —***v.i.*** to cry out with a strong, loud sound: *He yelled with pain.*
—***v.t.*** to say with a yell: *We yelled our good-bye to our friends as the bus moved away.*
—***n.*** **1** a strong, loud outcry. **2** *U.S.* a special shout or cheer, used by a school or college to encourage its sports team.
[Old English *gellan,* or *giellan*] —**yell′er,** *n.*

**yell²** (yel), *adj. Scottish.* yeld.

**yel|low** (yel′ō), *n., adj., v.* —***n.*** **1** the color of gold, butter, or ripe lemons. **2** a yellow pigment, dye, fabric, or other substance or object. **3** the yolk of an egg.
—***adj.*** **1** having a yellow color. **2a** having a yellowish skin, as the Mongolians do. **b** of the Mongolian race. **3** jealous, envious. **4** *Informal, Figurative.* cowardly. **5** characterized by sensational or lurid writing or presentation of the news: *yellow journalism, the yellow press.*
—***v.t., v.i.*** to turn or become yellow: *Buttercups yellowed the field* (v.t.).
[Old English *geolu*] —**yel′low|ly,** *adv.* —**yel′low-ness,** *n.*

**yellow arsenic,** = orpiment.

**yellow asphodel,** an asphodel native to Mediterranean regions, with yellow, fragrant flowers.

**yellow avens,** = herb bennet.

**yel|low-back** (yel′ō bak′), *n. Informal.* **1** shilling shocker. **2** *U.S.* a currency note printed on the back in a yellowish color.

**yel|low-bel|lied** (yel′ō bel′ēd), *adj.* **1** having a yellow belly or underside. **2** *Slang.* cowardly; craven.

**yellow-bellied flycatcher,** a small flycatcher of eastern North America with yellowish underparts.

**yellow-bellied sapsucker,** a North American woodpecker with a yellowish underside and a red throat and forehead.

**yel|low-bel|ly** (yel′ō bel′ē), *n., pl.* **-lies.** *Slang.* a coward: *Some of them called me a traitor and a yellow-belly—things like that* (Harper's).

**yellow bile,** = choler.

**yel|low-billed cuckoo** (yel′ō bild′), a North American cuckoo having a partly yellow bill.

**yellow birch,** a North American birch yielding a strong, light-brown wood: *When valuable yellow birch forests are cut in central Ontario the ensuing forest isn't yellow birch any more; it's a hardwood forest of maple, and usually a pretty poor one* (Maclean's).

**yel|low|bird** (yel′ō bėrd′), *n.* **1** the goldfinch of America. **2** the yellow warbler of North America. **3** any one of certain other yellow birds such as an oriole of Europe.

**yellow body,** = corpus luteum.

**yellow brass,** a malleable brass containing about 70 per cent copper and 30 per cent zinc, used when strength is not required; high brass.

**yel|low-breast|ed chat** (yel′ō bres′tid), a large North American warbler with an olive-green back and yellow breast.

**yellow buckeye,** a large horse chestnut tree with yellow flowers of the Ohio Valley and Appalachian Mountains.

**yellow cake,** a yellow powder obtained by processing uranium ore.

**yellow clover,** a hop clover with yellow flowers.

**yel|low-cov|ered** (yel′ō kuv′ərd), *adj.* **1** covered with yellow. **2** *Figurative.* cheap; trashy.

**yel|low-crowned night heron** (yel′ō kround′), a gray heron with a black and white head, chiefly of swamps of the southern United States and south to Brazil.

**yellow daisy,** **1** = black-eyed Susan. **2** any daisy or daisylike flower with yellow rays, such as anthemis.

**yellow dog,** *U.S. Slang.* **1** a worker who does not join or assist a labor union. **2** a despicable or worthless person.

**yel|low-dog contract** (yel′ō dôg′, -dog′), *U.S.* an agreement between employer and employee that the worker will not join or assist a labor union. The Norris-La Guardia Act of 1932 made such contracts illegal.

**yellow dwarf,** a virus disease of onion, barley, and soybean plants, which turns leaves yellow and stunts the plants.

**yellow enzyme,** = flavoprotein.

**yellow fat,** a condition caused by a deficiency of vitamin E in domestic animals.

**yellow fever,** a dangerous, infectious disease of warm climates, characterized by chills, high fever, jaundice, and often hemorrhaging; yellow jack. It is caused by a virus transmitted by the bite of a

**Pronunciation Key:** hat, āge, cãre, fär; let, ēqual, tėrm; it, īce; hot, ōpen, ôrder; **oil, out;** cup, pu̇t, rüle; **ch**ild; lo**ng**; **th**in; ᴛʜen; **zh,** measure; **ə** represents **a** in about, **e** in taken, **i** in pencil, **o** in lemon, **u** in circus.

mosquito. Yellow fever was once common in some southern parts of the United States.

**yel|low-fe|ver mosquito** (yel′ō fē′vər), the mosquito that transmits yellow fever and dengue; aëdes.

**yel|low|fin** (yel′ō fin′), *n.,* or **yellowfin tuna**, a tuna of the Atlantic and Pacific oceans that usually grows 6 feet long and weighs about 300 pounds.

**yellow flag**, **1** a flag flown by a ship in harbor indicating that the ship is in quarantine because of the presence of an infectious disease aboard; yellow jack; quarantine flag. **2** = yellow iris.

**yellow gentian**, a tall gentian of southern and central Europe whose yellowish-brown, bitter root is used as a tonic and as bitters.

**yellow gold**, an orange-yellow alloy of gold containing about nine parts gold to one part copper, used in jewelry.

**yel|low-green algae** (yel′ō grēn′), = green algae.

**yellow gum**, = eucalyptus.

**yel|low|ham|mer** (yel′ō ham′ər), *n.* **1** a European bunting with a bright-yellow head, throat, and breast. **2** *U.S.* the yellow-shafted flicker. [alteration of earlier *yelambre,* probably < Old English *geolu* yellow + Middle English *amore, omer,* or *emer* a kind of bird]

**Yellowhammer State**, a nickname for Alabama.

**yel|low-head|ed blackbird** (yel′ō hed′id), a blackbird of western North America, the male of which has a yellow head and breast.

**yellow iris**, a tall iris with bright yellow flowers, found in Europe, North America, and northern Africa.

**yel|low|ish** (yel′ō ish), *adj.* somewhat yellow.

**yellow jack**, **1** = yellow fever. **2** = yellow flag. **3** a fish of the West Indies and Florida, related to the pompano.

**yellow jacket**, **1** a small wasp marked with bright yellow. **2** *Slang.* a capsule of pentobarbital sodium (a sedative and hypnotic).

**yellow jasmine** or **jessamine**, a twining shrub of the southern United States having fragrant, yellow flowers; gelsemium. It is the floral emblem of South Carolina.

**yellow lead ore**, = wulfenite.

**yel|low|legs** (yel′ō legz′), *n.* either of two American shore birds with yellow legs, having a gray back marked with white and a white breast streaked with gray.

**yellow light**, a signal cautioning traffic to slow down, usually preceding a red light.

**yellow loosestrife**, a common loosestrife bearing clusters (racemes) of yellow flowers.

**yellow metal**, **1** gold. **2** a yellowish alloy containing copper (about 60 per cent) and zinc (about 40 per cent).

**Yellow New|town** (nü′toun′, nyü′-), = Albemarle pippin.

**yellow ocher**, a yellow variety of limonite mixed with clay, used as a pigment.

**yellow pages**, *U.S.* a telephone directory or a section of it, printed on pages of a yellow color, in which the names are classified according to types of business, services, and professions: *I opened the yellow pages and picked out the first restaurant listed* (New Yorker).

**yellow perch**, a North American perch having a golden yellow color and sides marked with several dark bars; ringed perch. It grows from 5 to 12 inches, weighing up to 4 pounds, and is much valued as a food and sport fish.

**yellow peril**, the alleged danger to the rest of the world, especially to Europe and America, from the growth and activities of Japan or China.

**yellow pine**, **1** any one of various American pines with yellow or yellowish wood. **2** the wood of any of these trees. **3** = tulip tree.

**yellow poplar**, = tulip tree.

**yellow puccoon**, = goldenseal.

**yellow race**, the Mongolian race.

**yellow rail**, a small, rare, yellowish rail of North America.

**yel|low|root** (yel′ō rüt′, -rů t′), *n.* = goldenseal.

**yel|lows** (yel′ōz), *n.pl.* (*often singular in use*). **1** *Botany.* any one of various unrelated diseases of plants in which the foliage turns yellow and growth is checked, as in peaches and cabbages. **2** jaundice, especially of horses and cattle. **3** *Obsolete.* jealousy.

**yellow sapphire**, = topaz.

**yel|low-shaft|ed flicker** (yel′ō shaf′tid; -shäf′-), a woodpecker of North America with yellow shafts in its wing and tail feathers; flicker; yellowhammer.

**yellow sponge**, a yellowish commercial sponge found especially in the warm waters off Florida, Cuba, and Haiti.

**yellow spot**, a yellowish depression on the retina, the region of most distinct vision.

**yellow streak**, **1** = cowardice. **2** an indication of cowardice.

**yel|low|tail** (yel′ō tāl′), *n., pl.* **-tails** or (*collectively*) **-tail**. **1** any one of various fishes with yellow tails, especially a game fish of the California coast and a snapper of the Atlantic coast of tropical America. **2** a large South African mackerel.

**yel|low-tailed** (yel′ō tāld′), *adj.* having the tail more or less yellow.

**yel|low|throat** (yel′ō thrōt′), *n.* any one of certain North American warblers, especially the Maryland yellowthroat, with olive-brown upper parts and yellow throat.

**yel|low-throat|ed vireo** (yel′ō thrō′tid), a North American vireo.

**yellow-throated warbler**, an American warbler with gray back, white belly, and yellow throat.

**yellow trefoil**, = black medic.

**yellow warbler**, a small American warbler; golden warbler; yellowbird. The male has yellow plumage, streaked with brown.

**yellow water lily**, any of various yellow-flowered aquatic plants, such as the water chinquapin and the spatterdock.

**yel|low|weed** (yel′ō wēd′), *n.* **1** the European ragwort. **2** = sneezeweed. **3** *U.S. Dialect.* any one of several coarse goldenrods. **4** *British Dialect.* weld.

**yel|low|wood** (yel′ō wůd′), *n.* **1** a tree of the pea family, bearing showy, white flowers; gopherwood. It is found in the southern United States. **2** its hard, yellow wood, which yields a clear yellow dye. **3** any one of several other trees yielding yellow wood or a yellow extract or dye, such as the Osage orange. **4** the wood of any of these trees.

**yel|low|y** (yel′ō ē), *adj.* = yellowish.

**yelp** (yelp), *n., v.* —*n.* a quick, sharp, shrill bark or cry of a dog or fox, especially a small or excited dog. [< verb]
—*v.i.* to give a quick, sharp, shrill bark or cry.
—*v.t.* to utter with a yelp. [Old English *gelpan,* or *gielpan* to boast] —**yelp′er**, *n.*

**Yem|e|ni** (yem′ə nē), *n., pl.* **-ni** or **-nis**, *adj.* = Yemenite.

**Yem|en|ite** (yem′ə nīt), *n., adj.* —*n.* a native or inhabitant of Yemen. —*adj.* of or having to do with Yemen or its people.

**yen**[1] (yen), *n., pl.* **yen**. **1** the unit of money of Japan, equal to 100 sen. **2** a former Japanese gold or silver coin. [< Japanese *yen* < Chinese *yüan* (literally) round object. See etym. of doublet **yuan**.]

**yen**[2] (yen), *n., v.,* **yenned, yen|ning**. *Informal.* —*n.* a sharp desire or hunger; urgent fancy: *a sudden yen to leave.* **SYN**: yearning.
—*v.i.* to have a yen; desire sharply or urgently.
**have a yen for**, to desire: *She had a yen for ice cream.*
[American English, perhaps < dialectal pronunciation of *yearn*]

**yen|ta** (yen′tə), *n. U.S. Slang.* a female gossip or busybody. [< Yiddish *yente* a plain woman, originally a woman's name]

**yeo.**, yeomanry.

**yeo|man** (yō′mən), *n., pl.* **-men**. **1** *U.S. Navy.* a petty officer who has charge of supplies and accounts and acts as a secretary or clerk. **2** *British.* a yeoman of the guard. **3** in Great Britain (chiefly historically): **a** a man who owned a small amount of land and ranked as a commoner; freeholder. A yeoman usually farmed the land himself. **b** a man who farms his own land, especially a man of respectable standing. **4** *Archaic.* **a** a servant or attendant of a lord or king. He was usually of superior grade, ranking between a sergeant and a groom, or a squire and a page. **b** an assistant to an official: *the sheriff's yeoman.* **5** *British.* a member of the yeomanry. [Middle English *yoman,* and *yeman;* origin uncertain. Compare Frisian *gāman* villager.]

**yeo|man|ette** (yō′mə net′), *n.* (formerly) a woman yeoman in the U.S. Naval Reserve.

**yeo|man|ly** (yō′mən lē), *adj., adv.* —*adj.* **1** having to do with a yeoman. **2** characteristic of a yeoman; sturdy; honest. **SYN**: dependable, trustworthy. **3** befitting a yeoman. **4** having the rank of a yeoman.
—*adv.* like a yeoman; bravely.

**yeoman of the guard**, a member of the bodyguard of the English sovereign, first appointed in 1485 by Henry VII and consisting of 100 men who still wear the uniform of the 1400's and whose duties are now purely ceremonial; beefeater.

**yeo|man|ry** (yō′mən rē), *n.* **1** a body of yeomen. **2** a British volunteer cavalry force organized for internal defense, incorporated in 1907 into the British Territorial Army.

**yeoman's** or **yeoman service**, good, efficient, or useful service, such as is rendered by a conscientious, unassuming servant or assistant; faithful support or assistance.

**yeo|wom|an** (yō′wům′ən), *n., pl.* **-wom|en**. a woman yeoman in the United States Navy.

**yep** (yep), *adv. U.S. Informal.* yes: *The only ethical thing to do was to return my salary. ... Yep, the whole estimated $200,000 salary* (Time). [alteration of *yes*]

**-yer**, *suffix.* the form of **-ier** after *w* or a vowel, as in *lawyer.*

**yer|ba maté** (yėr′bə), = maté. [< Spanish *yerba maté*]

**yerk** (yėrk), *n., v. Dialect.* —*n.* **1** a kick. **2** a jerk. **3** a sharp blow.
—*v.i.* **1** to draw stitches tight. **2** (of a whip) to crack. **3** to kick. **4** to spring. **5** to engage eagerly in some proceeding.
—*v.t.* **1** to bind. **2** to flog. **3** to jerk.

**Yerk|ish** (yėr′kish), *n.* an artificial language for communicating with chimpanzees, consisting of a number of geometric figures or lexigrams: *After five months of training Lana has mastered between 35 and 40 of the Yerkish symbols* (Science News). [< *Yerkes* Primate Research Center, Florida + *-ish*]

**yes** (yes), *adv., n., pl.* **yes|es**, *v.,* **yessed, yessing**. —*adv.* **1** a word used to show agreement, consent, or affirmation: *"Yes, five and two are seven," he said. Will you go? Yes.* **2** and what is more; in addition to that: *"Your work is good, yes, very good," said the teacher. The boy learned to endure—yes, even to enjoy—the hardships of a sailor's life.*
—*n.* **1** an answer that agrees, consents, or affirms: *You have my yes to that.* **SYN**: assent, affirmation, concurrence. **2** a vote for; person voting in favor of something: *The yesses won.*
—*v.i., v.t.* to say yes; approve of.
[Old English *gīse,* and *gēse* < *gēa, gīe* so, yea + *sī* be it]
▶ **Yes** and **no**, as adverbs, may modify a sentence (*Yes, you're right*) or may have the value of a coordinate clause (*No; but you should have told me*) or may stand as complete sentences (*"Do you really intend to go with him?" "Yes."*).

**ye'se** (yēs), *Scottish.* ye (you) shall.

**ye|shi|va** or **ye|shi|vah** (yə shē′və), *n., pl.* **ye-shi|vas, ye|shi|voth** (ye′shē vōt′). **1** a Jewish school for higher education, often a rabbinical seminary. **2** a Jewish elementary or high school in which both religious and secular subjects are taught. [< Hebrew *yeshībah* (literally) a sitting]

**yes-man** or **yes|man** (yes′man′), *n., pl.* **-men**. *Informal.* a person who habitually agrees with those of higher rank or greater authority than himself, without criticism: *You do not get good science as soon as you have reduced the scientists to yes-men* (Bulletin of Atomic Scientists).

**yes|ter** (yes′tər), *adj., adv.* —*adj. Archaic or Poetic.* of or belonging to yesterday.
—*adv. Obsolete.* yesterday.
[abstracted from *yesterday*]

**yester-**, *combining form.* **1** the ____ of the day before the present day: *Yestereve = yesterday evening.* **2** last; previous: *Yesteryear = last year.* [< *yester*]

**yes|ter|day** (yes′tər dē, -dā), *n., adv., adj.* —*n.* **1** the day before today: *Yesterday was cold and rainy.* **2** *Figurative.* the recent past; period not very long past: *We are often amused by fashions of yesterday.*
—*adv.* **1** on the day before today: *It rained yesterday.* **2** *Figurative.* a short time ago; only lately; recently.
—*adj. Obsolete.* belonging to yesterday or the immediate past; very recent.
[Old English *geostran dæg* < *geostra* of yesterday, probably (literally) the next day + *dæg* day]

**yes|ter|eve** (yes′tər ēv′), *n., adv. Archaic.* yesterday evening.

**yes|ter|eve|ning** (yes′tər ēv′ning), *n., adv. Archaic.* yesterday evening.

**yes|ter|morn** (yes′tər môrn′), *n., adv. Archaic.* yesterday morning.

**yes|ter|morn|ing** (yes′tər môr′ning), *n., adv. Archaic.* yesterday morning.

**yes|ter|night** (yes′tər nīt′), *n., adv. Archaic.* last night; the night before today: *I did yesternight dream a dreadful dream* (S. M. Ponniah).

**yes|ter|noon** (yes′tər nün′), *adv., n. Archaic.* yesterday noon.

**yes|ter|week** (yes′tər wēk′), *adv., n. Archaic.* last week.

**yes|ter|year** (yes′tər yir′), *n., adv. Archaic.* last year; the year before this.
**of yesteryear**, of yore. See under **yore**, *n.*

**yes|treen** (yes′trēn′), *n., adv. Scottish.* yesterday evening. [contraction of Scottish *yistrewin* < *yistir* yester + *ewin* evening]

**yet** (yet), *adv., conj.* —*adv.* **1** up to the present time; thus far; hitherto: *The work is not yet finished. The most important event that had yet occurred* (Henry T. Buckle). **2** at this time; so soon as this; now: *Don't go yet.* **3** at that time; then: *It was not yet dark.* **4** up to and at the present time; even now; still: *She is talking yet. It is yet*

*light.* **5** at some time in the future; before all is over or done; eventually; ultimately: *I may yet get rich. The thief will be caught yet. We may go there yet.* **6** in addition or continuation; also; again: *Yet once more I forbid you to go.* **7** as much as; even; moreover: *He won't do it for you nor yet for me.* **8** still; even; even more (used to strengthen comparatives): *The king spoke yet more harshly.* **9** in spite of that; nevertheless; however; but: *He was poor, yet honest. The story was strange, yet true.*
— ***conj.*** nevertheless; however; but: *The work is good, yet it could be better.* **SYN**: although.
**as yet**, up to this time; so far: *There were … extensions of this practice as yet but little noticed* (John P. Mahaffy).
[Old English *gēt,* or *gīet*]
► **Yet** is chiefly used as an adverb: *The books haven't come yet.* In rather formal English it is also used as a coordinating conjunction, equivalent to *but: His speech was almost unintelligible, yet for some unknown reason I enjoyed it.*

**Ye|ti** or **ye|ti** (ye′tē), *n., pl.* **-ti**. = Abominable Snowman: *For 60 years there have been stories about the Yeti, the hairy wild men who live in the eternal snows of the Himalayas* (Sunday Times). [< a Tibetan word]

**yeuk** or **yewk** (yük), *v.i., n. Scottish.* itch. [alteration of Middle English *yike,* Old English *gicce* itch]

**yeuk|y** or **yewk|y** (yü′kē), *adj. Scottish.* itchy.

**yew** (yü), *n.* **1** an evergreen tree native to Europe and Asia. Some kinds of yew are now widely grown in the United States as shrubs. The English yew has heavy, elastic wood, dense, dark-green foliage, and usually bright red fruit that look like berries. **2** the tough, elastic wood of any of these trees, especially as the material of bows for archers. Yew is also polished and made into tables. **3** an archer's bow made of this. [Old English *īw,* and *ēow*]

**yé-yé** (ye′ye′), *adj. Slang.* of or having to do with a style of teen-age dress, such as miniskirts and ankle-high boots, associated with discothèques, and rock'n'roll dancing, especially in the 1960's: *yé-yé fashions, yé-yé girls.* [< French Slang *yé-yé* < English *yeah, yeah,* refrain used by rock'n'roll singing groups]

**Yez|i|di** (yez′ə dē), *n., pl.* **-di** or **-dis**. a member of a religious sect in Kurdistan, Armenia, and the Caucasus, who believes in a Supreme God, but reveres the Devil as well: *He calls attention to the 70,000 devil worshippers still on earth, the heretical Moslem sect of Yezidi* (Newsweek). Also, **Yazidi**.

**Y|gerne** (i gern′), *n.* = Igraine.

**Ygg|dra|sil** or **Yg|dra|sil** (ig′drə sil), *n. Norse Mythology.* the ash tree whose branches and roots bind together earth, heaven, and hell. Also, **Igdrasil, Iggdrasil**. [< Old Icelandic (*askr*) *yggdrasils,* or *yggdrasill* (ash tree) of Yggdrasil < *yggr* a name of Odin, meaning "terrible, frightful"]

**YHWH** or **YHVH** (no periods), the Tetragrammaton.

**Yid|dish** (yid′ish), *n., adj.* — ***n.*** a language which developed from a dialect of German. Yiddish contains many Hebrew and Slavic words and is written in Hebrew characters. It is spoken mainly by Jews of eastern and central Europe and their descendants.
— ***adj.*** having to do with this language.
[< Yiddish *yidish* (*daytsh*) Jewish (German) < Middle High German *jüdisch* (*diutsch*)]

**Yid|dish|ism** (yid′i shiz əm), *n.* **1** devotion to the Yiddish language and literature. **2** a Yiddish word, phrase, or meaning: *Among Gentiles, it is becoming quite in to pepper one's talk with a Yiddishism or two ("what chutzpah!")* (Time).

**Yid|dish|ist** (yid′i shist), *n.* a person who is devoted to the Yiddish language and literature.

**yield** (yēld), *v., n.* — ***v.t.*** **1a** to produce; bear: *This land yields good crops. Mines yield ores.* **SYN**: furnish, supply. **b** to give in return; bring in: *an investment which yielded a large profit.* **c** to fill a need; furnish; afford: *The narrow valley … yielded fresh pasturage* (Washington Irving). **2** to give; grant: *to yield a point in an argument. Her mother yielded her consent to the plan.* **3** to give up; surrender: *to yield oneself up to the mercy of the enemy.* **4** *Archaic.* to pay; reward; remunerate.
— ***v.i.*** **1** to bear produce; be productive. **2** to give up; surrender: *The enemy yielded to our soldiers. The night has yielded to the morn* (Scott). **3** to give way: *The door yielded to his push. Theory should yield to fact* (Henry T. Buckle). **4** to give place: *We yield to nobody in love of freedom.*
— ***n.*** the amount produced; product: *This year's yield from the silver mine was very large.* **SYN**: harvest. See syn. under **crop**.
[Old English *geldan* or *gieldan* to pay] — **yield′er**, *n.*
— ***Syn.*** *v.i.* **2 Yield, submit** mean give in before a stronger force. **Yield** implies giving up a contest of any sort under pressure: *to yield to persuasive arguments.* **Submit** implies giving up all resistance and passively accepting defeat: *to submit to overwhelming forces, to submit to the inevitable.*

**yield|a|ble** (yēl′də bəl), *adj.* **1** that can be yielded. **2** *Obsolete.* inclined to yield; compliant.

**yield|ing** (yēl′ding), *adj.* **1** not resisting; submissive; compliant: *Mother has a yielding nature with her children.* **2** not stiff or rigid; easily bent, twisted, or shaped; flexible. — **yield′ing|ly**, *adv.*

**YIG** (yig), *n.* a synthetic garnet of yttrium and iron oxide having versatile magnetic properties, used especially in laser modulation. [< *Y*(ttrium) *I*(ron) *G*(arnet)]

**yill** (yil), *n. Scottish.* ale. [variant of *ale*]

**yin**[1] (yin), *n.* the passive principle or element in Chinese dualistic philosophy, representing the female qualities of darkness and cold, in constant interaction with its opposing principle (yang): *Light gives way to darkness, reason to feeling, yang to yin, the head to the heart* (Esquire). [< Chinese (Peking) *yin*]

**yin**[2] (yin), *n. Scottish.* one. [variant of *one*]

**yip** (yip), *v.,* **yipped, yip|ping**, *n. Informal.* — ***v.i.*** to bark briskly; yelp (used especially of dogs).
— ***n.*** a sharp barking sound.
[American English; imitative]

**yip|pee** (yip′ē), *interj.* a shout of joy: *The boss left this morning for Rotterdam. Marvellous. Field clear. Long lunch. Home. Yippee!* (London Times).

**Yip|pie** or **yip|pie** (yip′ē), *n.* a member of the Youth International Party, an organization of politically active hippies.

**yird** (yėrd), *n. Scottish.* earth. [variant of *earth*]

**yirr** (yėr), *n., v.i. Scottish.* snarl or growl. [imitative]

**Yiz|kor** (yiz′kər, yis′-), *n.* the Jewish memorial service for the dead, held in the synagogue on Yom Kippur, on the eighth day of Sukkoth, on the eighth day of Passover, and on the second day of Shabuoth. [< Hebrew *yizkōr* (literally) remember]

**-yl**, *combining form. Chemistry.* a radical composed of two or more elements (with one usually designated by the base word) acting like a simple element and forming the foundation of a series of compounds, as in *alkyl, acetyl, carbonyl.* [< French *-yle* < Greek *hȳlē* wood; stuff, matter]

**y|lang-y|lang** (ē′läng ē′läng), *n.* **1** a tree of the Philippines, Java, and other areas of eastern Asia, having fragrant, drooping, greenish-yellow flowers. **2** a fragrant oil or perfume obtained from its flowers. Also, **ilang-ilang**. [< Tagalog *ilang-ilang*]

**y|lem** (ī′ləm), *n.* a chaotic, dense, very hot mass of matter, the supposed original substance of the universe, believed to have consisted only of protons, neutrons, and electrons. [Middle English *ylem,* ultimately < Greek *hȳlē* substance, matter]

**Y-lev|el** (wī′lev′əl), *n.* a form of surveyor's level in which the telescope rests on two forked supports called Y's.

**Y.M.**, *Informal.* Young Men's Christian Association.

**Y.M.C.A.** or **YMCA** (no periods), Young Men's Christian Association (an organization for promoting the spiritual, intellectual, physical, and social well-being of young men, founded in London in 1844 by George Williams, 1821-1905).

**Y.M.Cath.A.**, Young Men's Catholic Association.

**Y.M.H.A.** or **YMHA** (no periods), Young Men's Hebrew Association (an organization for the moral, mental, physical, and social improvement of Jewish young men, founded in Baltimore in 1854).

**Y|mir** (ē′mir), *n. Norse Mythology.* a giant, formed from blocks of ice and sparks of fire, from whose body the gods made the universe. [< Old Icelandic *Ymir* (literally) noisemaker. Compare Old Icelandic *ymja* make a noise.]

**yob** (yob), *n. British Slang.* a coarse young man; boor. [reverse spelling of *boy*]

**yoc|co** (yok′ō), *n.* **1** a South American and African shrub, the bark of which is rich in caffeine, used to make a stimulating, nonintoxicating drink. **2** the drink made from this shrub: *Yocco, an African jungle drink, cuts hunger and fatigue* (Science News Letter). [< a native word]

**yock** (yok), *n., v. Slang.* — ***n.*** **1** a deep, hearty laugh: *Her laugh is one of those welcome, old-fashioned yocks* (Newsweek). **2** a joke or gag.
— ***v.i., v.t.*** to laugh or cause to laugh heartily: *Phil Napoleon's minions are yocking it up here* (New Yorker). Also, **yak, yuk**. [imitative]

**yod** (yōd, yůd), *n.* the tenth letter of the Hebrew alphabet. [< Hebrew *yōdh* (literally) hand]

**yo|del** (yō′dəl), *v.,* **-deled, -del|ing** or **-delled, -del|ling**, *n.* — ***v.t., v.i.*** to sing (a melody) with frequent, abrupt changes from the ordinary voice to a forced shrill voice and back again. Yodeling is typical for songs of mountaineers of Switzerland and the Tirol.
— ***n.*** an act or sound of yodeling.
[< German *jodeln* < *jo,* the name of a syllable used in the singing] — **yo′del|er, yo′del|ler**, *n.*

**yo|dle** (yō′dəl), *v.t., v.i.,* **-dled, -dling**, *n.* = yodel. — **yo′dler**, *n.*

**yo|ga** or **Yo|ga** (yō′gə), *n.* **1** a system of Hindu religious philosophy that requires intense mental and physical discipline as a means of attaining union with the universal spirit. **2** a system of physical exercises and positions used in yoga. [< Hindustani *yoga* < Sanskrit, union]

***yogh** (yōH), *n.* a letter of the Middle English alphabet, used to represent both a velar and a palatal fricative. [Middle English *yogh,* Old English *ēoh*]

***yogh**

| 3 | cniȝt=knight<br>ȝer=year |
|---|---|

**yo|ghourt** or **yo|ghurt** (yō′gərt), *n.* = yogurt.

**yo|gi** (yō′gē), *n., pl.* **-gis**. a person who practices or follows yoga. [< Hindustani *yogī* < Sanskrit *yogin* (nominative *yogī*) < *yoga* yoga]

**yo|gic** (yō′gik), *adj.* of or having to do with yogis or yoga: *yogic exercises.*

**yo|gin** (yō′gin), *n.* = yogi.

**yo|gism** (yō′giz əm), *n.* the doctrine or practice of the yogis.

**yo|gurt** (yō′gərt), *n.* a thickened, slightly fermented liquid food made from milk acted upon by bacteria. Yogurt was originally made in Turkey and other Oriental countries, and is now prepared commercially and sold widely in the United States and elsewhere. Also, **yoghourt, yoghurt, yohourt**. [< Turkish *yoğurt*]

**yo-heave-ho** (yō′hēv′hō′), *interj.* an exclamation used by sailors in pulling or lifting together, as when hauling at a rope or a capstan, or heaving an anchor up.

**yo|him|bé** (yō him′bā), *n.* a tropical African tree of the madder family, the bark of which is used to make yohimbine. [< a West African native word]

**yo|him|be|ho|a** (yō him′bā hō′ə), *n.* = yohimbé.

**yo|him|bine** (yō him′bēn, -bin), *n.* an alkaloid derived from the bark of the yohimbé tree, used as an aphrodisiac and as a stimulant in treating difficult breathing associated with certain heart conditions. *Formula:* $C_{21}H_{26}N_2O_3$

**yo-ho** (yō hō′), *interj., n., v.,* **-hoed, -ho|ing**.
— ***interj.*** a call or shout used especially by sailors to attract attention or accompany effort.
— ***n.*** a call or shout of "yo-ho."
— ***v.i.*** to shout "yo-ho": *the men … yo-hoing at their work* (Robert Louis Stevenson).

**yoh|ourt** (yō′ůrt), *n.* = yogurt.

**yoicks** (yoiks), *interj. Especially British.* a cry used to urge on the hounds in fox-hunting. [perhaps alteration of earlier *hoicks,* also *hoik,* variant of *hike*]

***yoke**
definition 1

***yoke** (yōk), *n., v.,* **yoked, yok|ing**. — ***n.*** **1** a wooden frame to fasten two oxen or other draft animals together for drawing a plow or vehicle. It usually consists of a crosspiece fitted with hoops (oxbow) which are placed around the animals' necks. **2** a pair of animals that are fastened together with a yoke (after a numeral the plural is usually *yoke*): *two yoke of oxen. The plow was drawn by a yoke of oxen.* **3** any frame connecting two other parts, such as a frame fitted to the neck and shoulders of a person for carrying a pair of pails or baskets: *The man carried two buckets on a yoke, one at each end.* **4** *Figurative.* **a** something that joins or unites; bond; tie: *the yoke of marriage.* **b** something that holds people in slavery or submission: *Throw off your yoke and be free.* **c** rule; dominion: *a country un-*

**Pronunciation Key:** hat, āge, cãre, fär; let, ēqual, tėrm; it, īce; hot, ōpen, ôrder; oil, out; cup, půt, rüle; child; long; thin; ᴛʜen; zh, measure; ə represents **a** in about, **e** in taken, **i** in pencil, **o** in lemon, **u** in circus.

*der the yoke of a dictator. Slaves are under the yoke of their masters.* **5** a part of a garment fitting the neck and shoulders closely. **6** a top piece to a skirt, fitting the hips. **7** a clamp which holds two parts firmly in place; double clamp. **8** a modified crosshead used instead of a connecting rod between the piston and crankshaft in certain small engines. **9** a crossbar at the top of the rudder of a boat, and having two lines or ropes attached for steering. **10** a crossbar connecting the tongue of a wagon, carriage, or other vehicle, to the collars, as of two horses or mules. **11** among the ancient Romans and others: **a** a contrivance similar to a yoke for oxen, placed on the neck of a captive. **b** a symbol of this consisting of two upright spears with a third placed across them, under which captives were forced to walk. **12** a steering column in certain aircraft, consisting of a wheel or the like mounted at the upper end of a lever, for controlling the aircraft in flight.

—*v.t.* **1** to put a yoke on; fasten with a yoke: *The farmer yoked the oxen before hitching them to the wagon.* **2** to harness or fasten a work animal or animals to: *The farmer yoked his plow.* **3** *Figurative.* to join; unite: *They are yoked in marriage.*

—*v.i.* to join; be or become united: *The care That yokes with empire* (Tennyson).

[Old English *geoc*]

**yoke|fel|low** (yōk′fel′ō), *n.* **1** a person associated with another in a task; fellow worker; partner. SYN: colleague. **2** a person joined in marriage to another; husband or wife; spouse. SYN: consort.

**yo|kel** (yō′kəl), *n.* a country fellow; bumpkin; rustic: *We don't want television cameras showing some yokel in the legislature reading a newspaper and smoking a cigar with his feet on a desk* (Wall Street Journal). [origin uncertain. Compare German *Jokel* a disparaging name for a farmer; (diminutive) < *Jakob* Jacob.]

**yo|kel|ish** (yō′kə lish), *adj.* characteristic of a yokel: *The Civil War had such a strangely civilian look—the shoddy, ill-matched uniforms; the pathetic, yokelish aspect of the fighting men* (New Yorker).

**yo|kel|ry** (yō′kəl rē), *n.* yokels as a group: *It seems a pity to waste so much elegant wit on so sluggish and easy a mark as the local yokelry* (Canadian Saturday Night).

**yoke|mate** (yōk′māt′), *n.* = yokefellow.

**Yo|kuts** (yō′kuts), *n.* a North American Indian linguistic family comprising a number of small tribes in California.

**yol|dring** (yol′dring, yōl′-; -drin), *n. Scottish.* the yellowhammer of Europe. [variant of obsolete *yowlring,* reduction of *yowlow* yellow + *ring*[1]]

**yolk**[1] (yōk, yōlk), *n.* **1** the yellow internal part of an egg of a bird or reptile, surrounded by the albumen or white, and serving as nourishment for the young before it is hatched; yellow. See picture under **egg**[1]. **2** the corresponding part in any animal ovum or egg cell, which serves for the nutrition of the embryo, together with the protoplasmic substances from which the embryo is developed. [Old English *geolca, geoloca* < *geolu* yellow]

**yolk**[2] (yōk, yōlk), *n.* the fat or grease in sheep's wool, secreted by the skin. [earlier *yoak,* unrecorded Old English *eowoca,* implied in *eowocig* yolky; spelling influenced by *yolk*[1]]

**yolked** (yōkt), *adj.* containing a yolk or yolks: *a double-yolked egg.*

**yolk sac,** a membranous sac filled with yolk, attached to and providing food for the embryo. In cephalopods and lower vertebrates, it is the only source of food for the embryo, for these animals do not develop a placenta.

**yolk stalk,** a narrow, ductlike part that unites the yolk sac to the middle of the embryo's digestive tract; vitelline duct.

**yolk|y** (yō′kē, yōl′kē), *adj.,* **yolk|i|er, yolk|i|est.** **1** resembling yolk. **2** consisting of yolk. **3** *British Dialect.* greasy or sticky, as unwashed wool.

**Yom Kip|pur** (yom kip′ər; yōm′ ki pür′), a Jewish fast day of atonement for sins; Day of Atonement, the most solemn day in the Jewish calendar, observed with complete fasting for 24 hours. It occurs ten days after Rosh Hashanah, the Jewish New Year, on the tenth day of Tishri (corresponding to September-October). [< Hebrew *yōm kippūr* day of atonement]

**yon** (yon), *adj., adv., pron.* —**adj., adv.** *Archaic.* yonder.

—*pron. Obsolete.* that or those (usually denoting an object or objects pointed out, at a distance but within view).

[Old English *geon,* adjective, that (over there)]

**yond** (yond), *adj., adv. Archaic.* yonder. [Old English *geondan,* preposition, adverb, throughout, yonder]

**yon|der** (yon′dər), *adv., adj.* —**adv.** within sight, but not near; over there: *Look at that wild duck yonder.*

—**adj.** **1** situated over there; being within sight, but not near: *On yonder hill stands a ruined castle.* **2** farther; more distant; other: *There is snow on the yonder side of the mountains.*

[Middle English *yonder.* See related etym. at **yon, yond.**]

**yo|ni** (yō′nē), *n.* a Hindu figure or symbol of the female genitals, representing the generative principle, used in the worship of Shakti. [< Sanskrit *yoni*]

**yoo-hoo** (yü′hü′), *interj., v.,* **-hooed, -hoo|ing.**

—*interj.* a call or shout used to attract someone's attention. —*v.i.* to shout yoo-hoo: *She yoo-hooed from her window to the deliveryman.*

**yop|on** (yop′ən), *n.* = yaupon.

**yor|dim** (yôr dēm′), *n.pl. Hebrew.* **1** Jewish emigrants from Israel: *Those who stay call those who leave yordim ... and look down on them as deserters* (Time). **2** (literally) those who descend. See also **olim.**

**yore** (yôr, yōr), *n., adv.* —*n.* **of yore, a** of time past; of long ago; former: *In days of yore how fortunately fared The Minstrel!* (Wordsworth). *He spoke of the trolley parties and picnics of yore* (James T. Farrell). **b** in time past; of old; formerly: *Here haunted of yore the fabulous Dragon of Wantley* (Scott).

—**adv.** *Obsolete.* long ago; years ago.

[Old English *gēara,* adverb; (originally) genitive plural of *gēar* year]

**york** (yôrk), *v.t. Cricket.* **1** to bowl (a batsman) out: *Soon Watson was yorked* (London Times). **2** to strike (the wicket) with a yorker. [back formation < *yorker*]

**York** (yôrk), *n.* the English royal house, a branch of the Plantagenets, descended from Richard, Duke of York, which reigned from 1461 to 1485. Its emblem was a white rose. The three kings of this house were Edward IV, Edward V, and Richard III.

**york|er** (yôr′kər), *n. Cricket.* a bowled ball that strikes the ground just barely in front of the bat. [probably < *York* + *-er*[2] (perhaps because the county had championship teams)]

**York Imperial,** a large yellow apple with red stripes, growing in mild climates.

**York|ist** (yôr′kist), *n., adj.* —*n.* a supporter or member of the royal house of York, especially in opposition to the Lancastrians in the Wars of the Roses. —**adj.** **1** of or having to do with the royal house of York. **2** of or having to do with the party that fought against the Lancastrians.

**York Rite,** one of the two branches of advanced Freemasonry.

**Yorks** (no period), Yorkshire.

**York|shire** (yôrk′shir, -shər), *n.* any one of a breed of white hogs with erect ears developed in the early 1800's in Yorkshire, England. [< *Yorkshire,* a county in England]

**York|shire|man** (yôrk′shir mən, -shər-), *n., pl.* **-men.** a native or resident of Yorkshire, England.

**Yorkshire pudding,** a batter cake made of milk, flour, egg, and salt, baked in the drippings of, and served with, roast beef.

**Yorkshire terrier,** any one of an English breed of small, shaggy dogs with a steel-blue coat, weighing four to eight pounds.

**yorsh** (yôrsh), *n. Russian.* a drink that is a mixture of vodka and beer.

**Yo|ru|ba** (yō′rù bä), *n., pl.* **-bas** or **-ba.** **1** a member of a large linguistic group of coastal West Africa. **2** the Sudanic language of this group.

**Yo|ru|ban** (yō′rù bən), *adj.* of or having to do with the Yoruba people or language.

**you** (yü; *unstressed* yu̇, yə), *pron. pl. or sing., poss.* **your** or **yours,** *obj.* **you.** **1** the person or persons spoken to: *Are you ready? Then you may go.* **2** one; anybody: *You never can tell. You push this button to turn on the light.* [Old English *ēow,* dative and accusative of *gē* ye[1]]

► **You** is used as an indefinite pronoun in informal English: *It's a good book, if you like detective stories.* In formal English *one* is more usual, though the prejudice against *you* has all but disappeared.

► **you all.** In Southern American *you all,* contracted to *y'all,* is frequently used as the plural of *you,* as in some other regions *yous* or *youse* is used. It is also used when addressing one person, usually regarded as one of a group, such as a family.

**you'd** (yüd; *unstressed* yu̇d, yəd), **1** you had. **2** you would.

**you'll** (yül; *unstressed* yu̇l, yəl), **1** you will. **2** you shall.

**young** (yung), *adj.,* **young|er** (yung′gər), **young|est** (yung′gist), *n.* —**adj.** **1** in the early part of life or growth; not old: *A puppy is a young dog.* SYN: immature, undeveloped. **2** having the looks, freshness, vigor, or other qualities of youth or a young person: *She looks and acts young for her age.* **3** of, having to do with, or belonging to youth; early: *In his young days he was very hot-tempered.* **4** not as old as another or the other; junior (used especially to distinguish the younger of two persons in the same family having the same name or title): *After graduating young Mr. Jones worked for his father.* **5** *Figurative.* **a** being in its early stage; not far advanced; lately begun, formed, introduced, or brought into use; recent; new: *a young firm, a young country. The night was still young when they left the party.* **b** without much experience or practice; green; raw: *I was too young in the trade to be successful.* **6** representing or favoring new and usually progressive or radical policies, tendencies, or the like. **7** *Physical Geography.* youthful.

—*n.* young animals, collectively; offspring: *An animal will fight to protect its young.*

**the young,** young people, collectively: *I have always lived with people older than myself, ... though it is very nice to be with the young* (Annie F. Hector).

**with young,** pregnant: *Goats grow fat when they are with young* (Edward Topsell).

[Old English *geong*] —**young′ness,** *n.*

—*Syn. adj.* **1, 3 Young, youthful, juvenile** mean of or like persons between childhood and adulthood. **Young,** the general term, is most often used to refer directly to a person's age: *They are too young to marry.* **Youthful** emphasizes having the qualities of a young person, especially the more appealing ones such as freshness, vitality, and optimism: *With youthful earnestness, the students debated the problems of the world.* **Juvenile** emphasizes immaturity: *That book is too juvenile for a high-school senior.*

**young|ber|ry** (yung′ber′ē, -bər-), *n., pl.* **-ries.** the large, sweet, purplish-black fruit of a trailing bramble, a hybrid between a blackberry and a dewberry, grown largely in the southwestern United States. [< B. M. *Young,* an American fruit grower]

**young blood, 1** young people. **2** *Figurative.* youthful vigor, energy, or enthusiasm.

**Young|er Edda** (yung′gər), a collection of old Norse legends, poems, and rules for writing poetry, written in the first half of the 1200's.

**young-eyed** (yung′īd′), *adj.* **1** having the outlook of one who is young; not cynical through age or experience. **2** having the bright or lively eyes of a young person.

**young|ish** (yung′ish), *adj.* rather young.

**young|ling** (yung′ling), *n., adj.* —*n.* **1** a young person, animal, or plant. **2** *Obsolete.* a novice; beginner.

—**adj.** young; youthful.

[Old English *geongling* < *geong* young + *-ling*]

**young man, 1** a man who is young or in early manhood. **2** a lover or fiancé.

**Young Men's Christian Association,** = Y.M.C.A.

**Young Men's Hebrew Association,** = Y.M.H.A.

**Young's modulus** (yungz), *Physics.* a measure of the rigidity or firmness of a material, defined as the ratio, within the elastic limit, of the stress in the material to the corresponding strain: *Silica glass lacks stiffness; in technical terms, silica glass has quite a low Young's modulus* (Scientific American). [< Thomas *Young,* 1773-1829, an English physicist]

**young|ster** (yung′stər), *n.* **1a** a person who is no longer an infant but not yet at the age of puberty; child: *a toy certain to please any youngster. He is a lively youngster.* **b** a person who is not yet an adult; one who is, or is viewed as being, still a youth; young person: *The old farmer was as spry as a youngster.* **2** *Figurative: Alberta is one of the youngsters of the Canadian family—it has been a province only since 1905* (Newsweek). **3** a young animal. **4** *U.S.* a midshipman in the second year at the United States Naval Academy. **5** *British.* a midshipman in grade less than four years.

**Young Turks, 1** the members of a group or party impatient with the existing organization and wishing to reform it: *I've heard some of the Young Turks on your editorial staff talk that way* (Esquire). **2** a reformist body of relatively young army officers, government functionaries, and intellectuals, that originated in Turkey in the 1800's. **3** the political group that grew out of this, active just before and during World War I, by which in large part Kemal Ataturk was enabled to seize the reins of power in Turkey.

**Young Women's Christian Association,** = Y.W.C.A.

**Young Women's Hebrew Association,** = Y.W.H.A.

**youn|ker** (yung′kər), *n.* **1** *Archaic or Informal.* a young fellow; youngster. **2** *Obsolete.* a young nobleman or gentleman. [< Middle Dutch *jonckher,* or *jonchere* < *jonc* young + *hēre* lord, master]

**your** (yu̇r; *unstressed* yər), *adj. possessive form of* **you.** **1** of or belonging to you: *Wash your* *hands.* **2** having to do with you: *We enjoyed your visit.* **3** that you know; well-known; that you speak of; that is spoken of: *your real lover of music, your average voter.* **4** *Your* is used as part of some titles: *Your Lordship, Your Highness, Your Honor, Mayor Jones. Abbr:* yr. [Old English *ēower,* genitive of *gē* ye[1]]

**you're** (yůr; *unstressed* yər), you are.

**yourn** (yůrn), *pron. Substandard or Dialect.* yours.

**yours** (yůrz), *pron. sing. and pl., possessive case of* **you**. **1** the one or ones belonging to or having to do with you: *This pencil is yours. My hands are clean; yours are dirty. I like ours better than yours.* **2** at your service: *I am yours to command.* **3** *Yours* is used at the end of a letter with some other word: *Sincerely yours.*

**of yours,** belonging to or having to do with you: *Is he a friend of yours?*

**your|self** (yůr self′, yər-), *pron., pl.* **-selves**. **1** the emphatic form of **you**: *You yourself know the story is not true.* **2** the reflexive form of **you**: *You will hurt yourself. Ask yourself what you really want. Try to do it by yourself.* **3** your real or true self: *You aren't yourself today.*

**your|selves** (yůr selvz′, yər-), *pron.* plural of **yourself**.

**yours truly,** **1** a phrase used at the end of a letter, before the signature. **2** *Informal.* I; me: *Yours truly, sir, has an eye for a ... fine horse* (Wilkie Collins).

**yous** or **youse** (yüz), *pron. Substandard or Dialect.* you (usually used in addressing two or more people).

**youth** (yüth), *n., pl.* **youths** (yüths, yüᴛʜz) or (*collectively*) **youth**. **1** the fact or quality of being young; youngness: *He has the vigor of youth. If I had youth and strength* (Edmund Burke). **2** the appearance, freshness or vigor, rashness, or other quality characteristic of the young: *She keeps her youth well.* **3** the time when one is young; early part of life. **4** the time between childhood and manhood or womanhood; period between puberty and maturity; adolescence. **SYN**: teens. **5** *Figurative.* the first or early stage of anything; early period of growth or development: *Many of our beliefs go back to the youth of this country.* **6** a young man between boyhood and adulthood. **SYN**: lad, stripling. **7** any young person or persons (used without article): *Almost everything that is great has been done by youth* (Benjamin Disraeli). **8** (*plural in use*) young people, collectively: *Now all the youth of England are on fire* (Shakespeare). [Old English *geoguth*]

**youth-and-old-age** (yüth′ən ōld′āj′), *n.* a zinnia that grows as high as three feet.

**youth|en** (yü′thən), *v.t.* to make youthful; impart a youthful appearance to: *No dress youthens a girl so much as white* (Evening Star). **—*v.i.*** to become youthful; acquire youthful qualities: *You will always be forty to strangers perhaps: and youthen as you get to know them* (C. H. Sorley).

**youth|ful** (yüth′fəl), *adj.* **1** young: *a youthful person.* **SYN**: immature. See syn. under **young**. **2** of youth; suitable for young people: *youthful enthusiasm, youthful pleasures.* **3** having the looks or qualities of youth; fresh and vigorous: *The old man had a very gay and youthful spirit.* **SYN**: lively. **4** *Figurative.* early; new. **5** *Physical Geography.* having eroded or been eroded for a relatively short time. **—youth′ful|ness,** *n.*

**youth|ful|ly** (yüth′fə lē), *adv.* in a youthful manner: *Your attire ... not youthfully wanton* (Samuel Richardson).

**youth hostel,** a supervised lodging place for young people on bicycle trips, hikes, and other outings; hostel.

**you've** (yüv; *unstressed* yův, yəv), you have.

**yow**[1] (you), *interj.* **1** an exclamation of vague meaning. **2** an imitation of the yelp or bark of a dog, or the meow of a cat.

**yow**[2] (yō, you), *n. Obsolete.* ewe.

**yowl** (youl), *n., v.* **—*n.*** a long, distressful, or dismal cry; howl.
**—*v.i., v.t.*** to howl: *That dog is always yowling.* [Middle English *yowlen;* imitative]

**yowl|er** (you′lər), *n.* a person or thing that yowls: *There are not many good girl singers these days, although there are plenty of echo chamber yowlers* (Time).

**yo|yo** or **yo-yo** (yō′yō), *n., pl.* **-yos**, *v.,* **-yoed**, **-yo|ing**. **—*n.*** **1** a small toy consisting of a deeply grooved disk which is spun out and reeled in by an attached string. **2** **Yo-yo**, a trademark for this toy. **3** *Aerospace.* a wide-swinging orbit around the earth by an artificial satellite. **4** *U.S. Slang.* a stupid person; jerk: *A yoyo is a gullible customer who can be sold second-hand goods as new* (New York Times).
**—*v.i.*** **1** to go back and forth, as if attached to a string. **2** *Figurative.* to waver in mind or opinion, especially from one point of view to the other: *There is plenty of room for debate on this point, because the Supreme Court has yoyoed on the issue of the right to travel* (New York Times). [American English; origin uncertain]

**y|per|ite** (ē′pə rīt), *n.* = mustard gas. [< French *ypérite* < *Ypres,* a town in Belgium, near where it was used in World War I + *-ite* -ite[1]]

**Y potential,** *Electricity.* the difference between the potential at a terminal and that at the neutral point in an armature activated by a three-phase alternating current.

**Y.P.S.C.E.,** Young People's Society of Christian Endeavor.

**Y|quem** (ē kem′), *n.* a kind of sauterne, considered by many to be the finest of all sauternes. [< French (*Château*) *Yquem* (originally) place where it is made]

**yr.,** **1** year or years. **2** younger. **3** your.

**yrs.,** **1** years. **2** yours.

**Y|seult** (i sült′), *n.* = Iseult.

**Yt** (no period), yttrium (chemical element).

**Y.T.,** Yukon Territory.

**Y-Teen** (wī′tēn′), *n.* a member of the Y.W.C.A. between the ages of 12 and 17.

**Y-track** (wī′trak′), *n.* a short track laid at right angles to a line of railroad, with which it is connected by two curved branches resembling the branches of the letter Y, used instead of a turntable for reversing engines or cars.

**yt|ter|bi|a** (i tėr′bē ə), *n.* a heavy, white powder, an oxide of ytterbium, which forms colorless salts. *Formula:* $Yb_2O_3$ [< New Latin *ytterbia* < *ytterbium;* see etym. under **ytterbium**]

**yt|ter|bic** (i tėr′bik), *adj.* **1** of ytterbium. **2** containing ytterbium.

**yt|ter|bic** (i tėr′bik), *adj.* of or containing ytterbium, especially with a valence of three.

**yt|ter|bite** (i tėr′bīt), *n. Mineralogy.* gadolinite.

***yt|ter|bi|um** (i tėr′bē əm), *n.* a metallic chemical element whose compounds resemble those of yttrium; neoytterbium. It is one of the rare earths, occurs with yttrium in gadolinite and various other minerals, and is used in making special alloys. [< New Latin *ytterbium* < *Ytterby,* a town in Sweden, where it was first discovered. Compare etym. under **erbium**, **terbium**.]

***ytterbium**

| symbol | atomic number | atomic weight | oxidation state |
|---|---|---|---|
| Yb | 70 | 173.04 | 2,3 |

**ytterbium metals,** = yttrium metals.

**yt|ter|bous** (i tėr′bəs), *adj.* of or containing ytterbium, especially with a valence of two.

**yt|tri|a** (it′rē ə), *n.* a heavy, white powder, an oxide of yttrium, obtained from gadolinite and other rare minerals. *Formula:* $Y_2O_3$ [< New Latin *yttria,* alteration (influenced by Swedish *ytterjord*) of *Ytterby;* see etym. under **ytterbium**]

**yt|tric** (it′rik), *adj.* **1** of yttrium. **2** having yttrium.

**yt|trif|er|ous** (i trif′ər əs), *adj.* containing or yielding yttrium.

***yt|tri|um** (it′rē əm), *n.* a dark-gray metallic chemical element resembling and associated with the rare earths, occurring in combination in gadolinite and various other minerals. It is used in making alloys and in removing impurities from metals. Yttrium compounds are used in making incandescent gas mantles. [< New Latin *yttrium* < *yttria* yttria]

***yttrium**

| symbol | atomic number | atomic weight | oxidation state |
|---|---|---|---|
| Y | 39 | 88.905 | 3 |

**yttrium metals,** a group of metals that include yttrium and the rare-earth metals dysprosium, erbium, holmium, lutetium, thulium, and ytterbium.

**yu|an** (yü än′), *n., pl.* **-an**. **1** the unit of money of the People's Republic of China, established in 1914 and equal to 10 chiao. **2** the dollar of Taiwan. [< Chinese *yüan* circle, round thing. See etym. of doublet **yen**[1].]

**Yu|an** (yü än′), *n.* the national assembly of Taiwan. Also, **Yuen**.

**Yü|an** (yü än′), *n., adj.* **—*n.*** the Mongol dynasty that ruled China from 1279 to 1368, founded by Kublai Khan. **—*adj.*** of this dynasty.

**yuan dollar,** = yuan.

**Yuc.,** Yucatan.

**yu|ca** (yü′kə), *n.* = cassava. [variant of *yucca*]

**Yu|ca|tec** (yü′kə tek), *n., pl.* **-tec** or **-tecs**. **1** a member of a tribe of American Indians of the Yucatán Peninsula, Mexico, descended from the Maya Indians and still observing some of the Mayan religious practices. **2** the Mayan language of this tribe.

**Yu|ca|tec|an** (yü′kə tek′ən), *adj., n.* **—*adj.*** of or having to do with Yucatán, a peninsula of southeastern Mexico.
**—*n.*** a native or inhabitant of Yucatán.

**Yu|ca|te|co** (yü′kə tā′kō), *n., pl.* **-cos**. = Yucatec.

**yuc|ca** (yuk′ə), *n.* **1** a plant found in dry, warm regions of North and Central America, having stiff, narrow, pointed leaves shaped like swords at its base and an upright cluster of white, bell-shaped flowers. Adam's-needle and Spanish bayonet are two kinds. Yucca belongs to the agave family. **2** its flower, the emblem of New Mexico. [< New Latin *Yucca* the genus name < Spanish *yuca*]

**yucca moth,** a small white moth that pollinates the flowers of the yucca plant when it lays its eggs inside the flower's ovary. The larvae feed on the seeds that grow from the pollination.

**Yu|en** (yü en′), *n.* = Yuan.

**Yu|ga** (yů′gə), *n.* any one of the four ages in the duration of the world, the four ages comprising 4,320,000 years and constituting a great Yuga in Hindu cosmology. [< Sanskrit *yuga* an age; (originally) a yoke]

**Yu|go|slav** (yü′gō släv′, -slav′), *n., adj.* **—*n.*** a person born or living in Yugoslavia.
**—*adj.*** of or having to do with Yugoslavia or its people. Also, **Jugoslav**, **Jugo-Slav**.

**Yu|go|sla|vi|an** (yü′gō slä′vē ən, -slav′ē-), *adj., n.* = Yugoslav.

**Yu|go|slav|ic** (yü′gō slä′vik, -slav′ik), *adj.* = Yugoslav. Also, **Jugoslavic**.

**Yu|it** (yü′it), *n., pl.* **-it** or **-its**. an Eskimo of Siberia. The Eskimos of North America are called Innuit. [< Eskimo *yuit, innuit* the people]

**yuk** (yuk), *n., v.i., v.t.,* **yukked**, **yuk|king**. = yock.

**yu|ka|ta** (yü kä′tä), *n., pl.* **-ta**. *Japanese.* a man's lightweight kimono: *They wear Western clothes to work, slip into cool yukata at home* (Time).

**yu-kin** (yü kin′), *n.* a Chinese four-stringed musical instrument with a large circular body and a short neck. [< Chinese *yukin*]

**Yu|kon|er** (yü′kon ər), *n.* a native or inhabitant of the Yukon Territory.

**Yukon Standard Time** (yü′kon), the standard time in the Yukon Territory and part of southern Alaska, one hour behind Pacific Standard Time.

**Yule** or **yule** (yül), *n.* **1** = Christmas. **SYN**: Noël. **2** the Christmas season; Yuletide. [Old English *geōl* < Scandinavian (compare Old Icelandic *jōl*)]

**Yule log, block,** or **clog,** a large log burned in the fireplace at Christmas.

**Yule|tide** or **yule|tide** (yül′tīd′), *n.* the season of Christmas; Christmastide.

**Yule|time** or **yule|time** (yül′tīm′), *n.* = Yuletide.

**Yu|ma** (yü′mə), *n., pl.* **-ma** or **-mas**. **1** a member of an American Indian tribe formerly of southwestern Arizona and now living chiefly in California. **2** the Yuman language of this tribe.

**Yu|man** (yü′mən), *adj., n.* **—*adj.*** of or having to do with an American Indian linguistic group of the southwestern United States and Mexico.
**—*n.*** this linguistic group.

**yum|my** (yum′ē), *adj.,* **-mi|er**, **-mi|est**, *n., pl.* **-mies**. *Slang.* **—*adj.*** very pleasing to the senses; delicious; delightful: *Take your pick of yummy pecans, butterflies, filled rings* (Maclean's).
**—*n.*** something delicious or delightful.

**yum-yum** (yum′yum′), *interj.* an expression of pleasure or delight, especially with reference to food. [imitative]

**yup** (yup), *adv. U.S. Informal.* yes. [variant of *yep*]

**yurt** (yůrt), *n.* a portable, tentlike dwelling made of a framework of branches covered with felt, used by nomadic Mongols in central Asia. [< Russian *jurta* < Turkic]

**yu|sho** (yü′shō), *n.* poisoning caused by the ingestion of polychlorinated biphenyl: *In 1968 more than 1000 Japanese ate rice oil seriously contaminated with PCB's ... The affected persons developed darkened skins, eye discharge, severe acne, and other symptoms ... known as yusho, oil disease* (George Harvey).

**Y.W.,** *Informal.* Young Women's Christian Association.

**Y.W.C.A.** or **YWCA** (no periods), Young Women's Christian Association (an organization for young women, which originated in England in 1855 simultaneously in two different bodies, united in 1877).

**Y.W.H.A.** or **YWHA** (no periods), Young Women's Hebrew Association (an organization of Jewish young women, especially the women's branch of the Y.M.H.A.).

**y|wis** (i wis′), *adv. Archaic.* certainly; indeed. [variant of *iwis*]

# Zz

***Z[1]** or **z** (zē; *especially British* zed), *n., pl.* **Z's** or **Zs, z's** or **zs. 1** the 26th and last letter of the English alphabet: *There are two z's in zigzag.* **2** any sound represented by this letter. **3** used as a symbol for: **a** the 26th, or more usually the 25th (of an actual or possible series, either *I* or *J* being omitted). **b** an unknown quantity, especially in algebraic equations.
**from A to Z.** See under **A**[1].

**Z[2]** (zē), *n., pl.* **Z's.** anything shaped like the letter Z: *The road winds in a series of Z's.*

**z.,** zone.

**Z** (no period), **1** atomic number. **2** zenith. **3** zenith distance.

**Z., 1** zaire (unit of money). **2** zone.

**za|ba|glio|ne** (zä'bäl yō'nā), *n.* a sweet mixture of sugar, egg yolks, and wine cooked slightly, served hot or cold as a dessert, or as a sauce on puddings, fruits, and pastry. [alteration of Italian *zabaione*]

**za|ba|io|ne** or **za|ba|jo|ne** (zä'bä yō'nē), *n.* = zabaglione.

**Zab|u|lon** (zab'yə lən), *n.* (in the Douay Bible) Zebulun.

**za|ca|tón** (sä'kä tōn', zak'ə-), *n.* any one of several coarse grasses of the dry regions of the southwestern United States; sacaton. [< Spanish *zacatón* < *zacate,* or *sacate* grass, hay < Nahuatl *zacatl*]

**Zac|che|us** or **Zac|chae|us** (za kē'əs), *n.* a tax collector so short he had to climb a tree, because of the crowd, to see Jesus, and who later entertained Him at dinner (in the Bible, Luke 19:1-10).

**Zach|a|ri|ah** (zak'ə rī'ə), *n.* **1** a king of Israel (in the Bible, II Kings 15:8-11). **2** = Zacharias.

**Zach|a|ri|as** (zak'ə rī'əs), *n.* **1** the father of John the Baptist (in the Bible, Luke 1:5). **2** a Jewish priest mentioned as a martyr, slain "between the temple and the altar" (in the Bible, Matthew 23:35). **3** in the Douay Bible: **a** = Zechariah. **b** = Zachariah.

**Zach|a|ry** (zak'ər ē), *n.* **1** = Zachariah. **2** = Zacharias.

**zad|dik** (tsä'dik), *n., pl.* **zad|dik|im** (tsä dē'kim). a holy man among the Jews; righteous or saintly man, especially a leader of the Hasidim. Also, **tsaddik.** [< Hebrew *ṣaddiq*]

**zaf|fer, zaf|fre,** or **zaf|fir** (zaf'ər), *n.* an impure oxide of cobalt, obtained by roasting cobalt ore, used as a blue coloring matter (cobalt blue) especially for pottery and glass. [< Italian *zaffera*]

**zaf|tig** (zäf'tik), *adj.* = zoftig.

**zag** (zag), *n., v.,* **zagged, zag|ging.** *Informal.* **—*n.*** a part, movement, or direction at an angle to that of a zig in a zigzag.
***—v.i.*** to move on the second turn of a zigzag: *When an American Communist functionary has nightmares, he dreams that he zigged when the party line zagged* (Newsweek).

**zai|bat|su** (zī bät'sü), *n.pl. or sing.* the leading families of Japan, who control and direct most of the country's industries. [< Japanese *zaibatsu* < *zai* property + *batsu* clan, family]

**Zai|di** (zī'dē), *n., pl.* **-di** or **-dis.** a member of a Shiitic sect of Yemen. Also, **Zaydi.** [< *Zaid* or *Zayd,* the founder of this sect]

**za|ire** (zä'ir, zä ir'), *n., pl.* **-ires** or **-ire.** the unit of money of Zaire (the former Democratic Republic of the Congo), equal to 100 makuta. [< French *zaïre* < *Zaïre* Zaire]

**Za|ir|i|an** or **Za|ire|an** (zä ir'ē ən, zī'rē ən), *adj., n.* **—*adj.*** of or having to do with Zaire, its people, or their language.
**—*n.*** a native or inhabitant of Zaire.

**za|kat** (zə kät'), *n.* a portion of a Moslem's yearly income required to be set aside for alms. [< Arabic *zakāt*]

**za|kus|ka** (zä küs'kə), *n., pl.* **-ki** (-kē). *Russian.* an hors d'oeuvre; appetizer.

**Zam|bi|an** (zam'bē ən), *adj., n.* **—*adj.*** of or having to do with Zambia (the former Northern Rhodesia), its people, or their language.
**—*n.*** a native or inhabitant of Zambia.

**zam|bo** (zam'bō), *n., pl.* **-bos. 1** the child of a Negro and an Indian in Spanish America. **2** *U.S. Obsolete.* sambo. [< American Spanish *zambo*]

**zam|bra** (zam'brə), *n.* a Spanish or Moorish dance. [< Spanish *zambra*]

**za|mi|a** (zā'mē ə), *n.* any one of a group of tropical and subtropical American cycads, having a short, thick trunk, a crown of palmlike leaves, and oblong cones. [< New Latin *Zamia* the genus name < *zamiae,* plural, apparently misreading of Latin *azāniae* pine nuts < Greek *azánein* to dry up]

**za|min|dar** (zə mēn'där'), *n.* in India: **1** (formerly) a native landlord who held land for which he paid tax directly to the British government. **2** (under Mogul rule) a collector of revenue, required to pay a fixed sum on the tract or district assigned to him. Also, **zemindar.** [< Hindustani *zamīndār* < Persian *zamīn* land + *-dār,* an agent suffix]

**za|min|da|ri** (zə mēn'dä'rē), *n.* **1** the status or jurisdiction of a zamindar. **2** the territory of a zamindar. **3** the system of landholding and revenue collection under zamindars. Also, **zemindary.** [< Hindustani *zamīndārī* < *zamīndār;* see etym. under **zamindar**]

**zan|der** (zan'dər), *n., pl.* **-ders** or (*collectively*) **-der.** a European perch valued as a food fish. [< German *Zander,* probably < Slavic]

**za|ni|ly** (zā'nə lē), *adv.* in a zany manner.

**za|ni|ness** (zā'nē nis), *n.* zany quality or behavior: *Ginsberg, for all his carefully cultivated (and natural) zaniness, is a writer far above Kerouac in my estimation* (John Ciardi).

**Zan|te currant** (zän'tē, zan'-), a dried, small, seedless raisin used in puddings and bakery products. [< *Zante,* an island and seaport in southwestern Greece]

**zan|thox|y|lum** (zan thok'sə ləm), *n.* the bark of various shrubs or small trees of the madder family, used medicinally. [alteration of New Latin *Xanthoxylum* the genus name < Greek *xanthós* yellow + *xýlon* wood]

**za|ny** (zā'nē), *n., pl.* **-nies,** *adj.,* **-ni|er, -ni|est. —*n.*** **1** a fool; simpleton. **2** a clown. **3** *Archaic or Historical.* an assistant or attendant to a clown, acrobat, etc., who imitates his master in a ludicrously awkward way.
**—*adj.*** that is, or is characteristic of, a zany; clownish; foolish; idiotic: [*He*] *deliriously festooned himself with pith helmets, monocles, drooping mustaches, sou'westers—a new and zanier assortment every show* (Maclean's).
[< French *zani* < Italian (Venetian) *Zanni,* variant of *Giovanni* John]

**za|ny|ish** (zā'nē ish), *adj.* like a zany; foolish.

**za|ny|ism** (zā'nē iz əm), *n.* fantastic folly; buffoonery.

**zan|za** (zan'zə), *n.* = sansa.

**Zan|zi|ba|ri** (zan'zi bä'rē), *adj., n.* **—*adj.*** of or having to do with Zanzibar, an island, now part of Tanzania, on the east coast of Africa, or its people. **—*n.*** a native or inhabitant of Zanzibar.

**zap** (zap), *interj., v.,* **zapped, zap|ping,** *n. Slang.*
**—*interj.*** **1** the sound of a sudden slap, blow, blast, etc. **2** an exclamation, as of surprise: *"Zap!" he thought. "Wrong vaccine"* (Time).
**—*v.t.*** **1** to hit with a hard blow. **2** to kill: *With its pistol grip and nubby barrel, the instrument looks like the handy ray gun with which Buck Rogers and Wilma used to zap Killer Kane* (Time). **3** to beat; defeat: *They'll need the Army to zap those hoodlums* (New York Times). **4** to move very fast. **5** to give force to.
**—*v.i.*** to move very fast; zip; zoom: *curious low cars blatting and zapping before us* (Atlantic).
**—*n.*** vitality; force; zip: *The heat's too much and the gin's lost its zap* (New York Times).
[imitative]

**za|pa|te|a|do** (zä'pə tä ä'dō; *Spanish* thä pä'tā ä'ᴛʜō, sä-), *n., pl.* **-dos.** a dance of flamenco origin, in which the rhythm is marked chiefly by tapping with the feet, usually danced by men. [< Spanish *zapateado,* ultimately < *zapato* shoe]

**za|po|te** (zə pō'tē; *Spanish* thä pō'tā, sä-), *n.* = sapota.

**Za|po|tec** (zä'pə tek), *n., pl.* **-tec** or **-tecs. 1** a member of an Indian people of southern Mexico whose culture shows both Mayan and Toltec influences: *The Maya, the Zapotecs, the Mixtecs, and the Aztecs evidently developed urban communities on a major scale* (Scientific American). **2** the Zapotecan language of this people.

**Za|po|tec|an** (zä'pə tek'ən), *n., adj.* **—*n.*** **1** a group of related Indian languages of southern Mexico and Guatemala. **2** any of various peoples speaking Zapotecan. **—*adj.*** of or having to do with the Zapotecs or their languages.

**zap pit,** a microscopic depression on surface rocks of the moon: *"Zap pits"... were caused by the solar wind, cosmic particles, and micrometeorites—impacts from which the earth is protected by its atmosphere* (V. Gornitz and R. Jastrow).

**zap|ti|ah** or **zap|ti|eh** (zup tē'ə), *n.* (in Turkey) a policeman. [earlier *zaptié* < Turkish *zaptiye* < Arabic *ḍabṭ* administration]

**Zar|a|thus|tri|an** (zar'ə thüs'trē ən), *adj., n.* = Zoroastrian.

**za|ra|tite** (zär'ə tīt), *n.* a hydrous carbonate of nickel, of a green color, found as an incrustation and in stalactites. [< Spanish *zaratita*]

**zar|a|zue|la** (zär'ə zwā'lə), *n.* = zarzuela.

**za|re|ba** or **za|ree|ba** (zə rē'bə), *n.* in the Sudan and adjacent parts of Africa: **1** a fence or enclosure, usually constructed of thornbushes, for defense against the attacks of enemies or wild beasts. **2** a camp protected by such a fence. [< Arabic *zarība* cattle pen, lair < *zaraba* he enclosed or penned up (cattle)]

**zarf** (zärf), *n.* a cup-shaped metal holder for a hot coffee cup without a handle, used in the Levant. Also, **zurf.** [< Arabic *ẓarf* vessel]

**zar|zue|la** (thär thwā'lä, sär swā'-), *n.* a short drama with incidental music, similar to an operetta or musical comedy. Also, **zarazuela.** [< Spanish *zarzuela* < the Palace of La *Zarzuela,* near Madrid, where festive dramas were presented]

**zas|tru|ga** (zäs trü'gə), *n., pl.* **-gi** (-gē). (in Siberia and elsewhere) one of a series of wavelike ridges formed in snow by the action of the wind, and running in the direction of the wind. Also, **sastruga.** [< Russian *zastruga* groove]

**zax** (zaks), *n.* a type of ax for shaping roofing slates, having a pointed peen for making nail holes: *Chicago's A to Z Rental ... rents everything for the home from axes to zaxes* (Time). [variant of *sax*[1]]

**z-ax|is** (zē'ak'sis), *n.* the third axis in a three-dimensional system of rectangular coordinates, the other two axes being the x-axis and y-axis.

**Zay|di** (zī'dē), *n., pl.* **-di** or **-dis.** = Zaidi.

**za|yin** (zä'yin, zī'ən), *n.* the seventh letter of the Hebrew alphabet. [< Hebrew *zayin*]

**za|zen** (zä'zen'), *n.* (in Zen Buddhism) omphaloskepsis. [< Japanese *zazen*]

**Z-bar** (zē'bär'), *n.* a steel bar used in constructing steel columns for buildings and other structures, consisting essentially of a web with two flanges at right angles to it, and having the cross section somewhat resembling the letter Z.

**ZBB** (no periods), zero-based budgeting: *ZBB critics point to its cost in management time, and the mind-boggling paper work involved* (Maclean's).

**zeal** (zēl), *n.* eager desire or effort; earnest enthusiasm; fervor: *religious zeal, to work with zeal for pollution control. A good citizen works with zeal for his country's interests.* [< Latin *zēlus* < Greek *zêlos*]

**zeal|ot** (zel'ət), *n.* a person who shows too much zeal; immoderate partisan; fanatic: *A band of zealots ... is pushing his candidacy hard* (Wall Street Journal). **SYN:** bigot. [< Latin *zēlōtēs* < Greek *zēlōtēs* < *zēloûn* be zealous < *zêlos* zeal]

**Zeal|ot** (zel'ət), *n.* a member of a strict, militant Jewish sect which fiercely resisted the Romans in Palestine until Jerusalem was destroyed in A.D. 70.

**zeal|ot|ry** (zel'ə trē), *n., pl.* **-ries. 1** action or feeling characteristic of a zealot; too great zeal; fanaticism. **2** an instance of this.

**zeal|ous** (zel'əs), *adj.* full of zeal; eager; earnest; actively enthusiastic: *The salesman seems very zealous to please. We made zealous efforts to clean up the house for the party.* **SYN:** ardent, fervent. [< Medieval Latin *zelosus* < Latin *zēlus* zeal] **—zeal'ous|ly,** *adv.* **—zeal'ous|ness,** *n.*

**ze|bec** or **ze|beck** (zē'bek), *n.* = xebec.

**Zeb|e|dee** (zeb'ə dē), *n.* the father of the Apostles James and John (in the Bible, Matthew 4:21).

**ze|bra** (zē'brə), *n., pl.* **-bras** or (*collectively*) **-bra.**

***Z[1]**
definition 1

Script letters look like examples of fine penmanship. They appear in many formal uses, such as invitations to social functions.

Handwritten letters, both manuscript or printed (left) and cursive (right), are easy for children to read and to write.

Roman letters have *serifs* (finishing strokes) adapted from the way Roman stonecutters carved their letters. This is *Times Roman* type.

Sans-serif letters are often called *gothic.* They have lines of even width and no serifs. This type face is called *Helvetica.*

Between roman and gothic, some letters have thick and thin lines with slight flares that suggest serifs. This type face is *Optima.*

Computer letters can be sensed by machines either from their shapes or from the magnetic ink with which they are printed.

a wild mammal of southern and eastern Africa, related to the horse and donkey but striped with dark bands on white. There are three species, the commonest being the Burchell's zebra or dauw. See picture at **horse**. [< Portuguese *zebra*, perhaps < the native Congo name]

**zebra butterfly**, a tropical American butterfly having black wings barred with yellow.

**zebra crossing**, *British.* a crosswalk painted black with white stripes, giving pedestrians right of way in crossing streets.

**zebra finch**, a waxbill very common in Australia and popular as a cage bird. It has black and white stripes and a chestnut patch on the cheek.

**zebra fish**, a percoid fish with dark stripes found in Australian waters.

**ze|brass** (zē′bras′), *n.* the offspring of a male zebra and a female ass.

**zebra swallowtail**, a large North American swallowtail butterfly having long tails and black wings banded with greenish or yellowish white.

**ze|bra-tailed lizard** (zē′brə tāld′), a lizard about 6 or 7 inches long, with a thick body, a small head, and a tapering tail. It lives in the deserts of southwestern United States and northern Mexico.

**ze|bra|wood** (zē′brə wu̇d′), *n.* **1** the hard, striped wood of a large tree of tropical America, used especially for cabinetwork. **2** this tree. **3** any one of several similar woods or the trees or shrubs yielding them.

**ze|brine** (zē′brīn, -brin), *adj.* **1** having to do with a zebra. **2** resembling a zebra.

**ze|broid** (zē′broid), *adj., n.* —***adj.*** resembling the zebra. —***n.*** a zebroid animal; cross between the zebra and the ass, or the zebra and the horse.

**ze|bru|la** (zē′bru̇ lə, zeb′rü-), *n.* the offspring of a male zebra and a female horse. [< *zebr*(a) + Latin (m)*ūla*, feminine of *mūlus* mule]

**ze|brule** (zē′brül), *n.* = zebrula.

**ze|bu** (zē′byü), *n., pl.* **-bus** or (*collectively*) **-bu**. a mammal like an ox but with a large, fatty hump over the shoulders, and a large dewlap. The zebu is a domestic animal in Asia and eastern Africa. [< French *zébu*]

**Zeb|u|lun** (zeb′yə lən), *n.* **1** tenth son of Jacob, by Leah (in the Bible, Genesis, 30:19, 20). **2** the tribe of Israel that claimed descent from him.

**zec|chin** (zek′in), *n.* a sequin, a former gold coin of Venice and Turkey: *If you don't choose to submit to be cheated by them out of a ducat here and a zecchin there, you will be cheated by them out of your picture* (John Ruskin). [< Italian *zecchino*. See etym. of doublet **sequin**.]

**zec|chi|no** (tsek kē′nō), *n., pl.* **-ni** (-nē). *Italian.* sequin, a former gold coin of Venice.

**Zech.**, Zechariah (book of the Old Testament).

**Zech|a|ri|ah** (zek′ə rī′ə), *n.* **1** a Hebrew prophet of the 500's B.C. **2** a prophetic book of the Old Testament attributed to him. *Abbr:* Zech.

**zech|in** (zek′in), *n.* = zecchin.

**zed** (zed), *n. Especially British.* a name for the letter *Z, z.* [< Middle French *zède*, learned borrowing from Late Latin *zēta* < Greek *zēta*. See etym. of doublet **zeta**.]

**Zed|e|ki|ah** (zed′ə kī′ə), *n.* the last king of Judah, whose reign lasted from 597 to 587 B.C. and ended with the Exile (in the Bible, II Kings 24:17-20).

**zed|o|ar|y** (zed′ō er′ē), *n.* **1** the aromatic tuberous root of one of two East Indian plants of the ginger family, used as a drug. **2** either of these plants. [< Medieval Latin *zedoaria*, or *zedoarium* < Arabic *zedwār*]

**zee** (zē), *n. Especially U.S.* a name for the letter *Z, z.*

**Zee|man effect** (zā′män), *Physics.* the separation of lines of the spectrum that occurs in light emanating from a source in a magnetic field. [< Pieter *Zeeman*, 1865-1943, a Dutch physicist]

**Zef|ran** (zef′ran), *n. Trademark.* a fabric of acrylic fiber used for clothing.

**ze|in** (zē′in), *n. Biochemistry.* a protein contained in corn, used in plastics, coatings, and adhesives. [< earlier *zea* (< New Latin *Zea* the maize genus < Latin *zēa* spelt < Greek *zeiá*) + *-in*]

**Zeiss planetarium** (zīs; *German* tsīs), an apparatus showing the movements of the sun, moon, planets, and stars by projecting lights on the inside of a dome shaped like a hemisphere; planetarium. [< Carl *Zeiss* Optical Works in Jena, Germany, which made the original planetarium]

**Zeiss projector**, = Zeiss planetarium.

**zeit|ge|ber** or **Zeit|ge|ber** (zīt′gā′bər; *German* tsīt′-), *n., pl.* **-ber** or **-bers**. *Biology.* any time indicator, such as light, dark, or temperature, that influences the workings of the biological clock: *The animal still must depend on Zeitgeber, or cues from the environment, to correct the clock and thus entrain its rhythm each year* (Scientific American). [< German *Zeitgeber* (literally) time giver]

**Zeit|geist** (zīt′gīst′; *German* tsīt′-), *n.* the characteristic thought or feeling of a period of time; spirit of the age: *Arthur Panter was not the sort of person who drifts along with the Zeitgeist* (New Yorker). [< German *Zeitgeist* (literally) spirit of the time < *Zeit* time + *Geist* spirit]

**Ze|lan** (zē′lan), *n. Trademark.* a chemical finish applied to fabrics to make them water- and stain-repellent.

**zel|ko|va** (zel kō′və), *n., pl.* **-vas** or **-va**. any one of a group of Asian trees or shrubs grown for shade or ornament, especially a tall, branching Japanese species often grown as a substitute for the elm. [< New Latin *Zelkova* the genus name < the native name in Crete]

**ze|mi** (zə mē′), *n., pl.* **-mis**. **1** a spirit worshipped by the ancient Arawak Indians and represented by a figure of wood, bone, or some other material. **2** the figure itself. Each Arawak Indian had at least one zemi in his home. [< Spanish *zemí* < Taino *zemi*]

**ze|min|dar** (zə mēn′där′), *n.* = zamindar.

**ze|min|da|ry** (zə mēn′dä′rē), *n., pl.* **-ries**. = zamindari.

**zem|stvo** (zem′stvō), *n., pl.* **-stvos**. a local elective assembly in Russia before the Revolution, which managed the affairs of a district. [< Russian *zemstvo* (originally) rural population, rural officials < *zem′*, variant of *zemlya* land]

**Zen** (zen), *n.* = Zen Buddhism. [< Japanese *zen* religious meditation]

**ze|na|na** (ze nä′nə), *n.* the part of a Moslem house set aside for the women in Pakistan, India, and certain other parts of Asia. [< Hindustani *zenana* < Persian *zanāna* < *zan* woman]

**Zen Buddhism**, a Japanese form of Buddhism that emphasizes meditation, introspection, and intuition as means of achieving a sense of self-control that leads to selflessness and identification with the spiritual world: *Hipsters go to Zen Buddhism, to extract from it whatever confirms them in their present convictions* (Harper's).

**Zen Buddhist**, a believer in Zen Buddhism.

**Zend** (zend), *n.* **1** the commentary usually accompanying the Zoroastrian Avesta. **2** the language of the Avesta; Avestan. [< French *zend* < Pahlavi *Zend*]

**Zend-A|ves|ta** (zend′ə ves′tə), *n.* the sacred writings of Zoroastrianism, consisting of the Avesta and the Zend. [alteration (influenced by Persian *zandawastā*) of Pahlavi *Avistāk va Zend* (literally) Avesta with Zend]

**zen|do** (zen′dō), *n.* a place for the study and practice of Zen Buddhism: *We gather in silence outside the zendo and do ... various forms of yoga and calisthenics* (Lawrence Shainberg). [< Japanese *zendō*]

**Ze|ner card** (zē′nər), any one of a set of 25 cards having five different symbols, such as a circle or cross, each symbol having its own color. Zener cards are used in experiments in extrasensory perception. [< Karl E. *Zener*, an American psychologist of the 1900's]

**ze|ner** or **Ze|ner diode** (zē′nər, zen′ər), a silicon semiconductor used as a voltage stabilizer: *The Zener diode is in effect a variable resistor that automatically maintains fixed voltage in a circuit* (Scientific American). [< Clarence M. *Zener*, born 1905, an American physicist]

***ze|nith** (zē′nith), *n.* **1a** the point in the heavens directly overhead; point where a vertical line would pierce the sky. It is opposite the nadir. To an observer at the North Pole, the North Star would be about at his zenith. **b** the point of highest altitude of a heavenly body, relative to a particular observer or place. **2** *Figurative.* highest point; apex: *At the zenith of its power, Rome ruled all the known world.* SYN: top, summit, acme, culmination, climax. [< Old French, or Medieval Latin *cenith* < Arabic *samt* (*ar-rās*) the way (over the head)]

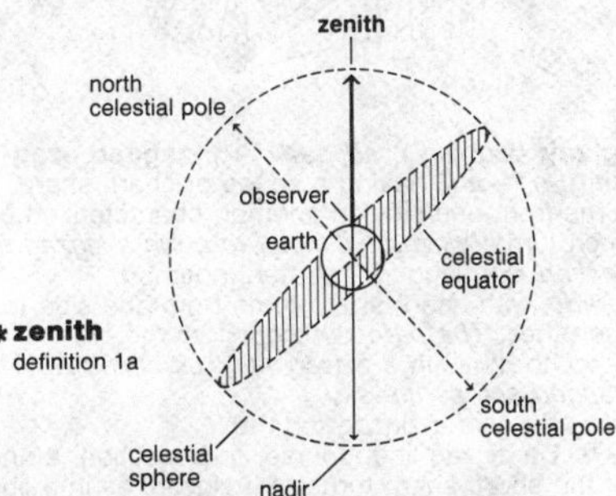

***zenith**
definition 1a

**ze|nith|al** (zē′nə thəl), *adj.* **1** of or having to do with the zenith. **2** occurring at the zenith.

**zenithal projection**, map projection having all points in true compass direction from the center of the map; azimuthal equidistant projection.

**zenith distance**, the distance of a heavenly body from the zenith of a particular observer or place, the complement of its altitude, measured in degrees along the vertical circle passing through the zenith and the body: *At the North Pole, the zenith distance of the North Star is about 0 degrees.*

**zenith telescope**, a telescope for measuring the difference of zenith distances of pairs of stars north and south of the zenith: *A zenith telescope ... is a telescope provided with a plumb line to ensure that it is vertical* (Listener).

**Zen|nist** (zen′ist), *n.* = Zen Buddhist.

**ze|o|lite** (zē′ə līt), *n.* any one of a large group of minerals consisting of hydrous silicates of aluminum with alkali metals, commonly found in the cavities of igneous rocks. Zeolites have their atoms arranged in an open crystal framework that can hold other atoms or molecules much as a sponge holds water. [< Swedish *zeolit* < Greek *zeîn* to boil + Swedish *-lit* -lite (because it boils or swells under the blowpipe)]

**ze|o|lit|ic** (zē′ə lit′ik), *adj.* **1** having to do with zeolite. **2** consisting of zeolite. **3** resembling zeolite.

**ze|ol|i|tize** (zē ol′ə tīz), *v.t.*, **-tized**, **-tiz|ing**. to change into a zeolite: *An unusual cave in zeolitized dolerite was found in Tasmania* (Gordon Warwick).

**Zeph.**, Zephaniah (book of the Old Testament).

**Zeph|a|ni|ah** (zef′ə nī′ə), *n.* **1** a Hebrew prophet of the 600's B.C. **2** a prophetic book of the Old Testament attributed to him, placed among the Minor Prophets. *Abbr:* Zeph.

**Zeph|i|ran Chloride** (zef′ə ran), *Trademark.* a mixture of alkyl-dimethyl-benzyl-ammonium chlorides, used as an antiseptic on skin and mucous membranes.

**Zeph|yr** (zef′ər), *n.* the west wind personified; Zephyrus. [< Latin *zephyrus* < Greek *zéphyros*]

**zeph|yr** (zef′ər), *n.* **1** any soft, gentle wind; mild breeze: *The flowers, the zephyrs, and the warblers of spring, returning after a tedious absence* (Washington Irving). **2** the west wind. **3** a fine, soft yarn or worsted. **4** a very light garment, such as a light shawl or light shirt. [< *Zephyr*]

**zephyr cloth**, a light kind of cassimere used for women's garments.

**zephyr lily**, a low-growing plant of the amaryllis family found in warm regions of the Western Hemisphere and often cultivated for its white, rose, or yellow flowers; fairy lily.

**Zeph|y|rus** (zef′ər əs), *n. Greek Mythology.* the god of the west wind, considered to be the mildest and gentlest of sylvan deities: *With voice Mild, as when Zephyrus on Flora breathes* (Milton).

**zephyr yarn** or **worsted**, a very light yarn or worsted, used for knitting and weaving.

***Zep|pe|lin** or **zep|pe|lin** (zep′ə lən, zep′lən; *German* tsep′ə lēn′), *n.* a large airship shaped like a cigar with pointed ends. It has a rigid frame of light metal within which are separate compartments filled with gas. The engines and freight or passenger compartments are contained in or slung from its bottom part. Zeppelins were mostly used between 1914 and 1937. [< German *Zeppelin* < Count Ferdinand von *Zeppelin*, 1838-1917, who invented it]

***Zeppelin**

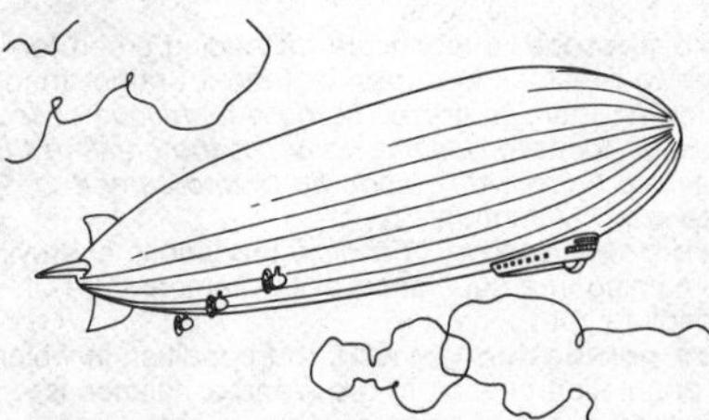

**ze|ro** (zir′ō), *n., pl.* **-ros** or **-roes**, *adj., v.*, **-roed**, **-ro|ing**. —***n.*** **1** the figure or digit 0; naught; cipher: *Add two zeros to 5 and get 500. There are three zeros in 40,006.* **2a** the point marked with a zero on the scale of a thermometer: *The numbers have faded; so you can't tell where zero is on that thermometer.* **b** the temperature that corresponds to zero on the scale of a thermometer: *At zero water is frozen solid.* **3** the complete absence of quantity; nothing: *Zero added to or subtracted from any number gives the original number* (Howard W. Eves). SYN: nullity, nil.

---

**Pronunciation Key:** hat, āge, cãre, fär; let, ēqual, tėrm; it, īce; hot, ōpen, ôrder; **oi**l, **ou**t; cup, pu̇t, rüle; **ch**ild; lo**ng**; **th**in; **ŧh**en; **zh**, measure; **ə** represents **a** in about, **e** in taken, **i** in pencil, **o** in lemon, **u** in circus.

4 *Figurative.* the lowest point or degree: *The team's spirit sank to zero after its fifth defeat.* SYN: nadir. 5 the correct sight setting of a rifle for elevation and windage at a given range.
—*adj.* 1 of or at zero: *the zero point of a thermometer, zero weather. The other team made zero score.* 2 none at all; not any: *Multiplication by zero gives a zero answer.* (*Figurative.*) *On a quiet Sunday there is zero probability of something happening around here.* 3 *Grammar.* lacking, absent, or weakly felt: *The second syllable of "zestful" has zero stress.* 4 *Meteorology, Aeronautics.* a denoting a ceiling not more than 50 feet high. b denoting visibility of not more than 165 feet in a horizontal direction: *The weather station announced zero visibility.*
—*v.t., v.i.* to adjust (an instrument or device) to zero point or line or to any given point from which readings will then be measured.
**zero in,** to adjust the sights of (a rifle) for a given range so a bullet will strike the center of the target: *He zeroed in his rifle at 50 yards.*
**zero in on, a** to get the range of (a target) by adjusting the sights or elevation of a firearm: *After settling in the prone position, Allen began zeroing in on a chuck at an estimated range of 400 yards* (New York Times). **b** to aim with precision toward (a target): *Like a plane zeroed in on target, the streamliner roared through a red signal* (Newsweek). **c** *Figurative.* to locate as a target; find the range of: *A new sound must repeat itself many times in a hinting rhythm before one can zero in on it* (Atlantic).
[< Italian *zero* < Arabic *ṣifr* empty. See etym. of doublet **cipher.**]

**Ze|ro** (zir′ō), *n., pl.* **-ros** or **-roes.** a Japanese fighter plane of World War II. [< Mitsubishi (the Japanese manufacturer), type *O,* designation]

**ze|ro-base budgeting** (zir′ō bās′), = zero-based budgeting: *As described by Mr. Pyhrr in the Advanced Management Journal, zero-base budgeting "informs top management about money needed to attain desired program ends by focusing on the dollars needed … rather than on the percentage increase or decrease from the previous year's budget"* (New York Times).

**ze|ro-based budgeting** (zir′ō bāst′), a system in which the budget of a government department, business, or the like, is drawn up each year anew, without reference to the budget of the previous year or years: *Zero-based budgeting … should be undertaken to eliminate swollen administrative costs and inequitable programs* (Tom Wicker).

**zero g,** = zero gravity.

**zero gravity,** the absence of gravity; a condition in which the effects of gravity are not felt; weightlessness. In an orbiting spacecraft, zero gravity is experienced as weightlessness.

**zero grazing,** *British.* zero pasture.

**zero hour,** 1 the time set for beginning an attack or some phase of an attack; H-hour. 2 a time set for any important action to begin; crucial moment. 3 midnight: *Zero hour … is the moment of beginning of the day, so that a new day is forever on its journey around the earth* (Bernhard, Bennett, and Rice).

**zero magnitude,** *Astronomy.* a measure of brilliance of certain stars, being 2½ times as bright as first magnitude.

**zero norm,** = nil norm.

**zero pasture,** a technique of feeding green forage to livestock in a barn or feed lot rather than allowing them to graze: *Using a technique called soilage, or zero pasture, they cut the grass in the pasture twice a day, chop it up, and carry it to the cows* (Atlantic).

**zero point energy,** *Physics.* the kinetic energy remaining in a substance at the temperature of absolute zero.

**zero population growth,** the condition in which a population ceases to grow and a balance is reached in the average number of births and deaths: *the ZPG* (*zero population growth*) *movement which advocates a halt in the U.S. growth rate* (Kingsley Davis).

**ze|ro-sum** (zir′ō sum′), *adj.* having to do with or characterized by a strategy in the theory of games in which the total winnings of one side equal the total losses of the other side.

**ze|roth** (zi′rōth), *adj.* of or at zero; being zero: $x^0 = x$ *to the zeroth power.*

**zero vowel,** = schwa.

**ze|ro-ze|ro** (zir′ō zir′ō), *adj. Meteorology.* of severely limited visibility in horizontal and vertical directions: *zero-zero landing conditions.*

**zest** (zest), *n., v.* —*n.* 1 keen enjoyment; relish; gusto: *a youthful zest for life. The hungry man ate with zest.* 2 a pleasant or exciting quality or flavor: *to give zest to food by the use of herbs. Wit gives zest to conversation.* SYN: piquancy.
—*v.t.* to give zest to; impart piquant quality to.
[< French *zeste* orange or lemon peel]

**zest|ful** (zest′fəl), *adj.* full of zest; characterized by keen relish or hearty enjoyment: *A zestful sort of place in which to spend a fortnight* (Fraser's Magazine). SYN: exhilarating. —**zest′ful|ly,** *adv.* —**zest′ful|ness,** *n.*

**zest|y** (zes′tē), *adj.* having much zest; full of zest: *Guests can shell their own* [*crustaceans*] *and dip them into a zesty mayonnaise* (New Yorker).

***ze|ta** (zā′tə, zē′-), *n.* the sixth letter of the Greek alphabet corresponding to English Z, z. [< Greek *zêta,* name of *z.* See etym. of doublet **zed.**]

***zeta**

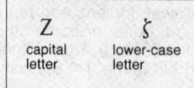

| Z | ζ |
|---|---|
| capital letter | lower-case letter |

**ze|tet|ic** (zə tet′ik), *adj.* 1 having to do with inquiry or investigation. 2 proceeding by inquiry or investigation. [< New Latin *zeteticus* < Greek *zētētikós* < *zēteîn* to seek, inquire]

**Ze|thus** (zē′thəs), *n. Greek Mythology.* the twin brother of Amphion.

**zeug|ma** (zūg′mə), *n. Grammar.* the use of a word to relate to two or more words in a sentence, when properly applying in sense to only one of them. [< Greek *zeûgma* (literally) a yoking < *zeugnýnai* to yoke, related to *zygón* a yoke]

**zeug|mat|ic** (zūg mat′ik), *adj. Grammar.* 1 having to do with zeugma. 2 of the nature of zeugma.

**Zeus** (zūs), *n.* the chief god of the ancient Greeks. He was the ruler of gods and men and the god of the sky and weather, son of Cronus and Rhea, and husband of Hera. The Romans called him Jupiter.

**Zhda|nov|ism** (zhdä′nə viz əm), *n.* a policy to purge Soviet literature of Western influence, especially during Stalin's regime. [< Andrei *Zhdanov,* 1888-1948, a Soviet official who implemented this policy + *-ism*]

**zho** (zhō), *n.* = dzo.

**zib|el|ine** or **zib|el|line** (zib′ə līn, -lin), *n., adj.* —*n.* 1 sable (the fur). 2 a woolen fabric with a slightly furry surface, used for dresses and coats. —*adj.* of or having to do with sable or the sable. [< Middle French *zebeline* or *zibeline* < Italian *zibellino,* ultimately < Slavic (compare Russian *sobol'* sable)]

**zib|et** or **zib|eth** (zib′it), *n.* a civet cat of India and the Malay Peninsula. [< Medieval Latin *zibethum* civet < Arabic *zabād.* See etym. of doublet **civet.**]

**zig** (zig), *n., v.,* **zigged, zig|ging.** *Informal.* —*n.* the first movement or turn of a zigzag: *The foreign parties slavishly followed every zig and zag of Kremlin maneuvering* (Wall Street Journal).
—*v.i.* to make the first movement or turn of a zigzag: *In the pursuit of this policy they zig and zag, change strategy and tactics, advance and retreat* (New York Times). [< *zig*(zag)]

***zig|gu|rat** (zig′ů rat), *n.* an ancient Assyrian and Babylonian temple in the form of a great pyramid having stories each smaller than that below it, so as to leave a terrace at each level. Also, **zikkurat, zikurat.** [< Akkadian *ziqquratu* temple tower; pinnacle, peak < *zaqāru* be high]

***ziggurat**

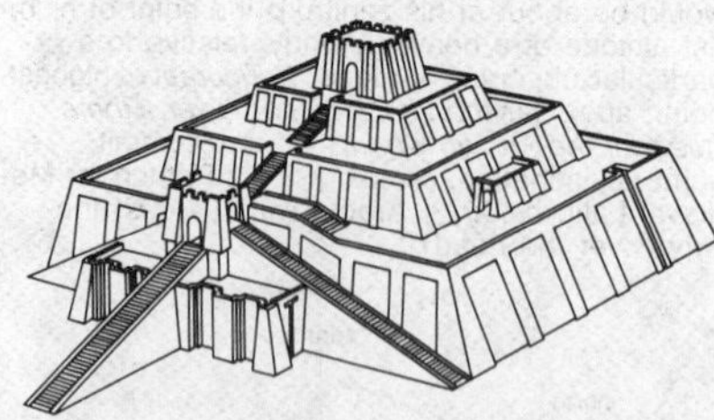

**zig|zag** (zig′zag′), *adj., adv., v.,* **-zagged, -zag|ging,** *n.* —*adj.* having a series of short, sharp turns from one side to another; characterized by such turns: *zigzag lightning, to go in a zigzag direction.* SYN: jagged, serrated, notched.
—*adv.* with short, sharp turns from one side to the other: *The path ran zigzag up the hill.*
—*v.i.* to move in a zigzag way: *Lightning zigzagged across the sky.*
—*v.t.* to give a zigzag form to.
—*n.* 1 a zigzag line, course, or projection. 2 one of the short, sharp turns of a zigzag, as in a line or path.
[(originally) noun < French *zigzag* < German *Zickzack,* perhaps varied reduplication of *Zacke* tooth, prong]

**zigzag stitch,** a stitch made with a sewing machine in a zigzag pattern, for joining two edges in places where a straight-line stitch is difficult or awkward.

**zik|ku|rat** or **zik|u|rat** (zik′ů rat), *n.* = ziggurat.

**zilch** (zilch), *n. U.S. Slang.* nothing at all; zero: *The Senator's lady … says she knows that her real political power is approximately zilch* (Harper's). [origin uncertain]

**zil|lah** (zil′ə), *n.* (formerly, in British India) an administrative division of a province. [< Hindustani *ḍilah* district; part; side < Arabic *ḍil'* part; rib]

**zil|lion** (zil′yən), *n., adj. Slang.* —*n.* any very large, indefinite number.
—*adj.* of such a number; very many; innumerable. [< *z* (last letter) + *-illion,* as in *million*]

**Zil|pah** (zil′pə), *n.* Leah's maid, mother of Gad and Asher (in the Bible, Genesis 30:9-13).

**Zim|bab|we|an** (zim bäb′wē ən), *n., adj.* —*n.* a native or inhabitant of Zimbabwe, the African nationalist name of Rhodesia: *To demonstrate on the Rhodesia question, the young Zimbabweans … raised hand-drawn posters in the gallery* (London Times). —*adj.* of or having to do with Zimbabwe or Zimbabweans.

**zim|ba|lon** (zim′bə lon), *n.* = cymbalom.

***zinc** (zingk), *n., v.,* **zincked** or **zinced** (zingkt), **zinck|ing** or **zinc|ing** (zing′king). —*n.* 1 a hard, bluish-white, metallic chemical element that is brittle and little affected by air and moisture at ordinary temperatures. It is used for coating or galvanizing iron, for roofing, in alloys such as brass, in electric batteries, in paint, and in medicine. 2 a piece of zinc used in a voltage cell.
—*v.t.* to coat or cover with zinc or compound.
[< German *Zink,* related to *Zinke* prong, point (perhaps because of the form which zinc assumes in blast furnaces)]

***zinc**
definition 1

| symbol | atomic number | atomic weight | oxidation state |
|---|---|---|---|
| Zn | 30 | 65.37 | 2 |

**zinc|ate** (zing′kāt), *n.* a salt of zinc hydroxide, such as $Zn(OH)_2$, when it acts as a feeble acid.

**zinc bacitracin,** the antibiotic bacitracin with 7 per cent zinc, used in medicine as flavoring, and as a silage preservative.

**zinc blende,** *Mineralogy.* = sphalerite.

**zinc chloride,** a water-soluble crystal or crystalline powder, used in galvanizing and electroplating and as a wood preservative, disinfectant, etc. *Formula:* $ZnCl_2$

**zinc dust,** a gray powder, usually containing zinc oxide, used as a reducing agent, a bleach, and in rust-resistant paints.

**zinc|ic** (zing′kik), *adj.* 1 having to do with zinc. 2 consisting of zinc. 3 containing zinc. 4 resembling zinc.

**zinc|if|er|ous** (zing kif′ər əs, zin sif′-), *adj.* 1 containing zinc. 2 producing zinc.

**zinc|i|fi|ca|tion** (zing′kə fə kā′shən), *n.* 1 the process of coating or impregnating an object with zinc. 2 the state resulting from such a process.

**zinc|i|fy** (zing′kə fī), *v.t.,* **-fied, -fy|ing.** to coat or impregnate with zinc; zinc.

**zinc|ite** (zing′kīt), *n. Mineralogy.* a native zinc oxide, of a deep-red or orange-yellow color, also called red oxide of zinc or red zinc ore. It is an important source of zinc. *Formula:* ZnO

**zinck|en|ite** (zing′kə nīt), *n.* = zinkenite.

**zinck|ic** (zing′kik), *adj.* = zincic.

**zinck|if|er|ous** (zing kif′ər əs), *adj.* = zinciferous.

**zinck|y** (zing′kē), *adj.* 1 having to do with zinc. 2 containing zinc. 3 resembling zinc.

**zin|co|graph** (zing′kə graf, -gräf), *n.* 1 the plate used in zincography. 2 a design or impression produced by zincography.

**zin|cog|ra|pher** (zing kog′rə fər), *n.* a person who makes zincographic plates.

**zin|co|graph|ic** (zing′kə graf′ik), *adj.* having to do with zincography.

**zin|co|graph|i|cal** (zing′kə graf′ə kəl), *adj.* = zincographic.

**zin|cog|ra|phy** (zing kog′rə fē), *n.* the art or process of etching or engraving designs on zinc, as on a zinc plate to print illustrations.

**zinc ointment,** a preparation containing 20 per cent zinc oxide, used in treating skin disorders.

**zin|co|type** (zing′kə tīp), *n.* = zincograph.

**zinc|ous** (zing′kəs), *adj. Chemistry.* 1 of zinc; zincic. 2 *Obsolete.* electropositive.

**zinc oxide,** a compound of zinc and oxygen, used in making paint, rubber, glass, cosmetics, and ointments. It is an insoluble white powder. *Formula:* ZnO

**zinc phosphide,** an insoluble, dark-gray powder, used chiefly as a rat poison. *Formula:* $Zn_3P_2$

**zinc sulfate,** = white vitriol.

**zinc sulfide,** a yellowish or white powder occurring naturally as sphalerite. Zinc sulfide is used as a pigment and as a phosphor in television screens and on watch faces. *Formula:* ZnS

**zinc white,** zinc oxide used as a white pigment in paints.

**zinc|y** (zing′kē), *adj.* = zincky.
**zin|eb** (zin′əb), *n.* a light tan organic fungicide and insecticide sprayed on the leaves of fruit trees and on vegetables and cereal grasses. [< *zin*(c) + *-eb* (as in *maneb*)]
**zin|fan|del** (zin′fən dəl), *n.* **1** a variety of wine grape much grown in California and of undetermined origin. **2** wine made from this grape. [American English; origin uncertain]
**zing** (zing), *n., interj., v.* — ***n.*** **1** a sharp humming sound: *Her cool presence silenced the customary zing and swish of hurled hardware* (Punch). **2** *Slang, Figurative.* liveliness; zest; spirit; vitality: *an exciting story with plenty of zing. The week's TV dramas were thin, talky, and without dramatic zing* (Time).
— ***interj.*** *Slang.* a sound used to express enthusiasm, spirit, or the like.
— ***v.i.*** to make a sharp humming sound, especially in going rapidly: *A bullet zinged past the ear of the Japanese consul from Manila* (New Yorker).
— ***v.t.*** *Slang.* **1** to bring forth with spirit or zest: *Whammy, we zing in a couple of great production numbers* (S. J. Perelman). **2** *Figurative.* to give zest to; liven up: *He claims to know by instinct how to "zing up" a face* (New Yorker). [imitative]
**zin|ga|ra** (tsēng′gä rä), *n., pl.* **-re** (-rā). *Italian.* a Gypsy girl or woman.
**zin|ga|ro** (tsēng′gä rō), *n., pl.* **-ri** (-rē). *Italian.* a Gypsy boy or man: *I am a zingaro, a Bohemian, an Egyptian, or whatever the Europeans ... may choose to call our people* (Scott).
**zing|el** (tsing′əl), *n. German.* a small fish of the perch family, found in the Danube.
**zing|er** (zing′ər), *n. Slang.* **1** a zingy person. **2** something that hits the mark: *His retort was a zinger.* **3** something of surpassing quality or size; corker: *Every actress needs one zinger of a part early in her career* (London Times).
**zin|gi|ber|a|ceous** (zin′jə bə rā′shəs), *adj.* belonging to the ginger family. Also, **zinziberaceous.** [< New Latin *Zingiberaceae* the family name (< Latin *zingiberi* ginger) + English *-ous*]
**zing|y** (zing′ē), *adj.,* **zing|i|er, zing|i|est.** *Slang.* full of vitality; lively; zesty: *A soupçon of wisdom, a lot of wit are laced into Jean Kerr's zingy comedy* (Time).
**Zin|jan|thro|pine** (zin′jan thrō′pēn, zin jan′thrə pēn), *n., adj.* — ***n.*** any one of the group of extinct primates represented by Zinjanthropus.
— ***adj.*** of or having to do with this group.
**Zin|jan|thro|pus** (zin′jan thrō′pəs, zin jan′thrə pəs), *n.* a prehistoric man of the Pleistocene epoch, with a large, deep jaw and low forehead, whose remains were discovered in Tanganyika in 1959. He was nicknamed "the Nutcracker Man" because of his huge teeth. *Leakey ... has abandoned his earlier opinion that Zinjanthropus, a manlike creature whose bones he found in Africa in 1959, was on the line of evolution to man* (Scientific American). [< New Latin *Zinjanthropus* the genus name < *zinj* East Africa + Greek *ánthrōpos* man]
**zin|ke** (zing′kə), *n.* a small cornet of wood or horn with finger holes and a cupped mouthpiece, formerly common in Europe; cornetto. [< German *Zinke*]
**zin|ken|ite** (zing′kə nīt), *n. Mineralogy.* a steel-gray sulfide of antimony and lead. *Formula:* $Pb_6Sb_{14}S_{27}$ Also, **zinckenite.** [< German *Zinkenit* < J. K. L. *Zinken,* director of the Anhalt mines + *-it* -ite[1]]
**zink|ite** (zing′kīt), *n.* = zincite.
**zink|y** (zing′kē), *adj.* = zincky.
**zin|ni|a** (zin′ē ə), *n.* **1** a garden plant grown for its showy flowers of many colors. It is a composite herb native to Mexico and the southwestern United States. **2** its flower. [< New Latin *Zinnia* the genus name < Johann G. *Zinn,* 1727-1759, a German botanist]
**zin|zi|ber|a|ceous** (zin′zə bə rā′shəs), *adj.* = zingiberaceous.
**Zi|on** (zī′ən), *n.* **1** a hill in Jerusalem on which the royal palace and the Temple stood. **2** Israel or the Israelites; the people of Israel, whose national religious life centered on Mount Zion. **3** heaven (as the final home of those who are virtuous and truly devout). **4** the Christian Church. Also, **Sion.** [Old English *Sion* < Late Latin *siōn* < Greek *Seiōn* < Hebrew *ṣiyyon* hill]
**Zi|on|ism** (zī′ə niz əm), *n.* a movement that started in the late 1800's to set up a Jewish national state in Palestine, and which now seeks to help maintain and develop the state of Israel.
**Zi|on|ist** (zī′ə nist), *n., adj.* — ***n.*** a person who supports or favors Zionism.
— ***adj.*** of or having to do with Zionists or Zionism.
**Zi|on|is|tic** (zī′ə nis′tik), *adj.* **1** of or having to do with Zionism. **2** like Zionism; resembling Zionism.
**Zi|on|ite** (zī′ə nīt), *n.* = Zionist.
**Zi|on|ward** (zī′ən wərd), *adv.* toward Zion.

**zip**[1] (zip), *v.,* **zipped, zip|ping,** *n.* — ***v.t.*** **1** to fasten or unfasten with a zipper: *Please help me zip up my dress. He zipped up his coat before going out.* **2** *Informal.* to move with energy. **3** *Informal.* to give vim or zest to: *This drink will zip you up.*
— ***v.i.*** **1** to make a sudden, brief hissing sound. **2** *Informal, Figurative.* to proceed with energy; move briskly. **3** to become fastened or unfastened with a zipper: *The jacket zips open easily.*
— ***n.*** **1** a sudden, brief hissing sound. **2** *Informal, Figurative.* energy or vim: *Satisfied with what's inside the can, the National Brewing Company is attempting to add a little zip to the outside* (New York Times). **3** *British.* a zipper. [imitative]
**zip**[2] or **Zip** (zip), *n. U.S. Informal.* = Zip Code.
**zip**[3] (zip), *n. U.S. Slang.* zero, especially in reference to a score in sports. [origin uncertain]
**Zi|pan|go** (zi pang′gō), *n.* = Cipango.
**Zi|pan|gu** (zi pang′gü), *n.* = Cipango.
**Zip Code, Zip code, zip code,** or **ZIP Code,** *U.S.* a five-digit number used to identify a mail-delivery zone in the United States. [< *ZIP,* abbreviation of *Zone Improvement Plan,* the U.S. Postal Service system of coding by zones for faster mail sorting and delivery, introduced in 1963]
**zip-code** (zip′kōd′), *v.t.,* **-cod|ed, -cod|ing.** to provide with the Zip Code: *to zip-code a letter, package, or address.*
**zip fastener,** *British.* zipper (def. 1).
**zip gun,** a crude gun made of metal tubing and a wooden handle. Rubber bands or a spring fire the cartridge.
**zip-in lining** (zip′in′), a removable lining that fits into a topcoat, raincoat, or other light coat or jacket, by means of a zipper.
**zip|per** (zip′ər), *n., v.* — ***n.*** **1** a sliding fastener for clothing, shoes, boots, bags, containers, and covers, consisting of two flexible parts interlocked or separated by an attached sliding device which is pulled along between them; slide fastener. A zipper is used in place of buttons, laces, etc. *He has a zipper on his coat.* **2** **Zipper.** a former trademark for this fastening. **3** *Surfing.* a howler.
— ***v.i., v.t.*** to fasten or close with a zipper: *Zipper your coat up before you go out in the cold. He was wearing a slate-blue flying suit zippered up to his chest* (New Yorker). [American English < *zip*[1] + *-er*[1]] — **zip′per|less,** *adj.*
**zipper bag,** a bag that opens or closes by means of a zipper.
**zip|pered** (zip′ərd), *adj.* furnished with a zipper: *a zippered closure.*
**zipper fleet,** *U.S.* ships taken out of active service and held in reserve; mothball fleet.
**zip|py** (zip′ē), *adj.,* **-pi|er, -pi|est.** *Informal.* full of energy; lively; gay.
**zip-top** (zip′top′), *adj.* having a top that may be removed by pulling a strip around its rim: *a zip-top beer can.*
**zirc|al|loy** or **zirc|a|loy** (zėrk′al′oi, zėr′kə loi′), *n.* an alloy of zirconium and some other metal or metals, widely used for its heat-resistant and corrosion-resistant properties, especially in reactors to separate the fuel from the coolant. [< *zirc*(onium) *alloy*]
**zir|con** (zėr′kon), *n.* a crystalline mineral, a silicate of zirconium, that occurs in tetragonal crystals, variously colored. Transparent zircon is used as a gem. The reddish-orange variety is sometimes called hyacinth in jewelry. The colorless, yellowish, or smoky zircon of Ceylon (Sri Lanka) is there called jargon. *Formula:* $ZrSiO_4$ [probably < French *zircon,* ultimately < Arabic *zarqūn* < Persian *zargūn* (literally) golden < *zar* gold. See etym. of doublet **jargon**[2].]
**zir|con|ate** (zėr′kə nāt), *n.* a salt of zirconium hydroxide when it acts as an acid.
**zir|co|ni|a** (zėr kō′nē ə), *n.* a dioxide of zirconium, usually obtained as a white, amorphous powder, used in making incandescent gas mantles and refractory utensils. *Formula:* $ZrO_2$ [< New Latin *zirconia* < *zircon* zircon]
**zir|con|ic** (zėr kon′ik), *adj.* **1** of or having to do with zirconia or zirconium. **2** containing zirconia or zirconium.

**∗zirconium**

| symbol | atomic number | atomic weight | oxidation state |
|---|---|---|---|
| Zr | 40 | 91.22 | 4 |

**∗zir|co|ni|um** (zėr kō′nē əm), *n.* a metallic chemical element commonly obtained from zircon as a black powder or as a grayish, crystalline substance. Zirconium has both acidic and basic properties. It is used in alloys for wires and filaments, in making steel, and in atomic reactors. [< New Latin *zirconium* < *zirconia* zirconia]
**zirconium hydroxide,** a white powder used in making pigments and dyes. *Formula:* $Zr(OH)_4$
**zirconium oxide,** = zirconia.
**zir|co|nyl** (zėr′kə nəl), *n.* a bivalent radical, ZrO-.
**zit** (zit), *n. U.S. Slang.* a pimple: (*Figurative.*) *Plans for redistricting featured districts ... with remarkable pimples in their boundary lines, zits that popped up to include the home of one liberal incumbent in the district of another* (Atlantic). [origin unknown]
**∗zith|er** (zith′ər, ziтн′-), *n.* a musical instrument having from 30 to 45 strings stretched over a shallow sounding box, played in a horizontal position with a plectrum and the fingers. [< German *Zither* < Latin *cithara.* See etym. of doublets **cithara, guitar.**]

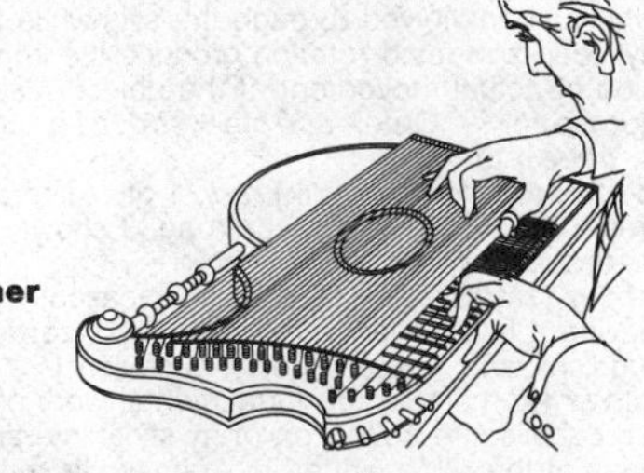
**∗zither**

**zith|er|ist** (zith′ər ist), *n.* a person who plays the zither.
**zith|ern** (zith′ərn), *n.* **1** = zither. **2** = cithern.
**zit|tern** (zit′ərn), *n.* = zithern.
**zi|zith** (tsē tsēt′, tsi′tsis), *n. pl.* the fringes of knotted threads at the four corners of the Jewish prayer shawl (tallith) or at the corners of a kind of scapular worn as an undergarment by Orthodox Jews. Also, **tzitzis.** [< Hebrew *ṣiṣith*]
**zizz** (ziz), *n., v. British Informal.* — ***n.*** **1** a humming sound; buzz. **2** a short sleep; nap or snooze.
— ***v.i.*** to make a humming or buzzing sound. [imitative]
**zl.,** zloty.
**zlo|ty** (zlō′tē), *n., pl.* **-tys** or (*collectively*) **-ty.** the basic Polish monetary unit, a coin or note worth 100 groszy. [< Polish *złoty* (literally) golden < *złoto* gold]
**Zn** (no period), zinc (chemical element).
**zo** (zō), *n., pl.* **zos** = zobo.
**zo-,** *combining form.* the form of **zoo-** before vowels, as in *zooid.*
**zo|a** (zō′ə), *n.* plural of **zoon.**
**Z.O.A.** or **ZOA** (no periods), Zionist Organization of America.
**zo|an|thar|i|an** (zō′an thãr′ē ən), *adj., n.* — ***adj.*** of or belonging to a division of the anthozoans having simple and usually many tentacles and parts arranged in sixes, such as the sea anemone.
— ***n.*** a zoantharian polyp.
[< New Latin *Zoantharia* the division or subclass name < *zo-* + Greek *ánthos* flower]
**zo|ar|i|al** (zō ãr′ē əl), *adj.* having to do with or constituting a zoarium.
**zo|ar|i|um** (zō ãr′ē əm), *n., pl.* **-ar|i|a** (-ãr′ē ə). *Zoology.* the colony or aggregate of individuals of a compound animal. [< New Latin *zoarium* < *zoon* animal < Greek *zôion*]
**zo|bo** (zō′bō), *n., pl.* **-bos.** a domesticated animal of eastern Asia that is a cross between a yak and a zebu. Also, **zo, zomo.** [< a native name]
**∗zo|di|ac** (zō′dē ak), *n.* **1** an imaginary belt of the heavens, extending about 8 degrees on both sides of the path of the sun and including the paths of the major planets and the moon. The zodiac is divided into 12 equal parts, called *signs,* named after 12 constellations. Each constellation now (because of the precession of the equinoxes) is in the sign named for the following constellation. **2** a diagram representing the zodiac, used in astrology. See the picture opposite on the following page. **3** *Figurative.* **a** a recurrent series, round, or course. **b** compass; range. **c** a set of twelve. **4** a girdle. [< Old French *zodiaque,* learned borrowing from Latin *zōdiacus* < Greek *zōidiakós* (*kýklos*) (circle) of the figures < *zôidion* zodiacal sign; (originally) sculptured figure of an animal; (diminutive) < *zôion* animal]
**zo|di|a|cal** (zō dī′ə kəl), *adj.* **1** of or having to do with the zodiac. **2** situated in the zodiac.
**zodiacal light,** an area of nebulous light in the sky, seen near the ecliptic at certain seasons of the year, either in the west after sunset or in the east before sunrise, and supposed to be the glow from a cloud of meteoric matter revolving around the sun.
**zo|e|a** (zō ē′ə), *n., pl.* **zo|e|ae** (zō ē′ē) or **zo|e|as.** a larval stage of development in crustaceans,

**Pronunciation Key:** hat, āge, cãre, fär; let, ēqual, tėrm; it, īce; hot, ōpen, ôrder; **oi**l, **ou**t; cup, pu̇t, rüle; **ch**ild; lo**ng**; **th**in; **ᴛʜ**en; **zh**, measure; **ə** represents **a** in about, **e** in taken, **i** in pencil, **o** in lemon, **u** in circus.

especially decapods such as crabs, characterized by spines on the carapace and rudimentary thoracic and abdominal limbs. [< New Latin *zoea* < Greek *zōē* life]

**zo|e|al** (zō ē′əl), *adj.* of or having to do with a zoea or zoeae.

**zo|e mou, sas a|ga|po** (zō′ē mü säs ä′gä pō′), *Greek.* my life, I love thee.

**zo|e|trope** (zō′ə trōp), *n.* an optical instrument consisting of a cylinder open at the top, with a series of slits in the circumference, and a series of figures representing successive positions of a moving object arranged along the inner surface, which when viewed through the slits while the cylinder is in rapid rotation produce the impression of actual movement of the object. Also, **zootrope.** [< Greek *zōē* life + *-tropos* a turning < *trépein* to turn]

**zo|e|trop|ic** (zō′ə trop′ik), *adj.* **1** of or like a zoetrope. **2** adapted to the zoetrope. **3** shown by the zoetrope.

**zof|tig** (zof′tik), *adj. U.S. Slang.* pleasantly plump; having a full, curvaceous figure. Also, **zaftig.** [< Yiddish *zaftig* (literally) juicy, succulent]

**Zo|har** (zō′här), *n.* the fundamental work of Jewish cabalism, a collection of mystical interpretations of the Bible written in Aramaic. Its author is unknown. [< Hebrew *zōhār* (literally) brightness]

**zo|ic** (zō′ik), *n.* of or having to do with living beings or animals; characterized by animal life. [< Greek *zōikós* < *zôion* animal]

**Zo|i|lus** (zō′ə ləs), *n.* a spiteful or malignant critic. [< *Zoilus,* a Greek grammarian of the 300's B.C., who was a severe critic of Homer]

**zois|ite** (zoi′sīt), *n.* a mineral, a silicate of aluminum and calcium, sometimes containing iron instead of aluminum. *Formula:* $HCa_2Al_3Si_3O_{13}$ [< German *Zoisit* < Baron von *Zois,* 1747-1819, the discoverer + *-ite*[1]]

**Zo|la|esque** (zō′lə esk′), *adj.* of or having to do with Émile Zola or Zolaism: *Somewhat Zolaesque in its fashion of realism and distinctly Jamesian in narrative method ...* (London Times).

**Zo|la|ism** (zō′lə iz əm), *n.* characteristic qualities of the works of the French novelist Émile Zola (1840-1902) noted for his unreserved realism or naturalism: *Set the maiden fancies wallowing in the troughs of Zolaism* (Tennyson).

**Zoll|ver|ein** (tsôl′fer īn′), *n.* **1** a union of various German states from 1834 to 1871 to promote free trade among themselves and uniform conditions of trade with other nations, the formation and existence of which was an important step in the unification of Germany. **2** any similar union of states or countries; customs union. [< German *Zollverein* customs union < *Zoll* toll, customs + *Verein* union]

**zom|bi** (zom′bē), *n., pl.* **-bis.** = zombie.

**zom|bie** (zom′bē), *n.* **1** a corpse supposedly brought back to a trancelike condition resembling life by a supernatural power. People who practice voodoo believe in zombies. **2** a supernatural power or force that supposedly makes the dead move and act. This power is alleged to be possessed by certain practitioners of West Indian voodoo. **3** the python god in certain West African voodoo cults. **4** the snake god of voodoo, derived from this. **5** an alcoholic drink of several kinds of rum, fruit juice, sugar, and brandy, served very cold and in a tall glass. **6** *Slang.* a very stupid, lethargic person. [American English < Creole *zōbi* < West African (compare Kongo *zumbi* fetish)] —**zom′bie|like′**, *adj.*

**zom|bi|ism** (zom′bē iz əm), *n.* the state or character of being a zombie.

**zo|mo** (zō′mō), *n., pl.* **-mos.** = zobo.

**zon|al** (zō′nəl), *adj.* **1** of a zone; having to do with zones. **2** divided into zones; characterized by or arranged in zones, circles, or rings. **3** of the nature of or forming a zone. **4** marked with zones or circular bands of color. Certain varieties of geranium have leaves so marked. —**zon′al|ly,** *adv.*

**zo|na pel|lu|ci|da** (zō′nə pe lü′sə də), *Embryology.* a thick, tough, transparent membrane surrounding the yolk of a developed mammalian ovum. [< New Latin *zona pellucida* (literally) pellucid zone]

**zon|a|ry** (zō′nər ē), *adj.* **1** occurring in a zone or zones. **2** having the form of a zone or girdle.

**zon|ate** (zō′nāt), *adj.* **1** marked with or divided into zones, rings, or bands of color; zoned. **2** *Botany.* arranged in one row.

**zon|at|ed** (zō′nā tid), *adj.* = zonate.

**zo|na|tion** (zō nā′shən), *n.* distribution in zones or regions of definite character: *Light penetration limits the distribution of plants, resulting in a zonation of the seaweeds: the green algae live in the uppermost, well-lighted zones; the brown algae in the intermediate zone; and the red algae at greatest depths* (Clarence J. Hylander).

**zon|da** (zon′də; *Spanish* sôn′dä), *n.* a wind of the foehn type in the Argentine pampas. [< American Spanish *zonda,* perhaps < a native word]

***zone**
definition 1

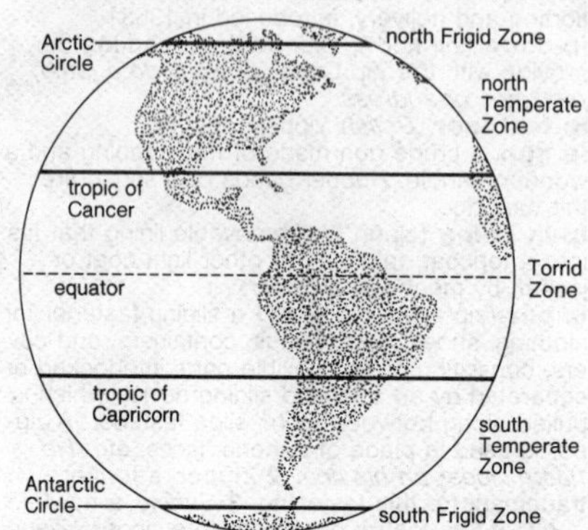


***zone** (zōn), *n., v.,* **zoned, zon|ing.** —*n.* **1** any one of the five great divisions of the earth's surface, bounded by imaginary lines going around the earth parallel to the equator. The zones are distinguished by differences of climate (the Torrid Zone, the two Temperate Zones, and the two Frigid Zones). **2** any region or area especially considered or set off. A combat zone is a district where fighting is going on. **3** a region or area characterized by certain forms of animal or vegetable life which are in turn determined by certain environmental conditions. **4** an area or district in a town or city under special restrictions as to building. **5a** a circular area or district within which the same rate of postage is charged for postal shipments from a particular place. **b** one of the sections into which a large city was formerly divided, each of which was assigned a number to be used on addresses in order to speed the sorting and delivery of mail. **6** an area, commonly circular, to all points within which a uniform rate prevails for transportation, telephone service, or some other service from a particular place. **7** the aggregate of railroad stations situated within a specific circumference around a particular shipping center. **8** *Geology.* a horizon. **9** *Mathematics.* a part of the surface of a sphere contained between two parallel planes. **10** *Archaic.* a girdle; belt. **11** an encircling or enclosing line, band, or ring, sometimes differing as in color or texture, from the surrounding medium.

—*v.t.* **1** to divide into zones, especially to divide (a town or city) into areas which are restricted, as to homes or businesses: *The city was zoned for factories and residences.* **2** to surround like a belt or girdle; encircle. **3** to surround with a belt or girdle. **4** to mark with rings or bands of color.

—*v.i.* to be formed or divided into zones.

[< Latin *zōna* < Greek *zṓnē* (originally) girdle < *zōnnýnai* to gird]

**zoned** (zōnd), *adj.* **1** marked with or having zones. **2** divided into zones.

**zone defense,** a defensive technique in which a team's defensive area is divided into zones, with each player assigned to a zone, used especially in basketball.

**zone electrophoresis,** electrophoresis conducted in a porous, solid, or semisolid medium, such as filter paper or a sheet of starch, whereby the components of a liquid can be separated ionically into various zones of the medium.

**zone|less** (zōn′lis), *adj.* **1** not marked with or divided into zones. **2** not confined by or wearing a zone or girdle: *The ruling goddess with the zoneless waist* (Cowper).

**zone melting** or **refining,** a method of purifying metals, semiconductors, and other materials, in which a high-temperature heat source is passed along the material to be purified, carrying off impurities and concentrating them at one or both ends of the treated material.

**Zon|i|an** (zō′nē ən), *n.* an American citizen who is a native or inhabitant of the Panama Canal Zone: *Many Zonians ... regard the Zone as something sacred* (Time).

**zon|ing** (zō′ning), *n.* the building restrictions in an area of a city or town.

**zonked** (zongkt), *adj. Slang.* intoxicated or dazed under the influence of alcohol or narcotics; stoned. [origin unknown]

**Zon|ti|an** (zon′tē ən), *n.* a member of Zonta International, a service club of executive business and professional women founded in 1919 to promote civic and social welfare, with emphasis on the advancement of girls and women.

**zon|ule** (zō′nyül), *n.* a little zone or band, as of tissue or ligament in an organism. [< New Latin *zonula* (diminutive) < Latin *zōna;* see etym. under **zone**]

**zoo** (zü), *n.* a place where animals are kept and shown; zoological garden: *There are often many tame animals in a children's zoo.* [short for *zoological* (*garden*)]

**zoo-,** *combining form.* a living being; animal or animals: *Zoology = the science of animals.* Also, **zo-** before vowels. [< Greek *zôion* animal]

**zoochem.,** zoochemistry.

**zo|o|chem|i|cal** (zō′ə kem′ə kəl), *adj.* of or having to do with zoochemistry.

**zo|o|chem|is|try** (zō′ə kem′ə strē), *n.* the chemistry of the components of animal bodies; animal chemistry.

**zo|o|dy|nam|ic** (zō′ə dī nam′ik), *adj.* of or having to do with zoodynamics.

**zo|o|dy|nam|ics** (zō′ə dī nam′iks), *n.* the branch of biology that deals with the vital force of animals; animal physiology.

**zoo|ful** (zü′fu̇l), *n., pl.* **-fuls.** as much or as many as a zoo will hold.

**zo|og|a|my** (zō og′ə mē), *n.* the coupling, mating, or pairing of animals of opposite sexes for the purpose of reproduction; sexual reproduction of animals.

**zo|o|gen|ic** (zō′ə jen′ik), *adj.* produced from animals; of animal origin: *Limestones formed from shells are zoogenic.*

**zo|og|e|nous** (zō oj′ə nəs), *adj.* = zoogenic.

**zo|og|e|ny** (zō oj′ə nē), *n.* the origin and development of animals.

**zoogeog.,** zoogeography.

**zo|o|ge|og|ra|pher** (zō′ə jē og′rə fər), *n.* an expert in zoogeography.

**zo|o|ge|o|graph|ic** (zō′ə jē′ə graf′ik), *adj.* of or having to do with zoogeography; faunistic; chorological.

**zo|o|ge|o|graph|i|cal** (zō′ə jē′ə graf′ə kəl), *adj.* = zoogeographic.

**zo|o|ge|o|graph|i|cal|ly** (zō′ə jē′ə graf′ə klē), *adv.* in relation to zoogeography.

**zo|o|ge|og|ra|phy** (zō′ə jē og′rə fē), *n.* **1** the study of the geographical distribution of animals. **2** the study of the causes and effects of such distribution and of the relationships between certain areas and the groups of animals inhabiting them.

**zo|o|ge|ol|o|gy** (zō′ə jē ol′ə jē), *n.* that branch of geology which deals with fossil animal remains; paleozoology.

**zo|o|gloe|a** (zō′ə glē′ə), *n.* a jellylike cluster of bacteria swollen by the absorption of water. [< New Latin *zoogloea* < Greek *zôion* animal + *gloiós* gelatinous substance]

**zo|o|gloe|al** (zō′ə glē′əl), *adj.* of or having to do with a zoogloea or zoogloeas.

**zo|o|gloe|ic** (zō′ə glē′ik), *adj.* = zoogloeal.

**zo|og|ra|pher** (zō og′rə fər), *n.* a person who describes or depicts animals, especially a descriptive zoologist.

**zo|o|graph|ic** (zō′ə graf′ik), *adj.* having to do with zoography.

**zo|o|graph|i|cal** (zō′ə graf′ə kəl), *adj.* = zoographic.

**zo|o|graph|i|cal|ly** (zō′ə graf′ə klē), *adv.* in relation to zoography.

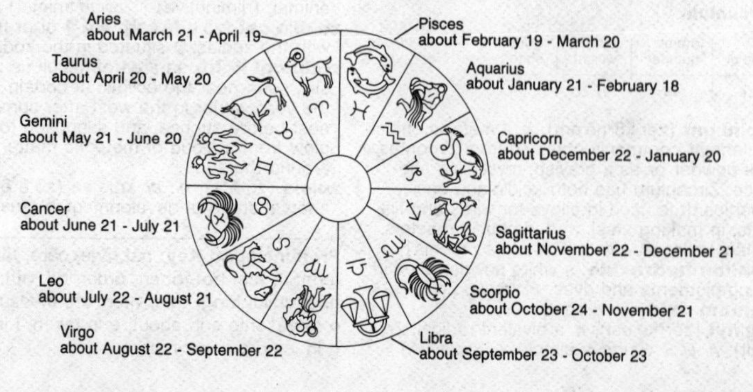


***zodiac**
definition 2

**zo|og|ra|phy** (zō og′rə fē), *n.* the branch of zoology dealing with the description of animals and animal habits; descriptive zoology.

**zo|oid** (zō′oid), *n., adj.* **—n. 1** *Biology.* a free-moving cell or other organism resembling an animal, although it is actually not one, such as a spermatozoan or antherozoid. **2** *Zoology.* **a** an independent organism produced by another asexually, as by budding or fission. **b** any individual which comes between the sexually produced organisms in the alternation of generations, such as various free-swimming medusae. **c** each of the distinct individuals which make up a colonial or compound animal organism.
**—*adj.*** resembling or having the character of an animal.
[< *zo-* + *-oid.* Compare Late Greek *zōioeidês* like an animal.]

**zo|oi|dal** (zō oi′dəl), *adj.* of, like, or being a zooid.

**zoo|keep|er** (zü′kē′pər), *n.* a person who owns or works in a zoo.

**zoo|keep|ing** (zü′kē′ping), *n.* the work or practice of keeping a zoo; occupation of a zookeeper.

**zooks** (zůks, züks), *interj. Archaic.* a mild oath or exclamation; Gadzooks.

**zool.**, **1** zoological. **2** zoology.

**zo|ol|a|ter** (zō ol′ə tər), *n.* a person who worships animals or practices zoolatry.

**zo|ol|a|trous** (zō ol′ə trəs), *adj.* **1** worshiping animals; practicing zoolatry. **2** of or relating to zoolatry.

**zo|ol|a|try** (zō ol′ə trē), *n.* the worship of animals. [< *zoo-* + Greek *latreíā* worship]

**zo|o|lite** (zō′ə līt), *n.* a fossil animal.

**zo|o|lith** (zō′ə lith), *n.* = zoolite.

**zo|o|log|ic** (zō′ə loj′ik), *adj.* = zoological.

**zo|o|log|i|cal** (zō′ə loj′ə kəl), *adj.* **1** of animals or animal life. **2** of or having to do with zoology. **—zo′o|log′i|cal|ly,** *adv.*

**zoological garden,** = zoo.

**zo|ol|o|gist** (zō ol′ə jist), *n.* an expert in zoology: *Zoologists are interested for the most part in the instinctive activities of animals drawn from the lower end of the evolutionary scale, since in them the mechanisms underlying behavior seem particularly accessible* (M. E. Bitterman).

**zo|ol|o|gy** (zō ol′ə jē), *n., pl.* **-gies. 1** the science of animals; study of animals and animal life, including their structure, physiology, development, and classification. Zoology and botany are the two main branches of biology. *Abbr:* zool. **2** the animals inhabiting a certain area. **3** the zoological facts or characteristics concerning a particular animal or group of animals: *the zoology of vertebrates.* **4** a treatise on zoology. [< New Latin *zoologia* < New Greek *zōiologiā* (originally) science of pharmaceuticals derived from animals < Greek *zôion* animal + *-logia* -logy]

**zoom** (züm), *v., n.* **—*v.i.* 1** to move suddenly upward. **2** to fly suddenly upward in a nearly vertical ascent at great speed, in or as if in an airplane: *The airplane zoomed.* **3** to make a continuous, low-pitched humming or buzzing sound. **4** to move or travel with a humming or buzzing sound. **5** to move rapidly from one focus to another, as with a zoom lens.
**—*v.t.*** to cause to move suddenly upward, especially to fly (an airplane) suddenly upward.
**—*n.*** an act of zooming; sudden upward flight: *The airplane made a zoom and left the mountain far below.*
[imitative] **—zoom′er,** *n.*

**Zoom|ar lens** (zü′mär), *Trademark.* a special zoom lens for television.

**zo|o|met|ric** (zō′ə met′rik), *adj.* of or having to do with zoometry.

**zo|om|e|try** (zō om′ə trē), *n.* the measurement of the dimensions and proportions of the bodies of animals.

**zoom|ing** (zü′ming), *adj.* rapidly rising; soaring: *Such periods were likely to be followed by other periods of zooming prices* (Atlantic).

**zoom lens,** a type of motion-picture camera lens which can be adjusted from wide-angle shots down to telephoto close-ups.

**zo|o|morph** (zō′ə môrf), *n.* a representation of an animal, as in primitive art; a zoomorphic image or design. [< *zoo-* + Greek *morphê* form, shape]

**zo|o|mor|phic** (zō′ə môr′fik), *adj.* **1** representing or using animal forms: *zoomorphic ornament.* **2** ascribing animal form or attributes to beings or things not animal; representing a deity in the form of an animal. **3** characterized by or involving such ascription or representation.

**zo|o|mor|phism** (zō′ə môr′fiz əm), *n.* the attribution of animal form or nature to a deity or superhuman being.

**zo|on** (zō′on), *n., pl.* **zo|a.** *Zoology.* **1** a completely developed individual that makes up a colonial or compound animal organism. **2** an animal which is the total product of an impregnated ovum. [< New Latin *zoon* < Greek *zôion* animal]

**zo|on|al** (zō′ə nəl), *adj.* **1** having to do with a zoon. **2** of the nature of a zoon.

**zo|on|o|my** (zō on′ə mē), *n.* the science treating of the causes and relations of the phenomena of living animals. [< New Latin *zoonomia* < Greek *zôion* animal + *nómos* law]

**zo|o|nose** (zō′ə nōs), *n.* = zoonosis.

**zo|o|no|sis** (zō′ə nō′sis), *n., pl.* **-ses** (-sēz). a disease or infection in animals that can be transmitted to man, such as tuberculosis, rabies, or parrot fever.

**zo|o|not|ic** (zō′ə not′ik), *adj.* of or having to do with a zoonosis.

**zo|o|par|a|site** (zō′ə par′ə sīt), *n.* a parasitic animal.

**zo|o|par|a|sit|ic** (zō′ə par ə sit′ik), *adj.* of or having to do with zooparasites.

**zo|o|pa|thol|o|gy** (zō′ə pə thol′ə jē), *n.* the science treating of the diseases of animals; veterinary pathology.

**zo|oph|a|gous** (zō of′ə gəs), *adj.* feeding on animals; carnivorous. [< *zoo-* + Greek *phageîn* to eat + English *-ous*]

**zo|o|phile** (zō′ə fīl), *n.* **1** a zoophilous plant. **2** the seed of such a plant. **3** a person who is extremely or excessively fond of animals. [< *zoo-* + *-phile*]

**zo|o|phil|ic** (zō′ə fil′ik), *adj.* of or having to do with a zoophile: *In England, presumably owing to the prevalence of zoophilic organizations such as the R.S.P.C.A., such practices are illegalised* (Alec Parker).

**zo|oph|i|list** (zō of′ə list), *n.* = zoophile.

**zo|oph|i|lous** (zō of′ə ləs), *adj.* **1** *Botany.* (of plants) adapted for being pollinated by animals. **2** that is extremely or excessively fond of animals.

**zo|o|pho|bi|a** (zō′ə fō′bē ə), *n.* a morbid or superstitious fear of animals. [< *zoo-* + *-phobia*]

**zo|o|phor|ic** (zō′ə fôr′ik, -for′-), *adj.* bearing a figure of a man or an animal, or more than one such figure: *a zoophoric column.*

**zo|o|phys|ics** (zō′ə fiz′iks), *n.* the study of the physical structure of animals; comparative anatomy as a branch of zoology.

**zo|o|phys|i|ol|o|gy** (zō′ə fiz′ē ol′ə jē), *n.* animal physiology.

**zo|o|phyte** (zō′ə fīt), *n.* any one of various invertebrate animals, being usually fixed and often having a branched or radiating structure, thus resembling plants or flowers, such as crinoids, sea anemones, corals, hydroids, and sponges. [< New Latin *zoophyton* < Greek *zōióphyton* a plant with animal qualities < *zôion* animal + *phytón* plant]

**zo|o|phyt|ic** (zō′ə fit′ik), *adj.* **1** of the nature of a zoophyte. **2** of or having to do with zoophytes; phytozoic.

**zo|o|phyt|i|cal** (zō′ə fit′ə kəl), *adj.* = zoophytic.

**zo|o|phy|tol|o|gy** (zō′ə fī tol′ə jē), *n.* the science that treats of zoophytes.

**zo|o|plank|ton** (zō′ə plangk′tən), *n.* the part of the plankton of any body of water which consists of animals: *The phytoplankton serves as food for tiny sea animals known as zooplankton, which in turn are eaten by fish, birds and other sea-going animals* (Science News Letter).

**zo|o|plank|ton|ic** (zō′ə plangk′ton′ik), *adj.* of or having to do with zooplankton: *zooplanktonic crops.*

**zo|o|plas|tic** (zō′ə plas′tik), *adj.* of or having to do with zooplasty.

**zo|o|plas|ty** (zō′ə plas′tē), *n., pl.* **-ties.** plastic surgery in which living tissue is transplanted from a lower animal to the human body.

**zo|o|psy|chol|o|gy** (zō′ə sī kol′ə jē), *n.* the psychology of animals other than man; animal psychology.

**zo|o|se|mi|ot|ics** (zō′ə sē′mē ot′iks), *n.* the study of communication among animals.

**zo|o|sperm** (zō′ə spėrm), *n.* **1** = spermatozoon. **2** = zoospore.

**zo|o|sper|mat|ic** (zō′ə spėr mat′ik), *adj.* = spermatozoic.

**zo|o|spo|ran|gi|al** (zō′ə spə ran′jē əl), *adj.* having to do with a zoosporangium.

**zo|o|spo|ran|gi|um** (zō′ə spə ran′jē əm), *n., pl.* **-gi|a** (-jē ə). *Botany.* a receptacle or sporangium in which zoospores are produced.

**zo|o|spore** (zō′ə spôr, -spōr), *n.* **1** *Botany.* an asexual spore that can move about by means of cilia or flagella, produced by some algae and fungi. **2** *Zoology.* any one of the minute, freely moving, flagellate or ameboid organisms released by the sporocyst of various protozoans.

**zo|o|spor|ic** (zō′ə spôr′ik, -spor′-), *adj.* **1** of the nature of a zoospore. **2** having to do with zoospores.

**zo|o|spo|rif|er|ous** (zō′ə spə rif′ər əs), *adj. Botany.* bearing or producing zoospores.

**zo|os|po|rous** (zō os′pər əs; zō′ə spôr′-, -spōr′-), *adj.* **1** producing zoospores. **2** of the nature of zoospores. **3** effected by zoospores.

**zo|os|ter|ol** (zō os′tə rōl, -rol), *n.* any sterol originating in animals, as distinguished from a phytosterol.

**zo|o|tech|nic** (zō′ə tek′nik), *adj.* of or having to do with zootechny.

**zo|o|tech|nics** (zō′ə tek′niks), *n.* = zootechny.

**zo|o|tech|ny** (zō′ə tek′nē), *n.* the keeping and breeding of animals in domestication. [< *zoo-* + Greek *téchnē* art, science]

**zo|o|the|ism** (zō′ə thē iz′əm), *n.* the attribution of deity to an animal; the worship of animals or animal forms.

**zo|o|the|ist** (zō′ə thē ist), *n.* a person who worships animals or animal forms.

**zo|o|the|is|tic** (zō′ə thē is′tik), *adj.* of or having to do with zootheism; relating to the worship of animals; zoolatrous.

**zo|o|tom|ic** (zō′ə tom′ik), *adj.* = zootomical.

**zo|o|tom|i|cal** (zō′ə tom′ə kəl), *adj.* of or having to do with zootomy. **—zo′o|tom′i|cal|ly,** *adv.*

**zo|ot|o|mist** (zō ot′ə mist), *n.* a person who dissects the bodies of animals, especially a comparative anatomist.

**zo|ot|o|my** (zō ot′ə mē), *n.* the anatomy of animals. [< *zoo-* + (ana)*tomy*]

**zo|o|trope** (zō′ə trōp), *n.* = zoetrope.

**zoot suit** (züt), a man's suit with a long, tight-fitting jacket having exaggerated, padded shoulders, and baggy trousers extending above the waist, tapering down to tight cuffs at the ankles. Zoot suits were especially popular in the early 1940's. [American English; origin uncertain]

**zoot-suit|ed** (züt′sü′tid), *adj.* wearing a zoot suit or zoot suits.

**zoot-suit|er** (züt′sü′tər), *n.* **1** a man wearing a zoot suit. 2 *Figurative.* a person who tries to dress fashionably, especially in cheap clothes.

**Zo|phi|el** (zō′fē əl), *n.* one of the archangels in Christian tradition.

**zop|po** (tsop′ō), *adj., adv. Music.* with syncopation. [< Italian *zoppo* (literally) limping]

**zo|ri** (zō′rē), *n., pl.* **-ri.** a flat sandal, usually made of woven straw, leather, or rubber. [< Japanese *zori*]

**zor|il** (zôr′əl, zor′-), *n.* a skunklike, carnivorous, South African mammal related to the weasel. [< French *zorille* < Spanish *zorillo,* (diminutive) < *zorra,* and *zorro* fox]

**zo|ril|la** (zə ril′ə), *n.* = zoril.

**Zorn's lemma** (zôrnz), *Mathematics.* the principle that if a set is partially ordered and each completely ordered subset has an upper bound, then the set has at least one element greater than any other element in the set. [< Max A. *Zorn,* born 1906, a German mathematician]

**Zo|ro|as|tri|an** (zôr′ō as′trē ən, zōr′-), *adj., n.* **—*adj.*** of or having to do with Zoroaster, a Persian religious teacher who lived about 600 B.C., or the religion founded by him.
**—*n.*** a person believing in the teachings of Zoroaster, now represented by the Ghebers and the Parsees. Also, **Zarathustrian.**

**Zo|ro|as|tri|an|ism** (zôr′ō as′trē ə niz′əm, zōr′-), *n.* the religion founded by Zoroaster and practiced in Persia until the Moslem conquest in the 600's. Zoroastrianism taught that there is an eternal struggle between the powers of light and the powers of darkness, or good and evil.

**Zo|ro|as|trism** (zôr′ō as′triz əm, zōr′-), *n.* = Zoroastrianism.

**zos|ter** (zos′tər), *n.* **1** = shingles. **2** a belt or girdle worn in ancient Greece, especially by men. [< Latin *zoster* shingles, a girdle < Greek *zōstêr* girdle < *zōnnýnai* to gird. Compare etym. under **zone.**]

***Zouave**
definition 1

***Zou|ave** (zü äv′, zwäv), *n.* **1** a member of any one of certain former light infantry regiments in the French army, noted for their bravery and dash and brilliant Oriental uniforms, and originally recruited from Algerian tribes. **2** a soldier of any unit patterned on these in style of uniform, especially a member of certain volunteer regiments in

**Pronunciation Key:** hat, āge, cãre, fär; let, ēqual, tėrm; it, īce; hot, ōpen, ôrder; **oi**l, **ou**t; cup, pů͡t, rüle; **ch**ild; lo**ng**; **th**in; **ᴛʜ**en; **zh**, measure; **ə** represents **a** in about, **e** in taken, **i** in pencil, **o** in lemon, **u** in circus.

the Union Army during the Civil War. [< French *Zouave* < *Zouaoua* the tribe < Kabyle *Zwawa*]

**Zouave jacket**, a short jacket ending at or above the waist and open in front.

**zounds** (zoundz), *interj. Archaic.* a mild oath expressing surprise, anger, or disappointment. [reduction of obsolete *God's wounds,* an oath]

**zow|ie** (zou′ē), *interj.* an exclamation as of wonder, surprise, or delight: *He snapped a cheroot in two. "Zowie!" he said* (Punch).

**zo|ys|i|a** (zō is′ē ə), *n.* a type of hardy lawn grass, for use in warm, dry climates: *Zoysias ... have tolerance to the hottest weather* (New York Times). [< New Latin *Zoysia* the genus name]

**ZPG** (no periods), zero population growth.

**Zr** (no period), zirconium (chemical element).

**zu|brow|ka** (zü′brev kə), *n.* a yellow-colored vodka flavored with a sweet grass or herb. [< Polish *żubrowka*]

**zuc|chet|to** (zü ket′ō; *Italian* tsük ket′tō), *n., pl.* **-tos,** *Italian* **-ti** (-tē). a small, round skullcap worn by Roman Catholic ecclesiastics. A priest wears black, a bishop violet, a cardinal red, and a pope white. [alteration of Italian *zucchetta* cap; small gourd (diminutive) < *zucca* gourd; head]

**zuc|chi|ni** (zü kē′nē), *n., pl.* **-ni** or **-nis. 1** a kind of dark-green summer squash shaped like a cucumber and sometimes striped or flecked with light green, turning yellow when mature. It is eaten as a vegetable while still green. **2** the plant it grows on. [American English < Italian *zucchino* (diminutive) < *zucca* squash, gourd]

**Zug|zwang** (tsük′tsfäng′), *n. Chess.* a situation in which a player is compelled to move against his will. [< German *Zugzwang* < *Zug* a drawing, pulling + *Zwang* force, compulsion]

**Zul|hij|jah** (zül hij′ä), *n.* the twelfth and last month of the Moslem year, during which the pilgrimage to Mecca must be made. It has 29 days, except during leap years, when it has 30 days. [< Arabic *Dhū*l-hijjah]

**Zul|ka|dah** (zül kä′dä, -kə dä′), *n.* the eleventh month of the Moslem year. It has 30 days. [< Arabic *Dhū'l-qa'dah*]

**Zu|lu¹** (zü′lü), *n., pl.* **-lus** or **-lu,** *adj.* —*n.* **1** a member of a large, (formerly) warlike, Bantu people of southeastern Africa chiefly in Natal, and resembling the Kaffirs. **2** their language.
—*adj.* of this people or their language.

**Zu|lu²** (zü′lü), *n. U.S.* a code name for the letter *z,* used in transmitting radio messages.

**Zum|pan|go** (zum pang′gō), *n.* = Cipango.

**Zu|ñi** (zün′yē, zü′nē), *n., pl.* **-ñis** or **-ñi,** *adj.* —*n.* **1** a member of a tribe of Pueblo Indians living in western New Mexico. **2** their language. —*adj.* of or having to do with this tribe or language.

**Zu|ñi|an** (zün′yē ən, zü′nē-), *adj., n.* = Zuñi.

**zurf** (zėrf), *n.* = zarf.

**Zwick|y galaxy** (zwik′ē), any one of a class of galaxies that recede at about the same speed, have relatively small masses, and concentrate most of their luminosity in a small area: *Efforts to find objects resembling Seyfert nuclei and quasars have led to the investigation of ... Zwicky compact galaxies and others* (Scientific American). [< Fritz *Zwicky,* 1898-1974, a Swiss-born American astronomer]

**zwie|back** (zwē′bäk′, swē′-, tswē′-), *n.* a kind of bread or cake which, after baking, is cut into slices and toasted brown and crisp in an oven. [American English < German *Zwieback* biscuit, rusk < *zwie-* twice + *backen* to bake, loan translation of Italian *biscotto.* Compare etym. under **biscuit.**]

**Zwing|li|an** (zwing′glē ən, tsving′lē-), *adj., n.* —*adj.* of or having to do with Ulrich Zwingli (1484-1531), a Swiss Protestant reformer, or his doctrines. —*n.* a follower of Ulrich Zwingli.

**Zwing|li|an|ism** (zwing′glē ə niz′əm, tsving′lē-), *n.* the doctrinal system of Ulrich Zwingli, Lutheran in essence but differing principally in denying the real presence of Christ in the Eucharist, which he maintained was a commemoration of the sacrifice of Christ rather than a renewal of it.

**Zwing|li|an|ist** (zwing′glē ə nist, tsving′lē-), *n., adj.* = Zwinglian.

**zwit|ter|i|on** (tsvit′ər ī′ən, swit′-), *n. Physics.* an ion which has both a positive and a negative charge, on opposite sides, as in certain protein molecules. [< German *Zwitterion* < *Zwitter* hybrid (< *zwie-* two, double) + *ion* ion]

**zwit|ter|i|on|ic** (tsvit′ər ī on′ik, swit′-), *adj.* of or having to do with a zwitterion.

**zyg-,** *combining form.* the form of **zygo-** before vowels, as in *zygapophysis.*

**zyg|ap|o|phys|e|al** or **zyg|ap|o|phys|i|al** (zig′ap ə fiz′ē əl), *adj.* of or having to do with a zygapophysis; articular, as a vertebral process.

**zyg|a|poph|y|sis** (zig′ə pof′ə sis, zī′gə-), *n., pl.* **-ses** (-sēz). *Anatomy.* one of the lateral processes upon the neural arch of a vertebra which interlock each vertebra with the one above and below. Each vertebra normally has four, two anterior and two posterior. [< *zyg-* + *apophysis*]

**zygo-,** *combining form.* **1** yoke; yoked or paired. *Zygodactyl = having the toes in pairs.*
**2** reproduction by zygosis, as in *zygospore.* Also, **zyg-** before vowels. [< Greek *zygón* yoke]

**zy|go|dac|tyl** (zī′gə dak′təl, zig′ə-), *adj., n.* —*adj.* having the toes arranged in pairs, with two before and two behind, as the feet of a climbing bird, or the bird itself.
—*n.* a zygodactyl bird, such as a parrot.
[< New Latin *Zygodactyles* the order name < Greek *zygón* yoke + *dáktylos* finger, toe]

**zy|go|dac|ty|lous** (zī′gə dak′tə ləs, zig′ə-), *adj.* = zygodactyl.

**zy|go|ma** (zī gō′mə, zi-), *n., pl.* **-ma|ta** (-mə tə). **1** the bony arch below the socket of the eye in vertebrates, formed by the zygomatic bone (cheekbone) and the zygomatic process of the temporal bone; zygomatic arch. **2** = zygomatic process. **3** = zygomatic bone. [< New Latin *zygoma* < Greek *zýgōma, -atos* < *zygón* yoke]

**zy|go|mat|ic** (zī′gə mat′ik, zig′ə-), *adj., n.* —*adj.* **1** of or having to do with the zygoma: *zygomatic muscle.* **2** constituting the zygoma.
—*n.* = zygomatic bone.

**zygomatic arch,** = zygoma.

**zygomatic bone,** the three-sided bone forming the lower boundary of the socket of the eye; cheekbone; malar bone; jugal bone; zygoma.

**zygomatic process,** a process of the temporal bone which articulates with the zygomatic bone to form the zygoma. See diagram under **face.**

**zy|go|mor|phic** (zī′gə môr′fik, zig′ə-), *adj. Botany.* (of a flower) divisible vertically into similar halves in only one way, as the sweet pea. [< *zygo-* + Greek *morphḗ* form + English *-ic*]

**zy|go|mor|phism** (zī′gə môr′fiz əm, zig′ə-), *n.* the character of being zygomorphic.

**zy|go|mor|phous** (zī′gə môr′fəs, zig′ə-), *adj.* = zygomorphic.

**zy|go|mor|phy** (zī′gə môr′fē, zig′ə-), *n.* = zygomorphism.

**zy|go|phyl|la|ceous** (zī′gə fə lā′shəs, zig′ə-), *adj.* belonging to a family of dicotyledonous herbs, shrubs, and trees typified by the bean caper, and including the creosote bush and lignum vitae. [< New Latin *Zygophyllaceae* the family name (< *Zygophyllum* the typical genus < Greek *zygón* a yoke + *phýllon* leaf) + English *-ous*]

**zy|go|phyte** (zī′gə fīt, zig′ə-), *n. Botany.* a plant in which reproduction consists of the fusion of two similar gametes (zygospores).

**zy|go|sis** (zī gō′sis, zi-), *n. Biology.* conjugation. [< New Latin *zygosis* < Greek *zýgōsis* a balancing < *zygoûn* to yoke < *zygón* a yoke]

**zy|go|spore** (zī′gə spôr, -spōr; zig′ə-), *n. Botany.* a spore formed by the union of two similar gametes, as in various algae and fungi. [< German *Zygospor* < Greek *zygón* a yoke + German *Spor* spore]

**zy|go|spor|ic** (zī′gə spôr′ik, -spōr′-; zig′ə-), *adj.* of or having to do with a zygospore.

**zy|gote** (zī′gōt, zig′ōt), *n.* **1** the cell formed by the union of two germ cells or gametes. A fertilized egg is a zygote. **2** the individual which develops from this cell. [< Greek *zygōtós* yoked < *zygoûn* to yoke < *zygón* a yoke]

**zy|go|tene** (zī′gə tēn), *n.* the stage of the prophase of meiosis in which homologous chromosomes become paired. [< *zygo-* + Greek *tainía* band]

**zy|got|ic** (zī got′ik, zi-), *adj.* **1** of a zygote or zygosis. **2** like a zygote or zygosis.

**zym-,** *combining form.* the form of **zymo-** before vowels, as in *zymoid.*

**zy|mase** (zī′mās), *n.* an enzyme complex in yeast which, in the absence of oxygen, changes sugar into alcohol and carbon dioxide or into lactic acid, or, in the presence of oxygen, changes sugar into carbon dioxide and water. [< French *zymase* < Greek *zýmē* leaven + French *-ase* -ase]

**zyme** (zīm), *n.* **1** the substance or principle causing a zymotic disease. **2** a substance causing fermentation; ferment. [< Greek *zýmē* leaven]

**zy|min** (zī′min), *n.* **1** a ferment; zyme. **2** a pancreatic extract, used to aid digestion.

**zymo-,** *combining form.* **1** fermentation: *Zymometer = an instrument that measures fermentation.*
**2** enzyme: *Zymolysis = the action of enzymes.* Also, **zym-** before vowels.
[< Greek *zýmē* leaven]

**zy|mo|gen** (zī′mə jən), *n.* **1** *Biochemistry.* a substance formed in an organism, from which, by some internal change, an enzyme is produced.
**2** *Biology.* any one of several enzyme-producing bacterial organisms. [< German *Zymogen* < *zymo-* zymo- + *-gen* -gen]

**zy|mo|gene** (zī′mə jēn), *n.* = zymogen.

**zy|mo|gen|e|sis** (zī′mə jen′ə sis), *n. Biochemistry.* the conversion of a zymogen into an enzyme. [< *zymo-* + *genesis*]

**zy|mo|gen|ic** (zī′mə jen′ik), *adj.* **1** of or relating to a zymogen. **2** causing fermentation.

**zymogenic organism,** any microorganism, as yeast, causing fermentative processes.

**zy|moid** (zī′moid), *adj.* resembling a zyme or ferment. [< *zym-* + *-oid*]

**zy|mo|log|ic** (zī′mə loj′ik), *adj.* of or having to do with zymology.

**zy|mo|log|i|cal** (zī′mə loj′ə kəl), *adj.* = zymologic.

**zy|mol|o|gist** (zī mol′ə jist), *n.* an expert in zymology.

**zy|mol|o|gy** (zī mol′ə jē), *n.* the study of fermentation and of ferments and their action.

**zy|mol|y|sis** (zī mol′ə sis), *n.* **1** the action of enzymes, as in digestion and fermentation. **2** fermentation or other changes produced by the action of enzymes. [< *zymo-* + Greek *lýsis* a loosening]

**zy|mo|lyt|ic** (zī′mə lit′ik), *adj.* = zymotic.

**zy|mom|e|ter** (zī mom′ə tər), *n.* an instrument for measuring the degree of fermentation of a fermenting liquid. [< *zymo-* + *-meter*]

**zy|mo|san** (zī′mə san), *n.* a drug, derived from the cell walls of yeast, used to raise the level of properdin in the blood and to guard against or promote immunity to infection and disease.

**zy|mo|sis** (zī mō′sis), *n.* **1** an infectious disease caused by a fungus. **2** an abnormal process considered analogous to fermentation, by which a zymotic disease was formerly supposed to be produced. **3** = fermentation. [< New Latin *zymosis* < Greek *zýmōsis* fermentation < *zymoûn* to leaven; ferment < *zýmē* leaven]

**zy|mot|ic** (zī mot′ik), *adj., n.* —*adj.* **1** of or having to do with fermentation. **2** causing fermentation. **3** caused by fermentation. **4** denoting or having to do with any infectious disease due to a fungus, originally regarded as being caused by a process analogous to fermentation.
—*n.* = zymotic disease. [< Greek *zymōtikós* causing fermentation < *zymoûn;* see etym. under **zymosis**] —**zy|mot′i|cal|ly,** *adv.*

**zymotic disease,** any one of various infectious and contagious diseases, such as smallpox and typhoid fever, which were formerly regarded as due to the presence in the system of a morbific principle acting in a manner analogous to the process of fermentation.

**zy|mur|gy** (zī′mėr jē), *n.* the branch of chemistry dealing with the processes of fermentation, as in brewing and the making of wine or yeast. [< Greek *zýmē* leaven + *-ourgos* making < *érgon* work. Compare Greek *zymourgós* a maker of leaven.]

**Zyr|i|an** (zir′ē ən), *n.* **1** a member of a Finno-Ugric people living in northeastern Russia. **2** the Finno-Ugric language or dialect of this people.